THE COMPLETE WORD GAME DICTIONARY

The Complete WORD GAME Dictionary

Tom Pulliam & Gorton Carruth

A Hudson Group Book

Facts On File Publications
New York, New York • Bicester, England

[redacted]

THE COMPLETE WORD GAME DICTIONARY

Library of Congress Cataloging in Publication Data
Carruth, Gorton.
The complete word game dictionary.
1. Word games—Dictionaries. 2. Scrabble (Game)—
Glossaries, vocabularies, etc. I. Pulliam, Tom.
II. Title.
GV1507.W8C37 1984 793.73 84-4190
ISBN 0-87196-112-1

Printed in United States of America
10 9 8 7 6 5 4 3 2 1

Contents

Preface

The Complete Word Game Dictionary is a unique dictionary. Its size and comprehensiveness put it in a class by itself. It is equally useful for tournament play and for family fun at home. It contains 240,000 words specially selected to help players of nearly all kinds of word games, from Anagrams to Superghost. It is designed to be used during play as the standard arbiter of the ever-present *"challenge,"* which lies at the heart of nearly every parlor word game. But **The Complete Word Game Dictionary** is also designed to be studied before and after play to increase one's knowledge of those words that help make a player a winner.

Millions play word games. Of all parlor games, word games are, perhaps, the first that children develop an interest in. Whole families play word games together, not only because of their sharp competitiveness—Americans are a nation of competitors—but also because of their educational value. Even in the solitary activity of the inveterate crossword puzzler, there is something sharply competitive: can the puzzle be broken? And surely all crossword puzzlers believe the new words they learn will prove useful. Nearly everyone would agree that a knowledge of words can help bring success in life.

Word games have been played in our families for as long as we can remember. We were drawn into them as children and, with the passage of time, have had neither the inclination nor the willpower to break away from their siren attraction.

The earliest in our memories—one that we still engage in now and then—had neither name nor title, to our knowledge. It consisted of nothing more complex than selecting, in random fashion, a standard word, from either a dictionary or newspaper, which became the "base" word for all players. Any number of players could, and did, play. With the "base" word boldly lettered at the top of a sheet of paper, and with an egg timer at hand, each player attempted to form new words from the letters contained in the "base" word. Each letter of the "base" word was taken in turn as the initial letter for the new words formed by the competitors.

Scoring, after time was called on each letter, was simplicity itself. For each word on our list, we were awarded a point for each competitor who failed to have it on his list.

It was anything but a quiet game—"chaotic" is the word! Debates were both numerous and loud, and a dictionary was consulted every few moments in an attempt to decide arguments as to the acceptability of words. One of our grandfathers, who has long since departed, had a well-deserved reputation for being a wily, shrewd swindler, given to flimflamming with both charm and persuasion.

A favorite place for word games was in the family car. Here, during a long ride, endless games of Ghost were conducted by us children, with our parents usually acting as referees by determining what is, and what isn't, an acceptable word. Or, perhaps, we should have written, "...what *was*, and what *wasn't*, an acceptable word," for language changes, after all, and what was not considered standard fifty years ago may well be standard now. And that is what **The Complete Word Game Dictionary** is all about: it contains the largest available list of words carefully chosen for their suitability in word games. It serves as your referee.

We do not want to saturate you with personal memories. Suffice to say that in many homes word games, be they simple or complex, are an ongoing activity. We know of no survey or in-depth study that has been conducted on such matters, but we venture to say that in today's average home, one or more of the following is still played: crossword puzzles; Anagrams; Hangman; Guggenheim; Ghost or Superghost; and the word games sold under the Scrabble® brand.* (Just because we are addicted to certain word games, we cannot presume they are equally familiar to you. Some of the games we have mentioned may be favorites of yours, others relative strangers.)

Of all present-day word games, none has the acknowledged stature of the Scrabble® brand crossword games. Since it was first invented, more than forty years ago, it captured interest, year by year, until it became both international and classic among today's gamesters. The Scrabble® brand set rests alongside the Monopoly® set in most family rooms. Because it challenges personal aptitudes ranging from structural visualization to "knowing how to spell," Scrabble® contains some inherent complexities not present in most other word games. In recognition of this, **The Complete Word Game Dictionary** has been organized in such a way that its greatest value will be for the Scrabble® player, whether neophyte or of tournament caliber.

The number of commercial family word games on the market is growing by leaps and bounds—practically all of them absorbing. It is not our intent to develop, to any length, the rules and conduct of these games. Each has its distinctive intricacies and individual traits.

Royalty® and Probe®, for example, depend upon using lettered cards to form words, with graduated rewards to the player for his skill in doing so. In the latter game, especially, which depends upon intuitive deduction of concealed words formed by opponents, a great deal of guile and bluff is a characteristic element.

Other word games, such as Scribbage®, Perquackey®, and Boggle®

*Scrabble® is the registered trademark of Selchow & Righter Co. for its line of word games and entertainment services. Permission obtained.

use a number of lettered dice. After the player has thrown these dice at random, there is a strictly measured time period during which he must form bona-fide words from the letters the random throw has bestowed upon him. In Perquackey® and several others the score depends on the number of words of differing word length that the player can construct within the allowable time frame. In Scribbage®, words formed will intersect with other words, in much the style of crossword puzzles or the Scrabble® brand crossword games.

Traditional word games have rules and procedures that are almost universally recognized and accepted, even though the games themselves have many forms and variations. We will briefly describe a few.

Anagrams is played with lettered cards or tiles. These are normally exposed one at a time in the center of the playing area. Within a specified time period any player may form acceptable words before him by withdrawing the required letters from the letter mass in the center. Words formed by any player are subject to "capture" by any other player. The condition for such "capture" of another player's word is that the word must be lengthened by addition of one or more letters from the center. Generally it is further agreed that some basic change in form and meaning of the word is a prerequisite for a "capture."

Guggenheim is equally well known by the name Categories. Each player, in turn, names aloud one category (color, country, tree, sport, etc.), and these categories are listed by each player in a vertical column on a piece of paper. Another word is then selected, either at random or by agreement. This latter word is normally not very long, contains no uncommon letters, and has no repeated letters (e.g., *table, comet, dingo*). Each player writes the letters of this selected word as captions for columns to the right of the previously listed categories. Within a specified time each player attempts to write acceptable words for each category that begin with the initial letters assigned to each column. Let us say that the selected word is *table* and that one of the categories is "color." A player might then enter such words as *tan, azure, blue, lilac,* and *ecru.* Restrictions and limitations to both categories and solution words are normally by group agreement.

In Ghost each player in turn names aloud a letter. Letters thus announced are mentally visualized by all players as being written in the order in which they are announced. From the fourth letter on, each player attempts to avoid completing a valid word. Regardless of the word envisioned by the preceding player, he attempts to continue the letter formation by adding another—while at the same time not ending a word. Each player is prepared to name, on demand, the word he has in mind which contains the letters already formed.

As an example, if the letters BEA are presented to a player, he obviously wishes to avoid ending a word by choosing D, M, N, R, T, or U. Instead, he will, perhaps, add a G, forming *beag,* because he has "beagle" in mind. This, of course, puts the onus on the succeeding players to avoid the trap thus set.

Normally, a player ending a word or caught in a bluff becomes "one-third of a ghost" and begins a new word. The next time he falls into error he becomes "two-thirds of a ghost." After three such losses, this player is eliminated, while the game continues among the survivors until a single winner remains.

Superghost is merely an embellishment of Ghost in which a player may add his letter either *after* or *before* the letter sequence with which he is faced. For example, if he is faced with *stabl* and concerned about an impending loss, he can escape by prefixing an N, to form *nstable* (having "unstable" in mind). The trap may not work, however. The succeeding player may deviously prefix an O, because he is considering "constable." As you can see, this calls for an agile mind and an ample vocabulary and one does not loosely "challenge" without weighing the caliber of his opponents!

Hangman is essentially a game for two and is relatively simple. One player thinks of a word. He then represents this word on paper by a series of dashes, a dash for each letter of his preselected word. The other player attempts to guess the hidden word by naming letters of the alphabet, in any order he desires. Whenever he "hits" a letter in the concealed word, this letter is written on the paper in its appropriate position(s). The object is simply to guess correctly the preselected word before being "hanged" by a given number of incorrect guesses.

The Complete Word Game Dictionary has been developed as an aid and a sharpener of wits for the many who indulge in these and other word games.

Part I: *The Comprehensive Word List*

In practically all competitive word games there arises what is known as the "challenge." Most such games would be mild and placid were it not for this device. The word "challenge" is self-explanatory. One player has made use of a word; the opponent disagrees with its spelling or validity, or his doubts are sufficiently strong in this respect to warrant a "challenge" to the word involved.

The rules of most games make reference to the "challenge" but are not overly specific as to the course of action that follows. Scrabble® brand rules, for example, inherently refer to the "challenge." In the standard set for the home all the directions and rules, although very practical for social, family play, are nonetheless sketchy in defining the steps used in resolving the "challenge." When one progresses to tournaments involving the Scrabble® brand games he finds that they have fully detailed rules of their own, containing principles for resolving the "challenge." There are strong punitive measures for the violator.

Less complex games, such as Anagrams, contain directions regarding the permissibility and correctness of words that might enter the play. The rules of most word games permit the use of practically any word "found in a standard dictionary."

Sounds simple, doesn't it? What actually happens, however, in the heat of a hard-fought game, which may very well hinge on the resolution of such a "challenge"? The opponents must reach mutual agreement, before the contest, as to *what* edition of *what* dictionary will be used to settle such differences. While I may place great weight on a pet dictionary that I'm very familiar with, can I persuade you, my opponent, to accept it as the arbitrating medium—or do you prefer to use a *different* dictionary?

Although admittedly of value for day-to-day normal uses, the desk dictionaries of today are found lacking as mediators for today's word games, which are becoming increasingly complex. The home dictionary, be it hardbound or paperback, will usually contain something under 60,000 entries. And, because of its age, may not include words of a more modern origin. It *may* serve to clarify your game query—or it may *not*.

Even after a dictionary has been selected, peripheral questions still hinder the progress of the game. Are proper names permitted? How about foreign words? Abbreviations? Past tenses? Illogical plurals? Irregular endings? And so it goes.

These problems lead us back to the basic premise and purpose of **The Complete Word Game Dictionary**. The greater part of it is devoted to a Comprehensive Word List, which serves, in the speediest way possible, to decide the acceptability of any word that arises during your game, be it Anagrams, Ghost, or what have you.

Does it have advantages over a dictionary that is mutually acceptable to all players? We believe it does.

In looking up any word in this Comprehensive Word List at the time of a "challenge," you have only to skim through a single alphabetical list of 185,000 words to the exact word in question, be it commonplace or esoteric.

Not so with a dictionary. The major objective of a dictionary is to define and clarify the meaning of words, and the bulk of its space is occupied by definitive and descriptive text. Valuable though such information may be, the impatient player must wade through it to arrive at the word under challenge—all in the interests of a word game in which meanings play no role!

So the Comprehensive Word List is, first of all, the easiest, quickest source for deciding on the acceptability of a questionable word.

Is it complete, however? The answer is an overwhelming Yes. The Comprehensive Word List is not based upon any *single* dictionary. And, containing 185,000 entry words, it goes well beyond the scope of any desktop dictionary.

If a word is found in one dictionary but not in others, is it any less a "word"? We think not. We will not launch into a philosophical discussion about "what is a word." It remains largely a matter of editorial judgment. And we are relieving you, the player of word games, of becoming embroiled in this morass of judgment. When a "challenge" arises you have the simplest of all methods for resolving it—simply consult the Comprehensive Word List!

Let us further examine this Comprehensive Word List to discover what it contains—and what it does not contain.

Proper Names

Consider, for example, the use of proper nouns. It is up to you, the user, to determine whether your word game permits the use of proper names. Most do not. A certain game, for instance, specifies that "capitalized" words are not acceptable. This immediately throws us on the mercy of a "dictionary of your choice." If this dictionary should be the *Oxford English Dictionary*, the progress of the game is immediately halted—because *each* word listed therein is capitalized! At the other extreme, let's assume you've agreed upon the *Merriam-Webster International Dictionary*, 3rd edition, an equally reputable tome. You are now overwhelmed to find that "the sky's the limit"—with very rare exceptions, *no* main entry is capitalized! One has to pore through the descriptive text to discover that a given word is "usually capitalized," "sometimes capitalized," etc.

So, to relieve you of this dilemma, we have established our own editorial criterion. Because most word games prohibit their use, we have *excluded* from the List all words that are always capitalized.

From chance thumbing through the Comprehensive Word List, you may exclaim: "Aha! Caught you! You've included such words as Argentine, Inverness, and Telamon!" Be aware of the injunction stated before—we have omitted only those words that are *always* capitalized. You are well aware that "china" need not be capitalized when referring to porcelain ware, that "argentine" means "silvery," that "inverness" is an overcoat, and that "telamon" is an architectural figure.

At this point it will be helpful to restate our editorial principle to guide your use of this List. If any word in the List appears to you, at first glance, to be a proper, or capitalized, word, be assured that it is listed as a common, or noncapitalized, word in at least one source. As such, it deserves inclusion and warrants your using it freely in word games.

Foreign Words

Most major word games have some stated prohibition against the use of words "designated as foreign words." But one has only to scan representative dictionaries to see that they differ in their manner of designating foreign words. Some use special symbols antecedent to the main entry; others place the burden on the etymology to indicate the degree of "foreignness."

In the heat of a hotly contested word game you should not have to be concerned with such interpretations and decisions. The foreign word of yesterday is the English word of today. Such words as *confetti*, *junta*, *dirndl*, and *houri* are commonplace to most game players, without thought as to their being foreign in the near past. So we have taken the view that the only foreign words are those that are *solely* foreign in their use. If a word appears in an authoritative English dictionary, regardless of foreign designation by either symbol or text, we have included it in the Comprehensive Word List and consider it quite acceptable for word play.

Variant and Archaic Forms

The same can be said for variant spellings and archaic and obsolete words. Eventually many of these will fade from current usage completely and will be, undoubtedly, dropped from reputable dictionaries. Until such time, we *have* included archaic and variant entries. Indeed, it has been our experience that they add spice to the game and have presented us with an escape outlet just when we were being painted into a corner in many tight crossword games.

Long Words

You will quickly note many long words in the Comprehensive Word List. Realizing that in a game such as the Scrabble® brand product you have only seven letters to play with, you may be doubtful as to the value of, say, the twelve-letter words.

Yet, as all top-notch players know, major scores are made by interconnecting with existing letters on the board, one or more. While admittedly they are uncommon in normal social games, words of twelve letters (and more) are conceivable and actually occur in Scrabble® game patterns.

Now, this does *not* mean that we have included willy-nilly all long words that exist in reputable sources. We have exercised editorial prerogative. If a long word is based upon an internal "root" word of common vintage, chances are we have included it. The expert player closely inspects all existing long words already played on the board to visualize the possiblities of adding his letters either fore or aft—or both. So, don't be frightened by the appearance of overlong words. They are there because the root word may easily be played in normal competition—and it can be elaborated on very easily by the canny player, with sizable dividends.

Verb Endings, Plurals, and Adverbial Forms

Let us now consider the treatment of verb endings, plurals, and adverbial forms. They customarily present a dilemma in all kinds of word play in which the "challenge" is a factor. The rules of most word games are not sufficiently explicit to gauge easily the permissibility of words in these categories. Are *forgetting, skillets,* and *nicely* acceptable? Some of our most heated word struggles have arisen during sharply contested battles of Superghost. In this game, perhaps more than others, the player who is trapped in an untenable position is strongly tempted to "weasel out" by use of a hastily contrived gerundive or participial form.

The Scrabble® brand crossword game product has progressed furthest in refining the rules covering word acceptability. At both the home and tournament level, normal inflected forms are acceptable, whether or not they are specifically printed in standard dictionaries.

These include the past tense, past participle, and present participle of verbs, and the plural of nouns. In most dictionaries such forms are entered in boldface only where there is some irregularity in spelling or form. This broad rule affords free license for the use of *-s, -es, -ed,* and *-ing;* they are understood to be permissible by the rules of normal usage and acceptance.

Comparative (*-er*) and superlative (*-est*) forms of adjectives are a somewhat different matter. One-syllable adjectives and their comparative and superlative forms (*strong, stronger, strongest*) are presumed to be acceptable, whether actually listed in the dictionary or not. Multisyllable adjectives (*healthy*) are permissible only if the comparative and superlative forms actually appear in the agreed-upon authority.

The Comprehensive Word List frees you from the need for personal interpretation and judgment. It does *not* list *all* simple plurals that can be formed merely by the addition of *-s* or *-es*, although a great many *are* included. But it liberally includes inflected forms and unusual plural forms, even those that you might have difficulty in ferreting out of your dictionary. For example, you can readily and quickly find the plural forms of such words as the following:

feis = feiseanna
os = ora
drostdy = drostden
boomslang = boomslange

To summarize briefly: we have compiled the List to serve as a handy, easy-to-use authority for *your* word game or games. It runs the gamut from the simple, short word to the longer, more exotic word. Its completeness ranges beyond the scope of any single standard dictionary that might otherwise serve as your arbiter. And the time saved by its use is significant. During a "challenge" a player does not normally have the time or patience to wade through extensive definitive text in order to resolve the question of permissibility. With **The Complete Word Game Dictionary** the player consults the List: it is either there or it is not—it's that simple!

Definitions

One immediately apparent characteristic of the Comprehensive Word List is the absence of definitions. This is due neither to oversight nor laziness, but to a decision on our part that was influenced by economy. We see no significant value or need for definitions in most word games. The basic consideration is: is the debatable word valid or not?

Some excellent books that serve as arbiters for word-game play do include definitions. But the users/players, to our knowledge, do not employ these definitions to edify the mind. The expressed purpose of the definitions is no more than to clarify the part of speech, consequently the admissibility of plurals or inflected forms. The Comprehensive Word List already contains most inflected forms as well as unusual plurals. Including definitions as well would have been, indeed, a labor of love without a corresponding benefit for the user.

Part II. *The High-Scoring Word Lists*

In recognition of the Scrabble® brand game's more complex play than that of other word games, **The Complete Word Game Dictionary** contains a number of Specialized Lists. They will have greatest value, no doubt, for the Scrabble® player; however, their value extends, to a lesser degree, to other word games as well.

The expert Scrabble® player is aware that his success, in large degree, hinges upon his judicious use and opportune placement of high-scoring letters. These are, of course: Z (10 points); Q (10 points); J (8 points); and X (8 points). Consequently, the high-scoring lists of Part II have been framed solely around words containing these four key letters.

Part II has four sections, one for J, Q, X, and Z, and each contains all words with that letter. Within these sections the lists are arranged first by word length and then by type of list. There are three types of lists: alphabetical, positional, and scoring, and they appear in that order.

Alphabetical Lists

For any one of these key letters—say, J —there first appear the *Alphabetical Lists,* by word length, of acceptable words containing that letter. Similar lists, of course, appear for Z, Q, and X.

Their greatest value to you, as a player, lies in your becoming familiar with as many of the two-letter and three-letter words as you can. Store them in the warehouse of your mind for quick retrieval and use under competitive conditions. Most experts will readily concede that familiarity with two- and three-letter words is a key factor in top-quality play. They represent the essential links in the interlocking process of forming new words in conjunction with those already appearing on the board.

Much depends, to be sure, on whether you are following an offensive or a defensive tack. Your game tactic may be to secure so tightly compacted a pattern on the board that your opponent is sorely strained to find a projecting cornice on which to hang his next contemplated word. Only with an extensive knowledge of two- and three-letter words can you fully accomplish this. So, scan the Lists often—make these short words a commonplace part of your playing arsenal!

Positional Lists

You will also find that for each of the key letters (Z, Q, J, and X) we have prepared *Positional Lists,* by word length. You can readily visualize the usefulness of such Lists beyond their obvious use in Scrabble®. Let us presume you are an avid crossword puzzler—yet one who is not above the use of research sources when you are in a quandary. If you are seeking an elusive six-letter word having Z in the fifth position, you can quickly find a number of prospects in these Positional Lists. Of the several words you thus locate, you can further pin down your specific word by seeing which of these has, say, L in the second position.

Scoring Order Lists

Finally we have included for each of the key letters a *Scoring Order List.* Here the words are listed in the order of the total Scrabble® score of all letters, arranged by word length.

A word of clarification may be in order here. In these Lists you may see a word such as "jazz." You may feel the impulse to exclaim: "Poor guys!

They don't seem to realize that there's only a single Z tile in a Scrabble® set!" But in any listed word that contains a given letter with greater frequency than permitted by the letter distribution in Scrabble®, we are presuming that the "excess" letter is formed by a blank (wild) tile. In such cases, this superfluous letter has *not* been included in the score for that word—just as during actual play a blank tile generates no score of its own.

To repeat, the user who familiarizes himself with a variety of two-letter and three-letter words, and further fortifies himself with an awareness of some of the higher-scoring words, is well on the way to becoming a more effective Scrabble® contestant.

Among the many variations of the Scrabble® brand product is solo or solitaire Scrabble®. It is not our intent to describe its nuances here, but many expert players are stimulated by spending hours alone at a board, contriving patterns and word combinations that will bear fruit in subsequent head-to-head competition. Many make a personal challenge of seeing just how artful they can become with such constructions and what heights in scoring they can achieve as a result.

Perhaps you are a true logophile—one whose interest in words extends well beyond the confines of any single word game. You and others like you are blessed with a quarterly publication of specialized appeal, *Word Ways: The Journal of Recreational Linguistics.* It is subscribed to, and read voraciously, by many who relish the appearance, spelling, derivation, sound, use, and peculiarities of words and word forms. Information relative to this publication can be secured by contacting the editor: A. Ross Eckler, Spring Valley Road, Morristown, New Jersey 07960. Many of the publication's readers and contributors have deeply involved themselves in the Scrabble® brand games in just the manner we described above, by examining the gaming possibilities of high-scoring words and interesting patterns. You and I, as average players, should not be unduly dismayed to learn that *Word Ways* contributors have constructed a theoretically possible Scrabble® crossword game with a combined score of 4,142 points for two players!

If that is not sufficient to boggle the senses, consider further that a *single play* can produce a score of 1804 points! (The key word is *benzoxycamphors.*)

The Complete Word Game Dictionary is intended to be used. In any word game in which the "challenge" arises, it is meant to be a handy, easy-to-use arbiter. If you familiarize yourself with the contents of this volume, and actually use it for its intended purposes, it cannot help but promote your progress as a gamester—without diluting the fun!

Tom Pulliam
Gorton Carruth

PART I

Comprehensive Word List

A

AA
AABEC
AAL
AALII
AAM
AAR
AARDVARK
AARDWOLF
AASVOGEL
ABA
ABACA
ABACATE
ABACAXI
ABACAY
ABACI
ABACINATE
ABACINATION
ABACISCUS
ABACIST
ABACK
ABACOT
ABACTINAL
ABACTINALLY
ABACTION
ABACTOR
ABACULI
ABACULUS
ABACUS
ABACUSES
ABAD
ABADA
ABADEJO
ABADENGO
ABADI
ABADIA
ABAFF
ABAFT
ABAISANCE
ABAISER
ABAISSE
ABAISSED
ABAKA
ABALIENATE
ABALIENATED
ABALIENATION
ABALONE
ABAMPERE
ABAND
ABANDON
ABANDONED
ABANDONEDLY
ABANDONER
ABANDONMENT
ABANDUM
ABANGA
ABAPTISTON
ABAPTISTUM
ABARTICULAR
ABARTICULATION
ABAS
ABASE
ABASED
ABASEDLY
ABASEDNESS
ABASEMENT
ABASER
ABASH
ABASHED
ABASHEDLY
ABASHING
ABASHLESS
ABASHLESSLY
ABASHMENT
ABASIA
ABASING
ABASIO
ABASK
ABASSI
ABASTARDIZE
ABATA
ABATABLE
ABATE
ABATED
ABATEMENT
ABATER
ABATI
ABATING
ABATIS
ABATON
ABATOR
ABATTIS
ABATTISED
ABATTOIR
ABATTOIRS
ABATTU
ABATTUE
ABATURE
ABAVE
ABAWE
ABAXIAL
ABAXILE
ABAYAH
ABAZE
ABB
ABBA
ABBACIES
ABBACY
ABBAS
ABBASI
ABBASSI
ABBATE
ABBATIAL
ABBATICAL
ABBAYE
ABBE
ABBESS
ABBEST
ABBEY
ABBEYS
ABBEYSTEDE
ABBOGADA
ABBOT
ABBOTCIES
ABBOTCY
ABBOTSHIP
ABBOZZO
ABBREVIATE
ABBREVIATED
ABBREVIATELY
ABBREVIATING
ABBREVIATION
ABBREVIATOR
ABBREVIATORY
ABBREVIATURE
ABCOULOMB
ABDAL
ABDALI
ABDAT
ABDEST
ABDICABLE
ABDICANT
ABDICATE
ABDICATED
ABDICATING
ABDICATION
ABDICATIVE
ABDICATOR
ABDITIVE
ABDITORY
ABDOMEN
ABDOMINAL
ABDOMINALES
ABDOMINALIAN
ABDOMINALLY
ABDOMINALS
ABDOMINOUS
ABDUCE
ABDUCENS
ABDUCENT
ABDUCT
ABDUCTED
ABDUCTION
ABDUCTOR
ABE
ABEAM
ABEAR
ABEARANCE
ABECEDAIRE
ABECEDARIA
ABECEDARIAN
ABECEDARIES
ABECEDARIUM
ABECEDARIUS
ABECEDARY
ABED
ABEEN
ABEGGE
ABEIGH
ABELE
ABELITE
ABELMOSK
ABELMUSK
ABELTREE
ABENTERIC
ABEPITHYMIA
ABERDAVINE
ABERDEVINE
ABERDUVINE
ABERR
ABERRANCE
ABERRANCY
ABERRANT
ABERRATE
ABERRATED
ABERRATING
ABERRATION
ABERRATIONAL
ABERRATOR
ABERROMETER
ABERROSCOPE
ABESSIVE
ABET
ABETMENT
ABETO
ABETTAL
ABETTED
ABETTER
ABETTING
ABETTOR
ABEVACUATION
ABEY
ABEYANCE
ABEYANCY
ABEYANT
ABFARAD
ABHAL
ABHENRY
ABHINAYA
ABHISEKA
ABHOMINABLE
ABHOR
ABHORRED
ABHORRENCE
ABHORRENCY
ABHORRENT
ABHORRENTLY
ABHORRER
ABHORRIBLE
ABHORRING
ABIDAL
ABIDANCE
ABIDDEN
ABIDE
ABIDED
ABIDER
ABIDING
ABIDINGLY
ABIDINGNESS
ABIEGH
ABIENCE
ABIETATE
ABIETENE
ABIETIC
ABIETINEOUS
ABIETINIC
ABIGAIL
ABIGAILSHIP
ABIGEI
ABIGEUS
ABILAO
ABILITIES
ABILITY
ABILLA
ABILO
ABIME
ABINTESTATE
ABIOGENESIS
ABIOGENETIC
ABIOGENIST
ABIOLOGICAL
ABIOLOGY
ABIOSIS
ABIOTIC
ABIOTROPHIC
ABIOTROPHY
ABIR
ABIRRITANT
ABIRRITATE
ABIRRITATED
ABIRRITATING
ABIRRITATION
ABIRRITATIVE
ABISTON
ABIURET
ABJECT
ABJECTEDNESS
ABJECTION
ABJECTIVE
ABJECTLY
ABJECTNESS
ABJOINT
ABJUDGE
ABJUDICATE
ABJUDICATION
ABJUDICATOR
ABJUNCTIVE
ABJURATION
ABJURATORY
ABJURE
ABJURED
ABJUREMENT
ABJURER
ABJURING
ABKAR
ABKARI
ABKARY
ABLACH
ABLACTATE
ABLACTATION
ABLARE
ABLASTEMIC
ABLASTIN
ABLASTOUS
ABLATE
ABLATION
ABLATITIOUS
ABLATIVAL
ABLATIVE
ABLATOR
ABLAUT
ABLAZE
ABLE
ABLEEZE
ABLEGATE
ABLEGATION
ABLENESS
ABLEPHARIA
ABLEPHAROUS
ABLEPSIA
ABLEPSY
ABLEPTICAL
ABLEPTICALLY
ABLER
ABLEST
ABLEWHACKETS
ABLINGS
ABLINS
ABLOOM
ABLOW
ABLUDE
ABLUENT
ABLUSH
ABLUTION
ABLUTIONARY
ABLY
ABNEGATE
ABNEGATED
ABNEGATING
ABNEGATION
ABNEGATIVE
ABNEGATOR
ABNERVAL
ABNET
ABNEURAL
ABNORMAL
ABNORMALITIES
ABNORMALITY
ABNORMALIZE
ABNORMALLY
ABNORMALNESS
ABNORMITIES
ABNORMITY
ABNORMOUS
ABOARD
ABOCOCKET
ABODAH
ABODE
ABODED
ABODEMENT
ABODING
ABOGADO
ABOGADOS
ABOHM
ABOIDEAU
ABOIDEAUS
ABOIDEAUX
ABOIL
ABOITEAU
ABOLETE
ABOLISH
ABOLISHABLE
ABOLISHED
ABOLISHER
ABOLISHING
ABOLISHMENT

ABOLITION
ABOLITIONARY
ABOLITIONISM
ABOLITIONIST
ABOLITIONIZE
ABOLLA
ABOLLAE
ABOMA
ABOMASUM
ABOMASUS
ABOMINABLE
ABOMINABLY
ABOMINATE
ABOMINATED
ABOMINATING
ABOMINATION
ABOMINATOR
ABONDANCE
ABONNE
ABONNEMENT
ABOO
ABOON
ABORAD
ABORAL
ABORALLY
ABORD
ABORIGINAL
ABORIGINALLY
ABORIGINARY
ABORIGINE
ABORIGINES
ABORT
ABORTED
ABORTICIDE
ABORTIENT
ABORTIN
ABORTION
ABORTIONAL
ABORTIONIST
ABORTIVE
ABORTIVELY
ABORTIVENESS
ABORTUS
ABOUCHEMENT
ABOUGHT
ABOULIA
ABOULIC
ABOUND
ABOUNDING
ABOUNDINGLY
ABOUT
ABOUTS
ABOVE
ABOVEBOARD
ABOVEDECK
ABOVEGROUND
ABOVEPROOF
ABOVESTAIRS
ABOW
ABOX
ABRA
ABRACADABRA
ABRACHIA
ABRADANT
ABRADE
ABRADED
ABRADER
ABRADING
ABRAID
ABRANCHIAL
ABRANCHIAN
ABRANCHIATE
ABRANCHIOUS
ABRASAX
ABRASE
ABRASED
ABRASH
ABRASING
ABRASIOMETER
ABRASION
ABRASIVE
ABRASIVES
ABRASTOL
ABRAUM
ABRAXAS
ABRAZO
ABREACT
ABREACTION
ABREAST
ABREED
ABREGE
ABREID
ABRENOUNCE
ABRENUNCIATE
ABRET
ABREUVOIR
ABRI
ABRICO
ABRICOT
ABRIDGABLE
ABRIDGE
ABRIDGEABLE
ABRIDGED
ABRIDGEDLY
ABRIDGEMENT
ABRIDGER
ABRIDGING
ABRIDGMENT
ABRIM
ABRIN
ABRINE
ABRIS
ABRISTLE
ABROACH
ABROAD
ABROCOME
ABROGABLE
ABROGATE
ABROGATED
ABROGATING
ABROGATION
ABROGATIVE
ABROGATOR
ABRONIA
ABROOD
ABROOK
ABROTANUM
ABROTIN
ABROTINE
ABRUPT
ABRUPTEDLY
ABRUPTION
ABRUPTLY
ABRUPTNESS
ABSAROKITE
ABSCESS
ABSCESSED
ABSCESSES
ABSCESSION
ABSCESSROOT
ABSCIND
ABSCISE
ABSCISED
ABSCISING
ABSCISS
ABSCISSA
ABSCISSAE
ABSCISSAS
ABSCISSION
ABSCONCE
ABSCOND
ABSCONDED
ABSCONDEDLY
ABSCONDENCE
ABSCONDER
ABSEIL
ABSENCE
ABSENT
ABSENTATION
ABSENTEE
ABSENTEEISM
ABSENTER
ABSENTLY
ABSENTMENT
ABSENTMINDED
ABSENTMINDEDNESS
ABSENTNESS
ABSINTH
ABSINTHE
ABSINTHIAL
ABSINTHIAN
ABSINTHIATE
ABSINTHIATED
ABSINTHIATING
ABSINTHIC
ABSINTHIIN
ABSINTHIN
ABSINTHINE
ABSINTHISM
ABSINTHISMIC
ABSINTHIUM
ABSISTOS
ABSIT
ABSOLUTE
ABSOLUTELY
ABSOLUTENESS
ABSOLUTION
ABSOLUTISM
ABSOLUTIST
ABSOLUTISTA
ABSOLUTISTIC
ABSOLUTIVE
ABSOLUTORY
ABSOLVABLE
ABSOLVATORY
ABSOLVE
ABSOLVED
ABSOLVENT
ABSOLVER
ABSOLVING
ABSOLVITOR
ABSOLVITORY
ABSONANT
ABSORB
ABSORBABILITY
ABSORBABLE
ABSORBANCY
ABSORBED
ABSORBEDLY
ABSORBEDNESS
ABSORBENCY
ABSORBENT
ABSORBER
ABSORBING
ABSORBINGLY
ABSORBITION
ABSORPT
ABSORPTANCE
ABSORPTION
ABSORPTIVE
ABSORPTIVITY
ABSQUATULATE
ABSTAIN
ABSTAINER
ABSTAINMENT
ABSTEMIOUS
ABSTEMIOUSLY
ABSTENTION
ABSTENTIOUS
ABSTERGE
ABSTERGED
ABSTERGENT
ABSTERGING
ABSTERSION
ABSTERSIVE
ABSTINENCE
ABSTINENCY
ABSTINENT
ABSTINENTIAL
ABSTINENTLY
ABSTORT
ABSTRACT
ABSTRACTED
ABSTRACTEDLY
ABSTRACTEDNESS
ABSTRACTER
ABSTRACTION
ABSTRACTIVE
ABSTRACTIVELY
ABSTRACTIVENESS
ABSTRACTLY
ABSTRACTNESS
ABSTRACTS
ABSTRAHENT
ABSTRICT
ABSTRICTED
ABSTRICTION
ABSTRUDE
ABSTRUSE
ABSTRUSELY
ABSTRUSENESS
ABSTRUSION
ABSTRUSITIES
ABSTRUSITY
ABSUME
ABSUMPTION
ABSURD
ABSURDITIES
ABSURDITY
ABSURDLY
ABSURDNESS
ABSURDUM
ABTERMINAL
ABTHANAGE
ABU
ABUCCO
ABULEIA
ABULIA
ABULIC
ABULOMANIA
ABULYEIT
ABUNA
ABUNDANCE
ABUNDANCY
ABUNDANT
ABUNDANTLY
ABUNE
ABURA
ABURABOZU
ABURAGIRI
ABURST
ABURTON
ABUSABLE
ABUSAGE
ABUSE
ABUSED
ABUSEE
ABUSER
ABUSING
ABUSION
ABUSIOUS
ABUSIVE
ABUSIVELY
ABUSIVENESS
ABUT
ABUTTAL
ABUTTALS
ABUTTED
ABUTTER
ABUTTING
ABUZZ
ABVOLT
ABWAB
ABWATT
ABY
ABYE
ABYSM
ABYSMAL
ABYSMALLY
ABYSS
ABYSSAL
ACACATECHIN
ACACATECHOL
ACACETIN
ACACIA
ACACIIN
ACACIN
ACACINE
ACADEME
ACADEMIA
ACADEMIAL
ACADEMIAN
ACADEMIC
ACADEMICAL
ACADEMICALLY
ACADEMICALS
ACADEMICIAN
ACADEMICISM
ACADEMIE
ACADEMIES
ACADEMISM
ACADEMIST
ACADEMITE
ACADEMIZE
ACADEMIZED
ACADEMIZING
ACADEMY
ACADIALITE
ACAENA
ACAJOU
ACALE
ACALEPH
ACALEPHAN
ACALEPHE
ACALEPHOID
ACALYCAL
ACALYCINE
ACALYCINOUS
ACALYCULATE
ACALYPTRATE
ACAMPSIA
ACANA
ACANACEOUS
ACANTH
ACANTHA
ACANTHACEOUS
ACANTHAD
ACANTHI
ACANTHIAL
ACANTHIN
ACANTHINE
ACANTHION
ACANTHITE
ACANTHODEAN
ACANTHODIAN
ACANTHOLOGY
ACANTHOLYSIS
ACANTHOMA
ACANTHON
ACANTHOPOD
ACANTHOPORE
ACANTHOSIS
ACANTHOUS
ACANTHUS
ACANTHUSES

ACAPNIA
ACAPNIAL
ACAPSULAR
ACAPU
ACAPULCO
ACARA
ACARDIA
ACARDIAC
ACARDITE
ACARI
ACARIAN
ACARIASIS
ACARIATRE
ACARICIDAL
ACARICIDE
ACARID
ACARIDOMATIA
ACARIFORM
ACARINE
ACAROCECIDIA
ACAROID
ACAROL
ACAROLOGIST
ACAROLOGY
ACAROPHILOUS
ACAROPHOBIA
ACAROTOXIC
ACARPELLOUS
ACARPELOUS
ACARPOUS
ACATALECTIC
ACATALEPSIA
ACATALEPSY
ACATALEPTIC
ACATAPHASIA
ACATAPOSIS
ACATASTASIA
ACATASTATIC
ACATE
ACATER
ACATERY
ACATES
ACATHARSIA
ACATHARSY
ACATHOLIC
ACAUDAL
ACAUDATE
ACAULESCENCE
ACAULESCENT
ACAULINE
ACAULOSE
ACAULOUS
ACCA
ACCABLE
ACCADEMIA
ACCEDE
ACCEDED
ACCEDENCE
ACCEDER
ACCEDING
ACCELERABLE
ACCELERANDO
ACCELERANT
ACCELERATE
ACCELERATED
ACCELERATEDLY
ACCELERATING
ACCELERATION
ACCELERATIVE
ACCELERATOR
ACCELERATORY
ACCEND
ACCENDIBLE
ACCENSION
ACCENSOR
ACCENT
ACCENTED
ACCENTOR
ACCENTUABLE
ACCENTUAL
ACCENTUALITY
ACCENTUALLY
ACCENTUATE
ACCENTUATED
ACCENTUATING
ACCENTUATION
ACCENTUATOR
ACCENTUS
ACCEPT
ACCEPTABILITY
ACCEPTABLE
ACCEPTABLENESS
ACCEPTABLY
ACCEPTANCE
ACCEPTANCY
ACCEPTANT
ACCEPTATION
ACCEPTED
ACCEPTEDLY
ACCEPTER
ACCEPTILATE
ACCEPTILATED
ACCEPTILATING
ACCEPTILATION
ACCEPTION
ACCEPTIVE
ACCEPTOR
ACCERSE
ACCERSITION
ACCERSITOR
ACCESS
ACCESSARILY
ACCESSARY
ACCESSIBILITY
ACCESSIBLE
ACCESSIBLY
ACCESSION
ACCESSIONAL
ACCESSIONED
ACCESSIONING
ACCESSIT
ACCESSIVE
ACCESSIVELY
ACCESSLESS
ACCESSORIAL
ACCESSORIES
ACCESSORII
ACCESSORILY
ACCESSORIUS
ACCESSORY
ACCIACCATURA
ACCIDENCE
ACCIDENCIES
ACCIDENCY
ACCIDENT
ACCIDENTAL
ACCIDENTALITY
ACCIDENTALLY
ACCIDENTARILY
ACCIDENTARY
ACCIDENTED
ACCIDENTIAL
ACCIDENTLY
ACCIDIA
ACCIDIE
ACCINGE
ACCINGED
ACCINGING
ACCIPITER
ACCIPITRAL
ACCIPITRARY
ACCIPITRINE
ACCIPTER
ACCISMUS
ACCITE
ACCLAIM
ACCLAIMABLE
ACCLAIMER
ACCLAMATION
ACCLAMATOR
ACCLAMATORY
ACCLIMATABLE
ACCLIMATE
ACCLIMATED
ACCLIMATING
ACCLIMATION
ACCLIMATIZE
ACCLIMATIZED
ACCLIMATIZER
ACCLIMATIZING
ACCLIMATURE
ACCLINAL
ACCLINATE
ACCLIVITIES
ACCLIVITOUS
ACCLIVITY
ACCLIVOUS
ACCLOY
ACCOAST
ACCOIL
ACCOLADE
ACCOLADED
ACCOLENT
ACCOLL
ACCOLLE
ACCOLLEE
ACCOMBINATION
ACCOMMODABLE
ACCOMMODATE
ACCOMMODATED
ACCOMMODATING
ACCOMMODATION
ACCOMMODATIVE
ACCOMMODATOR
ACCOMPANIED
ACCOMPANIER
ACCOMPANIMENT
ACCOMPANIST
ACCOMPANY
ACCOMPANYING
ACCOMPANYIST
ACCOMPLETIVE
ACCOMPLICE
ACCOMPLICITY
ACCOMPLISH
ACCOMPLISHED
ACCOMPLISHER
ACCOMPLISHING
ACCOMPLISHMENT
ACCOMPT
ACCON
ACCORD
ACCORDABLE
ACCORDANCE
ACCORDANCY
ACCORDANT
ACCORDANTLY
ACCORDATURA
ACCORDER
ACCORDING
ACCORDINGLY
ACCORDION
ACCORDIONIST
ACCORPORATE
ACCOST
ACCOSTABLE
ACCOSTED
ACCOUCHE
ACCOUCHEMENT
ACCOUCHEUR
ACCOUCHEUSE
ACCOUNT
ACCOUNTABILITY
ACCOUNTABLE
ACCOUNTABLY
ACCOUNTANCY
ACCOUNTANT
ACCOUNTING
ACCOUNTS
ACCOUPLE
ACCOUTER
ACCOUTERED
ACCOUTERING
ACCOUTERMENT
ACCOUTERMENTS
ACCOUTRE
ACCOUTRED
ACCOUTREMENT
ACCOUTRING
ACCOY
ACCOYED
ACCOYING
ACCREDIT
ACCREDITATION
ACCREDITED
ACCREDITING
ACCRESCE
ACCRESCENCE
ACCRESCENT
ACCRETE
ACCRETED
ACCRETING
ACCRETION
ACCRETIONARY
ACCRETIVE
ACCROACH
ACCROACHED
ACCROACHING
ACCRUAL
ACCRUE
ACCRUED
ACCRUEMENT
ACCRUER
ACCRUING
ACCUBATION
ACCUBITA
ACCUBITUM
ACCUBITUS
ACCUEIL
ACCULTURAL
ACCULTURATE
ACCULTURATION
ACCULTURIZE
ACCUMB
ACCUMBENCY
ACCUMBENT
ACCUMBER
ACCUMULABLE
ACCUMULATE
ACCUMULATED
ACCUMULATING
ACCUMULATION
ACCUMULATIVE
ACCUMULATIVELY
ACCUMULATIVENESS
ACCUMULATOR
ACCURACY
ACCURATE
ACCURATELY
ACCURATENESS
ACCURRE
ACCURSE
ACCURSED
ACCURSEDLY
ACCURSEDNESS
ACCURSING
ACCURST
ACCUSABLE
ACCUSABLY
ACCUSAL
ACCUSANT
ACCUSATION
ACCUSATIVAL
ACCUSATIVE
ACCUSATIVELY
ACCUSATORIAL
ACCUSATORY
ACCUSATRIX
ACCUSE
ACCUSED
ACCUSER
ACCUSING
ACCUSINGLY
ACCUSIVE
ACCUSTOM
ACCUSTOMED
ACCUSTOMEDLY
ACCUSTOMING
ACCUSTOMIZE
ACCUSTOMIZED
ACCUSTOMIZING
ACE
ACEANTHRENE
ACECAFFIN
ACECAFFINE
ACECONITIC
ACED
ACEDIA
ACEDIAMIN
ACEDIAMINE
ACEDIAST
ACEITE
ACEITUNA
ACELDAMA
ACEMILA
ACENAPHTHENE
ACENSUADA
ACENSUADOR
ACENTRIC
ACENTROUS
ACEOLOGIC
ACEOLOGY
ACEPHAL
ACEPHALINE
ACEPHALIST
ACEPHALOCYST
ACEPHALOUS
ACEPHALUS
ACEPOTS
ACEQUIA
ACEQUIADOR
ACERACEOUS
ACERATE
ACERATED
ACERATHERE
ACERATOSIS
ACERB
ACERBATE
ACERBATED
ACERBATING
ACERBIC
ACERBITIES
ACERBITUDE
ACERBITY
ACERDOL
ACERIN
ACEROLA
ACEROSE
ACEROUS
ACERRA
ACERTANNIN
ACERVAL
ACERVATE
ACERVATELY
ACERVATIM

ACERVATION
ACERVATIVE
ACERVOSE
ACERVULI
ACERVULINE
ACERVULUS
ACES
ACESCENCE
ACESCENCY
ACESCENT
ACESODYNE
ACETA
ACETABLE
ACETABULA
ACETABULAR
ACETABULUM
ACETAL
ACETALDEHYDE
ACETALDOL
ACETALIZE
ACETAMID
ACETAMIDE
ACETAMIDINE
ACETAMIDO
ACETAMINOL
ACETANILID
ACETANILIDE
ACETANION
ACETANISIDE
ACETARIOUS
ACETARSONE
ACETATE
ACETATED
ACETATION
ACETENYL
ACETIAM
ACETIC
ACETIFICATION
ACETIFIED
ACETIFIER
ACETIFY
ACETIFYING
ACETIMETER
ACETIMETRY
ACETIN
ACETINE
ACETOACETATE
ACETOACETIC
ACETOBENZOIC
ACETOCHLORAL
ACETOIN
ACETOL
ACETOLYSIS
ACETOLYTIC
ACETOMETER
ACETOMETRY
ACETOMORPHIN
ACETONAEMIA
ACETONAEMIC
ACETONATE
ACETONATION
ACETONE
ACETONEMIA
ACETONEMIC
ACETONIC
ACETONITRILE
ACETONIZATION
ACETONIZE
ACETONURIA
ACETONYL
ACETOPHENIN
ACETOPHENINE
ACETOPHENONE
ACETOPYRIN
ACETOPYRINE
ACETOSE
ACETOSITY
ACETOSOLUBLE
ACETOTOLUID
ACETOTOLUIDE
ACETOUS
ACETOXIM
ACETOXIME
ACETOXYL
ACETRACT
ACETTOLUIDE
ACETUM
ACETURIC
ACETYL
ACETYLAMINE
ACETYLATE
ACETYLATED
ACETYLATING
ACETYLATION
ACETYLATOR
ACETYLBIURET
ACETYLENE
ACETYLENIC
ACETYLENYL
ACETYLGLYCIN
ACETYLIC
ACETYLID
ACETYLIDE
ACETYLIODIDE
ACETYLIZABLE
ACETYLIZATION
ACETYLIZE
ACETYLIZER
ACETYLSALOL
ACETYLTHYMOL
ACETYLUREA
ACH
ACHAETOUS
ACHAFE
ACHAGE
ACHALASIA
ACHAR
ACHARNE
ACHARNEMENT
ACHARYA
ACHATE
ACHATES
ACHATOUR
ACHE
ACHED
ACHEILIA
ACHEILOUS
ACHEIRIA
ACHEIROUS
ACHEIRUS
ACHENE
ACHENIA
ACHENIAL
ACHENIUM
ACHENOCARP
ACHENODIA
ACHENODIUM
ACHER
ACHETE
ACHEWEED
ACHIEVABLE
ACHIEVE
ACHIEVED
ACHIEVEMENT
ACHIEVEMENTS
ACHIEVER
ACHIEVING
ACHIGAN
ACHILARY
ACHILL
ACHILLEIN
ACHILLEINE
ACHILLODYNIA
ACHIME
ACHING
ACHINGLY
ACHIOTE
ACHIR
ACHIRA
ACHLAMYDATE
ACHLAMYDEOUS
ACHLORHYDRIA
ACHLOROPSIA
ACHOLIA
ACHOLIC
ACHOLOUS
ACHOLURIA
ACHOLURIC
ACHONDRITE
ACHONDRITIC
ACHOR
ACHORDAL
ACHORDATE
ACHRAS
ACHREE
ACHROACYTE
ACHROGLOBIN
ACHROITE
ACHROMA
ACHROMACYTE
ACHROMASIA
ACHROMAT
ACHROMATE
ACHROMATIC
ACHROMATIN
ACHROMATINIC
ACHROMATISM
ACHROMATIZE
ACHROMATIZED
ACHROMATOPE
ACHROMATOSIS
ACHROMATOUS
ACHROMATURIA
ACHROMIA
ACHROMIC
ACHROMOUS
ACHROOUS
ACHROPSIA
ACHT
ACHTEHALBER
ACHTEL
ACHTELTHALER
ACHTER
ACHTERVELD
ACHUETE
ACHY
ACHYLIA
ACHYLOUS
ACHYMIA
ACHYMOUS
ACICHLORID
ACICHLORIDE
ACICULA
ACICULAE
ACICULAR
ACICULARLY
ACICULATE
ACICULATED
ACICULUM
ACICULUMS
ACID
ACIDAEMIA
ACIDEMIA
ACIDER
ACIDIC
ACIDIFEROUS
ACIDIFIABLE
ACIDIFIANT
ACIDIFIC
ACIDIFIED
ACIDIFIER
ACIDIFY
ACIDIFYING
ACIDIMETER
ACIDIMETRIC
ACIDIMETRY
ACIDITE
ACIDITIES
ACIDITY
ACIDIZE
ACIDLY
ACIDNESS
ACIDOLOGY
ACIDOPHIL
ACIDOPHILE
ACIDOPHILIC
ACIDOPHILOUS
ACIDOPHILUS
ACIDOSIS
ACIDOTIC
ACIDPROOF
ACIDULATE
ACIDULATED
ACIDULATING
ACIDULATION
ACIDULENT
ACIDULOUS
ACIER
ACIERAGE
ACIERATE
ACIERATED
ACIERATING
ACIERATION
ACIES
ACIFORM
ACINACEOUS
ACINACES
ACINACIFORM
ACINARIOUS
ACINETAE
ACING
ACINI
ACINIC
ACINIFORM
ACINOSE
ACINOTUBULAR
ACINOUS
ACINUS
ACIPENSERID
ACIPENSERINE
ACIPENSEROID
ACIURGY
ACKEE
ACKER
ACKEY
ACKMAN
ACKMEN
ACKNEW
ACKNOW
ACKNOWING
ACKNOWLEDGE
ACKNOWLEDGEABLE
ACKNOWLEDGED
ACKNOWLEDGEMENT
ACKNOWLEDGER
ACKNOWLEDGING
ACKNOWLEDGMENT
ACKNOWN
ACLASTIC
ACLE
ACLEIDIAN
ACLEISTOUS
ACLIDIAN
ACLINAL
ACLINIC
ACLOUD
ACLYDES
ACMAESTHESIA
ACMATIC
ACME
ACMESTHESIA
ACMIC
ACMITE
ACNE
ACNEFORM
ACNEIFORM
ACNEMIA
ACNODAL
ACNODE
ACOASMA
ACOCANTHERIN
ACOCK
ACOCKBILL
ACOCOTL
ACOEL
ACOELOMATE
ACOELOUS
ACOIN
ACOINE
ACOLD
ACOLOGIC
ACOLOGY
ACOLOUS
ACOLUTHIC
ACOLYTE
ACOLYTH
ACOLYTHATE
ACOMIA
ACOMOUS
ACON
ACONDYLOSE
ACONDYLOUS
ACONE
ACONIC
ACONIN
ACONINE
ACONITAL
ACONITE
ACONITIA
ACONITIC
ACONITIN
ACONITINE
ACONITUM
ACONTIA
ACONTIUM
ACONURESIS
ACOPIC
ACOPON
ACOR
ACOREA
ACORIA
ACORN
ACORNED
ACOSMIC
ACOSMISM
ACOSMIST
ACOSMISTIC
ACOST
ACOTYLEDON
ACOUASM
ACOUCHI
ACOUCHY
ACOUMETER
ACOUMETRY
ACOUOPHONIA
ACOUP
ACOUPA
ACOUPE
ACOUSMA
ACOUSMATA
ACOUSMATIC
ACOUSTIC
ACOUSTICAL
ACOUSTICALLY
ACOUSTICIAN

ACOUSTICS
ACQUAINT
ACQUAINTANCE
ACQUAINTANT
ACQUAINTED
ACQUENT
ACQUEREUR
ACQUEST
ACQUIESCE
ACQUIESCED
ACQUIESCENCE
ACQUIESCENT
ACQUIESCER
ACQUIESCING
ACQUIRABLE
ACQUIRE
ACQUIRED
ACQUIREMENT
ACQUIRENDA
ACQUIRER
ACQUIRING
ACQUISIBLE
ACQUISITA
ACQUISITE
ACQUISITED
ACQUISITION
ACQUISITIVE
ACQUISITIVELY
ACQUISITIVENESS
ACQUISITOR
ACQUISITUM
ACQUIST
ACQUIT
ACQUITAL
ACQUITMENT
ACQUITTAL
ACQUITTANCE
ACQUITTED
ACQUITTER
ACQUITTING
ACRACY
ACRAEIN
ACRALDEHYDE
ACRANIA
ACRANIAL
ACRANIATE
ACRASIA
ACRASPEDOTE
ACRASY
ACRATIA
ACRATURESIS
ACRAWL
ACRAZE
ACRE
ACREABLE
ACREAGE
ACREAK
ACREAM
ACRED
ACREMAN
ACREMEN
ACRES
ACRESTAFF
ACRID
ACRIDAN
ACRIDANE
ACRIDIAN
ACRIDIC
ACRIDID
ACRIDIN
ACRIDINE
ACRIDINIC
ACRIDINIUM
ACRIDITY
ACRIDLY
ACRIDNESS
ACRIDONE
ACRIDONIUM
ACRIDOPHAGUS
ACRIDYL
ACRIFLAVIN
ACRIFLAVINE
ACRIMONIES
ACRIMONIOUS
ACRIMONIOUSLY
ACRIMONY
ACRINDOLIN
ACRINDOLINE
ACRINYL
ACRISIA
ACRISY
ACRITAN
ACRITE
ACRITICAL
ACRITOL
ACRITY
ACROAMA
ACROAMATA
ACROAMATIC
ACROAMATICS
ACROASPHYXIA
ACROATAXIA
ACROATIC
ACROBACY
ACROBAT
ACROBATIC
ACROBATICAL
ACROBATICALLY
ACROBATICS
ACROBATISM
ACROBLAST
ACROBRYOUS
ACROBYSTITIS
ACROCARPOUS
ACROCEPHALIA
ACROCEPHALIC
ACROCEPHALY
ACROCHORDON
ACROCONIDIUM
ACROCORACOID
ACROCYANOSIS
ACROCYST
ACRODACTYLA
ACRODACTYLUM
ACRODONT
ACRODONTISM
ACRODROME
ACRODROMOUS
ACRODYNIA
ACROESTHESIA
ACROGAMOUS
ACROGAMY
ACROGEN
ACROGENIC
ACROGENOUS
ACROGENOUSLY
ACROGRAPHY
ACROGYNOUS
ACROLEIN
ACROLITH
ACROLITHAN
ACROLITHIC
ACROLOGIC
ACROLOGISM
ACROLOGUE
ACROLOGY
ACROMANIA
ACROMEGALIA
ACROMEGALIC
ACROMEGALY
ACROMELALGIA
ACROMETER
ACROMIA
ACROMIAL
ACROMICRIA
ACROMION
ACROMPHALUS
ACROMYODIAN
ACROMYODIC
ACROMYODOUS
ACROMYOTONIA
ACROMYOTONUS
ACRON
ACRONARCOTIC
ACRONEUROSIS
ACRONIC
ACRONICAL
ACRONICALLY
ACRONICHAL
ACRONICHALLY
ACRONYC
ACRONYCAL
ACRONYCALLY
ACRONYCH
ACRONYCHAL
ACRONYCHALLY
ACRONYCTOUS
ACRONYM
ACRONYX
ACROOK
ACROPATHY
ACROPETAL
ACROPETALLY
ACROPHOBIA
ACROPHONETIC
ACROPHONIC
ACROPHONY
ACROPODIA
ACROPODIUM
ACROPOLIS
ACROPOLISES
ACROPOLITAN
ACROPORE
ACRORHAGUS
ACRORRHEUMA
ACROSARC
ACROSARCA
ACROSARCUM
ACROSCOPIC
ACROSE
ACROSOME
ACROSPIRE
ACROSPIRED
ACROSPIRING
ACROSPORE
ACROSPOROUS
ACROSS
ACROSTIC
ACROSTICAL
ACROSTICALLY
ACROSTICHAL
ACROSTICHIC
ACROSTICHOID
ACROSTICISM
ACROTARSIAL
ACROTARSIUM
ACROTELEUTIC
ACROTER
ACROTERIAL
ACROTERIC
ACROTERIUM
ACROTIC
ACROTISM
ACROTOMOUS
ACROTROPHIC
ACRYL
ACRYLATE
ACRYLIC
ACRYLYL
ACT
ACTA
ACTABILITY
ACTABLE
ACTED
ACTIFICATION
ACTIFIER
ACTIFY
ACTIN
ACTINAL
ACTINALLY
ACTINE
ACTINENCHYMA
ACTING
ACTINIA
ACTINIAN
ACTINIARIAN
ACTINIC
ACTINICAL
ACTINICALLY
ACTINIDE
ACTINIFEROUS
ACTINIFORM
ACTININE
ACTINISM
ACTINIUM
ACTINOBRANCH
ACTINOCARP
ACTINOCARPIC
ACTINOCRINID
ACTINODROME
ACTINOGRAM
ACTINOGRAPH
ACTINOGRAPHY
ACTINOID
ACTINOLITE
ACTINOLITIC
ACTINOLOGOUS
ACTINOLOGUE
ACTINOLOGY
ACTINOMERE
ACTINOMERIC
ACTINOMETER
ACTINOMETRIC
ACTINOMETRY
ACTINOMORPHIC
ACTINOMORPHY
ACTINOMYCETE
ACTINOMYCOMA
ACTINON
ACTINOPHONE
ACTINOPHONIC
ACTINOPHORE
ACTINOPHRYAN
ACTINOPRAXIS
ACTINOSCOPY
ACTINOSOMA
ACTINOSOME
ACTINOST
ACTINOSTOMAL
ACTINOSTOME
ACTINOTROCHA
ACTINOZOAL
ACTINOZOAN
ACTINULA
ACTINULAE
ACTIO
ACTION
ACTIONABLE
ACTIONABLY
ACTIONAL
ACTIONARY
ACTIONER
ACTIONES
ACTIONIZE
ACTIONIZED
ACTIONIZING
ACTIONS
ACTIOUS
ACTIVATE
ACTIVATED
ACTIVATING
ACTIVATION
ACTIVATOR
ACTIVE
ACTIVELY
ACTIVENESS
ACTIVISM
ACTIVIST
ACTIVITAL
ACTIVITIES
ACTIVITY
ACTIVIZE
ACTLESS
ACTO
ACTON
ACTOR
ACTORISH
ACTORS
ACTORY
ACTOS
ACTRESS
ACTRESSY
ACTS
ACTU
ACTUAL
ACTUALISM
ACTUALIST
ACTUALISTIC
ACTUALITIES
ACTUALITY
ACTUALIZATION
ACTUALIZE
ACTUALIZED
ACTUALIZING
ACTUALLY
ACTUALNESS
ACTUARIAL
ACTUARIALLY
ACTUARIAN
ACTUARIES
ACTUARY
ACTUATE
ACTUATED
ACTUATES
ACTUATING
ACTUATION
ACTUATOR
ACTURE
ACTURIENCE
ACTUS
ACUATE
ACUATING
ACUATION
ACUCHI
ACUCLOSURE
ACUDUCTOR
ACUERDO
ACUERDOS
ACUITY
ACULEA
ACULEAE
ACULEATE
ACULEATED
ACULEI
ACULEIFORM
ACULEOLATE
ACULEUS
ACUMEN
ACUMINATE
ACUMINATED
ACUMINATING
ACUMINATION
ACUMINOSE
ACUMINOUS
ACUMINULATE

ACUPRESS
ACUPRESSURE
ACUPUNCTUATE
ACUPUNCTURATOR
ACUPUNCTURE
ACUPUNCTURED
ACUS
ACUSHLA
ACUTA
ACUTANGULAR
ACUTATE
ACUTE
ACUTELY
ACUTENESS
ACUTIATOR
ACUTIFOLIATE
ACUTILINGUAL
ACUTILOBATE
ACUTIPLANTAR
ACUTOGRAVE
ACUTONODOSE
ACUTORSION
ACXOYATL
ACYANOPSIA
ACYCLIC
ACYESIS
ACYETIC
ACYL
ACYLAL
ACYLASE
ACYLATE
ACYLATION
ACYLOGEN
ACYLOIN
ACYROLOGICAL
ACYROLOGY
ACYSTIA
AD
ADACTYLIA
ADACTYLOUS
ADAD
ADAGA
ADAGE
ADAGIAL
ADAGIETTO
ADAGIO
ADAGIOS
ADALAT
ADALID
ADAMANCY
ADAMANT
ADAMANTEAN
ADAMANTINE
ADAMANTINOMA
ADAMANTOID
ADAMANTOMA
ADAMAS
ADAMELLITE
ADAMINE
ADAMITE
ADAMSITE
ADAN
ADANCE
ADANGLE
ADAPID
ADAPT
ADAPTABILITY
ADAPTABLE
ADAPTABLENESS
ADAPTATION
ADAPTATIONAL
ADAPTATIVE
ADAPTED
ADAPTEDNESS
ADAPTER
ADAPTION
ADAPTIONISM
ADAPTITUDE
ADAPTIVE
ADAPTIVELY
ADAPTIVENESS
ADAPTOMETER
ADAPTOR
ADAPTORIAL
ADARME
ADARO
ADAT
ADATI
ADATIS
ADATOM
ADATY
ADAUNT
ADAW
ADAWE
ADAWLUT
ADAWN
ADAXIAL
ADAY
ADAYS
ADAZZLE
ADCRAFT
ADD
ADDA
ADDABLE
ADDAX
ADDEBTED
ADDED
ADDEEM
ADDEND
ADDENDA
ADDENDUM
ADDER
ADDERBOLT
ADDERSPIT
ADDERWORT
ADDIBILITY
ADDIBLE
ADDICE
ADDICENT
ADDICT
ADDICTED
ADDICTEDNESS
ADDICTION
ADDICTIVE
ADDIMENT
ADDING
ADDIO
ADDIS
ADDITA
ADDITAMENT
ADDITIMENT
ADDITION
ADDITIONAL
ADDITIONALLY
ADDITIONARY
ADDITIONS
ADDITITIOUS
ADDITIVE
ADDITIVELY
ADDITIVITY
ADDITORY
ADDITUM
ADDLE
ADDLEBRAIN
ADDLEBRAINED
ADDLED
ADDLEHEAD
ADDLEHEADED
ADDLEHEADEDLY
ADDLEPATE
ADDLEPATED
ADDLEPLOT
ADDLING
ADDLINGS
ADDLINS
ADDORSED
ADDOSSED
ADDRESS
ADDRESSED
ADDRESSEE
ADDRESSER
ADDRESSFUL
ADDRESSING
ADDRESSOR
ADDREST
ADDUCE
ADDUCEABLE
ADDUCED
ADDUCENT
ADDUCER
ADDUCIBLE
ADDUCING
ADDUCT
ADDUCTION
ADDUCTIVE
ADDUCTOR
ADDULCE
ADE
ADEAD
ADEEM
ADEEP
ADELANTADO
ADELANTE
ADELING
ADELITE
ADELOCODONIC
ADELOMORPHIC
ADELOPOD
ADELPHOGAMY
ADELPHOLITE
ADELPHOPHAGY
ADEMONIST
ADEMPT
ADEMPTED
ADEMPTION
ADENALGY
ADENASE
ADENASTHENIA
ADENECTOMIES
ADENECTOMY
ADENECTOPIA
ADENECTOPIC
ADENIA
ADENIFORM
ADENIN
ADENINE
ADENITIS
ADENIZATION
ADENOBLAST
ADENOCELE
ADENOCHROME
ADENOCYST
ADENODERMIA
ADENODYNIA
ADENOFIBROMA
ADENOFIBROSIS
ADENOGENESIS
ADENOGENOUS
ADENOGRAPHY
ADENOID
ADENOIDAL
ADENOIDISM
ADENOLIPOMA
ADENOLOGICAL
ADENOLOGY
ADENOMA
ADENOMALACIA
ADENOMATA
ADENOMATOUS
ADENOMYCOSIS
ADENOMYOMA
ADENOMYXOMA
ADENONCUS
ADENONEURAL
ADENONEURE
ADENOPATHY
ADENOPHORE
ADENOPHOREUS
ADENOPHYLLOUS
ADENOPHYMA
ADENOPODOUS
ADENOSARCOMA
ADENOSE
ADENOSINE
ADENOSIS
ADENOTOME
ADENOTOMIC
ADENOTOMY
ADENOTYPHOID
ADENOTYPHUS
ADENOUS
ADENYLIC
ADEPHAGAN
ADEPHAGOUS
ADEPS
ADEPT
ADEPTION
ADEPTLY
ADEPTNESS
ADEQUACY
ADEQUATE
ADEQUATELY
ADEQUATENESS
ADEQUATION
ADEQUATIVE
ADERMIA
ADERMIN
ADESPOTA
ADESPOTON
ADEVISM
ADEW
ADFIX
ADHAKA
ADHAMANT
ADHARMA
ADHERE
ADHERED
ADHERENCE
ADHERENCY
ADHEREND
ADHERENT
ADHERENTLY
ADHERER
ADHERESCENCE
ADHERESCENT
ADHERING
ADHESION
ADHESIONAL
ADHESIVE
ADHESIVELY
ADHESIVENESS
ADHI
ADHIBIT
ADHIBITED
ADHIBITING
ADHIBITION
ADHORT
ADIABAT
ADIABATIC
ADIABOLIST
ADIACTINIC
ADIAGNOSTIC
ADIANTIFORM
ADIANTUM
ADIAPHON
ADIAPHONON
ADIAPHORA
ADIAPHORAL
ADIAPHORESIS
ADIAPHORETIC
ADIAPHORISM
ADIAPHORIST
ADIAPHORITE
ADIAPHORON
ADIAPHOROUS
ADIATE
ADIATED
ADIATHERMAL
ADIATHERMIC
ADIATHETIC
ADIATING
ADIATION
ADIBASI
ADICITY
ADIENCE
ADIEU
ADIEUS
ADIEUX
ADIGHE
ADIGHT
ADINIDAN
ADINOLE
ADION
ADIOS
ADIPATE
ADIPESCENT
ADIPIC
ADIPINIC
ADIPOCELE
ADIPOCERE
ADIPOCEROUS
ADIPOFIBROMA
ADIPOGENIC
ADIPOGENOUS
ADIPOID
ADIPOLYSIS
ADIPOLYTIC
ADIPOMA
ADIPOMATA
ADIPOMATOUS
ADIPOMETER
ADIPOPEXIA
ADIPOPEXIS
ADIPOSE
ADIPOSENESS
ADIPOSIS
ADIPOSITY
ADIPOSURIA
ADIPOUS
ADIPSIA
ADIPSIC
ADIPSOUS
ADIPYL
ADIT
ADITAL
ADITIO
ADITUS
ADIVE
ADJAB
ADJACENCY
ADJACENT
ADJACENTLY
ADJAG
ADJECT
ADJECTION
ADJECTIONAL
ADJECTIVAL
ADJECTIVALLY
ADJECTIVE
ADJECTIVELY
ADJIGA
ADJIGER
ADJOIN
ADJOINED
ADJOINEDLY

ADJOINING
ADJOINT
ADJOURN
ADJOURNAL
ADJOURNMENT
ADJOUST
ADJUDGE
ADJUDGED
ADJUDGER
ADJUDGING
ADJUDICATE
ADJUDICATED
ADJUDICATING
ADJUDICATION
ADJUDICATIVE
ADJUDICATOR
ADJUDICATURE
ADJUGATE
ADJUMENT
ADJUNCT
ADJUNCTION
ADJUNCTIVE
ADJUNCTIVELY
ADJUNCTLY
ADJURATION
ADJURATORY
ADJURE
ADJURED
ADJURER
ADJURING
ADJUROR
ADJUST
ADJUSTABLE
ADJUSTAGE
ADJUSTED
ADJUSTER
ADJUSTIVE
ADJUSTMENT
ADJUSTOR
ADJUTAGE
ADJUTANCIES
ADJUTANCY
ADJUTANT
ADJUTANTSHIP
ADJUTOR
ADJUTORIOUS
ADJUTORY
ADJUTRICE
ADJUTRIX
ADJUVANT
ADJUVATE
ADLAY
ADLUMIDIN
ADLUMIDINE
ADLUMIN
ADLUMINE
ADMAN
ADMARGINATE
ADMAXILLARY
ADMEASURE
ADMEASURED
ADMEASURER
ADMEASURING
ADMEDIAL
ADMEDIAN
ADMEN
ADMI
ADMINICLE
ADMINICULAR
ADMINICULARY
ADMINICULATE
ADMINICULUM
ADMINISTER
ADMINISTERED
ADMINISTERIAL
ADMINISTRABLE
ADMINISTRANT
ADMINISTRATE
ADMINISTRATED
ADMINISTRATING
ADMINISTRATION
ADMINISTRATIONAL
ADMINISTRATIVE
ADMINISTRATOR
ADMIRABLE
ADMIRABLY
ADMIRAL
ADMIRALSHIP
ADMIRALTIES
ADMIRALTY
ADMIRATION
ADMIRATIVE
ADMIRATOR
ADMIRE
ADMIRED
ADMIREDLY
ADMIRER
ADMIRING
ADMIRINGLY
ADMISSIBLE
ADMISSIBLY
ADMISSION
ADMISSIVE
ADMISSORY
ADMIT
ADMITTABLE
ADMITTANCE
ADMITTATUR
ADMITTED
ADMITTEDLY
ADMITTEE
ADMITTER
ADMITTING
ADMITTY
ADMIX
ADMIXED
ADMIXING
ADMIXT
ADMIXTION
ADMIXTURE
ADMONISH
ADMONISHER
ADMONISHMENT
ADMONITION
ADMONITIVE
ADMONITIVELY
ADMONITOR
ADMONITORIAL
ADMONITORILY
ADMONITORY
ADMOVE
ADNASCENCE
ADNATE
ADNATION
ADNERVAL
ADNESCENT
ADNEURAL
ADNEX
ADNEXA
ADNEXAL
ADNEXED
ADNEXITIS
ADNEXOPEXY
ADNOMINAL
ADNOMINALLY
ADNOMINATION
ADNOUN
ADNUL
ADNUMBER
ADO
ADOBE
ADOLESCE
ADOLESCED
ADOLESCENCE
ADOLESCENCY
ADOLESCENT
ADOLESCENTLY
ADOLESCING
ADON
ADONIDIN
ADONIN
ADONIS
ADONITE
ADONITOL
ADONIZE
ADONIZED
ADONIZING
ADOORS
ADOPERATE
ADOPERATION
ADOPT
ADOPTABLE
ADOPTANT
ADOPTATIVE
ADOPTED
ADOPTEDLY
ADOPTEE
ADOPTER
ADOPTIAN
ADOPTIANISM
ADOPTIANIST
ADOPTION
ADOPTIONAL
ADOPTIONISM
ADOPTIONIST
ADOPTIOUS
ADOPTIVE
ADOPTIVELY
ADOR
ADORABILITY
ADORABLE
ADORABLENESS
ADORABLY
ADORAL
ADORALLY
ADORANT
ADORATION
ADORATORY
ADORE
ADORED
ADORER
ADORING
ADORN
ADORNED
ADORNER
ADORNMENT
ADOSCULATION
ADOULIE
ADOWN
ADOXACEOUS
ADOXIES
ADOXOGRAPHY
ADOXY
ADOZE
ADPRESS
ADPROMISSION
ADRAD
ADRADIAL
ADRADIALLY
ADRADIUS
ADREAD
ADREAM
ADREAMED
ADREAMT
ADRECTAL
ADRENAL
ADRENALIN
ADRENALINE
ADRENALIZE
ADRENALONE
ADRENCH
ADRENIN
ADRENINE
ADRENT
ADRIFT
ADRIP
ADROGATE
ADROIT
ADROITLY
ADROITNESS
ADROOP
ADROP
ADROSTRAL
ADROWSE
ADRUE
ADRY
ADSBUD
ADSCITITIOUS
ADSCRIPT
ADSCRIPTION
ADSCRIPTIVE
ADSESSOR
ADSIGNIFY
ADSMITH
ADSMITHING
ADSORB
ADSORBABLE
ADSORBATE
ADSORBENT
ADSORPTION
ADSORPTIVE
ADSORPTIVELY
ADSTIPULATE
ADSTIPULATED
ADSTIPULATOR
ADSUM
ADTERMINAL
ADUANA
ADUB
ADULAR
ADULARIA
ADULATE
ADULATED
ADULATING
ADULATION
ADULATOR
ADULATORY
ADULATRESS
ADULCE
ADULT
ADULTER
ADULTERANT
ADULTERATE
ADULTERATED
ADULTERATING
ADULTERATION
ADULTERATOR
ADULTERER
ADULTERESS
ADULTERIES
ADULTERINE
ADULTERIZE
ADULTEROUS
ADULTEROUSLY
ADULTERY
ADULTHOOD
ADULTNESS
ADULTOID
ADULTRESS
ADUMBRAL
ADUMBRANT
ADUMBRATE
ADUMBRATED
ADUMBRATING
ADUMBRATION
ADUMBRATIVE
ADUNC
ADUNCATE
ADUNCITY
ADUNCOUS
ADURE
ADURENT
ADUSK
ADUST
ADUSTION
ADUSTIOSIS
ADUSTIVE
ADVANCE
ADVANCED
ADVANCEMENT
ADVANCER
ADVANCES
ADVANCING
ADVANCIVE
ADVANTAGE
ADVANTAGED
ADVANTAGEOUS
ADVANTAGEOUSLY
ADVANTAGEOUSNESS
ADVANTAGING
ADVECTION
ADVECTITIOUS
ADVECTIVE
ADVEHENT
ADVENE
ADVENIENCE
ADVENIENT
ADVENT
ADVENTIAL
ADVENTITIA
ADVENTITIOUS
ADVENTIVE
ADVENTUAL
ADVENTURE
ADVENTURED
ADVENTURER
ADVENTURESOME
ADVENTURESS
ADVENTURING
ADVENTUROUS
ADVENTUROUSLY
ADVENTUROUSNES
ADVERB
ADVERBIAL
ADVERBIALIZE
ADVERBIALLY
ADVERBIATION
ADVERSARIA
ADVERSARIES
ADVERSARY
ADVERSATIVE
ADVERSE
ADVERSED
ADVERSELY
ADVERSENESS
ADVERSING
ADVERSITIES
ADVERSITY
ADVERSUS
ADVERT
ADVERTENCE
ADVERTENCY
ADVERTENT
ADVERTENTLY
ADVERTISE
ADVERTISED
ADVERTISEMENT
ADVERTISER
ADVERTISING
ADVERTIZE
ADVERTIZEMENT
ADVERTIZING
ADVICE
ADVICEFUL
ADVISABILITY

ADVISABLE
ADVISABLENESS
ADVISABLY
ADVISAL
ADVISATORY
ADVISE
ADVISED
ADVISEDLY
ADVISEDNESS
ADVISEE
ADVISEMENT
ADVISER
ADVISING
ADVISIVE
ADVISIVENESS
ADVISO
ADVISOR
ADVISORILY
ADVISORY
ADVITANT
ADVOCAAT
ADVOCACY
ADVOCATE
ADVOCATED
ADVOCATES
ADVOCATING
ADVOCATION
ADVOCATOR
ADVOCATORY
ADVOCATRESS
ADVOKE
ADVOLUTION
ADVOWEE
ADVOWSON
ADY
ADYNAMIA
ADYNAMIC
ADYNAMY
ADYT
ADYTA
ADYTON
ADYTUM
ADZ
ADZE
ADZER
ADZES
AE
AEA
AECIA
AECIAL
AECIDIA
AECIDIUM
AECIOSPORE
AECIOSTAGE
AECIOTELIA
AECIOTELIUM
AECIUM
AEDEAGI
AEDEAGUS
AEDES
AEDICULA
AEDICULAE
AEDILE
AEDILESHIP
AEDILIAN
AEDILIC
AEDILITIAN
AEDILITIES
AEDILITY
AEDOEOLOGY
AEGAGRI
AEGAGROPILA
AEGAGROPILAE
AEGAGROPILE
AEGAGROPILES
AEGAGRUS
AEGER
AEGERIAN
AEGERIID
AEGICRANIA
AEGILOPS
AEGIRINE
AEGIRINOLITE
AEGIRITE
AEGIS
AEGROTANT
AEGROTAT
AEGYPTILLA
AEGYRITE
AELODICON
AELUROPHOBE
AELUROPHOBIA
AELUROPODOUS
AENACH
AENEAN
AENEOLITHIC
AENEOUS
AENIGMATITE
AEOLIAN
AEOLID
AEOLIGHT
AEOLINE
AEOLIPILE
AEOLIPYLE
AEOLISTIC
AEOLODICON
AEOLOTROPIC
AEOLOTROPISM
AEOLOTROPY
AEOLSKLAVIER
AEON
AEONIAL
AEONIAN
AEONIC
AEQUOR
AEQUOREAL
AER
AERAGE
AERARIAN
AERARIUM
AERATE
AERATED
AERATING
AERATION
AERATOR
AERENCHYMA
AERIAL
AERIALIST
AERIALITY
AERIALLY
AERIALNESS
AERIC
AERICAL
AERIDES
AERIE
AERIED
AERIFACTION
AERIFEROUS
AERIFICATION
AERIFIED
AERIFORM
AERIFY
AERIFYING
AERO
AEROBATE
AEROBATED
AEROBATICS
AEROBATING
AEROBE
AEROBIAN
AEROBIC
AEROBICALLY
AEROBIOLOGY
AEROBIOSCOPE
AEROBIOSIS
AEROBIOTIC
AEROBIOUS
AEROBIUM
AEROBOAT
AEROBUS
AEROCAMERA
AEROCOLPOS
AEROCURVE
AEROCYST
AERODONE
AERODONETIC
AERODONETICS
AERODROME
AERODROMICS
AERODUCT
AERODYNAMIC
AERODYNAMICS
AERODYNE
AEROEMBOLISM
AEROFOIL
AEROGEL
AEROGEN
AEROGENES
AEROGENIC
AEROGEOLOGY
AEROGNOSY
AEROGRAM
AEROGRAMME
AEROGRAPH
AEROGRAPHER
AEROGRAPHIC
AEROGRAPHICS
AEROGRAPHIES
AEROGRAPHY
AEROGUN
AEROHYDROUS
AEROIDES
AEROLITE
AEROLITH
AEROLITIC
AEROLITICS
AEROLOGIC
AEROLOGICAL
AEROLOGIES
AEROLOGIST
AEROLOGY
AEROMANCY
AEROMARINE
AEROMECHANIC
AEROMEDICAL
AEROMEDICINE
AEROMETER
AEROMETRIC
AEROMETRY
AEROMOTOR
AERONAT
AERONAUT
AERONAUTIC
AERONAUTICAL
AERONAUTICS
AERONAUTISM
AERONEF
AERONEUROSIS
AEROPATHY
AEROPAUSE
AEROPHAGIA
AEROPHAGIST
AEROPHANE
AEROPHILE
AEROPHILOUS
AEROPHOBIA
AEROPHOBIC
AEROPHONE
AEROPHOR
AEROPHORE
AEROPHYSICAL
AEROPHYSICS
AEROPHYTE
AEROPLANE
AEROPLANER
AEROPLANIST
AEROPLEUSTIC
AEROPOROTOMY
AEROSCEPSIS
AEROSCEPSY
AEROSCOPE
AEROSCOPIC
AEROSCOPY
AEROSE
AEROSIDERITE
AEROSOL
AEROSPACE
AEROSPHERE
AEROSTAT
AEROSTATIC
AEROSTATICAL
AEROSTATICS
AEROSTATION
AEROSTEAM
AEROTAXIS
AEROTHERAPY
AEROTROPIC
AEROTROPISM
AEROVIEW
AEROYACHT
AERUGINOUS
AERUGO
AERY
AES
AESC
AESCULACEOUS
AESTHESIA
AESTHESIS
AESTHETE
AESTHETIC
AESTHETICAL
AESTHETICALLY
AESTHETICIAN
AESTHETICISM
AESTHETICIZE
AESTHETICS
AESTIVAL
AESTIVATE
AESTIVATED
AESTIVATING
AESTIVATION
AESTIVATOR
AESTUATE
AESTUATION
AESTUOUS
AESTURE
AESTUS
AETHALIA
AETHALIUM
AETHELING
AETHEOGAM
AETHEOGAMIC
AETHEOGAMOUS
AETHER
AETHERED
AETHOGEN
AETHRIOSCOPE
AETIOGENIC
AETIOLOGICAL
AETIOLOGUE
AETIOLOGY
AETIOPHYLLIN
AETIOTROPIC
AETITES
AETOSAUR
AEVIA
AEVUM
AFACE
AFAINT
AFALD
AFAR
AFARA
AFEAR
AFEARD
AFEARED
AFERNAN
AFETAL
AFF
AFFA
AFFABILITY
AFFABLE
AFFABLENESS
AFFABLY
AFFABROUS
AFFAIR
AFFAIRE
AFFAIRS
AFFAITE
AFFAMISH
AFFECT
AFFECTATION
AFFECTED
AFFECTEDLY
AFFECTEDNESS
AFFECTER
AFFECTIBILITY
AFFECTIBLE
AFFECTING
AFFECTINGLY
AFFECTION
AFFECTIONAL
AFFECTIONALLY
AFFECTIONATE
AFFECTIONATELY
AFFECTIONATENESS
AFFECTIONED
AFFECTIVE
AFFECTIVELY
AFFECTIVITY
AFFEEBLE
AFFEER
AFFEERER
AFFEERMENT
AFFEEROR
AFFEIR
AFFERE
AFFERENT
AFFETTUOSO
AFFIANCE
AFFIANCED
AFFIANCER
AFFIANCING
AFFIANT
AFFICHE
AFFIDATION
AFFIDAVIT
AFFIDAVY
AFFIED
AFFILE
AFFILIABLE
AFFILIATE
AFFILIATED
AFFILIATING
AFFILIATION
AFFINAGE
AFFINAL
AFFINATION
AFFINE
AFFINED
AFFINELY
AFFINITATIVE
AFFINITATIVELY
AFFINITE
AFFINITIES
AFFINITION

AFFINITIVE
AFFINITY
AFFIRM
AFFIRMABLE
AFFIRMABLY
AFFIRMANCE
AFFIRMANT
AFFIRMATION
AFFIRMATIVE
AFFIRMATIVELY
AFFIRMATORY
AFFIRMER
AFFIX
AFFIXAL
AFFIXATION
AFFIXED
AFFIXER
AFFIXING
AFFIXION
AFFIXT
AFFIXTURE
AFFLATE
AFFLATED
AFFLATION
AFFLATUS
AFFLICT
AFFLICTED
AFFLICTER
AFFLICTING
AFFLICTINGLY
AFFLICTION
AFFLICTIVE
AFFLICTIVELY
AFFLOOF
AFFLUENCE
AFFLUENT
AFFLUENTLY
AFFLUENTNESS
AFFLUX
AFFLUXION
AFFODILL
AFFORCE
AFFORCED
AFFORCEMENT
AFFORCING
AFFORD
AFFORDABLE
AFFOREST
AFFORESTMENT
AFFORMATIVE
AFFRANCHISE
AFFRANCHISED
AFFRAP
AFFRAY
AFFRAYED
AFFRAYER
AFFRAYING
AFFREIGHT
AFFREIGHTER
AFFRET
AFFRETTANDO
AFFREUX
AFFRICATE
AFFRICATED
AFFRICATION
AFFRICATIVE
AFFRIGHT
AFFRIGHTED
AFFRIGHTEDLY
AFFRIGHTER
AFFRIGHTFUL
AFFRIGHTMENT
AFFRONT
AFFRONTE
AFFRONTED
AFFRONTEDLY
AFFRONTEE
AFFRONTER
AFFRONTIVE
AFFRONTY
AFFUSE
AFFUSED
AFFUSING
AFFUSION
AFFY
AFFYDAVY
AFFYING
AFGHAN
AFGHANI
AFGHANIS
AFICIONADO
AFIELD
AFIKOMEN
AFIND
AFINE
AFIRE
AFLAGELLAR
AFLAME
AFLARE
AFLAT
AFLAUNT
AFLEY
AFLICKER
AFLIGHT
AFLOAT
AFLOW
AFLOWER
AFLUKING
AFLUSH
AFLUTTER
AFOAM
AFONG
AFOOT
AFORE
AFOREHAND
AFOREMENTIONED
AFORENAMED
AFORESAID
AFORETHOUGHT
AFORETIME
AFOUL
AFOUNDE
AFRAID
AFREET
AFRESCA
AFRESH
AFRET
AFRETE
AFRIT
AFRITE
AFRONT
AFROWN
AFT
AFTABA
AFTEN
AFTER
AFTERBAY
AFTERBEAT
AFTERBIRTH
AFTERBODY
AFTERBRAIN
AFTERBREAST
AFTERBURNER
AFTERBURNING
AFTERCARE
AFTERCAST
AFTERCHROME
AFTERCLAP
AFTERCOME
AFTERCOMER
AFTERCOOLER
AFTERCROP
AFTERDAMP
AFTERDATE
AFTERDATED
AFTERDECK
AFTERDINNER
AFTEREFFECT
AFTEREYE
AFTERFEED
AFTERFORM
AFTERFUTURE
AFTERGAME
AFTERGAS
AFTERGLOW
AFTERGRASS
AFTERGROWTH
AFTERGUARD
AFTERHAND
AFTERHATCH
AFTERHEND
AFTERHOLD
AFTERIMAGE
AFTERINGS
AFTERLIFE
AFTERLIGHT
AFTERMAST
AFTERMATH
AFTERMILK
AFTERMOST
AFTERNIGHT
AFTERNOON
AFTERNOONS
AFTERNOTE
AFTERPAIN
AFTERPAINS
AFTERPART
AFTERPEAK
AFTERPIECE
AFTERPLAY
AFTERRAKE
AFTERRIDER
AFTERS
AFTERSHAFT
AFTERSHAFTED
AFTERSHINE
AFTERSHOCK
AFTERSONG
AFTERSOUND
AFTERSPRING
AFTERSTORM
AFTERSUPPER
AFTERSWARM
AFTERTASTE
AFTERTHOUGHT
AFTERTIME
AFTERTOUCH
AFTERTURN
AFTERVISION
AFTERWALE
AFTERWARD
AFTERWARDS
AFTERWASH
AFTERWHILE
AFTERWISE
AFTERWIT
AFTERWITTED
AFTERWORLD
AFTERWRIST
AFTERYEARS
AFTMOST
AFTOSA
AFTWARD
AFTWARDS
AFUNCTION
AFUNCTIONAL
AFWILLITE
AGA
AGABANEE
AGACANT
AGACANTE
AGACELLA
AGACERIE
AGAIN
AGAINBUY
AGAINSAY
AGAINST
AGAL
AGALACTIC
AGALACTOUS
AGALAXIA
AGALAXY
AGALITE
AGALLOCH
AGALLOCHUM
AGALMA
AGALMATOLITE
AGALWOOD
AGAMA
AGAME
AGAMETE
AGAMI
AGAMIAN
AGAMIC
AGAMICALLY
AGAMID
AGAMIS
AGAMIST
AGAMOBIA
AGAMOBIUM
AGAMOGENESIS
AGAMOGENETIC
AGAMOID
AGAMONT
AGAMOSPORE
AGAMOUS
AGAMY
AGANGLIONIC
AGAPAE
AGAPANTHUS
AGAPE
AGAPETAE
AGAPETI
AGAPETID
AGAR
AGARIC
AGARICACEOUS
AGARICIC
AGARICIFORM
AGARICIN
AGARICINE
AGARICINIC
AGARICOID
AGARITA
AGAROID
AGARWAL
AGASP
AGAST
AGASTRIC
AGATA
AGATE
AGATEWARE
AGATHIN
AGATHISM
AGATHIST
AGATHODAEMON
AGATHODEMON
AGATHOLOGY
AGATIFEROUS
AGATIFORM
AGATINE
AGATIZE
AGATIZED
AGATIZING
AGATOID
AGATY
AGAVE
AGAVOSE
AGAZE
AGAZED
AGBA
AGE
AGEABLE
AGED
AGEDLY
AGEDNESS
AGEE
AGEING
AGELESS
AGELONG
AGEN
AGENCIES
AGENCY
AGENDA
AGENDUM
AGENESIA
AGENESIC
AGENESIS
AGENIZE
AGENNESIS
AGENNETIC
AGENT
AGENTESS
AGENTIAL
AGENTING
AGENTIVAL
AGENTIVE
AGENTRY
AGEOMETRICAL
AGER
AGERASIA
AGERATUM
AGEUSIA
AGEUSIC
AGGER
AGGERATE
AGGEROSE
AGGEST
AGGLOMERANT
AGGLOMERATE
AGGLOMERATED
AGGLOMERATIC
AGGLOMERATING
AGGLOMERATION
AGGLOMERATIVE
AGGLOMERATOR
AGGLUTINABLE
AGGLUTINANT
AGGLUTINATE
AGGLUTINATED
AGGLUTINATION
AGGLUTINATIVE
AGGLUTINATOR
AGGLUTININ
AGGLUTINIZE
AGGLUTINOGEN
AGGLUTINOID
AGGRACE
AGGRADATION
AGGRADATIONAL
AGGRADE
AGGRADED
AGGRADING
AGGRANDIZE
AGGRANDIZED
AGGRANDIZEMENT
AGGRANDIZER
AGGRANDIZING
AGGRATE
AGGRAVATE
AGGRAVATED
AGGRAVATING
AGGRAVATINGLY
AGGRAVATION
AGGRAVATIVE

AGGRAVATOR
AGGREGABLE
AGGREGANT
AGGREGATE
AGGREGATED
AGGREGATELY
AGGREGATENESS
AGGREGATING
AGGREGATION
AGGREGATIVE
AGGREGATOR
AGGREGATORY
AGGREGE
AGGRESS
AGGRESSED
AGGRESSIN
AGGRESSING
AGGRESSION
AGGRESSIVE
AGGRESSIVELY
AGGRESSIVENESS
AGGRESSOR
AGGRI
AGGRIEVANCE
AGGRIEVE
AGGRIEVED
AGGRIEVEDLY
AGGRIEVING
AGGROUP
AGGRY
AGGUR
AGHA
AGHANEE
AGHAST
AGHASTNESS
AGIBLE
AGILAWOOD
AGILE
AGILELY
AGILENESS
AGILITY
AGIN
AGING
AGIO
AGIOS
AGIOTAGE
AGIST
AGISTER
AGISTMENT
AGISTOR
AGITABLE
AGITANT
AGITATE
AGITATED
AGITATEDLY
AGITATING
AGITATION
AGITATIONAL
AGITATIVE
AGITATO
AGITATOR
AGITATORIAL
AGITATRIX
AGITPROP
AGITPUNKT
AGLA
AGLANCE
AGLAOZONIA
AGLARE
AGLEAF
AGLEAM
AGLEE
AGLET
AGLETHEAD
AGLEY
AGLIMMER
AGLINT
AGLISTEN
AGLITTER
AGLOBULIA
AGLOBULISM
AGLOSSAL
AGLOSSATE
AGLOSSIA
AGLOW
AGLUCON
AGLUCONE
AGLUTITION
AGLYCON
AGLYCONE
AGLYPHOUS
AGMA
AGMATINE
AGMATOLOGY
AGMINATE
AGMINATED
AGNAIL
AGNAME
AGNAMED
AGNAT
AGNATE
AGNATHIA
AGNATHIC
AGNATHOUS
AGNATIC
AGNATICAL
AGNATICALLY
AGNATION
AGNEAU
AGNEAUX
AGNEL
AGNI
AGNIFICATION
AGNITION
AGNIZE
AGNIZED
AGNIZING
AGNOIOLOGY
AGNOMEN
AGNOMICAL
AGNOMINA
AGNOMINAL
AGNOMINATION
AGNOSIA
AGNOSTIC
AGNOSTICAL
AGNOSTICALLY
AGNOSTICISM
AGNOSY
AGNUS
AGNUSES
AGO
AGOG
AGOGE
AGOGIC
AGOGICS
AGOHO
AGOING
AGOJO
AGOMENSIN
AGOMPHIASIS
AGOMPHIOUS
AGON
AGONAL
AGONE
AGONES
AGONIA
AGONIADA
AGONIADIN
AGONIATITE
AGONIC
AGONIED
AGONIES
AGONIST
AGONISTARCH
AGONISTIC
AGONISTICAL
AGONISTICS
AGONIUM
AGONIZE
AGONIZED
AGONIZER
AGONIZING
AGONOTHETE
AGONOTHETIC
AGONY
AGOOD
AGORA
AGORAE
AGORAMANIA
AGORANOME
AGORANOMUS
AGORAPHOBIA
AGORAS
AGOS
AGOSTADERO
AGOUARA
AGOUTA
AGOUTI
AGOUTIES
AGOUTIS
AGOUTY
AGPAITE
AGPAITIC
AGRAFE
AGRAFFE
AGRAH
AGRAL
AGRAMED
AGRAMMATISM
AGRAPHA
AGRAPHIA
AGRAPHIC
AGRARIAN
AGRARIANISM
AGRARIANIZE
AGRARIANLY
AGREAT
AGREE
AGREEABILITY
AGREEABLE
AGREEABLENESS
AGREEABLY
AGREED
AGREEING
AGREEINGLY
AGREEMENT
AGREER
AGREGATION
AGREGE
AGREMENS
AGREMENT
AGREMENTS
AGREST
AGRESTAL
AGRESTIAL
AGRESTIAN
AGRESTIC
AGRESTICAL
AGRI
AGRIA
AGRICERE
AGRICOLE
AGRICOLIST
AGRICOLITE
AGRICOLOUS
AGRICULTOR
AGRICULTURAL
AGRICULTURALLY
AGRICULTURE
AGRICULTURER
AGRICULTURIST
AGRIEF
AGRIMONIES
AGRIMONY
AGRIMOTOR
AGRIN
AGRIOLOGIST
AGRIOLOGY
AGRIONID
AGRIOTYPE
AGRISE
AGRISED
AGRISING
AGRITO
AGRITOS
AGROAN
AGROBIOLOGIC
AGROBIOLOGY
AGRODOLCE
AGROGEOLOGY
AGROLOGIC
AGROLOGICAL
AGROLOGY
AGROM
AGROMYZID
AGRONOME
AGRONOMIC
AGRONOMICAL
AGRONOMICS
AGRONOMIST
AGRONOMY
AGROOF
AGROPE
AGROSTEROL
AGROSTOLOGIC
AGROSTOLOGY
AGROTE
AGROTECHNY
AGROTYPE
AGROUND
AGRUFE
AGRUIF
AGRYPNIA
AGRYPNIAI
AGRYPNOTIC
AGSAM
AGUA
AGUACATE
AGUADA
AGUADOR
AGUAJI
AGUAMAS
AGUAMIEL
AGUARA
AGUARDIENTE
AGUAVINA
AGUE
AGUEPROOF
AGUEWEED
AGUEY
AGUGLIA
AGUILARITE
AGUILT
AGUINALDO
AGUINALDOS
AGUIRAGE
AGUISE
AGUISH
AGUISHLY
AGUISHNESS
AGUJA
AGUJON
AGUNAH
AGUSH
AGUST
AGY
AGYE
AGYIOMANIA
AGYNARIOUS
AGYNARY
AGYNOUS
AGYRATE
AGYRIA
AH
AHA
AHAAINA
AHAMKARA
AHANKARA
AHARTALAV
AHAU
AHAUNCH
AHEAD
AHEAP
AHEIGHT
AHEM
AHEY
AHIGH
AHIMSA
AHIND
AHL
AHLUWALIA
AHM
AHMADI
AHMAR
AHMEDI
AHOLD
AHOLE
AHOLT
AHONG
AHOO
AHORSEBACK
AHOY
AHSAN
AHU
AHUACA
AHUATLE
AHUEHUETE
AHULL
AHUM
AHUNG
AHUNGERED
AHUNGRY
AHUNT
AHURA
AHUREWA
AHUSH
AHUULA
AHWAL
AHYPNIA
AI
AIBLINS
AICHMOPHOBIA
AID
AIDANCE
AIDANT
AIDE
AIDED
AIDER
AIDFUL
AIDING
AIDLESS
AIDMAN
AIE
AIEL
AIERY
AIGIALOSAUR
AIGLET
AIGREMORE
AIGRET
AIGRETTE
AIGUIERE
AIGUILLE
AIGUILLETTE
AIKANE

AIKEN
AIKINITE
AIL
AILANTERY
AILANTHIC
AILANTHUS
AILANTINE
AILANTO
AILD
AILE
AILED
AILERON
AILETTE
AILING
AILLT
AILMENT
AILSYTE
AILUROID
AILUROMANIA
AILWEED
AIM
AIMARA
AIMED
AIMER
AIMFUL
AIMFULLY
AIMING
AIMLESS
AIMLESSLY
AIMLESSNESS
AIN
AINALEH
AINCE
AINE
AINEE
AINHUM
AINI
AINOI
AINSELL
AION
AIPI
AIPIM
AIR
AIRABLE
AIRAMPO
AIRAN
AIRBOAT
AIRBORNE
AIRBOUND
AIRBRUSH
AIRBURST
AIRCRAFT
AIRCRAFTMAN
AIRCRAFTMEN
AIRCRAFTSMAN
AIRCREW
AIRCREWMAN
AIRDOCK
AIRDROME
AIRDROP
AIRDROPPED
AIRDROPPING
AIRE
AIRED
AIRER
AIRFIELD
AIRFLOW
AIRFOIL
AIRFRAME
AIRGLOW
AIRGRAPH
AIRHEAD
AIRIER
AIRIEST
AIRIFEROUS
AIRIFIED
AIRIG
AIRILY
AIRINESS
AIRING
AIRISH
AIRLESS
AIRLIFT
AIRLIKE
AIRLINE
AIRLINER
AIRLING
AIRMAIL
AIRMAN
AIRMANSHIP
AIRMARK
AIRMONGER
AIROHYDROGEN
AIROMETER
AIRPARK
AIRPLANE
AIRPLANED
AIRPLANING
AIRPLANIST
AIRPORT
AIRPROOF
AIRS
AIRSCAPE
AIRSCREW
AIRSHEET
AIRSHIP
AIRSICK
AIRSICKNESS
AIRSOME
AIRSPACE
AIRSPEED
AIRSTREAM
AIRSTRIP
AIRT
AIRTH
AIRTIGHT
AIRTIGHTLY
AIRTIGHTNESS
AIRVIEW
AIRWARD
AIRWARDS
AIRWAVE
AIRWAY
AIRWAYMAN
AIRWISE
AIRWOMAN
AIRWOMEN
AIRWORTHY
AIRY
AIS
AISEWEED
AISLE
AISLED
AISLING
AISTEOIR
AISTOPOD
AIT
AITCH
AITCHBONE
AITCHES
AITCHLESS
AITEN
AITESIS
AITHOCHROI
AITION
AITIOTROPIC
AITIS
AITS
AITU
AIVER
AIWAIN
AIWAN
AIZLE
AIZOACEOUS
AJAJA
AJANGLE
AJAR
AJARI
AJAVA
AJAX
AJEE
AJENJO
AJHAR
AJI
AJIMEZ
AJITTER
AJIVA
AJIVIKA
AJO
AJOG
AJOINT
AJONJOLI
AJOUR
AJOURE
AJOURISE
AJOWAN
AJUTMENT
AK
AKA
AKAAKAI
AKABO
AKALA
AKALIMBA
AKAMAI
AKAMATSU
AKAROA
AKASA
AKAZGA
AKAZGIN
AKAZGINE
AKCHA
AKCHEH
AKE
AKEAKE
AKEBI
AKED
AKEE
AKEKI
AKELA
AKELE
AKELEY
AKEMBOLL
AKENBOLD
AKENE
AKENOBEITE
AKEPIRO
AKEPIROS
AKER
AKERITE
AKEY
AKH
AKHOOND
AKHROT
AKHUN
AKHUND
AKHUNDZADA
AKIA
AKIMBO
AKIN
AKINDLE
AKINESIA
AKINESIC
AKINESIS
AKINETE
AKING
AKKUM
AKLE
AKMUDDAR
AKO
AKOLOUTHIA
AKOLUTHIA
AKONGE
AKORI
AKOV
AKPEK
AKRA
AKROCHORDITE
AKROTER
AKROTERIA
AKROTERIAL
AKROTERION
AKU
AKUA
AKUAMMIN
AKUAMMINE
AKULE
AKUND
AKVAVIT
AL
ALA
ALABAMIDE
ALABAMINE
ALABANDITE
ALABARCH
ALABASTER
ALABASTRA
ALABASTRIAN
ALABASTRINE
ALABASTRUM
ALACHA
ALACHAH
ALACK
ALACKADAY
ALACRAN
ALACREATINE
ALACREATININ
ALACRIFY
ALACRIOUS
ALACRIOUSLY
ALACRITOUS
ALACRITY
ALADA
ALAE
ALAGAO
ALAGARTO
ALAGAU
ALAHEE
ALAI
ALAIHI
ALAITE
ALAKE
ALAL
ALALA
ALALI
ALALIA
ALALITE
ALALOI
ALALONGA
ALALUNGA
ALALUS
ALAMBIQUE
ALAMEDA
ALAMIQUI
ALAMIRE
ALAMO
ALAMODALITY
ALAMODE
ALAMORT
ALAMOS
ALAMOSITE
ALAN
ALAND
ALANE
ALANG
ALANGE
ALANGIN
ALANGINE
ALANI
ALANIN
ALANINE
ALANNAH
ALANT
ALANTIC
ALANTIN
ALANTOL
ALANTOLIC
ALANYL
ALAR
ALARE
ALARES
ALARM
ALARMABLE
ALARMED
ALARMEDLY
ALARMING
ALARMINGLY
ALARMISM
ALARMIST
ALARUM
ALARY
ALAS
ALASAS
ALASKAITE
ALASKITE
ALASTRIM
ALATE
ALATED
ALATERN
ALATERNUS
ALATION
ALAUDINE
ALAUND
ALAUNT
ALAY
ALAZOR
ALB
ALBA
ALBACEA
ALBACORA
ALBACORE
ALBACORES
ALBAE
ALBAHACA
ALBAM
ALBAN
ALBANITE
ALBARCO
ALBARDINE
ALBARELLO
ALBARIUM
ALBASPIDIN
ALBATA
ALBATROSS
ALBATROSSES
ALBE
ALBEDO
ALBEDOGRAPH
ALBEE
ALBEIT
ALBERCA
ALBERGATRICE
ALBERGE
ALBERGO
ALBERTIN
ALBERTITE
ALBERTTYPE
ALBERTYPE
ALBESCENCE
ALBESCENT
ALBESPINE
ALBESTON
ALBETAD
ALBICANT
ALBICATION
ALBICORE

ALBICULI
ALBIFICATION
ALBIFICATIVE
ALBIFIED
ALBIFLOROUS
ALBIFY
ALBIFYING
ALBINAL
ALBINESS
ALBINIC
ALBINISM
ALBINISTIC
ALBINO
ALBINOISM
ALBINOS
ALBINOTIC
ALBINURIA
ALBITE
ALBITIC
ALBITICAL
ALBITITE
ALBITIZATION
ALBITOPHYRE
ALBIZZIA
ALBOCRACY
ALBOLITE
ALBOLITH
ALBOPANNIN
ALBOPRUINOSE
ALBORADA
ALBORANITE
ALBRICIAS
ALBRONZE
ALBUGINEOUS
ALBUGINES
ALBUGINITIS
ALBUGO
ALBUM
ALBUMEAN
ALBUMEN
ALBUMENIZE
ALBUMENIZED
ALBUMENIZER
ALBUMENIZING
ALBUMENOID
ALBUMIMETER
ALBUMIN
ALBUMINATE
ALBUMINIFORM
ALBUMINIZE
ALBUMINIZED
ALBUMINIZING
ALBUMINOID
ALBUMINOIDAL
ALBUMINOSE
ALBUMINOSIS
ALBUMINOUS
ALBUMINURIA
ALBUMINURIC
ALBUMOSCOPE
ALBUMOSE
ALBUMOSURIA
ALBURN
ALBURNOUS
ALBURNUM
ALBUS
ALBUTANNIN
ALCABALA
ALCADE
ALCAICERIA
ALCAIDE
ALCALDE
ALCALDIA
ALCALIZATE
ALCAMINE
ALCANNA
ALCANTARA
ALCARRAZA
ALCATRAS
ALCAVALA
ALCAYDE
ALCAZABA
ALCAZAR
ALCAZAVA
ALCE
ALCELAPHINE
ALCHEMIC
ALCHEMICAL
ALCHEMICALLY
ALCHEMIST
ALCHEMISTER
ALCHEMISTIC
ALCHEMISTRY
ALCHEMIZE
ALCHEMIZED
ALCHEMIZING
ALCHEMY
ALCHERA
ALCHERINGA
ALCHITRAN
ALCHOCHODEN
ALCHORNEA
ALCHYMY
ALCIDINE
ALCINE
ALCLAD
ALCO
ALCOGEL
ALCOGENE
ALCOHOL
ALCOHOLATE
ALCOHOLATURE
ALCOHOLIC
ALCOHOLICALLY
ALCOHOLICITY
ALCOHOLISM
ALCOHOLIST
ALCOHOLIZATION
ALCOHOLIZE
ALCOHOLIZED
ALCOHOLIZING
ALCOHOLOMETER
ALCOHOLURIA
ALCOHOLYSIS
ALCOHOLYTIC
ALCORNOQUE
ALCOSOL
ALCOVE
ALCUMY
ALCYON
ALCYONACEAN
ALCYONARIAN
ALCYONIC
ALCYONIFORM
ALCYONOID
ALD
ALDAMIN
ALDAMINE
ALDANE
ALDAY
ALDEA
ALDEAMENT
ALDEHOL
ALDEHYDASE
ALDEHYDE
ALDEHYDIC
ALDEHYDINE
ALDEIA
ALDER
ALDERFLY
ALDERLIEFEST
ALDERMAN
ALDERMANATE
ALDERMANCY
ALDERMANESS
ALDERMANIC
ALDERMANITY
ALDERMANLIKE
ALDERMANLY
ALDERMANRY
ALDERMANSHIP
ALDERMEN
ALDERN
ALDERS
ALDERWOMAN
ALDERWOMEN
ALDIMIN
ALDIMINE
ALDINE
ALDITOL
ALDOL
ALDOLIZATION
ALDOLIZE
ALDOLIZED
ALDOLIZING
ALDOSE
ALDOXIME
ALDRIN
ALE
ALEAK
ALEATORY
ALEBENCH
ALEBERRY
ALEBUSH
ALEC
ALECITHAL
ALECIZE
ALECONNER
ALECOST
ALECTORIA
ALECTORIAE
ALECTORIDINE
ALECTORIOID
ALECUP
ALEE
ALEF
ALEFNULL
ALEFT
ALEFZERO
ALEGAR
ALEGER
ALEHOOF
ALEHOUSE
ALEIKOUM
ALEIKUM
ALEIPTES
ALEKNIGHT
ALEM
ALEMBIC
ALEMBICATE
ALEMBROTH
ALEMITE
ALEMMAL
ALEMONGER
ALEN
ALENGE
ALENGTH
ALENU
ALEPH
ALEPHS
ALEPIDOTE
ALEPINE
ALEPOLE
ALEPOT
ALERCE
ALERSE
ALERT
ALERTA
ALERTLY
ALERTNESS
ALESAN
ALESE
ALESHOT
ALESTAKE
ALETAP
ALETHIC
ALETHIOLOGY
ALETHOSCOPE
ALETTE
ALEUCAEMIC
ALEUCEMIC
ALEUKAEMIC
ALEUKEMIC
ALEURITIC
ALEUROMANCY
ALEUROMETER
ALEURONAT
ALEURONE
ALEURONIC
ALEUROSCOPE
ALEUTITE
ALEVIN
ALEW
ALEWHAP
ALEWIFE
ALEWIVES
ALEXANDERS
ALEXANDRITE
ALEXIA
ALEXIN
ALEXINE
ALEXINIC
ALEXIPHARMIC
ALEXIPYRETIC
ALEXITERIC
ALEY
ALEYARD
ALEYRODID
ALEZAN
ALEZE
ALFA
ALFAJE
ALFAKI
ALFALFA
ALFAQUI
ALFAQUIN
ALFARGA
ALFENIDE
ALFEREZ
ALFET
ALFILARIA
ALFILERIA
ALFILERILLO
ALFIN
ALFIONA
ALFIONE
ALFONCINO
ALFONSIN
ALFONSO
ALFORGE
ALFORJA
ALFRESCO
ALFRIDARIC
ALFRIDARY
ALGA
ALGAE
ALGAECIDE
ALGAESTHESIS
ALGAL
ALGALIA
ALGAROBA
ALGARROBA
ALGARROBILLA
ALGARROBIN
ALGATE
ALGATES
ALGAZEL
ALGEBRA
ALGEBRAIC
ALGEBRAICAL
ALGEBRAIST
ALGEBRAIZE
ALGEBRAIZED
ALGEBRAIZING
ALGEBRIZATION
ALGEDO
ALGEDONIC
ALGEDONICS
ALGEFACIENT
ALGERINE
ALGESIA
ALGESIC
ALGESIS
ALGESTHESIS
ALGETIC
ALGIC
ALGICIDE
ALGID
ALGIDITY
ALGIDNESS
ALGIFIC
ALGIN
ALGINATE
ALGINE
ALGINIC
ALGINURESIS
ALGIST
ALGIVOROUS
ALGOCYAN
ALGODON
ALGODONITE
ALGOGENIC
ALGOID
ALGOLAGNIA
ALGOLAGNIC
ALGOLAGNIST
ALGOLAGNY
ALGOLOGICAL
ALGOLOGIST
ALGOLOGY
ALGOMETER
ALGOMETRIC
ALGOMETRICAL
ALGOMETRY
ALGOPHILIA
ALGOPHOBIA
ALGOR
ALGORISM
ALGORISMIC
ALGORIST
ALGORITHM
ALGORITHMIC
ALGOSIS
ALGOUS
ALGOVITE
ALGUACIL
ALGUAZIL
ALGUM
ALHACENA
ALHENNA
ALHET
ALIAS
ALIASES
ALIBANGBANG
ALIBI
ALIBIED
ALIBIING
ALIBILITY
ALIBIS
ALIBLE
ALICHEL
ALICOCHE
ALICTISAL
ALICULA
ALICULAE

ALICYCLIC
ALIDAD
ALIDADA
ALIDADE
ALIEN
ALIENABILITY
ALIENABLE
ALIENAGE
ALIENATE
ALIENATED
ALIENATING
ALIENATION
ALIENATOR
ALIENE
ALIENED
ALIENEE
ALIENER
ALIENICOLA
ALIENICOLAE
ALIENIGENATE
ALIENING
ALIENISM
ALIENIST
ALIENOR
ALIETHMOID
ALIETHMOIDAL
ALIF
ALIFE
ALIFEROUS
ALIFORM
ALIGEROUS
ALIGHT
ALIGHTED
ALIGHTEN
ALIGHTING
ALIGN
ALIGNED
ALIGNER
ALIGNING
ALIGNMENT
ALIGREEK
ALII
ALIIPOE
ALIKE
ALIKENESS
ALILA
ALILONGHI
ALIM
ALIMA
ALIMENT
ALIMENTAL
ALIMENTALLY
ALIMENTARY
ALIMENTATION
ALIMENTATIVE
ALIMENTER
ALIMENTIC
ALIMENTIVE
ALIMONIED
ALIMONY
ALIN
ALINASAL
ALINE
ALINEATION
ALINED
ALINEMENT
ALINER
ALINING
ALINIT
ALINOTUM
ALINTATAO
ALIOFAR
ALIPATA
ALIPED
ALIPHATIC
ALIPIN
ALIPTAE
ALIPTES
ALIPTIC
ALIQUANT
ALIQUID
ALIQUOT
ALISANDERS
ALISEPTAL
ALISH
ALISIER
ALISMA
ALISMACEOUS
ALISMAD
ALISMAL
ALISMOID
ALISO
ALISON
ALISONITE
ALISOS
ALISP
ALISPHENOID
ALIST
ALIT
ALITE
ALITER
ALITRUNK
ALITURGIC
ALITURGICAL
ALIUD
ALIUNDE
ALIVE
ALIVENESS
ALIVINCULAR
ALIYAH
ALIZARATE
ALIZARI
ALIZARIN
ALIZARINE
ALJAMA
ALJAMADO
ALJAMIA
ALJAMIADO
ALJAMIAH
ALJOFAINA
ALK
ALKAHEST
ALKAHESTIC
ALKAHESTICAL
ALKALAMIDE
ALKALEMIA
ALKALESCENCE
ALKALESCENCY
ALKALESCENT
ALKALI
ALKALIC
ALKALIES
ALKALIFIABLE
ALKALIFIED
ALKALIFY
ALKALIFYING
ALKALIGEN
ALKALIMETER
ALKALIMETRIC
ALKALIMETRY
ALKALINE
ALKALINITY
ALKALINIZE
ALKALINIZED
ALKALINIZING
ALKALINURIA
ALKALIS
ALKALIZABLE
ALKALIZATE
ALKALIZATION
ALKALIZE
ALKALIZER
ALKALOID
ALKALOIDAL
ALKALOIDS
ALKALOMETRY
ALKALOSIS
ALKANAL
ALKANET
ALKANNA
ALKANNIN
ALKANOL
ALKAPTON
ALKAPTONE
ALKAPTONURIA
ALKAPTONURIC
ALKARSIN
ALKARSINE
ALKEKENGI
ALKENE
ALKENYL
ALKERMES
ALKID
ALKIDE
ALKIN
ALKINE
ALKITRAN
ALKOOL
ALKOXID
ALKOXIDE
ALKOXY
ALKOXYL
ALKY
ALKYD
ALKYL
ALKYLAMINE
ALKYLAMINO
ALKYLATE
ALKYLATED
ALKYLATING
ALKYLATION
ALKYLENE
ALKYLIC
ALKYLIDENE
ALKYLIZE
ALKYLOGEN
ALKYLOL
ALKYNE
ALL
ALLA
ALLABUTA
ALLACTITE
ALLAEANTHUS
ALLAGITE
ALLALINITE
ALLAMONTI
ALLAMOTH
ALLAMOTTI
ALLAN
ALLANITE
ALLANITIC
ALLANTIASIS
ALLANTOIC
ALLANTOID
ALLANTOIDAL
ALLANTOIDEAN
ALLANTOIDIAN
ALLANTOIN
ALLANTOIS
ALLANTURIC
ALLARGANDO
ALLASSOTONIC
ALLATIVE
ALLATRATE
ALLAY
ALLAYED
ALLAYER
ALLAYING
ALLAYMENT
ALLBE
ALLBONE
ALLECRET
ALLECT
ALLEE
ALLEGATE
ALLEGATION
ALLEGATOR
ALLEGE
ALLEGEABLE
ALLEGED
ALLEGEDLY
ALLEGEMENT
ALLEGER
ALLEGIANCE
ALLEGIANT
ALLEGING
ALLEGORIC
ALLEGORICAL
ALLEGORICALLY
ALLEGORIES
ALLEGORISM
ALLEGORIST
ALLEGORISTER
ALLEGORISTIC
ALLEGORIZATION
ALLEGORIZE
ALLEGORIZED
ALLEGORIZER
ALLEGORIZING
ALLEGORY
ALLEGRESSE
ALLEGRETTO
ALLEGRETTOS
ALLEGRO
ALLEGROS
ALLEL
ALLELE
ALLELOMORPH
ALLELOTROPY
ALLELUIA
ALLELUIAH
ALLELUIATIC
ALLELUJA
ALLEMAND
ALLEMANDE
ALLEMONTITE
ALLENARLY
ALLENE
ALLENTANDO
ALLENTATO
ALLER
ALLERGEN
ALLERGENIC
ALLERGIC
ALLERGIES
ALLERGIN
ALLERGIST
ALLERGY
ALLERION
ALLEVIATE
ALLEVIATED
ALLEVIATING
ALLEVIATION
ALLEVIATIVE
ALLEVIATOR
ALLEVIATORY
ALLEY
ALLEYED
ALLEYITE
ALLEYS
ALLEYWAY
ALLGOOD
ALLGOVITE
ALLHEAL
ALLIABLE
ALLIABLY
ALLIACEOUS
ALLIANCE
ALLIANCED
ALLIANCER
ALLIANCING
ALLIANT
ALLICHOLLY
ALLICIENCY
ALLICIENT
ALLICIN
ALLIED
ALLIES
ALLIGATE
ALLIGATION
ALLIGATOR
ALLIGATORED
ALLIGATORING
ALLINEATE
ALLINEATION
ALLIS
ALLISION
ALLITERAL
ALLITERATE
ALLITERATED
ALLITERATING
ALLITERATION
ALLITERATIVE
ALLITERATOR
ALLIUM
ALLIVALITE
ALLMOUTH
ALLNESS
ALLO
ALLOBAR
ALLOBARIC
ALLOCABLE
ALLOCAFFEINE
ALLOCATABLE
ALLOCATE
ALLOCATED
ALLOCATING
ALLOCATION
ALLOCATUR
ALLOCHEIRIA
ALLOCHETITE
ALLOCHEZIA
ALLOCHIRAL
ALLOCHIRALLY
ALLOCHIRIA
ALLOCHROIC
ALLOCHROITE
ALLOCHROOUS
ALLOCLASE
ALLOCLASITE
ALLOCOCHICK
ALLOCROTONIC
ALLOCRYPTIC
ALLOCTHONOUS
ALLOCUTE
ALLOCUTION
ALLOCUTIVE
ALLOCYANINE
ALLOD
ALLODELPHITE
ALLODESMISM
ALLODGE
ALLODIA
ALLODIAL
ALLODIALISM
ALLODIALIST
ALLODIALITY
ALLODIALLY
ALLODIAN
ALLODIARIES
ALLODIARY
ALLODIES
ALLODIUM
ALLODY
ALLOEOSIS

ALLOEOTIC
ALLOEROTIC
ALLOEROTISM
ALLOGAMOUS
ALLOGAMY
ALLOGENEITY
ALLOGENEOUS
ALLOGENIC
ALLOGRAPH
ALLOKINESIS
ALLOKINETIC
ALLOKURTIC
ALLOLALIA
ALLOLALIC
ALLOMERISM
ALLOMEROUS
ALLOMORPH
ALLOMORPHIC
ALLOMORPHISM
ALLOMORPHITE
ALLOMUCIC
ALLONGE
ALLONOMOUS
ALLONYM
ALLONYMOUS
ALLOPATH
ALLOPATHETIC
ALLOPATHIC
ALLOPATHIST
ALLOPATHY
ALLOPELAGIC
ALLOPHANAMID
ALLOPHANATES
ALLOPHANE
ALLOPHANIC
ALLOPHONE
ALLOPHORE
ALLOPHYLIAN
ALLOPHYTOID
ALLOPLASM
ALLOPLASMIC
ALLOPLAST
ALLOPLASTIC
ALLOPLASTY
ALLOPSYCHIC
ALLOQUIAL
ALLOQUIALISM
ALLOQUY
ALLOSAUR
ALLOSE
ALLOSEMATIC
ALLOSOME
ALLOT
ALLOTED
ALLOTELLURIC
ALLOTHEISM
ALLOTHIMORPH
ALLOTHOGENIC
ALLOTMENT
ALLOTRIURIA
ALLOTROPE
ALLOTROPIC
ALLOTROPICAL
ALLOTROPISM
ALLOTROPIZE
ALLOTROPOUS
ALLOTROPY
ALLOTRYLIC
ALLOTTED
ALLOTTEE
ALLOTTER
ALLOTTERY
ALLOTTING
ALLOTYPE
ALLOTYPICAL
ALLOVER
ALLOW
ALLOWABLE
ALLOWABLENESS
ALLOWABLY
ALLOWANCE
ALLOWANCED
ALLOWANCING
ALLOWED
ALLOWEDLY
ALLOWER
ALLOWING
ALLOXAN
ALLOXANATE
ALLOXANIC
ALLOXANTIN
ALLOXURIC
ALLOXY
ALLOY
ALLOYAGE
ALLOYED
ALLOYING
ALLOZOOID
ALLS
ALLSEED
ALLSPICE
ALLTHING
ALLTHORN
ALLTUD
ALLUDE
ALLUDED
ALLUDING
ALLUMETTE
ALLURE
ALLURED
ALLUREMENT
ALLURER
ALLURING
ALLURINGLY
ALLURINGNESS
ALLUSION
ALLUSIVE
ALLUSIVELY
ALLUSIVENESS
ALLUVIA
ALLUVIAL
ALLUVIATE
ALLUVIATION
ALLUVIO
ALLUVION
ALLUVIOUS
ALLUVIUM
ALLUVIUMS
ALLWHERE
ALLWHITHER
ALLWORK
ALLY
ALLYING
ALLYL
ALLYLAMINE
ALLYLATE
ALLYLATION
ALLYLENE
ALLYLIC
ALMA
ALMACEN
ALMACENISTA
ALMACIGA
ALMACIGO
ALMADIA
ALMADIE
ALMAGEST
ALMAGRA
ALMAH
ALMANAC
ALMANDER
ALMANDINE
ALMANDITE
ALME
ALMEH
ALMEIDINA
ALMEMAR
ALMEMOR
ALMENDRO
ALMENDRON
ALMERIITE
ALMICORE
ALMIGHTILY
ALMIGHTINESS
ALMIGHTY
ALMIQUE
ALMIRAH
ALMOCREBE
ALMOGAVAR
ALMOHAD
ALMOIGN
ALMOIN
ALMON
ALMOND
ALMONDY
ALMONER
ALMONING
ALMONRIES
ALMONRY
ALMOST
ALMOUS
ALMS
ALMSDEED
ALMSFOLK
ALMSGIVER
ALMSGIVING
ALMSHOUSE
ALMSMAN
ALMSMEN
ALMSMONEY
ALMSWOMAN
ALMSWOMEN
ALMUCANTAR
ALMUCE
ALMUD
ALMUDE
ALMUERZO
ALMUG
ALMURY
ALMUTEN
ALN
ALNAGE
ALNAGER
ALNAGERSHIP
ALNEIN
ALNICO
ALNIRESINOL
ALNOITE
ALNUIN
ALNUS
ALOCASIA
ALOCHIA
ALOD
ALODIAL
ALODIALISM
ALODIALIST
ALODIALITY
ALODIALLY
ALODIAN
ALODIARIES
ALODIARY
ALODIES
ALODIUM
ALODY
ALOE
ALOED
ALOEDARY
ALOEMODIN
ALOEROOT
ALOES
ALOESOL
ALOESWOOD
ALOETIC
ALOETICAL
ALOEWOOD
ALOFT
ALOGIA
ALOGICAL
ALOGICALLY
ALOGISM
ALOGY
ALOHA
ALOID
ALOIN
ALOISIITE
ALOJA
ALOMA
ALONE
ALONELY
ALONG
ALONGSHORE
ALONGSHOREMAN
ALONGSIDE
ALONGST
ALOOF
ALOOFE
ALOOFLY
ALOOFNESS
ALOOSE
ALOP
ALOPECIA
ALOPECIST
ALOPECOID
ALOPEKAI
ALOPEKE
ALOPHAS
ALOSE
ALOUATTE
ALOUD
ALOUT
ALOW
ALOWE
ALOYAU
ALOYSIA
ALP
ALPACA
ALPARGATA
ALPASOTES
ALPAX
ALPEEN
ALPENGLOW
ALPENHORN
ALPENSTOCK
ALPENSTOCKER
ALPESTRAL
ALPESTRIAN
ALPESTRINE
ALPHA
ALPHABET
ALPHABETARY
ALPHABETED
ALPHABETIC
ALPHABETICAL
ALPHABETICALLY
ALPHABETICS
ALPHABETIFORM
ALPHABETING
ALPHABETISM
ALPHABETIST
ALPHABETIZATION
ALPHABETIZE
ALPHABETIZED
ALPHABETIZER
ALPHABETIZING
ALPHATOLUIC
ALPHENIC
ALPHIN
ALPHOL
ALPHORN
ALPHOS
ALPHOSIS
ALPHYL
ALPHYN
ALPIEU
ALPIGENE
ALPINE
ALPINELY
ALPINERY
ALPINIA
ALPINISM
ALPINIST
ALPIST
ALPISTE
ALQUEIRE
ALQUIER
ALQUIFOU
ALRAUN
ALREADINESS
ALREADY
ALRIGHT
ALRIGHTY
ALROOT
ALRUNA
ALRUNE
ALS
ALSBACHITE
ALSIFILM
ALSIKE
ALSINACEOUS
ALSMEKILL
ALSO
ALSOON
ALSTONIDINE
ALSTONINE
ALSWEILL
ALSWITH
ALT
ALTAR
ALTARAGE
ALTARED
ALTARIST
ALTARLET
ALTARPIECE
ALTARWISE
ALTAZIMUTH
ALTEA
ALTER
ALTERABILITY
ALTERABLE
ALTERABLENESS
ALTERABLY
ALTERANT
ALTERATION
ALTERATIVE
ALTERCATE
ALTERCATED
ALTERCATING
ALTERCATION
ALTERCATIVE
ALTERED
ALTEREGOISM
ALTERER
ALTERING
ALTERITY
ALTERN
ALTERNACY
ALTERNAMENTE
ALTERNANCE
ALTERNANT
ALTERNARIOSE
ALTERNAT
ALTERNATE
ALTERNATED
ALTERNATELY
ALTERNATER

ALTERNATING
ALTERNATION
ALTERNATIVE
ALTERNATIVELY
ALTERNATIVENESS
ALTERNATIVITY
ALTERNATIVO
ALTERNATOR
ALTERNE
ALTERNIZE
ALTERUM
ALTESSE
ALTEZA
ALTEZZA
ALTHAEA
ALTHAEIN
ALTHEA
ALTHEIN
ALTHEINE
ALTHIONIC
ALTHO
ALTHORN
ALTHOUGH
ALTI
ALTIFY
ALTIGRAPH
ALTILIK
ALTILOQUENCE
ALTILOQUENT
ALTIMETER
ALTIMETRICAL
ALTIMETRY
ALTIN
ALTINCAR
ALTININCK
ALTIPLANICIE
ALTIPLANO
ALTISCOPE
ALTISONANT
ALTISSIMO
ALTITUDE
ALTITUDES
ALTITUDINAL
ALTO
ALTOCUMULUS
ALTOGETHER
ALTOIST
ALTOMETER
ALTOS
ALTOSTRATUS
ALTOUN
ALTRICES
ALTRICIAL
ALTROSE
ALTRUISM
ALTRUIST
ALTRUISTIC
ALTRUISTICALLY
ALTSCHIN
ALTUN
ALTURE
ALTUS
ALUDEL
ALULA
ALULAE
ALULAR
ALULET
ALUM
ALUMBLOOM
ALUMEN
ALUMETIZE
ALUMINA
ALUMINAPHONE
ALUMINATE
ALUMINE
ALUMINIC
ALUMINIDE
ALUMINIFORM
ALUMINITE
ALUMINIUM
ALUMINIZE
ALUMINIZED
ALUMINIZING
ALUMINOSE
ALUMINOSIS
ALUMINOSITY
ALUMINOTYPE
ALUMINOUS
ALUMINUM
ALUMINYL
ALUMITE
ALUMNA
ALUMNAE
ALUMNAL
ALUMNI
ALUMNIATE
ALUMNUS
ALUMROOT
ALUMSTONE
ALUNITE
ALUNOGEN
ALUPAG
ALURE
ALURGITE
ALUSHTITE
ALUTA
ALUTACEOUS
ALVAR
ALVEARIES
ALVEARIUM
ALVEARY
ALVEI
ALVELOS
ALVELOZ
ALVEOLA
ALVEOLAE
ALVEOLAR
ALVEOLARY
ALVEOLATE
ALVEOLATED
ALVEOLATION
ALVEOLE
ALVEOLI
ALVEOLIFORM
ALVEOLITE
ALVEOLONASAL
ALVEOLOTOMY
ALVEOLUS
ALVEUS
ALVIDUCOUS
ALVIN
ALVINE
ALVITE
ALVUS
ALWAY
ALWAYS
ALWISE
ALY
ALYMPHIA
ALYPIN
ALYPINE
ALYSSON
ALYSSUM
ALYTARCH
AM
AMA
AMAAS
AMABILE
AMABILITY
AMACRATIC
AMACRINAL
AMACRINE
AMADAVAT
AMADELPHOUS
AMADOU
AMAGA
AMAH
AMAIN
AMAINE
AMAIST
AMAISTER
AMAKEBE
AMALA
AMALAITA
AMALAKA
AMALETT
AMALGAM
AMALGAMABLE
AMALGAMATE
AMALGAMATED
AMALGAMATER
AMALGAMATING
AMALGAMATION
AMALGAMATIVE
AMALGAMATOR
AMALGAMIST
AMALGAMIZE
AMALTAS
AMAMAU
AMAND
AMANDIN
AMANG
AMANI
AMANIA
AMANITIN
AMANITINE
AMANORI
AMANOUS
AMANT
AMANTE
AMANUENSES
AMANUENSIS
AMAPA
AMAR
AMARANTH
AMARANTHINE
AMARANTHOID
AMARANTITE
AMARELLE
AMAREVOLE
AMARGOSA
AMARGOSO
AMARGOSOS
AMARILLO
AMARILLOS
AMARIN
AMARINE
AMARITY
AMAROID
AMAROIDAL
AMARTHRITIS
AMARYLLID
AMASESIS
AMASS
AMASSED
AMASSER
AMASSETTE
AMASSING
AMASSMENT
AMASTHENIC
AMASTIA
AMASTY
AMATE
AMATEUR
AMATEURISH
AMATEURISHLY
AMATEURISHNESS
AMATEURISM
AMATITO
AMATIVE
AMATIVELY
AMATIVENESS
AMATOL
AMATORIAL
AMATORIALLY
AMATORIAN
AMATORIES
AMATORIO
AMATORIOUS
AMATORY
AMATRICE
AMATUNGULA
AMAUROSIS
AMAUROTIC
AMAXOMANIA
AMAY
AMAZE
AMAZED
AMAZEFUL
AMAZEMENT
AMAZING
AMAZON
AMAZONITE
AMBA
AMBACH
AMBAGE
AMBAGES
AMBAGIOSITY
AMBAGIOUS
AMBAGIOUSLY
AMBAGITORY
AMBAK
AMBALAM
AMBAN
AMBAR
AMBAREE
AMBARELLA
AMBARI
AMBARY
AMBAS
AMBASH
AMBASSADE
AMBASSADOR
AMBASSADRESS
AMBASSY
AMBATCH
AMBAY
AMBE
AMBEER
AMBER
AMBERFISH
AMBERGRIS
AMBERIFEROUS
AMBERINA
AMBERITE
AMBERJACK
AMBEROID
AMBEROUS
AMBERY
AMBIANCE
AMBIDEXTER
AMBIDEXTERITY
AMBIDEXTRAL
AMBIDEXTROUS
AMBIENCE
AMBIENS
AMBIENT
AMBIER
AMBIGENOUS
AMBIGUITIES
AMBIGUITY
AMBIGUOUS
AMBIGUOUSLY
AMBIGUOUSNESS
AMBILATERAL
AMBILEVOUS
AMBILIAN
AMBIOPIA
AMBIPAROUS
AMBISINISTER
AMBIT
AMBITAL
AMBITENDENCY
AMBITION
AMBITIONIST
AMBITIONLESS
AMBITIOUS
AMBITIOUSLY
AMBITIOUSNESS
AMBITTY
AMBITUS
AMBIVALENCE
AMBIVALENCY
AMBIVALENT
AMBIVERSION
AMBIVERT
AMBLE
AMBLED
AMBLER
AMBLING
AMBLINGLY
AMBLOTIC
AMBLYGON
AMBLYGONITE
AMBLYOPE
AMBLYOPIA
AMBLYOPIC
AMBLYOSCOPE
AMBLYPOD
AMBLYSTEGITE
AMBO
AMBOCEPTOR
AMBOMALLEAL
AMBON
AMBONES
AMBONITE
AMBOS
AMBOSEXOUS
AMBRACAN
AMBRAIN
AMBRETTE
AMBRIES
AMBRITE
AMBROID
AMBROLOGY
AMBROSE
AMBROSIA
AMBROSIAC
AMBROSIAL
AMBROSIALLY
AMBROSIAN
AMBROSIATE
AMBROSIN
AMBROSINE
AMBROSTEROL
AMBROTYPE
AMBRY
AMBSACE
AMBULACRA
AMBULACRAL
AMBULACRUM
AMBULANCE
AMBULANCED
AMBULANCER
AMBULANCING
AMBULANT
AMBULATE
AMBULATED
AMBULATING
AMBULATION
AMBULATIVE
AMBULATOR
AMBULATORIA
AMBULATORIAL
AMBULATORIES

AMBULATORIUM
AMBULATORIUMS
AMBULATORY
AMBULIA
AMBULING
AMBULOMANCY
AMBURBIAL
AMBURY
AMBUSCADE
AMBUSCADED
AMBUSCADER
AMBUSCADING
AMBUSCADO
AMBUSCADOED
AMBUSH
AMBUSHER
AMBUSHMENT
AMCHOOR
AME
AMEBA
AMEBAE
AMEBAN
AMEBAS
AMEBIAN
AMEBIASIS
AMEBIC
AMEBICIDAL
AMEBICIDE
AMEBID
AMEBIFORM
AMEBOBACTER
AMEBOCYTE
AMEBOID
AMEBOIDISM
AMEBOUS
AMEBULA
AMEED
AMEEN
AMEER
AMEIOSIS
AMEL
AMELAND
AMELCORN
AMELET
AMELIORABLE
AMELIORANT
AMELIORATE
AMELIORATED
AMELIORATING
AMELIORATION
AMELIORATIVE
AMELIORATOR
AMELL
AMELLUS
AMELU
AMELUS
AMEN
AMENABILITY
AMENABLE
AMENABLENESS
AMENABLY
AMENAGE
AMENANCE
AMEND
AMENDABLE
AMENDATORY
AMENDE
AMENDER
AMENDING
AMENDMENT
AMENDS
AMENE
AMENITIES
AMENITY
AMENORRHEA
AMENORRHEAL
AMENORRHEIC
AMENORRHOEA
AMENORRHOEAL
AMENORRHOEIC
AMENT
AMENTA
AMENTACEOUS
AMENTAL
AMENTIA
AMENTIFEROUS
AMENTIFORM
AMENTULA
AMENTULUM
AMENTUM
AMENUSE
AMER
AMERCE
AMERCEABLE
AMERCED
AMERCEMENT
AMERCER
AMERCIAMENT
AMERCING
AMERICIUM
AMERIKANI
AMERISM
AMERISTIC
AMERVEIL
AMESACE
AMESE
AMESITE
AMETABOLE
AMETABOLIC
AMETABOLISM
AMETABOLOUS
AMETALLOUS
AMETHODICAL
AMETHYST
AMETHYSTINE
AMETRIA
AMETROMETER
AMETROPE
AMETROPIA
AMETROPIC
AMETROUS
AMGARN
AMHAR
AMHERSTITE
AMHRAN
AMI
AMIA
AMIABILITY
AMIABLE
AMIABLENESS
AMIABLY
AMIANTH
AMIANTHINE
AMIANTHOID
AMIANTHOIDAL
AMIANTHUS
AMIANTUS
AMIC
AMICABILITY
AMICABLE
AMICABLENESS
AMICABLY
AMICAL
AMICE
AMICED
AMICICIDE
AMICOUS
AMICROBIC
AMICRON
AMICTUS
AMID
AMIDASE
AMIDATE
AMIDATION
AMIDE
AMIDIC
AMIDIN
AMIDINE
AMIDO
AMIDOACETAL
AMIDOACETIC
AMIDOCAPRIC
AMIDOGEN
AMIDOHEXOSE
AMIDOKETONE
AMIDOL
AMIDOMYELIN
AMIDONE
AMIDOPHENOL
AMIDOPYRINE
AMIDOXIME
AMIDOXYL
AMIDRAZONE
AMIDSHIP
AMIDSHIPS
AMIDST
AMIDSTREAM
AMIDULIN
AMIE
AMIGA
AMIGO
AMIGOS
AMIL
AMIMIA
AMIN
AMINASE
AMINATE
AMINATION
AMINE
AMINI
AMINIC
AMINITY
AMINO
AMINOACETAL
AMINOACETONE
AMINOAZO
AMINOBENZENE
AMINOBENZOIC
AMINOCAPROIC
AMINOFORMIC
AMINOGEN
AMINOKETONE
AMINOLIPIN
AMINOLYSIS
AMINOLYTIC
AMINOMYELIN
AMINOPHENOL
AMINOPURINE
AMINOSIS
AMINOVALERIC
AMINOXYLOL
AMIR
AMIRAY
AMIS
AMISS
AMISSIBILITY
AMISSIBLE
AMISSION
AMIT
AMITATE
AMITIE
AMITIES
AMITOSIS
AMITOTIC
AMITOTICALLY
AMITY
AMIXIA
AMLA
AMLAH
AMLET
AMLI
AMLIKAR
AMLONG
AMMA
AMMAN
AMMELINE
AMMEOS
AMMER
AMMETER
AMMIACEOUS
AMMINE
AMMINOLYSIS
AMMINOLYTIC
AMMIOLITE
AMMO
AMMOBIUM
AMMOCETE
AMMOCHAETA
AMMOCHAETAE
AMMOCHRYSE
AMMOCOETE
AMMOCOETES
AMMOCOETID
AMMOCOETOID
AMMODYTE
AMMODYTOID
AMMONAL
AMMONATE
AMMONATION
AMMONIA
AMMONIAC
AMMONIACAL
AMMONIACUM
AMMONIAEMIA
AMMONIATE
AMMONIATED
AMMONIATING
AMMONIATION
AMMONIC
AMMONICAL
AMMONIEMIA
AMMONIFIER
AMMONIFY
AMMONION
AMMONITE
AMMONITIC
AMMONITOID
AMMONIUM
AMMONIURET
AMMONIURETED
AMMONIURIA
AMMONIZATION
AMMONOBASIC
AMMONOID
AMMONOIDEAN
AMMONOLYSIS
AMMONOLYTIC
AMMONOLYZE
AMMOPHILOUS
AMMORESLINOL
AMMOTHERAPY
AMMU
AMMUNITION
AMNEMONIC
AMNESIA
AMNESIC
AMNESTIC
AMNESTIES
AMNESTY
AMNIA
AMNIAC
AMNIC
AMNIOCHORIAL
AMNIOCLEPSIS
AMNIOMANCY
AMNION
AMNIONIC
AMNIONS
AMNIORRHEA
AMNIOS
AMNIOTE
AMNIOTIC
AMNIOTITIS
AMNIOTOME
AMOBARBITAL
AMOBER
AMOEBA
AMOEBAE
AMOEBAEA
AMOEBAEAN
AMOEBAEUM
AMOEBAN
AMOEBEAN
AMOEBEUM
AMOEBIAN
AMOEBIASIS
AMOEBIC
AMOEBICIDAL
AMOEBICIDE
AMOEBID
AMOEBIFORM
AMOEBOCYTE
AMOEBOID
AMOEBOIDISM
AMOEBOUS
AMOEBULA
AMOINDER
AMOK
AMOKE
AMOLE
AMOLILLA
AMOLISH
AMOLLISH
AMOMAL
AMOMUM
AMONG
AMONGST
AMONTILLADO
AMOR
AMORA
AMORADO
AMORAIC
AMORAIM
AMORAL
AMORALISM
AMORALITY
AMORALLY
AMORET
AMORETTI
AMORETTO
AMORINI
AMORINO
AMORISM
AMORIST
AMORISTIC
AMOROSA
AMOROSITY
AMOROSO
AMOROUS
AMOROUSLY
AMOROUSNESS
AMORPH
AMORPHA
AMORPHI
AMORPHIA
AMORPHIC
AMORPHINISM
AMORPHISM
AMORPHOPHYTE
AMORPHOTAE
AMORPHOUS
AMORPHOUSLY
AMORPHUS
AMORPHY
AMORT

AMORTISE
AMORTISSEUR
AMORTIZABLE
AMORTIZATION
AMORTIZE
AMORTIZED
AMORTIZEMENT
AMORTIZING
AMOSITE
AMOTION
AMOTUS
AMOULI
AMOUNT
AMOUR
AMOURET
AMOURETTE
AMOURIST
AMOVABILITY
AMOVABLE
AMOVE
AMOVED
AMOVING
AMPALAYA
AMPALEA
AMPANGABEITE
AMPARO
AMPASIMENITE
AMPASSY
AMPELITE
AMPELITIC
AMPELOGRAPHY
AMPELOPSIDIN
AMPELOPSIN
AMPELOPSIS
AMPER
AMPERAGE
AMPERE
AMPEREMETER
AMPEROMETER
AMPERSAND
AMPERY
AMPHANTHIA
AMPHANTHIUM
AMPHEROTOKY
AMPHETAMINE
AMPHIASTER
AMPHIB
AMPHIBALI
AMPHIBALUS
AMPHIBIA
AMPHIBIAL
AMPHIBIAN
AMPHIBIETY
AMPHIBIOLOGY
AMPHIBION
AMPHIBIOTIC
AMPHIBIOUS
AMPHIBIOUSLY
AMPHIBIUM
AMPHIBLASTIC
AMPHIBOLE
AMPHIBOLIA
AMPHIBOLIC
AMPHIBOLITE
AMPHIBOLITIC
AMPHIBOLOGY
AMPHIBOLOUS
AMPHIBOLY
AMPHIBRACH
AMPHIBRACHIC
AMPHIBRYOUS
AMPHICARPIA
AMPHICARPIC
AMPHICARPIUM
AMPHICENTRIC
AMPHICHROIC
AMPHICHROME
AMPHICHROMY
AMPHICOELOUS
AMPHICRANIA
AMPHICRIBRAL
AMPHICTYON
AMPHICTYONIC
AMPHICTYONY
AMPHICYRTIC
AMPHICYTULA
AMPHID
AMPHIDE
AMPHIDESMOUS
AMPHIDETIC
AMPHIDIPLOID
AMPHIDISC
AMPHIDISK
AMPHIEROTIC
AMPHIEROTISM
AMPHIGAEAN
AMPHIGAM
AMPHIGAMOUS
AMPHIGEAN
AMPHIGEN
AMPHIGENE
AMPHIGENESIS
AMPHIGENETIC
AMPHIGENOUS
AMPHIGONIA
AMPHIGONIC
AMPHIGONIUM
AMPHIGONOUS
AMPHIGONY
AMPHIGORIC
AMPHIGORIES
AMPHIGORY
AMPHIGOURI
AMPHIGOURIS
AMPHIKARYON
AMPHILOGISM
AMPHILOGY
AMPHIMACER
AMPHIMIXIS
AMPHIMORULA
AMPHIMORULAE
AMPHINEUROUS
AMPHINUCLEUS
AMPHIOXUS
AMPHIPHLOIC
AMPHIPLATYAN
AMPHIPNEUST
AMPHIPNEUSTIC
AMPHIPOD
AMPHIPODAL
AMPHIPODAN
AMPHIPODOUS
AMPHIPYRENIN
AMPHIRHINAL
AMPHIRHINE
AMPHISARCA
AMPHISBAENA
AMPHISBAENIC
AMPHISCIANS
AMPHISCII
AMPHISPORE
AMPHISTOME
AMPHISTOMOID
AMPHISTOMOUS
AMPHISTYLAR
AMPHISTYLIC
AMPHISTYLY
AMPHITENE
AMPHITHEATER
AMPHITHEATRE
AMPHITHECIA
AMPHITHECIAL
AMPHITHECIUM
AMPHITHECT
AMPHITHYRON
AMPHITOKAL
AMPHITOKOUS
AMPHITOKY
AMPHITRIAENE
AMPHITRICHA
AMPHITROPAL
AMPHITROPOUS
AMPHIVASAL
AMPHIVOROUS
AMPHODARCH
AMPHODELITE
AMPHOGENOUS
AMPHOLYTE
AMPHOPEPTONE
AMPHOPHILIC
AMPHOPHILOUS
AMPHORA
AMPHORAE
AMPHORAL
AMPHORE
AMPHORIC
AMPHORICITY
AMPHORILOQUY
AMPHOROPHONY
AMPHOROUS
AMPHOTERIC
AMPLE
AMPLECT
AMPLECTANT
AMPLENESS
AMPLEX
AMPLEXATION
AMPLEXICAUL
AMPLEXUS
AMPLIATE
AMPLIATION
AMPLIATIVE
AMPLICATIVE
AMPLIFICATE
AMPLIFICATION
AMPLIFICATIVE
AMPLIFICATOR
AMPLIFIED
AMPLIFIER
AMPLIFY
AMPLIFYING
AMPLITUDE
AMPLY
AMPOLLOSITY
AMPONGUE
AMPOULE
AMPTE
AMPUL
AMPULE
AMPULLA
AMPULLACEOUS
AMPULLAE
AMPULLAR
AMPULLARY
AMPULLATE
AMPULLATED
AMPULLIFORM
AMPULLITIS
AMPULLULA
AMPUTATE
AMPUTATED
AMPUTATING
AMPUTATION
AMPUTATIVE
AMPUTATOR
AMPUTEE
AMPYCES
AMPYX
AMPYXES
AMRA
AMREETA
AMREL
AMRELLE
AMRIT
AMRITA
AMSATH
AMSEL
AMSONIA
AMT
AMTER
AMTMAN
AMTMEN
AMTS
AMU
AMUCK
AMUGIS
AMUGUIS
AMULA
AMULAE
AMULAS
AMULET
AMULETIC
AMULLA
AMUNAM
AMURCA
AMURCOSITY
AMURCOUS
AMUSABLE
AMUSE
AMUSED
AMUSEDLY
AMUSEMENT
AMUSEMENTS
AMUSER
AMUSETTE
AMUSIA
AMUSING
AMUSINGLY
AMUSINGNESS
AMUSIVE
AMUSIVELY
AMUSIVENESS
AMUTTER
AMUYON
AMUYONG
AMUZE
AMVIS
AMY
AMYDON
AMYELIA
AMYELIC
AMYELINIC
AMYELONIC
AMYELOUS
AMYGDAL
AMYGDALA
AMYGDALAE
AMYGDALASE
AMYGDALATE
AMYGDALE
AMYGDALIC
AMYGDALIFORM
AMYGDALIN
AMYGDALINE
AMYGDALITIS
AMYGDALOID
AMYGDALOIDAL
AMYGDALOLITH
AMYGDALONCUS
AMYGDALOTOME
AMYGDALOTOMY
AMYGDOPHENIN
AMYGDULE
AMYL
AMYLACEOUS
AMYLAMINE
AMYLAN
AMYLASE
AMYLATE
AMYLEMIA
AMYLENE
AMYLIC
AMYLIDENE
AMYLIFEROUS
AMYLIN
AMYLO
AMYLOCLASTIC
AMYLODEXTRIN
AMYLOGEN
AMYLOGENESIS
AMYLOGENIC
AMYLOID
AMYLOIDAL
AMYLOIDOSIS
AMYLOLEUCITE
AMYLOLYSIS
AMYLOLYTIC
AMYLOM
AMYLOME
AMYLOMETER
AMYLON
AMYLOPECTIN
AMYLOPHAGIA
AMYLOPLAST
AMYLOPLASTIC
AMYLOPLASTID
AMYLOPSASE
AMYLOPSIN
AMYLOSE
AMYLOSIS
AMYLUM
AMYLURIA
AMYNODONT
AMYOSTHENIA
AMYOSTHENIC
AMYOTAXIA
AMYOTONIA
AMYOTROPHIA
AMYOTROPHIC
AMYOTROPHY
AMYOUS
AMYRIN
AMYROL
AMYROOT
AN
ANA
ANABAENA
ANABAENAS
ANABAPTIZED
ANABAPTIZING
ANABAS
ANABASES
ANABASIN
ANABASINE
ANABASIS
ANABASSE
ANABATA
ANABATHMOI
ANABATHMOS
ANABATIC
ANABEROGA
ANABIBAZON
ANABIOSIS
ANABIOTIC
ANABLEPS
ANABO
ANABOHITSITE
ANABOLIC
ANABOLIN
ANABOLISM
ANABOLITE
ANABOLIZE
ANABOLY
ANABONG
ANABRANCH

ANABROSIS
ANABROTIC
ANAC
ANACAHUITA
ANACAHUITE
ANACALYPSIS
ANACAMPSIS
ANACAMPTIC
ANACAMPTICS
ANACANTH
ANACANTHINE
ANACANTHOUS
ANACARA
ANACARD
ANACARDIC
ANACATHARSIS
ANACATHARTIC
ANACEPHALIZE
ANACHORISM
ANACHROMASIS
ANACHRONIC
ANACHRONICAL
ANACHRONICALLY
ANACHRONISM
ANACHRONIST
ANACHRONISTIC
ANACHRONIZE
ANACHRONOUS
ANACID
ANACIDITY
ANACK
ANACLASIS
ANACLASTIC
ANACLASTICS
ANACLETICA
ANACLETICUM
ANACLINAL
ANACLISIS
ANACLITIC
ANACOENOSIS
ANACOLUTHA
ANACOLUTHIC
ANACOLUTHON
ANACOLUTHONS
ANACONDA
ANACOUSTIC
ANACROGYNOUS
ANACROTIC
ANACROTISM
ANACRUSIS
ANACRUSTIC
ANACUSIA
ANACUSIC
ANACUSIS
ANADEM
ANADENIA
ANADICROTIC
ANADICROTISM
ANADIDYMUS
ANADIPLOSIS
ANADIPSIA
ANADIPSIC
ANADROM
ANADROMOUS
ANAEMATOSIS
ANAEMIA
ANAEMIC
ANAERETIC
ANAEROBATION
ANAEROBE
ANAEROBIA
ANAEROBIC
ANAEROBIOSIS
ANAEROBIOTIC
ANAEROBIUM
ANAEROPHYTE
ANAEROPLASTIC
ANAEROPLASTY
ANAESTHESIA
ANAESTHESIS
ANAESTHETIC
ANAESTHETIST
ANAESTHETIZE
ANAESTHETIZED
ANAESTHETIZER
ANAESTHETIZING
ANAESTHYL
ANAGALACTIC
ANAGAP
ANAGENESIS
ANAGENETIC
ANAGEP
ANAGLYPH
ANAGLYPHIC
ANAGLYPHICAL
ANAGLYPHY
ANAGLYPTIC
ANAGLYPTICS
ANAGLYPTON
ANAGNORISIS
ANAGNOST
ANAGNOSTES
ANAGOGE
ANAGOGIC
ANAGOGICAL
ANAGOGICALLY
ANAGOGICS
ANAGOGY
ANAGRAM
ANAGRAMMATIC
ANAGRAMS
ANAGRAPH
ANAGUA
ANAGYRINE
ANAHAO
ANAHAU
ANAI
ANAKINESIS
ANAKINETIC
ANAKTORON
ANAL
ANALABOS
ANALAV
ANALCIME
ANALCIMITE
ANALCITE
ANALCITITE
ANALECTA
ANALECTIC
ANALECTS
ANALEMMA
ANALEMMATIC
ANALEPSES
ANALEPSIS
ANALEPSY
ANALEPTIC
ANALGEN
ANALGENE
ANALGESIA
ANALGESIC
ANALGESIS
ANALGESIST
ANALGETIC
ANALGIA
ANALGIC
ANALGIZE
ANALLAGMATIC
ANALLANTOIC
ANALLERGIC
ANALLY
ANALOG
ANALOGA
ANALOGIC
ANALOGICAL
ANALOGICALLY
ANALOGICE
ANALOGIES
ANALOGION
ANALOGISM
ANALOGIST
ANALOGISTIC
ANALOGIZE
ANALOGIZED
ANALOGIZING
ANALOGON
ANALOGOUS
ANALOGOUSLY
ANALOGUE
ANALOGY
ANALPHABET
ANALPHABETE
ANALPHABETIC
ANALYSAND
ANALYSATION
ANALYSE
ANALYSED
ANALYSER
ANALYSES
ANALYSING
ANALYSIS
ANALYST
ANALYTIC
ANALYTICAL
ANALYTICALLY
ANALYTICS
ANALYZABLE
ANALYZATION
ANALYZE
ANALYZED
ANALYZER
ANALYZING
ANAM
ANAMA
ANAMESITE
ANAMIRTIN
ANAMMONIDE
ANAMNESIS
ANAMNESTIC
ANAMNIONIC
ANAMNIOTE
ANAMNIOTIC
ANAMORPHIC
ANAMORPHISM
ANAMORPHOSE
ANAMORPHOSES
ANAMORPHOSIS
ANAMORPHOTE
ANAMORPHOUS
ANAN
ANANA
ANANAS
ANANDA
ANANDRARIOUS
ANANDRIA
ANANDROUS
ANANEPIONIC
ANANGIOID
ANANKE
ANANTER
ANANTHERATE
ANANTHEROUS
ANANTHOUS
ANANYM
ANAPAEST
ANAPAESTIC
ANAPAESTICAL
ANAPAGANIZE
ANAPAITE
ANAPANAPA
ANAPEIRATIC
ANAPEST
ANAPESTIC
ANAPHASE
ANAPHIA
ANAPHORA
ANAPHORAL
ANAPHORIA
ANAPHORIC
ANAPHORICAL
ANAPHRODISIA
ANAPHRODITIC
ANAPHYLACTIC
ANAPHYLACTIN
ANAPHYLACTOID
ANAPHYLAXIS
ANAPHYTE
ANAPLASIA
ANAPLASIS
ANAPLASM
ANAPLASMOSIS
ANAPLASTIC
ANAPLASTY
ANAPLEROSIS
ANAPLEROTIC
ANAPNEA
ANAPNOGRAPH
ANAPNOIC
ANAPNOMETER
ANAPODEICTIC
ANAPOPHYSIAL
ANAPOPHYSIS
ANAPSID
ANAPSIDAN
ANAPTERYGOTE
ANAPTOTIC
ANAPTYCHI
ANAPTYCHUS
ANAPTYCTIC
ANAPTYCTICAL
ANAPTYXIS
ANAQUA
ANARCESTEAN
ANARCH
ANARCHIC
ANARCHICAL
ANARCHICALLY
ANARCHISM
ANARCHIST
ANARCHISTIC
ANARCHIZE
ANARCHY
ANARETA
ANARETIC
ANARETICAL
ANARGYROI
ANARGYROS
ANARTHRIA
ANARTHRIC
ANARTHROSIS
ANARTHROUS
ANARTHROUSLY
ANARTISMOS
ANARYA
ANASARCA
ANASARCOUS
ANASCHISTIC
ANASEISMIC
ANASPADIAS
ANASPALIN
ANASTALSIS
ANASTALTIC
ANASTASIMON
ANASTASIMOS
ANASTASIS
ANASTATE
ANASTATIC
ANASTIGMAT
ANASTIGMATIC
ANASTOMOSE
ANASTOMOSED
ANASTOMOSES
ANASTOMOSING
ANASTOMOSIS
ANASTOMOTIC
ANASTROPHE
ANASTROPHY
ANATASE
ANATEXIS
ANATHEMA
ANATHEMAS
ANATHEMATA
ANATHEMATIC
ANATHEMATISM
ANATHEMATIZE
ANATHEMIZE
ANATIFA
ANATIFAE
ANATIFER
ANATIFEROUS
ANATINE
ANATIRA
ANATMAN
ANATOCISM
ANATOMIC
ANATOMICAL
ANATOMICALLY
ANATOMIES
ANATOMISM
ANATOMIST
ANATOMIZE
ANATOMIZED
ANATOMIZER
ANATOMIZING
ANATOMY
ANATOPISM
ANATOXIN
ANATREPTIC
ANATRIPSIS
ANATRIPTIC
ANATRON
ANATROPAL
ANATROPOUS
ANATTA
ANATTO
ANAUDIA
ANAUNTER
ANAUNTERS
ANAUXITE
ANAXIAL
ANAXON
ANAXONE
ANAY
ANAZOTURIA
ANBA
ANBURY
ANCESTOR
ANCESTORIAL
ANCESTORS
ANCESTRAL
ANCESTRALLY
ANCESTRESS
ANCESTRIES
ANCESTRY
ANCHIETIN
ANCHIETINE
ANCHITHERE
ANCHITHERIOID
ANCHOR
ANCHORABLE
ANCHORAGE
ANCHORATE
ANCHORED
ANCHORER
ANCHORESS
ANCHORET

ANCHORETISM
ANCHORHOLD
ANCHORING
ANCHORITE
ANCHORITESS
ANCHORITIC
ANCHORITICAL
ANCHORITISM
ANCHORLESS
ANCHOVIES
ANCHOVY
ANCHUSA
ANCHUSIN
ANCHYLOSE
ANCHYLOSIS
ANCIENCE
ANCIENCY
ANCIENNETE
ANCIENT
ANCIENTISM
ANCIENTLY
ANCIENTNESS
ANCIENTRY
ANCIENTY
ANCILE
ANCILIA
ANCILLA
ANCILLARY
ANCIPITAL
ANCIPITOUS
ANCISTROID
ANCLE
ANCODONT
ANCOME
ANCON
ANCONA
ANCONAD
ANCONAGRA
ANCONAL
ANCONE
ANCONEAL
ANCONEI
ANCONES
ANCONEUS
ANCONITIS
ANCONOID
ANCONY
ANCORA
ANCYLOPOD
ANCYLOSE
ANCYLOSTOME
AND
ANDA
ANDABATA
ANDABATARIAN
ANDABATISM
ANDALUSITE
ANDANTE
ANDANTINO
ANDE
ANDERUN
ANDESINE
ANDESINITE
ANDESITE
ANDESITIC
ANDESYTE
ANDIRINE
ANDIROBA
ANDIRON
ANDORITE
ANDOUILLE
ANDOUILLET
ANDOUILLETTE
ANDRADITE
ANDRANATOMY
ANDRARCHY
ANDRENA
ANDRENID
ANDREWSITE
ANDRITE
ANDROCENTRIC
ANDROCLINIUM
ANDROCONIA
ANDROCONIUM
ANDROCRACY
ANDROCRATIC
ANDROCYTE
ANDROECIA
ANDROECIAL
ANDROECIUM
ANDROGEN
ANDROGENESIS
ANDROGENETIC
ANDROGENIC
ANDROGENOUS
ANDROGONIA
ANDROGONIAL
ANDROGYN
ANDROGYNAL
ANDROGYNARY
ANDROGYNE
ANDROGYNEITY
ANDROGYNIC
ANDROGYNISM
ANDROGYNOUS
ANDROGYNUS
ANDROGYNY
ANDROID
ANDROIDAL
ANDROIDES
ANDROKININ
ANDROL
ANDROLEPSIA
ANDROLEPSY
ANDROMANIA
ANDRON
ANDRONITIS
ANDROPETALAR
ANDROPHAGOUS
ANDROPHOBIA
ANDROPHORE
ANDROPHOROUS
ANDROPHORUM
ANDROPHYLL
ANDROSEME
ANDROSIN
ANDROSPHINX
ANDROSPORE
ANDROSTERONE
ANDROTAURIC
ANDS
ANE
ANEAR
ANEATH
ANECDOTA
ANECDOTAGE
ANECDOTAL
ANECDOTALISM
ANECDOTE
ANECDOTIC
ANECDOTICAL
ANECDOTIST
ANECHOIC
ANELE
ANELECTRIC
ANELED
ANELING
ANELYTROUS
ANEMATOSIS
ANEMI
ANEMIA
ANEMIC
ANEMOCHORD
ANEMOCHORE
ANEMOCLASTIC
ANEMOGRAM
ANEMOGRAPH
ANEMOGRAPHIC
ANEMOGRAPHY
ANEMOLOGIC
ANEMOLOGICAL
ANEMOLOGY
ANEMOMETER
ANEMOMETRIC
ANEMOMETRY
ANEMONAL
ANEMONE
ANEMONIN
ANEMONOL
ANEMOPATHY
ANEMOPHILE
ANEMOPHILOUS
ANEMOPHILY
ANEMOSCOPE
ANEMOSIS
ANEMOTAXIS
ANEMOTROPIC
ANEMOTROPISM
ANENCEPHALIA
ANENCEPHALIC
ANENCEPHALUS
ANENCEPHALY
ANEND
ANENERGIA
ANENST
ANENT
ANENTEROUS
ANEPIA
ANEPIGRAPHIC
ANEPIPLOIC
ANEPITHYMIA
ANERETHISIA
ANERETIC
ANERGIA
ANERGIC
ANERGY
ANERLY
ANEROID
ANEROTIC
ANESIS
ANESONE
ANESTHESIA
ANESTHESIANT
ANESTHESIOLOGIST
ANESTHESIOLOGY
ANESTHESIS
ANESTHETIC
ANESTHETIST
ANESTHETIZE
ANESTHETIZER
ANESTHYL
ANET
ANETH
ANETHOL
ANETHOLE
ANEUCH
ANEUPLOID
ANEUPLOIDY
ANEURIA
ANEURIC
ANEURILEMMIC
ANEURIN
ANEURISM
ANEURISMAL
ANEURISMALLY
ANEURISMATIC
ANEURYSM
ANEURYSMAL
ANEURYSMALLY
ANEURYSMATIC
ANEW
ANFEELD
ANFRACT
ANFRACTUOSE
ANFRACTUOUS
ANFRACTURE
ANGAKOK
ANGAKUT
ANGARALITE
ANGAREB
ANGAREEB
ANGAREP
ANGARIA
ANGARIATION
ANGARY
ANGEKKOK
ANGEKOK
ANGEKUT
ANGEL
ANGELATE
ANGELDOM
ANGELEEN
ANGELET
ANGELEYES
ANGELFISH
ANGELFISHES
ANGELHOOD
ANGELIC
ANGELICA
ANGELICAL
ANGELICALLY
ANGELICALNESS
ANGELICIZE
ANGELICO
ANGELIM
ANGELIN
ANGELINE
ANGELIQUE
ANGELITO
ANGELIZE
ANGELIZED
ANGELIZING
ANGELOCRACY
ANGELOGRAPHER
ANGELOLATER
ANGELOLATRY
ANGELOLOGIC
ANGELOLOGICAL
ANGELOLOGY
ANGELOMACHY
ANGELON
ANGELOPHANY
ANGELOT
ANGELS
ANGELUS
ANGER
ANGERED
ANGERING
ANGERLY
ANGERS
ANGEYOK
ANGIASTHENIA
ANGICO
ANGIECTASIS
ANGIECTOPIA
ANGIITIS
ANGILD
ANGILI
ANGINA
ANGINAL
ANGINIFORM
ANGINOID
ANGINOSE
ANGINOUS
ANGIOATAXIA
ANGIOBLAST
ANGIOBLASTIC
ANGIOCARP
ANGIOCARPIAN
ANGIOCARPIC
ANGIOCARPOUS
ANGIOCLAST
ANGIOCYST
ANGIOFIBROMA
ANGIOGENESIS
ANGIOGENIC
ANGIOGENY
ANGIOGLIOMA
ANGIOGRAPH
ANGIOGRAPHY
ANGIOID
ANGIOKINESIS
ANGIOKINETIC
ANGIOLIPOMA
ANGIOLITH
ANGIOLOGY
ANGIOMA
ANGIOMALACIA
ANGIOMAS
ANGIOMATA
ANGIOMATOSIS
ANGIOMATOUS
ANGIOMEGALY
ANGIOMETER
ANGIOMYOMA
ANGIONOMA
ANGIONOSIS
ANGIOPARESIS
ANGIOPATHY
ANGIOPHOROUS
ANGIOPLANY
ANGIOPLASTY
ANGIOPLEROSIS
ANGIOPOIETIC
ANGIORRHAGIA
ANGIORRHAPHY
ANGIORRHEA
ANGIORRHEXIS
ANGIOSARCOMA
ANGIOSCOPE
ANGIOSIS
ANGIOSPASM
ANGIOSPASTIC
ANGIOSPERM
ANGIOSPERMAL
ANGIOSPERMIC
ANGIOSPOROUS
ANGIOSTEOSIS
ANGIOSTOMIZE
ANGIOSTOMY
ANGIOSTROPHY
ANGIOTASIS
ANGIOTENOSIS
ANGIOTOME
ANGIOTOMY
ANGIOTONIC
ANGIOTRIBE
ANGIOTRIPSY
ANGIOTROPHIC
ANGKHAK
ANGLAISE
ANGLE
ANGLEBERRY
ANGLED
ANGLEDOG
ANGLEHOOK
ANGLEMETER
ANGLEPOD
ANGLER
ANGLES
ANGLESITE
ANGLESMITH
ANGLETOUCH
ANGLETWITCH
ANGLEWING

ANGLEWISE
ANGLEWORM
ANGLICIZE
ANGLICIZED
ANGLICIZING
ANGLIMANIAC
ANGLING
ANGO
ANGOISE
ANGOLAR
ANGOR
ANGOSTURA
ANGRIER
ANGRIEST
ANGRILY
ANGRINESS
ANGRITE
ANGRY
ANGST
ANGSTER
ANGSTROM
ANGUID
ANGUIFORM
ANGUILLIFORM
ANGUILLOID
ANGUINE
ANGUINEOUS
ANGUIPED
ANGUISH
ANGUISHED
ANGUISHOUS
ANGUISHOUSLY
ANGULA
ANGULAR
ANGULARE
ANGULARIA
ANGULARITIES
ANGULARITY
ANGULARIZATION
ANGULARIZE
ANGULARLY
ANGULARNESS
ANGULATE
ANGULATED
ANGULATELY
ANGULATENESS
ANGULATING
ANGULATION
ANGULE
ANGULIFEROUS
ANGULINERVED
ANGULOMETER
ANGULOSE
ANGULOSITY
ANGULOUS
ANGULUS
ANGURIA
ANGUS
ANGUST
ANGUSTATE
ANGUSTICLAVE
ANGWANTIBO
ANGWICH
ANHAEMATOSIS
ANHAEMOLYTIC
ANHALAMINE
ANHALINE
ANHALONIDINE
ANHALONIN
ANHALONINE
ANHANG
ANHARMONIC
ANHEDONIA
ANHEDRAL
ANHEDRON
ANHELATION
ANHELE
ANHELOSE
ANHELOUS
ANHEMATOSIS
ANHEMOLYTIC
ANHIDROSIS
ANHIDROTIC
ANHIMA
ANHINGA
ANHISTIC
ANHISTOUS
ANHUNGERED
ANHUNGRY
ANHYDRAEMIA
ANHYDRAEMIC
ANHYDRATE
ANHYDRATED
ANHYDRATING
ANHYDRATION
ANHYDREMIA
ANHYDREMIC
ANHYDRIDE
ANHYDRIDIZE
ANHYDRITE
ANHYDRIZE
ANHYDROUS
ANHYDROXIME
ANI
ANICCA
ANICONIC
ANICONISM
ANICULAR
ANICUT
ANIDIAN
ANIDROSIS
ANIENTE
ANIGH
ANIGHT
ANIGHTS
ANIL
ANILAO
ANILAU
ANILE
ANILENESS
ANILIC
ANILID
ANILIDE
ANILIDIC
ANILIDOXIME
ANILIID
ANILIN
ANILINE
ANILINISM
ANILINO
ANILITY
ANILLA
ANILOPYRIN
ANILOPYRINE
ANIMA
ANIMABILITY
ANIMABLE
ANIMABLENESS
ANIMADVERSION
ANIMADVERT
ANIMADVERTER
ANIMAL
ANIMALCULA
ANIMALCULAE
ANIMALCULAR
ANIMALCULE
ANIMALCULINE
ANIMALCULISM
ANIMALCULIST
ANIMALCULOUS
ANIMALCULUM
ANIMALIAN
ANIMALIC
ANIMALISH
ANIMALISM
ANIMALIST
ANIMALISTIC
ANIMALITY
ANIMALIZATION
ANIMALIZE
ANIMALIZED
ANIMALIZING
ANIMALLY
ANIMALS
ANIMANDO
ANIMASTIC
ANIMASTICAL
ANIMATE
ANIMATED
ANIMATEDLY
ANIMATELY
ANIMATENESS
ANIMATER
ANIMATING
ANIMATINGLY
ANIMATION
ANIMATISM
ANIMATISTIC
ANIMATIVE
ANIMATO
ANIMATOGRAPH
ANIMATOR
ANIME
ANIMETTA
ANIMIKITE
ANIMISM
ANIMIST
ANIMISTIC
ANIMIZE
ANIMO
ANIMOSE
ANIMOSENESS
ANIMOSITIES
ANIMOSITY
ANIMOSO
ANIMOUS
ANIMUS
ANION
ANIONIC
ANIRIDIA
ANIS
ANISADO
ANISAL
ANISALCOHOL
ANISALDEHYDE
ANISALDOXIME
ANISAMIDE
ANISANDROUS
ANISANILIDE
ANISATE
ANISE
ANISEED
ANISEIKONIA
ANISEIKONIC
ANISEROOT
ANISETTE
ANISIC
ANISIDINE
ANISIDINO
ANISIL
ANISILIC
ANISOCARPIC
ANISOCARPOUS
ANISOCERCAL
ANISOCHROMIA
ANISOCORIA
ANISOCOTYLY
ANISOCRATIC
ANISOCYCLE
ANISOCYTOSIS
ANISODACTYL
ANISODACTYLE
ANISODONT
ANISOGAMETE
ANISOGAMETES
ANISOGAMOUS
ANISOGAMY
ANISOGENOUS
ANISOGENY
ANISOGYNOUS
ANISOIN
ANISOL
ANISOLE
ANISOMELIA
ANISOMELUS
ANISOMERIC
ANISOMEROUS
ANISOMETRIC
ANISOMETROPE
ANISOMYARIAN
ANISOMYODIAN
ANISOMYODOUS
ANISOPHYLLY
ANISOPIA
ANISOPLEURAL
ANISOPTEROUS
ANISOSPORE
ANISOSTHENIC
ANISOSTOMOUS
ANISOTONIC
ANISOTROPAL
ANISOTROPE
ANISOTROPIC
ANISOTROPISM
ANISOTROPOUS
ANISOTROPY
ANISOYL
ANISUM
ANISURIA
ANISYL
ANISYLIDENE
ANITHER
ANITO
ANITOS
ANITROGENOUS
ANJAN
ANKARAMITE
ANKARATRITE
ANKEE
ANKER
ANKERHOLD
ANKERITE
ANKH
ANKLE
ANKLEBONE
ANKLEJACK
ANKLES
ANKLET
ANKLONG
ANKUS
ANKUSH
ANKUSHA
ANKYLENTERON
ANKYLODONTIA
ANKYLOMELE
ANKYLOMERISM
ANKYLOPHOBIA
ANKYLOPODIA
ANKYLOPOIETIC
ANKYLOSE
ANKYLOSED
ANKYLOSING
ANKYLOSIS
ANKYLOSTOMA
ANKYLOTIA
ANKYLOTIC
ANKYLOTOME
ANKYLOTOMY
ANKYROID
ANLACE
ANLAGE
ANLAGEN
ANLAGES
ANLAS
ANLAUT
ANLAUTE
ANLET
ANN
ANNA
ANNABERGITE
ANNAL
ANNALE
ANNALIA
ANNALINE
ANNALISM
ANNALIST
ANNALISTIC
ANNALIZE
ANNALS
ANNALY
ANNAT
ANNATES
ANNATTO
ANNEAL
ANNEALED
ANNEALER
ANNEALING
ANNECT
ANNECTANT
ANNECTENT
ANNELID
ANNELIDAN
ANNELIDIAN
ANNELIDOUS
ANNELISM
ANNELOID
ANNERODITE
ANNERRE
ANNET
ANNEX
ANNEXA
ANNEXABLE
ANNEXATION
ANNEXATIONAL
ANNEXATIONIST
ANNEXE
ANNEXED
ANNEXER
ANNEXING
ANNEXION
ANNEXIONIST
ANNEXIVE
ANNEXMENT
ANNEXURE
ANNICUT
ANNIDALIN
ANNIHILABLE
ANNIHILATE
ANNIHILATED
ANNIHILATING
ANNIHILATION
ANNIHILATIVE
ANNIHILATOR
ANNIHILATORY
ANNITE
ANNIVERSARIES
ANNIVERSARY
ANNIVERSE
ANNODATED
ANNONA
ANNONACEOUS
ANNONCE
ANNOTATE
ANNOTATED
ANNOTATING

ANNOTATION
ANNOTATIVE
ANNOTATOR
ANNOTATORY
ANNOTINE
ANNOTINOUS
ANNOTTO
ANNOUNCE
ANNOUNCED
ANNOUNCEMENT
ANNOUNCER
ANNOUNCING
ANNOY
ANNOYANCE
ANNOYANCER
ANNOYED
ANNOYER
ANNOYFUL
ANNOYING
ANNOYINGLY
ANNOYINGNESS
ANNOYMENT
ANNOYOUS
ANNOYOUSLY
ANNUAL
ANNUALIST
ANNUALIZE
ANNUALLY
ANNUARY
ANNUATION
ANNUELER
ANNUELLER
ANNUENT
ANNUITANT
ANNUITIES
ANNUITY
ANNUL
ANNULAR
ANNULARITY
ANNULARLY
ANNULARY
ANNULATE
ANNULATED
ANNULATION
ANNULE
ANNULET
ANNULETTEE
ANNULI
ANNULISM
ANNULLABLE
ANNULLATE
ANNULLATION
ANNULLED
ANNULLER
ANNULLING
ANNULMENT
ANNULOID
ANNULOSE
ANNULUS
ANNULUSES
ANNUNCIABLE
ANNUNCIATE
ANNUNCIATED
ANNUNCIATING
ANNUNCIATION
ANNUNCIATIVE
ANNUNCIATOR
ANNUNCIATORY
ANNUS
ANOA
ANOBING
ANOCARPOUS
ANOCIATION
ANOCOCCYGEAL
ANODAL
ANODE
ANODENDRON
ANODIC
ANODICALLY
ANODINE
ANODIZE
ANODIZED
ANODIZING
ANODONTIA
ANODOS
ANODYNE
ANODYNIA
ANODYNIC
ANODYNOUS
ANOEGENETIC
ANOESIA
ANOESIS
ANOESTROUS
ANOESTRUM
ANOESTRUS
ANOETIC
ANOGENIC
ANOGENITAL
ANOIA
ANOIL
ANOINE
ANOINT
ANOINTER
ANOINTMENT
ANOLE
ANOLI
ANOLIAN
ANOLYTE
ANOMALIES
ANOMALIPED
ANOMALIPOD
ANOMALISM
ANOMALIST
ANOMALISTIC
ANOMALONOMY
ANOMALOSCOPE
ANOMALOUS
ANOMALOUSLY
ANOMALURE
ANOMALY
ANOMER
ANOMIA
ANOMIC
ANOMIE
ANOMIES
ANOMITE
ANOMOCARPOUS
ANOMODONT
ANOMPHALOUS
ANOMURAL
ANOMURAN
ANOMUROUS
ANOMY
ANON
ANONANG
ANONCILLO
ANONOL
ANONYCHIA
ANONYM
ANONYMA
ANONYME
ANONYMITY
ANONYMOUS
ANONYMOUSLY
ANONYMOUSNESS
ANONYMUNCULE
ANOOPSIA
ANOPERINEAL
ANOPHELE
ANOPHELES
ANOPHELINE
ANOPHTHALMOS
ANOPHYTE
ANOPIA
ANOPLOTHERE
ANOPLOTHEROID
ANOPLURIFORM
ANOPSIA
ANOPUBIC
ANORAK
ANORCHI
ANORCHIA
ANORCHISM
ANORCHOUS
ANORCHUS
ANORECTAL
ANORECTIC
ANORECTOUS
ANOREXIA
ANOREXY
ANORGANA
ANORGANISM
ANORGANOLOGY
ANORMAL
ANORMALITY
ANORN
ANOROGENIC
ANORTH
ANORTHIC
ANORTHITE
ANORTHITIC
ANORTHITITE
ANORTHOCLASE
ANORTHOPHYRE
ANORTHOPIA
ANORTHOSCOPE
ANORTHOSE
ANORTHOSITE
ANOSCOPE
ANOSCOPY
ANOSMATIC
ANOSMIA
ANOSMIC
ANOSPHRASIA
ANOSPHRESIA
ANOSPINAL
ANOSTOSIS
ANOTERITE
ANOTHER
ANOTHERKINS
ANOTIA
ANOTUS
ANOUNOU
ANOVESICAL
ANOXAEMIA
ANOXAEMIC
ANOXEMIA
ANOXEMIC
ANOXIA
ANOXIC
ANOXIDATIVE
ANOXYBIOSIS
ANOXYBIOTIC
ANOXYSCOPE
ANQUERA
ANSA
ANSAE
ANSAR
ANSARIAN
ANSATE
ANSATED
ANSATION
ANSERATED
ANSERIN
ANSERINE
ANSEROUS
ANSU
ANSULATE
ANSWER
ANSWERABLE
ANSWERABLY
ANSWERED
ANSWERER
ANSWERINGLY
ANSWERLESS
ANSWERLESSLY
ANT
ANTA
ANTACID
ANTACRID
ANTADIFORM
ANTAE
ANTAGONISM
ANTAGONIST
ANTAGONISTIC
ANTAGONISTICAL
ANTAGONISTICALLY
ANTAGONIZATION
ANTAGONIZE
ANTAGONIZED
ANTAGONIZER
ANTAGONIZING
ANTAGONY
ANTAL
ANTALGESIC
ANTALGIC
ANTALGOL
ANTALKALI
ANTALKALIES
ANTALKALINE
ANTALKALIS
ANTANACLASIS
ANTANEMIC
ANTAPEX
ANTAPODOSIS
ANTAPOLOGY
ANTARCHISM
ANTARCHIST
ANTARCHISTIC
ANTARCHY
ANTARCTICA
ANTARCTICAL
ANTARCTICALLY
ANTARTHRITIC
ANTASPHYCTIC
ANTASTHENIC
ANTASTHMATIC
ANTATROPHIC
ANTBIRD
ANTE
ANTEAL
ANTEATER
ANTEBRACHIA
ANTEBRACHIAL
ANTEBRACHIUM
ANTECABINET
ANTECEDE
ANTECEDED
ANTECEDENCE
ANTECEDENCY
ANTECEDENT
ANTECEDENTAL
ANTECEDENTLY
ANTECEDING
ANTECESSOR
ANTECHAMBER
ANTECHAPEL
ANTECHOIR
ANTECHURCH
ANTECOLIC
ANTECORNU
ANTECOXAL
ANTED
ANTEDATE
ANTEDATED
ANTEDATING
ANTEDILUVIAL
ANTEDILUVIAN
ANTEDONIN
ANTEED
ANTEFIX
ANTEFIXA
ANTEFIXAL
ANTEFIXES
ANTEFLEXED
ANTEFLEXION
ANTEFURCA
ANTEFURCAE
ANTEFURCAL
ANTEGRADE
ANTEING
ANTELABIUM
ANTELOCATION
ANTELOPE
ANTELOPES
ANTELOPIAN
ANTELOPINE
ANTELUCAN
ANTELUDE
ANTEMARGINAL
ANTEMASK
ANTEMERIDIAN
ANTEMETIC
ANTEMINGENT
ANTEMUNDANE
ANTEMURAL
ANTENATAL
ANTENATI
ANTENATUS
ANTENAVE
ANTENNA
ANTENNAE
ANTENNAL
ANTENNARIID
ANTENNARY
ANTENNAS
ANTENNATE
ANTENNIFORM
ANTENNULA
ANTENNULAR
ANTENNULARY
ANTENNULE
ANTENUMBER
ANTENUPTIAL
ANTEOPERCLE
ANTEPAGMENTA
ANTEPAGMENTS
ANTEPALATAL
ANTEPASCHAL
ANTEPAST
ANTEPECTORAL
ANTEPECTUS
ANTEPENDIA
ANTEPENDIUM
ANTEPENUIT
ANTEPHIALTIC
ANTEPILEPTIC
ANTEPIRRHEMA
ANTEPONE
ANTEPORT
ANTEPOSITION
ANTER
ANTERETHIC
ANTERGIC
ANTERI
ANTERIAD
ANTERIN
ANTERIOR
ANTERIORITY
ANTERIORLY
ANTERIORNESS
ANTERODORSAL
ANTEROGRADE
ANTEROMEDIAL
ANTEROMEDIAN

ANTEROOM
ANTEROPYGAL
ANTEROSPINAL
ANTESCRIPT
ANTESIGNANI
ANTESTATURE
ANTESTERNAL
ANTESTERNUM
ANTETEMPLE
ANTETHEM
ANTETYPE
ANTEVENIENT
ANTEVERSION
ANTEVERT
ANTEVERTED
ANTEVERTING
ANTEVOCALIC
ANTEWAR
ANTHECOLOGY
ANTHELA
ANTHELAE
ANTHELIA
ANTHELICES
ANTHELION
ANTHELIONS
ANTHELIX
ANTHELMINTHIC
ANTHELMINTIC
ANTHEM
ANTHEMA
ANTHEMENE
ANTHEMIA
ANTHEMION
ANTHEMIS
ANTHEMWISE
ANTHEMY
ANTHER
ANTHERAL
ANTHERID
ANTHERIDIA
ANTHERIDIAL
ANTHERIDIUM
ANTHEROID
ANTHEROZOID
ANTHEROZOOID
ANTHESIS
ANTHESTERIN
ANTHESTEROL
ANTHEXIMETER
ANTHILL
ANTHINE
ANTHOBIOLOGY
ANTHOCARP
ANTHOCARPOUS
ANTHOCEROTE
ANTHOCHLOR
ANTHOCLINIUM
ANTHOCYAN
ANTHOCYANIN
ANTHODIA
ANTHODIUM
ANTHOECOLOGY
ANTHOGENESIS
ANTHOGENETIC
ANTHOGENOUS
ANTHOGRAPHY
ANTHOID
ANTHOLITE
ANTHOLOGICAL
ANTHOLOGIES
ANTHOLOGIST
ANTHOLOGIZE
ANTHOLOGIZED
ANTHOLOGIZING
ANTHOLOGY
ANTHOLYSIS
ANTHOMANIA
ANTHOMANIAC
ANTHOMEDUSAN
ANTHOMYIID
ANTHOPHAGOUS
ANTHOPHILE
ANTHOPHILIAN
ANTHOPHILOUS
ANTHOPHOBIA
ANTHOPHORE
ANTHOPHOROUS
ANTHOPHYTE
ANTHORINE
ANTHOTAXIS
ANTHOTAXY
ANTHOTROPIC
ANTHOTROPISM
ANTHOXANTHIN
ANTHOZOAN
ANTHOZOIC
ANTHOZOOID
ANTHOZOON
ANTHRACAEMIA
ANTHRACEMIA
ANTHRACENE
ANTHRACES
ANTHRACIA
ANTHRACIC
ANTHRACIN
ANTHRACITE
ANTHRACITIC
ANTHRACITISM
ANTHRACITOUS
ANTHRACNOSE
ANTHRACNOSIS
ANTHRACOCIDE
ANTHRACOID
ANTHRACONITE
ANTHRACOSIS
ANTHRACOTIC
ANTHRACYL
ANTHRADIOL
ANTHRAFLAVIC
ANTHRAGALLOL
ANTHRAMIN
ANTHRAMINE
ANTHRANIL
ANTHRANILATE
ANTHRANILIC
ANTHRANOL
ANTHRANONE
ANTHRANOYL
ANTHRANYL
ANTHRAQUINOL
ANTHRARUFIN
ANTHRATETROL
ANTHRATRIOL
ANTHRAX
ANTHRAXOLITE
ANTHRAXYLON
ANTHROIC
ANTHROL
ANTHRONE
ANTHROPIC
ANTHROPICAL
ANTHROPOGENY
ANTHROPOGLOT
ANTHROPOGONY
ANTHROPOID
ANTHROPOIDAL
ANTHROPOLITE
ANTHROPOLITH
ANTHROPOLOGIC
ANTHROPOLOGICAL
ANTHROPOLOGICALLY
ANTHROPOLOGIST
ANTHROPOLOGY
ANTHROPONOMY
ANTHROPOPHAGIT
ANTHROPOTOMY
ANTHROPOZOIC
ANTHROPURGIC
ANTHROXAN
ANTHROXANIC
ANTHRYL
ANTHRYLENE
ANTHURIUM
ANTI
ANTIABRIN
ANTIACID
ANTIADITIS
ANTIAE
ANTIAIRCRAFT
ANTIALBUMID
ANTIAR
ANTIARIN
ANTIBACCHIC
ANTIBACCHII
ANTIBACCHIUS
ANTIBACTERIAL
ANTIBARYON
ANTIBIONT
ANTIBIOSIS
ANTIBIOTIC
ANTIBLASTIC
ANTIBODIES
ANTIBODY
ANTIBROMIC
ANTIC
ANTICAL
ANTICARDIUM
ANTICATALASE
ANTICATALYST
ANTICATHODE
ANTICHANCE
ANTICHLOR
ANTICHLORINE
ANTICHRESES
ANTICHRESIS
ANTICHRETIC
ANTICHRIST
ANTICHTHON
ANTICIPANT
ANTICIPATE
ANTICIPATED
ANTICIPATING
ANTICIPATION
ANTICIPATIVE
ANTICIPATIVELY
ANTICIPATOR
ANTICIPATORY
ANTICIZE
ANTICK
ANTICKED
ANTICKER
ANTICKING
ANTICKT
ANTICLASTIC
ANTICLERICAL
ANTICLIMACTIC
ANTICLIMAX
ANTICLINAL
ANTICLINE
ANTICLINORIA
ANTICLY
ANTICNEMION
ANTICNESS
ANTICOAGULANT
ANTICOAGULIN
ANTICOR
ANTICOUS
ANTICREEP
ANTICREEPER
ANTICREEPING
ANTICROTALIC
ANTICRYPTIC
ANTICULARIA
ANTICUM
ANTICUS
ANTICYCLONE
ANTICYCLONIC
ANTIDACTYL
ANTIDETONANT
ANTIDORON
ANTIDOTAL
ANTIDOTALLY
ANTIDOTARY
ANTIDOTE
ANTIDOTED
ANTIDOTICAL
ANTIDOTING
ANTIDOTISM
ANTIDROMAL
ANTIDROMIC
ANTIDROMOUS
ANTIDROMY
ANTIENT
ANTIETHNIC
ANTIFEBRILE
ANTIFEDERAL
ANTIFOAM
ANTIFOGMATIC
ANTIFORMIN
ANTIFREEZE
ANTIFREEZING
ANTIFRICTION
ANTIGEN
ANTIGENE
ANTIGENIC
ANTIGLARE
ANTIGOD
ANTIGORITE
ANTIGRAPH
ANTIGRAVITY
ANTIGROPELOS
ANTIGUGGLER
ANTIHELICES
ANTIHELIX
ANTIHERO
ANTIHISTAMINE
ANTIHYDROPIN
ANTIKETOGEN
ANTIKETOGENIC
ANTIKNOCK
ANTILABORIST
ANTILEGALIST
ANTILEPSIS
ANTILEPTIC
ANTILIPOID
ANTILOBIUM
ANTILOG
ANTILOGIC
ANTILOGICAL
ANTILOGIES
ANTILOGISM
ANTILOGOUS
ANTILOGY
ANTILOQUY
ANTILUETIN
ANTILYSIN
ANTILYSIS
ANTILYSSIC
ANTILYTIC
ANTIMACASSAR
ANTIMASK
ANTIMASKER
ANTIMASQUE
ANTIMASQUER
ANTIMATTER
ANTIMELLIN
ANTIMENSIA
ANTIMENSION
ANTIMERE
ANTIMERIC
ANTIMERISM
ANTIMETABOLE
ANTIMETER
ANTIMINSIA
ANTIMINSION
ANTIMISSION
ANTIMNEMONIC
ANTIMONATE
ANTIMONIAL
ANTIMONIATED
ANTIMONIC
ANTIMONID
ANTIMONIDE
ANTIMONIOUS
ANTIMONITE
ANTIMONIUM
ANTIMONIURET
ANTIMONOUS
ANTIMONSOON
ANTIMONY
ANTIMONYL
ANTINEURITIC
ANTINEUTRINO
ANTINEUTRON
ANTINGANTING
ANTINIAL
ANTINION
ANTINODE
ANTINOME
ANTINOMIAN
ANTINOMIC
ANTINOMICAL
ANTINOMIES
ANTINOMIST
ANTINOMY
ANTIODONT
ANTIOPELMOUS
ANTIOXIDANT
ANTIOXYGEN
ANTIOXYGENIC
ANTIPARABEMA
ANTIPARALLEL
ANTIPART
ANTIPARTICLE
ANTIPASTIC
ANTIPASTO
ANTIPATHETIC
ANTIPATHIC
ANTIPATHIES
ANTIPATHIST
ANTIPATHIZE
ANTIPATHY
ANTIPEDAL
ANTIPEPSIN
ANTIPEPTONE
ANTIPERIODIC
ANTIPERTHITE
ANTIPETALOUS
ANTIPHARMIC
ANTIPHON
ANTIPHONA
ANTIPHONAL
ANTIPHONALLY
ANTIPHONARIES
ANTIPHONARY
ANTIPHONETIC
ANTIPHONIC
ANTIPHONICAL
ANTIPHONIES
ANTIPHONON
ANTIPHONY
ANTIPHRASES
ANTIPHRASIS
ANTIPHRASTIC
ANTIPLANET

ANTIPLASTIC
ANTIPLEION
ANTIPODAGRON
ANTIPODAL
ANTIPODE
ANTIPODEAN
ANTIPODES
ANTIPODIC
ANTIPODIST
ANTIPOINTS
ANTIPOLE
ANTIPOLEMIST
ANTIPOLO
ANTIPOPE
ANTIPRISM
ANTIPROTON
ANTIPTOSIS
ANTIPUDIC
ANTIPUTRID
ANTIPYIC
ANTIPYONIN
ANTIPYRESIS
ANTIPYRETIC
ANTIPYRIN
ANTIPYRINE
ANTIPYROTIC
ANTIPYRYL
ANTIQUA
ANTIQUARIAN
ANTIQUARIES
ANTIQUARISM
ANTIQUARY
ANTIQUATE
ANTIQUATED
ANTIQUATING
ANTIQUATION
ANTIQUE
ANTIQUED
ANTIQUELY
ANTIQUENESS
ANTIQUER
ANTIQUING
ANTIQUIST
ANTIQUITIES
ANTIQUITY
ANTIRACER
ANTIRACHITIC
ANTIRATTLER
ANTIRED
ANTIRENT
ANTIRENTER
ANTIRENTISM
ANTIRICIN
ANTIRRHINUM
ANTIS
ANTISALOON
ANTISCIA
ANTISCIANS
ANTISCII
ANTISCION
ANTISCOLIC
ANTISELENE
ANTISEPALOUS
ANTISEPSIS
ANTISEPTIC
ANTISEPTICAL
ANTISEPTICALLY
ANTISEPTICISM
ANTISEPTICIST
ANTISEPTICIZE
ANTISEPTION
ANTISERUM
ANTISIDERIC
ANTISIPHON
ANTISIPHONAL
ANTISLAVERY
ANTISNAPPER
ANTISOCIAL
ANTISOCIALIST
ANTISOCIALITY
ANTISOLAR
ANTISPACE
ANTISPADIX
ANTISPASMODIC
ANTISPAST
ANTISPASTIC
ANTISQUAMA
ANTISTES
ANTISTROPHAL
ANTISTROPHE
ANTISTROPHIC
ANTISTROPHON
ANTISUN
ANTITANK
ANTITHALIAN
ANTITHEFT
ANTITHEISM
ANTITHEIST
ANTITHEISTIC
ANTITHENAR
ANTITHERMIN
ANTITHESES
ANTITHESIS
ANTITHESISM
ANTITHESIZE
ANTITHET
ANTITHETIC
ANTITHETICAL
ANTITHETICS
ANTITOXIN
ANTITOXINE
ANTITRADE
ANTITRADES
ANTITRAGAL
ANTITRAGI
ANTITRAGIC
ANTITRAGICUS
ANTITRAGUS
ANTITROPE
ANTITROPIC
ANTITROPICAL
ANTITROPY
ANTITRUST
ANTITRYPSIN
ANTITRYPTIC
ANTITWILIGHT
ANTITYPAL
ANTITYPE
ANTITYPIC
ANTITYPICAL
ANTITYPY
ANTIVENENE
ANTIVENIN
ANTIVENINE
ANTIVIRAL
ANTIVIROTIC
ANTIWORLD
ANTIZOEA
ANTJAR
ANTLER
ANTLERED
ANTLERITE
ANTLERS
ANTLIA
ANTLIATE
ANTLING
ANTOECI
ANTOECIAN
ANTOECIANS
ANTONINIANI
ANTONINIANUS
ANTONOMASIA
ANTONOMASTIC
ANTONYM
ANTONYMOUS
ANTONYMY
ANTORBITAL
ANTRA
ANTRAL
ANTRALGIA
ANTRE
ANTRECTOMY
ANTRIN
ANTRITIS
ANTROCELE
ANTRONASAL
ANTROPHORE
ANTROPHOSE
ANTRORSE
ANTRORSELY
ANTROSCOPE
ANTROSCOPY
ANTROTOME
ANTROTOMY
ANTRUM
ANTRUSTION
ANTSHRIKE
ANTSY
ANUBIN
ANUBING
ANUKABIET
ANULOMA
ANUNDER
ANURAN
ANURESIS
ANURETIC
ANURIA
ANURIC
ANUROUS
ANURY
ANUS
ANUSIM
ANUSVARA
ANVIL
ANVILED
ANVILING
ANVILLED
ANVILLING
ANVILSMITH
ANVILTOP
ANXIETIES
ANXIETUDE
ANXIETY
ANXIOUS
ANXIOUSLY
ANXIOUSNESS
ANY
ANYBODIES
ANYBODY
ANYHOW
ANYMORE
ANYONE
ANYPLACE
ANYTHING
ANYWAY
ANYWAYS
ANYWHEN
ANYWHERE
ANYWHERENESS
ANYWHERES
ANYWHITHER
ANYWHY
ANYWISE
AO
AOGIRI
AONACH
AORIST
AORISTIC
AORISTICALLY
AORTA
AORTAE
AORTAL
AORTARCTIA
AORTAS
AORTECTASIA
AORTECTASIS
AORTIC
AORTICORENAL
AORTISM
AORTITIS
AORTOCLASIA
AORTOCLASIS
AORTOLITH
AORTOMALACIA
AORTOMALAXIS
AORTOPATHY
AORTOPTOSIA
AORTOPTOSIS
AORTORRHAPHY
AORTOTOMY
AOSMIC
AOUDAD
APA
APABHRAMSA
APACE
APACHE
APACHES
APACHISM
APACHITE
APADANA
APAESTHESIA
APAESTHETIC
APAESTHETIZE
APAESTICALLY
APAGOGE
APAGOGIC
APAGOGICAL
APAGOGICALLY
APAID
APALIT
APANAGE
APANAGED
APANAGING
APANDRY
APANG
APAR
APARA
APARAPHYSATE
APARDON
APAREJO
APAREJOS
APARITHMESIS
APART
APARTADO
APARTHEID
APARTHROSIS
APARTMENT
APARTMENTAL
APASOTE
APASS
APAST
APASTRON
APATAN
APATETIC
APATHETIC
APATHETICAL
APATHIA
APATHIC
APATHIES
APATHISM
APATHIST
APATHISTICAL
APATHOGENIC
APATHY
APATITE
APE
APEAK
APED
APEIRON
APELET
APELING
APELLOUS
APEPSIA
APEPSINIA
APEPSY
APEPTIC
APER
APERCH
APERCU
APERCUS
APEREA
APERIENT
APERIES
APERIODIC
APERISPERMIC
APERISTALSIS
APERITIF
APERITIVE
APERSEE
APERT
APERTION
APERTLY
APERTNESS
APERTOMETER
APERTURAL
APERTURE
APERTURED
APERULOSID
APERY
APESTHESIA
APESTHETIC
APESTHETIZE
APETALOID
APETALOSE
APETALOUS
APETALY
APEX
APEXED
APEXES
APEXING
APHAERESIS
APHAERETIC
APHAGIA
APHAKIA
APHAKIAL
APHAKIC
APHANESITE
APHANISIA
APHANISIS
APHANITE
APHANITIC
APHANITISM
APHANOPHYRE
APHASIA
APHASIAC
APHASIC
APHELIAN
APHELION
APHEMIA
APHEMIC
APHENGESCOPE
APHENGOSCOPE
APHENOSCOPE
APHERESIS
APHERETIC
APHESIS
APHETA
APHETIC
APHETICALLY
APHETISM
APHETIZE
APHID
APHIDES
APHIDIAN
APHIDICOLOUS

APHIDID
APHIDIOUS
APHIDIVOROUS
APHIDOLYSIN
APHIDOZER
APHIS
APHLEBIA
APHLOGISTIC
APHNOLOGY
APHODAL
APHODI
APHODIAN
APHODUS
APHONIA
APHONIC
APHONOUS
APHORIA
APHORISM
APHORISMATIC
APHORISMER
APHORISMIC
APHORISMICAL
APHORISMOS
APHORIST
APHORISTIC
APHORISTICAL
APHORIZE
APHORIZED
APHORIZER
APHORIZING
APHOTIC
APHOTOTACTIC
APHOTOTAXIS
APHOTOTROPIC
APHRASIA
APHRITE
APHRIZITE
APHRODISIA
APHRODISIAC
APHRODISIAN
APHRODITE
APHRODITIC
APHRODITOUS
APHROLITE
APHRONIA
APHTHA
APHTHAE
APHTHIC
APHTHITALITE
APHTHOID
APHTHONG
APHTHONGAL
APHTHONGIA
APHTHOUS
APHYLLOSE
APHYLLOUS
APHYLLY
APHYRIC
APIAN
APIARIAN
APIARIES
APIARIST
APIARY
APIATOR
APICAD
APICAL
APICALLY
APICES
APICIFIXED
APICILAR
APICILLARY
APICITIS
APICKABACK
APICKBACK
APICKPACK
APICOECTOMY
APICOLYSIS
APICULA
APICULATE
APICULATED
APICULATION
APICULI
APICULTURAL
APICULTURE
APICULTURIST
APICULUS
APIECE
APIECES
APIGENIN
APII
APIIN
APIKORES
APIKOROS
APIKORSIM
APILARY
APIMANIA
APINCH
APING
APINOID
APIO
APIOID
APIOIDAL
APIOL
APIOLE
APIOLIN
APIOLOGIST
APIOLOGY
APIONOL
APIOSE
APIPHOBIA
APISH
APISHAMORE
APISHLY
APISHNESS
APISM
APITONG
APITPAT
APIVOROUS
APJOHNITE
APLACENTAL
APLACOPHORAN
APLANAT
APLANATIC
APLANATISM
APLANOGAMETE
APLANOSPORE
APLASIA
APLASTIC
APLENTY
APLITE
APLITIC
APLOBASALT
APLODIORITE
APLOMB
APLOME
APLOTAXENE
APLOTOMY
APLUSTRA
APLUSTRE
APLUSTRIA
APNEA
APNEAL
APNEIC
APNEUMATIC
APNEUMATOSIS
APNEUMONOUS
APNEUSIS
APNEUSTIC
APNOEA
APNOEAL
APNOEIC
APOACONITINE
APOATROPINE
APOBIOTIC
APOBLAST
APOCAFFEINE
APOCALYPSE
APOCALYPST
APOCALYPT
APOCALYPTIC
APOCALYPTIST
APOCAMPHORIC
APOCARP
APOCARPOUS
APOCARPY
APOCATHARSIS
APOCENTER
APOCENTRE
APOCENTRIC
APOCHA
APOCHAE
APOCHOLIC
APOCHROMAT
APOCHROMATIC
APOCODEINE
APOCOPATE
APOCOPATED
APOCOPATING
APOCOPATION
APOCOPE
APOCOPIC
APOCRENIC
APOCRISIARY
APOCRUSTIC
APOCRYPH
APOCRYPHAL
APOCRYPHALLY
APOCRYPHATE
APOCYNACEOUS
APOCYNEOUS
APOCYTE
APOD
APODAN
APODE
APODEICTIC
APODEICTICAL
APODEIPNON
APODEMA
APODEMAL
APODEMATAL
APODEME
APODIA
APODICTIC
APODICTICAL
APODICTIVE
APODIXIS
APODOSES
APODOSIS
APODOUS
APODYTERIA
APODYTERIUM
APOEMBRYONY
APOFENCHENE
APOGAEIC
APOGAIC
APOGALACTEUM
APOGAMIC
APOGAMICALLY
APOGAMOUS
APOGAMOUSLY
APOGAMY
APOGEAL
APOGEAN
APOGEE
APOGENOUS
APOGENY
APOGEOTROPIC
APOGONID
APOGRAPH
APOGRAPHAL
APOHARMINE
APOHYAL
APOIKIA
APOISE
APOJOVE
APOKREA
APOKREOS
APOLAR
APOLARITY
APOLAUSTIC
APOLEGAMIC
APOLLONICON
APOLOG
APOLOGAL
APOLOGETE
APOLOGETIC
APOLOGETICAL
APOLOGETICALLY
APOLOGETICS
APOLOGIA
APOLOGIES
APOLOGIST
APOLOGIZE
APOLOGIZED
APOLOGIZER
APOLOGIZING
APOLOGUE
APOLOGY
APOLOUSIS
APOLUNE
APOLUSIS
APOLYSIS
APOLYTIKION
APOMECOMETER
APOMECOMETRY
APOMETABOLIC
APOMICT
APOMICTIC
APOMICTICAL
APOMIXIS
APOMORPHIA
APOMORPHIN
APOMORPHINE
APONEUROLOGY
APONEUROSES
APONEUROSIS
APONEUROTIC
APONEUROTOME
APONEUROTOMY
APONIA
APONIC
APOOP
APOPEMPTIC
APOPETALOUS
APOPHASIS
APOPHATIC
APOPHONIA
APOPHONIC
APOPHONY
APOPHTHEGM
APOPHYGE
APOPHYLACTIC
APOPHYLAXIS
APOPHYLLITE
APOPHYLLOUS
APOPHYSARY
APOPHYSATE
APOPHYSEAL
APOPHYSES
APOPHYSIAL
APOPHYSIS
APOPHYSITIS
APOPLECTIC
APOPLECTICAL
APOPLEX
APOPLEXIOUS
APOPLEXY
APOPYLE
APOQUININE
APORETIC
APORETICAL
APORHYOLITE
APORIA
APOROSE
APORPHIN
APORPHINE
APORRHAOID
APORRHEA
APORRHEGMA
APORT
APORTOISE
APOSAFRANINE
APOSATURN
APOSATURNIUM
APOSEMATIC
APOSEPALOUS
APOSIA
APOSIOPESIS
APOSIOPETIC
APOSITIA
APOSITIC
APOSORO
APOSPOROGONY
APOSPOROUS
APOSPORY
APOSTACY
APOSTASIES
APOSTASIS
APOSTASY
APOSTATE
APOSTATIC
APOSTATICAL
APOSTATISM
APOSTATIZE
APOSTATIZED
APOSTATIZING
APOSTAXIS
APOSTEMATE
APOSTEMATIC
APOSTEMATION
APOSTEMATOUS
APOSTEME
APOSTHIA
APOSTIL
APOSTILLE
APOSTLE
APOSTLES
APOSTLESHIP
APOSTOLATE
APOSTOLESS
APOSTOLI
APOSTOLIC
APOSTOLICAL
APOSTOLICISM
APOSTOLICITY
APOSTOLIZE
APOSTROPHAL
APOSTROPHE
APOSTROPHI
APOSTROPHIC
APOSTROPHIED
APOSTROPHIZE
APOSTROPHUS
APOTELESM
APOTHEC
APOTHECAL
APOTHECARIES
APOTHECARY
APOTHECE
APOTHECIA
APOTHECIAL
APOTHECIUM
APOTHEGM
APOTHEGMATIC
APOTHEM

APOTHEOSE
APOTHEOSES
APOTHEOSIS
APOTHEOSIZE
APOTHEOSIZED
APOTHESINE
APOTHESIS
APOTOME
APOTROPAIC
APOTROPAION
APOTROPAISM
APOTROPOUS
APOTURMERIC
APOTYPE
APOTYPIC
APOUT
APOXESIS
APOY
APOZEM
APOZEMA
APOZEMICAL
APPAIR
APPAL
APPALL
APPALLED
APPALLING
APPALLINGLY
APPALTO
APPANAGE
APPANAGED
APPANAGING
APPANAGIST
APPARATUS
APPARATUSES
APPAREL
APPARELED
APPARELING
APPARELLED
APPARELLING
APPARELMENT
APPARENCE
APPARENCY
APPARENT
APPARENTLY
APPARENTNESS
APPARITION
APPARITIONAL
APPARITOR
APPARTEMENT
APPASSIONATA
APPASSIONATO
APPAST
APPAUME
APPAUMEE
APPAY
APPEACH
APPEACHER
APPEACHMENT
APPEAL
APPEALABLE
APPEALED
APPEALER
APPEALING
APPEALINGLY
APPEALINGNESS
APPEAR
APPEARANCE
APPEARANCED
APPEARED
APPEARER
APPEARING
APPEASABLE
APPEASABLY
APPEASE
APPEASED
APPEASEMENT
APPEASER
APPEASING
APPEASINGLY
APPEASIVE
APPEL
APPELLABLE
APPELLANCY
APPELLANT
APPELLATION
APPELLATIVE
APPELLATIVED
APPELLATORY
APPELLEE
APPELLOR
APPENAGE
APPEND
APPENDAGE
APPENDAGED
APPENDALGIA
APPENDANCE
APPENDANCY
APPENDANT
APPENDECTOMIES
APPENDECTOMY
APPENDED
APPENDENT
APPENDICAL
APPENDICE
APPENDICEAL
APPENDICES
APPENDICITIS
APPENDICLE
APPENDICULAR
APPENDIX
APPENDIXED
APPENDIXES
APPENDIXING
APPENTICE
APPERCEIVE
APPERCEIVED
APPERCEIVING
APPERCEPTION
APPERCEPTIVE
APPERCIPIENT
APPERE
APPERIL
APPERT
APPERTAIN
APPERTISE
APPESTAT
APPET
APPETE
APPETENCE
APPETENCIES
APPETENCY
APPETENT
APPETENTLY
APPETIBILITY
APPETIBLE
APPETISER
APPETISING
APPETITE
APPETITION
APPETITIONAL
APPETITIOUS
APPETITIVE
APPETIZE
APPETIZED
APPETIZER
APPETIZING
APPETIZINGLY
APPINITE
APPLANATE
APPLANATION
APPLAUD
APPLAUDABLE
APPLAUDABLY
APPLAUDER
APPLAUDINGLY
APPLAUSE
APPLAUSIVE
APPLAUSIVELY
APPLE
APPLEBERRY
APPLEBLOSSOM
APPLECART
APPLED
APPLEDRANE
APPLEDRONE
APPLEGROWER
APPLEJACK
APPLEJOHN
APPLEMONGER
APPLENUT
APPLERINGIE
APPLERINGY
APPLEROOT
APPLES
APPLESAUCE
APPLEWIFE
APPLEWOMAN
APPLIABLE
APPLIABLENESS
APPLIABLY
APPLIANCE
APPLIANT
APPLICABLE
APPLICABLY
APPLICANCY
APPLICANT
APPLICATE
APPLICATION
APPLICATIVE
APPLICATOR
APPLICATORY
APPLIED
APPLIEDLY
APPLIER
APPLING
APPLIQUE
APPLIQUED
APPLIQUEING
APPLOSION
APPLOSIVE
APPLOT
APPLOTMENT
APPLY
APPLYING
APPLYINGLY
APPLYMENT
APPOGGIATURA
APPOGGIATURE
APPOINT
APPOINTE
APPOINTEE
APPOINTER
APPOINTIVE
APPOINTMENT
APPOINTOR
APPORT
APPORTION
APPORTIONER
APPORTIONMENT
APPOSABLE
APPOSE
APPOSED
APPOSER
APPOSING
APPOSITE
APPOSITELY
APPOSITENESS
APPOSITION
APPOSITIONAL
APPOSITIVE
APPOSITIVELY
APPRAISABLE
APPRAISAL
APPRAISE
APPRAISED
APPRAISEMENT
APPRAISER
APPRAISING
APPRAISIVE
APPRECIABLE
APPRECIABLY
APPRECIANT
APPRECIATE
APPRECIATED
APPRECIATING
APPRECIATION
APPRECIATIVE
APPRECIATIVELY
APPRECIATIVENESS
APPRECIATOR
APPRECIATORY
APPREHEND
APPREHENDED
APPREHENDER
APPREHENSIBLE
APPREHENSIBLY
APPREHENSION
APPREHENSIVE
APPREHENSIVELY
APPREHENSIVENESS
APPREND
APPRENTICE
APPRENTICED
APPRENTICESHIP
APPRENTICING
APPRESSED
APPRESSOR
APPRESSORIA
APPRESSORIAL
APPRESSORIUM
APPREST
APPRETEUR
APPRISE
APPRISED
APPRISING
APPRIZAL
APPRIZE
APPRIZEMENT
APPRIZER
APPRIZING
APPROACH
APPROACHABILITY
APPROACHABLE
APPROACHABLENESS
APPROACHER
APPROACHES
APPROACHING
APPROACHLESS
APPROACHMENT
APPROBATE
APPROBATED
APPROBATING
APPROBATION
APPROBATIVE
APPROBATOR
APPROBATORY
APPROOF
APPROPRE
APPROPRIABLE
APPROPRIATE
APPROPRIATED
APPROPRIATELY
APPROPRIATENES
APPROPRIATING
APPROPRIATION
APPROPRIATIVE
APPROPRIATOR
APPROVABLE
APPROVAL
APPROVANCE
APPROVE
APPROVED
APPROVEDLY
APPROVEMENT
APPROVER
APPROVING
APPROVINGLY
APPROXIMAL
APPROXIMATE
APPROXIMATED
APPROXIMATELY
APPROXIMATING
APPROXIMATION
APPROXIMATIVE
APPROXIMATOR
APPUI
APPULSE
APPULSION
APPULSIVE
APPULSIVELY
APPURTENANCE
APPURTENANT
APRAXIA
APRAXIC
APRENDIZ
APRES
APREYNTE
APRICATE
APRICATION
APRICKLE
APRICOT
APRIORISM
APRIORIST
APRIORISTIC
APRIORITY
APROCTIA
APROCTOUS
APRON
APRONEER
APRONLIKE
APROPOS
APROSEXIA
APROSOPIA
APROSOPOUS
APROTERODONT
APS
APSE
APSELAPHESIA
APSELAPHESIS
APSES
APSIDAL
APSIDALLY
APSIDES
APSIDIOLE
APSINTHION
APSIS
APSYCHIA
APSYCHICAL
APT
APTATE
APTERAL
APTERIA
APTERIAL
APTERIUM
APTEROID
APTEROUS
APTERYGIAL
APTERYGOTE
APTERYGOTOUS
APTERYLA
APTERYX
APTHA
APTITUDE
APTITUDINAL
APTITUDINALLY

APTLY
APTNESS
APTOTE
APTOTIC
APTYALIA
APTYALISM
APTYCHUS
APULMONIC
APULSE
APURPOSE
APUS
APYONIN
APYRASE
APYRENE
APYRETIC
APYREXIA
APYREXIAL
APYREXY
APYROTYPE
APYROUS
AQUA
AQUABIB
AQUACADE
AQUACULTURAL
AQUACULTURE
AQUAE
AQUAEMANALE
AQUAEMANALIA
AQUAFER
AQUAFORTIS
AQUAFORTIST
AQUAGE
AQUAGREEN
AQUALUNG
AQUAMARINE
AQUAMETER
AQUANAUT
AQUAPLANE
AQUAPLANED
AQUAPLANING
AQUAPUNCTURE
AQUARELLE
AQUARELLIST
AQUARIA
AQUARIAL
AQUARIAN
AQUARIIST
AQUARIST
AQUARIUM
AQUARIUMS
AQUARTER
AQUAS
AQUASCUTUM
AQUATE
AQUATIC
AQUATICAL
AQUATICALLY
AQUATICS
AQUATILE
AQUATINT
AQUATINTER
AQUATION
AQUATIVENESS
AQUATONE
AQUAVALENT
AQUAVIT
AQUEDUCT
AQUEITY
AQUEOGLACIAL
AQUEOIGNEOUS
AQUEOUS
AQUEOUSLY
AQUEOUSNESS
AQUICOLOUS
AQUICULTURAL
AQUICULTURE
AQUIFER
AQUIFEROUS
AQUIFORM
AQUIFUGE
AQUILA
AQUILAWOOD
AQUILEGE
AQUILEGIA
AQUILINE
AQUILINO
AQUIPAROUS
AQUIVER
AQUO
AQUOSE
AQUOSITY
AQUOTIZATION
AQUOTIZE
AR
ARA
ARABA
ARABAN
ARABESK
ARABESQUE
ARABESQUELY
ARABESQUERIE
ARABICA
ARABILITY
ARABIN
ARABINE
ARABINOSE
ARABINOSIC
ARABITE
ARABITOL
ARABLE
ARACA
ARACANGA
ARACARI
ARACE
ARACEOUS
ARACHE
ARACHIC
ARACHIDE
ARACHIDIC
ARACHIN
ARACHIS
ARACHNACTIS
ARACHNID
ARACHNIDAN
ARACHNIDIAL
ARACHNIDISM
ARACHNIDIUM
ARACHNISM
ARACHNITIS
ARACHNOID
ARACHNOIDAL
ARACHNOIDEA
ARACHNOIDEAN
ARACHNOLOGY
ARAD
ARADA
ARADID
ARADO
ARAGONITE
ARAGUANE
ARAGUATO
ARAH
ARAIN
ARAIRE
ARAK
ARAKE
ARAKI
ARALIA
ARALIACEOUS
ARALIAD
ARALIE
ARALKYL
ARALKYLATED
ARAMAYOITE
ARAMINA
ARANA
ARANEID
ARANEIDAN
ARANEIFORM
ARANEIN
ARANEOLOGIST
ARANEOLOGY
ARANEOSE
ARANEOUS
ARANGA
ARANGO
ARANGOES
ARANZADA
ARAPAHITE
ARAPAIMA
ARAPHOROSTIC
ARAPHOSTIC
ARAPONGA
ARAPUNGA
ARAR
ARARA
ARARAO
ARARAUNA
ARARIBA
ARAROBA
ARARU
ARAS
ARASE
ARATI
ARATINGA
ARATION
ARATORY
ARAUCARIA
ARAUCARIAN
ARAYNE
ARBA
ARBACIA
ARBACIN
ARBALEST
ARBALESTER
ARBALESTRE
ARBALIST
ARBALO
ARBALOS
ARBER
ARBITER
ARBITH
ARBITRABLE
ARBITRAGE
ARBITRAGER
ARBITRAGEUR
ARBITRAGIST
ARBITRAL
ARBITRAMENT
ARBITRARILY
ARBITRARINESS
ARBITRARY
ARBITRATE
ARBITRATED
ARBITRATING
ARBITRATION
ARBITRATIONAL
ARBITRATIVE
ARBITRATOR
ARBITREMENT
ARBITRER
ARBITRESS
ARBOLOCO
ARBOR
ARBORACEOUS
ARBORAL
ARBORARY
ARBORATOR
ARBOREAL
ARBOREALLY
ARBOREAN
ARBORED
ARBOREOUS
ARBORER
ARBORES
ARBORESCENCE
ARBORESCENT
ARBORESQUE
ARBORET
ARBORETA
ARBORETUM
ARBORETUMS
ARBORICAL
ARBORICOLE
ARBORICOLINE
ARBORICOLOUS
ARBORIFORM
ARBORISE
ARBORIST
ARBORIZATION
ARBORIZE
ARBORIZED
ARBORIZING
ARBOROID
ARBOROLATRY
ARBOROUS
ARBORS
ARBORVITAE
ARBORWAY
ARBOUR
ARBOURED
ARBUSCLE
ARBUSCULA
ARBUSCULAR
ARBUSCULE
ARBUSTA
ARBUSTERIN
ARBUSTEROL
ARBUSTUM
ARBUTE
ARBUTEAN
ARBUTIN
ARBUTUS
ARC
ARCA
ARCABUCERO
ARCADE
ARCADED
ARCADIAN
ARCADING
ARCAE
ARCANA
ARCANAL
ARCANE
ARCANUM
ARCATE
ARCATO
ARCATURE
ARCED
ARCELLA
ARCES
ARCH
ARCHA
ARCHAEOCYTE
ARCHAEOLATRY
ARCHAEOLOGER
ARCHAEOLOGIC
ARCHAEOLOGICAL
ARCHAEOLOGIST
ARCHAEOLOGY
ARCHAEUS
ARCHAI
ARCHAIC
ARCHAICAL
ARCHAICALLY
ARCHAICISM
ARCHAISE
ARCHAISM
ARCHAIST
ARCHAISTIC
ARCHAIZE
ARCHAIZED
ARCHAIZER
ARCHAIZING
ARCHANGEL
ARCHANGELIC
ARCHARIOS
ARCHBAND
ARCHBISHOP
ARCHBISHOPRIC
ARCHCHEMIC
ARCHDEACON
ARCHDEACONRY
ARCHDEAN
ARCHDIOCESAN
ARCHDIOCESE
ARCHDUCAL
ARCHDUCHESS
ARCHDUCHIES
ARCHDUCHY
ARCHDUKE
ARCHDUKEDOM
ARCHE
ARCHEAL
ARCHEBIOSIS
ARCHECENTRIC
ARCHED
ARCHEGONE
ARCHEGONIA
ARCHEGONIAL
ARCHEGONIATE
ARCHEGONIUM
ARCHEION
ARCHELOGY
ARCHENEMIES
ARCHENEMY
ARCHENTERIC
ARCHENTERON
ARCHEOCYTE
ARCHEOLITHIC
ARCHEOLOGIAN
ARCHEOLOGIC
ARCHEOLOGICAL
ARCHEOLOGIST
ARCHEOLOGY
ARCHEOPTERYX
ARCHEOSTOME
ARCHER
ARCHERFISH
ARCHERFISHES
ARCHERS
ARCHERY
ARCHES
ARCHESPORE
ARCHESPORIAL
ARCHESPORIUM
ARCHETYPAL
ARCHETYPALLY
ARCHETYPE
ARCHETYPIC
ARCHETYPICAL
ARCHETYPIST
ARCHEUS
ARCHFIEND
ARCHIATER
ARCHIBENTHAL
ARCHIBENTHIC
ARCHIBENTHOS
ARCHIBLAST
ARCHIBLASTIC
ARCHICAL
ARCHICARP
ARCHICEREBRA
ARCHICOELE
ARCHICYTE

ARCHICYTULA
ARCHIDOME
ARCHIE
ARCHIEREUS
ARCHIGENESIS
ARCHIKARYON
ARCHIL
ARCHILITHIC
ARCHILLA
ARCHILOWE
ARCHILUTE
ARCHIMAGE
ARCHIMAGUS
ARCHIMIME
ARCHIMORPHIC
ARCHIMORULA
ARCHIN
ARCHINE
ARCHINEURON
ARCHING
ARCHIPALLIAL
ARCHIPALLIUM
ARCHIPELAGIC
ARCHIPELAGO
ARCHIPELAGOES
ARCHIPELAGOS
ARCHIPHONEME
ARCHIPIN
ARCHIPLASM
ARCHIPLASMIC
ARCHISPERM
ARCHISPHERE
ARCHISPORE
ARCHISTOME
ARCHITECT
ARCHITECTIVE
ARCHITECTRESS
ARCHITECTURAL
ARCHITECTURALLY
ARCHITECTURE
ARCHITIS
ARCHITRAVAL
ARCHITRAVE
ARCHITRAVED
ARCHIVAL
ARCHIVAULT
ARCHIVE
ARCHIVED
ARCHIVES
ARCHIVING
ARCHIVIST
ARCHIVOLT
ARCHIZOIC
ARCHLUTE
ARCHLY
ARCHNESS
ARCHOCELE
ARCHOLOGY
ARCHON
ARCHONT
ARCHONTATE
ARCHONTIC
ARCHOPLASM
ARCHOPLASMA
ARCHOPLASMIC
ARCHOPTOMA
ARCHOPTOSIS
ARCHORRHAGIA
ARCHORRHEA
ARCHOSYRINX
ARCHPRIEST
ARCHPRIESTHOOD
ARCHPRIESTSHIP
ARCHSEE
ARCHWAY
ARCHWISE
ARCHY
ARCIFEROUS
ARCIFINIOUS
ARCIFORM
ARCING
ARCKED
ARCKING
ARCOCENTROUS
ARCOCENTRUM
ARCOGRAPH
ARCOSE
ARCOSOLIA
ARCOSOLIUM
ARCS
ARCT
ARCTATION
ARCTIAN
ARCTIC
ARCTICALLY
ARCTICIAN
ARCTICIZE
ARCTICIZED
ARCTICIZING
ARCTIID
ARCTOID
ARCTOIDEAN
ARCUAL
ARCUALE
ARCUALIA
ARCUATE
ARCUATED
ARCUATELY
ARCUATION
ARCULA
ARCULITE
ARCUS
ARD
ARDAB
ARDASSINE
ARDEB
ARDELIO
ARDELLA
ARDELLAE
ARDEN
ARDENCY
ARDENNITE
ARDENT
ARDENTLY
ARDENTNESS
ARDER
ARDILLA
ARDISH
ARDISIA
ARDITI
ARDITO
ARDOISE
ARDOO
ARDOR
ARDORS
ARDOUR
ARDRI
ARDRIGH
ARDU
ARDUINITE
ARDUOUS
ARDUOUSLY
ARDUOUSNESS
ARDURE
ARDUROUS
ARE
AREA
AREACH
AREAD
AREAE
AREAL
AREALITY
AREAR
AREAS
AREASON
AREAWAY
ARECA
ARECACEOUS
ARECHE
ARED
AREED
AREEK
AREEL
AREFACT
AREFACTION
AREFY
AREG
AREIC
AREITO
ARENA
ARENACEOUS
ARENAE
ARENARIAE
ARENARIOUS
ARENAS
ARENATION
AREND
ARENDALITE
ARENE
ARENG
ARENICOLITE
ARENICOLOUS
ARENILITIC
ARENITE
ARENOID
ARENOSE
ARENOSITY
AREOCENTRIC
AREOGRAPHER
AREOGRAPHIC
AREOGRAPHY
AREOLA
AREOLAE
AREOLAR
AREOLAS
AREOLATE
AREOLATED
AREOLATION
AREOLE
AREOLET
AREOLOGIC
AREOLOGICAL
AREOLOGIST
AREOLOGY
AREOMETER
AREOMETRIC
AREOMETRICAL
AREOMETRY
AREOPAGY
AREPA
ARERE
ARET
ARETAICS
ARETALOGY
ARETE
ARETHUSA
ARETTE
ARF
ARFVEDSONITE
ARGAL
ARGALA
ARGALI
ARGALIS
ARGASID
ARGEERS
ARGEL
ARGEMONE
ARGENOL
ARGENT
ARGENTAL
ARGENTAMID
ARGENTAMIDE
ARGENTAMIN
ARGENTAMINE
ARGENTARII
ARGENTARIUS
ARGENTATION
ARGENTEOUS
ARGENTER
ARGENTEUM
ARGENTIC
ARGENTIDE
ARGENTIN
ARGENTINE
ARGENTINO
ARGENTION
ARGENTITE
ARGENTOL
ARGENTOMETRY
ARGENTON
ARGENTOSE
ARGENTOUS
ARGENTUM
ARGH
ARGHAN
ARGHE
ARGHEL
ARGHOOL
ARGHOUL
ARGIFY
ARGIL
ARGILLACEOUS
ARGILLIC
ARGILLITE
ARGILLITIC
ARGILLOID
ARGILLOUS
ARGIN
ARGINASE
ARGINE
ARGININE
ARGLE
ARGO
ARGOL
ARGOLET
ARGOLETIER
ARGON
ARGONAUT
ARGONAUTIC
ARGONAUTID
ARGONAUTS
ARGOSIES
ARGOSY
ARGOT
ARGOTIC
ARGUABLE
ARGUE
ARGUED
ARGUENDO
ARGUER
ARGUFIED
ARGUFIER
ARGUFY
ARGUFYING
ARGUING
ARGUL
ARGUMENT
ARGUMENTA
ARGUMENTAL
ARGUMENTATION
ARGUMENTATIOUS
ARGUMENTATIVE
ARGUMENTATIVELY
ARGUMENTATIVENESS
ARGUMENTATOR
ARGUMENTATORY
ARGUMENTS
ARGUMENTUM
ARGUS
ARGUSFISH
ARGUSFISHES
ARGUTE
ARGUTELY
ARGUTENESS
ARGY
ARGYRANTHOUS
ARGYRIA
ARGYRIC
ARGYRITE
ARGYRODITE
ARGYROSE
ARGYRYTHROSE
ARHAR
ARHAT
ARIA
ARIBIN
ARIBINE
ARICIN
ARICINE
ARID
ARIDGE
ARIDIAN
ARIDITIES
ARIDITY
ARIDLY
ARIDNESS
ARIEGITE
ARIEL
ARIENZO
ARIES
ARIETATE
ARIETATION
ARIETINOUS
ARIETTA
ARIETTE
ARIGHT
ARIGHTLY
ARIGUE
ARIKI
ARIL
ARILED
ARILLARY
ARILLATE
ARILLATED
ARILLED
ARILLI
ARILLIFORM
ARILLODE
ARILLODIUM
ARILLOID
ARILLUS
ARIOLATE
ARIOLE
ARIOSE
ARIOSO
ARIOT
ARIPPLE
ARIS
ARISAID
ARISARD
ARISE
ARISEN
ARISING
ARISINGS
ARIST
ARISTA
ARISTAE
ARISTARCHIES
ARISTARCHY
ARISTATE
ARISTE
ARISTO
ARISTOCRACIES
ARISTOCRACY
ARISTOCRAT

ARISTOCRATIC
ARISTOCRATICAL
ARISTOCRATICALLY
ARISTOGENIC
ARISTOGENICS
ARISTOI
ARISTOLOGICAL
ARISTOLOGIST
ARISTOLOGY
ARISTOS
ARISTOTYPE
ARISTULATE
ARITE
ARITHMETIC
ARITHMETICAL
ARITHMETICALLY
ARITHMETICIAN
ARITHMETIZE
ARITHMOCRACY
ARITHMOGRAM
ARITHMOGRAPH
ARITHMOMANIA
ARITHMOMETER
ARITHROMANIA
ARIZONITE
ARJAN
ARJUN
ARK
ARKANSITE
ARKAR
ARKITE
ARKOSE
ARKOSIC
ARKSUTITE
ARLES
ARLING
ARLOUP
ARM
ARMADA
ARMADILLA
ARMADILLO
ARMADILLOS
ARMAGNAC
ARMAMENT
ARMAMENTARIA
ARMAMENTARY
ARMANGITE
ARMARIA
ARMARIUM
ARMATURE
ARMBAND
ARMBONE
ARMCHAIR
ARMCHAIRED
ARME
ARMED
ARMENIACEOUS
ARMENITE
ARMER
ARMET
ARMFUL
ARMFULS
ARMGAUNT
ARMGUARD
ARMHOLE
ARMHOOP
ARMIED
ARMIES
ARMIFEROUS
ARMIGER
ARMIGERAL
ARMIGERI
ARMIGEROUS
ARMIL
ARMILL
ARMILLA
ARMILLAE
ARMILLARY
ARMILLATE
ARMILLATED
ARMINE
ARMING
ARMIPOTENCE
ARMIPOTENT
ARMISONANT
ARMISONOUS
ARMISTICE
ARMITAS
ARMLET
ARMLOAD
ARMLOCK
ARMOIRE
ARMONICA
ARMOR
ARMORBEARER
ARMORED
ARMORER
ARMORIAL
ARMORIED
ARMORIES
ARMORIST
ARMORY
ARMOUR
ARMOURED
ARMOURER
ARMOURIES
ARMOURY
ARMOZEEN
ARMOZINE
ARMPIECE
ARMPIT
ARMPLATE
ARMRACK
ARMREST
ARMS
ARMSCYE
ARMSEYE
ARMSIZE
ARMURE
ARMY
ARMYWORM
ARN
ARNA
ARNATTA
ARNATTO
ARNBERRY
ARNEE
ARNEMENT
ARNI
ARNICA
ARNOTTO
ARNUT
AROAR
AROAST
AROCK
AROEIRA
AROID
AROIDEOUS
AROINT
AROLIA
AROLIUM
AROLLA
AROMA
AROMACITY
AROMADENDRIN
AROMAS
AROMATA
AROMATIC
AROMATICAL
AROMATICALLY
AROMATICITY
AROMATITAE
AROMATITE
AROMATITES
AROMATIZE
AROMATIZED
AROMATIZER
AROMATIZING
AROMATOUS
AROMO
AROOM
AROON
AROSE
AROUND
AROUSAL
AROUSE
AROUSED
AROUSER
AROUSING
AROW
AROXYL
AROYNT
ARPA
ARPEGGIANDO
ARPEGGIATION
ARPEGGIO
ARPEGGIOED
ARPEN
ARPENT
ARPENTEUR
ARQUEBUS
ARQUERITE
ARR
ARRA
ARRACACH
ARRACACHA
ARRACE
ARRACK
ARRAGE
ARRAH
ARRAIGN
ARRAIGNED
ARRAIGNER
ARRAIGNING
ARRAIGNMENT
ARRAME
ARRAND
ARRANGE
ARRANGED
ARRANGEMENT
ARRANGER
ARRANGING
ARRANT
ARRANTLY
ARRAS
ARRASED
ARRASENE
ARRASTRA
ARRASTRE
ARRATEL
ARRAU
ARRAY
ARRAYAL
ARRAYAN
ARRAYED
ARRAYER
ARRAYING
ARRAYMENT
ARREAR
ARREARAGE
ARREARS
ARRECT
ARRECTOR
ARRENT
ARRENTATION
ARREPTITIOUS
ARREST
ARRESTATION
ARRESTEE
ARRESTER
ARRESTING
ARRESTINGLY
ARRESTIVE
ARRESTMENT
ARRESTOR
ARRET
ARRHA
ARRHAL
ARRHENAL
ARRHENOTOKY
ARRHINIA
ARRHIZAL
ARRHIZOUS
ARRHYTHMIA
ARRHYTHMIC
ARRHYTHMICAL
ARRHYTHMICALLY
ARRHYTHMOUS
ARRHYTHMY
ARRIAGE
ARRIBA
ARRICCIO
ARRIDE
ARRIDGE
ARRIE
ARRIERE
ARRIERO
ARRIMBY
ARRIS
ARRISH
ARRISWAYS
ARRISWISE
ARRIVAGE
ARRIVAL
ARRIVE
ARRIVED
ARRIVER
ARRIVING
ARRIVISM
ARRIVIST
ARRIVISTE
ARROBA
ARRODE
ARROGANCE
ARROGANCY
ARROGANT
ARROGANTLY
ARROGANTNESS
ARROGATE
ARROGATED
ARROGATING
ARROGATION
ARROGATIVE
ARROGATOR
ARROJADITE
ARRONDI
ARROPE
ARROSION
ARROSIVE
ARROUND
ARROUSE
ARROW
ARROWBUSH
ARROWED
ARROWHEAD
ARROWHEADED
ARROWLEAF
ARROWLET
ARROWPLATE
ARROWROOT
ARROWS
ARROWSTONE
ARROWWEED
ARROWWOOD
ARROWWORM
ARROWY
ARROYA
ARROYO
ARROYOS
ARROYUELO
ARROZ
ARS
ARSANILIC
ARSE
ARSEDINE
ARSEFOOT
ARSENAL
ARSENATE
ARSENATION
ARSENETED
ARSENETTED
ARSENFAST
ARSENHEMOL
ARSENIASIS
ARSENIATE
ARSENIC
ARSENICAL
ARSENICALISM
ARSENICATE
ARSENICATED
ARSENICATING
ARSENICISM
ARSENICIZE
ARSENICKED
ARSENICKING
ARSENIDE
ARSENIDES
ARSENIFEROUS
ARSENILLO
ARSENIOUS
ARSENISM
ARSENITE
ARSENIUM
ARSENIURET
ARSENIURETED
ARSENIZATION
ARSENOFURAN
ARSENOLITE
ARSENOPHEN
ARSENOPHENOL
ARSENOPYRITE
ARSENOUS
ARSENOXIDE
ARSENYL
ARSES
ARSESMART
ARSHEEN
ARSHIN
ARSHINE
ARSHINS
ARSINE
ARSINIC
ARSINO
ARSIS
ARSLE
ARSNICKER
ARSOITE
ARSON
ARSONATE
ARSONATION
ARSONIC
ARSONIST
ARSONITE
ARSONIUM
ARSONO
ARSPHENAMINE
ARSYL
ARSYLENE
ART
ARTABA
ARTAL
ARTAR
ARTARIN
ARTARINE
ARTCRAFT

ARTEFAC
ARTEFACT
ARTEL
ARTEMIA
ARTEMISIA
ARTEMISIC
ARTEMISIN
ARTEMON
ARTER
ARTERIA
ARTERIAE
ARTERIAGRA
ARTERIAL
ARTERIALIZE
ARTERIALIZED
ARTERIALLY
ARTERIARCTIA
ARTERIASIS
ARTERIED
ARTERIES
ARTERIN
ARTERIOGRAM
ARTERIOGRAPH
ARTERIOLE
ARTERIOLITH
ARTERIOLOGY
ARTERIOMETER
ARTERIOMOTOR
ARTERIORENAL
ARTERIOSPASM
ARTERIOTOME
ARTERIOTOMY
ARTERIOUS
ARTERITIS
ARTERY
ARTERYING
ARTFUL
ARTFULLY
ARTFULNESS
ARTHA
ARTHEL
ARTHEMIS
ARTHRA
ARTHRAGRA
ARTHRAL
ARTHRALGIA
ARTHRALGIC
ARTHRECTOMY
ARTHREDEMA
ARTHRITIC
ARTHRITICAL
ARTHRITICINE
ARTHRITIDES
ARTHRITIS
ARTHRITISM
ARTHROBRANCH
ARTHROCACE
ARTHROCELE
ARTHROCLASIA
ARTHROCLISIS
ARTHRODERM
ARTHRODESIS
ARTHRODIA
ARTHRODIAE
ARTHRODIAL
ARTHRODIC
ARTHRODIRAN
ARTHRODIRE
ARTHRODIROUS
ARTHRODYMIC
ARTHRODYNIA
ARTHROGENOUS
ARTHROGRAPHY
ARTHROLITE
ARTHROLITH
ARTHROLOGY
ARTHROMERE
ARTHROMERIC
ARTHROMETER
ARTHROMETRY
ARTHRON
ARTHRONCUS
ARTHROPATHIC
ARTHROPATHY
ARTHROPHYMA
ARTHROPLASTY
ARTHROPLEURA
ARTHROPLEURE
ARTHROPOD
ARTHROPODAL
ARTHROPODAN
ARTHROPODOUS
ARTHROPYOSIS
ARTHROSES
ARTHROSIA
ARTHROSIS
ARTHROSPORE
ARTHROSPORIC
ARTHROSPOROUS
ARTHROSTOME
ARTHROSTOMY
ARTHROSYRINX
ARTHROTOME
ARTHROTOMIES
ARTHROTOMY
ARTHROTRAUMA
ARTHROTROPIC
ARTHROUS
ARTHROZOAN
ARTHROZOIC
ARTIAD
ARTICHOKE
ARTICLE
ARTICLED
ARTICLES
ARTICLING
ARTICULACY
ARTICULANT
ARTICULAR
ARTICULARE
ARTICULARLY
ARTICULARS
ARTICULATE
ARTICULATED
ARTICULATELY
ARTICULATENESS
ARTICULATING
ARTICULATION
ARTICULATIVE
ARTICULATOR
ARTICULATORY
ARTICULITE
ARTICULUS
ARTIFACT
ARTIFACTS
ARTIFEX
ARTIFICE
ARTIFICER
ARTIFICES
ARTIFICIAL
ARTIFICIALITIES
ARTIFICIALITY
ARTIFICIALLY
ARTIFICIALNESS
ARTILLER
ARTILLERIST
ARTILLERY
ARTILLERYMAN
ARTILLERYMEN
ARTILLERYSHIP
ARTINESS
ARTINITE
ARTIODACTYL
ARTIPHYLLOUS
ARTISAN
ARTISANRY
ARTISANSHIP
ARTIST
ARTISTE
ARTISTIC
ARTISTICAL
ARTISTICALLY
ARTISTRY
ARTLESS
ARTLESSLY
ARTLESSNESS
ARTLET
ARTLY
ARTOCARPAD
ARTOCARPEOUS
ARTOCARPOUS
ARTOLATER
ARTOPHAGOUS
ARTOPHORIA
ARTOPHORION
ARTOTYPE
ARTOTYPY
ARTS
ARTSMAN
ARTUS
ARTWARE
ARTWORK
ARTY
ARUI
ARUIN
ARUKE
ARUM
ARUMIN
ARUNDIFEROUS
ARUNDINEOUS
ARUPA
ARURA
ARUSA
ARUSHA
ARUSPEX
ARUSPICE
ARUSTLE
ARVAL
ARVEJON
ARVEL
ARVICOLE
ARVICOLINE
ARVICULTURE
ARX
ARY
ARYBALLOID
ARYBALLOS
ARYBALLUS
ARYL
ARYLAMINE
ARYLAMINO
ARYLATE
ARYLIDE
ARYTENOID
ARYTENOIDAL
ARZRUNITE
ARZUN
AS
ASADDLE
ASADO
ASAFETIDA
ASAFOETIDA
ASAK
ASAL
ASALE
ASAMBLEA
ASANA
ASAPHIA
ASAPHID
ASAR
ASARABACCA
ASARITE
ASARON
ASARONE
ASAROTUM
ASARUM
ASBEST
ASBESTIC
ASBESTIFORM
ASBESTINE
ASBESTINIZE
ASBESTOID
ASBESTOIDAL
ASBESTOS
ASBESTOSIS
ASBESTOUS
ASBESTUS
ASBOLAN
ASBOLANE
ASBOLIN
ASBOLITE
ASCAN
ASCARE
ASCARED
ASCARIASIS
ASCARICIDAL
ASCARICIDE
ASCARID
ASCARIDES
ASCARIDIASIS
ASCARIDOL
ASCARIDOLE
ASCARIS
ASCARON
ASCELLI
ASCELLUS
ASCEND
ASCENDABLE
ASCENDANCE
ASCENDANCY
ASCENDANT
ASCENDENCE
ASCENDENCY
ASCENDENT
ASCENDER
ASCENDIBLE
ASCENDING
ASCENDINGLY
ASCENSEUR
ASCENSION
ASCENSIONAL
ASCENSIVE
ASCENSOR
ASCENT
ASCERTAIN
ASCERTAINABLE
ASCERTAINABLY
ASCERTAINER
ASCERTAINMENT
ASCESIS
ASCETIC
ASCETICAL
ASCETICALLY
ASCETICISM
ASCHAFFITE
ASCHAM
ASCHER
ASCHISTIC
ASCI
ASCIAN
ASCIDIA
ASCIDIAN
ASCIDIATE
ASCIDICOLOUS
ASCIDIFEROUS
ASCIDIFORM
ASCIDIOID
ASCIDIOZOOID
ASCIDIUM
ASCIFEROUS
ASCIGEROUS
ASCII
ASCILL
ASCITES
ASCITIC
ASCITICAL
ASCITITIOUS
ASCLEPIAD
ASCLEPIDIN
ASCLEPIDOID
ASCLEPIN
ASCOCARP
ASCOCARPOUS
ASCOGENOUS
ASCOGONE
ASCOGONIAL
ASCOGONIDIA
ASCOGONIDIUM
ASCOGONIUM
ASCOLICHEN
ASCOMA
ASCOMATA
ASCOMYCETE
ASCOMYCETES
ASCOMYCETOUS
ASCON
ASCOPHORE
ASCOPHOROUS
ASCORBIC
ASCOSPORE
ASCOSPORIC
ASCOSPOROUS
ASCOT
ASCRIBABLE
ASCRIBE
ASCRIBED
ASCRIBING
ASCRIPT
ASCRIPTION
ASCRIPTITIOUS
ASCRIVE
ASCRY
ASCULA
ASCULAE
ASCUS
ASCYPHOUS
ASDIC
ASE
ASEA
ASEARCH
ASECRETORY
ASEETHE
ASEISMATIC
ASEISMIC
ASEISMICITY
ASEITAS
ASEITY
ASELAR
ASELGEIA
ASELLATE
ASELLUS
ASEM
ASEPSIS
ASEPTATE
ASEPTIC
ASEPTICALLY
ASEPTICISM
ASEPTICIZE
ASEPTICIZED
ASEPTICIZING
ASEPTIFY
ASEPTOL
ASEPTOLIN
ASEXUAL
ASEXUALITY

ASEXUALIZE
ASEXUALIZED
ASEXUALIZING
ASEXUALLY
ASH
ASHAKE
ASHAME
ASHAMED
ASHAMEDLY
ASHAMEDNESS
ASHAMNU
ASHBERRY
ASHCAKE
ASHCAN
ASHEN
ASHERAH
ASHERAHS
ASHERIES
ASHERIM
ASHERY
ASHES
ASHET
ASHFALL
ASHIER
ASHIEST
ASHILY
ASHIMMER
ASHINE
ASHINESS
ASHIPBOARD
ASHIVER
ASHKOKO
ASHLAR
ASHLARED
ASHLARING
ASHLER
ASHLERED
ASHLERING
ASHLING
ASHMAN
ASHMEN
ASHORE
ASHOT
ASHPAN
ASHPIT
ASHPLANT
ASHRAF
ASHRAFI
ASHRAM
ASHRAMA
ASHRE
ASHSTONE
ASHTRAY
ASHVAMEDHA
ASHWEED
ASHWORT
ASHY
ASIALIA
ASIDE
ASIDEHAND
ASIDEN
ASIENTO
ASIL
ASILID
ASIM
ASIMEN
ASIMMER
ASINEGO
ASINEGOES
ASININE
ASININELY
ASININITIES
ASININITY
ASIPHONATE
ASIS
ASITIA
ASK
ASKANCE
ASKANT
ASKAR
ASKAREL
ASKARI
ASKARIS
ASKER
ASKESIS
ASKEW
ASKI
ASKILE
ASKING
ASKINGLY
ASKIP
ASKOS
ASLAKE
ASLANT
ASLANTWISE
ASLAVER
ASLEEP
ASLOP
ASLOPE
ASLUMBER
ASMACK
ASMALTE
ASMEAR
ASMILE
ASMOKE
ASMOLDER
ASNIFFLE
ASNORT
ASOAK
ASOCIAL
ASOK
ASOKA
ASOMATOPHYTE
ASOMATOUS
ASONANT
ASONIA
ASOP
ASOR
ASOTE
ASOUTH
ASP
ASPACE
ASPALATHUS
ASPAR
ASPARAGIC
ASPARAGIN
ASPARAGINE
ASPARAGINIC
ASPARAGINOUS
ASPARAGUS
ASPARAGYL
ASPARKLE
ASPARTATE
ASPARTIC
ASPARTYL
ASPECT
ASPECTABLE
ASPECTANT
ASPECTION
ASPECTS
ASPEN
ASPER
ASPERATE
ASPERATED
ASPERATING
ASPERATION
ASPERGATION
ASPERGE
ASPERGER
ASPERGES
ASPERGILL
ASPERGILLA
ASPERGILLI
ASPERGILLIN
ASPERGILLUM
ASPERGILLUMS
ASPERGILLUS
ASPERITE
ASPERITIES
ASPERITY
ASPERMATIC
ASPERMATISM
ASPERMIA
ASPERMOUS
ASPEROUS
ASPEROUSLY
ASPERSE
ASPERSED
ASPERSER
ASPERSING
ASPERSION
ASPERSIONS
ASPERSIVE
ASPERSIVELY
ASPERSOR
ASPERSORIA
ASPERSORIUM
ASPERSORIUMS
ASPERSORY
ASPERULOSIDE
ASPERULOUS
ASPHALT
ASPHALTENE
ASPHALTER
ASPHALTIC
ASPHALTITE
ASPHALTUM
ASPHALTUS
ASPHETERISM
ASPHETERIZE
ASPHODEL
ASPHYCTIC
ASPHYCTOUS
ASPHYXIA
ASPHYXIAL
ASPHYXIANT
ASPHYXIATE
ASPHYXIATED
ASPHYXIATING
ASPHYXIATION
ASPHYXIATOR
ASPHYXIED
ASPHYXY
ASPIC
ASPIDATE
ASPIDE
ASPIDIARIA
ASPIDINOL
ASPIDISTRA
ASPIDIUM
ASPIDOMANCY
ASPIQUEE
ASPIRANT
ASPIRATA
ASPIRATAE
ASPIRATE
ASPIRATED
ASPIRATING
ASPIRATION
ASPIRATOR
ASPIRATORY
ASPIRE
ASPIRED
ASPIREE
ASPIRER
ASPIRIN
ASPIRING
ASPIRINGLY
ASPISH
ASPLANCHNIC
ASPLENIOID
ASPOROGENIC
ASPOROUS
ASPORT
ASPORTATION
ASPORULATE
ASPOUT
ASPRAWL
ASPREAD
ASPRING
ASPROUT
ASPY
ASQUARE
ASQUAT
ASQUEAL
ASQUINT
ASQUIRM
ASRAM
ASRAMA
ASS
ASSACU
ASSAFETIDA
ASSAFOETIDA
ASSAGAI
ASSAGAIED
ASSAGAIING
ASSAHY
ASSAI
ASSAIL
ASSAILABLE
ASSAILANT
ASSAILER
ASSAILMENT
ASSALTO
ASSAPAN
ASSAPANIC
ASSARION
ASSART
ASSARY
ASSASSIN
ASSASSINATE
ASSASSINATED
ASSASSINATING
ASSASSINATION
ASSASSINATIVE
ASSASSINATOR
ASSASSINATRESS
ASSASSINIST
ASSATE
ASSATION
ASSAULT
ASSAULTER
ASSAULTING
ASSAUT
ASSAY
ASSAYED
ASSAYER
ASSAYING
ASSBAA
ASSE
ASSEAL
ASSECURATION
ASSECURATOR
ASSEDAT
ASSEGAI
ASSEIZE
ASSELF
ASSEMBLABLE
ASSEMBLAGE
ASSEMBLE
ASSEMBLED
ASSEMBLEE
ASSEMBLER
ASSEMBLIES
ASSEMBLING
ASSEMBLY
ASSEMBLYMAN
ASSEMBLYMEN
ASSENT
ASSENTANEOUS
ASSENTATION
ASSENTATIOUS
ASSENTATORY
ASSENTED
ASSENTER
ASSENTIENT
ASSENTING
ASSENTIVE
ASSENTIVENESS
ASSENTOR
ASSERT
ASSERTA
ASSERTABLE
ASSERTATIVE
ASSERTER
ASSERTIBLE
ASSERTION
ASSERTIONAL
ASSERTIVE
ASSERTIVELY
ASSERTIVENESS
ASSERTOR
ASSERTORIAL
ASSERTORIC
ASSERTORICAL
ASSERTORILY
ASSERTORY
ASSERTRESS
ASSERTRIX
ASSERTUM
ASSERVE
ASSES
ASSESS
ASSESSABLE
ASSESSED
ASSESSEE
ASSESSING
ASSESSION
ASSESSIONARY
ASSESSMENT
ASSESSOR
ASSESSORIAL
ASSESSORY
ASSET
ASSETH
ASSETS
ASSEVER
ASSEVERATE
ASSEVERATED
ASSEVERATION
ASSEVERATIVE
ASSEVERATORY
ASSHEAD
ASSI
ASSIBILATE
ASSIBILATED
ASSIBILATING
ASSIBILATION
ASSIDENT
ASSIDUAL
ASSIDUALLY
ASSIDUITIES
ASSIDUITY
ASSIDUOUS
ASSIDUOUSLY
ASSIDUOUSNESS
ASSIEGE
ASSIENTIST
ASSIENTO
ASSIETTE
ASSIFY
ASSIGN
ASSIGNABLE
ASSIGNABLY
ASSIGNAT

ASSIGNATION
ASSIGNED
ASSIGNEE
ASSIGNER
ASSIGNMENT
ASSIGNOR
ASSILAG
ASSIMILABLE
ASSIMILATE
ASSIMILATED
ASSIMILATING
ASSIMILATION
ASSIMILATIVE
ASSIMILATOR
ASSIMILATORY
ASSIS
ASSISE
ASSISH
ASSISHLY
ASSISHNESS
ASSIST
ASSISTANCE
ASSISTANT
ASSISTANTED
ASSISTER
ASSISTFUL
ASSISTIVE
ASSISTLESS
ASSISTOR
ASSIZE
ASSIZED
ASSIZEMENT
ASSIZER
ASSIZES
ASSIZING
ASSMAN
ASSMANSHIP
ASSOCIABLE
ASSOCIATE
ASSOCIATED
ASSOCIATING
ASSOCIATION
ASSOCIATIVE
ASSOCIATIVELY
ASSOCIATIVENESS
ASSOCIATOR
ASSOCIE
ASSOIL
ASSOILMENT
ASSOILZIE
ASSOLUTO
ASSONANCE
ASSONANCED
ASSONANT
ASSONANTAL
ASSONANTIC
ASSONATE
ASSORT
ASSORTATIVE
ASSORTED
ASSORTER
ASSORTIVE
ASSORTMENT
ASSOT
ASSUADE
ASSUAGE
ASSUAGED
ASSUAGEMENT
ASSUAGER
ASSUAGING
ASSUASIVE
ASSUETUDE
ASSUMABLE
ASSUME
ASSUMED
ASSUMEDLY
ASSUMER
ASSUMING
ASSUMINGLY
ASSUMINGNESS
ASSUMMON
ASSUMPSIT
ASSUMPT
ASSUMPTION
ASSUMPTIOUS
ASSUMPTIVE
ASSUMPTIVELY
ASSURABLE
ASSURANCE
ASSURATE
ASSURD
ASSURE
ASSURED
ASSUREDLY
ASSUREDNESS
ASSURER
ASSURGE
ASSURGENCY
ASSURGENT
ASSURING
ASSURINGLY
ASSWAGE
ASSYNTITE
ASSYTH
ASSYTHMENT
ASTALK
ASTARBOARD
ASTARE
ASTART
ASTASIA
ASTATIC
ASTATICALLY
ASTATICISM
ASTATINE
ASTATIZE
ASTATIZED
ASTATIZER
ASTATIZING
ASTAY
ASTEAM
ASTEATOSIS
ASTEEP
ASTEER
ASTEISM
ASTELY
ASTER
ASTERACEOUS
ASTERIA
ASTERIAE
ASTERIAL
ASTERIATED
ASTERIN
ASTERION
ASTERISK
ASTERISKOS
ASTERISM
ASTERISMAL
ASTERN
ASTERNAL
ASTERNIA
ASTEROID
ASTEROIDAL
ASTEROIDEAN
ASTERT
ASTERWORT
ASTHENIA
ASTHENIC
ASTHENICAL
ASTHENOLOGY
ASTHENOPIA
ASTHENOPIC
ASTHENY
ASTHMA
ASTHMATIC
ASTHMATICAL
ASTHMATICALLY
ASTHMATOID
ASTHMOGENIC
ASTHORE
ASTHORIN
ASTICHOUS
ASTIGMATIC
ASTIGMATICAL
ASTIGMATISM
ASTIGMATIZER
ASTIGMIA
ASTIGMISM
ASTIGMOMETER
ASTIGMOMETRY
ASTILBE
ASTINT
ASTIPULATE
ASTIPULATION
ASTIR
ASTITE
ASTOGENY
ASTOMATAL
ASTOMATOUS
ASTOMIA
ASTOMOUS
ASTON
ASTOND
ASTONE
ASTONED
ASTONIED
ASTONISH
ASTONISHEDLY
ASTONISHER
ASTONISHING
ASTONISHINGLY
ASTONISHMENT
ASTONY
ASTONYING
ASTOOP
ASTORE
ASTOUND
ASTOUNDED
ASTOUNDING
ASTOUNDINGLY
ASTOUNDMENT
ASTRACHAN
ASTRADDLE
ASTRAEAN
ASTRAEID
ASTRAEIFORM
ASTRAGAL
ASTRAGALAR
ASTRAGALI
ASTRAGALUS
ASTRAIN
ASTRAKANITE
ASTRAKHAN
ASTRAL
ASTRALLY
ASTRAND
ASTRAPHOBIA
ASTRAY
ASTRE
ASTREAM
ASTRER
ASTRICT
ASTRICTION
ASTRICTIVE
ASTRICTIVELY
ASTRIDE
ASTRIER
ASTRIFEROUS
ASTRILD
ASTRINGE
ASTRINGED
ASTRINGENCY
ASTRINGENT
ASTRINGENTLY
ASTRINGER
ASTRINGING
ASTRION
ASTROBIOLOGY
ASTROBLAST
ASTROBOTANY
ASTROCHEMIST
ASTROCYTE
ASTROCYTOMA
ASTROCYTOMAS
ASTROCYTOMATA
ASTRODOME
ASTROFEL
ASTROFELL
ASTROGATE
ASTROGATED
ASTROGATING
ASTROGENY
ASTROGLIA
ASTROGNOSY
ASTROGONIC
ASTROGONY
ASTROGRAPH
ASTROGRAPHIC
ASTROGRAPHY
ASTROID
ASTROITE
ASTROLABE
ASTROLABICAL
ASTROLATER
ASTROLATRY
ASTROLOG
ASTROLOGE
ASTROLOGER
ASTROLOGIAN
ASTROLOGIC
ASTROLOGICAL
ASTROLOGICALLY
ASTROLOGISTIC
ASTROLOGIZE
ASTROLOGOUS
ASTROLOGY
ASTROMANCER
ASTROMANCY
ASTROMANTIC
ASTROMEDA
ASTROMETER
ASTROMETRY
ASTRONAUT
ASTRONAUTIC
ASTRONAUTICS
ASTRONOMER
ASTRONOMIC
ASTRONOMICAL
ASTRONOMICALLY
ASTRONOMICS
ASTRONOMIZE
ASTRONOMY
ASTROPHIL
ASTROPHOBIA
ASTROPHYSICS
ASTROSCOPE
ASTROSCOPY
ASTROSE
ASTROSPHERE
ASTRUT
ASTUCIOUS
ASTUCIOUSLY
ASTUCITY
ASTUTE
ASTUTELY
ASTUTENESS
ASTUTIOUS
ASTYLAR
ASUANG
ASUDDEN
ASUNDER
ASURA
ASWAIL
ASWARM
ASWASH
ASWAY
ASWEAT
ASWELL
ASWEVE
ASWIM
ASWING
ASWIRL
ASWOON
ASWOONED
ASYLA
ASYLLABIA
ASYLLABIC
ASYLLABICAL
ASYLUM
ASYLUMS
ASYMBOLIA
ASYMBOLIC
ASYMBOLICAL
ASYMMETRIC
ASYMMETRICAL
ASYMMETRICALLY
ASYMMETRY
ASYMPTOTE
ASYMPTOTIC
ASYMPTOTICAL
ASYNARTETE
ASYNARTETIC
ASYNCHRONISM
ASYNCHRONOUS
ASYNDETIC
ASYNDETON
ASYNERGIA
ASYNERGY
ASYNGAMIC
ASYNGAMY
ASYNTACTIC
ASYNTROPHY
ASYSTOLE
ASYSTOLIC
ASYSTOLISM
ASYZYGETIC
AT
ATA
ATABAL
ATABEG
ATABEK
ATABRINE
ATACAMITE
ATACTIC
ATACTIFORM
ATAGHAN
ATAJO
ATAKE
ATALAYA
ATAMAN
ATAMASCO
ATAME
ATANGLE
ATAP
ATAR
ATARACTIC
ATARAXIA
ATARAXIC
ATARAXY
ATATSCHITE
ATAUNT
ATAUNTO
ATAVI
ATAVIC
ATAVISM
ATAVIST

ATAVISTIC
ATAVUS
ATAXAPHASIA
ATAXIA
ATAXIAGRAM
ATAXIAGRAPH
ATAXIAMETER
ATAXIAPHASIA
ATAXIC
ATAXINOMIC
ATAXITE
ATAXONOMIC
ATAXOPHEMIA
ATAXY
ATAZIR
ATBASH
ATE
ATECHNIC
ATECHNICAL
ATECHNY
ATEES
ATEETER
ATEF
ATELECTASIS
ATELECTATIC
ATELESTITE
ATELIC
ATELIER
ATELIOSIS
ATELOCARDIA
ATELOGLOSSIA
ATELOGNATHIA
ATELOMITIC
ATELOMYELIA
ATELOPODIA
ATELOSTOMIA
ATEMOYA
ATEMPORAL
ATES
ATEUCHI
ATEUCHUS
ATHALAMOUS
ATHALLINE
ATHANASIA
ATHANASY
ATHANOR
ATHBASH
ATHECATE
ATHEISM
ATHEIST
ATHEISTIC
ATHEISTICAL
ATHEISTICALLY
ATHEIZE
ATHEIZER
ATHEL
ATHELIA
ATHELING
ATHEMATIC
ATHENAEUM
ATHENEUM
ATHENOR
ATHEOLOGICAL
ATHEOLOGY
ATHEOUS
ATHER
ATHERICERAN
ATHERICEROUS
ATHERINE
ATHERMANCY
ATHERMANOUS
ATHERMIC
ATHERMOUS
ATHEROMA
ATHEROMAS
ATHEROMASIA
ATHEROMATA
ATHEROMATOUS
ATHETESIS
ATHETIZE
ATHETIZED
ATHETIZING
ATHETOID
ATHETOSIC
ATHETOSIS
ATHIN
ATHING
ATHINK
ATHIRST
ATHLETE
ATHLETIC
ATHLETICAL
ATHLETICALLY
ATHLETICISM
ATHLETICS
ATHLETISM
ATHODYD
ATHOLD
ATHONITE
ATHREPSIA
ATHREPTIC
ATHRILL
ATHRIVE
ATHROB
ATHROGENIC
ATHRONG
ATHUMIA
ATHWART
ATHWARTHAWSE
ATHWARTSHIP
ATHWARTSHIPS
ATHWARTWISE
ATHYMIA
ATHYMIC
ATHYMY
ATHYREOSIS
ATHYRIA
ATHYRID
ATHYROID
ATHYROIDISM
ATI
ATILT
ATIMON
ATINGA
ATINGLE
ATINKLE
ATIP
ATIPTOE
ATIS
ATLANTAD
ATLANTAL
ATLANTES
ATLANTITE
ATLANTOAXIAL
ATLAS
ATLATL
ATLE
ATLEE
ATLOAXOID
ATLOID
ATLOIDEAN
ATLOIDOAXOID
ATMA
ATMAN
ATMIATRY
ATMID
ATMIDALBUMIN
ATMIDOMETER
ATMIDOMETRY
ATMOCAUSIS
ATMOCAUTERY
ATMOCLASTIC
ATMOGENIC
ATMOGRAPH
ATMOLOGIC
ATMOLOGICAL
ATMOLOGIST
ATMOLOGY
ATMOLYSIS
ATMOLYZATION
ATMOLYZE
ATMOLYZER
ATMOMETER
ATMOMETRIC
ATMOMETRY
ATMOSPHERE
ATMOSPHERIC
ATMOSPHERICAL
ATMOSPHERICALLY
ATMOSPHERICS
ATMOSTEA
ATMOSTEAL
ATMOSTEON
ATO
ATOCHA
ATOCIA
ATOKAL
ATOKE
ATOKOUS
ATOLE
ATOLL
ATOM
ATOMATIC
ATOMECHANICS
ATOMERG
ATOMIC
ATOMICAL
ATOMICALLY
ATOMICIAN
ATOMICISM
ATOMICITY
ATOMICS
ATOMIES
ATOMIFEROUS
ATOMISE
ATOMISM
ATOMIST
ATOMISTIC
ATOMISTICAL
ATOMISTICALLY
ATOMISTICS
ATOMITY
ATOMIZATION
ATOMIZE
ATOMIZED
ATOMIZER
ATOMIZING
ATOMOLOGY
ATOMS
ATOMY
ATONABLE
ATONAL
ATONALISM
ATONALISTIC
ATONALITY
ATONALLY
ATONE
ATONEABLE
ATONED
ATONEMENT
ATONENESS
ATONER
ATONIA
ATONIC
ATONICITY
ATONING
ATONINGLY
ATONY
ATOP
ATOPEN
ATOPIC
ATOPITE
ATOPY
ATOUR
ATRABILAIRE
ATRABILAR
ATRABILARIAN
ATRABILE
ATRABILIAR
ATRABILIARY
ATRABILIOUS
ATRACHEATE
ATRAGENE
ATRAIL
ATRAMENT
ATRAMENTAL
ATRAMENTARY
ATRAMENTOUS
ATRAUMATIC
ATREDE
ATREMATE
ATREMATOUS
ATREMBLE
ATRENNE
ATREPSY
ATREPTIC
ATRESIA
ATRESIC
ATRETIC
ATRIA
ATRIAL
ATRICHIA
ATRICHIC
ATRICHOUS
ATRICKLE
ATRIENSES
ATRIENSIS
ATRIO
ATRIOPORAL
ATRIOPORE
ATRIP
ATRIUM
ATROCE
ATROCHA
ATROCHAL
ATROCHOUS
ATROCIOUS
ATROCIOUSLY
ATROCIOUSNESS
ATROCITIES
ATROCITY
ATROLACTIC
ATROPACEOUS
ATROPAL
ATROPHIA
ATROPHIATED
ATROPHIC
ATROPHIED
ATROPHIES
ATROPHODERMA
ATROPHOUS
ATROPHY
ATROPHYING
ATROPIA
ATROPIC
ATROPIN
ATROPINE
ATROPINIZE
ATROPISM
ATROPOUS
ATRORUBENT
ATROUS
ATRY
ATRYPOID
ATSARA
ATT
ATTA
ATTABAL
ATTACCA
ATTACCO
ATTACH
ATTACHABLE
ATTACHE
ATTACHED
ATTACHEDLY
ATTACHER
ATTACHING
ATTACHMENT
ATTACK
ATTACKABLE
ATTACKER
ATTACKS
ATTACOLITE
ATTACUS
ATTAGEN
ATTAIN
ATTAINABILITY
ATTAINABLE
ATTAINABLENESS
ATTAINDER
ATTAINED
ATTAINER
ATTAINING
ATTAINMENT
ATTAINT
ATTAINTED
ATTAINTING
ATTAINTMENT
ATTAINTURE
ATTALEH
ATTAME
ATTAP
ATTAR
ATTARGUL
ATTASK
ATTASTE
ATTE
ATTEMPER
ATTEMPERANCE
ATTEMPERATE
ATTEMPERATOR
ATTEMPERED
ATTEMPERING
ATTEMPT
ATTEMPTABILITY
ATTEMPTABLE
ATTEMPTER
ATTEND
ATTENDANCE
ATTENDANCY
ATTENDANT
ATTENDANTLY
ATTENDANTS
ATTENDED
ATTENDEE
ATTENDING
ATTENDINGLY
ATTENDMENT
ATTENDRESS
ATTENSITY
ATTENT
ATTENTAT
ATTENTATE
ATTENTION
ATTENTIONAL
ATTENTIVE
ATTENTIVELY
ATTENTIVENESS
ATTENTLY
ATTENUABLE
ATTENUANT
ATTENUATE
ATTENUATED
ATTENUATING
ATTENUATION

ATTENUATOR
ATTER
ATTERCOP
ATTERMINE
ATTERN
ATTERR
ATTERY
ATTEST
ATTESTANT
ATTESTATION
ATTESTATIVE
ATTESTATOR
ATTESTED
ATTESTER
ATTESTIVE
ATTESTOR
ATTIC
ATTICE
ATTICISM
ATTICIST
ATTICIZE
ATTICIZED
ATTICIZING
ATTID
ATTIDAE
ATTINGE
ATTINGENCE
ATTINGENCY
ATTINGENT
ATTIRE
ATTIRED
ATTIREMENT
ATTIRER
ATTIRING
ATTITUDE
ATTITUDINAL
ATTITUDINISE
ATTITUDINIZE
ATTLE
ATTORN
ATTORNEY
ATTORNEYISM
ATTORNEYS
ATTORNEYSHIP
ATTORNMENT
ATTOUR
ATTOURNE
ATTRACT
ATTRACTABLE
ATTRACTANT
ATTRACTER
ATTRACTILE
ATTRACTINGLY
ATTRACTION
ATTRACTIVE
ATTRACTIVELY
ATTRACTIVENESS
ATTRACTIVITY
ATTRACTOR
ATTRAHENT
ATTRAP
ATTRIBUTABLE
ATTRIBUTAL
ATTRIBUTE
ATTRIBUTED
ATTRIBUTER
ATTRIBUTING
ATTRIBUTION
ATTRIBUTIVE
ATTRIBUTOR
ATTRIST
ATTRITE
ATTRITED
ATTRITION
ATTRITIVE
ATTRITUS
ATTRY
ATTUNE
ATTUNED
ATTUNELY
ATTUNEMENT
ATTUNING
ATTURN
ATU
ATUA
ATULE
ATUMBLE
ATUN
ATUNE
ATURN
ATWAIN
ATWEEL
ATWEEN
ATWIN
ATWIRL
ATWIST
ATWITCH
ATWITTER
ATWIXT
ATWO
ATYPIC
ATYPICAL
ATYPICALLY
ATYPY
AU
AUA
AUANTIC
AUBADE
AUBAIN
AUBAINE
AUBE
AUBERGE
AUBERGINE
AUBERGISTE
AUBIN
AUBRITE
AUBURN
AUCA
AUCHENIA
AUCHENIUM
AUCHLET
AUCHT
AUCTARY
AUCTION
AUCTIONARY
AUCTIONEER
AUCTIONING
AUCTOR
AUCTORIAL
AUCUBA
AUCUPATE
AUDACE
AUDACIOUS
AUDACIOUSLY
AUDACIOUSNESS
AUDACITY
AUDAD
AUDIBILITY
AUDIBLE
AUDIBLENESS
AUDIBLY
AUDIENCE
AUDIENCIA
AUDIENCIER
AUDIENT
AUDILE
AUDIO
AUDIOGRAM
AUDIOLOGICAL
AUDIOLOGY
AUDIOMETER
AUDIOMETRY
AUDION
AUDIOPHILE
AUDIPHONE
AUDIT
AUDITION
AUDITIVE
AUDITOR
AUDITORIA
AUDITORIAL
AUDITORIALLY
AUDITORILY
AUDITORIUM
AUDITORIUMS
AUDITORY
AUDITRESS
AUDITUAL
AUDIVISE
AUDIVISER
AUDIVISION
AUE
AUF
AUFAIT
AUFER
AUFGABE
AUFTAKT
AUGANITE
AUGE
AUGELITE
AUGEND
AUGER
AUGERER
AUGH
AUGHT
AUGHTLINS
AUGITE
AUGITIC
AUGITITE
AUGITOPHYRE
AUGMENT
AUGMENTABLE
AUGMENTATION
AUGMENTATIVE
AUGMENTED
AUGMENTEDLY
AUGMENTER
AUGMENTIVE
AUGRIM
AUGUR
AUGURAL
AUGURATE
AUGURATION
AUGURER
AUGURIES
AUGUROUS
AUGURY
AUGUST
AUGUSTAL
AUGUSTE
AUGUSTLY
AUGUSTNESS
AUH
AUHUHU
AUK
AUKLET
AUKSINAI
AUKSINAS
AUKSINU
AUL
AULA
AULARIAN
AULD
AULETE
AULETIC
AULETRIDES
AULETRIS
AULIC
AULICAL
AULICISM
AULLAY
AULOPHYTE
AULOS
AULOSTOMID
AULU
AUM
AUMAGA
AUMAIL
AUMAKUA
AUMIL
AUMILDAR
AUMONIERE
AUMOUS
AUMRIE
AUNCEL
AUNE
AUNT
AUNTER
AUNTERS
AUNTIE
AUNTRE
AUNTROUS
AUNTSARY
AUNTY
AUPAKA
AURA
AURAE
AURAL
AURALLY
AURAMIN
AURAMINE
AURANG
AURANTIA
AURANTIUM
AURAR
AURAS
AURATE
AURATED
AUREAL
AUREATE
AUREATELY
AUREATENESS
AUREATION
AUREI
AUREITY
AURELIA
AURELIAN
AURENE
AUREOLA
AUREOLE
AUREOLIN
AUREOLINE
AUREOMYCIN
AUREOUS
AUREOUSLY
AURES
AURESCA
AUREUS
AURIC
AURICHALCITE
AURICLE
AURICLED
AURICOMOUS
AURICULA
AURICULAE
AURICULAR
AURICULARE
AURICULARES
AURICULARIA
AURICULARIAE
AURICULARIAN
AURICULARIS
AURICULARLY
AURICULAS
AURICULATE
AURICULATED
AURICULATELY
AURIDE
AURIFEROUS
AURIFEX
AURIFIC
AURIFICATION
AURIFLAMME
AURIFORM
AURIFY
AURIGAL
AURIGATION
AURIGEROUS
AURIGO
AURILAVE
AURIN
AURINASAL
AURINE
AURIPHONE
AURIPHRYGIA
AURIPUNCTURE
AURIS
AURISCALP
AURISCOPE
AURISCOPY
AURIST
AURITE
AURIVOROUS
AUROAURIC
AUROBROMIDE
AUROCH
AUROCHS
AUROCYANIDE
AURODIAMINE
AUROPHOBIA
AUROPHORE
AURORA
AURORAL
AURORALLY
AURORE
AUROREAN
AURORIUM
AUROUS
AURRESCU
AURULENT
AURUM
AURUNG
AURURE
AURYL
AUSCULT
AUSCULTATE
AUSCULTATED
AUSCULTATING
AUSCULTATION
AUSCULTATOR
AUSCULTATORY
AUSLAUT
AUSPEX
AUSPICATE
AUSPICATED
AUSPICATING
AUSPICE
AUSPICES
AUSPICIAL
AUSPICIOUS
AUSPICIOUSLY
AUSPICIOUSNESS
AUSPICY
AUSTAUSCH
AUSTEMPER
AUSTENITE
AUSTENITIC
AUSTERE
AUSTERELY
AUSTERENESS
AUSTERITIES
AUSTERITY
AUSTRAL
AUSTRALENE
AUSTRALITE

AUSTRINE
AUSTRINGER
AUSTRIUM
AUSTROMANCY
AUSU
AUSUBO
AUTACOID
AUTACOIDAL
AUTANTITYPY
AUTARCH
AUTARCHIC
AUTARCHICAL
AUTARCHIES
AUTARCHY
AUTARKIC
AUTARKIK
AUTARKIKAL
AUTARKY
AUTE
AUTECHOSCOPE
AUTECOLOGY
AUTEM
AUTERE
AUTHENTIC
AUTHENTICAL
AUTHENTICALLY
AUTHENTICATE
AUTHENTICATED
AUTHENTICATING
AUTHENTICATION
AUTHENTICATOR
AUTHENTICITY
AUTHENTICLY
AUTHENTICNESS
AUTHIGENIC
AUTHIGENOUS
AUTHOR
AUTHORCRAFT
AUTHORESS
AUTHORIAL
AUTHORIALLY
AUTHORITARIAN
AUTHORITATIVE
AUTHORITATIVELY
AUTHORITATIVENESS
AUTHORITIES
AUTHORITY
AUTHORIZATION
AUTHORIZE
AUTHORIZED
AUTHORIZER
AUTHORIZING
AUTHORLESS
AUTHORLING
AUTHORLY
AUTHORS
AUTHORSHIP
AUTHOTYPE
AUTISM
AUTIST
AUTISTIC
AUTO
AUTOALARM
AUTOALLOGAMY
AUTOBAHN
AUTOBAHNEN
AUTOBAHNS
AUTOBASIDIA
AUTOBASIDIUM
AUTOBIOGRAPHAL
AUTOBIOGRAPHER
AUTOBIOGRAPHIC
AUTOBIOGRAPHICAL
AUTOBIOGRAPHICALLY
AUTOBIOGRAPHIES
AUTOBIOGRAPHIST
AUTOBIOGRAPHY
AUTOBLAST
AUTOBOAT
AUTOBOATING
AUTOBOLIDE
AUTOBUS
AUTOCAB
AUTOCAMP
AUTOCAMPER
AUTOCAMPING
AUTOCAR
AUTOCARIST
AUTOCARP
AUTOCARPIAN
AUTOCARPIC
AUTOCARPOUS
AUTOCATALYZE
AUTOCEPHALIA
AUTOCEPHALIC
AUTOCEPHALITY
AUTOCEPHALOUS
AUTOCEPHALY
AUTOCEPTIVE
AUTOCHROME
AUTOCHROMY
AUTOCHTHON
AUTOCHTHONAL
AUTOCHTHONES
AUTOCHTHONIC
AUTOCHTHONOUS
AUTOCHTHONS
AUTOCHTHONY
AUTOCIDE
AUTOCLASTIC
AUTOCLAVE
AUTOCOHERER
AUTOCOPIST
AUTOCOSM
AUTOCRACIES
AUTOCRACY
AUTOCRAT
AUTOCRATIC
AUTOCRATICAL
AUTOCRATICALLY
AUTOCRATOR
AUTOCRATORIC
AUTOCRATRIX
AUTODIDACT
AUTODIDACTIC
AUTODROME
AUTODYNAMIC
AUTODYNE
AUTOECIC
AUTOECIOUS
AUTOECIOUSLY
AUTOECISM
AUTOED
AUTOEROTIC
AUTOEROTISM
AUTOETTE
AUTOFRETTAGE
AUTOGAMIC
AUTOGAMOUS
AUTOGAMY
AUTOGAUGE
AUTOGENEAL
AUTOGENESIS
AUTOGENETIC
AUTOGENIC
AUTOGENOUS
AUTOGENOUSLY
AUTOGENY
AUTOGIRO
AUTOGIROS
AUTOGNOSIS
AUTOGNOSTIC
AUTOGRAFT
AUTOGRAFTING
AUTOGRAPH
AUTOGRAPHER
AUTOGRAPHIC
AUTOGRAPHICAL
AUTOGRAPHISM
AUTOGRAPHIST
AUTOGRAPHY
AUTOGRAVURE
AUTOGYRO
AUTOHEADER
AUTOHYPNOSIS
AUTOICOUS
AUTOIGNITION
AUTOING
AUTOIST
AUTOKINESIS
AUTOKINETIC
AUTOKRATOR
AUTOLITH
AUTOLOADING
AUTOLYSATE
AUTOLYSIN
AUTOLYSIS
AUTOLYTIC
AUTOLYZATE
AUTOLYZE
AUTOMA
AUTOMACY
AUTOMANIA
AUTOMANUAL
AUTOMAT
AUTOMATA
AUTOMATE
AUTOMATED
AUTOMATIC
AUTOMATICAL
AUTOMATICALLY
AUTOMATICITY
AUTOMATIN
AUTOMATING
AUTOMATISM
AUTOMATIST
AUTOMATIVE
AUTOMATIZATION
AUTOMATIZE
AUTOMATON
AUTOMATONS
AUTOMATOUS
AUTOMETRIC
AUTOMETRY
AUTOMOBILE
AUTOMOBILED
AUTOMOBILING
AUTOMOBILISM
AUTOMOBILIST
AUTOMOBILITY
AUTOMOLITE
AUTOMORPH
AUTOMORPHIC
AUTOMORPHISM
AUTOMOTIVE
AUTOMOWER
AUTOMPNE
AUTONOMIC
AUTONOMICAL
AUTONOMIES
AUTONOMIST
AUTONOMIZE
AUTONOMOUS
AUTONOMOUSLY
AUTONOMY
AUTONYM
AUTOPATHIC
AUTOPATHY
AUTOPELAGIC
AUTOPHAGI
AUTOPHAGIA
AUTOPHAGOUS
AUTOPHAGY
AUTOPHOBIA
AUTOPHOBY
AUTOPHON
AUTOPHONE
AUTOPHONOUS
AUTOPHONY
AUTOPHYTE
AUTOPHYTIC
AUTOPLASTIC
AUTOPLASTIES
AUTOPLASTY
AUTOPOLO
AUTOPOLOIST
AUTOPORE
AUTOPSIC
AUTOPSICAL
AUTOPSIES
AUTOPSY
AUTOPSYCHIC
AUTOPTIC
AUTOPTICAL
AUTOPTICALLY
AUTOPTICITY
AUTORAIL
AUTORISER
AUTOROTATION
AUTORRHAPHY
AUTOSCOPE
AUTOSCOPIC
AUTOSCOPY
AUTOSERUM
AUTOSIGHT
AUTOSITE
AUTOSITIC
AUTOSKELETON
AUTOSLED
AUTOSOMAL
AUTOSOME
AUTOSOTERIC
AUTOSOTERISM
AUTOSPORE
AUTOSPORIC
AUTOSPRAY
AUTOSTAGE
AUTOSTYLIC
AUTOSTYLISM
AUTOSTYLY
AUTOTELIC
AUTOTHEISM
AUTOTHEIST
AUTOTHERAPY
AUTOTOMIC
AUTOTOMIZE
AUTOTOMY
AUTOTOXAEMIA
AUTOTOXEMIA
AUTOTOXIC
AUTOTOXIN
AUTOTRACTOR
AUTOTROPHIC
AUTOTROPIC
AUTOTROPISM
AUTOTRUCK
AUTOTYPE
AUTOTYPIC
AUTOTYPY
AUTOVACCINE
AUTOVALVE
AUTOXIDATION
AUTOXIDATOR
AUTOXIDIZE
AUTOZOOID
AUTREFOIS
AUTUMN
AUTUMNAL
AUTUMNALLY
AUTUMNIAN
AUTUMNITY
AUTUNITE
AUWAI
AUX
AUXANOGRAM
AUXANOLOGY
AUXANOMETER
AUXESIS
AUXETIC
AUXETICAL
AUXETICALLY
AUXILIAR
AUXILIARIES
AUXILIARLY
AUXILIARY
AUXILIATE
AUXILIATION
AUXILIATOR
AUXILIATORY
AUXILIUM
AUXIMONE
AUXIN
AUXOACTION
AUXOAMYLASE
AUXOBLAST
AUXOBODY
AUXOCARDIA
AUXOCHROME
AUXOCHROMIC
AUXOCHROMISM
AUXOCHROMOUS
AUXOCYTE
AUXOFLORE
AUXOFLUOR
AUXOGRAPH
AUXOGRAPHIC
AUXOHORMONE
AUXOLOGY
AUXOMETER
AUXOSPORE
AUXOTONIC
AUXOTOX
AVA
AVADANA
AVADAVAT
AVADHUTA
AVAHI
AVAIL
AVAILABILITIES
AVAILABILITY
AVAILABLE
AVAILABLENESS
AVAILABLY
AVAILED
AVAILING
AVAILINGLY
AVAILS
AVAL
AVALANCHE
AVALANCHED
AVALANCHING
AVALE
AVALENT
AVALVULAR
AVANIA
AVANIOUS
AVANT
AVANTLAY
AVANYU
AVARAM
AVAREMOTEMO
AVARICE
AVARICIOUS
AVARICIOUSLY
AVAST

AVATAR
AVATARA
AVAUNT
AVE
AVEL
AVELL
AVELLAN
AVELLANE
AVELLANEOUS
AVELLANO
AVELONGE
AVELOZ
AVENACEOUS
AVENAGE
AVENALIN
AVENANT
AVENARY
AVENER
AVENERY
AVENGE
AVENGED
AVENGEFUL
AVENGEMENT
AVENGER
AVENGERESS
AVENGING
AVENGINGLY
AVENIDA
AVENIN
AVENINE
AVENOLITH
AVENOUS
AVENS
AVENTAIL
AVENTAYLE
AVENTRE
AVENTURIN
AVENTURINE
AVENUE
AVER
AVERA
AVERAGE
AVERAGED
AVERAGELY
AVERAGER
AVERAGING
AVERAH
AVERIL
AVERIN
AVERMENT
AVERRABLE
AVERRAL
AVERRED
AVERRING
AVERRUNCATE
AVERRUNCATOR
AVERSANT
AVERSATION
AVERSE
AVERSELY
AVERSENESS
AVERSION
AVERSIVE
AVERT
AVERTABLE
AVERTED
AVERTEDLY
AVERTER
AVERTIBLE
AVESTRUZ
AVEUGLE
AVGAS
AVIADOR
AVIAN
AVIANIZE
AVIARIST
AVIARY
AVIATE
AVIATED
AVIATIC
AVIATING
AVIATION
AVIATOR
AVIATORIAL
AVIATORY
AVIATRESS
AVIATRICE
AVIATRIX
AVICHI
AVICI
AVICIDE
AVICK
AVICOLOUS
AVICULAR
AVICULARIA
AVICULARIAN
AVICULARIUM
AVICULTURE
AVICULTURIST
AVID
AVIDIN
AVIDIOUS
AVIDIOUSLY
AVIDITY
AVIDLY
AVIDOUS
AVIDYA
AVIE
AVIEW
AVIFAUNA
AVIFAUNAL
AVIGATE
AVIGATION
AVIGATOR
AVIJJA
AVILE
AVILEMENT
AVINE
AVIOLITE
AVION
AVIONICS
AVIRULENCE
AVIRULENT
AVISION
AVISO
AVISOS
AVITAL
AVITAMINOSIS
AVITAMINOTIC
AVITIC
AVIVES
AVIZANDUM
AVO
AVOCADO
AVOCADOS
AVOCATE
AVOCATION
AVOCATIVE
AVOCATORY
AVOCET
AVODIRE
AVOGADRITE
AVOGRAM
AVOID
AVOIDABLE
AVOIDABLY
AVOIDANCE
AVOIDER
AVOIDLESS
AVOIDMENT
AVOIDS
AVOIRDUPOIS
AVOLATE
AVOLATION
AVONDBLOEM
AVOSET
AVOUCH
AVOUCHER
AVOUCHMENT
AVOUE
AVOURE
AVOURNEEN
AVOUTRY
AVOW
AVOWABLE
AVOWABLENESS
AVOWABLY
AVOWAL
AVOWANCE
AVOWANT
AVOWED
AVOWEDLY
AVOWEDNESS
AVOWER
AVOWRIES
AVOWRY
AVOY
AVOYER
AVOYERSHIP
AVULSE
AVULSION
AVUNCULAR
AVUNCULATE
AVYS
AVYSE
AW
AWA
AWABI
AWAFT
AWAG
AWAIT
AWAITER
AWAITING
AWAKE
AWAKED
AWAKEN
AWAKENER
AWAKENING
AWAKENINGLY
AWAKENMENT
AWAKING
AWALD
AWALE
AWALT
AWANE
AWANTING
AWANYU
AWAPUHI
AWARD
AWARDABLE
AWARDER
AWARDMENT
AWARE
AWARENESS
AWARP
AWARRANT
AWARUITE
AWASH
AWASTE
AWAT
AWATCH
AWATER
AWAVE
AWAY
AWAYNESS
AWBER
AWE
AWEARIED
AWEARY
AWEATHER
AWEBAND
AWED
AWEDE
AWEDNESS
AWEE
AWEEK
AWEEL
AWEIGH
AWEING
AWELESS
AWESOME
AWESOMELY
AWESOMENESS
AWEST
AWESTRUCK
AWETO
AWF
AWFUL
AWFULLY
AWFULNESS
AWHAPE
AWHEEL
AWHEFT
AWHET
AWHILE
AWHIR
AWHIRL
AWIDE
AWIGGLE
AWIKIWIKI
AWING
AWINK
AWIWI
AWK
AWKLY
AWKWARD
AWKWARDLY
AWKWARDNESS
AWL
AWLESS
AWLWORT
AWMER
AWMOUS
AWN
AWNED
AWNER
AWNIE
AWNING
AWNINGED
AWNLESS
AWNY
AWOKE
AWOKEN
AWONDER
AWORK
AWREAK
AWRIST
AWRONG
AWRY
AX
AXAL
AXAN
AXBREAKER
AXE
AXEBREAKER
AXED
AXEL
AXEMAN
AXEMASTER
AXENIC
AXES
AXHAMMER
AXHAMMERED
AXIAL
AXIALITY
AXIALLY
AXIATE
AXIFORM
AXIFUGAL
AXIL
AXILE
AXILEMMA
AXILEMMAS
AXILEMMATA
AXILLA
AXILLAE
AXILLANT
AXILLAR
AXILLARIES
AXILLARY
AXINE
AXINITE
AXINOMANCY
AXIOLITE
AXIOLITIC
AXIOLOGICAL
AXIOLOGIST
AXIOLOGY
AXIOM
AXIOMATIC
AXIOMATICAL
AXIOMATIZE
AXION
AXIOPISTY
AXIS
AXISYMMETRIC
AXITE
AXLE
AXLED
AXLESMITH
AXLETREE
AXLIKE
AXMAKER
AXMAKING
AXMAN
AXMANSHIP
AXMASTER
AXMEN
AXODENDRITE
AXOFUGAL
AXOGAMY
AXOID
AXOIDEAN
AXOLOTL
AXOLYSIS
AXOMETER
AXON
AXONAL
AXONE
AXONEME
AXONEURE
AXONEURON
AXONOLIPOUS
AXONOMETRIC
AXONOMETRY
AXONOPHOROUS
AXONOST
AXOPETAL
AXOPHYTE
AXOPLASM
AXOPODIUM
AXOSPERMOUS
AXOSTYLE
AXSEED
AXSTONE
AXTREE
AXUNGE
AXWEED
AY
AYA
AYACAHUITE
AYAH
AYAHAUSCA
AYAPANA
AYE

AYEGREEN
AYEL
AYELP
AYEN
AYENBITE
AYENS
AYENST
AYIN
AYLESS
AYLET
AYLLU
AYN
AYNE
AYOND
AYONT
AYOUS
AYRE
AYU
AYUDANTE
AYUNTAMIENTO
AYUNTAMIENTOS
AYUYU
AYWHERE
AZADIRACHTA
AZAFRAN
AZAFRIN
AZALEA
AZALEAMUM
AZAM
AZAN
AZAROLE
AZEDARACH
AZELAIC
AZELATE
AZEOTROPE
AZEOTROPIC
AZEOTROPISM
AZEOTROPY
AZEW
AZIDE
AZIETHANE
AZILUT
AZIMENE
AZIMETHYLENE
AZIMIN
AZIMINE
AZIMINO
AZIMUTH
AZIMUTHAL
AZIMUTHALLY
AZINE
AZIOLA
AZLACTONE
AZLON
AZO
AZOBENZENE
AZOBENZIL
AZOBENZOIC
AZOBENZOL
AZOBLACK
AZOCH
AZOCOCHINEAL
AZOCORALLINE
AZOCORINTH
AZOCYANIDE
AZOCYCLIC
AZODIPHENYL
AZOERYTHRIN
AZOFICATION
AZOFIER
AZOFORMIC
AZOFY
AZOGALLEIN
AZOGREEN
AZOHUMIC
AZOIC
AZOIMIDE
AZOLE
AZOLITMIN
AZOMETHINE
AZON
AZONAL
AZONIC
AZONIUM
AZOOSPERMIA
AZOPARAFFIN
AZOPHEN
AZOPHENETOLE
AZOPHENINE
AZOPHENOL
AZOPHENYL
AZOPHENYLENE
AZOPHOSPHIN
AZOPHOSPHORE
AZOPROTEIN
AZORITE
AZOSULPHINE
AZOSULPHONIC
AZOTATE
AZOTE
AZOTEA
AZOTED
AZOTEMIA
AZOTENESIS
AZOTETRAZOLE
AZOTH
AZOTHIONIUM
AZOTIC
AZOTIN
AZOTINE
AZOTITE
AZOTIZED
AZOTIZING
AZOTOBACTER
AZOTOLUENE
AZOTOMETER
AZOTORRHEA
AZOTORRHOEA
AZOTOUS
AZOTURIA
AZOVERNINE
AZOXINE
AZOXONIUM
AZOXY
AZOXYBENZENE
AZTECA
AZTHIONIUM
AZULEJO
AZULENE
AZULITE
AZUMBRE
AZURE
AZUREAN
AZURED
AZURINE
AZURITE
AZUROUS
AZURY
AZYGOMATOUS
AZYGOS
AZYGOSPERM
AZYGOSPORE
AZYGOTE
AZYGOUS
AZYM
AZYME
AZYMITE
AZYMOUS

B

BA
BAA
BAAED
BAAHLING
BAAING
BAAL
BAAN
BAAS
BABA
BABACOOTE
BABAI
BABAJAGA
BABAKOTO
BABASCO
BABASSU
BABAYLAN
BABAYLANES
BABBISHLY
BABBITT
BABBITTED
BABBITTER
BABBITTING
BABBLATIVE
BABBLE
BABBLED
BABBLEMENT
BABBLER
BABBLESOME
BABBLING
BABBLISH
BABBLY
BABBO
BABBY
BABE
BABERY
BABESHIP
BABESIASIS
BABICHE
BABIED
BABIES
BABIL
BABILLARD
BABINGTONITE
BABIROUSSA
BABIRUSA
BABIRUSSA
BABISH
BABISHED
BABISHLY
BABISHNESS
BABLAH
BABLOH
BABOEN
BABOO
BABOODOM
BABOOISM
BABOOL
BABOON
BABOONERY
BABOONROOT
BABOOS
BABOOSH
BABOUCHE
BABRACOT
BABROOT
BABU
BABUDOM
BABUINA
BABUISM
BABUL
BABURD
BABUS
BABUSHKA
BABY
BABYFIED
BABYHOOD
BABYHOUSE
BABYING
BABYISH
BABYISHLY
BABYISHNESS
BABYLIKE
BAC
BACABA
BACACH
BACALAO
BACALAOS
BACAO
BACAUAN
BACBAKIRI
BACCA
BACCACEOUS
BACCAE
BACCALAUREAN
BACCAR
BACCARA
BACCARAT
BACCARE
BACCATE
BACCATED
BACCHANAL
BACCHANALIA
BACCHANALIAN
BACCHANALIZE
BACCHANALS
BACCHANT
BACCHANTE
BACCHANTES
BACCHANTIC
BACCHANTS
BACCHAR
BACCHARIS
BACCHAROID
BACCHEION
BACCHIAC
BACCHIAN
BACCHIC
BACCHII
BACCHIUS
BACCIFEROUS
BACCIFORM
BACCIVOROUS
BACCO
BACCY
BACH
BACHE
BACHEL
BACHELOR
BACHELORHOOD
BACHELORIZE
BACHELORLY
BACHELORSHIP
BACHELORWISE
BACHELRY
BACILE
BACILLAR
BACILLARY
BACILLI
BACILLICIDAL
BACILLICIDE
BACILLICIDIC
BACILLIFORM
BACILLIGENIC
BACILLITE
BACILLOGENIC
BACILLOSIS
BACILLURIA
BACILLUS
BACK
BACKACHE
BACKACHY
BACKARE
BACKBAND
BACKBAR
BACKBEAR
BACKBEARING
BACKBENCHER
BACKBEND
BACKBERAND
BACKBEREND
BACKBIT
BACKBITE
BACKBITER
BACKBITING
BACKBITTEN
BACKBLOCKS
BACKBOARD
BACKBONE
BACKBONED
BACKBONELESS
BACKBRAND
BACKBREAKER
BACKBREAKING
BACKCAP
BACKCAST
BACKCHAIN
BACKCHAT
BACKCOUNTRY
BACKCOURT
BACKCROSS
BACKDOOR
BACKDOWN
BACKDROP
BACKED
BACKEN
BACKENED
BACKENING
BACKER
BACKET
BACKFALL
BACKFATTER
BACKFIELD
BACKFILL
BACKFILLER
BACKFILLING
BACKFIRE
BACKFIRED
BACKFIRING
BACKFLAP
BACKFLASH
BACKFLIP
BACKFLOW
BACKFOLD
BACKFRAME
BACKFRIEND
BACKFURROW
BACKGAME
BACKGAMMON
BACKGROUND
BACKHAND
BACKHANDED
BACKHANDEDLY
BACKHANDER
BACKHATCH
BACKHAUL
BACKHEEL
BACKHOE
BACKHOOKER
BACKHOUSE
BACKIE
BACKIEBIRD
BACKING
BACKINGS
BACKJAW
BACKJOINT
BACKLAND
BACKLANDS
BACKLASH
BACKLASHING
BACKLESS
BACKLET
BACKLIST
BACKLOG
BACKLOTTER
BACKMOST
BACKPACK
BACKPEDAL
BACKPIECE
BACKPLATE
BACKREST
BACKROPE
BACKRUN
BACKSAW
BACKSEAT
BACKSET
BACKSETTING
BACKSETTLER
BACKSEY
BACKSHEESH
BACKSHIFT
BACKSHISH
BACKSIDE
BACKSIGHT
BACKSLAP
BACKSLAPPER
BACKSLAPPING
BACKSLID
BACKSLIDDEN
BACKSLIDE
BACKSLIDER
BACKSLIDING
BACKSPACE
BACKSPACER
BACKSPANG
BACKSPEAR
BACKSPEER
BACKSPEIR
BACKSPIER
BACKSPIERER
BACKSPIN
BACKSPREAD
BACKSPRINGING
BACKSTAFF
BACKSTAGE
BACKSTAIR
BACKSTAIRS
BACKSTAMP
BACKSTAY
BACKSTER
BACKSTICK
BACKSTITCH
BACKSTOP
BACKSTRAP
BACKSTRETCH
BACKSTRING
BACKSTRIP
BACKSTROKE
BACKSTROKED
BACKSTROKING
BACKSTROMITE
BACKSWEPT
BACKSWING
BACKSWORD
BACKSWORDING
BACKSWORDMAN
BACKSWORDSMAN
BACKTACK
BACKTENTER
BACKTRACK
BACKTRACKER
BACKTRICK
BACKUP
BACKVELD
BACKVELDER
BACKWALL
BACKWARD
BACKWARDLY
BACKWARDNESS
BACKWARDS
BACKWASH
BACKWASHER
BACKWASHING
BACKWATER
BACKWATERED
BACKWAY
BACKWIND
BACKWOOD
BACKWOODS
BACKWOODSMAN
BACKWOODSY
BACKWORD
BACKWORM
BACKWORT
BACKY
BACKYARD
BACKYARDER
BACLIN
BACON
BACONER
BACONIZE
BACONWEED
BACONY
BACTERIA
BACTERIACEOUS
BACTERIAEMIA
BACTERIAL
BACTERIALLY
BACTERIAN
BACTERIC
BACTERICIDAL
BACTERICIDE
BACTERICIDIN
BACTERIEMIA
BACTERIFORM
BACTERIN
BACTERIOBLAST
BACTERIOCYTE
BACTERIOID
BACTERIOLOGIC
BACTERIOLOGICAL
BACTERIOLOGY
BACTERIOLYZE
BACTERIOSIS
BACTERIOSTAT
BACTERIOTOXIC
BACTERIOUS
BACTERITIC
BACTERIUM
BACTERIURIA
BACTERIZE
BACTERIZED
BACTERIZING
BACTEROID
BACTEROIDAL
BACTRITICONE
BACTRITOID
BACUBERT
BACULA
BACULE
BACULERE
BACULI
BACULIFEROUS
BACULIFORM
BACULINE
BACULITE

BACULITIC
BACULITICONE
BACULOID
BACULUS
BACURY
BAD
BADAK
BADAM
BADAN
BADAUD
BADAXE
BADCHAN
BADDELEYITE
BADDERLOCKS
BADDIE
BADDISH
BADDISHLY
BADDISHNESS
BADDOCK
BADDY
BADE
BADENITE
BADGE
BADGED
BADGEMAN
BADGEMEN
BADGER
BADGERER
BADGERLY
BADGERS
BADGERWEED
BADGING
BADGIR
BADHAN
BADIA
BADIAGA
BADIAN
BADIGEON
BADINAGE
BADINAGED
BADINAGING
BADINER
BADINERIE
BADINEUR
BADIOUS
BADJU
BADLAND
BADLANDS
BADLING
BADLY
BADMAN
BADMEN
BADMINTON
BADNESS
BADRANS
BAEL
BAETULI
BAETULUS
BAETYL
BAETYLIC
BAETYLUS
BAETZNER
BAFARO
BAFF
BAFFIES
BAFFLE
BAFFLED
BAFFLEPLATE
BAFFLER
BAFFLING
BAFFLINGLY
BAFFY
BAFT
BAFTA
BAFTAH
BAG
BAGA
BAGANI
BAGASS
BAGASSE
BAGATAWAY
BAGATELLE
BAGATINE
BAGATTINI
BAGATTINO
BAGEL
BAGFUL
BAGGAGE
BAGGAGEMAN
BAGGAGEMASTER
BAGGAGER
BAGGALA
BAGGE
BAGGED
BAGGER
BAGGIE
BAGGIER
BAGGIEST
BAGGILY
BAGGINESS
BAGGING
BAGGIT
BAGGY
BAGHOUSE
BAGLE
BAGLEAVES
BAGLIKE
BAGMAN
BAGMEN
BAGNE
BAGNES
BAGNET
BAGNIO
BAGNUT
BAGO
BAGONG
BAGOONG
BAGPIPE
BAGPIPER
BAGPIPES
BAGPOD
BAGRATIONITE
BAGRE
BAGREEF
BAGROOM
BAGS
BAGTIKAN
BAGUE
BAGUET
BAGUETTE
BAGUIO
BAGUIOS
BAGWIG
BAGWIGGED
BAGWORM
BAGWYN
BAH
BAHADA
BAHADUR
BAHAN
BAHAR
BAHAY
BAHERA
BAHI
BAHIA
BAHIAITE
BAHNUNG
BAHO
BAHOE
BAHR
BAHT
BAHTS
BAHU
BAHUR
BAHUT
BAHUVRIHI
BAIDAK
BAIDAR
BAIGNOIRE
BAIKALITE
BAIKERINITE
BAIKERITE
BAIKIE
BAIL
BAILABLE
BAILE
BAILEE
BAILER
BAILEY
BAILEYS
BAILIARIES
BAILIARY
BAILIE
BAILIERIES
BAILIERY
BAILIFF
BAILIFFRY
BAILIWICK
BAILLI
BAILLIAGE
BAILLONE
BAILMENT
BAILO
BAILOR
BAILOUT
BAILPIECE
BAILSMAN
BAILSMEN
BAILWOOD
BAIN
BAINITE
BAIOC
BAIOCCO
BAIRA
BAIRAGI
BAIRN
BAIRNIE
BAIRNISH
BAIRNISHNESS
BAIRNLINESS
BAIRNLY
BAIRNTEAM
BAIRNTEEM
BAIRNTIME
BAIT
BAITER
BAITFISH
BAITH
BAITING
BAITTLE
BAIZA
BAIZE
BAIZED
BAIZING
BAJADA
BAJOCCO
BAJOCHI
BAJOIRE
BAJONADO
BAJRA
BAJREE
BAJU
BAJULATE
BAK
BAKA
BAKAL
BAKE
BAKEAPPLE
BAKEBOARD
BAKED
BAKEHEAD
BAKEHOUSE
BAKELITE
BAKELIZE
BAKEMEAT
BAKEN
BAKEOUT
BAKEPAN
BAKER
BAKERIES
BAKERITE
BAKERLY
BAKERY
BAKESHOP
BAKESTONE
BAKEWARE
BAKIE
BAKING
BAKLAVA
BAKSHEESH
BAKSHI
BAKSHISH
BAKTUN
BAKU
BAKULA
BAKUPARI
BAL
BALABOS
BALACHAN
BALACHONG
BALADINE
BALAENID
BALAFO
BALAGAN
BALAGHAT
BALAGHAUT
BALAI
BALALAIKA
BALAM
BALANCE
BALANCEABLE
BALANCED
BALANCELLE
BALANCER
BALANCING
BALANDRA
BALANDRANA
BALANEUTICS
BALANGAY
BALANIC
BALANID
BALANIFEROUS
BALANISM
BALANITE
BALANITIS
BALANOCELE
BALANOID
BALANOPHORE
BALANOPHORIN
BALANOPLASTY
BALANOPS
BALANT
BALANTIDIAL
BALANTIDIC
BALAO
BALAPHON
BALARAO
BALAS
BALAT
BALATA
BALATE
BALATONG
BALATRON
BALATRONIC
BALATTE
BALAU
BALAUSTA
BALAUSTINE
BALAUSTRE
BALAYEUSE
BALBOA
BALBRIGGAN
BALBUSARD
BALBUTIATE
BALBUTIENT
BALBUTIES
BALCHE
BALCONE
BALCONET
BALCONETTE
BALCONIED
BALCONIES
BALCONY
BALD
BALDACCHINI
BALDACCHINO
BALDACHIN
BALDACHINED
BALDACHINO
BALDACHINOS
BALDAKIN
BALDAQUIN
BALDBERRY
BALDCROWN
BALDEN
BALDER
BALDERDASH
BALDFACED
BALDHEAD
BALDHEADED
BALDICOOT
BALDING
BALDISH
BALDLING
BALDLY
BALDMONEY
BALDMONEYS
BALDNESS
BALDPATE
BALDPATED
BALDRIB
BALDRIC
BALDRICK
BALDRICKED
BALDUCTA
BALDUCTUM
BALDY
BALE
BALEBOS
BALED
BALEEN
BALEFIRE
BALEFUL
BALEFULLY
BALEFULNESS
BALEI
BALEISE
BALER
BALESTRA
BALETE
BALEWORT
BALEYS
BALI
BALIAN
BALIBAGO
BALIMBING
BALINE
BALING
BALINGER
BALINGHASAY
BALISAUR
BALISIER
BALISTARII
BALISTARIUS
BALISTID

BALISTRARIA
BALITA
BALITAO
BALITI
BALK
BALKANIZE
BALKANIZED
BALKANIZING
BALKER
BALKIER
BALKIEST
BALKINGLY
BALKLINE
BALKY
BALL
BALLAD
BALLADE
BALLADEER
BALLADER
BALLADIC
BALLADICAL
BALLADIER
BALLADMONGER
BALLADROMIC
BALLADRY
BALLAHOO
BALLAHOU
BALLAM
BALLAN
BALLANT
BALLARAG
BALLARD
BALLAS
BALLAST
BALLASTAGE
BALLASTER
BALLASTING
BALLATA
BALLATOON
BALLCARRIER
BALLDRESS
BALLED
BALLER
BALLERINA
BALLERINAS
BALLERINE
BALLET
BALLETOMANE
BALLFLOWER
BALLHOOTER
BALLIAGE
BALLING
BALLISM
BALLIST
BALLISTA
BALLISTAE
BALLISTIC
BALLISTICALLY
BALLISTICIAN
BALLISTICS
BALLIUM
BALLMINE
BALLOCK
BALLOEN
BALLOGAN
BALLON
BALLONET
BALLONETTE
BALLONNE
BALLOON
BALLOONATION
BALLOONER
BALLOONERY
BALLOONET
BALLOONING
BALLOONIST
BALLOT
BALLOTADE
BALLOTAGE
BALLOTE
BALLOTED
BALLOTER
BALLOTING
BALLOTTEMENT
BALLOW
BALLPLAYER
BALLPROOF
BALLROOM
BALLS
BALLUP
BALLWEED
BALLY
BALLYHACK
BALLYHOO
BALLYHOOED
BALLYHOOER
BALLYHOOING
BALLYRAG
BALLYWACK
BALLYWRACK
BALM
BALMACAAN
BALMIER
BALMIEST
BALMILY
BALMINESS
BALMONIES
BALMONY
BALMORAL
BALMY
BALNEA
BALNEAE
BALNEAL
BALNEARY
BALNEATION
BALNEATORY
BALNEOGRAPHY
BALNEOLOGIC
BALNEOLOGY
BALNEUM
BALO
BALON
BALONEY
BALOO
BALOP
BALOTADE
BALOW
BALSA
BALSAM
BALSAMIC
BALSAMICAL
BALSAMICALLY
BALSAMINE
BALSAMITIC
BALSAMIZE
BALSAMO
BALSAMOUS
BALSAMROOT
BALSAMWEED
BALSAMY
BALSAS
BALTEI
BALTER
BALTEUS
BALTHEUS
BALTIMORITE
BALU
BALUSHAI
BALUSTER
BALUSTERED
BALUSTRADE
BALUSTRADED
BALUT
BALWARRA
BALZARINE
BAM
BAMAH
BAMBA
BAMBAN
BAMBINI
BAMBINO
BAMBINOS
BAMBOCCIADE
BAMBOCHE
BAMBOO
BAMBOOZLE
BAMBOOZLED
BAMBOOZLEMENT
BAMBOOZLER
BAMBOOZLING
BAMBOULA
BAMBUCO
BAMBUK
BAMIA
BAN
BANABA
BANAGO
BANAGOS
BANAK
BANAKITE
BANAL
BANALITIES
BANALITY
BANALLY
BANANA
BANANAS
BANANIST
BANANIVOROUS
BANAT
BANATE
BANATITE
BANAUSIC
BANC
BANCA
BANCAL
BANCALES
BANCHA
BANCO
BANCOS
BANCUS
BAND
BANDAGE
BANDAGED
BANDAGER
BANDAGING
BANDAGIST
BANDAITE
BANDAKA
BANDALA
BANDALORE
BANDANA
BANDANNA
BANDANNAED
BANDAR
BANDARLOG
BANDBOX
BANDBOXICAL
BANDBOXY
BANDCUTTER
BANDE
BANDEAU
BANDEAUX
BANDED
BANDELET
BANDELETTE
BANDENG
BANDER
BANDERILLA
BANDERILLAS
BANDERILLERO
BANDERILLEROS
BANDERLOG
BANDEROL
BANDEROLE
BANDEROLED
BANDEROLING
BANDERSNATCH
BANDFISH
BANDHAVA
BANDHOOK
BANDHU
BANDI
BANDICOOT
BANDICOY
BANDIDO
BANDIDOS
BANDIE
BANDIED
BANDIES
BANDIKAI
BANDING
BANDIT
BANDITRY
BANDITS
BANDITTI
BANDLE
BANDLEADER
BANDMAN
BANDMASTER
BANDO
BANDOG
BANDOLEER
BANDOLEERED
BANDOLERISMO
BANDOLERO
BANDOLEROS
BANDOLIER
BANDOLINE
BANDON
BANDONION
BANDORE
BANDOS
BANDS
BANDSMAN
BANDSMEN
BANDSTAND
BANDSTER
BANDSTRING
BANDURA
BANDURRIA
BANDURRIAS
BANDWAGON
BANDWORK
BANDWORM
BANDY
BANDYBALL
BANDYING
BANDYMAN
BANE
BANEBERRIES
BANEBERRY
BANED
BANEFUL
BANEFULLY
BANEFULNESS
BANEWORT
BANG
BANGA
BANGALAY
BANGALOW
BANGE
BANGER
BANGHY
BANGIACEOUS
BANGING
BANGKOK
BANGLE
BANGLED
BANGLING
BANGO
BANGOS
BANGS
BANGSTER
BANGTAIL
BANGTAILED
BANGY
BANI
BANIA
BANIAN
BANIG
BANILAD
BANING
BANISH
BANISHED
BANISHER
BANISHMENT
BANISTER
BANISTERINE
BANIYA
BANJARA
BANJO
BANJOES
BANJORE
BANJORINE
BANJOS
BANK
BANKABLE
BANKBOOK
BANKED
BANKER
BANKERA
BANKET
BANKFULL
BANKING
BANKMAN
BANKMEN
BANKRIDER
BANKROLL
BANKRUPT
BANKRUPTCIES
BANKRUPTCY
BANKRUPTISM
BANKRUPTLY
BANKRUPTURE
BANKS
BANKSHALL
BANKSIA
BANKSIDE
BANKSMAN
BANKSMEN
BANKWEED
BANKY
BANLIEU
BANLIEUE
BANNACK
BANNAT
BANNED
BANNER
BANNERED
BANNERER
BANNERET
BANNERETTE
BANNERFISH
BANNERMAN
BANNERMEN
BANNEROL
BANNEROLE
BANNET
BANNIMUS
BANNING
BANNISTER
BANNOCK
BANNS
BANNUT
BANOVINA

BANQUE
BANQUET
BANQUETED
BANQUETEER
BANQUETEERING
BANQUETER
BANQUETING
BANQUETTE
BANS
BANSALAGUE
BANSHEE
BANSHIE
BANSTICKLE
BANT
BANTAM
BANTAMIZE
BANTAMWEIGHT
BANTAY
BANTAYAN
BANTENG
BANTER
BANTERED
BANTERER
BANTERING
BANTERINGLY
BANTERY
BANTIN
BANTING
BANTINGIZE
BANTLING
BANTU
BANTY
BANUS
BANUYO
BANXRING
BANYA
BANYAN
BANZAI
BAOBAB
BAP
BAPISTERY
BAPTISIN
BAPTISM
BAPTISMAL
BAPTISMALLY
BAPTISTERIES
BAPTISTERY
BAPTISTIC
BAPTISTRIES
BAPTISTRY
BAPTIZE
BAPTIZED
BAPTIZEE
BAPTIZEMENT
BAPTIZER
BAPTIZING
BAPU
BAR
BARABARA
BARABORA
BARAD
BARADARI
BARAGNOSIS
BARAGOUIN
BARAITA
BARAJILLO
BARAMIN
BARANDOS
BARANGAY
BARANI
BARARITE
BARASINGHA
BARAT
BARATHEA
BARATHRA
BARATHRON
BARATHRUM
BARATO
BARATTE
BARB
BARBACOU
BARBAL
BARBARESQUE
BARBARIAN
BARBARIC
BARBARICAL
BARBARICALLY
BARBARIOUS
BARBARISM
BARBARITIES
BARBARITY
BARBARIZE
BARBARIZED
BARBARIZING
BARBAROUS
BARBAROUSLY
BARBARY
BARBAS
BARBASCO
BARBASTEL
BARBASTELLE
BARBATE
BARBATED
BARBATIMAO
BARBE
BARBEAU
BARBECUE
BARBECUED
BARBECUING
BARBED
BARBEIRO
BARBEL
BARBELL
BARBELLATE
BARBELLULA
BARBELLULAE
BARBELLULATE
BARBEQUE
BARBER
BARBERA
BARBERMONGER
BARBERO
BARBERRIES
BARBERRY
BARBERSHOP
BARBERY
BARBET
BARBETTE
BARBICAN
BARBICEL
BARBIGEROUS
BARBING
BARBION
BARBITA
BARBITAL
BARBITALISM
BARBITON
BARBITONE
BARBITURATE
BARBITURIC
BARBLESS
BARBLET
BARBOLA
BARBONE
BARBOTINE
BARBOTTE
BARBOY
BARBUDO
BARBUDOS
BARBULA
BARBULATE
BARBULE
BARBULYIE
BARBWIRE
BARCA
BARCAROLE
BARCAROLLE
BARCAS
BARCELLA
BARCELONA
BARCELONAS
BARCHAN
BARCHE
BARCOLONGO
BARD
BARDANE
BARDASH
BARDE
BARDEE
BARDEL
BARDELLE
BARDESS
BARDIC
BARDIE
BARDIGLIO
BARDILY
BARDINESS
BARDING
BARDINGS
BARDISH
BARDISM
BARDLET
BARDLING
BARDO
BARDS
BARDY
BARE
BAREBACK
BAREBACKED
BAREBONE
BARECA
BARED
BAREFACED
BAREFACEDLY
BAREFIT
BAREFOOT
BAREFOOTED
BAREGE
BAREHANDED
BAREHEAD
BAREHEADED
BAREKA
BARELEGGED
BARELY
BARENECKED
BARER
BARES
BARESARK
BARESMA
BARETTA
BARFF
BARFISH
BARFLIES
BARFLY
BARFUL
BARGAIN
BARGAINEE
BARGAINER
BARGAINING
BARGAINOR
BARGE
BARGEBOARD
BARGED
BARGEE
BARGEER
BARGEESE
BARGEHOUSE
BARGELIKE
BARGELLI
BARGELLO
BARGELOAD
BARGEMAN
BARGEMASTER
BARGEMEN
BARGER
BARGH
BARGHAM
BARGHEST
BARGING
BARGIR
BARGOOSE
BARHAL
BARHOP
BARI
BARIA
BARIC
BARID
BARIE
BARIL
BARILLA
BARIN
BARING
BARIOLAGE
BARIS
BARISH
BARIT
BARITE
BARITONE
BARIUM
BARK
BARKAN
BARKARY
BARKBOUND
BARKEEP
BARKEEPER
BARKEN
BARKENED
BARKENING
BARKENTINE
BARKER
BARKERY
BARKEVIKITE
BARKEVIKITIC
BARKEY
BARKHAN
BARKIER
BARKIEST
BARKING
BARKINGLY
BARKLE
BARKLYITE
BARKOMETER
BARKPEEL
BARKPEELER
BARKPEELING
BARKS
BARKSOME
BARKSTONE
BARKY
BARLA
BARLEY
BARLEYBIRD
BARLEYBRAKE
BARLEYBREAK
BARLEYCORN
BARLEYHOOD
BARLEYMOW
BARLEYSICK
BARLING
BARLOW
BARLY
BARM
BARMAID
BARMAN
BARMASTER
BARMBRACK
BARMCLOTH
BARMEN
BARMFEL
BARMIE
BARMIER
BARMIEST
BARMKIN
BARMOTE
BARMSKIN
BARMY
BARMYBRAINED
BARN
BARNACLE
BARNACLED
BARNACLING
BARNARD
BARNEY
BARNHARDTITE
BARNMAN
BARNMEN
BARNS
BARNSTORM
BARNSTORMER
BARNSTORMING
BARNY
BARNYARD
BARO
BAROCCO
BAROGNOSIS
BAROGRAM
BAROGRAPH
BAROGRAPHIC
BAROI
BAROLO
BAROLOGY
BAROMETER
BAROMETRIC
BAROMETRICAL
BAROMETRY
BAROMETZ
BAROMOTOR
BARON
BARONAGE
BARONESS
BARONET
BARONETAGE
BARONETCIES
BARONETCY
BARONETED
BARONETICAL
BARONETING
BARONG
BARONI
BARONIAL
BARONIES
BARONNE
BARONRIES
BARONRY
BARONY
BAROQUE
BAROSCOPE
BAROSCOPIC
BAROSCOPICAL
BAROSMIN
BAROSTAT
BAROTACTIC
BAROTAXIS
BAROTAXY
BAROTO
BAROUCHE
BAROUCHET
BAROUCHETTE
BAROXYTON
BARPOST
BARQUE
BARQUENTINE
BARQUEST
BARR
BARRA

BARRABLE
BARRABORA
BARRACAN
BARRACE
BARRACK
BARRACKER
BARRACKS
BARRACLADE
BARRACOON
BARRACOUTA
BARRACOUTAS
BARRACUDA
BARRACUDAS
BARRAD
BARRAGAN
BARRAGE
BARRAGED
BARRAGING
BARRAGON
BARRAMUNDA
BARRAMUNDAS
BARRAMUNDI
BARRAMUNDIES
BARRAMUNDIS
BARRANCA
BARRANCO
BARRANDITE
BARRAS
BARRAT
BARRATER
BARRATOR
BARRATRIES
BARRATROUS
BARRATROUSLY
BARRATRY
BARRE
BARRED
BARREL
BARRELAGE
BARRELED
BARRELER
BARRELET
BARRELFUL
BARRELFULS
BARRELHEAD
BARRELHOUSE
BARRELING
BARRELLED
BARRELLING
BARRELMAKER
BARRELMAKING
BARRELS
BARREN
BARRENER
BARRENLY
BARRENNESS
BARRENWORT
BARRER
BARRERA
BARRET
BARRETRY
BARRETTE
BARRETTER
BARRICADE
BARRICADED
BARRICADER
BARRICADING
BARRICO
BARRICOES
BARRICOS
BARRIER
BARRIERS
BARRIGUDA
BARRIGUDO
BARRIGUDOS
BARRIKIN
BARRING
BARRIO
BARRIOS
BARRISTER
BARRISTERIAL
BARRISTRESS
BARROOM
BARROW
BARROWCOAT
BARROWMAN
BARRULET
BARRULY
BARRY
BARS
BARSE
BARSOM
BARSPOON
BARSTOOL
BARTENDER
BARTENDING
BARTER
BARTERED
BARTERER
BARTERING
BARTH
BARTHITE
BARTHOLINITIS
BARTIZAN
BARTIZANED
BARTON
BARTREE
BARU
BARUKHZY
BARURIA
BARVEL
BARVELL
BARWAY
BARWAYS
BARWIN
BARWING
BARWISE
BARWOOD
BARYCENTER
BARYCENTRE
BARYCENTRIC
BARYE
BARYECOIA
BARYLITE
BARYON
BARYPHONIA
BARYPHONIC
BARYPHONY
BARYSILITE
BARYSPHERE
BARYTA
BARYTE
BARYTES
BARYTHYMIA
BARYTIC
BARYTINE
BARYTONE
BAS
BASAL
BASALE
BASALIA
BASALLY
BASALT
BASALTES
BASALTIC
BASALTIFORM
BASALTINE
BASALTOID
BASALTWARE
BASAN
BASANITE
BASAREE
BASCULE
BASCUNAN
BASE
BASEBALL
BASEBALLER
BASEBOARD
BASEBORN
BASEBRED
BASEBURNER
BASED
BASELARD
BASELESS
BASELESSLY
BASELESSNESS
BASELINER
BASELLACEOUS
BASELY
BASEMAN
BASEMEN
BASEMENT
BASENESS
BASENJI
BASEPLUG
BASER
BASES
BASEST
BASH
BASHA
BASHAW
BASHED
BASHER
BASHFUL
BASHFULLY
BASHFULNESS
BASHING
BASHLESS
BASHLIK
BASHLYK
BASI
BASIAL
BASIATE
BASIATION
BASIC
BASICALLY
BASICITY
BASICRANIAL
BASIDIA
BASIDIAL
BASIDIGITALE
BASIDIGITALIA
BASIDIOMYCETE
BASIDIOMYCETES
BASIDIOPHORE
BASIDIOSPORE
BASIDIUM
BASIDORSAL
BASIFACIAL
BASIFICATION
BASIFIED
BASIFIER
BASIFIXED
BASIFUGAL
BASIFY
BASIFYING
BASIG
BASIGAMOUS
BASIGAMY
BASIGENIC
BASIGENOUS
BASIHYAL
BASIL
BASILAR
BASILARY
BASILATERAL
BASILEIS
BASILEMMA
BASILEUS
BASILIC
BASILICA
BASILICAL
BASILICAN
BASILICAS
BASILICON
BASILINNA
BASILISCAN
BASILISCINE
BASILISK
BASILISSA
BASILWEED
BASILYSIS
BASILYST
BASIN
BASINASAL
BASINASIAL
BASINED
BASINET
BASING
BASION
BASIOPHITIC
BASIOTRIBE
BASIOTRIPSY
BASIPETAL
BASIPHOBIA
BASIPODITE
BASIPODITIC
BASIRADIAL
BASIRHINAL
BASIROSTRAL
BASIS
BASISCOPIC
BASISPHENOID
BASITEMPORAL
BASIVENTRAL
BASK
BASKER
BASKET
BASKETBALL
BASKETBALLER
BASKETING
BASKETMAKER
BASKETMAKING
BASKETRY
BASKETWARE
BASKETWOMAN
BASKETWOOD
BASKETWORK
BASOCYTE
BASON
BASOPHIL
BASOPHILE
BASOPHILIA
BASOPHILIC
BASOPHILOUS
BASOTE
BASOTHO
BASQUE
BASQUED
BASQUINE
BASS
BASSANELLO
BASSANITE
BASSARA
BASSARID
BASSARISK
BASSES
BASSET
BASSETED
BASSETING
BASSETITE
BASSETTA
BASSETTE
BASSI
BASSIE
BASSINE
BASSINET
BASSING
BASSIST
BASSO
BASSON
BASSOON
BASSOONIST
BASSORIN
BASSOS
BASSUS
BASSWOOD
BAST
BASTA
BASTANT
BASTARD
BASTARDA
BASTARDISM
BASTARDIZE
BASTARDIZED
BASTARDIZING
BASTARDLY
BASTARDY
BASTE
BASTED
BASTEN
BASTER
BASTIDE
BASTILE
BASTILLE
BASTINADE
BASTINADO
BASTINADOED
BASTINADOES
BASTINADOING
BASTING
BASTION
BASTIONARY
BASTIONED
BASTIONET
BASTITE
BASTNASITE
BASTO
BASTON
BASTONET
BASURAL
BASURALE
BAT
BATA
BATAAN
BATAD
BATAK
BATAKAN
BATALEUR
BATAMOTE
BATARA
BATARDE
BATARDEAU
BATATA
BATATILLA
BATCH
BATCHER
BATE
BATEA
BATEAU
BATEAUX
BATED
BATEFUL
BATEL
BATELEUR
BATEMAN
BATEMENT
BATER
BATES
BATETE
BATFISH
BATFOWL
BATFOWLER
BATFOWLING
BATFUL

BATH
BATHE
BATHEABLE
BATHED
BATHER
BATHETIC
BATHFLOWER
BATHHOUSE
BATHIC
BATHING
BATHKOL
BATHMAN
BATHMIC
BATHMISM
BATHMOTROPIC
BATHOCHROME
BATHOCHROMIC
BATHOCHROMY
BATHOFLORE
BATHOFLORIC
BATHOLITE
BATHOLITH
BATHOLITHIC
BATHOLITIC
BATHOMANIA
BATHOMETER
BATHOPHOBIA
BATHORSE
BATHOS
BATHQOL
BATHROBE
BATHROOM
BATHROOMED
BATHROOT
BATHS
BATHTUB
BATHUKOLPIAN
BATHVILLITE
BATHWORT
BATHYAL
BATHYBIAN
BATHYBIC
BATHYBIUS
BATHYCOLPIAN
BATHYCOLPIC
BATHYL
BATHYMETER
BATHYMETRIC
BATHYMETRY
BATHYPELAGIC
BATHYSCAPH
BATHYSCAPHE
BATHYSEISM
BATHYSMAL
BATHYSPHERE
BATIDACEOUS
BATIK
BATIKED
BATIKER
BATIKING
BATIKULIN
BATIKULING
BATING
BATINO
BATISTE
BATITINAN
BATLAN
BATLER
BATLET
BATLIKE
BATLING
BATLON
BATMAN
BATMEN
BATOID
BATON
BATONEER
BATONIST
BATONISTIC
BATONNE
BATONNIER
BATOPHOBIA
BATRACHIAN
BATRACHIATE
BATRACHITE
BATRACHOID
BATS
BATSMAN
BATSMANSHIP
BATSMEN
BATSWING
BATT
BATTA
BATTABLE
BATTAILOUS
BATTALIA
BATTALION
BATTE
BATTED
BATTEL
BATTELER
BATTEMENT
BATTEN
BATTENED
BATTENER
BATTENING
BATTENS
BATTER
BATTERCAKE
BATTERDOCK
BATTERED
BATTERER
BATTERFANG
BATTERIE
BATTERIES
BATTERING
BATTERMAN
BATTERY
BATTEUSE
BATTIER
BATTIES
BATTIEST
BATTIK
BATTING
BATTISH
BATTLE
BATTLED
BATTLEDORE
BATTLEDORED
BATTLEDORING
BATTLEFIELD
BATTLEFUL
BATTLEGROUND
BATTLEMENT
BATTLEMENTED
BATTLEPLANE
BATTLER
BATTLESHIP
BATTLESTEAD
BATTLEWAGON
BATTLING
BATTOLOGICAL
BATTOLOGIST
BATTOLOGIZE
BATTOLOGY
BATTON
BATTS
BATTU
BATTUE
BATTURE
BATTUTA
BATTY
BATTYCAKE
BATU
BATUKITE
BATULE
BATUQUE
BATWING
BATYPHONE
BATZ
BATZEN
BAUBEE
BAUBLE
BAUBLERY
BAUBLING
BAUCH
BAUCHLE
BAUCKIE
BAUD
BAUDEKIN
BAUDERY
BAUDRONS
BAUGH
BAUHINIA
BAUK
BAUL
BAULEA
BAULEAH
BAULK
BAULKY
BAUMHAUERITE
BAUMIER
BAUNO
BAUR
BAUSON
BAUSOND
BAUTA
BAUTTA
BAUXITE
BAUXITITE
BAVARDAGE
BAVAROISE
BAVAROY
BAVARY
BAVE
BAVENITE
BAVETTE
BAVIAN
BAVIN
BAVOSO
BAW
BAWARCHI
BAWBEE
BAWCOCK
BAWD
BAWDIER
BAWDIEST
BAWDILY
BAWDINESS
BAWDRIC
BAWDRICK
BAWDRY
BAWDSTROT
BAWDY
BAWDYHOUSE
BAWL
BAWLER
BAWLEY
BAWLING
BAWLY
BAWN
BAWNEEN
BAWREL
BAWSUNT
BAWTIE
BAWTY
BAXA
BAXTER
BAY
BAYA
BAYADEER
BAYADERE
BAYAL
BAYAMO
BAYAN
BAYANO
BAYARD
BAYARDLY
BAYBERRIES
BAYBERRY
BAYBOLT
BAYBUSH
BAYED
BAYETA
BAYETE
BAYGALL
BAYLET
BAYMAN
BAYMEN
BAYOG
BAYOK
BAYON
BAYONET
BAYONETED
BAYONETEER
BAYONETING
BAYONG
BAYOU
BAYOUS
BAYWOOD
BAZAAR
BAZAR
BAZE
BAZOO
BAZOOKA
BAZZITE
BB
BDELLID
BDELLIUM
BDELLOID
BDELLOTOMY
BE
BEACH
BEACHBOY
BEACHCOMB
BEACHCOMBER
BEACHCOMBING
BEACHDROPS
BEACHED
BEACHHEAD
BEACHIER
BEACHIEST
BEACHMAN
BEACHMASTER
BEACHMEN
BEACHY
BEACON
BEACONAGE
BEACONED
BEACONING
BEAD
BEADED
BEADER
BEADFLUSH
BEADHOUSE
BEADIER
BEADIEST
BEADILY
BEADINESS
BEADING
BEADLE
BEADLEDOM
BEADLERY
BEADMAN
BEADROLL
BEADROW
BEADS
BEADSMAN
BEADSWOMAN
BEADWORK
BEADY
BEAGLE
BEAGLING
BEAK
BEAKED
BEAKER
BEAKERMAN
BEAKERMEN
BEAKHEAD
BEAKIRON
BEAKLESS
BEAKLIKE
BEAKY
BEAL
BEALA
BEALACH
BEALING
BEALLACH
BEAM
BEAMAGE
BEAMBIRD
BEAMED
BEAMER
BEAMFILLING
BEAMFUL
BEAMHOUSE
BEAMIER
BEAMIEST
BEAMILY
BEAMINESS
BEAMING
BEAMINGLY
BEAMISH
BEAMLESS
BEAMLIKE
BEAMROOM
BEAMSMAN
BEAMSMEN
BEAMSTER
BEAMY
BEAN
BEANBAG
BEANBAGS
BEANBALL
BEANCOD
BEANERIES
BEANERY
BEANFEAST
BEANFEASTER
BEANFIELD
BEANIE
BEANIER
BEANIEST
BEANO
BEANPOLE
BEANS
BEANSETTER
BEANSHOOTER
BEANSTALK
BEANWEED
BEANY
BEAR
BEARABLE
BEARABLENESS
BEARABLY
BEARANCE
BEARBAITER
BEARBAITING
BEARBANE
BEARBERRIES
BEARBERRY
BEARBIND
BEARBINE
BEARCAT
BEARCOOT

BEARD
BEARDED
BEARDER
BEARDIE
BEARDING
BEARDLESS
BEARDLIKE
BEARDTONGUE
BEARDY
BEARER
BEARERS
BEARFOOT
BEARFOOTS
BEARHERD
BEARHOUND
BEARING
BEARINGS
BEARISH
BEARISHLY
BEARISHNESS
BEARLET
BEARM
BEARS
BEARSKIN
BEARWARD
BEARWOOD
BEARWORT
BEAST
BEASTIE
BEASTILY
BEASTLIER
BEASTLIEST
BEASTLIKE
BEASTLILY
BEASTLINESS
BEASTLINGS
BEASTLY
BEASTMAN
BEASTS
BEAT
BEATA
BEATAE
BEATEE
BEATEN
BEATER
BEATERMAN
BEATERMEN
BEATH
BEATI
BEATIFIC
BEATIFICAL
BEATIFICALLY
BEATIFICATE
BEATIFIED
BEATIFY
BEATIFYING
BEATILLE
BEATING
BEATITUDE
BEATNIK
BEATSTER
BEATUS
BEAU
BEAUED
BEAUETRY
BEAUFIN
BEAUING
BEAUISH
BEAUISM
BEAUPERE
BEAUS
BEAUSEANT
BEAUT
BEAUTEOUS
BEAUTEOUSLY
BEAUTEOUSNESS
BEAUTICIAN
BEAUTIED
BEAUTIES
BEAUTIFIED
BEAUTIFIER
BEAUTIFUL
BEAUTIFULLY
BEAUTIFY
BEAUTIFYING
BEAUTY
BEAUX
BEAVER
BEAVERBOARD
BEAVERED
BEAVERETTE
BEAVERIES
BEAVERITE
BEAVERIZE
BEAVERKIN
BEAVERPELT
BEAVERROOT
BEAVERTEEN
BEAVERWOOD
BEAVERY
BEBAY
BEBEERIN
BEBEERINE
BEBEERU
BEBILYA
BEBIZATION
BEBLED
BEBOG
BEBOP
BECAFICO
BECALL
BECALM
BECALMED
BECALMING
BECAME
BECARD
BECARVE
BECASSE
BECASSINE
BECAUSE
BECCAFICO
BECCAFICOS
BECCHI
BECCO
BECHAMEL
BECHANCE
BECHANCED
BECHANCING
BECHER
BECK
BECKELITE
BECKER
BECKET
BECKETT
BECKIRON
BECKON
BECKONED
BECKONER
BECKONING
BECKONINGLY
BECLAD
BECLAP
BECLIP
BECLOUD
BECLOUDED
BECLOUT
BECOME
BECOMED
BECOMES
BECOMING
BECOMINGLY
BECON
BECOOM
BECORESH
BECOUSINED
BECQUERELITE
BECREEP
BECROSS
BECRUSH
BECUIBA
BECUNA
BED
BEDA
BEDABBLE
BEDAD
BEDAFF
BEDAGGLE
BEDAMN
BEDANGLED
BEDASH
BEDAUB
BEDAWN
BEDAY
BEDAZE
BEDAZZLE
BEDAZZLED
BEDAZZLING
BEDAZZLINGLY
BEDBUG
BEDCHAIR
BEDCHAMBER
BEDCLOTHES
BEDCORD
BEDCOVER
BEDDED
BEDDER
BEDDING
BEDE
BEDECK
BEDECKED
BEDEEN
BEDEGAR
BEDEGUAR
BEDEHOUSE
BEDEL
BEDELL
BEDELVE
BEDEMAN
BEDEN
BEDENE
BEDESMAN
BEDESMEN
BEDEVIL
BEDEVILED
BEDEVILING
BEDEVILLED
BEDEVILLING
BEDEVILMENT
BEDEW
BEDEWED
BEDEWER
BEDFAST
BEDFELLOW
BEDFLOWER
BEDFRAME
BEDGERY
BEDGOWN
BEDIGHT
BEDIGHTED
BEDIGHTING
BEDIKAH
BEDIM
BEDIMMED
BEDIMMING
BEDIZEN
BEDIZENED
BEDIZENING
BEDIZENMENT
BEDKEY
BEDLAM
BEDLAMER
BEDLAMISM
BEDLAMITE
BEDLAMIZE
BEDLAR
BEDLIDS
BEDMAN
BEDMATE
BEDO
BEDOG
BEDOTE
BEDOWN
BEDOYO
BEDPAN
BEDPLATE
BEDPOST
BEDPOSTS
BEDQUILT
BEDRABBLE
BEDRAGGLE
BEDRAGGLED
BEDRAIL
BEDRAL
BEDRAPE
BEDREAD
BEDREL
BEDRESS
BEDRID
BEDRIDDEN
BEDRIGHT
BEDRIP
BEDRITE
BEDROCK
BEDROLL
BEDROOM
BEDROP
BEDS
BEDSIDE
BEDSITE
BEDSORE
BEDSPREAD
BEDSPRING
BEDSTAFF
BEDSTAND
BEDSTAVES
BEDSTEAD
BEDSTOCK
BEDSTRAW
BEDSWERVER
BEDTICK
BEDTIME
BEDU
BEDUB
BEDWARD
BEDWARDS
BEDWARMER
BEDWAY
BEDWELL
BEE
BEEBALL
BEEBEE
BEEBREAD
BEECH
BEECHDROPS
BEECHEN
BEECHES
BEECHNUT
BEECHNUTS
BEECHY
BEEF
BEEFCAKE
BEEFEATER
BEEFHEAD
BEEFHEADED
BEEFIER
BEEFIEST
BEEFILY
BEEFIN
BEEFINESS
BEEFISH
BEEFISHNESS
BEEFLESS
BEEFS
BEEFSTEAK
BEEFTONGUE
BEEFWOOD
BEEFY
BEEGERITE
BEEHEAD
BEEHEADED
BEEHERD
BEEHIVE
BEEHOUSE
BEEK
BEEKEEPER
BEEKEEPING
BEEKITE
BEELE
BEELINE
BEEMAN
BEEMASTER
BEEMEN
BEEN
BEENNUT
BEEP
BEEPER
BEER
BEERAGE
BEERBACHITE
BEERBIBBER
BEEREGAR
BEERHOUSE
BEERIER
BEERIEST
BEERILY
BEERINESS
BEERISH
BEERISHLY
BEERMAKER
BEERMAKING
BEERMONGER
BEEROCRACY
BEERPULL
BEERY
BEES
BEESTING
BEESTINGS
BEESWAX
BEESWING
BEET
BEETE
BEETEWK
BEETH
BEETIEST
BEETLE
BEETLED
BEETLEHEAD
BEETLEHEADED
BEETLER
BEETLESTOCK
BEETLESTONE
BEETLEWEED
BEETLING
BEETMISTER
BEETRAVE
BEETROOT
BEETROOTY
BEETS
BEETY
BEEVE
BEEVES
BEEVISH
BEEWARE
BEEWAY
BEEWEED

BEEWINGED
BEEWORT
BEEYARD
BEEZER
BEFALL
BEFALLEN
BEFALLING
BEFELL
BEFFROY
BEFILE
BEFIT
BEFITTED
BEFITTING
BEFITTINGLY
BEFLOUR
BEFLUM
BEFOG
BEFOGGED
BEFOGGING
BEFOOL
BEFOOLED
BEFOOLING
BEFORE
BEFOREHAND
BEFORETIME
BEFORTUNE
BEFOUL
BEFOULED
BEFOULER
BEFOULING
BEFOULMENT
BEFRET
BEFRIEND
BEFRIENDER
BEFUDDLE
BEFUDDLED
BEFUDDLEMENT
BEFUDDLER
BEFUDDLING
BEG
BEGA
BEGAD
BEGAN
BEGANI
BEGAR
BEGARI
BEGARIE
BEGARY
BEGASS
BEGAT
BEGATS
BEGATTAL
BEGEM
BEGEMMED
BEGEMMING
BEGET
BEGETTER
BEGETTING
BEGGAR
BEGGARDOM
BEGGARED
BEGGARER
BEGGARHOOD
BEGGARIES
BEGGARING
BEGGARLINESS
BEGGARLY
BEGGARMAN
BEGGARWEED
BEGGARWOMAN
BEGGARY
BEGGED
BEGGER
BEGGING
BEGILD
BEGIN
BEGINNER
BEGINNING
BEGIRD
BEGIRDED
BEGIRDING
BEGIRT
BEGLERBEG
BEGLERBEGLIC
BEGLERBEGLIK
BEGLERBEGLUC
BEGLEW
BEGNA
BEGNAW
BEGNAWED
BEGNAWN
BEGO
BEGOB
BEGOBS
BEGOD
BEGOHM
BEGONE
BEGONIA
BEGONIACEOUS
BEGORRA
BEGORRY
BEGOT
BEGOTTEN
BEGOWK
BEGRACE
BEGRIME
BEGRIMED
BEGRIMER
BEGRIMING
BEGRIPE
BEGRUDGE
BEGRUDGED
BEGRUDGING
BEGRUDGINGLY
BEGRUNTLE
BEGRUTTEN
BEGSTER
BEGTI
BEGUESS
BEGUILE
BEGUILED
BEGUILEMENT
BEGUILER
BEGUILING
BEGUIN
BEGUINE
BEGUM
BEGUMMED
BEGUN
BEGUNK
BEHALF
BEHALVES
BEHAR
BEHAVE
BEHAVED
BEHAVING
BEHAVIOR
BEHAVIORAL
BEHAVIORISM
BEHAVIORIST
BEHAVIOUR
BEHEAD
BEHEADAL
BEHEADED
BEHEADER
BEHEADING
BEHEAR
BEHEARS
BEHEIRA
BEHELD
BEHEMOTH
BEHEN
BEHENATE
BEHENIC
BEHEST
BEHEW
BEHIGHT
BEHIND
BEHINDHAND
BEHINDSIGHT
BEHN
BEHOLD
BEHOLDEN
BEHOLDER
BEHOLDING
BEHOOF
BEHOOVE
BEHOOVED
BEHOOVEFUL
BEHOOVEFULLY
BEHOOVES
BEHOOVING
BEHOVE
BEHOVED
BEHOVELY
BEHOVING
BEHOWL
BEHUNG
BEIGE
BEIGNET
BEIN
BEING
BEINGS
BEINLY
BEINNESS
BEIRA
BEISA
BEJABBERS
BEJABERS
BEJADE
BEJAN
BEJANT
BEJAPE
BEJEL
BEJESUS
BEJEWEL
BEJEWELED
BEJEWELING
BEJEWELLED
BEJEWELLING
BEJUCO
BEJUGGLE
BEKA
BEKAH
BEKEN
BEKING
BEKINKINITE
BEKISS
BEKKO
BEKNAVE
BEKNIGHT
BEKNOW
BEKNOWN
BEKRA
BEKTI
BEL
BELA
BELABOR
BELABOUR
BELACED
BELAGE
BELAH
BELAM
BELAMOUR
BELAMY
BELANDA
BELANDER
BELAR
BELAST
BELATE
BELATED
BELATEDLY
BELATEDNESS
BELATING
BELAUD
BELAY
BELAYED
BELAYING
BELCH
BELCHER
BELDAM
BELDAME
BELDER
BELDERROOT
BELDUQUE
BELE
BELEAGUER
BELEAGUERED
BELEAGUERER
BELEAGUERING
BELEAVE
BELEE
BELEED
BELEFT
BELEMNID
BELEMNITE
BELEMNITIC
BELEMNOID
BELETTER
BELEVE
BELFRIED
BELFRIES
BELFRY
BELGA
BELGARD
BELIBEL
BELIE
BELIED
BELIEF
BELIEFFUL
BELIEFFULNESS
BELIEFS
BELIER
BELIEVABLE
BELIEVE
BELIEVED
BELIEVER
BELIEVERS
BELIEVING
BELIEVINGLY
BELIGHT
BELIKE
BELIKELY
BELIME
BELITE
BELITTLE
BELITTLED
BELITTLER
BELITTLING
BELIVE
BELK
BELKNAP
BELL
BELLADONNA
BELLARMINE
BELLBIND
BELLBINDER
BELLBINE
BELLBIRD
BELLBOY
BELLE
BELLED
BELLEEK
BELLERIC
BELLETER
BELLETRIST
BELLETRISTIC
BELLFLOWER
BELLHANGING
BELLHOP
BELLHOUSE
BELLIC
BELLICAL
BELLICISM
BELLICOSE
BELLICOSELY
BELLICOSITY
BELLIED
BELLIES
BELLIFEROUS
BELLIGERENCE
BELLIGERENCY
BELLIGERENT
BELLING
BELLIPOTENT
BELLITE
BELLMAKER
BELLMAKING
BELLMAN
BELLMASTER
BELLMEN
BELLMOUTH
BELLMOUTHED
BELLONION
BELLOTA
BELLOTE
BELLOW
BELLOWER
BELLOWING
BELLOWS
BELLOWSMAKER
BELLOWSMAN
BELLPULL
BELLS
BELLTAIL
BELLTOPPER
BELLUINE
BELLUM
BELLWARE
BELLWAVER
BELLWEED
BELLWETHER
BELLWIND
BELLWINE
BELLWOOD
BELLWORT
BELLY
BELLYACHE
BELLYACHED
BELLYACHING
BELLYBAND
BELLYBUTTON
BELLYER
BELLYFISH
BELLYFUL
BELLYFULS
BELLYING
BELLYMAN
BELOEILITE
BELOID
BELOMANCY
BELONG
BELONGED
BELONGER
BELONGING
BELONGINGS
BELONID
BELONITE
BELONOID
BELOOK
BELORD
BELOTTE
BELOUKE
BELOVE
BELOVED

BELOW
BELOWSTAIRS
BELSIRE
BELT
BELTED
BELTER
BELTIE
BELTING
BELTMAKER
BELTMAKING
BELTMAN
BELTMEN
BELTON
BELTWAY
BELUE
BELUGA
BELUGITE
BELUTE
BELVE
BELVEDERE
BELVEDERED
BELY
BELYING
BELZEBUTH
BEMA
BEMASTER
BEMATA
BEMAUL
BEMAZED
BEME
BEMEAN
BEMEET
BEMENTITE
BEMETE
BEMIRE
BEMIRED
BEMIREMENT
BEMIRING
BEMIST
BEMOAN
BEMOANABLE
BEMOANER
BEMOCK
BEMOIL
BEMOL
BEMOON
BEMOURN
BEMOUTH
BEMUD
BEMUDDLE
BEMUDDLEMENT
BEMUSE
BEMUSED
BEMUSEDLY
BEMUSING
BEN
BENA
BENAB
BENADRYL
BENAME
BENAMED
BENAMEE
BENAMI
BENAMIDAR
BENAMING
BENASTY
BENBEN
BENCH
BENCHBOARD
BENCHER
BENCHES
BENCHFELLOW
BENCHING
BENCHLAND
BENCHMAN
BENCHMEN
BENCHWORK
BEND
BENDA
BENDAY
BENDED
BENDEE
BENDEL
BENDER
BENDERS
BENDING
BENDS
BENDSOME
BENDWAYS
BENDWISE
BENDY
BENE
BENEATH
BENECEPTION
BENECEPTIVE
BENECEPTOR
BENEDICITE
BENEDICK
BENEDICT
BENEDICTION
BENEDICTIVE
BENEDICTORY
BENEDIGHT
BENEFACTION
BENEFACTIVE
BENEFACTOR
BENEFACTORY
BENEFACTRESS
BENEFIC
BENEFICE
BENEFICED
BENEFICENCE
BENEFICENT
BENEFICENTLY
BENEFICIAIRE
BENEFICIAL
BENEFICIALLY
BENEFICIARIES
BENEFICIARY
BENEFICIATE
BENEFICING
BENEFICIUM
BENEFIT
BENEFITED
BENEFITER
BENEFITING
BENEGRO
BENEMPT
BENEMPTED
BENEPLACIT
BENEPLACITO
BENEPLACITY
BENET
BENETTED
BENETTING
BENEVOLENCE
BENEVOLENT
BENEVOLENTLY
BENEVOLIST
BENG
BENGALINE
BENIGHT
BENIGHTED
BENIGHTEDNESS
BENIGHTEN
BENIGHTER
BENIGHTING
BENIGN
BENIGNANCY
BENIGNANT
BENIGNANTLY
BENIGNITIES
BENIGNITY
BENIGNLY
BENISEED
BENISON
BENITIER
BENITOITE
BENJ
BENJAMIN
BENJAMINITE
BENJOIN
BENJY
BENK
BENMOST
BENN
BENNE
BENNEL
BENNET
BENNETWEED
BENNI
BENNIES
BENNISEED
BENNY
BENORTH
BENOTE
BENSAIL
BENSALL
BENSEL
BENSELL
BENSH
BENSIL
BENT
BENTANG
BENTHAL
BENTHIC
BENTHON
BENTHONIC
BENTHOS
BENTING
BENTLET
BENTONITE
BENTSTAR
BENTWOOD
BENTY
BENUMB
BENUMBED
BENUMBEDNESS
BENUMBING
BENUMBINGLY
BENUMBMENT
BENVENUTO
BENWARD
BENWEED
BENZAL
BENZALDEHYDE
BENZALDOXIME
BENZAMIDE
BENZAMIDO
BENZEDRINE
BENZEIN
BENZENE
BENZENOID
BENZENYL
BENZIDIN
BENZIDINE
BENZIDINO
BENZIL
BENZILIC
BENZIN
BENZINDULINE
BENZINE
BENZOATE
BENZOATED
BENZOBIS
BENZOCAINE
BENZOHYDROL
BENZOIC
BENZOIN
BENZOINATED
BENZOL
BENZOLATE
BENZOLE
BENZOLINE
BENZOLIZE
BENZONITRILE
BENZONITROL
BENZOPHENONE
BENZOPYRAN
BENZOXY
BENZOYL
BENZOYLATE
BENZOYLATION
BENZYL
BENZYLAMINE
BENZYLIC
BEO
BEPAINT
BEPAPER
BEPART
BEPRANKED
BEPRESS
BEPROSE
BEPUFFED
BEQAA
BEQUEATH
BEQUEATHAL
BEQUEATHER
BEQUEST
BEQUIRTLE
BER
BERAIN
BERAIROU
BERAKAH
BERAKOT
BERAKOTH
BERAT
BERATE
BERATED
BERATING
BERATTLE
BERAUNITE
BERAY
BERBAMINE
BERBE
BERBERID
BERBERIN
BERBERINE
BERBERRY
BERBERY
BERCEAU
BERCEUSE
BERCEUSES
BERDACHE
BERE
BEREAVE
BEREAVED
BEREAVEMENT
BEREAVEN
BEREAVER
BEREAVING
BEREDE
BEREFT
BERENDO
BERENGELITE
BERENGENA
BERESITE
BERG
BERGALITH
BERGAMIOL
BERGAMOT
BERGAPTENE
BERGER
BERGERE
BERGERETTE
BERGGYLT
BERGHAAN
BERGINIZATION
BERGINIZE
BERGSCHRUND
BERGUT
BERGY
BERGYLT
BERHYME
BERHYMED
BERHYMING
BERIBERI
BERIBERIC
BERIGORA
BERIME
BERIMED
BERIMING
BERINGITE
BERITH
BERKELIUM
BERLEY
BERLIN
BERLINE
BERLINITE
BERLOQUE
BERM
BERME
BERMUDITE
BERNICLE
BEROK
BERRENDO
BERRETTA
BERRETTINO
BERRI
BERRICHON
BERRICHONNE
BERRIED
BERRIES
BERRIGAN
BERRUGATE
BERRY
BERRYING
BERRYLIKE
BERSEEM
BERSERK
BERSERKER
BERSIM
BERTH
BERTHA
BERTHAGE
BERTHED
BERTHER
BERTHIERITE
BERTHING
BERTHS
BERTRANDITE
BERTRUM
BERUN
BERVIE
BERWICK
BERYCID
BERYCIFORM
BERYCINE
BERYCOID
BERYCOIDEAN
BERYL
BERYLLATE
BERYLLIA
BERYLLINE
BERYLLIUM
BERYLLOID
BERYLLONITE
BERYX
BERZELIANITE
BERZELIITE
BES
BESA
BESAGNE
BESAGUE
BESAIEL

BESAILE
BESAN
BESANT
BESAYLE
BESCREEN
BESEE
BESEECH
BESEECHED
BESEECHER
BESEECHING
BESEECHINGLY
BESEEM
BESEEMED
BESEEMING
BESEEMINGLY
BESEEMLINESS
BESEEMLY
BESEEN
BESEIGE
BESET
BESETMENT
BESETTER
BESETTING
BESHADE
BESHAG
BESHEAR
BESHINE
BESHLIK
BESHOW
BESHREW
BESICLOMETER
BESIDE
BESIDES
BESIEGE
BESIEGED
BESIEGEMENT
BESIEGER
BESIEGING
BESIEGINGLY
BESIN
BESING
BESIT
BESLAB
BESLAVER
BESLIME
BESLUBBER
BESLUIT
BESMEAR
BESMEARER
BESMIRCH
BESMIRCHER
BESMIRCHMENT
BESMOKE
BESMOTTERED
BESMUT
BESMUTTED
BESMUTTING
BESNOW
BESOIN
BESOM
BESOMER
BESOOTHE
BESOOTHEMENT
BESORT
BESOT
BESOTTED
BESOTTEDLY
BESOTTEDNESS
BESOTTING
BESOTTINGLY
BESOUGHT
BESPAKE
BESPANGLE
BESPANGLED
BESPANGLING
BESPATTER
BESPATTERED
BESPATTERER
BESPATTERING
BESPAWL
BESPEAK
BESPEAKER
BESPEAKING
BESPECKLE
BESPECTACLED
BESPELL
BESPETE
BESPIT
BESPOKE
BESPOKEN
BESPOT
BESPOTTED
BESPOTTING
BESPREAD
BESPREADING
BESPRENT
BESPRING
BESPRINKLE
BESPRINKLED
BESPRINKLER
BESPRINKLING
BESPRIZORNI
BESQUIRT
BESRA
BESSEMER
BESSEMERIZE
BESSEMERIZED
BESSEMERIZING
BESSES
BEST
BESTAIN
BESTAND
BESTEAD
BESTEAL
BESTED
BESTEER
BESTER
BESTIAL
BESTIALITIES
BESTIALITY
BESTIALIZE
BESTIALIZED
BESTIALIZING
BESTIALLY
BESTIALS
BESTIARIAN
BESTIARIES
BESTIARY
BESTICK
BESTICKING
BESTILL
BESTIR
BESTIRRED
BESTIRRING
BESTORM
BESTOW
BESTOWABLE
BESTOWAGE
BESTOWAL
BESTOWED
BESTOWER
BESTOWING
BESTOWMENT
BESTRADDLE
BESTRADDLED
BESTRADDLING
BESTRAUGHT
BESTREW
BESTREWED
BESTREWING
BESTREWN
BESTRID
BESTRIDDEN
BESTRIDE
BESTRIDING
BESTRODE
BESTRUT
BESTUCK
BESUGO
BESWINK
BET
BETA
BETACISM
BETACISMUS
BETAFITE
BETAINE
BETAINOGEN
BETAKE
BETAKEN
BETAKING
BETANAPHTHOL
BETEELA
BETEEM
BETEL
BETELNUT
BETERSCHAP
BETH
BETHABARA
BETHANKIT
BETHEL
BETHFLOWER
BETHINK
BETHINKING
BETHOUGHT
BETHROOT
BETHUMB
BETHUMP
BETHWACK
BETHYLID
BETID
BETIDE
BETIDED
BETIDING
BETIME
BETIMES
BETIS
BETISE
BETITLE
BETLE
BETOIL
BETOKEN
BETOKENED
BETOKENER
BETOKENING
BETON
BETONE
BETONGUE
BETONICA
BETONIES
BETONY
BETOOK
BETOSS
BETRAP
BETRAY
BETRAYAL
BETRAYED
BETRAYER
BETRAYING
BETRAYMENT
BETREND
BETRIM
BETROTH
BETROTHAL
BETROTHED
BETROTHING
BETROTHMENT
BETRUNK
BETRUST
BETS
BETSO
BETTED
BETTER
BETTERED
BETTERER
BETTERGATES
BETTERING
BETTERLY
BETTERMENT
BETTERMOST
BETTERNESS
BETTIES
BETTONG
BETTONGA
BETTOR
BETTY
BETULACEOUS
BETULIN
BETULINIC
BETULINOL
BETWEEN
BETWEENBRAIN
BETWEENITY
BETWEENMAID
BETWIXEN
BETWIXT
BEUDANITE
BEURRE
BEVARING
BEVATRON
BEVEL
BEVELED
BEVELER
BEVELING
BEVELLED
BEVELLER
BEVELLING
BEVER
BEVERAGE
BEVIES
BEVIL
BEVUE
BEVY
BEW
BEWAIL
BEWAILER
BEWAILING
BEWAILINGLY
BEWAKE
BEWARE
BEWARED
BEWARING
BEWED
BEWEEP
BEWEEPER
BEWEEPING
BEWEND
BEWEPT
BEWEST
BEWET
BEWHORE
BEWILDER
BEWILDERED
BEWILDEREDLY
BEWILDERING
BEWILDERMENT
BEWIT
BEWITCH
BEWITCHED
BEWITCHER
BEWITCHERY
BEWITCHING
BEWITCHINGLY
BEWITCHMENT
BEWITH
BEWONDER
BEWORK
BEWPERS
BEWRAP
BEWRAY
BEWRAYED
BEWRAYER
BEWRAYING
BEWRAYMENT
BEWREAK
BEY
BEYERITE
BEYLIC
BEYLICAL
BEYLIK
BEYOND
BEYRICHITE
BEZANT
BEZANTE
BEZANTEE
BEZANTY
BEZEL
BEZESTEEN
BEZETTA
BEZETTE
BEZIL
BEZIQUE
BEZOAR
BEZOARDIC
BEZONIAN
BEZZANT
BEZZLE
BEZZLED
BEZZLING
BEZZO
BHAGAT
BHAGAVAT
BHAGAVATA
BHAI
BHAIACHARA
BHAIYACHARA
BHAKTA
BHAKTI
BHALU
BHANDAR
BHANDARI
BHANG
BHANGI
BHARAL
BHARTI
BHAT
BHAVA
BHEESTIE
BHEESTY
BHIKSHU
BHISTI
BHISTIE
BHOKRA
BHOOSA
BHOY
BHUMIDAR
BHUNDER
BHUNGI
BHUNGINI
BHUSA
BHUT
BIABO
BIACETYL
BIACETYLENE
BIACUMINATE
BIACURU
BIAJAIBA
BIALATE
BIALLYL
BIALVEOLAR
BIALY
BIALYS
BIANCHITE
BIANCO
BIANGULAR
BIANGULATE

BIANGULATED
BIANGULOUS
BIANISIDINE
BIANNUAL
BIANNUALLY
BIARCHY
BIARCUATE
BIARCUATED
BIARTICULAR
BIARTICULATE
BIAS
BIASED
BIASES
BIASING
BIASSED
BIASSING
BIASTERIC
BIASWISE
BIATOMIC
BIAURICULAR
BIAURICULATE
BIAXAL
BIAXIAL
BIAXIALITY
BIAXIALLY
BIB
BIBACIOUS
BIBACITY
BIBASIC
BIBATION
BIBB
BIBBED
BIBBER
BIBBING
BIBBLE
BIBBLED
BIBBLER
BIBBLING
BIBBONS
BIBBY
BIBCOCK
BIBELOT
BIBENZYL
BIBERON
BIBI
BIBIONID
BIBIRI
BIBIRU
BIBITORY
BIBLE
BIBLICAL
BIBLIOCLASM
BIBLIOCLAST
BIBLIOFILM
BIBLIOGNOST
BIBLIOGONY
BIBLIOGRAPH
BIBLIOGRAPHIES
BIBLIOGRAPHY
BIBLIOKLEPT
BIBLIOLATER
BIBLIOLATRY
BIBLIOLOGIST
BIBLIOLOGY
BIBLIOMANCY
BIBLIOMANE
BIBLIOMANIA
BIBLIOMANIAC
BIBLIOMANIAN
BIBLIOPEGIC
BIBLIOPEGIST
BIBLIOPEGY
BIBLIOPHAGIC
BIBLIOPHIL
BIBLIOPHILE
BIBLIOPHILIC
BIBLIOPHOBIA
BIBLIOPOLAR
BIBLIOPOLE
BIBLIOPOLERY
BIBLIOPOLIC
BIBLIOPOLISM
BIBLIOPOLIST
BIBLIOPOLY
BIBLIOSOPH
BIBLIOTAPHIC
BIBLIOTHEC
BIBLIOTHECA
BIBLIOTHECAL
BIBLIOTHEKE
BIBLIOTHETIC
BIBLOS
BIBLUS
BIBULOSITY
BIBULOUS
BIBULOUSLY
BIBULOUSNESS
BICALCARATE
BICALVOUS
BICAMERAL
BICAMERIST
BICAPITATE
BICAPSULAR
BICARB
BICARBONATE
BICARBURETED
BICARBURETTED
BICARINATE
BICARPELLARY
BICARPELLATE
BICAUDAL
BICAUDATE
BICCHED
BICE
BICELLULAR
BICENTENARY
BICENTENNIAL
BICEPHALIC
BICEPHALOUS
BICEPS
BICEPSES
BICHLORIDE
BICHO
BICHORD
BICHOS
BICHROMATE
BICHROMATIC
BICHROME
BICHROMIC
BICHY
BICILIATE
BICILIATED
BICIPITAL
BICIPITOUS
BICIRCULAR
BICK
BICKER
BICKERED
BICKERER
BICKERING
BICKERN
BICKIRON
BICLINIA
BICLINIUM
BICOLLATERAL
BICOLLIGATE
BICOLOR
BICOLORED
BICOLOROUS
BICOLOUR
BICOLOURED
BICOLOUROUS
BICONCAVE
BICONCAVITY
BICONE
BICONIC
BICONICAL
BICONICALLY
BICONJUGATE
BICONVEX
BICORN
BICORNE
BICORNED
BICORNUATE
BICORNUOUS
BICORPORAL
BICORPORATE
BICORPOREAL
BICOSTATE
BICRENATE
BICROFARAD
BICRON
BICRURAL
BICULTURAL
BICURSAL
BICUSPID
BICUSPIDAL
BICUSPIDATE
BICYANIDE
BICYCLE
BICYCLED
BICYCLER
BICYCLIC
BICYCLICAL
BICYCLING
BICYCLISM
BICYCLIST
BICYCLO
BICYCULAR
BID
BIDAR
BIDARKA
BIDARKEE
BIDCOCK
BIDDABLE
BIDDABLENESS
BIDDABLY
BIDDANCE
BIDDEN
BIDDER
BIDDERY
BIDDIE
BIDDIES
BIDDING
BIDDY
BIDE
BIDED
BIDENE
BIDENT
BIDENTAL
BIDENTALIA
BIDENTATE
BIDER
BIDERY
BIDET
BIDI
BIDIGITATE
BIDING
BIDREE
BIDRI
BIDRY
BIDSTAND
BIDUOUS
BIEBERITE
BIEL
BIELBY
BIELD
BIELDY
BIELENITE
BIEN
BIENLY
BIENNE
BIENNESS
BIENNIA
BIENNIAL
BIENNIALLY
BIENNIUM
BIENSEANCE
BIENVENU
BIER
BIESTINGS
BIETLE
BIFACE
BIFACIAL
BIFANGED
BIFARA
BIFARIOUS
BIFARIOUSLY
BIFER
BIFEROUS
BIFF
BIFFIN
BIFFY
BIFID
BIFIDATE
BIFIDATED
BIFIDITY
BIFIDLY
BIFILAR
BIFILARLY
BIFISTULAR
BIFLABELLATE
BIFLAGELATE
BIFLECNODE
BIFLECTED
BIFLEX
BIFLORATE
BIFLOROUS
BIFLUORID
BIFLUORIDE
BIFOCAL
BIFOCALS
BIFOLD
BIFOLIA
BIFOLIATE
BIFOLIOLATE
BIFOLIUM
BIFOLLICULAR
BIFORATE
BIFORIN
BIFORINE
BIFORKED
BIFORM
BIFORMED
BIFORMITY
BIFRONT
BIFRONTAL
BIFRONTED
BIFURCAL
BIFURCATE
BIFURCATED
BIFURCATELY
BIFURCATING
BIFURCATION
BIFURCOUS
BIG
BIGA
BIGAMIC
BIGAMIST
BIGAMISTIC
BIGAMIZE
BIGAMOUS
BIGAMOUSLY
BIGAMY
BIGAN
BIGARADE
BIGAROON
BIGARREAU
BIGAS
BIGATE
BIGBLOOM
BIGBURY
BIGEMINAL
BIGEMINATE
BIGEMINATED
BIGENER
BIGENERIC
BIGENTIAL
BIGEYE
BIGG
BIGGED
BIGGEN
BIGGENED
BIGGENING
BIGGER
BIGGEST
BIGGETY
BIGGIE
BIGGIN
BIGGING
BIGGISH
BIGGITY
BIGGONET
BIGHA
BIGHEAD
BIGHEARTED
BIGHORN
BIGHORNS
BIGHT
BIGHTED
BIGHTING
BIGHTS
BIGLY
BIGMITT
BIGMOUTH
BIGMOUTHED
BIGNESS
BIGNONIA
BIGNONIAD
BIGNOU
BIGONIAC
BIGONIAL
BIGOT
BIGOTED
BIGOTEDLY
BIGOTHERO
BIGOTRIES
BIGOTRY
BIGOTTY
BIGRAM
BIGROOT
BIGTHATCH
BIGUANIDE
BIGUTTATE
BIGUTTULATE
BIGWIG
BIGWIGGED
BIGWIGGERY
BIGWIGGISM
BIHOURLY
BIJA
BIJASAL
BIJOU
BIJOUTERIE
BIJOUX
BIJUGATE
BIJUGOUS
BIJUGULAR
BIJWONER
BIKE
BIKER
BIKH
BIKIE
BIKINI
BIKKURIM

BILABE
BILABIAL
BILABIATE
BILALO
BILAMINAR
BILAMINATE
BILAMINATED
BILAN
BILAND
BILANDER
BILATERAL
BILATERALISM
BILATERALITY
BILATERALLY
BILBERRIES
BILBERRY
BILBI
BILBIE
BILBO
BILBOA
BILBOES
BILBOQUET
BILBY
BILCH
BILCOCK
BILDAR
BILDER
BILDERS
BILE
BILECTION
BILECTIONED
BILESTONE
BILEVE
BILGE
BILGED
BILGING
BILGY
BILHARZIAL
BILHARZIASIS
BILHARZIC
BILHARZIOSIS
BILIARY
BILIATE
BILIATION
BILIC
BILICYANIN
BILIFACTION
BILIFEROUS
BILIFICATION
BILIFUSCIN
BILIFY
BILIHUMIN
BILIMBI
BILIMBING
BILIMBIS
BILIMENT
BILINEAR
BILINGUAL
BILINGUALISM
BILINGUALLY
BILINGUIST
BILINIGRIN
BILINITE
BILIOUS
BILIOUSLY
BILIOUSNESS
BILIPRASIN
BILIPYRRHIN
BILIRUBIN
BILIRUBINIC
BILITERAL
BILITERALISM
BILITH
BILITHON
BILIVERDIN
BILK
BILKER
BILKIS
BILL
BILLABLE
BILLABONG
BILLAGE
BILLBACK
BILLBOARD
BILLBROKING
BILLBUG
BILLED
BILLER
BILLET
BILLETED
BILLETER
BILLETHEAD
BILLETING
BILLETTE
BILLETTY
BILLETY
BILLFISH
BILLFISHES
BILLFOLD
BILLHEAD
BILLHEADING
BILLHOLDER
BILLHOOK
BILLIAN
BILLIARD
BILLIARDIST
BILLIARDLY
BILLIARDS
BILLIE
BILLIES
BILLIKIN
BILLING
BILLINGS
BILLINGSGATE
BILLION
BILLIONAIRE
BILLIONISM
BILLIONTH
BILLMAN
BILLMEN
BILLON
BILLOT
BILLOW
BILLOWED
BILLOWIER
BILLOWIEST
BILLOWINESS
BILLOWING
BILLOWY
BILLPOSTER
BILLPOSTING
BILLS
BILLSTICKER
BILLSTICKING
BILLY
BILLYBOY
BILLYCAN
BILLYCOCK
BILLYER
BILLYHOOD
BILLYWIX
BILO
BILOBATE
BILOBATED
BILOBE
BILOBED
BILOBULAR
BILOCATION
BILOCELLATE
BILOCULAR
BILOCULATE
BILOCULINE
BILOPHODONT
BILOS
BILSH
BILSTED
BILTONG
BILTONGUE
BIMA
BIMACULATE
BIMACULATED
BIMAH
BIMANAL
BIMANE
BIMANOUS
BIMANUAL
BIMANUALLY
BIMARINE
BIMASTIC
BIMASTISM
BIMASTOID
BIMAXILLARY
BIMBASHI
BIMBIL
BIMBO
BIMEBY
BIMENSAL
BIMESTRIAL
BIMETAL
BIMETALISM
BIMETALLIC
BIMETALLIST
BIMILLENARY
BIMILLENIUM
BIMODAL
BIMODALITY
BIMOLECULAR
BIMONG
BIMONTHLY
BIMORPH
BIMOTORED
BIMOTORS
BIMUSCULAR
BIN
BINA
BINAL
BINAPTHYL
BINARIES
BINARY
BINATE
BINATELY
BINATION
BINAURAL
BINBASHI
BIND
BINDER
BINDERIES
BINDERY
BINDHEIMITE
BINDING
BINDINGLY
BINDINGNESS
BINDLE
BINDOREE
BINDWEB
BINDWEED
BINDWITH
BINDWOOD
BINE
BINERVATE
BINEWEED
BING
BINGE
BINGEE
BINGEY
BINGEYS
BINGHI
BINGIES
BINGLE
BINGO
BINGY
BINH
BINI
BINIOU
BINIT
BINK
BINMAN
BINMEN
BINNA
BINNACLE
BINNED
BINNING
BINNITE
BINNOGUE
BINNY
BINO
BINOCLE
BINOCULAR
BINOCULARITY
BINOCULARLY
BINOCULARS
BINOCULATE
BINODAL
BINODE
BINOMEN
BINOMIAL
BINOMIALISM
BINOMIALLY
BINOMINATED
BINOMINOUS
BINORMAL
BINOTIC
BINOTONOUS
BINOXALATE
BINOXIDE
BINT
BINTANGOR
BINTURONG
BINUCLEAR
BINUCLEATE
BINUCLEATED
BINUCLEOLATE
BINUKAU
BIOASSAY
BIOBLAST
BIOBLASTIC
BIOCATALYST
BIOCELLATE
BIOCENTRIC
BIOCHEMIC
BIOCHEMICAL
BIOCHEMICALLY
BIOCHEMICS
BIOCHEMIST
BIOCHEMISTRY
BIOCHEMY
BIOCHORE
BIOCHRON
BIOCIDE
BIOCOENOSE
BIOCOENOSES
BIOCOENOSIS
BIOCOENOTIC
BIOCYCLE
BIODYNAMIC
BIODYNAMICAL
BIODYNAMICS
BIOFLAVONOID
BIOGEN
BIOGENASE
BIOGENESIS
BIOGENESIST
BIOGENETIC
BIOGENETICAL
BIOGENOUS
BIOGENY
BIOGEOGRAPHY
BIOGNOSIS
BIOGRAPH
BIOGRAPHEE
BIOGRAPHER
BIOGRAPHIC
BIOGRAPHICAL
BIOGRAPHIES
BIOGRAPHIST
BIOGRAPHIZE
BIOGRAPHY
BIOHERM
BIOLITE
BIOLITH
BIOLOGIC
BIOLOGICAL
BIOLOGICALLY
BIOLOGIES
BIOLOGISM
BIOLOGIST
BIOLOGIZE
BIOLOGY
BIOLYSIS
BIOLYTIC
BIOME
BIOMETER
BIOMETRIC
BIOMETRICAL
BIOMETRICIAN
BIOMETRICIST
BIOMETRICS
BIOMETRY
BION
BIONERGY
BIONICS
BIONOMIC
BIONOMICAL
BIONOMICS
BIONOMIST
BIONOMY
BIONT
BIONTIC
BIOPHAGISM
BIOPHAGOUS
BIOPHAGY
BIOPHILOUS
BIOPHOR
BIOPHORE
BIOPHYSICAL
BIOPHYSICIST
BIOPHYSICS
BIOPHYTE
BIOPIC
BIOPLASM
BIOPLASMIC
BIOPLAST
BIOPLASTIC
BIOPOESIS
BIOPOTENTIAL
BIOPSIC
BIOPSIES
BIOPSY
BIOPSYCHIC
BIOPSYCHICAL
BIOPYRIBOLE
BIORDINAL
BIORGAN
BIOS
BIOSCOPE
BIOSCOPIC
BIOSCOPY
BIOSE
BIOSESTON
BIOSIS
BIOSOCIAL
BIOSOME
BIOSPHERE
BIOSTATIC
BIOSTATICAL

BIOSTATICS
BIOSTERIN
BIOSTEROL
BIOSTROME
BIOSYNTHESIS
BIOSYNTHETIC
BIOTA
BIOTAXY
BIOTIC
BIOTICAL
BIOTICS
BIOTIN
BIOTITE
BIOTITIC
BIOTOME
BIOTOMY
BIOTOPE
BIOTRON
BIOTYPE
BIOTYPIC
BIOZONE
BIPACK
BIPALEOLATE
BIPALMATE
BIPARASITIC
BIPARENTAL
BIPARIETAL
BIPAROUS
BIPARTED
BIPARTIBLE
BIPARTIENT
BIPARTILE
BIPARTISAN
BIPARTITE
BIPARTITELY
BIPARTITION
BIPECTINATE
BIPECTINATED
BIPED
BIPEDALITY
BIPELTATE
BIPENNIFORM
BIPETALOUS
BIPHASE
BIPHASIC
BIPHENOL
BIPHENYL
BIPHENYLENE
BIPINNARIA
BIPINNATE
BIPINNATED
BIPINNATELY
BIPLANAR
BIPLANE
BIPLICATE
BIPLICITY
BIPLOSION
BIPOD
BIPOLAR
BIPOLARITY
BIPOROSE
BIPOROUS
BIPRISM
BIPRONG
BIPROPELLANT
BIPUNCTAL
BIPUNCTATE
BIPUNCTUAL
BIPUPILLATE
BIPYRAMID
BIPYRAMIDAL
BIPYRIDINE
BIPYRIDYL
BIQUADRANTAL
BIQUADRATE
BIQUADRATIC
BIQUARTERLY
BIQUARTZ
BIQUINTILE
BIRADIAL
BIRADIATE
BIRADIATED
BIRAMOSE
BIRAMOUS
BIRATIONAL
BIRCH
BIRCHBARK
BIRCHEN
BIRCHES
BIRCHING
BIRCHMAN
BIRCHWOOD
BIRD
BIRDBANDER
BIRDBANDING
BIRDBATH
BIRDBERRY
BIRDBRAIN
BIRDCAGE
BIRDCALL
BIRDCLAPPER
BIRDEEN
BIRDER
BIRDEYE
BIRDGLUE
BIRDHOUSE
BIRDIE
BIRDIKIN
BIRDING
BIRDLIFE
BIRDLIME
BIRDLIMED
BIRDLIMING
BIRDLING
BIRDMAN
BIRDMEN
BIRDMOUTHED
BIRDNEST
BIRDS
BIRDSEED
BIRDSNEST
BIRDSONG
BIRDSTONE
BIRDWEED
BIRDWOMAN
BIRDY
BIREFRINGENT
BIREME
BIRETTA
BIRI
BIRIBA
BIRIMOSE
BIRK
BIRKEN
BIRKIE
BIRKREMITE
BIRKY
BIRL
BIRLE
BIRLER
BIRLING
BIRLINN
BIRMA
BIRN
BIRNE
BIRODO
BIROTATION
BIROTATORY
BIRR
BIRRED
BIRRING
BIRRUS
BIRSE
BIRSIT
BIRSLE
BIRSY
BIRTH
BIRTHBED
BIRTHDAY
BIRTHDOM
BIRTHING
BIRTHLAND
BIRTHLESS
BIRTHMARK
BIRTHMATE
BIRTHNIGHT
BIRTHPLACE
BIRTHRATE
BIRTHRIGHT
BIRTHROOT
BIRTHSTONE
BIRTHSTOOL
BIRTHWORT
BIRTHY
BIS
BISA
BISABOL
BISACROMIAL
BISAGRE
BISALT
BISAXILLARY
BISBEEITE
BISCAYEN
BISCHOFITE
BISCOTIN
BISCUIT
BISCUITING
BISCUITMAKER
BISCUITROOT
BISCUITS
BISE
BISECT
BISECTION
BISECTIONAL
BISECTOR
BISECTRICES
BISECTRIX
BISEGMENT
BISERIAL
BISERIALLY
BISERRATE
BISETOSE
BISETOUS
BISEXED
BISEXT
BISEXUAL
BISEXUALISM
BISEXUALITY
BISEXUALLY
BISEXUOUS
BISHOP
BISHOPDOM
BISHOPED
BISHOPESS
BISHOPING
BISHOPRIC
BISHOPSCAP
BISILIAC
BISILICATE
BISIMINE
BISINUATE
BISINUATION
BISISCHIADIC
BISISCHIATIC
BISK
BISKOP
BISMAR
BISMARINE
BISME
BISMER
BISMERPUND
BISMILLAH
BISMITE
BISMUTH
BISMUTHAL
BISMUTHATE
BISMUTHIC
BISMUTHIDE
BISMUTHINE
BISMUTHINITE
BISMUTHITE
BISMUTHOUS
BISMUTHYL
BISMUTITE
BISNAGA
BISON
BISONANT
BISONTINE
BISPINOSE
BISPINOUS
BISPORE
BISPOROUS
BISQUE
BISQUETTE
BISSABOL
BISSEXT
BISSEXTILE
BISSON
BIST
BISTER
BISTERED
BISTETRAZOLE
BISTI
BISTIPULAR
BISTIPULATE
BISTIPULED
BISTORT
BISTOURIES
BISTOURNAGE
BISTOURY
BISTRATAL
BISTRATOSE
BISTRE
BISTRED
BISTRIATE
BISTRIAZOLE
BISTRO
BISUBSTITUTED
BISULCATE
BISULCATED
BISULFATE
BISULFIDE
BISULFITE
BISULPHATE
BISULPHIDE
BISULPHITE
BISYLLABIC
BISYLLABISM
BISYMMETRIC
BISYMMETRY
BIT
BITABLE
BITANGENT
BITANGENTIAL
BITANHOL
BITARTRATE
BITBRACE
BITCH
BITCHERY
BITCHIER
BITCHIEST
BITCHY
BITE
BITEABLE
BITECHE
BITED
BITEMPORAL
BITEN
BITER
BITERNATE
BITERNATELY
BITEWING
BITHEISM
BITI
BITING
BITINGLY
BITINGNESS
BITO
BITOLYL
BITONALITY
BITORE
BITREADLE
BITRIPARTITE
BITRIPINNATIFID
BITRISEPTATE
BITS
BITSTALK
BITSTOCK
BITSY
BITT
BITTACLE
BITTE
BITTED
BITTEN
BITTER
BITTERBARK
BITTERBLAIN
BITTERBLOOM
BITTERBUR
BITTERBUSH
BITTERER
BITTEREST
BITTERHEAD
BITTERISH
BITTERISHNESS
BITTERLESS
BITTERLING
BITTERLY
BITTERN
BITTERNESS
BITTERNS
BITTERNUT
BITTERROOT
BITTERS
BITTERSWEET
BITTERWEED
BITTERWORM
BITTERWORT
BITTHEAD
BITTIE
BITTING
BITTOCK
BITTY
BITUBERCULAR
BITULITHIC
BITUME
BITUMED
BITUMEN
BITUMINIZE
BITUMINIZED
BITUMINIZING
BITUMINOID
BITUMINOUS
BITWISE
BITYITE
BITYPIC
BIUNE
BIUNIAL
BIUNITY
BIURATE
BIUREA
BIURET
BIVALENCE
BIVALENCY
BIVALENT

BIVALVE
BIVALVED
BIVALVES
BIVALVULAR
BIVARIANT
BIVASCULAR
BIVECTOR
BIVENTER
BIVENTRAL
BIVERBAL
BIVIOUS
BIVITTATE
BIVOCAL
BIVOCALIZED
BIVOLUMINOUS
BIVOUAC
BIVOUACKED
BIVOUACKING
BIWA
BIWEEKLY
BIXACEOUS
BIXBYITE
BIXIN
BIYEARLY
BIZ
BIZARDITE
BIZARRE
BIZARRELY
BIZARRENESS
BIZARRERIE
BIZE
BIZLE
BIZYGOMATIC
BIZZARRO
BLAA
BLAASOP
BLAB
BLABBED
BLABBER
BLABBERER
BLABBERMOUTH
BLABBING
BLACK
BLACKACRE
BLACKAMOOR
BLACKARM
BLACKBACK
BLACKBALL
BLACKBALLER
BLACKBERRIES
BLACKBERRY
BLACKBIRD
BLACKBIRDER
BLACKBIRDING
BLACKBOARD
BLACKBOY
BLACKBREAST
BLACKBRUSH
BLACKBUSH
BLACKBUTT
BLACKCAP
BLACKCOAT
BLACKCOCK
BLACKDAMP
BLACKEN
BLACKENED
BLACKENER
BLACKENING
BLACKER
BLACKEST
BLACKEY
BLACKEYE
BLACKEYES
BLACKFACE
BLACKFELLOW
BLACKFELLOWS
BLACKFIN
BLACKFIRE
BLACKFISH
BLACKFISHER
BLACKFISHES
BLACKFISHING
BLACKFLY
BLACKGUARD
BLACKGUARDISM
BLACKGUARDLY
BLACKGUARDRY
BLACKGUM
BLACKHEAD
BLACKHEADS
BLACKHEART
BLACKHEARTED
BLACKIE
BLACKIES
BLACKING
BLACKISH
BLACKISHLY
BLACKISHNESS
BLACKJACK
BLACKLAND
BLACKLEAD
BLACKLEG
BLACKLIST
BLACKLY
BLACKMAIL
BLACKMAILER
BLACKMAN
BLACKNEB
BLACKNECK
BLACKNESS
BLACKNOB
BLACKOUT
BLACKPOLL
BLACKPOT
BLACKPRINT
BLACKROOT
BLACKS
BLACKSHIRTED
BLACKSMITH
BLACKSNAKE
BLACKSTICK
BLACKSTRAP
BLACKTAIL
BLACKTHORN
BLACKTONGUE
BLACKTOP
BLACKTREE
BLACKWASH
BLACKWASHER
BLACKWATER
BLACKWEED
BLACKWOOD
BLACKWORK
BLACKWORT
BLACKY
BLAD
BLADDER
BLADDERET
BLADDERNOSE
BLADDERNUT
BLADDERSEED
BLADDERWEED
BLADDERWORT
BLADDERWRACK
BLADDERY
BLADE
BLADEBONE
BLADED
BLADELET
BLADER
BLADES
BLADESMITH
BLADING
BLADY
BLADYGRASS
BLAE
BLAEBERRY
BLAEWORT
BLAFF
BLAFFERT
BLAFLUM
BLAGGARD
BLAGUE
BLAH
BLAHLAUT
BLAIK
BLAIN
BLAIR
BLAIRMORITE
BLAKE
BLAKEBERYED
BLAKEITE
BLAMABLE
BLAMABLENESS
BLAMABLY
BLAME
BLAMEABLE
BLAMED
BLAMEFUL
BLAMEFULLY
BLAMEFULNESS
BLAMELESS
BLAMELESSLY
BLAMER
BLAMEWORTHY
BLAMING
BLAMINGLY
BLANC
BLANCA
BLANCARD
BLANCH
BLANCHED
BLANCHER
BLANCHING
BLANCHINGLY
BLANCMANGE
BLANCMANGER
BLANCO
BLAND
BLANDA
BLANDISH
BLANDISHER
BLANDISHING
BLANDISHMENT
BLANDLY
BLANDNESS
BLANK
BLANKBOOK
BLANKED
BLANKEEL
BLANKET
BLANKETED
BLANKETEER
BLANKETING
BLANKETRY
BLANKETY
BLANKING
BLANKISH
BLANKLY
BLANKNESS
BLANKS
BLANKY
BLANQUETTE
BLANQUILLO
BLARE
BLARED
BLARING
BLARNEY
BLARNEYER
BLART
BLAS
BLASE
BLASH
BLASHY
BLASPHEME
BLASPHEMED
BLASPHEMER
BLASPHEMIES
BLASPHEMING
BLASPHEMOUS
BLASPHEMY
BLAST
BLASTAEA
BLASTED
BLASTEMA
BLASTEMAL
BLASTEMATA
BLASTEMATIC
BLASTEMIC
BLASTER
BLASTHOLE
BLASTID
BLASTIE
BLASTING
BLASTMAN
BLASTMENT
BLASTOCELE
BLASTOCHEME
BLASTOCHYLE
BLASTOCOLLA
BLASTOCYST
BLASTOCYTE
BLASTODERM
BLASTODERMIC
BLASTODISC
BLASTODISK
BLASTOFF
BLASTOGENIC
BLASTOGENY
BLASTOID
BLASTOMA
BLASTOMATA
BLASTOMERE
BLASTOMERIC
BLASTOMYCETE
BLASTOPHITIC
BLASTOPHORAL
BLASTOPHORE
BLASTOPHORIC
BLASTOPORAL
BLASTOPORE
BLASTOPORIC
BLASTOSPHERE
BLASTOSTYLAR
BLASTOSTYLE
BLASTOZOOID
BLASTPLATE
BLASTULA
BLASTULAE
BLASTULAR
BLASTULATION
BLASTULE
BLASTY
BLAT
BLATANCY
BLATANT
BLATANTLY
BLATCH
BLATCHANG
BLATE
BLATELY
BLATENESS
BLATEROON
BLATHER
BLATHERER
BLATHERSKITE
BLATHERY
BLATIFORM
BLATJANG
BLATTA
BLATTED
BLATTER
BLATTERED
BLATTERER
BLATTERING
BLATTI
BLATTID
BLATTING
BLATTOID
BLAUBOK
BLAUBOKS
BLAVER
BLAW
BLAWORT
BLAY
BLAZE
BLAZED
BLAZER
BLAZES
BLAZING
BLAZON
BLAZONED
BLAZONER
BLAZONING
BLAZONMENT
BLAZONRY
BLAZY
BLEA
BLEACH
BLEACHED
BLEACHER
BLEACHERIES
BLEACHERITE
BLEACHERMAN
BLEACHERS
BLEACHERY
BLEACHFIELD
BLEACHHOUSE
BLEACHING
BLEACHMAN
BLEACHWORKS
BLEACHYARD
BLEAK
BLEAKISH
BLEAKLY
BLEAKNESS
BLEAKS
BLEAKY
BLEAR
BLEARED
BLEAREDNESS
BLEAREYE
BLEARIER
BLEARIEST
BLEARILY
BLEARINESS
BLEARY
BLEAT
BLEATER
BLEATING
BLEATINGLY
BLEAUNT
BLEB
BLEBBY
BLECHNOID
BLECK
BLED
BLEE
BLEED
BLEEDER
BLEEDING
BLEEKBOK
BLEERY
BLEEZE
BLEEZY

BLEIR
BLELLUM
BLEMISH
BLEMISHED
BLEMISHER
BLENCH
BLENCHER
BLENCHING
BLENCHINGLY
BLEND
BLENDCORN
BLENDE
BLENDED
BLENDER
BLENDING
BLENDURE
BLENK
BLENNIES
BLENNIID
BLENNIIFORM
BLENNIOID
BLENNORRHEA
BLENNORRHOEA
BLENNY
BLENS
BLENT
BLEO
BLEPHARA
BLEPHARAL
BLEPHARISM
BLEPHARITIS
BLEPHAROPLAST
BLESBOK
BLESBOKS
BLESBUCK
BLESMOL
BLESS
BLESSE
BLESSED
BLESSEDLY
BLESSEDNESS
BLESSER
BLESSING
BLESSINGLY
BLEST
BLET
BLETHE
BLETHER
BLETHERATION
BLETHERS
BLETTED
BLETTING
BLEU
BLEW
BLEWITS
BLIAUT
BLIBE
BLICK
BLICKEY
BLICKEYS
BLICKIE
BLICKIES
BLICKY
BLIGHT
BLIGHTBIRD
BLIGHTED
BLIGHTER
BLIGHTING
BLIGHTINGLY
BLIGHTY
BLIJVER
BLIMBING
BLIMP
BLIMY
BLIN
BLIND
BLINDAGE
BLINDBALL
BLINDED
BLINDEDLY
BLINDER
BLINDEST
BLINDEYES
BLINDFAST
BLINDFISH
BLINDFOLD
BLINDFOLDED
BLINDFOLDER
BLINDFOLDLY
BLINDING
BLINDINGLY
BLINDISM
BLINDLY
BLINDNESS
BLINDSTITCH
BLINDSTORIES
BLINDSTORY
BLINDWEED
BLINDWORM
BLINE
BLINGER
BLINK
BLINKARD
BLINKED
BLINKER
BLINKING
BLINKINGLY
BLINKS
BLINKY
BLINTER
BLINTZ
BLINTZE
BLIP
BLISS
BLISSFUL
BLISSFULLY
BLISSFULNESS
BLISSOM
BLIST
BLISTER
BLISTERED
BLISTERING
BLISTEROUS
BLISTERS
BLISTERWEED
BLISTERWORT
BLISTERY
BLITE
BLITHE
BLITHEFUL
BLITHEFULLY
BLITHELY
BLITHEMEAT
BLITHEN
BLITHENESS
BLITHER
BLITHERED
BLITHERING
BLITHESOME
BLITHESOMELY
BLITTER
BLITZ
BLIZZ
BLIZZARD
BLIZZARDLY
BLIZZARDOUS
BLIZZARDY
BLO
BLOAK
BLOAT
BLOATED
BLOATEDNESS
BLOATER
BLOATING
BLOB
BLOBBED
BLOBBER
BLOBBIER
BLOBBIEST
BLOBBING
BLOBBY
BLOC
BLOCAGE
BLOCK
BLOCKADE
BLOCKADED
BLOCKADER
BLOCKADING
BLOCKAGE
BLOCKBUSTER
BLOCKED
BLOCKER
BLOCKHEAD
BLOCKHEADED
BLOCKHEADISM
BLOCKHOLE
BLOCKHOLER
BLOCKHOUSE
BLOCKIER
BLOCKIEST
BLOCKING
BLOCKISH
BLOCKISHLY
BLOCKISHNESS
BLOCKLAYER
BLOCKLIKE
BLOCKLINE
BLOCKMAKER
BLOCKMAKING
BLOCKMAN
BLOCKOUT
BLOCKPATE
BLOCKS
BLOCKSHIP
BLOCKY
BLODE
BLODITE
BLOEDITE
BLOKE
BLOLLY
BLOND
BLONDE
BLONDENESS
BLONDINE
BLONDNESS
BLOO
BLOOD
BLOODALP
BLOODBERRY
BLOODBIRD
BLOODCURDLER
BLOODCURDLING
BLOODED
BLOODFIN
BLOODFLOWER
BLOODGUILT
BLOODGUILTY
BLOODHOUND
BLOODIED
BLOODIER
BLOODIEST
BLOODILY
BLOODINESS
BLOODING
BLOODLEAF
BLOODLESS
BLOODLESSLY
BLOODLETTER
BLOODLETTING
BLOODLINE
BLOODMOBILE
BLOODMONGER
BLOODNOUN
BLOODRIPE
BLOODROOT
BLOODSHED
BLOODSHEDDER
BLOODSHOT
BLOODSHOTTEN
BLOODSPILLER
BLOODSPILLING
BLOODSTAIN
BLOODSTAINED
BLOODSTANCH
BLOODSTOCK
BLOODSTONE
BLOODSUCK
BLOODSUCKER
BLOODSUCKING
BLOODTHIRST
BLOODTHIRSTER
BLOODTHIRSTY
BLOODWEED
BLOODWIT
BLOODWITE
BLOODWOOD
BLOODWORM
BLOODWORT
BLOODY
BLOODYBONES
BLOODYING
BLOOEY
BLOOIE
BLOOM
BLOOMAGE
BLOOMER
BLOOMERIES
BLOOMERS
BLOOMERY
BLOOMFELL
BLOOMING
BLOOMINGLY
BLOOMINGNESS
BLOOMY
BLOOP
BLOOPER
BLOOPING
BLOOTH
BLORE
BLOSMY
BLOSSOM
BLOSSOMBILL
BLOSSOMED
BLOSSOMING
BLOSSOMLESS
BLOSSOMRY
BLOSSOMS
BLOSSOMY
BLOT
BLOTCH
BLOTCHED
BLOTCHIER
BLOTCHIEST
BLOTCHINESS
BLOTCHING
BLOTCHY
BLOTE
BLOTLESS
BLOTTED
BLOTTER
BLOTTESQUE
BLOTTESQUELY
BLOTTING
BLOTTO
BLOTTY
BLOUSE
BLOUSED
BLOUSELIKE
BLOUSING
BLOUSY
BLOUT
BLOVIATE
BLOW
BLOWBACK
BLOWBALL
BLOWBY
BLOWBYS
BLOWCASE
BLOWDOWN
BLOWEN
BLOWER
BLOWFISH
BLOWFLIES
BLOWFLY
BLOWGUN
BLOWHARD
BLOWHOLE
BLOWIER
BLOWIEST
BLOWINESS
BLOWING
BLOWIRON
BLOWLAMP
BLOWLINE
BLOWN
BLOWOFF
BLOWOUT
BLOWPIPE
BLOWPIT
BLOWPOINT
BLOWPROOF
BLOWS
BLOWSPRAY
BLOWSY
BLOWTH
BLOWTORCH
BLOWTUBE
BLOWUP
BLOWY
BLOWZE
BLOWZED
BLOWZIER
BLOWZIEST
BLOWZING
BLOWZY
BLUB
BLUBBED
BLUBBER
BLUBBERED
BLUBBERER
BLUBBERING
BLUBBERMAN
BLUBBERY
BLUBBING
BLUCHER
BLUDE
BLUDGE
BLUDGEON
BLUDGEONED
BLUDGEONEER
BLUDGEONER
BLUDGER
BLUE
BLUEBACK
BLUEBALL
BLUEBEAD
BLUEBELL
BLUEBELLED
BLUEBERRIES
BLUEBERRY
BLUEBILL
BLUEBIRD
BLUEBLAW
BLUEBLOOD
BLUEBLOSSOM

BLUEBONNET
BLUEBOOK
BLUEBOTTLE
BLUEBREAST
BLUEBUCK
BLUEBUSH
BLUEBUTTON
BLUECAP
BLUECOAT
BLUECUP
BLUECURLS
BLUED
BLUEFIN
BLUEFISH
BLUEFISHES
BLUEGILL
BLUEGOWN
BLUEGRASS
BLUEGUM
BLUEHEARTS
BLUEING
BLUEISH
BLUEJACK
BLUEJACKET
BLUEJOINT
BLUELEGS
BLUELINE
BLUENESS
BLUENOSE
BLUENOSED
BLUEPOINT
BLUEPRINT
BLUEPRINTER
BLUER
BLUES
BLUESIDES
BLUEST
BLUESTEM
BLUESTOCKING
BLUESTONE
BLUESTONER
BLUET
BLUETICK
BLUETONGUE
BLUETOP
BLUETOPS
BLUEWEED
BLUEWING
BLUEWOOD
BLUEY
BLUEYS
BLUFF
BLUFFED
BLUFFER
BLUFFING
BLUFFLY
BLUFFNESS
BLUFFY
BLUFTER
BLUGGY
BLUID
BLUING
BLUISH
BLUISHNESS
BLUISNESS
BLUME
BLUMED
BLUMING
BLUNDER
BLUNDERBUSS
BLUNDERED
BLUNDERER
BLUNDERHEAD
BLUNDERING
BLUNDERINGLY
BLUNGE
BLUNGED
BLUNGER
BLUNGING
BLUNK
BLUNKER
BLUNKET
BLUNKS
BLUNT
BLUNTED
BLUNTER
BLUNTIE
BLUNTISH
BLUNTISHNESS
BLUNTLY
BLUNTNESS
BLUP
BLUR
BLURB
BLURBIST
BLURRED
BLURREDNESS
BLURRER
BLURRING
BLURRY
BLURT
BLUSH
BLUSHED
BLUSHER
BLUSHET
BLUSHFUL
BLUSHFULLY
BLUSHFULNESS
BLUSHINESS
BLUSHING
BLUSHINGLY
BLUSHT
BLUSHWORT
BLUSHY
BLUSTER
BLUSTERATION
BLUSTERED
BLUSTERER
BLUSTERING
BLUSTERINGLY
BLUSTEROUS
BLUSTEROUSLY
BLUSTERY
BLY
BLYPE
BO
BOA
BOAR
BOARD
BOARDED
BOARDER
BOARDING
BOARDINGHOUSE
BOARDLY
BOARDMAN
BOARDS
BOARDWALK
BOARDY
BOARFISH
BOARFISHES
BOARHOUND
BOARISH
BOARISHLY
BOARISHNESS
BOARS
BOART
BOARWOOD
BOAS
BOAST
BOASTER
BOASTFUL
BOASTFULLY
BOASTFULNESS
BOASTING
BOASTINGLY
BOAT
BOATABLE
BOATAGE
BOATBILL
BOATBUILDER
BOATBUILDING
BOATER
BOATHOOK
BOATHOUSE
BOATING
BOATION
BOATKEEPER
BOATLIP
BOATLOAD
BOATLOADER
BOATLOADING
BOATMAN
BOATMASTER
BOATMEN
BOATOWNER
BOATS
BOATSETTER
BOATSHOP
BOATSIDE
BOATSWAIN
BOATTAIL
BOATWRIGHT
BOB
BOBA
BOBAC
BOBACHE
BOBACHEE
BOBANCE
BOBBED
BOBBEJAAN
BOBBER
BOBBERIES
BOBBERY
BOBBIE
BOBBIES
BOBBIN
BOBBINER
BOBBINET
BOBBING
BOBBINS
BOBBISH
BOBBISHLY
BOBBLE
BOBBLED
BOBBLING
BOBBY
BOBBYSOXER
BOBCAT
BOBCATS
BOBCOAT
BOBECHE
BOBFLIES
BOBFLY
BOBIERRITE
BOBIZATION
BOBJEROM
BOBLET
BOBO
BOBOLINK
BOBOOTI
BOBOTEE
BOBOTIE
BOBSLED
BOBSLEDDED
BOBSLEDDING
BOBSLEIGH
BOBSTAY
BOBTAIL
BOBTAILED
BOBWHITE
BOBWOOD
BOCA
BOCACCIO
BOCAGE
BOCAL
BOCAN
BOCARDO
BOCASINE
BOCCA
BOCCALE
BOCCARELLA
BOCCARO
BOCCE
BOCCIE
BOCCONIA
BOCE
BOCHE
BOCHER
BOCHISM
BOCHUR
BOCK
BOCKEREL
BOCKERET
BOCKING
BOCO
BOCON
BOCOR
BOCOY
BOD
BODACH
BODACIOUS
BODACIOUSLY
BODAI
BODDAGH
BODDLE
BODE
BODED
BODEFUL
BODEGA
BODEGON
BODEMENT
BODEN
BODER
BODEWASH
BODEWORD
BODGE
BODGER
BODGERY
BODHI
BODHISAT
BODHISATTVA
BODHISATTWA
BODICE
BODICED
BODIED
BODIER
BODIERON
BODIES
BODIKIN
BODILESS
BODILESSNESS
BODILY
BODIMENT
BODING
BODINGLY
BODKIN
BODLE
BODOCK
BODONID
BODRAGE
BODSTICK
BODWORD
BODY
BODYBUILDER
BODYCHECK
BODYGUARD
BODYING
BODYKINS
BODYMAKER
BODYMAKING
BODYPLATE
BODYSHIRT
BODYWOOD
BODYWORK
BOE
BOEA
BOEG
BOEOTARCH
BOES
BOFF
BOFFIN
BOFFOLA
BOG
BOGA
BOGACH
BOGAN
BOGATYR
BOGBEAN
BOGBERRIES
BOGBERRY
BOGET
BOGEY
BOGEYMAN
BOGEYS
BOGFERN
BOGGARD
BOGGART
BOGGED
BOGGIER
BOGGIEST
BOGGIN
BOGGINESS
BOGGING
BOGGISH
BOGGISHNESS
BOGGLE
BOGGLEBO
BOGGLED
BOGGLER
BOGGLING
BOGGLISH
BOGGY
BOGHOLE
BOGIE
BOGIEMAN
BOGIER
BOGIES
BOGLAND
BOGLANDER
BOGLE
BOGLET
BOGMAN
BOGMIRE
BOGO
BOGONG
BOGOTANA
BOGSUCKER
BOGTROT
BOGTROTTER
BOGTROTTING
BOGUE
BOGUM
BOGUS
BOGWAY
BOGWOOD
BOGWORT
BOGY
BOH
BOHAWN
BOHEA
BOHIO
BOHMITE
BOHO
BOHOR
BOHORA

BOHUNK
BOID
BOIGID
BOIL
BOILDOWN
BOILED
BOILER
BOILERMAKER
BOILERY
BOILING
BOILOVER
BOILY
BOINA
BOIS
BOISSEAU
BOISSEAUX
BOIST
BOISTEROUS
BOISTEROUSLY
BOISTOUS
BOISTOUSLY
BOISTOUSNESS
BOITE
BOITHRIN
BOJITE
BOKADAM
BOKARD
BOKARK
BOKE
BOKO
BOKOM
BOLA
BOLAR
BOLAS
BOLBONAC
BOLD
BOLDEN
BOLDER
BOLDEST
BOLDFACE
BOLDHEARTED
BOLDIN
BOLDINE
BOLDLY
BOLDNESS
BOLDO
BOLDOINE
BOLE
BOLECTION
BOLECTIONED
BOLED
BOLEITE
BOLERO
BOLEROS
BOLETACEOUS
BOLETE
BOLETIC
BOLETUS
BOLEWEED
BOLEWORT
BOLIA
BOLICHE
BOLIDE
BOLIMBA
BOLIS
BOLITA
BOLIVAR
BOLIVARES
BOLIVARS
BOLIVIA
BOLIVIANO
BOLIVIANOS
BOLK
BOLL
BOLLARD
BOLLED
BOLLEN
BOLLER
BOLLIES
BOLLING
BOLLIX
BOLLIXED
BOLLIXING
BOLLO
BOLLOCK
BOLLWORM
BOLLY
BOLNE
BOLO
BOLOED
BOLOGNA
BOLOGRAPH
BOLOGRAPHIC
BOLOGRAPHY
BOLOING
BOLOISM
BOLOMAN
BOLOMEN
BOLOMETER
BOLOMETRIC
BOLONEY
BOLOROOT
BOLOS
BOLSA
BOLSHEVIK
BOLSHEVISM
BOLSHEVIST
BOLSHEVIZE
BOLSHEVIZED
BOLSHEVIZING
BOLSHIE
BOLSON
BOLSTER
BOLSTERED
BOLSTERER
BOLSTERING
BOLSTERWORK
BOLT
BOLTAGE
BOLTANT
BOLTEL
BOLTER
BOLTHEAD
BOLTHEADER
BOLTHEADING
BOLTI
BOLTIN
BOLTING
BOLTINGS
BOLTONIA
BOLTONITE
BOLTROPE
BOLTSTRAKE
BOLTY
BOLUS
BOLUSES
BOM
BOMA
BOMB
BOMBARD
BOMBARDE
BOMBARDELLE
BOMBARDER
BOMBARDIER
BOMBARDMAN
BOMBARDMEN
BOMBARDMENT
BOMBARDON
BOMBARDS
BOMBASINE
BOMBAST
BOMBASTER
BOMBASTIC
BOMBASTICAL
BOMBASTICALLY
BOMBASTRY
BOMBAZET
BOMBAZETTE
BOMBAZINE
BOMBE
BOMBED
BOMBER
BOMBERNICKEL
BOMBICCITE
BOMBILATE
BOMBILATION
BOMBILLA
BOMBINATE
BOMBINATION
BOMBLE
BOMBLINE
BOMBO
BOMBOLA
BOMBONNE
BOMBOUS
BOMBPROOF
BOMBS
BOMBSHELL
BOMBSIGHT
BOMBYCID
BOMBYCIFORM
BOMBYCINE
BOMBYX
BOMOS
BON
BONA
BONACE
BONACI
BONAGH
BONAGHT
BONAILIE
BONAIR
BONAIRE
BONAIRLY
BONAIRNESS
BONALLY
BONAMANO
BONANG
BONANZA
BONAO
BONASSUS
BONASUS
BONAUGHT
BONAV
BONAVIST
BONBON
BONBONNIERE
BONCE
BONCHIEF
BOND
BONDAGE
BONDAGER
BONDAR
BONDED
BONDER
BONDERMAN
BONDFOLK
BONDHOLDER
BONDHOLDING
BONDIEUSERIE
BONDING
BONDLAND
BONDMAID
BONDMAN
BONDMEN
BONDMINDER
BONDOC
BONDON
BONDSERVANT
BONDSHIP
BONDSLAVE
BONDSMAN
BONDSMEN
BONDSTONE
BONDSWOMAN
BONDUC
BONDUCNUT
BONDWOMAN
BONDWOMEN
BONE
BONEACHE
BONEBLACK
BONEBREAKER
BONED
BONEDOG
BONEEN
BONEFISH
BONEHEAD
BONEHEADED
BONELESS
BONELESSLY
BONELESSNESS
BONELET
BONER
BONES
BONESET
BONESETTER
BONESETTING
BONESHAKER
BONESHAVE
BONESHAW
BONETAIL
BONETE
BONEWOOD
BONEWORK
BONEWORT
BONEYARD
BONFIRE
BONG
BONGA
BONGAR
BONGO
BONGOS
BONGRACE
BONHOMIE
BONHOMMIE
BONIATA
BONIER
BONIEST
BONIFACE
BONIFICATION
BONIFORM
BONIFY
BONINESS
BONING
BONINITE
BONITA
BONITARIAN
BONITARY
BONITO
BONITOES
BONITOS
BONITY
BONK
BONKA
BONNAZ
BONNE
BONNET
BONNETED
BONNETING
BONNETMAN
BONNETMEN
BONNETS
BONNIBEL
BONNIE
BONNIER
BONNIEST
BONNILY
BONNINESS
BONNIVE
BONNOCK
BONNY
BONNYCLABBER
BONNYVIS
BONSAI
BONSER
BONSPELL
BONSPIEL
BONTE
BONTEBOK
BONTEBOKS
BONTEE
BONUM
BONUS
BONUSES
BONXIE
BONY
BONYFISH
BONYTAIL
BONZA
BONZE
BONZER
BONZERY
BONZIAN
BOO
BOOB
BOOBERY
BOOBIES
BOOBILY
BOOBOO
BOOBOOK
BOOBOOS
BOOBY
BOOBYALLA
BOOD
BOODIE
BOODLE
BOODLED
BOODLER
BOODLING
BOODY
BOOED
BOOER
BOOF
BOOGER
BOOGERMAN
BOOGEYMAN
BOOGIE
BOOGUM
BOOH
BOOHOO
BOOHOOED
BOOHOOING
BOOHOOS
BOOING
BOOJUM
BOOK
BOOKBINDER
BOOKBINDERIES
BOOKBINDERY
BOOKBINDING
BOOKBOARD
BOOKCASE
BOOKCASES
BOOKCRAFT
BOOKDEALER
BOOKED
BOOKEND
BOOKER
BOOKERY
BOOKFAIR
BOOKFOLD
BOOKHOLDER
BOOKIE
BOOKING

BOOKISH
BOOKISHLY
BOOKISHNESS
BOOKIT
BOOKKEEPER
BOOKKEEPING
BOOKLAND
BOOKLEAR
BOOKLESS
BOOKLET
BOOKLIFT
BOOKLORE
BOOKLOVER
BOOKMAKER
BOOKMAKING
BOOKMAN
BOOKMARK
BOOKMARKER
BOOKMATE
BOOKMEN
BOOKMOBILE
BOOKMONGER
BOOKPLATE
BOOKPRESS
BOOKRACK
BOOKREST
BOOKROOM
BOOKS
BOOKSELLER
BOOKSELLERISH
BOOKSELLERISM
BOOKSELLING
BOOKSHELF
BOOKSHELVES
BOOKSHOP
BOOKSTACK
BOOKSTALL
BOOKSTAND
BOOKSTORE
BOOKSY
BOOKWORK
BOOKWORM
BOOKWRIGHT
BOOKY
BOOL
BOOLEY
BOOLEYS
BOOLIES
BOOLY
BOOLYA
BOOM
BOOMAGE
BOOMAH
BOOMBOAT
BOOMDAS
BOOMER
BOOMERANG
BOOMINESS
BOOMING
BOOMINGLY
BOOMKIN
BOOMLET
BOOMORAH
BOOMSLANG
BOOMSLANGE
BOOMSTER
BOOMTOWN
BOOMY
BOON
BOONDOCK
BOONDOCKS
BOONDOGGLE
BOONDOGGLED
BOONDOGGLER
BOONDOGGLING
BOONG
BOONGARY
BOONK
BOOPIS
BOOR
BOORDLY
BOORISH
BOORISHLY
BOORISHNESS
BOORT
BOOS
BOOSE
BOOSIES
BOOST
BOOSTER
BOOSY
BOOT
BOOTBLACK
BOOTBOY
BOOTED
BOOTEE
BOOTER
BOOTERIES
BOOTERY
BOOTH
BOOTHAGE
BOOTHALE
BOOTHEEL
BOOTHER
BOOTHITE
BOOTHOLDER
BOOTHOSE
BOOTHS
BOOTIE
BOOTIED
BOOTIES
BOOTIKIN
BOOTING
BOOTJACK
BOOTJACKS
BOOTLACE
BOOTLE
BOOTLEG
BOOTLEGGED
BOOTLEGGER
BOOTLEGGING
BOOTLESS
BOOTLESSLY
BOOTLESSNESS
BOOTLICK
BOOTLICKER
BOOTMAKER
BOOTMAKING
BOOTMAN
BOOTS
BOOTSTRAP
BOOTY
BOOZE
BOOZED
BOOZER
BOOZILY
BOOZINESS
BOOZING
BOOZY
BOP
BOPEEP
BOPPED
BOPPER
BOPPING
BOPPIST
BOPSTER
BOPYRID
BOPYRIDIAN
BOR
BORA
BORACHIO
BORACIC
BORACIFEROUS
BORACITE
BORACOUS
BORAGE
BORAK
BORAL
BORANE
BORASCA
BORASCO
BORASQUE
BORATE
BORATED
BORAX
BORAZON
BORD
BORDAGE
BORDAR
BORDEL
BORDELLO
BORDER
BORDEREAU
BORDEREAUX
BORDERED
BORDERER
BORDERING
BORDERISM
BORDERLAND
BORDERLANDER
BORDERLINE
BORDRAG
BORDROOM
BORDUN
BORDURE
BORDURED
BORE
BOREAD
BOREAL
BOREALIS
BOREAN
BORECOLE
BORED
BOREDOM
BOREE
BOREEN
BOREGAT
BOREHOLE
BORELE
BORER
BORESOME
BORG
BORGH
BORGHI
BORGO
BORIC
BORICKITE
BORIDE
BORINE
BORING
BORINGLY
BORINGNESS
BORISH
BORISM
BORITH
BORITIES
BORITY
BORIZE
BORLASE
BORLEY
BORN
BORNANE
BORNE
BORNEOL
BORNING
BORNITE
BORNITIC
BORNYL
BORO
BOROCALCITE
BOROLANITE
BORON
BORONIC
BOROPHENOL
BOROSILICATE
BOROTUNGSTIC
BOROUGH
BORRACHA
BORRASCA
BORREL
BORRELIA
BORROW
BORROWED
BORROWER
BORROWING
BORSCH
BORSCHT
BORSHOLDER
BORSHT
BORSTAL
BORSTALL
BORT
BORTSCH
BORTZ
BORUN
BORWORT
BORYL
BORZOI
BOS
BOSA
BOSAL
BOSC
BOSCAGE
BOSCH
BOSCHBOK
BOSCHVARK
BOSCHVELD
BOSE
BOSER
BOSEY
BOSH
BOSHBOK
BOSHER
BOSHES
BOSHVARK
BOSK
BOSKAGE
BOSKER
BOSKET
BOSKINESS
BOSKY
BOSOM
BOSOMED
BOSOMER
BOSOMY
BOSON
BOSPORUS
BOSQUE
BOSQUET
BOSS
BOSSAGE
BOSSDOM
BOSSE
BOSSED
BOSSELATED
BOSSELATION
BOSSER
BOSSET
BOSSIER
BOSSIES
BOSSIEST
BOSSING
BOSSISM
BOSSY
BOST
BOSTAL
BOSTANGI
BOSTANJI
BOSTHOON
BOSTON
BOSTONITE
BOSTRYCHID
BOSTRYCHOID
BOSTRYX
BOSUN
BOT
BOTA
BOTANIC
BOTANICAL
BOTANICALLY
BOTANICS
BOTANIES
BOTANIST
BOTANIZE
BOTANIZED
BOTANIZER
BOTANIZING
BOTANY
BOTARGO
BOTARGOS
BOTCH
BOTCHED
BOTCHEDLY
BOTCHER
BOTCHERLY
BOTCHERY
BOTCHES
BOTCHIER
BOTCHIEST
BOTCHILY
BOTCHINESS
BOTCHING
BOTCHKA
BOTCHY
BOTE
BOTELER
BOTELLA
BOTEN
BOTEROL
BOTEROLL
BOTETE
BOTFLIES
BOTFLY
BOTH
BOTHER
BOTHERATION
BOTHERED
BOTHERER
BOTHERHEADED
BOTHERING
BOTHERMENT
BOTHERSOME
BOTHIE
BOTHIES
BOTHRENCHYMA
BOTHRIA
BOTHRIUM
BOTHROI
BOTHROPIC
BOTHROS
BOTHSIDED
BOTHWAY
BOTHY
BOTONE
BOTONEE
BOTONG
BOTONY
BOTOYAN
BOTRY
BOTRYOGEN
BOTRYOID
BOTRYOIDAL
BOTRYOIDALLY
BOTRYOLITE
BOTRYOMYCOMA

BOTRYOPTERID
BOTRYOSE
BOTS
BOTT
BOTTEGA
BOTTEGHE
BOTTEKIN
BOTTIER
BOTTINE
BOTTLE
BOTTLEBIRD
BOTTLED
BOTTLEFLOWER
BOTTLEHEAD
BOTTLEHOLDER
BOTTLEMAKER
BOTTLEMAKING
BOTTLEMAN
BOTTLENECK
BOTTLENEST
BOTTLENOSE
BOTTLER
BOTTLESTONE
BOTTLING
BOTTOM
BOTTOMED
BOTTOMER
BOTTOMING
BOTTOMLAND
BOTTOMLESS
BOTTOMLESSLY
BOTTOMMOST
BOTTOMRIED
BOTTOMRY
BOTTOMRYING
BOTTOMS
BOTTSTICK
BOTTU
BOTULIFORM
BOTULIN
BOTULINUS
BOTULISM
BOTULISMUS
BOUBA
BOUBAS
BOUBOU
BOUCAN
BOUCH
BOUCHAL
BOUCHALEEN
BOUCHARDE
BOUCHE
BOUCHEE
BOUCHER
BOUCHERISM
BOUCHERIZE
BOUCHETTE
BOUCHON
BOUCHONS
BOUCLE
BOUD
BOUDERIE
BOUDIN
BOUDOIR
BOUDOIRESQUE
BOUET
BOUFFANCY
BOUFFANT
BOUFFANTE
BOUFFE
BOUFFON
BOUGAR
BOUGE
BOUGEE
BOUGERON
BOUGET
BOUGH
BOUGHED
BOUGHPOT
BOUGHT
BOUGHTEN
BOUGHY
BOUGIE
BOUILLI
BOUILLON
BOUILLONE
BOUK
BOUKIT
BOUL
BOULANGERITE
BOULDER
BOULDERHEAD
BOULDERING
BOULDERS
BOULDERY
BOULE
BOULEUTERIA
BOULEUTERION
BOULEVARD
BOULEVARDIER
BOULIMIA
BOULLE
BOULT
BOULTEL
BOULTER
BOULTERER
BOUN
BOUNCE
BOUNCEABLE
BOUNCEABLY
BOUNCED
BOUNCER
BOUNCIER
BOUNCIEST
BOUNCILY
BOUNCING
BOUNCINGLY
BOUNCY
BOUND
BOUNDARIES
BOUNDARY
BOUNDED
BOUNDEN
BOUNDER
BOUNDING
BOUNDINGLY
BOUNDLESS
BOUNDLESSLY
BOUNDLY
BOUNDS
BOUNTEOUS
BOUNTEOUSLY
BOUNTIED
BOUNTIES
BOUNTIFUL
BOUNTIFULLY
BOUNTITH
BOUNTREE
BOUNTY
BOUQUET
BOUQUETIERE
BOUQUINISTE
BOURASQUE
BOURBON
BOURBONIZE
BOURD
BOURDER
BOURDON
BOURETTE
BOURG
BOURGADE
BOURGEOIS
BOURGEOISE
BOURGEOISIE
BOURGEON
BOURI
BOURN
BOURNE
BOURNONITE
BOUROCK
BOURRAN
BOURRE
BOURREAU
BOURREE
BOURRELET
BOURSE
BOURTREE
BOUSE
BOUSED
BOUSER
BOUSING
BOUSY
BOUT
BOUTADE
BOUTEFEU
BOUTELL
BOUTIQUE
BOUTO
BOUTON
BOUTONNIERE
BOUTRE
BOUTYLKA
BOUW
BOVARISM
BOVARYSM
BOVATE
BOVENLAND
BOVICIDE
BOVICULTURE
BOVID
BOVIFORM
BOVINE
BOVINELY
BOVINITY
BOVO
BOVOID
BOVOVACCINE
BOW
BOWABLE
BOWBACK
BOWBELLS
BOWBENT
BOWBOY
BOWDEN
BOWDITCH
BOWDLERISM
BOWDLERIZE
BOWDLERIZED
BOWDLERIZING
BOWED
BOWEL
BOWELED
BOWELING
BOWELLED
BOWELLING
BOWELS
BOWENITE
BOWER
BOWERBIRD
BOWERIES
BOWERLY
BOWERMAIDEN
BOWERMAY
BOWERWOMAN
BOWERY
BOWET
BOWFIN
BOWGRACE
BOWHEAD
BOWIE
BOWIEFUL
BOWING
BOWINGLY
BOWK
BOWKAIL
BOWKNOT
BOWL
BOWLA
BOWLDER
BOWLDERHEAD
BOWLDERING
BOWLDERY
BOWLED
BOWLEG
BOWLEGGED
BOWLER
BOWLIN
BOWLINE
BOWLING
BOWLMAKER
BOWLS
BOWLY
BOWMAKER
BOWMAKING
BOWMAN
BOWMEN
BOWN
BOWPIN
BOWPOT
BOWRALITE
BOWS
BOWSE
BOWSER
BOWSERY
BOWSHOT
BOWSIE
BOWSMAN
BOWSPRIT
BOWSSEN
BOWSTAVE
BOWSTRING
BOWSTRINGED
BOWSTRINGING
BOWSTRUNG
BOWTELL
BOWWOMAN
BOWWOOD
BOWWORT
BOWWOW
BOWWOWS
BOWYANG
BOWYER
BOX
BOXBERRIES
BOXBERRY
BOXBOARD
BOXBUSH
BOXCAR
BOXCARS
BOXEN
BOXER
BOXES
BOXFISH
BOXHAUL
BOXHEAD
BOXHOLDER
BOXING
BOXINGS
BOXKEEPER
BOXLIKE
BOXMAN
BOXROOM
BOXTHORN
BOXTREE
BOXTY
BOXWALLAH
BOXWOOD
BOXWORK
BOXY
BOY
BOYANG
BOYAR
BOYARD
BOYARDISM
BOYARISM
BOYAU
BOYAUS
BOYAUX
BOYCOTT
BOYCOTTAGE
BOYCOTTER
BOYER
BOYFRIEND
BOYHOOD
BOYISH
BOYISHLY
BOYISHNESS
BOYISM
BOYLA
BOYO
BOYSENBERRIES
BOYSENBERRY
BOZA
BOZAH
BOZAL
BOZINE
BOZO
BOZZE
BOZZETTO
BRA
BRAB
BRABAGIOUS
BRABANT
BRABBLE
BRABBLED
BRABBLEMENT
BRABBLER
BRABBLING
BRACA
BRACAE
BRACCAE
BRACCATE
BRACCIALE
BRACCIANITE
BRACCIO
BRACE
BRACED
BRACELET
BRACELETED
BRACER
BRACERO
BRACEROS
BRACES
BRACH
BRACHE
BRACHELYTROUS
BRACHERER
BRACHERING
BRACHET
BRACHIA
BRACHIAL
BRACHIALIS
BRACHIATE
BRACHIATED
BRACHIATING
BRACHIATION
BRACHIATOR
BRACHIOLARIA
BRACHIOPOD
BRACHIOSAUR
BRACHIUM
BRACHYAXIS
BRACHYCEPHAL
BRACHYCEPHALES
BRACHYCEPHALI

BRACHYCEROUS
BRACHYCRANIC
BRACHYDACTYL
BRACHYDONT
BRACHYGRAPHY
BRACHYLOGY
BRACHYPODINE
BRACHYPODOUS
BRACHYSKELIC
BRACHYSM
BRACHYTIC
BRACHYTMEMA
BRACHYTYPOUS
BRACHYURAL
BRACHYURAN
BRACHYURE
BRACHYUROUS
BRACING
BRACINGLY
BRACINGNESS
BRACK
BRACKED
BRACKEN
BRACKENED
BRACKER
BRACKET
BRACKETING
BRACKING
BRACKISH
BRACKISHNESS
BRACKMARD
BRACKY
BRACONID
BRACONNIERE
BRACOZZO
BRACT
BRACTEA
BRACTEAL
BRACTEATE
BRACTED
BRACTEIFORM
BRACTEOLATE
BRACTEOLE
BRACTEOSE
BRACTLET
BRAD
BRADAWL
BRADDED
BRADDING
BRADENHEAD
BRADOON
BRADSOT
BRADYCARDIA
BRADYCARDIC
BRADYCROTIC
BRADYPOD
BRADYPODE
BRADYPODOID
BRADYSEISM
BRADYSEISMAL
BRADYSEISMIC
BRADYTELY
BRAE
BRAEFACE
BRAEHEAD
BRAEMAN
BRAES
BRAESIDE
BRAG
BRAGAS
BRAGER
BRAGGADOCIAN
BRAGGADOCIO
BRAGGADOCIOS
BRAGGART
BRAGGARTISM
BRAGGARTLY
BRAGGARTRY
BRAGGED
BRAGGER
BRAGGERY
BRAGGET
BRAGGING
BRAGGINGLY
BRAGGISH
BRAGGISHLY
BRAGGITE
BRAGGLE
BRAGGY
BRAGITE
BRAGLY
BRAGOZZO
BRAGUETTE
BRAGWORT
BRAHMA
BRAHMACHARI
BRAID
BRAIDED
BRAIDER
BRAIDING
BRAIES
BRAIL
BRAILLE
BRAILLER
BRAILS
BRAIN
BRAINER
BRAINFAG
BRAINGE
BRAINIER
BRAINIEST
BRAINILY
BRAININESS
BRAINISH
BRAINLESS
BRAINLESSLY
BRAINPAN
BRAINPOWER
BRAINS
BRAINSICK
BRAINSICKLY
BRAINSTEM
BRAINSTORM
BRAINWASH
BRAINWASHING
BRAINWOOD
BRAINWORK
BRAINWORKER
BRAINY
BRAIRD
BRAIRDED
BRAIRDING
BRAIREAU
BRAIRO
BRAISE
BRAISED
BRAISING
BRAIZE
BRAK
BRAKE
BRAKEAGE
BRAKED
BRAKEHAND
BRAKEHEAD
BRAKELESS
BRAKEMAKER
BRAKEMAN
BRAKEMEN
BRAKER
BRAKESMAN
BRAKIE
BRAKIER
BRAKIEST
BRAKING
BRAKY
BRAMBLE
BRAMBLEBERRIES
BRAMBLEBERRY
BRAMBLEBUSH
BRAMBLED
BRAMBLIER
BRAMBLIEST
BRAMBLING
BRAMBLY
BRAME
BRAN
BRANCARD
BRANCARDIER
BRANCH
BRANCHAGE
BRANCHED
BRANCHER
BRANCHERY
BRANCHES
BRANCHIA
BRANCHIAE
BRANCHIAL
BRANCHIATE
BRANCHIER
BRANCHIER
BRANCHIEST
BRANCHIFORM
BRANCHIHYAL
BRANCHING
BRANCHIOMERE
BRANCHIOPOD
BRANCHIOSAUR
BRANCHIREME
BRANCHIUROUS
BRANCHLET
BRANCHLING
BRANCHMAN
BRANCHSTAND
BRANCHWAY
BRANCHY
BRAND
BRANDED
BRANDER
BRANDERING
BRANDIED
BRANDIES
BRANDING
BRANDISE
BRANDISH
BRANDISHER
BRANDISITE
BRANDLE
BRANDLIN
BRANDLING
BRANDRETH
BRANDS
BRANDSOLDER
BRANDY
BRANDYBALL
BRANDYING
BRANDYMAN
BRANDYWINE
BRANGLE
BRANGLED
BRANGLEMENT
BRANGLER
BRANGLING
BRANIAL
BRANK
BRANKIE
BRANKS
BRANKURSINE
BRANKY
BRANLE
BRANNER
BRANNERITE
BRANNIGAN
BRANNY
BRANSLE
BRANT
BRANTAIL
BRANTNESS
BRAROW
BRAS
BRASERO
BRASEROS
BRASH
BRASHIER
BRASHIEST
BRASHINESS
BRASHLY
BRASHNESS
BRASHY
BRASIER
BRASILETE
BRASILETTO
BRASQUE
BRASQUED
BRASQUING
BRASS
BRASSAGE
BRASSARD
BRASSART
BRASSBOUND
BRASSBOUNDER
BRASSE
BRASSER
BRASSERIE
BRASSES
BRASSEY
BRASSIDIC
BRASSIE
BRASSIER
BRASSIERE
BRASSIES
BRASSIEST
BRASSILY
BRASSINESS
BRASSY
BRAT
BRATCHET
BRATLING
BRATSTVA
BRATTACH
BRATTICE
BRATTICED
BRATTICER
BRATTICING
BRATTISH
BRATTLE
BRATTLED
BRATTLING
BRATWURST
BRAUL
BRAULA
BRAUNA
BRAUNITE
BRAVA
BRAVADE
BRAVADO
BRAVADOED
BRAVADOES
BRAVADOING
BRAVADOS
BRAVE
BRAVEHEARTED
BRAVELY
BRAVENESS
BRAVER
BRAVERIES
BRAVERY
BRAVEST
BRAVING
BRAVISSIMO
BRAVO
BRAVOES
BRAVOITE
BRAVOS
BRAVURA
BRAW
BRAWL
BRAWLER
BRAWLING
BRAWLINGLY
BRAWLY
BRAWN
BRAWNED
BRAWNEDNESS
BRAWNER
BRAWNIER
BRAWNIEST
BRAWNINESS
BRAWNY
BRAWS
BRAXIES
BRAXY
BRAY
BRAYED
BRAYER
BRAYERA
BRAYERIN
BRAYING
BRAYSTONE
BRAZA
BRAZE
BRAZED
BRAZEN
BRAZENED
BRAZENFACE
BRAZENFACED
BRAZENING
BRAZENLY
BRAZENNESS
BRAZER
BRAZERA
BRAZIER
BRAZIERY
BRAZIL
BRAZILEIN
BRAZILETTE
BRAZILITE
BRAZILWOOD
BRAZING
BREA
BREACH
BREACHER
BREACHY
BREAD
BREADBASKET
BREADBERRY
BREADBOARD
BREADBOX
BREADEARNER
BREADEARNING
BREADED
BREADEN
BREADFRUIT
BREADMAKER
BREADMAKING
BREADMAN
BREADNUT
BREADROOT
BREADS
BREADSELLER
BREADSTITCH
BREADSTUFF
BREADTH
BREADTHRIDERS
BREADTHWAYS
BREADTHWISE

BREADWINNER
BREADWINNING
BREAGHE
BREAK
BREAKABLE
BREAKABLY
BREAKAGE
BREAKAWAY
BREAKAX
BREAKAXE
BREAKBACK
BREAKBONE
BREAKBONES
BREAKDOWN
BREAKER
BREAKERMAN
BREAKERMEN
BREAKFAST
BREAKFASTER
BREAKFRONT
BREAKING
BREAKNECK
BREAKOFF
BREAKOUT
BREAKOVER
BREAKS
BREAKSTONE
BREAKTHROUGH
BREAKUP
BREAKWATER
BREAM
BREAMS
BREAN
BREARDS
BREAST
BREASTBAND
BREASTBEAM
BREASTBONE
BREASTED
BREASTER
BREASTHOOK
BREASTING
BREASTMARK
BREASTPIECE
BREASTPIN
BREASTPLATE
BREASTPLOUGH
BREASTPLOW
BREASTRAIL
BREASTROPE
BREASTS
BREASTSUMMER
BREASTWEED
BREASTWISE
BREASTWOOD
BREASTWORK
BREATH
BREATHABLE
BREATHE
BREATHED
BREATHER
BREATHIER
BREATHIEST
BREATHING
BREATHLESS
BREATHLESSLY
BREATHLESSNESS
BREATHSELLER
BREATHTAKING
BREATHY
BREBA
BRECCIA
BRECCIAL
BRECCIATED
BRECCIATION
BRECHAM
BRECHAN
BRECK
BRED
BREDBERGITE
BREDE
BREDESTITCH
BREDI
BREDSTITCH
BREE
BREECH
BREECHBLOCK
BREECHCLOTH
BREECHCLOUT
BREECHED
BREECHES
BREECHING
BREECHLOADER
BREECHLOADING
BREED
BREEDBATE
BREEDER
BREEDING
BREEDY
BREEKS
BREEKUMS
BREEM
BREENGE
BREER
BREEZE
BREEZED
BREEZEWAY
BREEZIER
BREEZIEST
BREEZILY
BREEZINESS
BREEZING
BREEZY
BREGMA
BREGMATA
BREGMATE
BREGMATIC
BREHON
BREI
BREIRD
BREISLAKITE
BREITHAUPTITE
BRELAN
BRELOQUE
BREME
BREMELY
BREMENESS
BREN
BRENNAGE
BRENNSCHLUSS
BRENT
BREPHIC
BRER
BREST
BRET
BRETELLE
BRETESSE
BRETH
BRETHEL
BRETHREN
BRETT
BREVA
BREVE
BREVET
BREVETCIES
BREVETCY
BREVETE
BREVETED
BREVETING
BREVETTED
BREVETTING
BREVIARIES
BREVIARY
BREVIATE
BREVIATURE
BREVICAUDATE
BREVICIPITID
BREVIER
BREVIFOLIATE
BREVIGER
BREVILINGUAL
BREVILOQUENT
BREVIPED
BREVIPEN
BREVIPENNATE
BREVIRADIATE
BREVIROSTRAL
BREVIT
BREVITIES
BREVITY
BREW
BREWAGE
BREWED
BREWER
BREWERIES
BREWERY
BREWHOUSE
BREWING
BREWIS
BREWMASTER
BREWSTER
BREWSTERITE
BREY
BRIAR
BRIARBERRY
BRIARED
BRIARROOT
BRIARWOOD
BRIARY
BRIBABLE
BRIBE
BRIBED
BRIBEE
BRIBEGIVER
BRIBEGIVING
BRIBEMONGER
BRIBER
BRIBERIES
BRIBERY
BRIBETAKER
BRIBETAKING
BRIBEWORTHY
BRIBING
BRICHETTE
BRICK
BRICKBAT
BRICKBATTED
BRICKBATTING
BRICKED
BRICKEN
BRICKFIELDER
BRICKIER
BRICKIEST
BRICKING
BRICKKILN
BRICKLAYING
BRICKLE
BRICKLENESS
BRICKLINER
BRICKLINING
BRICKLY
BRICKMAKER
BRICKMAKING
BRICKS
BRICKSET
BRICKSETTER
BRICKTIMBER
BRICKWORK
BRICKY
BRICKYARD
BRICOLE
BRIDAL
BRIDALE
BRIDALER
BRIDALLY
BRIDALTY
BRIDE
BRIDEBED
BRIDEBOWL
BRIDECAKE
BRIDECHAMBER
BRIDECUP
BRIDEGOD
BRIDEGROOM
BRIDEKNOT
BRIDELACE
BRIDELY
BRIDEMAIDEN
BRIDEMAN
BRIDESMAID
BRIDESMAIDING
BRIDESMAN
BRIDESMEN
BRIDESTAKE
BRIDEWAIN
BRIDEWEED
BRIDEWELL
BRIDEWORT
BRIDGE
BRIDGEABLE
BRIDGEBOARD
BRIDGEBUILDER
BRIDGEBUILDING
BRIDGED
BRIDGEHEAD
BRIDGEKEEPER
BRIDGEMAKER
BRIDGEMAKING
BRIDGEMAN
BRIDGEMASTER
BRIDGEMEN
BRIDGEPOT
BRIDGER
BRIDGETREE
BRIDGEWARD
BRIDGEWAY
BRIDGEWORK
BRIDGING
BRIDLE
BRIDLED
BRIDLEMAN
BRIDLER
BRIDLING
BRIDOON
BRIE
BRIEF
BRIEFCASE
BRIEFED
BRIEFING
BRIEFLESS
BRIEFLESSLY
BRIEFLY
BRIEFNESS
BRIEFS
BRIER
BRIERBERRY
BRIERED
BRIERROOT
BRIERS
BRIERWOOD
BRIERY
BRIEVE
BRIG
BRIGADE
BRIGADED
BRIGADIER
BRIGADING
BRIGALOW
BRIGAND
BRIGANDAGE
BRIGANDER
BRIGANDINE
BRIGANDISH
BRIGANDISHLY
BRIGANDISM
BRIGANTINE
BRIGBOTE
BRIGE
BRIGHT
BRIGHTEN
BRIGHTENER
BRIGHTER
BRIGHTEST
BRIGHTEYES
BRIGHTLY
BRIGHTNESS
BRIGHTS
BRIGHTSMITH
BRIGHTSOME
BRIGHTWORK
BRIGUE
BRIGUED
BRIGUER
BRIGUING
BRIKE
BRILL
BRILLANTE
BRILLIANCE
BRILLIANCY
BRILLIANDEER
BRILLIANT
BRILLIANTINE
BRILLIANTLY
BRILLS
BRIM
BRIMBORION
BRIMBORIUM
BRIMFUL
BRIMFULLY
BRIMFULNESS
BRIMING
BRIMLY
BRIMMED
BRIMMER
BRIMMERED
BRIMMERING
BRIMMING
BRIMMINGLY
BRIMSTONE
BRIMSTONY
BRIN
BRINCE
BRINDED
BRINDISI
BRINDLE
BRINDLED
BRINE
BRINED
BRINER
BRING
BRINGELA
BRINGER
BRINGING
BRINGS
BRINGSEL
BRINIE
BRINIER
BRINIEST
BRININESS
BRINING
BRINISH
BRINJAL
BRINJAREE
BRINJARRIES
BRINJARRY

BRINJAUL
BRINK
BRINKMANSHIP
BRINSELL
BRINSTON
BRINY
BRIO
BRIOCHE
BRIOLET
BRIOLETTE
BRIQUE
BRIQUET
BRIQUETTE
BRIS
BRISANCE
BRISANT
BRISCOLA
BRISE
BRISEMENT
BRISK
BRISKED
BRISKEN
BRISKENED
BRISKENING
BRISKET
BRISKING
BRISKLY
BRISKNESS
BRISKY
BRISLING
BRISQUE
BRISS
BRIST
BRISTLE
BRISTLEBIRD
BRISTLECONE
BRISTLED
BRISTLELIKE
BRISTLER
BRISTLES
BRISTLETAIL
BRISTLEWORT
BRISTLIER
BRISTLIEST
BRISTLINESS
BRISTLING
BRISTLY
BRISURE
BRIT
BRITANNIA
BRITCHEL
BRITCHES
BRITE
BRITH
BRITSKA
BRITT
BRITTEN
BRITTLE
BRITTLEBUSH
BRITTLELY
BRITTLENESS
BRITTLESTEM
BRITTLEWOOD
BRITTLEWORT
BRITTLING
BRITZKA
BRITZSKA
BRIZE
BRIZZ
BROACH
BROACHED
BROACHER
BROACHING
BROAD
BROADACRE
BROADAX
BROADAXE
BROADBILL
BROADBRIM
BROADCAST
BROADCASTED
BROADCASTER
BROADCASTING
BROADCLOTH
BROADEN
BROADENED
BROADENING
BROADEST
BROADGAGE
BROADHEAD
BROADHEARTED
BROADHORN
BROADLEAF
BROADLING
BROADLINGS
BROADLOOM
BROADLY
BROADNESS
BROADPIECE
BROADSHARE
BROADSHEET
BROADSIDE
BROADSWORD
BROADTAIL
BROADWAY
BROADWAYS
BROADWISE
BROB
BROCADE
BROCADED
BROCADING
BROCARD
BROCATEL
BROCATELLE
BROCCOLI
BROCH
BROCHAN
BROCHANT
BROCHANTITE
BROCHE
BROCHETTE
BROCHO
BROCHOPHONY
BROCHT
BROCHURE
BROCK
BROCKAGE
BROCKED
BROCKET
BROCKLE
BROD
BRODDER
BRODE
BRODEE
BRODEKIN
BRODEQUIN
BRODERER
BRODERIE
BRODIE
BRODYAGA
BRODYAGI
BROG
BROGAN
BROGGER
BROGGERITE
BROGGLE
BROGUE
BROGUED
BROGUENEER
BROGUER
BROGUES
BROGUING
BROH
BROIDER
BROIDERED
BROIDERER
BROIDERIES
BROIDERING
BROIDERY
BROIGNE
BROIL
BROILED
BROILER
BROILERY
BROILING
BROKAGE
BROKE
BROKEN
BROKENHEARTED
BROKENLY
BROKENNESS
BROKER
BROKERAGE
BROKERY
BROKES
BROKING
BROLETTI
BROLETTO
BROLGA
BROLL
BROLLIES
BROLLY
BROMA
BROMAL
BROMAMIDE
BROMARGYRITE
BROMATE
BROMATIUM
BROME
BROMEGRASS
BROMELIAD
BROMELIN
BROMELLITE
BROMHIDROSIS
BROMHYDRATE
BROMHYDRIC
BROMIC
BROMID
BROMIDE
BROMIDIC
BROMIDROSIS
BROMIN
BROMINATE
BROMINATED
BROMINATING
BROMINATION
BROMINE
BROMINISM
BROMISM
BROMITE
BROMIZATION
BROMIZE
BROMIZER
BROMLITE
BROMOACETONE
BROMOAURATES
BROMOBENZENE
BROMOCYANID
BROMOCYANIDE
BROMOFORM
BROMOHYDRATE
BROMOHYDRIN
BROMOIL
BROMOIODID
BROMOIODIDE
BROMOIODISM
BROMOIODIZED
BROMOL
BROMOMANIA
BROMOMETRIC
BROMOMETRY
BROMOPICRIN
BROMOPIKRIN
BROMOPROTEIN
BROMOTHYMOL
BROMOUS
BROMPICRIN
BROMTHYMOL
BROMURET
BROMVOEL
BROMVOGEL
BROMYRITE
BRON
BRONC
BRONCHI
BRONCHIA
BRONCHIAL
BRONCHIALLY
BRONCHILOQUY
BRONCHIOCELE
BRONCHIOLAR
BRONCHIOLE
BRONCHITIC
BRONCHITIS
BRONCHO
BRONCHOBUSTER
BRONCHOGENIC
BRONCHOS
BRONCHOSCOPE
BRONCHOSCOPY
BRONCHOTOMY
BRONCHUS
BRONCO
BRONCOBUSTER
BRONCOS
BRONGNIARDITE
BRONTEON
BRONTEPHOBIA
BRONTEUM
BRONTIDE
BRONTIDES
BRONTOGRAM
BRONTOGRAPH
BRONTOLITE
BRONTOLITH
BRONTOLOGY
BRONTOMETER
BRONTOPHOBIA
BRONTOSAUR
BRONTOSAURUS
BRONTOSAURUSES
BRONTOSCOPY
BRONZE
BRONZED
BRONZEN
BRONZER
BRONZESMITH
BRONZEWING
BRONZIFY
BRONZINE
BRONZING
BRONZITE
BRONZITITE
BRONZY
BROO
BROOCH
BROOCHED
BROOCHING
BROOD
BROODED
BROODER
BROODIER
BROODIEST
BROODING
BROODSAC
BROODY
BROOK
BROOKED
BROOKFLOWER
BROOKIE
BROOKIER
BROOKIEST
BROOKING
BROOKITE
BROOKLET
BROOKLIME
BROOKS
BROOKSIDE
BROOKWEED
BROOKY
BROOL
BROOM
BROOMBUSH
BROOMCORN
BROOMER
BROOMMAKER
BROOMMAKING
BROOMRAPE
BROOMROOT
BROOMSHANK
BROOMSTAFF
BROOMSTICK
BROOMSTRAW
BROOMTAIL
BROOMWEED
BROOMWOOD
BROOMWORT
BROOMY
BROON
BROOZLED
BROQUERY
BROQUINEER
BROSE
BROSOT
BROSSE
BROSY
BROT
BROTCHEN
BROTEL
BROTH
BROTHE
BROTHEL
BROTHER
BROTHERED
BROTHERHOOD
BROTHERING
BROTHERLY
BROTHERS
BROTHERWORT
BROTHY
BROTOCRYSTAL
BROTT
BROTULID
BROTULIFORM
BROUD
BROUETTE
BROUGH
BROUGHAM
BROUGHT
BROUHAHA
BROUILLON
BROUZE
BROW
BROWACHE
BROWBAND
BROWBEAT
BROWBEATEN
BROWBEATER
BROWBEATING
BROWBOUND
BROWDEN
BROWED
BROWET
BROWIS
BROWLESS

BROWMAN
BROWN
BROWNBACK
BROWNED
BROWNER
BROWNEST
BROWNIE
BROWNING
BROWNISH
BROWNNESS
BROWNNOSE
BROWNOUT
BROWNPRINT
BROWNSTONE
BROWNTAIL
BROWNTOP
BROWNWEED
BROWNWORT
BROWNY
BROWPIECE
BROWPOST
BROWSE
BROWSED
BROWSER
BROWSING
BROWST
BROWZER
BRUANG
BRUBRU
BRUCELLOSIS
BRUCHID
BRUCIA
BRUCIN
BRUCINA
BRUCINE
BRUCITE
BRUCKLE
BRUCKLED
BRUCKLENESS
BRUET
BRUGH
BRUH
BRUIN
BRUISE
BRUISED
BRUISER
BRUISEWORT
BRUISING
BRUIT
BRUITER
BRUJERIA
BRUJO
BRUKE
BRULEE
BRULOT
BRULYIE
BRULYIEMENT
BRULZIE
BRUM
BRUMAL
BRUMBEE
BRUMBIE
BRUMBIES
BRUMBY
BRUME
BRUMMAGEM
BRUMMER
BRUMMY
BRUMOUS
BRUNCH
BRUNE
BRUNET
BRUNETNESS
BRUNETTE
BRUNETTENESS
BRUNISSURE
BRUNIZEM
BRUNNEOUS
BRUNT
BRUSCUS
BRUSH
BRUSHBALL
BRUSHBIRD
BRUSHBUSH
BRUSHED
BRUSHER
BRUSHES
BRUSHET
BRUSHIER
BRUSHIEST
BRUSHING
BRUSHITE
BRUSHLAND
BRUSHMAKER
BRUSHMAKING
BRUSHMAN
BRUSHMEN
BRUSHOFF
BRUSHUP
BRUSHWOOD
BRUSHWORK
BRUSHY
BRUSK
BRUSQUE
BRUSQUELY
BRUSQUENESS
BRUSQUERIE
BRUSSEL
BRUSTLE
BRUSTLED
BRUSTLING
BRUT
BRUTAL
BRUTALITIES
BRUTALITY
BRUTALIZE
BRUTALIZED
BRUTALIZING
BRUTALLY
BRUTE
BRUTIFIED
BRUTIFY
BRUTIFYING
BRUTING
BRUTISH
BRUTISHLY
BRUTISHNESS
BRUTISM
BRUTTER
BRUXISM
BRUYERE
BRUZZ
BRYACEOUS
BRYNZA
BRYOGENIN
BRYOLOGICAL
BRYOLOGIST
BRYOLOGY
BRYONIA
BRYONIDIN
BRYONIES
BRYONIN
BRYONY
BRYOPHYTE
BRYOPHYTIC
BRYOZOAN
BRYOZOON
BRYOZOUM
BU
BUAL
BUAT
BUAZE
BUB
BUBA
BUBAL
BUBALE
BUBALINE
BUBALIS
BUBAS
BUBBER
BUBBIES
BUBBLE
BUBBLEBOW
BUBBLED
BUBBLER
BUBBLES
BUBBLIER
BUBBLIEST
BUBBLING
BUBBLINGLY
BUBBLY
BUBBY
BUBBYBUSH
BUBINGA
BUBO
BUBOED
BUBOES
BUBONALGIA
BUBONIC
BUBONOCELE
BUBU
BUBUD
BUBUKLE
BUCAN
BUCARE
BUCAYO
BUCCA
BUCCAL
BUCCAN
BUCCANED
BUCCANEER
BUCCANING
BUCCANNED
BUCCANNING
BUCCATE
BUCCHERO
BUCCIN
BUCCINA
BUCCINAE
BUCCINAL
BUCCINATOR
BUCCINATORY
BUCCINIFORM
BUCCINOID
BUCCO
BUCCOLINGUAL
BUCCULA
BUCCULAE
BUCENTAUR
BUCHITE
BUCHNERITE
BUCHONITE
BUCHU
BUCK
BUCKAROO
BUCKASS
BUCKAYRO
BUCKBEAN
BUCKBERRY
BUCKBOARD
BUCKBRUSH
BUCKBUSH
BUCKED
BUCKEEN
BUCKER
BUCKET
BUCKETED
BUCKETEER
BUCKETER
BUCKETING
BUCKETMAKER
BUCKETMAKING
BUCKETMAN
BUCKETY
BUCKEYE
BUCKEYED
BUCKHORN
BUCKHOUND
BUCKIE
BUCKING
BUCKISH
BUCKISHLY
BUCKISHNESS
BUCKISM
BUCKJUMP
BUCKLE
BUCKLED
BUCKLER
BUCKLING
BUCKLUM
BUCKO
BUCKOES
BUCKONE
BUCKPLATE
BUCKPOT
BUCKRA
BUCKRAM
BUCKRAMED
BUCKRAMING
BUCKS
BUCKSAW
BUCKSHEE
BUCKSHOT
BUCKSKIN
BUCKSKINNED
BUCKSTALL
BUCKSTAY
BUCKSTONE
BUCKTAIL
BUCKTHORN
BUCKTOOTH
BUCKTOOTHED
BUCKU
BUCKWAGON
BUCKWASH
BUCKWASHER
BUCKWASHING
BUCKWHEAT
BUCKWHEATER
BUCKY
BUCOLIAST
BUCOLIC
BUCOLICAL
BUCOLICALLY
BUCRANE
BUCRANIA
BUCRANIUM
BUD
BUDA
BUDBREAK
BUDDAGE
BUDDAH
BUDDED
BUDDER
BUDDHI
BUDDIE
BUDDIES
BUDDING
BUDDLE
BUDDLEIA
BUDDLER
BUDDY
BUDGE
BUDGED
BUDGER
BUDGEREE
BUDGEREEGAH
BUDGERIGAH
BUDGERIGAR
BUDGERO
BUDGEROW
BUDGERYGAH
BUDGET
BUDGETARY
BUDGETED
BUDGETEER
BUDGETER
BUDGETING
BUDGIE
BUDGING
BUDLET
BUDLING
BUDMASH
BUDTIME
BUDWOOD
BUDWORM
BUDZART
BUDZAT
BUF
BUFAGIN
BUFF
BUFFA
BUFFABLE
BUFFALO
BUFFALOBACK
BUFFALOED
BUFFALOES
BUFFALOING
BUFFALOS
BUFFBALL
BUFFBAR
BUFFCOAT
BUFFED
BUFFER
BUFFET
BUFFETED
BUFFETER
BUFFETING
BUFFI
BUFFIN
BUFFING
BUFFLE
BUFFLEHEAD
BUFFLEHORN
BUFFO
BUFFONE
BUFFONT
BUFFOON
BUFFOONERIES
BUFFOONERY
BUFFOONISH
BUFFOONISM
BUFFWARE
BUFFY
BUFIDIN
BUFO
BUFONID
BUFONITE
BUFOTALIN
BUG
BUGA
BUGABOO
BUGALA
BUGAN
BUGARA
BUGBANE
BUGBEAR
BUGBITE
BUGEYE
BUGFISH
BUGGANE
BUGGED
BUGGER
BUGGERY
BUGGIER

BUGGIES
BUGGIEST
BUGGINESS
BUGGING
BUGGY
BUGGYMAN
BUGGYMEN
BUGHEAD
BUGHOUSE
BUGHT
BUGHT
BUGIA
BUGLE
BUGLED
BUGLER
BUGLET
BUGLEWEED
BUGLING
BUGLOSS
BUGLOSSES
BUGOLOGIST
BUGOLOGY
BUGOR
BUGOUT
BUGRE
BUGS
BUGSEED
BUGWEED
BUGWORT
BUHL
BUHLBUHL
BUHLWORK
BUHR
BUHRMILL
BUHRSTONE
BUILD
BUILDER
BUILDING
BUILDINGS
BUILDRESS
BUILDUP
BUILT
BUIRD
BUIRDLY
BUIRE
BUISSON
BUIST
BUKE
BUKH
BUKID
BUKK
BUKSHEE
BUKSHI
BULAK
BULAQ
BULB
BULBACEOUS
BULBAR
BULBED
BULBI
BULBIER
BULBIEST
BULBIFEROUS
BULBIFORM
BULBIL
BULBILLA
BULBLET
BULBLIKE
BULBOSE
BULBOTUBER
BULBOUS
BULBS
BULBUL
BULBULE
BULBUS
BULBY
BULCH
BULCHIN
BULDER
BULE
BULGE
BULGED
BULGER
BULGIER
BULGIEST
BULGINESS
BULGING
BULGUR
BULGY
BULIES
BULIMIA
BULIMIAC
BULIMIC
BULIMIFORM
BULIMOID
BULIMY
BULK
BULKED
BULKER
BULKHEAD
BULKHEADED
BULKIER
BULKIEST
BULKILY
BULKINESS
BULKING
BULKY
BULL
BULLA
BULLACE
BULLAE
BULLAMACOW
BULLAN
BULLARIES
BULLARY
BULLATE
BULLATED
BULLATION
BULLBAITING
BULLBAT
BULLBEGGAR
BULLBERRY
BULLBIRD
BULLBOAT
BULLCOMBER
BULLDOG
BULLDOGGED
BULLDOGGER
BULLDOGGING
BULLDOGGY
BULLDOZE
BULLDOZED
BULLDOZER
BULLDOZING
BULLDUST
BULLED
BULLER
BULLET
BULLETED
BULLETHEAD
BULLETIN
BULLETINED
BULLETINING
BULLETMAKER
BULLETMAKING
BULLETPROOF
BULLETS
BULLETWOOD
BULLETY
BULLFICE
BULLFIGHT
BULLFIGHTER
BULLFIGHTING
BULLFINCH
BULLFIST
BULLFLOWER
BULLFOOT
BULLFROG
BULLGINE
BULLHEAD
BULLHEADED
BULLHEADEDLY
BULLHOOF
BULLHORN
BULLIED
BULLIES
BULLIFORM
BULLIMONG
BULLING
BULLION
BULLISH
BULLISHLY
BULLISHNESS
BULLISM
BULLNECK
BULLNECKED
BULLNOSE
BULLNUT
BULLOCK
BULLOCKER
BULLOCKMAN
BULLOCKY
BULLOSE
BULLOUS
BULLPATES
BULLPEN
BULLPOUT
BULLPUP
BULLRING
BULLROARER
BULLS
BULLSTICKER
BULLSUCKER
BULLTOAD
BULLULE
BULLWEED
BULLWHACK
BULLWHACKER
BULLWHIP
BULLWHIPPED
BULLWHIPPING
BULLWORK
BULLWORT
BULLY
BULLYBOY
BULLYHUFF
BULLYING
BULLYINGLY
BULLYRAG
BULLYRAGGED
BULLYRAGGER
BULLYRAGGING
BULLYROCK
BULLYROOK
BULREEDY
BULRUSH
BULSE
BULT
BULTEN
BULTER
BULTEY
BULTI
BULTO
BULTONG
BULTOW
BULWAND
BULWARK
BULWARKED
BULWARKING
BULWARKS
BUM
BUMAREE
BUMBAILIFF
BUMBARD
BUMBARGE
BUMBASS
BUMBASTE
BUMBAZE
BUMBEE
BUMBERSHOOT
BUMBLE
BUMBLEBEE
BUMBLEBERRY
BUMBLED
BUMBLEFOOT
BUMBLEKITE
BUMBLEPUPPY
BUMBLER
BUMBLING
BUMBO
BUMBOAT
BUMBOATMAN
BUMBOATWOMAN
BUMCLOCK
BUMF
BUMFEG
BUMICKY
BUMKIN
BUMMACK
BUMMALO
BUMMALOS
BUMMAREE
BUMMED
BUMMEL
BUMMER
BUMMERY
BUMMIL
BUMMING
BUMMLE
BUMMLER
BUMMOCK
BUMP
BUMPER
BUMPERED
BUMPERING
BUMPIER
BUMPIEST
BUMPILY
BUMPINESS
BUMPING
BUMPINGLY
BUMPITY
BUMPKIN
BUMPOLOGY
BUMPSY
BUMPTIOUS
BUMPTIOUSLY
BUMPY
BUMTRAP
BUMWOOD
BUN
BUNA
BUNCAL
BUNCE
BUNCH
BUNCHBERRIES
BUNCHBERRY
BUNCHED
BUNCHER
BUNCHFLOWER
BUNCHIER
BUNCHIEST
BUNCHILY
BUNCHINESS
BUNCHING
BUNCHY
BUNCO
BUNCOED
BUNCOING
BUNCOMBE
BUNCOS
BUND
BUNDER
BUNDIES
BUNDLE
BUNDLER
BUNDLET
BUNDOBUST
BUNDOC
BUNDOCKS
BUNDOOK
BUNDWEED
BUNDY
BUNEMOST
BUNG
BUNGALOID
BUNGALOW
BUNGARUM
BUNGED
BUNGEE
BUNGERLY
BUNGEY
BUNGFU
BUNGFULL
BUNGHOLE
BUNGING
BUNGLE
BUNGLED
BUNGLER
BUNGLING
BUNGLINGLY
BUNGMAKER
BUNGO
BUNGOS
BUNGS
BUNGTOWN
BUNGWALL
BUNGY
BUNION
BUNK
BUNKED
BUNKER
BUNKERMAN
BUNKERMEN
BUNKHOUSE
BUNKIE
BUNKING
BUNKLOAD
BUNKMATE
BUNKO
BUNKOED
BUNKOING
BUNKOS
BUNKS
BUNKUM
BUNN
BUNNELL
BUNNIA
BUNNIES
BUNNING
BUNNY
BUNNYMOUTH
BUNODONT
BUNSENITE
BUNT
BUNTAL
BUNTED
BUNTER
BUNTINE
BUNTING
BUNTLINE
BUNTON
BUNTS
BUNTY
BUNUELO

BUNYA
BUNYAH
BUNYIP
BUONAMANI
BUONAMANO
BUOY
BUOYAGE
BUOYANCE
BUOYANCIES
BUOYANCY
BUOYANT
BUOYANTLY
BUOYANTNESS
BUOYED
BUOYING
BUPHTHALMIA
BUPHTHALMIC
BUPHTHALMOS
BUPLEUROL
BUPLEVER
BUPRESTID
BUPRESTIDAN
BUR
BURA
BURAN
BURAO
BURBANKIAN
BURBARK
BURBLER
BURBLY
BURBOLT
BURBOT
BURBOTS
BURD
BURDASH
BURDEN
BURDENABLE
BURDENED
BURDENER
BURDENING
BURDENOUS
BURDENSOME
BURDENSOMELY
BURDIE
BURDOCK
BURDON
BURE
BUREAU
BUREAUCRACIES
BUREAUCRACY
BUREAUCRAT
BUREAUCRATIC
BUREAUS
BUREAUX
BUREL
BURELAGE
BURELE
BURELY
BUREO
BURET
BURETTE
BURFISH
BURG
BURGAGE
BURGALITY
BURGALL
BURGAMOT
BURGEE
BURGENSIC
BURGEON
BURGEONED
BURGEONING
BURGER
BURGESS
BURGH
BURGHAL
BURGHALPENNY
BURGHBOTE
BURGHER
BURGHMASTER
BURGHMOOT
BURGHMOTE
BURGI
BURGLAR
BURGLARIES
BURGLARIOUS
BURGLARIZE
BURGLARIZED
BURGLARIZING
BURGLARPROOF
BURGLARY
BURGLE
BURGLED
BURGLING
BURGOMASTER
BURGONET
BURGOO
BURGOOS
BURGOUT
BURGOYNE
BURGRAVE
BURGRAVIATE
BURGUL
BURGULLIAN
BURGUS
BURGWARE
BURGWERE
BURH
BURHEAD
BURHMOOT
BURI
BURIAL
BURIAN
BURIED
BURIER
BURIN
BURINIST
BURION
BURITI
BURK
BURKA
BURKE
BURKED
BURKER
BURKHA
BURKING
BURKITE
BURKUNDAUZE
BURKUNDAZ
BURL
BURLA
BURLAP
BURLAPS
BURLE
BURLED
BURLER
BURLESK
BURLESQUE
BURLESQUED
BURLESQUELY
BURLESQUER
BURLESQUING
BURLET
BURLETTA
BURLEY
BURLEYS
BURLIER
BURLIES
BURLIEST
BURLILY
BURLINESS
BURLING
BURLY
BURMITE
BURN
BURNABLE
BURNBEAT
BURNED
BURNER
BURNET
BURNETTIZE
BURNETTIZED
BURNETTIZING
BURNEWIN
BURNFIRE
BURNIE
BURNIEBEE
BURNING
BURNINGLY
BURNISH
BURNISHER
BURNISHING
BURNISHMENT
BURNOOSE
BURNOOSED
BURNOUS
BURNOUT
BURNOVER
BURNSIDE
BURNSIDES
BURNT
BURNUP
BURNUT
BURNWEED
BURNWOOD
BURNY
BURO
BURP
BURR
BURRA
BURRAH
BURRAWANG
BURRBARK
BURRED
BURREL
BURRER
BURRHEL
BURRIER
BURRIEST
BURRIO
BURRITO
BURRITOS
BURRKNOT
BURRO
BURROS
BURROW
BURROWED
BURROWEED
BURROWER
BURROWING
BURROWS
BURROWSTOWN
BURRSTONE
BURRY
BURSA
BURSAE
BURSAL
BURSAR
BURSARIAL
BURSARIES
BURSARY
BURSAS
BURSATE
BURSATI
BURSATTEE
BURSAUTEE
BURSE
BURSEED
BURSERACEOUS
BURSICLE
BURSICULATE
BURSIFORM
BURSITIS
BURST
BURSTED
BURSTER
BURSTING
BURSTONE
BURSTWORT
BURSULA
BURT
BURTHEN
BURTHENMAN
BURTON
BURTONIZATION
BURTONIZE
BURTREE
BURUCHA
BURWEED
BURY
BURYING
BUS
BUSBIES
BUSBOY
BUSBY
BUSCARL
BUSCARLE
BUSE
BUSED
BUSES
BUSH
BUSHBEATER
BUSHBOY
BUSHBUCK
BUSHED
BUSHEL
BUSHELED
BUSHELER
BUSHELING
BUSHELLED
BUSHELLER
BUSHELLING
BUSHELMAN
BUSHELS
BUSHELWOMAN
BUSHER
BUSHES
BUSHET
BUSHFIGHTER
BUSHFIGHTING
BUSHGOAT
BUSHGRASS
BUSHHAMMER
BUSHI
BUSHIDO
BUSHIER
BUSHIEST
BUSHILY
BUSHINESS
BUSHING
BUSHLAND
BUSHMAKER
BUSHMAKING
BUSHMASTER
BUSHMENT
BUSHPIG
BUSHRANGER
BUSHRANGING
BUSHROPE
BUSHTIT
BUSHVELD
BUSHWA
BUSHWACK
BUSHWAH
BUSHWHACK
BUSHWHACKER
BUSHWHACKING
BUSHWIFE
BUSHWOMAN
BUSHWOOD
BUSIED
BUSIER
BUSIEST
BUSILY
BUSINE
BUSINESS
BUSINESSES
BUSINESSLIKE
BUSINESSMAN
BUSINESSMEN
BUSINESSWOMAN
BUSING
BUSK
BUSKED
BUSKER
BUSKET
BUSKIN
BUSKINED
BUSKINS
BUSKLE
BUSMAN
BUSMEN
BUSS
BUSSE
BUSSED
BUSSER
BUSSES
BUSSING
BUSSOCK
BUSSU
BUSSY
BUST
BUSTARD
BUSTED
BUSTEE
BUSTER
BUSTHEAD
BUSTI
BUSTIAN
BUSTIC
BUSTICATE
BUSTING
BUSTLE
BUSTLED
BUSTLER
BUSTLING
BUSTLINGLY
BUSTO
BUSWAY
BUSY
BUSYBODIES
BUSYBODY
BUSYING
BUSYNESS
BUSYWORK
BUT
BUTADIENE
BUTANE
BUTANOL
BUTANONE
BUTCH
BUTCHA
BUTCHER
BUTCHERBIRD
BUTCHERBROOM
BUTCHERER
BUTCHERESS
BUTCHERIES
BUTCHERING
BUTCHERLY
BUTCHEROUS
BUTCHERY
BUTEIN
BUTENYL
BUTEONINE

BUTIN
BUTINE
BUTLER
BUTLERAGE
BUTLERIES
BUTLERY
BUTMENT
BUTOMACEOUS
BUTOR
BUTOXY
BUTOXYL
BUTS
BUTSUDAN
BUTT
BUTTAL
BUTTE
BUTTED
BUTTER
BUTTERACEOUS
BUTTERBACK
BUTTERBALL
BUTTERBILL
BUTTERBIRD
BUTTERBOUGH
BUTTERBOX
BUTTERBUMP
BUTTERBUR
BUTTERBURR
BUTTERBUSH
BUTTERCUP
BUTTERED
BUTTERFAT
BUTTERFISH
BUTTERFISHES
BUTTERFLIES
BUTTERFLOWER
BUTTERFLY
BUTTERHEAD
BUTTERIES
BUTTERINE
BUTTERIS
BUTTERJAGS
BUTTERMAN
BUTTERMILK
BUTTERMONGER
BUTTERNOSE
BUTTERNUT
BUTTERSCOTCH
BUTTERWEED
BUTTERWORKER
BUTTERWORT
BUTTERY
BUTTING
BUTTINSKY
BUTTLE
BUTTOCK
BUTTOCKED
BUTTOCKER
BUTTOCKS
BUTTON
BUTTONBALL
BUTTONBUR
BUTTONBUSH
BUTTONED
BUTTONER
BUTTONHOLD
BUTTONHOLDER
BUTTONHOLE
BUTTONHOLED
BUTTONHOLER
BUTTONHOLING
BUTTONHOOK
BUTTONING
BUTTONLIKE
BUTTONMOLD
BUTTONMOULD
BUTTONS
BUTTONWEED
BUTTONWOOD
BUTTONY
BUTTRESS
BUTTRESSED
BUTTRESSING
BUTTS
BUTTSTOCK
BUTTWOMAN
BUTTWOMEN
BUTTY
BUTTYMAN
BUTYL
BUTYLAMINE
BUTYLATION
BUTYLENE
BUTYLIC
BUTYNE
BUTYRACEOUS
BUTYRATE
BUTYRIC
BUTYRICALLY
BUTYRIN
BUTYRINASE
BUTYROMETER
BUTYROMETRIC
BUTYRONE
BUTYROUS
BUTYRYL
BUVETTE
BUXACEOUS
BUXERRIES
BUXERRY
BUXOM
BUXOMLY
BUXOMNESS
BUY
BUYABLE
BUYER
BUYING
BUYO
BUZANE
BUZZ
BUZZARD
BUZZARDLY
BUZZED
BUZZER
BUZZERPHONE
BUZZGLOAK
BUZZIER
BUZZIES
BUZZIEST
BUZZING
BUZZLE
BUZZWIG
BUZZY
BWANA
BWAZI
BY
BYARD
BYCOCKET
BYCOKET
BYE
BYEE
BYELAW
BYEMAN
BYERITE
BYERLITE
BYGO
BYGOING
BYGONE
BYHAND
BYLAND
BYLAW
BYLINA
BYLINER
BYLINY
BYNAME
BYNEDESTIN
BYON
BYOUS
BYOUSLY
BYPASS
BYPASSED
BYPASSER
BYPASSING
BYPAST
BYPATH
BYPLAY
BYRE
BYREMAN
BYREWOMAN
BYRL
BYRLADY
BYRLAW
BYRLAWMAN
BYRLAWMEN
BYRNIE
BYROAD
BYRRUS
BYRTHYNSAK
BYSEN
BYSMALITH
BYSPELL
BYSSACEOUS
BYSSAL
BYSSI
BYSSIFEROUS
BYSSIN
BYSSINE
BYSSOGENOUS
BYSSOID
BYSSOLITE
BYSSUS
BYSSUSES
BYSTANDER
BYSTREET
BYTH
BYTOWNITE
BYTOWNITITE
BYWALK
BYWALKER
BYWALKING
BYWAY
BYWONER
BYWORD
BYWORK
BYZANT
BYZEN

C

CAAM
CAAMA
CAAMING
CAAPEBA
CAAPI
CAATINGA
CAB
CABA
CABAAN
CABACK
CABAHO
CABAL
CABALA
CABALASSOU
CABALETTA
CABALIC
CABALISM
CABALIST
CABALISTIC
CABALISTICAL
CABALISTICALLY
CABALL
CABALLED
CABALLER
CABALLERIA
CABALLERO
CABALLEROS
CABALLINE
CABALLING
CABALLO
CABAN
CABANA
CABANE
CABARET
CABARETIER
CABAS
CABASA
CABASSET
CABASSOU
CABBAGE
CABBAGED
CABBAGEHEAD
CABBAGEWOOD
CABBAGING
CABBAGY
CABBALAH
CABBED
CABBER
CABBIES
CABBING
CABBLE
CABBLER
CABBY
CABDA
CABDRIVER
CABDRIVING
CABECERA
CABECUDO
CABELIAU
CABELLEROTE
CABER
CABERNET
CABESTRO
CABEZON
CABIE
CABILDO
CABILLIAU
CABIN
CABINED
CABINET
CABINETED
CABINETING
CABINETMAKER
CABINETMAKING
CABINETRY
CABINETTED
CABINETWORK
CABINETWORKER
CABINETWORKING
CABINING
CABINLIKE
CABIO
CABLE
CABLED
CABLEGRAM
CABLEMAN
CABLEMEN
CABLER
CABLES
CABLESE
CABLET
CABLEWAY
CABLING
CABMAN
CABOB
CABOCEER
CABOCHED
CABOCHON
CABOCLE
CABOCLO
CABOODLE
CABOOK
CABOOSE
CABOSHED
CABOT
CABOTAGE
CABOTIN
CABOTINAGE
CABOUCA
CABREE
CABRERITE
CABRESTA
CABRESTO
CABRET
CABRETTA
CABREUVA
CABRIE
CABRILLA
CABRIOLE
CABRIOLET
CABRIT
CABRITO
CABSTAND
CABUJA
CABULLA
CABURN
CABUYA
CACAESTHESIA
CACAFUEGO
CACAFUGO
CACAM
CACAO
CACAOS
CACAXTE
CACESTHESIA
CACESTHESIS
CACHACA
CACHAEMIA
CACHAEMIC
CACHALOT
CACHAZA
CACHE
CACHECTICAL
CACHED
CACHEMIA
CACHEMIC
CACHEPOT
CACHES
CACHET
CACHETIC
CACHEXIA
CACHEXIC
CACHEXY
CACHIBOU
CACHILA
CACHIMILLA
CACHINA
CACHING
CACHINNATE
CACHINNATION
CACHINNATOR
CACHINNATORY
CACHOEIRA
CACHOLONG
CACHOT
CACHOU
CACHRYS
CACHUA
CACHUCHA
CACHUCHO
CACHUNDE
CACIDROSIS
CACIOCAVALLO
CACIQUE
CACIQUISM
CACK
CACKEREL
CACKLE
CACKLED
CACKLER
CACKLING
CACO
CACOCHOLIA
CACOCHROIA
CACOCHYLIA
CACOCHYMIA
CACOCHYMIC
CACOCHYMICAL
CACOCHYMY
CACODAEMON
CACODEMON
CACODEMONIA
CACODEMONIAC
CACODEMONIAL
CACODEMONIC
CACODOXIAN
CACODOXICAL
CACODOXY
CACODYL
CACODYLIC
CACOECONOMY
CACOEPIST
CACOEPISTIC
CACOEPY
CACOETHES
CACOETHIC
CACOGALACTIA
CACOGASTRIC
CACOGENESIS
CACOGENIC
CACOGENICS
CACOGEUSIA
CACOGLOSSIA
CACOGRAPHER
CACOGRAPHIC
CACOGRAPHY
CACOLET
CACOLOGY
CACOMELIA
CACOMISTLE
CACOMIXL
CACOMIXLE
CACOMORPHIA
CACONYM
CACOON
CACOPATHY
CACOPHARYNGIA
CACOPHONIA
CACOPHONIC
CACOPHONICAL
CACOPHONICALLY
CACOPHONIST
CACOPHONIZE
CACOPHONOUS
CACOPHONOUSLY
CACOPHONY
CACOPLASIA
CACOPLASTIC
CACOPROCTIA
CACORHYTHMIC
CACORRHACHIS
CACORRHINIA
CACOSPERMIA
CACOSTOMIA
CACOTHELIN
CACOTHELINE
CACOTHYMIA
CACOTRICHIA
CACOTROPHIA
CACOTROPHY
CACOTYPE
CACOXENE
CACOXENITE
CACOZEAL
CACOZEALOUS
CACOZYME
CACTACEOUS
CACTAL
CACTI
CACTIFORM
CACTOID
CACTUS
CACTUSES
CACUMEN
CACUMINAL
CACUMINATE
CACUMINATION
CACUMINOUS
CACUR
CAD
CADALENE
CADAMBA
CADAR
CADASTER
CADASTRAL
CADASTRATION
CADASTRE
CADAVER
CADAVERIC
CADAVERIN
CADAVERINE
CADAVEROUS
CADAVEROUSLY
CADBAIT
CADBIT
CADBOTE
CADDED
CADDI
CADDICE
CADDICED
CADDIE
CADDIED
CADDIES
CADDING
CADDIS
CADDISED
CADDISH
CADDISHLY
CADDISHNESS
CADDLE
CADDOW
CADDY
CADDYING
CADE
CADEAU
CADELLE
CADENCE
CADENCED
CADENCIES
CADENCY
CADENETTE
CADENT
CADENTIAL
CADENZA
CADER
CADESSE
CADET
CADETCY
CADETSHIP
CADETTE
CADEW
CADGE
CADGED
CADGER
CADGILY
CADGINESS
CADGING
CADGY
CADI
CADIE
CADILESKER
CADILLO
CADINENE
CADIS
CADISH
CADJAN
CADLOCK
CADMIA
CADMIC
CADMIDE
CADMIFEROUS
CADMIUM
CADRANS
CADRE
CADUA
CADUAC
CADUCA
CADUCARY
CADUCE
CADUCEAN
CADUCEUS
CADUCIARY
CADUCIBRANCH
CADUCICORN
CADUCITY
CADUKE
CADUS
CADWEED
CADY
CAECA
CAECALLY
CAECECTOMY
CAECIFORM
CAECILIAN
CAECITIS
CAECOCOLIC
CAECOSTOMY
CAECOTOMY
CAECUM
CAELOMETER
CAENOSTYLIC
CAENOSTYLY
CAEOMA
CAESAREAN
CAESARIAN

CAESIOUS
CAESIUM
CAESPITOSE
CAESTUS
CAESURA
CAESURAE
CAESURAL
CAESURAS
CAESURIC
CAFARD
CAFARDISE
CAFE
CAFENEH
CAFENET
CAFETAL
CAFETERIA
CAFETIERE
CAFF
CAFFA
CAFFE
CAFFEATE
CAFFEIC
CAFFEIN
CAFFEINE
CAFFEINIC
CAFFEINISM
CAFFEISM
CAFFEOL
CAFFEONE
CAFFETANNIN
CAFFISO
CAFFLE
CAFFLED
CAFFLING
CAFFOLINE
CAFFOY
CAFILA
CAFIZ
CAFOY
CAFTA
CAFTAN
CAFTANED
CAFUSO
CAG
CAGE
CAGED
CAGELING
CAGEMAN
CAGEOT
CAGER
CAGESTER
CAGEWORK
CAGEY
CAGGY
CAGIER
CAGIEST
CAGIT
CAGMAG
CAHAR
CAHIER
CAHINCIC
CAHIZ
CAHOOT
CAHOOTS
CAHOT
CAHOW
CAHUITA
CAHUY
CAIARARA
CAID
CAILCEDRA
CAILLE
CAILLEACH
CAILLIACH
CAIMACAM
CAIMAKAM
CAIMAN
CAIMITILLO
CAIMITO
CAIN
CAINGIN
CAIQUE
CAIQUEJEE
CAIRD
CAIRN
CAIRNED
CAIRNGORM
CAIRNGORUM
CAIRNY
CAISSE
CAISSON
CAISSONED
CAITIF
CAITIFF
CAIXINHA
CAJA
CAJANG
CAJAPUT
CAJAVA
CAJEPUT
CAJETA
CAJI
CAJOLE
CAJOLED
CAJOLEMENT
CAJOLER
CAJOLERIES
CAJOLERY
CAJOLING
CAJOLINGLY
CAJON
CAJOO
CAJOU
CAJU
CAJUELA
CAJUN
CAJUPUT
CAJUPUTENE
CAJUPUTOL
CAKE
CAKEBOX
CAKEBREAD
CAKED
CAKEHOUSE
CAKEMAKER
CAKEMAKING
CAKER
CAKES
CAKETTE
CAKEWALK
CAKEY
CAKIER
CAKIEST
CAKING
CAKRA
CAKY
CAL
CALABA
CALABAR
CALABASH
CALABAZA
CALABAZILLA
CALABER
CALABOOSE
CALABOZO
CALABRASELLA
CALABRESE
CALABUR
CALADE
CALADIUM
CALAHAN
CALAITE
CALALU
CALAMANCOES
CALAMANCOS
CALAMANSI
CALAMARIAN
CALAMARIES
CALAMARIOID
CALAMAROID
CALAMARY
CALAMBAC
CALAMBOUR
CALAMI
CALAMIFORM
CALAMINE
CALAMINED
CALAMINING
CALAMINT
CALAMISTRAL
CALAMISTRUM
CALAMITE
CALAMITEAN
CALAMITIES
CALAMITOID
CALAMITOUS
CALAMITOUSLY
CALAMITY
CALAMONDIN
CALAMUS
CALAN
CALANDER
CALANDO
CALANDRE
CALANDRIA
CALANGAY
CALANID
CALANQUE
CALANTAS
CALANTHE
CALAO
CALAPITE
CALAPITTE
CALASCIONE
CALASH
CALATHEA
CALATHI
CALATHIDIA
CALATHIDIUM
CALATHISCI
CALATHISCUS
CALATHOS
CALATHUS
CALAVERITE
CALCAEMIA
CALCANEAL
CALCANEAN
CALCANEI
CALCANEUM
CALCANEUS
CALCAR
CALCARATE
CALCARATED
CALCAREOUS
CALCAREOUSLY
CALCARIA
CALCARIFORM
CALCARINE
CALCARIUM
CALCEATE
CALCED
CALCEDONY
CALCEIFORM
CALCEMIA
CALCEOLATE
CALCES
CALCEUS
CALCIC
CALCICLASE
CALCICOLOUS
CALCICOSIS
CALCIFEROL
CALCIFEROUS
CALCIFIC
CALCIFICATION
CALCIFIED
CALCIFORM
CALCIFUGAL
CALCIFUGE
CALCIFUGOUS
CALCIFY
CALCIFYING
CALCIGENOUS
CALCIGEROUS
CALCIMETER
CALCIMINE
CALCIMINED
CALCIMINER
CALCIMINING
CALCINATION
CALCINATORY
CALCINE
CALCINED
CALCINER
CALCINING
CALCINO
CALCIPEXY
CALCIPHILE
CALCIPHILIA
CALCIPHILOUS
CALCIPHYRE
CALCIPRIVIC
CALCITE
CALCITRANT
CALCITRATE
CALCITRATION
CALCIUM
CALCIVOROUS
CALCOGRAPHER
CALCOGRAPHIC
CALCOGRAPHY
CALCRETE
CALCSINTER
CALCSPAR
CALCTUFA
CALCTUFF
CALCULABLE
CALCULABLY
CALCULARY
CALCULATE
CALCULATED
CALCULATING
CALCULATION
CALCULATIONAL
CALCULATIVE
CALCULATOR
CALCULATORY
CALCULER
CALCULIFORM
CALCULIST
CALCULOUS
CALCULUS
CALCULUSES
CALDARIA
CALDARIUM
CALDEN
CALDERA
CALDRON
CALE
CALEAN
CALECHE
CALEDONITE
CALEFACIENT
CALEFACTION
CALEFACTIVE
CALEFACTOR
CALEFACTORY
CALELECTRIC
CALEMBOUR
CALENDAL
CALENDAR
CALENDARIAL
CALENDARIAN
CALENDARIC
CALENDER
CALENDERED
CALENDERER
CALENDERING
CALENDRIC
CALENDRICAL
CALENDRY
CALENDS
CALENDULA
CALENDULIN
CALENTURAL
CALENTURE
CALENTURED
CALENTURING
CALENTURIST
CALEPIN
CALESA
CALESCENCE
CALESCENT
CALESERO
CALESIN
CALF
CALFBOUND
CALFKILL
CALFLING
CALFSKIN
CALIBER
CALIBERED
CALIBOGUS
CALIBRATE
CALIBRATED
CALIBRATION
CALIBRATOR
CALIBRE
CALIBRED
CALICHE
CALICIFORM
CALICLE
CALICO
CALICOBACK
CALICOED
CALICOES
CALICOS
CALICULAR
CALID
CALIDITY
CALIDUCT
CALIF
CALIFORNITE
CALIFORNIUM
CALIGA
CALIGATED
CALIGINOSITY
CALIGINOUS
CALIGINOUSLY
CALIGO
CALIGRAPHY
CALIMANCO
CALIN
CALINDA
CALINE
CALINUT
CALIOLOGICAL
CALIOLOGIST
CALIOLOGY
CALIPASH
CALIPEE
CALIPER
CALIPERER
CALIPERS
CALIPH

CALIPHAL
CALIPHATE
CALISAYA
CALISTHENEUM
CALISTHENIC
CALISTHENICS
CALIVER
CALIX
CALK
CALKAGE
CALKER
CALKING
CALL
CALLA
CALLABLE
CALLAINITE
CALLAIS
CALLAN
CALLANT
CALLATE
CALLBOY
CALLE
CALLED
CALLER
CALLES
CALLET
CALLI
CALLID
CALLIDITY
CALLIDNESS
CALLIGRAPH
CALLIGRAPHER
CALLIGRAPHIC
CALLIGRAPHY
CALLING
CALLIOPE
CALLIOPHONE
CALLIOPSIS
CALLIPASH
CALLIPEE
CALLIPER
CALLIPERER
CALLIPHORID
CALLIPHORINE
CALLIPYGIAN
CALLIPYGOUS
CALLISECTION
CALLISTEIA
CALLISTHENIC
CALLISTHENICS
CALLITHUMP
CALLITYPE
CALLITYPED
CALLITYPING
CALLOP
CALLOSAL
CALLOSE
CALLOSITY
CALLOSUM
CALLOUS
CALLOUSED
CALLOUSING
CALLOUSLY
CALLOUSNESS
CALLOW
CALLOWER
CALLOWMAN
CALLUS
CALLUSES
CALM
CALMANT
CALMATIVE
CALMATO
CALMECAC
CALMER
CALMEST
CALMIERER
CALMLY
CALMNESS
CALMY
CALO
CALODAEMON
CALODEMON
CALODEMONIAL
CALOMBA
CALOMBIGAS
CALOMBO
CALOMEL
CALOOL
CALOR
CALORESCENCE
CALORESCENT
CALORIC
CALORICITY
CALORIE
CALORIFIC
CALORIFICAL
CALORIFICS
CALORIFIER
CALORIFY
CALORIGENIC
CALORIMETER
CALORIMETRIC
CALORIMETRY
CALORIMOTOR
CALORIS
CALORISATOR
CALORIST
CALORIZE
CALORIZER
CALOSOMA
CALOTIN
CALOTTE
CALOTYPE
CALOTYPIC
CALOTYPIST
CALOYER
CALP
CALPAC
CALPACK
CALPACKED
CALPOLLI
CALPUL
CALPULLI
CALQUE
CALSOUNS
CALTHROP
CALTRAP
CALTROP
CALTROPS
CALUMBA
CALUMET
CALUMNIATE
CALUMNIATED
CALUMNIATION
CALUMNIATIVE
CALUMNIATOR
CALUMNIATORY
CALUMNIES
CALUMNIOUS
CALUMNIOUSLY
CALUMNY
CALUSAR
CALVA
CALVAIRE
CALVARIA
CALVARIAL
CALVARIES
CALVARIUM
CALVARY
CALVE
CALVED
CALVER
CALVES
CALVING
CALVISH
CALVITIES
CALVITY
CALVOUS
CALX
CALXES
CALYCANTH
CALYCANTHEMY
CALYCANTHIN
CALYCANTHINE
CALYCATE
CALYCES
CALYCIFEROUS
CALYCIFLORAL
CALYCIFORM
CALYCINE
CALYCLE
CALYCLED
CALYCOID
CALYCOIDEOUS
CALYCOPHORAN
CALYCULAR
CALYCULATE
CALYCULATED
CALYCULE
CALYCULUS
CALYMMA
CALYPHYOMY
CALYPSO
CALYPTER
CALYPTRA
CALYPTRATE
CALYPTRIFORM
CALYPTROGEN
CALYX
CALZADA
CALZONERAS
CALZOONS
CAM
CAMACA
CAMACEY
CAMACHILE
CAMAGON
CAMAIEU
CAMAIL
CAMAILE
CAMAILED
CAMALIG
CAMALOTE
CAMAN
CAMANAY
CAMANSI
CAMARA
CAMARADA
CAMARADE
CAMARADERIE
CAMARERA
CAMARILLA
CAMARIN
CAMARON
CAMAS
CAMASS
CAMATA
CAMATINA
CAMAURO
CAMAY
CAMBAYE
CAMBER
CAMBERED
CAMBERING
CAMBIAL
CAMBIATA
CAMBIFORM
CAMBIO
CAMBISM
CAMBIST
CAMBISTRY
CAMBIUM
CAMBLET
CAMBOGIA
CAMBOOSE
CAMBOUIS
CAMBRESINE
CAMBRIC
CAMBUCA
CAME
CAMEIST
CAMEL
CAMELEER
CAMELHAIR
CAMELINE
CAMELISH
CAMELISHNESS
CAMELKEEPER
CAMELLIA
CAMELLIN
CAMELMAN
CAMELOID
CAMELOPARD
CAMELOT
CAMELRY
CAMEO
CAMEOGRAPH
CAMEOGRAPHY
CAMEOS
CAMERA
CAMERAE
CAMERAL
CAMERALISM
CAMERALIST
CAMERALISTIC
CAMERALISTICS
CAMERAMAN
CAMERAS
CAMERATE
CAMERATED
CAMERATION
CAMERIER
CAMERIERA
CAMERIERI
CAMERIST
CAMERLENGO
CAMERLINGO
CAMIAS
CAMILLA
CAMINO
CAMION
CAMIS
CAMISA
CAMISADE
CAMISADO
CAMISCIA
CAMISE
CAMISIA
CAMISOLE
CAMLET
CAMLETED
CAMLETEEN
CAMLETINE
CAMLETING
CAMMED
CAMMOCK
CAMMOCKY
CAMOGIE
CAMOIS
CAMOMILE
CAMOOCH
CAMOODI
CAMOODIE
CAMOTE
CAMOUDIE
CAMOUFLAGE
CAMOUFLAGED
CAMOUFLAGER
CAMOUFLAGING
CAMOUFLET
CAMOUFLEUR
CAMP
CAMPAGNA
CAMPAGNOL
CAMPAIGN
CAMPAIGNER
CAMPANA
CAMPANE
CAMPANELLA
CAMPANERO
CAMPANIFORM
CAMPANILE
CAMPANILES
CAMPANILLA
CAMPANINI
CAMPANIST
CAMPANISTIC
CAMPANOLOGER
CAMPANOLOGY
CAMPANULAR
CAMPANULATE
CAMPANULOUS
CAMPBELLITE
CAMPCRAFT
CAMPECHE
CAMPED
CAMPEPHAGINE
CAMPER
CAMPESINO
CAMPESTRAL
CAMPFIGHT
CAMPFIRE
CAMPGROUND
CAMPHANE
CAMPHANIC
CAMPHANONE
CAMPHANYL
CAMPHENE
CAMPHINE
CAMPHIRE
CAMPHOID
CAMPHOL
CAMPHOLIDE
CAMPHOR
CAMPHORATE
CAMPHORATED
CAMPHORATING
CAMPHORIC
CAMPHOROYL
CAMPHORWOOD
CAMPHORYL
CAMPHYLENE
CAMPIER
CAMPIEST
CAMPILAN
CAMPIMETER
CAMPIMETRY
CAMPING
CAMPIT
CAMPLE
CAMPMAN
CAMPMASTER
CAMPO
CAMPODEID
CAMPODEIFORM
CAMPODEOID
CAMPODY
CAMPONG
CAMPOO
CAMPOODY
CAMPOREE
CAMPSHED
CAMPSHEDDING
CAMPSHEETING

CAMPSHOT
CAMPSITE
CAMPSTOOL
CAMPTODROME
CAMPTONITE
CAMPUS
CAMPUSES
CAMPWARD
CAMPY
CAMPYLITE
CAMPYLODROME
CAMPYLOMETER
CAMSHACH
CAMSHACHLE
CAMSHAFT
CAMSTANE
CAMSTEARY
CAMSTEERY
CAMSTONE
CAMSTRARY
CAMUNING
CAMUS
CAMUSE
CAMUSED
CAMWOOD
CAN
CANABA
CANABAE
CANACUAS
CANADA
CANADITE
CANADOL
CANAFISTOLO
CANAFISTULA
CANAFISTULO
CANAGLIA
CANAIGRE
CANAILLE
CANAJONG
CANAKIN
CANAL
CANALBOAT
CANALE
CANALER
CANALETE
CANALI
CANALICULAR
CANALICULATE
CANALICULI
CANALICULUS
CANALIFEROUS
CANALIFORM
CANALING
CANALIS
CANALIZATION
CANALIZE
CANALIZED
CANALIZING
CANALLA
CANALLER
CANALLING
CANAMO
CANAO
CANAPE
CANAPINA
CANARD
CANARI
CANARIES
CANARIN
CANARINE
CANARY
CANASTER
CANAUT
CANAVALIN
CANCAN
CANCEL
CANCELABLE
CANCELATION
CANCELED
CANCELEER
CANCELER
CANCELIER
CANCELING
CANCELLARIAN
CANCELLARIUS
CANCELLATE
CANCELLATED
CANCELLATION
CANCELLED
CANCELLER
CANCELLI
CANCELLING
CANCELLOUS
CANCELS
CANCER
CANCERATE
CANCERATED
CANCERATING
CANCERATION
CANCERDROPS
CANCERED
CANCERIGENIC
CANCERISM
CANCERITE
CANCEROPHOBE
CANCEROUS
CANCEROUSLY
CANCERROOT
CANCERWEED
CANCERWORT
CANCH
CANCHA
CANCHALAGUA
CANCHITO
CANCION
CANCIONERO
CANCIONES
CANCRID
CANCRIFORM
CANCRINITE
CANCRISOCIAL
CANCRIVOROUS
CANCRIZANS
CANCROID
CANCRUM
CANCRUMS
CAND
CANDAREEN
CANDELABRA
CANDELABRAS
CANDELABRUM
CANDELABRUMS
CANDELILLA
CANDENCY
CANDENT
CANDESCENCE
CANDESCENT
CANDESCENTLY
CANDI
CANDID
CANDIDACIES
CANDIDACY
CANDIDATE
CANDIDATED
CANDIDATES
CANDIDATING
CANDIDATURE
CANDIDLY
CANDIDNESS
CANDIED
CANDIEL
CANDIER
CANDIES
CANDIFY
CANDIL
CANDIRU
CANDITE
CANDLE
CANDLEBALL
CANDLEBEAM
CANDLEBERRY
CANDLEBOMB
CANDLEBOX
CANDLED
CANDLEFISH
CANDLEHOLDER
CANDLELIGHT
CANDLELIGHTING
CANDLELIT
CANDLEMAKER
CANDLEMAKING
CANDLENUT
CANDLEPIN
CANDLEPOWER
CANDLER
CANDLERENT
CANDLES
CANDLESHINE
CANDLESHRIFT
CANDLESNUFFER
CANDLESTAND
CANDLESTICK
CANDLEWASTER
CANDLEWICK
CANDLEWICKING
CANDLEWOOD
CANDLEWRIGHT
CANDLING
CANDOCK
CANDOR
CANDOUR
CANDROY
CANDROYS
CANDUC
CANDY
CANDYING
CANDYMAKER
CANDYS
CANDYSTICK
CANDYTUFT
CANDYWEED
CANE
CANEBRAKE
CANED
CANEL
CANELA
CANELL
CANELLA
CANELLACEOUS
CANELLE
CANELO
CANEOLOGY
CANEPHOR
CANEPHORA
CANEPHORAE
CANEPHORI
CANEPHOROE
CANEPHOROI
CANEPHOROS
CANEPHORUS
CANEPIN
CANER
CANESCENT
CANETON
CANETTE
CANEWARE
CANEWORK
CANEZOU
CANFIELDITE
CANG
CANGAN
CANGIA
CANGLE
CANGUE
CANGY
CANHOOP
CANI
CANICULE
CANID
CANILLE
CANIN
CANINAL
CANINE
CANING
CANINIFORM
CANINITY
CANINUS
CANIONED
CANIONS
CANISTEL
CANISTER
CANITIES
CANK
CANKER
CANKERBERRY
CANKERBIRD
CANKEREAT
CANKERED
CANKEREDLY
CANKEREDNESS
CANKERFLOWER
CANKERFRET
CANKEROUS
CANKERROOT
CANKERWEED
CANKERWORM
CANKERWORT
CANKERY
CANMAN
CANN
CANNA
CANNABIC
CANNABIN
CANNABINE
CANNABIS
CANNABISM
CANNACEOUS
CANNACH
CANNAT
CANNE
CANNED
CANNEL
CANNELE
CANNELLATE
CANNELLATED
CANNELLE
CANNELLONI
CANNELON
CANNELURE
CANNELURED
CANNEQUIN
CANNER
CANNERIES
CANNERY
CANNET
CANNETILLE
CANNIBAL
CANNIBALIC
CANNIBALISM
CANNIBALISTIC
CANNIBALITY
CANNIBALIZE
CANNIBALIZED
CANNIBALIZING
CANNIBALLY
CANNIER
CANNIEST
CANNIKIN
CANNILY
CANNINESS
CANNING
CANNON
CANNONADE
CANNONADED
CANNONADING
CANNONED
CANNONEER
CANNONEERING
CANNONIER
CANNONPROOF
CANNONRY
CANNOPHORI
CANNOT
CANNULA
CANNULAR
CANNULATE
CANNULATED
CANNY
CANOE
CANOEING
CANOEIST
CANOELOAD
CANOEMAN
CANOES
CANOEWOOD
CANON
CANONCITO
CANONESS
CANONIC
CANONICAL
CANONICALLY
CANONICALS
CANONICATE
CANONICITY
CANONICS
CANONIST
CANONISTIC
CANONISTICAL
CANONIZANT
CANONIZATION
CANONIZE
CANONIZED
CANONIZER
CANONIZING
CANONRY
CANONS
CANONSHIP
CANOODLE
CANOPID
CANOPIED
CANOPIES
CANOPY
CANOPYING
CANOR
CANOROUS
CANOROUSLY
CANOROUSNESS
CANOS
CANOTIER
CANROY
CANROYER
CANSH
CANSO
CANSOS
CANST
CANT
CANTABANK
CANTABILE
CANTADOR
CANTALA
CANTALEVER
CANTALITE
CANTALOUP
CANTALOUPE
CANTANKEROUS

CANTAR
CANTARA
CANTARE
CANTARO
CANTATA
CANTATION
CANTATIVE
CANTATORY
CANTATRICE
CANTED
CANTEEN
CANTER
CANTERED
CANTERER
CANTERING
CANTHAL
CANTHARI
CANTHARIDAL
CANTHARIDATE
CANTHARIDEAN
CANTHARIDES
CANTHARIDIAN
CANTHARIDIN
CANTHARIDISM
CANTHARIDIZE
CANTHARIS
CANTHARUS
CANTHECTOMY
CANTHI
CANTHITIS
CANTHOLYSIS
CANTHOPLASTY
CANTHOTOMY
CANTHUS
CANTIC
CANTICLE
CANTICLES
CANTICO
CANTIGA
CANTIL
CANTILATED
CANTILATING
CANTILENA
CANTILENE
CANTILENES
CANTILEVER
CANTILLATE
CANTILLATION
CANTILY
CANTINA
CANTING
CANTINGLY
CANTINGNESS
CANTINO
CANTION
CANTLE
CANTLET
CANTLINE
CANTO
CANTON
CANTONAL
CANTONED
CANTONER
CANTONMENT
CANTOON
CANTOR
CANTORAL
CANTORIA
CANTORIAL
CANTORIS
CANTOROUS
CANTOS
CANTRAIP
CANTRAP
CANTRED
CANTREF
CANTRIP
CANTUS
CANTUT
CANTUTA
CANTY
CANULA
CANULATE
CANUN
CANVAS
CANVASBACK
CANVASBACKS
CANVASMAN
CANVASS
CANVASSED
CANVASSER
CANVASSING
CANY
CANYON
CANZON
CANZONA
CANZONE
CANZONET
CANZONI
CAOBA
CAOINE
CAOUTCHOUC
CAP
CAPA
CAPABILITIES
CAPABILITY
CAPABLE
CAPABLENESS
CAPABLY
CAPACIOUS
CAPACIOUSLY
CAPACITANCE
CAPACITATE
CAPACITATED
CAPACITATING
CAPACITATION
CAPACITATIVE
CAPACITIES
CAPACITIVE
CAPACITOR
CAPACITY
CAPANNA
CAPANNE
CAPARISON
CAPARISONED
CAPARISONING
CAPATAZ
CAPAX
CAPCASE
CAPE
CAPEADOR
CAPEL
CAPELET
CAPELIN
CAPELINE
CAPELLET
CAPER
CAPERBUSH
CAPERCAILLIE
CAPERCAILZIE
CAPERCUT
CAPERED
CAPERER
CAPERING
CAPERNOITED
CAPERNOITIE
CAPERNOITY
CAPERNUTIE
CAPERS
CAPERSOME
CAPERWORT
CAPES
CAPESKIN
CAPETTE
CAPEWEED
CAPFUL
CAPH
CAPHAR
CAPHITE
CAPIAS
CAPIASES
CAPIBARA
CAPICHA
CAPILACEOUS
CAPILLAIRE
CAPILLAMENT
CAPILLARIES
CAPILLARITIES
CAPILLARITY
CAPILLARY
CAPILLATION
CAPILLI
CAPILLIFORM
CAPILLITIA
CAPILLITIAL
CAPILLITIUM
CAPILLOSE
CAPILLUS
CAPILOTADE
CAPISTRATE
CAPITA
CAPITAL
CAPITALED
CAPITALING
CAPITALISM
CAPITALIST
CAPITALISTIC
CAPITALIZE
CAPITALIZED
CAPITALIZING
CAPITALLY
CAPITAN
CAPITANA
CAPITANO
CAPITATE
CAPITATED
CAPITATIM
CAPITATION
CAPITATIVE
CAPITATUM
CAPITE
CAPITELLA
CAPITELLAR
CAPITELLATE
CAPITELLUM
CAPITOL
CAPITOUL
CAPITOULATE
CAPITULANT
CAPITULAR
CAPITULARIES
CAPITULARY
CAPITULATE
CAPITULATED
CAPITULATING
CAPITULATION
CAPITULATOR
CAPITULATORY
CAPITULIFORM
CAPITULUM
CAPLE
CAPLIN
CAPLING
CAPLOCK
CAPMAKER
CAPMAKING
CAPMAN
CAPMINT
CAPNOMANCY
CAPOCCHIA
CAPOMO
CAPON
CAPONIER
CAPONIERE
CAPONIZE
CAPONIZER
CAPONNIERE
CAPORAL
CAPOT
CAPOTASTO
CAPOTE
CAPOUCH
CAPPA
CAPPADINE
CAPPAE
CAPPED
CAPPELENITE
CAPPER
CAPPIE
CAPPING
CAPPLE
CAPPO
CAPPY
CAPRATE
CAPRELLINE
CAPREOL
CAPREOLATE
CAPREOLINE
CAPRETTO
CAPRIC
CAPRICCETTO
CAPRICCETTOS
CAPRICCIO
CAPRICCIOS
CAPRICCIOSO
CAPRICE
CAPRICIOUS
CAPRICIOUSLY
CAPRICIOUSNESS
CAPRID
CAPRIFICATE
CAPRIFICATOR
CAPRIFIG
CAPRIFOIL
CAPRIFOLE
CAPRIFORM
CAPRIGENOUS
CAPRIMULGINE
CAPRIN
CAPRINE
CAPRINIC
CAPRIOLE
CAPRIOLED
CAPRIOLING
CAPRIPED
CAPRIPEDE
CAPRIZANT
CAPROATE
CAPROIC
CAPROIN
CAPRONE
CAPRONIC
CAPRONYL
CAPROYL
CAPRYL
CAPRYLATE
CAPRYLIC
CAPRYLIN
CAPRYLONE
CAPRYLYL
CAPS
CAPSA
CAPSAICIN
CAPSHEAF
CAPSHORE
CAPSICIN
CAPSICUM
CAPSID
CAPSIZAL
CAPSIZE
CAPSIZED
CAPSIZING
CAPSTAN
CAPSTONE
CAPSULA
CAPSULAR
CAPSULATE
CAPSULATED
CAPSULATION
CAPSULE
CAPSULECTOMY
CAPSULED
CAPSULER
CAPSULING
CAPSULITIS
CAPSULOTOME
CAPSULOTOMY
CAPSUMIN
CAPTACULA
CAPTACULUM
CAPTAIN
CAPTAINCIES
CAPTAINCY
CAPTAINESS
CAPTAINRIES
CAPTAINRY
CAPTAINSHIP
CAPTATION
CAPTION
CAPTIOUS
CAPTIOUSLY
CAPTIOUSNESS
CAPTIVATE
CAPTIVATED
CAPTIVATELY
CAPTIVATING
CAPTIVATION
CAPTIVATIVE
CAPTIVATOR
CAPTIVE
CAPTIVED
CAPTIVING
CAPTIVITIES
CAPTIVITY
CAPTOR
CAPTURE
CAPTURED
CAPTURER
CAPTURING
CAPUCHE
CAPUCHIN
CAPUCINE
CAPUL
CAPULI
CAPULIN
CAPUT
CAPUTIUM
CAPYBARA
CAR
CARA
CARABAO
CARABAOS
CARABEEN
CARABID
CARABIDAN
CARABIDEOUS
CARABIDOID
CARABIN
CARABINE
CARABINEER
CARABINERO
CARABINIER
CARABINIERE
CARABINIERI
CARABOID

CARABUS
CARAC
CARACAL
CARACARA
CARACK
CARACO
CARACOA
CARACOL
CARACOLE
CARACOLED
CARACOLER
CARACOLI
CARACOLING
CARACOLITE
CARACOLLER
CARACORA
CARACORE
CARACT
CARACTER
CARACUL
CARAFE
CARAFON
CARAGHEEN
CARAGUATA
CARAIBE
CARAIPE
CARAIPI
CARAJO
CARAJURA
CARAMBA
CARAMBOLA
CARAMBOLE
CARAMBOLED
CARAMBOLING
CARAMEL
CARAMELAN
CARAMELEN
CARAMELIN
CARAMELIZE
CARAMELIZED
CARAMELIZING
CARANCHA
CARANCHO
CARANDA
CARANDAY
CARANE
CARANGID
CARANGIN
CARANGOID
CARANNA
CARANX
CARAP
CARAPA
CARAPACE
CARAPACED
CARAPACIC
CARAPATO
CARAPAX
CARAPINE
CARAPO
CARAT
CARATCH
CARATS
CARAUNA
CARAUNDA
CARAVAN
CARAVANEER
CARAVANIST
CARAVANNER
CARAVANSARY
CARAVANSERAI
CARAVEL
CARAVELLE
CARAWAY
CARBAMATE
CARBAMIC
CARBAMIDE
CARBAMINE
CARBAMINO
CARBAMYL
CARBANIL
CARBANILIC
CARBANILID
CARBANILIDE
CARBARN
CARBASUS
CARBAZIC
CARBAZIDE
CARBAZIN
CARBAZINE
CARBAZOLE
CARBAZYLIC
CARBEEN
CARBENE
CARBERRY
CARBETHOXYL
CARBIDE
CARBIMIDE
CARBIN
CARBINE
CARBINEER
CARBINOL
CARBINYL
CARBO
CARBOAZOTINE
CARBOCER
CARBODIIMIDE
CARBOGELATIN
CARBOHYDRASE
CARBOHYDRATE
CARBOHYDRIDE
CARBOLATE
CARBOLATED
CARBOLIC
CARBOLINEATE
CARBOLIZE
CARBOLIZED
CARBOLIZING
CARBOLXYLOL
CARBON
CARBONA
CARBONACEOUS
CARBONADO
CARBONADOED
CARBONADOES
CARBONADOS
CARBONATE
CARBONATED
CARBONATING
CARBONATION
CARBONATOR
CARBONE
CARBONEMIA
CARBONERO
CARBONIC
CARBONIDE
CARBONIMETER
CARBONIMIDE
CARBONITE
CARBONITRIDE
CARBONIUM
CARBONIZE
CARBONIZED
CARBONIZER
CARBONIZING
CARBONOMETRY
CARBONOUS
CARBONURIA
CARBONYL
CARBONYLENE
CARBONYLIC
CARBOPHILOUS
CARBORA
CARBORUNDUM
CARBOSTYRIL
CARBOXIDE
CARBOXYL
CARBOXYLASE
CARBOXYLATE
CARBOXYLATED
CARBOXYLIC
CARBOY
CARBOYED
CARBOYS
CARBRO
CARBROMAL
CARBUNCLE
CARBUNCLED
CARBUNCULAR
CARBUNGI
CARBURAN
CARBURANT
CARBURATE
CARBURATED
CARBURATING
CARBURET
CARBURETANT
CARBURETED
CARBURETING
CARBURETION
CARBURETOR
CARBURETTED
CARBURETTER
CARBURETTING
CARBURETTOR
CARBURISE
CARBURIZE
CARBURIZED
CARBURIZER
CARBURIZING
CARBUROMETER
CARBYL
CARBYLAMINE
CARCAJOU
CARCAKE
CARCAN
CARCANET
CARCANETED
CARCANETTED
CARCASE
CARCASS
CARCASSED
CARCASSES
CARCASSING
CARCEAG
CARCEL
CARCER
CARCERAL
CARCERATE
CARCERATED
CARCERATING
CARCERATION
CARCHARIID
CARCHARIOID
CARCHARODONT
CARCINOGEN
CARCINOGENIC
CARCINOID
CARCINOLOGY
CARCINOLYSIN
CARCINOLYTIC
CARCINOMA
CARCINOMAS
CARCINOSIS
CARCINUS
CARCOON
CARD
CARDAISSIN
CARDAMOM
CARDAMUM
CARDANOL
CARDBOARD
CARDCASE
CARDE
CARDECU
CARDED
CARDEL
CARDER
CARDIA
CARDIAC
CARDIACAL
CARDIACEAN
CARDIAGRA
CARDIAGRAM
CARDIAGRAPH
CARDIAGRAPHY
CARDIAL
CARDIALGIA
CARDIALGIC
CARDIALGY
CARDIAMETER
CARDIANEURIA
CARDIANT
CARDIAPLEGIA
CARDIARCTIA
CARDIASTHMA
CARDIATAXIA
CARDIATOMY
CARDIAUXE
CARDIECTASIS
CARDIECTOMY
CARDIELCOSIS
CARDIFORM
CARDIN
CARDINAL
CARDINALATE
CARDINALATED
CARDINALIC
CARDINALIST
CARDINALLY
CARDINALS
CARDINES
CARDING
CARDIOBLAST
CARDIOCARPUM
CARDIOCELE
CARDIOCLASIA
CARDIODYNIA
CARDIOGENIC
CARDIOGRAM
CARDIOGRAPH
CARDIOGRAPHY
CARDIOID
CARDIOLITH
CARDIOLOGIST
CARDIOLOGY
CARDIOLYSIS
CARDIOMEGALY
CARDIOMETER
CARDIOMETRIC
CARDIOMETRY
CARDIONCUS
CARDIONEURAL
CARDIONOSUS
CARDIOPATHIC
CARDIOPATHY
CARDIOPHOBE
CARDIOPHOBIA
CARDIOPLASTY
CARDIOPLEGIA
CARDIOPTOSIS
CARDIORENAL
CARDIOSCOPE
CARDIOSPASM
CARDIOTOMY
CARDIOTONIC
CARDIOTOXIC
CARDITA
CARDITIC
CARDITIS
CARDMAKER
CARDMAKING
CARDO
CARDOL
CARDON
CARDONA
CARDONCILLO
CARDOOER
CARDOON
CARDOPHAGUS
CARDOSANTO
CARDPLAYER
CARDPLAYING
CARDS
CARDSHARP
CARDSHARPER
CARDSHARPING
CARDUACEOUS
CARE
CARECLOTH
CARED
CAREEN
CAREENAGE
CAREENED
CAREENER
CAREENING
CAREER
CAREERED
CAREERER
CAREERING
CAREERISM
CAREERIST
CAREFOX
CAREFREE
CAREFUL
CAREFULLY
CAREFULNESS
CARELESS
CARELESSLY
CARELESSNESS
CAREME
CARENE
CARER
CARESS
CARESSANT
CARESSED
CARESSER
CARESSING
CARESSINGLY
CARESSIVE
CARESSIVELY
CAREST
CARET
CARETAKER
CAREWORN
CAREX
CARF
CARFARE
CARFAX
CARFOUR
CARFUFFLE
CARFUFFLED
CARFUFFLING
CARGA
CARGADOR
CARGADORES
CARGASON
CARGO
CARGOES
CARGOOSE
CARGOS
CARHOP
CARHOUSE
CARIBE
CARIBOU

CARIBOUS
CARICACEOUS
CARICATURAL
CARICATURE
CARICATURED
CARICATURING
CARICATURIST
CARICETUM
CARICOGRAPHY
CARICOLOGIST
CARICOUS
CARID
CARIDEAN
CARIDEER
CARIDOID
CARIE
CARIEN
CARIES
CARILLON
CARILLONNED
CARILLONNEUR
CARILLONNING
CARINA
CARINAE
CARINAL
CARINATE
CARINATED
CARINATION
CARING
CARINIFORM
CARIOCA
CARIOLE
CARIOLING
CARIOSITY
CARIOUS
CARIOUSNESS
CARITAS
CARITATIVE
CARITIVE
CARK
CARKING
CARKINGLY
CARKLED
CARL
CARLAGE
CARLE
CARLET
CARLEY
CARLIN
CARLINA
CARLINE
CARLING
CARLINGS
CARLINO
CARLINS
CARLOAD
CARLOADING
CARLOADINGS
CARLOT
CARLS
CARMAGNOLE
CARMALUM
CARMAN
CARMELE
CARMELOITE
CARMEN
CARMETTA
CARMINATIVE
CARMINE
CARMINETTE
CARMINIC
CARMINITE
CARMOT
CARN
CARNAGE
CARNAL
CARNALITE
CARNALITIES
CARNALITY
CARNALIZE
CARNALIZED
CARNALIZING
CARNALLITE
CARNALLY
CARNAPTIOUS
CARNASSIAL
CARNATE
CARNATION
CARNATIONED
CARNATIONIST
CARNAUBA
CARNAUBYL
CARNEAU
CARNEL
CARNELIAN
CARNEOL
CARNEOUS
CARNET
CARNEY
CARNEYED
CARNIC
CARNIED
CARNIFEROUS
CARNIFERRIN
CARNIFEX
CARNIFEXES
CARNIFICES
CARNIFICIAL
CARNIFIED
CARNIFORM
CARNIFY
CARNIFYING
CARNIVAL
CARNIVALER
CARNIVALLER
CARNIVORAL
CARNIVORE
CARNIVORISM
CARNIVOROUS
CARNOSE
CARNOSIN
CARNOSINE
CARNOSITIES
CARNOSITY
CARNOTITE
CARNOUS
CARNY
CAROA
CAROACH
CAROB
CAROBA
CAROCH
CAROCHE
CAROL
CAROLE
CAROLED
CAROLER
CAROLIN
CAROLINE
CAROLING
CAROLLED
CAROLLER
CAROLLING
CAROLS
CAROLUS
CAROM
CAROMBOLETTE
CAROMS
CARONE
CAROOME
CAROON
CAROSELLA
CAROT
CAROTENE
CAROTENOID
CAROTIC
CAROTID
CAROTIDAL
CAROTIN
CAROTINAEMIA
CAROTINEMIA
CAROTINOID
CAROTOL
CAROTTE
CAROUBIER
CAROUSAL
CAROUSE
CAROUSED
CAROUSEL
CAROUSER
CAROUSING
CAROUSINGLY
CARP
CARPAINE
CARPAL
CARPALE
CARPALIA
CARPED
CARPEL
CARPELLARY
CARPELLATE
CARPELLUM
CARPELS
CARPENT
CARPENTER
CARPENTERING
CARPENTRY
CARPER
CARPET
CARPETBAG
CARPETBAGGER
CARPETBAGISM
CARPETBEATER
CARPETING
CARPETMAKING
CARPETMONGER
CARPETWEB
CARPETWEED
CARPETWORK
CARPETWOVEN
CARPHOLITE
CARPI
CARPID
CARPIDIUM
CARPINCHO
CARPING
CARPINGLY
CARPINTERO
CARPITIS
CARPOCACE
CARPOCARPAL
CARPOCERITE
CARPOGAM
CARPOGAMY
CARPOGENIC
CARPOGONE
CARPOGONIA
CARPOGONIUM
CARPOLITE
CARPOLITH
CARPOLOGICAL
CARPOLOGIST
CARPOLOGY
CARPOMANIA
CARPOPEDAL
CARPOPHORE
CARPOPHYL
CARPOPHYTE
CARPOPODITE
CARPOPTOSIS
CARPOS
CARPOSPERM
CARPOSPORE
CARPOSPORIC
CARPOSPOROUS
CARPOSTOME
CARPS
CARPSUCKER
CARPUS
CARQUAISE
CARR
CARRACK
CARRAGEEN
CARRAGEENIN
CARRAGHEEN
CARRE
CARREAU
CARREE
CARREFOUR
CARREL
CARRELL
CARRETA
CARRETELA
CARRETERA
CARRETON
CARRETTA
CARRIABLE
CARRIAGE
CARRIAGEABLE
CARRIAGEWAY
CARRICK
CARRIED
CARRIER
CARRIES
CARRIGEEN
CARRIOLE
CARRION
CARRITCH
CARRITCHES
CARRIWITCHET
CARRIZO
CARROCCI
CARROCCIO
CARROCH
CARROLLITE
CARROM
CARROMATA
CARRONADE
CARROON
CARROSSERIE
CARROT
CARROTAGE
CARROTER
CARROTIEST
CARROTIN
CARROTINESS
CARROTING
CARROTTOP
CARROTY
CARROUSEL
CARROW
CARROZZA
CARRY
CARRYABLE
CARRYALL
CARRYING
CARS
CARSE
CARSHOP
CARSICK
CARSMITH
CARSTONE
CART
CARTAGE
CARTE
CARTEL
CARTELISM
CARTELIST
CARTELIZE
CARTELLIST
CARTERLY
CARTHAME
CARTHAMIN
CARTIER
CARTIEST
CARTILAGE
CARTILAGINEAN
CARTILAGINEOUS
CARTILAGINOID
CARTILAGINOUS
CARTISANE
CARTLOAD
CARTMAKER
CARTMAKING
CARTMAN
CARTOGRAM
CARTOGRAPH
CARTOGRAPHER
CARTOGRAPHIC
CARTOGRAPHICAL
CARTOGRAPHY
CARTOMANCY
CARTON
CARTONER
CARTONNAGE
CARTOON
CARTOONED
CARTOONING
CARTOONIST
CARTOUCH
CARTOUCHE
CARTRIDGE
CARTSALE
CARTULARIES
CARTULARY
CARTWARE
CARTWAY
CARTWHEEL
CARTWHIP
CARTWRIGHT
CARTY
CARUAGE
CARUCAGE
CARUCAL
CARUCARIUS
CARUCATE
CARUCATED
CARUE
CARUNCLE
CARUNCULA
CARUNCULAR
CARUNCULATE
CARUNCULATED
CARUNCULOUS
CARUS
CARVACROL
CARVACRYL
CARVAL
CARVE
CARVED
CARVEL
CARVEN
CARVENE
CARVES
CARVESTRENE
CARVING
CARVOEIRA
CARVOL
CARVONE
CARVY
CARVYL
CARWITCHET
CARYATIC
CARYATID
CARYATIDAL

CARYATIDEAN
CARYL
CARYOPHYLLIN
CARYOPILITE
CARYOPSIS
CARYOTIN
CASA
CASABA
CASAL
CASALTY
CASAQUE
CASAQUIN
CASATE
CASAUN
CASCABEL
CASCABLE
CASCADE
CASCADED
CASCADING
CASCADITE
CASCADO
CASCALHO
CASCALOTE
CASCAN
CASCARA
CASCARILLA
CASCARON
CASCAVEL
CASCHROM
CASCO
CASCOL
CASCROM
CASCROME
CASE
CASEASE
CASEATE
CASEATED
CASEATING
CASEATION
CASEBOOK
CASEBOX
CASED
CASEFIED
CASEFY
CASEFYING
CASEHARDEN
CASEHARDENED
CASEIC
CASEIN
CASEINATE
CASEINE
CASEINOGEN
CASEKEEPER
CASELTY
CASEMAKER
CASEMAKING
CASEMATE
CASEMATED
CASEMENT
CASEMENTED
CASEOLYSIS
CASEOSE
CASEOUS
CASER
CASERIO
CASERIOS
CASERN
CASERNE
CASES
CASEWEED
CASEWOOD
CASEWORK
CASEWORKER
CASEWORM
CASH
CASHABLE
CASHAW
CASHBOOK
CASHBOX
CASHBOY
CASHED
CASHEL
CASHEW
CASHGIRL
CASHIER
CASHIERED
CASHIERER
CASHING
CASHKEEPER
CASHMERE
CASHMERETTE
CASHOO
CASIMERE
CASIMIRE
CASINA
CASINET
CASING
CASINO
CASINOS
CASIRI
CASITA
CASK
CASKET
CASKING
CASKS
CASQUE
CASQUED
CASQUET
CASQUETEL
CASQUETTE
CASS
CASSABA
CASSABANANA
CASSABULLY
CASSADA
CASSALTY
CASSAN
CASSARE
CASSAREEP
CASSATE
CASSATION
CASSAVA
CASSE
CASSELTY
CASSENA
CASSEROLE
CASSETTE
CASSIA
CASSICAN
CASSIDEOUS
CASSIDID
CASSIDONY
CASSIDULOID
CASSIE
CASSIMERE
CASSINA
CASSINE
CASSINETTE
CASSINO
CASSINOID
CASSIOBERRY
CASSIRI
CASSIS
CASSITERITE
CASSITES
CASSOCK
CASSOCKED
CASSOLETTE
CASSON
CASSONADE
CASSONE
CASSONS
CASSOON
CASSOWARIES
CASSOWARY
CASSUMUNAR
CASSUMUNIAR
CASSY
CAST
CASTAGNOLE
CASTANA
CASTANEAN
CASTANEOUS
CASTANET
CASTANIAN
CASTANO
CASTAWAY
CASTE
CASTELET
CASTELLAN
CASTELLANIES
CASTELLANO
CASTELLANY
CASTELLAR
CASTELLATE
CASTELLATED
CASTELLATION
CASTELLET
CASTEN
CASTER
CASTHOUSE
CASTICE
CASTIGABLE
CASTIGATE
CASTIGATED
CASTIGATING
CASTIGATION
CASTIGATIVE
CASTIGATOR
CASTIGATORIES
CASTIGATORY
CASTILE
CASTILIAN
CASTILLO
CASTING
CASTINGS
CASTLE
CASTLED
CASTLERY
CASTLET
CASTOCK
CASTOFF
CASTOR
CASTOREUM
CASTORIAL
CASTORIN
CASTORITE
CASTORIZED
CASTORY
CASTRAL
CASTRATE
CASTRATED
CASTRATER
CASTRATING
CASTRATION
CASTRATO
CASTRATOR
CASTRENSIAN
CASTRUM
CASTULI
CASUAL
CASUALISM
CASUALIST
CASUALLY
CASUALNESS
CASUALTY
CASUIST
CASUISTIC
CASUISTICAL
CASUISTICALLY
CASUISTRIES
CASUISTRY
CASULA
CASUS
CASWELLITE
CAT
CATABAPTIST
CATABASES
CATABASIS
CATABATIC
CATABIBAZON
CATABIOTIC
CATABOLIC
CATABOLICALLY
CATABOLIN
CATABOLISM
CATABOLITE
CATABOLIZE
CATABOLIZED
CATABOLIZING
CATACAUSTIC
CATACHRESES
CATACHRESIS
CATACHRESTIC
CATACHTHONIAN
CATACHTHONIC
CATACLASM
CATACLASMIC
CATACLASTIC
CATACLINAL
CATACLYSM
CATACLYSMAL
CATACLYSMIC
CATACLYSMIST
CATACOMB
CATACOROLLA
CATACOUSTICS
CATACROTIC
CATACUMBAL
CATADICROTIC
CATADIOPTRIC
CATADROMOUS
CATADUPE
CATAFALQUE
CATAGENESIS
CATAGENETIC
CATAGMATIC
CATAKINESIS
CATALASE
CATALECTA
CATALECTIC
CATALEPSY
CATALEPTIZE
CATALEXIS
CATALIN
CATALINA
CATALINETA
CATALINITE
CATALLACTIC
CATALLACTICS
CATALLUM
CATALO
CATALOES
CATALOG
CATALOGED
CATALOGER
CATALOGIC
CATALOGICAL
CATALOGING
CATALOGIST
CATALOGISTIC
CATALOGUE
CATALOGUED
CATALOGUER
CATALOGUING
CATALOGUIST
CATALOGUIZE
CATALOON
CATALOS
CATALOWNE
CATALPA
CATALUFA
CATALYSES
CATALYSIS
CATALYST
CATALYTE
CATALYTIC
CATALYZATOR
CATALYZE
CATALYZED
CATALYZER
CATALYZING
CATAMARAN
CATAMENIA
CATAMENIAL
CATAMITE
CATAMNESIS
CATAMOUNT
CATAMOUNTAIN
CATAN
CATAPAN
CATAPASM
CATAPETALOUS
CATAPHATIC
CATAPHORA
CATAPHORESIS
CATAPHORIA
CATAPHRACT
CATAPHRENIC
CATAPHYLL
CATAPHYLLARY
CATAPLASIA
CATAPLASIS
CATAPLASM
CATAPLEIITE
CATAPLEXY
CATAPULT
CATAPULTIC
CATAPULTIER
CATARACT
CATARACTAL
CATARACTED
CATARACTINE
CATARACTOUS
CATARIA
CATARINITE
CATARRH
CATARRHAL
CATARRHED
CATARRHINE
CATARRHINIAN
CATARRHOUS
CATASARKA
CATASTA
CATASTALTIC
CATASTASES
CATASTASIS
CATASTATE
CATASTATIC
CATASTERISM
CATASTROPHAL
CATASTROPHE
CATASTROPHIC
CATATHYMIC
CATATONIA
CATATONIAC
CATATONIC
CATAWAMPUS
CATBERRY
CATBIRD
CATBOAT
CATBRIER
CATCALL
CATCH
CATCHALL

CATCHCRY
CATCHED
CATCHER
CATCHFLY
CATCHIER
CATCHIEST
CATCHING
CATCHINGLY
CATCHINGNESS
CATCHLAND
CATCHMENT
CATCHPENNY
CATCHPLATE
CATCHPOLE
CATCHPOLED
CATCHPOLERY
CATCHPOLING
CATCHPOLL
CATCHPOLLED
CATCHPOLLERY
CATCHPOLLING
CATCHUP
CATCHWEED
CATCHWEIGHT
CATCHWORD
CATCHWORK
CATCHY
CATE
CATECHESES
CATECHESIS
CATECHETIC
CATECHETICAL
CATECHIN
CATECHISE
CATECHISED
CATECHISER
CATECHISING
CATECHISM
CATECHISMAL
CATECHIST
CATECHISTIC
CATECHISTICAL
CATECHIZATION
CATECHIZE
CATECHIZED
CATECHIZER
CATECHIZING
CATECHOL
CATECHU
CATECHUMEN
CATECHUMENAL
CATEGOREM
CATEGORIAL
CATEGORIC
CATEGORICAL
CATEGORIES
CATEGORIST
CATEGORIZE
CATEGORIZED
CATEGORIZING
CATEGORY
CATELLA
CATENA
CATENAE
CATENARIAN
CATENARIES
CATENARY
CATENATE
CATENATED
CATENATING
CATENATION
CATENOID
CATENULATE
CATEPUCE
CATER
CATERAN
CATERCAP
CATERCOUSIN
CATERED
CATERER
CATERESS
CATERING
CATERPILLAR
CATERPILLARS
CATERS
CATERVA
CATERWAUL
CATERWAULER
CATERWAULING
CATES
CATFACE
CATFACED
CATFALL
CATFIGHT
CATFISH
CATFISHES
CATFOOT
CATFOOTED
CATGUT
CATHARIZE
CATHARIZED
CATHARIZING
CATHARPING
CATHARSIS
CATHARTIC
CATHARTICAL
CATHEAD
CATHECTIC
CATHEDRA
CATHEDRAL
CATHEDRALIC
CATHEDRATIC
CATHEPSIN
CATHETER
CATHETERISM
CATHETERIZE
CATHETERIZED
CATHETOMETER
CATHETUS
CATHEXIS
CATHISMA
CATHODE
CATHODEGRAPH
CATHODIC
CATHODICAL
CATHODICALLY
CATHODOGRAPH
CATHOLE
CATHOLIC
CATHOLICAL
CATHOLICALLY
CATHOLICATE
CATHOLICISM
CATHOLICITY
CATHOLICIZE
CATHOLICIZED
CATHOLICIZING
CATHOLICLY
CATHOLICNESS
CATHOLICON
CATHOLICOS
CATHOLICUS
CATHOLYTE
CATHOP
CATHOUSE
CATION
CATIVO
CATJANG
CATKIN
CATKINATE
CATLA
CATLAP
CATLIKE
CATLIN
CATLINE
CATLING
CATLINITE
CATMALISON
CATMINT
CATNACHE
CATNEP
CATNIP
CATOBLEPAS
CATOCALID
CATOCTIN
CATODONT
CATOGENE
CATOGENIC
CATOPTRIC
CATOPTRICAL
CATOPTRICS
CATOPTRITE
CATOSTOMID
CATOSTOMOID
CATOUSE
CATPIECE
CATPIPE
CATS
CATSKIN
CATSKINNER
CATSLIDE
CATSO
CATSOS
CATSTANE
CATSTEP
CATSTICK
CATSTITCH
CATSTITCHER
CATSTONE
CATSUP
CATTABU
CATTAIL
CATTALO
CATTAN
CATTED
CATTER
CATTERIES
CATTERY
CATTIER
CATTIES
CATTIEST
CATTILY
CATTIMANDOO
CATTINESS
CATTISH
CATTISHLY
CATTISHNESS
CATTLE
CATTLEBUSH
CATTLEHIDE
CATTLEMAN
CATTLEYA
CATTLEYAK
CATTY
CATTYMAN
CATUR
CATVINE
CATWALK
CATWORT
CATYDID
CATZERIE
CAUBEEN
CAUBOGE
CAUCH
CAUCHEMAR
CAUCHILLO
CAUCHO
CAUCUS
CAUCUSED
CAUCUSING
CAUCUSSED
CAUCUSSING
CAUDA
CAUDAD
CAUDAL
CAUDALLY
CAUDATE
CAUDATED
CAUDATION
CAUDATORY
CAUDATUM
CAUDEX
CAUDEXES
CAUDICES
CAUDICLE
CAUDIFORM
CAUDILLO
CAUDLE
CAUDODORSAL
CAUDOFEMORAL
CAUDOLATERAL
CAUDOTIBIAL
CAUFLE
CAUGHT
CAUK
CAUKED
CAUKING
CAUL
CAULD
CAULDRIFE
CAULES
CAULESCENT
CAULICLE
CAULICOLOUS
CAULICULI
CAULICULUS
CAULIFLOROUS
CAULIFLORY
CAULIFLOWER
CAULIFORM
CAULIGENOUS
CAULINE
CAULIS
CAULOCARPIC
CAULOCARPOUS
CAULOME
CAULOMER
CAULOMIC
CAULOTAXY
CAULOTE
CAULP
CAUM
CAUMA
CAUMATIC
CAUP
CAUPONATE
CAUPONATION
CAUPONES
CAUPONIZE
CAUR
CAURALE
CAURE
CAUSA
CAUSABILITY
CAUSABLE
CAUSAE
CAUSAL
CAUSALGIA
CAUSALITIES
CAUSALITY
CAUSALLY
CAUSATA
CAUSATE
CAUSATION
CAUSATIONAL
CAUSATIONIST
CAUSATIVE
CAUSATIVELY
CAUSATUM
CAUSE
CAUSED
CAUSER
CAUSERIE
CAUSES
CAUSEUR
CAUSEUSE
CAUSEWAY
CAUSEWAYED
CAUSEWAYING
CAUSEWAYMAN
CAUSEY
CAUSEYS
CAUSIDICAL
CAUSING
CAUSINGNESS
CAUSSE
CAUSSON
CAUSTIC
CAUSTICAL
CAUSTICALLY
CAUSTICISER
CAUSTICISM
CAUSTICITY
CAUSTICIZE
CAUSTICIZED
CAUSTICIZER
CAUSTICIZING
CAUSTICLY
CAUSTICNESS
CAUSTIFIED
CAUSTIFY
CAUSTIFYING
CAUTEL
CAUTELA
CAUTELOUS
CAUTER
CAUTERANT
CAUTERIES
CAUTERIZATION
CAUTERIZE
CAUTERIZED
CAUTERIZING
CAUTERY
CAUTIO
CAUTION
CAUTIONARIES
CAUTIONARY
CAUTIONER
CAUTIONES
CAUTIONRY
CAUTIOUS
CAUTIOUSLY
CAUTIOUSNESS
CAVAL
CAVALCADE
CAVALCADED
CAVALCADING
CAVALIER
CAVALIERE
CAVALIERED
CAVALIERING
CAVALIERISM
CAVALIERLY
CAVALIERO
CAVALLA
CAVALRIES
CAVALRY
CAVALRYMAN
CAVASCOPE
CAVATE
CAVATINA
CAVAYARD
CAVE
CAVEA
CAVEAT

CAVEATEE
CAVEATOR
CAVEFISH
CAVEFISHES
CAVEKEEPER
CAVEL
CAVENDISH
CAVER
CAVERN
CAVERNAL
CAVERNED
CAVERNITIS
CAVERNOMA
CAVERNOUS
CAVERNOUSLY
CAVERNULOUS
CAVESON
CAVESSON
CAVETTO
CAVEY
CAVIAR
CAVIARE
CAVICORN
CAVIE
CAVIES
CAVIL
CAVILED
CAVILER
CAVILING
CAVILINGLY
CAVILINGNESS
CAVILLATION
CAVILLED
CAVILLINGLY
CAVING
CAVINGS
CAVITARY
CAVITATE
CAVITATED
CAVITATING
CAVITATION
CAVITENO
CAVITIED
CAVITIES
CAVITY
CAVIYA
CAVORT
CAVORTED
CAVORTING
CAVUM
CAVY
CAVYYARD
CAW
CAWF
CAWK
CAWKY
CAWL
CAWNEY
CAWNIE
CAWNY
CAWQUAW
CAXI
CAXIRI
CAXON
CAY
CAYAR
CAYENNE
CAYENNED
CAYMAN
CAYMANS
CAYNARD
CAYO
CAYOS
CAYUCA
CAYUCO
CAYUSE
CAZA
CAZIBI
CAZIMI
CAZIQUE
CAZY
CE
CEARIN
CEASE
CEASED
CEASELESS
CEASELESSLY
CEASING
CEASMIC
CEBELL
CEBID
CEBIL
CEBINE
CEBOID
CEBOLLITE
CEBUR
CECA
CECCHINE
CECIDIOLOGY
CECIDIUM
CECILITE
CECILS
CECITIS
CECITY
CECOGRAPH
CECOMORPHIC
CECOTOMY
CECUTIENCY
CEDAR
CEDARBIRD
CEDARED
CEDARN
CEDARWARE
CEDARWOOD
CEDE
CEDED
CEDENS
CEDENT
CEDILLA
CEDILLAS
CEDING
CEDOR
CEDRA
CEDRAT
CEDRATE
CEDRE
CEDRENE
CEDRIN
CEDRINE
CEDRIRET
CEDRIUM
CEDROL
CEDRON
CEDRY
CEDULA
CEDUOUS
CEE
CEEL
CEIBA
CEIBO
CEIL
CEILE
CEILED
CEILER
CEILIDH
CEILIDHE
CEILING
CEILINGED
CEILOMETER
CEINT
CEINTURE
CEL
CELADONITE
CELANDINE
CELARENT
CELATION
CELATIVE
CELATURE
CELEB
CELEBE
CELEBRANT
CELEBRATE
CELEBRATED
CELEBRATER
CELEBRATING
CELEBRATION
CELEBRATIVE
CELEBRATOR
CELEBRATORY
CELEBRIOUS
CELEBRIOUSLY
CELEBRITIES
CELEBRITY
CELEMIN
CELEMINES
CELEOMORPH
CELEOMORPHIC
CELER
CELERIAC
CELERITY
CELERY
CELESTA
CELESTE
CELESTIAL
CELESTIALITY
CELESTIALIZE
CELESTIALIZED
CELESTINA
CELESTINE
CELESTITE
CELIADELPHUS
CELIAGRA
CELIBACY
CELIBATAIRE
CELIBATARIAN
CELIBATE
CELIBATIC
CELIBATIST
CELIBATORY
CELIDOGRAPHY
CELIOCELE
CELIOCYESIS
CELIODYNIA
CELIOLYMPH
CELIOMYALGIA
CELIORRHAPHY
CELIORRHEA
CELIOSCHISIS
CELIOSCOPE
CELIOSCOPY
CELIOTOMY
CELITE
CELL
CELLA
CELLAE
CELLAR
CELLARAGE
CELLARED
CELLARER
CELLARESS
CELLARET
CELLARING
CELLARMAN
CELLAROUS
CELLARWAY
CELLARWOMAN
CELLATED
CELLED
CELLI
CELLIFORM
CELLIPETAL
CELLIST
CELLO
CELLOBIOSE
CELLOCUT
CELLOID
CELLOIDIN
CELLOIST
CELLOPHANE
CELLOS
CELLOSE
CELLS
CELLULAR
CELLULARITY
CELLULARLY
CELLULASE
CELLULATE
CELLULATED
CELLULATION
CELLULE
CELLULIFUGAL
CELLULIN
CELLULIPETAL
CELLULITIS
CELLULOID
CELLULOIDED
CELLULOSE
CELLULOSED
CELLULOSIC
CELLULOSING
CELLULOSITIES
CELLULOSITY
CELLULOUS
CELOM
CELOTOMIES
CELOTOMY
CELSIAN
CELSITUDE
CELT
CELTIFORM
CELTIUM
CELTUCE
CELURE
CEMBALIST
CEMBALO
CEMBALON
CEMBALOS
CEMENT
CEMENTAL
CEMENTATION
CEMENTATORY
CEMENTER
CEMENTIN
CEMENTITE
CEMENTITIOUS
CEMENTMAKER
CEMENTMAKING
CEMENTOBLAST
CEMENTOMA
CEMENTUM
CEMETERIAL
CEMETERIES
CEMETERY
CENA
CENACLE
CENACULUM
CENANTHOUS
CENANTHY
CENATION
CENATORY
CENCERRO
CENCERROS
CENESTHESIA
CENESTHESIS
CENESTHETIC
CENIZO
CENOBE
CENOBIAN
CENOBIES
CENOBITE
CENOBITIC
CENOBITICAL
CENOBITISM
CENOBIUM
CENOBY
CENOGENESIS
CENOGENETIC
CENOGONOUS
CENOSITE
CENOSITY
CENOTAPH
CENOTAPHIC
CENOTAPHIES
CENOTAPHY
CENOTE
CENOZOOLOGY
CENS
CENSE
CENSED
CENSER
CENSING
CENSITAIRE
CENSIVE
CENSO
CENSOR
CENSORATE
CENSORED
CENSORIAL
CENSORIAN
CENSORING
CENSORIOUS
CENSORIOUSLY
CENSORSHIP
CENSUAL
CENSURABLE
CENSURABLY
CENSURE
CENSURED
CENSURER
CENSURESHIP
CENSURING
CENSUS
CENSUSES
CENT
CENTAGE
CENTAL
CENTAS
CENTAUR
CENTAURIAL
CENTAURIAN
CENTAURIC
CENTAURIES
CENTAURY
CENTAVO
CENTAVOS
CENTENA
CENTENAR
CENTENARIAN
CENTENARIES
CENTENARY
CENTENIER
CENTENNIAL
CENTENNIUM
CENTER
CENTERBOARD
CENTERED
CENTEREDNESS
CENTERER
CENTERING
CENTERLESS
CENTERMOST
CENTERPIECE
CENTESIMAL
CENTESIMALLY
CENTESIMATE

CENTESIMI
CENTESIMO
CENTESIMOS
CENTESIS
CENTESM
CENTETID
CENTGENER
CENTIARE
CENTIBAR
CENTIDAY
CENTIFOLIOUS
CENTIGRADE
CENTIGRAM
CENTIGRAMME
CENTILE
CENTILITER
CENTILITRE
CENTILLION
CENTILLIONTH
CENTIME
CENTIMETER
CENTIMETRE
CENTIMOLAR
CENTINORMAL
CENTIPEDAL
CENTIPEDE
CENTIPLUME
CENTIPOISE
CENTISTERE
CENTISTOKE
CENTNER
CENTO
CENTON
CENTONICAL
CENTONISM
CENTOS
CENTRA
CENTRAD
CENTRAL
CENTRALISM
CENTRALIST
CENTRALISTIC
CENTRALITY
CENTRALIZE
CENTRALIZED
CENTRALIZER
CENTRALIZING
CENTRANTH
CENTRARCHOID
CENTRE
CENTREBOARD
CENTRED
CENTRELESS
CENTREMOST
CENTREPIECE
CENTRER
CENTRIC
CENTRICAL
CENTRICALITY
CENTRICALLY
CENTRICIPUT
CENTRICITY
CENTRIFFED
CENTRIFUGAL
CENTRIFUGATE
CENTRIFUGE
CENTRIFUGED
CENTRIFUGING
CENTRING
CENTRIOLE
CENTRIPETAL
CENTRISCID
CENTRIST
CENTRO
CENTROACINAR
CENTROBARIC
CENTROCLINAL
CENTRODE
CENTRODORSAL
CENTROID
CENTROIDAL
CENTROLINEAD
CENTROLINEAL
CENTROPLASM
CENTROSOME
CENTROSOMIC
CENTROSPHERE
CENTRUM
CENTRUMS
CENTRY
CENTS
CENTUM
CENTUMVIR
CENTUMVIRAL
CENTUMVIRATE
CENTUPLE
CENTUPLICATE
CENTUPLY
CENTURE
CENTURIAL
CENTURIATE
CENTURIATION
CENTURIATOR
CENTURIED
CENTURIES
CENTURION
CENTURY
CEORL
CEP
CEPA
CEPACEOUS
CEPE
CEPHAELINE
CEPHALAD
CEPHALAGRA
CEPHALALGIA
CEPHALALGIC
CEPHALALGY
CEPHALATE
CEPHALEMIA
CEPHALETRON
CEPHALIC
CEPHALIN
CEPHALINE
CEPHALISM
CEPHALITIS
CEPHALOB
CEPHALOCELE
CEPHALOCHORD
CEPHALOCLAST
CEPHALOCONE
CEPHALOCONIC
CEPHALOCYST
CEPHALOGRAM
CEPHALOGRAPH
CEPHALOID
CEPHALOLOGY
CEPHALOMANCY
CEPHALOMANT
CEPHALOMELUS
CEPHALOMENIA
CEPHALOMERE
CEPHALOMETER
CEPHALOMETRIC
CEPHALOMETRY
CEPHALOMOTOR
CEPHALON
CEPHALONASAL
CEPHALOPAGUS
CEPHALOPATHY
CEPHALOPHINE
CEPHALOPHYMA
CEPHALOPOD
CEPHALOPODAN
CEPHALOPODIC
CEPHALOSOME
CEPHALOSTYLE
CEPHALOTHECA
CEPHALOTOME
CEPHALOTOMY
CEPHALOTRIBE
CEPHALOUS
CEPHID
CEPTER
CEPTOR
CEQUI
CERACEOUS
CERAGO
CERAL
CERAMAL
CERAMBYCID
CERAMIACEOUS
CERAMIC
CERAMICITE
CERAMICS
CERAMIDIUM
CERAMIST
CERAMOGRAPHY
CERARGYRITE
CERAS
CERASEIN
CERASIN
CERASTES
CERATA
CERATE
CERATECTOMY
CERATED
CERATIASIS
CERATIID
CERATIOID
CERATION
CERATITE
CERATITIC
CERATITOID
CERATOBRANCHIA
CERATOHYAL
CERATOID
CERATOMANIA
CERATOPHYTE
CERATOPSIAN
CERATOPSID
CERATORHINE
CERATOTHECA
CERATOTHECAE
CERATOTHECAL
CERAUNIA
CERAUNICS
CERAUNOGRAM
CERAUNOGRAPH
CERAUNOMANCY
CERAUNOPHONE
CERAUNOSCOPE
CERAUNOSCOPY
CERCAL
CERCARIA
CERCARIAE
CERCARIAL
CERCARIAN
CERCARIFORM
CERCIS
CERCLE
CERCOMONAD
CERCOPID
CERCOPOD
CERCUS
CERE
CEREAL
CEREALIAN
CEREALISM
CEREALIST
CEREALS
CEREBELLA
CEREBELLAR
CEREBELLUM
CEREBELLUMS
CEREBRAL
CEREBRALGIA
CEREBRALISM
CEREBRALIST
CEREBRATE
CEREBRATED
CEREBRATING
CEREBRATION
CEREBRIC
CEREBRICITY
CEREBRIFORM
CEREBRIFUGAL
CEREBRIN
CEREBRIPETAL
CEREBRITIS
CEREBRIZE
CEREBROID
CEREBROLOGY
CEREBROMA
CEREBROMETER
CEREBRON
CEREBRONIC
CEREBROPATHY
CEREBROPEDAL
CEREBROSCOPE
CEREBROSCOPY
CEREBROSE
CEREBROSIDE
CEREBROSIS
CEREBROSURIA
CEREBROTOMY
CEREBRUM
CERECLOTH
CERED
CEREMENT
CEREMONIAL
CEREMONIALLY
CEREMONIES
CEREMONIOUS
CEREMONY
CEREOUS
CERER
CERESIN
CERESINE
CEREUS
CEREVIS
CEREZA
CERFOIL
CERIA
CERIANTHID
CERIANTHOID
CERIC
CERID
CERIDE
CERIFEROUS
CERILLO
CERIMAN
CERIN
CERINE
CERING
CERIOPS
CERIPH
CERISE
CERITE
CERITHIOID
CERIUM
CERN
CERNED
CERNING
CERNITURE
CERNUOUS
CERO
CEROGRAPH
CEROGRAPHIC
CEROGRAPHICAL
CEROGRAPHIES
CEROGRAPHIST
CEROGRAPHY
CEROID
CEROLINE
CEROLITE
CEROMA
CEROMANCY
CEROPHILOUS
CEROPLAST
CEROPLASTIC
CEROPLASTICS
CEROS
CEROTATE
CEROTE
CEROTENE
CEROTIC
CEROTIN
CEROTYPE
CEROUS
CEROXYLE
CERRERO
CERRIAL
CERRIS
CERRO
CERT
CERTAIN
CERTAINLY
CERTAINTIES
CERTAINTY
CERTES
CERTIE
CERTIFIABLE
CERTIFICATE
CERTIFICATED
CERTIFICATING
CERTIFICATION
CERTIFICATIVE
CERTIFICATOR
CERTIFICATORY
CERTIFIED
CERTIFIER
CERTIFY
CERTIFYING
CERTIORARI
CERTIORATE
CERTIORATING
CERTITUDE
CERTOSA
CERTOSE
CERTOSINA
CERTOSINO
CERTY
CERULE
CERULEAN
CERULEITE
CERULEOUS
CERULEUM
CERULIGNOL
CERULIGNONE
CERUMEN
CERUMINOUS
CERUSE
CERUSITE
CERUSSITE
CERVALET
CERVANTITE
CERVELAT
CERVELIERE
CERVICAL
CERVICECTOMY
CERVICES
CERVICITIS
CERVICONASAL
CERVICORN

CERVID
CERVINE
CERVISIA
CERVISIAL
CERVIX
CERVIXES
CERVOID
CERYL
CESAREAN
CESAREVITCH
CESARIAN
CESAROLITE
CESIOUS
CESIUM
CESPITITIOUS
CESPITOSE
CESPITOSELY
CESS
CESSANT
CESSATION
CESSATIVE
CESSAVIT
CESSE
CESSED
CESSER
CESSING
CESSIO
CESSION
CESSIONAIRE
CESSIONARIES
CESSIONARY
CESSOR
CESSPIPE
CESSPIT
CESSPOOL
CEST
CESTA
CESTODE
CESTODES
CESTOID
CESTON
CESTRUM
CESTUI
CESTUS
CESTUY
CETACEAN
CETACEOUS
CETACEUM
CETE
CETENE
CETERACH
CETIC
CETICIDE
CETIN
CETIOSAURIAN
CETOLOGICAL
CETOLOGIST
CETOLOGY
CETONIAN
CETORHINID
CETORHINOID
CETOTOLITE
CETRARIN
CETYL
CETYLENE
CETYLIC
CEVADILLA
CEVIAN
CEVICHE
CEVIN
CEVINE
CEYLANITE
CEYLONITE
CHA
CHAA
CHAAC
CHAB
CHABASIE
CHABASITE
CHABAZITE
CHABER
CHABO
CHABOT
CHABOUK
CHABUK
CHABUTRA
CHACATE
CHACCON
CHACE
CHACK
CHACKER
CHACKLE
CHACMA
CHACOLI
CHACONA
CHACONNE
CHACRA
CHACTE
CHADACRYST
CHADELLE
CHADLOCK
CHADOR
CHAETA
CHAETAE
CHAETIFEROUS
CHAETOGNATH
CHAETOPOD
CHAETOPODAN
CHAETOPTERIN
CHAETOSEMA
CHAETOTAXY
CHAFE
CHAFED
CHAFER
CHAFERY
CHAFEWAX
CHAFEWEED
CHAFF
CHAFFCUTTER
CHAFFED
CHAFFER
CHAFFERED
CHAFFERER
CHAFFERING
CHAFFERY
CHAFFIER
CHAFFIEST
CHAFFINCH
CHAFFING
CHAFFMAN
CHAFFSEED
CHAFFWAX
CHAFFWEED
CHAFFY
CHAFING
CHAFT
CHAGIGAH
CHAGOMA
CHAGRIN
CHAGRINED
CHAGRINING
CHAGRINS
CHAGUAR
CHAGUL
CHAHAR
CHAI
CHAIN
CHAINAGE
CHAINBEARER
CHAINED
CHAINER
CHAINETTE
CHAINING
CHAINLESS
CHAINLET
CHAINMAKER
CHAINMAKING
CHAINMAN
CHAINMEN
CHAINON
CHAINS
CHAINWORK
CHAIR
CHAIRER
CHAIRMAKER
CHAIRMAKING
CHAIRMAN
CHAIRMEN
CHAIRMENDER
CHAIRMENDING
CHAIRWARMER
CHAIRWAY
CHAIRWOMAN
CHAIRWOMEN
CHAIS
CHAISE
CHAITRA
CHAITYA
CHAITYAS
CHAJA
CHAK
CHAKAR
CHAKARI
CHAKAZI
CHAKDAR
CHAKOBU
CHAKRA
CHAKRAVARTIN
CHAKSI
CHAL
CHALACO
CHALANA
CHALASTIC
CHALAZA
CHALAZAE
CHALAZAL
CHALAZAS
CHALAZE
CHALAZIAN
CHALAZION
CHALAZIUM
CHALAZOGAM
CHALAZOGAMIC
CHALAZOGAMY
CHALAZOIDITE
CHALCANTHITE
CHALCEDONIC
CHALCEDONIES
CHALCEDONOUS
CHALCEDONY
CHALCEDONYX
CHALCHIHUITL
CHALCHUITE
CHALCID
CHALCIDICUM
CHALCIDID
CHALCIDIFORM
CHALCITES
CHALCOCITE
CHALCOGRAPH
CHALCOGRAPHY
CHALCOLITE
CHALCOLITHIC
CHALCOMANCY
CHALCOMENITE
CHALCON
CHALCONE
CHALCOPYRITE
CHALCOSINE
CHALCOTRIPT
CHALCUS
CHALDER
CHALDESE
CHALDRON
CHALET
CHALICE
CHALICED
CHALICOSIS
CHALICOTHERE
CHALININE
CHALK
CHALKBOARD
CHALKCUTTER
CHALKED
CHALKER
CHALKIER
CHALKIEST
CHALKINESS
CHALKING
CHALKOGRAPHY
CHALKONE
CHALKOS
CHALKOTHEKE
CHALKSTONE
CHALKWORKER
CHALKY
CHALLAH
CHALLENGE
CHALLENGED
CHALLENGEE
CHALLENGER
CHALLENGING
CHALLIS
CHALLOTE
CHALMER
CHALON
CHALONE
CHALOUPE
CHALQUE
CHALTA
CHALUKA
CHALUMEAU
CHALUMEAUX
CHALYBEATE
CHALYBEOUS
CHALYBITE
CHAM
CHAMADE
CHAMAERRHINE
CHAMAL
CHAMAR
CHAMBELLAN
CHAMBER
CHAMBERED
CHAMBERER
CHAMBERING
CHAMBERLAIN
CHAMBERLET
CHAMBERLETED
CHAMBERLETTED
CHAMBERMAID
CHAMBERWOMAN
CHAMBRANLE
CHAMBRAY
CHAMBUL
CHAMECEPHALY
CHAMELEON
CHAMELEONIC
CHAMELEONIZE
CHAMETZ
CHAMFER
CHAMFERER
CHAMFRAIN
CHAMFRON
CHAMISAL
CHAMISE
CHAMISO
CHAMITE
CHAMM
CHAMMA
CHAMMY
CHAMOIS
CHAMOISITE
CHAMOLINE
CHAMOTTE
CHAMP
CHAMPAC
CHAMPACA
CHAMPAGNE
CHAMPAGNED
CHAMPAGNING
CHAMPAGNIZE
CHAMPAGNIZED
CHAMPAGNIZING
CHAMPAIGN
CHAMPAIN
CHAMPAK
CHAMPART
CHAMPE
CHAMPED
CHAMPER
CHAMPERTIES
CHAMPERTOR
CHAMPERTOUS
CHAMPERTY
CHAMPIAN
CHAMPIGNON
CHAMPION
CHAMPIONED
CHAMPIONESS
CHAMPIONING
CHAMPIONSHIP
CHAMPLEVE
CHAMPY
CHAMSIN
CHAN
CHANCE
CHANCEABLE
CHANCEABLY
CHANCED
CHANCEFUL
CHANCEFULLY
CHANCEL
CHANCELED
CHANCELLED
CHANCELLERY
CHANCELLOR
CHANCELOR
CHANCELRY
CHANCER
CHANCERIES
CHANCERY
CHANCEY
CHANCHE
CHANCIER
CHANCIEST
CHANCILY
CHANCING
CHANCITO
CHANCO
CHANCRE
CHANCRIFORM
CHANCROID
CHANCROIDAL
CHANCROUS
CHANCY
CHANDALA
CHANDAM
CHANDELIER
CHANDI
CHANDLER
CHANDLERIES
CHANDLERING
CHANDLERLY
CHANDLERY

CHANDOO
CHANDRAKANTA
CHANDRAKHI
CHANDU
CHANDUL
CHANFRIN
CHANG
CHANGA
CHANGAR
CHANGE
CHANGEABLE
CHANGEABLENESS
CHANGEABLY
CHANGED
CHANGEFUL
CHANGEFULLY
CHANGELESS
CHANGELESSLY
CHANGELING
CHANGEOVER
CHANGER
CHANGES
CHANGING
CHANK
CHANKINGS
CHANNEL
CHANNELBILL
CHANNELED
CHANNELING
CHANNELIZE
CHANNELIZED
CHANNELIZING
CHANNELLED
CHANNELLING
CHANNELS
CHANNER
CHANOYU
CHANSON
CHANSONNETTE
CHANSONNIER
CHANT
CHANTAGE
CHANTANT
CHANTECLER
CHANTEFABLE
CHANTEPLEURE
CHANTER
CHANTERELLE
CHANTEUR
CHANTEUSE
CHANTEY
CHANTEYMAN
CHANTICLEER
CHANTIER
CHANTING
CHANTINGLY
CHANTLATE
CHANTMENT
CHANTOR
CHANTRESS
CHANTRY
CHANTY
CHAOGENOUS
CHAOLOGY
CHAOS
CHAOTIC
CHAOTICAL
CHAOTICALLY
CHAOUA
CHAOUSH
CHAP
CHAPAH
CHAPAPOTE
CHAPARAJOS
CHAPAREJOS
CHAPARRAL
CHAPARRO
CHAPATTI
CHAPATTIES
CHAPATTY
CHAPBOOK
CHAPE
CHAPEAU
CHAPEAUS
CHAPEAUX
CHAPEL
CHAPELED
CHAPELET
CHAPELGOER
CHAPELGOING
CHAPELING
CHAPELLANY
CHAPELLED
CHAPELLING
CHAPELMAN
CHAPELMASTER
CHAPELRIES
CHAPELRY
CHAPERNO
CHAPERON
CHAPERONAGE
CHAPERONED
CHAPERONING
CHAPFALLEN
CHAPFALLENLY
CHAPIN
CHAPITER
CHAPITRAL
CHAPLAIN
CHAPLAINCIES
CHAPLAINCY
CHAPLAINRY
CHAPLAINSHIP
CHAPLANRY
CHAPLESS
CHAPLET
CHAPLETED
CHAPMAN
CHAPON
CHAPOTE
CHAPOURNET
CHAPOURNETTED
CHAPPAUL
CHAPPE
CHAPPED
CHAPPER
CHAPPIE
CHAPPIES
CHAPPING
CHAPPOW
CHAPPY
CHAPRASI
CHAPS
CHAPT
CHAPTER
CHAPTERAL
CHAPTERED
CHAPTERING
CHAPTREL
CHAQUETA
CHAR
CHARABANC
CHARABANCER
CHARABANCS
CHARACEOUS
CHARACETUM
CHARACIN
CHARACINE
CHARACINID
CHARACINOID
CHARACT
CHARACTER
CHARACTERED
CHARACTERIAL
CHARACTERICAL
CHARACTERIES
CHARACTERING
CHARACTERISM
CHARACTERIST
CHARACTERISTIC
CHARACTERISTICALLY
CHARACTERIZATION
CHARACTERIZE
CHARACTERIZED
CHARACTERIZER
CHARACTERIZING
CHARACTERLESS
CHARACTERS
CHARACTERY
CHARADE
CHARADES
CHARADRINE
CHARADRIOID
CHARANGO
CHARAS
CHARBOCLE
CHARBON
CHARBONNIER
CHARCO
CHARCOAL
CHARCOALY
CHARCUTERIE
CHARCUTIER
CHARD
CHARDOCK
CHARE
CHARED
CHARELY
CHARER
CHARET
CHARETER
CHARETTE
CHARGE
CHARGEABLE
CHARGEABLY
CHARGED
CHARGEE
CHARGEFUL
CHARGEHOUSE
CHARGELING
CHARGEMAN
CHARGER
CHARGING
CHARIER
CHARIEST
CHARILY
CHARINESS
CHARIOT
CHARIOTED
CHARIOTEE
CHARIOTEER
CHARIOTEERS
CHARIOTMAN
CHARIOTRY
CHARISM
CHARISMATIC
CHARISTICARY
CHARITABLE
CHARITABLENESS
CHARITABLY
CHARITATIVE
CHARITIES
CHARITY
CHARIVARI
CHARIVARIS
CHARK
CHARKA
CHARKED
CHARKHA
CHARKHANA
CHARKING
CHARLADY
CHARLATAN
CHARLATANIC
CHARLATANISH
CHARLATANISM
CHARLATANRIES
CHARLATANRY
CHARLET
CHARLOCK
CHARLOTTE
CHARM
CHARMED
CHARMEDLY
CHARMER
CHARMEUSE
CHARMFUL
CHARMFULLY
CHARMING
CHARMINGLY
CHARNECO
CHARNEL
CHAROSES
CHARPIE
CHARPIT
CHARPOY
CHARQUE
CHARQUI
CHARR
CHARRE
CHARRED
CHARRIER
CHARRIEST
CHARRING
CHARRO
CHARRY
CHARS
CHARSHAF
CHART
CHARTA
CHARTACEOUS
CHARTER
CHARTERED
CHARTERER
CHARTERHOUSE
CHARTERING
CHARTERMASTER
CHARTHOUSE
CHARTLESS
CHARTOGRAPHY
CHARTOLOGY
CHARTOMETER
CHARTOPHYLAX
CHARTREUSE
CHARTROOM
CHARTS
CHARTULA
CHARTULAE
CHARTULARIES
CHARTULARY
CHARTULAS
CHARUK
CHARWOMAN
CHARWOMEN
CHARY
CHASE
CHASED
CHASER
CHASING
CHASM
CHASMA
CHASMAL
CHASMED
CHASMIC
CHASMOGAMIC
CHASMOGAMOUS
CHASMOGAMY
CHASMOPHYTE
CHASMY
CHASSE
CHASSED
CHASSEING
CHASSEPOT
CHASSEUR
CHASSIGNITE
CHASSIS
CHASTE
CHASTELY
CHASTEN
CHASTENER
CHASTENESS
CHASTISABLE
CHASTISE
CHASTISED
CHASTISEMENT
CHASTISER
CHASTISING
CHASTITY
CHASUBLE
CHASUBLED
CHAT
CHATAKA
CHATEAU
CHATEAUGRAY
CHATEAUX
CHATELAIN
CHATELAINE
CHATELAINRY
CHATHAMITE
CHATI
CHATON
CHATOYANCY
CHATOYANT
CHATS
CHATSOME
CHATTA
CHATTABLE
CHATTACK
CHATTAH
CHATTATION
CHATTED
CHATTEL
CHATTELISM
CHATTELIZE
CHATTELS
CHATTER
CHATTERATION
CHATTERBAG
CHATTERBOX
CHATTERED
CHATTERER
CHATTERING
CHATTERMAG
CHATTERY
CHATTIER
CHATTIES
CHATTIEST
CHATTILY
CHATTINESS
CHATTING
CHATTY
CHATWOOD
CHAUDRON
CHAUFER
CHAUFFAGE
CHAUFFER
CHAUFFEUR
CHAUFFEUSE
CHAUK
CHAUKIDARI
CHAULE
CHAULMAUGRA
CHAULMOOGRA
CHAULMOOGRIC
CHAULMUGRA

CHAUM
CHAUMER
CHAUMIERE
CHAUN
CHAURI
CHAUS
CHAUSSEE
CHAUSSEES
CHAUSSES
CHAUSSURE
CHAUTAUQUA
CHAUTE
CHAUTH
CHAUVE
CHAUVIN
CHAUVINISM
CHAUVINIST
CHAUVINISTIC
CHAVEL
CHAVENDER
CHAVER
CHAVIBETOL
CHAVICIN
CHAVICINE
CHAVICOL
CHAVISH
CHAVO
CHAW
CHAWAN
CHAWBACON
CHAWBONE
CHAWBUCK
CHAWDRON
CHAWER
CHAWK
CHAWL
CHAWLE
CHAWN
CHAWSTICK
CHAY
CHAYOTE
CHAZAN
CHAZANUT
CHAZZAN
CHAZZANUT
CHEAP
CHEAPEN
CHEAPENED
CHEAPENER
CHEAPENING
CHEAPER
CHEAPERY
CHEAPEST
CHEAPIE
CHEAPING
CHEAPISH
CHEAPLY
CHEAPNESS
CHEAPSKATE
CHEAT
CHEATED
CHEATEE
CHEATER
CHEATERS
CHEATERY
CHEATING
CHEATRIE
CHEATRY
CHEATS
CHEBEC
CHEBECK
CHEBEL
CHEBOG
CHEBULE
CHEBULIC
CHEBULINIC
CHECHAKO
CHECHEM
CHECHIA
CHECK
CHECKABLE
CHECKAGE
CHECKBIRD
CHECKBITE
CHECKBOOK
CHECKE
CHECKED
CHECKER
CHECKERBELLIES
CHECKERBELLY
CHECKERBERRIES
CHECKERBERRY
CHECKERBLOOM
CHECKERBOARD
CHECKERBREAST
CHECKERED
CHECKERING
CHECKERIST
CHECKERS
CHECKERWISE
CHECKERWORK
CHECKHOOK
CHECKING
CHECKLE
CHECKLESS
CHECKLINE
CHECKMAN
CHECKMATE
CHECKMATED
CHECKMATING
CHECKOFF
CHECKOUT
CHECKRACK
CHECKREIN
CHECKROLL
CHECKROOM
CHECKROPE
CHECKROW
CHECKROWER
CHECKS
CHECKSTONE
CHECKSTRAP
CHECKSTRING
CHECKWEIGHER
CHECKWORK
CHECKY
CHEDDAR
CHEDDARING
CHEDDITE
CHEDER
CHEDITE
CHEDLOCK
CHEE
CHEECHA
CHEECHACO
CHEECHAKO
CHEEK
CHEEKBONE
CHEEKER
CHEEKIER
CHEEKIEST
CHEEKILY
CHEEKINESS
CHEEKY
CHEENEY
CHEEP
CHEEPER
CHEEPIER
CHEEPIEST
CHEEPILY
CHEEPINESS
CHEER
CHEERED
CHEERER
CHEERFUL
CHEERFULIZE
CHEERFULLY
CHEERFULNESS
CHEERFULSOME
CHEERIER
CHEERIEST
CHEERILY
CHEERINESS
CHEERING
CHEERINGLY
CHEERIO
CHEERIOS
CHEERLEADER
CHEERLESS
CHEERLESSLY
CHEERLESSNESS
CHEERLY
CHEERO
CHEERS
CHEERY
CHEESE
CHEESEBURGER
CHEESECAKE
CHEESECLOTH
CHEESECURD
CHEESECUTTER
CHEESED
CHEESEFLOWER
CHEESELEP
CHEESELIP
CHEESEMONGER
CHEESEPARER
CHEESEPARING
CHEESER
CHEESERY
CHEESEWOOD
CHEESIER
CHEESIEST
CHEESINESS
CHEESING
CHEESY
CHEET
CHEETAH
CHEETAL
CHEETER
CHEEWINK
CHEF
CHEFE
CHEGOE
CHEGRE
CHEICERAL
CHEILION
CHEILITIS
CHEILOPLASTY
CHEIR
CHEIRAGRA
CHEIROGNOMY
CHEIROGRAPHY
CHEIROLIN
CHEIROLINE
CHEIROLOGY
CHEIROMANCY
CHEIROMEGALY
CHEIROPODIST
CHEIROPODY
CHEIROSOPHY
CHEIROSPASM
CHEK
CHEKAN
CHEKE
CHEKEN
CHEKI
CHEKKER
CHEKMAK
CHELA
CHELAE
CHELASHIP
CHELATE
CHELATED
CHELATION
CHELE
CHELEM
CHELERYTHRIN
CHELICERA
CHELICERATE
CHELIDON
CHELIDONATE
CHELIDONIAN
CHELIDONIC
CHELIDONIN
CHELIDONINE
CHELIFEROUS
CHELIFORM
CHELINGA
CHELINGAS
CHELINGO
CHELINGOS
CHELIPED
CHELODINE
CHELONE
CHELONIAN
CHELONID
CHELONIN
CHELOPHORE
CHELP
CHELYDROID
CHELYS
CHEMASTHENIA
CHEMAWINITE
CHEMESTHESIS
CHEMIATRIST
CHEMIATRY
CHEMIC
CHEMICAL
CHEMICALIZE
CHEMICALLY
CHEMICALS
CHEMICK
CHEMICKED
CHEMICKER
CHEMICKING
CHEMIGRAPH
CHEMIGRAPHIC
CHEMIGRAPHY
CHEMILOON
CHEMIN
CHEMINEE
CHEMIOTACTIC
CHEMIOTAXIC
CHEMIOTAXIS
CHEMIOTROPIC
CHEMIPHOTIC
CHEMIS
CHEMISE
CHEMISETTE
CHEMISM
CHEMIST
CHEMISTRIES
CHEMISTRY
CHEMITYPE
CHEMITYPIES
CHEMITYPY
CHEMIZO
CHEMMY
CHEMOCEPTOR
CHEMOKINESIS
CHEMOKINETIC
CHEMOLYSIS
CHEMOLYTIC
CHEMOLYZE
CHEMOREFLEX
CHEMOSES
CHEMOSIS
CHEMOSMOSES
CHEMOSMOSIS
CHEMOSMOTIC
CHEMOSPHERE
CHEMOSPHERIC
CHEMOSTAT
CHEMOTACTIC
CHEMOTAXIS
CHEMOTAXY
CHEMOTHERAPY
CHEMOTIC
CHEMOTROPIC
CHEMOTROPISM
CHEMURGIC
CHEMURGICAL
CHEMURGY
CHENA
CHENDE
CHENEAU
CHENET
CHENEVIXITE
CHENFISH
CHENG
CHENGAL
CHENICA
CHENIER
CHENILLE
CHENOPOD
CHEOPLASTIC
CHEPSTER
CHEQUE
CHEQUEEN
CHEQUER
CHEQUERBOARD
CHEQUERED
CHEQUERING
CHEQUERS
CHEQUERWISE
CHEQUERWORK
CHEQUIN
CHERCOCK
CHERE
CHERELY
CHERI
CHERIE
CHERIMOYA
CHERIMOYER
CHERISH
CHERISHED
CHERISHER
CHERISHING
CHERISHINGLY
CHERISHMENT
CHERMES
CHERNA
CHERNOZEM
CHEROGRIL
CHEROOT
CHERRIED
CHERRIES
CHERRY
CHERRYING
CHERRYSTONE
CHERSONESE
CHERT
CHERTE
CHERTY
CHERUB
CHERUBIC
CHERUBICAL
CHERUBICALLY
CHERUBIM
CHERUBIMIC
CHERUBIN
CHERUBS
CHERVIL
CHERVONETS

CHERVONETZ
CHERVONTSI
CHESBOLL
CHESIL
CHESON
CHESOUN
CHESS
CHESSART
CHESSBOARD
CHESSEL
CHESSER
CHESSET
CHESSMAN
CHESSMEN
CHESSNER
CHESSOM
CHESSTREE
CHESSYLITE
CHEST
CHESTER
CHESTERBED
CHESTERFIELD
CHESTERLITE
CHESTIER
CHESTIEST
CHESTILY
CHESTINESS
CHESTNUT
CHESTS
CHESTY
CHETAH
CHETH
CHETIF
CHETIVE
CHETOPOD
CHETTIK
CHETTY
CHETVERT
CHEUNG
CHEVACHIE
CHEVAGE
CHEVAL
CHEVALET
CHEVALINE
CHEVANCE
CHEVE
CHEVEE
CHEVELURE
CHEVENER
CHEVEREL
CHEVERIL
CHEVESAILE
CHEVESNE
CHEVET
CHEVEYS
CHEVIED
CHEVIES
CHEVILLE
CHEVIN
CHEVIOT
CHEVISANCE
CHEVISE
CHEVON
CHEVRET
CHEVRETTE
CHEVREUIL
CHEVRON
CHEVRONE
CHEVRONEL
CHEVRONELLY
CHEVRONWISE
CHEVRONY
CHEVROTAIN
CHEVVY
CHEVY
CHEVYING
CHEW
CHEWBARK
CHEWED
CHEWELER
CHEWER
CHEWET
CHEWIER
CHEWIEST
CHEWING
CHEWINK
CHEWSTICK
CHEWY
CHEYNEY
CHEYNEYS
CHEZ
CHHATRI
CHI
CHIA
CHIACK
CHIAROSCURIST
CHIAROSCURO
CHIAROSCUROS
CHIASM
CHIASMA
CHIASMAL
CHIASMATA
CHIASMATYPE
CHIASMATYPY
CHIASMIC
CHIASMUS
CHIASTIC
CHIASTOLITE
CHIASTONEURY
CHIAUS
CHIAVE
CHIAVETTA
CHIB
CHIBINITE
CHIBOUK
CHIBOUQUE
CHIBRIT
CHIC
CHICA
CHICADEE
CHICALOTE
CHICANE
CHICANED
CHICANER
CHICANERIES
CHICANERY
CHICANING
CHICARIC
CHICAYOTE
CHICH
CHICHA
CHICHARRA
CHICHICASTE
CHICHIMECAN
CHICHIPATE
CHICHIPE
CHICHITUNA
CHICK
CHICKABIDDY
CHICKADEE
CHICKAREE
CHICKASAW
CHICKEE
CHICKELL
CHICKEN
CHICKENBERRY
CHICKENBILL
CHICKENS
CHICKENWEED
CHICKENWORT
CHICKER
CHICKERY
CHICKIES
CHICKPEA
CHICKSTONE
CHICKWEED
CHICKWIT
CHICKY
CHICLE
CHICLERO
CHICNESS
CHICO
CHICORIES
CHICORY
CHICOS
CHICOT
CHICOTE
CHICQUED
CHICQUER
CHICQUING
CHID
CHIDDEN
CHIDE
CHIDED
CHIDER
CHIDING
CHIDINGLY
CHIDINGNESS
CHIDRA
CHIEF
CHIEFDOM
CHIEFERY
CHIEFLY
CHIEFRY
CHIEFTAIN
CHIEFTAINCY
CHIEFTAINESS
CHIEFTAINRIES
CHIEFTAINRY
CHIEFTAINSHIP
CHIEFTESS
CHIEFTY
CHIEL
CHIELD
CHIEN
CHIEVANCE
CHIEVE
CHIFFCHAFF
CHIFFER
CHIFFON
CHIFFONADE
CHIFFONIER
CHIFFONNIER
CHIFFOROBE
CHIFFRE
CHIGETAI
CHIGGA
CHIGGER
CHIGNON
CHIGOE
CHIH
CHIKARA
CHIKEE
CHIL
CHILACAYOTE
CHILALGIA
CHILARIA
CHILARIUM
CHILBLAIN
CHILD
CHILDAGE
CHILDBEARING
CHILDBED
CHILDBIRTH
CHILDCROWING
CHILDE
CHILDED
CHILDHOOD
CHILDING
CHILDISH
CHILDISHLY
CHILDISHNESS
CHILDKIND
CHILDLESS
CHILDLIER
CHILDLIEST
CHILDLIKE
CHILDLIKENESS
CHILDLY
CHILDNESS
CHILDREN
CHILDRENITE
CHILDRIDDEN
CHILDSHIP
CHILDWIFE
CHILE
CHILENITE
CHILI
CHILIAD
CHILIADAL
CHILIADIC
CHILIAEDRON
CHILIAGON
CHILIAHEDRON
CHILIARCH
CHILIARCHIA
CHILIARCHY
CHILIASM
CHILIAST
CHILIASTIC
CHILICOTE
CHILICOTHE
CHILIES
CHILIOMB
CHILITIS
CHILL
CHILLA
CHILLAGITE
CHILLED
CHILLER
CHILLI
CHILLIER
CHILLIEST
CHILLILY
CHILLINESS
CHILLING
CHILLINGLY
CHILLNESS
CHILLO
CHILLOES
CHILLROOM
CHILLSOME
CHILLUM
CHILLUMCHEE
CHILLY
CHILODON
CHILOGNATH
CHILOGNATHAN
CHILOMA
CHILOMATA
CHILONCUS
CHILOPLASTY
CHILOPOD
CHILOPODAN
CHILOPODOUS
CHILOTOMY
CHILTE
CHILVER
CHIMACHIMA
CHIMAERA
CHIMAERID
CHIMAEROID
CHIMANGO
CHIMB
CHIMBLE
CHIME
CHIMED
CHIMER
CHIMERA
CHIMERAL
CHIMERAS
CHIMERIC
CHIMERICAL
CHIMERICALLY
CHIMES
CHIMINAGE
CHIMING
CHIMLA
CHIMLEY
CHIMNEY
CHIMNEYLESS
CHIMO
CHIMOPELAGIC
CHIMP
CHIMPANZEE
CHIN
CHINA
CHINABERRIES
CHINABERRY
CHINAFISH
CHINAFY
CHINAMANIA
CHINAMANIAC
CHINAMPA
CHINANTA
CHINAPHTHOL
CHINAR
CHINAROOT
CHINAWARE
CHINCAPIN
CHINCH
CHINCHA
CHINCHAYOTE
CHINCHE
CHINCHER
CHINCHILLA
CHINCHY
CHINCOF
CHINCONA
CHINCOUGH
CHINDEE
CHINDI
CHINE
CHINED
CHINELA
CHINFEST
CHING
CHINGMA
CHINIK
CHINIKS
CHININ
CHINING
CHINIOFON
CHINK
CHINKARA
CHINKED
CHINKER
CHINKERS
CHINKING
CHINKLE
CHINKS
CHINKY
CHINNED
CHINNIER
CHINNIEST
CHINNING
CHINNY
CHINOA
CHINOISERIE
CHINOL
CHINOOK
CHINOS
CHINOTTI
CHINOTTO
CHINOVNIK

CHINPIECE
CHINQUAPIN
CHINSE
CHINTS
CHINTZ
CHINTZE
CHINTZES
CHINTZIER
CHINTZIEST
CHINTZY
CHINWOOD
CHIOCOCCINE
CHIOLITE
CHIONABLEPSIA
CHIP
CHIPCHOP
CHIPLET
CHIPLING
CHIPMUNK
CHIPOLATA
CHIPPABLE
CHIPPAGE
CHIPPED
CHIPPER
CHIPPERED
CHIPPERING
CHIPPIER
CHIPPIES
CHIPPIEST
CHIPPING
CHIPPINGS
CHIPPY
CHIPS
CHIPWOOD
CHIPYARD
CHIQUERO
CHIQUEST
CHIR
CHIRAGRA
CHIRAL
CHIRALGIA
CHIRALITY
CHIRAPSIA
CHIRATA
CHIRIMEN
CHIRIMIA
CHIRIMOYA
CHIRIMOYER
CHIRIPA
CHIRIVITA
CHIRK
CHIRKED
CHIRKING
CHIRL
CHIRM
CHIRO
CHIROGALE
CHIROGNOMIC
CHIROGNOMY
CHIROGNOSTIC
CHIROGRAPH
CHIROGRAPHER
CHIROGRAPHIC
CHIROGRAPHICAL
CHIROGRAPHY
CHIROGYMNAST
CHIROLOGICAL
CHIROLOGIST
CHIROLOGY
CHIROMANCE
CHIROMANCER
CHIROMANCIST
CHIROMANCY
CHIROMANT
CHIROMANTIC
CHIROMEGALY
CHIROMETER
CHIRONOMIC
CHIRONOMID
CHIRONOMY
CHIRONYM
CHIROPLASTY
CHIROPOD
CHIROPODIAL
CHIROPODIC
CHIROPODICAL
CHIROPODIST
CHIROPODISTRY
CHIROPODOUS
CHIROPODY
CHIROPRACTIC
CHIROPRACTOR
CHIROPRAXIS
CHIROPTER
CHIROPTERAN
CHIROPTERITE
CHIROS
CHIROSOPHIST
CHIROTHERIAN
CHIROTHESIA
CHIROTONSOR
CHIROTONSORY
CHIROTONY
CHIROTYPE
CHIRP
CHIRPED
CHIRPER
CHIRPIER
CHIRPIEST
CHIRPILY
CHIRPING
CHIRPINGLY
CHIRPLING
CHIRPY
CHIRR
CHIRRE
CHIRRED
CHIRRING
CHIRRUP
CHIRRUPED
CHIRRUPER
CHIRRUPING
CHIRRUPY
CHIRT
CHIRU
CHIRURGEON
CHIRURGEONLY
CHIRURGERY
CHIRURGIC
CHIRURGICAL
CHISEL
CHISELED
CHISELER
CHISELING
CHISELLED
CHISELLER
CHISELLING
CHISELLY
CHISELMOUTH
CHISTERA
CHISTKA
CHIT
CHITAL
CHITARRA
CHITARRINO
CHITARRONE
CHITCHAT
CHITCHATTY
CHITI
CHITIN
CHITINIZATION
CHITINIZED
CHITINOID
CHITINOUS
CHITLIN
CHITLING
CHITLINS
CHITON
CHITOSAMINE
CHITOSAN
CHITOSE
CHITRA
CHITS
CHITTACK
CHITTAK
CHITTAMWOOD
CHITTED
CHITTER
CHITTERLING
CHITTING
CHITTY
CHIURM
CHIV
CHIVAGE
CHIVALRESQUE
CHIVALRIC
CHIVALROUS
CHIVALROUSLY
CHIVALRY
CHIVARI
CHIVARRA
CHIVARRO
CHIVE
CHIVER
CHIVERET
CHIVEY
CHIVIATITE
CHIVIED
CHIVVY
CHIVY
CHIVYING
CHIZZ
CHIZZEL
CHKALIK
CHLADNITE
CHLAMYDATE
CHLAMYDEOUS
CHLAMYDOZOAN
CHLAMYPHORE
CHLAMYS
CHLAMYSES
CHLOANTHITE
CHLOASMA
CHLORAEMIA
CHLORAGEN
CHLORAGOGEN
CHLORAGOGUE
CHLORAL
CHLORALIDE
CHLORALISM
CHLORALIZATION
CHLORALIZE
CHLORALIZED
CHLORALIZING
CHLORALOSE
CHLORALUM
CHLORAMIDE
CHLORAMIN
CHLORAMINE
CHLORANAEMIA
CHLORANEMIA
CHLORANEMIC
CHLORANIL
CHLORANTHY
CHLORAPATITE
CHLORASTROLITE
CHLORATE
CHLORAZIDE
CHLORCOSANE
CHLORDANE
CHLORE
CHLORED
CHLORELLA
CHLOREMIA
CHLORENCHYMA
CHLORIC
CHLORIDATE
CHLORIDATED
CHLORIDE
CHLORIDIC
CHLORIDIZE
CHLORIDIZED
CHLORIDIZING
CHLORIN
CHLORINATE
CHLORINATED
CHLORINATING
CHLORINATION
CHLORINATOR
CHLORINE
CHLORINITY
CHLORINOUS
CHLORIODIDE
CHLORITE
CHLORITIC
CHLORITIZE
CHLORITOID
CHLOROACETIC
CHLOROAMIDE
CHLOROAMINE
CHLOROAURATE
CHLOROAURIC
CHLOROAURITE
CHLOROCHROUS
CHLOROCRESOL
CHLORODIZE
CHLORODIZED
CHLORODIZING
CHLOROFORM
CHLOROFORMED
CHLOROFORMIC
CHLOROGENIC
CHLOROGENINE
CHLOROHYDRIN
CHLOROIODIDE
CHLOROMA
CHLOROMATA
CHLOROMETER
CHLOROMETRIC
CHLOROMETRY
CHLOROPAL
CHLOROPHANE
CHLOROPHENOL
CHLOROPHYL
CHLOROPHYLL
CHLOROPICRIN
CHLOROPLAST
CHLOROPRENE
CHLOROPSIA
CHLOROSIS
CHLOROSPINEL
CHLOROTIC
CHLOROUS
CHLORPIKRIN
CHLORSALOL
CHLORYL
CHO
CHOACHYTE
CHOANA
CHOANATE
CHOANOCYTAL
CHOANOCYTE
CHOANOID
CHOANOSOME
CHOAR
CHOATE
CHOATY
CHOB
CHOBDAR
CHOBIE
CHOCA
CHOCALHO
CHOCARD
CHOCHO
CHOCHOS
CHOCK
CHOCKABLOCK
CHOCKER
CHOCKFUL
CHOCKS
CHOCOLATE
CHOCOLATIER
CHOCOLATIERE
CHOCOLATY
CHOEL
CHOENIX
CHOFFER
CHOGA
CHOGAK
CHOGSET
CHOICE
CHOICEFUL
CHOICELY
CHOICENESS
CHOICIER
CHOICIEST
CHOICY
CHOIL
CHOILE
CHOILER
CHOIR
CHOIRBOY
CHOIRMAN
CHOIRMASTER
CHOIRWISE
CHOKAGE
CHOKE
CHOKEBERRIES
CHOKEBERRY
CHOKEBORE
CHOKECHERRIES
CHOKECHERRY
CHOKED
CHOKEDAMP
CHOKER
CHOKERED
CHOKERMAN
CHOKES
CHOKEWEED
CHOKEY
CHOKIDAR
CHOKIER
CHOKIEST
CHOKING
CHOKINGLY
CHOKRA
CHOKY
CHOL
CHOLAEMIA
CHOLAGOGIC
CHOLAGOGUE
CHOLAM
CHOLANE
CHOLANGITIS
CHOLATE
CHOLD
CHOLEATE
CHOLECYANIN
CHOLECYANINE
CHOLECYST
CHOLECYSTIC
CHOLECYSTIS
CHOLEDOCH
CHOLEINE
CHOLELITH

CHOLELITHIC
CHOLEMIA
CHOLENT
CHOLEOKINASE
CHOLEPOIETIC
CHOLER
CHOLERA
CHOLERAIC
CHOLERIC
CHOLERICLY
CHOLERICNESS
CHOLERINE
CHOLEROID
CHOLERRHAGIA
CHOLESTANE
CHOLESTANOL
CHOLESTENE
CHOLESTERATE
CHOLESTERIC
CHOLESTERIN
CHOLESTEROL
CHOLESTERYL
CHOLETELIN
CHOLETHERAPY
CHOLI
CHOLIAMB
CHOLIAMBIC
CHOLIAMBIST
CHOLIC
CHOLICK
CHOLINE
CHOLINIC
CHOLLA
CHOLLER
CHOLLERS
CHOLO
CHOLOCHROME
CHOLOGENETIC
CHOLOLITH
CHOLOLITHIC
CHOLOPHAEIN
CHOLOPHEIN
CHOLORRHEA
CHOLOSCOPY
CHOLUM
CHOLURIA
CHOMAGE
CHOMER
CHOMP
CHON
CHONDRAL
CHONDRALGIA
CHONDRECTOMY
CHONDRIC
CHONDRIFIED
CHONDRIFY
CHONDRIGEN
CHONDRIN
CHONDRINOUS
CHONDRIOCONT
CHONDRIOMA
CHONDRIOME
CHONDRIOMITE
CHONDRIOSOME
CHONDRIOSOMES
CHONDRITE
CHONDRITIC
CHONDRITIS
CHONDROBLAST
CHONDROCELE
CHONDROCLAST
CHONDROCYTE
CHONDRODITE
CHONDRODITIC
CHONDRODYNIA
CHONDROFETAL
CHONDROGENY
CHONDROID
CHONDROITIN
CHONDROLOGY
CHONDROMA
CHONDROMAS
CHONDROMATA
CHONDROMYOMA
CHONDROPHORE
CHONDROPHYTE
CHONDROSIN
CHONDROSIS
CHONDROSTEAN
CHONDROTOME
CHONDROTOMY
CHONDRULE
CHONDRUS
CHONK
CHONOLITH
CHONTA
CHOOCHOO
CHOOK
CHOOKIE
CHOOP
CHOOSABLE
CHOOSE
CHOOSEABLE
CHOOSER
CHOOSEY
CHOOSIER
CHOOSIEST
CHOOSING
CHOOSINGLY
CHOOSY
CHOP
CHOPA
CHOPBOAT
CHOPDAR
CHOPFALLEN
CHOPHOUSE
CHOPIN
CHOPINE
CHOPLOGIC
CHOPPED
CHOPPER
CHOPPERS
CHOPPIER
CHOPPIEST
CHOPPIN
CHOPPINESS
CHOPPING
CHOPPY
CHOPS
CHOPSTICK
CHOPSTICKS
CHOR
CHORAGI
CHORAGIC
CHORAGION
CHORAGIUM
CHORAGUS
CHORAGY
CHORAL
CHORALCELO
CHORALE
CHORALIST
CHORALLY
CHORD
CHORDA
CHORDACEOUS
CHORDAL
CHORDATE
CHORDED
CHORDEE
CHORDITIS
CHORDOID
CHORDOTOMY
CHORDOTONAL
CHORDS
CHORE
CHOREA
CHOREAL
CHORED
CHOREE
CHOREGRAPHY
CHOREI
CHOREIC
CHOREIFORM
CHOREOGRAPHY
CHOREOID
CHOREOMANIA
CHOREUS
CHOREUTIC
CHORIAL
CHORIAMB
CHORIAMBI
CHORIAMBIC
CHORIAMBIZE
CHORIAMBUS
CHORIAMBUSES
CHORIC
CHORINE
CHORING
CHORIOCELE
CHORIOID
CHORIOMA
CHORION
CHORIONIC
CHORIOPTIC
CHORISIS
CHORISM
CHORIST
CHORISTATE
CHORISTER
CHORISTIC
CHORISTOMA
CHORISTRY
CHORIZATION
CHORIZONT
CHORIZONTES
CHORIZONTIC
CHORIZONTIST
CHOROGI
CHOROGRAPH
CHOROGRAPHER
CHOROGRAPHIC
CHOROGRAPHIES
CHOROGRAPHY
CHOROID
CHOROIDITIS
CHOROLOGICAL
CHOROLOGIST
CHOROLOGY
CHOROMANIA
CHOROMANIC
CHOROMETRY
CHOROOK
CHOROUS
CHORT
CHORTEN
CHORTLE
CHORTLED
CHORTLER
CHORTLING
CHORTOSTEROL
CHORUS
CHORUSED
CHORUSING
CHORUSSED
CHORUSSING
CHORYOS
CHOSE
CHOSEN
CHOTT
CHOU
CHOUCROUTE
CHOUETTE
CHOUFLEUR
CHOUGH
CHOUKA
CHOULTRY
CHOUNCE
CHOUP
CHOUPIC
CHOUQUETTE
CHOUS
CHOUSE
CHOUSED
CHOUSH
CHOUSING
CHOUT
CHOUX
CHOW
CHOWCHOW
CHOWDER
CHOWK
CHOWRIES
CHOWRY
CHOY
CHOZA
CHREMATIST
CHREMATISTIC
CHREOTECHNICS
CHRESARD
CHRESMOLOGY
CHRESTOMATHY
CHRIA
CHRIMSEL
CHRISM
CHRISMA
CHRISMAL
CHRISMALE
CHRISMARY
CHRISMATINE
CHRISMATION
CHRISMATITE
CHRISMATORY
CHRISMON
CHRISOM
CHRISROOT
CHRISTCROSS
CHRISTEN
CHRISTENER
CHRISTENING
CHRISTIANITE
CHROATOL
CHROMA
CHROMAFFIN
CHROMAFFINIC
CHROMAMAMIN
CHROMAMMINE
CHROMATE
CHROMATIC
CHROMATICALLY
CHROMATICIAN
CHROMATICISM
CHROMATICITY
CHROMATICS
CHROMATID
CHROMATIN
CHROMATINIC
CHROMATISM
CHROMATIST
CHROMATIZE
CHROMATOCYTE
CHROMATOID
CHROMATOLOGIES
CHROMATOLOGY
CHROMATOPHORE
CHROMATOPSIA
CHROMATOSIS
CHROMATROPE
CHROMATYPE
CHROME
CHROMED
CHROMIC
CHROMICIZE
CHROMICIZING
CHROMID
CHROMIDE
CHROMIDIAL
CHROMIDIUM
CHROMIDROSIS
CHROMIFEROUS
CHROMING
CHROMIOLE
CHROMITE
CHROMITITE
CHROMIUM
CHROMO
CHROMOBLAST
CHROMOCTYE
CHROMOGEN
CHROMOGENIC
CHROMOGENOUS
CHROMOGRAM
CHROMOGRAPH
CHROMOISOMER
CHROMOLIPOID
CHROMOLITH
CHROMOLITHIC
CHROMOMERE
CHROMOMETER
CHROMONE
CHROMOPAROUS
CHROMOPHANE
CHROMOPHIL
CHROMOPHILE
CHROMOPHILIC
CHROMOPHOBE
CHROMOPHOBIC
CHROMOPHOR
CHROMOPHORE
CHROMOPHORIC
CHROMOPHYL
CHROMOPHYLL
CHROMOPLASM
CHROMOPLAST
CHROMOPSIA
CHROMOS
CHROMOSCOPE
CHROMOSCOPIC
CHROMOSCOPY
CHROMOSOME
CHROMOSPHERE
CHROMOSPHERIC
CHROMOTROPE
CHROMOTROPIC
CHROMOTROPY
CHROMOTYPE
CHROMOTYPIC
CHROMOTYPY
CHROMOUS
CHROMY
CHROMYL
CHRONAL
CHRONANAGRAM
CHRONAXIA
CHRONAXIE
CHRONAXIES
CHRONAXY
CHRONIC
CHRONICA
CHRONICAL
CHRONICALLY
CHRONICITY
CHRONICLE
CHRONICLED
CHRONICLER

CHRONICLING
CHRONICON
CHRONIST
CHRONOCRATOR
CHRONODEIK
CHRONOGRAM
CHRONOGRAPH
CHRONOGRAPHIC
CHRONOGRAPHY
CHRONOLOGER
CHRONOLOGIC
CHRONOLOGICAL
CHRONOLOGIES
CHRONOLOGIST
CHRONOLOGIZE
CHRONOLOGIZED
CHRONOLOGIZING
CHRONOLOGY
CHRONOMANCY
CHRONOMANTIC
CHRONOMETER
CHRONOMETRIC
CHRONOMETRY
CHRONONOMY
CHRONOPHER
CHRONOSCOPIC
CHRONOSCOPY
CHRONOSEMIC
CHRONOTROPIC
CHROOCOCCOID
CHROTTA
CHRYSALID
CHRYSALIDAL
CHRYSALIDES
CHRYSALIDIAN
CHRYSALINE
CHRYSALIS
CHRYSALISES
CHRYSALOID
CHRYSAMMIC
CHRYSANILIN
CHRYSANILINE
CHRYSANISIC
CHRYSANTHEMUM
CHRYSANTHOUS
CHRYSAROBIN
CHRYSAZIN
CHRYSAZOL
CHRYSENE
CHRYSIN
CHRYSOBERYL
CHRYSOBULL
CHRYSOCHLORE
CHRYSOCHROUS
CHRYSOCOLLA
CHRYSOCRACY
CHRYSOERIOL
CHRYSOGEN
CHRYSOGRAPH
CHRYSOGRAPHY
CHRYSOIDINE
CHRYSOLITE
CHRYSOLITIC
CHRYSOLOGY
CHRYSOME
CHRYSOMELID
CHRYSOMONAD
CHRYSOPAL
CHRYSOPEE
CHRYSOPHAN
CHRYSOPHANE
CHRYSOPHANIC
CHRYSOPOEIA
CHRYSOPOETIC
CHRYSOPRASE
CHRYSOPRASUS
CHRYSORIN
CHRYSOSPERM
CHRYSOTILE
CHRYSTOCRENE
CHTHONIAN
CHUANA
CHUB
CHUBA
CHUBBED
CHUBBEDNESS
CHUBBIER
CHUBBIEST
CHUBBILY
CHUBBINESS
CHUBBY
CHUBS
CHUCHO
CHUCK
CHUCKAWALLA
CHUCKED
CHUCKER
CHUCKHOLE
CHUCKIE
CHUCKIES
CHUCKING
CHUCKINGLY
CHUCKLE
CHUCKLED
CHUCKLEHEAD
CHUCKLEHEADED
CHUCKLER
CHUCKLING
CHUCKLINGLY
CHUCKRAM
CHUCKSTONE
CHUCKWALLA
CHUCKY
CHUD
CHUDDAH
CHUDDAR
CHUDDER
CHUET
CHUFA
CHUFF
CHUFFIER
CHUFFIEST
CHUG
CHUGGED
CHUGGER
CHUGGING
CHUGHOLE
CHUHRA
CHUKAR
CHUKKA
CHUKKAR
CHUKKER
CHUKOR
CHULAN
CHULHA
CHULLO
CHULLPA
CHULO
CHULPA
CHULTUN
CHUM
CHUMAR
CHUMBLE
CHUMMAGE
CHUMMER
CHUMMERY
CHUMMIER
CHUMMIES
CHUMMIEST
CHUMMILY
CHUMMY
CHUMP
CHUMPA
CHUMPISH
CHUMPY
CHUNAM
CHUNARI
CHUNDARI
CHUNGA
CHUNK
CHUNKED
CHUNKHEAD
CHUNKIER
CHUNKIEST
CHUNKINESS
CHUNKING
CHUNKY
CHUNNER
CHUNO
CHUNTER
CHUPA
CHUPAK
CHUPON
CHUPRASSIE
CHUPRASSY
CHURCH
CHURCHANITY
CHURCHCRAFT
CHURCHGOER
CHURCHGOING
CHURCHIANITY
CHURCHIER
CHURCHIEST
CHURCHIFIED
CHURCHING
CHURCHITE
CHURCHLESS
CHURCHLIKE
CHURCHLINESS
CHURCHLY
CHURCHMAN
CHURCHMANLY
CHURCHMANSHIP
CHURCHMASTER
CHURCHMEN
CHURCHREEVE
CHURCHSCOT
CHURCHSHOT
CHURCHWARD
CHURCHWARDEN
CHURCHWARDS
CHURCHWAY
CHURCHWOMAN
CHURCHWOMEN
CHURCHY
CHURCHYARD
CHUREL
CHURINGA
CHURL
CHURLED
CHURLIER
CHURLIEST
CHURLISH
CHURLISHLY
CHURLISHNESS
CHURLY
CHURN
CHURNABILITY
CHURNED
CHURNING
CHURNMILK
CHURNSTAFF
CHURR
CHURRASCO
CHURRED
CHURRING
CHURRO
CHURRUCK
CHURRUS
CHURRWORM
CHUSE
CHUSER
CHUT
CHUTE
CHUTER
CHUTNEE
CHUTNEY
CHUTNEYS
CHUTZPAH
CHUZWI
CHWAS
CHYACK
CHYAK
CHYLACEOUS
CHYLE
CHYLIFACTION
CHYLIFACTIVE
CHYLIFACTORY
CHYLIFEROUS
CHYLIFIC
CHYLIFIED
CHYLIFORM
CHYLIFY
CHYLIFYING
CHYLOCAULOUS
CHYLOCAULY
CHYLOCELE
CHYLOMICRON
CHYLOPHYLLY
CHYLOPOETIC
CHYLOPOIESIS
CHYLOPOIETIC
CHYLOTHORAX
CHYLOUS
CHYLURIA
CHYMAQUEOUS
CHYME
CHYMIA
CHYMIC
CHYMIFEROUS
CHYMIFIED
CHYMIFY
CHYMIFYING
CHYMIST
CHYMOSIN
CHYMOUS
CHYPRE
CHYTRA
CHYTRID
CHYTRIDIAL
CHYTRIDIOSE
CHYTRIDIOSIS
CIBARIAL
CIBARIAN
CIBARIOUS
CIBATION
CIBOL
CIBOLERO
CIBOPHOBIA
CIBORIA
CIBORIUM
CIBOULE
CICAD
CICADA
CICADAE
CICADAS
CICADID
CICALA
CICATRICE
CICATRICES
CICATRICIAL
CICATRICLE
CICATRICOSE
CICATRICULA
CICATRICULAE
CICATRISATE
CICATRISIVE
CICATRIX
CICATRIXES
CICATRIZANT
CICATRIZATE
CICATRIZE
CICATRIZED
CICATRIZER
CICATRIZING
CICATROSE
CICELIES
CICELY
CICER
CICERO
CICERONAGE
CICERONE
CICERONES
CICERONI
CICERONING
CICERONISM
CICERONIZE
CICHAR
CICHLID
CICHLIDAE
CICHLIDS
CICHLOID
CICINDELID
CICISBEISM
CICISBEO
CICLATOUN
CICONIFORM
CICONIID
CICONINE
CICOREE
CICURATE
CICUTOXIN
CIDARID
CIDARIS
CIDER
CIDERIST
CIEL
CIENAGA
CIERGE
CIG
CIGALA
CIGALE
CIGAR
CIGARESQUE
CIGARET
CIGARETTE
CIGARETTES
CIGARFISH
CIGARILLO
CIGARILLOS
CIGARITO
CIGARITOS
CIGUA
CIGUATERA
CILERY
CILIA
CILIARY
CILIATE
CILIATED
CILIATELY
CILIATION
CILICE
CILICIOUS
CILIECTOMY
CILIELLA
CILIFEROUS
CILIFORM
CILIIFORM
CILIOGRADE
CILIOLA
CILIOLATE
CILIOLUM
CILIORETINAL
CILIOSCLERAL
CILIOSPINAL

CILIUM
CILLOSIS
CIMA
CIMAROON
CIMBAL
CIMBALOM
CIMBIA
CIMBORIO
CIMELIA
CIMETER
CIMEX
CIMICID
CIMICIDE
CIMICIFORM
CIMICIFUGIN
CIMICOID
CIMIER
CIMINITE
CIMLINE
CIMMARON
CIMOLITE
CINCH
CINCHA
CINCHER
CINCHOLOIPON
CINCHONA
CINCHONAMIN
CINCHONAMINE
CINCHONATE
CINCHONIA
CINCHONIC
CINCHONICIN
CINCHONICINE
CINCHONIDIA
CINCHONIN
CINCHONINE
CINCHONISM
CINCHONIZE
CINCHONIZED
CINCHONIZING
CINCHONOLOGY
CINCHOTINE
CINCINNAL
CINCINNI
CINCINNUS
CINCLIDES
CINCLIS
CINCT
CINCTURE
CINCTURED
CINCTURING
CINDER
CINDERED
CINDERING
CINDERMAN
CINDERS
CINDERY
CINEAST
CINEFACTION
CINEL
CINEMA
CINEMATIC
CINEMATICAL
CINEMATOGRAPH
CINEMIZE
CINEMOGRAPH
CINENCHYMA
CINENE
CINENEGATIVE
CINEOL
CINEOLE
CINEPHONE
CINERACEOUS
CINERARIA
CINERARIUM
CINERARY
CINERATION
CINERATOR
CINEREA
CINEREAL
CINEREOUS
CINERIN
CINERITIOUS
CINEROUS
CINEVARIETY
CINGLE
CINGULA
CINGULAR
CINGULATE
CINGULATED
CINGULUM
CINNABAR
CINNABARIC
CINNABARINE
CINNAMAL
CINNAMATE
CINNAMEIN
CINNAMIC
CINNAMOL
CINNAMON
CINNAMONED
CINNAMONIC
CINNAMONROOT
CINNAMONWOOD
CINNAMYL
CINNOLIN
CINNOLINE
CINQ
CINQFOIL
CINQUAIN
CINQUE
CINQUECENTO
CINQUEFOIL
CINQUEPACE
CINQUES
CINTER
CINTRE
CINURAN
CINUROUS
CION
CIONECTOMY
CIONITIS
CIONOCRANIAL
CIONOCRANIAN
CIONOPTOSIS
CIONOTOME
CIONOTOMY
CIOPPINO
CIPAYE
CIPHER
CIPHERED
CIPHERING
CIPO
CIPOLIN
CIPPI
CIPPUS
CIRC
CIRCA
CIRCADIAN
CIRCAR
CIRCINAL
CIRCINATE
CIRCINATELY
CIRCINATION
CIRCITER
CIRCLE
CIRCLED
CIRCLER
CIRCLES
CIRCLET
CIRCLETING
CIRCLINE
CIRCLING
CIRCOVARIAN
CIRCS
CIRCUE
CIRCUIT
CIRCUITAL
CIRCUITEER
CIRCUITER
CIRCUITIES
CIRCUITION
CIRCUITMAN
CIRCUITMEN
CIRCUITOR
CIRCUITOUS
CIRCUITOUSLY
CIRCUITRY
CIRCUITY
CIRCULABLE
CIRCULANT
CIRCULAR
CIRCULARITIES
CIRCULARITY
CIRCULARIZE
CIRCULARIZED
CIRCULARIZING
CIRCULARLY
CIRCULARNESS
CIRCULATE
CIRCULATED
CIRCULATING
CIRCULATION
CIRCULATIVE
CIRCULATOR
CIRCULATORIES
CIRCULATORY
CIRCULIN
CIRCULUS
CIRCUMANAL
CIRCUMARCTIC
CIRCUMAVIATE
CIRCUMAXIAL
CIRCUMAXILE
CIRCUMAXILLARY
CIRCUMBASAL
CIRCUMBOREAL
CIRCUMBUCCAL
CIRCUMBULBAR
CIRCUMCENTER
CIRCUMCINCT
CIRCUMCIRCLE
CIRCUMCISE
CIRCUMCISED
CIRCUMCISER
CIRCUMCISING
CIRCUMCISION
CIRCUMCLUDE
CIRCUMCLUSION
CIRCUMCONE
CIRCUMCONIC
CIRCUMCORNEAL
CIRCUMDUCE
CIRCUMDUCING
CIRCUMDUCT
CIRCUMDUCTED
CIRCUMFER
CIRCUMFERENCE
CIRCUMFERENT
CIRCUMFERENTOR
CIRCUMFLECT
CIRCUMFLEX
CIRCUMFLUENT
CIRCUMFLUOUS
CIRCUMFUSE
CIRCUMFUSILE
CIRCUMFUSING
CIRCUMFUSION
CIRCUMGYRATE
CIRCUMJACENT
CIRCUMLENTAL
CIRCUMLITIO
CIRCUMLOCUTE
CIRCUMLOCUTION
CIRCUMMURE
CIRCUMMURED
CIRCUMMURING
CIRCUMNATANT
CIRCUMNUTATE
CIRCUMOCULAR
CIRCUMORAL
CIRCUMORBITAL
CIRCUMPOLAR
CIRCUMPOSE
CIRCUMRENAL
CIRCUMROTATE
CIRCUMSAIL
CIRCUMSCRIBE
CIRCUMSCRIBED
CIRCUMSCRIBER
CIRCUMSCRIPT
CIRCUMSOLAR
CIRCUMSPECT
CIRCUMSPECTION
CIRCUMSPECTLY
CIRCUMSTANCE
CIRCUMSTANCED
CIRCUMSTANCES
CIRCUMSTANTIAL
CIRCUMSTANTIALLY
CIRCUMSTANTIATE
CIRCUMSTANTIATED
CIRCUMSTANTIATING
CIRCUMVENT
CIRCUMVENTED
CIRCUMVENTER
CIRCUMVENTING
CIRCUMVENTION
CIRCUMVIATE
CIRCUMVOLANT
CIRCUMVOLUTE
CIRCUMVOLVE
CIRCUMVOLVED
CIRCUMVOLVING
CIRCUS
CIRE
CIRL
CIRQUE
CIRRATE
CIRRATED
CIRRHOSED
CIRRHOSIS
CIRRHOTIC
CIRRHOUS
CIRRHUS
CIRRI
CIRRIBRANCH
CIRRIFEROUS
CIRRIFORM
CIRRIGEROUS
CIRRIPED
CIRRIPEDIAL
CIRROCUMULUS
CIRROLITE
CIRROPODOUS
CIRROSE
CIRROSTOME
CIRROSTRATUS
CIRROUS
CIRRUS
CIRSECTOMY
CIRSOID
CIRSOMPHALOS
CIRSOTOME
CIRSOTOMIES
CIRSOTOMY
CIRUELA
CISALPINE
CISANDINE
CISATLANTIC
CISCO
CISCOES
CISCOS
CISE
CISEAUX
CISELE
CISELEUR
CISELURE
CISGANGETIC
CISIUM
CISJURANE
CISLEITHAN
CISLUNAR
CISMARINE
CISMONTANE
CISOCEANIC
CISPADANE
CISPLATINE
CISPONTINE
CISRHENANE
CISSA
CISSING
CISSOID
CISSOIDAL
CIST
CISTACEOUS
CISTED
CISTERN
CISTERNA
CISTERNAL
CISTIC
CISTOPHORIC
CISTOPHORUS
CISTUS
CISTVAEN
CIT
CITABLE
CITADEL
CITAL
CITATION
CITATOR
CITATORY
CITE
CITEABLE
CITED
CITEE
CITER
CITHARA
CITHARIST
CITHAROEDIC
CITHAROEDUS
CITHER
CITHERN
CITIED
CITIES
CITIFICATION
CITIFIED
CITIFY
CITIGRADE
CITIZEN
CITIZENESS
CITIZENISM
CITIZENIZE
CITIZENIZED
CITIZENIZING
CITIZENLY
CITIZENRIES
CITIZENRY
CITIZENSHIP
CITO
CITOLA
CITOLE
CITOLER
CITOYEN
CITOYENNE

CITRACONATE
CITRACONIC
CITRAL
CITRAMIDE
CITRANGE
CITRANGEADE
CITRATE
CITRATED
CITREAN
CITRENE
CITREOUS
CITRIC
CITRICULTURE
CITRIL
CITRIN
CITRINATION
CITRINE
CITRININ
CITROCOLA
CITROMETER
CITRON
CITRONADE
CITRONELLA
CITRONELLAL
CITRONELLE
CITRONELLOL
CITRONIN
CITRONIZE
CITRONWOOD
CITROUS
CITRUL
CITRULLIN
CITRUS
CITTERN
CITTERNHEAD
CITUA
CITY
CITYCISM
CITYFIED
CITYSCAPE
CITYWARD
CIUDAD
CIVE
CIVET
CIVETONE
CIVIC
CIVICAL
CIVICALLY
CIVICISM
CIVICS
CIVIES
CIVIL
CIVILIAN
CIVILISE
CIVILIST
CIVILITE
CIVILITIES
CIVILITY
CIVILIZABLE
CIVILIZATION
CIVILIZATORY
CIVILIZE
CIVILIZED
CIVILIZEE
CIVILIZER
CIVILIZING
CIVISM
CIVITAS
CIVITE
CIVORY
CIVVIES
CIVVY
CIXIID
CLABBER
CLABBERY
CLACH
CLACHAN
CLACK
CLACKDISH
CLACKED
CLACKER
CLACKET
CLACKETY
CLACKING
CLACO
CLAD
CLADANTHOUS
CLADAUTOICOUS
CLADDING
CLADI
CLADINE
CLADOCARPOUS
CLADOCERAN
CLADOCEROUS
CLADODE
CLADODIAL
CLADODONT
CLADODONTID
CLADOGENOUS
CLADONIOID
CLADOPHYLL
CLADOPHYLLUM
CLADOPTOSIS
CLADOSE
CLADUS
CLAG
CLAGGUM
CLAGGY
CLAIK
CLAIM
CLAIMABLE
CLAIMANT
CLAIMER
CLAIMS
CLAIRAUDIENT
CLAIRCE
CLAIRE
CLAIRSCHACH
CLAIRVOYANCE
CLAIRVOYANT
CLAITH
CLAIVER
CLAM
CLAMANT
CLAMAROO
CLAMATORIAL
CLAMATORY
CLAMBAKE
CLAMBER
CLAMBERER
CLAMCRACKER
CLAME
CLAMEHEWIT
CLAMFLAT
CLAMJAMFERY
CLAMJAMFRY
CLAMJAMPHRIE
CLAMMED
CLAMMER
CLAMMERSOME
CLAMMIER
CLAMMIEST
CLAMMILY
CLAMMINESS
CLAMMING
CLAMMISH
CLAMMY
CLAMOR
CLAMORED
CLAMORER
CLAMORING
CLAMORIST
CLAMOROUS
CLAMOROUSLY
CLAMOROUSNESS
CLAMORSOME
CLAMOUR
CLAMOURED
CLAMOURER
CLAMOURING
CLAMOURIST
CLAMOUROUS
CLAMOURSOME
CLAMP
CLAMPED
CLAMPER
CLAMPING
CLAMSHELL
CLAMWORM
CLAN
CLANCULAR
CLANCULARLY
CLANDESTINE
CLANDESTINELY
CLANFELLOW
CLANG
CLANGOR
CLANGOROUS
CLANGOROUSLY
CLANGOUR
CLANK
CLANKED
CLANKETY
CLANKING
CLANKINGLY
CLANKINGNESS
CLANKUM
CLANNISH
CLANNISHLY
CLANNISHNESS
CLANSHIP
CLANSMAN
CLANSMEN
CLANSWOMAN
CLANSWOMEN
CLAP
CLAPBOARD
CLAPBOARDING
CLAPBREAD
CLAPCAKE
CLAPDISH
CLAPHOLT
CLAPMATCH
CLAPNEST
CLAPNET
CLAPPE
CLAPPED
CLAPPER
CLAPPERCLAW
CLAPPERED
CLAPPERING
CLAPPERS
CLAPPING
CLAPTRAP
CLAPWORT
CLAQUE
CLAQUEUR
CLARABELLA
CLARAIN
CLARENCE
CLARENDON
CLARET
CLARIBELLA
CLARIES
CLARIFIANT
CLARIFICATION
CLARIFIED
CLARIFIER
CLARIFY
CLARIFYING
CLARIGATION
CLARIGOLD
CLARIN
CLARINA
CLARINET
CLARINETIST
CLARINETTIST
CLARINO
CLARION
CLARIONET
CLARISSIMO
CLARITY
CLARO
CLAROS
CLARSACH
CLART
CLARTIER
CLARTIEST
CLARTY
CLARY
CLASH
CLASHED
CLASHEE
CLASHER
CLASHES
CLASHING
CLASHY
CLASMATOCYTE
CLASMATOSIS
CLASP
CLASPED
CLASPER
CLASPING
CLASPT
CLASS
CLASSBOOK
CLASSER
CLASSES
CLASSFELLOW
CLASSIC
CLASSICAL
CLASSICALISM
CLASSICALIST
CLASSICALITIES
CLASSICALITY
CLASSICALLY
CLASSICISM
CLASSICIST
CLASSICISTIC
CLASSICIZE
CLASSICIZED
CLASSICIZING
CLASSICS
CLASSIER
CLASSIEST
CLASSIFIABLE
CLASSIFIC
CLASSIFICATION
CLASSIFIED
CLASSIFIER
CLASSIFY
CLASSIFYING
CLASSIS
CLASSMAN
CLASSMATE
CLASSMEN
CLASSROOM
CLASSWORK
CLASSY
CLASTIC
CLAT
CLATCH
CLATCHY
CLATHRACEOUS
CLATHRARIAN
CLATHRATE
CLATHROID
CLATHROSE
CLATHRULATE
CLATTER
CLATTERED
CLATTERER
CLATTERING
CLATTERINGLY
CLATTERTRAPS
CLATTERY
CLATTY
CLAUBER
CLAUCHT
CLAUD
CLAUDENT
CLAUDETITE
CLAUDICANT
CLAUDICATE
CLAUDICATION
CLAUGHT
CLAUSAL
CLAUSE
CLAUSTHALITE
CLAUSTRA
CLAUSTRAL
CLAUSTRATION
CLAUSTRUM
CLAUSULA
CLAUSULAR
CLAUSULE
CLAUSURE
CLAUT
CLAVA
CLAVACIN
CLAVAE
CLAVAL
CLAVATE
CLAVATED
CLAVATELY
CLAVATIN
CLAVATION
CLAVE
CLAVECIN
CLAVECINIST
CLAVEL
CLAVELIZE
CLAVELLATED
CLAVER
CLAVES
CLAVIAL
CLAVIATURE
CLAVICEMBALO
CLAVICHORD
CLAVICITHERN
CLAVICLE
CLAVICOR
CLAVICORN
CLAVICORNATE
CLAVICOTOMY
CLAVICULAR
CLAVICULATE
CLAVICYMBAL
CLAVIER
CLAVIERIST
CLAVIFORM
CLAVIGER
CLAVIHARP
CLAVILUX
CLAVIOL
CLAVIOLE
CLAVIS
CLAVISES
CLAVODELTOID
CLAVUS
CLAVY
CLAW
CLAWBACK
CLAWED
CLAWER

CLAWK
CLAWKER
CLAWS
CLAWSICK
CLAY
CLAYBANK
CLAYBRAINED
CLAYED
CLAYEN
CLAYER
CLAYEY
CLAYIER
CLAYIEST
CLAYING
CLAYISH
CLAYMAN
CLAYMORE
CLAYPAN
CLAYTONIA
CLAYWARE
CLAYWEED
CLEACH
CLEAD
CLEADED
CLEADING
CLEAM
CLEAMER
CLEAN
CLEANABLE
CLEANED
CLEANER
CLEANEST
CLEANHANDED
CLEANING
CLEANLIER
CLEANLIEST
CLEANLILY
CLEANLINESS
CLEANLY
CLEANNESS
CLEANOUT
CLEANSE
CLEANSED
CLEANSER
CLEANSING
CLEANUP
CLEAR
CLEARABLE
CLEARAGE
CLEARANCE
CLEARCOLE
CLEARCOLED
CLEARCOLING
CLEARED
CLEAREDNESS
CLEARER
CLEAREST
CLEARHEADED
CLEARING
CLEARINGHOUSE
CLEARLY
CLEARNESS
CLEARS
CLEARSKINS
CLEARSTARCH
CLEARSTORIED
CLEARSTORY
CLEARWEED
CLEARWING
CLEAT
CLEATED
CLEATING
CLEATS
CLEAVABILITY
CLEAVABLE
CLEAVAGE
CLEAVE
CLEAVED
CLEAVER
CLEAVERS
CLEAVERWORT
CLEAVING
CLEAVINGLY
CLECHE
CLECHEE
CLECHY
CLECK
CLEDDE
CLEDGE
CLEDGY
CLEDONISM
CLEE
CLEECH
CLEED
CLEEK
CLEEKED
CLEEKING
CLEEKS
CLEEKY
CLEEVE
CLEF
CLEFT
CLEFTED
CLEG
CLEGG
CLEIDAGRA
CLEIDOCOSTAL
CLEIDOHYOID
CLEIDOIC
CLEIDOMANCY
CLEIDOTOMY
CLEIDOTRIPSY
CLEISTOCARP
CLEISTOGAMIC
CLEISTOGAMY
CLEISTOGENE
CLEITHRA
CLEITHRAL
CLEITHRUM
CLEM
CLEMATIS
CLEMATITE
CLEMENCE
CLEMENCIES
CLEMENCY
CLEMENT
CLEMENTLY
CLENCH
CLENCHED
CLENCHING
CLENK
CLEOID
CLEOME
CLEP
CLEPE
CLEPED
CLEPING
CLEPSYDRA
CLEPSYDRAE
CLEPSYDRAS
CLEPTOBIOSIS
CLEPTOBIOTIC
CLEPTOMANIA
CLERESTOREY
CLERESTORIED
CLERESTORIES
CLERESTORY
CLERGEON
CLERGESS
CLERGIAL
CLERGIES
CLERGION
CLERGY
CLERGYABLE
CLERGYMAN
CLERGYMEN
CLERGYWOMAN
CLERGYWOMEN
CLERIC
CLERICAL
CLERICALISM
CLERICALIST
CLERICALITY
CLERICALLY
CLERICATE
CLERICATURE
CLERICISM
CLERICITY
CLERID
CLERIHEW
CLERISY
CLERK
CLERKAGE
CLERKED
CLERKERY
CLERKESS
CLERKING
CLERKISH
CLERKLESS
CLERKLIER
CLERKLIEST
CLERKLIKE
CLERKLINESS
CLERKLY
CLERKSHIP
CLEROMANCY
CLERONOMY
CLERUCH
CLERUCHIAL
CLERUCHIC
CLERUCHIES
CLERUCHY
CLETCH
CLEUCH
CLEUGH
CLEUK
CLEVE
CLEVEITE
CLEVER
CLEVERALITY
CLEVERER
CLEVEREST
CLEVERISH
CLEVERISHLY
CLEVERLY
CLEVERNESS
CLEVIS
CLEVY
CLEW
CLEWED
CLEWING
CLIACK
CLIANTHUS
CLICHE
CLICK
CLICKED
CLICKER
CLICKET
CLICKING
CLICKY
CLIENCY
CLIENT
CLIENTAGE
CLIENTAL
CLIENTED
CLIENTELE
CLIENTRY
CLIER
CLIFF
CLIFFED
CLIFFHANGER
CLIFFHANGING
CLIFFING
CLIFFS
CLIFFSIDE
CLIFFSMAN
CLIFFY
CLIFT
CLIFTONITE
CLIFTY
CLIMACTER
CLIMACTERIC
CLIMACTERICAL
CLIMACTIC
CLIMACUS
CLIMATAL
CLIMATE
CLIMATH
CLIMATIC
CLIMATICAL
CLIMATICALLY
CLIMATIZE
CLIMATOLOGIC
CLIMATOLOGY
CLIMATOMETER
CLIMATURE
CLIMAX
CLIMAXED
CLIMAXING
CLIMB
CLIMBABLE
CLIMBED
CLIMBER
CLIMBERS
CLIMBING
CLIME
CLIMOGRAPH
CLINAMEN
CLINANDRIA
CLINANDRIUM
CLINANTHIA
CLINANTHIUM
CLINCH
CLINCHER
CLINE
CLINER
CLING
CLINGER
CLINGFISH
CLINGFISHES
CLINGING
CLINGINGLY
CLINGINGNESS
CLINGSTONE
CLINGY
CLINIA
CLINIC
CLINICAL
CLINICIAN
CLINIQUE
CLINIUM
CLINK
CLINKED
CLINKER
CLINKERER
CLINKERMAN
CLINKING
CLINKSTONE
CLINKUM
CLINOCEPHALY
CLINOCHLORE
CLINOCLASE
CLINOCLASITE
CLINODOMATIC
CLINODOME
CLINOEDRITE
CLINOGRAPH
CLINOGRAPHIC
CLINOHEDRAL
CLINOHEDRITE
CLINOHUMITE
CLINOID
CLINOLOGIC
CLINOLOGY
CLINOMETER
CLINOMETRIC
CLINOMETRY
CLINOSTAT
CLINQUANT
CLINT
CLINTONIA
CLINTONITE
CLINTY
CLIP
CLIPBOARD
CLIPEUS
CLIPPABLE
CLIPPED
CLIPPER
CLIPPING
CLIPS
CLIPSE
CLIPSHEET
CLIPSOME
CLIQUE
CLIQUED
CLIQUIER
CLIQUIEST
CLIQUING
CLIQUISH
CLIQUISHLY
CLIQUISHNESS
CLIQUISM
CLIQUY
CLISEOMETER
CLISTOCARP
CLISTOGAMIC
CLISTOGAMOUS
CLISTOGAMY
CLISTOGENE
CLIT
CLITCH
CLITE
CLITELLAR
CLITELLINE
CLITELLUM
CLITELLUS
CLITES
CLITHE
CLITHRIDIATE
CLITION
CLITORAL
CLITORIDAUXE
CLITORIDEAN
CLITORIDITIS
CLITORIS
CLITORISM
CLITORITIS
CLITTER
CLIVAL
CLIVE
CLIVERS
CLIVIS
CLIVOSE
CLIVUS
CLOACA
CLOACAE
CLOACAL
CLOACITIS
CLOAK
CLOAKAGE
CLOAKED
CLOAKEDLY
CLOAKING
CLOAKMAKER

CLOAKMAKING
CLOAKROOM
CLOAM
CLOAMEN
CLOAMER
CLOBBER
CLOBBERER
CLOCHAN
CLOCHE
CLOCHER
CLOCHETTE
CLOCK
CLOCKBIRD
CLOCKCASE
CLOCKED
CLOCKER
CLOCKFACE
CLOCKHOUSE
CLOCKING
CLOCKKEEPER
CLOCKMAKER
CLOCKMAKING
CLOCKMUTCH
CLOCKROOM
CLOCKSMITH
CLOCKWISE
CLOCKWORK
CLOCKWORKED
CLOD
CLODBREAKER
CLODDED
CLODDER
CLODDIER
CLODDIEST
CLODDILY
CLODDINESS
CLODDING
CLODDISH
CLODDISHLY
CLODDISHNESS
CLODDY
CLODHEAD
CLODHOPPER
CLODHOPPING
CLODPATE
CLODPATED
CLODPOLE
CLODPOLL
CLODS
CLOES
CLOFF
CLOG
CLOGDOGDO
CLOGGED
CLOGGER
CLOGGIER
CLOGGIEST
CLOGGILY
CLOGGINESS
CLOGGING
CLOGGY
CLOGHAD
CLOGHAUN
CLOGHEAD
CLOGMAKER
CLOGMAKING
CLOGWHEEL
CLOGWOOD
CLOGWYN
CLOINE
CLOISON
CLOISONNE
CLOISTER
CLOISTERAL
CLOISTERED
CLOISTERER
CLOISTERING
CLOISTERLY
CLOISTRAL
CLOISTRESS
CLOIT
CLOKY
CLOMB
CLONAL
CLONE
CLONIC
CLONICITY
CLONICOTONIC
CLONISM
CLONK
CLONOS
CLONUS
CLOOF
CLOOK
CLOOP
CLOOT
CLOOTIE
CLOP
CLOPPED
CLOPPING
CLOQUE
CLOS
CLOSE
CLOSED
CLOSEFISTED
CLOSEHANDED
CLOSELY
CLOSEMOUTH
CLOSEMOUTHED
CLOSEN
CLOSENESS
CLOSER
CLOSEST
CLOSESTOOL
CLOSET
CLOSEUP
CLOSH
CLOSING
CLOSISH
CLOSTER
CLOSTRIDIA
CLOSTRIDIAL
CLOSTRIDIUM
CLOSURE
CLOSURED
CLOSURING
CLOT
CLOTBUR
CLOTE
CLOTH
CLOTHE
CLOTHED
CLOTHES
CLOTHESBAG
CLOTHESBRUSH
CLOTHESHORSE
CLOTHESLINE
CLOTHESMAN
CLOTHESPIN
CLOTHESPRESS
CLOTHESYARD
CLOTHIER
CLOTHIFY
CLOTHING
CLOTHMAKER
CLOTHMAKING
CLOTHS
CLOTHWORKER
CLOTHY
CLOTS
CLOTTAGE
CLOTTED
CLOTTER
CLOTTY
CLOTURE
CLOTWEED
CLOU
CLOUD
CLOUDAGE
CLOUDBERRIES
CLOUDBERRY
CLOUDBURST
CLOUDCAP
CLOUDED
CLOUDIER
CLOUDIEST
CLOUDILY
CLOUDINESS
CLOUDING
CLOUDLAND
CLOUDLESSLY
CLOUDS
CLOUDY
CLOUE
CLOUEE
CLOUGH
CLOUR
CLOUT
CLOUTED
CLOUTER
CLOUTERLY
CLOUTY
CLOVE
CLOVEN
CLOVENE
CLOVER
CLOVERLAY
CLOVERLEAF
CLOVERLEAFS
CLOVERLEY
CLOVEROOT
CLOVERY
CLOVES
CLOVEWORT
CLOW
CLOWDER
CLOWE
CLOWER
CLOWN
CLOWNADE
CLOWNAGE
CLOWNERIES
CLOWNERY
CLOWNHEAL
CLOWNISH
CLOWNISHLY
CLOWNISHNESS
CLOWRE
CLOWRING
CLOY
CLOYED
CLOYEDNESS
CLOYER
CLOYING
CLOYINGLY
CLOYINGNESS
CLOYMENT
CLOYSOME
CLUB
CLUBABLE
CLUBBABILITY
CLUBBED
CLUBBER
CLUBBIER
CLUBBIEST
CLUBBILY
CLUBBING
CLUBBISH
CLUBBIST
CLUBBY
CLUBFEET
CLUBFELLOW
CLUBFIST
CLUBFISTED
CLUBFOOT
CLUBFOOTED
CLUBHAUL
CLUBHOUSE
CLUBIONID
CLUBLAND
CLUBMAN
CLUBMATE
CLUBMEN
CLUBMONGER
CLUBRIDDEN
CLUBROOM
CLUBROOT
CLUBS
CLUBSTART
CLUBSTER
CLUBWEED
CLUBWOMAN
CLUBWOMEN
CLUBWOOD
CLUCK
CLUCKED
CLUCKING
CLUE
CLUED
CLUF
CLUFE
CLUFF
CLUING
CLUM
CLUMBER
CLUMP
CLUMPER
CLUMPISH
CLUMPS
CLUMPST
CLUMPY
CLUMSE
CLUMSIER
CLUMSIEST
CLUMSILY
CLUMSINESS
CLUMSY
CLUNCH
CLUNG
CLUNK
CLUNTER
CLUPEID
CLUPEIFORM
CLUPEIN
CLUPEINE
CLUPEOID
CLUPIEN
CLUPPE
CLURICAUNE
CLUSE
CLUSIACEOUS
CLUSTER
CLUSTERBERRY
CLUSTERED
CLUSTERFIST
CLUSTERING
CLUSTERS
CLUSTERY
CLUTCH
CLUTCHED
CLUTCHING
CLUTHER
CLUTTER
CLUTTERED
CLUTTERER
CLUTTERING
CLUTTERY
CLY
CLYER
CLYERS
CLYFAKER
CLYPE
CLYPEAL
CLYPEASTROID
CLYPEATE
CLYPEATED
CLYPEI
CLYPEIFORM
CLYPEOLA
CLYPEOLAR
CLYPEOLATE
CLYPEOLE
CLYPEUS
CLYSIS
CLYSMA
CLYSMIAN
CLYSMIC
CLYSSUS
CLYSTER
CLYTE
CNAFE
CNEMIAL
CNEMIDIUM
CNEMIS
CNICIN
CNIDA
CNIDARIAN
CNIDOCELL
CNIDOCIL
CNIDOPHORE
CNIDOPOD
CNIDOSAC
CNIDOSIS
CO
COACERVATE
COACERVATION
COACH
COACHABILITY
COACHABLE
COACHBUILDER
COACHED
COACHEE
COACHER
COACHFELLOW
COACHING
COACHMAKER
COACHMAKING
COACHMAN
COACHMASTER
COACHMEN
COACHSMITH
COACHWAY
COACHWHIP
COACHWOMAN
COACHWORK
COACHWRIGHT
COACHY
COACT
COACTED
COACTING
COACTION
COACTIVE
COACTIVELY
COACTIVITY
COACTOR
COADAMITE
COADAPT
COADJACENCE
COADJACENT
COADJACENTLY
COADJUMENT
COADJUST
COADJUTANT
COADJUTATOR
COADJUTE

COADJUTEMENT
COADJUTIVE
COADJUTOR
COADJUTRESS
COADJUTRICE
COADJUTRICES
COADJUTRIX
COADJUVANT
COADMIT
COADSORBENT
COADUNATE
COADUNATED
COADUNATING
COADUNATION
COADUNATIVE
COADUNATIVELY
COADVENTURE
COADVENTURER
COAEVAL
COAGED
COAGEL
COAGMENT
COAGULA
COAGULABLE
COAGULANT
COAGULASE
COAGULATE
COAGULATED
COAGULATING
COAGULATION
COAGULATIVE
COAGULATOR
COAGULATORY
COAGULIN
COAGULOMETER
COAGULUM
COAITA
COAK
COAKUM
COAL
COALBAG
COALBAGGER
COALBIN
COALBOX
COALDEALER
COALED
COALER
COALESCE
COALESCED
COALESCENCE
COALESCENCY
COALESCENT
COALESCING
COALFIELD
COALFISH
COALFISHES
COALHEUGH
COALHOLE
COALIFY
COALING
COALITE
COALITION
COALITIONAL
COALITIONER
COALITIONIST
COALIZE
COALIZED
COALIZING
COALMONGER
COALMOUSE
COALPIT
COALRAKE
COALS
COALSACK
COALSHED
COALTERNATE
COALTITUDE
COALY
COALYARD
COAMING
COAPT
COAPTATE
COAPTATION
COAPTED
COAPTING
COARB
COARCT
COARCTATE
COARCTATION
COARCTED
COARCTING
COARSE
COARSELY
COARSEN
COARSENESS
COARSER
COARSEST
COART
COAST
COASTAL
COASTER
COASTING
COASTLAND
COASTLINE
COASTMAN
COASTMEN
COASTSIDE
COASTWAITER
COASTWARD
COASTWAYS
COASTWISE
COAT
COATED
COATEE
COATER
COATH
COATI
COATING
COATIS
COATLESS
COATRACK
COATROOM
COATS
COATTAIL
COATTAILED
COAX
COAXAL
COAXATION
COAXED
COAXER
COAXIAL
COAXIALLY
COAXING
COAXINGLY
COAXY
COAZERVATE
COAZERVATION
COB
COBAEA
COBALAMIN
COBALT
COBALTAMINE
COBALTAMMINE
COBALTIC
COBALTOUS
COBANG
COBB
COBBE
COBBER
COBBERER
COBBIN
COBBLE
COBBLED
COBBLER
COBBLERFISH
COBBLERY
COBBLES
COBBLESTONE
COBBLING
COBBLY
COBBRA
COBBY
COBCAB
COBEGO
COBERGER
COBHEAD
COBHOUSE
COBIA
COBIRON
COBISHOP
COBLE
COBLEMAN
COBLOAF
COBNUT
COBOLA
COBOSS
COBRA
COBRIDGEHEAD
COBRIFORM
COBROTHER
COBS
COBSTONE
COBURG
COBWEB
COBWEBBED
COBWEBBERY
COBWEBBING
COBWEBBY
COBWEBS
COBWORK
COCA
COCAIN
COCAINE
COCAINISM
COCAINIZE
COCAINIZED
COCAINIZING
COCAINOMANIA
COCASH
COCASHWEED
COCCACEOUS
COCCAGEE
COCCAL
COCCERIN
COCCI
COCCID
COCCIDIA
COCCIDIAL
COCCIDIAN
COCCIDIOIDAL
COCCIDIOSIS
COCCIDIUM
COCCIDOLOGY
COCCIFEROUS
COCCIFORM
COCCIGENIC
COCCINELLA
COCCIONELLA
COCCO
COCCOGONE
COCCOGONIUM
COCCOID
COCCOLITE
COCCOLITH
COCCOSPHERE
COCCOSTEAN
COCCOSTEID
COCCOUS
COCCYGALGIA
COCCYGEAL
COCCYGEAN
COCCYGECTOMY
COCCYGES
COCCYGEUS
COCCYGINE
COCCYGODYNIA
COCCYGOMORPH
COCCYGOTOMY
COCCYX
COCHAL
COCHER
COCHERO
COCHINEAL
COCHLEA
COCHLEAE
COCHLEAR
COCHLEARE
COCHLEATE
COCHLEATED
COCHLEIFORM
COCHLEITIS
COCHLEOUS
COCHLIODONT
COCHLITIS
COCHON
COCHYLIS
COCILLANA
COCINERA
COCINERO
COCIRCULAR
COCK
COCKADE
COCKADED
COCKAL
COCKALAN
COCKALEEKIE
COCKALORUM
COCKAMAMIE
COCKAMAMY
COCKANDY
COCKARD
COCKAROUSE
COCKATEEL
COCKATIEL
COCKATOO
COCKATOOS
COCKATRICE
COCKAWEE
COCKBELL
COCKBILL
COCKBIRD
COCKBOAT
COCKBRAIN
COCKCHAFER
COCKCROW
COCKCROWER
COCKCROWING
COCKED
COCKER
COCKEREL
COCKERIE
COCKERING
COCKERNONNIE
COCKERNONY
COCKEROUSE
COCKET
COCKETED
COCKETING
COCKEYE
COCKEYED
COCKEYES
COCKFIGHT
COCKFIGHTING
COCKHEAD
COCKHORSE
COCKIE
COCKIELEEKIE
COCKIER
COCKIES
COCKIEST
COCKILY
COCKINESS
COCKING
COCKISH
COCKISHLY
COCKISHNESS
COCKLE
COCKLEBOAT
COCKLEBUR
COCKLED
COCKLER
COCKLESHELL
COCKLEWIFE
COCKLIGHT
COCKLING
COCKLOCHE
COCKLOFT
COCKLY
COCKMASTER
COCKMATCH
COCKMATE
COCKNEIAN
COCKNEITY
COCKNEY
COCKNEYBRED
COCKNEYDOM
COCKNEYESE
COCKNEYESS
COCKNEYFY
COCKNEYFYING
COCKNEYISH
COCKNEYISM
COCKNEYIZE
COCKNEYLAND
COCKPADDLE
COCKPIT
COCKROACH
COCKSCOMB
COCKSCOMBED
COCKSFOOT
COCKSHEAD
COCKSHIES
COCKSHOOT
COCKSHOT
COCKSHUT
COCKSHY
COCKSHYING
COCKSPUR
COCKSURE
COCKSURENESS
COCKSURETY
COCKSWAIN
COCKSY
COCKTAIL
COCKTHROWING
COCKUP
COCKWEED
COCKY
COCLEA
COCO
COCOA
COCOANUT
COCOAWOOD
COCOBOLO
COCOMAT
COCONA
COCONSCIOUS
COCONUT
COCOON
COCOONERIES
COCOONERY
COCOONS
COCOPAN
COCORICO
COCOROOT

COCOTTE
COCOWOOD
COCOWORT
COCOYAM
COCT
COCTILE
COCTION
COCTO
COCTOANTIGEN
COCUISA
COCUIZA
COCULLO
COCUM
COCUSWOOD
COCUYO
COD
CODA
CODAMIN
CODAMINE
CODBANK
CODDED
CODDER
CODDING
CODDLE
CODDLED
CODDLER
CODDLING
CODDY
CODE
CODED
CODEIA
CODEIN
CODEINE
CODEN
CODER
CODETTA
CODEX
CODFISH
CODFISHER
CODFISHERIES
CODFISHERY
CODFISHES
CODFISHING
CODGER
CODHEAD
CODHEADED
CODIACEOUS
CODICAL
CODICES
CODICIL
CODICILIC
CODIFICATION
CODIFIED
CODIFIER
CODIFY
CODIFYING
CODILLA
CODING
CODINIAC
CODIST
CODLIN
CODLING
CODLINGS
CODMAN
CODOL
CODOMINANT
CODON
CODPIECE
CODPITCHINGS
CODS
CODSHEAD
CODWORM
COE
COED
COEDUCATION
COEDUCATIONAL
COEFFECT
COEFFICIENT
COEHORN
COELACANTH
COELACANTHID
COELAR
COELARIUM
COELELMINTH
COELENTERATE
COELENTERIC
COELENTERON
COELESTINE
COELHO
COELIA
COELIAC
COELIALGIA
COELIGENOUS
COELIN
COELIORRHEA
COELIORRHOEA
COELIOSCOPY
COELIOTOMY
COELOBLASTIC
COELODONT
COELOM
COELOMA
COELOMATA
COELOMATE
COELOMATIC
COELOMATOUS
COELOME
COELOMIC
COELOMOPORE
COELOPLANULA
COELOSPERM
COELOSTAT
COELOZOIC
COEMPT
COEMPTIO
COEMPTION
COEMPTIONAL
COEMPTIVE
COEMPTOR
COENA
COENACULOUS
COENANTHIUM
COENENCHYMA
COENENCHYMAL
COENENCHYMATA
COENENCHYME
COENESTHESIA
COENESTHESIS
COENOBE
COENOBIAR
COENOBIC
COENOBIOD
COENOBITE
COENOBIUM
COENOBLAST
COENOBLASTIC
COENOBY
COENOCENTRUM
COENOCYTE
COENOCYTIC
COENOECIAL
COENOECIC
COENOECIUM
COENOGAMETE
COENOGENESIS
COENOSARC
COENOSARCAL
COENOSARCOUS
COENOSTEAL
COENOSTEUM
COENOTROPE
COENOTYPE
COENURE
COENURUS
COENZYME
COEQUAL
COEQUALITY
COEQUALLY
COEQUALNESS
COEQUATE
COEQUATED
COEQUATION
COERCE
COERCED
COERCER
COERCIBILITY
COERCIBLE
COERCIBLY
COERCING
COERCION
COERCIONARY
COERCIONIST
COERCITIVE
COERCIVE
COERCIVELY
COERCIVENESS
COERCIVITY
COESSENTIAL
COESTATE
COETANEITY
COETANEOUS
COETANEOUSLY
COETERNALLY
COETERNITY
COETUS
COEVAL
COEVALLY
COEXIST
COEXISTENCE
COEXISTENCY
COEXISTENT
COEXTEND
COEXTENSION
COEXTENSIVE
COFACTOR
COFEOFFEE
COFF
COFFE
COFFEE
COFFEEBERRIES
COFFEEBERRY
COFFEEBUSH
COFFEECAKE
COFFEEGROWER
COFFEEHOUSE
COFFEELEAF
COFFEEMAN
COFFEEPOT
COFFEEROOM
COFFEEWEED
COFFEEWOOD
COFFER
COFFERDAM
COFFERED
COFFERER
COFFERING
COFFERWORK
COFFIN
COFFINED
COFFING
COFFINING
COFFINMAKER
COFFINMAKING
COFFLE
COFFLED
COFFLING
COFFRET
COFT
COG
COGBOAT
COGENCE
COGENCY
COGENER
COGENT
COGGED
COGGER
COGGERS
COGGIE
COGGING
COGGLE
COGGLEDY
COGGLETY
COGGLY
COGHLE
COGIDA
COGITABILITY
COGITABLE
COGITABUND
COGITABUNDLY
COGITANT
COGITATE
COGITATED
COGITATING
COGITATION
COGITATIVE
COGITATIVELY
COGITATIVITY
COGITATOR
COGITO
COGMAN
COGNAC
COGNATE
COGNATIC
COGNATION
COGNATUS
COGNISE
COGNITION
COGNITIONAL
COGNITIVE
COGNITIVELY
COGNITUM
COGNIZABLE
COGNIZABLY
COGNIZANCE
COGNIZANT
COGNIZE
COGNIZED
COGNIZEE
COGNIZER
COGNIZING
COGNIZOR
COGNOMEN
COGNOMENS
COGNOMINA
COGNOMINAL
COGNOMINALLY
COGNOMINATE
COGNOMINATED
COGNOSCE
COGNOSCENTE
COGNOSCIBLE
COGNOSCITIVE
COGON
COGONAL
COGRAIL
COGREDIENCY
COGREDIENT
COGROAD
COGUE
COGWAY
COGWHEEL
COGWOOD
COHAB
COHABIT
COHABITANCY
COHABITANT
COHABITATION
COHABITED
COHABITER
COHABITING
COHEIR
COHEIRESS
COHENITE
COHERE
COHERED
COHERENCE
COHERENCY
COHERENT
COHERENTLY
COHERER
COHERING
COHERITAGE
COHERITOR
COHERT
COHESIBILITY
COHESIBLE
COHESION
COHESIVE
COHESIVELY
COHESIVENESS
COHIBIT
COHIBITION
COHIBITIVE
COHIBITOR
COHITRE
COHO
COHOBA
COHOBATE
COHOBATED
COHOBATING
COHOBATION
COHOBATOR
COHOE
COHOL
COHORT
COHORTATION
COHORTATIVE
COHOSH
COHOW
COHU
COHUE
COHUNE
COIF
COIFED
COIFFE
COIFFEUR
COIFFEUSE
COIFFURE
COIFFURED
COIFFURING
COIFING
COIGN
COIGNE
COIGNY
COIGUE
COIL
COILED
COILER
COILING
COILS
COILSMITH
COILYEAR
COIMPLICANT
COIN
COINABLE
COINAGE
COINCIDE
COINCIDENCE
COINCIDENCY
COINCIDENT
COINCIDENTAL
COINCIDENTALLY
COINCIDENTLY
COINCIDER
COINCIDING

COINDICANT
COINDICATE
COINDICATION
COINED
COINER
COINHABIT
COINHABITOR
COINHERITOR
COINING
COINMAKER
COINMAKING
COINS
COINSURANCE
COINSURE
COINSURED
COINSURER
COINSURING
COINTENSE
COINTENSITY
COINTISE
COIR
COISTREL
COISTRIL
COITION
COITURE
COITUS
COIX
COJONES
COJUROR
COKE
COKEMAN
COKENEY
COKER
COKERNUT
COKERY
COKES
COKEWOLD
COKEY
COKIE
COL
COLA
COLAGE
COLALGIA
COLANDER
COLANE
COLATE
COLATION
COLATITUDE
COLATORIUM
COLATORY
COLATURE
COLAUXE
COLAZIONE
COLBERTER
COLBERTINE
COLCANNON
COLCHICIA
COLCHICIN
COLCHICINE
COLCHICUM
COLCOTHAR
COLD
COLDCOCK
COLDER
COLDFINCH
COLDHEARTED
COLDHEARTEDLY
COLDISH
COLDLY
COLDONG
COLE
COLECTOMIES
COLECTOMY
COLEGATEE
COLEMANITE
COLEOPTER
COLEOPTERA
COLEOPTERAL
COLEOPTERAN
COLEOPTERIST
COLEOPTEROID
COLEOPTERON
COLEOPTEROUS
COLEOPTILE
COLEOPTILUM
COLEORHIZA
COLESEED
COLESLAW
COLETIT
COLEUR
COLEUS
COLEWORT
COLF
COLFOX
COLI
COLIBERT
COLIBRI
COLIC
COLICAL
COLICHEMARDE
COLICIN
COLICKER
COLICKY
COLICROOT
COLICWEED
COLICWORT
COLIES
COLIFORM
COLIMA
COLIN
COLINEAR
COLING
COLISEUM
COLITIC
COLITIS
COLK
COLL
COLLABENT
COLLABORATE
COLLABORATED
COLLABORATING
COLLABORATOR
COLLAGEN
COLLAGENIC
COLLAGENOUS
COLLAPSABLE
COLLAPSE
COLLAPSED
COLLAPSIBLE
COLLAPSING
COLLAR
COLLARBAND
COLLARBIRD
COLLARBONE
COLLARD
COLLARED
COLLARET
COLLARETTE
COLLARMAN
COLLATE
COLLATED
COLLATEE
COLLATERAL
COLLATERALLY
COLLATING
COLLATION
COLLATIONER
COLLATITIOUS
COLLATIVE
COLLATOR
COLLATRESS
COLLAUD
COLLAUDATION
COLLEAGUE
COLLEAGUED
COLLEAGUING
COLLECT
COLLECTABLE
COLLECTANEA
COLLECTARIUM
COLLECTED
COLLECTEDLY
COLLECTIBLE
COLLECTION
COLLECTIONAL
COLLECTIONER
COLLECTIVE
COLLECTIVELY
COLLECTIVISM
COLLECTIVIST
COLLECTIVITY
COLLECTIVIZE
COLLECTIVIZED
COLLECTIVIZING
COLLECTOR
COLLECTORATE
COLLECTORSHIP
COLLEEN
COLLEGATARY
COLLEGE
COLLEGER
COLLEGIA
COLLEGIAL
COLLEGIALISM
COLLEGIALITY
COLLEGIAN
COLLEGIANER
COLLEGIATE
COLLEGIATELY
COLLEGIATION
COLLEGIUM
COLLEMBOLAN
COLLEMBOLE
COLLEMBOLIC
COLLEMBOLOUS
COLLEN
COLLENCHYMA
COLLENCHYME
COLLENCYTAL
COLLENCYTE
COLLERY
COLLET
COLLETER
COLLETERIA
COLLETERIAL
COLLETERIUM
COLLETIC
COLLETIN
COLLEY
COLLIBERT
COLLICLE
COLLICULATE
COLLICULUS
COLLIDE
COLLIDED
COLLIDIN
COLLIDINE
COLLIDING
COLLIE
COLLIED
COLLIER
COLLIERY
COLLIFORM
COLLIGATE
COLLIGATED
COLLIGATING
COLLIGATION
COLLIGATIVE
COLLIGIBLE
COLLIMATE
COLLIMATED
COLLIMATING
COLLIMATION
COLLIN
COLLINAL
COLLINE
COLLINEARITY
COLLINEARLY
COLLINEATE
COLLINEATION
COLLING
COLLINGUAL
COLLINSIA
COLLINSITE
COLLIQUATE
COLLIQUATION
COLLIQUATIVE
COLLIS
COLLISION
COLLISIONAL
COLLISIVE
COLLOBLAST
COLLOCAL
COLLOCATE
COLLOCATED
COLLOCATING
COLLOCATION
COLLOCK
COLLOCUTION
COLLOCUTOR
COLLOCUTORY
COLLODION
COLLODIONIZE
COLLODIOTYPE
COLLODIUM
COLLOGEN
COLLOGUE
COLLOGUED
COLLOGUING
COLLOID
COLLOIDAL
COLLOIDALITY
COLLOMIA
COLLOP
COLLOPED
COLLOPHANITE
COLLOPHORE
COLLOQUE
COLLOQUIAL
COLLOQUIALLY
COLLOQUIST
COLLOQUIUM
COLLOQUIZE
COLLOQUIZED
COLLOQUIZING
COLLOQUY
COLLOTYPE
COLLOTYPIC
COLLOTYPY
COLLOXYLIN
COLLUDE
COLLUDED
COLLUDER
COLLUDING
COLLUM
COLLUSION
COLLUSIVE
COLLUSIVELY
COLLUSORY
COLLUTORIES
COLLUTORIUM
COLLUTORY
COLLUVIAL
COLLUVIES
COLLY
COLLYBA
COLLYING
COLLYRIA
COLLYRIE
COLLYRITE
COLLYRIUM
COLLYRIUMS
COLLYWEST
COLLYWESTON
COLLYWOBBLES
COLMAR
COLMOSE
COLOBIN
COLOBIUM
COLOBOMA
COLOCENTESIS
COLOCLYSIS
COLOCOLA
COLOCOLIC
COLOCOLO
COLOCYNTH
COLOCYNTHIN
COLOGARITHM
COLOGNE
COLOLITE
COLOMBIER
COLOMBIN
COLOMETRIC
COLOMETRY
COLON
COLONATE
COLONEL
COLONELCIES
COLONELCY
COLONGITUDE
COLONIAL
COLONIALISM
COLONIC
COLONIES
COLONISE
COLONIST
COLONITIS
COLONIZATION
COLONIZE
COLONIZED
COLONIZER
COLONIZING
COLONNADE
COLONNADED
COLONNETTE
COLONOPATHY
COLONOPEXY
COLONOSCOPE
COLONOSCOPY
COLONS
COLONUS
COLONY
COLOPEXIA
COLOPEXOTOMY
COLOPEXY
COLOPHAN
COLOPHANE
COLOPHENE
COLOPHON
COLOPHONATE
COLOPHONIST
COLOPHONITE
COLOPHONY
COLOPLICATION
COLOPPE
COLOQUIES
COLOQUINTIDA
COLOR
COLORABILITY
COLORABLE
COLORABLY
COLORADO
COLORANT
COLORATE
COLORATION

COLORATIONAL
COLORATIVE
COLORATURA
COLORCAST
COLORED
COLORER
COLORFAST
COLORFUL
COLORIFIC
COLORIFICS
COLORIMETER
COLORIMETRIC
COLORIMETRY
COLORIN
COLORING
COLORISM
COLORIST
COLORISTIC
COLORIZATION
COLORIZE
COLORLESS
COLORMAKER
COLORMAKING
COLORMAN
COLOROTO
COLORRHAPHY
COLORS
COLORTYPE
COLORY
COLOSSAL
COLOSSALITY
COLOSSALLY
COLOSSEAN
COLOSSEUM
COLOSSO
COLOSSUS
COLOSTOMIES
COLOSTOMY
COLOSTRAL
COLOSTRIC
COLOSTROUS
COLOSTRUM
COLOTOMIES
COLOTOMY
COLOTYPHOID
COLOUR
COLOURABILITY
COLOURABLE
COLOURABLY
COLOURATION
COLOURATIVE
COLOURED
COLOURER
COLOURFUL
COLOURFULLY
COLOURFULNESS
COLOURIFIC
COLOURIFICS
COLOURING
COLOURIST
COLOURISTIC
COLOURIZE
COLOURLESS
COLOURLESSLY
COLOURMAN
COLOURTYPE
COLOURY
COLPENCHYMA
COLPEO
COLPEURYNTER
COLPEURYSIS
COLPHEG
COLPINDACH
COLPITIS
COLPOCELE
COLPOPLASTIC
COLPOPLASTY
COLPOPTOSIS
COLPORRHAGIA
COLPORRHAPHY
COLPORRHEA
COLPORRHEXIS
COLPORT
COLPORTAGE
COLPORTER
COLPORTEUR
COLPOSCOPE
COLPOSCOPY
COLPOSTAT
COLPOTOMY
COLT
COLTER
COLTISH
COLTPIXY
COLTS
COLTSFOOT
COLTSKIN
COLUBRID
COLUBRIFORM
COLUBRINE
COLUBROID
COLUGO
COLUGOS
COLUMBACEOUS
COLUMBARIA
COLUMBARIUM
COLUMBARY
COLUMBATE
COLUMBEION
COLUMBIAD
COLUMBIC
COLUMBIER
COLUMBIN
COLUMBINE
COLUMBITE
COLUMBIUM
COLUMBO
COLUMBOID
COLUMEL
COLUMELLA
COLUMELLAE
COLUMELLAR
COLUMELLATE
COLUMN
COLUMNAL
COLUMNAR
COLUMNATED
COLUMNEA
COLUMNED
COLUMNER
COLUMNIATION
COLUMNIFORM
COLUMNING
COLUMNIST
COLUMNS
COLUNAR
COLURE
COLUSITE
COLY
COLYBA
COLYMBIFORM
COLYMBION
COLYTIC
COLYUM
COLYUMIST
COLZA
COMA
COMACINE
COMAE
COMAL
COMALES
COMAMIE
COMARCA
COMART
COMAS
COMATE
COMATIC
COMATOSE
COMATOSELY
COMATOSENESS
COMATOSITY
COMATOUS
COMATULA
COMATULID
COMB
COMBARON
COMBASOU
COMBAT
COMBATABLE
COMBATANT
COMBATANTS
COMBATED
COMBATING
COMBATIVE
COMBATIVELY
COMBATIVITY
COMBATTED
COMBATTER
COMBATTING
COMBED
COMBER
COMBFISH
COMBFLOWER
COMBINABLE
COMBINANT
COMBINANTIVE
COMBINATE
COMBINATION
COMBINATIONS
COMBINATIVE
COMBINE
COMBINED
COMBINEDLY
COMBINEDNESS
COMBINEMENT
COMBINER
COMBING
COMBINGS
COMBINING
COMBITE
COMBLE
COMBMAKER
COMBMAKING
COMBO
COMBOLOIO
COMBOY
COMBURE
COMBURENT
COMBURGESS
COMBURIMETER
COMBURIMETRY
COMBUST
COMBUSTIBLE
COMBUSTIBLY
COMBUSTION
COMBUSTIOUS
COMBUSTIVE
COMBUSTOR
COMBWISE
COMBWRIGHT
COMBY
COME
COMEBACK
COMEDDLE
COMEDIA
COMEDIAL
COMEDIAN
COMEDIANT
COMEDIC
COMEDICAL
COMEDICALLY
COMEDIENNE
COMEDIES
COMEDIST
COMEDO
COMEDONES
COMEDOS
COMEDOWN
COMEDY
COMELIER
COMELIEST
COMELILY
COMELINESS
COMELING
COMELY
COMENDITE
COMEPHOROUS
COMER
COMES
COMESSATION
COMESTIBLE
COMESTION
COMET
COMETARIA
COMETARIUM
COMETARY
COMETHER
COMETIC
COMEUPANCE
COMEUPPANCE
COMFIT
COMFITURE
COMFORT
COMFORTABLE
COMFORTABLY
COMFORTED
COMFORTER
COMFORTING
COMFORTINGLY
COMFORTLESS
COMFREY
COMFREYS
COMFY
COMIC
COMICAL
COMICALITY
COMICALLY
COMICALNESS
COMICOCRATIC
COMICOGRAPHY
COMICRY
COMIDA
COMIFEROUS
COMING
COMINO
COMIQUE
COMISM
COMITAL
COMITANT
COMITATIVE
COMITATUS
COMITE
COMITES
COMITIA
COMITIAL
COMITIES
COMITIVA
COMITJE
COMITRAGEDY
COMITY
COMMA
COMMAES
COMMAING
COMMAND
COMMANDANT
COMMANDED
COMMANDEER
COMMANDER
COMMANDERY
COMMANDING
COMMANDINGLY
COMMANDMENT
COMMANDMENTS
COMMANDO
COMMANDOES
COMMANDOS
COMMANDRIES
COMMANDRY
COMMAS
COMMASSATION
COMMASSEE
COMMATA
COMMATIC
COMMATION
COMMATISM
COMMEASURE
COMMEASURED
COMMEASURING
COMMEM
COMMEMORABLE
COMMEMORATE
COMMEMORATED
COMMEMORATING
COMMEMORATION
COMMEMORATIVE
COMMEMORATOR
COMMEMORIZE
COMMEMORIZED
COMMEMORIZING
COMMENCE
COMMENCED
COMMENCEMENT
COMMENCER
COMMENCING
COMMEND
COMMENDA
COMMENDABLE
COMMENDABLY
COMMENDADOR
COMMENDAM
COMMENDATARY
COMMENDATION
COMMENDATOR
COMMENDATORIES
COMMENDATORY
COMMENDED
COMMENDER
COMMENDING
COMMENSAL
COMMENSALISM
COMMENSALIST
COMMENSALISTIC
COMMENSALITY
COMMENSALLY
COMMENSURABLE
COMMENSURABLY
COMMENSURATE
COMMENSURATED
COMMENSURATING
COMMENT
COMMENTARIAL
COMMENTARIES
COMMENTARY
COMMENTATE
COMMENTATION
COMMENTATOR
COMMENTER
COMMERCE
COMMERCED
COMMERCER
COMMERCIA
COMMERCIABLE
COMMERCIAL
COMMERCIALISM
COMMERCIALITY

COMMERCIALIZE
COMMERCIALIZED
COMMERCIALIZING
COMMERCIALLY
COMMERCING
COMMERCIUM
COMMERGE
COMMERS
COMMESSO
COMMINATE
COMMINATED
COMMINATING
COMMINATION
COMMINATIVE
COMMINATOR
COMMINATORY
COMMINGLE
COMMINGLER
COMMINISTER
COMMINUATE
COMMINUTE
COMMINUTED
COMMINUTING
COMMINUTION
COMMINUTOR
COMMIS
COMMISE
COMMISERABLE
COMMISERATE
COMMISERATED
COMMISERATING
COMMISERATION
COMMISERATIVE
COMMISERATOR
COMMISSAR
COMMISSARIAL
COMMISSARIAT
COMMISSARIES
COMMISSARY
COMMISSION
COMMISSIONAIRE
COMMISSIONAL
COMMISSIONARY
COMMISSIONATE
COMMISSIONATED
COMMISSIONATING
COMMISSIONER
COMMISSIVE
COMMISSIVELY
COMMISSURAL
COMMISSURE
COMMIT
COMMITMENT
COMMITTABLE
COMMITTAL
COMMITTED
COMMITTEE
COMMITTEEMAN
COMMITTEEMEN
COMMITTENT
COMMITTER
COMMITTIBLE
COMMITTING
COMMITTOR
COMMIX
COMMIXED
COMMIXING
COMMIXT
COMMIXTION
COMMIXTURE
COMMODATA
COMMODATARY
COMMODATE
COMMODATION
COMMODATUM
COMMODE
COMMODIOUS
COMMODIOUSLY
COMMODITIES
COMMODITY
COMMODORE
COMMON
COMMONABLE
COMMONAGE
COMMONALITIES
COMMONALITY
COMMONALTY
COMMONED
COMMONER
COMMONEY
COMMONING
COMMONLY
COMMONNESS
COMMONPLACE
COMMONPLACELY
COMMONPLACENES
COMMONS
COMMONTY
COMMONWEAL
COMMONWEALTH
COMMORANCY
COMMORANT
COMMORIENT
COMMORTH
COMMOS
COMMOT
COMMOTE
COMMOTION
COMMOTIONAL
COMMOVE
COMMOVED
COMMOVING
COMMUNAL
COMMUNALISM
COMMUNALIST
COMMUNALISTIC
COMMUNALITY
COMMUNALIZE
COMMUNALIZED
COMMUNALIZER
COMMUNALLY
COMMUNARD
COMMUNE
COMMUNED
COMMUNER
COMMUNICABLE
COMMUNICABLY
COMMUNICANT
COMMUNICATE
COMMUNICATED
COMMUNICATING
COMMUNICATION
COMMUNICATIVE
COMMUNICATOR
COMMUNICATORY
COMMUNING
COMMUNION
COMMUNIONABLE
COMMUNIONAL
COMMUNIONIST
COMMUNIQUE
COMMUNISM
COMMUNIST
COMMUNISTERIES
COMMUNISTERY
COMMUNISTIC
COMMUNISTICAL
COMMUNITAL
COMMUNITARIAN
COMMUNITARY
COMMUNITIES
COMMUNITIVE
COMMUNITY
COMMUNIZATION
COMMUNIZE
COMMUNIZED
COMMUNIZING
COMMUTABLE
COMMUTANT
COMMUTATE
COMMUTATED
COMMUTATING
COMMUTATION
COMMUTATIVE
COMMUTATOR
COMMUTE
COMMUTED
COMMUTER
COMMUTING
COMMUTUAL
COMMUTUALITY
COMMY
COMODATO
COMODO
COMOEDIA
COMOEDUS
COMOID
COMOLECULE
COMONTE
COMOQUER
COMORADO
COMOSE
COMOUS
COMP
COMPACT
COMPACTED
COMPACTEDLY
COMPACTER
COMPACTING
COMPACTION
COMPACTLY
COMPACTNESS
COMPACTURE
COMPADRE
COMPAGE
COMPAGES
COMPAGINATE
COMPANIED
COMPANIES
COMPANION
COMPANIONABLE
COMPANIONABLY
COMPANIONAGE
COMPANIONATE
COMPANIONED
COMPANIONING
COMPANIONIZE
COMPANIONIZED
COMPANIONIZING
COMPANIONSHIP
COMPANIONWAY
COMPANY
COMPANYING
COMPARABLE
COMPARABLY
COMPARATE
COMPARATIVAL
COMPARATIVE
COMPARATIVELY
COMPARATOR
COMPARE
COMPARED
COMPARER
COMPARING
COMPARISON
COMPAROGRAPH
COMPARSA
COMPART
COMPARTED
COMPARTING
COMPARTITION
COMPARTMENT
COMPARTMENTS
COMPASS
COMPASSABLE
COMPASSED
COMPASSER
COMPASSES
COMPASSING
COMPASSION
COMPASSIONATE
COMPASSIONATED
COMPASSIONATING
COMPASSIVE
COMPASSIVITY
COMPATERNITY
COMPATIBLE
COMPATIBLY
COMPATIENCE
COMPATIENT
COMPATRIOT
COMPATRIOTIC
COMPEAR
COMPEARANCE
COMPEARANT
COMPEER
COMPEL
COMPELLABLE
COMPELLABLY
COMPELLATION
COMPELLATIVE
COMPELLED
COMPELLENT
COMPELLER
COMPELLING
COMPELLINGLY
COMPEND
COMPENDENCY
COMPENDENT
COMPENDIA
COMPENDIARY
COMPENDIATE
COMPENDIOUS
COMPENDIUM
COMPENDIUMS
COMPENETRATE
COMPENSABLE
COMPENSATE
COMPENSATED
COMPENSATING
COMPENSATION
COMPENSATIVE
COMPENSATOR
COMPENSATORY
COMPENSE
COMPENSER
COMPERE
COMPERT
COMPESCE
COMPETE
COMPETED
COMPETENCE
COMPETENCY
COMPETENT
COMPETENTLY
COMPETIBLE
COMPETING
COMPETITION
COMPETITIVE
COMPETITIVELY
COMPETITOR
COMPETITORY
COMPETITRESS
COMPETITRIX
COMPILATION
COMPILATOR
COMPILATORY
COMPILE
COMPILED
COMPILEMENT
COMPILER
COMPILING
COMPITAL
COMPITUM
COMPLACENCE
COMPLACENCIES
COMPLACENCY
COMPLACENT
COMPLACENTLY
COMPLAIN
COMPLAINANT
COMPLAINED
COMPLAINER
COMPLAINING
COMPLAINT
COMPLAINTIVE
COMPLAISANCE
COMPLAISANT
COMPLAISANTLY
COMPLANATE
COMPLANATION
COMPLANT
COMPLECT
COMPLECTED
COMPLEMENT
COMPLEMENTAL
COMPLETE
COMPLETED
COMPLETELY
COMPLETENESS
COMPLETER
COMPLETING
COMPLETION
COMPLETIVE
COMPLETIVELY
COMPLETORIES
COMPLETORY
COMPLEX
COMPLEXIFY
COMPLEXION
COMPLEXIONAL
COMPLEXIONARY
COMPLEXIONED
COMPLEXITIES
COMPLEXITY
COMPLEXLY
COMPLEXNESS
COMPLEXUS
COMPLIABLE
COMPLIABLY
COMPLIANCE
COMPLIANCY
COMPLIANT
COMPLIANTLY
COMPLICACIES
COMPLICACY
COMPLICANT
COMPLICATE
COMPLICATED
COMPLICATING
COMPLICATION
COMPLICATIVE
COMPLICE
COMPLICITIES
COMPLICITOUS
COMPLICITY
COMPLIER
COMPLIMENT
COMPLIMENTAL
COMPLIMENTARY
COMPLIMENTER
COMPLIMENTS
COMPLIN
COMPLINE
COMPLINES

COMPLINS
COMPLISH
COMPLOT
COMPLOTTED
COMPLOTTER
COMPLOTTING
COMPLUVIUM
COMPLY
COMPLYING
COMPO
COMPOED
COMPOER
COMPOING
COMPONE
COMPONED
COMPONENCY
COMPONENDO
COMPONENT
COMPONENTAL
COMPONENTED
COMPONENTS
COMPONY
COMPORT
COMPORTABLE
COMPORTANCE
COMPORTMENT
COMPOS
COMPOSE
COMPOSED
COMPOSEDLY
COMPOSEDNESS
COMPOSER
COMPOSING
COMPOSIT
COMPOSITA
COMPOSITE
COMPOSITED
COMPOSITELY
COMPOSITING
COMPOSITION
COMPOSITIVE
COMPOSITOR
COMPOSITURE
COMPOSOGRAPH
COMPOSSIBLE
COMPOST
COMPOSTED
COMPOSTING
COMPOSTURE
COMPOSURE
COMPOT
COMPOTATION
COMPOTATOR
COMPOTATORY
COMPOTE
COMPOTOR
COMPOUND
COMPOUNDED
COMPOUNDER
COMPOUNDING
COMPRACHICO
COMPRACHICOS
COMPRADOR
COMPRADORE
COMPRECATION
COMPREHEND
COMPREHENDER
COMPREHENSE
COMPREHENSIBLE
COMPREHENSION
COMPREHENSIVE
COMPREHENSIVELY
COMPREHENSIVENESS
COMPREHENSOR
COMPRESBYTER
COMPRESENCE
COMPRESENT
COMPRESS
COMPRESSED
COMPRESSIBLE
COMPRESSING
COMPRESSION
COMPRESSIVE
COMPRESSIVELY
COMPRESSOR
COMPRESSURE
COMPREST
COMPRIEST
COMPRISABLE
COMPRISAL
COMPRISE
COMPRISED
COMPRISING
COMPRIZAL
COMPRIZE
COMPRIZED
COMPRIZING
COMPROBATE
COMPROBATION
COMPRODUCE
COMPROMISE
COMPROMISED
COMPROMISER
COMPROMISING
COMPROMIT
COMPROMITTED
COMPROMITTING
COMPT
COMPTER
COMPTIBLE
COMPTIE
COMPTLY
COMPTNESS
COMPTOIR
COMPTOMETER
COMPTROLLER
COMPULSATIVE
COMPULSATORY
COMPULSED
COMPULSION
COMPULSITOR
COMPULSIVE
COMPULSIVELY
COMPULSORILY
COMPULSORY
COMPUNCT
COMPUNCTION
COMPUNCTIOUS
COMPUNCTIVE
COMPURGATION
COMPURGATOR
COMPURGATORY
COMPURSION
COMPUTABLE
COMPUTABLY
COMPUTATION
COMPUTATIVE
COMPUTE
COMPUTED
COMPUTER
COMPUTING
COMPUTIST
COMPUTUS
COMRADE
COMRADELY
COMRADERY
COMRADESHIP
COMROGUE
COMSTOCKERIES
COMSTOCKERY
COMTE
COMTESSE
COMUNIDAD
CON
CONACASTE
CONACRE
CONAL
CONAMED
CONAND
CONARIAL
CONARIUM
CONATION
CONATIONAL
CONATIVE
CONATURAL
CONATUS
CONCAMERATE
CONCAMERATED
CONCANAVALIN
CONCAPTIVE
CONCASSATION
CONCATENARY
CONCATENATE
CONCATENATED
CONCATENATING
CONCATENATOR
CONCAUSE
CONCAVATION
CONCAVE
CONCAVED
CONCAVELY
CONCAVENESS
CONCAVER
CONCAVING
CONCAVITIES
CONCAVITY
CONCEAL
CONCEALED
CONCEALEDLY
CONCEALER
CONCEALING
CONCEALMENT
CONCEDE
CONCEDED
CONCEDEDLY
CONCEDER
CONCEDING
CONCEIT
CONCEITED
CONCEITEDLY
CONCEITING
CONCEITLESS
CONCEITY
CONCEIVABLE
CONCEIVABLY
CONCEIVE
CONCEIVED
CONCEIVER
CONCEIVING
CONCELEBRATE
CONCENT
CONCENTER
CONCENTERED
CONCENTERING
CONCENTIVE
CONCENTRATE
CONCENTRATED
CONCENTRATING
CONCENTRATION
CONCENTRATOR
CONCENTRE
CONCENTRED
CONCENTRIC
CONCENTRICAL
CONCENTRING
CONCENTUAL
CONCENTUS
CONCEPT
CONCEPTACLE
CONCEPTION
CONCEPTIONAL
CONCEPTISM
CONCEPTIVE
CONCEPTUAL
CONCEPTUALISM
CONCEPTUALITY
CONCEPTUALLY
CONCERN
CONCERNED
CONCERNEDLY
CONCERNING
CONCERNINGLY
CONCERNMENT
CONCERT
CONCERTATION
CONCERTED
CONCERTEDLY
CONCERTGOER
CONCERTI
CONCERTINA
CONCERTING
CONCERTINI
CONCERTINIST
CONCERTINO
CONCERTINOS
CONCERTION
CONCERTIST
CONCERTIZE
CONCERTIZED
CONCERTIZER
CONCERTIZING
CONCERTMASTER
CONCERTMEISTER
CONCERTO
CONCERTOS
CONCESSIBLE
CONCESSION
CONCESSIONAIRE
CONCESSIONAL
CONCESSIONER
CONCESSIVE
CONCESSIVELY
CONCESSOR
CONCESSORY
CONCETTI
CONCETTISM
CONCETTIST
CONCETTO
CONCH
CONCHA
CONCHAE
CONCHAL
CONCHATE
CONCHE
CONCHED
CONCHER
CONCHES
CONCHIES
CONCHIFEROUS
CONCHIFORM
CONCHININ
CONCHININE
CONCHIOLIN
CONCHITE
CONCHITIC
CONCHITIS
CONCHO
CONCHOID
CONCHOIDAL
CONCHOIDALLY
CONCHOLOGIST
CONCHOLOGIZE
CONCHOLOGY
CONCHOMETER
CONCHOMETRY
CONCHOTOME
CONCHS
CONCHY
CONCHYLIATED
CONCHYLIUM
CONCIERGE
CONCILE
CONCILIABLE
CONCILIABULE
CONCILIAR
CONCILIATE
CONCILIATED
CONCILIATING
CONCILIATION
CONCILIATIVE
CONCILIATOR
CONCILIATORY
CONCILIUM
CONCINNATE
CONCINNITIES
CONCINNITY
CONCINNOUS
CONCIO
CONCION
CONCIONAL
CONCIONARY
CONCIONATE
CONCIONATOR
CONCIONATORY
CONCIPIENCY
CONCIPIENT
CONCISE
CONCISELY
CONCISENESS
CONCISION
CONCITATION
CONCLAVE
CONCLAVIST
CONCLUDE
CONCLUDED
CONCLUDENCE
CONCLUDENCY
CONCLUDENT
CONCLUDENTLY
CONCLUDER
CONCLUDING
CONCLUDINGLY
CONCLUSION
CONCLUSIONAL
CONCLUSIVE
CONCLUSIVELY
CONCLUSORY
CONCOAGULATE
CONCOCT
CONCOCTER
CONCOCTION
CONCOCTIVE
CONCOCTOR
CONCOLOR
CONCOLOROUS
CONCOLOUR
CONCOMITANCE
CONCOMITANCY
CONCOMITANT
CONCOMITATE
CONCORD
CONCORDABLE
CONCORDABLY
CONCORDAL
CONCORDANCE
CONCORDANCER
CONCORDANCY
CONCORDANT
CONCORDANTLY
CONCORDAT
CONCORDATORY
CONCORDER
CONCORDIAL
CONCORDIST
CONCORDITY

CONCORDLY
CONCORPORATE
CONCORPORATED
CONCORPORATING
CONCOURS
CONCOURSE
CONCREATE
CONCREDIT
CONCREMATION
CONCREMENT
CONCRESCE
CONCRESCENCE
CONCRESCIBLE
CONCRESCIVE
CONCRETE
CONCRETED
CONCRETELY
CONCRETENESS
CONCRETER
CONCRETING
CONCRETION
CONCRETIONAL
CONCRETISM
CONCRETIVE
CONCRETIVELY
CONCRETIZE
CONCRETIZED
CONCRETIZING
CONCRETOR
CONCREW
CONCUBINAGE
CONCUBINAL
CONCUBINARY
CONCUBINE
CONCUBITANCY
CONCUBITANT
CONCUBITOUS
CONCUBITUS
CONCULCATE
CONCULCATION
CONCUMBENCY
CONCUPISCENCE
CONCUPISCENT
CONCUPY
CONCUR
CONCURRED
CONCURRENCE
CONCURRENCY
CONCURRENT
CONCURRENTLY
CONCURRING
CONCURRINGLY
CONCURSION
CONCURSO
CONCURSUS
CONCUSS
CONCUSSATION
CONCUSSED
CONCUSSING
CONCUSSION
CONCUSSIONAL
CONCUSSIVE
CONCUTIENT
CONCYCLIC
COND
CONDECENT
CONDEMN
CONDEMNATE
CONDEMNATION
CONDEMNATORY
CONDEMNED
CONDEMNER
CONDEMNING
CONDEMNINGLY
CONDEMNS
CONDENSABLE
CONDENSATE
CONDENSATION
CONDENSATIVE
CONDENSATOR
CONDENSE
CONDENSED
CONDENSER
CONDENSERY
CONDENSIBLE
CONDENSING
CONDENSITY
CONDER
CONDESCEND
CONDESCENDER
CONDESCENDING
CONDESCENSION
CONDESCENT
CONDICTION
CONDICTIOUS
CONDIDDLE
CONDIDDLED
CONDIDDLING
CONDIGN
CONDIGNITY
CONDIGNLY
CONDIGNNESS
CONDIMENT
CONDIMENTAL
CONDIMENTARY
CONDIMENTS
CONDISCIPLE
CONDITE
CONDITION
CONDITIONAL
CONDITIONALLY
CONDITIONATE
CONDITIONED
CONDITIONER
CONDITIONING
CONDIVISION
CONDOG
CONDOLATORY
CONDOLE
CONDOLED
CONDOLEMENT
CONDOLENCE
CONDOLENT
CONDOLER
CONDOLING
CONDOLINGLY
CONDOMINATE
CONDOMINIUM
CONDONANCE
CONDONATION
CONDONATIVE
CONDONE
CONDONED
CONDONER
CONDONING
CONDOR
CONDOTTIERE
CONDOTTIERI
CONDUCE
CONDUCED
CONDUCEMENT
CONDUCENT
CONDUCER
CONDUCIBLE
CONDUCIBLY
CONDUCING
CONDUCIVE
CONDUCT
CONDUCTA
CONDUCTANCE
CONDUCTED
CONDUCTIBLE
CONDUCTILITY
CONDUCTING
CONDUCTIO
CONDUCTION
CONDUCTIONAL
CONDUCTIVE
CONDUCTIVELY
CONDUCTIVITY
CONDUCTOR
CONDUCTORS
CONDUCTORY
CONDUCTRESS
CONDUCTUS
CONDUIT
CONDUPLICATE
CONDURANGIN
CONDYLAR
CONDYLARTH
CONDYLE
CONDYLION
CONDYLOID
CONDYLOMA
CONDYLOMATA
CONDYLOPOD
CONDYLOS
CONDYLURE
CONE
CONED
CONEEN
CONEFLOWER
CONEHEAD
CONEINE
CONELET
CONELRAD
CONEMAKER
CONEMAKING
CONENOSE
CONEPATE
CONEPATL
CONER
CONES
CONESSINE
CONEY
CONEYS
CONFAB
CONFABBED
CONFABBING
CONFABULAR
CONFABULATE
CONFABULATED
CONFABULATING
CONFACT
CONFARREATE
CONFARREATED
CONFATED
CONFECT
CONFECTION
CONFECTIONARIES
CONFECTIONARY
CONFECTIONER
CONFECTIONERIES
CONFECTIONERY
CONFECTORY
CONFECTURE
CONFEDER
CONFEDERACIES
CONFEDERACY
CONFEDERAL
CONFEDERALIST
CONFEDERATE
CONFEDERATED
CONFEDERATING
CONFEDERATIO
CONFEDERATION
CONFEDERATOR
CONFER
CONFEREE
CONFERENCE
CONFERENTIAL
CONFERMENT
CONFERRABLE
CONFERRED
CONFERREE
CONFERRER
CONFERRING
CONFERTED
CONFERVA
CONFERVAE
CONFERVAL
CONFERVAS
CONFERVOID
CONFERVOUS
CONFESS
CONFESSANT
CONFESSARIUS
CONFESSARY
CONFESSED
CONFESSEDLY
CONFESSER
CONFESSING
CONFESSION
CONFESSIONAL
CONFESSOR
CONFESSORY
CONFETTI
CONFIDANT
CONFIDANTE
CONFIDE
CONFIDED
CONFIDENCE
CONFIDENCES
CONFIDENCY
CONFIDENT
CONFIDENTIAL
CONFIDENTIALLY
CONFIDENTLY
CONFIDER
CONFIDING
CONFIDINGLY
CONFIGURAL
CONFIGURATE
CONFIGURATED
CONFIGURATING
CONFIGURATION
CONFIGURE
CONFIGURED
CONFIGURING
CONFINABLE
CONFINE
CONFINEABLE
CONFINED
CONFINEDLY
CONFINEDNESS
CONFINELESS
CONFINEMENT
CONFINER
CONFINES
CONFINING
CONFINITY
CONFIRM
CONFIRMABLE
CONFIRMAND
CONFIRMATION
CONFIRMATIVE
CONFIRMATORY
CONFIRMED
CONFIRMEDLY
CONFIRMEE
CONFIRMER
CONFIRMING
CONFIRMINGLY
CONFIRMITY
CONFIRMMENT
CONFIRMOR
CONFISCABLE
CONFISCATE
CONFISCATED
CONFISCATION
CONFISCATOR
CONFISCATORY
CONFISERIE
CONFISK
CONFISTICATING
CONFITENT
CONFITEOR
CONFITURE
CONFIX
CONFIXED
CONFIXING
CONFLAB
CONFLAGRANT
CONFLAGRATE
CONFLAGRATED
CONFLAGRATING
CONFLAGRATION
CONFLAGRATIVE
CONFLAGRATOR
CONFLATE
CONFLATED
CONFLATING
CONFLATION
CONFLICT
CONFLICTED
CONFLICTING
CONFLICTION
CONFLICTIVE
CONFLICTORY
CONFLICTS
CONFLOW
CONFLUENCE
CONFLUENT
CONFLUX
CONFLUXIBLE
CONFOCAL
CONFORM
CONFORMABLE
CONFORMABLY
CONFORMAL
CONFORMANCE
CONFORMANT
CONFORMATE
CONFORMATION
CONFORMATOR
CONFORMED
CONFORMER
CONFORMING
CONFORMIST
CONFORMITIES
CONFORMITY
CONFOUND
CONFOUNDED
CONFOUNDEDLY
CONFOUNDER
CONFOUNDING
CONFRATER
CONFRATERNAL
CONFRATERNITIES
CONFRATERNITY
CONFRERE
CONFRONT
CONFRONTAL
CONFRONTED
CONFRONTER
CONFRONTING
CONFRONTMENT
CONFUSABLE
CONFUSABLY
CONFUSE
CONFUSED
CONFUSEDLY
CONFUSEDNESS
CONFUSING
CONFUSINGLY

CONFUSION
CONFUSIONAL
CONFUSTICATE
CONFUTATION
CONFUTATIVE
CONFUTE
CONFUTED
CONFUTER
CONFUTING
CONGE
CONGEABLE
CONGEAL
CONGEALABLE
CONGEALED
CONGEALER
CONGEALING
CONGEALMENT
CONGED
CONGEE
CONGEING
CONGELATION
CONGENER
CONGENERACY
CONGENERIC
CONGENERICAL
CONGENEROUS
CONGENETIC
CONGENIAL
CONGENIALITY
CONGENIALIZE
CONGENIALLY
CONGENITAL
CONGENITALLY
CONGEON
CONGER
CONGEREE
CONGERIE
CONGERIES
CONGERY
CONGESSION
CONGEST
CONGESTED
CONGESTION
CONGESTIVE
CONGIARIES
CONGIARY
CONGIUS
CONGLACIATE
CONGLOBATE
CONGLOBATED
CONGLOBATELY
CONGLOBATING
CONGLOBATION
CONGLOBE
CONGLOBED
CONGLOBING
CONGLOBULATE
CONGLOMERATE
CONGLOMERATED
CONGLOMERATIC
CONGLOMERATING
CONGLOMERATION
CONGLUTIN
CONGLUTINANT
CONGLUTINATE
CONGLUTINATED
CONGLUTINATING
CONGO
CONGONI
CONGOU
CONGRATULANT
CONGRATULATE
CONGRATULATED
CONGRATULATING
CONGRATULATION
CONGREE
CONGREET
CONGREGABLE
CONGREGANIST
CONGREGANT
CONGREGATE
CONGREGATED
CONGREGATING
CONGREGATION
CONGREGATIVE
CONGREGATOR
CONGRESS
CONGRESSER
CONGRESSIONAL
CONGRESSIST
CONGRESSIVE
CONGRESSMAN
CONGRESSMEN
CONGRESSWOMAN
CONGRESSWOMEN
CONGRIO
CONGROID
CONGRUE
CONGRUENCE
CONGRUENCIES
CONGRUENCY
CONGRUENT
CONGRUENTIAL
CONGRUENTLY
CONGRUISM
CONGRUIST
CONGRUISTIC
CONGRUITIES
CONGRUITY
CONGRUOUS
CONGRUOUSLY
CONHYDRIN
CONHYDRINE
CONIC
CONICAL
CONICALITY
CONICALLY
CONICALNESS
CONICEIN
CONICEINE
CONICHALCITE
CONICINE
CONICITY
CONICLE
CONICOID
CONICOPOLY
CONICS
CONIDIA
CONIDIAL
CONIDIAN
CONIDIOID
CONIDIOPHORE
CONIDIOSPORE
CONIDIUM
CONIES
CONIFER
CONIFERIN
CONIFEROUS
CONIFERS
CONIFICATION
CONIFORM
CONIINE
CONIMA
CONIMENE
CONIN
CONING
CONIOLOGY
CONIROSTER
CONIROSTRAL
CONIUM
CONJECT
CONJECTIVE
CONJECTURAL
CONJECTURALLY
CONJECTURE
CONJECTURED
CONJECTURER
CONJECTURING
CONJEE
CONJOBBLE
CONJOIN
CONJOINED
CONJOINER
CONJOINING
CONJOINT
CONJOINTLY
CONJOINTNESS
CONJON
CONJUBILANT
CONJUGABLE
CONJUGACY
CONJUGAL
CONJUGALITY
CONJUGALLY
CONJUGANT
CONJUGATA
CONJUGATE
CONJUGATED
CONJUGATING
CONJUGATION
CONJUGATIVE
CONJUGATOR
CONJUGIAL
CONJUGIUM
CONJUNCT
CONJUNCTION
CONJUNCTIVAE
CONJUNCTIVAL
CONJUNCTIVAS
CONJUNCTIVE
CONJUNCTIVELY
CONJUNCTLY
CONJUNCTUR
CONJUNCTURAL
CONJUNCTURE
CONJURATION
CONJURATOR
CONJURE
CONJURED
CONJURER
CONJURING
CONJUROR
CONJURY
CONK
CONKER
CONKERS
CONKY
CONN
CONNACH
CONNARACEOUS
CONNARITE
CONNASCENCY
CONNASCENT
CONNATAL
CONNATE
CONNATELY
CONNATENESS
CONNATION
CONNATURAL
CONNATURALLY
CONNATURE
CONNECT
CONNECTED
CONNECTER
CONNECTING
CONNECTION
CONNECTIONAL
CONNECTIVAL
CONNECTIVE
CONNECTIVELY
CONNECTIVITY
CONNECTOR
CONNED
CONNELLITE
CONNER
CONNEX
CONNEXES
CONNEXION
CONNEXITIES
CONNEXITY
CONNEXIVA
CONNEXIVE
CONNEXIVUM
CONNEXUS
CONNING
CONNIPTION
CONNIVANCE
CONNIVANCY
CONNIVANT
CONNIVE
CONNIVED
CONNIVENCE
CONNIVENT
CONNIVER
CONNIVING
CONNOISSANCE
CONNOISSEUR
CONNOTATE
CONNOTATION
CONNOTATIVE
CONNOTE
CONNOTED
CONNOTING
CONNOTIVE
CONNOTIVELY
CONNU
CONNUBIAL
CONNUBIALITY
CONNUBIALLY
CONNUBIATE
CONNUBIUM
CONNUMERATE
CONOCLINIUM
CONOCUNEUS
CONODONT
CONOID
CONOIDAL
CONOIDALLY
CONOIDIC
CONOIDICAL
CONOIDICALLY
CONOPID
CONOPLAIN
CONOPODIUM
CONORMAL
CONOSCENTE
CONOSCENTI
CONOSCOPE
CONOURISH
CONPLANE
CONQUASSATE
CONQUEDLE
CONQUER
CONQUERABLE
CONQUERED
CONQUERING
CONQUERINGLY
CONQUEROR
CONQUEST
CONQUIAN
CONQUINAMINE
CONQUININE
CONQUISTADOR
CONQUISTADORES
CONRECTOR
CONRED
CONREY
CONS
CONSACRE
CONSANGUINE
CONSANGUINEOUS
CONSANGUINITY
CONSARCINATE
CONSARN
CONSARNED
CONSCIENCE
CONSCIENT
CONSCIENTIOUS
CONSCIENTIOUSLY
CONSCIENTIOUSNESS
CONSCIONABLE
CONSCIONABLY
CONSCIOUS
CONSCIOUSLY
CONSCIOUSNESS
CONSCIVE
CONSCRIBE
CONSCRIPT
CONSCRIPTION
CONSECRATE
CONSECRATED
CONSECRATER
CONSECRATING
CONSECRATION
CONSECRATIVE
CONSECRATOR
CONSECRATORY
CONSECTARY
CONSECUTE
CONSECUTION
CONSECUTIVE
CONSECUTIVELY
CONSECUTIVENESS
CONSECUTIVES
CONSENSION
CONSENSUAL
CONSENSUALLY
CONSENSUS
CONSENSUSES
CONSENT
CONSENTABLE
CONSENTANT
CONSENTED
CONSENTER
CONSENTFUL
CONSENTFULLY
CONSENTIENCE
CONSENTIENT
CONSENTIENTLY
CONSENTING
CONSENTINGLY
CONSENTIVE
CONSENTMENT
CONSEQUENCE
CONSEQUENT
CONSEQUENTIAL
CONSEQUENTLY
CONSERTAL
CONSERVABLE
CONSERVACY
CONSERVANCIES
CONSERVANCY
CONSERVANT
CONSERVATE
CONSERVATION
CONSERVATIONAL
CONSERVATISM
CONSERVATIST
CONSERVATIVE
CONSERVATIZE
CONSERVATOR
CONSERVATORIES
CONSERVATORY
CONSERVE
CONSERVED

CONSERVER
CONSERVING
CONSIDER
CONSIDERABLE
CONSIDERABLY
CONSIDERANCE
CONSIDERATE
CONSIDERATELY
CONSIDERATENESS
CONSIDERATION
CONSIDERATOR
CONSIDERED
CONSIDERER
CONSIDERING
CONSIGN
CONSIGNABLE
CONSIGNATARY
CONSIGNATION
CONSIGNED
CONSIGNEE
CONSIGNER
CONSIGNIFIED
CONSIGNIFY
CONSIGNIFYING
CONSIGNING
CONSIGNMENT
CONSIGNOR
CONSILIARY
CONSILIENCE
CONSILIENT
CONSIMILAR
CONSIMILATE
CONSIMILATED
CONSIMILATING
CONSIST
CONSISTENCE
CONSISTENCIES
CONSISTENCY
CONSISTENT
CONSISTENTLY
CONSISTORIAL
CONSISTORIAN
CONSISTORY
CONSOCIATE
CONSOCIATED
CONSOCIATING
CONSOCIATION
CONSOCIATIVE
CONSOCIES
CONSOL
CONSOLABLE
CONSOLATE
CONSOLATION
CONSOLATORY
CONSOLATRIX
CONSOLE
CONSOLED
CONSOLER
CONSOLIDANT
CONSOLIDATE
CONSOLIDATED
CONSOLIDATING
CONSOLIDATOR
CONSOLING
CONSOLS
CONSOLUTE
CONSOMME
CONSONANCE
CONSONANCY
CONSONANT
CONSONANTAL
CONSONANTIC
CONSONANTISM
CONSONANTIZE
CONSONANTLY
CONSONATE
CONSONOUS
CONSORT
CONSORTABLE
CONSORTED
CONSORTER
CONSORTIA
CONSORTIAL
CONSORTING
CONSORTION
CONSORTISM
CONSORTIUM
CONSOUND
CONSPECIES
CONSPECIFIC
CONSPECT
CONSPECTUS
CONSPECTUSES
CONSPERSE
CONSPERSION
CONSPICUITY
CONSPICUOUS
CONSPICUOUSLY
CONSPIRACIES
CONSPIRACY
CONSPIRANT
CONSPIRATIVE
CONSPIRATOR
CONSPIRE
CONSPIRED
CONSPIRER
CONSPIRING
CONSPIRINGLY
CONSPUE
CONSTABLE
CONSTABULAR
CONSTABULARIES
CONSTABULARY
CONSTANCE
CONSTANCY
CONSTANT
CONSTANTAN
CONSTANTLY
CONSTAT
CONSTATATION
CONSTATE
CONSTATORY
CONSTELLATE
CONSTELLATED
CONSTELLATING
CONSTELLATION
CONSTELLATORY
CONSTER
CONSTERNATE
CONSTERNATED
CONSTERNATING
CONSTERNATION
CONSTIPATE
CONSTIPATED
CONSTIPATING
CONSTIPATION
CONSTITUENCIES
CONSTITUENCY
CONSTITUENT
CONSTITUTE
CONSTITUTED
CONSTITUTER
CONSTITUTING
CONSTITUTION
CONSTITUTIONAL
CONSTITUTIVE
CONSTITUTIVELY
CONSTITUTOR
CONSTRAIN
CONSTRAINED
CONSTRAINER
CONSTRAINING
CONSTRAINT
CONSTRICT
CONSTRICTED
CONSTRICTING
CONSTRICTION
CONSTRICTIVE
CONSTRICTOR
CONSTRINGE
CONSTRINGED
CONSTRINGENT
CONSTRINGING
CONSTRUABLE
CONSTRUCT
CONSTRUCTED
CONSTRUCTER
CONSTRUCTION
CONSTRUCTIVE
CONSTRUCTIVELY
CONSTRUCTIVENESS
CONSTRUCTOR
CONSTRUE
CONSTRUED
CONSTRUER
CONSTRUING
CONSTUPRATE
CONSUETE
CONSUETUDE
CONSUL
CONSULAGE
CONSULAR
CONSULARITY
CONSULARY
CONSULATE
CONSULSHIP
CONSULT
CONSULTANT
CONSULTARY
CONSULTATION
CONSULTATIVE
CONSULTATORY
CONSULTEE
CONSULTER
CONSULTING
CONSULTIVE
CONSULTOR
CONSULTORY
CONSUMABLE
CONSUME
CONSUMED
CONSUMEDLY
CONSUMELESS
CONSUMER
CONSUMERS
CONSUMING
CONSUMINGLY
CONSUMMATE
CONSUMMATED
CONSUMMATELY
CONSUMMATING
CONSUMMATION
CONSUMMATIVE
CONSUMMATOR
CONSUMMATORY
CONSUMPT
CONSUMPTED
CONSUMPTIBLE
CONSUMPTION
CONSUMPTIVE
CONSUTE
CONTABESCENT
CONTACT
CONTACTOR
CONTACTUAL
CONTACTUALLY
CONTAGIA
CONTAGION
CONTAGIONED
CONTAGIONIST
CONTAGIOSITY
CONTAGIOUS
CONTAGIOUSLY
CONTAGIOUSNESS
CONTAGIUM
CONTAIN
CONTAINABLE
CONTAINED
CONTAINER
CONTAINING
CONTAINMENT
CONTAMINABLE
CONTAMINANT
CONTAMINATE
CONTAMINATED
CONTAMINATING
CONTAMINATION
CONTAMINATIVE
CONTAMINATOR
CONTAMINOUS
CONTANGO
CONTE
CONTECK
CONTECT
CONTECTION
CONTEK
CONTEKE
CONTEMN
CONTEMNED
CONTEMNER
CONTEMNING
CONTEMNINGLY
CONTEMNOR
CONTEMPER
CONTEMPERATE
CONTEMPLABLE
CONTEMPLAMEN
CONTEMPLANCE
CONTEMPLANT
CONTEMPLATE
CONTEMPLATED
CONTEMPLATING
CONTEMPLATION
CONTEMPLATIST
CONTEMPLATIVE
CONTEMPLATIVELY
CONTEMPLATOR
CONTEMPORANEOUS
CONTEMPORARY
CONTEMPORIZE
CONTEMPORIZED
CONTEMPORIZING
CONTEMPT
CONTEMPTFUL
CONTEMPTIBLE
CONTEMPTIBLENESS
CONTEMPTIBLY
CONTEMPTUOUS
CONTEMPTUOUSLY
CONTEND
CONTENDED
CONTENDER
CONTENDING
CONTENDINGLY
CONTENT
CONTENTATION
CONTENTED
CONTENTEDLY
CONTENTFUL
CONTENTING
CONTENTION
CONTENTIONAL
CONTENTIOUS
CONTENTLESS
CONTENTLY
CONTENTMENT
CONTENTNESS
CONTENTS
CONTENU
CONTERMINAL
CONTERMINANT
CONTERMINATE
CONTERMINE
CONTERMINOUS
CONTESSA
CONTEST
CONTESTABLE
CONTESTANT
CONTESTANTS
CONTESTATION
CONTESTER
CONTEUR
CONTEXT
CONTEXTUAL
CONTEXTUALLY
CONTEXTURAL
CONTEXTURE
CONTEXTURED
CONTICENT
CONTIGNATION
CONTIGUITIES
CONTIGUITY
CONTIGUOUS
CONTIGUOUSLY
CONTINENCE
CONTINENCY
CONTINENT
CONTINENTAL
CONTINENTLY
CONTINEU
CONTINGENCY
CONTINGENT
CONTINGENTLY
CONTINUABLE
CONTINUAL
CONTINUALITY
CONTINUALLY
CONTINUANCE
CONTINUANDO
CONTINUANT
CONTINUANTLY
CONTINUATE
CONTINUATELY
CONTINUATION
CONTINUATIVE
CONTINUATOR
CONTINUE
CONTINUED
CONTINUEDLY
CONTINUER
CONTINUING
CONTINUIST
CONTINUITY
CONTINUO
CONTINUOUS
CONTINUOUSLY
CONTINUUM
CONTISE
CONTLINE
CONTO
CONTOISE
CONTORNIATE
CONTORNIATES
CONTORNO
CONTORSIVE
CONTORT
CONTORTED
CONTORTEDLY
CONTORTING
CONTORTION
CONTORTIONAL
CONTORTIONED
CONTORTIONIST
CONTORTIVE
CONTOS

CONTOUR
CONTOURED
CONTOURING
CONTRABAND
CONTRABASS
CONTRABASSO
CONTRACIVIL
CONTRACT
CONTRACTANT
CONTRACTED
CONTRACTEDLY
CONTRACTER
CONTRACTIBLE
CONTRACTILE
CONTRACTILITY
CONTRACTING
CONTRACTION
CONTRACTIVE
CONTRACTOR
CONTRACTUAL
CONTRACTURE
CONTRACTURED
CONTRADA
CONTRADANCE
CONTRADE
CONTRADICT
CONTRADICTER
CONTRADICTION
CONTRADICTIVE
CONTRADICTOR
CONTRADICTORIES
CONTRADICTORY
CONTRADIVIDE
CONTRAFLOW
CONTRAFOCAL
CONTRAHENT
CONTRAIR
CONTRALTI
CONTRALTO
CONTRALTOS
CONTRAMARQUE
CONTRAOCTAVE
CONTRAPLEX
CONTRAPONEND
CONTRAPOSE
CONTRAPOSITA
CONTRAPTION
CONTRAPTIOUS
CONTRAPUNTAL
CONTRARIANT
CONTRARIES
CONTRARIETY
CONTRARILY
CONTRARINESS
CONTRARIOUS
CONTRARIOUSLY
CONTRARIWISE
CONTRARY
CONTRAST
CONTRASTABLE
CONTRASTED
CONTRASTING
CONTRASTIVE
CONTRASTY
CONTRATE
CONTRAVENE
CONTRAVENED
CONTRAVENER
CONTRAVENING
CONTRAVENTION
CONTRAYERVA
CONTREDANSE
CONTRETEMPS
CONTRIBUTE
CONTRIBUTED
CONTRIBUTING
CONTRIBUTION
CONTRIBUTIVE
CONTRIBUTOR
CONTRIBUTORIES
CONTRIBUTORY
CONTRIST
CONTRITE
CONTRITELY
CONTRITENESS
CONTRITION
CONTRITURATE
CONTRIVABLE
CONTRIVANCE
CONTRIVANCY
CONTRIVE
CONTRIVED
CONTRIVER
CONTRIVING
CONTROL
CONTROLLABLE
CONTROLLED
CONTROLLER
CONTROLLING
CONTROVERSIAL
CONTROVERSIALIST
CONTROVERSIALLY
CONTROVERSIES
CONTROVERSY
CONTROVERT
CONTROVERTED
CONTROVERTER
CONTRUDE
CONTUBERNAL
CONTUBERNIAL
CONTUBERNIUM
CONTUMACIES
CONTUMACIOUS
CONTUMACITIES
CONTUMACITY
CONTUMACY
CONTUMAX
CONTUMELIES
CONTUMELIOUS
CONTUMELY
CONTUND
CONTUNE
CONTURB
CONTURBATION
CONTUSE
CONTUSED
CONTUSING
CONTUSION
CONTUSIONED
CONTUSIVE
CONUBIUM
CONULE
CONUNDRUM
CONURBATION
CONURE
CONUS
CONUSES
CONVALESCE
CONVALESCED
CONVALESCENT
CONVALESCING
CONVALLARIN
CONVECT
CONVECTION
CONVECTIONAL
CONVECTIVE
CONVECTIVELY
CONVECTOR
CONVELL
CONVENABLE
CONVENABLY
CONVENANCE
CONVENE
CONVENED
CONVENER
CONVENERIES
CONVENERY
CONVENIENCE
CONVENIENCED
CONVENIENCY
CONVENIENT
CONVENIENTLY
CONVENING
CONVENT
CONVENTICAL
CONVENTICLE
CONVENTICLER
CONVENTION
CONVENTIONAL
CONVENTIONALIST
CONVENTIONALITY
CONVENTIONALIZE
CONVENTIONALIZED
CONVENTIONALIZING
CONVENTIONALLY
CONVENTIONER
CONVENTO
CONVENTUAL
CONVERGE
CONVERGED
CONVERGENCE
CONVERGENCY
CONVERGENT
CONVERGING
CONVERSABLE
CONVERSABLY
CONVERSANCE
CONVERSANCY
CONVERSANT
CONVERSANTLY
CONVERSATION
CONVERSATIONAL
CONVERSATIONALIST
CONVERSATIONALLY
CONVERSATIONIST
CONVERSATIVE
CONVERSE
CONVERSED
CONVERSELY
CONVERSER
CONVERSIBLE
CONVERSING
CONVERSION
CONVERSIONAL
CONVERSIVE
CONVERSO
CONVERT
CONVERTED
CONVERTEND
CONVERTER
CONVERTIBLE
CONVERTIBLY
CONVERTING
CONVERTISE
CONVERTITE
CONVERTIVE
CONVERTOR
CONVETH
CONVEX
CONVEXED
CONVEXEDLY
CONVEXEDNESS
CONVEXITIES
CONVEXITY
CONVEXLY
CONVEXNESS
CONVEY
CONVEYABLE
CONVEYAL
CONVEYANCE
CONVEYANCER
CONVEYANCING
CONVEYED
CONVEYER
CONVEYING
CONVEYOR
CONVICINITY
CONVICT
CONVICTABLE
CONVICTED
CONVICTIBLE
CONVICTING
CONVICTION
CONVICTIONAL
CONVICTISM
CONVICTIVE
CONVICTIVELY
CONVICTOR
CONVINCE
CONVINCED
CONVINCEMENT
CONVINCER
CONVINCIBLE
CONVINCING
CONVINCINGLY
CONVITE
CONVITO
CONVIVAL
CONVIVE
CONVIVIAL
CONVIVIALIST
CONVIVIALITY
CONVIVIALLY
CONVIVIO
CONVOCANT
CONVOCATE
CONVOCATED
CONVOCATING
CONVOCATION
CONVOCATIVE
CONVOCATOR
CONVOKE
CONVOKED
CONVOKER
CONVOKING
CONVOLUTE
CONVOLUTED
CONVOLUTELY
CONVOLUTING
CONVOLUTION
CONVOLUTIVE
CONVOLVE
CONVOLVED
CONVOLVING
CONVOLVULAD
CONVOLVULIN
CONVOLVULUS
CONVOY
CONVOYED
CONVOYING
CONVULSANT
CONVULSE
CONVULSED
CONVULSEDLY
CONVULSING
CONVULSION
CONVULSIONAL
CONVULSIVE
CONVULSIVELY
CONVULSIVENESS
CONY
CONYCATCHER
CONYGER
CONYNGE
CONYRIN
CONYRINE
COO
COOB
COOBA
COOBAH
COOCH
COODLE
COOED
COOEE
COOEED
COOEEING
COOER
COOEY
COOEYED
COOEYING
COOF
COOING
COOINGLY
COOJA
COOK
COOKABLE
COOKBOOK
COOKED
COOKEE
COOKEITE
COOKER
COOKERIES
COOKERY
COOKEY
COOKHOUSE
COOKIE
COOKIES
COOKING
COOKMAID
COOKROOM
COOKSHACK
COOKSHOP
COOKSTOVE
COOKY
COOL
COOLABAH
COOLAMAN
COOLANT
COOLED
COOLEN
COOLER
COOLEST
COOLEY
COOLHEADED
COOLHEADEDLY
COOLHOUSE
COOLIBAH
COOLIE
COOLIES
COOLIMAN
COOLING
COOLINGLY
COOLINGNESS
COOLISH
COOLLY
COOLNESS
COOLTH
COOLUNG
COOLWEED
COOLWORT
COOLY
COOM
COOMB
COOMBE
COOMY
COON
COONCAN
COONER
COONIER
COONIEST
COONILY
COONJINE
COONROOT
COONSKIN
COONTAIL

COONTIE
COONY
COOP
COOPED
COOPER
COOPERAGE
COOPERANCY
COOPERANT
COOPERATE
COOPERATED
COOPERATING
COOPERATION
COOPERATIVE
COOPERATIVELY
COOPERATOR
COOPERED
COOPERIES
COOPERING
COOPERY
COOPING
COOPT
COOPTATE
COOPTATION
COOPTATIVE
COOPTION
COOPTIVE
COORDAIN
COORDINAL
COORDINATE
COORDINATED
COORDINATELY
COORDINATING
COORDINATION
COORDINATIVE
COORDINATOR
COORDINATORY
COOREE
COORIE
COOSE
COOSER
COOSIFY
COOST
COOT
COOTCH
COOTER
COOTFOOT
COOTHAY
COOTIE
COOTY
COP
COPA
COPACETIC
COPAENE
COPAIBA
COPAIBIC
COPAIN
COPAIVA
COPAL
COPALCHE
COPALCHI
COPALCOCOTE
COPALINE
COPALITE
COPALJOCOTE
COPALM
COPARCENARY
COPARCENER
COPARCENY
COPART
COPARTNER
COPARTNERY
COPASETIC
COPATAIN
COPE
COPECK
COPED
COPEI
COPELIDINE
COPEMAN
COPEMATE
COPEN
COPEPOD
COPEPODAN
COPEPODOUS
COPER
COPEROSE
COPERTA
COPESETIC
COPESETTIC
COPESMATE
COPESTONE
COPHASAL
COPHOSIS
COPIA
COPIAPITE
COPIER
COPIHUE
COPING
COPIOSITY
COPIOUS
COPIOUSLY
COPIOUSNESS
COPIS
COPIST
COPLA
COPLANAR
COPLANARITY
COPOLYMER
COPOLYMERIZE
COPOLYMERIZED
COPOLYMERIZING
COPPA
COPPAELITE
COPPE
COPPED
COPPER
COPPERAH
COPPERAS
COPPERBOTTOM
COPPERED
COPPERHEAD
COPPERING
COPPERIZATION
COPPERIZE
COPPERLEAF
COPPERNOSE
COPPERNOSED
COPPERPLATE
COPPERPROOF
COPPERSKIN
COPPERSMITH
COPPERWING
COPPERWORKS
COPPERY
COPPET
COPPICE
COPPICED
COPPICING
COPPIN
COPPING
COPPLE
COPPLED
COPPRA
COPPY
COPRA
COPRAEMIA
COPRAEMIC
COPRAH
COPREMIA
COPREMIC
COPRODAEUM
COPROLAGNIA
COPROLAGNIST
COPROLALIA
COPROLALIAC
COPROLITE
COPROLITH
COPROLITIC
COPROLOGY
COPROPHAGAN
COPROPHAGIA
COPROPHAGIST
COPROPHAGOUS
COPROPHAGY
COPROPHILIA
COPROPHILIAC
COPROPHILIC
COPROPHILISM
COPROPHILOUS
COPROPHYTE
COPROSE
COPROSMA
COPROSTASIA
COPROSTASIS
COPROSTEROL
COPROZOIC
COPS
COPSE
COPSEWOOD
COPSEWOODED
COPSING
COPSY
COPTER
COPULA
COPULABLE
COPULAE
COPULAR
COPULARIUM
COPULAS
COPULATE
COPULATED
COPULATING
COPULATION
COPULATIVE
COPULATIVELY
COPULATORY
COPUNCTAL
COPUS
COPY
COPYBOOK
COPYCAT
COPYDESK
COPYGRAPH
COPYGRAPHED
COPYHOLD
COPYHOLDER
COPYHOLDING
COPYING
COPYIST
COPYMAN
COPYREAD
COPYREADER
COPYRIGHT
COPYRIGHTER
COPYWRITER
COQUE
COQUECIGRUE
COQUELICOT
COQUELUCHE
COQUET
COQUETOON
COQUETRIES
COQUETRY
COQUETTE
COQUETTED
COQUETTING
COQUETTISH
COQUETTISHLY
COQUILLE
COQUIMBITE
COQUIN
COQUINA
COQUITA
COQUITO
COR
CORACIIFORM
CORACINE
CORACLE
CORACLER
CORACOCOSTAL
CORACOHYOID
CORACOID
CORACOIDAL
CORADICATE
CORAGIO
CORAH
CORAL
CORALBERRY
CORALFLOWER
CORALIST
CORALITA
CORALLA
CORALLIC
CORALLIFORM
CORALLIN
CORALLINE
CORALLITE
CORALLOID
CORALLOIDAL
CORALLUM
CORALROOT
CORALWORT
CORAM
CORANCE
CORAVECA
CORB
CORBAN
CORBE
CORBEAU
CORBEIL
CORBEL
CORBELED
CORBELING
CORBELLED
CORBELLING
CORBET
CORBICULA
CORBICULAE
CORBICULATE
CORBIE
CORBINA
CORBLEU
CORBOVINUM
CORBULA
CORCASS
CORCHAT
CORCHORUS
CORCIR
CORCOPALI
CORD
CORDAGE
CORDAITALEAN
CORDAITEAN
CORDATE
CORDATELY
CORDAX
CORDE
CORDED
CORDEL
CORDELIERE
CORDELLE
CORDELLED
CORDELLING
CORDER
CORDIAL
CORDIALITIES
CORDIALITY
CORDIALLY
CORDIALNESS
CORDICEPS
CORDICOLE
CORDIFORM
CORDIGERI
CORDILLERA
CORDILLERAN
CORDING
CORDITE
CORDITIS
CORDLEAF
CORDMAKER
CORDOBA
CORDOBAN
CORDON
CORDONNET
CORDOVAN
CORDS
CORDUROY
CORDUROYED
CORDUROYING
CORDWAIN
CORDWAINER
CORDWAINERY
CORDWOOD
CORDY
CORE
COREBOX
CORED
COREDUCTASE
COREGONID
COREGONINE
COREGONOID
COREID
COREIGN
COREIGNER
CORELATION
CORELATIVE
CORELATIVELY
CORELESS
CORELIGIONIST
CORELLA
CORELYSIS
COREMAKER
COREMAKING
COREMIUM
COREOMETER
COREOPSIS
COREPLASTIC
COREPLASTY
CORER
CORESIDUAL
CORESPONDENT
CORETOMY
CORF
CORGE
CORIA
CORIACEOUS
CORIAL
CORIAMYRTIN
CORIANDER
CORIAUS
CORIIN
CORINDON
CORING
CORINNE
CORINTH
CORIUM
CORK
CORKAGE
CORKBOARD
CORKE
CORKED
CORKER
CORKIER
CORKIEST
CORKINESS

CORKING
CORKIR
CORKITE
CORKLINE
CORKMAKER
CORKSCREW
CORKSCREWY
CORKWING
CORKWOOD
CORKY
CORM
CORMEL
CORMI
CORMIDIUM
CORMOID
CORMOPHYTE
CORMOPHYTIC
CORMORANT
CORMOUS
CORMUS
CORN
CORNACEOUS
CORNADA
CORNAGE
CORNAMUTE
CORNBALL
CORNBELL
CORNBERRY
CORNBIN
CORNBIND
CORNBINKS
CORNBIRD
CORNBOLE
CORNBOTTLE
CORNBRASH
CORNCOB
CORNCOCKLE
CORNCRACKER
CORNCRAKE
CORNCRIB
CORNCRUSHER
CORNCUTTER
CORNCUTTING
CORNDODGER
CORNEA
CORNEAGEN
CORNEAL
CORNEAS
CORNED
CORNEIN
CORNEL
CORNELIAN
CORNEMUSE
CORNEOUS
CORNER
CORNERBIND
CORNERCAP
CORNERED
CORNERER
CORNERING
CORNERPIECE
CORNERS
CORNERSTONE
CORNERWAYS
CORNERWISE
CORNET
CORNETCIES
CORNETCY
CORNETER
CORNETFISH
CORNETIST
CORNETTER
CORNETTINO
CORNETTIST
CORNETTO
CORNEULE
CORNFIELD
CORNFLOOR
CORNFLOWER
CORNGROWER
CORNHUSK
CORNHUSKER
CORNHUSKING
CORNIC
CORNICE
CORNICED
CORNICING
CORNICLE
CORNICULATE
CORNICULER
CORNICULUM
CORNIER
CORNIEST
CORNIFIC
CORNIFIED
CORNIFORM
CORNIGEROUS
CORNIN
CORNING
CORNIPLUME
CORNLAND
CORNLOFT
CORNMASTER
CORNMEAL
CORNMONGER
CORNO
CORNOPEAN
CORNPIPE
CORNRICK
CORNROOT
CORNSACK
CORNSTALK
CORNSTALKS
CORNSTARCH
CORNSTOOK
CORNU
CORNUA
CORNUAL
CORNUATE
CORNUATED
CORNUBIANITE
CORNUCOPIA
CORNUCOPIAN
CORNUCOPIATE
CORNULE
CORNULITE
CORNUPETE
CORNUS
CORNUTE
CORNUTED
CORNUTIN
CORNUTINE
CORNUTO
CORNUTOS
CORNWALLIS
CORNWALLITE
CORNY
COROA
COROCLEISIS
CORODIARY
CORODIASTOLE
CORODIES
CORODY
COROJO
COROL
COROLLA
COROLLACEOUS
COROLLARIAL
COROLLARIES
COROLLARY
COROLLATE
COROLLATED
COROLLIFORM
COROLLINE
COROLLITIC
CORONA
CORONACH
CORONAD
CORONADITE
CORONAE
CORONAGRAPH
CORONAL
CORONALE
CORONALED
CORONALLED
CORONALLY
CORONAMEN
CORONARY
CORONAS
CORONATE
CORONATED
CORONATION
CORONATORIAL
CORONENE
CORONER
CORONERSHIP
CORONET
CORONETED
CORONETTED
CORONETTEE
CORONETTY
CORONIFORM
CORONILLIN
CORONILLO
CORONION
CORONITIS
CORONIUM
CORONIZE
CORONOFACIAL
CORONOID
CORONULE
COROPLAST
COROPLASTAE
COROPLASTIC
COROSCOPY
COROTOMY
COROZO
COROZOS
CORPORA
CORPORAL
CORPORALE
CORPORALISM
CORPORALITIES
CORPORALITY
CORPORALLY
CORPORALSHIP
CORPORAS
CORPORATE
CORPORATELY
CORPORATION
CORPORATIVE
CORPORATIVELY
CORPORATOR
CORPORATURE
CORPOREAL
CORPOREALIST
CORPOREALITY
CORPOREALIZE
CORPOREITY
CORPORIFY
CORPOROSITY
CORPOSANT
CORPS
CORPSBRUDER
CORPSE
CORPSMEN
CORPULENCE
CORPULENCY
CORPULENT
CORPULENTLY
CORPUS
CORPUSCLE
CORPUSCULAR
CORPUSCULE
CORRADE
CORRADED
CORRADIAL
CORRADIATE
CORRADIATED
CORRADIATING
CORRADIATION
CORRADING
CORRAL
CORRALLED
CORRALLING
CORRASION
CORRASIVE
CORREAL
CORREALITY
CORRECT
CORRECTABLE
CORRECTANT
CORRECTED
CORRECTEDNESS
CORRECTIBLE
CORRECTIFY
CORRECTING
CORRECTINGLY
CORRECTION
CORRECTIONAL
CORRECTIONER
CORRECTITUDE
CORRECTIVE
CORRECTIVELY
CORRECTLY
CORRECTNESS
CORRECTOR
CORRECTRESS
CORRECTRICE
CORREGIDOR
CORRELATE
CORRELATED
CORRELATING
CORRELATION
CORRELATIVE
CORREO
CORREPTION
CORRESOL
CORRESPOND
CORRESPONDED
CORRESPONDENCE
CORRESPONDENT
CORRESPONDER
CORRESPONDING
CORRESPONDINGLY
CORRIDA
CORRIDO
CORRIDOR
CORRIDORED
CORRIE
CORRIGE
CORRIGENDUM
CORRIGENT
CORRIGIBLE
CORRIGIBLY
CORRIVAL
CORRIVALITY
CORRIVALRY
CORRIVATE
CORRIVATION
CORRIVE
CORROBBOREE
CORROBER
CORROBORANT
CORROBORATE
CORROBORATED
CORROBORATING
CORROBORATOR
CORROBOREE
CORROBOREED
CORROBOREEING
CORROBORI
CORRODE
CORRODED
CORRODENT
CORRODER
CORRODIARY
CORRODIBLE
CORRODING
CORROSIBLE
CORROSION
CORROSIONAL
CORROSIVE
CORROSIVED
CORROSIVELY
CORROSIVING
CORROSIVITY
CORRUGATE
CORRUGATED
CORRUGATING
CORRUGATION
CORRUGATOR
CORRUMP
CORRUMPABLE
CORRUP
CORRUPABLE
CORRUPT
CORRUPTED
CORRUPTEDLY
CORRUPTER
CORRUPTFUL
CORRUPTIBLE
CORRUPTIBLY
CORRUPTING
CORRUPTINGLY
CORRUPTION
CORRUPTIVE
CORRUPTIVELY
CORRUPTLESS
CORRUPTLY
CORRUPTNESS
CORRUPTOR
CORRUPTRESS
CORSAC
CORSAGE
CORSAINT
CORSAIR
CORSAK
CORSE
CORSELET
CORSELETED
CORSELETING
CORSEQUE
CORSER
CORSET
CORSETIER
CORSETIERE
CORSETRY
CORSETS
CORSIE
CORSITE
CORSLET
CORSO
CORTA
CORTARO
CORTEGE
CORTEISE
CORTEX
CORTICAL
CORTICALLY
CORTICATE
CORTICATED
CORTICATING
CORTICATION
CORTICES

CORTICIFORM
CORTICIFUGAL
CORTICIPETAL
CORTICOLE
CORTICOLINE
CORTICOLOUS
CORTICOSE
CORTICOUS
CORTILE
CORTIN
CORTINA
CORTINAE
CORTINARIOUS
CORTINATE
CORTINE
CORTLANDTITE
CORUCO
CORUNDUM
CORUSCANT
CORUSCATE
CORUSCATED
CORUSCATING
CORUSCATION
CORVEE
CORVER
CORVES
CORVET
CORVETTE
CORVETTO
CORVIFORM
CORVILLOSUM
CORVINA
CORVINE
CORVISER
CORVISOR
CORVOID
CORVUS
CORYBANTIASM
CORYBANTIC
CORYDALIN
CORYDALINE
CORYDALIS
CORYDORA
CORYL
CORYLACEOUS
CORYLET
CORYLIN
CORYMB
CORYMBED
CORYMBIATE
CORYMBIATED
CORYMBIFORM
CORYMBOSE
CORYMBOSELY
CORYMBOUS
CORYPHAEI
CORYPHAENID
CORYPHAENOID
CORYPHAEUS
CORYPHEE
CORYPHENE
CORYPHODONT
CORYPHYLLY
CORYZA
COSALITE
COSAQUE
COSCET
COSCINOMANCY
COSCOROBA
COSEC
COSECANT
COSEISM
COSEISMAL
COSEISMIC
COSESSION
COSET
COSEY
COSH
COSHER
COSHERED
COSHERER
COSHERIES
COSHERING
COSHERY
COSIE
COSIER
COSIEST
COSIGNATORIES
COSIGNATORY
COSIGNER
COSILY
COSINAGE
COSINE
COSINESS
COSINGULAR
COSMECOLOGY
COSMESIS
COSMETIC
COSMETICAL
COSMETICALLY
COSMETICIAN
COSMETICS
COSMETISTE
COSMETOLOGY
COSMIC
COSMICAL
COSMICALITY
COSMICALLY
COSMINE
COSMISM
COSMIST
COSMOCRACY
COSMOCRAT
COSMOCRATIC
COSMOGENESIS
COSMOGENETIC
COSMOGONAL
COSMOGONIC
COSMOGONICAL
COSMOGONIES
COSMOGONIST
COSMOGONIZE
COSMOGONY
COSMOGRAPHER
COSMOGRAPHIC
COSMOGRAPHIES
COSMOGRAPHY
COSMOLABE
COSMOLATRY
COSMOLINE
COSMOLOGIC
COSMOLOGICAL
COSMOLOGICALLY
COSMOLOGIES
COSMOLOGIST
COSMOLOGY
COSMOMETRY
COSMONAUT
COSMOPATHIC
COSMOPLASTIC
COSMOPOIETIC
COSMOPOLICY
COSMOPOLIS
COSMOPOLITAN
COSMOPOLITE
COSMOPOLITIC
COSMORAMA
COSMORAMIC
COSMORGANIC
COSMOS
COSMOSCOPE
COSMOSOPHY
COSMOSPHERE
COSMOTHEISM
COSMOTHEIST
COSMOTHETIC
COSMOTRON
COSMOZOANS
COSMOZOIC
COSMOZOISM
COSO
COSPECIFIC
COSS
COSSAS
COSSET
COSSETTE
COSSETTED
COSSETTING
COSSHEN
COSSIC
COSSID
COSSNENT
COSSYRITE
COST
COSTA
COSTAE
COSTAGE
COSTAL
COSTALGIA
COSTALLY
COSTANDER
COSTAR
COSTARD
COSTARRED
COSTARRING
COSTATE
COSTATED
COSTEAN
COSTEANING
COSTECTOMY
COSTED
COSTEEN
COSTELLATE
COSTER
COSTERMONGER
COSTFUL
COSTIFEROUS
COSTIFORM
COSTING
COSTIVE
COSTIVELY
COSTIVENESS
COSTLESS
COSTLESSNESS
COSTLEW
COSTLIER
COSTLIEST
COSTLINESS
COSTLY
COSTMARY
COSTOAPICAL
COSTOCENTRAL
COSTOCHONDRAL
COSTOCOLIC
COSTOGENIC
COSTOINFERIOR
COSTOPHRENIC
COSTOPLEURAL
COSTOSTERNAL
COSTOTOME
COSTOTOMIES
COSTOTOMY
COSTOXIPHOID
COSTRAIGHT
COSTREL
COSTS
COSTULA
COSTULATION
COSTUME
COSTUMED
COSTUMER
COSTUMERY
COSTUMIC
COSTUMIER
COSTUMIERE
COSTUMING
COSTUMIST
COSTUSROOT
COSWEARER
COSY
COSYMMEDIAN
COT
COTANGENT
COTANGENTIAL
COTARIUS
COTARNIN
COTARNINE
COTBETTY
COTCH
COTE
COTEAU
COTED
COTEEN
COTELE
COTELINE
COTELLER
COTEMPORARY
COTENANCY
COTENANT
COTENURE
COTERELL
COTERIE
COTERMINOUS
COTH
COTHAMORE
COTHE
COTHISH
COTHON
COTHOUSE
COTHURN
COTHURNAL
COTHURNATE
COTHURNED
COTHURNI
COTHURNIAN
COTHURNUS
COTHY
COTICE
COTIDAL
COTILLAGE
COTILLION
COTILLON
COTING
COTINGA
COTINGID
COTINGOID
COTISE
COTISED
COTISING
COTITULAR
COTLAND
COTMAN
COTO
COTOIN
COTONIA
COTONIER
COTORO
COTOROS
COTQUEAN
COTRINE
COTRUSTEE
COTS
COTSET
COTSETLAND
COTSETLE
COTT
COTTA
COTTABUS
COTTAE
COTTAGE
COTTAGED
COTTAGER
COTTAGERS
COTTAR
COTTAS
COTTE
COTTED
COTTER
COTTERED
COTTEREL
COTTERING
COTTERITE
COTTERWAY
COTTID
COTTIER
COTTIFORM
COTTISE
COTTOID
COTTON
COTTONADE
COTTONED
COTTONEE
COTTONEER
COTTONER
COTTONING
COTTONIZE
COTTONMOUTH
COTTONOCRACY
COTTONSEED
COTTONTAIL
COTTONWEED
COTTONWOOD
COTTONY
COTTREL
COTTY
COTUIT
COTULA
COTUNNITE
COTYLA
COTYLAR
COTYLE
COTYLEDON
COTYLEDONAL
COTYLEDONAR
COTYLEDONARY
COTYLEDONOUS
COTYLIGEROUS
COTYLISCUS
COTYLOID
COTYLOIDAL
COTYLOPUBIC
COTYLOSACRAL
COTYLOSAUR
COTYLOSAURIAN
COTYPE
COUAC
COUCAL
COUCH
COUCHANCY
COUCHANT
COUCHE
COUCHED
COUCHEE
COUCHER
COUCHING
COUCHMAKER
COUCHMAKING
COUCHMATE
COUCHY
COUDE
COUDEE
COUGAR
COUGH
COUGHED
COUGHER

COUGHING
COUGHROOT
COUGHWEED
COUGNAR
COUHAGE
COUL
COULAGE
COULD
COULDNA
COULDST
COULE
COULEE
COULEUR
COULIE
COULIER
COULIS
COULISSE
COULOIR
COULOMB
COULOMETER
COULTER
COULTERNEB
COUMA
COUMALIN
COUMARAN
COUMARANE
COUMARATE
COUMARIC
COUMARIN
COUMARONE
COUMAROU
COUMBITE
COUNCIL
COUNCILLOR
COUNCILMAN
COUNCILMEN
COUNCILOR
COUNITE
COUNSEL
COUNSELED
COUNSELEE
COUNSELING
COUNSELLED
COUNSELLING
COUNSELLOR
COUNSELOR
COUNT
COUNTABLE
COUNTABLY
COUNTDOWN
COUNTED
COUNTENANCE
COUNTENANCED
COUNTENANCING
COUNTER
COUNTERACT
COUNTERACTANT
COUNTERACTED
COUNTERACTER
COUNTERACTING
COUNTERACTION
COUNTERACTIVE
COUNTERACTOR
COUNTERAPSE
COUNTERARCH
COUNTERBALANCE
COUNTERBALANCING
COUNTERBLAST
COUNTERBORE
COUNTERBRACE
COUNTERBRAND
COUNTERBUFF
COUNTERCHANGE
COUNTERCHANGED
COUNTERCHARGE
COUNTERCHARGED
COUNTERCHARGING
COUNTERCHECK
COUNTERCLAIM
COUNTERCLAIMING
COUNTERCLOCKWISE
COUNTERCOUPE
COUNTERCURRENT
COUNTERDIKE
COUNTERDRAIN
COUNTEREARTH
COUNTERFEIT
COUNTERFEITER
COUNTERFEITING
COUNTERFLORY
COUNTERFOIL
COUNTERFORT
COUNTERFUGUE
COUNTERGAGE
COUNTERGAGER
COUNTERGAUGE
COUNTERGLOW
COUNTERION
COUNTERIRRITANT
COUNTERLATH
COUNTERLATHED
COUNTERLODE
COUNTERMAN
COUNTERMAND
COUNTERMANDED
COUNTERMARCH
COUNTERMARK
COUNTERMINE
COUNTERMINED
COUNTERMINING
COUNTERMOVED
COUNTERMOVEMEN
COUNTERMOVING
COUNTERMURE
COUNTERPALY
COUNTERPANE
COUNTERPANED
COUNTERPART
COUNTERPLEA
COUNTERPLOT
COUNTERPLOTTED
COUNTERPLOTTING
COUNTERPOINT
COUNTERPOISE
COUNTERPOISED
COUNTERPOISING
COUNTERPOISON
COUNTERPOLE
COUNTERPROOF
COUNTERPROVE
COUNTERPUNCH
COUNTERRATE
COUNTERROLL
COUNTERROUND
COUNTERS
COUNTERSANK
COUNTERSCALE
COUNTERSEA
COUNTERSEAL
COUNTERSENSE
COUNTERSHADE
COUNTERSHAFT
COUNTERSIGN
COUNTERSIGNED
COUNTERSINK
COUNTERSINKING
COUNTERSLOPE
COUNTERSPY
COUNTERSTAIN
COUNTERSTAND
COUNTERSTOCK
COUNTERSTROKE
COUNTERSUN
COUNTERSUNK
COUNTERSUNKEN
COUNTERTAIL
COUNTERTALLY
COUNTERTENOR
COUNTERTERM
COUNTERTIME
COUNTERTURN
COUNTERTYPE
COUNTERVAIL
COUNTERVAILED
COUNTERVAILING
COUNTERVAIR
COUNTERVENE
COUNTERVIEW
COUNTERVOTE
COUNTERWALL
COUNTERWEIGH
COUNTERWEIGHED
COUNTERWEIGHING
COUNTERWEIGHT
COUNTERWHEEL
COUNTERWORD
COUNTERWORK
COUNTESS
COUNTIES
COUNTING
COUNTLESS
COUNTOR
COUNTOUR
COUNTRIES
COUNTRIFIED
COUNTRY
COUNTRYFIED
COUNTRYFOLK
COUNTRYMAN
COUNTRYMEN
COUNTRYSEAT
COUNTRYSIDE
COUNTRYWOMAN
COUNTRYWOMEN
COUNTS
COUNTY
COUP
COUPAGE
COUPE
COUPED
COUPEE
COUPELET
COUPER
COUPLE
COUPLED
COUPLER
COUPLERESS
COUPLET
COUPLETEER
COUPLING
COUPON
COUPS
COUPSTICK
COUPURE
COUR
COURAGE
COURAGEOUS
COURAGEOUSLY
COURAGER
COURANT
COURANTE
COURANTO
COURAP
COURATARI
COURB
COURBARIL
COURBE
COURE
COURGE
COURIDA
COURIE
COURIER
COURIL
COURLAN
COURONNE
COURSE
COURSED
COURSER
COURSES
COURSING
COURT
COURTAL
COURTBRED
COURTBY
COURTCRAFT
COURTEOUS
COURTEOUSLY
COURTEPY
COURTER
COURTESAN
COURTESIES
COURTESY
COURTEZAN
COURTHOUSE
COURTIER
COURTIERLY
COURTIERY
COURTIN
COURTING
COURTLET
COURTLIER
COURTLIEST
COURTLIKE
COURTLINESS
COURTLING
COURTLY
COURTMAN
COURTROOM
COURTS
COURTSHIP
COURTY
COURTYARD
COUS
COUSCOUS
COUSERANITE
COUSIN
COUSINAGE
COUSINHOOD
COUSINLY
COUSINRIES
COUSINRY
COUSINS
COUSINSHIP
COUSINY
COUTEAU
COUTEAUX
COUTEL
COUTELLE
COUTER
COUTH
COUTHE
COUTHIE
COUTHILY
COUTHINESS
COUTHLESS
COUTHLY
COUTHY
COUTIL
COUTILLE
COUTURE
COUTURIER
COUTURIERE
COUVADE
COUVERT
COUVERTE
COUVEUSE
COUXIA
COUXIO
COVADO
COVALENCE
COVALENCY
COVALENT
COVARIANT
COVARIATION
COVE
COVED
COVELLINE
COVELLITE
COVEN
COVENABLE
COVENABLY
COVENANT
COVENANTAL
COVENANTALLY
COVENANTED
COVENANTEE
COVENANTER
COVENANTING
COVENANTOR
COVENT
COVER
COVERAGE
COVERALLS
COVERCHIEF
COVERCLE
COVERED
COVERER
COVERING
COVERLET
COVERLID
COVERSINE
COVERSLUT
COVERT
COVERTICAL
COVERTLY
COVERTNESS
COVERTURE
COVET
COVETABLE
COVETED
COVETER
COVETING
COVETINGLY
COVETISE
COVETIVENESS
COVETOUS
COVETOUSLY
COVETOUSNESS
COVEY
COVEYS
COVID
COVIDO
COVIN
COVINE
COVING
COVINOUS
COVITE
COVOLUME
COW
COWAGE
COWAL
COWAN
COWARD
COWARDICE
COWARDISH
COWARDLINESS
COWARDLY
COWARDNESS
COWARDY
COWBANE
COWBELL
COWBERRIES
COWBERRY
COWBIND
COWBIRD

COWBOY
COWBRUTE
COWCATCHER
COWD
COWDIE
COWED
COWEEN
COWER
COWFISH
COWFISHES
COWGATE
COWGIRL
COWGRAM
COWGRASS
COWHAGE
COWHEART
COWHEARTED
COWHEEL
COWHERB
COWHERD
COWHIDE
COWHIDED
COWHIDING
COWHOUSE
COWISH
COWITCH
COWKEEPER
COWL
COWLE
COWLED
COWLEECH
COWLEECHING
COWLICK
COWLICKS
COWLIKE
COWLING
COWLSTAFF
COWMAN
COWMEN
COWP
COWPATH
COWPEA
COWPEN
COWPER
COWPERITIS
COWPOX
COWPUNCHER
COWQUAKE
COWR
COWRIE
COWRIES
COWROID
COWRY
COWS
COWSHARD
COWSHARN
COWSHED
COWSHOT
COWSHUT
COWSKIN
COWSLIP
COWSLIPPED
COWSON
COWSUCKER
COWTAIL
COWTHWORT
COWTONGUE
COWWEED
COWWHEAT
COWY
COWYARD
COX
COXA
COXAE
COXAL
COXALGIA
COXALGIC
COXALGY
COXARTHRITIS
COXBONES
COXCOMB
COXCOMBESS
COXCOMBICAL
COXCOMBRY
COXCOMBY
COXCOMICAL
COXIER
COXIEST
COXITE
COXITIS
COXOCERITE
COXOCERITIC
COXODYNIA
COXOFEMORAL
COXOPODITE
COXSWAIN
COXY
COY
COYAN
COYDOG
COYISH
COYLY
COYNE
COYNESS
COYNYE
COYO
COYOL
COYOS
COYOTE
COYOTES
COYOTING
COYPOU
COYPU
COYPUS
COYSTREL
COYURE
COZ
COZE
COZED
COZEN
COZENAGE
COZENER
COZENING
COZENINGLY
COZEY
COZIE
COZIER
COZIEST
COZILY
COZINESS
COZING
COZY
CRAAL
CRAB
CRABBED
CRABBEDLY
CRABBEDNESS
CRABBER
CRABBERY
CRABBIER
CRABBIEST
CRABBING
CRABBISH
CRABBIT
CRABBY
CRABCATCHER
CRABEATER
CRABER
CRABFISH
CRABHOLE
CRABMILL
CRABS
CRABSIDLE
CRABSTICK
CRABWEED
CRABWOOD
CRACCUS
CRACHOIR
CRACK
CRACKAJACK
CRACKBRAIN
CRACKBRAINED
CRACKDOWN
CRACKED
CRACKER
CRACKERBERRY
CRACKERS
CRACKHEMP
CRACKING
CRACKJAW
CRACKLE
CRACKLED
CRACKLEWARE
CRACKLING
CRACKLY
CRACKNEL
CRACKPOT
CRACKROPE
CRACKS
CRACKSMAN
CRACKSMEN
CRACKUP
CRACKY
CRACOVIENNE
CRACOWE
CRADDY
CRADGE
CRADLE
CRADLEBOARD
CRADLECHILD
CRADLED
CRADLEFELLOW
CRADLELAND
CRADLELIKE
CRADLEMAKER
CRADLEMAKING
CRADLEMAN
CRADLEMATE
CRADLEMEN
CRADLER
CRADLESIDE
CRADLESONG
CRADLETIME
CRADLING
CRAER
CRAFT
CRAFTIER
CRAFTIEST
CRAFTILY
CRAFTINESS
CRAFTLY
CRAFTSMAN
CRAFTSMANSHIP
CRAFTSMASTER
CRAFTSMEN
CRAFTSWOMAN
CRAFTWORK
CRAFTWORKER
CRAFTY
CRAG
CRAGGAN
CRAGGED
CRAGGEDNESS
CRAGGIER
CRAGGIEST
CRAGGINESS
CRAGGY
CRAGSMAN
CRAGSMEN
CRAICHY
CRAIGHLE
CRAIGMONTITE
CRAIN
CRAISEY
CRAIZEY
CRAKE
CRAKED
CRAKEFEET
CRAKING
CRAKOW
CRAL
CRAM
CRAMASIE
CRAMBAMBULEE
CRAMBAMBULI
CRAMBE
CRAMBID
CRAMBLE
CRAMBLY
CRAMBO
CRAME
CRAMMED
CRAMMEL
CRAMMER
CRAMMING
CRAMOISIE
CRAMOISY
CRAMP
CRAMPBIT
CRAMPED
CRAMPER
CRAMPET
CRAMPETTE
CRAMPFISH
CRAMPING
CRAMPIT
CRAMPON
CRAMPONNEE
CRAMPOON
CRAMPS
CRAMPY
CRAN
CRANAGE
CRANBERRIES
CRANBERRY
CRANCE
CRANCH
CRANDALL
CRANE
CRANEBILL
CRANED
CRANEMAN
CRANER
CRANES
CRANESBILL
CRANET
CRANEWAY
CRANEY
CRANG
CRANIA
CRANIAD
CRANIAL
CRANIALLY
CRANIAN
CRANIATE
CRANIC
CRANING
CRANIOCELE
CRANIOCLASIS
CRANIOCLASM
CRANIOCLAST
CRANIOFACIAL
CRANIOGNOMIC
CRANIOGNOMY
CRANIOGNOSY
CRANIOGRAPH
CRANIOGRAPHY
CRANIOLOGICAL
CRANIOLOGIST
CRANIOLOGY
CRANIOMETER
CRANIOMETRIC
CRANIOMETRY
CRANIOPAGUS
CRANIOPATHIC
CRANIOPATHY
CRANIOPHORE
CRANIOPLASTY
CRANIOSACRAL
CRANIOSCOPY
CRANIOSPINAL
CRANIOSTOSIS
CRANIOTABES
CRANIOTOME
CRANIOTOMIES
CRANIOTOMY
CRANIUM
CRANIUMS
CRANK
CRANKBIRD
CRANKCASE
CRANKED
CRANKER
CRANKERY
CRANKIER
CRANKIEST
CRANKILY
CRANKINESS
CRANKING
CRANKISH
CRANKLE
CRANKLED
CRANKLING
CRANKMAN
CRANKOUS
CRANKPIN
CRANKS
CRANKSHAFT
CRANKUM
CRANKY
CRANNAGE
CRANNEL
CRANNIED
CRANNIES
CRANNOCK
CRANNOG
CRANNOGE
CRANNOGER
CRANNY
CRANNYING
CRANREUCH
CRANSIER
CRANTARA
CRANTS
CRANY
CRAP
CRAPAUD
CRAPAUDINE
CRAPE
CRAPEFISH
CRAPEHANGER
CRAPETTE
CRAPON
CRAPPER
CRAPPIE
CRAPPIES
CRAPPIN
CRAPPLE
CRAPPO
CRAPPY
CRAPS
CRAPSHOOTER
CRAPULATE
CRAPULENCE
CRAPULENCY

CRAPULENT
CRAPULOUS
CRAPULOUSLY
CRAPWA
CRAPY
CRAQUELURE
CRARE
CRASES
CRASH
CRASHED
CRASHER
CRASHING
CRASIS
CRASPEDAL
CRASPEDON
CRASPEDOTAL
CRASPEDOTE
CRASPEDUM
CRASS
CRASSAMENTUM
CRASSIER
CRASSITUDE
CRASSLY
CRASSNESS
CRASSULACEOUS
CRATCH
CRATCHENS
CRATCHES
CRATCHINS
CRATE
CRATED
CRATEMAN
CRATEMEN
CRATER
CRATERAL
CRATERIFORM
CRATERKIN
CRATERLET
CRATEROUS
CRATICULAR
CRATING
CRATOMETER
CRATOMETRIC
CRATOMETRY
CRAUNCH
CRAVAT
CRAVATTED
CRAVATTING
CRAVE
CRAVED
CRAVEN
CRAVENETTE
CRAVENLY
CRAVENNESS
CRAVER
CRAVING
CRAVINGLY
CRAVINGNESS
CRAVO
CRAW
CRAWDAD
CRAWFISH
CRAWFISHES
CRAWFOOT
CRAWFOOTS
CRAWK
CRAWL
CRAWLED
CRAWLER
CRAWLIE
CRAWLIER
CRAWLIEST
CRAWLING
CRAWLINGLY
CRAWLY
CRAWM
CRAY
CRAYER
CRAYFISH
CRAYFISHES
CRAYLET
CRAYON
CRAYTHUR
CRAZE
CRAZED
CRAZEDLY
CRAZEDNESS
CRAZIER
CRAZIES
CRAZIEST
CRAZILY
CRAZINESS
CRAZING
CRAZY
CRAZYCAT
CRAZYWEED
CREA
CREACH
CREACHY
CREAGH
CREAGHT
CREAK
CREAKER
CREAKIER
CREAKIEST
CREAKILY
CREAKINESS
CREAKING
CREAKY
CREAM
CREAMCUPS
CREAMED
CREAMER
CREAMERIES
CREAMERY
CREAMERYMAN
CREAMERYMEN
CREAMFRUIT
CREAMIER
CREAMIEST
CREAMILY
CREAMINESS
CREAMING
CREAMMAKER
CREAMMAKING
CREAMOMETER
CREAMSACS
CREAMWARE
CREAMY
CREANCE
CREANCER
CREANT
CREASE
CREASED
CREASER
CREASHAKS
CREASIER
CREASIEST
CREASING
CREASOL
CREASY
CREAT
CREATE
CREATED
CREATIC
CREATIN
CREATINE
CREATING
CREATININ
CREATININE
CREATION
CREATIONAL
CREATIONARY
CREATIONISM
CREATIONIST
CREATIVE
CREATIVELY
CREATIVENESS
CREATIVITY
CREATOR
CREATORRHEA
CREATORSHIP
CREATOTOXISM
CREATURAL
CREATURE
CREATURELY
CREBRITY
CREBROUS
CRECHE
CREDDOCK
CREDENCE
CREDENCIVE
CREDENDA
CREDENDUM
CREDENS
CREDENSIVE
CREDENT
CREDENTIAL
CREDENZA
CREDIBILITY
CREDIBLE
CREDIBLENESS
CREDIBLY
CREDIT
CREDITABLE
CREDITABLY
CREDITED
CREDITIVE
CREDITOR
CREDNERITE
CREDO
CREDOS
CREDULITIES
CREDULITY
CREDULOUS
CREDULOUSLY
CREE
CREED
CREEDAL
CREEDALISM
CREEDALIST
CREEDED
CREEDITE
CREEDMORE
CREEDSMAN
CREEK
CREEKER
CREEKFISH
CREEKFISHES
CREEKS
CREEKSIDE
CREEKY
CREEL
CREELED
CREELER
CREELING
CREEM
CREEN
CREEP
CREEPAGE
CREEPER
CREEPERS
CREEPHOLE
CREEPIE
CREEPIER
CREEPIEST
CREEPILY
CREEPINESS
CREEPING
CREEPMOUSE
CREEPS
CREEPY
CREESE
CREESH
CREESHIE
CREESHY
CREIRGIST
CREMANT
CREMASTER
CREMASTERIAL
CREMASTERIC
CREMATE
CREMATED
CREMATING
CREMATION
CREMATIONISM
CREMATIONIST
CREMATOR
CREMATORIAL
CREMATORIES
CREMATORIUM
CREMATORY
CREMBALUM
CREME
CREMERIE
CREMNOPHOBIA
CREMOCARP
CREMOMETER
CREMOR
CREMULE
CRENA
CRENAE
CRENATE
CRENATED
CRENATELY
CRENATION
CRENATURE
CRENEL
CRENELATE
CRENELATED
CRENELATING
CRENELATION
CRENELE
CRENELED
CRENELEE
CRENELET
CRENELING
CRENELLATE
CRENELLATED
CRENELLATING
CRENELLATION
CRENELLE
CRENELLED
CRENELLING
CRENIC
CRENITIC
CRENOLOGY
CRENOTHERAPY
CRENULA
CRENULATE
CRENULATED
CRENULATION
CREODONT
CREOLE
CREOLEIZE
CREOLISM
CREOLITE
CREOLIZATION
CREOLIZE
CREOLIZED
CREOLIZING
CREOPHAGIA
CREOPHAGISM
CREOPHAGIST
CREOPHAGOUS
CREOPHAGY
CREOSOL
CREOSOTE
CREOSOTED
CREOSOTER
CREOSOTIC
CREOSOTING
CREPANCE
CREPE
CREPED
CREPEY
CREPINE
CREPINESS
CREPING
CREPITACULA
CREPITACULUM
CREPITANT
CREPITATE
CREPITATED
CREPITATING
CREPITATION
CREPITOUS
CREPITUS
CREPON
CREPT
CREPUSCLE
CREPUSCULAR
CREPUSCULINE
CREPUSCULUM
CREPY
CRESAMINE
CRESCENDO
CRESCENDOED
CRESCENDOING
CRESCENDOS
CRESCENT
CRESCENTADE
CRESCENTED
CRESCENTIC
CRESCENTING
CRESCENTLIKE
CRESCENTOID
CRESCIVE
CRESCOGRAPH
CRESOLIN
CRESOLINE
CRESORCIN
CRESORCINOL
CRESOTATE
CRESOTIC
CRESOTINATE
CRESOTINIC
CRESOXID
CRESOXIDE
CRESS
CRESSED
CRESSES
CRESSET
CRESSWEED
CRESSWORT
CRESSY
CREST
CRESTED
CRESTFALLEN
CRESTING
CRESTLESS
CRESTLINE
CRESTMOREITE
CRESYL
CRESYLATE
CRESYLENE
CRESYLIC
CRESYLITE
CRETA
CRETACEOUS
CRETACEOUSLY
CRETEFACTION
CRETIC
CRETIFY
CRETIN

CRETINIC
CRETINISM
CRETINOID
CRETINOUS
CRETION
CRETIONARY
CRETONNE
CREVALLE
CREVASS
CREVASSE
CREVASSED
CREVASSING
CREVET
CREVETTE
CREVICE
CREVICED
CREVICES
CREW
CREWE
CREWEL
CREWELIST
CREWELLERY
CREWELWORK
CREWER
CREWET
CREWMAN
CRIANCE
CRIANT
CRIB
CRIBBAGE
CRIBBED
CRIBBER
CRIBBING
CRIBBLE
CRIBBLED
CRIBELLA
CRIBELLUM
CRIBO
CRIBRAL
CRIBRATE
CRIBRATELY
CRIBRATION
CRIBRIFORM
CRIBROSE
CRIBWORK
CRIC
CRICETID
CRICETINE
CRICK
CRICKE
CRICKET
CRICKETER
CRICKETERS
CRICKETING
CRICKETINGS
CRICKETY
CRICKEY
CRICKLE
CRICOID
CRICOTHYROID
CRICOTOMY
CRIDDLE
CRIED
CRIER
CRIERS
CRIES
CRIEY
CRIG
CRIKE
CRIKEY
CRILE
CRIMBLE
CRIME
CRIMEFUL
CRIMES
CRIMINAL
CRIMINALISM
CRIMINALIST
CRIMINALITIES
CRIMINALITY
CRIMINALLY
CRIMINALOID
CRIMINALS
CRIMINATE
CRIMINATED
CRIMINATING
CRIMINATION
CRIMINATIVE
CRIMINATOR
CRIMINATORY
CRIMINE
CRIMINI
CRIMINOGENIC
CRIMINOLOGIC
CRIMINOLOGY
CRIMINOUS
CRIMINOUSLY
CRIMMY
CRIMOGENIC
CRIMP
CRIMPAGE
CRIMPED
CRIMPER
CRIMPIER
CRIMPIEST
CRIMPING
CRIMPLE
CRIMPLED
CRIMPLING
CRIMPNESS
CRIMPY
CRIMSON
CRIMSONLY
CRIMSONNESS
CRIN
CRINAL
CRINANITE
CRINATED
CRINATORY
CRINCH
CRINE
CRINED
CRINET
CRINGE
CRINGED
CRINGELING
CRINGER
CRINGING
CRINGINGLY
CRINGINGNESS
CRINGLE
CRINICULTURE
CRINIERE
CRINIFEROUS
CRINIGEROUS
CRINION
CRINIPAROUS
CRINITE
CRINITORY
CRINIVOROUS
CRINK
CRINKLE
CRINKLED
CRINKLEROOT
CRINKLIER
CRINKLIEST
CRINKLING
CRINKLY
CRINKUM
CRINOID
CRINOIDAL
CRINOIDEAN
CRINOLINE
CRINOSE
CRINOSITY
CRINULA
CRINUM
CRIOBOLIUM
CRIOBOLY
CRIOCERATITE
CRIOLLA
CRIOLLO
CRIOPHORE
CRIOSPHINX
CRIP
CRIPES
CRIPPLE
CRIPPLED
CRIPPLER
CRIPPLES
CRIPPLING
CRIPPLY
CRIPS
CRISE
CRISES
CRISIC
CRISIS
CRISLE
CRISP
CRISPATE
CRISPATED
CRISPATION
CRISPATURE
CRISPED
CRISPER
CRISPEST
CRISPIER
CRISPIEST
CRISPILY
CRISPINESS
CRISPING
CRISPLY
CRISPNESS
CRISPY
CRISS
CRISSA
CRISSAL
CRISSCROSS
CRISSCROSSED
CRISSET
CRISSUM
CRISTA
CRISTAE
CRISTATE
CRISTATED
CRISTIFORM
CRISTOBALITE
CRISTY
CRITCH
CRITERIA
CRITERIOLOGY
CRITERION
CRITERIONAL
CRITERIONS
CRITH
CRITHMENE
CRITHOMANCY
CRITIC
CRITICAL
CRITICALITY
CRITICALLY
CRITICALNESS
CRITICASTER
CRITICASTRY
CRITICISED
CRITICISER
CRITICISING
CRITICISM
CRITICIZABLE
CRITICIZE
CRITICIZED
CRITICIZER
CRITICIZING
CRITICKIN
CRITICULE
CRITIQUE
CRITIZE
CRITLING
CRITTER
CRIZZEL
CRIZZLE
CRO
CROAK
CROAKED
CROAKER
CROAKIER
CROAKIEST
CROAKILY
CROAKINESS
CROAKING
CROAKS
CROAKY
CROAPE
CROC
CROCARD
CROCEIN
CROCEINE
CROCEOUS
CROCETIN
CROCEUS
CROCHE
CROCHET
CROCHETED
CROCHETING
CROCI
CROCIARY
CROCIATE
CROCIDOLITE
CROCIN
CROCINE
CROCK
CROCKARD
CROCKED
CROCKER
CROCKERY
CROCKERYWARE
CROCKET
CROCKETED
CROCKETING
CROCKING
CROCKY
CROCODILE
CROCODILEAN
CROCODILIAN
CROCODILINE
CROCODILITY
CROCODILOID
CROCOISITE
CROCOITE
CROCONATE
CROCONIC
CROCUS
CROCUSED
CROCUSES
CROCUTA
CROFT
CROFTER
CROFTERIZE
CROFTING
CROFTLAND
CROIGHLE
CROISADE
CROISE
CROISEE
CROISES
CROISSANT
CROISSANTE
CROJIK
CROMA
CROMALTITE
CROMB
CROMBEC
CROME
CROMFORDITE
CROMLECH
CROMME
CROMMEL
CROMORNA
CROMORNE
CROMSTER
CRONE
CRONEBERRY
CRONET
CRONIED
CRONIES
CRONISH
CRONK
CRONKNESS
CRONSTEDTITE
CRONY
CRONYING
CROO
CROOCH
CROOD
CROODLE
CROOK
CROOKBACK
CROOKBACKED
CROOKBILLED
CROOKED
CROOKEDLY
CROOKEDNESS
CROOKEN
CROOKESITE
CROOKFINGERED
CROOKHEADED
CROOKING
CROOKKNEED
CROOKLE
CROOKLEGGED
CROOKNECK
CROOKNECKED
CROOKNOSED
CROOKS
CROOKSIDED
CROOKSTERNED
CROOKTOOTHED
CROOL
CROOM
CROON
CROONED
CROONER
CROONING
CROOSE
CROP
CROPE
CROPHEAD
CROPLAND
CROPMAN
CROPPA
CROPPED
CROPPER
CROPPIE
CROPPING
CROPPY
CROPS
CROPSHIN
CROPSICK
CROPSICKNESS
CROPWEED
CROQUET
CROQUETED
CROQUETING
CROQUETTE
CROQUIGNOLE

CROQUIS
CRORE
CROSA
CROSET
CROSHABELL
CROSIER
CROSIERED
CROSNE
CROSNES
CROSS
CROSSABILITY
CROSSABLE
CROSSARM
CROSSBAND
CROSSBAR
CROSSBARRED
CROSSBARRING
CROSSBEAK
CROSSBEAM
CROSSBELT
CROSSBILL
CROSSBIRTH
CROSSBITE
CROSSBONES
CROSSBOW
CROSSBOWMAN
CROSSBOWMEN
CROSSBRED
CROSSBREED
CROSSBREEDING
CROSSCHECK
CROSSCURRENT
CROSSCUT
CROSSCUTTER
CROSSCUTTING
CROSSE
CROSSED
CROSSER
CROSSES
CROSSETTE
CROSSFALL
CROSSFIRE
CROSSFIRED
CROSSFIRING
CROSSFISH
CROSSFLOWER
CROSSFOOT
CROSSHACKLE
CROSSHAND
CROSSHATCH
CROSSHATCHED
CROSSHATCHER
CROSSHATCHING
CROSSHAUL
CROSSHEAD
CROSSING
CROSSITE
CROSSJACK
CROSSLEGS
CROSSLET
CROSSLETED
CROSSLIGHT
CROSSLIGHTED
CROSSLINE
CROSSLY
CROSSNESS
CROSSOPODIA
CROSSOPT
CROSSOVER
CROSSPATCH
CROSSPIECE
CROSSPOINT
CROSSPOST
CROSSRAIL
CROSSROAD
CROSSROW
CROSSRUFF
CROSSTALK
CROSSTIE
CROSSTIED
CROSSTOES
CROSSTREE
CROSSWALK
CROSSWAY
CROSSWAYS
CROSSWEB
CROSSWEED
CROSSWIND
CROSSWISE
CROSSWORD
CROSSWORDER
CROSSWORT
CROST
CROSTARIE
CROT
CROTAL
CROTALIC
CROTALID
CROTALIFORM
CROTALIN
CROTALINE
CROTALISM
CROTALO
CROTALOID
CROTALUM
CROTAPHIC
CROTAPHION
CROTAPHITE
CROTAPHITIC
CROTCH
CROTCHED
CROTCHET
CROTCHETED
CROTCHETEER
CROTCHETINESS
CROTCHETING
CROTCHETY
CROTCHING
CROTCHY
CROTESCO
CROTIN
CROTON
CROTONATE
CROTONIC
CROTONYL
CROTTAL
CROTTELS
CROTTLE
CROTYL
CROUCH
CROUCHANT
CROUCHE
CROUCHED
CROUCHER
CROUCHIE
CROUCHING
CROUD
CROUKE
CROUP
CROUPADE
CROUPAL
CROUPE
CROUPERBUSH
CROUPIER
CROUPIEST
CROUPILY
CROUPINESS
CROUPON
CROUPOUS
CROUPY
CROUSE
CROUSELY
CROUSTADE
CROUT
CROUTE
CROUTH
CROUTON
CROW
CROWBAIT
CROWBAR
CROWBELL
CROWBERRIES
CROWBERRY
CROWBILL
CROWD
CROWDED
CROWDEDLY
CROWDEDNESS
CROWDER
CROWDING
CROWDLE
CROWDWEED
CROWDY
CROWED
CROWER
CROWFEET
CROWFLOWER
CROWFOOT
CROWFOOTED
CROWHOP
CROWING
CROWKEEPER
CROWL
CROWN
CROWNAL
CROWNBEARD
CROWNED
CROWNER
CROWNET
CROWNING
CROWNLAND
CROWNLESS
CROWNLET
CROWNLING
CROWNMENT
CROWNPIECE
CROWNWORK
CROWNWORT
CROWSTEP
CROWSTONE
CROWTOE
CROY
CROYDON
CROZE
CROZED
CROZER
CROZIER
CROZING
CROZLE
CROZZLE
CROZZLY
CRU
CRUB
CRUBEEN
CRUCE
CRUCES
CRUCETHOUSE
CRUCHE
CRUCIAL
CRUCIALITY
CRUCIALLY
CRUCIAN
CRUCIATE
CRUCIATED
CRUCIATELY
CRUCIATING
CRUCIATION
CRUCIBLE
CRUCIFER
CRUCIFEROUS
CRUCIFICIAL
CRUCIFIED
CRUCIFIER
CRUCIFIX
CRUCIFIXION
CRUCIFORM
CRUCIFORMITY
CRUCIFORMLY
CRUCIFY
CRUCIFYING
CRUCIGEROUS
CRUCIS
CRUCK
CRUDDLE
CRUDE
CRUDELY
CRUDENESS
CRUDER
CRUDEST
CRUDITIES
CRUDITY
CRUDWORT
CRUDY
CRUE
CRUEL
CRUELER
CRUELEST
CRUELIZE
CRUELLY
CRUELNESS
CRUELS
CRUELTIES
CRUELTY
CRUENT
CRUENTOUS
CRUET
CRUETY
CRUISE
CRUISED
CRUISER
CRUISING
CRUISKEEN
CRUISKEN
CRUIVE
CRUL
CRULL
CRULLER
CRUM
CRUMB
CRUMBABLE
CRUMBCLOTH
CRUMBED
CRUMBER
CRUMBIER
CRUMBIEST
CRUMBING
CRUMBLE
CRUMBLED
CRUMBLIER
CRUMBLIEST
CRUMBLINESS
CRUMBLING
CRUMBLINGS
CRUMBLY
CRUMBS
CRUMBY
CRUMEN
CRUMENA
CRUMENAL
CRUMMABLE
CRUMMER
CRUMMIE
CRUMMIER
CRUMMIEST
CRUMMOCK
CRUMMY
CRUMP
CRUMPER
CRUMPET
CRUMPLE
CRUMPLED
CRUMPLER
CRUMPLING
CRUMPLY
CRUMPY
CRUMSTER
CRUNCH
CRUNCHED
CRUNCHILY
CRUNCHINESS
CRUNCHING
CRUNCHINGLY
CRUNCHWEED
CRUNCHY
CRUNK
CRUNKLE
CRUNODAL
CRUNODE
CRUNT
CRUOR
CRUP
CRUPPEN
CRUPPER
CRUPPERED
CRUPPERING
CRURA
CRURAL
CRUROGENITAL
CRUROTARSAL
CRUS
CRUSADE
CRUSADED
CRUSADER
CRUSADERS
CRUSADING
CRUSADO
CRUSADOES
CRUSADOS
CRUSE
CRUSET
CRUSH
CRUSHABILITY
CRUSHABLE
CRUSHED
CRUSHER
CRUSHING
CRUSIE
CRUSILE
CRUSILEE
CRUSILY
CRUST
CRUSTA
CRUSTACEAN
CRUSTACEOUS
CRUSTADE
CRUSTAL
CRUSTALOGIST
CRUSTALOGY
CRUSTATE
CRUSTATED
CRUSTATION
CRUSTED
CRUSTEDLY
CRUSTER
CRUSTIER
CRUSTIEST
CRUSTIFIC
CRUSTILY
CRUSTINESS
CRUSTING
CRUSTOSE
CRUSTOSIS
CRUSTS
CRUSTY
CRUT

CRUTCH
CRUTCHED
CRUTCHER
CRUTCHING
CRUTCHLIKE
CRUTH
CRUTTER
CRUX
CRUXES
CRUZADO
CRUZEIRO
CRWTH
CRY
CRYABLE
CRYBABIES
CRYBABY
CRYER
CRYING
CRYINGLY
CRYMODYNIA
CRYMOTHERAPY
CRYOCHORE
CRYOCHORIC
CRYOCONITE
CRYOGEN
CRYOGENIC
CRYOGENY
CRYOHYDRATE
CRYOHYDRIC
CRYOLITE
CRYOLOGY
CRYOMETER
CRYOPHORIC
CRYOPHORUS
CRYOPHYLLITE
CRYOPLANKTON
CRYOSCOPE
CRYOSCOPIC
CRYOSCOPY
CRYOSEL
CRYOSTASE
CRYOSTAT
CRYOTHERAPY
CRYPT
CRYPTAL
CRYPTAMNESIC
CRYPTANALYST
CRYPTARCH
CRYPTARCHY
CRYPTED
CRYPTIC
CRYPTICAL
CRYPTICALLY
CRYPTOBRANCH
CRYPTOCARP
CRYPTOCARPIC
CRYPTOCARPOUS
CRYPTOCEROUS
CRYPTOCOCCI
CRYPTOCOCCIC
CRYPTODEIST
CRYPTODIRAN
CRYPTODIRE
CRYPTODIROUS
CRYPTODOUBLE
CRYPTOGAM
CRYPTOGAMIAN
CRYPTOGAMIC
CRYPTOGAMIST
CRYPTOGAMOUS
CRYPTOGAMY
CRYPTOGENIC
CRYPTOGENOUS
CRYPTOGLIOMA
CRYPTOGRAM
CRYPTOGRAPH
CRYPTOGRAPHER
CRYPTOGRAPHY
CRYPTOHERESY
CRYPTOLOGY
CRYPTOMERE
CRYPTOMEROUS
CRYPTOMNESIA
CRYPTOMNESIC
CRYPTOMONAD
CRYPTONEMA
CRYPTONYM
CRYPTONYMOUS
CRYPTOPAPIST
CRYPTOPHYTE
CRYPTOPIN
CRYPTOPINE
CRYPTORCHID
CRYPTOSCOPE
CRYPTOSCOPY
CRYPTOSTOMA
CRYPTOSTOME
CRYPTOUS
CRYPTOZOIC
CRYPTOZONATE
CRYPTOZYGOUS
CRYSTAL
CRYSTALED
CRYSTALING
CRYSTALITIC
CRYSTALLED
CRYSTALLIC
CRYSTALLIKE
CRYSTALLIN
CRYSTALLINE
CRYSTALLING
CRYSTALLITE
CRYSTALLIZE
CRYSTALLIZED
CRYSTALLIZER
CRYSTALLIZING
CRYSTALLOGRAPH
CRYSTALLOID
CRYSTALS
CRYSTALWORT
CRYSTE
CRYSTIC
CRYSTOGRAPH
CRYSTOLEUM
CRYSTOSPHENE
CSARDAS
CTENE
CTENIDIA
CTENIDIAL
CTENIDIUM
CTENIFORM
CTENII
CTENIZID
CTENOCYST
CTENODACTYL
CTENODONT
CTENOID
CTENOIDEAN
CTENOIDIAN
CTENOLIUM
CTENOPHORAL
CTENOPHORAN
CTENOPHORE
CTENOPHOROUS
CTENOSTOME
CTETOLOGY
CUADRA
CUADRILLA
CUAPINOLE
CUARENTA
CUARTA
CUARTEL
CUARTERON
CUARTILLA
CUARTILLO
CUARTINO
CUARTO
CUB
CUBA
CUBAGE
CUBALAYA
CUBANGLE
CUBANITE
CUBATION
CUBATORY
CUBATURE
CUBBIES
CUBBING
CUBBISH
CUBBISHLY
CUBBISHNESS
CUBBY
CUBBYHOLE
CUBBYHOUSE
CUBBYYEW
CUBE
CUBEB
CUBED
CUBELET
CUBER
CUBERA
CUBIC
CUBICA
CUBICAL
CUBICALLY
CUBICALNESS
CUBICITY
CUBICLE
CUBICONE
CUBICULA
CUBICULAR
CUBICULARY
CUBICULO
CUBICULUM
CUBIFORM
CUBING
CUBISM
CUBIST
CUBIT
CUBITAL
CUBITALE
CUBITALIA
CUBITED
CUBITIERE
CUBITO
CUBITOCARPAL
CUBITOPALMAR
CUBITORADIAL
CUBITUS
CUBMASTER
CUBOID
CUBOIDAL
CUBOIDES
CUBOMEDUSAN
CUCHIA
CUCK
CUCKHOLD
CUCKING
CUCKOLD
CUCKOLDED
CUCKOLDIZE
CUCKOLDLY
CUCKOLDOM
CUCKOLDRY
CUCKOO
CUCKOOFLOWER
CUCKOOMAID
CUCKOOMAIDEN
CUCKOOMATE
CUCKOOPINT
CUCKOOPINTLE
CUCKQUEAN
CUCKSTOOL
CUCOLINE
CUCULARIS
CUCULE
CUCULIFORM
CUCULINE
CUCULLA
CUCULLATE
CUCULLATED
CUCULLATELY
CUCULLIFORM
CUCULLUS
CUCULOID
CUCUMBER
CUCUMIFORM
CUCURB
CUCURBIT
CUCURBITE
CUCURBITINE
CUCUYO
CUD
CUDA
CUDAVA
CUDBEAR
CUDDEN
CUDDIE
CUDDIES
CUDDLE
CUDDLED
CUDDLESOME
CUDDLING
CUDDLY
CUDDY
CUDDYHOLE
CUDEIGH
CUDGEL
CUDGELED
CUDGELER
CUDGELING
CUDGELLED
CUDGELLER
CUDGELLING
CUDGERIE
CUDWEED
CUE
CUEBALL
CUECA
CUED
CUEIST
CUEMAN
CUEMANSHIP
CUEMEN
CUENA
CUER
CUERDA
CUERPO
CUESTA
CUFF
CUFFED
CUFFER
CUFFIN
CUFFING
CUFFLE
CUFFY
CUFFYISM
CUGGERMUGGER
CUICA
CUIDADO
CUIEJO
CUIF
CUINAGE
CUING
CUIR
CUIRASS
CUIRASSED
CUIRASSES
CUIRASSIER
CUISH
CUISINARY
CUISINE
CUISINIER
CUISSE
CUIT
CUITLE
CUITTLE
CUKE
CUL
CULBERT
CULBUT
CULCH
CULEBRA
CULERAGE
CULET
CULETT
CULGEE
CULICID
CULICIDE
CULICIFORM
CULICIFUGAL
CULICIFUGE
CULICINE
CULILAWAN
CULINARILY
CULINARY
CULL
CULLA
CULLAGE
CULLAS
CULLAY
CULLE
CULLED
CULLENDER
CULLER
CULLET
CULLIBLE
CULLIED
CULLIES
CULLING
CULLION
CULLIONLY
CULLIONRY
CULLIONS
CULLIS
CULLY
CULLYING
CULM
CULMEN
CULMICOLOUS
CULMIFEROUS
CULMINAL
CULMINANT
CULMINATE
CULMINATED
CULMINATING
CULMINATION
CULMS
CULMY
CULOT
CULOTTE
CULOTTES
CULOTTIC
CULOTTISM
CULP
CULPA
CULPABILITY
CULPABLE
CULPABLENESS
CULPABLY
CULPATE
CULPATORY
CULPEO
CULPON
CULPOSE

CULPRIT
CULT
CULTCH
CULTELLATION
CULTELLUS
CULTI
CULTIC
CULTIGEN
CULTIROSTRAL
CULTISM
CULTIST
CULTIVABLE
CULTIVABLY
CULTIVAR
CULTIVATABLE
CULTIVATE
CULTIVATED
CULTIVATING
CULTIVATION
CULTIVATOR
CULTIVE
CULTRATE
CULTRATED
CULTURABLE
CULTURAL
CULTURALIST
CULTURALLY
CULTURE
CULTURED
CULTURINE
CULTURIST
CULTUS
CULTUSES
CULVER
CULVERFOOT
CULVERHOUSE
CULVERIN
CULVERINEER
CULVERINER
CULVERKEY
CULVERS
CULVERT
CULVERTAGE
CULVERWORT
CUM
CUMACEAN
CUMACEOUS
CUMAL
CUMALDEHYDE
CUMALIN
CUMAPHYTE
CUMAPHYTIC
CUMAPHYTISM
CUMARU
CUMAY
CUMBENT
CUMBER
CUMBERED
CUMBERING
CUMBERSOME
CUMBERSOMELY
CUMBERWORLD
CUMBHA
CUMBLE
CUMBLY
CUMBRAITE
CUMBRANCE
CUMBRE
CUMBROUS
CUMBROUSLY
CUMBROUSNESS
CUMBU
CUMENE
CUMENGITE
CUMENYL
CUMFLUTTER
CUMHAL
CUMIC
CUMIDIN
CUMIDINE
CUMIN
CUMINOIN
CUMINSEED
CUMLY
CUMMER
CUMMERBUND
CUMMIN
CUMMOCK
CUMOL
CUMQUAT
CUMSHA
CUMSHAW
CUMULANT
CUMULAR
CUMULATE
CUMULATED
CUMULATELY
CUMULATING
CUMULATION
CUMULATIST
CUMULATIVE
CUMULATIVELY
CUMULENE
CUMULI
CUMULIFORM
CUMULITE
CUMULOCIRRUS
CUMULONIMBUS
CUMULOSE
CUMULOUS
CUMULUS
CUMYL
CUNABULA
CUNABULAR
CUNCTATION
CUNCTATIOUS
CUNCTATIVE
CUNCTATOR
CUNCTATORY
CUNCTIPOTENT
CUNDITE
CUNDUM
CUNDY
CUNEAL
CUNEATE
CUNEATED
CUNEATELY
CUNEATIC
CUNEATOR
CUNEI
CUNEIFORM
CUNEIFORMIST
CUNEOCUBOID
CUNETTE
CUNEUS
CUNGEBOI
CUNGEVOI
CUNIC
CUNICULAR
CUNICULI
CUNICULUS
CUNIFORM
CUNIT
CUNJAH
CUNJER
CUNJEVOI
CUNNE
CUNNER
CUNNING
CUNNINGLY
CUNNINGNESS
CUNNY
CUNONIACEOUS
CUNYE
CUNYIE
CUNZIE
CUORIN
CUP
CUPAY
CUPBEARER
CUPBOARD
CUPCAKE
CUPEL
CUPELED
CUPELER
CUPELING
CUPELLATION
CUPELLED
CUPELLER
CUPELLING
CUPFLOWER
CUPFUL
CUPHEAD
CUPHOLDER
CUPIDINOUS
CUPIDITY
CUPIDON
CUPIDONE
CUPIUBA
CUPMAKER
CUPMAKING
CUPMAN
CUPMATE
CUPOLA
CUPOLAED
CUPOLAING
CUPOLAMAN
CUPOLAR
CUPOLAS
CUPOLATED
CUPPED
CUPPEN
CUPPER
CUPPIER
CUPPIEST
CUPPIN
CUPPING
CUPPY
CUPRAMMONIUM
CUPREIN
CUPREINE
CUPRENE
CUPREOUS
CUPRIC
CUPRIDE
CUPRIFEROUS
CUPRITE
CUPROCYANIDE
CUPROID
CUPRONICKEL
CUPROSILICON
CUPROUS
CUPRUM
CUPS
CUPSEED
CUPSTONE
CUPULA
CUPULAR
CUPULATE
CUPULE
CUPULIFEROUS
CUPULIFORM
CUR
CURA
CURABILITY
CURABLE
CURABLENESS
CURABLY
CURACAO
CURACE
CURACIES
CURACY
CURARE
CURARI
CURARINE
CURARIZATION
CURARIZE
CURARIZED
CURARIZING
CURASSOW
CURATAGE
CURATE
CURATEL
CURATESS
CURATIAL
CURATIC
CURATICAL
CURATION
CURATIVE
CURATIVELY
CURATIVENESS
CURATOLATRY
CURATOR
CURATORIAL
CURATORIUM
CURATORSHIP
CURATORY
CURB
CURBASH
CURBING
CURBLINE
CURBSTONE
CURBSTONER
CURBY
CURCAS
CURCH
CURCHY
CURCUDDOCH
CURCULIO
CURCULIONID
CURCULIONIST
CURCULIOS
CURCUMA
CURCUMIN
CURD
CURDED
CURDINESS
CURDING
CURDLE
CURDLED
CURDLER
CURDLING
CURDLY
CURDOO
CURDWORT
CURDY
CURE
CURED
CURELESS
CUREMASTER
CURER
CURET
CURETTAGE
CURETTE
CURETTED
CURETTEMENT
CURETTING
CURFEW
CURIA
CURIAE
CURIAL
CURIALISM
CURIALIST
CURIALISTIC
CURIALITIES
CURIALITY
CURIARA
CURIATE
CURIBOCA
CURIE
CURIEGRAM
CURIESCOPY
CURIET
CURIETHERAPY
CURINE
CURING
CURIO
CURIOLOGIC
CURIOLOGICAL
CURIOLOGICS
CURIOLOGY
CURIOMANIAC
CURIOS
CURIOSA
CURIOSI
CURIOSITIES
CURIOSITY
CURIOSO
CURIOSOS
CURIOUS
CURIOUSLY
CURIOUSNESS
CURIOUSNESSES
CURITE
CURIUM
CURL
CURLED
CURLEDLY
CURLEDNESS
CURLER
CURLEW
CURLEWS
CURLICUE
CURLIER
CURLIEST
CURLIEWURLIE
CURLIEWURLY
CURLINESS
CURLING
CURLINGLY
CURLPAPER
CURLS
CURLY
CURLYCUE
CURLYHEAD
CURLYLOCKS
CURMUDGEON
CURMUDGEONLY
CURMURGING
CURMURRING
CURN
CURNEY
CURNEYS
CURNIE
CURNIES
CURPEL
CURPIN
CURPLE
CURR
CURRACH
CURRACK
CURRAGH
CURRAJONG
CURRAN
CURRANCE
CURRANE
CURRANT
CURRATOW
CURRAWANG
CURRAWONG
CURRENCIES
CURRENCY
CURRENT
CURRENTLY
CURRENTNESS

CURRENTWISE
CURRICLE
CURRICLED
CURRICLING
CURRICULA
CURRICULAR
CURRICULUM
CURRICULUMS
CURRIED
CURRIER
CURRIERIES
CURRIERY
CURRIES
CURRISH
CURRISHLY
CURRISHNESS
CURROCK
CURRY
CURRYCOMB
CURRYFAVEL
CURRYFAVOUR
CURRYING
CURSAL
CURSARO
CURSE
CURSED
CURSEDLY
CURSEDNESS
CURSER
CURSING
CURSITOR
CURSIVE
CURSIVELY
CURSIVENESS
CURSOR
CURSORARY
CURSORIAL
CURSORILY
CURSORINESS
CURSORIOUS
CURSORY
CURST
CURSTFUL
CURSTFULLY
CURSTLY
CURSTNESS
CURSUS
CURT
CURTAIL
CURTAILED
CURTAILEDLY
CURTAILER
CURTAILING
CURTAILMENT
CURTAIN
CURTAINED
CURTAINING
CURTAL
CURTATE
CURTATION
CURTAXE
CURTED
CURTESIES
CURTESY
CURTILAGE
CURTLAX
CURTLY
CURTNESS
CURTSEY
CURTSEYED
CURTSEYING
CURTSEYS
CURTSIED
CURTSIES
CURTSY
CURTSYING
CURUA
CURUBA
CURUCUCU
CURULE
CURUPAY
CURUPAYS
CURUPEY
CURURO
CURUROS
CURVACEOUS
CURVANT
CURVATE
CURVATED
CURVATION
CURVATURE
CURVE
CURVED
CURVEDLY
CURVEDNESS
CURVER
CURVES
CURVET
CURVETED
CURVETING
CURVETTED
CURVETTING
CURVEY
CURVICAUDATE
CURVICOSTATE
CURVIDENTATE
CURVIFOLIATE
CURVIFORM
CURVILINEAL
CURVILINEAR
CURVINERVATE
CURVINERVED
CURVING
CURVIROSTRAL
CURVISERIAL
CURVITAL
CURVITIES
CURVITY
CURVOGRAPH
CURVOMETER
CURVOUS
CURVULATE
CURVY
CURWHIBBLE
CURY
CUSCOHYGRIN
CUSCOHYGRINE
CUSCONIN
CUSCONINE
CUSCUTACEOUS
CUSEC
CUSELITE
CUSH
CUSHA
CUSHAG
CUSHAT
CUSHAW
CUSHIE
CUSHIER
CUSHIEST
CUSHION
CUSHIONED
CUSHIONING
CUSHIONLIKE
CUSHIONY
CUSHY
CUSIE
CUSINERO
CUSK
CUSKS
CUSP
CUSPAL
CUSPATE
CUSPATED
CUSPED
CUSPID
CUSPIDAL
CUSPIDATE
CUSPIDATED
CUSPIDATION
CUSPIDES
CUSPIDOR
CUSPING
CUSPIS
CUSPULE
CUSS
CUSSED
CUSSEDLY
CUSSEDNESS
CUSSER
CUSTARD
CUSTERITE
CUSTODEE
CUSTODIA
CUSTODIAL
CUSTODIAN
CUSTODIER
CUSTODIES
CUSTODY
CUSTOM
CUSTOMABLE
CUSTOMABLY
CUSTOMANCE
CUSTOMARIES
CUSTOMARILY
CUSTOMARY
CUSTOMED
CUSTOMER
CUSTOMHOUSE
CUSTOMING
CUSTOMLY
CUSTOMS
CUSTOS
CUSTREL
CUSTRON
CUSTROUN
CUSTUMAL
CUT
CUTANEAL
CUTANEOUS
CUTAWAY
CUTBACK
CUTBANK
CUTCH
CUTCHA
CUTCHER
CUTCHERIES
CUTCHERRIES
CUTCHERRY
CUTCHERY
CUTDOWN
CUTE
CUTELY
CUTENESS
CUTER
CUTEST
CUTGRASS
CUTHEAL
CUTICLE
CUTICOLOR
CUTICULA
CUTICULAR
CUTICULARIZE
CUTICULATE
CUTIDURE
CUTIDURIS
CUTIE
CUTIES
CUTIFICATION
CUTIGERAL
CUTIKIN
CUTIN
CUTINIZATION
CUTINIZE
CUTINIZED
CUTINIZING
CUTIREACTION
CUTIS
CUTISECTOR
CUTITIS
CUTIZATION
CUTLAS
CUTLASH
CUTLASS
CUTLER
CUTLERESS
CUTLERY
CUTLET
CUTLING
CUTLINGS
CUTLIPS
CUTOFF
CUTOUT
CUTOVER
CUTPURSE
CUTS
CUTTABLE
CUTTAGE
CUTTAIL
CUTTANEE
CUTTED
CUTTER
CUTTERHEAD
CUTTHROAT
CUTTIES
CUTTIKIN
CUTTING
CUTTINGLY
CUTTINGNESS
CUTTINGS
CUTTLE
CUTTLEBONE
CUTTLEFISH
CUTTLEFISHES
CUTTLER
CUTTOO
CUTTOOS
CUTTY
CUTTYHUNK
CUTUP
CUTUPS
CUTWATER
CUTWEED
CUTWORK
CUTWORM
CUVAGE
CUVEE
CUVETTE
CUVIES
CUVY
CUYA
CUYAS
CUZCENO
CWIERC
CWM
CYAMELID
CYAMELIDE
CYANACETIC
CYANAMID
CYANAMIDE
CYANATE
CYANAURATE
CYANAURIC
CYANBENZYL
CYANEAN
CYANEMIA
CYANEOUS
CYANFORMATE
CYANFORMIC
CYANHYDRATE
CYANHYDRIC
CYANHYDRIN
CYANICIDE
CYANID
CYANIDATION
CYANIDE
CYANIDED
CYANIDIN
CYANIDINE
CYANIDING
CYANIDROSIS
CYANIMIDE
CYANIN
CYANINE
CYANITE
CYANIZE
CYANIZED
CYANIZING
CYANOACETATE
CYANOACETIC
CYANOAURATE
CYANOAURIC
CYANOBENZENE
CYANOCHROIA
CYANOCHROIC
CYANODERMA
CYANOGEN
CYANOGENESIS
CYANOGENETIC
CYANOHYDRIN
CYANOMETER
CYANOMETRIC
CYANOMETRIES
CYANOMETRY
CYANOPATHIC
CYANOPATHY
CYANOPHIL
CYANOPHILE
CYANOPHILOUS
CYANOPHORIC
CYANOPHOSE
CYANOPHYCEAN
CYANOPIA
CYANOPLASTID
CYANOPSIA
CYANOSE
CYANOSIS
CYANOSITE
CYANOTIC
CYANOTYPE
CYANURAMIDE
CYANURET
CYANURIC
CYANUS
CYAPHENINE
CYATH
CYATHIFORM
CYATHIUM
CYATHOLITH
CYATHOS
CYATHOZOOID
CYATHUS
CYBERNETIC
CYBERNETICS
CYCAD
CYCADACEOUS
CYCADEAN
CYCADEOID
CYCADEOUS
CYCADIFORM
CYCADITE
CYCLADES
CYCLAMEN
CYCLAMIN
CYCLAMINE

CYCLANE
CYCLAR
CYCLAS
CYCLE
CYCLECAR
CYCLED
CYCLENE
CYCLER
CYCLESMITH
CYCLIAN
CYCLIC
CYCLICAL
CYCLICALLY
CYCLIDE
CYCLINDROID
CYCLING
CYCLIST
CYCLISTIC
CYCLITIS
CYCLIZATION
CYCLIZE
CYCLOALKANE
CYCLOCOELIC
CYCLOCOELOUS
CYCLODIOLEFIN
CYCLODIOLEFINE
CYCLOGANOID
CYCLOGRAM
CYCLOGRAPH
CYCLOGRAPHER
CYCLOHEPTANE
CYCLOHEXANE
CYCLOHEXANOL
CYCLOHEXENE
CYCLOHEXYL
CYCLOID
CYCLOIDAL
CYCLOIDALLY
CYCLOIDEAN
CYCLOIDIAN
CYCLOLITH
CYCLOMANIA
CYCLOMETER
CYCLOMETRIC
CYCLOMETRIES
CYCLOMETRY
CYCLOMYARIAN
CYCLONAL
CYCLONE
CYCLONIC
CYCLONICAL
CYCLONICALLY
CYCLONIST
CYCLONOLOGY
CYCLONOMETER
CYCLONOSCOPE
CYCLOOLEFIN
CYCLOOLEFINE
CYCLOPAEDIA
CYCLOPAEDIAS
CYCLOPAEDIC
CYCLOPAEDIST
CYCLOPE
CYCLOPEAN
CYCLOPEDIA
CYCLOPEDIAS
CYCLOPEDIC
CYCLOPEDICAL
CYCLOPEDIST
CYCLOPENTANE
CYCLOPENTENE
CYCLOPHORIA
CYCLOPHORIC
CYCLOPIA
CYCLOPISM
CYCLOPITE
CYCLOPLEGIA
CYCLOPLEGIC
CYCLOPOID
CYCLOPROPANE
CYCLOPTEROID
CYCLOPY
CYCLORAMA
CYCLORAMAS
CYCLORAMIC
CYCLOSCOPE
CYCLOSE
CYCLOSIS
CYCLOSPOROUS
CYCLOSTOMATE
CYCLOSTOME
CYCLOSTYLE
CYCLOTHEM
CYCLOTHYME
CYCLOTHYMIA
CYCLOTHYMIAC
CYCLOTHYMIC
CYCLOTOME
CYCLOTOMIC
CYCLOTOMY
CYCLOTRON
CYCLUS
CYDIPPIAN
CYDIPPID
CYDONIUM
CYESIOLOGY
CYESIS
CYGNEOUS
CYGNET
CYGNINE
CYKE
CYLICES
CYLINDER
CYLINDERED
CYLINDERER
CYLINDERING
CYLINDERS
CYLINDRIC
CYLINDRICAL
CYLINDRICULE
CYLINDRIFORM
CYLINDRITE
CYLINDROID
CYLINDROIDAL
CYLINDROMA
CYLINDROMATA
CYLINDRURIA
CYLIX
CYLLOSES
CYLLOSIS
CYMA
CYMAE
CYMAPHEN
CYMAR
CYMARIN
CYMAROSE
CYMATIA
CYMATION
CYMATIUM
CYMBA
CYMBAL
CYMBALED
CYMBALEER
CYMBALIST
CYMBALLED
CYMBALLING
CYMBALOM
CYMBALS
CYMBATE
CYMBID
CYMBIFORM
CYMBLIN
CYMBLING
CYMBOCEPHALY
CYME
CYMENE
CYMIFEROUS
CYMLIN
CYMLING
CYMOGENE
CYMOGRAPH
CYMOGRAPHIC
CYMOID
CYMOMETER
CYMOPHANE
CYMOPHANOUS
CYMOPHENOL
CYMOSCOPE
CYMOSE
CYMOSELY
CYMOTRICHY
CYMOUS
CYMRITE
CYMULE
CYMULOSE
CYNANCHE
CYNANTHROPY
CYNARACEOUS
CYNAREOUS
CYNAROID
CYNEBOT
CYNEGETIC
CYNEGETICS
CYNEGILD
CYNHYENA
CYNIATRIA
CYNIATRICS
CYNIC
CYNICAL
CYNICALLY
CYNICALNESS
CYNICISM
CYNICIST
CYNIPID
CYNIPIDOUS
CYNIPOID
CYNISM
CYNOCEPHALIC
CYNOCEPHALUS
CYNOCLEPT
CYNODON
CYNODONT
CYNOID
CYNOLOGY
CYNOMORPHIC
CYNOMORPHOUS
CYNOPHILE
CYNOPHILIC
CYNOPHILIST
CYNOPHOBE
CYNOPHOBIA
CYNOPODOUS
CYNORRHODA
CYNORRHODON
CYNOSURAL
CYNOSURE
CYNOTHERAPY
CYP
CYPERACEOUS
CYPHELLA
CYPHELLAE
CYPHELLATE
CYPHER
CYPHONAUTES
CYPHONISM
CYPRAEA
CYPRAEID
CYPRAEIFORM
CYPRE
CYPRES
CYPRESS
CYPRESSED
CYPRESSES
CYPRESSROOT
CYPRID
CYPRIDINOID
CYPRINE
CYPRINID
CYPRINIFORM
CYPRININ
CYPRININE
CYPRINODONT
CYPRINODONTOID
CYPRINOID
CYPRINOIDEAN
CYPRIPEDIUM
CYPSELA
CYPSELAE
CYPSELINE
CYPSELOID
CYPSELOMORPH
CYPSELOUS
CYRTOLITE
CYRTOMETER
CYRTOPIA
CYRTOSIS
CYRTOSTYLE
CYRUS
CYST
CYSTADENOMA
CYSTAL
CYSTALGIA
CYSTATROPHIA
CYSTATROPHY
CYSTECTASIA
CYSTECTASY
CYSTECTOMIES
CYSTECTOMY
CYSTED
CYSTEIN
CYSTEINE
CYSTEINIC
CYSTELCOSIS
CYSTENCHYMA
CYSTENCHYME
CYSTENCYTE
CYSTERETHISM
CYSTIC
CYSTICARPIC
CYSTICARPIUM
CYSTICERCI
CYSTICERCOID
CYSTICERCUS
CYSTICOLOUS
CYSTID
CYSTIDIA
CYSTIDIUM
CYSTIDIUMS
CYSTIFEROUS
CYSTIFORM
CYSTIGEROUS
CYSTIN
CYSTINE
CYSTINURIA
CYSTIRRHEA
CYSTIS
CYSTITIS
CYSTITOME
CYSTOADENOMA
CYSTOCARP
CYSTOCARPIC
CYSTOCELE
CYSTOCYTE
CYSTODYNIA
CYSTOFIBROMA
CYSTOGENESIS
CYSTOGRAM
CYSTOID
CYSTOIDEAN
CYSTOLITH
CYSTOLITHIC
CYSTOMA
CYSTOMATA
CYSTOMYOMA
CYSTOMYXOMA
CYSTONECTOUS
CYSTOPHORE
CYSTOPLASTY
CYSTOPLEGIA
CYSTOPTOSIS
CYSTORRHAGIA
CYSTORRHAPHY
CYSTORRHEA
CYSTOSARCOMA
CYSTOSCHISIS
CYSTOSCOPE
CYSTOSCOPIC
CYSTOSCOPY
CYSTOSE
CYSTOSPASM
CYSTOSPASTIC
CYSTOSTOMIES
CYSTOSTOMY
CYSTOSYRINX
CYSTOTOME
CYSTOTOMY
CYSTOUS
CYTASE
CYTASIC
CYTASTER
CYTE
CYTHERA
CYTIDINE
CYTIODERM
CYTIODERMA
CYTISINE
CYTITIS
CYTOBLAST
CYTOBLASTEMA
CYTOCHROME
CYTOCHYLEMA
CYTOCIDE
CYTOCLASIS
CYTOCLASTIC
CYTOCOCCI
CYTOCOCCUS
CYTOCYST
CYTODE
CYTODENDRITE
CYTODERM
CYTODIERESIS
CYTOGAMY
CYTOGENE
CYTOGENESIS
CYTOGENETIC
CYTOGENETICS
CYTOGENIC
CYTOGENOUS
CYTOGENY
CYTOGLOBIN
CYTOID
CYTOKINESIS
CYTOLIST
CYTOLOGIC
CYTOLOGICAL
CYTOLOGICALLY
CYTOLOGIES
CYTOLOGIST
CYTOLOGY
CYTOLYMPH
CYTOLYSIN
CYTOLYSIS
CYTOLYTIC
CYTOME
CYTOMERE

CYTOMETER
CYTON
CYTONE
CYTOPHAGOUS
CYTOPHARYNX
CYTOPHIL
CYTOPHYSICS
CYTOPHYSIOLOGY
CYTOPLASM
CYTOPLASMIC
CYTOPLAST
CYTOPLASTIC
CYTOPROCT
CYTOPYGE
CYTORYCTES
CYTOSIN
CYTOSINE
CYTOSOME
CYTOST
CYTOSTOMAL
CYTOSTOME
CYTOSTROMA
CYTOSTROMATIC
CYTOTACTIC
CYTOTAXIS
CYTOTOXIC
CYTOTOXIN
CYTOTROPHY
CYTOTROPIC
CYTOTROPISM
CYTOZOIC
CYTOZOON
CYTOZYMASE
CYTOZYME
CYTULA
CYTULAE
CYWYDD
CZAR
CZARDOM
CZAREVITCH
CZAREVNA
CZARINA
CZARINIAN
CZARISH
CZARISM
CZARIST
CZARISTIC
CZARITZA
CZIGANY

D

DA
DAALDER
DAB
DABB
DABBA
DABBED
DABBER
DABBING
DABBLE
DABBLED
DABBLER
DABBLING
DABBLINGLY
DABBLINGNESS
DABBY
DABCHICK
DABOIA
DABOYA
DABSTER
DABUH
DACE
DACELONINE
DACES
DACHA
DACHS
DACHSHUND
DACITE
DACITIC
DACKER
DACOIT
DACOITAGE
DACOITED
DACOITIES
DACOITING
DACOITS
DACOITY
DACRYOCYST
DACRYOLITE
DACRYOLITH
DACRYOMA
DACRYON
DACRYOPS
DACTYLAR
DACTYLATE
DACTYLIC
DACTYLICALLY
DACTYLIOLOGY
DACTYLION
DACTYLIST
DACTYLITIC
DACTYLITIS
DACTYLOGRAM
DACTYLOGRAPH
DACTYLOID
DACTYLOLOGY
DACTYLONOMY
DACTYLOPORE
DACTYLORHIZA
DACTYLOSCOPY
DACTYLOSE
DACTYLOTHECA
DACTYLOUS
DACTYLOZOOID
DACTYLUS
DAD
DADA
DADAISM
DADAIST
DADAISTIC
DADAP
DADDER
DADDING
DADDLE
DADDLED
DADDLING
DADDOCK
DADDOCKY
DADDY
DADDYNUT
DADE
DADED
DADENHUDD
DADING
DADO
DADOED
DADOES
DADOING
DADOUCHOS
DADUCHUS
DAEDAL
DAEDALOID
DAEKON
DAEMON
DAEMONES
DAEMONIC
DAEMONIES
DAEMONS
DAEMONURGIST
DAEMONURGY
DAEMONY
DAENA
DAER
DAEVA
DAFF
DAFFADILLY
DAFFED
DAFFERY
DAFFIER
DAFFIEST
DAFFING
DAFFISH
DAFFLE
DAFFLED
DAFFLING
DAFFODIL
DAFFODILLY
DAFFY
DAFT
DAFTAR
DAFTARDAR
DAFTBERRY
DAFTLY
DAFTNESS
DAG
DAGABA
DAGAME
DAGASSA
DAGESH
DAGG
DAGGA
DAGGAR
DAGGE
DAGGED
DAGGER
DAGGERBUSH
DAGGERED
DAGGERING
DAGGERS
DAGGING
DAGGLE
DAGGLED
DAGGLETAIL
DAGGLETAILED
DAGGLING
DAGGLY
DAGGY
DAGH
DAGHESH
DAGLOCK
DAGO
DAGOBA
DAGOES
DAGON
DAGOS
DAGS
DAGSWAIN
DAGUE
DAGUILLA
DAH
DAHABEAH
DAHABEEYAH
DAHABIAH
DAHABIEH
DAHABIYEH
DAHI
DAHIL
DAHLIA
DAHOMEY
DAHOON
DAIDLE
DAIDLED
DAIDLIE
DAIDLING
DAIDLY
DAIGH
DAIKER
DAIKON
DAILIES
DAILINESS
DAILY
DAIM
DAIMEN
DAIMIATE
DAIMIEL
DAIMIO
DAIMIOATE
DAIMIOS
DAIMIOTE
DAIMON
DAIMONIC
DAIMONION
DAIMONISTIC
DAIMYO
DAIN
DAINCHA
DAINCHAS
DAINFUL
DAINT
DAINTETH
DAINTIER
DAINTIES
DAINTIEST
DAINTIFIED
DAINTIFY
DAINTIFYING
DAINTILY
DAINTINESS
DAINTITH
DAINTREL
DAINTY
DAIQUIRI
DAIRA
DAIRI
DAIRIES
DAIROUS
DAIRT
DAIRY
DAIRYING
DAIRYMAID
DAIRYMAN
DAIRYMEN
DAIRYWOMAN
DAIRYWOMEN
DAIS
DAISED
DAISEE
DAISES
DAISIED
DAISIES
DAISING
DAISY
DAISYBUSH
DAITYA
DAIVA
DAK
DAKER
DAKHMA
DAKOIT
DAKOO
DAKTYLOS
DAKU
DAL
DALAG
DALAGA
DALAR
DALE
DALER
DALES
DALESFOLK
DALESMAN
DALESMEN
DALESPEOPLE
DALESWOMAN
DALETH
DALIS
DALK
DALLACK
DALLE
DALLES
DALLI
DALLIANCE
DALLIED
DALLIER
DALLIS
DALLOP
DALLY
DALLYING
DALLYINGLY
DALLYMAN
DALMATIC
DALO
DALT
DALTEEN
DAM
DAMA
DAMAGE
DAMAGEABLE
DAMAGEABLY
DAMAGED
DAMAGEOUS
DAMAGER
DAMAGES
DAMAGING
DAMAN
DAMAR
DAMAS
DAMASCENE
DAMASCENED
DAMASCENER
DAMASCENINE
DAMASCENING
DAMASK
DAMASKEEN
DAMASKIN
DAMASKINE
DAMASSE
DAMASSIN
DAMBO
DAMBOARD
DAMBONITOL
DAMBOSE
DAMBROD
DAME
DAMENIZATION
DAMEWORT
DAMFOOL
DAMIANA
DAMIE
DAMIER
DAMINE
DAMKJERNITE
DAMMAR
DAMMARET
DAMME
DAMMED
DAMMER
DAMMING
DAMMISH
DAMMIT
DAMN
DAMNABILITY
DAMNABLE
DAMNABLENESS
DAMNABLY
DAMNATION
DAMNATORY
DAMNDEST
DAMNED
DAMNEDEST
DAMNER
DAMNIFIED
DAMNIFY
DAMNIFYING
DAMNING
DAMNINGLY
DAMNINGNESS
DAMNOUS
DAMNOUSLY
DAMNUM
DAMOISEAU
DAMOISELLE
DAMONICO
DAMOSEL
DAMOURITE
DAMOZEL
DAMP
DAMPANG
DAMPED
DAMPEN
DAMPENED
DAMPENER
DAMPENING
DAMPER
DAMPEST
DAMPING
DAMPISH
DAMPLY
DAMPNESS
DAMPPROOF
DAMPPROOFING
DAMSEL
DAMSELFISH
DAMSITE
DAMSON
DAMYANKEE
DAN
DANAIDE
DANAINE
DANAITE
DANALITE
DANARO
DANBURITE
DANCALITE
DANCE
DANCED

DANCER
DANCERESS
DANCERS
DANCERY
DANCES
DANCETTE
DANCETTEE
DANCETTY
DANCING
DAND
DANDA
DANDELION
DANDER
DANDI
DANDIACAL
DANDIACALLY
DANDIE
DANDIER
DANDIES
DANDIEST
DANDIFIED
DANDIFY
DANDIFYING
DANDILLY
DANDILY
DANDIPRAT
DANDIS
DANDISETTE
DANDIZETTE
DANDLE
DANDLED
DANDLER
DANDLING
DANDRUFF
DANDRUFFY
DANDY
DANDYISH
DANDYISM
DANDYIZE
DANDYPRAT
DANEWORT
DANG
DANGER
DANGEROUS
DANGEROUSLY
DANGERSOME
DANGLE
DANGLEBERRY
DANGLED
DANGLER
DANGLIN
DANGLING
DANGLINGLY
DANICISM
DANIO
DANK
DANKER
DANKEST
DANKISH
DANKISHNESS
DANKLY
DANKNESS
DANLI
DANNEMORITE
DANNER
DANNOCK
DANSANT
DANSEUR
DANSEUSE
DANSEUSES
DANSY
DANTA
DANTON
DANZA
DANZON
DAO
DAOINE
DAP
DAPHNE
DAPHNETIN
DAPHNI
DAPHNID
DAPHNIN
DAPHNITE
DAPICHO
DAPICO
DAPIFER
DAPPED
DAPPER
DAPPERLING
DAPPERLY
DAPPERNESS
DAPPING
DAPPLE
DAPPLED
DAPPLING
DAPS
DAR
DARABUKKA
DARAC
DARAF
DARAK
DARAT
DARB
DARBHA
DARBIES
DARBUKKA
DARBY
DARCY
DARDANARIUS
DARDANIUM
DARDAOL
DARE
DAREALL
DARED
DAREDEVIL
DAREDEVILRY
DAREDEVILTRY
DAREFUL
DARER
DARES
DARESAY
DARG
DARGAH
DARGER
DARGSMAN
DARGUE
DARI
DARIBAH
DARIC
DARING
DARINGLY
DARINGNESS
DARIOLE
DARK
DARKED
DARKEN
DARKENED
DARKENER
DARKENING
DARKER
DARKEST
DARKEY
DARKEYS
DARKFUL
DARKIE
DARKIES
DARKING
DARKISH
DARKISHNESS
DARKLE
DARKLED
DARKLING
DARKLINGS
DARKLY
DARKMANS
DARKNESS
DARKROOM
DARKS
DARKSKIN
DARKSOME
DARKSOMENESS
DARKSUM
DARKY
DARLING
DARLINGLY
DARLINGNESS
DARN
DARNDEST
DARNED
DARNEDEST
DARNEL
DARNER
DARNEX
DARNING
DAROGA
DAROGAH
DAROGHA
DAROO
DARR
DARREIN
DARSHAN
DARSHANA
DARSO
DARST
DART
DARTARS
DARTED
DARTER
DARTING
DARTINGLY
DARTINGNESS
DARTLE
DARTLIKE
DARTMAN
DARTOS
DARTRE
DARTROSE
DARTS
DARWAN
DARWESH
DARZEE
DARZI
DAS
DASEIN
DASH
DASHBOARD
DASHED
DASHEDLY
DASHEE
DASHEEN
DASHEL
DASHER
DASHIER
DASHIEST
DASHING
DASHINGLY
DASHMAKER
DASHPLATE
DASHPOT
DASHT
DASHWHEEL
DASHY
DASI
DASS
DASSENT
DASSIE
DASSY
DAST
DASTARD
DASTARDIZE
DASTARDLY
DASTARDY
DASTUR
DASTURI
DASWEN
DASYMETER
DASYPAEDAL
DASYPAEDES
DASYURE
DASYURID
DASYURINE
DASYUROID
DATA
DATABLE
DATANA
DATARIA
DATARIES
DATARY
DATCH
DATCHA
DATE
DATED
DATELESS
DATELINE
DATEMARK
DATER
DATIL
DATING
DATIO
DATION
DATISCETIN
DATISCIN
DATISCOSID
DATISCOSIDE
DATIVAL
DATIVE
DATIVELY
DATO
DATOLITE
DATOLITIC
DATTO
DATTOCK
DATTOS
DATU
DATUM
DATURISM
DAUB
DAUBE
DAUBED
DAUBER
DAUBERY
DAUBING
DAUBREEITE
DAUBREELITE
DAUBREITE
DAUBRY
DAUBSTER
DAUBY
DAUD
DAUDED
DAUDING
DAUDIT
DAUERLAUF
DAUGHTER
DAUGHTERLY
DAUGHTERS
DAUKIN
DAULT
DAUNCH
DAUNCY
DAUNDER
DAUNER
DAUNT
DAUNTED
DAUNTER
DAUNTING
DAUNTINGLY
DAUNTINGNESS
DAUNTLESS
DAUNTLESSLY
DAUPHIN
DAUPHINE
DAUPHINESS
DAURNA
DAUT
DAUTIE
DAUW
DAVACH
DAVAINEA
DAVEN
DAVENPORT
DAVER
DAVERDY
DAVIDSONITE
DAVIELY
DAVIES
DAVIESITE
DAVIT
DAVOCH
DAVY
DAVYNE
DAW
DAWCOCK
DAWDLE
DAWDLED
DAWDLER
DAWDLING
DAWISH
DAWK
DAWKIN
DAWN
DAWNED
DAWNING
DAWNY
DAWPATE
DAWSONITE
DAWT
DAWTIE
DAWUT
DAY
DAYABHAGA
DAYAL
DAYAN
DAYBEAM
DAYBED
DAYBERRY
DAYBLUSH
DAYBOOK
DAYBREAK
DAYDAWN
DAYDREAM
DAYDREAMED
DAYDREAMER
DAYDREAMY
DAYDRUDGE
DAYFLOWER
DAYFLY
DAYLIGHT
DAYLIGHTED
DAYLIGHTING
DAYLIGHTS
DAYLILIES
DAYLILY
DAYLIT
DAYLONG
DAYMAN
DAYMARE
DAYMARK
DAYMEN
DAYMENT
DAYNET
DAYROOM
DAYS
DAYSHINE

DAYSIDE
DAYSMAN
DAYSPRING
DAYSTAR
DAYSTREAK
DAYTALE
DAYTIDE
DAYTIME
DAYTIMES
DAYWORK
DAYWORKER
DAYWRIT
DAZE
DAZED
DAZEDLY
DAZEDNESS
DAZING
DAZY
DAZZLE
DAZZLED
DAZZLER
DAZZLING
DAZZLINGLY
DE
DEACETYLATE
DEACON
DEACONAL
DEACONATE
DEACONESS
DEACONRIES
DEACONRY
DEACONSHIP
DEACTIVATE
DEACTIVATED
DEACTIVATING
DEACTIVATION
DEAD
DEADBEAT
DEADBORN
DEADEN
DEADENED
DEADENER
DEADENING
DEADER
DEADEYE
DEADFALL
DEADHEAD
DEADHEARTED
DEADHOUSE
DEADING
DEADISH
DEADISHLY
DEADISHNESS
DEADLATCH
DEADLIER
DEADLIEST
DEADLIGHT
DEADLINE
DEADLINESS
DEADLOCK
DEADLY
DEADMAN
DEADMELT
DEADNESS
DEADPAN
DEADPANNED
DEADPANNING
DEADPAY
DEADS
DEADTONGUE
DEADWOOD
DEADWORKS
DEADWORT
DEAERATE
DEAERATION
DEAERATOR
DEAF
DEAFEN
DEAFENED
DEAFENING
DEAFENINGLY
DEAFISH
DEAFLY
DEAFNESS
DEAL
DEALATE
DEALATED
DEALATION
DEALBATE
DEALBATION
DEALER
DEALERS
DEALFISH
DEALFISHES
DEALING
DEALKALIZE
DEALKYLATE
DEALKYLATION
DEALT
DEAMBULATION
DEAMBULATORY
DEAMIDASE
DEAMIDATE
DEAMINASE
DEAMINATE
DEAMINATION
DEAN
DEANER
DEANERIES
DEANERY
DEANESS
DEANSHIP
DEAR
DEARBORN
DEARER
DEAREST
DEARIE
DEARIES
DEARLING
DEARLY
DEARN
DEARNESS
DEARSENICATE
DEARTH
DEARTHFU
DEARWORTH
DEARWORTHILY
DEARY
DEAS
DEASIL
DEASPIRATE
DEASPIRATION
DEATH
DEATHBED
DEATHBLOW
DEATHCUP
DEATHDAY
DEATHFUL
DEATHIFY
DEATHIN
DEATHINESS
DEATHLESS
DEATHLESSLY
DEATHLIKE
DEATHLINESS
DEATHLY
DEATHROOT
DEATHSMAN
DEATHSMEN
DEATHTRAP
DEATHWATCH
DEATHWEED
DEATHWORM
DEATHY
DEAURATE
DEAVE
DEAVED
DEAVELY
DEAVING
DEBACLE
DEBAG
DEBAR
DEBARK
DEBARKATION
DEBARKMENT
DEBARMENT
DEBARRANCE
DEBARRASS
DEBARRATION
DEBARRED
DEBARRING
DEBASE
DEBASED
DEBASEMENT
DEBASER
DEBASING
DEBAT
DEBATABLE
DEBATE
DEBATEFUL
DEBATEFULLY
DEBATEMENT
DEBATER
DEBATING
DEBATINGLY
DEBATTER
DEBAUCH
DEBAUCHED
DEBAUCHEDLY
DEBAUCHEDNESS
DEBAUCHEE
DEBAUCHER
DEBAUCHERIES
DEBAUCHERY
DEBAUCHING
DEBAUCHMENT
DEBBIES
DEBEL
DEBELL
DEBELLATE
DEBELLATION
DEBELLATOR
DEBEN
DEBENTURE
DEBENTURED
DEBENZOLIZE
DEBILE
DEBILISSIMA
DEBILITANT
DEBILITATE
DEBILITATED
DEBILITATING
DEBILITATION
DEBILITATIVE
DEBILITY
DEBIND
DEBIT
DEBITED
DEBITEUSE
DEBITING
DEBITOR
DEBITUM
DEBLAI
DEBLATERATE
DEBLOCK
DEBOISE
DEBOIST
DEBONAIR
DEBONAIRE
DEBONAIRITY
DEBONAIRLY
DEBONAIRNESS
DEBONNAIRE
DEBORD
DEBORDMENT
DEBOSH
DEBOSHED
DEBOSS
DEBOUCH
DEBOUCHE
DEBOUCHMENT
DEBOUCHURE
DEBOUT
DEBOWEL
DEBRIDE
DEBRIDEMENT
DEBRIEF
DEBRIS
DEBRUISE
DEBT
DEBTED
DEBTEE
DEBTFUL
DEBTOR
DEBTS
DEBUG
DEBUGGED
DEBUGGING
DEBUNK
DEBUNKER
DEBUNKMENT
DEBURSE
DEBUS
DEBUT
DEBUTANT
DEBUTANTE
DEBUTED
DEBUTING
DEBYE
DECACHORD
DECAD
DECADAL
DECADALLY
DECADARY
DECADATION
DECADE
DECADENCE
DECADENCY
DECADENT
DECADENZA
DECADESCENT
DECADIANOME
DECADIC
DECADIST
DECADRACHMA
DECADRACHMAE
DECAEDRON
DECAFFEINIZE
DECAFID
DECAGON
DECAGONAL
DECAGONALLY
DECAGRAM
DECAGRAMME
DECAHEDRA
DECAHEDRAL
DECAHEDRON
DECAHEDRONS
DECAHYDRATE
DECAHYDRATED
DECAL
DECALAGE
DECALCIFIED
DECALCIFIER
DECALCIFY
DECALCIFYING
DECALCOMANIA
DECALESCENCE
DECALESCENT
DECALITER
DECALITRE
DECALOBATE
DECALVANT
DECALVATION
DECAMERAL
DECAMEROUS
DECAMETER
DECAMETER
DECAMETRE
DECAMP
DECAMPED
DECAMPING
DECAMPMENT
DECAN
DECANAL
DECANALLY
DECANATE
DECANDENTLY
DECANDROUS
DECANE
DECANI
DECANICALLY
DECANOL
DECANOYL
DECANT
DECANTATE
DECANTATION
DECANTER
DECANTIST
DECAPITABLE
DECAPITATE
DECAPITATED
DECAPITATING
DECAPITATION
DECAPITATOR
DECAPOD
DECAPODAL
DECAPODAN
DECAPODIFORM
DECAPODOUS
DECAPPER
DECAPSULATE
DECARBONATE
DECARBONATED
DECARBONATING
DECARBONATOR
DECARBONIZE
DECARBONIZED
DECARBONIZER
DECARBURIZE
DECARBURIZED
DECARCH
DECARCHIES
DECARCHY
DECARD
DECARE
DECARHINUS
DECARNATE
DECARNATED
DECASEMIC
DECAST
DECASTELLATE
DECASTERE
DECASTICH
DECASUALIZE
DECASYLLABIC
DECASYLLABLE
DECATE
DECATHLON
DECATING
DECATIZE
DECATIZER
DECATOIC
DECATYL
DECAUDATE

DECAUDATION
DECAY
DECAYED
DECAYEDNESS
DECAYER
DECAYING
DECEASE
DECEASED
DECEASING
DECEDE
DECEDENT
DECEIT
DECEITFUL
DECEITFULLY
DECEITFULNESS
DECEIVABLE
DECEIVABLY
DECEIVE
DECEIVED
DECEIVER
DECEIVING
DECEIVINGLY
DECELERATE
DECELERATED
DECELERATING
DECELERATION
DECELERATOR
DECEMVIR
DECEMVIRAL
DECEMVIRATE
DECEMVIRI
DECEMVIRS
DECENARY
DECENCE
DECENCIES
DECENCY
DECENE
DECENNAL
DECENNARY
DECENNIA
DECENNIAL
DECENNIALLY
DECENNIUM
DECENNIUMS
DECENT
DECENTER
DECENTERED
DECENTERING
DECENTLY
DECENTNESS
DECENTRALISM
DECENTRALIST
DECENTRALIZE
DECENTRATION
DECENTRE
DECENTRED
DECENTRING
DECENYL
DECEPTIBLE
DECEPTION
DECEPTIOUS
DECEPTIOUSLY
DECEPTITIOUS
DECEPTIVE
DECEPTIVELY
DECEPTIVENESS
DECEPTIVITY
DECEREBRATE
DECEREBRATED
DECEREBRATING
DECEREBRIZE
DECERN
DECERNITURE
DECERP
DECESS
DECESSION
DECHENITE
DECHORALIZE
DECIARE
DECIBEL
DECICERONIZE
DECIDABLE
DECIDE
DECIDED
DECIDEDLY
DECIDEDNESS
DECIDER
DECIDING
DECIDINGLY
DECIDUA
DECIDUAL
DECIDUARY
DECIDUATE
DECIDUITIS
DECIDUOMA
DECIDUOUS
DECIDUOUSLY
DECIGRAM
DECIGRAMME
DECIL
DECILE
DECILITER
DECILITRE
DECILLION
DECILLIONTH
DECIMA
DECIMAL
DECIMALISM
DECIMALIST
DECIMALIZE
DECIMALIZED
DECIMALIZING
DECIMALLY
DECIMATE
DECIMATED
DECIMATING
DECIMATION
DECIMATOR
DECIME
DECIMESTRIAL
DECIMETER
DECIMETRE
DECIMOLAR
DECIMOLE
DECIMOSEXTO
DECINE
DECINORMAL
DECIPHER
DECIPHERED
DECIPHERER
DECIPHERING
DECIPHERMENT
DECIPIUM
DECIPOLAR
DECISE
DECISION
DECISIONAL
DECISIVE
DECISIVELY
DECISIVENESS
DECISTERE
DECIVILIZE
DECK
DECKE
DECKED
DECKEL
DECKEN
DECKER
DECKHAND
DECKHEAD
DECKHOUSE
DECKIE
DECKING
DECKLE
DECKLOAD
DECKMAN
DECKS
DECLAIM
DECLAIMANT
DECLAIMED
DECLAIMER
DECLAIMING
DECLAMANDO
DECLAMATION
DECLAMATORY
DECLARANT
DECLARATION
DECLARATIVE
DECLARATOR
DECLARATORY
DECLARE
DECLARED
DECLAREDLY
DECLAREDNESS
DECLARER
DECLARING
DECLASS
DECLASSE
DECLASSED
DECLASSEE
DECLASSING
DECLENSION
DECLENSIONAL
DECLINABLE
DECLINAL
DECLINATE
DECLINATION
DECLINATIONS
DECLINATORY
DECLINATURE
DECLINE
DECLINED
DECLINER
DECLINING
DECLINOGRAPH
DECLINOMETER
DECLIVATE
DECLIVE
DECLIVITIES
DECLIVITOUS
DECLIVITY
DECLIVOUS
DECLUTCH
DECOCT
DECOCTION
DECOCTIVE
DECOCTUM
DECODE
DECODED
DECODER
DECODING
DECOHERE
DECOHERER
DECOIC
DECOKE
DECOLL
DECOLLATE
DECOLLATED
DECOLLATING
DECOLLATION
DECOLLATOR
DECOLLETAGE
DECOLLETE
DECOLOR
DECOLORANT
DECOLORATE
DECOLORATION
DECOLORIZE
DECOLORIZED
DECOLORIZER
DECOLORIZING
DECOLOUR
DECOLOURISE
DECOLOURIZE
DECOMMISSION
DECOMPENSATE
DECOMPLEX
DECOMPONIBLE
DECOMPOSABLE
DECOMPOSE
DECOMPOSED
DECOMPOSER
DECOMPOSING
DECOMPOSITE
DECOMPOSITION
DECOMPOSURE
DECOMPOUND
DECOMPRESS
DECONGESTIVE
DECONSIDER
DECONTROL
DECONTROLLED
DECOPED
DECOR
DECORAMENT
DECORATE
DECORATED
DECORATING
DECORATION
DECORATIVE
DECORATOR
DECORATORY
DECORE
DECOREMENT
DECORIST
DECOROUS
DECOROUSLY
DECOROUSNESS
DECORTICATE
DECORTICATED
DECORUM
DECOUPAGE
DECOY
DECOYED
DECOYER
DECOYING
DECOYMAN
DECOYMEN
DECOYS
DECRASSIFIED
DECRASSIFY
DECREASE
DECREASED
DECREASELESS
DECREASING
DECREASINGLY
DECREATION
DECREATIVE
DECREE
DECREED
DECREEING
DECREEMENT
DECREER
DECREET
DECREMENT
DECREMETER
DECREPID
DECREPIT
DECREPITATE
DECREPITATED
DECREPITLY
DECREPITNESS
DECREPITUDE
DECREPITY
DECRESCENCE
DECRESCENDO
DECRESCENT
DECRETAL
DECRETALIST
DECRETE
DECRETIST
DECRETIVE
DECRETIVELY
DECRETORIAL
DECRETORILY
DECRETORY
DECRETUM
DECREW
DECRIAL
DECRIED
DECRIER
DECROWN
DECRUSTATION
DECRY
DECRYING
DECRYPT
DECUBITAL
DECUBITUS
DECULTURATE
DECULTURATED
DECUMAN
DECUMANA
DECUMANI
DECUMANUS
DECUMARY
DECUMBENCE
DECUMBENCY
DECUMBENT
DECUMBITURE
DECUPLE
DECUPLED
DECUPLET
DECUPLING
DECURIA
DECURIES
DECURION
DECURIONATE
DECURRENCE
DECURRENCES
DECURRENCIES
DECURRENCY
DECURRENT
DECURRENTLY
DECURSION
DECURSIVE
DECURSIVELY
DECURT
DECURTATE
DECURVATION
DECURVE
DECURVED
DECURVING
DECURY
DECUS
DECUSSATE
DECUSSATED
DECUSSATELY
DECUSSATING
DECUSSATION
DECUSSION
DECUSSIS
DECUSSORIA
DECUSSORIUM
DECYL
DECYLENE
DECYLENIC
DECYLIC
DECYNE
DED
DEDAL
DEDANS
DEDDY
DEDE
DEDECORATE
DEDECORATION

DEDECOROUS
DEDENDA
DEDENDUM
DEDENTITION
DEDICATE
DEDICATED
DEDICATEE
DEDICATING
DEDICATION
DEDICATIONAL
DEDICATIVE
DEDICATOR
DEDICATORIAL
DEDICATORILY
DEDICATORY
DEDICATURE
DEDIMUS
DEDIT
DEDITICIAN
DEDITION
DEDO
DEDOLATION
DEDOLENCE
DEDOLENCY
DEDOLENT
DEDUCE
DEDUCED
DEDUCEMENT
DEDUCIBILITY
DEDUCIBLE
DEDUCIBLY
DEDUCING
DEDUCIVE
DEDUCT
DEDUCTED
DEDUCTIBLE
DEDUCTILE
DEDUCTING
DEDUCTIO
DEDUCTION
DEDUCTIONS
DEDUCTIVE
DEDUCTIVELY
DEDUCTORY
DEDUIT
DEE
DEECE
DEED
DEEDBOX
DEEDED
DEEDEED
DEEDFUL
DEEDFULLY
DEEDILY
DEEDINESS
DEEDING
DEEDLESS
DEEDS
DEEDY
DEEJAY
DEEL
DEEM
DEEMED
DEEMER
DEEMIE
DEEMING
DEEMSTER
DEEMSTERSHIP
DEEN
DEENER
DEENY
DEEP
DEEPEN
DEEPENER
DEEPENING
DEEPER
DEEPEST
DEEPFREEZE
DEEPFREEZED
DEEPFREEZING
DEEPFROZE
DEEPFROZEN
DEEPING
DEEPLY
DEEPMOST
DEEPMOUTHED
DEEPNESS
DEEPSOME
DEEPWATER
DEEPWATERMAN
DEEPWATERMEN
DEER
DEERBERRY
DEERDOG
DEERDRIVE
DEERFLY
DEERFOOD
DEERGRASS
DEERHAIR
DEERHERD
DEERHORN
DEERHOUND
DEERKILL
DEERLET
DEERSKIN
DEERSTALKER
DEERSTALKING
DEERSTAND
DEERTONGUE
DEERVETCH
DEERWEED
DEERWOOD
DEERYARD
DEES
DEESCALATE
DEESCALATED
DEESCALATING
DEESCALATION
DEESE
DEESIS
DEESS
DEEVE
DEEVEY
DEEVILICK
DEEWAN
DEFACE
DEFACED
DEFACEMENT
DEFACER
DEFACING
DEFACINGLY
DEFADE
DEFAIL
DEFAILANCE
DEFAILLANCE
DEFAILMENT
DEFAITISME
DEFAITISTE
DEFALCATE
DEFALCATED
DEFALCATING
DEFALCATION
DEFALCATOR
DEFALK
DEFAMATION
DEFAMATORY
DEFAME
DEFAMED
DEFAMER
DEFAMING
DEFAMINGLY
DEFAMOUS
DEFAMY
DEFASSA
DEFAT
DEFATIGABLE
DEFATIGATE
DEFATIGATED
DEFATIGATION
DEFATTED
DEFATTING
DEFAULT
DEFAULTANT
DEFAULTER
DEFAULTURE
DEFEASANCE
DEFEASANCED
DEFEASE
DEFEASIBLE
DEFEAT
DEFEATED
DEFEATER
DEFEATISM
DEFEATIST
DEFEATMENT
DEFEATURE
DEFECANT
DEFECATE
DEFECATED
DEFECATING
DEFECATION
DEFECATOR
DEFECT
DEFECTIBLE
DEFECTION
DEFECTIONIST
DEFECTIOUS
DEFECTIVE
DEFECTIVELY
DEFECTOR
DEFECTOSCOPE
DEFECTS
DEFEDATION
DEFEISE
DEFEIT
DEFEMINIZE
DEFENCE
DEFENCELESS
DEFEND
DEFENDABLE
DEFENDANT
DEFENDED
DEFENDER
DEFENDRESS
DEFENSATIVE
DEFENSE
DEFENSELESS
DEFENSER
DEFENSIBLE
DEFENSIBLY
DEFENSION
DEFENSIVE
DEFENSIVELY
DEFENSOR
DEFENSORY
DEFER
DEFERENCE
DEFERENT
DEFERENTIAL
DEFERENTITIS
DEFERMENT
DEFERRABLE
DEFERRAL
DEFERRED
DEFERRER
DEFERRING
DEFERRIZE
DEFERRIZED
DEFERRIZING
DEFERVESCE
DEFERVESCENT
DEFET
DEFI
DEFIABLE
DEFIAL
DEFIANCE
DEFIANT
DEFIANTLY
DEFIANTNESS
DEFIBER
DEFIBRINATE
DEFIBRINIZE
DEFICIENCE
DEFICIENCY
DEFICIENT
DEFICIENTLY
DEFICIT
DEFIED
DEFIER
DEFIES
DEFIGURATION
DEFIGURE
DEFILADE
DEFILADED
DEFILADING
DEFILE
DEFILED
DEFILEMENT
DEFILER
DEFILIATION
DEFILING
DEFILINGLY
DEFINABILITY
DEFINABLE
DEFINABLY
DEFINE
DEFINED
DEFINEDLY
DEFINEMENT
DEFINER
DEFINING
DEFINITE
DEFINITELY
DEFINITENESS
DEFINITION
DEFINITIONAL
DEFINITIVE
DEFINITIVELY
DEFINITIZE
DEFINITIZED
DEFINITIZING
DEFINITOR
DEFINITUDE
DEFIX
DEFLAGRABLE
DEFLAGRATE
DEFLAGRATED
DEFLAGRATING
DEFLAGRATION
DEFLAGRATOR
DEFLATE
DEFLATED
DEFLATING
DEFLATION
DEFLATIONARY
DEFLATIONIST
DEFLATOR
DEFLECT
DEFLECTED
DEFLECTING
DEFLECTION
DEFLECTIVE
DEFLECTOR
DEFLEX
DEFLEXED
DEFLEXING
DEFLEXION
DEFLEXURE
DEFLOCCULANT
DEFLOCCULATE
DEFLOCCULENT
DEFLORATE
DEFLORATION
DEFLORE
DEFLOWER
DEFLOWERER
DEFLUENT
DEFLUVIUM
DEFLUX
DEFLUXION
DEFOIL
DEFOLIATE
DEFOLIATED
DEFOLIATING
DEFOLIATION
DEFOLIATOR
DEFORCE
DEFORCED
DEFORCEMENT
DEFORCER
DEFORCIANT
DEFORCING
DEFOREST
DEFORESTER
DEFORM
DEFORMABLE
DEFORMATION
DEFORMATIVE
DEFORMED
DEFORMEDLY
DEFORMEDNESS
DEFORMER
DEFORMETER
DEFORMING
DEFORMISM
DEFORMITIES
DEFORMITY
DEFOUL
DEFRAUD
DEFRAUDATION
DEFRAUDED
DEFRAUDER
DEFRAUDING
DEFRAUDMENT
DEFRAY
DEFRAYAL
DEFRAYED
DEFRAYER
DEFRAYING
DEFRAYMENT
DEFROCK
DEFROST
DEFROSTER
DEFT
DEFTER
DEFTERDAR
DEFTEST
DEFTLY
DEFTNESS
DEFUNCT
DEFUNCTION
DEFUSE
DEFUSION
DEFY
DEFYING
DEG
DEGAGE
DEGAME
DEGAS
DEGASES
DEGASSED
DEGASSER
DEGASSES
DEGASSING
DEGAUSS

DEGELATION
DEGEN
DEGENDER
DEGENER
DEGENERACY
DEGENERATE
DEGENERATED
DEGENERATELY
DEGENERATING
DEGENERATION
DEGENERATIVE
DEGERM
DEGERMINATE
DEGGED
DEGGER
DEGGING
DEGLAZE
DEGLAZED
DEGLAZING
DEGLUTINATE
DEGLUTINATED
DEGLUTITION
DEGLUTITIVE
DEGLUTITORY
DEGOMME
DEGRADAND
DEGRADATION
DEGRADATIVE
DEGRADE
DEGRADED
DEGRADEDLY
DEGRADEDNESS
DEGRADEMENT
DEGRADER
DEGRADING
DEGRADINGLY
DEGRAIN
DEGRAS
DEGREASE
DEGREASED
DEGREASER
DEGREASING
DEGREE
DEGREED
DEGREEING
DEGREES
DEGREEWISE
DEGRESSION
DEGRESSIVE
DEGRESSIVELY
DEGRINGOLADE
DEGU
DEGUELIN
DEGUM
DEGUMMED
DEGUMMING
DEGUST
DEGUSTATE
DEGUSTATION
DEHA
DEHAIR
DEHAIRER
DEHEMATIZE
DEHEPATIZE
DEHISCE
DEHISCED
DEHISCENCE
DEHISCENT
DEHISCING
DEHNSTUFE
DEHORN
DEHORNER
DEHORS
DEHORT
DEHORTATION
DEHORTATIVE
DEHORTATORY
DEHORTED
DEHORTER
DEHORTING
DEHULL
DEHUMANIZE
DEHUMANIZED
DEHUMANIZING
DEHUMIDIFIED
DEHUMIDIFIER
DEHUMIDIFY
DEHUSK
DEHYDRANT
DEHYDRATE
DEHYDRATED
DEHYDRATING
DEHYDRATION
DEHYDRATOR
DEHYPNOTIZE
DEHYPNOTIZED
DEI
DEICE
DEICED
DEICER
DEICIDAL
DEICIDE
DEICING
DEICTIC
DEICTICALLY
DEIFIC
DEIFICAL
DEIFICATION
DEIFICATORY
DEIFIED
DEIFIER
DEIFORM
DEIFORMITY
DEIFY
DEIFYING
DEIGN
DEIGNED
DEIGNING
DEIGNOUS
DEIL
DEIN
DEINCRUSTANT
DEINOS
DEIONIZE
DEIPOTENT
DEIRID
DEISEAL
DEISM
DEIST
DEISTIC
DEISTICAL
DEISTICALLY
DEITIES
DEITY
DEJECT
DEJECTA
DEJECTED
DEJECTEDLY
DEJECTEDNESS
DEJECTILE
DEJECTION
DEJECTORY
DEJECTURE
DEJERATE
DEJEUNE
DEJEUNER
DEJUNKERIZE
DEKADRACHM
DEKAGRAM
DEKALITER
DEKALITRE
DEKAMETER
DEKAMETRE
DEKAN
DEKAPARSEC
DEKAPODE
DEKARCH
DEKASTERE
DEKE
DEKED
DEKING
DEKKO
DEL
DELACTATION
DELAINE
DELAMINATE
DELAMINATED
DELAMINATING
DELAMINATION
DELAPSE
DELAPSION
DELASSEMENT
DELATE
DELATED
DELATER
DELATING
DELATION
DELATOR
DELATORIAN
DELAVY
DELAWN
DELAY
DELAYAGE
DELAYED
DELAYER
DELAYING
DELAYINGLY
DELE
DELEAD
DELEATUR
DELECTABLE
DELECTABLY
DELECTATE
DELECTATED
DELECTATING
DELECTATION
DELECTUS
DELED
DELEERIT
DELEGABLE
DELEGACIES
DELEGACY
DELEGALIZE
DELEGANT
DELEGATE
DELEGATED
DELEGATEE
DELEGATING
DELEGATION
DELEGATIVE
DELEGATORY
DELEING
DELENDA
DELETE
DELETED
DELETERIOUS
DELETERY
DELETING
DELETION
DELETIVE
DELETORY
DELF
DELFT
DELFTWARE
DELIBATE
DELIBER
DELIBERANT
DELIBERATE
DELIBERATED
DELIBERATELY
DELIBERATENESS
DELIBERATING
DELIBERATION
DELIBERATIVE
DELIBERATOR
DELIBLE
DELICACIES
DELICACY
DELICATE
DELICATELY
DELICATENESS
DELICATESSEN
DELICE
DELICIAE
DELICIOSO
DELICIOUS
DELICIOUSLY
DELICIOUSNESS
DELICT
DELICTUM
DELIE
DELIERET
DELIGATED
DELIGATION
DELIGHT
DELIGHTABLE
DELIGHTED
DELIGHTEDLY
DELIGHTEDNESS
DELIGHTER
DELIGHTFUL
DELIGHTFULLY
DELIGHTFULNESS
DELIGHTING
DELIGHTINGLY
DELIGHTSOME
DELIGHTSOMELY
DELIGHTSOMENESS
DELIGNATE
DELIGNATED
DELIME
DELIMER
DELIMIT
DELIMITATE
DELIMITATED
DELIMITATING
DELIMITATION
DELIMITATIVE
DELIMITED
DELIMITER
DELIMITIZE
DELIMITIZED
DELIMITIZING
DELINE
DELINEABLE
DELINEATE
DELINEATED
DELINEATING
DELINEATION
DELINEATIVE
DELINEATOR
DELINEATORY
DELINEAVIT
DELINQUENCIES
DELINQUENCY
DELINQUENT
DELINQUENTLY
DELIQUESCE
DELIQUESCED
DELIQUESCENT
DELIQUESCING
DELIQUIUM
DELIRACY
DELIRAMENT
DELIRANT
DELIRATION
DELIRE
DELIRIA
DELIRIOUS
DELIRIOUSLY
DELIRIUM
DELIRIUMS
DELISK
DELITESCENCE
DELITESCENT
DELITOUS
DELIVER
DELIVERABLE
DELIVERANCE
DELIVERED
DELIVERER
DELIVERIES
DELIVERING
DELIVERLY
DELIVEROR
DELIVERY
DELIVERYMAN
DELIVERYMEN
DELK
DELL
DELLA
DELLENITE
DELLS
DELOCALIZE
DELOCALIZED
DELOCALIZING
DELOMORPHIC
DELOMORPHOUS
DELOUL
DELOUSE
DELOUSED
DELOUSING
DELPH
DELPHIN
DELPHINE
DELPHINIC
DELPHININ
DELPHININE
DELPHINITE
DELPHINIUM
DELPHINOID
DELT
DELTA
DELTAHEDRA
DELTAHEDRON
DELTAIC
DELTAITE
DELTAL
DELTATION
DELTHYRIA
DELTHYRIAL
DELTHYRIUM
DELTIC
DELTIDIA
DELTIDIAL
DELTIDIUM
DELTOHEDRA
DELTOHEDRON
DELTOID
DELTOIDAL
DELUBRUM
DELUDE
DELUDED
DELUDER
DELUDHER
DELUDING
DELUDINGLY
DELUGE
DELUGED
DELUGING
DELUL
DELUMINIZE
DELUNDUNG
DELUSION
DELUSIONAL

DELUSIONIST
DELUSIVE
DELUSIVELY
DELUSIVENESS
DELUSORY
DELUSTER
DELUXE
DELVE
DELVED
DELVER
DELVING
DEM
DEMAGNETIZE
DEMAGNETIZED
DEMAGNETIZER
DEMAGOG
DEMAGOGIC
DEMAGOGICAL
DEMAGOGISM
DEMAGOGUE
DEMAGOGUERY
DEMAGOGUISM
DEMAGOGY
DEMAIN
DEMAL
DEMAND
DEMANDABLE
DEMANDANT
DEMANDED
DEMANDER
DEMANDING
DEMANGANIZE
DEMANTOID
DEMARCATE
DEMARCATED
DEMARCATING
DEMARCATION
DEMARCH
DEMARCHE
DEMARCHY
DEMAREE
DEMARK
DEMARKATION
DEMARKED
DEMARKING
DEMAST
DEMATIACEOUS
DEME
DEMEAN
DEMEANED
DEMEANING
DEMEANOR
DEMEANOUR
DEMEGORIC
DEMELE
DEMEMBRATION
DEMENCY
DEMENT
DEMENTATE
DEMENTATION
DEMENTED
DEMENTEDLY
DEMENTEDNESS
DEMENTHOLIZE
DEMENTI
DEMENTIA
DEMEORE
DEMEPHITIZE
DEMERGE
DEMERIT
DEMEROL
DEMERSAL
DEMERSE
DEMERSED
DEMERSION
DEMESMAN
DEMESNE
DEMESNIAL
DEMETHYLATE
DEMI
DEMIBASTION
DEMIBATH
DEMIBRIGADE
DEMICADENCE
DEMICANNON
DEMICANTON
DEMICAPONIER
DEMICHAMFRON
DEMICIRCLE
DEMICIRCULAR
DEMICIVILIZED
DEMICUIRASS
DEMICULVERIN
DEMIDITONE
DEMIDOLMEN
DEMIES
DEMIGAUNTLET
DEMIGOD
DEMIGODDESS
DEMIGORGE
DEMIHAG
DEMIHAGBUT
DEMIHAGUE
DEMIHAKE
DEMIHAQUE
DEMIJAMBE
DEMIJOHN
DEMILANCE
DEMILANCER
DEMILEGATO
DEMILITARIZE
DEMILITARIZED
DEMILUNE
DEMIMARK
DEMIMETOPE
DEMIMONDAIN
DEMIMONDAINE
DEMIMONDE
DEMINERALIZE
DEMIOURGOI
DEMIPARALLEL
DEMIPAULDRON
DEMIPIKE
DEMIPIQUE
DEMIQUAVER
DEMIRACLE
DEMIRELIEF
DEMIREP
DEMIRHUMB
DEMIRILIEVO
DEMISABLE
DEMISANG
DEMISE
DEMISEASON
DEMISED
DEMISEMITONE
DEMISING
DEMISOLDE
DEMISPHERE
DEMISS
DEMISSION
DEMISSIONARY
DEMISSLY
DEMISSNESS
DEMISUIT
DEMIT
DEMITASSE
DEMITINT
DEMITOILET
DEMITONE
DEMITTED
DEMITTING
DEMIURGE
DEMIURGEOUS
DEMIURGIC
DEMIURGICAL
DEMIURGISM
DEMIURGOS
DEMIURGUS
DEMIVIERGE
DEMIVOL
DEMIVOLT
DEMIVOLTE
DEMIWOLF
DEMOB
DEMOBBED
DEMOBBING
DEMOBILIZE
DEMOBILIZED
DEMOBILIZING
DEMOCRACIES
DEMOCRACY
DEMOCRAT
DEMOCRATIAN
DEMOCRATIC
DEMOCRATICAL
DEMOCRATISM
DEMOCRATIZE
DEMOCRATIZED
DEMOCRAW
DEMODE
DEMODED
DEMODULATE
DEMODULATED
DEMODULATING
DEMODULATION
DEMODULATOR
DEMOGENIC
DEMOGRAPHER
DEMOGRAPHIC
DEMOGRAPHICAL
DEMOGRAPHIST
DEMOGRAPHY
DEMOID
DEMOISELLE
DEMOLISH
DEMOLISHER
DEMOLISHMENT
DEMOLITION
DEMOLOGICAL
DEMOLOGY
DEMON
DEMONASTERY
DEMONETIZE
DEMONETIZED
DEMONETIZING
DEMONIAC
DEMONIACAL
DEMONIACALLY
DEMONIACISM
DEMONIAL
DEMONIAN
DEMONIANISM
DEMONIAST
DEMONIC
DEMONICAL
DEMONIFUGE
DEMONIO
DEMONISM
DEMONIST
DEMONIZE
DEMONIZED
DEMONIZING
DEMONOLATER
DEMONOLATRY
DEMONOLOGER
DEMONOLOGIC
DEMONOLOGIST
DEMONOLOGY
DEMONRY
DEMONS
DEMONSTRABLE
DEMONSTRABLY
DEMONSTRANCE
DEMONSTRANT
DEMONSTRATE
DEMONSTRATED
DEMONSTRATION
DEMONSTRATIVE
DEMONSTRATOR
DEMOPHIL
DEMOPHILE
DEMOPHILISM
DEMOPHOBE
DEMORALIZE
DEMORALIZED
DEMORALIZER
DEMORALIZING
DEMORPHISM
DEMOS
DEMOTE
DEMOTED
DEMOTIC
DEMOTICS
DEMOTING
DEMOTION
DEMOTIST
DEMOUNT
DEMOUNTABLE
DEMPNE
DEMPSTER
DEMULCE
DEMULCEATE
DEMULCENT
DEMULSIFY
DEMULSION
DEMUR
DEMURE
DEMURELY
DEMURENESS
DEMUREST
DEMURITY
DEMURRABLE
DEMURRAGE
DEMURRAL
DEMURRANT
DEMURRED
DEMURRER
DEMURRING
DEMURRINGLY
DEMUTIZATION
DEMY
DEMYSHIP
DEN
DENAR
DENARI
DENARIES
DENARII
DENARIUS
DENARO
DENARY
DENAT
DENATURALIZE
DENATURANT
DENATURATE
DENATURATION
DENATURE
DENATURED
DENATURING
DENATURIZE
DENATURIZER
DENAY
DENAZIFIED
DENAZIFY
DENAZIFYING
DENDA
DENDRACHATE
DENDRAL
DENDRAXON
DENDRIC
DENDRIFORM
DENDRITE
DENDRITIC
DENDRITICAL
DENDRITIFORM
DENDROBE
DENDROCOELE
DENDRODONT
DENDROGRAPH
DENDROGRAPHY
DENDROID
DENDROIDAL
DENDROLITE
DENDROLOGIC
DENDROLOGIST
DENDROLOGY
DENDROMETER
DENDRON
DENE
DENEGATE
DENEGATION
DENEHOLE
DENERVATE
DENERVATION
DENGUE
DENIABLE
DENIABLY
DENIAL
DENICOTINE
DENICOTINIZE
DENIED
DENIER
DENIERAGE
DENIERER
DENIGRATE
DENIGRATED
DENIGRATING
DENIGRATION
DENIGRATOR
DENIM
DENIMS
DENITRATE
DENITRATED
DENITRATING
DENITRATION
DENITRATOR
DENITRIFIED
DENITRIFIER
DENITRIFY
DENITRIFYING
DENITRIZE
DENIZATE
DENIZATION
DENIZE
DENIZEN
DENIZENATION
DENIZENIZE
DENNED
DENNET
DENNING
DENOMINABLE
DENOMINATE
DENOMINATED
DENOMINATING
DENOMINATION
DENOMINATIONAL
DENOMINATIVE
DENOMINATOR
DENOTABLE
DENOTATE
DENOTATION
DENOTATIVE
DENOTATIVELY
DENOTE
DENOTED

DENOTEMENT
DENOTING
DENOTIVE
DENOUEMENT
DENOUNCE
DENOUNCED
DENOUNCEMENT
DENOUNCER
DENOUNCING
DENS
DENSATE
DENSATION
DENSE
DENSELY
DENSEN
DENSENESS
DENSER
DENSEST
DENSIFIED
DENSIFIER
DENSIFY
DENSIMETER
DENSIMETRIC
DENSIMETRY
DENSITIES
DENSITOMETER
DENSITY
DENT
DENTAGRA
DENTAL
DENTALE
DENTALISM
DENTALITY
DENTALIZE
DENTAPHONE
DENTARY
DENTATA
DENTATE
DENTATED
DENTATELY
DENTATION
DENTEL
DENTELATED
DENTELLATED
DENTELLE
DENTELLIERE
DENTELLO
DENTELURE
DENTEX
DENTICAL
DENTICATE
DENTICLE
DENTICULAR
DENTICULATE
DENTICULATED
DENTICULE
DENTIFORM
DENTIFRICE
DENTIGEROUS
DENTIL
DENTILABIAL
DENTILATED
DENTILATION
DENTILE
DENTILINGUAL
DENTILOGUY
DENTILOQUIST
DENTIMETER
DENTIN
DENTINAL
DENTINALGIA
DENTINASAL
DENTINE
DENTINITIS
DENTINOBLAST
DENTINOID
DENTINOMA
DENTIPAROUS
DENTIPHONE
DENTIROSTER
DENTIROSTRAL
DENTISCALP
DENTIST
DENTISTIC
DENTISTICAL
DENTISTRY
DENTITION
DENTOID
DENTOLOLABIAL
DENTONASAL
DENTURAL
DENTURE
DENTY
DENUDANT
DENUDATE
DENUDATED
DENUDATING
DENUDATION
DENUDATIVE
DENUDE
DENUDED
DENUDER
DENUDING
DENUM
DENUMERABLE
DENUMERABLY
DENUMERAL
DENUMERANT
DENUMERATION
DENUMERATIVE
DENUNCIABLE
DENUNCIANT
DENUNCIATE
DENUNCIATED
DENUNCIATING
DENUNCIATION
DENUNCIATIVE
DENUNCIATOR
DENUNCIATORY
DENUTRITION
DENY
DENYING
DEOBSTRUENT
DEOCULATE
DEODAND
DEODAR
DEODATE
DEODORANT
DEODORIZE
DEODORIZED
DEODORIZER
DEODORIZING
DEONTOLOGIST
DEONTOLOGY
DEOPERCULATE
DEOPPILANT
DEOPPILATE
DEOPPILATION
DEOPPILATIVE
DEORDINATION
DEORSUM
DEOTA
DEOXIDIZE
DEOXIDIZED
DEOXIDIZER
DEOXIDIZING
DEOXYGENATE
DEOXYGENATED
DEOXYGENIZE
DEOZONIZE
DEOZONIZER
DEPA
DEPAINT
DEPAINTED
DEPAINTING
DEPAIR
DEPARLIAMENT
DEPART
DEPARTED
DEPARTEMENT
DEPARTER
DEPARTING
DEPARTITION
DEPARTMENT
DEPARTMENTAL
DEPARTURE
DEPAS
DEPASCENT
DEPASS
DEPASTURABLE
DEPASTURAGE
DEPASTURE
DEPASTURED
DEPASTURING
DEPATRIATE
DEPAUPERATE
DEPAUPERIZE
DEPAUPERIZED
DEPAYSE
DEPAYSEE
DEPE
DEPECHE
DEPEL
DEPENCIL
DEPEND
DEPENDABILITY
DEPENDABLE
DEPENDABLY
DEPENDANCY
DEPENDANT
DEPENDED
DEPENDENCE
DEPENDENCIES
DEPENDENCY
DEPENDENT
DEPENDER
DEPENDING
DEPENDINGLY
DEPEOPLE
DEPERDITE
DEPERDITELY
DEPERDITION
DEPERITION
DEPERM
DEPERSONIZE
DEPETALIZE
DEPETER
DEPETTICOAT
DEPHASE
DEPHASED
DEPHASING
DEPHLEGMATE
DEPHLEGMATED
DEPHLEGMATOR
DEPICT
DEPICTED
DEPICTER
DEPICTING
DEPICTION
DEPICTIVE
DEPICTOR
DEPICTURE
DEPICTURED
DEPICTURING
DEPIGMENT
DEPIGMENTATE
DEPIGMENTIZE
DEPILATE
DEPILATED
DEPILATING
DEPILATION
DEPILATOR
DEPILATORY
DEPILITANT
DEPILOUS
DEPIT
DEPLACE
DEPLANE
DEPLANED
DEPLANING
DEPLANT
DEPLANTATION
DEPLENISH
DEPLETE
DEPLETED
DEPLETHORIC
DEPLETING
DEPLETION
DEPLETIVE
DEPLETORY
DEPLORABILIA
DEPLORABLE
DEPLORABLY
DEPLORATION
DEPLORE
DEPLORED
DEPLORER
DEPLORING
DEPLOY
DEPLOYMENT
DEPLUMATE
DEPLUMATED
DEPLUMATION
DEPLUME
DEPLUMED
DEPLUMING
DEPOH
DEPOLARIZE
DEPOLARIZED
DEPOLARIZER
DEPOLARIZING
DEPOLISH
DEPOLISHING
DEPOLYMERIZE
DEPONE
DEPONED
DEPONENT
DEPONER
DEPONING
DEPOPULATE
DEPOPULATED
DEPOPULATING
DEPOPULATION
DEPOPULATIVE
DEPOPULATOR
DEPORT
DEPORTATION
DEPORTE
DEPORTED
DEPORTEE
DEPORTER
DEPORTING
DEPORTMENT
DEPOSABLE
DEPOSAL
DEPOSE
DEPOSED
DEPOSER
DEPOSING
DEPOSIT
DEPOSITA
DEPOSITARIES
DEPOSITARY
DEPOSITATION
DEPOSITED
DEPOSITEE
DEPOSITING
DEPOSITION
DEPOSITIONAL
DEPOSITIVE
DEPOSITO
DEPOSITOR
DEPOSITORIES
DEPOSITORY
DEPOSITS
DEPOSITUM
DEPOSITURE
DEPOSURE
DEPOT
DEPOTENTIATE
DEPRAVATE
DEPRAVATION
DEPRAVE
DEPRAVED
DEPRAVEDLY
DEPRAVEDNESS
DEPRAVER
DEPRAVING
DEPRAVITIES
DEPRAVITY
DEPRECABLE
DEPRECATE
DEPRECATED
DEPRECATING
DEPRECATION
DEPRECATIVE
DEPRECATOR
DEPRECATORY
DEPRECIABLE
DEPRECIANT
DEPRECIATE
DEPRECIATED
DEPRECIATING
DEPRECIATION
DEPRECIATIVE
DEPRECIATOR
DEPRECIATORY
DEPREDATE
DEPREDATED
DEPREDATING
DEPREDATION
DEPREDATOR
DEPREDATORY
DEPREHEND
DEPREHENSION
DEPRESS
DEPRESSANT
DEPRESSED
DEPRESSING
DEPRESSINGLY
DEPRESSION
DEPRESSIVE
DEPRESSIVELY
DEPRESSOR
DEPREST
DEPRETER
DEPRINT
DEPRIORIZE
DEPRIVABLE
DEPRIVAL
DEPRIVATE
DEPRIVATION
DEPRIVATIVE
DEPRIVE
DEPRIVED
DEPRIVEMENT
DEPRIVER
DEPRIVING
DEPROME
DEPSID
DEPSIDE
DEPTH
DEPTHEN
DEPTHING
DEPTHLESS

DEPTHOMETER
DEPTHS
DEPULSE
DEPURANT
DEPURATE
DEPURATED
DEPURATING
DEPURATIVE
DEPURATOR
DEPUTATION
DEPUTATIVE
DEPUTATOR
DEPUTE
DEPUTED
DEPUTIES
DEPUTING
DEPUTIZE
DEPUTIZED
DEPUTIZING
DEPUTY
DEQUEEN
DER
DERACIALIZE
DERACINATE
DERACINATED
DERACINATING
DERACINATION
DERADELPHUS
DERADENITIS
DERADENONCUS
DERAH
DERAIGN
DERAIGNMENT
DERAIL
DERAILED
DERAILER
DERAILING
DERAILMENT
DERANGE
DERANGED
DERANGEMENT
DERANGER
DERANGING
DERAT
DERATE
DERATED
DERATER
DERATING
DERATIZATION
DERAY
DERBUKKA
DERBY
DERBYLITE
DERE
DERECHO
DERELICT
DERELICTION
DERELICTLY
DERELICTNESS
DERELIGION
DERERE
DERESINATE
DERESINIFY
DERESINIZE
DERF
DERFLY
DERFNESS
DERHAM
DERIC
DERIDE
DERIDED
DERIDER
DERIDING
DERIDINGLY
DERINGER
DERISIBLE
DERISION
DERISIVE
DERISIVELY
DERISIVENESS
DERISORY
DERIVABILITY
DERIVABLE
DERIVABLY
DERIVAL
DERIVANT
DERIVATE
DERIVATELY
DERIVATION
DERIVATIONAL
DERIVATIST
DERIVATIVE
DERIVE
DERIVED
DERIVEDLY
DERIVEDNESS
DERIVER
DERIVING
DERK
DERM
DERMA
DERMAD
DERMAHEMIA
DERMAL
DERMALITH
DERMAMYIASIS
DERMAPTERAN
DERMAPTEROUS
DERMASURGERY
DERMATALGIA
DERMATAUXE
DERMATHEMIA
DERMATIC
DERMATINE
DERMATITIS
DERMATOCELE
DERMATOCYST
DERMATODYNIA
DERMATOGEN
DERMATOGRAPH
DERMATOID
DERMATOLOGY
DERMATOLYSIS
DERMATOMA
DERMATOME
DERMATOMIC
DERMATOMYOMA
DERMATONOSUS
DERMATOPHONE
DERMATOPHONY
DERMATOPHYTE
DERMATOPLASM
DERMATOPLAST
DERMATOPSY
DERMATORRHEA
DERMATOSCOPY
DERMATOSIS
DERMATOTHERAPY
DERMATOTOMY
DERMATOZOON
DERMIC
DERMIS
DERMOBLAST
DERMOCHROME
DERMOCOCCUS
DERMOGASTRIC
DERMOGRAPHIA
DERMOGRAPHIC
DERMOHEMAL
DERMOHEMIA
DERMOID
DERMOIDAL
DERMOL
DERMOLYSIS
DERMONEURAL
DERMOOSSEOUS
DERMOPATHIC
DERMOPATHY
DERMOPHOBE
DERMOPHYTE
DERMOPHYTIC
DERMOPLASTY
DERMOPTERAN
DERMOPTEROUS
DERMOSTOSIS
DERMOTROPIC
DERMOVACCINE
DERMUTATION
DERN
DERNE
DERNED
DERNER
DERNFUL
DERNIER
DERNING
DERNLY
DERODIDYMUS
DEROGATE
DEROGATED
DEROGATELY
DEROGATING
DEROGATION
DEROGATIVE
DEROGATIVELY
DEROGATOR
DEROGATORILY
DEROGATORY
DEROUT
DERRICK
DERRICKING
DERRICKMAN
DERRICKMEN
DERRID
DERRIDE
DERRIERE
DERRIES
DERRINGER
DERRY
DERTRA
DERTROTHECA
DERTRUM
DERVISH
DERVISHHOOD
DERVISHISM
DERVISHLIKE
DESA
DESACRALIZE
DESALT
DESAND
DESATURATE
DESAURIN
DESAURINE
DESCALE
DESCAMISADO
DESCAMISADOS
DESCANT
DESCANTED
DESCANTER
DESCANTING
DESCEND
DESCENDABLE
DESCENDANCE
DESCENDANT
DESCENDED
DESCENDENCE
DESCENDENT
DESCENDENTAL
DESCENDER
DESCENDIBLE
DESCENDING
DESCENDINGLY
DESCENSION
DESCENSIONAL
DESCENSIVE
DESCENT
DESCLOIZITE
DESCORT
DESCRIAL
DESCRIBABLE
DESCRIBABLY
DESCRIBE
DESCRIBED
DESCRIBER
DESCRIBING
DESCRIED
DESCRIER
DESCRIPT
DESCRIPTION
DESCRIPTIVE
DESCRIPTORY
DESCRIVE
DESCRY
DESCRYING
DESCURE
DESEAM
DESECATE
DESECRATE
DESECRATED
DESECRATER
DESECRATING
DESECRATION
DESECRATOR
DESEED
DESEGREGATE
DESEGREGATED
DESEMER
DESENSITIZE
DESENSITIZER
DESERET
DESERT
DESERTED
DESERTEDLY
DESERTEDNESS
DESERTER
DESERTFUL
DESERTFULLY
DESERTIC
DESERTION
DESERTLESS
DESERTLESSLY
DESERTNESS
DESERTS
DESERVE
DESERVED
DESERVEDLY
DESERVEDNESS
DESERVER
DESERVING
DESERVINGLY
DESEX
DESEXUALIZE
DESEXUALIZED
DESH
DESHABILLE
DESI
DESIATIN
DESICCANT
DESICCATE
DESICCATED
DESICCATING
DESICCATION
DESICCATIVE
DESICCATOR
DESICCATORY
DESIDERANT
DESIDERATE
DESIDERATED
DESIDERATING
DESIDERATION
DESIDERATIVE
DESIDERATUM
DESIDERIUM
DESIGHT
DESIGHTMENT
DESIGN
DESIGNABLE
DESIGNADO
DESIGNATE
DESIGNATED
DESIGNATING
DESIGNATION
DESIGNATIVE
DESIGNATOR
DESIGNATORY
DESIGNED
DESIGNEDLY
DESIGNEDNESS
DESIGNEE
DESIGNER
DESIGNFUL
DESIGNFULLY
DESIGNING
DESIGNINGLY
DESILICATE
DESILICATED
DESILICATING
DESILICIFIED
DESILICIFY
DESILICONIZE
DESILVER
DESILVERIZE
DESILVERIZER
DESINENCE
DESINENT
DESINENTIAL
DESIPIENCE
DESIPIENCY
DESIPIENT
DESIRABILITY
DESIRABLE
DESIRABLY
DESIRE
DESIRED
DESIREDLY
DESIREDNESS
DESIREFUL
DESIRER
DESIRING
DESIROUS
DESIROUSLY
DESIROUSNESS
DESIST
DESISTANCE
DESISTENCE
DESISTIVE
DESITION
DESITIVE
DESIZE
DESK
DESKILL
DESKMAN
DESLIME
DESMA
DESMACHYME
DESMACYTE
DESMAN
DESMECTASIA
DESMIC
DESMID
DESMIDIAN
DESMIDIOLOGY
DESMINE
DESMITIS
DESMODONT
DESMODYNIA

DESMOGEN
DESMOID
DESMOLOGY
DESMOMA
DESMON
DESMONEME
DESMOPELMOUS
DESMOSE
DESMOSIS
DESMOSITE
DESMOTOMY
DESMOTROPE
DESMOTROPIC
DESMOTROPISM
DESMOTROPY
DESOEUVRE
DESOLATE
DESOLATED
DESOLATELY
DESOLATENESS
DESOLATER
DESOLATING
DESOLATINGLY
DESOLATION
DESOLATIVE
DESOLATOR
DESONATION
DESORPTION
DESOXALATE
DESPAIR
DESPAIRED
DESPAIRER
DESPAIRFUL
DESPAIRFULLY
DESPAIRING
DESPAIRINGLY
DESPATCH
DESPATCHER
DESPECT
DESPERACY
DESPERADO
DESPERADOES
DESPERADOS
DESPERATE
DESPERATELY
DESPERATION
DESPERT
DESPICABLE
DESPICABLY
DESPISAL
DESPISE
DESPISED
DESPISEMENT
DESPISER
DESPISING
DESPITE
DESPITED
DESPITEFUL
DESPITEFULLY
DESPITEOUS
DESPITEOUSLY
DESPITING
DESPOIL
DESPOILER
DESPOILMENT
DESPOLIATION
DESPOND
DESPONDENCE
DESPONDENCY
DESPONDENT
DESPONDENTLY
DESPONDER
DESPONDING
DESPONDINGLY
DESPOT
DESPOTIC
DESPOTICAL
DESPOTICALLY
DESPOTISM
DESPOTIST
DESPOTIZE
DESPOUSE
DESPUMATE
DESPUMATED
DESPUMATING
DESPUMATION
DESPUME
DESQUAMATE
DESQUAMATED
DESQUAMATING
DESQUAMATION
DESQUAMATIVE
DESQUAMATORY
DESRAY
DESS
DESSA
DESSE
DESSERT
DESSERTSPOON
DESSIATINE
DESSIL
DESSOUS
DESSUS
DESTERILIZE
DESTINATE
DESTINATION
DESTINE
DESTINED
DESTINEZITE
DESTINIES
DESTINING
DESTINISM
DESTINIST
DESTINY
DESTITUTE
DESTITUTELY
DESTITUTION
DESTO
DESTOOL
DESTOUR
DESTRER
DESTRIER
DESTROY
DESTROYED
DESTROYER
DESTROYING
DESTRUCT
DESTRUCTIBLE
DESTRUCTION
DESTRUCTIVE
DESTRUCTOR
DESTRUDO
DESUCRATION
DESUETE
DESUETUDE
DESUGAR
DESUGARIZE
DESULFURATE
DESULFURIZE
DESULFURIZED
DESULFURIZER
DESULPHUR
DESULPHURATE
DESULPHURIZE
DESULTOR
DESULTORILY
DESULTORY
DESUME
DESYL
DESYNONYMIZE
DETACH
DETACHABLE
DETACHE
DETACHED
DETACHEDLY
DETACHEDNESS
DETACHER
DETACHING
DETACHMENT
DETAIL
DETAILED
DETAILEDLY
DETAILEDNESS
DETAILER
DETAILING
DETAIN
DETAINAL
DETAINED
DETAINEE
DETAINER
DETAINING
DETAINMENT
DETASSEL
DETECT
DETECTABLE
DETECTAPHONE
DETECTER
DETECTIBLE
DETECTING
DETECTION
DETECTIVE
DETECTIVES
DETECTOR
DETENT
DETENTE
DETENTION
DETENTIVE
DETENU
DETER
DETERGE
DETERGED
DETERGENCE
DETERGENCY
DETERGENT
DETERGING
DETERIORATE
DETERIORATED
DETERIORATING
DETERIORATION
DETERIORATOR
DETERIORISM
DETERIORITY
DETERM
DETERMA
DETERMENT
DETERMINABLE
DETERMINABLY
DETERMINACY
DETERMINANT
DETERMINANTS
DETERMINATE
DETERMINATION
DETERMINATIVE
DETERMINE
DETERMINED
DETERMINEDLY
DETERMINER
DETERMINING
DETERMINISM
DETERMINIST
DETERMINOID
DETERRED
DETERRENCE
DETERRENT
DETERRING
DETERSION
DETERSIVE
DETERSIVELY
DETEST
DETESTABLE
DETESTABLY
DETESTATION
DETESTED
DETESTER
DETESTING
DETHRONE
DETHRONED
DETHRONEMENT
DETHRONER
DETHRONING
DETHYROIDISM
DETIN
DETINET
DETINUE
DETINUIT
DETONABLE
DETONATE
DETONATED
DETONATING
DETONATION
DETONATIVE
DETONATOR
DETONIZE
DETORSION
DETORT
DETOUR
DETOXICANT
DETOXICATE
DETOXICATED
DETOXICATING
DETOXICATION
DETOXICATOR
DETOXIFY
DETRACT
DETRACTED
DETRACTER
DETRACTING
DETRACTION
DETRACTIVE
DETRACTIVELY
DETRACTOR
DETRACTORY
DETRAIN
DETRAINMENT
DETRAQUE
DETRAY
DETRECT
DETRIBALIZE
DETRIMENT
DETRIMENTAL
DETRITAL
DETRITED
DETRITION
DETRITUS
DETRUCK
DETRUDE
DETRUDED
DETRUDING
DETRUNCATE
DETRUNCATED
DETRUNCATING
DETRUNCATION
DETRUSION
DETRUSIVE
DETRUSOR
DETUBATION
DETUMESCENCE
DETUNE
DETUNED
DETUNING
DETUR
DETURB
DETURN
DEUCE
DEUCED
DEUCEDLY
DEUL
DEUNAM
DEURWAARDER
DEUS
DEUSAN
DEUTERANOMAL
DEUTERIC
DEUTERIDE
DEUTERIUM
DEUTEROCONE
DEUTEROCONID
DEUTERODOME
DEUTEROGAMY
DEUTEROGENIC
DEUTERON
DEUTEROPATHY
DEUTEROPLASM
DEUTEROSCOPY
DEUTEROSTOMA
DEUTEROTOKY
DEUTEROTYPE
DEUTEROZOOID
DEUTOBROMIDE
DEUTOMALA
DEUTOMALAL
DEUTOMALAR
DEUTOMERITE
DEUTON
DEUTONYMPH
DEUTONYMPHAL
DEUTOPLASM
DEUTOPLASMIC
DEUTOPLASTIC
DEUTOVUM
DEUTSCHEMARK
DEUZAN
DEVA
DEVACHAN
DEVADASI
DEVAL
DEVALL
DEVALOKA
DEVALUATE
DEVALUATED
DEVALUATING
DEVALUATION
DEVALUE
DEVANCE
DEVANT
DEVAPORATE
DEVAPORATION
DEVARAJA
DEVARSHI
DEVAST
DEVASTATE
DEVASTATED
DEVASTATING
DEVASTATION
DEVASTATIVE
DEVASTATOR
DEVASTAVIT
DEVASTER
DEVATA
DEVAUL
DEVAUNT
DEVEIN
DEVEL
DEVELIN
DEVELOP
DEVELOPABLE
DEVELOPE
DEVELOPED
DEVELOPEMENT
DEVELOPER
DEVELOPING
DEVELOPMENT
DEVELOPMENTAL
DEVELOPOID
DEVELOPS

DEVER
DEVEST
DEVEX
DEVIABILITY
DEVIABLE
DEVIANT
DEVIATE
DEVIATED
DEVIATING
DEVIATION
DEVIATIONISM
DEVIATIONIST
DEVIATIVE
DEVIATOR
DEVIATORY
DEVICE
DEVICEFUL
DEVICEFULLY
DEVIL
DEVILBIRD
DEVILDOM
DEVILED
DEVILER
DEVILET
DEVILFISH
DEVILFISHES
DEVILING
DEVILISH
DEVILISHLY
DEVILISHNESS
DEVILISM
DEVILIZE
DEVILIZED
DEVILIZING
DEVILKIN
DEVILLED
DEVILMENT
DEVILRIES
DEVILRY
DEVILS
DEVILTRY
DEVILWOOD
DEVILY
DEVIOUS
DEVIOUSLY
DEVIOUSNESS
DEVIRGINATE
DEVIRGINATOR
DEVIRILIZE
DEVISABLE
DEVISAL
DEVISE
DEVISED
DEVISEE
DEVISER
DEVISING
DEVISOR
DEVITALIZE
DEVITALIZED
DEVITALIZING
DEVITAMINIZE
DEVITRIFIED
DEVITRIFY
DEVITRIFYING
DEVOCALIZE
DEVOCALIZED
DEVOCALIZING
DEVOCATE
DEVOCATION
DEVOICED
DEVOID
DEVOIR
DEVOIRS
DEVOLUTE
DEVOLUTION
DEVOLVE
DEVOLVED
DEVOLVEMENT
DEVOLVING
DEVONITE
DEVORATIVE
DEVOT
DEVOTARY
DEVOTE
DEVOTED
DEVOTEDLY
DEVOTEDNESS
DEVOTEE
DEVOTEEISM
DEVOTEMENT
DEVOTER
DEVOTING
DEVOTION
DEVOTIONAL
DEVOTIONALLY
DEVOTIONARY
DEVOTIONATE
DEVOTIONIST
DEVOTIONS
DEVOTO
DEVOUR
DEVOURED
DEVOURER
DEVOURING
DEVOURINGLY
DEVOUT
DEVOUTLY
DEVOUTNESS
DEVOVE
DEVOW
DEVULGARIZE
DEW
DEWA
DEWAN
DEWANEE
DEWANNY
DEWAR
DEWATA
DEWATER
DEWATERER
DEWAX
DEWBEAM
DEWBERRIES
DEWBERRY
DEWCAP
DEWCLAW
DEWCLAWED
DEWCUP
DEWDROP
DEWDROPPER
DEWER
DEWEYLITE
DEWFALL
DEWFLOWER
DEWIER
DEWIEST
DEWILY
DEWINESS
DEWLAP
DEWLAPPED
DEWOOL
DEWORM
DEWRET
DEWROT
DEWTRY
DEWY
DEXIOTROPE
DEXIOTROPIC
DEXIOTROPISM
DEXIOTROPOUS
DEXTER
DEXTERICAL
DEXTERITY
DEXTEROUS
DEXTEROUSLY
DEXTRAD
DEXTRAL
DEXTRALITY
DEXTRALLY
DEXTRAN
DEXTRANE
DEXTRAURAL
DEXTRIN
DEXTRINASE
DEXTRINATE
DEXTRINE
DEXTRINIZE
DEXTRINOUS
DEXTRO
DEXTROCARDIA
DEXTROCULAR
DEXTROGYRATE
DEXTROGYRE
DEXTRORSAL
DEXTRORSE
DEXTROSAZONE
DEXTROSE
DEXTROSURIA
DEXTROUS
DEXTROUSLY
DEXTROUSNESS
DEY
DEYHOUSE
DEYS
DEYWOMAN
DEZINC
DEZINCATION
DEZINCIFIED
DEZINCIFY
DEZINCIFYING
DEZINKIFY
DEZYMOTIZE
DGHAISA
DHA
DHABB
DHAI
DHAK
DHAL
DHAMAN
DHAMNOO
DHAN
DHANGAR
DHANUK
DHANUSH
DHAO
DHARANA
DHARANI
DHARMA
DHARMSALA
DHARNA
DHAURA
DHAURI
DHAVA
DHAW
DHER
DHERI
DHIKR
DHOBEE
DHOBEY
DHOBI
DHOBIE
DHOBIES
DHOBIS
DHOBY
DHOLE
DHOLES
DHOLL
DHONI
DHOON
DHOOTIE
DHOTEE
DHOTI
DHOTIS
DHOTY
DHOUL
DHOURRA
DHOW
DHU
DHURNA
DHURRA
DHURRIE
DHURRY
DHYAL
DHYANA
DI
DIA
DIABASE
DIABASIC
DIABETES
DIABETIC
DIABETICAL
DIABETOGENIC
DIABETOMETER
DIABLE
DIABLERIE
DIABLERY
DIABLO
DIABLOTIN
DIABOLARCH
DIABOLEPSY
DIABOLEPTIC
DIABOLIC
DIABOLICAL
DIABOLICALLY
DIABOLIFY
DIABOLISM
DIABOLIST
DIABOLIZE
DIABOLIZED
DIABOLIZING
DIABOLO
DIABOLOLOGY
DIABOLUS
DIABROSIS
DIABROTIC
DIACAUSTIC
DIACETATE
DIACETIC
DIACETURIA
DIACETYL
DIACETYLENE
DIACHORETIC
DIACHRONIC
DIACHYLON
DIACHYLUM
DIACID
DIACLASE
DIACLASIS
DIACLE
DIACLINAL
DIACODION
DIACODIUM
DIACOELE
DIACOELIA
DIACONAL
DIACONATE
DIACONIA
DIACONICON
DIACOPE
DIACRANTERIC
DIACRISIS
DIACRITIC
DIACRITICAL
DIACT
DIACTIN
DIACTINAL
DIACTINE
DIACTINIC
DIACTINISM
DIACULUM
DIAD
DIADELPHIAN
DIADELPHOUS
DIADEM
DIADERM
DIADERMIC
DIADOCHE
DIADOCHITE
DIADOUMENOS
DIADROME
DIADROMOUS
DIADUMENUS
DIAENE
DIAERESIS
DIAERETIC
DIAETETAE
DIAGENESIS
DIAGENETIC
DIAGEOTROPIC
DIAGLYPH
DIAGLYPHIC
DIAGLYPTIC
DIAGNOSE
DIAGNOSED
DIAGNOSES
DIAGNOSING
DIAGNOSIS
DIAGNOSTIC
DIAGNOSTICS
DIAGOMETER
DIAGONAL
DIAGONALITY
DIAGONALIZE
DIAGONALLY
DIAGONIC
DIAGRAM
DIAGRAMED
DIAGRAMING
DIAGRAMMATIC
DIAGRAMMED
DIAGRAMMETER
DIAGRAMMING
DIAGRAPH
DIAGRAPHIC
DIAGRAPHICAL
DIAGRAPHICS
DIAGREDIUM
DIAGRYDIUM
DIAKINESIS
DIAL
DIALCOHOL
DIALDEHYDE
DIALECT
DIALECTAL
DIALECTALIZE
DIALECTALLY
DIALECTIC
DIALECTICAL
DIALECTICALLY
DIALECTICIAN
DIALECTICISM
DIALECTICIZE
DIALECTICS
DIALECTOLOGY
DIALECTOR
DIALECTS
DIALED
DIALER
DIALIN
DIALING
DIALIST
DIALKYL
DIALKYLAMINE
DIALKYLIC
DIALLAGE

DIALLAGIC
DIALLAGITE
DIALLAGOID
DIALLED
DIALLEL
DIALLELA
DIALLELI
DIALLELON
DIALLELUS
DIALLER
DIALLING
DIALLIST
DIALOG
DIALOGER
DIALOGIC
DIALOGICAL
DIALOGICALLY
DIALOGISM
DIALOGIST
DIALOGISTIC
DIALOGITE
DIALOGIZE
DIALOGIZED
DIALOGIZING
DIALOGUE
DIALOGUED
DIALOGUER
DIALOGUING
DIALURIC
DIALYCARPOUS
DIALYSE
DIALYSES
DIALYSIS
DIALYSTELIC
DIALYTIC
DIALYTICALLY
DIALYZABLE
DIALYZATE
DIALYZATION
DIALYZATOR
DIALYZE
DIALYZED
DIALYZER
DIALYZING
DIAMAGNETIC
DIAMANTE
DIAMANTINE
DIAMANTOID
DIAMAT
DIAMB
DIAMBER
DIAMBIC
DIAMETER
DIAMETRAL
DIAMETRALLY
DIAMETRIC
DIAMETRICAL
DIAMICTON
DIAMIDE
DIAMIDO
DIAMIDOGEN
DIAMIN
DIAMINE
DIAMMONIUM
DIAMOND
DIAMONDBACK
DIAMONDED
DIAMONDING
DIAMONDIZE
DIAMONDIZED
DIAMONDIZING
DIAMONDS
DIAMORPHINE
DIAMYLOSE
DIAN
DIANDROUS
DIANITE
DIANODAL
DIANOETIC
DIANOETICAL
DIANOIA
DIANTRE
DIAPALMA
DIAPASE
DIAPASM
DIAPASON
DIAPASONAL
DIAPAUSE
DIAPEDESIS
DIAPEDETIC
DIAPENTE
DIAPER
DIAPERED
DIAPERING
DIAPERY
DIAPHANE
DIAPHANEITY
DIAPHANIE
DIAPHANOTYPE
DIAPHANOUS
DIAPHANOUSLY
DIAPHONE
DIAPHONIC
DIAPHONICAL
DIAPHONIES
DIAPHONY
DIAPHORESIS
DIAPHORETIC
DIAPHORITE
DIAPHOTE
DIAPHRAGM
DIAPHRAGMAL
DIAPHRAGMATIC
DIAPHRAGMED
DIAPHRAGMING
DIAPHTHERIN
DIAPHYSES
DIAPHYSIAL
DIAPHYSIS
DIAPIR
DIAPLASMA
DIAPLEXUS
DIAPNOIC
DIAPOPHYSES
DIAPOPHYSIS
DIAPOSITIVE
DIAPSID
DIAPSIDAN
DIAPYESIS
DIAPYETIC
DIARCH
DIARCHIAL
DIARCHIC
DIARCHIES
DIARCHY
DIARIAL
DIARIAN
DIARIST
DIARISTIC
DIARIZE
DIARRHEA
DIARRHEAL
DIARRHEIC
DIARRHETIC
DIARRHOEA
DIARRHOEAL
DIARRHOEIC
DIARRHOETIC
DIARSENIDE
DIARTHRODIAL
DIARTHROSIS
DIARTICULAR
DIARY
DIASCHISIS
DIASCHISMA
DIASCHISTIC
DIASCOPE
DIASCORD
DIASCORDIUM
DIASENE
DIASKEUASIS
DIASKEUAST
DIASPER
DIASPIDINE
DIASPIRIN
DIASPORE
DIASTALSES
DIASTALTIC
DIASTASE
DIASTASIC
DIASTASIS
DIASTATAXIC
DIASTATAXY
DIASTATIC
DIASTEM
DIASTEMA
DIASTEMATA
DIASTEMATIC
DIASTER
DIASTIMETER
DIASTOLE
DIASTOLIC
DIASTOMATIC
DIASTRAL
DIASTROPHE
DIASTROPHIC
DIASTROPHISM
DIASTYLE
DIASYNTHESIS
DIASYRM
DIATESSARON
DIATHERMACY
DIATHERMANCE
DIATHERMANCY
DIATHERMIA
DIATHERMIC
DIATHERMIES
DIATHERMY
DIATHESES
DIATHESIS
DIATHETIC
DIATOM
DIATOMACEAN
DIATOMACEOID
DIATOMACEOUS
DIATOMIC
DIATOMICITY
DIATOMIN
DIATOMINE
DIATOMITE
DIATOMOUS
DIATONIC
DIATONICAL
DIATONICALLY
DIATONICISM
DIATONOUS
DIATORIC
DIATREME
DIATRIBE
DIATROPIC
DIATROPISM
DIAULI
DIAULIC
DIAULOS
DIAVOLO
DIAXIAL
DIAXON
DIAXONE
DIAXONIC
DIAZENITHAL
DIAZEUTIC
DIAZEUXIS
DIAZID
DIAZIDE
DIAZIN
DIAZINE
DIAZO
DIAZOAMIN
DIAZOAMINE
DIAZOATE
DIAZOBENZENE
DIAZOIC
DIAZOIMIDE
DIAZOLE
DIAZOMA
DIAZOMETHANE
DIAZONIUM
DIAZOTATE
DIAZOTIC
DIAZOTIZE
DIAZOTIZED
DIAZOTIZING
DIAZOTYPE
DIB
DIBASE
DIBASIC
DIBASICITY
DIBATAG
DIBBED
DIBBER
DIBBING
DIBBLE
DIBBLED
DIBBLER
DIBBLING
DIBBUK
DIBENZOYL
DIBENZYL
DIBHOLE
DIBLASTULA
DIBRACH
DIBRANCH
DIBRANCHIATE
DIBROMID
DIBROMIDE
DIBS
DIBSTONE
DICACITY
DICAEOLOGY
DICARBONATE
DICARBOXYLIC
DICAST
DICASTERY
DICASTIC
DICATALECTIC
DICATALEXIS
DICE
DICEBOARD
DICEBOX
DICECUP
DICED
DICELLATE
DICEMAN
DICENTRIN
DICENTRINE
DICEPHALISM
DICEPHALOUS
DICEPHALUS
DICEPLAY
DICER
DICERION
DICEROUS
DICETYL
DICH
DICHAS
DICHASIA
DICHASIAL
DICHASIUM
DICHASTIC
DICHLONE
DICHLORAMIN
DICHLORAMINE
DICHLORIDE
DICHOCARPOUS
DICHOGAMIC
DICHOGAMOUS
DICHOGAMY
DICHONDRA
DICHOPTIC
DICHORD
DICHOREE
DICHOTIC
DICHOTOMAL
DICHOTOMIC
DICHOTOMIES
DICHOTOMIST
DICHOTOMIZE
DICHOTOMIZED
DICHOTOMOUS
DICHOTOMY
DICHROIC
DICHROISM
DICHROITE
DICHROITIC
DICHROMASIA
DICHROMASY
DICHROMAT
DICHROMATE
DICHROMATIC
DICHROMATISM
DICHROMIC
DICHROMISM
DICHRONOUS
DICHROOSCOPE
DICHROOUS
DICHROSCOPE
DICHROSCOPIC
DICHT
DICING
DICK
DICKCISSEL
DICKENS
DICKER
DICKERED
DICKERING
DICKEY
DICKEYBIRD
DICKEYS
DICKIES
DICKINSONITE
DICKTY
DICKY
DICKYBIRD
DICLINIC
DICLINISM
DICLINOUS
DICLINY
DICOCCOUS
DICODEINE
DICOELIOUS
DICOELOUS
DICOLIC
DICOLON
DICONDYLIAN
DICOPHANE
DICOT
DICOTYL
DICOTYLEDON
DICROTAL
DICROTIC
DICROTISM
DICROTOUS
DICT
DICTA
DICTAMEN

DICTAMINA
DICTAPHONE
DICTATE
DICTATED
DICTATING
DICTATINGLY
DICTATION
DICTATIONAL
DICTATIVE
DICTATOR
DICTATORIAL
DICTATORSHIP
DICTATORY
DICTATRESS
DICTATRIX
DICTATURE
DICTERY
DICTIC
DICTION
DICTIONARIES
DICTIONARY
DICTOGRAPH
DICTUM
DICTUMS
DICTY
DICTYNID
DICTYOGEN
DICTYOSOME
DICTYOSTELE
DICTYOSTELIC
DICTYOTIC
DICYANID
DICYANIDE
DICYANIN
DICYANINE
DICYCLE
DICYCLIC
DICYCLIST
DICYEMID
DID
DIDACTIC
DIDACTICAL
DIDACTICALLY
DIDACTICIAN
DIDACTICISM
DIDACTICITY
DIDACTICS
DIDACTIVE
DIDACTYL
DIDACTYLISM
DIDACTYLOUS
DIDAPPER
DIDASCALAR
DIDASCALIAE
DIDASCALIC
DIDASCALOS
DIDASCALY
DIDDER
DIDDERED
DIDDERING
DIDDEST
DIDDIES
DIDDLE
DIDDLED
DIDDLER
DIDDLING
DIDDY
DIDELPH
DIDELPHIAN
DIDELPHIC
DIDELPHID
DIDELPHINE
DIDELPHOUS
DIDEST
DIDIE
DIDINE
DIDLE
DIDLER
DIDNA
DIDRACHM
DIDRACHMA
DIDRACHMAL
DIDRACHMAS
DIDRIC
DIDROMIES
DIDROMY
DIDST
DIDUCE
DIDUCED
DIDUCING
DIDUCTION
DIDUCTOR
DIDY
DIDYM
DIDYMATE
DIDYMIA
DIDYMIUM
DIDYMOID
DIDYMOLITE
DIDYMOUS
DIDYMUS
DIDYNAMOUS
DIDYNAMY
DIE
DIEB
DIEBACK
DIECASE
DIECIOUS
DIECTASIS
DIED
DIEDRIC
DIEHARD
DIEING
DIELDRIN
DIELECTRIC
DIELECTRICAL
DIEM
DIEMAKING
DIENCEPHALIC
DIENCEPHALON
DIENE
DIENER
DIER
DIERESES
DIERESIS
DIERETIC
DIES
DIESEL
DIESELIZE
DIESES
DIESINKER
DIESINKING
DIESIS
DIESTOCK
DIESTRUM
DIESTRUS
DIET
DIETAL
DIETARIAN
DIETARIES
DIETARY
DIETER
DIETETIC
DIETETICAL
DIETETICALLY
DIETETICS
DIETETIST
DIETHER
DIETHYL
DIETHYLAMINE
DIETIC
DIETICAL
DIETICIAN
DIETICS
DIETINE
DIETING
DIETIST
DIETITIAN
DIETOTHERAPY
DIETOTOXIC
DIETRICHITE
DIETTED
DIETZEITE
DIEU
DIEUGARD
DIEWISE
DIEZEUGMENON
DIFERRION
DIFFA
DIFFAME
DIFFER
DIFFERED
DIFFERENCE
DIFFERENCED
DIFFERENCING
DIFFERENCY
DIFFERENT
DIFFERENTIA
DIFFERENTIAE
DIFFERENTIAL
DIFFERENTIATE
DIFFERENTIATION
DIFFERENTLY
DIFFERING
DIFFERINGLY
DIFFICILE
DIFFICULT
DIFFICULTIES
DIFFICULTY
DIFFIDATION
DIFFIDE
DIFFIDED
DIFFIDENCE
DIFFIDENT
DIFFIDENTLY
DIFFIDING
DIFFINITY
DIFFLUENCE
DIFFLUENT
DIFFORM
DIFFORME
DIFFORMED
DIFFORMITY
DIFFRACT
DIFFRACTED
DIFFRACTING
DIFFRACTION
DIFFRACTIVE
DIFFRANGIBLE
DIFFUGIENT
DIFFUND
DIFFUSATE
DIFFUSE
DIFFUSED
DIFFUSEDLY
DIFFUSEDNESS
DIFFUSELY
DIFFUSENESS
DIFFUSER
DIFFUSIBLE
DIFFUSIBLY
DIFFUSING
DIFFUSION
DIFFUSIONISM
DIFFUSIONIST
DIFFUSIVE
DIFFUSIVELY
DIFFUSIVITY
DIFFUSOR
DIG
DIGALLATE
DIGALLIC
DIGAMETIC
DIGAMIST
DIGAMMA
DIGAMMATE
DIGAMMATED
DIGAMOUS
DIGAMY
DIGASTRIC
DIGENESIS
DIGENETIC
DIGENITE
DIGENOUS
DIGENY
DIGERENT
DIGEST
DIGESTANT
DIGESTED
DIGESTEDLY
DIGESTEDNESS
DIGESTER
DIGESTIBLE
DIGESTIBLY
DIGESTING
DIGESTION
DIGESTIVE
DIGESTIVELY
DIGESTOR
DIGGED
DIGGER
DIGGING
DIGGINGS
DIGHT
DIGHTED
DIGHTER
DIGHTING
DIGIT
DIGITAL
DIGITALEIN
DIGITALIN
DIGITALIS
DIGITALISM
DIGITALIZE
DIGITALLY
DIGITATE
DIGITATED
DIGITATELY
DIGITATION
DIGITIFORM
DIGITIGRADE
DIGITIZE
DIGITIZED
DIGITIZER
DIGITIZING
DIGITOGENIN
DIGITONIN
DIGITORIUM
DIGITOXIN
DIGITOXOSE
DIGITULE
DIGITUS
DIGLADIATE
DIGLADIATED
DIGLADIATING
DIGLADIATION
DIGLADIATOR
DIGLOSSIA
DIGLOT
DIGLOTTIC
DIGLOTTISM
DIGLOTTIST
DIGLUCOSIDE
DIGLYPH
DIGLYPHIC
DIGMEAT
DIGNATION
DIGNE
DIGNIFIED
DIGNIFIEDLY
DIGNIFY
DIGNIFYING
DIGNITARIAL
DIGNITARIAN
DIGNITARIES
DIGNITARY
DIGNITAS
DIGNITIES
DIGNITY
DIGNOSCE
DIGONAL
DIGONEUTIC
DIGONEUTISM
DIGONOPOROUS
DIGONOUS
DIGOXIN
DIGRAM
DIGRAPH
DIGRAPHIC
DIGREDIENCY
DIGREDIENT
DIGRESS
DIGRESSED
DIGRESSING
DIGRESSION
DIGRESSIONAL
DIGRESSIVE
DIGRESSIVELY
DIGRESSORY
DIGS
DIGUE
DIHALID
DIHALIDE
DIHALO
DIHALOGEN
DIHEDRAL
DIHEDRON
DIHELIOS
DIHELIUM
DIHELY
DIHEXAGONAL
DIHEXAHEDRAL
DIHEXAHEDRON
DIHYBRID
DIHYBRIDISM
DIHYDRATE
DIHYDRATED
DIHYDRIC
DIHYDRIDE
DIHYDRITE
DIHYDROGEN
DIHYDROXY
DII
DIIAMB
DIIODID
DIIODIDE
DIIODO
DIIODOFORM
DIISATOGEN
DIJUDICATE
DIJUDICATION
DIK
DIKA
DIKAGE
DIKAMALI
DIKAMALLI
DIKARYON
DIKDIK
DIKE
DIKED
DIKEGRAVE
DIKELET
DIKER
DIKEREEVE
DIKERIA

DIKERION
DIKETENE
DIKETO
DIKETONE
DIKING
DIKKOP
DIKSHA
DIKTAT
DIKTYONITE
DILACERATE
DILACERATED
DILACERATING
DILACERATION
DILACTONE
DILAMBDODONT
DILAPIDATE
DILAPIDATED
DILAPIDATING
DILAPIDATION
DILAPIDATOR
DILATABILITY
DILATABLY
DILATANCY
DILATANT
DILATATE
DILATATION
DILATATIVE
DILATATOR
DILATE
DILATED
DILATEDLY
DILATEDNESS
DILATEMENT
DILATER
DILATING
DILATION
DILATIVE
DILATOMETER
DILATOMETRIC
DILATOMETRY
DILATOR
DILATORILY
DILATORINESS
DILATORY
DILDO
DILDOES
DILDOS
DILECTION
DILEMMA
DILEMMATIC
DILEMMIC
DILETANT
DILETTANIST
DILETTANTE
DILETTANTES
DILETTANTI
DILETTANTISH
DILETTANTISM
DILIGENCE
DILIGENT
DILIGENTIA
DILIGENTLY
DILIGENTNESS
DILIS
DILKER
DILL
DILLENIAD
DILLESK
DILLI
DILLIER
DILLIES
DILLIGROUT
DILLING
DILLIS
DILLISK
DILLSEED
DILLUE
DILLUER
DILLWEED
DILLY
DILLYDALLIED
DILLYDALLIER
DILLYDALLY
DILLYMAN
DILLYMEN
DILO
DILOGY
DILOS
DILUCID
DILUENDO
DILUENT
DILUTE
DILUTED
DILUTEDLY
DILUTEDNESS
DILUTEE
DILUTELY
DILUTENESS
DILUTENT
DILUTER
DILUTING
DILUTION
DILUTIVE
DILUVIA
DILUVIAL
DILUVIALIST
DILUVIAN
DILUVIANISM
DILUVIUM
DILUVIUMS
DILUVY
DILVE
DIM
DIMANGANION
DIMASTIGATE
DIMBER
DIMBLE
DIME
DIMEDON
DIMEDONE
DIMENSIBLE
DIMENSION
DIMENSIONAL
DIMENSIONED
DIMENSIONING
DIMENSIVE
DIMENSUM
DIMER
DIMERAN
DIMERCAPROL
DIMERCURION
DIMERIC
DIMERISM
DIMERIZATION
DIMEROUS
DIMES
DIMETALLIC
DIMETER
DIMETHOXY
DIMETHYL
DIMETRIA
DIMETRIC
DIMICATION
DIMIDIATE
DIMIDIATED
DIMIDIATING
DIMIDIATION
DIMINISH
DIMINISHED
DIMINISHER
DIMINISHING
DIMINISHMENT
DIMINUE
DIMINUENDO
DIMINUENDOED
DIMINUTAL
DIMINUTE
DIMINUTED
DIMINUTELY
DIMINUTING
DIMINUTION
DIMINUTIVAL
DIMINUTIVE
DIMINUTIVELY
DIMISS
DIMISSION
DIMISSORY
DIMIT
DIMITIES
DIMITTED
DIMITTING
DIMITY
DIMLY
DIMMED
DIMMER
DIMMERS
DIMMEST
DIMMET
DIMMING
DIMMISH
DIMMIT
DIMMY
DIMNESS
DIMOLECULAR
DIMORIC
DIMORPH
DIMORPHIC
DIMORPHISM
DIMORPHOUS
DIMPLE
DIMPLED
DIMPLEMENT
DIMPLIER
DIMPLIEST
DIMPLING
DIMPLY
DIMPS
DIMPSY
DIMWIT
DIMWITTED
DIMWITTEDLY
DIMYARIAN
DIN
DINAMODE
DINANDERIE
DINAPHTHYL
DINAR
DINDER
DINDLE
DINDLED
DINDLING
DINE
DINED
DINER
DINERGATE
DINERIC
DINERO
DINEROS
DINES
DINETTE
DINEURIC
DINEUTRON
DING
DINGAR
DINGBAT
DINGDONG
DINGE
DINGED
DINGEING
DINGER
DINGEY
DINGEYS
DINGHIES
DINGHY
DINGIER
DINGIES
DINGIEST
DINGILY
DINGINESS
DINGLE
DINGLEBERRY
DINGLED
DINGLEDANGLE
DINGLING
DINGLY
DINGMAN
DINGMAUL
DINGO
DINGOES
DINGTHRIFT
DINGUS
DINGWALL
DINGY
DINHEIRO
DINIC
DINICAL
DINING
DINITRATE
DINK
DINKED
DINKEY
DINKEYS
DINKIER
DINKIES
DINKIEST
DINKING
DINKUM
DINKY
DINMAN
DINMONT
DINNA
DINNED
DINNER
DINNERLY
DINNERTIME
DINNERWARE
DINNERY
DINNING
DINOCERAS
DINOMIC
DINOS
DINOSAUR
DINOSAURIAN
DINOTHERE
DINSOME
DINT
DINTED
DINTING
DINUS
DIOBELY
DIOBOL
DIOBOLON
DIOCESAN
DIOCESE
DIOCOEL
DIOCTAHEDRAL
DIODE
DIODONT
DIOECIAN
DIOECIOUS
DIOECIOUSLY
DIOECISM
DIOESTROUS
DIOESTRUM
DIOESTRUS
DIOGENITE
DIOICOUS
DIOL
DIOLEFIN
DIOLEFINE
DIOLEFINIC
DIOMATE
DIONISE
DIONYM
DIONYMAL
DIOPSIDE
DIOPTASE
DIOPTER
DIOPTOGRAPH
DIOPTOMETER
DIOPTOMETRY
DIOPTRA
DIOPTRAL
DIOPTRATE
DIOPTRE
DIOPTRIC
DIOPTRICAL
DIOPTRICALLY
DIOPTRICS
DIOPTROSCOPY
DIOPTRY
DIORAMA
DIORAMIC
DIORDINAL
DIORITE
DIORITIC
DIORTHOSIS
DIORTHOTIC
DIOSCOREIN
DIOSCORINE
DIOSE
DIOSMIN
DIOSMOSE
DIOSPHENOL
DIOTA
DIOTIC
DIOVULAR
DIOXAN
DIOXANE
DIOXIDE
DIOXIME
DIOXY
DIP
DIPARTITE
DIPARTITION
DIPASCHAL
DIPCOAT
DIPENTENE
DIPENTINE
DIPETALOUS
DIPHASE
DIPHASER
DIPHASIC
DIPHEAD
DIPHENAN
DIPHENOL
DIPHENYL
DIPHENYLENE
DIPHOSGENE
DIPHOSPHATE
DIPHOSPHID
DIPHOSPHIDE
DIPHOSPHORIC
DIPHRELATIC
DIPHTHERIA
DIPHTHERIAL
DIPHTHERIAN
DIPHTHERIC
DIPHTHERITIC
DIPHTHERITIS
DIPHTHEROID
DIPHTHONG
DIPHTHONGAL
DIPHTHONGED
DIPHTHONGIC

DIPHTHONGING
DIPHTHONGIZE
DIPHTHONGIZED
DIPHYCERCAL
DIPHYCERCY
DIPHYGENIC
DIPHYLETIC
DIPHYLLOUS
DIPHYODONT
DIPHYOZOOID
DIPLACUSIS
DIPLANETIC
DIPLANETISM
DIPLANTIDIAN
DIPLARTHRISM
DIPLARTHROUS
DIPLASIASMUS
DIPLASIC
DIPLASION
DIPLEGIA
DIPLEURA
DIPLEURAL
DIPLEURIC
DIPLEX
DIPLEXER
DIPLOBLASTIC
DIPLOCARDIA
DIPLOCARDIAC
DIPLOCEPHALY
DIPLOCOCCAL
DIPLOCOCCI
DIPLOCOCCIC
DIPLOCOCCUS
DIPLOCONICAL
DIPLOCORIA
DIPLODOCUS
DIPLOE
DIPLOETIC
DIPLOGENESIS
DIPLOGENETIC
DIPLOGENIC
DIPLOGRAPH
DIPLOGRAPHY
DIPLOHEDRAL
DIPLOHEDRON
DIPLOIC
DIPLOID
DIPLOIDIC
DIPLOIDION
DIPLOIDIZE
DIPLOIDY
DIPLOIS
DIPLOKARYON
DIPLOMA
DIPLOMACIES
DIPLOMACY
DIPLOMAED
DIPLOMAING
DIPLOMAT
DIPLOMATE
DIPLOMATIC
DIPLOMATICAL
DIPLOMATICS
DIPLOMATISM
DIPLOMATIST
DIPLOMATIZE
DIPLOMATIZED
DIPLOMYELIA
DIPLONEMA
DIPLONEURAL
DIPLONT
DIPLOPHASE
DIPLOPHYTE
DIPLOPIA
DIPLOPIAS
DIPLOPIC
DIPLOPLACULA
DIPLOPOD
DIPLOPODIC
DIPLOPODOUS
DIPLOSIS
DIPLOSOME
DIPLOSPHENAL
DIPLOTEGIA
DIPLOTENE
DIPLUMBIC
DIPMETER
DIPNEUST
DIPNOAN
DIPNOID
DIPNOOUS
DIPODE
DIPODIC
DIPODID
DIPODIES
DIPODY
DIPOLAR
DIPOLARIZE
DIPOLE
DIPOLSPHENE
DIPORPA
DIPPED
DIPPER
DIPPIER
DIPPIEST
DIPPING
DIPPY
DIPRIMARY
DIPRISMATIC
DIPROPYL
DIPSADES
DIPSAS
DIPSETIC
DIPSEY
DIPSIE
DIPSO
DIPSOMANIA
DIPSOMANIAC
DIPSOSIS
DIPSTICK
DIPSY
DIPT
DIPTER
DIPTERAL
DIPTERAN
DIPTERIST
DIPTEROCARP
DIPTEROLOGY
DIPTERON
DIPTEROS
DIPTEROUS
DIPTOTE
DIPTYCA
DIPTYCH
DIPTYCHON
DIPWARE
DIPYGI
DIPYGUS
DIPYLON
DIPYRE
DIPYRENOUS
DIRD
DIRDUM
DIRE
DIRECT
DIRECTABLE
DIRECTED
DIRECTER
DIRECTING
DIRECTION
DIRECTIONAL
DIRECTIONS
DIRECTITUDE
DIRECTIVE
DIRECTIVELY
DIRECTIVITY
DIRECTLY
DIRECTNESS
DIRECTOR
DIRECTORAL
DIRECTORATE
DIRECTORIAL
DIRECTORIES
DIRECTORSHIP
DIRECTORY
DIRECTRESS
DIRECTRICES
DIRECTRIX
DIRECTRIXES
DIREFUL
DIREFULLY
DIREFULNESS
DIRELY
DIREMPT
DIREMPTION
DIRENESS
DIREPTION
DIRER
DIREST
DIRGE
DIRGED
DIRGEFUL
DIRGELIKE
DIRGEMAN
DIRGIE
DIRGING
DIRGLER
DIRGY
DIRHAM
DIRHEM
DIRIGENT
DIRIGIBILITY
DIRIGIBLE
DIRIGO
DIRIGOMOTOR
DIRIMENT
DIRK
DIRKED
DIRKING
DIRL
DIRNDL
DIRT
DIRTBIRD
DIRTBOARD
DIRTEN
DIRTIED
DIRTIER
DIRTIEST
DIRTILY
DIRTINESS
DIRTPLATE
DIRTY
DIRTYING
DIS
DISABILITIES
DISABILITY
DISABLE
DISABLED
DISABLEMENT
DISABLENESS
DISABLING
DISABUSAL
DISABUSE
DISABUSED
DISABUSING
DISACCHARID
DISACCHARIDE
DISACCORD
DISACCORDANT
DISACCUSTOM
DISACCUSTOMED
DISACIDIFIED
DISACIDIFY
DISACKNOWLEDGE
DISACQUAINT
DISADJUST
DISADVANCE
DISADVANCED
DISADVANCING
DISADVANTAGE
DISADVANTAGEOUS
DISADVENTURE
DISADVISE
DISADVISED
DISADVISING
DISAFFECT
DISAFFECTED
DISAFFECTING
DISAFFECTION
DISAFFILIATE
DISAFFIRM
DISAFFOREST
DISAGIO
DISAGREE
DISAGREEABLE
DISAGREEABLENESS
DISAGREEABLY
DISAGREED
DISAGREEING
DISAGREEMENT
DISAGREER
DISALIGN
DISALIGNED
DISALIGNING
DISALIGNMENT
DISALLIEGE
DISALLOW
DISALLOWABLE
DISALLOWANCE
DISALLOWED
DISALLOWING
DISALLY
DISANCHOR
DISANIMATE
DISANIMATED
DISANIMATING
DISANIMATION
DISANNEX
DISANNUL
DISANNULLER
DISANOINT
DISAPPAREL
DISAPPEAR
DISAPPEARANCE
DISAPPEARED
DISAPPEARER
DISAPPEARING
DISAPPOINT
DISAPPOINTED
DISAPPOINTER
DISAPPOINTING
DISAPPOINTMENT
DISAPPROBATION
DISAPPROVAL
DISAPPROVE
DISAPPROVED
DISAPPROVER
DISAPPROVING
DISAPPROVINGLY
DISARD
DISARM
DISARMAMENT
DISARMATURE
DISARMED
DISARMER
DISARMING
DISARMINGLY
DISARRANGE
DISARRANGED
DISARRANGEMENT
DISARRANGING
DISARRAY
DISARRAYED
DISASINIZE
DISASSEMBLE
DISASSEMBLED
DISASSEMBLY
DISASSENT
DISASSIDUITY
DISASSOCIATE
DISASTER
DISASTERLY
DISASTROUS
DISASTROUSLY
DISATTAINT
DISATTIRE
DISAVAIL
DISAVOUCH
DISAVOW
DISAVOWAL
DISAVOWANCE
DISAVOWER
DISAVOWMENT
DISAWA
DISBALANCE
DISBAND
DISBANDED
DISBANDING
DISBANDMENT
DISBAR
DISBARK
DISBARMENT
DISBARRED
DISBARRING
DISBASE
DISBECOME
DISBELIEF
DISBELIEVE
DISBELIEVED
DISBELIEVER
DISBELIEVING
DISBENCH
DISBENCHED
DISBENCHING
DISBEND
DISBLAME
DISBOARD
DISBODIED
DISBODY
DISBOSOM
DISBOWEL
DISBRANCH
DISBRANCHED
DISBRANCHING
DISBUD
DISBUDDED
DISBUDDER
DISBUDDING
DISBURDEN
DISBURDENED
DISBURDENING
DISBURSABLE
DISBURSE
DISBURSED
DISBURSEMENT
DISBURSER
DISBURSING
DISBURTHEN
DISBURY
DISBUTTON
DISC
DISCAL
DISCALCEATE
DISCALCED
DISCAMP

DISCANDY
DISCANONIZE
DISCANONIZED
DISCANT
DISCARD
DISCARDED
DISCARDER
DISCARDING
DISCARNATE
DISCARNATION
DISCASE
DISCEDE
DISCEPT
DISCEPTATION
DISCEPTATOR
DISCERN
DISCERNED
DISCERNER
DISCERNIBLE
DISCERNIBLY
DISCERNING
DISCERNINGLY
DISCERNMENT
DISCERP
DISCERPED
DISCERPING
DISCERPTIBLE
DISCERPTION
DISCHARGE
DISCHARGED
DISCHARGER
DISCHARGING
DISCHARM
DISCHASE
DISCHURCH
DISCI
DISCIDE
DISCIFLORAL
DISCIFLOROUS
DISCINCT
DISCIND
DISCIPLE
DISCIPLED
DISCIPLESHIP
DISCIPLINAL
DISCIPLINANT
DISCIPLINARIAN
DISCIPLINARY
DISCIPLINE
DISCIPLINED
DISCIPLINER
DISCIPLING
DISCIPLINING
DISCIPULAR
DISCISSION
DISCITIS
DISCLAIM
DISCLAIMANT
DISCLAIMED
DISCLAIMER
DISCLAIMING
DISCLAMATION
DISCLAMATORY
DISCLOISTER
DISCLOSE
DISCLOSED
DISCLOSER
DISCLOSING
DISCLOSIVE
DISCLOSURE
DISCLOUD
DISCOAST
DISCOBLASTIC
DISCOBOLOS
DISCOBOLUS
DISCODACTYL
DISCOGRAPHY
DISCOID
DISCOIDAL
DISCOLICHEN
DISCOLITH
DISCOLOR
DISCOLORATE
DISCOLORATED
DISCOLORATION
DISCOLORED
DISCOLORING
DISCOLORMENT
DISCOLOUR
DISCOLOURED
DISCOLOURING
DISCOMEDUSAN
DISCOMFIT
DISCOMFITER
DISCOMFITURE
DISCOMFORT
DISCOMFORTED
DISCOMMEND
DISCOMMENDER
DISCOMMODE
DISCOMMODED
DISCOMMODING
DISCOMMODITY
DISCOMMON
DISCOMMONED
DISCOMMONING
DISCOMMUNITY
DISCOMORULA
DISCOMPOSE
DISCOMPOSED
DISCOMPOSING
DISCOMPOSURE
DISCOMPT
DISCOMYCETE
DISCONCERT
DISCONCERTED
DISCONGRUITY
DISCONNECT
DISCONNECTED
DISCONNECTER
DISCONNECTOR
DISCONSIDER
DISCONSOLATE
DISCONTENT
DISCONTENTED
DISCONTINUANCE
DISCONTINUE
DISCONTINUED
DISCONTINUEE
DISCONTINUER
DISCONTINUITY
DISCONTINUOR
DISCONTINUOUS
DISCONULA
DISCOPHILE
DISCOPHOROUS
DISCOPLASM
DISCOPODOUS
DISCORD
DISCORDANCE
DISCORDANCY
DISCORDANT
DISCORDANTLY
DISCORDER
DISCORDING
DISCORPORATE
DISCOTHEQUE
DISCOUNT
DISCOUNTABLE
DISCOUNTED
DISCOUNTER
DISCOUNTING
DISCOURAGE
DISCOURAGED
DISCOURAGEMENT
DISCOURAGER
DISCOURAGING
DISCOURSE
DISCOURSED
DISCOURSER
DISCOURSING
DISCOURSIVE
DISCOURTEOUS
DISCOURTEOUSLY
DISCOURTESY
DISCOUS
DISCOVER
DISCOVERABLE
DISCOVERED
DISCOVERER
DISCOVERIES
DISCOVERING
DISCOVERT
DISCOVERTURE
DISCOVERY
DISCREATE
DISCREATION
DISCREDIT
DISCREDITABLE
DISCREDITED
DISCREDITING
DISCREET
DISCREETER
DISCREETEST
DISCREETLY
DISCREETNESS
DISCREPANCE
DISCREPANCY
DISCREPANT
DISCREPANTLY
DISCREPATE
DISCREPATED
DISCREPATING
DISCRETE
DISCRETELY
DISCRETENESS
DISCRETION
DISCRETIONAL
DISCRETIVE
DISCRIMINAL
DISCRIMINANT
DISCRIMINATE
DISCRIMINATED
DISCRIMINATING
DISCRIMINATINGLY
DISCRIMINATION
DISCROWN
DISCULPATE
DISCULPATION
DISCULPATORY
DISCUMB
DISCUMBER
DISCURE
DISCUREN
DISCURRE
DISCURSATIVE
DISCURSIFY
DISCURSION
DISCURSIVE
DISCURSIVELY
DISCURSORY
DISCURSUS
DISCURTAIN
DISCUS
DISCUSES
DISCUSS
DISCUSSANT
DISCUSSED
DISCUSSER
DISCUSSIBLE
DISCUSSING
DISCUSSION
DISCUSSIONAL
DISCUSSIVE
DISCUTABLE
DISCUTE
DISDAIN
DISDAINED
DISDAINER
DISDAINFUL
DISDAINFULLY
DISDAINING
DISDAINLY
DISDAINOUS
DISDAR
DISDECEIVE
DISDIACLAST
DISDIAPASON
DISDIAZO
DISEASE
DISEASED
DISEASEDLY
DISEASEDNESS
DISEASEFUL
DISEASES
DISEASING
DISEASY
DISECONDARY
DISEDGE
DISEDIFY
DISELENID
DISELENIDE
DISEMATISM
DISEMBARK
DISEMBARKED
DISEMBARKING
DISEMBARRASS
DISEMBODIED
DISEMBODIMENT
DISEMBODY
DISEMBODYING
DISEMBOGUE
DISEMBOGUED
DISEMBOGUING
DISEMBOSOM
DISEMBOWEL
DISEMBOWELED
DISEMBURDEN
DISEME
DISEMIC
DISEMPLANE
DISEMPLANED
DISEMPLOY
DISENABLE
DISENABLED
DISENABLING
DISENACT
DISENCHANT
DISENCHANTED
DISENCHANTER
DISENCUMBER
DISENCUMBER
DISENDOW
DISENDOWER
DISENDOWMENT
DISENGAGE
DISENGAGED
DISENGAGING
DISENSOUL
DISENTAIL
DISENTANGLE
DISENTANGLED
DISENTANGLEMENT
DISENTANGLER
DISENTANGLING
DISENTHRALL
DISENTHRALLED
DISENTHRONE
DISENTHRONED
DISENTITLE
DISENTITLED
DISENTITLING
DISENTOMB
DISENTRACED
DISENTRAIN
DISENTRAINMENT
DISENTRANCE
DISENTWINE
DISENTWINED
DISEPALOUS
DISEQUALIZE
DISERT
DISESTABLISH
DISESTEEM
DISESTEEMED
DISESTEEMER
DISESTEEMING
DISEUR
DISEUSE
DISFAITH
DISFAME
DISFASHION
DISFAVOR
DISFAVORED
DISFAVORER
DISFAVORING
DISFAVOUR
DISFAVOURED
DISFAVOURER
DISFAVOURING
DISFEATURE
DISFEATURED
DISFEATURING
DISFEN
DISFIGURE
DISFIGURED
DISFIGUREMENT
DISFIGURER
DISFIGURING
DISFLESH
DISFOREST
DISFORM
DISFRANCHISE
DISFROCK
DISFURNISH
DISFURNISHED
DISFURNITURE
DISGAGE
DISGARNISH
DISGAVEL
DISGAVELED
DISGAVELING
DISGAVELLED
DISGAVELLING
DISGENERIC
DISGENIC
DISGLORY
DISGOOD
DISGORGE
DISGORGED
DISGORGER
DISGORGING
DISGOSPELIZE
DISGOWN
DISGRACE
DISGRACED
DISGRACEFUL
DISGRACER
DISGRACING
DISGRACIOUS
DISGRADE
DISGRADED
DISGRADING
DISGREGATE
DISGREGATION

DISGRESS
DISGRUNTLE
DISGRUNTLED
DISGRUNTLING
DISGUISAL
DISGUISE
DISGUISED
DISGUISEDLY
DISGUISER
DISGUISING
DISGULF
DISGUST
DISGUSTED
DISGUSTEDLY
DISGUSTER
DISGUSTFUL
DISGUSTFULLY
DISGUSTING
DISGUSTINGLY
DISH
DISHABILLE
DISHABIT
DISHABITUATE
DISHALLOW
DISHARMONIC
DISHARMONIES
DISHARMONIZE
DISHARMONY
DISHBOARD
DISHCLOTH
DISHCLOUT
DISHEART
DISHEARTEN
DISHEARTENED
DISHEARTENER
DISHEARTENING
DISHEATHING
DISHED
DISHEIR
DISHELM
DISHER
DISHERENT
DISHERISON
DISHERIT
DISHERITMENT
DISHES
DISHEVEL
DISHEVELED
DISHEVELING
DISHEVELLED
DISHEVELLING
DISHFUL
DISHING
DISHLIKE
DISHMAKER
DISHMAKING
DISHMONGER
DISHMOP
DISHONEST
DISHONESTIES
DISHONESTLY
DISHONESTY
DISHONOR
DISHONORABLE
DISHONORARY
DISHONORED
DISHONORER
DISHONORING
DISHONOUR
DISHONOURARY
DISHONOURED
DISHONOURER
DISHONOURING
DISHORSE
DISHPAN
DISHRAG
DISHTOWEL
DISHUMOR
DISHWASH
DISHWASHER
DISHWASHINGS
DISHWATER
DISHWATERY
DISHWIPER
DISIDENTIFY
DISILICID
DISILICIDE
DISILLUDE
DISILLUDED
DISILLUSION
DISILLUSIVE
DISIMAGINE
DISIMITATE
DISIMITATION
DISIMPRISON
DISINCLINATION
DISINCLINE
DISINCLINED
DISINCLINING
DISINFECT
DISINFECTANT
DISINFECTED
DISINFECTING
DISINFECTION
DISINFECTIVE
DISINFECTOR
DISINFEST
DISINFLATION
DISINGENUITY
DISINGENUOUS
DISINHERISON
DISINHERIT
DISINHUME
DISINTEGRANT
DISINTEGRATE
DISINTEGRATING
DISINTEGRATION
DISINTEGROUS
DISINTER
DISINTEREST
DISINTERESTED
DISINTERMENT
DISINTERRED
DISINTERRING
DISINTRENCH
DISINVEST
DISINVITE
DISINVOLVE
DISJASKED
DISJASKIT
DISJECT
DISJECTED
DISJECTING
DISJECTION
DISJEUNE
DISJOIN
DISJOINED
DISJOINING
DISJOINT
DISJOINTED
DISJOINTEDLY
DISJOINTING
DISJOINTLY
DISJOINTURE
DISJUNCT
DISJUNCTION
DISJUNCTIVE
DISJUNCTIVELY
DISJUNCTOR
DISJUNCTURE
DISJUNE
DISK
DISKELION
DISKER
DISKERY
DISKLESS
DISKLIKE
DISKOS
DISKS
DISLEAF
DISLEAFED
DISLEAFING
DISLEAL
DISLEAVE
DISLEAVED
DISLEAVING
DISLEVELMENT
DISLIKABLE
DISLIKE
DISLIKED
DISLIKEFUL
DISLIKEN
DISLIKER
DISLIKING
DISLIMB
DISLIMN
DISLINK
DISLOAD
DISLOCATE
DISLOCATED
DISLOCATING
DISLOCATION
DISLOCATOR
DISLOCATORY
DISLOCK
DISLODGE
DISLODGED
DISLODGEMENT
DISLODGING
DISLODGMENT
DISLOYAL
DISLOYALIST
DISLOYALLY
DISLOYALTIES
DISLOYALTY
DISLUSTER
DISLUSTERED
DISLUSTERING
DISLUSTRE
DISLUSTRED
DISLUSTRING
DISMAIL
DISMAIN
DISMAL
DISMALITIES
DISMALITY
DISMALLY
DISMALNESS
DISMALS
DISMANTLE
DISMANTLED
DISMANTLER
DISMANTLING
DISMARBLE
DISMARCH
DISMARK
DISMARKET
DISMARKETED
DISMARKETING
DISMASK
DISMAST
DISMASTED
DISMASTING
DISMAY
DISMAYED
DISMAYEDNESS
DISMAYFUL
DISMAYFULLY
DISMAYING
DISME
DISMEMBER
DISMEMBERED
DISMEMBERER
DISMEMBERING
DISMEMBRATE
DISMEMBRATED
DISMEMBRATOR
DISMISS
DISMISSAL
DISMISSED
DISMISSIBLE
DISMISSING
DISMISSION
DISMISSIVE
DISMIT
DISMODED
DISMOUNT
DISMOUNTABLE
DISMUTATION
DISNA
DISNATURE
DISNATURED
DISNATURING
DISOBEDIENCE
DISOBEDIENT
DISOBEY
DISOBEYAL
DISOBEYED
DISOBEYER
DISOBEYING
DISOBLIGE
DISOBLIGED
DISOBLIGER
DISOBLIGING
DISOCCUPIED
DISOCCUPY
DISOCCUPYING
DISOMATIC
DISOMATOUS
DISOMATY
DISOMUS
DISORB
DISORDER
DISORDERED
DISORDEREDLY
DISORDERING
DISORDERLY
DISORDERS
DISORDINATE
DISORDINATED
DISORGANIC
DISORGANIZE
DISORGANIZED
DISORGANIZER
DISORIENT
DISORIENTATE
DISOUR
DISOWN
DISOXYGENATE
DISPACE
DISPAIR
DISPAND
DISPAR
DISPARAGE
DISPARAGED
DISPARAGEMENT
DISPARAGER
DISPARAGING
DISPARATE
DISPARATELY
DISPARATION
DISPARATUM
DISPARISH
DISPARITIES
DISPARITY
DISPARK
DISPARPLE
DISPARPLED
DISPARPLING
DISPART
DISPARTMENT
DISPASSION
DISPASSIONATE
DISPASSIONED
DISPATCH
DISPATCHED
DISPATCHER
DISPATCHFUL
DISPATCHING
DISPATRIATED
DISPAUPER
DISPAUPERIZE
DISPEACE
DISPEACEFUL
DISPEED
DISPEL
DISPELLED
DISPELLER
DISPELLING
DISPEND
DISPENDER
DISPENDIOUS
DISPENDITURE
DISPENSABLE
DISPENSARIES
DISPENSARY
DISPENSATE
DISPENSATED
DISPENSATING
DISPENSATION
DISPENSATIVE
DISPENSATOR
DISPENSATORY
DISPENSATRIX
DISPENSE
DISPENSED
DISPENSER
DISPENSING
DISPEOPLE
DISPEOPLED
DISPEOPLER
DISPEOPLING
DISPERATO
DISPERGATE
DISPERGATED
DISPERGATING
DISPERGATION
DISPERGATOR
DISPERMIC
DISPERMOUS
DISPERSAL
DISPERSE
DISPERSED
DISPERSEDLY
DISPERSER
DISPERSIBLE
DISPERSING
DISPERSION
DISPERSITY
DISPERSIVE
DISPERSIVELY
DISPERSOID
DISPHENOID
DISPIECE
DISPIREM
DISPIREME
DISPIRIT
DISPIRITED
DISPIRITEDLY
DISPIRITING
DISPITEOUS
DISPITEOUSLY
DISPLACE
DISPLACED
DISPLACEMENT

DISPLACENCY
DISPLACER
DISPLACING
DISPLANT
DISPLAY
DISPLAYED
DISPLAYER
DISPLAYING
DISPLAYS
DISPLE
DISPLEASE
DISPLEASED
DISPLEASER
DISPLEASING
DISPLEASURE
DISPLENISH
DISPLICENCY
DISPLODE
DISPLODED
DISPLODING
DISPLUME
DISPLUMED
DISPLUMING
DISPLUVIATE
DISPOINT
DISPONDAIC
DISPONDEE
DISPONE
DISPONENT
DISPOROUS
DISPORT
DISPORTIVE
DISPORTMENT
DISPOSABLE
DISPOSAL
DISPOSE
DISPOSED
DISPOSEDLY
DISPOSEDNESS
DISPOSER
DISPOSING
DISPOSITION
DISPOSITIVE
DISPOSSESS
DISPOSSESSED
DISPOSSESSOR
DISPOST
DISPOSURE
DISPRAISE
DISPRAISED
DISPRAISER
DISPRAISING
DISPREAD
DISPREADER
DISPREADING
DISPREPARE
DISPRIVACIED
DISPRIZE
DISPRIZED
DISPRIZING
DISPROBATIVE
DISPROFIT
DISPROOF
DISPROPORTIONATE
DISPROVABLE
DISPROVAL
DISPROVE
DISPROVED
DISPROVEMENT
DISPROVEN
DISPROVER
DISPROVING
DISPUNCT
DISPUNGE
DISPUTABLE
DISPUTABLY
DISPUTANT
DISPUTATION
DISPUTATIOUS
DISPUTATIVE
DISPUTATOR
DISPUTE
DISPUTED
DISPUTER
DISPUTING
DISQUALIFIED
DISQUALIFY
DISQUIET
DISQUIETED
DISQUIETEDLY
DISQUIETER
DISQUIETING
DISQUIETLY
DISQUIETUDE
DISQUIPARANT
DISQUISIT
DISQUISITE
DISQUISITED
DISQUISITING
DISQUISITION
DISQUISITIVE
DISQUISITOR
DISQUISITORY
DISQUIXOTE
DISRANK
DISRATE
DISRATED
DISRATING
DISRAY
DISREALIZE
DISREGARD
DISREGARDED
DISREGARDER
DISREGARDFUL
DISREGARDING
DISRELATED
DISRELATION
DISRELISH
DISREMEMBER
DISREPAIR
DISREPUTABLE
DISREPUTABLENESS
DISREPUTABLY
DISREPUTE
DISRESPECT
DISRESPECTFUL
DISREST
DISROBE
DISROBED
DISROBEMENT
DISROBER
DISROBING
DISROOF
DISROOT
DISRUMP
DISRUPT
DISRUPTED
DISRUPTER
DISRUPTION
DISRUPTIVE
DISRUPTIVELY
DISRUPTMENT
DISRUPTOR
DISRUPTURE
DISS
DISSAIT
DISSATISFACTION
DISSATISFIED
DISSATISFY
DISSATURATE
DISSAVA
DISSCEPTER
DISSCEPTERED
DISSCEPTRE
DISSCEPTRED
DISSCEPTRING
DISSEAT
DISSECT
DISSECTED
DISSECTING
DISSECTION
DISSECTIONAL
DISSECTIVE
DISSECTOR
DISSEISE
DISSEISED
DISSEISEE
DISSEISIN
DISSEISOR
DISSEISORESS
DISSEIZE
DISSEIZED
DISSEIZEE
DISSEIZIN
DISSEIZING
DISSEIZOR
DISSEIZORESS
DISSEIZURE
DISSELBOOM
DISSEMBLANCE
DISSEMBLE
DISSEMBLED
DISSEMBLER
DISSEMBLIES
DISSEMBLING
DISSEMBLY
DISSEMINATE
DISSEMINATED
DISSEMINATOR
DISSEMINULE
DISSENSION
DISSENT
DISSENTED
DISSENTER
DISSENTIENCE
DISSENTIENT
DISSENTING
DISSENTINGLY
DISSENTIOUS
DISSENTIVE
DISSEPIMENT
DISSERT
DISSERTATE
DISSERTATED
DISSERTATING
DISSERTATION
DISSERTATIVE
DISSERTATOR
DISSERVE
DISSERVED
DISSERVICE
DISSERVING
DISSEVER
DISSEVERANCE
DISSEVERED
DISSEVERING
DISSHEATHE
DISSHEATHED
DISSIDENCE
DISSIDENT
DISSIDENTLY
DISSIGHT
DISSIGHTLY
DISSILIENCY
DISSILIENT
DISSIMILAR
DISSIMILARLY
DISSIMILARS
DISSIMILATE
DISSIMULATE
DISSIMULATED
DISSIMULATION
DISSIMULATOR
DISSIMULE
DISSIPABLE
DISSIPATE
DISSIPATED
DISSIPATEDLY
DISSIPATER
DISSIPATING
DISSIPATION
DISSIPATIVE
DISSIPATOR
DISSITE
DISSOCIABLE
DISSOCIABLY
DISSOCIAL
DISSOCIALITY
DISSOCIALIZE
DISSOCIANT
DISSOCIATE
DISSOCIATED
DISSOCIATING
DISSOCIATION
DISSOCIATIVE
DISSOCONCH
DISSOGENY
DISSOLUBLE
DISSOLUTE
DISSOLUTELY
DISSOLUTION
DISSOLUTIVE
DISSOLVABLE
DISSOLVE
DISSOLVED
DISSOLVENT
DISSOLVER
DISSOLVING
DISSONANCE
DISSONANCY
DISSONANT
DISSONANTLY
DISSONATE
DISSONOUS
DISSOUR
DISSPREAD
DISSUADE
DISSUADED
DISSUADER
DISSUADING
DISSUASION
DISSUASIVE
DISSUASIVELY
DISSUASORY
DISSUIT
DISSUITABLE
DISSUITED
DISSYLLABIC
DISSYLLABIFY
DISSYLLABISM
DISSYLLABIZE
DISSYLLABLE
DISSYMMETRIC
DISSYMMETRY
DISTAD
DISTAFF
DISTAFFS
DISTAIN
DISTAL
DISTALE
DISTALIA
DISTALLY
DISTANCE
DISTANCED
DISTANCING
DISTANCY
DISTANT
DISTANTLY
DISTANTNESS
DISTASTE
DISTASTED
DISTASTEFUL
DISTASTING
DISTAVES
DISTELFINK
DISTEMPER
DISTEMPERED
DISTEMPERING
DISTEND
DISTENDED
DISTENDER
DISTENDING
DISTENSIBLE
DISTENSION
DISTENSIVE
DISTENT
DISTENTION
DISTER
DISTHENE
DISTHRONE
DISTHRONED
DISTHRONING
DISTICH
DISTICHOUS
DISTICHOUSLY
DISTICHS
DISTIL
DISTILL
DISTILLABLE
DISTILLAGE
DISTILLATE
DISTILLATION
DISTILLATORY
DISTILLED
DISTILLER
DISTILLERY
DISTILLING
DISTILLMENT
DISTILMENT
DISTINCT
DISTINCTIFY
DISTINCTIO
DISTINCTION
DISTINCTIONAL
DISTINCTITY
DISTINCTIVE
DISTINCTIVENESS
DISTINCTLY
DISTINCTNESS
DISTINGUE
DISTINGUEE
DISTINGUISH
DISTINGUISHED
DISTINGUISHING
DISTOCLUSION
DISTOMATOUS
DISTOME
DISTOMIASIS
DISTORT
DISTORTED
DISTORTEDLY
DISTORTER
DISTORTING
DISTORTION
DISTORTIONAL
DISTORTIVE
DISTRACT
DISTRACTED
DISTRACTEDLY
DISTRACTER
DISTRACTIBLE
DISTRACTING
DISTRACTION
DISTRACTIVE
DISTRAIN

DISTRAINABLE
DISTRAINED
DISTRAINEE
DISTRAINER
DISTRAINING
DISTRAINMENT
DISTRAINOR
DISTRAINT
DISTRAIT
DISTRAITE
DISTRAUGHT
DISTRAUGHTED
DISTRESS
DISTRESSED
DISTRESSEDLY
DISTRESSFUL
DISTRESSING
DISTREST
DISTRIBUTARY
DISTRIBUTE
DISTRIBUTED
DISTRIBUTEE
DISTRIBUTER
DISTRIBUTING
DISTRIBUTION
DISTRIBUTIVE
DISTRIBUTIVELY
DISTRIBUTOR
DISTRICT
DISTRICTLY
DISTRICTS
DISTRINGAS
DISTRITO
DISTRITOS
DISTRUSS
DISTRUST
DISTRUSTED
DISTRUSTER
DISTRUSTFUL
DISTRUSTING
DISTURB
DISTURBANCE
DISTURBANT
DISTURBATIVE
DISTURBED
DISTURBER
DISTURBING
DISTURN
DISULFATE
DISULFID
DISULFIDE
DISULFOXID
DISULFOXIDE
DISULFURET
DISULPHATE
DISULPHID
DISULPHIDE
DISULPHONATE
DISULPHOXID
DISULPHOXIDE
DISULPHURET
DISUNIFORM
DISUNIFY
DISUNION
DISUNIONISM
DISUNIONIST
DISUNITE
DISUNITED
DISUNITER
DISUNITIES
DISUNITING
DISUNITY
DISUSAGE
DISUSE
DISUSED
DISUSING
DISUTILITY
DISVALUE
DISVALUED
DISVALUING
DISVELOP
DISVISAGE
DISVOUCH
DISWARREN
DISWARRENED
DISWARRENING
DISWASHING
DISWORSHIP
DISYLLABLE
DISYOKE
DISYOKED
DISYOKING
DIT
DITA
DITAL
DITALI
DITALINI
DITATION
DITCH
DITCHBANK
DITCHBUR
DITCHDIGGER
DITCHDOWN
DITCHED
DITCHER
DITCHING
DITCHSIDE
DITE
DITED
DITER
DITERTIARY
DITHECAL
DITHECOUS
DITHEISM
DITHEIST
DITHEISTIC
DITHEISTICAL
DITHER
DITHERED
DITHERING
DITHERY
DITHION
DITHIONATE
DITHIONIC
DITHYRAMB
DITHYRAMBIC
DITING
DITION
DITOKOUS
DITOLYL
DITONE
DITREMATOUS
DITREMID
DITRIGLYPH
DITRIGLYPHIC
DITRIGONAL
DITRIGONALLY
DITROCHEAN
DITROCHEE
DITROCHOUS
DITROITE
DITT
DITTAMY
DITTANDER
DITTANIES
DITTANY
DITTAY
DITTED
DITTIED
DITTIES
DITTING
DITTO
DITTOED
DITTOGRAM
DITTOGRAPH
DITTOGRAPHIC
DITTOGRAPHY
DITTOING
DITTOLOGIES
DITTOLOGY
DITTON
DITTOS
DITTY
DITTYING
DIURANATE
DIURESIS
DIURETIC
DIURETICAL
DIURETICALLY
DIURN
DIURNAL
DIURNALLY
DIURNALNESS
DIURNATION
DIURNE
DIURNULE
DIUTURNAL
DIUTURNITY
DIV
DIVA
DIVAGATE
DIVAGATED
DIVAGATING
DIVAGATION
DIVALENCE
DIVALENT
DIVAN
DIVARICATE
DIVARICATED
DIVARICATELY
DIVARICATING
DIVARICATION
DIVARICATOR
DIVAS
DIVATA
DIVE
DIVED
DIVEKEEPER
DIVEL
DIVELLED
DIVELLENT
DIVELLICATE
DIVELLING
DIVER
DIVERB
DIVERGE
DIVERGED
DIVERGENCE
DIVERGENCES
DIVERGENCIES
DIVERGENCY
DIVERGENT
DIVERGENTLY
DIVERGING
DIVERGINGLY
DIVERS
DIVERSE
DIVERSELY
DIVERSENESS
DIVERSIFIED
DIVERSIFIER
DIVERSIFORM
DIVERSIFY
DIVERSIFYING
DIVERSION
DIVERSIONAL
DIVERSIONARY
DIVERSITIES
DIVERSITY
DIVERSLY
DIVERSORY
DIVERT
DIVERTED
DIVERTEDLY
DIVERTER
DIVERTICLE
DIVERTICULAR
DIVERTICULUM
DIVERTIMENTO
DIVERTING
DIVERTINGLY
DIVERTISE
DIVERTISSANT
DIVERTIVE
DIVERTOR
DIVES
DIVEST
DIVESTED
DIVESTING
DIVESTITIVE
DIVESTITURE
DIVESTMENT
DIVESTURE
DIVI
DIVIDABLE
DIVIDANT
DIVIDE
DIVIDED
DIVIDEDLY
DIVIDEDNESS
DIVIDEND
DIVIDER
DIVIDERS
DIVIDING
DIVIDINGLY
DIVIDUAL
DIVIDUALLY
DIVIDUITY
DIVIDUOUS
DIVINAIL
DIVINATION
DIVINATOR
DIVINATORY
DIVINE
DIVINED
DIVINELY
DIVINENESS
DIVINER
DIVINERESS
DIVINESSE
DIVINEST
DIVING
DIVINIFIED
DIVINIFY
DIVINIFYING
DIVINING
DIVININGLY
DIVINISTRE
DIVINITIES
DIVINITY
DIVINIZATION
DIVINIZE
DIVINIZED
DIVINIZING
DIVINYL
DIVISA
DIVISI
DIVISIBILITY
DIVISIBLE
DIVISIBLENESS
DIVISIBLY
DIVISION
DIVISIONAL
DIVISIONALLY
DIVISIONARY
DIVISIONISM
DIVISIONIST
DIVISIVE
DIVISIVELY
DIVISIVENESS
DIVISOR
DIVISORIAL
DIVISORY
DIVISURAL
DIVORCE
DIVORCED
DIVORCEE
DIVORCEMENT
DIVORCER
DIVORCEUSE
DIVORCING
DIVORCIVE
DIVORT
DIVOT
DIVOTO
DIVULGATE
DIVULGATED
DIVULGATER
DIVULGATING
DIVULGATION
DIVULGATORY
DIVULGE
DIVULGED
DIVULGEMENT
DIVULGENCE
DIVULGER
DIVULGING
DIVULSE
DIVULSED
DIVULSING
DIVULSION
DIVULSIVE
DIVULSOR
DIVUS
DIVVIED
DIVVIES
DIVVY
DIVVYING
DIWAN
DIWANI
DIWATA
DIX
DIXAIN
DIXENITE
DIXI
DIXIE
DIXIT
DIXY
DIZAIN
DIZAINE
DIZDAR
DIZEN
DIZENED
DIZENING
DIZENMENT
DIZYGOTIC
DIZZARD
DIZZARDLY
DIZZEN
DIZZIED
DIZZIER
DIZZIEST
DIZZILY
DIZZINESS
DIZZY
DIZZYING
DJAGOONG
DJALMAITE
DJATI
DJEBEL
DJELFA
DJERIB
DJERSA
DJIBBAH
DJIN

DJINN
DJINNI
DJO
DO
DOAB
DOABLE
DOACH
DOARIUM
DOAT
DOATED
DOATER
DOATISH
DOATY
DOB
DOBBER
DOBBIE
DOBBIES
DOBBIN
DOBBY
DOBE
DOBIE
DOBLA
DOBLON
DOBLONES
DOBOS
DOBRA
DOBRAO
DOBRAS
DOBROES
DOBSON
DOBY
DOC
DOCENT
DOCENTSHIP
DOCETISM
DOCHMIAC
DOCHMIACAL
DOCHMIASIS
DOCHMII
DOCHMIUS
DOCHTER
DOCIBILITY
DOCIBLE
DOCIBLENESS
DOCILE
DOCILELY
DOCILITY
DOCIMASIES
DOCIMASTIC
DOCIMASTICAL
DOCIMASY
DOCIMOLOGY
DOCIOUS
DOCITY
DOCK
DOCKAGE
DOCKED
DOCKEN
DOCKER
DOCKET
DOCKHAND
DOCKHEAD
DOCKHOUSE
DOCKING
DOCKIZATION
DOCKIZE
DOCKMACKIE
DOCKMAN
DOCKMASTER
DOCKSIDE
DOCKYARD
DOCMAC
DOCOSANE
DOCTOR
DOCTORAL
DOCTORALLY
DOCTORATE
DOCTORBIRD
DOCTORED
DOCTORESS
DOCTORFISH
DOCTORIAL
DOCTORIALLY
DOCTORING
DOCTORIZE
DOCTORLY
DOCTORS
DOCTORSHIP
DOCTRESS
DOCTRINABLE
DOCTRINAIRE
DOCTRINAL
DOCTRINALISM
DOCTRINALIST
DOCTRINALITY
DOCTRINALLY
DOCTRINARIAN
DOCTRINARILY
DOCTRINARITY
DOCTRINARY
DOCTRINATE
DOCTRINE
DOCTRINES
DOCTRINISM
DOCTRINIST
DOCTRINIZE
DOCTRINIZED
DOCTRINIZING
DOCTUS
DOCUMENT
DOCUMENTAL
DOCUMENTARY
DOCUMENTIZE
DOD
DODA
DODAD
DODD
DODDARD
DODDART
DODDED
DODDER
DODDERED
DODDERER
DODDERING
DODDERY
DODDIE
DODDLE
DODDY
DODDYPOLL
DODECADE
DODECADRACHM
DODECAFID
DODECAGON
DODECAGONAL
DODECAHEDRA
DODECAHEDRAL
DODECAHEDRON
DODECAMEROUS
DODECANE
DODECANT
DODECAPHONIC
DODECARCH
DODECARCHY
DODECASEMIC
DODECASTYLE
DODECASTYLOS
DODECATEMORY
DODECATYL
DODECATYLIC
DODECUPLET
DODECYL
DODECYLENE
DODECYLIC
DODGASTED
DODGE
DODGED
DODGER
DODGERY
DODGILY
DODGINESS
DODGING
DODGY
DODKIN
DODLET
DODMAN
DODO
DODOES
DODOISM
DODOMA
DODOS
DODS
DODUNK
DOE
DOEBIRD
DOEGLING
DOELING
DOER
DOES
DOESKIN
DOEST
DOETH
DOFF
DOFFED
DOFFER
DOFFING
DOFTBERRY
DOFUNNY
DOG
DOGAL
DOGANA
DOGARESSA
DOGATE
DOGBANE
DOGBERRIES
DOGBERRY
DOGBITE
DOGBLOW
DOGBOAT
DOGBODY
DOGBOLT
DOGBUSH
DOGCART
DOGCATCHER
DOGDOM
DOGE
DOGEDOM
DOGELESS
DOGES
DOGESHIP
DOGFACE
DOGFALL
DOGFENNEL
DOGFIGHT
DOGFISH
DOGFISHES
DOGFOOT
DOGGED
DOGGEDLY
DOGGEDNESS
DOGGER
DOGGEREL
DOGGERELED
DOGGERELER
DOGGERELIZE
DOGGERELIZER
DOGGERELIZING
DOGGERELLED
DOGGERELLING
DOGGERIES
DOGGERY
DOGGESS
DOGGIE
DOGGIER
DOGGIES
DOGGIEST
DOGGING
DOGGISH
DOGGISHLY
DOGGISHNESS
DOGGLE
DOGGO
DOGGONE
DOGGONED
DOGGONING
DOGGREL
DOGGRELIZE
DOGGY
DOGHEAD
DOGHOLE
DOGHOUSE
DOGIE
DOGLEG
DOGLIKE
DOGLY
DOGMA
DOGMAN
DOGMAS
DOGMATA
DOGMATIC
DOGMATICAL
DOGMATICALLY
DOGMATICIAN
DOGMATICS
DOGMATISM
DOGMATIST
DOGMATIZE
DOGMATIZED
DOGMATIZER
DOGMATIZING
DOGMEAT
DOGMEN
DOGMOUTH
DOGPLATE
DOGS
DOGSHORE
DOGSKIN
DOGSLED
DOGSLEEP
DOGSTAIL
DOGSTONE
DOGTAIL
DOGTIE
DOGTOOTH
DOGTRICK
DOGTROT
DOGVANE
DOGWATCH
DOGWOOD
DOGY
DOH
DOHL
DOIGT
DOIGTE
DOILED
DOILIES
DOILY
DOINA
DOINE
DOING
DOINGS
DOIT
DOITED
DOITRIFIED
DOJO
DOKE
DOKHMA
DOL
DOLABRA
DOLABRATE
DOLABRIFORM
DOLCAN
DOLCE
DOLCIAN
DOLCINO
DOLCISSIMO
DOLD
DOLDRUM
DOLDRUMS
DOLE
DOLEANCE
DOLED
DOLEFISH
DOLEFUL
DOLEFULLY
DOLEFULNESS
DOLEFULS
DOLENT
DOLENTE
DOLENTISSIMO
DOLERITE
DOLERITIC
DOLESMAN
DOLESOME
DOLESS
DOLEY
DOLICHOBLOND
DOLICHURIC
DOLICHURUS
DOLINA
DOLINE
DOLING
DOLIOFORM
DOLISIE
DOLITE
DOLITTLE
DOLIUM
DOLL
DOLLAR
DOLLARBIRD
DOLLARDEE
DOLLARFISH
DOLLARFISHES
DOLLARLEAF
DOLLARS
DOLLBEER
DOLLEY
DOLLFACE
DOLLFISH
DOLLHOUSE
DOLLIE
DOLLIED
DOLLIER
DOLLIES
DOLLIN
DOLLINESS
DOLLISH
DOLLISHLY
DOLLISHNESS
DOLLMAKER
DOLLMAKING
DOLLOP
DOLLS
DOLLY
DOLLYING
DOLLYMAN
DOLLYWAY
DOLMAN
DOLMEN
DOLOMITE
DOLOMITIC
DOLOMITIZE
DOLOR
DOLORIFEROUS
DOLORIFIC
DOLORIFUGE

DOLORIMETRY
DOLOROSO
DOLOROUS
DOLOROUSLY
DOLOROUSNESS
DOLOS
DOLOSE
DOLOUR
DOLPHIN
DOLT
DOLTHEAD
DOLTISH
DOLTISHLY
DOLTISHNESS
DOLUS
DOM
DOMAIN
DOMAL
DOMANIAL
DOMATIUM
DOMBA
DOME
DOMED
DOMENT
DOMER
DOMESDAY
DOMESTIC
DOMESTICABLE
DOMESTICALLY
DOMESTICATE
DOMESTICATED
DOMESTICATOR
DOMESTICITY
DOMESTICIZE
DOMESTICIZED
DOMESTICS
DOMETT
DOMEYKITE
DOMIC
DOMICAL
DOMICALLY
DOMICIL
DOMICILE
DOMICILED
DOMICILIAR
DOMICILIARY
DOMICILIATE
DOMICILIATED
DOMICILING
DOMIFICATION
DOMIFY
DOMINA
DOMINAE
DOMINANCE
DOMINANCY
DOMINANT
DOMINANTLY
DOMINATE
DOMINATED
DOMINATING
DOMINATION
DOMINATIVE
DOMINATOR
DOMINE
DOMINEER
DOMINEERED
DOMINEERER
DOMINEERING
DOMING
DOMINI
DOMINIAL
DOMINICAL
DOMINIE
DOMINION
DOMINIONISM
DOMINIONIST
DOMINIONS
DOMINIUM
DOMINO
DOMINOES
DOMINOS
DOMINULE
DOMINUS
DOMITE
DOMITIC
DOMN
DOMNEI
DOMOID
DOMPT
DOMPTEUSE
DOMRA
DOMUS
DOMY
DON
DONA
DONABLE
DONACIFORM
DONACK
DONAH
DONARIES
DONARY
DONATARIES
DONATARY
DONATE
DONATED
DONATEE
DONATING
DONATIO
DONATION
DONATIVE
DONATIVELY
DONATOR
DONATORIES
DONATORY
DONATRESS
DONAX
DONCELLA
DONCY
DONDAINE
DONDINE
DONE
DONEE
DONEY
DONG
DONGA
DONGOLA
DONGON
DONI
DONICKER
DONJON
DONK
DONKEY
DONKEYBACK
DONKEYMAN
DONKEYMEN
DONKEYS
DONKEYWORK
DONNA
DONNE
DONNED
DONNEE
DONNERED
DONNERT
DONNICK
DONNING
DONNISH
DONNISHNESS
DONNISM
DONNOCK
DONNOT
DONNY
DONNYBROOK
DONOR
DONOUGHT
DONSHIP
DONSIE
DONSKY
DONSY
DONUM
DONUT
DONZEL
DONZELLA
DOO
DOOB
DOOCOT
DOODAB
DOODAD
DOODAH
DOODLE
DOODLEBUG
DOODLED
DOODLESACK
DOODLING
DOODSKOP
DOOHICKEY
DOOHICKEYS
DOOHICKUS
DOOHINKEY
DOOHINKUS
DOOK
DOOKET
DOOL
DOOLEE
DOOLEY
DOOLFU
DOOLI
DOOLIE
DOOLIES
DOOLY
DOOM
DOOMAGE
DOOMBOOK
DOOMED
DOOMER
DOOMFUL
DOOMING
DOOMLIKE
DOOMS
DOOMSDAY
DOOMSMAN
DOOMSTEAD
DOOMSTER
DOON
DOOPUTTY
DOOR
DOORBELL
DOORBOY
DOORBRAND
DOORCASE
DOORCHEEK
DOORED
DOORFRAME
DOORHAWK
DOORHEAD
DOORJAMB
DOORKEEPER
DOORKNOB
DOORMAID
DOORMAKER
DOORMAKING
DOORMAN
DOORMAT
DOORNAIL
DOORNBOOM
DOORPLATE
DOORPOST
DOORS
DOORSILL
DOORSTEAD
DOORSTEP
DOORSTONE
DOORSTOP
DOORWARD
DOORWAY
DOORWEED
DOORYARD
DOOSE
DOOZY
DOP
DOPA
DOPAMELANIN
DOPAOXIDASE
DOPATTA
DOPCHICK
DOPE
DOPEBOOK
DOPED
DOPEHEAD
DOPER
DOPESHEET
DOPESTER
DOPEY
DOPIER
DOPIEST
DOPING
DOPP
DOPPED
DOPPER
DOPPERBIRD
DOPPIA
DOPPING
DOPPIO
DOPPLERITE
DOPSTER
DOPY
DOR
DORAB
DORAD
DORADILLA
DORADO
DORALIUM
DORAY
DORBEETLE
DORBEL
DORBIE
DORBUG
DORCASTRY
DORE
DOREA
DOREE
DOREY
DORHAWK
DORIA
DORIES
DORIPPID
DORJE
DORLACH
DORLOT
DORM
DORMANCY
DORMANT
DORME
DORMER
DORMERED
DORMETTE
DORMEUSE
DORMICE
DORMIE
DORMIENT
DORMILONA
DORMITARY
DORMITION
DORMITIVE
DORMITORIES
DORMITORY
DORMOUSE
DORMY
DORN
DORNECK
DORNIC
DORNICK
DORNOCK
DORON
DOROSACRAL
DOROSCENTRAL
DOROSTERNAL
DORP
DORPER
DORR
DORRBEETLE
DORRE
DORSA
DORSAD
DORSAL
DORSALIS
DORSALLY
DORSALMOST
DORSE
DORSEL
DORSER
DORSICOLLAR
DORSICOLUMN
DORSICORNU
DORSIDUCT
DORSIFEROUS
DORSIFIXED
DORSIFLEX
DORSIFLEXION
DORSIFLEXOR
DORSIGRADE
DORSILATERAL
DORSILUMBAR
DORSIMEDIAN
DORSIMESAL
DORSIPAROUS
DORSIPINAL
DORSIVENTRAL
DORSO
DORSOCAUDAD
DORSOLATERAL
DORSOMEDIAL
DORSOMESAL
DORSONASAL
DORSONUCHAL
DORSOPLEURAL
DORSORADIAL
DORSOVENTRAD
DORSOVENTRAL
DORSULA
DORSULUM
DORSUM
DORSUMBONAL
DORT
DORTER
DORTINESS
DORTISHIP
DORTOUR
DORTS
DORTY
DORUCK
DORY
DORYLINE
DORYMAN
DORYPHOROS
DORYPHORUS
DOS
DOSA
DOSADH
DOSAGE
DOSAIN
DOSE
DOSED
DOSER
DOSES
DOSIMETER

DOSIMETRIC
DOSIMETRIST
DOSIMETRY
DOSING
DOSIOLOGY
DOSIS
DOSOLOGY
DOSS
DOSSAL
DOSSED
DOSSEL
DOSSENNUS
DOSSER
DOSSERET
DOSSETY
DOSSIER
DOSSIERE
DOSSIL
DOSSING
DOSSMAN
DOSSMEN
DOSSY
DOST
DOT
DOTAGE
DOTAL
DOTANT
DOTARD
DOTARDISM
DOTARDLY
DOTARDY
DOTATE
DOTATION
DOTCHIN
DOTE
DOTED
DOTER
DOTES
DOTH
DOTHER
DOTIER
DOTIEST
DOTINESS
DOTING
DOTINGLY
DOTINGNESS
DOTISH
DOTISHNESS
DOTKIN
DOTLET
DOTS
DOTTED
DOTTEL
DOTTER
DOTTEREL
DOTTERELS
DOTTI
DOTTIER
DOTTIEST
DOTTILY
DOTTINESS
DOTTING
DOTTLE
DOTTLED
DOTTLER
DOTTLING
DOTTREL
DOTTY
DOTY
DOUANE
DOUANIER
DOUAR
DOUBLE
DOUBLED
DOUBLEDAMN
DOUBLEGANGER
DOUBLELEAF
DOUBLENESS
DOUBLER
DOUBLES
DOUBLET
DOUBLETED
DOUBLETHINK
DOUBLETON
DOUBLETONE
DOUBLETREE
DOUBLETS
DOUBLETTE
DOUBLEYOU
DOUBLING
DOUBLOON
DOUBLURE
DOUBLY
DOUBT
DOUBTABLE
DOUBTANCE
DOUBTED
DOUBTEDLY
DOUBTER
DOUBTFUL
DOUBTFULLY
DOUBTFULNESS
DOUBTING
DOUBTINGLY
DOUBTINGNESS
DOUBTLESS
DOUBTLESSLY
DOUBTMONGER
DOUBTOUS
DOUBTSOME
DOUBTY
DOUC
DOUCE
DOUCELY
DOUCENESS
DOUCET
DOUCEUR
DOUCHE
DOUCHED
DOUCHING
DOUCIN
DOUCINE
DOUDLE
DOUF
DOUGH
DOUGHBOY
DOUGHFACE
DOUGHHEAD
DOUGHINESS
DOUGHMAKER
DOUGHMAKING
DOUGHMAN
DOUGHMEN
DOUGHNUT
DOUGHT
DOUGHTIER
DOUGHTIEST
DOUGHTILY
DOUGHTINESS
DOUGHTY
DOUGHY
DOULCE
DOULOCRACY
DOUM
DOUMA
DOUMAIST
DOUNDAKE
DOUP
DOUPER
DOUPING
DOUPION
DOUPIONI
DOUR
DOURA
DOURADE
DOURE
DOURICOULI
DOURINE
DOURLY
DOURNESS
DOUSE
DOUSED
DOUSER
DOUSING
DOUT
DOUTER
DOUTOUS
DOUX
DOUZAINE
DOUZAINIER
DOUZEPER
DOUZEPERS
DOVAP
DOVE
DOVECOT
DOVECOTE
DOVEFLOWER
DOVEFOOT
DOVEHOUSE
DOVEKEY
DOVEKIE
DOVELET
DOVELIKE
DOVELING
DOVER
DOVES
DOVETAIL
DOVETAILED
DOVETAILER
DOVETAILING
DOVEWEED
DOVEWOOD
DOVISH
DOW
DOWABLE
DOWAGE
DOWAGER
DOWCET
DOWCOTE
DOWD
DOWDIER
DOWDIES
DOWDIEST
DOWDILY
DOWDINESS
DOWDY
DOWDYISH
DOWDYISM
DOWED
DOWEL
DOWELED
DOWELING
DOWELLED
DOWELLING
DOWER
DOWERAL
DOWERED
DOWERESS
DOWERING
DOWERY
DOWF
DOWFART
DOWFF
DOWIE
DOWILY
DOWINESS
DOWING
DOWITCH
DOWITCHER
DOWITCHERS
DOWL
DOWLAS
DOWLE
DOWLESS
DOWLY
DOWN
DOWNA
DOWNBEAR
DOWNBEARD
DOWNBEAT
DOWNBEND
DOWNBENT
DOWNBY
DOWNBYE
DOWNCAST
DOWNCASTLY
DOWNCASTNESS
DOWNCOME
DOWNCOMER
DOWNCOMING
DOWNCRIED
DOWNCRY
DOWNCRYING
DOWNCURVED
DOWNCUT
DOWNDALE
DOWNDRAFT
DOWNDRAUGHT
DOWNED
DOWNER
DOWNFACE
DOWNFALL
DOWNFALLEN
DOWNFALLING
DOWNFEED
DOWNFLOW
DOWNFOLD
DOWNFOLDED
DOWNGATE
DOWNGONE
DOWNGRADE
DOWNGRADED
DOWNGRADING
DOWNGROWTH
DOWNGYVED
DOWNHANGING
DOWNHAUL
DOWNHEADED
DOWNHEARTED
DOWNHILL
DOWNIER
DOWNIEST
DOWNINESS
DOWNING
DOWNLAND
DOWNLIE
DOWNLIER
DOWNLIGGING
DOWNLINE
DOWNLOOKED
DOWNLOOKER
DOWNLYING
DOWNMOST
DOWNPIPE
DOWNPOUR
DOWNPOURING
DOWNRIGHT
DOWNRIGHTLY
DOWNRUSH
DOWNRUSHING
DOWNS
DOWNSET
DOWNSHORE
DOWNSIDE
DOWNSINKING
DOWNSITTING
DOWNSLIDING
DOWNSLIP
DOWNSLOPE
DOWNSMAN
DOWNSOME
DOWNSPOUT
DOWNSTAGE
DOWNSTAIR
DOWNSTAIRS
DOWNSTATE
DOWNSTATER
DOWNSTREAM
DOWNSTREET
DOWNSTROKE
DOWNSWING
DOWNTAKE
DOWNTHROW
DOWNTHROWN
DOWNTHRUST
DOWNTOWN
DOWNTREADING
DOWNTROD
DOWNTRODDEN
DOWNTURN
DOWNWARD
DOWNWARDLY
DOWNWARDNESS
DOWNWARDS
DOWNWARP
DOWNWASH
DOWNWAY
DOWNWEED
DOWNWEIGH
DOWNWEIGHT
DOWNWEIGHTED
DOWNWIND
DOWNWITH
DOWNY
DOWP
DOWRY
DOWSABEL
DOWSE
DOWSED
DOWSER
DOWSET
DOWSETS
DOWSING
DOWVE
DOWY
DOXASTIC
DOXASTICON
DOXIE
DOXIES
DOXOGRAPHER
DOXOGRAPHY
DOXOLOGICAL
DOXOLOGIES
DOXOLOGIZE
DOXOLOGIZED
DOXOLOGIZING
DOXOLOGY
DOXY
DOYEN
DOYENNE
DOYLEY
DOYLT
DOYLY
DOYST
DOZE
DOZED
DOZEN
DOZENED
DOZENER
DOZENS
DOZENT
DOZENTH
DOZER
DOZIER
DOZIEST

DOZILY
DOZINESS
DOZING
DOZY
DOZZLE
DOZZLED
DRA
DRAA
DRAB
DRABANT
DRABBED
DRABBER
DRABBEST
DRABBET
DRABBING
DRABBISH
DRABBLE
DRABBLED
DRABBLER
DRABBLETAIL
DRABBLING
DRABBY
DRABI
DRABLER
DRABLY
DRABNESS
DRACHEN
DRACHM
DRACHMA
DRACHMAE
DRACHMAI
DRACHMAL
DRACHMAS
DRACMA
DRACONIAN
DRACONITES
DRACONITIC
DRACONTIAN
DRACONTIASIS
DRACONTIC
DRACONTINE
DRACONTITES
DRACUNCULUS
DRAD
DRAFF
DRAFFISH
DRAFFMAN
DRAFFSACK
DRAFFY
DRAFT
DRAFTAGE
DRAFTED
DRAFTEE
DRAFTER
DRAFTIER
DRAFTILY
DRAFTINESS
DRAFTING
DRAFTS
DRAFTSMAN
DRAFTY
DRAG
DRAGADE
DRAGADED
DRAGADING
DRAGBAR
DRAGBOAT
DRAGBOLT
DRAGEE
DRAGEOIR
DRAGGED
DRAGGER
DRAGGIER
DRAGGIEST
DRAGGILY
DRAGGINESS
DRAGGING
DRAGGLE
DRAGGLED
DRAGGLETAIL
DRAGGLING
DRAGGLY
DRAGGY
DRAGHOUND
DRAGLINE
DRAGMAN
DRAGNET
DRAGO
DRAGOMAN
DRAGOMANATE
DRAGOMANIC
DRAGOMANISH
DRAGOMANS
DRAGOMEN
DRAGON
DRAGONESS
DRAGONET
DRAGONFISH
DRAGONFISHES
DRAGONFLIES
DRAGONFLY
DRAGONHEAD
DRAGONISM
DRAGONIZE
DRAGONKIND
DRAGONNADE
DRAGONNE
DRAGONROOT
DRAGONTAIL
DRAGONWORT
DRAGOON
DRAGOONAGE
DRAGOONED
DRAGOONER
DRAGOONING
DRAGROPE
DRAGSAW
DRAGSHOE
DRAGSMAN
DRAGSMEN
DRAGSTAFF
DRAGSTER
DRAIL
DRAILED
DRAILING
DRAIN
DRAINAGE
DRAINAGEWAY
DRAINBOARD
DRAINE
DRAINED
DRAINER
DRAINERMAN
DRAINERMEN
DRAINING
DRAINLESS
DRAINMAN
DRAINPIPE
DRAINS
DRAINTILE
DRAISENE
DRAISINE
DRAKE
DRAKELET
DRAKESTONE
DRAKONITE
DRAM
DRAMA
DRAMALOGUE
DRAMAMINE
DRAMATIC
DRAMATICAL
DRAMATICALLY
DRAMATICISM
DRAMATICS
DRAMATICULE
DRAMATISE
DRAMATISM
DRAMATIST
DRAMATIZATION
DRAMATIZE
DRAMATIZED
DRAMATIZER
DRAMATIZING
DRAMATURGE
DRAMATURGIC
DRAMATURGIST
DRAMATURGY
DRAME
DRAMM
DRAMMAGE
DRAMME
DRAMMED
DRAMMER
DRAMMING
DRAMMOCK
DRAMSELLER
DRAMSHOP
DRANE
DRANG
DRANK
DRANT
DRAP
DRAPE
DRAPEAU
DRAPED
DRAPER
DRAPERESS
DRAPERIED
DRAPERIES
DRAPERY
DRAPET
DRAPING
DRAPPIE
DRAPPY
DRASH
DRASHEL
DRASS
DRASSID
DRAST
DRASTIC
DRASTICALLY
DRASTY
DRAT
DRATCHELL
DRATE
DRATTED
DRATTING
DRAUGHT
DRAUGHTAGE
DRAUGHTBOARD
DRAUGHTED
DRAUGHTER
DRAUGHTHOUSE
DRAUGHTIER
DRAUGHTIEST
DRAUGHTILY
DRAUGHTINESS
DRAUGHTING
DRAUGHTS
DRAUGHTSMAN
DRAUGHTSMEN
DRAUGHTY
DRAUNT
DRAVE
DRAVITE
DRAW
DRAWABLE
DRAWARM
DRAWBACK
DRAWBAND
DRAWBAR
DRAWBEAM
DRAWBENCH
DRAWBOARD
DRAWBOLT
DRAWBORE
DRAWBORED
DRAWBORING
DRAWBOY
DRAWBRIDGE
DRAWCARD
DRAWCORD
DRAWCUT
DRAWCUTTING
DRAWDOWN
DRAWEE
DRAWER
DRAWERS
DRAWFILE
DRAWFILED
DRAWFILING
DRAWGATE
DRAWGEAR
DRAWGLOVE
DRAWGLOVES
DRAWHEAD
DRAWHORSE
DRAWING
DRAWK
DRAWKNIFE
DRAWKNIVES
DRAWKNOT
DRAWL
DRAWLATCH
DRAWLED
DRAWLER
DRAWLIER
DRAWLIEST
DRAWLING
DRAWLINGLY
DRAWLINGNESS
DRAWLINK
DRAWLOOM
DRAWLY
DRAWN
DRAWNET
DRAWOFF
DRAWOUT
DRAWPLATE
DRAWPOINT
DRAWROD
DRAWSHAVE
DRAWSHEET
DRAWSPAN
DRAWSPRING
DRAWSTOP
DRAWSTRING
DRAWTONGS
DRAWTUBE
DRAY
DRAYAGE
DRAYED
DRAYING
DRAYMAN
DRAYMEN
DRAZEL
DRAZIL
DREAD
DREADABLE
DREADED
DREADER
DREADFUL
DREADFULLY
DREADFULNESS
DREADING
DREADINGLY
DREADLESS
DREADLESSLY
DREADLY
DREADNAUGHT
DREADNESS
DREADNOUGHT
DREAM
DREAMED
DREAMER
DREAMERIES
DREAMERY
DREAMFUL
DREAMFULLY
DREAMFULNESS
DREAMHOLE
DREAMIER
DREAMIEST
DREAMILY
DREAMINESS
DREAMING
DREAMINGLY
DREAMLAND
DREAMLESS
DREAMLESSLY
DREAMLIKE
DREAMLIT
DREAMLORE
DREAMS
DREAMSILY
DREAMSINESS
DREAMSY
DREAMT
DREAMTIDE
DREAMTIME
DREAMWHILE
DREAMWORLD
DREAMY
DREAR
DREARIER
DREARIEST
DREARIHEAD
DREARIHOOD
DREARILY
DREARIMENT
DREARINESS
DREARING
DREARLY
DREARNESS
DREARY
DRECK
DREDDOUR
DREDGE
DREDGED
DREDGEMAN
DREDGER
DREDGIE
DREDGING
DREE
DREECH
DREED
DREEING
DREEL
DREELY
DREEN
DREEP
DREEPINESS
DREEPY
DREG
DREGGIER
DREGGIEST
DREGGILY
DREGGINESS
DREGGISH
DREGGY
DREGS
DREICH
DREIDEL
DREIE

DREIGH
DREILING
DRENCH
DRENCHED
DRENCHER
DRENCHING
DRENCHINGLY
DRENG
DRENGAGE
DRENGH
DREPANE
DREPANIA
DREPANID
DREPANIFORM
DREPANIUM
DREPANOID
DREPE
DRESS
DRESSAGE
DRESSED
DRESSER
DRESSES
DRESSIER
DRESSIEST
DRESSILY
DRESSINESS
DRESSING
DRESSMAKER
DRESSMAKERY
DRESSMAKING
DRESSY
DREST
DRETCH
DREW
DREWITE
DREY
DRIAS
DRIB
DRIBBED
DRIBBER
DRIBBING
DRIBBLE
DRIBBLED
DRIBBLER
DRIBBLET
DRIBBLING
DRIBLET
DRIDDER
DRIDDLE
DRIECH
DRIED
DRIEGH
DRIER
DRIERMAN
DRIES
DRIEST
DRIFT
DRIFTAGE
DRIFTBOLT
DRIFTED
DRIFTER
DRIFTIER
DRIFTIEST
DRIFTING
DRIFTINGLY
DRIFTLAND
DRIFTLESS
DRIFTLET
DRIFTMAN
DRIFTPIECE
DRIFTPIN
DRIFTWAY
DRIFTWEED
DRIFTWIND
DRIFTWOOD
DRIFTY
DRIGHTEN
DRIGHTIN
DRIKI
DRILL
DRILLED
DRILLER
DRILLET
DRILLING
DRILLMAN
DRILLMASTER
DRILLSTOCK
DRILVIS
DRILY
DRING
DRINGLE
DRINK
DRINKABILITY
DRINKABLE
DRINKABLY
DRINKER
DRINKERY
DRINKING
DRINKLESS
DRINKS
DRINKY
DRINN
DRIP
DRIPOLATOR
DRIPPED
DRIPPER
DRIPPIER
DRIPPIEST
DRIPPING
DRIPPLE
DRIPPY
DRIPSTICK
DRIPSTONE
DRIPT
DRISHEEN
DRISK
DRISSEL
DRIVABLE
DRIVAGE
DRIVE
DRIVEABLE
DRIVEAWAY
DRIVEBOAT
DRIVEBOLT
DRIVECAP
DRIVEHEAD
DRIVEL
DRIVELED
DRIVELER
DRIVELING
DRIVELINGLY
DRIVELLED
DRIVELLER
DRIVELLING
DRIVEN
DRIVEPIPE
DRIVER
DRIVESCREW
DRIVEWAY
DRIVING
DRIVINGLY
DRIZZLE
DRIZZLED
DRIZZLING
DRIZZLY
DROB
DROCHUIL
DRODDUM
DROFLAND
DROGER
DROGERMAN
DROGERMEN
DROGH
DROGHER
DROGHERMAN
DROGHLIN
DROGUE
DROGUET
DROICH
DROIL
DROIT
DROITS
DROITURAL
DROKE
DROLE
DROLERIE
DROLL
DROLLED
DROLLER
DROLLERIES
DROLLERY
DROLLEST
DROLLING
DROLLISH
DROLLISHNESS
DROLLIST
DROLLY
DROME
DROMED
DROMEDARIAN
DROMEDARIES
DROMEDARIST
DROMEDARY
DROMETER
DROMI
DROMIC
DROMICAL
DROMOGRAPH
DROMOMANIA
DROMOMETER
DROMON
DROMOND
DROMOS
DROMOTROPIC
DRONA
DRONAGE
DRONE
DRONED
DRONEL
DRONER
DRONET
DRONG
DRONGO
DRONGOS
DRONING
DRONISH
DRONISHLY
DRONISHNESS
DRONKGRASS
DRONY
DROOK
DROOL
DROOLED
DROOP
DROOPED
DROOPER
DROOPIER
DROOPIEST
DROOPILY
DROOPINESS
DROOPING
DROOPINGLY
DROOPINGNESS
DROOPT
DROOPY
DROP
DROPCLOTH
DROPFORGE
DROPFORGED
DROPFORGING
DROPHEAD
DROPKICK
DROPLET
DROPLIGHT
DROPLINE
DROPLING
DROPMAN
DROPMEAL
DROPOUT
DROPPED
DROPPER
DROPPING
DROPPY
DROPS
DROPSEED
DROPSICAL
DROPSICALLY
DROPSIED
DROPSIES
DROPSY
DROPT
DROPVIE
DROPWISE
DROPWORM
DROPWORT
DROSHKIES
DROSHKY
DROSKY
DROSOGRAPH
DROSOMETER
DROSOPHILA
DROSS
DROSSED
DROSSEL
DROSSER
DROSSIER
DROSSIEST
DROSSINESS
DROSSING
DROSSY
DROSTDEN
DROSTDY
DROUD
DROUGHERMEN
DROUGHT
DROUGHTINESS
DROUGHTY
DROUK
DROUKAN
DROUKED
DROUKET
DROUKING
DROUKIT
DROUMY
DROUTH
DROUTHY
DROVE
DROVED
DROVER
DROVING
DROVY
DROW
DROWK
DROWN
DROWNED
DROWNER
DROWNING
DROWSE
DROWSED
DROWSIER
DROWSIEST
DROWSIHEAD
DROWSIHOOD
DROWSILY
DROWSINESS
DROWSING
DROWSY
DROY
DROZE
DRUB
DRUBBED
DRUBBER
DRUBBING
DRUBBLE
DRUBLY
DRUCKEN
DRUDGE
DRUDGED
DRUDGER
DRUDGERIES
DRUDGERY
DRUDGING
DRUDGINGLY
DRUDGISM
DRUERY
DRUG
DRUGGE
DRUGGED
DRUGGER
DRUGGERIES
DRUGGERY
DRUGGET
DRUGGIER
DRUGGIEST
DRUGGING
DRUGGIST
DRUGGY
DRUGLESS
DRUGMAN
DRUGS
DRUGSHOP
DRUGSTORE
DRUID
DRUIDESS
DRUIDIC
DRUIDICAL
DRUIDISM
DRUIDRY
DRUK
DRUM
DRUMBEAT
DRUMBLE
DRUMBLED
DRUMBLEDORE
DRUMBLER
DRUMBLING
DRUMFIRE
DRUMFISH
DRUMFISHES
DRUMHEAD
DRUMHEADS
DRUMLER
DRUMLIN
DRUMLINE
DRUMLINOID
DRUMLOID
DRUMLOIDAL
DRUMLY
DRUMMED
DRUMMER
DRUMMING
DRUMMOCK
DRUMMY
DRUMS
DRUMSKIN
DRUMSLER
DRUMSTICK
DRUMWOOD
DRUN
DRUNG
DRUNGAR
DRUNK
DRUNKARD
DRUNKELEW
DRUNKEN

DRUNKENLY
DRUNKENNESS
DRUNKER
DRUNKERIES
DRUNKERY
DRUNKOMETER
DRUNT
DRUPACEOUS
DRUPAL
DRUPE
DRUPEL
DRUPELET
DRUPEOLE
DRUPETUM
DRUPIFEROUS
DRURY
DRUSE
DRUSED
DRUSH
DRUSY
DRUTHER
DRUTHERS
DRUTTLE
DRUVE
DRUVY
DRUXEY
DRUXINESS
DRUXY
DRY
DRYAD
DRYADES
DRYADIC
DRYAS
DRYASDUST
DRYBEARD
DRYER
DRYERMAN
DRYERMEN
DRYEST
DRYFIST
DRYFOOT
DRYGOODSMAN
DRYHOUSE
DRYING
DRYINID
DRYISH
DRYLOT
DRYLY
DRYNESS
DRYOPTEROID
DRYPOINT
DRYS
DRYSALTER
DRYSALTERIES
DRYSALTERY
DRYSNE
DRYSTER
DRYTH
DRYWORKER
DU
DUAB
DUAD
DUADIC
DUAL
DUALI
DUALIN
DUALISM
DUALIST
DUALISTIC
DUALITY
DUALIZATION
DUALIZE
DUALIZED
DUALIZING
DUAN
DUANT
DUAR
DUARCH
DUARCHY
DUB
DUBASH
DUBB
DUBBA
DUBBAH
DUBBED
DUBBEH
DUBBELTJE
DUBBER
DUBBIN
DUBBING
DUBBY
DUBIETIES
DUBIETY
DUBIOSITIES
DUBIOSITY
DUBIOUS
DUBIOUSLY
DUBIOUSNESS
DUBITABLE
DUBITABLY
DUBITANT
DUBITANTE
DUBITATE
DUBITATION
DUBITATIVE
DUBITATIVELY
DUBS
DUC
DUCAL
DUCALLY
DUCAPE
DUCAT
DUCATO
DUCATON
DUCATOON
DUCATUS
DUCDAME
DUCE
DUCES
DUCHAN
DUCHERY
DUCHESS
DUCHESSE
DUCHIES
DUCHN
DUCHY
DUCK
DUCKBILL
DUCKBLIND
DUCKBOARD
DUCKBOAT
DUCKED
DUCKER
DUCKERIES
DUCKERY
DUCKFOOT
DUCKHEARTED
DUCKHOUSE
DUCKHUNTING
DUCKIE
DUCKIER
DUCKIEST
DUCKING
DUCKISH
DUCKLAR
DUCKLET
DUCKLING
DUCKMEAT
DUCKMOLE
DUCKPIN
DUCKPINS
DUCKPOND
DUCKS
DUCKSTONE
DUCKTAIL
DUCKWEED
DUCKWIFE
DUCKWING
DUCKY
DUCT
DUCTIBILITY
DUCTIBLE
DUCTILE
DUCTILELY
DUCTILENESS
DUCTILIMETER
DUCTILITY
DUCTILIZE
DUCTILIZED
DUCTILIZING
DUCTION
DUCTOR
DUCTULE
DUCTURE
DUCTUS
DUD
DUDAIM
DUDDER
DUDDERY
DUDDIE
DUDDLE
DUDDY
DUDE
DUDEEN
DUDGEN
DUDGEON
DUDINE
DUDISH
DUDLER
DUDLEY
DUDLEYITE
DUDMAN
DUDS
DUE
DUEFUL
DUEL
DUELED
DUELER
DUELING
DUELIST
DUELISTIC
DUELLED
DUELLER
DUELLING
DUELLIST
DUELLISTIC
DUELLIZE
DUELLO
DUELLOS
DUENA
DUENAS
DUENNA
DUENNAS
DUES
DUET
DUETTED
DUETTING
DUETTINO
DUETTIST
DUETTO
DUFF
DUFFADAR
DUFFED
DUFFEL
DUFFER
DUFFIES
DUFFING
DUFFLE
DUFFY
DUFOIL
DUFRENITE
DUFRENOYSITE
DUFTER
DUFTERDAR
DUFTERY
DUFTITE
DUFTRY
DUG
DUGAL
DUGDUG
DUGGLER
DUGON
DUGONG
DUGOUT
DUGWAY
DUHAT
DUI
DUIKER
DUIKERBOK
DUIKERBOKS
DUIKERBUCK
DUIM
DUIME
DUINHEWASSEL
DUIT
DUJAN
DUKAN
DUKE
DUKEDOM
DUKELING
DUKELY
DUKERY
DUKES
DUKHN
DUKKER
DUKKERIPEN
DUKU
DUKUMA
DULBERT
DULCAMARA
DULCARNON
DULCE
DULCELY
DULCENESS
DULCET
DULCETLY
DULCETNESS
DULCIAN
DULCIANA
DULCID
DULCIFIED
DULCIFLUOUS
DULCIFY
DULCIFYING
DULCILOQUENT
DULCILOQUY
DULCIMER
DULCITE
DULCITOL
DULCITUDE
DULCITY
DULCOR
DULEDGE
DULER
DULIA
DULL
DULLARD
DULLARDISM
DULLARDNESS
DULLBRAINED
DULLED
DULLER
DULLERY
DULLEST
DULLHEAD
DULLHEARTED
DULLIFY
DULLING
DULLISH
DULLITY
DULLNESS
DULLPATE
DULLSOME
DULLY
DULNESS
DULOCRACY
DULOSIS
DULOTIC
DULSE
DULT
DULTIE
DULWILLY
DULY
DUMA
DUMAIST
DUMAL
DUMB
DUMBA
DUMBBELL
DUMBBELLER
DUMBCOW
DUMBFISH
DUMBFOUND
DUMBFOUNDED
DUMBHEAD
DUMBLE
DUMBLEDORE
DUMBLY
DUMBNESS
DUMBWAITER
DUMBY
DUMDUM
DUMFOUND
DUMFOUNDED
DUMKA
DUMKY
DUMMEL
DUMMERED
DUMMERER
DUMMIES
DUMMKOPF
DUMMY
DUMONTITE
DUMORTIERITE
DUMOSE
DUMOSITY
DUMOUS
DUMP
DUMPAGE
DUMPCART
DUMPED
DUMPER
DUMPIER
DUMPIES
DUMPIEST
DUMPILY
DUMPING
DUMPISH
DUMPISHLY
DUMPISHNESS
DUMPLE
DUMPLED
DUMPLER
DUMPLING
DUMPOKE
DUMPS
DUMPTY
DUMPY
DUN
DUNAIR
DUNAL
DUNAM
DUNAMIS
DUNBIRD
DUNCE

DUNCERY
DUNCH
DUNCICAL
DUNCIFY
DUNCIFYING
DUNCISH
DUNCISHLY
DUNCISHNESS
DUNDASITE
DUNDER
DUNDERFUNK
DUNDERHEAD
DUNDERHEADED
DUNDERPATE
DUNE
DUNES
DUNFISH
DUNG
DUNGA
DUNGANNONITE
DUNGAREE
DUNGARI
DUNGBECK
DUNGBIRD
DUNGED
DUNGEON
DUNGEONER
DUNGER
DUNGHILL
DUNGHILLY
DUNGING
DUNGON
DUNGY
DUNIEWASSAL
DUNITE
DUNK
DUNKADOO
DUNKER
DUNKING
DUNKLE
DUNKLED
DUNKLING
DUNLIN
DUNLINS
DUNNAGE
DUNNAGED
DUNNAGING
DUNNE
DUNNED
DUNNER
DUNNESS
DUNNIEWASSEL
DUNNING
DUNNISH
DUNNITE
DUNNOCK
DUNNY
DUNST
DUNSTABLE
DUNSTER
DUNT
DUNTED
DUNTING
DUNTLE
DUNUM
DUNY
DUNZIEKTE
DUO
DUOCOSANE
DUODECANE
DUODECENNIAL
DUODECILLION
DUODECIMAL
DUODECIMALITY
DUODECIMALLY
DUODECIMO
DUODECIMOLE
DUODECIMOS
DUODECUPLE
DUODENA
DUODENAL
DUODENARY
DUODENATE
DUODENATION
DUODENE
DUODENITIS
DUODENUM
DUODRAMA
DUOGRAPH
DUOLE
DUOLITERAL
DUOLOG
DUOLOGUE
DUOMACHY
DUOMI
DUOMO
DUOPOD
DUOS
DUOSECANT
DUOTONED
DUOTYPE
DUOVIRI
DUP
DUPABILITY
DUPABLE
DUPE
DUPED
DUPER
DUPERIES
DUPERY
DUPING
DUPION
DUPLATION
DUPLE
DUPLET
DUPLEX
DUPLEXED
DUPLEXER
DUPLEXES
DUPLEXING
DUPLEXITY
DUPLICABLE
DUPLICAND
DUPLICANDO
DUPLICATE
DUPLICATED
DUPLICATELY
DUPLICATING
DUPLICATION
DUPLICATIVE
DUPLICATOR
DUPLICATURE
DUPLICIDENT
DUPLICITAS
DUPLICITIES
DUPLICITY
DUPLIFIED
DUPLIFY
DUPLIFYING
DUPLONE
DUPLY
DUPONDIUS
DUPPER
DUPPIES
DUPPY
DUR
DURA
DURABILITIES
DURABILITY
DURABLE
DURABLENESS
DURABLY
DURACINE
DURAIN
DURAL
DURAMEN
DURANCE
DURANGITE
DURANT
DURANTE
DURAPLASTY
DURAQUARA
DURATION
DURATIONAL
DURATIVE
DURAX
DURBACHITE
DURBAR
DURDENITE
DURDUM
DURE
DUREE
DUREFUL
DURENOL
DURESS
DURESSOR
DUREZZA
DURGAH
DURGAN
DURGEN
DURIAN
DURICRUST
DURIDINE
DURING
DURINGLY
DURION
DURITY
DURMAST
DURN
DURNED
DURO
DUROMETER
DUROQUINONE
DUROS
DUROY
DURR
DURRA
DURRIE
DURRIES
DURRIN
DURRY
DURST
DURUKULI
DURUM
DURWAN
DURWAUN
DURYL
DURZEE
DUSACK
DUSCLE
DUSE
DUSH
DUSIO
DUSK
DUSKEN
DUSKIER
DUSKIEST
DUSKILY
DUSKINESS
DUSKINGTIDE
DUSKISH
DUSKLY
DUSKNESS
DUSKY
DUST
DUSTBAND
DUSTBIN
DUSTBLU
DUSTBOX
DUSTCLOTH
DUSTCOAT
DUSTED
DUSTEE
DUSTER
DUSTERMAN
DUSTERMEN
DUSTFALL
DUSTHEAP
DUSTIER
DUSTIEST
DUSTILY
DUSTINESS
DUSTING
DUSTLESS
DUSTLIKE
DUSTMAN
DUSTOOR
DUSTOORI
DUSTOUR
DUSTPAN
DUSTPOINT
DUSTPROOF
DUSTRAG
DUSTUCK
DUSTUK
DUSTUP
DUSTY
DUSTYFOOT
DUTCH
DUTCHED
DUTCHESS
DUTCHING
DUTCHMAN
DUTCHMEN
DUTEOUS
DUTEOUSLY
DUTEOUSNESS
DUTIABILITY
DUTIABLE
DUTIED
DUTIES
DUTIFUL
DUTIFULLY
DUTIFULNESS
DUTRA
DUTUBURI
DUTY
DUUMVIR
DUUMVIRAL
DUUMVIRATE
DUUMVIRI
DUUMVIRS
DUVEL
DUVET
DUVETINE
DUVETYN
DUVETYNE
DUX
DUXELLES
DUXES
DUYKER
DVAITA
DVANDVA
DVORNIK
DWAIBLE
DWAIBLY
DWAIN
DWALE
DWALL
DWALM
DWAM
DWANG
DWARF
DWARFED
DWARFING
DWARFISH
DWARFISHLY
DWARFISHNESS
DWARFISM
DWARFLING
DWARFNESS
DWARFS
DWARFY
DWARVES
DWAYBERRY
DWEEBLE
DWELL
DWELLED
DWELLER
DWELLING
DWELT
DWERE
DWINDLE
DWINDLED
DWINDLING
DWINE
DWINED
DWINING
DYAD
DYADIC
DYARCHIC
DYARCHICAL
DYARCHY
DYBBUK
DYCE
DYDE
DYE
DYEABLE
DYEBECK
DYED
DYEHOUSE
DYEING
DYELEAVES
DYER
DYESTER
DYESTUFF
DYEWARE
DYEWEED
DYEWOOD
DYGOGRAM
DYING
DYKAGE
DYKE
DYKEHOPPER
DYKER
DYKEREEVE
DYNAGRAPH
DYNAM
DYNAMETER
DYNAMETRIC
DYNAMETRICAL
DYNAMIC
DYNAMICAL
DYNAMICALLY
DYNAMICS
DYNAMIS
DYNAMISM
DYNAMIST
DYNAMISTIC
DYNAMITARD
DYNAMITE
DYNAMITED
DYNAMITER
DYNAMITIC
DYNAMITICAL
DYNAMITING
DYNAMITISM
DYNAMITIST
DYNAMIZATION
DYNAMIZE
DYNAMO
DYNAMOGENIC
DYNAMOGENOUS
DYNAMOMETER
DYNAMOMETRIC

DYNAMOMETRY
DYNAMONEURE
DYNAMOPHONE
DYNAMOSTATIC
DYNAMOTOR
DYNAST
DYNASTIC
DYNASTICAL
DYNASTICALLY
DYNASTID
DYNASTIDAN
DYNASTIES
DYNASTY
DYNATRON
DYNE
DYNODE
DYOPHONE
DYOTHEISM
DYPHONE
DYPNONE
DYSACOUSIA
DYSACOUSIS
DYSAESTHESIA
DYSANALYTE
DYSAPHIA
DYSARTHRIA
DYSARTHRIC
DYSARTHROSIS
DYSBULIA
DYSBULIC
DYSCHIRIA
DYSCHROA
DYSCHROIA
DYSCHRONOUS
DYSCRASE
DYSCRASED
DYSCRASIA
DYSCRASIC
DYSCRASING
DYSCRASITE
DYSCRATIC
DYSENTERIC
DYSENTERY
DYSERGASIA
DYSERGIA
DYSESTHESIA
DYSFUNCTION
DYSGENESIC
DYSGENESIS
DYSGENIC
DYSGENICS
DYSGEOGENOUS
DYSGNOSIA
DYSGRAPHIA
DYSIDROSIS
DYSKINESIA
DYSKINETIC
DYSLOGIA
DYSLOGISTIC
DYSLOGY
DYSLUITE
DYSLYSIN
DYSMENORRHEA
DYSMERISM
DYSMERISTIC
DYSMEROMORPH
DYSMNESIA
DYSMORPHISM
DYSNEURIA
DYSNOMY
DYSODILE
DYSOREXY
DYSOXIDATION
DYSOXIDIZE
DYSPATHETIC
DYSPATHY
DYSPEPSIA
DYSPEPSY
DYSPEPTIC
DYSPEPTICAL
DYSPHAGIA
DYSPHAGIC
DYSPHASIA
DYSPHASIC
DYSPHONIA
DYSPHONIC
DYSPHORIA
DYSPHORIC
DYSPHOTIC
DYSPHRASIA
DYSPHRENIA
DYSPNEA
DYSPNEAL
DYSPNEIC
DYSPNOEA
DYSPNOEAL
DYSPROSIA
DYSPROSIUM
DYSSNITE
DYSSYNERGIA
DYSSYNERGY
DYSSYSTOLE
DYSTAXIA
DYSTECTIC
DYSTELEOLOGY
DYSTHYMIA
DYSTOCIA
DYSTOCIAL
DYSTOME
DYSTOMIC
DYSTOMOUS
DYSTONIA
DYSTOPIA
DYSTROPHIA
DYSTROPHIC
DYSTROPHY
DYSURIA
DYSURIC
DYSYNTRIBITE
DYTE
DYTISCID
DYVOUR
DZEREN
DZERIN
DZERON
DZIGGETAI
DZO

E

EA
EACEWORM
EACH
EACHWHERE
EAGER
EAGERLY
EAGERNESS
EAGLE
EAGLESS
EAGLESTONE
EAGLET
EAGLEWOOD
EAGRASS
EAGRE
EALDERMAN
EALDORMAN
EAN
EANED
EANING
EANLING
EAR
EARABLE
EARACHE
EARBASH
EARBOB
EARCAP
EARCLIP
EARCOCKLE
EARD
EARDROP
EARDROPPER
EARDROPS
EARDRUM
EARED
EARFLAP
EARFLOWER
EARFUL
EARHEAD
EARHOLE
EARING
EARJEWEL
EARL
EARLAP
EARLDOM
EARLDUCK
EARLET
EARLIER
EARLIEST
EARLIKE
EARLINESS
EARLOBE
EARLOCK
EARLSHIP
EARLY
EARLYISH
EARMARK
EARMARKED
EARMARKING
EARMUFF
EARN
EARNED
EARNER
EARNEST
EARNESTLY
EARNESTNESS
EARNFUL
EARNING
EARNINGS
EAROCK
EARPHONE
EARPICK
EARPIECE
EARPLUG
EARREACH
EARRING
EARRINGED
EARS
EARSCREW
EARSHOT
EARSORE
EARSPLITTING
EARSPOOL
EARSTONE
EARTAB
EARTAG
EARTH
EARTHBOARD
EARTHBORN
EARTHBRED
EARTHDRAKE
EARTHED
EARTHEN
EARTHENHEARTED
EARTHENWARE
EARTHFALL
EARTHFAST
EARTHGALL
EARTHGRUBBER
EARTHIAN
EARTHIER
EARTHIEST
EARTHINESS
EARTHING
EARTHKIN
EARTHLESS
EARTHLIGHT
EARTHLIKE
EARTHLINESS
EARTHLING
EARTHLY
EARTHMAKER
EARTHMAKING
EARTHNUT
EARTHPEA
EARTHQUAKE
EARTHQUAKED
EARTHQUAKEN
EARTHQUAKING
EARTHQUAVE
EARTHS
EARTHSET
EARTHSHINE
EARTHSHOCK
EARTHSLIDE
EARTHSMOKE
EARTHSTAR
EARTHTONGUE
EARTHWARD
EARTHWARDS
EARTHWORK
EARTHWORM
EARTHY
EARWAX
EARWIG
EARWIGGED
EARWIGGINESS
EARWIGGING
EARWIGGY
EARWITNESS
EARWORM
EARWORT
EASE
EASED
EASEFUL
EASEFULLY
EASEFULNESS
EASEL
EASELED
EASELESS
EASEMENT
EASER
EASIER
EASIEST
EASILY
EASINESS
EASING
EASSEL
EAST
EASTABOUT
EASTBOUND
EASTED
EASTER
EASTERLING
EASTERLY
EASTERMOST
EASTERN
EASTERNER
EASTERNLY
EASTERNMOST
EASTING
EASTLAND
EASTLIN
EASTLING
EASTLINGS
EASTLINS
EASTMOST
EASTWARD
EASTWARDLY
EASTWARDS
EASY
EASYGOING
EASYLIKE
EAT
EATABILITY
EATABLE
EATABLENESS
EATABLES
EATAGE
EATBERRY
EATCHE
EATEN
EATER
EATERY
EATH
EATHLY
EATING
EATS
EAU
EAUX
EAVE
EAVEDROP
EAVEDROPPER
EAVEDROPPING
EAVER
EAVES
EAVESDRIP
EAVESDROP
EAVESDROPPER
EAVESING
EAWT
EBANO
EBAUCHE
EBB
EBBED
EBBET
EBBING
EBBMAN
EBENEOUS
EBO
EBOE
EBON
EBONIST
EBONITE
EBONIZE
EBONIZED
EBONIZING
EBONY
EBRACTEATE
EBRACTEOLATE
EBRIATE
EBRIATED
EBRIETY
EBRILLADE
EBRIOSE
EBRIOSITY
EBRIOUS
EBRIOUSLY
EBULLATE
EBULLIATE
EBULLIENCE
EBULLIENCY
EBULLIENT
EBULLIENTLY
EBULLIOMETER
EBULLIOSCOPE
EBULLIOSCOPIC
EBULLITION
EBULLITIVE
EBULUS
EBURATED
EBURE
EBURINE
EBURNATED
EBURNATION
EBURNEAN
EBURNEOID
EBURNEOUS
ECAD
ECALCARATE
ECANDA
ECARDINAL
ECARINATE
ECARTE
ECAUDATE
ECBASIS
ECBATIC
ECBLASTESIS
ECBOLE
ECBOLIC
ECCALEOBION
ECCE
ECCENTRATE
ECCENTRIC
ECCENTRICAL
ECCENTRICALLY
ECCENTRICITIES
ECCENTRICITY
ECCENTRING
ECCHONDROMA
ECCHYMOMA
ECCHYMOSE
ECCHYMOSES
ECCHYMOSIS
ECCHYMOTIC
ECCLE
ECCLESIA
ECCLESIAL
ECCLESIARCH
ECCLESIARCHY
ECCLESIAST
ECCLESIASTIC
ECCLESIASTICAL
ECCLESIASTICALLY
ECCLESIASTICIS
ECCLESIASTICS
ECCLESIASTRY
ECCLESIOLATER
ECCLESIOLOGIC
ECCOPROTIC
ECCRINOLOGY
ECCRISIS
ECCRITIC
ECCYCLEMA
ECCYESIS
ECDEMIC
ECDEMITE
ECDERON
ECDERONIC
ECDYSES
ECDYSIAST
ECDYSIS
ECE
ECESIC
ECESIS
ECGONIN
ECGONINE
ECHAPPE
ECHAPPEE
ECHARD
ECHE
ECHEA
ECHELETTE
ECHELLE
ECHELON
ECHENEID
ECHENEIDID
ECHEVIN
ECHIDNA
ECHIDNAE
ECHINACEA
ECHINAL
ECHINATE
ECHINATED
ECHINID
ECHINIDAN
ECHINIFORM
ECHINITAL
ECHINITE
ECHINOCHROME
ECHINOCOCCUS
ECHINODERM
ECHINODERMAL
ECHINODERMIC
ECHINOID
ECHINOLOGIST
ECHINOLOGY
ECHINOPSINE
ECHINULATE
ECHINULATION
ECHINULIFORM
ECHINUS
ECHITAMINE
ECHIUROID
ECHO
ECHOER
ECHOES
ECHOIC
ECHOISM
ECHOIZE
ECHOIZED
ECHOIZING
ECHOLALIA
ECHOLALIC
ECHOLOCATION
ECHOPRACTIC
ECHOPRAXIA
ECILIATE
ECIZE
ECKLE
ECLAIR
ECLAMPSIA
ECLAMPTIC
ECLAT
ECLATED
ECLATING

ECLECTIC
ECLECTICAL
ECLECTICALLY
ECLECTICISM
ECLEGM
ECLEGMA
ECLIPSAREON
ECLIPSE
ECLIPSED
ECLIPSER
ECLIPSING
ECLIPSIS
ECLIPTIC
ECLIPTICAL
ECLIPTICALLY
ECLOGITE
ECLOGUE
ECLOSION
ECMNESIA
ECOD
ECOID
ECOLE
ECOLOGIC
ECOLOGICAL
ECOLOGICALLY
ECOLOGIST
ECOLOGY
ECONOMETER
ECONOMETRIC
ECONOMETRICAL
ECONOMETRICS
ECONOMIC
ECONOMICAL
ECONOMICALLY
ECONOMICS
ECONOMIES
ECONOMISM
ECONOMIST
ECONOMIZATION
ECONOMIZE
ECONOMIZED
ECONOMIZER
ECONOMIZING
ECONOMY
ECOPHENE
ECOPHOBIA
ECORCHE
ECORTICATE
ECOSPECIES
ECOSTATE
ECOTIPICALLY
ECOTONE
ECOTYPE
ECOTYPIC
ECPHONESIS
ECPHORIA
ECPHORIAE
ECPHORIAS
ECPHORIZE
ECPHORY
ECPHRASIS
ECRASE
ECRASEUR
ECRASITE
ECRU
ECRUSTACEOUS
ECSTASIES
ECSTASY
ECSTATIC
ECSTATICA
ECSTATICAL
ECSTATICALLY
ECTAD
ECTAL
ECTALLY
ECTASIA
ECTASIS
ECTENE
ECTENTAL
ECTETHMOID
ECTETHMOIDAL
ECTHETICALLY
ECTHLIPSIS
ECTHYMA
ECTHYMATA
ECTIRIS
ECTOBATIC
ECTOBLAST
ECTOCARDIA
ECTOCARPOUS
ECTOCELIC
ECTOCINEREA
ECTOCINEREAL
ECTOCOELIC
ECTOCONDYLE
ECTOCONDYLOID
ECTOCORNEA
ECTOCRANIAL
ECTOCYST
ECTODERM
ECTODERMAL
ECTODERMIC
ECTODERMOSIS
ECTOENTAD
ECTOENZYM
ECTOENZYME
ECTOETHMOID
ECTOGENESIS
ECTOGENIC
ECTOGENOUS
ECTOGLIA
ECTOLECITHAL
ECTOLOPH
ECTOMERE
ECTOMERIC
ECTOMORPHIC
ECTOMORPHY
ECTOPARASITE
ECTOPATAGIA
ECTOPATAGIUM
ECTOPHLOIC
ECTOPHYTE
ECTOPHYTIC
ECTOPIA
ECTOPIC
ECTOPLACENTA
ECTOPLASM
ECTOPLASMIC
ECTOPLASY
ECTOPROCTAN
ECTOPROCTOUS
ECTORETINA
ECTORHINAL
ECTOSARC
ECTOSARCOUS
ECTOSKELETON
ECTOSOMAL
ECTOSOME
ECTOSPHERE
ECTOSTEAL
ECTOSTOSIS
ECTOTHECA
ECTOTHERM
ECTOTROPHIC
ECTOZOA
ECTOZOAN
ECTOZOIC
ECTRODACTYLY
ECTROGENIC
ECTROGENY
ECTROMELIA
ECTROMELIAN
ECTROMELIC
ECTROPION
ECTYPAL
ECTYPE
ECTYPOGRAPHY
ECU
ECUELLE
ECUELLING
ECUMENE
ECUMENIC
ECUMENICAL
ECUMENICALLY
ECUMENICITY
ECUMENISM
ECYPHELLATE
ECZEMA
ECZEMATOID
ECZEMATOSIS
ECZEMATOUS
EDACIOUS
EDACIOUSLY
EDACIOUSNESS
EDACITY
EDAPHIC
EDAPHOLOGY
EDAPHON
EDDER
EDDIED
EDDIES
EDDISH
EDDO
EDDY
EDDYING
EDDYROOT
EDEA
EDEAGRA
EDELWEISS
EDEMA
EDEMATA
EDEMATOUS
EDEMIC
EDENITE
EDENTAL
EDENTATE
EDENTULATE
EDENTULOUS
EDEODYNIA
EDEOLOGY
EDEOMANIA
EDEOSCOPY
EDEOTOMY
EDESTAN
EDESTIN
EDGE
EDGEBONE
EDGED
EDGELESS
EDGEMAKER
EDGEMAKING
EDGEMAN
EDGER
EDGERMAN
EDGES
EDGESHOT
EDGESTONE
EDGEWAYS
EDGEWEED
EDGEWISE
EDGINESS
EDGING
EDGINGLY
EDGREW
EDGROW
EDGY
EDH
EDI
EDIBILITY
EDIBLE
EDIBLENESS
EDICT
EDICTAL
EDICTALLY
EDICULE
EDIFICABLE
EDIFICATE
EDIFICATION
EDIFICATOR
EDIFICATORY
EDIFICE
EDIFICED
EDIFICES
EDIFICING
EDIFIED
EDIFY
EDIFYING
EDIFYINGLY
EDILE
EDILITY
EDINGTONITE
EDIT
EDITAL
EDITION
EDITOR
EDITORIAL
EDITORIALIZE
EDITORIALIZED
EDITORIALIZING
EDITORIALLY
EDITORSHIP
EDUCABILIAN
EDUCABILITY
EDUCABLE
EDUCAND
EDUCATABLE
EDUCATE
EDUCATED
EDUCATEE
EDUCATING
EDUCATION
EDUCATIONAL
EDUCATIONALLY
EDUCATIONARY
EDUCATIONIST
EDUCATIVE
EDUCATOR
EDUCATORY
EDUCE
EDUCED
EDUCIBLE
EDUCING
EDUCT
EDUCTION
EDUCTIVE
EDUCTOR
EDULCORATE
EDULCORATED
EDULCORATING
EDULCORATION
EDULCORATIVE
EDULCORATOR
EDULE
EE
EEBREE
EED
EEGRASS
EEL
EELBOAT
EELBOB
EELBOBBER
EELCAKE
EELCATCHER
EELED
EELER
EELERY
EELFARE
EELFISH
EELGRASS
EELING
EELPOT
EELPOUT
EELS
EELSHOP
EELSKIN
EELSPEAR
EELWARE
EELWORM
EELY
EEM
EEMIS
EEN
EENCE
EER
EERIE
EERILY
EERINESS
EERISOME
EEROCK
EERY
EES
EESOME
EF
EFECKS
EFF
EFFABLE
EFFACE
EFFACEABLE
EFFACED
EFFACEMENT
EFFACER
EFFACING
EFFATE
EFFATUM
EFFECT
EFFECTER
EFFECTFUL
EFFECTIBLE
EFFECTIVE
EFFECTIVELY
EFFECTIVENESS
EFFECTIVITY
EFFECTOR
EFFECTS
EFFECTUAL
EFFECTUALITY
EFFECTUALIZE
EFFECTUALLY
EFFECTUALNESS
EFFECTUATE
EFFECTUATED
EFFECTUATING
EFFECTUATION
EFFEIR
EFFEMINACY
EFFEMINATE
EFFEMINATED
EFFEMINATELY
EFFEMINATING
EFFEMINATION
EFFEMINATIZE
EFFEMINIZE
EFFEMINIZED
EFFEMINIZING
EFFENDI
EFFENDIS
EFFERENT
EFFERVESCE
EFFERVESCED
EFFERVESCENCE
EFFERVESCENCY
EFFERVESCENT
EFFERVESCENTLY
EFFERVESCING
EFFERVESCIVE

EFFET
EFFETE
EFFETMAN
EFFETMEN
EFFICACIES
EFFICACIOUS
EFFICACITY
EFFICACY
EFFICIENCE
EFFICIENCIES
EFFICIENCY
EFFICIENT
EFFICIENTLY
EFFIGIAL
EFFIGIATE
EFFIGIATION
EFFIGIES
EFFIGURATE
EFFIGURATION
EFFIGY
EFFLATE
EFFLATION
EFFLORESCE
EFFLORESCED
EFFLORESCENCE
EFFLORESCENCY
EFFLORESCENT
EFFLORESCING
EFFLOWER
EFFLUENCE
EFFLUENCY
EFFLUENT
EFFLUVE
EFFLUVIA
EFFLUVIAL
EFFLUVIOUS
EFFLUVIUM
EFFLUX
EFFLUXES
EFFODIENT
EFFORM
EFFORMATION
EFFORT
EFFORTLESS
EFFORTLESSLY
EFFORTLESSNESS
EFFOSSION
EFFRACTION
EFFRANCHISE
EFFRAY
EFFRONT
EFFRONTERIES
EFFRONTERY
EFFULGE
EFFULGED
EFFULGENCE
EFFULGENT
EFFULGENTLY
EFFULGING
EFFUME
EFFUND
EFFUSE
EFFUSED
EFFUSING
EFFUSION
EFFUSIVE
EFFUSIVENESS
EFFUVIATE
EFOVEOLATE
EFREET
EFT
EFTER
EFTEST
EFTSOON
EFTSOONS
EGAD
EGADI
EGAL
EGALITARIAN
EGALITARIANISM
EGALITE
EGALITY
EGALLY
EGENCE
EGENCY
EGER
EGERAN
EGEST
EGESTA
EGESTED
EGESTING
EGESTION
EGESTIVE
EGG
EGGAR
EGGBERRIES
EGGBERRY
EGGCUP
EGGCUPFUL
EGGEATER
EGGED
EGGER
EGGFISH
EGGFRUIT
EGGHEAD
EGGHOT
EGGING
EGGLER
EGGMENT
EGGNOG
EGGPLANT
EGGS
EGGSHELL
EGGY
EGILOPS
EGIS
EGLANDULAR
EGLANDULOSE
EGLANDULOUS
EGLANTINE
EGLATERE
EGLESTONITE
EGLING
EGMA
EGO
EGOCENTRIC
EGOCENTRICITY
EGOCENTRISM
EGOISM
EGOIST
EGOISTIC
EGOISTICAL
EGOISTICALLY
EGOITY
EGOIZE
EGOL
EGOLATROUS
EGOMANIA
EGOMANIAC
EGOMANIACAL
EGOPHONIC
EGOPHONY
EGOS
EGOSYNTONIC
EGOTHEISM
EGOTISM
EGOTIST
EGOTISTIC
EGOTISTICAL
EGOTISTICALLY
EGOTIZE
EGOTIZED
EGOTIZING
EGREGIOUS
EGREGIOUSLY
EGREGIOUSNESS
EGRESS
EGRESSES
EGRESSION
EGRESSOR
EGRET
EGRETS
EGRIMONY
EGROMANCY
EGUALMENTE
EGUEIITE
EGURGITATE
EGURGITATED
EGURGITATING
EH
EHEU
EHLITE
EHRWALDITE
EHTANETHIAL
EHUAWA
EICHBERGITE
EICOSANE
EIDE
EIDENT
EIDENTLY
EIDER
EIDERDOWN
EIDETIC
EIDOGRAPH
EIDOLIC
EIDOLISM
EIDOLOLOGY
EIDOLON
EIDOPTOMETRY
EIDOS
EIDOURANION
EIE
EIGHE
EIGHT
EIGHTEEN
EIGHTEENMO
EIGHTEENTH
EIGHTFOIL
EIGHTFOLD
EIGHTH
EIGHTHLY
EIGHTIETH
EIGHTLING
EIGHTS
EIGHTSCORE
EIGHTSMAN
EIGHTSMEN
EIGHTSOME
EIGHTVO
EIGHTY
EIGNE
EIK
EIKON
EILD
EILE
EIMER
EIMERIA
EINKORN
EIRACK
EIRE
EIRESIONE
EISEGESIS
EISEL
EISELL
EISTEDDFOD
EISTEDDFODAU
EISTEDDFODIC
EISTEDDFODS
EITH
EITHER
EJACULATE
EJACULATED
EJACULATING
EJACULATION
EJACULATIVE
EJACULATOR
EJACULATORY
EJECT
EJECTA
EJECTAMENTA
EJECTED
EJECTING
EJECTION
EJECTIVE
EJECTIVELY
EJECTIVITY
EJECTMENT
EJECTOR
EJICIENT
EJIDAL
EJIDO
EJOO
EJULATE
EJURATE
EKABORON
EKACAESIUM
EKAHA
EKAMANGANESE
EKASILICON
EKATANTALUM
EKE
EKEBERGITE
EKED
EKENAME
EKER
EKERITE
EKHIMI
EKING
EKKA
EKKI
EKPHORE
EKPHORIA
EKPHORIAS
EKPHORIZE
EKPHORY
EKTENE
EL
ELABOR
ELABORATE
ELABORATED
ELABORATELY
ELABORATENESS
ELABORATING
ELABORATION
ELABORATIVE
ELABORATOR
ELABORATORY
ELABRATE
ELAENIA
ELAEOBLAST
ELAEOBLASTIC
ELAEODOCHON
ELAEOPTEN
ELAEOPTENE
ELAEOTHESIUM
ELAIDATE
ELAIDIC
ELAIDIN
ELAIOLEUCITE
ELAIOPLAST
ELAIOSOME
ELAN
ELANCE
ELAND
ELANDS
ELANET
ELAPHINE
ELAPHURE
ELAPHURINE
ELAPID
ELAPINE
ELAPOID
ELAPSE
ELAPSED
ELAPSING
ELASMOBRANCH
ELASMOTHERE
ELASTANCE
ELASTASE
ELASTIC
ELASTICA
ELASTICALLY
ELASTICIAN
ELASTICIN
ELASTICITY
ELASTICIZE
ELASTICIZER
ELASTIN
ELASTIVITY
ELASTOMER
ELASTOMETER
ELASTOMETRY
ELASTOSE
ELATE
ELATED
ELATEDLY
ELATEDNESS
ELATER
ELATERID
ELATERIN
ELATERITE
ELATERIUM
ELATINACEOUS
ELATING
ELATION
ELATIVE
ELATOR
ELATROMETER
ELAYL
ELB
ELBOIC
ELBOW
ELBOWBOARD
ELBOWBUSH
ELBOWCHAIR
ELBOWED
ELBOWER
ELBOWPIECE
ELBOWROOM
ELBOWS
ELBOWY
ELBUCK
ELCAJA
ELCHEE
ELCHI
ELD
ELDER
ELDERBERRY
ELDERBUSH
ELDERLIES
ELDERLY
ELDERMAN
ELDERMEN
ELDERN
ELDERSHIP
ELDERWOMAN
ELDERWOMEN
ELDERWOOD
ELDERWORT
ELDEST
ELDIN
ELDING
ELDMOTHER
ELDRICH
ELDRITCH

ELE
ELEAN
ELECAMPANE
ELECT
ELECTANT
ELECTED
ELECTING
ELECTION
ELECTIONEER
ELECTIONEERER
ELECTIVE
ELECTIVELY
ELECTIVENESS
ELECTIVITY
ELECTO
ELECTOR
ELECTORATE
ELECTORIAL
ELECTRAGIST
ELECTRAL
ELECTRALIZE
ELECTRE
ELECTREPETER
ELECTRESS
ELECTRET
ELECTRIC
ELECTRICAL
ELECTRICALIZE
ELECTRICALLY
ELECTRICIAN
ELECTRICITY
ELECTRICIZE
ELECTRIFIED
ELECTRIFIER
ELECTRIFY
ELECTRIFYING
ELECTRIZE
ELECTRIZED
ELECTRIZER
ELECTRIZING
ELECTRO
ELECTROBATH
ELECTROBUS
ELECTROCUTE
ELECTROCUTED
ELECTROCUTING
ELECTROCUTION
ELECTRODE
ELECTRODEPOSIT
ELECTRODES
ELECTROED
ELECTROFORM
ELECTROFUSED
ELECTROGILT
ELECTROGRAPH
ELECTROING
ELECTROIONIC
ELECTROLIER
ELECTROLYSIS
ELECTROLYTE
ELECTROLYTIC
ELECTROLYZE
ELECTROLYZED
ELECTROLYZER
ELECTROLYZING
ELECTROMAGNET
ELECTROMAGNETIC
ELECTROMER
ELECTROMETER
ELECTROMETRY
ELECTROMOBILE
ELECTROMOTOR
ELECTRON
ELECTRONIC
ELECTRONICS
ELECTROPATHY
ELECTROPHONE
ELECTROPISM
ELECTROPLATE
ELECTROPLATED
ELECTROPLATING
ELECTROPOION
ELECTROPOLAR
ELECTROPOWER
ELECTROS
ELECTROSCOPE
ELECTROSHOCK
ELECTROSTATIC
ELECTROSTATICS
ELECTROSTEEL
ELECTROTAXIS
ELECTROTEST
ELECTROTONIC
ELECTROTONIZE
ELECTROTONUS
ELECTROTYPE
ELECTROTYPED
ELECTROTYPER
ELECTROTYPY
ELECTROVITAL
ELECTROWIN
ELECTRUM
ELECTUARY
ELEEMOSINAR
ELEEMOSYNAR
ELEEMOSYNARY
ELEGANCE
ELEGANCIES
ELEGANCY
ELEGANT
ELEGANTE
ELEGANTLY
ELEGIAC
ELEGIACAL
ELEGIAMBIC
ELEGIAMBUS
ELEGIAST
ELEGIES
ELEGIOUS
ELEGIST
ELEGIT
ELEGIZE
ELEGIZED
ELEGIZING
ELEGY
ELEIDIN
ELEME
ELEMENT
ELEMENTAL
ELEMENTALISM
ELEMENTALIST
ELEMENTALITY
ELEMENTARILY
ELEMENTARINESS
ELEMENTARITY
ELEMENTARY
ELEMENTOID
ELEMENTS
ELEMI
ELEMICIN
ELEMIN
ELEMOL
ELENCH
ELENCHI
ELENCHIZE
ELENCHUS
ELENCTIC
ELENCTICAL
ELENGE
ELENGELY
ELENGENESS
ELEOLITE
ELEOMARGARIC
ELEONORITE
ELEOPLAST
ELEOPTENE
ELEOTRID
ELEPAIO
ELEPHANT
ELEPHANTA
ELEPHANTIAC
ELEPHANTIASIS
ELEPHANTIC
ELEPHANTINE
ELEPHANTOID
ELEPHANTOIDAL
ELEPHANTOUS
ELEPHANTS
ELEUTHERISM
ELEVATE
ELEVATED
ELEVATEDLY
ELEVATEDNESS
ELEVATING
ELEVATINGLY
ELEVATIO
ELEVATION
ELEVATIONAL
ELEVATO
ELEVATOR
ELEVE
ELEVEN
ELEVENER
ELEVENS
ELEVENTH
ELEVON
ELF
ELFENFOLK
ELFIC
ELFIN
ELFISH
ELFISHLY
ELFISHNESS
ELFKIN
ELFLAND
ELFLIKE
ELFLOCK
ELFS
ELFT
ELFWORT
ELGER
ELIAD
ELIASITE
ELICIT
ELICITABLE
ELICITATE
ELICITATION
ELICITED
ELICITING
ELICITOR
ELICITORY
ELIDE
ELIDED
ELIDIBLE
ELIDING
ELIGENT
ELIGIBILITIES
ELIGIBILITY
ELIGIBLE
ELIMINABLE
ELIMINAND
ELIMINANT
ELIMINATE
ELIMINATED
ELIMINATING
ELIMINATION
ELIMINATIVE
ELIMINATOR
ELIMINATORY
ELIQUATE
ELIQUATED
ELIQUATING
ELIQUATION
ELISION
ELISOR
ELITE
ELIX
ELIXATE
ELIXATION
ELIXIR
ELK
ELKHOUND
ELKS
ELKSLIP
ELKWOOD
ELL
ELLACHICK
ELLAGATE
ELLAGIC
ELLAGITANNIN
ELLE
ELLECK
ELLER
ELLFISH
ELLIPSE
ELLIPSES
ELLIPSIS
ELLIPSOGRAPH
ELLIPSOID
ELLIPSOIDAL
ELLIPSONE
ELLIPTIC
ELLIPTICAL
ELLIPTICALLY
ELLIPTICALNESS
ELLIPTICITY
ELLIPTOID
ELLOPS
ELLWAND
ELM
ELMEN
ELMY
ELOCULAR
ELOCUTE
ELOCUTION
ELOCUTIONARY
ELOCUTIONER
ELOCUTIONIST
ELOD
ELOGE
ELOGIUM
ELOGY
ELOIGN
ELOIGNER
ELOIGNMENT
ELOINE
ELON
ELONG
ELONGATE
ELONGATED
ELONGATING
ELONGATION
ELONGATIVE
ELOPE
ELOPED
ELOPEMENT
ELOPER
ELOPING
ELOPS
ELOQUENCE
ELOQUENT
ELOQUENTIAL
ELOTILLO
ELPASOLITE
ELPIDITE
ELRITCH
ELS
ELSE
ELSEHOW
ELSEN
ELSEWARDS
ELSEWAYS
ELSEWHAT
ELSEWHEN
ELSEWHERE
ELSEWHERES
ELSEWHITHER
ELSEWISE
ELSHIN
ELSIN
ELSON
ELT
ELTROT
ELUATE
ELUCIDATE
ELUCIDATED
ELUCIDATING
ELUCIDATION
ELUCIDATIVE
ELUCIDATOR
ELUCIDATORY
ELUCTATE
ELUCUBRATE
ELUDE
ELUDED
ELUDER
ELUDING
ELUENT
ELUSION
ELUSIVE
ELUSIVELY
ELUSIVENESS
ELUSORINESS
ELUSORY
ELUTE
ELUTION
ELUTOR
ELUTRIATE
ELUTRIATED
ELUTRIATING
ELUTRIATION
ELUTRIATOR
ELUVIAL
ELUVIATION
ELUVIUM
ELVAN
ELVANITE
ELVANITIC
ELVEN
ELVER
ELVES
ELVISH
ELVISHLY
ELY
ELYDORIC
ELYNG
ELYTRA
ELYTRAL
ELYTRIFEROUS
ELYTRIFORM
ELYTRIGEROUS
ELYTRIN
ELYTROCELE
ELYTROCLASIA
ELYTROID
ELYTRON
ELYTROPLASTIC
ELYTROPTOSIS
ELYTRORHAGIA
ELYTROTOMY
ELYTROUS
ELYTRUM
EM
EMACIATE
EMACIATED

EMACIATING
EMACIATION
EMAGRAM
EMAIL
EMAJAGUA
EMANANT
EMANATE
EMANATED
EMANATING
EMANATION
EMANATIONAL
EMANATIONISM
EMANATIONIST
EMANATIVE
EMANATIVELY
EMANATOR
EMANATORY
EMANCIPATE
EMANCIPATED
EMANCIPATING
EMANCIPATIO
EMANCIPATION
EMANCIPATIONIST
EMANCIPATIVE
EMANCIPATOR
EMANCIPATORY
EMANCIPATRESS
EMANCIPIST
EMANDIBULATE
EMANE
EMANIUM
EMARCID
EMARGINATE
EMARGINATED
EMARGINATING
EMARGINATION
EMASCULATE
EMASCULATED
EMASCULATING
EMASCULATION
EMASCULATIVE
EMASCULATOR
EMASCULATORY
EMBAIN
EMBALE
EMBALL
EMBALM
EMBALMED
EMBALMER
EMBALMING
EMBALMMENT
EMBANK
EMBANKMENT
EMBAR
EMBARCATION
EMBARGO
EMBARGOED
EMBARGOES
EMBARGOING
EMBARK
EMBARKATION
EMBARKED
EMBARKING
EMBARKMENT
EMBARMENT
EMBARRAS
EMBARRASS
EMBARRASSED
EMBARRASSING
EMBARRASSINGLY
EMBARRASSMENT
EMBARRED
EMBARRING
EMBASE
EMBASSADOR
EMBASSAGE
EMBASSY
EMBATHE
EMBATTLE
EMBATTLED
EMBATTLING
EMBAY
EMBAYED
EMBAYING
EMBAYMENT
EMBED
EMBEDDED
EMBEDDING
EMBEDMENT
EMBELIF
EMBELIN
EMBELLISH
EMBELLISHED
EMBELLISHER
EMBELLISHING
EMBELLISHMENT
EMBER
EMBERGEESE
EMBERGOOSE
EMBERS
EMBEZZLE
EMBEZZLED
EMBEZZLEMENT
EMBEZZLER
EMBEZZLING
EMBIID
EMBIND
EMBIOTOCID
EMBIOTOCOID
EMBIRA
EMBITTER
EMBITTERED
EMBITTERER
EMBITTERING
EMBITTERMENT
EMBLANCH
EMBLAZE
EMBLAZED
EMBLAZER
EMBLAZING
EMBLAZON
EMBLAZONED
EMBLAZONER
EMBLAZONMENT
EMBLAZONRY
EMBLEM
EMBLEMA
EMBLEMATIC
EMBLEMATICAL
EMBLEMATICIZE
EMBLEMATIST
EMBLEMATIZE
EMBLEMATIZED
EMBLEMATIZING
EMBLEMENT
EMBLEMENTS
EMBLEMIST
EMBLEMIZE
EMBLEMIZED
EMBLEMIZING
EMBLIC
EMBLISS
EMBLOSSOM
EMBODIED
EMBODIER
EMBODIMENT
EMBODY
EMBODYING
EMBOG
EMBOITE
EMBOITEMENT
EMBOLDEN
EMBOLDENER
EMBOLE
EMBOLECTOMIES
EMBOLECTOMY
EMBOLEMIA
EMBOLIC
EMBOLIFORM
EMBOLISM
EMBOLISMIC
EMBOLITE
EMBOLIUM
EMBOLIZE
EMBOLO
EMBOLOLALIA
EMBOLOMERISM
EMBOLOMEROUS
EMBOLOMYCOTIC
EMBOLON
EMBOLUM
EMBOLUS
EMBOLY
EMBONPOINT
EMBORDER
EMBOSK
EMBOSOM
EMBOSS
EMBOSSED
EMBOSSER
EMBOSSING
EMBOSSMAN
EMBOSSMEN
EMBOSSMENT
EMBOST
EMBOUCHURE
EMBOUND
EMBOW
EMBOWED
EMBOWEL
EMBOWELED
EMBOWELER
EMBOWELING
EMBOWELLED
EMBOWELLER
EMBOWELLING
EMBOWER
EMBOWERED
EMBOWERING
EMBOWING
EMBOWMENT
EMBOX
EMBRACE
EMBRACED
EMBRACEMENT
EMBRACEOR
EMBRACER
EMBRACERY
EMBRACING
EMBRACIVE
EMBRAID
EMBRAKE
EMBRANCHMENT
EMBRANGLE
EMBRANGLED
EMBRANGLEMENT
EMBRANGLING
EMBRASE
EMBRASURE
EMBRASURED
EMBRASURING
EMBRAVE
EMBRAWN
EMBREATHE
EMBREW
EMBRIGHT
EMBRIGHTEN
EMBRITTLE
EMBRITTLEMENT
EMBROADEN
EMBROCATE
EMBROCATED
EMBROCATING
EMBROCATION
EMBROCHE
EMBROIDER
EMBROIDERED
EMBROIDERER
EMBROIDERESS
EMBROIDERIES
EMBROIDERING
EMBROIDERY
EMBROIL
EMBROILED
EMBROILER
EMBROILING
EMBROILMENT
EMBRONZE
EMBROSCOPIC
EMBROWN
EMBRUE
EMBRYECTOMY
EMBRYO
EMBRYOCARDIA
EMBRYOCTONY
EMBRYOFEROUS
EMBRYOGENIC
EMBRYOGENY
EMBRYOGONY
EMBRYOGRAPHY
EMBRYOID
EMBRYOLOGIC
EMBRYOLOGICAL
EMBRYOLOGICALLY
EMBRYOLOGIST
EMBRYOLOGY
EMBRYOMA
EMBRYOMAS
EMBRYOMATA
EMBRYON
EMBRYONAL
EMBRYONARY
EMBRYONATE
EMBRYONATED
EMBRYONIC
EMBRYONICALLY
EMBRYONIFORM
EMBRYONY
EMBRYOPHAGOUS
EMBRYOPHORE
EMBRYOPLASTIC
EMBRYOS
EMBRYOSCOPE
EMBRYOTEGA
EMBRYOTEGAE
EMBRYOTIC
EMBRYOTOME
EMBRYOTOMY
EMBRYOTROPHY
EMBRYOUS
EMBUE
EMBUIA
EMBUS
EMBUSK
EMBUSQUE
EMBUSSED
EMBUSSING
EMCEE
EMCUMBERING
EME
EMEER
EMEND
EMENDABLE
EMENDATE
EMENDATED
EMENDATELY
EMENDATING
EMENDATION
EMENDATOR
EMENDATORY
EMENDER
EMERALD
EMERANT
EMERAUDE
EMERGE
EMERGED
EMERGENCE
EMERGENCIES
EMERGENCY
EMERGENT
EMERGENTLY
EMERGENTNESS
EMERGING
EMERIED
EMERIL
EMERITED
EMERITI
EMERITUS
EMERIZE
EMEROD
EMERODS
EMEROID
EMERSED
EMERSION
EMERY
EMERYING
EMESIS
EMETIC
EMETICAL
EMETIN
EMETINE
EMETOLOGY
EMEU
EMEUTE
EMFORTH
EMGALLA
EMICTION
EMICTORY
EMIGRANT
EMIGRATE
EMIGRATED
EMIGRATING
EMIGRATION
EMIGRATIONAL
EMIGRATIVE
EMIGRATOR
EMIGRATORY
EMIGRE
EMIGREE
EMIGRES
EMINENCE
EMINENCIES
EMINENCY
EMINENT
EMINENTLY
EMIR
EMIRATE
EMISSARIA
EMISSARIUM
EMISSARY
EMISSILE
EMISSION
EMISSIVE
EMISSIVITY
EMIT
EMITTED
EMITTENT
EMITTER
EMITTING
EMMA
EMMARBLE
EMMARVEL
EMMELEIA
EMMENAGOGUE
EMMENIC

EMMENIOPATHY
EMMENOLOGY
EMMENSITE
EMMER
EMMET
EMMETROPE
EMMETROPIA
EMMETROPIC
EMODIN
EMOL
EMOLLESCENCE
EMOLLIATE
EMOLLIENT
EMOLOA
EMOLUMENT
EMOLUMENTAL
EMONY
EMORY
EMOTE
EMOTION
EMOTIONABLE
EMOTIONAL
EMOTIONALISM
EMOTIONALIST
EMOTIONALITY
EMOTIONALIZE
EMOTIONALIZED
EMOTIONED
EMOTIONIZE
EMOTIONLESS
EMOTIONS
EMOTIVE
EMOTIVELY
EMOTIVENESS
EMOTIVITY
EMPACKET
EMPAESTIC
EMPAISTIC
EMPALE
EMPANADA
EMPANEL
EMPANELMENT
EMPANOPLY
EMPAPER
EMPARADISE
EMPARK
EMPARL
EMPASM
EMPASMA
EMPATHIC
EMPATHICALLY
EMPATHIZE
EMPATHIZED
EMPATHIZING
EMPATHY
EMPATRON
EMPEARL
EMPEINE
EMPEIREMA
EMPENNAGE
EMPERESS
EMPERIES
EMPERIL
EMPEROR
EMPERORSHIP
EMPERY
EMPEST
EMPETRACEOUS
EMPEXA
EMPHASES
EMPHASIS
EMPHASIZE
EMPHASIZED
EMPHASIZING
EMPHATIC
EMPHATICAL
EMPHATICALLY
EMPHATICALNESS
EMPHEMERALNESS
EMPHLYSIS
EMPHRACTIC
EMPHRAXIS
EMPHYSEMA
EMPHYTEUSIS
EMPHYTEUTA
EMPHYTEUTIC
EMPICTURE
EMPID
EMPIECEMENT
EMPIGHT
EMPIRE
EMPIREMA
EMPIRIC
EMPIRICAL
EMPIRICALLY
EMPIRICALNESS
EMPIRICISM
EMPIRICIST
EMPIRICS
EMPIRISM
EMPIRISTIC
EMPIRY
EMPLACE
EMPLACEMENT
EMPLANE
EMPLANED
EMPLANING
EMPLASTIC
EMPLASTRA
EMPLASTRATION
EMPLASTRUM
EMPLECTITE
EMPLEOMANIA
EMPLOY
EMPLOYE
EMPLOYED
EMPLOYEE
EMPLOYER
EMPLOYING
EMPLOYMENT
EMPODIA
EMPODIUM
EMPOISON
EMPOISONED
EMPOISONER
EMPOISONING
EMPOISONMENT
EMPOLDER
EMPORETIC
EMPOREUTIC
EMPORIA
EMPORIAL
EMPORIUM
EMPORIUMS
EMPORTE
EMPORY
EMPOVER
EMPOVERISH
EMPOWER
EMPRESA
EMPRESARIO
EMPRESS
EMPRESSE
EMPRESSEMENT
EMPRISE
EMPRIZE
EMPT
EMPTIED
EMPTIER
EMPTIES
EMPTIEST
EMPTILY
EMPTINESS
EMPTINGS
EMPTINS
EMPTIO
EMPTION
EMPTOR
EMPTY
EMPTYHEARTED
EMPTYING
EMPTYSIS
EMPURPLE
EMPURPLED
EMPURPLING
EMPYEMA
EMPYEMATA
EMPYEMIC
EMPYESIS
EMPYOCELE
EMPYREAL
EMPYREAN
EMPYREUM
EMPYREUMA
EMPYREUMATA
EMPYREUMATIC
EMPYROMANCY
EMRAUD
EMU
EMULABLE
EMULANT
EMULATE
EMULATED
EMULATING
EMULATION
EMULATIVE
EMULATOR
EMULATORY
EMULATRESS
EMULE
EMULGE
EMULGENCE
EMULGENT
EMULOUS
EMULOUSLY
EMULOUSNESS
EMULSIBILITY
EMULSIBLE
EMULSIFIABILITY
EMULSIFIABLE
EMULSIFIED
EMULSIFIER
EMULSIFY
EMULSIFYING
EMULSIN
EMULSION
EMULSIONIZE
EMULSIVE
EMULSOID
EMULSOR
EMUNCTORY
EMUNDATION
EMUNGE
EMURE
EMYD
EMYDIAN
EN
ENABLE
ENABLED
ENABLER
ENABLING
ENACH
ENACT
ENACTION
ENACTIVE
ENACTMENT
ENACTOR
ENACTORY
ENACTURE
ENAENA
ENAGE
ENALID
ENALIOSAUR
ENALIOSAURIAN
ENALITE
ENALLAGE
ENALURON
ENALYRON
ENAM
ENAMDAR
ENAMEL
ENAMELED
ENAMELER
ENAMELING
ENAMELIST
ENAMELLED
ENAMELLER
ENAMELLING
ENAMELLIST
ENAMELOMA
ENAMELWARE
ENAMOR
ENAMORATO
ENAMORED
ENAMOREDNESS
ENAMORING
ENAMOUR
ENAMOURED
ENAMOUREDNESS
ENAMOURING
ENANTHEM
ENANTHEMA
ENANTHEMATOUS
ENANTHESIS
ENANTIOMORPH
ENANTIOPATHY
ENANTIOSIS
ENANTIOTROPY
ENARCHED
ENARGITE
ENARM
ENARME
ENARRATION
ENARTHRODIA
ENARTHRODIAL
ENARTHROSIS
ENATE
ENATIC
ENATION
ENBUSSHE
ENCAENIA
ENCAGE
ENCAGED
ENCAGING
ENCAMP
ENCAMPMENT
ENCANTHIS
ENCAPSULATE
ENCAPSULATED
ENCAPSULATING
ENCAPSULATION
ENCARNALIZE
ENCARNALIZED
ENCARNALIZING
ENCARPIUM
ENCARPUS
ENCASE
ENCASED
ENCASEMENT
ENCASH
ENCASHABLE
ENCASHMENT
ENCASTAGE
ENCASTRE
ENCASTREMENT
ENCAUMA
ENCAUSTES
ENCAUSTIC
ENCAUSTICALLY
ENCAVE
ENCEINT
ENCEINTE
ENCEPHALA
ENCEPHALIC
ENCEPHALIN
ENCEPHALITIC
ENCEPHALITIS
ENCEPHALOGRAM
ENCEPHALOGRAPH
ENCEPHALOID
ENCEPHALOLOGY
ENCEPHALOMA
ENCEPHALOMAS
ENCEPHALOMATA
ENCEPHALON
ENCEPHALOUS
ENCHAFE
ENCHAIN
ENCHAINED
ENCHAINING
ENCHAINMENT
ENCHANNEL
ENCHANT
ENCHANTED
ENCHANTER
ENCHANTING
ENCHANTINGLY
ENCHANTINGNESS
ENCHANTMENT
ENCHANTRESS
ENCHARGE
ENCHARGED
ENCHARGING
ENCHASE
ENCHASED
ENCHASER
ENCHASING
ENCHASTEN
ENCHEASON
ENCHEER
ENCHEQUER
ENCHESON
ENCHILADA
ENCHILADAS
ENCHIRIDION
ENCHODONTID
ENCHODONTOID
ENCHONDROMA
ENCHONDROMAS
ENCHONDROMATA
ENCHONDROSIS
ENCHORIAL
ENCHORIC
ENCHURCH
ENCHYLEMA
ENCHYMATOUS
ENCHYTRAE
ENCHYTRAEID
ENCINA
ENCINAL
ENCINCTURE
ENCINILLO
ENCIPHER
ENCIPHERED
ENCIPHERING
ENCIRCLE
ENCIRCLED
ENCIRCLEMENT
ENCIRCLER
ENCIRCLING
ENCLARET
ENCLASP
ENCLASPED
ENCLASPING
ENCLAVE

ENCLAVED
ENCLAVEMENT
ENCLAVING
ENCLEAR
ENCLISIS
ENCLITIC
ENCLITICAL
ENCLITICALLY
ENCLOAK
ENCLOG
ENCLOISTER
ENCLOSE
ENCLOSED
ENCLOSER
ENCLOSING
ENCLOSURE
ENCLOTHE
ENCLOUD
ENCODE
ENCODED
ENCODER
ENCODING
ENCOIGNURE
ENCOLLAR
ENCOLOR
ENCOLOUR
ENCOLPIA
ENCOLPION
ENCOLURE
ENCOMENDERO
ENCOMIA
ENCOMIAST
ENCOMIASTIC
ENCOMIC
ENCOMIENDA
ENCOMIOLOGIC
ENCOMIUM
ENCOMIUMS
ENCOMPASS
ENCOMPASSED
ENCOMPASSER
ENCOMPASSING
ENCOMY
ENCORBELMENT
ENCORE
ENCORED
ENCORING
ENCOUNTER
ENCOUNTERABLE
ENCOUNTERED
ENCOUNTERER
ENCOUNTERING
ENCOUNTERS
ENCOURAGE
ENCOURAGED
ENCOURAGEMENT
ENCOURAGER
ENCOURAGING
ENCOURAGINGLY
ENCRANIAL
ENCRATIC
ENCRATY
ENCRIMSON
ENCRINAL
ENCRINIC
ENCRINITAL
ENCRINITE
ENCRINITIC
ENCRINITICAL
ENCRINOID
ENCRISP
ENCROACH
ENCROACHED
ENCROACHER
ENCROACHING
ENCROACHMENT
ENCROTCHET
ENCRUST
ENCRUSTED
ENCRUSTMENT
ENCRYPT
ENCULTURATION
ENCUMBER
ENCUMBERED
ENCUMBERMENT
ENCUMBRANCE
ENCUMBRANCER
ENCURTAIN
ENCYCLIC
ENCYCLICAL
ENCYCLOPAEDIA
ENCYCLOPAEDIAC
ENCYCLOPAEDIAL
ENCYCLOPAEDIAN
ENCYCLOPAEDIC
ENCYCLOPAEDICAL
ENCYCLOPAEDICALLY
ENCYCLOPAEDISM
ENCYCLOPAEDIST
ENCYCLOPAEDIZE
ENCYCLOPEDIA
ENCYCLOPEDIAC
ENCYCLOPEDIACAL
ENCYCLOPEDIAL
ENCYCLOPEDIAN
ENCYCLOPEDIAST
ENCYCLOPEDIC
ENCYCLOPEDICAL
ENCYCLOPEDICALLY
ENCYCLOPEDISM
ENCYCLOPEDIST
ENCYCLOPEDIZE
ENCYRTID
ENCYST
ENCYSTATION
ENCYSTED
ENCYSTING
ENCYSTMENT
END
ENDAMAGE
ENDAMAGEABLE
ENDAMAGED
ENDAMAGEMENT
ENDAMAGING
ENDAMASK
ENDAMEBA
ENDAMEBIASIS
ENDAMEBIC
ENDAMOEBIASIS
ENDAMOEBIC
ENDANGER
ENDANGERED
ENDANGERER
ENDANGERING
ENDANGERMENT
ENDANGIUM
ENDAORTIC
ENDAORTITIS
ENDARCH
ENDARCHY
ENDARK
ENDARTERIAL
ENDARTERITIS
ENDARTERIUM
ENDASEH
ENDASPIDEAN
ENDAZE
ENDBALL
ENDBOARD
ENDBRAIN
ENDEAR
ENDEARANCE
ENDEARED
ENDEAREDLY
ENDEARING
ENDEARINGLY
ENDEARINGNESS
ENDEARMENT
ENDEAVOR
ENDEAVORED
ENDEAVORER
ENDEAVORING
ENDEAVOUR
ENDEAVOURED
ENDEAVOURER
ENDEAVOURING
ENDECHA
ENDED
ENDEICTIC
ENDELLIONITE
ENDEMIC
ENDEMICAL
ENDEMICALLY
ENDEMICITY
ENDEMIOLOGICAL
ENDEMIOLOGY
ENDEMISM
ENDENIZEN
ENDER
ENDERMATIC
ENDERMIC
ENDERON
ENDEW
ENDGATE
ENDIMANCHE
ENDING
ENDITE
ENDIVE
ENDLESS
ENDLESSLY
ENDLESSNESS
ENDLONG
ENDMOST
ENDOBLAST
ENDOBLASTIC
ENDOCARDIAC
ENDOCARDIAL
ENDOCARDITIC
ENDOCARDITIS
ENDOCARDIUM
ENDOCARP
ENDOCARPAL
ENDOCARPIC
ENDOCARPOID
ENDOCENTRIC
ENDOCHROME
ENDOCHYLOUS
ENDOCLINAL
ENDOCLINE
ENDOCOELAR
ENDOCOELE
ENDOCONE
ENDOCONIDIA
ENDOCONIDIUM
ENDOCRANIAL
ENDOCRANIUM
ENDOCRIN
ENDOCRINAL
ENDOCRINE
ENDOCRINIC
ENDOCRINISM
ENDOCRINOLOGY
ENDOCRINOUS
ENDOCRITIC
ENDOCYCLE
ENDOCYCLIC
ENDOCYEMATE
ENDOCYST
ENDODERM
ENDODERMAL
ENDODERMIC
ENDODERMIS
ENDODONTIA
ENDODONTICS
ENDOENZYME
ENDOGAMIC
ENDOGAMOUS
ENDOGAMY
ENDOGASTRIC
ENDOGEN
ENDOGENESIS
ENDOGENETIC
ENDOGENIC
ENDOGENOUS
ENDOGENOUSLY
ENDOGENY
ENDOGLOBULAR
ENDOGNATH
ENDOGNATHAL
ENDOGNATHION
ENDOLEMMA
ENDOLYMPH
ENDOLYMPHIC
ENDOLYSIN
ENDOMETRIAL
ENDOMETRITIS
ENDOMETRIUM
ENDOMETRY
ENDOMIXIS
ENDOMORPH
ENDOMORPHIC
ENDOMORPHISM
ENDOMORPHY
ENDOMYSIAL
ENDOMYSIUM
ENDONEURIUM
ENDONUCLEOLUS
ENDOPARASITE
ENDOPATHIC
ENDOPERIDIAL
ENDOPERIDIUM
ENDOPHAGOUS
ENDOPHAGY
ENDOPHRAGM
ENDOPHRAGMAL
ENDOPHYTAL
ENDOPHYTE
ENDOPHYTOUS
ENDOPLASM
ENDOPLASMA
ENDOPLASMIC
ENDOPLAST
ENDOPLASTULAR
ENDOPLASTULE
ENDOPLEURA
ENDOPLEURAL
ENDOPLEURITE
ENDOPLEURITIC
ENDOPOD
ENDOPODITE
ENDOPODITIC
ENDOPROCT
ENDOPROCTOUS
ENDOPSYCHIC
ENDORACHIS
ENDORAL
ENDORE
ENDORSABLE
ENDORSATION
ENDORSE
ENDORSED
ENDORSEE
ENDORSEMENT
ENDORSER
ENDORSING
ENDORSOR
ENDOSARC
ENDOSARCOUS
ENDOSCLERITE
ENDOSCOPE
ENDOSCOPY
ENDOSEPSIS
ENDOSKELETAL
ENDOSKELETON
ENDOSMOMETER
ENDOSMOSIC
ENDOSMOSIS
ENDOSMOTIC
ENDOSMOTICALLY
ENDOSOME
ENDOSPERM
ENDOSPERMIC
ENDOSPORE
ENDOSPORIUM
ENDOSPOROUS
ENDOSS
ENDOSTEAL
ENDOSTEALLY
ENDOSTEITIS
ENDOSTEOMA
ENDOSTEOMAS
ENDOSTEOMATA
ENDOSTERNITE
ENDOSTEUM
ENDOSTITIS
ENDOSTOMA
ENDOSTOMATA
ENDOSTOME
ENDOSTOSIS
ENDOSTRACAL
ENDOSTRACUM
ENDOSTYLAR
ENDOSTYLE
ENDOSTYLIC
ENDOTHECA
ENDOTHECAL
ENDOTHECIA
ENDOTHECIAL
ENDOTHECIUM
ENDOTHELIA
ENDOTHELIAL
ENDOTHELIOMA
ENDOTHELIUM
ENDOTHELOID
ENDOTHERM
ENDOTHERMAL
ENDOTHERMIC
ENDOTHERMOUS
ENDOTHERMY
ENDOTHORAX
ENDOTHYS
ENDOTOXIC
ENDOTOXIN
ENDOTROPHIC
ENDOTYS
ENDOUTE
ENDOW
ENDOWED
ENDOWER
ENDOWING
ENDOWMENT
ENDPAPERS
ENDPIECE
ENDPLATE
ENDRIN
ENDRUMPF
ENDS
ENDSEAL
ENDSHIP
ENDUE
ENDUED
ENDUING
ENDUNGEON
ENDURA
ENDURABILITY

ENDURABLE
ENDURABLENESS
ENDURABLY
ENDURANCE
ENDURANT
ENDURE
ENDURED
ENDURER
ENDURING
ENDURINGLY
ENDURINGNESS
ENDWAYS
ENDWISE
ENDYSIS
ENECATE
ENEMA
ENEMAS
ENEMATA
ENEMIED
ENEMIES
ENEMY
ENEMYING
ENEPIDERMIC
ENERGEIA
ENERGESIS
ENERGETIC
ENERGETICALLY
ENERGETICIST
ENERGETICS
ENERGETISTIC
ENERGIC
ENERGICO
ENERGID
ENERGIES
ENERGISM
ENERGIST
ENERGIZE
ENERGIZED
ENERGIZER
ENERGIZING
ENERGUMEN
ENERGY
ENERVATE
ENERVATED
ENERVATING
ENERVATION
ENERVATIVE
ENERVATOR
ENEW
ENFACE
ENFACED
ENFACEMENT
ENFACING
ENFAMISH
ENFANT
ENFARCE
ENFATICO
ENFAVOR
ENFEEBLE
ENFEEBLED
ENFEEBLEMENT
ENFEEBLER
ENFEEBLING
ENFELON
ENFEOFF
ENFEOFFED
ENFEOFFING
ENFEOFFMENT
ENFETTER
ENFILADE
ENFILADED
ENFILADING
ENFILE
ENFILED
ENFIN
ENFIRE
ENFIRM
ENFLAGELLATE
ENFLAGELLATION
ENFLAME
ENFLESH
ENFLEURAGE
ENFLOWER
ENFLOWERED
ENFLOWERING
ENFOLD
ENFOLDED
ENFOLDEN
ENFOLDING
ENFONCE
ENFONCED
ENFONCEE
ENFORCE
ENFORCEABLE
ENFORCED
ENFORCEDLY
ENFORCEMENT
ENFORCER
ENFORCING
ENFORCIVE
ENFORCIVELY
ENFORT
ENFORTH
ENFRAI
ENFRAME
ENFRAMED
ENFRAMEMENT
ENFRAMING
ENFRANCHISED
ENFRANCHISEMENT
ENFRANCHISER
ENFRANCHISING
ENFRENZY
ENFUME
ENG
ENGAGE
ENGAGED
ENGAGEDLY
ENGAGEDNESS
ENGAGEMENT
ENGAGER
ENGAGING
ENGAGINGLY
ENGAGINGNESS
ENGARDE
ENGARLAND
ENGARRISON
ENGASTRIMYTH
ENGASTRIMYTHIC
ENGAZE
ENGENDER
ENGENDERED
ENGENDERER
ENGENDERING
ENGENDERMENT
ENGENDRURE
ENGENDURE
ENGHLE
ENGHOSTED
ENGI
ENGILD
ENGINE
ENGINED
ENGINEER
ENGINEERED
ENGINEERING
ENGINEMAN
ENGINEMEN
ENGINERY
ENGINING
ENGINOUS
ENGIRD
ENGIRDED
ENGIRDING
ENGIRDLE
ENGIRDLED
ENGIRT
ENGLACIAL
ENGLEIM
ENGLISH
ENGLISHER
ENGLOBE
ENGLUE
ENGLUT
ENGLUTE
ENGLYN
ENGLYNS
ENGOBE
ENGORE
ENGORGE
ENGORGED
ENGORGEMENT
ENGORGING
ENGOUE
ENGOUEE
ENGOUEMENT
ENGOULED
ENGOUMENT
ENGRACE
ENGRACED
ENGRACING
ENGRAFF
ENGRAFFED
ENGRAFFING
ENGRAFT
ENGRAFTATION
ENGRAFTED
ENGRAFTER
ENGRAFTING
ENGRAFTMENT
ENGRAIL
ENGRAILED
ENGRAILING
ENGRAILMENT
ENGRAIN
ENGRAINED
ENGRAINEDLY
ENGRAINER
ENGRAINING
ENGRAM
ENGRAMMA
ENGRAMMATIC
ENGRAMME
ENGRAMMIC
ENGRANDIZE
ENGRAPHIA
ENGRAPHIC
ENGRAPHICALLY
ENGRAPHY
ENGRAVE
ENGRAVED
ENGRAVEMENT
ENGRAVER
ENGRAVING
ENGREGGE
ENGRIEVE
ENGROSS
ENGROSSED
ENGROSSEDLY
ENGROSSER
ENGROSSING
ENGROSSINGLY
ENGROSSINGNESS
ENGROSSMENT
ENGULF
ENGYSCOPE
ENHAEMOSPORE
ENHALO
ENHANCE
ENHANCED
ENHANCEMENT
ENHANCER
ENHANCING
ENHANCIVE
ENHARBOR
ENHARDEN
ENHARDY
ENHARMONIC
ENHARMONICAL
ENHARMONICALLY
ENHAUNT
ENHEART
ENHEARTEN
ENHEDGE
ENHEMOSPORE
ENHORROR
ENHYDRITE
ENHYDRITIC
ENHYDROUS
ENHYPOSTASIA
ENHYPOSTASIS
ENHYPOSTATIC
ENHYPOSTATIZE
ENIAC
ENIGMA
ENIGMAS
ENIGMATIC
ENIGMATICAL
ENIGMATICALLY
ENIGMATIST
ENIGMATIZE
ENIGMATIZED
ENIGMATIZING
ENIGMATOGRAPHER
ENIGMATOGRAPHY
ENIGUA
ENISLE
ENISLED
ENISLING
ENIUN
ENJAIL
ENJAMB
ENJAMBED
ENJAMBEMENT
ENJAMBMENT
ENJEOPARD
ENJEOPARDY
ENJEWEL
ENJOIN
ENJOINDER
ENJOINED
ENJOINER
ENJOINING
ENJOINMENT
ENJOY
ENJOYABLE
ENJOYABLENESS
ENJOYABLY
ENJOYED
ENJOYER
ENJOYING
ENJOYMENT
ENKINDLE
ENKINDLED
ENKINDLER
ENKINDLING
ENKO
ENLACE
ENLACED
ENLACEMENT
ENLACING
ENLARD
ENLARGE
ENLARGED
ENLARGEDLY
ENLARGEDNESS
ENLARGEMENT
ENLARGER
ENLARGING
ENLARGINGLY
ENLIGHT
ENLIGHTEN
ENLIGHTENED
ENLIGHTENER
ENLIGHTENING
ENLIGHTENMENT
ENLIMN
ENLINK
ENLINKED
ENLINKING
ENLINKMENT
ENLIST
ENLISTED
ENLISTER
ENLISTING
ENLISTMENT
ENLIVEN
ENLIVENED
ENLIVENER
ENLIVENING
ENLIVENINGLY
ENLIVENMENT
ENLOCK
ENLURE
ENLUTE
ENMESH
ENMESHED
ENMESHING
ENMESHMENT
ENMITIES
ENMITY
ENMOVE
ENMUFFLE
ENNEAD
ENNEADIC
ENNEAGON
ENNEAGONAL
ENNEAGYNOUS
ENNEAHEDRA
ENNEAHEDRAL
ENNEAHEDRIA
ENNEAHEDRON
ENNEAHEDRONS
ENNEASEMIC
ENNEASTYLE
ENNEASTYLOS
ENNEASYLLABIC
ENNEATIC
ENNOBLE
ENNOBLED
ENNOBLEMENT
ENNOBLER
ENNOBLING
ENNOMIC
ENNUE
ENNUI
ENNUIED
ENNUIS
ENNUYANT
ENNUYE
ENNUYEE
ENNUYING
ENODAL
ENODALLY
ENODATE
ENODATION
ENODE
ENOIL
ENOL
ENOLASE
ENOLATE
ENOLIC
ENOLIZABLE
ENOLIZATION
ENOLIZE

ENOLOGY
ENOMANIA
ENOMOTARCH
ENOMOTY
ENOPHTHALMOS
ENOPHTHALMUS
ENOPLAN
ENOPLION
ENOPTROMANCY
ENORGANIC
ENORM
ENORMITIES
ENORMITY
ENORMOUS
ENORMOUSLY
ENORMOUSNESS
ENOSIS
ENOSTOSIS
ENOUGH
ENOUNCE
ENOUNCED
ENOUNCEMENT
ENOUNCING
ENOW
ENPHYTOTIC
ENPLANE
ENPLANED
ENPLANING
ENQUIRE
ENQUIRER
ENQUIRY
ENRACE
ENRAGE
ENRAGED
ENRAGEDLY
ENRAGEDNESS
ENRAGING
ENRAMADA
ENRANGE
ENRANK
ENRAPT
ENRAPTURE
ENRAPTURED
ENRAPTURER
ENRAPTURING
ENRAVISH
ENRAVISHED
ENRAVISHING
ENRAVISHINGLY
ENREGIMENT
ENREGISTER
ENREGISTERED
ENREGISTERING
ENREGISTRATION
ENREGISTRY
ENRICH
ENRICHED
ENRICHER
ENRICHING
ENRICHINGLY
ENRICHMENT
ENRIDGED
ENRIGHT
ENRING
ENRINGED
ENRINGING
ENROBE
ENROBED
ENROBEMENT
ENROBER
ENROBING
ENROCKMENT
ENROL
ENROLL
ENROLLED
ENROLLER
ENROLLING
ENROLLMENT
ENROLMENT
ENROOT
ENROOTED
ENROOTING
ENROUGH
ENROUND
ENS
ENSAINT
ENSALADA
ENSAMPLE
ENSAMPLER
ENSANGUINE
ENSANGUINED
ENSANGUINING
ENSATE
ENSCENE
ENSCONCE
ENSCONCED
ENSCONCING
ENSCROLL
ENSE
ENSEAL
ENSEALED
ENSEALING
ENSEAM
ENSEAR
ENSEARCH
ENSEARCHER
ENSEAT
ENSEATED
ENSEATING
ENSELLURE
ENSEMBLE
ENSEPULCHER
ENSEPULCHERED
ENSEPULCHERING
ENSEPULCHRE
ENSETE
ENSHEATHE
ENSHIELD
ENSHIELDED
ENSHIELDING
ENSHRINE
ENSHRINED
ENSHRINEMENT
ENSHRINING
ENSHROUD
ENSIFORM
ENSIGN
ENSIGNCY
ENSIGNED
ENSIGNING
ENSIGNMENT
ENSIGNRY
ENSIGNSHIP
ENSILAGE
ENSILATE
ENSILATION
ENSILE
ENSILIST
ENSISTERNUM
ENSKIED
ENSKY
ENSKYED
ENSLAVE
ENSLAVED
ENSLAVEDNESS
ENSLAVEMENT
ENSLAVER
ENSLAVING
ENSLUMBER
ENSMALL
ENSNARE
ENSNARED
ENSNAREMENT
ENSNARER
ENSNARING
ENSNARINGLY
ENSNARL
ENSNOW
ENSORCEL
ENSORCELIZE
ENSORCELL
ENSORCERIZE
ENSOUL
ENSPHERE
ENSPHERED
ENSPHERING
ENSTAMP
ENSTAR
ENSTATE
ENSTATITE
ENSTATITIC
ENSTATITITE
ENSTATOLITE
ENSTEEP
ENSTOOL
ENSTORE
ENSTRANGED
ENSTYLE
ENSUABLE
ENSUANCE
ENSUANT
ENSUE
ENSUED
ENSUER
ENSUING
ENSURE
ENSURED
ENSURER
ENSURING
ENSWATHE
ENSWATHED
ENSWATHEMENT
ENSWATHING
ENSWEEP
ENTABLATURE
ENTABLATURED
ENTABLEMENT
ENTACH
ENTAD
ENTAIL
ENTAILED
ENTAILING
ENTAILMENT
ENTAL
ENTALENT
ENTAME
ENTAMEBIC
ENTAMOEBA
ENTAMOEBIC
ENTANGLE
ENTANGLED
ENTANGLEDLY
ENTANGLEDNESS
ENTANGLEMENT
ENTANGLER
ENTANGLING
ENTAPOPHYSIAL
ENTAPOPHYSIS
ENTARTHROTIC
ENTASIA
ENTASIS
ENTASTIC
ENTE
ENTELAM
ENTELECHIES
ENTELECHY
ENTELLUS
ENTELODONT
ENTEMPLE
ENTENTE
ENTER
ENTERA
ENTERADEN
ENTERAL
ENTERALGIA
ENTERATE
ENTERAUXE
ENTERCLOSE
ENTERECTOMY
ENTERED
ENTERER
ENTERGOGENIC
ENTERIC
ENTERICOID
ENTERING
ENTERITIDIS
ENTERITIS
ENTERMETE
ENTEROCELE
ENTEROCEPTOR
ENTEROCOELE
ENTEROCOELIC
ENTEROCOELOUS
ENTEROCYST
ENTERODYNIA
ENTEROGENOUS
ENTEROGRAM
ENTEROGRAPH
ENTEROGRAPHY
ENTEROID
ENTEROKINASE
ENTEROLITH
ENTEROLOGY
ENTEROLYSIS
ENTEROMERE
ENTERON
ENTEROPATHY
ENTEROPEXIA
ENTEROPLASTY
ENTEROPLEGIA
ENTEROPTOSIS
ENTEROPTOTIC
ENTERORRHEA
ENTEROSCOPE
ENTEROSCOPY
ENTEROSEPSIS
ENTEROSPASM
ENTEROSTASIS
ENTEROSTOMY
ENTEROTOMY
ENTEROTOXEMIA
ENTERPILLAR
ENTERPRISE
ENTERPRISED
ENTERPRISER
ENTERPRISING
ENTERPRISINGLY
ENTERTAIN
ENTERTAINED
ENTERTAINER
ENTERTAINING
ENTERTAININGLY
ENTERTAININGNESS
ENTERTAINMENT
ENTHALPY
ENTHEATE
ENTHELMINTHA
ENTHELMINTHES
ENTHEOS
ENTHETIC
ENTHRAL
ENTHRALL
ENTHRALLED
ENTHRALLER
ENTHRALLING
ENTHRALLINGLY
ENTHRALLMENT
ENTHRALMENT
ENTHRILL
ENTHRONE
ENTHRONED
ENTHRONG
ENTHRONING
ENTHRONIZATION
ENTHRONIZE
ENTHRONIZED
ENTHRONIZING
ENTHUSE
ENTHUSIASM
ENTHUSIAST
ENTHUSIASTIC
ENTHUSIASTICAL
ENTHUSIASTICALLY
ENTHUSIASTLY
ENTHYMEMATIC
ENTHYMEME
ENTIA
ENTICE
ENTICED
ENTICEMENT
ENTICER
ENTICING
ENTICINGLY
ENTICINGNESS
ENTIFICAL
ENTIFICATION
ENTIFY
ENTIRE
ENTIRELY
ENTIRENESS
ENTIRETY
ENTIRIS
ENTITATIVE
ENTITATIVELY
ENTITLE
ENTITLED
ENTITLING
ENTITY
ENTOBLAST
ENTOBLASTIC
ENTOCAROTID
ENTOCELE
ENTOCNEMIAL
ENTOCOELE
ENTOCOELIC
ENTOCONDYLE
ENTOCONE
ENTOCONID
ENTOCRANIAL
ENTOCYEMATE
ENTODERM
ENTODERMAL
ENTODERMIC
ENTOGASTRIC
ENTOGENOUS
ENTOGLOSSAL
ENTOIL
ENTOILED
ENTOILING
ENTOIRE
ENTOMB
ENTOMBED
ENTOMBING
ENTOMBMENT
ENTOMERE
ENTOMERIC
ENTOMICAL
ENTOMION
ENTOMOGENOUS
ENTOMOID
ENTOMOLITE
ENTOMOLOGIC
ENTOMOLOGICAL
ENTOMOLOGICALL
ENTOMOLOGIES

ENTOMOLOGIZE
ENTOMOLOGIZED
ENTOMOLOGIZING
ENTOMOLOGY
ENTOMOPHAGAN
ENTOMOPHILY
ENTOMOTAXY
ENTOMOTOMIST
ENTOMOTOMY
ENTOOLITIC
ENTOPHYTAL
ENTOPHYTE
ENTOPHYTIC
ENTOPHYTICALLY
ENTOPHYTOUS
ENTOPIC
ENTOPICAL
ENTOPLASM
ENTOPLASTIC
ENTOPLASTRAL
ENTOPLASTRON
ENTOPTICAL
ENTOPTICALLY
ENTOPTICS
ENTOPTOSCOPE
ENTOPTOSCOPIC
ENTOPTOSCOPY
ENTORETINA
ENTORGANISM
ENTOSPHERE
ENTOSTERNA
ENTOSTERNAL
ENTOSTERNITE
ENTOSTERNUM
ENTOTIC
ENTOTYMPANIC
ENTOURAGE
ENTOZOA
ENTOZOAL
ENTOZOAN
ENTOZOIC
ENTOZOOLOGY
ENTOZOON
ENTRADA
ENTRAIL
ENTRAILS
ENTRAIN
ENTRAINED
ENTRAINER
ENTRAINING
ENTRANCE
ENTRANCED
ENTRANCEMENT
ENTRANCEWAY
ENTRANCING
ENTRANCINGLY
ENTRANT
ENTRAP
ENTRAPMENT
ENTRAPPED
ENTRAPPER
ENTRAPPING
ENTREASURE
ENTREAT
ENTREATABLE
ENTREATED
ENTREATER
ENTREATFUL
ENTREATIES
ENTREATING
ENTREATMENT
ENTREATY
ENTRECHAT
ENTRECOTE
ENTREDEUX
ENTREE
ENTREFER
ENTREMES
ENTREMESS
ENTREMETS
ENTRENCH
ENTRENCHMENT
ENTREPAS
ENTREPOT
ENTREPRENANT
ENTREPRENEUR
ENTREPRENEUSE
ENTRER
ENTRESALLE
ENTRESOL
ENTRESSE
ENTREZ
ENTRIES
ENTRIKE
ENTROCHITE
ENTROPIES
ENTROPION
ENTROPY
ENTRUST
ENTRY
ENTRYMAN
ENTRYMEN
ENTRYWAY
ENTUM
ENTUNE
ENTWINE
ENTWINED
ENTWINING
ENTWIST
ENTWISTED
ENTWISTING
ENUCLEATE
ENUCLEATED
ENUCLEATING
ENUCLEATION
ENUCLEATOR
ENUMERABLE
ENUMERATE
ENUMERATED
ENUMERATING
ENUMERATION
ENUMERATIVE
ENUMERATOR
ENUNCIABILITY
ENUNCIABLE
ENUNCIATE
ENUNCIATED
ENUNCIATING
ENUNCIATION
ENUNCIATIVE
ENUNCIATIVELY
ENUNCIATOR
ENUNCIATORY
ENURE
ENURESIS
ENURNY
ENVASSAL
ENVASSALAGE
ENVAYE
ENVEIL
ENVELOP
ENVELOPE
ENVELOPED
ENVELOPER
ENVELOPING
ENVELOPMENT
ENVENOM
ENVENOMATION
ENVENOMED
ENVENOMING
ENVERGURE
ENVERMEIL
ENVIABLE
ENVIABLENESS
ENVIABLY
ENVIED
ENVIER
ENVIES
ENVINE
ENVIOUS
ENVIOUSLY
ENVIOUSNESS
ENVIRE
ENVIRON
ENVIRONAL
ENVIRONED
ENVIRONIC
ENVIRONING
ENVIRONMENT
ENVIRONMENTAL
ENVIRONMENTALI
ENVIRONMENTALI
ENVIRONS
ENVISAGE
ENVISAGED
ENVISAGEMENT
ENVISAGING
ENVISION
ENVOI
ENVOLUME
ENVOY
ENVY
ENVYING
ENVYINGLY
ENWHEEL
ENWIND
ENWOMB
ENWOMBED
ENWOMBING
ENWORTHY
ENWRAP
ENWRAPPED
ENWRAPPING
ENWRAPT
ENWREATHE
ENWROUGHT
ENZOOTIC
ENZYM
ENZYMATIC
ENZYME
ENZYMICALLY
ENZYMOLOGY
ENZYMOLYSIS
ENZYMOLYTIC
ENZYMOSIS
ENZYMOTIC
EOAN
EOBIONT
EODISCID
EOHIPPUS
EOLATION
EOLIAN
EOLIENNE
EOLIPILE
EOLITH
EOLITHIC
EOLOTROPIC
EON
EONIAN
EONISM
EOPHYTE
EOPHYTIC
EORHYOLITE
EORL
EOSATE
EOSIN
EOSINE
EOSINIC
EOSINOBLAST
EOSINOPHIL
EOSINOPHILE
EOSINOPHILIA
EOSINOPHILIC
EOSINOPHILOUS
EOSPHORITE
EOZOON
EOZOONAL
EP
EPACMAIC
EPACME
EPACRID
EPACRIDACEOUS
EPACT
EPACTAL
EPAGOGE
EPAGOGIC
EPAGOMENAE
EPAGOMENAL
EPAGOMENIC
EPAGOMENOUS
EPALPATE
EPANADIPLOSIS
EPANALEPSIS
EPANALEPTIC
EPANAPHORA
EPANAPHORAL
EPANASTROPHE
EPANODOS
EPANODY
EPANORTHOSIS
EPANTHOUS
EPAPILLATE
EPAPOPHYSIAL
EPAPOPHYSIS
EPAPPOSE
EPARC
EPARCH
EPARCHATE
EPARCHIAL
EPARCHIES
EPARCHY
EPARCUALE
EPARTERIAL
EPAULE
EPAULEMENT
EPAULET
EPAULETED
EPAULETTE
EPAULETTED
EPAULIERE
EPAXIAL
EPAXIALLY
EPEDAPHIC
EPEE
EPEEIST
EPEIRIC
EPEIROGENETIC
EPEIROGENIC
EPEIROGENY
EPEISODION
EPEMBRYONIC
EPENCEPHAL
EPENCEPHALIC
EPENCEPHALON
EPENDYMA
EPENDYMAL
EPENDYMOMA
EPENDYTES
EPENETIC
EPENTHESES
EPENTHESIS
EPENTHESIZE
EPENTHETIC
EPERGNE
EPERLAN
EPEROTESIS
EPERVA
EPEUS
EPEXEGESIS
EPEXEGETIC
EPEXEGETICAL
EPEXEGETICALLY
EPHA
EPHAH
EPHAPSE
EPHARMONIC
EPHARMONY
EPHEBE
EPHEBEION
EPHEBEUM
EPHEBIC
EPHEBOS
EPHEBUS
EPHECTIC
EPHEDRIN
EPHEDRINE
EPHELCYSTIC
EPHELIS
EPHEMERA
EPHEMERAE
EPHEMERAL
EPHEMERALITY
EPHEMERALLY
EPHEMERAN
EPHEMERAS
EPHEMERID
EPHEMERIDES
EPHEMERIS
EPHEMEROMORPHIC
EPHEMERON
EPHEMERONS
EPHEMEROUS
EPHERERIST
EPHESTIA
EPHETAE
EPHETE
EPHETIC
EPHIDROSIS
EPHIPPIA
EPHIPPIAL
EPHIPPIUM
EPHOD
EPHOR
EPHORAL
EPHORALTY
EPHORATE
EPHORI
EPHORIC
EPHORS
EPHORUS
EPHPHATHA
EPHTHIANURE
EPHYDRIAD
EPHYDRID
EPHYMNIUM
EPHYRA
EPHYRAE
EPHYRULA
EPI
EPIBASAL
EPIBATUS
EPIBENTHIC
EPIBENTHOS
EPIBIOTIC
EPIBLAST
EPIBLASTIC
EPIBLEMA
EPIBLEMATA
EPIBOLE
EPIBOLISM
EPIBOLY
EPIBRANCHIAL
EPIC
EPICAL
EPICALLY

EPICALYCES
EPICALYX
EPICALYXES
EPICANTHIC
EPICANTHUS
EPICARDIA
EPICARDIAC
EPICARDIAL
EPICARDIUM
EPICARID
EPICARIDAN
EPICARP
EPICE
EPICEDE
EPICEDIAL
EPICEDIUM
EPICENE
EPICENISM
EPICENITY
EPICENTER
EPICENTRA
EPICENTRAL
EPICENTRE
EPICENTRUM
EPICHEIREMA
EPICHEIREMATA
EPICHILE
EPICHILIA
EPICHILIUM
EPICHIREMA
EPICHONDROSIS
EPICHONDROTIC
EPICHORDAL
EPICHORIAL
EPICHORIC
EPICHORION
EPICHORISTIC
EPICIER
EPICISM
EPICIST
EPICLASTIC
EPICLEIDIAN
EPICLEIDIUM
EPICLESIS
EPICLY
EPICNEMIAL
EPICOELAR
EPICOELE
EPICOELIA
EPICOELIAC
EPICOELIAN
EPICOELOMA
EPICOELOUS
EPICOLIC
EPICONDYLE
EPICONDYLIAN
EPICONDYLIC
EPICONTINENTAL
EPICORACOID
EPICORACOIDAL
EPICORMIC
EPICOTYL
EPICRANIAL
EPICRANIUM
EPICRISES
EPICRISIS
EPICRITIC
EPICRYSTALLINE
EPICURE
EPICUREAN
EPICUREANISM
EPICYCLE
EPICYCLIC
EPICYCLICAL
EPICYCLOID
EPICYCLOIDAL
EPICYEMATE
EPICYESIS
EPICYSTOTOMY
EPICYTE
EPIDEICTIC
EPIDEICTICAL
EPIDEISTIC
EPIDEMIC
EPIDEMICAL
EPIDEMICALLY
EPIDEMICALNESS
EPIDEMICITY
EPIDEMIOGRAPHY
EPIDEMIOLOGY
EPIDEMY
EPIDENDRAL
EPIDENDRIC
EPIDERM
EPIDERMA
EPIDERMAL
EPIDERMATIC
EPIDERMATOID
EPIDERMIC
EPIDERMICAL
EPIDERMICALLY
EPIDERMIS
EPIDERMIZATION
EPIDERMOID
EPIDERMOIDAL
EPIDERMOLYSIS
EPIDERMOSE
EPIDERMOUS
EPIDESMINE
EPIDIALOGUE
EPIDIASCOPE
EPIDIDYMAL
EPIDIDYMIDES
EPIDIDYMIS
EPIDIDYMITE
EPIDIDYMITIS
EPIDIORITE
EPIDOSITE
EPIDOTE
EPIDOTIC
EPIDOTIZATION
EPIDURAL
EPIFOCAL
EPIGAMIC
EPIGASTER
EPIGASTRAL
EPIGASTRIA
EPIGASTRIAL
EPIGASTRIC
EPIGASTRICAL
EPIGASTRIUM
EPIGASTROCELE
EPIGEAL
EPIGEAN
EPIGEE
EPIGEIC
EPIGENE
EPIGENESIS
EPIGENESIST
EPIGENETIC
EPIGENETICALLY
EPIGENIC
EPIGENIST
EPIGENOUS
EPIGEOUS
EPIGEUM
EPIGLOTTAL
EPIGLOTTIDEAN
EPIGLOTTIDITIS
EPIGLOTTIS
EPIGLOTTITIS
EPIGNATHOUS
EPIGNE
EPIGONAL
EPIGONATION
EPIGONE
EPIGONIC
EPIGONIUM
EPIGONOUS
EPIGRAM
EPIGRAMMATIC
EPIGRAMMATICAL
EPIGRAMMATISM
EPIGRAMMATIST
EPIGRAMMATIZE
EPIGRAMMATIZED
EPIGRAMME
EPIGRAPH
EPIGRAPHER
EPIGRAPHIC
EPIGRAPHICAL
EPIGRAPHICALLY
EPIGRAPHIST
EPIGRAPHY
EPIGUANINE
EPIGYNE
EPIGYNOUS
EPIGYNUM
EPIGYNY
EPIHYAL
EPIKEIA
EPIKIA
EPIKLESIS
EPIKY
EPILABRA
EPILABRUM
EPILAMELLAR
EPILARYNGEAL
EPILATE
EPILATED
EPILATING
EPILATION
EPILATOR
EPILEGOMENON
EPILEMMA
EPILEMMAL
EPILEPSY
EPILEPTIC
EPILEPTICAL
EPILEPTICALLY
EPILEPTIFORM
EPILEPTOID
EPILIMNION
EPILOBE
EPILOG
EPILOGATION
EPILOGIC
EPILOGICAL
EPILOGISM
EPILOGIST
EPILOGIZE
EPILOGIZED
EPILOGIZING
EPILOGUE
EPILOIA
EPIMACUS
EPIMANDIBULAR
EPIMANIKIA
EPIMANIKION
EPIMER
EPIMERAL
EPIMERE
EPIMERITE
EPIMERITIC
EPIMERON
EPIMORPHA
EPIMORPHIC
EPIMORPHOSIS
EPIMYSIUM
EPIMYTH
EPINAOI
EPINAOS
EPINARD
EPINASTIC
EPINASTICALLY
EPINASTY
EPINEPHRIN
EPINEPHRINE
EPINETTE
EPINEURAL
EPINEURIAL
EPINEURIUM
EPINGLE
EPINGLETTE
EPINICIA
EPINICIAN
EPINICION
EPINIKIA
EPINIKIAN
EPINIKION
EPININE
EPIOPTICON
EPIOTIC
EPIPALEOLITHIC
EPIPARODOS
EPIPASTIC
EPIPERIPHERAL
EPIPETALOUS
EPIPHANOUS
EPIPHANY
EPIPHARYNGEAL
EPIPHARYNX
EPIPHLOEDAL
EPIPHLOEDIC
EPIPHONEMA
EPIPHORA
EPIPHRAGM
EPIPHRAGMAL
EPIPHYLL
EPIPHYLLINE
EPIPHYSARY
EPIPHYSEAL
EPIPHYSES
EPIPHYSIAL
EPIPHYSIS
EPIPHYSITIS
EPIPHYTAL
EPIPHYTE
EPIPHYTIC
EPIPHYTICAL
EPIPHYTICALLY
EPIPHYTOTIC
EPIPHYTOUS
EPIPIAL
EPIPLANKTON
EPIPLASM
EPIPLASMIC
EPIPLASTRAL
EPIPLASTRON
EPIPLECTIC
EPIPLEURA
EPIPLEURAE
EPIPLEURAL
EPIPLEXIS
EPIPLOCE
EPIPLOCELE
EPIPLOIC
EPIPLOITIS
EPIPLOON
EPIPLOPEXY
EPIPODIA
EPIPODIAL
EPIPODIALE
EPIPODIALIA
EPIPODITE
EPIPODIUM
EPIPOLISM
EPIPOLIZE
EPIPROCT
EPIPTERIC
EPIPTEROUS
EPIPTERYGOID
EPIPUBES
EPIPUBIC
EPIPUBIS
EPIRHIZOUS
EPIROGENIC
EPIROGENY
EPIROTULIAN
EPIRRHEMA
EPIRRHEMATIC
EPIRRHEME
EPISARCINE
EPISARKINE
EPISCENIA
EPISCENIUM
EPISCIA
EPISCLERA
EPISCLERAL
EPISCLERITIS
EPISCOPABLE
EPISCOPACIES
EPISCOPACY
EPISCOPAL
EPISCOPALIAN
EPISCOPALISM
EPISCOPALITY
EPISCOPALLY
EPISCOPATE
EPISCOPATION
EPISCOPATURE
EPISCOPE
EPISCOPICIDE
EPISCOPIZATION
EPISCOPIZE
EPISCOPIZED
EPISCOPIZING
EPISCOPOLATRY
EPISCOPY
EPISCOTISTER
EPISEMATIC
EPISEPALOUS
EPISIOCELE
EPISIOPLASTY
EPISIOTOMY
EPISKELETAL
EPISODAL
EPISODE
EPISODIC
EPISODICAL
EPISODICALLY
EPISPADIA
EPISPADIAC
EPISPADIAS
EPISPASTIC
EPISPERM
EPISPLENITIS
EPISPORE
EPISTAPEDIAL
EPISTASIS
EPISTATIC
EPISTAXIS
EPISTEME
EPISTEMIC
EPISTEMOLOG
EPISTEMOLOGY
EPISTEMONIC
EPISTEMONICAL
EPISTERNA
EPISTERNAL
EPISTERNALIA
EPISTERNITE
EPISTERNUM
EPISTILBITE
EPISTLE

EPISTLER
EPISTOLARIAN
EPISTOLARILY
EPISTOLATORY
EPISTOLER
EPISTOLET
EPISTOLIC
EPISTOLICAL
EPISTOLIST
EPISTOLIZABLE
EPISTOLIZATION
EPISTOLIZE
EPISTOLOGRAPHER
EPISTOLOGRAPHIST
EPISTOLOGRAPHY
EPISTOMA
EPISTOMAL
EPISTOMATA
EPISTOME
EPISTOMIAN
EPISTROPHE
EPISTROPHEAL
EPISTROPHEUS
EPISTROPHIC
EPISTROPHY
EPISTYLAR
EPISTYLE
EPISYLLOGISM
EPISYNALOEPHE
EPISYNTHETON
EPITACTIC
EPITAPH
EPITAPHER
EPITAPHIAL
EPITAPHIAN
EPITAPHIC
EPITAPHICAL
EPITAPHIZE
EPITASIS
EPITELA
EPITENDINEUM
EPITHALAMIA
EPITHALAMIC
EPITHALAMION
EPITHALAMIUM
EPITHALAMIUMS
EPITHALAMIZE
EPITHALAMUS
EPITHALAMY
EPITHALLINE
EPITHECA
EPITHECAL
EPITHECATE
EPITHECIA
EPITHECIUM
EPITHELIA
EPITHELIAL
EPITHELIOID
EPITHELIOMA
EPITHELIOMAS
EPITHELIOMATA
EPITHELIOSIS
EPITHELIUM
EPITHELIUMS
EPITHELIZATION
EPITHELIZE
EPITHELOID
EPITHEM
EPITHEMA
EPITHEME
EPITHESIS
EPITHET
EPITHETIC
EPITHETICAL
EPITHETICIAN
EPITHETON
EPITHYME
EPITHYMETIC
EPITIMESIS
EPITOKE
EPITOMATOR
EPITOMATORY
EPITOME
EPITOMES
EPITOMIC
EPITOMICAL
EPITOMICALLY
EPITOMISE
EPITOMIST
EPITOMIZATION
EPITOMIZE
EPITOMIZED
EPITOMIZER
EPITOMIZING
EPITONIC
EPITONION
EPITOXOID
EPITRICHIAL
EPITRICHIUM
EPITRITE
EPITRITIC
EPITROCHLEA
EPITROCHLEAR
EPITROCHOID
EPITROCHOIDAL
EPITROPE
EPITROPHIC
EPITROPHY
EPITYMPANIC
EPITYMPANUM
EPITYPHLITIS
EPITYPHLON
EPIURAL
EPIVALVE
EPIZEUXIS
EPIZOA
EPIZOAL
EPIZOAN
EPIZOIC
EPIZOON
EPIZOOTIC
EPIZOOTIOLOGY
EPIZOOTY
EPOCH
EPOCHA
EPOCHAL
EPOCHALLY
EPOCHE
EPOCHISM
EPOCHIST
EPODE
EPODIC
EPOLLICATE
EPONGE
EPONYCHIUM
EPONYM
EPONYMIC
EPONYMOUS
EPONYMY
EPOOPHORON
EPOPEE
EPOPOEAN
EPOPOEIA
EPOPOEIST
EPOPT
EPOPTAE
EPOPTIC
EPORNITIC
EPORNITICALLY
EPOS
EPOTE
EPOXIDE
EPOXY
EPRIS
EPRISE
EPRUINOSE
EPSILON
EPSOMITE
EPULARY
EPULATION
EPULIS
EPULO
EPULOID
EPULOSIS
EPULOTIC
EPUPILLATE
EPURAL
EPURATE
EPURATION
EPURE
EPYLLIA
EPYLLION
EQUABILITY
EQUABLE
EQUABLENESS
EQUABLY
EQUAEVAL
EQUAL
EQUALED
EQUALING
EQUALISE
EQUALIST
EQUALITARIAN
EQUALITARIANISM
EQUALITIES
EQUALITY
EQUALIZATION
EQUALIZE
EQUALIZED
EQUALIZER
EQUALIZING
EQUALLED
EQUALLING
EQUALLY
EQUALNESS
EQUANGULAR
EQUANIMITY
EQUANIMOUS
EQUANIMOUSLY
EQUANT
EQUATE
EQUATED
EQUATING
EQUATION
EQUATIONAL
EQUATIONALLY
EQUATIONISM
EQUATIONIST
EQUATIVE
EQUATOR
EQUATOREAL
EQUATORIAL
EQUATORIALLY
EQUERRIES
EQUERRY
EQUES
EQUESTRIAN
EQUESTRIENNE
EQUIANGULAR
EQUIAXED
EQUID
EQUIDISTANCE
EQUIDISTANT
EQUIDISTANTIAL
EQUIDISTANTLY
EQUIDIURNAL
EQUIFORM
EQUIFORMAL
EQUIFORMITY
EQUIGRANULAR
EQUIJACENT
EQUILATERAL
EQUILIBRANT
EQUILIBRATE
EQUILIBRATED
EQUILIBRATING
EQUILIBRATION
EQUILIBRATIVE
EQUILIBRATOR
EQUILIBRATORY
EQUILIBRIA
EQUILIBRIAL
EQUILIBRIATE
EQUILIBRIOUS
EQUILIBRIST
EQUILIBRISTAT
EQUILIBRISTIC
EQUILIBRITY
EQUILIBRIUM
EQUILIBRIUMS
EQUILIBRIZE
EQUILIN
EQUIMODAL
EQUIMOLAR
EQUIMOLECULAR
EQUIMOMENTAL
EQUIMULTIPLE
EQUINAL
EQUINATE
EQUINE
EQUINIA
EQUINITY
EQUINOCTIAL
EQUINOCTIALLY
EQUINOVARUS
EQUINOX
EQUINUS
EQUIP
EQUIPAGA
EQUIPAGE
EQUIPARANT
EQUIPARATE
EQUIPARATION
EQUIPARTILE
EQUIPARTITION
EQUIPEDAL
EQUIPLUVE
EQUIPMENT
EQUIPOISE
EQUIPOISED
EQUIPOISING
EQUIPOLLENCE
EQUIPOLLENCY
EQUIPOLLENT
EQUIPOLLENTLY
EQUIPONDERANT
EQUIPONDERATE
EQUIPONDERATED
EQUIPONDERATING
EQUIPOSTILE
EQUIPOTENTIAL
EQUIPPED
EQUIPPER
EQUIPPING
EQUIPROBABLE
EQUIPT
EQUISETA
EQUISETACEOUS
EQUISETIC
EQUISETUM
EQUISETUMS
EQUISIGNAL
EQUISON
EQUISONANCE
EQUISONANT
EQUITABLE
EQUITABLY
EQUITANT
EQUITATION
EQUITATIVE
EQUITES
EQUITIES
EQUITIST
EQUITY
EQUIVALENCE
EQUIVALENCED
EQUIVALENCY
EQUIVALENT
EQUIVALENTLY
EQUIVALVE
EQUIVOCACY
EQUIVOCAL
EQUIVOCALITY
EQUIVOCATE
EQUIVOCATED
EQUIVOCATING
EQUIVOCATION
EQUIVOCATOR
EQUIVOCATORY
EQUIVOKE
EQUIVOLUMINAL
EQUIVOQUE
EQUIVOROUS
EQUOID
EQUULEI
EQUULEUS
ER
ERA
ERADE
ERADIATE
ERADIATED
ERADIATING
ERADIATION
ERADICABLE
ERADICATE
ERADICATED
ERADICATING
ERADICATION
ERADICATIVE
ERADICATOR
ERADICATORY
ERADICULOSE
ERAL
ERANIST
ERASABLE
ERASE
ERASED
ERASER
ERASING
ERASION
ERASURE
ERBER
ERBIA
ERBIUM
ERD
ERDVARK
ERE
EREB
ERECT
ERECTED
ERECTER
ERECTILE
ERECTILITY
ERECTING
ERECTION
ERECTIVE
ERECTLY
ERECTNESS
ERECTOPATENT
ERECTOR
ERELONG
EREMACAUSIS
EREMIC
EREMITAL
EREMITE

EREMITIC
EREMITICAL
EREMITISH
EREMOLOGY
EREMOPHYTE
ERENACH
ERENOW
EREPSIN
EREPT
EREPTASE
EREPTIC
ERER
ERETHIC
ERETHISIA
ERETHISM
ERETHISMIC
ERETHISTIC
ERETHITIC
EREV
EREWHILE
ERF
ERG
ERGAL
ERGAMINE
ERGASIA
ERGASTERION
ERGASTIC
ERGASTOPLASM
ERGASTOPLASMIC
ERGASTULUM
ERGATANDROUS
ERGATANDRY
ERGATE
ERGATES
ERGATIVE
ERGATOCRACY
ERGATOGYNE
ERGATOGYNOUS
ERGATOGYNY
ERGATOID
ERGATOMORPH
ERGATOMORPHIC
ERGATOMORPHISM
ERGMETER
ERGO
ERGODIC
ERGOGRAM
ERGOGRAPH
ERGOISM
ERGOLOGY
ERGOMANIAC
ERGOMETER
ERGON
ERGOPHILE
ERGOPHOBIA
ERGOPHOBIAC
ERGOPLASM
ERGOSTAT
ERGOSTEROL
ERGOT
ERGOTAMINE
ERGOTAMININE
ERGOTED
ERGOTIC
ERGOTIN
ERGOTINE
ERGOTININE
ERGOTISM
ERGOTIST
ERGOTIZATION
ERGOTIZE
ERGOTIZED
ERGOTIZING
ERGOTOXINE
ERGUSIA
ERIA
ERIC
ERICACEOUS
ERICAD
ERICAL
ERICETAL
ERICHTHOID
ERICHTHUS
ERICINEOUS
ERICIUS
ERICOID
ERICOLIN
ERICOPHYTE
ERIGERON
ERIGIBLE
ERIGLOSSATE
ERIKA
ERIKITE
ERINACEOUS
ERINEUM
ERINGO
ERINITE
ERINOSE
ERIOMETER
ERIONITE
ERIOPHORUM
ERIOPHYLLOUS
ERISTIC
ERISTICAL
ERISTICALLY
ERIZO
ERK
ERLICHE
ERLKING
ERME
ERMELIN
ERMILINE
ERMIN
ERMINE
ERMINED
ERMINEE
ERMINES
ERMINING
ERMINITES
ERMINOIS
ERN
ERNE
ERODE
ERODED
ERODENT
ERODING
EROGATE
EROGENEITY
EROGENESIS
EROGENETIC
EROGENIC
EROGENOUS
EROSE
EROSIBLE
EROSION
EROSIONAL
EROSIONIST
EROSIVE
EROSTRATE
EROTEMA
EROTEME
EROTESIS
EROTETIC
EROTIC
EROTICA
EROTICAL
EROTICALLY
EROTICISM
EROTICOMANIA
EROTISM
EROTOGENIC
EROTOMANIA
EROTOMANIAC
EROTOPATH
EROTOPATHY
EROTYLID
ERR
ERRABILITY
ERRABLE
ERRABLENESS
ERRABUND
ERRANCY
ERRAND
ERRANT
ERRANTLY
ERRANTNESS
ERRANTRIES
ERRANTRY
ERRATA
ERRATIC
ERRATICAL
ERRATICALLY
ERRATICALNESS
ERRATUM
ERRED
ERRHINE
ERRING
ERRINGLY
ERRITE
ERRONEOUS
ERRONEOUSLY
ERRONEOUSNESS
ERROR
ERRORIST
ERS
ERSATZ
ERST
ERSTWHILE
ERSTWHILES
ERT
ERUB
ERUBESCENCE
ERUBESCENT
ERUC
ERUCA
ERUCIN
ERUCT
ERUCTATE
ERUCTATION
ERUCTATIVE
ERUDIT
ERUDITE
ERUDITELY
ERUDITENESS
ERUDITICAL
ERUDITION
ERUDITIONAL
ERUDITIONIST
ERUGATE
ERUGATION
ERUGATORY
ERUMPENT
ERUPT
ERUPTED
ERUPTING
ERUPTION
ERUPTIONAL
ERUPTIVE
ERUPTIVELY
ERUPTIVENESS
ERUPTIVITY
ERUPTURIENT
ERUV
ERVEN
ERVENHOLDER
ERVIL
ERYNGO
ERYOPID
ERYSIPELAS
ERYSIPELATOID
ERYSIPELOID
ERYTHEMA
ERYTHEMATIC
ERYTHEMATOUS
ERYTHEMIC
ERYTHRAEAN
ERYTHRAEMIA
ERYTHRASMA
ERYTHREAN
ERYTHREMIA
ERYTHRIN
ERYTHRINE
ERYTHRISM
ERYTHRISMAL
ERYTHRISTIC
ERYTHRITE
ERYTHRITIC
ERYTHRITOL
ERYTHROBLAST
ERYTHROCARPOUS
ERYTHROCYTOSIS
ERYTHRODERMIA
ERYTHROGENIC
ERYTHROGLUCIN
ERYTHROID
ERYTHROL
ERYTHROLEIN
ERYTHROLYSIN
ERYTHROLYSIS
ERYTHROLYTIC
ERYTHROMANIA
ERYTHRONIUM
ERYTHROPENIA
ERYTHROPHOBIA
ERYTHROPHORE
ERYTHROPHYLL
ERYTHROPIA
ERYTHROPSIA
ERYTHROPSIN
ERYTHROSCOPE
ERYTHROSE
ERYTHROSIN
ERYTHROSIS
ERYTHROZYME
ERYTHRULOSE
ERZAHLER
ES
ESAN
ESBAY
ESCA
ESCADRILLE
ESCALADE
ESCALADED
ESCALADER
ESCALADING
ESCALADO
ESCALAN
ESCALATE
ESCALATED
ESCALATING
ESCALATION
ESCALATOR
ESCALIER
ESCALLOP
ESCALLOPED
ESCALOP
ESCALOPED
ESCAMBIO
ESCAMBRON
ESCAMOTAGE
ESCAPABLE
ESCAPADE
ESCAPAGE
ESCAPE
ESCAPED
ESCAPEE
ESCAPEMENT
ESCAPER
ESCAPING
ESCAPISM
ESCAPIST
ESCARBUNCLE
ESCARGOT
ESCAROLE
ESCARP
ESCARPMENT
ESCHALOT
ESCHAR
ESCHARA
ESCHARINE
ESCHAROID
ESCHAROTIC
ESCHATOCOL
ESCHATOLOGY
ESCHAUFE
ESCHEAT
ESCHEATABLE
ESCHEATAGE
ESCHEATED
ESCHEATING
ESCHEATOR
ESCHEL
ESCHEW
ESCHEWAL
ESCHEWANCE
ESCHEWED
ESCHEWER
ESCHEWING
ESCHYNITE
ESCLANDRE
ESCLAVAGE
ESCOBA
ESCOBADURA
ESCOBILLA
ESCOBITA
ESCOLAR
ESCOLARS
ESCONSON
ESCOPET
ESCOPETA
ESCOPETTE
ESCORT
ESCORTED
ESCORTING
ESCOT
ESCRIBANO
ESCRIBE
ESCRIBED
ESCRIBIENTE
ESCRIBIENTES
ESCRIBING
ESCRIME
ESCRIPT
ESCRITOIRE
ESCRITORIAL
ESCROD
ESCROL
ESCROLL
ESCROW
ESCROWEE
ESCRY
ESCUAGE
ESCUDERO
ESCUDO
ESCUDOS
ESCULENT
ESCULETIN
ESCULIN
ESCUTCHEON
ESCUTCHEONED
ESCUTELLATE
ESEMPLASTIC
ESEMPLASY
ESEPTATE
ESERE

ESERIN
ESERINE
ESEXUAL
ESGUARD
ESHIN
ESILL
ESIPHONAL
ESK
ESKAR
ESKER
ESLABON
ESMERALDA
ESMERALDITE
ESNE
ESNECY
ESOANHYDRIDE
ESOCIFORM
ESODIC
ESOENTERITIS
ESOGASTRITIS
ESONARTHEX
ESONEURAL
ESOPHAGAL
ESOPHAGEAL
ESOPHAGEAN
ESOPHAGISM
ESOPHAGITIS
ESOPHAGOCELE
ESOPHAGOTOME
ESOPHAGOTOMY
ESOPHAGUS
ESOPHORIA
ESOTERIC
ESOTERICA
ESOTERICAL
ESOTERICALLY
ESOTERICISM
ESOTERICS
ESOTERISM
ESOTERIST
ESOTERIZE
ESOTERY
ESOTHYROPEXY
ESOTROPE
ESOTROPIA
ESOTROPIC
ESOX
ESP
ESPACEMENT
ESPADA
ESPADON
ESPADRILLE
ESPAGNOLETTE
ESPALIER
ESPALIERED
ESPALIERING
ESPANTOON
ESPARCET
ESPARTO
ESPATHATE
ESPAVE
ESPAVEL
ESPECE
ESPECIAL
ESPECIALLY
ESPECIALNESS
ESPEIRE
ESPERANCE
ESPHRESIS
ESPIAL
ESPIED
ESPIEGLE
ESPIEGLERIE
ESPIER
ESPINAL
ESPINEL
ESPINGOLE
ESPINO
ESPINOS
ESPIONAGE
ESPLANADE
ESPLEES
ESPOUSAL
ESPOUSE
ESPOUSED
ESPOUSER
ESPOUSING
ESPRESSIVO
ESPRESSOS
ESPRINGAL
ESPRISE
ESPRIT
ESPROVE
ESPUNDIA
ESPY
ESPYING
ESQUAMATE
ESQUAMULOSE
ESQUIRE
ESQUIRED
ESQUIRING
ESQUISSE
ESS
ESSANG
ESSART
ESSAY
ESSAYED
ESSAYER
ESSAYETTE
ESSAYICAL
ESSAYING
ESSAYIST
ESSAYISTIC
ESSAYISTICAL
ESSE
ESSED
ESSEDA
ESSEDE
ESSENCE
ESSENCED
ESSENCING
ESSENHOUT
ESSENTIA
ESSENTIAL
ESSENTIALITIES
ESSENTIALITY
ESSENTIALLY
ESSENTIATE
ESSENWOOD
ESSES
ESSEXITE
ESSIVE
ESSLING
ESSOIGN
ESSOIN
ESSOINED
ESSOINEE
ESSOINER
ESSOINING
ESSONITE
ESSORANT
EST
ESTABLISH
ESTABLISHED
ESTABLISHER
ESTABLISHING
ESTABLISHMENT
ESTACADE
ESTADAL
ESTADEL
ESTADIO
ESTADO
ESTAFA
ESTAFET
ESTAFETTE
ESTAFETTED
ESTAMENE
ESTAMIN
ESTAMINET
ESTAMP
ESTAMPAGE
ESTAMPEDE
ESTAMPEDERO
ESTAMPIE
ESTANCIA
ESTANCIERO
ESTANTION
ESTATE
ESTATED
ESTATES
ESTATESMAN
ESTATESMEN
ESTATING
ESTATS
ESTEEM
ESTEEMABLE
ESTEEMED
ESTEEMER
ESTEEMING
ESTER
ESTERASE
ESTERELLITE
ESTERIFEROUS
ESTERIFICATION
ESTERIFIED
ESTERIFY
ESTERIFYING
ESTERIZATION
ESTERIZE
ESTERIZING
ESTERLIN
ESTERO
ESTEROS
ESTEVIN
ESTHEMATOLOGY
ESTHERIAN
ESTHESIA
ESTHESIOGEN
ESTHESIOLOGY
ESTHESIS
ESTHETE
ESTHETIC
ESTHETICAL
ESTHETICALLY
ESTHETICIAN
ESTHETICISM
ESTHETICS
ESTHETOLOGY
ESTHETOPHORE
ESTHIOMENE
ESTHIOMENUS
ESTIMABLE
ESTIMABLY
ESTIMATE
ESTIMATED
ESTIMATING
ESTIMATINGLY
ESTIMATION
ESTIMATIVE
ESTIMATOR
ESTIPULATE
ESTIVAGE
ESTIVAL
ESTIVATE
ESTIVATED
ESTIVATING
ESTIVATION
ESTIVATOR
ESTIVE
ESTMARK
ESTOC
ESTOCADA
ESTOILE
ESTOLIDE
ESTOP
ESTOPPAGE
ESTOPPED
ESTOPPEL
ESTOPPING
ESTOQUE
ESTOVERS
ESTRADA
ESTRADAS
ESTRADE
ESTRADIOL
ESTRAGOL
ESTRAGOLE
ESTRAGON
ESTRANGE
ESTRANGED
ESTRANGEDNESS
ESTRANGEMENT
ESTRANGER
ESTRANGING
ESTRAPADE
ESTRAY
ESTRAYED
ESTRAYING
ESTRE
ESTREAT
ESTREATED
ESTREATING
ESTREPE
ESTREPEMENT
ESTRIATE
ESTRICHE
ESTRIF
ESTRIOL
ESTRO
ESTROGEN
ESTROGENIC
ESTRONE
ESTROUS
ESTRUAL
ESTRUM
ESTRUS
ESTUARIAL
ESTUARIAN
ESTUARIES
ESTUARINE
ESTUARY
ESTUATE
ESTUDY
ESTUFA
ESTUOUS
ESTURE
ESTUS
ESURIENCE
ESURIENCY
ESURIENT
ESURIENTLY
ESURINE
ET
ETA
ETAAC
ETABALLI
ETABELLI
ETACISM
ETAERIO
ETAGE
ETAGERE
ETALAGE
ETALON
ETAMINE
ETAPE
ETAS
ETATISM
ETATISME
ETCETERA
ETCETERAS
ETCH
ETCHANT
ETCHED
ETCHEMIN
ETCHER
ETCHING
ETEN
ETERN
ETERNAL
ETERNALIST
ETERNALIZATION
ETERNALIZE
ETERNALLY
ETERNALNESS
ETERNE
ETERNISH
ETERNITIES
ETERNITY
ETERNIZATION
ETERNIZE
ETERNIZED
ETERNIZING
ETESIAN
ETH
ETHAL
ETHALDEHYDE
ETHANAL
ETHANAMIDE
ETHANE
ETHANETHIOL
ETHANOL
ETHANOYL
ETHEL
ETHELING
ETHENE
ETHENOID
ETHENOIDAL
ETHENOL
ETHENYL
ETHEOSTOMOID
ETHER
ETHERATE
ETHEREAL
ETHEREALISM
ETHEREALITY
ETHEREALIZE
ETHEREALIZED
ETHEREALIZING
ETHEREALLY
ETHEREALNESS
ETHERED
ETHEREOUS
ETHERIC
ETHERICAL
ETHERIFIED
ETHERIFORM
ETHERIFY
ETHERIFYING
ETHERIN
ETHERION
ETHERISM
ETHERIZATION
ETHERIZE
ETHERIZED
ETHERIZER
ETHERIZING
ETHEROLATE
ETHEROUS
ETHIC
ETHICAL
ETHICALITY
ETHICALLY
ETHICALNESS
ETHICIAN
ETHICIST

ETHICIZE
ETHICIZED
ETHICIZING
ETHICS
ETHIDE
ETHIDENE
ETHINE
ETHINYL
ETHIODIDE
ETHIOPS
ETHIZE
ETHMOID
ETHMOIDAL
ETHMOIDITIS
ETHMOLITH
ETHMYPHITIS
ETHNARCH
ETHNARCHIES
ETHNARCHY
ETHNIC
ETHNICAL
ETHNICALLY
ETHNICISM
ETHNICIST
ETHNOBOTANY
ETHNOCENTRIC
ETHNOCENTRISM
ETHNOCRACY
ETHNODICY
ETHNOFLORA
ETHNOGENIC
ETHNOGENIES
ETHNOGENY
ETHNOGRAPHER
ETHNOGRAPHIC
ETHNOGRAPHIES
ETHNOGRAPHIST
ETHNOGRAPHY
ETHNOLOGER
ETHNOLOGIC
ETHNOLOGICAL
ETHNOLOGIST
ETHNOLOGY
ETHNOMANIAC
ETHNOPSYCHIC
ETHNOS
ETHNOZOOLOGY
ETHOGRAPHY
ETHOLIDE
ETHOLOGIC
ETHOLOGICAL
ETHOLOGY
ETHONOMIC
ETHONOMICS
ETHOPOEIA
ETHOS
ETHOXIDE
ETHOXYL
ETHROG
ETHYL
ETHYLAMIDE
ETHYLAMIME
ETHYLAMIN
ETHYLATE
ETHYLATED
ETHYLATING
ETHYLATION
ETHYLENE
ETHYLENIC
ETHYLIC
ETHYLIDENE
ETHYLIN
ETHYNE
ETHYNYL
ETHYSULPHURIC
ETIK
ETIOLATE
ETIOLATED
ETIOLATING
ETIOLATION
ETIOLIN
ETIOLIZE
ETIOLOGICAL
ETIOLOGICALLY
ETIOLOGIST
ETIOLOGUE
ETIOLOGY
ETIOPHYLLIN
ETIOTROPIC
ETIQUET
ETIQUETTE
ETIQUETTICAL
ETNA
ETOILE
ETOUFFE
ETOURDERIE
ETRENNE
ETROG
ETTERCAP
ETTLE
ETTLED
ETTLING
ETUDE
ETUI
ETWEE
ETWITE
ETYM
ETYMA
ETYMIC
ETYMOGRAPHY
ETYMOLOGER
ETYMOLOGIC
ETYMOLOGICAL
ETYMOLOGICON
ETYMOLOGIST
ETYMOLOGIZE
ETYMOLOGIZED
ETYMOLOGIZING
ETYMOLOGY
ETYMON
ETYMONS
ETYPIC
ETYPICAL
ETYPICALLY
EUANGIOTIC
EUASTER
EUBACTERIUM
EUCAINE
EUCAIRITE
EUCALYPT
EUCALYPTEOL
EUCALYPTI
EUCALYPTIAN
EUCALYPTIC
EUCALYPTOL
EUCALYPTOLE
EUCALYPTUS
EUCALYPTUSES
EUCATROPINE
EUCEPHALOUS
EUCHARIS
EUCHARIST
EUCHARISTIAL
EUCHARISTIC
EUCHARISTICAL
EUCHARISTIZE
EUCHARISTIZED
EUCHARISTIZING
EUCHLORHYDRIA
EUCHLORINE
EUCHOLOGION
EUCHOLOGY
EUCHRE
EUCHRED
EUCHRING
EUCHROITE
EUCHROME
EUCHROMOSOME
EUCLASE
EUCLEID
EUCOLITE
EUCONE
EUCONIC
EUCOSMID
EUCRASIA
EUCRASITE
EUCRASY
EUCRITE
EUCRYPTITE
EUCRYSTALLINE
EUCTICAL
EUCYCLIC
EUDAEMON
EUDAEMONIA
EUDAEMONIC
EUDAEMONICAL
EUDAEMONICS
EUDAEMONISM
EUDAEMONIST
EUDAEMONIZE
EUDAEMONY
EUDALENE
EUDEMON
EUDESMOL
EUDIAGNOSTIC
EUDIALYTE
EUDIDYMITE
EUDIOMETER
EUDIOMETRY
EUDIPLEURAL
EUGE
EUGENESIC
EUGENESIS
EUGENETIC
EUGENIC
EUGENICAL
EUGENICALLY
EUGENICIST
EUGENICS
EUGENISM
EUGENIST
EUGENOL
EUGENOLATE
EUGENY
EUGLENOID
EUGLOBULIN
EUGRANITIC
EUHARMONIC
EUHEDRAL
EUHEMERISM
EUHEMERIST
EUHEMERISTIC
EUHEMERIZE
EUHEMERIZED
EUHEMERIZING
EUHYOSTYLIC
EUHYOSTYLY
EUKTOLITE
EULACHAN
EULACHANS
EULACHON
EULACHONS
EULALIA
EULOGIA
EULOGIC
EULOGICAL
EULOGICALLY
EULOGIES
EULOGIOUS
EULOGISM
EULOGIST
EULOGISTIC
EULOGISTICAL
EULOGIUM
EULOGIUMS
EULOGIZATION
EULOGIZE
EULOGIZED
EULOGIZER
EULOGIZING
EULOGY
EULOPHID
EULYSITE
EULYTINE
EULYTITE
EUMEMORRHEA
EUMENID
EUMERISM
EUMERISTIC
EUMEROMORPH
EUMITOSIS
EUMITOTIC
EUMOIROUS
EUMOLPIQUE
EUMORPHOUS
EUMYCETE
EUMYCETIC
EUNICID
EUNOMY
EUNUCH
EUNUCHAL
EUNUCHOID
EUNUCHOIDISM
EUNUCHRY
EUOMPHALID
EUONYM
EUONYMIN
EUONYMOUS
EUONYMUS
EUONYMY
EUOSMITE
EUOUAE
EUPAD
EUPATHY
EUPATORIN
EUPATORIUM
EUPATORY
EUPATRID
EUPATRIDAE
EUPATRIDS
EUPEPSIA
EUPEPSY
EUPEPTIC
EUPEPTICISM
EUPEPTICITY
EUPHAUSID
EUPHEMIAN
EUPHEMIOUS
EUPHEMIOUSLY
EUPHEMISM
EUPHEMIST
EUPHEMISTIC
EUPHEMIZE
EUPHEMIZED
EUPHEMIZER
EUPHEMIZING
EUPHEMOUS
EUPHEMY
EUPHON
EUPHONE
EUPHONETIC
EUPHONETICS
EUPHONIA
EUPHONIC
EUPHONICAL
EUPHONICALLY
EUPHONIES
EUPHONIOUS
EUPHONIOUSLY
EUPHONISM
EUPHONIUM
EUPHONIZE
EUPHONIZED
EUPHONIZING
EUPHONON
EUPHONOUS
EUPHONY
EUPHONYM
EUPHORBIA
EUPHORBIAL
EUPHORBIUM
EUPHORIA
EUPHORIC
EUPHORY
EUPHRASY
EUPHROE
EUPHUISM
EUPHUIST
EUPHUISTIC
EUPHUISTICALLY
EUPHUIZE
EUPHUIZED
EUPHUIZING
EUPION
EUPIONE
EUPITTONE
EUPLASTIC
EUPLOID
EUPLOIDY
EUPNEA
EUPNOEA
EUPOLYZOAN
EUPRACTIC
EUPRAXIA
EUPSYCHICS
EUPYRCHROITE
EUPYRENE
EUPYRION
EURE
EUREKA
EURHODINE
EURHODOL
EURHYTHMIC
EURHYTHMICAL
EURHYTHMICS
EURHYTHMY
EURIPUS
EURITE
EURO
EUROBIN
EUROPIUM
EUROUS
EURYALIDAN
EURYBENTHIC
EURYCEPHALIC
EURYGNATHIC
EURYGNATHISM
EURYGNATHOUS
EURYHALINE
EURYLAIMOID
EURYON
EURYPROSOPIC
EURYPTERID
EURYPTEROID
EURYPYLOUS
EURYSCOPE
EURYTE
EURYTHERMAL
EURYTHERMIC
EURYTHMIC
EURYTHMICAL
EURYTHMICS
EURYTHMY
EURYTOMID
EURYZYGOUS

EUSOL
EUSTACY
EUSTATIC
EUSTELE
EUSTOMATOUS
EUSTYLE
EUSUCHIAN
EUSYNCHITE
EUTAXIC
EUTAXIE
EUTAXITE
EUTAXITIC
EUTAXY
EUTECHNIC
EUTECHNICS
EUTECTIC
EUTECTOID
EUTELEGENIC
EUTEXIA
EUTHANASIA
EUTHANASY
EUTHENICS
EUTHENIST
EUTHERMIC
EUTHYTROPIC
EUTOCIA
EUTOMOUS
EUTROPHIC
EUTROPHY
EUTROPIC
EUTROPOUS
EUXANTHATE
EUXANTHONE
EUXENITE
EVACUANT
EVACUATE
EVACUATED
EVACUATING
EVACUATION
EVACUATOR
EVACUE
EVACUEE
EVADABLE
EVADE
EVADED
EVADER
EVADIBLE
EVADING
EVAGATION
EVAGINABLE
EVAGINATE
EVAGINATED
EVAGINATING
EVAGINATION
EVALUABLE
EVALUATE
EVALUATED
EVALUATING
EVALUATION
EVALUATIVE
EVALUE
EVANESCE
EVANESCED
EVANESCENCE
EVANESCENCY
EVANESCENT
EVANESCENTLY
EVANESCIBLE
EVANESCING
EVANGEL
EVANGELIAN
EVANGELIC
EVANGELICAL
EVANGELICALLY
EVANGELICITY
EVANGELION
EVANGELISM
EVANGELIST
EVANGELISTARIES
EVANGELISTARY
EVANGELISTIC
EVANGELIUM
EVANGELIZE
EVANGELIZED
EVANGELIZER
EVANGELIZING
EVANID
EVANISH
EVANISHED
EVANISHING
EVANISHMENT
EVANSITE
EVAPORABLE
EVAPORATE
EVAPORATED
EVAPORATING
EVAPORATION
EVAPORATIVE
EVAPORATIVITY
EVAPORATOR
EVAPORIMETER
EVAPORIZE
EVASE
EVASIBLE
EVASION
EVASIONAL
EVASIVE
EVASIVELY
EVASIVENESS
EVE
EVECHURR
EVECK
EVECTION
EVECTIONAL
EVEJAR
EVEL
EVELIGHT
EVELONG
EVEN
EVENDOWN
EVENE
EVENED
EVENER
EVENFALL
EVENGLOME
EVENGLOW
EVENHAND
EVENHANDED
EVENHANDEDLY
EVENING
EVENK
EVENLONG
EVENLY
EVENMETE
EVENMINDED
EVENNESS
EVENOO
EVENS
EVENSONG
EVENT
EVENTAIL
EVENTFUL
EVENTFULLY
EVENTFULNESS
EVENTIDE
EVENTLESS
EVENTLESSLY
EVENTOGNATH
EVENTRATION
EVENTS
EVENTUAL
EVENTUALITIES
EVENTUALITY
EVENTUALIZE
EVENTUALLY
EVENTUATE
EVENTUATED
EVENTUATING
EVENWISE
EVEQUE
EVER
EVERBEARER
EVERBEARING
EVERBLOOMING
EVERDURING
EVERGLADE
EVERGLADES
EVERGREEN
EVERGREENERY
EVERGREENITE
EVERICH
EVERLASTING
EVERLASTINGLY
EVERLIVING
EVERLY
EVERMO
EVERMORE
EVERNIOID
EVERSE
EVERSIBLE
EVERSION
EVERSIVE
EVERSPORTING
EVERT
EVERTEBRAL
EVERTEBRATE
EVERTED
EVERTILE
EVERTING
EVERTOR
EVERWHICH
EVERWHO
EVERY
EVERYBODY
EVERYDAY
EVERYHOW
EVERYLIKE
EVERYONE
EVERYTHING
EVERYWHERE
EVERYWHERES
EVERYWHITHER
EVESTAR
EVET
EVETIDE
EVEWEED
EVIBRATE
EVICKE
EVICT
EVICTED
EVICTING
EVICTION
EVICTOR
EVIDENCE
EVIDENCED
EVIDENCING
EVIDENCIVE
EVIDENT
EVIDENTIAL
EVIDENTIALLY
EVIDENTIARY
EVIDENTLY
EVIL
EVILDOER
EVILHEARTED
EVILLY
EVILNESS
EVILSAYER
EVILSPEAKER
EVILSPEAKING
EVILWISHING
EVINCE
EVINCED
EVINCEMENT
EVINCIBLE
EVINCING
EVINCIVE
EVIRATE
EVIRATO
EVISCERATE
EVISCERATED
EVISCERATING
EVISCERATION
EVISITE
EVITABLE
EVITATE
EVITATION
EVITE
EVITTATE
EVOCABLE
EVOCATE
EVOCATED
EVOCATING
EVOCATION
EVOCATIVE
EVOCATOR
EVOCATORY
EVOE
EVOHE
EVOID
EVOKE
EVOKED
EVOKER
EVOKING
EVOLUTE
EVOLUTION
EVOLUTIONAL
EVOLUTIONARY
EVOLUTIONISM
EVOLUTIONIST
EVOLUTIONIZE
EVOLUTIVE
EVOLVABLE
EVOLVE
EVOLVEMENT
EVOLVENT
EVOME
EVOMIT
EVONYMUS
EVOVAE
EVULGATE
EVULGATION
EVULGE
EVULSE
EVULSION
EVZONE
EVZONES
EWAGE
EWDER
EWE
EWELEASE
EWER
EWERER
EWERIES
EWERY
EWEST
EWHOW
EWK
EWRY
EX
EXACERBATE
EXACERBATED
EXACERBATING
EXACERBATION
EXACT
EXACTA
EXACTABLE
EXACTED
EXACTER
EXACTING
EXACTINGLY
EXACTINGNESS
EXACTION
EXACTITUDE
EXACTIVE
EXACTIVENESS
EXACTLY
EXACTMENT
EXACTNESS
EXACTOR
EXACUATE
EXADVERSO
EXADVERSUM
EXAGGERATE
EXAGGERATED
EXAGGERATING
EXAGGERATION
EXAGGERATIVE
EXAGGERATOR
EXAGGERATORY
EXAGITATE
EXAIRESIS
EXALATE
EXALBUMINOSE
EXALBUMINOUS
EXALLOTRIOTE
EXALT
EXALTATE
EXALTATION
EXALTATIVE
EXALTE
EXALTED
EXALTEDLY
EXALTEDNESS
EXALTEE
EXALTER
EXALTING
EXAM
EXAMEN
EXAMINABLE
EXAMINANT
EXAMINATE
EXAMINATION
EXAMINATIONAL
EXAMINATIVE
EXAMINATOR
EXAMINATORY
EXAMINE
EXAMINED
EXAMINEE
EXAMINER
EXAMINING
EXAMPLE
EXAMPLED
EXAMPLING
EXANIMATE
EXANIMATION
EXANTHEM
EXANTHEMA
EXANTHEMAS
EXANTHEMATA
EXANTHEMATIC
EXANTLATE
EXANTLATION
EXARATE
EXARATION
EXARCH
EXARCHAL
EXARCHATE
EXARCHIST
EXARCHY
EXARTERITIS
EXARTICULATE
EXASPER
EXASPERATE

EXASPERATED
EXASPERATER
EXASPERATING
EXASPERATION
EXASPERATIVE
EXASPIDEAN
EXAUCTORATE
EXAUGURATE
EXAUGURATION
EXAUTHORIZE
EXCALATE
EXCALATION
EXCALCARATE
EXCALCEATE
EXCAMB
EXCAMBER
EXCAMBION
EXCANDESCENT
EXCANTATION
EXCARNATE
EXCARNATION
EXCATHEDRAL
EXCAUDATE
EXCAVATE
EXCAVATED
EXCAVATING
EXCAVATION
EXCAVATIONS
EXCAVATOR
EXCAVE
EXCECATE
EXCECATION
EXCEDENT
EXCEED
EXCEEDED
EXCEEDING
EXCEEDINGLY
EXCEL
EXCELENTE
EXCELLED
EXCELLENCE
EXCELLENCIES
EXCELLENCY
EXCELLENT
EXCELLENTLY
EXCELLING
EXCELS
EXCELSE
EXCELSIN
EXCELSIOR
EXCENTRAL
EXCENTRIC
EXCEPT
EXCEPTANT
EXCEPTED
EXCEPTER
EXCEPTING
EXCEPTIO
EXCEPTION
EXCEPTIONAL
EXCEPTIONALLY
EXCEPTIONARY
EXCEPTIONER
EXCEPTIOUS
EXCEPTIVE
EXCEPTIVELY
EXCERN
EXCERPT
EXCERPTA
EXCERPTED
EXCERPTIBLE
EXCERPTING
EXCERPTION
EXCERPTIVE
EXCERPTOR
EXCESS
EXCESSIVE
EXCESSIVELY
EXCESSIVENESS
EXCESSMAN
EXCESSMEN
EXCHANGE
EXCHANGEABLE
EXCHANGEABLY
EXCHANGED
EXCHANGER
EXCHANGING
EXCHEAT
EXCHEQUER
EXCIDE
EXCIDED
EXCIDING
EXCIPIENT
EXCIPLE
EXCIPULAR
EXCIPULE
EXCIPULIFORM
EXCIPULUM
EXCIRCLE
EXCISABLE
EXCISE
EXCISED
EXCISEMAN
EXCISEMEN
EXCISING
EXCISION
EXCISOR
EXCITABILITIES
EXCITABILITY
EXCITABLE
EXCITABLENESS
EXCITABLY
EXCITANCY
EXCITANT
EXCITATE
EXCITATION
EXCITATIVE
EXCITATOR
EXCITATORY
EXCITE
EXCITED
EXCITEDLY
EXCITEDNESS
EXCITEMENT
EXCITER
EXCITING
EXCITINGLY
EXCITIVE
EXCITOMOTOR
EXCITOMOTORY
EXCITON
EXCITOR
EXCITORY
EXCITRON
EXCLAIM
EXCLAIMED
EXCLAIMER
EXCLAIMING
EXCLAMATION
EXCLAMATIONAL
EXCLAMATIVE
EXCLAMATIVELY
EXCLAMATORILY
EXCLAMATORY
EXCLAVE
EXCLUDE
EXCLUDED
EXCLUDER
EXCLUDING
EXCLUSION
EXCLUSIONARY
EXCLUSIONER
EXCLUSIONISM
EXCLUSIONIST
EXCLUSIVE
EXCLUSIVELY
EXCLUSIVENESS
EXCLUSIVISM
EXCLUSIVITY
EXCLUSORY
EXCOCT
EXCOCTION
EXCOGITABLE
EXCOGITATE
EXCOGITATED
EXCOGITATING
EXCOGITATION
EXCOGITATIVE
EXCOGITATOR
EXCOMMUNICABLE
EXCOMMUNICANT
EXCOMMUNICATE
EXCOMMUNICATED
EXCOMMUNICATING
EXCOMMUNICATION
EXCOMMUNICATIVE
EXCOMMUNICATOR
EXCOMMUNICATORY
EXCOMMUNION
EXCONJUGANT
EXCORIABLE
EXCORIATE
EXCORIATED
EXCORIATING
EXCORIATION
EXCORIATOR
EXCORTICATE
EXCORTICATED
EXCORTICATING
EXCORTICATION
EXCREMENT
EXCREMENTAL
EXCREMENTARY
EXCREMENTIVE
EXCRESCE
EXCRESCENCE
EXCRESCENCES
EXCRESCENCIES
EXCRESCENCY
EXCRESCENT
EXCRESCENTIAL
EXCRETA
EXCRETAL
EXCRETE
EXCRETED
EXCRETER
EXCRETES
EXCRETING
EXCRETION
EXCRETIONARY
EXCRETIVE
EXCRETORY
EXCRIMINATE
EXCRUCIABLE
EXCRUCIATE
EXCRUCIATED
EXCRUCIATING
EXCRUCIATINGLY
EXCRUCIATION
EXCRUCIATOR
EXCUBANT
EXCUDATE
EXCUDERUNT
EXCUDIT
EXCULPABLE
EXCULPATE
EXCULPATED
EXCULPATING
EXCULPATION
EXCULPATIVE
EXCULPATORY
EXCUR
EXCURRENT
EXCURSE
EXCURSED
EXCURSING
EXCURSION
EXCURSIONAL
EXCURSIONARY
EXCURSIONER
EXCURSIONISM
EXCURSIONIST
EXCURSIONIZE
EXCURSIVE
EXCURSIVELY
EXCURSUS
EXCURVATE
EXCURVATED
EXCURVATURE
EXCURVED
EXCUSABILITY
EXCUSABLE
EXCUSABLENESS
EXCUSABLY
EXCUSAL
EXCUSATIVE
EXCUSATOR
EXCUSATORY
EXCUSE
EXCUSED
EXCUSER
EXCUSING
EXCUSIVE
EXCUSS
EXCUSSED
EXCUSSING
EXCYST
EXCYSTATION
EXCYSTED
EXCYSTMENT
EXEAT
EXEC
EXECRABLE
EXECRABLENESS
EXECRABLY
EXECRATE
EXECRATED
EXECRATING
EXECRATION
EXECRATIVE
EXECRATOR
EXECRATORY
EXECUTABLE
EXECUTANCY
EXECUTANT
EXECUTE
EXECUTED
EXECUTER
EXECUTING
EXECUTION
EXECUTIONAL
EXECUTIONEERING
EXECUTIONER
EXECUTIONERESS
EXECUTIONS
EXECUTIVE
EXECUTIVELY
EXECUTIVENESS
EXECUTOR
EXECUTORIAL
EXECUTORY
EXECUTRESS
EXECUTRICES
EXECUTRIX
EXECUTRIXES
EXECUTRY
EXEDE
EXEDENT
EXEDRA
EXEEM
EXEGESES
EXEGESIS
EXEGETE
EXEGETIC
EXEGETICAL
EXEGETICALLY
EXEGETICS
EXEGETIST
EXEME
EXEMPLA
EXEMPLAR
EXEMPLARIC
EXEMPLARILY
EXEMPLARINESS
EXEMPLARISM
EXEMPLARITY
EXEMPLARY
EXEMPLIFICATION
EXEMPLIFIED
EXEMPLIFIER
EXEMPLIFY
EXEMPLIFYING
EXEMPLUM
EXEMPT
EXEMPTIBLE
EXEMPTILE
EXEMPTION
EXEMPTIVE
EXENCEPHALIA
EXENCEPHALIC
EXENCEPHALUS
EXENTERATE
EXENTERATED
EXENTERATING
EXENTERATION
EXEQUATUR
EXEQUIAL
EXEQUIES
EXEQUY
EXERCE
EXERCENT
EXERCISABLE
EXERCISE
EXERCISED
EXERCISER
EXERCISES
EXERCISING
EXERCITANT
EXERCITATION
EXERCITOR
EXERCITORIAL
EXERESIS
EXERGUAL
EXERGUE
EXERT
EXERTED
EXERTING
EXERTION
EXERTIVE
EXES
EXESION
EXEUNT
EXFIGURATION
EXFIGURE
EXFILTRATION
EXFLAGELLATE
EXFLECT
EXFODIATE
EXFODIATION
EXFOLIATE
EXFOLIATED
EXFOLIATING
EXFOLIATION
EXFOLIATIVE
EXFOLIATORY

EXHALABLE
EXHALANT
EXHALATE
EXHALATION
EXHALATORY
EXHALE
EXHALED
EXHALING
EXHANCE
EXHAUST
EXHAUSTED
EXHAUSTEDLY
EXHAUSTEDNESS
EXHAUSTER
EXHAUSTIBLE
EXHAUSTING
EXHAUSTINGLY
EXHAUSTION
EXHAUSTIVE
EXHAUSTIVELY
EXHAUSTIVENESS
EXHAUSTLESS
EXHAUSTLESSLY
EXHEDRA
EXHIBIT
EXHIBITANT
EXHIBITED
EXHIBITING
EXHIBITION
EXHIBITIONAL
EXHIBITIONER
EXHIBITIONISM
EXHIBITIONIST
EXHIBITIONISTIC
EXHIBITIVE
EXHIBITIVELY
EXHIBITOR
EXHIBITORSHIP
EXHIBITORY
EXHIBITS
EXHILARANT
EXHILARATE
EXHILARATED
EXHILARATING
EXHILARATINGLY
EXHILARATION
EXHILARATIVE
EXHILARATOR
EXHILARATORY
EXHORT
EXHORTATION
EXHORTATIVE
EXHORTATIVELY
EXHORTATORY
EXHORTED
EXHORTER
EXHORTING
EXHUMATE
EXHUMATED
EXHUMATING
EXHUMATION
EXHUMATOR
EXHUMATORY
EXHUME
EXHUMED
EXHUMER
EXHUMING
EXIDO
EXIES
EXIGEANT
EXIGEANTE
EXIGENCE
EXIGENCIES
EXIGENCY
EXIGENT
EXIGENTER
EXIGENTLY
EXIGIBLE
EXIGUITY
EXIGUOUS
EXIGUOUSLY
EXIGUOUSNESS
EXILARCH
EXILARCHATE
EXILE
EXILED
EXILER
EXILIAN
EXILIC
EXILING
EXILITY
EXIMIOUS
EXIMIOUSLY
EXIMIOUSNESS
EXINANITE
EXINANITION
EXINE
EXINGUINAL
EXINITE
EXIST
EXISTED
EXISTENCE
EXISTENT
EXISTENTIAL
EXISTENTIALISM
EXISTENTIALIST
EXISTENTIALLY
EXISTENTLY
EXISTER
EXISTING
EXISTLESSNESS
EXIT
EXITE
EXITIAL
EXITION
EXITIOUS
EXITURE
EXITUS
EXLEX
EXOARTERITIS
EXOCARDIA
EXOCARDIAC
EXOCARDIAL
EXOCARP
EXOCCIPITAL
EXOCENTRIC
EXOCHORION
EXOCLINAL
EXOCLINE
EXOCOELAR
EXOCOELE
EXOCOELIC
EXOCOELOM
EXOCOELUM
EXOCOLITIS
EXOCONE
EXOCULATE
EXOCULATED
EXOCULATING
EXOCYCLIC
EXODE
EXODERM
EXODERMIS
EXODIC
EXODIST
EXODIUM
EXODONTIA
EXODROMIC
EXODROMY
EXODUS
EXODY
EXOENZYME
EXOGAMIC
EXOGAMOUS
EXOGAMY
EXOGASTRIC
EXOGASTRICALLY
EXOGASTRITIS
EXOGEN
EXOGENETIC
EXOGENIC
EXOGENOUS
EXOGENOUSLY
EXOGNATHION
EXOGNATHITE
EXOGRAPH
EXOLEMMA
EXOLETE
EXOLVE
EXOMETRITIS
EXOMION
EXOMIS
EXOMOLOGESIS
EXOMORPHIC
EXOMORPHISM
EXOMPHALOS
EXOMPHALOUS
EXOMPHALUS
EXON
EXONARTHEX
EXONER
EXONERATE
EXONERATED
EXONERATING
EXONERATION
EXONERATIVE
EXONERATOR
EXONERETUR
EXONEURAL
EXOPATHIC
EXOPERIDIUM
EXOPHAGOUS
EXOPHAGY
EXOPHORIA
EXOPHORIC
EXOPHTHALMIA
EXOPHTHALMIC
EXOPHTHALMOS
EXOPHTHALMUS
EXOPOD
EXOPODITE
EXOPODITIC
EXORABILITY
EXORABLE
EXORABLENESS
EXORATE
EXORBITAL
EXORBITANCE
EXORBITANCY
EXORBITANT
EXORBITANTLY
EXORBITATE
EXORBITATION
EXORCISATION
EXORCISE
EXORCISED
EXORCISEMENT
EXORCISER
EXORCISING
EXORCISM
EXORCISMAL
EXORCISORY
EXORCIST
EXORCISTIC
EXORCISTICAL
EXORCIZATION
EXORCIZE
EXORCIZED
EXORCIZEMENT
EXORCIZER
EXORCIZING
EXORDIAL
EXORDIUM
EXORDIUMS
EXORDIZE
EXORGANIC
EXORMIA
EXORN
EXORNATION
EXOSEPSIS
EXOSKELETAL
EXOSKELETON
EXOSMIC
EXOSMOSIS
EXOSMOTIC
EXOSPERM
EXOSPHERE
EXOSPHERIC
EXOSPORAL
EXOSPORE
EXOSPORIUM
EXOSPOROUS
EXOSTOME
EXOSTOSED
EXOSTOSES
EXOSTOSIS
EXOSTOTIC
EXOSTRA
EXOSTRACISM
EXOSTRACIZE
EXOSTRAE
EXOTERIC
EXOTERICAL
EXOTERICALLY
EXOTERICISM
EXOTERICS
EXOTHECA
EXOTHECAL
EXOTHECATE
EXOTHECIUM
EXOTHERMAL
EXOTHERMIC
EXOTHERMOUS
EXOTIC
EXOTICALLY
EXOTICALNESS
EXOTICISM
EXOTICIST
EXOTICITY
EXOTICNESS
EXOTISM
EXOTOSPORE
EXOTOXIC
EXOTOXIN
EXOTROPIA
EXOTROPISM
EXPALPATE
EXPAND
EXPANDED
EXPANDEDLY
EXPANDEDNESS
EXPANDER
EXPANDING
EXPANDINGLY
EXPANSE
EXPANSIBILITY
EXPANSIBLE
EXPANSIBLENESS
EXPANSIBLY
EXPANSILE
EXPANSION
EXPANSIONAL
EXPANSIONISM
EXPANSIONIST
EXPANSIVE
EXPANSIVELY
EXPANSIVENESS
EXPANSIVITY
EXPANSUM
EXPANSURE
EXPATIATE
EXPATIATED
EXPATIATER
EXPATIATING
EXPATIATION
EXPATIATIVE
EXPATIATOR
EXPATIATORY
EXPATRIATE
EXPATRIATED
EXPATRIATING
EXPATRIATION
EXPECT
EXPECTABLE
EXPECTANCE
EXPECTANCIES
EXPECTANCY
EXPECTANT
EXPECTANTLY
EXPECTATION
EXPECTATIVE
EXPECTED
EXPECTER
EXPECTING
EXPECTIVE
EXPECTORANT
EXPECTORATE
EXPECTORATED
EXPECTORATING
EXPECTORATION
EXPECTORATOR
EXPEDE
EXPEDED
EXPEDIATE
EXPEDIENCE
EXPEDIENCIES
EXPEDIENCY
EXPEDIENT
EXPEDIENTE
EXPEDIENTIAL
EXPEDIENTIALLY
EXPEDIENTIST
EXPEDIENTLY
EXPEDING
EXPEDITATE
EXPEDITATED
EXPEDITATING
EXPEDITATION
EXPEDITE
EXPEDITED
EXPEDITELY
EXPEDITENESS
EXPEDITER
EXPEDITING
EXPEDITION
EXPEDITIONARY
EXPEDITIONIST
EXPEDITIOUS
EXPEDITIOUSLY
EXPEDITIOUSNESS
EXPEDITOR
EXPEL
EXPELLABLE
EXPELLANT
EXPELLED
EXPELLEE
EXPELLENT
EXPELLER
EXPELLING
EXPEND
EXPENDABILITY
EXPENDABLE
EXPENDED
EXPENDER
EXPENDING

EXPENDITOR
EXPENDITRIX
EXPENDITURE
EXPENSE
EXPENSEFUL
EXPENSEFULNESS
EXPENSES
EXPENSILATION
EXPENSIVE
EXPENSIVELY
EXPENSIVENESS
EXPENTHESIS
EXPERIENCE
EXPERIENCED
EXPERIENCER
EXPERIENCES
EXPERIENCING
EXPERIENT
EXPERIENTIAL
EXPERIENTIALLY
EXPERIMENT
EXPERIMENTAL
EXPERIMENTALISM
EXPERIMENTALIST
EXPERIMENTALIZE
EXPERIMENTALLY
EXPERIMENTARIAN
EXPERIMENTATION
EXPERIMENTATIVE
EXPERIMENTATOR
EXPERIMENTED
EXPERIMENTEE
EXPERIMENTER
EXPERIMENTING
EXPERIMENTIST
EXPERIMENTIZE
EXPERIMENTLY
EXPERMENTIZED
EXPERT
EXPERTISE
EXPERTLY
EXPERTNESS
EXPIABLE
EXPIATE
EXPIATED
EXPIATING
EXPIATION
EXPIATIONAL
EXPIATIST
EXPIATIVE
EXPIATOR
EXPIATORINESS
EXPIATORY
EXPILATE
EXPILATION
EXPILATOR
EXPIRANT
EXPIRATE
EXPIRATION
EXPIRATOR
EXPIRATORY
EXPIRE
EXPIRED
EXPIREE
EXPIRER
EXPIRIES
EXPIRING
EXPIRY
EXPISCATE
EXPISCATED
EXPISCATING
EXPISCATION
EXPISCATOR
EXPISCATORY
EXPLAIN
EXPLAINABLE
EXPLAINED
EXPLAINER
EXPLAINING
EXPLANATE
EXPLANATION
EXPLANATIVE
EXPLANATIVELY
EXPLANATOR
EXPLANATORILY
EXPLANATORINES
EXPLANATORY
EXPLANT
EXPLANTATION
EXPLAT
EXPLEMENT
EXPLEMENTAL
EXPLETE
EXPLETIVE
EXPLETIVELY
EXPLETIVENESS
EXPLETORY
EXPLICABLE
EXPLICATE
EXPLICATED
EXPLICATING
EXPLICATION
EXPLICATIVE
EXPLICATOR
EXPLICATORY
EXPLICIT
EXPLICITLY
EXPLICITNESS
EXPLODE
EXPLODED
EXPLODENT
EXPLODER
EXPLODING
EXPLOIT
EXPLOITABLE
EXPLOITAGE
EXPLOITATION
EXPLOITATIONIST
EXPLOITATIVE
EXPLOITED
EXPLOITER
EXPLOITING
EXPLOITIVE
EXPLOITURE
EXPLORATION
EXPLORATIONAL
EXPLORATIVE
EXPLORATIVELY
EXPLORATIVENESS
EXPLORATOR
EXPLORATORY
EXPLORE
EXPLORED
EXPLOREMENT
EXPLORER
EXPLORING
EXPLOSIBILITY
EXPLOSIBLE
EXPLOSION
EXPLOSIONIST
EXPLOSIVE
EXPLOSIVELY
EXPLOSIVENESS
EXPLOSIVES
EXPONE
EXPONENCE
EXPONENT
EXPONENTIAL
EXPONENTIALLY
EXPONENTS
EXPONIBLE
EXPORT
EXPORTABILITY
EXPORTABLE
EXPORTATION
EXPORTED
EXPORTER
EXPORTING
EXPOSAL
EXPOSE
EXPOSED
EXPOSER
EXPOSING
EXPOSIT
EXPOSITION
EXPOSITIONAL
EXPOSITIONARY
EXPOSITIVE
EXPOSITIVELY
EXPOSITOR
EXPOSITORIAL
EXPOSITORIALLY
EXPOSITORILY
EXPOSITORINESS
EXPOSITORY
EXPOSTULATE
EXPOSTULATED
EXPOSTULATING
EXPOSTULATION
EXPOSTULATIVE
EXPOSTULATIVELY
EXPOSTULATOR
EXPOSTULATORY
EXPOSURE
EXPOUND
EXPOUNDED
EXPOUNDER
EXPOUNDING
EXPREME
EXPRESS
EXPRESSAGE
EXPRESSED
EXPRESSER
EXPRESSIBLE
EXPRESSING
EXPRESSION
EXPRESSIONAL
EXPRESSIONISM
EXPRESSIONIST
EXPRESSIONISTIC
EXPRESSIONLESS
EXPRESSIONLESSLY
EXPRESSIVE
EXPRESSIVELY
EXPRESSIVENESS
EXPRESSLESS
EXPRESSLY
EXPRESSMAN
EXPRESSWAY
EXPROBATE
EXPROBRATORY
EXPROMISSION
EXPROPRIATE
EXPROPRIATED
EXPROPRIATING
EXPROPRIATION
EXPROPRIATOR
EXPUGN
EXPUGNABLE
EXPUITION
EXPULSATORY
EXPULSE
EXPULSER
EXPULSION
EXPULSIVE
EXPULSORY
EXPUNCTION
EXPUNGE
EXPUNGED
EXPUNGER
EXPUNGING
EXPURGATE
EXPURGATED
EXPURGATING
EXPURGATION
EXPURGATIVE
EXPURGATOR
EXPURGATORIAL
EXPURGATORY
EXPURGE
EXQUIRE
EXQUISITE
EXQUISITELY
EXQUISITENESS
EXQUISITISM
EXQUISITIVELY
EXQUISITIVENES
EXRADIO
EXRADIUS
EXRUPEAL
EXSANGUINATE
EXSANGUINE
EXSANGUINOUS
EXSANGUIOUS
EXSCIND
EXSCINDED
EXSCINDING
EXSCRIBE
EXSCRIPT
EXSCRIPTURAL
EXSCULPTATE
EXSCUTELLATE
EXSECANT
EXSECT
EXSECTILE
EXSECTION
EXSECTOR
EXSERT
EXSERTED
EXSERTILE
EXSERTING
EXSERTION
EXSHEATH
EXSIBILATE
EXSICCATAE
EXSICCATE
EXSICCATED
EXSICCATING
EXSICCATION
EXSICCATIVE
EXSILIENCY
EXSOLVE
EXSOMATIC
EXSPUITION
EXSPUTORY
EXSTIPULATE
EXSTROPHY
EXSUCCOUS
EXSUCTION
EXSUFFLATE
EXSUFFLATION
EXSUFFLICATE
EXSURGE
EXSURGENT
EXTANCY
EXTANT
EXTEMPORAL
EXTEMPORALLY
EXTEMPORALNESS
EXTEMPORANEOUS
EXTEMPORANEOUSLY
EXTEMPORANEOUSNESS
EXTEMPORARILY
EXTEMPORARINESS
EXTEMPORARY
EXTEMPORE
EXTEMPORIZE
EXTEMPORIZED
EXTEMPORIZER
EXTEMPORIZING
EXTEND
EXTENDED
EXTENDEDLY
EXTENDEDNESS
EXTENDER
EXTENDIBILITY
EXTENDIBLE
EXTENDING
EXTENSE
EXTENSIBILITY
EXTENSIBLE
EXTENSIBLENESS
EXTENSILE
EXTENSIMETER
EXTENSION
EXTENSIONAL
EXTENSIONIST
EXTENSITY
EXTENSIVE
EXTENSIVELY
EXTENSIVENESS
EXTENSOMETER
EXTENSOR
EXTENSUM
EXTENT
EXTENUATE
EXTENUATED
EXTENUATING
EXTENUATINGLY
EXTENUATION
EXTENUATIVE
EXTENUATOR
EXTENUATORY
EXTER
EXTERIOR
EXTERIORATE
EXTERIORATION
EXTERIORITY
EXTERIORIZATION
EXTERIORIZE
EXTERIORIZED
EXTERIORIZING
EXTERIORLY
EXTERIORNESS
EXTERMINATE
EXTERMINATED
EXTERMINATING
EXTERMINATION
EXTERMINATIVE
EXTERMINATOR
EXTERMINATORY
EXTERMINE
EXTERN
EXTERNA
EXTERNAL
EXTERNALISM
EXTERNALIST
EXTERNALISTIC
EXTERNALITIES
EXTERNALITY
EXTERNALIZATION
EXTERNALIZE
EXTERNALLY
EXTERNAT
EXTERNATE
EXTERNATION
EXTERNE
EXTERNIZATION
EXTERNIZE
EXTERNUM
EXTEROCEPTIST
EXTEROCEPTIVE
EXTEROCEPTOR
EXTERRANEOUS
EXTERRESTRIAL

EXTERRITORIAL
EXTILL
EXTIMA
EXTIME
EXTINCT
EXTINCTEUR
EXTINCTION
EXTINCTIVE
EXTINCTOR
EXTINE
EXTINGUISH
EXTINGUISHED
EXTINGUISHER
EXTIRP
EXTIRPATE
EXTIRPATED
EXTIRPATING
EXTIRPATION
EXTIRPATIVE
EXTIRPATOR
EXTIRPATORY
EXTISPEX
EXTISPICES
EXTISPICIOUS
EXTISPICY
EXTOGENOUS
EXTOL
EXTOLL
EXTOLLATION
EXTOLLED
EXTOLLER
EXTOLLING
EXTOLLMENT
EXTOLMENT
EXTOOLITIC
EXTORSIVE
EXTORSIVELY
EXTORT
EXTORTED
EXTORTER
EXTORTING
EXTORTION
EXTORTIONARY
EXTORTIONATE
EXTORTIONER
EXTORTIONIST
EXTORTIVE
EXTRA
EXTRABOLD
EXTRABULBAR
EXTRACAPSULAR
EXTRACARPAL
EXTRACOSTAL
EXTRACT
EXTRACTABLE
EXTRACTED
EXTRACTIBLE
EXTRACTIFORM
EXTRACTING
EXTRACTION
EXTRACTIVE
EXTRACTOR
EXTRACTS
EXTRACURRICULAR
EXTRACYSTIC
EXTRADITABLE
EXTRADITE
EXTRADITED
EXTRADITING
EXTRADITION
EXTRADOS
EXTRADOSED
EXTRADOTAL
EXTRADUCTION
EXTRAENTERIC
EXTRAFORMAL
EXTRAGALACTIC
EXTRAJUDICIAL
EXTRALATERAL
EXTRALITE
EXTRALITY
EXTRAMUNDANE
EXTRAMURAL
EXTRAMURALLY
EXTRANEAN
EXTRANEITY
EXTRANEOUS
EXTRANEOUSLY
EXTRANEOUSNESS
EXTRAORDINARIES
EXTRAORDINARILY
EXTRAORDINARY
EXTRAPHYSICAL
EXTRAPOLAR
EXTRAPOLATE
EXTRAPOLATED
EXTRAPOLATING
EXTRAPOLATION
EXTRAPOLATIVE
EXTRAPOLATOR
EXTRARED
EXTRAREGULAR
EXTRARETINAL
EXTRASENSORY
EXTRASEROUS
EXTRASOLAR
EXTRASTAPEDIAL
EXTRASYSTOLE
EXTRATARSAL
EXTRATERRESTRIAL
EXTRATRIBAL
EXTRATUBAL
EXTRAUTERINE
EXTRAVAGANCE
EXTRAVAGANCIES
EXTRAVAGANCY
EXTRAVAGANT
EXTRAVAGANTLY
EXTRAVAGANTNESS
EXTRAVAGANZA
EXTRAVAGATE
EXTRAVAGATED
EXTRAVAGATING
EXTRAVAGATION
EXTRAVAGINAL
EXTRAVASATE
EXTRAVASATED
EXTRAVASATING
EXTRAVASATION
EXTRAVASCULAR
EXTRAVENTRICULAR
EXTRAVERSION
EXTRAVERT
EXTRAVIOLET
EXTRE
EXTREAT
EXTREME
EXTREMELY
EXTREMENESS
EXTREMER
EXTREMES
EXTREMEST
EXTREMISM
EXTREMIST
EXTREMISTIC
EXTREMITAL
EXTREMITIES
EXTREMITY
EXTREMUM
EXTRICABLE
EXTRICABLY
EXTRICATE
EXTRICATED
EXTRICATING
EXTRICATION
EXTRINSIC
EXTRINSICAL
EXTRINSICALLY
EXTRINSICATE
EXTROITIVE
EXTROPICAL
EXTRORSAL
EXTRORSE
EXTRORSELY
EXTROSPECT
EXTROSPECTION
EXTROSPECTIVE
EXTROVERSION
EXTROVERSIVE
EXTROVERT
EXTRUCT
EXTRUDE
EXTRUDED
EXTRUDER
EXTRUDING
EXTRUSILE
EXTRUSION
EXTRUSIVE
EXTRUSORY
EXTUBATE
EXTUBATION
EXTUMESCENCE
EXTUND
EXTURB
EXTUSION
EXUBERANCE
EXUBERANCY
EXUBERANT
EXUBERANTLY
EXUBERANTNESS
EXUBERATE
EXUBERATED
EXUBERATING
EXUBERATION
EXUDATE
EXUDATION
EXUDATIVE
EXUDATORY
EXUDE
EXUDED
EXUDENCE
EXUDING
EXUL
EXULATE
EXULCERATE
EXULCERATED
EXULCERATING
EXULCERATION
EXULCERATIVE
EXULCERATORY
EXULT
EXULTANCY
EXULTANT
EXULTANTLY
EXULTATION
EXULTED
EXULTET
EXULTING
EXULTINGLY
EXULULATE
EXUMBRAL
EXUMBRELLA
EXUMBRELLAR
EXUNDATE
EXUNDATION
EXURB
EXURBANITE
EXURBIA
EXUST
EXUTE
EXUVIABILITY
EXUVIABLE
EXUVIAE
EXUVIAL
EXUVIATE
EXUVIATED
EXUVIATING
EXUVIATION
EXZODIACAL
EY
EYAH
EYALET
EYAS
EYDENT
EYE
EYEABLE
EYEBALL
EYEBALM
EYEBAR
EYEBEAM
EYEBERRY
EYEBLINK
EYEBOLT
EYEBREE
EYEBRIDLED
EYEBRIGHT
EYEBROW
EYECUP
EYED
EYEDNESS
EYEDOT
EYEDROP
EYEFLAP
EYEFUL
EYEGLANCE
EYEGLASS
EYEGLASSES
EYEGROUND
EYEHOLE
EYEHOOK
EYEING
EYELASH
EYELAST
EYELESS
EYELET
EYELETED
EYELETEER
EYELETING
EYELETTER
EYELID
EYELIDS
EYELIGHT
EYELINE
EYEMARK
EYEN
EYEPIECE
EYEPIT
EYEPOINT
EYER
EYEREACH
EYEROOT
EYES
EYESALVE
EYESEED
EYESERVANT
EYESERVER
EYESERVICE
EYESHADE
EYESHIELD
EYESHINE
EYESHOT
EYESIGHT
EYESOME
EYESORE
EYESPOT
EYESS
EYESTALK
EYESTONE
EYESTRAIN
EYESTRING
EYETEETH
EYETOOTH
EYEWAITER
EYEWASH
EYEWATER
EYEWEAR
EYEWINK
EYEWINKER
EYEWITNESS
EYEWORT
EYEY
EYING
EYLE
EYLIAD
EYNE
EYOT
EYRA
EYRE
EYREN
EYRIE
EYRIR
EYRY
EYSOGE
EZBA

F

FA
FABA
FABACEOUS
FABE
FABELLA
FABES
FABIFORM
FABLE
FABLED
FABLEDOM
FABLEIST
FABLELAND
FABLEMAKER
FABLEMONGER
FABLER
FABLIAU
FABLIAUX
FABLING
FABRIC
FABRICANT
FABRICATE
FABRICATED
FABRICATES
FABRICATING
FABRICATION
FABRICATIVE
FABRICATOR
FABRICATURE
FABRICS
FABRIKOID
FABRILE
FABRIQUE
FABULA
FABULAR
FABULIST
FABULIZE
FABULOSITY
FABULOUS
FABULOUSLY
FABULOUSNESS
FABURDEN
FAC
FACADAL
FACADE
FACE
FACEABLE
FACEBOW
FACED
FACELESS
FACEMAKER
FACEMAKING
FACEMAN
FACEMARK
FACEPIECE
FACEPLATE
FACER
FACES
FACET
FACETE
FACETED
FACETELY
FACETENESS
FACETIAE
FACETIATION
FACETING
FACETIOUS
FACETIOUSLY
FACETIOUSNESS
FACETTE
FACEWORK
FACIA
FACIAL
FACIEND
FACIENT
FACIER
FACIES
FACIEST
FACILE
FACILELY
FACILENESS
FACILITATE
FACILITATED
FACILITATING
FACILITATION
FACILITATIVE
FACILITATOR
FACILITIES
FACILITY
FACING
FACINGLY
FACINOROUS
FACIOCERVICAL
FACIOPLEGIA
FACK
FACKELTANZ
FACKINS
FACON
FACONNE
FACSIMILE
FACSIMILED
FACSIMILEING
FACSIMILES
FACSIMILIST
FACSIMILIZE
FACT
FACTA
FACTABLE
FACTICE
FACTICIDE
FACTION
FACTIONAL
FACTIONALISM
FACTIONARIES
FACTIONARY
FACTIONATE
FACTIONEER
FACTIONISM
FACTIONIST
FACTIOUS
FACTIOUSLY
FACTIOUSNESS
FACTISH
FACTITIAL
FACTITIOUS
FACTITIOUSLY
FACTITIOUSNESS
FACTITIVE
FACTITIVELY
FACTITUDE
FACTIVE
FACTO
FACTOR
FACTORABILITY
FACTORABLE
FACTORAGE
FACTORED
FACTORIAL
FACTORIALLY
FACTORIES
FACTORING
FACTORIST
FACTORIZATION
FACTORIZE
FACTORIZED
FACTORIZING
FACTORS
FACTORSHIP
FACTORY
FACTORYSHIP
FACTOTUM
FACTRIX
FACTS
FACTUAL
FACTUALITY
FACTUALLY
FACTUALNESS
FACTUM
FACTURE
FACTY
FACULA
FACULAE
FACULAR
FACULOUS
FACULTATE
FACULTATIVE
FACULTATIVELY
FACULTIED
FACULTIES
FACULTIZE
FACULTY
FACUND
FACUNDITY
FACY
FAD
FADAISE
FADDINESS
FADDING
FADDISH
FADDISHNESS
FADDISM
FADDIST
FADDLE
FADDY
FADE
FADEAWAY
FADED
FADEDLY
FADEDNESS
FADELESS
FADELESSLY
FADER
FADGE
FADGED
FADGING
FADING
FADINGLY
FADINGNESS
FADME
FADO
FADS
FADY
FAE
FAECAL
FAECALITH
FAECES
FAECULA
FAENA
FAENUS
FAERIE
FAERY
FAEX
FAFF
FAFFLE
FAFFY
FAG
FAGACEOUS
FAGALD
FAGARA
FAGE
FAGER
FAGGED
FAGGER
FAGGERY
FAGGING
FAGGOT
FAGGOTED
FAGGOTY
FAGGY
FAGINE
FAGOPYRISM
FAGOT
FAGOTED
FAGOTER
FAGOTING
FAGOTT
FAGOTTE
FAGOTTINO
FAGOTTIST
FAGOTTO
FAGOTTONE
FAGOTY
FAHAM
FAHLBAND
FAHLERZ
FAHLORE
FAHLUNITE
FAIENCE
FAIK
FAIL
FAILANCE
FAILED
FAILING
FAILINGLY
FAILINGNESS
FAILLE
FAILURE
FAIN
FAINAIGUE
FAINAIGUED
FAINAIGUER
FAINAIGUING
FAINEANCE
FAINEANCY
FAINEANT
FAINEANTISE
FAINLY
FAINNESS
FAINS
FAINT
FAINTED
FAINTER
FAINTEST
FAINTFUL
FAINTHEART
FAINTHEARTED
FAINTHEARTEDLY
FAINTHEARTEDNESS
FAINTING
FAINTINGLY
FAINTISH
FAINTLING
FAINTLY
FAINTNESS
FAINTS
FAINTY
FAIPULE
FAIR
FAIRD
FAIRED
FAIRER
FAIREST
FAIRFIELDITE
FAIRGROUND
FAIRHEAD
FAIRIES
FAIRILY
FAIRING
FAIRISH
FAIRISHLY
FAIRLY
FAIRNESS
FAIRSHIP
FAIRSOME
FAIRWATER
FAIRWAY
FAIRY
FAIRYDOM
FAIRYFOLK
FAIRYHOOD
FAIRYISM
FAIRYLAND
FAIRYLIKE
FAIRYOLOGY
FAISCEAU
FAIT
FAITERY
FAITH
FAITHBREACH
FAITHBREAKER
FAITHFUL
FAITHFULLY
FAITHFULNESS
FAITHLESS
FAITHLESSLY
FAITHLESSNESS
FAITHWORTHINESS
FAITHWORTHY
FAITOR
FAITOUR
FAIZE
FAJA
FAKE
FAKED
FAKEER
FAKEMENT
FAKER
FAKERY
FAKING
FAKIR
FAKY
FALANAKA
FALBALA
FALBELO
FALCADE
FALCATE
FALCATED
FALCATION
FALCES
FALCHION
FALCIAL
FALCIFORM
FALCON
FALCONBILL
FALCONER
FALCONET
FALCONINE
FALCONOID
FALCONRY
FALCOPERN
FALCULA
FALCULAR
FALCULATE
FALDA
FALDAGE
FALDERAL
FALDEROL
FALDETTA
FALDFEE
FALDING
FALDISTORY
FALDSTOOL
FALDWORTH
FALK
FALL
FALLACIA

FALLACIES
FALLACIOUS
FALLACIOUSLY
FALLACIOUSNESS
FALLACY
FALLAGE
FALLAL
FALLALERY
FALLATION
FALLAWAY
FALLBACK
FALLECTOMY
FALLEN
FALLENCY
FALLER
FALLFISH
FALLFISHES
FALLIBILITY
FALLIBLE
FALLIBLENESS
FALLIBLY
FALLING
FALLOFF
FALLOSTOMY
FALLOUT
FALLOW
FALLOWED
FALLOWING
FALLOWNESS
FALLS
FALLTIME
FALLWAY
FALLY
FALSARY
FALSE
FALSEDAD
FALSEHEARTED
FALSEHEARTEDLY
FALSEHEARTEDNESS
FALSEHOOD
FALSEHOODS
FALSELY
FALSEN
FALSENESS
FALSER
FALSEST
FALSETTIST
FALSETTO
FALSETTOS
FALSEWORK
FALSIDICAL
FALSIE
FALSIES
FALSIFICATE
FALSIFICATION
FALSIFICATOR
FALSIFIED
FALSIFIER
FALSIFY
FALSIFYING
FALSISM
FALSITEIT
FALSITIES
FALSITY
FALSUM
FALTBOAT
FALTER
FALTERED
FALTERER
FALTERING
FALTERINGLY
FALUN
FALUS
FALX
FAM
FAMATINITE
FAMBLE
FAME
FAMED
FAMEFLOWER
FAMELESS
FAMELIC
FAMILIA
FAMILIAL
FAMILIAR
FAMILIARISM
FAMILIARITY
FAMILIARIZATION
FAMILIARIZE
FAMILIARIZED
FAMILIARIZER
FAMILIARIZING
FAMILIARIZINGLY
FAMILIARLY
FAMILIES
FAMILISM
FAMILIST
FAMILISTERE
FAMILISTIC
FAMILISTICAL
FAMILY
FAMINE
FAMING
FAMISH
FAMISHED
FAMISHING
FAMISHMENT
FAMOSE
FAMOUS
FAMOUSLY
FAMOUSNESS
FAMULAR
FAMULARY
FAMULI
FAMULUS
FAN
FANA
FANAKALO
FANAL
FANALOKA
FANAM
FANATIC
FANATICAL
FANATICALLY
FANATICALNESS
FANATICISM
FANATICIZE
FANATICIZED
FANATICIZING
FANATICS
FANBACK
FANBEARER
FANCICAL
FANCIED
FANCIER
FANCIES
FANCIEST
FANCIFUL
FANCIFULLY
FANCIFULNESS
FANCIFY
FANCILESS
FANCILY
FANCY
FANCYING
FANCYMONGER
FANCYWORK
FAND
FANDANGLE
FANDANGO
FANE
FANEGA
FANEGADA
FANFARE
FANFARON
FANFARONADE
FANFARONADING
FANFLOWER
FANFOLD
FANFOOT
FANG
FANGA
FANGED
FANGER
FANGING
FANGLE
FANGLED
FANGLESS
FANGLIKE
FANGLOMERATE
FANGO
FANGOT
FANGS
FANGY
FANHOUSE
FANIENTE
FANION
FANIONED
FANIT
FANJET
FANK
FANKLE
FANLIGHT
FANLIKE
FANMAKER
FANMAKING
FANMAN
FANNED
FANNEL
FANNELING
FANNER
FANNIER
FANNIES
FANNING
FANNINGS
FANNON
FANO
FANON
FANS
FANTAD
FANTADDISH
FANTAIL
FANTAISIE
FANTASIA
FANTASIED
FANTASIST
FANTASIZE
FANTASIZED
FANTASIZING
FANTASM
FANTASMAL
FANTASQUE
FANTASSIN
FANTAST
FANTASTIC
FANTASTICAL
FANTASTICALITY
FANTASTICALLY
FANTASTICALNESS
FANTASTICATE
FANTASTICATION
FANTASTICLY
FANTASTICNESS
FANTASTICO
FANTASTRY
FANTASY
FANTASYING
FANTEAGUE
FANTEEG
FANTIGUE
FANTOCCINI
FANTOCINE
FANTOD
FANTODDISH
FANTOM
FANUM
FANWEED
FANWORK
FANWORT
FANWRIGHT
FANZINE
FAON
FAP
FAPE
FAPESMO
FAQIH
FAQUIR
FAR
FARAD
FARADAIC
FARADAY
FARADIC
FARADISM
FARADIZATION
FARADIZE
FARADIZED
FARADIZER
FARADMETER
FARAND
FARANDINE
FARANDMAN
FARANDMEN
FARANDOLA
FARANDOLE
FARAON
FARASULA
FARAWAY
FARAWAYNESS
FARCE
FARCED
FARCER
FARCETTA
FARCEUR
FARCEUSE
FARCI
FARCIALIZE
FARCICAL
FARCICALITY
FARCICALLY
FARCICALNESS
FARCIE
FARCIED
FARCIFY
FARCIN
FARCING
FARCIST
FARCTATE
FARCY
FARD
FARDA
FARDAGE
FARDEL
FARDELS
FARDH
FARDO
FARE
FARED
FARER
FAREWELL
FARFARA
FARFEL
FARFET
FARFETCH
FARFETCHED
FARFETCHEDNESS
FARGOING
FARGOOD
FARINA
FARINACEOUS
FARINE
FARING
FARINHA
FARINOMETER
FARINOSE
FARINOSELY
FARINULENT
FARISH
FARKLEBERRY
FARL
FARLE
FARLEU
FARLEY
FARM
FARMAGE
FARMED
FARMER
FARMERESS
FARMERETTE
FARMERLY
FARMERY
FARMHAND
FARMHOLD
FARMHOUSE
FARMING
FARMLAND
FARMOST
FARMOUT
FARMPLACE
FARMSTEAD
FARMSTEADING
FARMTOWN
FARMWIFE
FARMY
FARMYARD
FARMYARDY
FARNESOL
FARNESS
FARO
FAROEISH
FAROL
FAROLITO
FAROUCHE
FARRAGE
FARRAGINOUS
FARRAGO
FARRAGOES
FARRAND
FARRANDLY
FARRANT
FARRANTLY
FARREL
FARRIER
FARRIERIES
FARRIERY
FARRISITE
FARROW
FARRUCA
FARSAKH
FARSANG
FARSE
FARSEEING
FARSEEINGNESS
FARSEER
FARSET
FARSIGHTED
FARSIGHTEDLY
FARSIGHTEDNESS
FARSTEPPED
FART
FARTHER
FARTHERMOST
FARTHEST
FARTHING
FARTHINGALE
FARTHINGS

FARWELTERED
FASCES
FASCET
FASCIA
FASCIAL
FASCIATE
FASCIATED
FASCIATELY
FASCIATION
FASCICLE
FASCICLED
FASCICULAR
FASCICULARLY
FASCICULATE
FASCICULATED
FASCICULATELY
FASCICULATION
FASCICULE
FASCICULI
FASCICULUS
FASCINATE
FASCINATED
FASCINATING
FASCINATINGLY
FASCINATION
FASCINATIVE
FASCINATOR
FASCINATRESS
FASCINE
FASCINERY
FASCINES
FASCIOLA
FASCIOLAE
FASCIOLAR
FASCIOLE
FASCIOLET
FASCIOLIASIS
FASCIOLOID
FASCIS
FASCISM
FASCIST
FASCISTIC
FASCISTICIZE
FASCISTIZE
FASELS
FASH
FASHER
FASHERIE
FASHERY
FASHION
FASHIONABILITY
FASHIONABLE
FASHIONABLENESS
FASHIONABLY
FASHIONATIVE
FASHIONED
FASHIONER
FASHIONING
FASHIONIST
FASHIONIZE
FASHIONMONGER
FASHIOUS
FASHIOUSNESS
FASIBITIKITE
FASINITE
FASNACHT
FASOLA
FASSAITE
FAST
FASTEN
FASTENED
FASTENER
FASTENING
FASTENINGS
FASTENS
FASTER
FASTEST
FASTHOLD
FASTI
FASTIDIOSITY
FASTIDIOUS
FASTIDIOUSLY
FASTIDIOUSNESS
FASTIDIUM
FASTIGATE
FASTIGIA
FASTIGIATE
FASTIGIATED
FASTIGIUM
FASTING
FASTINGLY
FASTLAND
FASTLY
FASTNESS
FASTUOUS
FASTUOUSLY
FASTUOUSNESS
FAT
FATAL
FATALISM
FATALIST
FATALISTIC
FATALISTICALLY
FATALITY
FATALIZE
FATALLY
FATBACK
FATBIRD
FATCAKE
FATE
FATED
FATEFUL
FATEFULLY
FATEFULNESS
FATES
FATHEAD
FATHEADED
FATHEADEDNESS
FATHEARTED
FATHER
FATHERED
FATHERHOOD
FATHERING
FATHERLAND
FATHERLESS
FATHERLESSNESS
FATHERLINESS
FATHERLY
FATHOM
FATHOMABLE
FATHOMAGE
FATHOMED
FATHOMER
FATHOMING
FATHOMLESS
FATHOMLESSLY
FATHOMLESSNESS
FATHOMS
FATIDIC
FATIDICAL
FATIDICALLY
FATIFEROUS
FATIGABILITY
FATIGABLE
FATIGABLENESS
FATIGATE
FATIGATION
FATIGUE
FATIGUED
FATIGUES
FATIGUESOME
FATIGUING
FATIHA
FATIHAH
FATILOQUENT
FATING
FATISCENCE
FATISCENT
FATLESS
FATLIKE
FATLING
FATLY
FATNESS
FATSIA
FATSO
FATSTOCK
FATTED
FATTEN
FATTENED
FATTENER
FATTENING
FATTER
FATTEST
FATTIER
FATTIEST
FATTILY
FATTINESS
FATTING
FATTISH
FATTISHNESS
FATTRELS
FATTY
FATUITIES
FATUITOUS
FATUITY
FATUOID
FATUOUS
FATUOUSLY
FATUOUSNESS
FATWOOD
FAUBOURG
FAUCAL
FAUCALIZE
FAUCES
FAUCET
FAUCHARD
FAUCIAL
FAUCITIS
FAUCONNIER
FAUCRE
FAUD
FAUGH
FAUJASITE
FAUJDAR
FAULD
FAULT
FAULTAGE
FAULTED
FAULTER
FAULTFIND
FAULTFINDER
FAULTFINDING
FAULTFUL
FAULTIER
FAULTIEST
FAULTILY
FAULTINESS
FAULTING
FAULTLESS
FAULTLESSLY
FAULTLESSNESS
FAULTSMAN
FAULTY
FAULX
FAUN
FAUNA
FAUNAE
FAUNAL
FAUNALLY
FAUNAS
FAUNCH
FAUNIST
FAUNISTIC
FAUNISTICAL
FAUNOLOGICAL
FAUNOLOGY
FAUNULA
FAUNULE
FAUR
FAURD
FAURED
FAUS
FAUSANT
FAUSE
FAUSEN
FAUSSEBRAIE
FAUSSEBRAYE
FAUSSEBRAYED
FAUST
FAUSTER
FAUTERER
FAUTEUIL
FAUTOR
FAUTORSHIP
FAUVE
FAUVETTE
FAUX
FAVA
FAVAGINOUS
FAVEL
FAVELIDIUM
FAVELLA
FAVELLOID
FAVEOLATE
FAVEOLUS
FAVI
FAVIFORM
FAVILLA
FAVILLAE
FAVILLOUS
FAVISM
FAVISSA
FAVISSAE
FAVONIAN
FAVOR
FAVORABLE
FAVORABLY
FAVORED
FAVOREDLY
FAVOREDNESS
FAVORER
FAVORESS
FAVORING
FAVORINGLY
FAVORITE
FAVORITISM
FAVORLESS
FAVORS
FAVOSE
FAVOSELY
FAVOSITE
FAVOSITOID
FAVOUR
FAVOURABLE
FAVOURABLENESS
FAVOURED
FAVOUREDLY
FAVOUREDNESS
FAVOURER
FAVOURESS
FAVOURING
FAVOURINGLY
FAVOURITE
FAVOURITISM
FAVOURLESS
FAVOUS
FAVUS
FAW
FAWN
FAWNED
FAWNER
FAWNERY
FAWNING
FAWNINGLY
FAWNINGNESS
FAWNY
FAX
FAXED
FAY
FAYALITE
FAYED
FAYING
FAYLES
FAZE
FAZED
FAZENDA
FAZENDEIRO
FAZING
FEABERRY
FEAGUE
FEAK
FEAKED
FEAKING
FEAL
FEALTIES
FEALTY
FEAR
FEARBABE
FEARED
FEAREDLY
FEAREDNESS
FEARER
FEARFUL
FEARFULLY
FEARFULNESS
FEARING
FEARINGLY
FEARLESS
FEARLESSLY
FEARLESSNESS
FEARNAUGHT
FEARNOUGHT
FEARSOME
FEARSOMELY
FEARSOMENESS
FEASANCE
FEASE
FEASIBILITY
FEASIBLE
FEASIBLENESS
FEASIBLY
FEASOR
FEAST
FEASTED
FEASTEN
FEASTER
FEASTFUL
FEASTFULLY
FEASTING
FEASTLY
FEAT
FEATER
FEATEST
FEATHER
FEATHERBACK
FEATHERBEDDED
FEATHERBEDDING
FEATHERBIRD
FEATHERBONE
FEATHERBRAIN
FEATHERBRAINED
FEATHERCUT
FEATHERDOM
FEATHERED
FEATHEREDGE

FEATHEREDGED
FEATHERER
FEATHERFEW
FEATHERFOIL
FEATHERHEAD
FEATHERHEADED
FEATHERINESS
FEATHERING
FEATHERLEAF
FEATHERMAN
FEATHERMONGER
FEATHERS
FEATHERSTITCH
FEATHERTOP
FEATHERWAY
FEATHERWEED
FEATHERWEIGHT
FEATHERWING
FEATHERWOOD
FEATHERWORK
FEATHERWORKER
FEATHERY
FEATISH
FEATISHLY
FEATISHNESS
FEATLESS
FEATLINESS
FEATLY
FEATOUS
FEATURAL
FEATURALLY
FEATURE
FEATURED
FEATUREFUL
FEATURELESS
FEATURELINESS
FEATURELY
FEATURES
FEATURING
FEATY
FEAZE
FEAZED
FEAZING
FEAZINGS
FEBRICANT
FEBRICIDE
FEBRICITY
FEBRICULA
FEBRIFACIENT
FEBRIFIC
FEBRIFUGAL
FEBRIFUGE
FEBRILE
FEBRILITY
FEBRIS
FEBRUATION
FECAL
FECALITH
FECALOID
FECCHE
FECES
FECIAL
FECIT
FECK
FECKET
FECKFUL
FECKFULLY
FECKLESS
FECKLESSLY
FECKLESSNESS
FECKLY
FECULA
FECULAE
FECULENCE
FECULENCY
FECULENT
FECUND
FECUNDATE
FECUNDATED
FECUNDATING
FECUNDATION
FECUNDATIVE
FECUNDATOR
FECUNDATORY
FECUNDIFY
FECUNDITY
FECUNDIZE
FED
FEDAI
FEDARIE
FEDAYEE
FEDDAN
FEDELINI
FEDERACIES
FEDERACY
FEDERAL
FEDERALISM
FEDERALIST
FEDERALISTIC
FEDERALIZATION
FEDERALIZE
FEDERALIZED
FEDERALIZING
FEDERALLY
FEDERALNESS
FEDERARY
FEDERATE
FEDERATED
FEDERATING
FEDERATION
FEDERATIVE
FEDERATIVELY
FEDERATOR
FEDIFRAGOUS
FEDITY
FEDORA
FEE
FEEB
FEEBLE
FEEBLEBRAINED
FEEBLEHEARTED
FEEBLEHEARTEDLY
FEEBLEHEARTEDNESS
FEEBLEMINDED
FEEBLENESS
FEEBLER
FEEBLEST
FEEBLISH
FEEBLY
FEED
FEEDBACK
FEEDBAG
FEEDBIN
FEEDBOARD
FEEDBOX
FEEDER
FEEDHEAD
FEEDING
FEEDLOT
FEEDMAN
FEEDS
FEEDSMAN
FEEDSTUFF
FEEDWAY
FEEDY
FEEING
FEEK
FEEL
FEELABLE
FEELER
FEELING
FEELINGLY
FEELINGNESS
FEELINGS
FEER
FEERE
FEERIE
FEERING
FEES
FEEST
FEET
FEEZE
FEFNICUTE
FEGARY
FEGS
FEHME
FEI
FEID
FEIGH
FEIGHER
FEIGN
FEIGNED
FEIGNEDLY
FEIGNEDNESS
FEIGNER
FEIGNING
FEIL
FEINT
FEINTER
FEIRIE
FEIS
FEISEANNA
FEIST
FEISTIER
FEISTIEST
FEISTY
FEKE
FELAPTON
FELD
FELDSHER
FELDSPAR
FELDSPARPHYRE
FELDSPATH
FELDSPATHIC
FELDSPATHOID
FELDSPATHOSE
FELF
FELICIDE
FELICIFIC
FELICIFY
FELICITATE
FELICITATED
FELICITATING
FELICITATION
FELICITATOR
FELICITIES
FELICITOUS
FELICITOUSLY
FELICITOUSNESS
FELICITY
FELID
FELIFORM
FELINE
FELINELY
FELINENESS
FELINITY
FELINOPHILE
FELINOPHOBE
FELIS
FELL
FELLABLE
FELLAGE
FELLAGHA
FELLAH
FELLAHEEN
FELLAHIN
FELLAHS
FELLATA
FELLED
FELLEN
FELLER
FELLFARE
FELLIC
FELLIES
FELLIFLUOUS
FELLING
FELLMONGER
FELLNESS
FELLOE
FELLOW
FELLOWCRAFT
FELLOWED
FELLOWING
FELLOWLIKE
FELLOWLY
FELLOWMAN
FELLOWS
FELLOWSHIP
FELLOWSHIPED
FELLOWSHIPING
FELLOWSHIPPED
FELLOWSHIPPING
FELLSIDE
FELLY
FELO
FELOID
FELON
FELONIES
FELONIOUS
FELONIOUSLY
FELONIOUSNESS
FELONOUS
FELONRY
FELONSETTER
FELONWEED
FELONWOOD
FELONWORT
FELONY
FELS
FELSITE
FELSITIC
FELSOBANYITE
FELSOPHYRE
FELSOPHYRIC
FELSPAR
FELSPATH
FELSTONE
FELT
FELTED
FELTER
FELTING
FELTLIKE
FELTMAKER
FELTMAKING
FELTMAN
FELTMONGER
FELTWORK
FELTWORT
FELTY
FELTYFARE
FELTYFLIER
FELUCCA
FELWORT
FELZE
FEMALE
FEMALELY
FEMALENESS
FEMALIST
FEMALITY
FEMCEE
FEME
FEMEREIL
FEMERELL
FEMIC
FEMICIDE
FEMINACY
FEMINAL
FEMINALITY
FEMINATE
FEMINEITY
FEMINIE
FEMINILITY
FEMININ
FEMININE
FEMININELY
FEMININENESS
FEMININITY
FEMINISM
FEMINIST
FEMINISTIC
FEMINITY
FEMINIZATION
FEMINIZE
FEMME
FEMORA
FEMORAL
FEMUR
FEMURS
FEN
FENAGLE
FENBANK
FENBERRY
FENCE
FENCED
FENCEFUL
FENCELESS
FENCELESSNESS
FENCEPLAY
FENCER
FENCHENE
FENCHOL
FENCHONE
FENCHYL
FENCIBLE
FENCING
FEND
FENDABLE
FENDED
FENDER
FENDERING
FENDING
FENDY
FENERATION
FENESTELLA
FENESTER
FENESTRA
FENESTRAE
FENESTRAL
FENESTRATE
FENESTRATED
FENESTRATION
FENESTRATO
FENESTRONE
FENESTRULE
FENETRE
FENITE
FENKS
FENLAND
FENLANDER
FENMAN
FENMAN
FENNEC
FENNEL
FENNELFLOWER
FENNER
FENNIG
FENNISH
FENNY
FENOUILLET
FENOUILLETTE
FENS
FENSTER
FENT
FENTER
FENUGREEK

FEOD
FEODAL
FEODALITY
FEODARY
FEODATORY
FEODUM
FEOFF
FEOFFED
FEOFFEE
FEOFFEESHIP
FEOFFER
FEOFFING
FEOFFMENT
FEOFFOR
FER
FERACIOUS
FERACITY
FERAL
FERASH
FERBAM
FERBERITE
FERDWIT
FERE
FERETORIES
FERETORY
FERETRA
FERETRUM
FERFEL
FERGANITE
FERGUSITE
FERGUSONITE
FERIA
FERIAE
FERIAL
FERIDJEE
FERIDJI
FERIE
FERIGEE
FERIJEE
FERINE
FERINELY
FERINENESS
FERIO
FERISON
FERITY
FERK
FERLIE
FERLIED
FERLIES
FERLING
FERLY
FERLYING
FERM
FERMAIL
FERMATA
FERME
FERMENT
FERMENTABILITY
FERMENTABLE
FERMENTARIAN
FERMENTATION
FERMENTATIVE
FERMENTATIVELY
FERMENTATIVENESS
FERMENTATORY
FERMENTED
FERMENTER
FERMENTING
FERMENTIVE
FERMENTOLOGY
FERMENTOR
FERMENTUM
FERMERER
FERMERY
FERMI
FERMION
FERMIUM
FERMORITE
FERN
FERNBIRD
FERNBRAKE
FERNED
FERNENT
FERNERIES
FERNERY
FERNGALE
FERNGROWER
FERNINST
FERNLAND
FERNLEAF
FERNLIKE
FERNSHAW
FERNSICK
FERNTICKLE
FERNTICKLED
FERNWORT
FERNY
FERNYEAR
FEROCE
FEROCIOUS
FEROCIOUSLY
FEROCIOUSNESS
FEROCITIES
FEROCITY
FEROHER
FERRAMENT
FERRASH
FERRATE
FERRATED
FERRATIN
FERRE
FERREIRO
FERREL
FERREOUS
FERRER
FERRET
FERRETED
FERRETER
FERRETING
FERRETTO
FERRETY
FERRI
FERRIAGE
FERRIC
FERRICYANIC
FERRICYANIDE
FERRIED
FERRIER
FERRIES
FERRIFEROUS
FERRING
FERRITE
FERRITIN
FERRIVOROUS
FERROALLOY
FERROBORON
FERROCALCITE
FERROCERIUM
FERROCHROME
FERROCONCRETE
FERROCYANIC
FERROCYANIDE
FERROINCLAVE
FERROMAGNETIC
FERROMAGNETISM
FERRONATRITE
FERRONICKEL
FERROPRINT
FERROSILICON
FERROTYPE
FERROTYPER
FERROUS
FERRUGINATE
FERRUGINATED
FERRUGINATING
FERRUGINEAN
FERRUGINEOUS
FERRUGINOUS
FERRUGO
FERRULE
FERRULED
FERRULER
FERRULING
FERRUM
FERRUMINATE
FERRUMINATED
FERRUMINATING
FERRY
FERRYAGE
FERRYBOAT
FERRYHOUSE
FERRYING
FERRYMAN
FERRYMEN
FERRYWAY
FERS
FERSMITE
FERTILE
FERTILELY
FERTILENESS
FERTILITIES
FERTILITY
FERTILIZABLE
FERTILIZATION
FERTILIZATIONAL
FERTILIZE
FERTILIZED
FERTILIZER
FERTILIZIN
FERTILIZING
FERU
FERULA
FERULACEOUS
FERULAE
FERULAS
FERULE
FERULED
FERULIC
FERULING
FERVANITE
FERVENCIES
FERVENCY
FERVENT
FERVENTLY
FERVENTNESS
FERVESCENCE
FERVESCENT
FERVID
FERVIDITY
FERVIDLY
FERVIDNESS
FERVOR
FERVOROUS
FERVOUR
FESAPO
FESCENNINITY
FESCUE
FESH
FESS
FESSE
FESSEWISE
FESSWAYS
FESSWISE
FEST
FESTA
FESTAL
FESTALLY
FESTER
FESTERED
FESTERING
FESTERMENT
FESTILOGIES
FESTILOGY
FESTINATE
FESTINATED
FESTINATELY
FESTINATING
FESTINATION
FESTINE
FESTINO
FESTIVAL
FESTIVALLY
FESTIVE
FESTIVELY
FESTIVENESS
FESTIVITIES
FESTIVITY
FESTIVOUS
FESTOLOGY
FESTON
FESTOON
FESTOONED
FESTOONERIES
FESTOONERY
FESTOONING
FESTOONY
FESTUCA
FESTUCINE
FESTY
FET
FETA
FETAL
FETALISM
FETATION
FETCH
FETCHED
FETCHER
FETCHING
FETCHINGLY
FETE
FETED
FETERITA
FETIAL
FETIALES
FETIALIS
FETICH
FETICHIC
FETICHISM
FETICHIST
FETICHISTIC
FETICHIZE
FETICHRY
FETICIDAL
FETICIDE
FETID
FETIDLY
FETIDNESS
FETIFEROUS
FETII
FETING
FETIPAROUS
FETIS
FETISH
FETISHEER
FETISHER
FETISHIC
FETISHISM
FETISHIST
FETISHISTIC
FETISHIZE
FETISHRY
FETLOCK
FETLOCKED
FETLOW
FETOGRAPHY
FETOMETRY
FETOR
FETTED
FETTER
FETTERBUSH
FETTERED
FETTERER
FETTERING
FETTERLOCK
FETTERS
FETTICUS
FETTING
FETTLE
FETTLED
FETTLER
FETTLING
FETTUCINI
FETURE
FETUS
FETUSES
FEU
FEUAGE
FEUAR
FEUCHT
FEUD
FEUDAL
FEUDALISM
FEUDALIST
FEUDALISTIC
FEUDALITY
FEUDALIZATION
FEUDALIZE
FEUDALIZED
FEUDALIZING
FEUDALLY
FEUDARIES
FEUDARY
FEUDATORIAL
FEUDATORIES
FEUDATORY
FEUDEE
FEUDIST
FEUDUM
FEUED
FEUILLAGE
FEUILLE
FEUILLETON
FEUING
FEUTE
FEUTER
FEVER
FEVERBERRIES
FEVERBERRY
FEVERBUSH
FEVERCUP
FEVERED
FEVERET
FEVERFEW
FEVERGUM
FEVERING
FEVERISH
FEVERISHLY
FEVERISHNESS
FEVERLESS
FEVEROUS
FEVEROUSLY
FEVERROOT
FEVERTRAP
FEVERTWIG
FEVERWEED
FEVERWORT
FEVERY
FEW
FEWER
FEWEST
FEWMAND
FEWMET
FEWNESS
FEWSOME
FEWTER

FEWTERER
FEWTRILS
FEY
FEZ
FEZZED
FEZZES
FEZZY
FIACRE
FIADOR
FIANCAILLES
FIANCE
FIANCED
FIANCEE
FIANCHETTI
FIANCHETTO
FIANCING
FIANT
FIANTS
FIAR
FIARD
FIASCO
FIASCOES
FIASCOS
FIAT
FIB
FIBBED
FIBBER
FIBBERY
FIBBING
FIBER
FIBERBOARD
FIBERED
FIBERIZE
FIBERIZER
FIBERS
FIBRA
FIBRATION
FIBRE
FIBREBOARD
FIBRED
FIBRIFORM
FIBRIL
FIBRILLA
FIBRILLAE
FIBRILLAR
FIBRILLARY
FIBRILLATE
FIBRILLATED
FIBRILLATION
FIBRILLED
FIBRILLIFORM
FIBRILLOSE
FIBRILLOUS
FIBRILS
FIBRIN
FIBRINATE
FIBRINATION
FIBRINE
FIBRINOGEN
FIBRINOGENIC
FIBRINOLYSIN
FIBRINOLYSIS
FIBRINOLYTIC
FIBRINOSE
FIBRINOSIS
FIBRINOUS
FIBROADENIA
FIBROADENOMA
FIBROADIPOSE
FIBROAREOLAR
FIBROBLAST
FIBROBLASTIC
FIBROCARTILAGE
FIBROCASEOSE
FIBROCELLULAR
FIBROCYST
FIBROCYSTIC
FIBROCYSTOMA
FIBROCYTE
FIBROELASTIC
FIBROFATTY
FIBROFERRITE
FIBROGLIA
FIBROGLIOMA
FIBROID
FIBROIN
FIBROLIPOMA
FIBROLITIC
FIBROMA
FIBROMAS
FIBROMATA
FIBROMATOID
FIBROMATOSIS
FIBROMATOUS
FIBROMUCOUS
FIBROMYITIS
FIBROMYOMA
FIBROMYOTOMY
FIBROMYXOMA
FIBRONEUROMA
FIBRONUCLEAR
FIBROPLASIA
FIBROPLASTIC
FIBROPOLYPUS
FIBROSARCOMA
FIBROSE
FIBROSEROUS
FIBROSIS
FIBROSITIS
FIBROTIC
FIBROUS
FIBROUSLY
FIBROUSNESS
FIBROVASAL
FIBRY
FIBSTER
FIBULA
FIBULAE
FIBULAR
FIBULARE
FIBULARIA
FIBULAS
FICARIES
FICARY
FICCHE
FICE
FICELLE
FICHAT
FICHE
FICHTELITE
FICHU
FICIFORM
FICK
FICKLE
FICKLEHEARTED
FICKLENESS
FICKLETY
FICKLY
FICO
FICOES
FICOID
FICOIDAL
FICTATION
FICTIL
FICTILE
FICTILENESS
FICTILITY
FICTION
FICTIONAL
FICTIONALIZATION
FICTIONALIZED
FICTIONALIZING
FICTIONALLY
FICTIONARY
FICTIONEER
FICTIONER
FICTIONIST
FICTIONISTIC
FICTIONIZE
FICTIONIZED
FICTIONIZING
FICTIOUS
FICTITIOUS
FICTITIOUSLY
FICTITIOUSNESS
FICTIVE
FICTIVELY
FICTOR
FID
FIDAI
FIDALGO
FIDATE
FIDATION
FIDAWI
FIDDED
FIDDING
FIDDLE
FIDDLEBACK
FIDDLECOME
FIDDLED
FIDDLEDEEDEE
FIDDLEFACED
FIDDLEHEAD
FIDDLEHEADED
FIDDLENECK
FIDDLER
FIDDLERFISH
FIDDLERFISHES
FIDDLERY
FIDDLESTICK
FIDDLESTICKS
FIDDLESTRING
FIDDLEWOOD
FIDDLEY
FIDDLEYS
FIDDLIES
FIDDLING
FIDE
FIDEICOMMISS
FIDEISM
FIDEIST
FIDEJUSSION
FIDEJUSSOR
FIDEJUSSORY
FIDELITIES
FIDELITY
FIDEOS
FIDFAD
FIDGE
FIDGED
FIDGET
FIDGETATION
FIDGETED
FIDGETER
FIDGETILY
FIDGETINESS
FIDGETING
FIDGETINGLY
FIDGETY
FIDGING
FIDICINAL
FIDICINALES
FIDICULA
FIDICULAE
FIDUCIA
FIDUCIAL
FIDUCIALLY
FIDUCIARIES
FIDUCIARILY
FIDUCIARY
FIE
FIEDLERITE
FIEF
FIELD
FIELDBIRD
FIELDED
FIELDEN
FIELDER
FIELDFARE
FIELDFIGHT
FIELDIE
FIELDING
FIELDMAN
FIELDMEN
FIELDPIECE
FIELDS
FIELDSMAN
FIELDSMEN
FIELDSTONE
FIELDWORK
FIELDWORKER
FIELDWORT
FIELDY
FIEND
FIENDFUL
FIENDFULLY
FIENDHEAD
FIENDISH
FIENDISHLY
FIENDISHNESS
FIENDLIKE
FIENDLINESS
FIENDLY
FIENDSHIP
FIENT
FIER
FIERASFEROID
FIERCE
FIERCEHEARTED
FIERCELY
FIERCEN
FIERCENED
FIERCENESS
FIERCENING
FIERCER
FIERCEST
FIERDING
FIERIER
FIERIEST
FIERILY
FIERINESS
FIERY
FIESTA
FIFE
FIFED
FIFER
FIFIE
FIFING
FIFISH
FIFTEEN
FIFTEENER
FIFTEENTH
FIFTEENTHLY
FIFTH
FIFTHLY
FIFTIES
FIFTIETH
FIFTY
FIG
FIGARY
FIGBIRD
FIGBOY
FIGEATER
FIGENT
FIGGED
FIGGERY
FIGGING
FIGGLE
FIGGY
FIGHT
FIGHTABLE
FIGHTER
FIGHTING
FIGHTINGLY
FIGHTWITE
FIGMENT
FIGMENTAL
FIGO
FIGPECKER
FIGS
FIGSHELL
FIGULATE
FIGULATED
FIGULINE
FIGURA
FIGURABILITY
FIGURABLE
FIGURAE
FIGURAL
FIGURANT
FIGURANTE
FIGURATE
FIGURATELY
FIGURATION
FIGURATIVE
FIGURATIVELY
FIGURATIVENESS
FIGURATO
FIGURE
FIGURED
FIGUREDLY
FIGUREHEAD
FIGURER
FIGURES
FIGURESOME
FIGURETTE
FIGURIAL
FIGURINE
FIGURING
FIGURISM
FIGURIST
FIGURIZE
FIGURY
FIGWORM
FIGWORT
FIKE
FIKERY
FIKEY
FIKIE
FIKY
FIL
FILA
FILACE
FILACEOUS
FILACER
FILAGREE
FILAMENT
FILAMENTAR
FILAMENTARY
FILAMENTED
FILAMENTOID
FILAMENTOSE
FILAMENTOUS
FILAMENTS
FILAMENTULE
FILANDER
FILANDERS
FILAO
FILAR
FILAREE
FILARIA
FILARIAE
FILARIAL
FILARIAN
FILARIASIS

FILARICIDAL
FILARIFORM
FILARIID
FILARIOUS
FILASSE
FILATE
FILATOR
FILATURE
FILAZER
FILBERT
FILCH
FILCHED
FILCHER
FILCHERY
FILCHING
FILCHINGLY
FILE
FILED
FILEFISH
FILEFISHES
FILEMAKER
FILEMAKING
FILEMOT
FILER
FILET
FILETED
FILETING
FILI
FILIAL
FILIALITY
FILIALLY
FILIALNESS
FILIATE
FILIATED
FILIATING
FILIATION
FILIBEG
FILIBRANCH
FILIBRANCHIATE
FILIBUSTER
FILIBUSTERED
FILIBUSTERER
FILIBUSTERING
FILIBUSTERISM
FILIBUSTEROUS
FILIBUSTROUS
FILICAL
FILICAULINE
FILICIDAL
FILICIDE
FILICIFORM
FILICIN
FILICINEAN
FILICINIAN
FILICITE
FILICOID
FILID
FILIETY
FILIFEROUS
FILIFORM
FILIFORMED
FILIGEROUS
FILIGRAIN
FILIGRAINED
FILIGRANE
FILIGRANED
FILIGREE
FILIGREED
FILIGREEING
FILII
FILING
FILINGS
FILIONYMIC
FILIOQUE
FILIP
FILIPPI
FILIPPIC
FILIPPO
FILIPUNCTURE
FILITE
FILIUS
FILL
FILLAGREE
FILLE
FILLED
FILLER
FILLERCAP
FILLET
FILLETED
FILLETER
FILLETING
FILLETS
FILLIES
FILLING
FILLINGLY
FILLINGNESS
FILLIP
FILLIPED
FILLIPEEN
FILLIPING
FILLISTER
FILLMASS
FILLOCK
FILLOWITE
FILLY
FILM
FILMED
FILMGOER
FILMGOING
FILMIC
FILMIER
FILMIEST
FILMIFORM
FILMILY
FILMINESS
FILMING
FILMISH
FILMIST
FILMIZE
FILMIZED
FILMIZING
FILMLAND
FILMLIKE
FILMOGEN
FILMS
FILMSLIDE
FILMY
FILO
FILOPLUME
FILOPODIA
FILOPODIUM
FILOSE
FILOSELLE
FILS
FILTER
FILTERABILITY
FILTERABLE
FILTERABLENESS
FILTERED
FILTERER
FILTERING
FILTERMAN
FILTERMEN
FILTH
FILTHIER
FILTHIEST
FILTHIFIED
FILTHIFY
FILTHIFYING
FILTHILY
FILTHINESS
FILTHY
FILTRABILITY
FILTRABLE
FILTRATABLE
FILTRATE
FILTRATED
FILTRATING
FILTRATION
FILUM
FIMBLE
FIMBRIA
FIMBRIAE
FIMBRIAL
FIMBRIATE
FIMBRIATED
FIMBRIATING
FIMBRIATION
FIMBRICATE
FIMBRICATED
FIMBRILLA
FIMBRILLAE
FIMBRILLATE
FIMBRILLOSE
FIME
FIMETIC
FIMICOLOUS
FIN
FINABLE
FINABLENESS
FINAGLE
FINAGLED
FINAGLER
FINAGLING
FINAL
FINALE
FINALIS
FINALISM
FINALIST
FINALITIES
FINALITY
FINALIZE
FINALIZED
FINALIZING
FINALLY
FINANCE
FINANCED
FINANCIAL
FINANCIALIST
FINANCIALLY
FINANCIER
FINANCIERED
FINANCIERING
FINANCIERY
FINANCING
FINANCIST
FINBACK
FINBONE
FINCA
FINCAS
FINCH
FINCHBACKED
FINCHED
FINCHERY
FINCHES
FIND
FINDAL
FINDER
FINDFAULT
FINDING
FINDJAN
FINE
FINEABLE
FINEBENT
FINECOMB
FINED
FINELEAF
FINELESS
FINELY
FINEMENT
FINENESS
FINER
FINERIES
FINERY
FINES
FINESPUN
FINESSE
FINESSED
FINESSER
FINESSING
FINEST
FINESTILL
FINESTILLER
FINETOP
FINEW
FINEWED
FINFISH
FINFOOTS
FINGAN
FINGENT
FINGER
FINGERBERRY
FINGERBOARD
FINGERED
FINGERER
FINGERFISH
FINGERFISHES
FINGERFLOWER
FINGERHOLD
FINGERHOOK
FINGERING
FINGERLEAF
FINGERLING
FINGERNAIL
FINGERNAILS
FINGERPARTED
FINGERPRINT
FINGERPRINTING
FINGERROOT
FINGERS
FINGERSMITH
FINGERSPIN
FINGERSTALL
FINGERSTONE
FINGERTIP
FINGERWORK
FINGERY
FINGIAN
FINGRIGO
FINIAL
FINIALED
FINICAL
FINICALITY
FINICALLY
FINICALNESS
FINICISM
FINICK
FINICKILY
FINICKING
FINICKINGLY
FINICKY
FINIFIC
FINIFY
FINIKIN
FINIKING
FINING
FINIS
FINISES
FINISH
FINISHED
FINISHER
FINISHES
FINISHING
FINITE
FINITELY
FINITENESS
FINITESIMAL
FINITISM
FINITIVE
FINITUDE
FINITY
FINJAN
FINK
FINKEL
FINLAND
FINLESS
FINLET
FINNAC
FINNACK
FINNED
FINNER
FINNESKO
FINNICK
FINNICKING
FINNICKY
FINNING
FINNIP
FINNOC
FINNY
FINO
FINOCHIO
FINTA
FINTADORES
FIORD
FIORDED
FIORIN
FIORITE
FIORITURA
FIORITURE
FIP
FIPENNY
FIPPLE
FIQUE
FIR
FIRCA
FIRE
FIREARM
FIREBACK
FIREBALL
FIREBED
FIREBIRD
FIREBLENDE
FIREBOARD
FIREBOAT
FIREBOLT
FIREBOLTED
FIREBOOT
FIREBOTE
FIREBOX
FIREBOY
FIREBRAND
FIREBRAT
FIREBREAK
FIREBRICK
FIREBUG
FIRECLAY
FIRECOAT
FIRECRACKER
FIRECREST
FIRED
FIREDAMP
FIREDOG
FIREDRAGON
FIREDRAKE
FIREFALL
FIREFANG
FIREFANGED
FIREFANGING
FIREFIGHTER
FIREFLAUGHT
FIREFLIES
FIREFLIRT
FIREFLOWER
FIREFLY
FIREGUARD

FIREHALL
FIREHOUSE
FIRELESS
FIRELIGHT
FIRELIT
FIRELOCK
FIREMAN
FIREMASTER
FIREMEN
FIREPAN
FIREPINK
FIREPLACE
FIREPLOUGH
FIREPLOW
FIREPLUG
FIREPOT
FIREPOWER
FIREPROOF
FIREPROOFED
FIREPROOFING
FIREPROOFNESS
FIRER
FIREROOM
FIRESAFE
FIRESAFENESS
FIRESAFETY
FIRESHINE
FIRESIDE
FIRESIDER
FIRESIDESHIP
FIRESPOUT
FIRESTONE
FIRESTOPPING
FIRETAIL
FIRETHORN
FIRETOP
FIRETRAP
FIREWARD
FIREWARDEN
FIREWATER
FIREWEED
FIREWOOD
FIREWORK
FIREWORKLESS
FIREWORKS
FIREWORKY
FIREWORM
FIRING
FIRK
FIRKED
FIRKER
FIRKIN
FIRKING
FIRLOT
FIRM
FIRMA
FIRMAMENT
FIRMAMENTAL
FIRMAN
FIRMANS
FIRMARII
FIRMARIUS
FIRMED
FIRMER
FIRMEST
FIRMHEARTED
FIRMING
FIRMISTERNAL
FIRMISTERNIAL
FIRMISTERNOUS
FIRMLAND
FIRMLY
FIRMNESS
FIRMS
FIRN
FIRRY
FIRS
FIRST
FIRSTBORN
FIRSTCOMER
FIRSTER
FIRSTLING
FIRSTLY
FIRTH
FISC
FISCAL
FISCALITY
FISCALIZATION
FISCALIZE
FISCALIZED
FISCALIZING
FISCHERITE
FISCUS
FISETIN
FISH
FISHABLE
FISHBACK
FISHBED
FISHBERRIES
FISHBERRY
FISHBOLT
FISHBONE
FISHBOWL
FISHEATER
FISHED
FISHER
FISHERBOAT
FISHERBOY
FISHERFOLK
FISHERGIRL
FISHERIES
FISHERMAN
FISHERMEN
FISHERPEOPLE
FISHERS
FISHERWOMAN
FISHERY
FISHES
FISHET
FISHEYE
FISHFALL
FISHGARTH
FISHGIG
FISHGRASS
FISHHOLD
FISHHOOK
FISHHOOKS
FISHHOUSE
FISHIER
FISHIEST
FISHIFIED
FISHIFY
FISHIFYING
FISHILY
FISHINESS
FISHING
FISHLIKE
FISHLINE
FISHMAN
FISHMEAL
FISHMEN
FISHMONGER
FISHMOUTH
FISHNET
FISHPLATE
FISHPOLE
FISHPOND
FISHPOOL
FISHPOT
FISHPOTTER
FISHPOUND
FISHSKIN
FISHSPEAR
FISHTAIL
FISHTAILS
FISHWAY
FISHWEED
FISHWEIR
FISHWIFE
FISHWIVES
FISHWOMAN
FISHWOOD
FISHWORKER
FISHWORKS
FISHWORM
FISHY
FISHYARD
FISK
FISNOGA
FISSATE
FISSILE
FISSILINGUAL
FISSILITY
FISSION
FISSIONABLE
FISSIPALMATE
FISSIPARISM
FISSIPARITY
FISSIPAROUS
FISSIPED
FISSIPEDAL
FISSIPEDATE
FISSIPEDIAL
FISSIROSTRAL
FISSIVE
FISSLE
FISSURA
FISSURAL
FISSURATION
FISSURE
FISSURED
FISSURIFORM
FISSURING
FISSURY
FIST
FISTED
FISTER
FISTFIGHT
FISTFUL
FISTFULS
FISTIANA
FISTIC
FISTICAL
FISTICUFF
FISTICUFFED
FISTICUFFER
FISTICUFFERY
FISTICUFFING
FISTIFY
FISTINESS
FISTING
FISTLE
FISTMELE
FISTNOTE
FISTUCA
FISTULA
FISTULAE
FISTULAR
FISTULAS
FISTULATOME
FISTULATOUS
FISTULIFORM
FISTULIZE
FISTULOSE
FISTULOUS
FISTY
FIT
FITCH
FITCHE
FITCHEE
FITCHER
FITCHERED
FITCHERING
FITCHERY
FITCHES
FITCHET
FITCHEW
FITE
FITFUL
FITFULLY
FITFULNESS
FITIFIED
FITLY
FITMENT
FITMENTS
FITNESS
FITOUT
FITROOT
FITS
FITTABLE
FITTAGE
FITTED
FITTEDNESS
FITTEN
FITTER
FITTERS
FITTEST
FITTIER
FITTIEST
FITTILY
FITTINESS
FITTING
FITTINGLY
FITTINGNESS
FITTIT
FITTY
FITTYFIED
FITTYWAYS
FITTYWISE
FITWEED
FIVE
FIVEBAR
FIVEFOLD
FIVELING
FIVEPENCE
FIVEPENNY
FIVEPINS
FIVER
FIVES
FIVESCORE
FIVESOME
FIVESTONES
FIX
FIXABLE
FIXAGE
FIXATE
FIXATED
FIXATIF
FIXATING
FIXATION
FIXATIVE
FIXATOR
FIXATURE
FIXED
FIXEDLY
FIXEDNESS
FIXER
FIXIDITY
FIXING
FIXINGS
FIXITIES
FIXITY
FIXT
FIXTURE
FIXURE
FIXY
FIZ
FIZELYITE
FIZGIG
FIZZ
FIZZED
FIZZER
FIZZIER
FIZZIEST
FIZZING
FIZZLE
FIZZLED
FIZZLING
FIZZY
FJALL
FJELD
FJORD
FJORDED
FLAB
FLABBERGAST
FLABBERGASTED
FLABBERGASTING
FLABBIER
FLABBIEST
FLABBILY
FLABBINESS
FLABBY
FLABEL
FLABELLA
FLABELLATE
FLABELLATION
FLABELLIFORM
FLABELLUM
FLABRA
FLABRUM
FLACCID
FLACCIDITY
FLACCIDLY
FLACCIDNESS
FLACHERIE
FLACHERY
FLACK
FLACKED
FLACKER
FLACKET
FLACON
FLAE
FLAFF
FLAFFER
FLAG
FLAGARIE
FLAGBOAT
FLAGELLA
FLAGELLANT
FLAGELLAR
FLAGELLATE
FLAGELLATED
FLAGELLATING
FLAGELLATION
FLAGELLATIVE
FLAGELLATOR
FLAGELLATORY
FLAGELLIFORM
FLAGELLIST
FLAGELLOSIS
FLAGELLULA
FLAGELLULAE
FLAGELLUM
FLAGELLUMS
FLAGEOLET
FLAGFALL
FLAGFISH
FLAGGED
FLAGGER
FLAGGERY
FLAGGIER
FLAGGIEST
FLAGGILY
FLAGGINESS
FLAGGING

FLAGGINGLY
FLAGGISH
FLAGGY
FLAGITATE
FLAGITATION
FLAGITIOUS
FLAGITIOUSLY
FLAGLEAF
FLAGLESS
FLAGLIKE
FLAGMAKER
FLAGMAKING
FLAGMAN
FLAGON
FLAGONET
FLAGPOLE
FLAGRANCE
FLAGRANCY
FLAGRANT
FLAGRANTLY
FLAGRANTNESS
FLAGROOT
FLAGS
FLAGSHIP
FLAGSTAFF
FLAGSTAFFS
FLAGSTAVES
FLAGSTICK
FLAGSTONE
FLAGWORM
FLAIL
FLAILED
FLAILING
FLAIR
FLAITE
FLAITH
FLAITHSHIP
FLAJOLOTITE
FLAK
FLAKAGE
FLAKE
FLAKED
FLAKER
FLAKIER
FLAKIEST
FLAKILY
FLAKINESS
FLAKING
FLAKY
FLAM
FLAMANT
FLAMB
FLAMBAGE
FLAMBANT
FLAMBE
FLAMBEAU
FLAMBEAUS
FLAMBEAUX
FLAMBEE
FLAMBERG
FLAMBERGE
FLAMBOYANCE
FLAMBOYANCY
FLAMBOYANT
FLAMBOYANTISM
FLAMBOYANTIZE
FLAMBOYANTLY
FLAME
FLAMED
FLAMELET
FLAMEN
FLAMENCO
FLAMENS
FLAMEOUT
FLAMEPROOF
FLAMER
FLAMFEW
FLAMIER
FLAMIEST
FLAMINEOUS
FLAMINES
FLAMING
FLAMINGLY
FLAMINGO
FLAMINGOES
FLAMINGOS
FLAMINICA
FLAMINICAL
FLAMMABILITY
FLAMMABLE
FLAMMANT
FLAMMED
FLAMMEOUS
FLAMMING
FLAMMULATED
FLAMMULATION
FLAMMULE
FLAMY
FLAN
FLANCARD
FLANCH
FLANCHARD
FLANCHE
FLANCHED
FLANCONADE
FLANCONNADE
FLANDAN
FLANERIE
FLANEUR
FLANG
FLANGE
FLANGED
FLANGER
FLANGEWAY
FLANGING
FLANK
FLANKARD
FLANKED
FLANKER
FLANKING
FLANNED
FLANNEL
FLANNELBUSH
FLANNELED
FLANNELET
FLANNELETTE
FLANNELFLOWER
FLANNELLEAF
FLANNELLED
FLANNELLY
FLANNELMOUTH
FLANNELMOUTHED
FLANNELS
FLANNING
FLAP
FLAPCAKE
FLAPDOCK
FLAPDOODLE
FLAPDRAGON
FLAPJACK
FLAPMOUTHED
FLAPPED
FLAPPER
FLAPPERDOM
FLAPPERED
FLAPPERHOOD
FLAPPERING
FLAPPERISH
FLAPPERISM
FLAPPET
FLAPPING
FLAPPY
FLAPS
FLARE
FLAREBACK
FLAREBOARD
FLARED
FLARER
FLARING
FLARINGLY
FLARY
FLASER
FLASH
FLASHBACK
FLASHBOARD
FLASHED
FLASHER
FLASHET
FLASHGUN
FLASHIER
FLASHIEST
FLASHILY
FLASHINESS
FLASHING
FLASHINGLY
FLASHLIGHT
FLASHLIKE
FLASHLY
FLASHNESS
FLASHOVER
FLASHPAN
FLASHPROOF
FLASHTESTER
FLASHY
FLASK
FLASKER
FLASKET
FLASKLET
FLASQUE
FLAT
FLATBED
FLATBOAT
FLATBOTTOM
FLATBROD
FLATCAP
FLATCAR
FLATDOM
FLATED
FLATFISH
FLATFISHES
FLATFOOT
FLATH
FLATHE
FLATHEAD
FLATIRON
FLATLAND
FLATLET
FLATLING
FLATLINGS
FLATLONG
FLATLY
FLATMAN
FLATMEN
FLATNESS
FLATNOSE
FLATS
FLATTEN
FLATTENED
FLATTENER
FLATTENING
FLATTER
FLATTERABLE
FLATTERCAP
FLATTERDOCK
FLATTERED
FLATTERER
FLATTERESS
FLATTERIES
FLATTERING
FLATTERINGLY
FLATTERINGNESS
FLATTEROUS
FLATTERY
FLATTEST
FLATTIE
FLATTING
FLATTISH
FLATTOP
FLATTY
FLATULENCE
FLATULENCY
FLATULENT
FLATULENTLY
FLATULENTNESS
FLATUOUS
FLATUS
FLATUSES
FLATWARE
FLATWAY
FLATWAYS
FLATWEED
FLATWISE
FLATWOODS
FLATWORK
FLATWORM
FLAUCHT
FLAUGHT
FLAUGHTBRED
FLAUGHTER
FLAUGHTS
FLAUNT
FLAUNTED
FLAUNTER
FLAUNTIER
FLAUNTIEST
FLAUNTILY
FLAUNTINESS
FLAUNTING
FLAUNTINGLY
FLAUNTY
FLAUTATO
FLAUTINO
FLAUTIST
FLAUTO
FLAVANILIN
FLAVANILINE
FLAVANTHRENE
FLAVANTHRONE
FLAVE
FLAVEDO
FLAVESCENCE
FLAVESCENT
FLAVIC
FLAVICANT
FLAVID
FLAVIN
FLAVINE
FLAVONE
FLAVONOL
FLAVOPROTEIN
FLAVOR
FLAVORED
FLAVORER
FLAVORFUL
FLAVORING
FLAVORLESS
FLAVOROUS
FLAVORSOME
FLAVORY
FLAVOUR
FLAVOURED
FLAVOURER
FLAVOURING
FLAVOUROUS
FLAVOURSOME
FLAVOURY
FLAW
FLAWED
FLAWFLOWER
FLAWIER
FLAWIEST
FLAWING
FLAWLESS
FLAWLESSLY
FLAWLESSNESS
FLAWN
FLAWS
FLAWY
FLAX
FLAXBIRD
FLAXBOARD
FLAXBUSH
FLAXDROP
FLAXEN
FLAXIER
FLAXIEST
FLAXMAN
FLAXSEED
FLAXTAIL
FLAXWEED
FLAXWENCH
FLAXWIFE
FLAXWOMAN
FLAXWORT
FLAXY
FLAY
FLAYER
FLAYFLINT
FLEA
FLEABAG
FLEABANE
FLEABITE
FLEABITING
FLEADOCK
FLEAK
FLEAM
FLEAS
FLEASEED
FLEAWEED
FLEAWOOD
FLEAWORT
FLEAY
FLEBILE
FLECH
FLECHE
FLECHETTE
FLECHETTES
FLECK
FLECKED
FLECKER
FLECKERED
FLECKERING
FLECKIER
FLECKIEST
FLECKINESS
FLECKING
FLECKLED
FLECKY
FLECNODE
FLECTION
FLECTIONAL
FLECTOR
FLED
FLEDGE
FLEDGED
FLEDGELESS
FLEDGELING
FLEDGING
FLEDGLING
FLEDGY
FLEE
FLEECE
FLEECED
FLEECEFLOWER
FLEECER

FLEECH
FLEECHMENT
FLEECIER
FLEECIEST
FLEECILY
FLEECINESS
FLEECING
FLEECY
FLEEING
FLEEM
FLEER
FLEERED
FLEERER
FLEERING
FLEERINGLY
FLEERISH
FLEET
FLEETER
FLEETEST
FLEETING
FLEETINGLY
FLEETINGNESS
FLEETINGS
FLEETLY
FLEETNESS
FLEETWING
FLEG
FLEME
FLEMER
FLEMISH
FLENCH
FLENSE
FLENSED
FLENSER
FLENSING
FLENTES
FLERRIED
FLERRY
FLERRYING
FLESH
FLESHBRUSH
FLESHED
FLESHEN
FLESHER
FLESHFUL
FLESHHOOK
FLESHIER
FLESHIEST
FLESHINESS
FLESHING
FLESHINGS
FLESHLESS
FLESHLILY
FLESHLINESS
FLESHLY
FLESHMENT
FLESHPOT
FLESHQUAKE
FLESHY
FLET
FLETCH
FLETCHED
FLETCHER
FLETCHING
FLETHER
FLETTON
FLEUR
FLEURET
FLEURETTEE
FLEURETTY
FLEURON
FLEURONEE
FLEURONNE
FLEURONNEE
FLEURY
FLEW
FLEWED
FLEWIT
FLEWS
FLEX
FLEXANIMOUS
FLEXED
FLEXIBILITY
FLEXIBLE
FLEXIBLENESS
FLEXIBLY
FLEXILE
FLEXILITY
FLEXING
FLEXION
FLEXIONAL
FLEXIVE
FLEXOR
FLEXUOSE
FLEXUOSITIES
FLEXUOSITY
FLEXUOUS
FLEXUOUSLY
FLEXUOUSNESS
FLEXURA
FLEXURAL
FLEXURE
FLEXURED
FLEY
FLEYEDLY
FLEYEDNESS
FLEYLAND
FLEYSOME
FLIC
FLICFLAC
FLICHTER
FLICHTERED
FLICK
FLICKED
FLICKER
FLICKERED
FLICKERING
FLICKERS
FLICKERTAIL
FLICKERY
FLICKING
FLICKS
FLICKY
FLIDDER
FLIED
FLIER
FLIERS
FLIES
FLIEST
FLIFFUS
FLIGGED
FLIGGER
FLIGHT
FLIGHTED
FLIGHTER
FLIGHTFUL
FLIGHTHEAD
FLIGHTIER
FLIGHTIEST
FLIGHTILY
FLIGHTINESS
FLIGHTING
FLIGHTLESS
FLIGHTS
FLIGHTSHOT
FLIGHTWORTHY
FLIGHTY
FLIMFLAM
FLIMFLAMMED
FLIMFLAMMER
FLIMFLAMMERY
FLIMFLAMMING
FLIMMER
FLIMP
FLIMSIER
FLIMSIES
FLIMSIEST
FLIMSILY
FLIMSINESS
FLIMSY
FLINCH
FLINCHED
FLINCHER
FLINCHING
FLINCHINGLY
FLINDER
FLINDERS
FLINDOSA
FLINDOSY
FLING
FLINGDUST
FLINGER
FLINGING
FLINGY
FLINKITE
FLINT
FLINTED
FLINTER
FLINTHEAD
FLINTHEARTED
FLINTIER
FLINTIEST
FLINTIFIED
FLINTIFY
FLINTIFYING
FLINTILY
FLINTINESS
FLINTING
FLINTLOCK
FLINTS
FLINTWOOD
FLINTWORK
FLINTWORKER
FLINTY
FLIOMA
FLIP
FLIPE
FLIPED
FLIPING
FLIPJACK
FLIPPANCE
FLIPPANCIES
FLIPPANCY
FLIPPANT
FLIPPANTLY
FLIPPANTNESS
FLIPPED
FLIPPER
FLIPPERLING
FLIPPERY
FLIPPING
FLIRD
FLIRE
FLIRT
FLIRTABLE
FLIRTATION
FLIRTATIONAL
FLIRTATIOUS
FLIRTATIOUSLY
FLIRTATIOUSNESS
FLIRTED
FLIRTER
FLIRTIER
FLIRTIEST
FLIRTIGIG
FLIRTING
FLIRTISH
FLIRTISHNESS
FLIRTY
FLISK
FLISKED
FLISKIER
FLISKIEST
FLISKING
FLISKMAHOY
FLISKY
FLIT
FLITCH
FLITCHED
FLITCHEN
FLITCHING
FLITE
FLITED
FLITFOLD
FLITING
FLITTED
FLITTER
FLITTERBAT
FLITTERED
FLITTERING
FLITTERMICE
FLITTERMOUSE
FLITTERN
FLITTERS
FLITTINESS
FLITTING
FLITTINGLY
FLITTY
FLITWITE
FLIVVER
FLIX
FLIXWEED
FLO
FLOAT
FLOATABILITY
FLOATABLE
FLOATAGE
FLOATATION
FLOATATIVE
FLOATBOARD
FLOATED
FLOATER
FLOATERS
FLOATIER
FLOATIEST
FLOATINESS
FLOATING
FLOATINGLY
FLOATIVE
FLOATS
FLOATSMAN
FLOATSMEN
FLOATSTONE
FLOATY
FLOB
FLOC
FLOCCI
FLOCCILATION
FLOCCIPEND
FLOCCOSE
FLOCCOSELY
FLOCCULABLE
FLOCCULAR
FLOCCULATE
FLOCCULATED
FLOCCULATING
FLOCCULATION
FLOCCULATOR
FLOCCULE
FLOCCULENCE
FLOCCULENCY
FLOCCULENT
FLOCCULENTLY
FLOCCULI
FLOCCULOSE
FLOCCULOUS
FLOCCULUS
FLOCCUS
FLOCK
FLOCKED
FLOCKER
FLOCKET
FLOCKIER
FLOCKIEST
FLOCKING
FLOCKLING
FLOCKMAN
FLOCKMASTER
FLOCKMEAL
FLOCKMEN
FLOCKOWNER
FLOCKS
FLOCKWISE
FLOCKY
FLOCOON
FLODGE
FLOE
FLOEBERG
FLOG
FLOGGABLE
FLOGGED
FLOGGER
FLOGGING
FLOGMASTER
FLOGSTER
FLOIT
FLOKITE
FLONG
FLOOD
FLOODAGE
FLOODBOARD
FLOODCOCK
FLOODED
FLOODER
FLOODGATE
FLOODING
FLOODLIGHT
FLOODLIGHTED
FLOODLIGHTING
FLOODLIT
FLOODMARK
FLOODOMETER
FLOODPLAIN
FLOODTIME
FLOODWATER
FLOODWAY
FLOODWOOD
FLOODY
FLOOEY
FLOOKAN
FLOOR
FLOORAGE
FLOORBOARD
FLOORCLOTH
FLOORED
FLOORER
FLOORHEAD
FLOORING
FLOORMAN
FLOORMEN
FLOORS
FLOORWALKER
FLOORWAY
FLOOSY
FLOOZIES
FLOOZY
FLOP
FLOPEROO
FLOPHOUSE
FLOPOVER
FLOPPED
FLOPPER
FLOPPERS
FLOPPIER
FLOPPIEST

FLOPPILY
FLOPPINESS
FLOPPING
FLOPPY
FLOPWING
FLOR
FLORA
FLORAE
FLORAISON
FLORAL
FLORALIZE
FLORALLY
FLORAMOR
FLORAMOUR
FLORAN
FLORAS
FLORATE
FLOREAL
FLOREATE
FLOREATED
FLOREATING
FLORENCE
FLORENT
FLORENTIUM
FLORES
FLORESCENCE
FLORESCENT
FLORESSENCE
FLORET
FLORETA
FLORETED
FLORETTY
FLORETUM
FLORIATE
FLORIATED
FLORIATION
FLORIBUNDA
FLORICAN
FLORICIN
FLORICULTURE
FLORID
FLORIDEAN
FLORIDEOUS
FLORIDITIES
FLORIDITY
FLORIDLY
FLORIDNESS
FLORIFEROUS
FLORIFEROUSLY
FLORIFEROUSNESS
FLORIFICATION
FLORIFORM
FLORIGEN
FLORIGRAPHY
FLORILEGE
FLORILEGIA
FLORILEGIUM
FLORIMANIA
FLORIMANIST
FLORIN
FLORIPAROUS
FLORIPONDIO
FLORISCOPE
FLORIST
FLORISTIC
FLORISTICALLY
FLORISTICS
FLORISTRY
FLORISUGENT
FLORIZINE
FLOROON
FLOROSCOPE
FLORUIT
FLORULA
FLORULAE
FLORULAS
FLORULENT
FLORY
FLOSCULAR
FLOSCULARIAN
FLOSCULE
FLOSCULOSE
FLOSCULOUS
FLOSH
FLOSS
FLOSSA
FLOSSER
FLOSSFLOWER
FLOSSIE
FLOSSIER
FLOSSIES
FLOSSIEST
FLOSSING
FLOSSY
FLOT
FLOTA
FLOTAGE
FLOTANT
FLOTATION
FLOTATIVE
FLOTE
FLOTILLA
FLOTS
FLOTSAM
FLOTSAN
FLOTSEN
FLOTSON
FLOTTER
FLOUNCE
FLOUNCED
FLOUNCING
FLOUNCY
FLOUNDER
FLOUNDERED
FLOUNDERING
FLOUNDERINGLY
FLOUNDERS
FLOUR
FLOURED
FLOURING
FLOURISH
FLOURISHED
FLOURISHER
FLOURISHES
FLOURISHING
FLOURISHINGLY
FLOURISHY
FLOURY
FLOUSE
FLOUSH
FLOUT
FLOUTED
FLOUTER
FLOUTING
FLOUTINGLY
FLOW
FLOWAGE
FLOWED
FLOWER
FLOWERAGE
FLOWERED
FLOWERER
FLOWERET
FLOWERFENCE
FLOWERFLY
FLOWERIER
FLOWERIEST
FLOWERILY
FLOWERINESS
FLOWERING
FLOWERIST
FLOWERLET
FLOWERPECKER
FLOWERPOT
FLOWERS
FLOWERWORK
FLOWERY
FLOWING
FLOWINGLY
FLOWINGNESS
FLOWMETER
FLOWN
FLOWOFF
FLU
FLUATE
FLUAVIL
FLUAVILE
FLUB
FLUBBED
FLUBBING
FLUBDUB
FLUBDUBBERIES
FLUBDUBBERY
FLUCAN
FLUCTUABILITY
FLUCTUABLE
FLUCTUANT
FLUCTUATE
FLUCTUATED
FLUCTUATING
FLUCTUATION
FLUCTUOSITY
FLUCTUOUS
FLUE
FLUED
FLUELLEN
FLUELLIN
FLUELLITE
FLUEMAN
FLUEMEN
FLUENCE
FLUENCIES
FLUENCY
FLUENT
FLUENTLY
FLUENTNESS
FLUER
FLUEWORK
FLUEY
FLUFF
FLUFFED
FLUFFER
FLUFFIER
FLUFFIEST
FLUFFILY
FLUFFINESS
FLUFFING
FLUFFY
FLUGEL
FLUGELHORN
FLUGELMAN
FLUGELMEN
FLUIBLE
FLUID
FLUIDAL
FLUIDALLY
FLUIDEXTRACT
FLUIDIC
FLUIDICS
FLUIDIFICATION
FLUIDIFIED
FLUIDIFIER
FLUIDIFY
FLUIDIFYING
FLUIDIMETER
FLUIDISM
FLUIDIST
FLUIDITY
FLUIDIZATION
FLUIDIZE
FLUIDIZED
FLUIDIZING
FLUIDLY
FLUIDNESS
FLUIDRACHM
FLUIDRAM
FLUIGRAM
FLUIGRAMME
FLUING
FLUITANT
FLUKE
FLUKED
FLUKES
FLUKEWORT
FLUKEY
FLUKIER
FLUKIEST
FLUKILY
FLUKINESS
FLUKING
FLUKY
FLUM
FLUMDIDDLE
FLUME
FLUMED
FLUMERIN
FLUMING
FLUMINOSE
FLUMINOUS
FLUMMER
FLUMMERIES
FLUMMERY
FLUMMOX
FLUMMOXED
FLUMMOXING
FLUMP
FLUMPED
FLUMPING
FLUNG
FLUNK
FLUNKED
FLUNKER
FLUNKEY
FLUNKEYISM
FLUNKEYISTIC
FLUNKEYITE
FLUNKEYS
FLUNKIES
FLUNKING
FLUNKY
FLUNKYISM
FLUNKYISTIC
FLUNKYITE
FLUOARSENATE
FLUOBORATE
FLUOBORIC
FLUOBORITE
FLUOCERINE
FLUOCERITE
FLUOHYDRIC
FLUOR
FLUORAN
FLUORANE
FLUORANTHENE
FLUORAPATITE
FLUORATE
FLUORENE
FLUORESAGE
FLUORESCE
FLUORESCED
FLUORESCEIN
FLUORESCEINE
FLUORESCENCE
FLUORESCENT
FLUORESCIN
FLUORESCING
FLUORHYDRIC
FLUORIC
FLUORID
FLUORIDATE
FLUORIDATED
FLUORIDATING
FLUORIDATION
FLUORIDE
FLUORIN
FLUORINATE
FLUORINATION
FLUORINDIN
FLUORINE
FLUORITE
FLUORMETER
FLUOROBORATE
FLUOROCARBON
FLUOROFORM
FLUOROFORMOL
FLUOROGEN
FLUOROGENIC
FLUOROGRAPHY
FLUOROID
FLUOROMETER
FLUOROSCOPE
FLUOROSCOPIC
FLUOROSCOPY
FLUOROTYPE
FLUORSPAR
FLUORYL
FLUOSILICATE
FLUOSILICIC
FLUOTANTALIC
FLURN
FLURR
FLURRIED
FLURRIEDLY
FLURRIES
FLURRIMENT
FLURRY
FLURRYING
FLUSH
FLUSHBOARD
FLUSHED
FLUSHER
FLUSHERMAN
FLUSHERMEN
FLUSHEST
FLUSHGATE
FLUSHING
FLUSHINGLY
FLUSHNESS
FLUSHY
FLUSK
FLUSKER
FLUSTER
FLUSTERATE
FLUSTERATION
FLUSTERED
FLUSTERER
FLUSTERING
FLUSTERY
FLUSTRATE
FLUSTRATION
FLUSTRINE
FLUSTROID
FLUSTRUM
FLUTE
FLUTEBIRD
FLUTED
FLUTEMOUTH
FLUTER
FLUTES
FLUTEWORK
FLUTHER
FLUTIER
FLUTIEST
FLUTINA
FLUTING

FLUTINGS
FLUTIST
FLUTTER
FLUTTERATION
FLUTTERED
FLUTTERER
FLUTTERING
FLUTTERINGLY
FLUTTERSOME
FLUTTERY
FLUTY
FLUVANNA
FLUVIAL
FLUVIALIST
FLUVIATIC
FLUVIATILE
FLUVICOLINE
FLUVIOGRAPH
FLUVIOLOGY
FLUVIOMARINE
FLUVIOSE
FLUVIOUS
FLUX
FLUXATION
FLUXED
FLUXER
FLUXIBILITY
FLUXIBLE
FLUXIBLENESS
FLUXIBLY
FLUXILE
FLUXILITY
FLUXING
FLUXION
FLUXIONAL
FLUXIONALLY
FLUXIONARY
FLUXIONIST
FLUXIVE
FLUXMETER
FLUXROOT
FLUXURE
FLUXWEED
FLY
FLYABLE
FLYAWAY
FLYBACK
FLYBALL
FLYBANE
FLYBELT
FLYBLEW
FLYBLOW
FLYBLOWN
FLYBOAT
FLYBOY
FLYBRUSH
FLYBY
FLYCATCHER
FLYEATER
FLYER
FLYFLAP
FLYFLAPPER
FLYFLOWER
FLYING
FLYINGLY
FLYINGS
FLYLEAF
FLYLEAVES
FLYMAN
FLYMEN
FLYNESS
FLYOVER
FLYPAPER
FLYPE
FLYPROOF
FLYSPECK
FLYSWAT
FLYTAIL
FLYTE
FLYTED
FLYTIER
FLYTIME
FLYTING
FLYTRAP
FLYWAY
FLYWEIGHT
FLYWHEEL
FLYWINCH
FLYWIRE
FLYWORT
FNESE
FOAL
FOALED
FOALFOOT
FOALFOOTS
FOALING
FOALY
FOAM
FOAMBOW
FOAMED
FOAMER
FOAMFLOWER
FOAMIER
FOAMIEST
FOAMILY
FOAMINESS
FOAMING
FOAMY
FOB
FOBBED
FOBBING
FOCAL
FOCALIZATION
FOCALIZE
FOCALIZED
FOCALIZING
FOCALLY
FOCALOID
FOCI
FOCIMETER
FOCIMETRY
FOCKLE
FOCOIDS
FOCOMETER
FOCOMETRY
FOCSLE
FOCUS
FOCUSED
FOCUSER
FOCUSES
FOCUSING
FOCUSSED
FOCUSSING
FODDA
FODDER
FODDERED
FODDERER
FODDERING
FODE
FODGE
FODGEL
FODIENT
FOE
FOEDERATI
FOEDERATUS
FOEHN
FOEHOOD
FOEMAN
FOEMANSHIP
FOEMEN
FOETAL
FOETALISM
FOETATION
FOETICIDAL
FOETICIDE
FOETIFEROUS
FOETIPAROUS
FOETOR
FOETURE
FOETUS
FOETUSES
FOFARRAW
FOG
FOGAS
FOGBOUND
FOGBOW
FOGDOG
FOGE
FOGEATER
FOGEY
FOGFRUIT
FOGGAGE
FOGGARA
FOGGED
FOGGER
FOGGIER
FOGGIEST
FOGGILY
FOGGINESS
FOGGING
FOGGY
FOGHORN
FOGIE
FOGIES
FOGLE
FOGLIETTO
FOGMAN
FOGMEN
FOGO
FOGON
FOGOU
FOGRAM
FOGRAMITE
FOGRAMITY
FOGRUM
FOGSCOFFER
FOGUS
FOGY
FOGYDOM
FOGYISH
FOGYISM
FOH
FOHAT
FOHN
FOIBLE
FOIE
FOIL
FOILED
FOILER
FOILING
FOILSMAN
FOILSMEN
FOIN
FOINED
FOINING
FOISON
FOISONLESS
FOISONS
FOIST
FOISTED
FOISTER
FOISTINESS
FOISTING
FOISTY
FOITER
FOLCGEMOT
FOLD
FOLDAGE
FOLDBOAT
FOLDCOURSE
FOLDED
FOLDEDLY
FOLDEN
FOLDER
FOLDEROL
FOLDING
FOLDOUT
FOLDS
FOLDSKIRT
FOLDURE
FOLDY
FOLEYE
FOLIA
FOLIACEOUS
FOLIAGE
FOLIAGED
FOLIAGEOUS
FOLIAGING
FOLIAL
FOLIAR
FOLIARY
FOLIATE
FOLIATED
FOLIATING
FOLIATION
FOLIATURE
FOLIE
FOLIICOLOUS
FOLIIFEROUS
FOLIIFORM
FOLIO
FOLIOBRANCH
FOLIOED
FOLIOING
FOLIOLATE
FOLIOLE
FOLIOLOSE
FOLIOS
FOLIOSE
FOLIOSITY
FOLIOT
FOLIOUS
FOLIOUSLY
FOLIUM
FOLIUMS
FOLK
FOLKCRAFT
FOLKFREE
FOLKLAND
FOLKLORE
FOLKLORIC
FOLKLORISH
FOLKLORISM
FOLKLORIST
FOLKLORISTIC
FOLKMOOT
FOLKMOOTER
FOLKMOT
FOLKMOTE
FOLKMOTER
FOLKRIGHT
FOLKS
FOLKSEY
FOLKSIER
FOLKSIEST
FOLKSINESS
FOLKSY
FOLKWAY
FOLKWAYS
FOLKY
FOLLE
FOLLER
FOLLES
FOLLETTI
FOLLETTO
FOLLICLE
FOLLICULAR
FOLLICULATE
FOLLICULATED
FOLLICULE
FOLLICULITIS
FOLLICULOSE
FOLLICULOSIS
FOLLICULOUS
FOLLIED
FOLLIES
FOLLIFUL
FOLLILY
FOLLIS
FOLLOW
FOLLOWED
FOLLOWER
FOLLOWERSHIP
FOLLOWING
FOLLOWS
FOLLY
FOLLYER
FOLLYING
FOLO
FOMENT
FOMENTATION
FOMENTED
FOMENTER
FOMENTING
FOMENTO
FOMES
FOMITES
FON
FOND
FONDA
FONDACO
FONDANT
FONDATEUR
FONDER
FONDEST
FONDISH
FONDLE
FONDLED
FONDLER
FONDLING
FONDLY
FONDNESS
FONDOUK
FONDU
FONDUE
FONDUK
FONIO
FONO
FONS
FONT
FONTAL
FONTALLY
FONTANEL
FONTANELLE
FONTANGE
FONTED
FONTES
FONTICULUS
FONTINA
FONTINAL
FOO
FOOD
FOODER
FOODLESS
FOODS
FOODSTUFF
FOODY
FOOFARAW
FOOL
FOOLED
FOOLER
FOOLERIES
FOOLERY
FOOLESS
FOOLFISH

FOOLFISHES
FOOLHARDIER
FOOLHARDIEST
FOOLHARDIHOOD
FOOLHARDILY
FOOLHARDINESS
FOOLHARDY
FOOLHEAD
FOOLIFY
FOOLING
FOOLISH
FOOLISHLY
FOOLISHNESS
FOOLMONGER
FOOLOCRACY
FOOLPROOF
FOOLPROOFNESS
FOOLSCAP
FOONER
FOOSTER
FOOSTERER
FOOT
FOOTAGE
FOOTBACK
FOOTBALL
FOOTBALLER
FOOTBALLIST
FOOTBAND
FOOTBEAT
FOOTBLOWER
FOOTBOARD
FOOTBOARDS
FOOTBOY
FOOTBREADTH
FOOTBRIDGE
FOOTCLOTH
FOOTCLOTHS
FOOTED
FOOTEITE
FOOTER
FOOTFALL
FOOTFARER
FOOTFAULT
FOOTFEED
FOOTFOLK
FOOTFUL
FOOTGANGER
FOOTGEAR
FOOTGELD
FOOTGLOVE
FOOTGRIP
FOOTH
FOOTHALT
FOOTHILL
FOOTHOLD
FOOTHOOK
FOOTHOT
FOOTIER
FOOTIEST
FOOTING
FOOTINGLY
FOOTINGS
FOOTLE
FOOTLED
FOOTLER
FOOTLESS
FOOTLICKER
FOOTLIGHT
FOOTLIGHTS
FOOTLIKE
FOOTLING
FOOTLINING
FOOTLOCK
FOOTLOCKER
FOOTLOG
FOOTLOOSE
FOOTMAKER
FOOTMAN
FOOTMANHOOD
FOOTMANRY
FOOTMANSHIP
FOOTMARK
FOOTMEN
FOOTNOTE
FOOTNOTED
FOOTNOTING
FOOTPACE
FOOTPAD
FOOTPADDERY
FOOTPATH
FOOTPICK
FOOTPLATE
FOOTPRINT
FOOTRAIL
FOOTREST
FOOTRILL
FOOTROOM
FOOTROPE
FOOTS
FOOTSCALD
FOOTSLOG
FOOTSLOGGER
FOOTSORE
FOOTSORENESS
FOOTSTALK
FOOTSTALL
FOOTSTEP
FOOTSTICK
FOOTSTOCK
FOOTSTONE
FOOTSTOOL
FOOTWALK
FOOTWALL
FOOTWAY
FOOTWEAR
FOOTWORK
FOOTWORN
FOOTY
FOOYOUNG
FOOYUNG
FOOZLE
FOOZLED
FOOZLER
FOOZLING
FOP
FOPDOODLE
FOPLING
FOPPERIES
FOPPERLY
FOPPERY
FOPPISH
FOPPISHLY
FOPPISHNESS
FOPPY
FOPSHIP
FOR
FORA
FORAGE
FORAGED
FORAGEMENT
FORAGER
FORAGERS
FORAGING
FORALITE
FORAM
FORAMEN
FORAMENS
FORAMINA
FORAMINATE
FORAMINATED
FORAMINATION
FORAMINIFER
FORAMINOSE
FORAMINOUS
FORAMINULATE
FORAMINULE
FORAMINULOSE
FORAMINULOUS
FORANE
FORANEOUS
FORASTERO
FORAY
FORAYED
FORAYER
FORAYING
FORB
FORBAD
FORBADE
FORBAR
FORBARE
FORBARRED
FORBEAR
FORBEARABLE
FORBEARANCE
FORBEARANT
FORBEARANTLY
FORBEARER
FORBEARING
FORBESITE
FORBID
FORBIDDAL
FORBIDDANCE
FORBIDDEN
FORBIDDENLY
FORBIDDENNESS
FORBIDDER
FORBIDDING
FORBIDDINGLY
FORBIDDINGNESS
FORBITE
FORBLED
FORBLOW
FORBODE
FORBORE
FORBORNE
FORBREAK
FORBY
FORBYE
FORBYSEN
FORBYSENING
FORCAT
FORCE
FORCEABLE
FORCED
FORCEDLY
FORCEDNESS
FORCEFUL
FORCEFULLY
FORCEFULNESS
FORCELET
FORCEMEAT
FORCEMENT
FORCENE
FORCEPS
FORCEPSES
FORCEPUT
FORCER
FORCET
FORCHASE
FORCHES
FORCIBILITY
FORCIBLE
FORCIBLENESS
FORCIBLY
FORCING
FORCIPATE
FORCIPATED
FORCIPES
FORCIPIFORM
FORCIPRESSURE
FORCIPULATE
FORCIVE
FORCUT
FORCY
FORD
FORDABLE
FORDEAL
FORDID
FORDING
FORDO
FORDOING
FORDONE
FORDULL
FORDWINE
FORDY
FORE
FOREARM
FOREBACKWARDLY
FOREBAR
FOREBAY
FOREBEAR
FOREBITT
FOREBITTER
FOREBOARD
FOREBODE
FOREBODED
FOREBODER
FOREBODING
FOREBODINGLY
FOREBODINGNESS
FOREBODY
FOREBOOM
FOREBOOT
FOREBOW
FOREBOWELS
FOREBOWS
FOREBRACE
FOREBRAIN
FOREBREAST
FOREBROADS
FOREBUSH
FOREBY
FOREBYE
FORECABIN
FORECAR
FORECARRIAGE
FORECAST
FORECASTED
FORECASTER
FORECASTING
FORECASTLE
FORECASTLEHEAD
FORECASTLEMAN
FORECASTLEMEN
FORECHASE
FORECHURCH
FORECLOSABLE
FORECLOSE
FORECLOSED
FORECLOSING
FORECLOSURE
FORECOME
FORECOMINGNESS
FORECOOL
FORECOOLER
FORECOURSE
FORECOURT
FOREDATE
FOREDATED
FOREDATING
FOREDAWN
FOREDAY
FOREDAYS
FOREDECK
FOREDEEM
FOREDEEP
FOREDESTINE
FOREDESTINED
FOREDESTINING
FOREDESTINY
FOREDO
FOREDONE
FOREDOOM
FOREDOOMED
FOREDOOMER
FOREDOOMING
FOREDOOR
FOREDUNE
FOREFACE
FOREFATHER
FOREFATHERLY
FOREFEEL
FOREFEELING
FOREFEELINGLY
FOREFEET
FOREFELT
FOREFEND
FOREFIELD
FOREFINGER
FOREFOOT
FOREFRONT
FOREGAME
FOREGANGER
FOREGATE
FOREGATHER
FOREGIFT
FOREGIRTH
FOREGLANCE
FOREGLEAM
FOREGLIMPSE
FOREGO
FOREGOER
FOREGOING
FOREGONE
FOREGONENESS
FOREGROUND
FOREGUT
FOREHALL
FOREHAMMER
FOREHAND
FOREHANDED
FOREHANDEDNESS
FOREHARD
FOREHEAD
FOREHEADED
FOREHEARTH
FOREHEATER
FOREHENT
FOREHOLD
FOREHOOF
FOREHOOK
FOREIGN
FOREIGNEERING
FOREIGNER
FOREIGNISM
FOREIGNNESS
FOREIRON
FOREJUDGE
FOREJUDGED
FOREJUDGER
FOREJUDGING
FOREKNEW
FOREKNOW
FOREKNOWER
FOREKNOWING
FOREKNOWLEDGE
FOREKNOWN
FOREL
FORELADIES
FORELADY
FORELAID
FORELAND
FORELAY
FORELAYING
FORELEECH

FORELEG
FORELIMB
FORELOCK
FORELOOK
FORELOOP
FORELOOPER
FORELOPER
FORELOUPER
FOREMAN
FOREMANSHIP
FOREMARCH
FOREMAST
FOREMASTHAND
FOREMASTMAN
FOREMASTMEN
FOREMEN
FOREMILK
FOREMIND
FOREMISTRESS
FOREMOST
FOREMOTHER
FORENAME
FORENAMED
FORENENT
FORENIGHT
FORENOON
FORENOTE
FORENSAL
FORENSIC
FORENSICAL
FORENSICALITY
FORENSICALLY
FOREORDAIN
FOREORDAINMENT
FOREORDINATE
FOREORDINATED
FOREORDINATING
FOREORDINATION
FOREPALE
FOREPALED
FOREPALING
FOREPARENT
FOREPARENTS
FOREPART
FOREPASS
FOREPASSED
FOREPAST
FOREPEAK
FOREPIECE
FOREPLOT
FOREPOINT
FOREPOINTER
FOREPOLE
FOREPOLED
FOREPOLING
FOREPOST
FOREPRISE
FOREPRIZE
FOREQUARTER
FORERAN
FORERANK
FOREREACH
FOREREACHING
FORERIBS
FORERIGHT
FOREROOM
FORERUN
FORERUNNER
FORERUNNING
FORERUNNINGS
FORES
FORESADDLE
FORESAID
FORESAIL
FORESAW
FORESAY
FORESAYING
FORESCENT
FORESCRIPT
FORESEE
FORESEEING
FORESEEINGLY
FORESEEN
FORESEER
FORESET
FORESEY
FORESHADOW
FORESHADOWER
FORESHAFT
FORESHEET
FORESHIFT
FORESHIP
FORESHOCK
FORESHORE
FORESHORTEN
FORESHORTENING
FORESHOT
FORESHOW
FORESHOWED
FORESHOWER
FORESHOWING
FORESHOWN
FORESIDE
FORESIGHT
FORESIGHTED
FORESIGHTEDLY
FORESIGHTEDNESS
FORESIGHTFUL
FORESIGN
FORESIGNIFY
FORESINGER
FORESKIN
FORESLEEVE
FORESLOW
FORESOUND
FORESPAKE
FORESPEAK
FORESPEAKER
FORESPEAKING
FORESPEECH
FORESPEED
FORESPOKE
FORESPOKEN
FOREST
FORESTAFF
FORESTAGE
FORESTAIR
FORESTAL
FORESTALL
FORESTALLED
FORESTALLER
FORESTALLING
FORESTARLING
FORESTATION
FORESTAY
FORESTAYSAIL
FORESTCRAFT
FORESTED
FORESTEM
FORESTEP
FORESTER
FORESTIAL
FORESTICK
FORESTINE
FORESTING
FORESTLESS
FORESTOLOGY
FORESTRAL
FORESTRESS
FORESTRY
FORESTS
FORESTSIDE
FORESTY
FORESWEAT
FORETACK
FORETACKLE
FORETAKE
FORETALK
FORETALKING
FORETASTE
FORETASTED
FORETASTER
FORETASTING
FORETEETH
FORETELL
FORETELLER
FORETELLING
FORETHINK
FORETHINKER
FORETHINKING
FORETHOUGHT
FORETHOUGHTED
FORETHOUGHTFUL
FORETHOUGHTFULLY
FORETHOUGHTFULNESS
FORETIME
FORETOKEN
FORETOKENED
FORETOKENING
FORETOLD
FORETOOTH
FORETOP
FORETOPMAN
FORETOPMAST
FORETOPMEN
FORETOPSAIL
FORETURN
FORETYPE
FOREVER
FOREVERMORE
FOREWARD
FOREWARM
FOREWARMER
FOREWARN
FOREWARNED
FOREWARNER
FOREWARNING
FOREWATERS
FOREWENT
FOREWING
FOREWINNING
FOREWISDOM
FOREWIT
FOREWOMAN
FOREWOMEN
FOREWORD
FOREWORLD
FOREWORN
FOREYARD
FORFAIRN
FORFAR
FORFARE
FORFARS
FORFAULT
FORFAULTURE
FORFEIT
FORFEITABLE
FORFEITED
FORFEITER
FORFEITING
FORFEITS
FORFEITURE
FORFEND
FORFENDED
FORFENDING
FORFEX
FORFICATE
FORFICATED
FORFICATION
FORFICIFORM
FORFICULATE
FORFOUCHTEN
FORFOUGHEN
FORFOUGHTEN
FORGAB
FORGAINST
FORGAT
FORGATHER
FORGATHERED
FORGATHERING
FORGAVE
FORGE
FORGED
FORGEFUL
FORGEMAN
FORGEMEN
FORGER
FORGERIES
FORGERY
FORGET
FORGETFUL
FORGETFULLY
FORGETFULNESS
FORGETIVE
FORGETNESS
FORGETT
FORGETTABLE
FORGETTE
FORGETTER
FORGETTING
FORGETTINGLY
FORGIFT
FORGING
FORGIVABLE
FORGIVE
FORGIVELESS
FORGIVEN
FORGIVENESS
FORGIVER
FORGIVING
FORGIVINGLY
FORGIVINGNESS
FORGO
FORGOER
FORGOING
FORGONE
FORGOT
FORGOTTEN
FORGROW
FORGROWN
FORHAILE
FORHEED
FORHOO
FORHOOIE
FORHOOY
FORHOW
FORINSEC
FORINT
FORJASKIT
FORJESKET
FORJUDGE
FORJUDGED
FORJUDGER
FORJUDGING
FORK
FORKBEARD
FORKED
FORKEDLY
FORKEDNESS
FORKER
FORKHEAD
FORKINESS
FORKING
FORKLIFT
FORKMAN
FORKMEN
FORKSMITH
FORKTAIL
FORKY
FORLAIN
FORLANA
FORLAY
FORLEAVE
FORLEAVING
FORLEFT
FORLEIT
FORLESE
FORLET
FORLETTING
FORLIE
FORLIVE
FORLOIN
FORLORN
FORLORNITY
FORLORNLY
FORLORNNESS
FORM
FORMA
FORMAL
FORMALAZINE
FORMALDEHYD
FORMALDEHYDE
FORMALDOXIME
FORMALESQUE
FORMALISM
FORMALIST
FORMALISTIC
FORMALITER
FORMALITH
FORMALITIES
FORMALITY
FORMALIZATION
FORMALIZE
FORMALIZED
FORMALIZER
FORMALIZING
FORMALLY
FORMAMIDE
FORMAMIDINE
FORMANILIDE
FORMANT
FORMAT
FORMATE
FORMATION
FORMATIONAL
FORMATIVE
FORMATIVELY
FORMATIVENESS
FORMATURE
FORMAZAN
FORMAZYL
FORMBY
FORME
FORMED
FORMEDON
FORMEE
FORMEL
FORMELT
FORMENE
FORMENIC
FORMER
FORMERET
FORMERLY
FORMFUL
FORMIATE
FORMIC
FORMICA
FORMICARIAN
FORMICARIES
FORMICARY
FORMICATE
FORMICATED
FORMICATING
FORMICATION
FORMICATIVE

FORMICID
FORMICIDE
FORMICINE
FORMIDABILITY
FORMIDABLE
FORMIDABLENESS
FORMIDABLY
FORMIN
FORMING
FORMISM
FORMITY
FORMLESS
FORMLESSLY
FORMLESSNESS
FORMLY
FORMOLIT
FORMOLITE
FORMONITRILE
FORMOSE
FORMOSITY
FORMOUS
FORMS
FORMULA
FORMULABLE
FORMULAE
FORMULAIC
FORMULAR
FORMULARIES
FORMULARISM
FORMULARIST
FORMULARIZATION
FORMULARIZE
FORMULARIZED
FORMULARIZING
FORMULARY
FORMULAS
FORMULATE
FORMULATED
FORMULATING
FORMULATION
FORMULATOR
FORMULATORY
FORMULE
FORMULISM
FORMULIST
FORMULISTIC
FORMULIZATION
FORMULIZE
FORMULIZED
FORMULIZER
FORMULIZING
FORMWORK
FORMY
FORMYL
FORMYLATE
FORMYLATED
FORMYLATING
FORMYLATION
FORNACIC
FORNAXID
FORNCAST
FORNE
FORNENST
FORNENT
FORNICAL
FORNICATE
FORNICATED
FORNICATING
FORNICATION
FORNICATOR
FORNICATRICES
FORNICATRIX
FORNINST
FORNIX
FOROLD
FORPASS
FORPET
FORPINE
FORPINED
FORPINING
FORPIT
FORPRISE
FORREL
FORRIL
FORRIT
FORRITSOME
FORSADO
FORSAKE
FORSAKEN
FORSAKENLY
FORSAKENNESS
FORSAKER
FORSAKES
FORSAKING
FORSAR
FORSAY
FORSEEK
FORSET
FORSHAPE
FORSLACK
FORSLAKE
FORSLOW
FORSOOK
FORSOOTH
FORSPEAK
FORSPEAKING
FORSPEND
FORSPENT
FORSPOKE
FORSPOKEN
FORSTAND
FORSTEAL
FORSTERITE
FORSUNG
FORSWEAR
FORSWEARER
FORSWEARING
FORSWORE
FORSWORN
FORSWORNNESS
FORT
FORTAKE
FORTALICE
FORTE
FORTEMENTE
FORTEPIANO
FORTES
FORTESCUE
FORTESCURE
FORTH
FORTHBRING
FORTHBRINGER
FORTHBRINGING
FORTHBROUGHT
FORTHBY
FORTHCALL
FORTHCAME
FORTHCOME
FORTHCOMER
FORTHCOMING
FORTHFARE
FORTHGAZE
FORTHGO
FORTHGOING
FORTHINK
FORTHINKING
FORTHON
FORTHOUGHT
FORTHPUTTING
FORTHRIGHT
FORTHRIGHTLY
FORTHRIGHTNESS
FORTHRIGHTS
FORTHSET
FORTHTELL
FORTHTELLER
FORTHWARD
FORTHWITH
FORTHY
FORTIES
FORTIETH
FORTIFIABLE
FORTIFICATION
FORTIFICATIONS
FORTIFIED
FORTIFIER
FORTIFY
FORTIFYING
FORTIFYINGLY
FORTIN
FORTIS
FORTISSIMI
FORTISSIMO
FORTISSIMOS
FORTITUDE
FORTITUDINOUS
FORTLET
FORTNIGHT
FORTNIGHTLY
FORTO
FORTRAVAIL
FORTREAD
FORTRESS
FORTRESSED
FORTRESSING
FORTUITIES
FORTUITISM
FORTUITIST
FORTUITOUS
FORTUITOUSLY
FORTUITOUSNESS
FORTUITY
FORTUNATE
FORTUNATELY
FORTUNATENESS
FORTUNATION
FORTUNE
FORTUNED
FORTUNEL
FORTUNETELL
FORTUNETELLER
FORTUNETELLING
FORTUNING
FORTUNITE
FORTY
FORUM
FORUMIZE
FORUMS
FORVAY
FORWAKE
FORWAKED
FORWALK
FORWANDER
FORWARD
FORWARDAL
FORWARDATION
FORWARDED
FORWARDER
FORWARDING
FORWARDLY
FORWARDNESS
FORWARDS
FORWARN
FORWASTE
FORWEAN
FORWEAR
FORWEARIED
FORWEARY
FORWEARYING
FORWEEND
FORWELK
FORWENT
FORWHY
FORWODEN
FORWORDEN
FORWORE
FORWORK
FORWORN
FORWRAP
FORYIELD
FORZANDO
FORZATO
FOSH
FOSS
FOSSA
FOSSAE
FOSSAGE
FOSSANE
FOSSARIAN
FOSSE
FOSSES
FOSSETTE
FOSSICK
FOSSICKED
FOSSICKER
FOSSICKING
FOSSIFIED
FOSSIFORM
FOSSIL
FOSSILAGE
FOSSILATED
FOSSILATION
FOSSILED
FOSSILFYING
FOSSILIFEROUS
FOSSILIFICATION
FOSSILIFY
FOSSILIST
FOSSILIZATION
FOSSILIZE
FOSSILIZED
FOSSILIZING
FOSSILOGIST
FOSSILOGY
FOSSILOLOGIST
FOSSILOLOGY
FOSSILS
FOSSOR
FOSSORES
FOSSORIAL
FOSSORIOUS
FOSSORS
FOSSULA
FOSSULAE
FOSSULATE
FOSSULE
FOSSULET
FOSTELL
FOSTER
FOSTERAGE
FOSTERED
FOSTERER
FOSTERING
FOSTERINGLY
FOSTERITE
FOSTERLAND
FOSTERLING
FOSTRESS
FOT
FOTCH
FOTCHED
FOTHER
FOTHERED
FOTHERING
FOTMAL
FOTUI
FOU
FOUCH
FOUD
FOUDROYANT
FOUETTE
FOUETTEE
FOUGADE
FOUGASSE
FOUGHT
FOUGHTEN
FOUGHTY
FOUGUE
FOUJDAR
FOUJDARRY
FOUJDARY
FOUL
FOULAGE
FOULARD
FOULDRE
FOULE
FOULED
FOULER
FOULEST
FOULING
FOULLY
FOULMART
FOULMOUTHED
FOULMOUTHEDLY
FOULMOUTHEDNESS
FOULNESS
FOULSOME
FOUMART
FOUN
FOUNCE
FOUND
FOUNDATION
FOUNDATIONAL
FOUNDATIONALLY
FOUNDATIONARY
FOUNDATIONER
FOUNDED
FOUNDER
FOUNDERED
FOUNDERING
FOUNDEROUS
FOUNDING
FOUNDLING
FOUNDRIES
FOUNDRY
FOUNDRYMAN
FOUNDRYMEN
FOUNT
FOUNTAIN
FOUNTAINED
FOUNTAINEER
FOUNTAINHEAD
FOUNTAINOUS
FOUNTAINOUSLY
FOUNTE
FOUNTFUL
FOUR
FOURB
FOURBE
FOURBLE
FOURCHE
FOURCHEE
FOURCHER
FOURCHET
FOURCHETTE
FOURCHITE
FOURER
FOURFLUSHER
FOURFOLD
FOURGON
FOURHANDED
FOURLING
FOURPENCE
FOURPENNY
FOURPOUNDER

FOURQUINE
FOURRAGERE
FOURRE
FOURRIER
FOURS
FOURSCORE
FOURSCORTH
FOURSOME
FOURSQUARE
FOURSQUARELY
FOURSQUARENESS
FOURSTRAND
FOURTEEN
FOURTEENER
FOURTEENTH
FOURTEENTHLY
FOURTH
FOURTHER
FOURTHLY
FOUSSA
FOUTE
FOUTER
FOUTH
FOUTRA
FOUTRE
FOUTY
FOVEA
FOVEAE
FOVEAL
FOVEATE
FOVEATED
FOVEATION
FOVEIFORM
FOVENT
FOVEOLA
FOVEOLAE
FOVEOLARIOUS
FOVEOLATE
FOVEOLATED
FOVEOLE
FOVEOLET
FOW
FOWD
FOWL
FOWLED
FOWLER
FOWLERITE
FOWLERY
FOWLFOOT
FOWLING
FOWLS
FOX
FOXBANE
FOXBERRIES
FOXBERRY
FOXCHOP
FOXED
FOXER
FOXERY
FOXES
FOXFEET
FOXFIRE
FOXFISH
FOXGLOVE
FOXHOLE
FOXHOUND
FOXIER
FOXIEST
FOXILY
FOXINESS
FOXING
FOXISH
FOXLIKE
FOXSKIN
FOXTAIL
FOXTAILED
FOXTROT
FOXY
FOY
FOYAITE
FOYAITIC
FOYBOAT
FOYER
FOYLE
FOZE
FOZINESS
FOZY
FRA
FRAB
FRABBIT
FRABJOUS
FRABJOUSLY
FRABOUS
FRACAS
FRACASES
FRACEDINOUS
FRACHE
FRACID
FRACK
FRACT
FRACTABLE
FRACTABLING
FRACTED
FRACTILE
FRACTION
FRACTIONAL
FRACTIONALISM
FRACTIONALIZE
FRACTIONALLY
FRACTIONARY
FRACTIONATE
FRACTIONATED
FRACTIONATING
FRACTIONATION
FRACTIONATOR
FRACTIONED
FRACTIONING
FRACTIONIZATION
FRACTIONIZE
FRACTIONIZED
FRACTIONIZING
FRACTIOUS
FRACTIOUSLY
FRACTIOUSNESS
FRACTUOSITY
FRACTUR
FRACTURAL
FRACTURE
FRACTURED
FRACTURING
FRADICIN
FRAE
FRAENA
FRAENULAR
FRAENULUM
FRAENUM
FRAENUMS
FRAG
FRAGE
FRAGGING
FRAGHAN
FRAGILE
FRAGILELY
FRAGILENESS
FRAGILITIES
FRAGILITY
FRAGMENT
FRAGMENTAL
FRAGMENTALLY
FRAGMENTARILY
FRAGMENTARINESS
FRAGMENTARY
FRAGMENTATION
FRAGMENTED
FRAGMENTIST
FRAGMENTITIOUS
FRAGMENTIZE
FRAGMENTS
FRAGOR
FRAGRANCE
FRAGRANCIES
FRAGRANCY
FRAGRANT
FRAGRANTLY
FRAGRANTNESS
FRAICHEUR
FRAID
FRAIK
FRAIL
FRAILE
FRAILEJON
FRAILER
FRAILES
FRAILEST
FRAILLY
FRAILNESS
FRAILTIES
FRAILTY
FRAIM
FRAIN
FRAISE
FRAISED
FRAISING
FRAIST
FRAKE
FRAM
FRAMBESIA
FRAMBOESIA
FRAME
FRAMEA
FRAMEAE
FRAMED
FRAMER
FRAMES
FRAMESMITH
FRAMEWORK
FRAMING
FRAMMIT
FRAMPLER
FRAMPOLD
FRANC
FRANCHISE
FRANCHISEMENT
FRANCHISER
FRANCISC
FRANCISCA
FRANCIUM
FRANCO
FRANCOLIN
FRANCOLITE
FRANGENT
FRANGIBILITY
FRANGIBLE
FRANGIBLENESS
FRANGIPANE
FRANGIPANI
FRANGULA
FRANGULIC
FRANGULIN
FRANGULINIC
FRANION
FRANK
FRANKALMOIGN
FRANKALMOIGNE
FRANKALMOIN
FRANKED
FRANKENIACEOUS
FRANKER
FRANKEST
FRANKFORT
FRANKFORTER
FRANKFURT
FRANKFURTER
FRANKHEARTED
FRANKHEARTEDLY
FRANKHEARTNESS
FRANKINCENSE
FRANKINCENSED
FRANKING
FRANKLANDITE
FRANKLIN
FRANKLINITE
FRANKLY
FRANKMARRIAGE
FRANKNESS
FRANKPLEDGE
FRANSERIA
FRANTIC
FRANTICALLY
FRANTICLY
FRANTICNESS
FRAP
FRAPE
FRAPLE
FRAPLER
FRAPPE
FRAPPED
FRAPPEED
FRAPPEING
FRAPPING
FRARY
FRASE
FRASER
FRASIER
FRASS
FRAT
FRATCH
FRATCHED
FRATCHEOUS
FRATCHER
FRATCHETY
FRATCHY
FRATE
FRATER
FRATERIES
FRATERNAL
FRATERNALISM
FRATERNALIST
FRATERNALITY
FRATERNALLY
FRATERNATE
FRATERNATION
FRATERNISM
FRATERNITIES
FRATERNITY
FRATERNIZATION
FRATERNIZE
FRATERNIZED
FRATERNIZER
FRATERNIZING
FRATERY
FRATI
FRATRICIDAL
FRATRICIDE
FRATRIES
FRATRY
FRAUD
FRAUDER
FRAUDFUL
FRAUDFULLY
FRAUDLESS
FRAUDLESSLY
FRAUDLESSNESS
FRAUDULENCE
FRAUDULENCY
FRAUDULENT
FRAUDULENTLY
FRAUDULENTNESS
FRAUEN
FRAUGHT
FRAUGHTED
FRAUGHTING
FRAUNCH
FRAVASHI
FRAWN
FRAXETIN
FRAXIN
FRAXINELLA
FRAY
FRAYED
FRAYING
FRAYN
FRAYNE
FRAZE
FRAZER
FRAZIL
FRAZZLE
FRAZZLED
FRAZZLING
FREAK
FREAKED
FREAKERY
FREAKFUL
FREAKIER
FREAKIEST
FREAKILY
FREAKINESS
FREAKING
FREAKISH
FREAKISHLY
FREAKISHNESS
FREAKPOT
FREAKY
FREAM
FREATH
FRECK
FRECKEN
FRECKET
FRECKLE
FRECKLED
FRECKLEDNESS
FRECKLING
FRECKLY
FREDAINE
FREDDO
FREDERIK
FREDRICITE
FREE
FREEBOARD
FREEBOOT
FREEBOOTED
FREEBOOTER
FREEBOOTERY
FREEBOOTING
FREEBOOTY
FREEBORN
FREED
FREEDMAN
FREEDMEN
FREEDOM
FREEDWOMAN
FREEDWOMEN
FREEHAND
FREEHANDED
FREEHANDEDLY
FREEHANDEDNESS
FREEHEARTED
FREEHOLD
FREEHOLDER
FREEHOLDING
FREEING
FREELAGE
FREELOAD
FREELOADER
FREELY

FREEMAN
FREEMARTIN
FREEMASON
FREEMASONIC
FREEMASONICAL
FREEMASONISM
FREEMASONS
FREEMEN
FREENESS
FREER
FREESIA
FREEST
FREESTANDING
FREESTONE
FREESTYLE
FREESTYLER
FREET
FREETHINKER
FREETHINKING
FREETRADER
FREETY
FREEWARD
FREEWAY
FREEWHEEL
FREEWHEELER
FREEWHEELING
FREEWILL
FREEWOMAN
FREEWOMEN
FREEZABLE
FREEZE
FREEZER
FREEZING
FREEZY
FREIBERGITE
FREIGHT
FREIGHTAGE
FREIGHTED
FREIGHTER
FREIGHTING
FREIJO
FREINAGE
FREIT
FREITH
FREITY
FREKE
FREM
FREMD
FREMDLY
FREMDNESS
FREMESCENCE
FREMESCENT
FREMITUS
FREMT
FRENA
FRENAL
FRENATE
FRENCHED
FRENCHEN
FRENCHIFY
FRENCHING
FRENETIC
FRENETICAL
FRENETICALLY
FRENNE
FRENULA
FRENULAR
FRENULUM
FRENUM
FRENUMS
FRENZIED
FRENZIEDLY
FRENZIES
FRENZILY
FRENZY
FRENZYING
FREQUENCE
FREQUENCIES
FREQUENCY
FREQUENT
FREQUENTABLE
FREQUENTAGE
FREQUENTATION
FREQUENTATIVE
FREQUENTED
FREQUENTER
FREQUENTING
FREQUENTLY
FREQUENTNESS
FRERE
FRERES
FRESCADE
FRESCO
FRESCOED
FRESCOER
FRESCOES
FRESCOING
FRESCOIST
FRESCOS
FRESE
FRESH
FRESHEN
FRESHENER
FRESHER
FRESHEST
FRESHET
FRESHHEARTED
FRESHING
FRESHLY
FRESHMAN
FRESHMANIC
FRESHMEN
FRESHNESS
FRESNE
FRESNEL
FRET
FRETA
FRETFUL
FRETFULLY
FRETFULNESS
FRETISH
FRETIZE
FRETSAW
FRETSOME
FRETT
FRETTAGE
FRETTATION
FRETTE
FRETTED
FRETTEN
FRETTER
FRETTIER
FRETTIEST
FRETTING
FRETTINGLY
FRETTY
FRETUM
FRETWORK
FRETWORKED
FREYALITE
FRIABILITY
FRIABLE
FRIABLENESS
FRIAND
FRIANDISE
FRIAR
FRIARBIRD
FRIARIES
FRIARLY
FRIARY
FRIATION
FRIB
FRIBBLE
FRIBBLED
FRIBBLER
FRIBBLERY
FRIBBLING
FRIBBY
FRIBORG
FRIBOURG
FRICACE
FRICANDEAU
FRICANDEAUX
FRICANDEL
FRICANDELLE
FRICANDO
FRICASSEE
FRICASSEED
FRICASSEEING
FRICATION
FRICATIVE
FRICATRICE
FRICK
FRICTION
FRICTIONAL
FRICTIONALLY
FRICTIONIZE
FRICTIONIZED
FRICTIONIZING
FRICTIONLESS
FRIDGE
FRIDSTOOL
FRIE
FRIED
FRIEDCAKE
FRIEDELITE
FRIEND
FRIENDED
FRIENDING
FRIENDLESS
FRIENDLESSNESS
FRIENDLIER
FRIENDLIES
FRIENDLIEST
FRIENDLILY
FRIENDLINESS
FRIENDLY
FRIENDS
FRIENDSHIP
FRIER
FRIESEITE
FRIEZE
FRIEZED
FRIEZER
FRIEZING
FRIEZY
FRIG
FRIGATE
FRIGATOON
FRIGGLE
FRIGHT
FRIGHTED
FRIGHTEN
FRIGHTENED
FRIGHTENEDLY
FRIGHTENEDNESS
FRIGHTENER
FRIGHTENING
FRIGHTENINGLY
FRIGHTER
FRIGHTFUL
FRIGHTFULLY
FRIGHTFULNESS
FRIGHTING
FRIGHTSOME
FRIGHTY
FRIGID
FRIGIDARIA
FRIGIDARIUM
FRIGIDITIES
FRIGIDITY
FRIGIDLY
FRIGIDNESS
FRIGIFEROUS
FRIGO
FRIGOLABILE
FRIGOR
FRIGORIC
FRIGORIFIC
FRIGORIFICAL
FRIGORIFICO
FRIGORIFY
FRIGORIMETER
FRIGOSTABLE
FRIGOTHERAPY
FRIJOL
FRIJOLE
FRIJOLES
FRIJOLILLO
FRIKE
FRILAL
FRILL
FRILLBACK
FRILLED
FRILLER
FRILLERY
FRILLIER
FRILLIES
FRILLIEST
FRILLILY
FRILLINESS
FRILLING
FRILLY
FRIM
FRIMITTS
FRINGE
FRINGED
FRINGEFLOWER
FRINGEFOOT
FRINGENT
FRINGEPOD
FRINGES
FRINGIER
FRINGIEST
FRINGILLACEOUS
FRINGILLINE
FRINGILLOID
FRINGING
FRINGY
FRIPPER
FRIPPERER
FRIPPERIES
FRIPPERY
FRISADO
FRISCA
FRISCAL
FRISCH
FRISCO
FRISE
FRISETTE
FRISEUR
FRISK
FRISKER
FRISKEST
FRISKET
FRISKFUL
FRISKIER
FRISKIEST
FRISKILY
FRISKIN
FRISKINESS
FRISKING
FRISKINGLY
FRISKLE
FRISKY
FRISOLEE
FRISON
FRISS
FRISSON
FRIST
FRISURE
FRISZKA
FRIT
FRITH
FRITHBORGH
FRITHBORH
FRITHBOT
FRITHLES
FRITHSOKEN
FRITHSTOOL
FRITHWORK
FRITHY
FRITILLARIES
FRITILLARY
FRITT
FRITTATA
FRITTED
FRITTER
FRITTERED
FRITTERER
FRITTERING
FRITTERS
FRITTING
FRIVOL
FRIVOLED
FRIVOLER
FRIVOLISM
FRIVOLITIES
FRIVOLITY
FRIVOLIZE
FRIVOLIZED
FRIVOLIZING
FRIVOLLED
FRIVOLLER
FRIVOLOUS
FRIVOLOUSLY
FRIVOLOUSNESS
FRIZ
FRIZADO
FRIZE
FRIZEL
FRIZER
FRIZETTE
FRIZZ
FRIZZED
FRIZZEN
FRIZZER
FRIZZES
FRIZZIER
FRIZZIEST
FRIZZILY
FRIZZINESS
FRIZZING
FRIZZLE
FRIZZLED
FRIZZLER
FRIZZLING
FRIZZLY
FRIZZY
FRO
FROCK
FROCKING
FROCKMAKER
FROE
FROEMAN
FROG
FROGBIT
FROGEATER
FROGEYE
FROGFACE
FROGFISH
FROGFISHES
FROGFLOWER
FROGFOOT
FROGGED

FROGGER
FROGGERY
FROGGIER
FROGGIES
FROGGIEST
FROGGINESS
FROGGING
FROGGISH
FROGGY
FROGHOPPER
FROGLAND
FROGLEAF
FROGLET
FROGMAN
FROGMEN
FROGMOUTH
FROGNOSE
FROGS
FROGSKIN
FROGSTOOL
FROGTONGUE
FROGWORT
FROHLICH
FROIDEUR
FROISE
FROISSE
FROKIN
FROLIC
FROLICFUL
FROLICKED
FROLICKER
FROLICKING
FROLICKY
FROLICLY
FROLICNESS
FROLICSOME
FROLICSOMELY
FROLICSOMENESS
FROM
FROMAGE
FROMENTY
FROMWARD
FROMWARDS
FROND
FRONDAGE
FRONDED
FRONDENT
FRONDESCE
FRONDESCED
FRONDESCENCE
FRONDESCENT
FRONDESCING
FRONDIFEROUS
FRONDIFORM
FRONDIGEROUS
FRONDIVOROUS
FRONDLET
FRONDOSE
FRONDOSELY
FRONDOUS
FRONS
FRONT
FRONTAD
FRONTAGE
FRONTAGER
FRONTAL
FRONTALIS
FRONTALITY
FRONTED
FRONTER
FRONTES
FRONTIER
FRONTIERMAN
FRONTIERSMAN
FRONTIERSMEN
FRONTING
FRONTIS
FRONTISPIECE
FRONTISPIECED
FRONTISPIECING
FRONTLESS
FRONTLESSLY
FRONTLESSNESS
FRONTLET
FRONTOLYSIS
FRONTOMALAR
FRONTOMENTAL
FRONTON
FRONTONASAL
FRONTPIECE
FRONTSMAN
FRONTSTALL
FRONTURE
FROOM
FROPPISH
FRORE
FROREN
FRORY
FROSH
FROSK
FROST
FROSTATION
FROSTBIRD
FROSTBIT
FROSTBITE
FROSTBITING
FROSTBITTEN
FROSTBOW
FROSTED
FROSTER
FROSTFISH
FROSTFISHES
FROSTFLOWER
FROSTIER
FROSTIEST
FROSTILY
FROSTINESS
FROSTING
FROSTLESS
FROSTPROOFING
FROSTROOT
FROSTWEED
FROSTWORK
FROSTY
FROT
FROTH
FROTHED
FROTHER
FROTHIER
FROTHIEST
FROTHILY
FROTHINESS
FROTHING
FROTHY
FROTTAGE
FROTTED
FROTTING
FROTTOLA
FROTTON
FROUD
FROUFROU
FROUGH
FROUGHY
FROUNCE
FROUNCED
FROUNCING
FROUST
FROUSTY
FROUZE
FROUZY
FROW
FROWARD
FROWARDLY
FROWARDNESS
FROWER
FROWL
FROWN
FROWNED
FROWNER
FROWNING
FROWNY
FROWST
FROWSTIER
FROWSTIEST
FROWSTY
FROWSY
FROWY
FROWZE
FROWZIER
FROWZIEST
FROWZILY
FROWZINESS
FROWZLED
FROWZY
FROZE
FROZEN
FROZENLY
FROZENNESS
FRUB
FRUBBISH
FRUCTED
FRUCTESCENCE
FRUCTESCENT
FRUCTICULTURAL
FRUCTIFEROUS
FRUCTIFIED
FRUCTIFIER
FRUCTIFORM
FRUCTIFY
FRUCTIFYING
FRUCTIPAROUS
FRUCTIVOROUS
FRUCTOSE
FRUCTOSIDE
FRUCTUARIUS
FRUCTUOSE
FRUCTUOSITY
FRUCTUOUS
FRUCTUOUSLY
FRUCTUOUSNESS
FRUGAL
FRUGALISM
FRUGALIST
FRUGALITIES
FRUGALITY
FRUGALLY
FRUGALNESS
FRUGGAN
FRUGGIN
FRUGIFEROUS
FRUGIFEROUSNESS
FRUGIVOROUS
FRUIT
FRUITADE
FRUITAGE
FRUITARIAN
FRUITARIANISM
FRUITCAKE
FRUITED
FRUITER
FRUITERER
FRUITERESS
FRUITERIES
FRUITERY
FRUITFUL
FRUITFULLY
FRUITFULNESS
FRUITGROWER
FRUITGROWING
FRUITIER
FRUITIEST
FRUITINESS
FRUITING
FRUITION
FRUITIST
FRUITIVE
FRUITLESS
FRUITLESSLY
FRUITLESSNESS
FRUITLET
FRUITS
FRUITSTALK
FRUITTIME
FRUITWISE
FRUITWOMAN
FRUITWOMEN
FRUITWORM
FRUITY
FRUM
FRUMARYL
FRUMENT
FRUMENTATION
FRUMENTUM
FRUMENTY
FRUMETY
FRUMP
FRUMPERIES
FRUMPERY
FRUMPIER
FRUMPIEST
FRUMPILY
FRUMPINESS
FRUMPISH
FRUMPISHLY
FRUMPISHNESS
FRUMPLE
FRUMPLED
FRUMPLING
FRUMPS
FRUMPY
FRUNDEL
FRUSH
FRUST
FRUSTA
FRUSTRANEOUS
FRUSTRATE
FRUSTRATED
FRUSTRATELY
FRUSTRATER
FRUSTRATES
FRUSTRATING
FRUSTRATION
FRUSTRATIVE
FRUSTRATORY
FRUSTULE
FRUSTULENT
FRUSTULOSE
FRUSTUM
FRUSTUMS
FRUTESCENCE
FRUTESCENT
FRUTEX
FRUTICES
FRUTICETA
FRUTICETUM
FRUTICOSE
FRUTICOUS
FRUTICULOSE
FRUTICULTURE
FRUTIFY
FRUTILLA
FRY
FRYER
FRYING
FRYPAN
FU
FUANG
FUB
FUBBERY
FUBBY
FUBSIER
FUBSIEST
FUBSY
FUCACEOUS
FUCATE
FUCATION
FUCATIOUS
FUCHSIA
FUCHSIN
FUCHSINE
FUCHSINOPHIL
FUCHSITE
FUCHSONE
FUCI
FUCINITA
FUCIPHAGOUS
FUCIVOROUS
FUCOID
FUCOIDAL
FUCOIDIN
FUCOSAN
FUCOSE
FUCOUS
FUCOXANTHIN
FUCUS
FUCUSED
FUCUSES
FUD
FUDDLE
FUDDLED
FUDDLER
FUDDLING
FUDER
FUDGE
FUDGED
FUDGER
FUDGING
FUDGY
FUEL
FUELED
FUELER
FUELING
FUELIZER
FUELLED
FUELLER
FUELLING
FUERO
FUERTE
FUFF
FUFFIT
FUFFLE
FUFFY
FUG
FUGA
FUGACIOUS
FUGACIOUSLY
FUGACIOUSNESS
FUGACITIES
FUGACITY
FUGACY
FUGAL
FUGALLY
FUGARA
FUGATO
FUGGY
FUGI
FUGIE
FUGIENT
FUGITATE
FUGITATED
FUGITATING
FUGITATION
FUGITIVE
FUGITIVELY
FUGITIVENESS

FUGITIVITY
FUGLE
FUGLED
FUGLEMAN
FUGLEMEN
FUGLER
FUGLING
FUGU
FUGUE
FUGUIST
FUIDHIR
FUIRDAYS
FUJI
FULCIFORM
FULCRA
FULCRAL
FULCRATE
FULCRUM
FULCRUMAGE
FULCRUMED
FULCRUMING
FULCRUMS
FULFIL
FULFILL
FULFILLED
FULFILLER
FULFILLING
FULFILLMENT
FULFILMENT
FULGENCE
FULGENCY
FULGENT
FULGENTLY
FULGENTNESS
FULGID
FULGIDE
FULGIDITY
FULGOR
FULGORID
FULGOROUS
FULGOUR
FULGOUROUS
FULGURAL
FULGURANT
FULGURANTLY
FULGURATA
FULGURATE
FULGURATED
FULGURATING
FULGURATION
FULGURITE
FULGUROUS
FULHAM
FULICINE
FULIGINOSITY
FULIGINOUS
FULIGINOUSLY
FULIGINOUSNESS
FULIGULINE
FULK
FULL
FULLAM
FULLBACK
FULLDO
FULLED
FULLER
FULLERBOARD
FULLERED
FULLERIES
FULLERING
FULLERY
FULLFACE
FULLHEARTED
FULLING
FULLMOUTH
FULLMOUTHED
FULLMOUTHEDLY
FULLNESS
FULLOM
FULLY
FULMAR
FULMEN
FULMINA
FULMINANCY
FULMINANT
FULMINATE
FULMINATED
FULMINATING
FULMINATION
FULMINATOR
FULMINATORY
FULMINE
FULMINED
FULMINEOUS
FULMINING
FULMINOUS
FULMINURATE
FULMINURIC
FULNESS
FULSOME
FULSOMELY
FULSOMENESS
FULTH
FULTZ
FULVENE
FULVESCENT
FULVID
FULVIDNESS
FULVOUS
FULWA
FULYIE
FULZIE
FUM
FUMACIOUS
FUMADO
FUMADOS
FUMAGE
FUMAGINE
FUMARASE
FUMARATE
FUMARIA
FUMARIC
FUMARINE
FUMARIUM
FUMAROID
FUMAROIDAL
FUMAROLE
FUMAROLIC
FUMATORIA
FUMATORIES
FUMATORIUM
FUMATORIUMS
FUMATORY
FUMBA
FUMBLE
FUMBLED
FUMBLER
FUMBLING
FUMBULATOR
FUME
FUMED
FUMER
FUMEROOT
FUMET
FUMETTE
FUMEWORT
FUMID
FUMIDITY
FUMIDUCT
FUMIER
FUMIEST
FUMIFEROUS
FUMIGANT
FUMIGATE
FUMIGATED
FUMIGATING
FUMIGATION
FUMIGATOR
FUMIGATORIES
FUMIGATORY
FUMILY
FUMINESS
FUMING
FUMINGLY
FUMISH
FUMISHLY
FUMISHNESS
FUMISTERY
FUMITORIES
FUMITORY
FUMMEL
FUMMLE
FUMOSE
FUMOSITY
FUMOUS
FUMOUSLY
FUMULI
FUMULUS
FUMY
FUN
FUNA
FUNAMBULATE
FUNAMBULATED
FUNAMBULATING
FUNAMBULATION
FUNAMBULATORY
FUNAMBULIC
FUNAMBULISM
FUNAMBULIST
FUNAMBULO
FUNAMBULOES
FUNCTION
FUNCTIONAL
FUNCTIONALISM
FUNCTIONALIST
FUNCTIONALITY
FUNCTIONALIZE
FUNCTIONALIZED
FUNCTIONALIZIN
FUNCTIONALLY
FUNCTIONARIES
FUNCTIONARISM
FUNCTIONARY
FUNCTIONATE
FUNCTIONATED
FUNCTIONATING
FUNCTIONATION
FUNCTIONED
FUNCTIONING
FUNCTIONIZE
FUNCTIONLESS
FUNCTOR
FUND
FUNDA
FUNDAL
FUNDAMENT
FUNDAMENTAL
FUNDAMENTALISM
FUNDAMENTALIST
FUNDAMENTALITY
FUNDAMENTALLY
FUNDATORIAL
FUNDATRICES
FUNDATRIX
FUNDED
FUNDER
FUNDHOLDER
FUNDI
FUNDIC
FUNDIFORM
FUNDING
FUNDITOR
FUNDITORES
FUNDMONGER
FUNDMONGERING
FUNDO
FUNDS
FUNDUCK
FUNDULINE
FUNDUS
FUNEBRE
FUNEBRIAL
FUNEBRIOUS
FUNEBROUS
FUNERAL
FUNERALIZE
FUNERALLY
FUNERALS
FUNERARY
FUNERATE
FUNERATION
FUNEREAL
FUNEREALLY
FUNEST
FUNESTAL
FUNFEST
FUNGACEOUS
FUNGAL
FUNGATE
FUNGATED
FUNGATING
FUNGE
FUNGI
FUNGIAN
FUNGIBILITY
FUNGIBLE
FUNGIC
FUNGICIDAL
FUNGICIDE
FUNGID
FUNGIFORM
FUNGIFY
FUNGILLIFORM
FUNGIN
FUNGISTAT
FUNGISTATIC
FUNGO
FUNGOES
FUNGOID
FUNGOIDAL
FUNGOLOGICAL
FUNGOLOGIST
FUNGOLOGY
FUNGOSE
FUNGOSITY
FUNGOUS
FUNGUS
FUNGUSED
FUNGUSES
FUNGUSY
FUNICLE
FUNICULAR
FUNICULATE
FUNICULI
FUNICULITIS
FUNICULUS
FUNIFORM
FUNIS
FUNK
FUNKED
FUNKER
FUNKIER
FUNKIEST
FUNKINESS
FUNKING
FUNKY
FUNMAKER
FUNNED
FUNNEL
FUNNELED
FUNNELFORM
FUNNELING
FUNNELLED
FUNNELLIKE
FUNNELLING
FUNNIER
FUNNIES
FUNNIEST
FUNNILY
FUNNIMENT
FUNNINESS
FUNNING
FUNNY
FUNNYMAN
FUNNYMEN
FUNORI
FUNORIN
FUNSTER
FUNT
FUR
FURACANA
FURACIOUS
FURACIOUSNESS
FURACITY
FURAL
FURAN
FURANE
FURANOSE
FURBEARER
FURBELOW
FURBELOWED
FURBELOWING
FURBISH
FURBISHED
FURBISHER
FURBISHING
FURCA
FURCAE
FURCAL
FURCATE
FURCATED
FURCATELY
FURCATING
FURCATION
FURCELLATE
FURCIFERINE
FURCIFEROUS
FURCIFORM
FURCILIA
FURCRAEA
FURCULA
FURCULAE
FURCULAR
FURCULE
FURCULUM
FURDEL
FURDLE
FURE
FURFUR
FURFURACEOUS
FURFURAL
FURFURAMID
FURFURAMIDE
FURFURAN
FURFURATION
FURFURES
FURFURINE
FURFUROID
FURFUROL
FURFUROLE
FURFUROUS
FURFURYL
FURIAL
FURIANT
FURIBUND

FURICANE
FURIED
FURIES
FURIFY
FURIL
FURILE
FURILIC
FURIOSO
FURIOUS
FURIOUSITY
FURIOUSLY
FURIOUSNESS
FURISON
FURL
FURLANA
FURLED
FURLER
FURLING
FURLONG
FURLOUGH
FURLOUGHED
FURLOUGHING
FURMENTY
FURMETY
FURMITY
FURNACE
FURNACED
FURNACEMAN
FURNACEMEN
FURNACER
FURNACING
FURNACITE
FURNAGE
FURNER
FURNISH
FURNISHED
FURNISHER
FURNISHING
FURNISHINGS
FURNISHMENT
FURNISHNESS
FURNITURE
FUROATE
FUROID
FUROIN
FUROL
FUROLE
FUROMONAZOLE
FUROR
FURORE
FURPHY
FURR
FURRED
FURRIER
FURRIERED
FURRIERIES
FURRIERY
FURRIEST
FURRILY
FURRINESS
FURRING
FURROW
FURROWED
FURROWER
FURROWING
FURROWS
FURROWY
FURRURE
FURRY
FURS
FURTHER
FURTHERANCE
FURTHERED
FURTHERER
FURTHERING
FURTHERLY
FURTHERMORE
FURTHERMOST
FURTHERSOME
FURTHEST
FURTHY
FURTIVE
FURTIVELY
FURTIVENESS
FURTUM
FURUNCLE
FURUNCULAR
FURUNCULOID
FURUNCULOSIS
FURUNCULOUS
FURWA
FURY
FURYL
FURZE
FURZECHAT
FURZED
FURZERY
FURZETOP
FURZY
FUSAIN
FUSARIAL
FUSARIOSE
FUSARIOSIS
FUSAROLE
FUSATE
FUSC
FUSCESCENT
FUSCIN
FUSCOHYALINE
FUSCOUS
FUSE
FUSEAU
FUSEBOARD
FUSED
FUSEE
FUSEL
FUSELAGE
FUSEPLUG
FUSIBILITY
FUSIBLE
FUSIBLENESS
FUSIBLY
FUSIFORM
FUSIL
FUSILADED
FUSILADING
FUSILE
FUSILEER
FUSILIER
FUSILLADE
FUSILLY
FUSING
FUSINIST
FUSINITE
FUSION
FUSIONAL
FUSIONISM
FUSIONIST
FUSIONLESS
FUSOID
FUSS
FUSSED
FUSSER
FUSSIER
FUSSIEST
FUSSIFICATION
FUSSIFY
FUSSILY
FUSSINESS
FUSSING
FUSSLE
FUSSOCK
FUSSY
FUST
FUSTANELLA
FUSTANELLE
FUSTEE
FUSTER
FUSTERIC
FUSTET
FUSTIAN
FUSTIANIST
FUSTIC
FUSTIE
FUSTIER
FUSTIEST
FUSTIGATE
FUSTIGATED
FUSTIGATING
FUSTIGATION
FUSTIGATOR
FUSTIGATORY
FUSTILUGS
FUSTILY
FUSTIN
FUSTINESS
FUSTLE
FUSTOC
FUSTY
FUSULA
FUSUMA
FUSURE
FUT
FUTCHEL
FUTCHELL
FUTE
FUTHARC
FUTHARK
FUTHORC
FUTHORK
FUTILE
FUTILELY
FUTILENESS
FUTILITARIAN
FUTILITIES
FUTILITY
FUTILOUS
FUTTAH
FUTTER
FUTTERET
FUTTOCK
FUTURAL
FUTURAMA
FUTURE
FUTURELESS
FUTURELY
FUTURISM
FUTURIST
FUTURISTIC
FUTURITIES
FUTURITION
FUTURITY
FUTWA
FUYE
FUZE
FUZEE
FUZIL
FUZZ
FUZZBALL
FUZZIER
FUZZIEST
FUZZILY
FUZZINESS
FUZZLE
FUZZTAIL
FUZZY
FYCE
FYKE
FYLE
FYLFOT
FYLGJA
FYLGJUR
FYLKE
FYLKER
FYND
FYRD
FYRDUNG

G

GA
GAAL
GAATCH
GAB
GABARDINE
GABARI
GABARIT
GABBACK
GABBAI
GABBARD
GABBART
GABBED
GABBER
GABBIER
GABBIEST
GABBING
GABBLE
GABBLED
GABBLEMENT
GABBLER
GABBLING
GABBRO
GABBROIC
GABBROID
GABBROITIC
GABBROS
GABBY
GABE
GABELER
GABELLE
GABELLED
GABELLEMAN
GABELLER
GABERDINE
GABERLUNZIE
GABGAB
GABI
GABION
GABIONADE
GABIONAGE
GABIONED
GABLATORES
GABLE
GABLEBOARD
GABLET
GABLEWISE
GABLOCK
GABY
GACHUPIN
GAD
GADABOUT
GADBEE
GADBUSH
GADDED
GADDER
GADDI
GADDING
GADDINGLY
GADDISH
GADDISHNESS
GADE
GADES
GADFLY
GADGE
GADGER
GADGET
GADGETRY
GADHI
GADID
GADININE
GADLING
GADMAN
GADOID
GADOLINIA
GADOLINIC
GADOLINITE
GADOLINIUM
GADROON
GADROONAGE
GADSMAN
GADUIN
GADWALL
GADWELL
GAE
GAED
GAEDOWN
GAET
GAFF
GAFFE
GAFFED
GAFFER
GAFFING
GAFFLE
GAFFLET
GAFFSAIL
GAFFSMAN
GAG
GAGA
GAGATE
GAGE
GAGED
GAGEE
GAGEITE
GAGEL
GAGER
GAGES
GAGGED
GAGGER
GAGGERY
GAGGING
GAGGLE
GAGGLED
GAGGLER
GAGGLING
GAGING
GAGMAN
GAGOR
GAGROOT
GAGTOOTH
GAHE
GAHNITE
GAIAC
GAIASSA
GAIETY
GAIG
GAIL
GAILLARD
GAILY
GAIN
GAINAGE
GAINBIRTH
GAINCALL
GAINCOME
GAINCOPE
GAINE
GAINED
GAINER
GAINFUL
GAINFULLY
GAINFULNESS
GAINGIVING
GAINING
GAINLESS
GAINLINESS
GAINLY
GAINOR
GAINPAIN
GAINS
GAINSAY
GAINSAYER
GAINSET
GAINSOME
GAINSPEAKER
GAINSPEAKING
GAINST
GAINSTAND
GAINSTRIVE
GAINTURN
GAINTWIST
GAINWARD
GAINYIELD
GAIR
GAIRFISH
GAIRFOWL
GAIST
GAIT
GAITED
GAITER
GAITING
GAITT
GAIZE
GAJO
GAL
GALA
GALABEAH
GALABIA
GALABIEH
GALACTAGOG
GALACTAGOGUE
GALACTAN
GALACTASE
GALACTEMIA
GALACTIC
GALACTIN
GALACTITE
GALACTOCELE
GALACTOGOGUE
GALACTOHEMIA
GALACTOID
GALACTOLYSIS
GALACTOLYTIC
GALACTOMETER
GALACTONIC
GALACTOPATHY
GALACTOPHORE
GALACTOPYRA
GALACTOSCOPE
GALACTOSE
GALACTOSIDE
GALACTOSIS
GALACTOSURIA
GALACTURIA
GALAGALA
GALAH
GALANAS
GALANGAL
GALANGIN
GALANT
GALANTE
GALANTINE
GALAPAGO
GALATEA
GALAVANT
GALAXIAN
GALAXY
GALBAN
GALBANUM
GALBE
GALBULUS
GALD
GALE
GALEA
GALEAE
GALEAGE
GALEATE
GALEATED
GALECHE
GALEE
GALEENY
GALEGINE
GALEID
GALEIFORM
GALEMPONG
GALENA
GALENIC
GALENICAL
GALENITE
GALENOID
GALEOID
GALERA
GALERICULATE
GALERIE
GALERUM
GALERUS
GALESAUR
GALET
GALETTE
GALEWORT
GALGAL
GALI
GALIANES
GALILEE
GALIMATIAS
GALINGALE
GALIONGEE
GALIONJI
GALIOT
GALIPOT
GALIVANT
GALJOEN
GALL
GALLA
GALLACH
GALLAH
GALLANILIDE
GALLANT
GALLANTLY
GALLANTNESS
GALLANTRY
GALLATE
GALLATURE
GALLBERRY
GALLBUSH
GALLEASS
GALLED
GALLEIN
GALLEINE
GALLEON
GALLER
GALLERA
GALLERIAN
GALLERIES
GALLERY
GALLET
GALLETA
GALLEY
GALLEYMAN
GALLEYS
GALLEYWORM
GALLFLOWER
GALLFLY
GALLIAMBIC
GALLIAMBUS
GALLIARD
GALLIARDISE
GALLIARDLY
GALLIARDNESS
GALLIASS
GALLIC
GALLICIZER
GALLICOLA
GALLICOLOUS
GALLIFEROUS
GALLIFORM
GALLIGASKIN
GALLIGASKINS
GALLIMAUFRY
GALLINACEAN
GALLINACEOUS
GALLINAZO
GALLINE
GALLINEY
GALLING
GALLINGLY
GALLINGNESS
GALLINIPPER
GALLINULE
GALLINULINE
GALLIOT
GALLIPOT
GALLISH
GALLIUM
GALLIVANT
GALLIVANTER
GALLIVAT
GALLIVOROUS
GALLIWASP
GALLIZE
GALLNUT
GALLOFLAVIN
GALLOFLAVINE
GALLOGLASS
GALLON
GALLONAGE
GALLOON
GALLOONED
GALLOOT
GALLOP
GALLOPADE
GALLOPED
GALLOPER
GALLOPING
GALLOPTIOUS
GALLOTANNATE
GALLOTANNIN
GALLOUS
GALLOW
GALLOWAY
GALLOWGLASS
GALLOWS
GALLOWSNESS
GALLSTONE
GALLUSES
GALLWEED
GALLWORT
GALLY
GALLYBAGGER
GALLYBEGGAR
GALLYCROW
GALLYGASKINS
GALLYWASP
GALON
GALOOT
GALOP
GALOPADE
GALOPED
GALOPIN
GALOPING
GALORE
GALOSH
GALOSHE
GALOUBET
GALP
GALRAVAGE
GALRAVITCH

GALT
GALTRAP
GALUCHAT
GALUMPH
GALUMPTIOUS
GALUT
GALUTH
GALVANIC
GALVANICAL
GALVANICALLY
GALVANISE
GALVANISM
GALVANIST
GALVANIZATION
GALVANIZE
GALVANIZED
GALVANIZER
GALVANIZING
GALVANOGRAPH
GALVANOLOGY
GALVANOMETER
GALVANOMETRY
GALVANOSCOPE
GALVANOSCOPY
GALVANOTAXIS
GALVAYNE
GALVAYNED
GALVAYNING
GALYAC
GALYAK
GAM
GAMAHE
GAMARI
GAMASHES
GAMB
GAMBA
GAMBADE
GAMBADO
GAMBANG
GAMBE
GAMBEER
GAMBEERED
GAMBEERING
GAMBESON
GAMBET
GAMBETTE
GAMBIAE
GAMBIER
GAMBIR
GAMBIST
GAMBIT
GAMBLE
GAMBLED
GAMBLER
GAMBLERS
GAMBLING
GAMBO
GAMBOGE
GAMBOGIAN
GAMBOISED
GAMBOL
GAMBOLED
GAMBOLING
GAMBOLLED
GAMBOLLING
GAMBONE
GAMBREL
GAMBRELED
GAMBRELLED
GAMBROON
GAMDEBOO
GAME
GAMEBAG
GAMEBALL
GAMECOCK
GAMECRAFT
GAMED
GAMEFUL
GAMEKEEPER
GAMEKEEPING
GAMELAN
GAMELANG
GAMELIN
GAMELOTE
GAMELOTTE
GAMELY
GAMENE
GAMENESS
GAMER
GAMES
GAMESOME
GAMESOMELY
GAMESOMENESS
GAMEST
GAMESTER
GAMETAL
GAMETANGIUM
GAMETE
GAMETIC
GAMETICALLY
GAMETOCYST
GAMETOCYTE
GAMETOGENIC
GAMETOGENOUS
GAMETOGENY
GAMETOGONIUM
GAMETOID
GAMETOPHORE
GAMETOPHYLL
GAMETOPHYTE
GAMEY
GAMIC
GAMIE
GAMIER
GAMIEST
GAMILY
GAMIN
GAMINE
GAMINESS
GAMING
GAMLA
GAMMA
GAMMACISM
GAMMADION
GAMMARID
GAMMAROID
GAMMATION
GAMME
GAMMELOST
GAMMER
GAMMERSTANG
GAMMICK
GAMMOCK
GAMMON
GAMMONER
GAMMONING
GAMMY
GAMOBIUM
GAMODEME
GAMODESMIC
GAMODESMY
GAMOGAMY
GAMOGENESIS
GAMOGENETIC
GAMOGENY
GAMOND
GAMONT
GAMOPETALOUS
GAMOPHAGIA
GAMOPHYLLOUS
GAMORI
GAMOSEPALOUS
GAMOSTELE
GAMOSTELIC
GAMOSTELY
GAMP
GAMPHREL
GAMUT
GAMY
GAN
GANAM
GANANCIAL
GANANCIALES
GANANCIAS
GANCH
GANCHED
GANCHING
GANDER
GANDERESS
GANDERGOOSE
GANDERMOONER
GANDERTEETH
GANDI
GANDOURA
GANDUL
GANDUM
GANDURAH
GANE
GANEF
GANG
GANGA
GANGAVA
GANGBOARD
GANGE
GANGED
GANGER
GANGEREL
GANGFLOWER
GANGGANG
GANGING
GANGION
GANGLAND
GANGLANDER
GANGLIA
GANGLIAC
GANGLIAL
GANGLIAR
GANGLIATE
GANGLIATED
GANGLIFORM
GANGLING
GANGLIOBLAST
GANGLIOCYTE
GANGLIOFORM
GANGLIOMA
GANGLIOMAS
GANGLIOMATA
GANGLION
GANGLIONARY
GANGLIONATE
GANGLIONATED
GANGLIONIC
GANGLIONITIS
GANGLIONS
GANGLY
GANGMAN
GANGMASTER
GANGPLANK
GANGPLOW
GANGREL
GANGRENATE
GANGRENE
GANGRENED
GANGRENING
GANGRENOUS
GANGSA
GANGSMAN
GANGSTER
GANGSTERISM
GANGTIDE
GANGUE
GANGWA
GANGWAY
GANGWAYMAN
GANGWAYMEN
GANISTER
GANJA
GANNER
GANNET
GANNETRY
GANNETS
GANOF
GANOID
GANOIDAL
GANOIDEAN
GANOIDIAN
GANOIN
GANOMALITE
GANOPHYLLITE
GANOSIS
GANSEL
GANSEY
GANSH
GANSY
GANT
GANTA
GANTANG
GANTANGS
GANTLET
GANTLETED
GANTLETING
GANTLINE
GANTLOPE
GANTRIES
GANTRY
GANTRYMAN
GANYIE
GANZA
GANZIE
GAOL
GAOLAGE
GAOLBIRD
GAOLER
GAOLERING
GAOLERNESS
GAOLORING
GAP
GAPE
GAPED
GAPER
GAPES
GAPESEED
GAPEWORM
GAPING
GAPINGSTOCK
GAPO
GAPPED
GAPPER
GAPPIER
GAPPIEST
GAPPING
GAPPY
GAPS
GAPY
GAR
GARABATO
GARAD
GARAGE
GARAGED
GARAGEMAN
GARAGING
GARANCE
GARANCIN
GARAPATA
GARAPATO
GARAU
GARAVA
GARAVANCE
GARAWI
GARB
GARBAGE
GARBANZO
GARBILL
GARBLE
GARBLED
GARBLER
GARBLING
GARBLINGS
GARBOARD
GARBOIL
GARBURE
GARCE
GARCON
GARD
GARDANT
GARDE
GARDEBRAS
GARDEEN
GARDEN
GARDENED
GARDENER
GARDENIN
GARDENING
GARDENIZE
GARDENS
GARDENY
GARDEROBE
GARDEVIANCE
GARDEVIN
GARDEVISURE
GARDINOL
GARDNAP
GARDON
GARDY
GARDYLOO
GARE
GAREFOWL
GAREH
GARETTA
GAREWAITE
GARFISH
GARFISHES
GARGANEY
GARGET
GARGETY
GARGIL
GARGLE
GARGLED
GARGLING
GARGOYLE
GARGOYLEY
GARIAL
GARIBA
GARIBALDI
GARIGUE
GARISH
GARISHLY
GARISHNESS
GARLAND
GARLANDAGE
GARLANDED
GARLANDING
GARLANDRY
GARLE
GARLIC
GARLICKY
GARLION
GARLOPA
GARMENT
GARMENTED
GARMENTING
GARMENTMAKER
GARMENTS
GARMENTURE
GARN

GARNEL
GARNER
GARNERED
GARNERING
GARNET
GARNETBERRY
GARNETER
GARNETT
GARNETWORK
GARNETZ
GARNI
GARNIEC
GARNIERITE
GARNISH
GARNISHED
GARNISHEE
GARNISHEED
GARNISHEEING
GARNISHER
GARNISHING
GARNISHMENT
GARNISHRY
GARNITURE
GAROO
GAROOKUH
GAROTE
GAROTTE
GAROTTED
GAROTTER
GARPIKE
GARR
GARRAFA
GARRAN
GARRAT
GARRE
GARRETEER
GARRICK
GARRIDGE
GARRIGUE
GARRISON
GARRON
GARROO
GARROT
GARROTE
GARROTED
GARROTER
GARROTING
GARROTTE
GARROTTING
GARRULINE
GARRULITY
GARRULOUS
GARRULOUSLY
GARRUPA
GARSE
GARSIL
GARSTON
GARTEN
GARTER
GARTERED
GARTERING
GARTERS
GARTH
GARTHMAN
GARUM
GARVANCE
GARVANZO
GARVEY
GARVIE
GARVOCK
GAS
GASALIER
GASBAG
GASBOAT
GASCHECK
GASCON
GASCONADE
GASCONADED
GASCONADER
GASCONADING
GASCONISM
GASEITY
GASELIER
GASEOSITY
GASEOUS
GASEOUSNESS
GASH
GASHED
GASHES
GASHFUL
GASHING
GASHLINESS
GASHLY
GASHOLDER
GASHOUSE
GASHY
GASIFIABLE
GASIFICATION
GASIFIED
GASIFIER
GASIFORM
GASIFY
GASIFYING
GASKET
GASKIN
GASKING
GASKINS
GASLIGHT
GASLIGHTED
GASLIGHTING
GASLIT
GASLOCK
GASMAN
GASMEN
GASOGEN
GASOGENE
GASOLIER
GASOLIERY
GASOLINE
GASOLINER
GASOMETER
GASOMETRIC
GASOMETRICAL
GASOMETRY
GASP
GASPARILLO
GASPER
GASPEREAU
GASPERGOU
GASPING
GASPY
GASSER
GASSES
GASSING
GASSY
GAST
GASTALDITE
GASTALDO
GASTER
GASTERALGIA
GASTERIA
GASTEROPOD
GASTEROSTEID
GASTEROTHECA
GASTEROZOOID
GASTFUL
GASTIGHT
GASTIGHTNESS
GASTNESS
GASTRAEA
GASTRAEAL
GASTRAEUM
GASTRAL
GASTRALGIA
GASTRALGIC
GASTRECTOMY
GASTRELCOSIS
GASTRIC
GASTRICISM
GASTRIMARGY
GASTRIN
GASTRITIC
GASTRITIS
GASTROATONIA
GASTROCELE
GASTROCOEL
GASTROCOELE
GASTROCOLIC
GASTROCYSTIS
GASTRODISK
GASTRODYNIA
GASTROGRAPH
GASTROID
GASTROLATER
GASTROLIENAL
GASTROLITH
GASTROLOGER
GASTROLOGIST
GASTROLOGY
GASTROLYSIS
GASTROMANCY
GASTROMELUS
GASTROMENIA
GASTROMYCES
GASTRONOME
GASTRONOMER
GASTRONOMIC
GASTRONOMIST
GASTRONOMY
GASTRONOSUS
GASTROPEXY
GASTROPHILE
GASTROPLASTY
GASTROPOD
GASTROPODAN
GASTROPORE
GASTROPTOSIS
GASTRORRHEA
GASTROSCOPE
GASTROSCOPIC
GASTROSCOPY
GASTROSOPH
GASTROSOPHER
GASTROSOPHY
GASTROSPASM
GASTROSTEGAL
GASTROSTEGE
GASTROSTOMY
GASTROTAXIS
GASTROTHECA
GASTROTHECAL
GASTROTOME
GASTROTOMIC
GASTROTOMY
GASTROXYNSIS
GASTROZOOID
GASTRULA
GASTRULATE
GASTRULATION
GASWORKER
GASWORKS
GAT
GATA
GATCH
GATCHWORK
GATE
GATEADO
GATEAGE
GATEAU
GATED
GATEFOLD
GATEHOUSE
GATEKEEPER
GATEMAKER
GATEMAN
GATEPOST
GATER
GATES
GATETENDER
GATEWARD
GATEWAY
GATEWAYMAN
GATEWAYMEN
GATEWOMAN
GATEWORKS
GATEWRIGHT
GATHER
GATHERED
GATHERER
GATHERING
GATHERUM
GATING
GATO
GATOR
GATTER
GATTINE
GAU
GAUB
GAUCHE
GAUCHELY
GAUCHENESS
GAUCHERIE
GAUCIE
GAUCY
GAUD
GAUDEAMUS
GAUDERY
GAUDFUL
GAUDIER
GAUDIES
GAUDIEST
GAUDILY
GAUDINESS
GAUDISH
GAUDSMAN
GAUDY
GAUE
GAUFFER
GAUFFERED
GAUFFERER
GAUFFERING
GAUFFRE
GAUFFRED
GAUFRE
GAUFRETTE
GAUFRETTES
GAUG
GAUGE
GAUGEABLE
GAUGED
GAUGER
GAUGING
GAULDING
GAULE
GAULIN
GAULOISERIE
GAULSH
GAULT
GAULTER
GAULTHERASE
GAULTHERIA
GAULTHERIN
GAULTHERINE
GAUM
GAUMISH
GAUMLESS
GAUMLIKE
GAUMY
GAUN
GAUNCH
GAUNT
GAUNTED
GAUNTER
GAUNTEST
GAUNTLET
GAUNTLETED
GAUNTLY
GAUNTNESS
GAUNTRY
GAUNTY
GAUP
GAUPUS
GAUR
GAURIC
GAURIE
GAUS
GAUSS
GAUSSAGE
GAUSSBERGITE
GAUSTER
GAUSTERER
GAUT
GAUTEITE
GAUZE
GAUZELIKE
GAUZEWING
GAUZIER
GAUZIEST
GAUZILY
GAUZINESS
GAUZY
GAV
GAVAGE
GAVALL
GAVE
GAVEL
GAVELAGE
GAVELER
GAVELKIND
GAVELKINDER
GAVELLER
GAVELMAN
GAVELMEN
GAVELOCK
GAVIAL
GAVIALOID
GAVOT
GAVOTTE
GAVYUTI
GAW
GAWCEY
GAWD
GAWISH
GAWK
GAWKHAMMER
GAWKIER
GAWKIEST
GAWKILY
GAWKINESS
GAWKISH
GAWKY
GAWN
GAWNEY
GAWP
GAWSIE
GAWSY
GAY
GAYAL
GAYALS
GAYATRI
GAYBINE
GAYCAT
GAYDIANG
GAYER
GAYEST

GAYETY
GAYLIES
GAYLUSSITE
GAYLY
GAYMENT
GAYNESS
GAYSOME
GAYWAY
GAYWINGS
GAYYOU
GAZ
GAZABO
GAZABOES
GAZABOS
GAZANGABIN
GAZE
GAZEBO
GAZEBOES
GAZEBOS
GAZED
GAZEHOUND
GAZEL
GAZELESS
GAZELLE
GAZELLES
GAZEMENT
GAZER
GAZET
GAZETTAL
GAZETTE
GAZETTED
GAZETTEER
GAZETTEERAGE
GAZETTING
GAZI
GAZING
GAZINGLY
GAZINGSTOCK
GAZOGENE
GAZON
GAZOO
GAZOOK
GAZOZ
GAZPACHO
GAZY
GAZZETTA
GBO
GEAL
GEAN
GEANTICLINAL
GEANTICLINE
GEAR
GEARBOX
GEARCASE
GEARE
GEARED
GEARING
GEARKSUTITE
GEARLESS
GEARMAN
GEARS
GEARSET
GEARSHIFT
GEARWHEEL
GEASON
GEAST
GEBANG
GEBANGA
GEBBIE
GEBUR
GECK
GECKO
GECKOES
GECKOS
GED
GEDACT
GEDANITE
GEDD
GEDDA
GEDDER
GEDECKT
GEDECKTWORK
GEDRITE
GEDUNK
GEE
GEEBUNG
GEED
GEEING
GEEK
GEELBEC
GEELBECK
GEELBEK
GEELHOUT
GEEPOUND
GEERAH
GEES
GEESE
GEEST
GEET
GEEZER
GEFULLTEFISH
GEG
GEGENION
GEGENSCHEIN
GEGG
GEGGEE
GEGGER
GEGGERY
GEHLENITE
GEIG
GEIGE
GEIGER
GEIKIELITE
GEIN
GEIR
GEIRA
GEISHA
GEISHAS
GEISON
GEISOTHERM
GEISOTHERMAL
GEISTLICH
GEITJIE
GEITONOGAMY
GEKKONID
GEKKONOID
GEL
GELABLE
GELADA
GELANDESPRUNG
GELASTIC
GELATE
GELATIA
GELATIN
GELATINATE
GELATINATED
GELATINATING
GELATINATION
GELATINE
GELATINED
GELATINITY
GELATINIZE
GELATINIZED
GELATINIZER
GELATINIZING
GELATINOID
GELATINOTYPE
GELATINOUS
GELATINOUSLY
GELATION
GELATOSE
GELD
GELDANT
GELDED
GELDER
GELDING
GELEE
GELEEM
GELID
GELIDITY
GELIDLY
GELIDNESS
GELIGNITE
GELILAH
GELINOTTE
GELL
GELLED
GELLING
GELLY
GELOFER
GELOFRE
GELOGENIC
GELONG
GELOSCOPY
GELOSE
GELOSIN
GELOSINE
GELOTHERAPY
GELOTOSCOPY
GELSEMIN
GELSEMINE
GELSEMININE
GELSEMIUM
GELT
GEM
GEMATRIA
GEMATRICAL
GEMATRIOT
GEMAUVE
GEMEINDE
GEMEL
GEMELED
GEMELLED
GEMELLION
GEMELLUS
GEMELS
GEMINATE
GEMINATED
GEMINATELY
GEMINATING
GEMINATION
GEMINATIVE
GEMINIFORM
GEMINOUS
GEMLIKE
GEMMA
GEMMACEOUS
GEMMAE
GEMMAN
GEMMARY
GEMMATE
GEMMATED
GEMMATING
GEMMATION
GEMMATIVE
GEMMED
GEMMEL
GEMMEOUS
GEMMER
GEMMIFEROUS
GEMMIFORM
GEMMILY
GEMMINESS
GEMMING
GEMMIPARA
GEMMIPARES
GEMMIPARITY
GEMMIPAROUS
GEMMOID
GEMMOLOGY
GEMMULA
GEMMULATION
GEMMULE
GEMMY
GEMOLOGY
GEMOT
GEMOTE
GEMSBOK
GEMSBUCK
GEMSHORN
GEMSTONE
GEMUL
GEMUTLICH
GEMWORK
GEN
GENA
GENAE
GENAL
GENAPP
GENAPPE
GENAPPER
GENARCH
GENARCHA
GENDARME
GENDARMERIE
GENDARMERY
GENDERED
GENDERER
GENDERING
GENDERLESS
GENE
GENEAL
GENEALOGIC
GENEALOGICAL
GENEALOGIES
GENEALOGIST
GENEALOGIZE
GENEALOGIZER
GENEALOGY
GENEAT
GENEKI
GENEPI
GENER
GENERA
GENERABILITY
GENERABLE
GENERAL
GENERALATE
GENERALCIES
GENERALCY
GENERALE
GENERALIA
GENERALIFIC
GENERALISM
GENERALIST
GENERALISTIC
GENERALITER
GENERALITY
GENERALIZABLE
GENERALIZATION
GENERALIZE
GENERALIZED
GENERALIZER
GENERALL
GENERALLY
GENERALNESS
GENERALSHIP
GENERALTY
GENERANT
GENERATE
GENERATED
GENERATING
GENERATION
GENERATIONAL
GENERATIVE
GENERATOR
GENERATRICES
GENERATRIX
GENERIC
GENERICAL
GENERICALLY
GENEROSITIES
GENEROSITY
GENEROUS
GENEROUSLY
GENEROUSNESS
GENESERIN
GENESERINE
GENESES
GENESIAL
GENESIC
GENESIOLOGY
GENESIS
GENESIURGIC
GENET
GENETHLIAC
GENETHLIC
GENETIC
GENETICAL
GENETICALLY
GENETICISM
GENETICIST
GENETICS
GENETOR
GENETOUS
GENETRIX
GENETTE
GENEVOISE
GENIAL
GENIALITY
GENIALIZE
GENIALLY
GENIC
GENICULATE
GENICULATED
GENICULATELY
GENICULUM
GENIE
GENII
GENIN
GENIO
GENIOGLOSSAL
GENIOGLOSSUS
GENIOHYOID
GENIOLATRY
GENION
GENIOPLASTY
GENIP
GENIPAP
GENIPAPADA
GENISARO
GENISTEIN
GENISTIN
GENITAL
GENITALIA
GENITALS
GENITIVAL
GENITIVALLY
GENITIVE
GENITOCRURAL
GENITOR
GENITORIAL
GENITORY
GENITURE
GENIUS
GENIUSES
GENIZAH
GENOBLAST
GENOBLASTIC
GENOCIDE
GENOME
GENOS
GENOTYPE
GENOTYPIC
GENOTYPICAL

GENOUILLERE
GENOVINO
GENRE
GENRO
GENROS
GENS
GENSON
GENT
GENTE
GENTEEL
GENTEELISM
GENTEELLY
GENTEELNESS
GENTES
GENTHITE
GENTIAN
GENTIANELLA
GENTIANOSE
GENTIANWORT
GENTIL
GENTILE
GENTILES
GENTILESSE
GENTILIC
GENTILISH
GENTILISM
GENTILITIAL
GENTILITIAN
GENTILITIES
GENTILITIOUS
GENTILITY
GENTILIZE
GENTIOBIOSE
GENTIOPICRIN
GENTISEIN
GENTISIN
GENTLE
GENTLED
GENTLEFOLK
GENTLEFOLKS
GENTLEHOOD
GENTLEMAN
GENTLEMANLY
GENTLEMEN
GENTLENESS
GENTLER
GENTLESHIP
GENTLEST
GENTLEWOMAN
GENTLEWOMEN
GENTLING
GENTLY
GENTMAN
GENTRICE
GENTRY
GENTY
GENU
GENUA
GENUAL
GENUCLAST
GENUFLECT
GENUFLECTED
GENUFLECTING
GENUFLECTION
GENUFLECTOR
GENUFLECTORY
GENUFLEXION
GENUFLEXUOUS
GENUINE
GENUINELY
GENUINENESS
GENUS
GENUSES
GEO
GEOBIOLOGIC
GEOBIOLOGY
GEOBIONT
GEOBIOS
GEOBLAST
GEOBOTANY
GEOCARPIC
GEOCENTRIC
GEOCENTRICAL
GEOCERITE
GEOCHEMICAL
GEOCHEMIST
GEOCHEMISTRY
GEOCHRONIC
GEOCHRONY
GEOCLINE
GEOCORONIUM
GEOCRATIC
GEOCRONITE
GEOCYCLIC
GEODAESIA
GEODE
GEODESIA
GEODESIC
GEODESICAL
GEODESIST
GEODESY
GEODETE
GEODETIC
GEODETICAL
GEODETICALLY
GEODETICS
GEODIC
GEODIFEROUS
GEODIST
GEODUCK
GEODYNAMIC
GEODYNAMICAL
GEODYNAMICS
GEOETHNIC
GEOFORM
GEOGEN
GEOGENESIS
GEOGENETIC
GEOGENIC
GEOGENOUS
GEOGENY
GEOGLYPHIC
GEOGNOSIS
GEOGNOSIST
GEOGNOST
GEOGNOSTIC
GEOGNOSTICAL
GEOGNOSY
GEOGONIC
GEOGONICAL
GEOGONY
GEOGRAPHER
GEOGRAPHIC
GEOGRAPHICAL
GEOGRAPHICS
GEOGRAPHIES
GEOGRAPHIZED
GEOGRAPHY
GEOHYDROLOGY
GEOID
GEOIDAL
GEOLATRY
GEOLOGER
GEOLOGIAN
GEOLOGIC
GEOLOGICAL
GEOLOGICALLY
GEOLOGIES
GEOLOGIST
GEOLOGIZE
GEOLOGIZED
GEOLOGIZING
GEOLOGY
GEOM
GEOMAGNETIC
GEOMAGNETICS
GEOMAGNETISM
GEOMALIC
GEOMALISM
GEOMANCE
GEOMANCER
GEOMANCY
GEOMANT
GEOMANTIC
GEOMANTICAL
GEOMEDICINE
GEOMETER
GEOMETRIC
GEOMETRICAL
GEOMETRICIAN
GEOMETRICIZE
GEOMETRID
GEOMETRIES
GEOMETRIZE
GEOMETRIZED
GEOMETRIZING
GEOMETRY
GEOMOROI
GEOMORPHIC
GEOMORPHIST
GEOMORPHY
GEOMYID
GEONEGATIVE
GEOPHAGIA
GEOPHAGISM
GEOPHAGIST
GEOPHAGOUS
GEOPHAGY
GEOPHILID
GEOPHILOUS
GEOPHYSICAL
GEOPHYSICIST
GEOPHYSICS
GEOPHYTE
GEOPHYTIC
GEOPOLAR
GEOPOLITIC
GEOPOLITICAL
GEOPOLITICS
GEOPONIC
GEOPONICAL
GEOPONICS
GEOPONY
GEOPOSITIVE
GEORAMA
GEORG
GEORGIC
GEORGICAL
GEOSCOPIC
GEOSCOPY
GEOSELENIC
GEOSPHERE
GEOSTATIC
GEOSTATICS
GEOSTROPHIC
GEOSYNCLINAL
GEOSYNCLINE
GEOTACTIC
GEOTAXIS
GEOTAXY
GEOTECHNICS
GEOTECTOLOGY
GEOTECTONIC
GEOTHERM
GEOTHERMAL
GEOTHERMIC
GEOTONIC
GEOTONUS
GEOTROPIC
GEOTROPISM
GEOTROPY
GEPHYREAN
GER
GERA
GERAERA
GERAH
GERANIACEOUS
GERANIAL
GERANIOL
GERANIUM
GERANYL
GERARA
GERARDIA
GERASTIAN
GERATE
GERATED
GERATELY
GERATIC
GERATOLOGY
GERB
GERBE
GERBIL
GERBILLE
GERCROW
GERE
GEREAGLE
GEREFA
GERENDUM
GERENT
GERENUK
GERFALCON
GERFUL
GERHARDTITE
GERIATRIC
GERIATRICIAN
GERIATRICS
GERIATRIST
GERIP
GERKIN
GERM
GERMAL
GERMAN
GERMANDER
GERMANE
GERMANIC
GERMANITE
GERMANITY
GERMANIUM
GERMANIZE
GERMANOUS
GERMANYL
GERMARIUM
GERMEN
GERMENS
GERMFREE
GERMICIDAL
GERMICIDE
GERMIFUGE
GERMIN
GERMINABLE
GERMINAL
GERMINALLY
GERMINANCE
GERMINANCY
GERMINANT
GERMINATE
GERMINATED
GERMINATING
GERMINATION
GERMINATIVE
GERMINATOR
GERMING
GERMINOGONY
GERMIPARITY
GERMLING
GERMON
GERMPROOF
GERMS
GERMULE
GEROCOMIA
GEROCOMICAL
GEROCOMY
GERODERMA
GERODERMIA
GEROMORPHISM
GERONTAL
GERONTES
GERONTIC
GERONTINE
GERONTISM
GERONTOCRACY
GERONTOGEOUS
GERONTOLOGY
GERONTOXON
GEROUSIA
GERRYMANDER
GERS
GERSDORFFITE
GERSUM
GERTRUDE
GERUND
GERUNDIAL
GERUNDIALLY
GERUNDIVAL
GERUNDIVE
GERUNDIVELY
GERUSIA
GERVAO
GERY
GERYONID
GESITH
GESITHCUND
GESNERAD
GESSERON
GESSO
GEST
GESTALT
GESTALTEN
GESTALTER
GESTALTIST
GESTALTS
GESTANT
GESTATE
GESTATED
GESTATING
GESTATION
GESTATIONAL
GESTATIVE
GESTATORIAL
GESTATORIUM
GESTATORY
GESTE
GESTED
GESTEN
GESTENING
GESTER
GESTIC
GESTICAL
GESTICULANT
GESTICULAR
GESTICULATE
GESTICULATED
GESTICULATOR
GESTIO
GESTION
GESTNING
GESTONIE
GESTURAL
GESTURE
GESTURED
GESTURER
GESTURES
GESTURING
GESWARP
GET

GETA
GETAN
GETAS
GETAWAY
GETHSEMANE
GETLING
GETPENNY
GETT
GETTABLE
GETTER
GETTING
GETUP
GEULAH
GEVE
GEWGAW
GEWGAWED
GEWGAWISH
GEWGAWRY
GEY
GEYAN
GEYERITE
GEYLIES
GEYSER
GEYSERAL
GEYSERIC
GEYSERINE
GEYSERITE
GEYZE
GEZ
GEZERAH
GHAFFIR
GHAFIR
GHALVA
GHARIAL
GHARNAO
GHARRI
GHARRIES
GHARRY
GHAST
GHASTFUL
GHASTFULLY
GHASTFULNESS
GHASTILY
GHASTLIER
GHASTLIEST
GHASTLILY
GHASTLINESS
GHASTLY
GHAT
GHATS
GHATWAL
GHAUT
GHAWAZEE
GHAWAZI
GHAZAL
GHAZEL
GHAZI
GHAZIES
GHEBETA
GHEE
GHELD
GHENTING
GHERKIN
GHETCHOO
GHETTO
GHI
GHILLIE
GHIZITE
GHOL
GHOOM
GHOR
GHORKHAR
GHOST
GHOSTCRAFT
GHOSTDOM
GHOSTED
GHOSTER
GHOSTFISH
GHOSTFLOWER
GHOSTIFIED
GHOSTILY
GHOSTING
GHOSTISM
GHOSTLAND
GHOSTLIER
GHOSTLIEST
GHOSTLIFY
GHOSTLIKE
GHOSTLY
GHOSTMONGER
GHOSTOLOGY
GHOSTS
GHOSTSHIP
GHOSTWEED
GHOSTWRITE
GHOSTWRITER
GHOSTWRITING
GHOSTWRITTEN
GHOSTWROTE
GHOSTY
GHOUL
GHOULIE
GHOULISH
GHOULISHLY
GHOULISHNESS
GHURRY
GHYLL
GI
GIALLOLINO
GIANSAR
GIANT
GIANTESS
GIANTISM
GIANTIZE
GIANTKIND
GIANTLY
GIANTRY
GIANTS
GIAOUR
GIARDIASIS
GIB
GIBARO
GIBBALS
GIBBAR
GIBBARTAS
GIBBED
GIBBER
GIBBERED
GIBBERELLIN
GIBBERGUNYAH
GIBBERING
GIBBERISH
GIBBEROSE
GIBBEROSITY
GIBBERT
GIBBET
GIBBETED
GIBBETING
GIBBLEGABLE
GIBBLES
GIBBOL
GIBBON
GIBBOSE
GIBBOSITIES
GIBBOSITY
GIBBOUS
GIBBOUSLY
GIBBOUSNESS
GIBBSITE
GIBBUS
GIBBY
GIBE
GIBED
GIBEL
GIBELITE
GIBER
GIBETTING
GIBING
GIBINGLY
GIBLEH
GIBLET
GIBLETS
GIBOIA
GIBSTAFF
GIBUS
GID
GIDDAP
GIDDIED
GIDDIER
GIDDIEST
GIDDIFY
GIDDILY
GIDDINESS
GIDDY
GIDDYBERRY
GIDDYBRAIN
GIDDYHEAD
GIDDYING
GIDE
GIDGEA
GIDGEE
GIDIA
GIDJEE
GIDYA
GIDYEA
GIE
GIER
GIESECKITE
GIF
GIFBLAAR
GIFFGAFF
GIFT
GIFTBOOK
GIFTED
GIFTEDLY
GIFTEDNESS
GIFTIE
GIFTING
GIFTS
GIFTURE
GIFTWARE
GIG
GIGA
GIGACYCLE
GIGANT
GIGANTAL
GIGANTEAN
GIGANTESQUE
GIGANTIC
GIGANTICAL
GIGANTICALLY
GIGANTICIDAL
GIGANTICIDE
GIGANTICNESS
GIGANTISM
GIGANTIZE
GIGANTOBLAST
GIGANTOCYTE
GIGANTOLITE
GIGANTOLOGY
GIGATON
GIGBACK
GIGELIRA
GIGERIUM
GIGGE
GIGGED
GIGGER
GIGGING
GIGGISH
GIGGIT
GIGGLE
GIGGLED
GIGGLER
GIGGLIER
GIGGLIEST
GIGGLING
GIGGLY
GIGLET
GIGLIATO
GIGLIO
GIGLOT
GIGMAN
GIGMANESS
GIGMANHOOD
GIGMANIA
GIGMANIC
GIGMANICALLY
GIGMANISM
GIGMANITY
GIGNATE
GIGNITIVE
GIGOLO
GIGOT
GIGSMAN
GIGSMEN
GIGSTER
GIGTREE
GIGUE
GIGUNU
GIKE
GIL
GILBERT
GILBERTAGE
GILBERTITE
GILD
GILDABLE
GILDED
GILDEN
GILDER
GILDING
GILDSHIP
GILDSMAN
GILENYER
GILENYIE
GILET
GILGAI
GILGAMES
GILGAMESH
GILGUL
GILGUY
GILIAK
GILL
GILLAR
GILLAROO
GILLED
GILLER
GILLFLIRT
GILLHOOTER
GILLIE
GILLIED
GILLIES
GILLING
GILLIVER
GILLNET
GILLOT
GILLOTAGE
GILLOTYPE
GILLS
GILLSTOUP
GILLY
GILLYFLOWER
GILLYGAUPUS
GILLYING
GILO
GILOE
GILP
GILPEY
GILPY
GILRAVAGE
GILRAVAGER
GILSONITE
GILT
GILTCUP
GILTEN
GILTHEAD
GILTTAIL
GILVER
GIM
GIMBAL
GIMBALED
GIMBALJAWED
GIMBALS
GIMBERJAWED
GIMBLE
GIMBRI
GIMCRACK
GIMCRACKERY
GIMCRACKY
GIME
GIMEL
GIMLET
GIMLETEYED
GIMLETY
GIMMAL
GIMMALED
GIMME
GIMMER
GIMMERINGLY
GIMMICK
GIMMICKRY
GIMMICKY
GIMMOR
GIMP
GIMPER
GIMPIER
GIMPIEST
GIMPING
GIMPY
GIN
GINEP
GINETE
GING
GINGAL
GINGALL
GINGE
GINGELEY
GINGELI
GINGELLY
GINGELY
GINGER
GINGERADE
GINGERBERRY
GINGERBREAD
GINGERBREADY
GINGERIN
GINGERLEAF
GINGERLINE
GINGERLY
GINGERNUT
GINGEROL
GINGEROUS
GINGERROOT
GINGERSNAP
GINGERSPICE
GINGERWORK
GINGERWORT
GINGERY
GINGHAM
GINGHAMED
GINGILI
GINGIVA
GINGIVAL
GINGIVALGIA
GINGIVECTOMY
GINGIVITIS

GINGKO
GINGLYFORM
GINGLYMOID
GINGLYMUS
GINGRAS
GINHOUSE
GINK
GINNED
GINNEL
GINNER
GINNERIES
GINNERS
GINNERY
GINNING
GINNLE
GINNY
GINORITE
GINSENG
GIO
GIOCOSO
GIOJOSO
GIORNATA
GIP
GIPON
GIPPED
GIPPER
GIPPING
GIPPO
GIPSEIAN
GIPSER
GIPSIES
GIPSIOLOGIST
GIPSIRE
GIPSOLOGY
GIPSY
GIPSYDOM
GIPSYFY
GIPSYHEAD
GIPSYRY
GIPSYWEED
GIPSYWORT
GIR
GIRAFFE
GIRAFFES
GIRAFFINE
GIRAFFOID
GIRANDOLE
GIRASOL
GIRASOLE
GIRBA
GIRD
GIRDED
GIRDER
GIRDERAGE
GIRDING
GIRDLE
GIRDLECAKE
GIRDLED
GIRDLER
GIRDLESTEAD
GIRDLING
GIRDLINGLY
GIREH
GIRG
GIRL
GIRLEEN
GIRLERY
GIRLFULLY
GIRLHOOD
GIRLIE
GIRLING
GIRLISH
GIRLISHLY
GIRLISHNESS
GIRLY
GIRN
GIRNAL
GIRNEL
GIRNIE
GIRNY
GIRO
GIRON
GIROSOL
GIROUETTE
GIROUETTISM
GIRR
GIRRIT
GIRSE
GIRSH
GIRT
GIRTED
GIRTH
GIRTING
GIRTLINE
GISANT
GISARME
GISE
GISH
GISLER
GISMO
GISMONDITE
GISMOS
GISPIN
GIST
GISTS
GIT
GITALIGENIN
GITALIN
GITANA
GITANEMUK
GITANO
GITANOS
GITE
GITERNE
GITH
GITONIN
GITOXIGENIN
GITOXIN
GITTER
GITTERN
GITTITH
GIULIO
GIUSTAMENTE
GIUSTINA
GIUSTO
GIVE
GIVEAWAY
GIVEN
GIVER
GIVEY
GIVING
GIZMO
GIZZ
GIZZARD
GIZZEN
GIZZENED
GIZZERN
GJEDOST
GJOLL
GLABELLA
GLABELLAE
GLABELLAR
GLABELLOUS
GLABRATE
GLABRESCENT
GLABROUS
GLACE
GLACIABLE
GLACIAL
GLACIALISM
GLACIALIST
GLACIALLY
GLACIARIUM
GLACIATE
GLACIATION
GLACIER
GLACIERED
GLACIERET
GLACIERIST
GLACIOLOGIC
GLACIOLOGIST
GLACIOLOGY
GLACIOMARINE
GLACIOMETER
GLACIONATANT
GLACIS
GLACK
GLACON
GLAD
GLADDED
GLADDEN
GLADDENED
GLADDENER
GLADDENING
GLADDER
GLADDEST
GLADDING
GLADDON
GLADDY
GLADE
GLADEN
GLADES
GLADEYE
GLADFUL
GLADFULLY
GLADFULNESS
GLADHEARTED
GLADIATE
GLADIATOR
GLADIATORIAL
GLADIFY
GLADIOLA
GLADIOLAR
GLADIOLI
GLADIOLUS
GLADIOLUSES
GLADITE
GLADIUS
GLADKAITE
GLADLESS
GLADLY
GLADNESS
GLADSHIP
GLADSOME
GLADSOMELY
GLADSOMENESS
GLADY
GLAGA
GLAGAH
GLAIEUL
GLAIK
GLAIKET
GLAIKETNESS
GLAIKIT
GLAIKITNESS
GLAIKS
GLAIR
GLAIRED
GLAIREOUS
GLAIRIER
GLAIRIEST
GLAIRINESS
GLAIRING
GLAIRY
GLAISTER
GLAISTIG
GLAIVE
GLAIZIE
GLAKED
GLAKY
GLAM
GLAMBERRY
GLAME
GLAMOR
GLAMORIZE
GLAMORIZED
GLAMORIZING
GLAMOROUS
GLAMOROUSLY
GLAMOUR
GLAMOURED
GLAMOURIE
GLAMOURING
GLAMOUROUS
GLAMOUROUS
GLAMOUROUSLY
GLAMOURY
GLAMP
GLANCE
GLANCED
GLANCER
GLANCING
GLANCINGLY
GLAND
GLANDACEOUS
GLANDERED
GLANDEROUS
GLANDERS
GLANDES
GLANDIFEROUS
GLANDIFORM
GLANDULA
GLANDULAR
GLANDULE
GLANDULOSE
GLANDULOUS
GLANIS
GLANS
GLAR
GLARE
GLAREOLE
GLAREOUS
GLAREWORM
GLARIER
GLARIEST
GLARILY
GLARINESS
GLARING
GLARINGLY
GLARINGNESS
GLARRY
GLARY
GLASHAN
GLASS
GLASSBLOWER
GLASSBLOWING
GLASSED
GLASSEN
GLASSER
GLASSES
GLASSEYE
GLASSFUL
GLASSHOUSE
GLASSIE
GLASSIER
GLASSIEST
GLASSILY
GLASSIN
GLASSINE
GLASSINESS
GLASSING
GLASSMAKER
GLASSMAKING
GLASSMAN
GLASSMEN
GLASSTEEL
GLASSWARE
GLASSWEED
GLASSWORK
GLASSWORKER
GLASSWORKERS
GLASSWORKING
GLASSWORKS
GLASSWORM
GLASSWORT
GLASSY
GLAUBERITE
GLAUCESCENCE
GLAUCESCENT
GLAUCINE
GLAUCODOT
GLAUCOLITE
GLAUCOMA
GLAUCOMATOUS
GLAUCONITE
GLAUCONITIC
GLAUCOPHANE
GLAUCOUS
GLAUM
GLAUMRIE
GLAUR
GLAVE
GLAVER
GLAVERED
GLAVERING
GLAZE
GLAZED
GLAZEN
GLAZER
GLAZEWORK
GLAZIER
GLAZIERS
GLAZIERY
GLAZIEST
GLAZILY
GLAZINESS
GLAZING
GLAZY
GLEAD
GLEAM
GLEAMED
GLEAMIER
GLEAMIEST
GLEAMILY
GLEAMINESS
GLEAMING
GLEAMY
GLEAN
GLEANER
GLEANING
GLEARY
GLEAVE
GLEBA
GLEBE
GLEBOUS
GLEBY
GLED
GLEDE
GLEDGE
GLEDY
GLEE
GLEED
GLEEDS
GLEEFUL
GLEEFULLY
GLEEFULNESS
GLEEK
GLEEMAIDEN
GLEEMAN
GLEEMEN
GLEEN
GLEESOME
GLEESOMELY
GLEESOMENESS
GLEET

GLEETY
GLEG
GLEGLY
GLEGNESS
GLEIT
GLEN
GLENE
GLENOHUMERAL
GLENOID
GLENOIDAL
GLENT
GLESSITE
GLET
GLETTY
GLEW
GLEY
GLEYD
GLEYDE
GLIA
GLIADIN
GLIAL
GLIB
GLIBBER
GLIBBERY
GLIBBEST
GLIBLY
GLIBNESS
GLIDDER
GLIDDERY
GLIDE
GLIDED
GLIDELESS
GLIDENESS
GLIDER
GLIDERPORT
GLIDEWORT
GLIDING
GLIDINGLY
GLIFF
GLIFFING
GLIFFY
GLIM
GLIMA
GLIME
GLIMMER
GLIMMERED
GLIMMERING
GLIMMERITE
GLIMMEROUS
GLIMMERS
GLIMMERY
GLIMPSE
GLIMPSED
GLIMPSER
GLIMPSING
GLIMS
GLIN
GLINK
GLINSE
GLINT
GLINTED
GLINTING
GLIOCYTE
GLIOMA
GLIOMAS
GLIOMATA
GLIOMATOUS
GLIOSA
GLIOSIS
GLIRIFORM
GLIRINE
GLISK
GLISKY
GLISS
GLISSADE
GLISSADED
GLISSADER
GLISSADING
GLISSANDO
GLISSETTE
GLIST
GLISTEN
GLISTENED
GLISTENING
GLISTER
GLISTERED
GLISTERING
GLIT
GLITTER
GLITTERANCE
GLITTERED
GLITTERING
GLITTERINGLY
GLITTERY
GLOAM
GLOAMING
GLOAT
GLOATED
GLOATER
GLOATING
GLOATINGLY
GLOB
GLOBAL
GLOBALLY
GLOBATE
GLOBATED
GLOBE
GLOBED
GLOBEFISH
GLOBEFLOWER
GLOBEHOLDER
GLOBETROTTER
GLOBICAL
GLOBIFEROUS
GLOBIGERINA
GLOBIN
GLOBING
GLOBOID
GLOBOSE
GLOBOSELY
GLOBOSENESS
GLOBOSITE
GLOBOSITY
GLOBOUS
GLOBOUSLY
GLOBOUSNESS
GLOBULAR
GLOBULARITY
GLOBULARLY
GLOBULARNESS
GLOBULE
GLOBULET
GLOBULICIDE
GLOBULIN
GLOBULITE
GLOBULITIC
GLOBULOID
GLOBULOSE
GLOBULOUS
GLOBULYSIS
GLOBY
GLOCHID
GLOCHIDEOUS
GLOCHIDIAL
GLOCHIDIATE
GLOCHIDIUM
GLOCHIS
GLOCK
GLOCKENSPIEL
GLODE
GLOEA
GLOEAL
GLOEOCAPSOID
GLOFF
GLOGG
GLOM
GLOME
GLOMERA
GLOMERATE
GLOMERATION
GLOMERULAR
GLOMERULATE
GLOMERULE
GLOMERULOSE
GLOMERULUS
GLOMMOX
GLOMUS
GLONOIN
GLONOINE
GLOOM
GLOOMED
GLOOMFUL
GLOOMFULLY
GLOOMIER
GLOOMIEST
GLOOMILY
GLOOMINESS
GLOOMING
GLOOMINGLY
GLOOMS
GLOOMTH
GLOOMY
GLOP
GLOPNEN
GLOPPEN
GLOR
GLORE
GLORIATION
GLORIED
GLORIETTE
GLORIFICATION
GLORIFIED
GLORIFIER
GLORIFY
GLORIFYING
GLORIOLE
GLORIOSO
GLORIOUS
GLORIOUSLY
GLORIOUSNESS
GLORY
GLORYFUL
GLORYLESS
GLOSE
GLOSS
GLOSSA
GLOSSAGRA
GLOSSAL
GLOSSALGIA
GLOSSALGY
GLOSSARIAL
GLOSSARIALLY
GLOSSARIAN
GLOSSARIES
GLOSSARIST
GLOSSARY
GLOSSATE
GLOSSATOR
GLOSSATORIAL
GLOSSECTOMY
GLOSSED
GLOSSER
GLOSSIC
GLOSSIER
GLOSSIEST
GLOSSILY
GLOSSINESS
GLOSSING
GLOSSIST
GLOSSITIC
GLOSSITIS
GLOSSMETER
GLOSSOCELE
GLOSSOCOMA
GLOSSOCOMON
GLOSSODYNIA
GLOSSOGRAPH
GLOSSOGRAPHER
GLOSSOGRAPHY
GLOSSOHYAL
GLOSSOID
GLOSSOLABIAL
GLOSSOLALIA
GLOSSOLALIST
GLOSSOLALY
GLOSSOLOGIST
GLOSSOLOGY
GLOSSOPATHY
GLOSSOPETRA
GLOSSOPHYTIA
GLOSSOPLASTY
GLOSSOPLEGIA
GLOSSOPODIUM
GLOSSOPTOSIS
GLOSSOSCOPIA
GLOSSOSCOPY
GLOSSOSPASM
GLOSSOTOMY
GLOSSOTYPE
GLOSSY
GLOST
GLOTTAL
GLOTTALITE
GLOTTALIZE
GLOTTIC
GLOTTID
GLOTTIDEAN
GLOTTIDES
GLOTTIS
GLOTTISCOPE
GLOTTISES
GLOTTOGONIC
GLOTTOGONIST
GLOTTOGONY
GLOTTOLOGIC
GLOTTOLOGICAL
GLOTTOLOGIST
GLOTTOLOGY
GLOTUM
GLOUP
GLOUT
GLOVE
GLOVEMAKER
GLOVEMAKING
GLOVEMAN
GLOVER
GLOVERESS
GLOVING
GLOW
GLOWBIRD
GLOWED
GLOWER
GLOWERER
GLOWERING
GLOWERINGLY
GLOWFLIES
GLOWFLY
GLOWING
GLOWINGLY
GLOWWORM
GLOX
GLOY
GLOZE
GLOZED
GLOZER
GLOZING
GLUB
GLUCAEMIA
GLUCASE
GLUCEMIA
GLUCIDE
GLUCINA
GLUCINE
GLUCINIC
GLUCINIUM
GLUCINUM
GLUCK
GLUCKE
GLUCOKININ
GLUCOSAMIN
GLUCOSAMINE
GLUCOSAN
GLUCOSAZONE
GLUCOSE
GLUCOSIC
GLUCOSIDAL
GLUCOSIDE
GLUCOSIDIC
GLUCOSINE
GLUCOSONE
GLUCOSURIA
GLUCURONIC
GLUE
GLUED
GLUEMAKER
GLUEMAKING
GLUEMAN
GLUEPOT
GLUER
GLUEY
GLUEYNESS
GLUG
GLUGGLUG
GLUHWEIN
GLUING
GLUISH
GLUISHNESS
GLUM
GLUMA
GLUMACEOUS
GLUMAL
GLUME
GLUMES
GLUMIFEROUS
GLUMLY
GLUMMER
GLUMMEST
GLUMMY
GLUMNESS
GLUMOSE
GLUMOSITY
GLUMOUS
GLUMP
GLUMPIER
GLUMPIEST
GLUMPILY
GLUMPINESS
GLUMPISH
GLUMPY
GLUNCH
GLUSIDE
GLUT
GLUTAMIC
GLUTAMINE
GLUTAMINIC
GLUTARIC
GLUTATHIONE
GLUTCH
GLUTEAL
GLUTELIN
GLUTEN
GLUTENIN
GLUTENOUS
GLUTEUS
GLUTIN

GLUTINATE
GLUTINATION
GLUTINATIVE
GLUTINIZE
GLUTINOSE
GLUTINOSITY
GLUTINOUS
GLUTINOUSLY
GLUTITION
GLUTOID
GLUTOSE
GLUTTED
GLUTTER
GLUTTERY
GLUTTING
GLUTTON
GLUTTONIES
GLUTTONIZE
GLUTTONIZED
GLUTTONIZING
GLUTTONOUS
GLUTTONOUSLY
GLUTTONY
GLY
GLYCAN
GLYCERATE
GLYCERIC
GLYCERIDE
GLYCERIN
GLYCERINATE
GLYCERINE
GLYCERINIZE
GLYCERITE
GLYCERIZE
GLYCEROGEL
GLYCEROL
GLYCEROLATE
GLYCEROSE
GLYCERYL
GLYCID
GLYCIDE
GLYCIDIC
GLYCIDOL
GLYCIN
GLYCININ
GLYCOCHOLATE
GLYCOCHOLIC
GLYCOCIN
GLYCOCOLL
GLYCOGELATIN
GLYCOGEN
GLYCOGENESIS
GLYCOGENETIC
GLYCOGENIC
GLYCOGENOUS
GLYCOGENY
GLYCOL
GLYCOLATE
GLYCOLIC
GLYCOLIDE
GLYCOLIPID
GLYCOLIPIDE
GLYCOLIPIN
GLYCOLIPINE
GLYCOLURIL
GLYCOLYL
GLYCOLYSIS
GLYCOLYTIC
GLYCOLYTICALLY
GLYCONIC
GLYCONIN
GLYCOPROTEIN
GLYCOSE
GLYCOSIDE
GLYCOSIN
GLYCOSINE
GLYCOSURIA
GLYCOSURIC
GLYCURESIS
GLYCYL
GLYCYPHYLLIN
GLYCYRRHIZIN
GLYDE
GLYN
GLYOXAL
GLYOXALASE
GLYOXALIC
GLYOXALINE
GLYOXIME
GLYOXYL
GLYOXYLIC
GLYPH
GLYPHIC
GLYPHOGRAPH
GLYPHOGRAPHY
GLYPTIC
GLYPTICAL
GLYPTICIAN
GLYPTICS
GLYPTODONT
GLYPTOGRAPH
GLYPTOGRAPHY
GLYPTOLOGY
GLYPTOTHECA
GMELINITE
GNABBLE
GNAP
GNAR
GNARE
GNARL
GNARLED
GNARLIER
GNARLIEST
GNARLINESS
GNARLING
GNARLY
GNARR
GNARRED
GNARRING
GNASH
GNASHED
GNASHING
GNAT
GNATCATCHER
GNATFLOWER
GNATHAL
GNATHIC
GNATHIDIUM
GNATHION
GNATHISM
GNATHITE
GNATHOBASE
GNATHOBASIC
GNATHOMETER
GNATHONIC
GNATHONICAL
GNATHONIZE
GNATHOPOD
GNATHOPODITE
GNATHOSTOME
GNATHOTHECA
GNATLING
GNATSNAP
GNATSNAPPER
GNATTER
GNATTY
GNATWORM
GNAW
GNAWED
GNAWER
GNAWING
GNAWINGLY
GNAWINGS
GNAWN
GNEDE
GNEDELY
GNEISS
GNEISSIC
GNEISSITIC
GNEISSOID
GNEISSOSE
GNEISSY
GNIB
GNOCCHETTI
GNOCCHI
GNOF
GNOFF
GNOME
GNOMED
GNOMIC
GNOMICAL
GNOMICALLY
GNOMIDE
GNOMISH
GNOMIST
GNOMOLOGIC
GNOMOLOGICAL
GNOMOLOGIST
GNOMOLOGY
GNOMON
GNOMONIC
GNOMONICS
GNOMONOLOGY
GNOSIOLOGY
GNOSIS
GNOSTIC
GNOSTICAL
GNOSTICALLY
GNOSTICITY
GNU
GO
GOA
GOAD
GOADED
GOADING
GOADMAN
GOADSMAN
GOADSTER
GOAF
GOAI
GOAL
GOALAGE
GOALEE
GOALIE
GOALKEEPER
GOALKEEPING
GOALLESS
GOALMOUTH
GOALTENDER
GOAM
GOANA
GOANNA
GOAT
GOATBEARD
GOATBRUSH
GOATBUSH
GOATEE
GOATEED
GOATFISH
GOATFISHES
GOATHERD
GOATHERDESS
GOATISH
GOATISHLY
GOATISHNESS
GOATLAND
GOATLING
GOATLY
GOATROOT
GOATSBANE
GOATSBEARD
GOATSFOOT
GOATSFOOTS
GOATSKIN
GOATSTONE
GOATSUCKER
GOATWEED
GOATY
GOAVE
GOB
GOBACK
GOBAN
GOBANG
GOBBE
GOBBER
GOBBET
GOBBIN
GOBBING
GOBBLE
GOBBLED
GOBBLEDYGOOK
GOBBLER
GOBBLING
GOBBO
GOBBY
GOBELIN
GOBERNADOR
GOBERNADORA
GOBIERNO
GOBIES
GOBIID
GOBIIFORM
GOBIOID
GOBLET
GOBLETED
GOBLIN
GOBLINE
GOBLINRY
GOBMOUTHED
GOBO
GOBONATED
GOBONE
GOBONY
GOBOS
GOBSTICK
GOBURRA
GOBY
GOCART
GOD
GODCHILD
GODDAM
GODDAMN
GODDAMNED
GODDARD
GODDAUGHTER
GODDESS
GODDIZE
GODE
GODET
GODFATHER
GODFORSAKEN
GODHEAD
GODHOOD
GODIVEAU
GODKIN
GODLESS
GODLESSLY
GODLESSNESS
GODLET
GODLIER
GODLIEST
GODLIKE
GODLIKENESS
GODLILY
GODLINESS
GODLING
GODLY
GODMAMMA
GODMOTHER
GODOWN
GODPAPA
GODPARENT
GODPHERE
GODROON
GODS
GODSEND
GODSHIP
GODSON
GODSONSHIP
GODWIT
GOEL
GOELAND
GOELISM
GOER
GOES
GOETHITE
GOETIC
GOETY
GOFE
GOFER
GOFF
GOFFER
GOFFERED
GOFFERER
GOFFERING
GOFFLE
GOG
GOGA
GOGGA
GOGGAN
GOGGANS
GOGGLE
GOGGLED
GOGGLER
GOGGLES
GOGGLING
GOGGLY
GOGLET
GOGO
GOH
GOI
GOIABADA
GOING
GOINGS
GOITCHO
GOITER
GOITERED
GOITRE
GOITRED
GOITROUS
GOL
GOLA
GOLACH
GOLADAR
GOLAH
GOLANDAAS
GOLANDAUSE
GOLANDAUZE
GOLD
GOLDARN
GOLDBACK
GOLDBEATER
GOLDBEATING
GOLDBRICK
GOLDBUG
GOLDCREST
GOLDCUP
GOLDE
GOLDEN
GOLDENBACK
GOLDENEYE
GOLDENEYES
GOLDENFLEECE
GOLDENLOCKS
GOLDENLY

GOLDENNESS
GOLDENPERT
GOLDENROD
GOLDENSEAL
GOLDENTOP
GOLDENWING
GOLDER
GOLDEYE
GOLDFIELDER
GOLDFINCH
GOLDFINNIES
GOLDFINNY
GOLDFISH
GOLDFISHES
GOLDFLOWER
GOLDHAMMER
GOLDHEAD
GOLDIE
GOLDILOCKS
GOLDIN
GOLDING
GOLDMIST
GOLDNEY
GOLDSMITH
GOLDSMITHERY
GOLDSMITHING
GOLDSMITHRY
GOLDSPINK
GOLDSTONE
GOLDTAIL
GOLDTHREAD
GOLDTIT
GOLDURN
GOLDWATER
GOLDWEED
GOLDWORK
GOLDWORKER
GOLDY
GOLE
GOLEE
GOLEM
GOLES
GOLF
GOLFER
GOLFING
GOLI
GOLIAD
GOLIARD
GOLIARDERY
GOLIARDIC
GOLILLA
GOLKAKRA
GOLL
GOLLAND
GOLLAR
GOLLER
GOLLIWOG
GOLLIWOGG
GOLLOP
GOLLY
GOLOCH
GOLOE
GOLOKA
GOLOSH
GOLP
GOLPE
GOLUNDAUZE
GOM
GOMARI
GOMART
GOMASHTA
GOMASTA
GOMAVEL
GOMBAY
GOMBEEN
GOMBO
GOMBROON
GOME
GOMER
GOMERAL
GOMEREL
GOMERIL
GOMLAH
GOMMIER
GOMPHODONT
GOMPHOSIS
GOMUKHI
GOMUTI
GON
GONAD
GONADAL
GONADIAL
GONADIC
GONADUCT
GONAGRA
GONAKE
GONAKIE
GONAL
GONALGIA
GONAPOD
GONAPOPHYSAL
GONAPOPHYSIS
GONARTHRITIS
GONCALO
GONDANG
GONDITE
GONDOLA
GONDOLET
GONDOLIER
GONE
GONENESS
GONEOCLINIC
GONEPOIESIS
GONEPOIETIC
GONER
GONESOME
GONEY
GONFALON
GONFALONIER
GONFANON
GONG
GONGMAN
GONGORISTIC
GONIAC
GONIAL
GONIALE
GONID
GONIDANGIUM
GONIDIA
GONIDIAL
GONIDIOSE
GONIDIOSPORE
GONIDIUM
GONIMIC
GONIMOBLAST
GONIMOLOBE
GONIMOUS
GONIOMETER
GONIOMETRIC
GONIOMETRY
GONION
GONIOSTAT
GONIOTHECA
GONIOTROPOUS
GONITIS
GONIUM
GONNARDITE
GONOBLAST
GONOBLASTIC
GONOCALYX
GONOCHORISM
GONOCOCCI
GONOCOCCUS
GONOCOEL
GONOCOELE
GONOCYTE
GONOECIUM
GONOF
GONOMERE
GONOMERY
GONOPH
GONOPHORE
GONOPHORIC
GONOPHOROUS
GONOPLASM
GONOPOD
GONOPOIETIC
GONORRHEA
GONORRHEAL
GONORRHEIC
GONORRHOEA
GONORRHOEAL
GONORRHOEIC
GONOSOMAL
GONOSOME
GONOSPHERE
GONOSTYLE
GONOTHECA
GONOTHECAL
GONOTOCONT
GONOTOKONT
GONOTOME
GONOTYL
GONOTYPE
GONOZOOID
GONY
GONYALGIA
GONYDEAL
GONYDIAL
GONYOCELE
GONYONCUS
GONYS
GONYTHECA
GONZALO
GOO
GOOBER
GOOD
GOODHAP
GOODHEARTED
GOODIES
GOODING
GOODISH
GOODISHNESS
GOODLIER
GOODLIEST
GOODLIHEAD
GOODLIKE
GOODLINESS
GOODLY
GOODMAN
GOODNESS
GOODS
GOODSIRE
GOODWIFE
GOODWILL
GOODWILLIT
GOODWILLY
GOODWIVES
GOODY
GOODYEAR
GOOEY
GOOF
GOOFA
GOOFAH
GOOFBALL
GOOFER
GOOFIER
GOOFIEST
GOOFILY
GOOFINESS
GOOFY
GOOG
GOOGLY
GOOGOL
GOOGOLPLEX
GOOGUL
GOOIER
GOOIEST
GOOK
GOOL
GOOLAH
GOOLDE
GOOLS
GOOM
GOOMA
GOOMBAY
GOON
GOONCH
GOONDA
GOONDIE
GOONEY
GOONIE
GOONY
GOOR
GOORAL
GOORANUT
GOOSANDER
GOOSE
GOOSEBEAK
GOOSEBERRY
GOOSEBILL
GOOSEBIRD
GOOSEBONE
GOOSEBOY
GOOSECAP
GOOSED
GOOSEFLESH
GOOSEFLOWER
GOOSEFOOT
GOOSEGIRL
GOOSEGOG
GOOSEGRASS
GOOSEHERD
GOOSEHOUSE
GOOSEMOUTH
GOOSENECK
GOOSERIES
GOOSERUMPED
GOOSERY
GOOSES
GOOSESKIN
GOOSETONGUE
GOOSEWEED
GOOSEWING
GOOSEWINGED
GOOSEY
GOOSIER
GOOSIEST
GOOSING
GOOSISH
GOOSISHLY
GOOSISHNESS
GOOSY
GOOTE
GOOTEE
GOOZLE
GOPAK
GOPE
GOPHER
GOPHERBERRY
GOPHERMAN
GOPHERROOT
GOPHERWOOD
GOPURA
GOR
GORA
GORACCO
GORAH
GORAL
GORALOG
GORALS
GORAN
GORB
GORBELLIES
GORBELLY
GORBET
GORBIT
GORBLE
GORBLIMY
GORBLIN
GORCE
GORCOCK
GORCROW
GORDIID
GORDIOID
GORDOLOBO
GORDUNITE
GORE
GORED
GOREFISH
GORER
GOREVAN
GORFLY
GORGE
GORGED
GORGEDLY
GORGELET
GORGEOUS
GORGEOUSLY
GORGEOUSNESS
GORGER
GORGERIN
GORGES
GORGET
GORGETED
GORGIA
GORGING
GORGIO
GORGON
GORGONACEAN
GORGONESQUE
GORGONEUM
GORGONIAN
GORGONIN
GORGONIZE
GORGONIZED
GORHEN
GORIC
GORILLA
GORILLAS
GORILLIAN
GORILLOID
GORILY
GORINESS
GORING
GORKUN
GORLIN
GORLING
GORM
GORMA
GORMAND
GORMANDIZE
GORMANDIZER
GORMAW
GORMED
GORRAF
GORREL
GORSE
GORSEBIRD
GORSECHAT
GORSEDD
GORSEHATCH
GORSIER
GORSIEST
GORST

GORSY
GORY
GOS
GOSAIN
GOSCHENS
GOSH
GOSHAWK
GOSHENITE
GOSLARITE
GOSLET
GOSLING
GOSMORE
GOSPEL
GOSPELER
GOSPELIZE
GOSPELLER
GOSPELLIKE
GOSPELLY
GOSPODAR
GOSPODIN
GOSPORT
GOSSAMER
GOSSAMERED
GOSSAMERY
GOSSAMPINE
GOSSAN
GOSSARD
GOSSIP
GOSSIPED
GOSSIPER
GOSSIPHOOD
GOSSIPINESS
GOSSIPING
GOSSIPINGLY
GOSSIPMONGER
GOSSIPPED
GOSSIPPING
GOSSIPRED
GOSSIPRY
GOSSIPY
GOSSOON
GOSSY
GOSSYPIN
GOSSYPINE
GOSSYPOL
GOSTER
GOSTHER
GOT
GOTA
GOTCH
GOTCHED
GOTCHY
GOTE
GOTHIC
GOTHITE
GOTHS
GOTRA
GOTRAJA
GOTTEN
GOUACHE
GOUAREE
GOUFF
GOUGE
GOUGED
GOUGER
GOUGING
GOUJAT
GOUJON
GOUK
GOUL
GOULASH
GOULDIAN
GOUM
GOUMI
GOUMIER
GOUNAU
GOUND
GOUNDOU
GOUPEN
GOUPIN
GOUR
GOURA
GOURAMI
GOURD
GOURDE
GOURDED
GOURDHEAD
GOURDINESS
GOURDING
GOURDY
GOURMAND
GOURMANDER
GOURMANDERIE
GOURMANDISE
GOURMET
GOUROUNUT
GOURY
GOUSTIE
GOUSTROUS
GOUSTY
GOUT
GOUTER
GOUTIER
GOUTIEST
GOUTIFY
GOUTILY
GOUTINESS
GOUTISH
GOUTTE
GOUTWEED
GOUTWORT
GOUTY
GOUVERNANTE
GOVE
GOVERN
GOVERNABLE
GOVERNAIL
GOVERNANCE
GOVERNED
GOVERNESS
GOVERNING
GOVERNMENT
GOVERNMENTAL
GOVERNOR
GOVERNORATE
GOVERNORS
GOVERNORSHIP
GOW
GOWAN
GOWANED
GOWANY
GOWD
GOWDIE
GOWDNIE
GOWDNOOK
GOWDY
GOWF
GOWFF
GOWIDDIE
GOWK
GOWKED
GOWKEDLY
GOWKEDNESS
GOWKIT
GOWL
GOWLAN
GOWLAND
GOWN
GOWNED
GOWNING
GOWNSMAN
GOWP
GOWPEN
GOWPIN
GOWT
GOY
GOYAL
GOYAZITE
GOYIM
GOYIN
GOYISH
GOYLE
GOZELL
GOZILL
GOZZAN
GOZZARD
GRA
GRAAL
GRAAP
GRAB
GRABBED
GRABBER
GRABBING
GRABBLE
GRABBLER
GRABBLING
GRABBOTS
GRABBY
GRABEN
GRABHOOK
GRABMAN
GRABOUCHE
GRACE
GRACED
GRACEFUL
GRACEFULLY
GRACEFULNESS
GRACELESS
GRACELESSLY
GRACER
GRACES
GRACILARIID
GRACILE
GRACILENESS
GRACILESCENT
GRACILIS
GRACILITY
GRACING
GRACIOSITY
GRACIOSO
GRACIOUS
GRACIOUSLY
GRACIOUSNESS
GRACKLE
GRACY
GRAD
GRADAL
GRADATE
GRADATED
GRADATIM
GRADATING
GRADATION
GRADATIONAL
GRADATIVE
GRADATORY
GRADDAN
GRADE
GRADED
GRADEFINDER
GRADELY
GRADER
GRADES
GRADGRIND
GRADIENT
GRADIENTER
GRADIN
GRADINE
GRADING
GRADINO
GRADIOMETER
GRADIOMETRIC
GRADO
GRADOMETER
GRADUAL
GRADUALE
GRADUALISM
GRADUALIST
GRADUALISTIC
GRADUALITY
GRADUALLY
GRADUALNESS
GRADUAND
GRADUATE
GRADUATED
GRADUATICAL
GRADUATING
GRADUATION
GRADUS
GRAFF
GRAFFAGE
GRAFFER
GRAFFITO
GRAFT
GRAFTAGE
GRAFTED
GRAFTER
GRAFTING
GRAFTONITE
GRAGER
GRAHAM
GRAHAMITE
GRAIL
GRAILER
GRAILING
GRAILLE
GRAIN
GRAINAGE
GRAINE
GRAINED
GRAINER
GRAINERING
GRAINERY
GRAINFIELD
GRAINIER
GRAINIEST
GRAININESS
GRAINING
GRAINLAND
GRAINLESS
GRAINMAN
GRAINS
GRAINSICK
GRAINSICKNESS
GRAINSMAN
GRAINSMEN
GRAINY
GRAIP
GRAISSE
GRAITH
GRAITHLY
GRALLATORIAL
GRALLATORY
GRALLIC
GRALLINE
GRALLOCH
GRAM
GRAMA
GRAMARY
GRAMARYE
GRAME
GRAMENITE
GRAMERCY
GRAMINEAL
GRAMINEOUS
GRAMINIFORM
GRAMININ
GRAMINIVORE
GRAMINOLOGY
GRAMINOUS
GRAMMA
GRAMMALOGUE
GRAMMAR
GRAMMARIAN
GRAMMATES
GRAMMATICAL
GRAMMATICALLY
GRAMMATICISM
GRAMMATICIZE
GRAMMATICS
GRAMMATIST
GRAMME
GRAMMEL
GRAMOCHES
GRAMOPHONE
GRAMOPHONIC
GRAMP
GRAMPS
GRAMPUS
GRAMY
GRAN
GRANA
GRANADILLA
GRANADILLO
GRANAGE
GRANAM
GRANARY
GRANAT
GRANATE
GRANATUM
GRANCH
GRAND
GRANDAD
GRANDADA
GRANDADDY
GRANDAM
GRANDAME
GRANDAUNT
GRANDCHILD
GRANDDAD
GRANDDADA
GRANDDADDY
GRANDDAM
GRANDDAUGHTER
GRANDE
GRANDEE
GRANDER
GRANDESQUE
GRANDEST
GRANDEUR
GRANDEVAL
GRANDEVITY
GRANDEZA
GRANDFATHER
GRANDFER
GRANDFILIAL
GRANDGORE
GRANDILOQUENT
GRANDIOSE
GRANDIOSELY
GRANDIOSITY
GRANDIOSO
GRANDISONANT
GRANDISONOUS
GRANDITY
GRANDLY
GRANDMA
GRANDMAMA
GRANDMAMMA
GRANDMATERNAL
GRANDMOTHER
GRANDNEPHEW
GRANDNESS
GRANDNIECE
GRANDO
GRANDPA

GRANDPAPA
GRANDPARENT
GRANDPARENTS
GRANDPATERNAL
GRANDSIR
GRANDSIRE
GRANDSON
GRANDSTAND
GRANDSTANDER
GRANDUNCLE
GRANE
GRANES
GRANET
GRANGE
GRANGER
GRANGERISM
GRANGERITE
GRANGERIZE
GRANI
GRANIFEROUS
GRANIFORM
GRANILLA
GRANITA
GRANITE
GRANITEWARE
GRANITIC
GRANITICAL
GRANITITE
GRANITIZE
GRANITOID
GRANITOIDAL
GRANIVORE
GRANIVOROUS
GRANJENO
GRANK
GRANNAM
GRANNIE
GRANNOM
GRANNY
GRANNYBUSH
GRANNYKNOT
GRANO
GRANOBLASTIC
GRANODIORITE
GRANOGABBRO
GRANOLITH
GRANOLITHIC
GRANOMERITE
GRANOPHYRE
GRANOPHYRIC
GRANOSE
GRANOSPHERITE
GRANT
GRANTABLE
GRANTED
GRANTEE
GRANTER
GRANTHI
GRANTING
GRANTOR
GRANTS
GRANULA
GRANULAR
GRANULARITY
GRANULARLY
GRANULARY
GRANULATE
GRANULATED
GRANULATER
GRANULATING
GRANULATION
GRANULATIVE
GRANULATOR
GRANULE
GRANULET
GRANULITE
GRANULITIC
GRANULITIS
GRANULITIZE
GRANULIZE
GRANULOCYTE
GRANULOMA
GRANULOMAS
GRANULOMATA
GRANULOSE
GRANUM
GRANZA
GRAO
GRAPE
GRAPED
GRAPEFLOWER
GRAPEFRUIT
GRAPEFRUITS
GRAPELET
GRAPELIKE
GRAPENUTS
GRAPEROOT
GRAPERY
GRAPES
GRAPESHOT
GRAPESKIN
GRAPESTALK
GRAPESTONE
GRAPEVINE
GRAPEWORT
GRAPH
GRAPHALLOY
GRAPHIC
GRAPHICAL
GRAPHICALLY
GRAPHICLY
GRAPHICNESS
GRAPHICS
GRAPHIOLOGY
GRAPHITE
GRAPHITER
GRAPHITIC
GRAPHITIZE
GRAPHITIZED
GRAPHITOID
GRAPHITOIDAL
GRAPHOLOGIC
GRAPHOLOGIST
GRAPHOLOGY
GRAPHOMETER
GRAPHOMETRIC
GRAPHOMETRY
GRAPHOMOTOR
GRAPHOPHONE
GRAPHOPHONIC
GRAPHORRHEA
GRAPHOSCOPE
GRAPHOSPASM
GRAPHOSTATIC
GRAPHOTYPE
GRAPHY
GRAPIER
GRAPIEST
GRAPING
GRAPLIN
GRAPLINE
GRAPNEL
GRAPPA
GRAPPLE
GRAPPLED
GRAPPLER
GRAPPLING
GRAPSOID
GRAPTOLITE
GRAPTOLITIC
GRAPTOMANCY
GRAPY
GRASH
GRASNI
GRASO
GRASP
GRASPABLE
GRASPED
GRASPER
GRASPING
GRASPINGLY
GRASPINGNESS
GRASPLESS
GRASS
GRASSANT
GRASSATION
GRASSBIRD
GRASSCHAT
GRASSCUT
GRASSCUTTER
GRASSED
GRASSER
GRASSERIE
GRASSET
GRASSEYE
GRASSFLAT
GRASSFLOWER
GRASSHOP
GRASSHOPPER
GRASSHOUSE
GRASSIE
GRASSIER
GRASSIEST
GRASSILY
GRASSINESS
GRASSING
GRASSLAND
GRASSLESS
GRASSLIKE
GRASSMAN
GRASSMEN
GRASSNUT
GRASSPLAT
GRASSPLOT
GRASSQUIT
GRASSROOTS
GRASSWEED
GRASSWIDOW
GRASSWORK
GRASSWORM
GRASSY
GRAT
GRATE
GRATED
GRATEFUL
GRATEFULLY
GRATEFULNESS
GRATEMAN
GRATER
GRATHER
GRATICULATE
GRATICULE
GRATIFICATION
GRATIFIED
GRATIFIEDLY
GRATIFIER
GRATIFY
GRATIFYING
GRATIFYINGLY
GRATILITY
GRATILLITY
GRATIN
GRATINATE
GRATINATED
GRATINATING
GRATING
GRATINGLY
GRATINGS
GRATIOLIN
GRATIOSOLIN
GRATIS
GRATITUDE
GRATTEN
GRATTERS
GRATTOIR
GRATTON
GRATUITANT
GRATUITIES
GRATUITO
GRATUITOUS
GRATUITOUSLY
GRATUITY
GRATULANT
GRATULATE
GRATULATED
GRATULATION
GRATULATORY
GRAUPEL
GRAVAMEN
GRAVAMINA
GRAVAMINOUS
GRAVAT
GRAVATA
GRAVE
GRAVECLOD
GRAVECLOTH
GRAVECLOTHES
GRAVED
GRAVEDIGGER
GRAVEDO
GRAVEGARTH
GRAVEL
GRAVELED
GRAVELING
GRAVELLED
GRAVELLINESS
GRAVELLING
GRAVELLY
GRAVELSTONE
GRAVELWEED
GRAVELY
GRAVEMAKER
GRAVEMAKING
GRAVEMAN
GRAVEMASTER
GRAVEN
GRAVENESS
GRAVEOLENCE
GRAVEOLENCY
GRAVEOLENT
GRAVER
GRAVERY
GRAVES
GRAVESHIP
GRAVESIDE
GRAVEST
GRAVESTEAD
GRAVESTONE
GRAVETTE
GRAVEWARD
GRAVEWARDS
GRAVEYARD
GRAVIC
GRAVID
GRAVIDA
GRAVIDATE
GRAVIDATION
GRAVIDITY
GRAVIDLY
GRAVIDNESS
GRAVIERS
GRAVIFIC
GRAVIGRADE
GRAVILEA
GRAVIMETER
GRAVIMETRIC
GRAVIMETRY
GRAVING
GRAVIPAUSE
GRAVISPHERIC
GRAVITATE
GRAVITATED
GRAVITATER
GRAVITATING
GRAVITATION
GRAVITATIONAL
GRAVITATIVE
GRAVITIES
GRAVITY
GRAVURE
GRAVY
GRAWLS
GRAY
GRAYBACK
GRAYBEARD
GRAYCOAT
GRAYED
GRAYER
GRAYEST
GRAYFISH
GRAYFLY
GRAYHEAD
GRAYHOUND
GRAYISH
GRAYLAG
GRAYLAGS
GRAYLING
GRAYLINGS
GRAYLY
GRAYMILL
GRAYNESS
GRAYOUT
GRAYPATE
GRAYS
GRAYSBY
GRAYWACKE
GRAYWALL
GRAYWARE
GRAYWETHER
GRAZE
GRAZED
GRAZIER
GRAZIERY
GRAZING
GRAZINGLY
GRAZIOSO
GREABLE
GREABLY
GREASE
GREASEBUSH
GREASED
GREASEHORN
GREASER
GREASEWOOD
GREASIER
GREASIEST
GREASILY
GREASINESS
GREASING
GREASY
GREAT
GREATCOAT
GREATCOATED
GREATEN
GREATER
GREATEST
GREATHEAD
GREATHEART
GREATHEARTED
GREATLY
GREATMOUTHED
GREATNESS
GREAVE
GREAVES
GREBE

GREBES
GRECE
GRECQUE
GREDE
GREE
GREED
GREEDIER
GREEDIEST
GREEDILY
GREEDINESS
GREEDLESS
GREEDSOME
GREEDY
GREEDYGUT
GREEDYGUTS
GREEGREE
GREEN
GREENALITE
GREENBACK
GREENBELT
GREENBOARD
GREENBONE
GREENBRIER
GREENBUL
GREENCOAT
GREENED
GREENER
GREENERIES
GREENERY
GREENEY
GREENFINCH
GREENFISH
GREENFLY
GREENGAGE
GREENGILL
GREENGROCER
GREENGROCERY
GREENHEAD
GREENHEADED
GREENHEART
GREENHEW
GREENHIDE
GREENHORN
GREENHOUSE
GREENIER
GREENIEST
GREENING
GREENISH
GREENISHNESS
GREENKEEPER
GREENKEEPING
GREENLANDITE
GREENLEEK
GREENLET
GREENLING
GREENLY
GREENNESS
GREENOCKITE
GREENOVITE
GREENROOM
GREENS
GREENSAND
GREENSAUCE
GREENSHANK
GREENSICK
GREENSICKNESS
GREENSIDE
GREENSTONE
GREENSWARD
GREENSWARDED
GREENTH
GREENUK
GREENWAX
GREENWEED
GREENWING
GREENWITHE
GREENWOOD
GREENY
GREENYARD
GREESAGH
GREESE
GREESHOCH
GREET
GREETED
GREETER
GREETING
GREETINGLY
GREFFE
GREFFIER
GREFFOTOME
GREGAL
GREGALE
GREGALOID
GREGARIAN
GREGARIANISM
GREGARINE
GREGARINIDAL
GREGARINOSIS
GREGARINOUS
GREGARIOUS
GREGARIOUSLY
GREGARITIC
GREGATIM
GREGE
GREGGLE
GREGO
GREIGE
GREILLADE
GREIN
GREISEN
GREKING
GRELOT
GREMIAL
GREMIALE
GREMIO
GREMLIN
GRENADE
GRENADES
GRENADIER
GRENADIERIAL
GRENADIERLY
GRENADIN
GRENADINE
GRENADO
GRENAT
GRENIER
GRES
GRESIL
GRESSORIAL
GRESSORIOUS
GRETH
GREUND
GREW
GREWHOUND
GREWSOME
GREWSOMELY
GREWSOMENESS
GREWT
GREX
GREY
GREYBACK
GREYBEARD
GREYCOAT
GREYER
GREYEST
GREYFISH
GREYFLIES
GREYFLY
GREYHOUND
GREYHOUNDS
GREYLAG
GREYLY
GREYNESS
GREYPATE
GREYS
GREYSKIN
GREYWACKE
GREYWARE
GREYWETHER
GRI
GRIBANE
GRIBBLE
GRICE
GRID
GRIDDER
GRIDDLE
GRIDDLECAKE
GRIDDLED
GRIDDLER
GRIDDLING
GRIDE
GRIDELIN
GRIDING
GRIDIRON
GRIEBEN
GRIECE
GRIECED
GRIEF
GRIEFFUL
GRIEGE
GRIEKO
GRIEN
GRIESHOCH
GRIESHUCKLE
GRIEVANCE
GRIEVE
GRIEVED
GRIEVER
GRIEVESHIP
GRIEVING
GRIEVINGLY
GRIEVOUS
GRIEVOUSLY
GRIEVOUSNESS
GRIFF
GRIFFADE
GRIFFADO
GRIFFAUN
GRIFFE
GRIFFIN
GRIFFINAGE
GRIFFITHITE
GRIFFON
GRIFFONAGE
GRIFT
GRIFTER
GRIG
GRIGGLES
GRIGNET
GRIGRI
GRIGS
GRIHYASUTRA
GRIKE
GRIL
GRILL
GRILLADE
GRILLAGE
GRILLE
GRILLED
GRILLEE
GRILLER
GRILLING
GRILLROOM
GRILLWORK
GRILLY
GRILSE
GRILSES
GRIM
GRIMACE
GRIMACED
GRIMACER
GRIMACING
GRIMACINGLY
GRIMALKIN
GRIME
GRIMED
GRIMFUL
GRIMGRIBBER
GRIMIER
GRIMIEST
GRIMILY
GRIMINESS
GRIMING
GRIMLY
GRIMME
GRIMMER
GRIMMEST
GRIMNESS
GRIMOIRE
GRIMP
GRIMSIR
GRIMSIRE
GRIMY
GRIN
GRINAGOG
GRINCH
GRINCOME
GRIND
GRINDAL
GRINDED
GRINDER
GRINDERMAN
GRINDERS
GRINDERY
GRINDING
GRINDLE
GRINDSTONE
GRINGO
GRINGOLE
GRINGOLEE
GRINNED
GRINNER
GRINNIE
GRINNING
GRINNINGLY
GRINNY
GRINT
GRINTER
GRINTERN
GRIOTTE
GRIP
GRIPE
GRIPED
GRIPEFUL
GRIPER
GRIPES
GRIPGRASS
GRIPH
GRIPHE
GRIPHITE
GRIPHUS
GRIPIER
GRIPIEST
GRIPING
GRIPINGLY
GRIPLESS
GRIPMAN
GRIPPAL
GRIPPE
GRIPPED
GRIPPER
GRIPPERS
GRIPPING
GRIPPINGLY
GRIPPINGNESS
GRIPPIT
GRIPPLE
GRIPPLENESS
GRIPPOTOXIN
GRIPPY
GRIPS
GRIPSACK
GRIPT
GRIPY
GRIQUAITE
GRIS
GRISAILLE
GRISARD
GRISBET
GRISE
GRISEOUS
GRISETTE
GRISETTISH
GRISKIN
GRISLIER
GRISLIEST
GRISLINESS
GRISLY
GRISON
GRISONS
GRISOUNITE
GRISOUTINE
GRISP
GRISPING
GRISSEN
GRISSET
GRIST
GRISTBITE
GRISTER
GRISTLE
GRISTLINESS
GRISTLY
GRISTMILL
GRISTMILLER
GRISTMILLING
GRISTY
GRIT
GRITH
GRITHBREACH
GRITHMAN
GRITROCK
GRITS
GRITTED
GRITTEN
GRITTER
GRITTIE
GRITTIER
GRITTIEST
GRITTILY
GRITTINESS
GRITTING
GRITTLE
GRITTY
GRIVE
GRIVET
GRIVNA
GRIVOIS
GRIVOISE
GRIZARD
GRIZZLE
GRIZZLED
GRIZZLER
GRIZZLIER
GRIZZLIES
GRIZZLIEST
GRIZZLING
GRIZZLY
GRIZZLYMAN
GROAK
GROAN
GROANED
GROANER
GROANFUL
GROANING
GROANINGLY

GROAT
GROATS
GROATSWORTH
GROBIAN
GROBIANISM
GROCER
GROCERIES
GROCERLY
GROCERY
GROFF
GROG
GROGGED
GROGGER
GROGGERIES
GROGGERY
GROGGIER
GROGGIEST
GROGGILY
GROGGINESS
GROGGING
GROGGY
GROGNARD
GROGRAM
GROGSHOP
GROIN
GROINED
GROINERY
GROINING
GROM
GROMATIC
GROMATICAL
GROMATICS
GROMET
GROMMET
GROMWELL
GROMYL
GRONDWET
GRONT
GROOF
GROOM
GROOMED
GROOMER
GROOMING
GROOMLET
GROOMSMAN
GROOMSMEN
GROOMY
GROOP
GROOSE
GROOT
GROOTY
GROOVE
GROOVED
GROOVER
GROOVERHEAD
GROOVIER
GROOVIEST
GROOVING
GROOVY
GROPE
GROPED
GROPER
GROPING
GROPINGLY
GROPPLE
GRORUDITE
GROS
GROSBEAK
GROSCHEN
GROSER
GROSET
GROSGRAIN
GROSGRAINED
GROSS
GROSSEN
GROSSER
GROSSES
GROSSEST
GROSSIERETE
GROSSIFY
GROSSLY
GROSSO
GROSSULAR
GROSSULARITE
GROSZ
GROSZY
GROT
GROTE
GROTEN
GROTESCO
GROTESQUE
GROTESQUELY
GROTESQUERIE
GROTESQUERY
GROTHINE
GROTHITE
GROTTO
GROTTOED
GROTTOWORK
GROTZEN
GROUCH
GROUCHIER
GROUCHIEST
GROUCHILY
GROUCHINESS
GROUCHY
GROUF
GROUGH
GROUND
GROUNDABLE
GROUNDAGE
GROUNDBERRY
GROUNDBIRD
GROUNDED
GROUNDEDLY
GROUNDEDNESS
GROUNDEN
GROUNDENELL
GROUNDER
GROUNDHOG
GROUNDING
GROUNDLESS
GROUNDLESSLY
GROUNDLINE
GROUNDLINESS
GROUNDLING
GROUNDLY
GROUNDMAN
GROUNDMASS
GROUNDNEEDLE
GROUNDNUT
GROUNDS
GROUNDSEL
GROUNDSILL
GROUNDSMAN
GROUNDWALL
GROUNDWARD
GROUNDWARDS
GROUNDWOOD
GROUNDWORK
GROUNDY
GROUP
GROUPAGE
GROUPED
GROUPER
GROUPIE
GROUPING
GROUPMENT
GROUPS
GROUSE
GROUSED
GROUSER
GROUSING
GROUSY
GROUT
GROUTED
GROUTER
GROUTHEAD
GROUTIER
GROUTIEST
GROUTING
GROUTITE
GROUTS
GROUTY
GROUZE
GROVE
GROVED
GROVEL
GROVELED
GROVELER
GROVELING
GROVELINGLY
GROVELINGS
GROVELLED
GROVELLER
GROVELLING
GROVELLINGLY
GROVELLINGS
GROVET
GROVY
GROW
GROWAN
GROWER
GROWING
GROWL
GROWLED
GROWLER
GROWLERIES
GROWLERY
GROWLING
GROWLY
GROWN
GROWNUP
GROWS
GROWSE
GROWSOME
GROWTH
GROWTHINESS
GROWTHY
GROWZE
GROYNE
GROZART
GROZER
GRU
GRUB
GRUBBED
GRUBBER
GRUBBERIES
GRUBBERY
GRUBBIER
GRUBBIEST
GRUBBILY
GRUBBINESS
GRUBBING
GRUBBLE
GRUBBY
GRUBROOT
GRUBS
GRUBSTAKE
GRUBSTAKER
GRUBSTREET
GRUBWORM
GRUDGE
GRUDGED
GRUDGER
GRUDGERY
GRUDGING
GRUDGINGLY
GRUE
GRUEL
GRUELED
GRUELER
GRUELING
GRUELLED
GRUELLER
GRUELLING
GRUELLY
GRUESOME
GRUESOMELY
GRUESOMENESS
GRUF
GRUFF
GRUFFER
GRUFFEST
GRUFFILY
GRUFFINESS
GRUFFLY
GRUFFNESS
GRUFFS
GRUFFY
GRUFT
GRUFTED
GRUG
GRUGOUS
GRUGRU
GRUIFORM
GRUINE
GRULLA
GRUM
GRUMBLE
GRUMBLED
GRUMBLER
GRUMBLING
GRUMBLINGLY
GRUMBLY
GRUME
GRUMLY
GRUMMEL
GRUMMELS
GRUMMER
GRUMMEST
GRUMMET
GRUMMETER
GRUMNESS
GRUMOSE
GRUMOUS
GRUMOUSNESS
GRUMP
GRUMPH
GRUMPHIE
GRUMPHY
GRUMPIER
GRUMPIEST
GRUMPILY
GRUMPINESS
GRUMPISH
GRUMPS
GRUMPY
GRUN
GRUNCH
GRUNDY
GRUNERITE
GRUNION
GRUNT
GRUNTER
GRUNTING
GRUNTLE
GRUNTLED
GRUNTLING
GRUNZIE
GRUP
GRUPPETTO
GRUPPO
GRUSH
GRUSHIE
GRUSS
GRUTCH
GRY
GRYLLE
GRYLLI
GRYLLID
GRYLLOS
GRYLLUS
GRYPANIAN
GRYPHON
GRYPOSIS
GRYS
GRYSBOK
GUACA
GUACACOA
GUACHAMACA
GUACHARO
GUACHIPILIN
GUACIMO
GUACIN
GUACO
GUACONIZE
GUADUA
GUAGUANCHE
GUAHIVO
GUAIAC
GUAIACOL
GUAIACUM
GUAIASANOL
GUAICAN
GUAIOCUM
GUAIOL
GUAJILLO
GUAJIRA
GUAKO
GUALE
GUAMA
GUAN
GUANA
GUANABANA
GUANABANO
GUANACO
GUANAJUATITE
GUANAMINE
GUANARE
GUANASE
GUANAY
GUANEIDE
GUANGO
GUANIDINE
GUANIFEROUS
GUANINE
GUANIZE
GUANO
GUANOPHORE
GUANOSINE
GUANYL
GUAO
GUAPENA
GUAPILLA
GUAPINOL
GUAR
GUARA
GUARABU
GUARACHA
GUARACHE
GUARAGUAO
GUARANA
GUARAND
GUARANINE
GUARANTEE
GUARANTEED
GUARANTEES
GUARANTIED
GUARANTIES
GUARANTOR
GUARANTY
GUARANTYING
GUARAPO
GUARAPUCU

GUARD
GUARDAGE
GUARDANT
GUARDED
GUARDEDLY
GUARDEDNESS
GUARDEE
GUARDER
GUARDFUL
GUARDFULLY
GUARDHOUSE
GUARDIAN
GUARDIANCY
GUARDIANLY
GUARDIANSHIP
GUARDING
GUARDO
GUARDRAIL
GUARDROOM
GUARDS
GUARDSMAN
GUARDSMEN
GUARDSTONE
GUARIBA
GUARICO
GUARINITE
GUARISH
GUARRI
GUARY
GUASA
GUASO
GUATAMBU
GUATIBERO
GUATIVERE
GUAVA
GUAVABERRY
GUAVINA
GUAXIMA
GUAYABA
GUAYABI
GUAYABO
GUAYACAN
GUAYROTO
GUAYULE
GUAZA
GUAZUTI
GUB
GUBAT
GUBBERTUSH
GUBBIN
GUBBINGS
GUBBINS
GUBBO
GUBERNATION
GUBERNATIVE
GUBERNATOR
GUBERNATRIX
GUBERNIA
GUBERNIYA
GUCK
GUCKED
GUDAME
GUDDA
GUDDLE
GUDE
GUDEMOTHER
GUDESIRE
GUDEWIFE
GUDGE
GUDGEON
GUDGET
GUDOK
GUE
GUEBUCU
GUEJARITE
GUEMAL
GUEMUL
GUENON
GUEPARD
GUEPARDE
GUERDON
GUERDONER
GUEREBA
GUEREZA
GUERIDON
GUERILLA
GUERISON
GUERITE
GUERNSEYED
GUERNSEYS
GUERRILLA
GUESS
GUESSED
GUESSER
GUESSING
GUESSTIMATE
GUESSWORK
GUESSWORKER
GUEST
GUESTCHAMBER
GUESTED
GUESTEN
GUESTER
GUESTHOUSE
GUESTING
GUESTIVE
GUESTMASTER
GUETRE
GUF
GUFA
GUFF
GUFFAW
GUFFER
GUFFIN
GUFFY
GUGAL
GUGGLE
GUGGLET
GUGLET
GUGLIA
GUGLIO
GUGU
GUGUL
GUHR
GUIB
GUIBA
GUICHET
GUID
GUIDA
GUIDABLE
GUIDAGE
GUIDANCE
GUIDE
GUIDEBOARD
GUIDEBOOK
GUIDECRAFT
GUIDED
GUIDELINE
GUIDEPOST
GUIDER
GUIDERESS
GUIDESHIP
GUIDEWAY
GUIDING
GUIDMAN
GUIDON
GUIDSIRE
GUIDWIFE
GUIGE
GUIGNE
GUIJO
GUILD
GUILDER
GUILDHALL
GUILDIC
GUILDITE
GUILDRY
GUILDSHIP
GUILDSMAN
GUILDSMEN
GUILE
GUILEFUL
GUILEFULLY
GUILEFULNESS
GUILELESS
GUILELESSLY
GUILER
GUILERY
GUILLEMET
GUILLEMOT
GUILLEVAT
GUILLOCHE
GUILLOCHEE
GUILLOTINADE
GUILLOTINE
GUILLOTINED
GUILLOTINER
GUILLOTINING
GUILLOTINISM
GUILLOTINIST
GUILT
GUILTFUL
GUILTIER
GUILTIEST
GUILTILY
GUILTINESS
GUILTLESS
GUILTLESSLY
GUILTSICK
GUILTY
GUILY
GUIMBARD
GUIMPE
GUINEA
GUIPURE
GUIRO
GUISE
GUISED
GUISER
GUISING
GUITAR
GUITARFISH
GUITARIST
GUITERMANITE
GUITGUIT
GUJERAT
GUL
GULA
GULAMAN
GULANCHA
GULAR
GULARIS
GULASH
GULCH
GULDEN
GULE
GULES
GULF
GULFWEED
GULFY
GULGUL
GULINULA
GULINULAR
GULIX
GULL
GULLAGE
GULLED
GULLER
GULLERIES
GULLERY
GULLET
GULLEY
GULLIBILITY
GULLIBLE
GULLIBLY
GULLIED
GULLIES
GULLING
GULLION
GULLISH
GULLISHLY
GULLISHNESS
GULLY
GULLYGUT
GULLYHOLE
GULLYING
GULMOHAR
GULOC
GULOSE
GULOSITY
GULP
GULPED
GULPER
GULPH
GULPIN
GULPING
GULPINGLY
GULPS
GULPY
GULSACH
GULY
GUM
GUMBE
GUMBO
GUMBOIL
GUMBOTIL
GUMBY
GUMCHEWER
GUMDIGGER
GUMDIGGING
GUMDROP
GUME
GUMFIELD
GUMFLOWER
GUMHAR
GUMIHAN
GUMLAH
GUMLY
GUMMA
GUMMAGE
GUMMAKER
GUMMAS
GUMMATA
GUMMATOUS
GUMMED
GUMMER
GUMMIER
GUMMIEST
GUMMIFEROUS
GUMMINESS
GUMMING
GUMMITE
GUMMOSE
GUMMOSIS
GUMMOSITY
GUMMOUS
GUMMY
GUMP
GUMPHEON
GUMPHION
GUMPTION
GUMPUS
GUMS
GUMSHOE
GUMSHOED
GUMSHOEING
GUMTREE
GUMWEED
GUMWOOD
GUN
GUNA
GUNATE
GUNATED
GUNATING
GUNATION
GUNBOAT
GUNBOATS
GUNBUILDER
GUNCOTTON
GUNDA
GUNDALOW
GUNDECK
GUNDELOW
GUNDI
GUNDIE
GUNDOG
GUNDY
GUNDYGUT
GUNFIGHT
GUNFIRE
GUNFLINT
GUNGE
GUNHOUSE
GUNITER
GUNJ
GUNJA
GUNJAH
GUNK
GUNKHOLE
GUNLAYER
GUNLAYING
GUNLINE
GUNLOCK
GUNMAKER
GUNMAKING
GUNMAN
GUNMEN
GUNMETAL
GUNNAGE
GUNNED
GUNNEL
GUNNELS
GUNNER
GUNNERY
GUNNIES
GUNNING
GUNNUNG
GUNNY
GUNNYSACK
GUNOCRACY
GUNONG
GUNPAPER
GUNPLAY
GUNPORT
GUNPOWDER
GUNPOWDEROUS
GUNPOWER
GUNRACK
GUNREACH
GUNRUNNER
GUNRUNNING
GUNS
GUNSEL
GUNSHIP
GUNSHOP
GUNSHOT
GUNSMAN
GUNSMITH
GUNSMITHERY
GUNSMITHING
GUNSTER
GUNSTICK
GUNSTOCK
GUNSTOCKER
GUNSTOCKING

GUNSTONE
GUNTER
GUNTUB
GUNUNG
GUNWALE
GUNYAH
GUNYANG
GUNYEH
GUP
GUPPIES
GUPPY
GUPTAVIDYA
GUR
GURDFISH
GURDWARA
GURDY
GURGE
GURGEONS
GURGES
GURGITATION
GURGLE
GURGLED
GURGLET
GURGLING
GURGLINGLY
GURGLY
GURGULATION
GURGULIO
GURJAN
GURJUN
GURK
GURL
GURLET
GURLY
GURNARD
GURNARDS
GURNEY
GURR
GURRAH
GURRY
GURT
GURU
GUSAIN
GUSH
GUSHED
GUSHER
GUSHET
GUSHIER
GUSHIEST
GUSHILY
GUSHINESS
GUSHING
GUSHINGLY
GUSHINGNESS
GUSHY
GUSLA
GUSLE
GUSLEE
GUSLI
GUSS
GUSSET
GUSSIE
GUST
GUSTABLE
GUSTATION
GUSTATIVE
GUSTATORY
GUSTFUL
GUSTFULLY
GUSTFULNESS
GUSTIER
GUSTIEST
GUSTILY
GUSTINESS
GUSTO
GUSTOSO
GUSTY
GUT
GUTBUCKET
GUTLESS
GUTLING
GUTS
GUTSIER
GUTSIEST
GUTSY
GUTT
GUTTA
GUTTAE
GUTTATE
GUTTATED
GUTTATIM
GUTTE
GUTTED
GUTTEE
GUTTER
GUTTERAL
GUTTERBLOOD
GUTTERED
GUTTERING
GUTTERLING
GUTTERMAN
GUTTERS
GUTTERSNIPE
GUTTERY
GUTTIDE
GUTTIE
GUTTIFEROUS
GUTTIFORM
GUTTING
GUTTLE
GUTTLED
GUTTLER
GUTTLING
GUTTULA
GUTTULAR
GUTTULATE
GUTTULE
GUTTULOUS
GUTTUR
GUTTURAL
GUTTURALISM
GUTTURALITY
GUTTURALIZE
GUTTURALIZING
GUTTURALLY
GUTTURALNESS
GUTTUS
GUTTY
GUTWEED
GUTWORT
GUV
GUY
GUYED
GUYER
GUYING
GUYO
GUYOT
GUYTRASH
GUYVER
GUZ
GUZE
GUZERAT
GUZZLE
GUZZLED
GUZZLER
GUZZLING
GWAG
GWANTUS
GWEDUC
GWEDUCK
GWEED
GWEEON
GWELY
GWERZIOU
GWINIAD
GWYNIAD
GYANI
GYASCUTUS
GYASSA
GYBE
GYLE
GYM
GYMEL
GYMKHANA
GYMNANTHOUS
GYMNASIA
GYMNASIAL
GYMNASIARCH
GYMNASIARCHY
GYMNASIAST
GYMNASIC
GYMNASIUM
GYMNAST
GYMNASTIC
GYMNASTICAL
GYMNASTICS
GYMNETROUS
GYMNIC
GYMNICAL
GYMNICS
GYMNITE
GYMNOBLASTIC
GYMNOCARPIC
GYMNOCARPOUS
GYMNOCIDIUM
GYMNODONT
GYMNOGENOUS
GYMNOGLOSSATE
GYMNOGYNOUS
GYMNOPAEDIC
GYMNOPLAST
GYMNORHINAL
GYMNOSOPH
GYMNOSOPHIST
GYMNOSOPHY
GYMNOSPERM
GYMNOSPERMY
GYMNOSPORE
GYMNOSPOROUS
GYMNOSTOMOUS
GYMNOTID
GYMNOTOKOUS
GYMNURE
GYMNURINE
GYMPIE
GYN
GYNAECEUM
GYNAECIUM
GYNAECOCRACY
GYNAECOCRAT
GYNAECOLOGIC
GYNAECOLOGY
GYNAECONITIS
GYNAEOCRACY
GYNAEOLATER
GYNAEOLATRY
GYNANDER
GYNANDRARCHY
GYNANDRIA
GYNANDRIAN
GYNANDRISM
GYNANDROID
GYNANDROUS
GYNANDRY
GYNANTHEROUS
GYNARCHIC
GYNARCHIES
GYNARCHY
GYNE
GYNECIC
GYNECIDAL
GYNECIDE
GYNECIUM
GYNECOCRACY
GYNECOCRAT
GYNECOCRATIC
GYNECOID
GYNECOLATRY
GYNECOLOGIC
GYNECOLOGIST
GYNECOLOGY
GYNECOMASTIA
GYNECOMASTY
GYNECOMAZIA
GYNECONITIS
GYNECOPATHIC
GYNECOPATHY
GYNECOTELIC
GYNECRATIC
GYNEE
GYNEOCRACY
GYNEOLATER
GYNEOLATRY
GYNETHUSIA
GYNETYPE
GYNIATRICS
GYNICS
GYNOBASE
GYNOBASEOUS
GYNOBASIC
GYNOCARDIC
GYNOCRACY
GYNOCRATIC
GYNOECIUM
GYNOGENESIS
GYNOPARA
GYNOPHAGITE
GYNOPHORE
GYNOPHORIC
GYNOSTEGIUM
GYOKURO
GYP
GYPE
GYPPED
GYPPERY
GYPPING
GYPS
GYPSEIAN
GYPSIED
GYPSIES
GYPSIFEROUS
GYPSINE
GYPSIOLOGIST
GYPSITE
GYPSOGRAPHY
GYPSOLOGIST
GYPSOLOGY
GYPSOPLAST
GYPSOUS
GYPSUM
GYPSUMED
GYPSUMING
GYPSY
GYPSYFY
GYPSYHEAD
GYPSYING
GYPSYRY
GYPSYWEED
GYPSYWORT
GYRAL
GYRALLY
GYRANT
GYRATE
GYRATED
GYRATING
GYRATION
GYRATIONAL
GYRATOR
GYRATORY
GYRE
GYRED
GYRENE
GYRFALCON
GYRING
GYRINID
GYRO
GYROCAR
GYROCERACONE
GYROCERAN
GYROCHROME
GYROCOMPASS
GYRODYNE
GYROGONITE
GYROGRAPH
GYROHORIZON
GYROIDAL
GYROIDALLY
GYROLITE
GYROLITH
GYROMA
GYROMAGNETIC
GYROMANCY
GYROMELE
GYROMETER
GYRON
GYRONNY
GYROPIGEON
GYROPLANE
GYROSCOPE
GYROSCOPIC
GYROSE
GYROSTAT
GYROSTATIC
GYROSTATICS
GYROUS
GYROVAGUES
GYROWHEEL
GYRTH
GYRUS
GYTE
GYTLING
GYTRASH
GYTTJA
GYVE
GYVED
GYVING

H

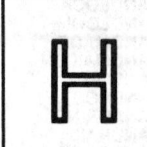

HA
HAAB
HAAF
HAAK
HAAR
HABBLE
HABDALAH
HABEAS
HABENA
HABENAL
HABENAR
HABENDUM
HABENULA
HABENULAR
HABERDASH
HABERDASHER
HABERDASHERY
HABERDINE
HABERGEON
HABI
HABIL
HABILABLE
HABILE
HABILIMENT
HABILIMENTAL
HABILIMENTARY
HABILIMENTATIO
HABILIMENTED
HABILITATE
HABILITATION
HABILITATOR
HABILITY
HABILLE
HABIT
HABITABLE
HABITABLY
HABITACLE
HABITACULE
HABITALLY
HABITAN
HABITANCE
HABITANT
HABITAT
HABITATAL
HABITATE
HABITATIO
HABITATION
HABITATIVE
HABITUAL
HABITUALITY
HABITUALLY
HABITUALNESS
HABITUATE
HABITUATED
HABITUATION
HABITUDE
HABITUE
HABITUS
HABNAB
HABOOB
HABRO
HABRONEMIC
HABROWNE
HABU
HABUKA
HABUTAI
HABUTAYE
HACCUCAL
HACEK
HACHE
HACHIS
HACHMENT
HACHT
HACHURE
HACIENDA
HACK
HACKAMORE
HACKBARROW
HACKBERRY
HACKBOLT
HACKBUSH
HACKBUT
HACKBUTEER
HACKBUTTER
HACKED
HACKEE
HACKEEM
HACKER
HACKERY
HACKEYMAL
HACKIA
HACKIE
HACKIN
HACKING
HACKINGLY
HACKLE
HACKLEBACK
HACKLER
HACKLES
HACKLET
HACKLOG
HACKLY
HACKMACK
HACKMALL
HACKMAN
HACKMATACK
HACKNEY
HACKNEYED
HACKNEYER
HACKNEYMAN
HACKSAW
HACKSILBER
HACKSTER
HACKTHORN
HACKTREE
HACKWOOD
HACKY
HAD
HADADA
HADBOT
HADBOTE
HADDEN
HADDER
HADDIE
HADDIN
HADDO
HADDOCK
HADDOCKER
HADE
HADES
HADING
HADIT
HADJ
HADJI
HADLAND
HADNA
HADROM
HADROME
HADROSAUR
HAE
HAEC
HAECCEITY
HAEM
HAEMAD
HAEMATHERM
HAEMATHERMAL
HAEMATHERMOUS
HAEMATID
HAEMATITE
HAEMONY
HAEMOPHILE
HAEMOPOD
HAEMOSTAT
HAEN
HAEREMAI
HAERES
HAET
HAFF
HAFFET
HAFFIT
HAFFLE
HAFFLINS
HAFIZ
HAFLIN
HAFNIUM
HAFNYL
HAFT
HAFTARAH
HAFTER
HAG
HAGADA
HAGADIST
HAGBERRY
HAGBOAT
HAGBOLT
HAGBORN
HAGBUSH
HAGBUT
HAGDEN
HAGDIN
HAGDON
HAGDOWN
HAGEEN
HAGEIN
HAGFISH
HAGG
HAGGADAL
HAGGADAY
HAGGADIC
HAGGADIST
HAGGARD
HAGGARDLY
HAGGARDNESS
HAGGED
HAGGEIS
HAGGIOGRAPHAL
HAGGIS
HAGGISH
HAGGISHLY
HAGGISHNESS
HAGGLE
HAGGLER
HAGGLING
HAGGLY
HAGGY
HAGI
HAGIA
HAGIARCHY
HAGIGAH
HAGIOCRACY
HAGIOGRAPHER
HAGIOGRAPHIC
HAGIOGRAPHIST
HAGIOGRAPHY
HAGIOLATER
HAGIOLATROUS
HAGIOLATRY
HAGIOLITH
HAGIOLOGIC
HAGIOLOGIST
HAGIOLOGY
HAGIOSCOPE
HAGLET
HAGLIKE
HAGLIN
HAGMALL
HAGMENA
HAGRIDDEN
HAGRIDE
HAGROPE
HAGSEED
HAGSTONE
HAGTAPER
HAGWEED
HAGWORM
HAH
HAHAM
HAHR
HAI
HAIARI
HAICK
HAIK
HAIKAI
HAIKAL
HAIKU
HAIKUN
HAIKWAN
HAIL
HAILER
HAILL
HAILPROOF
HAILSE
HAILSHOT
HAILSTONE
HAILSTORM
HAILWEED
HAIM
HAIMSUCKEN
HAIN
HAINBERRY
HAINCH
HAINE
HAINED
HAIR
HAIRBALL
HAIRBAND
HAIRBEARD
HAIRBELL
HAIRBIRD
HAIRBRAIN
HAIRBRAINED
HAIRBREADTH
HAIRBRUSH
HAIRCAP
HAIRCLOTH
HAIRCUT
HAIRDO
HAIRDRESS
HAIRDRESSER
HAIRDRESSING
HAIRE
HAIRED
HAIREN
HAIRHOOF
HAIRHOUND
HAIRIF
HAIRINESS
HAIRLACE
HAIRLESS
HAIRLIKE
HAIRLINE
HAIRLOCK
HAIRMONEERING
HAIRMONGER
HAIRN
HAIROF
HAIRPIECE
HAIRPIN
HAIRS
HAIRSBREADTH
HAIRSE
HAIRSPLITTER
HAIRSPLITTING
HAIRSPRING
HAIRST
HAIRSTANE
HAIRSTONE
HAIRSTREAK
HAIRTAIL
HAIRUP
HAIRWEAVE
HAIRWEAVING
HAIRWEED
HAIRWORK
HAIRWORM
HAIRY
HAIT
HAITH
HAITSAI
HAIVER
HAJ
HAJE
HAJI
HAJIB
HAJILIJ
HAJJ
HAJJI
HAK
HAKA
HAKAFOTH
HAKAM
HAKAMIM
HAKDAR
HAKE
HAKED
HAKEEM
HAKH
HAKIM
HAKO
HAKU
HAL
HALA
HALACHA
HALACHAH
HALACHIST
HALAKA
HALAKAH
HALAKIC
HALAKIST
HALAL
HALALCOR
HALAPEPE
HALAS
HALATION
HALAZONE
HALBE
HALBERD
HALBERDIER
HALBERDMAN
HALBERDS
HALBERT
HALCH
HALCYON
HALDI
HALDU
HALE
HALEBI
HALECRET
HALEDAY
HALELY
HALENESS
HALER
HALERZ
HALES
HALESOME

HALEWEED
HALF
HALFA
HALFBACK
HALFBEAK
HALFCOCK
HALFCOCKED
HALFEN
HALFHEADED
HALFHEARTED
HALFHEARTEDLY
HALFHEARTEDNESS
HALFLANG
HALFLIN
HALFLING
HALFLINGS
HALFLY
HALFMAN
HALFNESS
HALFPACE
HALFPACED
HALFPENCE
HALFPENNIES
HALFPENNY
HALFWAY
HALFWISE
HALFY
HALIBIOS
HALIBIU
HALIBUT
HALIBUTER
HALID
HALIDE
HALIDOM
HALIDOME
HALIEUTIC
HALIEUTICAL
HALIEUTICALLY
HALIEUTICS
HALIMOT
HALIMOUS
HALINOUS
HALIOTOID
HALIPLID
HALITE
HALITOSIS
HALITUOUS
HALITUS
HALK
HALKE
HALL
HALLAGE
HALLAH
HALLALCOR
HALLALI
HALLAN
HALLBOY
HALLCIST
HALLE
HALLEBARDIER
HALLECRET
HALLEL
HALLELUIAH
HALLIARD
HALLICET
HALLIDOME
HALLING
HALLION
HALLMAN
HALLMARK
HALLMARKER
HALLMOOT
HALLMOTE
HALLO
HALLOA
HALLOCK
HALLOO
HALLOW
HALLOWD
HALLOWED
HALLOWEDLY
HALLOWEDNESS
HALLOWER
HALLUCES
HALLUCINATE
HALLUCINATION
HALLUCINED
HALLUX
HALLWAY
HALM
HALMA
HALMALILLE
HALO
HALOBIOS
HALOBIOTIC
HALOESQUE
HALOGEN
HALOGENATION
HALOID
HALOLIKE
HALOMETER
HALOPHILE
HALOPHYTE
HALOPHYTIC
HALOSCOPE
HALOSERE
HALPACE
HALPER
HALS
HALSE
HALSEN
HALSFANG
HALSH
HALT
HALTER
HALTERBREAK
HALTERE
HALTERES
HALTING
HALTINGLY
HALTINGNESS
HALTLESS
HALUCKET
HALUKKAH
HALURGIST
HALURGY
HALUTZ
HALUTZIM
HALVANER
HALVANS
HALVE
HALVED
HALVELINGS
HALVER
HALVERS
HALVES
HALVING
HALWE
HALY
HALYARD
HAM
HAMADA
HAMADRYAD
HAMAL
HAMALD
HAMAMELIN
HAMARTIA
HAMARTITE
HAMATE
HAMATED
HAMATUM
HAMAUL
HAMBER
HAMBLE
HAMBO
HAMBONE
HAMBURGER
HAMDMAID
HAME
HAMEIL
HAMEL
HAMELT
HAMESOKEN
HAMESUCKEN
HAMETZ
HAMEWITH
HAMFARE
HAMFAT
HAMFATTER
HAMHUNG
HAMI
HAMIFORM
HAMILT
HAMINGJA
HAMINOEA
HAMLAH
HAMLET
HAMLETED
HAMLETEER
HAMLETIZE
HAMLINE
HAMLINITE
HAMMAID
HAMMAL
HAMMER
HAMMERABLE
HAMMERBIRD
HAMMERCLOTH
HAMMERDRESS
HAMMERED
HAMMERER
HAMMERFISH
HAMMERHEAD
HAMMERHEADED
HAMMERING
HAMMERKOP
HAMMERLESS
HAMMERLIKE
HAMMERMAN
HAMMERSMITH
HAMMERSTONE
HAMMERTOE
HAMMERWORT
HAMMOCK
HAMMY
HAMOSE
HAMOTZI
HAMOUS
HAMP
HAMPER
HAMPERED
HAMPERER
HAMPERING
HAMPERMAN
HAMRONGITE
HAMSA
HAMSHACKLE
HAMSTER
HAMSTRING
HAMULAR
HAMULATE
HAMULE
HAMULOSE
HAMULOUS
HAMULUS
HAMUS
HAMZA
HAMZAH
HAN
HANAHILL
HANAP
HANAPER
HANASTER
HANCE
HANCED
HANCH
HANCOCKITE
HAND
HANDARM
HANDBAG
HANDBALL
HANDBALLER
HANDBANK
HANDBANKER
HANDBARROW
HANDBELL
HANDBILL
HANDBLOW
HANDBOLT
HANDBOOK
HANDBOW
HANDBREADTH
HANDBREED
HANDCAR
HANDCART
HANDCLAP
HANDCLASP
HANDCLOTH
HANDCRAFT
HANDCUFF
HANDED
HANDEDNESS
HANDER
HANDERSOME
HANDFAST
HANDFASTING
HANDFASTLY
HANDFASTNESS
HANDFISH
HANDFLAG
HANDFLOWER
HANDFUL
HANDGRAVURE
HANDGRIP
HANDGRIPING
HANDGUN
HANDHAVING
HANDHOLD
HANDHOLE
HANDICAP
HANDICAPPED
HANDICAPPER
HANDICRAFT
HANDICRAFTSMAN
HANDICRAFTSWOMAN
HANDICUFF
HANDIER
HANDIEST
HANDILY
HANDINESS
HANDING
HANDIRON
HANDISTROKE
HANDIWORK
HANDJAR
HANDKERCHER
HANDLAID
HANDLE
HANDLEABLE
HANDLEBAR
HANDLED
HANDLER
HANDLES
HANDLESS
HANDLIKE
HANDLING
HANDLOAD
HANDLOADING
HANDLOCK
HANDLOOM
HANDMADE
HANDMAIDEN
HANDOUT
HANDPOST
HANDPRINT
HANDRAIL
HANDRAILING
HANDREADER
HANDREADING
HANDREST
HANDS
HANDSALE
HANDSAW
HANDSCRAPE
HANDSEL
HANDSELLER
HANDSET
HANDSHAKE
HANDSHAKER
HANDSHAKING
HANDSLED
HANDSMOOTH
HANDSOME
HANDSOMELY
HANDSOMENESS
HANDSPADE
HANDSPAN
HANDSPEC
HANDSPIKE
HANDSPOKE
HANDSPRING
HANDSTAFF
HANDSTAND
HANDSTONE
HANDSTROKE
HANDTRAP
HANDWALED
HANDWHEEL
HANDWHILE
HANDWORK
HANDWORKMAN
HANDWORM
HANDWRIST
HANDWRIT
HANDWRITE
HANDWRITING
HANDY
HANDYBLOW
HANDYBOOK
HANDYCUFF
HANDYFIGHT
HANDYFRAME
HANDYGRIP
HANDYGRIPE
HANDYMAN
HANG
HANGABLE
HANGALAI
HANGAR
HANGBIRD
HANGBY
HANGDOG
HANGE
HANGEE
HANGER
HANGFIRE
HANGI
HANGIE
HANGING
HANGKANG
HANGLE
HANGMAN
HANGMENT
HANGNAIL
HANGNEST

HANGOUT
HANGOVER
HANGTAG
HANGUL
HANGUP
HANGWORM
HANGWORTHY
HANIF
HANIFISM
HANIFITE
HANIFIYA
HANK
HANKER
HANKERER
HANKERING
HANKERINGLY
HANKIE
HANKING
HANKLE
HANKS
HANKSITE
HANKT
HANKUL
HANKY
HANNA
HANNAYITE
HANOLOGATE
HANSA
HANSE
HANSEL
HANSELIN
HANSGRAVE
HANSOM
HANT
HANTLE
HANUM
HANUMAN
HAO
HAOLE
HAOMA
HAP
HAPALOTE
HAPHAZARD
HAPHAZARDLY
HAPHAZARDNESS
HAPHTARAH
HAPITON
HAPLESS
HAPLESSLY
HAPLESSNESS
HAPLITE
HAPLITIC
HAPLODONT
HAPLODONTY
HAPLOID
HAPLOIDIC
HAPLOIDY
HAPLOLALY
HAPLOLOGIC
HAPLOLOGY
HAPLOMA
HAPLOME
HAPLOMID
HAPLONT
HAPLOPHASE
HAPLOSCOPE
HAPLOSIS
HAPLOTYPE
HAPLY
HAPPEN
HAPPENING
HAPPER
HAPPIER
HAPPIEST
HAPPIFY
HAPPILESS
HAPPILY
HAPPINESS
HAPPING
HAPPY
HAPS
HAPT
HAPTERA
HAPTERE
HAPTERON
HAPTIC
HAPTICS
HAPTOMETER
HAPTOR
HAPTOTROPIC
HAPU
HAPUKU
HAQUETON
HAR
HARACE
HARAKEKE
HARANG
HARANGUE
HARANGUEFUL
HARANGUER
HARAS
HARASS
HARASSED
HARASSEDLY
HARASSER
HARASSING
HARASSINGLY
HARASSMENT
HARAST
HARATCH
HARATEEN
HARAUCANA
HARBERGAGE
HARBI
HARBINGE
HARBINGER
HARBORAGE
HARBORER
HARBORLESS
HARBORMASTER
HARBORSIDE
HARBOUR
HARBOURAGE
HARBOURER
HARBOURSIDE
HARD
HARDANGER
HARDBACK
HARDBAKE
HARDBALL
HARDBEAM
HARDBERRY
HARDCASE
HARDEN
HARDENED
HARDENER
HARDENING
HARDENITE
HARDER
HARDEST
HARDFERN
HARDFIST
HARDFISTED
HARDHACK
HARDHANDED
HARDHEAD
HARDHEADED
HARDHEADEDLY
HARDHEADEDNESS
HARDHEARTED
HARDHEARTEDLY
HARDHEARTEDNESS
HARDHEWER
HARDIE
HARDIER
HARDIES
HARDIESSE
HARDIEST
HARDIHEAD
HARDIHOOD
HARDILY
HARDIM
HARDIMENT
HARDINESS
HARDISH
HARDLY
HARDMOUTH
HARDMOUTHED
HARDNESS
HARDOCK
HARDPAN
HARDS
HARDSALT
HARDSET
HARDSHIP
HARDSTAND
HARDTACK
HARDTAIL
HARDTOP
HARDWARE
HARDWAY
HARDWEED
HARDWOOD
HARDWORKING
HARDY
HARDYHEAD
HARE
HAREBELL
HAREBOTTLE
HAREBRAIN
HAREBRAINED
HAREBUR
HAREEM
HAREFOOT
HAREFOOTED
HAREHEARTED
HAREHOUND
HARELIKE
HARELIP
HARELIPPED
HAREM
HAREMISM
HAREMLIK
HARENUT
HARES
HAREWOOD
HARFANG
HARIANA
HARICO
HARICOT
HARIER
HARIF
HARIFFE
HARIGALDS
HARIOLATE
HARIOLATION
HARISH
HARK
HARKA
HARKEN
HARKENER
HARL
HARLE
HARLEQUIN
HARLEQUINA
HARLEQUINADE
HARLEQUINESQUE
HARLEQUINIC
HARLEQUINIZE
HARLING
HARLOCK
HARLOT
HARLOTRIES
HARLOTRY
HARM
HARMAL
HARMALA
HARMALIN
HARMALINE
HARMAN
HARMATTAN
HARMEL
HARMER
HARMFUL
HARMFULLY
HARMFULNESS
HARMIN
HARMINE
HARMLESS
HARMLESSLY
HARMLESSNESS
HARMONIA
HARMONIACAL
HARMONIC
HARMONICA
HARMONICAL
HARMONICALLY
HARMONICI
HARMONICON
HARMONICS
HARMONIES
HARMONIOUS
HARMONIOUSLY
HARMONIOUSNESS
HARMONIST
HARMONISTIC
HARMONISTICALLY
HARMONIUM
HARMONIZE
HARMONIZER
HARMONIZING
HARMONY
HARMOOT
HARMOST
HARMOTOME
HARMOUT
HARN
HARNESS
HARNESSED
HARNESSER
HARNESSRY
HARNPAN
HARO
HAROSET
HARP
HARPAGO
HARPAGON
HARPE
HARPER
HARPIER
HARPIES
HARPIN
HARPINGS
HARPINS
HARPIST
HARPLESS
HARPLIKE
HARPOON
HARPOONED
HARPOONEER
HARPOONER
HARPSICAL
HARPSICHON
HARPSICHORD
HARPULA
HARPWISE
HARPY
HARQUEBUS
HARQUEBUSS
HARR
HARRAGE
HARRATEEN
HARRID
HARRIDAN
HARRIED
HARRIER
HARRISITE
HARROW
HARROWED
HARROWER
HARROWING
HARROWINGLY
HARROWINGNESS
HARROWMENT
HARROWTRY
HARRUMPH
HARRY
HARRYCANE
HARSH
HARSHISH
HARSHLY
HARSHNESS
HARSK
HARSLET
HARST
HARSTIGITE
HARSTRANG
HARSTRONG
HART
HARTAIL
HARTAKE
HARTAL
HARTALL
HARTBERRY
HARTEBEEST
HARTEN
HARTH
HARTIN
HARTITE
HARTLY
HARTSHORN
HARTSTONGUE
HARTTITE
HARUSPEX
HARUSPICAL
HARUSPICE
HARUSPICES
HARVEST
HARVESTER
HARVESTING
HARVESTLESS
HARVESTMAN
HARVESTRY
HARVESTTIME
HARZBURGITE
HAS
HASAN
HASARD
HASEL
HASH
HASHAB
HASHABI
HASHEESH
HASHER
HASHISH
HASHT
HASHY
HASK
HASKARD
HASKNESS
HASKWORT
HASKY
HASLET
HASLOCK
HASP

HASPICOL
HASS
HASSAR
HASSEL
HASSING
HASSLE
HASSLET
HASSOCK
HASSOCKY
HASTA
HASTATE
HASTATED
HASTATELY
HASTATI
HASTE
HASTEFUL
HASTEFULLY
HASTEN
HASTENER
HASTER
HASTIER
HASTIEST
HASTIF
HASTIFLY
HASTIFNESS
HASTILUDE
HASTILY
HASTINESS
HASTINGS
HASTINGSITE
HASTISH
HASTIVE
HASTLER
HASTULA
HASTY
HAT
HATABLE
HATBAND
HATBOX
HATCH
HATCHABLE
HATCHED
HATCHEL
HATCHELER
HATCHELLER
HATCHER
HATCHERIES
HATCHERY
HATCHERYMAN
HATCHET
HATCHETBACK
HATCHETLIKE
HATCHETTINE
HATCHETTITE
HATCHETY
HATCHGATE
HATCHING
HATCHITE
HATCHLING
HATCHMAN
HATCHMENT
HATCHWAY
HATCHWAYMAN
HATE
HATEABLE
HATEFUL
HATEFULLY
HATEFULNESS
HATEL
HATEN
HATER
HATFUL
HATH
HATHERLITE
HATHI
HATLESS
HATLIKE
HATMAKER
HATMAKING
HATPIN
HATRACK
HATRAIL
HATRED
HATRESS
HATS
HATSTAND
HATT
HATTE
HATTED
HATTER
HATTERIA
HATTERY
HATTING
HATTOCK
HATTY
HAU
HAUBERGEON
HAUBERGET
HAUBERK
HAUD
HAUERITE
HAUF
HAUFLIN
HAUGH
HAUGHLAND
HAUGHT
HAUGHTILY
HAUGHTINESS
HAUGHTONITE
HAUGHTY
HAUL
HAULABOUT
HAULAGE
HAULAGEWAY
HAULAWAY
HAULBACK
HAULD
HAULE
HAULER
HAULIER
HAULING
HAULM
HAULMY
HAULSTER
HAULT
HAULYARD
HAUN
HAUNCH
HAUNCHED
HAUNCHER
HAUNCHES
HAUNCHING
HAUNCHLESS
HAUNCHY
HAUNT
HAUNTED
HAUNTER
HAUNTING
HAUNTINGLY
HAUNTY
HAUPIA
HAURIANT
HAURIENT
HAURN
HAUSE
HAUSEN
HAUSSE
HAUSTELLA
HAUSTELLATE
HAUSTELLATED
HAUSTELLUM
HAUSTORIUM
HAUSTRAL
HAUSTRUM
HAUSTUS
HAUT
HAUTAIN
HAUTBOIS
HAUTBOY
HAUTBOYIST
HAUTESSE
HAUTEUR
HAUYNE
HAUYNITE
HAVAGE
HAVANCE
HAVE
HAVEAGE
HAVEL
HAVELESS
HAVELOCK
HAVEN
HAVENAGE
HAVENER
HAVENET
HAVER
HAVERAL
HAVERCAKE
HAVEREL
HAVERER
HAVERGRASS
HAVERING
HAVERMEAL
HAVERS
HAVERSACK
HAVERSINE
HAVIER
HAVILDAR
HAVING
HAVINGNESS
HAVINGS
HAVIOR
HAVIORED
HAVIOUR
HAVIOURED
HAVLAGAH
HAVOC
HAVOCKER
HAW
HAWAIITE
HAWBUCK
HAWCUBITE
HAWEBAKE
HAWER
HAWFINCH
HAWK
HAWKBILL
HAWKBIT
HAWKED
HAWKER
HAWKERY
HAWKEY
HAWKIE
HAWKING
HAWKINS
HAWKISH
HAWKNOSE
HAWKNOSED
HAWKNUT
HAWKS
HAWKSBILL
HAWKSHAW
HAWKWEED
HAWKY
HAWM
HAWN
HAWOK
HAWSE
HAWSEHOLE
HAWSEMAN
HAWSEPIECE
HAWSEPIPE
HAWSER
HAWTHORN
HAWTHORNY
HAY
HAYA
HAYBAND
HAYBIRD
HAYBOTE
HAYBURNER
HAYCAP
HAYCOCK
HAYDENITE
HAYE
HAYEY
HAYFIELD
HAYFORK
HAYING
HAYLOFT
HAYMAKER
HAYMAKING
HAYMARKET
HAYMOW
HAYNE
HAYRACK
HAYRICK
HAYRIDE
HAYS
HAYSEED
HAYSEL
HAYSHOCK
HAYSTACK
HAYSUCK
HAYWARD
HAYWEED
HAYWIRE
HAYZ
HAZAN
HAZANUT
HAZARD
HAZARDER
HAZARDOUS
HAZARDOUSLY
HAZARDOUSNESS
HAZARDRY
HAZE
HAZEL
HAZELED
HAZELLY
HAZELNUT
HAZEN
HAZER
HAZIER
HAZIEST
HAZILY
HAZINESS
HAZING
HAZLE
HAZNADAR
HAZY
HAZZAN
HAZZANUT
HE
HEAD
HEADACHE
HEADACHY
HEADBAND
HEADBANDER
HEADBOARD
HEADBOROUGH
HEADBOX
HEADCAP
HEADCHAIR
HEADCHEESE
HEADCHUTE
HEADCLOTH
HEADDRESS
HEADED
HEADENDER
HEADER
HEADFAST
HEADFIRST
HEADFISH
HEADFOREMOST
HEADFRAME
HEADFUL
HEADGEAR
HEADHUNT
HEADHUNTER
HEADIER
HEADIEST
HEADILY
HEADINESS
HEADING
HEADINGS
HEADLAND
HEADLE
HEADLEDGE
HEADLESS
HEADLIGHT
HEADLIGHTING
HEADLINE
HEADLINER
HEADLING
HEADLOAD
HEADLOCK
HEADLONG
HEADLONGLY
HEADLONGNESS
HEADLY
HEADMAN
HEADMARK
HEADMASTER
HEADMASTERLY
HEADMISTRESS
HEADMOLD
HEADMOST
HEADMOULD
HEADNOTE
HEADPENNY
HEADPHONE
HEADPIECE
HEADPIN
HEADPLATE
HEADPOST
HEADQUARTER
HEADQUARTERS
HEADRAIL
HEADREACH
HEADRENT
HEADREST
HEADRIG
HEADRIGHT
HEADRING
HEADROOM
HEADROPE
HEADS
HEADSAIL
HEADSAW
HEADSET
HEADSHAKE
HEADSHIP
HEADSILL
HEADSKIN
HEADSMAN
HEADSPACE
HEADSPRING
HEADSTALL
HEADSTAND
HEADSTICK
HEADSTOCK
HEADSTONE
HEADSTREAM
HEADSTRONG

HEADSTRONGLY
HEADSTRONGNESS
HEADTIRE
HEADWAITER
HEADWALL
HEADWARD
HEADWARDS
HEADWARK
HEADWATER
HEADWATERS
HEADWAY
HEADWEAR
HEADWORK
HEADWORKER
HEADWORKING
HEADY
HEAF
HEAL
HEALD
HEALDER
HEALED
HEALER
HEALFUL
HEALING
HEALINGLY
HEALLESS
HEALSOME
HEALSOMENESS
HEALTH
HEALTHCRAFT
HEALTHFUL
HEALTHFULLY
HEALTHFULNESS
HEALTHGUARD
HEALTHIER
HEALTHIEST
HEALTHLESS
HEALTHSOME
HEALTHY
HEAM
HEAP
HEAPED
HEAPER
HEAPING
HEAPS
HEAPSTEAD
HEAPY
HEAR
HEARD
HEARER
HEARING
HEARKEN
HEARKENER
HEARSAY
HEARSE
HEARSECLOTH
HEARST
HEART
HEARTACHE
HEARTACHING
HEARTBEAT
HEARTBIRD
HEARTBLOCK
HEARTBLOOD
HEARTBREAK
HEARTBREAKER
HEARTBREAKING
HEARTBROKEN
HEARTBROKENLY
HEARTBROKENNESS
HEARTBURN
HEARTBURNING
HEARTDEEP
HEARTEASE
HEARTED
HEARTEDLY
HEARTEN
HEARTENER
HEARTENING
HEARTFELT
HEARTFUL
HEARTFULLY
HEARTFULNESS
HEARTGRIEF
HEARTH
HEARTHMAN
HEARTHPENNY
HEARTHRUG
HEARTHS
HEARTHSTONE
HEARTHWARD
HEARTHWARMING
HEARTIER
HEARTIES
HEARTIEST
HEARTIKIN
HEARTILY
HEARTINESS
HEARTING
HEARTLEAF
HEARTLESS
HEARTLESSLY
HEARTLESSNESS
HEARTLY
HEARTNUT
HEARTPEA
HEARTQUAKE
HEARTROOT
HEARTROT
HEARTS
HEARTSCALD
HEARTSEASE
HEARTSEED
HEARTSETTE
HEARTSICK
HEARTSOME
HEARTSOMELY
HEARTSORE
HEARTSTRING
HEARTSTRINGS
HEARTTHROB
HEARTWATER
HEARTWEED
HEARTWOOD
HEARTWORM
HEARTWORT
HEARTY
HEAT
HEATDROPS
HEATED
HEATEDLY
HEATEN
HEATER
HEATERMAN
HEATH
HEATHBERRY
HEATHBIRD
HEATHEN
HEATHENDOM
HEATHENESSE
HEATHENISH
HEATHENISHLY
HEATHENISHNESS
HEATHENISM
HEATHENIST
HEATHENIZE
HEATHENLY
HEATHENRY
HEATHER
HEATHERED
HEATHERINESS
HEATHERY
HEATHIER
HEATHIEST
HEATHLIKE
HEATHWORT
HEATHY
HEATING
HEATINGLY
HEATLESS
HEATSMAN
HEATSTROKE
HEAUME
HEAUMER
HEAUTARIT
HEAVE
HEAVEN
HEAVENLY
HEAVENS
HEAVENWARD
HEAVENWARDLY
HEAVENWARDNESS
HEAVENWARDS
HEAVER
HEAVES
HEAVIER
HEAVIES
HEAVIEST
HEAVILY
HEAVINESS
HEAVING
HEAVISOME
HEAVITY
HEAVY
HEAVYBACK
HEAVYSET
HEAVYWEIGHT
HEAZY
HEBAMIC
HEBDOMAD
HEBDOMADAL
HEBDOMADALLY
HEBDOMADARY
HEBDOMADER
HEBEANTHOUS
HEBECARPOUS
HEBECLADOUS
HEBENON
HEBEPHRENIC
HEBETATE
HEBETATION
HEBETATIVE
HEBETE
HEBETIC
HEBETUDE
HECATOMB
HECATOMPED
HECCEITY
HECCO
HECH
HECHIMA
HECHSHER
HECK
HECKIMAL
HECKLE
HECKLER
HECTARE
HECTE
HECTIC
HECTICAL
HECTICALLY
HECTIVE
HECTOGRAM
HECTOGRAMME
HECTOGRAPH
HECTOGRAPHIC
HECTOLITER
HECTOLITRE
HECTOR
HECTORED
HECTORING
HECTORLY
HECTOSTERE
HECTOWATT
HED
HEDDE
HEDDLE
HEDDLER
HEDDLES
HEDEBO
HEDER
HEDERACEOUS
HEDERATED
HEDERIC
HEDERIN
HEDEROSE
HEDGE
HEDGEBERRY
HEDGEBETTY
HEDGEBOTE
HEDGEHOG
HEDGEHOGGY
HEDGEHOP
HEDGEPIG
HEDGER
HEDGEROW
HEDGES
HEDGESMITH
HEDGESTRAW
HEDGETAPER
HEDGING
HEDGINGLY
HEDGY
HEDONIC
HEDONICAL
HEDONICALLY
HEDONICS
HEDONISM
HEDONIST
HEDONISTIC
HEDONISTICALLY
HEDROCELE
HEDRUMITE
HEDYPHANE
HEE
HEED
HEEDER
HEEDFUL
HEEDFULLY
HEEDFULNESS
HEEDILY
HEEDINESS
HEEDLESS
HEEDLESSLY
HEEDLESSNESS
HEEDY
HEEHAW
HEEL
HEELBALL
HEELCAP
HEELD
HEELED
HEELER
HEELING
HEELPATH
HEELPIECE
HEELPLATE
HEELPOST
HEELS
HEELSTRAP
HEELTAP
HEELTREE
HEELWORK
HEEMRAAD
HEEMRAAT
HEER
HEEZE
HEFT
HEFTER
HEFTIER
HEFTIEST
HEFTILY
HEFTINESS
HEFTY
HEG
HEGEMON
HEGEMONIC
HEGEMONICAL
HEGEMONIST
HEGEMONY
HEGIRA
HEGUMEN
HEGUMENESS
HEGUMENOS
HEGUMENY
HEIAU
HEIFER
HEIGH
HEIGHT
HEIGHTEN
HEIGHTENER
HEIGHTH
HEII
HEIL
HEIMIN
HEIMLICH
HEIN
HEINOUS
HEINOUSLY
HEINOUSNESS
HEIR
HEIRDOM
HEIRESS
HEIRLOOM
HEIRMOS
HEIRSHIP
HEIST
HEISTER
HEITIKI
HEJIRA
HEKTEUS
HEL
HELAS
HELBEH
HELCOID
HELCOLOGY
HELCOPLASTY
HELCOSIS
HELCOTIC
HELD
HELDER
HELENIN
HELEPOLE
HELER
HELIAC
HELIACAL
HELIACALLY
HELIANTHUS
HELIAST
HELIASTIC
HELICAL
HELICALLY
HELICED
HELICINE
HELICITIC
HELICLINE
HELICOGRAPH
HELICOGYRE
HELICOID
HELICOIDAL
HELICOIDALLY
HELICOMETRY
HELICON
HELICONIST
HELICOPROTEIN

HELICOPTER
HELICORUBIN
HELICOTREMA
HELICTITE
HELID
HELIDE
HELIO
HELIOCENTRIC
HELIOCENTRICAL
HELIOCENTRICITY
HELIOCHROME
HELIOCHROMIC
HELIOCHROMY
HELIOCULTURE
HELIODON
HELIODOR
HELIOELECTRIC
HELIOFUGAL
HELIOGRAM
HELIOGRAPH
HELIOGRAPHER
HELIOGRAPHIC
HELIOGRAPHY
HELIOGRAVURE
HELIOID
HELIOLATER
HELIOLATOR
HELIOLATROUS
HELIOLATRY
HELIOLITE
HELIOMETER
HELIOMETRIC
HELIOMETRY
HELIOSCOPE
HELIOSIS
HELIOSTAT
HELIOTACTIC
HELIOTAXIS
HELIOTHERAPY
HELIOTROPE
HELIOTROPIC
HELIOTROPISM
HELIOTROPY
HELIOTYPE
HELIOZOAN
HELIPORT
HELIUM
HELIX
HELIXIN
HELL
HELLBENDER
HELLBOX
HELLBROTH
HELLCAT
HELLDOG
HELLEBORE
HELLEBOREIN
HELLEBORIC
HELLEBORIN
HELLER
HELLERI
HELLERY
HELLFIRE
HELLGRAMMITE
HELLHAG
HELLHOLE
HELLHOUND
HELLICAT
HELLICATE
HELLIER
HELLIM
HELLION
HELLISH
HELLISHLY
HELLISHNESS
HELLKITE
HELLO
HELLROOT
HELLSHIP
HELLUO
HELLVINE
HELLWEED
HELLY
HELM
HELMAGE
HELMED
HELMET
HELMETED
HELMETFLOWER
HELMETLIKE
HELMETPOD
HELMINTH
HELMINTHIC
HELMINTHISM
HELMSMAN
HELO
HELOBIOUS
HELODES
HELOE
HELOMA
HELONIN
HELOSIS
HELOT
HELOTISM
HELOTOMY
HELOTRY
HELP
HELPER
HELPFUL
HELPFULLY
HELPFULNESS
HELPING
HELPLESS
HELPLESSLY
HELPLESSNESS
HELPLY
HELPMATE
HELPMEET
HELPSOME
HELPWORTHY
HELVE
HELVELL
HELVELLIC
HELVIN
HELVINE
HELVITE
HELZEL
HEM
HEMACHATE
HEMACHROME
HEMACITE
HEMAD
HEMAGOG
HEMAGOGIC
HEMAGOGUE
HEMAL
HEMAMEBA
HEMAPOD
HEMATAL
HEMATEIN
HEMATIC
HEMATID
HEMATIN
HEMATINE
HEMATINIC
HEMATITE
HEMATITIC
HEMATOCELE
HEMATOID
HEMATOLIN
HEMATOMA
HEMATOMETER
HEMATOSCOPE
HEMATOSE
HEMATOSIN
HEMATOSIS
HEMATOZOON
HEMATURIA
HEME
HEMEL
HEMEN
HEMERA
HEMERALOPE
HEMERALOPIA
HEMERALOPIC
HEMIACETAL
HEMIALGIA
HEMIAMB
HEMIAUXIN
HEMIBRANCH
HEMIC
HEMICARDIA
HEMICARP
HEMICENTRUM
HEMICHORDATE
HEMICOLLIN
HEMICRANE
HEMICRANIA
HEMICYCLE
HEMICYCLIC
HEMIDITONE
HEMIDOME
HEMIEPES
HEMIFACIAL
HEMIFORM
HEMIGLYPH
HEMIHEDRAL
HEMIHEDRIC
HEMIKARYON
HEMIMELLITIC
HEMIMELUS
HEMIMORPH
HEMIMORPHIC
HEMIMORPHITE
HEMIN
HEMINA
HEMINE
HEMINEE
HEMIOLA
HEMIOLIA
HEMIOLIC
HEMIONUS
HEMIOPE
HEMIOPIA
HEMIOPIC
HEMIOPSIA
HEMIPENIS
HEMIPHRASE
HEMIPIC
HEMIPLEGIA
HEMIPLEGIC
HEMIPLEGY
HEMIPOD
HEMIPODE
HEMIPPE
HEMIPRISM
HEMIPROTEIN
HEMIPTER
HEMIPTERAL
HEMIPTERAN
HEMIPTERON
HEMIPTEROUS
HEMISECT
HEMISPHERAL
HEMISPHERE
HEMISPHERED
HEMISTATER
HEMISTICH
HEMITERATA
HEMITERIA
HEMITERY
HEMITONE
HEMITROPAL
HEMITROPE
HEMITROPIC
HEMITYPE
HEMITYPIC
HEML
HEMLOCK
HEMMEL
HEMMER
HEMMING
HEMOBLAST
HEMOCHROME
HEMOCONIA
HEMOCYTE
HEMOFUSCIN
HEMOGASTRIC
HEMOGLOBIN
HEMOGRAM
HEMOID
HEMOL
HEMOLYSIN
HEMOLYSIS
HEMOLYZE
HEMOPHILE
HEMOPHILIA
HEMOPHILIAC
HEMOPHILIC
HEMOPTOE
HEMORRHAGE
HEMORRHOID
HEMOSCOPE
HEMOSCOPY
HEMOSTASIA
HEMOSTASIS
HEMOSTAT
HEMOSTATIC
HEMOTHORAX
HEMOTOXIC
HEMOTOXIN
HEMOTROPHE
HEMOTROPIC
HEMOZOON
HEMP
HEMPBUSH
HEMPEN
HEMPHERDS
HEMPIE
HEMPIER
HEMPIEST
HEMPSEED
HEMPSTRING
HEMPWEED
HEMPWORT
HEMPY
HEMSELF
HEMSTITCH
HEMSTITCHER
HEN
HENAD
HENBANE
HENBILL
HENBIT
HENCE
HENCEFORTH
HENCEFORWARDS
HENCH
HENCHBOY
HENCHMAN
HENCOOP
HEND
HENDE
HENDECAGON
HENDECANE
HENDECOIC
HENDECYL
HENDIADYS
HENEQUEN
HENFISH
HENHEARTED
HENHUSSIES
HENHUSSY
HENISM
HENNA
HENNERIES
HENNERY
HENNIN
HENNISH
HENNY
HENOTIC
HENPECK
HENPECKED
HENPEN
HENRIES
HENRYS
HENS
HENT
HENWARE
HENWILE
HENWOODITE
HEO
HEP
HEPAR
HEPARIN
HEPATIC
HEPATICAE
HEPATICAL
HEPATITE
HEPATITIS
HEPATIZE
HEPATOID
HEPATOMA
HEPPEN
HEPPER
HEPTACHORD
HEPTACOLIC
HEPTAD
HEPTAGLOT
HEPTAGON
HEPTAGONAL
HEPTAHEDRAL
HEPTAHEDRON
HEPTAL
HEPTAMETER
HEPTANE
HEPTANGULAR
HEPTANONE
HEPTAPLOID
HEPTAPODY
HEPTARCH
HEPTARCHAL
HEPTARCHIC
HEPTARCHIES
HEPTARCHIST
HEPTARCHY
HEPTASTICH
HEPTENE
HEPTERIS
HEPTITE
HEPTITOL
HEPTOIC
HEPTORITE
HEPTOSE
HEPTOXIDE
HEPTYL
HEPTYLENE
HEPTYLIC
HEPTYNE
HER
HERALD
HERALDIC
HERALDICAL
HERALDIST
HERALDIZE

HERALDRIES
HERALDRY
HERB
HERBACEOUS
HERBAGE
HERBAGED
HERBAGER
HERBAGIOUS
HERBAL
HERBALIST
HERBALIZE
HERBARISM
HERBARIZE
HERBARY
HERBBANE
HERBER
HERBESCENT
HERBICIDE
HERBIFEROUS
HERBIVORE
HERBLET
HERBMAN
HERBORIST
HERBORIZE
HERBOSE
HERBS
HERBWIFE
HERBWOMAN
HERBY
HERCULEAN
HERCYNITE
HERD
HERDBOOK
HERDBOY
HERDER
HERDERITE
HERDIC
HERDING
HERDSMAN
HERDSMEN
HERDSWOMAN
HERDWICK
HERE
HEREABOUT
HEREABOUTS
HEREADAYS
HEREAFTER
HEREAFTERWARD
HEREAGAIN
HEREAGAINST
HEREAMONG
HEREANENT
HEREAT
HEREAWAY
HEREBEFORE
HEREBY
HEREDIA
HEREDITABLE
HEREDITAL
HEREDITAMENT
HEREDITARY
HEREDITAS
HEREDITIES
HEREDITISM
HEREDITIST
HEREDITY
HEREDOLUES
HEREFORE
HEREFROM
HEREGELD
HEREGILD
HEREHENCE
HEREIN
HEREINABOVE
HEREINAFTER
HEREINBEFORE
HEREINTO
HEREM
HERENACH
HERENIGING
HEREOF
HEREON
HEREOUT
HERERIGHT
HERES
HERESIARCH
HERESIES
HERESIMACH
HERESIOLOGER
HERESIOLOGY
HERESY
HERETIC
HERETICAL
HERETICALLY
HERETICALNESS
HERETICATE
HERETICATED
HERETICATION
HERETICATOR
HERETICIDE
HERETICIZE
HERETO
HERETOFORE
HERETOGA
HEREUNDER
HEREUNTO
HEREUPON
HEREWITH
HEREWITHAL
HEREZELD
HERIF
HERILE
HERIOT
HERIOTABLE
HERISSON
HERITABLE
HERITABLY
HERITAGE
HERITANCE
HERITOR
HERITRIX
HERL
HERLING
HERM
HERMA
HERMAE
HERMAEAN
HERMAI
HERMAIC
HERMANDAD
HERMAPHRODITE
HERMAPHRODITIC
HERMAPHRODITISM
HERME
HERMELE
HERMENEUT
HERMENEUTIC
HERMETIC
HERMETICAL
HERMIDIN
HERMIT
HERMITAGE
HERMITARY
HERMITIC
HERMITICAL
HERMITRY
HERN
HERNE
HERNIA
HERNIAE
HERNIAL
HERNIARIN
HERNIARY
HERNIATE
HERNIATED
HERNIATION
HERO
HERODIAN
HEROES
HEROESS
HEROIC
HEROICAL
HEROICITY
HEROICOMIC
HEROICS
HEROID
HEROIFY
HEROIN
HEROINE
HEROISM
HEROISTIC
HEROLA
HERON
HERONBILL
HERONER
HERONITE
HERONRY
HERONS
HERONSEW
HEROOGONY
HEROOLOGY
HERPES
HERPESTINE
HERPETIC
HERRING
HERRINGBONE
HERRINGER
HERRINGS
HERRY
HERS
HERSALL
HERSCHELITE
HERSE
HERSED
HERSELF
HERSHIP
HERSIR
HERTZ
HERTZIAN
HERY
HESH
HESITANCE
HESITANCY
HESITANT
HESITANTLY
HESITATE
HESITATER
HESITATING
HESITATION
HESITATIVE
HESITATOR
HESPED
HESPEL
HESPERIDATE
HESPERIDENE
HESPERIDIN
HESSITE
HESSONITE
HEST
HET
HETAERA
HETAERIA
HETAERIO
HETAERISM
HETAERIST
HETAERY
HETAIRIA
HETAIRY
HETE
HETERAKID
HETERIC
HETERISM
HETERIZE
HETEROCENTRIC
HETEROCERC
HETEROCERCAL
HETEROCHIRAL
HETEROCHROME
HETEROCLINE
HETEROCLITE
HETEROCLITIC
HETEROCYCLE
HETEROCYCLIC
HETEROCYST
HETERODONT
HETERODOX
HETERODOXIES
HETERODOXY
HETERODYNE
HETEROECY
HETEROEROTISM
HETEROGAMETE
HETEROGAMIC
HETEROGAMY
HETEROGENE
HETEROGENEOUS
HETEROGONY
HETEROGRAFT
HETEROGRAPHIES
HETEROGRAPHY
HETEROGYNAL
HETEROLATERAL
HETEROLITH
HETEROLOGICAL
HETEROLOGIES
HETEROLOGY
HETEROLYSIS
HETEROLYTIC
HETEROMORPHIC
HETERONOMOUS
HETERONOMY
HETERONUCLEAR
HETERONYM
HETERONYMOUS
HETEROPATHIC
HETEROPATHY
HETEROPLASM
HETEROPLASTIC
HETEROPLASTIES
HETEROPLASTY
HETEROPOLAR
HETEROPTICS
HETEROSCOPE
HETEROSEXUAL
HETEROSIS
HETEROSPHERE
HETEROSTATIC
HETEROTACTIC
HETEROTAXIA
HETEROTAXIC
HETEROTAXIS
HETEROTELIC
HETEROTOPIA
HETEROTOPIC
HETEROTOPY
HETEROTROPAL
HETEROTROPHIC
HETEROTYPIC
HETEROXENOUS
HETEROZYGOTE
HETEROZYGOUS
HETHEN
HETHING
HETMAN
HETTER
HEU
HEUCH
HEUGH
HEURETIC
HEURT
HEUVEL
HEVEN
HEVER
HEVI
HEW
HEWE
HEWEL
HEWER
HEWGAG
HEWHALL
HEWHOLE
HEWN
HEWT
HEX
HEXABASIC
HEXABIOSE
HEXABROMID
HEXABROMIDE
HEXACHORD
HEXACID
HEXACOLIC
HEXACOSANE
HEXACTINAL
HEXACYCLIC
HEXAD
HEXADE
HEXADECANE
HEXADECYL
HEXADIC
HEXADIENE
HEXADIINE
HEXADIYNE
HEXAEMERIC
HEXAEMERON
HEXAFOIL
HEXAFOOS
HEXAGLOT
HEXAGON
HEXAGONAL
HEXAGONALLY
HEXAGRAM
HEXAGYN
HEXAGYNOUS
HEXAHEDRA
HEXAHEDRAL
HEXAHEDRON
HEXAHYDRIC
HEXAMER
HEXAMERAL
HEXAMERISM
HEXAMERON
HEXAMEROUS
HEXAMETER
HEXAMETRAL
HEXAMETRIC
HEXAMINE
HEXAMMIN
HEXAMMINE
HEXANAL
HEXANDRIC
HEXANDROUS
HEXANDRY
HEXANE
HEXANGULAR
HEXAPED
HEXAPLA
HEXAPLAR
HEXAPLARIC
HEXAPLOID
HEXAPOD
HEXAPODIES
HEXAPODY
HEXARADIAL
HEXARCHIES
HEXARCHY

HEXASEME
HEXASEMIC
HEXASTER
HEXASTICH
HEXASTICHIC
HEXASTICHY
HEXASTIGM
HEXASTYLOS
HEXATHLON
HEXATOMIC
HEXATRIOSE
HEXAVALENT
HEXAXON
HEXENE
HEXER
HEXEREI
HEXERIS
HEXINE
HEXIS
HEXITOL
HEXOBARBITAL
HEXODE
HEXOIC
HEXONE
HEXONIC
HEXOSAN
HEXOSE
HEXPARTITE
HEXT
HEXYL
HEXYLENE
HEXYLIC
HEXYNE
HEY
HEYDAY
HEYDEGUY
HEYDEY
HEYRAT
HEYT
HI
HIA
HIANT
HIATAL
HIATE
HIATION
HIATUS
HIBACHI
HIBBIN
HIBERNAL
HIBERNATE
HIBERNATING
HIBERNATION
HIC
HICACO
HICAN
HICATEE
HICCAN
HICCOUGH
HICCUP
HICHT
HICHU
HICK
HICKEY
HICKORY
HICKWALL
HICKWAY
HICKY
HID
HIDAGE
HIDALGO
HIDATED
HIDATION
HIDDELS
HIDDEN
HIDDENITE
HIDE
HIDEAWAY
HIDEBIND
HIDEBOUND
HIDEBOUNDNESS
HIDED
HIDEL
HIDELAND
HIDELING
HIDEOSITY
HIDEOUS
HIDEOUSLY
HIDEOUSNESS
HIDEOUT
HIDER
HIDES
HIDING
HIDLING
HIDLINGS
HIDLINS
HIDROSIS
HIDROTIC
HIE
HIEDER
HIELAMAN
HIELAMEN
HIELD
HIELMITE
HIEMAL
HIEMATION
HIEMS
HIEN
HIER
HIERA
HIERAPICRA
HIERARCH
HIERARCHAL
HIERARCHIC
HIERARCHICAL
HIERARCHICALLY
HIERARCHISM
HIERARCHIST
HIERARCHIZE
HIERARCHY
HIERATIC
HIERATICAL
HIERATICALLY
HIERATITE
HIEROCRACIES
HIEROCRACY
HIEROCRATIC
HIEROCRATICAL
HIERODULE
HIEROGAMY
HIEROGLYPH
HIEROGLYPHER
HIEROGLYPHIC
HIEROGRAM
HIEROGRAPH
HIEROGRAPHER
HIEROGRAPHIC
HIEROGRAPHY
HIEROLATRY
HIEROLOGIC
HIEROLOGIST
HIEROLOGY
HIEROMACHY
HIEROMANCY
HIEROMNEMON
HIEROMONACH
HIERON
HIEROPATHIC
HIEROPHANCY
HIEROPHANT
HIEROS
HIEROSCOPY
HIERURGY
HIFALUTIN
HIGDON
HIGGAION
HIGGLE
HIGGLEHAGGLE
HIGGLER
HIGGLERY
HIGH
HIGHBALL
HIGHBINDER
HIGHBORN
HIGHBOY
HIGHBRED
HIGHBROW
HIGHBROWED
HIGHBROWISM
HIGHCHAIR
HIGHDAY
HIGHER
HIGHERMOST
HIGHEST
HIGHFALUTIN
HIGHFALUTING
HIGHFLIER
HIGHFLYER
HIGHFLYING
HIGHHANDED
HIGHHEARTED
HIGHHOLE
HIGHJACK
HIGHJACKER
HIGHLAND
HIGHLANDER
HIGHLIGHT
HIGHLINE
HIGHLOW
HIGHLY
HIGHMAN
HIGHMOOR
HIGHMOST
HIGHNESS
HIGHROAD
HIGHT
HIGHTAIL
HIGHTIDE
HIGHTOBY
HIGHTOP
HIGHVELD
HIGHWAY
HIGHWAYMAN
HIGRE
HIGUERO
HIJACK
HIJACKER
HIJINKS
HIKE
HIKER
HIKU
HIKULI
HILARIOUS
HILARIOUSLY
HILARIOUSNESS
HILARITY
HILASMIC
HILCH
HILDING
HILL
HILLBILLIES
HILLBILLY
HILLBIRD
HILLER
HILLET
HILLMAN
HILLO
HILLOA
HILLOCK
HILLOCKED
HILLOCKY
HILLS
HILLSALE
HILLSALESMAN
HILLSIDE
HILLSMAN
HILLTOP
HILLTROT
HILLWORT
HILLY
HILSA
HILSAH
HILT
HILUM
HILUS
HIM
HIMATIA
HIMATION
HIMENE
HIMMING
HIMP
HIMPLE
HIMSELF
HIN
HINAU
HINCH
HIND
HINDBERRY
HINDBRAIN
HINDCAST
HINDDECK
HINDER
HINDERANCE
HINDERED
HINDERER
HINDEREST
HINDERFUL
HINDERFULLY
HINDERLY
HINDERMENT
HINDERMOST
HINDERSOME
HINDGUT
HINDHAND
HINDHEAD
HINDMOST
HINDQUARTER
HINDQUARTERS
HINDRANCE
HINDS
HINDSADDLE
HINDSIGHT
HINE
HING
HINGE
HINGECORNER
HINGED
HINGEFLOWER
HINGLE
HINK
HINNA
HINNER
HINNIBLE
HINNIES
HINNY
HINOID
HINOIDEOUS
HINOKI
HINSDALITE
HINT
HINTERLAND
HIODONT
HIP
HIPBERRY
HIPBONE
HIPE
HIPHALT
HIPHAPE
HIPLINE
HIPMOLD
HIPPARCH
HIPPED
HIPPEN
HIPPIAN
HIPPIATER
HIPPIATRIC
HIPPIATRY
HIPPIC
HIPPIE
HIPPING
HIPPISH
HIPPLE
HIPPO
HIPPOBOSCID
HIPPOCAMPAL
HIPPOCAMPUS
HIPPOCAUST
HIPPOCERF
HIPPOCRAS
HIPPODROME
HIPPOGRIFF
HIPPOGRYPH
HIPPOID
HIPPOLITH
HIPPOLOGY
HIPPOMANES
HIPPONOUS
HIPPOPHILE
HIPPOPOD
HIPPOPOTAMIC
HIPPOPOTAMUS
HIPPOTOMY
HIPPURATE
HIPPURIC
HIPPURID
HIPPURITE
HIPPUS
HIPPY
HIPS
HIPSHOT
HIPSTER
HIRABLE
HIRAGANA
HIRCARRA
HIRCH
HIRCINE
HIRCINOUS
HIRCUS
HIRE
HIRED
HIRELING
HIRER
HIRING
HIRLING
HIRMOS
HIRO
HIRONDELLE
HIRPLE
HIRR
HIRRIENT
HIRSE
HIRSEL
HIRSELED
HIRSELING
HIRSELLED
HIRSELLING
HIRSH
HIRSLE
HIRST
HIRSUTE
HIRSUTENESS
HIRSUTIES
HIRSUTISM
HIRTCH
HIRUDINEAN
HIRUDINOID

HIRUNDINE
HIS
HISH
HISINGERITE
HISLOPITE
HISN
HISPID
HISPIDITY
HISPIDULATE
HISPIDULOUS
HISS
HISSEL
HISSELF
HISSER
HISSING
HISSY
HIST
HISTAMINE
HISTAMINIC
HISTER
HISTIDINE
HISTIE
HISTOBLAST
HISTOCHEMIC
HISTOCHEMICAL
HISTOCLASTIC
HISTOGEN
HISTOGENESIS
HISTOGENETIC
HISTOGENIC
HISTOGENOUS
HISTOGENY
HISTOGRAM
HISTOGRAPHIC
HISTOGRAPHY
HISTOID
HISTOLOGIC
HISTOLOGICAL
HISTOLOGIES
HISTOLOGIST
HISTOLOGY
HISTOLYSIS
HISTON
HISTONAL
HISTONE
HISTONOMY
HISTORIAL
HISTORIAN
HISTORIC
HISTORICAL
HISTORICALNESS
HISTORICS
HISTORIED
HISTORIER
HISTORIES
HISTORIETTE
HISTORIFY
HISTORIOGRAPH
HISTORIOGRAPHER
HISTORIOUS
HISTORISM
HISTORIZE
HISTORY
HISTOTOME
HISTOTOMY
HISTOTROPHIC
HISTOTROPHY
HISTOTROPIC
HISTRIO
HISTRION
HISTRIONIC
HISTRIONICAL
HISTRIONICALLY
HISTRIONICS
HIT
HITCH
HITCHER
HITCHHIKE
HITCHHIKER
HITCHILY
HITCHING
HITCHY
HITHE
HITHER
HITHERMOST
HITHERTILLS
HITHERTO
HITHERTOWARD
HITHERUNTO
HITHERWARD
HITTABLE
HITTER
HIVE
HIVER
HIVES
HIYA
HIYAKKIN
HIZ
HIZZ
HIZZIE
HO
HOACTZIN
HOAR
HOARD
HOARDED
HOARDER
HOARDING
HOARDWARD
HOARFROST
HOARHEAD
HOARHEADED
HOARHOUND
HOARINESS
HOARISH
HOARSE
HOARSELY
HOARSEN
HOARSENESS
HOARSTONE
HOARWORT
HOARY
HOAST
HOASTMAN
HOATZIN
HOAX
HOAXEE
HOAXER
HOAXPROOF
HOB
HOBB
HOBBER
HOBBET
HOBBIL
HOBBINOLL
HOBBIT
HOBBLE
HOBBLEBUSH
HOBBLEDEHOY
HOBBLER
HOBBLES
HOBBLING
HOBBLY
HOBBY
HOBBYHORSE
HOBBYISM
HOBBYIST
HOBGOBLIN
HOBHOUCHIN
HOBLIKE
HOBLOB
HOBNAIL
HOBNAILED
HOBNAILER
HOBNOB
HOBO
HOBOISM
HOBTHRUSH
HOC
HOCCO
HOCH
HOCK
HOCKELTY
HOCKER
HOCKET
HOCKEY
HOCKING
HOCKSHIN
HOCKY
HOCUS
HOD
HODAG
HODDEN
HODDER
HODDLE
HODDY
HODENING
HODFUL
HODGEPODGE
HODIERNAL
HODJA
HODMAN
HODMANDOD
HODOGRAPH
HODOMETER
HODOMETRICAL
HODOSCOPE
HODURE
HOE
HOECAKE
HOEDOWN
HOER
HOERNESITE
HOG
HOGA
HOGAN
HOGBACK
HOGBUSH
HOGCHOKER
HOGCOTE
HOGFISH
HOGFRAME
HOGG
HOGGASTER
HOGGED
HOGGEE
HOGGER
HOGGEREL
HOGGERY
HOGGET
HOGGIE
HOGGIN
HOGGING
HOGGINS
HOGGISH
HOGGISHLY
HOGGISHNESS
HOGGLER
HOGGY
HOGHEAD
HOGHERD
HOGLING
HOGMACE
HOGMANAY
HOGNOSE
HOGNUT
HOGO
HOGREEVE
HOGS
HOGSHEAD
HOGSHOUTHER
HOGSKIN
HOGSTEER
HOGSUCKER
HOGTON
HOGWARD
HOGWASH
HOGWEED
HOGWORT
HOI
HOICK
HOICKS
HOIDEN
HOIGH
HOIHERE
HOIN
HOISE
HOIST
HOISTAWAY
HOISTED
HOISTER
HOISTING
HOISTMAN
HOISTWAY
HOIT
HOJA
HOJU
HOK
HOKE
HOKER
HOKERER
HOKERLY
HOKEY
HOKKU
HOKUM
HOL
HOLA
HOLARCTIC
HOLARD
HOLCAD
HOLCODONT
HOLD
HOLDALL
HOLDBACK
HOLDE
HOLDENITE
HOLDER
HOLDFAST
HOLDING
HOLDINGS
HOLDMAN
HOLDOUT
HOLDOVER
HOLDSMAN
HOLDUP
HOLE
HOLEABLE
HOLEMAN
HOLER
HOLES
HOLEWORT
HOLEY
HOLIA
HOLIDAY
HOLIDAYER
HOLIES
HOLILY
HOLINESS
HOLING
HOLISHKES
HOLISM
HOLISTIC
HOLISTICALLY
HOLL
HOLLA
HOLLAITE
HOLLANDAISE
HOLLEKE
HOLLER
HOLLIN
HOLLIPER
HOLLO
HOLLOA
HOLLOCK
HOLLONG
HOLLOW
HOLLOWED
HOLLOWER
HOLLOWFACED
HOLLOWFOOT
HOLLOWHEARTED
HOLLOWLY
HOLLOWNESS
HOLLOWROOT
HOLLUSCHICK
HOLLY
HOLLYHOCK
HOLLYLEAF
HOLM
HOLMBERRY
HOLMES
HOLMGANG
HOLMIA
HOLMIC
HOLMIUM
HOLMOS
HOLOBAPTIST
HOLOBENTHIC
HOLOBLASTIC
HOLOBRANCH
HOLOCAINE
HOLOCARPIC
HOLOCAUST
HOLOCAUSTAL
HOLOCAUSTIC
HOLOCHORDATE
HOLOCHROAL
HOLOCLASTIC
HOLOGAMOUS
HOLOGAMY
HOLOGRAM
HOLOGRAPH
HOLOGRAPHIC
HOLOGRAPHY
HOLOHEDRAL
HOLOHEDRIC
HOLOHEDRON
HOLOKU
HOLOMETER
HOLOMORPH
HOLOMORPHIC
HOLOMORPHISM
HOLOMORPHY
HOLOPARASITE
HOLOPHOTAL
HOLOPHOTE
HOLOPHRASE
HOLOPHRASM
HOLOPHRASTIC
HOLOPHYTE
HOLOPHYTIC
HOLOPLEXIA
HOLOPTIC
HOLORHINAL
HOLOSIDE
HOLOSIDERITE
HOLOSTEAN
HOLOSTERIC
HOLOSTOME
HOLOSTYLIC
HOLOTHURIAN
HOLOTONY
HOLOTYPE
HOLOTYPIC
HOLOUR
HOLOZOIC

HOLP
HOLSOM
HOLSTER
HOLSTERED
HOLSTERS
HOLT
HOLY
HOLYDAY
HOLYSTONE
HOLYTIDE
HOMA
HOMAGE
HOMAGEABLE
HOMAGER
HOMALOID
HOMARD
HOMATOMIC
HOMAXIAL
HOME
HOMEBODY
HOMEBORN
HOMEBOUND
HOMEBRED
HOMECOMING
HOMECRAFT
HOMECROFT
HOMEFELT
HOMEKEEPER
HOMEKEEPING
HOMELAND
HOMELESS
HOMELIFE
HOMELIKE
HOMELIKENESS
HOMELILY
HOMELINESS
HOMELING
HOMELY
HOMELYN
HOMEMADE
HOMEMAKER
HOMEMAKING
HOMEOID
HOMEOIDAL
HOMEOPATH
HOMEOPOLAR
HOMEOSIS
HOMEOSTASIS
HOMEOSTATIC
HOMEOTIC
HOMEOTYPE
HOMEOTYPIC
HOMEOWNER
HOMER
HOMEROOM
HOMESEEKER
HOMESICK
HOMESICKLY
HOMESICKNESS
HOMESITE
HOMESOME
HOMESPUN
HOMESTALL
HOMESTEAD
HOMESTEADER
HOMESTER
HOMESTRETCH
HOMETOWN
HOMEWARD
HOMEWARDLY
HOMEWARDS
HOMEWORK
HOMEWORKER
HOMEWORT
HOMEY
HOMEYNESS
HOMICIDAL
HOMICIDALLY
HOMICIDE
HOMICULTURE
HOMILETE
HOMILETIC
HOMILETICAL
HOMILETICS
HOMILIST
HOMILITE
HOMILIZE
HOMILY
HOMINAL
HOMINESS
HOMING
HOMINID
HOMININE
HOMINOID
HOMINY
HOMISH
HOMISHNESS
HOMME
HOMO
HOMOBARIC
HOMOBLASTIC
HOMOBLASTY
HOMOCENTRIC
HOMOCENTRICAL
HOMOCERC
HOMOCERCAL
HOMOCERCY
HOMOCEREBRIN
HOMOCHIRAL
HOMOCHROME
HOMOCHROMIC
HOMOCHRONOUS
HOMOCLINE
HOMOCYCLIC
HOMODERMIC
HOMODERMY
HOMODONT
HOMODOX
HOMODROMAL
HOMODROME
HOMODROMY
HOMODYNAMIC
HOMODYNE
HOMOEOMERIC
HOMOEOMERY
HOMOGAMY
HOMOGEN
HOMOGENE
HOMOGENEAL
HOMOGENEITY
HOMOGENEOUS
HOMOGENESIS
HOMOGENETIC
HOMOGENIZE
HOMOGENIZER
HOMOGENOUS
HOMOGENY
HOMOGLOT
HOMOGONE
HOMOGONY
HOMOGRAPH
HOMOGRAPHIC
HOMOGRAPHY
HOMOHEDRAL
HOMOLATERAL
HOMOLOG
HOMOLOGATE
HOMOLOGIC
HOMOLOGICAL
HOMOLOGIES
HOMOLOGIZE
HOMOLOGON
HOMOLOGOUS
HOMOLOGUE
HOMOLOGY
HOMOLOSINE
HOMOMERAL
HOMOMEROUS
HOMOMORPH
HOMOMORPHIC
HOMOMORPHISM
HOMOMORPHY
HOMONID
HOMONYM
HOMONYMIC
HOMONYMOUS
HOMONYMY
HOMOPATHY
HOMOPHENE
HOMOPHONE
HOMOPHONIC
HOMOPHONY
HOMOPHYLIC
HOMOPHYLY
HOMOPLASIS
HOMOPLASMIC
HOMOPLASMY
HOMOPLASSY
HOMOPLAST
HOMOPLASTIC
HOMOPLASY
HOMOPOLAR
HOMOPOLIC
HOMOPTER
HOMORGANIC
HOMOSEXUAL
HOMOSEXUALITY
HOMOSTYLED
HOMOSTYLIC
HOMOSTYLY
HOMOTACTIC
HOMOTATIC
HOMOTAXIS
HOMOTAXY
HOMOTHALLIC
HOMOTHETIC
HOMOTHETY
HOMOTONIC
HOMOTONY
HOMOTOPIC
HOMOTROPAL
HOMOTYPAL
HOMOTYPE
HOMOTYPIC
HOMOTYPY
HOMOZYGOTE
HOMOZYGOUS
HOMUNCIO
HOMUNCLE
HOMY
HON
HONAN
HONDA
HONDO
HONE
HONEST
HONESTLY
HONESTONE
HONESTY
HONEWORT
HONEY
HONEYBALLS
HONEYBEE
HONEYBEES
HONEYBERRY
HONEYBIND
HONEYBLOB
HONEYBLOOM
HONEYBUN
HONEYCOMB
HONEYCOMBED
HONEYCOMBING
HONEYCUP
HONEYDEW
HONEYDEWED
HONEYED
HONEYEDNESS
HONEYFALL
HONEYFLOWER
HONEYFOGLE
HONEYFUGLE
HONEYLIPPED
HONEYMONTH
HONEYMOON
HONEYMOONY
HONEYMOUTHED
HONEYPOD
HONEYPOT
HONEYS
HONEYSUCK
HONEYSUCKER
HONEYSUCKLE
HONEYSUCKLED
HONEYSWEET
HONEYWARE
HONEYWOOD
HONEYWORT
HONG
HONIED
HONK
HONKER
HONKIE
HONKIES
HONKY
HONOR
HONORABILITY
HONORABLE
HONORABLENESS
HONORABLY
HONORANCE
HONORARIUM
HONORARY
HONORED
HONORER
HONORIFIC
HONORIFICALLY
HONORS
HONOUR
HONOURABILITY
HONOURABLE
HONOURABLY
HONOURER
HONOURS
HONTISH
HONTOUS
HOO
HOOCH
HOOD
HOODCAP
HOODED
HOODIE
HOODING
HOODLUM
HOODMAN
HOODMOLD
HOODOO
HOODSHY
HOODSHYNESS
HOODWINK
HOODWINKER
HOODWORT
HOODY
HOOEY
HOOF
HOOFBEAT
HOOFBOUND
HOOFED
HOOFER
HOOFLET
HOOFPRINT
HOOFS
HOOFWORM
HOOGAARS
HOOK
HOOKA
HOOKAH
HOOKAROON
HOOKED
HOOKEDNESS
HOOKER
HOOKERS
HOOKHEAL
HOOKLAND
HOOKLET
HOOKLIKE
HOOKMAN
HOOKNOSE
HOOKS
HOOKSHOP
HOOKTIP
HOOKUM
HOOKUP
HOOKUPU
HOOKWEED
HOOKWORM
HOOKWORMER
HOOKWORMY
HOOKY
HOOLAKIN
HOOLAULEA
HOOLEY
HOOLIE
HOOLIGAN
HOOLIHAN
HOOLOCK
HOOLY
HOON
HOONDEE
HOONDI
HOOP
HOOPED
HOOPER
HOOPING
HOOPLA
HOOPLE
HOOPLIKE
HOOPMAKER
HOOPMAN
HOOPOE
HOOPS
HOOPSKIRT
HOOPSTER
HOOPSTICK
HOOPWOOD
HOORAH
HOORAY
HOOROOSH
HOOSE
HOOSEGOW
HOOSH
HOOT
HOOTAY
HOOTER
HOOTS
HOOVE
HOOVEY
HOOZE
HOP
HOPBIND
HOPBINE
HOPBUSH
HOPCALITE
HOPCREASE
HOPE
HOPED

HOPEFUL
HOPEFULLY
HOPEFULNESS
HOPEITE
HOPELESS
HOPELESSLY
HOPELESSNESS
HOPER
HOPHEAD
HOPLITE
HOPLITIC
HOPLOLOGY
HOPLOMACHIC
HOPLOMACHY
HOPO
HOPOFF
HOPPE
HOPPED
HOPPER
HOPPERBURN
HOPPERDOZER
HOPPERETTE
HOPPERINGS
HOPPERMAN
HOPPERS
HOPPESTERE
HOPPET
HOPPING
HOPPITY
HOPPLE
HOPPO
HOPPY
HOPS
HOPSACK
HOPSACKING
HOPSAGE
HOPSCOTCH
HOPTOAD
HOPVINE
HOPYARD
HORA
HORAL
HORARY
HORBACHITE
HORDARIAN
HORDARY
HORDE
HORDEACEOUS
HORDEATE
HORDEIFORM
HORDEIN
HORDENINE
HORDEOLUM
HORDOCK
HORE
HOREHOUND
HORISMOLOGY
HORIZOMETER
HORIZON
HORIZONTAL
HORIZONTALITY
HORIZONTALIZE
HORIZONTALLY
HORIZONTIC
HORIZONTICAL
HORIZONTICALLY
HORKEY
HORME
HORMIC
HORMIGO
HORMION
HORMISM
HORMIST
HORMONE
HORMONES
HORMOS
HORN
HORNADA
HORNBEAM
HORNBILL
HORNBLENDE
HORNBLOWER
HORNBOOK
HORNED
HORNER
HORNERAH
HORNERO
HORNET
HORNETY
HORNFAIR
HORNFELS
HORNFISH
HORNGELD
HORNIFY
HORNING
HORNIST
HORNITO
HORNKECK
HORNLESS
HORNLIKE
HORNOTINE
HORNPIE
HORNPIPE
HORNPLANT
HORNS
HORNSLATE
HORNSMAN
HORNSTAY
HORNSTONE
HORNSWOGGLE
HORNTAIL
HORNTHUMB
HORNTIP
HORNWEED
HORNWOOD
HORNWORK
HORNWORM
HORNWORT
HORNY
HORNYHANDED
HORNYHEAD
HOROGRAPH
HOROGRAPHER
HOROGRAPHY
HOROKAKA
HOROLOGE
HOROLOGER
HOROLOGIC
HOROLOGICAL
HOROLOGICALLY
HOROLOGIST
HOROLOGIUM
HOROLOGUE
HOROLOGY
HOROMETRY
HOROPITO
HOROPTER
HOROPTERIC
HOROPTERY
HOROSCOPAL
HOROSCOPE
HOROSCOPER
HOROSCOPICAL
HOROSCOPIST
HOROSCOPY
HOROTELY
HORRAL
HORRENDOUS
HORRENDOUSLY
HORRENT
HORRESCENT
HORREUM
HORRIBLE
HORRIBLENESS
HORRIBLES
HORRIBLY
HORRID
HORRIDITY
HORRIDLY
HORRIFIC
HORRIFICATION
HORRIFIED
HORRIFY
HORRIFYING
HORRIPILANT
HORRIPILATE
HORRISONANT
HORROR
HORROROUS
HORRORS
HORRORSOME
HORRY
HORS
HORSE
HORSEBACK
HORSEBACKER
HORSEBANE
HORSEBLOCK
HORSEBOY
HORSEBREAKER
HORSEBUSH
HORSECAR
HORSECLOTH
HORSEDRAWING
HORSEFAIR
HORSEFIGHT
HORSEFISH
HORSEFLESH
HORSEFLIES
HORSEFLOWER
HORSEFLY
HORSEFOOT
HORSEGATE
HORSEHAIR
HORSEHAIRED
HORSEHEAD
HORSEHEAL
HORSEHEEL
HORSEHIDE
HORSEHOOF
HORSEKEEPER
HORSEKEEPING
HORSELAUGH
HORSELAUGHTER
HORSELEACH
HORSELEECH
HORSELESS
HORSELOAD
HORSELOCK
HORSELY
HORSEMAN
HORSEMANSHIP
HORSEMEN
HORSEMINT
HORSENAIL
HORSEPIPE
HORSEPOND
HORSEPOWER
HORSEPOX
HORSER
HORSERADISH
HORSES
HORSESHOE
HORSESHOER
HORSETAIL
HORSETONGUE
HORSETREE
HORSEWAY
HORSEWEED
HORSEWHIP
HORSEWHIPPER
HORSEWOMAN
HORSEWOMANSHIP
HORSEWOOD
HORSFORDITE
HORSIFY
HORSINESS
HORSING
HORST
HORSTE
HORSY
HORSYISM
HORTATION
HORTATIVE
HORTATOR
HORTATORILY
HORTATORY
HORTENSIAL
HORTESIAN
HORTICULTURAL
HORTICULTURALLY
HORTICULTURE
HORTITE
HORTONOLITE
HORTULAN
HORTYARD
HORY
HOSANNA
HOSE
HOSEBIRD
HOSED
HOSEL
HOSEMAN
HOSEN
HOSEPIPE
HOSIER
HOSIERY
HOSIOMARTYR
HOSPICE
HOSPITABLE
HOSPITABLENESS
HOSPITABLY
HOSPITAGE
HOSPITAL
HOSPITALARY
HOSPITALER
HOSPITALISM
HOSPITALITY
HOSPITALIZATION
HOSPITALIZE
HOSPITALLER
HOSPITANT
HOSPITATE
HOSPITIUM
HOSPODAR
HOSPODARIAT
HOSPODARIATE
HOSS
HOST
HOSTAGE
HOSTAGER
HOSTEL
HOSTELER
HOSTELRY
HOSTER
HOSTESS
HOSTILE
HOSTILELY
HOSTILENESS
HOSTILITIES
HOSTILITY
HOSTING
HOSTLE
HOSTLER
HOSTLERWIFE
HOSTLY
HOSTRY
HOT
HOTBED
HOTBLOOD
HOTBOX
HOTCH
HOTCHA
HOTCHPOT
HOTCHPOTCH
HOTCHPOTCHLY
HOTE
HOTEL
HOTELIER
HOTELKEEPER
HOTFOOT
HOTHEAD
HOTHEADED
HOTHEADEDLY
HOTHEADEDNESS
HOTHOUSE
HOTI
HOTLY
HOTMELT
HOTMOUTHED
HOTNESS
HOTPRESS
HOTSPUR
HOTSPURRED
HOTT
HOTTER
HOTTERY
HOTTLE
HOUBARA
HOUGH
HOUGHER
HOUGHITE
HOUGHMAGANDY
HOUGHSINEW
HOUHERE
HOUNCE
HOUND
HOUNDER
HOUNDFISH
HOUNDING
HOUNDMAN
HOUNDS
HOUNDSBANE
HOUNDSBERRY
HOUNDSHARK
HOUNDY
HOUPPELANDE
HOUR
HOURGLASS
HOURI
HOURLY
HOUSAGE
HOUSAL
HOUSE
HOUSEBALL
HOUSEBOAT
HOUSEBOATING
HOUSEBOTE
HOUSEBOUND
HOUSEBOY
HOUSEBREAK
HOUSEBREAKER
HOUSEBROKE
HOUSEBROKEN
HOUSEBUG
HOUSEBUILDER
HOUSECARL
HOUSECOAT
HOUSEDRESS
HOUSEFAST
HOUSEFATHER
HOUSEFLY
HOUSEFUL
HOUSEHOLD
HOUSEHOLDER

HOUSEHOLDING
HOUSEHOLDRY
HOUSEKEEP
HOUSEKEEPER
HOUSEKEEPERLY
HOUSEKEEPING
HOUSEL
HOUSELEEK
HOUSELESS
HOUSELINE
HOUSELING
HOUSEMAID
HOUSEMAIDENLY
HOUSEMAIDY
HOUSEMAN
HOUSEMASTER
HOUSEMATE
HOUSEMINDER
HOUSEMISTRESS
HOUSEMOTHER
HOUSER
HOUSERIDDEN
HOUSEROOM
HOUSES
HOUSESMITH
HOUSETOP
HOUSEWARES
HOUSEWARM
HOUSEWARMING
HOUSEWIFE
HOUSEWIFELY
HOUSEWIFERY
HOUSEWIVES
HOUSEWORK
HOUSEWRIGHT
HOUSING
HOUSINGS
HOUSTONIA
HOUSTY
HOUSY
HOUTING
HOUTOU
HOUVARI
HOUVE
HOVEDANCE
HOVEL
HOVELER
HOVELLER
HOVEN
HOVER
HOVERCRAFT
HOVERER
HOVERING
HOVERINGLY
HOVERLY
HOW
HOWADJI
HOWARDITE
HOWBEIT
HOWD
HOWDAH
HOWDER
HOWDIE
HOWDY
HOWE
HOWEL
HOWEVER
HOWF
HOWFF
HOWFING
HOWGATES
HOWISH
HOWITZ
HOWITZER
HOWK
HOWKIT
HOWL
HOWLER
HOWLET
HOWLING
HOWLINGLY
HOWLITE
HOWSO
HOWSOEVER
HOWSOMEVER
HOWSOUR
HOX
HOY
HOYDEN
HOYMAN
HSIEN
HSIN
HU
HUACA
HUACO
HUAJILLO
HUAMUCHIL
HUAPANGO
HUARACHE
HUARACHO
HUARIZO
HUB
HUBAM
HUBB
HUBBA
HUBBABOO
HUBBER
HUBBLE
HUBBLY
HUBBUB
HUBBUBOO
HUBBY
HUBCAP
HUBNERITE
HUBRIS
HUBRISTIC
HUBSHI
HUCCATOON
HUCH
HUCHEN
HUCHO
HUCK
HUCKABACK
HUCKLE
HUCKLEBACK
HUCKLEBACKED
HUCKLEBERRIES
HUCKLEBERRY
HUCKLEBONE
HUCKMUCK
HUCKSTER
HUCKSTERER
HUCKSTERISM
HUCKSTERY
HUD
HUDDERON
HUDDLE
HUDDLER
HUDDLING
HUDDOCK
HUDDROUN
HUDDUP
HUDE
HUDGE
HUDSONIA
HUE
HUED
HUEFUL
HUEHUETL
HUEL
HUELESS
HUELESSNESS
HUEMUL
HUER
HUERTA
HUFFCAP
HUFFER
HUFFILY
HUFFINESS
HUFFINGLY
HUFFISH
HUFFISHLY
HUFFISHNESS
HUFFLE
HUFFLER
HUFFY
HUG
HUGE
HUGELITE
HUGELY
HUGENESS
HUGEOUS
HUGEOUSLY
HUGEOUSNESS
HUGGABLE
HUGGER
HUGGING
HUGGLE
HUGMATEE
HUGONIS
HUH
HUHU
HUI
HUIA
HUILA
HUIPIL
HUIPILLA
HUISACHE
HUISCOYOL
HUISHER
HUISQUIL
HUISSIER
HUITAIN
HUITRE
HUKE
HULA
HULCH
HULCHY
HULDEE
HULDI
HULK
HULKAGE
HULKING
HULKY
HULL
HULLABALOO
HULLED
HULLER
HULLING
HULLO
HULLOCK
HULLOO
HULLS
HULSITE
HULSTER
HULU
HULVER
HULVERHEAD
HULVERHEADED
HULWORT
HUM
HUMAN
HUMANE
HUMANELY
HUMANENESS
HUMANIFY
HUMANISM
HUMANIST
HUMANISTIC
HUMANITARIAN
HUMANITARY
HUMANITIES
HUMANITY
HUMANIZE
HUMANIZER
HUMANKIND
HUMANLY
HUMANOID
HUMATE
HUMATION
HUMBIRD
HUMBLE
HUMBLEBEE
HUMBLED
HUMBLENESS
HUMBLER
HUMBLESSO
HUMBLIE
HUMBLING
HUMBLY
HUMBO
HUMBOLDTITE
HUMBUG
HUMBUGGER
HUMBUZZ
HUMDINGER
HUMDRUM
HUMECT
HUMECTANT
HUMECTATE
HUMERAL
HUMERUS
HUMET
HUMETTEE
HUMETTY
HUMHUM
HUMIC
HUMID
HUMIDATE
HUMIDIFIER
HUMIDIFY
HUMIDITY
HUMIDLY
HUMIDNESS
HUMIDOR
HUMIFIC
HUMIFUSE
HUMIFY
HUMILIANT
HUMILIATE
HUMILIATED
HUMILIATION
HUMILITIES
HUMILITY
HUMIN
HUMIT
HUMITE
HUMLIE
HUMMAUL
HUMMEL
HUMMELER
HUMMER
HUMMIE
HUMMING
HUMMINGBIRD
HUMMINGLY
HUMMOCK
HUMMOCKY
HUMMUM
HUMOR
HUMORAL
HUMORALISM
HUMORALIST
HUMORED
HUMORESQUE
HUMORISM
HUMORIST
HUMORISTIC
HUMORIZE
HUMOROUS
HUMOROUSLY
HUMOROUSNESS
HUMORS
HUMOUR
HUMOURAL
HUMOURIST
HUMOURIZE
HUMOURS
HUMOUS
HUMP
HUMPBACK
HUMPBACKED
HUMPED
HUMPH
HUMPINESS
HUMPTY
HUMPY
HUMSTRUM
HUMULENE
HUMULON
HUMULONE
HUMUS
HUNCH
HUNCHBACK
HUNCHBACKED
HUNCHET
HUNCHY
HUNDER
HUNDI
HUNDRED
HUNDREDAL
HUNDREDER
HUNDREDFOLD
HUNDREDPENNY
HUNDREDTH
HUNDREDWEIGHT
HUNDREDWORK
HUNFYSH
HUNG
HUNGARITE
HUNGER
HUNGERINGLY
HUNGERLY
HUNGERROOT
HUNGERWEED
HUNGRIER
HUNGRIEST
HUNGRIFY
HUNGRILY
HUNGRINESS
HUNGRY
HUNH
HUNIA
HUNK
HUNKER
HUNKEROUS
HUNKERS
HUNKIES
HUNKS
HUNKY
HUNNER
HUNT
HUNTER
HUNTILITE
HUNTING
HUNTRESS
HUNTSMAN
HUNTSWOMAN
HUP
HUPP
HURA
HURCHEON
HURDIES
HURDIS
HURDLE

HURDLEMAN
HURDLER
HURDLES
HURDS
HURE
HUREAULITE
HUREEK
HURGILA
HURKLE
HURL
HURLBARROW
HURLBAT
HURLED
HURLEMENT
HURLER
HURLEY
HURLEYHACKET
HURLEYHOUSE
HURLIES
HURLING
HURLOCK
HURLY
HURON
HURR
HURRAH
HURRAY
HURRER
HURRICANE
HURRICANIZE
HURRICANO
HURRIED
HURRIEDLY
HURRIEDNESS
HURRIER
HURRIES
HURRISOME
HURROCK
HURROO
HURROOSH
HURRY
HURSE
HURST
HURT
HURTER
HURTFUL
HURTFULLY
HURTFULNESS
HURTING
HURTINGEST
HURTLE
HURTLEBERRY
HURTLESS
HURTLESSLY
HURTLESSNESS
HURTLING
HURTSOME
HURTY
HUSBAND
HUSBANDAGE
HUSBANDED
HUSBANDER
HUSBANDFIELD
HUSBANDLAND
HUSBANDLY
HUSBANDMAN
HUSBANDRESS
HUSBANDRY
HUSCARL
HUSE
HUSH
HUSHABY
HUSHCLOTH
HUSHED
HUSHEEN
HUSHEL
HUSHER
HUSHFUL
HUSHING
HUSHION
HUSHPUPPIES
HUSHPUPPY
HUSI
HUSK
HUSKANAW
HUSKED
HUSKENED
HUSKER
HUSKIER
HUSKIEST
HUSKING
HUSKROOT
HUSKS
HUSKWORT
HUSKY
HUSO
HUSPEL
HUSPIL
HUSS
HUSSAR
HUSSIES
HUSSY
HUST
HUSTING
HUSTINGS
HUSTLE
HUSTLECAP
HUSTLEMENT
HUSTLER
HUSTLING
HUT
HUTCH
HUTCHER
HUTCHET
HUTHOLD
HUTIA
HUTKEEPER
HUTMENT
HUTS
HUTTONING
HUTTONWEED
HUTUKHTU
HUTUKTU
HUTUNG
HUTZPAH
HUURDER
HUVELYK
HUXEN
HUZ
HUZOOR
HUZZ
HUZZA
HUZZAH
HUZZARD
HUZZY
HWAN
HY
HYACINTH
HYACINTHINE
HYAENA
HYAENID
HYAHYA
HYALESCENCE
HYALESCENT
HYALIN
HYALINE
HYALINIZE
HYALITE
HYALITHE
HYALITIS
HYALOGEN
HYALOGRAPH
HYALOGRAPHER
HYALOGRAPHY
HYALOID
HYALOLIPARITE
HYALOLITH
HYALOMUCOID
HYALOPLASM
HYALOPLASMA
HYALOPLASMIC
HYALOPSITE
HYALOSIDERITE
HYALOTEKITE
HYALOTYPE
HYBODONT
HYBOSIS
HYBRID
HYBRIDAL
HYBRIDATION
HYBRIDISM
HYBRIDITY
HYBRIDIZABLE
HYBRIDIZATION
HYBRIDIZE
HYBRIDIZER
HYBRIDOUS
HYBRIS
HYDANTOIC
HYDANTOIN
HYDATHODE
HYDATID
HYDATIFORM
HYDATOGENESIS
HYDATOGENIC
HYDATOID
HYDATOMORPHIC
HYDNOID
HYDRA
HYDRACID
HYDRACORAL
HYDRACRYLATE
HYDRACRYLIC
HYDRAE
HYDRAGOG
HYDRAGOGUE
HYDRAGOGY
HYDRAMINE
HYDRANGEA
HYDRANT
HYDRANTH
HYDRARCH
HYDRASE
HYDRASTINE
HYDRATE
HYDRATED
HYDRATION
HYDRATOR
HYDRAULIC
HYDRAULICS
HYDRAZIN
HYDRAZINE
HYDRAZOATE
HYDRAZOIC
HYDRAZONE
HYDRIA
HYDRIC
HYDRIDE
HYDRIFORM
HYDRIODIC
HYDRION
HYDRO
HYDROA
HYDROAERIC
HYDROAROMATIC
HYDROBENZOIN
HYDROBIOLOGY
HYDROBIOSIS
HYDROBIPLANE
HYDROBROMATE
HYDROBROMIC
HYDROBROMID
HYDROBROMIDE
HYDROCARBON
HYDROCARBONATE
HYDROCARBONIC
HYDROCAULINE
HYDROCAULUS
HYDROCELE
HYDROCEPHALIC
HYDROCEPHALY
HYDROCERAMIC
HYDROCHLORATE
HYDROCHLORIC
HYDROCHLORID
HYDROCHLORIDE
HYDROCLADIUM
HYDROCLASTIC
HYDROCOELE
HYDROCONION
HYDROCYANIC
HYDROCYANIDE
HYDROCYCLE
HYDROCYCLIC
HYDROCYCLIST
HYDROCYST
HYDROCYSTIC
HYDRODYNAMIC
HYDRODYNAMICS
HYDROELECTRIC
HYDROEXTRACT
HYDROEXTRACTOR
HYDROFLUATE
HYDROFLUORIC
HYDROFOIL
HYDROFUGE
HYDROGEL
HYDROGEN
HYDROGENASE
HYDROGENATE
HYDROGENATOR
HYDROGENIC
HYDROGENIZE
HYDROGEOLOGY
HYDROGLIDER
HYDROGNOSY
HYDROGODE
HYDROGRAPH
HYDROGRAPHER
HYDROGRAPHIC
HYDROGRAPHY
HYDROHALID
HYDROHALIDE
HYDROHEMATITE
HYDROID
HYDROKINETIC
HYDROL
HYDROLASE
HYDROLATRY
HYDROLOGIC
HYDROLOGICAL
HYDROLOGICALLY
HYDROLOGIST
HYDROLYSIS
HYDROLYST
HYDROLYTE
HYDROLYTIC
HYDROLYZATE
HYDROLYZE
HYDROMANIA
HYDROMANIAC
HYDROMANTIC
HYDROME
HYDROMEL
HYDROMETER
HYDROMETRA
HYDROMETRIC
HYDROMETRID
HYDROMETRY
HYDROMICA
HYDROMOTOR
HYDROMYOMA
HYDRONE
HYDRONITRIC
HYDRONIUM
HYDROPATH
HYDROPATHIC
HYDROPATHY
HYDROPERIOD
HYDROPHANE
HYDROPHANOUS
HYDROPHID
HYDROPHIL
HYDROPHILE
HYDROPHILIC
HYDROPHILID
HYDROPHILY
HYDROPHOBE
HYDROPHOBIA
HYDROPHOBIC
HYDROPHOBICAL
HYDROPHOBIST
HYDROPHOBOUS
HYDROPHONE
HYDROPHORIA
HYDROPHYLL
HYDROPHYLLIUM
HYDROPHYTE
HYDROPHYTIC
HYDROPHYTON
HYDROPIC
HYDROPICAL
HYDROPLANE
HYDROPOLYP
HYDROPONIC
HYDROPONICS
HYDROPOT
HYDROPS
HYDROPSY
HYDROPTIC
HYDROPULT
HYDROQUININE
HYDROQUINONE
HYDRORHIZA
HYDRORHIZAL
HYDRORRHEA
HYDRORRHOEA
HYDRORUBBER
HYDROSALT
HYDROSCOPE
HYDROSCOPIC
HYDROSELENIDE
HYDROSOL
HYDROSOLE
HYDROSOMA
HYDROSOME
HYDROSORBIC
HYDROSPHERE
HYDROSPIRE
HYDROSPIRIC
HYDROSTAT
HYDROSTATIC
HYDROSTATICS
HYDROSTOME
HYDROSULFATE
HYDROTALCITE
HYDROTAXIS
HYDROTECHNIC
HYDROTECHNY
HYDROTERPENE
HYDROTHECA
HYDROTHECAL
HYDROTHERAPY
HYDROTHERMAL
HYDROTHORAX
HYDROTYPE

HYDROUS
HYDROVANE
HYDROXIDE
HYDROZINCITE
HYDROZOAL
HYDROZOAN
HYDROZOIC
HYDROZOON
HYDRULA
HYE
HYENA
HYENIA
HYENIC
HYENINE
HYENOID
HYETAL
HYETOGRAPH
HYETOGRAPHIC
HYETOGRAPHY
HYGEEN
HYGEIST
HYGEISTIC
HYGIEIST
HYGIENE
HYGIENIC
HYGIENICS
HYGIENIST
HYGIENIZE
HYGRE
HYGRIC
HYGRIN
HYGRINE
HYGRODEIK
HYGROGRAPH
HYGROMA
HYGROMETER
HYGROMETRIC
HYGROMETRY
HYGROPHOBIA
HYGROPHYTE
HYGROPLASM
HYGROSCOPE
HYGROSCOPIC
HYGROSCOPY
HYGROSTAT
HYGROSTATICS
HYGROSTOMIA
HYGROTHERMAL
HYINGLY
HYKE
HYLA
HYLACTIC
HYLE
HYLEAN
HYLEG
HYLEGIACAL
HYLIC
HYLICIST
HYLID
HYLISM
HYLOID
HYLOLOGY
HYLOTHEISM
HYLOTHEIST
HYLOZOIC
HYLOZOISM
HYLOZOIST
HYMEN
HYMENAL
HYMENEAL
HYMENEALS
HYMENEAN
HYMENIAL
HYMENIC
HYMENIUM
HYMENOID
HYMN
HYMNAL
HYMNARY
HYMNBOOK
HYMNER
HYMNIC
HYMNIST
HYMNODE
HYMNODIST
HYMNODY
HYMNOLOGY
HYNDE
HYNE
HYOID
HYOIDES
HYOMENTAL
HYOPLASTRAL
HYOPLASTRON
HYOSCINE
HYOSTERNAL
HYOSTERNUM
HYOSTYLIC
HYOSTYLY
HYOTHERE
HYP
HYPALGIA
HYPALLAGE
HYPANTRUM
HYPASPIST
HYPATE
HYPATON
HYPAXIAL
HYPE
HYPER
HYPERABELIAN
HYPERACUSIA
HYPERALGESIA
HYPERALGESIC
HYPERALGESIS
HYPERAPHIA
HYPERAPHIC
HYPERBARIC
HYPERBARISM
HYPERBATIC
HYPERBATON
HYPERBOLA
HYPERBOLAS
HYPERBOLE
HYPERBOLIC
HYPERBOLISM
HYPERBOLIZE
HYPERBOLIZED
HYPERBOLIZING
HYPERBOREAL
HYPERBOREAN
HYPERBULIA
HYPERCONE
HYPERCORACOID
HYPERCORRECT
HYPERCRITIC
HYPERCRITICAL
HYPERCUBE
HYPERCYCLE
HYPERCYLINDER
HYPERDACTYL
HYPERDIAPASON
HYPERDIAPENTE
HYPERDITONE
HYPERDULIA
HYPERDULIC
HYPERELLIPTIC
HYPEREMESIS
HYPEREMIA
HYPEREMIC
HYPERESSENCE
HYPERESTHESIA
HYPERESTHETIC
HYPEREUTECTIC
HYPERFOCAL
HYPERGAMY
HYPERGEOMETRY
HYPERGOLIC
HYPERIN
HYPERKINESIA
HYPERKINESIS
HYPERKINETIC
HYPERMETER
HYPERMETRIC
HYPERMETRICAL
HYPERMORPH
HYPERNIC
HYPERON
HYPEROON
HYPEROPIC
HYPEROSMIA
HYPEROSMIC
HYPEROSTOSIS
HYPEROSTOTIC
HYPEROTRETAN
HYPEROXIDE
HYPERPENCIL
HYPERPER
HYPERPHORIA
HYPERPHORIC
HYPERPIESIA
HYPERPIESIS
HYPERPIETIC
HYPERPLANE
HYPERPLASIA
HYPERPLASTIC
HYPERPLOID
HYPERPLOIDY
HYPERPNEA
HYPERPRISM
HYPERPYRAMID
HYPERPYRETIC
HYPERSOLID
HYPERSONIC
HYPERSONICS
HYPERSPACE
HYPERSPHERE
HYPERTELY
HYPERTHESIS
HYPERTHETIC
HYPERTHYROID
HYPERTONIA
HYPERTONIC
HYPERTONUS
HYPERTROPHY
HYPERTROPIA
HYPERTYPE
HYPERTYPIC
HYPERTYPICAL
HYPETHRAL
HYPHA
HYPHAE
HYPHAL
HYPHEMA
HYPHEMIA
HYPHEN
HYPHENATE
HYPHENATED
HYPHENED
HYPHO
HYPHODROME
HYPNALE
HYPNOBATE
HYPNOCYST
HYPNODY
HYPNOETIC
HYPNOID
HYPNOIDAL
HYPNOIDIZE
HYPNOLOGIC
HYPNOLOGY
HYPNOSIS
HYPNOSPORE
HYPNOSPORIC
HYPNOTIC
HYPNOTISM
HYPNOTIST
HYPNOTIZE
HYPNOTOID
HYPO
HYPOADENIA
HYPOADRENIA
HYPOBARIC
HYPOBARISM
HYPOBASAL
HYPOBLAST
HYPOBLASTIC
HYPOBOLE
HYPOBROMITES
HYPOBROMOUS
HYPOBULIA
HYPOBULIC
HYPOCARP
HYPOCAUST
HYPOCENTER
HYPOCENTRUM
HYPOCHIL
HYPOCHNOSE
HYPOCHONDRIA
HYPOCHONDRIAC
HYPOCHORDAL
HYPOCHROMIA
HYPOCHROSIS
HYPOCIST
HYPOCONE
HYPOCORISTIC
HYPOCOTYL
HYPOCRATER
HYPOCRISIS
HYPOCRISY
HYPOCRITAL
HYPOCRITE
HYPOCRITIC
HYPOCRITICAL
HYPOCRITICALLY
HYPOCRIZE
HYPOCYCLOID
HYPOCYTOSIS
HYPODERM
HYPODERMA
HYPODERMAL
HYPODERMIC
HYPODERMIS
HYPODITONE
HYPOEUTECTIC
HYPOGAMY
HYPOGASTRIC
HYPOGEAL
HYPOGEAN
HYPOGEE
HYPOGEIC
HYPOGENE
HYPOGENESIS
HYPOGENIC
HYPOGEOUS
HYPOGEUM
HYPOGLOSSAL
HYPOGLOSSUS
HYPOGLOTTIS
HYPOGYNIC
HYPOGYNIUM
HYPOHALOUS
HYPOHEMIA
HYPOHIDROSIS
HYPOHYAL
HYPOID
HYPOMANIA
HYPOMANIC
HYPOMERAL
HYPOMERE
HYPOMORPH
HYPONASTIC
HYPONASTY
HYPONITRITE
HYPONOIA
HYPONOME
HYPONYM
HYPOPHARE
HYPOPHARYNX
HYPOPHONIC
HYPOPHORA
HYPOPHORIA
HYPOPHRENIA
HYPOPHYGE
HYPOPHYLL
HYPOPHYSE
HYPOPLASIA
HYPOPLASTIC
HYPOPLASTRAL
HYPOPLASTRON
HYPOPLOID
HYPOPNEA
HYPOPODIUM
HYPOPRAXIA
HYPOPTERAL
HYPOPTERON
HYPOPTILUM
HYPOPUS
HYPOPYON
HYPORADIAL
HYPORADIUS
HYPORHINED
HYPORIT
HYPOSCLERAL
HYPOSCOPE
HYPOSKELETAL
HYPOSMIA
HYPOSPADIAC
HYPOSPADIAS
HYPOSPHENE
HYPOSTASIS
HYPOSTATIC
HYPOSTATICAL
HYPOSTATIZE
HYPOSTHENIA
HYPOSTIGMA
HYPOSTILBITE
HYPOSTOMA
HYPOSTOME
HYPOSTYLE
HYPOSTYPSIS
HYPOSTYPTIC
HYPOTARSAL
HYPOTARSUS
HYPOTAXIA
HYPOTAXIC
HYPOTAXIS
HYPOTENSION
HYPOTENSIVE
HYPOTENSOR
HYPOTENUSE
HYPOTHEC
HYPOTHECA
HYPOTHECARY
HYPOTHECATE
HYPOTHECIAL
HYPOTHENAL
HYPOTHENAR
HYPOTHENIC
HYPOTHERMAL
HYPOTHERMIA
HYPOTHERMIC
HYPOTHESIS
HYPOTHETICAL
HYPOTONIC

HYPOTOXICITY
HYPOTRACHELIUM
HYPOTROPHY
HYPOTYPE
HYPOTYPIC
HYPOVALVE
HYPOVANADATE
HYPOVANADIC
HYPOXANTHIC
HYPOXANTHINE
HYPOZEUGMA
HYPOZEUXIS
HYPOZOAN
HYPOZOIC
HYPPISH
HYPSIPYLE
HYPSOMETER
HYPSOMETRIC
HYPSOMETRY
HYPSOPHOBIA
HYPSOPHYLL
HYPURAL
HYRACEUM
HYRACID
HYRAX
HYRST
HYSON
HYSSOP
HYSTERIA
HYSTERIAC
HYSTERIC
HYSTERICAL
HYSTERICALLY
HYSTERICS
HYSTERIFORM
HYSTEROGEN
HYSTEROGENETIC
HYSTEROGENIC
HYSTEROID
HYSTEROLITH
HYSTEROLOGY
HYSTEROMANIA
HYSTEROMETER
HYSTEROMETRY
HYSTEROPATHY
HYSTEROSCOPE
HYSTEROTOME
HYTE

I

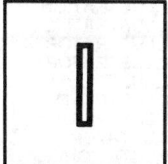

IAMATOLOGY
IAMB
IAMBELEGUS
IAMBIC
IAMBICAL
IAMBICALLY
IAMBIST
IAMBIZE
IAMBOGRAPHER
IAMBUS
IANTHINE
IANTHINITE
IAO
IATRALIPTIC
IATRALIPTICS
IATRIC
IATRICAL
IATROCHEMICAL
IATROCHEMISTRY
IATROGENIC
IATROLOGICAL
IATROLOGY
IATROPHYSICS
IATROTECHNICS
IBA
IBE
IBERITE
IBEX
IBEXES
IBICES
IBID
IBIDEM
IBIS
IBISBILL
IBISES
IBIT
IBOLIUM
IBOTA
ICACINACEOUS
ICACO
ICE
ICEBERG
ICEBLINK
ICEBOAT
ICEBONE
ICEBOUND
ICEBOX
ICEBREAKER
ICECAP
ICECRAFT
ICED
ICEFALL
ICEFISH
ICEFISHES
ICEHOUSE
ICELAND
ICELEAF
ICEMAN
ICEMEN
ICEQUAKE
ICER
ICEROOT
ICEWORK
ICH
ICHAM
ICHEBU
ICHIBU
ICHNEUMON
ICHNEUMONED
ICHNEUMOUS
ICHNEUTIC
ICHNITE
ICHNOGRAPHIC
ICHNOGRAPHY
ICHNOLITE
ICHNOLITIC
ICHNOLOGICAL
ICHNOLOGY
ICHNOMANCY
ICHO
ICHOGLAN
ICHOR
ICHOROUS
ICHORRHAEMIA
ICHORRHEA
ICHORRHEMIA
ICHORRHOEA
ICHTHULIN
ICHTHULINIC
ICHTHUS
ICHTHYAL
ICHTHYIC
ICHTHYISM
ICHTHYISMUS
ICHTHYIZATION
ICHTHYIZED
ICHTHYOCOL
ICHTHYOCOLLA
ICHTHYODIAN
ICHTHYODONT
ICHTHYOFAUNA
ICHTHYOID
ICHTHYOIDAL
ICHTHYOLATRY
ICHTHYOLITE
ICHTHYOLOGIC
ICHTHYOLOGY
ICHTHYOMANIA
ICHTHYOPHAGI
ICHTHYOPHAGY
ICHTHYOPSID
ICHTHYOSAUR
ICHTHYOSIS
ICHTHYOSISM
ICHTHYOTOMY
ICHTHYOTOXIN
ICHTHYS
ICHU
ICHULLE
ICICA
ICICLE
ICICLED
ICIER
ICIEST
ICILY
ICINESS
ICING
ICK
ICKER
ICKLE
ICKY
ICON
ICONES
ICONIC
ICONICAL
ICONISM
ICONOCLASM
ICONOCLAST
ICONOCLASTIC
ICONODULE
ICONODULIC
ICONODULIST
ICONODULY
ICONOGRAPH
ICONOGRAPHER
ICONOGRAPHIC
ICONOGRAPHIST
ICONOGRAPHY
ICONOLATER
ICONOLATROUS
ICONOLATRY
ICONOLOGICAL
ICONOLOGIST
ICONOLOGY
ICONOMACHAL
ICONOMACHIST
ICONOMACHY
ICONOMANIA
ICONOMATIC
ICONOMATICISM
ICONOMETER
ICONOMETRIC
ICONOMETRICAL
ICONOMETRY
ICONOPHILE
ICONOPHILISM
ICONOPHILIST
ICONOPHILY
ICONOPLAST
ICONOSCOPE
ICONOSTAS
ICONOSTASES
ICONOSTASION
ICONOSTASIS
ICONOTYPE
ICONS
ICOSAHEDRA
ICOSAHEDRAL
ICOSAHEDRON
ICOSASEMIC
ICOSIAN
ICOSTEID
ICOSTEINE
ICOTYPE
ICRE
ICTERIC
ICTERICAL
ICTERINE
ICTERITIOUS
ICTERITOUS
ICTERODE
ICTEROGENIC
ICTEROHEMATURIA
ICTEROID
ICTERUS
ICTIC
ICTUATE
ICTUS
ICTUSES
ICY
ID
IDAEIN
IDALIA
IDANT
IDDAT
IDE
IDEA
IDEAED
IDEAGENOUS
IDEAL
IDEALISM
IDEALIST
IDEALISTIC
IDEALISTICAL
IDEALISTICALLY
IDEALITIES
IDEALITY
IDEALIZATION
IDEALIZE
IDEALIZED
IDEALIZER
IDEALIZING
IDEALLY
IDEAS
IDEATE
IDEATED
IDEATING
IDEATION
IDEATIONAL
IDEATIONALLY
IDEATIVE
IDEATUM
IDEE
IDEIN
IDEIST
IDEM
IDEMPOTENT
IDENT
IDENTIC
IDENTICAL
IDENTICALISM
IDENTICALLY
IDENTIFICATION
IDENTIFIED
IDENTIFIER
IDENTIFY
IDENTIFYING
IDENTISM
IDENTITIES
IDENTITY
IDEOGENICAL
IDEOGENY
IDEOGLYPH
IDEOGRAM
IDEOGRAMMIC
IDEOGRAPH
IDEOGRAPHIC
IDEOGRAPHY
IDEOLOGIC
IDEOLOGICAL
IDEOLOGICALLY
IDEOLOGIES
IDEOLOGIST
IDEOLOGY
IDEOMANIA
IDEOMOTION
IDEOMOTOR
IDEOPHONE
IDEOPHONOUS
IDEOPLASTIA
IDEOPLASTIC
IDEOPLASTICS
IDEOPLASTY
IDEOPRAXIST
IDEOTYPE
IDES
IDESIA
IDGAH
IDIASM
IDIGBO
IDIOBLAST
IDIOBLASTIC
IDIOCRASIES
IDIOCRASIS
IDIOCRASY
IDIOCRATIC
IDIOCRATICAL
IDIOCY
IDIOELECTRIC
IDIOGENOUS
IDIOGLOSSIA
IDIOGLOTTIC
IDIOGRAM
IDIOGRAPH
IDIOGRAPHIC
IDIOGRAPHICAL
IDIOLATRY
IDIOLECT
IDIOLOGISM
IDIOM
IDIOMATIC
IDIOMATICAL
IDIOMATICALLY
IDIOMATICALNESS
IDIOMELON
IDIOMETER
IDIOMOGRAPHY
IDIOMOLOGY
IDIOMORPHIC
IDIOMORPHOUS
IDIOMUSCULAR
IDIOPATHETIC
IDIOPATHIC
IDIOPATHICAL
IDIOPATHICALLY
IDIOPATHIES
IDIOPATHY
IDIOPHANISM
IDIOPHANOUS
IDIOPHONE
IDIOPHONIC
IDIOPLASM
IDIOPLASMATIC
IDIOPLASMIC
IDIORETINAL
IDIOSOME
IDIOSPASM
IDIOSPASTIC
IDIOSTATIC
IDIOSYNCRASIES
IDIOSYNCRASY
IDIOSYNCRATIC
IDIOSYNCRATICA
IDIOT
IDIOTCIES
IDIOTCY
IDIOTHERMIC
IDIOTHERMOUS
IDIOTHERMY
IDIOTIC
IDIOTICAL
IDIOTICALLY
IDIOTICON
IDIOTISM
IDIOTROPIAN
IDIOTRY
IDIOTYPE
IDIOTYPIC
IDIOZOME
IDITE
IDITOL
IDLE
IDLEBY
IDLED
IDLEFUL
IDLEHEADED
IDLEHOOD
IDLEMAN
IDLEMEN
IDLENESS
IDLER
IDLESET
IDLESHIP
IDLESSE
IDLEST
IDLING
IDLY
IDOCRASE
IDOL
IDOLA
IDOLASTER
IDOLASTRE
IDOLATER
IDOLATRIC
IDOLATRICAL

IDOLATRIES
IDOLATRIZE
IDOLATRIZED
IDOLATRIZER
IDOLATRIZING
IDOLATROUS
IDOLATROUSLY
IDOLATRY
IDOLET
IDOLIFY
IDOLISH
IDOLISM
IDOLIST
IDOLISTIC
IDOLIZATION
IDOLIZE
IDOLIZED
IDOLIZER
IDOLIZING
IDOLOCLAST
IDOLOCLASTIC
IDOLODULIA
IDOLOMANCY
IDOLOMANIA
IDOLON
IDOLOTHYTE
IDOLOTHYTIC
IDOLOUS
IDOLUM
IDONEAL
IDONEITY
IDONEOUS
IDONEOUSNESS
IDORGAN
IDOSACCHARIC
IDOSE
IDRIALIN
IDRIALINE
IDRIALITE
IDROSIS
IDRYL
IDYL
IDYLER
IDYLIAN
IDYLIST
IDYLL
IDYLLER
IDYLLIA
IDYLLIAN
IDYLLIC
IDYLLICAL
IDYLLICALLY
IDYLLICISM
IDYLLION
IDYLLIST
IDYLLIUM
IE
IEROE
IF
IFE
IFFEN
IFFY
IFIL
IFRIT
IGAD
IGARAPE
IGELSTROMITE
IGITUR
IGLESIA
IGLOO
IGLU
IGNAME
IGNARO
IGNATIA
IGNAVIA
IGNAVY
IGNEOUS
IGNESCENT
IGNICOLIST
IGNIFEROUS
IGNIFIED
IGNIFORM
IGNIFUGE
IGNIFY
IGNIFYING
IGNIGENOUS
IGNIPOTENT
IGNIPUNCTURE
IGNITE
IGNITED
IGNITER
IGNITING
IGNITION
IGNITIVE
IGNITOR
IGNITRON
IGNIVOMOUS
IGNOBILITY
IGNOBLE
IGNOBLESSE
IGNOBLY
IGNOMINIES
IGNOMINIOUS
IGNOMINIOUSLY
IGNOMINY
IGNOMIOUS
IGNORAMUS
IGNORAMUSES
IGNORANCE
IGNORANT
IGNORANTISM
IGNORANTIST
IGNORANTLY
IGNORATION
IGNORE
IGNORED
IGNORER
IGNORING
IGNOTE
IGUANA
IGUANODONT
IGUANOID
IHI
IHLEITE
IHRAM
IIWI
IJMA
IJMAA
IJOLITE
IJUSSITE
IKARY
IKAT
IKBAL
IKEY
IKEYNESS
IKMO
IKON
IKONA
IL
ILD
ILE
ILEAC
ILEECTOMY
ILEITIS
ILEOCAECAL
ILEOCECAL
ILEOCOLIC
ILEOCOLITIS
ILEOSTOMIES
ILEOSTOMY
ILEOTOMY
ILESITE
ILEUM
ILEUS
ILEX
ILEXES
ILIAC
ILIACUS
ILIAHI
ILIAL
ILIAU
ILICACEOUS
ILICIC
ILICIN
ILIMA
ILIOCAUDALIS
ILION
ILIOPSOAS
ILIOPSOATIC
ILK
ILKA
ILKANE
ILL
ILLABORATE
ILLAPSABLE
ILLAPSE
ILLAPSED
ILLAPSING
ILLAPSIVE
ILLAQUEATE
ILLATION
ILLATIVE
ILLATIVELY
ILLAUDABLE
ILLAUDABLY
ILLAUDATION
ILLAUDATORY
ILLBRED
ILLE
ILLECEBROUS
ILLECK
ILLEGAL
ILLEGALITIES
ILLEGALITY
ILLEGALIZE
ILLEGALIZED
ILLEGALIZING
ILLEGALLY
ILLEGALNESS
ILLEGIBILITY
ILLEGIBLE
ILLEGIBLY
ILLEGITIMACIES
ILLEGITIMACY
ILLEGITIMATE
ILLEGITIMATED
ILLEGITIMATING
ILLEISM
ILLEIST
ILLER
ILLFARE
ILLGUIDE
ILLGUIDED
ILLGUIDING
ILLIBERAL
ILLIBERALITY
ILLIBERALLY
ILLICIT
ILLICITLY
ILLICITNESS
ILLIMITABLE
ILLIMITABLY
ILLIMITATE
ILLIMITATION
ILLIMITED
ILLINITION
ILLINIUM
ILLIPENE
ILLIQUATION
ILLIQUID
ILLIQUIDLY
ILLISH
ILLISION
ILLITE
ILLITERACIES
ILLITERACY
ILLITERAL
ILLITERATE
ILLITERATELY
ILLITERATURE
ILLIUM
ILLNESS
ILLOCAL
ILLOCALITY
ILLOCALLY
ILLOGIC
ILLOGICAL
ILLOGICALITY
ILLOGICIAN
ILLOGICITY
ILLORICATE
ILLOYAL
ILLTH
ILLUCIDATE
ILLUCIDATION
ILLUCIDATIVE
ILLUDE
ILLUDED
ILLUDER
ILLUDING
ILLUK
ILLUME
ILLUMED
ILLUMER
ILLUMINANCE
ILLUMINANT
ILLUMINATE
ILLUMINATED
ILLUMINATI
ILLUMINATING
ILLUMINATION
ILLUMINATISM
ILLUMINATIVE
ILLUMINATO
ILLUMINATOR
ILLUMINATORY
ILLUMINATUS
ILLUMINE
ILLUMINED
ILLUMINEE
ILLUMINER
ILLUMING
ILLUMINING
ILLUMINIST
ILLUMINOMETER
ILLUMINOUS
ILLUPI
ILLURE
ILLUREMENT
ILLUSIBLE
ILLUSION
ILLUSIONABLE
ILLUSIONAL
ILLUSIONARY
ILLUSIONED
ILLUSIONISM
ILLUSIONIST
ILLUSIVE
ILLUSIVELY
ILLUSIVENESS
ILLUSOR
ILLUSORILY
ILLUSORINESS
ILLUSORY
ILLUSTRABLE
ILLUSTRATE
ILLUSTRATED
ILLUSTRATING
ILLUSTRATION
ILLUSTRATIVE
ILLUSTRATOR
ILLUSTRATORY
ILLUSTRE
ILLUSTRICITY
ILLUSTRIOUS
ILLUTATE
ILLUTATION
ILLUVIAL
ILLUVIATION
ILLY
ILMENITE
ILMENORUTILE
ILOT
ILVAITE
ILYSIOID
IMAGE
IMAGED
IMAGER
IMAGERIAL
IMAGERIALLY
IMAGERY
IMAGES
IMAGINABLE
IMAGINAL
IMAGINANT
IMAGINARILY
IMAGINARY
IMAGINATE
IMAGINATED
IMAGINATING
IMAGINATION
IMAGINATIONAL
IMAGINATIVE
IMAGINATOR
IMAGINE
IMAGINED
IMAGINER
IMAGINES
IMAGING
IMAGINING
IMAGINIST
IMAGINOUS
IMAGISM
IMAGIST
IMAGISTIC
IMAGO
IMAGOES
IMAMAH
IMAMATE
IMAMBARA
IMAMBARAH
IMAMBARRA
IMAMIC
IMANLAUT
IMARET
IMAUM
IMAUMBARAH
IMBALANCE
IMBALM
IMBAN
IMBAND
IMBANNERED
IMBARGE
IMBARK
IMBARKATION
IMBARN
IMBASED
IMBASTARDIZE
IMBAT
IMBAUBA
IMBE
IMBECILE
IMBECILELY
IMBECILITATE
IMBECILITATED

IMBECILITIES
IMBECILITY
IMBED
IMBEDDED
IMBEDDING
IMBELLIC
IMBELLIOUS
IMBER
IMBERBE
IMBIBE
IMBIBED
IMBIBER
IMBIBING
IMBIBITION
IMBIBITIONAL
IMBIBITORY
IMBIRUSSU
IMBITTER
IMBLAZE
IMBODY
IMBOLDEN
IMBOLISH
IMBONDO
IMBONITY
IMBORDURE
IMBORSATION
IMBOSCATA
IMBOSK
IMBOSOM
IMBOST
IMBOWER
IMBREATHE
IMBREVIATE
IMBREVIATED
IMBREVIATING
IMBREX
IMBRICATE
IMBRICATED
IMBRICATELY
IMBRICATING
IMBRICATION
IMBRICATIVE
IMBRICES
IMBRIER
IMBROGLIO
IMBROGLIOS
IMBROIN
IMBROWN
IMBRUE
IMBRUED
IMBRUING
IMBRUTE
IMBRUTED
IMBRUTING
IMBUE
IMBUED
IMBUIA
IMBUING
IMBURSE
IMBURSED
IMBURSING
IMELLE
IMI
IMID
IMIDAZOL
IMIDAZOLE
IMIDAZOLYL
IMIDE
IMIDIC
IMIDO
IMIDOGEN
IMIN
IMINE
IMINO
IMITABILITY
IMITABLE
IMITANCY
IMITANT
IMITATE
IMITATED
IMITATEE
IMITATING
IMITATION
IMITATIONAL
IMITATIONIST
IMITATIVE
IMITATIVELY
IMITATOR
IMMACULACY
IMMACULANCE
IMMACULATE
IMMACULATELY
IMMALLEABLE
IMMANACLE
IMMANACLED
IMMANACLING
IMMANATION
IMMANE
IMMANELY
IMMANENCE
IMMANENCY
IMMANENESS
IMMANENT
IMMANENTAL
IMMANENTISM
IMMANENTIST
IMMANENTLY
IMMANIFEST
IMMANITY
IMMANTLE
IMMANTLED
IMMANTLING
IMMARBLE
IMMARGINATE
IMMASK
IMMATCHABLE
IMMATCHLESS
IMMATERIAL
IMMATERIALISM
IMMATERIALIST
IMMATERIALITIES
IMMATERIALITY
IMMATERIALIZE
IMMATERIALS
IMMATERIATE
IMMATRICULATE
IMMATURE
IMMATURED
IMMATURELY
IMMATURENESS
IMMATURITIES
IMMATURITY
IMMEABILITY
IMMEASURABLE
IMMEASURABLY
IMMEASURED
IMMECHANICAL
IMMEDIACY
IMMEDIAL
IMMEDIATE
IMMEDIATELY
IMMEDIATENESS
IMMEDIATISM
IMMEDIATIST
IMMEDICABLE
IMMEDICABLY
IMMELODIOUS
IMMEMBER
IMMEMORABLE
IMMEMORIAL
IMMENSE
IMMENSELY
IMMENSENESS
IMMENSIBLE
IMMENSITIES
IMMENSITY
IMMENSIVE
IMMENSURABLE
IMMENSURATE
IMMERD
IMMERGE
IMMERGED
IMMERGENCE
IMMERGENT
IMMERGING
IMMERIT
IMMERITED
IMMERITORIOUS
IMMERSE
IMMERSED
IMMERSIBLE
IMMERSING
IMMERSION
IMMERSIONISM
IMMERSIONIST
IMMERSIVE
IMMESH
IMMETHODIC
IMMETHODIZE
IMMEW
IMMI
IMMIE
IMMIGRANT
IMMIGRANTS
IMMIGRATE
IMMIGRATED
IMMIGRATING
IMMIGRATION
IMMIGRATOR
IMMIGRATORY
IMMIND
IMMINENCE
IMMINENCY
IMMINENT
IMMINENTLY
IMMINGLE
IMMINUTION
IMMIS
IMMISCIBLE
IMMISCIBLY
IMMISS
IMMISSION
IMMIT
IMMITIGABLE
IMMITIGABLY
IMMITTED
IMMITTING
IMMIX
IMMIXT
IMMIXTURE
IMMOBILE
IMMOBILITY
IMMOBILIZATION
IMMOBILIZE
IMMOBILIZED
IMMOBILIZING
IMMODERACY
IMMODERATE
IMMODERATENESS
IMMODERATION
IMMODEST
IMMODESTY
IMMOLATE
IMMOLATED
IMMOLATING
IMMOLATION
IMMOLATOR
IMMOMENT
IMMONASTERED
IMMORAL
IMMORALISM
IMMORALIST
IMMORALITIES
IMMORALITY
IMMORIGEROUS
IMMORTABLE
IMMORTAL
IMMORTALISM
IMMORTALIST
IMMORTALITY
IMMORTALIZE
IMMORTALIZED
IMMORTALIZER
IMMORTALIZING
IMMORTALLY
IMMORTELLE
IMMORTIFIED
IMMOTE
IMMOTILE
IMMOTIONED
IMMOTIVE
IMMOUND
IMMOVABILITY
IMMOVABLE
IMMOVABLY
IMMOVED
IMMUND
IMMUNDITY
IMMUNE
IMMUNIST
IMMUNITIES
IMMUNITY
IMMUNIZATION
IMMUNIZE
IMMUNIZED
IMMUNOGENIC
IMMUNOLOGY
IMMUNOREACTION
IMMUNOTOXIN
IMMURATION
IMMURE
IMMURED
IMMURING
IMMUSICAL
IMMUSICALLY
IMMUTABILITY
IMMUTABLE
IMMUTABLY
IMMUTATION
IMMUTE
IMMUTILATE
IMMUTUAL
IMO
IMONIUM
IMP
IMPACABLE
IMPACK
IMPACT
IMPACTED
IMPACTER
IMPACTING
IMPACTION
IMPACTIONIZE
IMPACTMENT
IMPACTOR
IMPACTUAL
IMPAGES
IMPAINT
IMPAIR
IMPAIRED
IMPAIRER
IMPAIRING
IMPAIRMENT
IMPALA
IMPALACE
IMPALE
IMPALED
IMPALEMENT
IMPALER
IMPALING
IMPALM
IMPALPABLE
IMPALPABLY
IMPALSY
IMPALUDISM
IMPANATE
IMPANATED
IMPANATION
IMPANATOR
IMPANE
IMPANEL
IMPANELED
IMPANELING
IMPANELLED
IMPANELLING
IMPAPYRATE
IMPAPYRATED
IMPAR
IMPARADISE
IMPARALLELED
IMPARASITIC
IMPARDONABLE
IMPARITY
IMPARK
IMPARKATION
IMPARKED
IMPARKING
IMPARL
IMPARLANCE
IMPARLED
IMPARLING
IMPARSONEE
IMPART
IMPARTABLE
IMPARTANCE
IMPARTATION
IMPARTED
IMPARTER
IMPARTIAL
IMPARTIALITY
IMPARTIALLY
IMPARTIBLE
IMPARTIBLY
IMPARTICIPABLE
IMPARTING
IMPARTITE
IMPARTIVE
IMPARTIVITY
IMPARTMENT
IMPASSABLE
IMPASSABLY
IMPASSE
IMPASSES
IMPASSIBLE
IMPASSIBLY
IMPASSION
IMPASSIONATE
IMPASSIONED
IMPASSIONING
IMPASSIVE
IMPASSIVELY
IMPASSIVENESS
IMPASTATION
IMPASTE
IMPASTED
IMPASTING
IMPASTO
IMPASTURE
IMPATERNATE
IMPATIBLE
IMPATIENCE
IMPATIENCY
IMPATIENS
IMPATIENT
IMPATIENTLY

IMPATRONIZE
IMPAVE
IMPAVID
IMPAVIDITY
IMPAVIDLY
IMPAWN
IMPAWNED
IMPAWNING
IMPAYABLE
IMPEACH
IMPEACHABLE
IMPEACHED
IMPEACHER
IMPEACHING
IMPEACHMENT
IMPEARL
IMPEARLED
IMPEARLING
IMPECCABLE
IMPECCABLY
IMPECCANCE
IMPECCANCY
IMPECCANT
IMPECTINATE
IMPECUNIARY
IMPECUNIOUS
IMPEDANCE
IMPEDE
IMPEDED
IMPEDER
IMPEDIBILITY
IMPEDIBLE
IMPEDIENT
IMPEDIMENT
IMPEDIMENTA
IMPEDIMENTAL
IMPEDIMENTARY
IMPEDING
IMPEDINGLY
IMPEDITE
IMPEDITION
IMPEDITIVE
IMPEDOMETER
IMPEDOR
IMPEEVISH
IMPEL
IMPELLED
IMPELLENT
IMPELLER
IMPELLING
IMPEN
IMPEND
IMPENDED
IMPENDENCE
IMPENDENCY
IMPENDENT
IMPENDING
IMPENETRABILITY
IMPENETRABLE
IMPENETRABLY
IMPENETRATE
IMPENITENCE
IMPENITENCY
IMPENITENT
IMPENITENTLY
IMPENITIBLE
IMPENNATE
IMPENT
IMPERANCE
IMPERANT
IMPERATE
IMPERATION
IMPERATIVE
IMPERATIVELY
IMPERATOR
IMPERATORIAL
IMPERATORY
IMPERATRICE
IMPERATRIX
IMPERCEIVED
IMPERCEPTIBLE
IMPERCEPTION
IMPERCEPTIVE
IMPERCIPIENT
IMPERENT
IMPERFECT
IMPERFECTED
IMPERFECTIBLE
IMPERFECTION
IMPERFECTIOUS
IMPERFECTIVE
IMPERFECTLY
IMPERFORABLE
IMPERFORATE
IMPERFORATED
IMPERFORATION
IMPERIA
IMPERIAL
IMPERIALIN
IMPERIALINE
IMPERIALISM
IMPERIALIST
IMPERIALISTIC
IMPERIALITIES
IMPERIALITY
IMPERIALIZE
IMPERIALIZED
IMPERIALIZING
IMPERIALTY
IMPERIL
IMPERILED
IMPERILING
IMPERILLED
IMPERILLING
IMPERIOUS
IMPERIOUSLY
IMPERISH
IMPERISHABLE
IMPERITE
IMPERIUM
IMPERMANENCE
IMPERMANENT
IMPERMEABLE
IMPERMEABLY
IMPERMEATOR
IMPERMISSIBLE
IMPERMIXT
IMPERMUTABLE
IMPERSONABLE
IMPERSONAL
IMPERSONALITIES
IMPERSONALITY
IMPERSONALIZE
IMPERSONALIZED
IMPERSONALIZING
IMPERSONATE
IMPERSONATED
IMPERSONATING
IMPERSONATION
IMPERSONATIVE
IMPERSONATOR
IMPERSUADABLE
IMPERSUASIBLE
IMPERTINACY
IMPERTINENCE
IMPERTINENCES
IMPERTINENCIES
IMPERTINENCY
IMPERTINENT
IMPERTRANSIBLE
IMPERTURBABILITY
IMPERTURBABLE
IMPERTURBABLY
IMPERTURBED
IMPERVERSE
IMPERVERTIBLE
IMPERVIABLE
IMPERVIAL
IMPERVIOUS
IMPERVIOUSLY
IMPEST
IMPESTATION
IMPESTER
IMPETICOS
IMPETIGINOUS
IMPETIGO
IMPETITION
IMPETRATE
IMPETRATED
IMPETRATING
IMPETRATION
IMPETRATIVE
IMPETRATOR
IMPETRATORY
IMPETRE
IMPETULANT
IMPETUOSITY
IMPETUOSO
IMPETUOUS
IMPETUOUSLY
IMPETUS
IMPETUSES
IMPHEE
IMPI
IMPICTURE
IMPIERCEABLE
IMPIETIES
IMPIETY
IMPIGNORATE
IMPIGNORATED
IMPIGNORATING
IMPING
IMPINGE
IMPINGED
IMPINGEMENT
IMPINGENCE
IMPINGENT
IMPINGER
IMPINGING
IMPINGUATE
IMPIOUS
IMPIOUSLY
IMPIOUSNESS
IMPISH
IMPISHLY
IMPISHNESS
IMPITEOUS
IMPITIABLY
IMPLACABLE
IMPLACABLY
IMPLACEMENT
IMPLACENTAL
IMPLACENTATE
IMPLANT
IMPLANTATION
IMPLANTED
IMPLANTER
IMPLANTING
IMPLASTIC
IMPLATE
IMPLAUSIBILITY
IMPLAUSIBLE
IMPLEACH
IMPLEAD
IMPLEADABLE
IMPLEADER
IMPLEDGE
IMPLEMENT
IMPLEMENTAL
IMPLETE
IMPLETION
IMPLETIVE
IMPLEX
IMPLIABLE
IMPLIAL
IMPLICANT
IMPLICATE
IMPLICATED
IMPLICATELY
IMPLICATING
IMPLICATION
IMPLICATIONAL
IMPLICATIVE
IMPLICATORY
IMPLICIT
IMPLICITLY
IMPLICITNESS
IMPLIED
IMPLIEDLY
IMPLODE
IMPLODED
IMPLODENT
IMPLODING
IMPLORATION
IMPLORATOR
IMPLORATORY
IMPLORE
IMPLORED
IMPLORER
IMPLORING
IMPLORINGLY
IMPLOSION
IMPLOSIVE
IMPLOSIVELY
IMPLUME
IMPLUNGE
IMPLUVIA
IMPLUVIUM
IMPLY
IMPLYING
IMPOCKET
IMPOFO
IMPOLICY
IMPOLISHED
IMPOLITE
IMPOLITELY
IMPOLITENESS
IMPOLITIC
IMPOLITICAL
IMPOLITICLY
IMPOLLUTE
IMPONDERABILIA
IMPONDERABLE
IMPONDERABLY
IMPONDEROUS
IMPONE
IMPONENT
IMPOOR
IMPOROSITY
IMPOROUS
IMPORT
IMPORTABLE
IMPORTABLY
IMPORTANCE
IMPORTANT
IMPORTATION
IMPORTED
IMPORTER
IMPORTING
IMPORTLESS
IMPORTMENT
IMPORTRAITURE
IMPORTRAY
IMPORTUNACY
IMPORTUNANCE
IMPORTUNATE
IMPORTUNATELY
IMPORTUNATOR
IMPORTUNE
IMPORTUNED
IMPORTUNELY
IMPORTUNEMENT
IMPORTUNER
IMPORTUNING
IMPORTUNITIES
IMPORTUNITY
IMPOSAL
IMPOSE
IMPOSED
IMPOSEMENT
IMPOSER
IMPOSING
IMPOSINGLY
IMPOSINGNESS
IMPOSITION
IMPOSITIONAL
IMPOSSIBILIST
IMPOSSIBILITIES
IMPOSSIBILITY
IMPOSSIBLE
IMPOSSIBLY
IMPOST
IMPOSTED
IMPOSTER
IMPOSTEROUS
IMPOSTHUMATE
IMPOSTHUME
IMPOSTING
IMPOSTOR
IMPOSTRIX
IMPOSTROUS
IMPOSTUMATE
IMPOSTUME
IMPOSTURE
IMPOSTUROUS
IMPOSURE
IMPOT
IMPOTENCE
IMPOTENCY
IMPOTENT
IMPOTENTLY
IMPOTENTNESS
IMPOUND
IMPOUNDAGE
IMPOUNDED
IMPOUNDER
IMPOUNDING
IMPOUNDMENT
IMPOVERISH
IMPOVERISHED
IMPOVERISHER
IMPOVERISHING
IMPOWER
IMPRACTICABLE
IMPRACTICAL
IMPRECANT
IMPRECATE
IMPRECATED
IMPRECATING
IMPRECATION
IMPRECATOR
IMPRECATORY
IMPRECISE
IMPRECISELY
IMPRECISION
IMPREDICABLE
IMPREGN
IMPREGNABILITY
IMPREGNABLE
IMPREGNABLY
IMPREGNANT
IMPREGNATE
IMPREGNATED
IMPREGNATING
IMPREGNATION

IMPREGNATIVE
IMPREGNATOR
IMPREGNATORY
IMPREJUDICE
IMPREMEDITATE
IMPREPARATION
IMPRESA
IMPRESARI
IMPRESARIO
IMPRESARIOS
IMPRESCIENCE
IMPRESE
IMPRESS
IMPRESSED
IMPRESSEDLY
IMPRESSER
IMPRESSIBLE
IMPRESSIBLY
IMPRESSING
IMPRESSION
IMPRESSIONABLE
IMPRESSIONARY
IMPRESSIONISM
IMPRESSIONIST
IMPRESSIONISTIC
IMPRESSIVE
IMPRESSIVELY
IMPRESSMENT
IMPRESSOR
IMPRESSURE
IMPREST
IMPRESTED
IMPRESTING
IMPREVISION
IMPREVU
IMPRIMATUR
IMPRIME
IMPRIMENT
IMPRIMERIE
IMPRIMERY
IMPRIMIS
IMPRIMITIVE
IMPRINT
IMPRINTED
IMPRINTER
IMPRINTING
IMPRISON
IMPRISONED
IMPRISONER
IMPRISONING
IMPRISONMENT
IMPROBABILITIES
IMPROBABILITY
IMPROBABILIZE
IMPROBABLE
IMPROBABLY
IMPROBATION
IMPROBATIVE
IMPROBATORY
IMPROBITY
IMPROCREANT
IMPRODUCIBLE
IMPROFICIENCY
IMPROMPT
IMPROMPTITUDE
IMPROMPTU
IMPROOF
IMPROPER
IMPROPERATION
IMPROPERLY
IMPROPRIATE
IMPROPRIATED
IMPROPRIATING
IMPROPRIATION
IMPROPRIATOR
IMPROPRIATRICE
IMPROPRIATRIX
IMPROPRIETIES
IMPROPRIETY
IMPROVABLE
IMPROVABLY
IMPROVE
IMPROVED
IMPROVEMENT
IMPROVER
IMPROVIDENCE
IMPROVIDENT
IMPROVING
IMPROVINGLY
IMPROVISATE
IMPROVISATION
IMPROVISATOR
IMPROVISATORY
IMPROVISE
IMPROVISED
IMPROVISER
IMPROVISING
IMPROVISO
IMPRUDENCE
IMPRUDENT
IMPRUDENTIAL
IMPRUDENTLY
IMPUBERAL
IMPUBERATE
IMPUBERTY
IMPUBIC
IMPUDENCE
IMPUDENCIES
IMPUDENCY
IMPUDENT
IMPUDENTLY
IMPUDENTNESS
IMPUDICITY
IMPUGN
IMPUGNABLE
IMPUGNATION
IMPUGNED
IMPUGNER
IMPUGNING
IMPUISSANCE
IMPUISSANT
IMPULSE
IMPULSES
IMPULSION
IMPULSIVE
IMPULSIVELY
IMPULSIVITY
IMPULSOR
IMPULSORY
IMPUNIBLE
IMPUNITY
IMPURE
IMPURELY
IMPURENESS
IMPURIFY
IMPURITAN
IMPURITIES
IMPURITY
IMPUT
IMPUTABILITY
IMPUTABLE
IMPUTABLY
IMPUTATION
IMPUTATIVE
IMPUTATIVELY
IMPUTE
IMPUTED
IMPUTER
IMPUTING
IMPUTRESCENCE
IMPY
IMSHI
IMSONIC
IMU
IN
INA
INABILITY
INABORDABLE
INACCEPTABLE
INACCESSIBILITY
INACCESSIBLE
INACCESSIBLY
INACCURACIES
INACCURACY
INACCURATE
INACCURATELY
INACHID
INACHOID
INACTION
INACTIONIST
INACTIVATE
INACTIVATION
INACTIVE
INACTIVELY
INACTIVENESS
INACTIVITY
INACTUATE
INACTUATION
INADAPTABLE
INADAPTATION
INADEQUACY
INADEQUATE
INADEQUATELY
INADEQUATION
INADMISSIBLE
INADVERTENCE
INADVERTENCES
INADVERTENCY
INADVERTENT
INADVERTENTLY
INADVISABLE
INADVISEDLY
INAESTHETIC
INAFFABILITY
INAFFABLE
INAFFABLY
INAGGLUTINABLE
INAJA
INALACRITY
INALIENABLE
INALIENABLY
INALTERABLE
INALTERABLY
INAM
INAMIA
INAMISSIBLE
INAMORATA
INAMORATE
INAMORATION
INAMORATO
INAMORATOS
INAMOVABLE
INANE
INANELY
INANGA
INANIMATE
INANIMATED
INANIMATELY
INANIMATION
INANITIES
INANITION
INANITY
INANTHERATE
INAPPEASABLE
INAPPETENCE
INAPPETENCY
INAPPETENT
INAPPLICABLE
INAPPLICABLY
INAPPLICATION
INAPPOSITE
INAPPOSITELY
INAPPRECIABLE
INAPPROPRIATE
INAPT
INAPTITUDE
INAPTLY
INAPTNESS
INARCH
INARCHING
INARCULUM
INARM
INARTICULACY
INARTICULATE
INARTICULATED
INARTICULATELY
INARTICULATION
INARTIFICIAL
INARTISTIC
INASMUCH
INASSIMILATION
INATTENTION
INATTENTIVE
INAUDIBILITY
INAUDIBLE
INAUDIBLY
INAUGUR
INAUGURAL
INAUGURATE
INAUGURATED
INAUGURATING
INAUGURATION
INAUGURATIVE
INAUGURATOR
INAUGURATORY
INAUGURER
INAURATE
INAURATION
INAUSPICIOUS
INAUTHENTIC
INAXON
INBASSAT
INBE
INBEAMING
INBEARING
INBEING
INBENDING
INBENT
INBIRTH
INBLOW
INBLOWING
INBLOWN
INBOARD
INBODY
INBOND
INBORN
INBOUND
INBOW
INBREAD
INBREAK
INBREAKING
INBREATHE
INBREATHED
INBREATHER
INBREATHING
INBRED
INBREED
INBREEDING
INBRING
INBRINGER
INBRINGING
INBROUGHT
INBUILT
INBURNING
INBURNT
INBURST
INBUSH
INBY
INBYE
INCAGE
INCALCULABLE
INCALCULABLY
INCALESCENT
INCALICULATE
INCALVER
INCALVING
INCAMERATION
INCAMP
INCANDENT
INCANDESCE
INCANDESCED
INCANDESCENCE
INCANDESCENT
INCANDESCING
INCANOUS
INCANT
INCANTATION
INCANTATOR
INCANTATORY
INCANTON
INCAPABILITY
INCAPABLE
INCAPABLY
INCAPACIOUS
INCAPACITATE
INCAPACITATED
INCAPACITATING
INCAPACITATION
INCAPACITIES
INCAPACITY
INCAPSULATE
INCAPSULATED
INCAPSULATING
INCAPSULATION
INCAPTIVATE
INCARCERATE
INCARCERATED
INCARCERATING
INCARCERATOR
INCARDINATE
INCARMINED
INCARN
INCARNADINE
INCARNADINED
INCARNADINING
INCARNANT
INCARNATE
INCARNATED
INCARNATING
INCARNATION
INCARNATIONAL
INCARNATIONIST
INCARNATIVE
INCASE
INCASED
INCASEMENT
INCASING
INCASK
INCAST
INCASTELLATE
INCATENATE
INCATENATION
INCAUTION
INCAUTIOUS
INCAUTIOUSLY
INCAVATE
INCAVATED
INCAVATION
INCAVERN
INCAVO
INCEDE
INCEDINGLY
INCELEBRITY
INCEND
INCENDIARIES

INCENDIARISM
INCENDIARY
INCENDIUM
INCENDIVITY
INCENSATION
INCENSE
INCENSED
INCENSER
INCENSING
INCENSION
INCENSOR
INCENSORIES
INCENSORY
INCENTER
INCENTIVE
INCENTIVELY
INCENTOR
INCENTRE
INCEPT
INCEPTED
INCEPTING
INCEPTION
INCEPTIVE
INCEPTIVELY
INCEPTOR
INCERATE
INCERATION
INCERTITUDE
INCESSABLE
INCESSABLY
INCESSANCY
INCESSANT
INCESSANTLY
INCESSION
INCEST
INCESTUOUS
INCESTUOUSLY
INCH
INCHAIN
INCHED
INCHER
INCHES
INCHLING
INCHMEAL
INCHOACY
INCHOANT
INCHOATE
INCHOATED
INCHOATELY
INCHOATENESS
INCHOATING
INCHOATION
INCHOATIVE
INCHPIN
INCHWORM
INCIDE
INCIDENCE
INCIDENT
INCIDENTAL
INCIDENTALLY
INCIENSO
INCINERABLE
INCINERATE
INCINERATED
INCINERATING
INCINERATION
INCINERATOR
INCIPIENCE
INCIPIENCY
INCIPIENT
INCIPIENTLY
INCIPIT
INCIRCLET
INCISAL
INCISE
INCISED
INCISELY
INCISIFORM
INCISING
INCISION
INCISIVE
INCISIVELY
INCISIVENESS
INCISOR
INCISORIAL
INCISORY
INCISURA
INCISURE
INCITABILITY
INCITABLE
INCITAMENTUM
INCITANT
INCITATE
INCITATION
INCITE
INCITED
INCITEMENT
INCITER
INCITING
INCITIVE
INCIVIL
INCIVILITIES
INCIVILITY
INCIVILIZATION
INCIVILLY
INCIVISM
INCLASP
INCLASPED
INCLASPING
INCLE
INCLEMENCIES
INCLEMENCY
INCLEMENT
INCLEMENTLY
INCLINABLE
INCLINABLENESS
INCLINATION
INCLINATOR
INCLINATORY
INCLINE
INCLINED
INCLINER
INCLINING
INCLINOGRAPH
INCLINOMETER
INCLIP
INCLOSE
INCLOSURE
INCLUDE
INCLUDED
INCLUDER
INCLUDING
INCLUSA
INCLUSE
INCLUSION
INCLUSIVE
INCLUSIVELY
INCLUSORY
INCLUSUS
INCOALESCENCE
INCOERCIBLE
INCOG
INCOGITABLE
INCOGITANCY
INCOGITANT
INCOGITANTLY
INCOGITATIVE
INCOGNITA
INCOGNITE
INCOGNITO
INCOGNITOS
INCOGNIZABLE
INCOGNIZANCE
INCOGNIZANT
INCOGNOSCENT
INCOGNOSCIBILITY
INCOHERENCE
INCOHERENCES
INCOHERENCIES
INCOHERENCY
INCOHERENT
INCOHERENTIFIC
INCOHERENTLY
INCOHERENTNESS
INCOHERING
INCOLANT
INCOMBUSTIBLE
INCOME
INCOMER
INCOMING
INCOMMENSURABILITY
INCOMMENSURABLE
INCOMMENSURABLENESS
INCOMMENSURABLY
INCOMMENSURATE
INCOMMISCIBLE
INCOMMODATE
INCOMMODATION
INCOMMODE
INCOMMODED
INCOMMODING
INCOMMODIOUS
INCOMMODITIES
INCOMMODITY
INCOMMUNICABLE
INCOMMUTABILITY
INCOMMUTABLE
INCOMPACT
INCOMPACTLY
INCOMPARABILITY
INCOMPARABLE
INCOMPARABLY
INCOMPARED
INCOMPATIBILITY
INCOMPATIBLE
INCOMPATIBLY
INCOMPENSATION
INCOMPETENCE
INCOMPETENCY
INCOMPETENT
INCOMPLETABLE
INCOMPLETE
INCOMPLETED
INCOMPLETELY
INCOMPLETENESS
INCOMPLETION
INCOMPLEX
INCOMPLIANCE
INCOMPLIANCY
INCOMPLIANT
INCOMPLIANTLY
INCOMPOSED
INCOMPOSEDLY
INCOMPOSEDNESS
INCOMPOSITE
INCOMPOSSIBLE
INCOMPREHENSIBLE
INCOMPREHENSIBLY
INCOMPRESSIBLE
INCOMPT
INCOMPUTABLE
INCONCEIVABILITY
INCONCEIVABLE
INCONCINNATE
INCONCINNITY
INCONCINNOUS
INCONCLUDENT
INCONCLUDING
INCONCLUSION
INCONCLUSIVE
INCONDENSABLE
INCONDENSIBLE
INCONDITE
INCONFORMITY
INCONFUSED
INCONFUSEDLY
INCONFUSION
INCONGEALABLE
INCONGRUENCE
INCONGRUENT
INCONGRUENTLY
INCONGRUITIES
INCONGRUITY
INCONGRUOUS
INCONJOINABLE
INCONJUNCT
INCONNU
INCONSCIENCE
INCONSCIENT
INCONSCIENTLY
INCONSCIOUS
INCONSEQUENCE
INCONSEQUENT
INCONSEQUENTIAL
INCONSEQUENTLY
INCONSEQUENTNESS
INCONSIDERABLE
INCONSIDERABLY
INCONSIDERATE
INCONSIDERATELY
INCONSIDERATION
INCONSIDERED
INCONSISTENCE
INCONSISTENCIES
INCONSISTENCY
INCONSISTENT
INCONSISTENTLY
INCONSOLABLE
INCONSOLABLY
INCONSOLATE
INCONSONANCE
INCONSONANT
INCONSPICUOUS
INCONSPICUOUSLY
INCONSPICUOUSNESS
INCONSTANCY
INCONSTANT
INCONSTANTLY
INCONSTANTNESS
INCONSUMABLE
INCONSUMABLY
INCONTAMINATE
INCONTESTABLE
INCONTESTABLY
INCONTINENCE
INCONTINENCY
INCONTINENT
INCONTINENTLY
INCONTINUITY
INCONTINUOUS
INCONTRACTILE
INCONTRACTION
INCONTROLLABLE
INCONTROLLABLY
INCONTROVERTIBLE
INCONVENIENCE
INCONVENIENCY
INCONVENIENT
INCONVERSABLE
INCONVERTIBLE
INCONVINCIBLE
INCONY
INCOORDINATION
INCORONATE
INCORONATED
INCORONATION
INCORPORABLE
INCORPORAL
INCORPORALITY
INCORPORALLY
INCORPORALNESS
INCORPORATE
INCORPORATED
INCORPORATING
INCORPORATION
INCORPORATIVE
INCORPORATOR
INCORPOREAL
INCORPOREITIES
INCORPOREITY
INCORPOREOUS
INCORPSE
INCORRECT
INCORRECTION
INCORRECTLY
INCORRECTNESS
INCORRIGIBLE
INCORRIGIBLENESS
INCORRIGIBLY
INCORRUPT
INCORRUPTED
INCORRUPTIBILITY
INCORRUPTIBLE
INCORRUPTION
INCORRUPTLY
INCOUP
INCOURSE
INCOURTEOUS
INCOURTEOUSLY
INCRASH
INCRASSATE
INCRASSATED
INCRASSATING
INCRASSATION
INCREASE
INCREASED
INCREASEMENT
INCREASER
INCREASING
INCREASINGLY
INCREATE
INCREATELY
INCREATIVE
INCREDIBILITIES
INCREDIBILITY
INCREDIBLE
INCREDIBLENESS
INCREDIBLY
INCREDULITY
INCREDULOUS
INCREDULOUSLY
INCREEP
INCREEPING
INCREMATE
INCREMATED
INCREMATING
INCREMATION
INCREMENT
INCREMENTAL
INCREPATION
INCREPT
INCRESCENCE
INCRESCENT
INCREST
INCRETION
INCRETIONARY
INCRETORY
INCRIMINATE
INCRIMINATED
INCRIMINATING
INCRIMINATION
INCRIMINATOR
INCRIMINATORY
INCROSS
INCROSSING

INCROTCHET
INCROYABLE
INCRUENT
INCRUENTAL
INCRUENTOUS
INCRUST
INCRUSTANT
INCRUSTATE
INCRUSTATED
INCRUSTATING
INCRUSTATION
INCRUSTATOR
INCRUSTED
INCRUSTING
INCRUSTIVE
INCRUSTMENT
INCRYSTAL
INCUBATE
INCUBATED
INCUBATING
INCUBATION
INCUBATIONAL
INCUBATIVE
INCUBATOR
INCUBATORIUM
INCUBATORY
INCUBE
INCUBI
INCUBOUS
INCUBUS
INCUBUSES
INCUDAL
INCUDATE
INCUDECTOMY
INCUDES
INCULCATE
INCULCATED
INCULCATING
INCULCATION
INCULCATIVE
INCULCATOR
INCULCATORY
INCULK
INCULPABLE
INCULPABLY
INCULPATE
INCULPATED
INCULPATING
INCULPATION
INCULPATIVE
INCULPATORY
INCULT
INCULTURE
INCUMBENCE
INCUMBENCIES
INCUMBENCY
INCUMBENT
INCUMBENTLY
INCUMBER
INCUMBRANCE
INCUNABLE
INCUNABULA
INCUNABULAR
INCUNABULIST
INCUNABULUM
INCUNEATION
INCUR
INCURABILITY
INCURABLE
INCURABLENESS
INCURABLY
INCURIOSITY
INCURIOUS
INCURIOUSLY
INCURRED
INCURRENCE
INCURRENT
INCURRING
INCURSE
INCURSION
INCURSIONIST
INCURSIVE
INCURVATE
INCURVATED
INCURVATING
INCURVATION
INCURVATURE
INCURVE
INCURVED
INCUS
INCUSE
INCUSED
INCUSING
INCUSS
INCUTE
INCUTTING
INDABA
INDACONITIN
INDACONITINE
INDAGATE
INDAGATION
INDAGATIVE
INDAGATOR
INDAGATORY
INDAMIN
INDAMINE
INDAN
INDANE
INDART
INDAZOL
INDAZOLE
INDEBT
INDEBTED
INDEBTEDNESS
INDEBTING
INDEBTMENT
INDECENCE
INDECENCIES
INDECENCY
INDECENT
INDECENTLY
INDECENTNESS
INDECIDUATE
INDECIDUOUS
INDECISION
INDECISIVE
INDECISIVELY
INDECISIVENESS
INDECLINABLE
INDECLINABLY
INDECOROUS
INDECOROUSLY
INDECORUM
INDEED
INDEFATIGABLE
INDEFEASIBLE
INDEFEASIBLY
INDEFECTIBLE
INDEFECTIBLY
INDEFECTIVE
INDEFENSIBLE
INDEFICIENCY
INDEFICIENT
INDEFICIENTLY
INDEFINABLE
INDEFINABLY
INDEFINITE
INDEFINITELY
INDEFINITY
INDEFLECTIBLE
INDEHISCENCE
INDEHISCENT
INDELECTABLE
INDELIBERATE
INDELIBILITY
INDELIBLE
INDELIBLY
INDELICACIES
INDELICACY
INDELICATE
INDELICATELY
INDEMNIFICATION
INDEMNIFIED
INDEMNIFIER
INDEMNIFY
INDEMNIFYING
INDEMNITEE
INDEMNITIES
INDEMNITOR
INDEMNITY
INDEMONIATE
INDEMONSTRABLE
INDENE
INDENIZE
INDENT
INDENTATION
INDENTED
INDENTEDLY
INDENTEE
INDENTER
INDENTING
INDENTION
INDENTMENT
INDENTOR
INDENTURE
INDENTURED
INDENTURING
INDENTWISE
INDEPENDENCE
INDEPENDENCIES
INDEPENDENCY
INDEPENDENT
INDEPENDENTLY
INDERITE
INDESCRIBABLE
INDESCRIPT
INDESERT
INDESIGNATE
INDESTRUCTIBLE
INDETERMINACY
INDETERMINATE
INDEVOTION
INDEX
INDEXED
INDEXER
INDEXES
INDEXICAL
INDEXICALLY
INDEXING
INDEXTERITY
INDIANAITE
INDICAN
INDICANT
INDICANURIA
INDICATE
INDICATED
INDICATING
INDICATION
INDICATIVE
INDICATIVELY
INDICATOR
INDICATORY
INDICATRIX
INDICAVIT
INDICE
INDICES
INDICIA
INDICIAL
INDICIBLE
INDICO
INDICOLITE
INDICT
INDICTABLE
INDICTABLY
INDICTED
INDICTEE
INDICTER
INDICTING
INDICTION
INDICTIONAL
INDICTIVE
INDICTMENT
INDICTOR
INDIENNE
INDIFEROUS
INDIFFERENCE
INDIFFERENCIES
INDIFFERENCY
INDIFFERENT
INDIFFERENTIAL
INDIFFERENTISM
INDIFFERENTIST
INDIFFERENTLY
INDIGENA
INDIGENAE
INDIGENAL
INDIGENATE
INDIGENCE
INDIGENCY
INDIGENE
INDIGENEITY
INDIGENITY
INDIGENOUS
INDIGENT
INDIGENTLY
INDIGEST
INDIGESTED
INDIGESTIBLE
INDIGESTIBLY
INDIGESTION
INDIGESTIVE
INDIGITATE
INDIGITATION
INDIGN
INDIGNANCE
INDIGNANCY
INDIGNANT
INDIGNANTLY
INDIGNATION
INDIGNATORY
INDIGNIFIED
INDIGNIFY
INDIGNIFYING
INDIGNITIES
INDIGNITY
INDIGNLY
INDIGO
INDIGOES
INDIGOFEROUS
INDIGOID
INDIGOS
INDIGOTIC
INDIGOTIN
INDIGOTINE
INDIMENSIBLE
INDIMPLE
INDIO
INDIRECT
INDIRECTION
INDIRECTLY
INDIRECTNESS
INDIRUBIN
INDIRUBINE
INDISCERNIBLE
INDISCERNIBLY
INDISCIPLINE
INDISCREET
INDISCREETLY
INDISCRETE
INDISCRETELY
INDISCRETION
INDISCRIMINATE
INDISCRIMINATED
INDISCRIMINATELY
INDISCRIMINATING
INDISCRIMINATION
INDISCRIMINATIVE
INDISPENSABLE
INDISPOSE
INDISPOSED
INDISPOSING
INDISPOSITION
INDISPUTABLE
INDISPUTABLY
INDISSOLUBLE
INDISSOLUBLY
INDISSOLUTE
INDISSOLVABLE
INDISTINCT
INDISTINCTION
INDISTINCTIVE
INDISTINCTLY
INDISTINCTNESS
INDISTORTABLE
INDISTURBANCE
INDITE
INDITED
INDITEMENT
INDITER
INDITING
INDIUM
INDIVERTIBLE
INDIVERTIBLY
INDIVIDUA
INDIVIDUAL
INDIVIDUALISM
INDIVIDUALIST
INDIVIDUALITIES
INDIVIDUALITY
INDIVIDUALIZE
INDIVIDUALIZED
INDIVIDUALIZING
INDIVIDUALLY
INDIVIDUATE
INDIVIDUATED
INDIVIDUATING
INDIVIDUATION
INDIVIDUATOR
INDIVIDUITY
INDIVIDUUM
INDIVIDUUMS
INDIVINABLE
INDIVISIBLE
INDIVISIBLY
INDIVISIM
INDIVISION
INDOCIBLE
INDOCILE
INDOCILITY
INDOCTRINATE
INDOCTRINATED
INDOCTRINATING
INDOCTRINE
INDOCTRINIZE
INDOGEN
INDOGENIDE
INDOL
INDOLE
INDOLENCE
INDOLENT
INDOLENTLY
INDOLES
INDOLIN
INDOLINE
INDOLOID

INDOMITABLE
INDONE
INDOOR
INDOORS
INDOPHENIN
INDOPHENOL
INDORSATION
INDORSE
INDORSED
INDORSING
INDOXYL
INDOXYLIC
INDRAFT
INDRAPE
INDRAUGHT
INDRAWAL
INDRAWING
INDRAWN
INDRENCH
INDRI
INDUBIOUS
INDUBIOUSLY
INDUBITABLE
INDUBITABLY
INDUCE
INDUCED
INDUCEMENT
INDUCER
INDUCIAE
INDUCIBLE
INDUCING
INDUCIVE
INDUCT
INDUCTANCE
INDUCTED
INDUCTEE
INDUCTEOUS
INDUCTILE
INDUCTILITY
INDUCTING
INDUCTION
INDUCTIONAL
INDUCTIVE
INDUCTIVELY
INDUCTIVITY
INDUCTOMETER
INDUCTOPHONE
INDUCTOR
INDUCTORY
INDUCTOSCOPE
INDUE
INDUED
INDUING
INDULGE
INDULGED
INDULGENCE
INDULGENCED
INDULGENCY
INDULGENT
INDULGENTIAL
INDULGENTLY
INDULGENTNESS
INDULGER
INDULGING
INDULGINGLY
INDULIN
INDULINE
INDULT
INDULTO
INDULTS
INDUMENT
INDUMENTUM
INDUNA
INDUPLICATE
INDUPLICATION
INDUPLICATIVE
INDURATE
INDURATED
INDURATING
INDURATION
INDURATIVE
INDURE
INDURITE
INDUSIA
INDUSIAL
INDUSIATE
INDUSIATED
INDUSIFORM
INDUSIOID
INDUSIUM
INDUSTRIAL
INDUSTRIALLY
INDUSTRIES
INDUSTRIOUS
INDUSTRY
INDUVIAE
INDUVIAL
INDUVIATE
INDWELL
INDWELLER
INDWELLING
INDWELT
INDYL
INDYLIC
INEARTH
INEBRIACY
INEBRIANT
INEBRIATE
INEBRIATED
INEBRIATING
INEBRIATION
INEBRIATIVE
INEBRIETY
INEBRIOUS
INEDIBILITY
INEDIBLE
INEDITA
INEDITED
INEDUCATION
INEE
INEFFABILITY
INEFFABLE
INEFFABLY
INEFFACEABLE
INEFFACEABLY
INEFFECTIBLE
INEFFECTIBLY
INEFFECTIVE
INEFFECTIVELY
INEFFECTUAL
INEFFICACITY
INEFFICACY
INEFFICIENCE
INEFFICIENCY
INEFFICIENT
INELASTIC
INELASTICATE
INELASTICITY
INELEGANCE
INELEGANCES
INELEGANCIES
INELEGANCY
INELEGANT
INELEGANTLY
INELIGIBLE
INELIGIBLY
INELOQUENCE
INELOQUENT
INELUCTABLE
INELUCTABLY
INELUDIBLE
INENARRABLE
INENUBILABLE
INEPT
INEPTITUDE
INEPTLY
INEPTNESS
INEQUAL
INEQUALITARIAN
INEQUALITIES
INEQUALITY
INEQUALLY
INEQUALNESS
INEQUATION
INEQUITABLE
INEQUITABLY
INEQUITIES
INEQUITY
INEQUIVALVE
INERADICABLE
INERASABLE
INERASABLY
INERM
INERMOUS
INERRABLE
INERRANCY
INERRANT
INERRANTLY
INERRATIC
INERRING
INERRINGLY
INERT
INERTIA
INERTION
INERTLY
INERTNESS
INERUDITE
INERUDITELY
INERUDITION
INESCAPABLE
INESCATE
INESCATION
INESCULENT
INESCUTCHEON
INESITE
INESSENTIAL
INESTHETIC
INESTIMABLE
INESTIMABLY
INEUNT
INEVAPORABLE
INEVASIBLE
INEVIDENCE
INEVIDENT
INEVITABILITY
INEVITABLE
INEVITABLY
INEXACT
INEXACTITUDE
INEXACTLY
INEXACTNESS
INEXCUSABLE
INEXCUSABLY
INEXECUTION
INEXERTION
INEXHAUSTIBLE
INEXHAUSTIVE
INEXIST
INEXISTENCE
INEXISTENCY
INEXISTENT
INEXORABLE
INEXORABLY
INEXPECTED
INEXPECTEDLY
INEXPEDIENCY
INEXPEDIENT
INEXPENSIVE
INEXPERIENCE
INEXPERIENCED
INEXPERT
INEXPERTLY
INEXPERTNESS
INEXPIABLE
INEXPIABLENESS
INEXPIABLY
INEXPIATE
INEXPLICABLE
INEXPLICABLES
INEXPLICABLY
INEXPLICIT
INEXPLICITLY
INEXPRESS
INEXPRESSIBLE
INEXPRESSIVE
INEXPUGNABLE
INEXTENSIVE
INEXTERMINABLE
INEXTIRPABLE
INEXTRICABLE
INEXTRICABLY
INEYE
INFACE
INFAIR
INFALL
INFALLIBILIST
INFALLIBILITY
INFALLIBLE
INFALLIBLY
INFALLID
INFALLING
INFAME
INFAMED
INFAMIES
INFAMIZE
INFAMIZED
INFAMIZING
INFAMONIZE
INFAMOUS
INFAMOUSLY
INFAMOUSNESS
INFAMY
INFANCIES
INFANCY
INFAND
INFANDOUS
INFANG
INFANGLEMENT
INFANGTHEF
INFANGTHIEF
INFANS
INFANT
INFANTA
INFANTADO
INFANTE
INFANTICIDAL
INFANTICIDE
INFANTILE
INFANTILISM
INFANTILITY
INFANTINE
INFANTRIES
INFANTRY
INFANTRYMAN
INFANTS
INFARCT
INFARCTATE
INFARCTED
INFARCTION
INFARE
INFATUATE
INFATUATED
INFATUATEDLY
INFATUATING
INFATUATION
INFATUATOR
INFAUST
INFAUSTING
INFEASIBLE
INFECT
INFECTANT
INFECTED
INFECTEDNESS
INFECTING
INFECTION
INFECTIOUS
INFECTIVE
INFECTIVENESS
INFECTIVITY
INFECTOR
INFECTUM
INFECTUOUS
INFECUND
INFEED
INFEFT
INFEFTING
INFEFTMENT
INFELICIFIC
INFELICITIES
INFELICITOUS
INFELICITY
INFELT
INFEOFF
INFEOFFMENT
INFER
INFERABLE
INFERENCE
INFERENT
INFERENTIAL
INFERENTIALISM
INFERENTIALLY
INFERI
INFERIAE
INFERIAL
INFERIOR
INFERIORITY
INFERN
INFERNAL
INFERNALITY
INFERNALLY
INFERNALRY
INFERNO
INFERNOS
INFERRED
INFERRER
INFERRIBLE
INFERRING
INFERTILE
INFERTILELY
INFERTILITY
INFEST
INFESTANT
INFESTATION
INFESTED
INFESTER
INFESTING
INFESTIOUS
INFESTIVE
INFESTIVITY
INFESTMENT
INFEUDATION
INFIBULATE
INFIBULATION
INFICETE
INFIDEL
INFIDELIC
INFIDELICAL
INFIDELITIES
INFIDELITY
INFIELD
INFIELDER
INFIGHTER
INFIGHTING
INFILE
INFILL

INFILLING
INFILM
INFILTER
INFILTERED
INFILTERING
INFILTRATE
INFILTRATED
INFILTRATING
INFILTRATION
INFILTRATIVE
INFINITANT
INFINITARILY
INFINITARY
INFINITATE
INFINITATED
INFINITATING
INFINITATION
INFINITE
INFINITELY
INFINITENESS
INFINITESIMAL
INFINITETH
INFINITIES
INFINITIETH
INFINITIVAL
INFINITIVE
INFINIT!VELY
INFINITO
INFINITUDE
INFINITUM
INFINITUPLE
INFINITY
INFIRM
INFIRMARER
INFIRMARESS
INFIRMARIAN
INFIRMARIES
INFIRMARY
INFIRMATE
INFIRMATION
INFIRMATIVE
INFIRMED
INFIRMING
INFIRMITIES
INFIRMITY
INFIT
INFITTER
INFIX
INFIXED
INFIXES
INFIXING
INFIXION
INFLAME
INFLAMED
INFLAMEDLY
INFLAMEDNESS
INFLAMER
INFLAMING
INFLAMINGLY
INFLAMMABILITY
INFLAMMABLE
INFLAMMABLENESS
INFLAMMABLY
INFLAMMATION
INFLAMMATIVE
INFLAMMATORY
INFLATE
INFLATED
INFLATEDLY
INFLATEDNESS
INFLATER
INFLATILE
INFLATING
INFLATION
INFLATIONARY
INFLATIONISM
INFLATIONIST
INFLATIVE
INFLATUS
INFLECT
INFLECTED
INFLECTING
INFLECTION
INFLECTIONAL
INFLECTIVE
INFLECTOR
INFLEX
INFLEXED
INFLEXIBILITY
INFLEXIBLE
INFLEXIBLY
INFLEXION
INFLEXIVE
INFLICT
INFLICTED
INFLICTER
INFLICTING
INFLICTION
INFLICTIVE
INFLOOD
INFLORESCENCE
INFLORESCENT
INFLOW
INFLUENCE
INFLUENCED
INFLUENCER
INFLUENCES
INFLUENCING
INFLUENCIVE
INFLUENT
INFLUENTIAL
INFLUENZA
INFLUENZAL
INFLUENZIC
INFLUX
INFLUXION
INFLUXIONISM
INFLUXIVE
INFO
INFOLD
INFOLDED
INFOLDER
INFOLDING
INFOLIATE
INFORM
INFORMAL
INFORMALITIES
INFORMALITY
INFORMALIZE
INFORMALLY
INFORMANT
INFORMATION
INFORMATIONAL
INFORMATIVE
INFORMATIVELY
INFORMATORY
INFORMED
INFORMEDLY
INFORMER
INFORMIDABLE
INFORMING
INFORMITY
INFORTIATE
INFORTITUDE
INFORTUNATE
INFORTUNE
INFOUND
INFRA
INFRABASAL
INFRACENTRAL
INFRACLUSION
INFRACOSTAL
INFRACT
INFRACTED
INFRACTING
INFRACTION
INFRACTOR
INFRADENTARY
INFRAGLACIAL
INFRAGLENOID
INFRAGULAR
INFRAHUMAN
INFRAHYOID
INFRALABIAL
INFRALITTORAL
INFRAMEDIAN
INFRANATURAL
INFRANGIBLE
INFRAPOSE
INFRAPOSED
INFRAPOSING
INFRAPROTEIN
INFRARED
INFRASONIC
INFRASPINAL
INFRASPINATUS
INFRASPINOUS
INFRATEMPORAL
INFRAVENTRAL
INFREQUENCE
INFREQUENCY
INFREQUENT
INFRIGIDATE
INFRINGE
INFRINGED
INFRINGEMENT
INFRINGER
INFRINGIBLE
INFRINGING
INFRUCTUOSE
INFRUCTUOUS
INFRUNITE
INFULA
INFULAE
INFUMATE
INFUMATED
INFUND
INFUNDIBULAR
INFUNDIBULUM
INFURIATE
INFURIATED
INFURIATELY
INFURIATING
INFURIATION
INFUSCATE
INFUSCATED
INFUSCATION
INFUSE
INFUSED
INFUSER
INFUSIBILITY
INFUSIBLE
INFUSING
INFUSION
INFUSIONISM
INFUSIONIST
INFUSIVE
INFUSORIAL
INFUSORIAN
INFUSORIES
INFUSORY
INGALLANTRY
INGANG
INGANGS
INGATE
INGATES
INGATHER
INGATHERED
INGATHERER
INGATHERING
INGE
INGEMINATE
INGEMINATED
INGEMINATING
INGENDER
INGENE
INGENERABLE
INGENERABLY
INGENERATE
INGENERATED
INGENERATING
INGENERATION
INGENIER
INGENIOSITY
INGENIOUS
INGENIOUSLY
INGENIT
INGENITAL
INGENITE
INGENT
INGENUE
INGENUITIES
INGENUITY
INGENUOUS
INGENUOUSLY
INGENUOUSNESS
INGENY
INGERMINATE
INGEST
INGESTA
INGESTED
INGESTER
INGESTIBLE
INGESTING
INGESTION
INGESTIVE
INGINE
INGIVER
INGIVING
INGLE
INGLENOOK
INGLES
INGLESA
INGLESIDE
INGLOBATE
INGLOBE
INGLOBED
INGLOBING
INGLORIOUS
INGLORIOUSLY
INGLORIOUSNESS
INGLUTITION
INGLUVIAL
INGLUVIES
INGLUVIITIS
INGOING
INGOT
INGOTED
INGOTING
INGOTMAN
INGOTMEN
INGOTS
INGRAFT
INGRAIN
INGRAINED
INGRAINEDLY
INGRAINING
INGRAMNESS
INGRANDIZE
INGRATE
INGRATEFUL
INGRATEFULNESS
INGRATELY
INGRATIATE
INGRATIATED
INGRATIATING
INGRATIATION
INGRATIATORY
INGRATITUDE
INGRAVESCENT
INGRAVIDATE
INGREAT
INGREDIENCE
INGREDIENT
INGRESS
INGRESSION
INGRESSIVE
INGROSS
INGROUP
INGROW
INGROWING
INGROWN
INGROWTH
INGRUENT
INGUEN
INGUINAL
INGULF
INGULFMENT
INGURGITATE
INGURGITATED
INGURGITATING
INGUSTABLE
INGYRE
INHABILE
INHABIT
INHABITABILITY
INHABITABLE
INHABITANCE
INHABITANCY
INHABITANT
INHABITATE
INHABITATION
INHABITATIVE
INHABITED
INHABITER
INHABITING
INHABITRESS
INHALANT
INHALATION
INHALE
INHALED
INHALENT
INHALER
INHALING
INHAME
INHARMONIC
INHARMONIOUS
INHARMONY
INHAUL
INHAULER
INHAUST
INHAUSTION
INHEARSE
INHEAVEN
INHELDE
INHERE
INHERED
INHERENCE
INHERENCIES
INHERENCY
INHERENT
INHERENTLY
INHERING
INHERIT
INHERITABLE
INHERITABLY
INHERITAGE
INHERITANCE
INHERITED
INHERITING
INHERITOR
INHESION
INHIATE
INHIBIT
INHIBITABLE

INHIBITED
INHIBITER
INHIBITION
INHIBITIONIST
INHIBITIONS
INHIBITIVE
INHIBITOR
INHIBITORY
INHOLDER
INHONEST
INHOOP
INHOSPITABLE
INHOSPITABLY
INHOSPITALITY
INHUMAN
INHUMANE
INHUMANELY
INHUMANITIES
INHUMANITY
INHUMANLY
INHUMANNESS
INHUMATE
INHUMATION
INHUMATIONIST
INHUME
INHUMED
INHUMER
INHUMING
INIAL
INIMICABLE
INIMICAL
INIMICALITY
INIMICALLY
INIMICALNESS
INIMICITIOUS
INIMICOUS
INIMITABILITY
INIMITABLE
INIMITABLY
INIOME
INIOMOUS
INION
INIQUITABLE
INIQUITIES
INIQUITOUS
INIQUITOUSLY
INIQUITY
INIRRITABILITY
INIRRITABLE
INISSUABLE
INITIAL
INITIALED
INITIALER
INITIALING
INITIALIST
INITIALLED
INITIALLY
INITIANT
INITIARY
INITIATE
INITIATED
INITIATING
INITIATION
INITIATIVE
INITIATIVELY
INITIATOR
INITIATORILY
INITIATORY
INITION
INJECT
INJECTED
INJECTING
INJECTION
INJECTOR
INJELLY
INJOINT
INJUDICIAL
INJUDICIALLY
INJUDICIOUS
INJUDICIOUSLY
INJUDICIOUSNESS
INJUNCT
INJUNCTION
INJUNCTIVE
INJUNCTIVELY
INJURE
INJURED
INJUREDLY
INJUREDNESS
INJURER
INJURIA
INJURIES
INJURING
INJURIOUS
INJURIOUSLY
INJURY
INJUST
INJUSTICE
INJUSTLY
INK
INKBERRIES
INKBERRY
INKBLOT
INKED
INKEN
INKER
INKET
INKFISH
INKHOLDER
INKHORN
INKHORNISM
INKHORNIST
INKHORNIZE
INKHORNIZER
INKIER
INKIEST
INKINDLE
INKING
INKLE
INKLING
INKMAN
INKNIT
INKNOT
INKOS
INKOSI
INKPOT
INKROOT
INKS
INKSHED
INKSLINGER
INKSLINGING
INKSTAND
INKSTANDISH
INKSTONE
INKWEED
INKWELL
INKWOOD
INKWRITER
INKY
INLAGATION
INLAID
INLAIK
INLAKE
INLAND
INLANDER
INLANDISH
INLAPIDATE
INLARD
INLAUT
INLAW
INLAWRY
INLAY
INLAYER
INLAYING
INLEAGUE
INLEAGUED
INLEAGUING
INLEAK
INLEAKAGE
INLESS
INLET
INLETTING
INLIER
INLIKE
INLOOK
INLOOKER
INLOOKING
INLY
INLYING
INMATE
INMEATS
INMESH
INMIXTURE
INMORE
INMOST
INN
INNAM
INNARDS
INNASCIBLE
INNATE
INNATELY
INNATENESS
INNATISM
INNATIVE
INNATURAL
INNATURALITY
INNATURALLY
INNEITY
INNER
INNERLY
INNERMORE
INNERMOST
INNERVATE
INNERVATED
INNERVATING
INNERVATION
INNERVATIONAL
INNERVE
INNERVED
INNERVING
INNESS
INNEST
INNET
INNHOLDER
INNING
INNINGS
INNINMORITE
INNITENCY
INNKEEPER
INNOCENCE
INNOCENCIES
INNOCENCY
INNOCENT
INNOCENTLY
INNOCENTNESS
INNOCUITY
INNOCUOUS
INNOCUOUSLY
INNOCUOUSNESS
INNODATE
INNOMINABLE
INNOMINABLES
INNOMINATA
INNOMINATE
INNOMINATUM
INNOVANT
INNOVATE
INNOVATED
INNOVATING
INNOVATION
INNOVATIVE
INNOVATOR
INNOVATORY
INNOXIOUS
INNOXIOUSLY
INNUATE
INNUENDO
INNUENDOED
INNUENDOES
INNUENDOING
INNUMERABLE
INNUMERABLY
INNUMEROUS
INNUTRIENT
INNUTRITION
INNUTRITIOUS
INNYARD
INOBEDIENCE
INOBEDIENT
INOBNOXIOUS
INOBSCURABLE
INOBSERVANCE
INOBSERVANCY
INOBSERVANT
INOBSERVANTLY
INOBSERVATION
INOBTAINABLE
INOBTRUSIVE
INOCCUPATION
INOCULABILITY
INOCULABLE
INOCULANT
INOCULAR
INOCULATE
INOCULATED
INOCULATING
INOCULATION
INOCULATIVE
INOCULATOR
INOCULUM
INODIATE
INODOROUS
INODOROUSLY
INODOROUSNESS
INOFFENSIVE
INOFFICIOSITY
INOFFICIOUS
INOFFICIOUSNESS
INOGEN
INOMA
INOMINOUS
INONE
INOPERABLE
INOPERATIVE
INOPERCULAR
INOPERCULATE
INOPINABLE
INOPINATE
INOPINATELY
INOPINE
INOPPORTUNE
INOPPORTUNELY
INOPPORTUNIST
INOPPORTUNITY
INOPULENT
INORB
INORDINACY
INORDINATE
INORDINATELY
INORDINATENESS
INORDINATION
INORGANIC
INORGANIZATION
INORIGINATE
INORNATE
INOSCULATED
INOSCULATING
INOSINE
INOSITE
INOSITOL
INOTROPIC
INOWER
INOXIDIZE
INOXIDIZED
INOXIDIZING
INPARFIT
INPATIENT
INPAYMENT
INPENSIONER
INPHASE
INPORT
INPOUR
INPOURING
INPUSH
INPUT
INQUAINTANCE
INQUARTATION
INQUEST
INQUESTUAL
INQUIET
INQUIETLY
INQUIETNESS
INQUIETUDE
INQUILINE
INQUILINISM
INQUILINITY
INQUILINOUS
INQUINATE
INQUINATED
INQUINATING
INQUINATION
INQUIRABLE
INQUIRATION
INQUIRE
INQUIRED
INQUIRENDO
INQUIRENT
INQUIRER
INQUIRIES
INQUIRING
INQUIRINGLY
INQUIRY
INQUISIT
INQUISITE
INQUISITION
INQUISITIONAL
INQUISITIONIST
INQUISITIVE
INQUISITOR
INQUISITORIAL
INQUISITORY
INRADIUS
INRIGGED
INRIGGER
INRIGHTED
INRING
INRO
INROAD
INROADER
INROLL
INROOTED
INRUB
INRUN
INRUNNING
INRUPTION
INRUSH
INS
INSACK
INSAGACITY
INSALIVATE
INSALIVATED
INSALIVATING
INSALIVATION
INSALUBRIOUS
INSALUBRITY

INSAME
INSANE
INSANELY
INSANENESS
INSANIFY
INSANITARY
INSANITATION
INSANITY
INSATIABLE
INSATIABLY
INSATIATE
INSATIATED
INSATIATELY
INSATIETY
INSATISFACTION
INSATURABLE
INSCENATION
INSCIENCE
INSCIENT
INSCIOUS
INSCRIBABLE
INSCRIBE
INSCRIBED
INSCRIBER
INSCRIBING
INSCRIPT
INSCRIPTIBLE
INSCRIPTION
INSCRIPTIONED
INSCRIPTIVE
INSCRIPTURED
INSCROLL
INSCROLLED
INSCROLLING
INSCRUTABLE
INSCRUTABLES
INSCRUTABLY
INSCULP
INSCULPTURE
INSEA
INSEAM
INSEAMER
INSECT
INSECTAN
INSECTARIA
INSECTARIES
INSECTARIUM
INSECTARIUMS
INSECTARY
INSECTEAN
INSECTED
INSECTICIDAL
INSECTICIDE
INSECTILE
INSECTION
INSECTIVAL
INSECTIVORE
INSECTIVOROUS
INSECTMONGER
INSECTOLOGER
INSECTOLOGY
INSECTS
INSECURE
INSECURELY
INSECURENESS
INSECURITIES
INSECURITY
INSEE
INSEEING
INSEER
INSELBERG
INSELBERGE
INSEMINATE
INSEMINATED
INSEMINATING
INSEMINATION
INSENESCIBLE
INSENSATE
INSENSATELY
INSENSE
INSENSED
INSENSIBILITY
INSENSIBILIZE
INSENSIBLE
INSENSIBLY
INSENSING
INSENSITIVE
INSENSUOUS
INSENTIENCE
INSENTIENCY
INSENTIENT
INSEPARABLE
INSEPARABLY
INSEPARATE
INSEPARATELY
INSEQUENT
INSERT
INSERTED
INSERTER
INSERTING
INSERTION
INSERTIONAL
INSERTIVE
INSERVIENT
INSESSION
INSESSOR
INSESSORIAL
INSET
INSETTER
INSEVERABLE
INSEVERABLY
INSHAVE
INSHEATHE
INSHEATHED
INSHEATHING
INSHELL
INSHINING
INSHIP
INSHOE
INSHOOT
INSHORE
INSHRINE
INSIDE
INSIDENT
INSIDER
INSIDES
INSIDIATE
INSIDIATION
INSIDIATOR
INSIDIOSITY
INSIDIOUS
INSIDIOUSLY
INSIGHT
INSIGHTED
INSIGHTFUL
INSIGNE
INSIGNIA
INSIGNIFICANCE
INSIGNIFICANCIES
INSIGNIFICANCY
INSIGNIFICANT
INSIGNIFICANTLY
INSIMPLICITY
INSINCERE
INSINCERELY
INSINCERITIES
INSINCERITY
INSINEW
INSINKING
INSINUANT
INSINUATE
INSINUATED
INSINUATING
INSINUATION
INSINUATIVE
INSINUATOR
INSINUATORY
INSINUENDO
INSIPID
INSIPIDITIES
INSIPIDITY
INSIPIDLY
INSIPIDNESS
INSIPIENCE
INSIPIENT
INSIPIENTLY
INSIST
INSISTED
INSISTENCE
INSISTENCY
INSISTENT
INSISTENTLY
INSISTER
INSISTING
INSISTIVE
INSISTURE
INSITE
INSITION
INSITITIOUS
INSNARE
INSNAREMENT
INSNARER
INSOBRIETY
INSOCIABILITY
INSOCIABLE
INSOCIABLY
INSOCIAL
INSOCIALLY
INSOLATE
INSOLATED
INSOLATING
INSOLATION
INSOLE
INSOLENCE
INSOLENCY
INSOLENT
INSOLENTLY
INSOLENTNESS
INSOLID
INSOLIDITY
INSOLITE
INSOLUBILITY
INSOLUBLE
INSOLUBLY
INSOLVABLE
INSOLVABLY
INSOLVENCE
INSOLVENCIES
INSOLVENCY
INSOLVENT
INSOMNIA
INSOMNIAC
INSOMNIOUS
INSOMNOLENCE
INSOMNOLENCY
INSOMNOLENT
INSOMUCH
INSOOTH
INSORB
INSORDID
INSOUCIANCE
INSOUCIANT
INSOUCIANTLY
INSOUL
INSPAKE
INSPAN
INSPANNED
INSPANNING
INSPEAK
INSPEAKING
INSPECT
INSPECTED
INSPECTING
INSPECTION
INSPECTIONAL
INSPECTIONEER
INSPECTIVE
INSPECTOR
INSPECTORAL
INSPECTORATE
INSPECTORIAL
INSPECTRESS
INSPECTRIX
INSPEXIMUS
INSPHERATION
INSPHERE
INSPIRABILITY
INSPIRABLE
INSPIRANT
INSPIRATION
INSPIRATIONAL
INSPIRATIVE
INSPIRATOR
INSPIRATORY
INSPIRE
INSPIRED
INSPIREDLY
INSPIRER
INSPIRING
INSPIRINGLY
INSPIRIT
INSPIRITED
INSPIRITER
INSPIRITING
INSPIRITINGLY
INSPIROMETER
INSPISSANT
INSPISSATE
INSPISSATED
INSPISSATING
INSPISSATION
INSPISSATOR
INSPISSOSIS
INSPOKE
INSPOKEN
INSPREITH
INSTABILITIES
INSTABILITY
INSTABLE
INSTAL
INSTALL
INSTALLANT
INSTALLATION
INSTALLED
INSTALLER
INSTALLING
INSTALLMENT
INSTANCE
INSTANCED
INSTANCING
INSTANCY
INSTANDING
INSTANT
INSTANTANEITY
INSTANTANEOUS
INSTANTER
INSTANTIAL
INSTANTLY
INSTAR
INSTARRED
INSTARRING
INSTATE
INSTATED
INSTATING
INSTAURATE
INSTAURATION
INSTAURATOR
INSTEAD
INSTEALING
INSTEAM
INSTEEP
INSTELLATION
INSTEP
INSTIGANT
INSTIGATE
INSTIGATED
INSTIGATING
INSTIGATION
INSTIGATIVE
INSTIGATOR
INSTIL
INSTILL
INSTILLATION
INSTILLATOR
INSTILLATORY
INSTILLED
INSTILLER
INSTILLING
INSTINCT
INSTINCTION
INSTINCTIVE
INSTINCTIVELY
INSTINCTIVIST
INSTINCTIVITY
INSTINCTUAL
INSTIPULATE
INSTITOR
INSTITORIAL
INSTITORY
INSTITUE
INSTITUTE
INSTITUTED
INSTITUTING
INSTITUTION
INSTITUTIONAL
INSTITUTIVE
INSTITUTOR
INSTONEMENT
INSTOP
INSTORE
INSTRATIFIED
INSTRENGTHEN
INSTRESSED
INSTROKE
INSTRUCT
INSTRUCTED
INSTRUCTING
INSTRUCTION
INSTRUCTIONAL
INSTRUCTIVE
INSTRUCTOR
INSTRUMENT
INSTRUMENTAL
INSTRUMENTALIST
INSTRUMENTALITIES
INSTRUMENTALITY
INSTRUMENTATE
INSTRUMENTED
INSTRUMENTS
INSTYLE
INSUAVITY
INSUBJECTION
INSUBMISSION
INSUBORDINATE
INSUBORDINATION
INSUBSTANTIAL
INSUBSTANTIALITY
INSUBSTANTIATE
INSUCCATION
INSUCCESS
INSUCCESSFUL
INSUCKEN
INSUETUDE
INSUFFERABLE
INSUFFERABLY

INSUFFICIENCE
INSUFFICIENCY
INSUFFICIENT
INSUFFICIENTLY
INSUFFLATE
INSUFFLATED
INSUFFLATION
INSUFFLATOR
INSULA
INSULAE
INSULANCE
INSULANT
INSULAR
INSULARITY
INSULARY
INSULATE
INSULATED
INSULATING
INSULATION
INSULATOR
INSULIN
INSULIZE
INSULPHURED
INSULSE
INSULSITY
INSULT
INSULTANT
INSULTATION
INSULTED
INSULTER
INSULTING
INSULTINGLY
INSUME
INSUNK
INSUPER
INSUPERABLE
INSUPERABLY
INSUPPORTABLE
INSUPPRESSIVE
INSURABILITY
INSURABLE
INSURANCE
INSURANT
INSURE
INSURED
INSUREDS
INSURER
INSURGE
INSURGENCE
INSURGENCY
INSURGENT
INSURGESCENCE
INSURING
INSURMOUNTABLE
INSURRECT
INSURRECTION
INSURRECTO
INSURRECTORY
INSUSCEPTIBLE
INSWARMING
INSWATHE
INSWATHEMENT
INSWEEPING
INSWELL
INSWEPT
INSWING
INSWINGER
INTABULATE
INTACT
INTACTILE
INTACTLY
INTACTNESS
INTAGLI
INTAGLIATED
INTAGLIO
INTAGLIOED
INTAGLIOING
INTAGLIOS
INTAKE
INTAKER
INTANGIBLE
INTANGIBLY
INTARISSABLE
INTARSIA
INTARSIATE
INTARSIST
INTEGER
INTEGERS
INTEGRABLE
INTEGRAL
INTEGRALITY
INTEGRANT
INTEGRAPH
INTEGRATE
INTEGRATED
INTEGRATING
INTEGRATION
INTEGRATIVE
INTEGRATOR
INTEGRIOUS
INTEGRIOUSLY
INTEGRITY
INTEGUMENT
INTEGUMENTAL
INTEIND
INTELLECT
INTELLECTATION
INTELLECTED
INTELLECTIBLE
INTELLECTION
INTELLECTIVE
INTELLECTUAL
INTELLIGENCE
INTELLIGENCY
INTELLIGENT
INTELLIGENTLY
INTELLIGENTSIA
INTELLIGIBLE
INTELLIGIBLY
INTELLIGIZE
INTEMERATE
INTEMERATELY
INTEMERATION
INTEMPERANCE
INTEMPERANCY
INTEMPERATE
INTEMPERATURE
INTEMPESTIVE
INTEMPORAL
INTEMPORALLY
INTEND
INTENDANCE
INTENDANCIES
INTENDANCY
INTENDANT
INTENDED
INTENDEDLY
INTENDEDNESS
INTENDENCE
INTENDENCIA
INTENDENTE
INTENDER
INTENDIBLE
INTENDING
INTENDINGLY
INTENDIT
INTENDMENT
INTENERATE
INTENERATED
INTENERATING
INTENERATION
INTENIBLE
INTENSATE
INTENSATION
INTENSATIVE
INTENSE
INTENSELY
INTENSIFIED
INTENSIFIER
INTENSIFY
INTENSIFYING
INTENSION
INTENSIONAL
INTENSIONALLY
INTENSITIES
INTENSITIVE
INTENSITY
INTENSIVE
INTENSIVELY
INTENSIVENESS
INTENT
INTENTED
INTENTION
INTENTIONAL
INTENTIONALITY
INTENTIONED
INTENTIVE
INTENTIVELY
INTENTLY
INTER
INTERACINOUS
INTERACT
INTERACTION
INTERACTIONISM
INTERACTIVE
INTERADDITIVE
INTERAGENT
INTERALLIED
INTERAMNIAN
INTERATOMIC
INTERAXAL
INTERAXIAL
INTERAXIS
INTERBANDED
INTERBED
INTERBEDDED
INTERBLEND
INTERBLENDED
INTERBLENDING
INTERBLENT
INTERBONDING
INTERBOROUGH
INTERBOURSE
INTERBRAIN
INTERBREED
INTERBREEDING
INTERCADENCE
INTERCADENT
INTERCALARE
INTERCALARIUM
INTERCALARY
INTERCALATE
INTERCALATED
INTERCALATING
INTERCALATION
INTERCANAL
INTERCARDINAL
INTERCAROTID
INTERCARPAL
INTERCEDE
INTERCEDED
INTERCEDER
INTERCEDING
INTERCENSAL
INTERCENTRA
INTERCENTRAL
INTERCENTRUM
INTERCEPT
INTERCEPTED
INTERCEPTER
INTERCEPTING
INTERCEPTION
INTERCEPTIVE
INTERCEPTOR
INTERCESS
INTERCESSION
INTERCESSIVE
INTERCESSOR
INTERCESSORY
INTERCHANGE
INTERCHANGEABLE
INTERCHANGED
INTERCHANGER
INTERCHANGING
INTERCHURCH
INTERCILIARY
INTERCILIUM
INTERCISION
INTERCIVIC
INTERCLAVICLE
INTERCLOUD
INTERCLUDE
INTERCLUSION
INTERCOASTAL
INTERCOLLEGE
INTERCOLLINE
INTERCOLONIAL
INTERCOLUMNIATION
INTERCOM
INTERCOMMON
INTERCOMMONED
INTERCOMMONING
INTERCOMMUNE
INTERCOMMUNED
INTERCOMMUNICATION
INTERCOMMUNING
INTERCONNECTED
INTERCONNECTING
INTERCONNECTION
INTERCOOLER
INTERCOOLING
INTERCOSMIC
INTERCOSTAL
INTERCOURSE
INTERCROP
INTERCROPPED
INTERCROPPING
INTERCROSS
INTERCROSSED
INTERCROSSING
INTERCUR
INTERCURRENT
INTERCUT
INTERDEAL
INTERDEALER
INTERDENTAL
INTERDENTIL
INTERDEPEND
INTERDEPENDENT
INTERDICT
INTERDICTION
INTERDICTIVE
INTERDICTOR
INTERDICTORY
INTERDIGITATE
INTERDIGITATED
INTERDIGITATING
INTERDOME
INTERESS
INTERESSE
INTERESSEE
INTEREST
INTERESTED
INTERESTER
INTERESTING
INTERESTINGLY
INTERESTS
INTERFACE
INTERFACIAL
INTERFECTOR
INTERFERANT
INTERFERE
INTERFERED
INTERFERENCE
INTERFERENT
INTERFERER
INTERFERING
INTERFEROMETER
INTERFERON
INTERFERRIC
INTERFERTILE
INTERFILAR
INTERFINGER
INTERFLANGE
INTERFLOW
INTERFLUENCE
INTERFLUENT
INTERFLUOUS
INTERFLUVE
INTERFLUVIAL
INTERFOLD
INTERFOLIATE
INTERFRET
INTERFRETTED
INTERFRONTAL
INTERFUSE
INTERFUSED
INTERFUSING
INTERFUSION
INTERGLACIAL
INTERGLYPH
INTERGRADE
INTERGRADED
INTERGRADING
INTERGRAFT
INTERGRAVE
INTERGROW
INTERGROWN
INTERGROWTH
INTERGULAR
INTERHAEMAL
INTERHEMAL
INTERHYAL
INTERIEUR
INTERIM
INTERIMIST
INTERIMISTIC
INTERIONIC
INTERIOR
INTERIORITY
INTERJACENCE
INTERJACENT
INTERJECT
INTERJECTED
INTERJECTING
INTERJECTION
INTERJECTOR
INTERJECTORY
INTERJOIN
INTERJOIST
INTERJUNCTION
INTERKINESIS
INTERKINETIC
INTERKNIT
INTERKNOT
INTERKNOW
INTERLACE
INTERLACED
INTERLACEDLY
INTERLACEMENT
INTERLACERY
INTERLACING
INTERLAID
INTERLAMINATE
INTERLAMINATED

INTERLAMINATING
INTERLAP
INTERLAPSE
INTERLARD
INTERLARDED
INTERLARDING
INTERLAY
INTERLAYING
INTERLEAF
INTERLEAGUE
INTERLEAVE
INTERLEAVED
INTERLEAVER
INTERLEAVES
INTERLEAVING
INTERLIBEL
INTERLINE
INTERLINEAL
INTERLINEAR
INTERLINEARLY
INTERLINEARY
INTERLINEATE
INTERLINED
INTERLINER
INTERLINGUAL
INTERLINING
INTERLINK
INTERLINKED
INTERLOCAL
INTERLOCATE
INTERLOCK
INTERLOCKED
INTERLOCKER
INTERLOCKING
INTERLOCULUS
INTERLOCUTION
INTERLOCUTIVE
INTERLOCUTOR
INTERLOCUTORY
INTERLOPE
INTERLOPED
INTERLOPER
INTERLOPING
INTERLOT
INTERLUCENT
INTERLUDE
INTERLUDER
INTERLUDIAL
INTERLUNAR
INTERLUNARY
INTERLUNATION
INTERMARRIED
INTERMARRY
INTERMARRYING
INTERMASTOID
INTERMEDDLE
INTERMEDDLED
INTERMEDDLER
INTERMEDDLING
INTERMEDE
INTERMEDIA
INTERMEDIACY
INTERMEDIAE
INTERMEDIAL
INTERMEDIARIES
INTERMEDIARY
INTERMEDIATE
INTERMEDIATED
INTERMEDIATING
INTERMEDIATOR
INTERMEDIUM
INTERMEDIUS
INTERMEMBRAL
INTERMENT
INTERMENTION
INTERMESH
INTERMESSAGE
INTERMEW
INTERMEWED
INTERMEWER
INTERMEZZI
INTERMEZZO
INTERMEZZOS
INTERMINABLE
INTERMINANT
INTERMINATE
INTERMINATED
INTERMINE
INTERMINED
INTERMINGLE
INTERMINGLED
INTERMINGLING
INTERMINING
INTERMISSION
INTERMISSIVE
INTERMIT
INTERMITTED
INTERMITTENT
INTERMITTENTLY
INTERMITTING
INTERMIX
INTERMIXED
INTERMIXEDLY
INTERMIXING
INTERMIXT
INTERMIXTLY
INTERMIXTURE
INTERMURAL
INTERMUTATION
INTERMUTUAL
INTERN
INTERNAL
INTERNALITIES
INTERNALITY
INTERNALIZE
INTERNALLY
INTERNALNESS
INTERNARIAL
INTERNASAL
INTERNATION
INTERNATIONAL
INTERNE
INTERNECINE
INTERNECION
INTERNECIVE
INTERNECT
INTERNECTION
INTERNED
INTERNEE
INTERNETTED
INTERNEURAL
INTERNEURON
INTERNING
INTERNIST
INTERNMENT
INTERNOBASAL
INTERNODAL
INTERNODE
INTERNODIA
INTERNODIAL
INTERNODIAN
INTERNODIUM
INTERNSHIP
INTERNUCLEAR
INTERNUNCIAL
INTERNUNCIO
INTERNUNCIOS
INTERNUPTIAL
INTERNUPTIALS
INTEROCEPTOR
INTEROCULAR
INTEROLIVARY
INTEROPERCLE
INTEROPTIC
INTEROSCULANT
INTEROSCULATE
INTEROSCULATED
INTEROSCULATING
INTEROSSEAL
INTEROSSEI
INTEROSSEOUS
INTEROSSEUS
INTERPAGE
INTERPASS
INTERPAUSE
INTERPEAL
INTERPEL
INTERPELLANT
INTERPELLATE
INTERPELLATED
INTERPELLATING
INTERPELLATION
INTERPELLED
INTERPELLING
INTERPENDENT
INTERPENETRATE
INTERPENETRATE
INTERPHASE
INTERPIECE
INTERPLACE
INTERPLAIT
INTERPLAY
INTERPLEA
INTERPLEAD
INTERPLEADER
INTERPLEURAL
INTERPLICATE
INTERPOINT
INTERPOLABLE
INTERPOLAR
INTERPOLARY
INTERPOLATE
INTERPOLATED
INTERPOLATER
INTERPOLATING
INTERPOLATION
INTERPOLATOR
INTERPOLE
INTERPOLISH
INTERPOLITY
INTERPONE
INTERPORTAL
INTERPOSAL
INTERPOSE
INTERPOSED
INTERPOSER
INTERPOSING
INTERPOSURE
INTERPRET
INTERPRETABLE
INTERPRETATE
INTERPRETATION
INTERPRETED
INTERPRETER
INTERPRETING
INTERPRETIVE
INTERPUBIC
INTERRACIAL
INTERRADIAL
INTERRADII
INTERRADIUM
INTERRADIUS
INTERRAMAL
INTERRED
INTERREGAL
INTERREGES
INTERREGNA
INTERREGNAL
INTERREGNUM
INTERREIGN
INTERRELATE
INTERRELATED
INTERRELATING
INTERRELATION
INTERRELATIONS
INTERRENAL
INTERRER
INTERREX
INTERRIGHT
INTERRING
INTERROGANT
INTERROGATE
INTERROGATED
INTERROGATEE
INTERROGATING
INTERROGATION
INTERROGATOR
INTERROGEE
INTERRUPT
INTERRUPTED
INTERRUPTER
INTERRUPTING
INTERRUPTION
INTERRUPTIVE
INTERRUPTOR
INTERSCRIBE
INTERSEAMED
INTERSECT
INTERSECTANT
INTERSECTED
INTERSECTING
INTERSECTION
INTERSEPTAL
INTERSERTAL
INTERSESSION
INTERSEX
INTERSEXUAL
INTERSEXUALITY
INTERSHOCK
INTERSHOOT
INTERSOCIAL
INTERSOMNIAL
INTERSOW
INTERSPACE
INTERSPATIAL
INTERSPEAKER
INTERSPERSAL
INTERSPERSE
INTERSPERSED
INTERSPERSING
INTERSPHERE
INTERSPINAL
INTERSPINOUS
INTERSPORAL
INTERSTADIAL
INTERSTAGE
INTERSTATE
INTERSTELLAR
INTERSTERILE
INTERSTERNAL
INTERSTICE
INTERSTICED
INTERSTICES
INTERSTITIAL
INTERSTRATIFY
INTERSTRIAL
INTERTALK
INTERTANGLE
INTERTEAR
INTERTERGAL
INTERTEX
INTERTEXTURE
INTERTIDAL
INTERTIE
INTERTILL
INTERTILLAGE
INTERTISSUED
INTERTONE
INTERTONGUE
INTERTONIC
INTERTRAGIAN
INTERTRIBAL
INTERTRIGO
INTERTROPIC
INTERTROPICS
INTERTRUDE
INTERTWINE
INTERTWINED
INTERTWINING
INTERTWIST
INTERTWISTED
INTERTWISTING
INTERURBAN
INTERVAL
INTERVALE
INTERVALED
INTERVALING
INTERVALLED
INTERVALLIC
INTERVALLING
INTERVALS
INTERVEIN
INTERVEINAL
INTERVEINED
INTERVEINING
INTERVENANT
INTERVENE
INTERVENED
INTERVENER
INTERVENIENT
INTERVENING
INTERVENIUM
INTERVENOR
INTERVENT
INTERVENTION
INTERVENTIVE
INTERVENTOR
INTERVENULAR
INTERVERBAL
INTERVERSION
INTERVERT
INTERVERTED
INTERVERTING
INTERVIEW
INTERVIEWED
INTERVIEWEE
INTERVIEWER
INTERVIEWING
INTERVILLOUS
INTERVISIT
INTERVITAL
INTERVOCAL
INTERVOCALIC
INTERVOLVE
INTERVOLVED
INTERVOLVING
INTERWEAVE
INTERWEAVED
INTERWEAVER
INTERWEAVING
INTERWED
INTERWIND
INTERWINDING
INTERWORK
INTERWORKED
INTERWORKING
INTERWOUND
INTERWOVE
INTERWOVEN
INTERWREATHE
INTERWREATHED
INTERWREATHING
INTERWROUGHT
INTERXYLARY
INTERZONAL

INTESTABLE
INTESTACIES
INTESTACY
INTESTATE
INTESTATION
INTESTINAL
INTESTINE
INTESTINES
INTEXINE
INTEXT
INTEXTINE
INTEXTURE
INTHRAL
INTHRALL
INTHRALLMENT
INTHRALMENT
INTHRONE
INTHRONG
INTHRONISTIC
INTHRONIZATE
INTHRONIZE
INTHROW
INTHRUST
INTIL
INTILL
INTIMA
INTIMACIES
INTIMACY
INTIMADO
INTIMADOS
INTIMAE
INTIMAL
INTIMATE
INTIMATED
INTIMATELY
INTIMATENESS
INTIMATER
INTIMATING
INTIMATION
INTIME
INTIMIDATE
INTIMIDATED
INTIMIDATING
INTIMIDATION
INTIMIDATOR
INTIMISM
INTIMITY
INTINCT
INTINCTION
INTINE
INTISY
INTITLE
INTITULE
INTITULED
INTITULING
INTO
INTOED
INTOLERABLE
INTOLERABLY
INTOLERANCE
INTOLERANCY
INTOLERANT
INTOLERANTLY
INTOLERATING
INTOLERATION
INTOMB
INTONABLE
INTONACO
INTONATE
INTONATED
INTONATING
INTONATION
INTONATOR
INTONE
INTONED
INTONER
INTONING
INTOOTHED
INTORSION
INTORT
INTORTED
INTORTILLAGE
INTORTING
INTOWER
INTOWN
INTOXATION
INTOXICABLE
INTOXICANT
INTOXICATE
INTOXICATED
INTOXICATING
INTOXICATION
INTOXICATIVE
INTOXICATOR
INTRA
INTRABIONTIC
INTRABRED
INTRACARDIAC
INTRACHORDAL
INTRACISTERN
INTRACOASTAL
INTRACTABLE
INTRACTABLY
INTRACTILE
INTRADA
INTRADO
INTRADOS
INTRADURAL
INTRAFUSAL
INTRAGANTES
INTRAGLACIAL
INTRAGROUP
INTRAGROUPAL
INTRAIL
INTRAIT
INTRALOGICAL
INTRAMENTAL
INTRAMONTANE
INTRAMUNDANE
INTRAMURAL
INTRAMURALLY
INTRANATAL
INTRANEOUS
INTRANSIENT
INTRANSIGENT
INTRANSITABLE
INTRANSITIVE
INTRANT
INTRAPIAL
INTRAPOLAR
INTRAPSYCHIC
INTRASTATE
INTRATE
INTRATHECAL
INTRATHYROID
INTRAUTERINE
INTRAVAGINAL
INTRAVENOUS
INTRAVITAL
INTRAXYLARY
INTREAT
INTRENCH
INTRENCHANT
INTRENCHED
INTRENCHER
INTRENCHING
INTREPID
INTREPIDITY
INTREPIDLY
INTREPIDNESS
INTRICACIES
INTRICACY
INTRICATE
INTRICATELY
INTRIGANT
INTRIGANTE
INTRIGANTS
INTRIGO
INTRIGUE
INTRIGUED
INTRIGUER
INTRIGUERY
INTRIGUING
INTRIGUINGLY
INTRINE
INTRINSE
INTRINSIC
INTRINSICAL
INTRINSICALLY
INTRINSICATE
INTRO
INTROCEPTIVE
INTRODDEN
INTRODUCE
INTRODUCED
INTRODUCEE
INTRODUCER
INTRODUCING
INTRODUCTION
INTRODUCTIVE
INTRODUCTOR
INTRODUCTORY
INTROFACTION
INTROFIED
INTROFIER
INTROFLEX
INTROFLEXION
INTROFY
INTROFYING
INTROIT
INTROITUS
INTROJECTION
INTROMISSION
INTROMISSIVE
INTROMIT
INTROMITTED
INTROMITTENT
INTROMITTER
INTROMITTING
INTROPULSIVE
INTRORSE
INTRORSELY
INTROSPECT
INTROSPECTED
INTROSPECTING
INTROSPECTION
INTROSPECTOR
INTROSUSCEPT
INTROVENIENT
INTROVERSE
INTROVERSION
INTROVERSIVE
INTROVERT
INTROVERTED
INTROVERTING
INTROVERTIVE
INTRUDANCE
INTRUDE
INTRUDED
INTRUDER
INTRUDING
INTRUDINGLY
INTRUS
INTRUSE
INTRUSION
INTRUSIONAL
INTRUSIONIST
INTRUSIVE
INTRUSIVELY
INTRUSO
INTRUST
INTUBATE
INTUBATION
INTUBATOR
INTUBE
INTUE
INTUENT
INTUICITY
INTUIT
INTUITABLE
INTUITION
INTUITIONAL
INTUITIONISM
INTUITIONIST
INTUITIVE
INTUITIVELY
INTUITIVISM
INTUITIVIST
INTUMESCE
INTUMESCED
INTUMESCENCE
INTUMESCENT
INTUMESCING
INTURBIDATE
INTURN
INTURNED
INTURNING
INTUSE
INTUSSUSCEPT
INTWINE
INTWIST
INUKSHUK
INULA
INULACEOUS
INULASE
INULIN
INULOID
INUMBRATE
INUNCT
INUNCTION
INUNCTUM
INUND
INUNDABLE
INUNDANT
INUNDATE
INUNDATED
INUNDATING
INUNDATION
INUNDATOR
INUNDATORY
INURBANE
INURBANITY
INURE
INURED
INUREDNESS
INURING
INURN
INURNED
INURNING
INUSITATE
INUSITATION
INUSTION
INUTILE
INUTILELY
INUTILITIES
INUTILITY
INUTTERABLE
INVACCINATE
INVADE
INVADED
INVADER
INVADERS
INVADING
INVAGINABLE
INVAGINATE
INVAGINATED
INVAGINATING
INVAGINATION
INVALESCENCE
INVALID
INVALIDATE
INVALIDATED
INVALIDATING
INVALIDATOR
INVALIDED
INVALIDING
INVALIDISM
INVALIDITY
INVALUABLE
INVALUABLY
INVALUED
INVARIABLE
INVARIABLENESS
INVARIABLY
INVARIANCE
INVARIANCY
INVARIANT
INVARIANTIVE
INVARIANTLY
INVARIED
INVASION
INVASIVE
INVECT
INVECTED
INVECTION
INVECTIVE
INVECTIVELY
INVEIGH
INVEIGHED
INVEIGHER
INVEIGHING
INVEIGLE
INVEIGLED
INVEIGLER
INVEIGLING
INVEIL
INVENIENT
INVENIT
INVENT
INVENTARY
INVENTED
INVENTER
INVENTIBLE
INVENTING
INVENTION
INVENTIONAL
INVENTIVE
INVENTIVELY
INVENTIVENESS
INVENTOR
INVENTORIAL
INVENTORIED
INVENTORIES
INVENTORY
INVENTORYING
INVERACITY
INVERITY
INVERMINATE
INVERSE
INVERSED
INVERSEDLY
INVERSELY
INVERSION
INVERSIVE
INVERT
INVERTASE
INVERTEBRAL
INVERTEBRATE
INVERTED
INVERTEDLY
INVERTEND
INVERTER
INVERTIBLE
INVERTILE
INVERTIN

INVERTING
INVERTOR
INVEST
INVESTED
INVESTIENT
INVESTIGABLE
INVESTIGATE
INVESTIGATED
INVESTIGATING
INVESTIGATION
INVESTIGATOR
INVESTING
INVESTITIVE
INVESTITOR
INVESTITURE
INVESTMENT
INVESTOR
INVETERACY
INVETERATE
INVETERATELY
INVIABLE
INVIABLY
INVICT
INVICTED
INVICTIVE
INVIDIOUS
INVIDIOUSLY
INVIGILATE
INVIGILATION
INVIGILATOR
INVIGORANT
INVIGORATE
INVIGORATED
INVIGORATING
INVIGORATION
INVIGORATIVE
INVIGORATOR
INVINATE
INVINATION
INVINCIBLE
INVINCIBLY
INVIOLABILITY
INVIOLABLE
INVIOLABLY
INVIOLACY
INVIOLATE
INVIOLATELY
INVIOUS
INVIOUSNESS
INVIRTUATE
INVISCATE
INVISED
INVISIBILITY
INVISIBLE
INVISIBLY
INVITANT
INVITATION
INVITATIONAL
INVITATORY
INVITE
INVITED
INVITEE
INVITER
INVITING
INVITINGLY
INVITINGNESS
INVIVID
INVOCABLE
INVOCANT
INVOCATE
INVOCATION
INVOCATIVE
INVOCATOR
INVOCATORY
INVOICE
INVOICED
INVOICING
INVOKE
INVOKED
INVOKER
INVOKING
INVOLUCEL
INVOLUCRA
INVOLUCRAL
INVOLUCRATE
INVOLUCRE
INVOLUCRED
INVOLUCRUM
INVOLUNTARY
INVOLUTE
INVOLUTED
INVOLUTEDLY
INVOLUTION
INVOLUTIONAL
INVOLUTORIAL
INVOLUTORY
INVOLVE
INVOLVED
INVOLVEMENT
INVOLVENT
INVOLVER
INVOLVING
INVULNERABLE
INVULNERABLY
INVULTUATION
INWALE
INWALL
INWANDERING
INWARD
INWARDLY
INWARDNESS
INWARDS
INWEAVE
INWEDGED
INWEED
INWEIGHT
INWICK
INWIND
INWINDING
INWIT
INWITH
INWORK
INWORKS
INWORN
INWOUND
INWOVEN
INWRAP
INWRAPPED
INWRAPPING
INWRAPT
INWREATHE
INWRIT
INWRITTEN
INWROUGHT
INYALA
INYOITE
INYOKE
IOA
IOD
IODATE
IODATED
IODATING
IODATION
IODIC
IODID
IODIDE
IODIN
IODINATE
IODINATION
IODINE
IODINOPHIL
IODINOPHILE
IODINOPHILIC
IODISM
IODIZATION
IODIZE
IODIZED
IODIZER
IODIZING
IODO
IODOBEHENATE
IODOBENZENE
IODOBROMITE
IODOCASEIN
IODOCHLORID
IODOCHLORIDE
IODOCRESOL
IODODERMA
IODOETHANE
IODOFORM
IODOGALLICIN
IODOHYDRIN
IODOL
IODOMETHANE
IODOMETRIC
IODOMETRY
IODONIUM
IODOSO
IODOSPONGIN
IODOTHERAPY
IODOTHYRIN
IODOUS
IODOXY
IODYRITE
IOLITE
ION
IONIC
IONICAL
IONIUM
IONIZABLE
IONIZATION
IONIZE
IONIZER
IONOGEN
IONOGENIC
IONONE
IONOPAUSE
IONOSPHERE
IOTA
IOTACISM
IOTACISMUS
IOTACIST
IOTAS
IOTIZATION
IOTIZE
IOTIZED
IOTIZING
IPECAC
IPECACUANHA
IPECACUANHIC
IPETE
IPI
IPID
IPIL
IPILIPIL
IPITI
IPO
IPOMEA
IPOMOEIN
IPSE
IPSEAND
IPSEITY
IR
IRACUND
IRACUNDITY
IRACUNDULOUS
IRADE
IRASCENT
IRASCIBILITY
IRASCIBLE
IRASCIBLY
IRATE
IRATELY
IRBIS
IRCHIN
IRE
IREFUL
IREFULLY
IREFULNESS
IRENARCH
IRENIC
IRENICA
IRENICAL
IRENICALLY
IRENICISM
IRENICIST
IRENICON
IRENICS
IREOS
IRIAN
IRID
IRIDACEOUS
IRIDAL
IRIDATE
IRIDECTOMIES
IRIDECTOMY
IRIDEOUS
IRIDES
IRIDESCE
IRIDESCENCE
IRIDESCENCY
IRIDESCENT
IRIDESCENTLY
IRIDIATE
IRIDIC
IRIDICAL
IRIDIN
IRIDINE
IRIDIOUS
IRIDITE
IRIDIUM
IRIDIZATION
IRIDIZE
IRIDIZED
IRIDIZING
IRIDOCYTE
IRIDODESIS
IRIDODONESIS
IRIDOPHORE
IRIDOPLEGIA
IRIDOSMINE
IRIDOTASIS
IRIDOTOMIES
IRIDOTOMY
IRIRI
IRIS
IRISATED
IRISATION
IRISCOPE
IRISED
IRISES
IRISIN
IRISING
IRISROOT
IRITIC
IRITIS
IRK
IRKED
IRKING
IRKSOME
IRKSOMELY
IRKSOMENESS
IRNE
IROK
IROKO
IRON
IRONBACK
IRONBARK
IRONBOUND
IRONBUSH
IRONCLAD
IRONE
IRONED
IRONER
IRONFISTED
IRONFLOWER
IRONHANDED
IRONHARD
IRONHEAD
IRONHEADED
IRONHEARTED
IRONIC
IRONICAL
IRONICALLY
IRONICALNESS
IRONICE
IRONIES
IRONING
IRONIOUSLY
IRONISH
IRONISM
IRONIST
IRONIZE
IRONLESS
IRONLIKE
IRONLY
IRONMAN
IRONMASTER
IRONMEN
IRONMONGER
IRONMONGERY
IRONNESS
IRONS
IRONSHOD
IRONSHOT
IRONSIDE
IRONSIDED
IRONSIDES
IRONSMITH
IRONSTONE
IRONWARE
IRONWEED
IRONWOOD
IRONWORK
IRONWORKED
IRONWORKER
IRONWORKING
IRONWORKS
IRONWORT
IRONY
IROUS
IRPE
IRRADIANCE
IRRADIANCY
IRRADIANT
IRRADIATE
IRRADIATED
IRRADIATING
IRRADIATION
IRRADIATIVE
IRRADIATOR
IRRADICABLE
IRRADICATE
IRRAREFIABLE
IRRATIONABLE
IRRATIONAL
IRRATIONALLY
IRREALITY
IRREALIZABLE
IRREBUTTABLE
IRRECEPTIVE
IRRECIPROCAL
IRRECLAIMED
IRRECONCILE
IRRECORDABLE

IRRECUSABLE
IRREDEEMABLE
IRREDEEMABLY
IRREDENTA
IRREDENTIAL
IRREDRESSIBLE
IRREDUCIBLE
IRREDUCIBLY
IRREDUCTIBLE
IRREDUCTION
IRREFERABLE
IRREFLECTION
IRREFLECTIVE
IRREFLEXIVE
IRREFORMABLE
IRREFRAGABLE
IRREFRANGIBLE
IRREFUSABLE
IRREFUTABLE
IRREGARDLESS
IRREGENERACY
IRREGENERATE
IRREGULAR
IRREGULARIST
IRREGULARITIES
IRREGULARITY
IRREGULARIZE
IRREGULARLY
IRREGULATE
IRREGULATED
IRREGULOUS
IRRELATE
IRRELATED
IRRELATION
IRRELATIVE
IRRELATIVELY
IRRELEVANCE
IRRELEVANCIES
IRRELEVANCY
IRRELEVANT
IRRELEVANTLY
IRRELIEVABLE
IRRELIGION
IRRELIGIOUS
IRRELUCTANT
IRREMEABLE
IRREMEABLY
IRREMEDIABLE
IRREMEDIABLY
IRREMEDILESS
IRREMISSIBLE
IRREMISSIBLY
IRREMISSIVE
IRREMOVABLE
IRREMOVABLY
IRRENDERABLE
IRRENEWABLE
IRREPAIR
IRREPAIRABLE
IRREPARABLE
IRREPARABLY
IRREPASSABLE
IRREPEALABLE
IRREPEALABLY
IRREPENTANCE
IRREPENTANT
IRREPORTABLE
IRREPRESSIVE
IRREPROACHABLE
IRREPROVABLE
IRREPROVABLY
IRREPTITIOUS
IRRESILIENT
IRRESISTANCE
IRRESISTIBLE
IRRESISTIBLY
IRRESOLUBLE
IRRESOLUTE
IRRESOLUTELY
IRRESOLUTION
IRRESOLVABLE
IRRESOLVED
IRRESOLVEDLY
IRRESONANCE
IRRESONANT
IRRESPECTABLE
IRRESPECTFUL
IRRESPECTIVE
IRRESPIRABLE
IRRESPONSIBLE
IRRESPONSIVE
IRRESTRICTIVE
IRRESULTIVE
IRRETENTION
IRRETENTIVE
IRRETICENCE
IRRETICENT
IRRETRACEABLE
IRRETRACTABLE
IRRETRACTILE
IRRETRIEVABLE
IRRETURNABLE
IRREVEALABLE
IRREVEALABLY
IRREVERENCE
IRREVEREND
IRREVERENDLY
IRREVERENT
IRREVERENTLY
IRREVERSIBLE
IRREVERSIBLY
IRREVERTIBLE
IRREVISABLE
IRREVOCABLE
IRREVOCABLY
IRREVOLUBLE
IRRIDE
IRRIGABLE
IRRIGABLY
IRRIGANT
IRRIGATE
IRRIGATED
IRRIGATING
IRRIGATION
IRRIGATIONAL
IRRIGATIVE
IRRIGATOR
IRRIGATORY
IRRIGUOUS
IRRISION
IRRISOR
IRRISORY
IRRITABILITIES
IRRITABILITY
IRRITABLE
IRRITABLY
IRRITAMENT
IRRITANCIES
IRRITANCY
IRRITANT
IRRITATE
IRRITATED
IRRITATING
IRRITATINGLY
IRRITATION
IRRITATIVE
IRRITATOR
IRRITATORY
IRRITE
IRRITOMOTILE
IRROGATE
IRRORATE
IRRORATION
IRROTATIONAL
IRRUBRICAL
IRRUGATE
IRRUPT
IRRUPTED
IRRUPTIBLE
IRRUPTING
IRRUPTION
IRRUPTIVE
IRRUPTIVELY
IRUL
IRY
IS
ISABELINA
ISABELITA
ISABELITE
ISABNORMAL
ISACOUSTIC
ISADELPHOUS
ISAGOGE
ISAGOGIC
ISAGOGICAL
ISAGOGICALLY
ISAGOGICS
ISAGON
ISALLOBAR
ISALLOTHERM
ISAMIN
ISAMINE
ISANDROUS
ISANEMONE
ISANOMAL
ISANOMALOUS
ISANTHOUS
ISAPOSTOLIC
ISARIOID
ISATATE
ISATIC
ISATID
ISATIDE
ISATIN
ISATINE
ISATOGEN
ISATOGENIC
ISBA
ISCHAR
ISCHEMIA
ISCHIA
ISCHIAC
ISCHIADIC
ISCHIALGIA
ISCHIALGIC
ISCHIATIC
ISCHIDROSIS
ISCHIOCERITE
ISCHIOPODITE
ISCHIOPUBIS
ISCHIUM
ISCHOCHOLIA
ISCHURETIC
ISCHURIA
ISCHURY
ISE
ISEL
ISENERGIC
ISENTROPIC
ISEPIPTESIAL
ISEPIPTESIS
ISERINE
ISERITE
ISETHIONATE
ISH
ISHPINGO
ISIDIA
ISIDIOID
ISIDIOSE
ISIDIUM
ISING
ISINGLASS
ISLAND
ISLANDED
ISLANDER
ISLANDIC
ISLANDING
ISLANDMAN
ISLANDMEN
ISLANDRY
ISLANDS
ISLANDY
ISLAY
ISLE
ISLED
ISLEMAN
ISLESMEN
ISLET
ISLETED
ISLING
ISLOT
ISM
ISMAL
ISMATIC
ISMATICAL
ISMY
ISNAD
ISO
ISOAMID
ISOAMIDE
ISOAMYL
ISOBAR
ISOBARE
ISOBARIC
ISOBARISM
ISOBASE
ISOBATH
ISOBATHIC
ISOBORNEOL
ISOBRONT
ISOBRONTON
ISOBUTYRIC
ISOCARPIC
ISOCARPOUS
ISOCELLULAR
ISOCEPHALIC
ISOCEPHALISM
ISOCEPHALY
ISOCERCAL
ISOCERCY
ISOCHASM
ISOCHASMIC
ISOCHEIM
ISOCHEIMAL
ISOCHEIMENAL
ISOCHEIMIC
ISOCHELA
ISOCHLOR
ISOCHOR
ISOCHORE
ISOCHORIC
ISOCHROMATIC
ISOCHRONAL
ISOCHRONALLY
ISOCHRONE
ISOCHRONIC
ISOCHRONISM
ISOCHRONIZE
ISOCHRONIZED
ISOCHRONIZING
ISOCHRONON
ISOCHRONOUS
ISOCHROOUS
ISOCLASITE
ISOCLINAL
ISOCLINE
ISOCLINIC
ISOCOLA
ISOCOLIC
ISOCOLON
ISOCORIA
ISOCRACY
ISOCRAT
ISOCRATIC
ISOCRYMAL
ISOCRYME
ISOCRYMIC
ISOCYANATE
ISOCYANIC
ISOCYANID
ISOCYANIDE
ISOCYANIN
ISOCYANINE
ISOCYANO
ISOCYTIC
ISODACTYLOUS
ISODIABATIC
ISODIAMETRIC
ISODOMON
ISODOMOUS
ISODOMUM
ISODONT
ISODONTOUS
ISODRIN
ISODROME
ISODYNAMIA
ISODYNAMIC
ISOELECTRIC
ISOENERGETIC
ISOEUGENOL
ISOGAM
ISOGAMETE
ISOGAMETIC
ISOGAMETISM
ISOGAMIC
ISOGAMOUS
ISOGAMY
ISOGEN
ISOGENESIS
ISOGENETIC
ISOGENIC
ISOGENOTYPE
ISOGENOUS
ISOGENY
ISOGEOTHERM
ISOGLOSS
ISOGLOSSAL
ISOGLOSSES
ISOGNATHISM
ISOGNATHOUS
ISOGON
ISOGONAL
ISOGONALITY
ISOGONALLY
ISOGONIC
ISOGONIOSTAT
ISOGONISM
ISOGRAFT
ISOGRAM
ISOGRAPH
ISOGRAPHIC
ISOGRAPHY
ISOGRIV
ISOGYNOUS
ISOGYRE
ISOHALSINE
ISOHEL
ISOHYDRIC
ISOHYET
ISOHYETAL
ISOKERAUNIC
ISOKONTAN
ISOLABILITY
ISOLABLE
ISOLATE

ISOLATED
ISOLATING
ISOLATION
ISOLATIONISM
ISOLATIONIST
ISOLATIVE
ISOLATOR
ISOLEAD
ISOLETTE
ISOLEUCINE
ISOLICHENIN
ISOLINE
ISOLOG
ISOLOGOUS
ISOLOGUE
ISOLOGY
ISOLYSIN
ISOLYSIS
ISOMAGNETIC
ISOMALTOSE
ISOMASTIGATE
ISOMER
ISOMERE
ISOMERIC
ISOMERICAL
ISOMERICALLY
ISOMERIDE
ISOMERISM
ISOMERIZE
ISOMEROUS
ISOMERY
ISOMETRIC
ISOMETRICAL
ISOMETROGRAPH
ISOMETROPIA
ISOMETRY
ISOMORPH
ISOMORPHIC
ISOMORPHISM
ISOMORPHOUS
ISOMYARIAN
ISONEPH
ISONEPHELIC
ISONIAZID
ISONITRIL
ISONITRILE
ISONITRO
ISONITROSO
ISONOMIC
ISONOMOUS
ISONOMY
ISONUCLEAR
ISONYM
ISONYMIC
ISONYMY
ISOOCTANE
ISOPACHOUS
ISOPAG
ISOPARAFFIN
ISOPERIMETER
ISOPERIMETRY
ISOPETALOUS
ISOPHANAL
ISOPHANE
ISOPHASAL
ISOPHENE
ISOPHORIA
ISOPHOTE
ISOPHTHALIC
ISOPHTHALYL
ISOPHYLLOUS
ISOPHYLLY
ISOPIESTIC
ISOPLERE
ISOPLETH
ISOPOD
ISOPODAN
ISOPODIFORM
ISOPODOUS
ISOPOGONOUS
ISOPOLITE
ISOPOLITICAL
ISOPOLITY
ISOPOLY
ISOPRENE
ISOPROPENYL
ISOPROPYL
ISOPSEPHIC
ISOPSEPHISM
ISOPTEROUS
ISOPTIC
ISOPYCNIC
ISOPYRE
ISOQUINOLINE
ISORHYTHM
ISORITHM
ISORRHYTHMIC
ISORROPIC
ISOSCELE
ISOSCELES
ISOSCOPE
ISOSEISMAL
ISOSEISMIC
ISOSMOTIC
ISOSPORE
ISOSPORIC
ISOSPOROUS
ISOSPORY
ISOSTASIST
ISOSTASY
ISOSTATIC
ISOSTATICAL
ISOSTEMONY
ISOSTER
ISOSTERE
ISOSTERIC
ISOSTERISM
ISOTAC
ISOTACH
ISOTE
ISOTELES
ISOTELY
ISOTHERAL
ISOTHERE
ISOTHERM
ISOTHERMAL
ISOTHERMIC
ISOTHERMICAL
ISOTHERMOUS
ISOTHIOCYANO
ISOTOME
ISOTOMOUS
ISOTONE
ISOTONIA
ISOTONIC
ISOTONICITY
ISOTOPE
ISOTOPIC
ISOTOPISM
ISOTOPY
ISOTRON
ISOTROPE
ISOTROPIC
ISOTROPISM
ISOTROPOUS
ISOTROPY
ISOTYPE
ISOTYPIC
ISOTYPICAL
ISOVALERATE
ISOXAZOLE
ISOZOOID
ISPAGHUL
ISPRAYNIK
ISSITE
ISSUABLE
ISSUANCE
ISSUANT
ISSUE
ISSUED
ISSUER
ISSUING
IST
ISTHMI
ISTHMIAN
ISTHMIATE
ISTHMIC
ISTHMOID
ISTHMUS
ISTHMUSES
ISTLE
ISURETINE
ISUROID
IT
ITABIRITE
ITAC
ITACISM
ITACIST
ITACISTIC
ITACOLUMITE
ITACONIC
ITALIC
ITALICIZE
ITALICIZED
ITALICIZING
ITALICS
ITALITE
ITAUBA
ITCH
ITCHED
ITCHEOGLAN
ITCHIER
ITCHIEST
ITCHING
ITCHINGLY
ITCHLESS
ITCHREED
ITCHWEED
ITCHWOOD
ITCHY
ITCZE
ITEM
ITEMING
ITEMIZATION
ITEMIZE
ITEMIZED
ITEMIZER
ITEMIZING
ITEMS
ITEMY
ITER
ITERABLE
ITERANCE
ITERANCY
ITERANT
ITERATE
ITERATED
ITERATELY
ITERATING
ITERATION
ITERATIVE
ITERATIVELY
ITERS
ITERUM
ITHAGINE
ITHAND
ITHER
ITHOMIID
ITHYPHALLIC
ITINERACY
ITINERANCY
ITINERANT
ITINERANTLY
ITINERARIAN
ITINERARIES
ITINERARY
ITINERATE
ITINERATED
ITINERATING
ITINERATION
ITMO
ITOUBOU
ITR
ITS
ITSELF
ITZEBU
IUS
IVA
IVIED
IVIES
IVIN
IVORIED
IVORIES
IVORINE
IVORINESS
IVORIST
IVORY
IVORYTYPE
IVRAY
IVRESSE
IVY
IVYBELLS
IVYBERRY
IVYFLOWER
IVYING
IVYWOOD
IVYWORT
IWA
IWAIWA
IWAN
IWEARTH
IWIS
IWORTH
IWURCHE
IWURTHEN
IXODIAN
IXODIC
IXODID
IXTLE
IYA
IYO
IZAFAT
IZAR
IZARD
IZBA
IZLE
IZOTE
IZTLE
IZTLI
IZVOZCHIK
IZZARD
IZZAT

J

JA
JAB
JABBED
JABBER
JABBERED
JABBERER
JABBERING
JABBERINGLY
JABBERMENT
JABBING
JABBLE
JABERS
JABIA
JABIRU
JABORANDI
JABORIN
JABORINE
JABOT
JABOTICABA
JABOTS
JABUL
JABULES
JACA
JACAL
JACALES
JACAMAR
JACAMEROPINE
JACAMIN
JACANA
JACARANDA
JACARE
JACATE
JACATOO
JACCHUS
JACCONET
JACCONOT
JACENT
JACINTH
JACINTHE
JACITARA
JACK
JACKAL
JACKALS
JACKANAPES
JACKAROO
JACKASH
JACKASS
JACKASSERY
JACKBIRD
JACKBOOT
JACKBOX
JACKBOY
JACKDAW
JACKED
JACKEEN
JACKER
JACKEROO
JACKEROOS
JACKET
JACKETED
JACKETING
JACKETY
JACKFISH
JACKFISHES
JACKFRUIT
JACKHAMMER
JACKHEAD
JACKING
JACKKNIFE
JACKKNIVES
JACKLEG
JACKLIGHT
JACKMAN
JACKMEN
JACKO
JACKPLANE
JACKPOT
JACKPOTS
JACKPUDDING
JACKROD
JACKROLL
JACKS
JACKSAW
JACKSCREW
JACKSHAFT
JACKSHAY
JACKSHEA
JACKSLAVE
JACKSMELT
JACKSMITH
JACKSNIPE
JACKSNIPES
JACKSTAY
JACKSTOCK
JACKSTONE
JACKSTRAW
JACKTAN
JACKWEED
JACKWOOD
JACKY
JACOBAEA
JACOBIN
JACOBSITE
JACOBUS
JACOBY
JACOLATT
JACONET
JACOUNCE
JACQUARD
JACQUERIE
JACTANCE
JACTANCY
JACTANT
JACTATION
JACTITATE
JACTITATED
JACTITATING
JACTITATION
JACTURE
JACU
JACUARU
JACULATE
JACULATED
JACULATING
JACULATION
JACULATIVE
JACULATOR
JACULATORIAL
JACULATORY
JACULIFEROUS
JACUTINGA
JAD
JADDED
JADDER
JADDING
JADE
JADED
JADEDLY
JADEDNESS
JADEITE
JADERY
JADING
JADISH
JADISHLY
JADISHNESS
JADOO
JADU
JADY
JAEGER
JAELA
JAG
JAGAT
JAGEER
JAGER
JAGG
JAGGAR
JAGGARY
JAGGED
JAGGEDLY
JAGGEDNESS
JAGGER
JAGGERY
JAGGHERY
JAGGIER
JAGGIEST
JAGGING
JAGGY
JAGHEER
JAGHEERDAR
JAGHIR
JAGHIRDAR
JAGHIRE
JAGHIREDAR
JAGIR
JAGIRDAR
JAGLA
JAGONG
JAGRA
JAGRATA
JAGS
JAGUA
JAGUAR
JAGUARETE
JAGUARONDI
JAGUARS
JAGUARUNDI
JAGUEY
JAIL
JAILAGE
JAILBIRD
JAILED
JAILER
JAILERESS
JAILERING
JAILHOUSE
JAILKEEPER
JAILMATE
JAILOR
JAILORING
JAILYARD
JAK
JAKE
JAKES
JAKEY
JAKFRUIT
JAKO
JAKOS
JALAP
JALAPA
JALAPENO
JALAPIC
JALAPIN
JALEO
JALET
JALKAR
JALLOPED
JALOP
JALOPIES
JALOPPY
JALOPY
JALOUSE
JALOUSED
JALOUSIE
JALOUSIED
JALOUSING
JALPAITE
JAM
JAMA
JAMAH
JAMAN
JAMB
JAMBA
JAMBALAYA
JAMBE
JAMBEAU
JAMBEAUX
JAMBEE
JAMBER
JAMBO
JAMBOLAN
JAMBOLANA
JAMBON
JAMBONE
JAMBOOL
JAMBOREE
JAMBOSA
JAMBSTONE
JAMBUL
JAMDANEE
JAMDANI
JAMESONITE
JAMI
JAMMED
JAMMER
JAMMING
JAMMY
JAMNUT
JAMOKE
JAMON
JAMPAN
JAMPANEE
JAMPANI
JAMROSADE
JAMTLAND
JAMWOOD
JAN
JANAPA
JANAPAN
JANAPUM
JANDERS
JANE
JANG
JANGADA
JANGAR
JANGKAR
JANGLE
JANGLED
JANGLER
JANGLING
JANGLY
JANICEPS
JANISARY
JANISSARY
JANITOR
JANITORIAL
JANITRESS
JANITRIX
JANIZARIES
JANIZARY
JANK
JANKER
JANKERS
JANN
JANNER
JANNOCK
JANTEE
JANTU
JANTY
JANUA
JAOB
JAOUR
JAP
JAPACONIN
JAPACONINE
JAPACONITIN
JAPACONITINE
JAPAN
JAPANNED
JAPANNER
JAPANNERY
JAPANNING
JAPE
JAPED
JAPER
JAPERIES
JAPERY
JAPING
JAPISH
JAPISHLY
JAPISHNESS
JAPONICA
JAPYGID
JAPYGOID
JAQUETTE
JAQUIMA
JAR
JARA
JARABE
JARAGUA
JARANA
JARARACA
JARARACUSSU
JARBIRD
JARBLE
JARBOT
JARDE
JARDINIERE
JAREED
JARFLY
JARFUL
JARG
JARGON
JARGONAL
JARGONED
JARGONEL
JARGONELLE
JARGONER
JARGONIC
JARGONING
JARGONISH
JARGONIST
JARGONIUM
JARGONIZE
JARGONIZED
JARGONIZING
JARGONNELLE
JARGOON
JARHEAD
JARINA
JARK
JARKMAN
JARL
JARLESS
JARLITE
JARNUT
JAROOL
JAROSITE
JAROVIZATION
JAROVIZE
JAROVIZED
JAROVIZING
JARRA
JARRAH
JARRED
JARRET

JARRING
JARRY
JARVEY
JARVEYS
JASEY
JASEYED
JASEYS
JASK
JASM
JASMIN
JASMINE
JASMINED
JASMINEWOOD
JASMONE
JASPACHATE
JASPAGATE
JASPE
JASPER
JASPERATED
JASPERED
JASPERITE
JASPERIZE
JASPERIZED
JASPERIZING
JASPEROID
JASPERY
JASPIDEAN
JASPIDEOUS
JASPILITE
JASPILYTE
JASPIS
JASPOID
JASPONYX
JASPOPAL
JASS
JASSID
JATACO
JATAMANSI
JATEORHIZIN
JATEORHIZINE
JATHA
JATI
JATO
JATOBA
JATROPHIC
JAUD
JAUDIE
JAUG
JAUK
JAUN
JAUNCE
JAUNDER
JAUNDERS
JAUNDICE
JAUNDICED
JAUNDICEROOT
JAUNDICING
JAUNE
JAUNER
JAUNT
JAUNTED
JAUNTIE
JAUNTIER
JAUNTIEST
JAUNTILY
JAUNTINESS
JAUNTING
JAUNTY
JAUP
JAUPS
JAVA
JAVALI
JAVEL
JAVELIN
JAVELINA
JAVELINEER
JAVELOT
JAVER
JAVVER
JAW
JAWAB
JAWBATION
JAWBONE
JAWBREAKER
JAWBREAKING
JAWBREAKINGLY
JAWCRUSHER
JAWED
JAWFALL
JAWFALLEN
JAWFEET
JAWFISH
JAWFISHES
JAWFOOT
JAWFOOTED
JAWHOLE
JAWING
JAWS
JAWSMITH
JAWY
JAY
JAYGEE
JAYHAWK
JAYHAWKER
JAYPIE
JAYPIET
JAYVEE
JAYWALK
JAYWALKER
JAYWALKING
JAZEL
JAZERAN
JAZERANT
JAZZ
JAZZBOW
JAZZER
JAZZIER
JAZZIEST
JAZZILY
JAZZINESS
JAZZY
JEALOUS
JEALOUSE
JEALOUSIES
JEALOUSLY
JEALOUSNESS
JEALOUSY
JEAN
JEANS
JEBAT
JEBEL
JECORAL
JECORIN
JECORIZE
JED
JEDCOCK
JEDDOCK
JEDGE
JEE
JEEL
JEEP
JEEPERS
JEEPNEY
JEER
JEERED
JEERER
JEERING
JEERINGLY
JEERS
JEERY
JEETEE
JEEZ
JEFE
JEFF
JEFFERISITE
JEFFERSONITE
JEHAD
JEHUP
JEJUNA
JEJUNAL
JEJUNATOR
JEJUNE
JEJUNELY
JEJUNENESS
JEJUNITIS
JEJUNITY
JEJUNOSTOMY
JEJUNOTOMY
JEJUNUM
JELAB
JELERANG
JELICK
JELL
JELLAB
JELLICA
JELLICO
JELLIED
JELLIEDNESS
JELLIES
JELLIFICATION
JELLIFIED
JELLIFY
JELLIFYING
JELLILY
JELLO
JELLOID
JELLY
JELLYBEAN
JELLYFISH
JELLYFISHES
JELLYING
JELLYLEAF
JELLYLIKE
JELOTONG
JELUTONG
JEMADAR
JEMBLE
JEMIDAR
JEMMIES
JEMMILY
JEMMINESS
JEMMY
JEN
JENKIN
JENNA
JENNERIZE
JENNET
JENNETING
JENNIER
JENNIES
JENNY
JENOAR
JENTACULAR
JEOFAIL
JEOPARD
JEOPARDED
JEOPARDER
JEOPARDIED
JEOPARDING
JEOPARDIOUS
JEOPARDIZE
JEOPARDIZED
JEOPARDIZING
JEOPARDOUS
JEOPARDOUSLY
JEOPARDY
JEOPARDYING
JEQUERITY
JEQUIRITIES
JEQUIRITY
JERBOA
JEREED
JEREMIAD
JEREZ
JERIB
JERICAN
JERK
JERKED
JERKER
JERKIER
JERKIEST
JERKILY
JERKIN
JERKINED
JERKINESS
JERKING
JERKISH
JERKS
JERKSOME
JERKWATER
JERKY
JERL
JERM
JERMONAL
JERMOONAL
JERNIE
JEROBOAM
JERQUE
JERQUED
JERQUER
JERQUING
JERRICAN
JERRID
JERRIES
JERRY
JERRYBUILD
JERRYBUILDING
JERRYBUILT
JERRYISM
JERSEY
JERSEYED
JERSEYS
JERT
JERVIA
JERVIN
JERVINA
JERVINE
JES
JESS
JESSAKEED
JESSAMIES
JESSAMINE
JESSAMY
JESSANT
JESSED
JESSING
JESSUR
JEST
JESTBOOK
JESTED
JESTEE
JESTER
JESTING
JESTINGLY
JESTINGSTOCK
JESTWORD
JET
JETBEAD
JETE
JETEE
JETLINER
JETON
JETPORT
JETSAM
JETTAGE
JETTATORE
JETTATURA
JETTEAU
JETTED
JETTER
JETTIED
JETTIES
JETTINESS
JETTING
JETTISON
JETTO
JETTON
JETTRU
JETTY
JETTYHEAD
JETWARE
JEU
JEUNESSE
JEUX
JEW
JEWBIRD
JEWBUSH
JEWEL
JEWELED
JEWELER
JEWELHOUSE
JEWELING
JEWELLED
JEWELLER
JEWELLERY
JEWELLING
JEWELLY
JEWELRY
JEWELS
JEWELSMITH
JEWELWEED
JEWELY
JEWFISH
JEWFISHES
JEWING
JEZAIL
JEZEKITE
JEZIA
JEZIAH
JHANA
JHARAL
JHEEL
JHIL
JHOOL
JHOOM
JHOW
JHUM
JIB
JIBBA
JIBBAH
JIBBED
JIBBEH
JIBBER
JIBBING
JIBBINGS
JIBBOOM
JIBE
JIBED
JIBER
JIBHEAD
JIBI
JIBING
JIBMAN
JIBMEN
JIBOA
JIBOYA
JIBSTAY
JICAMA
JICARA
JIFF
JIFFIES
JIFFLE
JIFFY
JIG
JIGAMAREE

JIGGED
JIGGER
JIGGERED
JIGGERER
JIGGERMAN
JIGGERS
JIGGET
JIGGETY
JIGGINESS
JIGGING
JIGGISH
JIGGIT
JIGGLE
JIGGLED
JIGGLING
JIGGLY
JIGGUMBOB
JIGGY
JIGMAN
JIGMEN
JIGOTE
JIGSAW
JIGUA
JIHAD
JIKUNGU
JILL
JILLET
JILLFLIRT
JILLING
JILLION
JILT
JILTED
JILTEE
JILTER
JILTING
JIMBANG
JIMBERJAW
JIMBERJAWED
JIMCRACK
JIMJAM
JIMJAMS
JIMMER
JIMMIED
JIMMIES
JIMMY
JIMMYING
JIMMYWEED
JIMP
JIMPLY
JIMPNESS
JIMPRICUTE
JIMPY
JIMSEDGE
JIMSON
JINA
JINETE
JING
JINGAL
JINGALL
JINGBANG
JINGLE
JINGLEBOB
JINGLED
JINGLEJANGLE
JINGLER
JINGLET
JINGLING
JINGLINGLY
JINGLY
JINGO
JINGOED
JINGOES
JINGOING
JINGOISH
JINGOISM
JINGOIST
JINGOISTIC
JINJA
JINJILI
JINK
JINKED
JINKER
JINKET
JINKING
JINKLE
JINKS
JINN
JINNEE
JINNESTAN
JINNI
JINNIES
JINNIWINK
JINNIYEH
JINNY
JINNYWINK
JINRICKSHA
JINRIKI
JINRIKIMAN
JINRIKIMEN
JINRIKISHA
JINSHA
JINSHANG
JINSING
JINX
JIPIJAPA
JIPPER
JIPPO
JIQUE
JIQUI
JIRBLE
JIRD
JIRGA
JIRGAH
JIRKINET
JIRT
JITI
JITNEUR
JITNEUSE
JITNEY
JITNEYMAN
JITNEYS
JITTER
JITTERBUG
JITTERS
JITTERY
JIUJITSU
JIUJUTSU
JIVA
JIVATMA
JIVE
JIXIE
JIZ
JIZYA
JIZYAH
JIZZEN
JNANA
JNANAMARGA
JNANASHAKTI
JNANAYOGA
JNANENDRIYA
JNANI
JO
JOANNES
JOAQUINITE
JOB
JOBADE
JOBARBE
JOBATION
JOBBED
JOBBER
JOBBERIES
JOBBERNOWL
JOBBERY
JOBBING
JOBBISH
JOBBLE
JOBE
JOBHOLDER
JOBLESS
JOBLESSNESS
JOBMAN
JOBMASTER
JOBMEN
JOBMISTRESS
JOBMONGER
JOBO
JOBS
JOBSITE
JOBSMITH
JOBSON
JOCANT
JOCATORY
JOCH
JOCK
JOCKER
JOCKEY
JOCKEYED
JOCKEYING
JOCKEYISM
JOCKEYS
JOCKO
JOCKOS
JOCKS
JOCKSTRAP
JOCKTELEG
JOCO
JOCOQUE
JOCOQUI
JOCOSE
JOCOSELY
JOCOSENESS
JOCOSERIOUS
JOCOSITIES
JOCOSITY
JOCOTE
JOCTELEG
JOCU
JOCULAR
JOCULARITY
JOCULARLY
JOCULARNESS
JOCULATOR
JOCULATORY
JOCUM
JOCUMA
JOCUND
JOCUNDITIES
JOCUNDITY
JOCUNDLY
JOCUNDNESS
JOCUNDRY
JOD
JODEL
JODHPURS
JOE
JOEBUSH
JOES
JOEWOOD
JOEY
JOG
JOGGED
JOGGER
JOGGING
JOGGLE
JOGGLED
JOGGLER
JOGGLETY
JOGGLEWORK
JOGGLING
JOGGLY
JOGI
JOGTROTTISM
JOHANNES
JOHANNITE
JOHN
JOHNBOAT
JOHNIN
JOHNNYCAKE
JOHNSTRUPITE
JOIN
JOINANT
JOINDER
JOINED
JOINER
JOINERED
JOINERING
JOINERY
JOINHAND
JOINING
JOININGLY
JOINT
JOINTAGE
JOINTED
JOINTEDLY
JOINTEDNESS
JOINTER
JOINTING
JOINTIST
JOINTLY
JOINTRESS
JOINTS
JOINTURE
JOINTURED
JOINTURESS
JOINTURING
JOINTWEED
JOINTWOOD
JOINTWORM
JOINTY
JOISE
JOIST
JOISTED
JOISTING
JOJOBA
JOKE
JOKED
JOKELET
JOKER
JOKESMITH
JOKESOME
JOKESOMENESS
JOKESTER
JOKEY
JOKIER
JOKIEST
JOKING
JOKINGLY
JOKISH
JOKIST
JOKUL
JOKY
JOLE
JOLI
JOLIE
JOLL
JOLLIED
JOLLIER
JOLLIES
JOLLIEST
JOLLIFICATION
JOLLIFIED
JOLLIFY
JOLLIFYING
JOLLILY
JOLLIMENT
JOLLINESS
JOLLITIES
JOLLITRY
JOLLITY
JOLLOP
JOLLOPED
JOLLY
JOLLYHEAD
JOLLYING
JOLT
JOLTED
JOLTER
JOLTERHEAD
JOLTERHEADED
JOLTHEAD
JOLTHEADED
JOLTINESS
JOLTING
JOLTY
JONDLA
JONG
JONGLERY
JONGLEUR
JONK
JONQUIL
JONQUILLE
JOOKERIE
JOOLA
JOOM
JOPY
JORAM
JORDAN
JORDANITE
JORDANON
JORDEN
JOREE
JORNADA
JOROPO
JORRAM
JORUM
JOSEF
JOSEFITE
JOSEITE
JOSEPH
JOSEPHINITE
JOSEY
JOSH
JOSHER
JOSHI
JOSIE
JOSKIN
JOSS
JOSSA
JOSSER
JOSTLE
JOSTLED
JOSTLEMENT
JOSTLER
JOSTLING
JOSUP
JOT
JOTA
JOTATION
JOTI
JOTISARU
JOTISI
JOTTED
JOTTER
JOTTING
JOTTY
JOUBARB
JOUG
JOUGH
JOUGS
JOUISSANCE
JOUK
JOUKERY
JOULE
JOULEAN
JOULEMETER

JOUNCE
JOUNCED
JOUNCING
JOURNAL
JOURNALED
JOURNALESE
JOURNALING
JOURNALISE
JOURNALISM
JOURNALIST
JOURNALISTIC
JOURNALIZE
JOURNALIZED
JOURNALIZER
JOURNALIZING
JOURNALLED
JOURNALLING
JOURNEY
JOURNEYCAKE
JOURNEYED
JOURNEYER
JOURNEYING
JOURNEYMAN
JOURNEYMEN
JOURNEYS
JOURNEYWOMAN
JOURNEYWOMEN
JOURNEYWORK
JOURS
JOUST
JOUSTER
JOUSTING
JOUSTS
JOUTES
JOVIAL
JOVIALIST
JOVIALISTIC
JOVIALITY
JOVIALIZE
JOVIALIZED
JOVIALIZING
JOVIALLY
JOVIALNESS
JOVIALTY
JOVILABE
JOVY
JOW
JOWAR
JOWARI
JOWEL
JOWER
JOWERY
JOWL
JOWLER
JOWLOP
JOWLY
JOWPY
JOWSER
JOWTER
JOY
JOYANCE
JOYANCY
JOYANT
JOYED
JOYFUL
JOYFULLY
JOYFULNESS
JOYHOP
JOYHOUSE
JOYING
JOYLEAF
JOYLESS
JOYLESSLY
JOYLESSNESS
JOYOUS
JOYOUSLY
JOYOUSNESS
JOYPOPPER
JOYRIDE
JOYSOME
JOYWEED
JUAMAVE
JUB
JUBA
JUBARB
JUBARTAS
JUBARTES
JUBATE
JUBBAH
JUBBE
JUBE
JUBEROUS
JUBHAH
JUBILANCE
JUBILANCY
JUBILANT
JUBILANTLY
JUBILARIAN
JUBILATE
JUBILATED
JUBILATING
JUBILATIO
JUBILATION
JUBILATORY
JUBILE
JUBILEAN
JUBILEE
JUBILIST
JUBILIZATION
JUBILIZE
JUBILUS
JUBO
JUBUS
JUCHART
JUCK
JUCKIES
JUCUNDITY
JUD
JUDAIZER
JUDCOCK
JUDD
JUDDER
JUDDOCK
JUDEX
JUDGE
JUDGED
JUDGEMENT
JUDGER
JUDGING
JUDGMATIC
JUDGMATICAL
JUDGMENT
JUDGMENTS
JUDICABLE
JUDICATE
JUDICATION
JUDICATIVE
JUDICATOR
JUDICATORIAL
JUDICATORIES
JUDICATORY
JUDICATURE
JUDICES
JUDICIABLE
JUDICIAL
JUDICIALITY
JUDICIALIZE
JUDICIALLY
JUDICIARIES
JUDICIARILY
JUDICIARY
JUDICIOUS
JUDICIOUSLY
JUDICIOUSNESS
JUDICIUM
JUDKA
JUDO
JUDOPHOBIA
JUECES
JUEY
JUEZ
JUFFER
JUFTI
JUFTS
JUG
JUGA
JUGAL
JUGALE
JUGATE
JUGATED
JUGATION
JUGER
JUGFUL
JUGGED
JUGGER
JUGGERNAUT
JUGGING
JUGGINS
JUGGLE
JUGGLED
JUGGLEMENT
JUGGLER
JUGGLERIES
JUGGLERY
JUGGLING
JUGGLINGLY
JUGHEAD
JUGLANDIN
JUGLAR
JUGLONE
JUGULA
JUGULAR
JUGULATE
JUGULATED
JUGULATING
JUGULATION
JUGULUM
JUGUM
JUGUMS
JUICE
JUICER
JUICIER
JUICIEST
JUICILY
JUICINESS
JUICY
JUISE
JUJITSU
JUJU
JUJUBE
JUJUISM
JUJUIST
JUJUTSU
JUKE
JUKEBOX
JUKES
JULEP
JULID
JULIDAN
JULIENITE
JULIENNE
JULIETT
JULIO
JULOID
JULOIDIAN
JULOL
JULOLE
JULOLIDIN
JULOLIDINE
JULOLIN
JULOLINE
JUM
JUMART
JUMBA
JUMBIE
JUMBLE
JUMBLED
JUMBLEMENT
JUMBLER
JUMBLING
JUMBLY
JUMBO
JUMBOISM
JUMBOS
JUMBUCK
JUMBY
JUMELLE
JUMENT
JUMENTOUS
JUMFRU
JUMILLITE
JUMMA
JUMP
JUMPED
JUMPER
JUMPERS
JUMPIER
JUMPIEST
JUMPINESS
JUMPING
JUMPOFF
JUMPROCK
JUMPROCKS
JUMPS
JUMPSCRAPE
JUMPSEED
JUMPSOME
JUMPY
JUNCACEOUS
JUNCIFORM
JUNCITE
JUNCO
JUNCOS
JUNCOUS
JUNCTION
JUNCTIONAL
JUNCTIVE
JUNCTLY
JUNCTURE
JUNCUS
JUNDIE
JUNDY
JUNE
JUNECTOMY
JUNEFISH
JUNGLE
JUNGLED
JUNGLESIDE
JUNGLEWOOD
JUNGLI
JUNGLIER
JUNGLIEST
JUNGLY
JUNIATA
JUNIOR
JUNIORATE
JUNIORITY
JUNIPER
JUNK
JUNKBOARD
JUNKDEALER
JUNKER
JUNKERDOM
JUNKERISM
JUNKET
JUNKETED
JUNKETER
JUNKETING
JUNKIE
JUNKING
JUNKMAN
JUNKMEN
JUNKY
JUNKYARD
JUNT
JUNTA
JUNTAS
JUNTO
JUNTOS
JUPATI
JUPE
JUPES
JUPON
JUR
JURA
JURAL
JURALLY
JURAMENT
JURAMENTA
JURAMENTADO
JURAMENTAL
JURAMENTALLY
JURAMENTUM
JURANT
JURARA
JURAT
JURATA
JURATION
JURATIVE
JURATOR
JURATORIAL
JURATORY
JURE
JUREL
JURIDIC
JURIDICAL
JURIDICALLY
JURIDICIAL
JURIES
JURING
JURISCONSULT
JURISDICTION
JURISDICTIVE
JURISPRUDENCE
JURISPRUDENT
JURIST
JURISTIC
JURISTICAL
JURISTICALLY
JURM
JUROR
JURORS
JURR
JURT
JURUPAITE
JURY
JURYMAN
JURYMEN
JURYWOMAN
JUS
JUSI
JUSLIK
JUSSAL
JUSSEL
JUSSHELL
JUSSION
JUSSIVE
JUSSORY
JUST
JUSTAUCORPS
JUSTEN
JUSTER
JUSTICE
JUSTICED
JUSTICEHOOD

JUSTICER
JUSTICESHIP
JUSTICEWEED
JUSTICIABLE
JUSTICIAL
JUSTICIAR
JUSTICIARY
JUSTICIER
JUSTICIES
JUSTICING
JUSTICO
JUSTIFIABLE
JUSTIFIABLY
JUSTIFICATION
JUSTIFICATIVE
JUSTIFICATOR
JUSTIFIED
JUSTIFIER
JUSTIFY
JUSTIFYING
JUSTIFYINGLY
JUSTITIA
JUSTLE
JUSTLER
JUSTLY
JUSTMENT
JUSTMENTS
JUSTNESS
JUSTO
JUT
JUTE
JUTES
JUTIA
JUTKA
JUTTED
JUTTIES
JUTTING
JUTTINGLY
JUTTY
JUVENAL
JUVENATE
JUVENESCENCE
JUVENESCENT
JUVENILE
JUVENILELY
JUVENILENESS
JUVENILIA
JUVENILIFY
JUVENILISM
JUVENILITIES
JUVENILITY
JUVENT
JUVENTUDE
JUVIA
JUVITE
JUWISE
JUXTA
JUXTAMARINE
JUXTAPOSE
JUXTAPOSED
JUXTAPOSING
JUXTAPOSIT
JUXTAPOSITION
JUXTAPYLORIC
JUXTASPINAL
JUZAIL
JYNGINE
JYNX

K

KA
KAAMA
KAAS
KAB
KABAKA
KABALA
KABAR
KABAYA
KABBALA
KABEL
KABELJOU
KABERU
KABIET
KABOB
KABUKI
KACHIN
KACHINA
KADDER
KADE
KADEIN
KADI
KADIKANE
KADINE
KADISCHI
KADOS
KADSURA
KADY
KAE
KAEMPFEROL
KAFERITA
KAFFIR
KAFFIRS
KAFFIYEH
KAFIR
KAFIRIN
KAFIZ
KAFTAN
KAGO
KAGU
KAGURA
KAHA
KAHAL
KAHALA
KAHAR
KAHAU
KAHAWAI
KAHIKATEA
KAHILI
KAHU
KAHUNA
KAI
KAIAK
KAID
KAIF
KAIK
KAIKA
KAIKARA
KAIKAWAKA
KAIL
KAILS
KAILYARD
KAILYARDER
KAILYARDISM
KAIN
KAINGA
KAINGIN
KAINIT
KAINITE
KAINSI
KAIO
KAIR
KAIRI
KAIRIN
KAIRINE
KAIROLIN
KAIROLINE
KAIROS
KAISER
KAISERDOM
KAISERISM
KAITAKA
KAIVALYA
KAIWHIRIA
KAIWI
KAJAWAH
KAJEPUT
KAJUGARU
KAKA
KAKAPO
KAKAR
KAKARALI
KAKARALLI
KAKARIKI
KAKAWAHIE
KAKEL
KAKEMONO
KAKI
KAKIDROSIS
KAKISTOCRACY
KAKKAK
KAKKE
KAKORTOKITE
KAKU
KAKUR
KAL
KALA
KALAC
KALACH
KALADANA
KALAM
KALAMANSANAI
KALAMKARI
KALAN
KALASIE
KALE
KALEIDOPHON
KALEIDOPHONE
KALEIDOSCOPE
KALEMA
KALENDS
KALEWIFE
KALEWIVES
KALEYARD
KALI
KALIAN
KALIDIUM
KALIF
KALIFORM
KALIGENOUS
KALIJ
KALINITE
KALIOPHILITE
KALIPAYA
KALIPH
KALIUM
KALKVIS
KALLAH
KALLEGE
KALLILITE
KALLITYPE
KALMIA
KALMUCK
KALMUK
KALO
KALOKAGATHIA
KALON
KALONG
KALPAK
KALPIS
KALSOMINE
KALUA
KALUMPANG
KALUMPIT
KALUNTI
KALYMMOCYTE
KALYPTRA
KAM
KAMAAINA
KAMACHI
KAMACHILE
KAMACITE
KAMAHI
KAMALA
KAMALOKA
KAMANCHILE
KAMANI
KAMAO
KAMAREZITE
KAMARUPA
KAMARUPIC
KAMAS
KAMASS
KAMASSI
KAMAVACHARA
KAMBAL
KAMBOH
KAMBOU
KAME
KAMEEL
KAMEELDOORN
KAMEELTHORN
KAMELA
KAMELAUKION
KAMERAD
KAMI
KAMIAN
KAMIAS
KAMICHI
KAMIK
KAMIKA
KAMIKAZE
KAMIKS
KAMIS
KAMLEIKA
KAMMALAN
KAMMERERITE
KAMMEU
KAMPERITE
KAMPONG
KAMPTOMORPH
KAMSEEN
KAMSIN
KAN
KANA
KANAE
KANAF
KANAFF
KANAGI
KANAIMA
KANARA
KANARI
KANAT
KANCHIL
KANDE
KANDH
KANDJAR
KANE
KANEH
KANGA
KANGANI
KANGANY
KANGAROO
KANGAROOER
KANGAROOS
KANGAYAM
KANGLA
KANGRI
KANIN
KANKEDORT
KANKIE
KANKREJ
KANNA
KANNE
KANNEN
KANNU
KANNUME
KANONE
KANOON
KANS
KANT
KANTAR
KANTELA
KANTELE
KANTELETAR
KANTEN
KANTIARA
KANUKA
KANYAW
KANZU
KAOLIANG
KAOLIN
KAOLINATE
KAOLINE
KAOLINIC
KAOLINITE
KAOLINIZE
KAORI
KAPA
KAPAI
KAPEIKA
KAPH
KAPOK
KAPOR
KAPOTE
KAPP
KAPPA
KAPPARAH
KAPPE
KAPPIE
KAPPLAND
KAPU
KAPUKA
KAPUR
KAPUT
KAPUTT
KARABINER
KARAGAN
KARAKA
KARAKUL
KARAKULE
KARAKURT
KARAMU
KARAO
KARAT
KARATAS
KARATE
KARATTO
KARAYA
KARBI
KARCH
KAREAO
KAREAU
KAREETA
KARELA
KAREWA
KAREZ
KARI
KARINGHOTA
KARITE
KARITI
KARMA
KARMADHARAYA
KARMIC
KARMOUTH
KARN
KARO
KAROO
KAROOS
KAROSS
KAROU
KARPAS
KARREE
KARREN
KARRI
KARROO
KARROOS
KARRUSEL
KARSHA
KARST
KARSTIC
KARTEL
KARTOS
KARUNA
KARVAR
KARWAR
KARYOCHROME
KARYOGAMIC
KARYOGAMY
KARYOKINESIS
KARYOKINETIC
KARYOLYMPH
KARYOLYSIS
KARYOLYTIC
KARYOMERE
KARYOMERITE
KARYOMITOIC
KARYOMITOME
KARYOMITOSIS
KARYOMITOTIC
KARYON
KARYOPLASM
KARYOPLASMA
KARYOPLASMIC
KARYORRHEXIS
KARYOSOMA
KARYOSOME
KARYOTIN
KAS
KASA
KASBA
KASBEKE
KASCAMIOL
KASHA
KASHER
KASHGA
KASHI
KASHIM
KASHIMA
KASHMIR
KASHRUTH
KASIDA
KASM
KASOLITE
KASSABAH
KASSU
KASTURA
KASWA
KAT
KATA
KATABASES
KATABASIS
KATABATIC
KATABELLA
KATABOLIC
KATABOLISM

KATABOLITE
KATABOLIZE
KATABOTHRA
KATABOTHRON
KATACROTIC
KATACROTISM
KATAGENESIS
KATAGENETIC
KATAKANA
KATAKINESIS
KATAKINETIC
KATAKIRIBORI
KATALASE
KATALYSIS
KATALYST
KATALYTIC
KATALYZE
KATAMORPHISM
KATANA
KATAPHORESIS
KATAPHORETIC
KATAPHORIC
KATAPHRENIA
KATAPLASIA
KATAPLECTIC
KATAPLEXY
KATAR
KATASTATE
KATASTATIC
KATATONIA
KATATONIC
KATATYPE
KATCHUNG
KATCINA
KATE
KATEL
KATH
KATHA
KATHAK
KATHAKALI
KATHAL
KATHAROMETER
KATHARSIS
KATHARTIC
KATHODE
KATI
KATIN
KATION
KATIPO
KATJEPIERING
KATMON
KATOGLE
KATONKEL
KATSU
KATUKA
KATUN
KATURAI
KATYDID
KATZENJAMMER
KAURI
KAURY
KAVA
KAVAKAVA
KAVASS
KAVIKA
KAVVANAH
KAVYA
KAW
KAWA
KAWAKA
KAWAKAWA
KAY
KAYA
KAYAK
KAYAKER
KAYLE
KAYLES
KAYO
KAYS
KAZAK
KAZI
KAZOO
KAZY
KEA
KEACH
KEACORN
KEAWE
KEBAR
KEBBIE
KEBBOCK
KEBBUCK
KEBBY
KEBOB
KEBYAR
KECHEL
KECHIL
KECK
KECKLE
KECKLING
KECKSY
KECKY
KED
KEDDAH
KEDGE
KEDGER
KEDGEREE
KEDGY
KEDIRI
KEDJAVE
KEDLOCK
KEDUSHAH
KEECH
KEEF
KEEK
KEEKER
KEEKERS
KEEL
KEELAGE
KEELBACK
KEELBILL
KEELBIRD
KEELBLOCK
KEELBOAT
KEELBOATMAN
KEELED
KEELER
KEELFAT
KEELHALE
KEELHAUL
KEELIE
KEELING
KEELIVINE
KEELMAN
KEELS
KEELSON
KEELVAT
KEEN
KEENA
KEENED
KEENER
KEENLY
KEENNESS
KEEP
KEEPER
KEEPERING
KEEPING
KEEPS
KEEPSAKE
KEEPSAKY
KEEPWORTHY
KEEROGUE
KEESH
KEESHOND
KEESHONDEN
KEESLIP
KEEST
KEESTER
KEET
KEETH
KEEVE
KEF
KEFFEL
KEFIR
KEFIRIC
KEG
KEGLER
KEGLING
KEGMEG
KEHAYA
KEHILLAH
KEHILLOTH
KEHOEITE
KEIKI
KEILHAUITE
KEIR
KEIRI
KEIST
KEISTER
KEITLOA
KELCHIN
KELCHYN
KELD
KELDER
KELE
KELEBE
KELECTOME
KELEH
KELEK
KELEP
KELK
KELL
KELLA
KELLECK
KELLEG
KELLIN
KELLION
KELLUPWEED
KELLY
KELOID
KELP
KELPER
KELPFISH
KELPIE
KELPWARE
KELPWORT
KELPY
KELSON
KELT
KELTER
KELTIE
KELTY
KELVIN
KELYPHITE
KEM
KEMANCHA
KEMB
KEMIRI
KEMP
KEMPAS
KEMPER
KEMPERYMAN
KEMPITE
KEMPLE
KEMPSTER
KEMPT
KEMPY
KEN
KENAF
KENCH
KENDIR
KENDNA
KENDO
KENDYR
KENEMA
KENLORE
KENMARK
KENNA
KENNEBUNKER
KENNED
KENNEL
KENNELED
KENNELING
KENNELLED
KENNELLING
KENNELLY
KENNELMAN
KENNELMEN
KENNER
KENNET
KENNING
KENNINGWORT
KENNO
KENO
KENOGENESIS
KENOSIS
KENOTIC
KENOTICISM
KENOTICIST
KENOTISM
KENOTIST
KENOTOXIN
KENOTRON
KENSCOFF
KENSINGTON
KENSPECK
KENSPECKLE
KENT
KENTALLENITE
KENTIA
KENTLEDGE
KENTROGON
KENTROLITE
KENYTE
KEOUT
KEP
KEPE
KEPHIR
KEPI
KEPT
KERALITE
KERAMIC
KERAMICS
KERANA
KERAPHYLLOUS
KERASIN
KERASINE
KERAT
KERATALGIA
KERATECTASIA
KERATECTOMY
KERATIN
KERATINIZE
KERATINOSE
KERATINOUS
KERATITIS
KERATOCELE
KERATOCONUS
KERATODE
KERATODERMIA
KERATOGENIC
KERATOGENOUS
KERATOGLOBUS
KERATOHYAL
KERATOID
KERATOIRITIS
KERATOL
KERATOLYSIS
KERATOLYTIC
KERATOMA
KERATOME
KERATOMETER
KERATOMETRY
KERATONCUS
KERATONOSUS
KERATONYXIS
KERATOPHYRE
KERATOPLASTY
KERATOSCOPE
KERATOSCOPY
KERATOSE
KERATOSES
KERATOSIS
KERATOTOME
KERATOTOMY
KERATTO
KERAULOPHON
KERAULOPHONE
KERAUNIA
KERAUNION
KERAUNOGRAPH
KERAUNOPHONE
KERB
KERBAU
KERBSTONE
KERCHER
KERCHIEF
KERCHIEFED
KERCHIEFT
KERCHOO
KERCHUG
KERCHUNK
KERE
KEREL
KERF
KERFLAP
KERFLOP
KERFLUMMOX
KERI
KERIAH
KERION
KERITE
KERLOCK
KERMES
KERMESITE
KERMESS
KERMIS
KERN
KERNE
KERNEL
KERNELED
KERNELLATE
KERNELLED
KERNELLY
KERNER
KERNETTY
KERNISH
KERNITE
KERNOI
KERNOS
KEROGEN
KEROSENE
KEROSINE
KERPLUNK
KERRANA
KERRIL
KERRITE
KERRY
KERS
KERSANNE
KERSANTITE
KERSE
KERSENNEH
KERSEY
KERSEYMERE
KERSEYS

KERSLAM
KERSLOSH
KERSMASH
KERUGMA
KERUING
KERWHAM
KERYGMA
KERYGMATIC
KERYKEION
KERYSTIC
KESSLERMAN
KESTREL
KET
KETA
KETAL
KETAPANG
KETATE
KETCH
KETCHCRAFT
KETCHUP
KETCHY
KETEMBILLA
KETEN
KETENE
KETHIB
KETHIBH
KETIB
KETIMID
KETIMIDE
KETIMIN
KETIMINE
KETIPATE
KETIPIC
KETMIE
KETOGEN
KETOGENESIS
KETOGENIC
KETOHEPTOSE
KETOL
KETOLE
KETOLYSIS
KETOLYTIC
KETONAEMIA
KETONE
KETONEMIA
KETONIC
KETONIZATION
KETONIZE
KETONURIA
KETOSE
KETOSIDE
KETOSIS
KETOXIME
KETTE
KETTLE
KETTLECASE
KETTLEDRUM
KETTLER
KETTRIN
KETTY
KETUBA
KETUBAH
KETUPA
KETYL
KEUP
KEURBOOM
KEVALIN
KEVAZINGO
KEVEL
KEVELHEAD
KEVUTZAH
KEVUTZOTH
KEWEENAWITE
KEWPIE
KEX
KEXY
KEY
KEYAKI
KEYBOARD
KEYED
KEYER
KEYHOLE
KEYLOCK
KEYMAN
KEYMOVE
KEYNOTE
KEYNOTER
KEYSEAT
KEYSEATER
KEYSERLICK
KEYSLOT
KEYSMITH
KEYSTER
KEYSTONE
KEYSTONED
KEYWAY
KHADDAR
KHADI
KHAGIARITE
KHAIKI
KHAIR
KHAJA
KHAJUR
KHAKAN
KHAKHAM
KHAKI
KHAKIED
KHAKIS
KHAL
KHALAL
KHALAT
KHALIF
KHALIFA
KHALIFAT
KHALSA
KHALSAH
KHAMAL
KHAMSEEN
KHAMSIN
KHAN
KHANATE
KHANDA
KHANDAIT
KHANJAR
KHANJEE
KHANKAH
KHANSAMA
KHANSAMAH
KHANSAMAN
KHANUM
KHAR
KHARAJ
KHARIF
KHAROUBA
KHARUA
KHARWA
KHAS
KHASS
KHAT
KHATIB
KHATIN
KHATRI
KHAUR
KHAYA
KHAZEN
KHEDAH
KHEDIVE
KHEDIVIAH
KHEDIVIAL
KHEDIVIATE
KHELLA
KHELLIN
KHEPESH
KHESARI
KHET
KHIDMATGAR
KHIDMUTGAR
KHILAT
KHIR
KHIRKA
KHIRKAH
KHOA
KHODJA
KHOJA
KHOJAH
KHOKA
KHOR
KHOT
KHUBBER
KHUD
KHULA
KHUR
KHUSKHUS
KHUTBA
KHUTBAH
KHVAT
KI
KIABOOCA
KIACK
KIAK
KIAKI
KIALEE
KIANG
KIAUGH
KIBBE
KIBBEH
KIBBER
KIBBLE
KIBBLER
KIBBLERMAN
KIBBUTZ
KIBBUTZIM
KIBE
KIBITKA
KIBITZ
KIBITZER
KIBLA
KIBLAH
KIBOSH
KIBSEY
KIBY
KICHEL
KICK
KICKBACK
KICKBALL
KICKDOWN
KICKER
KICKING
KICKISH
KICKOFF
KICKOUT
KICKS
KICKSEYS
KICKSHAW
KICKSIES
KICKUP
KICKXIA
KICKY
KID
KIDANG
KIDCOTE
KIDDED
KIDDER
KIDDIE
KIDDIER
KIDDIES
KIDDING
KIDDISH
KIDDLE
KIDDUSH
KIDDUSHIN
KIDDY
KIDLET
KIDNAP
KIDNAPER
KIDNAPING
KIDNAPPER
KIDNEY
KIDNEYLIPPED
KIDNEYROOT
KIDNEYS
KIDNEYWORT
KIDSKIN
KIDSMAN
KIEF
KIEFEKIL
KIEKIE
KIELBASA
KIER
KIESELGUHR
KIESELGUR
KIESERITE
KIESTER
KIESTLESS
KIEVE
KIF
KIKAR
KIKE
KIKEPA
KIKI
KIKORI
KIKU
KIKUEL
KIKUMON
KIL
KILADJA
KILAH
KILDEE
KILDERKIN
KILE
KILEH
KILERG
KILEY
KILHIG
KILIARE
KILIM
KILL
KILLABLE
KILLADAR
KILLAS
KILLBUCK
KILLCALF
KILLCROP
KILLCU
KILLDEE
KILLDEER
KILLED
KILLEEKILLEE
KILLEEN
KILLER
KILLICK
KILLIFISH
KILLIG
KILLIKINICK
KILLING
KILLINGLY
KILLINGNESS
KILLINITE
KILLJOY
KILLOCK
KILLOGIE
KILLOW
KILLWEED
KILLWORT
KILLY
KILN
KILNEYE
KILNHOLE
KILNRIB
KILNSTICK
KILNTREE
KILO
KILOAMPERE
KILOBAR
KILOCALORIE
KILOCYCLE
KILODYNE
KILOGAUSS
KILOGRAM
KILOGRAMME
KILOJOULE
KILOLITER
KILOLITRE
KILOLUMEN
KILOMETER
KILOMETRE
KILOMETRIC
KILOMETRICAL
KILOPARSEC
KILOS
KILOTON
KILOVAR
KILOVOLT
KILOWARE
KILOWATT
KILP
KILT
KILTED
KILTER
KILTIE
KILTIES
KILTING
KILTY
KIM
KIMBERLIN
KIMBERLITE
KIMBO
KIMCHI
KIMIGAYO
KIMMER
KIMNEL
KIMONO
KIMONOED
KIMRI
KIN
KINA
KINAESTHESIA
KINAESTHESIS
KINAH
KINASE
KINBOOT
KINBOT
KINBOTE
KINCH
KINCHIN
KINCHINMORT
KINCOB
KIND
KINDAL
KINDERGARTEN
KINDHEART
KINDHEARTED
KINDLE
KINDLER
KINDLESOME
KINDLESS
KINDLESSLY
KINDLIER
KINDLIEST
KINDLINESS
KINDLING
KINDLY
KINDNESS
KINDRED
KINDREDLY

KINDREDNESS
KINE
KINEMATIC
KINEMATICAL
KINEMATICS
KINEMOMETER
KINEPLASTY
KINEPOX
KINESALGIA
KINESCOPE
KINESIATRIC
KINESIATRICS
KINESIC
KINESIMETER
KINESIOMETER
KINESIS
KINESODIC
KINESTHESIA
KINESTHESIS
KINESTHETIC
KINETIC
KINETICAL
KINETICALLY
KINETICS
KINETOGENESIS
KINETOGENIC
KINETOGRAM
KINETOGRAPH
KINETOPHONE
KINETOSCOPE
KINETOSCOPIC
KINETOSIS
KINFOLK
KING
KINGBIRD
KINGBOLT
KINGCOB
KINGCRAFT
KINGCUP
KINGDOM
KINGDOMED
KINGDOMSHIP
KINGFISH
KINGFISHER
KINGHEAD
KINGHOOD
KINGHUNTER
KINGKLIP
KINGLESS
KINGLESSNESS
KINGLET
KINGLIER
KINGLIEST
KINGLIHOOD
KINGLIKE
KINGLILY
KINGLINESS
KINGLING
KINGLY
KINGMAKER
KINGMAKING
KINGPIECE
KINGPIN
KINGSHIP
KINGSMAN
KINGWEED
KINGWOOD
KINIC
KININ
KINK
KINKAJOU
KINKCOUGH
KINKER
KINKHAB
KINKHAUST
KINKHOST
KINKIER
KINKIEST
KINKILY
KINKINESS
KINKING
KINKLE
KINKLED
KINKSBUSH
KINKY
KINNERY
KINNIKINIC
KINNIKINNICK
KINNOR
KINO
KINOFLUOUS
KINOLOGY
KINOPLASM
KINOPLASMIC
KINOSPORE
KINOT
KINOTANNIC
KINSEN
KINSFOLK
KINSHIP
KINSMAN
KINSMANLY
KINSMEN
KINSPEOPLE
KINSWOMAN
KINTAR
KINTRA
KINTRY
KINURA
KIO
KIOEA
KIORE
KIOSK
KIOTOME
KIP
KIPE
KIPFEL
KIPP
KIPPAGE
KIPPEEN
KIPPER
KIPPERER
KIPPIN
KIPPY
KIPSEY
KIPSKIN
KIPUKA
KIRBY
KIRI
KIRIMON
KIRK
KIRKER
KIRKIFY
KIRKMAN
KIRKTON
KIRKTOWN
KIRKYARD
KIRMESS
KIRMEW
KIRN
KIROMBO
KIRPAN
KIRSCH
KIRSCHWASSER
KIRSEN
KIRTLE
KIRTLED
KIRVE
KIRVER
KIRVI
KISAENG
KISAN
KISANG
KISH
KISHEN
KISHKE
KISI
KISKADEE
KISKATOM
KISKATOMAS
KISKITOM
KISKITOMAS
KISM
KISMET
KISRA
KISS
KISSAGE
KISSAR
KISSER
KISSES
KISSING
KISSINGLY
KIST
KISTFUL
KISTVAEN
KISWA
KISWAH
KIT
KITAB
KITABI
KITAR
KITCAT
KITCHEN
KITCHENER
KITCHENET
KITCHENETTE
KITCHENMAID
KITCHENMAN
KITCHENRY
KITCHENWARE
KITCHENY
KITCHIE
KITE
KITEFLIER
KITEFLYING
KITES
KITH
KITHARA
KITHE
KITHOGUE
KITISH
KITLING
KITMAN
KITMUDGAR
KITT
KITTAR
KITTE
KITTEL
KITTEN
KITTENISH
KITTENISHLY
KITTER
KITTEREEN
KITTHOGE
KITTIE
KITTIWAKE
KITTLE
KITTLEPINS
KITTLES
KITTLISH
KITTLY
KITTOCK
KITTOOL
KITTUL
KITTY
KITTYSOL
KITUL
KIUTLE
KIVA
KIVER
KIVIKIVI
KIVU
KIVVER
KIWACH
KIWI
KIYAS
KIYI
KJELDAHLIZE
KLAFTER
KLAM
KLATSCH
KLAVERN
KLAXON
KLEENEBOC
KLEENEX
KLEG
KLEINITE
KLEPHT
KLEPHTIC
KLEPHTISM
KLEPTIC
KLEPTISTIC
KLEPTOMANIA
KLEPTOMANIAC
KLEPTOMANIST
KLEPTOPHOBIA
KLEZMER
KLICKET
KLINK
KLIP
KLIPBOK
KLIPDAS
KLIPFISH
KLIPHAAS
KLIPPE
KLIPPEN
KLIPSPRINGER
KLISMOS
KLISTER
KLOCKMANNITE
KLOM
KLOMP
KLONG
KLOOCH
KLOOF
KLOOTCHMAN
KLOP
KLOPS
KLOSH
KLOWET
KLUCKER
KLYSTRON
KMET
KNAB
KNABBLE
KNACK
KNACKAWAY
KNACKEBROD
KNACKER
KNACKERY
KNACKIER
KNACKIEST
KNACKWURST
KNACKY
KNAG
KNAGGED
KNAGGIER
KNAGGIEST
KNAGGY
KNAIDEL
KNAP
KNAPE
KNAPPAN
KNAPPE
KNAPPER
KNAPPISH
KNAPPISHLY
KNAPPLE
KNAPSACK
KNAPSACKED
KNAPSACKING
KNAPSCAP
KNAPSCULL
KNAPWEED
KNAR
KNARK
KNARL
KNARRED
KNARRY
KNASH
KNATCH
KNATTE
KNAUR
KNAVE
KNAVERY
KNAVESHIP
KNAVISH
KNAVISHLY
KNAVISHNESS
KNAW
KNAWEL
KNEAD
KNEADER
KNEADING
KNEADINGLY
KNEBELITE
KNECK
KNEE
KNEEBRUSH
KNEECAP
KNEED
KNEEHOLE
KNEEL
KNEELER
KNEELET
KNEELING
KNEELINGLY
KNEEPAD
KNEEPAN
KNEEPIECE
KNEESTONE
KNELL
KNELT
KNETCH
KNEVEL
KNEW
KNEZ
KNEZI
KNIAZ
KNICK
KNICKER
KNICKERED
KNICKERS
KNICKKNACK
KNICKKNACKED
KNICKKNACKET
KNICKKNACKY
KNICKPOINT
KNIFE
KNIFEBOARD
KNIFEFUL
KNIFELIKE
KNIFEMAN
KNIFER
KNIFESMITH
KNIFEWAY
KNIGHT
KNIGHTAGE
KNIGHTESS
KNIGHTHEAD
KNIGHTHOOD
KNIGHTLESS
KNIGHTLIKE
KNIGHTLINESS
KNIGHTLY

KNIP
KNISH
KNIT
KNITBACK
KNITCH
KNITTED
KNITTER
KNITTING
KNITTLE
KNITWEAR
KNITWEED
KNITWORK
KNIVE
KNIVED
KNIVES
KNIVEY
KNOB
KNOBBED
KNOBBER
KNOBBIER
KNOBBIEST
KNOBBLE
KNOBBLER
KNOBBLIER
KNOBBLIEST
KNOBBLY
KNOBBY
KNOBKERRY
KNOBLIKE
KNOBSTICK
KNOBSTONE
KNOBULAR
KNOBWEED
KNOBWOOD
KNOCK
KNOCKABOUT
KNOCKAWAY
KNOCKDOWN
KNOCKEMDOWN
KNOCKER
KNOCKING
KNOCKOFF
KNOCKOUT
KNOCKSTONE
KNOCKUP
KNOCKWURST
KNOIT
KNOLL
KNOLLER
KNOLLY
KNOP
KNOPITE
KNOPPED
KNOPPER
KNOPPIE
KNOPPY
KNORHAAN
KNOSP
KNOSPED
KNOT
KNOTBERRY
KNOTGRASS
KNOTHEAD
KNOTHOLE
KNOTHORN
KNOTROOT
KNOTS
KNOTTED
KNOTTER
KNOTTIER
KNOTTIEST
KNOTTINESS
KNOTTING
KNOTTY
KNOTWEED
KNOTWORK
KNOTWORT
KNOUT
KNOW
KNOWABILITY
KNOWABLE
KNOWABLENESS
KNOWE
KNOWER
KNOWING
KNOWINGLY
KNOWINGNESS
KNOWLEDGE
KNOWLEDGEABLE
KNOWLEDGED
KNOWLEDGEMENT
KNOWLEDGING
KNOWN
KNUB
KNUBBIER
KNUBBIEST
KNUBBLY
KNUBBY
KNUCK
KNUCKLE
KNUCKLEBONE
KNUCKLED
KNUCKLER
KNUCKLESOME
KNUCKLING
KNUCKLY
KNUCKS
KNULLING
KNUR
KNURL
KNURLED
KNURLIER
KNURLIEST
KNURLIN
KNURLING
KNURLY
KNURR
KNURRY
KNUT
KNYAZ
KNYSNA
KO
KOA
KOAE
KOALA
KOALI
KOAN
KOB
KOBA
KOBAN
KOBANG
KOBELLITE
KOBIL
KOBIRD
KOBOLD
KOBONG
KOBU
KOCHIA
KODA
KODAK
KODAKED
KODAKER
KODAKING
KODAKIST
KODAKKED
KODAKKING
KODAKRY
KODKOD
KODRA
KODURITE
KOECHLINITE
KOEL
KOENENITE
KOFF
KOFT
KOFTGAR
KOFTGARI
KOGASIN
KOGON
KOHEKOHE
KOHEMP
KOHL
KOHLRABI
KOHLRABIES
KOHUA
KOI
KOIL
KOILON
KOIMESIS
KOINE
KOINON
KOINONIA
KOJI
KOK
KOKAKO
KOKAM
KOKAMA
KOKAN
KOKANEE
KOKERBOOM
KOKIL
KOKILA
KOKIO
KOKKO
KOKLA
KOKLAS
KOKO
KOKOON
KOKOONA
KOKOPU
KOKOWAI
KOKRA
KOKSTAD
KOKTAITE
KOKU
KOKUM
KOKUMIN
KOLA
KOLACH
KOLAMI
KOLATTAM
KOLEA
KOLEK
KOLEL
KOLEROGA
KOLINSKI
KOLINSKY
KOLKHOS
KOLKHOZ
KOLKOZ
KOLLER
KOLLERGANG
KOLM
KOLO
KOLOBIA
KOLOBION
KOLOKOLO
KOLS
KOLSKITE
KOLSUN
KOLTUNNA
KOM
KOMARCH
KOMATIK
KOMBO
KOMBU
KOMINUTER
KOMITADJI
KOMITAJI
KOMMETJE
KOMMOS
KOMONDOR
KOMPENI
KOMPOW
KOMTOK
KON
KONA
KONAK
KONFYT
KONG
KONGONI
KONGSBERGITE
KONGU
KONIMETER
KONINCKITE
KONINI
KONIOLOGY
KONISCOPE
KONJAK
KONK
KONOHIKI
KONSEAL
KONZE
KOODOO
KOODOOS
KOOKA
KOOKABURRA
KOOKIE
KOOKIER
KOOKIEST
KOOKINESS
KOOKY
KOOLAH
KOOLAU
KOOLETAH
KOOLIMAN
KOOLOKAMBA
KOOMBAR
KOOMKIE
KOONTI
KOOP
KOOPBRIEF
KOORAJONG
KOORHAAN
KOORKA
KOOSIN
KOOTCHA
KOOTCHAR
KOP
KOPECK
KOPEK
KOPH
KOPI
KOPJE
KOPPA
KOPPEN
KOPPIE
KOPPITE
KOR
KORA
KORADJI
KORAIT
KORAKAN
KORARI
KORDAX
KORE
KOREC
KORERO
KORHAAN
KORI
KORIMAKO
KORIN
KORNERUPINE
KORO
KOROMIKA
KOROMIKO
KORONA
KOROVA
KORREL
KORRIGAN
KORRIGUM
KORUMBURRA
KORUN
KORUNA
KORUNY
KORZEC
KOS
KOSAM
KOSHARE
KOSHER
KOSIN
KOSMOKRATOR
KOSO
KOSONG
KOSOTOXIN
KOSS
KOSSO
KOSWITE
KOTAL
KOTO
KOTOITE
KOTSCHUBEITE
KOTTIGITE
KOTUKU
KOTUKUTUKU
KOTWAL
KOTWALEE
KOTYLE
KOU
KOUBA
KOULAN
KOUMISS
KOUMYS
KOUPREY
KOUPROH
KOURBASH
KOUROS
KOUS
KOUSE
KOUSIN
KOUSSIN
KOUSSO
KOUZA
KOVIL
KOWBIRD
KOWHAI
KOWL
KOWTOW
KOWTOWER
KOY
KOYEMSHI
KOZO
KRA
KRAAL
KRAFT
KRAGEROITE
KRAIT
KRAKEN
KRAKOWIAK
KRAL
KRAN
KRANG
KRANS
KRANTZ
KRANTZITE
KRAPFEN
KRAS
KRASIS
KRATER
KRATOGEN
KRATOGENIC
KRAUSEN
KRAUSITE
KRAUT
KRAUTHEAD

KRAUTWEED
KRAVERS
KREEF
KREESE
KREIS
KREISTLE
KREITONITE
KRELOS
KREMERSITE
KREMLIN
KREMS
KRENG
KRENNERITE
KREPLACH
KREPLECH
KREUTZER
KREUZER
KREX
KRIEGSPIEL
KRIEKER
KRIGIA
KRILL
KRIMMER
KRIS
KRISS
KRITARCHY
KRITRIMA
KROBYLOI
KROBYLOS
KROCKET
KROHNKITE
KROMESKI
KROMESKY
KROMOGRAM
KROMSKOP
KRONA
KRONE
KRONEN
KRONER
KRONOR
KRONOS
KRONUR
KROON
KROONI
KROONS
KROSA
KROUCHKA
KROUSHKA
KRUBI
KRUBUT
KRULLER
KRUMHORN
KRUMMHORN
KRYOKONITE
KRYOLITE
KRYOLITH
KRYPSIS
KRYPTIC
KRYPTICISM
KRYPTOL
KRYPTON
KTHIB
KTHIBH
KUAN
KUBA
KUBBA
KUBONG
KUBUKLION
KUCHEN
KUDIZE
KUDOS
KUDU
KUDZU
KUE
KUEI
KUERR
KUFA
KUGE
KUGEL
KUGELHOF
KUICHUA
KUJAWIAK
KUKERI
KUKRI
KUKU
KUKUI
KUKUPA
KULA
KULAH
KULAITE
KULAK
KULAKISM
KULAN
KULANG
KULKARNI
KULLAITE
KULM
KULMET
KULP
KUMARA
KUMBI
KUMBUK
KUMHAR
KUMISS
KUMKUM
KUMMEL
KUMMERBUND
KUMQUAT
KUMRAH
KUMYS
KUNAI
KUNG
KUNK
KUNKUR
KUNMIUT
KUNZITE
KUPFERNICKEL
KUPFFERITE
KUPHAR
KUPPER
KURBASH
KURCHICINE
KURCHINE
KURGAN
KURI
KURK
KURRAJONG
KURSI
KURTOSIS
KURUMA
KURUMAYA
KURUNG
KURUNJ
KURVEY
KURVEYOR
KUSA
KUSAM
KUSHA
KUSIMANSE
KUSIMANSEL
KUSKITE
KUSKUS
KUSSO
KUSTI
KUSU
KUSUM
KUTAI
KUTCH
KUTCHA
KUTTAB
KUTTAR
KUVASZ
KVARNER
KVAS
KVASS
KVINT
KVUTZA
KVUTZAH
KWAN
KWARTA
KWASHIORKOR
KWATUMA
KWAZOKU
KWEEK
KWEI
KWIEN
KWINTRA
KYAAK
KYACK
KYAH
KYANG
KYANISE
KYANITE
KYANIZATION
KYANIZE
KYAR
KYAT
KYATHOS
KYAUNG
KYE
KYKE
KYL
KYLE
KYLIE
KYLIKES
KYLIN
KYLITE
KYLIX
KYMATOLOGY
KYMBALON
KYMOGRAM
KYMOGRAPH
KYMOGRAPHIC
KYNURENIC
KYNURIN
KYNURINE
KYOODLE
KYPHOSIS
KYPHOTIC
KYPOO
KYRIAL
KYRIALE
KYRIELLE
KYRIN
KYRINE
KYRIOS
KYSCHTYMITE
KYTE
KYTHE

L

LA
LAAGER
LAAGTE
LAANG
LAAP
LAARP
LAB
LABARA
LABARIA
LABARUM
LABBA
LABBER
LABDACISM
LABDACISMUS
LABDANUM
LABEFACT
LABEFACTION
LABEFIED
LABEFY
LABEFYING
LABEL
LABELED
LABELER
LABELING
LABELLATE
LABELLED
LABELLER
LABELLING
LABELLOID
LABELLUM
LABIA
LABIAL
LABIALISM
LABIALISMUS
LABIALITY
LABIALIZE
LABIALIZED
LABIALIZING
LABIALLY
LABIATE
LABIATED
LABIE
LABIELLA
LABILE
LABILITY
LABILIZATION
LABILIZE
LABIODENTAL
LABIOGLOSSAL
LABIOGRAPH
LABIOLINGUAL
LABIOMANCY
LABIOMENTAL
LABIONASAL
LABIOPALATAL
LABIOPLASTY
LABIOSE
LABIOVELAR
LABIOVERSION
LABIS
LABITE
LABIUM
LABLAB
LABOR
LABORAGE
LABORANT
LABORATORIAL
LABORATORIAN
LABORATORIES
LABORATORY
LABORED
LABOREDLY
LABOREDNESS
LABORER
LABORES
LABORESS
LABORING
LABORINGLY
LABORIOUS
LABORIOUSLY
LABORIOUSNESS
LABORISM
LABORIST
LABORITE
LABOROUS
LABORSAVING
LABORSOME
LABORSOMELY
LABOUR
LABOURAGE
LABOURED
LABOUREDLY
LABOUREDNESS
LABOURER
LABOURESS
LABOURING
LABOURINGLY
LABOURISM
LABOURIST
LABOURITE
LABOURSAVING
LABOURSOME
LABOURSOMELY
LABRA
LABRADORITE
LABRADORITIC
LABRAL
LABRAS
LABRET
LABRETIFERY
LABRID
LABROID
LABROSAURID
LABROSAUROID
LABROSE
LABRUM
LABRUSCA
LABRYS
LABURNUM
LABYRINTH
LABYRINTHAL
LABYRINTHALLY
LABYRINTHED
LABYRINTHIAN
LABYRINTHIC
LABYRINTHICAL
LABYRINTHICALLY
LABYRINTHINE
LAC
LACATAN
LACCA
LACCASE
LACCOL
LACCOLITE
LACCOLITH
LACCOLITHIC
LACCOLITIC
LACE
LACEBARK
LACED
LACEFLOWER
LACELEAF
LACEMAKER
LACEMAKING
LACEMAN
LACEMEN
LACEPIECE
LACEPOD
LACER
LACERABILITY
LACERABLE
LACERANT
LACERATE
LACERATED
LACERATELY
LACERATING
LACERATION
LACERATIVE
LACERT
LACERTIAN
LACERTIFORM
LACERTILIAN
LACERTILOID
LACERTINE
LACERTOID
LACERY
LACET
LACEWING
LACEWOMAN
LACEWOMEN
LACEWOOD
LACEWORK
LACEWORKER
LACHE
LACHES
LACHRYMA
LACHRYMAL
LACHRYMALLY
LACHRYMARY
LACHRYMATION
LACHRYMATOR
LACHRYMATORY
LACHRYMIFORM
LACHRYMIST
LACHRYMOSAL
LACHRYMOSE
LACHRYMOSELY
LACHRYMOSITY
LACHRYMOUS
LACHSA
LACIER
LACIEST
LACILY
LACINESS
LACING
LACINIA
LACINIATE
LACINIATED
LACINIATION
LACINIFORM
LACINIOSE
LACINIOUS
LACINULA
LACINULAS
LACINULATE
LACINULOSE
LACIS
LACK
LACKADAISICAL
LACKADAISY
LACKADAY
LACKED
LACKER
LACKERER
LACKERING
LACKEY
LACKEYED
LACKEYING
LACKEYS
LACKIES
LACKING
LACKLAND
LACKLUSTER
LACKLUSTRE
LACKLUSTROUS
LACKWIT
LACKWITTEDLY
LACKWITTEDNESS
LACMOID
LACMUS
LACONIC
LACONICAL
LACONICALLY
LACONICISM
LACONICS
LACONICUM
LACONISM
LACONIZE
LACONIZED
LACONIZER
LACONIZING
LACQUER
LACQUERED
LACQUERER
LACQUERING
LACQUERIST
LACQUERWORK
LACQUEY
LACRIMAL
LACRIMATOR
LACROIXITE
LACROSSE
LACROSSER
LACTALBUMIN
LACTAM
LACTAMIDE
LACTANT
LACTARENE
LACTARINE
LACTARIUM
LACTARY
LACTASE
LACTATE
LACTATED
LACTATING
LACTATION
LACTEAL
LACTEAN
LACTENIN
LACTEOUS
LACTESCE
LACTESCENCE
LACTESCENCY
LACTESCENT
LACTIC
LACTICINIA
LACTID
LACTIDE
LACTIFEROUS
LACTIFIC
LACTIFICAL
LACTIFIED
LACTIFLOROUS
LACTIFLUOUS
LACTIFORM
LACTIFUGE
LACTIFY
LACTIFYING
LACTIGENIC
LACTIGENOUS
LACTIGEROUS
LACTIM
LACTIMIDE
LACTINATE
LACTIVOROUS
LACTO
LACTOCHROME
LACTOCITRATE
LACTOFLAVIN
LACTOGEN
LACTOGENIC
LACTOID
LACTOL
LACTOMETER
LACTONE
LACTONIC
LACTONIZE
LACTOPROTEID
LACTOPROTEIN
LACTOSCOPE
LACTOSE
LACTOSID
LACTOSIDE
LACTOSURIA
LACTOTOXIN
LACTUCARIUM
LACTUCERIN
LACTUCIN
LACTUCOL
LACTUCON
LACTYL
LACUNA
LACUNAE
LACUNAL
LACUNAR
LACUNARIA
LACUNARS
LACUNARY
LACUNAS
LACUNE
LACUNOME
LACUNOSE
LACUNOSITY
LACUNULE
LACUNULOSE
LACUSCULAR
LACUSTRAL
LACUSTRIAN
LACUSTRINE
LACWORK
LACY
LAD
LADANG
LADANIGEROUS
LADANUM
LADDER
LADDERED
LADDERING
LADDERWAY
LADDERY
LADDESS
LADDIE
LADDIKIE
LADDISH
LADDOCK
LADE
LADED
LADEMAN
LADEN
LADENED
LADENING
LADER
LADIES
LADIFIED
LADIFY
LADIFYING
LADING
LADKIN
LADLE
LADLED
LADLEFUL
LADLER
LADLEWOOD
LADLING
LADRONE

LADRONISM
LADRONIZE
LADY
LADYBIRD
LADYBUG
LADYCLOCK
LADYFINGER
LADYFISH
LADYFLIES
LADYFLY
LADYFY
LADYHOOD
LADYKIN
LADYKIND
LADYLIKE
LADYLIKELY
LADYLING
LADYLOVE
LADYPALM
LADYSFINGER
LADYSHIP
LADYSLIPPER
LAEMODIPOD
LAEMODIPODAN
LAEN
LAENDER
LAEOTROPIC
LAEOTROPISM
LAEOTROPOUS
LAET
LAETATION
LAETI
LAETIC
LAEVO
LAEVODUCTION
LAEVOGYRATE
LAEVOGYRE
LAEVOVERSION
LAFAYETTE
LAFE
LAFT
LAG
LAGAN'
LAGE
LAGEN
LAGENA
LAGENAE
LAGEND
LAGER
LAGERED
LAGERING
LAGETTO
LAGGAR
LAGGARD
LAGGARDLY
LAGGARDNESS
LAGGED
LAGGEN
LAGGER
LAGGIN
LAGGING
LAGLAST
LAGNA
LAGNAPPE
LAGNIAPPE
LAGO
LAGOMORPH
LAGOMORPHIC
LAGOMORPHOUS
LAGONITE
LAGOON
LAGOONAL
LAGOPODE
LAGOPODOUS
LAGOPOUS
LAGOSTOMA
LAGS
LAGUNA
LAGUNE
LAGWORT
LAHAR
LAHN
LAI
LAIC
LAICAL
LAICALITY
LAICALLY
LAICH
LAICISM
LAICITY
LAICIZATION
LAICIZE
LAICIZED
LAICIZER
LAICIZING
LAID
LAIDE
LAIDLY
LAIGH
LAIN
LAINAGE
LAINE
LAINER
LAIOSE
LAIR
LAIRAGE
LAIRD
LAIRDESS
LAIRDIE
LAIRDLY
LAIRDOCRACY
LAIRDSHIP
LAIRED
LAIRING
LAIRMAN
LAIRMEN
LAIRSTONE
LAIRY
LAISSE
LAIT
LAITANCE
LAITH
LAITHE
LAITHLY
LAITIES
LAITY
LAK
LAKARPITE
LAKATAN
LAKATOI
LAKE
LAKED
LAKELAND
LAKELANDER
LAKELET
LAKEMANSHIP
LAKER
LAKES
LAKESHORE
LAKEWEED
LAKEY
LAKH
LAKIE
LAKIER
LAKIEST
LAKIN
LAKING
LAKISH
LAKISHNESS
LAKISM
LAKIST
LAKMUS
LAKY
LALA
LALANG
LALAPALOOZA
LALAQUI
LALI
LALLAPALOOZA
LALLATION
LALLING
LALLYGAG
LALO
LALONEUROSIS
LALOPATHY
LALOPHOBIA
LALOPLEGIA
LAM
LAMA
LAMAIC
LAMANTIN
LAMANY
LAMASERIES
LAMASERY
LAMB
LAMBA
LAMBACK
LAMBALE
LAMBAST
LAMBASTE
LAMBASTED
LAMBASTING
LAMBDA
LAMBDACISM
LAMBDOID
LAMBDOIDAL
LAMBEAU
LAMBENCIES
LAMBENCY
LAMBENT
LAMBENTLY
LAMBER
LAMBERT
LAMBIE
LAMBINESS
LAMBISH
LAMBITIVE
LAMBKILL
LAMBKIN
LAMBLIASIS
LAMBLIKE
LAMBLING
LAMBOYS
LAMBREQUIN
LAMBS
LAMBSDOWN
LAMBSKIN
LAMDAN
LAMDEN
LAME
LAMED
LAMEDH
LAMEL
LAMELLA
LAMELLAE
LAMELLAR
LAMELLARY
LAMELLAS
LAMELLATE
LAMELLATED
LAMELLATELY
LAMELLATION
LAMELLICORN
LAMELLIFORM
LAMELLOID
LAMELLOSE
LAMELLOSITY
LAMELLULE
LAMELY
LAMENESS
LAMENT
LAMENTABLE
LAMENTABLY
LAMENTATION
LAMENTATORY
LAMENTED
LAMENTEDLY
LAMENTER
LAMENTFUL
LAMENTING
LAMENTINGLY
LAMENTIVE
LAMENTORY
LAMER
LAMEST
LAMESTER
LAMETER
LAMETTA
LAMIA
LAMIACEOUS
LAMIAE
LAMIAS
LAMIGER
LAMIID
LAMIN
LAMINA
LAMINABILITY
LAMINABLE
LAMINAE
LAMINAL
LAMINAR
LAMINARIAN
LAMINARIN
LAMINARIOID
LAMINARITE
LAMINARY
LAMINAS
LAMINATE
LAMINATED
LAMINATING
LAMINATION
LAMINBOARD
LAMINECTOMY
LAMING
LAMINIFEROUS
LAMINIFORM
LAMINITIS
LAMINOSE
LAMINOUS
LAMISH
LAMITER
LAMM
LAMMAS
LAMMED
LAMMER
LAMMERGEIER
LAMMERGEIR
LAMMERGEYER
LAMMIE
LAMMING
LAMMOCK
LAMMY
LAMNID
LAMNOID
LAMP
LAMPAD
LAMPADARIES
LAMPADARY
LAMPADEDROMY
LAMPADEPHORE
LAMPADITE
LAMPARA
LAMPAS
LAMPATIA
LAMPBLACK
LAMPBLACKED
LAMPBLACKING
LAMPED
LAMPER
LAMPERN
LAMPERS
LAMPFLOWER
LAMPFLY
LAMPFUL
LAMPHOLE
LAMPING
LAMPION
LAMPIST
LAMPISTRY
LAMPLESS
LAMPLET
LAMPLIGHT
LAMPLIGHTED
LAMPLIGHTER
LAMPLIT
LAMPMAKER
LAMPMAKING
LAMPMAN
LAMPMEN
LAMPOON
LAMPOONED
LAMPOONER
LAMPOONERY
LAMPOONING
LAMPOONIST
LAMPPOST
LAMPREL
LAMPRET
LAMPREY
LAMPREYS
LAMPROPHONY
LAMPROPHYRE
LAMPROPHYRIC
LAMPROTYPE
LAMPS
LAMPSHADE
LAMPSTAND
LAMPWICK
LAMPYRID
LAMPYRINE
LAMSIEKTE
LAMSTER
LAMZIEKTE
LAN
LANA
LANAC
LANAI
LANAMETER
LANARKITE
LANAS
LANATE
LANATED
LANAZ
LANCE
LANCED
LANCEGAY
LANCEGAYE
LANCELET
LANCELY
LANCEMAN
LANCEMEN
LANCEOLATE
LANCEOLATED
LANCEOLATELY
LANCEOLATION
LANCEPESADE
LANCEPOD
LANCEPRISADO
LANCER
LANCERS
LANCES
LANCET
LANCETED
LANCETEER
LANCEWOOD

LANCHA
LANCHARA
LANCIERS
LANCIFEROUS
LANCIFORM
LANCINATE
LANCINATED
LANCINATING
LANCINATION
LANCING
LAND
LANDAGE
LANDAMMAN
LANDAU
LANDAULET
LANDAULETTE
LANDBLINK
LANDBOC
LANDBOOK
LANDDROST
LANDDROSTEN
LANDE
LANDED
LANDER
LANDESITE
LANDFALL
LANDFANG
LANDFAST
LANDFLOOD
LANDFOLK
LANDFORM
LANDGAFOL
LANDGATE
LANDGATES
LANDGRAVE
LANDGRAVESS
LANDGRAVIATE
LANDGRAVINE
LANDHOLDER
LANDHOLDING
LANDIMERE
LANDING
LANDIRON
LANDLADIES
LANDLADY
LANDLEAPER
LANDLER
LANDLESS
LANDLESSNESS
LANDLINE
LANDLOCK
LANDLOCKED
LANDLOOK
LANDLOOKER
LANDLOPER
LANDLOPING
LANDLORD
LANDLORDISM
LANDLORDLY
LANDLORDRY
LANDLORDSHIP
LANDLOUPER
LANDLOUPING
LANDLUBBER
LANDLUBBERISH
LANDLUBBERLY
LANDLUBBING
LANDMAN
LANDMARK
LANDMASS
LANDMEN
LANDOCRACY
LANDOCRAT
LANDOWNER
LANDOWNERSHIP
LANDOWNING
LANDPLANE
LANDRACE
LANDRAKER
LANDREEVE
LANDRIGHT
LANDS
LANDSALE
LANDSCAPE
LANDSCAPED
LANDSCAPING
LANDSCAPIST
LANDSHARD
LANDSHIP
LANDSICK
LANDSIDE
LANDSKIP
LANDSLIDE
LANDSLIP
LANDSMAN
LANDSMEN
LANDSPOUT
LANDSPRINGY
LANDSTORM
LANDTROST
LANDWAITER
LANDWARD
LANDWARDS
LANDWASH
LANDWAY
LANDWAYS
LANDWHIN
LANDWIRE
LANDWRACK
LANDWRECK
LANDYARD
LANE
LANELY
LANER
LANESOME
LANETE
LANEWAY
LANEY
LANG
LANGAHA
LANGARAI
LANGBANITE
LANGBEINITE
LANGCA
LANGEL
LANGI
LANGITE
LANGKA
LANGLAUF
LANGLAUFER
LANGLE
LANGOON
LANGOOTY
LANGOSTA
LANGOUSTE
LANGRAGE
LANGREL
LANGRET
LANGRIDGE
LANGSETTLE
LANGSHAN
LANGSPIEL
LANGSPIL
LANGSYNE
LANGUAGE
LANGUAGED
LANGUAGES
LANGUAGING
LANGUE
LANGUENT
LANGUESCENT
LANGUET
LANGUETTE
LANGUID
LANGUIDLY
LANGUIDNESS
LANGUISH
LANGUISHED
LANGUISHER
LANGUISHING
LANGUISHINGLY
LANGUISHMENT
LANGUOR
LANGUORMENT
LANGUOROUS
LANGUOROUSLY
LANGUR
LANIA
LANIARD
LANIARIES
LANIARIFORM
LANIARY
LANIATE
LANIFEROUS
LANIFIC
LANIFICE
LANIFLOROUS
LANIFORM
LANIGEROUS
LANIIFORM
LANISTA
LANISTAE
LANITAL
LANK
LANKER
LANKEST
LANKET
LANKIER
LANKIEST
LANKILY
LANKINESS
LANKLY
LANKNESS
LANKY
LANNER
LANNERET
LANOLIN
LANOLINE
LANOSE
LANOSITY
LANSA
LANSAT
LANSDOWNE
LANSEH
LANSFORDITE
LANSQUENET
LANT
LANTACA
LANTAKA
LANTANA
LANTCHA
LANTERLOO
LANTERN
LANTERNED
LANTERNING
LANTERNLEAF
LANTERNMAN
LANTERNS
LANTHANA
LANTHANIA
LANTHANID
LANTHANIDE
LANTHANITE
LANTHANON
LANTHANUM
LANTHOPIN
LANTHOPINE
LANTHORN
LANTUM
LANUGINOSE
LANUGINOUS
LANUGO
LANUGOS
LANUM
LANX
LANYARD
LANZON
LAODAH
LAP
LAPACHO
LAPACHOL
LAPACTIC
LAPAN
LAPARECTOMY
LAPAROCELE
LAPAROMYITIS
LAPAROSCOPY
LAPAROSTICT
LAPAROTOME
LAPAROTOMIST
LAPAROTOMIZE
LAPAROTOMY
LAPBOARD
LAPCOCK
LAPDOG
LAPEL
LAPELER
LAPELLED
LAPFUL
LAPFULS
LAPICIDE
LAPIDARIAN
LAPIDARIES
LAPIDARIST
LAPIDARY
LAPIDATE
LAPIDATED
LAPIDATING
LAPIDATION
LAPIDATOR
LAPIDEON
LAPIDEOUS
LAPIDES
LAPIDESCENCE
LAPIDESCENT
LAPIDICOLOUS
LAPIDIFIC
LAPIDIFICAL
LAPIDIFIED
LAPIDIFY
LAPIDIFYING
LAPIDIST
LAPIDITY
LAPIDOSE
LAPIES
LAPILLI
LAPILLIFORM
LAPILLO
LAPILLUS
LAPIN
LAPIS
LAPLING
LAPON
LAPPACEOUS
LAPPAGE
LAPPED
LAPPER
LAPPET
LAPPETED
LAPPETHEAD
LAPPING
LAPPISH
LAPSABILITY
LAPSABLE
LAPSATION
LAPSE
LAPSED
LAPSER
LAPSI
LAPSIBILITY
LAPSIBLE
LAPSING
LAPSINGLY
LAPSTONE
LAPSTRAKE
LAPSTREAK
LAPSTREAKED
LAPSTREAKER
LAPSUS
LAPULAPU
LAPWING
LAPWORK
LAQUEAR
LAQUEARIA
LAQUEARIAN
LAQUEUS
LAR
LARARIUM
LARB
LARBOARD
LARBOLINS
LARBOWLINES
LARCENER
LARCENIC
LARCENIES
LARCENISH
LARCENIST
LARCENOUS
LARCENOUSLY
LARCENY
LARCH
LARCIN
LARCINRY
LARD
LARDACEIN
LARDACEOUS
LARDED
LARDER
LARDERELLITE
LARDERER
LARDIFORM
LARDINER
LARDING
LARDITE
LARDON
LARDOON
LARDRY
LARDY
LAREABELL
LARES
LARGAMENTE
LARGANDO
LARGE
LARGEBRAINED
LARGEHEARTED
LARGEHEARTEDNESS
LARGELY
LARGEMOUTHED
LARGEN
LARGENESS
LARGEOUR
LARGEOUS
LARGER
LARGESS
LARGESSE
LARGEST
LARGHETTO
LARGHETTOS
LARGHISSIMO
LARGHISSIMOS
LARGIFICAL
LARGISH
LARGITION
LARGITIONAL
LARGO

LARGY
LARI
LARIAT
LARIATED
LARIATING
LARICK
LARID
LARIDINE
LARIGO
LARIGOT
LARIID
LARIN
LARINE
LARIOT
LARIX
LARIXIN
LARK
LARKED
LARKER
LARKING
LARKINGLY
LARKISH
LARKISHNESS
LARKS
LARKSOME
LARKSPUR
LARKY
LARM
LARME
LARMIER
LARMOYANT
LARNAKES
LARNAX
LAROID
LARON
LARREE
LARRIES
LARRIGAN
LARRIKIN
LARRIKINESS
LARRIKINISM
LARRIMAN
LARRUP
LARRUPED
LARRUPING
LARRY
LARS
LARSENITE
LARUM
LARVA
LARVAE
LARVAL
LARVARIA
LARVARIUM
LARVARIUMS
LARVATE
LARVATED
LARVE
LARVICIDAL
LARVICIDE
LARVICOLOUS
LARVIFORM
LARVIGEROUS
LARVIPAROUS
LARVIPOSIT
LARVIPOSITION
LARVIVOROUS
LARVULE
LARY
LARYNGAL
LARYNGALGIA
LARYNGEAL
LARYNGEAN
LARYNGEATING
LARYNGECTOMY
LARYNGES
LARYNGIC
LARYNGISMAL
LARYNGISMUS
LARYNGITIC
LARYNGITIS
LARYNGOCELE
LARYNGOGRAPH
LARYNGOLOGY
LARYNGOMETRY
LARYNGOPATHY
LARYNGOPHONY
LARYNGORRHEA
LARYNGOSCOPE
LARYNGOSCOPY
LARYNGOSTOMY
LARYNGOTOME
LARYNGOTOMY
LARYNX
LARYNXES
LAS
LASAGNA
LASAGNE
LASCAR
LASCHETY
LASCIVIENT
LASCIVIENTLY
LASCIVIOUS
LASCIVIOUSLY
LASCIVIOUSNESS
LASER
LASERWORT
LASH
LASHED
LASHER
LASHES
LASHING
LASHINGS
LASHINS
LASHLESS
LASHLIGHT
LASHLITE
LASHNESS
LASHORN
LASIOCAMPID
LASIOCARPOUS
LASK
LASKE
LASKET
LASKING
LASPRING
LASQUE
LASS
LASSET
LASSIE
LASSIKY
LASSITUDE
LASSLORN
LASSO
LASSOCK
LASSOCKIE
LASSOED
LASSOER
LASSOES
LASSOING
LASSOS
LASSU
LAST
LASTAGE
LASTER
LASTEX
LASTING
LASTINGLY
LASTINGNESS
LASTLY
LASTRE
LASTY
LASYA
LAT
LATA
LATAH
LATANIER
LATCH
LATCHED
LATCHER
LATCHET
LATCHING
LATCHKEY
LATCHMAN
LATCHMEN
LATCHSTRING
LATE
LATEBRA
LATEBRICOLE
LATECOMER
LATECOMING
LATED
LATEEN
LATEENER
LATELINESS
LATELY
LATEMOST
LATEN
LATENCE
LATENCIES
LATENCY
LATENESS
LATENT
LATENTLY
LATER
LATERA
LATERAD
LATERAL
LATERALITY
LATERALIZE
LATERALIZED
LATERALIZING
LATERALLY
LATERAN
LATERIFLORAL
LATERIGRADE
LATERITE
LATERITIC
LATERIZATION
LATEROCAUDAL
LATERODORSAL
LATERONUCHAL
LATESCENCE
LATESCENT
LATESOME
LATEST
LATEWARD
LATEWHILE
LATEWHILES
LATEWOOD
LATEX
LATEXES
LATEXOSIS
LATH
LATHE
LATHED
LATHEE
LATHEMAN
LATHEN
LATHER
LATHERED
LATHEREEVE
LATHERER
LATHERIN
LATHERING
LATHERWORT
LATHERY
LATHESMAN
LATHESMEN
LATHI
LATHIE
LATHIER
LATHIEST
LATHING
LATHREEVE
LATHS
LATHWORK
LATHY
LATHYRIC
LATHYRISM
LATI
LATIBULIZE
LATICES
LATICIFEROUS
LATICLAVE
LATICOSTATE
LATIDENTATE
LATIFOLIATE
LATIFOLIOUS
LATIFUNDIA
LATIFUNDIAN
LATIFUNDIUM
LATIGO
LATINISM
LATINIZE
LATION
LATIPENNATE
LATIPENNINE
LATIPLANTAR
LATIROSTRAL
LATIROSTROUS
LATISEPT
LATISEPTAL
LATISEPTATE
LATISH
LATISTERNAL
LATITANCY
LATITANT
LATITAT
LATITE
LATITUDE
LATITUDINAL
LATITUDINALLY
LATITUDINARIAN
LATITUDINARY
LATITUDINOUS
LATIVE
LATKE
LATOMIA
LATOMY
LATOSOL
LATRANT
LATRATION
LATREDE
LATREUTIC
LATREUTICAL
LATRIA
LATRIAL
LATRIALLY
LATRIAN
LATRINE
LATRO
LATROBE
LATROBITE
LATROCINIUM
LATROCINY
LATRON
LATS
LATTEN
LATTENER
LATTENS
LATTER
LATTERLY
LATTERMATH
LATTERMOST
LATTICE
LATTICED
LATTICELEAF
LATTICEWORK
LATTICING
LATTICINIO
LATTIN
LATU
LATUS
LAUAN
LAUBANITE
LAUD
LAUDABILITY
LAUDABLE
LAUDABLENESS
LAUDABLY
LAUDANIDINE
LAUDANIN
LAUDANINE
LAUDANOSINE
LAUDANUM
LAUDATION
LAUDATIVE
LAUDATORILY
LAUDATORY
LAUDED
LAUDER
LAUDIFICATION
LAUDING
LAUDIST
LAUDS
LAUGH
LAUGHABLE
LAUGHABLENESS
LAUGHABLY
LAUGHED
LAUGHEE
LAUGHER
LAUGHFUL
LAUGHING
LAUGHINGLY
LAUGHINGSTOCK
LAUGHS
LAUGHSOME
LAUGHTER
LAUGHWORTHY
LAUGHY
LAUHALA
LAUIA
LAUK
LAULAU
LAUMONITE
LAUMONTITE
LAUN
LAUNCE
LAUNCH
LAUNCHED
LAUNCHER
LAUNCHING
LAUND
LAUNDER
LAUNDERED
LAUNDERER
LAUNDERETTE
LAUNDERING
LAUNDRESS
LAUNDRIES
LAUNDROMAT
LAUNDRY
LAUNDRYMAID
LAUNDRYMAN
LAUNDRYMEN
LAUNDRYOWNER
LAUNDRYWOMAN
LAUNDRYWOMEN
LAUNEDDAS
LAURA
LAURACEOUS
LAURAE
LAURALDEHYDE

LAURAS
LAURATE
LAURDALITE
LAURE
LAUREATE
LAUREATED
LAUREATESHIP
LAUREATING
LAUREATION
LAUREL
LAURELED
LAURELING
LAURELLED
LAURELLING
LAURELS
LAURELSHIP
LAURELWOOD
LAUREOLE
LAURIC
LAURIN
LAURINOXYLON
LAURIONITE
LAURITE
LAURONE
LAURUSTINE
LAURUSTINUS
LAURVIKITE
LAURY
LAURYL
LAUTARITE
LAUTER
LAUTITE
LAUTITIOUS
LAUTU
LAUWINE
LAVA
LAVABO
LAVABOES
LAVACRE
LAVADERO
LAVAGE
LAVALIER
LAVALIERE
LAVAMENT
LAVANDERA
LAVANDERAS
LAVANDERO
LAVANDEROS
LAVANDIN
LAVANGA
LAVANT
LAVARET
LAVASH
LAVATIC
LAVATION
LAVATIONAL
LAVATORIES
LAVATORY
LAVE
LAVED
LAVEER
LAVEMENT
LAVENDER
LAVENDERED
LAVENDERING
LAVENITE
LAVER
LAVEROCK
LAVETTE
LAVIALITE
LAVING
LAVISH
LAVISHED
LAVISHER
LAVISHING
LAVISHINGLY
LAVISHLY
LAVISHNESS
LAVOLTA
LAVROCK
LAVROFFITE
LAVROVITE
LAVY
LAW
LAWBOOK
LAWBREAKER
LAWBREAKERS
LAWBREAKING
LAWFUL
LAWFULLY
LAWFULNESS
LAWGIVER
LAWGIVING
LAWINE
LAWING
LAWISH
LAWK
LAWKS
LAWLANTS
LAWLESS
LAWLESSLY
LAWLESSNESS
LAWLIKE
LAWMAKER
LAWMAKING
LAWMAN
LAWMEN
LAWMONGER
LAWN
LAWNED
LAWNER
LAWNLEAF
LAWNLET
LAWNLIKE
LAWNY
LAWPROOF
LAWRENCITE
LAWRENCIUM
LAWRIGHTMAN
LAWRIGHTMEN
LAWS
LAWSONE
LAWSONITE
LAWSUIT
LAWSUITING
LAWTER
LAWYER
LAWYERLIKE
LAWYERLY
LAWYERY
LAX
LAXATE
LAXATION
LAXATIVE
LAXATIVELY
LAXATIVENESS
LAXER
LAXEST
LAXIFLOROUS
LAXIFOLIATE
LAXIFOLIOUS
LAXISM
LAXIST
LAXITY
LAXLY
LAXNESS
LAY
LAYAWAY
LAYBACK
LAYBOY
LAYER
LAYERAGE
LAYERED
LAYERING
LAYERS
LAYERY
LAYETTE
LAYFOLK
LAYING
LAYLAND
LAYLIGHT
LAYLOCK
LAYMAN
LAYMANSHIP
LAYMEN
LAYNE
LAYOFF
LAYOUT
LAYOVER
LAYROCK
LAYSTALL
LAYSTOW
LAYWOMAN
LAYWOMEN
LAZAR
LAZARET
LAZARETTE
LAZARETTO
LAZARETTOS
LAZARLY
LAZAROLE
LAZARONE
LAZAROUS
LAZARY
LAZE
LAZED
LAZIER
LAZIEST
LAZILY
LAZINESS
LAZING
LAZO
LAZULE
LAZULI
LAZULITE
LAZULITIC
LAZURITE
LAZY
LAZYBACK
LAZYBED
LAZYBIRD
LAZYBONE
LAZYBONES
LAZYBOOTS
LAZYLEGS
LAZZARONE
LAZZARONI
LAZZO
LE
LEA
LEACH
LEACHATE
LEACHED
LEACHER
LEACHIER
LEACHIEST
LEACHING
LEACHMAN
LEACHMEN
LEACHY
LEAD
LEADAGE
LEADBACK
LEADED
LEADEN
LEADENLY
LEADENNESS
LEADER
LEADERETTE
LEADERS
LEADERSHIP
LEADHILLITE
LEADIN
LEADING
LEADMAN
LEADOFF
LEADOFFS
LEADOUT
LEADPLANT
LEADS
LEADSMAN
LEADSMEN
LEADWAY
LEADWOOD
LEADWORK
LEADWORT
LEADY
LEAF
LEAFAGE
LEAFBIRD
LEAFBOY
LEAFCUP
LEAFDOM
LEAFED
LEAFEN
LEAFER
LEAFERY
LEAFGIRL
LEAFHOPPER
LEAFIER
LEAFIEST
LEAFINESS
LEAFING
LEAFIT
LEAFLESS
LEAFLET
LEAFLETEER
LEAFLIKE
LEAFMOLD
LEAFSTALK
LEAFWOOD
LEAFWORK
LEAFWORM
LEAFY
LEAG
LEAGUE
LEAGUED
LEAGUER
LEAGUERER
LEAGUING
LEAK
LEAKAGE
LEAKANCE
LEAKED
LEAKER
LEAKIER
LEAKIEST
LEAKINESS
LEAKING
LEAKY
LEAL
LEALAND
LEALLY
LEALNESS
LEALTY
LEAM
LEAMER
LEAN
LEANED
LEANER
LEANING
LEANLY
LEANNESS
LEANT
LEANY
LEAP
LEAPED
LEAPER
LEAPFROG
LEAPFROGGER
LEAPFROGGING
LEAPING
LEAPINGLY
LEAPS
LEAPT
LEAR
LEARN
LEARNED
LEARNEDLY
LEARNEDNESS
LEARNER
LEARNING
LEARNT
LEARY
LEASE
LEASEBACK
LEASED
LEASEHOLD
LEASEHOLDER
LEASEHOLDING
LEASEMONGER
LEASER
LEASH
LEASING
LEASOW
LEAST
LEASTWAYS
LEASTWISE
LEAT
LEATH
LEATHER
LEATHERBACK
LEATHERBARK
LEATHERBOARD
LEATHERCOAT
LEATHERER
LEATHERETTE
LEATHERFISH
LEATHERFISHES
LEATHERFLOWER
LEATHERHEAD
LEATHERINE
LEATHERINESS
LEATHERING
LEATHERIZE
LEATHERJACKET
LEATHERLEAF
LEATHERN
LEATHERNECK
LEATHEROID
LEATHERS
LEATHERSIDE
LEATHERWARE
LEATHERWING
LEATHERWOOD
LEATHERWORK
LEATHERWORKER
LEATHERWORKING
LEATHERY
LEATHWAKE
LEATMAN
LEATMEN
LEAVE
LEAVED
LEAVELESS
LEAVELOOKER
LEAVEN
LEAVENED
LEAVENING
LEAVENOUS
LEAVER
LEAVES
LEAVIER
LEAVIEST
LEAVING

LEAVINGS
LEAVY
LEAWILL
LEAZE
LEBAN
LEBBAN
LEBBEK
LEBEN
LEBHAFT
LEBO
LEBRANCHO
LEBU
LECAMA
LECANIID
LECANINE
LECANOMANCER
LECANOMANCY
LECANOMANTIC
LECANORINE
LECANOROID
LECANOSCOPIC
LECANOSCOPY
LECCE
LECH
LECHER
LECHERER
LECHERIES
LECHEROUS
LECHEROUSLY
LECHEROUSNESS
LECHERY
LECHOSA
LECHRIODONT
LECHUGUILLA
LECHWE
LECIDEIFORM
LECIDEINE
LECIDIOID
LECITHAL
LECITHALITY
LECITHIN
LECITHOBLAST
LECK
LECKER
LECONTITE
LECOTROPAL
LECTERN
LECTION
LECTIONARIES
LECTIONARY
LECTOR
LECTORATE
LECTORIAL
LECTOTYPE
LECTRESS
LECTRICE
LECTUAL
LECTUARY
LECTURE
LECTURED
LECTURER
LECTURESHIP
LECTURETTE
LECTURING
LECYTH
LECYTHI
LECYTHID
LECYTHOI
LECYTHOID
LECYTHUS
LED
LEDE
LEDEN
LEDERHOSEN
LEDERITE
LEDGE
LEDGED
LEDGEMAN
LEDGEMENT
LEDGER
LEDGERED
LEDGERING
LEDGES
LEDGIER
LEDGIEST
LEDGING
LEDGMENT
LEDGY
LEDOL
LEE
LEEANGLE
LEEBOARD
LEECH
LEECHCRAFT
LEECHDOM
LEECHEATER
LEECHED
LEECHER
LEECHERY
LEECHES
LEECHING
LEECHMAN
LEECHWORT
LEED
LEEFANG
LEEFANGE
LEEFTAIL
LEEFUL
LEEFULLY
LEEFULNESS
LEEGTE
LEEK
LEEKY
LEELANE
LEELANG
LEEM
LEEN
LEEP
LEEPIT
LEER
LEERED
LEERFISH
LEERIER
LEERIEST
LEERING
LEERISH
LEERNESS
LEERY
LEES
LEESE
LEESER
LEESING
LEESOME
LEESOMELY
LEET
LEETLE
LEETMAN
LEETMEN
LEEVE
LEEWAN
LEEWARD
LEEWARDLY
LEEWARDMOST
LEEWAY
LEEWILL
LEFSE
LEFSEL
LEFSEN
LEFT
LEFTISM
LEFTIST
LEFTMENTS
LEFTOVER
LEFTWARD
LEFTWARDLY
LEFTWARDS
LEFTY
LEG
LEGACIES
LEGACY
LEGAL
LEGALESE
LEGALISE
LEGALISM
LEGALIST
LEGALISTIC
LEGALISTICALLY
LEGALITIES
LEGALITY
LEGALIZATION
LEGALIZE
LEGALIZED
LEGALIZING
LEGALLY
LEGANTINE
LEGATARY
LEGATE
LEGATEE
LEGATESHIP
LEGATI
LEGATINE
LEGATION
LEGATIONARY
LEGATIVE
LEGATO
LEGATOR
LEGATORIAL
LEGATOS
LEGATUS
LEGBAR
LEGEND
LEGENDA
LEGENDARIAN
LEGENDARY
LEGENDIC
LEGENDRY
LEGENDS
LEGER
LEGERDEMAIN
LEGERDEMAINIST
LEGERETE
LEGERITY
LEGES
LEGGE
LEGGED
LEGGER
LEGGIER
LEGGIERO
LEGGIEST
LEGGINESS
LEGGING
LEGGINGED
LEGGINGS
LEGGY
LEGHORN
LEGIBILITY
LEGIBLE
LEGIBLENESS
LEGIBLY
LEGIFER
LEGIFIC
LEGION
LEGIONARIES
LEGIONARY
LEGIONED
LEGIONER
LEGIONNAIRE
LEGIONRY
LEGISLATE
LEGISLATED
LEGISLATING
LEGISLATION
LEGISLATIONAL
LEGISLATIVE
LEGISLATIVELY
LEGISLATOR
LEGISLATORIAL
LEGISLATRESS
LEGISLATRIX
LEGISLATURE
LEGIST
LEGISTER
LEGIT
LEGITIM
LEGITIMACY
LEGITIMATE
LEGITIMATED
LEGITIMATELY
LEGITIMATENESS
LEGITIMATING
LEGITIMATION
LEGITIMATIST
LEGITIMATIZE
LEGITIMATIZED
LEGITIMATIZING
LEGITIME
LEGITIMISM
LEGITIMIST
LEGITIMISTIC
LEGITIMITY
LEGITIMIZATION
LEGITIMIZE
LEGITIMIZED
LEGITIMIZING
LEGLEN
LEGLESS
LEGLET
LEGMAN
LEGOA
LEGONG
LEGPIECE
LEGPULL
LEGPULLER
LEGPULLING
LEGROOM
LEGS
LEGUA
LEGUAN
LEGULEIAN
LEGULEIOUS
LEGUME
LEGUMELIN
LEGUMEN
LEGUMIN
LEGUMINIFORM
LEGUMINOSE
LEGUMINOUS
LEGWORK
LEHAYIM
LEHIITE
LEHR
LEHRBACHITE
LEHRMAN
LEHRMEN
LEHRSMAN
LEHRSMEN
LEHUA
LEI
LEIE
LEIF
LEIFITE
LEIGHTON
LEIMTYPE
LEIOCOME
LEIOMYOMA
LEIOMYOMATA
LEIOTRICHINE
LEIOTRICHOUS
LEIOTRICHY
LEIOTROPIC
LEIR
LEIS
LEISHMANIA
LEISHMANIASIS
LEISS
LEISTER
LEISTERER
LEISURABLE
LEISURABLY
LEISURE
LEISURED
LEISURELINESS
LEISURELY
LEITMOTIF
LEITMOTIV
LEK
LEKACH
LEKANAI
LEKANE
LEKIN
LEKYTHOS
LELWEL
LEMAN
LEMANRY
LEMANS
LEMEL
LEMMA
LEMMAS
LEMMATA
LEMMING
LEMMINGS
LEMMOBLASTIC
LEMMOCYTE
LEMMON
LEMNACEOUS
LEMNAD
LEMNISCATA
LEMNISCATE
LEMNISCATIC
LEMNISCI
LEMNISCUS
LEMOGRAPHY
LEMOLOGY
LEMON
LEMONADE
LEMONADO
LEMONGRASS
LEMONWEED
LEMONWOOD
LEMONY
LEMPIRA
LEMUR
LEMURES
LEMURIFORM
LEMURINE
LEMUROID
LEMURS
LENA
LENAD
LENARD
LENCH
LENCHEON
LEND
LENDE
LENDER
LENDING
LENE
LENES
LENG
LENGTH
LENGTHEN
LENGTHENED
LENGTHENING
LENGTHER
LENGTHIER

LENGTHIEST
LENGTHILY
LENGTHINESS
LENGTHS
LENGTHSMAN
LENGTHSMEN
LENGTHWAYS
LENGTHWISE
LENGTHY
LENIATE
LENIENCE
LENIENCY
LENIENT
LENIENTLY
LENIFY
LENIS
LENITIC
LENITIES
LENITION
LENITIVE
LENITIVELY
LENITIVENESS
LENITUDE
LENITY
LENNILITE
LENNOACEOUS
LENNOW
LENO
LENOS
LENS
LENSED
LENSES
LENSLESS
LENSMAN
LENT
LENTAMENTE
LENTANDO
LENTEN
LENTICEL
LENTICELLATE
LENTICLE
LENTICONUS
LENTICULA
LENTICULAE
LENTICULAR
LENTICULARE
LENTICULARIS
LENTICULARLY
LENTICULAS
LENTICULATE
LENTICULE
LENTIFORM
LENTIGEROUS
LENTIGINES
LENTIGINOSE
LENTIGINOUS
LENTIGO
LENTIL
LENTILE
LENTINER
LENTISCINE
LENTISCUS
LENTISSIMO
LENTITUDE
LENTNER
LENTO
LENTOID
LENTOR
LENTOUS
LENVOY
LEODICID
LEONCITO
LEONHARDITE
LEONINE
LEONINELY
LEONINES
LEONITE
LEONTIASIS
LEOPARD
LEOPARDE
LEOPARDESS
LEOPARDITE
LEOTARD
LEOTARDS
LEP
LEPADID
LEPADOID
LEPER
LEPERED
LEPERO
LEPID
LEPIDIN
LEPIDINE
LEPIDITY
LEPIDLY
LEPIDOBLASTIC
LEPIDOID
LEPIDOLITE
LEPIDOMELANE
LEPIDOPHYTE
LEPIDOPHYTIC
LEPIDOPTER
LEPIDOPTERA
LEPIDOPTERAL
LEPIDOPTERAN
LEPIDOPTERID
LEPIDOPTERIST
LEPIDOPTERON
LEPIDOPTEROUS
LEPIDOSIREN
LEPIDOSIS
LEPIDOSTEOID
LEPIDOTE
LEPOCYTA
LEPOCYTE
LEPORID
LEPORIDE
LEPORIFORM
LEPORINE
LEPOTHRIX
LEPPER
LEPPY
LEPRA
LEPRECHAUN
LEPRIC
LEPRID
LEPROID
LEPROLOGIC
LEPROLOGIST
LEPROLOGY
LEPROMA
LEPROMATOUS
LEPROSARIA
LEPROSARIUM
LEPROSARIUMS
LEPROSE
LEPROSED
LEPROSERIES
LEPROSERY
LEPROSIED
LEPROSIS
LEPROSITY
LEPROSY
LEPROUS
LEPROUSLY
LEPROUSNESS
LEPRY
LEPTA
LEPTANDRIN
LEPTENE
LEPTID
LEPTINOLITE
LEPTITE
LEPTOBOS
LEPTOCARDIAN
LEPTOCENTRIC
LEPTOCERCAL
LEPTOCHROA
LEPTOCHROUS
LEPTOCLASE
LEPTODACTYL
LEPTODERMOUS
LEPTOFORM
LEPTOLOGY
LEPTOMATIC
LEPTOME
LEPTOMEDUSAN
LEPTOMETER
LEPTOMONAD
LEPTON
LEPTONEMA
LEPTONS
LEPTOPELLIC
LEPTOPROSOPE
LEPTOPROSOPY
LEPTORRHIN
LEPTORRHINE
LEPTOSOME
LEPTOSPERM
LEPTOSPIROSIS
LEPTOSTRACAN
LEPTOTENE
LEPTUS
LEPTYNITE
LERE
LERED
LERER
LERNAEAN
LEROT
LERP
LERRET
LES
LESBIAN
LESBIANISM
LESCHE
LESE
LESED
LESHEY
LESHY
LESION
LESIY
LESKEACEOUS
LESS
LESSE
LESSEE
LESSEN
LESSENED
LESSENER
LESSENING
LESSER
LESSES
LESSEST
LESSIVE
LESSNESS
LESSON
LESSONED
LESSONING
LESSOR
LEST
LESTIWARITE
LESTOBIOSIS
LESTOBIOTIC
LESTRAD
LET
LETCH
LETCHY
LETDOWN
LETGAME
LETHAL
LETHALITY
LETHARGIC
LETHARGICAL
LETHARGICALLY
LETHARGIZE
LETHARGIZED
LETHARGIZING
LETHARGUS
LETHARGY
LETHIED
LETHIFEROUS
LETHOLOGICA
LETOFF
LETON
LETTED
LETTEN
LETTER
LETTERED
LETTERER
LETTERET
LETTERGAE
LETTERGRAM
LETTERHEAD
LETTERING
LETTERLEAF
LETTERMAN
LETTERMEN
LETTERPRESS
LETTERS
LETTERSPACE
LETTERWEIGHT
LETTICE
LETTIGA
LETTING
LETTRURE
LETTUCE
LETUP
LEU
LEUCAETHIOP
LEUCAETHIOPES
LEUCAETHIOPIC
LEUCANILINE
LEUCANTHOUS
LEUCAUGITE
LEUCAURIN
LEUCIN
LEUCINE
LEUCITE
LEUCITIC
LEUCITIS
LEUCITITE
LEUCITOID
LEUCITOPHYRE
LEUCO
LEUCOBASALT
LEUCOBLAST
LEUCOBLASTIC
LEUCOCARPOUS
LEUCOCHOLIC
LEUCOCHOLY
LEUCOCHROIC
LEUCOCIDIC
LEUCOCIDIN
LEUCOCRATE
LEUCOCRATIC
LEUCOCYAN
LEUCOCYTE
LEUCOCYTIC
LEUCOCYTOID
LEUCOCYTOSIS
LEUCOCYTOTIC
LEUCODERMA
LEUCODERMIA
LEUCODERMIC
LEUCOGENIC
LEUCOID
LEUCOMA
LEUCOMAINE
LEUCOMATOUS
LEUCOMELANIC
LEUCON
LEUCONES
LEUCOPENIA
LEUCOPENIC
LEUCOPHANE
LEUCOPHANITE
LEUCOPHORE
LEUCOPHYRE
LEUCOPLAKIA
LEUCOPLAKIAL
LEUCOPLAST
LEUCOPLASTID
LEUCOPOIESIS
LEUCOPYRITE
LEUCORRHEA
LEUCORRHEAL
LEUCORRHOEA
LEUCORRHOEAL
LEUCORYX
LEUCOSPHERE
LEUCOSPHERIC
LEUCOSTASIS
LEUCOSYENITE
LEUCOTOME
LEUCOTOXIC
LEUCOUS
LEUCOXENE
LEUCYL
LEUD
LEUDES
LEUDS
LEUGH
LEUKAEMIA
LEUKAEMIC
LEUKEMIA
LEUKEMIC
LEUKEMID
LEUKOCIDIC
LEUKOCIDIN
LEUKOCYTE
LEUKOCYTOSIS
LEUKOCYTOTIC
LEUKODERMA
LEUKODERMIC
LEUKOMA
LEUKOPENIA
LEUKOPENIC
LEUKORRHEA
LEUKOSIS
LEUMA
LEV
LEVA
LEVADE
LEVAN
LEVANCE
LEVANCY
LEVANT
LEVANTER
LEVANTINE
LEVATION
LEVATOR
LEVATORES
LEVATORS
LEVE
LEVEE
LEVEED
LEVEEING
LEVEL
LEVELED
LEVELER
LEVELHEADED
LEVELHEADEDLY
LEVELHEADEDNESS
LEVELING
LEVELISM
LEVELLED

LEVELLER
LEVELLING
LEVELLY
LEVELMAN
LEVELNESS
LEVER
LEVERAGE
LEVERED
LEVERER
LEVERET
LEVERING
LEVERMAN
LEVERS
LEVESEL
LEVET
LEVIABLE
LEVIATHAN
LEVIED
LEVIER
LEVIES
LEVIGABLE
LEVIGATE
LEVIGATION
LEVIGATOR
LEVIN
LEVINING
LEVIR
LEVIRATE
LEVIRATIC
LEVIRATICAL
LEVIRATION
LEVITANT
LEVITATE
LEVITATED
LEVITATING
LEVITATION
LEVITATIONAL
LEVITATIVE
LEVITATOR
LEVITIES
LEVITY
LEVODUCTION
LEVOGYRATE
LEVOGYRE
LEVOROTATION
LEVOROTATORY
LEVOVERSION
LEVULIN
LEVULINIC
LEVULOSE
LEVULOSURIA
LEVY
LEVYING
LEVYIST
LEVYNE
LEVYNITE
LEW
LEWAN
LEWD
LEWDER
LEWDEST
LEWDLY
LEWDNESS
LEWIS
LEWISITE
LEWISSON
LEWTH
LEWTY
LEX
LEXIA
LEXIC
LEXICAL
LEXICALIC
LEXICALITY
LEXICOGRAPHY
LEXICOLOGIC
LEXICOLOGICAL
LEXICOLOGIST
LEXICOLOGY
LEXICON
LEXICONIST
LEXICONIZE
LEXIGRAPHIC
LEXIGRAPHICAL
LEXIGRAPHY
LEXIPHANIC
LEY
LEYE
LEYLAND
LEYSING
LEZA
LHERZITE
LI
LIABILITIES
LIABILITY
LIABLE
LIABLENESS
LIAISON
LIAMBA
LIANA
LIANE
LIANG
LIANGLE
LIAR
LIARD
LIB
LIBAMENT
LIBANIFEROUS
LIBANT
LIBATE
LIBATED
LIBATING
LIBATION
LIBATIONARY
LIBATIONER
LIBATORY
LIBBARD
LIBBER
LIBBET
LIBBRA
LIBECCIO
LIBEL
LIBELANT
LIBELED
LIBELEE
LIBELER
LIBELING
LIBELIST
LIBELLANT
LIBELLARY
LIBELLATE
LIBELLED
LIBELLEE
LIBELLER
LIBELLING
LIBELLIST
LIBELLOUS
LIBELLOUSLY
LIBELLULID
LIBELLULOID
LIBELOUS
LIBELOUSLY
LIBER
LIBERAL
LIBERALISM
LIBERALIST
LIBERALISTIC
LIBERALITES
LIBERALITY
LIBERALIZATION
LIBERALIZE
LIBERALIZED
LIBERALIZER
LIBERALIZING
LIBERALLY
LIBERALNESS
LIBERATE
LIBERATED
LIBERATING
LIBERATION
LIBERATIONISM
LIBERATIONIST
LIBERATIVE
LIBERATOR
LIBERATORY
LIBERATRESS
LIBERATRICE
LIBERATRIX
LIBEROMOTOR
LIBERTARIAN
LIBERTARIANISM
LIBERTICIDAL
LIBERTICIDE
LIBERTIES
LIBERTINAGE
LIBERTINE
LIBERTINISM
LIBERTY
LIBETHENITE
LIBIDIBI
LIBIDINAL
LIBIDINALLY
LIBIDINOSITY
LIBIDINOUS
LIBIDINOUSLY
LIBIDINOUSNESS
LIBIDO
LIBKEN
LIBKIN
LIBRA
LIBRAE
LIBRAL
LIBRARIAN
LIBRARIANESS
LIBRARIANSHIP
LIBRARIES
LIBRARII
LIBRARIOUS
LIBRARIUS
LIBRARY
LIBRAS
LIBRATE
LIBRATED
LIBRATING
LIBRATION
LIBRATORY
LIBRETTI
LIBRETTIST
LIBRETTO
LIBRETTOS
LIBRIFORM
LIBROPLAST
LICAREOL
LICCA
LICE
LICENCE
LICENCED
LICENCEE
LICENCER
LICENSABLE
LICENSE
LICENSED
LICENSEE
LICENSER
LICENSING
LICENSOR
LICENSURE
LICENTIATE
LICENTIATION
LICENTIOUS
LICENTIOUSLY
LICENTIOUSNESS
LICET
LICH
LICHAM
LICHANOS
LICHEE
LICHEN
LICHENACEOUS
LICHENED
LICHENIAN
LICHENIASIS
LICHENIC
LICHENIFORM
LICHENIN
LICHENISM
LICHENIST
LICHENIZATION
LICHENIZE
LICHENOID
LICHENOLOGY
LICHENOSE
LICHENOUS
LICHENS
LICHI
LICHT
LICHWAKE
LICIT
LICITATION
LICITLY
LICITNESS
LICK
LICKED
LICKER
LICKERISH
LICKERISHLY
LICKERISHNESS
LICKING
LICKPENNY
LICKSPIT
LICKSPITTLE
LICORICE
LICORN
LICORNE
LICTOR
LICTORIAN
LICURI
LICURY
LID
LIDDED
LIDDER
LIDDERON
LIDFLOWER
LIDGATE
LIDLESS
LIE
LIEBENERITE
LIEBIGITE
LIEBLICH
LIED
LIEDER
LIEDERKRANZ
LIEF
LIEFER
LIEFEST
LIEFLY
LIEFSOME
LIEGE
LIEGEFUL
LIEGEFULLY
LIEGELESS
LIEGELY
LIEGEMAN
LIEGEMEN
LIEGER
LIEGEWOMAN
LIEN
LIENAL
LIENCULI
LIENCULUS
LIENEE
LIENIC
LIENITIS
LIENOCELE
LIENOGASTRIC
LIENOR
LIENORENAL
LIENOTOXIN
LIENTERIC
LIENTERY
LIEPOT
LIER
LIERNE
LIERRE
LIES
LIESPFUND
LIEU
LIEUE
LIEUTENANCY
LIEUTENANT
LIEVE
LIEVER
LIEVEST
LIEVRITE
LIFE
LIFEBLOOD
LIFEBOAT
LIFEBOATMAN
LIFEBOATMEN
LIFEDAY
LIFEDROP
LIFEFUL
LIFEFULLY
LIFEFULNESS
LIFEGUARD
LIFEHOLD
LIFEHOLDER
LIFEHOOD
LIFELEAF
LIFELESS
LIFELESSLY
LIFELESSNESS
LIFELET
LIFELIKE
LIFELIKENESS
LIFELINE
LIFELONG
LIFER
LIFERENT
LIFERENTED
LIFERENTER
LIFERENTING
LIFERENTRIX
LIFEROOT
LIFESAVER
LIFESAVING
LIFESOME
LIFESOMELY
LIFESOMENESS
LIFESPRING
LIFETIME
LIFEWAY
LIFEWORK
LIFEY
LIFT
LIFTED
LIFTER
LIFTING
LIFTMAN
LIFTMEN
LIFTOFF
LIG
LIGABLE
LIGAMENT
LIGAMENTA

LIGAMENTAL
LIGAMENTARY
LIGAMENTOUS
LIGAMENTOUSLY
LIGAMENTS
LIGAMENTUM
LIGAN
LIGAND
LIGAS
LIGATE
LIGATED
LIGATING
LIGATION
LIGATIVE
LIGATOR
LIGATORY
LIGATURE
LIGATURED
LIGATURING
LIGE
LIGEANCE
LIGER
LIGG
LIGGAT
LIGGER
LIGHT
LIGHTBOAT
LIGHTED
LIGHTEN
LIGHTENED
LIGHTENER
LIGHTENING
LIGHTER
LIGHTERAGE
LIGHTERMAN
LIGHTERMEN
LIGHTEST
LIGHTFACE
LIGHTFOOT
LIGHTFUL
LIGHTHEADED
LIGHTHEADEDLY
LIGHTHEADEDNESS
LIGHTHEARTEDLY
LIGHTHEARTEDNESS
LIGHTHOUSE
LIGHTHOUSES
LIGHTING
LIGHTISH
LIGHTKEEPER
LIGHTLESS
LIGHTLY
LIGHTMAN
LIGHTMANSHIP
LIGHTMEN
LIGHTMOUTHED
LIGHTNESS
LIGHTNING
LIGHTPROOF
LIGHTROOM
LIGHTS
LIGHTSCOT
LIGHTSHIP
LIGHTSMAN
LIGHTSMEN
LIGHTSOME
LIGHTSOMELY
LIGHTSOMENESS
LIGHTWEIGHT
LIGHTWOOD
LIGNALOES
LIGNE
LIGNEOUS
LIGNESCENT
LIGNICOLE
LIGNICOLINE
LIGNICOLOUS
LIGNIFEROUS
LIGNIFICATION
LIGNIFIED
LIGNIFORM
LIGNIFY
LIGNIFYING
LIGNIN
LIGNIPERDOUS
LIGNITE
LIGNITIC
LIGNITIZE
LIGNIVOROUS
LIGNOCERIC
LIGNOGRAPHY
LIGNONE
LIGNOSE
LIGNOSITY
LIGNOUS
LIGNUM
LIGROIN
LIGROINE
LIGULA
LIGULAE
LIGULAR
LIGULAS
LIGULATE
LIGULE
LIGULIFORM
LIGULIN
LIGULOID
LIGURE
LIGURITE
LIGURITION
LIGURRITION
LIIN
LIJA
LIKABILITY
LIKABLE
LIKABLENESS
LIKE
LIKEABILITY
LIKEABLE
LIKEABLENESS
LIKED
LIKEFUL
LIKELIER
LIKELIEST
LIKELIHEAD
LIKELIHOOD
LIKELY
LIKEN
LIKENED
LIKENESS
LIKENING
LIKER
LIKEROUS
LIKES
LIKESOME
LIKEST
LIKEWAYS
LIKEWISE
LIKEWISELY
LIKEWISENESS
LIKIN
LIKING
LIKINGLY
LIKNA
LIKNON
LIL
LILAC
LILACEOUS
LILACIN
LILACKY
LILACTHROAT
LILACTIDE
LILAS
LILBURNE
LILE
LILES
LILIACEOUS
LILIAL
LILIATED
LILIED
LILIES
LILIFORM
LILIUM
LILL
LILLIANITE
LILLIBULLERO
LILT
LILTED
LILTING
LILY
LILYFY
LILYWORT
LIM
LIMA
LIMACEL
LIMACELLE
LIMACEOUS
LIMACIFORM
LIMACINE
LIMACINID
LIMACOID
LIMACON
LIMAIL
LIMAILLE
LIMAN
LIMATION
LIMB
LIMBA
LIMBATE
LIMBATION
LIMBEC
LIMBECK
LIMBED
LIMBER
LIMBERED
LIMBERER
LIMBEREST
LIMBERHAM
LIMBERING
LIMBERLY
LIMBERNESS
LIMBERS
LIMBIC
LIMBIFEROUS
LIMBING
LIMBMEAL
LIMBO
LIMBOS
LIMBOUS
LIMBURGER
LIMBURGITE
LIMBUS
LIMBY
LIME
LIMEADE
LIMEBERRIES
LIMEBERRY
LIMEBUSH
LIMED
LIMEHOUSE
LIMEKILN
LIMELIGHT
LIMELIGHTER
LIMEMAN
LIMEN
LIMENS
LIMEQUAT
LIMER
LIMERICK
LIMES
LIMESTONE
LIMETTIN
LIMEWASH
LIMEWATER
LIMEWORT
LIMEY
LIMEYS
LIMICOLINE
LIMICOLOUS
LIMIER
LIMIEST
LIMINA
LIMINAL
LIMINARY
LIMING
LIMIT
LIMITABLE
LIMITAL
LIMITARIAN
LIMITARIES
LIMITARY
LIMITATE
LIMITATION
LIMITATIVE
LIMITATIVELY
LIMITED
LIMITEDLY
LIMITEDNESS
LIMITER
LIMITES
LIMITING
LIMITIVE
LIMITLESS
LIMITLESSLY
LIMITLESSNESS
LIMITROPHE
LIMITS
LIMITY
LIMIVOROUS
LIMMA
LIMMATA
LIMMER
LIMMOCK
LIMMU
LIMN
LIMNAL
LIMNANTH
LIMNED
LIMNER
LIMNERY
LIMNETIC
LIMNIAD
LIMNIMETER
LIMNIMETRIC
LIMNING
LIMNITE
LIMNOBIOLOGY
LIMNOBIOS
LIMNOGRAPH
LIMNOLOGIC
LIMNOLOGICAL
LIMNOLOGIST
LIMNOLOGY
LIMNOMETER
LIMNOPHIL
LIMNOPHILE
LIMNOPHILID
LIMNOPHILOUS
LIMNORIOID
LIMON
LIMONCILLO
LIMONCITO
LIMONENE
LIMONIAD
LIMONIN
LIMONITE
LIMONITIC
LIMONIUM
LIMOSE
LIMOUS
LIMOUSINE
LIMP
LIMPA
LIMPED
LIMPER
LIMPEST
LIMPET
LIMPHAULT
LIMPID
LIMPIDITY
LIMPIDLY
LIMPIDNESS
LIMPIN
LIMPING
LIMPINGLY
LIMPINGNESS
LIMPKIN
LIMPLY
LIMPNESS
LIMPSY
LIMPY
LIMSY
LIMU
LIMULID
LIMULOID
LIMULUS
LIMURITE
LIMY
LIN
LINA
LINABLE
LINACEOUS
LINAGA
LINAGE
LINALOA
LINALOE
LINALOOL
LINALYL
LINAMARIN
LINARITE
LINCH
LINCHBOLT
LINCHET
LINCHPIN
LINCHPINNED
LINCLOTH
LINCTUS
LIND
LINDACKERITE
LINDANE
LINDEN
LINDER
LINDO
LINDOITE
LINDWORM
LINE
LINEA
LINEABLE
LINEAGE
LINEAGED
LINEAL
LINEALITY
LINEALLY
LINEAMENT
LINEAMENTAL
LINEAMETER
LINEAR
LINEARITY
LINEARIZATION
LINEARIZE
LINEARLY
LINEARY
LINEAS
LINEATE
LINEATED

LINEATION
LINEATURE
LINEBACKER
LINEBACKING
LINECUT
LINED
LINEIFORM
LINELESS
LINELET
LINEMAN
LINEMEN
LINEN
LINENER
LINENETTE
LINENIZE
LINENIZER
LINENMAN
LINENS
LINEOGRAPH
LINEOLATE
LINEOLATED
LINER
LINES
LINESIDES
LINESMAN
LINESMEN
LINEUP
LINEWALKER
LINEWORK
LINEY
LING
LINGA
LINGAM
LINGBERRIES
LINGBERRY
LINGBIRD
LINGCOD
LINGE
LINGEL
LINGENBERRY
LINGER
LINGERED
LINGERER
LINGERIE
LINGERING
LINGERINGLY
LINGET
LINGLE
LINGO
LINGOE
LINGOES
LINGONBERRIES
LINGONBERRY
LINGOT
LINGS
LINGSTER
LINGTOW
LINGTOWMAN
LINGUA
LINGUACIOUS
LINGUADENTAL
LINGUAE
LINGUAL
LINGUALE
LINGUALIS
LINGUALITY
LINGUALIZE
LINGUANASAL
LINGUATULOID
LINGUET
LINGUIDENTAL
LINGUIFORM
LINGUISHED
LINGUIST
LINGUISTER
LINGUISTIC
LINGUISTICAL
LINGUISTICALLY
LINGUISTICIAN
LINGUISTICS
LINGUISTRY
LINGULA
LINGULAE
LINGULATE
LINGULATED
LINGULID
LINGULIFORM
LINGULOID
LINGUODENTAL
LINGUODISTAL
LINGWORT
LINGY
LINHA
LINHAY
LINIE
LINIER
LINIEST
LINIMENT
LININ
LINING
LININGS
LINITIS
LINIYA
LINJA
LINJE
LINK
LINKAGE
LINKBOY
LINKED
LINKER
LINKIER
LINKIEST
LINKING
LINKMAN
LINKMEN
LINKS
LINKSMITH
LINKSTER
LINKWORK
LINKY
LINN
LINNAEITE
LINNEON
LINNET
LINO
LINOLATE
LINOLEATE
LINOLEIC
LINOLEIN
LINOLENATE
LINOLENIC
LINOLENIN
LINOLEUM
LINOMETER
LINON
LINOTYPE
LINOTYPED
LINOTYPER
LINOTYPING
LINOTYPIST
LINQUISH
LINS
LINSANG
LINSEED
LINSEY
LINSTOCK
LINT
LINTEL
LINTELED
LINTELING
LINTELLED
LINTELLING
LINTEN
LINTER
LINTERN
LINTERS
LINTIE
LINTIER
LINTIEST
LINTONITE
LINTSEED
LINTWHITE
LINTY
LINWOOD
LINY
LIODERMIA
LIOMYOMA
LION
LIONCEL
LIONESS
LIONET
LIONHEART
LIONHEARTED
LIONHEARTEDNESS
LIONISM
LIONIZABLE
LIONIZATION
LIONIZE
LIONIZED
LIONIZER
LIONIZING
LIONLIKE
LIONLY
LIONS
LIOS
LIP
LIPA
LIPARIAN
LIPAROCELE
LIPAROID
LIPAROUS
LIPASE
LIPE
LIPID
LIPIDE
LIPIN
LIPOBLAST
LIPOBLASTOMA
LIPOCELE
LIPOCERATOUS
LIPOCERE
LIPOCHROME
LIPOCLASIS
LIPOCLASTIC
LIPOCYTE
LIPOFEROUS
LIPOFIBROMA
LIPOGENESIS
LIPOGENETIC
LIPOGENIC
LIPOGENOUS
LIPOGRAM
LIPOGRAPHY
LIPOHEMIA
LIPOID
LIPOIDAEMIA
LIPOIDAL
LIPOIDEMIA
LIPOIDIC
LIPOLYSIS
LIPOLYTIC
LIPOMA
LIPOMAS
LIPOMATA
LIPOMATOSIS
LIPOMATOUS
LIPOMYOMA
LIPOMYXOMA
LIPOPEXIA
LIPOPHAGIC
LIPOPHORE
LIPOPOD
LIPOPROTEIN
LIPOSARCOMA
LIPOSIS
LIPOSOME
LIPOSTOMY
LIPOTHYMIA
LIPOTHYMIAL
LIPOTHYMIC
LIPOTHYMY
LIPOTROPHIC
LIPOTROPHY
LIPOTROPIC
LIPOTROPY
LIPOTYPE
LIPOVACCINE
LIPOXENOUS
LIPOXENY
LIPPED
LIPPEN
LIPPER
LIPPIE
LIPPIER
LIPPIEST
LIPPINESS
LIPPING
LIPPITUDE
LIPPITUDO
LIPPY
LIPS
LIPSANOTHECA
LIPSTICK
LIPURIA
LIPWORK
LIQUABLE
LIQUAMEN
LIQUATE
LIQUATED
LIQUATING
LIQUATION
LIQUEFACIENT
LIQUEFACTION
LIQUEFACTIVE
LIQUEFIABLE
LIQUEFIED
LIQUEFIER
LIQUEFY
LIQUEFYING
LIQUESCE
LIQUESCENCE
LIQUESCENCY
LIQUESCENT
LIQUET
LIQUEUR
LIQUEURED
LIQUEURING
LIQUID
LIQUIDABLE
LIQUIDAMBAR
LIQUIDAMBER
LIQUIDATE
LIQUIDATED
LIQUIDATING
LIQUIDATION
LIQUIDATOR
LIQUIDITY
LIQUIDIZE
LIQUIDIZED
LIQUIDIZING
LIQUIDLY
LIQUIDNESS
LIQUIDOGENIC
LIQUIDS
LIQUIDUS
LIQUIDY
LIQUIFORM
LIQUIFY
LIQUOR
LIQUORED
LIQUORER
LIQUORICE
LIQUORING
LIQUORISH
LIQUORISHLY
LIQUORISHNESS
LIQUORIST
LIQUORS
LIQUORY
LIRA
LIRAS
LIRATE
LIRATION
LIRE
LIRELLA
LIRELLATE
LIRELLIFORM
LIRELLINE
LIRELLOUS
LIRIODENDRON
LIRIPIPE
LIRIPOOP
LIRK
LIROCONITE
LIRP
LIS
LISERE
LISETTE
LISH
LISI
LISIERE
LISK
LISLE
LISP
LISPED
LISPER
LISPING
LISPOUND
LISPUND
LISS
LISSE
LISSES
LISSOM
LISSOME
LISSOMELY
LISSOMENESS
LISSOTRICHAN
LISSOTRICHY
LIST
LISTABLE
LISTED
LISTEDNESS
LISTEL
LISTEN
LISTENED
LISTENER
LISTENERS
LISTENING
LISTER
LISTERIA
LISTFUL
LISTING
LISTLESS
LISTLESSLY
LISTLESSNESS
LISTRED
LISTS
LISTWORK
LISTY
LIT
LITAI
LITANEUTICAL
LITANIES
LITANY
LITAS

LITATION
LITCH
LITCHI
LITE
LITER
LITERACY
LITERAL
LITERALISM
LITERALIST
LITERALISTIC
LITERALITIES
LITERALITY
LITERALIZATION
LITERALIZE
LITERALIZED
LITERALIZER
LITERALIZING
LITERALLY
LITERALNESS
LITERARIAN
LITERARILY
LITERARINESS
LITERARY
LITERATE
LITERATED
LITERATI
LITERATIM
LITERATION
LITERATIST
LITERATO
LITERATOR
LITERATOS
LITERATURE
LITERATURED
LITERATUS
LITEROSE
LITEROSITY
LITH
LITHAEMIA
LITHAEMIC
LITHAGOGUE
LITHANGIURIA
LITHANTHRAX
LITHARGE
LITHATE
LITHATIC
LITHE
LITHECTASY
LITHECTOMY
LITHELY
LITHEMIA
LITHEMIC
LITHENESS
LITHER
LITHERLY
LITHERNESS
LITHESOME
LITHESOMENESS
LITHEST
LITHI
LITHIA
LITHIASIS
LITHIASTIC
LITHIATE
LITHIC
LITHIFICATION
LITHIFIED
LITHIFY
LITHIFYING
LITHITE
LITHIUM
LITHLESS
LITHO
LITHOBIID
LITHOBIOID
LITHOCENOSIS
LITHOCHROMIC
LITHOCHROMY
LITHOCLASE
LITHOCLAST
LITHOCULTURE
LITHOCYST
LITHODESMA
LITHODID
LITHODOMOUS
LITHOFELLIC
LITHOFELLINIC
LITHOFRACTEUR
LITHOFRACTOR
LITHOGENESIS
LITHOGENESY
LITHOGENETIC
LITHOGENOUS
LITHOGENY
LITHOGLYPH
LITHOGLYPHER
LITHOGLYPHIC
LITHOGLYPTIC
LITHOGLYPTICS
LITHOGRAPH
LITHOGRAPHED
LITHOGRAPHER
LITHOGRAPHIC
LITHOGRAPHING
LITHOGRAPHY
LITHOGRAVURE
LITHOID
LITHOIDAL
LITHOIDITE
LITHOLABE
LITHOLAPAXY
LITHOLATROUS
LITHOLATRY
LITHOLOGIC
LITHOLOGICAL
LITHOLOGIST
LITHOLOGY
LITHOLYSIS
LITHOLYTE
LITHOLYTIC
LITHOMANCY
LITHOMARGE
LITHOMETER
LITHONEPHRIA
LITHONTRIPTIC
LITHOPAEDION
LITHOPAEDIUM
LITHOPEDION
LITHOPEDIUM
LITHOPHAGOUS
LITHOPHANE
LITHOPHANIC
LITHOPHANY
LITHOPHILOUS
LITHOPHONE
LITHOPHYL
LITHOPHYLL
LITHOPHYSA
LITHOPHYSAE
LITHOPHYSAL
LITHOPHYTE
LITHOPHYTIC
LITHOPHYTOUS
LITHOPONE
LITHOSCOPE
LITHOSIAN
LITHOSIID
LITHOSIS
LITHOSPERM
LITHOSPERMON
LITHOSPHERE
LITHOTINT
LITHOTOME
LITHOTOMIC
LITHOTOMICAL
LITHOTOMIES
LITHOTOMIST
LITHOTOMIZE
LITHOTOMOUS
LITHOTOMY
LITHOTONY
LITHOTRESIS
LITHOTRIPSY
LITHOTRITE
LITHOTRITIC
LITHOTRITIES
LITHOTRITIST
LITHOTRITOR
LITHOTRITY
LITHOTYPE
LITHOTYPED
LITHOTYPIC
LITHOTYPING
LITHOTYPY
LITHOUS
LITHOXYL
LITHOXYLE
LITHOXYLITE
LITHSMAN
LITHURESIS
LITHURIA
LITHY
LITI
LITIGABLE
LITIGANT
LITIGATE
LITIGATED
LITIGATING
LITIGATION
LITIGATOR
LITIGATORY
LITIGIOSITY
LITIGIOUS
LITIGIOUSLY
LITIGIOUSNESS
LITISCONTEST
LITMUS
LITORINOID
LITOTES
LITRA
LITRE
LITRO
LITS
LITTEN
LITTER
LITTERATEUR
LITTERATIM
LITTERBUG
LITTERED
LITTERER
LITTERING
LITTERY
LITTLE
LITTLENECK
LITTLENESS
LITTLER
LITTLEST
LITTLEWALE
LITTLIN
LITTLING
LITTORAL
LITTRESS
LITU
LITUATE
LITUI
LITUIFORM
LITUITE
LITUITOID
LITUOLINE
LITUOLOID
LITURATE
LITURGIC
LITURGICAL
LITURGICALLY
LITURGICIAN
LITURGICS
LITURGIES
LITURGIOLOGY
LITURGISM
LITURGIST
LITURGIZE
LITURGY
LITUS
LITUUS
LITZ
LIVABILITY
LIVABLE
LIVABLENESS
LIVE
LIVEABLE
LIVED
LIVEDO
LIVELIER
LIVELIEST
LIVELIHOOD
LIVELINESS
LIVELONG
LIVELY
LIVEN
LIVENER
LIVER
LIVERANCE
LIVERBERRY
LIVERED
LIVERIED
LIVERIES
LIVERING
LIVERISH
LIVERISHNESS
LIVERLEAF
LIVERWORT
LIVERWURST
LIVERY
LIVERYMAN
LIVERYMEN
LIVES
LIVESTOCK
LIVETIN
LIVEYER
LIVID
LIVIDITY
LIVIDLY
LIVIDNESS
LIVIER
LIVING
LIVINGS
LIVISH
LIVISHLY
LIVOR
LIVRE
LIVRES
LIVYER
LIWA
LIWAN
LIXIVIAL
LIXIVIATE
LIXIVIATED
LIXIVIATING
LIXIVIATION
LIXIVIATOR
LIXIVIOUS
LIXIVIUM
LIZA
LIZARD
LIZARDTAIL
LIZARY
LLAMA
LLAMAS
LLANERO
LLANO
LLANOS
LLARETA
LLAUTU
LLYN
LO
LOA
LOACH
LOACHES
LOAD
LOADED
LOADEN
LOADER
LOADING
LOADPENNY
LOADS
LOADSOME
LOADSTAR
LOADSTONE
LOADUM
LOAF
LOAFER
LOAFING
LOAFINGLY
LOAGHTAN
LOAIASIS
LOAM
LOAMIER
LOAMIEST
LOAMILY
LOAMINESS
LOAMING
LOAMY
LOAN
LOANABLE
LOANBLEND
LOANED
LOANER
LOANGE
LOANIN
LOANING
LOANMONGER
LOANSHIFT
LOANWORD
LOASACEOUS
LOATH
LOATHE
LOATHED
LOATHER
LOATHFUL
LOATHFULLY
LOATHFULNESS
LOATHING
LOATHINGLY
LOATHLINESS
LOATHLY
LOATHSOME
LOATHSOMELY
LOATHSOMENESS
LOATHY
LOAVE
LOAVES
LOB
LOBA
LOBAL
LOBAR
LOBATE
LOBATED
LOBATION
LOBBED
LOBBER
LOBBIED
LOBBIES
LOBBING
LOBBISH
LOBBY

LOBBYER
LOBBYGOW
LOBBYING
LOBBYISM
LOBBYIST
LOBBYMAN
LOBBYMEN
LOBCOCK
LOBCOKT
LOBE
LOBECTOMY
LOBED
LOBEFOOT
LOBEFOOTED
LOBEFOOTS
LOBELIA
LOBELIACEOUS
LOBELIN
LOBELINE
LOBELLATED
LOBFIG
LOBI
LOBIFORM
LOBIGEROUS
LOBING
LOBIPED
LOBLOLLIES
LOBLOLLY
LOBO
LOBOLA
LOBOPODIUM
LOBOS
LOBOSE
LOBOTOMIES
LOBOTOMY
LOBSCOURSE
LOBSCOUSE
LOBSCOUSER
LOBSTER
LOBSTERING
LOBSTERPROOF
LOBSTERS
LOBSTICK
LOBTAIL
LOBULAR
LOBULARLY
LOBULATE
LOBULATED
LOBULATION
LOBULE
LOBULETTE
LOBULI
LOBULOSE
LOBULOUS
LOBULUS
LOBUS
LOBWORM
LOCA
LOCABLE
LOCAL
LOCALE
LOCALED
LOCALING
LOCALISM
LOCALIST
LOCALISTIC
LOCALITIES
LOCALITY
LOCALIZABLE
LOCALIZATION
LOCALIZE
LOCALIZED
LOCALIZER
LOCALIZING
LOCALLED
LOCALLING
LOCALLY
LOCALNESS
LOCANDA
LOCATABLE
LOCATE
LOCATED
LOCATER
LOCATING
LOCATIO
LOCATION
LOCATIONAL
LOCATIONS
LOCATIVE
LOCATOR
LOCELLATE
LOCELLUS
LOCH
LOCHAGUS
LOCHAN
LOCHE
LOCHETIC
LOCHI
LOCHIA
LOCHIAL
LOCHIOCOLPOS
LOCHIOCYTE
LOCHIOMETRA
LOCHIOPYRA
LOCHIORRHEA
LOCHOPYRA
LOCHUS
LOCHY
LOCI
LOCK
LOCKABLE
LOCKAGE
LOCKBOX
LOCKED
LOCKER
LOCKERMAN
LOCKERMEN
LOCKET
LOCKFAST
LOCKFUL
LOCKHOLE
LOCKING
LOCKJAW
LOCKLESS
LOCKLET
LOCKMAKER
LOCKMAN
LOCKNUT
LOCKOUT
LOCKPIN
LOCKRAM
LOCKRUM
LOCKSMAN
LOCKSMITH
LOCKSMITHERY
LOCKSMITHING
LOCKSPIT
LOCKUP
LOCKWORK
LOCKY
LOCKYER
LOCO
LOCOED
LOCOFOCO
LOCOFOCOS
LOCOING
LOCOISM
LOCOMOBILE
LOCOMOBILITY
LOCOMOTE
LOCOMOTILITY
LOCOMOTION
LOCOMOTIVE
LOCOMOTIVELY
LOCOMOTIVEMAN
LOCOMOTIVEMEN
LOCOMOTIVITY
LOCOMOTOR
LOCOMOTORY
LOCOMUTATION
LOCOS
LOCOWEED
LOCULAMENT
LOCULAR
LOCULATE
LOCULATED
LOCULATION
LOCULE
LOCULI
LOCULICIDAL
LOCULOSE
LOCULOUS
LOCULUS
LOCUM
LOCUPLETE
LOCUPLETELY
LOCUS
LOCUST
LOCUSTA
LOCUSTBERRY
LOCUSTELLE
LOCUSTID
LOCUSTING
LOCUTION
LOCUTOR
LOCUTORIES
LOCUTORSHIP
LOCUTORY
LOD
LODE
LODEMAN
LODEMANAGE
LODEN
LODESMAN
LODESMEN
LODESTAR
LODESTONE
LODESTUFF
LODGE
LODGED
LODGEMAN
LODGEMENT
LODGEPOLE
LODGER
LODGING
LODGINGHOUSE
LODGMENT
LODICULA
LODICULE
LOESS
LOESSAL
LOESSIAL
LOESSIC
LOESSLAND
LOESSOID
LOF
LOFT
LOFTED
LOFTER
LOFTIER
LOFTIEST
LOFTILY
LOFTINESS
LOFTING
LOFTMAN
LOFTMEN
LOFTSMAN
LOFTSMEN
LOFTY
LOG
LOGAN
LOGANBERRIES
LOGANBERRY
LOGANIACEOUS
LOGANIN
LOGAOEDIC
LOGARITHM
LOGARITHMAL
LOGARITHMIC
LOGARITHMICAL
LOGARITHMICALLY
LOGBOOK
LOGCOCK
LOGE
LOGEIA
LOGEION
LOGGAT
LOGGATS
LOGGED
LOGGER
LOGGERHEAD
LOGGERHEADED
LOGGERHEADS
LOGGET
LOGGIA
LOGGIAS
LOGGIN
LOGGING
LOGGY
LOGHE
LOGHEAD
LOGHEADED
LOGIA
LOGIC
LOGICAL
LOGICALIST
LOGICALITY
LOGICALIZATION
LOGICALIZE
LOGICALLY
LOGICALNESS
LOGICASTER
LOGICIAN
LOGICIANER
LOGICISM
LOGICITY
LOGICIZE
LOGICS
LOGIE
LOGIER
LOGIEST
LOGIN
LOGION
LOGIS
LOGISTIC
LOGISTICAL
LOGISTICIAN
LOGISTICS
LOGJAM
LOGMAN
LOGOCRACY
LOGODAEDALY
LOGOGOGUE
LOGOGRAM
LOGOGRAPH
LOGOGRAPHER
LOGOGRAPHIC
LOGOGRAPHICAL
LOGOGRAPHY
LOGOGRIPH
LOGOGRIPHIC
LOGOLATRY
LOGOLOGY
LOGOMACH
LOGOMACHER
LOGOMACHIC
LOGOMACHICAL
LOGOMACHIES
LOGOMACHIST
LOGOMACHIZE
LOGOMACHY
LOGOMANCY
LOGOMANIAC
LOGOMETER
LOGOMETRIC
LOGOMETRICAL
LOGOPEDIA
LOGOPEDICS
LOGORRHEA
LOGORRHOEA
LOGOS
LOGOTHETE
LOGOTYPE
LOGOTYPY
LOGROLL
LOGROLLER
LOGROLLING
LOGS
LOGWAY
LOGWOOD
LOGWORK
LOGY
LOHAN
LOHOCH
LOHOCK
LOI
LOIMIC
LOIMOGRAPHY
LOIMOLOGY
LOIN
LOINCLOTH
LOINED
LOINS
LOIR
LOITER
LOITERED
LOITERER
LOITERING
LOKA
LOKAO
LOKAPALA
LOKE
LOKELANI
LOKIEC
LOKSHEN
LOLL
LOLLAPALOOSA
LOLLAPALOOZA
LOLLED
LOLLER
LOLLIES
LOLLING
LOLLINGITE
LOLLIPOP
LOLLOP
LOLLOPY
LOLLUP
LOLLY
LOLLYGAG
LOLLYPOP
LOMA
LOMASTOME
LOMATA
LOMATINE
LOMATINOUS
LOMBOY
LOMENT
LOMENTACEOUS
LOMENTUM
LOMILOMI
LOMITA
LOMONITE
LONE
LONEFUL
LONELIER

LONELIEST
LONELIHOOD
LONELILY
LONELINESS
LONELY
LONENESS
LONER
LONESOME
LONESOMELY
LONESOMENESS
LONG
LONGA
LONGACRE
LONGAN
LONGANIMITIES
LONGANIMITY
LONGANIMOUS
LONGBEAK
LONGBEARD
LONGBILL
LONGBOAT
LONGBOW
LONGCLOTH
LONGE
LONGEAR
LONGED
LONGER
LONGERON
LONGEST
LONGEVAL
LONGEVE
LONGEVITY
LONGEVOUS
LONGFIN
LONGFUL
LONGHAIR
LONGHAND
LONGHEAD
LONGHEADED
LONGHEADEDLY
LONGHEADEDNESS
LONGHORN
LONGICAUDAL
LONGICAUDATE
LONGICONE
LONGICORN
LONGILATERAL
LONGILINGUAL
LONGIMANOUS
LONGIMETRIC
LONGIMETRY
LONGING
LONGINGLY
LONGINQUITY
LONGIPENNATE
LONGIPENNINE
LONGIROSTRAL
LONGIROSTRATE
LONGISH
LONGITUDE
LONGITUDINAL
LONGITUDINALLY
LONGJAW
LONGJAWS
LONGLEAF
LONGLEGS
LONGLICK
LONGLINE
LONGLINER
LONGLINERMAN
LONGLINERMEN
LONGNECK
LONGNOSE
LONGPOD
LONGROOT
LONGS
LONGSHANKS
LONGSHORE
LONGSHOREMAN
LONGSHOREMEN
LONGSHUCKS
LONGSOME
LONGSOMELY
LONGSOMENESS
LONGSPUR
LONGTAIL
LONGTIMER
LONGUE
LONGUEUR
LONGULITE
LONGUS
LONGWALL
LONGWAYS
LONGWISE
LONGWOOD
LONGWOOL
LONGWORK
LONGYI
LONQUHARD
LONTAR
LOO
LOOBIES
LOOBILY
LOOBY
LOOCH
LOOD
LOOED
LOOF
LOOFA
LOOFAH
LOOFIE
LOOING
LOOK
LOOKED
LOOKER
LOOKING
LOOKOUT
LOOKOUTS
LOOKUM
LOOL
LOOM
LOOMED
LOOMER
LOOMERY
LOOMFIXER
LOOMING
LOOMS
LOON
LOONERY
LOONEY
LOONIER
LOONIES
LOONIEST
LOONY
LOOP
LOOPED
LOOPER
LOOPFUL
LOOPHOLE
LOOPHOLED
LOOPHOLING
LOOPIER
LOOPIEST
LOOPING
LOOPIST
LOOPS
LOOPY
LOORY
LOOS
LOOSE
LOOSED
LOOSELY
LOOSEN
LOOSENED
LOOSENER
LOOSENESS
LOOSENING
LOOSER
LOOSEST
LOOSESTRIFE
LOOSING
LOOT
LOOTED
LOOTER
LOOTIE
LOOTIEWALLAH
LOOTING
LOOTSMAN
LOOTSMANS
LOP
LOPE
LOPED
LOPER
LOPESKONCE
LOPHEAVY
LOPHIID
LOPHIN
LOPHINE
LOPHIODONT
LOPHOBRANCH
LOPHOCERCAL
LOPHODONT
LOPHOPHORAL
LOPHOPHORE
LOPHOPHORINE
LOPHOSTEA
LOPHOSTEON
LOPHOSTEONS
LOPHOTRIAENE
LOPING
LOPOLITH
LOPPARD
LOPPE
LOPPED
LOPPER
LOPPET
LOPPIER
LOPPIEST
LOPPING
LOPPY
LOPSEED
LOPSIDED
LOPSIDEDLY
LOPSIDEDNESS
LOPSTICK
LOQUACIOUS
LOQUACIOUSLY
LOQUACIOUSNESS
LOQUACITY
LOQUAT
LOQUENCE
LOQUENCY
LOQUENT
LOQUENTLY
LOQUITUR
LOR
LORA
LORAE
LORAL
LORAN
LORANDITE
LORANSKITE
LORARII
LORARIUS
LORATE
LORCHA
LORD
LORDAN
LORDED
LORDING
LORDINGS
LORDLESS
LORDLIER
LORDLIEST
LORDLIKE
LORDLINESS
LORDLING
LORDLY
LORDOLATRY
LORDOMA
LORDOSIS
LORDOTIC
LORDSHIP
LORDSWIKE
LORDWOOD
LORE
LOREAL
LORED
LOREL
LORENZENITE
LORETIN
LORETTOITE
LORGNETTE
LORGNON
LORIC
LORICA
LORICAE
LORICARIAN
LORICARIOID
LORICATE
LORICATED
LORICATING
LORICATION
LORICOID
LORIES
LORIKEET
LORILET
LORIMER
LORINER
LORING
LORIOT
LORIS
LORISES
LORMERY
LORN
LORO
LOROS
LORRE
LORRIES
LORRIKER
LORRY
LORS
LORUM
LORY
LOSABLE
LOSE
LOSEL
LOSELRY
LOSENGER
LOSER
LOSH
LOSING
LOSINGLY
LOSS
LOSSE
LOSSENITE
LOSSER
LOSSFUL
LOST
LOT
LOTA
LOTAH
LOTASE
LOTE
LOTEBUSH
LOTEWOOD
LOTH
LOTHE
LOTIC
LOTIFORM
LOTION
LOTIUM
LOTMENT
LOTONG
LOTOPHAGOUS
LOTOS
LOTRITE
LOTS
LOTTED
LOTTER
LOTTERIES
LOTTERY
LOTTING
LOTTO
LOTUS
LOTUSIN
LOUCH
LOUCHE
LOUCHETTES
LOUD
LOUDEN
LOUDERING
LOUDISH
LOUDLY
LOUDMOUTHED
LOUDNESS
LOUDSPEAKER
LOUEY
LOUGH
LOUGHEEN
LOUIS
LOUISINE
LOUK
LOUKE
LOUKOUM
LOUKOUMI
LOULU
LOUN
LOUND
LOUNDER
LOUNDERER
LOUNGE
LOUNGED
LOUNGER
LOUNGING
LOUNGY
LOUP
LOUPE
LOUR
LOURD
LOURDISH
LOURDY
LOURE
LOURED
LOURIE
LOURING
LOURINGLY
LOURINGNESS
LOURY
LOUSE
LOUSEBERRIES
LOUSEBERRY
LOUSED
LOUSEWORT
LOUSIER
LOUSIEST
LOUSILY
LOUSINESS
LOUSING
LOUSTER
LOUSY
LOUT
LOUTER
LOUTHER
LOUTISH

LOUTISHLY
LOUTISHNESS
LOUTRE
LOUTROPHOROS
LOUTY
LOUVAR
LOUVER
LOUVERED
LOUVERWORK
LOVABILITY
LOVABLE
LOVABLENESS
LOVABLY
LOVAGE
LOVANENTY
LOVAT
LOVE
LOVEABLE
LOVEBIRD
LOVED
LOVEFLOWER
LOVEHOOD
LOVELASS
LOVELESS
LOVELESSLY
LOVELESSNESS
LOVELIER
LOVELIEST
LOVELIHEAD
LOVELILY
LOVELINESS
LOVELING
LOVELOCK
LOVELORN
LOVELORNNESS
LOVELY
LOVEMAKING
LOVEMAN
LOVEMANS
LOVEMATE
LOVEMONGER
LOVER
LOVERED
LOVERING
LOVERLINESS
LOVERLY
LOVESICK
LOVESICKNESS
LOVESOME
LOVESOMELY
LOVESOMENESS
LOVEVINE
LOVING
LOVINGLY
LOVINGNESS
LOW
LOWA
LOWABLE
LOWAN
LOWANCE
LOWBALL
LOWBELL
LOWBORN
LOWBOY
LOWBRED
LOWBROW
LOWBROWISM
LOWDAH
LOWDER
LOWDOWN
LOWE
LOWED
LOWEITE
LOWER
LOWERCLASSMAN
LOWERCLASSMEN
LOWERED
LOWERER
LOWERING
LOWERINGLY
LOWERINGNESS
LOWERMOST
LOWERY
LOWEST
LOWIGITE
LOWING
LOWLAND
LOWLANDER
LOWLIER
LOWLIEST
LOWLIHEAD
LOWLY
LOWMEN
LOWMOST
LOWN
LOWNESS
LOWRIE
LOWRY
LOWSE
LOWSIN
LOWTH
LOWWOOD
LOWY
LOX
LOXIA
LOXOCLASE
LOXOCOSM
LOXODOGRAPH
LOXODONT
LOXODROME
LOXODROMIC
LOXODROMICS
LOXODROMISM
LOXODROMY
LOXOSOMA
LOXOTIC
LOXOTOMY
LOY
LOYAL
LOYALISM
LOYALIST
LOYALLY
LOYALNESS
LOYALTIES
LOYALTY
LOYN
LOZEN
LOZENGE
LOZENGED
LOZENGER
LOZENGY
LUAU
LUBBER
LUBBERCOCK
LUBBERLINESS
LUBBERLY
LUBRA
LUBRIC
LUBRICAL
LUBRICANT
LUBRICATE
LUBRICATED
LUBRICATING
LUBRICATION
LUBRICATIONAL
LUBRICATIVE
LUBRICATOR
LUBRICATORY
LUBRICIOUS
LUBRICITIES
LUBRICITY
LUBRICOUS
LUBRIFY
LUBRITORIAN
LUBRITORIUM
LUBRITORY
LUCANID
LUCARNE
LUCBAN
LUCE
LUCENCE
LUCENCY
LUCENT
LUCENTLY
LUCERN
LUCERNAL
LUCERNE
LUCES
LUCET
LUCIBLE
LUCID
LUCIDA
LUCIDITY
LUCIDLY
LUCIDNESS
LUCIFER
LUCIFERASE
LUCIFERIN
LUCIFEROID
LUCIFEROUS
LUCIFEROUSLY
LUCIFIC
LUCIFORM
LUCIFUGAL
LUCIFUGOUS
LUCIGEN
LUCIMETER
LUCINOID
LUCIVEE
LUCK
LUCKEN
LUCKFUL
LUCKIE
LUCKIER
LUCKIES
LUCKIEST
LUCKILY
LUCKINESS
LUCKLESS
LUCKLESSLY
LUCKLESSNESS
LUCKLY
LUCKY
LUCOMBE
LUCRATION
LUCRATIVE
LUCRATIVELY
LUCRATIVENESS
LUCRE
LUCRIFEROUS
LUCRIFIC
LUCRIFY
LUCROUS
LUCTATION
LUCTIFEROUS
LUCTUAL
LUCUBRATE
LUCUBRATED
LUCUBRATING
LUCUBRATION
LUCUBRATOR
LUCUBRATORY
LUCULE
LUCULENT
LUCULENTLY
LUCULLITE
LUCUMIA
LUCUMONY
LUCY
LUD
LUDDEN
LUDDY
LUDI
LUDIBRIOUS
LUDIBRY
LUDICROSITIES
LUDICROSITY
LUDICROUS
LUDICROUSLY
LUDICROUSNESS
LUDIFICATION
LUDLAMITE
LUDO
LUDWIGITE
LUE
LUES
LUETIC
LUETICALLY
LUFF
LUFFA
LUFFED
LUFFER
LUFFING
LUG
LUGE
LUGER
LUGGAGE
LUGGAR
LUGGARD
LUGGED
LUGGER
LUGGIE
LUGGING
LUGHDOAN
LUGMARK
LUGS
LUGSAIL
LUGSOME
LUGUBRIOSITY
LUGUBRIOUS
LUGUBRIOUSLY
LUGUBRIOUSNESS
LUGUBROUS
LUGWORM
LUHINGA
LUIGINI
LUIGINO
LUJAURITE
LUJAVRITE
LUJULA
LUKE
LUKET
LUKEWARD
LUKEWARM
LUKEWARMLY
LUKEWARMNESS
LUKEWARMTH
LULAB
LULL
LULLABIES
LULLABY
LULLAY
LULLED
LULLER
LULLILOO
LULLILOOED
LULLILOOING
LULLING
LULLY
LULU
LULUAI
LUM
LUMACHEL
LUMACHELLA
LUMACHELLE
LUMBAGINOUS
LUMBAGO
LUMBANG
LUMBAR
LUMBAYAO
LUMBER
LUMBERDAR
LUMBERED
LUMBERER
LUMBERING
LUMBERINGLY
LUMBERJACK
LUMBERJACKET
LUMBERLY
LUMBERMAN
LUMBERMEN
LUMBERYARD
LUMBODYNIA
LUMBOSACRAL
LUMBRICAL
LUMBRICALES
LUMBRICALIS
LUMBRICID
LUMBRICIFORM
LUMBRICINE
LUMBRICOID
LUMBRICOSIS
LUMBROUS
LUMEN
LUMENS
LUMINA
LUMINAIRE
LUMINAL
LUMINANCE
LUMINANT
LUMINARIES
LUMINARIOUS
LUMINARISM
LUMINARIST
LUMINARY
LUMINATE
LUMINATION
LUMINATIVE
LUMINATOR
LUMINE
LUMINESCE
LUMINESCED
LUMINESCENCE
LUMINESCENT
LUMINESCING
LUMINIFEROUS
LUMINIFICENT
LUMINISM
LUMINIST
LUMINISTE
LUMINOSITIES
LUMINOSITY
LUMINOUS
LUMINOUSLY
LUMINOUSNESS
LUMM
LUMMOX
LUMMY
LUMP
LUMPED
LUMPEN
LUMPER
LUMPET
LUMPFISH
LUMPFISHES
LUMPIER
LUMPIEST
LUMPILY
LUMPINESS
LUMPING
LUMPINGLY
LUMPISH
LUMPISHLY
LUMPISHNESS
LUMPKIN

LUMPMAN
LUMPMEN
LUMPS
LUMPSUCKER
LUMPY
LUMUT
LUNA
LUNACIES
LUNACY
LUNAMBULISM
LUNAR
LUNARE
LUNARIA
LUNARIAN
LUNARIST
LUNARIUM
LUNARY
LUNATA
LUNATE
LUNATED
LUNATELLUS
LUNATELY
LUNATIC
LUNATICAL
LUNATICALLY
LUNATION
LUNATIZE
LUNATUM
LUNCH
LUNCHEON
LUNCHEONER
LUNCHEONETTE
LUNCHER
LUNCHROOM
LUNDYFOOT
LUNE
LUNES
LUNET
LUNETS
LUNETTE
LUNETTES
LUNG
LUNGE
LUNGED
LUNGEE
LUNGEOUS
LUNGER
LUNGFISH
LUNGFISHES
LUNGFLOWER
LUNGI
LUNGIE
LUNGING
LUNGIS
LUNGMOTOR
LUNGOOR
LUNGS
LUNGSICK
LUNGWORM
LUNGWORT
LUNGY
LUNICURRENT
LUNIES
LUNIFORM
LUNISOLAR
LUNISTICE
LUNISTITIAL
LUNITIDAL
LUNKER
LUNKHEAD
LUNKHEADED
LUNN
LUNOID
LUNT
LUNULA
LUNULAE
LUNULAR
LUNULATE
LUNULATED
LUNULE
LUNULET
LUNULITE
LUNY
LUNYIE
LUPANAR
LUPANARIAN
LUPANIN
LUPANINE
LUPE
LUPEOL
LUPEOSE
LUPETIDIN
LUPETIDINE
LUPICIDE
LUPIFORM
LUPIN
LUPINASTER
LUPINE
LUPININ
LUPININE
LUPINOSIS
LUPINOUS
LUPIS
LUPOID
LUPOUS
LUPULIN
LUPULINE
LUPULINIC
LUPULINOUS
LUPULUS
LUPUS
LUR
LURA
LURACAN
LURCH
LURCHER
LURCHING
LURDAN
LURDANE
LURE
LURED
LUREMENT
LURER
LURG
LURGWORM
LURID
LURIDITY
LURIDLY
LURIDNESS
LURING
LURK
LURKED
LURKER
LURKING
LURKINGLY
LURKY
LURRIER
LURRIES
LURRY
LUSCIOUS
LUSCIOUSLY
LUSCIOUSNESS
LUSH
LUSHBURG
LUSHER
LUSHLY
LUSHNESS
LUSHY
LUSK
LUSKISH
LUSKY
LUSORY
LUST
LUSTED
LUSTER
LUSTERED
LUSTERER
LUSTERING
LUSTERLESS
LUSTERWARE
LUSTFUL
LUSTFULLY
LUSTFULNESS
LUSTICK
LUSTIER
LUSTIEST
LUSTIHOOD
LUSTILY
LUSTING
LUSTLESS
LUSTLY
LUSTRA
LUSTRAL
LUSTRANT
LUSTRATE
LUSTRATED
LUSTRATING
LUSTRATION
LUSTRATIVE
LUSTRATORY
LUSTRE
LUSTRED
LUSTREWARE
LUSTRICAL
LUSTRIFY
LUSTRINE
LUSTRING
LUSTROUS
LUSTROUSLY
LUSTROUSNESS
LUSTRUM
LUSTRUMS
LUSTY
LUSUS
LUTACEOUS
LUTANIST
LUTANY
LUTATION
LUTE
LUTEAL
LUTECIA
LUTECIUM
LUTED
LUTEIN
LUTENIST
LUTEOFULVOUS
LUTEOFUSCOUS
LUTEOLIN
LUTEOLOUS
LUTEOMA
LUTEOUS
LUTER
LUTESCENT
LUTETIUM
LUTEUM
LUTFISK
LUTH
LUTHERN
LUTHIER
LUTIANID
LUTIANOID
LUTIDIN
LUTIDINE
LUTIDINIC
LUTING
LUTIST
LUTJANID
LUTONG
LUTOSE
LUTRIN
LUTRINE
LUTULENCE
LUTULENT
LUTZ
LUX
LUXATE
LUXATED
LUXATING
LUXATION
LUXE
LUXES
LUXIVE
LUXULLIANITE
LUXUR
LUXURIANCE
LUXURIANCY
LUXURIANT
LUXURIANTLY
LUXURIANTNESS
LUXURIATE
LUXURIATED
LUXURIATING
LUXURIATION
LUXURIES
LUXURIOUS
LUXURIOUSLY
LUXURIOUSNESS
LUXURIST
LUXURITY
LUXURY
LUXUS
LY
LYAM
LYANCE
LYARD
LYART
LYCAENID
LYCANTHROPE
LYCANTHROPIC
LYCANTHROPY
LYCEA
LYCEAL
LYCEE
LYCEUM
LYCEUMS
LYCHEE
LYCHNIS
LYCHNOMANCY
LYCHNOSCOPE
LYCHNOSCOPIC
LYCID
LYCODOID
LYCOPENE
LYCOPERDOID
LYCOPIN
LYCOPOD
LYCOPODE
LYCOPODIUM
LYCORINE
LYCOSID
LYCTID
LYDDITE
LYDITE
LYE
LYED
LYERY
LYFKIE
LYGAEID
LYGUS
LYING
LYINGLY
LYKEWAKE
LYM
LYMANTRIID
LYME
LYMNAEAN
LYMNAEID
LYMPH
LYMPHAD
LYMPHADENIA
LYMPHADENOID
LYMPHADENOMA
LYMPHAEMIA
LYMPHAGOGUE
LYMPHANGIAL
LYMPHANGIOMA
LYMPHANGIOMATA
LYMPHANGITIC
LYMPHANGITIS
LYMPHATIC
LYMPHATICAL
LYMPHATION
LYMPHATISM
LYMPHATITIS
LYMPHECTASIA
LYMPHEDEMA
LYMPHEMIA
LYMPHOBLAST
LYMPHOBLASTIC
LYMPHOCELE
LYMPHOCYST
LYMPHOCYTE
LYMPHOCYTIC
LYMPHOCYTOSIS
LYMPHOCYTOTIC
LYMPHODERMIA
LYMPHODUCT
LYMPHOEDEMA
LYMPHOGENIC
LYMPHOID
LYMPHOLOGY
LYMPHOMA
LYMPHOMATOUS
LYMPHOPATHY
LYMPHOPENIAL
LYMPHORRHAGE
LYMPHORRHEA
LYMPHOSTASIS
LYMPHOTOME
LYMPHOTOMY
LYMPHOTOXIN
LYMPHOTROPHY
LYMPHOUS
LYMPHURIA
LYMPHY
LYN
LYNCEAN
LYNCH
LYNCHED
LYNCHER
LYNCHET
LYNCHING
LYNCINE
LYNE
LYNNHAVEN
LYNX
LYNXES
LYOMEROUS
LYONETIID
LYONNAISE
LYOPHIL
LYOPHILE
LYOPHILIC
LYOPHOBE
LYOPHOBIC
LYOTROPE
LYOTROPIC
LYPEMANIA
LYPOTHYMIA
LYRA
LYRATE
LYRATED
LYRATELY
LYRAWAY
LYRE

LYREBIRD
LYREMAN
LYRETAIL
LYRIC
LYRICAL
LYRICALLY
LYRICALNESS
LYRICHORD
LYRICISM
LYRICIST
LYRICKED
LYRICKING
LYRIFORM
LYRISM
LYRIST
LYSATE
LYSE
LYSED
LYSIDIN
LYSIDINE
LYSIGENIC
LYSIGENOUS
LYSIGENOUSLY
LYSIMETER
LYSIN
LYSINE
LYSING
LYSIS
LYSOGEN
LYSOGENESIS
LYSOGENETIC
LYSOGENIC
LYSSA
LYSSIC
LYTERIAN
LYTHE
LYTHRACEOUS
LYTIC
LYTTA
LYTTAE
LYXOSE

M

MA
MAA
MAABARA
MAAL
MAAR
MAARAD
MAARIB
MAASS
MAATJE
MAB
MABE
MABI
MABOLO
MABUTI
MABYER
MAC
MACAASIM
MACABER
MACABI
MACABRE
MACAC
MACACO
MACACOS
MACADAM
MACADAMER
MACADAMIA
MACADAMITE
MACADAMIZE
MACADAMIZED
MACADAMIZER
MACADAMIZING
MACAN
MACANA
MACAO
MACAQUE
MACARISM
MACARIZE
MACARIZED
MACARIZING
MACARON
MACARONI
MACARONIC
MACARONICAL
MACARONICALLY
MACARONICISM
MACARONIES
MACARONIS
MACARONISM
MACAROON
MACAW
MACCABOY
MACCHIA
MACCHIE
MACCO
MACCOBOY
MACCUS
MACE
MACEBEARER
MACEDOINE
MACEHEAD
MACELLUM
MACEMAN
MACER
MACERABLE
MACERAL
MACERATE
MACERATED
MACERATER
MACERATING
MACERATION
MACERATOR
MACH
MACHAIR
MACHAIRODONT
MACHAN
MACHAON
MACHAR
MACHEER
MACHETE
MACHI
MACHICOLATE
MACHICOLATED
MACHILA
MACHIN
MACHINA
MACHINABLE
MACHINAL
MACHINAMENT
MACHINATE
MACHINATED
MACHINATING
MACHINATION
MACHINATOR
MACHINE
MACHINED
MACHINELY
MACHINEMAN
MACHINEMEN
MACHINER
MACHINERY
MACHINING
MACHINISM
MACHINIST
MACHINULE
MACHISMO
MACHMETER
MACHOPOLYP
MACHREE
MACIES
MACILENCE
MACILENCY
MACILENT
MACINTOSH
MACK
MACKALLOW
MACKAYBEAN
MACKENBOY
MACKEREL
MACKERELER
MACKERELING
MACKERELS
MACKINAW
MACKINBOY
MACKINS
MACKINTOSH
MACKINTOSHITE
MACKLE
MACKLED
MACKLIKE
MACKLING
MACLE
MACLED
MACLURIN
MACO
MACONITE
MACONNE
MACRADENOUS
MACRAME
MACRANDER
MACRANDRE
MACRANDROUS
MACRIO
MACROANALYST
MACROBIAN
MACROBIOSIS
MACROBIOTE
MACROBIOTICS
MACROCEPHALY
MACROCHAETA
MACROCHAETAE
MACROCHIRAN
MACROCLIMATE
MACROCOSM
MACROCOSMIC
MACROCOSMOS
MACROCYST
MACROCYTE
MACROCYTIC
MACROCYTOSIS
MACRODONT
MACRODONTIA
MACRODONTISM
MACROGAMETE
MACROGAMY
MACROGRAPH
MACROGRAPHIC
MACROGRAPHY
MACROLOGY
MACROMANIA
MACROMERAL
MACROMERE
MACROMERIC
MACROMERITE
MACROMERITIC
MACROMETER
MACROMETHOD
MACROMYELON
MACRON
MACRONUCLEAR
MACRONUCLEUS
MACROPHAGE
MACROPHAGUS
MACROPHYSICS
MACROPODIAN
MACROPODINE
MACROPODOUS
MACROPSIA
MACROPSY
MACROPTEROUS
MACROSCIAN
MACROSCOPIC
MACROSEISM
MACROSEISMIC
MACROSMATIC
MACROSPECIES
MACROSPORE
MACROSPORIC
MACROSTRUCTURE
MACROSTYLE
MACROSTYLOUS
MACROTHERE
MACROTHERM
MACROTIA
MACROTIN
MACROTOME
MACROTOUS
MACROURID
MACRURAL
MACRURAN
MACRUROID
MACRUROUS
MACTATION
MACTROID
MACUCA
MACULA
MACULAE
MACULAR
MACULATE
MACULATED
MACULATING
MACULATION
MACULE
MACULED
MACULICOLE
MACULICOLOUS
MACULIFEROUS
MACULING
MACULOSE
MACUPA
MACUPI
MACUSHLA
MACUTA
MACUTE
MAD
MADAM
MADAME
MADAMS
MADAPOLAM
MADAPOLAN
MADAPOLLAM
MADAR
MADAROSIS
MADAROTIC
MADBRAIN
MADBRAINED
MADCAP
MADDED
MADDEN
MADDENED
MADDENING
MADDENINGLY
MADDER
MADDERISH
MADDERWORT
MADDEST
MADDING
MADDINGLY
MADDISH
MADDLE
MADDOCK
MADE
MADEFACTION
MADEFY
MADELEINE
MADELINE
MADEMOISELLE
MADESCENT
MADHAB
MADHOUSE
MADHUCA
MADID
MADIDANS
MADISTERIUM
MADLING
MADLY
MADMAN
MADMEN
MADNEP
MADNESS
MADO
MADONNA
MADOQUA
MADOR
MADRAGUE
MADRAS
MADRASA
MADRASAH
MADRASSAH
MADRASSEH
MADRE
MADREPERL
MADREPORAL
MADREPORE
MADREPORIAN
MADREPORIC
MADREPORITE
MADREPORITIC
MADRIER
MADRIGAL
MADRIGALER
MADRIGALETTO
MADRIGALIAN
MADRIGALIST
MADRIH
MADRILENE
MADRONA
MADRONO
MADSTONE
MADURO
MADWEED
MADWOMAN
MADWOMEN
MADWORT
MAE
MAEANDER
MAEANDRINE
MAEANDRINOID
MAEANDROID
MAEGBOT
MAEGBOTE
MAELSTROM
MAENAD
MAENADES
MAENADIC
MAENADICALLY
MAENADISM
MAENADS
MAENAITE
MAESTIVE
MAESTOSO
MAESTRA
MAESTRO
MAESTROS
MAFEY
MAFFIA
MAFFICK
MAFFICKED
MAFFICKER
MAFFICKING
MAFFIOSO
MAFFLE
MAFFLER
MAFFLIN
MAFIA
MAFIC
MAFIOSO
MAFOO
MAFTIR
MAFU
MAFURA
MAFURRA
MAG
MAGADIS
MAGADIZE
MAGANI
MAGAS
MAGAZINABLE
MAGAZINAGE
MAGAZINE
MAGAZINED
MAGAZINER
MAGAZINING
MAGAZINISM
MAGAZINIST
MAGAZINY
MAGBOTE
MAGDALEN
MAGE
MAGENTA
MAGERFUL
MAGG
MAGGED
MAGGID
MAGGIORE
MAGGLE

MAGGOT
MAGGOTINESS
MAGGOTPIE
MAGGOTRY
MAGGOTY
MAGHZEN
MAGI
MAGIC
MAGICAL
MAGICALLY
MAGICIAN
MAGICKED
MAGICKING
MAGILP
MAGIRIC
MAGIRICS
MAGIRIST
MAGIRISTIC
MAGIROLOGIST
MAGIROLOGY
MAGISTER
MAGISTERIAL
MAGISTERIES
MAGISTERIUM
MAGISTERY
MAGISTRACIES
MAGISTRACY
MAGISTRAL
MAGISTRALITY
MAGISTRALLY
MAGISTRAND
MAGISTRANT
MAGISTRATE
MAGISTRATIVE
MAGISTRATURE
MAGMA
MAGMAS
MAGMATA
MAGMATIC
MAGNA
MAGNALE
MAGNANERIE
MAGNANIME
MAGNANIMITY
MAGNANIMOUS
MAGNANIMOUSLY
MAGNASCOPE
MAGNASCOPIC
MAGNATE
MAGNELECTRIC
MAGNEOPTIC
MAGNES
MAGNESIA
MAGNESIAL
MAGNESIAN
MAGNESIC
MAGNESITE
MAGNESIUM
MAGNET
MAGNETA
MAGNETIC
MAGNETICAL
MAGNETICALLY
MAGNETICIAN
MAGNETICS
MAGNETIFY
MAGNETIMETER
MAGNETISM
MAGNETIST
MAGNETITE
MAGNETITIC
MAGNETIZABLE
MAGNETIZATION
MAGNETIZE
MAGNETIZED
MAGNETIZER
MAGNETIZING
MAGNETO
MAGNETOBELL
MAGNETOGRAM
MAGNETOGRAPH
MAGNETOID
MAGNETOLYSIS
MAGNETOMETER
MAGNETOMETRY
MAGNETOMOTOR
MAGNETON
MAGNETOOPTIC
MAGNETOPHONE
MAGNETOS
MAGNETOSCOPE
MAGNETRON
MAGNETS
MAGNICAUDATE
MAGNIFIABLE
MAGNIFIC
MAGNIFICAL
MAGNIFICALLY
MAGNIFICATE
MAGNIFICATION
MAGNIFICE
MAGNIFICENCE
MAGNIFICENT
MAGNIFICENTLY
MAGNIFICO
MAGNIFICOES
MAGNIFIED
MAGNIFIER
MAGNIFIQUE
MAGNIFY
MAGNIFYING
MAGNILOQUENT
MAGNIPOTENCE
MAGNIPOTENT
MAGNISONANT
MAGNITUDE
MAGNITUDES
MAGNITUDINOUS
MAGNOLIA
MAGNUM
MAGOT
MAGPIE
MAGPIED
MAGRIM
MAGSMAN
MAGUARI
MAGUEY
MAHA
MAHAJAN
MAHAJUN
MAHAL
MAHALA
MAHALAMAT
MAHALEB
MAHALLA
MAHALY
MAHAN
MAHANT
MAHAR
MAHARAJA
MAHARAJAH
MAHARAJRANA
MAHARANA
MAHARANEE
MAHARANI
MAHARAO
MAHARAWAL
MAHARAWAT
MAHARMAH
MAHARSHI
MAHAT
MAHATMA
MAHATMAISM
MAHBUB
MAHIMAHI
MAHJONG
MAHJONGG
MAHLSTICK
MAHMAL
MAHMUDI
MAHO
MAHOE
MAHOGANIES
MAHOGANIZE
MAHOGANY
MAHOITRE
MAHOLI
MAHOLTINE
MAHONE
MAHOUT
MAHR
MAHSEER
MAHSIR
MAHSUR
MAHUA
MAHUANG
MAHWA
MAHZOR
MAI
MAIAN
MAID
MAIDAN
MAIDCHILD
MAIDEN
MAIDENCHILD
MAIDENHAIR
MAIDENHEAD
MAIDENHOOD
MAIDENLINESS
MAIDENLY
MAIDENWEED
MAIDHEAD
MAIDHOOD
MAIDIN
MAIDISM
MAIDKIN
MAIDLY
MAIDSERVANT
MAIDY
MAIEUTIC
MAIEUTICAL
MAIEUTICS
MAIG
MAIGRE
MAIHEM
MAIID
MAIL
MAILABLE
MAILBAG
MAILBOX
MAILCATCHER
MAILCLAD
MAILE
MAILED
MAILER
MAILGUARD
MAILIE
MAILING
MAILL
MAILLE
MAILLECHORT
MAILLOT
MAILMAN
MAILMEN
MAILPLANE
MAILPOUCH
MAIM
MAIMED
MAIMEDLY
MAIMEDNESS
MAIMER
MAIMING
MAIMON
MAIMUL
MAIN
MAINE
MAINFERRE
MAINLAND
MAINLANDER
MAINLINE
MAINLINED
MAINLINER
MAINLINING
MAINLY
MAINMAST
MAINMORTABLE
MAINOR
MAINOUR
MAINPAST
MAINPERNABLE
MAINPERNOR
MAINPIN
MAINPORT
MAINPOST
MAINPRISE
MAINPRIZE
MAINPRIZER
MAINS
MAINSAIL
MAINSHEET
MAINSPRING
MAINSTAY
MAINSTREAM
MAINT
MAINTAIN
MAINTAINED
MAINTAINER
MAINTAINING
MAINTAINOR
MAINTENANCE
MAINTOP
MAINTOPMAN
MAINTOPMAST
MAINTOPMEN
MAINTOPSAIL
MAINWARD
MAIOLICA
MAIPO
MAIRATOUR
MAIRE
MAIRIE
MAISON
MAISONETTE
MAIST
MAISTRY
MAITLANDITE
MAITRE
MAITRESSE
MAITRISE
MAIZE
MAIZEBIRD
MAIZER
MAJA
MAJAGUA
MAJAS
MAJESTIC
MAJESTICAL
MAJESTICALLY
MAJESTIES
MAJESTIOUS
MAJESTY
MAJID
MAJIDIEH
MAJO
MAJOE
MAJOLICA
MAJOLIST
MAJOON
MAJOR
MAJORAT
MAJORATE
MAJORATION
MAJORDOMO
MAJORETTE
MAJORITIES
MAJORITY
MAJORIZE
MAJOS
MAJUSCULAE
MAJUSCULAR
MAJUSCULE
MAK
MAKADOO
MAKAHIKI
MAKAI
MAKALE
MAKAR
MAKARA
MAKATEA
MAKE
MAKEBATE
MAKEDOM
MAKEFAST
MAKELESS
MAKER
MAKEREADY
MAKERESS
MAKERS
MAKES
MAKESHIFT
MAKESHIFTY
MAKEWEIGHT
MAKHORKA
MAKHZAN
MAKHZEN
MAKI
MAKIMONO
MAKIN
MAKING
MAKINGS
MAKLUK
MAKO
MAKOMAKO
MAKOPA
MAKOUA
MAKRAN
MAKROSKELIC
MAKUK
MAKUTU
MAL
MALA
MALAANONANG
MALABATHRUM
MALACANTHID
MALACEOUS
MALACHITE
MALACIA
MALACODERM
MALACOID
MALACOLITE
MALACOLOGIST
MALACOLOGY
MALACON
MALACONE
MALACTIC
MALADAPTATION
MALADDRESS
MALADE
MALADIES
MALADIVE
MALADJUSTED
MALADJUSTMENT
MALADROIT
MALADROITLY
MALADVENTURE

MALADY
MALAGMA
MALAHACK
MALAISE
MALAKIN
MALAKON
MALAMBO
MALAMUTE
MALANDERED
MALANDERS
MALANDROUS
MALANGA
MALAPAHO
MALAPERT
MALAPERTLY
MALAPERTNESS
MALAPROP
MALAPROPIAN
MALAPROPISM
MALAPROPOS
MALAR
MALARIA
MALARIAL
MALARIAN
MALARIN
MALARIOID
MALARIOLOGY
MALARIOUS
MALARKEY
MALARKY
MALATE
MALATI
MALAX
MALAXABLE
MALAXAGE
MALAXATE
MALAXATION
MALAXATOR
MALAXED
MALAXERMAN
MALAXERMEN
MALAXING
MALBROUCK
MALCHITE
MALCONDUCT
MALCONTENT
MALCONTENTED
MALCONTENTEDLY
MALCONTENTISM
MALCONTENTLY
MALCONTENTMENT
MALDOCCHIO
MALDONITE
MALDUCK
MALE
MALEABILITY
MALEASE
MALEATE
MALEDICENT
MALEDICT
MALEDICTION
MALEDICTIVE
MALEDICTORY
MALEFACTION
MALEFACTOR
MALEFACTORY
MALEFACTRESS
MALEFIC
MALEFICAL
MALEFICALLY
MALEFICE
MALEFICENCE
MALEFICENT
MALEFICIAL
MALEFICIATE
MALEIC
MALEINOID
MALEINOIDAL
MALELLA
MALELLAE
MALEMIUT
MALEMUTE
MALENESS
MALENGINE
MALENTENDU
MALEO
MALEOS
MALETOTE
MALEVOLENCE
MALEVOLENCY
MALEVOLENT
MALEVOLENTLY
MALEVOLOUS
MALFEASANCE
MALFEASANT
MALFEASOR
MALFORMATION
MALFORMED
MALFUNCTION
MALGRACE
MALGRADO
MALGRE
MALGUZAR
MALGUZARI
MALHEUR
MALI
MALIC
MALICE
MALICEFUL
MALICIOUS
MALICIOUSLY
MALICORIUM
MALIFEROUS
MALIFORM
MALIGN
MALIGNANCE
MALIGNANCIES
MALIGNANCY
MALIGNANT
MALIGNANTLY
MALIGNATION
MALIGNED
MALIGNER
MALIGNIFIED
MALIGNIFY
MALIGNIFYING
MALIGNING
MALIGNITIES
MALIGNITY
MALIGNLY
MALIGNMENT
MALIHINI
MALIK
MALIKANA
MALINCHE
MALINE
MALINES
MALINGER
MALINGERED
MALINGERER
MALINGERING
MALINGERY
MALINOWSKITE
MALINTENT
MALISM
MALISON
MALIST
MALISTIC
MALKIN
MALL
MALLADRITE
MALLANGONG
MALLARD
MALLARDITE
MALLARDS
MALLEABLE
MALLEABLEIZE
MALLEABLEIZED
MALLEABLEIZING
MALLEABLIZE
MALLEABLY
MALLEAL
MALLEATE
MALLEATED
MALLEATING
MALLEATION
MALLED
MALLEE
MALLEI
MALLEIFEROUS
MALLEIFORM
MALLEIN
MALLEINIZE
MALLEMUCK
MALLENDERS
MALLEOINCUDAL
MALLEOLABLE
MALLEOLAR
MALLEOLI
MALLEOLUS
MALLET
MALLETED
MALLETING
MALLEUS
MALLING
MALLOPHAGAN
MALLOPHAGOUS
MALLOSEISMIC
MALLOW
MALLOWWORT
MALLUM
MALLUS
MALM
MALMARSH
MALMED
MALMIGNATTE
MALMING
MALMOCK
MALMSEY
MALMSEYS
MALMSTONE
MALMY
MALNUTRITE
MALNUTRITION
MALO
MALOCA
MALOCCHIO
MALOCCLUDED
MALOCCLUSION
MALODOR
MALODOROUS
MALODOROUSLY
MALODOUR
MALONATE
MALONIC
MALONYL
MALONYLUREA
MALOUAH
MALPAIS
MALPOSED
MALPOSITION
MALPRACTICE
MALPRACTITIONER
MALPRAXIS
MALPROPRIETY
MALT
MALTASE
MALTED
MALTER
MALTHA
MALTHOUSE
MALTIER
MALTIEST
MALTING
MALTMAN
MALTOLTE
MALTOSE
MALTREAT
MALTREATED
MALTREATING
MALTREATMENT
MALTREATOR
MALTSTER
MALTWORM
MALTY
MALUM
MALURINE
MALVACEOUS
MALVASIA
MALVASIAN
MALVERSATION
MALVERSE
MALVIN
MALVOISIE
MAMA
MAMALOI
MAMAMU
MAMBA
MAMBO
MAMBOS
MAMBU
MAMELIERE
MAMELON
MAMELUCO
MAMEYES
MAMEYS
MAMILLA
MAMLATDAR
MAMLUTDAR
MAMMA
MAMMAE
MAMMAL
MAMMALGIA
MAMMALIAN
MAMMALITY
MAMMALOGICAL
MAMMALOGIST
MAMMALOGY
MAMMARY
MAMMATE
MAMMATUS
MAMME
MAMMEE
MAMMER
MAMMET
MAMMEY
MAMMIE
MAMMIES
MAMMIFER
MAMMIFEROUS
MAMMIFORM
MAMMILATE
MAMMILATED
MAMMILLA
MAMMILLAE
MAMMILLAR
MAMMILLARY
MAMMILLATION
MAMMILLIFORM
MAMMILLOID
MAMMITIS
MAMMOCK
MAMMOCKED
MAMMOCKING
MAMMON
MAMMONI
MAMMONIACAL
MAMMONISH
MAMMONISM
MAMMONIST
MAMMONISTIC
MAMMONITE
MAMMONITISH
MAMMONIZATION
MAMMONIZE
MAMMONOLATRY
MAMMOSE
MAMMOTH
MAMMOTHREPT
MAMMULA
MAMMULAE
MAMMULAR
MAMMY
MAMO
MAMONA
MAMOTY
MAMPALON
MAMPUS
MAMRY
MAMUSHI
MAMZER
MAN
MANA
MANACLE
MANACLED
MANACLES
MANACLING
MANADA
MANAGE
MANAGEABILITY
MANAGEABLE
MANAGEABLENESS
MANAGEABLY
MANAGED
MANAGELESS
MANAGEMENT
MANAGEMENTAL
MANAGER
MANAGERESS
MANAGERIAL
MANAGERIALLY
MANAGERSHIP
MANAGERY
MANAGES
MANAGING
MANAI
MANAKIN
MANAL
MANANA
MANARVEL
MANAS
MANATEE
MANATI
MANATINE
MANATION
MANATOID
MANAVEL
MANAVELINS
MANAVILINS
MANBARKLAK
MANBIRD
MANBOT
MANBOTE
MANCALA
MANCANDO
MANCHE
MANCHET
MANCHINEEL
MANCINISM
MANCIPABLE
MANCIPANT
MANCIPATE
MANCIPATION
MANCIPATIVE
MANCIPATORY

MANCIPEE
MANCIPIA
MANCIPIUM
MANCIPLE
MANCIPULAR
MANCO
MANCONO
MANCUS
MAND
MANDALA
MANDAMENT
MANDAMUS
MANDAMUSED
MANDAMUSING
MANDAPA
MANDAR
MANDARAH
MANDARIN
MANDARINATE
MANDARINED
MANDARINESS
MANDARINIC
MANDARINING
MANDARINISM
MANDAT
MANDATARIES
MANDATARY
MANDATE
MANDATED
MANDATEE
MANDATING
MANDATION
MANDATIVE
MANDATOR
MANDATORIES
MANDATORILY
MANDATORY
MANDATS
MANDATUM
MANDELATE
MANDELIC
MANDIBLE
MANDIBULAR
MANDIBULARY
MANDIBULATE
MANDIBULATED
MANDIL
MANDILION
MANDIR
MANDLEN
MANDOER
MANDOLA
MANDOLIN
MANDOLINIST
MANDOLUTE
MANDORA
MANDORE
MANDORLA
MANDORLE
MANDRA
MANDRAGON
MANDRAGORA
MANDRAKE
MANDREL
MANDRIARCH
MANDRIL
MANDRILL
MANDRIN
MANDRITTA
MANDRUKA
MANDS
MANDUA
MANDUCABLE
MANDUCATE
MANDUCATED
MANDUCATING
MANDUCATION
MANDUCATORY
MANDYAS
MANE
MANED
MANEGE
MANEH
MANEI
MANELESS
MANENT
MANERIAL
MANES
MANESHEET
MANESS
MANET
MANEUVER
MANEUVERABLE
MANEUVERED
MANEUVERER
MANEUVERING
MANEUVRABLE
MANEUVRE
MANEUVRED
MANEUVRING
MANEY
MANFISH
MANFUL
MANFULLY
MANFULNESS
MANG
MANGA
MANGABEIRA
MANGABEY
MANGABY
MANGANA
MANGANATE
MANGANBLENDE
MANGANEISEN
MANGANESE
MANGANESIAN
MANGANESIC
MANGANETIC
MANGANIC
MANGANITE
MANGANIUM
MANGANIZE
MANGANOSITE
MANGANOUS
MANGE
MANGEAO
MANGEL
MANGELIN
MANGER
MANGERITE
MANGERY
MANGI
MANGIER
MANGIEST
MANGILY
MANGINESS
MANGLE
MANGLED
MANGLEMAN
MANGLER
MANGLING
MANGLINGLY
MANGO
MANGOES
MANGOLD
MANGONA
MANGONEL
MANGONISM
MANGONIZE
MANGORO
MANGOS
MANGOSTEEN
MANGOUR
MANGRASS
MANGRATE
MANGROVE
MANGUE
MANGWE
MANGY
MANHANDLE
MANHANDLED
MANHANDLING
MANHEAD
MANHOLE
MANHOOD
MANHUNT
MANHUNTER
MANHUNTING
MANI
MANIA
MANIABLE
MANIAC
MANIACAL
MANIACALLY
MANIC
MANICATE
MANICHORDON
MANICOLE
MANICON
MANICORD
MANICURE
MANICURED
MANICURING
MANICURIST
MANID
MANIFEST
MANIFESTABLE
MANIFESTANT
MANIFESTATION
MANIFESTED
MANIFESTER
MANIFESTING
MANIFESTIVE
MANIFESTLY
MANIFESTO
MANIFESTOES
MANIFESTOS
MANIFOLD
MANIFOLDED
MANIFOLDER
MANIFOLDING
MANIFOLDLY
MANIFOLDNESS
MANIFORM
MANIFY
MANIHOT
MANIKIN
MANIKINISM
MANILA
MANILLA
MANILLE
MANINI
MANIOC
MANIPLE
MANIPULABLE
MANIPULAR
MANIPULARY
MANIPULATE
MANIPULATED
MANIPULATING
MANIPULATION
MANIPULATIVE
MANIPULATOR
MANIPULATORY
MANISM
MANIST
MANISTIC
MANITO
MANITOU
MANITRUNK
MANITU
MANIU
MANJACK
MANJAK
MANJEET
MANJEL
MANK
MANKEEPER
MANKIE
MANKILLER
MANKILLING
MANKIN
MANKIND
MANKINDLY
MANKY
MANLESS
MANLESSLY
MANLESSNESS
MANLIER
MANLIEST
MANLIHOOD
MANLIKE
MANLIKELY
MANLIKENESS
MANLILY
MANLINESS
MANLY
MANMADE
MANNA
MANNAIA
MANNAN
MANNED
MANNEQUIN
MANNER
MANNERABLE
MANNERED
MANNERING
MANNERISM
MANNERIST
MANNERISTIC
MANNERIZE
MANNERLESS
MANNERLINESS
MANNERLY
MANNERS
MANNERSOME
MANNESS
MANNET
MANNIE
MANNIFEROUS
MANNIFY
MANNIKIN
MANNIKINISM
MANNING
MANNISH
MANNISHLY
MANNISHNESS
MANNITAN
MANNITE
MANNITIC
MANNITOL
MANNITOSE
MANNOHEPTITE
MANNOHEPTITOL
MANNOHEPTOSE
MANNONIC
MANNOSAN
MANNOSE
MANNY
MANO
MANOC
MANOEUVER
MANOEUVRE
MANOEUVRER
MANOGRAPH
MANOIR
MANOMETER
MANOMETRIC
MANOMETRICAL
MANOMETRY
MANOMIN
MANOR
MANORIAL
MANORIALISM
MANORIALIZE
MANOSCOPE
MANPOWER
MANQUE
MANQUEE
MANRED
MANRENT
MANROOT
MANROPE
MANSARD
MANSARDED
MANSE
MANSERVANT
MANSHIP
MANSION
MANSIONAL
MANSIONARY
MANSIONED
MANSIONRY
MANSLAUGHTER
MANSLAUGHTERER
MANSLAUGHTERING
MANSLAYER
MANSLAYING
MANSO
MANSTEALER
MANSTEALING
MANSTOPPER
MANSTOPPING
MANSUETE
MANSUETELY
MANSUETUDE
MANSWEAR
MANSWORN
MANT
MANTA
MANTAL
MANTEAU
MANTEAUS
MANTEAUX
MANTEEL
MANTEGAR
MANTEL
MANTELET
MANTELLETTA
MANTELLONE
MANTELPIECE
MANTELSHELF
MANTELTREE
MANTER
MANTES
MANTEVIL
MANTIC
MANTICISM
MANTICORA
MANTICORE
MANTID
MANTILLA
MANTIS
MANTISES
MANTISPID
MANTISSA
MANTISTIC
MANTLE
MANTLED
MANTLEROCK
MANTLET
MANTLING
MANTO
MANTOID
MANTOLOGIST

MANTOLOGY
MANTRA
MANTRAM
MANTRAP
MANTUA
MANTUAMAKER
MANTUAMAKING
MANTY
MANU
MANUAL
MANUALII
MANUALIST
MANUALITER
MANUALLY
MANUAO
MANUARY
MANUBALISTE
MANUBRIA
MANUBRIAL
MANUBRIATED
MANUBRIUM
MANUBRIUMS
MANUCAPTION
MANUCAPTOR
MANUCAPTURE
MANUCODE
MANUCODIATA
MANUDUCE
MANUDUCT
MANUDUCTION
MANUDUCTIVE
MANUDUCTOR
MANUDUCTORY
MANUFACT
MANUFACTION
MANUFACTOR
MANUFACTORY
MANUFACTURAL
MANUFACTURE
MANUFACTURED
MANUFACTURER
MANUFACTURING
MANUKA
MANUL
MANUMA
MANUMEA
MANUMISABLE
MANUMISE
MANUMISSION
MANUMISSIVE
MANUMIT
MANUMITTED
MANUMITTER
MANUMITTING
MANUMOTIVE
MANUPRISOR
MANURABLE
MANURAGE
MANURANCE
MANURE
MANURED
MANUREMENT
MANURER
MANURIAL
MANURIALLY
MANURING
MANUS
MANUSCRIPT
MANUSCRIPTAL
MANUSCRIPTION
MANUSINA
MANUTAGI
MANUTERGIUM
MANWARD
MANWARDS
MANWAY
MANWEED
MANWISE
MANY
MANYATTA
MANYBERRY
MANYFOLD
MANYPLIES
MANYROOT
MANYWHERE
MANZANA
MANZANILLA
MANZANILLO
MANZANITA
MANZIL
MAO
MAOMAO
MAORMOR
MAP
MAPACH
MAPACHE
MAPAU
MAPLAND
MAPLE
MAPLEFACE
MAPLES
MAPO
MAPPED
MAPPEMONDE
MAPPEN
MAPPER
MAPPING
MAPPIST
MAPPY
MAPS
MAPWISE
MAQUAHUITL
MAQUETTE
MAQUI
MAQUIS
MAR
MARABOTIN
MARABOU
MARABOUT
MARABUTO
MARACA
MARACAN
MARACOCK
MARAE
MARAI
MARAKAPAS
MARAL
MARAN
MARANAO
MARANG
MARANON
MARANTACEOUS
MARANTIC
MARARA
MARARIE
MARAS
MARASCA
MARASCHINO
MARASMIC
MARASMOID
MARASMOUS
MARASMUS
MARATHON
MARATHONER
MARAUD
MARAUDED
MARAUDER
MARAUDING
MARAVEDI
MARAY
MARBELIZE
MARBLE
MARBLED
MARBLEHEAD
MARBLEHEADER
MARBLEIZE
MARBLEIZED
MARBLEIZER
MARBLEIZING
MARBLER
MARBLES
MARBLEWOOD
MARBLING
MARBLY
MARBRINUS
MARC
MARCANDO
MARCANTANT
MARCASITE
MARCASITIC
MARCASITICAL
MARCATISSIMO
MARCATO
MARCEL
MARCELINE
MARCELLA
MARCELLED
MARCELLER
MARCELLING
MARCELLO
MARCESCENCE
MARCESCENT
MARCH
MARCHAND
MARCHED
MARCHER
MARCHESA
MARCHESE
MARCHESI
MARCHET
MARCHETTI
MARCHETTO
MARCHING
MARCHIONESS
MARCHITE
MARCHLAND
MARCHMAN
MARCHMEN
MARCHPANE
MARCID
MARCO
MARCONI
MARCONIGRAM
MARCONIGRAPH
MARCOR
MARCOT
MARCOTTAGE
MARDY
MARE
MAREBLOB
MARECHAL
MARECHALE
MAREKANITE
MAREMMA
MAREMMATIC
MAREMME
MAREMMESE
MARENGO
MARENNIN
MARES
MARFIRE
MARGA
MARGARATE
MARGARIC
MARGARIN
MARGARINE
MARGARITA
MARGARITAE
MARGARITE
MARGARITIC
MARGARODITE
MARGAY
MARGE
MARGELINE
MARGENT
MARGIN
MARGINAL
MARGINALIA
MARGINALITY
MARGINALIZE
MARGINALLY
MARGINATE
MARGINATED
MARGINATING
MARGINATION
MARGINED
MARGINIFORM
MARGINING
MARGINOPLASTY
MARGINS
MARGOSA
MARGRAVATE
MARGRAVE
MARGRAVELY
MARGRAVIAL
MARGRAVIATE
MARGRAVINE
MARGUERITE
MARGULLIE
MARHALA
MARIA
MARIACHI
MARIALITE
MARIANA
MARIANNA
MARIANNE
MARICA
MARICOLOUS
MARID
MARIGENOUS
MARIGOLD
MARIGRAM
MARIGRAPH
MARIGRAPHIC
MARIHUANA
MARIJUANA
MARIKINA
MARIMBA
MARIMONDA
MARINA
MARINADE
MARINADED
MARINADING
MARINAL
MARINATE
MARINATED
MARINATING
MARINE
MARINER
MARINERSHIP
MARINHEIRO
MARINIST
MARINORAMA
MARIONET
MARIONETTE
MARIPOSITE
MARIS
MARISH
MARISHNESS
MARISHY
MARITA
MARITAGE
MARITAGIUM
MARITAL
MARITALITY
MARITALLY
MARITICIDAL
MARITICIDE
MARITIMAL
MARITIMATE
MARITIME
MARITIMES
MARITORIOUS
MARIUPOLITE
MARJORAM
MARK
MARKA
MARKABLE
MARKAZ
MARKAZES
MARKDOWN
MARKED
MARKEDLY
MARKEDNESS
MARKER
MARKERY
MARKET
MARKETABILITY
MARKETABLE
MARKETABLY
MARKETED
MARKETEER
MARKETER
MARKETING
MARKETMAN
MARKETPLACE
MARKETSTEAD
MARKFIELDITE
MARKHOOR
MARKHOR
MARKING
MARKINGLY
MARKINGS
MARKKA
MARKKAA
MARKLAND
MARKMAN
MARKMEN
MARKMOOT
MARKMOTE
MARKS
MARKSHOT
MARKSMAN
MARKSMANLY
MARKSMANSHIP
MARKSMEN
MARKSTONE
MARKSWOMAN
MARKSWOMEN
MARKUP
MARKWEED
MARKWORTHY
MARL
MARLACEOUS
MARLBERRY
MARLED
MARLER
MARLET
MARLI
MARLIN
MARLINE
MARLINESPIKE
MARLING
MARLINGSPIKE
MARLINSPIKE
MARLITE
MARLITIC
MARLOCK
MARLPIT
MARLY
MARM
MARMALADE
MARMALADY
MARMARITIN
MARMARIZE

MARMARIZED
MARMARIZING
MARMAROSIS
MARMATITE
MARMELOS
MARMENNILL
MARMION
MARMIT
MARMITE
MARMOLITE
MARMOR
MARMORACEOUS
MARMORATE
MARMOREAL
MARMOREALLY
MARMOREAN
MARMORIC
MARMOSE
MARMOSET
MARMOT
MARO
MAROCAIN
MAROK
MAROON
MAROONED
MAROONER
MAROONING
MAROQUIN
MAROR
MAROS
MAROTTE
MARPLOT
MARPLOTRY
MARQUE
MARQUEE
MARQUESS
MARQUETERIE
MARQUETRY
MARQUIS
MARQUISAL
MARQUISATE
MARQUISDOM
MARQUISE
MARQUISESS
MARQUISETTE
MARQUISINA
MARQUISOTTE
MARQUITO
MARRAINE
MARRAM
MARRANISM
MARRANIZE
MARRANO
MARRED
MARREE
MARRER
MARRIABLE
MARRIAGE
MARRIAGEABLE
MARRIED
MARRIER
MARRING
MARROCK
MARRON
MARROT
MARROW
MARROWBONE
MARROWED
MARROWFAT
MARROWING
MARROWSKY
MARROWSKYER
MARROWY
MARRUBE
MARRY
MARRYER
MARRYING
MARRYMUFFE
MARSE
MARSEILLE
MARSEILLES
MARSH
MARSHAL
MARSHALATE
MARSHALCY
MARSHALED
MARSHALER
MARSHALESS
MARSHALING
MARSHALLED
MARSHALLER
MARSHALLING
MARSHALMAN
MARSHALSHIP
MARSHBERRIES
MARSHBERRY
MARSHBUCK
MARSHFIRE
MARSHFLOWER
MARSHIER
MARSHIEST
MARSHINESS
MARSHITE
MARSHLAND
MARSHLANDER
MARSHLOCKS
MARSHMALLOW
MARSHMAN
MARSHMEN
MARSHWORT
MARSHY
MARSOON
MARSUPIA
MARSUPIAL
MARSUPIALIAN
MARSUPIALIZE
MARSUPIAN
MARSUPIATE
MARSUPIUM
MART
MARTAGON
MARTEL
MARTELINE
MARTELLATE
MARTELLATO
MARTELLEMENT
MARTELLO
MARTEN
MARTENIKO
MARTENOT
MARTENS
MARTENSITE
MARTENSITIC
MARTEXT
MARTIAL
MARTIALISM
MARTIALIST
MARTIALITY
MARTIALIZE
MARTIALLY
MARTIALNESS
MARTILOGE
MARTIN
MARTINET
MARTINETA
MARTINETISM
MARTINGAL
MARTINGALE
MARTINI
MARTINICO
MARTINIS
MARTINOE
MARTITE
MARTLET
MARTRIX
MARTYR
MARTYRDOM
MARTYRED
MARTYRER
MARTYRESS
MARTYRIES
MARTYRING
MARTYRIUM
MARTYRIZE
MARTYRIZED
MARTYRIZER
MARTYRIZING
MARTYRLY
MARTYROLATRY
MARTYROLOGE
MARTYROLOGIC
MARTYROLOGICAL
MARTYROLOGY
MARTYRY
MARU
MARUA
MARUM
MARVEL
MARVELED
MARVELING
MARVELLED
MARVELLING
MARVELLOUS
MARVELLOUSLY
MARVELOUS
MARVELOUSLY
MARVELRY
MARVER
MARY
MARYBUD
MARYSOLE
MARZIPAN
MAS
MASA
MASARID
MASARIDID
MASCAGNINE
MASCAGNITE
MASCALLY
MASCARA
MASCARON
MASCLE
MASCLED
MASCON
MASCOT
MASCOTISM
MASCOTRY
MASCOTTE
MASCULARITY
MASCULATE
MASCULATION
MASCULINE
MASCULINELY
MASCULINENESS
MASCULINISM
MASCULINIST
MASCULINITY
MASCULY
MASDEU
MASER
MASH
MASHA
MASHAK
MASHAL
MASHALLAH
MASHAM
MASHED
MASHELTON
MASHER
MASHGIAH
MASHIE
MASHIER
MASHIES
MASHIEST
MASHING
MASHLOCH
MASHLUM
MASHMAN
MASHMEN
MASHRU
MASHY
MASI
MASJID
MASK
MASKALONGE
MASKED
MASKEG
MASKELYNITE
MASKER
MASKERY
MASKETTE
MASKFLOWER
MASKING
MASKINONGE
MASKOID
MASLIN
MASOCHISM
MASOCHIST
MASOCHISTIC
MASON
MASONED
MASONER
MASONIC
MASONING
MASONITE
MASONRIED
MASONRIES
MASONRY
MASONRYING
MASONS
MASONWORK
MASOOKA
MASOOLA
MASQUE
MASQUER
MASQUERADE
MASQUERADED
MASQUERADER
MASQUERADING
MASS
MASSA
MASSACRE
MASSACRED
MASSACRER
MASSACRING
MASSACROUS
MASSAGE
MASSAGED
MASSAGER
MASSAGEUSE
MASSAGING
MASSAGIST
MASSARANDUBA
MASSASAUGA
MASSE
MASSEBAH
MASSECUITE
MASSED
MASSEL
MASSELGEM
MASSER
MASSES
MASSETER
MASSETERIC
MASSETERINE
MASSEUR
MASSEURS
MASSEUSE
MASSEUSES
MASSICOT
MASSIER
MASSIEST
MASSIF
MASSIG
MASSINESS
MASSIVE
MASSIVELY
MASSIVENESS
MASSIVITY
MASSOTHERAPY
MASSOY
MASSULA
MASSY
MASSYMORE
MAST
MASTABA
MASTABAH
MASTADENITIS
MASTADENOMA
MASTAGE
MASTALGIA
MASTATROPHIA
MASTATROPHY
MASTAUXE
MASTAX
MASTECTOMIES
MASTECTOMY
MASTED
MASTER
MASTERATE
MASTERDOM
MASTERED
MASTERER
MASTERFAST
MASTERFUL
MASTERFULLY
MASTERFULNESS
MASTERHOOD
MASTERIES
MASTERING
MASTERLESS
MASTERLILY
MASTERLINESS
MASTERLY
MASTERMAN
MASTERMEN
MASTERMIND
MASTEROUS
MASTERPIECE
MASTERSHIP
MASTERSINGER
MASTERSINGERS
MASTERSTROKE
MASTERWORK
MASTERWORT
MASTERY
MASTFUL
MASTHEAD
MASTIC
MASTICABLE
MASTICATE
MASTICATED
MASTICATING
MASTICATION
MASTICATOR
MASTICATORIES
MASTICATORY
MASTICIC
MASTICUROUS
MASTIFF
MASTIGATE
MASTIGIA
MASTIGIUM
MASTIGONEME
MASTIGOPOD

MASTIGOTE
MASTIGURE
MASTING
MASTITIS
MASTMAN
MASTMEN
MASTODON
MASTODONT
MASTODONTIC
MASTODONTINE
MASTODONTOID
MASTODYNIA
MASTOID
MASTOIDALE
MASTOIDITIS
MASTOIDOTOMY
MASTOLOGICAL
MASTOLOGIST
MASTOLOGY
MASTOMENIA
MASTOPATHY
MASTOPEXY
MASTOPLASTIA
MASTORRHAGIA
MASTOTOMY
MASTS
MASTURBATE
MASTURBATED
MASTURBATING
MASTURBATION
MASTURBATOR
MASTURBATORY
MASTWOOD
MASTY
MASU
MASURIUM
MAT
MATA
MATACHIN
MATACHINA
MATACHINAS
MATACO
MATADERO
MATADOR
MATAEOLOGUE
MATAEOLOGY
MATAEOTECHNY
MATAGASSE
MATAGORY
MATAI
MATAJUELO
MATALAN
MATAMATA
MATAMORO
MATANZA
MATAPAN
MATAPI
MATARA
MATASANO
MATAX
MATBOARD
MATCH
MATCHABLE
MATCHABLY
MATCHBOARD
MATCHBOARDING
MATCHBOOK
MATCHBOX
MATCHCLOTH
MATCHCOAT
MATCHED
MATCHER
MATCHING
MATCHLESS
MATCHLESSLY
MATCHLESSNESS
MATCHLOCK
MATCHMAKER
MATCHMAKING
MATCHMARK
MATCHSAFE
MATCHSTALK
MATCHSTICK
MATCHWOOD
MATCHY
MATE
MATED
MATEE
MATEGRIFFON
MATELASSE
MATELEY
MATELOT
MATELOTAGE
MATELOTE
MATELOTTE
MATER
MATERFAMILIAS
MATERIA
MATERIABLE
MATERIAL
MATERIALISM
MATERIALIST
MATERIALISTIC
MATERIALITY
MATERIALIZATION
MATERIALIZE
MATERIALIZED
MATERIALIZER
MATERIALIZING
MATERIALLY
MATERIALMAN
MATERIALMEN
MATERIALNESS
MATERIALS
MATERIATE
MATERIATION
MATERIEL
MATERNAL
MATERNALITY
MATERNALIZE
MATERNALLY
MATERNALNESS
MATERNITIES
MATERNITY
MATERNOLOGY
MATEY
MATEZITE
MATFELLON
MATFELON
MATGRASS
MATH
MATHE
MATHEMATIC
MATHEMATICAL
MATHEMATICALLY
MATHEMATICALS
MATHEMATICIAN
MATHEMATICS
MATHEMATIZE
MATHEMEG
MATHER
MATHES
MATHESIS
MATHETIC
MATHS
MATICO
MATIE
MATIES
MATILDITE
MATIN
MATINA
MATINAL
MATINEE
MATING
MATINS
MATIPO
MATKA
MATKAH
MATLOCKITE
MATLOW
MATMAKER
MATMAKING
MATMAN
MATRA
MATRACE
MATRAH
MATRAL
MATRANEE
MATRASS
MATREED
MATRIARCH
MATRIARCHAL
MATRIARCHATE
MATRIARCHIC
MATRIARCHIES
MATRIARCHIST
MATRIARCHY
MATRIC
MATRICAL
MATRICE
MATRICES
MATRICIDAL
MATRICIDE
MATRICULA
MATRICULABLE
MATRICULAE
MATRICULANT
MATRICULAR
MATRICULATE
MATRICULATED
MATRICULATING
MATRICULATION
MATRICULATOR
MATRICULATORY
MATRIHERITAGE
MATRIHERITAL
MATRILINEAL
MATRILINEAR
MATRILINY
MATRILOCAL
MATRIMONIAL
MATRIMONIES
MATRIMONIOUS
MATRIMONY
MATRIOTISM
MATRIS
MATRIX
MATRIXES
MATROCLINAL
MATROCLINIC
MATROCLINOUS
MATROCLINY
MATRON
MATRONAGE
MATRONAL
MATRONIZE
MATRONIZED
MATRONIZING
MATRONLIKE
MATRONLINESS
MATRONLY
MATRONYMIC
MATROSS
MATSTER
MATSU
MATSUE
MATSURI
MATTA
MATTAMORE
MATTARO
MATTE
MATTED
MATTEDLY
MATTEDNESS
MATTER
MATTERED
MATTERING
MATTERS
MATTERY
MATTI
MATTIN
MATTING
MATTO
MATTOCK
MATTOID
MATTOIR
MATTRASS
MATTRESS
MATTULLA
MATURABLE
MATURATE
MATURATED
MATURATING
MATURATION
MATURATIVE
MATURE
MATURED
MATURELY
MATURENESS
MATURER
MATURESCENCE
MATURESCENT
MATUREST
MATURING
MATURITY
MATUTINAL
MATUTINALLY
MATUTINARY
MATUTINE
MATUTINELY
MATWEED
MATY
MATZO
MATZOH
MATZOON
MATZOS
MATZOT
MATZOTH
MAU
MAUCACO
MAUCHERITE
MAUD
MAUDELINE
MAUDLE
MAUDLIN
MAUDLINISM
MAUDLINLY
MAUGER
MAUGH
MAUGHT
MAUGRE
MAUKA
MAUKIN
MAUL
MAULA
MAULANA
MAULED
MAULER
MAULEY
MAULING
MAULSTICK
MAULVI
MAUM
MAUMET
MAUMETRY
MAUN
MAUNA
MAUNCHE
MAUND
MAUNDER
MAUNDERED
MAUNDERER
MAUNDERING
MAUNDFUL
MAUNDY
MAUNGE
MAUNNA
MAURICIO
MAUSOLE
MAUSOLEA
MAUSOLEAL
MAUSOLEAN
MAUSOLEUM
MAUSOLEUMS
MAUT
MAUTHER
MAUVE
MAUVEIN
MAUVETTE
MAUVINE
MAUX
MAVERICK
MAVIE
MAVIS
MAVOURNEEN
MAVOURNIN
MAVRODAPHNE
MAW
MAWALI
MAWBOUND
MAWK
MAWKIN
MAWKISH
MAWKISHLY
MAWKISHNESS
MAWKS
MAWKY
MAWMISH
MAWP
MAWTHER
MAWWORM
MAX
MAXILLA
MAXILLAE
MAXILLARIES
MAXILLARY
MAXILLIFORM
MAXILLIPED
MAXILLIPEDARY
MAXILLIPEDE
MAXILLOJUGAL
MAXILLOLABIAL
MAXIM
MAXIMA
MAXIMAL
MAXIMALLY
MAXIMATE
MAXIMATION
MAXIMED
MAXIMIST
MAXIMISTIC
MAXIMITE
MAXIMIZATION
MAXIMIZE
MAXIMIZED
MAXIMIZER
MAXIMIZING
MAXIMUM
MAXIMUMS
MAXIMUS
MAXIXE
MAXWELL
MAY
MAYA
MAYACACEOUS

MAYAPIS
MAYAPPLE
MAYBE
MAYBERRY
MAYBUSH
MAYCOCK
MAYDAY
MAYDUKE
MAYENCE
MAYEST
MAYFISH
MAYFISHES
MAYFLOWER
MAYFLY
MAYHAP
MAYHAPPEN
MAYHAPS
MAYHEM
MAYNE
MAYONNAISE
MAYOR
MAYORAL
MAYORALTY
MAYORESS
MAYORSHIP
MAYPOLE
MAYPOP
MAYSIN
MAYST
MAYTEN
MAYTHE
MAYTHES
MAYWEED
MAZA
MAZAGRAN
MAZALGIA
MAZAME
MAZAPILITE
MAZAR
MAZARD
MAZARINE
MAZDOOR
MAZE
MAZED
MAZEDLY
MAZEDNESS
MAZEFUL
MAZER
MAZIC
MAZIER
MAZIEST
MAZILY
MAZINESS
MAZING
MAZODYNIA
MAZOLYSIS
MAZOLYTIC
MAZOPATHIA
MAZOPATHIC
MAZOPEXY
MAZOURKA
MAZUCA
MAZUMA
MAZURKA
MAZUT
MAZY
MAZZARD
MBORI
ME
MEABLE
MEACHING
MEACOCK
MEAD
MEADER
MEADOW
MEADOWED
MEADOWER
MEADOWING
MEADOWINK
MEADOWLAND
MEADOWLARK
MEADOWS
MEADOWSWEET
MEADOWY
MEADSMAN
MEADWORT
MEAGER
MEAGERLY
MEAGERNESS
MEAGRE
MEAGRELY
MEAGRENESS
MEAK
MEAL
MEALABLE
MEALED
MEALER
MEALIE
MEALIER
MEALIES
MEALIEST
MEALILY
MEALINESS
MEALING
MEALMAN
MEALMEN
MEALMONGER
MEALMOUTH
MEALMOUTHED
MEALOCK
MEALS
MEALTIDE
MEALTIME
MEALY
MEALYBUG
MEALYMOUTH
MEALYMOUTHED
MEALYWING
MEAN
MEANDER
MEANDERED
MEANDERER
MEANDERING
MEANDRITE
MEANDROUS
MEANED
MEANER
MEANEST
MEANIE
MEANING
MEANINGFUL
MEANINGFULLY
MEANINGFULNESS
MEANINGLESS
MEANINGLY
MEANINGNESS
MEANLESS
MEANLY
MEANNESS
MEANS
MEANT
MEANTIME
MEANTONE
MEANWHILE
MEANY
MEAR
MEARE
MEARSTONE
MEASE
MEASLE
MEASLED
MEASLEDNESS
MEASLES
MEASLIER
MEASLIEST
MEASLY
MEASONDUE
MEASURABILITY
MEASURABLE
MEASURABLY
MEASURAGE
MEASURATION
MEASURE
MEASURED
MEASUREDLY
MEASUREDNESS
MEASURELESS
MEASURELY
MEASUREMENT
MEASURER
MEASURES
MEASURING
MEAT
MEATAL
MEATBALL
MEATBIRD
MEATCUTTER
MEATED
MEATH
MEATHE
MEATHOOK
MEATIC
MEATIER
MEATIEST
MEATINESS
MEATLESS
MEATMAN
MEATMEN
MEATOMETER
MEATORRHAPHY
MEATOSCOPE
MEATOSCOPY
MEATOTOME
MEATOTOMY
MEATURE
MEATUS
MEATUSES
MEATWORKS
MEATY
MEBBE
MEBOS
MECATE
MECCA
MECHANALITY
MECHANALIZE
MECHANIC
MECHANICAL
MECHANICALLY
MECHANICIAN
MECHANICS
MECHANISM
MECHANIST
MECHANISTIC
MECHANIZATION
MECHANIZE
MECHANIZER
MECHANOLATER
MECHANOLOGY
MECHOACAN
MECKELECTOMY
MECODONT
MECOMETER
MECOMETRY
MECON
MECONIC
MECONIDIUM
MECONIN
MECONIOID
MECONIUM
MECONOLOGY
MECOPTERAN
MECOPTERON
MECOPTEROUS
MEDA
MEDAL
MEDALED
MEDALET
MEDALING
MEDALIST
MEDALIZE
MEDALLARY
MEDALLED
MEDALLIC
MEDALLICALLY
MEDALLING
MEDALLION
MEDALLIONED
MEDALLIONING
MEDALLIONIST
MEDDLE
MEDDLECOME
MEDDLED
MEDDLER
MEDDLESOME
MEDDLESOMELY
MEDDLING
MEDENAGAN
MEDIA
MEDIACID
MEDIACY
MEDIAD
MEDIAE
MEDIAEVAL
MEDIAEVALISM
MEDIAEVALIST
MEDIAL
MEDIALIZE
MEDIALKALINE
MEDIALLY
MEDIAN
MEDIANIC
MEDIANIMIC
MEDIANIMITY
MEDIANISM
MEDIANITY
MEDIANLY
MEDIANT
MEDIASTINA
MEDIASTINAL
MEDIASTINE
MEDIASTINUM
MEDIATE
MEDIATED
MEDIATELY
MEDIATING
MEDIATINGLY
MEDIATION
MEDIATIVE
MEDIATIZE
MEDIATIZED
MEDIATIZING
MEDIATOR
MEDIATORIAL
MEDIATORIOUS
MEDIATORY
MEDIATRESS
MEDIATRICE
MEDIATRIX
MEDIC
MEDICABLE
MEDICAL
MEDICALLY
MEDICAMENT
MEDICAMENTAL
MEDICARE
MEDICASTER
MEDICATE
MEDICATED
MEDICATING
MEDICATION
MEDICATIVE
MEDICATOR
MEDICATORY
MEDICINABLE
MEDICINAL
MEDICINARY
MEDICINE
MEDICINED
MEDICINER
MEDICINING
MEDICK
MEDICO
MEDICODENTAL
MEDICOLEGAL
MEDICOMORAL
MEDICOS
MEDIETY
MEDIEVAL
MEDIEVALISM
MEDIEVALIST
MEDIEVALLY
MEDIFIXED
MEDIGLACIAL
MEDILLE
MEDIMNO
MEDIMNOS
MEDIMNUS
MEDIN
MEDINE
MEDINO
MEDIO
MEDIOCARPAL
MEDIOCRAL
MEDIOCRE
MEDIOCRITIES
MEDIOCRITY
MEDIOCUBITAL
MEDIODIGITAL
MEDIODORSAL
MEDIOFRONTAL
MEDIOLATERAL
MEDIOPALATAL
MEDIOPASSIVE
MEDIOPONTINE
MEDIOSILICIC
MEDIOTARSAL
MEDIOVENTRAL
MEDISANCE
MEDISECT
MEDISECTION
MEDITABUND
MEDITANCE
MEDITANT
MEDITATE
MEDITATED
MEDITATER
MEDITATING
MEDITATION
MEDITATIST
MEDITATIVE
MEDITATIVELY
MEDITATOR
MEDITERRANE
MEDITERRANEAN
MEDITHORAX
MEDITULLIUM
MEDIUM
MEDIUMISTIC
MEDIUMIZE
MEDIUMS
MEDIUS
MEDJIDIE
MEDJIDIEH
MEDLAR
MEDLEY

MEDLEYED
MEDLEYING
MEDLEYS
MEDLIED
MEDREGAL
MEDRICK
MEDRINACKS
MEDRINACLES
MEDRINAQUE
MEDULLA
MEDULLAE
MEDULLAR
MEDULLARY
MEDULLAS
MEDULLATE
MEDULLATED
MEDULLATION
MEDULLITIS
MEDULLOSE
MEDULLOUS
MEDUSA
MEDUSAE
MEDUSAL
MEDUSAN
MEDUSAS
MEDUSIFEROUS
MEDUSIFORM
MEDUSOID
MEEBOS
MEECH
MEECHER
MEECHING
MEED
MEEDLESS
MEEK
MEEKEN
MEEKER
MEEKEST
MEEKHEARTED
MEEKLY
MEEKNESS
MEER
MEERED
MEERKAT
MEERSCHAUM
MEES
MEESE
MEET
MEETEN
MEETER
MEETERLY
MEETHELP
MEETHELPER
MEETING
MEETINGER
MEETINGHOUSE
MEETINGS
MEETLY
MEG
MEGABAR
MEGACEPHALIA
MEGACEPHALIC
MEGACEPHALY
MEGACERINE
MEGACEROTINE
MEGACHILID
MEGACOLON
MEGACURIE
MEGACYCLE
MEGADONT
MEGADYNAMICS
MEGADYNE
MEGAFARAD
MEGAFOG
MEGAGAMETE
MEGALEME
MEGALESTHETE
MEGALITH
MEGALITHIC
MEGALOBLAST
MEGALOBLASTIC
MEGALOCARDIA
MEGALOCORNEA
MEGALOCYTE
MEGALOGRAPH
MEGALOGRAPHY
MEGALOMANIA
MEGALOMANIAC
MEGALOMELIA
MEGALOPENIS
MEGALOPHONIC
MEGALOPIC
MEGALOPINE
MEGALOPOLIS
MEGALOPORE
MEGALOPS
MEGALOPSYCHY
MEGALOSAUR
MEGALOSCOPE
MEGALOSCOPY
MEGALOSPHERE
MEGAMETER
MEGAMETRE
MEGAMPERE
MEGAPHONE
MEGAPHONED
MEGAPHONIC
MEGAPHONING
MEGAPOD
MEGAPODE
MEGAPOLIS
MEGAPROSOPOUS
MEGAPTERINE
MEGARON
MEGASCLERE
MEGASCLERIC
MEGASCLEROUS
MEGASCLERUM
MEGASCOPE
MEGASCOPIC
MEGASCOPICAL
MEGASEISM
MEGASEISMIC
MEGASPORANGE
MEGASPORE
MEGASPORIC
MEGASS
MEGASSE
MEGATHERE
MEGATHERIAN
MEGATHERINE
MEGATHERIOID
MEGATHERIUM
MEGATHERM
MEGATHERMIC
MEGATHEROID
MEGATON
MEGATYPE
MEGATYPY
MEGAVOLT
MEGAZOOID
MEGAZOOSPORE
MEGILP
MEGILPH
MEGOHM
MEGOHMIT
MEGOHMMETER
MEGOMIT
MEGOTALC
MEGRIM
MEGRIMS
MEGUILP
MEHALLA
MEHARI
MEHARIS
MEHARIST
MEHMANDAR
MEHTAR
MEHTARSHIP
MEILE
MEILER
MEIN
MEINIE
MEINIES
MEINY
MEIO
MEIOBAR
MEIONITE
MEIOPHYLLY
MEIOSIS
MEIOTAXY
MEIOTIC
MEISJE
MEITH
MEIZOSEISMAL
MEIZOSEISMIC
MEJORANA
MEKE
MEKIL
MEKILTA
MEKOMETER
MEL
MELA
MELACONITE
MELADA
MELADIORITE
MELAENA
MELAENIC
MELAGABBRO
MELAGRA
MELAGRANITE
MELALGIA
MELAM
MELAMED
MELAMIN
MELAMINE
MELAMMED
MELAMPOD
MELAMPODE
MELAMPODIUM
MELAMPYRIN
MELAMPYRITE
MELAMPYRITOL
MELANAEMIA
MELANAEMIC
MELANAGOGAL
MELANAGOGUE
MELANCHOLIA
MELANCHOLIAC
MELANCHOLIC
MELANCHOLIES
MELANCHOLIOUS
MELANCHOLIST
MELANCHOLIZE
MELANCHOLY
MELANEMIA
MELANEMIC
MELANGE
MELANGER
MELANGES
MELANGEUR
MELANIAN
MELANIC
MELANIFEROUS
MELANIN
MELANISM
MELANISTIC
MELANITE
MELANITIC
MELANIZE
MELANO
MELANOBLAST
MELANOCERITE
MELANOCHROIC
MELANOCOMOUS
MELANOCRATE
MELANOCRATIC
MELANODERMA
MELANODERMIA
MELANODERMIC
MELANOGEN
MELANOID
MELANOMA
MELANOMAS
MELANOMATA
MELANOPATHIA
MELANOPATHY
MELANOPHORE
MELANOPLAKIA
MELANORRHEA
MELANOSCOPE
MELANOSE
MELANOSED
MELANOSITY
MELANOTEKITE
MELANOTIC
MELANOUS
MELANTERITE
MELANTHY
MELANURE
MELANURENIC
MELANURESIS
MELANURIA
MELANURIC
MELAPHYRE
MELASMA
MELASMIC
MELASSIGENIC
MELASTOMAD
MELASTOME
MELATOPE
MELAXUMA
MELCH
MELD
MELDER
MELDOMETER
MELDROP
MELE
MELEAGRINE
MELEE
MELENA
MELENE
MELENIC
MELEZITASE
MELEZITOSE
MELIACEOUS
MELIATIN
MELIBIOSE
MELIC
MELICERA
MELICERIC
MELICERIS
MELICEROUS
MELICHROUS
MELICITOSE
MELICRATE
MELICRATON
MELICRATORY
MELICRATUM
MELILITE
MELILITITE
MELILOT
MELINE
MELINITE
MELIORABILITY
MELIORABLE
MELIORANT
MELIORATE
MELIORATED
MELIORATER
MELIORATING
MELIORATION
MELIORATIVE
MELIORATOR
MELIORISM
MELIORIST
MELIORISTIC
MELIORITY
MELIPHAGOUS
MELIPHANITE
MELIPONINE
MELIS
MELISMA
MELISMATA
MELISMATIC
MELISMATICS
MELITAEMIA
MELITEMIA
MELITHAEMIA
MELITHEMIA
MELITIS
MELITTOLOGIST
MELITTOLOGY
MELITURIA
MELITURIC
MELKHOUT
MELL
MELLAGINOUS
MELLAH
MELLATE
MELLAY
MELLEOUS
MELLER
MELLIFEROUS
MELLIFICATE
MELLIFICATION
MELLIFLUATE
MELLIFLUENCE
MELLIFLUENT
MELLIFLUENTLY
MELLIFLUOUS
MELLILOT
MELLISONANT
MELLISUGENT
MELLIT
MELLITATE
MELLITE
MELLITIC
MELLIVOROUS
MELLON
MELLONE
MELLONIDES
MELLOPHONE
MELLOW
MELLOWED
MELLOWER
MELLOWEST
MELLOWING
MELLOWLY
MELLOWNESS
MELLOWY
MELLSMAN
MELOCOTON
MELOCOTOON
MELODEON
MELODIA
MELODIAL
MELODIALLY
MELODIC
MELODICA
MELODICAL
MELODICALLY
MELODICS
MELODIED
MELODIES

MELODION
MELODIOUS
MELODIOUSLY
MELODIOUSNESS
MELODISM
MELODIST
MELODIZE
MELODIZED
MELODIZER
MELODIZING
MELODRAMA
MELODRAMATIC
MELODRAMATICAL
MELODRACTICALLY
MELODRAMATICS
MELODRAMATIST
MELODRAMATIZE
MELODY
MELODYING
MELOE
MELOGRAM
MELOGRAPH
MELOGRAPHIC
MELOID
MELOLOGUE
MELOLONTHINE
MELOMAME
MELOMANIA
MELOMANIAC
MELOMANIC
MELON
MELONCUS
MELONGENA
MELONGROWER
MELONIST
MELONITE
MELONLIKE
MELONMONGER
MELONRY
MELOPHONE
MELOPHONIC
MELOPHONIST
MELOPIANO
MELOPIANOS
MELOPLAST
MELOPLASTIC
MELOPLASTY
MELOPOEIA
MELOPOEIC
MELOS
MELOTE
MELOTRAGEDY
MELOTRAGIC
MELOTROPE
MELPELL
MELSH
MELT
MELTABILITY
MELTABLE
MELTAGE
MELTED
MELTEIGITE
MELTER
MELTERS
MELTETH
MELTING
MELTINGLY
MELTINGNESS
MELTITH
MELTON
MELTWATER
MELVIE
MEM
MEMBER
MEMBERED
MEMBERS
MEMBERSHIP
MEMBRACID
MEMBRACINE
MEMBRAL
MEMBRALLY
MEMBRANA
MEMBRANATE
MEMBRANE
MEMBRANED
MEMBRANELLA
MEMBRANELLE
MEMBRANIFORM
MEMBRANIN
MEMBRANOID
MEMBRANOLOGY
MEMBRANOSIS
MEMBRANOUS
MEMBRANOUSLY
MEMBRANULA
MEMBRANULE
MEMBRETTE
MEMBRETTO
MEMEL
MEMENTO
MEMENTOES
MEMENTOS
MEMINNA
MEMO
MEMOIR
MEMOIRISM
MEMOIRIST
MEMOIRS
MEMORABILE
MEMORABILIA
MEMORABILITY
MEMORABLE
MEMORABLY
MEMORANDA
MEMORANDIST
MEMORANDIZE
MEMORANDUM
MEMORANDUMS
MEMORATE
MEMORATION
MEMORATIVE
MEMORIA
MEMORIAL
MEMORIALIST
MEMORIALIZE
MEMORIALIZED
MEMORIALIZER
MEMORIALIZING
MEMORIALLY
MEMORIED
MEMORIES
MEMORIOUS
MEMORIST
MEMORITER
MEMORIZATION
MEMORIZE
MEMORIZED
MEMORIZER
MEMORIZING
MEMORY
MEMOS
MEN
MENACE
MENACED
MENACER
MENACING
MENACINGLY
MENACME
MENAGE
MENAGERIE
MENAGERIST
MENALD
MENARCHE
MENAT
MEND
MENDACIOUS
MENDACIOUSLY
MENDACITIES
MENDACITY
MENDED
MENDEE
MENDELEVIUM
MENDER
MENDICANCY
MENDICANT
MENDICATE
MENDICATED
MENDICATING
MENDICATION
MENDICITY
MENDIGO
MENDING
MENDINGS
MENDIPITE
MENDOLE
MENDOZITE
MENDY
MENE
MENEGHINITE
MENEHUNE
MENEL
MENFOLK
MENFOLKS
MENG
MENHADEN
MENHADENS
MENHIR
MENIAL
MENIALISM
MENIALITY
MENIALLY
MENIALTY
MENILITE
MENINGEAL
MENINGES
MENINGIC
MENINGINA
MENINGISM
MENINGISMUS
MENINGITIC
MENINGITIDES
MENINGITIS
MENINGOCELE
MENINGORRHEA
MENINGOSIS
MENINTING
MENINX
MENISCAL
MENISCATE
MENISCI
MENISCIFORM
MENISCITIS
MENISCOID
MENISCOIDAL
MENISCUS
MENISCUSES
MENISE
MENISON
MENISPERM
MENISPERMIN
MENISPERMINE
MENKIND
MENNOM
MENNON
MENNUET
MENO
MENOGNATH
MENOGNATHOUS
MENOLOGIES
MENOLOGY
MENOMINEE
MENOPAUSE
MENOPAUSIC
MENOPHANIA
MENOPLANIA
MENORRHAGIA
MENORRHAGIC
MENORRHAGY
MENORRHEA
MENORRHEIC
MENORRHOEA
MENORRHOEIC
MENOSCHESIS
MENOSCHETIC
MENOSEPSIS
MENOSTASIA
MENOSTASIS
MENOSTATIC
MENOSTAXIS
MENOTYPHLIC
MENOXENIA
MENSA
MENSAE
MENSAL
MENSALIZE
MENSE
MENSEFUL
MENSELESS
MENSERVANTS
MENSES
MENSHEVIK
MENSK
MENSTRUA
MENSTRUAL
MENSTRUANT
MENSTRUATE
MENSTRUATED
MENSTRUATING
MENSTRUATION
MENSTRUOSITY
MENSTRUOUS
MENSTRUUM
MENSTRUUMS
MENSUAL
MENSURABLE
MENSURABLY
MENSURAL
MENSURALIST
MENSURATE
MENSURATION
MENSURATIVE
MENT
MENTA
MENTAGRA
MENTAL
MENTALIS
MENTALISM
MENTALIST
MENTALISTIC
MENTALITIES
MENTALITY
MENTALLY
MENTATION
MENTERY
MENTHACEOUS
MENTHADIENE
MENTHAN
MENTHANE
MENTHE
MENTHENE
MENTHENOL
MENTHENONE
MENTHOL
MENTHOLATED
MENTHONE
MENTHYL
MENTICULTURE
MENTIFEROUS
MENTIFORM
MENTIGEROUS
MENTIMETER
MENTION
MENTIONABLE
MENTIONED
MENTIONER
MENTIONING
MENTOHYOID
MENTOLABIAL
MENTONIERE
MENTONNIERE
MENTOR
MENTORIAL
MENTUM
MENU
MENUS
MEOW
MEPHITIC
MEPHITICAL
MEPHITINE
MEPHITIS
MEPHITISM
MEPROBAMATE
MER
MERAI
MERALGIA
MERALINE
MERBABY
MERCANTILE
MERCANTILELY
MERCANTILISM
MERCANTILIST
MERCANTILISTIC
MERCANTILITY
MERCAPTAL
MERCAPTAN
MERCAPTIDES
MERCAPTIDS
MERCAPTO
MERCAPTOL
MERCAPTOLE
MERCATORIAL
MERCATURE
MERCE
MERCEMENT
MERCENARIAN
MERCENARIES
MERCENARILY
MERCENARY
MERCER
MERCERESS
MERCERIES
MERCERIZE
MERCERIZED
MERCERIZER
MERCERIZING
MERCERY
MERCH
MERCHANDISABLE
MERCHANDISE
MERCHANDISED
MERCHANDISER
MERCHANDIZE
MERCHANDRISE
MERCHANDRY
MERCHANDY
MERCHANT
MERCHANTABLE
MERCHANTEER
MERCHANTER
MERCHANTLIKE
MERCHANTLY
MERCHANTMAN
MERCHANTMEN
MERCHANTRY
MERCHANTSHIP

MERCHET
MERCI
MERCIABLE
MERCIABLELY
MERCIABLY
MERCIES
MERCIFUL
MERCIFULLY
MERCIFULNESS
MERCIFY
MERCILESS
MERCILESSLY
MERCILESSNESS
MERCIMENT
MERCURATE
MERCURATION
MERCURIAL
MERCURIALISM
MERCURIALIST
MERCURIALITY
MERCURIALIZE
MERCURIALLY
MERCURIATE
MERCURIC
MERCURID
MERCURIDE
MERCURIES
MERCURIFIED
MERCURIFY
MERCURIFYING
MERCURIZE
MERCURIZED
MERCURIZING
MERCUROUS
MERCURY
MERCY
MERD
MERDA
MERDIVOROUS
MERDURINOUS
MERE
MERED
MEREL
MERELS
MERELY
MERENCHYMA
MERESMAN
MERESMEN
MEREST
MERESTONE
MERESWINE
MERETRICES
MERETRICIOUS
MERETRIX
MERFOLD
MERFOLK
MERGANSER
MERGE
MERGED
MERGENCE
MERGER
MERGH
MERGING
MERIAH
MERICARP
MERICE
MERIDIAN
MERIDIONAL
MERIDIONALLY
MERINGUE
MERINGUED
MERINO
MERINOS
MERIQUINONE
MERIQUINONIC
MERISM
MERISMATIC
MERISMOID
MERIST
MERISTELE
MERISTEM
MERISTEMATIC
MERISTIC
MERISTICALLY
MERIT
MERITABLE
MERITED
MERITEDLY
MERITER
MERITING
MERITMONGER
MERITMONGERY
MERITORIOUS
MERITORY
MERKHET
MERKIN
MERL
MERLE
MERLETTE
MERLIGO
MERLIN
MERLON
MERMAID
MERMAIDEN
MERMAN
MERMEN
MERMITHANER
MERMITHIZED
MERMITHOGYNE
MERMOTHER
MERO
MEROBLASTIC
MEROCELE
MEROCELIC
MEROCERITE
MEROCERITIC
MEROCYTE
MEROGAMY
MEROGASTRULA
MEROGENESIS
MEROGENETIC
MEROGENIC
MEROGNATHITE
MEROGONIC
MEROGONY
MEROHEDRAL
MEROHEDRIC
MEROHEDRISM
MEROISTIC
MEROMORPHIC
MEROP
MEROPIA
MEROPIC
MEROPIDAN
MEROPLANKTON
MEROPODITE
MEROPODITIC
MERORGANIZE
MEROS
MEROSOMAL
MEROSOMATOUS
MEROSOME
MEROSTHENIC
MEROSTOME
MEROTOMIZE
MEROTOMY
MEROTROPISM
MEROTROPY
MEROXENE
MEROZOITE
MERPEOPLE
MERRIER
MERRIEST
MERRILESS
MERRILY
MERRIMENT
MERRINESS
MERROW
MERROWES
MERRY
MERRYMAKE
MERRYMAKER
MERRYMAKING
MERRYMAN
MERRYMEETING
MERRYMEN
MERRYTHOUGHT
MERRYTROTTER
MERRYWING
MERSE
MERSION
MERULIOID
MERVEILLEUX
MERWINITE
MERWOMAN
MERYCISM
MES
MESA
MESABITE
MESACONATE
MESACONIC
MESADENIA
MESAIL
MESAL
MESALLIANCE
MESALLY
MESAMEBOID
MESANGE
MESAORTITIS
MESARAIC
MESARAICAL
MESARCH
MESARTERITIC
MESARTERITIS
MESATICEPHAL
MESATISKELIC
MESAXONIC
MESCAL
MESCALISM
MESCHANT
MESCHANTLY
MESDAMES
MESE
MESECTODERM
MESEEMS
MESEL
MESELED
MESELEDNESS
MESELRY
MESELY
MESEM
MESEMBRYO
MESEMBRYONIC
MESENCHYMA
MESENCHYMAL
MESENCHYME
MESENDODERM
MESENNA
MESENTERA
MESENTERIAL
MESENTERIC
MESENTERICAL
MESENTERIES
MESENTERITIC
MESENTERITIS
MESENTERIUM
MESENTERON
MESENTERONIC
MESENTERY
MESEPIMERAL
MESEPIMERON
MESETHMOID
MESETHMOIDAL
MESH
MESHED
MESHING
MESHRABIYEH
MESHREBEEYEH
MESHUGGA
MESHUMMAD
MESHWORK
MESHY
MESIAD
MESIAL
MESIALLY
MESIAN
MESIC
MESILLA
MESIODISTAL
MESIOINCISAL
MESIOLABIAL
MESIOLINGUAL
MESIOPULPAL
MESITINE
MESITITE
MESITYL
MESITYLENE
MESKED
MESMERIAN
MESMERIC
MESMERICAL
MESMERICALLY
MESMERISE
MESMERISM
MESMERIST
MESMERITE
MESMERIZATION
MESMERIZE
MESMERIZED
MESMERIZEE
MESMERIZER
MESMERIZING
MESNALITY
MESNALTIES
MESNALTY
MESNE
MESO
MESOAPPENDIX
MESOARIAL
MESOARIUM
MESOBAR
MESOBENTHOS
MESOBLAST
MESOBLASTEM
MESOBLASTEMA
MESOBLASTIC
MESOBREGMATE
MESOCAECAL
MESOCAECUM
MESOCARDIA
MESOCARDIUM
MESOCARP
MESOCENTROUS
MESOCEPHAL
MESOCEPHALIC
MESOCEPHALON
MESOCEPHALOUS
MESOCEPHALY
MESOCHILIUM
MESOCHROIC
MESOCOELE
MESOCOELIA
MESOCOELIAN
MESOCOELIC
MESOCOLIC
MESOCOLON
MESOCORACOID
MESOCRANIAL
MESOCRATIC
MESODE
MESODERM
MESODERMAL
MESODERMIC
MESODIC
MESODONT
MESOFURCA
MESOFURCAL
MESOGASTER
MESOGASTRAL
MESOGASTRIC
MESOGASTRIUM
MESOGLOEA
MESOGLOEAL
MESOGNATHIC
MESOGNATHION
MESOGNATHISM
MESOGNATHOUS
MESOGNATHY
MESOGYRATE
MESOHEPAR
MESOLABE
MESOLE
MESOLECITHAL
MESOLIMNION
MESOLITE
MESOLITHIC
MESOLOGIC
MESOLOGY
MESOMERE
MESOMETRAL
MESOMETRIC
MESOMETRIUM
MESOMORPH
MESOMORPHIC
MESOMORPHOUS
MESOMORPHY
MESOMYODIAN
MESOMYODOUS
MESON
MESONASAL
MESONEPHRIC
MESONEPHROS
MESONOTAL
MESONOTUM
MESOPAUSE
MESOPETALUM
MESOPHIL
MESOPHILE
MESOPHILIC
MESOPHILOUS
MESOPHRAGMA
MESOPHRAGMAL
MESOPHRYON
MESOPHYL
MESOPHYLL
MESOPHYLLUM
MESOPHYTE
MESOPHYTIC
MESOPHYTISM
MESOPIC
MESOPLANKTON
MESOPLAST
MESOPLASTIC
MESOPLASTRA
MESOPLASTRAL
MESOPLASTRON
MESOPLEURA
MESOPLEURAL
MESOPLEURON
MESOPLODONT
MESOPODIA
MESOPODIAL
MESOPODIALE
MESOPODIALIA
MESOPODIUM

MESOPOTAMIA
MESOPROSOPIC
MESORCHIAL
MESORCHIUM
MESORECTAL
MESORECTUM
MESORHIN
MESORHINAL
MESORHINE
MESORHINIAN
MESORHINISM
MESORHINIUM
MESORHINY
MESORRHIN
MESORRHINAL
MESORRHINIAN
MESORRHINISM
MESORRHINIUM
MESORRHINY
MESOSALPINX
MESOSAUR
MESOSCAPULA
MESOSCAPULAR
MESOSCUTAL
MESOSCUTUM
MESOSEISMAL
MESOSEME
MESOSIGMOID
MESOSOMA
MESOSOMATA
MESOSOMATIC
MESOSPERM
MESOSPHERE
MESOSPHERIC
MESOSPORE
MESOSPORIC
MESOSTASIS
MESOSTERNA
MESOSTERNAL
MESOSTERNUM
MESOSTETHIUM
MESOSTOMID
MESOSTYLOUS
MESOSUCHIAN
MESOTARSAL
MESOTHELIAL
MESOTHELIUM
MESOTHERM
MESOTHERMAL
MESOTHESIS
MESOTHETIC
MESOTHETICAL
MESOTHORACIC
MESOTHORAX
MESOTHORIUM
MESOTONIC
MESOTROCH
MESOTROCHA
MESOTROCHAL
MESOTROCHOUS
MESOTRON
MESOTROPIC
MESOTYPE
MESOVARIA
MESOVARIAN
MESOVARIUM
MESOVENTRAL
MESOVENTRALLY
MESOXALATE
MESOXALIC
MESOXALYL
MESOZOAN
MESPIL
MESQUIN
MESQUITA
MESQUITE
MESS
MESSAGE
MESSAGED
MESSAGERY
MESSAGING
MESSALINE
MESSAN
MESSE
MESSED
MESSELITE
MESSENGER
MESSER
MESSET
MESSIER
MESSIEST
MESSIEURS
MESSILY
MESSIN
MESSINESS
MESSING
MESSIRE
MESSMAN
MESSMATE
MESSMEN
MESSOR
MESSROOM
MESSTIN
MESSUAGE
MESSY
MESTA
MESTEE
MESTENO
MESTESO
MESTFULL
MESTINO
MESTIZA
MESTIZO
MESTIZOES
MESTIZOS
MESTLEN
MESTO
MESTOME
MESYMNION
MET
META
METABASES
METABASIS
METABASITE
METABATIC
METABIOLOGICAL
METABIOLOGY
METABIOSIS
METABIOTIC
METABLETIC
METABOLE
METABOLIAN
METABOLIC
METABOLICAL
METABOLISM
METABOLITE
METABOLIZE
METABOLIZED
METABOLIZING
METABOLON
METABOLOUS
METABOLY
METABORATE
METABORIC
METABRANCHIAL
METABRUSHITE
METABULAR
METACARPAL
METACARPALE
METACARPUS
METACENTER
METACENTRAL
METACENTRE
METACENTRIC
METACHEMIC
METACHEMICAL
METACHEMISTRY
METACHROME
METACHRONISM
METACHROSIS
METACISM
METACLASE
METACNEME
METACOELE
METACONAL
METACONE
METACONID
METACONULE
METACORACOID
METACRASIS
METACROMIAL
METACROMION
METACRYST
METACYCLIC
METAD
METADROMOUS
METAE
METAFLUIDAL
METAGALACTIC
METAGALAXIES
METAGALAXY
METAGASTER
METAGASTRIC
METAGASTRULA
METAGE
METAGELATIN
METAGELATINE
METAGENESIS
METAGENETIC
METAGENIC
METAGEOMETER
METAGEOMETRY
METAGNATH
METAGNATHISM
METAGNATHOUS
METAGNOMY
METAGNOSTIC
METAGRAM
METAGRAPHIC
METAGRAPHY
METAIGNEOUS
METAIRIE
METAKINESIS
METAKINETIC
METAL
METALCRAFT
METALDEHYDE
METALED
METALEPSES
METALEPSIS
METALEPTIC
METALEPTICAL
METALER
METALINE
METALINED
METALING
METALISE
METALIST
METALIZATION
METALIZE
METALIZED
METALIZING
METALLARY
METALLED
METALLEITY
METALLER
METALLIC
METALLICAL
METALLICALLY
METALLICITY
METALLICLY
METALLICS
METALLIDE
METALLIFORM
METALLIFY
METALLIK
METALLINE
METALLING
METALLISH
METALLIST
METALLIZATION
METALLIZE
METALLOGENIC
METALLOGENY
METALLOGRAPH
METALLOID
METALLOIDAL
METALLOMETER
METALLOPHONE
METALLURGIC
METALLURGICAL
METALLURGIST
METALLURGY
METALOGIC
METALOGICAL
METALOPH
METALORGANIC
METALOSCOPE
METALOSCOPY
METALS
METALUMINATE
METALWARE
METALWORK
METALWORKER
METALWORKING
METALWORKS
METAMER
METAMERAL
METAMERE
METAMERIC
METAMERIDE
METAMERISM
METAMERIZED
METAMEROUS
METAMERY
METAMORPHIC
METAMORPHISM
METAMORPHIZE
METAMORPHOSE
METAMORPHOSED
METAMORPHOSING
METAMORPHOSIS
METAMORPHOSY
METAMORPHOUS
METAMORPHY
METANALYSIS
METANAUPLIUS
METANEPHRIC
METANEPHRITIC
METANEPHRON
METANEPHROS
METANEPIONIC
METANILINE
METANOMEN
METANOTAL
METANOTUM
METANYM
METAPEPTONE
METAPHASE
METAPHLOEM
METAPHONICAL
METAPHONIZE
METAPHONY
METAPHOR
METAPHORIC
METAPHORICAL
METAPHORICALLY
METAPHORIST
METAPHRAGM
METAPHRAGMA
METAPHRAGMAL
METAPHRASE
METAPHRASED
METAPHRASING
METAPHRAST
METAPHRASTIC
METAPHYSEAL
METAPHYSIC
METAPHYSICAL
METAPHYSICALLY
METAPHYSICIAN
METAPHYSICIST
METAPHYSICS
METAPHYSIS
METAPHYTE
METAPLASIA
METAPLASIS
METAPLASM
METAPLASMIC
METAPLAST
METAPLASTIC
METAPLEUR
METAPLEURA
METAPLEURAL
METAPLEURE
METAPLEURON
METAPNEUSTIC
METAPODIA
METAPODIAL
METAPODIALE
METAPODIUM
METAPOLITIC
METAPOLITICAL
METAPOLITICIAN
METAPOLITICS
METAPOPHYSIS
METAPORE
METAPROTEIN
METAPSYCHIC
METAPSYCHICAL
METAPSYCHICS
METAPSYCHISM
METAPSYCHIST
METAPSYCHOLOGY
METAROSSITE
METASCUTUM
METASOMA
METASOMASIS
METASOMATA
METASOMATIC
METASOMATISM
METASPERM
METASPERMIC
METASPERMOUS
METASTABLE
METASTANNATE
METASTASES
METASTASIS
METASTASIZE
METASTASIZED
METASTATIC
METASTATICAL
METASTATICALLY
METASTERNAL
METASTERNUM
METASTHENIC
METASTIBNITE
METASTOMA
METASTOMATA
METASTROPHE
METASTROPHIC
METATARSAL
METATARSALE
METATARSE
METATARSI

METATARSUS
METATATIC
METATATICAL
METATAXIC
METATAXIS
METATE
METATHALAMUS
METATHESES
METATHESIS
METATHETIC
METATHETICAL
METATHORACIC
METATHORAX
METATHORAXES
METATITANATE
METATROPHIC
METATYPE
METATYPIC
METAVANADATE
METAVAUXITE
METAVOLTINE
METAXITE
METAXYLEM
METAYAGE
METAYER
METAZOAL
METAZOAN
METAZOEA
METAZOIC
METAZOON
METE
METED
METEL
METEMPIRIC
METEMPIRICAL
METEMPIRICS
METEMPSYCHIC
METEMPSYCHOSIS
METEMPTOSIS
METENTERON
METENTERONIC
METEOR
METEORGRAPH
METEORIC
METEORICAL
METEORICALLY
METEORISM
METEORIST
METEORISTIC
METEORITAL
METEORITE
METEORITICS
METEORIZE
METEORLIKE
METEOROGRAM
METEOROGRAPH
METEOROID
METEOROIDAL
METEOROLITE
METEOROLITIC
METEOROLOGIC
METEOROLOGICAL
METEOROLOGICALLY
METEOROLOGIST
METEOROLOGY
METEOROMETER
METEOROSCOPY
METEOROUS
METEORSCOPE
METEPIMERON
METER
METERAGE
METERED
METERER
METERGRAM
METERING
METERMAN
METESTICK
METEWAND
METEYARD
METHACRYLATE
METHACRYLIC
METHADONE
METHANAL
METHANATE
METHANATED
METHANATING
METHANE
METHANOIC
METHANOL
METHANOMETER
METHE
METHEGLIN
METHENAMINE
METHENE
METHENYL
METHER
METHIDE
METHINE
METHINKS
METHIODIDE
METHIONIC
METHIONINE
METHOD
METHODIC
METHODICAL
METHODICALLY
METHODICALNESS
METHODICS
METHODISM
METHODIST
METHODIZE
METHODIZED
METHODIZER
METHODIZING
METHODLESS
METHODOLOGICAL
METHODOLOGICALLY
METHODOLOGIST
METHODOLOGY
METHODS
METHONE
METHOUGHT
METHOXY
METHOXYL
METHRONIC
METHYL
METHYLAL
METHYLAMINE
METHYLATE
METHYLATED
METHYLATING
METHYLATION
METHYLATOR
METHYLENE
METHYLENITAN
METHYLIC
METHYLOSIS
METHYLOTIC
METIC
METICULOSITY
METICULOUS
METICULOUSLY
METIER
METIF
METING
METIS
METISSE
METOCHOUS
METOCHY
METOESTROUS
METOESTRUM
METONYM
METONYMIC
METONYMICAL
METONYMOUS
METONYMOUSLY
METONYMY
METOPE
METOPIC
METOPION
METOPISM
METOPOMANCY
METOPON
METOPOSCOPIC
METOPOSCOPY
METORGANISM
METOSTEAL
METOSTEON
METRA
METRALGIA
METRAN
METRANEMIA
METRATONIA
METRAZOL
METRE
METRECTASIA
METRECTATIC
METRECTOMY
METRECTOPIA
METRECTOPIC
METRECTOPY
METREGRAM
METREME
METRETA
METRETES
METREZA
METRIA
METRIC
METRICAL
METRICALLY
METRICIAN
METRICISM
METRICIST
METRICIZE
METRICS
METRIFIED
METRIFIER
METRIFY
METRIFYING
METRIST
METRITIS
METRO
METROLOGICAL
METROLOGIST
METROLOGUE
METROLOGY
METROMANIA
METROMANIAC
METRONOME
METRONOMIC
METRONOMICAL
METRONYM
METRONYMIC
METRONYMY
METROPOLE
METROPOLEIS
METROPOLIC
METROPOLIS
METROPOLISES
METROPOLITAN
METROPOLITE
METRORRHAGIA
METRORRHAGIC
METRORTHOSIS
METROSTYLE
METTAR
METTLE
METTLED
METTLESOME
METTLESOMELY
METUMP
METUSIA
METWAND
METZE
MEUBLES
MEUM
MEURE
MEUSE
MEUTE
MEW
MEWED
MEWER
MEWING
MEWL
MEWLED
MEWLER
MEWLING
MEWS
MEXICAL
MEZCAL
MEZCALINE
MEZEREON
MEZEREUM
MEZQUIT
MEZQUITE
MEZUZA
MEZUZAH
MEZUZAHS
MEZUZOTH
MEZZA
MEZZANINE
MEZZO
MEZZOGRAPH
MEZZOS
MEZZOTINT
MEZZOTINTED
MEZZOTINTER
MEZZOTINTING
MEZZOTINTO
MHO
MHOMETER
MHORR
MI
MIAMIA
MIAN
MIANG
MIAOU
MIAOW
MIAOWER
MIARGYRITE
MIAROLITIC
MIAS
MIASCITE
MIASKITE
MIASM
MIASMA
MIASMAL
MIASMAS
MIASMATA
MIASMATIC
MIASMATICAL
MIASMATOLOGY
MIASMATOUS
MIASMIC
MIASMOLOGY
MIASMOUS
MIAUER
MIAUL
MIAULED
MIAULER
MIAULING
MIAUW
MIB
MICA
MICACEOUS
MICACIOUS
MICACITE
MICASIZATION
MICASIZE
MICATE
MICATION
MICE
MICELL
MICELLA
MICELLAR
MICELLE
MICH
MICHE
MICHED
MICHER
MICHERY
MICHING
MICK
MICKERY
MICKEY
MICKEYS
MICKLE
MICKLENESS
MICO
MICONCAVE
MICRA
MICRACOUSTIC
MICRAESTHETE
MICRAMOCK
MICRANDER
MICRANDROUS
MICRANER
MICRESTHETE
MICRIFIED
MICRIFY
MICRIFYING
MICRO
MICROAMMETER
MICROANALYSIS
MICROANALYST
MICROBAL
MICROBALANCE
MICROBATTERY
MICROBE
MICROBEPROOF
MICROBIAL
MICROBIAN
MICROBIC
MICROBICIDE
MICROBIOSIS
MICROBIOTA
MICROBIOTIC
MICROBIOUS
MICROBISM
MICROBOTANY
MICROBURNER
MICROCARPOUS
MICROCENTRUM
MICROCEPHAL
MICROCEPHALI
MICROCEPHALY
MICROCHAETA
MICROCHAETAE
MICROCIRCUIT
MICROCLASTIC
MICROCLIMATE
MICROCLINE
MICROCOAT
MICROCOCCAL
MICROCOCCI
MICROCOCCUS
MICROCOPIED
MICROCOPIES
MICROCOPY
MICROCOPYING
MICROCOSM
MICROCOSMAL
MICROCOSMIAN
MICROCOSMIC

MICROCOSMOS
MICROCRANOUS
MICROCRITH
MICROCYST
MICROCYTE
MICROCYTOSIS
MICRODONT
MICRODONTISM
MICRODONTOUS
MICRODRAWING
MICRODRIVE
MICROFELSITE
MICROFICHE
MICROFILARIA
MICROFILM
MICROFLUIDAL
MICROFORM
MICROGAMETE
MICROGAMY
MICROGLIA
MICROGRAM
MICROGRAMME
MICROGRANITE
MICROGRAPH
MICROGRAPHER
MICROGRAPHIC
MICROGRAPHY
MICROGRAVER
MICROGROOVE
MICROHMMETER
MICROINCH
MICROLEVEL
MICROLITE
MICROLITH
MICROLITHIC
MICROLITIC
MICROLOGIC
MICROLOGICAL
MICROLOGUE
MICROLOGY
MICROMANIA
MICROMANIAC
MICROMELIA
MICROMELIC
MICROMELUS
MICROMERAL
MICROMERE
MICROMERIC
MICROMERISM
MICROMERITIC
MICROMETER
MICROMETHOD
MICROMETRIC
MICROMETRY
MICROMHO
MICROMICRON
MICROMODULE
MICROMOTION
MICRON
MICRONOMETER
MICRONUCLEAR
MICRONUCLEI
MICRONUCLEUS
MICROORGANIC
MICROORGANISM
MICROORGANISMS
MICROPHAGE
MICROPHAGOUS
MICROPHAGY
MICROPHONE
MICROPHONIC
MICROPHONICS
MICROPHYSICS
MICROPHYTAL
MICROPHYTE
MICROPHYTIC
MICROPIN
MICROPIPET
MICROPIPETTE
MICROPLAKITE
MICROPODAL
MICROPODOUS
MICROPORE
MICROPRINT
MICROPSIA
MICROPSY
MICROPTERISM
MICROPTEROUS
MICROPYLAR
MICROPYLE
MICRORHABDUS
MICROSAURIAN
MICROSCLERE
MICROSCLEROUS
MICROSCLERUM
MICROSCOPE
MICROSCOPIC
MICROSCOPICAL
MICROSCOPICS
MICROSCOPIST
MICROSCOPIZE
MICROSCOPY
MICROSECOND
MICROSEISM
MICROSEISMIC
MICROSEPTUM
MICROSMATIC
MICROSMATISM
MICROSOMA
MICROSOME
MICROSOMMITE
MICROSPECIES
MICROSPHERE
MICROSPHERIC
MICROSPORE
MICROSPORIC
MICROSPOROUS
MICROSTAT
MICROSTHENE
MICROSTOME
MICROSTOMOUS
MICROSTYLOUS
MICROTECHNIC
MICROTHEOS
MICROTHERM
MICROTHERMIC
MICROTHORAX
MICROTIA
MICROTOME
MICROTOMIC
MICROTOMICAL
MICROTOMIST
MICROTOMY
MICROTONE
MICROTYPAL
MICROTYPE
MICROTYPICAL
MICROVOLUME
MICROWATT
MICROWAVE
MICROZOA
MICROZOAL
MICROZOAN
MICROZOARIA
MICROZOARIAN
MICROZOARY
MICROZOIC
MICROZONE
MICROZOOID
MICROZOON
MICROZYMA
MICROZYME
MICROZYMIAN
MICRURGIC
MICRURGICAL
MICRURGIST
MICRURGY
MICTION
MICTURATE
MICTURATED
MICTURATING
MICTURITION
MID
MIDAFTERNOON
MIDAIR
MIDBRAIN
MIDCARPAL
MIDDAY
MIDDEN
MIDDENSTEAD
MIDDES
MIDDIES
MIDDLE
MIDDLEBROW
MIDDLECLASS
MIDDLED
MIDDLELAND
MIDDLEMAN
MIDDLEMEN
MIDDLEMOST
MIDDLER
MIDDLES
MIDDLETONE
MIDDLEWAY
MIDDLEWEIGHT
MIDDLEWOMAN
MIDDLEWOMEN
MIDDLING
MIDDLINGLY
MIDDLINGNESS
MIDDY
MIDE
MIDEWIN
MIDEWIWIN
MIDGE
MIDGET
MIDGETY
MIDGUT
MIDGY
MIDHEAVEN
MIDINETTE
MIDIRON
MIDLAND
MIDMAIN
MIDMORN
MIDMOST
MIDNIGHT
MIDNIGHTLY
MIDNOON
MIDPARENT
MIDPARENTAGE
MIDPARENTAL
MIDPOINT
MIDRASH
MIDRASHIC
MIDRASHIM
MIDRASHOTH
MIDRIB
MIDRIBBED
MIDRIFF
MIDS
MIDSHIP
MIDSHIPMAN
MIDSHIPMEN
MIDSHIPMITE
MIDSHIPS
MIDST
MIDSTEAD
MIDSTYLED
MIDSUMMER
MIDSUMMERY
MIDTARSAL
MIDTERM
MIDTOWN
MIDVEIN
MIDVENTRAL
MIDWARD
MIDWATCH
MIDWAY
MIDWEEK
MIDWEEKLY
MIDWIFE
MIDWIFED
MIDWIFERY
MIDWIFING
MIDWINTER
MIDWINTERLY
MIDWINTRY
MIDWISE
MIDWIVED
MIDWIVES
MIDWIVING
MIDYEAR
MIEN
MIERSITE
MIFF
MIFFED
MIFFIER
MIFFIEST
MIFFINESS
MIFFY
MIG
MIGALE
MIGGLE
MIGGLES
MIGHT
MIGHTED
MIGHTFUL
MIGHTFULLY
MIGHTFULNESS
MIGHTIER
MIGHTIEST
MIGHTILY
MIGHTINESS
MIGHTLESS
MIGHTLY
MIGHTS
MIGHTY
MIGLIO
MIGMATITE
MIGNIARD
MIGNIARDISE
MIGNIARDIZE
MIGNON
MIGNONETTE
MIGNONNE
MIGRAINE
MIGRAINOID
MIGRAINOUS
MIGRANS
MIGRANT
MIGRATE
MIGRATED
MIGRATING
MIGRATION
MIGRATIONAL
MIGRATIONIST
MIGRATIVE
MIGRATOR
MIGRATORIAL
MIGRATORY
MIHARAITE
MIHRAB
MIJAKITE
MIJNHEER
MIKADO
MIKADOATE
MIKADOS
MIKE
MIKER
MIKRA
MIKRON
MIKVAH
MIL
MILA
MILACRE
MILADI
MILADIES
MILADY
MILAGE
MILAN
MILARITE
MILCH
MILCHER
MILCHIGS
MILCHY
MILD
MILDEN
MILDENED
MILDENING
MILDER
MILDEST
MILDEW
MILDEWER
MILDEWY
MILDFUL
MILDFULNESS
MILDHEARTED
MILDLY
MILDNESS
MILE
MILEAGE
MILEPOST
MILER
MILES
MILESIMA
MILESTONE
MILEWAY
MILFOIL
MILHA
MILIA
MILIACEOUS
MILIARENSES
MILIARENSIS
MILIARIA
MILIARIUM
MILIARY
MILICE
MILIEU
MILIOLIFORM
MILIOLINE
MILIOLITE
MILIOLITIC
MILITANCY
MILITANT
MILITANTLY
MILITANTNESS
MILITAR
MILITARILY
MILITARISM
MILITARIST
MILITARISTIC
MILITARISTICAL
MILITARIZATION
MILITARIZE
MILITARIZED
MILITARIZING
MILITARY
MILITARYISM
MILITARYMENT
MILITASTER
MILITATE
MILITATED
MILITATING
MILITATION

MILITIA
MILITIAMAN
MILITIAMEN
MILITIATE
MILIUM
MILJEE
MILK
MILKBUSH
MILKED
MILKEN
MILKER
MILKERESS
MILKFISH
MILKFISHES
MILKGRASS
MILKIER
MILKIEST
MILKILY
MILKINESS
MILKING
MILKLESS
MILKMAID
MILKMAN
MILKMEN
MILKNESS
MILKSHED
MILKSICK
MILKSOP
MILKSOPPING
MILKSOPPISH
MILKSOPPY
MILKSTONE
MILKTOAST
MILKWEED
MILKWOOD
MILKWORT
MILKY
MILL
MILLA
MILLAGE
MILLANARE
MILLBOARD
MILLCLAPPER
MILLCOURSE
MILLDAM
MILLDOLL
MILLE
MILLED
MILLEFIORE
MILLEFIORI
MILLEFLEURS
MILLEFLOROUS
MILLEFOLIATE
MILLENARIAN
MILLENARIES
MILLENARIST
MILLENARY
MILLENIUM
MILLENNIA
MILLENNIAL
MILLENNIALLY
MILLENNIAN
MILLENNIARY
MILLENNIUMS
MILLEPED
MILLEPEDE
MILLEPORE
MILLEPORINE
MILLEPORITE
MILLEPOROUS
MILLER
MILLERESS
MILLERING
MILLERITE
MILLESIMAL
MILLET
MILLFEED
MILLHOUSE
MILLIAD
MILLIAMMETER
MILLIAMPERE
MILLIARD
MILLIARDAIRE
MILLIARY
MILLIBAR
MILLICRON
MILLICURIE
MILLIEME
MILLIER
MILLIFARAD
MILLIFOLD
MILLIFORM
MILLIGRADE
MILLIGRAM
MILLIGRAMAGE
MILLIGRAMME
MILLIHENRY
MILLILAMBERT
MILLILE
MILLILITER
MILLILITRE
MILLILUX
MILLIMETER
MILLIMETRE
MILLIMICRON
MILLIMOL
MILLIMOLAR
MILLIMOLE
MILLINCOST
MILLINE
MILLINER
MILLINERIAL
MILLINERING
MILLINERY
MILLING
MILLINORMAL
MILLIOCTAVE
MILLIOERSTED
MILLION
MILLIONAIRE
MILLIONAIRESS
MILLIONARY
MILLIONED
MILLIONER
MILLIONFOLD
MILLIONISM
MILLIONIST
MILLIONIZE
MILLIONNAIRE
MILLIONS
MILLIONTH
MILLIPED
MILLIPEDE
MILLIPHOT
MILLIPOISE
MILLISECOND
MILLISTERE
MILLITHRUM
MILLIVOLT
MILLIWATT
MILLIWEBER
MILLKEN
MILLMAN
MILLMEN
MILLOCRACY
MILLOCRAT
MILLOCRATISM
MILLOWNER
MILLPOND
MILLPOOL
MILLPOST
MILLRACE
MILLRIND
MILLRYND
MILLS
MILLSITE
MILLSTOCK
MILLSTONE
MILLSTONES
MILLSTREAM
MILLTAIL
MILLWARD
MILLWORK
MILLWORKER
MILLWRIGHT
MILLY
MILN
MILNER
MILO
MILORD
MILPA
MILQUETOAST
MILREIS
MILRIND
MILSEY
MILSIE
MILT
MILTED
MILTER
MILTING
MILTSICK
MILTY
MILVINE
MILVINOUS
MILWELL
MIM
MIMA
MIMAE
MIMAMSA
MIMBAR
MIMBLE
MIME
MIMED
MIMEOGRAPH
MIMEOGRAPHED
MIMEOGRAPHIC
MIMEOGRAPHING
MIMER
MIMESIS
MIMESTER
MIMETENE
MIMETESITE
MIMETIC
MIMETICALLY
MIMETISM
MIMETITE
MIMIAMBI
MIMIAMBIC
MIMIAMBICS
MIMIC
MIMICAL
MIMICALLY
MIMICISM
MIMICKED
MIMICKER
MIMICKING
MIMICRIES
MIMICRY
MIMINE
MIMING
MIMINYPIMINY
MIMMATION
MIMMED
MIMMING
MIMMOCK
MIMMOCKING
MIMMOCKY
MIMMOUTHED
MIMODRAMA
MIMOGRAPHER
MIMOGRAPHY
MIMOLOGIST
MIMOSA
MIMOSACEOUS
MIMOSITE
MIMOTYPE
MIMOTYPIC
MIMP
MIMSEY
MIMZY
MIN
MINA
MINACIOUS
MINACIOUSLY
MINACIOUSNESS
MINACITY
MINAE
MINAL
MINAR
MINARET
MINARETED
MINARGENT
MINAS
MINASRAGRITE
MINATORIAL
MINATORIALLY
MINATORIES
MINATORILY
MINATORY
MINAUDERIE
MINAWAY
MINBAR
MINBU
MINCE
MINCED
MINCEMEAT
MINCER
MINCHAH
MINCHEN
MINCHERY
MINCHIATE
MINCING
MINCINGLY
MINCINGNESS
MINCIO
MIND
MINDED
MINDEDNESS
MINDER
MINDFUL
MINDFULLY
MINDFULNESS
MINDING
MINDLESS
MINDLESSLY
MINDLESSNESS
MINDLY
MINDSIGHT
MINE
MINED
MINEFIELD
MINELAYER
MINEOWNER
MINER
MINERAL
MINERALIZATION
MINERALIZE
MINERALIZED
MINERALIZER
MINERALIZING
MINERALOGIC
MINERALOGIES
MINERALOGIST
MINERALOGIZE
MINERALOGY
MINERALS
MINERS
MINERVAL
MINERY
MINES
MINESTRA
MINESTRONE
MINESWEEPER
MINETTE
MINEWORKER
MING
MINGE
MINGIE
MINGLE
MINGLED
MINGLER
MINGLING
MINGUETITE
MINGWORT
MINGY
MINHAG
MINHAH
MINIACEOUS
MINIATE
MINIATED
MINIATING
MINIATOR
MINIATOUS
MINIATURE
MINIATURED
MINIATURING
MINIATURIST
MINIATURIZE
MINIATURIZED
MINIBUS
MINICAM
MINIFICATION
MINIFIED
MINIFY
MINIFYING
MINIKEN
MINIKIN
MINIKINLY
MINIM
MINIMA
MINIMACID
MINIMAL
MINIMALIST
MINIMALLY
MINIMETRIC
MINIMI
MINIMIFIDIAN
MINIMISE
MINIMISM
MINIMISTIC
MINIMIZATION
MINIMIZE
MINIMIZED
MINIMIZER
MINIMIZING
MINIMUM
MINIMUMS
MINIMUS
MINIMUSCULAR
MINING
MINION
MINIONETTE
MINIONLY
MINISH
MINISHED
MINISHER
MINISHING
MINISHMENT
MINISKIRT
MINISTER
MINISTERED
MINISTERIAL
MINISTERING
MINISTERIUM
MINISTERSHIP

MINISTRABLE
MINISTRANT
MINISTRATE
MINISTRATION
MINISTRATIVE
MINISTRATOR
MINISTRER
MINISTRIES
MINISTRY
MINITANT
MINITRACK
MINIUM
MINIVER
MINIVET
MINK
MINKERY
MINKS
MINNESINGER
MINNESONG
MINNIE
MINNIEBUSH
MINNING
MINNOW
MINNOWS
MINNY
MINO
MINOIZE
MINOR
MINORAGE
MINORATE
MINORATION
MINORESS
MINORITY
MINOT
MINSITIVE
MINSTER
MINSTERYARD
MINSTREL
MINSTRELESS
MINSTRELSY
MINT
MINTAGE
MINTBUSH
MINTED
MINTER
MINTING
MINTMAN
MINTMASTER
MINTWEED
MINTY
MINUEND
MINUET
MINUETIC
MINUETISH
MINUS
MINUSCULAR
MINUSCULE
MINUTARY
MINUTATION
MINUTE
MINUTED
MINUTELY
MINUTEMAN
MINUTEMEN
MINUTENESS
MINUTER
MINUTES
MINUTHESIS
MINUTIA
MINUTIAE
MINUTIAL
MINUTING
MINUTIOSE
MINUTIOUS
MINUTIOUSLY
MINUTISSIMIC
MINVERITE
MINX
MINXES
MINY
MINYAN
MIOCARDIA
MIOMBO
MIOPLASMIA
MIOSIS
MIOTHERMIC
MIOTIC
MIQRA
MIQUELET
MIR
MIRABILIA
MIRABILIARY
MIRABILITE
MIRABLE
MIRAC
MIRACH
MIRACIDIUM
MIRACLE
MIRACLED
MIRACLING
MIRACLIST
MIRACULAR
MIRACULIST
MIRACULIZE
MIRACULOSITY
MIRACULOUS
MIRACULOUSLY
MIRADOR
MIRAGE
MIRAGY
MIRANDOUS
MIRATE
MIRCROBICIDAL
MIRD
MIRDAHA
MIRDHA
MIRE
MIRED
MIREPOIS
MIREPOIX
MIRESNIPE
MIRID
MIRIER
MIRIEST
MIRIFIC
MIRIFICAL
MIRIKI
MIRING
MIRISH
MIRK
MIRKILY
MIRKINESS
MIRKISH
MIRKLY
MIRKNESS
MIRKSOME
MIRKY
MIRLED
MIRLIGO
MIRLITON
MIRLY
MIRO
MIRROR
MIRRORED
MIRRORING
MIRRORSCOPE
MIRRORY
MIRTH
MIRTHFUL
MIRTHFULLY
MIRTHFULNESS
MIRTHLESS
MIRTHLESSLY
MIRY
MIRYACHIT
MIRZA
MIS
MISACCEPT
MISACCEPTION
MISADVENTURE
MISADVISE
MISADVISED
MISADVISEDLY
MISADVISING
MISAFFECT
MISALLIANCE
MISALLIED
MISALLY
MISALLYING
MISANDRY
MISANTHROPE
MISANTHROPI
MISANTHROPIC
MISANTHROPOS
MISANTHROPY
MISAPPLIED
MISAPPLIER
MISAPPLY
MISAPPLYING
MISAPPREHEND
MISAPPREHENSION
MISAPPREHENSIVE
MISARCHISM
MISARCHIST
MISARRANGE
MISARRANGED
MISARRANGEMENT
MISARRANGING
MISATTEND
MISAUNTER
MISBAPTIZE
MISBEAR
MISBECAME
MISBECOME
MISBECOMING
MISBEDE
MISBEFALL
MISBEFALLEN
MISBEGET
MISBEGOT
MISBEGOTTEN
MISBEHAVE
MISBEHAVED
MISBEHAVING
MISBEHAVIOR
MISBEHAVIOUR
MISBEHOLDEN
MISBELIEF
MISBELIEVE
MISBELIEVED
MISBELIEVER
MISBELIEVING
MISBIRTH
MISBODE
MISBORN
MISBRAND
MISCAL
MISCALCULATE
MISCALCULATED
MISCALCULATING
MISCALCULATION
MISCALCULATOR
MISCALL
MISCALLED
MISCALLER
MISCALLING
MISCARRIAGE
MISCARRIED
MISCARRY
MISCARRYING
MISCAST
MISCASTING
MISCASUALTY
MISCE
MISCEABILITY
MISCEGENATE
MISCEGENATION
MISCEGENATOR
MISCEGENETIC
MISCEGENIST
MISCEGINE
MISCELLANE
MISCELLANEA
MISCELLANEAL
MISCELLANEOUS
MISCELLANIES
MISCELLANIST
MISCELLANY
MISCHANCE
MISCHANCY
MISCHIEF
MISCHIEFFUL
MISCHIEVE
MISCHIEVOUS
MISCHIEVOUSLY
MISCHIEVOUSNESS
MISCHIO
MISCHOICE
MISCHOOSE
MISCHOOSING
MISCHOSE
MISCHOSEN
MISCIBILITY
MISCIBLE
MISCOGNIZANT
MISCOLOR
MISCOLOUR
MISCONCEIVE
MISCONCEIVED
MISCONCEIVER
MISCONCEIVING
MISCONCEPTION
MISCONDUCT
MISCONDUCTED
MISCONDUCTING
MISCONSTRUCT
MISCONSTRUCTIO
MISCONSTRUE
MISCONSTRUED
MISCONSTRUER
MISCONVEY
MISCORRECT
MISCORRECTED
MISCORRECTING
MISCOUNSEL
MISCOUNSELED
MISCOUNSELING
MISCOUNSELLED
MISCOUNSELLING
MISCOUNT
MISCREANCE
MISCREANCY
MISCREANT
MISCREATE
MISCREATED
MISCREATING
MISCREATION
MISCREATIVE
MISCREATOR
MISCREED
MISCROP
MISCUE
MISCUED
MISCUING
MISDATE
MISDATED
MISDATEFUL
MISDATING
MISDEAL
MISDEALER
MISDEALING
MISDEALT
MISDEED
MISDEEM
MISDEEMED
MISDEEMFUL
MISDEEMING
MISDEMEAN
MISDEMEANANT
MISDEMEANED
MISDEMEANING
MISDEMEANIST
MISDEMEANOR
MISDEMEANOUR
MISDERIVE
MISDERIVED
MISDERIVING
MISDESCRIBE
MISDESCRIBED
MISDESCRIBER
MISDESERT
MISDESERVE
MISDID
MISDIRECT
MISDIRECTED
MISDIRECTING
MISDIRECTION
MISDIVISION
MISDO
MISDOER
MISDOING
MISDONE
MISDOUBT
MISDOUBTED
MISDOUBTING
MISDREAD
MISE
MISEASE
MISEASED
MISEMPHASIS
MISEMPHASIZE
MISEMPLOY
MISEMPLOYED
MISEMPLOYING
MISENITE
MISENTREAT
MISER
MISERABILISM
MISERABILIST
MISERABILITY
MISERABLE
MISERABLY
MISERE
MISERERE
MISERICORD
MISERICORDE
MISERICORDIA
MISERIES
MISERISM
MISERLINESS
MISERLY
MISERY
MISES
MISESTEEM
MISESTEEMED
MISESTEEMING
MISESTIMATE
MISESTIMATED
MISFAITH
MISFALL
MISFARE
MISFATE
MISFEASANCE
MISFEASOR
MISFEATURE

MISFEIGN
MISFIELD
MISFIGURE
MISFIRE
MISFIRED
MISFIRING
MISFIT
MISFITTED
MISFITTING
MISFORGIVE
MISFORTUNATE
MISFORTUNE
MISFORTUNED
MISFORTUNER
MISGAVE
MISGIVE
MISGIVEN
MISGIVING
MISGIVINGLY
MISGO
MISGOTTEN
MISGOVERN
MISGOVERNED
MISGOVERNING
MISGOVERNOR
MISGRAFF
MISGROWTH
MISGUGGLE
MISGUIDANCE
MISGUIDE
MISGUIDED
MISGUIDEDLY
MISGUIDER
MISGUIDING
MISGUIDINGLY
MISGUISE
MISHANDLE
MISHANDLED
MISHANDLING
MISHANTER
MISHAP
MISHAPPEN
MISHARA
MISHAVE
MISHEAR
MISHEARD
MISHEARING
MISHIT
MISHMASH
MISHMEE
MISHMI
MISIMPROVE
MISIMPROVED
MISIMPROVING
MISINFORM
MISINFORMANT
MISINFORMED
MISINFORMER
MISINFORMING
MISINTERPRET
MISINTERPRETATION
MISIONES
MISJOINDER
MISJUDGE
MISJUDGED
MISJUDGEMENT
MISJUDGER
MISJUDGING
MISJUDGINGLY
MISJUDGMENT
MISKAL
MISKEN
MISKENNING
MISKNEW
MISKNOW
MISKNOWLEDGE
MISKNOWN
MISKY
MISLAID
MISLAY
MISLAYER
MISLAYING
MISLE
MISLEAD
MISLEADER
MISLEADING
MISLEADINGLY
MISLEAR
MISLEARED
MISLED
MISLEERED
MISLEST
MISLIKE
MISLIKED
MISLIKEN
MISLIKER
MISLIKING
MISLIKINGLY
MISLIPPEN
MISLUCK
MISMADE
MISMAKE
MISMANAGE
MISMANAGEABLE
MISMANAGED
MISMANAGEMENT
MISMANAGER
MISMANAGING
MISMANNERED
MISMANNERS
MISMARRIAGE
MISMARRY
MISMATCH
MISMATCHMENT
MISMATE
MISMATED
MISMATING
MISMAZE
MISMEAN
MISMOVE
MISNAME
MISNAMED
MISNAMING
MISNOMED
MISNOMER
MISO
MISOCAPNIC
MISOCAPNIST
MISOGALLIC
MISOGAMIC
MISOGAMIST
MISOGAMY
MISOGYNE
MISOGYNIC
MISOGYNICAL
MISOGYNISM
MISOGYNIST
MISOGYNISTIC
MISOGYNOUS
MISOGYNY
MISOHELLENE
MISOLOGIST
MISOLOGY
MISOMATH
MISONEISM
MISONEIST
MISONEISTIC
MISOPAEDIA
MISOPAEDISM
MISOPAEDIST
MISOPATERIST
MISOPEDIA
MISOPEDISM
MISOPEDIST
MISORDER
MISOSCOPIST
MISOSOPHER
MISOSOPHIST
MISOSOPHY
MISOTHEISM
MISOTHEIST
MISOTHEISTIC
MISOTYRANNY
MISOXENE
MISOXENY
MISPAID
MISPAY
MISPAYING
MISPICK
MISPICKEL
MISPLACE
MISPLACED
MISPLACEMENT
MISPLACING
MISPLANT
MISPLAY
MISPLEAD
MISPLEADED
MISPLEADING
MISPLED
MISPRAISE
MISPRINT
MISPRISAL
MISPRISE
MISPRISION
MISPRIZE
MISPRIZED
MISPRIZER
MISPRIZING
MISPROFESS
MISPRONOUNCE
MISPRONOUNCED
MISPRONUNCIATI
MISPROUD
MISPUT
MISQUOTATION
MISQUOTE
MISQUOTED
MISQUOTER
MISQUOTING
MISREAD
MISREADER
MISREADING
MISRECKON
MISRECKONED
MISRECKONING
MISREMEMBER
MISREPORT
MISREPORTER
MISREPRESENT
MISREPRESENTATION
MISRULE
MISRULED
MISRULING
MISRUN
MISS
MISSAID
MISSAL
MISSARY
MISSATICAL
MISSAY
MISSAYING
MISSCRIPT
MISSED
MISSEEM
MISSEL
MISSERVE
MISSERVICE
MISSES
MISSET
MISSETTING
MISSHAPE
MISSHAPED
MISSHAPEN
MISSHAPENLY
MISSHAPING
MISSI
MISSIBLE
MISSIES
MISSILE
MISSILEMAN
MISSILEMEN
MISSILERY
MISSILES
MISSILRY
MISSING
MISSINGLY
MISSION
MISSIONAL
MISSIONARIES
MISSIONARIZE
MISSIONARY
MISSIONER
MISSIONIZER
MISSIS
MISSISH
MISSIT
MISSIVE
MISSMARK
MISSMENT
MISSOURITE
MISSOUT
MISSPEAK
MISSPEAKING
MISSPEECH
MISSPEED
MISSPELL
MISSPELLED
MISSPELLING
MISSPEND
MISSPENDER
MISSPENDING
MISSPENT
MISSPOKE
MISSTATE
MISSTATED
MISSTATEMENT
MISSTATER
MISSTATING
MISSTAY
MISSTEP
MISSUADE
MISSUS
MISSY
MIST
MISTAKABLE
MISTAKABLY
MISTAKE
MISTAKEN
MISTAKENLY
MISTAKENNESS
MISTAKER
MISTAKING
MISTAKINGLY
MISTAL
MISTASSINI
MISTASTE
MISTAUGHT
MISTBOW
MISTEACH
MISTEACHER
MISTED
MISTELL
MISTELLING
MISTEMPER
MISTEMPERED
MISTER
MISTERED
MISTERING
MISTERS
MISTETCH
MISTEUK
MISTFALL
MISTFLOWER
MISTHINK
MISTHINKING
MISTHOUGHT
MISTIC
MISTICO
MISTIDE
MISTIER
MISTIEST
MISTIFY
MISTIGRI
MISTIGRIS
MISTILY
MISTIME
MISTIMED
MISTIMING
MISTINESS
MISTING
MISTION
MISTLE
MISTLETOE
MISTOLD
MISTONE
MISTONUSK
MISTOOK
MISTRADITION
MISTRAIN
MISTRAL
MISTRANSLATE
MISTREAT
MISTREATMENT
MISTRESS
MISTRESSLY
MISTRIAL
MISTRIST
MISTROW
MISTRUST
MISTRUSTER
MISTRUSTFUL
MISTRUSTFULLY
MISTRUSTFULNESS
MISTRUSTING
MISTRUSTINGLY
MISTRY
MISTRYST
MISTURE
MISTURN
MISTY
MISUNDERSTAND
MISUNDERSTANDI
MISUNDERSTOOD
MISURA
MISUSAGE
MISUSE
MISUSED
MISUSING
MISVALUATION
MISVALUE
MISVALUED
MISVALUING
MISVENTURE
MISVENTUROUS
MISVOUCH
MISWED
MISWEND
MISWERN
MISWISH
MISWOMAN
MISWORD
MISWORDED
MISWORDING
MISWORSHIP

MISWORSHIPER
MISWREST
MISWRITE
MISWRITING
MISWRITTEN
MISWROTE
MISY
MISZEALOUS
MIT
MITAPSIS
MITCHBOARD
MITE
MITER
MITERED
MITERER
MITERFLOWER
MITERING
MITERWORT
MITHAN
MITHER
MITHRIDATE
MITHRIDATIC
MITHRIDATISM
MITHRIDATIZE
MITIGABLE
MITIGANT
MITIGATE
MITIGATED
MITIGATING
MITIGATION
MITIGATIVE
MITIGATOR
MITIGATORY
MITING
MITIS
MITOCHONDRIA
MITOGENETIC
MITOME
MITOSIS
MITOSOME
MITOTIC
MITOTICALLY
MITRA
MITRAILLE
MITRAILLEUR
MITRAILLEUSE
MITRAL
MITRATE
MITRE
MITRED
MITREFLOWER
MITRER
MITREWORT
MITRIFORM
MITRING
MITSUMATA
MITSVAH
MITSVOTH
MITT
MITTELHAND
MITTEN
MITTENED
MITTIMUS
MITTLE
MITTY
MITY
MITZVAH
MITZVAHS
MITZVOTH
MIURUS
MIX
MIXABLE
MIXBLOOD
MIXED
MIXEN
MIXER
MIXERESS
MIXHILL
MIXIBLE
MIXILINEAL
MIXING
MIXITE
MIXOBARBARIC
MIXOTROPHIC
MIXT
MIXTIFORM
MIXTILINEAR
MIXTION
MIXTURE
MIXUP
MIXY
MIZENMAST
MIZMAZE
MIZRACH
MIZZEN
MIZZENMAST
MIZZENTOPMAN
MIZZENTOPMEN
MIZZLE
MIZZLED
MIZZLING
MIZZLY
MIZZONITE
MIZZY
MKS
MLECHCHHA
MNEME
MNEMONIC
MNEMONICAL
MNEMONICALLY
MNEMONICON
MNEMONICS
MNEMONISM
MNEMONIST
MNEMONIZE
MNEMONIZED
MNEMONIZING
MNEMOTECHNY
MNESIC
MNESTIC
MNIACEOUS
MNIOID
MO
MOA
MOAB
MOALA
MOAN
MOANED
MOANFUL
MOANFULLY
MOANING
MOANO
MOAT
MOATHILL
MOB
MOBBED
MOBBER
MOBBIE
MOBBING
MOBBISH
MOBBISHLY
MOBBISHNESS
MOBBISM
MOBBIST
MOBBY
MOBCAP
MOBED
MOBILE
MOBILIANER
MOBILIARY
MOBILISE
MOBILITIES
MOBILITY
MOBILIZATION
MOBILIZE
MOBILIZED
MOBILIZING
MOBILOMETER
MOBLE
MOBOCRACIES
MOBOCRACY
MOBOCRAT
MOBOCRATIC
MOBOCRATICAL
MOBOLATRY
MOBSMAN
MOBSMEN
MOBSTER
MOCCASIN
MOCCENIGO
MOCH
MOCHA
MOCHILA
MOCHRAS
MOCHUDI
MOCHY
MOCK
MOCKADO
MOCKAGE
MOCKBIRD
MOCKED
MOCKER
MOCKERIES
MOCKERNUT
MOCKERY
MOCKETER
MOCKGROUND
MOCKING
MOCKINGBIRD
MOCKINGLY
MOCKINGSTOCK
MOCKISH
MOCKUP
MOCMAIN
MOCO
MOCOCK
MOCOMOCO
MOCUCK
MODAL
MODALIST
MODALISTIC
MODALITIES
MODALITY
MODALIZE
MODALLY
MODDER
MODE
MODEL
MODELED
MODELER
MODELESS
MODELESSNESS
MODELING
MODELIST
MODELIZE
MODELLED
MODELLER
MODELLING
MODELMAKER
MODELMAKING
MODENA
MODER
MODERANT
MODERANTISM
MODERANTIST
MODERATE
MODERATED
MODERATELY
MODERATENESS
MODERATING
MODERATION
MODERATISM
MODERATIST
MODERATO
MODERATOR
MODERN
MODERNER
MODERNISM
MODERNIST
MODERNISTIC
MODERNITIES
MODERNITY
MODERNIZATION
MODERNIZE
MODERNIZED
MODERNIZER
MODERNIZING
MODERNLY
MODERNNESS
MODEST
MODESTIES
MODESTLY
MODESTNESS
MODESTY
MODIATION
MODICA
MODICITY
MODICUM
MODICUMS
MODIFIABLE
MODIFIABLY
MODIFICABLE
MODIFICATION
MODIFICATIVE
MODIFICATOR
MODIFICATORY
MODIFIED
MODIFIER
MODIFY
MODIFYING
MODILLION
MODIOLAR
MODIOLI
MODIOLUS
MODISH
MODISHLY
MODISHNESS
MODIST
MODISTE
MODISTRY
MODS
MODULABILITY
MODULANT
MODULAR
MODULATE
MODULATED
MODULATING
MODULATION
MODULATIVE
MODULATOR
MODULATORY
MODULE
MODULET
MODULI
MODULIZE
MODULO
MODULUS
MODUR
MODUS
MODY
MOE
MOELLON
MOERITHERE
MOERITHERIAN
MOEURS
MOFETTE
MOFF
MOFFETTE
MOFFLE
MOFUSSIL
MOFUSSILITE
MOG
MOGADORE
MOGGAN
MOGGED
MOGGI
MOGGIES
MOGGING
MOGGIO
MOGGY
MOGIGRAPHIC
MOGIGRAPHY
MOGILALIA
MOGILALISM
MOGIPHONIA
MOGITOCIA
MOGO
MOGOTE
MOGUEY
MOGUL
MOHA
MOHABAT
MOHAIR
MOHAR
MOHATRA
MOHAWKITE
MOHEL
MOHNSEED
MOHO
MOHOE
MOHOS
MOHR
MOHUR
MOHWA
MOIDER
MOIDORE
MOIETER
MOIETIES
MOIETY
MOIL
MOILED
MOILER
MOILES
MOILING
MOILINGLY
MOILSOME
MOINE
MOINEAU
MOIO
MOIRE
MOIREED
MOIREING
MOIRETTE
MOISE
MOISON
MOISSANITE
MOIST
MOISTEN
MOISTENED
MOISTENER
MOISTENING
MOISTFUL
MOISTIFY
MOISTLESS
MOISTLY
MOISTNESS
MOISTURE
MOISTY
MOIT
MOITY
MOJARRA
MOJO
MOJOS
MOKADDAM
MOKAMOKA

MOKE
MOKI
MOKIHANA
MOKIHI
MOKO
MOKSHA
MOKUM
MOKY
MOL
MOLA
MOLAL
MOLALITY
MOLAR
MOLARIFORM
MOLARIMETER
MOLARITY
MOLARY
MOLASSES
MOLASSIED
MOLASSY
MOLAVE
MOLD
MOLDABLE
MOLDAVITE
MOLDBOARD
MOLDED
MOLDER
MOLDERED
MOLDERING
MOLDERY
MOLDINESS
MOLDING
MOLDINGS
MOLDMADE
MOLDWARP
MOLDY
MOLE
MOLECAST
MOLECULA
MOLECULAR
MOLECULARIST
MOLECULARITY
MOLECULE
MOLED
MOLEHEAD
MOLEHEAP
MOLEHILL
MOLEHILLISH
MOLEHILLY
MOLEISM
MOLENDINAR
MOLENDINARY
MOLESKIN
MOLEST
MOLESTATION
MOLESTED
MOLESTER
MOLESTFUL
MOLESTFULLY
MOLESTIE
MOLESTING
MOLESTIOUS
MOLET
MOLIES
MOLIMEN
MOLIMINOUS
MOLINARY
MOLINE
MOLINET
MOLING
MOLITION
MOLKA
MOLLA
MOLLAH
MOLLAND
MOLLE
MOLLES
MOLLESCENCE
MOLLESCENT
MOLLETON
MOLLICHOP
MOLLICRUSH
MOLLIE
MOLLIENISIA
MOLLIENT
MOLLIFIABLE
MOLLIFIED
MOLLIFIER
MOLLIFY
MOLLIFYING
MOLLIFYINGLY
MOLLIGRANT
MOLLIPILOSE
MOLLISIOSE
MOLLISOL
MOLLITIES
MOLLITIOUS
MOLLITUDE
MOLLUSC
MOLLUSCAN
MOLLUSCOID
MOLLUSCOIDAL
MOLLUSCOUS
MOLLUSCUM
MOLLUSK
MOLLY
MOLLYCODDLE
MOLLYCODDLED
MOLLYCODDLER
MOLLYCOSSET
MOLLYCOT
MOLMAN
MOLMEN
MOLOCH
MOLOCKER
MOLOID
MOLOKER
MOLOMPI
MOLOSSIC
MOLOSSINE
MOLOSSOID
MOLOSSUS
MOLPE
MOLROOKEN
MOLT
MOLTED
MOLTEN
MOLTENLY
MOLTER
MOLTING
MOLTO
MOLY
MOLYBDATE
MOLYBDENA
MOLYBDENIC
MOLYBDENITE
MOLYBDENOUS
MOLYBDENUM
MOLYBDIC
MOLYBDITE
MOLYBDOCOLIC
MOLYBDOMANCY
MOLYBDONOSUS
MOLYBDOSIS
MOLYBDOUS
MOLYSITE
MOM
MOMBIN
MOMBLE
MOME
MOMENT
MOMENTA
MOMENTAL
MOMENTALLY
MOMENTANEITY
MOMENTANEOUS
MOMENTANEOUSLY
MOMENTARILY
MOMENTARY
MOMENTLY
MOMENTOUS
MOMENTOUSLY
MOMENTOUSNESS
MOMENTUM
MOMENTUMS
MOMI
MOMIOLOGY
MOMISH
MOMISM
MOMIST
MOMMA
MOMME
MOMMY
MOMO
MOMUS
MOMUSES
MON
MONA
MONACANTHID
MONACANTHINE
MONACANTHOUS
MONACH
MONACHAL
MONACHATE
MONACHISM
MONACHIST
MONACHIZE
MONACID
MONACT
MONACTIN
MONACTINAL
MONACTINE
MONAD
MONADELPH
MONADELPHIAN
MONADELPHOUS
MONADES
MONADIC
MONADICAL
MONADICALLY
MONADIFORM
MONADIGEROUS
MONADISM
MONADISTIC
MONADNOCK
MONADOLOGY
MONAL
MONAMNIOTIC
MONANDER
MONANDRIAN
MONANDRIC
MONANDROUS
MONANDRY
MONANTHOUS
MONAPHASE
MONAPSAL
MONARCH
MONARCHAL
MONARCHALLY
MONARCHIAN
MONARCHIC
MONARCHICAL
MONARCHIES
MONARCHISM
MONARCHIST
MONARCHISTIC
MONARCHIZE
MONARCHIZED
MONARCHIZER
MONARCHIZING
MONARCHY
MONARDA
MONARTICULAR
MONAS
MONASCIDIAN
MONASE
MONASTER
MONASTERIAL
MONASTERIES
MONASTERY
MONASTIC
MONASTICAL
MONASTICALLY
MONASTICISM
MONATOMIC
MONATOMICITY
MONATOMISM
MONAUL
MONAULI
MONAULOS
MONAURAL
MONAX
MONAXIAL
MONAXON
MONAXONIAL
MONAXONIC
MONAZITE
MONCHIQUITE
MONDAINE
MONDE
MONDEGO
MONDIAL
MONDO
MONDSEE
MONE
MONECIOUS
MONEMBRYONIC
MONEMBRYONY
MONEPIC
MONEPISCOPAL
MONEPISCOPUS
MONER
MONERA
MONERAL
MONERAN
MONERGIC
MONERGISM
MONERGIST
MONERGISTIC
MONERIC
MONERON
MONERONS
MONERULA
MONESIA
MONETARILY
MONETARY
MONETITE
MONETIZATION
MONETIZE
MONETIZED
MONETIZING
MONEY
MONEYAGE
MONEYBAG
MONEYBAGS
MONEYCHANGER
MONEYED
MONEYER
MONEYGRUB
MONEYGRUBBER
MONEYING
MONEYLENDER
MONEYLENDING
MONEYMAKER
MONEYMAKING
MONEYMAN
MONEYMONGER
MONEYS
MONEYSAVING
MONEYWORT
MONG
MONGER
MONGERING
MONGERY
MONGLER
MONGO
MONGOE
MONGOOSE
MONGOOSES
MONGREL
MONGRELDOM
MONGRELISH
MONGRELISM
MONGRELITY
MONGRELIZE
MONGRELLY
MONGRELNESS
MONHEIMITE
MONIAL
MONICA
MONICKER
MONIE
MONIER
MONIES
MONIKER
MONILATED
MONILETHRIX
MONILIACEOUS
MONILICORN
MONILIFORM
MONILIFORMLY
MONILIOID
MONIMENT
MONIMIACEOUS
MONIMOLITE
MONIMOSTYLIC
MONISH
MONISHER
MONISHMENT
MONISM
MONIST
MONISTIC
MONISTICAL
MONISTICALLY
MONITION
MONITIVE
MONITOR
MONITORIAL
MONITORIALLY
MONITORSHIP
MONITORY
MONITRESS
MONK
MONKBIRD
MONKCRAFT
MONKERIES
MONKERY
MONKESS
MONKEY
MONKEYBOARD
MONKEYFIED
MONKEYFY
MONKEYFYING
MONKEYING
MONKEYNUT
MONKEYPOD
MONKEYPOT
MONKEYRY
MONKEYS
MONKEYSHINE
MONKEYTAIL
MONKFISH
MONKFISHES
MONKFLOWER
MONKHOOD

MONKISH
MONKISHLY
MONKISHNESS
MONKISM
MONKLINESS
MONKLY
MONKMONGER
MONKS
MONKSHOOD
MONMOUTHITE
MONNIKER
MONO
MONOACETATE
MONOACID
MONOACIDIC
MONOAMID
MONOAMIDE
MONOAMIN
MONOAMINE
MONOAMINO
MONOAZO
MONOBASE
MONOBASIC
MONOBASICITY
MONOBLASTIC
MONOBLEPSIA
MONOBLEPSIS
MONOBLOC
MONOBROMATED
MONOBROMIDE
MONOCARBONIC
MONOCARDIAN
MONOCARP
MONOCARPAL
MONOCARPELLARY
MONOCARPIAN
MONOCARPIC
MONOCARPOUS
MONOCELLULAR
MONOCENTRIC
MONOCERCOUS
MONOCEROS
MONOCEROUS
MONOCHASIAL
MONOCHASIUM
MONOCHLOR
MONOCHLORIDE
MONOCHLORO
MONOCHORD
MONOCHORDIST
MONOCHORDIZE
MONOCHROIC
MONOCHROMASY
MONOCHROMAT
MONOCHROMATE
MONOCHROME
MONOCHROMIC
MONOCHROMIST
MONOCHROMOUS
MONOCHROMY
MONOCHRONIC
MONOCILIATED
MONOCLE
MONOCLED
MONOCLEID
MONOCLEIDE
MONOCLINAL
MONOCLINALLY
MONOCLINE
MONOCLINIAN
MONOCLINIC
MONOCLINISM
MONOCLINOUS
MONOCONDYLAR
MONOCOQUE
MONOCORMIC
MONOCOT
MONOCOTYL
MONOCRACY
MONOCRAT
MONOCRATIC
MONOCROTIC
MONOCROTISM
MONOCULAR
MONOCULARITY
MONOCULARLY
MONOCULE
MONOCULOUS
MONOCULTURE
MONOCULUS
MONOCYCLE
MONOCYCLIC
MONOCYSTIC
MONOCYTE
MONOCYTIC
MONODACTYL
MONODACTYLE
MONODACTYLY
MONODELPHIAN
MONODELPHIC
MONODELPHOUS
MONODERMIC
MONODIC
MONODICAL
MONODICALLY
MONODIES
MONODIMETRIC
MONODIST
MONODIZE
MONODOMOUS
MONODONT
MONODONTAL
MONODRAM
MONODRAMA
MONODRAME
MONODROMIC
MONODROMY
MONODY
MONODYNAMIC
MONODYNAMISM
MONOECIAN
MONOECIOUS
MONOECIOUSLY
MONOECISM
MONOEIDIC
MONOESTROUS
MONOGAMIAN
MONOGAMIC
MONOGAMIST
MONOGAMISTIC
MONOGAMOUS
MONOGAMOUSLY
MONOGAMY
MONOGASTRIC
MONOGENE
MONOGENEITY
MONOGENEOUS
MONOGENESIS
MONOGENESIST
MONOGENESY
MONOGENETIC
MONOGENIC
MONOGENISM
MONOGENIST
MONOGENISTIC
MONOGENOUS
MONOGENY
MONOGLOT
MONOGONEUTIC
MONOGONY
MONOGRAM
MONOGRAMING
MONOGRAMMED
MONOGRAMMIC
MONOGRAMMING
MONOGRAPH
MONOGRAPHED
MONOGRAPHER
MONOGRAPHIC
MONOGRAPHING
MONOGRAPHIST
MONOGRAPHY
MONOGRAPTID
MONOGYNIC
MONOGYNIOUS
MONOGYNIST
MONOGYNOUS
MONOGYNY
MONOHYBRID
MONOHYDRATE
MONOHYDRATED
MONOHYDRIC
MONOHYDROGEN
MONOICOUS
MONOID
MONOLATER
MONOLATRIST
MONOLATROUS
MONOLATRY
MONOLAYER
MONOLINE
MONOLINGUAL
MONOLINGUIST
MONOLITERAL
MONOLITH
MONOLITHIC
MONOLITHS
MONOLOBULAR
MONOLOCULAR
MONOLOG
MONOLOGIAN
MONOLOGIC
MONOLOGICAL
MONOLOGIST
MONOLOGIZE
MONOLOGIZED
MONOLOGIZING
MONOLOGUE
MONOLOGUIST
MONOLOGY
MONOMACHIST
MONOMACHY
MONOMANIA
MONOMANIAC
MONOMANIACAL
MONOMER
MONOMERIC
MONOMEROUS
MONOMETALISM
MONOMETALIST
MONOMETALLIC
MONOMETER
MONOMETHYL
MONOMETHYLIC
MONOMETRIC
MONOMETRICAL
MONOMIAL
MONOMICT
MONOMINERAL
MONOMORPHIC
MONOMORPHISM
MONOMORPHOUS
MONOMYARIAN
MONONCH
MONONEURAL
MONONITRATE
MONONITRATED
MONONOMIAL
MONONOMIAN
MONONT
MONONUCLEAR
MONONYCHOUS
MONONYM
MONONYMIC
MONONYMIZE
MONONYMY
MONOOUSIAN
MONOOUSIOUS
MONOPARENTAL
MONOPARESIS
MONOPERSONAL
MONOPETALOUS
MONOPHAGIA
MONOPHAGISM
MONOPHAGOUS
MONOPHAGY
MONOPHASIC
MONOPHOBIA
MONOPHONE
MONOPHONIC
MONOPHONOUS
MONOPHOTAL
MONOPHOTE
MONOPHTHONG
MONOPHTHONGAL
MONOPHTHONGIZE
MONOPHYLETIC
MONOPHYLITE
MONOPHYLLOUS
MONOPHYODONT
MONOPLACULA
MONOPLACULAR
MONOPLANE
MONOPLANIST
MONOPLAST
MONOPLASTIC
MONOPLEGIA
MONOPLEGIC
MONOPODE
MONOPODIA
MONOPODIAL
MONOPODIALLY
MONOPODIC
MONOPODIES
MONOPODIUM
MONOPODOUS
MONOPODY
MONOPOLAR
MONOPOLARIC
MONOPOLARITY
MONOPOLE
MONOPOLIES
MONOPOLISE
MONOPOLISM
MONOPOLIST
MONOPOLISTIC
MONOPOLIZE
MONOPOLIZED
MONOPOLIZER
MONOPOLIZING
MONOPOLOUS
MONOPOLY
MONOPRIONID
MONOPSYCHISM
MONOPTERAL
MONOPTEROUS
MONOPTIC
MONOPTICAL
MONOPTOTE
MONOPTOTIC
MONOPYRENOUS
MONORAIL
MONORAILROAD
MONORAILWAY
MONORCHID
MONORCHIDISM
MONORCHIS
MONORCHISM
MONORGANIC
MONORHYME
MONORHYMED
MONORHYTHMIC
MONOSACCHARIDE
MONOSCHEMIC
MONOSE
MONOSEMIC
MONOSEPALOUS
MONOSERVICE
MONOSILANE
MONOSIPHONIC
MONOSKI
MONOSPERM
MONOSPERMAL
MONOSPERMIC
MONOSPERMOUS
MONOSPORE
MONOSPORED
MONOSPOROUS
MONOSTELE
MONOSTELIC
MONOSTELOUS
MONOSTELY
MONOSTICH
MONOSTICHOUS
MONOSTOME
MONOSTOMOUS
MONOSTROPHE
MONOSTROPHIC
MONOSTYLOUS
MONOSULPHIDE
MONOSYLLABIC
MONOSYLLABLE
MONOSYMMETRY
MONOTHALAMAN
MONOTHECAL
MONOTHEISM
MONOTHEIST
MONOTHEISTIC
MONOTHELIOUS
MONOTHETIC
MONOTIC
MONOTINT
MONOTOCOUS
MONOTOMOUS
MONOTONE
MONOTONIC
MONOTONICAL
MONOTONIST
MONOTONIZE
MONOTONOUS
MONOTONOUSLY
MONOTONY
MONOTREMAL
MONOTREMATE
MONOTREME
MONOTREMOUS
MONOTRICHIC
MONOTRICHOUS
MONOTRIGLYPH
MONOTROCHAL
MONOTROCHIAN
MONOTROCHOUS
MONOTROPHIC
MONOTROPIC
MONOTROPY
MONOTYPAL
MONOTYPE
MONOTYPIC
MONOTYPICAL
MONOTYPOUS
MONOVALENCE
MONOVALENCY
MONOVALENT
MONOVARIANT
MONOVOLTINE

MONOVULAR
MONOXENOUS
MONOXIDE
MONOXYLA
MONOXYLE
MONOXYLIC
MONOXYLON
MONOXYLOUS
MONOZOAN
MONOZOIC
MONOZYGOTIC
MONROLITE
MONS
MONSEIGNEUR
MONSIEUR
MONSIGNOR
MONSIGNORE
MONSIGNORIAL
MONSOON
MONSOONAL
MONSPERMY
MONSTER
MONSTRANCE
MONSTRICIDE
MONSTRIFY
MONSTROSITIES
MONSTROSITY
MONSTROUS
MONSTROUSLY
MONT
MONTABYN
MONTAGE
MONTANAS
MONTANE
MONTANITE
MONTANT
MONTANTO
MONTBRETIA
MONTE
MONTEGRE
MONTEITH
MONTEM
MONTERA
MONTERO
MONTEROS
MONTES
MONTGOLFIER
MONTH
MONTHLIES
MONTHLY
MONTHON
MONTHS
MONTICELLITE
MONTICLE
MONTICOLINE
MONTICULATE
MONTICULE
MONTICULOSE
MONTICULOUS
MONTICULUS
MONTIFORM
MONTIGENEOUS
MONTILLA
MONTJOY
MONTJOYE
MONTMARTRITE
MONTON
MONTRE
MONTROYDITE
MONTURE
MONTUVIO
MONUMENT
MONUMENTAL
MONUMENTALLY
MONUMENTARY
MONUMENTED
MONUMENTING
MONY
MONZODIORITE
MONZOGABBRO
MONZONITE
MONZONITIC
MOO
MOOCAH
MOOCH
MOOCHA
MOOCHER
MOOD
MOODER
MOODIER
MOODIEST
MOODILY
MOODINESS
MOODIR
MOODISH
MOODISHLY
MOODISHNESS
MOODS
MOODY
MOOED
MOOING
MOOKHTAR
MOOKTAR
MOOL
MOOLAH
MOOLEY
MOOLINGS
MOOLS
MOOLUM
MOON
MOONACK
MOONAL
MOONBEAM
MOONBILL
MOONBLIND
MOONBLINK
MOONCALF
MOONCREEPER
MOONDOG
MOONDOWN
MOONDROP
MOONED
MOONER
MOONERY
MOONET
MOONEYE
MOONFACE
MOONFACED
MOONFALL
MOONFISH
MOONFISHES
MOONFLOWER
MOONGLADE
MOONGLOW
MOONHEAD
MOONIE
MOONIER
MOONIEST
MOONING
MOONISH
MOONITE
MOONJA
MOONLET
MOONLIGHT
MOONLIGHTED
MOONLIGHTER
MOONLIGHTING
MOONLING
MOONLIT
MOONLITTEN
MOONMAN
MOONMEN
MOONPATH
MOONPENNY
MOONRAKER
MOONRAKING
MOONRAT
MOONRISE
MOONSAIL
MOONSEED
MOONSET
MOONSHADE
MOONSHEE
MOONSHINE
MOONSHINER
MOONSHINING
MOONSHINY
MOONSHOT
MOONSICK
MOONSICKNESS
MOONSTONE
MOONSTRICKEN
MOONSTRUCK
MOONTIDE
MOONWORT
MOONY
MOOP
MOOR
MOORAGE
MOORBALL
MOORBAND
MOORBERRIES
MOORBERRY
MOORBIRD
MOORBURN
MOORBURNER
MOORBURNING
MOORED
MOORFLOWER
MOORFOWL
MOORHEN
MOORIER
MOORIEST
MOORING
MOORISH
MOORLAND
MOORLANDER
MOORMAN
MOORMEN
MOORPAN
MOORPUNKY
MOORS
MOORSTONE
MOORTETTER
MOORUP
MOORWORT
MOORY
MOOS
MOOSA
MOOSE
MOOSEBERRIES
MOOSEBERRY
MOOSEBIRD
MOOSEBUSH
MOOSECALL
MOOSEFLOWER
MOOSEMILK
MOOSETONGUE
MOOSEWOOD
MOOSEY
MOOST
MOOT
MOOTCH
MOOTED
MOOTER
MOOTH
MOOTING
MOOTMAN
MOOTMEN
MOOTSTEAD
MOOTSUDDY
MOOTWORTHY
MOP
MOPANE
MOPANI
MOPBOARD
MOPE
MOPED
MOPEHAWK
MOPER
MOPERY
MOPES
MOPH
MOPHEAD
MOPHEADED
MOPING
MOPISH
MOPISHLY
MOPISHNESS
MOPLA
MOPLAH
MOPOKE
MOPPED
MOPPER
MOPPET
MOPPY
MOPS
MOPSEY
MOPSTICK
MOPSY
MOPUS
MOPUSES
MOPUSSES
MOQUETTE
MORA
MORABIT
MORACEOUS
MORADA
MORAE
MORAINAL
MORAINE
MORAINIC
MORAL
MORALE
MORALER
MORALISE
MORALISM
MORALIST
MORALISTIC
MORALITIES
MORALITY
MORALIZATION
MORALIZE
MORALIZED
MORALIZER
MORALIZING
MORALLER
MORALLY
MORALS
MORAS
MORASS
MORASSIC
MORASSWEED
MORASSY
MORAT
MORATE
MORATION
MORATORIA
MORATORIUM
MORATORY
MORAVITE
MORAY
MORB
MORBID
MORBIDEZZA
MORBIDITIES
MORBIDITY
MORBIDLY
MORBIDNESS
MORBIFERAL
MORBIFEROUS
MORBIFIC
MORBIFICAL
MORBIFICALLY
MORBIFY
MORBILLARY
MORBILLI
MORBILLIFORM
MORBILLOUS
MORBLEU
MORBOSE
MORBUS
MORCEAU
MORCEAUX
MORCELLATE
MORCELLATED
MORCELLATING
MORCELLATION
MORDACIOUS
MORDACIOUSLY
MORDACITY
MORDANCY
MORDANT
MORDANTED
MORDANTING
MORDELLID
MORDELLOID
MORDENITE
MORDENT
MORDICATE
MORDICATION
MORDICATIVE
MORDIEU
MORDISHEEN
MORDORE
MORDU
MORE
MOREEN
MOREISH
MOREL
MORELLA
MORELLE
MORELLO
MORENA
MORENCITE
MORENDO
MORENESS
MORENITA
MORENOSITE
MOREOVER
MOREPEON
MOREPORK
MORES
MORFOND
MORFOUND
MORFOUNDER
MORFREY
MORG
MORGA
MORGANATIC
MORGANATICAL
MORGANIC
MORGANITE
MORGANIZE
MORGAY
MORGEN
MORGENS
MORGLAY
MORGUE
MORIBUND
MORIBUNDITY
MORIBUNDLY
MORICHE
MORIFORM
MORIGERATE

MORIGERATION
MORIGEROUS
MORIGEROUSLY
MORIGLIO
MORILLON
MORIN
MORINDIN
MORINDONE
MORINEL
MORINGACEOUS
MORINGAD
MORINGUID
MORINGUOID
MORION
MORKIN
MORLING
MORLOP
MORMAER
MORMAL
MORMAOR
MORMAORDOM
MORMAORSHIP
MORMO
MORMON
MORMORANDO
MORMYR
MORMYRE
MORMYRIAN
MORMYRID
MORMYROID
MORN
MORNE
MORNED
MORNETTE
MORNING
MORNINGLY
MORNINGS
MORNINGTIDE
MORNTIME
MORO
MOROC
MOROCAIN
MOROCCO
MOROCOTA
MOROLOGICAL
MOROLOGIST
MOROLOGY
MOROMANCY
MORON
MORONCY
MORONES
MORONG
MORONIC
MORONICALLY
MORONISM
MORONITY
MORONRY
MOROR
MOROSAURIAN
MOROSAUROID
MOROSE
MOROSELY
MOROSENESS
MOROSIS
MOROSITY
MOROSOPH
MOROXITE
MORPH
MORPHALLAXIS
MORPHEA
MORPHEME
MORPHEMES
MORPHEMIC
MORPHETIC
MORPHEW
MORPHIA
MORPHIATE
MORPHIC
MORPHICALLY
MORPHIN
MORPHINE
MORPHINIC
MORPHINISM
MORPHINIST
MORPHINIZE
MORPHIOMANIA
MORPHOGENIC
MORPHOGENY
MORPHOGRAPHY
MORPHOLIN
MORPHOLINE
MORPHOLOGIC
MORPHOLOGICAL
MORPHOLOGIES
MORPHOLOGIST
MORPHOLOGY
MORPHOMETRY
MORPHON
MORPHONOMIC
MORPHONOMY
MORPHOPHYLY
MORPHOPLASM
MORPHOSIS
MORPHOTIC
MORPHOTROPIC
MORPHOTROPY
MORPHOUS
MORPHREY
MORPION
MORPUNKEE
MORRAL
MORRHUATE
MORRHUIN
MORRICER
MORRION
MORRIS
MORRO
MORROS
MORROW
MORROWING
MORROWMASS
MORROWSPEECH
MORSAL
MORSE
MORSEL
MORSELED
MORSELING
MORSELIZE
MORSELLED
MORSELLING
MORSING
MORSURE
MORT
MORTACIOUS
MORTAL
MORTALISM
MORTALIST
MORTALITIES
MORTALITY
MORTALIZE
MORTALIZED
MORTALIZING
MORTALLY
MORTAR
MORTARBOARD
MORTARED
MORTARING
MORTARWARE
MORTARY
MORTBELL
MORTCLOTH
MORTERSHEEN
MORTGAGE
MORTGAGED
MORTGAGEE
MORTGAGER
MORTGAGING
MORTGAGOR
MORTH
MORTHWYRTHA
MORTICE
MORTICED
MORTICER
MORTICIAN
MORTICING
MORTIER
MORTIFEROUS
MORTIFIC
MORTIFICATION
MORTIFIED
MORTIFIEDLY
MORTIFY
MORTIFYING
MORTIFYINGLY
MORTISE
MORTISED
MORTISER
MORTISING
MORTLAKE
MORTLING
MORTMAIN
MORTMAINER
MORTORIO
MORTREUX
MORTREWES
MORTUARIES
MORTUARY
MORTUOUS
MORULA
MORULAE
MORULAR
MORULATION
MORULOID
MORVIN
MORWONG
MOS
MOSAIC
MOSAICAL
MOSAICALLY
MOSAICIST
MOSAICKED
MOSAICKING
MOSAIST
MOSANDRITE
MOSASAUR
MOSASAURIAN
MOSASAURID
MOSASAUROID
MOSCH
MOSCHATE
MOSCHATEL
MOSCHIFEROUS
MOSCHINE
MOSE
MOSESITE
MOSEY
MOSEYED
MOSEYING
MOSHAV
MOSK
MOSKENEER
MOSKER
MOSLINGS
MOSQUE
MOSQUITAL
MOSQUITO
MOSQUITOBILL
MOSQUITOES
MOSQUITOEY
MOSQUITOS
MOSS
MOSSBACK
MOSSBACKED
MOSSBANKER
MOSSBERRY
MOSSBUNKER
MOSSED
MOSSER
MOSSERY
MOSSES
MOSSHEAD
MOSSHORN
MOSSIER
MOSSIEST
MOSSINESS
MOSSING
MOSSO
MOSSTROOPER
MOSSTROOPERY
MOSSWORT
MOSSY
MOST
MOSTDEAL
MOSTLIKE
MOSTLINGS
MOSTLY
MOSTRA
MOSTWHAT
MOT
MOTACIL
MOTACILLID
MOTACILLINE
MOTATORIOUS
MOTATORY
MOTE
MOTED
MOTEL
MOTER
MOTET
MOTETTIST
MOTETUS
MOTEY
MOTH
MOTHBALL
MOTHED
MOTHER
MOTHERED
MOTHERER
MOTHERGATE
MOTHERHOOD
MOTHERING
MOTHERLAND
MOTHERLESS
MOTHERLINESS
MOTHERLY
MOTHERWORT
MOTHERY
MOTHIER
MOTHIEST
MOTHPROOF
MOTHPROOFED
MOTHPROOFING
MOTHS
MOTHWORM
MOTHY
MOTIF
MOTIFIC
MOTILE
MOTILITY
MOTION
MOTIONABLE
MOTIONAL
MOTIONED
MOTIONER
MOTIONING
MOTIONIST
MOTIONLESS
MOTIONLESSLY
MOTIONS
MOTITATION
MOTIVATE
MOTIVATED
MOTIVATING
MOTIVATION
MOTIVATIONAL
MOTIVE
MOTIVED
MOTIVENESS
MOTIVING
MOTIVITY
MOTLEY
MOTLEYER
MOTLEYEST
MOTLEYNESS
MOTMOT
MOTO
MOTOFACIENT
MOTOGRAPH
MOTOGRAPHIC
MOTOMAGNETIC
MOTONEURON
MOTOPHONE
MOTOR
MOTORABLE
MOTORBIKE
MOTORBOAT
MOTORBOATMAN
MOTORBUS
MOTORCAB
MOTORCADE
MOTORCAR
MOTORCYCLE
MOTORCYCLED
MOTORCYCLING
MOTORCYCLIST
MOTORDROME
MOTORED
MOTORING
MOTORISM
MOTORIST
MOTORIUM
MOTORIZATION
MOTORIZE
MOTORIZED
MOTORIZING
MOTORMAN
MOTORMEN
MOTORNEER
MOTORPHOBE
MOTORPHOBIA
MOTORPHOBIAC
MOTORSHIP
MOTORTRUCK
MOTORWAY
MOTRE
MOTRICITY
MOTT
MOTTE
MOTTLE
MOTTLED
MOTTLEDNESS
MOTTLEMENT
MOTTLER
MOTTLING
MOTTO
MOTTOED
MOTTOES
MOTTOS
MOTTRAMITE
MOTTY
MOTU
MOTYKA
MOU
MOUCH
MOUCHARABIES

MOUCHARABY
MOUCHARD
MOUCHARDISM
MOUCHE
MOUCHOIR
MOUDIE
MOUDIEMAN
MOUDY
MOUE
MOUFFLON
MOUFLON
MOUFLONS
MOUILLATION
MOUILLE
MOUILLURE
MOUJIK
MOUL
MOULAGE
MOULD
MOULDBOARD
MOULDED
MOULDER
MOULDERED
MOULDERING
MOULDERY
MOULDIER
MOULDIEST
MOULDING
MOULDMADE
MOULDWARP
MOULDY
MOULE
MOULIN
MOULINAGE
MOULINET
MOULLEEN
MOULRUSH
MOULS
MOULT
MOULTED
MOULTER
MOULTING
MOULY
MOUND
MOUNDED
MOUNDING
MOUNDSMAN
MOUNDWORK
MOUNT
MOUNTABLE
MOUNTAIN
MOUNTAINED
MOUNTAINEER
MOUNTAINEERING
MOUNTAINET
MOUNTAINETTE
MOUNTAINOUS
MOUNTAINS
MOUNTAINSIDE
MOUNTAINTOP
MOUNTAINY
MOUNTANCE
MOUNTANT
MOUNTEBANK
MOUNTEBANKED
MOUNTEBANKLY
MOUNTED
MOUNTEE
MOUNTER
MOUNTIE
MOUNTING
MOUNTINGLY
MOUNTS
MOUNTURE
MOUNTY
MOUP
MOURN
MOURNE
MOURNED
MOURNER
MOURNFUL
MOURNFULLY
MOURNFULNESS
MOURNING
MOURNINGLY
MOURNIVAL
MOUSE
MOUSEBANE
MOUSEBIRD
MOUSED
MOUSEFISH
MOUSEFISHES
MOUSEHAWK
MOUSEHOLE
MOUSEHOUND
MOUSELET
MOUSELING
MOUSEMILL
MOUSEPROOF
MOUSER
MOUSERIES
MOUSERY
MOUSETAIL
MOUSETRAP
MOUSETRAPPED
MOUSEWEB
MOUSEY
MOUSIER
MOUSIEST
MOUSILY
MOUSINESS
MOUSING
MOUSLE
MOUSLINGLY
MOUSME
MOUSMEE
MOUSQUETAIRE
MOUSSE
MOUSSELINE
MOUSSEUX
MOUSTACHE
MOUSTACHED
MOUSTACHIAL
MOUSTACHIO
MOUSTOC
MOUSY
MOUTAN
MOUTH
MOUTHABLE
MOUTHBREEDER
MOUTHED
MOUTHER
MOUTHFUL
MOUTHFULS
MOUTHIER
MOUTHIEST
MOUTHILY
MOUTHINESS
MOUTHING
MOUTHISHLY
MOUTHLIKE
MOUTHPART
MOUTHPIECE
MOUTHPIPE
MOUTHS
MOUTHWASH
MOUTHY
MOUTON
MOUTONEED
MOUTONNEE
MOUZAH
MOUZOUNA
MOVABILITY
MOVABLE
MOVABLENESS
MOVABLY
MOVANT
MOVE
MOVEABILITY
MOVEABLE
MOVEABLENESS
MOVEABLY
MOVED
MOVELESS
MOVELESSLY
MOVELESSNESS
MOVEMENT
MOVEMENTS
MOVENT
MOVER
MOVES
MOVIE
MOVIEGOER
MOVIEGOING
MOVIELAND
MOVING
MOVINGLY
MOW
MOWABLE
MOWANA
MOWBURN
MOWBURNT
MOWE
MOWED
MOWER
MOWHA
MOWHAY
MOWIE
MOWING
MOWLAND
MOWN
MOWRA
MOWS
MOWSTEAD
MOWTH
MOXA
MOXIE
MOXIEBERRY
MOY
MOYEN
MOYENANT
MOYENER
MOYENNE
MOYITE
MOYLE
MOYO
MOZAMBIQUE
MOZEMIZE
MOZETTA
MOZING
MOZO
MOZZARELLA
MOZZETTA
MPRET
MU
MUABLE
MUANCE
MUANG
MUBARAT
MUCAGO
MUCARO
MUCEDIN
MUCEDINE
MUCEDINEOUS
MUCEDINOUS
MUCH
MUCHACHA
MUCHACHO
MUCHACHOS
MUCHLY
MUCHNESS
MUCHWHAT
MUCID
MUCIDITY
MUCIDNESS
MUCIFEROUS
MUCIFIC
MUCIFORM
MUCIGEN
MUCIGENOUS
MUCILAGE
MUCILAGINOUS
MUCIN
MUCINOGEN
MUCINOID
MUCINOUS
MUCIPAROUS
MUCIVORE
MUCIVOROUS
MUCK
MUCKAMUCK
MUCKED
MUCKENDER
MUCKER
MUCKERER
MUCKET
MUCKHILL
MUCKIBUS
MUCKIER
MUCKIEST
MUCKILY
MUCKINESS
MUCKING
MUCKITE
MUCKLE
MUCKMAN
MUCKMENT
MUCKMIDDEN
MUCKNA
MUCKRAKE
MUCKRAKED
MUCKRAKER
MUCKRAKING
MUCKSWEAT
MUCKSY
MUCKTHRIFT
MUCKWEED
MUCKWORM
MUCKY
MUCOCELE
MUCODERMAL
MUCOFIBROUS
MUCOID
MUCOIDAL
MUCOPROTEIN
MUCOPURULENT
MUCOPUS
MUCOR
MUCORACEOUS
MUCORINE
MUCORIOID
MUCORMYCOSIS
MUCORRHEA
MUCORRHOEA
MUCOSA
MUCOSAL
MUCOSE
MUCOSEROUS
MUCOSITY
MUCOUS
MUCRO
MUCRONATE
MUCRONATED
MUCRONATELY
MUCRONATION
MUCRONES
MUCRONIFORM
MUCRONULATE
MUCULENT
MUCUS
MUCUSIN
MUD
MUDAR
MUDBANK
MUDCAP
MUDCAPPED
MUDCAPPING
MUDCAT
MUDDEN
MUDDER
MUDDIED
MUDDIER
MUDDIEST
MUDDIFY
MUDDILY
MUDDINESS
MUDDISH
MUDDLE
MUDDLED
MUDDLEDOM
MUDDLEHEAD
MUDDLEHEADED
MUDDLER
MUDDLESOME
MUDDLING
MUDDY
MUDDYBRAINED
MUDDYBREAST
MUDDYHEADED
MUDDYING
MUDFISH
MUDFISHES
MUDFLOW
MUDGE
MUDGUARD
MUDHEAD
MUDHOLE
MUDHOOK
MUDIR
MUDIRIA
MUDIRIEH
MUDLAND
MUDLARK
MUDLARKER
MUDRA
MUDROCK
MUDSILL
MUDSKIPPER
MUDSLINGER
MUDSLINGING
MUDSPATE
MUDSTAIN
MUDSTONE
MUDSUCKER
MUDTRACK
MUDWEED
MUDWORT
MUEDDIN
MUERMO
MUET
MUETTE
MUEZZIN
MUFASAL
MUFF
MUFFED
MUFFET
MUFFETEE
MUFFIN
MUFFINEER
MUFFING
MUFFLE
MUFFLED
MUFFLEMAN
MUFFLEMEN
MUFFLER

MUFFLIN
MUFFLING
MUFFY
MUFTI
MUFTIS
MUFTY
MUG
MUGA
MUGEARITE
MUGG
MUGGA
MUGGAR
MUGGED
MUGGER
MUGGET
MUGGIER
MUGGIEST
MUGGINESS
MUGGING
MUGGINS
MUGGISH
MUGGLES
MUGGS
MUGGUR
MUGGY
MUGHOPINE
MUGHOUSE
MUGIENCE
MUGIENCY
MUGIENT
MUGILIFORM
MUGILOID
MUGS
MUGUET
MUGWEED
MUGWET
MUGWORT
MUGWUMP
MUGWUMPERY
MUGWUMPIAN
MUGWUMPISM
MUHAMMADI
MUHLIES
MUHLY
MUID
MUIR
MUIRBURN
MUIRCOCK
MUIRFOWL
MUISHOND
MUJER
MUJERES
MUJIK
MUJTAHID
MUKHTAR
MUKLUK
MUKTAR
MUKTATMA
MUKTEAR
MUKTI
MUKTUK
MULADA
MULADI
MULAPRAKRITI
MULATTO
MULATTOES
MULBERRIES
MULBERRY
MULCH
MULCHED
MULCHING
MULCT
MULCTABLE
MULCTARY
MULCTATION
MULCTATIVE
MULCTATORY
MULCTED
MULCTUARY
MULE
MULEBACK
MULEFOOT
MULEFOOTED
MULEMAN
MULEMEN
MULES
MULET
MULETA
MULETEER
MULETRESS
MULETTA
MULEWORT
MULEY
MULGA
MULIEBRAL
MULIEBRIA
MULIEBRILE
MULIEBRITY
MULIEBROUS
MULIER
MULIERINE
MULIERLY
MULIEROSE
MULIEROSITY
MULISH
MULISHLY
MULISHNESS
MULITA
MULK
MULL
MULLA
MULLAH
MULLAR
MULLED
MULLEIN
MULLEN
MULLENIZE
MULLER
MULLET
MULLETRY
MULLETS
MULLEY
MULLID
MULLIGAN
MULLIGATAWNY
MULLIGRUBS
MULLING
MULLION
MULLIONED
MULLIONING
MULLOCK
MULLOCKER
MULLOCKY
MULLOID
MULLOWAY
MULM
MULMUL
MULSE
MULT
MULTANGLE
MULTANGULAR
MULTANGULOUS
MULTANGULUM
MULTANIMOUS
MULTEITY
MULTIBREAK
MULTICOLORED
MULTICYCLE
MULTIFARIOUS
MULTIFARIOUSNE
MULTIFEROUS
MULTIFID
MULTIFIDLY
MULTIFIDOUS
MULTIFIDUS
MULTIFLOW
MULTIFOIL
MULTIFOILED
MULTIFOLD
MULTIFORM
MULTIFORMED
MULTIFORMITY
MULTIGAP
MULTIGRAPH
MULTIGRAPHER
MULTILATERAL
MULTILINGUAL
MULTILITERAL
MULTILITH
MULTILOCATION
MULTILOQUENT
MULTILOQUOUS
MULTILOQUY
MULTIMARBLE
MULTIMEDIA
MULTIMODAL
MULTINOMIAL
MULTIPARA
MULTIPARAE
MULTIPARITY
MULTIPAROUS
MULTIPARTITE
MULTIPED
MULTIPEDE
MULTIPHASE
MULTIPHASER
MULTIPLANE
MULTIPLE
MULTIPLET
MULTIPLEX
MULTIPLIABLE
MULTIPLICAND
MULTIPLICATE
MULTIPLICATION
MULTIPLICITY
MULTIPLIED
MULTIPLIER
MULTIPLY
MULTIPLYING
MULTIPOLAR
MULTIPOLE
MULTIPOTENT
MULTIPRESENT
MULTISCIENCE
MULTISECT
MULTISECTOR
MULTISENSUAL
MULTISONANT
MULTISONOUS
MULTISTAGE
MULTITARIAN
MULTITHEISM
MULTITUBE
MULTITUDE
MULTITUDINAL
MULTITUDINOUS
MULTITURN
MULTIVAGANT
MULTIVALENCE
MULTIVALENCY
MULTIVALENT
MULTIVALVE
MULTIVARIANT
MULTIVARIOUS
MULTIVERSANT
MULTIVERSE
MULTIVIOUS
MULTIVOCAL
MULTIVOLENT
MULTIVOLTINE
MULTIWALL
MULTOCULAR
MULTUM
MULTUNGULATE
MULTURE
MULTURER
MULVEL
MUM
MUMBLE
MUMBLEBEE
MUMBLED
MUMBLEMENT
MUMBLER
MUMBLING
MUMBLINGLY
MUMBUDGET
MUMCHANCE
MUME
MUMHOUSE
MUMJUMA
MUMM
MUMMED
MUMMER
MUMMERIES
MUMMERY
MUMMIA
MUMMICHOG
MUMMICK
MUMMIED
MUMMIES
MUMMIFIED
MUMMIFORM
MUMMIFY
MUMMIFYING
MUMMING
MUMMY
MUMMYING
MUMMYLIKE
MUMP
MUMPED
MUMPER
MUMPHEAD
MUMPING
MUMPISH
MUMPISHLY
MUMPISHNESS
MUMPS
MUMPSIMUS
MUMRUFFIN
MUMU
MUN
MUNA
MUNCH
MUNCHED
MUNCHEE
MUNCHEEL
MUNCHER
MUNCHET
MUNCHING
MUND
MUNDAL
MUNDANE
MUNDANELY
MUNDANENESS
MUNDANISM
MUNDANITY
MUNDATORY
MUNDIC
MUNDIFICANT
MUNDIFIER
MUNDIFY
MUNDIL
MUNDIVAGANT
MUNDLE
MUNDUNGO
MUNDUNGUS
MUNG
MUNGA
MUNGCORN
MUNGE
MUNGER
MUNGEY
MUNGO
MUNGOFA
MUNGOOSE
MUNGOOSES
MUNGUBA
MUNGY
MUNI
MUNICIPAL
MUNICIPALISM
MUNICIPALIST
MUNICIPALITIES
MUNICIPALITY
MUNICIPALIZE
MUNICIPALIZED
MUNICIPALIZING
MUNICIPALLY
MUNICIPIA
MUNICIPIUM
MUNIFIC
MUNIFICENCE
MUNIFICENCY
MUNIFICENT
MUNIFICENTLY
MUNIFY
MUNIMENT
MUNIMENTS
MUNITE
MUNITION
MUNITIONARY
MUNITIONEER
MUNITIONER
MUNITY
MUNJ
MUNJEET
MUNJISTIN
MUNK
MUNNION
MUNSHI
MUNSIFF
MUNTIN
MUNTING
MUNTJAC
MUNTJAK
MUON
MUR
MURA
MURAENOID
MURAGE
MURAL
MURALED
MURALIST
MURARIUM
MURASAKITE
MURCHY
MURCIANA
MURDER
MURDERED
MURDERER
MURDERESS
MURDERING
MURDERINGLY
MURDEROUS
MURDEROUSLY
MURDRUM
MURE
MURED
MURENGER
MURES
MUREX
MUREXAN
MUREXES
MUREXID
MUREXIDE

MURGEON
MURIATE
MURIATED
MURIATIC
MURICATE
MURICATED
MURICES
MURICID
MURICIFORM
MURICINE
MURICOID
MURICULATE
MURID
MURIE
MURIFORM
MURIFORMLY
MURINE
MURING
MURINUS
MURIONITRIC
MURIUM
MURK
MURKIER
MURKIEST
MURKILY
MURKINESS
MURKISH
MURKLY
MURKNESS
MURKSOME
MURKY
MURL
MURLACK
MURLAIN
MURLEMEWES
MURLIN
MURLOCK
MURLY
MURMUR
MURMURATION
MURMURATOR
MURMURED
MURMURER
MURMURING
MURMURINGLY
MURMURISH
MURMUROUS
MURMUROUSLY
MURNIVAL
MUROID
MUROMONTITE
MURON
MURPHIES
MURPHY
MURR
MURRA
MURRAH
MURRAIN
MURRAL
MURRAY
MURRE
MURRELET
MURRES
MURREY
MURRHA
MURRHINE
MURRHUINE
MURRINA
MURRNONG
MURRY
MURSHID
MURTHER
MURTHERER
MURUMURU
MURUP
MURVA
MURZA
MUSACEOUS
MUSAF
MUSAL
MUSANG
MUSAR
MUSARD
MUSARDRY
MUSCA
MUSCADE
MUSCADEL
MUSCADIN
MUSCADINE
MUSCAE
MUSCARDINE
MUSCARIFORM
MUSCARINE
MUSCAT
MUSCATEL
MUSCAVADA
MUSCICAPINE
MUSCICIDE
MUSCICOLE
MUSCICOLINE
MUSCICOLOUS
MUSCID
MUSCIFORM
MUSCLE
MUSCLED
MUSCLEMAN
MUSCLES
MUSCLING
MUSCLY
MUSCOID
MUSCOLOGIC
MUSCOLOGIST
MUSCOLOGY
MUSCONE
MUSCOSE
MUSCOSENESS
MUSCOSITY
MUSCOVADE
MUSCOVADITE
MUSCOVADO
MUSCOVITE
MUSCOVITIZE
MUSCOVITIZED
MUSCOVY
MUSCULAR
MUSCULARITY
MUSCULARIZE
MUSCULARLY
MUSCULATION
MUSCULATURE
MUSCULE
MUSCULI
MUSCULIN
MUSCULUS
MUSE
MUSED
MUSEE
MUSEFUL
MUSEFULLY
MUSELESS
MUSELESSNESS
MUSEOGRAPHER
MUSEOGRAPHY
MUSEOLOGIST
MUSEOLOGY
MUSER
MUSERY
MUSES
MUSET
MUSETTE
MUSEUM
MUSH
MUSHA
MUSHAA
MUSHED
MUSHER
MUSHHEAD
MUSHHEADED
MUSHIER
MUSHIEST
MUSHILY
MUSHINESS
MUSHING
MUSHLA
MUSHMELON
MUSHROOM
MUSHROOMER
MUSHROOMIC
MUSHROOMING
MUSHROOMY
MUSHRU
MUSHRUMP
MUSHY
MUSIC
MUSICA
MUSICAL
MUSICALE
MUSICALITY
MUSICALIZE
MUSICALLY
MUSICALNESS
MUSICATE
MUSICIAN
MUSICIANER
MUSICIANLY
MUSICIANS
MUSICIANSHIP
MUSICKER
MUSICLESS
MUSICMONGER
MUSICO
MUSICOGRAPHY
MUSICOLOGIES
MUSICOLOGIST
MUSICOLOGY
MUSICOMANIA
MUSICOPHOBIA
MUSICOPOETIC
MUSICRY
MUSIMON
MUSING
MUSINGLY
MUSION
MUSIVE
MUSJID
MUSK
MUSKALLUNGE
MUSKEG
MUSKEGGY
MUSKELLUNGE
MUSKELLUNGES
MUSKET
MUSKETADE
MUSKETEER
MUSKETOON
MUSKETRY
MUSKGRASS
MUSKIE
MUSKIER
MUSKIEST
MUSKIFIED
MUSKILY
MUSKINESS
MUSKISH
MUSKIT
MUSKMELON
MUSKRAT
MUSKRATS
MUSKROOT
MUSKWOOD
MUSKY
MUSLIN
MUSLINED
MUSLINET
MUSLINETTE
MUSNUD
MUSOPHAGINE
MUSPIKE
MUSQUASH
MUSQUASHROOT
MUSQUASHWEED
MUSQUASPEN
MUSQUAW
MUSROL
MUSROOMED
MUSS
MUSSACK
MUSSAL
MUSSALCHEE
MUSSED
MUSSEL
MUSSELCRACKER
MUSSELED
MUSSELER
MUSSICK
MUSSIER
MUSSIEST
MUSSILY
MUSSINESS
MUSSING
MUSSITATE
MUSSITATION
MUSSUCK
MUSSUK
MUSSURANA
MUSSY
MUST
MUSTACHE
MUSTACHED
MUSTACHIAL
MUSTACHIO
MUSTACHIOED
MUSTAFINA
MUSTAFUZ
MUSTANG
MUSTANGER
MUSTARD
MUSTARDER
MUSTED
MUSTEE
MUSTELID
MUSTELIN
MUSTELINE
MUSTELINOUS
MUSTELOID
MUSTER
MUSTERED
MUSTERER
MUSTERING
MUSTERMASTER
MUSTERS
MUSTH
MUSTIER
MUSTIEST
MUSTIFY
MUSTILY
MUSTINESS
MUSTING
MUSTULENT
MUSTY
MUSUMEE
MUT
MUTA
MUTABILITY
MUTABLE
MUTABLENESS
MUTABLY
MUTAGE
MUTAGEN
MUTANT
MUTAROTATE
MUTAROTATION
MUTASE
MUTATE
MUTATED
MUTATING
MUTATION
MUTATIONAL
MUTATIONALLY
MUTATIONISM
MUTATIONIST
MUTATIVE
MUTATORY
MUTAWALLI
MUTAWALLIS
MUTCH
MUTCHKIN
MUTE
MUTED
MUTELY
MUTENESS
MUTER
MUTESCENCE
MUTESSARIF
MUTESSARIFAT
MUTH
MUTHMANNITE
MUTI
MUTIC
MUTICOUS
MUTILATE
MUTILATED
MUTILATING
MUTILATION
MUTILATIVE
MUTILATOR
MUTILATORY
MUTILLID
MUTILOUS
MUTINADO
MUTINE
MUTINEER
MUTINEERS
MUTING
MUTINIED
MUTINIES
MUTINOUS
MUTINOUSLY
MUTINOUSNESS
MUTINY
MUTINYING
MUTISM
MUTIST
MUTISTIC
MUTIVE
MUTIVITY
MUTOSCOPE
MUTOSCOPIC
MUTSJE
MUTSUDDY
MUTT
MUTTER
MUTTERED
MUTTERER
MUTTERING
MUTTERINGLY
MUTTON
MUTTONBIRD
MUTTONCHOP
MUTTONCHOPS
MUTTONFISH
MUTTONFISHES
MUTTONHEAD
MUTTONHEADED
MUTTONMONGER

MUTTONWOOD
MUTUA
MUTUAL
MUTUALISM
MUTUALIST
MUTUALISTIC
MUTUALITY
MUTUALIZE
MUTUALIZED
MUTUALIZING
MUTUALLY
MUTUARY
MUTUATE
MUTUATITIOUS
MUTUEL
MUTULE
MUTUUM
MUTWALLI
MUUMUU
MUVULE
MUX
MUY
MUYUSA
MUZHIK
MUZJIK
MUZOONA
MUZZ
MUZZIER
MUZZIEST
MUZZLE
MUZZLED
MUZZLELOADER
MUZZLELOADING
MUZZLER
MUZZLEWOOD
MUZZLING
MUZZY
MWAMI
MY
MYAL
MYALGIA
MYALGIC
MYALISM
MYALL
MYARIAN
MYASTHENIA
MYASTHENIC
MYATONIA
MYATONIC
MYATONY
MYATROPHY
MYCELE
MYCELIAL
MYCELIAN
MYCELIOID
MYCELIUM
MYCELOID
MYCETISM
MYCETOCYTE
MYCETOGENIC
MYCETOGENOUS
MYCETOID
MYCETOLOGY
MYCETOMA
MYCETOMATA
MYCETOMATOUS
MYCETOME
MYCETOUS
MYCETOZOAN
MYCETOZOON
MYCOCECIDIUM
MYCODERM
MYCODERMA
MYCODERMIC
MYCODOMATIUM
MYCOID
MYCOLOGIC
MYCOLOGICAL
MYCOLOGIES
MYCOLOGIST
MYCOLOGIZE
MYCOLOGY
MYCOMYCETE
MYCOMYCETOUS
MYCOPHAGIST
MYCOPHAGOUS
MYCOPHAGY
MYCOPLASM
MYCOPLASMA
MYCORHIZA
MYCORHIZAL
MYCORRHIZA
MYCORRHIZAL
MYCORRHIZIC
MYCOSE
MYCOSIN
MYCOSIS
MYCOSTEROL
MYCOTIC
MYCOTROPHIC
MYCTERIC
MYCTERISM
MYCTOPHID
MYDALEINE
MYDATOXINE
MYDINE
MYDRIASINE
MYDRIASIS
MYDRIATIC
MYDRIATINE
MYECTOMIZE
MYECTOMY
MYECTOPIA
MYECTOPY
MYELALGIA
MYELAPOPLEXY
MYELASTHENIA
MYELATROPHY
MYELAUXE
MYELEMIA
MYELIC
MYELIN
MYELINATE
MYELINATED
MYELINATION
MYELINE
MYELINIC
MYELINOGENY
MYELITIC
MYELITIS
MYELOBLAST
MYELOBLASTIC
MYELOCELE
MYELOCOELE
MYELOCYST
MYELOCYSTIC
MYELOCYTE
MYELOCYTIC
MYELOCYTOSIS
MYELOGENESIS
MYELOGENETIC
MYELOGENOUS
MYELOGONIUM
MYELOIC
MYELOID
MYELOMA
MYELOMALACIA
MYELOMAS
MYELOMATA
MYELOMATOID
MYELOMATOSIS
MYELOMENIA
MYELON
MYELONAL
MYELONIC
MYELOPATHIC
MYELOPATHY
MYELOPETAL
MYELOPLAST
MYELOPLASTIC
MYELOPLAX
MYELOPLAXES
MYELOPLEGIA
MYELOPOIESIS
MYELOPOIETIC
MYELORRHAGIA
MYELORRHAPHY
MYELOSARCOMA
MYELOSPASM
MYELOTHERAPY
MYENTASIS
MYENTERIC
MYENTERON
MYGALE
MYGALID
MYGALOID
MYIASIS
MYIODESOPSIA
MYKISS
MYLODONT
MYLOHYOID
MYLOHYOIDEAN
MYLONITE
MYLONITIC
MYMARID
MYNA
MYNAH
MYNHEER
MYNPACHT
MYOALBUMIN
MYOALBUMOSE
MYOATROPHY
MYOBLAST
MYOBLASTIC
MYOCARDIAC
MYOCARDIAL
MYOCARDITIC
MYOCARDITIS
MYOCARDIUM
MYOCLONIC
MYOCLONUS
MYOCOEL
MYOCOELE
MYOCOELOM
MYOCOLPITIS
MYOCOMMA
MYOCOMMATA
MYOCYTE
MYODIASTASIS
MYODYNAMIA
MYODYNAMIC
MYODYNAMICS
MYOEDEMA
MYOELECTRIC
MYOENOTOMY
MYOFIBRIL
MYOFIBRILLA
MYOFIBROMA
MYOGEN
MYOGENESIS
MYOGENETIC
MYOGENIC
MYOGENOUS
MYOGLOBIN
MYOGLOBULIN
MYOGRAM
MYOGRAPH
MYOGRAPHER
MYOGRAPHIC
MYOGRAPHICAL
MYOGRAPHIST
MYOGRAPHY
MYOHAEMATIN
MYOHEMATIN
MYOID
MYOKINESIS
MYOLEMMA
MYOLIPOMA
MYOLIPOSIS
MYOLOGIC
MYOLOGICAL
MYOLOGIST
MYOLOGY
MYOLYSIS
MYOMA
MYOMALACIA
MYOMANCY
MYOMANTIC
MYOMATA
MYOMATOUS
MYOMECTOMIES
MYOMECTOMY
MYOMELANOSIS
MYOMERE
MYOMETRITIS
MYOMETRIUM
MYOMORPH
MYOMORPHIC
MYOMOTOMY
MYONEMA
MYONEME
MYONEURAL
MYONEURALGIA
MYONEURE
MYONEUROMA
MYONEUROSIS
MYONOSUS
MYOPACHYNSIS
MYOPARALYSIS
MYOPARESIS
MYOPATHIA
MYOPATHIC
MYOPATHY
MYOPE
MYOPHAN
MYOPHORE
MYOPHOROUS
MYOPHYSICAL
MYOPHYSICS
MYOPIA
MYOPIC
MYOPICAL
MYOPICALLY
MYOPLASM
MYOPLASTIC
MYOPLASTY
MYOPOLAR
MYOPORACEOUS
MYOPORAD
MYOPROTEID
MYOPROTEIN
MYOPROTEOSE
MYOPS
MYOPY
MYORRHAPHY
MYORRHEXIS
MYOSARCOMA
MYOSCLEROSIS
MYOSCOPE
MYOSEPTUM
MYOSIN
MYOSIS
MYOSITIC
MYOSITIS
MYOSOTE
MYOSOTIS
MYOSPASM
MYOSPASMIA
MYOSUTURE
MYOSYNIZESIS
MYOTASIS
MYOTHERMIC
MYOTIC
MYOTOME
MYOTOMIC
MYOTOMY
MYOTONIA
MYOTROPHY
MYOWUN
MYOXINE
MYRCENE
MYRIACOULOMB
MYRIAD
MYRIADED
MYRIADLY
MYRIAGRAM
MYRIAGRAMME
MYRIALITER
MYRIALITRE
MYRIAMETER
MYRIAMETRE
MYRIAPOD
MYRIAPODAN
MYRIAPODOUS
MYRIARCH
MYRIARCHY
MYRIARE
MYRICA
MYRICACEOUS
MYRICETIN
MYRICIN
MYRICYL
MYRICYLIC
MYRINGA
MYRINGECTOMY
MYRINGITIS
MYRINGOTOME
MYRINGOTOMY
MYRIOLOGIST
MYRIOLOGUE
MYRIORAMA
MYRIOSCOPE
MYRIOSPOROUS
MYRIOTHEISM
MYRISTATE
MYRISTIC
MYRISTIN
MYRISTONE
MYRMECOBIINE
MYRMECOCHORY
MYRMECOID
MYRMECOIDY
MYRMECOLOGY
MYRMECOPHILE
MYRMECOPHILY
MYRMECOPHYTE
MYRMEKITE
MYRMICID
MYRMICINE
MYRMICOID
MYRMIDON
MYRMOTHERINE
MYROBALAN
MYRONATE
MYROPOLIST
MYROSIN
MYRRH
MYRRHED
MYRRHIC
MYRRHINE
MYRRHOL
MYRRHOPHORE
MYRRHY
MYRSINACEOUS
MYRSINAD

MYRT
MYRTACEOUS
MYRTAL
MYRTIFORM
MYRTLE
MYRTLEBERRY
MYRTOL
MYSELF
MYSEN
MYSID
MYSIDEAN
MYSOID
MYSOPHOBIA
MYSOST
MYST
MYSTACAL
MYSTACIAL
MYSTACINE
MYSTACINOUS
MYSTAGOG
MYSTAGOGIC
MYSTAGOGICAL
MYSTAGOGUE
MYSTAGOGY
MYSTAX
MYSTERIAL
MYSTERIARCH
MYSTERIES
MYSTERIOUS
MYSTERIOUSLY
MYSTERIZE
MYSTERY
MYSTES
MYSTIC
MYSTICAL
MYSTICALITY
MYSTICALLY
MYSTICALNESS
MYSTICETE
MYSTICISM
MYSTICITY
MYSTIFICALLY
MYSTIFICATOR
MYSTIFIED
MYSTIFIER
MYSTIFY
MYSTIFYING
MYSTIFYINGLY
MYSTIQUE
MYTACISM
MYTH
MYTHE
MYTHIC
MYTHICAL
MYTHICALISM
MYTHICALITY
MYTHICALLY
MYTHICALNESS
MYTHICISM
MYTHICIST
MYTHICIZE
MYTHICIZED
MYTHICIZER
MYTHICIZING
MYTHIFY
MYTHIST
MYTHOCLAST
MYTHOCLASTIC
MYTHOGENESIS
MYTHOGENY
MYTHOGONIC
MYTHOGONY
MYTHOGRAPHER
MYTHOGRAPHY
MYTHOGREEN
MYTHOHEROIC
MYTHOLOGEMA
MYTHOLOGER
MYTHOLOGIAN
MYTHOLOGIC
MYTHOLOGICAL
MYTHOLOGIES
MYTHOLOGISE
MYTHOLOGIST
MYTHOLOGIZE
MYTHOLOGIZED
MYTHOLOGIZER
MYTHOLOGIZING
MYTHOLOGUE
MYTHOLOGY
MYTHOMANIA
MYTHOMANIAC
MYTHOMETER
MYTHONOMY
MYTHOPEIC
MYTHOPEIST
MYTHOPOEIA
MYTHOPOEIC
MYTHOPOEISM
MYTHOPOEIST
MYTHOPOEM
MYTHOPOESIS
MYTHOPOESY
MYTHOPOET
MYTHOPOETIC
MYTHOPOETIZE
MYTHOPOETRY
MYTHOS
MYTILACEAN
MYTILACEOUS
MYTILID
MYTILIFORM
MYTILOID
MYTILOTOXINE
MYXA
MYXADENITIS
MYXADENOMA
MYXAEMIA
MYXAMOEBA
MYXANGITIS
MYXASTHENIA
MYXEDEMA
MYXEDEMATOUS
MYXEDEMIC
MYXEMIA
MYXINOID
MYXO
MYXOBLASTOMA
MYXOCYSTOMA
MYXOCYTE
MYXOEDEMA
MYXOEDEMIC
MYXOFIBROMA
MYXOGASTER
MYXOGLIOMA
MYXOID
MYXOINOMA
MYXOLIPOMA
MYXOMA
MYXOMAS
MYXOMATA
MYXOMATOSIS
MYXOMATOUS
MYXOMYCETE
MYXOMYCETOUS
MYXOMYOMA
MYXONEUROMA
MYXOPODIA
MYXOPODIUM
MYXORRHEA
MYXOSARCOMA
MYXOSPORE
MYXOSPOROUS
MYXOTHECA
MYZONT
MYZOSTOMID
MYZOSTOMIDAN
MYZOSTOMOUS

N

NA
NAAM
NAARTJE
NAB
NABAK
NABAM
NABBED
NABBER
NABBING
NABBUK
NABBY
NABCHEAT
NABEE
NABK
NABLA
NABLE
NABLUS
NABO
NABOB
NABOBERY
NABOBESS
NABOBICAL
NABOBISH
NABOBISHLY
NABOBISM
NABOBRY
NABS
NACARAT
NACARINE
NACE
NACELLE
NACHTMAAL
NACK
NACKET
NACRE
NACRED
NACREOUS
NACRINE
NACROUS
NACRY
NADA
NADDER
NADIR
NADIRAL
NADORITE
NAE
NAEGAIT
NAEGATE
NAEGATES
NAEL
NAEVE
NAEVOID
NAEVUS
NAG
NAGA
NAGAIKA
NAGAMI
NAGANA
NAGARA
NAGATELITE
NAGGAR
NAGGED
NAGGER
NAGGIN
NAGGING
NAGGINGLY
NAGGINGNESS
NAGGISH
NAGGLE
NAGGLY
NAGGY
NAGHT
NAGID
NAGKASSAR
NAGMAAL
NAGMAN
NAGOR
NAGSMAN
NAGSTER
NAGUAL
NAGUALISM
NAGUALIST
NAGYAGITE
NAHIE
NAHOOR
NAIAD
NAIANT
NAIB
NAID
NAIF
NAIFLY
NAIG
NAIGUE
NAIK
NAIL
NAILED
NAILER
NAILERY
NAILHEAD
NAILING
NAILLESS
NAILROD
NAILS
NAILSICK
NAILWORT
NAILY
NAINSEL
NAINSELL
NAINSOOK
NAIO
NAIQUE
NAIRY
NAIS
NAISH
NAISSANCE
NAISSANT
NAIT
NAITLY
NAIVE
NAIVELY
NAIVENESS
NAIVETE
NAIVETY
NAK
NAKE
NAKED
NAKEDIZE
NAKEDLY
NAKEDNESS
NAKEDWOOD
NAKER
NAKHLITE
NAKHOD
NAKHODA
NAKONG
NAKOO
NAL
NALL
NALLAH
NALLE
NAMABILITY
NAMABLE
NAMAQUA
NAMAYCUSH
NAMAZ
NAMAZLIK
NAMBY
NAMDA
NAME
NAMEABILITY
NAMEABLE
NAMEBOARD
NAMED
NAMELESS
NAMELESSLY
NAMELESSNESS
NAMELING
NAMELY
NAMEPLATE
NAMER
NAMESAKE
NAMING
NAMMAD
NAN
NANA
NANANDER
NANAWOOD
NANCA
NANCY
NANDIN
NANDINE
NANDOW
NANDU
NANDUTI
NANE
NANES
NANGA
NANGCA
NANGER
NANGKA
NANIGO
NANISM
NANITIC
NANIZATION
NANKEEN
NANKEENS
NANKIN
NANKINS
NANMU
NANNANDER
NANNIE
NANNIES
NANNINOSE
NANNY
NANOCEPHALIA
NANOCEPHALIC
NANOCEPHALUS
NANOCEPHALY
NANOID
NANOMELIA
NANOMELOUS
NANOMELUS
NANOPLANKTON
NANOSOMA
NANOSOMUS
NANPIE
NANSOMIA
NANT
NANTLE
NANTOKITE
NANTS
NAO
NAOLOGICAL
NAOLOGY
NAOMETRY
NAOS
NAP
NAPA
NAPAL
NAPALM
NAPE
NAPEAD
NAPECREST
NAPELLUS
NAPERER
NAPERIES
NAPERY
NAPHTHA
NAPHTHACENE
NAPHTHALATE
NAPHTHALENE
NAPHTHALENIC
NAPHTHALIC
NAPHTHALIZE
NAPHTHAMINE
NAPHTHENE
NAPHTHENIC
NAPHTHIONATE
NAPHTHOIC
NAPHTHOL
NAPHTHOLATE
NAPHTHOUS
NAPHTHYL
NAPHTHYLENE
NAPHTHYLIC
NAPIFORM
NAPKIN
NAPKINED
NAPKINING
NAPKINS
NAPLESS
NAPLESSNESS
NAPOLEON
NAPOO
NAPOOH
NAPPE
NAPPED
NAPPER
NAPPIE
NAPPINESS
NAPPING
NAPPISHNESS
NAPPY
NAPRAPATHY
NAPRON
NAPU
NAR
NARCEIN
NARCEINE
NARCISM
NARCISSISM
NARCISSIST
NARCISSISTIC
NARCISSUS
NARCIST
NARCISTIC
NARCOHYPNIA
NARCOLEPSY
NARCOLEPTIC
NARCOMA
NARCOMANIA
NARCOMANIAC
NARCOMANIACAL
NARCOMAS
NARCOMATA
NARCOMEDUSAN
NARCOSE
NARCOSIS
NARCOTIA
NARCOTIC
NARCOTICAL
NARCOTICALLY
NARCOTICISM
NARCOTICS
NARCOTIN
NARCOTINA
NARCOTINE
NARCOTINIC
NARCOTISM
NARCOTIST
NARCOTIZE
NARCOTIZED
NARCOTIZING
NARD
NARDINE
NARDO
NARDOO
NARDU
NARE
NARES
NARGHILE
NARGIL
NARGILE
NARGILEH
NARIAL
NARICA
NARICORN
NARIFORM
NARINE
NARINGENIN
NARINGIN
NARIS
NARK
NARKY
NARR
NARRA
NARRANTE
NARRAS
NARRATABLE
NARRATE
NARRATION
NARRATIONAL
NARRATIVE
NARRATIVELY
NARRATOR
NARRATORY
NARRATRESS
NARRAWOOD
NARROW
NARROWED
NARROWER
NARROWEST
NARROWING
NARROWLY
NARROWNESS
NARROWY
NARSARSUKITE
NARSINGA
NARTHECAL
NARTHEX
NARWAL
NARWHAL
NARWHALE
NARY
NAS
NASAB
NASAL
NASALIS
NASALISM
NASALITY
NASALIZATION
NASALIZE
NASALIZED
NASALIZING
NASALLY
NASARD
NASAT
NASAUMP
NASCENCE
NASCENCY
NASCENT
NASCH
NASE
NASEBERRY
NASETHMOID

NASH
NASHGAB
NASHGOB
NASI
NASIAL
NASICORN
NASICORNOUS
NASIFORM
NASILABIAL
NASILLATE
NASILLATION
NASION
NASITIS
NASOANTRAL
NASOBASILAR
NASOBUCCAL
NASOCILIARY
NASOFRONTAL
NASOLABIAL
NASOLOGICAL
NASOLOGIST
NASOLOGY
NASOMALAR
NASONITE
NASOORBITAL
NASOPALATAL
NASOPALATINE
NASOPHARYNX
NASOROSTRAL
NASOSCOPE
NASOSEPTAL
NASOSINUITIS
NASOSUBNASAL
NASROL
NASSOLOGY
NAST
NASTALIQ
NASTIC
NASTIER
NASTIEST
NASTIKA
NASTILY
NASTINESS
NASTURTIUM
NASTY
NASUS
NASUTE
NASUTENESS
NASUTIFORM
NAT
NATA
NATABILITY
NATAKA
NATAL
NATALITIAL
NATALITY
NATANT
NATANTLY
NATATION
NATATOR
NATATORIAL
NATATORIOUS
NATATORIUM
NATATORY
NATCH
NATCHBONE
NATCHNEE
NATE
NATED
NATES
NATHE
NATHER
NATHLESS
NATICIFORM
NATICINE
NATICOID
NATIFORM
NATION
NATIONAL
NATIONALISM
NATIONALIST
NATIONALISTIC
NATIONALISTICALLY
NATIONALITY
NATIONALIZATION
NATIONALIZE
NATIONALIZED
NATIONALIZER
NATIONALIZING
NATIONALLY
NATIONALNESS
NATIONS
NATIVE
NATIVELY
NATIVISM
NATIVIST
NATIVISTIC
NATIVITIES
NATIVITY
NATR
NATRIUM
NATROCHALCITE
NATROJAROSITE
NATROLITE
NATRON
NATTE
NATTER
NATTERED
NATTEREDNESS
NATTERJACK
NATTIER
NATTIEST
NATTILY
NATTLE
NATTOCK
NATTY
NATUARY
NATURA
NATURAL
NATURALESQUE
NATURALIA
NATURALISE
NATURALISM
NATURALIST
NATURALISTIC
NATURALITY
NATURALIZE
NATURALIZED
NATURALIZER
NATURALIZING
NATURALLY
NATURALNESS
NATURATA
NATURE
NATURECRAFT
NATURED
NATURING
NATURISM
NATURIST
NATURISTIC
NATURIZE
NATUROPATH
NATUROPATHIC
NATUROPATHY
NATYA
NAU
NAUCORID
NAUCRAR
NAUCRARY
NAUFRAGE
NAUFRAGOUS
NAUGER
NAUGHT
NAUGHTIER
NAUGHTIEST
NAUGHTILY
NAUGHTINESS
NAUGHTY
NAUJAITE
NAUKRAR
NAULUM
NAUMACHIA
NAUMACHIAE
NAUMACHIAS
NAUMACHIES
NAUMACHY
NAUMANNITE
NAUMK
NAUMKEAG
NAUMKEAGER
NAUNT
NAUNTLE
NAUPATHIA
NAUPLIAL
NAUPLIIFORM
NAUPLIOID
NAUPLIUS
NAUROPOMETER
NAUSCOPY
NAUSEA
NAUSEANT
NAUSEATE
NAUSEATED
NAUSEATING
NAUSEATION
NAUSEOUS
NAUSEOUSLY
NAUSEOUSNESS
NAUSITY
NAUT
NAUTCH
NAUTHER
NAUTIC
NAUTICAL
NAUTICALITY
NAUTICALLY
NAUTICS
NAUTIFORM
NAUTILACEAN
NAUTILI
NAUTILICONE
NAUTILIFORM
NAUTILITE
NAUTILOID
NAUTILOIDEAN
NAUTILUS
NAUTILUSES
NAVAL
NAVALISM
NAVALIST
NAVALISTIC
NAVARCH
NAVARCHY
NAVARHO
NAVARIN
NAVE
NAVEL
NAVELED
NAVELWORT
NAVET
NAVETA
NAVETTE
NAVEW
NAVIA
NAVICELLA
NAVICERT
NAVICULA
NAVICULAR
NAVICULARE
NAVICULOID
NAVIES
NAVIFORM
NAVIGABILITY
NAVIGABLE
NAVIGABLENESS
NAVIGABLY
NAVIGANT
NAVIGATE
NAVIGATED
NAVIGATING
NAVIGATION
NAVIGATIONAL
NAVIGATOR
NAVIGEROUS
NAVIPENDULAR
NAVIPENDULUM
NAVITE
NAVVIE
NAVVIES
NAVVY
NAVY
NAW
NAWAB
NAWOB
NAWT
NAY
NAYAK
NAYAUR
NAYSAY
NAYWARD
NAYWORD
NAZARD
NAZE
NAZI
NAZIFICATION
NAZIFIED
NAZIFY
NAZIFYING
NAZIM
NAZIR
NAZIS
NE
NEAKES
NEAL
NEALLOTYPE
NEANIC
NEAP
NEAPED
NEAR
NEARABOUT
NEARABOUTS
NEARAWAY
NEARAWAYS
NEARBY
NEARED
NEARER
NEAREST
NEARING
NEARISH
NEARLIER
NEARLIEST
NEARLY
NEARMOST
NEARNESS
NEARSIGHT
NEARSIGHTED
NEARSIGHTEDLY
NEARSIGHTEDNESS
NEARTHROSIS
NEASCUS
NEAT
NEATEN
NEATER
NEATEST
NEATH
NEATHERD
NEATHERDESS
NEATHMOST
NEATIFY
NEATLY
NEATNESS
NEAVIL
NEB
NEBACK
NEBALIOID
NEBBED
NEBBUCK
NEBBUK
NEBBY
NEBENKERN
NEBRIS
NEBRODI
NEBUK
NEBULA
NEBULAE
NEBULAR
NEBULARIZATION
NEBULARIZE
NEBULAS
NEBULATED
NEBULATION
NEBULE
NEBULESCENT
NEBULIFEROUS
NEBULITE
NEBULIUM
NEBULIZATION
NEBULIZE
NEBULIZED
NEBULIZER
NEBULIZING
NEBULON
NEBULOSE
NEBULOSITY
NEBULOUS
NEBULOUSLY
NEBULOUSNESS
NECESSAR
NECESSARIES
NECESSARILY
NECESSARY
NECESSE
NECESSISM
NECESSIST
NECESSITARIAN
NECESSITATE
NECESSITATED
NECESSITATING
NECESSITATIVE
NECESSITIES
NECESSITOUS
NECESSITUDE
NECESSITY
NECK
NECKAR
NECKATEE
NECKBAND
NECKCLOTH
NECKED
NECKENGER
NECKER
NECKERCHER
NECKERCHIEF
NECKGUARD
NECKING
NECKINGER
NECKLACE
NECKLACED
NECKLACEWEED
NECKLET
NECKLINE
NECKMOLD
NECKMOULD
NECKPIECE
NECKTIE

NECKWEAR
NECKWEED
NECRAEMIA
NECRECTOMY
NECREMIA
NECROBIOSIS
NECROBIOTIC
NECROGENIC
NECROGENOUS
NECROLATRY
NECROLOGICAL
NECROLOGIST
NECROLOGUE
NECROLOGY
NECROMANCER
NECROMANCING
NECROMANCY
NECROMANIA
NECROMANTIC
NECRONITE
NECROPATHY
NECROPHAGOUS
NECROPHIL
NECROPHILE
NECROPHILIA
NECROPHILIC
NECROPHILOUS
NECROPHOBIA
NECROPHOBIC
NECROPOLEIS
NECROPOLIS
NECROPOLISES
NECROPOLITAN
NECROPSIES
NECROPSY
NECROSCOPIC
NECROSCOPY
NECROSE
NECROSED
NECROSES
NECROSING
NECROSIS
NECROTIC
NECROTIZE
NECROTOMIC
NECROTOMIES
NECROTOMIST
NECROTOMY
NECROTYPE
NECROTYPIC
NECTAR
NECTAREAL
NECTAREAN
NECTARED
NECTAREOUS
NECTAREOUSLY
NECTARIAL
NECTARIAN
NECTARIED
NECTARIES
NECTARIFEROUS
NECTARIN
NECTARINE
NECTARIOUS
NECTARIUM
NECTARIZE
NECTAROUS
NECTARY
NECTIFEROUS
NECTOCALYCES
NECTOCALYCINE
NECTOCALYX
NECTON
NECTOPHORE
NECTOPOD
NECTRON
NEDDER
NEDDIES
NEDDY
NEE
NEED
NEEDER
NEEDFIRE
NEEDFUL
NEEDFULLY
NEEDFULNESS
NEEDGATES
NEEDIER
NEEDIEST
NEEDINESS
NEEDING
NEEDLE
NEEDLEBILL
NEEDLEBOOK
NEEDLEBUSH
NEEDLECASE
NEEDLED
NEEDLEFISH
NEEDLEFISHES
NEEDLEFUL
NEEDLELIKE
NEEDLEMAKER
NEEDLEMAKING
NEEDLEMAN
NEEDLEMEN
NEEDLEMONGER
NEEDLEPOINT
NEEDLEPROOF
NEEDLER
NEEDLES
NEEDLESS
NEEDLESSLY
NEEDLESSNESS
NEEDLESTONE
NEEDLEWOMAN
NEEDLEWOOD
NEEDLEWORK
NEEDLEWORKER
NEEDLING
NEEDLY
NEEDMENTS
NEEDS
NEEDSOME
NEEDY
NEELE
NEEM
NEEMBA
NEEN
NEENCEPHALIC
NEENCEPHALON
NEEP
NEER
NEESE
NEEZE
NEF
NEFANDOUS
NEFARIOUS
NEFARIOUSLY
NEFAS
NEFAST
NEFFY
NEFTE
NEFTGIL
NEGARA
NEGATE
NEGATED
NEGATING
NEGATION
NEGATIONAL
NEGATIONIST
NEGATIVE
NEGATIVED
NEGATIVELY
NEGATIVENESS
NEGATIVER
NEGATIVING
NEGATIVISM
NEGATIVIST
NEGATIVISTIC
NEGATIVITY
NEGATOR
NEGATORY
NEGER
NEGINOTH
NEGLECT
NEGLECTABLE
NEGLECTED
NEGLECTER
NEGLECTFUL
NEGLECTFULLY
NEGLECTFULNESS
NEGLECTING
NEGLECTION
NEGLECTIVE
NEGLECTOR
NEGLIGEE
NEGLIGENCE
NEGLIGENCY
NEGLIGENT
NEGLIGENTLY
NEGLIGIBILITY
NEGLIGIBLE
NEGLIGIBLY
NEGOCE
NEGOTIABLE
NEGOTIANT
NEGOTIATE
NEGOTIATED
NEGOTIATING
NEGOTIATION
NEGOTIATOR
NEGOTIATORY
NEGOTIATRESS
NEGOTIATRIX
NEGRILLO
NEGRINE
NEGRITA
NEGRITUDE
NEGRO
NEGROHEAD
NEGROS
NEGUS
NEHILOTH
NEHU
NEI
NEIF
NEIFE
NEIGH
NEIGHBOR
NEIGHBORED
NEIGHBORER
NEIGHBORESS
NEIGHBORHOOD
NEIGHBORHOODS
NEIGHBORING
NEIGHBORLY
NEIGHBORS
NEIGHBOUR
NEIGHBOURED
NEIGHBOURER
NEIGHBOURESS
NEIGHBOURHOOD
NEIGHBOURING
NEIGHBOURLY
NEIGHED
NEIGHER
NEIGHING
NEILAH
NEIPER
NEIST
NEITHER
NEKTON
NELLY
NELMA
NELSONITE
NELUMBIAN
NELUMBO
NEMA
NEMALINE
NEMALITE
NEMATHECE
NEMATHECIAL
NEMATHECIUM
NEMATOBLAST
NEMATOCERAN
NEMATOCIDE
NEMATOCYST
NEMATOCYSTIC
NEMATODE
NEMATODIASIS
NEMATOGEN
NEMATOGENE
NEMATOGENIC
NEMATOGONE
NEMATOIDEAN
NEMATOLOGIST
NEMATOLOGY
NEMATOPHYTON
NEMATOZOOID
NEMBUTSU
NEMEA
NEMERTEAN
NEMERTIAN
NEMERTINE
NEMERTINEAN
NEMERTOID
NEMESIC
NEMESIS
NEMME
NEMN
NEMOPHILIST
NEMOPHILOUS
NEMOPHILY
NEMORAL
NEMORICOLE
NEMORICOLINE
NEMORICOLOUS
NEMPNE
NENE
NENTA
NENUPHAR
NEO
NEOBLASTIC
NEOCEROTIC
NEOCLASSIC
NEOCLASSICISM
NEOCOSMIC
NEOCRACY
NEOCRITICISM
NEOCYANINE
NEOCYTE
NEOCYTOSIS
NEODAMODE
NEODIDYMIUM
NEODYMIUM
NEOFETAL
NEOFETUS
NEOFORMATION
NEOFORMATIVE
NEOGAMOUS
NEOGAMY
NEOGENESIS
NEOGENETIC
NEOGNATHIC
NEOGNATHOUS
NEOGRAPHIC
NEOIMPRESSIONISM
NEOLATER
NEOLATRY
NEOLITH
NEOLITHIC
NEOLOGIAN
NEOLOGIC
NEOLOGICAL
NEOLOGICALLY
NEOLOGISM
NEOLOGIST
NEOLOGISTIC
NEOLOGISTICAL
NEOLOGIZE
NEOLOGIZED
NEOLOGIZING
NEOLOGY
NEOMENIA
NEOMENIAN
NEOMIRACLE
NEOMODAL
NEOMORPH
NEOMORPHIC
NEOMORPHISM
NEOMYCIN
NEON
NEONATAL
NEONATUS
NEONOMIAN
NEONOMIANISM
NEONYCHIUM
NEOORTHODOXY
NEOPAGAN
NEOPAGANISM
NEOPAGANIZE
NEOPALLIAL
NEOPALLIUM
NEOPHILISM
NEOPHOBIA
NEOPHOBIC
NEOPHRASTIC
NEOPHYTE
NEOPHYTIC
NEOPHYTISH
NEOPHYTISM
NEOPINE
NEOPLASIA
NEOPLASM
NEOPLASMS
NEOPLASTIC
NEOPLASTIES
NEOPLASTY
NEOPRENE
NEORAMA
NEOSSIN
NEOSSOLOGY
NEOSSOPTILE
NEOSTRIATUM
NEOSTYLE
NEOTEINIA
NEOTENIA
NEOTENY
NEOTERIC
NEOTERICAL
NEOTERICALLY
NEOTERISM
NEOTERIST
NEOTERISTIC
NEOTERIZE
NEOTHALAMUS
NEOTYPE
NEOVITALISM
NEOVOLCANIC
NEOYTTERBIUM
NEP
NEPAL
NEPE
NEPENTHE
NEPENTHEAN

NEPENTHES
NEPER
NEPHALISM
NEPHALIST
NEPHELINE
NEPHELINIC
NEPHELINITE
NEPHELINITIC
NEPHELITE
NEPHELOGNOSY
NEPHELOID
NEPHELOMETER
NEPHELOSCOPE
NEPHESH
NEPHEW
NEPHIONIC
NEPHOGRAM
NEPHOGRAPH
NEPHOLOGICAL
NEPHOLOGIST
NEPHOLOGY
NEPHOSCOPE
NEPHRALGIA
NEPHRALGIC
NEPHRATONIA
NEPHRAUXE
NEPHRECTASIA
NEPHRECTASIS
NEPHRECTOMIES
NEPHRECTOMY
NEPHRELCOSIS
NEPHREMIA
NEPHRIA
NEPHRIC
NEPHRIDIA
NEPHRIDIAL
NEPHRIDIUM
NEPHRISM
NEPHRITE
NEPHRITIC
NEPHRITICAL
NEPHRITIS
NEPHROCELE
NEPHROCOELE
NEPHROCOLIC
NEPHROCYTE
NEPHRODINIC
NEPHROGENIC
NEPHROGENOUS
NEPHROID
NEPHROLITH
NEPHROLITHIC
NEPHROLOGY
NEPHROLYSIN
NEPHROLYSIS
NEPHROLYTIC
NEPHROMERE
NEPHRON
NEPHRONCUS
NEPHROPATHY
NEPHROPEXY
NEPHROPORE
NEPHROPTOSIA
NEPHROPTOSIS
NEPHROPYOSIS
NEPHROS
NEPHROSIS
NEPHROSTOME
NEPHROTIC
NEPHROTOME
NEPHROTOMY
NEPHROTOXIC
NEPHROTOXIN
NEPHROTYPHUS
NEPID
NEPIONIC
NEPMAN
NEPMEN
NEPOTAL
NEPOTE
NEPOTIC
NEPOTIOUS
NEPOTISM
NEPOTIST
NEPOTISTICAL
NEPOUITE
NEPTUNISM
NEPTUNIUM
NER
NERAL
NERE
NEREITE
NERITE
NERITIC
NERITOID
NERKA
NEROL
NEROLI
NERTEROLOGY
NERVAL
NERVATE
NERVATION
NERVATURE
NERVE
NERVED
NERVELESS
NERVELESSLY
NERVELESSNESS
NERVELET
NERVER
NERVEROOT
NERVES
NERVI
NERVID
NERVIDUCT
NERVIER
NERVIEST
NERVIMOTION
NERVIMOTOR
NERVINE
NERVING
NERVISH
NERVISM
NERVOSE
NERVOSISM
NERVOSITY
NERVOUS
NERVOUSLY
NERVOUSNESS
NERVULAR
NERVULE
NERVULET
NERVULOSE
NERVURATION
NERVURE
NERVUS
NERVY
NESCIENCE
NESCIENT
NESE
NESH
NESIOTE
NESLAVE
NESLE
NESLIA
NESQUEHONITE
NESS
NESSBERRY
NESSLERIZE
NESSLERIZED
NEST
NESTABLE
NESTAGE
NESTED
NESTER
NESTIATRIA
NESTING
NESTITHERAPY
NESTLE
NESTLED
NESTLER
NESTLING
NESTORINE
NESTY
NET
NETBALL
NETBRAIDER
NETBUSH
NETCHA
NETER
NETHE
NETHEIST
NETHER
NETHERMORE
NETHERMOST
NETHERSTOCK
NETHERSTONE
NETHERWARD
NETHERWORLD
NETI
NETLEAF
NETLIKE
NETMAKER
NETMAKING
NETMAN
NETMONGER
NETOP
NETS
NETSMAN
NETSUKE
NETTABLE
NETTED
NETTER
NETTING
NETTLE
NETTLEBIRD
NETTLED
NETTLEFIRE
NETTLEFOOT
NETTLEMONGER
NETTLER
NETTLESOME
NETTLEWORT
NETTLING
NETTLY
NETTY
NETWORK
NEU
NEUCK
NEUGROSCHEN
NEUM
NEUMATIC
NEUMATIZE
NEUME
NEUMIC
NEURAD
NEURAL
NEURALGIA
NEURALGIAC
NEURALGIC
NEURALGIFORM
NEURALGY
NEURALIST
NEURASTHENIA
NEURASTHENIC
NEURASTHENICAL
NEURATAXIA
NEURATAXY
NEURATION
NEURATROPHIA
NEURATROPHIC
NEURATROPHY
NEURAXIS
NEURAXON
NEURAXONE
NEURECTASIA
NEURECTASIS
NEURECTASY
NEURECTOME
NEURECTOMIC
NEURECTOMY
NEURECTOPIA
NEURECTOPY
NEURENTERIC
NEURERGIC
NEURHYPNOTIST
NEURIC
NEURILEMMA
NEURILEMMAL
NEURILITY
NEURIN
NEURINE
NEURINOMA
NEURINOMAS
NEURINOMATA
NEURISM
NEURITE
NEURITIC
NEURITIDES
NEURITIS
NEUROBLAST
NEUROCANAL
NEUROCARDIAC
NEUROCENTRAL
NEUROCENTRUM
NEUROCHITIN
NEUROCHORD
NEUROCITY
NEUROCLONIC
NEUROCOELE
NEUROCYTE
NEUROCYTOMA
NEURODYNIA
NEUROFIBRIL
NEUROFIBROMA
NEUROFIL
NEUROGASTRIC
NEUROGENESIS
NEUROGENETIC
NEUROGENIC
NEUROGENOUS
NEUROGLIA
NEUROGLIAC
NEUROGLIAL
NEUROGLIAR
NEUROGLIOMA
NEUROGLIOSIS
NEUROGRAM
NEUROGRAPHY
NEUROID
NEUROKERATIN
NEUROKYME
NEUROLOGICAL
NEUROLOGIST
NEUROLOGIZE
NEUROLOGY
NEUROLYMPH
NEUROLYSIS
NEUROMA
NEUROMALACIA
NEUROMALAKIA
NEUROMATOSIS
NEUROMATOUS
NEUROMERE
NEUROMERISM
NEUROMEROUS
NEUROMOTOR
NEURON
NEURONIC
NEURONISM
NEURONYM
NEURONYMY
NEUROPATH
NEUROPATHIC
NEUROPATHIST
NEUROPATHY
NEUROPHILE
NEUROPHILIC
NEUROPIL
NEUROPILE
NEUROPILEM
NEUROPLASM
NEUROPLASMIC
NEUROPLASTY
NEUROPLEXUS
NEUROPODIUM
NEUROPODOUS
NEUROPORE
NEUROPSYCHIC
NEUROPTERIST
NEUROPTEROID
NEUROPTERON
NEUROSAL
NEUROSES
NEUROSIS
NEUROSKELETAL
NEUROSOME
NEUROSPASM
NEUROSPAST
NEUROSTHENIA
NEUROSURGEON
NEUROSURGERY
NEUROSUTURE
NEUROSYNAPSE
NEUROTENSION
NEUROTHERAPY
NEUROTIC
NEUROTICALLY
NEUROTICISM
NEUROTOME
NEUROTOMICAL
NEUROTOMIST
NEUROTOMIZE
NEUROTOMY
NEUROTONIC
NEUROTOXIA
NEUROTOXIC
NEUROTOXIN
NEUROTRIPSY
NEUROTROPHIC
NEUROTROPHY
NEUROTROPIC
NEUROTROPISM
NEUROTROPY
NEUROVACCINE
NEURULA
NEURYPNOLOGY
NEUSTON
NEUTER
NEUTERDOM
NEUTERED
NEUTERING
NEUTERLY
NEUTERNESS
NEUTRAL
NEUTRALISE
NEUTRALISM
NEUTRALIST
NEUTRALITIES
NEUTRALITY
NEUTRALIZE
NEUTRALIZED
NEUTRALIZER
NEUTRALIZING
NEUTRALLY

NEUTRALNESS
NEUTRIA
NEUTRINO
NEUTRON
NEUTROPHIL
NEUTROPHILE
NEUTROPHILIA
NEVADITE
NEVAT
NEVE
NEVEL
NEVELL
NEVEN
NEVER
NEVERMASS
NEVERMORE
NEVERTHELESS
NEVES
NEVOID
NEVOY
NEVUS
NEVYANSKITE
NEW
NEWBERYITE
NEWBORN
NEWCAL
NEWCOME
NEWCOMER
NEWEL
NEWELTY
NEWER
NEWEST
NEWFANGLE
NEWFANGLED
NEWFISH
NEWING
NEWISH
NEWLANDITE
NEWLIGHT
NEWLINGS
NEWLINS
NEWLY
NEWLYWED
NEWMARKET
NEWMOWN
NEWNESS
NEWS
NEWSAGENT
NEWSBILL
NEWSBOARD
NEWSBOAT
NEWSBOY
NEWSCAST
NEWSCASTER
NEWSDEALER
NEWSIER
NEWSIEST
NEWSINESS
NEWSLETTER
NEWSMAGAZINE
NEWSMAN
NEWSMEN
NEWSMONGER
NEWSMONGERING
NEWSMONGERY
NEWSPAPER
NEWSPAPERMAN
NEWSPAPERMEN
NEWSPAPERWOMAN
NEWSPAPERWOMEN
NEWSPAPERY
NEWSPRINT
NEWSREADER
NEWSREEL
NEWSROOM
NEWSSHEET
NEWSSTAND
NEWSTELLER
NEWSWORTHY
NEWSY
NEWT
NEWTAKE
NEWTON
NEWTONITE
NEXAL
NEXT
NEXTLY
NEXTNESS
NEXUM
NEXUS
NEXUSES
NEY
NEYANDA
NGAI
NGAIO
NGAN
NGAPI
NGU
NI
NIACIN
NIATA
NIB
NIBBED
NIBBER
NIBBLE
NIBBLED
NIBBLER
NIBBLING
NIBBY
NIBLIC
NIBLICK
NIBONG
NIBS
NIBSOME
NIBUNG
NICCOLIC
NICCOLITE
NICCOLO
NICCOLOUS
NICE
NICELING
NICELY
NICENESS
NICER
NICEST
NICETIES
NICETISH
NICETY
NICHE
NICHED
NICHELINO
NICHEVO
NICHIL
NICHING
NICHT
NICK
NICKED
NICKEL
NICKELBLOOM
NICKELIC
NICKELIFEROUS
NICKELINE
NICKELIZE
NICKELODEON
NICKELOUS
NICKELTYPE
NICKER
NICKERPECKER
NICKERY
NICKEY
NICKING
NICKLE
NICKNACK
NICKNAME
NICKNAMED
NICKNAMEE
NICKNAMER
NICKNAMING
NICKPOT
NICKSTICK
NICKUM
NICKY
NICOLAYITE
NICOLO
NICOTIA
NICOTIAN
NICOTIANIN
NICOTIN
NICOTINA
NICOTINE
NICOTINEAN
NICOTINED
NICOTINIAN
NICOTINIC
NICOTINISM
NICOTINIZE
NICOTISM
NICOTIZE
NICTATE
NICTATED
NICTATING
NICTATION
NICTITANT
NICTITATE
NICTITATED
NICTITATING
NICTITATION
NID
NIDAL
NIDAMENTAL
NIDANA
NIDARY
NIDATION
NIDATORY
NIDDER
NIDDERING
NIDDICK
NIDDICOCK
NIDDLE
NIDE
NIDERING
NIDGE
NIDGET
NIDGETY
NIDI
NIDICOLOUS
NIDIFICANT
NIDIFICATE
NIDIFICATED
NIDIFICATING
NIDIFICATION
NIDIFICATIONAL
NIDIFIED
NIDIFUGOUS
NIDIFY
NIDIFYING
NIDING
NIDIOT
NIDOLOGIST
NIDOLOGY
NIDOR
NIDOROSE
NIDOROSITY
NIDOROUS
NIDORULENT
NIDULANT
NIDULATE
NIDULATION
NIDULI
NIDULUS
NIDUS
NIDUSES
NIE
NIECE
NIEF
NIELLATED
NIELLED
NIELLI
NIELLIST
NIELLO
NIELLOED
NIELLOING
NIELLOS
NIEPA
NIESHOUT
NIEVE
NIEVETA
NIEVLING
NIF
NIFE
NIFESIMA
NIFFER
NIFIC
NIFLE
NIFLING
NIFTIER
NIFTIEST
NIFTY
NIG
NIGGARD
NIGGARDLY
NIGGER
NIGGERED
NIGGERFISH
NIGGERFISHES
NIGGERGOOSE
NIGGERHEAD
NIGGERISH
NIGGERISM
NIGGERLING
NIGGERTOE
NIGGERWEED
NIGGERY
NIGGET
NIGGLE
NIGGLED
NIGGLER
NIGGLING
NIGGLINGLY
NIGGLY
NIGGOT
NIGGUN
NIGH
NIGHED
NIGHER
NIGHEST
NIGHING
NIGHLY
NIGHT
NIGHTCAP
NIGHTCAPPED
NIGHTCAPS
NIGHTCLOTHES
NIGHTCLUB
NIGHTDRESS
NIGHTED
NIGHTERY
NIGHTFALL
NIGHTFISH
NIGHTFLIT
NIGHTFOWL
NIGHTGALE
NIGHTGLASS
NIGHTGOWN
NIGHTHAWK
NIGHTIE
NIGHTIES
NIGHTING
NIGHTINGALE
NIGHTINGALIZE
NIGHTISH
NIGHTJAR
NIGHTLONG
NIGHTLY
NIGHTMAN
NIGHTMARE
NIGHTMARISH
NIGHTMARISHLY
NIGHTMARY
NIGHTMEN
NIGHTRIDER
NIGHTS
NIGHTSHADE
NIGHTSHIRT
NIGHTSPOT
NIGHTSTICK
NIGHTTIDE
NIGHTTIME
NIGHTWAKE
NIGHTWALKER
NIGHTWALKING
NIGHTWARD
NIGHTWEAR
NIGHTWORK
NIGHTWORKER
NIGHTY
NIGNAY
NIGNYE
NIGON
NIGORI
NIGRE
NIGRESCENCE
NIGRESCENT
NIGRESCITE
NIGRICANT
NIGRIFICATION
NIGRIFIED
NIGRIFY
NIGRIFYING
NIGRINE
NIGRITIES
NIGRITUDE
NIGROSIN
NIGROSINE
NIGROUS
NIGS
NIGUA
NIGUN
NIHIL
NIHILIANISM
NIHILIFICATION
NIHILIFY
NIHILISM
NIHILIST
NIHILISTIC
NIHILITIC
NIHILITIES
NIHILITY
NIHILOBSTAT
NIHILUM
NIKAU
NIKENO
NIKLESITE
NIL
NILGAI
NILGAIS
NILGAU
NILL
NILPOTENT
NIM
NIMB
NIMBATED
NIMBI
NIMBIFEROUS
NIMBIFICATION

NIMBLE
NIMBLEBRAINED
NIMBLENESS
NIMBLER
NIMBLEST
NIMBLY
NIMBOSE
NIMBOSTRATUS
NIMBUS
NIMBUSED
NIMBUSES
NIMIETY
NIMINY
NIMIOUS
NIMMED
NIMMER
NIMMING
NIMSHI
NINCOM
NINCOMPOOP
NINCOMPOOPERY
NINCOMPOOPHOOD
NINCOMPOOPISH
NINCUM
NINE
NINEBARK
NINEFOLD
NINEHOLES
NINEPEGS
NINEPENCE
NINEPENCES
NINEPENNIES
NINEPENNY
NINEPIN
NINEPINS
NINESCORE
NINETED
NINETEEN
NINETEENTH
NINETEENTHLY
NINETIETH
NINETY
NINGLE
NINNIES
NINNY
NINNYHAMMER
NINNYISH
NINNYISM
NINNYSHIP
NINNYWATCH
NINO
NINOS
NINTH
NINTHLY
NINTU
NINUT
NIOBATE
NIOBIC
NIOBITE
NIOBIUM
NIOBOUS
NIOG
NIOTA
NIP
NIPA
NIPCHEESE
NIPE
NIPER
NIPMUCK
NIPPED
NIPPER
NIPPERKIN
NIPPERS
NIPPIER
NIPPIEST
NIPPING
NIPPINGLY
NIPPITATE
NIPPITATO
NIPPITATUM
NIPPITATY
NIPPLE
NIPPLED
NIPPLEWORT
NIPPLING
NIPPONIUM
NIPPY
NIPS
NIPTER
NIRIS
NIRLES
NIRLS
NIRMANAKAYA
NIRVANA
NIRVANIC
NIS
NISBERRY
NISHIKI
NISI
NISNAS
NISPERO
NISSE
NISUS
NIT
NITCH
NITCHEVO
NITCHIE
NITE
NITENCY
NITENT
NITER
NITERED
NITERING
NITHER
NITHING
NITID
NITIDOUS
NITO
NITON
NITOR
NITOS
NITRAMIN
NITRAMINE
NITRANILIC
NITRATE
NITRATED
NITRATINE
NITRATING
NITRATION
NITRATOR
NITRE
NITRED
NITRIARIES
NITRIARY
NITRIC
NITRID
NITRIDATION
NITRIDE
NITRIDING
NITRIDIZATION
NITRIDIZE
NITRIFACTION
NITRIFEROUS
NITRIFIABLE
NITRIFICATION
NITRIFIED
NITRIFIER
NITRIFY
NITRIFYING
NITRIL
NITRILE
NITRITE
NITRO
NITROAMINE
NITROANILIN
NITROANILINE
NITROBACTERIA
NITROBARITE
NITROBENZENE
NITROCALCITE
NITROCOTTON
NITROFORM
NITROGELATIN
NITROGELATINE
NITROGEN
NITROGENATE
NITROGENATION
NITROGENIZATION
NITROGENIZE
NITROGENIZED
NITROGENIZING
NITROGENOUS
NITROGLYCERIN
NITROGLYCERINE
NITROLAMINE
NITROLIC
NITROMAGNESITE
NITROMETER
NITROMURIATE
NITROPARAFFIN
NITROPHENOL
NITROPHILOUS
NITROPHYTE
NITROPHYTIC
NITROPRUSSIC
NITROSAMIN
NITROSAMINE
NITROSATE
NITROSIFY
NITROSITE
NITROSTARCH
NITROSULPHATE
NITROSYL
NITROTOLUENE
NITROTOLUOL
NITROUS
NITROXYL
NITRYL
NITTE
NITTER
NITTY
NITWIT
NIVAL
NIVATION
NIVEAU
NIVELLATE
NIVELLATION
NIVELLATOR
NIVELLIZATION
NIVENITE
NIVEOUS
NIVER
NIVERNAISE
NIVICOLOUS
NIVOSITY
NIX
NIXE
NIXEN
NIXES
NIXIE
NIXTAMAL
NIXY
NIYANDA
NIYO
NIYOGA
NIZ
NIZAMAT
NIZAMATE
NIZAMUT
NIZEY
NIZY
NJAVE
NO
NOA
NOANCE
NOB
NOBBER
NOBBIER
NOBBIEST
NOBBLE
NOBBLED
NOBBLER
NOBBLING
NOBBUT
NOBBY
NOBELIUM
NOBILIARY
NOBILITATE
NOBILITIES
NOBILITY
NOBLE
NOBLED
NOBLEHEARTED
NOBLEMAN
NOBLEMANLY
NOBLEMEN
NOBLENESS
NOBLER
NOBLESSE
NOBLEST
NOBLEWOMAN
NOBLEWOMEN
NOBLEY
NOBLIFY
NOBLING
NOBLY
NOBOB
NOBODIES
NOBODY
NOBODYNESS
NOBS
NOBUT
NOCAKE
NOCENCE
NOCENT
NOCERITE
NOCHT
NOCICEPTIVE
NOCICEPTOR
NOCIVE
NOCK
NOCKED
NOCKERL
NOCKET
NOCKING
NOCKTAT
NOCTAMBULANT
NOCTAMBULE
NOCTIDIAL
NOCTIDIURNAL
NOCTILUCA
NOCTILUCAN
NOCTILUCENCE
NOCTILUCENT
NOCTILUCIN
NOCTILUCINE
NOCTILUCOUS
NOCTIMANIA
NOCTIVAGANT
NOCTIVAGATION
NOCTIVAGOUS
NOCTOGRAPH
NOCTOVISION
NOCTUID
NOCTUIDEOUS
NOCTUIDOUS
NOCTUIFORM
NOCTULE
NOCTUOID
NOCTURIA
NOCTURN
NOCTURNAL
NOCTURNALLY
NOCTURNE
NOCUMENT
NOCUOUS
NOCUOUSLY
NOCUOUSNESS
NOD
NODAL
NODALITY
NODALLY
NODATED
NODDED
NODDER
NODDIES
NODDING
NODDLE
NODDLEBONE
NODDLED
NODDLING
NODDY
NODE
NODED
NODIAK
NODICAL
NODICORN
NODIFEROUS
NODIFLOROUS
NODIFORM
NODOSARIAN
NODOSARIFORM
NODOSARINE
NODOSAUR
NODOSE
NODOSITIES
NODOSITY
NODOUS
NODULAR
NODULATE
NODULATED
NODULATION
NODULE
NODULED
NODULES
NODULIZE
NODULIZED
NODULIZING
NODULOSE
NODUS
NOED
NOEGENESIS
NOEGENETIC
NOEL
NOEMATICAL
NOESIS
NOETIC
NOETICS
NOEUD
NOG
NOGADA
NOGAI
NOGAKU
NOGAL
NOGG
NOGGED
NOGGEN
NOGGIN
NOGGING
NOGHEAD
NOGHEADED
NOH
NOHOW
NOI
NOIBWOOD

NOIL
NOILAGE
NOILER
NOILY
NOING
NOINT
NOIO
NOIR
NOISANCE
NOISE
NOISED
NOISEFUL
NOISEFULLY
NOISELESS
NOISELESSLY
NOISELESSNESS
NOISEMAKER
NOISEMAKING
NOISES
NOISETTE
NOISIER
NOISIEST
NOISILY
NOISINESS
NOISING
NOISOME
NOISOMELY
NOISOMENESS
NOISY
NOIT
NOIX
NOKI
NOKIN
NOKTA
NOLA
NOLD
NOLITION
NOLL
NOLLEITY
NOLO
NOM
NOMA
NOMAD
NOMADE
NOMADIAN
NOMADIC
NOMADICAL
NOMADICALLY
NOMADISM
NOMAN
NOMANCY
NOMARCH
NOMARCHIES
NOMARCHY
NOMARTHRAL
NOMBLES
NOMBRIL
NOME
NOMEN
NOMENCLATE
NOMENCLATIVE
NOMENCLATOR
NOMENCLATORIAL
NOMENCLATORY
NOMENCLATURAL
NOMENCLATURE
NOMENCLATURIST
NOMEUS
NOMIAL
NOMIC
NOMINA
NOMINABLE
NOMINAL
NOMINALISM
NOMINALIST
NOMINALISTIC
NOMINALITY
NOMINALLY
NOMINATE
NOMINATED
NOMINATELY
NOMINATING
NOMINATION
NOMINATIVE
NOMINATOR
NOMINATRIX
NOMINATURE
NOMINEE
NOMINEEISM
NOMINY
NOMISM
NOMISMA
NOMISMATA
NOMISTIC
NOMOCANON
NOMOCRACY
NOMOGENIST
NOMOGENOUS
NOMOGENY
NOMOGRAM
NOMOGRAPH
NOMOGRAPHER
NOMOGRAPHIC
NOMOGRAPHICAL
NOMOGRAPHIES
NOMOGRAPHY
NOMOLOGICAL
NOMOLOGIST
NOMOLOGY
NOMOPELMOUS
NOMOPHYLAX
NOMOPHYLLOUS
NOMOS
NOMOTHETE
NOMOTHETES
NOMOTHETIC
NOMOTHETICAL
NON
NONA
NONABILITY
NONABJURER
NONACCESS
NONACOSANE
NONACT
NONADDRESS
NONADDRESSER
NONADECANE
NONADJUSTIVE
NONAGE
NONAGENARIAN
NONAGENARIES
NONAGENARY
NONAGESIMAL
NONAGON
NONAGREEMENT
NONAHYDRATE
NONAMINO
NONAN
NONANE
NONAPPEARANCE
NONARCHING
NONARCKING
NONARY
NONASPIRATE
NONBEING
NONBELIEVER
NONBEVERAGE
NONCALLABLE
NONCASTE
NONCE
NONCERTAIN
NONCHALANCE
NONCHALANT
NONCHALANTLY
NONCHALANTNESS
NONCITIZEN
NONCLAIM
NONCLERICAL
NONCOMBATANT
NONCOMBUSTIBLE
NONCOME
NONCOMMISSIONED
NONCOMMITALLY
NONCOMMITTAL
NONCOMMITTALNESS
NONCOMMUNION
NONCOMMUTATIVE
NONCOMPEARANCE
NONCOMPLIANCE
NONCOMPOS
NONCOMPOSES
NONCOMPOUNDER
NONCON
NONCONDENSING
NONCONDUCTING
NONCONDUCTOR
NONCONFORM
NONCONFORMABLE
NONCONFORMABLY
NONCONFORMER
NONCONFORMING
NONCONFORMISM
NONCONFORMIST
NONCONFORMITY
NONCONTENT
NONCONTINUOUS
NONCONTRADICTION
NONCOOPERATION
NONCURANTIST
NONDA
NONDECIDUATE
NONDENUMERABLE
NONDEPENDENT
NONDESCRIPT
NONDETINET
NONDISCLOSURE
NONDISJUNCT
NONDISJUNCTION
NONDISTINCTIVE
NONDO
NONDUALISM
NONDUMPING
NONE
NONEFFECTIVE
NONEGO
NONELASTIC
NONENE
NONENT
NONENTITIES
NONENTITIVE
NONENTITIZE
NONENTITY
NONENTITYISM
NONENTRES
NONENTRESSE
NONENTRY
NONES
NONESSENTIAL
NONESUCH
NONET
NONETHELESS
NONETTO
NONEXISTENCE
NONEXISTENT
NONFEASANCE
NONFEASOR
NONFERROUS
NONFICTION
NONFICTIONALLY
NONFLAMMABLE
NONGYPSY
NONHARMONIC
NONHEARER
NONIC
NONILLION
NONINCREASING
NONINDUCTIVE
NONINDUCTIVELY
NONINDUCTIVITY
NONINJURY
NONINTRUSION
NONION
NONISOBARIC
NONISSUABLE
NONIUS
NONJOINDER
NONJURANCY
NONJURANT
NONJURANTISM
NONJURING
NONJUROR
NONLEGAL
NONLEGATO
NONLICET
NONMAGNETIC
NONMETAL
NONMETALLIC
NONMODAL
NONMORAL
NONMORALITY
NONNAT
NONNATURAL
NONNATURALISM
NONNATURALITY
NONNATURALS
NONNY
NONOBJECTIVE
NONOBJECTIVITY
NONOIC
NONOPENING
NONPAREIL
NONPAROUS
NONPARTICIPATING
NONPARTISAN
NONPARTIZAN
NONPASSERINE
NONPAYMENT
NONPERMANENT
NONPHENOMENAL
NONPLACET
NONPLANE
NONPLUS
NONPLUSATION
NONPLUSED
NONPLUSING
NONPLUSSATION
NONPLUSSED
NONPLUSSING
NONPOISONOUS
NONPOLAR
NONPOSITIVE
NONPRODUCTIVE
NONPRODUCTIVELY
NONPRODUCTIVENESS
NONPROFESSIONAL
NONPROFIT
NONPROTEIN
NONQUOTA
NONREACTIVE
NONREDUCING
NONREGENT
NONREGULATION
NONRESIDENCE
NONRESIDENCY
NONRESIDENT
NONRESIDENTER
NONRESIDENTIARY
NONRESIDENTOR
NONRESISTANCE
NONRESISTANT
NONRESTRAINT
NONRESTRICTIVE
NONRIGID
NONROTATING
NONSCRIPTURAL
NONSECTARIAN
NONSENSE
NONSENSICAL
NONSENSICALITY
NONSENSICALLY
NONSENSICALNESS
NONSENSIFICATION
NONSENSIFY
NONSENTENCE
NONSEPARATIST
NONSIPHONAGE
NONSKED
NONSKID
NONSKIDDING
NONSPORED
NONSTANDARD
NONSTELLAR
NONSTOP
NONSTRIATED
NONSUBSCRIBER
NONSUBSTANTIALISM
NONSUBSTANTIALIST
NONSUCH
NONSUGAR
NONSUIT
NONSUPPORT
NONSWEARER
NONSWEARING
NONSYLLABIC
NONSYLLABICNESS
NONSYMBIOTIC
NONSYMBIOTICALLY
NONSYNC
NONTENURE
NONTERM
NONTERMINATING
NONTHEMATIC
NONTRONITE
NONUMBILICATE
NONUNIFORM
NONUNIFORMIST
NONUNIFORMLY
NONUNION
NONUNIONISM
NONUNIONIST
NONUPLE
NONUPLET
NONUPLICATE
NONUSER
NONVALENT
NONVIBRATORY
NONVIOLENCE
NONVOLUNTARY
NONVORTICAL
NONVORTICALLY
NONWHITE
NONYA
NONYL
NONYLENE
NONYLIC
NOO
NOODLE
NOOK
NOOKED
NOOKERY
NOOKIER
NOOKIEST
NOOKING
NOOKY
NOOLOGICAL

NOOLOGIST
NOOLOGY
NOOMETRY
NOON
NOONDAY
NOONED
NOONFLOWER
NOONING
NOONLIGHT
NOONLIT
NOONMEAT
NOONSTEAD
NOONTIDE
NOONTIME
NOOP
NOOSCOPIC
NOOSE
NOOSED
NOOSER
NOOSING
NOOT
NOPAL
NOPALRY
NOPE
NOPINENE
NOR
NORATE
NORATION
NORBERGITE
NORCAMPHANE
NORDCAPER
NORDMARKITE
NORGINE
NORI
NORIA
NORICE
NORIE
NORIMON
NORIT
NORITE
NORITO
NORKYN
NORLAND
NORLANDER
NORLANDISM
NORLEUCINE
NORM
NORMA
NORMAL
NORMALCY
NORMALISM
NORMALIST
NORMALITY
NORMALIZATION
NORMALIZE
NORMALIZED
NORMALIZER
NORMALIZING
NORMALLY
NORMALNESS
NORMATED
NORMATIVE
NORMATIVENESS
NORMOCYTE
NORRY
NORSEL
NORSELED
NORSELING
NORSELLED
NORSELLING
NORSH
NORTELRY
NORTH
NORTHBOUND
NORTHEAST
NORTHEASTER
NORTHEASTERLY
NORTHEASTERN
NORTHEASTWARD
NORTHEASTWARDLY
NORTHEASTWARDS
NORTHEN
NORTHER
NORTHERED
NORTHERING
NORTHERLINESS
NORTHERLY
NORTHERN
NORTHERNER
NORTHERNLY
NORTHEST
NORTHING
NORTHLAND
NORTHLANDER
NORTHLIGHT
NORTHMOST
NORTHNESS
NORTHUPITE
NORTHWARD
NORTHWARDLY
NORTHWARDS
NORTHWEST
NORTHWESTER
NORTHWESTERLY
NORTHWESTERN
NORTHWESTWARD
NORTHWESTWARDLY
NORTHWESTWARDS
NORWARD
NORWARDS
NORWESTER
NOSARIAN
NOSE
NOSEAN
NOSEANITE
NOSEBAG
NOSEBAND
NOSEBLEED
NOSEBONE
NOSEBURN
NOSED
NOSEGAY
NOSEHOLE
NOSELITE
NOSEPIECE
NOSEPINCH
NOSER
NOSESMART
NOSETHIRL
NOSETIOLOGY
NOSEWING
NOSEWISE
NOSEWORT
NOSEY
NOSIER
NOSIEST
NOSILY
NOSINE
NOSINESS
NOSING
NOSISM
NOSITE
NOSOCOMIUM
NOSOGENESIS
NOSOGENETIC
NOSOGENIC
NOSOGENY
NOSOGRAPHER
NOSOGRAPHIC
NOSOGRAPHIES
NOSOGRAPHY
NOSOHAEMIA
NOSOHEMIA
NOSOLOGICAL
NOSOLOGICALLY
NOSOLOGIES
NOSOLOGIST
NOSOLOGY
NOSOMANIA
NOSOMYCOSIS
NOSONOMY
NOSOPHOBIA
NOSOPHYTE
NOSOPOETIC
NOSOPOIETIC
NOSOTAXY
NOSOTROPHY
NOSSEL
NOSTALGIA
NOSTALGIC
NOSTIC
NOSTOC
NOSTOCACEOUS
NOSTOLOGY
NOSTOMANIA
NOSTRIFICATE
NOSTRIFICATION
NOSTRIL
NOSTRILED
NOSTRILITY
NOSTRILLED
NOSTRUM
NOSTRUMS
NOSY
NOT
NOTA
NOTABILIA
NOTABILITIES
NOTABILITY
NOTABLE
NOTABLENESS
NOTABLY
NOTACANTHID
NOTACANTHOID
NOTACANTHOUS
NOTAEAL
NOTAEUM
NOTAL
NOTALGIA
NOTALGIC
NOTALIA
NOTAM
NOTAN
NOTANDUDA
NOTANDUM
NOTANDUMS
NOTAR
NOTARIAL
NOTARIALLY
NOTARIATE
NOTARIES
NOTARIKON
NOTARIZATION
NOTARIZE
NOTARIZED
NOTARIZING
NOTARY
NOTATE
NOTATION
NOTATIONAL
NOTATIVE
NOTATOR
NOTAULIX
NOTCH
NOTCHBOARD
NOTCHED
NOTCHEL
NOTCHER
NOTCHES
NOTCHING
NOTCHWEED
NOTCHWING
NOTCHWORT
NOTCHY
NOTE
NOTEBOOK
NOTECASE
NOTED
NOTEDLY
NOTEDNESS
NOTEHEAD
NOTEHOLDER
NOTELESS
NOTELESSLY
NOTELESSNESS
NOTEMAN
NOTEMIGGE
NOTEMUGGE
NOTER
NOTES
NOTEWORTHILY
NOTEWORTHY
NOTHAL
NOTHARCTID
NOTHER
NOTHING
NOTHINGARIAN
NOTHINGISM
NOTHINGIST
NOTHINGIZE
NOTHINGLESS
NOTHINGLY
NOTHINGNESS
NOTHOSAUR
NOTHOSAURIAN
NOTHOUS
NOTICE
NOTICEABILITY
NOTICEABLE
NOTICEABLY
NOTICED
NOTICER
NOTICING
NOTIDANIAN
NOTIFIABLE
NOTIFICATION
NOTIFIED
NOTIFIER
NOTIFY
NOTIFYING
NOTING
NOTION
NOTIONABLE
NOTIONAL
NOTIONALIST
NOTIONALITY
NOTIONALLY
NOTIONALNESS
NOTIONARY
NOTIONATE
NOTIONED
NOTIONIST
NOTIONS
NOTIST
NOTITIA
NOTITION
NOTOCENTRUM
NOTOCHORD
NOTODONTIAN
NOTODONTID
NOTODONTOID
NOTOIRE
NOTONECTID
NOTOPODIAL
NOTOPODIUM
NOTOPTERID
NOTOPTEROID
NOTORHIZAL
NOTORIETIES
NOTORIETY
NOTORIOUS
NOTORIOUSLY
NOTORIOUSNESS
NOTORNIS
NOTOTRIBE
NOTOUNGULATE
NOTOUR
NOTOURLY
NOTSELF
NOTT
NOTUM
NOTUNGULATE
NOTWITHSTANDING
NOUCH
NOUCHE
NOUE
NOUGAT
NOUGATINE
NOUGHT
NOUGHTILY
NOUGHTINESS
NOUGHTLY
NOUGHTY
NOUILLE
NOUILLES
NOUMEA
NOUMEAITE
NOUMEITE
NOUMENAL
NOUMENALISM
NOUMENALIST
NOUMENALITY
NOUMENALLY
NOUMENISM
NOUMENON
NOUMMOS
NOUN
NOUNAL
NOUNALLY
NOUNIZE
NOUNS
NOUP
NOURISH
NOURISHABLE
NOURISHED
NOURISHER
NOURISHING
NOURISHINGLY
NOURISHMENT
NOURITURE
NOUS
NOUTHER
NOUVEAU
NOUVEAUTE
NOUVELLE
NOUVELLES
NOVA
NOVACULITE
NOVAE
NOVALE
NOVALIA
NOVANTIQUE
NOVAS
NOVATE
NOVATIVE
NOVATOR
NOVATORY
NOVATRIX
NOVCIC
NOVEL
NOVELA
NOVELANT
NOVELCRAFT
NOVELET
NOVELETIST

NOVELETTE
NOVELETTER
NOVELISM
NOVELIST
NOVELISTIC
NOVELISTICALLY
NOVELIZATION
NOVELIZE
NOVELIZED
NOVELIZING
NOVELLA
NOVELLAE
NOVELLAS
NOVELLE
NOVELRY
NOVELTIES
NOVELTY
NOVELWRIGHT
NOVENA
NOVENAE
NOVENARY
NOVENDIAL
NOVENE
NOVENNIAL
NOVERCAL
NOVERINT
NOVICE
NOVICEHOOD
NOVICERY
NOVICIATE
NOVILLADA
NOVILLO
NOVILUNAR
NOVITIAL
NOVITIATE
NOVITIATION
NOVITY
NOVOCAIN
NOVOCAINE
NOVODAMUS
NOVUM
NOW
NOWADAYS
NOWANIGHTS
NOWAY
NOWAYS
NOWDER
NOWED
NOWEL
NOWHAT
NOWHEN
NOWHENCE
NOWHERE
NOWHERES
NOWHIT
NOWHITHER
NOWISE
NOWN
NOWNESS
NOWT
NOWTHE
NOWTHER
NOWTHERD
NOWY
NOXA
NOXAE
NOXAL
NOXIAL
NOXIOUS
NOXIOUSLY
NOXIOUSNESS
NOY
NOYADE
NOYADED
NOYADING
NOYANCE
NOYANT
NOYAU
NOYFUL
NOYOUS
NOZZLE
NOZZLER
NRITTA
NTH
NU
NUADU
NUANCE
NUANCED
NUANCES
NUANCING
NUB
NUBBIN
NUBBLE
NUBBLING
NUBBLY
NUBECULA
NUBECULAE
NUBIA
NUBILATE
NUBILATION
NUBILE
NUBILITY
NUBILOSE
NUBILOUS
NUBK
NUCAL
NUCAMENT
NUCELLAR
NUCELLI
NUCELLUS
NUCHA
NUCHAE
NUCHAL
NUCHALE
NUCHALGIA
NUCHE
NUCICULTURE
NUCIFEROUS
NUCIFORM
NUCIN
NUCIVOROUS
NUCK
NUCLEAL
NUCLEAR
NUCLEARY
NUCLEASE
NUCLEATE
NUCLEATED
NUCLEATING
NUCLEATION
NUCLEATOR
NUCLEI
NUCLEIFORM
NUCLEIN
NUCLEINASE
NUCLEOALBUMIN
NUCLEOFUGAL
NUCLEOHISTONE
NUCLEOID
NUCLEOLAR
NUCLEOLATE
NUCLEOLATED
NUCLEOLE
NUCLEOLI
NUCLEOLINI
NUCLEOLINUS
NUCLEOLOID
NUCLEOLUS
NUCLEOLYSIS
NUCLEON
NUCLEONE
NUCLEONIC
NUCLEONICS
NUCLEONS
NUCLEOPLASM
NUCLEOPLASMIC
NUCLEOPROTEIN
NUCLEOSID
NUCLEOSIDE
NUCLEOTIDE
NUCLEUS
NUCLEUSES
NUCULANE
NUCULANIA
NUCULANIUM
NUCULE
NUCULIFORM
NUCULOID
NUD
NUDATE
NUDDLE
NUDE
NUDELY
NUDENESS
NUDGE
NUDGED
NUDGING
NUDIBRANCH
NUDICAUDATE
NUDICAUL
NUDICAULOUS
NUDIFIER
NUDIFLOROUS
NUDIPED
NUDISM
NUDIST
NUDITARIAN
NUDITY
NUDNICK
NUE
NUGACIOUS
NUGACIOUSNESS
NUGACITIES
NUGACITY
NUGAE
NUGAMENT
NUGATOR
NUGATORILY
NUGATORINESS
NUGATORY
NUGGAR
NUGGET
NUGGETY
NUGIFY
NUGILOGUE
NUIK
NUISANCE
NUISANCER
NUISOME
NUIT
NUKE
NUL
NULL
NULLA
NULLABLE
NULLAH
NULLED
NULLIBICITY
NULLIBIETY
NULLIBILITY
NULLIBIQUITOUS
NULLIBIST
NULLIFICATION
NULLIFICATOR
NULLIFIDIAN
NULLIFIED
NULLIFIER
NULLIFY
NULLIFYING
NULLING
NULLIPARA
NULLIPARAE
NULLIPARITY
NULLIPAROUS
NULLIPENNATE
NULLIPLEX
NULLIPORE
NULLIPOROUS
NULLITIES
NULLITY
NULLIVERSE
NULLO
NUMB
NUMBAT
NUMBED
NUMBEDNESS
NUMBER
NUMBERED
NUMBERER
NUMBERFUL
NUMBERING
NUMBERLESS
NUMBEROUS
NUMBERS
NUMBERSOME
NUMBFISH
NUMBFISHES
NUMBING
NUMBINGLY
NUMBLE
NUMBLES
NUMBLY
NUMBNESS
NUMDA
NUMDAH
NUMEN
NUMERABLE
NUMERABLY
NUMERAL
NUMERALLY
NUMERALS
NUMERANT
NUMERARY
NUMERATE
NUMERATED
NUMERATING
NUMERATION
NUMERATIVE
NUMERATOR
NUMERIC
NUMERICAL
NUMERICALLY
NUMERICALNESS
NUMERIST
NUMERO
NUMEROLOGY
NUMEROS
NUMEROSITY
NUMEROUS
NUMEROUSLY
NUMEROUSNESS
NUMINA
NUMINISM
NUMINOUS
NUMINOUSLY
NUMISMATIC
NUMISMATICAL
NUMISMATICALLY
NUMISMATICS
NUMISMATIST
NUMMARY
NUMMIFORM
NUMMULAR
NUMMULARY
NUMMULATION
NUMMULINE
NUMMULITE
NUMMULITIC
NUMMULOIDAL
NUMMUS
NUMNAH
NUMPS
NUMSKULL
NUMSKULLED
NUMSKULLISM
NUN
NUNATAK
NUNATAKS
NUNBIRD
NUNCE
NUNCHEON
NUNCHION
NUNCIATE
NUNCIATIVE
NUNCIATORY
NUNCIATURE
NUNCIO
NUNCIOS
NUNCLE
NUNCUPATE
NUNCUPATION
NUNCUPATIVE
NUNCUPATIVELY
NUNDINAL
NUNDINATION
NUNDINE
NUNKY
NUNLET
NUNNARI
NUNNATION
NUNNED
NUNNERIES
NUNNERY
NUNNI
NUNNIFY
NUNNING
NUNNISH
NUNNISHNESS
NUNRY
NUNTING
NUNTIUS
NUPSON
NUPTIAL
NUPTIALITY
NUPTIALIZE
NUPTIALLY
NUQUE
NUR
NURAGH
NURAGHE
NURL
NURLY
NURRY
NURSE
NURSED
NURSEGIRL
NURSEHOUND
NURSEMAID
NURSER
NURSERIES
NURSERY
NURSERYMAID
NURSERYMAN
NURSERYMEN
NURSETENDER
NURSING
NURSINGLY
NURSLE
NURSLING
NURSY
NURTURAL
NURTURE
NURTURED
NURTURER
NURTURING

NUSFIAH
NUSS
NUSUB
NUT
NUTANT
NUTARIAN
NUTATE
NUTATED
NUTATING
NUTATION
NUTATIONAL
NUTBREAKER
NUTBROWN
NUTCAKE
NUTCRACK
NUTCRACKER
NUTCRACKERS
NUTCRACKERY
NUTGALL
NUTGRASS
NUTHATCH
NUTHOOK
NUTJOBBER
NUTLET
NUTLIKE
NUTMEG
NUTMEGGED
NUTMEGGY
NUTPECKER
NUTPICK
NUTRAMIN
NUTRIA
NUTRICE
NUTRICIAL
NUTRICISM
NUTRIENT
NUTRIFY
NUTRIMENT
NUTRIMENTAL
NUTRITION
NUTRITIONAL
NUTRITIONALLY
NUTRITIONARY
NUTRITIONIST
NUTRITIOUS
NUTRITIOUSLY
NUTRITIVE
NUTRITIVELY
NUTRITIVENESS
NUTRITORY
NUTS
NUTSHELL
NUTTED
NUTTER
NUTTERY
NUTTIER
NUTTIEST
NUTTILY
NUTTINESS
NUTTING
NUTTY
NUTWOOD
NUWAB
NUZZER
NUZZLE
NUZZLED
NUZZLING
NYALA
NYANZA
NYAS
NYASA
NYCE
NYCHTHEMERON
NYCTALOPE
NYCTALOPIA
NYCTALOPIC
NYCTALOPS
NYCTERIBIID
NYCTIPELAGIC
NYCTITROPIC
NYCTITROPISM
NYCTOPHOBIA
NYCTURIA
NYE
NYET
NYLAST
NYLGAU
NYLON
NYMIL
NYMPH
NYMPHA
NYMPHAE
NYMPHAEA
NYMPHAEUM
NYMPHAL
NYMPHALINE
NYMPHEAL
NYMPHEAN
NYMPHET
NYMPHEUM
NYMPHIC
NYMPHICAL
NYMPHID
NYMPHINE
NYMPHITIS
NYMPHLIN
NYMPHOLEPSIA
NYMPHOLEPSY
NYMPHOLEPT
NYMPHOLEPTIC
NYMPHOMANIA
NYMPHOMANIAC
NYMPHOSIS
NYMPHOTOMY
NYMSS
NYSTAGMIC
NYSTAGMUS
NYSTATIN
NYTRIL
NYXIS

O

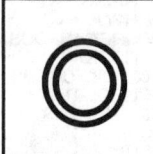

OADAL
OADE
OAF
OAFDOM
OAFISH
OAFISHLY
OAFISHNESS
OAFS
OAK
OAKBERRY
OAKEN
OAKENSHAW
OAKER
OAKMOSS
OAKS
OAKUM
OAKWEB
OAKWOOD
OAKY
OAM
OAR
OARAGE
OARCOCK
OARED
OARFISH
OARFISHES
OARIALGIA
OARING
OARIOCELE
OARIOPATHIC
OARIOPATHY
OARIOTOMY
OARITIC
OARITIS
OARIUM
OARLOCK
OARLOP
OARS
OARSMAN
OARSMANSHIP
OARSMEN
OARSWOMAN
OARSWOMEN
OARWEED
OARY
OASAL
OASEAN
OASES
OASIS
OASITIC
OAST
OASTHOUSE
OASY
OAT
OATCAKE
OATEAR
OATEN
OATENMEAL
OATFOWL
OATH
OATHAY
OATHED
OATHS
OATLAND
OATMEAL
OATS
OATSEED
OATY
OAVES
OB
OBA
OBAMBULATE
OBAMBULATION
OBAMBULATORY
OBAN
OBANG
OBARNE
OBARNI
OBBA
OBBLIGATI
OBBLIGATO
OBBLIGATOS
OBCLAVATE
OBCLUDE
OBCOMPRESSED
OBCONIC
OBCONICAL
OBCORDATE
OBCORDIFORM
OBCUNEATE
OBDELTOID
OBDORMITION
OBDUCTION
OBDURACY
OBDURATE
OBDURATELY
OBDURATENESS
OBDURATION
OBDURE
OBE
OBEAHISM
OBECHE
OBEDIENCE
OBEDIENCY
OBEDIENT
OBEDIENTIAL
OBEDIENTIALLY
OBEDIENTIAR
OBEDIENTIARIES
OBEDIENTIARY
OBEDIENTLY
OBEISANCE
OBEISANT
OBEISANTLY
OBEISH
OBEISM
OBELI
OBELIA
OBELIAC
OBELIAL
OBELION
OBELISCAL
OBELISCAR
OBELISK
OBELISKED
OBELISKING
OBELISKOID
OBELISM
OBELIZE
OBELIZED
OBELIZING
OBELUS
OBESE
OBESELY
OBESENESS
OBESITY
OBEX
OBEY
OBEYED
OBEYER
OBEYING
OBFUSCABLE
OBFUSCATE
OBFUSCATED
OBFUSCATING
OBFUSCATION
OBFUSCATOR
OBFUSCITY
OBFUSCOUS
OBFUSK
OBI
OBIA
OBIAH
OBIISM
OBIIT
OBISPO
OBIT
OBITAL
OBITER
OBITUAL
OBITUARIAN
OBITUARIES
OBITUARIST
OBITUARIZE
OBITUARY
OBJECT
OBJECTABLE
OBJECTATION
OBJECTATIVE
OBJECTED
OBJECTEE
OBJECTIFICATION
OBJECTIFIED
OBJECTIFY
OBJECTIFYING
OBJECTING
OBJECTION
OBJECTIONABILITY
OBJECTIONABLE
OBJECTIONABLY
OBJECTIONAL
OBJECTIONER
OBJECTIONIST
OBJECTIONS
OBJECTIVAL
OBJECTIVATE
OBJECTIVATED
OBJECTIVATING
OBJECTIVATION
OBJECTIVE
OBJECTIVELY
OBJECTIVENESS
OBJECTIVISM
OBJECTIVIST
OBJECTIVISTIC
OBJECTIVITY
OBJECTIVIZE
OBJECTIVIZED
OBJECTIVIZING
OBJECTIZATION
OBJECTIZE
OBJECTIZED
OBJECTIZING
OBJECTLESS
OBJECTOR
OBJECTS
OBJICIENT
OBJURATION
OBJURE
OBJURGATE
OBJURGATED
OBJURGATING
OBJURGATION
OBJURGATIVE
OBJURGATIVELY
OBJURGATOR
OBJURGATORILY
OBJURGATORY
OBJURGATRIX
OBLANCEOLATE
OBLAST
OBLAT
OBLATA
OBLATE
OBLATED
OBLATELY
OBLATENESS
OBLATING
OBLATIO
OBLATION
OBLATIONAL
OBLATIONARY
OBLATORY
OBLECTATE
OBLECTATION
OBLEY
OBLICQUE
OBLIGABLE
OBLIGANCY
OBLIGANT
OBLIGATE
OBLIGATED
OBLIGATING
OBLIGATION
OBLIGATIONAL
OBLIGATIONARY
OBLIGATIVE
OBLIGATIVENESS
OBLIGATO
OBLIGATOR
OBLIGATORILY
OBLIGATORINESS
OBLIGATORY
OBLIGATUM
OBLIGE
OBLIGED
OBLIGEDLY
OBLIGEDNESS
OBLIGEE
OBLIGEMENT
OBLIGER
OBLIGING
OBLIGINGLY
OBLIGINGNESS
OBLIGISTIC
OBLIGOR
OBLIQUATE
OBLIQUATION
OBLIQUE
OBLIQUED
OBLIQUELY
OBLIQUENESS
OBLIQUING
OBLIQUITIES
OBLIQUITOUS
OBLIQUITY
OBLIQUUS
OBLITERABLE
OBLITERATE
OBLITERATED
OBLITERATING
OBLITERATION
OBLITERATIVE
OBLITERATOR
OBLIVESCENCE
OBLIVIAL
OBLIVIALITY
OBLIVION
OBLIVIONATE
OBLIVIONIZE
OBLIVIOUS
OBLIVIOUSLY
OBLIVIOUSNESS
OBLIVISCENCE
OBLIVISCIBLE
OBLOCUTOR
OBLONG
OBLONGATA
OBLONGATAL
OBLONGATED
OBLONGITUDE
OBLONGITUDINAL
OBLONGLY
OBLONGNESS
OBLOQUIAL
OBLOQUIES
OBLOQUIOUS
OBLOQUY
OBMIT
OBMUTESCENCE
OBMUTESCENT
OBNEBULATE
OBNOUNCE
OBNOXIETY
OBNOXIOUS
OBNOXIOUSLY
OBNOXIOUSNESS
OBNUBILATE
OBNUBILATION
OBOE
OBOIST
OBOL
OBOLARY
OBOLE
OBOLI
OBOLOS
OBOLUS
OBOMEGOID
OBOVAL
OBOVATE
OBOVOID
OBPYRAMIDAL
OBPYRIFORM
OBREPTION
OBREPTITIOUS
OBREPTITIOUSLY
OBRIZE
OBROGATE
OBROGATION
OBROK
OBROTUND
OBSCENE
OBSCENELY
OBSCENENESS
OBSCENITIES
OBSCENITY
OBSCURANCY
OBSCURANT
OBSCURANTIC
OBSCURANTISM
OBSCURANTIST
OBSCURATION
OBSCURATIVE
OBSCURE
OBSCURED
OBSCURELY
OBSCUREMENT
OBSCURENESS
OBSCURER
OBSCUREST
OBSCURING
OBSCURITIES
OBSCURITY
OBSECRATE
OBSECRATED
OBSECRATING
OBSECRATION
OBSECRATIONARY
OBSECRATORY
OBSEDE
OBSEQUENCE
OBSEQUENT
OBSEQUIAL
OBSEQUIES
OBSEQUIOUS

OBSEQUIOUSLY
OBSEQUITY
OBSEQUY
OBSERVABILITY
OBSERVABLE
OBSERVABLENESS
OBSERVABLY
OBSERVANCE
OBSERVANDA
OBSERVANDUM
OBSERVANT
OBSERVANTLY
OBSERVANTNESS
OBSERVATION
OBSERVATIONAL
OBSERVATIONALLY
OBSERVATIVE
OBSERVATORIAL
OBSERVATORIES
OBSERVATORY
OBSERVE
OBSERVED
OBSERVER
OBSERVING
OBSERVINGLY
OBSESS
OBSESSED
OBSESSING
OBSESSION
OBSESSIONAL
OBSESSIVE
OBSESSOR
OBSIDE
OBSIDIAN
OBSIDIANITE
OBSIDIONAL
OBSIDIONARY
OBSIDIOUS
OBSIGN
OBSIGNATE
OBSIGNATION
OBSIGNATORY
OBSOLESCE
OBSOLESCED
OBSOLESCENCE
OBSOLESCENT
OBSOLESCENTLY
OBSOLESCING
OBSOLETE
OBSOLETELY
OBSOLETENESS
OBSOLETION
OBSOLETISM
OBSTACLE
OBSTANCY
OBSTANT
OBSTETRIC
OBSTETRICAL
OBSTETRICALLY
OBSTETRICATE
OBSTETRICATED
OBSTETRICATING
OBSTETRICIAN
OBSTETRICS
OBSTETRICY
OBSTETRIST
OBSTETRIX
OBSTINACIES
OBSTINACIOUS
OBSTINACY
OBSTINANCE
OBSTINANCY
OBSTINATE
OBSTINATELY
OBSTINATENESS
OBSTINATION
OBSTINATIVE
OBSTIPANT
OBSTIPATION
OBSTREPERATE
OBSTREPEROUS
OBSTREPEROUSLY
OBSTRICTION
OBSTRINGE
OBSTRUCT
OBSTRUCTANT
OBSTRUCTED
OBSTRUCTER
OBSTRUCTING
OBSTRUCTION
OBSTRUCTIONISM
OBSTRUCTIONIST
OBSTRUCTIVE
OBSTRUCTIVELY
OBSTRUCTIVENESS
OBSTRUCTIVITY
OBSTRUCTOR
OBSTRUENT
OBSTRUSE
OBTAIN
OBTAINABLE
OBTAINAL
OBTAINANCE
OBTAINED
OBTAINER
OBTAINING
OBTAINMENT
OBTECT
OBTECTED
OBTEMPER
OBTEND
OBTENEBRATE
OBTENEBRATION
OBTENT
OBTENTION
OBTEST
OBTESTATION
OBTESTED
OBTESTING
OBTRECT
OBTRIANGULAR
OBTRUDE
OBTRUDED
OBTRUDER
OBTRUDING
OBTRUNCATE
OBTRUNCATION
OBTRUNCATOR
OBTRUSION
OBTRUSIONIST
OBTRUSIVE
OBTRUSIVELY
OBTRUSIVENESS
OBTUND
OBTUNDED
OBTUNDENT
OBTUNDER
OBTUNDING
OBTUNDITY
OBTURATE
OBTURATED
OBTURATING
OBTURATION
OBTURATOR
OBTURATORY
OBTURBINATE
OBTUSE
OBTUSELY
OBTUSENESS
OBTUSER
OBTUSEST
OBTUSIFID
OBTUSILOBOUS
OBTUSION
OBTUSITY
OBUMBRANT
OBUMBRATE
OBUMBRATION
OBUS
OBVALLATE
OBVELATION
OBVENTION
OBVERSE
OBVERSELY
OBVERSION
OBVERT
OBVERTED
OBVERTEND
OBVERTING
OBVIABLE
OBVIATE
OBVIATED
OBVIATING
OBVIATION
OBVIATOR
OBVIOUS
OBVIOUSLY
OBVIOUSNESS
OBVOLUTE
OBVOLUTED
OBVOLUTION
OBVOLUTIVE
OBVOLVE
OBVOLVENT
OC
OCA
OCARINA
OCCAMY
OCCASION
OCCASIONAL
OCCASIONALISM
OCCASIONALIST
OCCASIONALISTIC
OCCASIONALITY
OCCASIONALLY
OCCASIONARY
OCCASIONED
OCCASIONER
OCCASIONING
OCCASIVE
OCCIDENT
OCCIDENTAL
OCCIDENTALITY
OCCIDENTALLY
OCCIPITA
OCCIPITAL
OCCIPITALIS
OCCIPITOOTIC
OCCIPUT
OCCISION
OCCITONE
OCCLUDE
OCCLUDED
OCCLUDENT
OCCLUDING
OCCLUSAL
OCCLUSE
OCCLUSION
OCCLUSIVE
OCCLUSOMETER
OCCLUSOR
OCCULT
OCCULTATE
OCCULTATION
OCCULTED
OCCULTER
OCCULTING
OCCULTISM
OCCULTIST
OCCULTLY
OCCULTNESS
OCCUPANCE
OCCUPANCIES
OCCUPANCY
OCCUPANT
OCCUPATION
OCCUPATIONAL
OCCUPATIONALIST
OCCUPATIONALLY
OCCUPATIVE
OCCUPIED
OCCUPIER
OCCUPY
OCCUPYING
OCCUR
OCCURRED
OCCURRENCE
OCCURRENT
OCCURRING
OCCURSE
OCEAN
OCEANED
OCEANET
OCEANIC
OCEANITY
OCEANOGRAPHER
OCEANOGRAPHIC
OCEANOGRAPHICAL
OCEANOGRAPHICALLY
OCEANOGRAPHIST
OCEANOGRAPHY
OCEANOUS
OCEANSIDE
OCELLANA
OCELLAR
OCELLATE
OCELLATED
OCELLATION
OCELLI
OCELLICYST
OCELLICYSTIC
OCELLIFEROUS
OCELLIFORM
OCELLIGEROUS
OCELLUS
OCELOID
OCELOT
OCELOTS
OCH
OCHAVA
OCHAVO
OCHE
OCHER
OCHERED
OCHERING
OCHERISH
OCHEROUS
OCHERY
OCHIDORE
OCHLESIS
OCHLESITIC
OCHLETIC
OCHLOCRACY
OCHLOCRAT
OCHLOCRATIC
OCHLOCRATICAL
OCHLOMANIA
OCHLOPHOBIA
OCHLOPHOBIST
OCHNACEOUS
OCHONE
OCHRA
OCHRACEOUS
OCHRE
OCHREA
OCHRED
OCHREISH
OCHREOUS
OCHRING
OCHRO
OCHROCARPOUS
OCHROID
OCHROLEUCOUS
OCHROLITE
OCHRONOSIS
OCHRONOTIC
OCHROUS
OCHRY
OCK
OCKER
OCKSTER
OCOTE
OCOTILLO
OCQUE
OCRACY
OCREA
OCREACEOUS
OCREAE
OCREATE
OCREATED
OCTACHLORIDE
OCTACHORD
OCTACHORDAL
OCTACOLIC
OCTACTINAL
OCTACTINE
OCTAD
OCTADECANE
OCTADECYL
OCTADIC
OCTADRACHM
OCTADRACHMA
OCTAECHOS
OCTAEMERA
OCTAEMERON
OCTAETERIC
OCTAETERID
OCTAETERIS
OCTAGON
OCTAGONAL
OCTAGONALLY
OCTAHEDRA
OCTAHEDRAL
OCTAHEDRIC
OCTAHEDRICAL
OCTAHEDRITE
OCTAHEDROID
OCTAHEDRON
OCTAHEDROUS
OCTAHYDRATE
OCTAHYDRATED
OCTAMERISM
OCTAMEROUS
OCTAMETER
OCTAN
OCTANDRIAN
OCTANDRIOUS
OCTANE
OCTANGLE
OCTANGULAR
OCTANGULARNESS
OCTANT
OCTANTAL
OCTAPLA
OCTAPLOID
OCTAPLOIDIC
OCTAPLOIDY
OCTAPODIC
OCTAPODY
OCTARCH
OCTARCHIES
OCTARCHY
OCTARIUS
OCTASEMIC
OCTASTICH

OCTASTICHON
OCTASTROPHIC
OCTASTYLOS
OCTATEUCH
OCTAVAL
OCTAVALENT
OCTAVARIA
OCTAVARIUM
OCTAVE
OCTAVIC
OCTAVINA
OCTAVO
OCTAVOS
OCTENE
OCTENNIAL
OCTENNIALLY
OCTET
OCTETTE
OCTIC
OCTILLION
OCTILLIONTH
OCTINE
OCTOAD
OCTOALLOY
OCTOATE
OCTOBASS
OCTOCOTYLOID
OCTODACTYL
OCTODACTYLE
OCTODE
OCTODECIMAL
OCTODECIMO
OCTODECIMOS
OCTODENTATE
OCTODIANOME
OCTODONT
OCTOECHOS
OCTOFID
OCTOFOIL
OCTOFOILED
OCTOGAMY
OCTOGENARIAN
OCTOGENARIES
OCTOGENARY
OCTOGILD
OCTOGLOT
OCTOGYNIAN
OCTOGYNIOUS
OCTOGYNOUS
OCTOHEDRAL
OCTOIC
OCTOID
OCTOLATERAL
OCTOLOCULAR
OCTOMERAL
OCTOMEROUS
OCTONAL
OCTONARE
OCTONARIAN
OCTONARIES
OCTONARIUS
OCTONARY
OCTONEMATOUS
OCTONION
OCTONOCULAR
OCTOON
OCTOPARTITE
OCTOPEAN
OCTOPED
OCTOPEDE
OCTOPETALOUS
OCTOPHYLLOUS
OCTOPI
OCTOPINE
OCTOPOD
OCTOPODAN
OCTOPODES
OCTOPODOUS
OCTOPOLAR
OCTOPUS
OCTOPUSES
OCTORADIAL
OCTORADIATE
OCTORADIATED
OCTOREME
OCTOROON
OCTOSE
OCTOSEPALOUS
OCTOSPERMOUS
OCTOSPORE
OCTOSPOROUS
OCTOSTICHOUS
OCTOSYLLABIC
OCTOSYLLABLE
OCTOVALENT
OCTOYL
OCTROI
OCTROY
OCTUOR
OCTUPLE
OCTUPLED
OCTUPLET
OCTUPLEX
OCTUPLICATE
OCTUPLICATION
OCTUPLING
OCTUPLY
OCTYL
OCTYLENE
OCTYNE
OCUBY
OCULAR
OCULARIST
OCULARLY
OCULARY
OCULATE
OCULATED
OCULAUDITORY
OCULI
OCULIFEROUS
OCULIFORM
OCULIGEROUS
OCULINID
OCULINOID
OCULIST
OCULISTIC
OCULOFACIAL
OCULOFRONTAL
OCULOMOTOR
OCULOMOTORY
OCULONASAL
OCULOSPINAL
OCULUS
OCYDROME
OCYDROMINE
OCYME
OCYPODAN
OCYPODIAN
OCYPODOID
OD
ODA
ODACOID
ODAL
ODALBORN
ODALISK
ODALISQUE
ODALLER
ODD
ODDBALL
ODDER
ODDEST
ODDITIES
ODDITY
ODDLEGS
ODDLY
ODDMAN
ODDMENT
ODDMENTS
ODDNESS
ODDS
ODDSMAN
ODE
ODEA
ODEL
ODELET
ODEON
ODEUM
ODHAL
ODIBLE
ODIC
ODICALLY
ODINISM
ODINITE
ODIOMETER
ODIOUS
ODIOUSLY
ODIOUSNESS
ODIST
ODIUM
ODLING
ODOGRAPH
ODOLOGY
ODOMETER
ODOMETRICAL
ODOMETRY
ODONTOTRIPSIS
ODONTAGRA
ODONTALGIA
ODONTALGIC
ODONTATROPHY
ODONTEXESIS
ODONTIASIS
ODONTIC
ODONTIST
ODONTITIS
ODONTOBLAST
ODONTOBLASTIC
ODONTOCELE
ODONTOCETE
ODONTOCETOUS
ODONTOCLASIS
ODONTOCLAST
ODONTODYNIA
ODONTOGEN
ODONTOGENESIS
ODONTOGENIC
ODONTOGENY
ODONTOGRAPH
ODONTOGRAPHIC
ODONTOGRAPHY
ODONTOID
ODONTOLCATE
ODONTOLCOUS
ODONTOLITE
ODONTOLITH
ODONTOLOGICAL
ODONTOLOGIST
ODONTOLOGY
ODONTOLOXIA
ODONTOMA
ODONTOMOUS
ODONTOPATHY
ODONTOPHORAL
ODONTOPHORE
ODONTOSCOPE
ODONTOTECHNY
ODOOM
ODOPHONE
ODOR
ODORABLE
ODORANT
ODORATE
ODORATOR
ODORED
ODORIFERANT
ODORIFEROUS
ODORIFEROUSLY
ODORIFIC
ODORIPHOR
ODORIPHORE
ODORIVECTOR
ODORIZE
ODORLESS
ODORLESSLY
ODORLESSNESS
ODOROMETER
ODOROSITY
ODOROUS
ODOROUSLY
ODOROUSNESS
ODORS
ODOUR
ODOURED
ODSO
ODUM
ODYL
ODYLE
ODYLIC
ODYLISM
ODYLIST
ODYLIZATION
ODYLIZE
ODYSSEYS
OE
OECIST
OECODOMIC
OECOID
OECONOMUS
OECOPARASITE
OECOPARASITISM
OECUMENIAN
OECUMENIC
OECUMENICAL
OECUMENICITY
OECUS
OEDEMA
OEDEMERID
OEDICNEMINE
OEILLADE
OEKIST
OELET
OENANTHATE
OENANTHIC
OENANTHYL
OENANTHYLATE
OENIN
OENOCHOAE
OENOCHOE
OENOCYTE
OENOCYTIC
OENOLIN
OENOLOGICAL
OENOLOGIES
OENOLOGIST
OENOLOGY
OENOMANCY
OENOMEL
OENOMETER
OENOPHILIST
OENOPHOBIST
OENOPOETIC
OERSTED
OESOPHAGAL
OESOPHAGEAL
OESOPHAGEAN
OESOPHAGISM
OESOPHAGITIS
OESOPHAGUS
OESTRIAN
OESTRIASIS
OESTRID
OESTRIN
OESTRIOL
OESTROGEN
OESTROID
OESTRONE
OESTROUS
OESTRUAL
OESTRUATE
OESTRUATION
OESTRUM
OESTRUS
OEUVRE
OEUVRES
OF
OFAY
OFF
OFFAL
OFFALING
OFFBEAT
OFFBREAK
OFFCAST
OFFCOME
OFFCUT
OFFED
OFFENCE
OFFENCELESS
OFFENCELESSLY
OFFEND
OFFENDANT
OFFENDED
OFFENDEDLY
OFFENDEDNESS
OFFENDER
OFFENDERS
OFFENDING
OFFENDRESS
OFFENSE
OFFENSELESS
OFFENSELESSLY
OFFENSIBLE
OFFENSIVE
OFFENSIVELY
OFFENSIVENESS
OFFER
OFFERED
OFFERER
OFFERING
OFFERINGS
OFFEROR
OFFERTORIAL
OFFERTORIES
OFFERTORY
OFFGOING
OFFGRADE
OFFHAND
OFFHANDED
OFFHANDEDLY
OFFHANDEDNESS
OFFICARIES
OFFICE
OFFICEHOLDER
OFFICER
OFFICERAGE
OFFICERED
OFFICERESS
OFFICERIAL
OFFICERING
OFFICERS
OFFICIAL
OFFICIALDOM
OFFICIALISM
OFFICIALITIES
OFFICIALITY
OFFICIALIZE

OFFICIALLY
OFFICIANT
OFFICIARY
OFFICIATE
OFFICIATED
OFFICIATING
OFFICIATION
OFFICIATOR
OFFICINA
OFFICINAL
OFFICINALLY
OFFICIOUS
OFFICIOUSLY
OFFICIOUSNESS
OFFING
OFFISH
OFFISHLY
OFFISHNESS
OFFLAP
OFFLET
OFFLOOK
OFFPRINT
OFFSADDLE
OFFSCAPE
OFFSCOUR
OFFSCOURER
OFFSCOURING
OFFSCOURINGS
OFFSCUM
OFFSET
OFFSHOOT
OFFSHORE
OFFSIDE
OFFSIDER
OFFSPRING
OFFTAKE
OFFTYPE
OFFUSCATE
OFFUSCATION
OFFWARD
OFFWARDS
OFICINA
OFLAG
OFLETE
OFT
OFTEN
OFTENNESS
OFTENS
OFTENTIME
OFTENTIMES
OFTHINK
OFTLY
OFTNESS
OFTTIME
OFTTIMES
OFTWHILES
OGAM
OGAMIC
OGDOAD
OGDOAS
OGEE
OGEED
OGGANITION
OGHAM
OGHAMIC
OGIVAL
OGIVE
OGIVED
OGLE
OGLED
OGLER
OGLING
OGLIO
OGRE
OGREISH
OGRESS
OGRISH
OGTIERN
OGUM
OH
OHED
OHELO
OHIA
OHING
OHM
OHMAGE
OHMIC
OHMMETER
OHNE
OHO
OHONE
OIDIA
OIDIOID
OIDIOMYCOSIS
OIDIOMYCOTIC
OII
OIKOLOGY
OIKOMANIA
OIKOPLAST
OIL
OILBERRIES
OILBERRY
OILBIRD
OILCAN
OILCASE
OILCLOTH
OILCOAT
OILDOM
OILED
OILER
OILERY
OILFISH
OILFISHES
OILHOLE
OILIER
OILIEST
OILILY
OILINESS
OILISH
OILLESS
OILLESSNESS
OILLET
OILMAN
OILMEN
OILMONGER
OILMONGERY
OILOMETER
OILPAPER
OILPROOF
OILPROOFING
OILSEED
OILSKIN
OILSKINNED
OILSTOCK
OILSTONE
OILSTONED
OILSTONING
OILSTOVE
OILTIGHT
OILTIGHTNESS
OILWAY
OILWELL
OILY
OIME
OIMEE
OINOCHOE
OINOLOGY
OINOMANCY
OINOMANIA
OINOMEL
OINT
OINTMENT
OISIVITY
OITA
OITAVA
OJO
OK
OKA
OKAPI
OKAPIS
OKAY
OKE
OKEE
OKEH
OKENITE
OKET
OKEYDOKE
OKI
OKIA
OKIE
OKIEH
OKOLEHAO
OKONITE
OKOUME
OKOW
OKRA
OKRO
OKROOG
OKRUG
OKRUZI
OKSHOOFD
OKTHABAH
OLA
OLACACEOUS
OLACAD
OLAM
OLAY
OLD
OLDEN
OLDENED
OLDENING
OLDER
OLDERMOST
OLDERS
OLDEST
OLDFANGLED
OLDFANGLEDNESS
OLDHAMITE
OLDHEARTED
OLDISH
OLDLAND
OLDNESS
OLDS
OLDSTER
OLDWENCH
OLDWIFE
OLDWIVES
OLE
OLEACEOUS
OLEAGINOUS
OLEAGINOUSLY
OLEANA
OLEANDER
OLEANDRIN
OLEASE
OLEASTER
OLEATE
OLECRANAL
OLECRANON
OLEFIANT
OLEFIN
OLEFINE
OLEFINIC
OLEIC
OLEIFEROUS
OLEIN
OLEINE
OLEN
OLENA
OLENELLIDIAN
OLENID
OLENIDIAN
OLENT
OLEO
OLEOCELLOSIS
OLEOCYST
OLEODUCT
OLEOGRAPH
OLEOGRAPHER
OLEOGRAPHIC
OLEOGRAPHY
OLEOMARGARIN
OLEOMARGARINE
OLEOMETER
OLEOPTENE
OLEORESIN
OLEORESINOUS
OLEOSE
OLEOSITY
OLEOSTEARATE
OLEOSTEARIN
OLEOSTEARINE
OLEOTHORAX
OLEOUS
OLEPI
OLEPY
OLER
OLERACEOUS
OLERICULTURE
OLETHREUTID
OLEUM
OLFACT
OLFACTABLE
OLFACTIBLE
OLFACTION
OLFACTOLOGY
OLFACTOMETER
OLFACTOMETRIC
OLFACTOMETRY
OLFACTOR
OLFACTORIES
OLFACTORILY
OLFACTORY
OLFACTY
OLIBAN
OLIBANUM
OLID
OLIGAEMIA
OLIGANDROUS
OLIGANTHOUS
OLIGARCH
OLIGARCHAL
OLIGARCHIC
OLIGARCHICAL
OLIGARCHIES
OLIGARCHISM
OLIGARCHIST
OLIGARCHIZE
OLIGARCHY
OLIGEMIA
OLIGIDRIA
OLIGIST
OLIGISTIC
OLIGISTICAL
OLIGOCARPOUS
OLIGOCHAETE
OLIGOCHETE
OLIGOCHOLIA
OLIGOCHROME
OLIGOCHYLIA
OLIGOCLASE
OLIGOCLASITE
OLIGOCYSTIC
OLIGODIPSIA
OLIGODONTOUS
OLIGODYNAMIC
OLIGOHEMIA
OLIGOLACTIA
OLIGOMEROUS
OLIGOMERY
OLIGOMYODIAN
OLIGOMYOID
OLIGONEPHRIC
OLIGONITE
OLIGOPEPSIA
OLIGOPHAGOUS
OLIGOPHRENIA
OLIGOPHRENIC
OLIGOPLASMIA
OLIGOPNEA
OLIGOPOLIST
OLIGOPOLY
OLIGOPSYCHIA
OLIGOPYRENE
OLIGORHIZOUS
OLIGOSIALIA
OLIGOSITE
OLIGOSPERMIA
OLIGOTOKEUS
OLIGOTRICHIA
OLIGOTROPHIC
OLIGOTROPHY
OLIGURESIA
OLIGURESIS
OLIGURETIC
OLIGURIA
OLIO
OLIOS
OLIPHANT
OLIPRANCE
OLITORY
OLIVA
OLIVACEOUS
OLIVARY
OLIVASTER
OLIVE
OLIVED
OLIVENESS
OLIVENITE
OLIVERMAN
OLIVERMEN
OLIVERSMITH
OLIVES
OLIVESCENT
OLIVET
OLIVETTE
OLIVEWOOD
OLIVIFEROUS
OLIVIFORM
OLIVIL
OLIVILE
OLIVILIN
OLIVINE
OLIVINEFELS
OLIVINIC
OLIVINITE
OLIVINITIC
OLLA
OLLAE
OLLAMH
OLLAPOD
OLLAV
OLLENITE
OLLOCK
OLLUCK
OLM
OLOGICAL
OLOGIST
OLOGISTIC
OLOGY
OLOMAO
OLONA
OLOROSO
OLP
OLPAE

OLPE
OLPH
OLTONDE
OLTUNNA
OLYCOOK
OLYKOEK
OM
OMADAWN
OMADHAUN
OMAGRA
OMALGIA
OMAO
OMARTHRITIS
OMASA
OMASUM
OMBER
OMBRE
OMBRETTE
OMBRIFUGE
OMBROGRAPH
OMBROLOGICAL
OMBROLOGY
OMBROMETER
OMBROPHIL
OMBROPHILE
OMBROPHILIC
OMBROPHILOUS
OMBROPHILY
OMBROPHOBE
OMBROPHOBOUS
OMBROPHOBY
OMBROPHYTE
OMBUDSMAN
OMBUDSMEN
OMDA
OMDEH
OMEGA
OMEGOID
OMEL
OMELET
OMELETTE
OMELIE
OMEN
OMENED
OMENOLOGY
OMENTA
OMENTAL
OMENTECTOMY
OMENTITIS
OMENTOCELE
OMENTOPEXY
OMENTOPLASTY
OMENTOTOMY
OMENTULUM
OMENTUM
OMER
OMICRON
OMIKRON
OMINATE
OMINOUS
OMINOUSLY
OMINOUSNESS
OMISSIBLE
OMISSION
OMISSIVE
OMISSIVELY
OMIT
OMITIS
OMITTED
OMITTER
OMITTING
OMLAH
OMMATEA
OMMATEAL
OMMATEUM
OMMATIDIA
OMMATIDIAL
OMMATIDIUM
OMMATOPHORE
OMNEITY
OMNES
OMNIACTIVE
OMNIANA
OMNIARCH
OMNIBUS
OMNIBUSES
OMNIBUSMAN
OMNIERUDITE
OMNIESSENCE
OMNIFACIAL
OMNIFARIOUS
OMNIFEROUS
OMNIFIC
OMNIFICENT
OMNIFIDEL
OMNIFIED
OMNIFORM
OMNIFORMAL
OMNIFORMITY
OMNIFY
OMNIFYING
OMNIGENOUS
OMNIGERENT
OMNIGRAPH
OMNIHUMAN
OMNIHUMANITY
OMNILEGENT
OMNILINGUAL
OMNILOQUENT
OMNILUCENT
OMNIMENTAL
OMNIMETER
OMNIMODE
OMNIMODOUS
OMNINESCIENT
OMNIPARENT
OMNIPARIENT
OMNIPARITY
OMNIPAROUS
OMNIPATIENT
OMNIPERFECT
OMNIPOTENCE
OMNIPOTENCY
OMNIPOTENT
OMNIPOTENTLY
OMNIPRESENCE
OMNIPRESENT
OMNIPRUDENCE
OMNIPRUDENT
OMNIRANGE
OMNIREGENCY
OMNIREGENT
OMNISCIENCE
OMNISCIENCY
OMNISCIENT
OMNISCIENTLY
OMNISCOPE
OMNISCRIBENT
OMNISENTIENT
OMNISPECTIVE
OMNIST
OMNITEMPORAL
OMNITENENT
OMNITOLERANT
OMNITONAL
OMNITONALITY
OMNITONIC
OMNITUDE
OMNIUM
OMNIVAGANT
OMNIVALENCE
OMNIVALENT
OMNIVALOUS
OMNIVARIOUS
OMNIVIDENCE
OMNIVIDENT
OMNIVISION
OMNIVOLENT
OMNIVORACITY
OMNIVORE
OMNIVOROUS
OMNIVOROUSLY
OMODYNIA
OMOHYOID
OMOIDEUM
OMOPHAGIA
OMOPHAGIC
OMOPHAGIST
OMOPHAGOUS
OMOPHAGY
OMOPHORIA
OMOPHORION
OMOPLATE
OMOSTEGITE
OMOSTERNAL
OMOSTERNUM
OMPHACINE
OMPHACITE
OMPHACY
OMPHALECTOMY
OMPHALI
OMPHALIC
OMPHALISM
OMPHALITIS
OMPHALOCELE
OMPHALODE
OMPHALODIA
OMPHALODIUM
OMPHALOID
OMPHALOMA
OMPHALONCUS
OMPHALORRHEA
OMPHALOS
OMPHALOSITE
OMPHALOTOMY
OMPHALUS
OMRAH
ON
ONA
ONAGER
ONAGERS
ONAGRA
ONAGRACEOUS
ONAGRI
ONANISM
ONANIST
ONANISTIC
ONCA
ONCE
ONCET
ONCETTA
ONCIA
ONCIN
ONCOGRAPH
ONCOGRAPHY
ONCOLOGIC
ONCOLOGICAL
ONCOLOGY
ONCOME
ONCOMETER
ONCOMETRIC
ONCOMETRY
ONCOMING
ONCOSIMETER
ONCOSIS
ONCOSPHERE
ONCOST
ONCOSTMAN
ONCOTOMY
ONDAGRAM
ONDAGRAPH
ONDAMETER
ONDASCOPE
ONDATRA
ONDE
ONDINE
ONDOGRAM
ONDOGRAPH
ONDOMETER
ONDOSCOPE
ONDOYANT
ONDULE
ONE
ONEBERRY
ONEFOLD
ONEFOLDNESS
ONEGITE
ONEHOOD
ONEHOW
ONEIRIC
ONEIROCRITIC
ONEIROCRITICS
ONEIRODYNIA
ONEIROLOGIST
ONEIROLOGY
ONEIROMANCER
ONEIROMANCY
ONEIROSCOPIC
ONEIROSCOPY
ONEIROTIC
ONEISM
ONEMENT
ONENESS
ONER
ONERARY
ONERATE
ONERATIVE
ONEROSE
ONEROSITY
ONEROUS
ONEROUSLY
ONEROUSNESS
ONERY
ONESELF
ONETHE
ONETIME
ONEWHERE
ONEYER
ONFALL
ONFLEMED
ONFLOW
ONFLOWING
ONGARO
ONGLE
ONGOING
ONHANGER
ONI
ONIOMANIA
ONIOMANIAC
ONION
ONIONET
ONIONIZED
ONIONPEEL
ONIONS
ONIONSKIN
ONIONY
ONIROTIC
ONISCIFORM
ONISCOID
ONISCOIDEAN
ONKILONITE
ONKOS
ONLAP
ONLAY
ONLEPY
ONLESS
ONLINESS
ONLOOK
ONLOOKER
ONLOOKING
ONLY
ONMARCH
ONOCENTAUR
ONOCROTAL
ONOFRITE
ONOLATRY
ONOMANCY
ONOMASTIC
ONOMASTICAL
ONOMASTICON
ONOMASTICS
ONOMATOLOGY
ONOMATOPE
ONOMATOPLASM
ONOMATOPOEIA
ONOMATOPOEIC
ONOMATOPOESY
ONOMATOPY
ONOMATOUS
ONON
ONOTOGENIC
ONRUSH
ONRUSHING
ONS
ONSET
ONSETTER
ONSHORE
ONSIDE
ONSIGHT
ONSLAUGHT
ONSTAND
ONSTANDING
ONSTEAD
ONSWEEP
ONSWEEPING
ONTAL
ONTIC
ONTO
ONTOCYCLE
ONTOCYCLIC
ONTOGENAL
ONTOGENESIS
ONTOGENETIC
ONTOGENIST
ONTOGENY
ONTOGRAPHY
ONTOLOGIC
ONTOLOGICAL
ONTOLOGICALLY
ONTOLOGIES
ONTOLOGISM
ONTOLOGIST
ONTOLOGISTIC
ONTOLOGIZE
ONTOLOGY
ONUS
ONWAITING
ONWARD
ONWARDLY
ONWARDNESS
ONWARDS
ONY
ONYCHA
ONYCHAUXIS
ONYCHIA
ONYCHIN
ONYCHITE
ONYCHITIS
ONYCHIUM
ONYCHOID
ONYCHOLYSIS
ONYCHOPATHIC
ONYCHOPATHY
ONYCHOPHAGIA
ONYCHOPHAGY

ONYCHOPHORAN
ONYCHOPHYMA
ONYCHOPTOSIS
ONYCHOSIS
ONYCHOTROPHY
ONYM
ONYMAL
ONYMATIC
ONYMITY
ONYMIZE
ONYMOUS
ONYMY
ONYX
ONYXES
ONYXIS
ONZA
OO
OOANGIUM
OOBLAST
OOBLASTIC
OOCYESIS
OOCYST
OOCYSTACEOUS
OOCYSTIC
OOCYTE
OODLES
OODLINS
OOECIA
OOECIAL
OOECIUM
OOF
OOFBIRD
OOFIER
OOFIEST
OOFTISH
OOFY
OOGAMETE
OOGAMOUS
OOGAMY
OOGENESIS
OOGENETIC
OOGENY
OOGLEA
OOGLOEA
OOGONE
OOGONIA
OOGONIAL
OOGONIOPHORE
OOGONIUM
OOGONIUMS
OOGRAPH
OOID
OOIDAL
OOK
OOKINESIS
OOKINETE
OOKINETIC
OOLACHAN
OOLAK
OOLEMMA
OOLITE
OOLITIC
OOLLIES
OOLLY
OOLOGIC
OOLOGICAL
OOLOGICALLY
OOLOGIST
OOLOGIZE
OOLOGY
OOLONG
OOM
OOMANCY
OOMANTIA
OOMETER
OOMETRIC
OOMETRY
OOMIAC
OOMIAK
OOMPAH
OOMPH
OOMYCETE
OOMYCETES
OOMYCETOUS
OON
OONS
OONT
OOP
OOPACK
OOPAK
OOPHORALGIA
OOPHORAUXE
OOPHORE
OOPHORECTOMY
OOPHORIC
OOPHORIDIA
OOPHORIDIUM
OOPHORIDIUMS
OOPHORITIS
OOPHOROCELE
OOPHOROMA
OOPHOROMANIA
OOPHORON
OOPHOROPEXY
OOPHOROSTOMY
OOPHOROTOMY
OOPHYTE
OOPHYTIC
OOPLASM
OOPLASMIC
OOPLAST
OOPOD
OOPODAL
OOPORPHYRIN
OOPUHUE
OORALI
OORD
OORIAL
OORIE
OOSCOPE
OOSCOPY
OOSPERM
OOSPHERE
OOSPORANGIA
OOSPORANGIUM
OOSPORE
OOSPORIC
OOSPOROUS
OOSTEGITE
OOSTEGITIC
OOT
OOTHECA
OOTHECAL
OOTID
OOTOCOID
OOTOCOIDEAN
OOTOCOUS
OOTWITH
OOTYPE
OOZE
OOZED
OOZEL
OOZIER
OOZIEST
OOZILY
OOZINESS
OOZING
OOZOID
OOZY
OPACATE
OPACIFIER
OPACIFY
OPACITE
OPACITIES
OPACITY
OPACOUS
OPACOUSNESS
OPAH
OPAL
OPALED
OPALESCE
OPALESCED
OPALESCENCE
OPALESCENT
OPALESCING
OPALEYE
OPALINE
OPALINID
OPALININE
OPALIZE
OPALIZED
OPALIZING
OPALOID
OPAQUE
OPAQUED
OPAQUELY
OPAQUENESS
OPAQUING
OPDALITE
OPE
OPED
OPEIDOSCOPE
OPELET
OPELU
OPEN
OPENBAND
OPENBEAK
OPENBILL
OPENCAST
OPENCUT
OPENED
OPENER
OPENEST
OPENHANDED
OPENHANDEDLY
OPENHEAD
OPENHEARTED
OPENHEARTEDLY
OPENING
OPENINGS
OPENLY
OPENMOUTHED
OPENNESS
OPENSIDE
OPENWORK
OPERA
OPERABILITY
OPERABLE
OPERABLY
OPERAGOER
OPERALOGUE
OPERAMETER
OPERANCE
OPERANCY
OPERAND
OPERANT
OPERARY
OPERAS
OPERATABLE
OPERATE
OPERATED
OPERATEE
OPERATIC
OPERATICAL
OPERATICALLY
OPERATING
OPERATION
OPERATIONAL
OPERATIONS
OPERATIVE
OPERATIVELY
OPERATIVENESS
OPERATIVITY
OPERATIZE
OPERATOR
OPERATORY
OPERATRICES
OPERATRIX
OPERCELE
OPERCLE
OPERCLED
OPERCULA
OPERCULAR
OPERCULATE
OPERCULATED
OPERCULE
OPERCULIFORM
OPERCULUM
OPERETTIST
OPERETTA
OPERETTAS
OPERETTE
OPEROSE
OPEROSELY
OPEROSENESS
OPHELIMITY
OPHIASIS
OPHIC
OPHICALCITE
OPHICHTHYOID
OPHICLEIDE
OPHICLEIDEAN
OPHICLEIDIST
OPHIDIAN
OPHIDIOID
OPHIDIOMANIA
OPHIDIOUS
OPHIOGRAPHY
OPHIOID
OPHIOLATER
OPHIOLATROUS
OPHIOLATRY
OPHIOLITE
OPHIOLITIC
OPHIOLOGIC
OPHIOLOGICAL
OPHIOLOGIST
OPHIOLOGY
OPHIOMANCY
OPHIOMORPHIC
OPHIONID
OPHIONINE
OPHIOPHAGOUS
OPHIOPHILISM
OPHIOPHILIST
OPHIOPHOBE
OPHIOPHOBIA
OPHIOPHOBY
OPHIOPLUTEUS
OPHIOURIDE
OPHITE
OPHITIC
OPHIURAN
OPHIURID
OPHIUROID
OPHIUROIDEAN
OPHRYON
OPHTHALMAGRA
OPHTHALMIA
OPHTHALMIAC
OPHTHALMIATER
OPHTHALMIC
OPHTHALMIOUS
OPHTHALMIST
OPHTHALMITE
OPHTHALMITIC
OPHTHALMITIS
OPHTHALMOPOD
OPHTHALMY
OPIANE
OPIANIC
OPIANYL
OPIATE
OPIATED
OPIATIC
OPIATING
OPIE
OPIFEX
OPIFICE
OPIFICER
OPIHI
OPIISM
OPILIACEOUS
OPIME
OPINABILITY
OPINABLE
OPINABLY
OPINANT
OPINATIVE
OPINATIVELY
OPINATOR
OPINE
OPINED
OPINER
OPING
OPINIATE
OPINIATED
OPINIATEDLY
OPINIATER
OPINIATIVE
OPINIATIVELY
OPINIATRE
OPINIATRETY
OPINICUS
OPINING
OPINION
OPINIONABLE
OPINIONAL
OPINIONATE
OPINIONATED
OPINIONATEDLY
OPINIONATELY
OPINIONATIVE
OPINIONED
OPINIONIST
OPINIONS
OPIOMANIA
OPIOMANIAC
OPIOPHAGISM
OPIOPHAGY
OPISOMETER
OPISTHENAR
OPISTHION
OPISTHOCOME
OPISTHODETIC
OPISTHODOME
OPISTHODONT
OPISTHOGRAPH
OPISTHOSOMAL
OPISTHOTIC
OPISTHOTONIC
OPISTHOTONOS
OPIUM
OPIUMISM
OPOBALSAM
OPOBALSAMUM
OPODELDOC
OPODIDYMUS
OPOPANAX
OPOSSUM
OPOSSUMS
OPPIDA
OPPIDAN
OPPIDUM
OPPIGNERATE

OPPIGNORATE
OPPILANT
OPPILATE
OPPILATED
OPPILATING
OPPILATION
OPPILATIVE
OPPLETE
OPPLETION
OPPO
OPPONENCY
OPPONENS
OPPONENT
OPPORTUNE
OPPORTUNELY
OPPORTUNISM
OPPORTUNIST
OPPORTUNISTIC
OPPORTUNITIES
OPPORTUNITY
OPPOSABILITY
OPPOSABLE
OPPOSAL
OPPOSE
OPPOSED
OPPOSELESS
OPPOSER
OPPOSING
OPPOSINGLY
OPPOSIT
OPPOSITE
OPPOSITELY
OPPOSITENESS
OPPOSITION
OPPOSITIONAL
OPPOSITIOUS
OPPOSITIVE
OPPOSITIVELY
OPPOSURE
OPPRESS
OPPRESSED
OPPRESSING
OPPRESSION
OPPRESSIVE
OPPRESSIVELY
OPPRESSIVENESS
OPPRESSOR
OPPROBRIATE
OPPROBRIOUS
OPPROBRIUM
OPPROBRY
OPPUGN
OPPUGNACY
OPPUGNANCE
OPPUGNANCY
OPPUGNANT
OPPUGNATE
OPPUGNATION
OPPUGNED
OPPUGNER
OPPUGNING
OPSIGAMY
OPSIMATH
OPSIMATHY
OPSISFORM
OPSISTYPE
OPSONIA
OPSONIC
OPSONIFEROUS
OPSONIFIED
OPSONIFY
OPSONIFYING
OPSONIN
OPSONIST
OPSONIUM
OPSONIZATION
OPSONIZE
OPSONOGEN
OPSONOID
OPSONOMETRY
OPSONOPHILIA
OPSONOPHILIC
OPSONOPHORIC
OPSONOTHERAPY
OPT
OPTABLE
OPTABLENESS
OPTABLY
OPTANT
OPTATE
OPTATION
OPTATIVE
OPTATIVELY
OPTED
OPTIC
OPTICAL
OPTICALLY
OPTICIAN
OPTICIST
OPTICITY
OPTICS
OPTIGRAPH
OPTIMA
OPTIMACY
OPTIMAL
OPTIMATE
OPTIMATES
OPTIME
OPTIMISM
OPTIMIST
OPTIMISTIC
OPTIMISTICAL
OPTIMISTICALLY
OPTIMITY
OPTIMIZATION
OPTIMIZE
OPTIMIZED
OPTIMIZING
OPTIMUM
OPTIMUMS
OPTING
OPTION
OPTIONAL
OPTIONALITY
OPTIONALIZE
OPTIONALLY
OPTIONARY
OPTIONEE
OPTIONOR
OPTIVE
OPTOBLAST
OPTOGRAM
OPTOGRAPHY
OPTOLOGICAL
OPTOLOGIST
OPTOLOGY
OPTOMENINX
OPTOMETER
OPTOMETRICAL
OPTOMETRIST
OPTOMETRY
OPTOPHONE
OPTOTYPE
OPULENCE
OPULENCY
OPULENT
OPULENTLY
OPULUS
OPUNTIA
OPUNTIOID
OPUS
OPUSCLE
OPUSCULAR
OPUSCULE
OPUSCULUM
OQUASSA
OQUE
OQUI
OR
ORA
ORABASSU
ORACH
ORACHE
ORACLE
ORACLER
ORACULA
ORACULAR
ORACULARITY
ORACULARLY
ORACULARNESS
ORACULATE
ORACULOUS
ORACULOUSLY
ORACULOUSNESS
ORACULUM
ORAD
ORAGE
ORAGIOUS
ORAL
ORALE
ORALER
ORALISM
ORALIST
ORALITY
ORALLY
ORALOGIST
ORALOGY
ORANG
ORANGE
ORANGEADE
ORANGEADO
ORANGEAT
ORANGEBERRIES
ORANGEBERRY
ORANGEBIRD
ORANGELEAF
ORANGER
ORANGEROOT
ORANGERY
ORANGEWOMAN
ORANGEWOOD
ORANGEY
ORANGIST
ORANGITE
ORANGIZE
ORANGOUTANG
ORANGUTAN
ORANS
ORANT
ORANTE
ORANTES
ORARIA
ORARIAN
ORARION
ORARY
ORAS
ORATE
ORATED
ORATING
ORATION
ORATIONAL
ORATIONER
ORATOR
ORATORIAL
ORATORIALLY
ORATORIAN
ORATORIC
ORATORICAL
ORATORICALLY
ORATORIES
ORATORIO
ORATORIOS
ORATORIZE
ORATORY
ORATRESS
ORATRICES
ORATRIX
ORB
ORBAL
ORBATE
ORBED
ORBELL
ORBIC
ORBICAL
ORBICLE
ORBICULAR
ORBICULARIS
ORBICULARITY
ORBICULARLY
ORBICULATE
ORBICULATED
ORBICULATELY
ORBICULATION
ORBIFIC
ORBING
ORBIT
ORBITAL
ORBITALE
ORBITAR
ORBITARY
ORBITE
ORBITELAR
ORBITELARIAN
ORBITELE
ORBITELOUS
ORBITER
ORBITOLITE
ORBITOMALAR
ORBITONASAL
ORBITOSTAT
ORBITOTOMY
ORBITUDE
ORBITY
ORBY
ORC
ORCANET
ORCANETTE
ORCEIN
ORCHAMUS
ORCHANET
ORCHARD
ORCHARDING
ORCHARDIST
ORCHARDMAN
ORCHARDMEN
ORCHEITIS
ORCHEN
ORCHESIS
ORCHESTIAN
ORCHESTIC
ORCHESTIID
ORCHESTRA
ORCHESTRAL
ORCHESTRALLY
ORCHESTRATE
ORCHESTRATED
ORCHESTRATER
ORCHESTRATING
ORCHESTRATION
ORCHESTRATOR
ORCHESTRIC
ORCHESTRION
ORCHIALGIA
ORCHIC
ORCHICHOREA
ORCHID
ORCHIDACEAN
ORCHIDACEOUS
ORCHIDALGIA
ORCHIDECTOMY
ORCHIDIST
ORCHIDITIS
ORCHIDOCELE
ORCHIDOLOGIST
ORCHIDOLOGY
ORCHIDOPEXY
ORCHIDOTOMY
ORCHIDS
ORCHIECTOMY
ORCHIL
ORCHILLA
ORCHILYTIC
ORCHIOCELE
ORCHIODYNIA
ORCHIONCUS
ORCHIOPEXY
ORCHIOPLASTY
ORCHIOTOMY
ORCHIS
ORCHISES
ORCHITIC
ORCHITIS
ORCHOTOMY
ORCIN
ORCINE
ORCINOL
ORDAIN
ORDAINABLE
ORDAINED
ORDAINER
ORDAINING
ORDAINMENT
ORDALIAN
ORDALIUM
ORDANCHITE
ORDEAL
ORDENE
ORDER
ORDERABLE
ORDERED
ORDEREDNESS
ORDERER
ORDERING
ORDERLESS
ORDERLIES
ORDERLINESS
ORDERLY
ORDERS
ORDINABILITY
ORDINABLE
ORDINAL
ORDINANCE
ORDINAND
ORDINANT
ORDINAR
ORDINARIES
ORDINARILY
ORDINARINESS
ORDINARY
ORDINATE
ORDINATED
ORDINATING
ORDINATION
ORDINATIVE
ORDINATOR
ORDINEE
ORDINES
ORDNANCE
ORDO
ORDONNANCE
ORDONNANT
ORDOS
ORDOSITE
ORDU
ORDURE

ORDUROUS
ORE
OREAD
ORECCHION
ORECTIC
ORECTIVE
OREGANO
OREIDE
OREILET
OREILLER
OREILLETTE
OREJON
ORELLIN
OREMUS
ORENDA
ORENDITE
OREOPHASINE
OREOPITHECUS
OREOTRAGINE
ORES
OREWEED
OREWOOD
OREXIS
ORF
ORFE
ORFEVRERIE
ORFGILD
ORFRAY
ORGAMENT
ORGAMY
ORGAN
ORGANA
ORGANAL
ORGANBIRD
ORGANDIE
ORGANDIES
ORGANDY
ORGANELLA
ORGANELLAE
ORGANELLE
ORGANER
ORGANETTE
ORGANIC
ORGANICAL
ORGANICALLY
ORGANICISM
ORGANICISMAL
ORGANICIST
ORGANICISTIC
ORGANICITY
ORGANIFIC
ORGANIFIER
ORGANIFY
ORGANING
ORGANISATION
ORGANISE
ORGANISM
ORGANISMAL
ORGANISMIC
ORGANISMS
ORGANIST
ORGANISTIC
ORGANISTRUM
ORGANITY
ORGANIZABLE
ORGANIZATION
ORGANIZATIONAL
ORGANIZATORY
ORGANIZE
ORGANIZED
ORGANIZER
ORGANIZING
ORGANOGEL
ORGANOGEN
ORGANOGENIC
ORGANOGENIST
ORGANOGENY
ORGANOGRAPHY
ORGANOID
ORGANOLEPTIC
ORGANOLOGIC
ORGANOLOGIST
ORGANOLOGY
ORGANON
ORGANONOMIC
ORGANONOMY
ORGANONS
ORGANONYMAL
ORGANONYMIC
ORGANONYMY
ORGANONYN
ORGANOPATHY
ORGANOPHONE
ORGANOPHONIC
ORGANOPHYLY
ORGANOSCOPY
ORGANOSOL
ORGANOTROPY
ORGANRY
ORGANULE
ORGANUM
ORGANUMS
ORGANY
ORGANZA
ORGANZINE
ORGANZINED
ORGANZINING
ORGASM
ORGASMIC
ORGASTIC
ORGEAT
ORGIA
ORGIAC
ORGIACS
ORGIASM
ORGIAST
ORGIASTIC
ORGIASTICAL
ORGIC
ORGIES
ORGONE
ORGUE
ORGUEIL
ORGUIL
ORGUINETTE
ORGUL
ORGULOUS
ORGULOUSLY
ORGY
ORGYIA
ORHAMWOOD
ORIBATID
ORIBI
ORIBIS
ORICHALC
ORICHALCEOUS
ORICHALCH
ORICHALCUM
ORIEL
ORIENCY
ORIENT
ORIENTAL
ORIENTALISM
ORIENTALIST
ORIENTALITY
ORIENTALIZE
ORIENTALIZED
ORIENTALIZING
ORIENTALLY
ORIENTATE
ORIENTATED
ORIENTATING
ORIENTATION
ORIENTATIVE
ORIENTATOR
ORIENTED
ORIENTING
ORIENTITE
ORIENTIZE
ORIENTNESS
ORIFACIAL
ORIFICE
ORIFICIAL
ORIFLAMB
ORIFLAMME
ORIFORM
ORIGAMI
ORIGAN
ORIGANIZED
ORIGIN
ORIGINABLE
ORIGINAL
ORIGINALIST
ORIGINALITIES
ORIGINALITY
ORIGINALLY
ORIGINANT
ORIGINARILY
ORIGINARY
ORIGINATE
ORIGINATED
ORIGINATING
ORIGINATION
ORIGINATIVE
ORIGINATIVELY
ORIGINATOR
ORIGINATRESS
ORIGINES
ORIGINIST
ORIGNAL
ORIHON
ORILLON
ORINASAL
ORINASALITY
ORIOLE
ORISHA
ORISMOLOGIC
ORISMOLOGY
ORISON
ORISTIC
ORKEY
ORKYN
ORLAGE
ORLE
ORLEAN
ORLET
ORLO
ORLOP
ORMER
ORMOLU
ORMUZINE
ORN
ORNA
ORNAMENT
ORNAMENTAL
ORNAMENTALLY
ORNAMENTARY
ORNAMENTATION
ORNAMENTED
ORNAMENTER
ORNAMENTING
ORNAMENTIST
ORNAMENTS
ORNARY
ORNATE
ORNATELY
ORNATENESS
ORNATION
ORNATURE
ORNE
ORNERINESS
ORNERY
ORNES
ORNIFY
ORNIS
ORNISCOPIC
ORNISCOPIST
ORNISCOPY
ORNITHIC
ORNITHICHNITE
ORNITHINE
ORNITHOGAL
ORNITHOID
ORNITHOLITE
ORNITHOLITIC
ORNITHOLOGIC
ORNITHOLOGIST
ORNITHOLOGY
ORNITHOMANCY
ORNITHOMANIA
ORNITHON
ORNITHOPHILE
ORNITHOPHILY
ORNITHOPOD
ORNITHOPTER
ORNITHOSCOPY
ORNITHOSIS
ORNITHOTOMY
ORNITHURIC
ORNITHUROUS
ORNOITE
ORO
OROANAL
OROBANCHEOUS
OROCRATIC
OROGEN
OROGENESIS
OROGENESY
OROGENETIC
OROGENIC
OROGENY
OROGRAPH
OROGRAPHIC
OROGRAPHICAL
OROGRAPHY
OROIDE
OROLOGICAL
OROLOGIST
OROLOGY
OROMETER
OROMETRIC
OROMETRY
ORONOCO
ORONOKO
ORONOOKO
OROPHARYNGES
OROPHARYNX
OROPHARYNXES
OROTUND
OROTUNDITY
ORP
ORPED
ORPHAN
ORPHANAGE
ORPHANED
ORPHANHOOD
ORPHANING
ORPHANRY
ORPHARION
ORPHEON
ORPHEONIST
ORPHEUM
ORPHIC
ORPHICAL
ORPHICALLY
ORPHREY
ORPHREYED
ORPHREYS
ORPIMENT
ORPIN
ORPINE
ORPIT
ORRA
ORRERIES
ORRERY
ORRHOID
ORRHOLOGY
ORRHOTHERAPY
ORRICE
ORRIS
ORRISROOT
ORROW
ORSEDE
ORSEDUE
ORSEILLE
ORSEILLINE
ORSEL
ORSELLER
ORSELLINATE
ORSELLINIC
ORT
ORTALID
ORTALIDIAN
ORTERDE
ORTHAL
ORTHIAN
ORTHICON
ORTHID
ORTHITE
ORTHITIC
ORTHO
ORTHOBIOSIS
ORTHOBORATE
ORTHOCARPOUS
ORTHOCENTER
ORTHOCENTRE
ORTHOCENTRIC
ORTHOCLASE
ORTHOCLASITE
ORTHOCLASTIC
ORTHOCYMENE
ORTHODIAGRAM
ORTHODONTIA
ORTHODONTIC
ORTHODONTICS
ORTHODONTIST
ORTHODOX
ORTHODOXAL
ORTHODOXALLY
ORTHODOXIAN
ORTHODOXICAL
ORTHODOXIES
ORTHODOXISM
ORTHODOXIST
ORTHODOXLY
ORTHODOXNESS
ORTHODOXY
ORTHODROMIC
ORTHODROMICS
ORTHODROMY
ORTHOEPIC
ORTHOEPICAL
ORTHOEPIST
ORTHOEPISTIC
ORTHOEPY
ORTHOGENESIS
ORTHOGENETIC
ORTHOGENIC
ORTHOGNATHIC
ORTHOGNATHUS
ORTHOGNATHY
ORTHOGONAL
ORTHOGONALLY
ORTHOGONIAL
ORTHOGRADE

ORTHOGRANITE
ORTHOGRAPH
ORTHOGRAPHER
ORTHOGRAPHIC
ORTHOGRAPHIES
ORTHOGRAPHY
ORTHOLOGER
ORTHOLOGIAN
ORTHOLOGICAL
ORTHOLOGY
ORTHOMETOPIC
ORTHOMETRIC
ORTHOMETRY
ORTHOPAEDIA
ORTHOPAEDIC
ORTHOPAEDICS
ORTHOPAEDIST
ORTHOPAEDY
ORTHOPATH
ORTHOPATHIC
ORTHOPATHY
ORTHOPEDIA
ORTHOPEDIC
ORTHOPEDICS
ORTHOPEDIST
ORTHOPEDY
ORTHOPHONIC
ORTHOPHONY
ORTHOPHORIA
ORTHOPHORIC
ORTHOPHYRE
ORTHOPHYRIC
ORTHOPLASTIC
ORTHOPLASY
ORTHOPNEA
ORTHOPNEIC
ORTHOPNOEA
ORTHOPNOEIC
ORTHOPRAXY
ORTHOPRISM
ORTHOPTER
ORTHOPTERAL
ORTHOPTERAN
ORTHOPTERIST
ORTHOPTEROID
ORTHOPTERON
ORTHOPTEROUS
ORTHOPTIC
ORTHOPTICS
ORTHORHOMBIC
ORTHORRHAPHY
ORTHOSCOPE
ORTHOSCOPIC
ORTHOSE
ORTHOSILICIC
ORTHOSIS
ORTHOSITE
ORTHOSOMATIC
ORTHOSTATIC
ORTHOSTICHIES
ORTHOSTICHY
ORTHOSTYLE
ORTHOTACTIC
ORTHOTECTIC
ORTHOTIC
ORTHOTOMIC
ORTHOTONE
ORTHOTONESIS
ORTHOTONIC
ORTHOTONUS
ORTHOTROPAL
ORTHOTROPIC
ORTHOTROPISM
ORTHOTROPOUS
ORTHOTROPY
ORTHOTYPE
ORTHOTYPOUS
ORTHRON
ORTHROS
ORTIGA
ORTIVE
ORTOLAN
ORTS
ORTSTALER
ORTSTEIN
ORTYGAN
ORTYGINE
ORVET
ORVIETAN
ORVIETITE
ORY
ORYCTICS
ORYCTOGNOSY
ORYCTOLOGIC
ORYCTOLOGIST
ORYCTOLOGY
ORYSSID
ORYX
ORYXES
ORYZANIN
ORYZANINE
ORYZENIN
ORYZIVOROUS
OS
OSAMINE
OSAR
OSAZONE
OSCELLA
OSCHEITIS
OSCHEOCELE
OSCHEOLITH
OSCHEOMA
OSCHEONCUS
OSCHEOPLASTY
OSCILLANCE
OSCILLANCY
OSCILLANT
OSCILLATE
OSCILLATED
OSCILLATING
OSCILLATION
OSCILLATIVE
OSCILLATOR
OSCILLATORY
OSCILLOGRAM
OSCILLOGRAPH
OSCILLOMETER
OSCILLOMETRY
OSCILLOSCOPE
OSCIN
OSCINE
OSCINIAN
OSCININE
OSCITANCE
OSCITANCIES
OSCITANCY
OSCITANT
OSCITANTLY
OSCITATE
OSCITATION
OSCNODE
OSCULA
OSCULABLE
OSCULANT
OSCULAR
OSCULARITY
OSCULATE
OSCULATED
OSCULATING
OSCULATION
OSCULATORIES
OSCULATORY
OSCULATRIX
OSCULATRIXES
OSCULE
OSCULIFEROUS
OSCULUM
OSCURANTIST
OSE
OSELA
OSELE
OSELLA
OSELLE
OSHAC
OSID
OSIDE
OSIER
OSIERED
OSIERIES
OSIERS
OSIERY
OSITE
OSKEN
OSMATE
OSMATIC
OSMATISM
OSMAZOMATIC
OSMAZOMATOUS
OSMAZOME
OSMESIS
OSMETERIA
OSMETERIUM
OSMIC
OSMICS
OSMIDROSIS
OSMIN
OSMIOUS
OSMIRIDIUM
OSMIUM
OSMOGENE
OSMOGRAPH
OSMOLAGNIA
OSMOLOGY
OSMOMETER
OSMOMETRIC
OSMOMETRY
OSMOND
OSMONDITE
OSMOSCOPE
OSMOSE
OSMOSED
OSMOSING
OSMOSIS
OSMOTACTIC
OSMOTAXIS
OSMOTHERAPY
OSMOTIC
OSMOTICALLY
OSMOUS
OSMUND
OSMUNDACEOUS
OSMUNDINE
OSNABURG
OSOBERRIES
OSOBERRY
OSONE
OSOPHIES
OSOPHY
OSPHRADIA
OSPHRADIAL
OSPHRADIUM
OSPHRESIS
OSPHRETIC
OSPHYALGIA
OSPHYALGIC
OSPHYITIS
OSPHYOCELE
OSPREY
OSPREYS
OSS
OSSA
OSSAL
OSSARIUM
OSSATURE
OSSE
OSSEIN
OSSELET
OSSEMENTS
OSSEOMUCOID
OSSEOUS
OSSEOUSLY
OSSIA
OSSICLE
OSSICULA
OSSICULAR
OSSICULATE
OSSICULATED
OSSICULE
OSSICULOTOMY
OSSICULUM
OSSIFEROUS
OSSIFIC
OSSIFICATION
OSSIFIED
OSSIFIER
OSSIFLUENCE
OSSIFLUENT
OSSIFORM
OSSIFRAGE
OSSIFRANGENT
OSSIFY
OSSIFYING
OSSIVOROUS
OSSUARIES
OSSUARIUM
OSSUARY
OSSYPITE
OSTALGIA
OSTARTHRITIS
OSTE
OSTEAL
OSTEALGIA
OSTECTOMY
OSTEECTOMY
OSTEECTOPIA
OSTEECTOPY
OSTEIN
OSTEITIC
OSTEITIS
OSTEMIA
OSTEMPYESIS
OSTEND
OSTENSIBLE
OSTENSIBLY
OSTENSION
OSTENSIVE
OSTENSIVELY
OSTENSORIA
OSTENSORIES
OSTENSORIUM
OSTENSORY
OSTENT
OSTENTATE
OSTENTATION
OSTENTATIOUS
OSTENTATIOUSLY
OSTEOBLAST
OSTEOBLASTIC
OSTEOCELE
OSTEOCLASIA
OSTEOCLASIS
OSTEOCLAST
OSTEOCLASTIC
OSTEOCLASTY
OSTEOCOLLA
OSTEOCOMMA
OSTEOCRANIUM
OSTEOCYSTOMA
OSTEODENTINE
OSTEODERM
OSTEODERMAL
OSTEODERMIA
OSTEODERMIS
OSTEODERMOUS
OSTEODYNIA
OSTEOFIBROUS
OSTEOGEN
OSTEOGENESIS
OSTEOGENETIC
OSTEOGENIC
OSTEOGENIST
OSTEOGENOUS
OSTEOGENY
OSTEOGLOSSID
OSTEOGRAPHER
OSTEOGRAPHY
OSTEOID
OSTEOLITE
OSTEOLOGIC
OSTEOLOGICAL
OSTEOLOGIST
OSTEOLOGY
OSTEOLYSIS
OSTEOLYTIC
OSTEOMA
OSTEOMALACIA
OSTEOMALACIC
OSTEOMANCY
OSTEOMANTY
OSTEOMAS
OSTEOMATA
OSTEOMATOID
OSTEOME
OSTEOMERE
OSTEOMETRIC
OSTEOMETRY
OSTEONCUS
OSTEOPATH
OSTEOPATHIC
OSTEOPATHIST
OSTEOPATHY
OSTEOPHAGIA
OSTEOPHONE
OSTEOPHONY
OSTEOPHORE
OSTEOPHYMA
OSTEOPHYTE
OSTEOPHYTIC
OSTEOPLAQUE
OSTEOPLAST
OSTEOPLASTIC
OSTEOPLASTIES
OSTEOPLASTY
OSTEOPOROSIS
OSTEOPOROTIC
OSTEORRHAPHY
OSTEOSARCOMA
OSTEOSCOPE
OSTEOSTIXIS
OSTEOSTOMOUS
OSTEOTOME
OSTEOTOMIES
OSTEOTOMIST
OSTEOTOMY
OSTEOTRIBE
OSTEOTRITE
OSTEOTROPHY
OSTERIA
OSTIA
OSTIAL
OSTIARIES
OSTIARY
OSTIATE
OSTINATO
OSTIOLAR

OSTIOLATE
OSTIOLE
OSTITIS
OSTIUM
OSTLER
OSTLERESS
OSTMARK
OSTOMATID
OSTOSIS
OSTRACA
OSTRACEAN
OSTRACEOUS
OSTRACINE
OSTRACIOID
OSTRACISE
OSTRACISM
OSTRACITE
OSTRACIZATION
OSTRACIZE
OSTRACIZED
OSTRACIZER
OSTRACIZING
OSTRACOD
OSTRACODE
OSTRACODERM
OSTRACODOUS
OSTRACON
OSTRACOPHORE
OSTRACUM
OSTRAITE
OSTREACEOUS
OSTREGER
OSTREIFORM
OSTREOID
OSTREOPHAGE
OSTRICH
OSTRICHES
OSTRICHLIKE
OTACOUSTIC
OTACOUSTICON
OTACUST
OTALGIA
OTALGIC
OTALGY
OTARIAN
OTARIES
OTARIINE
OTARINE
OTARIOID
OTARY
OTATE
OTECTOMY
OTELCOSIS
OTHAEMATOMA
OTHELCOSIS
OTHEMATOMA
OTHEMATOMATA
OTHEMORRHEA
OTHEOSCOPE
OTHER
OTHEREST
OTHERGATES
OTHERGUESS
OTHERGUISE
OTHERHOW
OTHERISM
OTHERIST
OTHERNESS
OTHERS
OTHERSOME
OTHERTIME
OTHERTIMES
OTHERWHENCE
OTHERWHERE
OTHERWHERES
OTHERWHILE
OTHERWHILES
OTHERWHITHER
OTHERWISE
OTHERWORLDLY
OTHMANY
OTHYGROMA
OTIANT
OTIATRIC
OTIATRICS
OTIATRY
OTIC
OTICODINIA
OTIDIA
OTIDIFORM
OTIDINE
OTIDIUM
OTIORHYNCHID
OTIOSE
OTIOSELY
OTIOSENESS
OTIOSITY
OTITIC
OTITIS
OTIUM
OTKON
OTOANTRITIS
OTOCARIASIS
OTOCLEISIS
OTOCONIA
OTOCONIAL
OTOCONITE
OTOCONIUM
OTOCRANIAL
OTOCRANIC
OTOCRANIUM
OTOCYST
OTOCYSTIC
OTODYNIA
OTODYNIC
OTOGENIC
OTOGENOUS
OTOGRAPHICAL
OTOGRAPHY
OTOLITE
OTOLITH
OTOLITIC
OTOLOGICAL
OTOLOGIST
OTOLOGY
OTOMASSAGE
OTOMYCES
OTOMYCOSIS
OTONEURALGIA
OTOPATHIC
OTOPATHY
OTOPHONE
OTOPIESIS
OTOPLASTIC
OTOPLASTY
OTOPOLYPUS
OTOPYORRHEA
OTOPYOSIS
OTORRHAGIA
OTORRHEA
OTORRHOEA
OTOSCLEROSIS
OTOSCOPE
OTOSCOPIC
OTOSCOPY
OTOSIS
OTOSTEAL
OTOSTEON
OTOTOI
OTOTOMY
OTTAJANITE
OTTAR
OTTAVA
OTTAVARIMA
OTTAVE
OTTAVINO
OTTER
OTTERER
OTTERHOUND
OTTETTO
OTTINGER
OTTO
OTTOMAN
OTTRELITE
OTTROYE
OU
OUABAIN
OUABAIO
OUABE
OUACHITITE
OUAKARI
OUANANICHE
OUANGA
OUBLIANCE
OUBLIET
OUBLIETTE
OUCH
OUD
OUDENARDE
OUED
OUENITE
OUF
OUGH
OUGHT
OUGHTLINGS
OUGHTLINS
OUGLE
OUIJA
OUISTITI
OUK
OUKIA
OULAP
OULK
OUNCE
OUNDING
OUNDY
OUPH
OUPHE
OUR
OURANG
OURARI
OURE
OUREBI
OURICURY
OURIE
OUROUB
OURS
OURSEL
OURSELF
OURSELS
OURSELVES
OUSEL
OUSIA
OUST
OUSTED
OUSTEE
OUSTER
OUSTING
OUT
OUTACT
OUTADMIRAL
OUTAGE
OUTAMBUSH
OUTARDE
OUTARGUE
OUTAS
OUTASK
OUTBABBLE
OUTBACK
OUTBACKER
OUTBADE
OUTBAKE
OUTBALANCE
OUTBANTER
OUTBARGAIN
OUTBARK
OUTBAWL
OUTBEAM
OUTBEAR
OUTBEARING
OUTBEG
OUTBEGGAR
OUTBELCH
OUTBELLOW
OUTBETTER
OUTBID
OUTBIDDEN
OUTBIDDER
OUTBIDDING
OUTBIRTH
OUTBLACKEN
OUTBLAZE
OUTBLEAT
OUTBLESS
OUTBLOOM
OUTBLOSSOM
OUTBLOWN
OUTBLUFF
OUTBLUNDER
OUTBLUSH
OUTBLUSTER
OUTBOARD
OUTBOAST
OUTBOND
OUTBOOK
OUTBORE
OUTBORN
OUTBORNE
OUTBOUND
OUTBOWL
OUTBOX
OUTBRAG
OUTBRAID
OUTBRAVE
OUTBRAVED
OUTBRAVING
OUTBRAZEN
OUTBREAK
OUTBREAKING
OUTBREATHE
OUTBREATHER
OUTBRED
OUTBREED
OUTBREEDING
OUTBRIBE
OUTBUILD
OUTBUILDING
OUTBULK
OUTBULLY
OUTBURN
OUTBURST
OUTBUY
OUTBUZZ
OUTBY
OUTBYE
OUTCAME
OUTCANT
OUTCAPER
OUTCAROL
OUTCARRY
OUTCASE
OUTCAST
OUTCASTE
OUTCASTED
OUTCASTING
OUTCASTS
OUTCAVIL
OUTCEPT
OUTCHAMBER
OUTCHARM
OUTCHATTER
OUTCHEAT
OUTCHIDE
OUTCLASS
OUTCLIMB
OUTCOME
OUTCOMER
OUTCOMING
OUTCOMPASS
OUTCOMPLETE
OUTCOUNTRY
OUTCRAWL
OUTCRICKET
OUTCRIED
OUTCRIER
OUTCRIES
OUTCROP
OUTCROPPED
OUTCROPPER
OUTCROPPING
OUTCROSS
OUTCROSSING
OUTCROW
OUTCRY
OUTCRYING
OUTCURE
OUTCURSE
OUTCURVE
OUTCURVED
OUTCURVING
OUTDANCE
OUTDARE
OUTDATE
OUTDATED
OUTDATING
OUTDAZZLE
OUTDEVIL
OUTDID
OUTDISPATCH
OUTDISTANCE
OUTDISTANCED
OUTDISTANCING
OUTDO
OUTDODGE
OUTDOER
OUTDOING
OUTDONE
OUTDOOR
OUTDOORS
OUTDOORSMAN
OUTDOORSMEN
OUTDRAFT
OUTDRAGON
OUTDRAUGHT
OUTDREAM
OUTDRESS
OUTDRINK
OUTDRIVE
OUTDURE
OUTDWELLER
OUTE
OUTEAT
OUTECHO
OUTED
OUTEN
OUTER
OUTERLY
OUTERMOST
OUTERWEAR
OUTFABLE
OUTFACE
OUTFACED
OUTFACING
OUTFALL
OUTFAME

OUTFAST
OUTFAWN
OUTFEAST
OUTFEAT
OUTFERRET
OUTFICTION
OUTFIELD
OUTFIELDER
OUTFIELDSMAN
OUTFIELDSMEN
OUTFIGHT
OUTFIGHTER
OUTFIGHTING
OUTFISH
OUTFIT
OUTFITTED
OUTFITTER
OUTFITTING
OUTFLANK
OUTFLANKER
OUTFLANKING
OUTFLATTER
OUTFLING
OUTFLOAT
OUTFLOW
OUTFLUNKY
OUTFLUSH
OUTFLUX
OUTFLY
OUTFOOL
OUTFOOT
OUTFORM
OUTFORT
OUTFORTH
OUTFOX
OUTFRONT
OUTFROWN
OUTGABBLE
OUTGAIN
OUTGALLOP
OUTGAMBLE
OUTGAME
OUTGANG
OUTGARTH
OUTGATE
OUTGAUGE
OUTGAZE
OUTGENERAL
OUTGENERALED
OUTGENERALING
OUTGENERALLED
OUTGENERALLING
OUTGIVE
OUTGIVING
OUTGLAD
OUTGLARE
OUTGLITTER
OUTGLOW
OUTGNAW
OUTGO
OUTGOER
OUTGOES
OUTGOING
OUTGONE
OUTGREEN
OUTGREW
OUTGRIN
OUTGROWING
OUTGROWN
OUTGROWTH
OUTGUARD
OUTGUESS
OUTGUN
OUTGUSH
OUTHAMMER
OUTHASTEN
OUTHAUL
OUTHAULER
OUTHEAR
OUTHECTOR
OUTHEEL
OUTHER
OUTHIT
OUTHOLD
OUTHORN
OUTHORROR
OUTHOUSE
OUTHOUSING
OUTHOWL
OUTHUE
OUTHUMOR
OUTHUNT
OUTHUT
OUTHYMN
OUTIMAGE
OUTING
OUTINVENT
OUTISH
OUTJAZZ
OUTJINX
OUTJOCKEY
OUTJOURNEY
OUTJUGGLE
OUTJUMP
OUTJUT
OUTKEEPER
OUTKICK
OUTKILL
OUTKING
OUTKISS
OUTKNAVE
OUTKNEE
OUTLABOR
OUTLAND
OUTLANDER
OUTLANDISH
OUTLANDISHLY
OUTLASH
OUTLAST
OUTLAUGH
OUTLAW
OUTLAWED
OUTLAWING
OUTLAWRIES
OUTLAWRY
OUTLAY
OUTLEAP
OUTLEARN
OUTLEGEND
OUTLER
OUTLET
OUTLIE
OUTLIER
OUTLIGHTEN
OUTLIMN
OUTLINE
OUTLINEAR
OUTLINED
OUTLINER
OUTLINGER
OUTLINING
OUTLIVE
OUTLIVED
OUTLIVER
OUTLIVING
OUTLODGING
OUTLOOK
OUTLOOKER
OUTLOPE
OUTLORD
OUTLOVE
OUTLUNG
OUTLUSTER
OUTLY
OUTLYING
OUTMAGIC
OUTMALAPROP
OUTMAN
OUTMANEUVER
OUTMANNED
OUTMANNING
OUTMANTLE
OUTMARCH
OUTMARRIAGE
OUTMARRY
OUTMASTER
OUTMATCH
OUTMATE
OUTMEASURE
OUTMIRACLE
OUTMODE
OUTMODED
OUTMOST
OUTMOUNT
OUTMOUTH
OUTMOVE
OUTNAME
OUTNESS
OUTNIGHT
OUTNOISE
OUTNUMBER
OUTPAGE
OUTPAINT
OUTPARAGON
OUTPARAMOUR
OUTPARISH
OUTPART
OUTPARTS
OUTPASS
OUTPASSION
OUTPATIENT
OUTPAYMENT
OUTPEER
OUTPENSION
OUTPENSIONER
OUTPERFORM
OUTPICK
OUTPICKET
OUTPIPE
OUTPITCH
OUTPITY
OUTPLACE
OUTPLAN
OUTPLAY
OUTPLAYED
OUTPLEASE
OUTPLOD
OUTPLOT
OUTPOCKETING
OUTPOINT
OUTPOISE
OUTPOISON
OUTPOLL
OUTPOMP
OUTPOPULATE
OUTPORT
OUTPORTER
OUTPORTION
OUTPOST
OUTPOUR
OUTPOURED
OUTPOURER
OUTPOURING
OUTPRACTICE
OUTPRAISE
OUTPRAY
OUTPREACH
OUTPREEN
OUTPRICE
OUTPRODIGY
OUTPRODUCE
OUTPROMISE
OUTPRY
OUTPULL
OUTPURL
OUTPURSE
OUTPUSH
OUTPUT
OUTPUTTER
OUTQUEEN
OUTQUESTION
OUTQUIBBLE
OUTQUOTE
OUTRACE
OUTRAGE
OUTRAGED
OUTRAGELY
OUTRAGEOUS
OUTRAGEOUSLY
OUTRAGER
OUTRAGING
OUTRAIL
OUTRAKE
OUTRAN
OUTRANCE
OUTRANGE
OUTRANK
OUTRANT
OUTRAP
OUTRATE
OUTRAVE
OUTRAY
OUTRAZE
OUTRE
OUTREACH
OUTREASON
OUTRECKON
OUTREDDEN
OUTREIGN
OUTRELIEF
OUTREMER
OUTRHYME
OUTRIDDEN
OUTRIDE
OUTRIDER
OUTRIDING
OUTRIG
OUTRIGGED
OUTRIGGER
OUTRIGGERED
OUTRIGGING
OUTRIGHT
OUTRIGHTLY
OUTRIGHTNESS
OUTRIVAL
OUTRIVE
OUTROAD
OUTROAR
OUTRODE
OUTROGUE
OUTROLL
OUTROMANCE
OUTROOP
OUTROOPER
OUTROOT
OUTROVE
OUTROW
OUTROYAL
OUTRUN
OUTRUNNER
OUTRUNNING
OUTRUSH
OUTS
OUTSAIL
OUTSAINT
OUTSAT
OUTSATISFY
OUTSAVOR
OUTSCAPE
OUTSCENT
OUTSCOLD
OUTSCORE
OUTSCORN
OUTSCOUR
OUTSCOURING
OUTSCOUT
OUTSCREAM
OUTSEA
OUTSEE
OUTSELL
OUTSELLING
OUTSEND
OUTSENTINEL
OUTSENTRY
OUTSERT
OUTSET
OUTSETTING
OUTSHADOW
OUTSHAKE
OUTSHAME
OUTSHARP
OUTSHARPEN
OUTSHEATHE
OUTSHIFTS
OUTSHINE
OUTSHINER
OUTSHINING
OUTSHONE
OUTSHOOT
OUTSHOOTING
OUTSHOT
OUTSHOUT
OUTSHOWER
OUTSHRIEK
OUTSHUT
OUTSIDE
OUTSIDED
OUTSIDER
OUTSIDES
OUTSIGHT
OUTSIN
OUTSING
OUTSIT
OUTSITTING
OUTSIZE
OUTSIZED
OUTSKILL
OUTSKIP
OUTSKIRMISH
OUTSKIRT
OUTSKIRTER
OUTSKIRTS
OUTSLANDER
OUTSLANG
OUTSLEEP
OUTSLING
OUTSLIP
OUTSMART
OUTSMILE
OUTSNORE
OUTSOAR
OUTSOLD
OUTSOLE
OUTSOLER
OUTSONNET
OUTSOUND
OUTSPAN
OUTSPANNED
OUTSPANNING
OUTSPARKLE
OUTSPEAK
OUTSPEAKER
OUTSPEAKING
OUTSPEECH
OUTSPEED

OUTSPEND
OUTSPENT
OUTSPIT
OUTSPLENDOR
OUTSPOKE
OUTSPOKEN
OUTSPOKENLY
OUTSPORT
OUTSPOUT
OUTSPREAD
OUTSPREADING
OUTSPRINT
OUTSTAGGER
OUTSTAID
OUTSTAND
OUTSTANDER
OUTSTANDING
OUTSTANDINGLY
OUTSTARE
OUTSTART
OUTSTARTER
OUTSTATE
OUTSTATION
OUTSTATURE
OUTSTAY
OUTSTAYED
OUTSTAYING
OUTSTEP
OUTSTING
OUTSTINK
OUTSTOOD
OUTSTORM
OUTSTRETCH
OUTSTRETCHED
OUTSTRETCHER
OUTSTRETCHING
OUTSTRIDE
OUTSTRIP
OUTSTRIPPED
OUTSTRIPPING
OUTSTRIVE
OUTSTROKE
OUTSTRUT
OUTSTUDY
OUTSTUNT
OUTSUBTLE
OUTSUCKEN
OUTSUFFER
OUTSUITOR
OUTSULK
OUTSUM
OUTSWAGGER
OUTSWEAR
OUTSWEEPING
OUTSWEETEN
OUTSWELL
OUTSWIFT
OUTSWIM
OUTSWINDLE
OUTTAKE
OUTTAKEN
OUTTALENT
OUTTALK
OUTTASK
OUTTASTE
OUTTEASE
OUTTELL
OUTTELLING
OUTTHIEVE
OUTTHINK
OUTTHREATEN
OUTTHROB
OUTTHROUGH
OUTTHROW
OUTTHRUST
OUTTHWACK
OUTTOIL
OUTTOLD
OUTTONGUE
OUTTOP
OUTTOPPED
OUTTOPPING
OUTTOWER
OUTTRADE
OUTTRAIL
OUTTRAVEL
OUTTRICK
OUTTROT
OUTTRUMP
OUTTURN
OUTTURNED
OUTTWINE
OUTTYRANNIZE
OUTUSURE
OUTVALUE
OUTVAUNT
OUTVELVET
OUTVENOM
OUTVICTOR
OUTVIE
OUTVILLAIN
OUTVOICE
OUTVOTE
OUTVOTER
OUTWAIT
OUTWAKE
OUTWALE
OUTWALK
OUTWALL
OUTWALLOP
OUTWAR
OUTWARBLE
OUTWARD
OUTWARDLY
OUTWARDS
OUTWASH
OUTWASTE
OUTWATCH
OUTWAY
OUTWEALTH
OUTWEAPON
OUTWEAR
OUTWEARING
OUTWEARY
OUTWEIGH
OUTWEIGHT
OUTWENT
OUTWHIRL
OUTWICK
OUTWILE
OUTWILL
OUTWIN
OUTWIND
OUTWING
OUTWISH
OUTWIT
OUTWITH
OUTWITTAL
OUTWITTED
OUTWITTER
OUTWITTING
OUTWOE
OUTWOMAN
OUTWORD
OUTWORE
OUTWORK
OUTWORKED
OUTWORKING
OUTWORLD
OUTWORN
OUTWORTH
OUTWRANGLE
OUTWREST
OUTWRESTLE
OUTWRIGGLE
OUTWRITE
OUTWRITING
OUTWRITTEN
OUTWROTE
OUTWROUGHT
OUTYELP
OUTYIELD
OUTZANY
OUVERT
OUVERTE
OUVRAGE
OUVRIER
OUVRIERE
OUYEZD
OUZEL
OUZO
OVA
OVAL
OVALBUMIN
OVALIFORM
OVALIZATION
OVALIZE
OVALNESS
OVALOID
OVALWISE
OVANT
OVARIA
OVARIAL
OVARIAN
OVARIECTOMY
OVARIES
OVARIN
OVARIOCELE
OVARIOCYESIS
OVARIOLE
OVARIOSTOMY
OVARIOTOMIES
OVARIOTOMIST
OVARIOTOMIZE
OVARIOTOMY
OVARIOUS
OVARITIS
OVARIUM
OVARY
OVATE
OVATECONICAL
OVATED
OVATELY
OVATION
OVATIONAL
OVATOCONICAL
OVATOCORDATE
OVATODELTOID
OVATOGLOBOSE
OVATOOBLONG
OVATOSERRATE
OVEN
OVENBIRD
OVENDRY
OVENED
OVENING
OVENLY
OVENMAN
OVENMEN
OVENPEEL
OVENS
OVENSMAN
OVENSTONE
OVENWARE
OVENWISE
OVER
OVERABUNDANCE
OVERABUNDANT
OVERACT
OVERAGE
OVERALL
OVERALLED
OVERALLS
OVERARCH
OVERARM
OVERATE
OVERAWE
OVERAWED
OVERAWING
OVERBADE
OVERBALANCE
OVERBANK
OVERBARISH
OVERBEAR
OVERBEARANCE
OVERBEARER
OVERBEARING
OVERBEARINGLY
OVERBEND
OVERBERG
OVERBID
OVERBIDDEN
OVERBIDDING
OVERBIDE
OVERBIT
OVERBITE
OVERBLEW
OVERBLOUSE
OVERBLOW
OVERBLOWING
OVERBLOWN
OVERBOARD
OVERBODY
OVERBOIL
OVERBOOK
OVERBORE
OVERBORNE
OVERBOUGHT
OVERBOWED
OVERBOWL
OVERBREATHE
OVERBRIBE
OVERBRIDGE
OVERBRIM
OVERBRIMMED
OVERBRIMMING
OVERBROOD
OVERBROW
OVERBUILD
OVERBUILDING
OVERBUILT
OVERBURDEN
OVERBURN
OVERBURST
OVERBUSY
OVERBUY
OVERBUYING
OVERBY
OVERCALL
OVERCAME
OVERCARRY
OVERCAST
OVERCASTING
OVERCATCH
OVERCERTIFY
OVERCHARGE
OVERCHARGED
OVERCHARGER
OVERCHARGING
OVERCHECK
OVERCLOTHES
OVERCLOUD
OVERCOAT
OVERCOATED
OVERCOATING
OVERCOIL
OVERCOME
OVERCOMER
OVERCOMING
OVERCOMPOUND
OVERCONFIDENT
OVERCOOK
OVERCORRECT
OVERCOUNT
OVERCOVER
OVERCROP
OVERCROW
OVERCROWD
OVERCURRENT
OVERCUT
OVERDARE
OVERDATED
OVERDECK
OVERDECORATED
OVERDEN
OVERDEVELOP
OVERDEVELOPED
OVERDID
OVERDO
OVERDOER
OVERDOING
OVERDONE
OVERDOOR
OVERDOSAGE
OVERDOSE
OVERDRAFT
OVERDRAPE
OVERDRAPERY
OVERDRAUGHT
OVERDRAW
OVERDRAWER
OVERDRAWING
OVERDRAWN
OVERDRESS
OVERDREW
OVERDRIED
OVERDRIVE
OVERDRIVEN
OVERDRIVING
OVERDROVE
OVERDUE
OVERDYE
OVERDYED
OVERDYEING
OVEREAGER
OVEREAT
OVEREATEN
OVEREATING
OVERED
OVEREDUCATED
OVERELABORATE
OVERENTER
OVERENTRY
OVEREST
OVERESTIMATE
OVERESTIMATED
OVERESTIMATING
OVEREXERT
OVEREXPOSE
OVEREXPOSED
OVEREXPOSING
OVEREXPOSURE
OVEREYE
OVERFACE
OVERFALL
OVERFALLEN
OVERFALLING
OVERFASTIDIOUS
OVERFED
OVERFEED
OVERFELL
OVERFINE
OVERFISH
OVERFLEW
OVERFLIGHT

OVERFLOAT
OVERFLOOD
OVERFLOURISH
OVERFLOW
OVERFLOWED
OVERFLOWER
OVERFLOWING
OVERFLOWN
OVERFLUSH
OVERFLUTTER
OVERFLY
OVERFLYING
OVERFOLD
OVERFOOT
OVERFREIGHT
OVERFRET
OVERFRIEZE
OVERFULL
OVERGANG
OVERGARMENT
OVERGAZE
OVERGET
OVERGETTING
OVERGILD
OVERGIVE
OVERGLANCE
OVERGLAZE
OVERGLAZED
OVERGLAZING
OVERGLIDE
OVERGLOOM
OVERGO
OVERGOING
OVERGONE
OVERGOT
OVERGOTTEN
OVERGOVERN
OVERGRAIN
OVERGRAINER
OVERGRAZE
OVERGREW
OVERGROUND
OVERGROW
OVERGROWING
OVERGROWN
OVERGROWTH
OVERHAIL
OVERHAIR
OVERHALE
OVERHAND
OVERHANDED
OVERHANG
OVERHANGING
OVERHAUL
OVERHAULED
OVERHAULER
OVERHAULING
OVERHEAD
OVERHEAP
OVERHEAR
OVERHEARD
OVERHEARER
OVERHEARING
OVERHEAT
OVERHEAVE
OVERHIE
OVERHIP
OVERHIT
OVERHUNG
OVERINFORM
OVERING
OVERINSURE
OVERISSUE
OVERISSUED
OVERISSUING
OVERJOY
OVERJUDGE
OVERJUMP
OVERKEEP
OVERKILL
OVERKING
OVERKNEE
OVERKNOW
OVERLABOR
OVERLABORED
OVERLABORING
OVERLABOUR
OVERLABOURED
OVERLABOURING
OVERLADE
OVERLADED
OVERLADEN
OVERLADING
OVERLAID
OVERLAIN
OVERLAND
OVERLANDER
OVERLAP
OVERLAPPED
OVERLAPPING
OVERLASH
OVERLAUNCH
OVERLAVE
OVERLAY
OVERLAYER
OVERLAYING
OVERLEAD
OVERLEAF
OVERLEAP
OVERLEAPED
OVERLEAPING
OVERLEAPT
OVERLEATHER
OVERLEAVE
OVERLEAVEN
OVERLICK
OVERLIE
OVERLIER
OVERLIFT
OVERLINE
OVERLING
OVERLIP
OVERLISTEN
OVERLIVE
OVERLIVER
OVERLOAD
OVERLOADED
OVERLOCK
OVERLOCKER
OVERLONG
OVERLOOK
OVERLOOKED
OVERLOOKER
OVERLOOKING
OVERLORD
OVERLOUP
OVERLOVE
OVERLOVER
OVERLY
OVERLYING
OVERMAN
OVERMANTLE
OVERMARCH
OVERMARK
OVERMARKING
OVERMASK
OVERMAST
OVERMASTER
OVERMATCH
OVERMATURITY
OVERMEASURE
OVERMEN
OVERMICKLE
OVERMIND
OVERMODEST
OVERMORE
OVERMOST
OVERMOUNT
OVERMOUNTS
OVERMUCH
OVERMUSE
OVERNAME
OVERNET
OVERNICE
OVERNICELY
OVERNICETY
OVERNIGHT
OVERNOISE
OVERNUMBER
OVERPAID
OVERPAINT
OVERPART
OVERPARTED
OVERPARTY
OVERPASS
OVERPASSED
OVERPASSING
OVERPAY
OVERPAYING
OVERPAYMENT
OVERPEER
OVERPENDING
OVERPEOPLE
OVERPERSUADE
OVERPERSUADED
OVERPERSUADING
OVERPICK
OVERPICTURE
OVERPITCH
OVERPITCHED
OVERPLAY
OVERPLIED
OVERPLUS
OVERPLY
OVERPLYING
OVERPOLE
OVERPOPULATE
OVERPOPULATED
OVERPOPULATING
OVERPOST
OVERPOT
OVERPOUR
OVERPOWER
OVERPOWERED
OVERPOWERING
OVERPREACH
OVERPRECISE
OVERPRESS
OVERPRICE
OVERPRICED
OVERPRICING
OVERPRINT
OVERPRIZE
OVERPRIZED
OVERPRIZER
OVERPRIZING
OVERPRODUCE
OVERPRODUCED
OVERPRODUCING
OVERPROOF
OVERPROTECT
OVERPURCHASE
OVERPUT
OVERQUELL
OVERRACK
OVERRAKE
OVERRAKED
OVERRAKING
OVERRAN
OVERRATE
OVERRATED
OVERRATING
OVERRAUGHT
OVERREACH
OVERREACHED
OVERREACHER
OVERREACHING
OVERREAD
OVERREADER
OVERREADING
OVERREADY
OVERRECKON
OVERREFINED
OVERREGISTER
OVERRENT
OVERRID
OVERRIDDEN
OVERRIDE
OVERRIDER
OVERRIDING
OVERRIGHT
OVERRIM
OVERRIOT
OVERRIPE
OVERRIPENESS
OVERRISE
OVERRISEN
OVERRISING
OVERRODE
OVERROLL
OVERROOF
OVERROSE
OVERRUFF
OVERRULE
OVERRULED
OVERRULER
OVERRULING
OVERRUN
OVERRUNNER
OVERRUNNING
OVERS
OVERSAID
OVERSAIL
OVERSANDED
OVERSAW
OVERSAY
OVERSCENTED
OVERSCORE
OVERSCORED
OVERSCORING
OVERSCURF
OVERSCUTCHED
OVERSEA
OVERSEAM
OVERSEAMER
OVERSEARCH
OVERSEAS
OVERSEE
OVERSEEING
OVERSEEN
OVERSEER
OVERSELL
OVERSELLING
OVERSENSITIVE
OVERSENTIMENTAL
OVERSET
OVERSETTER
OVERSETTING
OVERSEW
OVERSEWED
OVERSEWING
OVERSEWN
OVERSEXED
OVERSHADE
OVERSHADED
OVERSHADING
OVERSHADOW
OVERSHADOWED
OVERSHADOWER
OVERSHADOWING
OVERSHAVE
OVERSHINE
OVERSHINING
OVERSHIRT
OVERSHOE
OVERSHOES
OVERSHONE
OVERSHOOT
OVERSHOOTING
OVERSHOT
OVERSIDE
OVERSIGHT
OVERSIGNED
OVERSILE
OVERSIZE
OVERSIZED
OVERSKIP
OVERSKIPPER
OVERSKIRT
OVERSLAUGH
OVERSLAUGHED
OVERSLAUGHING
OVERSLEEP
OVERSLEEPING
OVERSLEPT
OVERSLID
OVERSLIDDEN
OVERSLIDE
OVERSLIDING
OVERSLIP
OVERSLIPPED
OVERSLIPPING
OVERSLOP
OVERSMOKE
OVERSNOW
OVERSOFT
OVERSOLD
OVERSOUL
OVERSOUND
OVERSOW
OVERSOWED
OVERSOWING
OVERSOWN
OVERSPAN
OVERSPANNED
OVERSPANNING
OVERSPARRED
OVERSPEAK
OVERSPEAKING
OVERSPEND
OVERSPENDING
OVERSPENT
OVERSPILL
OVERSPIN
OVERSPOKE
OVERSPOKEN
OVERSPREAD
OVERSPREADING
OVERSPRING
OVERSPRUNG
OVERSPUN
OVERSTAID
OVERSTAND
OVERSTANDING
OVERSTATE
OVERSTATED
OVERSTATEMENT
OVERSTATING
OVERSTAY
OVERSTAYAL
OVERSTAYED
OVERSTAYING
OVERSTEP
OVERSTEPPED
OVERSTEPPING

OVERSTITCH
OVERSTOCK
OVERSTOOD
OVERSTOPING
OVERSTORY
OVERSTRAIN
OVERSTRAINED
OVERSTRAINING
OVERSTRAITEN
OVERSTRETCH
OVERSTREW
OVERSTREWED
OVERSTREWING
OVERSTREWN
OVERSTRICKEN
OVERSTRIDDEN
OVERSTRIDE
OVERSTRIDING
OVERSTRIKE
OVERSTRIKING
OVERSTRING
OVERSTRINGING
OVERSTRODE
OVERSTRUCK
OVERSTRUNG
OVERSTUDIED
OVERSTUDY
OVERSTUFF
OVERSUM
OVERSUPPLIED
OVERSUPPLY
OVERSUPPLYING
OVERSWARM
OVERSWAY
OVERSWELL
OVERSWELLED
OVERSWELLING
OVERSWOLLEN
OVERT
OVERTAKE
OVERTAKEN
OVERTAKER
OVERTAKING
OVERTASK
OVERTAX
OVERTAXATION
OVERTAXED
OVERTAXING
OVERTEEM
OVERTELL
OVERTELLING
OVERTEST
OVERTHINK
OVERTHREW
OVERTHROW
OVERTHROWAL
OVERTHROWER
OVERTHROWING
OVERTHROWN
OVERTHRUST
OVERTHWART
OVERTHWARTLY
OVERTIDE
OVERTILT
OVERTIME
OVERTIMED
OVERTIMER
OVERTIMING
OVERTITLE
OVERTLY
OVERTOE
OVERTOIL
OVERTOISE
OVERTOLD
OVERTONE
OVERTOOK
OVERTOP
OVERTOWER
OVERTRACE
OVERTRACK
OVERTRADE
OVERTRADED
OVERTRADER
OVERTRADING
OVERTRAIN
OVERTRAINED
OVERTRAINING
OVERTRAVEL
OVERTREAD
OVERTREADING
OVERTRICK
OVERTROD
OVERTRODDEN
OVERTRUMP
OVERTUMBLE
OVERTURE
OVERTURED
OVERTURING
OVERTURN
OVERTURNED
OVERTURNING
OVERTYPE
OVERUSE
OVERVAULT
OVERVEIL
OVERVIEW
OVERVOLTAGE
OVERVOTE
OVERWADE
OVERWAGES
OVERWAKE
OVERWALK
OVERWART
OVERWASH
OVERWATCH
OVERWATCHER
OVERWEAR
OVERWEARIED
OVERWEARING
OVERWEARY
OVERWEARYING
OVERWEATHER
OVERWEEN
OVERWEENED
OVERWEENER
OVERWEENING
OVERWEEP
OVERWEIGH
OVERWEIGHT
OVERWELT
OVERWEND
OVERWENT
OVERWHELM
OVERWHELMER
OVERWHELMING
OVERWHELMINGLY
OVERWIN
OVERWIND
OVERWINDING
OVERWING
OVERWINNING
OVERWINTER
OVERWIPED
OVERWOMAN
OVERWON
OVERWOOD
OVERWORD
OVERWORE
OVERWORK
OVERWORKED
OVERWORKING
OVERWORN
OVERWOUND
OVERWREST
OVERWRITE
OVERWRITING
OVERWRITTEN
OVERWROTE
OVERWROUGHT
OVERYEAR
OVERZEALOUS
OVEST
OVEY
OVIBOS
OVIBOVINE
OVICAPSULAR
OVICAPSULE
OVICELL
OVICELLULAR
OVICIDAL
OVICIDE
OVICULAR
OVICULATED
OVICULUM
OVICYST
OVICYSTIC
OVIDUCAL
OVIDUCT
OVIDUCTAL
OVIFEROUS
OVIFICATION
OVIFORM
OVIGENESIS
OVIGENETIC
OVIGENIC
OVIGENOUS
OVIGER
OVIGERM
OVIGEROUS
OVILE
OVIN
OVINE
OVINIA
OVIPARA
OVIPARAL
OVIPARITY
OVIPAROUS
OVIPAROUSLY
OVIPOSIT
OVIPOSITED
OVIPOSITING
OVIPOSITION
OVIPOSITOR
OVISAC
OVISM
OVIST
OVISTIC
OVIVOROUS
OVOCYTE
OVOELLIPTIC
OVOGENESIS
OVOGENETIC
OVOGENOUS
OVOGONIUM
OVOID
OVOIDAL
OVOLI
OVOLO
OVOLOGICAL
OVOLOGIST
OVOLOGY
OVOLYTIC
OVOMUCOID
OVOPLASM
OVOPLASMIC
OVOPYRIFORM
OVORHOMBOID
OVOTESTIS
OVULA
OVULAR
OVULARIAN
OVULARY
OVULATE
OVULATED
OVULATING
OVULATION
OVULE
OVULIFEROUS
OVULIGEROUS
OVULITE
OVULUM
OVUM
OW
OWE
OWED
OWELTY
OWER
OWERANCE
OWHERE
OWING
OWL
OWLER
OWLERIES
OWLERY
OWLET
OWLHEAD
OWLING
OWLISH
OWLISHLY
OWLISHNESS
OWLLIGHT
OWLY
OWN
OWNABLE
OWNED
OWNER
OWNERLESS
OWNERSHIP
OWNHOOD
OWNING
OWNNESS
OWNWAYISH
OWRE
OWRECOME
OWREHIP
OWRELAY
OWSE
OWSEN
OWTCHAH
OWYHEEITE
OWZEL
OX
OXADIAZOLE
OXALACETIC
OXALAEMIA
OXALATE
OXALATO
OXALEMIA
OXALIC
OXALIS
OXALURAMID
OXALURAMIDE
OXALURATE
OXALURIA
OXALURIC
OXALYL
OXALYLUREA
OXAMATE
OXAMETHANE
OXAMIC
OXAMIDE
OXAMIDIN
OXAMIDINE
OXAMMITE
OXAN
OXANE
OXANILATE
OXANILIC
OXANILIDE
OXAZIN
OXAZINE
OXAZOLE
OXBANE
OXBERRIES
OXBERRY
OXBIRD
OXBITER
OXBLOOD
OXBOW
OXBOY
OXBRAKE
OXCART
OXCHEEK
OXDIAZOLE
OXEA
OXEATE
OXEN
OXEOTE
OXER
OXEYE
OXFLY
OXFORD
OXGALL
OXGANG
OXGATE
OXGOAD
OXHARROW
OXHEAD
OXHEAL
OXHEART
OXHIDE
OXHOFT
OXHORN
OXHOUSE
OXHUVUD
OXID
OXIDABILITY
OXIDABLE
OXIDANT
OXIDASE
OXIDASIC
OXIDATE
OXIDATED
OXIDATING
OXIDATION
OXIDATIONAL
OXIDATIVE
OXIDATOR
OXIDE
OXIDIMETRIC
OXIDIMETRY
OXIDISE
OXIDIZABLE
OXIDIZE
OXIDIZED
OXIDIZER
OXIDIZING
OXIDO
OXIDULATED
OXIM
OXIMATE
OXIMATION
OXIME
OXLAND
OXLIKE
OXLIP
OXMAN
OXMANSHIP
OXMEN
OXO
OXONIUM
OXOZONE
OXOZONIDES
OXPECKER
OXREIM

OXSHOE
OXSKIN
OXTAIL
OXTER
OXTONGUE
OXWORT
OXY
OXYACANTHIN
OXYACANTHINE
OXYACANTHOUS
OXYACETYLENE
OXYACID
OXYALDEHYDE
OXYAMINE
OXYAPHIA
OXYASTER
OXYAZO
OXYBAPHA
OXYBENZYL
OXYBERBERINE
OXYBLEPSIA
OXYBROMIDE
OXYBUTYRIA
OXYCALCIUM
OXYCAMPHOR
OXYCAPROIC
OXYCARBONATE
OXYCELLULOSE
OXYCEPHALIC
OXYCEPHALISM
OXYCEPHALOUS
OXYCEPHALY
OXYCHLORATE
OXYCHLORIC
OXYCHLORID
OXYCHLORIDE
OXYCHLORINE
OXYCHROMATIC
OXYCHROMATIN
OXYCINNAMIC
OXYCOPAIVIC
OXYCOUMARIN
OXYCRATE
OXYCYANIDE
OXYDACTYL
OXYDIACT
OXYESTHESIA
OXYETHER
OXYETHYL
OXYGEN
OXYGENANT
OXYGENATE
OXYGENATED
OXYGENATING
OXYGENATOR
OXYGENERATOR
OXYGENIC
OXYGENICITY
OXYGENIUM
OXYGENIZABLE
OXYGENIZE
OXYGENIZED
OXYGENIZER
OXYGENIZING
OXYGENOUS
OXYGEUSIA
OXYGNATHOUS
OXYGON
OXYGONAL
OXYGONIAL
OXYHAEMATIN
OXYHALIDE
OXYHALOID
OXYHEMATIN
OXYHEXACTINE
OXYHEXASTER
OXYHYDRATE
OXYHYDRIC
OXYHYDROGEN
OXYIODIDE
OXYKETONE
OXYL
OXYLUCIFERIN
OXYMEL
OXYMETHYLENE
OXYMORA
OXYMORON
OXYMURIATE
OXYMURIATIC
OXYNEURIN
OXYNEURINE
OXYNITRATE
OXYNTIC
OXYOPHITIC
OXYOPIA
OXYOPY
OXYOSPHRESIA
OXYPETALOUS
OXYPHENOL
OXYPHENYL
OXYPHIL
OXYPHILE
OXYPHILIC
OXYPHILOUS
OXYPHONIA
OXYPHONY
OXYPHOSPHATE
OXYPHTHALIC
OXYPHYLLOUS
OXYPHYTE
OXYPICRIC
OXYPROLINE
OXYPROPIONIC
OXYPURINE
OXYPYCNOS
OXYQUINOLINE
OXYQUINONE
OXYRHINE
OXYRHINOUS
OXYRHYNCH
OXYRHYNCHID
OXYRHYNCHOUS
OXYRRHYNCHID
OXYSALICYLIC
OXYSALT
OXYSTEARIC
OXYSTOMATOUS
OXYSTOME
OXYSULFID
OXYSULFIDE
OXYSULPHATE
OXYSULPHID
OXYSULPHIDE
OXYTERPENE
OXYTOCIA
OXYTOCIC
OXYTOCIN
OXYTOCOUS
OXYTOLUENE
OXYTOLUIC
OXYTONE
OXYTONESIS
OXYTONICAL
OXYTONIZE
OXYTYLOTATE
OXYTYLOTE
OXYURIASIS
OXYURICIDE
OXYURID
OXYUROUS
OXYWELDING
OY
OYAPOCK
OYE
OYER
OYES
OYEZ
OYSTER
OYSTERAGE
OYSTERBIRD
OYSTERER
OYSTERFISH
OYSTERFISHES
OYSTERGREEN
OYSTERHOUSE
OYSTERING
OYSTERLING
OYSTERMAN
OYSTERMEN
OYSTEROUS
OYSTERROOT
OYSTERS
OYSTERSEED
OYSTERSHELL
OYSTERWIFE
OYSTERWOMAN
OZAENA
OZARKITE
OZENA
OZOBROME
OZOCERITE
OZOENA
OZONATE
OZONATION
OZONE
OZONED
OZONER
OZONIC
OZONID
OZONIDE
OZONIFEROUS
OZONIFY
OZONIZATION
OZONIZE
OZONIZED
OZONIZER
OZONIZING
OZONOMETER
OZONOMETRY
OZONOSCOPE
OZONOSCOPIC
OZONOSPHERE
OZONOSPHERIC
OZONOUS
OZOSTOMIA
OZOTYPE

P

PA
PAAGE
PAAL
PAAR
PAAUW
PAB
PABBLE
PABLO
PABULAR
PABULARY
PABULATION
PABULATORY
PABULOUS
PABULUM
PAC
PACA
PACABLE
PACANE
PACATE
PACATELY
PACATION
PACATIVE
PACAY
PACAYA
PACCIOLI
PACE
PACEBOARD
PACED
PACEMAKER
PACEMAKING
PACER
PACHA
PACHAK
PACHALIC
PACHINKO
PACHISI
PACHNOLITE
PACHOULI
PACHUCO
PACHYDACTYL
PACHYDACTYLY
PACHYDERM
PACHYDERMA
PACHYDERMAL
PACHYDERMIA
PACHYDERMIAL
PACHYDERMIC
PACHYDERMOID
PACHYDERMOUS
PACHYGLOSSAL
PACHYLOSIS
PACHYMENIA
PACHYMENIC
PACHYMENINX
PACHYMETER
PACHYNEMA
PACHYNSIS
PACHYNTIC
PACHYSANDRA
PACHYTENE
PACIFIABLE
PACIFIC
PACIFICAL
PACIFICALLY
PACIFICATE
PACIFICATED
PACIFICATING
PACIFICATION
PACIFICATOR
PACIFICATORY
PACIFICITY
PACIFICO
PACIFICOS
PACIFIED
PACIFIER
PACIFISM
PACIFIST
PACIFISTIC
PACIFY
PACIFYING
PACING
PACK
PACKAGE
PACKAGED
PACKAGING
PACKALL
PACKBUILDER
PACKCLOTH
PACKED
PACKER
PACKERIES
PACKERY
PACKET
PACKETED
PACKETING
PACKHORSE
PACKHOUSE
PACKING
PACKINGHOUSE
PACKLESS
PACKLY
PACKMAN
PACKMEN
PACKNESS
PACKSACK
PACKSADDLE
PACKSTAFF
PACKSTAVES
PACKTHREAD
PACKTONG
PACKWARE
PACKWAX
PACKWAY
PACO
PACOS
PACOTA
PACOURYUVA
PACT
PACTA
PACTION
PACTIONAL
PACTIONALLY
PACTUM
PAD
PADANG
PADASHA
PADAUK
PADCLOTH
PADDED
PADDER
PADDING
PADDLE
PADDLED
PADDLEFISH
PADDLEFISHES
PADDLER
PADDLEWOOD
PADDLING
PADDO
PADDOCK
PADDOCKED
PADDOCKING
PADDOCKRIDE
PADDOCKSTONE
PADDOCKSTOOL
PADDY
PADDYBIRD
PADDYMELON
PADDYWACK
PADDYWATCH
PADDYWHACK
PADELION
PADELLA
PADEMELON
PADFOOT
PADGE
PADI
PADISHAH
PADLE
PADLOCK
PADLOCKED
PADLOCKING
PADMASANA
PADMELON
PADNAG
PADOU
PADRE
PADRES
PADRI
PADRINO
PADROADIST
PADROADO
PADRONA
PADRONE
PADRONES
PADRONI
PADRONISM
PADS
PADSHAH
PADSTONE
PADTREE
PADUASOY
PAEAN
PAEANISM
PAEANIZE
PAEANIZED
PAEANIZING
PAEDARCHY
PAEDATROPHIA
PAEDATROPHY
PAEDERAST
PAEDERASTIC
PAEDERASTY
PAEDIATRIC
PAEDIATRICS
PAEDOBAPTISM
PAEDOBAPTIST
PAEDOGENESIS
PAEDOGENETIC
PAEDOLOGICAL
PAEDOLOGIST
PAEDOLOGY
PAEDOMETER
PAEDOMORPHIC
PAEDONYMIC
PAEDONYMY
PAEDOTRIBE
PAEDOTROPHIC
PAEDOTROPHY
PAEGEL
PAEGL
PAEGLE
PAELLA
PAENULA
PAENULAE
PAEON
PAEONIC
PAEPAE
PAGA
PAGADOR
PAGAN
PAGANDOM
PAGANIC
PAGANICAL
PAGANICALLY
PAGANISH
PAGANISM
PAGANIST
PAGANISTIC
PAGANITY
PAGANIZATION
PAGANIZE
PAGANIZED
PAGANIZER
PAGANIZING
PAGANRY
PAGE
PAGEANT
PAGEANTED
PAGEANTEER
PAGEANTIC
PAGEANTRIES
PAGEANTRY
PAGEBOY
PAGED
PAGER
PAGES
PAGGLE
PAGINA
PAGINAE
PAGINAL
PAGINARY
PAGINATE
PAGINATED
PAGINATING
PAGINATION
PAGINE
PAGING
PAGLE
PAGNE
PAGODA
PAGODAS
PAGOSCOPE
PAGRUS
PAGURIAN
PAGURID
PAGURINE
PAGUROID
PAGUS
PAH
PAHA
PAHAUTEA
PAHI
PAHLAVI
PAHLEVI
PAHMI
PAHO
PAHOEHOE
PAHUA
PAHUTAN
PAI
PAICHE
PAID
PAIDEIA
PAIDEUTIC
PAIDEUTICS
PAIDLE
PAIDOLOGICAL
PAIDOLOGIST
PAIDOLOGY
PAIK
PAIL
PAILETTE
PAILFUL
PAILLASSE
PAILLES
PAILLETTE
PAILLETTED
PAILLETTES
PAILLON
PAILLONS
PAILOLO
PAILOO
PAILOU
PAILOW
PAIN
PAINCH
PAINDEMAINE
PAINED
PAINFUL
PAINFULLY
PAINFULNESS
PAINING
PAININGLY
PAINKILLER
PAINLESS
PAINLESSLY
PAINLESSNESS
PAINS
PAINSTAKER
PAINSTAKING
PAINSWORTHY
PAINT
PAINTBOX
PAINTBRUSH
PAINTED
PAINTER
PAINTERLY
PAINTIER
PAINTIEST
PAINTINESS
PAINTING
PAINTINGNESS
PAINTINGS
PAINTLESS
PAINTPOT
PAINTRESS
PAINTRY
PAINTS
PAINTURE
PAINTY
PAIOCK
PAIOCKE
PAIP
PAIR
PAIRED
PAIREDNESS
PAIRER
PAIRIAL
PAIRING
PAIRMENT
PAIRS
PAIRT
PAIS
PAISA
PAISANITE
PAISANO
PAISE
PAIWARI
PAJAHUELLO
PAJAK
PAJAMA
PAJAMAED
PAJAMAS
PAJAROELLO
PAJERO
PAJOCK
PAKCHOI
PAKE
PAKEHA
PAKKA
PAKTONG
PAL
PALA
PALABRA

PALACE
PALACED
PALACEOUS
PALACH
PALADIN
PALAEOBOTANY
PALAEOCYCLIC
PALAEOETHNIC
PALAEOGLYPH
PALAEOGRAPH
PALAEOGRAPHY
PALAEOLATRY
PALAEOLITH
PALAEOLITHIC
PALAEOLITHY
PALAEOLOGIST
PALAEOLOGY
PALAEOPHYTIC
PALAEOPLAIN
PALAEOSOPHY
PALAEOSTYLIC
PALAEOSTYLY
PALAEOTYPE
PALAESTRA
PALAESTRAE
PALAESTRAL
PALAESTRIAN
PALAESTRIC
PALAESTRICS
PALAETIOLOGY
PALAFITTE
PALAGONITE
PALAGONITIC
PALAIOTYPE
PALAIS
PALAISTE
PALAITE
PALAKA
PALAMA
PALAMAE
PALAMATE
PALAME
PALAMPORE
PALANDER
PALANKA
PALANKEEN
PALANKEENED
PALANKEENING
PALANQUIN
PALANQUINED
PALANQUINING
PALAPALA
PALAPALAI
PALAR
PALAS
PALATABILITY
PALATABLE
PALATABLY
PALATAL
PALATALISM
PALATALITY
PALATALIZE
PALATE
PALATED
PALATEFUL
PALATIAL
PALATIALLY
PALATIALNESS
PALATIAN
PALATIC
PALATINAL
PALATINATE
PALATINE
PALATINITE
PALATION
PALATIST
PALATITIS
PALATIVE
PALATIZATION
PALATIZE
PALATODENTAL
PALATOGRAM
PALATOGRAPH
PALATOGRAPHY
PALATOMETER
PALAVER
PALAVERED
PALAVERER
PALAVERING
PALAVERIST
PALAVERMENT
PALAVEROUS
PALAY
PALAYAN
PALAZZI
PALAZZO
PALBERRY
PALCH
PALE
PALEA
PALEACEOUS
PALEAE
PALEANTHROPIC
PALEATE
PALEBELLY
PALEBREAST
PALEBUCK
PALED
PALEDNESS
PALEFACE
PALEGOLD
PALEHEARTED
PALEIFORM
PALELY
PALENESS
PALEOATAVISM
PALEOBIOLOGY
PALEOBOTANIC
PALEOBOTANY
PALEOCOSMIC
PALEOCRYSTAL
PALEOCRYSTIC
PALEOCYCLIC
PALEOECOLOGY
PALEOETHNIC
PALEOFAUNA
PALEOGENETIC
PALEOGLYPH
PALEOGRAPH
PALEOGRAPHER
PALEOGRAPHY
PALEOKINETIC
PALEOLA
PALEOLATE
PALEOLATRY
PALEOLITH
PALEOLITHIC
PALEOLITHIST
PALEOLITHOID
PALEOLITHY
PALEOLOGIST
PALEOLOGY
PALEONTOLOGY
PALEOPHYTIC
PALEOPICRITE
PALEOPLAIN
PALEOPSYCHIC
PALEOSTYLIC
PALEOSTYLY
PALEOTECHNIC
PALEOTHERMAL
PALEOTHERMIC
PALEOZOOLOGY
PALER
PALERON
PALEST
PALESTRA
PALESTRAE
PALESTRAL
PALESTRIAN
PALESTRIC
PALET
PALETIOLOGY
PALETOT
PALETTE
PALETZ
PALEW
PALEWISE
PALFRENIER
PALFREY
PALFREYED
PALFREYS
PALFRY
PALGAT
PALI
PALIER
PALIEST
PALIFICATION
PALIFORM
PALIKAR
PALIKINESIA
PALILA
PALILALIA
PALILOGETIC
PALILOGY
PALIMBACCHIC
PALIMPSEST
PALINAL
PALINDROME
PALINDROMIC
PALINDROMIST
PALING
PALINGENESIS
PALINGENETIC
PALINGENIST
PALINGENY
PALINODE
PALINODED
PALINODIAL
PALINODIC
PALINODIST
PALINODY
PALIPHRASIA
PALIRRHEA
PALIS
PALISADE
PALISADED
PALISADING
PALISADO
PALISADOES
PALISADOING
PALISH
PALISANDER
PALISTROPHIA
PALKEE
PALKI
PALL
PALLA
PALLADAMMIN
PALLADAMMINE
PALLADIC
PALLADIUM
PALLADIUMIZE
PALLADIZE
PALLADOUS
PALLAE
PALLAH
PALLALL
PALLAR
PALLASITE
PALLBEARER
PALLE
PALLED
PALLESCENCE
PALLESCENT
PALLESTHESIA
PALLET
PALLETING
PALLETIZE
PALLETIZED
PALLETIZING
PALLETTE
PALLHOLDER
PALLI
PALLIA
PALLIAL
PALLIARD
PALLIASSE
PALLIATA
PALLIATE
PALLIATED
PALLIATING
PALLIATION
PALLIATIVE
PALLIATIVELY
PALLIATOR
PALLIATORY
PALLID
PALLIDITY
PALLIDLY
PALLIDNESS
PALLIER
PALLIES
PALLIEST
PALLINESS
PALLING
PALLION
PALLIOPEDAL
PALLISER
PALLIUM
PALLIUMS
PALLOGRAPH
PALLOGRAPHIC
PALLOMETRIC
PALLONE
PALLOR
PALLY
PALM
PALMA
PALMACEOUS
PALMAD
PALMAR
PALMARIAN
PALMARIS
PALMARY
PALMATE
PALMATED
PALMATELY
PALMATIFID
PALMATIFORM
PALMATILOBED
PALMATION
PALMATISECT
PALMATURE
PALMCRIST
PALMED
PALMELLOID
PALMER
PALMERIES
PALMERITE
PALMERY
PALMETTE
PALMETTO
PALMETTOES
PALMETTOS
PALMETUM
PALMFUL
PALMI
PALMICOLEUS
PALMIER
PALMIEST
PALMIFEROUS
PALMIFORM
PALMIGRADE
PALMILLA
PALMILLO
PALMILOBATE
PALMILOBATED
PALMILOBED
PALMINERVATE
PALMINERVED
PALMING
PALMIPED
PALMIRA
PALMIST
PALMISTRY
PALMITATE
PALMITE
PALMITIC
PALMITIN
PALMITINE
PALMITO
PALMITONE
PALMITOS
PALMIVEINED
PALMIVOROUS
PALMO
PALMODIC
PALMOSCOPY
PALMOSPASMUS
PALMS
PALMULA
PALMUS
PALMWISE
PALMWOOD
PALMY
PALMYRA
PALO
PALOLO
PALOMA
PALOMBINO
PALOMETA
PALOMINO
PALOMINOS
PALOOKA
PALOSAPIS
PALOUR
PALOUSER
PALOVERDE
PALP
PALPABILITY
PALPABLE
PALPABLENESS
PALPABLY
PALPACLE
PALPAL
PALPATE
PALPATED
PALPATING
PALPATION
PALPATORY
PALPEBRA
PALPEBRAE
PALPEBRAL
PALPEBRATE
PALPEBRATION
PALPEBRITIS
PALPED
PALPI
PALPIFER
PALPIFEROUS
PALPIFORM
PALPIGER
PALPIGEROUS
PALPITANT

PALPITATE
PALPITATED
PALPITATING
PALPITATION
PALPOCIL
PALPON
PALPULUS
PALPUS
PALSGRAVE
PALSGRAVINE
PALSIED
PALSIES
PALSIFY
PALSTAFF
PALSTAVE
PALSTER
PALSY
PALSYING
PALT
PALTER
PALTERED
PALTERER
PALTERING
PALTERLY
PALTOCK
PALTRIER
PALTRIEST
PALTRILY
PALTRINESS
PALTRY
PALU
PALUDAL
PALUDAMENT
PALUDE
PALUDIAL
PALUDIC
PALUDICOLE
PALUDICOLINE
PALUDICOLOUS
PALUDIFEROUS
PALUDINAL
PALUDINE
PALUDINOUS
PALUDISM
PALUDOSE
PALUDOUS
PALULE
PALULI
PALULUS
PALUS
PALUSTRAL
PALUSTRIAN
PALUSTRINE
PALY
PALYNOLOGY
PAM
PAMBANMANCHE
PAMBY
PAMENT
PAMMENT
PAMPA
PAMPANITO
PAMPAS
PAMPEAN
PAMPER
PAMPERED
PAMPEREDLY
PAMPEREDNESS
PAMPERER
PAMPERING
PAMPERIZE
PAMPERO
PAMPEROS
PAMPHAGOUS
PAMPHARMACON
PAMPHLET
PAMPHLETAGE
PAMPHLETARY
PAMPHLETEER
PAMPHLETER
PAMPHLETIC
PAMPHLETICAL
PAMPHLETIZE
PAMPHYSIC
PAMPHYSICAL
PAMPHYSICISM
PAMPILION
PAMPINIFORM
PAMPINOCELE
PAMPLEGIA
PAMPOOTEE
PAMPOOTIE
PAMPRE
PAMPRODACTYL
PAMPSYCHISM
PAMPSYCHIST
PAN
PANABASE
PANACE
PANACEA
PANACEAN
PANACEIST
PANACHE
PANACHED
PANACHURE
PANADA
PANADE
PANAESTHESIA
PANAESTHETIC
PANAGIARION
PANAMA
PANAPOSPORY
PANARCHIC
PANARCHY
PANARIS
PANARITIUM
PANARTERITIS
PANARTHRITIS
PANARY
PANATELA
PANATROPHY
PANAX
PANCAKE
PANCAKED
PANCAKING
PANCARDITIS
PANCHAMA
PANCHART
PANCHAX
PANCHAYAT
PANCHAYET
PANCHEON
PANCHION
PANCHRESTON
PANCHROMATIC
PANCHWAY
PANCOSMIC
PANCOSMISM
PANCOSMIST
PANCRATIAN
PANCRATIAST
PANCRATIC
PANCRATICAL
PANCRATISM
PANCRATIST
PANCRATIUM
PANCREAS
PANCREATIC
PANCREATIN
PANCREATISM
PANCREATITIC
PANCREATITIS
PANCREATIZE
PANCREATOID
PANCREATOMY
PAND
PANDA
PANDAL
PANDAN
PANDAR
PANDARAM
PANDAS
PANDATION
PANDAVA
PANDECT
PANDEMIA
PANDEMIC
PANDEMICITY
PANDEMONIAC
PANDEMONIC
PANDEMONISM
PANDEMONIUM
PANDEMY
PANDER
PANDERAGE
PANDERED
PANDERER
PANDERESS
PANDERING
PANDERISM
PANDERIZE
PANDERLY
PANDERMITE
PANDEROUS
PANDIED
PANDIES
PANDIT
PANDITA
PANDLE
PANDLEWHEW
PANDOOR
PANDORA
PANDORE
PANDOUR
PANDOWDY
PANDROP
PANDURA
PANDURATE
PANDURIFORM
PANDY
PANDYING
PANE
PANED
PANEE
PANEGOISM
PANEGOIST
PANEGYRE
PANEGYRIC
PANEGYRICA
PANEGYRICAL
PANEGYRICIZE
PANEGYRICON
PANEGYRICUM
PANEGYRIS
PANEGYRIST
PANEGYRIZE
PANEGYRIZED
PANEGYRIZER
PANEGYRIZING
PANEITY
PANEL
PANELA
PANELATION
PANELED
PANELER
PANELING
PANELIST
PANELLATION
PANELLING
PANELWORK
PANENTHEISM
PANESTHESIA
PANESTHETIC
PANETELA
PANETELLA
PANETIERE
PANFIL
PANFISH
PANFRY
PANG
PANGA
PANGAMIC
PANGAMOUS
PANGAMOUSLY
PANGAMY
PANGANE
PANGARA
PANGASI
PANGEN
PANGENE
PANGENESIS
PANGENETIC
PANGENIC
PANGENS
PANGERANG
PANGLESS
PANGLESSLY
PANGLIMA
PANGOLIN
PANGUINGUI
PANHANDLE
PANHANDLED
PANHANDLER
PANHANDLING
PANHARMONIC
PANHAS
PANHEAD
PANHEADED
PANHIDROSIS
PANHUMAN
PANHYGROUS
PANHYPEREMIA
PANIC
PANICKED
PANICKING
PANICKY
PANICLE
PANICLED
PANICMONGER
PANICULATE
PANICULATED
PANICULATELY
PANIDROSIS
PANIER
PANIFICATION
PANIME
PANIMMUNITY
PANINI
PANIOLO
PANION
PANISC
PANISCUS
PANISK
PANIVOROUS
PANJANDRUM
PANK
PANKIN
PANLOGICAL
PANLOGISM
PANMAN
PANMELODION
PANMERISM
PANMERISTIC
PANMIXIA
PANMIXY
PANMNESIA
PANMUG
PANNADE
PANNAG
PANNAGE
PANNAM
PANNE
PANNED
PANNEL
PANNER
PANNERY
PANNEURITIC
PANNEURITIS
PANNICLE
PANNICULAR
PANNICULITIS
PANNICULUS
PANNIER
PANNIERED
PANNIERMAN
PANNIKIN
PANNING
PANNOSE
PANNOSELY
PANNUM
PANNUS
PANOCHA
PANOCHE
PANOCOCO
PANOISTIC
PANOMPHAEAN
PANOMPHAIC
PANOMPHEAN
PANOMPHIC
PANOPLIED
PANOPLIES
PANOPLIST
PANOPLY
PANOPLYING
PANOPTIC
PANOPTICAL
PANOPTICON
PANORAM
PANORAMA
PANORAMIC
PANORAMICAL
PANORAMIST
PANORPID
PANOSTEITIS
PANOSTITIS
PANOTITIS
PANOWIE
PANPHARMACON
PANPLEGIA
PANPOLISM
PANPSYCHIC
PANPSYCHISM
PANPSYCHIST
PANS
PANSCIENTIST
PANSCLEROSIS
PANSCLEROTIC
PANSE
PANSEXUAL
PANSEXUALISM
PANSEXUALIST
PANSEXUALITY
PANSEXUALIZE
PANSHARD
PANSIDE
PANSIDEMAN
PANSIED
PANSIERE
PANSIES
PANSIL
PANSINUITIS
PANSINUSITIS
PANSIT
PANSMITH
PANSOPHIC

PANSOPHICAL
PANSOPHISM
PANSOPHIST
PANSOPHY
PANSPERMIA
PANSPERMY
PANSY
PANT
PANTACOSM
PANTAGAMY
PANTAGOGUE
PANTAGRAPH
PANTAGRAPHIC
PANTALAN
PANTALEON
PANTALET
PANTALETS
PANTALETTE
PANTALETTED
PANTALETTES
PANTALGIA
PANTALON
PANTALOON
PANTALOONED
PANTALOONERY
PANTALOONS
PANTAMETER
PANTAMORPH
PANTAMORPHIA
PANTAMORPHIC
PANTANEMONE
PANTAPHOBIA
PANTARBE
PANTARCHY
PANTAS
PANTASCOPE
PANTASCOPIC
PANTATROPHIA
PANTATROPHY
PANTATYPE
PANTECHNIC
PANTECHNICON
PANTED
PANTELEPHONE
PANTELLERITE
PANTER
PANTERER
PANTH
PANTHEA
PANTHEIC
PANTHEISM
PANTHEIST
PANTHEISTIC
PANTHELISM
PANTHEOLOGY
PANTHEON
PANTHEONIC
PANTHEONIZE
PANTHER
PANTHERESS
PANTHERINE
PANTHERS
PANTHERWOOD
PANTHEUM
PANTIES
PANTILE
PANTILED
PANTILING
PANTINE
PANTING
PANTINGLY
PANTISOCRACY
PANTISOCRAT
PANTLE
PANTLER
PANTO
PANTOCHROME
PANTOCHROMIC
PANTOFFLE
PANTOFLE
PANTOGLOT
PANTOGRAPH
PANTOGRAPHER
PANTOGRAPHIC
PANTOGRAPHY
PANTOLOGIC
PANTOLOGICAL
PANTOLOGIST
PANTOLOGY
PANTOMANCER
PANTOMANIA
PANTOMETER
PANTOMETRY
PANTOMIME
PANTOMIMIC
PANTOMIMICAL
PANTOMIMICRY
PANTOMIMIST
PANTOMNESIA
PANTOMNESIC
PANTOMORPH
PANTOMORPHIA
PANTOMORPHIC
PANTON
PANTOON
PANTOPHAGIC
PANTOPHAGIST
PANTOPHAGY
PANTOPHILE
PANTOPHOBIA
PANTOPHOBIC
PANTOPHOBOUS
PANTOPTEROUS
PANTOSCOPE
PANTOSCOPIC
PANTOTACTIC
PANTOTHENATE
PANTOTYPE
PANTOUM
PANTRIES
PANTRY
PANTRYMAN
PANTRYWOMAN
PANTS
PANTSUIT
PANTUN
PANTYWAIST
PANUELO
PANUELOS
PANUNG
PANURE
PANURGIC
PANURGY
PANYAR
PANZER
PANZOISM
PANZOOTIA
PANZOOTIC
PANZOOTY
PAOLI
PAOLO
PAON
PAOPAO
PAP
PAPA
PAPABILITY
PAPABLE
PAPABOT
PAPABOTE
PAPACIES
PAPACY
PAPAGALLO
PAPAGAYO
PAPAIN
PAPAIO
PAPAL
PAPALISM
PAPALIST
PAPALISTIC
PAPALIZATION
PAPALIZE
PAPALIZER
PAPALOI
PAPALTY
PAPANE
PAPAPHOBIA
PAPAPHOBIST
PAPARCHICAL
PAPARCHY
PAPAVERIN
PAPAVERINE
PAPAVEROUS
PAPAW
PAPAYA
PAPAYOTIN
PAPBOAT
PAPE
PAPELON
PAPELONNE
PAPER
PAPERBACK
PAPERBARK
PAPERBOARD
PAPERED
PAPERER
PAPERHANGER
PAPERHANGING
PAPERING
PAPERKNIFE
PAPERKNIVES
PAPERMAKER
PAPERMAKING
PAPERMOUTH
PAPERN
PAPERS
PAPERSHELL
PAPERWEIGHT
PAPERWORK
PAPERY
PAPETERIE
PAPEY
PAPICOLAR
PAPICOLIST
PAPIER
PAPILLA
PAPILLAE
PAPILLAR
PAPILLARY
PAPILLATE
PAPILLECTOMY
PAPILLEDEMA
PAPILLIFORM
PAPILLITIS
PAPILLOEDEMA
PAPILLOMA
PAPILLOMAS
PAPILLOMATA
PAPILLON
PAPILLOSE
PAPILLOSITY
PAPILLOTE
PAPILLOUS
PAPILLULATE
PAPILLULE
PAPINGO
PAPION
PAPIOPIO
PAPISH
PAPISHER
PAPISM
PAPIST
PAPISTIC
PAPISTICAL
PAPISTICALLY
PAPISTRY
PAPIZE
PAPLESS
PAPMEAT
PAPOLATER
PAPOLATROUS
PAPOLATRY
PAPOOSE
PAPOOSEROOT
PAPOULA
PAPPESCENT
PAPPI
PAPPIER
PAPPIES
PAPPIEST
PAPPIFEROUS
PAPPIFORM
PAPPOOSE
PAPPOSE
PAPPOUS
PAPPOX
PAPPUS
PAPPY
PAPREG
PAPRICA
PAPRIKA
PAPULA
PAPULAE
PAPULAN
PAPULAR
PAPULATE
PAPULATED
PAPULATION
PAPULE
PAPULIFEROUS
PAPULOSE
PAPULOUS
PAPYRACEOUS
PAPYRAL
PAPYRI
PAPYRIAN
PAPYRIN
PAPYRINE
PAPYRITIOUS
PAPYROCRACY
PAPYROGRAPH
PAPYROLOGIST
PAPYROLOGY
PAPYROPHOBIA
PAPYROTAMIA
PAPYROTINT
PAPYROTYPE
PAPYRUS
PAR
PARA
PARABANATE
PARABANIC
PARABAPTISM
PARABASIC
PARABASIS
PARABEMA
PARABEMATA
PARABEMATIC
PARABIEN
PARABIOSIS
PARABIOTIC
PARABLAST
PARABLASTIC
PARABLE
PARABLED
PARABLEPSIA
PARABLEPSIS
PARABLEPSY
PARABLEPTIC
PARABLING
PARABOLA
PARABOLANUS
PARABOLAS
PARABOLIC
PARABOLICAL
PARABOLIFORM
PARABOLIST
PARABOLIZE
PARABOLIZED
PARABOLIZER
PARABOLIZING
PARABOLOID
PARABOLOIDAL
PARABOTULISM
PARABRANCHIA
PARABULIA
PARABULIC
PARACARMINE
PARACENTESIS
PARACENTRAL
PARACENTRIC
PARACEPHALUS
PARACHOLIA
PARACHOR
PARACHORDAL
PARACHROMA
PARACHRONISM
PARACHROSE
PARACHUTE
PARACHUTED
PARACHUTIC
PARACHUTING
PARACHUTISM
PARACHUTIST
PARACHUTISTS
PARACLETE
PARACME
PARACOELE
PARACOELIAN
PARACOLPITIS
PARACOLPIUM
PARACONE
PARACONID
PARACOROLLA
PARACROSTIC
PARACUSIA
PARACUSIC
PARACUSIS
PARACYANOGEN
PARACYESIS
PARACYSTIC
PARACYSTITIS
PARACYSTIUM
PARADE
PARADED
PARADENTAL
PARADENTIUM
PARADER
PARADERM
PARADIASTOLE
PARADIDYMAL
PARADIDYMIS
PARADIGM
PARADIGMATIC
PARADING
PARADINGLY
PARADISAIC
PARADISAICAL
PARADISAL
PARADISE
PARADISEAN
PARADISIAC
PARADISIACAL
PARADISIAL
PARADISIAN
PARADISIC

PARADISICAL
PARADO
PARADOS
PARADOSES
PARADOX
PARADOXAL
PARADOXER
PARADOXIAL
PARADOXIC
PARADOXICAL
PARADOXICIAN
PARADOXIDIAN
PARADOXIST
PARADOXOLOGY
PARADOXURE
PARADOXY
PARADROMIC
PARADROP
PARAENESIS
PARAENESIZE
PARAENETIC
PARAENETICAL
PARAESTHESIA
PARAESTHETIC
PARAFFIN
PARAFFINE
PARAFFINED
PARAFFINER
PARAFFINIC
PARAFFINING
PARAFFINOID
PARAFFLE
PARAFLE
PARAFORM
PARAFRONT
PARAGANGLION
PARAGASTER
PARAGASTRAL
PARAGASTRIC
PARAGASTRULA
PARAGE
PARAGENESIA
PARAGENESIS
PARAGENETIC
PARAGENIC
PARAGERONTIC
PARAGEUSIA
PARAGEUSIC
PARAGEUSIS
PARAGLENAL
PARAGLOSSA
PARAGLOSSAE
PARAGLOSSAL
PARAGLOSSATE
PARAGLOSSIA
PARAGNATH
PARAGNATHISM
PARAGNATHOUS
PARAGNATHS
PARAGNATHUS
PARAGNOSIA
PARAGOGE
PARAGOGIC
PARAGOGICAL
PARAGOGIZE
PARAGON
PARAGONED
PARAGONING
PARAGONITE
PARAGONITIC
PARAGRAM
PARAGRAPH
PARAGRAPHED
PARAGRAPHER
PARAGRAPHIA
PARAGRAPHIC
PARAGRAPHING
PARAGRAPHIST
PARAH
PARAHEMATIN
PARAHEPATIC
PARAHOPEITE
PARAHORMONE
PARAHYPNOSIS
PARAIBA
PARAKEET
PARAKILYA
PARAKINESIA
PARAKINESIS
PARAKINETIC
PARALALIA
PARALDEHYDE
PARALEIPSIS
PARALEPSIS
PARALEXIA
PARALEXIC
PARALGESIA
PARALGESIC
PARALIAN
PARALININ
PARALIPOMENA
PARALIPSIS
PARALITICAL
PARALLACTIC
PARALLAX
PARALLEL
PARALLELED
PARALLELER
PARALLELING
PARALLELISM
PARALLELIST
PARALLELITH
PARALLELIZE
PARALLELIZED
PARALLELIZER
PARALLELLED
PARALLELLING
PARALLELLY
PARALLELOGRAM
PARALLELS
PARALOGIC
PARALOGICAL
PARALOGISM
PARALOGIST
PARALOGISTIC
PARALOGIZE
PARALOGY
PARALUMINITE
PARALYSES
PARALYSIS
PARALYTIC
PARALYTICAL
PARALYZANT
PARALYZATION
PARALYZE
PARALYZED
PARALYZER
PARALYZING
PARAMAGNET
PARAMAGNETIC
PARAMASTITIS
PARAMASTOID
PARAMATTA
PARAMECIUM
PARAMEDIAN
PARAMENIA
PARAMENT
PARAMERE
PARAMERIC
PARAMESE
PARAMESIAL
PARAMETER
PARAMETRAL
PARAMETRIC
PARAMETRICAL
PARAMETRITIC
PARAMETRITIS
PARAMID
PARAMIDE
PARAMILITARY
PARAMIMIA
PARAMITA
PARAMITOM
PARAMITOME
PARAMNESIA
PARAMO
PARAMORPH
PARAMORPHIC
PARAMORPHISM
PARAMORPHOUS
PARAMOS
PARAMOUNT
PARAMOUNTCY
PARAMOUNTLY
PARAMOUR
PARAMOURS
PARAMUTHETIC
PARAMYELIN
PARAMYOTONE
PARAMYOTONIA
PARANASAL
PARANATELLON
PARANEMA
PARANEMATIC
PARANEPHROS
PARANEPIONIC
PARANETE
PARANG
PARANGI
PARANJA
PARANOEAC
PARANOIA
PARANOIAC
PARANOID
PARANOIDAL
PARANOIDISM
PARANOMIA
PARANOSIC
PARANTHELION
PARANUCLEAR
PARANUCLEATE
PARANUCLEI
PARANUCLEIC
PARANUCLEIN
PARANUCLEUS
PARANYMPH
PARANYMPHAL
PARAO
PARAPARESIS
PARAPARETIC
PARAPEGM
PARAPEGMA
PARAPEGMATA
PARAPET
PARAPETALOUS
PARAPETED
PARAPH
PARAPHASIA
PARAPHASIC
PARAPHED
PARAPHEMIA
PARAPHERNA
PARAPHERNAL
PARAPHIA
PARAPHIMOSIS
PARAPHING
PARAPHONIA
PARAPHONIC
PARAPHRASE
PARAPHRASED
PARAPHRASER
PARAPHRASIA
PARAPHRASING
PARAPHRAST
PARAPHRASTIC
PARAPHRENIA
PARAPHRENIC
PARAPHYLLIA
PARAPHYLLIUM
PARAPHYSATE
PARAPHYSICAL
PARAPHYSIS
PARAPLASM
PARAPLASMIC
PARAPLASTIC
PARAPLASTIN
PARAPLECTIC
PARAPLEGIA
PARAPLEGIC
PARAPLEGY
PARAPLEURUM
PARAPOD
PARAPODIAL
PARAPODIUM
PARAPRAXES
PARAPRAXIA
PARAPRAXIS
PARAPROCTIUM
PARAPSIDAL
PARAPSIS
PARAPSYCHISM
PARAPTERA
PARAPTERAL
PARAPTERON
PARAPTERUM
PARAQUADRATE
PARAQUET
PARAREKA
PARARTHRIA
PARASANG
PARASCENIUM
PARASCEVE
PARASELENAE
PARASELENE
PARASELENIC
PARASHAH
PARASHIOTH
PARASHOTH
PARASITAL
PARASITARY
PARASITE
PARASITES
PARASITIC
PARASITICAL
PARASITICIDE
PARASITISM
PARASITIZE
PARASITOID
PARASITOLOGY
PARASITOSIS
PARASOL
PARASOLED
PARASOLETTE
PARASPECIFIC
PARASPHENOID
PARASTADES
PARASTAS
PARASTATIC
PARASTEMON
PARASTEMONAL
PARASTERNAL
PARASTERNUM
PARASTICHIES
PARASTICHY
PARASTYLE
PARASYNAPSIS
PARASYNAPTIC
PARASYNDESIS
PARASYNESIS
PARASYNETIC
PARASYPHILIS
PARASYSTOLE
PARATACTIC
PARATACTICAL
PARATAXIS
PARATE
PARATERMINAL
PARATHESIS
PARATHETIC
PARATHORMONE
PARATHYROID
PARATITLA
PARATITLES
PARATITLON
PARATOMIAL
PARATOMIUM
PARATONIC
PARATONNERRE
PARATORIUM
PARATORY
PARATRIPTIC
PARATROOPER
PARATROOPS
PARATROPHIC
PARATROPHY
PARATYPE
PARATYPHOID
PARATYPIC
PARATYPICAL
PARAVAIL
PARAVANE
PARAVANT
PARAVAUXITE
PARAVENT
PARAVESICAL
PARAXIAL
PARAXIALLY
PARAXON
PARAXONIC
PARAZONIUM
PARBAKE
PARBOIL
PARBOILED
PARBOILING
PARBREAK
PARBUCKLE
PARBUCKLED
PARBUCKLING
PARCEL
PARCELED
PARCELING
PARCELLED
PARCELLING
PARCELS
PARCENARY
PARCENER
PARCH
PARCHED
PARCHEESI
PARCHEMIN
PARCHER
PARCHESI
PARCHING
PARCHINGLY
PARCHISI
PARCHMENT
PARCHMENTIZE
PARCHY
PARCIDENTATE
PARCILOQUY
PARCITY
PARCLOSE
PARCOOK
PARD
PARDAL

PARDALE
PARDALOTE
PARDAO
PARDAOS
PARDE
PARDED
PARDEE
PARDESI
PARDHAN
PARDI
PARDIE
PARDIEU
PARDINE
PARDNER
PARDO
PARDON
PARDONABLE
PARDONABLY
PARDONED
PARDONEE
PARDONER
PARDONING
PARDONMONGER
PARDY
PARE
PAREA
PARECIOUS
PARED
PAREGAL
PAREGORIC
PAREGORICAL
PAREIRA
PAREJA
PAREL
PARELL
PARELLA
PARELLE
PAREN
PARENCHYM
PARENCHYMA
PARENCHYMAL
PARENCHYME
PARENCHYMOUS
PARENESIS
PARENESIZE
PARENETIC
PARENETICAL
PARENT
PARENTAGE
PARENTAL
PARENTALISM
PARENTALITY
PARENTALLY
PARENTATE
PARENTATION
PARENTELA
PARENTELIC
PARENTERAL
PARENTERALLY
PARENTHESES
PARENTHESIS
PARENTHESIZE
PARENTHETIC
PARENTHOOD
PARENTICIDE
PARER
PARERETHESIS
PARERGAL
PARERGIC
PARERGON
PARESES
PARESIS
PARESTHESIA
PARESTHETIC
PARETIC
PARETICALLY
PAREU
PAREUNIA
PAREVE
PARFAIT
PARFEY
PARFILAGE
PARFLECHE
PARFLESH
PARFOCAL
PARGANA
PARGANNA
PARGASITE
PARGE
PARGET
PARGETED
PARGETER
PARGETING
PARGETTED
PARGETTING
PARGO
PARGOS
PARHELIA
PARHELIACAL
PARHELIC
PARHELION
PARHELIUM
PARHOMOLOGY
PARHYPATE
PARI
PARIAH
PARIAL
PARIAN
PARICA
PARIDIGITATE
PARIDROSIS
PARIES
PARIET
PARIETAL
PARIETARY
PARIETES
PARIETOJUGAL
PARIFY
PARIGENIN
PARIGLIN
PARILLIN
PARIMUTUEL
PARINE
PARING
PARINGS
PARIPINNATE
PARISH
PARISHED
PARISHEN
PARISHIONAL
PARISHIONATE
PARISHIONER
PARISIA
PARISIS
PARISOLOGY
PARISON
PARISONIC
PARISTHMIC
PARISTHMION
PARISYLLABIC
PARITIES
PARITOR
PARITY
PARIVINCULAR
PARK
PARKA
PARKED
PARKEE
PARKER
PARKIN
PARKING
PARKLAND
PARKLEAVES
PARKWAY
PARKY
PARLANCE
PARLANDO
PARLATORY
PARLAY
PARLE
PARLEMENT
PARLESIE
PARLEY
PARLEYED
PARLEYER
PARLEYING
PARLEYS
PARLIAMENT
PARLIAMENTAL
PARLIAMENTARIAN
PARLIAMENTARY
PARLIAMENTER
PARLING
PARLISH
PARLOR
PARLORMAID
PARLOUR
PARLOUS
PARLOUSLY
PARLOUSNESS
PARLY
PARMA
PARMACETY
PARMACK
PARMAK
PARMENTIER
PARNAS
PARNEL
PARO
PAROARION
PAROARIUM
PAROCCIPITAL
PAROCH
PAROCHIAL
PAROCHIALISM
PAROCHIALIST
PAROCHIAN
PAROCHIN
PAROCHINE
PARODE
PARODI
PARODIABLE
PARODIAL
PARODIC
PARODICAL
PARODIED
PARODIES
PARODINIA
PARODIST
PARODISTIC
PARODONTITIS
PARODOS
PARODUS
PARODY
PARODYING
PAROECIOUS
PAROECIOUSLY
PAROECISM
PAROECY
PAROEMIA
PAROEMIAC
PAROEMIOLOGY
PAROICOUS
PAROL
PAROLABLE
PAROLE
PAROLED
PAROLEE
PAROLI
PAROLING
PAROLIST
PAROMOEON
PAROMOLOGIA
PAROMOLOGY
PARONOMASIA
PARONOMASIAN
PARONOMASTIC
PARONYCHIA
PARONYCHIAL
PARONYCHIUM
PARONYM
PARONYMIC
PARONYMIZE
PARONYMOUS
PARONYMY
PAROO
PAROOPHORON
PAROPSIS
PAROPTESIS
PAROPTIC
PAROQUET
PAROREXIA
PAROSMIA
PAROSMIC
PAROSTEAL
PAROSTEITIS
PAROSTEOSIS
PAROSTOSIS
PAROSTOTIC
PAROTIC
PAROTID
PAROTIDITIS
PAROTIS
PAROTITIC
PAROTITIS
PAROTOID
PAROUS
PAROUSIA
PAROVARIAN
PAROVARIUM
PAROXYSM
PAROXYSMAL
PAROXYSMALLY
PAROXYSMIC
PAROXYTONE
PAROXYTONIC
PARPAL
PARPEN
PARQUET
PARQUETED
PARQUETING
PARQUETRY
PARR
PARRAH
PARRAKEET
PARRAL
PARRALL
PARRAMATTA
PARRED
PARREL
PARRHESIA
PARRICIDAL
PARRICIDALLY
PARRICIDE
PARRICIDED
PARRICIDIAL
PARRIDGE
PARRIED
PARRIER
PARRIES
PARRING
PARRITCH
PARROCK
PARROKET
PARROQUET
PARROT
PARROTBEAK
PARROTBILL
PARROTED
PARROTER
PARROTING
PARROTLET
PARROTRY
PARROTY
PARRS
PARRY
PARRYING
PARS
PARSE
PARSEC
PARSED
PARSER
PARSIMONIOUS
PARSIMONY
PARSING
PARSLEY
PARSLEYWORT
PARSNIP
PARSON
PARSONAGE
PARSONARCHY
PARSONED
PARSONESE
PARSONESS
PARSONET
PARSONIC
PARSONICAL
PARSONICALLY
PARSONING
PARSONITY
PARSONLY
PARSONOLATRY
PARSONOLOGY
PARSONRY
PARSONS
PARSONSITE
PART
PARTABLE
PARTAGE
PARTAKE
PARTAKEN
PARTAKER
PARTAKING
PARTAN
PARTANFULL
PARTED
PARTEN
PARTER
PARTERRE
PARTERRED
PARTES
PARTHENIAD
PARTHENIAN
PARTHENIC
PARTHENOGENY
PARTHENOLOGY
PARTI
PARTIAL
PARTIALIST
PARTIALITIES
PARTIALITY
PARTIALLY
PARTIALNESS
PARTIARY
PARTIBILITY
PARTIBLE
PARTICIPABLE
PARTICIPANCE
PARTICIPANCY
PARTICIPANT
PARTICIPATE
PARTICIPATED
PARTICIPATOR
PARTICIPIAL
PARTICIPLE

PARTICLE
PARTICLES
PARTICULAR
PARTICULARLY
PARTICULATE
PARTICULE
PARTIES
PARTIGEN
PARTILE
PARTIM
PARTIMEN
PARTIMENTO
PARTING
PARTINIUM
PARTISAN
PARTISANSHIP
PARTITA
PARTITE
PARTITION
PARTITIONAL
PARTITIONARY
PARTITIONED
PARTITIONER
PARTITIONING
PARTITIONIST
PARTITIVE
PARTITURA
PARTIVERSAL
PARTIVITY
PARTIZAN
PARTLESS
PARTLET
PARTLY
PARTNER
PARTNERSHIP
PARTOOK
PARTRIDGE
PARTRIDGES
PARTRIDGING
PARTS
PARTSCHINITE
PARTURE
PARTURIATE
PARTURIENCE
PARTURIENCY
PARTURIENT
PARTURITION
PARTURITIVE
PARTY
PARTYISM
PARTYIST
PARTYMONGER
PARULIS
PARUMBILICAL
PARURA
PARURE
PARURIA
PARVANIMITY
PARVE
PARVENU
PARVENUISM
PARVIFLOROUS
PARVIFOLIATE
PARVIFOLIOUS
PARVIPOTENT
PARVIS
PARVISCIENT
PARVITUDE
PARVOLIN
PARVOLINE
PARVULE
PARYPHODROME
PAS
PASA
PASAN
PASANG
PASAR
PASCHAL
PASCHALIST
PASCHFLOWER
PASCOITE
PASCOLA
PASCUAGE
PASCUAL
PASCUOUS
PASEAR
PASENG
PASEO
PASEWA
PASH
PASHA
PASHALIC
PASHALIK
PASHED
PASHIM
PASHING
PASHM
PASHMINA
PASI
PASIG
PASIGRAPHIC
PASIGRAPHY
PASILALY
PASILLO
PASIN
PASIS
PASMO
PASO
PASQUEFLOWER
PASQUIL
PASQUILANT
PASQUILER
PASQUILIC
PASQUILLANT
PASQUILLER
PASQUILLIC
PASQUIN
PASQUINADE
PASQUINADED
PASQUINADER
PASQUINADING
PASS
PASSABLE
PASSABLENESS
PASSABLY
PASSACAGLIA
PASSACAGLIO
PASSADE
PASSADO
PASSADOES
PASSADOS
PASSAGE
PASSAGEABLE
PASSAGED
PASSAGER
PASSAGEWAY
PASSAGGI
PASSAGGIO
PASSAGING
PASSAGIO
PASSAMENT
PASSANGRAHAN
PASSANT
PASSAREE
PASSATA
PASSAY
PASSBACK
PASSBOOK
PASSE
PASSED
PASSEE
PASSEGARDE
PASSEL
PASSEMEASURE
PASSEMENT
PASSEMENTED
PASSEMENTING
PASSEMEZZO
PASSEN
PASSENGER
PASSEPIED
PASSER
PASSERBY
PASSERINE
PASSERS
PASSES
PASSEWA
PASSGANG
PASSIBILITY
PASSIBLE
PASSIBLENESS
PASSIM
PASSING
PASSINGLY
PASSION
PASSIONAL
PASSIONATE
PASSIONATELY
PASSIONATIVE
PASSIONATO
PASSIONED
PASSIONFLOWER
PASSIONLESS
PASSIONWORT
PASSIR
PASSIVAL
PASSIVATE
PASSIVATION
PASSIVE
PASSIVELY
PASSIVENESS
PASSIVISM
PASSIVIST
PASSIVITY
PASSKEY
PASSLESS
PASSMAN
PASSOMETER
PASSOUT
PASSOVER
PASSPENNY
PASSPORT
PASSULATE
PASSULATION
PASSUS
PASSWAY
PASSWORD
PAST
PASTA
PASTE
PASTEBOARD
PASTEBOARDY
PASTED
PASTEDOWN
PASTEL
PASTELIST
PASTELLIST
PASTER
PASTERER
PASTERN
PASTERNED
PASTEURELLA
PASTEURISE
PASTEURISM
PASTEURIZE
PASTEURIZED
PASTEURIZER
PASTEURIZING
PASTICCIO
PASTICHE
PASTICHEUR
PASTIER
PASTIES
PASTIEST
PASTIL
PASTILE
PASTILED
PASTILING
PASTILLE
PASTILLED
PASTILLING
PASTIME
PASTIMER
PASTINESS
PASTING
PASTLER
PASTNESS
PASTOPHOR
PASTOPHORION
PASTOPHORIUM
PASTOPHORUS
PASTOR
PASTORA
PASTORAL
PASTORALE
PASTORALES
PASTORALI
PASTORALIST
PASTORALITY
PASTORALIZE
PASTORALLY
PASTORALNESS
PASTORATE
PASTORITA
PASTORIUM
PASTORIUMS
PASTORIZE
PASTORLY
PASTORSHIP
PASTOSE
PASTOSITY
PASTOUR
PASTOURELLE
PASTRAMI
PASTRIES
PASTRY
PASTRYMAN
PASTURABLE
PASTURAGE
PASTURAL
PASTURE
PASTURED
PASTURELAND
PASTURER
PASTURES
PASTURING
PASTY
PASUL
PAT
PATA
PATACA
PATACAO
PATACHE
PATACO
PATACOON
PATAGIA
PATAGIAL
PATAGIATE
PATAGIUM
PATAGON
PATAGONIA
PATAKA
PATAMAR
PATANA
PATAND
PATAO
PATAPAT
PATAQUE
PATART
PATAS
PATASHTE
PATATA
PATAVINITY
PATBALL
PATBALLER
PATCH
PATCHABLE
PATCHCOCK
PATCHED
PATCHER
PATCHERIES
PATCHERY
PATCHES
PATCHHEAD
PATCHIER
PATCHIEST
PATCHILY
PATCHINESS
PATCHING
PATCHLEAF
PATCHOULI
PATCHOULY
PATCHWORD
PATCHWORK
PATCHY
PATE
PATEFY
PATEL
PATELLA
PATELLAE
PATELLAR
PATELLAROID
PATELLATE
PATELLIFORM
PATELLINE
PATELLOID
PATELLULA
PATELLULAE
PATELLULATE
PATEN
PATENCY
PATENER
PATENT
PATENTABLE
PATENTABLY
PATENTE
PATENTED
PATENTEE
PATENTING
PATENTLY
PATENTOR
PATER
PATERA
PATERAE
PATERERO
PATERIFORM
PATERISSA
PATERNAL
PATERNALISM
PATERNALIST
PATERNALITY
PATERNALIZE
PATERNALLY
PATERNITY
PATERNOSTER
PATESI
PATESIATE
PATETICO
PATH
PATHBREAKER
PATHED
PATHEMA
PATHEMATIC
PATHETIC
PATHETICAL

PATHETICALLY
PATHETICATE
PATHFARER
PATHFINDER
PATHFINDING
PATHIC
PATHLESS
PATHLESSNESS
PATHMENT
PATHOANATOMY
PATHOBIOLOGY
PATHOCHEMISTRY
PATHODONTIA
PATHOGEN
PATHOGENE
PATHOGENESIS
PATHOGENESY
PATHOGENETIC
PATHOGENIC
PATHOGENOUS
PATHOGENY
PATHOGERM
PATHOGERMIC
PATHOGNOMIC
PATHOGNOMY
PATHOGNOSTIC
PATHOGRAPHY
PATHOLOGIC
PATHOLOGICAL
PATHOLOGIST
PATHOLOGY
PATHOLYSIS
PATHOLYTIC
PATHOMANIA
PATHOMIMESIS
PATHOMIMICRY
PATHONOMIA
PATHONOMY
PATHOPHOBIA
PATHOPHORIC
PATHOPLASTIC
PATHOPOEIA
PATHOPOIESIS
PATHOPOIETIC
PATHOS
PATHOSOCIAL
PATHS
PATHWAY
PATHY
PATIBLE
PATIBULARY
PATIBULATE
PATIENCE
PATIENCY
PATIENT
PATIENTLY
PATIENTNESS
PATIN
PATINA
PATINAE
PATINATE
PATINATION
PATINE
PATINED
PATINIZE
PATINOUS
PATIO
PATIOS
PATISE
PATISSERIE
PATNIDAR
PATO
PATOIS
PATOLA
PATONCE
PATRIA
PATRIAL
PATRIARCH
PATRIARCHAL
PATRIARCHATE
PATRIARCHESS
PATRIARCHIC
PATRIARCHIST
PATRIARCHY
PATRICIAN
PATRICIANLY
PATRICIATE
PATRICIDAL
PATRICIDE
PATRICK
PATRICO
PATRIDGE
PATRILINEAL
PATRILINEAR
PATRILINY
PATRILOCAL
PATRIMONIAL
PATRIMONIES
PATRIMONY
PATRIN
PATRIOLATRY
PATRIOT
PATRIOTEER
PATRIOTIC
PATRIOTICAL
PATRIOTICS
PATRIOTISM
PATRIST
PATRISTIC
PATRISTICAL
PATRISTICISM
PATRISTICS
PATRIX
PATRIZATE
PATRIZATION
PATROCINIUM
PATROCLINIC
PATROCLINOUS
PATROCLINY
PATROGENESIS
PATROL
PATROLE
PATROLLED
PATROLLER
PATROLLING
PATROLMAN
PATROLOGIC
PATROLOGICAL
PATROLOGIST
PATROLOGY
PATRON
PATRONAGE
PATRONAL
PATRONATE
PATRONESS
PATRONITE
PATRONIZE
PATRONIZED
PATRONIZER
PATRONIZING
PATRONLY
PATRONNE
PATRONYM
PATRONYMIC
PATRONYMY
PATROON
PATROONRY
PATROULLART
PATRUITY
PATSY
PATT
PATTA
PATTAMAR
PATTARA
PATTE
PATTED
PATTEE
PATTEN
PATTENED
PATTENER
PATTER
PATTERED
PATTERER
PATTERING
PATTERIST
PATTERN
PATTERNED
PATTERNER
PATTERNING
PATTERNIZE
PATTERNMAKER
PATTERNS
PATTERNY
PATTI
PATTIDARI
PATTIE
PATTIES
PATTING
PATTOO
PATTU
PATTY
PATTYPAN
PATU
PATUCA
PATULENT
PATULIN
PATULOUS
PATULOUSLY
PATULOUSNESS
PATWARI
PATY
PAU
PAUA
PAUCIDENTATE
PAUCIFLOROUS
PAUCIFOLIATE
PAUCIFOLIOUS
PAUCIFY
PAUCIJUGATE
PAUCILOCULAR
PAUCILOQUENT
PAUCILOQUY
PAUCINERVATE
PAUCIPINNATE
PAUCIPLICATE
PAUCIRADIATE
PAUCISPIRAL
PAUCITIES
PAUCITY
PAUGHTY
PAUK
PAUKPAN
PAUKY
PAUL
PAULAR
PAULDRON
PAULIE
PAULIN
PAULOPAST
PAULOPOST
PAULOSPORE
PAUN
PAUNCH
PAUNCHE
PAUNCHED
PAUNCHFUL
PAUNCHILY
PAUNCHINESS
PAUNCHY
PAUNE
PAUP
PAUPER
PAUPERAGE
PAUPERATE
PAUPERED
PAUPERESS
PAUPERISM
PAUPERITIC
PAUPERIZE
PAUPERIZED
PAUPERIZING
PAURAQUE
PAUROPOD
PAUSABLY
PAUSAL
PAUSATION
PAUSE
PAUSED
PAUSEMENT
PAUSER
PAUSING
PAUSSID
PAUT
PAUXI
PAVADE
PAVAGE
PAVAN
PAVANE
PAVE
PAVED
PAVEED
PAVEMENT
PAVEMENTAL
PAVEN
PAVER
PAVESTONE
PAVID
PAVIDITY
PAVIE
PAVIES
PAVILION
PAVILLON
PAVING
PAVIOR
PAVIOUR
PAVIS
PAVISADE
PAVISADO
PAVISE
PAVISER
PAVISOR
PAVISSE
PAVOIS
PAVONATED
PAVONAZZO
PAVONE
PAVONIAN
PAVONINE
PAVONIZE
PAVY
PAW
PAWAW
PAWDITE
PAWED
PAWER
PAWING
PAWK
PAWKERY
PAWKIER
PAWKIEST
PAWKILY
PAWKINESS
PAWKRIE
PAWKY
PAWL
PAWN
PAWNABLE
PAWNAGE
PAWNBROKER
PAWNBROKERY
PAWNBROKING
PAWNE
PAWNED
PAWNEE
PAWNER
PAWNIE
PAWNING
PAWNOR
PAWNS
PAWNSHOP
PAWPAW
PAX
PAXILLA
PAXILLAE
PAXILLAR
PAXILLARY
PAXILLATE
PAXILLI
PAXILLIFORM
PAXILLOSE
PAXILLUS
PAXIUBA
PAXWAX
PAY
PAYABILITY
PAYABLE
PAYABLY
PAYBOX
PAYCHECK
PAYDAY
PAYED
PAYEE
PAYER
PAYING
PAYLOAD
PAYMASTER
PAYMENT
PAYMISTRESS
PAYNIM
PAYNIMHOOD
PAYNIMRIE
PAYNIMRY
PAYOFF
PAYOLA
PAYONG
PAYROLL
PAYSAGE
PAYSAGIST
PAYSANNE
PAYYETAN
PAZAREE
PE
PEA
PEABERRY
PEABIRD
PEABUSH
PEACE
PEACEABLE
PEACEABLY
PEACEBREAKER
PEACEFUL
PEACEFULLY
PEACEFULNESS
PEACELESS
PEACEMAKER
PEACEMAKING
PEACEMAN
PEACEMONGER
PEACETIME
PEACH
PEACHBERRY
PEACHBLOOM
PEACHBLOSSOM
PEACHBLOW
PEACHEN

PEACHER
PEACHERY
PEACHICK
PEACHIER
PEACHIEST
PEACHIFY
PEACHINESS
PEACHLET
PEACHWOOD
PEACHWORT
PEACHY
PEACK
PEACOAT
PEACOCK
PEACOCKERY
PEACOCKISH
PEACOCKISHLY
PEACOCKS
PEACOCKY
PEACOD
PEAFOWL
PEAFOWLS
PEAG
PEAGE
PEAGOOSE
PEAHEN
PEAI
PEAIISM
PEAK
PEAKED
PEAKEDLY
PEAKEDNESS
PEAKER
PEAKGOOSE
PEAKILY
PEAKINESS
PEAKING
PEAKISH
PEAKISHLY
PEAKISHNESS
PEAKY
PEAL
PEALED
PEALER
PEALIKE
PEALING
PEAN
PEANE
PEANUT
PEAPOD
PEAR
PEARCE
PEARCEITE
PEARCH
PEARL
PEARLASH
PEARLBERRY
PEARLBIRD
PEARLBUSH
PEARLED
PEARLER
PEARLET
PEARLFISH
PEARLIER
PEARLIEST
PEARLIN
PEARLING
PEARLINGS
PEARLISH
PEARLITE
PEARLITIC
PEARLSIDES
PEARLSPAR
PEARLWEED
PEARLWORT
PEARLY
PEARMAIN
PEARMONGER
PEARS
PEART
PEARTEN
PEARWOOD
PEAS
PEASANT
PEASANTIZE
PEASANTLIKE
PEASANTLY
PEASANTRY
PEASCOD
PEASE
PEASECOD
PEASEWEEP
PEASHOOTER
PEASOUPER
PEASTAKE
PEASTAKING
PEASTICK
PEASTICKING
PEASTONE
PEASY
PEAT
PEATERY
PEATHOUSE
PEATIER
PEATIEST
PEATMAN
PEATMEN
PEATSHIP
PEATSTACK
PEATWEED
PEATWOOD
PEATY
PEAU
PEAUDER
PEAVEY
PEAVIE
PEAVINE
PEAVY
PEBA
PEBBLE
PEBBLED
PEBBLES
PEBBLESTONE
PEBBLEWARE
PEBBLIER
PEBBLIEST
PEBBLING
PEBBLY
PEBRINE
PEBRINOUS
PECA
PECAN
PECCABILITY
PECCABLE
PECCADILLO
PECCADILLOES
PECCADILLOS
PECCANCIES
PECCANCY
PECCANT
PECCANTLY
PECCANTNESS
PECCARIES
PECCARY
PECCATION
PECCAVI
PECE
PECH
PECHAN
PECHAY
PECHILI
PECHT
PECHYS
PECIFY
PECITE
PECK
PECKAGE
PECKED
PECKER
PECKERWOOD
PECKET
PECKHAMITE
PECKIER
PECKIEST
PECKINESS
PECKING
PECKISH
PECKISHLY
PECKISHNESS
PECKLE
PECKLED
PECKLY
PECKY
PECORINO
PECTASE
PECTATE
PECTEN
PECTIC
PECTIN
PECTINACEOUS
PECTINAL
PECTINASE
PECTINATE
PECTINATED
PECTINATELY
PECTINATION
PECTINEAL
PECTINES
PECTINEUS
PECTINID
PECTINIFORM
PECTINITE
PECTINOUS
PECTIZABLE
PECTIZATION
PECTIZE
PECTIZED
PECTIZING
PECTOLITE
PECTORAL
PECTORALGIA
PECTORALIS
PECTORALIST
PECTORILOQUE
PECTORILOQUY
PECTOUS
PECTRON
PECTUNCULATE
PECTUS
PECUL
PECULATE
PECULATED
PECULATING
PECULATION
PECULATOR
PECULIAR
PECULIARISM
PECULIARITY
PECULIARIZE
PECULIARIZED
PECULIARLY
PECULIUM
PECUNIARY
PECUNIOSITY
PECUNIOUS
PED
PEDA
PEDAGE
PEDAGESE
PEDAGOG
PEDAGOGIC
PEDAGOGICAL
PEDAGOGICS
PEDAGOGISM
PEDAGOGIST
PEDAGOGUE
PEDAGOGUERY
PEDAGOGUISH
PEDAGOGY
PEDAL
PEDALED
PEDALER
PEDALFER
PEDALIAN
PEDALIER
PEDALING
PEDALIST
PEDALITER
PEDALITY
PEDALLED
PEDALLER
PEDANT
PEDANTESS
PEDANTIC
PEDANTICAL
PEDANTICALLY
PEDANTICISM
PEDANTISM
PEDANTIZE
PEDANTOCRACY
PEDANTOCRAT
PEDANTRY
PEDARY
PEDATE
PEDATED
PEDATELY
PEDATIFID
PEDATIFORM
PEDATILOBATE
PEDATILOBED
PEDATINERVED
PEDATISECT
PEDATISECTED
PEDATROPHIA
PEDATROPHY
PEDDER
PEDDLE
PEDDLED
PEDDLER
PEDDLERY
PEDDLING
PEDDLINGLY
PEDEE
PEDELION
PEDERAST
PEDERASTIC
PEDERASTY
PEDERERO
PEDES
PEDESIS
PEDESTAL
PEDESTALED
PEDESTALING
PEDESTALLED
PEDESTALLING
PEDESTRIAL
PEDESTRIALLY
PEDESTRIAN
PEDETENTOUS
PEDIAL
PEDIALGIA
PEDIATRIC
PEDIATRICIAN
PEDIATRICS
PEDIATRIST
PEDIATRY
PEDICAB
PEDICEL
PEDICELED
PEDICELLAR
PEDICELLARIA
PEDICELLATE
PEDICELLATED
PEDICELLED
PEDICLE
PEDICULAR
PEDICULATE
PEDICULATED
PEDICULE
PEDICULICIDE
PEDICULOSIS
PEDICULOUS
PEDICURE
PEDICURED
PEDICURING
PEDICURISM
PEDICURIST
PEDIFORM
PEDIGEROUS
PEDIGRAIC
PEDIGREE
PEDIGREED
PEDILUVIUM
PEDIMENT
PEDIMENTAL
PEDIMENTED
PEDIMENTUM
PEDION
PEDIONOMITE
PEDIPALP
PEDIPALPAL
PEDIPALPATE
PEDIPALPUS
PEDIPULATE
PEDIPULATION
PEDIPULATOR
PEDIWAK
PEDLAR
PEDLARY
PEDLER
PEDOBAPTISM
PEDOBAPTIST
PEDODONTIA
PEDODONTIC
PEDODONTIST
PEDOGRAPH
PEDOLOGICAL
PEDOLOGIST
PEDOLOGY
PEDOMANCY
PEDOMANIA
PEDOMETER
PEDOMETRICAL
PEDOMETRIST
PEDOMORPHIC
PEDOMORPHISM
PEDOMOTIVE
PEDOMOTOR
PEDOPHILIA
PEDOPHILIC
PEDOSPHERE
PEDOSPHERIC
PEDOTRIBE
PEDOTROPHIC
PEDOTROPHIST
PEDOTROPHY
PEDRAIL
PEDREGAL
PEDRERO
PEDRO
PEDROS
PEDULE
PEDUM
PEDUNCLE
PEDUNCLED

PEDUNCULAR
PEDUNCULATE
PEDUNCULATED
PEDUNCULI
PEDUNCULUS
PEE
PEEBEEN
PEEBLES
PEED
PEEING
PEEK
PEEKABOO
PEEKED
PEEKING
PEEL
PEELCROW
PEELE
PEELED
PEELEDNESS
PEELER
PEELHOUSE
PEELING
PEELMAN
PEELS
PEEN
PEENED
PEENGE
PEENING
PEEOY
PEEP
PEEPED
PEEPER
PEEPEYE
PEEPHOLE
PEEPING
PEEPUL
PEEPY
PEER
PEERAGE
PEERDOM
PEERED
PEERESS
PEERIE
PEERING
PEERLESS
PEERLESSLY
PEERLESSNESS
PEERLING
PEERLY
PEERT
PEERY
PEES
PEESASH
PEESEWEEP
PEESOREH
PEESWEEP
PEETWEET
PEEVE
PEEVED
PEEVEDLY
PEEVEDNESS
PEEVER
PEEVERS
PEEVING
PEEVISH
PEEVISHLY
PEEVISHNESS
PEEWEE
PEEWEEP
PEG
PEGA
PEGADOR
PEGALL
PEGANITE
PEGBOARD
PEGBOX
PEGGED
PEGGER
PEGGING
PEGGLE
PEGGY
PEGGYMAST
PEGH
PEGMA
PEGMAN
PEGMATITE
PEGMATITIC
PEGMATIZE
PEGMATOID
PEGMATOPHYRE
PEGME
PEGMEN
PEGOLOGY
PEGOMANCY
PEGROOTS
PEGWOOD
PEHO
PEIGNOIR
PEIKTHA
PEINE
PEIRAMETER
PEIRASTIC
PEIS
PEISAGE
PEISANT
PEISE
PEISER
PEIXERE
PEIXEREY
PEIZE
PEJERREY
PEJORATE
PEJORATION
PEJORATIVE
PEJORATIVELY
PEJORISM
PEJORIST
PEJORITY
PEKAN
PEKIN
PEKOE
PEKOK
PEL
PELA
PELADE
PELADIC
PELADO
PELADORE
PELAGE
PELAGIAL
PELAGIAN
PELAGIC
PELAGRA
PELAMYD
PELANOS
PELARGIC
PELARGONATE
PELARGONIC
PELARGONIDIN
PELARGONIN
PELARGONIUM
PELEAN
PELECAN
PELELITH
PELELIU
PELENG
PELERIN
PELERINE
PELETRE
PELF
PELICAN
PELICANRY
PELICK
PELICOMETER
PELIKE
PELIOM
PELIOMA
PELIOSIS
PELISSE
PELITE
PELITIC
PELL
PELLAGE
PELLAGRA
PELLAGRIN
PELLAGROSE
PELLAGROUS
PELLAR
PELLARD
PELLAS
PELLATE
PELLATION
PELLER
PELLET
PELLETED
PELLETIERINE
PELLETING
PELLETS
PELLETY
PELLICLE
PELLICULAR
PELLICULATE
PELLILE
PELLITORIES
PELLITORY
PELLMELL
PELLOCK
PELLOTIN
PELLOTINE
PELLUCID
PELLUCIDLY
PELLUCIDNESS
PELMA
PELMATA
PELMATIC
PELMATOGRAM
PELMET
PELOG
PELOID
PELOK
PELON
PELOPEA
PELORIA
PELORIAN
PELORIATE
PELORIC
PELORISM
PELORIZATION
PELORIZE
PELORUS
PELOTA
PELOTAS
PELOTHERAPY
PELOTON
PELT
PELTA
PELTAE
PELTAST
PELTATE
PELTATED
PELTATELY
PELTATION
PELTER
PELTERER
PELTIFEROUS
PELTIFOLIOUS
PELTIFORM
PELTIGERINE
PELTIGEROUS
PELTINERVATE
PELTINERVED
PELTING
PELTINGLY
PELTISH
PELTMONGER
PELTRIES
PELTRY
PELU
PELUDO
PELURE
PELVES
PELVIC
PELVIFORM
PELVIGRAPH
PELVIGRAPHY
PELVIMETER
PELVIMETRIC
PELVIMETRY
PELVIOPLASTY
PELVIOSCOPY
PELVIOTOMY
PELVIRECTAL
PELVIS
PELVISES
PELVISTERNAL
PELVISTERNUM
PELYCOGRAM
PELYCOGRAPHY
PELYCOLOGY
PELYCOMETER
PELYCOMETRY
PEMBINA
PEMBROKE
PEMICAN
PEMMICAN
PEMMICANIZE
PEMPHIGOID
PEMPHIGOUS
PEMPHIGUS
PEMPHIX
PEN
PENACUTE
PENAL
PENALISE
PENALIST
PENALITY
PENALIZATION
PENALIZE
PENALIZED
PENALIZING
PENALLY
PENALTIES
PENALTY
PENANCE
PENANCED
PENANCER
PENANCING
PENANCY
PENANG
PENANNULAR
PENATES
PENBARD
PENCATITE
PENCE
PENCEL
PENCEY
PENCH
PENCHANT
PENCHE
PENCHUTE
PENCIL
PENCILED
PENCILER
PENCILIFORM
PENCILING
PENCILLED
PENCILLER
PENCILLIKE
PENCILLING
PENCILRY
PENCILWOOD
PENCLERK
PENCRAFT
PEND
PENDA
PENDANT
PENDANTED
PENDANTING
PENDELOQUE
PENDENCY
PENDENT
PENDENTIVE
PENDENTLY
PENDICLE
PENDICLER
PENDING
PENDLE
PENDOM
PENDRAGON
PENDRAGONISH
PENDULANT
PENDULAR
PENDULATE
PENDULE
PENDULINE
PENDULOSITY
PENDULOUS
PENDULOUSLY
PENDULUM
PENDULUMS
PENE
PENEID
PENEPLAIN
PENEPLANE
PENES
PENESEISMIC
PENEST
PENETRABLE
PENETRABLY
PENETRAL
PENETRALIA
PENETRALIAN
PENETRANCE
PENETRANCY
PENETRANT
PENETRATE
PENETRATED
PENETRATING
PENETRATION
PENETRATIVE
PENETRATOR
PENETROLOGY
PENETROMETER
PENFIELDITE
PENFUL
PENGHULU
PENGO
PENGOS
PENGUIN
PENGUINERY
PENGUN
PENHEAD
PENHOLDER
PENIAL
PENIBLE
PENICILLATE
PENICILLATED
PENICILLIN
PENICILLIUM
PENIDE
PENILE
PENINSULA
PENINSULAR
PENINSULATE
PENINTIME

PENINVARIANT
PENIS
PENISES
PENISTONE
PENITENCE
PENITENCER
PENITENT
PENITENTIAL
PENITENTIARIES
PENITENTIARY
PENITENTLY
PENK
PENKEEPER
PENKNIFE
PENKNIVES
PENLITE
PENLOP
PENMAKER
PENMAKING
PENMAN
PENMANSHIP
PENMASTER
PENMEN
PENNA
PENNACEOUS
PENNAE
PENNAGE
PENNANT
PENNATE
PENNATED
PENNATULID
PENNATULOID
PENNED
PENNEECH
PENNEECK
PENNER
PENNI
PENNIA
PENNIED
PENNIES
PENNIFEROUS
PENNIFORM
PENNIGEROUS
PENNILESS
PENNILESSLY
PENNILL
PENNINE
PENNINERVATE
PENNINERVED
PENNING
PENNINITE
PENNIPOTENT
PENNIS
PENNIVEINED
PENNON
PENNONCEL
PENNONCELLE
PENNONED
PENNOPLUMA
PENNOPLUME
PENNORTH
PENNY
PENNYBIRD
PENNYCRESS
PENNYEARTH
PENNYFLOWER
PENNYHOLE
PENNYLAND
PENNYLEAF
PENNYROT
PENNYROYAL
PENNYSILLER
PENNYSTONE
PENNYWEIGHT
PENNYWINKLE
PENNYWORT
PENNYWORTH
PENOCHI
PENOLOGIC
PENOLOGICAL
PENOLOGIES
PENOLOGIST
PENOLOGY
PENONCEL
PENORCON
PENOUN
PENRACK
PENROSEITE
PENS
PENSCRIPT
PENSE
PENSEE
PENSEFUL
PENSEFULNESS
PENSEROSO
PENSHIP
PENSIL
PENSILE
PENSILENESS
PENSILITY
PENSION
PENSIONABLE
PENSIONARIES
PENSIONARY
PENSIONED
PENSIONER
PENSIONING
PENSIONNAIRE
PENSIONNAT
PENSIVE
PENSIVED
PENSIVELY
PENSIVENESS
PENSTEMON
PENSTER
PENSTICK
PENSTOCK
PENSUM
PENSY
PENT
PENTABASIC
PENTABROMIDE
PENTACAPSULAR
PENTACARBON
PENTACE
PENTACETATE
PENTACHENIUM
PENTACHLORIDE
PENTACHORD
PENTACHROMIC
PENTACID
PENTACLE
PENTACOCCOUS
PENTACONTANE
PENTACOSANE
PENTACRINITE
PENTACRINOID
PENTACRON
PENTACROSTIC
PENTACTINAL
PENTACTINE
PENTACULAR
PENTACYCLIC
PENTAD
PENTADACTYL
PENTADACTYLE
PENTADECAGON
PENTADECANE
PENTADECOIC
PENTADECYL
PENTADICITY
PENTADRACHM
PENTADRACHMA
PENTAFID
PENTAGAMIST
PENTAGLOSSAL
PENTAGLOT
PENTAGON
PENTAGONAL
PENTAGONALLY
PENTAGONOID
PENTAGONON
PENTAGRAM
PENTAGYN
PENTAGYNIAN
PENTAGYNOUS
PENTAHALIDE
PENTAHEDRA
PENTAHEDRAL
PENTAHEDROID
PENTAHEDRON
PENTAHEDROUS
PENTAHYDRATE
PENTAHYDRIC
PENTAIL
PENTAIODIDE
PENTALOBATE
PENTALOGUE
PENTALOGY
PENTALPHA
PENTAMERAL
PENTAMERAN
PENTAMERID
PENTAMERISM
PENTAMEROID
PENTAMEROUS
PENTAMERY
PENTAMETER
PENTAMETRIST
PENTAMETRIZE
PENTANDER
PENTANDRIAN
PENTANDROUS
PENTANE
PENTANGLE
PENTANGULAR
PENTANITRATE
PENTANOLIDE
PENTANONE
PENTAPLOID
PENTAPLOIDIC
PENTAPLOIDY
PENTAPODY
PENTAPOLIS
PENTAPOLITAN
PENTAPTEROUS
PENTAPTOTE
PENTAPTYCH
PENTARCH
PENTARCHICAL
PENTARCHIES
PENTARCHY
PENTASILICATE
PENTASPHERIC
PENTASTICH
PENTASTICHY
PENTASTYLE
PENTASTYLOS
PENTATEUCHAL
PENTATHIONIC
PENTATHLETE
PENTATHLON
PENTATHLOS
PENTATOMIC
PENTATOMID
PENTATONE
PENTATONIC
PENTAVALENCE
PENTAVALENCY
PENTAVALENT
PENTECONTER
PENTECOSTAL
PENTECOSTYS
PENTENE
PENTETERIC
PENTHEMIMER
PENTHIOPHENE
PENTHOUSE
PENTHOUSED
PENTHOUSING
PENTICLE
PENTILE
PENTIMENTO
PENTINE
PENTIT
PENTITOL
PENTLANDITE
PENTODE
PENTOIC
PENTOMIC
PENTOSAN
PENTOSANE
PENTOSE
PENTOSID
PENTOSIDE
PENTOSURIA
PENTOXIDE
PENTREMITAL
PENTREMITE
PENTROUGH
PENTSTEMON
PENTSTOCK
PENTYL
PENTYLENE
PENTYLIC
PENTYNE
PENUCHE
PENUCHI
PENUCHLE
PENUCKLE
PENULT
PENULTIMA
PENULTIMATE
PENUMBRA
PENUMBRAE
PENUMBRAL
PENUMBRAS
PENUMBROUS
PENURIOUS
PENURIOUSLY
PENURY
PENWIPER
PENWOMAN
PENWOMANSHIP
PENWOMEN
PENWORK
PENWORKER
PENWRIGHT
PEON
PEONAGE
PEONES
PEONIES
PEONISM
PEONY
PEOPLE
PEOPLED
PEOPLEIZE
PEOPLER
PEOPLES
PEOPLET
PEOPLING
PEOPLISH
PEOTOMY
PEP
PEPEREK
PEPERINE
PEPERINO
PEPERONI
PEPINELLA
PEPINO
PEPLOS
PEPLOSED
PEPLUM
PEPLUMS
PEPLUS
PEPO
PEPON
PEPONIDA
PEPONIUM
PEPOS
PEPPED
PEPPER
PEPPERBOX
PEPPERCORN
PEPPERED
PEPPERER
PEPPERGRASS
PEPPERIDGE
PEPPERING
PEPPERMINT
PEPPERONI
PEPPERROOT
PEPPERS
PEPPERWEED
PEPPERWOOD
PEPPERWORT
PEPPERY
PEPPILY
PEPPIN
PEPPINESS
PEPPING
PEPPY
PEPSIN
PEPSINATE
PEPSINATED
PEPSINATING
PEPSINE
PEPSINOGEN
PEPSIS
PEPTIC
PEPTICAL
PEPTICITY
PEPTIDASE
PEPTIDE
PEPTIZABLE
PEPTIZATION
PEPTIZE
PEPTIZED
PEPTIZER
PEPTIZING
PEPTOGASTER
PEPTONATE
PEPTONE
PEPTONIC
PEPTONIZE
PEPTONIZED
PEPTONIZER
PEPTONIZING
PEPTONOID
PEPTOTOXINE
PER
PERACEPHALUS
PERACID
PERACIDITE
PERACIDITY
PERACT
PERACUTE
PERADVENTURE
PERAGRATE
PERAGRATION
PERAMBLE
PERAMBULANT
PERAMBULATE
PERAMBULATED
PERAMBULATION

PERAMBULATOR
PERAMELINE
PERAMELOID
PERAU
PERBORATE
PERBROMIDE
PERCALE
PERCALINE
PERCARBONIC
PERCASE
PERCEANT
PERCEIVABLE
PERCEIVABLY
PERCEIVANCE
PERCEIVE
PERCEIVED
PERCEIVER
PERCEIVING
PERCENTABLE
PERCENTABLY
PERCENTAGE
PERCENTAGED
PERCENTAL
PERCENTILE
PERCENTS
PERCENTUAL
PERCENTUM
PERCEPT
PERCEPTIBLE
PERCEPTIBLY
PERCEPTION
PERCEPTIONAL
PERCEPTIVE
PERCEPTIVELY
PERCEPTIVITY
PERCEPTUAL
PERCEPTUALLY
PERCEPTUM
PERCESOCINE
PERCH
PERCHANCE
PERCHE
PERCHED
PERCHER
PERCHES
PERCHING
PERCHLORATE
PERCHLORIC
PERCHLORIDE
PERCHROMATE
PERCHROMIC
PERCID
PERCIFORM
PERCIPI
PERCIPIENCE
PERCIPIENCY
PERCIPIENT
PERCLOSE
PERCNOSOME
PERCOCT
PERCOID
PERCOIDEAN
PERCOLATE
PERCOLATION
PERCOLATIVE
PERCOLATOR
PERCOMORPH
PERCONTATION
PERCONTATORIAL
PERCRIBRATE
PERCRIBRATION
PERCULSION
PERCULSIVE
PERCUR
PERCURRATION
PERCURRENT
PERCURSORY
PERCUSS
PERCUSSION
PERCUSSIONAL
PERCUSSIONER
PERCUSSIVE
PERCUSSIVELY
PERCUSSOR
PERCUTANEOUS
PERCUTIENT
PERCYLITE
PERDENDO
PERDENDOSI
PERDIE
PERDILIGENCE
PERDILIGENT
PERDIT
PERDITION
PERDRICIDE
PERDRIGON
PERDU
PERDUE
PERDUELLION
PERDURABLE
PERDURABLY
PERDURANCE
PERDURANT
PERDURE
PERDURED
PERDURING
PERDURINGLY
PERDY
PERE
PEREGRIN
PEREGRINA
PEREGRINATE
PEREGRINATED
PEREGRINATOR
PEREGRINE
PEREGRINITY
PEREGRINOID
PEREGRINUS
PEREION
PEREIOPOD
PEREIRA
PEREIRINE
PEREJONET
PEREJONETTE
PEREMPT
PEREMPTION
PEREMPTORILY
PEREMPTORY
PERENDINANT
PERENDINATE
PERENDURE
PERENNATE
PERENNATION
PERENNIAL
PERENNIALITY
PERENNIALIZE
PERENNIALLY
PERENNIBRANCH
PEREQUITATE
PERES
PEREUNDEM
PEREZONE
PERFAY
PERFECT
PERFECTATION
PERFECTED
PERFECTER
PERFECTI
PERFECTIBLE
PERFECTING
PERFECTION
PERFECTIONER
PERFECTIONIST
PERFECTISM
PERFECTIST
PERFECTIVE
PERFECTIVELY
PERFECTIVIZE
PERFECTLY
PERFECTNESS
PERFECTO
PERFECTOR
PERFECTOS
PERFERVENT
PERFERVID
PERFERVIDLY
PERFICIENT
PERFIDIES
PERFIDIOUS
PERFIDIOUSLY
PERFIDY
PERFILOGRAPH
PERFINS
PERFIX
PERFLATE
PERFLATION
PERFLUENT
PERFOLIATE
PERFOLIATION
PERFORABLE
PERFORANT
PERFORATE
PERFORATED
PERFORATING
PERFORATION
PERFORATIONS
PERFORATIVE
PERFORATOR
PERFORATORY
PERFORCE
PERFORM
PERFORMABLE
PERFORMANCE
PERFORMANCES
PERFORMANT
PERFORMATIVE
PERFORMED
PERFORMER
PERFORMING
PERFRICATION
PERFUMATORY
PERFUME
PERFUMED
PERFUMER
PERFUMERY
PERFUMES
PERFUMING
PERFUMY
PERFUNCTORY
PERFUSATE
PERFUSE
PERFUSED
PERFUSING
PERFUSION
PERFUSIVE
PERGAMENEOUS
PERGAMYN
PERGE
PERGOLA
PERGOLAS
PERHALIDE
PERHALOGEN
PERHAPS
PERHAZARD
PERHORRESCE
PERI
PERIACINAL
PERIACTUS
PERIADENITIS
PERIANAL
PERIANGIOMA
PERIANGITIS
PERIANTH
PERIANTHIAL
PERIANTHIUM
PERIAORTIC
PERIAORTITIS
PERIAPICAL
PERIAPT
PERIAREUM
PERIARTERIAL
PERIARTERITIS
PERIARTHRIC
PERIARTHRITIS
PERIARTICULAR
PERIASTRAL
PERIASTRON
PERIASTRUM
PERIATRIAL
PERIAXIAL
PERIAXILLARY
PERIAXONAL
PERIBLASTIC
PERIBLASTULA
PERIBLEM
PERIBOLOS
PERIBOLUS
PERIBULBAR
PERIBURSAL
PERICAECAL
PERICAECITIS
PERICAPSULAR
PERICARDIA
PERICARDIAC
PERICARDIAL
PERICARDIAN
PERICARDITIS
PERICARDIUM
PERICARP
PERICARPIAL
PERICARPIC
PERICECAL
PERICECITIS
PERICELLULAR
PERICEMENTAL
PERICEMENTUM
PERICENTER
PERICENTRAL
PERICENTRE
PERICENTRIC
PERICEPHALIC
PERICEREBRAL
PERICHAETE
PERICHAETIAL
PERICHAETIUM
PERICHETE
PERICHONDRAL
PERICHORD
PERICHORDAL
PERICHORESIS
PERICHYLOUS
PERICLADIUM
PERICLASE
PERICLASITE
PERICLINAL
PERICLINALLY
PERICLINE
PERICLINIUM
PERICLITATE
PERICOLITIS
PERICOLPITIS
PERICONCHAL
PERICOPAL
PERICOPE
PERICOPE
PERICOPIC
PERICORNEAL
PERICOXITIS
PERICRANIA
PERICRANIAL
PERICRANITIS
PERICRANIUM
PERICRISTATE
PERICULANT
PERICULUM
PERICYCLE
PERICYCLIC
PERICYCLOID
PERICYCLONE
PERICYCLONIC
PERICYSTIC
PERICYSTITIS
PERICYSTIUM
PERICYTIAL
PERIDERM
PERIDERMAL
PERIDERMIC
PERIDESM
PERIDESMIC
PERIDESMITIS
PERIDESMIUM
PERIDIA
PERIDIAL
PERIDIASTOLE
PERIDIDYMIS
PERIDIIFORM
PERIDINIAL
PERIDINIAN
PERIDINID
PERIDIOLE
PERIDIOLUM
PERIDIUM
PERIDOT
PERIDOTIC
PERIDOTITE
PERIDOTITIC
PERIDUCTAL
PERIEGESIS
PERIEGETIC
PERIELESIS
PERIENTERIC
PERIENTERON
PERIERGY
PERIFISTULAR
PERIFOLIARY
PERIGASTRIC
PERIGASTRULA
PERIGEAL
PERIGEAN
PERIGEE
PERIGEMMAL
PERIGENESIS
PERIGENITAL
PERIGEUM
PERIGLIAL
PERIGLOEA
PERIGLOTTIC
PERIGLOTTIS
PERIGNATHIC
PERIGON
PERIGONADIAL
PERIGONE
PERIGONIAL
PERIGONIUM
PERIGRAPH
PERIGRAPHIC
PERIGYNIAL
PERIGYNIUM
PERIGYNOUS
PERIGYNY
PERIHELIA
PERIHELIAL
PERIHELIAN
PERIHELION
PERIHEPATIC

PERIHERNIAL
PERIHYSTERIC
PERIJOVE
PERIKARYA
PERIKARYON
PERIL
PERILED
PERILING
PERILLED
PERILLING
PERILOBAR
PERILOUS
PERILOUSLY
PERILOUSNESS
PERILUNE
PERILYMPH
PERIMASTITIS
PERIMETER
PERIMETRIC
PERIMETRICAL
PERIMETRITIC
PERIMETRITIS
PERIMETRIUM
PERIMETRY
PERIMORPH
PERIMORPHIC
PERIMORPHISM
PERIMORPHOUS
PERIMYELITIS
PERIMYSIAL
PERIMYSIUM
PERINAEUM
PERINE
PERINEAL
PERINEOCELE
PERINEOSTOMY
PERINEOTOMY
PERINEPHRAL
PERINEPHRIAL
PERINEPHRIC
PERINEPHRIUM
PERINEUM
PERINEURAL
PERINEURIA
PERINEURIAL
PERINEURITIS
PERINEURIUM
PERINIUM
PERINUCLEAR
PERIOCULAR
PERIOD
PERIODATE
PERIODIC
PERIODICAL
PERIODICALLY
PERIODICALNESS
PERIODICITY
PERIODID
PERIODIDE
PERIODOGRAM
PERIODOLOGY
PERIODONTAL
PERIODONTIA
PERIODONTIC
PERIODONTICS
PERIODONTIST
PERIODONTIUM
PERIODOSCOPE
PERIOECI
PERIOECIC
PERIOECID
PERIOMPHALIC
PERIONYCHIA
PERIONYCHIUM
PERIOPLE
PERIOPLIC
PERIOQUE
PERIORAL
PERIORBIT
PERIORBITA
PERIORBITAL
PERIORCHITIS
PERIOSTEAL
PERIOSTEOMA
PERIOSTEOUS
PERIOSTEUM
PERIOSTITIC
PERIOSTITIS
PERIOSTOSIS
PERIOSTRACAL
PERIOSTRACUM
PERIOTIC
PERIOVULAR
PERIPATETIC
PERIPATIZE
PERIPATOID
PERIPENIAL
PERIPETALOUS
PERIPETASMA
PERIPETEIA
PERIPETIA
PERIPETY
PERIPHACITIS
PERIPHERAD
PERIPHERAL
PERIPHERALLY
PERIPHERIAL
PERIPHERIC
PERIPHERICAL
PERIPHERIES
PERIPHERY
PERIPHRACTIC
PERIPHRASE
PERIPHRASED
PERIPHRASES
PERIPHRASING
PERIPHRASIS
PERIPHRASTIC
PERIPHRAXY
PERIPHYLLUM
PERIPHYSIS
PERIPLASM
PERIPLAST
PERIPLASTIC
PERIPLEURAL
PERIPLUS
PERIPNEUSTIC
PERIPOLAR
PERIPORTAL
PERIPROCT
PERIPROCTAL
PERIPROCTOUS
PERIPTER
PERIPTERAL
PERIPTEROI
PERIPTEROS
PERIPTEROUS
PERIPTERY
PERIPYLORIC
PERIQUE
PERIRECTAL
PERIRECTITIS
PERIRENAL
PERIRHINAL
PERIS
PERISARC
PERISARCAL
PERISARCOUS
PERISCIANS
PERISCII
PERISCOPAL
PERISCOPE
PERISCOPIC
PERISCOPICAL
PERISH
PERISHABLE
PERISHABLY
PERISHED
PERISHING
PERISHINGLY
PERISINUITIS
PERISINUOUS
PERISOMA
PERISOMAL
PERISOMATIC
PERISOME
PERISOMIAL
PERISPERM
PERISPERMAL
PERISPERMIC
PERISPHERE
PERISPHERIC
PERISPLENIC
PERISPOMENA
PERISPOMENON
PERISPORE
PERISSAD
PERISSOLOGIC
PERISSOLOGY
PERISTALITH
PERISTALSIS
PERISTALTIC
PERISTELE
PERISTERITE
PERISTERONIC
PERISTEROPOD
PERISTETHIUM
PERISTOLE
PERISTOMA
PERISTOMAL
PERISTOMATIC
PERISTOME
PERISTOMIAL
PERISTOMIUM
PERISTREPHIC
PERISTYLAR
PERISTYLE
PERISTYLOS
PERISYNOVIAL
PERISYSTOLE
PERISYSTOLIC
PERIT
PERITE
PERITECTIC
PERITHECE
PERITHECIAL
PERITHECIUM
PERITHELIAL
PERITHELIOMA
PERITHELIUM
PERITHORACIC
PERITOMIZE
PERITOMOUS
PERITOMY
PERITONAEA
PERITONAEAL
PERITONAEUM
PERITONEA
PERITONEAL
PERITONEALLY
PERITONEUM
PERITONISM
PERITONITAL
PERITONITIC
PERITONITIS
PERITRACHEAL
PERITREMA
PERITREME
PERITRICH
PERITRICHA
PERITRICHAN
PERITRICHIC
PERITRICHOUS
PERITROCH
PERITROCHAL
PERITROPAL
PERITROPHIC
PERITROPOUS
PERITYPHLIC
PERIUNGUAL
PERIURETERIC
PERIURETHRAL
PERIUTERINE
PERIUVULAR
PERIVAGINAL
PERIVASCULAR
PERIVENOUS
PERIVESICAL
PERIVISCERAL
PERIVITELLIN
PERIWIG
PERIWIGPATED
PERIWINKLE
PERIWINKLED
PERIWINKLER
PERIZONIUM
PERJINK
PERJINKETY
PERJINKITIES
PERJINKLY
PERJURE
PERJURED
PERJUREDLY
PERJUREDNESS
PERJURER
PERJURIES
PERJURING
PERJURIOUS
PERJURIOUSLY
PERJURY
PERK
PERKIER
PERKIEST
PERKILY
PERKIN
PERKINESS
PERKING
PERKISH
PERKNITE
PERKY
PERLACEOUS
PERLE
PERLECHE
PERLECTION
PERLID
PERLIGENOUS
PERLINGUAL
PERLINGUALLY
PERLITE
PERLITIC
PERLOIR
PERLUSTRATE
PERLUSTRATOR
PERMAFROST
PERMALLOY
PERMANENCE
PERMANENCY
PERMANENT
PERMANENTLY
PERMANGANATE
PERMANGANIC
PERMANSIVE
PERMEABILITY
PERMEABLE
PERMEABLY
PERMEAMETER
PERMEANCE
PERMEANT
PERMEATE
PERMEATED
PERMEATING
PERMEATION
PERMEATIVE
PERMEATOR
PERMILLAGE
PERMIRIFIC
PERMISS
PERMISSIBLE
PERMISSIBLY
PERMISSION
PERMISSIONED
PERMISSIVE
PERMISSIVELY
PERMISSORY
PERMIT
PERMITTABLE
PERMITTED
PERMITTEDLY
PERMITTEE
PERMITTER
PERMITTIVITY
PERMIX
PERMIXABLE
PERMIXTION
PERMIXTIVE
PERMIXTURE
PERMORALIZE
PERMUTABLE
PERMUTABLY
PERMUTATE
PERMUTATION
PERMUTATOR
PERMUTATORY
PERMUTE
PERMUTED
PERMUTER
PERMUTING
PERN
PERNANCY
PERNASAL
PERNAVIGATE
PERNICIOUS
PERNICIOUSLY
PERNICKETTY
PERNICKETY
PERNICKITY
PERNINE
PERNIO
PERNOCTATE
PERNOCTATION
PERNOR
PERO
PEROBA
PEROCHIRUS
PERODACTYLUS
PEROMELOUS
PEROMELUS
PERONATE
PERONEAL
PERONEUS
PERONIAL
PERONIUM
PEROPOD
PEROPODOUS
PEROPUS
PERORAL
PERORALLY
PERORATE
PERORATED
PERORATING
PERORATION
PERORATIONAL
PERORATIVE
PERORATOR
PERORATORY

PEROSMATE
PEROSOMUS
PEROVSKITE
PEROXIDASE
PEROXIDE
PEROXIDED
PEROXIDIC
PEROXIDING
PEROXIDIZE
PEROXY
PEROXYL
PERPEND
PERPENDICLE
PERPENDICULAR
PERPENDICULARITY
PERPENDICULARLY
PERPENSE
PERPENT
PERPERA
PERPET
PERPETRABLE
PERPETRATE
PERPETRATED
PERPETRATING
PERPETRATION
PERPETRATOR
PERPETUABLE
PERPETUAL
PERPETUALIST
PERPETUALLY
PERPETUANA
PERPETUANCE
PERPETUANT
PERPETUATE
PERPETUATED
PERPETUATING
PERPETUATION
PERPETUATOR
PERPETUITY
PERPLANTAR
PERPLEX
PERPLEXED
PERPLEXEDLY
PERPLEXER
PERPLEXING
PERPLEXINGLY
PERPLEXITIES
PERPLEXITY
PERPLICATION
PERQUADRAT
PERQUEER
PERQUEERLY
PERQUEIR
PERQUEST
PERQUISITE
PERQUISITION
PERQUISITOR
PERRADIAL
PERRADIALLY
PERRADIATE
PERRADIUS
PERRIE
PERRIER
PERRON
PERRUCHE
PERRUQUIER
PERRUTHENATE
PERRY
PERRYMAN
PERSALT
PERSCRIBE
PERSCRUTATE
PERSCRUTATOR
PERSE
PERSECUTE
PERSECUTED
PERSECUTEE
PERSECUTING
PERSECUTION
PERSECUTIVE
PERSECUTOR
PERSECUTORY
PERSEITE
PERSEITOL
PERSEITY
PERSEVERANCE
PERSEVERANT
PERSEVERATE
PERSEVERE
PERSEVERED
PERSEVERING
PERSICARIA
PERSICARY
PERSICO
PERSICOT
PERSIENNE
PERSIENNES
PERSIFLAGE
PERSIFLATE
PERSIFLEUR
PERSILICIC
PERSILLADE
PERSIMMON
PERSIO
PERSIS
PERSIST
PERSISTENCE
PERSISTENCY
PERSISTENT
PERSISTENTLY
PERSISTER
PERSISTINGLY
PERSISTIVE
PERSISTIVELY
PERSNICKETY
PERSOLVE
PERSON
PERSONA
PERSONABLE
PERSONABLY
PERSONAE
PERSONAGE
PERSONAL
PERSONALIA
PERSONALISM
PERSONALIST
PERSONALITY
PERSONALIZE
PERSONALIZED
PERSONALLY
PERSONALTIES
PERSONALTY
PERSONATE
PERSONATED
PERSONATING
PERSONATION
PERSONATIVE
PERSONATOR
PERSONED
PERSONEITY
PERSONIFIANT
PERSONIFICATION
PERSONIFY
PERSONIFYING
PERSONIZE
PERSONNEL
PERSONS
PERSPECTIVE
PERSPECTIVED
PERSPICACIOUS
PERSPICACITY
PERSPICUITY
PERSPICUOUS
PERSPIRABLE
PERSPIRANT
PERSPIRATION
PERSPIRATIVE
PERSPIRATORY
PERSPIRE
PERSPIRED
PERSPIRING
PERSPIRY
PERSTAND
PERSTRINGE
PERSTRINGED
PERSUADABLE
PERSUADABLY
PERSUADE
PERSUADED
PERSUADER
PERSUADING
PERSUASIBLE
PERSUASIBLY
PERSUASION
PERSUASIVE
PERSUASIVELY
PERSUASORY
PERSUE
PERSULFATE
PERSULPHATE
PERSULPHIDE
PERSULPHURIC
PERT
PERTAIN
PERTAINING
PERTEN
PERTENENCIA
PERTHITE
PERTHOSITE
PERTINACIOUS
PERTINACITY
PERTINENCE
PERTINENCY
PERTINENT
PERTINENTIA
PERTINENTLY
PERTLY
PERTNESS
PERTURB
PERTURBABLE
PERTURBANCE
PERTURBANCY
PERTURBANT
PERTURBATE
PERTURBATION
PERTURBATIVE
PERTURBATOR
PERTURBATORY
PERTURBED
PERTURBEDLY
PERTURBER
PERTURBING
PERTUSE
PERTUSED
PERTUSION
PERTUSSAL
PERTUSSIS
PERUKE
PERUKER
PERUKERY
PERUKIER
PERULA
PERULATE
PERULE
PERUSABLE
PERUSAL
PERUSE
PERUSED
PERUSER
PERUSING
PERVADE
PERVADED
PERVADENCE
PERVADER
PERVADING
PERVADINGLY
PERVAGATE
PERVAGATION
PERVALVAR
PERVASION
PERVASIVE
PERVASIVELY
PERVENCHE
PERVERSE
PERVERSELY
PERVERSENESS
PERVERSION
PERVERSITIES
PERVERSITY
PERVERSIVE
PERVERT
PERVERTED
PERVERTEDLY
PERVERTER
PERVERTIBLE
PERVERTIBLY
PERVERTING
PERVERTIVE
PERVIAL
PERVICACIOUS
PERVICACITY
PERVIGILIUM
PERVIOUS
PERVIOUSLY
PERVIOUSNESS
PERVULGATE
PERWICK
PERWITSKY
PERY
PES
PESA
PESADE
PESAGE
PESANTE
PESCOD
PESETA
PESHKAR
PESHKASH
PESHWA
PESKIER
PESKIEST
PESKILY
PESKINESS
PESKY
PESO
PESOS
PESS
PESSA
PESSARIES
PESSARY
PESSIMISM
PESSIMIST
PESSIMISTIC
PESSIMIZE
PESSONER
PESSULAR
PESSULUS
PEST
PESTE
PESTER
PESTERED
PESTERER
PESTERING
PESTEROUS
PESTFUL
PESTHOLE
PESTHOUSE
PESTICIDAL
PESTICIDE
PESTIDUCT
PESTIFEROUS
PESTIFUGOUS
PESTIFY
PESTILENCE
PESTILENT
PESTILENTIAL
PESTILENTLY
PESTIS
PESTLE
PESTLED
PESTLING
PESTO
PESTOLOGICAL
PESTOLOGIST
PESTOLOGY
PET
PETA
PETAL
PETALAGE
PETALED
PETALIFEROUS
PETALINE
PETALING
PETALISM
PETALITE
PETALLED
PETALLING
PETALOCEROUS
PETALODIC
PETALODONT
PETALODONTID
PETALODY
PETALOID
PETALOIDEOUS
PETALON
PETALOUS
PETALY
PETARA
PETARD
PETARDING
PETASMA
PETASOS
PETASUS
PETATE
PETAURINE
PETAURIST
PETCHARY
PETCOCK
PETE
PETECA
PETECHIA
PETECHIAE
PETECHIAL
PETECHIATE
PETEGREU
PETEMAN
PETER
PETERED
PETERERO
PETERING
PETERMAN
PETERMEN
PETERNET
PETERSHAM
PETFUL
PETHER
PETIOLAR
PETIOLATE
PETIOLATED
PETIOLE
PETIOLED
PETIOLI
PETIOLULAR
PETIOLULATE
PETIOLULE

PETIOLUS
PETIT
PETITE
PETITGRAIN
PETITION
PETITIONAL
PETITIONARY
PETITIONED
PETITIONEE
PETITIONER
PETITIONING
PETITIONIST
PETITOR
PETITORY
PETKIN
PETLING
PETO
PETRARY
PETRE
PETREAN
PETREITY
PETREL
PETRESCENCE
PETRESCENCY
PETRESCENT
PETRICOLOUS
PETRIE
PETRIFACTION
PETRIFACTIVE
PETRIFIABLE
PETRIFIC
PETRIFIED
PETRIFIER
PETRIFY
PETRIFYING
PETRISSAGE
PETROGENESIS
PETROGENIC
PETROGENY
PETROGLYPH
PETROGLYPHIC
PETROGLYPHY
PETROGRAPH
PETROGRAPHER
PETROGRAPHIC
PETROGRAPHY
PETROHYOID
PETROL
PETROLAGE
PETROLATUM
PETROLEAN
PETROLENE
PETROLEOUS
PETROLEUM
PETROLEUR
PETROLEUSE
PETROLIC
PETROLIFIC
PETROLIST
PETROLITHIC
PETROLIZE
PETROLIZED
PETROLIZING
PETROLOGIC
PETROLOGICAL
PETROLOGIST
PETROLOGY
PETROMASTOID
PETRONEL
PETRONELLA
PETRONELLIER
PETROSA
PETROSAL
PETROSILEX
PETROSTEARIN
PETROUS
PETROXOLIN
PETTABLE
PETTAH
PETTED
PETTEDLY
PETTEDNESS
PETTER
PETTI
PETTIAGUA
PETTICHAPS
PETTICOAT
PETTICOATED
PETTICOATERY
PETTICOATING
PETTICOATISM
PETTIER
PETTIEST
PETTIFOG
PETTIFOGGED
PETTIFOGGER
PETTIFOGGERY
PETTIFOGGING
PETTILY
PETTINESS
PETTING
PETTISH
PETTISHLY
PETTISHNESS
PETTITOES
PETTLE
PETTLED
PETTLING
PETTO
PETTY
PETTYFOG
PETTYGOD
PETULANCE
PETULANCY
PETULANT
PETULANTLY
PETUN
PETUNE
PETUNIA
PETUNSE
PETUNTZE
PETWOOD
PETZITE
PEUCITES
PEUGH
PEULVAN
PEVA
PEW
PEWAGE
PEWEE
PEWFELLOW
PEWHOLDER
PEWING
PEWIT
PEWKE
PEWMATE
PEWTER
PEWTERER
PEWTERWORT
PEWTERY
PEWY
PEY
PEYOTE
PEYOTISM
PEYOTL
PEYTON
PEZANTIC
PEZIZACEOUS
PEZIZAEFORM
PEZIZIFORM
PEZIZOID
PEZOGRAPH
PEZZO
PFEFFERNUSS
PFENNIG
PFENNIGE
PFENNIGS
PFIFF
PFUI
PFUND
PFUNDE
PHACELITE
PHACELLA
PHACELLITE
PHACELLUS
PHACITIS
PHACOCELE
PHACOCHERE
PHACOCHOERE
PHACOCYST
PHACOID
PHACOIDAL
PHACOLITE
PHACOLITH
PHACOLYSIS
PHACOMETER
PHACOPID
PHACOSCOPE
PHAEISM
PHAENANTHERY
PHAENOLOGY
PHAEOCHROUS
PHAEOPHORE
PHAEOPHYL
PHAEOPHYLL
PHAEOPHYTIN
PHAEOPLAST
PHAEOSPORE
PHAEOSPOROUS
PHAET
PHAETON
PHAGEDAENA
PHAGEDAENIC
PHAGEDAENICAL
PHAGEDAENOUS
PHAGEDENA
PHAGEDENIC
PHAGEDENICAL
PHAGEDENOUS
PHAGOCYTABLE
PHAGOCYTAL
PHAGOCYTE
PHAGOCYTER
PHAGOCYTIC
PHAGOCYTISM
PHAGOCYTIZE
PHAGOCYTOSE
PHAGOCYTOSED
PHAGOCYTOSIS
PHAGOLYSIS
PHAGOMANIA
PHALACROSIS
PHALAENOPSID
PHALANGAL
PHALANGE
PHALANGEAL
PHALANGEAN
PHALANGER
PHALANGES
PHALANGETTE
PHALANGIAN
PHALANGID
PHALANGIDAN
PHALANGIDEAN
PHALANGIFORM
PHALANGIST
PHALANGITE
PHALANSTERIC
PHALANSTERY
PHALANX
PHALANXED
PHALANXES
PHALARICA
PHALAROPE
PHALERA
PHALERAE
PHALERATE
PHALERATED
PHALLACEOUS
PHALLALGIA
PHALLEPHORIC
PHALLIC
PHALLICAL
PHALLICISM
PHALLICIST
PHALLIN
PHALLISM
PHALLIST
PHALLITIS
PHALLODYNIA
PHALLOID
PHALLONCUS
PHALLOPLASTY
PHALLUS
PHAN
PHANERIC
PHANERITE
PHANEROCRYST
PHANEROGAM
PHANEROGAMY
PHANEROGENIC
PHANEROMERE
PHANEROSCOPE
PHANEROSIS
PHANEROZOIC
PHANIC
PHANO
PHANSIGAR
PHANTASCOPE
PHANTASIA
PHANTASIES
PHANTASIZE
PHANTASM
PHANTASMA
PHANTASMAL
PHANTASMALLY
PHANTASMATA
PHANTASMATIC
PHANTASMIC
PHANTAST
PHANTASY
PHANTIC
PHANTOM
PHANTOMATIC
PHANTOMIC
PHANTOMIZE
PHANTOMIZER
PHANTOMRY
PHANTOMY
PHANTOSCOPE
PHARE
PHARISAICAL
PHARISAISM
PHARISEE
PHARMACAL
PHARMACEUTIC
PHARMACIC
PHARMACIES
PHARMACIST
PHARMACITE
PHARMACOLITE
PHARMACOLOGY
PHARMACON
PHARMACY
PHARMAKOI
PHARMAKOS
PHARMIC
PHARO
PHAROLOGY
PHAROS
PHARYNGAL
PHARYNGEAL
PHARYNGES
PHARYNGIC
PHARYNGISMUS
PHARYNGITIS
PHARYNGOCELE
PHARYNGOLITH
PHARYNGOLOGY
PHARYNGOTOME
PHARYNGOTOMY
PHARYNX
PHARYNXES
PHASCACEOUS
PHASCOLOME
PHASE
PHASEAL
PHASED
PHASELIN
PHASEMETER
PHASEMY
PHASEOLIN
PHASEOLOUS
PHASES
PHASIANIC
PHASIANID
PHASIANINE
PHASIANOID
PHASIC
PHASING
PHASIS
PHASM
PHASMA
PHASMATID
PHASMATOID
PHASMATROPE
PHASOGENEOUS
PHASOR
PHASOTROPY
PHAT
PHEAL
PHEALE
PHEARSE
PHEASANT
PHEASANTRY
PHEASANTS
PHEBE
PHEEAL
PHEER
PHELLANDRENE
PHELLEM
PHELLODERM
PHELLODERMAL
PHELLOGEN
PHELLOGENIC
PHELLOPLASTIC
PHEMIC
PHENACAINE
PHENACETIN
PHENACETINE
PHENACETURIC
PHENACITE
PHENACYL
PHENAKISM
PHENANTHRENE
PHENANTHROL
PHENARSINE
PHENAZIN
PHENAZINE
PHENAZONE
PHENE
PHENENE
PHENETHYL
PHENETIDINE
PHENETOL

PHENETOLE
PHENGITE
PHENGITICAL
PHENIC
PHENICATE
PHENICIOUS
PHENICOPTER
PHENIN
PHENINE
PHENIX
PHENMIAZINE
PHENOBARBITOL
PHENOCOLL
PHENOCOPY
PHENOCRYST
PHENOGENESIS
PHENOGENETIC
PHENOL
PHENOLATE
PHENOLIC
PHENOLIZE
PHENOLOGIC
PHENOLOGICAL
PHENOLOGIST
PHENOLOGY
PHENOMENA
PHENOMENAL
PHENOMENALLY
PHENOMENON
PHENOQUINONE
PHENOSAL
PHENOSOL
PHENOSPERMY
PHENOTYPE
PHENOTYPIC
PHENOTYPICAL
PHENOXAZINE
PHENOXIDE
PHENYL
PHENYLACETIC
PHENYLAMIDE
PHENYLAMINE
PHENYLATE
PHENYLATED
PHENYLATION
PHENYLENE
PHENYLIC
PHEON
PHEOPHYTIN
PHERETRER
PHEW
PHI
PHIAL
PHIALE
PHIALED
PHIALINE
PHIALING
PHIALLED
PHIALLING
PHILABEG
PHILADELPHITE
PHILADELPHY
PHILALETHIST
PHILAMOT
PHILANDER
PHILANDERED
PHILANDERER
PHILANDERING
PHILANTHID
PHILANTHROPE
PHILANTHROPIC
PHILANTHROPIST
PHILANTHROPY
PHILANTOMBA
PHILARCHAIST
PHILATELIC
PHILATELIST
PHILATELY
PHILATHLETIC
PHILAUTY
PHILHARMONIC
PHILHELLENE
PHILHELLENIC
PHILHIPPIC
PHILHYMNIC
PHILIA
PHILIATER
PHILIBEG
PHILINE
PHILIPPICIZE
PHILIPPIZE
PHILIPPIZER
PHILIPPUS
PHILLILEW
PHILLILOO
PHILLIPEENER
PHILLIPSINE
PHILLIPSITE
PHILLYRIN
PHILOBIBLIAN
PHILOBIBLIC
PHILOBIBLICAL
PHILOBIBLIST
PHILOBOTANIC
PHILOBRUTISH
PHILOCALIC
PHILOCALIST
PHILOCALY
PHILOCOMAL
PHILOCUBIST
PHILOCYNIC
PHILOCYNICAL
PHILOCYNY
PHILODEMIC
PHILODENDRON
PHILODESPOT
PHILODOX
PHILODOXER
PHILODOXICAL
PHILOFELIST
PHILOFELON
PHILOGARLIC
PHILOGASTRIC
PHILOGEANT
PHILOGRAPH
PHILOGRAPHIC
PHILOGYNIST
PHILOGYNOUS
PHILOGYNY
PHILOKLEPTIC
PHILOLOGER
PHILOLOGIC
PHILOLOGICAL
PHILOLOGIST
PHILOLOGIZE
PHILOLOGUE
PHILOLOGY
PHILOMATH
PHILOMATHIC
PHILOMATHY
PHILOME
PHILOMEL
PHILOMELIAN
PHILOMUSE
PHILOMUSICAL
PHILOMYSTIC
PHILOMYTHIA
PHILOMYTHIC
PHILONATURAL
PHILONEISM
PHILONIST
PHILONIUM
PHILONOIST
PHILOPAGAN
PHILOPATER
PHILOPATRIAN
PHILOPENA
PHILOPIG
PHILOPOET
PHILOPOGON
PHILOPOLEMIC
PHILOPORNIST
PHILORADICAL
PHILORNITHIC
PHILOSOPH
PHILOSOPHE
PHILOSOPHEME
PHILOSOPHER
PHILOSOPHERESS
PHILOSOPHESS
PHILOSOPHIC
PHILOSOPHICAL
PHILOSOPHIES
PHILOSOPHISM
PHILOSOPHIST
PHILOSOPHIZE
PHILOSOPHY
PHILOTADPOLE
PHILOTECHNIC
PHILOTHEISM
PHILOTHEIST
PHILOTHERIAN
PHILOZOIC
PHILOZOIST
PHILOZOONIST
PHILP
PHILTER
PHILTERED
PHILTERER
PHILTERING
PHILTRE
PHILTRED
PHILTRING
PHILTRUM
PHIMOSED
PHIMOSIS
PHIMOTIC
PHIP
PHIPPE
PHIT
PHITONES
PHIZ
PHIZOG
PHLEBALGIA
PHLEBECTASIA
PHLEBECTASIS
PHLEBECTASY
PHLEBECTOMY
PHLEBECTOPIA
PHLEBECTOPY
PHLEBENTERIC
PHLEBITIS
PHLEBOGRAM
PHLEBOGRAPH
PHLEBOGRAPHY
PHLEBOID
PHLEBOIDAL
PHLEBOLITE
PHLEBOLITH
PHLEBOLITHIC
PHLEBOLITIC
PHLEBOLOGY
PHLEBOPEXY
PHLEBOPLASTY
PHLEBORRHAGE
PHLEBORRHEXIS
PHLEBOSTASIA
PHLEBOSTASIS
PHLEBOTOME
PHLEBOTOMIC
PHLEBOTOMIST
PHLEBOTOMIZE
PHLEBOTOMY
PHLEGM
PHLEGMA
PHLEGMAGOGUE
PHLEGMASIA
PHLEGMATIC
PHLEGMATICAL
PHLEGMATICLY
PHLEGMATISM
PHLEGMATIST
PHLEGMATOUS
PHLEGMON
PHLEGMONIC
PHLEGMONOID
PHLEGMONOUS
PHLEGMY
PHLOBAPHENE
PHLOBATANNIN
PHLOEM
PHLOEOTERMA
PHLOEUM
PHLOGISTIAN
PHLOGISTIC
PHLOGISTON
PHLOGOGENIC
PHLOGOPITE
PHLOGOSED
PHLOGOSIN
PHLOGOSIS
PHLOGOTIC
PHLORETIN
PHLORHIZIN
PHLORIDZIN
PHLORINA
PHLORIZIN
PHLOROL
PHLYCTAENA
PHLYCTAENULA
PHLYCTENA
PHLYCTENAE
PHLYCTENOID
PHLYCTENULA
PHLYCTENULE
PHLYZACIOUS
PHLYZACIUM
PHO
PHOBIA
PHOBIAC
PHOBIC
PHOBIES
PHOBISM
PHOBIST
PHOBIST
PHOBY
PHOCA
PHOCACEAN
PHOCACEOUS
PHOCAENINE
PHOCAL
PHOCENIN
PHOCID
PHOCIFORM
PHOCINE
PHOCODONT
PHOCOID
PHOCOMELIA
PHOCOMELUS
PHOEBADS
PHOEBE
PHOENICEAN
PHOENICOPTER
PHOENICUROUS
PHOENIGM
PHOENIX
PHOENIXES
PHOENIXITY
PHOLAD
PHOLADIAN
PHOLADID
PHOLADOID
PHOLCID
PHOLCOID
PHOLIDOLITE
PHOLIDOTE
PHON
PHONAL
PHONATE
PHONATED
PHONATING
PHONATION
PHONATORY
PHONAUTOGRAM
PHONE
PHONED
PHONEME
PHONEMIC
PHONEMICALLY
PHONEMICS
PHONES
PHONESIS
PHONETIC
PHONETICAL
PHONETICALLY
PHONETICIAN
PHONETICISM
PHONETICIST
PHONETICIZE
PHONETICS
PHONETISM
PHONETIST
PHONETIZATION
PHONETIZE
PHONEY
PHONGHI
PHONIATRICS
PHONIATRY
PHONIC
PHONICS
PHONIER
PHONIES
PHONIEST
PHONIKON
PHONING
PHONO
PHONOCAMPTIC
PHONODEIK
PHONOGLYPH
PHONOGRAM
PHONOGRAMIC
PHONOGRAMMIC
PHONOGRAPH
PHONOGRAPHER
PHONOGRAPHIC
PHONOGRAPHY
PHONOLITE
PHONOLITIC
PHONOLOGER
PHONOLOGIC
PHONOLOGICAL
PHONOLOGIST
PHONOLOGY
PHONOMANIA
PHONOMETER
PHONOMETRY
PHONOMIMIC
PHONOMOTOR
PHONON
PHONOPATHY
PHONOPHONE
PHONOPHORE
PHONOPHORIC
PHONOPHOROUS
PHONOPHOTE

PHONOPLEX
PHONOSCOPE
PHONOTYPE
PHONOTYPER
PHONOTYPIC
PHONOTYPIST
PHONOTYPY
PHONY
PHOO
PHOOEY
PHOOKA
PHORANTHIUM
PHORBIN
PHORESIS
PHORESY
PHORIA
PHORID
PHORMINX
PHOROMETER
PHOROMETRIC
PHOROMETRY
PHORONE
PHORONID
PHORONOMIA
PHORONOMIC
PHORONOMICS
PHORONOMY
PHOROSCOPE
PHOROZOOID
PHORRHEA
PHOS
PHOSE
PHOSGENE
PHOSGENITE
PHOSIS
PHOSPHAGEN
PHOSPHAM
PHOSPHAMIDE
PHOSPHATASE
PHOSPHATE
PHOSPHATED
PHOSPHATEMIA
PHOSPHATESE
PHOSPHATIC
PHOSPHATIDE
PHOSPHATION
PHOSPHATIZE
PHOSPHATIZED
PHOSPHATIZING
PHOSPHATURIA
PHOSPHATURIC
PHOSPHENE
PHOSPHENYL
PHOSPHID
PHOSPHIDE
PHOSPHINATE
PHOSPHINE
PHOSPHINIC
PHOSPHITE
PHOSPHOLIPID
PHOSPHONATE
PHOSPHONIC
PHOSPHONIUM
PHOSPHOR
PHOSPHORATE
PHOSPHORE
PHOSPHOREAL
PHOSPHORENT
PHOSPHOREOUS
PHOSPHORESCE
PHOSPHORESCENCE
PHOSPHORESCENT
PHOSPHORETED
PHOSPHORI
PHOSPHORIC
PHOSPHORICAL
PHOSPHORISM
PHOSPHORITE
PHOSPHORITIC
PHOSPHORIZE
PHOSPHOROGEN
PHOSPHOROGENE
PHOSPHOROUS
PHOSPHORUS
PHOSPHORYL
PHOSPHURIA
PHOSPHYL
PHOSS
PHOSSY
PHOT
PHOTA
PHOTAL
PHOTALGIA
PHOTECHY
PHOTEOLIC
PHOTIC
PHOTICS
PHOTISM
PHOTISTIC
PHOTO
PHOTOACTINIC
PHOTOBATHIC
PHOTOBIOTIC
PHOTOBROMIDE
PHOTOCAMPSIS
PHOTOCATHODE
PHOTOCHEMIST
PHOTOCHLORIDE
PHOTOCHROME
PHOTOCHROMY
PHOTOCOMPOSE
PHOTOCOPIER
PHOTOCOPY
PHOTOCRAYON
PHOTOCURRENT
PHOTODRAMA
PHOTODROME
PHOTODROMY
PHOTODYNAMIC
PHOTOELECTRIC
PHOTOENGRAVE
PHOTOENGRAVED
PHOTOENGRAVER
PHOTOENGRAVING
PHOTOETCH
PHOTOETCHED
PHOTOETCHER
PHOTOETCHING
PHOTOGELATIN
PHOTOGEN
PHOTOGENE
PHOTOGENIC
PHOTOGENY
PHOTOGEOLOGY
PHOTOGLYPH
PHOTOGLYPHIC
PHOTOGLYPHY
PHOTOGRAM
PHOTOGRAPH
PHOTOGRAPHEE
PHOTOGRAPHER
PHOTOGRAPHIC
PHOTOGRAPHY
PHOTOGRAVURE
PHOTOGYRIC
PHOTOHALIDE
PHOTOKINESIS
PHOTOLITH
PHOTOLOGIC
PHOTOLOGICAL
PHOTOLOGIST
PHOTOLOGY
PHOTOLYSIS
PHOTOLYTIC
PHOTOMA
PHOTOMAP
PHOTOMAPPER
PHOTOMETEOR
PHOTOMETER
PHOTOMETRIC
PHOTOMETRY
PHOTOMONTAGE
PHOTOMURAL
PHOTON
PHOTONASTY
PHOTONIC
PHOTONOSUS
PHOTONUCLEAR
PHOTOPATHIC
PHOTOPATHY
PHOTOPERIOD
PHOTOPHANE
PHOTOPHILE
PHOTOPHILIC
PHOTOPHILOUS
PHOTOPHILY
PHOTOPHOBE
PHOTOPHOBIA
PHOTOPHOBIC
PHOTOPHOBOUS
PHOTOPHONE
PHOTOPHONIC
PHOTOPHONY
PHOTOPHORE
PHOTOPHYGOUS
PHOTOPIA
PHOTOPIC
PHOTOPILE
PHOTOPLAY
PHOTOPLAYER
PHOTOPRINT
PHOTOPRINTER
PHOTORADIO
PHOTORELIEF
PHOTOSALT
PHOTOSCOPE
PHOTOSCOPIC
PHOTOSCOPY
PHOTOSPHERE
PHOTOSPHERIC
PHOTOSTABLE
PHOTOSTAT
PHOTOSTATED
PHOTOSTATIC
PHOTOSTATING
PHOTOSTATTED
PHOTOSTATTING
PHOTOSYNTAX
PHOTOTACTIC
PHOTOTACTISM
PHOTOTAXIS
PHOTOTAXY
PHOTOTHERAPY
PHOTOTHERMIC
PHOTOTIMER
PHOTOTONIC
PHOTOTONUS
PHOTOTROPE
PHOTOTROPIC
PHOTOTROPISM
PHOTOTUBE
PHOTOTYPE
PHOTOTYPIC
PHOTOTYPY
PHOTOVISUAL
PHOTOVOLTAIC
PHOTURIA
PHOUSDAR
PHRAGMA
PHRAGMOID
PHRAGMOSIS
PHRAMPEL
PHRASABLE
PHRASAL
PHRASALLY
PHRASE
PHRASEABLE
PHRASED
PHRASELESS
PHRASEMAKER
PHRASEMAKING
PHRASEMAN
PHRASEMONGER
PHRASEOGRAM
PHRASEOGRAPH
PHRASEOLOGIES
PHRASEOLOGY
PHRASER
PHRASINESS
PHRASING
PHRASY
PHRATOR
PHRATRAL
PHRATRIAC
PHRATRIAL
PHRATRIC
PHRATRIES
PHRATRY
PHREATIC
PHREATOPHYTE
PHREN
PHRENESIA
PHRENESIAC
PHRENESIS
PHRENETIC
PHRENETICAL
PHRENIC
PHRENICOTOMY
PHRENICS
PHRENITIC
PHRENITIS
PHRENOCARDIA
PHRENOGRAM
PHRENOGRAPH
PHRENOGRAPHY
PHRENOLOGER
PHRENOLOGIST
PHRENOLOGIZE
PHRENOLOGY
PHRENOPATHIC
PHRENOPATHY
PHRENOPLEGIA
PHRENOSIN
PHRENOSINIC
PHRENOTROPIC
PHRENSY
PHRONESIS
PHRYGANEID
PHRYGANEOID
PHRYGIA
PHRYGIUM
PHRYNID
PHRYNIN
PHTHALACENE
PHTHALAN
PHTHALATE
PHTHALEIN
PHTHALEINE
PHTHALIC
PHTHALIDE
PHTHALIMIDE
PHTHALIN
PHTHALYL
PHTHANITE
PHTHINOID
PHTHIRIASIS
PHTHISIC
PHTHISICAL
PHTHISICKY
PHTHISIS
PHTHONGAL
PHTHOR
PHTHORIC
PHTOR
PHU
PHUGOID
PHUL
PHULKARI
PHULWARA
PHUT
PHYCITE
PHYCITID
PHYCITOL
PHYCOCHROM
PHYCOCHROME
PHYCOCYANIN
PHYCOGRAPHY
PHYCOLOGICAL
PHYCOLOGIST
PHYCOLOGY
PHYCOMYCETE
PHYCOMYCETES
PHYCOPHAEIN
PHYLA
PHYLACTERIC
PHYLACTERIED
PHYLACTERIES
PHYLACTERIZE
PHYLACTERY
PHYLACTIC
PHYLARCH
PHYLARCHIC
PHYLARCHICAL
PHYLARCHY
PHYLE
PHYLEPHEBIC
PHYLESIS
PHYLETIC
PHYLETICALLY
PHYLETISM
PHYLIC
PHYLLADE
PHYLLARY
PHYLLIFORM
PHYLLIN
PHYLLINE
PHYLLITE
PHYLLITIC
PHYLLOCARID
PHYLLOCERATE
PHYLLOCLAD
PHYLLOCLADE
PHYLLOCYST
PHYLLOCYSTIC
PHYLLODE
PHYLLODIA
PHYLLODIAL
PHYLLODINOUS
PHYLLODIUM
PHYLLODY
PHYLLOGENOUS
PHYLLOID
PHYLLOIDAL
PHYLLOMANCY
PHYLLOMANIA
PHYLLOME
PHYLLOMIC
PHYLLOMORPH
PHYLLOMORPHY
PHYLLOPHORE
PHYLLOPOD
PHYLLOPODAN
PHYLLOPODE
PHYLLOPODOUS
PHYLLOPTOSIS

PHYLLORHINE
PHYLLOSOMA
PHYLLOSOME
PHYLLOTACTIC
PHYLLOTAXIS
PHYLLOTAXY
PHYLLOUS
PHYLLOXERA
PHYLLOXERAN
PHYLLOXERIC
PHYLLOZOOID
PHYLOGENESIS
PHYLOGENETIC
PHYLOGENY
PHYLON
PHYLUM
PHYMA
PHYMATA
PHYMATIC
PHYMATOID
PHYMATOSIS
PHYSAGOGUE
PHYSALIAN
PHYSALITE
PHYSCIOID
PHYSETEROID
PHYSIATRIC
PHYSIATRICS
PHYSIC
PHYSICAL
PHYSICALIST
PHYSICALITY
PHYSICALLY
PHYSICALNESS
PHYSICIAN
PHYSICIANCY
PHYSICIANED
PHYSICIANER
PHYSICIANING
PHYSICIANLY
PHYSICISM
PHYSICIST
PHYSICKED
PHYSICKER
PHYSICKING
PHYSICKY
PHYSICOLOGIC
PHYSICOMORPH
PHYSICS
PHYSID
PHYSIFORM
PHYSIOCRACY
PHYSIOCRAT
PHYSIOCRATIC
PHYSIOGENIC
PHYSIOGENY
PHYSIOGNOMIC
PHYSIOGNOMY
PHYSIOGONY
PHYSIOGRAPHY
PHYSIOLATER
PHYSIOLATRY
PHYSIOLOGER
PHYSIOLOGIAN
PHYSIOLOGIC
PHYSIOLOGICAL
PHYSIOLOGIST
PHYSIOLOGIZE
PHYSIOLOGUE
PHYSIOLOGUS
PHYSIOLOGY
PHYSIOSOPHIC
PHYSIOSOPHY
PHYSIQUE
PHYSIQUED
PHYSIS
PHYSITHEISM
PHYSITISM
PHYSIURGIC
PHYSIURGY
PHYSOCARPOUS
PHYSOCELE
PHYSOCLIST
PHYSOCLISTIC
PHYSOGASTRIC
PHYSOGASTRY
PHYSOMETRA
PHYSONECTOUS
PHYSOPOD
PHYSOSTIGMINE
PHYSOSTOME
PHYSOSTOMOUS
PHYTASE
PHYTATE
PHYTIC
PHYTIN
PHYTIVOROUS
PHYTOBEZOAR
PHYTOCHLORE
PHYTOCHLORIN
PHYTOGAMY
PHYTOGENESIS
PHYTOGENETIC
PHYTOGENIC
PHYTOGENY
PHYTOGNOMY
PHYTOGRAPH
PHYTOGRAPHER
PHYTOGRAPHIC
PHYTOGRAPHY
PHYTOID
PHYTOKININ
PHYTOL
PHYTOLOGIC
PHYTOLOGICAL
PHYTOLOGIST
PHYTOLOGY
PHYTOMA
PHYTOME
PHYTOMER
PHYTOMERA
PHYTOMETER
PHYTOMONAD
PHYTON
PHYTONIC
PHYTOPHAGAN
PHYTOPHAGIC
PHYTOPHAGOUS
PHYTOPHAGY
PHYTOPHILOUS
PHYTOPSYCHE
PHYTOPTID
PHYTOPTOSE
PHYTOPTOSIS
PHYTORHODIN
PHYTOSAUR
PHYTOSAURIAN
PHYTOSIS
PHYTOSTEROL
PHYTOSTROTE
PHYTOTOMIST
PHYTOTOMY
PHYTOTOXIC
PHYTOTOXIN
PHYTOTRON
PHYTOZOAN
PHYTOZOON
PHYTYL
PI
PIA
PIABA
PIACABA
PIACEVOLE
PIACHE
PIACLE
PIACULA
PIACULAR
PIACULARITY
PIACULARLY
PIACULUM
PIAFFE
PIAFFED
PIAFFER
PIAFFING
PIALYN
PIAN
PIANET
PIANETA
PIANETTE
PIANGENDO
PIANI
PIANIC
PIANINO
PIANISM
PIANISSIMO
PIANISSIMOS
PIANIST
PIANISTE
PIANISTIC
PIANNET
PIANO
PIANOFORTE
PIANOGRAPH
PIANOLA
PIANOLIST
PIANOLOGUE
PIANOS
PIANOSA
PIARHAEMIC
PIARHEMIC
PIASABA
PIASAVA
PIASSABA
PIASSAVA
PIASTER
PIASTRE
PIAT
PIATION
PIATTI
PIAY
PIAZIN
PIAZZA
PIAZZAED
PIAZZETTA
PIAZZIAN
PIBCORN
PIBGORN
PIBLOCKTO
PIBLOKTO
PIBROCH
PIC
PICA
PICACHO
PICACHOS
PICADOR
PICADURA
PICAL
PICAMAR
PICARA
PICARD
PICAREL
PICARESQUE
PICARIAN
PICARO
PICAROON
PICAYUNE
PICAYUNISH
PICAYUNISHLY
PICCADILL
PICCADILLY
PICCAGE
PICCALILLI
PICCANINNY
PICCIOTTO
PICCOLO
PICCOLOIST
PICCOLOS
PICE
PICEIN
PICENE
PICEOUS
PICEWORTH
PICHI
PICHICIAGO
PICHICIAGOS
PICHICIEGO
PICHURIC
PICHURIM
PICIFORM
PICINE
PICK
PICKABACK
PICKADIL
PICKAGE
PICKANINNIES
PICKANINNY
PICKAROON
PICKAX
PICKAXE
PICKBACK
PICKED
PICKEDEVANT
PICKEDLY
PICKEDNESS
PICKEER
PICKEERED
PICKEERING
PICKEL
PICKER
PICKEREL
PICKERELS
PICKERELWEED
PICKERING
PICKERINGITE
PICKERY
PICKET
PICKETEER
PICKETER
PICKI
PICKING
PICKLE
PICKLED
PICKLEMAN
PICKLER
PICKLES
PICKLEWEED
PICKLEWORM
PICKLING
PICKLOCK
PICKMAN
PICKMAW
PICKMEN
PICKOFF
PICKOUT
PICKOVER
PICKPENNY
PICKPOCKET
PICKPOCKETRY
PICKPOLE
PICKPURSE
PICKSMAN
PICKSMITH
PICKSOME
PICKSOMENESS
PICKTHANK
PICKTHATCH
PICKTOOTH
PICKUP
PICKWICK
PICKY
PICNIC
PICNICKED
PICNICKER
PICNICKERY
PICNICKING
PICNICKY
PICO
PICOID
PICOLINE
PICOLINIC
PICORY
PICOT
PICOTAH
PICOTE
PICOTEE
PICOTITE
PICOTS
PICOTTAH
PICQUET
PICQUETER
PICRA
PICRASMIN
PICRATE
PICRATED
PICRIC
PICRITE
PICROCARMINE
PICROL
PICROLITE
PICROMERITE
PICRORHIZA
PICRORHIZIN
PICROTIN
PICROTOXIC
PICROTOXIN
PICRY
PICRYL
PICT
PICTARNIE
PICTOGRAM
PICTOGRAPH
PICTOGRAPHIC
PICTOGRAPHY
PICTORIAL
PICTORIALLY
PICTORIC
PICTORICAL
PICTORICALLY
PICTUN
PICTURABLE
PICTURABLY
PICTURAL
PICTURE
PICTURED
PICTUREDOM
PICTUREDROME
PICTURELY
PICTURER
PICTURESQUE
PICTURING
PICTURIZE
PICTURY
PICUCULE
PICUDA
PICUDILLA
PICUDO
PICUL
PICULE
PICULET
PICULS
PICULULE
PIDAN
PIDDLE
PIDDLED
PIDDLER

PIDDLING
PIDDOCK
PIDGIN
PIE
PIEBALD
PIEBALDLY
PIEBALDNESS
PIECE
PIECEABLE
PIECED
PIECEMEAL
PIECEN
PIECENER
PIECER
PIECES
PIECETTE
PIECEWORK
PIECEWORKER
PIECING
PIECRUST
PIED
PIEDE
PIEDFORT
PIEDLY
PIEDMONT
PIEDMONTITE
PIEDNESS
PIEDRA
PIEDROIT
PIEHOUSE
PIEING
PIEMAG
PIEMAN
PIEMARKER
PIEN
PIENA
PIENANNY
PIEND
PIENO
PIENTAO
PIEPAN
PIEPLANT
PIEPOUDRE
PIEPOWDER
PIEPRINT
PIER
PIERCE
PIERCED
PIERCEL
PIERCER
PIERCING
PIERCINGLY
PIERCINGNESS
PIERDROP
PIERHEAD
PIERID
PIERIDINE
PIERINE
PIERRETTE
PIERROT
PIERROTIC
PIERT
PIESHOP
PIET
PIETAS
PIETIC
PIETIES
PIETISM
PIETIST
PIETISTIC
PIETISTICAL
PIETON
PIETOSE
PIETOSO
PIETY
PIEWIFE
PIEWIPE
PIEWOMAN
PIEZO
PIEZOMETER
PIEZOMETRIC
PIEZOMETRY
PIFERO
PIFF
PIFFERO
PIFFLE
PIFFLED
PIFFLING
PIG
PIGBELLY
PIGBOAT
PIGDAN
PIGEON
PIGEONABLE
PIGEONBERRY
PIGEONEER
PIGEONER
PIGEONFOOT
PIGEONGRAM
PIGEONHOLE
PIGEONRY
PIGEONS
PIGEONTAIL
PIGEONWEED
PIGEONWING
PIGEONWOOD
PIGFACE
PIGFISH
PIGFISHES
PIGFLOWER
PIGFOOT
PIGGED
PIGGERIES
PIGGERY
PIGGIE
PIGGIN
PIGGING
PIGGISH
PIGGISHLY
PIGGISHNESS
PIGGLE
PIGGY
PIGGYBACK
PIGGYBACKING
PIGHEAD
PIGHEADED
PIGHEADEDLY
PIGHERD
PIGHTEL
PIGHTLE
PIGLET
PIGLIKE
PIGLING
PIGLY
PIGMAKER
PIGMAKING
PIGMAN
PIGMENT
PIGMENTARY
PIGMENTATION
PIGMENTIZE
PIGMENTOSE
PIGMEW
PIGMY
PIGNOLIA
PIGNON
PIGNORA
PIGNORATE
PIGNORATION
PIGNORATIVE
PIGNUS
PIGNUT
PIGPEN
PIGRITIA
PIGROOT
PIGROOTS
PIGS
PIGSKIN
PIGSNEY
PIGSNIES
PIGSTICK
PIGSTICKER
PIGSTICKING
PIGSTIES
PIGSTY
PIGTAIL
PIGTAILED
PIGWASH
PIGWEED
PIGWIDGEON
PIGWIDGIN
PIGWIGEON
PIGYARD
PIITIS
PIJA
PIK
PIKA
PIKAKE
PIKE
PIKED
PIKEL
PIKELET
PIKEMAN
PIKEMEN
PIKEMONGER
PIKER
PIKES
PIKESTAFF
PIKESTAVES
PIKETAIL
PIKEY
PIKI
PIKING
PIKLE
PIKOL
PIKY
PIL
PILA
PILAF
PILAFF
PILAGE
PILANDITE
PILAPIL
PILAR
PILARY
PILASTER
PILASTERED
PILASTERING
PILASTRADE
PILASTRADED
PILASTRIC
PILAU
PILAUED
PILAW
PILCH
PILCHARD
PILCHER
PILCHERD
PILCORN
PILCROW
PILE
PILEA
PILEATA
PILEATE
PILEATED
PILED
PILEIFORM
PILELESS
PILEOLATED
PILEOLI
PILEOLUS
PILEORHIZA
PILEORHIZE
PILEOUS
PILER
PILES
PILEUM
PILEUS
PILEWEED
PILEWORK
PILEWORM
PILEWORT
PILFER
PILFERAGE
PILFERER
PILFERING
PILFERY
PILFRE
PILGARLIC
PILGARLICKY
PILGER
PILGRIM
PILGRIMAGE
PILGRIMAGER
PILGRIMATIC
PILGRIMER
PILGRIMESS
PILGRIMIZE
PILI
PILIDIUM
PILIFER
PILIFEROUS
PILIFORM
PILIGAN
PILIGANIN
PILIGANINE
PILIKAI
PILIKIA
PILILLOO
PILIMICTION
PILINE
PILING
PILITICO
PILK
PILKINS
PILL
PILLAGE
PILLAGED
PILLAGER
PILLAGERS
PILLAGING
PILLAR
PILLARED
PILLARET
PILLARING
PILLARIST
PILLARLET
PILLARLIKE
PILLARY
PILLAS
PILLBOX
PILLED
PILLEDNESS
PILLER
PILLERY
PILLET
PILLEUS
PILLICOCK
PILLION
PILLIVER
PILLIWINKS
PILLMAKER
PILLMAKING
PILLMONGER
PILLORIED
PILLORIES
PILLORIZE
PILLORY
PILLORYING
PILLOW
PILLOWBEER
PILLOWBER
PILLOWBERE
PILLOWCASE
PILLOWING
PILLOWMADE
PILLOWWORK
PILLOWY
PILLS
PILLULE
PILLWORM
PILLWORT
PILM
PILMY
PILOCARPIN
PILOCARPINE
PILOCYSTIC
PILOERECTION
PILOMOTOR
PILON
PILONCILLO
PILONIDAL
PILORI
PILOSE
PILOSIN
PILOSINE
PILOSIS
PILOSISM
PILOSITY
PILOT
PILOTAGE
PILOTAXITIC
PILOTED
PILOTHOUSE
PILOTING
PILOTISM
PILOTMAN
PILOTRY
PILOTWEED
PILOUS
PILPUL
PILPULIST
PILPULISTIC
PILSENER
PILSNER
PILT
PILTOCK
PILULA
PILULAR
PILULE
PILULIST
PILULOUS
PILUM
PILUS
PILWILLET
PILY
PIMA
PIMBINA
PIMELATE
PIMELIC
PIMELITE
PIMELITIS
PIMENT
PIMENTO
PIMENTON
PIMENTOS
PIMGENET
PIMIENTA
PIMIENTO
PIMIENTOS
PIMLICO
PIMOLA
PIMP
PIMPED
PIMPERNEL

PIMPERY
PIMPING
PIMPLE
PIMPLEBACK
PIMPLED
PIMPLIER
PIMPLIEST
PIMPLINESS
PIMPLING
PIMPLO
PIMPLY
PIN
PINA
PINABETE
PINACEOUS
PINACHROME
PINACLE
PINACOCYTAL
PINACOCYTE
PINACOID
PINACOIDAL
PINACOL
PINACOLATE
PINACOLIN
PINACOLINE
PINACULUM
PINAFORE
PINAG
PINAKIOLITE
PINAKOID
PINAKOIDAL
PINAKOTHEKE
PINANG
PINAS
PINASTER
PINATA
PINAVERDOL
PINAX
PINAYUSA
PINBALL
PINBEFORE
PINBONE
PINBUSH
PINCASE
PINCEMENT
PINCER
PINCERLIKE
PINCERS
PINCETTE
PINCH
PINCHBACK
PINCHBECK
PINCHBUG
PINCHCOCK
PINCHE
PINCHED
PINCHEDLY
PINCHEDNESS
PINCHEM
PINCHER
PINCHFIST
PINCHFISTED
PINCHGUT
PINCHING
PINCHPENNY
PINCPINC
PINCUSHION
PINCUSHIONY
PIND
PINDA
PINDAL
PINDARICAL
PINDARICALLY
PINDARICS
PINDER
PINDJAJAP
PINDLING
PINDY
PINE
PINEAL
PINEALISM
PINEALOMA
PINEAPPLE
PINEBANK
PINECONE
PINED
PINEDROPS
PINELAND
PINENE
PINER
PINERIES
PINERY
PINES
PINESAP
PINETA
PINETUM
PINEWEED
PINEWOODS
PINEY
PINFALL
PINFEATHER
PINFEATHERED
PINFEATHERER
PINFEATHERY
PINFIRE
PINFISH
PINFISHES
PINFOLD
PING
PINGE
PINGED
PINGING
PINGLE
PINGLER
PINGO
PINGRASS
PINGSTER
PINGUE
PINGUECULA
PINGUEDINOUS
PINGUEFACTION
PINGUEFY
PINGUESCENCE
PINGUESCENT
PINGUICULA
PINGUID
PINGUIDITY
PINGUIN
PINGUITE
PINGUITUDE
PINHEAD
PINHEADED
PINHOLD
PINHOLE
PINHOOK
PINIC
PINIER
PINIEST
PINING
PININGLY
PININGS
PINION
PINIONED
PINIONING
PINIPICRIN
PINITE
PINITOL
PINJANE
PINJRA
PINK
PINKANY
PINKBERRY
PINKED
PINKEEN
PINKEN
PINKENY
PINKER
PINKEYE
PINKFISH
PINKFISHES
PINKIE
PINKIFIED
PINKIFY
PINKIFYING
PINKING
PINKISH
PINKROOT
PINKSOME
PINKWEED
PINKWOOD
PINKWORT
PINKY
PINLOCK
PINMAKER
PINMAKING
PINMAN
PINNA
PINNACE
PINNACLE
PINNACLED
PINNACLING
PINNAE
PINNAGE
PINNAGLOBIN
PINNAL
PINNAS
PINNATE
PINNATED
PINNATELY
PINNATIFID
PINNATIFIDLY
PINNATION
PINNATIPED
PINNATISECT
PINNATULATE
PINNED
PINNEL
PINNER
PINNET
PINNIGRADE
PINNING
PINNIPED
PINNIPEDIAN
PINNOCK
PINNOITE
PINNOTERE
PINNOTHERE
PINNOTHERIAN
PINNULA
PINNULAE
PINNULAR
PINNULATE
PINNULATED
PINNULE
PINNULET
PINNY
PINNYWINKLE
PINO
PINOCHLE
PINOCLE
PINOLE
PINOLEUM
PINOLIA
PINOLIN
PINON
PINOT
PINPATCH
PINPILLOW
PINPOINT
PINPRICK
PINPROOF
PINRAIL
PINROWED
PINS
PINSCHER
PINSETTER
PINSON
PINSONS
PINT
PINTA
PINTADERA
PINTADO
PINTADOES
PINTADOITE
PINTADOS
PINTAIL
PINTAILS
PINTANO
PINTANOS
PINTE
PINTID
PINTLE
PINTO
PINTURA
PINUELA
PINULUS
PINUP
PINWEED
PINWHEEL
PINWORK
PINWORM
PINXIT
PINY
PINYL
PINYON
PIOLET
PION
PIONED
PIONEER
PIONEERED
PIONEERING
PIONERY
PIONNOTES
PIOSCOPE
PIOTED
PIOTINE
PIOTTY
PIOUPIOU
PIOURY
PIOUS
PIOUSLY
PIOUSNESS
PIP
PIPA
PIPAGE
PIPAL
PIPE
PIPEAGE
PIPECOLIN
PIPECOLINE
PIPECOLINIC
PIPED
PIPEFISH
PIPEFISHES
PIPEFITTER
PIPEFITTING
PIPEFUL
PIPEFULS
PIPELAYER
PIPELAYING
PIPELESS
PIPELIKE
PIPELINE
PIPEMAN
PIPEMOUTH
PIPER
PIPERACEOUS
PIPERATE
PIPERAZINE
PIPERIDE
PIPERIDEINE
PIPERIDGE
PIPERIDID
PIPERIDIDE
PIPERIDIN
PIPERIDINE
PIPERINE
PIPERITIOUS
PIPERITONE
PIPERLY
PIPERONAL
PIPERONYL
PIPERY
PIPERYLENE
PIPES
PIPESTAPPLE
PIPESTEM
PIPESTONE
PIPET
PIPETTE
PIPEWALKER
PIPEWOOD
PIPEWORK
PIPEWORT
PIPEY
PIPI
PIPID
PIPIER
PIPIEST
PIPIKAULA
PIPING
PIPINGLY
PIPINGNESS
PIPIRI
PIPISTREL
PIPISTRELLE
PIPIT
PIPKIN
PIPPED
PIPPEN
PIPPER
PIPPIER
PIPPIEST
PIPPIN
PIPPINER
PIPPINFACE
PIPPING
PIPPLE
PIPPY
PIPRINE
PIPROID
PIPSISSEWA
PIPUNCULID
PIPY
PIQUABLE
PIQUANCY
PIQUANT
PIQUANTLY
PIQUANTNESS
PIQUE
PIQUED
PIQUERO
PIQUET
PIQUETTE
PIQUEUR
PIQUIA
PIQUIERE
PIQUING
PIQURE
PIR
PIRACIES
PIRACY
PIRAGUA
PIRAI
PIRANA

PIRANHA
PIRARUCU
PIRATE
PIRATED
PIRATERY
PIRATIC
PIRATICAL
PIRATICALLY
PIRATING
PIRATISM
PIRATRY
PIRATY
PIRAYA
PIRCA
PIRE
PIRIJIRI
PIRIPIRI
PIRIRIGUA
PIRL
PIRLIE
PIRN
PIRNED
PIRNER
PIRNIE
PIRNY
PIROGEN
PIROGUE
PIROJKI
PIROL
PIROOT
PIROPLASM
PIROPLASMOSIS
PIROSHKI
PIROT
PIROUETTE
PIROUETTED
PIROUETTER
PIROUETTIST
PIRR
PIRRAURA
PIRRAURU
PIRRMAW
PIRSSONITE
PIRY
PISACA
PISACHA
PISACHEE
PISACHI
PISANG
PISANITE
PISAY
PISCARIES
PISCARY
PISCATION
PISCATOLOGY
PISCATOR
PISCATORIAL
PISCATORIAN
PISCATORIOUS
PISCATORY
PISCIAN
PISCICAPTURE
PISCICOLOUS
PISCICULTURE
PISCIFAUNA
PISCIFEROUS
PISCIFORM
PISCINA
PISCINAL
PISCINE
PISCINITY
PISCIVOROUS
PISCO
PISE
PISH
PISHAUG
PISHOGUE
PISHPASH
PISHU
PISIFORM
PISK
PISKUN
PISKY
PISMIRE
PISMIRISM
PISO
PISOLITE
PISOLITIC
PISOTE
PISS
PISSABED
PISSANT
PISSED
PISSING
PIST
PISTACHE
PISTACHIO
PISTACHIOS
PISTACITE
PISTAREEN
PISTE
PISTEOLOGY
PISTIC
PISTICK
PISTIL
PISTILLAR
PISTILLARY
PISTILLATE
PISTILLID
PISTILLIDIUM
PISTILLINE
PISTILLODE
PISTILLODY
PISTILLOID
PISTILS
PISTIOLOGY
PISTLE
PISTLER
PISTOL
PISTOLADE
PISTOLE
PISTOLED
PISTOLEER
PISTOLET
PISTOLETER
PISTOLETIER
PISTOLGRAM
PISTOLGRAPH
PISTOLIER
PISTOLING
PISTOLLED
PISTOLLING
PISTOLOGY
PISTOLPROOF
PISTON
PISTONHEAD
PISTRICES
PISTRIX
PIT
PITA
PITAHAYA
PITANGA
PITANGUA
PITAPAT
PITAPATATION
PITARAH
PITAU
PITBIRD
PITCH
PITCHBLENDE
PITCHED
PITCHER
PITCHERED
PITCHERY
PITCHFIELD
PITCHFORK
PITCHHOLE
PITCHI
PITCHIER
PITCHIEST
PITCHILY
PITCHINESS
PITCHING
PITCHMAN
PITCHOMETER
PITCHPIKE
PITCHSTONE
PITCHWORK
PITCHY
PITE
PITEIRA
PITEOUS
PITEOUSLY
PITEOUSNESS
PITFALL
PITFOLD
PITH
PITHANOLOGY
PITHEAD
PITHECAN
PITHECIAN
PITHECIINE
PITHECISM
PITHECOID
PITHECOLOGY
PITHECUS
PITHED
PITHIER
PITHIEST
PITHILY
PITHINESS
PITHING
PITHLESS
PITHOI
PITHOLE
PITHOS
PITHSOME
PITHY
PITIABILITY
PITIABLE
PITIABLENESS
PITIABLY
PITIED
PITIER
PITIES
PITIFUL
PITIFULLY
PITIFULNESS
PITIKINS
PITILESS
PITILESSLY
PITILESSNESS
PITIRRI
PITMAN
PITMANS
PITMEN
PITMIRK
PITO
PITOMETER
PITOMIE
PITON
PITPAN
PITPIT
PITPROP
PITSAW
PITSIDE
PITTACAL
PITTANCE
PITTANCER
PITTARD
PITTED
PITTER
PITTICITE
PITTINE
PITTING
PITTITE
PITTO
PITTOID
PITTOSPORE
PITUITAL
PITUITARIES
PITUITARY
PITUITE
PITUITOUS
PITURI
PITWOOD
PITWORK
PITWRIGHT
PITY
PITYING
PITYINGLY
PITYOCAMPA
PITYOCAMPE
PITYRIASIC
PITYRIASIS
PITYROID
PIU
PIUI
PIUPIU
PIURA
PIURI
PIVA
PIVOT
PIVOTAL
PIVOTALLY
PIVOTED
PIVOTER
PIVOTING
PIX
PIXIE
PIXIES
PIXILATED
PIXY
PIYYUT
PIZE
PIZZA
PIZZERIA
PIZZICATO
PIZZLE
PLACABILITY
PLACABLE
PLACABLENESS
PLACABLY
PLACARD
PLACARDED
PLACARDER
PLACARDING
PLACATE
PLACATED
PLACATER
PLACATING
PLACATION
PLACATIVE
PLACATORY
PLACCATE
PLACE
PLACEBO
PLACEBOES
PLACEBOS
PLACED
PLACEHOLDER
PLACEMAKER
PLACEMAN
PLACEMEN
PLACEMENT
PLACEMONGER
PLACENT
PLACENTA
PLACENTAE
PLACENTAL
PLACENTALIAN
PLACENTARY
PLACENTAS
PLACENTATE
PLACENTATION
PLACENTIFORM
PLACENTITIS
PLACENTOID
PLACENTOMA
PLACER
PLACET
PLACID
PLACIDAMENTE
PLACIDITY
PLACIDLY
PLACIDNESS
PLACING
PLACIT
PLACITUM
PLACK
PLACKET
PLACKLESS
PLACODE
PLACODERM
PLACODERMAL
PLACODERMOID
PLACODONT
PLACOID
PLACOIDAL
PLACOIDEAN
PLACOPLAST
PLACULA
PLADAROMA
PLAFOND
PLAGA
PLAGAL
PLAGATE
PLAGE
PLAGIAPLITE
PLAGIARICAL
PLAGIARIES
PLAGIARISE
PLAGIARISM
PLAGIARIST
PLAGIARISTIC
PLAGIARIZE
PLAGIARIZED
PLAGIARIZER
PLAGIARIZING
PLAGIARY
PLAGIHEDRAL
PLAGIOCLASE
PLAGIOCLINAL
PLAGIODONT
PLAGIOGRAPH
PLAGIONITE
PLAGIOPHYRE
PLAGIOSTOME
PLAGIOTROPIC
PLAGIUM
PLAGOSE
PLAGOSITY
PLAGUE
PLAGUED
PLAGUER
PLAGUESOME
PLAGUEY
PLAGUILY
PLAGUING
PLAGULA
PLAGUY
PLAICE
PLAID
PLAIDED
PLAIDMAN

PLAIDOYER
PLAIK
PLAIN
PLAINBACK
PLAINBACKS
PLAINED
PLAINER
PLAINEST
PLAINFUL
PLAINING
PLAINLY
PLAINNESS
PLAINS
PLAINSCRAFT
PLAINSFOLK
PLAINSMAN
PLAINSMEN
PLAINSOLED
PLAINSONG
PLAINSTONES
PLAINSWOMAN
PLAINSWOMEN
PLAINT
PLAINTAIL
PLAINTEXT
PLAINTIFF
PLAINTILE
PLAINTIVE
PLAINTIVELY
PLAINWARD
PLAINY
PLAISTER
PLAIT
PLAITED
PLAITER
PLAITING
PLAITWORK
PLAKAT
PLAN
PLANAEA
PLANAR
PLANARIAN
PLANARIFORM
PLANARIOID
PLANARITY
PLANATE
PLANATION
PLANCH
PLANCHE
PLANCHEITE
PLANCHER
PLANCHET
PLANCHETTE
PLANCHING
PLANCIER
PLANDOK
PLANE
PLANED
PLANER
PLANES
PLANET
PLANETA
PLANETABLE
PLANETABLER
PLANETAL
PLANETARIA
PLANETARIAN
PLANETARIES
PLANETARIUM
PLANETARIUMS
PLANETARY
PLANETED
PLANETESIMAL
PLANETFALL
PLANETIC
PLANETICOSE
PLANETING
PLANETOGENY
PLANETOID
PLANETOIDAL
PLANETOLOGIC
PLANETOLOGY
PLANETS
PLANFORM
PLANFUL
PLANFULLY
PLANFULNESS
PLANG
PLANGENCY
PLANGENT
PLANGENTLY
PLANGI
PLANGOR
PLANGOROUS
PLANICIPITAL
PLANIFOLIOUS
PLANIFORM
PLANIGRAPH
PLANILLA
PLANIMETER
PLANIMETRIC
PLANIMETRY
PLANING
PLANIPENNATE
PLANIPENNINE
PLANIROSTAL
PLANISCOPE
PLANISCOPIC
PLANISH
PLANISHED
PLANISHER
PLANISHING
PLANISPHERAL
PLANISPHERE
PLANISPHERIC
PLANISPIRAL
PLANK
PLANKAGE
PLANKED
PLANKER
PLANKING
PLANKS
PLANKTER
PLANKTOLOGY
PLANKTON
PLANKTONIC
PLANKTONT
PLANKWAYS
PLANKWISE
PLANLESS
PLANLESSLY
PLANLESSNESS
PLANNED
PLANNER
PLANNING
PLANOBLAST
PLANOBLASTIC
PLANOFERRITE
PLANOGAMETE
PLANOGRAPH
PLANOGRAPHIC
PLANOGRAPHY
PLANOMETER
PLANOMETRY
PLANOMILLER
PLANONT
PLANORBIFORM
PLANORBINE
PLANORBOID
PLANOSOME
PLANOSPORE
PLANT
PLANTA
PLANTAD
PLANTAGE
PLANTAIN
PLANTAL
PLANTANO
PLANTAR
PLANTARIS
PLANTARIUM
PLANTATION
PLANTATOR
PLANTED
PLANTER
PLANTERLY
PLANTIGRADE
PLANTIGRADY
PLANTING
PLANTIVOROUS
PLANTLET
PLANTLING
PLANTOCRACY
PLANTS
PLANTSMAN
PLANTULAE
PLANTULAR
PLANTULE
PLANULA
PLANULAE
PLANULAN
PLANULAR
PLANULATE
PLANULIFORM
PLANULOID
PLANUM
PLANURIA
PLANXTY
PLAP
PLAPPERT
PLAQUE
PLAQUETTE
PLASH
PLASHED
PLASHER
PLASHET
PLASHING
PLASHY
PLASM
PLASMA
PLASMASE
PLASMATIC
PLASMATICAL
PLASMATION
PLASMIC
PLASMOCHIN
PLASMOCYTE
PLASMODESM
PLASMODESMUS
PLASMODIA
PLASMODIAL
PLASMODIATE
PLASMODIUM
PLASMOGEN
PLASMOID
PLASMOLYSIS
PLASMOLYTIC
PLASMOLYZE
PLASMOMA
PLASMOMATA
PLASMON
PLASMOPHAGY
PLASMOPTYSIS
PLASMOQUIN
PLASMOQUINE
PLASMOSOMA
PLASMOSOMATA
PLASMOSOME
PLASMOTOMY
PLASOME
PLASS
PLASSON
PLASTEIN
PLASTER
PLASTERBILL
PLASTERBOARD
PLASTERED
PLASTERER
PLASTERINESS
PLASTERING
PLASTERWORK
PLASTERY
PLASTIC
PLASTICALLY
PLASTICINE
PLASTICISM
PLASTICITY
PLASTICIZE
PLASTICIZED
PLASTICIZER
PLASTICIZING
PLASTICLY
PLASTICS
PLASTID
PLASTIDIUM
PLASTIDOME
PLASTIDULAR
PLASTIDULE
PLASTIFY
PLASTIN
PLASTINOID
PLASTIQUE
PLASTOGAMIC
PLASTOGAMY
PLASTOMERE
PLASTOMETER
PLASTOSOME
PLASTOTYPE
PLASTRAL
PLASTRON
PLASTRUM
PLAT
PLATALEIFORM
PLATALEINE
PLATAN
PLATANE
PLATANIST
PLATANNA
PLATANO
PLATBAND
PLATCH
PLATE
PLATEA
PLATEASM
PLATEAU
PLATEAUS
PLATEAUX
PLATED
PLATEFUL
PLATEFULS
PLATEHOLDER
PLATEIASMUS
PLATELAYER
PLATELET
PLATEMAKER
PLATEMAKING
PLATEMAN
PLATEMEN
PLATEN
PLATER
PLATERER
PLATERESQUE
PLATERY
PLATES
PLATEWAY
PLATEWORK
PLATFORM
PLATFORMALLY
PLATFORMIST
PLATIC
PLATICLY
PLATIE
PLATILLA
PLATINA
PLATINAMIN
PLATINAMINE
PLATINAMMIN
PLATINAMMINE
PLATINATE
PLATINE
PLATING
PLATINIC
PLATINIZE
PLATINIZED
PLATINIZING
PLATINOID
PLATINOTYPE
PLATINOUS
PLATINUM
PLATITUDE
PLATITUDINAL
PLATLY
PLATODE
PLATOID
PLATONICALLY
PLATOON
PLATOPIC
PLATTED
PLATTEN
PLATTER
PLATTERFACE
PLATTING
PLATTNERITE
PLATTY
PLATUROUS
PLATY
PLATYBASIC
PLATYCARPOUS
PLATYCELIAN
PLATYCELOUS
PLATYCEPHALY
PLATYCHEIRIA
PLATYCNEMIA
PLATYCNEMIC
PLATYCOELIAN
PLATYCOELOUS
PLATYCORIA
PLATYCRANIA
PLATYCRANIAL
PLATYDACTYL
PLATYDACTYLE
PLATYFISH
PLATYGLOSSAL
PLATYGLOSSIA
PLATYHIERIC
PLATYLOBATE
PLATYMERIA
PLATYMETER
PLATYMYOID
PLATYNITE
PLATYNOTAL
PLATYODONT
PLATYOPE
PLATYOPIA
PLATYOPIC
PLATYPELLIC
PLATYPOD
PLATYPODIA
PLATYPODOUS
PLATYPUS
PLATYPUSES
PLATYPYGOUS
PLATYRRHIN
PLATYRRHINE
PLATYRRHINY

PLATYSMA
PLATYSOMID
PLATYSTERNAL
PLATYTROPE
PLAUD
PLAUDATION
PLAUDIT
PLAUDITE
PLAUDITOR
PLAUDITORY
PLAUENITE
PLAUSIBILITY
PLAUSIBLE
PLAUSIBLY
PLAUSIVE
PLAUSTRAL
PLAY
PLAYA
PLAYABILITY
PLAYABLE
PLAYAS
PLAYBACK
PLAYBILL
PLAYBOOK
PLAYBOX
PLAYBOY
PLAYBROKER
PLAYDAY
PLAYDOWN
PLAYED
PLAYER
PLAYERESS
PLAYFELLOW
PLAYFERE
PLAYFIELD
PLAYFUL
PLAYFULLY
PLAYFULNESS
PLAYGOER
PLAYGOING
PLAYGROUND
PLAYHOUSE
PLAYING
PLAYINGLY
PLAYLET
PLAYMAKER
PLAYMAKING
PLAYMAN
PLAYMARE
PLAYMATE
PLAYMONGER
PLAYOCK
PLAYOFF
PLAYPEN
PLAYREADER
PLAYROOM
PLAYSCRIPT
PLAYSOME
PLAYSOMELY
PLAYSOMENESS
PLAYSTEAD
PLAYSTOW
PLAYTE
PLAYTHING
PLAYTIME
PLAYWARD
PLAYWOMAN
PLAYWOMEN
PLAYWORK
PLAYWRIGHT
PLAYWRITER
PLAYWRITING
PLAZA
PLAZOLITE
PLEA
PLEACH
PLEACHED
PLEACHER
PLEACHING
PLEAD
PLEADABLE
PLEADED
PLEADER
PLEADING
PLEADINGLY
PLEADINGNESS
PLEASANCE
PLEASANT
PLEASANTLY
PLEASANTNESS
PLEASANTRY
PLEASANTSOME
PLEASAUNCE
PLEASE
PLEASED
PLEASEDLY
PLEASEDNESS
PLEASEMAN
PLEASEMEN
PLEASER
PLEASHIP
PLEASING
PLEASINGLY
PLEASINGNESS
PLEASURABLE
PLEASURABLY
PLEASURE
PLEASURED
PLEASUREFUL
PLEASUREMAN
PLEASUREMENT
PLEASURER
PLEASURING
PLEASURIST
PLEASUROUS
PLEAT
PLEATED
PLEATER
PLEATS
PLEB
PLEBE
PLEBEIAN
PLEBEIANISM
PLEBEIANIZE
PLEBEIANIZED
PLEBEIANLY
PLEBEIANNESS
PLEBEITY
PLEBES
PLEBICOLAR
PLEBICOLIST
PLEBICOLOUS
PLEBIFY
PLEBISCITARY
PLEBISCITE
PLEBISCITIC
PLEBISCITUM
PLEBS
PLECK
PLECOPTERAN
PLECOPTERID
PLECOPTEROUS
PLECOTINE
PLECTOGNATH
PLECTRA
PLECTRE
PLECTRIDIAL
PLECTRIDIUM
PLECTRON
PLECTRUM
PLECTRUMS
PLED
PLEDGE
PLEDGED
PLEDGEE
PLEDGEOR
PLEDGER
PLEDGESHOP
PLEDGET
PLEDGING
PLEDGOR
PLEE
PLEGAPHONIA
PLEGOMETER
PLEIN
PLEIOBAR
PLEIOCHROMIA
PLEIOCHROMIC
PLEIOMEROUS
PLEIOMERY
PLEION
PLEIONIAN
PLEIOPHYLLY
PLEIOTAXIS
PLEISTOSEIST
PLEMOCHOE
PLENA
PLENAL
PLENARILY
PLENARINESS
PLENARIUM
PLENARTY
PLENARY
PLENICORN
PLENILUNAL
PLENILUNE
PLENIPO
PLENIPOTENCE
PLENIPOTENT
PLENISH
PLENISHING
PLENISHMENT
PLENISM
PLENIST
PLENITUDE
PLENITY
PLENTEOUS
PLENTEOUSLY
PLENTIES
PLENTIFUL
PLENTIFULLY
PLENTIFULNESS
PLENTY
PLENUM
PLENUMS
PLENY
PLEOCHROIC
PLEOCHROISM
PLEOCHROOUS
PLEODONT
PLEOMASTIA
PLEOMASTIC
PLEOMETROSIS
PLEOMETROTIC
PLEOMORPHIC
PLEOMORPHIST
PLEOMORPHY
PLEON
PLEONASM
PLEONAST
PLEONASTE
PLEONASTIC
PLEONASTICAL
PLEONECTIC
PLEONEXIA
PLEONIC
PLEOPOD
PLEOPODITE
PLERERGATE
PLEROCERCOID
PLEROMA
PLEROMATIC
PLEROME
PLEROMORPH
PLEROPHORIC
PLEROPHORY
PLEROSIS
PLEROTIC
PLESIOBIOSIS
PLESIOSAUR
PLESIOSAURUS
PLESIOTYPE
PLESSIGRAPH
PLESSOR
PLET
PLETE
PLETHORA
PLETHORIC
PLETHORICAL
PLETHOROUS
PLETHORY
PLETHRON
PLETHRUM
PLEURA
PLEURAE
PLEURAL
PLEURIC
PLEURISY
PLEURITIC
PLEURITIS
PLEUROBRANCH
PLEUROCARP
PLEUROCELE
PLEUROCEROID
PLEURODONT
PLEUROGENIC
PLEUROLITH
PLEURON
PLEURONECTID
PLEUROPEDAL
PLEUROPODIUM
PLEUROSTEAL
PLEUROSTICT
PLEUROTOMIES
PLEUROTOMY
PLEUROTRIBE
PLEURUM
PLEUSTON
PLEVIN
PLEW
PLEWCH
PLEWE
PLEWGH
PLEX
PLEXAL
PLEXICOSE
PLEXIFORM
PLEXIGLAS
PLEXIGLASS
PLEXIMETER
PLEXIMETRIC
PLEXIMETRY
PLEXIPPUS
PLEXODONT
PLEXOR
PLEXURE
PLEXUS
PLEXUSES
PLIABILITY
PLIABLE
PLIABLENESS
PLIABLY
PLIANCY
PLIANT
PLIANTLY
PLIANTNESS
PLICA
PLICABLE
PLICAE
PLICAL
PLICATE
PLICATED
PLICATELY
PLICATENESS
PLICATINE
PLICATION
PLICATOR
PLICATULATE
PLICATURE
PLICIFEROUS
PLICIFORM
PLIED
PLIER
PLIERS
PLIES
PLIGHT
PLIGHTED
PLIGHTER
PLIGHTING
PLIM
PLIMSOLL
PLINTH
PLINTHER
PLINTHIFORM
PLIOSAUR
PLIOSAURIAN
PLIOTHERMIC
PLISKIE
PLISKY
PLISSE
PLITCH
PLOAT
PLOCE
PLOCEIFORM
PLOCK
PLOD
PLODDED
PLODDER
PLODDERLY
PLODDING
PLODDINGLY
PLODDINGNESS
PLODGE
PLOESTI
PLOIMATE
PLOMB
PLONK
PLOOK
PLOP
PLOPPED
PLOPPING
PLORATION
PLORATORY
PLOSH
PLOSION
PLOSIVE
PLOT
PLOTCH
PLOTCOCK
PLOTFUL
PLOTOSID
PLOTPROOF
PLOTT
PLOTTAGE
PLOTTED
PLOTTER
PLOTTERY
PLOTTING
PLOTTINGLY
PLOTTON
PLOTTY
PLOUGH
PLOUGHBOY
PLOUGHED
PLOUGHFISH

PLOUGHFOOT
PLOUGHGANG
PLOUGHGATE
PLOUGHHEAD
PLOUGHING
PLOUGHJOGGER
PLOUGHLAND
PLOUGHLINE
PLOUGHMAN
PLOUGHMELL
PLOUGHPOINT
PLOUGHSHARE
PLOUGHSHOE
PLOUGHSTAFF
PLOUGHSTILT
PLOUGHTAIL
PLOUGHWISE
PLOUGHWRIGHT
PLOUK
PLOUNCE
PLOUSIOCRACY
PLOUT
PLOUTER
PLOVER
PLOVERS
PLOVERY
PLOW
PLOWABLE
PLOWBOTE
PLOWBOY
PLOWED
PLOWER
PLOWFISH
PLOWFOOT
PLOWGANG
PLOWGATE
PLOWGRAITH
PLOWHEAD
PLOWING
PLOWJOGGER
PLOWLAND
PLOWLIGHT
PLOWLINE
PLOWMAKER
PLOWMAKING
PLOWMAN
PLOWMELL
PLOWMEN
PLOWPOINT
PLOWSHARE
PLOWSHOE
PLOWSTAFF
PLOWSTILT
PLOWTAIL
PLOWTER
PLOWWISE
PLOWWOMAN
PLOWWRIGHT
PLOY
PLOYMENT
PLUCK
PLUCKED
PLUCKER
PLUCKIER
PLUCKIEST
PLUCKILY
PLUCKINESS
PLUCKING
PLUCKY
PLUD
PLUFF
PLUFFER
PLUFFY
PLUG
PLUGBOARD
PLUGDRAWER
PLUGGABLE
PLUGGED
PLUGGER
PLUGGING
PLUGGINGLY
PLUGGY
PLUGHOLE
PLUGMAN
PLUGMEN
PLUGS
PLUGTRAY
PLUKE
PLUM
PLUMA
PLUMACEOUS
PLUMACH
PLUMADE
PLUMAGE
PLUMAGED
PLUMAGERY
PLUMASITE
PLUMASSIER
PLUMATE
PLUMATELLID
PLUMATELLOID
PLUMB
PLUMBAGE
PLUMBAGINE
PLUMBAGINOUS
PLUMBAGO
PLUMBAGOS
PLUMBATE
PLUMBEAN
PLUMBED
PLUMBEOUS
PLUMBER
PLUMBERIES
PLUMBERY
PLUMBET
PLUMBIC
PLUMBING
PLUMBISM
PLUMBITE
PLUMBLESS
PLUMBNESS
PLUMBOG
PLUMBOUS
PLUMBUM
PLUMCOT
PLUME
PLUMED
PLUMELET
PLUMEMAKER
PLUMEMAKING
PLUMEOUS
PLUMER
PLUMERY
PLUMET
PLUMETE
PLUMETIS
PLUMETTE
PLUMICORN
PLUMIER
PLUMIERIDE
PLUMIEST
PLUMING
PLUMIPED
PLUMIPEDE
PLUMIST
PLUMLIKE
PLUMMER
PLUMMET
PLUMMETED
PLUMMETLESS
PLUMMIER
PLUMMIEST
PLUMMING
PLUMMY
PLUMOSE
PLUMOSELY
PLUMOSENESS
PLUMOSITY
PLUMOUS
PLUMP
PLUMPEN
PLUMPER
PLUMPEST
PLUMPING
PLUMPLY
PLUMPNESS
PLUMPS
PLUMPY
PLUMROCK
PLUMULA
PLUMULACEOUS
PLUMULAR
PLUMULARIAN
PLUMULATE
PLUMULE
PLUMULIFORM
PLUMULOSE
PLUMY
PLUNDER
PLUNDERAGE
PLUNDERBUND
PLUNDERED
PLUNDERER
PLUNDERESS
PLUNDERING
PLUNDERINGLY
PLUNDEROUS
PLUNDERPROOF
PLUNGE
PLUNGED
PLUNGEON
PLUNGER
PLUNGING
PLUNGY
PLUNK
PLUNKED
PLUNKING
PLUNTHER
PLUPATRIOTIC
PLUPERFECT
PLUPERFECTLY
PLURAL
PLURALISM
PLURALIST
PLURALISTIC
PLURALITIES
PLURALITY
PLURALIZE
PLURALIZED
PLURALIZER
PLURALIZING
PLURALLY
PLURATIVE
PLUREL
PLURENNIAL
PLURIAXIAL
PLURICIPITAL
PLURICUSPID
PLURIES
PLURIFACIAL
PLURIFOLIATE
PLURIFY
PLURILATERAL
PLURILINGUAL
PLURILOCULAR
PLURINOMINAL
PLURIPARA
PLURIPARITY
PLURIPAROUS
PLURIPARTITE
PLURIPOTENCE
PLURIPOTENT
PLURISEPTATE
PLURISERIAL
PLURISERIATE
PLURISETOSE
PLURISPIRAL
PLURISPOROUS
PLURISY
PLURIVALENT
PLURIVALVE
PLURIVOROUS
PLURIVORY
PLUS
PLUSES
PLUSH
PLUSHED
PLUSHETTE
PLUSHIER
PLUSHIEST
PLUSHILY
PLUSHINESS
PLUSHY
PLUSQUAM
PLUSSAGE
PLUTEAL
PLUTEAN
PLUTEI
PLUTEIFORM
PLUTEUS
PLUTEUSES
PLUTOCRACIES
PLUTOCRACY
PLUTOCRAT
PLUTOCRATIC
PLUTOCRATICAL
PLUTOLATRY
PLUTOLOGICAL
PLUTOLOGIST
PLUTOLOGY
PLUTOMANIA
PLUTONIAN
PLUTONIC
PLUTONISM
PLUTONIST
PLUTONITE
PLUTONIUM
PLUTONOMIC
PLUTONOMIST
PLUTONOMY
PLUTTER
PLUVIAL
PLUVIALINE
PLUVINE
PLUVIOGRAPH
PLUVIOGRAPHY
PLUVIOMETER
PLUVIOMETRIC
PLUVIOMETRY
PLUVIOSCOPE
PLUVIOSITY
PLUVIOUS
PLY
PLYER
PLYGAIN
PLYING
PLYWOOD
PNEOGRAPH
PNEOMETER
PNEOMETRY
PNEOSCOPE
PNEUMA
PNEUMATIC
PNEUMATICAL
PNEUMATICITY
PNEUMATICS
PNEUMATISM
PNEUMATIST
PNEUMATIZE
PNEUMATIZED
PNEUMATOCELE
PNEUMATOCYST
PNEUMATOGRAM
PNEUMATOLOGY
PNEUMATOSIS
PNEUMATURIA
PNEUME
PNEUMECTOMY
PNEUMOCELE
PNEUMOCOCCUS
PNEUMODERMA
PNEUMOGASTRIC
PNEUMOGRAM
PNEUMOGRAPH
PNEUMOLITH
PNEUMOLOGY
PNEUMOLYSIS
PNEUMONALGIA
PNEUMONIA
PNEUMONIC
PNEUMONITIC
PNEUMONOCACE
PNEUMONOCELE
PNEUMONOLITH
PNEUMONOPEXY
PNEUMONOSIS
PNEUMOPEXY
PNEUMOTHORAX
PNEUMOTOMY
PNEUMOTOXIN
PO
POACEOUS
POACH
POACHED
POACHER
POACHIER
POACHIEST
POACHINESS
POACHING
POACHY
POAK
POAKE
POALI
POALO
POAP
POB
POBBIES
POBBY
POBEDY
POBLACION
POBS
POCAN
POCHADE
POCHARD
POCHAY
POCHE
POCHETTE
POCHETTINO
POCHISMO
POCHOIR
POCHOTE
POCILLIFORM
POCK
POCKET
POCKETABLE
POCKETBOOK
POCKETED
POCKETER
POCKETFUL
POCKETFULS
POCKETING
POCKETKNIFE
POCKETKNIVES
POCKETS
POCKETY

POCKHOUSE
POCKIER
POCKIEST
POCKMANKY
POCKMARK
POCKWEED
POCKWOOD
POCKY
POCO
POCOCURANTE
POCOSIN
POCULARY
POCULATION
POCULENT
POCULIFORM
POD
PODAGRA
PODAGRAL
PODAGRIC
PODAGRICAL
PODAGROUS
PODAGRY
PODAL
PODALGIA
PODALIC
PODANGER
PODARGUE
PODARTHRITIS
PODARTHRUM
PODATUS
PODDED
PODDER
PODDIDGE
PODDIGE
PODDING
PODDISH
PODDLE
PODDOCK
PODDY
PODE
PODELCOMA
PODEON
PODESTA
PODESTERATE
PODETIIFORM
PODETIUM
PODEX
PODGE
PODGER
PODGIER
PODGIEST
PODGILY
PODGINESS
PODGY
PODIA
PODIAL
PODIATRIST
PODIATRY
PODICAL
PODILEGOUS
PODITE
PODITIC
PODITTI
PODIUM
PODLER
PODLEY
PODO
PODOBRANCH
PODOCARP
PODODERM
PODODYNIA
PODOGYN
PODOGYNE
PODOGYNIUM
PODOLITE
PODOLOGY
PODOMANCY
PODOMERE
PODOPHYLLIC
PODOPHYLLIN
PODOPHYLLOUS
PODOS
PODOSCAPH
PODOSCAPHER
PODOSCOPY
PODOSPERM
PODOTHECA
PODOTHECAL
PODS
PODSOL
PODURAN
PODURID
PODWARE
PODZOL
PODZOLIC
POE
POEBIRD
POECHORE
POECHORIC
POECILITIC
POECILOGONY
POECILOMERE
POECILONYM
POECILONYMIC
POECILONYMY
POECILOPOD
POEM
POEMATIC
POEMS
POENOLOGY
POEPHAGOUS
POESIS
POESY
POET
POETASTER
POETASTERING
POETASTERY
POETASTRIC
POETASTRICAL
POETASTRY
POETESQUE
POETESS
POETIC
POETICAL
POETICALITY
POETICALLY
POETICIZE
POETICS
POETICULE
POETITO
POETIZATION
POETIZE
POETIZED
POETIZER
POETIZING
POETLING
POETLY
POETOMACHIA
POETRY
POFFLE
POGAMOGGAN
POGEY
POGGE
POGGIES
POGGY
POGIE
POGIES
POGO
POGONIA
POGONIASIS
POGONIATE
POGONION
POGONIP
POGONITE
POGONOLOGIST
POGONOLOGY
POGONOTOMY
POGONOTROPHY
POGROM
POGROMIST
POGUE
POGY
POH
POHA
POHICKORY
POHUTUKAWA
POI
POIESIS
POIETIC
POIGNADO
POIGNANCE
POIGNANCIES
POIGNANCY
POIGNANT
POIGNANTLY
POIGNET
POIKILE
POIKILITIC
POIKILOBLAST
POIKILOCYTE
POIKILOTHERM
POIKILOTHERMAL
POIL
POILU
POIMENIC
POIMENICS
POINADO
POINARD
POINCIANA
POIND
POINDABLE
POINDER
POINDING
POING
POINT
POINTABLE
POINTAGE
POINTAL
POINTBLANK
POINTE
POINTED
POINTEDLY
POINTEDNESS
POINTEL
POINTER
POINTES
POINTIER
POINTIEST
POINTILLE
POINTILLISM
POINTILLIST
POINTING
POINTINGLY
POINTLESS
POINTLESSLY
POINTLET
POINTLETED
POINTMAKER
POINTMAKING
POINTMAN
POINTMEN
POINTMENT
POINTS
POINTSMAN
POINTURE
POINTWAYS
POINTWISE
POINTY
POIS
POISE
POISED
POISER
POISING
POISON
POISONABLE
POISONBERRY
POISONBUSH
POISONED
POISONER
POISONING
POISONMAKER
POISONOUS
POISONOUSLY
POISONWEED
POISONWOOD
POISSARDE
POISSON
POISTER
POISURE
POIT
POITRAIL
POITREL
POITRINAIRE
POIVRADE
POIZE
POKAL
POKE
POKEBERRY
POKED
POKEFUL
POKELOKEN
POKER
POKERISH
POKERISHLY
POKERISHNESS
POKEROOT
POKEWEED
POKEY
POKIES
POKING
POKKE
POKOMOO
POKUNT
POKY
POLACCA
POLACRE
POLAK
POLAR
POLARIC
POLARIMETER
POLARIMETRIC
POLARIMETRY
POLARISCOPE
POLARISCOPY
POLARISE
POLARISTIC
POLARITY
POLARIZABLE
POLARIZATION
POLARIZE
POLARIZED
POLARIZER
POLARIZING
POLARON
POLARY
POLATOUCHE
POLAXIS
POLDAVIS
POLDAVY
POLDER
POLDERBOY
POLDERLAND
POLDERMAN
POLDOODY
POLDRON
POLE
POLEARM
POLEAX
POLEAXE
POLEAXER
POLEBURN
POLECAT
POLECATS
POLED
POLEHEAD
POLEMAN
POLEMARCH
POLEMIC
POLEMICAL
POLEMICALLY
POLEMICIAN
POLEMICIST
POLEMICS
POLEMIST
POLEMIZE
POLEMOSCOPE
POLENTA
POLER
POLES
POLESAW
POLESETTER
POLESTAR
POLEWARD
POLEWARDS
POLEY
POLEYN
POLEYNE
POLI
POLIAD
POLIADIC
POLIANITE
POLICE
POLICED
POLICEMAN
POLICEMEN
POLICEWOMAN
POLICEWOMEN
POLICIAL
POLICIES
POLICING
POLICIZE
POLICIZER
POLICLINIC
POLICY
POLICYHOLDER
POLIES
POLIGAR
POLIGARSHIP
POLILLA
POLING
POLIO
POLIORCETIC
POLIOSIS
POLIS
POLISH
POLISHED
POLISHER
POLISHING
POLISHINGS
POLISHMENT
POLISSOIR
POLISTA
POLITARCH
POLITARCHIC
POLITE
POLITEFUL
POLITEIA
POLITELY
POLITENESS
POLITER
POLITESSE
POLITEST
POLITIC
POLITICAL
POLITICALISM

POLITICALIZE
POLITICALLY
POLITICIAN
POLITICIOUS
POLITICIST
POLITICIZE
POLITICIZED
POLITICIZER
POLITICIZING
POLITICK
POLITICLY
POLITICOS
POLITICS
POLITIED
POLITIES
POLITIST
POLITIZE
POLITURE
POLITY
POLITZERIZE
POLJE
POLK
POLKA
POLKAED
POLKAING
POLL
POLLABLE
POLLACK
POLLAGE
POLLAKIURIA
POLLAM
POLLAN
POLLARCHY
POLLARD
POLLARDED
POLLARDING
POLLBOOK
POLLE
POLLED
POLLEE
POLLEN
POLLENATE
POLLENATION
POLLENED
POLLENITE
POLLENT
POLLER
POLLERA
POLLET
POLLETEN
POLLETTE
POLLEX
POLLICAL
POLLICAR
POLLICES
POLLICITATION
POLLINAR
POLLINARIUM
POLLINATE
POLLINATED
POLLINATING
POLLINATION
POLLINATOR
POLLINCTOR
POLLINCTURE
POLLING
POLLINIC
POLLINIUM
POLLINIZE
POLLINIZER
POLLINODIAL
POLLINODIUM
POLLINOID
POLLINOSE
POLLINOSIS
POLLIWOG
POLLOCK
POLLSTER
POLLUCITE
POLLUTANT
POLLUTE
POLLUTED
POLLUTER
POLLUTING
POLLUTION
POLLYWOG
POLO
POLOCONIC
POLOIST
POLONAISE
POLONICK
POLONIUM
POLONY
POLOS
POLSKA
POLSTER
POLT
POLTERGEIST
POLTFOOT
POLTFOOTED
POLTINA
POLTINIK
POLTOPHAGIC
POLTOPHAGIST
POLTOPHAGY
POLTROON
POLTROONERY
POLTROONISH
POLTROONISM
POLVERINE
POLY
POLYACID
POLYACOUSTIC
POLYACT
POLYACTINAL
POLYACTINE
POLYAD
POLYADELPH
POLYADENIA
POLYADIC
POLYAEMIA
POLYAEMIC
POLYALCOHOL
POLYAMIDE
POLYAMYLOSE
POLYANDRIA
POLYANDRIAN
POLYANDRIC
POLYANDRISM
POLYANDRIST
POLYANDRIUM
POLYANDROUS
POLYANDRY
POLYANTHA
POLYANTHUS
POLYARCH
POLYARCHAL
POLYARCHICAL
POLYARCHIST
POLYARCHY
POLYAXON
POLYAXONE
POLYBASIC
POLYBASICITY
POLYBASITE
POLYBLAST
POLYBORINE
POLYBRID
POLYBUNOUS
POLYBUNY
POLYCARPIC
POLYCARPOUS
POLYCARPY
POLYCENTRISM
POLYCENTRIST
POLYCHAETAL
POLYCHAETAN
POLYCHAETE
POLYCHAETOUS
POLYCHASIAL
POLYCHASIUM
POLYCHLORIDE
POLYCHOERANY
POLYCHORD
POLYCHREST
POLYCHRESTIC
POLYCHRESTY
POLYCHROIC
POLYCHROMATE
POLYCHROME
POLYCHROMIA
POLYCHROMIC
POLYCHROMISM
POLYCHROMIZE
POLYCHROMOUS
POLYCHROMY
POLYCLAD
POLYCLADINE
POLYCLINIC
POLYCONIC
POLYCOTYL
POLYCRACY
POLYCRASE
POLYCRATIC
POLYCROTIC
POLYCROTISM
POLYCYCLIC
POLYCYESIS
POLYDACTYL
POLYDACTYLE
POLYDACTYLY
POLYDEMIC
POLYDIPSIA
POLYDISPERSE
POLYDOMOUS
POLYDYMITE
POLYDYNAMIC
POLYEIDIC
POLYEIDISM
POLYEMIA
POLYEMIC
POLYERGIC
POLYESTHESIA
POLYETHNIC
POLYETHYLENE
POLYGALIN
POLYGAM
POLYGAMIAN
POLYGAMIC
POLYGAMICAL
POLYGAMIST
POLYGAMIZE
POLYGAMOUS
POLYGAMY
POLYGAR
POLYGENE
POLYGENESIC
POLYGENESIS
POLYGENESIST
POLYGENETIC
POLYGENIC
POLYGENISM
POLYGENIST
POLYGENOUS
POLYGENY
POLYGLOSSARY
POLYGLOT
POLYGLOTRY
POLYGLOTTAL
POLYGLOTTED
POLYGLOTTER
POLYGLOTTERY
POLYGLOTTIC
POLYGLOTTING
POLYGLOTTISM
POLYGLOTTIST
POLYGLYCEROL
POLYGON
POLYGONAL
POLYGONALLY
POLYGONEUTIC
POLYGONIC
POLYGONOID
POLYGONOUS
POLYGONUM
POLYGONY
POLYGRAM
POLYGRAPH
POLYGRAPHER
POLYGRAPHIC
POLYGRAPHY
POLYGYN
POLYGYNAIKY
POLYGYNIAN
POLYGYNIST
POLYGYNOUS
POLYGYNY
POLYGYRAL
POLYGYRIA
POLYHAEMIA
POLYHAEMIC
POLYHALIDE
POLYHALITE
POLYHARMONIC
POLYHARMONY
POLYHEDRA
POLYHEDRAL
POLYHEDRIC
POLYHEDRICAL
POLYHEDROID
POLYHEDRON
POLYHEDRONS
POLYHEDROUS
POLYHEMIA
POLYHEMIC
POLYHIDROSIS
POLYHISTOR
POLYHISTORIC
POLYHISTORY
POLYHYBRID
POLYHYDRIC
POLYHYDROXY
POLYIDEIC
POLYIDEISM
POLYIDROSIS
POLYLEMMA
POLYLEPIDOUS
POLYLITH
POLYLITHIC
POLYLOGY
POLYLOQUENT
POLYMAGNET
POLYMANIA
POLYMASTIA
POLYMASTIC
POLYMASTISM
POLYMASTY
POLYMATH
POLYMATHIC
POLYMATHIST
POLYMATHY
POLYMAZIA
POLYMELIA
POLYMELIAN
POLYMELY
POLYMER
POLYMERE
POLYMERIA
POLYMERIC
POLYMERISE
POLYMERISM
POLYMERIZE
POLYMEROUS
POLYMETER
POLYMETOCHIC
POLYMICRIAN
POLYMICROBIC
POLYMIGNITE
POLYMIXIID
POLYMNITE
POLYMNY
POLYMORPH
POLYMORPHIC
POLYMORPHISM
POLYMORPHOUS
POLYMORPHY
POLYMYARIAN
POLYMYODIAN
POLYMYODOUS
POLYMYOID
POLYMYOSITIS
POLYMYTHIC
POLYMYTHY
POLYNEE
POLYNEMID
POLYNEMOID
POLYNESIC
POLYNEURITIC
POLYNEURITIS
POLYNICES
POLYNOID
POLYNOMIAL
POLYNOMIC
POLYNUCLEAR
POLYNUCLEATE
POLYNYA
POLYODON
POLYODONT
POLYODONTAL
POLYODONTIA
POLYODONTOID
POLYOECIOUS
POLYOECISM
POLYOICOUS
POLYOL
POLYONOMOUS
POLYONOMY
POLYONYCHIA
POLYONYM
POLYONYMAL
POLYONYMIC
POLYONYMIST
POLYONYMOUS
POLYONYMY
POLYOPIA
POLYORAMA
POLYORGANIC
POLYOSE
POLYOXIDE
POLYP
POLYPARIA
POLYPARIAN
POLYPARIES
POLYPARIUM
POLYPAROUS
POLYPARY
POLYPEAN
POLYPED
POLYPEPTIDE
POLYPETAL
POLYPETALOUS
POLYPETALY
POLYPHAGE
POLYPHAGIA
POLYPHAGIAN

POLYPHAGIC
POLYPHAGIST
POLYPHAGOUS
POLYPHAGY
POLYPHARMACY
POLYPHARMIC
POLYPHASAL
POLYPHASE
POLYPHASER
POLYPHEMIAN
POLYPHEMIC
POLYPHEMUS
POLYPHENOL
POLYPHOBIA
POLYPHONE
POLYPHONED
POLYPHONIC
POLYPHONICAL
POLYPHONIES
POLYPHONISM
POLYPHONIST
POLYPHONIUM
POLYPHONOUS
POLYPHONY
POLYPHORE
POLYPHOTAL
POLYPHOTE
POLYPHYLESIS
POLYPHYLETIC
POLYPHYLLINE
POLYPHYLY
POLYPHYODONT
POLYPIAN
POLYPIDE
POLYPIDOM
POLYPIFEROUS
POLYPIGEROUS
POLYPITE
POLYPLASTIC
POLYPLOID
POLYPLOIDIC
POLYPLOIDY
POLYPNOEA
POLYPOD
POLYPODIA
POLYPODIES
POLYPODY
POLYPOID
POLYPOIDAL
POLYPORE
POLYPORITE
POLYPOROID
POLYPOSE
POLYPOSIS
POLYPOTOME
POLYPOUS
POLYPRAGMACY
POLYPRAGMATY
POLYPRAGMON
POLYPRENE
POLYPRISM
POLYPSYCHIC
POLYPSYCHISM
POLYPTERID
POLYPTEROID
POLYPTOTE
POLYPTOTON
POLYPTYCH
POLYPUS
POLYRHYTHMIC
POLYSACCHARIDE
POLYSARCIA
POLYSARCOUS
POLYSCOPE
POLYSCOPIC
POLYSEMANT
POLYSEMANTIC
POLYSEMEIA
POLYSEMIA
POLYSEMY
POLYSENSUOUS
POLYSIPHONIC
POLYSOMIA
POLYSOMITIC
POLYSPAST
POLYSPASTON
POLYSPERMIA
POLYSPERMIC
POLYSPERMY
POLYSPONDYLY
POLYSPORE
POLYSPORED
POLYSPORIC
POLYSPOROUS
POLYSTAURION
POLYSTELE
POLYSTELLIC
POLYSTICHOID
POLYSTOME
POLYSTOMIUM
POLYSTYLE
POLYSTYLOUS
POLYSTYRENE
POLYSULFIDE
POLYSULPHID
POLYSULPHIDE
POLYSYLLABIC
POLYSYLLABLE
POLYSYNDETIC
POLYSYNDETON
POLYTECHNIC
POLYTECHNICS
POLYTECHNIST
POLYTHEISM
POLYTHEIST
POLYTHEISTIC
POLYTHEIZE
POLYTHELIA
POLYTHIONIC
POLYTOCOUS
POLYTOMOUS
POLYTOMY
POLYTONAL
POLYTONALISM
POLYTONALITY
POLYTONE
POLYTONIC
POLYTONY
POLYTOPE
POLYTOPIC
POLYTOPICAL
POLYTRICHIA
POLYTRICHOUS
POLYTROCHAL
POLYTROCHOUS
POLYTROPE
POLYTROPHIC
POLYTYPE
POLYTYPED
POLYTYPIC
POLYTYPICAL
POLYTYPING
POLYTYPY
POLYURESIS
POLYURETHANE
POLYURIA
POLYURIC
POLYVALENCE
POLYVALENT
POLYVE
POLYVINYL
POLYVIRULENT
POLYVOLTINE
POLYZOAN
POLYZOARIA
POLYZOARIAL
POLYZOARIUM
POLYZOARY
POLYZOIC
POLYZOISM
POLYZONAL
POLYZOOID
POLYZOON
POLZENITE
POM
POMACE
POMACENTRID
POMACENTROID
POMACEOUS
POMADA
POMADE
POMADED
POMADING
POMANDER
POMANE
POMARINE
POMARIUM
POMARY
POMATE
POMATO
POMATOES
POMATOMID
POMATORHINE
POMATUM
POMBE
POMBO
POME
POMEGRANATE
POMELO
POMELY
POMERIA
POMERIUM
POMEROY
POMESHCHIK
POMEWATER
POMEY
POMEYS
POMFRET
POMICULTURE
POMIFEROUS
POMIFORM
POMIVOROUS
POMMADO
POMMAGE
POMME
POMMEE
POMMEL
POMMELED
POMMELER
POMMELING
POMMELION
POMMELLED
POMMELLER
POMMELLING
POMMELO
POMMER
POMMIES
POMMY
POMOERIUM
POMOLO
POMOLOGICAL
POMOLOGIST
POMOLOGY
POMONAL
POMONIC
POMP
POMPA
POMPADOUR
POMPAL
POMPANO
POMPANOS
POMPELMOOSE
POMPELMOUS
POMPERKIN
POMPHOLIX
POMPHOLYX
POMPHUS
POMPIER
POMPILID
POMPILOID
POMPION
POMPIST
POMPLESS
POMPON
POMPOON
POMPOSITY
POMPOSO
POMPOUS
POMPOUSLY
POMPOUSNESS
POMSTER
PON
PONCE
PONCEAU
PONCELET
PONCHO
PONCHOED
PONCHOS
POND
PONDAGE
PONDBUSH
PONDER
PONDERABILITY
PONDERABLE
PONDERAL
PONDERANCE
PONDERANCY
PONDERANT
PONDERARY
PONDERATE
PONDERATION
PONDERATIVE
PONDERED
PONDERER
PONDERING
PONDERINGLY
PONDERLING
PONDEROSITY
PONDEROUS
PONDEROUSLY
PONDEROUSNESS
PONDFISH
PONDFISHES
PONDGRASS
PONDMAN
PONDOK
PONDOKKIE
PONDUS
PONDWEED
PONDWORT
PONDY
PONE
PONENT
PONERID
PONERINE
PONEROID
PONEROLOGY
PONEY
PONG
PONGA
PONGEE
PONGID
PONGO
PONHAWS
PONIARD
PONIARDED
PONIARDING
PONICA
PONIER
PONIES
PONJA
PONOR
PONS
PONT
PONTAGE
PONTAL
PONTEE
PONTES
PONTIC
PONTICELLO
PONTICULAR
PONTICULUS
PONTIFEX
PONTIFF
PONTIFIC
PONTIFICAL
PONTIFICALLY
PONTIFICATE
PONTIFICATED
PONTIFICES
PONTIFICIAL
PONTIFY
PONTIL
PONTILE
PONTIN
PONTINE
PONTIST
PONTLEVIS
PONTON
PONTONIER
PONTOON
PONTUS
PONTVOLANT
PONY
PONYTAIL
PONZITE
POO
POOA
POOAH
POOCH
POOD
POODLE
POODLER
POOGYE
POOH
POOJA
POOJAH
POOK
POOKA
POOKAUN
POOKAWN
POOKHAUN
POOKOO
POOL
POOLER
POOLI
POOLROOM
POOLROOT
POOLWORT
POOLY
POON
POONA
POONAC
POONGEE
POONGHEE
POONGHIE
POOP
POOPED
POOPHYTE
POOPHYTIC
POOR
POORER
POOREST
POORHOUSE
POORISH

POORLINESS
POORLING
POORLY
POORLYISH
POORMASTER
POORNESS
POORT
POORTITH
POORWILL
POOSE
POOT
POOTHER
POOTY
POP
POPADAM
POPAL
POPCORN
POPDOCK
POPE
POPEDOM
POPEHOLY
POPEHOOD
POPEISM
POPEL
POPELER
POPELINE
POPELING
POPELY
POPERY
POPEYE
POPEYED
POPGLOVE
POPGUN
POPGUNNER
POPGUNNERY
POPINAC
POPINJAY
POPISH
POPISHLY
POPISHNESS
POPJOY
POPLAR
POPLARED
POPLEMAN
POPLESIE
POPLET
POPLIN
POPLINETTE
POPLITAEAL
POPLITEAL
POPLITEUS
POPLITIC
POPLOLLY
POPOMASTIC
POPOVER
POPPA
POPPABILITY
POPPABLE
POPPEAN
POPPED
POPPER
POPPET
POPPETHEAD
POPPIED
POPPIES
POPPIN
POPPING
POPPLE
POPPLED
POPPLING
POPPLY
POPPY
POPPYCOCK
POPPYCOCKISH
POPPYFISH
POPPYFISHES
POPPYHEAD
POPPYWORT
POPSHOP
POPSICLE
POPSKULL
POPULACE
POPULACY
POPULAR
POPULARES
POPULARISE
POPULARISM
POPULARITY
POPULARIZE
POPULARIZED
POPULARIZER
POPULARIZING
POPULARLY
POPULARNESS
POPULATE
POPULATED
POPULATING
POPULATION
POPULATIONAL
POPULATOR
POPULEON
POPULICIDE
POPULIN
POPULOUS
POPULOUSLY
POPULOUSNESS
POPWEED
PORAIL
PORAL
PORBEAGLE
PORCATE
PORCATED
PORCELAIN
PORCELAINIZE
PORCELAINLIKE
PORCELAINOUS
PORCELANEOUS
PORCELANIC
PORCELANITE
PORCELANOUS
PORCELLANIAN
PORCELLANIC
PORCELLANID
PORCELLANITE
PORCELLANIZE
PORCELLANOUS
PORCH
PORCHED
PORCHING
PORCINE
PORCUPINE
PORCUPINISH
PORE
PORED
PORER
PORES
PORET
PORETT
PORGE
PORGER
PORGIES
PORGY
PORI
PORICIDAL
PORIFERAL
PORIFERAN
PORIFEROUS
PORIFORM
PORINA
PORINESS
PORING
PORION
PORISM
PORISMATIC
PORISTIC
PORISTICAL
PORITE
PORITOID
PORK
PORKEATER
PORKER
PORKERY
PORKET
PORKFISH
PORKFISHES
PORKIER
PORKIES
PORKIEST
PORKIN
PORKISH
PORKLING
PORKMAN
PORKPEN
PORKPIE
PORKWOOD
PORKY
PORNERASTIC
PORNO
PORNOCRACY
PORNOCRAT
PORNOGRAPHER
PORNOGRAPHIC
PORNOGRAPHIES
PORNOGRAPHY
PORNOLOGICAL
PORO
PORODINE
PORODITE
POROGAM
POROGAMIC
POROGAMOUS
POROGAMY
POROMA
POROMAS
POROMATA
POROMETER
POROPLASTIC
POROPORO
POROROCA
POROS
POROSCOPE
POROSCOPIC
POROSCOPY
POROSE
POROSENESS
POROSIMETER
POROSIS
POROSITIES
POROSITY
POROTIC
POROTYPE
POROUS
POROUSLY
POROUSNESS
PORPENTINE
PORPHYRATIN
PORPHYRIAN
PORPHYRIES
PORPHYRIN
PORPHYRINE
PORPHYRION
PORPHYRITE
PORPHYRITIC
PORPHYROID
PORPHYROUS
PORPHYRY
PORPITOID
PORPOISE
PORPOISES
PORPORATE
PORR
PORRACEOUS
PORRECT
PORRET
PORRIDGE
PORRIDGY
PORRIGINOUS
PORRIGO
PORRINGER
PORRY
PORT
PORTA
PORTABILITY
PORTABLE
PORTABLENESS
PORTABLY
PORTAGE
PORTAGUE
PORTAL
PORTALED
PORTALLED
PORTAMENTI
PORTAMENTO
PORTANCE
PORTAS
PORTASS
PORTATILE
PORTATIVE
PORTATO
PORTATOR
PORTCRAYON
PORTCULLIS
PORTCULLISED
PORTCULLISING
PORTEACID
PORTED
PORTEND
PORTENDANCE
PORTENDED
PORTENDING
PORTENSION
PORTENT
PORTENTION
PORTENTIVE
PORTENTOSITY
PORTENTOUS
PORTENTOUSLY
PORTEOUS
PORTER
PORTERAGE
PORTERESS
PORTERHOUSE
PORTERLY
PORTESSE
PORTFIRE
PORTFOLIO
PORTFOLIOS
PORTGLAIVE
PORTGLAVE
PORTGRAVE
PORTGREVE
PORTHOLE
PORTHOOK
PORTHORS
PORTHOUSE
PORTICO
PORTICOED
PORTICOES
PORTICOS
PORTICUS
PORTIERE
PORTIERED
PORTIFY
PORTING
PORTIO
PORTION
PORTIONAL
PORTIONALLY
PORTIONED
PORTIONER
PORTIONING
PORTIONIST
PORTIONLESS
PORTITOR
PORTLAST
PORTLET
PORTLIGATURE
PORTLIGHT
PORTLILY
PORTLINESS
PORTLY
PORTMAN
PORTMANMOTE
PORTMANTEAU
PORTMANTLE
PORTMENT
PORTMOOT
PORTMOTE
PORTO
PORTOISE
PORTOLANO
PORTPAYNE
PORTRAIT
PORTRAITIST
PORTRAITURE
PORTRAY
PORTRAYABLE
PORTRAYAL
PORTRAYED
PORTRAYER
PORTRAYING
PORTRAYIST
PORTRAYMENT
PORTREEVE
PORTRESS
PORTSALE
PORTSIDE
PORTSIDER
PORTSMAN
PORTSOKEN
PORTUGAIS
PORTULACA
PORTUNIAN
PORTUNID
PORTURE
PORTY
PORULE
PORULOSE
PORULOUS
PORUS
PORWIGLE
PORY
POS
POSADA
POSADAS
POSCA
POSCHAY
POSE
POSED
POSEMENT
POSER
POSEUR
POSEUSE
POSEY
POSH
POSIED
POSIES
POSING
POSIT
POSITED
POSITING
POSITION
POSITIONAL
POSITIONED
POSITIONER

POSITIONING
POSITIVAL
POSITIVE
POSITIVELY
POSITIVENESS
POSITIVISM
POSITIVIST
POSITIVISTIC
POSITIVITY
POSITIVIZE
POSITOR
POSITRINO
POSITRON
POSITRONIUM
POSITUM
POSITURE
POSNET
POSOL
POSOLE
POSOLOGIC
POSOLOGICAL
POSOLOGIST
POSOLOGY
POSOSTEMAD
POSPOLITE
POSS
POSSE
POSSEMAN
POSSEMEN
POSSESS
POSSESSED
POSSESSEDLY
POSSESSING
POSSESSION
POSSESSIONAL
POSSESSIONED
POSSESSIONER
POSSESSIONS
POSSESSIVE
POSSESSOR
POSSESSORIAL
POSSESSORY
POSSET
POSSIBILE
POSSIBILIST
POSSIBILITY
POSSIBLE
POSSIBLENESS
POSSIBLY
POSSIE
POSSODIE
POSSUM
POSSUMHAW
POST
POSTABDOMEN
POSTABLE
POSTADJUNCT
POSTAGE
POSTAL
POSTALVEOLAR
POSTAMENT
POSTANTENNAL
POSTASPIRATE
POSTAXIAD
POSTAXIAL
POSTAXIALLY
POSTBAG
POSTBOOK
POSTBOX
POSTBOY
POSTCARD
POSTCARDINAL
POSTCARNATE
POSTCART
POSTCAVA
POSTCAVAL
POSTCENAL
POSTCENTRAL
POSTCENTRUM
POSTCIBAL
POSTCLASSIC
POSTCLAVICLE
POSTCLIVAL
POSTCOENAL
POSTCOLONIAL
POSTCOMITIAL
POSTCONTACT
POSTCORNU
POSTCOSMIC
POSTCRIBRATE
POSTDATE
POSTDATED
POSTDATING
POSTDENTAL
POSTDICROTIC
POSTDILUVIAL
POSTDILUVIAN
POSTE
POSTEA
POSTED
POSTEEN
POSTEL
POSTENTRIES
POSTENTRY
POSTER
POSTERIAD
POSTERIAL
POSTERIOR
POSTERIORI
POSTERIORIC
POSTERIORITY
POSTERIORLY
POSTERIORS
POSTERIORUMS
POSTERIST
POSTERITY
POSTERIZE
POSTERN
POSTETERNITY
POSTEXILIAN
POSTEXILIC
POSTEXIST
POSTEXISTENT
POSTFACE
POSTFACT
POSTFIX
POSTFIXED
POSTFLECTION
POSTFLEXION
POSTFRONTAL
POSTFURCA
POSTFURCAL
POSTGEMINUM
POSTGENITURE
POSTGLACIAL
POSTGLENOID
POSTGRACILE
POSTGRADUATE
POSTHABIT
POSTHASTE
POSTHITIS
POSTHOLDER
POSTHOLE
POSTHOUSE
POSTHUMA
POSTHUME
POSTHUMOUS
POSTHUMOUSLY
POSTHYPNOTIC
POSTIC
POSTICAL
POSTICALLY
POSTICHE
POSTICOUS
POSTICUM
POSTICUS
POSTIL
POSTILER
POSTILION
POSTILIONED
POSTILLATE
POSTILLATION
POSTILLATOR
POSTILLER
POSTILLION
POSTILLIONED
POSTILS
POSTIN
POSTING
POSTINGLY
POSTIQUE
POSTJACENT
POSTLIMINARY
POSTLIMINIUM
POSTLIMINOUS
POSTLIMINY
POSTLUDE
POSTLUDIUM
POSTMAN
POSTMARITAL
POSTMARK
POSTMARRIAGE
POSTMASTER
POSTMATURITY
POSTMEDIA
POSTMEDIAL
POSTMEDIAN
POSTMEN
POSTMERIDIAN
POSTMINERAL
POSTMISTRESS
POSTMORTAL
POSTMORTEM
POSTMORTUARY
POSTMUNDANE
POSTMUTATIVE
POSTNARIAL
POSTNARIS
POSTNASAL
POSTNATAL
POSTNATE
POSTNATI
POSTNATUS
POSTNUPTIAL
POSTOCULAR
POSTORBITAL
POSTOTIC
POSTPAGAN
POSTPAID
POSTPALATAL
POSTPALATINE
POSTPARIETAL
POSTPARTUM
POSTPHRAGMA
POSTPLACE
POSTPONABLE
POSTPONE
POSTPONED
POSTPONEMENT
POSTPONENCE
POSTPONER
POSTPONING
POSTPOSE
POSTPOSITED
POSTPOSITION
POSTPOSITIVE
POSTPRANDIAL
POSTPROPHESY
POSTPUBIC
POSTPUBIS
POSTRAMUS
POSTREMOTE
POSTRIDER
POSTRORSE
POSTS
POSTSCAPULA
POSTSCAPULAR
POSTSCENIUM
POSTSCHOOL
POSTSCRIBE
POSTSCRIPT
POSTSCRIPTUM
POSTSPHENOID
POSTSYNAPTIC
POSTSYSTOLIC
POSTTEMPORAL
POSTTONIC
POSTTYMPANIC
POSTULANCY
POSTULANT
POSTULATE
POSTULATED
POSTULATING
POSTULATION
POSTULATOR
POSTULATORY
POSTULATUM
POSTURAL
POSTURE
POSTURED
POSTURER
POSTURING
POSTURIST
POSTURIZE
POSTURIZED
POSTURIZING
POSTVELAR
POSTVERBAL
POSTVIDE
POSTVOCALIC
POSTWAR
POSTWARD
POSTWISE
POSTWOMAN
POSTWOMEN
POSTYARD
POSY
POT
POTABILITY
POTABLE
POTABLENESS
POTAGE
POTAGER
POTAGERE
POTAGERIE
POTAGERY
POTAIL
POTAMIC
POTAMOLOGIST
POTAMOLOGY
POTAMOMETER
POTASH
POTASHERY
POTASS
POTASSA
POTASSAMIDE
POTASSIC
POTASSIUM
POTATE
POTATION
POTATIVE
POTATO
POTATOES
POTATOR
POTATORY
POTBANK
POTBELLIED
POTBELLY
POTBOIL
POTBOILER
POTBOY
POTBOYDOM
POTCH
POTCHER
POTCHERMAN
POTCHERMEN
POTDAR
POTE
POTECARY
POTEEN
POTENCE
POTENCIES
POTENCY
POTENT
POTENTACY
POTENTATE
POTENTIAL
POTENTIALITY
POTENTIALIZE
POTENTIALLY
POTENTIATE
POTENTIATION
POTENTILLA
POTENTIZE
POTENTLY
POTENTNESS
POTER
POTESTAL
POTESTAS
POTESTATE
POTESTATIVE
POTEYE
POTFUL
POTGUN
POTHANGER
POTHEAD
POTHECARIES
POTHECARY
POTHEEN
POTHER
POTHERB
POTHERED
POTHERING
POTHERMENT
POTHERY
POTHOLE
POTHOOK
POTHOOKERY
POTHOOKS
POTHOUSE
POTHOUSEY
POTHUNT
POTHUNTED
POTHUNTER
POTHUNTING
POTICHE
POTICHES
POTIFER
POTIN
POTION
POTLACH
POTLACHE
POTLATCH
POTLEG
POTLICKER
POTLID
POTLIKKER
POTLINE
POTLING
POTLUCK
POTMAN
POTMEN
POTOMANIA
POTOMATO
POTOMETER

POTONG
POTOO
POTOROO
POTPIE
POTPOURRI
POTRACK
POTRERO
POTRO
POTS
POTSHARD
POTSHAW
POTSHERD
POTSHOOT
POTSHOOTER
POTSHOT
POTSIE
POTSTICK
POTSTONE
POTSY
POTT
POTTAGE
POTTAH
POTTARO
POTTED
POTTER
POTTERED
POTTERER
POTTERIES
POTTERING
POTTERINGLY
POTTERN
POTTERY
POTTIES
POTTING
POTTINGER
POTTLE
POTTLED
POTTO
POTTOS
POTTUR
POTTY
POTWALLER
POTWALLING
POTWARE
POTWHISKY
POTWORK
POTWORT
POTYCARY
POU
POUAH
POUCE
POUCER
POUCEY
POUCH
POUCHED
POUCHING
POUCY
POUDRET
POUDRETTE
POUF
POUFFE
POUL
POULAINE
POULARD
POULARDIZE
POULDRON
POULE
POULET
POULETTE
POULP
POULPE
POULT
POULTER
POULTERER
POULTICE
POULTICED
POULTICING
POULTRY
POULTRYMAN
POUNAMU
POUNCE
POUNCED
POUNCER
POUNCET
POUNCING
POUNCY
POUND
POUNDAGE
POUNDAL
POUNDCAKE
POUNDER
POUNDING
POUNDKEEPER
POUNDMAN
POUNDMASTER
POUNDMEAL
POUNDS
POUNDSTONE
POUNDWORTH
POUNE
POUR
POURBOIRE
POURED
POURER
POURIE
POURING
POURPARLER
POURPARLEY
POURPOINT
POURPOINTER
POURPRISE
POURVETE
POUS
POUSE
POUSER
POUSSE
POUSSETTE
POUSSETTED
POUSSETTING
POUSSIE
POUSSIN
POUSTIE
POUSY
POUT
POUTED
POUTER
POUTFUL
POUTING
POUTINGLY
POUTY
POVERISH
POVERISHMENT
POVERTY
POVERTYWEED
POVIE
POW
POWAN
POWCAT
POWDER
POWDERED
POWDERER
POWDERING
POWDERIZE
POWDERIZER
POWDERMAN
POWDERY
POWDIKE
POWELLITE
POWER
POWERABLE
POWERABLY
POWERBOAT
POWERED
POWERFUL
POWERFULLY
POWERFULNESS
POWERHOUSE
POWERLESS
POWERLESSLY
POWERMONGER
POWERS
POWHEAD
POWITCH
POWLDOODY
POWNIE
POWNY
POWSODDY
POWSOWDY
POWT
POWWOW
POWWOWER
POWWOWISM
POX
POXY
POY
POYBIRD
POYOU
POZ
POZZOLANA
POZZOLANIC
POZZUOLANA
POZZUOLANIC
PRAAM
PRABBLE
PRABHU
PRACTIC
PRACTICABLE
PRACTICABLY
PRACTICAL
PRACTICALISM
PRACTICALIST
PRACTICALITY
PRACTICALIZE
PRACTICALIZED
PRACTICALLY
PRACTICALNESS
PRACTICANT
PRACTICE
PRACTICED
PRACTICER
PRACTICIAN
PRACTICING
PRACTICO
PRACTICUM
PRACTISANT
PRACTISE
PRACTISED
PRACTISER
PRACTISING
PRACTITIONAL
PRACTITIONER
PRACTIVE
PRAD
PRADHANA
PRAEABDOMEN
PRAEANAL
PRAECAVA
PRAECIPE
PRAECIPUUM
PRAECOCES
PRAECOCIAL
PRAECORACOID
PRAECORDIA
PRAECORDIAL
PRAECORDIUM
PRAECORNU
PRAECOX
PRAECUNEUS
PRAEDIAL
PRAEDIALIST
PRAEDIALITY
PRAEDIUM
PRAEFECT
PRAEFECTORIAL
PRAEFECTUS
PRAEFERVID
PRAEHALLUX
PRAELABRUM
PRAELECT
PRAELECTION
PRAELECTOR
PRAELECTRESS
PRAELUDIUM
PRAEMAXILLA
PRAEMOLAR
PRAEMUNIRE
PRAENARIAL
PRAENEURAL
PRAENOMEN
PRAENOMINA
PRAENOMINAL
PRAEPOSITOR
PRAEPOSITURE
PRAEPOSITUS
PRAEPOSTER
PRAEPUBIS
PRAEPUCE
PRAESCUTUM
PRAESERTIM
PRAESES
PRAESIDIUM
PRAESPHENOID
PRAESTERNAL
PRAESTERNUM
PRAESTOMIUM
PRAESYSTOLIC
PRAETAXATION
PRAETEXTA
PRAETOR
PRAETORIAL
PRAETORIAN
PRAETORIUM
PRAETORSHIP
PRAGMATIC
PRAGMATICA
PRAGMATICAL
PRAGMATICISM
PRAGMATISM
PRAGMATIST
PRAGMATISTIC
PRAGMATIZE
PRAGMATIZER
PRAHAM
PRAHU
PRAIRIE
PRAIRIED
PRAIRIEWEED
PRAIRILLON
PRAISABLE
PRAISABLY
PRAISE
PRAISED
PRAISEFUL
PRAISEFULLY
PRAISER
PRAISES
PRAISEWORTHY
PRAISING
PRAISINGLY
PRAISS
PRAJNA
PRAKRITI
PRALINE
PRALLTRILLER
PRAM
PRANA
PRANCE
PRANCED
PRANCER
PRANCING
PRANCINGLY
PRANCOME
PRANDIAL
PRANG
PRANK
PRANKED
PRANKER
PRANKIER
PRANKIEST
PRANKING
PRANKINGLY
PRANKISH
PRANKISHLY
PRANKISHNESS
PRANKLE
PRANKS
PRANKSOME
PRANKSTER
PRANKT
PRANKY
PRASE
PRASEOLITE
PRASINE
PRASKEEN
PRASOID
PRASOPHAGOUS
PRASOPHAGY
PRASTHA
PRAT
PRATAL
PRATE
PRATED
PRATEMENT
PRATENSIAN
PRATER
PRATEY
PRATFALL
PRATILOMA
PRATINCOLE
PRATINCOLINE
PRATINCOLOUS
PRATING
PRATINGLY
PRATIQUE
PRATTLE
PRATTLED
PRATTLEMENT
PRATTLER
PRATTLING
PRATTLINGLY
PRATTLY
PRATTY
PRAU
PRAVE
PRAVILEGE
PRAVITY
PRAVOUS
PRAWN
PRAWNER
PRAWNY
PRAXINOSCOPE
PRAXIOLOGY
PRAXIS
PRAXITHEA
PRAY
PRAYA
PRAYABLE
PRAYED
PRAYER
PRAYERFUL
PRAYERFULLY
PRAYERMAKER
PRAYERMAKING
PRAYERS
PRAYFUL

PRAYING
PREACE
PREACH
PREACHED
PREACHER
PREACHERESS
PREACHERIZE
PREACHIER
PREACHIEST
PREACHIFIED
PREACHIFY
PREACHIFYING
PREACHILY
PREACHING
PREACHMAN
PREACHMENT
PREACHY
PREADAMIC
PREADAMITE
PREADAMITIC
PREADAMITISM
PREADJUNCT
PREADMISSION
PREAGONAL
PREAGONY
PREALLABLE
PREALLABLY
PREALVEOLAR
PREAMBLE
PREAMBLED
PREAMBLING
PREAMBULARY
PREAMBULATE
PREAMP
PREAMPLIFIER
PREANIMISM
PREANTERIOR
PREARRANGE
PREARRANGED
PREASEPTIC
PREATAXIC
PREAUDIENCE
PREAXIAL
PREAXIALLY
PREBACILLARY
PREBELLUM
PREBEND
PREBENDAL
PREBENDARIES
PREBENDARY
PREBENDATE
PREBRACHIAL
PREBRACHIUM
PREBRONCHIAL
PRECANCEL
PRECANCELED
PRECANCELING
PRECANCELLED
PRECANCELLING
PRECANCEROUS
PRECANONICAL
PRECANT
PRECANTATION
PRECARIOUS
PRECARIOUSLY
PRECARIUM
PRECARTILAGE
PRECARY
PRECAST
PRECATION
PRECATIVE
PRECATIVELY
PRECATORY
PRECAUSATION
PRECAUTION
PRECAUTIONAL
PRECAUTIOUS
PRECAVA
PRECEDABLE
PRECEDANEOUS
PRECEDE
PRECEDED
PRECEDENCE
PRECEDENCIES
PRECEDENCY
PRECEDENT
PRECEDENTARY
PRECEDENTED
PRECEDENTIAL
PRECEDER
PRECEDING
PRECEL
PRECENT
PRECENTOR
PRECENTORIAL
PRECENTORY
PRECENTRAL
PRECENTRESS
PRECENTRUM
PRECEPT
PRECEPTION
PRECEPTIST
PRECEPTIVE
PRECEPTIVELY
PRECEPTOR
PRECEPTORAL
PRECEPTORATE
PRECEPTORIAL
PRECEPTORY
PRECEPTRESS
PRECEPTUAL
PRECEPTUALLY
PRECERAMIC
PRECES
PRECESS
PRECESSED
PRECESSING
PRECESSION
PRECESSIONAL
PRECHORDAL
PRECIATION
PRECIDE
PRECIEUSE
PRECIEUX
PRECINCT
PRECINCTION
PRECINCTIVE
PRECIOSITIES
PRECIOSITY
PRECIOUS
PRECIOUSLY
PRECIOUSNESS
PRECIPE
PRECIPICE
PRECIPICED
PRECIPITABLE
PRECIPITANCE
PRECIPITANCY
PRECIPITANT
PRECIPITATE
PRECIPITATED
PRECIPITATELY
PRECIPITATION
PRECIPITATOR
PRECIPITIN
PRECIPITOUS
PRECIPITOUSLY
PRECIS
PRECISE
PRECISELY
PRECISENESS
PRECISIAN
PRECISIANISM
PRECISIANIST
PRECISION
PRECISIONAL
PRECISIONER
PRECISIONIST
PRECISIVE
PRECISO
PRECLARE
PRECLINICAL
PRECLIVAL
PRECLUDE
PRECLUDED
PRECLUDING
PRECLUSION
PRECLUSIVE
PRECOCIAL
PRECOCIOUS
PRECOCIOUSLY
PRECOCITY
PRECOGITATE
PRECOGNITION
PRECOGNITIVE
PRECOGNIZE
PRECOGNOSCE
PRECOMPOSE
PRECONCEIVE
PRECONCEIVED
PRECONCEIVING
PRECONCEPT
PRECONCERT
PRECONCERTED
PRECONDITION
PRECONIZE
PRECONIZED
PRECONIZER
PRECONIZING
PRECONQUEST
PRECONSCIOUS
PRECONSIGN
PRECONTACT
PRECONY
PRECOOK
PRECOOL
PRECOOLER
PRECOOLING
PRECORACOID
PRECORDIA
PRECORDIAL
PRECORDIALLY
PRECORNU
PRECOSTAL
PRECOURSE
PRECOX
PRECRITICAL
PRECRURAL
PRECULE
PRECUNEATE
PRECUNEUS
PRECURRENT
PRECURRER
PRECURSAL
PRECURSE
PRECURSIVE
PRECURSOR
PRECURSORY
PREDABLE
PREDACEAN
PREDACEOUS
PREDACIOUS
PREDACITY
PREDATE
PREDATED
PREDATING
PREDATION
PREDATISM
PREDATIVE
PREDATOR
PREDATORILY
PREDATORY
PREDAZZITE
PREDE
PREDECAY
PREDECEASE
PREDECEASER
PREDECESS
PREDECESSOR
PREDEFINE
PREDEFINITE
PREDELLA
PREDENTARY
PREDENTATE
PREDESIGNATE
PREDESTINATE
PREDESTINATION
PREDESTINE
PREDESTINED
PREDESTINING
PREDESTINY
PREDETERMINE
PREDETERMINED
PREDEVOTE
PREDIAL
PREDIALIST
PREDIALITY
PREDIASTOLIC
PREDIATORY
PREDICABLE
PREDICABLY
PREDICAMENT
PREDICANT
PREDICATE
PREDICATED
PREDICATING
PREDICATION
PREDICATIVE
PREDICATOR
PREDICATORY
PREDICROTIC
PREDICT
PREDICTABLE
PREDICTABLY
PREDICTED
PREDICTING
PREDICTION
PREDICTIONAL
PREDICTIVE
PREDICTIVELY
PREDICTOR
PREDICTORY
PREDIGEST
PREDIGESTION
PREDIKANT
PREDILECT
PREDILECTED
PREDILECTION
PREDISPONENT
PREDISPOSE
PREDISPOSED
PREDISPOSITION
PREDOMINANCE
PREDOMINANT
PREDOMINATE
PREDOMINATING
PREDOMINATOR
PREDOOM
PREDY
PREDYNASTIC
PREE
PREED
PREEING
PREEMINENCE
PREEMINENT
PREEMINENTLY
PREEMPT
PREEMPTION
PREEMPTIVE
PREEMPTOR
PREEMPTORY
PREEN
PREENED
PREENER
PREENING
PREEXILIAN
PREEXILIC
PREEXIST
PREEXISTENCE
PREEXISTENT
PREFABRICATE
PREFABRICATED
PREFABRICATING
PREFACE
PREFACED
PREFACER
PREFACIAL
PREFACING
PREFACIST
PREFACTOR
PREFATOR
PREFATORIAL
PREFATORILY
PREFATORY
PREFECT
PREFECTLY
PREFECTORAL
PREFECTORIAL
PREFECTORIAN
PREFECTUAL
PREFECTURAL
PREFECTURE
PREFER
PREFERABLE
PREFERABLY
PREFERENCE
PREFERENT
PREFERENTIAL
PREFERMENT
PREFERRED
PREFERREDLY
PREFERRER
PREFERRING
PREFERVID
PREFET
PREFIGURATE
PREFIGURE
PREFIGURED
PREFIGURING
PREFILTER
PREFINAL
PREFINE
PREFIX
PREFIXAL
PREFIXALLY
PREFIXATION
PREFIXED
PREFIXEDLY
PREFIXION
PREFIXTURE
PREFLECTION
PREFLEXION
PREFLIGHT
PREFORM
PREFORMATION
PREFORMATIVE
PREFORMED
PREFORMISM
PREFORMIST
PREFORMISTIC
PREFORMULATE
PREFRACT
PREFRONTAL
PREFULGENCE
PREFULGENCY

PREFULGENT
PREGEMINUM
PREGENIAL
PREGENICULUM
PREGENITAL
PREGHIERA
PREGLACIAL
PREGLOBULIN
PREGNABILITY
PREGNABLE
PREGNANCE
PREGNANCIES
PREGNANCY
PREGNANT
PREGNANTLY
PREGNANTNESS
PREGRACILE
PREGUST
PREGUSTANT
PREGUSTATION
PREGUSTATOR
PREGUSTIC
PREHALLUX
PREHALTER
PREHALTERES
PREHEND
PREHENSIBLE
PREHENSILE
PREHENSILITY
PREHENSION
PREHENSIVE
PREHENSOR
PREHENSORIAL
PREHENSORY
PREHEPATIC
PREHEPATICUS
PREHISTORIAN
PREHISTORIC
PREHISTORICS
PREHISTORY
PREHNITE
PREHUMAN
PREHYDRATION
PREIGNITION
PREINCARNATE
PREINDICANT
PREINDICATE
PREINSTRUCT
PREINSULA
PREINSULAR
PREINTONE
PREIOTIZE
PREJACENT
PREJUDGE
PREJUDGED
PREJUDGEMENT
PREJUDGER
PREJUDGING
PREJUDGMENT
PREJUDICATE
PREJUDICATOR
PREJUDICE
PREJUDICED
PREJUDICEDLY
PREJUDICIAL
PREJUDICING
PREJUDICIOUS
PREKE
PRELABRUM
PRELACHRYMAL
PRELACIES
PRELACTEAL
PRELACY
PRELAPSARIAN
PRELATE
PRELATEITY
PRELATESHIP
PRELATESS
PRELATIAL
PRELATIC
PRELATICAL
PRELATICALLY
PRELATION
PRELATISH
PRELATISM
PRELATIST
PRELATIZE
PRELATRY
PRELATURE
PRELE
PRELECT
PRELECTION
PRELECTOR
PRELECTRESS
PRELEGACY
PRELEGATE
PRELEGATEE
PRELIBATION
PRELIM
PRELIMINARY
PRELIMIT
PRELIMITATE
PRELINGUAL
PRELITERATE
PRELITHIC
PRELOGIC
PRELOGICAL
PRELORAL
PRELOREAL
PRELUDE
PRELUDED
PRELUDER
PRELUDIAL
PRELUDING
PRELUDIO
PRELUDIOUS
PRELUDIOUSLY
PRELUDIUM
PRELUDIZE
PRELUMBAR
PRELUSION
PRELUSIVE
PRELUSIVELY
PRELUSORILY
PRELUSORY
PREMAN
PREMATERNITY
PREMATURE
PREMATURELY
PREMATURITY
PREMAXILLA
PREMAXILLARY
PREMED
PREMEDIA
PREMEDIAL
PREMEDIAN
PREMEDIC
PREMEDICAL
PREMEDITATE
PREMEDITATED
PREMEDITATOR
PREMENSTRUAL
PREMERIDIAN
PREMETALLIC
PREMIAL
PREMIANT
PREMIATED
PREMIATING
PREMIE
PREMIER
PREMIERAL
PREMIERE
PREMIERED
PREMIERESS
PREMIERING
PREMIERSHIP
PREMIO
PREMIOUS
PREMISAL
PREMISE
PREMISED
PREMISING
PREMISORY
PREMISS
PREMIUM
PREMIUMS
PREMIXED
PREMOLAR
PREMONISH
PREMONITION
PREMONITIVE
PREMONITOR
PREMONITORY
PREMORSE
PREMOTION
PREMOVE
PREMOVEMENT
PREMOVER
PREMULTIPLY
PREMUNDANE
PREMUNE
PREMUNITORY
PREMUTATIVE
PRENAME
PRENARIAL
PRENASAL
PRENATAL
PRENATALIST
PRENDER
PRENDRE
PRENEPHRITIC
PRENEURAL
PRENOBLE
PRENODAL
PRENOMEN
PRENOMINATE
PRENOMINATED
PRENOTATION
PRENOTE
PRENOTICE
PRENOTIFY
PRENOTION
PRENTICE
PRENTICESHIP
PRENUNCIAL
PRENUPTIAL
PRENZIE
PREOCCUPANCY
PREOCCUPATE
PREOCCUPATION
PREOCCUPIED
PREOCCUPIER
PREOCCUPY
PREOCCUPYING
PREOCULAR
PREOPERATIVE
PREOPERCLE
PREOPERCULAR
PREOPERCULUM
PREOPINION
PREOPTION
PREORAL
PREORBITAL
PREORDAIN
PREORDER
PREORGANIC
PREP
PREPACKAGE
PREPACKAGED
PREPACKAGING
PREPAID
PREPALATAL
PREPARATEUR
PREPARATION
PREPARATIVE
PREPARATOR
PREPARATORY
PREPARDON
PREPARE
PREPARED
PREPAREDLY
PREPAREDNESS
PREPAREMENT
PREPARENTAL
PREPARER
PREPARIETAL
PREPARING
PREPARINGLY
PREPATELLAR
PREPAY
PREPAYING
PREPAYMENT
PREPEND
PREPENIAL
PREPENSE
PREPENSELY
PREPERCEIVE
PREPERFECT
PREPHRAGMA
PREPLACENTAL
PREPOLLENCE
PREPOLLENCY
PREPOLLENT
PREPOLLEX
PREPONDER
PREPONDERANCE
PREPONDERANT
PREPONDERATE
PREPONDERATING
PREPONDEROUS
PREPONTINE
PREPOSE
PREPOSED
PREPOSING
PREPOSITION
PREPOSITIVE
PREPOSITOR
PREPOSITURE
PREPOSSESS
PREPOSSESSED
PREPOSSESSION
PREPOSTER
PREPOSTEROUS
PREPOSTOR
PREPOTENCE
PREPOTENCY
PREPOTENT
PREPOTENTIAL
PREPOTENTLY
PREPRINT
PREPUBERTAL
PREPUBERTY
PREPUBESCENT
PREPUBIC
PREPUBIS
PREPUCE
PREPUPA
PREPUPAL
PREPUTIAL
PREPUTIUM
PRERAMUS
PREREDUCTION
PREREGAL
PREREGNANT
PRERELEASE
PREREMOTE
PREREPTION
PREREQUISITE
PREROGATIVAL
PREROGATIVE
PREROGATIVED
PRERUPT
PRES
PRESA
PRESAGE
PRESAGED
PRESAGEFUL
PRESAGEFULLY
PRESAGEMENT
PRESAGER
PRESAGIENT
PRESAGING
PRESAID
PRESANCTIFY
PRESAY
PRESAYING
PRESBYOPE
PRESBYOPIA
PRESBYOPIC
PRESBYTE
PRESBYTER
PRESBYTERAL
PRESBYTERATE
PRESBYTERE
PRESBYTERESS
PRESBYTERIAL
PRESBYTERIAN
PRESBYTERY
PRESBYTIA
PRESBYTIC
PRESCAPULA
PRESCAPULAR
PRESCHOOL
PRESCIENCE
PRESCIENT
PRESCIENTLY
PRESCIND
PRESCINDENT
PRESCISSION
PRESCRIBE
PRESCRIBED
PRESCRIBER
PRESCRIBING
PRESCRIPT
PRESCRIPTION
PRESCRIPTIVE
PRESCUTAL
PRESCUTUM
PRESE
PRESEMINAL
PRESEMINARY
PRESENCE
PRESENCED
PRESENCELESS
PRESENILE
PRESENILITY
PRESENSION
PRESENT
PRESENTABLE
PRESENTABLY
PRESENTAL
PRESENTATION
PRESENTATIVE
PRESENTED
PRESENTEE
PRESENTER
PRESENTIAL
PRESENTIENT
PRESENTIMENT
PRESENTING
PRESENTIST
PRESENTIVE
PRESENTIVELY
PRESENTLY
PRESENTMENT

PRESERVABLE
PRESERVAL
PRESERVATION
PRESERVATIVE
PRESERVATIZE
PRESERVATORY
PRESERVE
PRESERVED
PRESERVER
PRESERVING
PRESES
PRESEXUAL
PRESHOW
PRESIDE
PRESIDED
PRESIDENCE
PRESIDENCIA
PRESIDENCY
PRESIDENT
PRESIDENTE
PRESIDENTES
PRESIDENTIAL
PRESIDENTS
PRESIDER
PRESIDIAL
PRESIDIARY
PRESIDING
PRESIDIO
PRESIDIOS
PRESIDIUM
PRESIDY
PRESIGNIFIED
PRESIGNIFY
PRESIGNIFYING
PRESIMIAN
PRESOCIAL
PRESPHENOID
PRESPHYGMIC
PRESS
PRESSBOARD
PRESSED
PRESSEL
PRESSER
PRESSFAT
PRESSGANG
PRESSING
PRESSINGLY
PRESSION
PRESSIROSTRAL
PRESSIVE
PRESSLY
PRESSMAN
PRESSMARK
PRESSMASTER
PRESSMEN
PRESSOR
PRESSPACK
PRESSROOM
PRESSURAGE
PRESSURAL
PRESSURE
PRESSURIZE
PRESSURIZED
PRESSURIZING
PRESSWOMAN
PRESSWOMEN
PRESSWORK
PRESSWORKER
PREST
PRESTABILISM
PRESTABLE
PRESTANT
PRESTATE
PRESTATED
PRESTATING
PRESTATION
PRESTER
PRESTERNAL
PRESTERNUM
PRESTEZZA
PRESTIDIGITATOR
PRESTIGE
PRESTIGIATE
PRESTIGIATOR
PRESTIGIOUS
PRESTISSIMO
PRESTLY
PRESTO
PRESTOMIAL
PRESTOMIUM
PRESUBICULUM
PRESUL
PRESUMABLE
PRESUMABLY
PRESUME
PRESUMED
PRESUMEDLY
PRESUMER
PRESUMING
PRESUMPTION
PRESUMPTIVE
PRESUMPTUOUS
PRESUMPTUOUSLY
PRESUPPOSAL
PRESUPPOSE
PRESURMISE
PRESYLVIAN
PRESYNAPSIS
PRESYNAPTIC
PRESYSTOLE
PRESYSTOLIC
PRET
PRETA
PRETAN
PRETANNAGE
PRETANNED
PRETANNING
PRETEMPORAL
PRETENCE
PRETEND
PRETENDANT
PRETENDED
PRETENDEDLY
PRETENDER
PRETENDING
PRETENSE
PRETENSES
PRETENSION
PRETENSIONAL
PRETENSIVE
PRETENSIVELY
PRETENTIOUS
PRETENTIOUSNESS
PRETER
PRETERCANINE
PRETEREQUINE
PRETERGRESS
PRETERHUMAN
PRETERIENCE
PRETERIENT
PRETERIST
PRETERIT
PRETERITE
PRETERITION
PRETERITIVE
PRETERLEGAL
PRETERLETHAL
PRETERMIT
PRETERMITTED
PRETERMITTER
PRETERMITTING
PRETERNATIVE
PRETERNATURAL
PRETERROYAL
PRETERVECTION
PRETEST
PRETEXT
PRETEXTED
PRETEXTUOUS
PRETHORACIC
PRETIL
PRETIUM
PRETONE
PRETONIC
PRETOR
PRETORIAL
PRETORIAN
PRETORIUM
PRETREAT
PRETREATMENT
PRETREATY
PRETREMATIC
PRETTIER
PRETTIES
PRETTIEST
PRETTIFIED
PRETTIFIER
PRETTIFY
PRETTIFYING
PRETTIKIN
PRETTILY
PRETTINESS
PRETTY
PRETTYFACE
PRETTYISM
PRETYMPANIC
PRETYPIFY
PRETZEL
PREU
PREUX
PREVAIL
PREVAILED
PREVAILING
PREVAILINGLY
PREVAILMENT
PREVALENCE
PREVALENCIES
PREVALENCY
PREVALENT
PREVALENTLY
PREVALESCENT
PREVARICATE
PREVARICATED
PREVARICATOR
PREVASCULAR
PREVE
PREVELAR
PREVENANCE
PREVENANT
PREVENE
PREVENED
PREVENIENCE
PREVENIENT
PREVENING
PREVENT
PREVENTABLE
PREVENTATIVE
PREVENTED
PREVENTER
PREVENTIBLE
PREVENTING
PREVENTION
PREVENTIVE
PREVENTIVELY
PREVENTORIUM
PREVERNAL
PREVESICAL
PREVIDE
PREVIDENCE
PREVIEW
PREVIOUS
PREVIOUSLY
PREVIOUSNESS
PREVISE
PREVISED
PREVISING
PREVISION
PREVISIONAL
PREVISIVE
PREVISOR
PREVOCALIC
PREVOMER
PREVOST
PREVOT
PREVOTAL
PREVOYANCE
PREVOYANT
PREVUE
PREWAR
PREWARN
PREWE
PREX
PREXIES
PREXY
PREY
PREYED
PREYER
PREYFUL
PREYING
PREYINGLY
PREZONAL
PREZONE
PRIACANTHID
PRIAPISM
PRIAPUS
PRIBBLE
PRICE
PRICED
PRICEITE
PRICELESS
PRICER
PRICES
PRICING
PRICK
PRICKADO
PRICKANT
PRICKED
PRICKER
PRICKET
PRICKFOOT
PRICKING
PRICKISH
PRICKLE
PRICKLED
PRICKLIER
PRICKLIEST
PRICKLING
PRICKLINGLY
PRICKLOUSE
PRICKLY
PRICKMADAM
PRICKSEAM
PRICKSHOT
PRICKSPUR
PRICKTIMBER
PRICKWOOD
PRICKY
PRIDE
PRIDED
PRIDEFUL
PRIDEFULLY
PRIDEFULNESS
PRIDELING
PRIDIAN
PRIDING
PRIDY
PRIE
PRIED
PRIER
PRIES
PRIEST
PRIESTAL
PRIESTCAP
PRIESTCRAFT
PRIESTEEN
PRIESTERY
PRIESTESS
PRIESTFISH
PRIESTHOOD
PRIESTIANITY
PRIESTISM
PRIESTLIER
PRIESTLIEST
PRIESTLIKE
PRIESTLINESS
PRIESTLING
PRIESTLY
PRIESTS
PRIESTSHIRE
PRIG
PRIGGED
PRIGGER
PRIGGERY
PRIGGING
PRIGGISH
PRIGGISHLY
PRIGGISHNESS
PRIGGISM
PRIGMAN
PRIGSTER
PRILL
PRILLION
PRIM
PRIMA
PRIMACY
PRIMAGE
PRIMAL
PRIMALITY
PRIMAR
PRIMARIAN
PRIMARIED
PRIMARIES
PRIMARILY
PRIMARY
PRIMATAL
PRIMATE
PRIMATESHIP
PRIMATIAL
PRIMATIC
PRIMATICAL
PRIMATOLOGY
PRIMAVERA
PRIMAVERAL
PRIME
PRIMED
PRIMELY
PRIMENESS
PRIMER
PRIMERO
PRIMEROLE
PRIMEUR
PRIMEVAL
PRIMEVALLY
PRIMEVERIN
PRIMEVEROSE
PRIMEVITY
PRIMEVOUS
PRIMI
PRIMICES
PRIMIGENE
PRIMIGENIAL
PRIMIGENIAN
PRIMIGRAVIDA
PRIMINE
PRIMING

PRIMIPARA
PRIMIPARAE
PRIMIPARITY
PRIMIPAROUS
PRIMIPILAR
PRIMITIAE
PRIMITIAL
PRIMITIVE
PRIMITIVELY
PRIMITIVENESS
PRIMITIVISM
PRIMITIVITY
PRIMITY
PRIMLY
PRIMMED
PRIMMER
PRIMMEST
PRIMMING
PRIMNESS
PRIMO
PRIMOGENIAL
PRIMOGENITOR
PRIMOGENOUS
PRIMOMO
PRIMOPRIME
PRIMORDIAL
PRIMORDIALLY
PRIMORDIATE
PRIMORDIUM
PRIMOSITY
PRIMOST
PRIMP
PRIMPED
PRIMPING
PRIMPRINT
PRIMROSE
PRIMROSED
PRIMROSETIDE
PRIMROSETIME
PRIMROSY
PRIMSIE
PRIMULACEOUS
PRIMULAVERIN
PRIMULINE
PRIMUS
PRIMWORT
PRIMY
PRIN
PRINCE
PRINCEAGE
PRINCECRAFT
PRINCEDOM
PRINCEHOOD
PRINCEKIN
PRINCELET
PRINCELIER
PRINCELIEST
PRINCELIKE
PRINCELINESS
PRINCELING
PRINCELY
PRINCEPS
PRINCES
PRINCESS
PRINCESSE
PRINCESSLY
PRINCEWOOD
PRINCIFIED
PRINCIFY
PRINCIPAL
PRINCIPALITY
PRINCIPALLY
PRINCIPATE
PRINCIPE
PRINCIPES
PRINCIPIA
PRINCIPIANT
PRINCIPIUM
PRINCIPLE
PRINCIPLED
PRINCIPLES
PRINCIPLING
PRINCOCK
PRINCOD
PRINCOX
PRINE
PRINGLE
PRINK
PRINKED
PRINKER
PRINKING
PRINKLE
PRINKY
PRINOS
PRINT
PRINTABILITY
PRINTABLE
PRINTED
PRINTER
PRINTERIES
PRINTERY
PRINTING
PRINTLESS
PRINTLINE
PRINTSCRIPT
PRINTWORKS
PRIODONT
PRION
PRIONID
PRIONINE
PRIONODONT
PRIONOPINE
PRIOR
PRIORACY
PRIORAL
PRIORATE
PRIORESS
PRIORIES
PRIORISTIC
PRIORITE
PRIORITIES
PRIORITY
PRIORLY
PRIORSHIP
PRIORY
PRISABLE
PRISAGE
PRISAL
PRISCAN
PRISE
PRISM
PRISMAL
PRISMATIC
PRISMATICAL
PRISMATIZE
PRISMATOID
PRISMATOIDAL
PRISMED
PRISMOID
PRISMOIDAL
PRISMY
PRISOMETER
PRISON
PRISONER
PRISONERS
PRISONMENT
PRISONOUS
PRISS
PRISSIER
PRISSIES
PRISSIEST
PRISSILY
PRISSINESS
PRISSY
PRISTANE
PRISTAV
PRISTAW
PRISTINE
PRITCH
PRITCHEL
PRITHEE
PRITTLE
PRIUS
PRIVACIES
PRIVACITY
PRIVACY
PRIVADO
PRIVANT
PRIVATE
PRIVATEER
PRIVATEERED
PRIVATEERING
PRIVATELY
PRIVATENESS
PRIVATION
PRIVATIVE
PRIVATIVELY
PRIVE
PRIVET
PRIVIES
PRIVILEGE
PRIVILEGED
PRIVILEGER
PRIVILEGING
PRIVILY
PRIVITIES
PRIVITY
PRIVY
PRIX
PRIZABLE
PRIZE
PRIZEABLE
PRIZED
PRIZEFIGHT
PRIZEFIGHTER
PRIZEHOLDER
PRIZEMAN
PRIZEMEN
PRIZER
PRIZERY
PRIZES
PRIZETAKER
PRIZING
PRO
PROA
PROACH
PROAERESIS
PROAIRESIS
PROAL
PROAMBIENT
PROAMNION
PROAMNIOTIC
PROANAPHORA
PROANAPHORAL
PROANTHROPOS
PROATLAS
PROAULION
PROAVIAN
PROB
PROBABILISM
PROBABILIST
PROBABILITY
PROBABILIZE
PROBABLE
PROBABLY
PROBAL
PROBANG
PROBANT
PROBATE
PROBATED
PROBATING
PROBATION
PROBATIONAL
PROBATIONARY
PROBATIONER
PROBATIONISM
PROBATIONIST
PROBATIVE
PROBATOR
PROBATORY
PROBE
PROBEABLE
PROBED
PROBER
PROBING
PROBITY
PROBLEM
PROBLEMATIC
PROBLEMATICAL
PROBLEMATIST
PROBLEMATIZE
PROBLEMIST
PROBLEMISTIC
PROBLEMIZE
PROBOSCIDAL
PROBOSCIDATE
PROBOSCIDEAN
PROBOSCIDES
PROBOSCIDIAL
PROBOSCIDIAN
PROBOSCIFORM
PROBOSCIS
PROBOSCISES
PROBOULEUTIC
PROCACCIA
PROCACCIO
PROCACIOUS
PROCACIOUSLY
PROCACITY
PROCAINE
PROCAMBIAL
PROCAMBIUM
PROCARP
PROCARPIUM
PROCATARCTIC
PROCATARXIS
PROCATHEDRAL
PROCEDENDO
PROCEDURAL
PROCEDURE
PROCEED
PROCEEDED
PROCEEDER
PROCEEDING
PROCEEDINGS
PROCEEDS
PROCELLAS
PROCELLOSE
PROCELLOUS
PROCEPHALIC
PROCERCOID
PROCERE
PROCEREBRAL
PROCEREBRUM
PROCERES
PROCERITE
PROCERITY
PROCERUS
PROCESS
PROCESSAL
PROCESSED
PROCESSER
PROCESSING
PROCESSION
PROCESSIONAL
PROCESSIONER
PROCESSIVE
PROCESSOR
PROCESSUAL
PROCESSUS
PROCHAIN
PROCHEIN
PROCHLORITE
PROCHONDRAL
PROCHOOS
PROCHORDAL
PROCHORION
PROCHRONIC
PROCHRONISM
PROCHRONIZE
PROCIDENCE
PROCIDENT
PROCINCT
PROCK
PROCLAIM
PROCLAIMANT
PROCLAIMED
PROCLAIMER
PROCLAIMING
PROCLAMATION
PROCLAMATOR
PROCLINE
PROCLISIS
PROCLITIC
PROCLIVE
PROCLIVITIES
PROCLIVITOUS
PROCLIVITY
PROCLIVOUS
PROCNEMIAL
PROCOELIA
PROCOELIAN
PROCOELOUS
PROCONSUL
PROCONSULAR
PROCONSULATE
PROCRASTINATE
PROCRASTINATION
PROCREANT
PROCREATE
PROCREATED
PROCREATING
PROCREATION
PROCREATIVE
PROCREATOR
PROCREATORY
PROCTALGIA
PROCTALGY
PROCTATRESIA
PROCTATRESY
PROCTECTASIA
PROCTECTOMY
PROCTITIS
PROCTOCELE
PROCTOCLYSIS
PROCTOCOLITIS
PROCTODAEAL
PROCTODAEUM
PROCTODYNIA
PROCTOLOGIC
PROCTOLOGICAL
PROCTOLOGIST
PROCTOLOGY
PROCTOPLASTY
PROCTOPLEGIA
PROCTOPTOSIS
PROCTOR
PROCTORAGE
PROCTORAL
PROCTORIAL
PROCTORIALLY
PROCTORICAL
PROCTORIZE
PROCTORRHEA
PROCTORSHIP

PROCTOSCOPE
PROCTOSCOPIC
PROCTOSCOPY
PROCTOSPASM
PROCTOSTOMY
PROCTOTOME
PROCTOTOMY
PROCTOTRESIA
PROCULCATE
PROCULCATION
PROCUMBENT
PROCURABLE
PROCURACIES
PROCURACY
PROCURAL
PROCURANCE
PROCURATE
PROCURATION
PROCURATIVE
PROCURATOR
PROCURATORY
PROCURATRIX
PROCURE
PROCURED
PROCUREMENT
PROCURER
PROCURESS
PROCUREUR
PROCURING
PROCURRENT
PROCURSIVE
PROCURVATION
PROCURVED
PROCYONINE
PROD
PRODATARY
PRODD
PRODDED
PRODDER
PRODDING
PRODDLE
PRODELISION
PRODENTINE
PRODIALOGUE
PRODIGAL
PRODIGALISH
PRODIGALISM
PRODIGALITY
PRODIGALIZE
PRODIGALLY
PRODIGIOSITY
PRODIGIOUS
PRODIGIOUSLY
PRODIGUS
PRODIGY
PRODITION
PRODITOR
PRODITORIOUS
PRODROMAL
PRODROME
PRODROMOUS
PRODROMUS
PRODUCE
PRODUCEABLE
PRODUCED
PRODUCEMENT
PRODUCENT
PRODUCER
PRODUCIBLE
PRODUCING
PRODUCT
PRODUCTED
PRODUCTIBLE
PRODUCTID
PRODUCTILE
PRODUCTION
PRODUCTIONAL
PRODUCTIVE
PRODUCTIVELY
PRODUCTIVITY
PRODUCTOID
PRODUCTOR
PRODUCTORY
PRODUCTS
PROEGUMENAL
PROEM
PROEMBRYO
PROEMBRYONIC
PROEMIAL
PROEMIUM
PROEMPTOSIS
PROEPIMERON
PROETHICAL
PROETHNIC
PROETID
PROETTE
PROF
PROFACE
PROFANATION
PROFANATORY
PROFANE
PROFANED
PROFANELY
PROFANEMENT
PROFANENESS
PROFANER
PROFANING
PROFANISM
PROFANITIES
PROFANITY
PROFANIZE
PROFECTION
PROFECTIONAL
PROFER
PROFERMENT
PROFERT
PROFESS
PROFESSED
PROFESSEDLY
PROFESSION
PROFESSIONAL
PROFESSIONALLY
PROFESSIVE
PROFESSIVELY
PROFESSOR
PROFESSORATE
PROFESSORIAL
PROFESSORSHIP
PROFESSORY
PROFFER
PROFFERED
PROFFERER
PROFFERING
PROFICHI
PROFICIENCE
PROFICIENCY
PROFICIENT
PROFICIENTLY
PROFICUOUS
PROFICUOUSLY
PROFILE
PROFILED
PROFILER
PROFILING
PROFILIST
PROFILOGRAPH
PROFIT
PROFITABLE
PROFITABLY
PROFITED
PROFITEER
PROFITEERING
PROFITER
PROFITING
PROFITLESS
PROFITMONGER
PROFITS
PROFLATED
PROFLAVINE
PROFLIGACIES
PROFLIGACY
PROFLIGATE
PROFLIGATED
PROFLIGATELY
PROFLUENCE
PROFLUENT
PROFLUVIOUS
PROFLUVIUM
PROFONDE
PROFOUND
PROFOUNDLY
PROFOUNDNESS
PROFRE
PROFUGATE
PROFULGENT
PROFUNDA
PROFUNDITY
PROFUSE
PROFUSELY
PROFUSENESS
PROFUSER
PROFUSION
PROFUSIVELY
PROG
PROGAMETE
PROGAMIC
PROGANOSAUR
PROGENERATE
PROGENIES
PROGENITAL
PROGENITIVE
PROGENITOR
PROGENITRIX
PROGENITURE
PROGENITY
PROGENY
PROGERIA
PROGESTIN
PROGG
PROGGED
PROGGER
PROGGING
PROGLOTTIC
PROGLOTTID
PROGLOTTIDES
PROGLOTTIS
PROGNATHI
PROGNATHIC
PROGNATHISM
PROGNATHOUS
PROGNATHY
PROGNE
PROGNOSE
PROGNOSIS
PROGNOSTIC
PROGNOSTICAL
PROGNOSTICATE
PROGNOSTICATION
PROGNOSTICATOR
PROGONEATE
PROGRAM
PROGRAMATIC
PROGRAMED
PROGRAMER
PROGRAMING
PROGRAMIST
PROGRAMISTIC
PROGRAMMA
PROGRAMMATIC
PROGRAMMED
PROGRAMMER
PROGRAMMING
PROGRAMMIST
PROGREDE
PROGREDIENCY
PROGREDIENT
PROGRESS
PROGRESSED
PROGRESSER
PROGRESSING
PROGRESSION
PROGRESSISM
PROGRESSIST
PROGRESSIVE
PROGRESSIVELY
PROGRESSOR
PROHEIM
PROHIBIT
PROHIBITED
PROHIBITER
PROHIBITING
PROHIBITION
PROHIBITIONIST
PROHIBITIVE
PROHIBITOR
PROHIBITORY
PROJACIENT
PROJECT
PROJECTEDLY
PROJECTILE
PROJECTING
PROJECTINGLY
PROJECTION
PROJECTIONAL
PROJECTIVE
PROJECTIVITY
PROJECTOR
PROJECTRIX
PROJECTURE
PROJET
PROJICIENCE
PROJICIENT
PROJICIENTLY
PROKE
PROKEIMENON
PROKER
PROLABIUM
PROLACTIN
PROLAMIN
PROLAMINE
PROLAPSE
PROLAPSED
PROLAPSING
PROLAPSION
PROLAPSUS
PROLATE
PROLATELY
PROLATENESS
PROLATION
PROLATIVE
PROLEAGUE
PROLEAGUER
PROLEG
PROLEGATE
PROLEGOMENAL
PROLEGOMENON
PROLEPSES
PROLEPSIS
PROLEPTIC
PROLEPTICAL
PROLEPTICS
PROLES
PROLETAIRE
PROLETAIRISM
PROLETARIAN
PROLETARIAT
PROLETARIATE
PROLETARIZE
PROLETARY
PROLETCULT
PROLETKULT
PROLICIDAL
PROLICIDE
PROLIFERANT
PROLIFERATE
PROLIFEROUS
PROLIFIC
PROLIFICACY
PROLIFICAL
PROLIFICALLY
PROLIFICATE
PROLIFICATED
PROLIFICATING
PROLIFICITY
PROLIFICNESS
PROLIFY
PROLIGEROUS
PROLIN
PROLINE
PROLIX
PROLIXITY
PROLIXLY
PROLIXNESS
PROLLER
PROLOCUTION
PROLOCUTOR
PROLOCUTRIX
PROLOG
PROLOGIST
PROLOGIZE
PROLOGIZER
PROLOGUE
PROLOGUIST
PROLOGUIZE
PROLOGUIZER
PROLONG
PROLONGATE
PROLONGATION
PROLONGE
PROLONGED
PROLONGER
PROLONGING
PROLONGMENT
PROLUSION
PROLUSIONIZE
PROLUSORY
PROLYL
PROM
PROMACHOS
PROMENADE
PROMENADED
PROMENADER
PROMENADING
PROMERISTEM
PROMERIT
PROMETHIUM
PROMIC
PROMINENCE
PROMINENCY
PROMINENT
PROMINENTLY
PROMISCUITY
PROMISCUOUS
PROMISCUOUSLY
PROMISE
PROMISED
PROMISEE
PROMISER
PROMISING
PROMISINGLY
PROMISOR
PROMISS
PROMISSIVE
PROMISSOR
PROMISSORY

PROMIT
PROMITOSIS
PROMITTOR
PROMNESIA
PROMONTORIES
PROMONTORY
PROMORPH
PROMOTE
PROMOTED
PROMOTER
PROMOTING
PROMOTION
PROMOTIONAL
PROMOTIVE
PROMOTORIAL
PROMOVAL
PROMOVE
PROMOVENT
PROMPT
PROMPTBOOK
PROMPTER
PROMPTING
PROMPTITUDE
PROMPTIVE
PROMPTLY
PROMPTNESS
PROMPTUARY
PROMPTURE
PROMULGATE
PROMULGATED
PROMULGATING
PROMULGATION
PROMULGE
PROMULGED
PROMULGER
PROMULGING
PROMUSCIDATE
PROMUSCIS
PROMYCELIAL
PROMYCELIUM
PRONAOS
PRONATE
PRONATED
PRONATING
PRONATION
PRONATOR
PRONE
PRONELY
PRONENESS
PRONEPHRIC
PRONEPHROS
PRONEUR
PRONG
PRONGBUCK
PRONGED
PRONGER
PRONGHORN
PRONGHORNS
PRONGY
PRONIC
PRONITY
PRONOGRADE
PRONOMINAL
PRONOMINALLY
PRONONCE
PRONOTUM
PRONOUN
PRONOUNAL
PRONOUNCE
PRONOUNCEABLE
PRONOUNCED
PRONOUNCEDLY
PRONOUNCEMENT
PRONOUNCER
PRONOUNCING
PRONTO
PRONUBA
PRONUBIAL
PRONUCLEAR
PRONUCLEI
PRONUCLEUS
PRONUNCIABLE
PRONUNCIAL
PRONUNCIATION
PRONUNCIATOR
PRONYMPH
PRONYMPHAL
PROO
PROODE
PROOEMIAC
PROOEMION
PROOEMIUM
PROOF
PROOFER
PROOFFUL
PROOFING
PROOFLESS
PROOFLESSLY
PROOFREAD
PROOFREADER
PROOFREADING
PROOFROOM
PROOFY
PROP
PROPAEDEUTIC
PROPAGABLE
PROPAGANDA
PROPAGANDIC
PROPAGANDISM
PROPAGANDIST
PROPAGANDIZE
PROPAGATE
PROPAGATED
PROPAGATING
PROPAGATION
PROPAGATIVE
PROPAGATOR
PROPAGATORY
PROPAGINES
PROPAGO
PROPAGULE
PROPAGULUM
PROPALE
PROPALINAL
PROPANE
PROPANEDIOL
PROPARENT
PROPARGYL
PROPARGYLIC
PROPARIAN
PROPASSION
PROPATAGIAL
PROPATAGIAN
PROPATAGIUM
PROPEL
PROPELLANT
PROPELLED
PROPELLENT
PROPELLER
PROPELLING
PROPELMENT
PROPEND
PROPENDENT
PROPENE
PROPENSE
PROPENSELY
PROPENSENESS
PROPENSION
PROPENSITIES
PROPENSITY
PROPENYL
PROPENYLIC
PROPER
PROPERISPOME
PROPERLY
PROPERNESS
PROPERTIED
PROPERTIES
PROPERTY
PROPERTYSHIP
PROPHASE
PROPHASIS
PROPHECIES
PROPHECY
PROPHESIED
PROPHESIER
PROPHESY
PROPHESYING
PROPHET
PROPHETESS
PROPHETHOOD
PROPHETIC
PROPHETICAL
PROPHETICISM
PROPHETICLY
PROPHETISM
PROPHETIZE
PROPHETRY
PROPHLOEM
PROPHORIC
PROPHYLACTIC
PROPHYLAXIS
PROPHYLL
PROPHYLLUM
PROPINATION
PROPINE
PROPINED
PROPINING
PROPINQUANT
PROPINQUE
PROPINQUITY
PROPINQUOUS
PROPIO
PROPIOLATE
PROPIOLIC
PROPIONATE
PROPIONE
PROPIONIC
PROPIONYL
PROPITIABLE
PROPITIAL
PROPITIATE
PROPITIATED
PROPITIATING
PROPITIATION
PROPITIATIVE
PROPITIATOR
PROPITIATORY
PROPITIOUS
PROPITIOUSLY
PROPJET
PROPLASM
PROPLASTIC
PROPLEURON
PROPLEX
PROPLEXUS
PROPODEAL
PROPODEUM
PROPODIAL
PROPODIALE
PROPODITE
PROPODITIC
PROPODIUM
PROPOLIS
PROPOLIZE
PROPOMA
PROPOMATA
PROPONE
PROPONED
PROPONEMENT
PROPONENT
PROPONER
PROPONING
PROPONS
PROPORT
PROPORTION
PROPORTIONAL
PROPORTIONATENESS
PROPORTIONED
PROPORTIONER
PROPOSAL
PROPOSANT
PROPOSE
PROPOSED
PROPOSEDLY
PROPOSER
PROPOSING
PROPOSITIO
PROPOSITION
PROPOSITUS
PROPOUND
PROPOUNDED
PROPOUNDER
PROPOUNDING
PROPOUNDMENT
PROPOXY
PROPPAGE
PROPPED
PROPPER
PROPPING
PROPRAETOR
PROPRETOR
PROPRIATION
PROPRIATORY
PROPRIETAGE
PROPRIETARY
PROPRIETIES
PROPRIETOR
PROPRIETORY
PROPRIETOUS
PROPRIETRESS
PROPRIETY
PROPRIUM
PROPROCTOR
PROPS
PROPTERYGIAL
PROPTERYGIUM
PROPTOSED
PROPTOSES
PROPTOSIS
PROPUGN
PROPUGNACLED
PROPUGNATION
PROPUGNATOR
PROPULSATION
PROPULSATORY
PROPULSE
PROPULSION
PROPULSITY
PROPULSIVE
PROPULSOR
PROPULSORY
PROPUPA
PROPUPAL
PROPWOOD
PROPYGIDIUM
PROPYL
PROPYLAEA
PROPYLAEUM
PROPYLAMINE
PROPYLATION
PROPYLENE
PROPYLIC
PROPYLIDENE
PROPYLITE
PROPYLON
PROPYNE
PROQUAESTOR
PRORATA
PRORATABLE
PRORATE
PRORATED
PRORATING
PRORATION
PRORE
PROREAN
PRORECTOR
PRORECTORATE
PROREPTION
PROREX
PRORHINAL
PROROGATE
PROROGATION
PROROGATOR
PROROGUE
PROROGUED
PROROGUER
PROROGUING
PRORRHESIS
PRORSA
PRORSAL
PRORUMP
PRORUPTION
PROS
PROSAIC
PROSAICAL
PROSAICALLY
PROSAICISM
PROSAICNESS
PROSAISM
PROSAIST
PROSAL
PROSAPY
PROSAR
PROSCAPULA
PROSCAPULAR
PROSCENIA
PROSCENIUM
PROSCIND
PROSCIUTTO
PROSCOLECINE
PROSCOLEX
PROSCOLICES
PROSCRIBE
PROSCRIBED
PROSCRIBER
PROSCRIBING
PROSCRIPT
PROSCRIPTION
PROSCRIPTIVE
PROSE
PROSECT
PROSECTION
PROSECTOR
PROSECUTE
PROSECUTED
PROSECUTING
PROSECUTION
PROSECUTOR
PROSED
PROSELENIC
PROSELYTE
PROSELYTED
PROSELYTER
PROSELYTICAL
PROSELYTING
PROSELYTISM
PROSELYTIST
PROSELYTIZE
PROSELYTIZED
PROSELYTIZER
PROSEMAN
PROSEMINAR
PROSEMINARY
PROSEMINATE

PROSENCHYMA
PROSER
PROSETHMOID
PROSEUCHA
PROSEUCHE
PROSIER
PROSIEST
PROSIFY
PROSILIENCY
PROSILIENT
PROSILIENTLY
PROSILY
PROSIMIAN
PROSINESS
PROSING
PROSIPHON
PROSIPHONAL
PROSIPHONATE
PROSISH
PROSIT
PROSLAVER
PROSLAVERY
PROSNEUSIS
PROSO
PROSOBRANCH
PROSOCELE
PROSOCOELE
PROSODE
PROSODEMIC
PROSODETIC
PROSODIAC
PROSODIAL
PROSODIAN
PROSODIC
PROSODICAL
PROSODICALLY
PROSODION
PROSODIST
PROSODUS
PROSODY
PROSOGASTER
PROSOGYRATE
PROSOMA
PROSOMAL
PROSOMATIC
PROSONOMASIA
PROSOPIC
PROSOPICALLY
PROSOPITE
PROSOPLASIA
PROSOPOLEPSY
PROSOPON
PROSOPYLE
PROSORUS
PROSPECT
PROSPECTED
PROSPECTING
PROSPECTIVE
PROSPECTOR
PROSPECTUS
PROSPER
PROSPERED
PROSPERER
PROSPERING
PROSPERITY
PROSPEROUS
PROSPEROUSLY
PROSPICE
PROSPICIENCE
PROSS
PROSSY
PROSTATE
PROSTATIC
PROSTATISM
PROSTATOLITH
PROSTATOTOMY
PROSTERN
PROSTERNAL
PROSTERNUM
PROSTHECA
PROSTHENIC
PROSTHESES
PROSTHESIS
PROSTHETIC
PROSTHETICS
PROSTHETIST
PROSTHION
PROSTHIONIC
PROSTITUTE
PROSTITUTED
PROSTITUTING
PROSTITUTION
PROSTITUTOR
PROSTOMIAL
PROSTOMIATE
PROSTOMIUM
PROSTRATE
PROSTRATED
PROSTRATING
PROSTRATION
PROSTRATIVE
PROSTRATOR
PROSTYLE
PROSTYLOS
PROSY
PROSYLLOGISM
PROTACTIC
PROTACTINIUM
PROTAGON
PROTAGONISM
PROTAGONIST
PROTAMIN
PROTAMINE
PROTANDRIC
PROTANDRISM
PROTANDROUS
PROTANDRY
PROTANOMAL
PROTANOPE
PROTANOPIA
PROTANOPIC
PROTARSAL
PROTARSUS
PROTASIS
PROTASPIS
PROTATIC
PROTATICALLY
PROTAXIAL
PROTAXIS
PROTE
PROTEAD
PROTEAN
PROTEASE
PROTECT
PROTECTED
PROTECTIBLE
PROTECTING
PROTECTINGLY
PROTECTION
PROTECTIONAL
PROTECTIVE
PROTECTIVELY
PROTECTOR
PROTECTORAL
PROTECTORATE
PROTECTORIAN
PROTECTORIES
PROTECTORY
PROTECTRESS
PROTEGE
PROTEGEE
PROTEGULUM
PROTEIC
PROTEID
PROTEIDE
PROTEIFORM
PROTEIN
PROTEINASE
PROTEINOUS
PROTEINS
PROTEINURIA
PROTEND
PROTENDED
PROTENDING
PROTENSE
PROTENSION
PROTENSITY
PROTENSIVE
PROTENSIVELY
PROTEOLYSIS
PROTEOLYTIC
PROTEOPECTIC
PROTEOPEXIC
PROTEOPEXIS
PROTEOPEXY
PROTEOSE
PROTEOSOMAL
PROTEOSOME
PROTEOSURIA
PROTERANDRY
PROTEROBASE
PROTEROGLYPH
PROTEROGYNY
PROTEROTYPE
PROTERVE
PROTERVITY
PROTEST
PROTESTANCY
PROTESTANT
PROTESTATION
PROTESTATOR
PROTESTATORY
PROTESTED
PROTESTER
PROTESTING
PROTESTINGLY
PROTESTIVE
PROTEXT
PROTHALAMION
PROTHALAMIUM
PROTHALLIAL
PROTHALLINE
PROTHALLIUM
PROTHALLOID
PROTHALLUS
PROTHECA
PROTHESES
PROTHESIS
PROTHETIC
PROTHETICAL
PROTHONOTARY
PROTHORACES
PROTHORACIC
PROTHORAX
PROTHORAXES
PROTHROMBIN
PROTHYSTERON
PROTID
PROTIDE
PROTIST
PROTISTAN
PROTISTIC
PROTISTOLOGY
PROTISTON
PROTOBLAST
PROTOBLASTIC
PROTOCITIZEN
PROTOCLASTIC
PROTOCNEME
PROTOCOCCOID
PROTOCOL
PROTOCOLAR
PROTOCOLARY
PROTOCOLED
PROTOCOLING
PROTOCOLIST
PROTOCOLIZE
PROTOCOLLED
PROTOCOLLING
PROTOCONCH
PROTOCONCHAL
PROTOCONE
PROTOCONID
PROTOCONULE
PROTOCORM
PROTODEACON
PROTODERM
PROTODEVIL
PROTODONATAN
PROTODONATE
PROTODONT
PROTOGENAL
PROTOGENES
PROTOGENESIS
PROTOGENETIC
PROTOGENIC
PROTOGENIST
PROTOGINE
PROTOGOD
PROTOGONOUS
PROTOGRAPH
PROTOGYNOUS
PROTOGYNY
PROTOHOMO
PROTOHUMAN
PROTOLITHIC
PROTOLOG
PROTOLOGIST
PROTOMA
PROTOMALA
PROTOMALAL
PROTOMALAR
PROTOMARTYR
PROTOME
PROTOMERITE
PROTOMERITIC
PROTOMETALS
PROTOMORPH
PROTOMORPHIC
PROTON
PROTONE
PROTONEGROID
PROTONEMA
PROTONEMAL
PROTONEMATA
PROTONEMATAL
PROTONEME
PROTONEPHROS
PROTONEUTRON
PROTONIC
PROTONOTARY
PROTONOTATER
PROTONYM
PROTONYMPH
PROTONYMPHAL
PROTOPAPAS
PROTOPARENT
PROTOPATHIC
PROTOPATHY
PROTOPECTIN
PROTOPEPSIA
PROTOPHLOEM
PROTOPHYTE
PROTOPHYTIC
PROTOPINE
PROTOPLASM
PROTOPLASMAL
PROTOPLASMIC
PROTOPLAST
PROTOPLASTIC
PROTOPOD
PROTOPODIAL
PROTOPODITE
PROTOPODITIC
PROTOPOPE
PROTOPRISM
PROTORE
PROTOREBEL
PROTOSALT
PROTOSINNER
PROTOSOCIAL
PROTOSPASM
PROTOSPORE
PROTOSTELE
PROTOSTELIC
PROTOSTOME
PROTOTHECA
PROTOTHECAL
PROTOTHEME
PROTOTHERE
PROTOTRAITOR
PROTOTROCH
PROTOTROPHIC
PROTOTYPAL
PROTOTYPE
PROTOTYPIC
PROTOTYPICAL
PROTOVILLAIN
PROTOVUM
PROTOXID
PROTOXIDE
PROTOXIDIZE
PROTOXIDIZED
PROTOXYLEM
PROTOZOAL
PROTOZOAN
PROTOZOEA
PROTOZOEAN
PROTOZOIASIS
PROTOZOIC
PROTOZOON
PROTOZOONAL
PROTRACT
PROTRACTED
PROTRACTEDLY
PROTRACTER
PROTRACTILE
PROTRACTING
PROTRACTION
PROTRACTIVE
PROTRACTOR
PROTREPTIC
PROTREPTICAL
PROTRIAENE
PROTRUDE
PROTRUDED
PROTRUDENT
PROTRUDING
PROTRUSIBLE
PROTRUSILE
PROTRUSION
PROTRUSIVE
PROTRUSIVELY
PROTUBERANCE
PROTUBERANCES
PROTUBERANT
PROTUBERATE
PROTUBERATED
PROTUBEROUS
PROTURAN
PROTUTOR
PROTUTORY
PROTYL
PROTYLE
PROTYPE

PROUD
PROUDER
PROUDEST
PROUDFUL
PROUDHEARTED
PROUDISH
PROUDISHLY
PROUDLING
PROUDLY
PROUSTITE
PROVABILITY
PROVABLE
PROVABLENESS
PROVABLY
PROVAND
PROVANT
PROVE
PROVECT
PROVECTION
PROVED
PROVEDITOR
PROVEDOR
PROVEDORE
PROVEN
PROVENANCE
PROVEND
PROVENDER
PROVENE
PROVENIENCE
PROVENIENT
PROVENLY
PROVENT
PROVER
PROVERB
PROVERBIAL
PROVERBIALLY
PROVERBIC
PROVERBIZE
PROVES
PROVIANT
PROVICAR
PROVICARIATE
PROVIDANCE
PROVIDE
PROVIDED
PROVIDENCE
PROVIDENT
PROVIDENTIAL
PROVIDENTLY
PROVIDER
PROVIDING
PROVIDORE
PROVINCE
PROVINCES
PROVINCIAL
PROVINCIALLY
PROVINCIATE
PROVINCULUM
PROVINE
PROVING
PROVINGLY
PROVISION
PROVISIONAL
PROVISIONARY
PROVISIONER
PROVISIONS
PROVISIVE
PROVISO
PROVISOES
PROVISOR
PROVISORILY
PROVISORY
PROVISOS
PROVITAMIN
PROVO
PROVOCANT
PROVOCATION
PROVOCATIVE
PROVOCATOR
PROVOCATORY
PROVOKE
PROVOKED
PROVOKEE
PROVOKER
PROVOKING
PROVOKINGLY
PROVOLA
PROVOST
PROVOSTAL
PROVOSTRY
PROVOSTSHIP
PROW
PROWED
PROWER
PROWERSITE
PROWESS
PROWESSED
PROWL
PROWLED
PROWLER
PROWLING
PROWLINGLY
PROX
PROXENET
PROXENETE
PROXENETISM
PROXENOS
PROXENUS
PROXENY
PROXICALLY
PROXIED
PROXIES
PROXIMAD
PROXIMAL
PROXIMATE
PROXIMATELY
PROXIMATION
PROXIME
PROXIMITY
PROXIMO
PROXY
PROXYING
PROXYSM
PROZYMITE
PRUDE
PRUDELY
PRUDENCE
PRUDENT
PRUDENTIAL
PRUDENTIALLY
PRUDENTLY
PRUDERIES
PRUDERY
PRUDISH
PRUDISHLY
PRUDISHNESS
PRUDIST
PRUDITY
PRUINESCENCE
PRUINOSE
PRUINOUS
PRULAURASIN
PRUNABLE
PRUNABLENESS
PRUNABLY
PRUNASE
PRUNASIN
PRUNE
PRUNED
PRUNELL
PRUNELLA
PRUNELLE
PRUNELLO
PRUNER
PRUNING
PRUNITRIN
PRUNT
PRUNTED
PRURIENCE
PRURIENCY
PRURIENT
PRURIENTLY
PRURIGINOUS
PRURIGO
PRURIOUSNESS
PRURITIC
PRURITUS
PRUSIANO
PRUSSIATE
PRUSSIC
PRUSSIN
PRUSSINE
PRUT
PRY
PRYER
PRYING
PRYINGLY
PRYINGNESS
PRYLER
PRYS
PRYSE
PRYTANEUM
PRYTANIS
PRYTANIZE
PRYTANY
PSALIS
PSALLOID
PSALM
PSALMIC
PSALMIST
PSALMISTRY
PSALMODIAL
PSALMODIC
PSALMODICAL
PSALMODIES
PSALMODIST
PSALMODIZE
PSALMODY
PSALMOGRAPH
PSALMY
PSALOID
PSALTER
PSALTERER
PSALTERIA
PSALTERIAL
PSALTERIAN
PSALTERIST
PSALTERIUM
PSALTERY
PSAMMITE
PSAMMITIC
PSAMMOLITHIC
PSAMMOLOGY
PSAMMOMA
PSAMMOPHILE
PSAMMOUS
PSCHENT
PSELLISM
PSELLISMUS
PSEPHISM
PSEPHISMA
PSEPHITE
PSEPHITIC
PSEPHOLOGIST
PSEPHOLOGY
PSEPHOMANCY
PSEUDACONIN
PSEUDACONINE
PSEUDACUSIS
PSEUDANDRY
PSEUDAPHIA
PSEUDAPOSTLE
PSEUDATOLL
PSEUDAXIS
PSEUDHAEMAL
PSEUDHEMAL
PSEUDIMAGO
PSEUDO
PSEUDOACACIA
PSEUDOALUM
PSEUDOANGINA
PSEUDOAQUATIC
PSEUDOBRANCH
PSEUDOBULB
PSEUDOBULBAR
PSEUDOBULBIL
PSEUDOCARP
PSEUDOCHINA
PSEUDOCLASSIC
PSEUDOCONE
PSEUDOCORTEX
PSEUDOCUMYL
PSEUDOCYST
PSEUDODERM
PSEUDODONT
PSEUDODOX
PSEUDODOXAL
PSEUDOFARCY
PSEUDOGALENA
PSEUDOGLIOMA
PSEUDOGRAPH
PSEUDOGRAPHY
PSEUDOGYNE
PSEUDOGYNY
PSEUDOISM
PSEUDOLALIA
PSEUDOLATRY
PSEUDOLICHEN
PSEUDOLOGICAL
PSEUDOLOGIST
PSEUDOLOGUE
PSEUDOLOGY
PSEUDOMANCY
PSEUDOMANIA
PSEUDOMANTIC
PSEUDOMITOTIC
PSEUDOMORPH
PSEUDOMUCIN
PSEUDONITROL
PSEUDONYM
PSEUDONYMAL
PSEUDONYMIC
PSEUDONYMITY
PSEUDONYMOUS
PSEUDOPLASM
PSEUDOPOD
PSEUDOPODAL
PSEUDOPODE
PSEUDOPODIAL
PSEUDOPODIUM
PSEUDOPORE
PSEUDOPSIA
PSEUDOPTICS
PSEUDOPTOSIS
PSEUDOPUPA
PSEUDOPUPAL
PSEUDORABIES
PSEUDORAMOSE
PSEUDOSALT
PSEUDOSCININE
PSEUDOSCOPE
PSEUDOSCOPIC
PSEUDOSCOPY
PSEUDOSMIA
PSEUDOSOPH
PSEUDOSOPHER
PSEUDOSPERM
PSEUDOSPHERE
PSEUDOSPORE
PSEUDOSTOMA
PSEUDOSUCHIAN
PSEUDOTABES
PSEUDOVUM
PSHA
PSHAW
PSHAWED
PSHAWING
PSHEM
PSI
PSILANTHROPIC
PSILANTHROPY
PSILATRO
PSILOCERAN
PSILOCERATAN
PSILOCERATID
PSILOI
PSILOLOGY
PSILOMELANE
PSILOMELANIC
PSILOPHYTE
PSILOSIS
PSILOSOPHER
PSILOSOPHY
PSILOTACEOUS
PSILOTHRUM
PSILOTIC
PSITHURISM
PSITTACEOUS
PSITTACINE
PSITTACINITE
PSITTACISM
PSITTACISTIC
PSITTACOSIS
PSOAS
PSOATIC
PSOCID
PSOCINE
PSOITIS
PSOMOPHAGIST
PSOMOPHAGY
PSORA
PSORIASIFORM
PSORIASIS
PSORIATIC
PSOROID
PSOROPTIC
PSOROSIS
PSOROSPERM
PSOROSPERMIC
PSOROUS
PSOVIE
PST
PSYCHAGOGIC
PSYCHAGOGOS
PSYCHAGOGUE
PSYCHAGOGY
PSYCHAL
PSYCHALGIA
PSYCHE
PSYCHEDELIC
PSYCHEOMETRY
PSYCHIASIS
PSYCHIATER
PSYCHIATRIC
PSYCHIATRIST
PSYCHIATRIZE
PSYCHIATRY
PSYCHIC
PSYCHICAL
PSYCHICALLY
PSYCHICISM
PSYCHICIST
PSYCHICS
PSYCHID
PSYCHISM

PSYCHO
PSYCHOANALYST
PSYCHOCLINIC
PSYCHODRAMA
PSYCHOFUGAL
PSYCHOGENESIS
PSYCHOGENETIC
PSYCHOGENIC
PSYCHOGENY
PSYCHOGNOSIS
PSYCHOGNOSY
PSYCHOGRAM
PSYCHOGRAPH
PSYCHOGRAPHY
PSYCHOID
PSYCHOKINESIA
PSYCHOKYME
PSYCHOLEPSY
PSYCHOLEPTIC
PSYCHOLOGER
PSYCHOLOGIC
PSYCHOLOGICAL
PSYCHOLOGICS
PSYCHOLOGISM
PSYCHOLOGIST
PSYCHOLOGIZE
PSYCHOLOGUE
PSYCHOLOGY
PSYCHOMACHY
PSYCHOMANCY
PSYCHOMETER
PSYCHOMETRIC
PSYCHOMETRY
PSYCHOMOTOR
PSYCHON
PSYCHONOMIC
PSYCHONOMICS
PSYCHOPATH
PSYCHOPATHIC
PSYCHOPATHY
PSYCHOPETAL
PSYCHOPHOBIA
PSYCHOPLASM
PSYCHOPOMP
PSYCHOPOMPOS
PSYCHOREFLEX
PSYCHOSES
PSYCHOSEXUAL
PSYCHOSIS
PSYCHOSOCIAL
PSYCHOSOME
PSYCHOSOPHY
PSYCHOSTATIC
PSYCHOTAXIS
PSYCHOTHEISM
PSYCHOTIC
PSYCHOTRINE
PSYCHOTROPIC
PSYCHROGRAPH
PSYCHROMETER
PSYCHROMETRY
PSYCHROPHILE
PSYCHROPHOBIA
PSYCHROPHORE
PSYCHROPHYTE
PSYCHURGY
PSYKTER
PSYLLID
PSYLLIUM
PSYWAR
PTARMIC
PTARMICAL
PTARMIGAN
PTARMIGANS
PTERANODONT
PTERASPID
PTERERGATE
PTERIC
PTERIDEOUS
PTERIDIUM
PTERIDOID
PTERIDOLOGY
PTERIDOPHYTE
PTERIDOSPERM
PTERIN
PTERION
PTERNA
PTEROCARPOUS
PTERODACTYL
PTEROGRAPHY
PTEROID
PTEROMA
PTEROMALID
PTERON
PTEROPAEDES
PTEROPEGAL
PTEROPEGOUS
PTEROPEGUM
PTEROPID
PTEROPINE
PTEROPOD
PTEROPODAL
PTEROPODAN
PTEROPODIAL
PTEROPODIUM
PTEROPODOUS
PTEROSAUR
PTEROSAURIAN
PTEROSTIGMA
PTEROSTIGMAL
PTEROTHECA
PTEROTHORAX
PTEROTIC
PTERYGIAL
PTERYGIUM
PTERYGIUMS
PTERYGODE
PTERYGODUM
PTERYGOID
PTERYGOIDAL
PTERYGOIDEAN
PTERYGOPHORE
PTERYGOTE
PTERYGOTOUS
PTERYLA
PTERYLAE
PTERYLOGRAPHY
PTERYLOLOGY
PTERYLOSIS
PTILINAL
PTILINUM
PTILOPAEDES
PTILOPAEDIC
PTILOSIS
PTINID
PTINOID
PTISAN
PTOCHOCRACY
PTOCHOGONY
PTOCHOLOGY
PTOMAIN
PTOMAINE
PTOMAINIC
PTOMATROPINE
PTOSIS
PTOTIC
PTYALAGOGUE
PTYALIN
PTYALISM
PTYALIZE
PTYALIZED
PTYALIZING
PTYALOCELE
PTYALOGENIC
PTYALOLITH
PTYALORRHEA
PTYXIS
PU
PUAN
PUB
PUBAL
PUBBLE
PUBERAL
PUBERTAL
PUBERTIC
PUBERTY
PUBERULENT
PUBES
PUBESCENCE
PUBESCENCY
PUBESCENT
PUBIAN
PUBIGEROUS
PUBIOTOMY
PUBIS
PUBLIC
PUBLICAN
PUBLICANISM
PUBLICATE
PUBLICATION
PUBLICE
PUBLICISM
PUBLICIST
PUBLICITY
PUBLICIZE
PUBLICIZED
PUBLICIZING
PUBLICLY
PUBLICNESS
PUBLISH
PUBLISHABLE
PUBLISHED
PUBLISHER
PUBLISHING
PUBLISHMENT
PUBOFEMORAL
PUBOILIAC
PUBOISCHIAC
PUBOISCHIAL
PUBORECTALIS
PUBOTIBIAL
PUCCA
PUCCOON
PUCE
PUCELAGE
PUCELLAGE
PUCELLE
PUCERON
PUCHERA
PUCHERITE
PUCHERO
PUCK
PUCKA
PUCKBALL
PUCKER
PUCKERBUSH
PUCKERED
PUCKEREL
PUCKERER
PUCKERIER
PUCKERIEST
PUCKERING
PUCKERMOUTH
PUCKERY
PUCKFIST
PUCKFOIST
PUCKISH
PUCKISHLY
PUCKISHNESS
PUCKNEEDLE
PUCKREL
PUCKSEY
PUCKSTER
PUD
PUDDEE
PUDDENING
PUDDER
PUDDING
PUDDINGBERRY
PUDDINGHEAD
PUDDINGHEADED
PUDDINGHOUSE
PUDDINGWIFE
PUDDINGWIVES
PUDDINGY
PUDDLE
PUDDLEBALL
PUDDLEBAR
PUDDLED
PUDDLER
PUDDLING
PUDDLY
PUDDOCK
PUDDY
PUDENCY
PUDENDAL
PUDENDOUS
PUDENDUM
PUDENT
PUDER
PUDGE
PUDGIER
PUDGIEST
PUDGILY
PUDGINESS
PUDGY
PUDIANO
PUDIBUND
PUDIBUNDITY
PUDIC
PUDICAL
PUDICITIA
PUDICITY
PUDOR
PUDU
PUE
PUEBLITO
PUEBLO
PUEBLOS
PUER
PUERARIA
PUERICULTURE
PUERILE
PUERILELY
PUERILENESS
PUERILISM
PUERILITIES
PUERILITY
PUERPERA
PUERPERAL
PUERPERALISM
PUERPERANT
PUERPERIUM
PUERPEROUS
PUFF
PUFFBACK
PUFFBALL
PUFFBIRD
PUFFED
PUFFER
PUFFERIES
PUFFERY
PUFFIER
PUFFIEST
PUFFIN
PUFFINESS
PUFFINET
PUFFING
PUFFS
PUFFWIG
PUFFY
PUG
PUGENELLO
PUGGAREE
PUGGED
PUGGER
PUGGI
PUGGING
PUGGISH
PUGGLE
PUGGREE
PUGGRY
PUGGY
PUGH
PUGIL
PUGILANT
PUGILISM
PUGILIST
PUGILISTIC
PUGILISTICAL
PUGLIANITE
PUGMARK
PUGMILL
PUGMILLER
PUGNACIOUS
PUGNACIOUSLY
PUGNACITY
PUGREE
PUGUA
PUHA
PUIRTITH
PUISNE
PUISNY
PUISSANCE
PUISSANT
PUISSANTLY
PUISSANTNESS
PUIST
PUIT
PUJA
PUKA
PUKATEA
PUKATEINE
PUKE
PUKED
PUKEKA
PUKEKO
PUKER
PUKEWEED
PUKING
PUKISH
PUKISHNESS
PUKKA
PUKRAS
PUKU
PUKY
PUL
PULAHAN
PULAHANES
PULAHANISM
PULAJAN
PULAS
PULASAN
PULASKITE
PULCHRIFY
PULCHRITUDE
PULE
PULED
PULEGOL
PULEGONE
PULER
PULEYN
PULGADA
PULI
PULICARIOUS

PULICAT
PULICATE
PULICENE
PULICID
PULICIDAL
PULICIDE
PULICINE
PULICOID
PULICOSE
PULICOSITY
PULICOUS
PULIJAN
PULING
PULINGLY
PULIOL
PULISH
PULK
PULKA
PULL
PULLABLE
PULLAILE
PULLALUE
PULLBACK
PULLBOAT
PULLDEVIL
PULLDOO
PULLDOWN
PULLED
PULLEN
PULLER
PULLERIES
PULLERY
PULLET
PULLEY
PULLEYS
PULLICAT
PULLING
PULLISEE
PULLOCK
PULLOUT
PULLOVER
PULLSHOVEL
PULLULANT
PULLULATE
PULLULATED
PULLULATING
PULLULATION
PULLULATIVE
PULLUS
PULMENT
PULMOGASTRIC
PULMOMETER
PULMOMETRY
PULMONAR
PULMONARIAN
PULMONARY
PULMONATE
PULMONIC
PULMONICAL
PULMONITIS
PULMOTOR
PULP
PULPACEOUS
PULPAL
PULPALGIA
PULPATONE
PULPATOON
PULPBOARD
PULPECTOMY
PULPED
PULPEFACTION
PULPER
PULPERIA
PULPIER
PULPIEST
PULPIFIED
PULPIFIER
PULPIFY
PULPIFYING
PULPILY
PULPINESS
PULPING
PULPIT
PULPITAL
PULPITARIAN
PULPITEER
PULPITER
PULPITIC
PULPITICAL
PULPITICALLY
PULPITIS
PULPITLESS
PULPITLY
PULPITRY
PULPOTOMY
PULPOUS
PULPOUSNESS
PULPSTONE
PULPWOOD
PULPY
PULQUE
PULSANT
PULSAR
PULSATE
PULSATED
PULSATILE
PULSATING
PULSATION
PULSATIONAL
PULSATIVE
PULSATIVELY
PULSATOR
PULSATORY
PULSE
PULSED
PULSEJET
PULSELESS
PULSELESSLY
PULSELLUM
PULSIDGE
PULSIFIC
PULSIMETER
PULSING
PULSION
PULSIVE
PULSOMETER
PULSUS
PULTACEOUS
PULTON
PULTUN
PULTURE
PULU
PULVERABLE
PULVERACEOUS
PULVERANT
PULVERATE
PULVERATED
PULVERATING
PULVEREOUS
PULVERIN
PULVERINE
PULVERIZATE
PULVERIZATOR
PULVERIZE
PULVERIZED
PULVERIZER
PULVERIZING
PULVEROUS
PULVERULENCE
PULVERULENT
PULVIL
PULVILLAR
PULVILLI
PULVILLIFORM
PULVILLUS
PULVINAR
PULVINARIAN
PULVINATE
PULVINATED
PULVINATION
PULVINIFORM
PULVINO
PULVINULUS
PULVINUS
PULVIPLUME
PULWAR
PULY
PUMA
PUMEX
PUMICATE
PUMICATED
PUMICATING
PUMICE
PUMICED
PUMICEOUS
PUMICER
PUMICIFORM
PUMICITE
PUMICOSE
PUMIE
PUMMEL
PUMMELED
PUMMELING
PUMMELLED
PUMMELLING
PUMMICE
PUMP
PUMPAGE
PUMPELLYITE
PUMPER
PUMPERNICKEL
PUMPET
PUMPHANDLE
PUMPING
PUMPKIN
PUMPKINIFY
PUMPKINITY
PUMPKINSEED
PUMPKNOT
PUMPMAN
PUMPS
PUMPWRIGHT
PUN
PUNA
PUNAISE
PUNALUA
PUNALUAN
PUNAMU
PUNATOO
PUNCH
PUNCHABLE
PUNCHAYET
PUNCHBOARD
PUNCHED
PUNCHEON
PUNCHER
PUNCHINELLO
PUNCHINESS
PUNCHING
PUNCHY
PUNCT
PUNCTAL
PUNCTATE
PUNCTATED
PUNCTATIM
PUNCTATION
PUNCTATOR
PUNCTICULAR
PUNCTICULOSE
PUNCTIFORM
PUNCTILIAR
PUNCTILIO
PUNCTILIOS
PUNCTILIOUS
PUNCTION
PUNCTIST
PUNCTUAL
PUNCTUALIST
PUNCTUALITY
PUNCTUALLY
PUNCTUATE
PUNCTUATED
PUNCTUATING
PUNCTUATION
PUNCTUATIVE
PUNCTUATOR
PUNCTUIST
PUNCTULATE
PUNCTULATED
PUNCTULATION
PUNCTULE
PUNCTULUM
PUNCTUM
PUNCTURATION
PUNCTURE
PUNCTURER
PUNCTURING
PUNCTUS
PUND
PUNDIGRION
PUNDIT
PUNDITA
PUNDITIC
PUNDITICALLY
PUNDITRY
PUNDONOR
PUNDUM
PUNECA
PUNEE
PUNESE
PUNG
PUNGAPUNG
PUNGAR
PUNGE
PUNGENCE
PUNGENCY
PUNGENT
PUNGENTLY
PUNGER
PUNGEY
PUNGI
PUNGLE
PUNGLED
PUNGY
PUNGYI
PUNICACEOUS
PUNICEOUS
PUNICIAL
PUNICIN
PUNIER
PUNIEST
PUNILY
PUNINESS
PUNISH
PUNISHABLE
PUNISHED
PUNISHER
PUNISHING
PUNISHMENT
PUNITION
PUNITIONAL
PUNITIONALLY
PUNITIVE
PUNITIVELY
PUNITIVENESS
PUNITORY
PUNJUM
PUNK
PUNKA
PUNKAH
PUNKER
PUNKETTO
PUNKIE
PUNKIES
PUNKISH
PUNKLING
PUNKT
PUNKWOOD
PUNKY
PUNNABLE
PUNNAGE
PUNNED
PUNNER
PUNNET
PUNNIC
PUNNICAL
PUNNIGRAM
PUNNING
PUNNINGLY
PUNNOLOGY
PUNSTER
PUNT
PUNTA
PUNTABOUT
PUNTAL
PUNTELLO
PUNTER
PUNTI
PUNTIES
PUNTILLA
PUNTIST
PUNTO
PUNTOUT
PUNTSMAN
PUNTY
PUNY
PUNYISM
PUNYSHIP
PUP
PUPA
PUPAE
PUPAL
PUPARIAL
PUPARIUM
PUPAS
PUPATE
PUPATED
PUPATING
PUPATION
PUPELO
PUPIFEROUS
PUPIFORM
PUPIGENOUS
PUPIL
PUPILABILITY
PUPILAGE
PUPILAR
PUPILARITY
PUPILARY
PUPILATE
PUPILED
PUPILIZE
PUPILLAGE
PUPILLAR
PUPILLARITY
PUPILLARY
PUPILLATE
PUPILLED
PUPILLIZE
PUPILLONIAN
PUPILMONGER
PUPIPAROUS
PUPIVORE
PUPIVOROUS
PUPPED

PUPPET
PUPPETEER
PUPPETHEAD
PUPPETISM
PUPPETIZE
PUPPETMAN
PUPPETMASTER
PUPPETRY
PUPPIED
PUPPIES
PUPPIFY
PUPPILY
PUPPING
PUPPY
PUPPYDOM
PUPPYFISH
PUPPYFOOT
PUPPYHOOD
PUPPYING
PUPPYISM
PUPULO
PUPUNHA
PUR
PURAQUE
PURAU
PURBLIND
PURBLINDLY
PURBLINDNESS
PURCHASABLE
PURCHASE
PURCHASED
PURCHASER
PURCHASERY
PURCHASING
PURDAH
PURDY
PURE
PUREAYN
PUREBLOOD
PUREBRED
PURED
PUREDEE
PUREE
PURELY
PURENESS
PURER
PUREST
PUREY
PURFLE
PURFLED
PURFLER
PURFLING
PURFLY
PURGA
PURGAMENT
PURGATION
PURGATIVE
PURGATORIAL
PURGATORIAN
PURGATORY
PURGE
PURGED
PURGER
PURGERY
PURGING
PURIFICANT
PURIFICATION
PURIFICATOR
PURIFICATORY
PURIFIED
PURIFIER
PURIFORM
PURIFY
PURIFYING
PURIN
PURINE
PURIRI
PURISM
PURIST
PURISTIC
PURISTICAL
PURITAN
PURITANIC
PURITANICAL
PURITANISM
PURITANO
PURITY
PURL
PURLED
PURLER
PURLHOUSE
PURLICUE
PURLICUES
PURLIEU
PURLIEUMAN
PURLIEUMEN
PURLIEUS
PURLIN
PURLINE
PURLING
PURLMAN
PURLOIN
PURLOINER
PURO
PURPARTY
PURPENSE
PURPIE
PURPLE
PURPLED
PURPLEHEART
PURPLELY
PURPLES
PURPLESCENT
PURPLEWORT
PURPLING
PURPLISH
PURPLISHNESS
PURPLY
PURPORT
PURPORTED
PURPORTEDLY
PURPORTING
PURPOSE
PURPOSED
PURPOSEDLY
PURPOSEFUL
PURPOSEFULLY
PURPOSELESS
PURPOSELIKE
PURPOSELY
PURPOSER
PURPOSES
PURPOSING
PURPOSIVE
PURPOSIVELY
PURPOSIVISM
PURPRESTURE
PURPRISE
PURPRISION
PURPURA
PURPURACEOUS
PURPURATE
PURPURE
PURPUREAL
PURPUREAN
PURPURESCENT
PURPURIC
PURPURIN
PURPURINE
PURPURITE
PURPURIZE
PURPUROID
PURR
PURRAH
PURRE
PURRED
PURREE
PURREL
PURRER
PURRING
PURRONE
PURRY
PURSE
PURSED
PURSEFUL
PURSELIKE
PURSER
PURSES
PURSET
PURSIER
PURSIEST
PURSINESS
PURSING
PURSIVE
PURSLANE
PURSLEY
PURSUABLE
PURSUAL
PURSUANCE
PURSUANT
PURSUANTLY
PURSUE
PURSUED
PURSUER
PURSUING
PURSUIT
PURSUITMETER
PURSUIVANT
PURSY
PURTENANCE
PURTY
PURULENCE
PURULENCY
PURULENT
PURULENTLY
PURULOID
PURUSHA
PURUSHARTHA
PURVEY
PURVEYABLE
PURVEYAL
PURVEYANCE
PURVEYANCER
PURVEYED
PURVEYING
PURVEYOR
PURVIEW
PURVOE
PURWANNAH
PUS
PUSH
PUSHBALL
PUSHCARD
PUSHCART
PUSHED
PUSHER
PUSHFUL
PUSHFULLY
PUSHFULNESS
PUSHIER
PUSHIEST
PUSHILY
PUSHINESS
PUSHING
PUSHINGLY
PUSHINGNESS
PUSHMOBILE
PUSHOVER
PUSHPIN
PUSHUM
PUSHWAINLING
PUSHY
PUSIL
PUSILL
PUSILLANIMOUS
PUSS
PUSSCAT
PUSSIER
PUSSIES
PUSSIEST
PUSSLEY
PUSSLY
PUSSY
PUSSYCAT
PUSSYFOOT
PUSSYFOOTED
PUSSYFOOTER
PUSSYFOOTING
PUSSYFOOTISM
PUSSYTOE
PUSTULANT
PUSTULAR
PUSTULATE
PUSTULATED
PUSTULATING
PUSTULATION
PUSTULATOUS
PUSTULE
PUSTULED
PUSTULIFORM
PUSTULOSE
PUSTULOUS
PUSZTA
PUT
PUTAGE
PUTAIN
PUTAMEN
PUTAMINOUS
PUTANISM
PUTATION
PUTATIONARY
PUTATIVE
PUTATIVELY
PUTBACK
PUTCHEN
PUTCHER
PUTE
PUTEAL
PUTELEE
PUTELI
PUTHERY
PUTID
PUTIDLY
PUTIDNESS
PUTING
PUTLOCK
PUTLOG
PUTOIS
PUTREDINOUS
PUTREFACIENT
PUTREFACTION
PUTREFACTIVE
PUTREFIED
PUTREFIER
PUTREFY
PUTREFYING
PUTRESCE
PUTRESCENCE
PUTRESCENCY
PUTRESCENT
PUTRESCIBLE
PUTRESCINE
PUTRICIDE
PUTRID
PUTRIDITY
PUTRIDLY
PUTRIDNESS
PUTRIFACTED
PUTRIFORM
PUTRILAGE
PUTSCHISM
PUTSCHIST
PUTT
PUTTAN
PUTTEE
PUTTER
PUTTERER
PUTTERINGLY
PUTTI
PUTTIED
PUTTIER
PUTTING
PUTTO
PUTTOCK
PUTTOO
PUTTY
PUTTYBLOWER
PUTTYHEARTED
PUTTYING
PUTTYROOT
PUTURE
PUTZ
PUUD
PUXY
PUY
PUZZLE
PUZZLEATION
PUZZLED
PUZZLEDLY
PUZZLEDNESS
PUZZLEHEAD
PUZZLEHEADED
PUZZLEMAN
PUZZLEMENT
PUZZLEPATE
PUZZLEPATED
PUZZLER
PUZZLING
PUZZLINGLY
PUZZLINGNESS
PYAEMIA
PYAEMIC
PYAL
PYARTHROSIS
PYAT
PYCHE
PYCNIAL
PYCNIC
PYCNID
PYCNIDIOSPORE
PYCNIDIUM
PYCNIOSPORE
PYCNITE
PYCNIUM
PYCNODONT
PYCNOGONID
PYCNOGONOID
PYCNOMETER
PYCNOSIS
PYCNOSPORE
PYCNOSPORIC
PYCNOSTYLE
PYCNOTIC
PYE
PYELECTASIS
PYELIC
PYELITIC
PYELITIS
PYELOGRAM
PYELOGRAPHIC
PYELOGRAPHY
PYEMESIS
PYEMIA
PYEMIC
PYENGADU

PYGAL
PYGARG
PYGARGUS
PYGIDID
PYGIDIUM
PYGMAEAN
PYGMEAN
PYGMIES
PYGMOID
PYGMY
PYGMYWEED
PYGOFER
PYGON
PYGOPAGUS
PYGOPOD
PYGOPODINE
PYGOPODOUS
PYGOSTYLE
PYGOSTYLED
PYGOSTYLOUS
PYIC
PYIN
PYJAMA
PYJAMAED
PYJAMAS
PYKAR
PYKE
PYKNATOM
PYKNIC
PYLA
PYLAGORE
PYLANGIAL
PYLANGIUM
PYLAR
PYLIC
PYLON
PYLORALGIA
PYLORIC
PYLORITIS
PYLOROPLASTY
PYLOROPTOSIS
PYLOROSCOPY
PYLOROSPASM
PYLORUS
PYNE
PYNOT
PYNUNG
PYOCELE
PYOCTANIN
PYOCTANINE
PYOCYANASE
PYOCYANIN
PYOCYST
PYOCYTE
PYODERMIA
PYODERMIC
PYOGENESIS
PYOGENETIC
PYOGENIC
PYOGENIN
PYOGENOUS
PYOID
PYOLYMPH
PYOMETRA
PYOMETRITIS
PYONEPHRITIS
PYONEPHROTIC
PYOPHAGIA
PYOPHTHALMIA
PYOPLANIA
PYOPOIESIS
PYOPOIETIC
PYOPTYSIS
PYORRHEAL
PYORRHOEAL
PYOSALPINX
PYOSIS
PYOSPERMIA
PYOT
PYOTHERAPY
PYOTHORAX
PYOURETER
PYOXANTHOSE
PYR
PYRACANTH
PYRACANTHA
PYRACENE
PYRAL
PYRALIDAN
PYRALIDID
PYRALIDIFORM
PYRALIS
PYRALOID
PYRAMID
PYRAMIDAIRE
PYRAMIDAL
PYRAMIDALE
PYRAMIDALIS
PYRAMIDALLY
PYRAMIDATE
PYRAMIDED
PYRAMIDELLID
PYRAMIDER
PYRAMIDIA
PYRAMIDIC
PYRAMIDICAL
PYRAMIDING
PYRAMIDION
PYRAMIDOIDAL
PYRAMIDS
PYRAMOIDAL
PYRAN
PYRANOMETER
PYRANOSE
PYRANYL
PYRARGYRITE
PYRAZIN
PYRAZINE
PYRAZOLE
PYRAZOLINE
PYRAZOLONE
PYRAZOLYL
PYRE
PYRECTIC
PYRENA
PYRENE
PYRENIN
PYRENOCARP
PYRENODEAN
PYRENODEOUS
PYRENOID
PYRENOLICHEN
PYRETHRIN
PYRETHRUM
PYRETIC
PYRETICOSIS
PYRETOGENIC
PYRETOGENOUS
PYRETOGRAPHY
PYRETOLOGY
PYRETOLYSIS
PYREX
PYREXIA
PYREXIAL
PYREXIC
PYREXICAL
PYRGEOMETER
PYRGOIDAL
PYRGOLOGIST
PYRGOM
PYRIBOLE
PYRIDAZINE
PYRIDIC
PYRIDINE
PYRIDINIUM
PYRIDINIZE
PYRIDONE
PYRIDOXINE
PYRIDYL
PYRIFORM
PYRIFORMIS
PYRIMIDIN
PYRIMIDINE
PYRIMIDYL
PYRITACEOUS
PYRITE
PYRITES
PYRITIC
PYRITICAL
PYRITIFEROUS
PYRITIZE
PYRITOHEDRAL
PYRITOHEDRON
PYRITOID
PYRITOLOGY
PYRITOUS
PYROACETIC
PYROARSENATE
PYROARSENIC
PYROARSENITE
PYROBALLOGY
PYROBELONITE
PYROBORATE
PYROBORIC
PYROCATECHIN
PYROCATECHOL
PYROCHEMICAL
PYROCHLORE
PYROCITRIC
PYROCLASTIC
PYROCOLL
PYROCOTTON
PYROELECTRIC
PYROGALLATE
PYROGALLIC
PYROGALLOL
PYROGEN
PYROGENATION
PYROGENESIA
PYROGENESIS
PYROGENIC
PYROGENOUS
PYROGNOMIC
PYROGNOSTIC
PYROGNOSTICS
PYROGRAPH
PYROGRAPHER
PYROGRAPHIC
PYROGRAPHY
PYROGRAVURE
PYROGUAIACIN
PYROID
PYROLACEOUS
PYROLATER
PYROLATRY
PYROLIGNEOUS
PYROLIGNIC
PYROLIGNITE
PYROLIGNOUS
PYROLITE
PYROLOGICAL
PYROLOGIST
PYROLOGY
PYROLUSITE
PYROLYSIS
PYROLYTIC
PYROMACHY
PYROMAGNETIC
PYROMANCER
PYROMANCY
PYROMANIA
PYROMANIACAL
PYROMANTIC
PYROMELLITIC
PYROMETER
PYROMETRIC
PYROMETRICAL
PYROMETRY
PYROMORPHITE
PYROMORPHOUS
PYROMOTOR
PYROMUCATE
PYROMUCIC
PYROMUCYL
PYRONAPHTHA
PYRONE
PYRONOMICS
PYRONYXIS
PYROPE
PYROPEN
PYROPHANITE
PYROPHANOUS
PYROPHILE
PYROPHILOUS
PYROPHOBIA
PYROPHONE
PYROPHORIC
PYROPHOROUS
PYROPHORUS
PYROPHYLLITE
PYROPUNCTURE
PYROPUS
PYROSCOPE
PYROSCOPY
PYROSIS
PYROSMALITE
PYROSPHERE
PYROSTAT
PYROSTILPNITE
PYROSULPHATE
PYROSULPHITE
PYROTARTARIC
PYROTARTRATE
PYROTECHNIAN
PYROTECHNIC
PYROTECHNICS
PYROTECHNIST
PYROTECHNY
PYROTEREBIC
PYROTIC
PYROTOXIN
PYROTRITARIC
PYROURIC
PYROVANADIC
PYROXANTHIN
PYROXENE
PYROXENIC
PYROXENITE
PYROXMANGITE
PYROXYLIC
PYROXYLIN
PYROXYLINE
PYRRHIC
PYRRHICHIAN
PYRRHICHIUS
PYRRHICIST
PYRRHOTINE
PYRRHOTISM
PYRRHOTITE
PYRRHOUS
PYRRHULOXIA
PYRRHUS
PYRRODIAZOLE
PYRROL
PYRROLE
PYRROLIC
PYRROLIDINE
PYRROLIDONE
PYRROLIDYL
PYRROLINE
PYRROPHYLLIN
PYRROYL
PYRRYL
PYRRYLENE
PYRUVATE
PYRUVIC
PYRUVYL
PYRYLIUM
PYSE
PYTHOGENIC
PYTHON
PYTHONESS
PYTHONIC
PYTHONICAL
PYTHONID
PYTHONIFORM
PYTHONINE
PYTHONISM
PYTHONIST
PYTHONIZE
PYTHONOID
PYTHONOMORPH
PYURIA
PYX
PYXIDATE
PYXIDES
PYXIDIUM
PYXIE
PYXIS

Q

QABBALA
QABBALAH
QADARITE
QADI
QAID
QAIMAQAM
QANEH
QANTAR
QASAB
QAT
QAZAQ
QERI
QIBLA
QINAH
QIYAS
QOBAR
QRI
QU
QUA
QUAA
QUAB
QUABIRD
QUACHIL
QUACK
QUACKED
QUACKERIES
QUACKERY
QUACKHOOD
QUACKING
QUACKISH
QUACKISHLY
QUACKISHNESS
QUACKISM
QUACKLE
QUACKSALVER
QUACKSTER
QUACKY
QUAD
QUADDED
QUADDLE
QUADE
QUADER
QUADLE
QUADRA
QUADRABLE
QUADRAE
QUADRAGESIMAL
QUADRAL
QUADRANGLE
QUADRANGLED
QUADRANGULAR
QUADRANGULED
QUADRANS
QUADRANT
QUADRANTAL
QUADRANTILE
QUADRAPHONIC
QUADRAT
QUADRATE
QUADRATED
QUADRATIC
QUADRATICAL
QUADRATICS
QUADRATING
QUADRATRIX
QUADRATUM
QUADRATURE
QUADRATUS
QUADREL
QUADRENNIA
QUADRENNIAL
QUADRENNIUM
QUADRENNIUMS
QUADRIAD
QUADRIC
QUADRICEPS
QUADRICINIUM
QUADRICIPITAL
QUADRICONE
QUADRICYCLE
QUADRICYCLER
QUADRIENNIUM
QUADRIFID
QUADRIFILAR
QUADRIFOCAL
QUADRIFOLIUM
QUADRIFORM
QUADRIFRONS
QUADRIGA
QUADRIGAE
QUADRIGAMIST
QUADRIGATE
QUADRIGATUS
QUADRIHYBRID
QUADRIJUGAL
QUADRILATERAL
QUADRILLE
QUADRILLED
QUADRILLES
QUADRILLING
QUADRILLION
QUADRILOGY
QUADRIMUM
QUADRIN
QUADRINE
QUADRINOMIAL
QUADRIPAROUS
QUADRIPLANAR
QUADRISECT
QUADRIURATE
QUADRIVALENT
QUADRIVIA
QUADRIVIAL
QUADRIVIOUS
QUADRIVIUM
QUADROON
QUADRUAL
QUADRUM
QUADRUMANAL
QUADRUMANE
QUADRUMANOUS
QUADRUPED
QUADRUPEDAL
QUADRUPEDAN
QUADRUPEDANT
QUADRUPEDATE
QUADRUPEDOUS
QUADRUPLANE
QUADRUPLATE
QUADRUPLATOR
QUADRUPLE
QUADRUPLED
QUADRUPLET
QUADRUPLEX
QUADRUPLING
QUAEDAM
QUAERE
QUAESITA
QUAESITUM
QUAESTIO
QUAESTIONES
QUAESTOR
QUAESTORIAL
QUAESTORIAN
QUAESTORSHIP
QUAESTUARY
QUAFF
QUAFFED
QUAFFER
QUAFFING
QUAG
QUAGGA
QUAGGAS
QUAGGIER
QUAGGIEST
QUAGGLE
QUAGGY
QUAGMIRE
QUAGMIRED
QUAGMIRY
QUAHAUG
QUAHOG
QUAI
QUAICH
QUAIFE
QUAIGH
QUAIL
QUAILED
QUAILERIES
QUAILERY
QUAILHEAD
QUAILING
QUAILY
QUAINT
QUAINTANCE
QUAINTER
QUAINTEST
QUAINTISE
QUAINTLY
QUAINTNESS
QUAIR
QUAIS
QUAKE
QUAKED
QUAKER
QUAKERBIRD
QUAKETAIL
QUAKIER
QUAKIEST
QUAKILY
QUAKINESS
QUAKING
QUAKINGLY
QUAKY
QUALE
QUALIA
QUALIFIABLE
QUALIFICATION
QUALIFICATOR
QUALIFIED
QUALIFIEDLY
QUALIFIER
QUALIFY
QUALIFYING
QUALIMETER
QUALITATIVE
QUALITIED
QUALITIES
QUALITY
QUALLY
QUALM
QUALMISH
QUALMISHLY
QUALMISHNESS
QUALMY
QUALTAGH
QUAMASH
QUAN
QUANDANG
QUANDARIES
QUANDARY
QUANDONG
QUANDY
QUANNET
QUANT
QUANTA
QUANTIC
QUANTICAL
QUANTIFIED
QUANTIFIER
QUANTIFY
QUANTIFYING
QUANTIMETER
QUANTITATE
QUANTITATIVE
QUANTITIED
QUANTITIES
QUANTITIVE
QUANTITIVELY
QUANTITY
QUANTIVALENT
QUANTIZATION
QUANTIZE
QUANTIZED
QUANTIZING
QUANTOMETER
QUANTONG
QUANTULUM
QUANTUM
QUAP
QUAQUAVERSAL
QUAR
QUARANTINE
QUARANTINED
QUARANTINER
QUARANTINING
QUARANTY
QUARDEEL
QUARE
QUARENDEN
QUARENDER
QUARENTENE
QUARESMA
QUARION
QUARK
QUARL
QUARLE
QUARLES
QUARRED
QUARREL
QUARRELED
QUARRELING
QUARRELLED
QUARRELLING
QUARRELLOUS
QUARRELOUS
QUARRELOUSLY
QUARRELSOME
QUARRELSOMENESS
QUARRIED
QUARRIER
QUARRIES
QUARRION
QUARROME
QUARRY
QUARRYING
QUARRYMAN
QUARRYMEN
QUARRYSTONE
QUART
QUARTA
QUARTAN
QUARTANE
QUARTANO
QUARTATION
QUARTAUT
QUARTE
QUARTER
QUARTERAGE
QUARTERBACK
QUARTERED
QUARTERER
QUARTERFOIL
QUARTERING
QUARTERLAND
QUARTERLIES
QUARTERLY
QUARTERMAN
QUARTERMASTER
QUARTERMEN
QUARTERN
QUARTERNIGHT
QUARTERNION
QUARTERON
QUARTERPACE
QUARTERS
QUARTERSAW
QUARTERSAWED
QUARTERSAWING
QUARTERSAWN
QUARTERSTAFF
QUARTERSTAVES
QUARTET
QUARTETTE
QUARTIC
QUARTILE
QUARTIN
QUARTINE
QUARTINHO
QUARTIPAROUS
QUARTO
QUARTOLE
QUARTOS
QUARTZ
QUARTZIC
QUARTZITE
QUARTZITIC
QUARTZOID
QUARTZOSE
QUARTZOUS
QUARTZY
QUAS
QUASAR
QUASH
QUASHED
QUASHEY
QUASHING
QUASHY
QUASI
QUASKIES
QUASKY
QUASS
QUASSATION
QUASSATIVE
QUASSIA
QUASSIIN
QUASSIN
QUAT
QUATCH
QUATE
QUATENUS
QUATERN
QUATERNARIES
QUATERNARIUS
QUATERNARY
QUATERNATE
QUATERNION
QUATERNIONIC
QUATERNITIES
QUATERNITY
QUATERON
QUATERS
QUATERTENSES
QUATORZAIN
QUATORZE

QUATRAIN
QUATRAL
QUATRAYLE
QUATRE
QUATREBLE
QUATREFOIL
QUATREFOILED
QUATRIBLE
QUATRIN
QUATTIE
QUATTRINI
QUATTRINO
QUATTROCENTO
QUATTY
QUATUOR
QUAVER
QUAVERED
QUAVERER
QUAVERING
QUAVERINGLY
QUAVEROUS
QUAVERY
QUAVIVER
QUAW
QUAWK
QUAX
QUAY
QUAYAGE
QUAYED
QUAYING
QUAYSIDE
QUAYSIDER
QUEACH
QUEACHIER
QUEACHIEST
QUEACHY
QUEAK
QUEAL
QUEAN
QUEANISH
QUEASE
QUEASIER
QUEASIEST
QUEASILY
QUEASINESS
QUEASOM
QUEASY
QUEAZEN
QUEBRACHITE
QUEBRACHITOL
QUEBRACHO
QUEBRADA
QUEBRADILLA
QUEBRITH
QUECH
QUED
QUEDE
QUEDLY
QUEDNESS
QUEDSHIP
QUEE
QUEECHY
QUEED
QUEEL
QUEEN
QUEENCAKE
QUEENCRAFT
QUEENCUP
QUEENFISH
QUEENFISHES
QUEENING
QUEENITE
QUEENLET
QUEENLIER
QUEENLIEST
QUEENLIKE
QUEENLINESS
QUEENLY
QUEENRIGHT
QUEENROOT
QUEENS
QUEENSBERRIES
QUEENSBERRY
QUEENWEED
QUEENWOOD
QUEER
QUEERER
QUEEREST
QUEERITY
QUEERLY
QUEERNESS
QUEERSOME
QUEERY
QUEEST
QUEET
QUEEVE
QUEI
QUEINTISE
QUELCH
QUELITE
QUELL
QUELLED
QUELLER
QUELLING
QUELLIO
QUELLUNG
QUELME
QUELT
QUEMADO
QUEME
QUEMEFUL
QUEMELY
QUENA
QUENCH
QUENCHABLE
QUENCHED
QUENCHER
QUENCHING
QUENCHLESS
QUENCHLESSLY
QUENDA
QUENELLE
QUENSELITE
QUENT
QUENTISE
QUERCETIC
QUERCETIN
QUERCETUM
QUERCIC
QUERCIN
QUERCINE
QUERCITANNIN
QUERCITE
QUERCITOL
QUERCITRIN
QUERCITRON
QUERCIVOROUS
QUERELA
QUERELAE
QUERELE
QUERENCIA
QUERENT
QUERIDA
QUERIDAS
QUERIDO
QUERIDOS
QUERIED
QUERIER
QUERIES
QUERIMAN
QUERIMANS
QUERIMONIES
QUERIMONIOUS
QUERIMONY
QUERIST
QUERKEN
QUERL
QUERN
QUERNAL
QUERNSTONE
QUERRE
QUERULENT
QUERULENTIAL
QUERULIST
QUERULITY
QUERULOSITY
QUERULOUS
QUERULOUSLY
QUERY
QUERYING
QUERYINGLY
QUESAL
QUESITED
QUESITIVE
QUEST
QUESTED
QUESTER
QUESTEUR
QUESTHOUSE
QUESTING
QUESTION
QUESTIONABLE
QUESTIONABLY
QUESTIONARIES
QUESTIONARY
QUESTIONED
QUESTIONEE
QUESTIONER
QUESTIONING
QUESTIONIST
QUESTIONLESS
QUESTIONNAIRE
QUESTIONS
QUESTMAN
QUESTMEN
QUESTMONGER
QUESTOR
QUESTORIAL
QUESTRIST
QUET
QUETCH
QUETENITE
QUETHE
QUETSCH
QUETZAL
QUEUE
QUEY
QUEZAL
QUEZALES
QUI
QUIAPO
QUIAQUIA
QUIB
QUIBBLE
QUIBBLED
QUIBBLER
QUIBBLING
QUIBLET
QUICA
QUICK
QUICKBEAM
QUICKBORN
QUICKED
QUICKEN
QUICKENANCE
QUICKENBEAM
QUICKENED
QUICKENER
QUICKENING
QUICKER
QUICKEST
QUICKFOOT
QUICKHATCH
QUICKIE
QUICKING
QUICKLIME
QUICKLY
QUICKNESS
QUICKSAND
QUICKSANDY
QUICKSET
QUICKSIDE
QUICKSILVER
QUICKSILVERY
QUICKSTEP
QUICKTHORN
QUICKWATER
QUICKWORK
QUID
QUIDAM
QUIDDANY
QUIDDATIVE
QUIDDER
QUIDDIT
QUIDDITATIVE
QUIDDITIES
QUIDDITY
QUIDDLE
QUIDDLED
QUIDDLER
QUIDDLING
QUIDNUNC
QUIENAL
QUIESCE
QUIESCED
QUIESCENCE
QUIESCENCY
QUIESCENT
QUIESCENTLY
QUIESCING
QUIET
QUIETAGE
QUIETED
QUIETEN
QUIETENER
QUIETER
QUIETEST
QUIETING
QUIETISM
QUIETIST
QUIETISTIC
QUIETIVE
QUIETLIKE
QUIETLY
QUIETNESS
QUIETSOME
QUIETUDE
QUIETUS
QUIFF
QUIINACEOUS
QUILA
QUILATE
QUILE
QUILECES
QUILES
QUILESES
QUILEZ
QUILISMA
QUILK
QUILKIN
QUILL
QUILLAI
QUILLAIC
QUILLAJIC
QUILLBACK
QUILLED
QUILLER
QUILLET
QUILLETED
QUILLFISH
QUILLFISHES
QUILLING
QUILLITY
QUILLON
QUILLTAIL
QUILLWORK
QUILLWORT
QUILLY
QUILT
QUILTED
QUILTER
QUILTING
QUIM
QUIN
QUINA
QUINACRINE
QUINALDIC
QUINALDIN
QUINALDINE
QUINALDINIC
QUINALDINIUM
QUINALDYL
QUINAMICIN
QUINAMICINE
QUINAMIDIN
QUINAMIDINE
QUINAMIN
QUINAMINE
QUINANISOLE
QUINAQUINA
QUINARIAN
QUINARIES
QUINARIUS
QUINARY
QUINAS
QUINATE
QUINATOXIN
QUINATOXINE
QUINAZOLIN
QUINAZOLINE
QUINAZOLYL
QUINCE
QUINCEWORT
QUINCH
QUINCUNCIAL
QUINCUNX
QUINCUNXES
QUINCUNXIAL
QUINDECAD
QUINDECAGON
QUINDECEMVIR
QUINDECEMVIRI
QUINDECIM
QUINDECIMA
QUINDECIMVIR
QUINDENE
QUINE
QUINELLA
QUINET
QUINETUM
QUINHYDRONE
QUINIA
QUINIBLE
QUINIC
QUINICIN
QUINICINE
QUINIDIN
QUINIDINE
QUINIELA
QUININ
QUININA
QUININE
QUININISM
QUININIZE
QUINIRETIN

QUINISEXT
QUINISEXTINE
QUINITE
QUINITOL
QUINIZARIN
QUINK
QUINNAT
QUINNET
QUINOA
QUINOFORM
QUINOGEN
QUINOID
QUINOIDAL
QUINOIDATION
QUINOIDIN
QUINOIDINE
QUINOL
QUINOLAS
QUINOLIN
QUINOLINE
QUINOLINIUM
QUINOLINYL
QUINOLOGIST
QUINOLOGY
QUINOLYL
QUINOMETRY
QUINON
QUINONE
QUINONIC
QUINONIMIN
QUINONIMINE
QUINONIZE
QUINONOID
QUINONYL
QUINOPYRIN
QUINOVATE
QUINOVIN
QUINOVOSE
QUINOXALIN
QUINOXALINE
QUINOXALYL
QUINOYL
QUINQUENNIA
QUINQUENNIAD
QUINQUENNIAL
QUINQUENNIUM
QUINQUENNIUMS
QUINQUERTIUM
QUINQUEVIR
QUINQUEVIRS
QUINQUINA
QUINQUINO
QUINSE
QUINSIED
QUINSY
QUINSYBERRIES
QUINSYBERRY
QUINSYWORT
QUINT
QUINTA
QUINTAD
QUINTADENA
QUINTADENE
QUINTAIN
QUINTAL
QUINTAN
QUINTANT
QUINTARY
QUINTE
QUINTELEMENT
QUINTERNION
QUINTESSENCE
QUINTET
QUINTETTE
QUINTETTO
QUINTFOIL
QUINTIC
QUINTILE
QUINTILLION
QUINTIN
QUINTIPED
QUINTO
QUINTOLE
QUINTON
QUINTROON
QUINTUPLE
QUINTUPLED
QUINTUPLET
QUINTUPLING
QUINTUS
QUINUCLIDINE
QUINYIE
QUINYL
QUINZAINE
QUINZE
QUINZIEME
QUIP
QUIPO
QUIPPE
QUIPPED
QUIPPER
QUIPPING
QUIPPISH
QUIPPISHNESS
QUIPPU
QUIPPY
QUIPSOME
QUIPSTER
QUIPU
QUIPUS
QUIRA
QUIRCAL
QUIRE
QUIRED
QUIREWISE
QUIRING
QUIRITARIAN
QUIRK
QUIRKED
QUIRKIER
QUIRKIEST
QUIRKING
QUIRKSEY
QUIRKSOME
QUIRKY
QUIRL
QUIRQUINCHO
QUIRT
QUIS
QUISBY
QUISCOS
QUISLING
QUISLINGISM
QUISQUEITE
QUISQUILIAN
QUISQUILIARY
QUISQUILIOUS
QUISQUOUS
QUIST
QUISTRON
QUISUTSCH
QUIT
QUITANTIE
QUITCH
QUITCLAIM
QUITCLAIMED
QUITCLAIMING
QUITE
QUITELY
QUITEVE
QUITRENT
QUITS
QUITTANCE
QUITTED
QUITTER
QUITTERBONE
QUITTING
QUITTOR
QUIVER
QUIVERED
QUIVERER
QUIVERFUL
QUIVERING
QUIVERLEAF
QUIVERY
QUIXOTIC
QUIXOTICAL
QUIXOTISM
QUIXOTIZE
QUIXOTRY
QUIZ
QUIZZACIOUS
QUIZZATORIAL
QUIZZED
QUIZZEE
QUIZZER
QUIZZERY
QUIZZICAL
QUIZZICALITY
QUIZZICALLY
QUIZZIFY
QUIZZING
QUIZZISH
QUIZZISM
QUIZZITY
QUIZZY
QUO
QUOAD
QUOCK
QUOD
QUODDED
QUODDIES
QUODDING
QUODDITY
QUODLIBET
QUODLIBETARY
QUODLIBETIC
QUODLING
QUOG
QUOILERS
QUOIN
QUOINED
QUOINING
QUOIT
QUOITER
QUOITS
QUOKKA
QUOMINUS
QUOMODO
QUONDAM
QUONIAM
QUONK
QUONKING
QUOP
QUORUM
QUORUMS
QUOT
QUOTA
QUOTABILITY
QUOTABLE
QUOTABLENESS
QUOTABLY
QUOTAS
QUOTATION
QUOTATIONAL
QUOTATIONIST
QUOTATIVE
QUOTE
QUOTED
QUOTEE
QUOTELESS
QUOTENNIAL
QUOTER
QUOTEWORTHY
QUOTH
QUOTHA
QUOTIDIAN
QUOTIDIANLY
QUOTIENT
QUOTIETIES
QUOTIETY
QUOTING
QUOTINGLY
QUOTITY
QUOTT
QUOTUM
QUOY
QUOZ
QUYTE

R

RA
RAAD
RAADZAAL
RAAN
RAASCH
RAASH
RAB
RABAND
RABANNA
RABAT
RABATINE
RABATO
RABATTE
RABATTED
RABATTEMENT
RABATTING
RABBAN
RABBET
RABBETED
RABBETING
RABBI
RABBIES
RABBIN
RABBINATE
RABBINIC
RABBINICAL
RABBINICALLY
RABBINISM
RABBINIST
RABBINISTIC
RABBINISTICAL
RABBINITE
RABBINITIC
RABBINIZE
RABBIS
RABBISH
RABBIT
RABBITBERRIES
RABBITBERRY
RABBITER
RABBITEYE
RABBITFISH
RABBITMOUTH
RABBITRIES
RABBITROOT
RABBITRY
RABBITS
RABBITSKIN
RABBITWEED
RABBITWOOD
RABBITY
RABBLE
RABBLED
RABBLEMENT
RABBLEPROOF
RABBLER
RABBLESOME
RABBLING
RABBONI
RABDOMANCY
RABFAK
RABI
RABIATOR
RABIC
RABID
RABIDITY
RABIDLY
RABIDNESS
RABIES
RABIETIC
RABIFIC
RABIFORM
RABIGENIC
RABINET
RABIOUS
RABIRUBIA
RABITIC
RABLIN
RABULISTIC
RABULOUS
RACA
RACAHOUT
RACALLABLE
RACCHE
RACCOON
RACCOONBERRY
RACCOONS
RACE
RACEABOUT
RACECOURSE
RACED
RACEGOER
RACEGOING
RACEHORSE
RACEHORSES
RACELIKE
RACELINE
RACEMASE
RACEMATE
RACEMATION
RACEME
RACEMED
RACEMIC
RACEMIFEROUS
RACEMIFORM
RACEMISM
RACEMIZATION
RACEMIZE
RACEMIZED
RACEMIZING
RACEMOID
RACEMOSE
RACEMOSELY
RACEMOUS
RACEMULE
RACEMULOSE
RACER
RACES
RACETRACK
RACETTE
RACEWAY
RACH
RACHE
RACHES
RACHIAL
RACHIALGIA
RACHIALGIC
RACHICENTESIS
RACHIDES
RACHIDIAN
RACHIFORM
RACHIGRAPH
RACHILLA
RACHILLAE
RACHIODONT
RACHIODYNIA
RACHIOMETER
RACHIOPLEGIA
RACHIOTOME
RACHIOTOMY
RACHIPAGUS
RACHIS
RACHISCHISIS
RACHISES
RACHITIC
RACHITIS
RACHITISM
RACHITOGENIC
RACHITOME
RACHITOMOUS
RACHITOMY
RACIAL
RACIALISM
RACIALIST
RACIALITY
RACIALIZATION
RACIALIZE
RACIALLY
RACILY
RACINESS
RACING
RACION
RACISM
RACIST
RACK
RACKABONES
RACKAN
RACKAPEE
RACKBONE
RACKED
RACKER
RACKET
RACKETEER
RACKETEERING
RACKETER
RACKETRY
RACKETT
RACKETY
RACKING
RACKLE
RACKMAN
RACKWAY
RACKWORK
RACLOIR
RACON
RACONTEUR
RACOON
RACQUET
RACY
RAD
RADA
RADAR
RADARSCOPE
RADDLE
RADDLED
RADDLEMAN
RADDLEMEN
RADDLING
RADDLINGS
RADE
RADEAU
RADECTOMY
RADEUR
RADEVORE
RADFORD
RADIABILITY
RADIABLE
RADIAL
RADIALE
RADIALITY
RADIALIZATION
RADIALIZE
RADIALLY
RADIAN
RADIANCE
RADIANCY
RADIANT
RADIANTLY
RADIANTNESS
RADIATE
RADIATED
RADIATIFORM
RADIATING
RADIATION
RADIATIONAL
RADIATIVE
RADIATOR
RADIATORS
RADIATORY
RADIATURE
RADICAL
RADICALISM
RADICALITY
RADICALIZATION
RADICALIZE
RADICALLY
RADICALNESS
RADICAND
RADICANT
RADICATE
RADICATED
RADICATING
RADICATION
RADICEL
RADICES
RADICICOLA
RADICLE
RADICOLOUS
RADICOSE
RADICULA
RADICULAR
RADICULE
RADICULECTOMY
RADICULITIS
RADICULOSE
RADIENT
RADIESCENT
RADIFEROUS
RADII
RADIO
RADIOACOUSTICS
RADIOACTINIUM
RADIOACTIVATE
RADIOACTIVE
RADIOACTIVITY
RADIOBIOLOGY
RADIOBSERVER
RADIOCARBON
RADIOCARPAL
RADIOCHEMICAL
RADIOCHEMISTRY
RADIOCONDUCTOR
RADIODATING
RADIODE
RADIODETECTOR
RADIODIGITAL
RADIODONTIA
RADIODONTIC
RADIODONTIST
RADIODYNAMIC
RADIODYNAMICS
RADIOED
RADIOELEMENT
RADIOGRAM
RADIOGRAPH
RADIOGRAPHER
RADIOGRAPHIC
RADIOGRAPHICAL
RADIOGRAPHICALLY
RADIOGRAPHY
RADIOHUMERAL
RADIOING
RADIOISOTOPE
RADIOLARIAN
RADIOLEAD
RADIOLITE
RADIOLITIC
RADIOLOCATION
RADIOLOGIC
RADIOLOGICAL
RADIOLOGIST
RADIOLOGY
RADIOLUCENCY
RADIOLUCENT
RADIOMAN
RADIOMEN
RADIOMETER
RADIOMETRIC
RADIOMETRICALLY
RADIOMETRY
RADIOMICROMETER
RADIOMOVIES
RADIONIC
RADIOPACITY
RADIOPALMAR
RADIOPAQUE
RADIOPHARE
RADIOPHONE
RADIOPHONIC
RADIOPHONY
RADIOPHOTOGRAPH
RADIOPHOTOGRAPHY
RADIOPRAXIS
RADIOS
RADIOSCOPE
RADIOSCOPIC
RADIOSCOPICAL
RADIOSCOPY
RADIOSENSIBILITY
RADIOSENSITIVE
RADIOSENSITIVITY
RADIOSONDE
RADIOSONIC
RADIOSYMMETRICAL
RADIOTECHNOLOGY
RADIOTELEGRAM
RADIOTELEGRAPH
RADIOTELEGRAPHY
RADIOTELEPHONE
RADIOTELEPHONIC
RADIOTELEPHONY
RADIOTHALLIUM
RADIOTHERAPEUTIC
RADIOTHERAPEUTICS
RADIOTHERAPEUTIST
RADIOTHERAPIST
RADIOTHERAPY
RADIOTHERMY
RADIOTHORIUM
RADIOTOXIC
RADIOTRANSPARENCY
RADIOTRANSPARENT
RADIOTRICIAN
RADIOTROPIC
RADIOTROPISM
RADIOUS
RADIOVISION
RADISH
RADIUM
RADIUMIZATION
RADIUMIZE
RADIUS
RADIUSES
RADIX
RADKNIGHT
RADLY
RADMAN
RADOME
RADON
RADULA
RADULAE
RADULAR
RADULATE
RADULIFEROUS
RADULIFORM

RADZIMIR
RAE
RAFALE
RAFF
RAFFE
RAFFEE
RAFFIA
RAFFINASE
RAFFING
RAFFINOSE
RAFFISH
RAFFISHLY
RAFFISHNESS
RAFFLE
RAFFLED
RAFFLER
RAFFLESIA
RAFFLESIACEOUS
RAFFLING
RAFFMAN
RAFT
RAFTAGE
RAFTER
RAFTINESS
RAFTMAN
RAFTSMAN
RAFTSMEN
RAFTY
RAG
RAGA
RAGABASH
RAGABRASH
RAGAMUFFIN
RAGAMUFFINLY
RAGBAG
RAGE
RAGED
RAGEOUS
RAGEOUSLY
RAGEOUSNESS
RAGERY
RAGFISH
RAGGED
RAGGEDLY
RAGGEDNESS
RAGGEE
RAGGER
RAGGERY
RAGGETY
RAGGI
RAGGIL
RAGGILY
RAGGING
RAGGLE
RAGGLED
RAGGY
RAGHOUSE
RAGI
RAGING
RAGINGLY
RAGLAN
RAGLANITE
RAGLET
RAGLIN
RAGMAN
RAGMEN
RAGONDIN
RAGOUT
RAGOUTED
RAGOUTING
RAGPICKER
RAGS
RAGSELLER
RAGSHAG
RAGSORTER
RAGSTONE
RAGTAG
RAGTIME
RAGTIMER
RAGTIMEY
RAGULE
RAGULY
RAGUSYE
RAGWEED
RAGWORT
RAH
RAHDAR
RAHDAREE
RAHDARI
RAIA
RAID
RAIDER
RAIK
RAIL
RAILAGE
RAILBIRD
RAILED
RAILER
RAILHEAD
RAILING
RAILLERY
RAILLEUR
RAILLY
RAILMAN
RAILMEN
RAILROAD
RAILROADER
RAILROADING
RAILWAY
RAIM
RAIMENT
RAIN
RAINBAND
RAINBIRD
RAINBOUND
RAINBOW
RAINBOWY
RAINBURST
RAINCOAT
RAINDROP
RAINER
RAINES
RAINFALL
RAINFOWL
RAINIER
RAINIEST
RAINILY
RAININESS
RAINLESS
RAINLIGHT
RAINMAKER
RAINMAKING
RAINOUT
RAINPROOF
RAINPROOFER
RAINSPOUT
RAINSTORM
RAINTIGHT
RAINWASH
RAINWATER
RAINWORM
RAINY
RAIOID
RAIR
RAIS
RAISE
RAISED
RAISER
RAISIN
RAISINE
RAISING
RAISINS
RAISINY
RAISONNE
RAIT
RAITH
RAIYAT
RAJ
RAJA
RAJAH
RAJAS
RAJBANSI
RAJOGUNA
RAK
RAKA
RAKAH
RAKAN
RAKE
RAKEAGE
RAKED
RAKEE
RAKEHELL
RAKEHELLISH
RAKEHELLY
RAKELY
RAKEOFF
RAKER
RAKERY
RAKESTEEL
RAKESTELE
RAKH
RAKI
RAKIA
RAKIJA
RAKILY
RAKING
RAKING
RAKISH
RAKISHLY
RAKISHNESS
RAKIT
RAKSHASA
RALE
RALISH
RALLENTANDO
RALLERY
RALLIANCE
RALLIER
RALLIES
RALLIFORM
RALLINE
RALLY
RALLYING
RALO
RALPH
RALSTONITE
RAM
RAMACK
RAMADA
RAMAGE
RAMARAMA
RAMARK
RAMASS
RAMATE
RAMBARRE
RAMBEH
RAMBERGE
RAMBLA
RAMBLE
RAMBLED
RAMBLER
RAMBLING
RAMBLINGLY
RAMBONG
RAMBOOZE
RAMBUNCTIOUS
RAMBURE
RAMBUTAN
RAME
RAMEAL
RAMEE
RAMEKIN
RAMELLOSE
RAMENT
RAMENTA
RAMENTACEOUS
RAMENTAL
RAMENTUM
RAMEOUS
RAMEQUIN
RAMEX
RAMFEEZLED
RAMFORCE
RAMGUNSHOCH
RAMHEAD
RAMI
RAMICORN
RAMIE
RAMIFICATE
RAMIFICATION
RAMIFIED
RAMIFORM
RAMIFY
RAMIFYING
RAMILLIE
RAMISECTION
RAMISECTOMY
RAMLINE
RAMMACK
RAMMAGE
RAMMASS
RAMMED
RAMMEL
RAMMELSBERGITE
RAMMER
RAMMERMAN
RAMMERMEN
RAMMING
RAMMISH
RAMMISHNESS
RAMMY
RAMON
RAMONEUR
RAMOSE
RAMOUS
RAMP
RAMPACIOUS
RAMPACIOUSLY
RAMPAGE
RAMPAGED
RAMPAGEOUS
RAMPAGEOUSLY
RAMPAGEOUSNESS
RAMPAGER
RAMPAGING
RAMPAGIOUS
RAMPANCY
RAMPANT
RAMPANTLY
RAMPART
RAMPARTED
RAMPARTING
RAMPER
RAMPICK
RAMPIER
RAMPIKE
RAMPION
RAMPIRE
RAMPISH
RAMPLER
RAMPLOR
RAMPOLE
RAMRACE
RAMROD
RAMRODDY
RAMSCALLION
RAMSCH
RAMSHACKLE
RAMSHACKLENESS
RAMSON
RAMSTAM
RAMSTEAD
RAMTIL
RAMULAR
RAMULIFEROUS
RAMULOSE
RAMULOUS
RAMULUS
RAMUS
RAMVERSE
RAN
RANA
RANAL
RANARIA
RANARIAN
RANARIUM
RANCE
RANCEL
RANCELLOR
RANCELMAN
RANCELMEN
RANCER
RANCESCENT
RANCH
RANCHE
RANCHER
RANCHERIA
RANCHERO
RANCHEROS
RANCHMAN
RANCHMEN
RANCHO
RANCHOS
RANCHWOMAN
RANCID
RANCIDIFICATION
RANCIDIFY
RANCIDITY
RANCIDLY
RANCIDNESS
RANCIO
RANCOR
RANCOROUS
RANCOROUSLY
RANCOUR
RAND
RANDALL
RANDAN
RANDANNITE
RANDEM
RANDER
RANDERS
RANDIE
RANDING
RANDIR
RANDOM
RANDOMIZE
RANDOMIZED
RANDOMIZING
RANDOMLY
RANDOMNESS
RANDOMWISE
RANDON
RANDORI
RANDY
RANE
RANEE
RANFORCE
RANG
RANGALE
RANGDOODLES
RANGE
RANGED
RANGEHEADS
RANGEMAN

RANGEMEN
RANGER
RANGERSHIP
RANGEWORK
RANGIER
RANGIEST
RANGING
RANGLE
RANGY
RANI
RANINE
RANINIAN
RANK
RANKER
RANKET
RANKING
RANKISH
RANKLE
RANKLED
RANKLING
RANKLY
RANKNESS
RANKS
RANKSMAN
RANKSMEN
RANN
RANNEL
RANNIGAL
RANNY
RANPIKE
RANSACK
RANSACKER
RANSEL
RANSELMEN
RANSES
RANSOM
RANSOMER
RANSOMLESS
RANSTEAD
RANT
RANTAN
RANTANKEROUS
RANTEPOLE
RANTER
RANTING
RANTIPOLE
RANTISM
RANTIZE
RANTOCK
RANTOON
RANTREE
RANTY
RANULA
RANUNCULI
RANUNCULUS
RANUNCULUSES
RAOB
RAP
RAPACEUS
RAPACIOUS
RAPACIOUSLY
RAPACITY
RAPAKIVI
RAPATEACEOUS
RAPE
RAPED
RAPEFUL
RAPELY
RAPER
RAPESEED
RAPEYE
RAPHAE
RAPHANIA
RAPHANUS
RAPHANY
RAPHE
RAPHIA
RAPHIDE
RAPHIDES
RAPHIDIFEROUS
RAPHIS
RAPHUS
RAPIC
RAPID
RAPIDAMENTE
RAPIDE
RAPIDITY
RAPIDLY
RAPIDNESS
RAPIDO
RAPIDS
RAPIER
RAPIERED
RAPILLO
RAPIN
RAPINE
RAPING
RAPINIC
RAPIST
RAPLOCH
RAPORT
RAPPAGE
RAPPAREE
RAPPE
RAPPED
RAPPEE
RAPPEL
RAPPELLED
RAPPELLING
RAPPEN
RAPPER
RAPPING
RAPPINI
RAPPIST
RAPPORT
RAPSCALLION
RAPSCALLIONISM
RAPSCALLIONLY
RAPSCALLIONRY
RAPT
RAPTATORIAL
RAPTER
RAPTLY
RAPTNESS
RAPTOR
RAPTORIAL
RAPTORIOUS
RAPTRIL
RAPTURE
RAPTURED
RAPTURIST
RAPTURIZE
RAPTUROUS
RAPTUROUSLY
RAPTUROUSNESS
RAPTUS
RAQUET
RARE
RAREBIT
RAREFACTION
RAREFACTIONAL
RAREFACTIVE
RAREFIABLE
RAREFICATION
RAREFIED
RAREFIER
RAREFY
RAREFYING
RARELY
RARENESS
RARER
RARERIPE
RAREST
RARICONSTANT
RARIETY
RARING
RARIORA
RARISH
RARITIES
RARITY
RAS
RASA
RASAMALA
RASANT
RASBORA
RASCACIO
RASCAL
RASCALITIES
RASCALITY
RASCALLY
RASCALRY
RASCETA
RASE
RASED
RASEE
RASEN
RASER
RASGADO
RASH
RASHBUSS
RASHER
RASHFUL
RASHING
RASHLY
RASHNESS
RASING
RASION
RASOIR
RASON
RASOR
RASORIAL
RASOUR
RASP
RASPATORY
RASPBERRY
RASPED
RASPER
RASPIER
RASPIEST
RASPING
RASPINGLY
RASPINGNESS
RASPIS
RASPISH
RASPITE
RASPY
RASSASY
RASSE
RASSLE
RASTIK
RASTY
RASURE
RAT
RATA
RATABLE
RATABLENESS
RATABLY
RATAFEE
RATAFIA
RATAL
RATAN
RATANY
RATAPLAN
RATAPLANNED
RATAPLANNING
RATBAG
RATBITE
RATCATCHER
RATCH
RATCHEL
RATCHER
RATCHET
RATCHETY
RATE
RATEABILITY
RATEABLE
RATED
RATEL
RATEPAYER
RATEPAYING
RATER
RATERO
RATES
RATFISH
RATH
RATHA
RATHE
RATHELY
RATHENESS
RATHER
RATHERIPE
RATHERISH
RATHERLY
RATHEST
RATHITE
RATHOLE
RATHRIPE
RATHSKELLER
RATI
RATIFIA
RATIFICATION
RATIFICATIONIST
RATIFIED
RATIFY
RATIFYING
RATIHABITION
RATINE
RATING
RATIO
RATIOCINANT
RATIOCINATE
RATIOCINATED
RATIOCINATING
RATIOCINATION
RATIOCINATIVE
RATIOCINATOR
RATIOCINATORY
RATIOMETER
RATION
RATIONABLE
RATIONAL
RATIONALE
RATIONALISM
RATIONALIST
RATIONALISTIC
RATIONALITIES
RATIONALITY
RATIONALIZE
RATIONALIZED
RATIONALIZER
RATIONALLY
RATIONALNESS
RATIONATE
RATIONING
RATIONS
RATIOS
RATITE
RATIUNCLE
RATLINE
RATLINER
RATO
RATON
RATOON
RATS
RATSBANE
RATTAIL
RATTAN
RATTAREE
RATTATTOO
RATTED
RATTEEN
RATTEL
RATTEN
RATTENED
RATTENER
RATTENING
RATTER
RATTERY
RATTI
RATTINET
RATTING
RATTINGLY
RATTISH
RATTLE
RATTLEBAG
RATTLEBONES
RATTLEBOX
RATTLEBRAIN
RATTLEBRAINED
RATTLEBUSH
RATTLED
RATTLEHEAD
RATTLEHEADED
RATTLEJACK
RATTLEMOUSE
RATTLENUT
RATTLEPATE
RATTLEPATED
RATTLER
RATTLERAN
RATTLEROOT
RATTLERTREE
RATTLES
RATTLESKULL
RATTLESKULLED
RATTLESNAKE
RATTLESOME
RATTLETRAP
RATTLEWEED
RATTLEWORT
RATTLING
RATTLINGNESS
RATTLY
RATTON
RATTONER
RATTOON
RATTRAP
RATTY
RATWA
RATWOOD
RAUCID
RAUCIDITY
RAUCITY
RAUCOUS
RAUCOUSLY
RAUCOUSNESS
RAUGRAVE
RAUK
RAULI
RAUN
RAUNCHY
RAUNGE
RAUNPICK
RAUPO
RAURACI
RAURIKI
RAVAGE
RAVAGED
RAVAGEMENT
RAVAGER
RAVAGING
RAVE
RAVED
RAVEHOOK
RAVEL

RAVELED
RAVELER
RAVELIN
RAVELING
RAVELLED
RAVELLER
RAVELLING
RAVELLY
RAVELMENT
RAVEN
RAVENER
RAVENING
RAVENINGLY
RAVENLING
RAVENOUS
RAVENOUSLY
RAVENOUSNESS
RAVENRY
RAVENSTONE
RAVER
RAVERY
RAVIGOTE
RAVIN
RAVINATE
RAVINE
RAVINED
RAVINEMENT
RAVINEY
RAVING
RAVIOLI
RAVISH
RAVISHED
RAVISHER
RAVISHING
RAVISHINGLY
RAVISHMENT
RAVISON
RAVISSANT
RAW
RAWBONE
RAWBONED
RAWBONES
RAWED
RAWHEAD
RAWHIDE
RAWHIDER
RAWIN
RAWING
RAWISH
RAWISHNESS
RAWKY
RAWLY
RAWNESS
RAWNIE
RAX
RAY
RAYA
RAYAGE
RAYAH
RAYAT
RAYED
RAYGRASS
RAYING
RAYLESS
RAYLESSLY
RAYLESSNESS
RAYNE
RAYON
RAYONNANCE
RAYONNANT
RAYS
RAZE
RAZED
RAZEE
RAZEED
RAZEEING
RAZING
RAZON
RAZOO
RAZOR
RAZORBACK
RAZORBILL
RAZOREDGE
RAZORMAKER
RAZORMAKING
RAZORMAN
RAZORSTROP
RAZOUR
RAZZ
RAZZBERRIES
RAZZBERRY
RAZZIA
RAZZING
RAZZLY
RE
REA
REAAL
REABLE
REACCESS
REACH
REACHED
REACHER
REACHING
REACHLESS
REACHY
REACQUIRE
REACT
REACTANCE
REACTANT
REACTION
REACTIONAL
REACTIONALLY
REACTIONARIES
REACTIONARINESS
REACTIONARISM
REACTIONARIST
REACTIONARY
REACTIONARYISM
REACTIONISM
REACTIONIST
REACTIVATE
REACTIVATED
REACTIVATING
REACTIVATION
REACTIVATOR
REACTIVE
REACTIVELY
REACTIVENESS
REACTIVITY
REACTOLOGICAL
REACTOLOGY
REACTOR
REACTUALIZATION
REACTUALIZE
REACTUATE
READ
READABILITY
READABLE
READABLENESS
READABLY
READDRESS
READEPT
READER
READERSHIP
READIED
READIER
READIEST
READILY
READINESS
READING
READINGDOM
READJUST
READJUSTABLE
READJUSTER
READJUSTMENT
READMISSION
READMIT
READMITTANCE
READMITTED
READMITTING
READS
READVERTENCY
READY
READYING
REAFFIRM
REAFFIRMANCE
REAFFIRMER
REAGENCY
REAGENT
REAGGRAVATE
REAGGRAVATION
REAGIN
REAK
REAKS
REAL
REALES
REALEST
REALGAR
REALIA
REALIGN
REALIGNMENT
REALISM
REALIST
REALISTIC
REALISTICALLY
REALISTICIZE
REALITIES
REALITY
REALIZABLE
REALIZATION
REALIZE
REALIZED
REALIZER
REALIZING
REALLY
REALM
REALNESS
REALS
REALTIES
REALTOR
REALTY
REAM
REAMAGE
REAME
REAMER
REAMERER
REAMY
REAN
REANIMATE
REANIMATED
REANIMATING
REANIMATION
REANSWER
REAP
REAPABLE
REAPDOLE
REAPER
REAPERS
REAPING
REAPPEAR
REAPPEARANCE
REAR
REARDOSS
REARED
REARER
REARHORSE
REARING
REARLING
REARLY
REARM
REARMAMENT
REARMED
REARMOST
REARMOUSE
REARRANGE
REARRANGED
REARRANGEMENT
REARRANGING
REARWARD
REARWARDS
REASINESS
REASON
REASONABILITY
REASONABLE
REASONABLENESS
REASONABLY
REASONAL
REASONED
REASONER
REASONING
REASONLESS
REASONLESSLY
REASONLESSNESS
REASONS
REASSEMBLE
REASSERT
REASSERTION
REASSERTOR
REASSIGN
REASSOCIATION
REASSUME
REASSUMPTION
REASSURANCE
REASSURE
REASSURED
REASSUREDLY
REASSUREMENT
REASSURER
REASSURING
REASSURINGLY
REASTINESS
REASTY
REASY
REATUS
REAUTE
REAVE
REAVED
REAVER
REAVERY
REAVING
REB
REBAB
REBACK
REBAIT
REBAN
REBAPTISM
REBAPTISMAL
REBAPTIZATION
REBAPTIZE
REBAPTIZER
REBAR
REBARBATIVE
REBATE
REBATED
REBATEMENT
REBATER
REBATING
REBATO
REBBE
REBEAT
REBEC
REBECK
REBEL
REBELDOM
REBELLED
REBELLING
REBELLION
REBELLIOUS
REBELLIOUSLY
REBELLIOUSNESS
REBELLY
REBIA
REBID
REBILLING
REBIND
REBIRTH
REBOANT
REBOANTIC
REBOATION
REBOIL
REBOISE
REBOISEMENT
REBOKE
REBOLERA
REBOLT
REBORN
REBOTE
REBOUND
REBOUNDER
REBOUNDING
REBOZO
REBROADCAST
REBUFF
REBUILD
REBUILDER
REBUILT
REBUKABLE
REBUKE
REBUKED
REBUKER
REBUKING
REBUN
REBURSE
REBUS
REBUSED
REBUSES
REBUSING
REBUT
REBUTE
REBUTTAL
REBUTTED
REBUTTER
REBUTTING
RECADENCY
RECADO
RECALCITRANCE
RECALCITRANCY
RECALCITRANT
RECALCITRATE
RECALCITRATION
RECALESCE
RECALESCED
RECALESCENCE
RECALESCENT
RECALESCING
RECALL
RECALLED
RECALLING
RECALLIST
RECALLMENT
RECAMERA
RECANT
RECANTATION
RECANTED
RECANTER
RECANTING
RECAP
RECAPITALIZATION
RECAPITALIZE
RECAPITALIZED
RECAPITALIZING
RECAPITULATE
RECAPITULATED
RECAPITULATING
RECAPITULATION

RECAPPED
RECAPPER
RECAPPING
RECAPTION
RECAPTOR
RECAPTURE
RECAPTURED
RECAPTURING
RECARBON
RECARBONIZE
RECARBONIZER
RECARBURIZATION
RECARBURIZE
RECARBURIZER
RECAST
RECASTER
RECASTING
RECAULESCENCE
RECCE
RECCHE
RECCO
RECCY
RECEDE
RECEDED
RECEDENCE
RECEDENT
RECEDER
RECEDING
RECEIPT
RECEIPTED
RECEIPTER
RECEIPTING
RECEIPTMENT
RECEIPTOR
RECEIVABILITY
RECEIVABLE
RECEIVABLENESS
RECEIVABLES
RECEIVAL
RECEIVE
RECEIVED
RECEIVEDNESS
RECEIVER
RECEIVERSHIP
RECEIVING
RECENCY
RECENSE
RECENSION
RECENSURE
RECENT
RECENTLY
RECENTNESS
RECEPT
RECEPTACLE
RECEPTACULAR
RECEPTANT
RECEPTIBILITY
RECEPTIBLE
RECEPTION
RECEPTIONISM
RECEPTIONIST
RECEPTITIOUS
RECEPTIVE
RECEPTIVELY
RECEPTIVENESS
RECEPTIVITY
RECEPTOR
RECEPTORAL
RECEPTORIAL
RECEPTUAL
RECEPTUALLY
RECERCELEE
RECESS
RECESSED
RECESSER
RECESSION
RECESSIONAL
RECESSIONARY
RECESSIVE
RECESSIVELY
RECHANGE
RECHARGE
RECHARTER
RECHASE
RECHASER
RECHATE
RECHAUFFE
RECHE
RECHEAT
RECHERCHE
RECIDE
RECIDIVATE
RECIDIVATION
RECIDIVE
RECIDIVISM
RECIDIVIST
RECIDIVISTIC
RECIDIVITY
RECIDIVOUS
RECIPE
RECIPIANGLE
RECIPIENCE
RECIPIENCY
RECIPIEND
RECIPIENDARY
RECIPIENT
RECIPIOMOTOR
RECIPROCABLE
RECIPROCAL
RECIPROCALITY
RECIPROCALIZE
RECIPROCALLY
RECIPROCANT
RECIPROCANTIVE
RECIPROCATE
RECIPROCATED
RECIPROCATING
RECIPROCATION
RECIPROCATIVE
RECIPROCATOR
RECIPROCATORY
RECIPROCITY
RECISION
RECIT
RECITAL
RECITALIST
RECITANDO
RECITATION
RECITATIONIST
RECITATIVE
RECITE
RECITED
RECITEMENT
RECITER
RECITING
RECK
RECKLA
RECKLESS
RECKLESSLY
RECKLESSNESS
RECKLING
RECKON
RECKONED
RECKONER
RECKONING
RECLAIM
RECLAIMABLE
RECLAIMABLENES
RECLAIMABLY
RECLAIMANT
RECLAIMED
RECLAIMER
RECLAIMLESS
RECLAIMMENT
RECLAMA
RECLAMATION
RECLAME
RECLINABLE
RECLINATE
RECLINATED
RECLINATION
RECLINE
RECLINED
RECLINER
RECLINING
RECLOSE
RECLUDE
RECLUSE
RECLUSELY
RECLUSENESS
RECLUSERY
RECLUSION
RECLUSIVE
RECLUSIVENESS
RECOCT
RECOCTION
RECOGITATE
RECOGITATION
RECOGNITA
RECOGNITION
RECOGNITIVE
RECOGNITOR
RECOGNITORY
RECOGNIZABLE
RECOGNIZABLY
RECOGNIZANCE
RECOGNIZANT
RECOGNIZE
RECOGNIZED
RECOGNIZEE
RECOGNIZER
RECOGNIZING
RECOGNIZOR
RECOGNOSCE
RECOIL
RECOILED
RECOILING
RECOILLESS
RECOILMENT
RECOIN
RECOINAGE
RECOLLECT
RECOLLECTED
RECOLLECTEDLY
RECOLLECTEDNESS
RECOLLECTION
RECOLLECTIVE
RECOLLECTIVELY
RECOLLECTIVENESS
RECOLLET
RECOMBINATION
RECOMEMBER
RECOMFORT
RECOMMAND
RECOMMENCE
RECOMMENCEMENT
RECOMMENCER
RECOMMEND
RECOMMENDABILITY
RECOMMENDABLE
RECOMMENDABLENESS
RECOMMENDABLY
RECOMMENDATION
RECOMMENDATORY
RECOMMENDEE
RECOMMENDER
RECOMMIT
RECOMMITING
RECOMMITMENT
RECOMMITTAL
RECOMMITTED
RECOMPENSABLE
RECOMPENSATION
RECOMPENSE
RECOMPENSED
RECOMPENSER
RECOMPENSING
RECOMPENSIVE
RECOMPOSE
RECOMPOSED
RECOMPOSER
RECOMPOSING
RECOMPOSITION
RECOMPRESS
RECOMPRESSION
RECONCENTRADO
RECONCENTRATE
RECONCENTRATION
RECONCILABILITY
RECONCILABLE
RECONCILABLENESS
RECONCILABLY
RECONCILE
RECONCILED
RECONCILEE
RECONCILELESS
RECONCILEMENT
RECONCILER
RECONCILIABILITY
RECONCILIABLE
RECONCILIATE
RECONCILIATION
RECONCILIATIVE
RECONCILIATOR
RECONCILIATORY
RECONCILING
RECONCILINGLY
RECOND
RECONDITE
RECONDITELY
RECONDITENESS
RECONDITION
RECONDUCT
RECONDUCTION
RECONNAISSANCE
RECONNOITER
RECONNOITERED
RECONNOITERER
RECONNOITERING
RECONSIDER
RECONSIDERATIO
RECONSIGN
RECONSIGNMENT
RECONSTITUENT
RECONSTITUTE
RECONSTITUTION
RECONSTRUCT
RECONSTRUCTED
RECONSTRUCTION
RECONSTRUCTIONAL
RECONSTRUCTIONARY
RECONSTRUCTIONIST
RECONSTRUCTIVE
RECONSTRUCTIVENESS
RECONSTRUCTOR
RECONTER
RECONVENTION
RECONVENTIONAL
RECONVERT
RECONVERTIBLE
RECONVEY
RECONVEYANCE
RECOPILATION
RECORD
RECORDANT
RECORDATION
RECORDATIVE
RECORDATIVELY
RECORDATORY
RECORDED
RECORDER
RECORDING
RECORDIST
RECORDS
RECOUNT
RECOUNTAL
RECOUNTED
RECOUNTER
RECOUNTING
RECOUNTMENT
RECOUP
RECOUPABLE
RECOUPE
RECOUPED
RECOUPER
RECOUPING
RECOUPLING
RECOUPMENT
RECOUR
RECOURSE
RECOVER
RECOVERABILITY
RECOVERABLE
RECOVERABLENES
RECOVERANCE
RECOVERED
RECOVEREE
RECOVERER
RECOVERIES
RECOVERY
RECRAYED
RECREANCE
RECREANCY
RECREANT
RECREANTLY
RECREANTNESS
RECREATE
RECREATED
RECREATING
RECREATION
RECREATIONAL
RECREATIONIST
RECREATIVE
RECREATIVELY
RECREATIVENESS
RECREATOR
RECREDENTIAL
RECREMENT
RECREMENTAL
RECREMENTITIAL
RECREMENTITIOUS
RECRESCENCE
RECREW
RECRIMINATE
RECRIMINATOR
RECRUDENCY
RECRUDESCE
RECRUDESCED
RECRUDESCENCE
RECRUDESCENCY
RECRUDESCENT
RECRUDESCING
RECRUIT
RECRUITAGE
RECRUITAL
RECRUITEE
RECRUITER
RECRUITING
RECRUITMENT
RECRUSHER
RECRYSTALLIZE
RECT
RECTAL
RECTANGLE
RECTANGLED

RECTANGULAR
RECTANGULARLY
RECTANGULARNESS
RECTANGULATE
RECTIFIABLE
RECTIFICATION
RECTIFICATIVE
RECTIFICATOR
RECTIFIED
RECTIFIER
RECTIFY
RECTIFYING
RECTIGRADE
RECTILINEAL
RECTILINEALLY
RECTILINEAR
RECTILINEAR
RECTILINEARITY
RECTILINEARNESS
RECTINERVED
RECTION
RECTIROSTRAL
RECTISERIAL
RECTITUDE
RECTITUDINOUS
RECTO
RECTOCELE
RECTOCLYSIS
RECTOCOLITIC
RECTOCOLONIC
RECTOGENITAL
RECTOPEXY
RECTOPLASTY
RECTOR
RECTORAL
RECTORATE
RECTORIAL
RECTORRHAPHY
RECTORY
RECTOS
RECTOSCOPE
RECTOSCOPY
RECTOSIGMOID
RECTOSTOMY
RECTOTOME
RECTOTOMY
RECTOVESICAL
RECTRESS
RECTRICES
RECTRICIAL
RECTRIX
RECTUM
RECTUS
RECU
RECUBANT
RECUBATE
RECUBATION
RECUEIL
RECUEILLEMENT
RECULADE
RECULE
RECUMB
RECUMBENCE
RECUMBENCY
RECUMBENT
RECUMBENTLY
RECUPERANCE
RECUPERATE
RECUPERATED
RECUPERATING
RECUPERATION
RECUPERATIVE
RECUPERATOR
RECUPERATORY
RECUR
RECURE
RECURRED
RECURRENCE
RECURRENCY
RECURRENT
RECURRENTLY
RECURRER
RECURRING
RECURRINGLY
RECURSE
RECURSION
RECURSIVE
RECURVANT
RECURVATE
RECURVATION
RECURVATURE
RECURVE
RECURVED
RECURVING
RECURVOUS
RECUSANCE
RECUSANCY
RECUSANT
RECUSATION
RECUSATIVE
RECUSATOR
RECUSE
RECUSED
RECUSING
RECUSSION
RECUTTING
RECYCLE
RED
REDACT
REDACTED
REDACTEUR
REDACTING
REDACTION
REDACTIONAL
REDACTOR
REDACTORIAL
REDAMATION
REDAME
REDAN
REDARGUE
REDARGUED
REDARGUING
REDARGUTION
REDARGUTIVE
REDARGUTORY
REDBACK
REDBAITING
REDBAY
REDBEARD
REDBELLY
REDBERRY
REDBILL
REDBIRD
REDBONE
REDBREAST
REDBRUSH
REDBUCK
REDBUD
REDCAP
REDCOAT
REDCOLL
REDD
REDDE
REDDED
REDDEN
REDDENDA
REDDENDO
REDDENDUM
REDDER
REDDEST
REDDING
REDDINGITE
REDDISH
REDDISHLY
REDDISHNESS
REDDITION
REDDITIVE
REDDLE
REDDLED
REDDLEMEN
REDDLING
REDDOCK
REDDSMAN
REDDY
REDE
REDEAR
REDECORATE
REDECORATED
REDECORATING
REDECORATION
REDECUSSATE
REDEEM
REDEEMABLE
REDEEMABLY
REDEEMER
REDEEMING
REDEEMLESS
REDELESS
REDELIVER
REDELIVERANCE
REDELIVERER
REDELIVERY
REDELY
REDEMAND
REDEMANDABLE
REDEMPTIBLE
REDEMPTION
REDEMPTIONAL
REDEMPTIONER
REDEMPTIVE
REDEMPTIVELY
REDEMPTOR
REDEMPTORIAL
REDEMPTORY
REDEMPTRESS
REDEMPTRICE
REDESMAN
REDETERMINE
REDEVELOP
REDEVELOPER
REDEYE
REDFIN
REDFINCH
REDFISH
REDHEAD
REDHEADEDLY
REDHEARTED
REDHIBITION
REDHIBITORY
REDHOOP
REDHORSE
REDIA
REDIENT
REDIF
REDINGOTE
REDINTEGRATE
REDINTEGRATED
REDINTEGRATION
REDINTEGRATIVE
REDINTEGRATOR
REDIRECT
REDIRECTION
REDISCOUNT
REDISSEIZE
REDISTILL
REDISTRIBUTE
REDISTRICT
REDITION
REDIVIVE
REDIVIVOUS
REDIVIVUS
REDJACKET
REDKNEES
REDLEG
REDLEGS
REDLINE
REDLY
REDMOUTH
REDNECK
REDNESS
REDO
REDOLENCE
REDOLENCY
REDOLENT
REDOLENTLY
REDONDILLA
REDOUBLE
REDOUBLED
REDOUBLEMENT
REDOUBLER
REDOUBLING
REDOUBT
REDOUBTABLE
REDOUBTABLENESS
REDOUBTABLY
REDOUBTED
REDOUBTING
REDOUND
REDOUNDED
REDOUNDING
REDOUTE
REDOWA
REDPOLL
REDRAFT
REDRAW
REDRAWER
REDRESS
REDRESSAL
REDRESSED
REDRESSER
REDRESSING
REDRESSIVE
REDRESSOR
REDROOT
REDSEAR
REDSHANK
REDSHIRT
REDSKIN
REDSTART
REDSTREAK
REDTAB
REDTAIL
REDTOP
REDUB
REDUBBER
REDUCCION
REDUCE
REDUCED
REDUCED
REDUCEMENT
REDUCENT
REDUCER
REDUCIBILITY
REDUCIBLE
REDUCIBLENESS
REDUCIBLY
REDUCING
REDUCT
REDUCTANT
REDUCTASE
REDUCTIBILITY
REDUCTIO
REDUCTION
REDUCTIONAL
REDUCTIONIST
REDUCTIVE
REDUCTIVELY
REDUCTOR
REDUCTORIAL
REDUE
REDUIT
REDUNDANCE
REDUNDANCIES
REDUNDANCY
REDUNDANT
REDUNDANTLY
REDUPLICATE
REDUPLICATED
REDUPLICATING
REDUPLICATION
REDUPLICATIVE
REDUPLICATIVELY
REDUPLICATORY
REDUPLICATURE
REDUX
REDWARD
REDWARE
REDWEED
REDWING
REDWITHE
REDWOOD
REDYE
REE
REECH
REECHO
REECHY
REED
REEDBIRD
REEDBUCK
REEDBUSH
REEDED
REEDEN
REEDER
REEDIER
REEDIEST
REEDINESS
REEDING
REEDISH
REEDLESS
REEDLIKE
REEDLING
REEDMAKER
REEDMAKING
REEDPLOT
REEDS
REEDWORK
REEDY
REEF
REEFABLE
REEFED
REEFER
REEFING
REEFY
REEK
REEKED
REEKER
REEKIER
REEKIEST
REEKING
REEKY
REEL
REELABLE
REELED
REELER
REELING
REELRALL
REEM
REEMISH
REENFORCE
REENFORCEMENT
REENLISTMENT
REENTER
REENTERING
REENTRANT
REENTRY

REEPER
REERE
REESE
REESHIE
REESHLE
REESK
REESLE
REEST
REESTER
REESTLE
REESTY
REET
REEVALUATE
REEVALUATED
REEVALUATING
REEVALUATION
REEVE
REEVED
REEVELAND
REEVING
REEVOKE
REEXAMINE
REEXPORT
REF
REFACE
REFAIT
REFATHERED
REFECT
REFECTION
REFECTIONARY
REFECTIONER
REFECTIVE
REFECTORER
REFECTORIAL
REFECTORIAN
REFECTORY
REFEL
REFER
REFERABLE
REFEREE
REFEREED
REFEREEING
REFERENCE
REFERENDAL
REFERENDARIES
REFERENDARY
REFERENDUM
REFERENT
REFERENTIAL
REFERENTLY
REFERRABLE
REFERRAL
REFERRED
REFERRER
REFERRIBLE
REFERRING
REFETE
REFFO
REFIGURE
REFILL
REFILTER
REFINAGE
REFINANCE
REFINE
REFINED
REFINEDLY
REFINEDNESS
REFINEMENT
REFINER
REFINERIES
REFINERY
REFINING
REFININGLY
REFINISH
REFIT
REFITMENT
REFITTED
REFITTING
REFLAIR
REFLATE
REFLATED
REFLATING
REFLATION
REFLECT
REFLECTANCE
REFLECTED
REFLECTEDLY
REFLECTENT
REFLECTER
REFLECTING
REFLECTINGLY
REFLECTION
REFLECTIONAL
REFLECTIONING
REFLECTIVE
REFLECTIVELY
REFLECTIVITY
REFLECTOR
REFLET
REFLEX
REFLEXED
REFLEXIBLE
REFLEXIONAL
REFLEXISM
REFLEXIVE
REFLEXIVELY
REFLEXIVITY
REFLEXOLOGY
REFLORESCENT
REFLOURISH
REFLOW
REFLUENCE
REFLUENCY
REFLUENT
REFLUOUS
REFLUX
REFLUXED
REFOCILLATE
REFONT
REFOREST
REFORESTIZE
REFORGE
REFORGER
REFORM
REFORMADO
REFORMANDA
REFORMANDUM
REFORMATION
REFORMATIVE
REFORMATORY
REFORMED
REFORMER
REFORMING
REFORMISM
REFORMIST
REFORMISTIC
REFOUND
REFOUNDER
REFRACT
REFRACTED
REFRACTEDLY
REFRACTILE
REFRACTILITY
REFRACTING
REFRACTION
REFRACTIONAL
REFRACTIVE
REFRACTIVELY
REFRACTIVITY
REFRACTOR
REFRACTORIES
REFRACTORILY
REFRACTORY
REFRACTURE
REFRAGABLE
REFRAIN
REFRAINER
REFRAINMENT
REFRANGENT
REFRANGIBLE
REFREID
REFREIT
REFRENATION
REFRESCO
REFRESH
REFRESHANT
REFRESHED
REFRESHER
REFRESHFUL
REFRESHFULLY
REFRESHING
REFRESHINGLY
REFRESHMENT
REFRIGERANT
REFRIGERATE
REFRIGERATED
REFRIGERATION
REFRIGERATOR
REFRINGE
REFRINGENCE
REFRINGENCY
REFRINGENT
REFROID
REFT
REFUEL
REFUELED
REFUELING
REFUELLED
REFUELLING
REFUGE
REFUGED
REFUGEE
REFUGEEISM
REFUGING
REFULGE
REFULGENCE
REFULGENCY
REFULGENT
REFULGENTLY
REFULGENTNESS
REFUND
REFUNDED
REFUNDER
REFUNDING
REFURBISH
REFURBISHMENT
REFUSABLE
REFUSAL
REFUSE
REFUSED
REFUSER
REFUSING
REFUSION
REFUSIVE
REFUTABILITY
REFUTABLE
REFUTABLY
REFUTAL
REFUTATION
REFUTATIVE
REFUTATORY
REFUTE
REFUTED
REFUTER
REFUTING
REG
REGAIN
REGAINER
REGAL
REGALADO
REGALD
REGALE
REGALED
REGALEMENT
REGALER
REGALIA
REGALIAN
REGALING
REGALIO
REGALISM
REGALIST
REGALITIES
REGALITY
REGALIZE
REGALLY
REGALO
REGARD
REGARDANCE
REGARDANCY
REGARDANT
REGARDED
REGARDER
REGARDFUL
REGARDFULLY
REGARDING
REGARDLESS
REGARDLESSLY
REGATTA
REGELATE
REGELATED
REGELATING
REGELATION
REGENCE
REGENCIES
REGENCY
REGENERABLE
REGENERACY
REGENERANCE
REGENERANT
REGENERATE
REGENERATED
REGENERATING
REGENERATION
REGENERATIVE
REGENERATOR
REGENESIS
REGENT
REGENTAL
REGES
REGEST
REGIA
REGIAN
REGICIDAL
REGICIDE
REGICIDISM
REGIDOR
REGIE
REGIFUGE
REGIME
REGIMEN
REGIMENAL
REGIMENT
REGIMENTAL
REGIMENTALED
REGIMENTALLED
REGIMENTALS
REGIMENTARY
REGIMENTATION
REGIMENTED
REGIMENTING
REGIMINAL
REGIN
REGINA
REGINAL
REGION
REGIONAL
REGIONALISM
REGIONALIST
REGIONALISTIC
REGIONALIZE
REGIONALLY
REGIONARY
REGIONED
REGIONS
REGISSEUR
REGISTER
REGISTERED
REGISTERER
REGISTERING
REGISTRABILITY
REGISTRABLE
REGISTRAL
REGISTRANT
REGISTRAR
REGISTRARSHIP
REGISTRARY
REGISTRATE
REGISTRATION
REGISTRATOR
REGISTRER
REGISTRY
REGITIVE
REGIUS
REGLE
REGLEMENTARY
REGLEMENTIST
REGLET
REGLOW
REGMA
REGMACARP
REGMATA
REGNAL
REGNANCY
REGNANT
REGNUM
REGOLITH
REGORGE
REGORGED
REGORGING
REGOSOL
REGRACY
REGRADATION
REGRADE
REGRADED
REGRADING
REGRANT
REGRASS
REGRATE
REGRATED
REGRATER
REGRATING
REGREDE
REGREET
REGRESS
REGRESSED
REGRESSING
REGRESSION
REGRESSIVE
REGRESSIVELY
REGRESSIVITY
REGRESSOR
REGRET
REGRETFUL
REGRETFULLY
REGRETTABLE
REGRETTABLY
REGRETTED
REGRETTER
REGRETTING
REGULA
REGULABLE
REGULAR
REGULARISE
REGULARITIES
REGULARITY

REGULARIZATION
REGULARIZE
REGULARIZED
REGULARIZER
REGULARLY
REGULARNESS
REGULATE
REGULATED
REGULATES
REGULATING
REGULATION
REGULATIVE
REGULATOR
REGULATORY
REGULI
REGULINE
REGULIZE
REGULUS
REGUR
REGURGITANT
REGURGITATE
REGURGITATED
REH
REHABILITATE
REHABILITATION
REHAIR
REHANDLING
REHARMONIZE
REHASH
REHAYTE
REHBOC
REHEARD
REHEARING
REHEARSAL
REHEARSE
REHEARSED
REHEARSER
REHEARSING
REHEAT
REHEATED
REHEATER
REHETE
REHOUSE
REI
REICHSGULDEN
REICHSMARK
REICHSPFENNIG
REICHSTALER
REIF
REIFICATION
REIFIED
REIFIER
REIFY
REIFYING
REIGN
REIGNED
REIGNER
REIGNING
REIK
REIMBURSABLE
REIMBURSE
REIMBURSED
REIMBURSEMENT
REIMBURSER
REIMBURSING
REIMBUSH
REIMBUSHMENT
REIMKENNAR
REIMMIGRANT
REIMPEL
REIMPLANT
REIMPORT
REIMPOSE
REIMPOSITION
REIMPOSURE
REIMPRESSION
REIN
REINA
REINCARNATE
REINCARNATED
REINCENSE
REINCIDENCE
REINCIDENCY
REINCRUDATE
REINDEER
REINDICTMENT
REINETTE
REINFECT
REINFECTION
REINFECTIOUS
REINFORCE
REINFORCED
REINFORCEMENT
REINFORCER
REINLESS
REINS
REINSMAN
REINSTALL
REINSTALMENT
REINSTATE
REINSTATED
REINSTATING
REINSTATION
REINSTATOR
REINSURANCE
REINSURE
REINSURED
REINSURER
REINSURING
REINTEGRATE
REINTHRONE
REINVERSION
REINVEST
REINVESTMENT
REINVIGORATE
REIS
REISE
REISSUE
REISSUING
REISTER
REIT
REITBOK
REITER
REITERABLE
REITERANCE
REITERANT
REITERATE
REITERATED
REITERATING
REITERATION
REITERATIVE
REIVE
REIVER
REJA
REJECT
REJECTAGE
REJECTAMENTA
REJECTED
REJECTER
REJECTING
REJECTION
REJECTIVE
REJECTOR
REJOICE
REJOICED
REJOICEFUL
REJOICEMENT
REJOICER
REJOICING
REJOIN
REJOINDER
REJOINED
REJOINING
REJOLT
REJON
REJONEADOR
REJONEO
REJOUNCE
REJOURN
REJUDGE
REJUNCTION
REJUVENANT
REJUVENATE
REJUVENATED
REJUVENATING
REJUVENATION
REJUVENATIVE
REJUVENATOR
REJUVENESCE
REJUVENIZE
REKE
REKHTI
REKINDLE
REKINDLER
REL
RELACHE
RELAIS
RELAPSE
RELAPSED
RELAPSER
RELAPSING
RELAST
RELASTER
RELATA
RELATABILITY
RELATABLE
RELATE
RELATED
RELATEDNESS
RELATER
RELATING
RELATION
RELATIONAL
RELATIONALLY
RELATIONARY
RELATIONISM
RELATIONIST
RELATIONS
RELATIONSHIP
RELATIONSHIPS
RELATIVAL
RELATIVE
RELATIVELY
RELATIVENESS
RELATIVES
RELATIVISM
RELATIVIST
RELATIVISTIC
RELATIVITY
RELATOR
RELATRIX
RELATUM
RELAX
RELAXABLE
RELAXANT
RELAXATION
RELAXATIVE
RELAXATORY
RELAXED
RELAXEDLY
RELAXEDNESS
RELAXER
RELAXIN
RELAXING
RELAY
RELAYER
RELAYMAN
RELBUN
RELEARN
RELEASE
RELEASED
RELEASEE
RELEASEMENT
RELEASER
RELEASING
RELEASOR
RELECTION
RELEGABLE
RELEGATE
RELEGATED
RELEGATING
RELEGATION
RELENT
RELENTED
RELENTING
RELENTINGLY
RELENTLESS
RELENTLESSLY
RELENTMENT
RELES
RELESSEE
RELESSOR
RELEVANCE
RELEVANCY
RELEVANT
RELEVANTLY
RELEVATE
RELEVATION
RELEVATOR
RELEVE
RELIABILITY
RELIABLE
RELIABLENESS
RELIABLY
RELIANCE
RELIANT
RELIANTLY
RELIC
RELICARY
RELICMONGER
RELICS
RELICT
RELICTED
RELICTION
RELIDE
RELIED
RELIEF
RELIER
RELIEVABLE
RELIEVE
RELIEVED
RELIEVEDLY
RELIEVER
RELIEVING
RELIEVINGLY
RELIEVO
RELIGATE
RELIGATION
RELIGIEUSE
RELIGIEUSES
RELIGIO
RELIGION
RELIGIONARY
RELIGIONATE
RELIGIONER
RELIGIONISM
RELIGIONIST
RELIGIONIZE
RELIGIOSE
RELIGIOSITY
RELIGIOSO
RELIGIOUS
RELIGIOUSLY
RELINQUENT
RELINQUISH
RELINQUISHED
RELINQUISHER
RELIQUAIRE
RELIQUARIES
RELIQUARY
RELIQUE
RELIQUIAE
RELIQUIAN
RELIQUISM
RELISH
RELISHABLE
RELISHED
RELISHER
RELISHING
RELISHINGLY
RELISHY
RELIVE
RELIVED
RELIVING
RELOCABLE
RELOCATE
RELOCATION
RELOCATOR
RELONG
RELUCE
RELUCENT
RELUCT
RELUCTANCE
RELUCTANCY
RELUCTANT
RELUCTANTLY
RELUCTATE
RELUCTATION
RELUCTIVITY
RELUME
RELUMED
RELUMINE
RELUMING
RELY
RELYING
REM
REMAIN
REMAINDER
REMAINDERMAN
REMAINDERMEN
REMAINED
REMAINER
REMAINING
REMAINS
REMAN
REMANATION
REMANCIPATE
REMAND
REMANDMENT
REMANENCE
REMANENCY
REMANENT
REMANET
REMANIE
REMANNED
REMANNING
REMARGIN
REMARK
REMARKABILITY
REMARKABLE
REMARKABLENESS
REMARKABLY
REMARKED
REMARKER
REMARKING
REMARQUE
REMARRIAGE
REMARRIED
REMARRY
REMARRYING
REMATCH
REMBLAI
REMBLE
REMBLERE
REME

REMEANT
REMEDE
REMEDIABLE
REMEDIABLENESS
REMEDIABLY
REMEDIAL
REMEDIALLY
REMEDIATION
REMEDIED
REMEDIES
REMEDILESS
REMEDILESSLY
REMEDILESSNESS
REMEDY
REMEDYING
REMEMBER
REMEMBERABLE
REMEMBERED
REMEMBERER
REMEMBERING
REMEMBRANCE
REMEMBRANCER
REMEMORATE
REMEMORATION
REMEMORATIVE
REMENE
REMERCY
REMEX
REMICLE
REMIGATE
REMIGES
REMIGIAL
REMIGRANT
REMIGRATE
REMIGRATION
REMIND
REMINDAL
REMINDER
REMINDFUL
REMINISCE
REMINISCED
REMINISCENCE
REMINISCENT
REMINISCENTLY
REMINISCING
REMIPED
REMISE
REMISED
REMISING
REMISS
REMISSFUL
REMISSIBLE
REMISSION
REMISSIVE
REMISSIVELY
REMISSNESS
REMISSORY
REMIT
REMITMENT
REMITTABLE
REMITTAL
REMITTANCE
REMITTANCER
REMITTED
REMITTEE
REMITTENCE
REMITTENCY
REMITTENT
REMITTENTLY
REMITTER
REMITTING
REMITTITUR
REMITTOR
REMNANT
REMNANTAL
REMNANTS
REMODEL
REMODELED
REMODELER
REMODELING
REMODELLED
REMODELLER
REMODELLING
REMODELMENT
REMOLADE
REMONETIZATION
REMONETIZE
REMONSTRANCE
REMONSTRANT
REMONSTRATE
REMONSTRATED
REMONSTRATING
REMONSTRATOR
REMONTADO
REMONTANT
REMONTOIR
REMORA
REMORD
REMORE
REMORSE
REMORSEFUL
REMORSEFULLY
REMORSEFULNESS
REMORSELESS
REMOTE
REMOTELY
REMOTENESS
REMOTER
REMOTEST
REMOTION
REMOTIVE
REMOULADE
REMOUNT
REMOVABILITY
REMOVABLE
REMOVABLY
REMOVAL
REMOVE
REMOVED
REMOVEDLY
REMOVEDNESS
REMOVELESS
REMOVEMENT
REMOVER
REMOVES
REMOVING
REMUABLE
REMUDA
REMUE
REMUNERABLE
REMUNERABLY
REMUNERATE
REMUNERATED
REMUNERATING
REMUNERATION
REMUNERATIVE
REMUNERATOR
REMUNERATORY
REMURMUR
REMUTATION
RENA
RENABLE
RENABLY
RENAIL
RENAISSANCE
RENAL
RENAME
RENASCENCE
RENASCENCY
RENASCENT
RENASCIBLE
RENATURE
RENAY
RENCH
RENCONTRE
RENCOUNTER
RENCOUNTERED
RENCOUNTERING
REND
RENDEMENT
RENDER
RENDERABLE
RENDERED
RENDERER
RENDERING
RENDERSET
RENDEZVOUS
RENDING
RENDITION
RENDLEWOOD
RENDOUN
RENDROCK
RENDU
RENDZINA
RENEGADE
RENEGADO
RENEGATION
RENEGE
RENEGED
RENEGER
RENEGING
RENERVE
RENES
RENETTE
RENEW
RENEWABLE
RENEWAL
RENEWED
RENEWING
RENEWMENT
RENGE
RENGUE
RENGUERA
RENICULUS
RENIFORM
RENIG
RENIN
RENIPORTAL
RENISH
RENISHLY
RENITENCE
RENITENCY
RENITENT
RENK
RENKY
RENNE
RENNER
RENNET
RENNIN
RENNINOGEN
RENOGASTRIC
RENOGRAPHY
RENOMEE
RENOMINATE
RENOMME
RENOMMEE
RENONE
RENOUNCE
RENOUNCED
RENOUNCEMENT
RENOUNCER
RENOUNCING
RENOVATE
RENOVATED
RENOVATER
RENOVATING
RENOVATION
RENOVATIVE
RENOVATOR
RENOVATORY
RENOVE
RENOVIZE
RENOWN
RENOWNED
RENOWNEDLY
RENOWNEDNESS
RENOWNER
RENOWNFUL
RENSH
RENT
RENTABLE
RENTAGE
RENTAL
RENTE
RENTED
RENTEE
RENTER
RENTIER
RENTING
RENTLESS
RENTRANT
RENTREE
RENUMERATE
RENUMERATION
RENUNCIABLE
RENUNCIANCE
RENUNCIANT
RENUNCIATE
RENUNCIATION
RENUNCIATIVE
RENUNCIATOR
RENUNCIATORY
RENVERSE
RENVERSEMENT
RENVOI
RENVOY
REOCCUPY
REOCCUR
REOIL
REOMETER
REOPEN
REOPHORE
REORDER
REORDINATION
REORGANISE
REORGANIZATION
REORGANIZE
REORGANIZED
REORGANIZER
REORGANIZING
REORIENT
REP
REPACE
REPAID
REPAINT
REPAIR
REPAIRABLE
REPAIRED
REPAIRER
REPAIRING
REPAIRMAN
REPAIRMEN
REPAIRS
REPAND
REPANDLY
REPANDOUS
REPARABILITY
REPARABLE
REPARABLY
REPARATE
REPARATION
REPARATIVE
REPARATORY
REPAREL
REPART
REPARTABLE
REPARTEE
REPARTITION
REPASS
REPASSAGE
REPASSER
REPAST
REPASTURE
REPATENCY
REPATRIATE
REPATRIATED
REPATRIATING
REPATRIATION
REPAY
REPAYABLE
REPAYAL
REPAYING
REPAYMENT
REPEAL
REPEALABLE
REPEALED
REPEALER
REPEALING
REPEALIST
REPEAT
REPEATABLE
REPEATAL
REPEATED
REPEATEDLY
REPEATER
REPEATING
REPEL
REPELLED
REPELLENCE
REPELLENCY
REPELLENT
REPELLER
REPELLING
REPENT
REPENTANCE
REPENTANT
REPENTANTLY
REPENTED
REPENTER
REPENTING
REPEOPLE
REPERCEPT
REPERCUSS
REPERCUSSION
REPERCUSSIVE
REPERCUSSOR
REPERCUTIENT
REPERIBLE
REPERTOIRE
REPERTORIAL
REPERTORILY
REPERTORIUM
REPERTORY
REPETEND
REPETITION
REPETITIONAL
REPETITIOUS
REPETITIOUSLY
REPETITIVE
REPETITIVELY
REPETITORY
REPHRASE
REPHRASED
REPHRASING
REPINE
REPINED
REPINEMENT
REPINER
REPINING
REPIQUE
REPIQUED
REPIQUING
REPKIE
REPLACE
REPLACEABLE

REPLACED
REPLACEMENT
REPLACER
REPLACING
REPLANT
REPLANTATION
REPLANTER
REPLEADER
REPLEDGE
REPLEDGER
REPLENISH
REPLENISHED
REPLENISHER
REPLENISHING
REPLETE
REPLETION
REPLETIVE
REPLETIVELY
REPLETORY
REPLEVIABLE
REPLEVIED
REPLEVIN
REPLEVISABLE
REPLEVISOR
REPLEVY
REPLEVYING
REPLIAL
REPLIANT
REPLICA
REPLICATE
REPLICATED
REPLICATILE
REPLICATION
REPLICATIVE
REPLICATIVELY
REPLICATORY
REPLIED
REPLIER
REPLIES
REPLIQUE
REPLOT
REPLOTMENT
REPLOTTER
REPLUM
REPLUME
REPLY
REPLYING
REPOLON
REPONE
REPOPE
REPORT
REPORTABLE
REPORTAGE
REPORTED
REPORTEDLY
REPORTER
REPORTING
REPORTINGLY
REPORTORIAL
REPORTORIALLY
REPORTS
REPOSAL
REPOSE
REPOSED
REPOSEDLY
REPOSEDNESS
REPOSEFUL
REPOSEFULLY
REPOSER
REPOSING
REPOSIT
REPOSITION
REPOSITOR
REPOSITORY
REPOSOIR
REPOSSESS
REPOSSESSION
REPOSSESSOR
REPOST
REPOSTPONE
REPOSURE
REPOUSSAGE
REPOUSSE
REPP
REPPED
REPREHEND
REPREHENDED
REPREHENDER
REPREHENDING
REPREHENSIBLE
REPREHENSION
REPREHENSORY
REPRESENT
REPRESENTAMEN
REPRESENTANT
REPRESENTATION
REPRESENTATIVE
REPRESENTED
REPRESENTER
REPRESENTING
REPRESENTMENT
REPRESENTS
REPRESS
REPRESSED
REPRESSEDLY
REPRESSER
REPRESSIBLE
REPRESSIBLY
REPRESSING
REPRESSION
REPRESSIVE
REPRESSIVELY
REPRESSOR
REPRESSORY
REPRESSURE
REPRIEVABLE
REPRIEVAL
REPRIEVE
REPRIEVED
REPRIEVER
REPRIEVING
REPRIMAND
REPRIMANDED
REPRIMANDER
REPRIMANDING
REPRIME
REPRIMER
REPRINT
REPRINTER
REPRISAL
REPRISE
REPRISTINATE
REPROACH
REPROACHABLE
REPROACHABLY
REPROACHED
REPROACHER
REPROACHES
REPROACHFUL
REPROACHING
REPROBACY
REPROBANCE
REPROBATE
REPROBATED
REPROBATER
REPROBATING
REPROBATION
REPROBATIVE
REPROBATOR
REPROBATORY
REPRODUCE
REPRODUCEABLE
REPRODUCED
REPRODUCER
REPRODUCIBLE
REPRODUCING
REPRODUCTION
REPRODUCTIVE
REPRODUCTORY
REPROFFER
REPROOF
REPROVABLE
REPROVABLY
REPROVAL
REPROVE
REPROVED
REPROVER
REPROVING
REPROVINGLY
REPRY
REPTANT
REPTATION
REPTATORIAL
REPTATORY
REPTILE
REPTILIAN
REPTILIARY
REPTILIOUS
REPTILISM
REPTILITY
REPTILOID
REPUBLIC
REPUBLICAL
REPUBLICAN
REPUBLISH
REPUBLISHER
REPUDIABLE
REPUDIATE
REPUDIATED
REPUDIATING
REPUDIATION
REPUDIATIVE
REPUDIATOR
REPUDIATORY
REPUGN
REPUGNABLE
REPUGNANCE
REPUGNANCY
REPUGNANT
REPUGNATE
REPUGNER
REPULLULATE
REPULPIT
REPULSE
REPULSED
REPULSELESS
REPULSER
REPULSING
REPULSION
REPULSIVE
REPULSIVELY
REPULSORY
REPURCHASE
REPURCHASER
REPUTABILITY
REPUTABLE
REPUTABLY
REPUTATION
REPUTATIVE
REPUTATIVELY
REPUTE
REPUTED
REPUTEDLY
REPUTELESS
REPUTING
REQUEEN
REQUEST
REQUESTER
REQUIEM
REQUIESCAT
REQUIESCENCE
REQUIN
REQUINS
REQUIRABLE
REQUIRE
REQUIRED
REQUIREMENT
REQUIRER
REQUIRING
REQUISITE
REQUISITELY
REQUISITION
REQUISITOR
REQUISITORY
REQUITABLE
REQUITAL
REQUITATIVE
REQUITE
REQUITED
REQUITELESS
REQUITEMENT
REQUITER
REQUITING
RERADIATION
RERAILER
RERD
RERDE
REREAD
REREBRACE
RERECORD
REREDOS
REREE
REREFIEF
REREMOUSE
RERESUPPER
REROLL
RERUN
RERUNNING
RES
RESACA
RESAI
RESAIL
RESAK
RESALABLE
RESALE
RESAW
RESAWER
RESAWYER
RESAY
RESCIND
RESCINDABLE
RESCINDED
RESCINDER
RESCINDING
RESCISSIBLE
RESCISSION
RESCISSORY
RESCORE
RESCRIBE
RESCRIPT
RESCRIPTION
RESCRIPTIVE
RESCUABLE
RESCUE
RESCUED
RESCUER
RESCUING
RESE
RESEAL
RESEARCH
RESEARCHER
RESEARCHFUL
RESEARCHIST
RESEAT
RESEAU
RESEAUX
RESECATE
RESECT
RESECTION
RESECTIONAL
RESEDA
RESEDACEOUS
RESEISER
RESEIZE
RESEIZER
RESEIZURE
RESELL
RESELLING
RESEMBLANCE
RESEMBLANT
RESEMBLE
RESEMBLED
RESEMBLER
RESEMBLING
RESEMINATE
RESEND
RESENDING
RESENE
RESENT
RESENTED
RESENTER
RESENTFUL
RESENTFULLY
RESENTIENCE
RESENTING
RESENTIVE
RESENTLESS
RESENTMENT
RESERATE
RESERPINE
RESERVABLE
RESERVAL
RESERVATION
RESERVATIVE
RESERVATORY
RESERVE
RESERVED
RESERVEDLY
RESERVEDNESS
RESERVEE
RESERVER
RESERVERY
RESERVING
RESERVIST
RESERVOIR
RESERVOIRED
RESET
RESETTER
RESETTING
RESGAT
RESH
RESHIP
RESHIPMENT
RESHIPPED
RESHIPPER
RESHIPPING
RESIANCE
RESIANCY
RESIANT
RESICCATE
RESIDE
RESIDENCE
RESIDENCER
RESIDENCIA
RESIDENCIES
RESIDENCY
RESIDENT
RESIDENTAL
RESIDENTER
RESIDENTIAL
RESIDENTIARY
RESIDER
RESIDING
RESIDUA
RESIDUAL

RESIDUARY
RESIDUATION
RESIDUE
RESIDUENT
RESIDUOUS
RESIDUUM
RESIGN
RESIGNATARY
RESIGNATION
RESIGNED
RESIGNEDLY
RESIGNEDNESS
RESIGNEE
RESIGNER
RESIGNFUL
RESIGNMENT
RESILE
RESILED
RESILEMENT
RESILIA
RESILIAL
RESILIATE
RESILIENCE
RESILIENCY
RESILIENT
RESILIENTLY
RESILIFER
RESILING
RESILIOMETER
RESILITION
RESILIUM
RESILVER
RESIN
RESINA
RESINACEOUS
RESINATE
RESINATED
RESINATING
RESINBUSH
RESINER
RESINIC
RESINIFEROUS
RESINIFLUOUS
RESINIFORM
RESINIFY
RESINIZE
RESINOGENOUS
RESINOID
RESINOL
RESINOPHORE
RESINOSIS
RESINOUS
RESINOUSLY
RESINOUSNESS
RESINY
RESIPISCENCE
RESIPISCENT
RESIST
RESISTABLE
RESISTANCE
RESISTANT
RESISTED
RESISTER
RESISTFUL
RESISTIBLE
RESISTIBLY
RESISTING
RESISTINGLY
RESISTIVE
RESISTIVELY
RESISTIVITY
RESISTLESS
RESISTLESSLY
RESISTOR
RESITTING
RESIZE
RESIZED
RESIZER
RESIZING
RESKEW
RESNATRON
RESOJET
RESOLE
RESOLED
RESOLING
RESOLUBILITY
RESOLUBLE
RESOLUTE
RESOLUTELY
RESOLUTENESS
RESOLUTION
RESOLUTIONER
RESOLUTIVE
RESOLUTORY
RESOLVABLE
RESOLVANCY
RESOLVE
RESOLVED
RESOLVEDLY
RESOLVEDNESS
RESOLVENT
RESOLVER
RESOLVIBLE
RESOLVING
RESON
RESONANCE
RESONANCIES
RESONANCY
RESONANT
RESONANTLY
RESONATE
RESONATED
RESONATING
RESONATOR
RESONATORY
RESORB
RESORBENCE
RESORBENT
RESORCIN
RESORCINAL
RESORCINISM
RESORCINOL
RESORCINUM
RESORCYLIC
RESORPTION
RESORPTIVE
RESORT
RESORTED
RESORTER
RESORUFIN
RESOUND
RESOUNDER
RESOUNDING
RESOURCE
RESOURCEFUL
RESOURCEFULLY
RESOURCEFULNESS
RESOURCES
RESOWN
RESP
RESPASSE
RESPEAK
RESPECT
RESPECTABILITY
RESPECTABLE
RESPECTABLY
RESPECTANT
RESPECTED
RESPECTER
RESPECTFUL
RESPECTFULLY
RESPECTING
RESPECTIVE
RESPECTIVELY
RESPECTLESS
RESPECTUOUS
RESPELL
RESPERSIVE
RESPIRABLE
RESPIRATION
RESPIRATIVE
RESPIRATOR
RESPIRATORY
RESPIRE
RESPIRED
RESPIRING
RESPIRIT
RESPIROMETER
RESPITE
RESPITED
RESPITING
RESPLEND
RESPLENDENCE
RESPLENDENCY
RESPLENDENT
RESPOND
RESPONDE
RESPONDENCE
RESPONDENCY
RESPONDENT
RESPONDENTIA
RESPONDER
RESPONSABLE
RESPONSAL
RESPONSARY
RESPONSE
RESPONSER
RESPONSIBILITY
RESPONSIBLE
RESPONSIBLY
RESPONSION
RESPONSIVE
RESPONSIVELY
RESPONSIVENESS
RESPONSIVITY
RESPONSORIAL
RESPONSORY
RESPUE
RESSAIDAR
RESSALA
RESSAUT
RESSORT
REST
RESTANT
RESTATE
RESTATEMENT
RESTAUR
RESTAURANT
RESTAURATE
RESTAURATEUR
RESTAURATION
RESTBALK
RESTED
RESTER
RESTERILIZE
RESTES
RESTFUL
RESTFULLY
RESTFULNESS
RESTHARROW
RESTHOUSE
RESTIAD
RESTIFORM
RESTING
RESTIS
RESTITUE
RESTITUTE
RESTITUTION
RESTITUTIVE
RESTITUTOR
RESTITUTORY
RESTIVE
RESTIVELY
RESTIVENESS
RESTLESS
RESTLESSLY
RESTLESSNESS
RESTOCK
RESTORAL
RESTORATION
RESTORATIVE
RESTORATOR
RESTORATORY
RESTORE
RESTORED
RESTORER
RESTORING
RESTRAIN
RESTRAINABLE
RESTRAINED
RESTRAINEDLY
RESTRAINER
RESTRAINING
RESTRAINT
RESTRESS
RESTRICT
RESTRICTED
RESTRICTING
RESTRICTION
RESTRICTIVE
RESTRICTIVELY
RESTRIKE
RESTRINGE
RESTRINGENCY
RESTRINGENT
RESTY
RESTYLE
RESUDATION
RESUE
RESUING
RESULT
RESULTANCE
RESULTANCY
RESULTANT
RESULTATIVE
RESULTED
RESULTING
RESULTIVE
RESUMABLE
RESUME
RESUMED
RESUMEING
RESUMER
RESUMING
RESUMMON
RESUMMONS
RESUMPTION
RESUMPTIVE
RESUMPTIVELY
RESUPINATE
RESUPINATED
RESUPINATION
RESUPINE
RESURFACE
RESURFACED
RESURFACING
RESURGAM
RESURGE
RESURGED
RESURGENCE
RESURGENCY
RESURGENT
RESURGING
RESURRECT
RESURRECTION
RESURRECTIVE
RESURRECTOR
RESURVEY
RESUSCITABLE
RESUSCITANT
RESUSCITATE
RESUSCITATED
RESUSCITATION
RESUSCITATOR
RESYNTHESIS
RET
RETABLE
RETABLO
RETAIL
RETAILER
RETAIN
RETAINABLE
RETAINAL
RETAINED
RETAINER
RETAINING
RETAKE
RETAKEN
RETAKER
RETAKING
RETALIATE
RETALIATED
RETALIATING
RETALIATION
RETALIATIVE
RETALIATOR
RETALIATORY
RETAMA
RETAN
RETARD
RETARDANCE
RETARDANT
RETARDATE
RETARDATION
RETARDATIVE
RETARDED
RETARDER
RETARDING
RETARDIVE
RETARDMENT
RETARDURE
RETCH
RETE
RETECIOUS
RETELL
RETELLING
RETEM
RETENE
RETENT
RETENTION
RETENTIVE
RETENTIVELY
RETENTIVITIES
RETENTIVITY
RETENTOR
RETENUE
RETEPORE
RETEXTURE
RETHE
RETHENESS
RETHER
RETIA
RETIARIAN
RETIARII
RETIARIUS
RETIARY
RETICELLA
RETICENCE
RETICENCIES
RETICENCY
RETICENT
RETICENTLY
RETICLE
RETICULA
RETICULAR

RETICULARIAN
RETICULARY
RETICULATE
RETICULATED
RETICULATING
RETICULATION
RETICULE
RETICULED
RETICULIN
RETICULITIS
RETICULOCYTE
RETICULOSE
RETICULUM
RETIFORM
RETINA
RETINACULA
RETINACULAR
RETINACULATE
RETINACULUM
RETINAL
RETINASPHALT
RETINENE
RETINERVED
RETINIAN
RETINISPORA
RETINITE
RETINITIS
RETINIZE
RETINOID
RETINOL
RETINOPHORAL
RETINOPHORE
RETINOSCOPE
RETINOSCOPIC
RETINOSCOPIST
RETINOSCOPY
RETINUE
RETINULA
RETINULAE
RETINULE
RETIP
RETIRACIED
RETIRACY
RETIRADE
RETIRAL
RETIRE
RETIRED
RETIREMENT
RETIRING
RETIRINGLY
RETIRINGNESS
RETOLD
RETOLERATE
RETOLERATION
RETOMB
RETONATION
RETOOK
RETORSION
RETORT
RETORTED
RETORTER
RETORTING
RETORTION
RETORTIVE
RETORTS
RETOUCH
RETOUCHER
RETOUCHING
RETOUCHMENT
RETOUR
RETRACE
RETRACEABLE
RETRACED
RETRACEMENT
RETRACT
RETRACTABLE
RETRACTATION
RETRACTED
RETRACTIBLE
RETRACTILE
RETRACTILITY
RETRACTING
RETRACTION
RETRACTIVE
RETRACTIVELY
RETRACTOR
RETRAD
RETRADITION
RETRAHENT
RETRAIT
RETRAL
RETRALLY
RETRAXIT
RETREAD
RETREADED
RETREADING
RETREAT
RETREATED
RETREATER
RETREATFUL
RETREATING
RETREATIVE
RETREATMENT
RETREE
RETRENCH
RETRENCHED
RETRENCHER
RETRENCHING
RETRENCHMENT
RETRIAL
RETRIBUTE
RETRIBUTION
RETRIBUTIVE
RETRIBUTOR
RETRIBUTORY
RETRICKED
RETRIED
RETRIEVABLE
RETRIEVABLY
RETRIEVAL
RETRIEVE
RETRIEVED
RETRIEVELESS
RETRIEVEMENT
RETRIEVER
RETRIEVING
RETRIM
RETRIMMER
RETROACT
RETROACTION
RETROACTIVE
RETROBUCCAL
RETROBULBAR
RETROCAECAL
RETROCEDE
RETROCEDENCE
RETROCEDENT
RETROCESSION
RETROCESSIVE
RETROCHOIR
RETROCLUSION
RETROCOLIC
RETROCOSTAL
RETROCURVED
RETRODATE
RETRODUCTION
RETRODURAL
RETROFIRE
RETROFLECTED
RETROFLEX
RETROFLEXED
RETROFLEXION
RETROFRACT
RETROFRACTED
RETROFRONTAL
RETROGASTRIC
RETROGRADE
RETROGRADED
RETROGRADELY
RETROGRADING
RETROGRADISM
RETROGRADIST
RETROGRESS
RETROGRESSION
RETROHEPATIC
RETROINSULAR
RETROIRIDIAN
RETROJECT
RETROJECTION
RETROJUGULAR
RETROLENTAL
RETROLINGUAL
RETROMINGENT
RETRONASAL
RETROPOSED
RETROPUBIC
RETROPULSION
RETROPULSIVE
RETRORECTAL
RETRORENAL
RETROROCKET
RETRORSE
RETRORSELY
RETROSERRATE
RETROSPECT
RETROSPLENIC
RETROSTALSIS
RETROSTALTIC
RETROSTERNAL
RETROTARSAL
RETROTHYROID
RETROUSSAGE
RETROUSSE
RETROVACCINE
RETROVERSE
RETROVERSION
RETROVERT
RETROXIPHOID
RETRUDE
RETRUSIBLE
RETRUSION
RETRY
RETRYING
RETTE
RETTED
RETTER
RETTERIES
RETTERY
RETTI
RETTING
RETTORY
RETUND
RETUNDED
RETUNDING
RETURN
RETURNABLE
RETURNED
RETURNER
RETURNING
RETURNLESS
RETURNLESSLY
RETURNS
RETUSE
RETZIAN
REUNE
REUNIFY
REUNION
REUNIONISM
REUNIONIST
REUNIONISTIC
REUNITE
REUNITED
REUNITER
REUNITING
REUNITION
REUNITIVE
REUS
REUT
REUTE
REV
REVACCINATE
REVALENTA
REVALESCENCE
REVALESCENT
REVALIDATE
REVALIDATION
REVALORIZE
REVALUATE
REVALUATED
REVALUATING
REVALUATION
REVALUE
REVALUED
REVALUING
REVAMP
REVAMPER
REVAMPMENT
REVANCHE
REVANCHISM
REVANCHIST
REVAY
REVE
REVEAL
REVEALABLE
REVEALED
REVEALER
REVEALING
REVEALMENT
REVEILLE
REVEL
REVELABILITY
REVELANT
REVELATION
REVELATIONAL
REVELATIONER
REVELATIVE
REVELATOR
REVELATORY
REVELED
REVELER
REVELING
REVELLED
REVELLENT
REVELLER
REVELLER
REVELLING
REVELLY
REVELMENT
REVELOUS
REVELROUS
REVELROUT
REVELRY
REVELS
REVENANT
REVENDICATE
REVENEER
REVENGE
REVENGEABLE
REVENGED
REVENGEFUL
REVENGEFULLY
REVENGEMENT
REVENGER
REVENGING
REVENUAL
REVENUE
REVENUED
REVENUER
REVENUES
REVERB
REVERBATORY
REVERBERANT
REVERBERATE
REVERBERATING
REVERBERATION
REVERBERATIONS
REVERBERATIVE
REVERBERATOR
REVERBRATE
REVERDI
REVERDURE
REVERE
REVERED
REVEREE
REVERENCE
REVERENCED
REVERENCER
REVERENCING
REVEREND
REVERENDLY
REVERENT
REVERENTIAL
REVERENTLY
REVERER
REVERIE
REVERIES
REVERIFY
REVERING
REVERIST
REVERS
REVERSAL
REVERSE
REVERSED
REVERSEDLY
REVERSEFUL
REVERSELESS
REVERSELY
REVERSEMENT
REVERSER
REVERSI
REVERSIBLE
REVERSIBLY
REVERSING
REVERSINGLY
REVERSION
REVERSIONABLE
REVERSIONAL
REVERSIONARY
REVERSIONER
REVERSIONIST
REVERSIST
REVERSIVE
REVERSO
REVERT
REVERTAL
REVERTED
REVERTER
REVERTIBLE
REVERTING
REVERTIVE
REVERTIVELY
REVERY
REVEST
REVESTIARY
REVESTRY
REVET
REVETMENT
REVETTED
REVETTING
REVICTUAL
REVICTUALED
REVICTUALING
REVICTUALLED
REVICTUALLING
REVIE

REVIEW
REVIEWAGE
REVIEWAL
REVIEWED
REVIEWER
REVIEWING
REVIGOR
REVIGORATE
REVIGORATION
REVIGOUR
REVILE
REVILED
REVILEMENT
REVILER
REVILING
REVILING
REVILINGLY
REVINCE
REVINDICATE
REVIRADO
REVIRESCENCE
REVIRESCENT
REVISAL
REVISE
REVISED
REVISER
REVISING
REVISION
REVISIONAL
REVISIONARY
REVISIONISM
REVISIONIST
REVISIT
REVISITANT
REVISITATION
REVITALIZE
REVITALIZED
REVITALIZER
REVITALIZING
REVIVAL
REVIVALISM
REVIVALIST
REVIVALISTIC
REVIVATORY
REVIVE
REVIVED
REVIVEMENT
REVIVER
REVIVIFIED
REVIVIFIER
REVIVIFY
REVIVIFYING
REVIVING
REVIVINGLY
REVIVISCENCE
REVIVISCENCY
REVIVISCENT
REVIVISCIBLE
REVIVOR
REVOCABILITY
REVOCABLE
REVOCABLY
REVOCATE
REVOCATION
REVOCATIVE
REVOCATORY
REVOICE
REVOICED
REVOICING
REVOKABLE
REVOKE
REVOKED
REVOKEMENT
REVOKER
REVOKING
REVOLANT
REVOLT
REVOLTED
REVOLTER
REVOLTING
REVOLTINGLY
REVOLUBILITY
REVOLUBLE
REVOLUBLY
REVOLUTE
REVOLUTION
REVOLUTIONAL
REVOLUTIONARY
REVOLUTIONER
REVOLUTIONIST
REVOLVABLE
REVOLVE
REVOLVED
REVOLVENCY
REVOLVER
REVOLVES
REVOLVING
REVOLVINGLY
REVS
REVUE
REVUETTE
REVUIST
REVULSANT
REVULSE
REVULSED
REVULSION
REVULSIONARY
REVULSIVE
REVULSIVELY
REVVED
REVVING
REW
REWARD
REWARDED
REWARDER
REWARDING
REWARDINGLY
REWCH
REWE
REWED
REWEIGHT
REWET
REWIND
REWINDER
REWIRE
REWIRED
REWIRING
REWME
REWORD
REWORKED
REWRITE
REWRITER
REWRITTEN
REWROTE
REX
REXEN
REXINE
REY
REYE
REYLE
REYOUTH
REYSON
REZAI
REZBANYITE
RH
RHABDITE
RHABDITIFORM
RHABDIUM
RHABDOID
RHABDOLITH
RHABDOM
RHABDOMAL
RHABDOMANCER
RHABDOMANCY
RHABDOMANTIC
RHABDOME
RHABDOMYOMA
RHABDOPHANE
RHABDOPOD
RHABDOS
RHABDOSOME
RHABDOSOPHY
RHABDOSPHERE
RHABDUS
RHACHIS
RHAEBOSIS
RHAGADES
RHAGADIFORM
RHAGIONID
RHAGITE
RHAGON
RHAGONATE
RHAGOSE
RHAMN
RHAMNACEOUS
RHAMNAL
RHAMNETIN
RHAMNINASE
RHAMNINOSE
RHAMNITE
RHAMNITOL
RHAMNOHEXITE
RHAMNOHEXOSE
RHAMNONIC
RHAMNOSE
RHAMNOSIDE
RHAMPHOID
RHAMPHOTHECA
RHAPHE
RHAPONTIC
RHAPONTICIN
RHAPONTIN
RHAPSODE
RHAPSODIC
RHAPSODICAL
RHAPSODIES
RHAPSODISM
RHAPSODIST
RHAPSODISTIC
RHAPSODIZE
RHAPSODIZED
RHAPSODIZING
RHAPSODY
RHASON
RHASOPHORE
RHATANIA
RHATANY
RHATIKON
RHE
RHEA
RHEADINE
RHEBOK
RHEBOSIS
RHEEBOK
RHEEN
RHEGMATYPE
RHEGMATYPY
RHEIM
RHEINBERRY
RHEINGOLD
RHEMA
RHEMATIC
RHEMATOLOGY
RHEME
RHENEA
RHENIUM
RHEOBASE
RHEOCRAT
RHEOLOGIST
RHEOLOGY
RHEOMETER
RHEOMETRIC
RHEOMETRY
RHEOPHILE
RHEOPHORE
RHEOPHORIC
RHEOPLANKTON
RHEOSCOPE
RHEOSCOPIC
RHEOSTAT
RHEOSTATIC
RHEOSTATICS
RHEOTACTIC
RHEOTAN
RHEOTAXIS
RHEOTOME
RHEOTROPE
RHEOTROPIC
RHEOTROPISM
RHESIAN
RHESIS
RHESUS
RHETOR
RHETORIC
RHETORICAL
RHETORICALLY
RHETORICALS
RHETORICIAN
RHETORIZE
RHEUM
RHEUMATALGIA
RHEUMATIC
RHEUMATICAL
RHEUMATICKY
RHEUMATISM
RHEUMATISMAL
RHEUMATIVE
RHEUMATIZ
RHEUMATIZE
RHEUMATOID
RHEUMATOIDAL
RHEUMED
RHEUMIC
RHEUMILY
RHEUMINESS
RHEUMY
RHEXIS
RHIGOLENE
RHIGOSIS
RHIGOTIC
RHINAL
RHINALGIA
RHINARIUM
RHINCOSPASM
RHIND
RHINESTONE
RHINEURYNTER
RHINION
RHINITIS
RHINO
RHINOBYON
RHINOCAUL
RHINOCELE
RHINOCELIAN
RHINOCERINE
RHINOCEROID
RHINOCEROS
RHINOCEROSES
RHINOCEROTIC
RHINOCOELE
RHINOCOELIAN
RHINODYNIA
RHINOGENOUS
RHINOLALIA
RHINOLITH
RHINOLITHIC
RHINOLOGIST
RHINOLOGY
RHINOPHARYNX
RHINOPHORE
RHINOPHYMA
RHINOPLASTIC
RHINOPLASTY
RHINOPOLYPUS
RHINORRHAGIA
RHINORRHEA
RHINORRHEAL
RHINORRHOEA
RHINOS
RHINOSCOPE
RHINOSCOPIC
RHINOSCOPY
RHINOTHECA
RHINOTHECAL
RHIPIDATE
RHIPIDION
RHIPIDISTIAN
RHIPIDIUM
RHIPIPHORID
RHIZANTHOUS
RHIZINE
RHIZINOUS
RHIZOBIA
RHIZOBIUM
RHIZOCARP
RHIZOCARPIC
RHIZOCARPOUS
RHIZOCAUL
RHIZOCAULUS
RHIZOCORM
RHIZODERMIS
RHIZOGEN
RHIZOGENETIC
RHIZOGENIC
RHIZOGENOUS
RHIZOID
RHIZOIDAL
RHIZOMA
RHIZOMATIC
RHIZOMATOUS
RHIZOME
RHIZOMELIC
RHIZOMIC
RHIZOMORPH
RHIZOMORPHIC
RHIZONEURE
RHIZOPHAGOUS
RHIZOPHILOUS
RHIZOPHORE
RHIZOPHYTE
RHIZOPLAST
RHIZOPOD
RHIZOPODAL
RHIZOPODAN
RHIZOPODIST
RHIZOPODOUS
RHIZOSTOME
RHIZOSTOMOUS
RHIZOTAXIS
RHIZOTAXY
RHIZOTE
RHIZOTIC
RHIZOTOMI
RHIZOTOMY
RHO
RHODA
RHODAMIN
RHODAMINE
RHODANATE
RHODANINE
RHODANTHE
RHODEOSE
RHODESWOOD
RHODIC
RHODING

RHODINOL
RHODITE
RHODIUM
RHODIZITE
RHODIZONIC
RHODOCYTE
RHODODAPHNE
RHODODENDRON
RHODOLITE
RHODONITE
RHODOPHANE
RHODOPHYLL
RHODOPLAST
RHODOPSIN
RHODORA
RHODOSPERM
RHODOSPERMIN
RHOMB
RHOMBI
RHOMBIC
RHOMBICAL
RHOMBIFORM
RHOMBOCLASE
RHOMBOGANOID
RHOMBOGENE
RHOMBOGENIC
RHOMBOGENOUS
RHOMBOHEDRA
RHOMBOHEDRAL
RHOMBOHEDRIC
RHOMBOHEDRON
RHOMBOID
RHOMBOIDAL
RHOMBOIDALLY
RHOMBOIDES
RHOMBOIDEUS
RHOMBOIDLY
RHOMBOS
RHOMBOVATE
RHOMBUS
RHOMBUSES
RHONCHAL
RHONCHIAL
RHONCHUS
RHOPALIC
RHOPALISM
RHOPALIUM
RHOTACISM
RHOTACISMUS
RHOTACIST
RHUBARB
RHUBARBY
RHUM
RHUMB
RHUMBA
RHYACOLITE
RHYME
RHYMED
RHYMEMAKER
RHYMEMAKING
RHYMER
RHYMERY
RHYMESTER
RHYMIC
RHYMING
RHYMY
RHYNCHODONT
RHYNCHOLITE
RHYNIA
RHYOBASALT
RHYODACITE
RHYOLITE
RHYOLITIC
RHYOTAXITIC
RHYPOGRAPHY
RHYPTIC
RHYPTICAL
RHYSIMETER
RHYTHM
RHYTHMAL
RHYTHMIC
RHYTHMICAL
RHYTHMICALLY
RHYTHMICITY
RHYTHMICIZE
RHYTHMICS
RHYTHMIST
RHYTHMIZABLE
RHYTHMIZE
RHYTHMOMETER
RHYTHMUS
RHYTIDOME
RHYTINA
RHYTON
RI
RIA
RIAL
RIALTY
RIANT
RIANTLY
RIATA
RIB
RIBALD
RIBALDISH
RIBALDRIES
RIBALDROUS
RIBALDRY
RIBAND
RIBANDMAKER
RIBANDRY
RIBAT
RIBAUDEQUIN
RIBAUDRED
RIBAZUBA
RIBBAND
RIBBED
RIBBER
RIBBET
RIBBING
RIBBLE
RIBBON
RIBBONBACK
RIBBONER
RIBBONFISH
RIBBONFISHES
RIBBONLIKE
RIBBONMAKER
RIBBONS
RIBBONWOOD
RIBBONY
RIBBY
RIBE
RIBGRASS
RIBIBE
RIBLESS
RIBOFLAVIN
RIBONIC
RIBONUCLEASE
RIBOSE
RIBOSOMAL
RIBOSOME
RIBROAST
RIBROASTER
RIBROASTING
RIBS
RIBSKIN
RIBWORT
RIBZUBA
RICASSO
RICE
RICEBIRD
RICEGRASS
RICER
RICERCARE
RICERCATA
RICEY
RICH
RICHARD
RICHDOM
RICHE
RICHELLITE
RICHEN
RICHER
RICHES
RICHESSE
RICHEST
RICHLING
RICHLY
RICHNESS
RICHT
RICHTERITE
RICHWEED
RICIN
RICINELAIDIC
RICININE
RICINIUM
RICINOLEATE
RICINOLEIC
RICINOLEIN
RICK
RICKARDITE
RICKER
RICKETIER
RICKETIEST
RICKETILY
RICKETINESS
RICKETISH
RICKETS
RICKETTSIA
RICKETTSIAE
RICKETTSIAL
RICKETY
RICKEYS
RICKLE
RICKMATIC
RICKRACK
RICKSHAW
RICKSTADDLE
RICKSTAND
RICKSTICK
RICKYARD
RICO
RICOCHET
RICOCHETED
RICOCHETING
RICOCHETTED
RICOLETTAITE
RICOTTA
RICRAC
RICTAL
RICTUS
RID
RIDABLE
RIDDAM
RIDDANCE
RIDDED
RIDDEL
RIDDEN
RIDDER
RIDDING
RIDDLE
RIDDLED
RIDDLEMEREE
RIDDLER
RIDDLING
RIDDLINGLY
RIDDLINGS
RIDE
RIDEN
RIDENT
RIDER
RIDERED
RIDGE
RIDGEBAND
RIDGEBONE
RIDGED
RIDGELING
RIDGEPOLE
RIDGEPOLED
RIDGER
RIDGEROPE
RIDGEROPE
RIDGES
RIDGIER
RIDGIEST
RIDGIL
RIDGING
RIDGLING
RIDGY
RIDIBUND
RIDICULE
RIDICULED
RIDICULER
RIDICULING
RIDICULOSITY
RIDICULOUS
RIDICULOUSLY
RIDING
RIDINGMAN
RIDINGMEN
RIDOTTO
RIDOTTOS
RIE
RIEBECKITE
RIEL
RIEM
RIEMPIE
RIER
RIEVER
RIFACIMENTO
RIFART
RIFE
RIFELY
RIFENESS
RIFER
RIFEST
RIFF
RIFFLE
RIFFLED
RIFFLER
RIFFRAFF
RIFLE
RIFLEBIRD
RIFLED
RIFLEMAN
RIFLEMANSHIP
RIFLEMEN
RIFLEPROOF
RIFLER
RIFLERY
RIFLESHOT
RIFLING
RIFT
RIFTER
RIFTY
RIG
RIGADIG
RIGADON
RIGADOON
RIGAMAJIG
RIGAMAROLE
RIGAUDON
RIGBANE
RIGESCENCE
RIGESCENT
RIGGAL
RIGGED
RIGGER
RIGGING
RIGGISH
RIGGOT
RIGHT
RIGHTABOUT
RIGHTEN
RIGHTEOUS
RIGHTEOUSLY
RIGHTEOUSNESS
RIGHTER
RIGHTEST
RIGHTFORTH
RIGHTFUL
RIGHTFULLY
RIGHTFULNESS
RIGHTHAND
RIGHTHEADED
RIGHTHEARTED
RIGHTIST
RIGHTLE
RIGHTLESS
RIGHTLY
RIGHTMOST
RIGHTNESS
RIGHTO
RIGHTS
RIGHTSHIP
RIGHTWARD
RIGHTWARDLY
RIGHTWARDS
RIGHTY
RIGID
RIGIDIFIED
RIGIDIFY
RIGIDIFYING
RIGIDIST
RIGIDITIES
RIGIDITY
RIGIDLY
RIGIDNESS
RIGIDULOUS
RIGINAL
RIGLET
RIGLING
RIGMAREE
RIGMAROLE
RIGMAROLERY
RIGNUM
RIGO
RIGODON
RIGOL
RIGOLE
RIGOLETTE
RIGOR
RIGORISM
RIGORIST
RIGORISTIC
RIGOROUS
RIGOROUSLY
RIGOROUSNESS
RIGOUR
RIGOURISM
RIGOURISTIC
RIGSBY
RIGSDALER
RIGWIDDIE
RIGWIDDY
RIGWOODIE
RIKK
RIKSDAALDER
RILAWA
RILE
RILED
RILEY
RILIEVO
RILING
RILL

RILLE
RILLET
RILLETT
RILLETTE
RILLOCK
RILLOW
RILLS
RILLSTONE
RILY
RIM
RIMA
RIMAL
RIMAS
RIMATE
RIMBASE
RIME
RIMED
RIMER
RIMERY
RIMESTER
RIMFIRE
RIMIC
RIMIER
RIMIEST
RIMIFORM
RIMING
RIMLESS
RIMMAKER
RIMMAKING
RIMMED
RIMMER
RIMOSE
RIMOSELY
RIMOSITY
RIMOUS
RIMPI
RIMPLE
RIMPLED
RIMPLING
RIMPTION
RIMROCK
RIMU
RIMULA
RIMULOSE
RIMUR
RIMY
RIN
RINCEAU
RINCON
RIND
RINDED
RINDERPEST
RINDLE
RINDS
RINDY
RINE
RINFORZANDO
RING
RINGBILL
RINGBIRD
RINGBOLT
RINGBONE
RINGBONED
RINGCRAFT
RINGDOVE
RINGE
RINGED
RINGENT
RINGER
RINGEYE
RINGGIVER
RINGGIVING
RINGGOER
RINGHALS
RINGHALSES
RINGHEAD
RINGINESS
RINGING
RINGINGLY
RINGITE
RINGLE
RINGLEAD
RINGLEADER
RINGLET
RINGLETED
RINGLETS
RINGLETY
RINGLIKE
RINGMAKER
RINGMAKING
RINGMAN
RINGMASTER
RINGNECK
RINGS
RINGSAIL
RINGSIDE
RINGSIDER
RINGSTER
RINGSTICK
RINGSTRAKED
RINGTAIL
RINGTAW
RINGTIME
RINGTOSS
RINGWALK
RINGWALL
RINGWISE
RINGWORM
RINGY
RINK
RINKA
RINKER
RINKITE
RINN
RINNEITE
RINNER
RINNING
RINSE
RINSED
RINSER
RINSING
RINTHEREOUT
RIO
RIOT
RIOTED
RIOTER
RIOTING
RIOTINGLY
RIOTISE
RIOTIST
RIOTISTIC
RIOTOCRACY
RIOTOUS
RIOTOUSLY
RIOTOUSNESS
RIOTRY
RIP
RIPA
RIPAL
RIPARIAL
RIPARIAN
RIPARIOUS
RIPCORD
RIPE
RIPED
RIPELY
RIPEN
RIPENED
RIPENER
RIPENESS
RIPENING
RIPENINGLY
RIPER
RIPEST
RIPGUT
RIPICOLOUS
RIPIDOLITE
RIPIENIST
RIPIENO
RIPIER
RIPON
RIPOST
RIPOSTE
RIPOSTED
RIPOSTING
RIPPABLE
RIPPED
RIPPER
RIPPERMAN
RIPPERMEN
RIPPET
RIPPIER
RIPPING
RIPPINGLY
RIPPINGNESS
RIPPIT
RIPPLE
RIPPLED
RIPPLER
RIPPLES
RIPPLET
RIPPLING
RIPPLINGLY
RIPPLY
RIPPON
RIPRAP
RIPRAPPED
RIPRAPPING
RIPSACK
RIPSAW
RIPSNORTER
RIPSNORTING
RIPTIDE
RIPUP
RIRORIRO
RISALA
RISALDAR
RISBERM
RISCO
RISDALER
RISE
RISEN
RISER
RISH
RISHI
RISHTADAR
RISIBILITIES
RISIBILITY
RISIBLE
RISIBLENESS
RISIBLES
RISIBLY
RISING
RISK
RISKED
RISKER
RISKFUL
RISKFULNESS
RISKIER
RISKIEST
RISKILY
RISKINESS
RISKING
RISKISH
RISKLESS
RISKY
RISOM
RISORGIMENTO
RISORIAL
RISORIUS
RISORSE
RISOTTO
RISP
RISPER
RISPETTO
RISPOSTA
RISQUE
RISSER
RISSLE
RISSOID
RISSOLE
RISSOM
RIST
RISTORI
RISUS
RIT
RITARD
RITARDANDO
RITARDANDOS
RITE
RITELY
RITENUTO
RITES
RITHE
RITMASTER
RITORNEL
RITORNELLE
RITORNELLO
RITRATTO
RITSU
RITTINGERITE
RITTOCK
RITUAL
RITUALISM
RITUALIST
RITUALISTIC
RITUALITIES
RITUALITY
RITUALLY
RITUS
RITZ
RITZIER
RITZIEST
RITZY
RIVA
RIVAGE
RIVAL
RIVALED
RIVALING
RIVALISM
RIVALITY
RIVALIZE
RIVALLED
RIVALLING
RIVALRIES
RIVALROUS
RIVALRY
RIVE
RIVED
RIVEL
RIVELED
RIVELING
RIVELL
RIVEN
RIVER
RIVERAIN
RIVERBANK
RIVERBED
RIVERBOAT
RIVERDAMP
RIVERED
RIVERET
RIVERHEAD
RIVERINE
RIVERISH
RIVERLET
RIVERLING
RIVERLY
RIVERMAN
RIVERMEN
RIVERS
RIVERSIDE
RIVERSIDER
RIVERWASH
RIVERWAY
RIVERWEED
RIVERY
RIVET
RIVETED
RIVETER
RIVETING
RIVETS
RIVIERE
RIVING
RIVO
RIVOSE
RIVULATION
RIVULET
RIVULETS
RIVULOSE
RIX
RIXATRIX
RIXDALER
RIXY
RIYAL
RIZIFORM
RIZZAR
RIZZER
RIZZLE
RIZZOM
RIZZOMED
RO
ROACH
ROACHBACK
ROACHED
ROACHING
ROAD
ROADABILITY
ROADBED
ROADBLOCK
ROADBOOK
ROADCRAFT
ROADED
ROADER
ROADFELLOW
ROADHEAD
ROADHOUSE
ROADING
ROADITE
ROADMAN
ROADMASTER
ROADRUNNER
ROADS
ROADSIDE
ROADSIDER
ROADSTEAD
ROADSTER
ROADSTONE
ROADWAY
ROADWEED
ROADWISE
ROADWORK
ROADWORTHY
ROAG
ROAM
ROAMAGE
ROAMED
ROAMER
ROAMING
ROAMINGLY
ROAN
ROAR
ROARED
ROARER
ROARING

ROARINGLY
ROAST
ROASTABLE
ROASTED
ROASTER
ROASTING
ROASTINGLY
ROB
ROBALITO
ROBALO
ROBAND
ROBBED
ROBBER
ROBBERY
ROBBIN
ROBBING
ROBE
ROBED
ROBER
ROBERD
ROBERT
ROBHAH
ROBIN
ROBINET
ROBING
ROBININ
ROBLE
ROBORANT
ROBORATE
ROBORATION
ROBORATIVE
ROBOREAN
ROBOREOUS
ROBOT
ROBOTESQUE
ROBOTIAN
ROBOTISM
ROBOTISTIC
ROBOTIZATION
ROBOTIZE
ROBOTRY
ROBUR
ROBURITE
ROBUST
ROBUSTFUL
ROBUSTFULLY
ROBUSTIC
ROBUSTICITY
ROBUSTIOUS
ROBUSTIOUSLY
ROBUSTITY
ROBUSTLY
ROBUSTNESS
ROC
ROCAILLE
ROCAMBOLE
ROCCA
ROCCELLIN
ROCCELLINE
ROCHE
ROCHELIME
ROCHER
ROCHET
ROCK
ROCKABLE
ROCKABLY
ROCKABY
ROCKABYE
ROCKALLITE
ROCKAT
ROCKBELL
ROCKBIRD
ROCKBORN
ROCKBRUSH
ROCKCIST
ROCKCRAFT
ROCKELAY
ROCKER
ROCKERTHON
ROCKERY
ROCKET
ROCKETED
ROCKETER
ROCKETING
ROCKETRY
ROCKETS
ROCKETSONDE
ROCKETY
ROCKFALL
ROCKFISH
ROCKFISHES
ROCKFOIL
ROCKHAIR
ROCKHEARTED
ROCKIER
ROCKIEST
ROCKINESS
ROCKING
ROCKINGLY
ROCKISH
ROCKLAY
ROCKLING
ROCKLINGS
ROCKMAN
ROCKOON
ROCKRIBBED
ROCKROSE
ROCKS
ROCKSHAFT
ROCKSLIDE
ROCKSTAFF
ROCKTREE
ROCKWEED
ROCKWOOD
ROCKWORK
ROCKY
ROCOCO
ROCOLO
ROCTA
ROD
RODD
RODDEN
RODDIKIN
RODDIN
RODDING
RODE
RODENT
RODENTIAL
RODENTIALLY
RODENTIAN
RODEO
RODGE
RODHAM
RODING
RODINGITE
RODLESS
RODLIKE
RODMAKER
RODMAN
RODNEY
RODOMONTADE
RODOMONTADOR
RODS
RODSMAN
RODSTER
RODWOOD
ROEBLINGITE
ROEBUCK
ROED
ROEDE
ROENENG
ROENTGEN
ROENTGENISM
ROENTGENIZE
ROER
ROESTONE
ROEY
ROG
ROGAN
ROGATION
ROGATIVE
ROGATORY
ROGER
ROGERIAN
ROGERSITE
ROGGLE
ROGNON
ROGNONS
ROGUE
ROGUED
ROGUERIES
ROGUERY
ROGUING
ROGUISH
ROGUISHLY
ROGUISHNESS
ROGUY
ROHAN
ROHOB
ROHU
ROHUN
ROHUNA
ROI
ROID
ROIL
ROILED
ROILIER
ROILIEST
ROILING
ROILY
ROIN
ROINISH
ROIS
ROIST
ROISTER
ROISTERER
ROISTERING
ROISTERLY
ROISTEROUS
ROISTEROUSLY
ROIT
ROITELET
ROJO
ROKA
ROKE
ROKEAGE
ROKEE
ROKELAY
ROKER
ROKEY
ROKY
ROLA
ROLE
ROLEO
ROLL
ROLLABLE
ROLLAWAY
ROLLBACK
ROLLED
ROLLEJEE
ROLLER
ROLLERMAKER
ROLLERMAKING
ROLLERMAN
ROLLEY
ROLLEYWAY
ROLLEYWAYMAN
ROLLICHE
ROLLICHIE
ROLLICK
ROLLICKED
ROLLICKER
ROLLICKING
ROLLICKINGLY
ROLLICKSOME
ROLLICKY
ROLLING
ROLLIX
ROLLMOP
ROLLTOP
ROLLWAY
ROLOWAY
ROLP
ROLPENS
ROM
ROMAIKA
ROMAINE
ROMAL
ROMAN
ROMANCE
ROMANCEALIST
ROMANCEAN
ROMANCED
ROMANCER
ROMANCES
ROMANCICAL
ROMANCING
ROMANCIST
ROMANCY
ROMANESQUE
ROMANIUM
ROMANTIC
ROMANTICAL
ROMANTICALLY
ROMANTICISM
ROMANTICIST
ROMANTICITY
ROMANTICIZE
ROMANTICLY
ROMANTICNESS
ROMANTISM
ROMANTIST
ROMANZA
ROMAUNT
ROMBLE
ROMBOS
ROMBOWLINE
ROMEITE
ROMERILLO
ROMERO
ROMI
ROMMACK
ROMNI
ROMP
ROMPED
ROMPER
ROMPERS
ROMPING
ROMPINGLY
ROMPISH
ROMPISHLY
ROMPISHNESS
ROMPU
ROMPY
RON
RONCADOR
RONCET
RONCHO
RONCO
ROND
RONDACHE
RONDACHER
RONDAWEL
RONDE
RONDEAU
RONDEAUX
RONDEL
RONDELET
RONDELIER
RONDELLE
RONDELLIER
RONDINO
RONDLE
RONDO
RONDOLETTO
RONDOS
RONDURE
RONE
RONEO
RONG
RONGEUR
RONIER
RONIN
RONION
RONQUIL
RONTGENISM
RONYON
ROO
ROOD
ROODEBOK
ROODLES
ROODSTONE
ROOF
ROOFAGE
ROOFED
ROOFER
ROOFING
ROOFLESS
ROOFLET
ROOFMAN
ROOFMEN
ROOFTREE
ROOFWARD
ROOFY
ROOIBOK
ROOINEK
ROOK
ROOKED
ROOKER
ROOKERIED
ROOKERY
ROOKIE
ROOKING
ROOKS
ROOKUS
ROOKY
ROOL
ROOM
ROOMAGE
ROOMER
ROOMETTE
ROOMFUL
ROOMIE
ROOMIER
ROOMIEST
ROOMILY
ROOMINESS
ROOMING
ROOMKEEPER
ROOMMATE
ROOMS
ROOMSOME
ROOMSTEAD
ROOMTH
ROOMTHILY
ROOMTHINESS
ROOMTHY
ROOMWARD
ROOMY
ROON
ROOP
ROORBACK
ROOSA
ROOSE
ROOSEVELT

ROOST
ROOSTED
ROOSTER
ROOSTERFISH
ROOSTERS
ROOSTY
ROOT
ROOTAGE
ROOTCAP
ROOTED
ROOTEDLY
ROOTEDNESS
ROOTER
ROOTERY
ROOTFAST
ROOTFASTNESS
ROOTHOLD
ROOTIER
ROOTIEST
ROOTINESS
ROOTLE
ROOTLESS
ROOTLESSNESS
ROOTLET
ROOTLIKE
ROOTLING
ROOTS
ROOTSTALK
ROOTSTOCK
ROOTWALT
ROOTWORM
ROOTY
ROOVE
ROOYEBOK
ROPABLE
ROPAND
ROPANI
ROPE
ROPEBAND
ROPEBARK
ROPED
ROPEDANCE
ROPEDANCER
ROPEDANCING
ROPELAYER
ROPELAYING
ROPEMAKER
ROPEMAKING
ROPEMAN
ROPEMEN
ROPER
ROPERIPE
ROPERY
ROPES
ROPESMITH
ROPEWALK
ROPEWALKER
ROPEWAY
ROPEWORK
ROPEY
ROPIER
ROPIEST
ROPILY
ROPINESS
ROPING
ROPISH
ROPISHNESS
ROPLOCH
ROPY
ROQUE
ROQUELAURE
ROQUET
ROQUETED
ROQUETING
ROQUETTE
ROQUILLE
ROQUIST
RORAL
RORATORIO
RORIC
RORID
RORIFEROUS
RORIFLUENT
RORITORIOUS
RORQUAL
RORT
RORTY
RORULENT
ROSACE
ROSACEAN
ROSACEOUS
ROSAKER
ROSANILINE
ROSARIAN
ROSARIES
ROSARIUM
ROSARUBY
ROSARY
ROSATED
ROSCHERITE
ROSCID
ROSCOELITE
ROSE
ROSEAL
ROSEATE
ROSEATELY
ROSEBAY
ROSEBUD
ROSEBUSH
ROSED
ROSEDROP
ROSEFISH
ROSEFISHES
ROSEHEAD
ROSEHILL
ROSEHILLER
ROSEI
ROSEINE
ROSEL
ROSELET
ROSELITE
ROSELLA
ROSELLATE
ROSELLE
ROSEMARIES
ROSEMARY
ROSEN
ROSENBUSCHITE
ROSEOLA
ROSEOLAR
ROSEOLIFORM
ROSEOLOUS
ROSEOUS
ROSER
ROSEROOT
ROSES
ROSET
ROSETAN
ROSETANGLE
ROSETIME
ROSETTE
ROSETTED
ROSETTY
ROSETTY
ROSETUM
ROSETY
ROSEWAYS
ROSEWISE
ROSEWOOD
ROSEWORT
ROSIED
ROSIER
ROSIERESITE
ROSIEST
ROSILLA
ROSILLO
ROSILY
ROSIN
ROSINESS
ROSING
ROSINOUS
ROSINWEED
ROSINY
ROSLAND
ROSMARINE
ROSOLIC
ROSOLIO
ROSOLITE
ROSORIAL
ROSSER
ROSSITE
ROSTEL
ROSTELLA
ROSTELLAR
ROSTELLATE
ROSTELLIFORM
ROSTELLUM
ROSTER
ROSTRA
ROSTRAL
ROSTRALLY
ROSTRATE
ROSTRATED
ROSTRIFEROUS
ROSTRIFORM
ROSTROID
ROSTRULAR
ROSTRULATE
ROSTRULUM
ROSTRUM
ROSTRUMS
ROSULAR
ROSULATE
ROSY
ROT
ROTA
ROTACISM
ROTAL
ROTALIAN
ROTALIFORM
ROTAMAN
ROTAMEN
ROTAMETER
ROTAN
ROTANG
ROTARIANIZE
ROTARY
ROTATABLE
ROTATE
ROTATED
ROTATING
ROTATION
ROTATIONAL
ROTATIVE
ROTATIVELY
ROTATIVISM
ROTATOPLANE
ROTATOR
ROTATORES
ROTATORY
ROTCH
ROTCHE
ROTE
ROTELLA
ROTENONE
ROTGE
ROTGUT
ROTHER
ROTHERMUCK
ROTI
ROTIFER
ROTIFERAL
ROTIFEROUS
ROTIFORM
ROTISSERIE
ROTL
ROTN
ROTO
ROTOGRAPH
ROTOGRAVURE
ROTONDE
ROTOR
ROTTA
ROTTAN
ROTTE
ROTTED
ROTTEN
ROTTENLY
ROTTENNESS
ROTTENSTONE
ROTTER
ROTTING
ROTTLE
ROTTLERA
ROTTLERIN
ROTTOCK
ROTTOLO
ROTULA
ROTULAD
ROTULAR
ROTULET
ROTULIAN
ROTULIFORM
ROTULUS
ROTUND
ROTUNDA
ROTUNDATE
ROTUNDITIES
ROTUNDITY
ROTUNDLY
ROTUNDNESS
ROTURIER
ROTURIERS
ROUB
ROUBLE
ROUBOUH
ROUCH
ROUCHE
ROUCOU
ROUDAS
ROUE
ROUERIE
ROUGE
ROUGEAU
ROUGED
ROUGEMONTITE
ROUGEOT
ROUGH
ROUGHAGE
ROUGHCAST
ROUGHCASTER
ROUGHCASTING
ROUGHDRAFT
ROUGHDRAW
ROUGHDRESS
ROUGHDRIED
ROUGHDRY
ROUGHDRYING
ROUGHEN
ROUGHENED
ROUGHENER
ROUGHER
ROUGHET
ROUGHHEW
ROUGHHEWED
ROUGHHEWER
ROUGHHEWING
ROUGHHEWN
ROUGHHOUSE
ROUGHHOUSER
ROUGHHOUSING
ROUGHHOUSY
ROUGHIE
ROUGHINGS
ROUGHISH
ROUGHISHLY
ROUGHISHNESS
ROUGHLEG
ROUGHLY
ROUGHNECK
ROUGHNESS
ROUGHOMETER
ROUGHRIDE
ROUGHRIDER
ROUGHROOT
ROUGHSCUFF
ROUGHSETTER
ROUGHSHOD
ROUGHSLANT
ROUGHSOME
ROUGHSTRING
ROUGHSTUFF
ROUGHT
ROUGHTAILED
ROUGHWORK
ROUGHWROUGHT
ROUGHY
ROUGING
ROUKY
ROULADE
ROULEAU
ROULEAUS
ROULEAUX
ROULETTE
ROUN
ROUNCE
ROUNCEVAL
ROUNCY
ROUND
ROUNDABOUT
ROUNDABOUTLY
ROUNDED
ROUNDEL
ROUNDELAY
ROUNDELEER
ROUNDER
ROUNDERS
ROUNDHEADED
ROUNDHOUSE
ROUNDING
ROUNDISH
ROUNDISHNESS
ROUNDLET
ROUNDLINE
ROUNDLY
ROUNDNESS
ROUNDNOSE
ROUNDNOSED
ROUNDS
ROUNDSMAN
ROUNDTAIL
ROUNDTOP
ROUNDUP
ROUNDWORM
ROUNDY
ROUNGE
ROUNSPIK
ROUNTREE
ROUP
ROUPET
ROUPIE
ROUPIT
ROUPY
ROUSE
ROUSEABOUT

ROUSED
ROUSEMENT
ROUSER
ROUSETTE
ROUSING
ROUSINGLY
ROUSSEAU
ROUST
ROUSTABOUT
ROUSTING
ROUT
ROUTE
ROUTED
ROUTER
ROUTH
ROUTHERCOCK
ROUTHY
ROUTIER
ROUTINARY
ROUTINE
ROUTINEER
ROUTINELY
ROUTING
ROUTINISH
ROUTINISM
ROUTINIST
ROUTINIZE
ROUTINIZED
ROUTINIZING
ROUTIVARITE
ROUTOUS
ROUTOUSLY
ROUVILLITE
ROUX
ROVE
ROVED
ROVER
ROVESCIO
ROVET
ROVETTO
ROVING
ROVINGLY
ROVINGNESS
ROW
ROWABLE
ROWAN
ROWANBERRIES
ROWANBERRY
ROWBOAT
ROWDILY
ROWDINESS
ROWDY
ROWDYDOW
ROWDYISH
ROWDYISHLY
ROWDYISM
ROWED
ROWEL
ROWELED
ROWELHEAD
ROWELING
ROWELLED
ROWELLING
ROWEN
ROWER
ROWET
ROWINESS
ROWING
ROWK
ROWLANDITE
ROWLET
ROWLOCK
ROWN
ROWP
ROWPORT
ROWS
ROWTH
ROWTY
ROWY
ROX
ROXY
ROY
ROYAL
ROYALE
ROYALET
ROYALISM
ROYALIST
ROYALISTIC
ROYALIZATION
ROYALIZE
ROYALLY
ROYALMAST
ROYALME
ROYALTIES
ROYALTY
ROYD
ROYET
ROYETNESS
ROYETOUS
ROYETOUSLY
ROYLE
ROYNOUS
ROYT
ROZUM
RSI
RUACH
RUADE
RUANA
RUAY
RUB
RUBABOO
RUBACE
RUBAIYAT
RUBAN
RUBASSE
RUBATO
RUBBABOO
RUBBED
RUBBEE
RUBBER
RUBBERIZE
RUBBERIZED
RUBBERIZING
RUBBERNECK
RUBBERNOSE
RUBBERS
RUBBERSTONE
RUBBERY
RUBBING
RUBBIO
RUBBISHING
RUBBISHINGLY
RUBBISHLY
RUBBISHRY
RUBBISHY
RUBBLE
RUBBLER
RUBBLES
RUBBLESTONE
RUBBLEWORK
RUBBLY
RUBDOWN
RUBEDINOUS
RUBEDITY
RUBEFACIENCE
RUBEFACIENT
RUBEFACTION
RUBELET
RUBELLA
RUBELLE
RUBELLITE
RUBEOLA
RUBEOLAR
RUBEOLOID
RUBERYTHRIC
RUBESCENCE
RUBESCENT
RUBIACEOUS
RUBIANIC
RUBIATE
RUBIATOR
RUBIBLE
RUBICAN
RUBICUND
RUBICUNDITY
RUBIDIC
RUBIDINE
RUBIDIUM
RUBIED
RUBIES
RUBIFIC
RUBIFICATION
RUBIFICATIVE
RUBIFY
RUBIGINOUS
RUBIGO
RUBIJERVINE
RUBIN
RUBINE
RUBINEOUS
RUBIOUS
RUBLE
RUBLIS
RUBOR
RUBRIC
RUBRICAL
RUBRICALITY
RUBRICALLY
RUBRICATE
RUBRICATED
RUBRICATING
RUBRICATION
RUBRICATOR
RUBRICIAN
RUBRICISM
RUBRICIST
RUBRICITY
RUBRICIZE
RUBRICOSE
RUBRIFIC
RUBRIFY
RUBROSPINAL
RUBSTONE
RUBY
RUBYING
RUBYTAIL
RUCERVINE
RUCERVUS
RUCHE
RUCHING
RUCK
RUCKLE
RUCKSACK
RUCKSEY
RUCKUS
RUCKY
RUCTION
RUCTIOUS
RUD
RUDAS
RUDBECKIA
RUDD
RUDDER
RUDDERFISH
RUDDERHEAD
RUDDERHOLE
RUDDERLESS
RUDDERPOST
RUDDERSTOCK
RUDDIED
RUDDIER
RUDDIEST
RUDDINESS
RUDDISH
RUDDLE
RUDDLED
RUDDLEMAN
RUDDLEMEN
RUDDLING
RUDDOCK
RUDDY
RUDE
RUDELY
RUDENESS
RUDENTED
RUDER
RUDERA
RUDERAL
RUDERATE
RUDESBY
RUDEST
RUDGE
RUDIMENT
RUDIMENTAL
RUDIMENTARY
RUDISH
RUDITY
RUDLOFF
RUDOUS
RUE
RUED
RUEFUL
RUEFULLY
RUEFULNESS
RUELLE
RUELY
RUEN
RUER
RUESOME
RUESOMENESS
RUEWORT
RUF
RUFESCENCE
RUFESCENT
RUFF
RUFFE
RUFFED
RUFFER
RUFFIAN
RUFFIANAGE
RUFFIANISH
RUFFIANISM
RUFFIANIZE
RUFFIANLY
RUFFING
RUFFLE
RUFFLED
RUFFLER
RUFFLINESS
RUFFLING
RUFFLY
RUFFMANS
RUFOUS
RUFULOUS
RUFUS
RUG
RUGA
RUGAE
RUGATE
RUGG
RUGGED
RUGGEDLY
RUGGEDNESS
RUGGING
RUGGLE
RUGGY
RUGINE
RUGOSE
RUGOSITY
RUGOUS
RUIN
RUINABLE
RUINATE
RUINATED
RUINATING
RUINATION
RUINATIOUS
RUINATOR
RUINED
RUINER
RUING
RUINIFORM
RUINOUS
RUINOUSLY
RUINOUSNESS
RUINPROOF
RUINS
RUKH
RULE
RULED
RULEMONGER
RULER
RULERS
RULERSHIP
RULES
RULING
RULINGLY
RULL
RULLER
RULLION
RULLOCK
RUM
RUMAL
RUMBA
RUMBARGE
RUMBELOW
RUMBLE
RUMBLED
RUMBLEGARIE
RUMBLEGUMPTION
RUMBLEMENT
RUMBLER
RUMBLING
RUMBLINGLY
RUMBLY
RUMBO
RUMBOOZE
RUMBOWLINE
RUMBOWLING
RUMBULLION
RUMBUMPTIOUS
RUMBUSTICAL
RUMBUSTIOUS
RUMCHUNDER
RUMEN
RUMENITIS
RUMENOTOMY
RUMFUSTIAN
RUMGUMPTION
RUMGUMPTIOUS
RUMINA
RUMINAL
RUMINANT
RUMINANTLY
RUMINANTS
RUMINATE
RUMINATED
RUMINATING
RUMINATINGLY
RUMINATION
RUMINATIVE
RUMINATIVELY
RUMINATOR
RUMKIN
RUMMAGE

RUMMAGED
RUMMAGER
RUMMAGING
RUMMAGY
RUMMER
RUMMES
RUMMIER
RUMMIEST
RUMMILY
RUMMINESS
RUMMLE
RUMMY
RUMNESS
RUMNEY
RUMOR
RUMORED
RUMORER
RUMORING
RUMORMONGER
RUMOROUS
RUMOUR
RUMOURED
RUMOURER
RUMOURING
RUMP
RUMPAD
RUMPADE
RUMPLE
RUMPLED
RUMPLING
RUMPUS
RUMPY
RUMRUNNER
RUMSHOP
RUMTYTOO
RUN
RUNABOUT
RUNAGADO
RUNAGATE
RUNAROUND
RUNAWAY
RUNBACK
RUNBY
RUNCH
RUNCHWEED
RUNCINATE
RUND
RUNDALE
RUNDEL
RUNDLE
RUNDLET
RUNDOWN
RUNE
RUNECRAFT
RUNEFOLK
RUNER
RUNES
RUNESMITH
RUNESTAFF
RUNEWORD
RUNFISH
RUNG
RUNGHEAD
RUNHOLDER
RUNIC
RUNIFORM
RUNITE
RUNKEEPER
RUNKLE
RUNLET
RUNMAN
RUNN
RUNNEL
RUNNER
RUNNERS
RUNNET
RUNNING
RUNNY
RUNOFF
RUNOLOGIST
RUNOLOGY
RUNOUT
RUNOVER
RUNRIG
RUNROUND
RUNS
RUNSY
RUNT
RUNTED
RUNTEE
RUNTIER
RUNTIEST
RUNTINESS
RUNTISH
RUNTISHLY
RUNTISHNESS
RUNTY
RUNWAY
RUPA
RUPEE
RUPELLARY
RUPESTRAL
RUPESTRIAN
RUPESTRINE
RUPIA
RUPIAH
RUPICOLINE
RUPICOLOUS
RUPIE
RUPITIC
RUPTILE
RUPTION
RUPTIVE
RUPTUARY
RUPTURABLE
RUPTURE
RUPTURED
RUPTUREWORT
RUPTURING
RURAL
RURALISM
RURALIST
RURALITE
RURALITIES
RURALITY
RURALIZATION
RURALIZE
RURALIZED
RURALIZING
RURALLY
RURIC
RURIDECANAL
RURIGENOUS
RURU
RUSE
RUSH
RUSHBUSH
RUSHED
RUSHEN
RUSHER
RUSHES
RUSHIER
RUSHIEST
RUSHINESS
RUSHING
RUSHLAND
RUSHLIGHT
RUSHLIGHTED
RUSHLIKE
RUSHY
RUSINE
RUSK
RUSKY
RUSMA
RUSOT
RUSPONE
RUSSEL
RUSSELET
RUSSET
RUSSETING
RUSSETISH
RUSSUD
RUST
RUSTIC
RUSTICAL
RUSTICALLY
RUSTICALNESS
RUSTICATE
RUSTICATED
RUSTICATING
RUSTICATION
RUSTICATOR
RUSTICIAL
RUSTICISM
RUSTICITIES
RUSTICITY
RUSTICIZE
RUSTICOAT
RUSTICWORK
RUSTIER
RUSTIEST
RUSTINESS
RUSTLE
RUSTLED
RUSTLER
RUSTLING
RUSTLINGLY
RUSTLY
RUSTRE
RUSTRED
RUSTY
RUSTYISH
RUSWUT
RUT
RUTAB
RUTABAGA
RUTACEOUS
RUTE
RUTELIAN
RUTH
RUTHE
RUTHENATE
RUTHENIC
RUTHENIOUS
RUTHENIUM
RUTHENOUS
RUTHER
RUTHERFORD
RUTHFUL
RUTHFULLY
RUTHFULNESS
RUTHLESS
RUTHLESSLY
RUTHLESSNESS
RUTIC
RUTIDOSIS
RUTILANT
RUTILATE
RUTILATED
RUTILATION
RUTILE
RUTILOUS
RUTIN
RUTINOSE
RUTTEE
RUTTER
RUTTIER
RUTTIEST
RUTTINESS
RUTTING
RUTTISH
RUTTISHNESS
RUTTLE
RUTTY
RUTYL
RUTYLENE
RUVID
RUX
RYAL
RYBAT
RYDER
RYE
RYEGRASS
RYEL
RYEN
RYFT
RYG
RYKE
RYKED
RYKING
RYME
RYND
RYNT
RYOT
RYOTWAR
RYOTWARI
RYPE
RYPECK
RYTIDOSIS

S

SA
SAA
SAAH
SAAME
SAB
SABA
SABADILLA
SABADIN
SABADINE
SABAKHA
SABALO
SABALOTE
SABANA
SABATON
SABAYON
SABBAT
SABBATICAL
SABBATINE
SABBATISM
SABBATON
SABBEKA
SABBITHA
SABBY
SABDARIFFA
SABE
SABECA
SABED
SABEING
SABELLAN
SABELLID
SABELLOID
SABER
SABERBILL
SABERED
SABERING
SABERTOOTH
SABHA
SABIACEOUS
SABICU
SABIN
SABINA
SABINE
SABINO
SABIO
SABLA
SABLE
SABLEFISH
SABLEFISHES
SABLENESS
SABLES
SABLY
SABORA
SABORAIM
SABOT
SABOTAGE
SABOTAGED
SABOTAGING
SABOTED
SABOTEUR
SABOTIER
SABOTINE
SABRE
SABREBILL
SABRETACHE
SABRETOOTH
SABREUR
SABRING
SABULINE
SABULITE
SABULOSE
SABULOSITY
SABULOUS
SABULUM
SABURRA
SABURRAL
SABURRATE
SABURRATION
SABUTAN
SABZI
SAC
SACALAIT
SACALINE
SACATE
SACATON
SACATRA
SACBROOD
SACCADE
SACCADGE
SACCADIC
SACCAGE
SACCATE
SACCATED
SACCHARATE
SACCHARATED
SACCHARIC
SACCHARIDE
SACCHARIFIED
SACCHARIFIER
SACCHARIFY
SACCHARIFYING
SACCHARILLA
SACCHARIN
SACCHARINATE
SACCHARINE
SACCHARINELY
SACCHARINIC
SACCHARINITY
SACCHARIZE
SACCHARIZED
SACCHARIZING
SACCHAROID
SACCHAROIDAL
SACCHARONATE
SACCHARONE
SACCHARONIC
SACCHAROSE
SACCHAROSURIA
SACCODERM
SACCOON
SACCOS
SACCULAR
SACCULATE
SACCULATED
SACCULATION
SACCULE
SACCULUS
SACCUS
SACE
SACELLA
SACELLUM
SACER
SACERDOCY
SACERDOS
SACERDOTAGE
SACERDOTAL
SACERDOTALLY
SACERDOTICAL
SACERDOTISM
SACERDOTIUM
SACHEM
SACHEMDOM
SACHEMIC
SACHET
SACK
SACKAGE
SACKBAG
SACKBUT
SACKBUTT
SACKCLOTH
SACKCLOTHED
SACKDOUDLE
SACKED
SACKEN
SACKER
SACKET
SACKFUL
SACKING
SACKLESS
SACKMAKER
SACKMAKING
SACKS
SACO
SACOPE
SACQUE
SACRA
SACRAD
SACRAL
SACRALGIA
SACRAMENT
SACRAMENTAL
SACRAMENTALISM
SACRAMENTALIST
SACRAMENTALITY
SACRAMENTALLY
SACRAMENTARIAN
SACRAMENTARY
SACRAMENTER
SACRAMENTIZE
SACRAMENTUM
SACRARIA
SACRARIAL
SACRARIUM
SACRARY
SACRATE
SACRE
SACRECTOMY
SACRED
SACREDLY
SACREDNESS
SACRI
SACRIFICATION
SACRIFICATOR
SACRIFICATORY
SACRIFICATURE
SACRIFICE
SACRIFICED
SACRIFICER
SACRIFICES
SACRIFICIAL
SACRIFICIALLY
SACRIFICING
SACRIFICINGLY
SACRILEGE
SACRILEGER
SACRILEGIOUS
SACRILEGIOUSLY
SACRILEGIST
SACRING
SACRIST
SACRISTAN
SACRISTIES
SACRISTY
SACRO
SACROCOCCYX
SACROCOXITIS
SACRODORSAL
SACRODYNIA
SACROILIAC
SACROSANCT
SACROSCIATIC
SACROSPINOUS
SACROTUBEROUS
SACRUM
SACRY
SAD
SADD
SADDEN
SADDENED
SADDENING
SADDER
SADDEST
SADDHU
SADDIK
SADDISH
SADDLE
SADDLEBACK
SADDLEBAG
SADDLEBOW
SADDLECLOTH
SADDLED
SADDLELEAF
SADDLELESS
SADDLELIKE
SADDLEMAKER
SADDLENOSE
SADDLER
SADDLERIES
SADDLERY
SADDLES
SADDLESICK
SADDLESORE
SADDLETREE
SADDLETREES
SADDLING
SADE
SADH
SADHANA
SADHE
SADHEARTED
SADHU
SADIC
SADIRON
SADISM
SADIST
SADISTIC
SADISTICALLY
SADLY
SADNESS
SADO
SADOO
SADR
SADWARE
SAE
SAEBEINS
SAECULAR
SAECULUM
SAER
SAERNAITE
SAETER
SAEX
SAFARI
SAFE
SAFEBLOWER
SAFEBLOWING
SAFEBREAKER
SAFEBREAKING
SAFECRACKER
SAFECRACKING
SAFEGUARD
SAFEGUARDER
SAFEHOLD
SAFEKEEPER
SAFEKEEPING
SAFELIGHT
SAFELY
SAFEMAKER
SAFENER
SAFENESS
SAFER
SAFEST
SAFETIES
SAFETY
SAFFI
SAFFIAN
SAFFIOR
SAFFLOR
SAFFLORITE
SAFFLOW
SAFFLOWER
SAFFO
SAFFRON
SAFFRONED
SAFFRONWOOD
SAFFRONY
SAFIE
SAFIR
SAFRANIN
SAFRANINE
SAFRANOPHIL
SAFRANOPHILE
SAFROL
SAFROLE
SAFTLY
SAG
SAGA
SAGACIATE
SAGACIOUS
SAGACIOUSLY
SAGACIOUSNESS
SAGACITY
SAGAIE
SAGAMAN
SAGAMITE
SAGAMORE
SAGANASH
SAGAPEN
SAGAPENUM
SAGATHY
SAGE
SAGEBRUSH
SAGEBRUSHER
SAGEER
SAGELEAF
SAGELY
SAGENE
SAGENESS
SAGENITE
SAGENITIC
SAGER
SAGEROSE
SAGESHIP
SAGESSE
SAGEST
SAGEWOOD
SAGGAR
SAGGARD
SAGGED
SAGGER
SAGGING
SAGGON
SAGGY
SAGHAVART
SAGIER
SAGIEST
SAGINATE
SAGINATION
SAGING
SAGITTA
SAGITTAE
SAGITTAL
SAGITTALLY
SAGITTARII
SAGITTARIUS
SAGITTARY
SAGITTATE

SAGITTIFORM
SAGITTOCYST
SAGITTOID
SAGO
SAGOIN
SAGOS
SAGOWEER
SAGUARO
SAGUAROS
SAGUING
SAGUM
SAGURAN
SAGURANES
SAGVANDITE
SAGWIRE
SAGY
SAH
SAHEB
SAHH
SAHIB
SAHLITE
SAHME
SAHRAS
SAHU
SAI
SAIBLING
SAIC
SAICE
SAID
SAIDE
SAIF
SAIGA
SAIL
SAILABLE
SAILAGE
SAILBOAT
SAILCLOTH
SAILED
SAILER
SAILFIN
SAILFISH
SAILFISHES
SAILING
SAILMAKER
SAILMAKING
SAILOR
SAILORING
SAILORIZING
SAILORLY
SAILORMAN
SAILOUR
SAILPLANE
SAILS
SAILSHIP
SAILSMAN
SAILY
SAILYE
SAIM
SAIMIRI
SAIMY
SAIN
SAINDOUX
SAINFOIN
SAINT
SAINTE
SAINTED
SAINTHOOD
SAINTING
SAINTISH
SAINTISM
SAINTLIER
SAINTLIEST
SAINTLIKE
SAINTLINESS
SAINTLY
SAINTS
SAINTSHIP
SAIR
SAIRVE
SAIS
SAITHE
SAIYID
SAJ
SAJOU
SAKE
SAKEBER
SAKEEN
SAKER
SAKHA
SAKI
SAKIA
SAKIEH
SAKIYEH
SAKKOS
SAKULYA
SAL
SALA
SALAAM
SALABILITY
SALABLE
SALABLENESS
SALABLY
SALACIOUS
SALACIOUSLY
SALACIOUSNESS
SALACITY
SALACOT
SALAD
SALADA
SALADANG
SALADE
SALADERO
SALADIN
SALADING
SALAGO
SALAGRAMA
SALAL
SALAM
SALAMANDARIN
SALAMANDER
SALAMANDRA
SALAMANDRINE
SALAMANDROID
SALAMAT
SALAMBAO
SALAME
SALAMI
SALAMO
SALAMPORE
SALANGANE
SALANGID
SALAR
SALARIAT
SALARIED
SALARIEGO
SALARIES
SALARY
SALARYING
SALAT
SALAY
SALBAND
SALCHOW
SALDID
SALE
SALEABLE
SALEB
SALEEITE
SALEGOER
SALELE
SALEM
SALEMA
SALEP
SALERATUS
SALEROOM
SALES
SALESCLERK
SALESGIRL
SALESITE
SALESLADIES
SALESLADY
SALESMAN
SALESMANSHIP
SALESMEN
SALESPEOPLE
SALESPERSON
SALESROOM
SALESWOMAN
SALESWOMEN
SALEW
SALEWARE
SALEWORK
SALEYARD
SALFERN
SALIANT
SALIC
SALICACEOUS
SALICETUM
SALICIN
SALICIONAL
SALICORN
SALICYL
SALICYLAL
SALICYLATE
SALICYLIC
SALICYLIDE
SALICYLISM
SALICYLIZE
SALICYLURIC
SALICYLYL
SALIENCE
SALIENCY
SALIENT
SALIENTIAN
SALIENTLY
SALIENTNESS
SALIFEROUS
SALIFIABLE
SALIFICATION
SALIFIED
SALIFY
SALIFYING
SALIGENIN
SALIGENOL
SALIGOT
SALIGRAM
SALINA
SALINAS
SALINATION
SALINE
SALINELLE
SALINIFORM
SALINITY
SALINIZE
SALINOMETER
SALINOMETRY
SALITE
SALITED
SALIVA
SALIVANT
SALIVARY
SALIVATE
SALIVATED
SALIVATING
SALIVATION
SALIVATOR
SALIVATORY
SALIVOUS
SALL
SALLE
SALLEE
SALLEEMAN
SALLEEMEN
SALLENDERS
SALLET
SALLIED
SALLIER
SALLIES
SALLO
SALLOO
SALLOW
SALLOWED
SALLOWER
SALLOWING
SALLOWISH
SALLOWNESS
SALLOWY
SALLY
SALLYING
SALLYMAN
SALLYMEN
SALLYWOOD
SALM
SALMA
SALMAGUNDI
SALMARY
SALMI
SALMIAC
SALMIN
SALMINE
SALMIS
SALMON
SALMONBERRIES
SALMONBERRY
SALMONELLOSIS
SALMONET
SALMONID
SALMONIFORM
SALMONOID
SALMONSITE
SALMWOOD
SALNATRON
SALOL
SALOMETER
SALOMETRY
SALOMON
SALON
SALONIKA
SALONS
SALOON
SALOONIST
SALOONKEEPER
SALOOP
SALOP
SALOPIAN
SALP
SALPACEAN
SALPIAN
SALPICON
SALPID
SALPIFORM
SALPINGES
SALPINGIAN
SALPINGION
SALPINGITIS
SALPINGOCELE
SALPINX
SALPOID
SALSE
SALSIFIES
SALSIFY
SALSILLA
SALSO
SALSODA
SALSUGINOSE
SALSUGINOUS
SALT
SALTA
SALTANDO
SALTANT
SALTARELLO
SALTARY
SALTATE
SALTATION
SALTATIVENESS
SALTATO
SALTATORIAL
SALTATORIC
SALTATORY
SALTATRAS
SALTBOX
SALTBRUSH
SALTBUSH
SALTCAT
SALTCATCH
SALTCELLAR
SALTEAUX
SALTED
SALTEE
SALTEN
SALTER
SALTERETTO
SALTERN
SALTERY
SALTEST
SALTFAT
SALTFOOT
SALTHOUSE
SALTICID
SALTIE
SALTIER
SALTIERRA
SALTIERWISE
SALTIEST
SALTIGRADE
SALTILY
SALTIMBANCO
SALTINE
SALTINESS
SALTING
SALTIRE
SALTIREWISE
SALTISH
SALTMAKING
SALTMAN
SALTMOUTH
SALTNESS
SALTO
SALTOMETER
SALTOREL
SALTPAN
SALTPANS
SALTPETER
SALTPETRE
SALTS
SALTSHAKER
SALTSPOONFUL
SALTSPRINKLER
SALTUS
SALTWEED
SALTWORK
SALTWORKER
SALTWORKS
SALTWORT
SALTY
SALUBRIFY
SALUBRIOUS
SALUBRIOUSLY
SALUBRITY
SALUDA
SALUE
SALUKI
SALUNG
SALUS
SALUTARILY
SALUTARINESS

SALUTARY
SALUTATION
SALUTATIONAL
SALUTATIOUS
SALUTATORIAN
SALUTATORIES
SALUTATORY
SALUTE
SALUTER
SALUTES
SALVABILITY
SALVABLE
SALVABLY
SALVAGE
SALVAGEABLE
SALVAGED
SALVAGEE
SALVAGER
SALVAGING
SALVARSAN
SALVATELLA
SALVATION
SALVATIONAL
SALVATIONISM
SALVATIONIST
SALVATOR
SALVATORY
SALVE
SALVED
SALVER
SALVERFORM
SALVIA
SALVIANIN
SALVIFIC
SALVIFICAL
SALVING
SALVIOL
SALVO
SALVOES
SALVOR
SALVOS
SALVY
SALWE
SALWIN
SAM
SAMA
SAMADH
SAMADHI
SAMAJ
SAMAN
SAMARA
SAMARIA
SAMARIFORM
SAMARIUM
SAMAROID
SAMARSKITE
SAMBA
SAMBAL
SAMBAQUI
SAMBAQUIS
SAMBAR
SAMBARS
SAMBAS
SAMBEL
SAMBHAR
SAMBHUR
SAMBO
SAMBOS
SAMBOUK
SAMBOUSE
SAMBUCA
SAMBUK
SAMBUKE
SAMBUL
SAMBUNIGRIN
SAMBUR
SAME
SAMECH
SAMEK
SAMEKH
SAMEL
SAMELY
SAMEN
SAMENESS
SAMESOME
SAMGHA
SAMH
SAMHITA
SAMIEL
SAMIRESITE
SAMIRI
SAMISEN
SAMITE
SAMKARA
SAMKHYA
SAMLET
SAMM
SAMMEL
SAMMER
SAMMIER
SAMMY
SAMNANI
SAMOGON
SAMOGONKA
SAMOHU
SAMORY
SAMOTHERE
SAMOVAR
SAMP
SAMPAGUITA
SAMPALOC
SAMPAN
SAMPHIRE
SAMPI
SAMPLE
SAMPLED
SAMPLEMAN
SAMPLEMEN
SAMPLER
SAMPLERY
SAMPLES
SAMPLING
SAMSARA
SAMSHU
SAMSKARA
SAMSONITE
SAMUIN
SAMUM
SAMURAI
SAMVAT
SAN
SANA
SANABILITY
SANABLE
SANAD
SANAI
SANATION
SANATIVE
SANATIVENESS
SANATORIUM
SANATORIUMS
SANATORY
SANBENITO
SANCHO
SANCORD
SANCT
SANCTA
SANCTANIMITY
SANCTIFICATE
SANCTIFICATION
SANCTIFIED
SANCTIFIEDLY
SANCTIFIER
SANCTIFY
SANCTIFYING
SANCTILOGY
SANCTILOQUENT
SANCTIMONIAL
SANCTIMONIOUS
SANCTIMONIOUSLY
SANCTIMONIOUSNESS
SANCTIMONY
SANCTION
SANCTIONARY
SANCTIONATIVE
SANCTIONED
SANCTIONER
SANCTITIES
SANCTITUDE
SANCTITY
SANCTOLOGIST
SANCTORIUM
SANCTUARIED
SANCTUARIES
SANCTUARIZE
SANCTUARY
SANCTUM
SANCTUMS
SANCYITE
SAND
SANDAK
SANDAL
SANDALED
SANDALIFORM
SANDALING
SANDALLED
SANDALLING
SANDALWOOD
SANDALWORT
SANDAN
SANDARAC
SANDARACIN
SANDASTRA
SANDASTROS
SANDBAG
SANDBAGGED
SANDBAGGER
SANDBAGGING
SANDBANK
SANDBAR
SANDBLAST
SANDBLASTER
SANDBLIND
SANDBOARD
SANDBOX
SANDBOY
SANDBUR
SANDBURR
SANDCLUB
SANDED
SANDER
SANDERLING
SANDERS
SANDERSWOOD
SANDFISH
SANDGOBY
SANDHEAT
SANDHI
SANDHOG
SANDIA
SANDIER
SANDIES
SANDIEST
SANDING
SANDIVER
SANDIX
SANDKEY
SANDLAPPER
SANDLING
SANDLOT
SANDMAN
SANDMITE
SANDNATTER
SANDPAPER
SANDPAPERER
SANDPEEP
SANDPILE
SANDPIPER
SANDPIPERS
SANDRA
SANDROCK
SANDSHOE
SANDSOAP
SANDSPIT
SANDSPUR
SANDSTAY
SANDSTONE
SANDSTORM
SANDUNGA
SANDUST
SANDWEED
SANDWICH
SANDWICHED
SANDWICHING
SANDWOOD
SANDWORM
SANDWORT
SANDY
SANDYISH
SANDYX
SANE
SANELY
SANENESS
SANER
SANEST
SANG
SANGA
SANGAH
SANGAMON
SANGAR
SANGAREE
SANGFROID
SANGGAU
SANGH
SANGHA
SANGIL
SANGLANT
SANGLEY
SANGLIER
SANGREEROOT
SANGREL
SANGU
SANGUICOLOUS
SANGUIFEROUS
SANGUIFIER
SANGUIMOTOR
SANGUIMOTORY
SANGUINARY
SANGUINE
SANGUINELESS
SANGUINELY
SANGUINENESS
SANGUINEOUS
SANGUINITY
SANGUINOLENT
SANGUINOUS
SANGUISUGE
SANGUISUGENT
SANGUISUGOUS
SANICLE
SANIDINE
SANIDINITE
SANIES
SANIFICATION
SANIFY
SANIOUS
SANITARIA
SANITARIAN
SANITARIES
SANITARIST
SANITARIUM
SANITARIUMS
SANITARY
SANITATE
SANITATED
SANITATING
SANITATION
SANITIZE
SANITIZED
SANITY
SANJAK
SANJAKBEG
SANK
SANKH
SANKHA
SANN
SANNA
SANNAITE
SANNHEMP
SANNUP
SANNYASI
SANNYASIN
SANS
SANSAR
SANSARA
SANSCULOT
SANSERIF
SANSHACH
SANSI
SANT
SANTA
SANTAL
SANTALACEOUS
SANTALIN
SANTALOL
SANTAPEE
SANTAR
SANTENE
SANTIMS
SANTIR
SANTO
SANTOL
SANTON
SANTONICA
SANTONIN
SANTONINE
SANTORINITE
SANTOS
SANTOUR
SANTY
SANUKITE
SAO
SAORA
SAP
SAPA
SAPAJOU
SAPAN
SAPANWOOD
SAPBUSH
SAPE
SAPEC
SAPEK
SAPFUL
SAPHEAD
SAPHEADED
SAPHEADEDNESS
SAPHENA
SAPHENAE
SAPHENAL
SAPHENOUS
SAPHIE
SAPIAO
SAPID
SAPIDITY
SAPIDNESS

SAPIENCE
SAPIENCY
SAPIENT
SAPIENTIAL
SAPIENTIALLY
SAPIENTIZE
SAPIENTLY
SAPIN
SAPINDA
SAPINDACEOUS
SAPINDASHIP
SAPINDUS
SAPIT
SAPIUTAN
SAPLE
SAPLESS
SAPLESSNESS
SAPLING
SAPO
SAPODILLA
SAPODILLO
SAPOGENIN
SAPONACEOUS
SAPONACITY
SAPONARIN
SAPONARY
SAPONIFIABLE
SAPONIFIED
SAPONIFIER
SAPONIFY
SAPONIFYING
SAPONIN
SAPONINE
SAPONITE
SAPONUL
SAPONULE
SAPOPHORIC
SAPOR
SAPORIFIC
SAPOROSITY
SAPOROUS
SAPOTACEOUS
SAPOTE
SAPOTOXIN
SAPPANWOOD
SAPPARE
SAPPED
SAPPER
SAPPHIRE
SAPPHIRED
SAPPHIRINE
SAPPIER
SAPPIEST
SAPPILY
SAPPING
SAPPLES
SAPPY
SAPRAEMIA
SAPREMIA
SAPREMIC
SAPRIN
SAPRINE
SAPROCOLL
SAPRODIL
SAPRODONTIA
SAPROGEN
SAPROGENIC
SAPROGENOUS
SAPROLITE
SAPROLITIC
SAPROPEL
SAPROPELIC
SAPROPELITE
SAPROPHAGAN
SAPROPHAGOUS
SAPROPHILOUS
SAPROPHYTE
SAPROPHYTIC
SAPROPHYTISM
SAPROPLANKTON
SAPROSTOMOUS
SAPROZOIC
SAPS
SAPSAGO
SAPSAP
SAPSUCK
SAPSUCKER
SAPUCAIA
SAPUCAINHA
SAPWOOD
SAPWORT
SARAAD
SARABAND
SARAF
SARAFAN
SARAN
SARANGI
SARANGOUSTY
SARAPE
SARAVAN
SARAWAKITE
SARBACANE
SARCASM
SARCAST
SARCASTIC
SARCASTICAL
SARCASTICALLY
SARCASTICNESS
SARCEL
SARCELLE
SARCELLY
SARCENET
SARCILIS
SARCITIS
SARCLE
SARCLER
SARCOBLAST
SARCOCARP
SARCOCELE
SARCOCOL
SARCOCOLLIN
SARCOCYTE
SARCODE
SARCODERM
SARCODERMA
SARCODES
SARCODIC
SARCOGENIC
SARCOGENOUS
SARCOGLIA
SARCOID
SARCOLEMMA
SARCOLEMMIC
SARCOLEMMOUS
SARCOLINE
SARCOLITE
SARCOLOGIC
SARCOLOGICAL
SARCOLOGIST
SARCOLOGY
SARCOLYSIS
SARCOLYTE
SARCOLYTIC
SARCOMA
SARCOMATA
SARCOMATOID
SARCOMATOSIS
SARCOMATOUS
SARCOMERE
SARCOPHAGAL
SARCOPHAGI
SARCOPHAGIC
SARCOPHAGID
SARCOPHAGIZE
SARCOPHAGOUS
SARCOPHAGUS
SARCOPHAGY
SARCOPHILE
SARCOPHILOUS
SARCOPLASM
SARCOPLASMA
SARCOPLASMIC
SARCOPLAST
SARCOPLASTIC
SARCOPTIC
SARCOPTID
SARCOSEPSIS
SARCOSINE
SARCOSIS
SARCOSOMA
SARCOSOME
SARCOSPERM
SARCOSPORID
SARCOSTOSIS
SARCOSTYLE
SARCOTHECA
SARCOTIC
SARCOUS
SARD
SARDACHATE
SARDANA
SARDAR
SARDEL
SARDELLE
SARDINE
SARDINES
SARDIUS
SARDONIC
SARDONICALLY
SARDONICISM
SARDONYX
SAREE
SARGASSO
SARGASSUM
SARGE
SARGO
SARGOS
SARGUS
SARI
SARIGUE
SARIN
SARINDA
SARIP
SARIS
SARK
SARKFUL
SARKICAL
SARKING
SARKINITE
SARKIT
SARKLESS
SARLAK
SARLYK
SARMATIER
SARMENT
SARMENTA
SARMENTOSE
SARMENTOUS
SARMENTUM
SARNA
SAROD
SARON
SARONG
SARONIC
SARONIDE
SAROS
SAROTHRUM
SARPE
SARPLER
SARPO
SARRA
SARRAZIN
SARRE
SARROW
SARRUSOPHONE
SARSA
SARSAPARILLA
SARSAR
SARSEN
SARSENET
SARSNET
SARSON
SARTOR
SARTORIAD
SARTORIAL
SARTORIALLY
SARTORIAN
SARTORITE
SARTORIUS
SARUS
SARWAN
SASAN
SASANI
SASANQUA
SASARARA
SASH
SASHAY
SASHED
SASHERIES
SASHERY
SASHES
SASHIMI
SASHING
SASHOON
SASIN
SASINE
SASKATOON
SASS
SASSABIES
SASSABY
SASSAFRAS
SASSAGUM
SASSANDRA
SASSE
SASSIER
SASSIEST
SASSOLIN
SASSOLINE
SASSWOOD
SASSY
SASSYBARK
SASSYWOOD
SASTRA
SASTRUGA
SASTRUGI
SAT
SATANG
SATANIC
SATANICAL
SATANICALLY
SATANIST
SATANIZE
SATARA
SATCHEL
SATCHELED
SATE
SATED
SATEEN
SATEENWOOD
SATELLES
SATELLITE
SATELLITED
SATELLITIAN
SATELLITIC
SATELLITIOUS
SATELLITIUM
SATELLITOID
SATELLITORY
SATELLOID
SATI
SATIABILITY
SATIABLE
SATIABLENESS
SATIABLY
SATIATE
SATIATED
SATIATING
SATIATION
SATIENT
SATIETIES
SATIETY
SATIN
SATINAY
SATINBUSH
SATINE
SATINED
SATINET
SATINETTE
SATINFIN
SATINFLOWER
SATING
SATINING
SATINITE
SATINITY
SATINIZE
SATINLEAF
SATINPOD
SATINWOOD
SATINY
SATION
SATIRE
SATIRIC
SATIRICAL
SATIRICALLY
SATIRICALNESS
SATIRIST
SATIRIZABLE
SATIRIZE
SATIRIZED
SATIRIZER
SATIRIZING
SATISDATION
SATISDICTION
SATISFACTION
SATISFACTIONAL
SATISFACTIVE
SATISFACTORILY
SATISFACTORY
SATISFIED
SATISFIEDLY
SATISFIEDNESS
SATISFIER
SATISFY
SATISFYING
SATISFYINGLY
SATISPASSION
SATIVE
SATLIJK
SATORI
SATRAP
SATRAPATE
SATRAPESS
SATRAPIC
SATRAPICAL
SATRAPIES
SATRAPY
SATRON
SATSOP
SATTAR
SATTIE
SATTVA
SATURA
SATURABILITY
SATURABLE
SATURANT

SATURATE
SATURATED
SATURATER
SATURATING
SATURATION
SATURATOR
SATURITY
SATURNIID
SATURNINE
SATURNINELY
SATURNINITY
SATURNISM
SATURNIST
SATURNIZE
SATURY
SATYAGRAHA
SATYASHODAK
SATYR
SATYRESQUE
SATYRESS
SATYRIASIS
SATYRIC
SATYRICAL
SATYRID
SATYRINE
SATYRION
SATYRISM
SATYROMANIAC
SAUCE
SAUCEBOAT
SAUCEBOX
SAUCEDISH
SAUCEMAN
SAUCEMEN
SAUCEPAN
SAUCEPOT
SAUCER
SAUCERLEAF
SAUCERLIKE
SAUCERY
SAUCH
SAUCIER
SAUCIEST
SAUCILY
SAUCINESS
SAUCISSE
SAUCY
SAUERBRATEN
SAUERKRAUT
SAUGER
SAUGH
SAUGHEN
SAUGHT
SAUK
SAUL
SAULGE
SAULIE
SAULT
SAUM
SAUMON
SAUMONT
SAUNA
SAUNDERS
SAUNT
SAUNTER
SAUNTERED
SAUNTERER
SAUNTERING
SAUQUI
SAUR
SAUREL
SAURIAN
SAURIOSIS
SAURISCHIAN
SAURLESS
SAURODONT
SAUROID
SAUROPOD
SAUROPSID
SAUROPSIDAN
SAURY
SAUSAGE
SAUSINGER
SAUSSURITE
SAUTE
SAUTEED
SAUTEING
SAUTER
SAUTEREAU
SAUTERELLE
SAUTERNE
SAUTERNES
SAUTEUR
SAUTOIR
SAUTREE
SAUVE
SAVABLE
SAVABLENESS
SAVAGE
SAVAGED
SAVAGEDOM
SAVAGELY
SAVAGENESS
SAVAGER
SAVAGERIES
SAVAGEROUS
SAVAGERY
SAVAGESS
SAVAGEST
SAVAGING
SAVAGISM
SAVAGIZE
SAVANILLA
SAVANNA
SAVANNAH
SAVANT
SAVARIN
SAVATE
SAVATION
SAVE
SAVED
SAVELHA
SAVELOY
SAVEMENT
SAVER
SAVEY
SAVILE
SAVIN
SAVINE
SAVING
SAVINGLY
SAVINGNESS
SAVINGS
SAVIOR
SAVIORESS
SAVIOUR
SAVIOURESS
SAVOLA
SAVOR
SAVORED
SAVORER
SAVORILY
SAVORINESS
SAVORING
SAVORLESS
SAVORLY
SAVOROUS
SAVORY
SAVOUR
SAVOURIER
SAVOURIEST
SAVOURY
SAVOY
SAVOYED
SAVOYING
SAVSSAT
SAVVIED
SAVVY
SAVVYING
SAW
SAWAH
SAWALI
SAWBACK
SAWBELLY
SAWBILL
SAWBONES
SAWBUCK
SAWBWA
SAWDER
SAWDUST
SAWDUSTISH
SAWDUSTY
SAWED
SAWER
SAWFISH
SAWFISHES
SAWFLIES
SAWFLOM
SAWFLY
SAWHORSE
SAWING
SAWINGS
SAWLIKE
SAWLOG
SAWLSHOT
SAWMAN
SAWMILL
SAWMONT
SAWN
SAWNEB
SAWNEY
SAWNIE
SAWNY
SAWSETTER
SAWSMITH
SAWT
SAWTOOTH
SAWWAY
SAWWORT
SAWYER
SAX
SAXATILE
SAXAUL
SAXBOARD
SAXCORNET
SAXHORN
SAXICOLE
SAXICOLINE
SAXICOLOUS
SAXIFRAGANT
SAXIFRAGOUS
SAXIFRAX
SAXIGENOUS
SAXON
SAXONITE
SAXOPHONE
SAXOPHONIC
SAXOPHONIST
SAXOTROMBA
SAXTUBA
SAY
SAYA
SAYER
SAYETTE
SAYID
SAYING
SAYINGS
SAYNAY
SAYNETE
SAYON
SAYONARA
SAYYID
SAZEN
SAZERAC
SBIRRO
SCAB
SCABBADO
SCABBARD
SCABBED
SCABBEDNESS
SCABBERY
SCABBIER
SCABBIEST
SCABBILY
SCABBINESS
SCABBING
SCABBLE
SCABBLED
SCABBLER
SCABBLING
SCABBY
SCABELLUM
SCABERULOUS
SCABETIC
SCABIA
SCABIES
SCABIETIC
SCABINE
SCABINUS
SCABIOSA
SCABIOSITY
SCABIOUS
SCABISH
SCABLAND
SCABRATE
SCABRESCENT
SCABRID
SCABRIDITY
SCABRIDULOUS
SCABRIN
SCABRITIES
SCABROCK
SCABROUS
SCABROUSLY
SCABROUSNESS
SCABWORT
SCACCHIC
SCAD
SCADDLE
SCADS
SCAENA
SCAFF
SCAFFER
SCAFFERY
SCAFFIE
SCAFFLE
SCAFFOLD
SCAFFOLDAGE
SCAFFOLDED
SCAFFOLDER
SCAFFOLDING
SCAFFY
SCAGLIA
SCAGLIOLA
SCAGLIOLIST
SCAIFE
SCALA
SCALABLE
SCALADE
SCALADO
SCALAE
SCALAGE
SCALAR
SCALARE
SCALARIFORM
SCALARWISE
SCALARY
SCALAWAG
SCALAWAGGERY
SCALAWAGGY
SCALD
SCALDBERRY
SCALDED
SCALDER
SCALDFISH
SCALDIC
SCALDING
SCALDINI
SCALDINO
SCALDWEED
SCALDY
SCALE
SCALEBACK
SCALEBARK
SCALEBOARD
SCALED
SCALEDRAKE
SCALEFISH
SCALEFUL
SCALEMAN
SCALEMEN
SCALENE
SCALENON
SCALENOUS
SCALENUM
SCALENUS
SCALEPAN
SCALER
SCALES
SCALESMITH
SCALET
SCALETAIL
SCALEWING
SCALEWORK
SCALFE
SCALIER
SCALIEST
SCALIGER
SCALINESS
SCALING
SCALL
SCALLAGE
SCALLAWAG
SCALLED
SCALLION
SCALLOM
SCALLOP
SCALLOPED
SCALLOPER
SCALLOPING
SCALLYWAG
SCALMA
SCALOPPINE
SCALP
SCALPED
SCALPEEN
SCALPEL
SCALPELLAR
SCALPELLIC
SCALPELLUM
SCALPER
SCALPING
SCALPLESS
SCALPRA
SCALPRIFORM
SCALPRUM
SCALPTURE
SCALY
SCAM
SCAMBLE
SCAMBLED
SCAMBLER
SCAMBLING
SCAMILLUS
SCAMMEL

SCAMMONIATE
SCAMMONY
SCAMP
SCAMPAVIA
SCAMPER
SCAMPERED
SCAMPERER
SCAMPERING
SCAMPI
SCAMPING
SCAMPISH
SCAMPISHLY
SCAMPISHNESS
SCAN
SCANCE
SCANDAL
SCANDALED
SCANDALING
SCANDALIZATION
SCANDALIZE
SCANDALIZED
SCANDALIZING
SCANDALLED
SCANDALLING
SCANDALMONGER
SCANDALOUS
SCANDALOUSLY
SCANDALOUSNESS
SCANDAROON
SCANDENT
SCANDIA
SCANDIC
SCANDICUS
SCANDIUM
SCANMAG
SCANNABLE
SCANNED
SCANNER
SCANNING
SCANNINGLY
SCANSION
SCANSIONIST
SCANSORIAL
SCANSORIOUS
SCANSORY
SCANT
SCANTED
SCANTER
SCANTEST
SCANTIER
SCANTIES
SCANTIEST
SCANTILY
SCANTINESS
SCANTING
SCANTITY
SCANTLE
SCANTLET
SCANTLING
SCANTLINGED
SCANTLY
SCANTNESS
SCANTY
SCAPE
SCAPEGOAT
SCAPEGRACE
SCAPEL
SCAPELESS
SCAPETHRIFT
SCAPHA
SCAPHE
SCAPHION
SCAPHISM
SCAPHITE
SCAPHITOID
SCAPHOCERITE
SCAPHOCERITIC
SCAPHOID
SCAPHOLUNAR
SCAPHOPOD
SCAPHOPODOUS
SCAPI
SCAPIFORM
SCAPIGEROUS
SCAPOID
SCAPOLITE
SCAPOSE
SCAPPLE
SCAPPLER
SCAPULA
SCAPULAR
SCAPULARE
SCAPULARY
SCAPULATED
SCAPULET
SCAPULETTE
SCAPULIMANCY
SCAPULOPEXY
SCAPUS
SCAR
SCARAB
SCARABAEAN
SCARABAEI
SCARABAEID
SCARABAEOID
SCARABAEUS
SCARABAEUSES
SCARABEE
SCARABOID
SCARCE
SCARCELINS
SCARCELY
SCARCEMENT
SCARCEN
SCARCENESS
SCARCER
SCARCEST
SCARCITY
SCARCY
SCARE
SCAREBABE
SCAREBUG
SCARECROW
SCARECROWISH
SCARECROWY
SCARED
SCAREFUL
SCAREHEAD
SCAREMONGER
SCAREMONGERING
SCARER
SCAREY
SCARF
SCARFE
SCARFED
SCARFER
SCARFING
SCARFPIN
SCARFS
SCARFSKIN
SCARID
SCARIER
SCARIEST
SCARIFICATION
SCARIFICATOR
SCARIFIED
SCARIFIER
SCARIFY
SCARIFYING
SCARING
SCARINGLY
SCARIOLE
SCARIOSE
SCARIOUS
SCARLATINA
SCARLATINAL
SCARLATINOID
SCARLET
SCARLETBERRY
SCARLETSEED
SCARLETY
SCARN
SCAROID
SCAROLA
SCARP
SCARPA
SCARPE
SCARPED
SCARPER
SCARPETTI
SCARPH
SCARPINES
SCARPING
SCARPLET
SCARR
SCARRED
SCARRER
SCARRING
SCARROW
SCARRY
SCARS
SCART
SCARTH
SCARUS
SCARVED
SCARVES
SCARY
SCAT
SCATBACK
SCATCH
SCATH
SCATHE
SCATHED
SCATHEFUL
SCATHELESS
SCATHELESSLY
SCATHFUL
SCATHING
SCATHINGLY
SCATHY
SCATLAND
SCATOLOGIA
SCATOLOGIC
SCATOLOGICAL
SCATOLOGIST
SCATOLOGY
SCATOPHAGOUS
SCATOPHAGY
SCATOSCOPY
SCATT
SCATTED
SCATTER
SCATTERATION
SCATTERAWAY
SCATTERBRAIN
SCATTERBRAINED
SCATTERBRAINS
SCATTERED
SCATTERER
SCATTERGOOD
SCATTERING
SCATTERINGLY
SCATTERLING
SCATTERMOUCH
SCATTERY
SCATTIER
SCATTIEST
SCATTING
SCATTY
SCATULA
SCATURIENT
SCAUD
SCAUM
SCAUP
SCAUPER
SCAUPS
SCAUR
SCAURIE
SCAUT
SCAVAGE
SCAVAGER
SCAVAGERY
SCAVENAGE
SCAVENGE
SCAVENGED
SCAVENGER
SCAVENGERY
SCAVENGING
SCAW
SCAWTITE
SCAZON
SCAZONTIC
SCEAR
SCEAT
SCEGGER
SCELERAT
SCELOTYRBE
SCENA
SCENARIO
SCENARIOS
SCENARIST
SCENARIZE
SCENARIZING
SCENARY
SCEND
SCENE
SCENECRAFT
SCENERY
SCENES
SCENESHIFTER
SCENEWRIGHT
SCENIC
SCENICAL
SCENIST
SCENITE
SCENOGRAPH
SCENOGRAPHER
SCENOGRAPHIC
SCENOGRAPHY
SCENSION
SCENT
SCENTED
SCENTER
SCENTFUL
SCENTING
SCENTLESS
SCENTWOOD
SCEPSIS
SCEPTER
SCEPTERDOM
SCEPTERED
SCEPTERING
SCEPTERLESS
SCEPTIC
SCEPTICAL
SCEPTICISM
SCEPTICIZE
SCEPTICIZED
SCEPTICIZING
SCEPTRAL
SCEPTRE
SCEPTRED
SCEPTREDOM
SCEPTRELESS
SCEPTRING
SCEPTROSOPHY
SCEPTRY
SCERNE
SCETE
SCEUOPHYLAX
SCEWING
SCHADCHAN
SCHAIRERITE
SCHAL
SCHALMEI
SCHALMEY
SCHALSTEIN
SCHANZ
SCHAPPE
SCHAPPING
SCHAPSKA
SCHARF
SCHATCHEN
SCHEAT
SCHEDIASM
SCHEDULAR
SCHEDULATE
SCHEDULE
SCHEDULED
SCHEDULING
SCHEDULIZE
SCHEELIN
SCHEELITE
SCHEFFEL
SCHEFFERITE
SCHEL
SCHELLING
SCHELLY
SCHELM
SCHELTOPUSIK
SCHEMA
SCHEMATA
SCHEMATIC
SCHEMATICAL
SCHEMATICALLY
SCHEMATISM
SCHEMATIST
SCHEMATIZE
SCHEMATOGRAM
SCHEMATOGRAPH
SCHEMATONICS
SCHEME
SCHEMED
SCHEMER
SCHEMERY
SCHEMING
SCHEMIST
SCHEMOZZLE
SCHEMY
SCHENE
SCHEPEL
SCHEPEN
SCHERM
SCHERZANDO
SCHERZI
SCHERZO
SCHERZOS
SCHESIS
SCHIAVONE
SCHIFFLI
SCHIH
SCHILLER
SCHILLERFELS
SCHILLERIZE
SCHILLERIZED
SCHILLERIZING
SCHILLING
SCHILLU
SCHIMMEL
SCHIPPERKE
SCHISM
SCHISMA
SCHISMATIC
SCHISMATICAL
SCHISMATICALLY

SCHISMATISM
SCHISMATIST
SCHISMATIZE
SCHISMATIZED
SCHISMATIZING
SCHISMIC
SCHIST
SCHISTACEOUS
SCHISTIC
SCHISTOCYTE
SCHISTOID
SCHISTOSCOPE
SCHISTOSE
SCHISTOSITY
SCHISTOSOME
SCHISTOUS
SCHIZAXON
SCHIZOCARP
SCHIZOCARPIC
SCHIZOCHROAL
SCHIZOCOELE
SCHIZODINIC
SCHIZOGAMY
SCHIZOGENESIS
SCHIZOGENETIC
SCHIZOGENIC
SCHIZOGENOUS
SCHIZOGNATH
SCHIZOGONIC
SCHIZOGONY
SCHIZOID
SCHIZOIDISM
SCHIZOLITE
SCHIZOMYCETE
SCHIZOMYCETES
SCHIZONT
SCHIZOPELMOUS
SCHIZOPHASIA
SCHIZOPHRENE
SCHIZOPHRENIA
SCHIZOPHYTE
SCHIZOPOD
SCHIZOPODAL
SCHIZOPODOUS
SCHIZORHINAL
SCHIZOSPORE
SCHIZOSTELE
SCHIZOSTELIC
SCHIZOSTELY
SCHIZOTHECAL
SCHIZOTHYME
SCHIZOTHYMIA
SCHIZOTHYMIC
SCHIZOTRICHIA
SCHIZTIC
SCHIZZO
SCHLEMIEL
SCHLENTER
SCHLEPP
SCHLIEREN
SCHLOCK
SCHLOOP
SCHMALTZ
SCHMALZ
SCHMALZY
SCHMEISS
SCHMELZ
SCHMO
SCHMOOSE
SCHMOOZE
SCHMUCK
SCHNAPPER
SCHNAPPS
SCHNAUZER
SCHNEIDER
SCHNELL
SCHNITZ
SCHNITZEL
SCHNOOK
SCHNORRER
SCHNOZZLE
SCHO
SCHOCHE
SCHOENANTH
SCHOENOBATIC
SCHOKKER
SCHOLA
SCHOLAPTITUDE
SCHOLAR
SCHOLARCH
SCHOLARIAN
SCHOLARISM
SCHOLARLIKE
SCHOLARLY
SCHOLARS
SCHOLARSHIP
SCHOLASM
SCHOLASTIC
SCHOLASTICAL
SCHOLASTICALLY
SCHOLASTICATE
SCHOLASTICISM
SCHOLASTICLY
SCHOLASTICUS
SCHOLIA
SCHOLIAST
SCHOLIASTIC
SCHOLION
SCHOLIUM
SCHOLIUMS
SCHONE
SCHONFELSITE
SCHOOL
SCHOOLABLE
SCHOOLAGE
SCHOOLBOOK
SCHOOLBOOKISH
SCHOOLBOY
SCHOOLBOYDOM
SCHOOLBOYISH
SCHOOLBOYISHLY
SCHOOLBOYISM
SCHOOLCRAFT
SCHOOLDAME
SCHOOLED
SCHOOLER
SCHOOLERY
SCHOOLFELLOW
SCHOOLGIRL
SCHOOLGIRLHOOD
SCHOOLGIRLISH
SCHOOLGIRLISHLY
SCHOOLGIRLISM
SCHOOLGIRLY
SCHOOLHOUSE
SCHOOLING
SCHOOLINGLY
SCHOOLISH
SCHOOLKEEPER
SCHOOLMAN
SCHOOLMARM
SCHOOLMASTER
SCHOOLMASTERING
SCHOOLMASTERISM
SCHOOLMASTERLY
SCHOOLMASTERY
SCHOOLMATE
SCHOOLMEN
SCHOOLMISTRESS
SCHOOLMISTRESSY
SCHOOLROOM
SCHOOLTEACHER
SCHOOLTIME
SCHOOLWARD
SCHOOLWARDS
SCHOOLWORK
SCHOOLYARD
SCHOON
SCHOONER
SCHOPPEN
SCHORL
SCHORLACEOUS
SCHORLOMITE
SCHORLOUS
SCHORLY
SCHOTTISCHE
SCHOUT
SCHOUW
SCHRADAN
SCHREINER
SCHRIK
SCHROTHER
SCHRUND
SCHTICK
SCHUH
SCHUIT
SCHUL
SCHULE
SCHULTENITE
SCHUNGITE
SCHUSS
SCHUYT
SCHWA
SCHWABACHER
SCHWANPAN
SCHWARZ
SCHYL
SCIAENID
SCIAENIFORM
SCIAENOID
SCIAGRAPH
SCIAGRAPHED
SCIAGRAPHIC
SCIAGRAPHING
SCIALYTIC
SCIAMACHIES
SCIAMACHY
SCIAMETRY
SCIAPOD
SCIAPODOUS
SCIARID
SCIASCOPE
SCIASCOPY
SCIATH
SCIATHERIC
SCIATHERICAL
SCIATIC
SCIATICA
SCIATICAL
SCIATICALLY
SCIATICKY
SCIBILE
SCIENCE
SCIENCED
SCIENT
SCIENTER
SCIENTIA
SCIENTIAL
SCIENTIARUM
SCIENTIFIC
SCIENTIFICAL
SCIENTIFICALLY
SCIENTISM
SCIENTIST
SCIENTISTIC
SCIENTIZE
SCIENTOLISM
SCILICET
SCILLAIN
SCILLIPICRIN
SCILLITIN
SCILLITINE
SCILLITOXIN
SCIMETAR
SCIMITAR
SCIMITARED
SCIMITARPOD
SCIMITER
SCIMITERED
SCIMITERPOD
SCINCID
SCINCIDOID
SCINCIFORM
SCINCOID
SCINCOIDIAN
SCIND
SCINIPH
SCINK
SCINTIL
SCINTILLA
SCINTILLANT
SCINTILLANTLY
SCINTILLATE
SCINTILLATED
SCINTILLATING
SCINTILLATINGLY
SCINTILLATION
SCINTILLATOR
SCINTILLESCENT
SCINTILLOMETER
SCINTILLOSCOPE
SCINTILLOSE
SCINTILLOUS
SCINTILLOUSLY
SCINTLE
SCINTLED
SCINTLER
SCINTLING
SCIOLISM
SCIOLIST
SCIOLISTIC
SCIOLOUS
SCIOLTO
SCIOMACHY
SCIOMANCY
SCION
SCIOPHILOUS
SCIOPHYTE
SCIOPTIC
SCIOPTICON
SCIOPTICS
SCIOPTRIC
SCIOSOPHIST
SCIOSOPHY
SCIOTHEISM
SCIOUS
SCIRENGA
SCIRRHI
SCIRRHOID
SCIRRHOSIS
SCIRRHOSITIES
SCIRRHOSITY
SCIRRHOUS
SCIRRHUS
SCIRRHUSES
SCIRTOPOD
SCIRTOPODOUS
SCISCITATION
SCISSEL
SCISSIBLE
SCISSIL
SCISSILE
SCISSION
SCISSOR
SCISSORBILL
SCISSORBIRD
SCISSORED
SCISSORER
SCISSORIA
SCISSORING
SCISSORIUM
SCISSORS
SCISSORTAIL
SCISSURA
SCISSURE
SCITUATE
SCIURID
SCIURINE
SCIUROID
SCLAFF
SCLAFFED
SCLAFFER
SCLAFFERT
SCLAFFING
SCLAT
SCLATCH
SCLAW
SCLERA
SCLERAL
SCLERANTH
SCLERE
SCLEREDEMA
SCLEREID
SCLEREMA
SCLERENCHYMA
SCLERENCHYME
SCLERERYTHRIN
SCLERETINITE
SCLERIASIS
SCLERIFY
SCLERITE
SCLERITIC
SCLERITIS
SCLERIZED
SCLEROBASE
SCLEROBASIC
SCLEROBLAST
SCLEROBLASTIC
SCLEROCAULY
SCLERODERM
SCLERODERMA
SCLERODERMIA
SCLERODERMIC
SCLERODERMITE
SCLEROGEN
SCLEROGENIC
SCLEROGENOUS
SCLEROID
SCLEROMA
SCLEROMATA
SCLEROMERE
SCLEROMETER
SCLERONYCHIA
SCLERONYXIS
SCLEROPHYLL
SCLEROPHYLLY
SCLEROPROTEIN
SCLEROSAL
SCLEROSE
SCLEROSED
SCLEROSEPTUM
SCLEROSES
SCLEROSIS
SCLEROTAL
SCLEROTE
SCLEROTIA
SCLEROTIAL
SCLEROTIC
SCLEROTICA
SCLEROTICAL
SCLEROTINIAL
SCLEROTIOID
SCLEROTITIC
SCLEROTITIS
SCLEROTIUM

SCLEROTIZED
SCLEROTOID
SCLEROTOME
SCLEROTOMIC
SCLEROTOMIES
SCLEROTOMY
SCLEROUS
SCLIFF
SCLIMB
SCLUM
SCLY
SCOAD
SCOB
SCOBBY
SCOBE
SCOBICULAR
SCOBIFORM
SCOBS
SCODGY
SCOFF
SCOFFED
SCOFFER
SCOFFERY
SCOFFING
SCOFFLAW
SCOG
SCOGGAN
SCOGGER
SCOGGIN
SCOGIE
SCOKE
SCOLD
SCOLDED
SCOLDENORE
SCOLDER
SCOLDING
SCOLDINGLY
SCOLECES
SCOLECIASIS
SCOLECID
SCOLECIFORM
SCOLECITE
SCOLECOID
SCOLERYNG
SCOLEX
SCOLEY
SCOLIA
SCOLICES
SCOLIID
SCOLIOGRAPTIC
SCOLIOMETER
SCOLION
SCOLIOSIS
SCOLIOTIC
SCOLIOTONE
SCOLITE
SCOLLOP
SCOLLOPER
SCOLOC
SCOLOG
SCOLOPENDRID
SCOLOPHORE
SCOLYTID
SCOLYTOID
SCOLYTUS
SCOMBRID
SCOMBRIFORM
SCOMBRINE
SCOMBROID
SCOMBRONE
SCOMFIT
SCOMM
SCON
SCONCE
SCONCED
SCONCER
SCONCHEON
SCONCIBLE
SCONCING
SCONE
SCOOCH
SCOON
SCOOP
SCOOPED
SCOOPER
SCOOPFUL
SCOOPING
SCOOR
SCOOT
SCOOTER
SCOOTERS
SCOOTS
SCOP
SCOPA
SCOPARIN
SCOPARIUS
SCOPATE
SCOPE
SCOPELISM
SCOPHONY
SCOPIC
SCOPINE
SCOPIOUS
SCOPIPED
SCOPOLA
SCOPOLAMIN
SCOPOLAMINE
SCOPOLEINE
SCOPOLETIN
SCOPOLINE
SCOPONE
SCOPPERIL
SCOPS
SCOPTICAL
SCOPULA
SCOPULARIAN
SCOPULATE
SCOPULIPED
SCOPULITE
SCORBUCH
SCORBUTE
SCORBUTIC
SCORBUTICAL
SCORBUTIZE
SCORBUTUS
SCORCE
SCORCH
SCORCHED
SCORCHER
SCORCHING
SCORCHINGLY
SCORCHINGNESS
SCORDATO
SCORDATURA
SCORDIUM
SCORE
SCORED
SCOREKEEPER
SCORELESS
SCORER
SCORES
SCORIA
SCORIAC
SCORIACEOUS
SCORIAE
SCORIFICATION
SCORIFIED
SCORIFIER
SCORIFORM
SCORIFY
SCORIFYING
SCORING
SCORIOUS
SCORKLE
SCORN
SCORNED
SCORNER
SCORNFUL
SCORNFULLY
SCORNFULNESS
SCORNING
SCORNY
SCORODITE
SCORPAENID
SCORPAENOID
SCORPENE
SCORPER
SCORPIOID
SCORPIOIDAL
SCORPION
SCORPIONIC
SCORPIONID
SCORPIONWORT
SCORSE
SCORSER
SCORTATION
SCORTATORY
SCORZA
SCOT
SCOTAL
SCOTALE
SCOTCH
SCOTCHED
SCOTCHER
SCOTCHING
SCOTCHMAN
SCOTE
SCOTER
SCOTERS
SCOTIA
SCOTINO
SCOTODINIA
SCOTOGRAM
SCOTOGRAPH
SCOTOGRAPHIC
SCOTOGRAPHY
SCOTOMA
SCOTOMATOUS
SCOTOMIA
SCOTOMIC
SCOTOMY
SCOTOPHOBIA
SCOTOPIA
SCOTOPIC
SCOTOSCOPE
SCOTOSIS
SCOTT
SCOUCH
SCOUNDREL
SCOUNDRELISH
SCOUNDRELLY
SCOUP
SCOUR
SCOURAGE
SCOURED
SCOURER
SCOURFISH
SCOURFISHES
SCOURGE
SCOURGED
SCOURGER
SCOURGING
SCOURGINGLY
SCOURING
SCOURINGS
SCOURWAY
SCOURWEED
SCOURWORT
SCOURY
SCOUSE
SCOUT
SCOUTCRAFT
SCOUTED
SCOUTER
SCOUTH
SCOUTHER
SCOUTHOOD
SCOUTING
SCOUTMASTER
SCOUTS
SCOUTWATCH
SCOVE
SCOVEL
SCOVY
SCOW
SCOWBANK
SCOWBANKER
SCOWDER
SCOWL
SCOWLED
SCOWLER
SCOWLING
SCOWLINGLY
SCOWMAN
SCOWMEN
SCOWTHER
SCRAB
SCRABBLE
SCRABBLED
SCRABBLER
SCRABBLING
SCRABBLY
SCRABE
SCRABER
SCRAE
SCRAFFLE
SCRAG
SCRAGGED
SCRAGGEDLY
SCRAGGEDNESS
SCRAGGER
SCRAGGIER
SCRAGGIEST
SCRAGGINESS
SCRAGGING
SCRAGGLE
SCRAGGLED
SCRAGGLING
SCRAGGLY
SCRAGGY
SCRAICH
SCRAIGH
SCRAILY
SCRAM
SCRAMASAX
SCRAMBLE
SCRAMBLED
SCRAMBLER
SCRAMBLING
SCRAMBLINGLY
SCRAMBLY
SCRAMMED
SCRAMMING
SCRAMPUM
SCRAN
SCRANCH
SCRANK
SCRANKY
SCRANNEL
SCRANNIER
SCRANNIEST
SCRANNING
SCRANNY
SCRAP
SCRAPABLE
SCRAPBOOK
SCRAPE
SCRAPED
SCRAPEPENNY
SCRAPER
SCRAPIE
SCRAPING
SCRAPINGLY
SCRAPMAN
SCRAPMONGER
SCRAPPAGE
SCRAPPER
SCRAPPET
SCRAPPIER
SCRAPPIEST
SCRAPPILY
SCRAPPINESS
SCRAPPLE
SCRAPPY
SCRAPS
SCRAPY
SCRAT
SCRATCH
SCRATCHBOARD
SCRATCHBRUSH
SCRATCHCARDING
SCRATCHCAT
SCRATCHED
SCRATCHER
SCRATCHES
SCRATCHIER
SCRATCHIEST
SCRATCHING
SCRATCHWEED
SCRATCHY
SCRATTER
SCRATTLE
SCRATTLING
SCRAUCHLE
SCRAW
SCRAWK
SCRAWL
SCRAWLED
SCRAWLER
SCRAWLIER
SCRAWLIEST
SCRAWLINESS
SCRAWLING
SCRAWLY
SCRAWM
SCRAWNIER
SCRAWNIEST
SCRAWNILY
SCRAWNINESS
SCRAWNY
SCRAY
SCRAYE
SCRAZE
SCREAK
SCREAKED
SCREAKING
SCREAKY
SCREAM
SCREAMED
SCREAMER
SCREAMINESS
SCREAMING
SCREAMINGLY
SCREAMY
SCREAR
SCREE
SCREECH
SCREECHBIRD
SCREECHED
SCREECHER
SCREECHIER
SCREECHIEST
SCREECHING
SCREECHY
SCREED

SCREEK
SCREEL
SCREEMAN
SCREEN
SCREENABLE
SCREENAGE
SCREENED
SCREENER
SCREENING
SCREENINGS
SCREENMAN
SCREENO
SCREENPLAY
SCREENSMAN
SCREENY
SCREEVE
SCREEVED
SCREEVER
SCREEVING
SCREW
SCREWBALL
SCREWBARREL
SCREWDRIVER
SCREWED
SCREWER
SCREWING
SCREWLESS
SCREWMAN
SCREWPILE
SCREWPOD
SCREWSMAN
SCREWSTOCK
SCREWWORM
SCREWY
SCRIB
SCRIBABLE
SCRIBACIOUS
SCRIBAL
SCRIBATIOUS
SCRIBBET
SCRIBBLAGE
SCRIBBLATIVE
SCRIBBLATORY
SCRIBBLE
SCRIBBLED
SCRIBBLEMENT
SCRIBBLER
SCRIBBLING
SCRIBBLINGLY
SCRIBBLY
SCRIBE
SCRIBED
SCRIBER
SCRIBING
SCRIBISM
SCRIDE
SCRIEVE
SCRIEVED
SCRIEVER
SCRIEVING
SCRIGGLE
SCRIGGLY
SCRIKE
SCRIM
SCRIME
SCRIMER
SCRIMMAGE
SCRIMMAGED
SCRIMMAGER
SCRIMMAGING
SCRIMP
SCRIMPED
SCRIMPER
SCRIMPIER
SCRIMPIEST
SCRIMPINESS
SCRIMPING
SCRIMPIT
SCRIMPTION
SCRIMPY
SCRIMSHANK
SCRIMSHAW
SCRIMY
SCRIN
SCRINCH
SCRINE
SCRINGE
SCRINIARY
SCRIP
SCRIPEE
SCRIPPAGE
SCRIPSIT
SCRIPT
SCRIPTER
SCRIPTION
SCRIPTITIOUS
SCRIPTITORY
SCRIPTIVE
SCRIPTOR
SCRIPTORIAL
SCRIPTORIUM
SCRIPTORY
SCRIPTURAL
SCRIPTURALLY
SCRIPTURE
SCRIPTURIENT
SCRIPTWRITER
SCRIPULUM
SCRIT
SCRITCH
SCRITE
SCRITHE
SCRIVAN
SCRIVANO
SCRIVE
SCRIVED
SCRIVELLO
SCRIVELLOES
SCRIVELLOS
SCRIVEN
SCRIVENER
SCRIVENERY
SCRIVENING
SCRIVER
SCRIVING
SCROB
SCROBBLE
SCROBE
SCROBICULA
SCROBICULAR
SCROBICULATE
SCROBICULE
SCROBICULUS
SCROBIS
SCROD
SCRODGILL
SCROFF
SCROFULA
SCROFULAROOT
SCROFULAWEED
SCROFULISM
SCROFULITIC
SCROFULODERM
SCROFULOSIS
SCROFULOUS
SCROFULOUSLY
SCROG
SCROGGED
SCROGGIE
SCROGGY
SCROGIE
SCROGS
SCROINOCH
SCROINOGH
SCROLAR
SCROLL
SCROLLED
SCROLLERY
SCROLLHEAD
SCROLLING
SCROLLWORK
SCROLLY
SCRONACH
SCROO
SCROOCH
SCROOP
SCROTAL
SCROTIFORM
SCROTUM
SCROUGE
SCROUGER
SCROUNGE
SCROUNGED
SCROUNGING
SCROUT
SCROW
SCROYLE
SCRUB
SCRUBBED
SCRUBBER
SCRUBBING
SCRUBBIRD
SCRUBBLY
SCRUBBOARD
SCRUBBY
SCRUBGRASS
SCRUBLAND
SCRUFF
SCRUFFLE
SCRUFFMAN
SCRUFFY
SCRUM
SCRUMMAGE
SCRUMMAGED
SCRUMMAGER
SCRUMMAGING
SCRUMP
SCRUMPLE
SCRUMPTIOUS
SCRUMPTIOUSLY
SCRUNCH
SCRUNCHY
SCRUNGE
SCRUNT
SCRUNTY
SCRUPLE
SCRUPLED
SCRUPLER
SCRUPLING
SCRUPULAR
SCRUPULIST
SCRUPULOSITY
SCRUPULOUS
SCRUPULOUSLY
SCRUSH
SCRUTABILITY
SCRUTABLE
SCRUTATE
SCRUTATION
SCRUTATOR
SCRUTATORY
SCRUTINANT
SCRUTINATE
SCRUTINEER
SCRUTINIZE
SCRUTINIZED
SCRUTINIZER
SCRUTINIZING
SCRUTINOUS
SCRUTINOUSLY
SCRUTINY
SCRUTO
SCRUTOIRE
SCRUZE
SCRY
SCRYER
SCRYING
SCUBA
SCUD
SCUDDALER
SCUDDAWN
SCUDDED
SCUDDER
SCUDDICK
SCUDDING
SCUDDLE
SCUDDY
SCUDI
SCUDO
SCUDS
SCUFE
SCUFF
SCUFFED
SCUFFER
SCUFFING
SCUFFLE
SCUFFLED
SCUFFLER
SCUFFLING
SCUFFY
SCUFT
SCUFTER
SCUG
SCUGGERY
SCULCH
SCULDUDDERIES
SCULDUDDERY
SCULL
SCULLED
SCULLER
SCULLERIES
SCULLERY
SCULLING
SCULLION
SCULLOG
SCULLOGUE
SCULLS
SCULP
SCULPIN
SCULPINS
SCULPSIT
SCULPT
SCULPTILE
SCULPTITORY
SCULPTOGRAPH
SCULPTOR
SCULPTRESS
SCULPTURAL
SCULPTURE
SCULPTURED
SCULPTURER
SCULPTURESQUE
SCULPTURING
SCULT
SCUM
SCUMBER
SCUMBLE
SCUMBLED
SCUMBLING
SCUMBOARD
SCUMFISH
SCUMMED
SCUMMER
SCUMMIER
SCUMMIEST
SCUMMING
SCUMMY
SCUN
SCUNDER
SCUNGILI
SCUNGILLI
SCUNNER
SCUP
SCUPPAUG
SCUPPER
SCUPPERNONG
SCUPPERS
SCUPPET
SCUPPIT
SCUPPLER
SCUR
SCURDY
SCURF
SCURFER
SCURFIER
SCURFIEST
SCURFINESS
SCURFY
SCURLING
SCURRIED
SCURRIER
SCURRIL
SCURRILE
SCURRILITY
SCURRILOUS
SCURRILOUSLY
SCURRY
SCURRYING
SCURVIED
SCURVILY
SCURVINESS
SCURVISH
SCURVY
SCUSE
SCUSIN
SCUT
SCUTA
SCUTAGE
SCUTAL
SCUTATE
SCUTATED
SCUTATIFORM
SCUTATION
SCUTCH
SCUTCHEON
SCUTCHER
SCUTCHING
SCUTE
SCUTELLA
SCUTELLAE
SCUTELLAR
SCUTELLARIN
SCUTELLATE
SCUTELLATED
SCUTELLATION
SCUTELLIFORM
SCUTELLUM
SCUTIFER
SCUTIFEROUS
SCUTIFORM
SCUTIGER
SCUTIGERAL
SCUTIGEROUS
SCUTIPED
SCUTTER
SCUTTLE
SCUTTLEBUTT
SCUTTLED
SCUTTLEMAN
SCUTTLER
SCUTTLING
SCUTTOCK
SCUTTY
SCUTULA
SCUTULAR

SCUTULATE
SCUTULUM
SCUTUM
SCYBALUM
SCYE
SCYELITE
SCYLD
SCYLLITE
SCYLLITOL
SCYPHA
SCYPHATE
SCYPHIFORM
SCYPHISTOMA
SCYPHOPHORE
SCYPHOSE
SCYPHOZOAN
SCYPHULA
SCYPHULUS
SCYPHUS
SCYTALE
SCYTHE
SCYTHED
SCYTHEMAN
SCYTHESMITH
SCYTHESTONE
SCYTHING
SDAIN
SDEIGN
SDRUCCIOLA
SE
SEA
SEABAG
SEABEACH
SEABEARD
SEABED
SEABERRY
SEABIRD
SEABOARD
SEABOOT
SEABORDERER
SEACANNIE
SEACATCH
SEACOAST
SEACONNY
SEACRAFT
SEACRAFTY
SEACROSS
SEACUNNY
SEADOG
SEADROME
SEAFARE
SEAFARER
SEAFARING
SEAFLOOD
SEAFLOWER
SEAFOAM
SEAFOLK
SEAFOOD
SEAFOWL
SEAGIRT
SEAGOER
SEAGOING
SEAH
SEAHOUND
SEAK
SEAL
SEALABLE
SEALCH
SEALED
SEALER
SEALERIES
SEALERY
SEALET
SEALIKE
SEALINE
SEALING
SEALKIE
SEALLESS
SEALS
SEALSKIN
SEALSKINS
SEALWORT
SEAM
SEAMAN
SEAMANITE
SEAMANLIKE
SEAMANLY
SEAMANSHIP
SEAMARK
SEAMBITER
SEAMED
SEAMEN
SEAMER
SEAMIER
SEAMIEST
SEAMINESS
SEAMING
SEAMLESS
SEAMLET
SEAMLIKE
SEAMOST
SEAMOUNT
SEAMREND
SEAMROG
SEAMS
SEAMSTER
SEAMSTRESS
SEAMY
SEANCE
SEAPIECE
SEAPLANE
SEAPOOSE
SEAPORT
SEAPOST
SEAQUAKE
SEAR
SEARCE
SEARCER
SEARCH
SEARCHABLE
SEARCHANT
SEARCHER
SEARCHFUL
SEARCHING
SEARCHINGLY
SEARCHINGNESS
SEARCHLESS
SEARCHLIGHT
SEARED
SEARER
SEARING
SEARY
SEAS
SEASCAPE
SEASCOUTING
SEASHELL
SEASHINE
SEASHORE
SEASICK
SEASICKNESS
SEASIDE
SEASIDER
SEASON
SEASONABLE
SEASONABLY
SEASONAL
SEASONALITY
SEASONALLY
SEASONED
SEASONER
SEASONING
SEAT
SEATANG
SEATED
SEATER
SEATING
SEATRAIN
SEATRON
SEATS
SEATSTONE
SEAVE
SEAVY
SEAWALL
SEAWAN
SEAWARD
SEAWARDLY
SEAWARDS
SEAWARE
SEAWATER
SEAWAY
SEAWEED
SEAWIFE
SEAWORN
SEAWORTHINESS
SEAWORTHY
SEAX
SEBACATE
SEBACEOUS
SEBACIC
SEBAGO
SEBAIT
SEBASTIANITE
SEBAT
SEBEL
SEBESTEN
SEBIC
SEBIFEROUS
SEBIFIC
SEBILLA
SEBKA
SEBKHA
SEBOLITH
SEBORRHAGIA
SEBORRHEA
SEBORRHEAL
SEBORRHOEA
SEBUM
SEBUNDY
SEC
SECABLE
SECALIN
SECALINE
SECALOSE
SECANCY
SECANT
SECANTLY
SECATEUR
SECCHIO
SECCO
SECEDE
SECEDED
SECEDER
SECEDING
SECERN
SECERNED
SECERNING
SECERNMENT
SECESH
SECESHER
SECESS
SECESSION
SECESSIONAL
SECESSIONALIST
SECESSIONISM
SECESSIONIST
SECK
SECLE
SECLUDE
SECLUDED
SECLUDEDLY
SECLUDEDNESS
SECLUDING
SECLUSE
SECLUSION
SECLUSIONIST
SECLUSIVE
SECLUSIVELY
SECODONT
SECOHM
SECOND
SECONDAR
SECONDARILY
SECONDARY
SECONDE
SECONDER
SECONDHAND
SECONDINE
SECONDLY
SECONDO
SECONDS
SECOURS
SECQUE
SECRECY
SECRET
SECRETA
SECRETAGE
SECRETAIRE
SECRETAR
SECRETARIAL
SECRETARIAN
SECRETARIAT
SECRETARIES
SECRETARY
SECRETE
SECRETED
SECRETIN
SECRETING
SECRETION
SECRETIONAL
SECRETIONARY
SECRETITIOUS
SECRETIVE
SECRETIVELY
SECRETIVENESS
SECRETLY
SECRETOR
SECRETORY
SECRETS
SECRETUM
SECT
SECTA
SECTARIAL
SECTARIAN
SECTARIANISM
SECTARIANIZE
SECTARIANIZED
SECTARIANIZING
SECTARIANLY
SECTARIES
SECTARISM
SECTARIST
SECTARY
SECTATOR
SECTILE
SECTILITY
SECTION
SECTIONAL
SECTIONALISM
SECTIONALIST
SECTIONALIZE
SECTIONALIZED
SECTIONALIZING
SECTIONALLY
SECTIONARY
SECTIONIZE
SECTISM
SECTIST
SECTOR
SECTORAL
SECTORIAL
SECTUARY
SECULAR
SECULARISM
SECULARIST
SECULARISTIC
SECULARITIES
SECULARITY
SECULARIZE
SECULARIZED
SECULARIZING
SECULUM
SECUND
SECUNDINE
SECUNDIPARA
SECUNDLY
SECUNDUM
SECURABLE
SECURE
SECURED
SECUREFUL
SECURELY
SECUREMENT
SECURENESS
SECURER
SECURING
SECURITIES
SECURITY
SECUS
SECUTOR
SEDAN
SEDANIER
SEDATE
SEDATELY
SEDATENESS
SEDATION
SEDATIVE
SEDENT
SEDENTARILY
SEDENTARINESS
SEDENTARY
SEDENTATION
SEDERUNT
SEDGE
SEDGELIKE
SEDGY
SEDILE
SEDILIA
SEDILIUM
SEDIMENT
SEDIMENTAL
SEDIMENTARIES
SEDIMENTARY
SEDIMENTATE
SEDIMENTATION
SEDIMENTOUS
SEDIMETRIC
SEDITION
SEDITIONARY
SEDITIONIST
SEDITIOUS
SEDITIOUSLY
SEDITIOUSNESS
SEDJADEH
SEDUCE
SEDUCEABLE
SEDUCED
SEDUCEE
SEDUCEMENT
SEDUCER
SEDUCIBLE
SEDUCING
SEDUCIVE
SEDUCT
SEDUCTION
SEDUCTIONIST

SEDUCTIVE
SEDUCTIVELY
SEDUCTIVENESS
SEDUCTRESS
SEDULITY
SEDULOUS
SEDULOUSLY
SEDULOUSNESS
SEDUM
SEE
SEECATCH
SEECATCHIE
SEECAWK
SEECHELT
SEED
SEEDAGE
SEEDBALL
SEEDBED
SEEDBIRD
SEEDBOX
SEEDCAKE
SEEDCASE
SEEDEATER
SEEDED
SEEDER
SEEDFUL
SEEDGALL
SEEDIER
SEEDIEST
SEEDILY
SEEDINESS
SEEDING
SEEDKIN
SEEDLEAF
SEEDLESS
SEEDLET
SEEDLING
SEEDLINGS
SEEDLIP
SEEDMAN
SEEDNESS
SEEDS
SEEDSMAN
SEEDSMEN
SEEDSTALK
SEEDSTER
SEEDTIME
SEEDY
SEEGE
SEEING
SEEINGLY
SEEINGNESS
SEEK
SEEKER
SEEKING
SEEL
SEELED
SEELFUL
SEELILY
SEELINESS
SEELING
SEELY
SEEM
SEEMABLE
SEEMER
SEEMING
SEEMINGLY
SEEMINGNESS
SEEMLESS
SEEMLIER
SEEMLIEST
SEEMLIHEAD
SEEMLILY
SEEMLINESS
SEEMLY
SEEN
SEENIL
SEEP
SEEPAGE
SEEPED
SEEPWEED
SEEPY
SEER
SEERBAND
SEERESS
SEERFISH
SEERHAND
SEERPAW
SEERSUCKER
SEESAW
SEESAWINESS
SEESEE
SEET
SEETHE
SEETHED
SEETHER
SEETHING
SEETHINGLY
SEEWEE
SEG
SEGA
SEGAR
SEGATHY
SEGE
SEGETAL
SEGG
SEGGE
SEGGED
SEGGIO
SEGGIOLA
SEGGROM
SEGGY
SEGHOL
SEGHOLATE
SEGMENT
SEGMENTAL
SEGMENTALLY
SEGMENTARY
SEGMENTATE
SEGMENTATION
SEGMENTED
SEGMENTS
SEGNI
SEGNO
SEGO
SEGOL
SEGOLATE
SEGOS
SEGOU
SEGRA
SEGREANT
SEGREGABLE
SEGREGATE
SEGREGATED
SEGREGATING
SEGREGATION
SEGREGATIONAL
SEGREGATIONIST
SEGREGATIVE
SEGREGATOR
SEGUE
SEGUENDO
SEGUIDILLA
SEI
SEICENTO
SEICHE
SEID
SEIDEL
SEIF
SEIGNEUR
SEIGNEURESS
SEIGNEURIAL
SEIGNEURY
SEIGNIOR
SEIGNIORAGE
SEIGNIORAL
SEIGNIORALTY
SEIGNIORIES
SEIGNIORY
SEIGNORAGE
SEIGNORAL
SEIGNORIAL
SEIGNORIZE
SEIGNORY
SEIL
SEIMAS
SEIN
SEINE
SEINED
SEINER
SEINING
SEIROSPORE
SEIROSPORIC
SEISE
SEISM
SEISMAL
SEISMATICAL
SEISMETIC
SEISMIC
SEISMICAL
SEISMICALLY
SEISMICITY
SEISMISM
SEISMOGRAM
SEISMOGRAPH
SEISMOGRAPHER
SEISMOGRAPHY
SEISMOLOGIC
SEISMOLOGICAL
SEISMOLOGIST
SEISMOLOGUE
SEISMOLOGY
SEISMOMETER
SEISMOMETRIC
SEISMOMETRY
SEISMOSCOPE
SEISMOTECTONIC
SEISMOTHERAPY
SEISMOTIC
SEISOR
SEIT
SEITH
SEITY
SEIZABLE
SEIZE
SEIZED
SEIZER
SEIZIN
SEIZING
SEIZOR
SEIZURE
SEJANT
SEJEANT
SEJERO
SEJOIN
SEJOINED
SEJOUR
SEJUGATE
SEJUGOUS
SEJUNCT
SEJUNCTION
SEJUNCTIVE
SEJUNCTIVELY
SEJUNCTLY
SEKERE
SEL
SELACHIAN
SELACHOID
SELACHOSTOME
SELADANG
SELAGINELLA
SELAGITE
SELAH
SELAMIN
SELAMLIK
SELBERGITE
SELCOUTH
SELD
SELDEN
SELDOM
SELDOMCY
SELDOMLY
SELDSEEN
SELE
SELECT
SELECTED
SELECTEDLY
SELECTEE
SELECTING
SELECTION
SELECTIONISM
SELECTIONIST
SELECTIVE
SELECTIVITY
SELECTMAN
SELECTMEN
SELECTNESS
SELECTOR
SELENATE
SELENIAN
SELENIATE
SELENIC
SELENIDE
SELENIFEROUS
SELENION
SELENIOUS
SELENITE
SELENITIC
SELENITICAL
SELENIUM
SELENODONT
SELENODONTY
SELENOGRAPH
SELENOGRAPHER
SELENOGRAPHIC
SELENOGRAPHY
SELENOLOGICAL
SELENOLOGIST
SELENOLOGY
SELENOMANCY
SELENOSCOPE
SELENOTROPISM
SELENOTROPY
SELENSILVER
SELENSULPHUR
SELETAR
SELETY
SELEUCIA
SELF
SELFDOM
SELFFUL
SELFHEAL
SELFHOOD
SELFISH
SELFISHLY
SELFISHNESS
SELFISM
SELFIST
SELFLESS
SELFLESSLY
SELFLESSNESS
SELFLIKE
SELFLY
SELFNESS
SELFSAID
SELFSAME
SELFSAMENESS
SELI
SELICTAR
SELIGMANNITE
SELIHOTH
SELING
SELION
SELL
SELLA
SELLABLE
SELLAITE
SELLAR
SELLARY
SELLATE
SELLE
SELLER
SELLING
SELLOUT
SELLY
SELSOVIET
SELT
SELTZER
SELTZOGENE
SELVA
SELVAGE
SELVAGED
SELVAGEE
SELVEDGE
SELVEDGED
SELVES
SELY
SEMANG
SEMANTEME
SEMANTIC
SEMANTICALLY
SEMANTICIST
SEMANTICS
SEMANTOLOGY
SEMANTRON
SEMAPHORE
SEMAPHORIST
SEMAR
SEMARUM
SEMASIOLOGIST
SEMASIOLOGY
SEMATEME
SEMATOGRAPHY
SEMATOLOGY
SEMATROPE
SEMBE
SEMBLABLE
SEMBLABLY
SEMBLANCE
SEMBLANT
SEMBLATIVE
SEMBLE
SEME
SEMEE
SEMEED
SEMEIA
SEMEIOGRAPHY
SEMEIOLOGY
SEMEION
SEMEIOTIC
SEMEIOTICS
SEMELFACTIVE
SEMEME
SEMEN
SEMENCE
SEMENCINAE
SEMENCONTRA
SEMENTERA
SEMESE
SEMESTER
SEMESTRAL
SEMESTRIAL
SEMI
SEMIAN
SEMIANNA

SEMIANTHRACITE
SEMIANTIQUE
SEMIAPE
SEMIAQUATIC
SEMIARCH
SEMIBASTION
SEMIBEAM
SEMIBEJAN
SEMIBREVE
SEMIBULL
SEMIC
SEMICADENCE
SEMICELL
SEMICENTENNIAL
SEMICHA
SEMICHORIC
SEMICHORUS
SEMICIRCLE
SEMICIRCLED
SEMICIRCULAR
SEMICIRQUE
SEMICIVILIZED
SEMICLASSIC
SEMICLIMBING
SEMICOKE
SEMICOLON
SEMICOLUMN
SEMICOMA
SEMICONDUCTOR
SEMICONSCIOUS
SEMICOPE
SEMICUBICAL
SEMICUPE
SEMICURSIVE
SEMICYCLIC
SEMIDARKNESS
SEMIDEPONENT
SEMIDETACHED
SEMIDIAMETER
SEMIDIAPASON
SEMIDIAPENTE
SEMIDINE
SEMIDITONE
SEMIDIURNAL
SEMIDIVINE
SEMIDOLE
SEMIDOME
SEMIDOMED
SEMIDOUBLE
SEMIDRESS
SEMIDRYING
SEMIEDUCATED
SEMIEFFIGY
SEMIELISION
SEMIFIGURE
SEMIFINAL
SEMIFINALIST
SEMIFINISHED
SEMIFLEXIBLE
SEMIFLORET
SEMIFLOSCULE
SEMIFLUID
SEMIFLUIDIC
SEMIFORM
SEMIFORMAL
SEMIFRATER
SEMIFY
SEMIGIRDER
SEMIGLOSS
SEMIHIATUS
SEMIHORAL
SEMIJUBILEE
SEMIKAH
SEMILIQUID
SEMILOCULAR
SEMILOR
SEMILUNAR
SEMILUNATE
SEMILUNE
SEMIMACHINE
SEMIMEMBER
SEMIMETAL
SEMIMETALLIC
SEMIMINIM
SEMIMONTHLY
SEMIMUTE
SEMINAL
SEMINALITY
SEMINALLY
SEMINAR
SEMINARIAL
SEMINARIAN
SEMINARIST
SEMINARISTIC
SEMINARIZE
SEMINARY
SEMINASE
SEMINATE
SEMINATED
SEMINATING
SEMINATION
SEMINATIVE
SEMINIFERAL
SEMINIFEROUS
SEMINIFIC
SEMINIFICAL
SEMINIST
SEMINIUM
SEMINIVOROUS
SEMINOMA
SEMINOMAS
SEMINOMATA
SEMINOSE
SEMINULE
SEMINURIA
SEMINVARIANT
SEMIOFFICIAL
SEMIOFFICIALLY
SEMIOGRAPHY
SEMIOLOGIST
SEMIOLOGY
SEMIOPAL
SEMIOPAQUE
SEMIOTIC
SEMIOTICAL
SEMIOTICS
SEMIOVIPAROUS
SEMIPALMATE
SEMIPALMATION
SEMIPED
SEMIPEDAL
SEMIPERMEABLE
SEMIPLUME
SEMIPORCELAIN
SEMIPORTABLE
SEMIPOSTAL
SEMIPRECIOUS
SEMIPRIVATE
SEMIPRO
SEMIPROOF
SEMIPUPA
SEMIQUARTILE
SEMIQUAVER
SEMIQUIETIST
SEMIQUOTE
SEMIREGULAR
SEMIRIGID
SEMIRING
SEMIROTARY
SEMIROTATING
SEMIROUND
SEMIS
SEMISAGITTATE
SEMISERIOUS
SEMISERVILE
SEMISEVERE
SEMISEVERELY
SEMISEXTILE
SEMISHRUB
SEMISHRUBBY
SEMISKILLED
SEMISOFT
SEMISOLEMN
SEMISOLID
SEMISOUN
SEMISPINALIS
SEMISQUARE
SEMISTEEL
SEMISTOCK
SEMISUCCESSFUL
SEMITA
SEMITAL
SEMITANDEM
SEMITANGENT
SEMITAUR
SEMITERTIAN
SEMITONAL
SEMITONE
SEMITONIC
SEMITRAILER
SEMIUNCIAL
SEMIVOCAL
SEMIVOCALIC
SEMIVOWEL
SEMIWEEKLY
SEMIYEARLY
SEMMEL
SEMMET
SEMMIT
SEMOIS
SEMOLA
SEMOLELLA
SEMOLINA
SEMOLOGY
SEMOTED
SEMOULE
SEMPER
SEMPERIDEM
SEMPERVIRENT
SEMPERVIRID
SEMPITERN
SEMPITERNAL
SEMPITERNITY
SEMPITERNIZE
SEMPITERNOUS
SEMPLE
SEMPLICE
SEMPRE
SEMPSTER
SEMPSTRESS
SEMPSTRY
SEMSEM
SEMUL
SEMUNCIA
SEMUNCIAL
SEMY
SEN
SENACHIE
SENAGE
SENAITE
SENAL
SENAM
SENARIAN
SENARIUS
SENARMONTITE
SENARY
SENATE
SENATOR
SENATORIAL
SENATORIAN
SENATORSHIP
SENATORY
SENATRESS
SENATRIX
SENATUS
SENCIO
SENCION
SEND
SENDA
SENDAL
SENDER
SENDING
SENDLE
SENDOFF
SENE
SENECIOID
SENECIONINE
SENECTITUDE
SENECTUDE
SENECTUOUS
SENEGA
SENEGIN
SENESCE
SENESCENCE
SENESCENCY
SENESCENT
SENESCHAL
SENGE
SENGREEN
SENHOR
SENHORA
SENHORITA
SENICIDE
SENILE
SENILISM
SENILITY
SENIOR
SENIORITY
SENIORY
SENIT
SENIUM
SENN
SENNA
SENNE
SENNET
SENNETT
SENNIGHT
SENNIT
SENNITE
SENOCULAR
SENOR
SENORA
SENORES
SENORITA
SENOUFO
SENS
SENSABLE
SENSAL
SENSATE
SENSATED
SENSATING
SENSATION
SENSATIONAL
SENSATIONALISM
SENSATIONALIST
SENSATIONALISTIC
SENSATIONARY
SENSATIONISM
SENSATIONIST
SENSATIONISTIC
SENSATORIAL
SENSATORY
SENSE
SENSED
SENSEFUL
SENSELESS
SENSELESSLY
SENSELESSNESS
SENSES
SENSIBILITIES
SENSIBILITIST
SENSIBILITOUS
SENSIBILITY
SENSIBILIZATION
SENSIBILIZE
SENSIBLE
SENSIBLENESS
SENSIBLY
SENSICAL
SENSIFACIENT
SENSIFIC
SENSIFICATORY
SENSIFICS
SENSIFY
SENSILE
SENSILLA
SENSILLAE
SENSING
SENSION
SENSISM
SENSIST
SENSISTIC
SENSITIVE
SENSITIVELY
SENSITIVENESS
SENSITIVITY
SENSITIZATION
SENSITIZE
SENSITIZED
SENSITIZER
SENSITIZING
SENSITOMETER
SENSITORY
SENSIVE
SENSO
SENSOR
SENSORIA
SENSORIAL
SENSORIES
SENSORIMOTOR
SENSORIUM
SENSORIUMS
SENSORY
SENSUAL
SENSUALISE
SENSUALISM
SENSUALIST
SENSUALISTIC
SENSUALITIES
SENSUALITY
SENSUALIZE
SENSUALIZED
SENSUALIZING
SENSUALLY
SENSUALNESS
SENSUISM
SENSUIST
SENSUM
SENSUOSITY
SENSUOUS
SENSUOUSLY
SENSUOUSNESS
SENSUS
SENT
SENTENCE
SENTENCED
SENTENCER
SENTENCING
SENTENTIAL
SENTENTIALLY
SENTENTIARIST
SENTENTIARY
SENTENTIOSITY
SENTENTIOUS
SENTENTIOUSLY

SENTIENCE
SENTIENCY
SENTIENDUM
SENTIENT
SENTIMENT
SENTIMENTAL
SENTIMENTALISM
SENTIMENTALIST
SENTIMENTALITIES
SENTIMENTALITY
SENTIMENTALIZE
SENTIMENTALIZED
SENTIMENTALIZER
SENTIMENTALIZING
SENTIMENTALLY
SENTIMENTER
SENTIMENTO
SENTINE
SENTINEL
SENTINELED
SENTINELING
SENTINELLED
SENTINELLING
SENTISECTION
SENTITION
SENTRIES
SENTRY
SENUFO
SENVY
SENYE
SEPAD
SEPAL
SEPALED
SEPALINE
SEPALODY
SEPALOID
SEPALOUS
SEPARABILITY
SEPARABLE
SEPARABLENESS
SEPARABLY
SEPARATE
SEPARATED
SEPARATELY
SEPARATENESS
SEPARATICAL
SEPARATING
SEPARATION
SEPARATISM
SEPARATIST
SEPARATISTIC
SEPARATIVE
SEPARATIVELY
SEPARATIVENESS
SEPARATOR
SEPARATORY
SEPARATRIX
SEPARTE
SEPAWN
SEPHEN
SEPHIRA
SEPHIRAH
SEPIA
SEPIACEOUS
SEPIAE
SEPIAN
SEPIARIAN
SEPIARY
SEPIAS
SEPICOLOUS
SEPIMENT
SEPIOLITE
SEPION
SEPIOSTAIRE
SEPIUM
SEPON
SEPONE
SEPOSE
SEPOY
SEPPUKU
SEPS
SEPSID
SEPSIN
SEPSINE
SEPSIS
SEPT
SEPTA
SEPTAL
SEPTAN
SEPTANE
SEPTANGLE
SEPTANGLED
SEPTARIA
SEPTARIAN
SEPTARIATE
SEPTARIUM
SEPTATE
SEPTATED
SEPTATION
SEPTAVE
SEPTECTOMY
SEPTEMVIOUS
SEPTEMVIR
SEPTENAR
SEPTENARIES
SEPTENARIUS
SEPTENARY
SEPTENATE
SEPTENNATE
SEPTENNIAL
SEPTENNIUM
SEPTENTRION
SEPTET
SEPTETTE
SEPTFOIL
SEPTIC
SEPTICAL
SEPTICALLY
SEPTICEMIA
SEPTICEMIC
SEPTICIDAL
SEPTICIDE
SEPTICITY
SEPTICIZATION
SEPTIER
SEPTIFOLIOUS
SEPTIFRAGAL
SEPTILATERAL
SEPTILE
SEPTILLION
SEPTILLIONTH
SEPTIMAL
SEPTIME
SEPTIMOLE
SEPTINSULAR
SEPTIVALENT
SEPTLEVA
SEPTOCOSTA
SEPTOIC
SEPTONASAL
SEPTOTOMY
SEPTUAGENARY
SEPTULA
SEPTULATE
SEPTULUM
SEPTUM
SEPTUNCIAL
SEPTUOR
SEPTUPLE
SEPTUPLET
SEPTUPLICATE
SEPULCHER
SEPULCHERED
SEPULCHERING
SEPULCHRAL
SEPULCHRALLY
SEPULCHRE
SEPULCHRED
SEPULCHRING
SEPULCHROUS
SEPULT
SEPULTURAL
SEPULTURE
SEQUA
SEQUACES
SEQUACIOUS
SEQUACIOUSLY
SEQUACITY
SEQUEL
SEQUELA
SEQUELAE
SEQUELANT
SEQUENCE
SEQUENCER
SEQUENT
SEQUENTIAL
SEQUENTIALITY
SEQUEST
SEQUESTER
SEQUESTERED
SEQUESTERING
SEQUESTERMENT
SEQUESTRA
SEQUESTRABLE
SEQUESTRAL
SEQUESTRANT
SEQUESTRATE
SEQUESTRATED
SEQUESTRATING
SEQUESTRATION
SEQUESTRATOR
SEQUESTRUM
SEQUIN
SEQUITUR
SEQUOIA
SER
SERA
SERAB
SERAC
SERAGLI
SERAGLIO
SERAHULI
SERAI
SERAIL
SERAING
SERAL
SERAPE
SERAPH
SERAPHIC
SERAPHICAL
SERAPHICALLY
SERAPHICISM
SERAPHICNESS
SERAPHIM
SERAPHINE
SERAPHISM
SERAPHS
SERAPHTIDE
SERASKER
SERASKIER
SERASKIERAT
SERAU
SERAYA
SERCIAL
SERDAB
SERE
SEREH
SEREIN
SEREMENT
SERENA
SERENADE
SERENADED
SERENADER
SERENADING
SERENATA
SERENATAS
SERENATE
SERENDIBITE
SERENDIPITY
SERENDITE
SERENE
SERENED
SERENELY
SERENENESS
SERENIFY
SERENISSIMO
SERENITIES
SERENITY
SERENIZE
SERENO
SERF
SERFAGE
SERFDOM
SERFHOOD
SERFISM
SERFS
SERFSHIP
SERGE
SERGEANCY
SERGEANT
SERGEANTRY
SERGEANTSHIP
SERGEANTY
SERGEDESOY
SERGEDUSOY
SERGELIM
SERGER
SERGETTE
SERGING
SERGIPE
SERGLOBULIN
SERIAL
SERIALISM
SERIALITY
SERIALIZATION
SERIALIZE
SERIALIZED
SERIALIZING
SERIALLY
SERIARY
SERIATE
SERIATELY
SERIATIM
SERIATION
SERIAUNT
SERICATE
SERICATED
SERICEA
SERICEOUS
SERICICULTURE
SERICIN
SERICON
SERICTERIES
SERICTERY
SERICULTURE
SERIEMA
SERIES
SERIF
SERIFIC
SERIFORM
SERIGRAPH
SERIGRAPHER
SERIGRAPHIC
SERIGRAPHY
SERIMETER
SERIMPI
SERIN
SERINE
SERINETTE
SERINGA
SERINGAL
SERINGHI
SERIO
SERIOCOMIC
SERIOLINE
SERIOSITIES
SERIOSITY
SERIOSO
SERIOUS
SERIOUSLY
SERIOUSNESS
SERIPOSITOR
SERIR
SERJEANCY
SERJEANT
SERJEANTRY
SERJEANTY
SERMENT
SERMO
SERMON
SERMONEER
SERMONER
SERMONET
SERMONIC
SERMONICAL
SERMONICALLY
SERMONICS
SERMONISH
SERMONISM
SERMONIST
SERMONIZE
SERMONIZED
SERMONIZER
SERMONIZING
SERMONOID
SERMONOLOGY
SERMUNCLE
SERNAMBY
SERO
SEROLEMMA
SEROLIN
SEROLOGIC
SEROLOGICAL
SEROLOGIST
SEROLOGY
SERON
SERONEGATIVE
SEROON
SEROOT
SEROPOSITIVE
SEROPURULENT
SEROSA
SEROSE
SEROSITIES
SEROSITIS
SEROSITY
SEROTINAL
SEROTINE
SEROTINOUS
SEROTONIN
SEROTYPE
SEROUS
SEROUSNESS
SEROVACCINE
SEROW
SEROZEM
SERPEDINOUS
SERPENT
SERPENTARIA
SERPENTARIUM
SERPENTARY
SERPENTEAU
SERPENTESS
SERPENTILE
SERPENTIN

SERPENTINE
SERPENTINIC
SERPENTINIZE
SERPENTINOID
SERPENTINOUS
SERPENTIZE
SERPENTLIKE
SERPENTLY
SERPENTOID
SERPENTRY
SERPENTWOOD
SERPETTE
SERPHID
SERPHOID
SERPIERITE
SERPIGINOUS
SERPIGO
SERPIVOLANT
SERPOLET
SERPULAN
SERPULID
SERPULIDAN
SERPULINE
SERPULITE
SERPULOID
SERR
SERRA
SERRADELLA
SERRAE
SERRAGE
SERRAI
SERRAN
SERRANA
SERRANID
SERRANO
SERRANOID
SERRANOS
SERRATE
SERRATED
SERRATIA
SERRATIC
SERRATILE
SERRATION
SERRATURE
SERRATUS
SERRICORN
SERRIED
SERRIEDLY
SERRIEDNESS
SERRIFEROUS
SERRIFORM
SERRING
SERRIPED
SERRULA
SERRULATE
SERRULATED
SERRULATION
SERRURERIE
SERRY
SERRYING
SERT
SERTA
SERTO
SERTULARIAN
SERTULARIOID
SERTULAROID
SERTULE
SERTULUM
SERTUM
SERULE
SERUM
SERUMAL
SERUMS
SERVABLE
SERVAGE
SERVAL
SERVALINE
SERVANT
SERVANTS
SERVATION
SERVE
SERVED
SERVENTE
SERVER
SERVERY
SERVES
SERVET
SERVETTE
SERVIABLE
SERVICE
SERVICEABLE
SERVICEABLY
SERVICEBERRIES
SERVICEBERRY
SERVICED
SERVICELESS
SERVICEMAN
SERVICEMEN
SERVICING
SERVIENT
SERVIETTE
SERVILE
SERVILELY
SERVILENESS
SERVILISM
SERVILITIES
SERVILITY
SERVING
SERVINGMAN
SERVIST
SERVITEUR
SERVITIAL
SERVITIUM
SERVITOR
SERVITORIAL
SERVITRIX
SERVITUDE
SERVITURE
SERVO
SERVOMECHANISM
SERVOMOTOR
SERVOS
SERVOTAB
SERVULATE
SERVUS
SERWAMBY
SESAME
SESAMIN
SESAMINE
SESAMOID
SESAMOIDAL
SESAMOIDITIS
SESAMOL
SESCUPLE
SESI
SESKIN
SESMA
SESPERAL
SESQUI
SESQUIALTER
SESQUIALTERA
SESQUIALTERAL
SESQUICENTENNIAL
SESQUINONA
SESQUINONAL
SESQUIOCTAVA
SESQUIPEDAL
SESQUIPLICATE
SESQUIQUARTA
SESQUIQUINTA
SESQUISEXTAL
SESQUITERPENE
SESQUITERTIA
SESS
SESSA
SESSILE
SESSILITY
SESSION
SESSIONAL
SESSIONALLY
SESSIONARY
SESSIONS
SESSPOOL
SESTERCE
SESTERCES
SESTERTIA
SESTERTIUM
SESTERTIUS
SESTET
SESTETTO
SESTI
SESTIAD
SESTINA
SESTINE
SESTOLE
SESTOLET
SESTON
SESTUOR
SET
SETA
SETACEOUS
SETACEOUSLY
SETAE
SETAL
SETARID
SETARIOUS
SETATION
SETBACK
SETBOLT
SETDOWN
SETE
SETER
SETH
SETHEAD
SETIER
SETIFEROUS
SETIFORM
SETIGER
SETLINE
SETLING
SETNESS
SETNET
SETOFF
SETON
SETOSE
SETOUS
SETOUT
SETOVER
SETSCREW
SETSMAN
SETT
SETTAINE
SETTE
SETTECENTO
SETTEE
SETTER
SETTERGRASS
SETTERS
SETTERWORT
SETTIMA
SETTIMO
SETTING
SETTLE
SETTLED
SETTLEMENT
SETTLEMENTS
SETTLER
SETTLERS
SETTLING
SETTLOR
SETTSMAN
SETULA
SETULE
SETULIFORM
SETULOSE
SETULOUS
SETUP
SETWALL
SETWISE
SETWORK
SETWORKS
SEUCH
SEUDAH
SEUGH
SEVE
SEVEN
SEVENBARK
SEVENER
SEVENFOLD
SEVENFOLDED
SEVENSCORE
SEVENTEEN
SEVENTEENTH
SEVENTH
SEVENTHLY
SEVENTIES
SEVENTIETH
SEVENTY
SEVER
SEVERABLE
SEVERAL
SEVERALITY
SEVERALIZE
SEVERALLY
SEVERALTY
SEVERANCE
SEVERATE
SEVERATION
SEVERE
SEVERED
SEVERELY
SEVERENESS
SEVERER
SEVEREST
SEVERING
SEVERISH
SEVERITY
SEVERIZE
SEVERY
SEVIER
SEVILLANAS
SEVUM
SEW
SEWAGE
SEWAN
SEWED
SEWELLEL
SEWEN
SEWER
SEWERAGE
SEWERED
SEWERMAN
SEWERY
SEWIN
SEWING
SEWLESS
SEWN
SEWROUND
SEWSTER
SEX
SEXADECIMAL
SEXAGENARIAN
SEXAGENARY
SEXAGESIMAL
SEXANGLE
SEXANGLED
SEXANGULAR
SEXANGULARLY
SEXCENTENARY
SEXDIGITAL
SEXDIGITATE
SEXDIGITATED
SEXDIGITISM
SEXED
SEXENARY
SEXENNIAL
SEXENNIUM
SEXERN
SEXIER
SEXIEST
SEXISM
SEXIST
SEXISYLLABLE
SEXLESS
SEXLESSLY
SEXLESSNESS
SEXLIKE
SEXLY
SEXOLOGIC
SEXOLOGICAL
SEXOLOGIST
SEXOLOGY
SEXPARTITE
SEXPLOITATION
SEXT
SEXTACTIC
SEXTAIN
SEXTAN
SEXTANS
SEXTANT
SEXTANTAL
SEXTARIUS
SEXTENNIAL
SEXTERN
SEXTET
SEXTETTE
SEXTIC
SEXTILE
SEXTILLION
SEXTILLIONTH
SEXTIPARA
SEXTIPARTITE
SEXTIPLY
SEXTIPOLAR
SEXTO
SEXTOLE
SEXTOLET
SEXTON
SEXTRY
SEXTUOR
SEXTUPLE
SEXTUPLED
SEXTUPLET
SEXTUPLICATE
SEXTUPLICATED
SEXTUPLICATING
SEXTUPLING
SEXTUPLY
SEXTUR
SEXUAL
SEXUALE
SEXUALISM
SEXUALIST
SEXUALITY
SEXUALIZE
SEXUALLY
SEXUOUS
SEXUPARA
SEXUPAROUS
SEXY
SEY
SEYBERTITE
SEYID
SFERICS
SFOGATO

SFORZANDO
SFORZANDOS
SFORZATO
SFUMATO
SGABELLO
SGRAFFIATO
SGRAFFITO
SHA
SHAATNEZ
SHAB
SHABANDAR
SHABASH
SHABBAT
SHABBED
SHABBIER
SHABBIEST
SHABBIFY
SHABBILY
SHABBINESS
SHABBLE
SHABBOS
SHABBY
SHABEQUE
SHABRACK
SHABROON
SHABUNDER
SHACHLE
SHACK
SHACKANITE
SHACKATORY
SHACKBOLT
SHACKLE
SHACKLEBONE
SHACKLED
SHACKLER
SHACKLING
SHACKLY
SHACKY
SHAD
SHADBELLY
SHADBERRIES
SHADBERRY
SHADBIRD
SHADBLOW
SHADBUSH
SHADCHAN
SHADDOCK
SHADE
SHADED
SHADER
SHADES
SHADETAIL
SHADFLOWER
SHADIER
SHADIEST
SHADILY
SHADINE
SHADINESS
SHADING
SHADKAN
SHADOOF
SHADOW
SHADOWBOX
SHADOWED
SHADOWER
SHADOWGRAM
SHADOWGRAPH
SHADOWINESS
SHADOWING
SHADOWIST
SHADOWLAND
SHADOWLESS
SHADOWLY
SHADOWS
SHADOWY
SHADRACH
SHADS
SHADUF
SHADY
SHAFFLE
SHAFII
SHAFT
SHAFTED
SHAFTER
SHAFTING
SHAFTMAN
SHAFTMENT
SHAFTSMAN
SHAFTWAY
SHAFTY
SHAG
SHAGANAPPI
SHAGANAPPY
SHAGBARK
SHAGBUSH
SHAGGED
SHAGGEDNESS
SHAGGIER
SHAGGIEST
SHAGGILY
SHAGGINESS
SHAGGING
SHAGGY
SHAGLET
SHAGRAG
SHAGREEN
SHAGREENED
SHAGROON
SHAGTAIL
SHAH
SHAHARIT
SHAHARITH
SHAHDOM
SHAHEE
SHAHEEN
SHAHI
SHAHIDI
SHAHIN
SHAHZADA
SHAHZADAH
SHAIKH
SHAIKHI
SHAIRD
SHAIRN
SHAITAN
SHAKABLE
SHAKE
SHAKEABLE
SHAKEDOWN
SHAKEFORK
SHAKEN
SHAKEOUT
SHAKEPROOF
SHAKER
SHAKES
SHAKESCENE
SHAKEUP
SHAKHA
SHAKIER
SHAKIEST
SHAKILY
SHAKINESS
SHAKING
SHAKINGS
SHAKO
SHAKOS
SHAKSHEER
SHAKTIS
SHAKU
SHAKY
SHAL
SHALDER
SHALE
SHALED
SHALEE
SHALEMAN
SHALL
SHALLAL
SHALLON
SHALLOON
SHALLOP
SHALLOT
SHALLOW
SHALLOWER
SHALLOWEST
SHALLOWLY
SHALLOWNESS
SHALLOWPATE
SHALLOWPATED
SHALLU
SHALLY
SHALM
SHALOM
SHALWAR
SHALY
SHAM
SHAMA
SHAMAL
SHAMAN
SHAMANESS
SHAMANIC
SHAMANISM
SHAMANIST
SHAMANISTIC
SHAMATEUR
SHAMATEURISM
SHAMBA
SHAMBLE
SHAMBLED
SHAMBLES
SHAMBLING
SHAMBRIER
SHAME
SHAMED
SHAMEFACE
SHAMEFACED
SHAMEFACEDLY
SHAMEFACEDNESS
SHAMEFAST
SHAMEFASTLY
SHAMEFASTNESS
SHAMEFUL
SHAMEFULLY
SHAMEFULNESS
SHAMELESS
SHAMELESSLY
SHAMELESSNESS
SHAMER
SHAMES
SHAMIANAH
SHAMING
SHAMMAS
SHAMMASH
SHAMMED
SHAMMER
SHAMMING
SHAMMISH
SHAMMOCK
SHAMMOCKING
SHAMMOS
SHAMMY
SHAMPOO
SHAMPOOED
SHAMPOOER
SHAMPOOING
SHAMROCK
SHAMROOT
SHAMSHEER
SHAMUS
SHANACHAS
SHANACHIE
SHANACHUS
SHAND
SHANDITE
SHANDRY
SHANDRYDAN
SHANDY
SHANDYGAFF
SHANGAN
SHANGHAI
SHANGHAIED
SHANGHAIING
SHANGY
SHANK
SHANKED
SHANKER
SHANKING
SHANKINGS
SHANKPIECE
SHANKS
SHANNA
SHANNY
SHANT
SHANTEY
SHANTIES
SHANTUNG
SHANTY
SHANTYMAN
SHANTYMEN
SHANTYTOWN
SHAPABLE
SHAPE
SHAPED
SHAPEFUL
SHAPELESS
SHAPELESSLY
SHAPELESSNESS
SHAPELIER
SHAPELIEST
SHAPELINESS
SHAPELY
SHAPEN
SHAPER
SHAPEUP
SHAPIER
SHAPIEST
SHAPING
SHAPINGLY
SHAPOMETER
SHAPOO
SHAPY
SHAR
SHARD
SHARDY
SHARE
SHAREBONE
SHAREBROKER
SHARECROPPER
SHARED
SHAREEF
SHAREHOLDER
SHAREMAN
SHAREPENNY
SHARER
SHARES
SHAREWORT
SHARGAR
SHARGER
SHARGOSS
SHARIAT
SHARING
SHARK
SHARKED
SHARKER
SHARKI
SHARKING
SHARKISH
SHARKLET
SHARKSKIN
SHARKY
SHARN
SHARNBUD
SHARNBUG
SHARNY
SHARON
SHARP
SHARPED
SHARPEN
SHARPENED
SHARPENER
SHARPENING
SHARPER
SHARPERS
SHARPEST
SHARPIE
SHARPING
SHARPISH
SHARPITE
SHARPLING
SHARPLY
SHARPNESS
SHARPS
SHARPSAW
SHARPSHOD
SHARPSHOOTER
SHARPTAIL
SHARPWARE
SHARPY
SHARRY
SHASLIK
SHASTAITE
SHASTRA
SHASTRAIK
SHASTRAS
SHASTRI
SHASTRIK
SHAT
SHATHMONT
SHATTER
SHATTERBRAIN
SHATTERED
SHATTERER
SHATTERING
SHATTERPATED
SHATTERPROOF
SHATTERWIT
SHATTERY
SHATTUCKITE
SHAUCHLE
SHAUGH
SHAUL
SHAUP
SHAURI
SHAVE
SHAVED
SHAVEE
SHAVELING
SHAVEN
SHAVER
SHAVERY
SHAVESTER
SHAVETAIL
SHAVIE
SHAVING
SHAVINGS
SHAW
SHAWABTI
SHAWFOWL
SHAWL
SHAWLED
SHAWLING
SHAWM
SHAWNEEWOOD
SHAWNY
SHAY

SHAYED
SHAYKH
SHCHI
SHE
SHEA
SHEADING
SHEAF
SHEAFAGE
SHEAFY
SHEAL
SHEALING
SHEAR
SHEARBILL
SHEARED
SHEARER
SHEARERS
SHEARGRASS
SHEARHOG
SHEARING
SHEARLING
SHEARMAN
SHEARMOUSE
SHEARS
SHEARTAIL
SHEARWATER
SHEARWATERS
SHEATFISH
SHEATFISHES
SHEATH
SHEATHBILL
SHEATHE
SHEATHED
SHEATHER
SHEATHERY
SHEATHING
SHEATHS
SHEAVE
SHEAVED
SHEAVEMAN
SHEAVES
SHEAVING
SHEBANG
SHEBAR
SHEBEEN
SHEBEENER
SHECHITA
SHED
SHEDDED
SHEDDER
SHEDDING
SHEDER
SHEDHAND
SHEDIM
SHEDMAN
SHEDU
SHEE
SHEEFISH
SHEELING
SHEEN
SHEENLY
SHEENY
SHEEP
SHEEPBACK
SHEEPBACKS
SHEEPBERRY
SHEEPBINE
SHEEPBITER
SHEEPBITING
SHEEPCOT
SHEEPCOTE
SHEEPCROOK
SHEEPFACED
SHEEPFOLD
SHEEPFOOT
SHEEPFOOTS
SHEEPGATE
SHEEPHEADED
SHEEPHERDER
SHEEPHERDING
SHEEPHOOK
SHEEPIFIED
SHEEPIFY
SHEEPIFYING
SHEEPISH
SHEEPISHLY
SHEEPISHNESS
SHEEPKILL
SHEEPLIKE
SHEEPMAN
SHEEPMASTER
SHEEPMEN
SHEEPMINT
SHEEPNOSE
SHEEPNUT
SHEEPPEN
SHEEPSHEAD
SHEEPSHEADS
SHEEPSHEAR
SHEEPSHEARER
SHEEPSHEARING
SHEEPSKIN
SHEEPSKINS
SHEEPSPLIT
SHEEPSTEAL
SHEEPWALK
SHEEPWALKER
SHEEPWEED
SHEEPY
SHEER
SHEERING
SHEERLY
SHEERNESS
SHEERS
SHEET
SHEETAGE
SHEETED
SHEETER
SHEETFLOOD
SHEETING
SHEETLET
SHEETS
SHEETWASH
SHEETWAYS
SHEETWISE
SHEETWORK
SHEETY
SHEEVE
SHEGETZ
SHEHITA
SHEIK
SHEIKDOM
SHEIKH
SHEIKHDOM
SHEIKHLY
SHEIKLY
SHEILING
SHEITAN
SHEITEL
SHEKEL
SHELA
SHELAH
SHELD
SHELDER
SHELDFOWL
SHELDRAKE
SHELDRAKES
SHELDUCK
SHELF
SHELL
SHELLAC
SHELLACK
SHELLACKED
SHELLACKING
SHELLAK
SHELLAPPLE
SHELLBACK
SHELLBARK
SHELLBLOW
SHELLBOUND
SHELLBURST
SHELLEATER
SHELLED
SHELLER
SHELLFIRE
SHELLFISH
SHELLFISHERIES
SHELLFISHERY
SHELLFISHES
SHELLFLOWER
SHELLHEAD
SHELLIER
SHELLING
SHELLMAN
SHELLMEN
SHELLMONGER
SHELLPAD
SHELLPOT
SHELLPROOF
SHELLS
SHELLUM
SHELLWORK
SHELLY
SHELLYCOAT
SHELM
SHELTA
SHELTER
SHELTERAGE
SHELTERED
SHELTERER
SHELTERING
SHELTERLESS
SHELTERWOOD
SHELTERY
SHELTIE
SHELTIES
SHELTRON
SHELTY
SHELVE
SHELVED
SHELVER
SHELVES
SHELVING
SHELVY
SHENANIGAN
SHEND
SHENDFUL
SHENDING
SHENG
SHENT
SHEOGUE
SHEOL
SHEOLIC
SHEP
SHEPE
SHEPHERD
SHEPHERDESS
SHEPHERDISM
SHEPHERDS
SHEPHERDY
SHEPPECK
SHEPPERDING
SHEPPEY
SHEPPHERDED
SHEPPICK
SHEPSTARE
SHEPSTER
SHER
SHERARDIZE
SHERARDIZED
SHERARDIZING
SHERBACHA
SHERBET
SHERBETLEE
SHERBETZIDE
SHERD
SHERE
SHEREEF
SHERIAT
SHERIF
SHERIFATE
SHERIFF
SHERIFFDOM
SHERIFFESS
SHERIFFRY
SHERIFFWICK
SHERIFIAN
SHERISTADAR
SHERLOCK
SHEROOT
SHERRIES
SHERRIS
SHERRY
SHERRYVALLIES
SHERWANI
SHETH
SHEUCH
SHEUGH
SHEVEL
SHEVELED
SHEVRI
SHEW
SHEWBREAD
SHEWEL
SHEWER
SHEYLE
SHI
SHIBAH
SHIBAR
SHIBBOLETH
SHIBUICHI
SHICE
SHICER
SHICK
SHICKER
SHICKERED
SHICKSA
SHIDE
SHIED
SHIEL
SHIELD
SHIELDED
SHIELDER
SHIELDFERN
SHIELDFLOWER
SHIELDING
SHIELDLESS
SHIELDLESSLY
SHIELDLESSNESS
SHIELDMAY
SHIELDS
SHIELDTAIL
SHIELING
SHIER
SHIEST
SHIFT
SHIFTED
SHIFTER
SHIFTFUL
SHIFTFULNESS
SHIFTIER
SHIFTIEST
SHIFTINESS
SHIFTING
SHIFTINGLY
SHIFTLESS
SHIFTLESSLY
SHIFTLESSNESS
SHIFTMAN
SHIFTS
SHIFTY
SHIGGAION
SHIGIONOTH
SHIGRAM
SHIH
SHIKAR
SHIKARA
SHIKAREE
SHIKARGAH
SHIKARI
SHIKASTA
SHIKII
SHIKIMI
SHIKIMOL
SHIKIMOTOXIN
SHIKKEN
SHIKO
SHIKRA
SHIKSE
SHILF
SHILFA
SHILL
SHILLA
SHILLABER
SHILLALA
SHILLALAH
SHILLELAGH
SHILLER
SHILLET
SHILLETY
SHILLIBEER
SHILLING
SHILLOO
SHILLY
SHILP
SHILPIT
SHIM
SHIMAL
SHIMMED
SHIMMER
SHIMMERED
SHIMMERING
SHIMMERY
SHIMMEY
SHIMMIED
SHIMMING
SHIMMY
SHIMMYING
SHIMOSE
SHIMPER
SHIN
SHINARUMP
SHINBONE
SHINDIG
SHINDLE
SHINDY
SHINE
SHINED
SHINER
SHING
SHINGLE
SHINGLED
SHINGLER
SHINGLES
SHINGLEWOOD
SHINGLING
SHINGLY
SHINGON
SHINIER
SHINIEST
SHININESS
SHINING
SHININGLY
SHININGNESS
SHINLEAF
SHINNER

SHINNERIES
SHINNERY
SHINNIED
SHINNY
SHINNYING
SHINPLASTER
SHINS
SHINTAI
SHINTIYAN
SHINTY
SHINTYAN
SHINWOOD
SHINY
SHINZA
SHIP
SHIPBOARD
SHIPBOY
SHIPBUILDER
SHIPBUILDING
SHIPFERD
SHIPFITTER
SHIPFUL
SHIPFULS
SHIPHIRE
SHIPHOLDER
SHIPKEEPER
SHIPLAP
SHIPLET
SHIPLOAD
SHIPMAN
SHIPMANSHIP
SHIPMAST
SHIPMASTER
SHIPMATE
SHIPMEN
SHIPMENT
SHIPOWNER
SHIPPABLE
SHIPPAGE
SHIPPED
SHIPPEN
SHIPPER
SHIPPING
SHIPPLANE
SHIPPO
SHIPPON
SHIPPY
SHIPRADE
SHIPS
SHIPSHAPE
SHIPSIDE
SHIPWAY
SHIPWORM
SHIPWRECK
SHIPWRECKY
SHIPWRIGHT
SHIPYARD
SHIR
SHIRALEE
SHIRE
SHIREHOUSE
SHIREMAN
SHIREMEN
SHIRK
SHIRKER
SHIRL
SHIRPIT
SHIRR
SHIRRA
SHIRRED
SHIRREL
SHIRRER
SHIRRING
SHIRT
SHIRTBAND
SHIRTING
SHIRTLESS
SHIRTLESSNESS
SHIRTMAKER
SHIRTMAKING
SHIRTMAN
SHIRTMEN
SHIRTS
SHIRTTAIL
SHIRTWAIST
SHIRTY
SHISH
SHISHAM
SHISN
SHIST
SHITA
SHITHER
SHITTAH
SHITTEN
SHITTIMWOOD
SHITTLE
SHIV
SHIVA
SHIVAREE
SHIVE
SHIVER
SHIVERED
SHIVEREENS
SHIVERING
SHIVERINGLY
SHIVERS
SHIVERWEED
SHIVERY
SHIVEY
SHIVOO
SHIVVY
SHIZOKU
SHLEMIEL
SHO
SHOADER
SHOAL
SHOALBRAIN
SHOALER
SHOALIER
SHOALIEST
SHOALINESS
SHOALNESS
SHOALY
SHOAR
SHOAT
SHOCHET
SHOCK
SHOCKABLE
SHOCKED
SHOCKER
SHOCKHEAD
SHOCKHEADED
SHOCKING
SHOCKINGLY
SHOCKINGNESS
SHOCKS
SHOD
SHODDIED
SHODDIER
SHODDIES
SHODDIEST
SHODDY
SHODDYING
SHODE
SHODER
SHOE
SHOEBILL
SHOEBINDER
SHOEBINDERY
SHOEBINDING
SHOEBIRD
SHOEBLACK
SHOEBOY
SHOECRAFT
SHOEFLOWER
SHOEHORN
SHOEING
SHOEINGSMITH
SHOELACE
SHOEMAKE
SHOEMAKER
SHOEMAKING
SHOEMAN
SHOEPAC
SHOEPACK
SHOER
SHOES
SHOESHINE
SHOESTRING
SHOETREE
SHOFAR
SHOFUL
SHOG
SHOGGIE
SHOGGLE
SHOGGLY
SHOGI
SHOGUN
SHOHET
SHOJI
SHOLA
SHOLE
SHOMA
SHONDE
SHONE
SHONEEN
SHONEENS
SHONKINITE
SHOO
SHOOD
SHOOFA
SHOOFLIES
SHOOFLY
SHOOGLE
SHOOH
SHOOI
SHOOK
SHOOL
SHOON
SHOOP
SHOOT
SHOOTER
SHOOTING
SHOOTIST
SHOOTMAN
SHOP
SHOPBOARD
SHOPBOOK
SHOPBOY
SHOPBREAKER
SHOPBREAKING
SHOPGIRL
SHOPHAR
SHOPKEEPER
SHOPKEEPERY
SHOPKEEPING
SHOPLIFT
SHOPLIFTER
SHOPLIFTING
SHOPLIKE
SHOPMAID
SHOPMAN
SHOPMARK
SHOPMATE
SHOPOCRACY
SHOPOCRAT
SHOPPE
SHOPPED
SHOPPER
SHOPPIER
SHOPPIEST
SHOPPING
SHOPPINI
SHOPPISH
SHOPPY
SHOPSTER
SHOPTALK
SHOPWALKER
SHOPWEAR
SHOPWINDOW
SHOPWORK
SHOPWORKER
SHOPWORN
SHOQ
SHOR
SHORAN
SHORE
SHOREBERRY
SHOREBIRD
SHORED
SHOREFISH
SHORELAND
SHORELESS
SHORELINE
SHOREMAN
SHORER
SHORESMAN
SHOREWARD
SHOREWARDS
SHOREYER
SHORING
SHORL
SHORN
SHORT
SHORTAGE
SHORTBREAD
SHORTCAKE
SHORTCHANGE
SHORTCHANGED
SHORTCHANGER
SHORTCHANGING
SHORTCOAT
SHORTCOMER
SHORTCOMING
SHORTCUT
SHORTEN
SHORTENED
SHORTENER
SHORTENING
SHORTER
SHORTEST
SHORTFALL
SHORTHAND
SHORTHANDED
SHORTHEAD
SHORTHEELS
SHORTHORN
SHORTIA
SHORTIE
SHORTISH
SHORTITE
SHORTLY
SHORTNESS
SHORTS
SHORTSIGHTED
SHORTSIGHTEDLY
SHORTSOME
SHORTSTAFF
SHORTSTOP
SHORTY
SHOSHONITE
SHOT
SHOTBUSH
SHOTCRETE
SHOTE
SHOTGUN
SHOTMAKER
SHOTMAN
SHOTS
SHOTSHELL
SHOTSTAR
SHOTT
SHOTTED
SHOTTEN
SHOTTY
SHOU
SHOUGH
SHOULD
SHOULDER
SHOULDERED
SHOULDERER
SHOULDERETTE
SHOULDERING
SHOULDERS
SHOULDEST
SHOULDNA
SHOULDST
SHOULERD
SHOUT
SHOUTED
SHOUTER
SHOUTHER
SHOUTING
SHOUTS
SHOVAL
SHOVE
SHOVED
SHOVEL
SHOVELBILL
SHOVELBOARD
SHOVELED
SHOVELER
SHOVELFISH
SHOVELHEAD
SHOVELLED
SHOVELLING
SHOVELNOSE
SHOVELWEED
SHOVER
SHOVING
SHOW
SHOWABLE
SHOWANCE
SHOWBIRD
SHOWBOARD
SHOWBOAT
SHOWBREAD
SHOWCASE
SHOWD
SHOWDOWN
SHOWED
SHOWER
SHOWERED
SHOWERER
SHOWERIER
SHOWERIEST
SHOWERING
SHOWERY
SHOWFUL
SHOWIER
SHOWIEST
SHOWILY
SHOWINESS
SHOWING
SHOWISH
SHOWMAN
SHOWMANSHIP
SHOWN
SHOWOFF
SHOWPIECE
SHOWROOM
SHOWSHOP
SHOWUP
SHOWY
SHOYA

SHOYU
SHRAB
SHRADD
SHRADDHA
SHRAG
SHRAM
SHRAME
SHRAMMED
SHRANK
SHRAP
SHRAPE
SHRAPNEL
SHRAVE
SHRAVEY
SHRED
SHREDCOCK
SHREDDED
SHREDDER
SHREDDING
SHREDDY
SHREDS
SHREE
SHREEVE
SHREND
SHREW
SHREWD
SHREWDER
SHREWDEST
SHREWDLY
SHREWDNESS
SHREWDY
SHREWISH
SHREWISHLY
SHREWISHNESS
SHREWMOUSE
SHREWSTRUCK
SHRI
SHRIDE
SHRIEK
SHRIEKED
SHRIEKER
SHRIEKERY
SHRIEKING
SHRIEKY
SHRIEVAL
SHRIEVALTIES
SHRIEVALTY
SHRIEVE
SHRIFT
SHRIKE
SHRILL
SHRILLED
SHRILLER
SHRILLEST
SHRILLING
SHRILLY
SHRIMP
SHRIMPER
SHRIMPFISH
SHRIMPI
SHRIMPISH
SHRIMPISHNESS
SHRIMPY
SHRINAL
SHRINE
SHRINED
SHRINING
SHRINK
SHRINKABLE
SHRINKAGE
SHRINKER
SHRINKING
SHRINKINGLY
SHRIP
SHRITE
SHRIVE
SHRIVED
SHRIVEL
SHRIVELED
SHRIVELING
SHRIVELLED
SHRIVELLING
SHRIVEN
SHRIVER
SHRIVING
SHROFF
SHROG
SHROGS
SHROUD
SHROUDED
SHROUDING
SHROUDS
SHROUDY
SHROVE
SHROVED
SHROVER
SHROVING
SHROVY
SHRUB
SHRUBBED
SHRUBBERIES
SHRUBBERY
SHRUBBIER
SHRUBBIEST
SHRUBBINESS
SHRUBBY
SHRUBLET
SHRUBS
SHRUBWOOD
SHRUFF
SHRUG
SHRUGGED
SHRUGGING
SHRUNK
SHRUNKEN
SHRUPS
SHRUTI
SHTCHEE
SHTETEL
SHTETL
SHTICK
SHUBA
SHUBUNKIN
SHUCK
SHUCKED
SHUCKER
SHUCKING
SHUCKS
SHUD
SHUDDER
SHUDDERED
SHUDDERING
SHUDDERSOME
SHUDDERY
SHUDE
SHUDNA
SHUFF
SHUFFLE
SHUFFLEBOARD
SHUFFLECAP
SHUFFLED
SHUFFLER
SHUFFLEWING
SHUFFLING
SHUG
SHUILER
SHUL
SHULER
SHULWAURS
SHUMAN
SHUN
SHUNE
SHUNLESS
SHUNNABLE
SHUNNED
SHUNNER
SHUNNING
SHUNPIKE
SHUNT
SHUNTED
SHUNTER
SHUNTING
SHURE
SHURF
SHURGEE
SHUSH
SHUT
SHUTDOWN
SHUTE
SHUTEYE
SHUTOFF
SHUTOUT
SHUTTER
SHUTTERBUG
SHUTTERING
SHUTTING
SHUTTLE
SHUTTLECOCK
SHUTTLECOCKED
SHUTTLECOCKING
SHUTTLER
SHUTTLEWISE
SHWA
SHWANPAN
SHWEBO
SHY
SHYER
SHYING
SHYISH
SHYLY
SHYNESS
SHYSTER
SI
SIACALLE
SIAFU
SIAK
SIAL
SIALAGOGIC
SIALAGOGUE
SIALIC
SIALID
SIALIDAN
SIALOID
SIAMANG
SIAMESE
SIAMOISE
SIAPO
SIAULIAI
SIB
SIBBED
SIBBENDY
SIBBENS
SIBBING
SIBERITE
SIBILANCE
SIBILANCY
SIBILANT
SIBILANTLY
SIBILATE
SIBILATOR
SIBILATORY
SIBILI
SIBILOUS
SIBILUS
SIBLING
SIBNESS
SIBREDE
SIBRIT
SIBSHIP
SIBUCAO
SIBYL
SIBYLIC
SIBYLLA
SIBYLLAE
SIBYLLIC
SIBYLLINE
SIBYLLISM
SIBYLLIST
SIC
SICARIAN
SICARII
SICARIOUS
SICARIUS
SICCA
SICCANEOUS
SICCANT
SICCAR
SICCATE
SICCATED
SICCATING
SICCATION
SICCATIVE
SICCIMETER
SICCITY
SICE
SICER
SICHT
SICILIENNE
SICINNIAN
SICK
SICKBAY
SICKBED
SICKED
SICKEN
SICKENED
SICKENER
SICKENING
SICKENINGLY
SICKER
SICKEST
SICKET
SICKING
SICKISH
SICKISHLY
SICKISHNESS
SICKLE
SICKLEBILL
SICKLED
SICKLEMAN
SICKLEMEN
SICKLEMIA
SICKLEPOD
SICKLER
SICKLERITE
SICKLEWORT
SICKLIED
SICKLIER
SICKLIEST
SICKLILY
SICKLING
SICKLY
SICKLYING
SICKNESS
SICKROOM
SICLIKE
SICSAC
SICU
SICULA
SICULAR
SIDDER
SIDDOW
SIDDUR
SIDE
SIDEAGE
SIDEARM
SIDEBAND
SIDEBAR
SIDEBOARD
SIDEBONE
SIDEBONES
SIDEBOX
SIDEBURNS
SIDECAR
SIDECHECK
SIDED
SIDEFLASH
SIDEHEAD
SIDEHILL
SIDEHOLD
SIDEKICK
SIDELANG
SIDELIGHT
SIDELINE
SIDELINED
SIDELING
SIDELINGS
SIDELINING
SIDELINS
SIDELOCK
SIDELONG
SIDEMAN
SIDENESS
SIDENOTE
SIDEPIECE
SIDER
SIDERAL
SIDERATE
SIDERATED
SIDERATION
SIDEREAL
SIDEREALIZE
SIDEREALLY
SIDEREAN
SIDERISM
SIDERITE
SIDERITIC
SIDEROGNOST
SIDEROGRAPHY
SIDEROLITE
SIDEROLOGY
SIDEROMANCY
SIDEROMELANE
SIDERONATRITE
SIDERONYM
SIDEROSCOPE
SIDEROSE
SIDEROSIS
SIDEROSTAT
SIDEROSTATIC
SIDEROUS
SIDES
SIDESADDLE
SIDESHAKE
SIDESHOW
SIDESLIP
SIDESMAN
SIDESMEN
SIDESPIN
SIDESPLITTER
SIDESPLITTING
SIDESTEP
SIDESTEPPED
SIDESTEPPER
SIDESTEPPING
SIDESWAY
SIDESWIPE
SIDESWIPED
SIDESWIPER
SIDESWIPING
SIDETONE
SIDETRACK
SIDETRACKED
SIDETRACKING
SIDEWALK
SIDEWALL

SIDEWARD
SIDEWARDS
SIDEWASH
SIDEWAY
SIDEWAYS
SIDEWINDER
SIDEWISE
SIDHE
SIDI
SIDING
SIDLE
SIDLED
SIDLER
SIDLING
SIDLINGLY
SIDLINS
SIDTH
SIDY
SIE
SIECLE
SIEGE
SIEGED
SIEGENITE
SIEGER
SIEGEWORK
SIEGING
SIENITE
SIENITIC
SIENNA
SIER
SIEROZEM
SIERRA
SIERRAN
SIESTA
SIEUR
SIEVE
SIEVED
SIEVEFUL
SIEVELIKE
SIEVER
SIEVING
SIEVINGS
SIEVY
SIFAC
SIFAKA
SIFE
SIFF
SIFFILATE
SIFFLE
SIFFLEMENT
SIFFLET
SIFFLEUR
SIFFLEURS
SIFFLEUSE
SIFFLEUSES
SIFFLOT
SIFT
SIFTAGE
SIFTED
SIFTER
SIFTING
SIG
SIGATOKA
SIGGER
SIGH
SIGHED
SIGHER
SIGHFUL
SIGHING
SIGHINGLY
SIGHINGNESS
SIGHT
SIGHTED
SIGHTEN
SIGHTENING
SIGHTER
SIGHTFUL
SIGHTFULNESS
SIGHTHOLE
SIGHTING
SIGHTLESS
SIGHTLESSLY
SIGHTLESSNESS
SIGHTLIER
SIGHTLY
SIGHTPROOF
SIGHTS
SIGHTSEEING
SIGHTSMAN
SIGHTY
SIGIL
SIGILLARIAN
SIGILLARID
SIGILLARIOID
SIGILLARIST
SIGILLARY
SIGILLATE
SIGILLATED
SIGILLATION
SIGILLATIVE
SIGILLISTIC
SIGILLOGRAPHY
SIGILLUM
SIGLA
SIGLARIAN
SIGLOS
SIGLUM
SIGMA
SIGMASPIRE
SIGMATE
SIGMATIC
SIGMATION
SIGMODONT
SIGMOID
SIGMOIDAL
SIGMOIDALLY
SIGMOIDITIS
SIGN
SIGNABLE
SIGNACLE
SIGNAL
SIGNALED
SIGNALER
SIGNALETIC
SIGNALETICS
SIGNALING
SIGNALIST
SIGNALITIES
SIGNALITY
SIGNALIZE
SIGNALIZED
SIGNALIZING
SIGNALLER
SIGNALLING
SIGNALLY
SIGNALMAN
SIGNALMENT
SIGNANCE
SIGNARY
SIGNATE
SIGNATION
SIGNATOR
SIGNATORY
SIGNATURAL
SIGNATURE
SIGNATURIST
SIGNBOARD
SIGNED
SIGNEE
SIGNER
SIGNET
SIGNEURY
SIGNIFER
SIGNIFIABLE
SIGNIFICAL
SIGNIFICANCE
SIGNIFICANCY
SIGNIFICANT
SIGNIFICANTLY
SIGNIFICATE
SIGNIFICATION
SIGNIFICATIVE
SIGNIFICATOR
SIGNIFICATORY
SIGNIFICATURE
SIGNIFICAVIT
SIGNIFICIAN
SIGNIFICS
SIGNIFIE
SIGNIFIED
SIGNIFIER
SIGNIFY
SIGNIFYING
SIGNING
SIGNIOR
SIGNIST
SIGNITOR
SIGNLESS
SIGNMAN
SIGNOR
SIGNORA
SIGNORE
SIGNORIA
SIGNORIAL
SIGNORINA
SIGNORINE
SIGNORINO
SIGNORY
SIGNPOST
SIGNS
SIGNUM
SIGNWRITER
SIGRIM
SIJIL
SIJILL
SIKA
SIKAR
SIKARA
SIKE
SIKER
SIKERLY
SIKHARA
SIKIMI
SIKSIKA
SIKU
SIL
SILAGE
SILANE
SILANGA
SILCRETE
SILD
SILE
SILEN
SILENACEOUS
SILENCE
SILENCED
SILENCER
SILENCING
SILENIC
SILENT
SILENTIAL
SILENTIARY
SILENTIOUS
SILENTIUM
SILENTLY
SILENTNESS
SILENTS
SILENUS
SILESIA
SILEX
SILEXITE
SILGREEN
SILHOUETTE
SILHOUETTED
SILHOUETTING
SILHOUETTIST
SILICA
SILICAM
SILICATE
SILICATION
SILICATIZATION
SILICEAN
SILICEOUS
SILICIC
SILICIDE
SILICIDIZE
SILICIFEROUS
SILICIFIED
SILICIFY
SILICIFYING
SILICIOPHITE
SILICIOUS
SILICIUM
SILICIZE
SILICLE
SILICON
SILICONE
SILICONIZE
SILICOSIS
SILICOTIC
SILICULA
SILICULAR
SILICULE
SILICULOSE
SILICULOUS
SILICYL
SILIQUA
SILIQUE
SILIQUOSE
SILK
SILKALENE
SILKALINE
SILKED
SILKEN
SILKER
SILKFLOWER
SILKGROWER
SILKIE
SILKIER
SILKIEST
SILKILY
SILKINESS
SILKMAN
SILKMEN
SILKNESS
SILKSMAN
SILKTAIL
SILKWEED
SILKWOMAN
SILKWOOD
SILKWORK
SILKWORKER
SILKWORKS
SILKWORM
SILKY
SILL
SILLABUB
SILLADAR
SILLANDAR
SILLAR
SILLER
SILLIER
SILLIES
SILLIEST
SILLILY
SILLINESS
SILLOCK
SILLOGRAPH
SILLOGRAPHER
SILLOMETER
SILLON
SILLY
SILLYHOW
SILLYTON
SILO
SILOED
SILOING
SILOS
SILOXANE
SILPHID
SILPHIUM
SILT
SILTAGE
SILTATION
SILTED
SILTING
SILTY
SILUNDUM
SILURID
SILUROID
SILVA
SILVAN
SILVANITY
SILVANRY
SILVENDY
SILVER
SILVERBACK
SILVERBELLY
SILVERBERRIES
SILVERBERRY
SILVERBIDDY
SILVERBILL
SILVERBUSH
SILVERED
SILVERER
SILVERFIN
SILVERFISH
SILVERFISHES
SILVERIER
SILVERIEST
SILVERINESS
SILVERING
SILVERITE
SILVERIZE
SILVERLEAF
SILVERLING
SILVERLY
SILVERN
SILVERROD
SILVERSIDE
SILVERSIDES
SILVERSKIN
SILVERSMITH
SILVERSMITHING
SILVERSMITHS
SILVERSPOT
SILVERTAIL
SILVERTIP
SILVERTOP
SILVERVINE
SILVERWARE
SILVERWEED
SILVERWING
SILVERWOOD
SILVERWORK
SILVERY
SILVICAL
SILVICOLOUS
SILVICS
SILVICULTURE
SIM
SIMA
SIMAGRE
SIMAL
SIMAR

SIMARA
SIMARRE
SIMARUBA
SIMBA
SIMBALL
SIMBIL
SIMBLIN
SIMBLING
SIMBLOT
SIME
SIMIAD
SIMIAL
SIMIAN
SIMIANITY
SIMIESQUE
SIMIID
SIMILAR
SIMILARITY
SIMILARLY
SIMILATE
SIMILATIVE
SIMILE
SIMILIMUM
SIMILITER
SIMILITIVE
SIMILITUDE
SIMILITUDINIZE
SIMILIZE
SIMILOR
SIMIOID
SIMIOUS
SIMIOUSNESS
SIMIR
SIMITAR
SIMITY
SIMKIN
SIMLIN
SIMLING
SIMMER
SIMMERED
SIMMERING
SIMMON
SIMMONS
SIMNEL
SIMOLEON
SIMONIAC
SIMONIACAL
SIMONIOUS
SIMONISM
SIMONIST
SIMONIZE
SIMONY
SIMOOM
SIMOON
SIMOUS
SIMP
SIMPAI
SIMPATICO
SIMPER
SIMPERED
SIMPERER
SIMPERING
SIMPERINGLY
SIMPLE
SIMPLED
SIMPLER
SIMPLES
SIMPLEST
SIMPLETON
SIMPLETONIAN
SIMPLETONIC
SIMPLEX
SIMPLEXED
SIMPLEXITY
SIMPLICIST
SIMPLICITER
SIMPLICITIES
SIMPLICITY
SIMPLICIZE
SIMPLIFICATION
SIMPLIFICATIVE
SIMPLIFICATOR
SIMPLIFIED
SIMPLIFIEDLY
SIMPLIFIER
SIMPLIFY
SIMPLIFYING
SIMPLING
SIMPLISM
SIMPLIST
SIMPLISTIC
SIMPLUM
SIMPLY
SIMPSON
SIMRI
SIMSON
SIMULACRA
SIMULACRAL
SIMULACRE
SIMULACRIZE
SIMULACRUM
SIMULANCE
SIMULANT
SIMULAR
SIMULATE
SIMULATED
SIMULATING
SIMULATION
SIMULATIVE
SIMULATIVELY
SIMULATOR
SIMULATORY
SIMULCAST
SIMULE
SIMULIID
SIMULIZE
SIMULTANEOUS
SIMULTANEOUSLY
SIMULTY
SIMURG
SIMURGH
SIN
SINA
SINAITE
SINAL
SINALBIN
SINAMAY
SINAMIN
SINAMINE
SINAPATE
SINAPIC
SINAPIN
SINAPINE
SINAPISM
SINAPIZE
SINAPOLINE
SINAWA
SINCALINE
SINCAMAS
SINCE
SINCERE
SINCERELY
SINCERENESS
SINCERER
SINCEREST
SINCERITY
SINCIPITAL
SINCIPUT
SINDER
SINDLE
SINDON
SINE
SINEBADA
SINECURAL
SINECURE
SINECURED
SINECURING
SINECURISM
SINECURIST
SINEW
SINEWED
SINEWING
SINEWLESS
SINEWOUS
SINEWY
SINFONIA
SINFUL
SINFULLY
SINFULNESS
SING
SINGABLE
SINGALLY
SINGARIP
SINGE
SINGED
SINGEING
SINGEINGLY
SINGER
SINGERESS
SINGERIE
SINGERS
SINGH
SINGILLATIM
SINGING
SINGKAMAS
SINGLE
SINGLEBAR
SINGLED
SINGLEHANDED
SINGLEHANDEDLY
SINGLEHANDEDNESS
SINGLEHEARTED
SINGLEHEARTEDLY
SINGLEHEARTEDNESS
SINGLEHOOD
SINGLENESS
SINGLER
SINGLES
SINGLESTICK
SINGLET
SINGLETON
SINGLETREE
SINGLING
SINGLY
SINGSONG
SINGSPIEL
SINGSTRESS
SINGULAR
SINGULARISM
SINGULARIST
SINGULARITIES
SINGULARITY
SINGULARIZATION
SINGULARIZE
SINGULARIZED
SINGULARIZING
SINGULARLY
SINGULARNESS
SINGULT
SINGULTOUS
SINGULTUS
SINHASAN
SINIGRIN
SINISTER
SINISTERLY
SINISTERNESS
SINISTRA
SINISTRAD
SINISTRAL
SINISTRALITY
SINISTRALLY
SINISTRATION
SINISTRIN
SINISTRORSAL
SINISTRORSE
SINISTROUS
SINISTROUSLY
SINJER
SINK
SINKAGE
SINKBOAT
SINKBOX
SINKER
SINKHEAD
SINKHOLE
SINKING
SINKLESS
SINKROOM
SINKSTONE
SINKY
SINLESS
SINLESSLY
SINLESSNESS
SINNED
SINNER
SINNET
SINNING
SINNOWED
SINOMENINE
SINOPIA
SINOPITE
SINOPLE
SINSRING
SINSYNE
SINTER
SINTOC
SINUATE
SINUATED
SINUATEDENTATE
SINUATELY
SINUATING
SINUATION
SINUITIS
SINUOSE
SINUOSITIES
SINUOSITY
SINUOUS
SINUOUSLY
SINUOUSNESS
SINUPALLIAL
SINUPALLIATE
SINUS
SINUSAL
SINUSITIS
SINUSOID
SINUSOIDAL
SINUSOIDALLY
SINZER
SIOL
SION
SIP
SIPAGE
SIPAPU
SIPE
SIPER
SIPERS
SIPHAC
SIPHON
SIPHONACEOUS
SIPHONAGE
SIPHONAL
SIPHONATED
SIPHONEOUS
SIPHONET
SIPHONIA
SIPHONIC
SIPHONIFORM
SIPHONIUM
SIPHONOGAM
SIPHONOGAMIC
SIPHONOGLYPH
SIPHONOPHORAN
SIPHONOPHORE
SIPHONOPLAX
SIPHONOSOME
SIPHONOSTELE
SIPHONOSTELIC
SIPHONOSTELY
SIPHONOSTOME
SIPHONOZOOID
SIPHONULA
SIPHORHINAL
SIPHUNCLE
SIPHUNCLED
SIPHUNCULAR
SIPID
SIPIDITY
SIPING
SIPLING
SIPO
SIPPED
SIPPER
SIPPET
SIPPING
SIPPIO
SIPPLE
SIPUNCULID
SIPUNCULOID
SIPYLITE
SIR
SIRCAR
SIRDAR
SIRE
SIRED
SIRELESS
SIREN
SIRENE
SIRENIAN
SIRENIC
SIRENICAL
SIRENICALLY
SIRENING
SIRENIZE
SIRENOID
SIRENOMELUS
SIRENY
SIREX
SIRGANG
SIRI
SIRIAN
SIRICID
SIRIH
SIRING
SIRIOMETER
SIRKAR
SIRKEER
SIRKI
SIRKY
SIRLOIN
SIRLOINY
SIRMARK
SIROCCO
SIROS
SIRPEA
SIRPLE
SIRPOON
SIRRAH
SIRREE
SIRS
SIRSE
SIRUABALLI
SIRUELAS
SIRUP
SIRUPED
SIRUPER

SIRUPY
SIRVENT
SIS
SISAL
SISALANA
SISCOWET
SISE
SISEL
SISERARA
SISERARY
SISH
SISI
SISITH
SISKIN
SISS
SISSIES
SISSIFICATION
SISSIFIED
SISSONE
SISSONNE
SISSOO
SISSU
SISSY
SIST
SISTEN
SISTER
SISTERHOOD
SISTERING
SISTERIZE
SISTERLINESS
SISTERLY
SISTERN
SISTERS
SISTERSHIP
SISTLE
SISTOMENSIN
SISTREN
SISTROID
SISTRUM
SIT
SITAO
SITAR
SITATUNGA
SITATUNGAS
SITE
SITFAST
SITH
SITHE
SITHENCE
SITHENS
SITHES
SITIENT
SITIO
SITOLOGY
SITOMANIA
SITOSTERIN
SITOSTEROL
SITOTOXISM
SITREP
SITTER
SITTINE
SITTING
SITTRINGY
SITU
SITUAL
SITUATE
SITUATED
SITUATION
SITUATIONAL
SITULA
SITUS
SITZ
SITZMARK
SIVE
SIVER
SIVVENS
SIWASH
SIWASHED
SIWASHING
SIX
SIXAIN
SIXER
SIXFOLD
SIXMO
SIXPENCE
SIXPENCES
SIXPENNY
SIXPENNYWORTH
SIXSCORE
SIXSOME
SIXTE
SIXTEEN
SIXTEENER
SIXTEENMO
SIXTEENTH
SIXTH
SIXTIES
SIXTIETH
SIXTY
SIZABLE
SIZABLENESS
SIZABLY
SIZAR
SIZARSHIP
SIZE
SIZEABLE
SIZED
SIZEINE
SIZEMAN
SIZER
SIZES
SIZIER
SIZIEST
SIZINESS
SIZING
SIZINGS
SIZY
SIZYGIUM
SIZZ
SIZZARD
SIZZING
SIZZLE
SIZZLED
SIZZLER
SIZZLING
SIZZLINGLY
SJAMBOK
SJOMIL
SJOMILA
SKAALPUND
SKAAMOOG
SKADDLE
SKAFF
SKAFFIE
SKAG
SKAIF
SKAIL
SKAILLIE
SKAINSMATE
SKAIR
SKAITBIRD
SKAITHY
SKALAWAG
SKALD
SKALDIC
SKALPUND
SKANDHAS
SKARN
SKAT
SKATE
SKATED
SKATER
SKATES
SKATIKAS
SKATING
SKATIST
SKATOL
SKATOLE
SKATOLOGY
SKATOSINE
SKATOXYL
SKEAN
SKEANOCKLE
SKEAT
SKED
SKEDADDLE
SKEDADDLED
SKEDADDLER
SKEDADDLING
SKEDGE
SKEDLOCK
SKEE
SKEED
SKEEG
SKEEING
SKEEL
SKEELING
SKEENYIE
SKEER
SKEERED
SKEERY
SKEES
SKEESICKS
SKEET
SKEETER
SKEEZIX
SKEG
SKEGGER
SKEICH
SKEIF
SKEIGH
SKEIN
SKEINER
SKELB
SKELDER
SKELDOCK
SKELDRAKE
SKELET
SKELETAL
SKELETIN
SKELETON
SKELETONIAN
SKELETONIC
SKELETONIZATION
SKELETONIZE
SKELETONIZED
SKELETONIZER
SKELETONIZING
SKELETONY
SKELF
SKELGOOSE
SKELL
SKELLAT
SKELLER
SKELLOCH
SKELLUM
SKELLY
SKELP
SKELPED
SKELPER
SKELPIN
SKELPING
SKELTER
SKELVY
SKEMMEL
SKEMP
SKEN
SKENAI
SKENE
SKEO
SKEOUGH
SKEP
SKEPFUL
SKEPPE
SKEPPIST
SKEPPUND
SKEPSIS
SKEPTIC
SKEPTICAL
SKEPTICALLY
SKEPTICALNESS
SKEPTICISM
SKEPTICIZE
SKEPTICIZED
SKEPTICIZING
SKERM
SKERRICK
SKERRIES
SKERRY
SKETCH
SKETCHABLE
SKETCHBOOK
SKETCHED
SKETCHER
SKETCHIER
SKETCHIEST
SKETCHILY
SKETCHINESS
SKETCHING
SKETCHIST
SKETCHY
SKETE
SKETIOTAI
SKEUOMORPH
SKEVISH
SKEW
SKEWBACK
SKEWBACKED
SKEWBALD
SKEWED
SKEWER
SKEWERED
SKEWERER
SKEWERING
SKEWERWOOD
SKEWING
SKEWINGS
SKEWL
SKEWNESS
SKEWWISE
SKEWY
SKEY
SKEYTING
SKHIAN
SKI
SKIAGRAM
SKIAGRAPH
SKIAGRAPHED
SKIAGRAPHIC
SKIAGRAPHING
SKIAMETER
SKIAMETRY
SKIAPOD
SKIAPODOUS
SKIASCOPE
SKIASCOPY
SKIBBET
SKIBBY
SKICE
SKID
SKIDDED
SKIDDER
SKIDDING
SKIDDOO
SKIDDY
SKIDDYCOCK
SKIDOO
SKIDPAN
SKIDPROOF
SKIDS
SKIDWAY
SKIED
SKIEGH
SKIEPPE
SKIER
SKIES
SKIEUR
SKIFF
SKIFFLE
SKIFFLED
SKIFFLING
SKIFT
SKIING
SKIJORE
SKIJORER
SKIJORING
SKIL
SKILDER
SKILDFEL
SKILFISH
SKILFUL
SKILFULLY
SKILL
SKILLAGALEE
SKILLED
SKILLET
SKILLFUL
SKILLFULLY
SKILLFULNESS
SKILLING
SKILLION
SKILLO
SKILLS
SKILLY
SKILPOT
SKILTS
SKILTY
SKIM
SKIMBACK
SKIME
SKIMMED
SKIMMER
SKIMMING
SKIMMINGS
SKIMMINGTON
SKIMMITY
SKIMP
SKIMPIER
SKIMPIEST
SKIMPILY
SKIMPINESS
SKIMPY
SKIN
SKINBALL
SKINBOUND
SKINCH
SKINFLICK
SKINFLINT
SKINFLINTILY
SKINFLINTINESS
SKINFLINTY
SKINFUL
SKINFULS
SKINHEAD
SKINK
SKINKED
SKINKER
SKINKING
SKINKLE
SKINLESS
SKINNED
SKINNER
SKINNERS
SKINNERY
SKINNIER

SKINNIEST
SKINNING
SKINNY
SKINS
SKINTIGHT
SKINWORM
SKIOGRAM
SKIOGRAPH
SKIP
SKIPBRAIN
SKIPDENT
SKIPJACK
SKIPJACKLY
SKIPJACKS
SKIPKENNEL
SKIPMAN
SKIPPED
SKIPPER
SKIPPERED
SKIPPERSHIP
SKIPPERY
SKIPPET
SKIPPING
SKIPPLE
SKIPPUND
SKIPPY
SKIPS
SKIPTAIL
SKIRL
SKIRLCOCK
SKIRLING
SKIRM
SKIRMISH
SKIRMISHED
SKIRMISHER
SKIRMISHING
SKIRP
SKIRR
SKIRREH
SKIRRET
SKIRT
SKIRTBOARD
SKIRTED
SKIRTER
SKIRTING
SKIRTS
SKIRTY
SKIS
SKISE
SKISH
SKIT
SKITE
SKITER
SKITHER
SKITTER
SKITTERY
SKITTISH
SKITTISHLY
SKITTISHNESS
SKITTLE
SKITTLED
SKITTLES
SKITTLING
SKITTY
SKITTYBOOT
SKIV
SKIVE
SKIVED
SKIVER
SKIVERWOOD
SKIVIE
SKIVING
SKIVVIES
SKIVVY
SKLENT
SKLEROPELITE
SKLIM
SKLINTER
SKOAL
SKOGBOLITE
SKOKIAAN
SKOLLY
SKOMERITE
SKOOKUM
SKOOT
SKOUT
SKRAELLING
SKREEL
SKREIGH
SKRIKE
SKRUPUL
SKRYER
SKUA
SKUG
SKULDUGGERY
SKULK
SKULKED
SKULKER
SKULKING
SKULL
SKULLBANKER
SKULLCAP
SKULLERY
SKULLFISH
SKULLY
SKUNK
SKUNKBILL
SKUNKBUSH
SKUNKERY
SKUNKISH
SKUNKTOP
SKUNKWEED
SKUNKY
SKURRY
SKUTTERUDITE
SKY
SKYBAL
SKYBALD
SKYCOACH
SKYCRAFT
SKYED
SKYER
SKYEY
SKYFTE
SKYHOOK
SKYHOOT
SKYING
SKYISH
SKYJACK
SKYJACKING
SKYLARK
SKYLARKED
SKYLARKER
SKYLARKING
SKYLESS
SKYLIGHT
SKYLINE
SKYLOOK
SKYMAN
SKYME
SKYPHOS
SKYPORT
SKYR
SKYRE
SKYRGALIARD
SKYRIN
SKYROCKET
SKYROCKETY
SKYSAIL
SKYSCAPE
SKYSCRAPER
SKYSCRAPING
SKYSHINE
SKYSTONE
SKYT
SKYUGLE
SKYWARD
SKYWARDS
SKYWAY
SKYWRITE
SKYWRITER
SKYWRITING
SLA
SLAB
SLABBED
SLABBER
SLABBERED
SLABBERER
SLABBERING
SLABBERY
SLABBINESS
SLABBING
SLABBY
SLABMAN
SLABS
SLABSTONE
SLABWOOD
SLACK
SLACKAGE
SLACKED
SLACKEN
SLACKENED
SLACKENING
SLACKER
SLACKEST
SLACKIE
SLACKING
SLACKLY
SLACKNESS
SLACKS
SLAD
SLADE
SLAG
SLAGGED
SLAGGING
SLAGGY
SLAIN
SLAINTE
SLAISTER
SLAISTERY
SLAIT
SLAKE
SLAKED
SLAKELESS
SLAKER
SLAKIER
SLAKIEST
SLAKIN
SLAKING
SLAKY
SLALOM
SLAM
SLAMBANG
SLAMMED
SLAMMING
SLAMMOCK
SLAMMOCKING
SLAMMOCKY
SLAMP
SLAMPAMP
SLAMPANT
SLANDER
SLANDERER
SLANDERING
SLANDEROUS
SLANDEROUSLY
SLANDEROUSNESS
SLANE
SLANG
SLANGED
SLANGIER
SLANGIEST
SLANGILY
SLANGINESS
SLANGING
SLANGISH
SLANGISHLY
SLANGISM
SLANGKOP
SLANGOUS
SLANGRELL
SLANGSTER
SLANGUAGE
SLANGULAR
SLANGY
SLANK
SLANT
SLANTED
SLANTER
SLANTING
SLANTINGLY
SLANTLY
SLANTWAYS
SLANTWISE
SLAP
SLAPDAB
SLAPDASH
SLAPDASHERIES
SLAPDASHERY
SLAPE
SLAPHAPPIER
SLAPHAPPIEST
SLAPHAPPY
SLAPJACK
SLAPPED
SLAPPER
SLAPPING
SLAPPY
SLAPSTICK
SLARE
SLART
SLARTH
SLASH
SLASHED
SLASHER
SLASHERS
SLASHING
SLASHINGLY
SLASHY
SLAT
SLATCH
SLATE
SLATED
SLATELIKE
SLATER
SLATES
SLATH
SLATHER
SLATIER
SLATIEST
SLATIFIED
SLATIFY
SLATIFYING
SLATING
SLATISH
SLATS
SLATTED
SLATTER
SLATTERED
SLATTERING
SLATTERN
SLATTERNISH
SLATTERNLINESS
SLATTERNLY
SLATTERY
SLATTING
SLATY
SLAUGHTER
SLAUGHTERDOM
SLAUGHTERED
SLAUGHTERER
SLAUGHTERHOUSE
SLAUGHTERING
SLAUGHTERMAN
SLAUGHTEROUS
SLAUGHTEROUSLY
SLAUM
SLAVE
SLAVED
SLAVEHOLDER
SLAVEHOLDING
SLAVELET
SLAVELING
SLAVER
SLAVERED
SLAVERER
SLAVERING
SLAVERY
SLAVES
SLAVEY
SLAVIKITE
SLAVIN
SLAVING
SLAVISH
SLAVOCRACY
SLAVOCRAT
SLAVOCRATIC
SLAW
SLAWBANK
SLAY
SLAYER
SLEATHY
SLEAVE
SLEAVED
SLEAVING
SLEAZINESS
SLEAZY
SLED
SLEDDED
SLEDDER
SLEDDING
SLEDGE
SLEDGED
SLEDGEHAMMER
SLEDGEMETER
SLEDGER
SLEDGING
SLEE
SLEECH
SLEECHY
SLEEK
SLEEKED
SLEEKEN
SLEEKENED
SLEEKENING
SLEEKER
SLEEKIER
SLEEKING
SLEEKIT
SLEEKLY
SLEEKNESS
SLEEKY
SLEEP
SLEEPER
SLEEPERED
SLEEPIER
SLEEPIEST
SLEEPIFY
SLEEPING
SLEEPISH
SLEEPLESS
SLEEPLESSLY
SLEEPLESSNESS
SLEEPMARKEN
SLEEPRY

SLEEPWALK
SLEEPWALKER
SLEEPWALKING
SLEEPWORT
SLEEPY
SLEEPYHEAD
SLEER
SLEET
SLEETED
SLEETIER
SLEETIEST
SLEETING
SLEETY
SLEEVE
SLEEVED
SLEEVEEN
SLEEVEFISH
SLEEVELESS
SLEEVELET
SLEEVER
SLEEVES
SLEEVING
SLEEZY
SLEIDED
SLEIGH
SLEIGHER
SLEIGHING
SLEIGHT
SLEIGHTNESS
SLEIGHTY
SLENDANG
SLENDER
SLENDERER
SLENDEREST
SLENDERISH
SLENDERIZE
SLENDERIZED
SLENDERIZING
SLENDERLY
SLENDERNESS
SLENT
SLEPEZ
SLEUTH
SLEUTHED
SLEUTHHOUND
SLEUTHING
SLEW
SLEWED
SLEWER
SLEWING
SLEWTH
SLEY
SLEYED
SLEYING
SLIBBERSAUCE
SLICE
SLICED
SLICER
SLICES
SLICING
SLICINGLY
SLICK
SLICKED
SLICKENS
SLICKENSIDE
SLICKENSIDED
SLICKER
SLICKERED
SLICKERY
SLICKEST
SLICKING
SLICKLY
SLID
SLIDAGE
SLIDDEN
SLIDDER
SLIDDERNESS
SLIDDERY
SLIDDRY
SLIDE
SLIDEGROAT
SLIDEHEAD
SLIDEKNOT
SLIDEMAN
SLIDER
SLIDEWAY
SLIDING
SLIDOMETER
SLIER
SLIEST
SLIFTER
SLIGGEEN
SLIGHT
SLIGHTED
SLIGHTER
SLIGHTEST
SLIGHTIER
SLIGHTIEST
SLIGHTING
SLIGHTINGLY
SLIGHTLY
SLIGHTNESS
SLIGHTY
SLIKE
SLILY
SLIM
SLIME
SLIMED
SLIMEMAN
SLIMEMEN
SLIMER
SLIMIER
SLIMIEST
SLIMILY
SLIMINESS
SLIMING
SLIMISH
SLIMISHNESS
SLIMLY
SLIMMED
SLIMMER
SLIMMEST
SLIMMING
SLIMMISH
SLIMNESS
SLIMPSY
SLIMSIER
SLIMSIEST
SLIMSY
SLIMY
SLINE
SLING
SLINGE
SLINGER
SLINGING
SLINGSHOT
SLINGSMAN
SLINGSMEN
SLINGSTONE
SLINK
SLINKER
SLINKIER
SLINKIEST
SLINKING
SLINKINGLY
SLINKSKIN
SLINKWEED
SLINKY
SLIP
SLIPBACK
SLIPBAND
SLIPBOARD
SLIPBODIES
SLIPBODY
SLIPCASE
SLIPCOAT
SLIPCOTE
SLIPCOVER
SLIPE
SLIPES
SLIPHALTER
SLIPHORN
SLIPHOUSE
SLIPKNOT
SLIPMAN
SLIPOVER
SLIPPAGE
SLIPPED
SLIPPER
SLIPPERED
SLIPPERFLOWER
SLIPPERIER
SLIPPERIEST
SLIPPERILY
SLIPPERINESS
SLIPPERWEED
SLIPPERWORT
SLIPPERY
SLIPPERYBACK
SLIPPERYROOT
SLIPPIER
SLIPPIEST
SLIPPINESS
SLIPPING
SLIPPINGLY
SLIPPROOF
SLIPPY
SLIPRAIL
SLIPS
SLIPSHEET
SLIPSHOD
SLIPSHOE
SLIPSKIN
SLIPSLAP
SLIPSLOP
SLIPSLOPPISH
SLIPSLOPPISM
SLIPSOLE
SLIPSTICK
SLIPSTREAM
SLIPSTRING
SLIPT
SLIPTOPPED
SLIPUP
SLIPWARE
SLIPWAY
SLIRT
SLISH
SLIT
SLITE
SLITHER
SLITHERING
SLITHEROO
SLITHERS
SLITHERY
SLITING
SLITSHELL
SLITTED
SLITTER
SLITTING
SLITTY
SLITWORK
SLIVE
SLIVER
SLIVERED
SLIVERER
SLIVERING
SLIVERS
SLIVERY
SLIVING
SLIVOVIC
SLIVOVITZ
SLIVVER
SLO
SLOAK
SLOAN
SLOAT
SLOB
SLOBBER
SLOBBERCHOPS
SLOBBERER
SLOBBERS
SLOBBERY
SLOBBY
SLOCK
SLOCKEN
SLOCKER
SLOCKINGSTONE
SLOCKSTER
SLOD
SLODDER
SLODGE
SLODGER
SLOE
SLOEBERRIES
SLOEBERRY
SLOEBUSH
SLOETREE
SLOG
SLOGAN
SLOGANEER
SLOGGED
SLOGGER
SLOGGING
SLOGWOOD
SLOID
SLOJD
SLOKA
SLOKE
SLOKED
SLOKEN
SLOKING
SLOMMACK
SLON
SLONE
SLONK
SLOO
SLOOM
SLOOMY
SLOOP
SLOOPMAN
SLOOPMEN
SLOOSH
SLOOT
SLOP
SLOPE
SLOPED
SLOPER
SLOPEWAYS
SLOPING
SLOPINGLY
SLOPINGNESS
SLOPMAKER
SLOPMAKING
SLOPPAGE
SLOPPED
SLOPPERIES
SLOPPERY
SLOPPIER
SLOPPIEST
SLOPPILY
SLOPPINESS
SLOPPING
SLOPPY
SLOPS
SLOPSELLER
SLOPSELLING
SLOPSHOP
SLOPSTONE
SLOPWORK
SLOPWORKER
SLOPY
SLORP
SLOSH
SLOSHED
SLOSHER
SLOSHILY
SLOSHINESS
SLOSHING
SLOSHY
SLOT
SLOTE
SLOTH
SLOTHFUL
SLOTHFULLY
SLOTHFULNESS
SLOTTED
SLOTTEN
SLOTTER
SLOTTERY
SLOTTING
SLOUBBIE
SLOUCH
SLOUCHED
SLOUCHER
SLOUCHIER
SLOUCHIEST
SLOUCHILY
SLOUCHINESS
SLOUCHING
SLOUCHINGLY
SLOUCHY
SLOUGH
SLOUGHED
SLOUGHING
SLOUGHY
SLOUM
SLOUNGE
SLOUNGER
SLOUR
SLOVEN
SLOVENLIER
SLOVENLIEST
SLOVENLINESS
SLOVENLY
SLOW
SLOWBACK
SLOWBELLIED
SLOWBELLIES
SLOWBELLY
SLOWDOWN
SLOWED
SLOWER
SLOWEST
SLOWFUL
SLOWGOING
SLOWHEADED
SLOWHEARTED
SLOWING
SLOWISH
SLOWLY
SLOWMOUTHED
SLOWNESS
SLOWPOKE
SLOWRIE
SLOWS
SLOWWITTED
SLOWWITTEDLY
SLOWWORM
SLOYD
SLUB
SLUBBED
SLUBBER
SLUBBERED
SLUBBERER

SLUBBERING
SLUBBERINGLY
SLUBBERY
SLUBBING
SLUBBY
SLUD
SLUDDER
SLUDDERY
SLUDE
SLUDGE
SLUDGED
SLUDGER
SLUDGING
SLUDGY
SLUE
SLUED
SLUER
SLUFF
SLUG
SLUGABED
SLUGFEST
SLUGGARD
SLUGGARDING
SLUGGARDIZE
SLUGGARDLY
SLUGGED
SLUGGER
SLUGGING
SLUGGINGLY
SLUGGISH
SLUGGISHLY
SLUGGISHNESS
SLUGGY
SLUGHORN
SLUICE
SLUICED
SLUICER
SLUICEWAY
SLUICING
SLUICY
SLUIG
SLUING
SLUIT
SLUM
SLUMBER
SLUMBERED
SLUMBERER
SLUMBERING
SLUMBERINGLY
SLUMBERLAND
SLUMBERLESS
SLUMBEROUS
SLUMBEROUSLY
SLUMBERY
SLUMBROUS
SLUMDOM
SLUMGULLION
SLUMGUM
SLUMLAND
SLUMLORD
SLUMMAGE
SLUMMED
SLUMMER
SLUMMIER
SLUMMIEST
SLUMMING
SLUMMOCK
SLUMMOCKY
SLUMMY
SLUMP
SLUMPED
SLUMPING
SLUMPWORK
SLUMPY
SLUMS
SLUNG
SLUNGBODIES
SLUNGBODY
SLUNGE
SLUNGSHOT
SLUNK
SLUNKEN
SLUP
SLUR
SLURBOW
SLURP
SLURRED
SLURRIED
SLURRIES
SLURRING
SLURRY
SLURRYING
SLUSH
SLUSHED
SLUSHER
SLUSHIER
SLUSHIEST
SLUSHING
SLUSHPIT
SLUSHY
SLUT
SLUTCH
SLUTCHY
SLUTE
SLUTHER
SLUTTED
SLUTTER
SLUTTERED
SLUTTERING
SLUTTERY
SLUTTING
SLUTTISH
SLUTTISHLY
SLUTTISHNESS
SLUTTY
SLY
SLYBOOTS
SLYER
SLYEST
SLYISH
SLYLY
SLYNESS
SLYPE
SMA
SMACH
SMACHRIE
SMACK
SMACKED
SMACKEE
SMACKER
SMACKING
SMACKINGLY
SMACKSMAN
SMACKSMEN
SMAD
SMAIK
SMAIL
SMAK
SMALL
SMALLAGE
SMALLCLOTHES
SMALLCOAL
SMALLEN
SMALLER
SMALLEST
SMALLHEARTED
SMALLHOLDER
SMALLING
SMALLISH
SMALLMOUTH
SMALLMOUTHED
SMALLNESS
SMALLNESSES
SMALLPOX
SMALLS
SMALLSWORD
SMALLTIME
SMALLWARE
SMALLY
SMALM
SMALMED
SMALMING
SMALT
SMALTER
SMALTI
SMALTINE
SMALTITE
SMALTO
SMALTZ
SMARAGD
SMARAGDE
SMARAGDINE
SMARAGDITE
SMARM
SMARMIER
SMARMIEST
SMARMY
SMART
SMARTED
SMARTEN
SMARTER
SMARTEST
SMARTIES
SMARTING
SMARTINGLY
SMARTISM
SMARTLESS
SMARTLY
SMARTNESS
SMARTWEED
SMARTY
SMASH
SMASHAGE
SMASHED
SMASHER
SMASHERY
SMASHING
SMASHINGLY
SMASHUP
SMATCH
SMATCHET
SMATTER
SMATTERED
SMATTERER
SMATTERING
SMATTERINGLY
SMATTERY
SMAZE
SMEAR
SMEARCASE
SMEARED
SMEARER
SMEARIER
SMEARIEST
SMEARINESS
SMEARING
SMEARLESS
SMEARY
SMECTIC
SMECTITE
SMEDDUM
SMEE
SMEECH
SMEEK
SMEEKY
SMEER
SMEETH
SMEGMA
SMEGMATIC
SMEIR
SMELL
SMELLAGE
SMELLED
SMELLER
SMELLFUL
SMELLIE
SMELLIER
SMELLIEST
SMELLING
SMELLY
SMELT
SMELTED
SMELTER
SMELTERIES
SMELTERY
SMELTING
SMELTS
SMERK
SMERVY
SMETHE
SMEU
SMEUSE
SMEUTH
SMEW
SMICH
SMICKER
SMICKET
SMICKLY
SMIDDY
SMIDGE
SMIDGEN
SMIDGEON
SMIDGIN
SMIFT
SMIGGINS
SMILACACEOUS
SMILAX
SMILE
SMILED
SMILEFUL
SMILEFULNESS
SMILEMAKER
SMILEMAKING
SMILER
SMILEY
SMILING
SMILINGLY
SMILINGNESS
SMILO
SMILY
SMINTHURID
SMIRCH
SMIRCHED
SMIRCHER
SMIRCHING
SMIRCHY
SMIRIS
SMIRK
SMIRKED
SMIRKER
SMIRKING
SMIRKINGLY
SMIRKISH
SMIRKLE
SMIRKY
SMIRR
SMIRTLE
SMIT
SMITABLE
SMITCH
SMITE
SMITER
SMITH
SMITHCRAFT
SMITHER
SMITHEREENS
SMITHERIES
SMITHERS
SMITHERY
SMITHIED
SMITHIER
SMITHIES
SMITHING
SMITHITE
SMITHSONITE
SMITHUM
SMITHWORK
SMITHY
SMITHYDANDER
SMITHYING
SMITING
SMITTEN
SMITTER
SMITTING
SMITTLE
SMITTLEISH
SMITTLISH
SMOCK
SMOCKED
SMOCKER
SMOCKFACE
SMOCKING
SMOCKLESS
SMOG
SMOKABLES
SMOKE
SMOKEBOX
SMOKEBUSH
SMOKED
SMOKEHOUSE
SMOKEJACK
SMOKEJUMPER
SMOKELESS
SMOKELESSLY
SMOKELESSNESS
SMOKEPOT
SMOKEPROOF
SMOKER
SMOKERY
SMOKES
SMOKESTACK
SMOKESTONE
SMOKETIGHT
SMOKEWOOD
SMOKEY
SMOKIER
SMOKIEST
SMOKILY
SMOKINESS
SMOKING
SMOKISH
SMOKO
SMOKY
SMOKYSEEMING
SMOLDER
SMOLDERED
SMOLDERING
SMOLT
SMOOCH
SMOOCHY
SMOODGE
SMOODGER
SMOOGE
SMOOR
SMOORICH
SMOOT
SMOOTH
SMOOTHBOOTS
SMOOTHBORE
SMOOTHBORED
SMOOTHCOAT
SMOOTHED
SMOOTHEN
SMOOTHER
SMOOTHEST

SMOOTHIE
SMOOTHIFY
SMOOTHING
SMOOTHINGLY
SMOOTHLY
SMOOTHNESS
SMOOTHPATE
SMOOTHY
SMOPPLE
SMORE
SMORGASBORD
SMORZANDO
SMORZATO
SMOT
SMOTE
SMOTHER
SMOTHERATION
SMOTHERED
SMOTHERER
SMOTHERINESS
SMOTHERING
SMOTHERINGLY
SMOTHERY
SMOTTER
SMOUCH
SMOUCHER
SMOULDER
SMOULDERED
SMOULDERING
SMOUS
SMOUSE
SMOUSER
SMOUT
SMRITI
SMRTI
SMUDDER
SMUDGE
SMUDGED
SMUDGEDLY
SMUDGER
SMUDGIER
SMUDGIEST
SMUDGILY
SMUDGINESS
SMUDGING
SMUDGY
SMUG
SMUGGER
SMUGGERY
SMUGGEST
SMUGGISH
SMUGGISHLY
SMUGGISHNESS
SMUGGLE
SMUGGLED
SMUGGLER
SMUGGLERY
SMUGGLING
SMUGLY
SMUGNESS
SMUISTY
SMUR
SMURR
SMURRY
SMURTLE
SMUSE
SMUSH
SMUT
SMUTCH
SMUTCHED
SMUTCHIN
SMUTCHING
SMUTCHY
SMUTTED
SMUTTER
SMUTTIER
SMUTTIEST
SMUTTILY
SMUTTINESS
SMUTTING
SMUTTY
SMY
SMYTH
SMYTRIE
SNA
SNAB
SNABBIE
SNABBLE
SNABBY
SNACK
SNACKLE
SNACKY
SNAFF
SNAFFLE
SNAFFLEBIT
SNAFFLED
SNAFFLES
SNAFFLING
SNAFU
SNAFUED
SNAFUING
SNAFUS
SNAG
SNAGBUSH
SNAGGED
SNAGGER
SNAGGIER
SNAGGIEST
SNAGGING
SNAGGLE
SNAGGLED
SNAGGLETEETH
SNAGGLETOOTH
SNAGGLETOOTHED
SNAGGY
SNAGLINE
SNAGREL
SNAIL
SNAILEATER
SNAILERY
SNAILFLOWER
SNAILISH
SNAILISHLY
SNAILY
SNAKE
SNAKEBARK
SNAKEBERRY
SNAKEBIRD
SNAKEBITE
SNAKED
SNAKEFISH
SNAKEFISHES
SNAKEFLOWER
SNAKEHEAD
SNAKEHOLING
SNAKELET
SNAKELIKE
SNAKEMOUTH
SNAKENECK
SNAKEOLOGY
SNAKEPIECE
SNAKEPIPE
SNAKER
SNAKEROOT
SNAKERY
SNAKES
SNAKESKIN
SNAKESTONE
SNAKEWEED
SNAKEWOOD
SNAKEWORM
SNAKEWORT
SNAKEY
SNAKIER
SNAKIEST
SNAKILY
SNAKINESS
SNAKING
SNAKISH
SNAKY
SNAP
SNAPBACK
SNAPBAG
SNAPBERRY
SNAPDRAGON
SNAPE
SNAPER
SNAPHAAN
SNAPHANCE
SNAPHEAD
SNAPHOLDER
SNAPJACK
SNAPLESS
SNAPPAGE
SNAPPED
SNAPPER
SNAPPIER
SNAPPIEST
SNAPPILY
SNAPPINESS
SNAPPING
SNAPPINGLY
SNAPPISH
SNAPPISHLY
SNAPPISHNESS
SNAPPY
SNAPS
SNAPSACK
SNAPSHARE
SNAPSHOT
SNAPSHOTTED
SNAPSHOTTER
SNAPSHOTTING
SNAPWEED
SNAPWOOD
SNAPWORT
SNAPY
SNARE
SNARED
SNARER
SNARING
SNARK
SNARL
SNARLED
SNARLER
SNARLEYOW
SNARLEYYOW
SNARLING
SNARLINGLY
SNARLISH
SNARLY
SNARY
SNASH
SNAST
SNASTE
SNASTY
SNATCH
SNATCHED
SNATCHER
SNATCHIER
SNATCHIEST
SNATCHING
SNATCHINGLY
SNATCHY
SNATH
SNATHE
SNATTOCK
SNAVEL
SNAVVLE
SNAW
SNAZZY
SNEAD
SNEAK
SNEAKED
SNEAKER
SNEAKIER
SNEAKIEST
SNEAKILY
SNEAKINESS
SNEAKING
SNEAKINGLY
SNEAKINGNESS
SNEAKISH
SNEAKISHLY
SNEAKISHNESS
SNEAKSBY
SNEAKY
SNEAP
SNEATH
SNEB
SNECK
SNECKDRAW
SNECKDRAWING
SNECKDRAWN
SNECKED
SNECKER
SNECKET
SNECKING
SNED
SNEDDED
SNEDDING
SNEE
SNEER
SNEERED
SNEERER
SNEERFUL
SNEERFULNESS
SNEERING
SNEERINGLY
SNEERY
SNEESH
SNEESHIN
SNEESHING
SNEEST
SNEESTY
SNEEZE
SNEEZED
SNEEZER
SNEEZEWEED
SNEEZEWOOD
SNEEZEWORT
SNEEZING
SNEEZY
SNEG
SNELL
SNELLY
SNERP
SNEW
SNIB
SNIBBLE
SNIBBLED
SNIBBLER
SNIBEL
SNICK
SNICKDRAW
SNICKED
SNICKER
SNICKERED
SNICKERING
SNICKERINGLY
SNICKERSNEE
SNICKET
SNICKEY
SNICKING
SNICKLE
SNIDDLE
SNIDE
SNIDENESS
SNIDERY
SNIFF
SNIFFED
SNIFFER
SNIFFIER
SNIFFIEST
SNIFFILY
SNIFFINESS
SNIFFING
SNIFFINGLY
SNIFFISH
SNIFFISHNESS
SNIFFLE
SNIFFLED
SNIFFLER
SNIFFLES
SNIFFLING
SNIFFY
SNIFT
SNIFTED
SNIFTER
SNIFTERS
SNIFTING
SNIFTY
SNIG
SNIGGER
SNIGGERER
SNIGGERING
SNIGGERS
SNIGGLE
SNIGGLED
SNIGGLER
SNIGGLING
SNIGGORINGLY
SNIGHT
SNIGS
SNIP
SNIPE
SNIPEBILL
SNIPED
SNIPEFISH
SNIPEFISHES
SNIPER
SNIPERSCOPE
SNIPES
SNIPING
SNIPISH
SNIPJACK
SNIPOCRACY
SNIPPED
SNIPPER
SNIPPERADO
SNIPPERTY
SNIPPET
SNIPPETY
SNIPPIER
SNIPPIEST
SNIPPING
SNIPPY
SNIPS
SNIPTIOUS
SNIPY
SNIRL
SNIRT
SNIRTLE
SNIT
SNITCH
SNITCHER
SNITE
SNITHE
SNITHY
SNITS
SNITTLE
SNITZ
SNIVEL
SNIVELED
SNIVELER

SNIVELING
SNIVELLED
SNIVELLER
SNIVELLING
SNIVELLY
SNIVELS
SNIVELY
SNIVEY
SNIVY
SNOB
SNOBBER
SNOBBERY
SNOBBING
SNOBBISH
SNOBBISHLY
SNOBBISHNESS
SNOBBISM
SNOBBY
SNOBISM
SNOBOCRACY
SNOBOCRAT
SNOBOGRAPHER
SNOBOGRAPHY
SNOBOLOGIST
SNOBONOMER
SNOBS
SNOBSCAT
SNOCAT
SNOCHER
SNOCK
SNOCKER
SNOD
SNODE
SNODLY
SNOEK
SNOEKING
SNOGA
SNOOD
SNOODED
SNOODING
SNOOK
SNOOKER
SNOOKERED
SNOOKS
SNOOL
SNOOP
SNOOPER
SNOOPIER
SNOOPIEST
SNOOPY
SNOOT
SNOOTFUL
SNOOTIER
SNOOTIEST
SNOOTY
SNOOVE
SNOOZE
SNOOZED
SNOOZER
SNOOZING
SNOOZLE
SNOOZY
SNOP
SNORE
SNORED
SNORER
SNORING
SNORINGLY
SNORK
SNORKEL
SNORKELED
SNORKELING
SNORKER
SNORT
SNORTED
SNORTER
SNORTING
SNORTINGLY
SNORTLE
SNORTY
SNOT
SNOTTER
SNOTTERY
SNOTTIE
SNOTTIER
SNOTTIEST
SNOTTY
SNOUCH
SNOUT
SNOUTED
SNOUTER
SNOUTFAIR
SNOUTISH
SNOUTY
SNOVE
SNOW
SNOWBALL
SNOWBALLED
SNOWBALLING
SNOWBANK
SNOWBELL
SNOWBERG
SNOWBERRIES
SNOWBERRY
SNOWBIRD
SNOWBLINK
SNOWBLOWER
SNOWBOUND
SNOWBREAK
SNOWBROTH
SNOWBUSH
SNOWCAP
SNOWCRAFT
SNOWDRIFT
SNOWDROP
SNOWED
SNOWFALL
SNOWFLAKE
SNOWFLIGHT
SNOWFLOWER
SNOWFOWL
SNOWHAMMER
SNOWHOUSE
SNOWIER
SNOWIEST
SNOWILY
SNOWINESS
SNOWING
SNOWK
SNOWL
SNOWLAND
SNOWLESS
SNOWLIKE
SNOWMAN
SNOWMELT
SNOWMEN
SNOWMOBILE
SNOWPACK
SNOWPLOUGH
SNOWPLOW
SNOWS
SNOWSCAPE
SNOWSHADE
SNOWSHED
SNOWSHINE
SNOWSHOE
SNOWSHOED
SNOWSHOEING
SNOWSHOER
SNOWSLIDE
SNOWSLIP
SNOWSTORM
SNOWSUIT
SNOWTHROWER
SNOWWORM
SNOWY
SNOZZLE
SNUB
SNUBBED
SNUBBEE
SNUBBER
SNUBBING
SNUBBINGLY
SNUBBISH
SNUBBISHLY
SNUBBISHNESS
SNUBBY
SNUCK
SNUDGE
SNUDGERY
SNUFF
SNUFFBOX
SNUFFBOXER
SNUFFCOLORED
SNUFFED
SNUFFER
SNUFFERS
SNUFFIER
SNUFFIEST
SNUFFILY
SNUFFINESS
SNUFFING
SNUFFINGLY
SNUFFISH
SNUFFKIN
SNUFFLE
SNUFFLED
SNUFFLER
SNUFFLES
SNUFFLESS
SNUFFLINESS
SNUFFLING
SNUFFLINGLY
SNUFFLY
SNUFFMAN
SNUFFY
SNUG
SNUGGED
SNUGGER
SNUGGERIES
SNUGGERY
SNUGGEST
SNUGGIES
SNUGGING
SNUGGISH
SNUGGLE
SNUGGLED
SNUGGLING
SNUGIFY
SNUGLY
SNUGNESS
SNUM
SNUP
SNUPPER
SNUR
SNURL
SNURLY
SNURP
SNURT
SNUSH
SNUZZLE
SNY
SNYE
SNYED
SNYING
SO
SOA
SOAK
SOAKAGE
SOAKAWAY
SOAKED
SOAKEN
SOAKER
SOAKERS
SOAKING
SOAKINGLY
SOAKY
SOAL
SOALLIES
SOALLY
SOAM
SOAP
SOAPBARK
SOAPBERRIES
SOAPBERRY
SOAPBOX
SOAPBOXER
SOAPBUBBLY
SOAPBUSH
SOAPED
SOAPER
SOAPERIES
SOAPERY
SOAPFISH
SOAPFISHES
SOAPIER
SOAPIEST
SOAPING
SOAPLEES
SOAPLESS
SOAPMAKER
SOAPMAKING
SOAPROCK
SOAPROOT
SOAPSTONE
SOAPSTONER
SOAPSUDDY
SOAPSUDS
SOAPSUDSY
SOAPWEED
SOAPWOOD
SOAPWORT
SOAPY
SOAR
SOARABILITY
SOARABLE
SOARED
SOARER
SOARING
SOARINGLY
SOARY
SOAVE
SOAVEMENTE
SOB
SOBBED
SOBBER
SOBBING
SOBBINGLY
SOBBY
SOBEIT
SOBER
SOBERED
SOBERER
SOBEREST
SOBERING
SOBERINGLY
SOBERIZE
SOBERLY
SOBERNESS
SOBERSIDED
SOBERSIDES
SOBFUL
SOBOL
SOBOLE
SOBOLES
SOBOLIFEROUS
SOBOR
SOBPROOF
SOBRALITE
SOBREVEST
SOBRIETIES
SOBRIETY
SOBRIQUET
SOC
SOCAGE
SOCAGER
SOCCAGE
SOCCER
SOCCERIST
SOCCERITE
SOCE
SOCIABILITIES
SOCIABILITY
SOCIABLE
SOCIABLENESS
SOCIABLY
SOCIAL
SOCIALISM
SOCIALIST
SOCIALISTIC
SOCIALITE
SOCIALITIES
SOCIALITY
SOCIALIZATION
SOCIALIZE
SOCIALIZED
SOCIALIZER
SOCIALIZING
SOCIALLY
SOCIATE
SOCIATION
SOCIATIVE
SOCIES
SOCIETAL
SOCIETALLY
SOCIETARIAN
SOCIETARY
SOCIETAS
SOCIETE
SOCIETEIT
SOCIETIES
SOCIETIFIED
SOCIETISM
SOCIETIST
SOCIETOLOGIST
SOCIETOLOGY
SOCIETY
SOCIETYISH
SOCII
SOCIOCENTRIC
SOCIOCRACY
SOCIOCRAT
SOCIOCRATIC
SOCIOCULTURAL
SOCIOECONOMIC
SOCIOECONOMICALLY
SOCIOEDUCATIONAL
SOCIOGENESIS
SOCIOGENETIC
SOCIOGENY
SOCIOGRAPHY
SOCIOLATRY
SOCIOLEGAL
SOCIOLOGIAN
SOCIOLOGIC
SOCIOLOGICAL
SOCIOLOGICALLY
SOCIOLOGIST
SOCIOLOGISTIC
SOCIOLOGY
SOCIOMEDICAL
SOCIOMETRIC
SOCIOMETRY
SOCIONOMIC
SOCIONOMY

SOCIOPHAGOUS
SOCIOPOLITICAL
SOCIORELIGIOUS
SOCIOROMANTIC
SOCIOSTATIC
SOCIOTECHNICAL
SOCIUS
SOCK
SOCKDOLAGER
SOCKDOLOGER
SOCKER
SOCKEROO
SOCKET
SOCKETED
SOCKETING
SOCKEYE
SOCKHEAD
SOCKMAKER
SOCKMAKING
SOCKMAN
SOCKO
SOCKS
SOCKY
SOCLE
SOCMAN
SOCMANRY
SOCMEN
SOCO
SOD
SODA
SODACLASE
SODAIC
SODALIST
SODALITE
SODALITHITE
SODALITIES
SODALITY
SODAMID
SODAMIDE
SODAR
SODBUSTER
SODDED
SODDEN
SODDENLY
SODDENNESS
SODDIER
SODDIES
SODDIEST
SODDING
SODDITE
SODDY
SODIC
SODIOAUROUS
SODIOCITRATE
SODIOHYDRIC
SODIUM
SODOKU
SODOMITE
SODOMITIC
SODOMITICAL
SODOMITICALLY
SODOMY
SODS
SODWORK
SOE
SOEVER
SOFA
SOFANE
SOFAR
SOFFARID
SOFFIONE
SOFFIONI
SOFFIT
SOFI
SOFKEE
SOFT
SOFTA
SOFTBALL
SOFTCOAL
SOFTEN
SOFTENED
SOFTENER
SOFTENING
SOFTER
SOFTEST
SOFTHEAD
SOFTHEARTED
SOFTHEARTEDLY
SOFTHEARTEDNESS
SOFTHORN
SOFTIE
SOFTIES
SOFTISH
SOFTLING
SOFTLY
SOFTNESS
SOFTS
SOFTTACK
SOFTWARE
SOFTWOOD
SOFTY
SOG
SOGA
SOGGARTH
SOGGED
SOGGENDALITE
SOGGIER
SOGGIEST
SOGGILY
SOGGINESS
SOGGING
SOGGY
SOH
SOHO
SOIGNE
SOIGNEE
SOIL
SOILAGE
SOILED
SOILIER
SOILIEST
SOILING
SOILS
SOILURE
SOILY
SOIREE
SOIXANTINE
SOJA
SOJOURN
SOJOURNED
SOJOURNER
SOJOURNING
SOJOURNMENT
SOK
SOKA
SOKE
SOKEMAN
SOKEMANEMOT
SOKEMANRIES
SOKEMANRY
SOKEN
SOL
SOLA
SOLACE
SOLACED
SOLACEMENT
SOLACER
SOLACH
SOLACING
SOLAH
SOLAK
SOLAN
SOLANACEOUS
SOLANAL
SOLAND
SOLANDER
SOLANDRA
SOLANEIN
SOLANEINE
SOLANEOUS
SOLANIDIN
SOLANIDINE
SOLANIN
SOLANINE
SOLANO
SOLANOS
SOLANUM
SOLAR
SOLARIA
SOLARIEGO
SOLARIMETER
SOLARISM
SOLARIST
SOLARISTIC
SOLARISTICALLY
SOLARISTICS
SOLARIUM
SOLARIUMS
SOLARIZATION
SOLARIZE
SOLARIZED
SOLARIZING
SOLAROMETER
SOLARY
SOLATE
SOLATIA
SOLATION
SOLATIUM
SOLAY
SOLD
SOLDADO
SOLDADOES
SOLDADOS
SOLDAN
SOLDANEL
SOLDANELLE
SOLDANRIE
SOLDAT
SOLDATESQUE
SOLDER
SOLDERED
SOLDERER
SOLDERING
SOLDI
SOLDIER
SOLDIERBIRD
SOLDIERBUSH
SOLDIERED
SOLDIERFARE
SOLDIERFISH
SOLDIERFISHES
SOLDIERHEARTED
SOLDIERIES
SOLDIERING
SOLDIERLIKE
SOLDIERLINESS
SOLDIERLY
SOLDIERPROOF
SOLDIERS
SOLDIERWOOD
SOLDIERY
SOLDO
SOLE
SOLEA
SOLECISE
SOLECISM
SOLECIST
SOLECISTIC
SOLECISTICAL
SOLECISTICALLY
SOLECIZE
SOLECIZED
SOLECIZER
SOLECIZING
SOLED
SOLEIFORM
SOLEIL
SOLEIN
SOLELESS
SOLELY
SOLEMN
SOLEMNCHOLY
SOLEMNESS
SOLEMNIFIED
SOLEMNIFY
SOLEMNIFYING
SOLEMNISE
SOLEMNITIES
SOLEMNITUDE
SOLEMNITY
SOLEMNIZATION
SOLEMNIZE
SOLEMNIZED
SOLEMNIZER
SOLEMNIZING
SOLEMNLY
SOLEMNNESS
SOLENACEAN
SOLENACEOUS
SOLENETTE
SOLENIAL
SOLENITE
SOLENITIS
SOLENIUM
SOLENNE
SOLENNEMENTE
SOLENOCYTE
SOLENODONT
SOLENOGASTER
SOLENOGLYPH
SOLENOID
SOLENOIDAL
SOLENOIDALLY
SOLENOSTELE
SOLENOSTELIC
SOLENOSTOMID
SOLENTINE
SOLEPIECE
SOLEPLATE
SOLEPRINT
SOLER
SOLERET
SOLERT
SOLES
SOLEUS
SOLEYN
SOLEYNE
SOLFATARA
SOLFATARIC
SOLFEGE
SOLFEGGI
SOLFEGGIARE
SOLFEGGIO
SOLFEGGIOS
SOLFERINO
SOLI
SOLICIT
SOLICITANT
SOLICITATION
SOLICITED
SOLICITEE
SOLICITER
SOLICITING
SOLICITOR
SOLICITOUS
SOLICITOUSLY
SOLICITOUSNESS
SOLICITUDE
SOLID
SOLIDAGO
SOLIDAGOS
SOLIDARE
SOLIDARIC
SOLIDARISM
SOLIDARIST
SOLIDARISTIC
SOLIDARITIES
SOLIDARITY
SOLIDARIZE
SOLIDARIZED
SOLIDARIZING
SOLIDARY
SOLIDATE
SOLIDATED
SOLIDATING
SOLIDEO
SOLIDER
SOLIDEST
SOLIDI
SOLIDIFICATION
SOLIDIFIED
SOLIDIFIER
SOLIDIFORM
SOLIDIFY
SOLIDIFYING
SOLIDISM
SOLIDIST
SOLIDISTIC
SOLIDITIES
SOLIDITY
SOLIDLY
SOLIDNESS
SOLIDUM
SOLIDUNGULAR
SOLIDUS
SOLIFIDIAN
SOLIFIDIANISM
SOLIFLUCTION
SOLIFORM
SOLIFUGE
SOLILOQUACIOUS
SOLILOQUIES
SOLILOQUISE
SOLILOQUIST
SOLILOQUIZE
SOLILOQUIZED
SOLILOQUIZER
SOLILOQUIZING
SOLILOQUIZINGLY
SOLILOQUY
SOLILUNAR
SOLING
SOLION
SOLIPED
SOLIPEDAL
SOLIPEDOUS
SOLIPSISM
SOLIPSISMAL
SOLIPSIST
SOLIPSISTIC
SOLIQUID
SOLISTE
SOLITAIRE
SOLITARIAN
SOLITARIES
SOLITARILY
SOLITARINESS
SOLITARY
SOLITIDAL
SOLITUDE
SOLITUDINIZE
SOLITUDINIZED
SOLITUDINIZING
SOLITUDINOUS
SOLIVAGANT

SOLIVAGOUS
SOLLAR
SOLLER
SOLLERET
SOLMIZATE
SOLMIZATION
SOLO
SOLOED
SOLOING
SOLOIST
SOLONETZ
SOLONIST
SOLOS
SOLOTH
SOLPUGID
SOLS
SOLSTICE
SOLSTICION
SOLSTITIAL
SOLSTITIALLY
SOLUBILITIES
SOLUBILITY
SOLUBILIZE
SOLUBLE
SOLUBLENESS
SOLUBLY
SOLUM
SOLUS
SOLUTE
SOLUTIO
SOLUTION
SOLUTIONAL
SOLUTIONER
SOLUTIONIST
SOLUTIONS
SOLUTIVE
SOLUTORY
SOLVABILITY
SOLVABLE
SOLVABLENESS
SOLVATE
SOLVATION
SOLVE
SOLVED
SOLVENCIES
SOLVENCY
SOLVEND
SOLVENT
SOLVENTLY
SOLVER
SOLVING
SOLVOLYSIS
SOLVOLYTIC
SOLVOLYZE
SOLVOLYZED
SOLVOLYZING
SOLVSBERGITE
SOLVUS
SOMA
SOMACULE
SOMAL
SOMALO
SOMAPLASM
SOMATA
SOMATEN
SOMATENES
SOMATIC
SOMATICAL
SOMATICALLY
SOMATISM
SOMATIST
SOMATOCHROME
SOMATOCYST
SOMATOCYSTIC
SOMATODERM
SOMATOGENIC
SOMATOGNOSIS
SOMATOLOGIC
SOMATOLOGIST
SOMATOLOGY
SOMATOME
SOMATOMIC
SOMATOPHYTE
SOMATOPHYTIC
SOMATOPLASM
SOMATOPLEURE
SOMATOTROPIC
SOMBER
SOMBERISH
SOMBERLY
SOMBERNESS
SOMBRE
SOMBREISH
SOMBREITE
SOMBRELY
SOMBRENESS
SOMBRERO
SOMBREROED
SOMBREROS
SOMBROUS
SOMBROUSLY
SOMBROUSNESS
SOMDEL
SOMDIEL
SOME
SOMEBODIES
SOMEBODY
SOMEDAY
SOMEDEAL
SOMEGATE
SOMEHOW
SOMEONE
SOMEPART
SOMEPLACE
SOMER
SOMERS
SOMERSAULT
SOMERSET
SOMERVILLITE
SOMESTHESIA
SOMESTHESIS
SOMESTHETIC
SOMETHING
SOMETIME
SOMETIMES
SOMEWAY
SOMEWAYS
SOMEWHAT
SOMEWHATLY
SOMEWHATNESS
SOMEWHEN
SOMEWHENCE
SOMEWHERE
SOMEWHERES
SOMEWHILE
SOMEWHILES
SOMEWHITHER
SOMEWHY
SOMEWISE
SOMITAL
SOMITE
SOMITIC
SOMLER
SOMMA
SOMMAITE
SOMME
SOMMELIER
SOMMITE
SOMNAMBULANCE
SOMNAMBULANCY
SOMNAMBULANT
SOMNAMBULAR
SOMNAMBULARY
SOMNAMBULATE
SOMNAMBULATED
SOMNAMBULATING
SOMNAMBULATION
SOMNAMBULATOR
SOMNAMBULE
SOMNAMBULENCY
SOMNAMBULIC
SOMNAMBULICALLY
SOMNAMBULISM
SOMNAMBULIST
SOMNAMBULISTIC
SOMNAMBULIZE
SOMNAMBULOUS
SOMNIAL
SOMNIATE
SOMNIATIVE
SOMNIFACIENT
SOMNIFEROUS
SOMNIFIC
SOMNIFUGE
SOMNIFUGOUS
SOMNIFY
SOMNILOQUENCE
SOMNILOQUENT
SOMNILOQUISM
SOMNILOQUIST
SOMNILOQUOUS
SOMNILOQUY
SOMNIPATHIST
SOMNIPATHY
SOMNIVOLENCY
SOMNIVOLENT
SOMNO
SOMNOLENCE
SOMNOLENCY
SOMNOLENT
SOMNOLENTLY
SOMNOLESCENT
SOMNOLISM
SOMNORIFIC
SOMNUS
SOMPAY
SOMPNE
SOMPNER
SON
SONABLE
SONANCE
SONANT
SONANTAL
SONANTIC
SONAR
SONARMAN
SONATA
SONATINA
SONATINAS
SONATINE
SONATION
SONCY
SONDAGE
SONDATION
SONDE
SONDELI
SONDER
SONDERCLASS
SONE
SONED
SONERI
SONG
SONGBIRD
SONGBOOK
SONGCRAFT
SONGER
SONGFUL
SONGFULLY
SONGFULNESS
SONGISH
SONGLAND
SONGLE
SONGLESS
SONGLET
SONGMAN
SONGS
SONGSTER
SONGSTRESS
SONGWRIGHT
SONGWRITER
SONGY
SONIC
SONICA
SONICS
SONIFEROUS
SONIFICATION
SONING
SONIOU
SONK
SONLY
SONNET
SONNETARY
SONNETED
SONNETEER
SONNETIC
SONNETING
SONNETIST
SONNETIZE
SONNETRY
SONNETTED
SONNETTING
SONNY
SONOBUOY
SONORANT
SONORESCENCE
SONORESCENT
SONORIC
SONORIFEROUS
SONORIFIC
SONORITIES
SONORITY
SONORIZE
SONOROPHONE
SONOROUS
SONOROUSLY
SONOROUSNESS
SONOVOX
SONS
SONSE
SONSHIP
SONSIE
SONSY
SONTAG
SOO
SOOCHONG
SOODLE
SOODLED
SOODLING
SOODLY
SOOEY
SOOGAN
SOOGEE
SOOK
SOOKIE
SOOKY
SOOL
SOOLOOS
SOOM
SOON
SOOND
SOONER
SOONEST
SOONISH
SOOP
SOOPER
SOOR
SOORAWN
SOOREYN
SOORKEE
SOORKI
SOORKY
SOORMA
SOOSOO
SOOT
SOOTED
SOOTER
SOOTERKIN
SOOTH
SOOTHE
SOOTHED
SOOTHER
SOOTHERER
SOOTHEST
SOOTHFAST
SOOTHFASTLY
SOOTHFUL
SOOTHING
SOOTHINGLY
SOOTHINGNESS
SOOTHLY
SOOTHSAID
SOOTHSAW
SOOTHSAY
SOOTHSAYER
SOOTHSAYING
SOOTIED
SOOTIER
SOOTIEST
SOOTILY
SOOTINESS
SOOTING
SOOTISH
SOOTY
SOOTYING
SOP
SOPE
SOPH
SOPHEME
SOPHENE
SOPHER
SOPHIC
SOPHICAL
SOPHICALLY
SOPHIOLOGIC
SOPHIOLOGY
SOPHISM
SOPHIST
SOPHISTER
SOPHISTIC
SOPHISTICAL
SOPHISTICALLY
SOPHISTICALNESS
SOPHISTICANT
SOPHISTICATE
SOPHISTICATED
SOPHISTICATING
SOPHISTICATION
SOPHISTICATIVE
SOPHISTICATOR
SOPHISTICISM
SOPHISTRIES
SOPHISTRY
SOPHOMORE
SOPHOMORIC
SOPHOMORICAL
SOPHOMORICALLY
SOPHORIA
SOPHRONIZE
SOPHRONIZED
SOPHRONIZING
SOPHTA
SOPHY
SOPIE
SOPITE
SOPITED

SOPITING
SOPITION
SOPOR
SOPORATE
SOPORIFEROUS
SOPORIFIC
SOPORIFICAL
SOPOROSE
SOPPED
SOPPER
SOPPIER
SOPPIEST
SOPPING
SOPPY
SOPRA
SOPRANI
SOPRANINO
SOPRANIST
SOPRANO
SOPRANOS
SOPT
SORA
SORAGE
SORAL
SORANCE
SORB
SORBATE
SORBEFACIENT
SORBENT
SORBET
SORBIC
SORBILE
SORBITAN
SORBITE
SORBITIC
SORBITIZE
SORBITOL
SORBOSE
SORBOSID
SORBOSIDE
SORCER
SORCERER
SORCERESS
SORCERIES
SORCERING
SORCEROUS
SORCEROUSLY
SORCERY
SORD
SORDA
SORDAVALITE
SORDAWALITE
SORDELLINA
SORDES
SORDID
SORDIDITY
SORDIDLY
SORDIDNESS
SORDINE
SORDINO
SORDO
SORDOR
SORE
SOREDIA
SOREDIAL
SOREDIATE
SOREDIFEROUS
SOREDIFORM
SOREDIOID
SOREDIUM
SOREFALCON
SOREFOOT
SOREHAWK
SOREHEAD
SOREHEADED
SOREHEADEDLY
SOREHEADEDNESS
SOREHEARTED
SOREHON
SOREL
SORELY
SOREMA
SORENESS
SORER
SOREST
SORGE
SORGHE
SORGHO
SORGHUM
SORGO
SORGOS
SORI
SORICID
SORICIDENT
SORICINE
SORICOID
SORIFEROUS
SORITE
SORITES
SORITIC
SORITICAL
SORN
SORNARI
SORNER
SOROBAN
SOROCHE
SORORAL
SORORATE
SORORIAL
SORORIALLY
SORORICIDAL
SORORICIDE
SORORITIES
SORORITY
SORORIZE
SOROSE
SOROSES
SOROSIS
SOROSPHERE
SORPTION
SORRA
SORRANCE
SORREL
SORREN
SORRENTO
SORRIER
SORRIEST
SORRILY
SORRINESS
SORROW
SORROWED
SORROWER
SORROWFUL
SORROWFULLY
SORROWFULNESS
SORROWING
SORROWINGLY
SORRY
SORRYHEARTED
SORRYISH
SORS
SORT
SORTABLE
SORTABLY
SORTAL
SORTANCE
SORTATION
SORTED
SORTER
SORTES
SORTIARY
SORTIE
SORTILEGE
SORTILEGER
SORTILEGI
SORTILEGIC
SORTILEGIOUS
SORTILEGUS
SORTIMENT
SORTING
SORTITA
SORTITION
SORTLY
SORTMENT
SORTS
SORTY
SORUS
SORVA
SORY
SOSH
SOSHED
SOSIE
SOSO
SOSOISH
SOSPIRO
SOSQUIL
SOSS
SOSSIEGO
SOSSLE
SOSTENENDO
SOSTENENTE
SOSTENUTI
SOSTENUTO
SOSTENUTOS
SOSTINENTE
SOSTINENTO
SOT
SOTERIOLOGIC
SOTERIOLOGY
SOTH
SOTIE
SOTNIA
SOTNIK
SOTOL
SOTS
SOTTAGE
SOTTED
SOTTER
SOTTERY
SOTTING
SOTTISE
SOTTISH
SOTTISHLY
SOTTISHNESS
SOTTO
SOTWEED
SOU
SOUARI
SOUBISE
SOUBRETTE
SOUBRETTISH
SOUBRIQUET
SOUCAR
SOUCE
SOUCH
SOUCHIE
SOUCHONG
SOUD
SOUDAGUR
SOUDAN
SOUFFLE
SOUFFLEED
SOUFFLEUR
SOUGAN
SOUGH
SOUGHED
SOUGHER
SOUGHING
SOUGHT
SOUK
SOUL
SOULACK
SOULCAKE
SOULDIE
SOULE
SOULED
SOULFUL
SOULFULLY
SOULFULNESS
SOULHEAL
SOULHEALTH
SOULICAL
SOULISH
SOULLESS
SOULLESSLY
SOULLESSNESS
SOULPENCE
SOULPENNY
SOULS
SOULTER
SOULTRE
SOULX
SOULY
SOULZ
SOUM
SOUMAK
SOUMANSITE
SOUND
SOUNDABLE
SOUNDAGE
SOUNDBOARD
SOUNDED
SOUNDER
SOUNDFUL
SOUNDHEADED
SOUNDHEADEDNESS
SOUNDHEARTED
SOUNDHEARTEDNESS
SOUNDING
SOUNDINGLY
SOUNDINGNESS
SOUNDLESS
SOUNDLESSLY
SOUNDLESSNESS
SOUNDLY
SOUNDNESS
SOUNDPROOF
SOUNDPROOFING
SOUNDS
SOUNE
SOUP
SOUPBONE
SOUPCON
SOUPER
SOUPFIN
SOUPIER
SOUPIEST
SOUPLE
SOUPLED
SOUPLESS
SOUPLIKE
SOUPLING
SOUPSPOON
SOUPY
SOUR
SOURBALL
SOURBELLIES
SOURBELLY
SOURBERRIES
SOURBERRY
SOURBREAD
SOURBUSH
SOURCE
SOURCROUT
SOURD
SOURDINE
SOURDOOK
SOURDOUGH
SOURDRE
SOURED
SOUREDNESS
SOUREN
SOURER
SOUREST
SOURING
SOURJACK
SOURLING
SOURLY
SOURNESS
SOUROCK
SOURPUSS
SOURSOP
SOURTOP
SOURVELD
SOURWEED
SOURWOOD
SOURY
SOUS
SOUSAPHONE
SOUSAPHONIST
SOUSE
SOUSED
SOUSER
SOUSEWIFE
SOUSING
SOUSLIK
SOUTACHE
SOUTAGE
SOUTANE
SOUTAR
SOUTENU
SOUTER
SOUTERLY
SOUTERRAIN
SOUTH
SOUTHARD
SOUTHBOUND
SOUTHEAST
SOUTHEASTER
SOUTHEASTERLY
SOUTHEASTERN
SOUTHEASTERNMOST
SOUTHEASTWARD
SOUTHEASTWARDLY
SOUTHEASTWARDS
SOUTHED
SOUTHER
SOUTHERLAND
SOUTHERLIES
SOUTHERLINESS
SOUTHERLY
SOUTHERMOST
SOUTHERN
SOUTHERNER
SOUTHERNEST
SOUTHERNISM
SOUTHERNIZE
SOUTHERNLINESS
SOUTHERNLY
SOUTHERNMOST
SOUTHERNWOOD
SOUTHING
SOUTHLAND
SOUTHLANDER
SOUTHMOST
SOUTHNESS
SOUTHPAW
SOUTHRON
SOUTHWARD
SOUTHWARDLY
SOUTHWARDS
SOUTHWEST
SOUTHWESTER
SOUTHWESTERLIES
SOUTHWESTERLY

SOUTHWESTERN
SOUTHWESTERNMOST
SOUTHWESTWARD
SOUTHWESTWARDLY
SOUTHWESTWARDS
SOUVENIR
SOUVERAIN
SOV
SOVENEZ
SOVEREIGN
SOVEREIGNESS
SOVEREIGNIZE
SOVEREIGNLY
SOVEREIGNNESS
SOVEREIGNTIES
SOVEREIGNTY
SOVERTY
SOVIET
SOVIETIC
SOVIETISM
SOVIETIST
SOVIETISTIC
SOVIETIZATION
SOVIETIZE
SOVIETIZED
SOVIETIZING
SOVIK
SOVITE
SOVKHOS
SOVKHOSE
SOVKHOZ
SOVPRENE
SOVRAN
SOVRANLY
SOVRANTY
SOW
SOWAN
SOWAR
SOWARREE
SOWARRY
SOWBACK
SOWBACKED
SOWBANE
SOWBELLY
SOWBREAD
SOWCAR
SOWCE
SOWD
SOWDER
SOWDONES
SOWED
SOWEL
SOWENS
SOWER
SOWF
SOWFF
SOWFOOT
SOWING
SOWISH
SOWL
SOWLE
SOWLTH
SOWN
SOWP
SOWSE
SOWTH
SOX
SOY
SOYA
SOYATE
SOYBEAN
SOYL
SOYLE
SOYLED
SOZIN
SOZOLIC
SOZZLE
SOZZLED
SOZZLY
SPA
SPAAD
SPACE
SPACEBAND
SPACECRAFT
SPACED
SPACEFUL
SPACELESS
SPACEMAN
SPACEMANSHIP
SPACEMEN
SPACEPORT
SPACER
SPACES
SPACESHIP
SPACEWALK
SPACIAL
SPACINESS
SPACING
SPACIOSITY
SPACIOUS
SPACIOUSLY
SPACIOUSNESS
SPACK
SPACKLE
SPACKLED
SPACKLING
SPACY
SPAD
SPADAITE
SPADASSIN
SPADDLE
SPADE
SPADEBONE
SPADED
SPADEFISH
SPADEFOOT
SPADEFUL
SPADEMAN
SPADEMEN
SPADER
SPADES
SPADESMAN
SPADEWORK
SPADGER
SPADIARD
SPADICEOUS
SPADICES
SPADICIFORM
SPADICOSE
SPADILLA
SPADILLE
SPADILLO
SPADING
SPADISH
SPADIX
SPADO
SPADONES
SPADONIC
SPADONISM
SPADROON
SPAE
SPAEBOOK
SPAECRAFT
SPAED
SPAEDOM
SPAEING
SPAEMAN
SPAER
SPAEWIFE
SPAEWOMAN
SPAEWORK
SPAEWRIGHT
SPAGHETTI
SPAGNUOLO
SPAGYRIC
SPAGYRICAL
SPAGYRIST
SPAHEE
SPAHI
SPAHIS
SPAIL
SPAIN
SPAIR
SPAIRGE
SPAIT
SPAK
SPAKE
SPAKED
SPALACID
SPALACINE
SPALD
SPALDER
SPALDING
SPALE
SPALL
SPALLATION
SPALLED
SPALLER
SPALLING
SPALPEEN
SPALT
SPAN
SPANAEMIA
SPANAEMIC
SPANCEL
SPANCELED
SPANCELING
SPANCELLED
SPANCELLING
SPANDEX
SPANDLE
SPANDREL
SPANDRIL
SPANDY
SPANE
SPANED
SPANEMIA
SPANEMIC
SPANEMY
SPANG
SPANGED
SPANGHEW
SPANGING
SPANGLE
SPANGLED
SPANGLER
SPANGLET
SPANGLIER
SPANGLIEST
SPANGLING
SPANGLY
SPANGOLITE
SPANIEL
SPANING
SPANIPELAGIC
SPANK
SPANKED
SPANKER
SPANKILY
SPANKING
SPANKINGLY
SPANKLED
SPANKY
SPANLESS
SPANN
SPANNED
SPANNER
SPANNERMAN
SPANNERMEN
SPANNING
SPANOPNEA
SPANOPNOEA
SPANPIECE
SPANSPEK
SPANULE
SPANWORM
SPAR
SPARABLE
SPARADA
SPARADRAP
SPARAGE
SPARASSODONT
SPARCH
SPARE
SPARED
SPAREFUL
SPARELESS
SPARELY
SPARENESS
SPARER
SPARERIB
SPARESOME
SPAREST
SPARGANUM
SPARGE
SPARGED
SPARGER
SPARGING
SPARGOSIS
SPARHAWK
SPARID
SPARILY
SPARING
SPARINGLY
SPARINGNESS
SPARK
SPARKBACK
SPARKED
SPARKER
SPARKIER
SPARKIEST
SPARKINESS
SPARKING
SPARKINGLY
SPARKISH
SPARKISHLY
SPARKISHNESS
SPARKLE
SPARKLEBERRY
SPARKLED
SPARKLER
SPARKLET
SPARKLINESS
SPARKLING
SPARKLINGNESS
SPARKLY
SPARKPLUG
SPARKPLUGGED
SPARKPLUGGING
SPARKS
SPARKY
SPARLING
SPAROID
SPARPLE
SPARPLED
SPARPLING
SPARRED
SPARRER
SPARRIER
SPARRIEST
SPARRING
SPARRINGLY
SPARROW
SPARROWCIDE
SPARROWGRASS
SPARROWISH
SPARROWWORT
SPARROWY
SPARRY
SPARRYGRASS
SPARSE
SPARSEDLY
SPARSELY
SPARSENESS
SPARSER
SPARSEST
SPARSILE
SPARSIM
SPARSIOPLAST
SPARSITY
SPART
SPARTACIST
SPARTEIN
SPARTEINE
SPARTERIE
SPARTH
SPARTLE
SPARTLED
SPARTLING
SPARVER
SPARY
SPASM
SPASMATIC
SPASMATICAL
SPASMED
SPASMIC
SPASMODIC
SPASMODICAL
SPASMODICALLY
SPASMODICALNESS
SPASMODISM
SPASMODIST
SPASMOPHILIA
SPASMOPHILIC
SPASMOTIN
SPASMOTOXIN
SPASMOTOXINE
SPASMOUS
SPASMUS
SPASTIC
SPASTICALLY
SPASTICITY
SPAT
SPATALAMANCY
SPATANGOID
SPATCHCOCK
SPATE
SPATED
SPATH
SPATHA
SPATHACEOUS
SPATHAE
SPATHAL
SPATHE
SPATHED
SPATHIC
SPATHILLA
SPATHILLAE
SPATHOSE
SPATHOUS
SPATHULATE
SPATIAL
SPATIALITY
SPATIALIZATION
SPATIALIZE
SPATIALLY
SPATIATE
SPATIATION
SPATILOMANCY
SPATING
SPATIUM
SPATTANIA
SPATTED
SPATTER
SPATTERDASH

SPATTERDOCK
SPATTERED
SPATTERING
SPATTERINGLY
SPATTERWORK
SPATTING
SPATTLE
SPATTLED
SPATTLEHOE
SPATTLING
SPATULA
SPATULAMANCY
SPATULAR
SPATULATE
SPATULATION
SPATULE
SPATULIFORM
SPATULOSE
SPATULOUS
SPATZLE
SPAUGHT
SPAUL
SPAULD
SPAULDROCHY
SPAVER
SPAVIE
SPAVIED
SPAVIET
SPAVIN
SPAVINE
SPAVINED
SPAVIT
SPAWL
SPAWLER
SPAWN
SPAWNEATER
SPAWNED
SPAWNER
SPAWNING
SPAWNY
SPAY
SPAYAD
SPAYARD
SPAYED
SPAYING
SPEAK
SPEAKABLE
SPEAKABLENESS
SPEAKABLY
SPEAKEASIES
SPEAKEASY
SPEAKER
SPEAKERESS
SPEAKERSHIP
SPEAKHOUSE
SPEAKIES
SPEAKING
SPEAKINGLY
SPEAKINGNESS
SPEAKLESS
SPEAKLESSLY
SPEAL
SPEALBONE
SPEAN
SPEAR
SPEARED
SPEARER
SPEAREYE
SPEARFISH
SPEARFISHES
SPEARFLOWER
SPEARHEAD
SPEARING
SPEARMAN
SPEARMANSHIP
SPEARMEN
SPEARMINT
SPEARPROOF
SPEARSMAN
SPEARSMEN
SPEARWOOD
SPEARWORT
SPEARY
SPEAVE
SPEC
SPECCHIE
SPECE
SPECH
SPECIAL
SPECIALISE
SPECIALISM
SPECIALIST
SPECIALISTIC
SPECIALITIES
SPECIALITY
SPECIALIZATION
SPECIALIZE
SPECIALIZED
SPECIALIZER
SPECIALIZING
SPECIALLY
SPECIALNESS
SPECIALTIES
SPECIALTY
SPECIATE
SPECIATION
SPECIE
SPECIES
SPECIFIABLE
SPECIFIC
SPECIFICAL
SPECIFICALITY
SPECIFICALLY
SPECIFICATE
SPECIFICATION
SPECIFICATIVE
SPECIFICATIVELY
SPECIFICITY
SPECIFICIZE
SPECIFICLY
SPECIFIED
SPECIFIER
SPECIFIST
SPECIFY
SPECIFYING
SPECIMEN
SPECIMENIZE
SPECIMENIZED
SPECIMENS
SPECIOLOGY
SPECIOSITIES
SPECIOSITY
SPECIOUS
SPECIOUSLY
SPECIOUSNESS
SPECK
SPECKED
SPECKEDNESS
SPECKFALL
SPECKIER
SPECKIEST
SPECKING
SPECKLE
SPECKLEBELLY
SPECKLEBREAST
SPECKLED
SPECKLEDBILL
SPECKLEDY
SPECKLEHEAD
SPECKLESS
SPECKLESSLY
SPECKLESSNESS
SPECKLING
SPECKLY
SPECKS
SPECKSIONEER
SPECKY
SPECS
SPECTACLE
SPECTACLED
SPECTACLES
SPECTACULAR
SPECTACULARISM
SPECTACULARITY
SPECTACULARLY
SPECTATE
SPECTATOR
SPECTATORIAL
SPECTATORY
SPECTATRESS
SPECTATRIX
SPECTER
SPECTERED
SPECTERLIKE
SPECTRA
SPECTRAL
SPECTRALISM
SPECTRALITY
SPECTRALLY
SPECTRALNESS
SPECTRE
SPECTRED
SPECTROGRAM
SPECTROGRAPH
SPECTROLOGY
SPECTROMETER
SPECTROMETRIC
SPECTROMETRY
SPECTROPHOBY
SPECTROPHONE
SPECTROSCOPE
SPECTROSCOPY
SPECTRUM
SPECTRUMS
SPECTRY
SPECULA
SPECULAR
SPECULARLY
SPECULATE
SPECULATED
SPECULATING
SPECULATION
SPECULATIST
SPECULATIVE
SPECULATIVELY
SPECULATIVENESS
SPECULATOR
SPECULATORY
SPECULATRICES
SPECULATRIX
SPECULIST
SPECULUM
SPECULUMS
SPECUS
SPED
SPEECE
SPEECH
SPEECHCRAFT
SPEECHER
SPEECHFUL
SPEECHFULNESS
SPEECHIFICATION
SPEECHIFIED
SPEECHIFIER
SPEECHIFY
SPEECHIFYING
SPEECHING
SPEECHLESS
SPEECHLESSLY
SPEECHLESSNESS
SPEECHLORE
SPEECHMAKER
SPEECHMAKING
SPEECHMENT
SPEED
SPEEDBALL
SPEEDBOAT
SPEEDBOATING
SPEEDBOATMAN
SPEEDED
SPEEDER
SPEEDFUL
SPEEDFULLY
SPEEDFULNESS
SPEEDGUN
SPEEDIER
SPEEDIEST
SPEEDILY
SPEEDINESS
SPEEDING
SPEEDINGLY
SPEEDLY
SPEEDOMETER
SPEEDSTER
SPEEDUP
SPEEDWAY
SPEEDWELL
SPEEDY
SPEEL
SPEELLESS
SPEER
SPEERED
SPEERING
SPEERINGS
SPEIGHT
SPEIR
SPEISE
SPEISKOBALT
SPEISS
SPEISSCOBALT
SPEKBOOM
SPEKT
SPELAEAN
SPELD
SPELDER
SPELDING
SPELDRIN
SPELDRING
SPELDRON
SPELE
SPELEAN
SPELEOLOGIST
SPELEOLOGY
SPELK
SPELL
SPELLBIND
SPELLBINDER
SPELLBINDING
SPELLBOUND
SPELLCRAFT
SPELLDOWN
SPELLED
SPELLER
SPELLFUL
SPELLING
SPELLINGDOWN
SPELLINGLY
SPELLKEN
SPELLMONGER
SPELLPROOF
SPELLWORD
SPELLWORK
SPELMAN
SPELT
SPELTER
SPELTERMAN
SPELTERMEN
SPELTOID
SPELTZ
SPELUNCAR
SPELUNCEAN
SPELUNK
SPELUNKER
SPELUNKING
SPENCE
SPENCER
SPENCERITE
SPENCIE
SPENCY
SPEND
SPENDER
SPENDFUL
SPENDIBLE
SPENDING
SPENDLESS
SPENDTHRIFT
SPENDTHRIFTY
SPENSE
SPENT
SPEOS
SPERAGE
SPERATE
SPERE
SPERK
SPERKET
SPERLING
SPERM
SPERMA
SPERMACETI
SPERMADUCT
SPERMALIST
SPERMAPHYTE
SPERMAPHYTIC
SPERMARIES
SPERMARIUM
SPERMARY
SPERMATA
SPERMATHECA
SPERMATHECAE
SPERMATHECAL
SPERMATIA
SPERMATIC
SPERMATID
SPERMATIN
SPERMATISM
SPERMATIST
SPERMATITIS
SPERMATIUM
SPERMATIZE
SPERMATOCELE
SPERMATOCYST
SPERMATOCYTE
SPERMATOGENY
SPERMATOID
SPERMATOVA
SPERMATOVUM
SPERMATOZOA
SPERMATOZOAL
SPERMATOZOAN
SPERMATOZOIC
SPERMATOZOID
SPERMATOZOON
SPERMATURIA
SPERMIC
SPERMIDIN
SPERMIDINE
SPERMIDUCAL
SPERMIDUCT
SPERMIGEROUS
SPERMIN
SPERMINE
SPERMISM
SPERMIST
SPERMOBLAST
SPERMOCARP

SPERMODERM
SPERMODUCT
SPERMOGENOUS
SPERMOGONE
SPERMOGONIA
SPERMOGONIUM
SPERMOGONOUS
SPERMOLOGER
SPERMOLOGIST
SPERMOLOGY
SPERMOPHILE
SPERMOPHORE
SPERMOSPHERE
SPERMOTHECA
SPERMOTOXIN
SPERMOUS
SPERMULE
SPERMY
SPERON
SPERONARA
SPERONARAS
SPERONARES
SPERONARO
SPERONAROES
SPERONAROS
SPERONE
SPERPLE
SPERRYLITE
SPERSE
SPES
SPESSARTINE
SPESSARTITE
SPET
SPETCH
SPETCHES
SPEUCHAN
SPEW
SPEWED
SPEWER
SPEWIER
SPEWIEST
SPEWINESS
SPEWING
SPEWY
SPEX
SPEY
SPEYERIA
SPHACEL
SPHACELATE
SPHACELATED
SPHACELATING
SPHACELATION
SPHACELIA
SPHACELIAL
SPHACELISM
SPHACELOUS
SPHACELUS
SPHAERIDIA
SPHAERIDIAL
SPHAERIDIUM
SPHAERITE
SPHAEROBLAST
SPHAEROSOME
SPHAEROSPORE
SPHAGIA
SPHAGION
SPHAGNACEOUS
SPHAGNOLOGY
SPHAGNOUS
SPHAGNUM
SPHALERITE
SPHALM
SPHALMA
SPHECID
SPHECIUS
SPHECOID
SPHENDONE
SPHENE
SPHENETHMOID
SPHENIC
SPHENION
SPHENISCINE
SPHENODON
SPHENODONT
SPHENOGRAM
SPHENOGRAPHY
SPHENOID
SPHENOIDAL
SPHENOIDITIS
SPHENOLITH
SPHENOMALAR
SPHENOTIC
SPHENOTRIBE
SPHENOTRIPSY
SPHERABLE
SPHERADIAN
SPHERAL
SPHERALITY
SPHERASTER
SPHERATION
SPHERE
SPHERED
SPHERELESS
SPHERIC
SPHERICAL
SPHERICALITY
SPHERICALLY
SPHERICALNESS
SPHERICIST
SPHERICITIES
SPHERICITY
SPHERICLE
SPHERICS
SPHERIER
SPHERIEST
SPHERIFORM
SPHERIFY
SPHERING
SPHEROGRAPH
SPHEROID
SPHEROIDAL
SPHEROIDALLY
SPHEROIDIC
SPHEROIDICAL
SPHEROIDISM
SPHEROIDITY
SPHEROIDIZE
SPHEROME
SPHEROMERE
SPHEROMETER
SPHERULA
SPHERULAR
SPHERULATE
SPHERULE
SPHERULITE
SPHERULITIC
SPHERULITIZE
SPHERY
SPHETERIZE
SPHEXIDE
SPHINCTER
SPHINCTERAL
SPHINCTERATE
SPHINCTERIAL
SPHINCTERIC
SPHINDID
SPHINGAL
SPHINGES
SPHINGID
SPHINGIFORM
SPHINGINE
SPHINGOMETER
SPHINGOSIN
SPHINGOSINE
SPHINX
SPHINXES
SPHINXIAN
SPHINXINE
SPHINXLIKE
SPHRAGIDE
SPHRAGISTIC
SPHRAGISTICS
SPHYGMIA
SPHYGMIC
SPHYGMODIC
SPHYGMOGRAM
SPHYGMOGRAPH
SPHYGMOID
SPHYGMOLOGY
SPHYGMOMETER
SPHYGMOPHONE
SPHYGMUS
SPIAL
SPICA
SPICAE
SPICANT
SPICATE
SPICATED
SPICCATO
SPICE
SPICEBERRIES
SPICEBERRY
SPICEBUSH
SPICECAKE
SPICED
SPICEFUL
SPICEHOUSE
SPICELAND
SPICER
SPICERIES
SPICERY
SPICES
SPICEWOOD
SPICIER
SPICIEST
SPICIFEROUS
SPICIFORM
SPICIGEROUS
SPICILEGE
SPICILY
SPICINESS
SPICING
SPICK
SPICKET
SPICKLE
SPICKNEL
SPICOSE
SPICOSITY
SPICOUS
SPICOUSNESS
SPICULA
SPICULAR
SPICULATE
SPICULATED
SPICULATION
SPICULE
SPICULIFORM
SPICULOFIBER
SPICULOSE
SPICULOUS
SPICULUM
SPICY
SPIDER
SPIDERED
SPIDERFLOWER
SPIDERISH
SPIDERLING
SPIDERLY
SPIDERWEB
SPIDERWORK
SPIDERWORT
SPIDERY
SPIDGER
SPIED
SPIEGEL
SPIEGELEISEN
SPIEL
SPIELER
SPIER
SPIES
SPIFF
SPIFFED
SPIFFIER
SPIFFIEST
SPIFFILY
SPIFFINESS
SPIFFING
SPIFFLICATE
SPIFFLICATED
SPIFFLICATION
SPIFFY
SPIFLICATE
SPIFLICATED
SPIFLICATION
SPIG
SPIGGOTY
SPIGNEL
SPIGNET
SPIGNUT
SPIGOT
SPIKE
SPIKEBILL
SPIKED
SPIKEDNESS
SPIKEFISH
SPIKEFISHES
SPIKEHOLE
SPIKEHORN
SPIKELET
SPIKELIKE
SPIKENARD
SPIKER
SPIKES
SPIKETAIL
SPIKETOP
SPIKEWEED
SPIKIER
SPIKIEST
SPIKILY
SPIKINESS
SPIKING
SPIKY
SPILE
SPILED
SPILEHOLE
SPILER
SPILEWORM
SPILI
SPILIKIN
SPILING
SPILITE
SPILITIC
SPILL
SPILLAGE
SPILLED
SPILLER
SPILLET
SPILLIKIN
SPILLING
SPILLOVER
SPILLWAY
SPILLY
SPILOMA
SPILOMAS
SPILOSITE
SPILT
SPILTH
SPILUS
SPIN
SPINA
SPINACEOUS
SPINACH
SPINACHLIKE
SPINAE
SPINAGE
SPINAL
SPINALES
SPINALIS
SPINALLY
SPINATE
SPINDER
SPINDLAGE
SPINDLE
SPINDLEAGE
SPINDLED
SPINDLEHEAD
SPINDLELEGS
SPINDLER
SPINDLETAIL
SPINDLEWOOD
SPINDLIER
SPINDLIEST
SPINDLINESS
SPINDLING
SPINDLY
SPINDRIFT
SPINE
SPINEBILL
SPINEBONE
SPINED
SPINEFINNED
SPINEL
SPINELESS
SPINELESSLY
SPINELESSNESS
SPINELET
SPINELLE
SPINES
SPINESCENCE
SPINESCENT
SPINET
SPINETAIL
SPINGEL
SPINIBULBAR
SPINICARPOUS
SPINIDENTATE
SPINIER
SPINIEST
SPINIFEROUS
SPINIFEX
SPINIFORM
SPINIFUGAL
SPINIGEROUS
SPINIGRADE
SPININESS
SPINIPETAL
SPINITIS
SPINK
SPINNABLE
SPINNAKER
SPINNEL
SPINNER
SPINNERET
SPINNERETTE
SPINNERIES
SPINNERS
SPINNERULAR
SPINNERULE
SPINNERY
SPINNEY
SPINNEYS
SPINNIES
SPINNING
SPINNINGLY
SPINNY

SPINOBULBAR
SPINODE
SPINOGLENOID
SPINOID
SPINONEURAL
SPINOR
SPINOSE
SPINOSELY
SPINOSENESS
SPINOSITY
SPINOTECTAL
SPINOUS
SPINSTER
SPINSTERHOOD
SPINSTERIAL
SPINSTERISH
SPINSTERISHLY
SPINSTERLY
SPINSTEROUS
SPINSTRESS
SPINSTRY
SPINTEXT
SPINTHERISM
SPINTRY
SPINTURNIX
SPINULA
SPINULATE
SPINULATED
SPINULATION
SPINULE
SPINULESCENT
SPINULIFORM
SPINULOSE
SPINULOSELY
SPINULOUS
SPINY
SPION
SPIONID
SPIRABLE
SPIRACLE
SPIRACULA
SPIRACULAR
SPIRACULATE
SPIRACULUM
SPIRAEA
SPIRAL
SPIRALE
SPIRALED
SPIRALIFORM
SPIRALING
SPIRALISM
SPIRALITY
SPIRALIZATION
SPIRALIZE
SPIRALLED
SPIRALLING
SPIRALLY
SPIRALOID
SPIRALTAIL
SPIRAN
SPIRANE
SPIRANT
SPIRANTHIC
SPIRANTHY
SPIRANTIZE
SPIRASTER
SPIRATE
SPIRATED
SPIRATION
SPIRE
SPIREA
SPIRED
SPIREGRASS
SPIRELET
SPIREM
SPIREME
SPIRICLE
SPIRIFERID
SPIRIFEROID
SPIRIFEROUS
SPIRIFORM
SPIRILLA
SPIRILLAR
SPIRILLOSIS
SPIRILLUM
SPIRING
SPIRIT
SPIRITALLY
SPIRITED
SPIRITEDLY
SPIRITEDNESS
SPIRITER
SPIRITFUL
SPIRITFULLY
SPIRITFULNESS
SPIRITING
SPIRITISM
SPIRITIST
SPIRITISTIC
SPIRITIZE
SPIRITLAND
SPIRITLEAF
SPIRITLESS
SPIRITLESSLY
SPIRITLESSNESS
SPIRITLIKE
SPIRITOSO
SPIRITOUS
SPIRITS
SPIRITSOME
SPIRITUAL
SPIRITUALISE
SPIRITUALISM
SPIRITUALIST
SPIRITUALISTIC
SPIRITUALISTICALLY
SPIRITUALITIES
SPIRITUALITY
SPIRITUALIZATION
SPIRITUALIZE
SPIRITUALIZED
SPIRITUALIZER
SPIRITUALIZING
SPIRITUALLY
SPIRITUALNESS
SPIRITUALTY
SPIRITUEL
SPIRITUELLE
SPIRITUOSITY
SPIRITUOUS
SPIRITUOUSLY
SPIRITUOUSNESS
SPIRITUS
SPIRITWEED
SPIRITY
SPIRIVALVE
SPIRKET
SPIRKETING
SPIRLIE
SPIRO
SPIROCHAETAL
SPIROCHAETE
SPIROCHETAL
SPIROCHETE
SPIROCHETIC
SPIROGRAM
SPIROGRAPH
SPIROGRAPHIC
SPIROGRAPHIN
SPIROGRAPHY
SPIROGYRA
SPIROID
SPIROIDAL
SPIROILIC
SPIROL
SPIROLE
SPIROMETER
SPIROMETRIC
SPIROMETRY
SPIROSCOPE
SPIROUS
SPIRT
SPIRTLE
SPIRULA
SPIRULAE
SPIRULATE
SPIRY
SPISE
SPISS
SPISSATED
SPISSITUDE
SPISSY
SPIT
SPITAL
SPITBALL
SPITBALLER
SPITBOX
SPITCHCOCK
SPITCHCOCKED
SPITCHCOCKING
SPITE
SPITED
SPITEFUL
SPITEFULLY
SPITEFULNESS
SPITFIRE
SPITFROG
SPITFUL
SPITHAME
SPITING
SPITISH
SPITKID
SPITKIT
SPITOUS
SPITPOISON
SPITSCOCKED
SPITSTICK
SPITSTICKER
SPITTED
SPITTER
SPITTING
SPITTLE
SPITTLEFORK
SPITTLEMAN
SPITTLEMEN
SPITTLESTAFF
SPITTOON
SPITZ
SPITZENBERG
SPITZENBURG
SPITZER
SPITZFLUTE
SPITZKOP
SPIV
SPLACHNOID
SPLACKNUCK
SPLAIRGE
SPLAKE
SPLANCHNIC
SPLASH
SPLASHBOARD
SPLASHDOWN
SPLASHED
SPLASHER
SPLASHIER
SPLASHIEST
SPLASHING
SPLASHPROOF
SPLASHWING
SPLASHY
SPLAT
SPLATCH
SPLATCHER
SPLATHER
SPLATHERING
SPLATTER
SPLATTERDASH
SPLATTERER
SPLATTERFACED
SPLATTERWORK
SPLAY
SPLAYED
SPLAYER
SPLAYFEET
SPLAYFOOT
SPLAYFOOTED
SPLAYMOUTH
SPLAYMOUTHED
SPLAYMOUTHS
SPLEEN
SPLEENED
SPLEENFUL
SPLEENFULLY
SPLEENIER
SPLEENIEST
SPLEENING
SPLEENISH
SPLEENISHLY
SPLEENISHNESS
SPLEENLESS
SPLEENWORT
SPLEENY
SPLEET
SPLENADENOMA
SPLENALGIA
SPLENALGIC
SPLENALGY
SPLENATROPHY
SPLENAUXE
SPLENCULI
SPLENCULUS
SPLENDACEOUS
SPLENDACIOUS
SPLENDACIOUSLY
SPLENDATIOUS
SPLENDENT
SPLENDENTLY
SPLENDESCENT
SPLENDID
SPLENDIDER
SPLENDIDEST
SPLENDIDLY
SPLENDIDNESS
SPLENDIFEROUS
SPLENDOR
SPLENDOROUS
SPLENDOUR
SPLENDROUS
SPLENECTAMA
SPLENECTASIS
SPLENECTOMIES
SPLENECTOMY
SPLENECTOPIA
SPLENECTOPY
SPLENELCOSIS
SPLENEMIA
SPLENEOLUS
SPLENETIC
SPLENETICAL
SPLENETIVE
SPLENIA
SPLENIAL
SPLENIC
SPLENICAL
SPLENICTERUS
SPLENIFORM
SPLENII
SPLENITIS
SPLENITIVE
SPLENIUM
SPLENIUS
SPLENIZATION
SPLENOBLAST
SPLENOCELE
SPLENOCLEISIS
SPLENOCOLIC
SPLENOCYTE
SPLENODYNIA
SPLENOGRAPHY
SPLENOHEMIA
SPLENOID
SPLENOLOGY
SPLENOLYMPH
SPLENOLYSIN
SPLENOLYSIS
SPLENOMA
SPLENOMEGALY
SPLENONCUS
SPLENOPATHY
SPLENOPEXIA
SPLENOPEXIS
SPLENOPEXY
SPLENOPTOSIA
SPLENOPTOSIS
SPLENOTOMY
SPLENOTOXIN
SPLENT
SPLENULUS
SPLEUCHAN
SPLICE
SPLICED
SPLICER
SPLICING
SPLINE
SPLINED
SPLINING
SPLINT
SPLINTAGE
SPLINTED
SPLINTER
SPLINTERED
SPLINTERING
SPLINTERNEW
SPLINTERPROOF
SPLINTERY
SPLINTING
SPLINTS
SPLINTWOOD
SPLINTY
SPLIT
SPLITBEAK
SPLITE
SPLITFINGER
SPLITFRUIT
SPLITMOUTH
SPLITNEW
SPLITNUT
SPLITSAW
SPLITTAIL
SPLITTED
SPLITTER
SPLITTERMAN
SPLITTING
SPLITWORM
SPLODGE
SPLOIT
SPLORE
SPLOSH
SPLOSHY
SPLOTCH
SPLOTCHED
SPLOTCHIER
SPLOTCHIEST
SPLOTCHILY
SPLOTCHINESS

SPLOTCHING
SPLOTCHY
SPLOTHER
SPLUNGE
SPLUNT
SPLURGE
SPLURGED
SPLURGILY
SPLURGING
SPLURGY
SPLURT
SPLUTHER
SPLUTTER
SPLUTTERED
SPLUTTERER
SPLUTTERING
SPOACH
SPODE
SPODIOSITE
SPODIUM
SPODOGENIC
SPODOGENOUS
SPODOMANCY
SPODOMANTIC
SPODUMENE
SPOFFISH
SPOFFLE
SPOFFY
SPOGEL
SPOIL
SPOILAGE
SPOILATION
SPOILED
SPOILER
SPOILFIVE
SPOILFUL
SPOILING
SPOILMENT
SPOILS
SPOILSMAN
SPOILSMEN
SPOILSMONGER
SPOILSPORT
SPOILT
SPOKE
SPOKED
SPOKEN
SPOKES
SPOKESHAVE
SPOKESMAN
SPOKESMEN
SPOKESTER
SPOKESWOMAN
SPOKESWOMEN
SPOKING
SPOKY
SPOLIA
SPOLIARIA
SPOLIARIUM
SPOLIARY
SPOLIATE
SPOLIATED
SPOLIATING
SPOLIATION
SPOLIATIVE
SPOLIATOR
SPOLIATORY
SPOLIUM
SPONDAIC
SPONDAICAL
SPONDAIZE
SPONDEAN
SPONDEE
SPONDIL
SPONDULICKS
SPONDULICS
SPONDULIX
SPONDYL
SPONDYLE
SPONDYLIC
SPONDYLIOID
SPONDYLITIC
SPONDYLITIS
SPONDYLIUM
SPONDYLIZEMA
SPONDYLOCACE
SPONDYLOID
SPONDYLOSIS
SPONDYLOTOMY
SPONDYLOUS
SPONDYLUS
SPONE
SPONG
SPONGE
SPONGECAKE
SPONGED
SPONGEOUS
SPONGER
SPONGEWOOD
SPONGIAN
SPONGICOLOUS
SPONGIER
SPONGIEST
SPONGIFEROUS
SPONGIFORM
SPONGILLID
SPONGILLINE
SPONGILY
SPONGIN
SPONGINBLAST
SPONGINESS
SPONGING
SPONGIOBLAST
SPONGIOCYTE
SPONGIOLE
SPONGIOLIN
SPONGIOPILIN
SPONGIOSE
SPONGIOSITY
SPONGIOUS
SPONGIOUSNESS
SPONGOBLAST
SPONGOID
SPONGOLOGY
SPONGOPHORE
SPONGY
SPONK
SPONSAL
SPONSALIA
SPONSION
SPONSIONAL
SPONSON
SPONSOR
SPONSORIAL
SPONSORSHIP
SPONSPECK
SPONTANEITIES
SPONTANEITY
SPONTANEOUS
SPONTANEOUSLY
SPONTANEOUSNESS
SPONTON
SPONTOON
SPOOF
SPOOFED
SPOOFER
SPOOFERIES
SPOOFERY
SPOOFING
SPOOFISH
SPOOK
SPOOKERIES
SPOOKERY
SPOOKIER
SPOOKIES
SPOOKIEST
SPOOKILY
SPOOKINESS
SPOOKISH
SPOOKISM
SPOOKIST
SPOOKOLOGIST
SPOOKOLOGY
SPOOKY
SPOOL
SPOOLED
SPOOLER
SPOOLING
SPOOLWOOD
SPOON
SPOONBILL
SPOONBREAD
SPOONDRIFT
SPOONED
SPOONER
SPOONERISM
SPOONEY
SPOONEYISM
SPOONEYLY
SPOONEYNESS
SPOONEYS
SPOONFUL
SPOONFULS
SPOONHUTCH
SPOONIER
SPOONIES
SPOONIEST
SPOONILY
SPOONINESS
SPOONING
SPOONISM
SPOONMAKER
SPOONMAKING
SPOONWAYS
SPOONWISE
SPOONWOOD
SPOONY
SPOONYISM
SPOOR
SPOORED
SPOORER
SPOORING
SPOORN
SPORABOLA
SPORACEOUS
SPORADES
SPORADIAL
SPORADIC
SPORADICAL
SPORADICALLY
SPORADICALNESS
SPORADICITY
SPORADIN
SPORADISM
SPORAL
SPORANGE
SPORANGIA
SPORANGIAL
SPORANGIFORM
SPORANGIOID
SPORANGIOLA
SPORANGIOLE
SPORANGIOLUM
SPORANGITE
SPORANGIUM
SPORATION
SPORE
SPORED
SPOREFORMER
SPOREFORMING
SPORELING
SPORES
SPORICIDE
SPORID
SPORIDESM
SPORIDIA
SPORIDIAL
SPORIDIOLE
SPORIDIOLUM
SPORIDIUM
SPORIFEROUS
SPORING
SPORIPARITY
SPORIPAROUS
SPOROBLAST
SPOROCARP
SPOROCARPIA
SPOROCARPIUM
SPOROCYST
SPOROCYSTIC
SPOROCYSTID
SPOROCYTE
SPORODERM
SPORODOCHIA
SPORODOCHIUM
SPORODUCT
SPOROGEN
SPOROGENESIS
SPOROGENIC
SPOROGENOUS
SPOROGENY
SPOROGONE
SPOROGONIA
SPOROGONIAL
SPOROGONIC
SPOROGONIUM
SPOROGONY
SPOROID
SPOROLOGIST
SPOROMYCOSIS
SPORONT
SPOROPHORE
SPOROPHORIC
SPOROPHOROUS
SPOROPHYDIUM
SPOROPHYL
SPOROPHYLL
SPOROPHYLLUM
SPOROPHYTE
SPOROPHYTIC
SPOROPLASM
SPOROSAC
SPOROSTEGIUM
SPOROSTROTE
SPOROUS
SPOROZOAL
SPOROZOAN
SPOROZOIC
SPOROZOID
SPOROZOITE
SPOROZOOID
SPOROZOON
SPORRAN
SPORT
SPORTABILITY
SPORTABLE
SPORTANCE
SPORTED
SPORTER
SPORTFUL
SPORTFULLY
SPORTFULNESS
SPORTIER
SPORTIEST
SPORTILY
SPORTINESS
SPORTING
SPORTIVE
SPORTIVELY
SPORTIVENESS
SPORTLING
SPORTS
SPORTSCAST
SPORTSCASTER
SPORTSMAN
SPORTSMANLIKE
SPORTSMANLY
SPORTSMANSHIP
SPORTSMEN
SPORTSOME
SPORTSWEAR
SPORTSWOMAN
SPORTULA
SPORTULAE
SPORTY
SPORULAR
SPORULATE
SPORULATED
SPORULATING
SPORULATION
SPORULE
SPORULOID
SPOSH
SPOSHY
SPOT
SPOTLESS
SPOTLESSLY
SPOTLESSNESS
SPOTLIGHT
SPOTLIGHTER
SPOTRUMP
SPOTS
SPOTSMAN
SPOTSMEN
SPOTTABLE
SPOTTAIL
SPOTTED
SPOTTELDY
SPOTTER
SPOTTIER
SPOTTIEST
SPOTTILY
SPOTTINESS
SPOTTING
SPOTTLE
SPOTTY
SPOTWELDER
SPOUCHER
SPOUSAGE
SPOUSAL
SPOUSALLY
SPOUSE
SPOUSED
SPOUSEHOOD
SPOUSING
SPOUT
SPOUTED
SPOUTER
SPOUTINESS
SPOUTING
SPOUTLESS
SPOUTY
SPOW
SPOWE
SPRACHLE
SPRACK
SPRACKLY
SPRACKNESS
SPRADDLE
SPRAG
SPRAGGED
SPRAGGER
SPRAGGING
SPRAGGLY
SPRAGMAN

SPRAICH
SPRAIN
SPRAINED
SPRAING
SPRAINING
SPRAINTS
SPRAITH
SPRANG
SPRANGLE
SPRANGLY
SPRANK
SPRAT
SPRATTED
SPRATTER
SPRATTING
SPRATTLE
SPRATTLED
SPRATTLING
SPRATTY
SPRAUCHLE
SPRAWL
SPRAWLED
SPRAWLER
SPRAWLIER
SPRAWLIEST
SPRAWLING
SPRAWLINGLY
SPRAWLY
SPRAY
SPRAYBOARD
SPRAYED
SPRAYER
SPRAYEY
SPRAYING
SPRAYS
SPREAD
SPREADATION
SPREADBOARD
SPREADER
SPREADHEAD
SPREADING
SPREADINGLY
SPREADINGNESS
SPREADOVER
SPREADY
SPREAGH
SPREAGHERY
SPREATH
SPRECKLE
SPREE
SPREED
SPREEING
SPREEUW
SPRENG
SPRENGE
SPRENGING
SPRENT
SPRET
SPRETTY
SPREW
SPRIDHOGUE
SPRIER
SPRIEST
SPRIG
SPRIGGED
SPRIGGER
SPRIGGIER
SPRIGGIEST
SPRIGGING
SPRIGGY
SPRIGHT
SPRIGHTED
SPRIGHTFUL
SPRIGHTFULLY
SPRIGHTFULNESS
SPRIGHTLIER
SPRIGHTLIEST
SPRIGHTLILY
SPRIGHTLINESS
SPRIGHTLY
SPRIGHTY
SPRIGTAIL
SPRINDGE
SPRING
SPRINGAL
SPRINGALD
SPRINGBOARD
SPRINGBOK
SPRINGBOKS
SPRINGBUCK
SPRINGE
SPRINGED
SPRINGEING
SPRINGER
SPRINGERLE
SPRINGFINGER
SPRINGFISH
SPRINGFISHES
SPRINGFUL
SPRINGHAAS
SPRINGHALT
SPRINGHEAD
SPRINGHOUSE
SPRINGIER
SPRINGIEST
SPRINGILY
SPRINGINESS
SPRINGING
SPRINGINGLY
SPRINGLE
SPRINGLED
SPRINGLESS
SPRINGLET
SPRINGLIKE
SPRINGLING
SPRINGLY
SPRINGMAKER
SPRINGMAKING
SPRINGS
SPRINGTAIL
SPRINGTIDE
SPRINGTIME
SPRINGTRAP
SPRINGWOOD
SPRINGWORM
SPRINGWORT
SPRINGY
SPRINK
SPRINKLE
SPRINKLED
SPRINKLER
SPRINKLERED
SPRINKLING
SPRINT
SPRINTED
SPRINTER
SPRINTING
SPRIT
SPRITE
SPRITELY
SPRITISH
SPRITSAIL
SPRITTAIL
SPRITTED
SPRITTING
SPRITTY
SPRITZ
SPRITZER
SPROAT
SPROCKET
SPROD
SPROGUE
SPROIL
SPRONG
SPROSE
SPROT
SPROTTLE
SPROTY
SPROUT
SPROUTAGE
SPROUTED
SPROUTER
SPROUTING
SPROUTLAND
SPROUTLING
SPROUTS
SPROWSY
SPRUCE
SPRUCED
SPRUCELY
SPRUCENESS
SPRUCER
SPRUCERY
SPRUCEST
SPRUCIFICATION
SPRUCIFY
SPRUCING
SPRUE
SPRUER
SPRUG
SPRUIKER
SPRUIT
SPRUNG
SPRUNK
SPRUNNY
SPRUNT
SPRUNTLY
SPRUSADO
SPRUSH
SPRY
SPRYER
SPRYEST
SPRYLY
SPRYNESS
SPUD
SPUDDED
SPUDDER
SPUDDING
SPUDDLE
SPUDDY
SPUDS
SPUE
SPUFFLE
SPUG
SPUILZIE
SPULE
SPULYIEMENT
SPULZIE
SPUME
SPUMED
SPUMESCENCE
SPUMESCENT
SPUMIER
SPUMIEST
SPUMIFEROUS
SPUMIFORM
SPUMING
SPUMOID
SPUMONE
SPUMONI
SPUMOSE
SPUMOUS
SPUMY
SPUN
SPUNG
SPUNGE
SPUNK
SPUNKIE
SPUNKIER
SPUNKIEST
SPUNKILY
SPUNKINESS
SPUNKY
SPUNNIES
SPUNNY
SPUR
SPURDIE
SPURDOG
SPURFLOWER
SPURGALL
SPURGE
SPURIA
SPURIAE
SPURIOUS
SPURIOUSLY
SPURIOUSNESS
SPURL
SPURLESS
SPURLET
SPURLIKE
SPURMAKER
SPURMONEY
SPURN
SPURNED
SPURNER
SPURNING
SPURNPOINT
SPURNWATER
SPURRED
SPURRER
SPURREY
SPURRIER
SPURRIES
SPURRING
SPURRINGS
SPURRITE
SPURRY
SPURS
SPURT
SPURTED
SPURTER
SPURTING
SPURTIVE
SPURTIVELY
SPURTLE
SPURTLEBLADE
SPURTS
SPURWAY
SPURWING
SPURWORT
SPUT
SPUTA
SPUTATIVE
SPUTE
SPUTNIK
SPUTTER
SPUTTERED
SPUTTERER
SPUTTERING
SPUTTERINGLY
SPUTTERY
SPUTUM
SPUTUMARY
SPUTUMOSE
SPUTUMOUS
SPY
SPYBOAT
SPYER
SPYGLASS
SPYING
SQUAB
SQUABASH
SQUABASHER
SQUABBED
SQUABBER
SQUABBIER
SQUABBIEST
SQUABBING
SQUABBISH
SQUABBLE
SQUABBLED
SQUABBLER
SQUABBLING
SQUABBLINGLY
SQUABBLY
SQUABBY
SQUACCO
SQUACCOS
SQUAD
SQUADDED
SQUADDING
SQUADDY
SQUADER
SQUADRATE
SQUADRISM
SQUADROL
SQUADRON
SQUADRONE
SQUADRONED
SQUADRONING
SQUAGGA
SQUAIL
SQUAILER
SQUAILS
SQUALENE
SQUALID
SQUALIDITY
SQUALIDLY
SQUALIDNESS
SQUALIFORM
SQUALL
SQUALLED
SQUALLER
SQUALLERY
SQUALLIER
SQUALLIEST
SQUALLING
SQUALLY
SQUALODONT
SQUALOID
SQUALOR
SQUAM
SQUAMA
SQUAMACEOUS
SQUAMAE
SQUAMATE
SQUAMATED
SQUAMATINE
SQUAMATION
SQUAME
SQUAMELLA
SQUAMELLAE
SQUAMELLATE
SQUAMEOUS
SQUAMIFEROUS
SQUAMIFORM
SQUAMIFY
SQUAMIGEROUS
SQUAMISH
SQUAMOID
SQUAMOSA
SQUAMOSAL
SQUAMOSE
SQUAMOSELY
SQUAMOSENESS
SQUAMOSITY
SQUAMOUS
SQUAMOUSLY
SQUAMOUSNESS
SQUAMULA
SQUAMULAE
SQUAMULATE
SQUAMULATION
SQUAMULE
SQUAMULOSE

SQUAMY
SQUANDER
SQUANDERED
SQUANDERER
SQUANDERING
SQUANDERINGLY
SQUANTUM
SQUAP
SQUARE
SQUAREAGE
SQUARECAP
SQUARED
SQUAREFACE
SQUAREHEAD
SQUARELY
SQUAREMAN
SQUAREMEN
SQUARENESS
SQUARER
SQUARES
SQUARETAIL
SQUARIER
SQUARING
SQUARISH
SQUARISHLY
SQUARK
SQUARROSE
SQUARROSELY
SQUARROUS
SQUARRULOSE
SQUARSON
SQUARSONRY
SQUARY
SQUASH
SQUASHBERRY
SQUASHED
SQUASHER
SQUASHIER
SQUASHIEST
SQUASHILY
SQUASHINESS
SQUASHING
SQUASHY
SQUAT
SQUATAROLE
SQUATEROLE
SQUATINID
SQUATINOID
SQUATLY
SQUATMORE
SQUATNESS
SQUATTAGE
SQUATTED
SQUATTER
SQUATTIER
SQUATTIEST
SQUATTILY
SQUATTINESS
SQUATTING
SQUATTISH
SQUATTLE
SQUATTOCRACY
SQUATTY
SQUAW
SQUAWBERRIES
SQUAWBERRY
SQUAWBUSH
SQUAWFISH
SQUAWFISHES
SQUAWFLOWER
SQUAWK
SQUAWKED
SQUAWKER
SQUAWKIE
SQUAWKIER
SQUAWKIEST
SQUAWKING
SQUAWKINGLY
SQUAWKY
SQUAWL
SQUAWROOT
SQUAWWEED
SQUDGE
SQUDGY
SQUEAK
SQUEAKED
SQUEAKER
SQUEAKERY
SQUEAKILY
SQUEAKINESS
SQUEAKING
SQUEAKINGLY
SQUEAKY
SQUEAL
SQUEALED
SQUEALER
SQUEALING
SQUEAM
SQUEAMISH
SQUEAMISHLY
SQUEAMISHNESS
SQUEEF
SQUEEGE
SQUEEGEE
SQUEEGEED
SQUEEGEEING
SQUEEL
SQUEEZABLE
SQUEEZE
SQUEEZED
SQUEEZEMAN
SQUEEZER
SQUEEZING
SQUEEZINGLY
SQUEEZY
SQUEG
SQUELCH
SQUELCHED
SQUELCHER
SQUELCHIER
SQUELCHIEST
SQUELCHILY
SQUELCHINESS
SQUELCHING
SQUELCHINGLY
SQUELCHINGNESS
SQUELCHY
SQUELETTE
SQUET
SQUETEAGUE
SQUETEE
SQUIB
SQUIBBED
SQUIBBER
SQUIBBERY
SQUIBBING
SQUIBBISH
SQUIBCRACK
SQUIBSTER
SQUID
SQUIDDED
SQUIDDER
SQUIDDING
SQUIDDLE
SQUIDGE
SQUIDGEREEN
SQUIDGIER
SQUIDGIEST
SQUIDGY
SQUIDS
SQUIFFED
SQUIFFER
SQUIFFIER
SQUIFFIEST
SQUIFFY
SQUIGGLE
SQUIGGLIER
SQUIGGLIEST
SQUIGGLY
SQUILGEE
SQUILGEED
SQUILGEEING
SQUILGEER
SQUILL
SQUILLA
SQUILLAGEE
SQUILLGEE
SQUILLIAN
SQUILLID
SQUILLITIC
SQUIN
SQUINACY
SQUINANCE
SQUINANT
SQUINCH
SQUINNY
SQUINT
SQUINTED
SQUINTER
SQUINTING
SQUINTINGLY
SQUINTINGNESS
SQUINTY
SQUIR
SQUIRAGE
SQUIRALTY
SQUIRARCH
SQUIRARCHAL
SQUIRARCHY
SQUIRE
SQUIREARCH
SQUIREARCHAL
SQUIREARCHIES
SQUIREARCHY
SQUIRED
SQUIREEN
SQUIRELING
SQUIRELY
SQUIRESS
SQUIRET
SQUIRING
SQUIRISH
SQUIRK
SQUIRL
SQUIRM
SQUIRMED
SQUIRMER
SQUIRMIER
SQUIRMIEST
SQUIRMINESS
SQUIRMING
SQUIRMINGLY
SQUIRR
SQUIRREL
SQUIRRELFISH
SQUIRRELFISHES
SQUIRRELTAIL
SQUIRRELY
SQUIRT
SQUIRTED
SQUIRTER
SQUIRTINESS
SQUIRTING
SQUIRTINGLY
SQUIRTISH
SQUIRTS
SQUIRTY
SQUISH
SQUISHED
SQUISHING
SQUISHY
SQUISS
SQUIT
SQUITCH
SQUITTER
SQUIZ
SQUSH
SQUSHY
SQUUSH
SQUUSHY
SRADDHA
SRADH
SRADHA
SRAMANA
SRAVAKA
SRI
SRUTI
SSU
STAAB
STAATSRAAD
STAB
STABBED
STABBER
STABBING
STABBINGLY
STABILATE
STABILE
STABILIFY
STABILISE
STABILIST
STABILITATE
STABILITIES
STABILITY
STABILIZATION
STABILIZATOR
STABILIZE
STABILIZED
STABILIZER
STABILIZING
STABLE
STABLEBOY
STABLED
STABLEKEEPER
STABLEMAN
STABLEMEAL
STABLEMEN
STABLENESS
STABLER
STABLES
STABLESTAND
STABLING
STABLISH
STABLY
STABOY
STABWORT
STACCATO
STACCATOS
STACHER
STACHYDRIN
STACHYDRINE
STACHYOSE
STACK
STACKAGE
STACKED
STACKENCLOUD
STACKER
STACKET
STACKFREED
STACKGARTH
STACKING
STACKMAN
STACKMEN
STACKS
STACKSTAND
STACKYARD
STACTE
STACTOMETER
STAD
STADDA
STADDLE
STADDLING
STADE
STADHOLDER
STADHOUSE
STADIA
STADIAL
STADIC
STADIE
STADIMETER
STADIOMETER
STADION
STADIUM
STADTHOLDER
STAFETTE
STAFF
STAFFAGE
STAFFED
STAFFELITE
STAFFER
STAFFIER
STAFFING
STAFFISH
STAFFMAN
STAFFMEN
STAFFS
STAFFSTRIKER
STAG
STAGBUSH
STAGE
STAGECOACH
STAGECOACHING
STAGECRAFT
STAGED
STAGEHAND
STAGEHOUSE
STAGELAND
STAGELIKE
STAGEMAN
STAGEMEN
STAGER
STAGERY
STAGES
STAGEWORTHY
STAGEY
STAGGARD
STAGGART
STAGGED
STAGGER
STAGGERBUSH
STAGGERED
STAGGERER
STAGGERING
STAGGERINGLY
STAGGERS
STAGGERWEED
STAGGERWORT
STAGGERY
STAGGIE
STAGGING
STAGGY
STAGHEAD
STAGHORN
STAGHOUND
STAGHUNT
STAGHUNTER
STAGHUNTING
STAGIARY
STAGIER
STAGIEST
STAGILY
STAGINESS
STAGING
STAGION
STAGMOMETER
STAGNANCY

STAGNANT
STAGNANTLY
STAGNANTNESS
STAGNATE
STAGNATED
STAGNATING
STAGNATION
STAGNATORY
STAGNE
STAGNICOLOUS
STAGNUM
STAGS
STAGSKIN
STAGWORM
STAGY
STAID
STAIDLY
STAIDNESS
STAIG
STAIL
STAIN
STAINABLE
STAINED
STAINER
STAINIERITE
STAINING
STAINLESS
STAINLESSLY
STAIO
STAIR
STAIRBEAK
STAIRBUILDER
STAIRBUILDING
STAIRCASE
STAIRHEAD
STAIRS
STAIRSTEP
STAIRWAY
STAIRWELL
STAIRWORK
STAITH
STAITHMAN
STAITHMEN
STAIVER
STAKE
STAKED
STAKEHEAD
STAKEHOLDER
STAKEMASTER
STAKEOUT
STAKER
STAKING
STALACE
STALACTIC
STALACTICAL
STALACTIFORM
STALACTITAL
STALACTITE
STALACTITES
STALACTITIC
STALACTITIED
STALAG
STALAGMITE
STALAGMITIC
STALDER
STALE
STALED
STALELY
STALEMATE
STALEMATED
STALEMATING
STALENESS
STALER
STALEST
STALING
STALK
STALKED
STALKER
STALKIER
STALKIEST
STALKING
STALKINGLY
STALKLESS
STALKLET
STALKLIKE
STALKO
STALKOES
STALKS
STALKY
STALL
STALLAGE
STALLAND
STALLAR
STALLARY
STALLBOARD
STALLBOAT
STALLED
STALLENGER
STALLER
STALLING
STALLINGER
STALLINGKEN
STALLION
STALLIONIZE
STALLKEEPER
STALLMAN
STALLMEN
STALLMENT
STALLON
STALLS
STALWART
STALWARTISM
STALWARTIZE
STALWARTLY
STALWARTNESS
STALWORTH
STALWORTHLY
STALWORTHNESS
STAM
STAMBHA
STAMBOULINE
STAMEN
STAMENED
STAMENS
STAMIN
STAMINA
STAMINAL
STAMINATE
STAMINEAL
STAMINEOUS
STAMINODE
STAMINODIA
STAMINODIUM
STAMINODY
STAMMEL
STAMMER
STAMMERER
STAMMERING
STAMMERINGLY
STAMMERINGNESS
STAMMERWORT
STAMNOS
STAMP
STAMPAGE
STAMPED
STAMPEDE
STAMPEDED
STAMPEDER
STAMPEDING
STAMPEDO
STAMPEE
STAMPER
STAMPERY
STAMPHEAD
STAMPING
STAMPLE
STAMPMAN
STAMPMEN
STAMPS
STAMPSMAN
STAMPSMEN
STAMPWEED
STANCE
STANCH
STANCHED
STANCHEL
STANCHELED
STANCHER
STANCHEST
STANCHING
STANCHION
STAND
STANDAGE
STANDARD
STANDARDBRED
STANDARDIZABLE
STANDARDIZATION
STANDARDIZE
STANDARDIZED
STANDARDIZER
STANDARDIZING
STANDBY
STANDBYS
STANDEE
STANDEL
STANDELWELKS
STANDELWORT
STANDER
STANDERGRASS
STANDERWORT
STANDFAST
STANDING
STANDISH
STANDOFF
STANDOFFISH
STANDOFFISHNESS
STANDOUT
STANDPAT
STANDPATISM
STANDPATTER
STANDPATTISM
STANDPIPE
STANDPOINT
STANDPOST
STANDSTILL
STANDUP
STANE
STANG
STANHOPE
STANINE
STANITSA
STANITZA
STANJEN
STANK
STANKIE
STANN
STANNANE
STANNARIES
STANNARY
STANNATE
STANNATOR
STANNEL
STANNER
STANNERS
STANNERY
STANNIC
STANNID
STANNIDE
STANNIFEROUS
STANNITE
STANNO
STANNOTYPE
STANNOUS
STANNUM
STANNYL
STANZA
STANZAED
STANZAIC
STANZAICAL
STANZAICALLY
STANZAS
STANZE
STANZO
STAP
STAPEDECTOMY
STAPEDES
STAPEDIAL
STAPEDIFORM
STAPEDIUS
STAPELIA
STAPES
STAPH
STAPHISAGRIA
STAPHYLE
STAPHYLEDEMA
STAPHYLIC
STAPHYLINE
STAPHYLINIC
STAPHYLINID
STAPHYLION
STAPHYLITIS
STAPHYLOMA
STAPHYLONCUS
STAPHYLOSIS
STAPHYLOTOME
STAPHYLOTOMY
STAPLE
STAPLED
STAPLER
STAPLING
STAPP
STAPPLE
STAR
STARBLIND
STARBLOOM
STARBOARD
STARBOLINS
STARBOWLINES
STARBRIGHT
STARCH
STARCHBOARD
STARCHED
STARCHER
STARCHFLOWER
STARCHIER
STARCHIEST
STARCHILY
STARCHINESS
STARCHING
STARCHLY
STARCHMAKER
STARCHMAKING
STARCHMAN
STARCHMEN
STARCHROOT
STARCHWORKS
STARCHWORT
STARCHY
STARCRAFT
STARDOM
STARDUST
STARE
STARED
STAREE
STARER
STARETS
STARFISH
STARFISHES
STARFLOWER
STARFRUIT
STARGAZE
STARGAZED
STARGAZER
STARGAZING
STARIK
STARING
STARK
STARKEN
STARKER
STARKEST
STARKLE
STARKY
STARLESS
STARLESSLY
STARLESSNESS
STARLET
STARLIGHT
STARLIGHTED
STARLIGHTS
STARLIKE
STARLING
STARLIT
STARLITE
STARLITTEN
STARMONGER
STARN
STARNEL
STARNIE
STARNOSE
STARNY
STAROST
STAROSTA
STAROSTI
STAROSTY
STARR
STARRED
STARRIER
STARRIEST
STARRIFY
STARRILY
STARRINESS
STARRING
STARRINGLY
STARRY
STARS
STARSHAKE
STARSHINE
STARSHIP
STARSHOOT
STARSHOT
STARSTONE
STARSTROKE
START
STARTED
STARTER
STARTFUL
STARTFULNESS
STARTHROAT
STARTING
STARTINGLY
STARTISH
STARTLE
STARTLED
STARTLER
STARTLING
STARTLINGLY
STARTLINGNESS
STARTLISH
STARTLISHNESS
STARTLY
STARTS
STARTY
STARVATION
STARVE
STARVEACRE

STARVED
STARVEDLY
STARVELING
STARVEN
STARVER
STARVING
STARVY
STARWISE
STARWORM
STARWORT
STARY
STASES
STASH
STASHIE
STASIDIA
STASIDION
STASIMA
STASIMETRIC
STASIMON
STASIMORPHY
STASIPHOBIA
STASIS
STASSFURTITE
STATABLE
STATANT
STATARY
STATCOULOMB
STATE
STATECRAFT
STATED
STATEDLY
STATEFUL
STATEFULLY
STATEFULNESS
STATELESS
STATELET
STATELIER
STATELIEST
STATELINESS
STATELY
STATEMENT
STATEMENTS
STATEMONGER
STATEQUAKE
STATER
STATERA
STATEROOM
STATESBOY
STATESIDE
STATESMAN
STATESMANLIKE
STATESMANLY
STATESMANSHIP
STATESMEN
STATESMONGER
STATESWOMAN
STATESWOMEN
STATEWAY
STATFARAD
STATHMOS
STATIC
STATICAL
STATICALLY
STATICS
STATING
STATION
STATIONAL
STATIONARIES
STATIONARILY
STATIONARINESS
STATIONARY
STATIONED
STATIONER
STATIONERY
STATIONING
STATIONMAN
STATIONMASTER
STATISM
STATIST
STATISTIC
STATISTICAL
STATISTICALLY
STATISTICIAN
STATISTICIZE
STATISTICS
STATISTOLOGY
STATIVE
STATIZE
STATOBLAST
STATOCRACY
STATOCYST
STATOHM
STATOLATRY
STATOLITH
STATOLITHIC
STATOMETER
STATOR
STATORHAB
STATOSCOPE
STATOSPORE
STATUA
STATUARIES
STATUARISM
STATUARIST
STATUARY
STATUE
STATUECRAFT
STATUED
STATUELIKE
STATUES
STATUESQUE
STATUESQUELY
STATUESQUENESS
STATUETTE
STATUING
STATURE
STATURED
STATUS
STATUSES
STATUTABLE
STATUTABLY
STATUTE
STATUTORILY
STATUTORY
STATUTUM
STATVOLT
STAUMREL
STAUNCH
STAUNCHED
STAUNCHER
STAUNCHEST
STAUNCHING
STAUNCHLY
STAUNCHNESS
STAUP
STAURACIN
STAURAXONIA
STAURAXONIAL
STAURION
STAUROLATRIES
STAUROLATRY
STAUROLITE
STAUROLITIC
STAUROPEGIAL
STAUROPEGION
STAUROSCOPE
STAUROSCOPIC
STAUROTIDE
STAVE
STAVED
STAVER
STAVERS
STAVERWORT
STAVES
STAVESACRE
STAVEWOOD
STAVING
STAVRITE
STAW
STAWSOME
STAXIS
STAY
STAYED
STAYER
STAYING
STAYLACE
STAYLESS
STAYLESSNESS
STAYMAKER
STAYMAKING
STAYNIL
STAYPAK
STAYS
STAYSAIL
STAYSHIP
STCHI
STEAD
STEADABLE
STEADFAST
STEADFASTLY
STEADFASTNESS
STEADIED
STEADIER
STEADIEST
STEADILY
STEADIMENT
STEADINESS
STEADING
STEADITE
STEADMAN
STEADY
STEADYING
STEADYINGLY
STEAK
STEAKHOUSE
STEAL
STEALAGE
STEALER
STEALING
STEALINGLY
STEALTH
STEALTHIER
STEALTHIEST
STEALTHILY
STEALTHINESS
STEALTHLIKE
STEALTHY
STEALY
STEAM
STEAMBOAT
STEAMBOATING
STEAMBOATMAN
STEAMBOATMEN
STEAMCAR
STEAMED
STEAMER
STEAMERLOAD
STEAMFITTER
STEAMFITTING
STEAMIER
STEAMIEST
STEAMILY
STEAMINESS
STEAMING
STEAMPIPE
STEAMROLLER
STEAMSHIP
STEAMTIGHT
STEAMY
STEAN
STEANING
STEAPSIN
STEARATE
STEARIC
STEARIFORM
STEARIN
STEARINE
STEARONE
STEAROPTENE
STEARRHEA
STEARRHOEA
STEARYL
STEATIN
STEATITE
STEATITIC
STEATOCELE
STEATOGENOUS
STEATOLYSIS
STEATOLYTIC
STEATOMA
STEATOMAS
STEATOMATA
STEATOMATOUS
STEATOPATHIC
STEATOPYGA
STEATOPYGIA
STEATOPYGIC
STEATOPYGOUS
STEATOPYGY
STEATORRHEA
STEATORRHOEA
STEATOSES
STEATOSIS
STECH
STECHADOS
STECHLING
STECKLING
STEDFAST
STEDFASTLY
STEDFASTNESS
STEE
STEED
STEEK
STEEKKAN
STEEL
STEELBOW
STEELE
STEELED
STEELEN
STEELER
STEELHEAD
STEELHEADS
STEELHEARTED
STEELIER
STEELIEST
STEELIFICATION
STEELIFIED
STEELIFY
STEELIFYING
STEELINESS
STEELING
STEELMAKER
STEELMAKING
STEELPROOF
STEELWARE
STEELWORK
STEELWORKER
STEELWORKING
STEELWORKS
STEELY
STEELYARD
STEELYARDS
STEEM
STEEN
STEENBOK
STEENBRAS
STEENBRASS
STEENING
STEENKIRK
STEEP
STEEPDOWN
STEEPED
STEEPEN
STEEPER
STEEPEST
STEEPGRASS
STEEPING
STEEPISH
STEEPLE
STEEPLEBUSH
STEEPLECHASE
STEEPLECHASER
STEEPLECHASING
STEEPLED
STEEPLEJACK
STEEPLETOP
STEEPLY
STEEPNESS
STEEPWEED
STEEPWORT
STEEPY
STEER
STEERABLE
STEERAGE
STEERAGEWAY
STEERED
STEERER
STEERING
STEERLING
STEERSMAN
STEERSMATE
STEERSMEN
STEERY
STEEVE
STEEVED
STEEVELY
STEEVER
STEEVING
STEFLY
STEG
STEGANOGRAM
STEGH
STEGNOSIS
STEGNOTIC
STEGOCARPOUS
STEGODON
STEGODONS
STEGODONT
STEGODONTINE
STEGOMYIA
STEGOSAUR
STEGOSAURI
STEGOSAURIAN
STEGOSAUROID
STEGOSAURUS
STEIN
STEINBOK
STEINBUCK
STEINKIRK
STELA
STELAE
STELAR
STELE
STELENE
STELES
STELIC
STELL
STELLAR
STELLARATOR
STELLARY
STELLATE
STELLATED
STELLATELY
STELLATION
STELLATURE

STELLED
STELLERINE
STELLIFEROUS
STELLIFORM
STELLIFY
STELLING
STELLIONATE
STELLISCRIPT
STELLULAR
STELLULARLY
STELLULATE
STELOGRAPHY
STEM
STEMBOK
STEMFORM
STEMHEAD
STEMLESS
STEMLET
STEMMA
STEMMAS
STEMMATA
STEMMATOUS
STEMMED
STEMMER
STEMMERIES
STEMMERY
STEMMIER
STEMMIEST
STEMMING
STEMMY
STEMONACEOUS
STEMPEL
STEMPLE
STEMPOST
STEMSON
STEMWARE
STEN
STENCH
STENCHIER
STENCHIEST
STENCHING
STENCHY
STENCIL
STENCILED
STENCILER
STENCILING
STENCILLED
STENCILLER
STENCILLING
STENCILMAKER
STENCILMAKING
STEND
STENGAH
STENIA
STENION
STENO
STENOBENTHIC
STENOBREGMA
STENOCARDIA
STENOCARDIAC
STENOCEPHALY
STENOCHORIA
STENOCHROME
STENOCHROMY
STENOCRANIAL
STENOGASTRIC
STENOGASTRY
STENOGRAPH
STENOGRAPHED
STENOGRAPHER
STENOGRAPHIC
STENOGRAPHING
STENOGRAPHIST
STENOGRAPHY
STENOHALINE
STENOMETER
STENOPAEIC
STENOPAIC
STENOPEIC
STENOSED
STENOSIS
STENOSPHERE
STENOSTOMIA
STENOTHERMAL
STENOTHORAX
STENOTIC
STENOTROPIC
STENOTYPE
STENOTYPIC
STENOTYPIST
STENOTYPY
STENT
STENTER
STENTERER
STENTING
STENTMASTER
STENTON
STENTOR
STENTORIAN
STENTORIANLY
STENTORINE
STENTORIOUS
STENTORONIC
STENTREL
STEP
STEPAUNT
STEPBAIRN
STEPBROTHER
STEPCHILD
STEPDAME
STEPDAUGHTER
STEPFATHER
STEPFATHERLY
STEPGRANDCHILD
STEPGRANDFATHER
STEPGRANDMOTHER
STEPGRANDSON
STEPHANE
STEPHANIAL
STEPHANIC
STEPHANION
STEPHANITE
STEPHANOME
STEPHANOS
STEPLADDER
STEPMINNIE
STEPMOTHER
STEPMOTHERLINESS
STEPMOTHERLY
STEPNEPHEW
STEPNIECE
STEPONY
STEPPARENT
STEPPE
STEPPED
STEPPER
STEPPING
STEPPINGSTONE
STEPRELATION
STEPS
STEPSIRE
STEPSISTER
STEPSON
STEPSTONE
STEPT
STEPUNCLE
STEPWAY
STEPWISE
STERACLE
STERAD
STERADIAN
STERCOLIN
STERCORAEMIA
STERCORAL
STERCORARIES
STERCORARY
STERCORATE
STERCORATION
STERCOREMIA
STERCORITE
STERCOROL
STERCOROUS
STERCOVOROUS
STERCULIAD
STERE
STEREAGNOSIS
STEREID
STEREO
STEREOBATE
STEREOBATIC
STEREOCAMERA
STEREOCHEMIC
STEREOCHROME
STEREOCHROMY
STEREOED
STEREOGNOSIS
STEREOGRAM
STEREOGRAPH
STEREOGRAPHY
STEREOING
STEREOISOMER
STEREOM
STEREOMATRIX
STEREOME
STEREOMERIC
STEREOMETER
STEREOMETRIC
STEREOMETRY
STEREONEURAL
STEREOPHONE
STEREOPHONIC
STEREOPHONY
STEREOPHYSICS
STEREOPICTURE
STEREOPLASM
STEREOPSIS
STEREOPTICON
STEREOS
STEREOSCOPE
STEREOSCOPIC
STEREOSCOPY
STEREOSTATIC
STEREOSTATICS
STEREOTACTIC
STEREOTAXIS
STEREOTAXY
STEREOTOMIC
STEREOTOMIST
STEREOTOMY
STEREOTROPIC
STEREOTYPE
STEREOTYPED
STEREOTYPER
STEREOTYPERY
STEREOTYPIC
STEREOTYPICAL
STEREOTYPING
STEREOTYPIST
STEREOTYPY
STEREOVISION
STERIC
STERICAL
STERICALLY
STERID
STERIDE
STERIGMA
STERIGMATA
STERIGMATIC
STERILANT
STERILE
STERILELY
STERILENESS
STERILISE
STERILITIES
STERILITY
STERILIZATION
STERILIZE
STERILIZED
STERILIZER
STERILIZING
STERIN
STERLET
STERLING
STERLINGLY
STERLINGNESS
STERN
STERNA
STERNAD
STERNAGE
STERNAL
STERNALIS
STERNBERGITE
STERNCASTLE
STERNEBER
STERNEBRA
STERNEBRAL
STERNER
STERNEST
STERNFOREMOST
STERNFUL
STERNFULLY
STERNITE
STERNKNEE
STERNLY
STERNMAN
STERNMEN
STERNMOST
STERNNESS
STERNOCOSTAL
STERNOFACIAL
STERNOHYOID
STERNOMANCY
STERNONUCHAL
STERNOTHERE
STERNOTRIBE
STERNPOST
STERNSON
STERNUM
STERNUMS
STERNUTATION
STERNUTATIVE
STERNUTATOR
STERNUTATORY
STERNWARD
STERNWARDS
STERNWAY
STERNWAYS
STERNWORKS
STERO
STEROID
STEROL
STERRINCK
STERTOR
STERTORIOUS
STERTOROUS
STERTOROUSLY
STET
STETHAL
STETHOMETER
STETHOMETRIC
STETHOMETRY
STETHOPHONE
STETHOSCOPE
STETHOSCOPIC
STETHOSCOPY
STETHOSPASM
STETHY
STETTED
STETTING
STEVE
STEVEDORAGE
STEVEDORE
STEVEDORED
STEVEDORING
STEVEL
STEVEN
STEW
STEWARD
STEWARDESS
STEWARDLY
STEWARDRY
STEWARDSHIP
STEWART
STEWARTRY
STEWBUM
STEWED
STEWHOUSE
STEWING
STEWISH
STEWPAN
STEWPOND
STEWPOT
STEWY
STEY
STEYN
STEYNING
STHENE
STHENIA
STHENIC
STHENOCHIRE
STIACCIATO
STIB
STIBBLE
STIBBLER
STIBBLERIG
STIBIAL
STIBIALISM
STIBIATE
STIBIATED
STIBICONITE
STIBINE
STIBIUM
STIBNITE
STIBONIUM
STIBOPHEN
STICCADO
STICH
STICHADO
STICHARION
STICHEL
STICHERON
STICHIC
STICHICALLY
STICHID
STICHIDIA
STICHIDIUM
STICHOI
STICHOMANCY
STICHOMETRIC
STICHOMETRY
STICHOMYTHIC
STICHOMYTHY
STICHOS
STICHWORT
STICK
STICKAGE
STICKBALL
STICKED
STICKER
STICKERS
STICKERY
STICKFAST
STICKFUL
STICKFULS
STICKIER

STICKIEST
STICKILY
STICKINESS
STICKING
STICKIT
STICKJAW
STICKLE
STICKLEAF
STICKLEBACK
STICKLED
STICKLER
STICKLING
STICKLY
STICKMAN
STICKPIN
STICKS
STICKSEED
STICKTAIL
STICKTIGHT
STICKUM
STICKUP
STICKWEED
STICKWORK
STICKY
STICTIFORM
STIDDY
STIED
STIFE
STIFF
STIFFEN
STIFFENED
STIFFENER
STIFFENING
STIFFER
STIFFEST
STIFFHEARTED
STIFFISH
STIFFLEG
STIFFLER
STIFFLY
STIFFNECK
STIFFNESS
STIFFRUMP
STIFFTAIL
STIFLE
STIFLED
STIFLEDLY
STIFLER
STIFLING
STIFLINGLY
STIGMA
STIGMAI
STIGMAL
STIGMARIA
STIGMARIAE
STIGMARIAN
STIGMARIOID
STIGMAS
STIGMASTEROL
STIGMATA
STIGMATAL
STIGMATIC
STIGMATICAL
STIGMATICALLY
STIGMATICALNESS
STIGMATIFORM
STIGMATISE
STIGMATISM
STIGMATIST
STIGMATIZATION
STIGMATIZE
STIGMATIZED
STIGMATIZER
STIGMATIZING
STIGMATOID
STIGMATOSE
STIGME
STIGMEOLOGY
STIGMES
STIGMONOSE
STIGONOMANCY
STILB
STILBENE
STILBESTROL
STILBITE
STILE
STILEMAN
STILEMEN
STILET
STILETTE
STILETTO
STILETTOED
STILETTOES
STILETTOING
STILETTOS
STILL
STILLAGE
STILLATORY
STILLBIRTH
STILLBORN
STILLED
STILLER
STILLERY
STILLEST
STILLHOUSE
STILLICIDE
STILLICIDIUM
STILLIER
STILLIEST
STILLIFORM
STILLING
STILLION
STILLISH
STILLMAN
STILLMEN
STILLNESS
STILLROOM
STILLSTAND
STILLY
STILO
STILT
STILTED
STILTEDLY
STILTEDNESS
STILTER
STILTIER
STILTIEST
STILTIFIED
STILTIFY
STILTIFYING
STILTINESS
STILTING
STILTISH
STILTY
STIM
STIME
STIMPART
STIMULABILITY
STIMULABLE
STIMULANCE
STIMULANCY
STIMULANT
STIMULATE
STIMULATED
STIMULATER
STIMULATING
STIMULATION
STIMULATIVE
STIMULATOR
STIMULATORY
STIMULATRESS
STIMULATRIX
STIMULI
STIMULUS
STIMY
STING
STINGAREE
STINGAREEING
STINGBULL
STINGE
STINGER
STINGFISH
STINGFISHES
STINGIER
STINGIEST
STINGILY
STINGINESS
STINGING
STINGINGLY
STINGINGNESS
STINGLESS
STINGO
STINGRAY
STINGTAIL
STINGY
STINK
STINKARD
STINKARDLY
STINKBALL
STINKBERRIES
STINKBERRY
STINKBIRD
STINKBUG
STINKBUSH
STINKDAMP
STINKER
STINKHORN
STINKING
STINKINGLY
STINKINGNESS
STINKO
STINKPOT
STINKS
STINKSTONE
STINKWEED
STINKWOOD
STINKWORT
STINKY
STINT
STINTED
STINTEDLY
STINTEDNESS
STINTER
STINTING
STINTS
STINTY
STIPATE
STIPE
STIPED
STIPEL
STIPELLATE
STIPEND
STIPENDIA
STIPENDIAL
STIPENDIARIES
STIPENDIARY
STIPENDIATE
STIPENDIUM
STIPENDIUMS
STIPES
STIPIFORM
STIPITATE
STIPITES
STIPITIFORM
STIPITURE
STIPPEN
STIPPLE
STIPPLED
STIPPLER
STIPPLING
STIPPLY
STIPULA
STIPULABLE
STIPULACEOUS
STIPULAR
STIPULARY
STIPULATE
STIPULATED
STIPULATING
STIPULATIO
STIPULATION
STIPULATOR
STIPULATORY
STIPULE
STIPULED
STIPULIFORM
STIR
STIRABOUT
STIRIA
STIRK
STIRLESS
STIRLESSLY
STIRLESSNESS
STIRLING
STIRP
STIRPES
STIRPS
STIRRA
STIRRAGE
STIRRED
STIRRER
STIRRING
STIRRINGLY
STIRRUP
STITCH
STITCHBIRD
STITCHDOWN
STITCHED
STITCHER
STITCHERY
STITCHES
STITCHING
STITCHWHILE
STITCHWORK
STITCHWORT
STITE
STITH
STITHE
STITHIED
STITHIES
STITHLY
STITHY
STITHYING
STIVE
STIVER
STIVY
STOA
STOACH
STOAE
STOAK
STOAS
STOAT
STOATER
STOATING
STOATS
STOB
STOBBALL
STOBBED
STOBBING
STOCAH
STOCCADO
STOCCATA
STOCHASTIC
STOCHASTICAL
STOCK
STOCKADE
STOCKADED
STOCKADING
STOCKADO
STOCKAGE
STOCKANNET
STOCKBOW
STOCKBREEDER
STOCKBREEDING
STOCKBROKER
STOCKBROKERAGE
STOCKBROKING
STOCKCAR
STOCKED
STOCKER
STOCKFATHER
STOCKFISH
STOCKFISHES
STOCKHOLDER
STOCKHOLDING
STOCKHOUSE
STOCKIER
STOCKIEST
STOCKILY
STOCKINESS
STOCKINET
STOCKINETTE
STOCKING
STOCKINGED
STOCKINGER
STOCKINGING
STOCKINGLESS
STOCKINGS
STOCKISH
STOCKISHLY
STOCKISHNESS
STOCKJOBBER
STOCKJOBBERY
STOCKJOBBING
STOCKJUDGING
STOCKKEEPER
STOCKKEEPING
STOCKMAKER
STOCKMAKING
STOCKMAN
STOCKMEN
STOCKOWNER
STOCKPILE
STOCKPILED
STOCKPILING
STOCKPOT
STOCKPROOF
STOCKRIDER
STOCKRIDING
STOCKROOM
STOCKS
STOCKSTONE
STOCKTAKER
STOCKTAKING
STOCKWORK
STOCKWRIGHT
STOCKY
STOCKYARD
STOD
STODE
STODGE
STODGED
STODGER
STODGERY
STODGIER
STODGIEST
STODGILY
STODGINESS
STODGING
STODGY
STODTONE
STOECHIOLOGY
STOEP
STOF
STOFF

STOG
STOGA
STOGIE
STOGIES
STOGY
STOIC
STOICAL
STOICALLY
STOICALNESS
STOICHIOLOGY
STOICISM
STOIT
STOITER
STOKE
STOKED
STOKEHOLD
STOKEHOLE
STOKER
STOKES
STOKESITE
STOKING
STOKROOS
STOKVIS
STOLA
STOLAE
STOLE
STOLED
STOLEN
STOLENLY
STOLENNESS
STOLENWISE
STOLID
STOLIDITY
STOLIDLY
STOLIDNESS
STOLIST
STOLKJAERRE
STOLLEN
STOLO
STOLON
STOLONATE
STOLZITE
STOMA
STOMACACE
STOMACH
STOMACHABLE
STOMACHACHE
STOMACHAL
STOMACHED
STOMACHER
STOMACHFUL
STOMACHFULLY
STOMACHFULNESS
STOMACHIC
STOMACHICAL
STOMACHICALLY
STOMACHING
STOMACHLESS
STOMACHLESSNESS
STOMACHY
STOMATA
STOMATAL
STOMATE
STOMATIC
STOMATITIC
STOMATITIS
STOMATOCACE
STOMATODE
STOMATOGRAPH
STOMATOLOGIC
STOMATOLOGY
STOMATOMENIA
STOMATOMY
STOMATOPATHY
STOMATOPOD
STOMATOSCOPE
STOMATOSCOPY
STOMATOSE
STOMATOTOMY
STOMATOUS
STOMION
STOMIUM
STOMODAEA
STOMODAEAL
STOMODAEUM
STOMODEAL
STOMODEUM
STOMOXYS
STOMP
STOMPER
STONAGE
STONE
STONEBASS
STONEBIRD
STONEBITER
STONEBOAT
STONEBOW
STONEBRASH
STONEBREAK
STONEBROOD
STONECAST
STONECAT
STONECHAT
STONECROP
STONECUTTER
STONECUTTING
STONED
STONEFISH
STONEGALE
STONEGALL
STONEHAND
STONEHATCH
STONEHEAD
STONEHEARTED
STONEITE
STONELAYER
STONELAYING
STONELIKE
STONEMAN
STONEMASON
STONEMASONRY
STONEMEN
STONEMINT
STONEN
STONEPECKER
STONEPUT
STONER
STONEROOT
STONES
STONESHOT
STONESMATCH
STONESMITCH
STONESMITH
STONEWALL
STONEWALLED
STONEWALLER
STONEWALLING
STONEWALLY
STONEWARE
STONEWEED
STONEWISE
STONEWOOD
STONEWORK
STONEWORKER
STONEWORT
STONEY
STONEYARD
STONIER
STONIEST
STONIFIABLE
STONIFY
STONILY
STONINESS
STONING
STONISH
STONISHMENT
STONK
STONKER
STONY
STONYHEARTED
STOOD
STOODED
STOOF
STOOGE
STOOGED
STOOGING
STOOK
STOOKER
STOOKIE
STOOL
STOOLBALL
STOOLED
STOOLIE
STOOLING
STOOP
STOOPED
STOOPER
STOOPGALLANT
STOOPING
STOOPINGLY
STOOR
STOOREY
STOORY
STOOTER
STOOTH
STOOTHING
STOP
STOPA
STOPBACK
STOPBLOCK
STOPBOARD
STOPCOCK
STOPDICE
STOPE
STOPED
STOPEN
STOPER
STOPGAP
STOPHOUND
STOPING
STOPLESS
STOPLESSNESS
STOPLIGHT
STOPOVER
STOPPABILITY
STOPPABLE
STOPPABLY
STOPPAGE
STOPPED
STOPPEL
STOPPER
STOPPERED
STOPPERING
STOPPING
STOPPLE
STOPPLED
STOPPLING
STOPS
STOPSHIP
STOPT
STOPWATCH
STOPWATER
STOPWORK
STOR
STORABLE
STORAGE
STORAX
STORE
STORED
STOREEN
STOREHOUSE
STOREKEEP
STOREKEEPER
STOREKEEPING
STOREMAN
STOREMASTER
STOREMEN
STORER
STOREROOM
STORES
STORESHIP
STOREY
STOREYED
STOREYS
STORGE
STORIAL
STORIATE
STORIATION
STORIED
STORIER
STORIES
STORIETTE
STORIFIED
STORIFY
STORIFYING
STORING
STORIOLOGIST
STORIOLOGY
STORK
STORKEN
STORKLIKE
STORKS
STORKSBILL
STORM
STORMABLE
STORMBELT
STORMBIRD
STORMBOUND
STORMCOCK
STORMED
STORMER
STORMFUL
STORMFULLY
STORMFULNESS
STORMIER
STORMIEST
STORMILY
STORMINESS
STORMING
STORMINGLY
STORMISH
STORMPROOF
STORMS
STORMWIND
STORMY
STORNELLI
STORNELLO
STORY
STORYBOOK
STORYING
STORYMAKER
STORYMONGER
STORYTELLER
STORYTELLING
STORYWORK
STOSH
STOSS
STOSSTON
STOT
STOTER
STOTINKA
STOTINKI
STOTT
STOTTER
STOUN
STOUND
STOUNDMEAL
STOUP
STOUR
STOURE
STOURIE
STOURING
STOURLINESS
STOURLY
STOURNESS
STOURY
STOUSH
STOUT
STOUTEN
STOUTER
STOUTEST
STOUTH
STOUTHEARTED
STOUTHEARTEDLY
STOUTHEARTEDNESS
STOUTHRIEF
STOUTLY
STOUTNESS
STOUTWOOD
STOUTY
STOVE
STOVEBRUSH
STOVED
STOVEHOUSE
STOVEMAKER
STOVEMAKING
STOVEMAN
STOVEMEN
STOVEN
STOVEPIPE
STOVER
STOVEWOOD
STOVIES
STOVING
STOW
STOWAGE
STOWAWAY
STOWBALL
STOWBOARD
STOWBORD
STOWBORDMAN
STOWBORDMEN
STOWCE
STOWDOWN
STOWED
STOWER
STOWING
STOWL
STOWLINS
STOWNET
STOWP
STOWSE
STOWTH
STOWWOOD
STRABISM
STRABISMAL
STRABISMALLY
STRABISMIC
STRABISMICAL
STRABISMUS
STRABOMETER
STRABOMETRY
STRABOTOME
STRABOTOMIES
STRABOTOMY
STRACKLING
STRACT
STRAD
STRADDLE
STRADDLEBACK
STRADDLEBUG
STRADDLED
STRADDLER
STRADDLING
STRADDLINGLY

STRADICO
STRADINE
STRADIOT
STRADLINGS
STRAFE
STRAFED
STRAFER
STRAFING
STRAG
STRAGE
STRAGGLE
STRAGGLED
STRAGGLER
STRAGGLIER
STRAGGLIEST
STRAGGLING
STRAGGLINGLY
STRAGGLY
STRAGULAR
STRAGULUM
STRAIGHT
STRAIGHTAWAY
STRAIGHTEDGE
STRAIGHTEDGED
STRAIGHTEDGING
STRAIGHTEN
STRAIGHTENED
STRAIGHTENER
STRAIGHTENING
STRAIGHTER
STRAIGHTEST
STRAIGHTFORWARD
STRAIGHTFORWARDLY
STRAIGHTFORWARDNESS
STRAIGHTFORWARDS
STRAIGHTHEAD
STRAIGHTLY
STRAIGHTNESS
STRAIGHTWAY
STRAIGHTWAYS
STRAIGHTWISE
STRAIK
STRAIKE
STRAIL
STRAIN
STRAINABLE
STRAINABLY
STRAINED
STRAINEDLY
STRAINEDNESS
STRAINER
STRAINERMAN
STRAINERMEN
STRAINING
STRAININGLY
STRAINSLIP
STRAINT
STRAIT
STRAITEN
STRAITENED
STRAITENING
STRAITER
STRAITEST
STRAITJACKET
STRAITLACED
STRAITLACING
STRAITLY
STRAITNESS
STRAITSMAN
STRAITSMEN
STRAITWORK
STRAKE
STRAKED
STRAKES
STRAKY
STRALET
STRAM
STRAMASH
STRAMAZON
STRAMINEOUS
STRAMMEL
STRAMMER
STRAMONIUM
STRAMONY
STRAMP
STRAN
STRAND
STRANDAGE
STRANDED
STRANDER
STRANDING
STRANDLOOPER
STRANDS
STRANG
STRANGE
STRANGELING
STRANGELY
STRANGENESS
STRANGER
STRANGEST
STRANGLE
STRANGLEABLE
STRANGLED
STRANGLEHOLD
STRANGLEMENT
STRANGLER
STRANGLES
STRANGLETARE
STRANGLEWEED
STRANGLING
STRANGULATE
STRANGULATED
STRANGULATING
STRANGULATION
STRANGULATIVE
STRANGULLION
STRANGURIOUS
STRANGURY
STRANNER
STRANY
STRAP
STRAPHANG
STRAPHANGER
STRAPHEAD
STRAPLESS
STRAPPABLE
STRAPPADO
STRAPPADOES
STRAPPED
STRAPPER
STRAPPING
STRAPPLE
STRAPS
STRAPWORK
STRAPWORT
STRASS
STRATA
STRATAGEM
STRATAGEMS
STRATAL
STRATAMETER
STRATEGE
STRATEGETIC
STRATEGETICAL
STRATEGETICS
STRATEGI
STRATEGIAN
STRATEGIC
STRATEGICAL
STRATEGICALLY
STRATEGICS
STRATEGIES
STRATEGIST
STRATEGIZE
STRATEGOI
STRATEGOS
STRATEGUS
STRATEGY
STRATH
STRATHSPEY
STRATI
STRATIC
STRATICULATE
STRATIFICATION
STRATIFIED
STRATIFORM
STRATIFY
STRATIFYING
STRATIGRAPHER
STRATIGRAPHIC
STRATIGRAPHY
STRATLIN
STRATOCRACIES
STRATOCRACY
STRATOCRAT
STRATOCRATIC
STRATOGRAPHIC
STRATOGRAPHY
STRATONIC
STRATOPAUSE
STRATOSE
STRATOSPHERE
STRATOSPHERIC
STRATOUS
STRATUM
STRATUMS
STRATUS
STRAUGHT
STRAVAGANT
STRAVAGE
STRAVAGED
STRAVAGING
STRAVAGUE
STRAVAIG
STRAVAIGER
STRAW
STRAWBERRIES
STRAWBERRY
STRAWBILL
STRAWBOARD
STRAWBREADTH
STRAWEN
STRAWER
STRAWFLOWER
STRAWFORK
STRAWHAT
STRAWIER
STRAWIEST
STRAWMOTE
STRAWSMEAR
STRAWSTACK
STRAWSTACKER
STRAWWALKER
STRAWWORK
STRAWWORM
STRAWY
STRAWYARD
STRAY
STRAYAWAY
STRAYED
STRAYER
STRAYING
STREAK
STREAKED
STREAKEDLY
STREAKEDNESS
STREAKER
STREAKIER
STREAKIEST
STREAKILY
STREAKINESS
STREAKING
STREAKS
STREAKY
STREAM
STREAMED
STREAMER
STREAMIER
STREAMIEST
STREAMING
STREAMINGLY
STREAMLET
STREAMLINE
STREAMLINED
STREAMLING
STREAMLINING
STREAMS
STREAMWAY
STREAMWORT
STREAMY
STRECK
STRECKLY
STREEK
STREEL
STREELER
STREEN
STREEP
STREET
STREETAGE
STREETCAR
STREETS
STREETWALKER
STREETWALKING
STREETWARD
STREETWAY
STREIT
STREITE
STREMMA
STREMMAS
STRENGITE
STRENGTH
STRENGTHEN
STRENGTHENED
STRENGTHENER
STRENGTHENING
STRENGTHENINGLY
STRENGTHILY
STRENGTHLESS
STRENGTHLESSLY
STRENGTHLESSNESS
STRENGTHY
STRENT
STRENUITY
STRENUOSITY
STRENUOUS
STRENUOUSLY
STRENUOUSNESS
STREPENT
STREPERA
STREPEROUS
STREPHONADE
STREPITANT
STREPITANTLY
STREPITATION
STREPITOSO
STREPITOUS
STREPOR
STREPSINEMA
STREPSIPTERAL
STREPSIPTERON
STREPSIS
STREPSITENE
STREPTASTER
STREPTOCOCCI
STREPTOLYSIN
STREPTOMYCIN
STRESS
STRESSED
STRESSER
STRESSFUL
STRESSING
STRESSLESS
STRETCH
STRETCHABLE
STRETCHBERRY
STRETCHED
STRETCHER
STRETCHERMAN
STRETCHINESS
STRETCHING
STRETCHNECK
STRETCHPANTS
STRETCHY
STRETMAN
STRETMEN
STRETTA
STRETTAS
STRETTE
STRETTI
STRETTO
STRETTOS
STREUSEL
STREW
STREWED
STREWER
STREWING
STREWMENT
STREWN
STRIA
STRIAE
STRIAL
STRIATE
STRIATED
STRIATING
STRIATION
STRIATURE
STRICH
STRICK
STRICKEN
STRICKENLY
STRICKENNESS
STRICKER
STRICKLE
STRICKLED
STRICKLER
STRICKLING
STRICT
STRICTER
STRICTEST
STRICTION
STRICTLY
STRICTNESS
STRICTURE
STRICTURED
STRID
STRIDDEN
STRIDDLE
STRIDE
STRIDELEG
STRIDELEGS
STRIDENCE
STRIDENCY
STRIDENT
STRIDENTLY
STRIDER
STRIDES
STRIDEWAYS
STRIDHAN
STRIDHANA
STRIDHANUM
STRIDING
STRIDLING
STRIDLINS
STRIDOR
STRIDULANT

STRIDULATE
STRIDULATED
STRIDULATING
STRIDULATION
STRIDULATOR
STRIDULATORY
STRIDULENT
STRIDULOUS
STRIDULOUSLY
STRIE
STRIFE
STRIFFEN
STRIFT
STRIG
STRIGA
STRIGAE
STRIGAL
STRIGATE
STRIGGLE
STRIGIL
STRIGILATE
STRIGILATION
STRIGILATOR
STRIGILES
STRIGILIS
STRIGILLOSE
STRIGINE
STRIGOSE
STRIGOUS
STRIGOVITE
STRIKE
STRIKEBOUND
STRIKEBREAKER
STRIKEBREAKING
STRIKEOUT
STRIKER
STRIKES
STRIKING
STRIKINGLY
STRIKINGNESS
STRIND
STRING
STRINGBOARD
STRINGCOURSE
STRINGED
STRINGENCIES
STRINGENCY
STRINGENDO
STRINGENDOS
STRINGENT
STRINGENTLY
STRINGENTNESS
STRINGER
STRINGHALT
STRINGHALTED
STRINGHALTY
STRINGIER
STRINGIEST
STRINGILY
STRINGINESS
STRINGING
STRINGMAKER
STRINGMAKING
STRINGMAN
STRINGMEN
STRINGPIECE
STRINGS
STRINGSMAN
STRINGSMEN
STRINGWAYS
STRINGWOOD
STRINGY
STRINGYBARK
STRINKLE
STRIOLA
STRIOLAE
STRIOLATE
STRIOLATED
STRIOLET
STRIP
STRIPE
STRIPED
STRIPER
STRIPES
STRIPIER
STRIPIEST
STRIPING
STRIPLIGHT
STRIPLING
STRIPPAGE
STRIPPED
STRIPPER
STRIPPING
STRIPPLER
STRIPS
STRIPT
STRIPTEASE
STRIPTEASER
STRIPY
STRIT
STRIVE
STRIVED
STRIVEN
STRIVER
STRIVING
STRIX
STROAM
STROBE
STROBIC
STROBIL
STROBILA
STROBILAE
STROBILATE
STROBILATION
STROBILE
STROBILI
STROBILIFORM
STROBILINE
STROBILOID
STROBILUS
STROBOSCOPE
STROBOSCOPIC
STROBOSCOPY
STROCKLE
STROIL
STROKE
STROKED
STROKER
STROKES
STROKESMAN
STROKING
STROKINGS
STROKY
STROLL
STROLLED
STROLLER
STROLLING
STROM
STROMA
STROMAL
STROMATA
STROMATEOID
STROMATIC
STROMATIFORM
STROMATOLOGY
STROMATOUS
STROMB
STROMBIFORM
STROMBITE
STROMBOID
STROMBOLIAN
STROME
STROMEYERITE
STROMMING
STROMUHR
STROND
STRONE
STRONG
STRONGBACK
STRONGBARK
STRONGBOX
STRONGER
STRONGEST
STRONGFULLY
STRONGHAND
STRONGHANDED
STRONGHEADED
STRONGHEARTED
STRONGHOLD
STRONGISH
STRONGLY
STRONGMAN
STRONGMEN
STRONGNESS
STRONGPOINT
STRONGROOM
STRONGYL
STRONGYLATE
STRONGYLE
STRONGYLID
STRONGYLOID
STRONGYLON
STRONGYLOSIS
STRONTIA
STRONTIAN
STRONTIANITE
STRONTIC
STRONTION
STRONTITIC
STRONTIUM
STROOT
STROP
STROPHAIC
STROPHANTHIN
STROPHE
STROPHES
STROPHIC
STROPHICAL
STROPHICALLY
STROPHIOLATE
STROPHIOLE
STROPHOID
STROPHOMENID
STROPHOSIS
STROPHOTAXIS
STROPHULUS
STROPPED
STROPPER
STROPPING
STROPPINGS
STROSSER
STROTH
STROTHER
STROUD
STROUDING
STROUNGE
STROUP
STROUT
STROVE
STROW
STROWD
STROWED
STROWING
STROWN
STROY
STROYER
STROYGOOD
STRUB
STRUBBLY
STRUCION
STRUCK
STRUCKEN
STRUCTURAL
STRUCTURALISM
STRUCTURALIST
STRUCTURALIZATION
STRUCTURALIZE
STRUCTURALLY
STRUCTURATION
STRUCTURE
STRUCTURED
STRUCTURELESS
STRUCTURELESSNESS
STRUCTURELY
STRUCTURES
STRUCTURIST
STRUDE
STRUDEL
STRUE
STRUGGLE
STRUGGLED
STRUGGLER
STRUGGLING
STRUGGLINGLY
STRUIS
STRUISSLE
STRUM
STRUMA
STRUMAE
STRUMATIC
STRUMECTOMY
STRUMIFEROUS
STRUMIFORM
STRUMIPRIVIC
STRUMITIS
STRUMMED
STRUMMER
STRUMMING
STRUMOSE
STRUMOUS
STRUMOUSNESS
STRUMPET
STRUMPETRY
STRUMSTRUM
STRUMULOSE
STRUNG
STRUNT
STRUSE
STRUT
STRUTHIAN
STRUTHIFORM
STRUTHIIFORM
STRUTHIIN
STRUTHIN
STRUTHIOID
STRUTHIONINE
STRUTHIOUS
STRUTTED
STRUTTER
STRUTTING
STRUTTINGLY
STRUVITE
STRY
STRYCH
STRYCHNIA
STRYCHNIC
STRYCHNIN
STRYCHNINE
STRYCHNINISM
STRYCHNINIZE
STRYPE
STUB
STUBACHITE
STUBB
STUBBED
STUBBER
STUBBIER
STUBBIEST
STUBBILY
STUBBINESS
STUBBING
STUBBLE
STUBBLEBERRY
STUBBLED
STUBBLES
STUBBLIER
STUBBLIEST
STUBBLING
STUBBLY
STUBBORN
STUBBORNLY
STUBBORNNESS
STUBBY
STUBCHEN
STUBE
STUBRUNNER
STUCCO
STUCCOED
STUCCOER
STUCCOES
STUCCOING
STUCCOS
STUCCOWORK
STUCCOWORKER
STUCK
STUCKEN
STUCKING
STUCKLING
STUD
STUDBOOK
STUDDED
STUDDER
STUDDERY
STUDDIE
STUDDING
STUDDINGSAIL
STUDDLE
STUDDY
STUDENT
STUDENTRY
STUDENTS
STUDENTSHIP
STUDERITE
STUDFISH
STUDFISHES
STUDHORSE
STUDIA
STUDIED
STUDIEDLY
STUDIEDNESS
STUDIER
STUDIES
STUDIO
STUDIOS
STUDIOUS
STUDIOUSLY
STUDIOUSNESS
STUDIUM
STUDWORK
STUDY
STUDYING
STUE
STUFA
STUFE
STUFF
STUFFAGE
STUFFATA
STUFFED
STUFFENDER
STUFFER
STUFFIER
STUFFIEST
STUFFILY
STUFFINESS
STUFFING

STUFFY
STUG
STUGGY
STUIVER
STULL
STULLER
STULM
STULP
STULTIFIED
STULTIFIER
STULTIFY
STULTIFYING
STULTILOQUY
STULTY
STUM
STUMBLE
STUMBLEBUM
STUMBLED
STUMBLER
STUMBLING
STUMBLINGLY
STUMBLY
STUMER
STUMMED
STUMMEL
STUMMER
STUMMING
STUMMY
STUMOR
STUMOUR
STUMP
STUMPAGE
STUMPED
STUMPER
STUMPIER
STUMPIEST
STUMPINESS
STUMPING
STUMPISH
STUMPLING
STUMPNOSE
STUMPS
STUMPSUCKER
STUMPY
STUN
STUNG
STUNK
STUNKARD
STUNNED
STUNNER
STUNNING
STUNNINGLY
STUNPOLL
STUNSAIL
STUNT
STUNTED
STUNTEDLY
STUNTEDNESS
STUNTER
STUNTINESS
STUNTING
STUNTIST
STUNTNESS
STUNTY
STUP
STUPA
STUPE
STUPED
STUPEFACIENT
STUPEFACTION
STUPEFACTIVE
STUPEFIED
STUPEFIEDNESS
STUPEFIER
STUPEFY
STUPEFYING
STUPEND
STUPENDLY
STUPENDOUS
STUPENDOUSLY
STUPENDOUSNESS
STUPENT
STUPEOUS
STUPEX
STUPHE
STUPID
STUPIDHEAD
STUPIDITIES
STUPIDITY
STUPIDLY
STUPIDNESS
STUPING
STUPOR
STUPORIFIC
STUPOROSE
STUPOROUS
STUPOSE
STUPP
STUPRATE
STUPRATED
STUPRATING
STUPRATION
STUPRUM
STUPULOSE
STURBLE
STURDIED
STURDIER
STURDIEST
STURDILY
STURDINESS
STURDY
STURGEON
STURGEONS
STURIN
STURINE
STURNIFORM
STURNINE
STURNOID
STUROCH
STURSHUM
STURT
STURTAN
STURTE
STURTIN
STURTION
STURTITE
STUSS
STUT
STUTTER
STUTTERER
STUTTERING
STUTTERINGLY
STY
STYAN
STYANY
STYCA
STYCERIN
STYCERINOL
STYCHOMYTHIA
STYE
STYFZIEKTE
STYGIAN
STYING
STYKE
STYLAR
STYLATE
STYLE
STYLEBOOK
STYLED
STYLEDOM
STYLER
STYLET
STYLEWORT
STYLI
STYLIFEROUS
STYLIFORM
STYLINE
STYLING
STYLION
STYLISH
STYLISHLY
STYLISHNESS
STYLIST
STYLISTIC
STYLISTICAL
STYLISTICALLY
STYLISTICS
STYLITE
STYLITISM
STYLIZATION
STYLIZE
STYLIZED
STYLIZER
STYLIZING
STYLO
STYLOBATE
STYLOGLOSSAL
STYLOGLOSSUS
STYLOGRAPH
STYLOGRAPHIC
STYLOGRAPHY
STYLOHYAL
STYLOHYOID
STYLOID
STYLOLITE
STYLOLITIC
STYLOMASTOID
STYLOMETER
STYLOPID
STYLOPIZED
STYLOPOD
STYLOPODIA
STYLOPODIUM
STYLOSPORE
STYLOSPOROUS
STYLOSTEGIUM
STYLOSTEMON
STYLOTYPITE
STYLUS
STYLUSES
STYME
STYMIE
STYMIED
STYMYING
STYPHNATE
STYPHNIC
STYPSIS
STYPTIC
STYPTICAL
STYPTICITY
STYPTICNESS
STYRACACEOUS
STYRACIN
STYRENE
STYROFOAM
STYROGALLOL
STYROL
STYRONE
STYRYL
STYRYLIC
STYTH
STYTHE
SUABILITY
SUABLE
SUABLY
SUADE
SUAHARO
SUANT
SUANTLY
SUASIBLE
SUASION
SUASIONIST
SUASIVE
SUASIVELY
SUASIVENESS
SUASORIA
SUASORY
SUAVE
SUAVELY
SUAVENESS
SUAVEOLENT
SUAVIFY
SUAVILOQUENT
SUAVITIES
SUAVITY
SUB
SUBABDOMINAL
SUBACID
SUBACIDITY
SUBACIDLY
SUBACIDNESS
SUBACT
SUBACTION
SUBACUTE
SUBACUTELY
SUBADAR
SUBADULT
SUBAERIAL
SUBAERIALLY
SUBAGE
SUBAGENCY
SUBAGENT
SUBAH
SUBAHDAR
SUBAHDARY
SUBAHSHIP
SUBAID
SUBALARY
SUBALBID
SUBALKALINE
SUBALMONER
SUBALPINE
SUBALTERN
SUBALTERNANT
SUBALTERNATE
SUBALTERNITY
SUBAMARE
SUBANGLED
SUBANGULAR
SUBANGULATE
SUBANGULATED
SUBANTARCTIC
SUBAPICAL
SUBAPOSTOLIC
SUBAPTEROUS
SUBAQUATIC
SUBAQUEAN
SUBAQUEOUS
SUBARACHNOID
SUBARCH
SUBARCTIC
SUBARCUATE
SUBARCUATED
SUBARCUATION
SUBAREA
SUBAREOLAR
SUBARID
SUBARMALE
SUBARMOR
SUBARRATION
SUBARRHATION
SUBASHI
SUBASSEMBLY
SUBASTRAL
SUBATOM
SUBATOMIC
SUBAUD
SUBAUDIBLE
SUBAUDITION
SUBAUDITUR
SUBAURAL
SUBAURICULAR
SUBAXILLAR
SUBAXILLARY
SUBBASAL
SUBBASE
SUBBASEMENT
SUBBASS
SUBBASSA
SUBBIFID
SUBBING
SUBBOREAL
SUBBOURDON
SUBBRACHIAL
SUBBRACHIAN
SUBBRACHIATE
SUBBRANCH
SUBBRANCHED
SUBBREED
SUBBRIGADIER
SUBCALCARINE
SUBCALIBER
SUBCALIBRE
SUBCALLOSAL
SUBCANTOR
SUBCAPSULAR
SUBCAPTION
SUBCARBIDE
SUBCARBONATE
SUBCARDINAL
SUBCAST
SUBCASTE
SUBCAUDAL
SUBCAUDATE
SUBCELESTIAL
SUBCELLAR
SUBCENTER
SUBCENTRAL
SUBCENTRALLY
SUBCENTRE
SUBCHAIRMAN
SUBCHANTER
SUBCHASER
SUBCHELA
SUBCHELAE
SUBCHELATE
SUBCHIEF
SUBCHLORIDE
SUBCHONDRAL
SUBCHORDAL
SUBCHORIOID
SUBCHORIONIC
SUBCINCTORIUM
SUBCLAIM
SUBCLASS
SUBCLAUSE
SUBCLAVIAN
SUBCLAVIUS
SUBCLIMACTIC
SUBCLIMAX
SUBCLINICAL
SUBCLONE
SUBCOASTAL
SUBCOAT
SUBCOLUMNAR
SUBCOMMIT
SUBCOMMITTEE
SUBCONSCIOUS
SUBCONSCIOUSLY
SUBCONSCIOUSNESS
SUBCONSTABLE
SUBCONTINENT
SUBCONTRACT
SUBCONTRACTED
SUBCONTRACTOR

SUBCONTRARIES
SUBCONTRARY
SUBCOOL
SUBCORNEOUS
SUBCORTEX
SUBCORTICAL
SUBCORTICES
SUBCOSTA
SUBCOSTAL
SUBCOSTALIS
SUBCREPITANT
SUBCRITICAL
SUBCRUREAL
SUBCRUREUS
SUBCRUST
SUBCRUSTAL
SUBCULTURE
SUBCULTURED
SUBCULTURING
SUBCUTANEOUS
SUBCUTIS
SUBDEACON
SUBDEACONATE
SUBDEACONESS
SUBDEACONRY
SUBDEAN
SUBDEANERY
SUBDEB
SUBDEBUTANTE
SUBDECANAL
SUBDECIMAL
SUBDECUPLE
SUBDELEGATE
SUBDELEGATED
SUBDELIRIUM
SUBDENTED
SUBDERMAL
SUBDIACONAL
SUBDIACONATE
SUBDIAL
SUBDICHOTOMY
SUBDIT
SUBDITITIOUS
SUBDIVERSIFY
SUBDIVIDE
SUBDIVIDED
SUBDIVIDER
SUBDIVIDING
SUBDIVISIBLE
SUBDIVISION
SUBDIVISIVE
SUBDOLOUS
SUBDOLOUSLY
SUBDOMINANT
SUBDORSAL
SUBDORSALLY
SUBDOUBLE
SUBDRAIN
SUBDRAINAGE
SUBDRILL
SUBDUABLE
SUBDUABLY
SUBDUAL
SUBDUCE
SUBDUCED
SUBDUCING
SUBDUCT
SUBDUCTION
SUBDUE
SUBDUED
SUBDUEDLY
SUBDUEDNESS
SUBDUEMENT
SUBDUER
SUBDUING
SUBDUINGLY
SUBDUPLE
SUBDUPLICATE
SUBDURAL
SUBDURALLY
SUBDURE
SUBDWARF
SUBEDIT
SUBEDITOR
SUBEDITORIAL
SUBELAPHINE
SUBELECTRON
SUBENFEOFF
SUBENTITLE
SUBER
SUBERATE
SUBERECT
SUBEREOUS
SUBERIC
SUBERIFEROUS
SUBERIFORM
SUBERIN
SUBERINE
SUBERINIZE
SUBERITE
SUBERIZATION
SUBERIZE
SUBERIZED
SUBERIZING
SUBEROSE
SUBEROUS
SUBETH
SUBEXCITE
SUBFACTORIAL
SUBFAMILIES
SUBFAMILY
SUBFEBRILE
SUBFEU
SUBFEUDATION
SUBFEUDATORY
SUBFIEF
SUBFIX
SUBFLAVOR
SUBFLAVOUR
SUBFLOOR
SUBFLOORING
SUBFLORA
SUBFLUVIAL
SUBFOCAL
SUBFRESHMAN
SUBFUNCTIONAL
SUBFUSC
SUBFUSCOUS
SUBFUSK
SUBGALEA
SUBGALLATE
SUBGENERA
SUBGENERIC
SUBGENERICAL
SUBGENITAL
SUBGENUAL
SUBGENUS
SUBGENUSES
SUBGIANT
SUBGLACIAL
SUBGLACIALLY
SUBGLENOID
SUBGLOSSITIS
SUBGOVERNOR
SUBGRADE
SUBGROUP
SUBHARMONIC
SUBHASTATION
SUBHEAD
SUBHEADING
SUBHEDRAL
SUBHUMAN
SUBHYMENIAL
SUBHYMENIUM
SUBICTERIC
SUBICULAR
SUBICULUM
SUBIMAGINAL
SUBIMAGO
SUBINCIDENT
SUBINCISE
SUBINCISION
SUBINDEX
SUBINDICATE
SUBINDICATED
SUBINDICATING
SUBINDICATION
SUBINDICATIVE
SUBINDICES
SUBINDIVIDUAL
SUBINDUCE
SUBINFEUD
SUBINFEUDATE
SUBINGUINAL
SUBINSPECTOR
SUBINTENT
SUBINVOLUTED
SUBIRRIGATE
SUBIRRIGATED
SUBIRRIGATING
SUBIRRIGATION
SUBITANE
SUBITANEOUS
SUBITANY
SUBITO
SUBITOUS
SUBJACENCY
SUBJACENT
SUBJECT
SUBJECTED
SUBJECTEDLY
SUBJECTEDNESS
SUBJECTIFY
SUBJECTILE
SUBJECTING
SUBJECTION
SUBJECTIONAL
SUBJECTIVE
SUBJECTIVELY
SUBJECTIVENESS
SUBJECTIVISM
SUBJECTIVIST
SUBJECTIVITY
SUBJICIBLE
SUBJOIN
SUBJOINDER
SUBJOINED
SUBJOINING
SUBJOINT
SUBJUGABLE
SUBJUGAL
SUBJUGATE
SUBJUGATED
SUBJUGATING
SUBJUGATION
SUBJUGATOR
SUBJUGULAR
SUBJUNCT
SUBJUNCTION
SUBJUNCTIVE
SUBJUNCTIVELY
SUBKINGDOM
SUBLABIAL
SUBLANGUAGE
SUBLAPSARIAN
SUBLAPSARY
SUBLATE
SUBLATED
SUBLATERAL
SUBLATING
SUBLATION
SUBLATIVE
SUBLEADER
SUBLEASE
SUBLEASED
SUBLEASING
SUBLESSEE
SUBLESSOR
SUBLET
SUBLETHAL
SUBLETTABLE
SUBLETTER
SUBLETTING
SUBLEVATE
SUBLEVATION
SUBLICENSEE
SUBLIEUTENANT
SUBLIGATION
SUBLIMANT
SUBLIMATE
SUBLIMATED
SUBLIMATING
SUBLIMATION
SUBLIMATIONAL
SUBLIMATIONIST
SUBLIMATOR
SUBLIMATORY
SUBLIME
SUBLIMED
SUBLIMELY
SUBLIMENESS
SUBLIMER
SUBLIMEST
SUBLIMIFICATION
SUBLIMINAL
SUBLIMINALLY
SUBLIMING
SUBLIMITIES
SUBLIMITY
SUBLINE
SUBLINEATION
SUBLINGUA
SUBLINGUAE
SUBLINGUAL
SUBLITTORAL
SUBLOBULAR
SUBLUNAR
SUBLUNARY
SUBLUXATE
SUBLUXATION
SUBMAIN
SUBMAN
SUBMARGINAL
SUBMARGINALLY
SUBMARGINATE
SUBMARGINED
SUBMARINE
SUBMARINED
SUBMARINER
SUBMARINING
SUBMARINISM
SUBMARINIST
SUBMAXILLA
SUBMAXILLAE
SUBMAXILLARY
SUBMAXIMAL
SUBMEDIAL
SUBMEDIAN
SUBMEDIANT
SUBMEN
SUBMENTA
SUBMENTAL
SUBMENTUM
SUBMERGE
SUBMERGED
SUBMERGEMENT
SUBMERGENCE
SUBMERGIBILITY
SUBMERGIBLE
SUBMERGING
SUBMERSE
SUBMERSED
SUBMERSIBILITY
SUBMERSIBLE
SUBMERSION
SUBMETER
SUBMETERING
SUBMICRON
SUBMILIARY
SUBMINIATURE
SUBMINIMAL
SUBMINISTER
SUBMISS
SUBMISSIBLE
SUBMISSION
SUBMISSIONIST
SUBMISSIVE
SUBMISSIVELY
SUBMISSIVENESS
SUBMIT
SUBMITTAL
SUBMITTED
SUBMITTER
SUBMITTING
SUBMONTAGNE
SUBMONTANE
SUBMONTANELY
SUBMORPHOUS
SUBMOTIVE
SUBMUCOSA
SUBMUCOSAE
SUBMUCOSAL
SUBMUCOUS
SUBMULTIPLE
SUBNASAL
SUBNASCENT
SUBNATURAL
SUBNECT
SUBNEURAL
SUBNITRATE
SUBNIVEAL
SUBNIVEAN
SUBNORMAL
SUBNORMALITY
SUBNUBILAR
SUBNUCLEUS
SUBNUVOLAR
SUBOCCIPITAL
SUBOCEANIC
SUBOCTAVE
SUBOCTILE
SUBOCTUPLE
SUBOCULAR
SUBOFFICER
SUBOPERCLE
SUBOPERCULAR
SUBOPERCULUM
SUBOPPOSITE
SUBOPTIMAL
SUBORBITAL
SUBORBITAR
SUBORBITARY
SUBORDAIN
SUBORDER
SUBORDINACY
SUBORDINAL
SUBORDINARY
SUBORDINATE
SUBORDINATED
SUBORDINATELY
SUBORDINATENESS
SUBORDINATING
SUBORDINATION
SUBORDINATIVE
SUBORN

SUBORNATION
SUBORNATIVE
SUBORNED
SUBORNER
SUBORNING
SUBOVAL
SUBOXID
SUBOXIDATION
SUBOXIDE
SUBPASSAGE
SUBPENA
SUBPERMANENT
SUBPETIOLAR
SUBPHRENIC
SUBPHYLAR
SUBPHYLUM
SUBPIAL
SUBPLAT
SUBPLATE
SUBPLEURAL
SUBPLINTH
SUBPLOT
SUBPOENA
SUBPOENAED
SUBPOENAING
SUBPOENAL
SUBPOTENCIES
SUBPOTENCY
SUBPOTENT
SUBPRESS
SUBPRINCIPAL
SUBPRIOR
SUBPUNCH
SUBPURCHASER
SUBPURLIN
SUBQUINTUPLE
SUBRACE
SUBRADIAL
SUBRADIUS
SUBRATIONAL
SUBREADER
SUBREGION
SUBREGIONAL
SUBREGULI
SUBREGULUS
SUBRENT
SUBREPTARY
SUBREPTION
SUBRESIN
SUBRIDENT
SUBRIDENTLY
SUBRISION
SUBRISIVE
SUBRISORY
SUBROGATE
SUBROGATED
SUBROGATING
SUBROGATION
SUBROUND
SUBSARTORIAL
SUBSCALE
SUBSCAPULAR
SUBSCAPULARY
SUBSCLERAL
SUBSCLEROTIC
SUBSCRIBE
SUBSCRIBED
SUBSCRIBER
SUBSCRIBING
SUBSCRIPT
SUBSCRIPTION
SUBSCRIPTIONIST
SUBSCRIPTIVE
SUBSCRIVE
SUBSCRIVER
SUBSEA
SUBSECIVE
SUBSECT
SUBSECTION
SUBSECUTE
SUBSECUTIVE
SUBSEGMENT
SUBSELLA
SUBSELLIA
SUBSELLIUM
SUBSEMIFUSA
SUBSEMITONE
SUBSENSIBLE
SUBSEPTUPLE
SUBSEQUENCE
SUBSEQUENCY
SUBSEQUENT
SUBSEQUENTIAL
SUBSEQUENTIALLY
SUBSEQUENTLY
SUBSEQUENTNESS
SUBSEROSA
SUBSEROUS
SUBSERVE
SUBSERVED
SUBSERVIATE
SUBSERVIENCE
SUBSERVIENCY
SUBSERVIENT
SUBSERVIENTLY
SUBSERVIENTNESS
SUBSERVING
SUBSESQUI
SUBSESSILE
SUBSET
SUBSEXTUPLE
SUBSHRUB
SUBSHRUBBY
SUBSICIVE
SUBSIDE
SUBSIDED
SUBSIDENCE
SUBSIDENCY
SUBSIDENT
SUBSIDER
SUBSIDIARIE
SUBSIDIARIES
SUBSIDIARILY
SUBSIDIARINESS
SUBSIDIARY
SUBSIDIES
SUBSIDING
SUBSIDISE
SUBSIDIST
SUBSIDIUM
SUBSIDIZATION
SUBSIDIZE
SUBSIDIZED
SUBSIDIZER
SUBSIDIZING
SUBSIDY
SUBSIGN
SUBSILICIC
SUBSILL
SUBSIMILATION
SUBSIMPLE
SUBSIST
SUBSISTED
SUBSISTENCE
SUBSISTENCY
SUBSISTENT
SUBSISTER
SUBSISTING
SUBSIZAR
SUBSOIL
SUBSOILER
SUBSOLAR
SUBSONIC
SUBSPACE
SUBSPECIES
SUBSPECIFIC
SUBSPECIFICALLY
SUBSPINOUS
SUBSTAGE
SUBSTANCE
SUBSTANCH
SUBSTANDARD
SUBSTANT
SUBSTANTIA
SUBSTANTIAL
SUBSTANTIALISM
SUBSTANTIALIST
SUBSTANTIALITY
SUBSTANTIALIZE
SUBSTANTIALLY
SUBSTANTIALNESS
SUBSTANTIATE
SUBSTANTIATED
SUBSTANTIATING
SUBSTANTIATION
SUBSTANTIATIVE
SUBSTANTIATOR
SUBSTANTIFY
SUBSTANTIOUS
SUBSTANTIVAL
SUBSTANTIVALLY
SUBSTANTIVE
SUBSTANTIVELY
SUBSTANTIVENESS
SUBSTANTIVITY
SUBSTANTIVIZE
SUBSTANTIVIZED
SUBSTANTIVIZING
SUBSTANTIZE
SUBSTATION
SUBSTILE
SUBSTITUENT
SUBSTITUTE
SUBSTITUTED
SUBSTITUTER
SUBSTITUTING
SUBSTITUTION
SUBSTITUTIONAL
SUBSTITUTIONALLY
SUBSTITUTIVE
SUBSTITUTIVELY
SUBSTORY
SUBSTRAT
SUBSTRATA
SUBSTRATAL
SUBSTRATE
SUBSTRATIVE
SUBSTRATOSE
SUBSTRATUM
SUBSTRATUMS
SUBSTREAM
SUBSTRUCT
SUBSTRUCTION
SUBSTRUCTIONAL
SUBSTRUCTURAL
SUBSTRUCTURE
SUBSTYLAR
SUBSTYLE
SUBSULPHATE
SUBSULT
SUBSULTORILY
SUBSULTORY
SUBSULTUS
SUBSUMABLE
SUBSUME
SUBSUMED
SUBSUMING
SUBSUMPTION
SUBSUMPTIVE
SUBSURFACE
SUBTACK
SUBTACKSMAN
SUBTACKSMEN
SUBTANGENT
SUBTARGET
SUBTARTAREAN
SUBTECTACLE
SUBTECTAL
SUBTEEN
SUBTEGMINAL
SUBTEMPERATE
SUBTENANCY
SUBTENANT
SUBTEND
SUBTENDED
SUBTENDING
SUBTENSE
SUBTENURE
SUBTERFLUENT
SUBTERFLUOUS
SUBTERFUGE
SUBTERHUMAN
SUBTERJACENT
SUBTERMARINE
SUBTERPOSE
SUBTERRANE
SUBTERRANEAL
SUBTERRANEAN
SUBTERRENE
SUBTERRESTRIAL
SUBTHALAMIC
SUBTHALAMUS
SUBTHORACIC
SUBTILE
SUBTILELY
SUBTILENESS
SUBTILIATE
SUBTILIATION
SUBTILIN
SUBTILISM
SUBTILIST
SUBTILITIES
SUBTILITY
SUBTILIZATION
SUBTILIZED
SUBTILIZER
SUBTILIZING
SUBTILTIES
SUBTILTY
SUBTITLE
SUBTITULAR
SUBTLE
SUBTLENESS
SUBTLER
SUBTLEST
SUBTLETIES
SUBTLETY
SUBTLIST
SUBTLY
SUBTONE
SUBTONIC
SUBTORRID
SUBTOTAL
SUBTRACT
SUBTRACTED
SUBTRACTER
SUBTRACTING
SUBTRACTION
SUBTRACTIVE
SUBTRAHEND
SUBTRAY
SUBTREASURER
SUBTREASURIES
SUBTREASURY
SUBTRIBE
SUBTRIST
SUBTROPIC
SUBTROPICAL
SUBTROPICS
SUBTRUDE
SUBTUBERANT
SUBTUNIC
SUBTURBARY
SUBTYPE
SUBTYPICAL
SUBUCULA
SUBULATE
SUBULATED
SUBULICORN
SUBULIFORM
SUBUMBONAL
SUBUMBRAL
SUBUMBRELLA
SUBUMBRELLAR
SUBUNGUAL
SUBUNGUIAL
SUBUNGULATE
SUBURB
SUBURBAN
SUBURBANITE
SUBURBANITIES
SUBURBANITY
SUBURBANIZATION
SUBURBANIZE
SUBURBED
SUBURBIA
SUBURBICAN
SUBURBS
SUBVAGINAL
SUBVALUATION
SUBVARIETAL
SUBVARIETY
SUBVENDEE
SUBVENE
SUBVENED
SUBVENING
SUBVENTION
SUBVENTIONED
SUBVENTIVE
SUBVERSAL
SUBVERSION
SUBVERSIONARY
SUBVERSIVE
SUBVERSIVELY
SUBVERT
SUBVERTED
SUBVERTER
SUBVERTIBLE
SUBVERTING
SUBVIRATE
SUBVIRILE
SUBVISIBLE
SUBVITALIZED
SUBVITREOUS
SUBVOCAL
SUBVOLA
SUBWATER
SUBWAY
SUBWEIGHT
SUBZONAL
SUBZONE
SUCCADE
SUCCAH
SUCCEDANEA
SUCCEDANEOUS
SUCCEDANEUM
SUCCEDANEUMS
SUCCEDENT
SUCCEED
SUCCEEDED
SUCCEEDER
SUCCEEDING
SUCCEEDINGLY
SUCCENT
SUCCENTOR

SUCCESS
SUCCESSFUL
SUCCESSFULLY
SUCCESSFULNESS
SUCCESSION
SUCCESSIONAL
SUCCESSIONALLY
SUCCESSIONIST
SUCCESSIVE
SUCCESSIVELY
SUCCESSIVENESS
SUCCESSIVITY
SUCCESSOR
SUCCESSORAL
SUCCIN
SUCCINAMATE
SUCCINAMIC
SUCCINAMIDE
SUCCINANIL
SUCCINATE
SUCCINCT
SUCCINCTLY
SUCCINCTNESS
SUCCINCTORIA
SUCCINCTURE
SUCCINIC
SUCCINIMID
SUCCINIMIDE
SUCCINITE
SUCCINOUS
SUCCINUM
SUCCINYL
SUCCISE
SUCCOR
SUCCORABLE
SUCCORED
SUCCORER
SUCCORING
SUCCORRHEA
SUCCORRHOEA
SUCCORY
SUCCOSE
SUCCOTASH
SUCCOUR
SUCCOURABLE
SUCCOURED
SUCCOURER
SUCCOURING
SUCCOUS
SUCCUBA
SUCCUBAE
SUCCUBI
SUCCUBINE
SUCCUBOUS
SUCCUBUS
SUCCUBUSES
SUCCUDRY
SUCCULA
SUCCULENCE
SUCCULENCIES
SUCCULENCY
SUCCULENT
SUCCULENTLY
SUCCULENTNESS
SUCCULOUS
SUCCUMB
SUCCUMBED
SUCCUMBENCE
SUCCUMBENCY
SUCCUMBENT
SUCCUMBER
SUCCUMBING
SUCCURSAL
SUCCURSALE
SUCCUS
SUCCUSS
SUCCUSSATION
SUCCUSSATORY
SUCCUSSION
SUCCUSSIVE
SUCH
SUCHLIKE
SUCHNESS
SUCHWISE
SUCK
SUCKABOB
SUCKAUHOCK
SUCKED
SUCKEN
SUCKENER
SUCKER
SUCKERED
SUCKEREL
SUCKERFISH
SUCKERFISHES
SUCKERING
SUCKFISH
SUCKFISHES
SUCKHOLE
SUCKING
SUCKLE
SUCKLEBUSH
SUCKLED
SUCKLER
SUCKLING
SUCKSTONE
SUCLAT
SUCRAMIN
SUCRAMINE
SUCRASE
SUCRATE
SUCRE
SUCRIER
SUCROACID
SUCROSE
SUCTION
SUCTIONAL
SUCTORIAL
SUCTORIAN
SUCTORIOUS
SUCUPIRA
SUCURI
SUCURIU
SUCURUJU
SUCURY
SUD
SUDADERO
SUDAMEN
SUDAMINA
SUDAMINAL
SUDARIA
SUDARIUM
SUDARY
SUDATE
SUDATION
SUDATORIA
SUDATORIES
SUDATORIUM
SUDATORY
SUDBURITE
SUDD
SUDDEN
SUDDENLY
SUDDENNESS
SUDDENTY
SUDDER
SUDDLE
SUDIFORM
SUDOR
SUDORAL
SUDORESIS
SUDORIC
SUDORIFEROUS
SUDORIFIC
SUDORIPAROUS
SUDOROUS
SUDS
SUDSIER
SUDSIEST
SUDSMAN
SUDSMEN
SUDSY
SUE
SUED
SUEDE
SUEDINE
SUENT
SUER
SUERTE
SUET
SUETY
SUFF
SUFFARI
SUFFECT
SUFFECTION
SUFFER
SUFFERABLE
SUFFERABLENESS
SUFFERABLY
SUFFERANCE
SUFFERANT
SUFFERED
SUFFERER
SUFFERING
SUFFERINGLY
SUFFETE
SUFFETES
SUFFICE
SUFFICED
SUFFICER
SUFFICIENCIES
SUFFICIENCY
SUFFICIENT
SUFFICIENTLY
SUFFICIENTNESS
SUFFICING
SUFFICINGLY
SUFFICINGNESS
SUFFICTION
SUFFIX
SUFFIXAL
SUFFIXATION
SUFFIXED
SUFFIXING
SUFFIXION
SUFFIXMENT
SUFFLATE
SUFFLATED
SUFFLATING
SUFFLATION
SUFFLUE
SUFFOCATE
SUFFOCATED
SUFFOCATING
SUFFOCATINGLY
SUFFOCATION
SUFFOCATIVE
SUFFRAGAN
SUFFRAGANAL
SUFFRAGANATE
SUFFRAGANCY
SUFFRAGATORY
SUFFRAGE
SUFFRAGETTE
SUFFRAGIAL
SUFFRAGISM
SUFFRAGIST
SUFFRAGISTIC
SUFFRAGO
SUFFRAIN
SUFFRONT
SUFFRUTEX
SUFFRUTICES
SUFFRUTICOSE
SUFFRUTICOUS
SUFFUMIGATE
SUFFUMIGATED
SUFFUSE
SUFFUSED
SUFFUSEDLY
SUFFUSING
SUFFUSION
SUFFUSIVE
SUG
SUGAMO
SUGAN
SUGANN
SUGAR
SUGARBERRIES
SUGARBERRY
SUGARBIRD
SUGARBUSH
SUGARED
SUGARELLY
SUGARER
SUGARHOUSE
SUGARIES
SUGARINESS
SUGARING
SUGARLESS
SUGARPLATE
SUGARPLUM
SUGARSOP
SUGARSWEET
SUGARWORKS
SUGARY
SUGAT
SUGENT
SUGESCENT
SUGGAN
SUGGEST
SUGGESTA
SUGGESTED
SUGGESTER
SUGGESTIBILITY
SUGGESTIBLE
SUGGESTIBLENESS
SUGGESTIBLY
SUGGESTING
SUGGESTINGLY
SUGGESTION
SUGGESTIVE
SUGGESTIVELY
SUGGESTIVENESS
SUGGESTIVITY
SUGGESTUM
SUGGIL
SUGGILLATE
SUGGILLATION
SUGH
SUGI
SUGSLOOT
SUHA
SUICIDAL
SUICIDALLY
SUICIDE
SUICIDED
SUICIDING
SUICIDISM
SUICISM
SUID
SUIDIAN
SUIFORM
SUIKERBOSCH
SUILINE
SUIMATE
SUING
SUINGLY
SUINT
SUISIMILAR
SUISSE
SUIST
SUIT
SUITABILITY
SUITABLE
SUITABLENESS
SUITABLY
SUITCASE
SUITE
SUITED
SUITHOLD
SUITING
SUITLY
SUITOR
SUITORESS
SUITY
SUIVANTE
SUIVEZ
SUJEE
SUJI
SUK
SUKIYAKI
SUKKAH
SUKKENYE
SUL
SULBASUTRA
SULCAL
SULCALIZATION
SULCALIZE
SULCATE
SULCATED
SULCATION
SULCI
SULCIFORM
SULCULAR
SULCULATE
SULCULUS
SULCUS
SULD
SULEA
SULFA
SULFACID
SULFADIAZINE
SULFAMATE
SULFAMIC
SULFAMIDATE
SULFAMIDE
SULFAMIDIC
SULFAMINE
SULFAMINIC
SULFAMYL
SULFANILIC
SULFARSENIDE
SULFARSENITE
SULFATASE
SULFATE
SULFATED
SULFATIC
SULFATING
SULFATIZE
SULFATIZED
SULFATIZING
SULFATO
SULFAZIDE
SULFHYDRATE
SULFHYDRIC
SULFHYDRYL
SULFID
SULFIDE
SULFINATE
SULFINDYLIC
SULFINE
SULFINIC
SULFINIDE
SULFINYL

SULFION
SULFIONIDE
SULFITE
SULFITIC
SULFITO
SULFOACID
SULFOAMIDE
SULFOBENZIDE
SULFOBENZOIC
SULFOBORITE
SULFOCYAN
SULFOCYANIDE
SULFOHALITE
SULFOHYDRATE
SULFOLEIC
SULFOLYSIS
SULFONAL
SULFONAMIC
SULFONAMIDE
SULFONATE
SULFONATED
SULFONATING
SULFONATION
SULFONATOR
SULFONE
SULFONIC
SULFONIUM
SULFONYL
SULFORICINIC
SULFOUREA
SULFOVINATE
SULFOVINIC
SULFOXIDE
SULFOXISM
SULFOXYLATE
SULFOXYLIC
SULFUR
SULFURAGE
SULFURAN
SULFURATE
SULFURATION
SULFURATOR
SULFUREA
SULFURED
SULFUREOUS
SULFUREOUSLY
SULFURET
SULFURET
SULFURETED
SULFURETING
SULFURETTED
SULFURETTING
SULFURIC
SULFURING
SULFURIZE
SULFURIZED
SULFURIZING
SULFUROSYL
SULFUROUS
SULFURY
SULFURYL
SULK
SULKA
SULKED
SULKER
SULKIER
SULKIES
SULKIEST
SULKILY
SULKINESS
SULKING
SULKS
SULKY
SULL
SULLA
SULLAGE
SULLEN
SULLENLY
SULLENNESS
SULLENS
SULLIED
SULLIES
SULLOW
SULLY
SULLYING
SULPHA
SULPHACID
SULPHAMATE
SULPHAMIC
SULPHAMID
SULPHAMIDATE
SULPHAMIDE
SULPHAMIDIC
SULPHAMIN
SULPHAMINE
SULPHAMINIC
SULPHAMINO
SULPHAMYL
SULPHANILIC
SULPHARSENIC
SULPHARSENID
SULPHATASE
SULPHATE
SULPHATED
SULPHATIC
SULPHATING
SULPHATION
SULPHATIZE
SULPHATIZED
SULPHATIZING
SULPHATO
SULPHAZID
SULPHAZIDE
SULPHAZOTIZE
SULPHETHYLIC
SULPHID
SULPHIDATION
SULPHIDE
SULPHIDIC
SULPHIDIZE
SULPHIMIDE
SULPHIN
SULPHINATE
SULPHINE
SULPHINIC
SULPHINIDE
SULPHINYL
SULPHITATION
SULPHITE
SULPHITIC
SULPHITO
SULPHO
SULPHOBENZID
SULPHOBORITE
SULPHOCYAN
SULPHOCYANIC
SULPHOFY
SULPHOGALLIC
SULPHOGEL
SULPHOHALITE
SULPHOHALOID
SULPHOLEATE
SULPHOLIPIN
SULPHOLYSIS
SULPHONAL
SULPHONALISM
SULPHONAMID
SULPHONAMIDE
SULPHONAMIDO
SULPHONAMINE
SULPHONATE
SULPHONATED
SULPHONATING
SULPHONATION
SULPHONATOR
SULPHONE
SULPHONIC
SULPHONIUM
SULPHONYL
SULPHOPHENYL
SULPHOSOL
SULPHOTANNIC
SULPHOTOLUIC
SULPHOUREA
SULPHOVINATE
SULPHOVINIC
SULPHOXID
SULPHOXIDE
SULPHOXISM
SULPHOXYLIC
SULPHUR
SULPHURAGE
SULPHURAN
SULPHURATE
SULPHURATED
SULPHURATING
SULPHURATION
SULPHURATOR
SULPHUREA
SULPHURED
SULPHUREITY
SULPHUREOUS
SULPHURET
SULPHURETED
SULPHURETING
SULPHURETTED
SULPHURETTING
SULPHURIC
SULPHURING
SULPHURIZE
SULPHURIZED
SULPHURIZING
SULPHUROSYL
SULPHUROUS
SULPHUROUSLY
SULPHURWEED
SULPHURWORT
SULPHURY
SULPHURYL
SULPHYDRATE
SULPHYDRYL
SULTAM
SULTAN
SULTANA
SULTANATE
SULTANE
SULTANESS
SULTANIC
SULTANIN
SULTANISM
SULTANIST
SULTANIZE
SULTANSHIP
SULTANY
SULTONE
SULTRIER
SULTRIEST
SULTRILY
SULTRINESS
SULTRY
SULUNG
SULVANITE
SULVASUTRA
SUM
SUMAC
SUMACH
SUMAGE
SUMBAL
SUMBUL
SUMBULIC
SUMEN
SUMI
SUMLESS
SUMLESSNESS
SUMMA
SUMMABILITY
SUMMABLE
SUMMAE
SUMMAGE
SUMMAND
SUMMAR
SUMMARIES
SUMMARILY
SUMMARINESS
SUMMARISE
SUMMARIST
SUMMARIZATION
SUMMARIZE
SUMMARIZED
SUMMARIZER
SUMMARIZING
SUMMARY
SUMMAT
SUMMATE
SUMMATED
SUMMATING
SUMMATION
SUMMATIONAL
SUMMATIVE
SUMMATORY
SUMMED
SUMMER
SUMMERBIRD
SUMMERCASTLE
SUMMERED
SUMMERER
SUMMERGAME
SUMMERHEAD
SUMMERHOUSE
SUMMERING
SUMMERINGS
SUMMERLAND
SUMMERLAY
SUMMERLINESS
SUMMERLING
SUMMERLY
SUMMERROOM
SUMMERSAULT
SUMMERSET
SUMMERTIDE
SUMMERTIME
SUMMERWARD
SUMMERWOOD
SUMMERY
SUMMING
SUMMIST
SUMMIT
SUMMITAL
SUMMITLESS
SUMMITRY
SUMMITY
SUMMON
SUMMONED
SUMMONER
SUMMONING
SUMMONS
SUMMONSED
SUMMONSES
SUMMONSING
SUMMULA
SUMMULAE
SUMMULIST
SUMNER
SUMP
SUMPAGE
SUMPER
SUMPH
SUMPHISH
SUMPHISHLY
SUMPHISHNESS
SUMPHY
SUMPIT
SUMPITAN
SUMPLE
SUMPMAN
SUMPSIMUS
SUMPT
SUMPTER
SUMPTION
SUMPTUARY
SUMPTUOSITY
SUMPTUOUS
SUMPTUOUSLY
SUMPTUOUSNESS
SUMPTURE
SUMPWEED
SUN
SUNBATHER
SUNBATHING
SUNBEAM
SUNBEAMED
SUNBEAMY
SUNBERRY
SUNBIRD
SUNBLIND
SUNBLINK
SUNBONNET
SUNBOW
SUNBREAK
SUNBURN
SUNBURNED
SUNBURNING
SUNBURNT
SUNBURNTNESS
SUNBURST
SUNCHERCHOR
SUNCK
SUNCKE
SUNCUP
SUNDAE
SUNDANG
SUNDARI
SUNDER
SUNDERANCE
SUNDERED
SUNDERER
SUNDERING
SUNDERLY
SUNDERMENT
SUNDEW
SUNDIAL
SUNDIK
SUNDOG
SUNDOWN
SUNDOWNER
SUNDOWNING
SUNDRESS
SUNDRI
SUNDRIES
SUNDRILY
SUNDRINESS
SUNDROPS
SUNDRY
SUNDRYMAN
SUNDRYMEN
SUNFALL
SUNFAST
SUNFISH
SUNFISHER
SUNFISHERY
SUNFISHES
SUNFLOWER
SUNFOIL
SUNG
SUNGAR

SUNGLADE
SUNGLASS
SUNGLASSES
SUNGLO
SUNGLOW
SUNK
SUNKE
SUNKEN
SUNKET
SUNKIE
SUNKLAND
SUNLAMP
SUNLAND
SUNLESS
SUNLESSNESS
SUNLET
SUNLIGHT
SUNLIGHTED
SUNLIT
SUNN
SUNNA
SUNNED
SUNNIER
SUNNIEST
SUNNILY
SUNNINESS
SUNNING
SUNNUD
SUNNY
SUNNYASEE
SUNNYHEARTED
SUNPROOF
SUNQUAKE
SUNRAY
SUNRISE
SUNRISING
SUNROOM
SUNROSE
SUNSCALD
SUNSCORCH
SUNSET
SUNSETTING
SUNSETTY
SUNSHADE
SUNSHINE
SUNSHINY
SUNSMIT
SUNSMITTEN
SUNSPOT
SUNSPOTTED
SUNSPOTTERY
SUNSPOTTY
SUNSQUALL
SUNSTAY
SUNSTEAD
SUNSTONE
SUNSTRICKEN
SUNSTROKE
SUNSTRUCK
SUNT
SUNTAN
SUNTANS
SUNUP
SUNWARD
SUNWARDS
SUNWAYS
SUNWEED
SUNWISE
SUNYATA
SUNYIE
SUP
SUPA
SUPARI
SUPAWN
SUPE
SUPELLECTILE
SUPELLEX
SUPER
SUPERABILITY
SUPERABLE
SUPERABLY
SUPERABOUND
SUPERABUNDANCE
SUPERABUNDANT
SUPERABUNDANTLY
SUPERACID
SUPERADD
SUPERALBAL
SUPERALTAR
SUPERANAL
SUPERANNATE
SUPERANNUATE
SUPERANNUATED
SUPERANNUATING
SUPERARCTIC
SUPERATE
SUPERAURAL
SUPERAVIT
SUPERB
SUPERBIOUS
SUPERBITY
SUPERBLY
SUPERBNESS
SUPERBOMB
SUPERCARGO
SUPERCARGOES
SUPERCARGOS
SUPERCARPAL
SUPERCARRIER
SUPERCENTRAL
SUPERCHARGE
SUPERCHARGED
SUPERCHARGER
SUPERCHARGING
SUPERCILIA
SUPERCILIARY
SUPERCILIOUS
SUPERCILIOUSLY
SUPERCILIOUSNESS
SUPERCILIUM
SUPERCLASS
SUPERCOMBING
SUPERCONSCIOUS
SUPERCONSCIOUSNESS
SUPERCOOL
SUPERCRUST
SUPERDUPER
SUPERDURAL
SUPEREDIFY
SUPEREGO
SUPEREMINENT
SUPEREROGANT
SUPEREROGATE
SUPEREXIST
SUPERFAMILY
SUPERFAT
SUPERFECTA
SUPERFEMALE
SUPERFETATE
SUPERFETATED
SUPERFICIAL
SUPERFICIALISM
SUPERFICIALIST
SUPERFICIALITIES
SUPERFICIALITY
SUPERFICIALIZE
SUPERFICIALLY
SUPERFICIALNESS
SUPERFICIARIES
SUPERFICIARY
SUPERFICIES
SUPERFINE
SUPERFINISH
SUPERFIX
SUPERFLEXION
SUPERFLUENT
SUPERFLUID
SUPERFLUITIES
SUPERFLUITY
SUPERFLUOUS
SUPERFLUOUSLY
SUPERFLUOUSNESS
SUPERFLUX
SUPERFRONTAL
SUPERFUSE
SUPERFUSED
SUPERFUSING
SUPERFUSION
SUPERGENE
SUPERGENERIC
SUPERGENUAL
SUPERGLACIAL
SUPERGLOTTAL
SUPERHEAT
SUPERHEATED
SUPERHEATER
SUPERHEATING
SUPERHIGHWAY
SUPERHUMAN
SUPERHUMANLY
SUPERHUMERAL
SUPERI
SUPERIAL
SUPERIMPOSE
SUPERIMPOSED
SUPERIMPOSING
SUPERIMPOSITION
SUPERIMPOSURE
SUPERINDUCE
SUPERINDUCED
SUPERINDUCING
SUPERINDUCT
SUPERINDUE
SUPERINFUSE
SUPERINTEND
SUPERINTENDED
SUPERINTENDENCE
SUPERINTENDENCY
SUPERINTENDENT
SUPERINTENDING
SUPERIOR
SUPERIORESS
SUPERIORITY
SUPERIORLY
SUPERIUS
SUPERJACENT
SUPERLABIAL
SUPERLATION
SUPERLATIVE
SUPERLATIVELY
SUPERLATIVENESS
SUPERLUNAR
SUPERLUNARY
SUPERMALE
SUPERMAN
SUPERMANLY
SUPERMARINE
SUPERMARKET
SUPERMAXILLA
SUPERMEDIAL
SUPERMEN
SUPERMUSCAN
SUPERNACULAR
SUPERNACULUM
SUPERNAL
SUPERNALLY
SUPERNATANT
SUPERNATURAL
SUPERNATURALIST
SUPERNATURALIZE
SUPERNATURALLY
SUPERNATURALNESS
SUPERNATURE
SUPERNORMAL
SUPERNOVA
SUPERNOVAE
SUPERNOVAS
SUPEROCTAVE
SUPEROCULAR
SUPERODORSAL
SUPERORBITAL
SUPERORDER
SUPERORDINAL
SUPERORDINATE
SUPERORDINATION
SUPERORGANIC
SUPERPARTICULAR
SUPERPHYSICAL
SUPERPLANT
SUPERPLUS
SUPERPOSABLE
SUPERPOSE
SUPERPOSED
SUPERPOSING
SUPERPOSITION
SUPERPOWER
SUPERPOWERED
SUPERRENAL
SUPERROYAL
SUPERSACRAL
SUPERSALIENCY
SUPERSALIENT
SUPERSALT
SUPERSATURATE
SUPERSATURATED
SUPERSATURATING
SUPERSATURATION
SUPERSCRIBE
SUPERSCRIBED
SUPERSCRIBING
SUPERSCRIPT
SUPERSCRIPTION
SUPERSEDE
SUPERSEDEAS
SUPERSEDED
SUPERSEDENCE
SUPERSEDER
SUPERSEDERE
SUPERSEDING
SUPERSEDURE
SUPERSENSIBLE
SUPERSENSIBLY
SUPERSENSORY
SUPERSENSUAL
SUPERSEPTAL
SUPERSESSION
SUPERSESSIVE
SUPERSEX
SUPERSEXUAL
SUPERSISTENT
SUPERSOCIAL
SUPERSOLID
SUPERSONANT
SUPERSONIC
SUPERSONICS
SUPERSTATE
SUPERSTITION
SUPERSTITIONIST
SUPERSTITIOUS
SUPERSTITIOUSLY
SUPERSTITIOUSNESS
SUPERSTRATA
SUPERSTRATUM
SUPERSTRUCT
SUPERSTRUCTED
SUPERSTRUCTING
SUPERSTRUCTION
SUPERSTRUCTIVE
SUPERSTRUCTOR
SUPERSTRUCTORY
SUPERSTRUCTRAL
SUPERSTRUCTURE
SUPERSUBTLE
SUPERTAX
SUPERTERRENE
SUPERTONIC
SUPERTUNIC
SUPERVENE
SUPERVENED
SUPERVENIENT
SUPERVENING
SUPERVENTION
SUPERVISAL
SUPERVISANCE
SUPERVISE
SUPERVISED
SUPERVISING
SUPERVISION
SUPERVISIONARY
SUPERVISIVE
SUPERVISOR
SUPERVISORY
SUPERVISURE
SUPERVOLUTE
SUPERWEENING
SUPINATE
SUPINATED
SUPINATING
SUPINATION
SUPINATOR
SUPINE
SUPINELY
SUPINENESS
SUPPABLE
SUPPAGE
SUPPED
SUPPEDANEA
SUPPEDANEOUS
SUPPEDANEUM
SUPPEDIT
SUPPER
SUPPERING
SUPPERLESS
SUPPERTIME
SUPPERWARD
SUPPERWARDS
SUPPING
SUPPLACE
SUPPLANT
SUPPLANTED
SUPPLANTER
SUPPLANTING
SUPPLE
SUPPLED
SUPPLEJACK
SUPPLELY
SUPPLEMENT
SUPPLEMENTAL
SUPPLEMENTARY
SUPPLEMENTATION
SUPPLEMENTED
SUPPLEMENTER
SUPPLEMENTING
SUPPLENESS
SUPPLER
SUPPLETORIES
SUPPLETORILY
SUPPLETORY
SUPPLIAL
SUPPLIANCE
SUPPLIANCY
SUPPLIANT
SUPPLIANTLY
SUPPLIANTNESS
SUPPLICANCY

SUPPLICANT
SUPPLICANTLY
SUPPLICAT
SUPPLICATE
SUPPLICATED
SUPPLICATING
SUPPLICATION
SUPPLICATOR
SUPPLICATORY
SUPPLICAVIT
SUPPLICE
SUPPLIED
SUPPLIER
SUPPLIES
SUPPLING
SUPPLY
SUPPLYING
SUPPONE
SUPPORT
SUPPORTABILITY
SUPPORTABLE
SUPPORTABLENES
SUPPORTABLY
SUPPORTANCE
SUPPORTASSE
SUPPORTED
SUPPORTER
SUPPORTING
SUPPORTINGLY
SUPPORTIVE
SUPPOSABLE
SUPPOSABLENESS
SUPPOSABLY
SUPPOSAL
SUPPOSE
SUPPOSED
SUPPOSEDLY
SUPPOSER
SUPPOSING
SUPPOSITAL
SUPPOSITION
SUPPOSITIONAL
SUPPOSITITIOUS
SUPPOSITIVE
SUPPOSITIVELY
SUPPOSITORIES
SUPPOSITORY
SUPPOSITUM
SUPPOST
SUPPRESS
SUPPRESSAL
SUPPRESSED
SUPPRESSEDLY
SUPPRESSER
SUPPRESSIBLE
SUPPRESSING
SUPPRESSION
SUPPRESSIVE
SUPPRESSIVELY
SUPPRESSOR
SUPPRIME
SUPPRISE
SUPPURANT
SUPPURATE
SUPPURATED
SUPPURATING
SUPPURATION
SUPPURATIVE
SUPPUTE
SUPRA
SUPRABUCCAL
SUPRACAECAL
SUPRACAUDAL
SUPRACILIARY
SUPRACLAVICLE
SUPRACLUSION
SUPRACOSTAL
SUPRACOXAL
SUPRACRANIAL
SUPRADENTAL
SUPRADORSAL
SUPRADURAL
SUPRAFINE
SUPRAFOLIAR
SUPRAGLACIAL
SUPRAGLENOID
SUPRAGLOTTIC
SUPRAHEPATIC
SUPRAHUMAN
SUPRAHUMANITY
SUPRAILIAC
SUPRAILIUM
SUPRAJURAL
SUPRALABIAL
SUPRALATERAL
SUPRALEGAL
SUPRALIMINAL
SUPRALINEAL
SUPRALINEAR
SUPRALOCAL
SUPRALOCALLY
SUPRALORAL
SUPRALUNAR
SUPRALUNARY
SUPRAMAMMARY
SUPRAMARINE
SUPRAMASTOID
SUPRAMAXILLA
SUPRAMAXIMAL
SUPRAMEATAL
SUPRAMEDIAL
SUPRAMENTAL
SUPRAMORAL
SUPRAMORTAL
SUPRAMUNDANE
SUPRANASAL
SUPRANATIONAL
SUPRANATURAL
SUPRANATURE
SUPRANERVIAN
SUPRANEURAL
SUPRANORMAL
SUPRANUCLEAR
SUPRAOCULAR
SUPRAOPTIMAL
SUPRAOPTIONAL
SUPRAORAL
SUPRAORBITAL
SUPRAORBITAR
SUPRAORDINARY
SUPRAPEDAL
SUPRAPROTEST
SUPRAPUBIAN
SUPRAPUBIC
SUPRAPYGAL
SUPRARATIONAL
SUPRARENAL
SUPRARENALIN
SUPRARENIN
SUPRARENINE
SUPRARIMAL
SUPRASCAPULA
SUPRASCRIPT
SUPRASENSUAL
SUPRASEPTAL
SUPRASOLAR
SUPRASPINAL
SUPRASPINATE
SUPRASPINOUS
SUPRASTATE
SUPRASTERNAL
SUPRASTIGMAL
SUPRASUBTLE
SUPRAVAGINAL
SUPRAVERSION
SUPRAVITAL
SUPRAWORLD
SUPREMACIES
SUPREMACY
SUPREME
SUPREMELY
SUPREMENESS
SUPREMITY
SUPTION
SUQ
SUR
SURA
SURADDITION
SURAH
SURAHEE
SURAHI
SURAL
SURAMIN
SURANAL
SURANGULAR
SURAT
SURBASE
SURBASED
SURBASEMENT
SURBATE
SURBATER
SURBED
SURBEDDED
SURBEDDING
SURCEASE
SURCEASED
SURCEASING
SURCHARGE
SURCHARGED
SURCHARGER
SURCHARGING
SURCINGLE
SURCINGLED
SURCINGLING
SURCLE
SURCLOY
SURCOAT
SURCRUE
SURCULI
SURCULOSE
SURCULOUS
SURCULUS
SURD
SURDATION
SURDENT
SURDIMUTISM
SURDITY
SURDOMUTE
SURE
SUREFIRE
SURELY
SUREMENT
SURENESS
SURER
SURES
SURESBY
SUREST
SURETIES
SURETTE
SURETY
SURETYSHIP
SURF
SURFACE
SURFACED
SURFACEDLY
SURFACELESS
SURFACELY
SURFACEMAN
SURFACEMEN
SURFACER
SURFACING
SURFACTANT
SURFACY
SURFBIRD
SURFBOARD
SURFBOARDING
SURFBOAT
SURFBOATMAN
SURFCASTER
SURFCASTING
SURFEIT
SURFEITED
SURFEITER
SURFEITING
SURFER
SURFICIAL
SURFING
SURFLE
SURFMAN
SURFMANSHIP
SURFMEN
SURFRAPPE
SURFRIDING
SURFUSE
SURFUSION
SURFY
SURGE
SURGED
SURGENCY
SURGENT
SURGEON
SURGEONCIES
SURGEONCY
SURGEONFISH
SURGEONFISHES
SURGER
SURGERIES
SURGERIZE
SURGERY
SURGICAL
SURGICALLY
SURGIER
SURGIEST
SURGING
SURGY
SURHAI
SURICAT
SURICATE
SURIGA
SURINAMINE
SURIQUE
SURLIER
SURLIEST
SURLILY
SURLINESS
SURLY
SURMA
SURMARK
SURMASTER
SURMENAGE
SURMISAL
SURMISANT
SURMISE
SURMISED
SURMISEDLY
SURMISER
SURMISING
SURMIT
SURMOUNT
SURMOUNTABLE
SURMOUNTAL
SURMOUNTED
SURMOUNTER
SURMOUNTING
SURMULLET
SURMULLETS
SURN
SURNAI
SURNAME
SURNAMED
SURNAMER
SURNAMING
SURNAP
SURNAPE
SURNAY
SURNOMINAL
SURNOUN
SURPASS
SURPASSABLE
SURPASSED
SURPASSER
SURPASSING
SURPASSINGLY
SURPASSINGNESS
SURPHUL
SURPLICE
SURPLICED
SURPLICIAN
SURPLUS
SURPLUSAGE
SURPLUSES
SURPOOSE
SURPRINT
SURPRISABLE
SURPRISAL
SURPRISE
SURPRISED
SURPRISEDLY
SURPRISEMENT
SURPRISER
SURPRISING
SURPRISINGLY
SURPRISINGNESS
SURPRIZAL
SURQUEDRY
SURQUIDRY
SURQUIDY
SURRA
SURRAH
SURREALISM
SURREALIST
SURREALISTIC
SURREALISTICALLY
SURREBOUND
SURREBUT
SURREBUTTAL
SURREBUTTER
SURRECTION
SURREIN
SURREJOIN
SURREJOINDER
SURRENDER
SURRENDERED
SURRENDEREE
SURRENDERER
SURRENDERING
SURRENDEROR
SURREPT
SURREPTION
SURREPTITIOUS
SURREPTITIOUSLY
SURREPTITIOUSNESS
SURREVERENCE
SURREY
SURROGATE
SURROGATED
SURROGATING
SURROGATION
SURROSION
SURROUND
SURROUNDED
SURROUNDEDLY
SURROUNDER
SURROUNDING
SURROYAL

SURSISE
SURSIZE
SURSOLID
SURSTYLE
SURTAX
SURTAXED
SURTAXING
SURTOUT
SURTURBRAND
SURUCUCU
SURVEILLANCE
SURVEILLANT
SURVEY
SURVEYAGE
SURVEYAL
SURVEYANCE
SURVEYED
SURVEYING
SURVEYOR
SURVEYORSHIP
SURVIEW
SURVIGROUS
SURVISE
SURVIVAL
SURVIVALISM
SURVIVALIST
SURVIVANCE
SURVIVANCY
SURVIVE
SURVIVED
SURVIVER
SURVIVING
SURVIVOR
SURVIVORSHIP
SUSANEE
SUSCEPT
SUSCEPTANCE
SUSCEPTIBILITY
SUSCEPTIBLE
SUSCEPTIBLENESS
SUSCEPTIBLY
SUSCEPTION
SUSCEPTIVE
SUSCEPTIVENESS
SUSCEPTIVITY
SUSCEPTOR
SUSCITATE
SUSCITATION
SUSCITE
SUSI
SUSLIK
SUSOTOXIN
SUSPECT
SUSPECTED
SUSPECTEDNESS
SUSPECTER
SUSPECTFUL
SUSPECTFULNESS
SUSPECTING
SUSPECTOR
SUSPEND
SUSPENDED
SUSPENDER
SUSPENDIBILITY
SUSPENDIBLE
SUSPENDING
SUSPENSATION
SUSPENSE
SUSPENSION
SUSPENSIVE
SUSPENSIVELY
SUSPENSIVENESS
SUSPENSOID
SUSPENSOR
SUSPENSORIA
SUSPENSORIAL
SUSPENSORIUM
SUSPENSORY
SUSPICION
SUSPICIONAL
SUSPICIOUS
SUSPICIOUSLY
SUSPICIOUSNESS
SUSPIRAL
SUSPIRATION
SUSPIRATIOUS
SUSPIRATIVE
SUSPIRE
SUSPIRED
SUSPIRING
SUSPIRIOUS
SUSS
SUSSEXITE
SUSSULTATORY
SUSSULTORIAL
SUSSY
SUSTAIN
SUSTAINABLE
SUSTAINED
SUSTAINEDLY
SUSTAINER
SUSTAINING
SUSTAININGLY
SUSTAINMENT
SUSTENANCE
SUSTENANT
SUSTENTATE
SUSTENTATION
SUSTENTATIVE
SUSTENTATOR
SUSTENTION
SUSTENTIVE
SUSTENTOR
SUSTINENT
SUSU
SUSURR
SUSURRANT
SUSURRATE
SUSURRATED
SUSURRATING
SUSURRATION
SUSURRINGLY
SUSURROUS
SUSURRUS
SUTE
SUTEL
SUTERBERRIES
SUTERBERRY
SUTHER
SUTILE
SUTLER
SUTLERAGE
SUTLERSHIP
SUTLERY
SUTOR
SUTORIAL
SUTORIAN
SUTORIOUS
SUTRA
SUTRAS
SUTTA
SUTTEE
SUTTEEISM
SUTTER
SUTTLE
SUTURAL
SUTURALLY
SUTURATION
SUTURE
SUTURED
SUTURING
SUUM
SUWAR
SUWARRO
SUZ
SUZERAIN
SUZERAINTY
SUZU
SVABITE
SVAMI
SVAMIN
SVARABHAKTI
SVARABHAKTIC
SVARAJ
SVASTIKA
SVEDBERG
SVELT
SVELTE
SVIATONOSITE
SWAB
SWABBED
SWABBER
SWABBERLY
SWABBING
SWABBLE
SWABBY
SWACK
SWACKED
SWACKEN
SWACKING
SWAD
SWADDER
SWADDISH
SWADDLE
SWADDLEBILL
SWADDLED
SWADDLER
SWADDLING
SWADDY
SWADE
SWAG
SWAGBELLIED
SWAGBELLIES
SWAGBELLY
SWAGE
SWAGED
SWAGER
SWAGGED
SWAGGER
SWAGGERED
SWAGGERER
SWAGGERING
SWAGGERINGLY
SWAGGIE
SWAGGING
SWAGGY
SWAGING
SWAGMAN
SWAGMEN
SWAGSMAN
SWAGSMEN
SWAIL
SWAIMOUS
SWAIN
SWAINISH
SWAINISHNESS
SWAINMOTE
SWAIRD
SWAK
SWALE
SWALER
SWALING
SWALINGLY
SWALLET
SWALLO
SWALLOW
SWALLOWABLE
SWALLOWED
SWALLOWER
SWALLOWING
SWALLOWPIPE
SWALLOWS
SWALLOWTAIL
SWALLOWWORT
SWAM
SWAMI
SWAMIS
SWAMP
SWAMPABLE
SWAMPBERRIES
SWAMPBERRY
SWAMPED
SWAMPER
SWAMPHEN
SWAMPIER
SWAMPIEST
SWAMPINE
SWAMPING
SWAMPISH
SWAMPISHNESS
SWAMPLAND
SWAMPWEED
SWAMPWOOD
SWAMPY
SWAMY
SWAN
SWANFLOWER
SWANG
SWANGY
SWANHERD
SWANIMOTE
SWANK
SWANKER
SWANKEY
SWANKIE
SWANKIER
SWANKIEST
SWANKILY
SWANKINESS
SWANKING
SWANKY
SWANLIKE
SWANMARK
SWANMARKER
SWANMARKING
SWANMOTE
SWANNECK
SWANNECKED
SWANNERIES
SWANNERY
SWANNET
SWANNISH
SWANNY
SWANPAN
SWANS
SWANSDOWN
SWANSKIN
SWANWEED
SWANWORT
SWAP
SWAPE
SWAPPED
SWAPPER
SWAPPING
SWARAJ
SWARAJISM
SWARAJIST
SWARBIE
SWARD
SWARDED
SWARDING
SWARDY
SWARE
SWARF
SWARGA
SWARM
SWARMED
SWARMER
SWARMING
SWARMY
SWART
SWARTBACK
SWARTH
SWARTHIER
SWARTHIEST
SWARTHILY
SWARTHINESS
SWARTHNESS
SWARTHY
SWARTISH
SWARTNESS
SWARTRUTTER
SWARTRUTTING
SWARTY
SWARVE
SWASH
SWASHBUCKLE
SWASHBUCKLER
SWASHBUCKLING
SWASHED
SWASHER
SWASHING
SWASHINGLY
SWASHWAY
SWASHWORK
SWASHY
SWASTICA
SWASTIKA
SWAT
SWATCH
SWATCHER
SWATH
SWATHE
SWATHED
SWATHER
SWATHING
SWATHY
SWATS
SWATTED
SWATTER
SWATTING
SWATTLE
SWAVER
SWAY
SWAYBACK
SWAYED
SWAYER
SWAYING
SWAYINGLY
SWAYLESS
SWEAL
SWEAM
SWEAR
SWEARER
SWEARING
SWEARINGLY
SWEARWORD
SWEAT
SWEATBAND
SWEATBOX
SWEATED
SWEATER
SWEATFUL
SWEATH
SWEATHOUSE
SWEATIER
SWEATIEST
SWEATILY
SWEATINESS
SWEATING
SWEATS
SWEATSHOP
SWEATWEED
SWEATY
SWEB

SWEDE
SWEDGE
SWEDGER
SWEDRU
SWEE
SWEEK
SWEEL
SWEENS
SWEENY
SWEEP
SWEEPAGE
SWEEPBACK
SWEEPBOARD
SWEEPDOM
SWEEPER
SWEEPING
SWEEPINGLY
SWEEPINGNESS
SWEEPSTAKE
SWEEPSTAKES
SWEEPUP
SWEEPWASHER
SWEEPY
SWEER
SWEERT
SWEESWEE
SWEET
SWEETBERRY
SWEETBREAD
SWEETBRIAR
SWEETBRIER
SWEETBRIERY
SWEETCLOVER
SWEETEN
SWEETENED
SWEETENER
SWEETENING
SWEETER
SWEETEST
SWEETFISH
SWEETFUL
SWEETHEART
SWEETHEARTING
SWEETIE
SWEETING
SWEETISH
SWEETISHLY
SWEETISHNESS
SWEETLEAF
SWEETLY
SWEETMAKER
SWEETMEAT
SWEETNESS
SWEETROOT
SWEETS
SWEETSHOP
SWEETSOP
SWEETWATER
SWEETWEED
SWEETWOOD
SWEETWORT
SWEETY
SWEGO
SWELCHIE
SWELL
SWELLAGE
SWELLDOM
SWELLDOODLE
SWELLED
SWELLER
SWELLFISH
SWELLFISHES
SWELLING
SWELLISH
SWELLISHNESS
SWELLMOBSMAN
SWELLNESS
SWELLTOAD
SWELLY
SWELP
SWELT
SWELTER
SWELTERED
SWELTERING
SWELTERINGLY
SWELTH
SWELTRY
SWELTY
SWEPE
SWEPT
SWEPTBACK
SWEPTWING
SWERVE
SWERVED
SWERVER
SWERVILY
SWERVING
SWEVEN
SWEYN
SWICH
SWICK
SWIDDEN
SWIDGE
SWIFT
SWIFTEN
SWIFTER
SWIFTEST
SWIFTFOOT
SWIFTLET
SWIFTLIER
SWIFTLIEST
SWIFTLY
SWIFTNESS
SWIFTY
SWIG
SWIGGED
SWIGGER
SWIGGING
SWIGGLE
SWIKE
SWILE
SWILK
SWILKIE
SWILL
SWILLBOWL
SWILLED
SWILLER
SWILLING
SWILLTUB
SWIM
SWIMBEL
SWIMMER
SWIMMERET
SWIMMING
SWIMMINGLY
SWIMMIST
SWIMMY
SWIMSUIT
SWIMY
SWINDLE
SWINDLED
SWINDLER
SWINDLERS
SWINDLERY
SWINDLING
SWINE
SWINEBREAD
SWINECOTE
SWINEHEAD
SWINEHERD
SWINEHERDSHIP
SWINEHULL
SWINELY
SWINEPIPE
SWINEPOX
SWINERY
SWINESTONE
SWINESTY
SWINEY
SWING
SWINGBACK
SWINGDEVIL
SWINGDINGLE
SWINGE
SWINGED
SWINGEING
SWINGEINGLY
SWINGEL
SWINGEOUR
SWINGER
SWINGING
SWINGINGLY
SWINGKNIFE
SWINGLE
SWINGLEBAR
SWINGLED
SWINGLETAIL
SWINGLETREE
SWINGLING
SWINGMAN
SWINGSTOCK
SWINGTREE
SWINGY
SWINISH
SWINISHLY
SWINISHNESS
SWINK
SWINKER
SWINKING
SWINNEY
SWIP
SWIPE
SWIPED
SWIPES
SWIPING
SWIPLE
SWIPPER
SWIPPLE
SWIPY
SWIRE
SWIRL
SWIRLED
SWIRLING
SWIRLY
SWIRRING
SWISH
SWISHED
SWISHER
SWISHING
SWISHINGLY
SWISHY
SWISS
SWISSING
SWITCH
SWITCHBACK
SWITCHBACKER
SWITCHBOARD
SWITCHED
SWITCHEL
SWITCHER
SWITCHGEAR
SWITCHING
SWITCHKEEPER
SWITCHLIKE
SWITCHMAN
SWITCHMEN
SWITCHTAIL
SWITCHY
SWITCHYARD
SWITH
SWITHE
SWITHEN
SWITHER
SWITHLY
SWIVE
SWIVEL
SWIVELED
SWIVELEYE
SWIVELEYED
SWIVELING
SWIVELLED
SWIVELLIKE
SWIVELLING
SWIVER
SWIVET
SWIVETTY
SWIVVET
SWIZ
SWIZZ
SWIZZLE
SWIZZLER
SWOB
SWOBBER
SWOLLEN
SWONK
SWOON
SWOONED
SWOONING
SWOONINGLY
SWOONY
SWOOP
SWOOPED
SWOOPER
SWOOPING
SWOOSH
SWOP
SWOPE
SWORD
SWORDBILL
SWORDCRAFT
SWORDER
SWORDFISH
SWORDFISHERMAN
SWORDFISHERY
SWORDFISHES
SWORDFISHING
SWORDICK
SWORDING
SWORDKNOT
SWORDMAKER
SWORDMAKING
SWORDMAN
SWORDMANSHIP
SWORDPLAY
SWORDPLAYER
SWORDPROOF
SWORDSLIPPER
SWORDSMAN
SWORDSMANSHIP
SWORDSMEN
SWORDSMITH
SWORDSTICK
SWORDSWOMAN
SWORDTAIL
SWORDWEED
SWORE
SWORL
SWORN
SWOSH
SWOT
SWOTTER
SWOUGH
SWOUN
SWOUND
SWOUNDS
SWOUNS
SWOW
SWUM
SWUNG
SWY
SWYTHE
SY
SYAGUSH
SYBARITICAL
SYBIL
SYBO
SYBOES
SYBOTIC
SYBOTISM
SYBOW
SYCAMINE
SYCAMORE
SYCE
SYCEE
SYCHEE
SYCITE
SYCOCK
SYCOMA
SYCOMANCY
SYCONARIAN
SYCONATE
SYCONES
SYCONIA
SYCONID
SYCONIUM
SYCONOID
SYCONUS
SYCOPHANCIES
SYCOPHANCY
SYCOPHANT
SYCOPHANTIC
SYCOPHANTISH
SYCOPHANTISM
SYCOPHANTIZE
SYCOPHANTRY
SYCOSIFORM
SYCOSIS
SYDDIR
SYE
SYENITE
SYENITIC
SYENODIORITE
SYENOGABBRO
SYKE
SYKER
SYKERLY
SYLE
SYLENE
SYLIB
SYLING
SYLLAB
SYLLABARIES
SYLLABARIUM
SYLLABARY
SYLLABATIM
SYLLABATION
SYLLABE
SYLLABI
SYLLABIC
SYLLABICAL
SYLLABICALLY
SYLLABICATE
SYLLABICATED
SYLLABICATING
SYLLABICNESS
SYLLABIFIED
SYLLABIFY
SYLLABIFYING
SYLLABISM
SYLLABIZE
SYLLABIZED
SYLLABIZING
SYLLABLE
SYLLABLED
SYLLABLES

SYLLABLING
SYLLABUB
SYLLABUS
SYLLABUSES
SYLLEPSES
SYLLEPSIS
SYLLEPTIC
SYLLEPTICAL
SYLLID
SYLLIDIAN
SYLLOGE
SYLLOGISM
SYLLOGIST
SYLLOGISTIC
SYLLOGISTICAL
SYLLOGISTICALL
SYLLOGISTICS
SYLLOGIZE
SYLLOGIZED
SYLLOGIZER
SYLLOGIZING
SYLPH
SYLPHID
SYLPHIDINE
SYLPHISH
SYLPHLIKE
SYLPHY
SYLVA
SYLVAE
SYLVAGE
SYLVAN
SYLVANITE
SYLVANITIC
SYLVANITY
SYLVANRY
SYLVAS
SYLVATE
SYLVATIC
SYLVATICAL
SYLVESTER
SYLVESTRAL
SYLVESTRENE
SYLVESTRIAN
SYLVIID
SYLVIINE
SYLVIN
SYLVINE
SYLVINITE
SYLVITE
SYMAR
SYMBASIC
SYMBASICAL
SYMBASICALLY
SYMBASIS
SYMBION
SYMBIONT
SYMBIONTIC
SYMBIOSIS
SYMBIOT
SYMBIOTE
SYMBIOTIC
SYMBIOTICAL
SYMBIOTICALLY
SYMBIOTICS
SYMBIOTISM
SYMBLEPHARON
SYMBOL
SYMBOLATER
SYMBOLIC
SYMBOLICAL
SYMBOLICALLY
SYMBOLICALNESS
SYMBOLICS
SYMBOLISE
SYMBOLISM
SYMBOLIST
SYMBOLISTIC
SYMBOLISTICAL
SYMBOLISTICALLY
SYMBOLIZATION
SYMBOLIZE
SYMBOLIZED
SYMBOLIZER
SYMBOLIZING
SYMBOLOGICAL
SYMBOLOGIST
SYMBOLOGY
SYMBOLOLATRY
SYMBOLOLOGY
SYMBOLRY
SYMBOLS
SYMBOLUM
SYMBOULEUTIC
SYMBRANCH
SYMBRANCHOID
SYMBRANCHOUS
SYMMACHY
SYMMEDIAN
SYMMELUS
SYMMETALLISM
SYMMETRAL
SYMMETRIAN
SYMMETRIC
SYMMETRICAL
SYMMETRICALITY
SYMMETRICALLY
SYMMETRICALNESS
SYMMETRIES
SYMMETRIST
SYMMETRIZE
SYMMETRIZED
SYMMETRIZING
SYMMETROID
SYMMETRY
SYMMIST
SYMPATHETIC
SYMPATHETICAL
SYMPATHETICALLY
SYMPATHIES
SYMPATHIN
SYMPATHIQUE
SYMPATHISE
SYMPATHISM
SYMPATHIST
SYMPATHIZE
SYMPATHIZED
SYMPATHIZER
SYMPATHIZING
SYMPATHIZINGLY
SYMPATHY
SYMPATRIC
SYMPATRY
SYMPETALOUS
SYMPHILE
SYMPHILIC
SYMPHILOUS
SYMPHILY
SYMPHOGENOUS
SYMPHONETIC
SYMPHONIA
SYMPHONIC
SYMPHONICALLY
SYMPHONIES
SYMPHONION
SYMPHONIOUS
SYMPHONIOUSLY
SYMPHONIST
SYMPHONIZE
SYMPHONIZED
SYMPHONIZING
SYMPHONOUS
SYMPHONY
SYMPHRASE
SYMPHYLAN
SYMPHYLLOUS
SYMPHYLOUS
SYMPHYNOTE
SYMPHYSEAL
SYMPHYSES
SYMPHYSION
SYMPHYSIS
SYMPHYSY
SYMPHYTIC
SYMPHYTISM
SYMPHYTIZE
SYMPLASM
SYMPLAST
SYMPLECTIC
SYMPLESITE
SYMPLOCE
SYMPLOCIUM
SYMPODE
SYMPODIA
SYMPODIAL
SYMPODIALLY
SYMPODIUM
SYMPOSIA
SYMPOSIAC
SYMPOSIACAL
SYMPOSIAL
SYMPOSIARCH
SYMPOSIAST
SYMPOSION
SYMPOSIUM
SYMPOSIUMS
SYMPTOM
SYMPTOMATIC
SYMPTOMATICAL
SYMPTOMATICALLY
SYMPTOMATICS
SYMPTOMATIZE
SYMPTOMS
SYMPTOSIS
SYMPUS
SYN
SYNACME
SYNACMIC
SYNACMY
SYNACTIC
SYNADELPHITE
SYNAERESIS
SYNAESTHESIA
SYNAGOG
SYNAGOGAL
SYNAGOGICAL
SYNAGOGUE
SYNALEPHA
SYNALEPHE
SYNALLACTIC
SYNALOEPHA
SYNALOEPHE
SYNANGE
SYNANGIA
SYNANGIAL
SYNANGIC
SYNANGIUM
SYNANTHEMA
SYNANTHEROUS
SYNANTHESIS
SYNANTHETIC
SYNANTHIC
SYNANTHOUS
SYNANTHROSE
SYNANTHY
SYNAPHEA
SYNAPHEIA
SYNAPSE
SYNAPSES
SYNAPSID
SYNAPSIDAN
SYNAPSIS
SYNAPTAI
SYNAPTASE
SYNAPTE
SYNAPTEROUS
SYNAPTIC
SYNAPTICAL
SYNAPTICALLY
SYNAPTICULA
SYNAPTICULAR
SYNAPTICULUM
SYNAPTID
SYNAPTYCHUS
SYNARCHICAL
SYNARCHY
SYNARMOGOID
SYNARTESIS
SYNARTETE
SYNARTETIC
SYNARTHRODIA
SYNARTHROSES
SYNARTHROSIS
SYNASTRY
SYNAXAR
SYNAXARION
SYNAXARIST
SYNAXARY
SYNAXIS
SYNCARP
SYNCARPIA
SYNCARPIUM
SYNCARPOUS
SYNCARPY
SYNCARYON
SYNCEPHALIC
SYNCEPHALUS
SYNCEREBRAL
SYNCEREBRUM
SYNCHITIC
SYNCHORESIS
SYNCHRO
SYNCHROMESH
SYNCHRONAL
SYNCHRONE
SYNCHRONIC
SYNCHRONICAL
SYNCHRONISM
SYNCHRONIZATION
SYNCHRONIZE
SYNCHRONIZED
SYNCHRONIZER
SYNCHRONIZING
SYNCHRONOUS
SYNCHRONOUSLY
SYNCHRONY
SYNCHROSCOPE
SYNCHROTRON
SYNCHYSIS
SYNCLADOUS
SYNCLASTIC
SYNCLINAL
SYNCLINALLY
SYNCLINE
SYNCLINICAL
SYNCLINORIAL
SYNCLINORIAN
SYNCLINORIUM
SYNCLITIC
SYNCLITICISM
SYNCLITISM
SYNCOELOM
SYNCOPAL
SYNCOPATE
SYNCOPATED
SYNCOPATING
SYNCOPATION
SYNCOPATOR
SYNCOPE
SYNCOPES
SYNCOPIC
SYNCOPISM
SYNCOPIST
SYNCOPIZE
SYNCRANIATE
SYNCRANTERIC
SYNCRASY
SYNCRETIC
SYNCRETICAL
SYNCRETICISM
SYNCRETION
SYNCRETISM
SYNCRETIST
SYNCRETISTIC
SYNCRETIZE
SYNCRETIZED
SYNCRETIZING
SYNCRISIS
SYNCRYPTIC
SYNCYTIA
SYNCYTIAL
SYNCYTIOMA
SYNCYTIOMAS
SYNCYTIOMATA
SYNCYTIUM
SYNDACTYL
SYNDACTYLE
SYNDACTYLIA
SYNDACTYLIC
SYNDACTYLISM
SYNDACTYLOUS
SYNDACTYLY
SYNDERESIS
SYNDESIS
SYNDESMITIS
SYNDESMOLOGY
SYNDESMOMA
SYNDESMOSES
SYNDESMOSIS
SYNDESMOTIC
SYNDESMOTOMY
SYNDET
SYNDETIC
SYNDETICAL
SYNDETICALLY
SYNDIC
SYNDICAL
SYNDICALISM
SYNDICALIST
SYNDICALIZE
SYNDICAT
SYNDICATE
SYNDICATED
SYNDICATEER
SYNDICATING
SYNDICATION
SYNDICATOR
SYNDROME
SYNDROMIC
SYNDYASMIAN
SYNE
SYNECDOCHE
SYNECDOCHIC
SYNECDOCHISM
SYNECHIA
SYNECHIAE
SYNECHIOLOGY
SYNECHOLOGY
SYNECHOTOMY
SYNECHTHRAN
SYNECHTHRY
SYNECIOUS
SYNECOLOGY
SYNECTIC
SYNECTICITY
SYNEDRAL

SYNEDRIAL
SYNEDRIAN
SYNEIDESIS
SYNEMA
SYNEMATA
SYNEMMENON
SYNENTOGNATH
SYNERESIS
SYNERGASTIC
SYNERGETIC
SYNERGIA
SYNERGIC
SYNERGID
SYNERGIDAE
SYNERGIDAL
SYNERGISM
SYNERGIST
SYNERGISTIC
SYNERGIZE
SYNERGY
SYNERIZE
SYNESIS
SYNESTHESIA
SYNESTHETIC
SYNETHNIC
SYNEZISIS
SYNGAMIC
SYNGAMOUS
SYNGAMY
SYNGENESIAN
SYNGENESIOUS
SYNGENESIS
SYNGENETIC
SYNGENISM
SYNGENITE
SYNGNATHID
SYNGNATHOID
SYNGNATHOUS
SYNGRAPH
SYNIZESIS
SYNKARYON
SYNKINESIS
SYNKINETIC
SYNNEMA
SYNNEUROSIS
SYNOCHAL
SYNOCHOUS
SYNOCHUS
SYNOCREATE
SYNOD
SYNODAL
SYNODALIST
SYNODALLY
SYNODIAN
SYNODIC
SYNODICAL
SYNODICALLY
SYNODICON
SYNODIST
SYNODITE
SYNODONTID
SYNODONTOID
SYNODSMAN
SYNODSMEN
SYNOECETE
SYNOECIOSIS
SYNOECIOUS
SYNOECIOUSLY
SYNOECISM
SYNOECIZE
SYNOECY
SYNOEKY
SYNOICOUS
SYNOMOSY
SYNONYM
SYNONYMATIC
SYNONYME
SYNONYMIC
SYNONYMICAL
SYNONYMICON
SYNONYMICS
SYNONYMIES
SYNONYMIST
SYNONYMITY
SYNONYMIZE
SYNONYMIZED
SYNONYMIZING
SYNONYMOUS
SYNONYMOUSLY
SYNONYMY
SYNOPSES
SYNOPSIS
SYNOPSIZE
SYNOPSY
SYNOPTIC
SYNOPTICAL
SYNOPTICALLY
SYNORCHIDISM
SYNORCHISM
SYNOSTEOLOGY
SYNOSTEOSES
SYNOSTEOSIS
SYNOSTOSE
SYNOSTOSES
SYNOSTOSIS
SYNOSTOTIC
SYNOSTOTICAL
SYNOUSIACS
SYNOVECTOMY
SYNOVIA
SYNOVIAL
SYNOVIALLY
SYNOVIPAROUS
SYNOVITIC
SYNOVITIS
SYNPELMOUS
SYNSACRAL
SYNSACRUM
SYNSEPALOUS
SYNSPERMOUS
SYNSPOROUS
SYNTACTIC
SYNTACTICAL
SYNTACTICALLY
SYNTACTICIAN
SYNTAGMA
SYNTAN
SYNTAX
SYNTAXIS
SYNTAXIST
SYNTECHNIC
SYNTECTIC
SYNTECTICAL
SYNTENOSIS
SYNTERESIS
SYNTEXIS
SYNTHEME
SYNTHERMAL
SYNTHESES
SYNTHESIS
SYNTHESISE
SYNTHESISM
SYNTHESIST
SYNTHESIZE
SYNTHESIZED
SYNTHESIZER
SYNTHESIZING
SYNTHETE
SYNTHETIC
SYNTHETICAL
SYNTHETICALLY
SYNTHETICISM
SYNTHETIST
SYNTHETIZATION
SYNTHETIZE
SYNTHETIZER
SYNTHOL
SYNTHRONI
SYNTHRONOI
SYNTHRONOS
SYNTHRONUS
SYNTOMIA
SYNTOMY
SYNTONE
SYNTONIC
SYNTONICAL
SYNTONICALLY
SYNTONIN
SYNTONIZE
SYNTONIZED
SYNTONIZER
SYNTONIZING
SYNTONOUS
SYNTONY
SYNTROPE
SYNTROPHIC
SYNTROPICAL
SYNTROPY
SYNTYPE
SYNTYPIC
SYNTYPICISM
SYNURA
SYNURAE
SYNUSIAST
SYPH
SYPHER
SYPHERED
SYPHERING
SYPHILID
SYPHILIDE
SYPHILIS
SYPHILITIC
SYPHILIZE
SYPHILIZED
SYPHILIZING
SYPHILODERM
SYPHILOGENY
SYPHILOID
SYPHILOLOGY
SYPHILOMA
SYPHILOPHOBE
SYPHILOSIS
SYPHON
SYRETTE
SYRINGA
SYRINGE
SYRINGEAL
SYRINGED
SYRINGES
SYRINGIN
SYRINGING
SYRINGITIS
SYRINGIUM
SYRINGOCELE
SYRINGOCOELE
SYRINGOTOME
SYRINGOTOMY
SYRINX
SYRINXES
SYRMA
SYRPHID
SYRT
SYRTIC
SYRUP
SYRUPED
SYRUPER
SYRUPY
SYRUS
SYSE
SYSSARCOSIC
SYSSARCOSIS
SYSSARCOTIC
SYSSEL
SYSSELMAN
SYSSITIA
SYSSITION
SYSTALTIC
SYSTASIS
SYSTATIC
SYSTEM
SYSTEMATIC
SYSTEMATICAL
SYSTEMATICALITY
SYSTEMATICALLY
SYSTEMATICIAN
SYSTEMATICS
SYSTEMATISE
SYSTEMATISM
SYSTEMATIST
SYSTEMATIZATION
SYSTEMATIZE
SYSTEMATIZED
SYSTEMATIZER
SYSTEMATIZING
SYSTEMIC
SYSTEMICALLY
SYSTEMIZATION
SYSTEMIZE
SYSTEMIZED
SYSTEMIZER
SYSTEMIZING
SYSTILIUS
SYSTOLATED
SYSTOLE
SYSTOLIC
SYSTYLE
SYSTYLOUS
SYZYGAL
SYZYGETIC
SYZYGIA
SYZYGIAL
SYZYGIES
SYZYGIUM
SYZYGY
SZAIBELYITE
SZLACHTA
SZOPELKA

T

TA
TAA
TAAR
TAB
TABAC
TABACIN
TABACOSIS
TABACUM
TABAGIE
TABANID
TABANUCO
TABARD
TABARDED
TABARDILLO
TABARET
TABASHEER
TABASHIR
TABATIERE
TABBER
TABBIES
TABBINET
TABBY
TABEFACTION
TABEFY
TABELLA
TABELLION
TABER
TABERDAR
TABERNA
TABERNACLE
TABERNACLED
TABERNACLER
TABERNACLING
TABERNACULAR
TABERNAE
TABES
TABESCENCE
TABESCENT
TABET
TABETIC
TABETIFORM
TABETLESS
TABI
TABIA
TABID
TABIDLY
TABIDNESS
TABIFIC
TABIFICAL
TABINET
TABITUDE
TABLA
TABLAS
TABLATURE
TABLE
TABLEAU
TABLEAUS
TABLEAUX
TABLECLOTH
TABLECLOTHY
TABLED
TABLEITY
TABLELAND
TABLEMAID
TABLEMAKER
TABLEMAKING
TABLEMAN
TABLEMATE
TABLER
TABLES
TABLESPOON
TABLESPOONFUL
TABLESPOONFULS
TABLET
TABLETARY
TABLETOP
TABLEWARE
TABLEWISE
TABLIER
TABLINA
TABLING
TABLINUM
TABLITA
TABLOID
TABOG
TABOO
TABOOS
TABOPARALYSIS
TABOPARESIS
TABOPARETIC
TABOPHOBIA
TABOR
TABORED
TABORER
TABORET
TABORIN
TABORINE
TABORING
TABOUR
TABOURED
TABOURER
TABOURET
TABOURINE
TABOURING
TABRET
TABS
TABU
TABULA
TABULABLE
TABULAE
TABULAR
TABULARE
TABULARIA
TABULARIUM
TABULARIZE
TABULARIZED
TABULARIZING
TABULARLY
TABULARY
TABULATE
TABULATED
TABULATING
TABULATION
TABULATOR
TABULATORY
TABULE
TABUN
TABUS
TABUT
TACAHOUT
TACAMAHAC
TACAMAHACA
TACAMAHACK
TACCACEOUS
TACCADA
TACE
TACET
TACH
TACHE
TACHEOGRAPHY
TACHEOMETER
TACHEOMETRIC
TACHEOMETRY
TACHETURE
TACHHYDRITE
TACHIBANA
TACHINA
TACHINARIAN
TACHINID
TACHIOL
TACHOGRAM
TACHOGRAPH
TACHOMETER
TACHOMETRIC
TACHOMETRY
TACHOSCOPE
TACHYCARDIA
TACHYCARDIAC
TACHYGEN
TACHYGENESIS
TACHYGENETIC
TACHYGLOSSAL
TACHYGRAPH
TACHYGRAPHER
TACHYGRAPHIC
TACHYGRAPHY
TACHYLITE
TACHYLYTE
TACHYLYTIC
TACHYMETER
TACHYMETRIC
TACHYMETRY
TACHYSCOPE
TACHYTYPE
TACIT
TACITLY
TACITNESS
TACITURN
TACITURNIST
TACITURNITY
TACITURNLY
TACK
TACKED
TACKER
TACKET
TACKETY
TACKEY
TACKIER
TACKIEST
TACKING
TACKINGLY
TACKLE
TACKLED
TACKLEMAN
TACKLER
TACKLES
TACKLESS
TACKLING
TACKSMAN
TACKSMEN
TACKY
TACLOCUS
TACMAHACK
TACNODE
TACON
TACONITE
TACSO
TACT
TACTFUL
TACTFULLY
TACTFULNESS
TACTIC
TACTICAL
TACTICALLY
TACTICIAN
TACTICS
TACTILE
TACTILIST
TACTILITIES
TACTILITY
TACTION
TACTITE
TACTLESS
TACTLESSLY
TACTLESSNESS
TACTOMETER
TACTOR
TACTUAL
TACTUALITY
TACTUALLY
TACTUS
TACUACINE
TAD
TADBHAVA
TADPOLE
TAE
TAEL
TAENIA
TAENIACIDAL
TAENIACIDE
TAENIAE
TAENIAFUGE
TAENIAL
TAENIAN
TAENIASIS
TAENIATE
TAENICIDE
TAENIDIA
TAENIDIUM
TAENIFORM
TAENIFUGE
TAENIIFORM
TAENIOID
TAENIOSOME
TAENIOSOMOUS
TAENITE
TAENNIN
TAEPO
TAFFAREL
TAFFEREL
TAFFETA
TAFFETY
TAFFIA
TAFFLE
TAFFRAIL
TAFFY
TAFIA
TAFT
TAFWIZ
TAG
TAGASASTE
TAGATOSE
TAGBOARD
TAGETOL
TAGETONE
TAGGE
TAGGED
TAGGER
TAGGERS
TAGGING
TAGGLE
TAGGY
TAGHAIRM
TAGILITE
TAGLIA
TAGLIONI
TAGLOCK
TAGMEME
TAGRAG
TAGRAGGERY
TAGSORE
TAGSTER
TAGTAIL
TAGUA
TAGUAN
TAGWERK
TAHA
TAHALI
TAHANUN
TAHARAH
TAHEEN
TAHGOOK
TAHIN
TAHKHANA
TAHLI
TAHONA
TAHR
TAHSEELDAR
TAHSIL
TAHSILDAR
TAHUA
TAI
TAIAHA
TAIGA
TAIGLE
TAIGLESOME
TAIHOA
TAIKIH
TAIKUN
TAIL
TAILAGE
TAILBAND
TAILBOARD
TAILED
TAILENDER
TAILER
TAILET
TAILFIRST
TAILFLOWER
TAILFOREMOST
TAILGATE
TAILGATED
TAILGATING
TAILGUNNER
TAILHEAD
TAILING
TAILINGS
TAILLE
TAILLESS
TAILLEUR
TAILLIGHT
TAILLOIR
TAILOR
TAILORAGE
TAILORBIRD
TAILORED
TAILORING
TAILORISM
TAILORLY
TAILORS
TAILORY
TAILPIECE
TAILPIN
TAILPIPE
TAILRACE
TAILSKID
TAILSPIN
TAILSTOCK
TAILWISE
TAILY
TAILYE
TAILZEE
TAILZIE
TAILZIED
TAIMEN
TAIMYRITE
TAIN
TAINT
TAINTE
TAINTED
TAINTING
TAINTMENT
TAINTOR
TAINTURE
TAINTWORM

TAIPAN
TAIPO
TAIRA
TAIRGE
TAIS
TAISCH
TAISSLE
TAISTREL
TAISTRIL
TAIT
TAIVER
TAIVERS
TAIVERT
TAJ
TAJO
TAKABLE
TAKAHE
TAKAR
TAKE
TAKEDOWN
TAKEFUL
TAKEN
TAKEOFF
TAKEOUT
TAKER
TAKIN
TAKING
TAKINGLY
TAKINGNESS
TAKKANAH
TAKOSIS
TAKROURI
TAKT
TAKY
TAKYR
TAL
TALA
TALABON
TALAJE
TALAK
TALALGIA
TALANTON
TALAO
TALAPOIN
TALAR
TALARI
TALARIA
TALARIC
TALAYOT
TALAYOTI
TALBOT
TALC
TALCED
TALCER
TALCING
TALCKED
TALCKING
TALCKY
TALCOID
TALCOSE
TALCOUS
TALCUM
TALE
TALEBEARER
TALEBEARING
TALEBOOK
TALECARRIER
TALECARRYING
TALEMASTER
TALEMONGER
TALENT
TALENTED
TALENTER
TALENTING
TALEPYET
TALER
TALES
TALESMAN
TALESMEN
TALETELLER
TALETELLING
TALEWISE
TALI
TALIATION
TALIERA
TALIGRADE
TALION
TALIONIC
TALIPED
TALIPEDIC
TALIPES
TALIPOMANUS
TALIPOT
TALISAY
TALISMAN
TALISMANIC
TALISMANICAL
TALISMANNI
TALISMANS
TALITE
TALITOL
TALK
TALKABILITY
TALKABLE
TALKATHON
TALKATIVE
TALKATIVELY
TALKATIVENESS
TALKED
TALKER
TALKFEST
TALKIE
TALKIER
TALKIEST
TALKING
TALKWORTHY
TALKY
TALL
TALLAGE
TALLAGEABLE
TALLAGED
TALLAGING
TALLAPOI
TALLATE
TALLBOY
TALLEGALANE
TALLER
TALLERO
TALLEST
TALLET
TALLIABLE
TALLIAR
TALLIATE
TALLIATED
TALLIATING
TALLIED
TALLIER
TALLIES
TALLIS
TALLISH
TALLIT
TALLITH
TALLNESS
TALLOL
TALLOTE
TALLOW
TALLOWBERRIES
TALLOWBERRY
TALLOWED
TALLOWER
TALLOWINESS
TALLOWING
TALLOWMAKER
TALLOWMAKING
TALLOWMAN
TALLOWROOT
TALLOWWEED
TALLOWWOOD
TALLOWY
TALLWOOD
TALLY
TALLYHO
TALLYHOS
TALLYING
TALLYMAN
TALLYMEN
TALLYWAG
TALLYWALKA
TALLYWOMAN
TALLYWOMEN
TALMA
TALMAS
TALMOUSE
TALO
TALOFIBULAR
TALON
TALONED
TALONID
TALOSE
TALOTIBIAL
TALPACOTI
TALPATATE
TALPETATE
TALPICIDE
TALPID
TALPIFORM
TALPIFY
TALPINE
TALPOID
TALSHIDE
TALTER
TALTHIB
TALUK
TALUKA
TALUKDAR
TALUKDARI
TALUS
TALUTO
TALWOOD
TAM
TAMABLE
TAMALE
TAMANDU
TAMANDUA
TAMANOAS
TAMANOIR
TAMANOWUS
TAMANU
TAMARA
TAMARACK
TAMARAITE
TAMARAO
TAMARAU
TAMARIN
TAMARIND
TAMARISK
TAMAS
TAMASHA
TAMBAC
TAMBAROORA
TAMBER
TAMBO
TAMBOOKIE
TAMBOR
TAMBOUR
TAMBOURA
TAMBOURED
TAMBOURER
TAMBOURET
TAMBOURGI
TAMBOURIN
TAMBOURINE
TAMBOURING
TAMBOURIST
TAMBREET
TAMBURA
TAMBURAN
TAMBURELLO
TAMBURONE
TAME
TAMEABLE
TAMED
TAMEHEARTED
TAMEIN
TAMELESS
TAMELESSNESS
TAMELY
TAMEN
TAMENES
TAMER
TAMEST
TAMIDINE
TAMIN
TAMINE
TAMING
TAMINY
TAMIS
TAMISE
TAMLUNG
TAMMAR
TAMMIE
TAMMIES
TAMMY
TAMP
TAMPALA
TAMPAN
TAMPANG
TAMPED
TAMPER
TAMPERED
TAMPERER
TAMPERING
TAMPING
TAMPION
TAMPIONED
TAMPOE
TAMPON
TAMPONADE
TAMPONAGE
TAMPONMENT
TAMPOON
TAMPOY
TAMURE
TAN
TANA
TANACETIN
TANACETYL
TANACH
TANADAR
TANAGER
TANAGRINE
TANAK
TANAN
TANBARK
TANBUR
TANCEL
TANDAN
TANDAVA
TANDEM
TANDEMER
TANDEMIST
TANDEMIZE
TANDEMWISE
TANDLE
TANDSTICKA
TANEGA
TANEKAHA
TANG
TANGA
TANGALUNG
TANGANTANGAN
TANGE
TANGED
TANGEITE
TANGELO
TANGELOS
TANGENCE
TANGENCIES
TANGENCY
TANGENT
TANGENTAL
TANGENTALLY
TANGENTIAL
TANGENTIALLY
TANGENTLY
TANGERINE
TANGFISH
TANGFISHES
TANGHAN
TANGHIN
TANGHININ
TANGI
TANGIBILITY
TANGIBLE
TANGIBLENESS
TANGIBLY
TANGIE
TANGIER
TANGIEST
TANGILIN
TANGING
TANGKA
TANGLAD
TANGLE
TANGLEBERRIES
TANGLEBERRY
TANGLED
TANGLEFISH
TANGLEFISHES
TANGLEFOOT
TANGLEHEAD
TANGLER
TANGLEROOT
TANGLING
TANGLY
TANGO
TANGOS
TANGRAM
TANGUE
TANGUILE
TANGUIN
TANGUM
TANGUN
TANGY
TANHA
TANIA
TANICA
TANIER
TANIKO
TANIST
TANISTIC
TANISTRY
TANISTSHIP
TANJIB
TANJONG
TANK
TANKA
TANKAGE
TANKAH
TANKARD
TANKED
TANKER
TANKERABOGUS
TANKETTE
TANKFUL

TANKIE
TANKING
TANKLE
TANKODROME
TANKS
TANLING
TANNA
TANNADAR
TANNAGE
TANNAIC
TANNAIM
TANNAITIC
TANNAKIN
TANNASE
TANNATE
TANNED
TANNER
TANNERIES
TANNERY
TANNIC
TANNID
TANNIDE
TANNIFEROUS
TANNIGEN
TANNIN
TANNINED
TANNING
TANNOGEN
TANNOID
TANNOMETER
TANNY
TANNYL
TANOA
TANQUAM
TANQUEN
TANREC
TANSEL
TANSEY
TANSIES
TANSY
TANTA
TANTADLIN
TANTALATE
TANTALIC
TANTALISE
TANTALITE
TANTALIZE
TANTALIZED
TANTALIZER
TANTALIZING
TANTALUM
TANTAMOUNT
TANTARA
TANTARARA
TANTI
TANTIEME
TANTIVIES
TANTIVY
TANTLE
TANTO
TANTRA
TANTRIC
TANTRIK
TANTRISM
TANTRIST
TANTRUM
TANTUM
TANWOOD
TANYA
TANYSTOME
TAO
TAOS
TAOTAI
TAOYIN
TAP
TAPA
TAPACULO
TAPADERA
TAPADERO
TAPALO
TAPALOS
TAPAMAKER
TAPAMAKING
TAPAS
TAPASVI
TAPE
TAPED
TAPELESS
TAPELINE
TAPEMAN
TAPEMEN
TAPEN
TAPER
TAPERED
TAPERER
TAPERING
TAPERINGLY
TAPERY
TAPESIUM
TAPESTER
TAPESTRIED
TAPESTRIES
TAPESTRY
TAPESTRYING
TAPET
TAPETA
TAPETAL
TAPETI
TAPETIS
TAPETUM
TAPEWORM
TAPHEPHOBIA
TAPHOLE
TAPHOUSE
TAPIA
TAPIDERO
TAPING
TAPINOSIS
TAPIOCA
TAPIR
TAPIRIDIAN
TAPIRINE
TAPIROID
TAPIRS
TAPIS
TAPISER
TAPISM
TAPISSERIE
TAPISSIER
TAPIST
TAPIT
TAPLASH
TAPLET
TAPLING
TAPNET
TAPOA
TAPOTEMENT
TAPOUN
TAPPA
TAPPABLE
TAPPABLENESS
TAPPALL
TAPPAUL
TAPPED
TAPPEN
TAPPER
TAPPET
TAPPING
TAPPISH
TAPPIT
TAPPOON
TAPROOM
TAPROOT
TAPROOTED
TAPS
TAPSALTEERIE
TAPSMAN
TAPSTER
TAPSTRESS
TAPT
TAPU
TAPUL
TAPWORT
TAQIYA
TAQLID
TAR
TARA
TARABOOKA
TARADIDDLE
TARAF
TARAFDAR
TARAGE
TARAIRI
TARAKIHI
TARAMELLITE
TARAN
TARAND
TARANTARIZE
TARANTAS
TARANTASS
TARANTELLA
TARANTELLE
TARANTISM
TARANTIST
TARANTULA
TARANTULAE
TARANTULAR
TARANTULAS
TARANTULATED
TARANTULID
TARANTULITE
TARANTULOUS
TARASSIS
TARATA
TARATAH
TARATANTARA
TARAU
TARAXACUM
TARBAGAN
TARBET
TARBLE
TARBOARD
TARBOOSH
TARBOX
TARBOY
TARBRUSH
TARBUSH
TARBUTTITE
TARCEL
TARCHON
TARDAMENTE
TARDANDO
TARDANT
TARDE
TARDIER
TARDIEST
TARDIGRADE
TARDILOQUENT
TARDILOQUOUS
TARDILOQUY
TARDILY
TARDINESS
TARDITY
TARDIVE
TARDLE
TARDO
TARDY
TARE
TAREA
TARED
TAREFA
TAREFITCH
TARENTE
TARENTISM
TARES
TARFA
TARFE
TARFLOWER
TARGE
TARGED
TARGEMAN
TARGER
TARGET
TARGETED
TARGETEER
TARGETIER
TARGETING
TARGING
TARHOOD
TARI
TARIE
TARIFF
TARIFFED
TARIFFING
TARIFFIST
TARIFFITE
TARIFFIZE
TARIN
TARING
TARIQA
TARIQAT
TARIRIC
TARIRINIC
TARISH
TARKASHI
TARKEEAN
TARKHAN
TARLATAN
TARLATANED
TARLEATHER
TARLETAN
TARLIES
TARLTONIZE
TARMAC
TARMOSINED
TARN
TARNAL
TARNALLY
TARNATION
TARNISH
TARNISHABLE
TARNISHED
TARNISHER
TARNISHING
TARO
TAROCCO
TAROGATO
TAROPATCH
TAROS
TAROT
TARP
TARPAN
TARPAPER
TARPAULIAN
TARPAULIN
TARPON
TARPONS
TARPOT
TARR
TARRABA
TARRACK
TARRADIDDLE
TARRADIDDLER
TARRAGON
TARRAGONA
TARRASS
TARRED
TARRER
TARRI
TARRIANCE
TARRIED
TARRIER
TARRIEST
TARRILY
TARRINESS
TARRING
TARRISH
TARROCK
TARROW
TARRY
TARRYING
TARRYINGLY
TARRYINGNESS
TARS
TARSAL
TARSALE
TARSALIA
TARSE
TARSECTOMY
TARSI
TARSIA
TARSIER
TARSIOID
TARSO
TARSOME
TARSOMETATARSUS
TARSONEMID
TARSOTARSAL
TARSUS
TART
TARTAGO
TARTAN
TARTANA
TARTAR
TARTAREOUS
TARTARET
TARTARIC
TARTARIN
TARTARINE
TARTARISH
TARTARIZE
TARTARIZED
TARTARIZING
TARTARLY
TARTAROUS
TARTARUM
TARTE
TARTEN
TARTINE
TARTISH
TARTISHLY
TARTLE
TARTLET
TARTLY
TARTNESS
TARTRAMATE
TARTRAMID
TARTRAMIDE
TARTRATE
TARTRATED
TARTRAZIN
TARTRAZINE
TARTRAZINIC
TARTRO
TARTRONATE
TARTRONIC
TARTRONYL
TARTROUS
TARTRYL
TARTRYLIC
TARTUFE
TARTUFERY
TARTUFFE
TARTUFFERY
TARTUFFIAN

TARTUFFISH
TARTUFFISHLY
TARTUFFISM
TARTUFIAN
TARTUFISH
TARTUFISHLY
TARTUFISM
TARTWOMAN
TARTWOMEN
TARVE
TARWEED
TARWHINE
TARWOOD
TARZAN
TASAJILLO
TASAJO
TASBIH
TASCAL
TASCO
TASH
TASHERIFF
TASHIE
TASHLIK
TASHREEF
TASHRIF
TASIMETER
TASIMETRIC
TASIMETRY
TASK
TASKAGE
TASKED
TASKER
TASKING
TASKIT
TASKMASTER
TASKMISTRESS
TASKSETTER
TASKSETTING
TASKWORK
TASMANITE
TASS
TASSARD
TASSE
TASSEL
TASSELED
TASSELER
TASSELFISH
TASSELING
TASSELLED
TASSELLUS
TASSELS
TASSELY
TASSES
TASSET
TASSIE
TASSOO
TASTABLE
TASTE
TASTED
TASTEFUL
TASTEFULLY
TASTEFULNESS
TASTELESS
TASTELESSLY
TASTEN
TASTER
TASTIER
TASTIEST
TASTILY
TASTINESS
TASTING
TASTINGLY
TASTO
TASTY
TASU
TAT
TATA
TATAMI
TATAUPA
TATBEB
TATCH
TATCHY
TATE
TATER
TATH
TATHATA
TATINEK
TATLER
TATMJOLK
TATOU
TATOUAY
TATPURUSHA
TATS
TATSMAN
TATT
TATTED
TATTER
TATTERED
TATTEREDLY
TATTEREDNESS
TATTERING
TATTERLY
TATTERSALL
TATTERWAG
TATTERWALLOP
TATTERY
TATTIED
TATTIES
TATTING
TATTLE
TATTLED
TATTLER
TATTLERY
TATTLETALE
TATTLING
TATTLINGLY
TATTOO
TATTOOAGE
TATTOOED
TATTOOER
TATTOOING
TATTOOIST
TATTOOMENT
TATTOOS
TATTVA
TATTY
TATU
TATUASU
TATUKIRA
TAU
TAUGA
TAUGHT
TAULA
TAULCH
TAUM
TAUN
TAUNT
TAUNTED
TAUNTER
TAUNTING
TAUNTINGLY
TAUNTINGNESS
TAUNTRESS
TAUPE
TAUPO
TAUPOU
TAURANGA
TAUREAN
TAURIAN
TAURIC
TAURICIDE
TAURICORNOUS
TAURIFEROUS
TAURIFORM
TAURIN
TAURINE
TAURITE
TAUROBOLIA
TAUROBOLIUM
TAUROCHOLATE
TAUROCHOLIC
TAUROCOL
TAUROCOLLA
TAURODONT
TAUROESQUE
TAUROLATRY
TAUROMACHIA
TAUROMACHIAN
TAUROMACHIC
TAUROMACHY
TAUROMORPHIC
TAUROPHILE
TAUROPHOBE
TAURYL
TAUT
TAUTAUG
TAUTED
TAUTEGORICAL
TAUTEGORY
TAUTEN
TAUTIRITE
TAUTLY
TAUTNESS
TAUTOCHRONE
TAUTOCHRONISM
TAUTOCHRONOUS
TAUTOG
TAUTOLOGIC
TAUTOLOGIES
TAUTOLOGISM
TAUTOLOGIST
TAUTOLOGIZE
TAUTOLOGIZED
TAUTOLOGIZER
TAUTOLOGIZING
TAUTOLOGY
TAUTOMER
TAUTOMERAL
TAUTOMERIC
TAUTOMERISM
TAUTOMERIZE
TAUTOMERS
TAUTOMETER
TAUTOMETRIC
TAUTONYM
TAUTONYMIC
TAUTONYMIES
TAUTONYMY
TAUTOOUSIAN
TAUTOPHONIC
TAUTOPHONY
TAUTOPODIC
TAUTOPODY
TAUTOTYPE
TAUTOZONAL
TAV
TAVE
TAVELL
TAVER
TAVERN
TAVERNER
TAVERNIZE
TAVERNLY
TAVERNOUS
TAVERNRY
TAVERS
TAVERT
TAVESTOCK
TAVISTOCKITE
TAVOLA
TAVOLATITE
TAVOY
TAW
TAWA
TAWDERED
TAWDRIER
TAWDRIES
TAWDRIEST
TAWDRILY
TAWDRINESS
TAWDRY
TAWED
TAWER
TAWERY
TAWHAI
TAWHID
TAWIE
TAWING
TAWITE
TAWKEE
TAWKIN
TAWN
TAWNEY
TAWNIE
TAWNIER
TAWNIEST
TAWNINESS
TAWNY
TAWPIE
TAWPY
TAWS
TAWSE
TAX
TAXABILITY
TAXABLE
TAXABLENESS
TAXABLY
TAXACEOUS
TAXAMETER
TAXASPIDEAN
TAXATION
TAXATIONAL
TAXATIVE
TAXATIVELY
TAXATOR
TAXEATER
TAXEATING
TAXED
TAXEL
TAXEME
TAXEOPOD
TAXEOPODOUS
TAXEOPODY
TAXER
TAXES
TAXGATHERER
TAXGATHERING
TAXI
TAXIARCH
TAXIAUTO
TAXIBUS
TAXICAB
TAXIDERMAL
TAXIDERMIC
TAXIDERMIST
TAXIDERMIZE
TAXIDERMY
TAXIED
TAXIMAN
TAXIMETER
TAXIMETERED
TAXINE
TAXING
TAXINGLY
TAXIPLANE
TAXIS
TAXITE
TAXITIC
TAXMAN
TAXODONT
TAXOLOGY
TAXOMETER
TAXON
TAXONOMER
TAXONOMIC
TAXONOMICAL
TAXONOMIST
TAXONOMY
TAXOR
TAXPAID
TAXPAYER
TAXPAYING
TAXY
TAXYING
TAY
TAYASSUID
TAYER
TAYIR
TAYLORITE
TAYRA
TAYSAAM
TAZEEA
TAZIA
TAZZA
TCH
TCHA
TCHAI
TCHAPAN
TCHAST
TCHE
TCHEIREK
TCHERVONETS
TCHERVONETZ
TCHI
TCHICK
TCHIN
TCHINCOU
TCHU
TCK
TE
TEA
TEABERRIES
TEABERRY
TEABOARD
TEABOX
TEABOY
TEACAKE
TEACART
TEACH
TEACHABILITY
TEACHABLE
TEACHABLENESS
TEACHABLY
TEACHE
TEACHED
TEACHER
TEACHERAGE
TEACHERESS
TEACHERLY
TEACHERY
TEACHES
TEACHING
TEACHINGLY
TEACHLESS
TEACHY
TEACUP
TEACUPFUL
TEACUPFULS
TEADISH
TEAED
TEAER
TEAEY
TEAGARDENY
TEAGLE
TEAHOUSE

TEAING
TEAK
TEAKETTLE
TEAKWOOD
TEAL
TEALEAFY
TEALLITE
TEALS
TEAM
TEAMAKER
TEAMAKING
TEAMAN
TEAMED
TEAMEO
TEAMING
TEAMLAND
TEAMMAN
TEAMMATE
TEAMSTER
TEAMWORK
TEAN
TEANAL
TEAP
TEAPOT
TEAPOY
TEAR
TEARAGE
TEARCAT
TEARDOWN
TEARDROP
TEARER
TEARFUL
TEARFULLY
TEARFULNESS
TEARIER
TEARIEST
TEARING
TEARLESS
TEARLESSLY
TEARLESSNESS
TEAROOM
TEARPIT
TEARS
TEARSTAIN
TEART
TEARTHUMB
TEARY
TEASE
TEASED
TEASEHOLE
TEASEL
TEASELED
TEASELER
TEASELING
TEASELLED
TEASELLER
TEASELLING
TEASELS
TEASELWORT
TEASER
TEASHOP
TEASING
TEASINGLY
TEASLE
TEASPOON
TEASPOONFUL
TEASPOONFULS
TEASY
TEAT
TEATASTER
TEATED
TEATFISH
TEATIME
TEATLING
TEATMAN
TEATY
TEAVE
TEAZE
TEAZEL
TEAZLE
TEBBAD
TEBELDI
TEC
TECA
TECALI
TECH
TECHIER
TECHIEST
TECHNE
TECHNETIUM
TECHNIC
TECHNICA
TECHNICAL
TECHNICALISM
TECHNICALIST
TECHNICALITIES
TECHNICALITY
TECHNICALIZE
TECHNICALLY
TECHNICIAN
TECHNICISM
TECHNICIST
TECHNICOLOGY
TECHNICOLOR
TECHNICON
TECHNICS
TECHNIPHONE
TECHNIQUE
TECHNISM
TECHNOCAUSIS
TECHNOCRACIES
TECHNOCRACY
TECHNOCRAT
TECHNOCRATIC
TECHNOGRAPHY
TECHNOLITHIC
TECHNOLOGIC
TECHNOLOGICAL
TECHNOLOGIES
TECHNOLOGIST
TECHNOLOGY
TECHNONOMY
TECHOUS
TECHY
TECK
TECOMIN
TECON
TECT
TECTAL
TECTIBRANCH
TECTIFORM
TECTOCEPHALY
TECTOLOGY
TECTONIC
TECTONICS
TECTORIAL
TECTORIUM
TECTOSPHERE
TECTOSPINAL
TECTRICES
TECTRICIAL
TECTRIX
TECTUM
TECTURE
TECUM
TED
TEDDED
TEDDER
TEDDIES
TEDDING
TEDDY
TEDESCA
TEDESCHE
TEDESCHI
TEDESCO
TEDGE
TEDIOSITY
TEDIOUS
TEDIOUSLY
TEDIOUSNESS
TEDIOUSOME
TEDISOME
TEDIUM
TEE
TEECALL
TEED
TEEDLE
TEEING
TEEKA
TEEL
TEEM
TEEMED
TEEMER
TEEMFUL
TEEMFULNESS
TEEMING
TEEMINGLY
TEEMINGNESS
TEEMLESS
TEEMS
TEEN
TEENAGER
TEENET
TEENFUL
TEENFULLY
TEENIER
TEENIEST
TEENS
TEENSY
TEENY
TEENYBOPPER
TEEPEE
TEER
TEES
TEEST
TEET
TEETAN
TEETEE
TEETER
TEETERBOARD
TEETERER
TEETERTAIL
TEETH
TEETHE
TEETHED
TEETHIER
TEETHIEST
TEETHING
TEETHLESS
TEETHRIDGE
TEETHY
TEETING
TEETOTAL
TEETOTALED
TEETOTALER
TEETOTALING
TEETOTALISM
TEETOTALIST
TEETOTALLED
TEETOTALLER
TEETOTALLING
TEETOTALLY
TEETOTUM
TEETOTUMISM
TEETOTUMIZE
TEETSOOK
TEEWHAAP
TEFF
TEFILLIN
TEG
TEGG
TEGMEN
TEGMENT
TEGMENTA
TEGMENTAL
TEGMENTUM
TEGMINA
TEGMINAL
TEGS
TEGU
TEGUA
TEGUEXIN
TEGULA
TEGULAE
TEGULAR
TEGULARLY
TEGULATED
TEGUMEN
TEGUMENT
TEGUMENTAL
TEGUMENTARY
TEGURIA
TEGURIUM
TEHOO
TEHSIL
TEICHER
TEIGLACH
TEIGLECH
TEIHTE
TEIID
TEIL
TEIND
TEINDABLE
TEINDER
TEINLAND
TEINOSCOPE
TEIOID
TEJANO
TEJON
TEJU
TEK
TEKE
TEKIAH
TEKKE
TEKNONYMOUS
TEKNONYMY
TEKTITE
TEKYA
TEL
TELA
TELACOUSTIC
TELAE
TELAESTHESIA
TELAKUCHA
TELAMON
TELAMONES
TELANGIOSIS
TELAR
TELARIAN
TELARLY
TELAUTOGRAM
TELAUTOGRAPH
TELD
TELEBLEM
TELECAST
TELECASTED
TELECASTING
TELECHEMIC
TELECODE
TELEDU
TELEGA
TELEGNOSIS
TELEGNOSTIC
TELEGONIC
TELEGONOUS
TELEGONY
TELEGRAF
TELEGRAM
TELEGRAMMIC
TELEGRAPH
TELEGRAPHED
TELEGRAPHEME
TELEGRAPHER
TELEGRAPHESE
TELEGRAPHIC
TELEGRAPHING
TELEGRAPHIST
TELEGRAPHONE
TELEGRAPHY
TELEIANTHOUS
TELEIOSIS
TELEKINESIS
TELEKINETIC
TELELECTRIC
TELEMARK
TELEMECHANIC
TELEMETER
TELEMETERING
TELEMETRIC
TELEMETRICAL
TELEMETRIST
TELEMETRY
TELEMOTOR
TELENCEPHALON
TELENERGIC
TELENERGY
TELENEURITE
TELENEURON
TELENGISCOPE
TELEODONT
TELEOLOGIC
TELEOLOGICAL
TELEOLOGIES
TELEOLOGISM
TELEOLOGIST
TELEOLOGY
TELEOPHOBIA
TELEOPHORE
TELEOPHYTE
TELEOPTILE
TELEORGANIC
TELEOSAUR
TELEOST
TELEOSTEAN
TELEOSTEOUS
TELEOSTOME
TELEOSTOMOUS
TELEOZOIC
TELEOZOON
TELEPATH
TELEPATHIC
TELEPATHIST
TELEPATHIZE
TELEPATHY
TELEPHEME
TELEPHONE
TELEPHONED
TELEPHONER
TELEPHONIC
TELEPHONING
TELEPHONIST
TELEPHONY
TELEPHOTE
TELEPHOTO
TELEPLASM
TELEPLASMIC
TELEPLASTIC
TELEPOST
TELEPRINTER
TELEPROMPTER
TELERAN
TELERGIC
TELERGICAL
TELERGICALLY
TELERGY

TELESCOPE
TELESCOPED
TELESCOPIC
TELESCOPICAL
TELESCOPING
TELESCOPIST
TELESCOPY
TELESCRIBE
TELESCRIPT
TELESCRIPTOR
TELESEISM
TELESEISMIC
TELESEME
TELESIA
TELESIS
TELESIURGIC
TELESM
TELESMATIC
TELESMATICAL
TELESMETER
TELESOMATIC
TELESTERION
TELESTHESIA
TELESTHETIC
TELESTIC
TELESTICH
TELETACTILE
TELETACTOR
TELETAPE
TELETHERAPY
TELETHON
TELETYPE
TELETYPED
TELETYPER
TELETYPING
TELEUTO
TELEUTOSORUS
TELEUTOSPORE
TELEVIEW
TELEVIEWER
TELEVISE
TELEVISED
TELEVISING
TELEVISION
TELEVISIONAL
TELEVISOR
TELEVISUAL
TELEVOCAL
TELEVOX
TELEX
TELFER
TELFERAGE
TELFORD
TELFORDIZE
TELFORDIZED
TELFORDIZING
TELHARMONIC
TELHARMONIUM
TELHARMONY
TELI
TELIA
TELIAL
TELIC
TELICAL
TELICALLY
TELIFEROUS
TELIOSPORE
TELIOSPORIC
TELIOSTAGE
TELIUM
TELL
TELLABLE
TELLACH
TELLE
TELLER
TELLERSHIP
TELLIES
TELLIGRAPH
TELLINACEAN
TELLINACEOUS
TELLING
TELLINGLY
TELLINOID
TELLSOME
TELLTALE
TELLTALELY
TELLTRUTH
TELLURAL
TELLURATE
TELLURETED
TELLURETHYL
TELLURETTED
TELLURIAN
TELLURIC
TELLURIDE
TELLURION
TELLURISM
TELLURIST
TELLURITE
TELLURIUM
TELLURIZE
TELLURIZED
TELLURIZING
TELLURONIUM
TELLUROUS
TELLY
TELMATOLOGY
TELOBLAST
TELOBLASTIC
TELODENDRIA
TELODENDRION
TELODYNAMIC
TELOKINESIS
TELOLECITHAL
TELOLEMMA
TELOLEMMATA
TELOMITIC
TELONISM
TELOPHASE
TELOPSIS
TELOPTIC
TELOS
TELOSYNAPSIS
TELOSYNAPTIC
TELOTROCH
TELOTROCHA
TELOTROCHAL
TELOTROCHOUS
TELOTYPE
TELPHER
TELPHERAGE
TELPHERIC
TELPHERMAN
TELPHERMEN
TELPHERWAY
TELSON
TELSONIC
TELURGY
TELYN
TEMA
TEMACHA
TEMADAU
TEMALACATL
TEMAN
TEMBE
TEMBEITERA
TEMBETA
TEMBETARA
TEMBLOR
TEMBLORES
TEMBLORS
TEME
TEMENE
TEMENOS
TEMERARIOUS
TEMERATE
TEMERITOUS
TEMERITY
TEMEROUS
TEMEROUSLY
TEMEROUSNESS
TEMESCAL
TEMIAK
TEMIN
TEMP
TEMPER
TEMPERA
TEMPERABLE
TEMPERABLY
TEMPERALITY
TEMPERAMENT
TEMPERAMENTAL
TEMPERANCE
TEMPERATE
TEMPERATELY
TEMPERATIVE
TEMPERATURE
TEMPERED
TEMPEREDLY
TEMPEREDNESS
TEMPERER
TEMPERING
TEMPERSOME
TEMPERY
TEMPEST
TEMPESTICAL
TEMPESTIVE
TEMPESTIVELY
TEMPESTIVITY
TEMPESTUOUS
TEMPESTY
TEMPETE
TEMPI
TEMPLAR
TEMPLARDOM
TEMPLARISM
TEMPLARY
TEMPLATE
TEMPLATER
TEMPLE
TEMPLED
TEMPLES
TEMPLET
TEMPLIZE
TEMPLUM
TEMPO
TEMPORAL
TEMPORALE
TEMPORALIS
TEMPORALISM
TEMPORALIST
TEMPORALITIES
TEMPORALITY
TEMPORALIZE
TEMPORALLY
TEMPORALTIES
TEMPORALTY
TEMPORANEOUS
TEMPORARIES
TEMPORARILY
TEMPORARY
TEMPORATOR
TEMPORE
TEMPORISE
TEMPORIZE
TEMPORIZED
TEMPORIZER
TEMPORIZING
TEMPOS
TEMPRE
TEMPS
TEMPT
TEMPTABLE
TEMPTATION
TEMPTATIONAL
TEMPTATIOUS
TEMPTATORY
TEMPTED
TEMPTER
TEMPTING
TEMPTINGLY
TEMPTINGNESS
TEMPTRESS
TEMPTSOME
TEMPURA
TEMPUS
TEMS
TEMSE
TEMSEBREAD
TEMSELOAF
TEMULENCE
TEMULENCY
TEMULENT
TEMULENTIVE
TEMULENTLY
TEN
TENA
TENABILITY
TENABLE
TENABLENESS
TENABLY
TENACE
TENACIOUS
TENACIOUSLY
TENACIOUSNESS
TENACITY
TENACLE
TENACULA
TENACULUM
TENACY
TENAI
TENAIL
TENAILLE
TENAILLON
TENALGIA
TENANCIES
TENANCY
TENANT
TENANTABLE
TENANTED
TENANTER
TENANTING
TENANTLESS
TENANTLIKE
TENANTRIES
TENANTRY
TENANTS
TENANTSHIP
TENCH
TENCHES
TENCHWEED
TEND
TENDANCE
TENDED
TENDEJON
TENDENCE
TENDENCIES
TENDENCIOUS
TENDENCY
TENDENT
TENDENTIAL
TENDENTIOUS
TENDER
TENDEREE
TENDERER
TENDEREST
TENDERFEET
TENDERFOOT
TENDERFUL
TENDERFULLY
TENDERHEART
TENDERHEARTED
TENDERIZE
TENDERIZED
TENDERIZER
TENDERIZING
TENDERLING
TENDERLOIN
TENDERLY
TENDERNESS
TENDERSOME
TENDICLE
TENDIDO
TENDINAL
TENDINEAL
TENDING
TENDINGLY
TENDINOUS
TENDMENT
TENDO
TENDOMUCOID
TENDON
TENDONOUS
TENDONS
TENDOOR
TENDOPLASTY
TENDOTOME
TENDOTOMY
TENDOUR
TENDRAC
TENDRE
TENDREL
TENDRESSE
TENDRIL
TENDRILED
TENDRILLAR
TENDRILLED
TENDRILOUS
TENDRON
TENDRY
TENEBRA
TENEBRES
TENEBRIFIC
TENEBRION
TENEBRIONID
TENEBRIOUS
TENEBRIOUSLY
TENEBRITY
TENEBROSE
TENEBROSI
TENEBROSITY
TENEBROUS
TENEBROUSLY
TENEMENT
TENEMENTAL
TENEMENTARY
TENEMENTER
TENEMENTIZE
TENENDA
TENENDAS
TENENDUM
TENENT
TENER
TENERAL
TENERAMENTE
TENERITY
TENESMIC
TENESMUS
TENET
TENEZ
TENFOLD
TENFOLDNESS
TENG
TENGERE
TENGERITE

TENGU
TENIA
TENIACIDAL
TENIACIDE
TENIAFUGE
TENIASIS
TENIENTE
TENIO
TENMANTALE
TENNANTITE
TENNE
TENNER
TENNIS
TENNISY
TENNU
TENON
TENONECTOMY
TENONED
TENONER
TENONING
TENONITIS
TENONTOLOGY
TENONTOTOMY
TENOR
TENORE
TENORINO
TENORIST
TENORITE
TENOROON
TENORRHAPHIES
TENORRHAPHY
TENOSITIS
TENOTOMIES
TENOTOMIST
TENOTOMIZE
TENOTOMY
TENPENCE
TENPENNY
TENPIN
TENPINS
TENPOUNDER
TENREC
TENS
TENSAS
TENSAW
TENSE
TENSED
TENSELY
TENSENESS
TENSER
TENSES
TENSEST
TENSIBILITY
TENSIBLE
TENSIBLENESS
TENSIBLY
TENSIFY
TENSILE
TENSILELY
TENSILENESS
TENSILITY
TENSIMETER
TENSING
TENSIOMETER
TENSION
TENSIONAL
TENSIONED
TENSIONING
TENSITY
TENSIVE
TENSOME
TENSON
TENSOR
TENSORSHIP
TENSURE
TENT
TENTABILITY
TENTACLE
TENTACLED
TENTACULA
TENTACULAR
TENTACULATE
TENTACULATED
TENTACULITE
TENTACULOID
TENTACULUM
TENTAGE
TENTAMEN
TENTATION
TENTATIVE
TENTATIVELY
TENTED
TENTER
TENTERBELLY
TENTERER
TENTERHOOK
TENTFUL
TENTH
TENTHLY
TENTHMETER
TENTHMETRE
TENTHREDINID
TENTICLE
TENTIE
TENTIFORM
TENTIGO
TENTILLA
TENTILLUM
TENTILY
TENTLESS
TENTLET
TENTMAKER
TENTMAKING
TENTMATE
TENTOR
TENTORIAL
TENTORIUM
TENTORY
TENTS
TENTURE
TENTWORK
TENTWORT
TENTY
TENUATE
TENUE
TENUES
TENUIFLOROUS
TENUIFOLIOUS
TENUIROSTER
TENUIROSTRAL
TENUIS
TENUISTRIATE
TENUITY
TENUOUS
TENUOUSLY
TENUOUSNESS
TENURE
TENURIAL
TENURIALLY
TENURY
TENUTO
TENZON
TEOCALLI
TEOCALLIS
TEOPAN
TEOSINTE
TEPACHE
TEPAL
TEPARIES
TEPARY
TEPEE
TEPEFACTION
TEPEFIED
TEPEFY
TEPEFYING
TEPETATE
TEPHILLIN
TEPHRAMANCY
TEPHRITE
TEPHRITIC
TEPHROITE
TEPHROSIS
TEPID
TEPIDARIA
TEPIDARIUM
TEPIDITY
TEPIDLY
TEPIDNESS
TEPONAZTLI
TEPOR
TEQUILA
TEQUILLA
TER
TERA
TERAGLIN
TERAKIHI
TERAMORPHOUS
TERAP
TERAPH
TERAPHIM
TERAS
TERATA
TERATICAL
TERATISM
TERATOGENIC
TERATOGENY
TERATOID
TERATOLOGIC
TERATOLOGIST
TERATOLOGY
TERATOMA
TERATOMAS
TERATOMATA
TERATOMATOUS
TERATOSCOPY
TERATOSIS
TERBIA
TERBIC
TERBIUM
TERCE
TERCEL
TERCELET
TERCENTENARIES
TERCENTENARY
TERCER
TERCERON
TERCET
TERCHLORIDE
TERCIA
TERCINE
TERCIO
TERDIURNAL
TEREBATE
TEREBELLA
TEREBELLID
TEREBELLOID
TEREBELLUM
TEREBENE
TEREBENTHENE
TEREBIC
TEREBINTH
TEREBINTHIC
TEREBINTHINA
TEREBINTHINE
TEREBRA
TEREBRAE
TEREBRAL
TEREBRANT
TEREBRAS
TEREBRATE
TEREBRATION
TEREBRATULAR
TEREBRATULID
TEREDINES
TEREDO
TEREDOS
TEREK
TEREPHAH
TEREPHTHALLIC
TERETE
TERETIAL
TERETISM
TEREU
TERFA
TERFEZ
TERGA
TERGAL
TERGANT
TERGEMINAL
TERGEMINATE
TERGIFEROUS
TERGITE
TERGITIC
TERGIVERSANT
TERGIVERSATE
TERGIVERSATED
TERGIVERSATING
TERGIVERSATION
TERGIVERSE
TERGOLATERAL
TERGUM
TERIN
TERLINGUAITE
TERM
TERMA
TERMAGANCY
TERMAGANT
TERMAGANTISH
TERMAGANTISM
TERMAGANTLY
TERMAGE
TERMAL
TERMATIC
TERMED
TERMEN
TERMER
TERMIN
TERMINABLE
TERMINABLY
TERMINAL
TERMINALLY
TERMINANT
TERMINATE
TERMINATED
TERMINATING
TERMINATION
TERMINATIVE
TERMINATOR
TERMINATORY
TERMINE
TERMINER
TERMING
TERMINI
TERMININE
TERMINISM
TERMINIST
TERMINISTIC
TERMINIZE
TERMINO
TERMINOLOGIES
TERMINOLOGY
TERMINUS
TERMINUSES
TERMITAL
TERMITARIA
TERMITARIUM
TERMITARY
TERMITE
TERMITIC
TERMITOPHILE
TERMLESS
TERMLY
TERMON
TERMOR
TERMS
TERMTIME
TERN
TERNA
TERNAL
TERNAR
TERNARIANT
TERNARIES
TERNARIOUS
TERNARY
TERNATE
TERNATELY
TERNE
TERNED
TERNEPLATE
TERNER
TERNERY
TERNING
TERNION
TERNLET
TERNO
TERP
TERPADIENE
TERPANE
TERPEN
TERPENE
TERPHENYL
TERPILENE
TERPINENE
TERPINEOL
TERPINOL
TERPINOLENE
TERPODION
TERRA
TERRACE
TERRACED
TERRACEOUS
TERRACER
TERRACETTE
TERRACEWORK
TERRACIFORM
TERRACING
TERRAEFILIAL
TERRAEFILIAN
TERRAGE
TERRAIN
TERRAL
TERRAMARA
TERRAMARE
TERRAMYCIN
TERRANE
TERRANEAN
TERRANEOUS
TERRAPIN
TERRAQUEAN
TERRAQUEOUS
TERRAR
TERRARIA
TERRARIUM
TERRARIUMS
TERRAS
TERRASSE
TERRAZZO
TERRE
TERREEN
TERREITY
TERRELLA
TERREMOTIVE
TERRENE
TERRENELY
TERRENENESS

TERRENO
TERREOUS
TERREPLEIN
TERRESTRIAL
TERRESTRIALLY
TERRESTRIFY
TERRET
TERRIBLE
TERRIBLENESS
TERRIBLY
TERRICOLINE
TERRICOLIST
TERRICOLOUS
TERRIE
TERRIER
TERRIES
TERRIFIC
TERRIFICALLY
TERRIFICLY
TERRIFICNESS
TERRIFIED
TERRIFIER
TERRIFY
TERRIFYING
TERRIFYINGLY
TERRIGENE
TERRIGENOUS
TERRINE
TERRITORIAL
TERRITORIALISM
TERRITORIAN
TERRITORIED
TERRITORIES
TERRITORY
TERRON
TERROR
TERRORFUL
TERRORIFIC
TERRORISE
TERRORISM
TERRORIST
TERRORISTIC
TERRORIZE
TERRORIZED
TERRORIZER
TERRORIZING
TERRORSOME
TERRY
TERSE
TERSELY
TERSENESS
TERSER
TERSEST
TERSION
TERSULFID
TERSULFIDE
TERSULPHATE
TERSULPHID
TERSULPHIDE
TERSULPHURET
TERTIA
TERTIAL
TERTIAN
TERTIANA
TERTIANSHIP
TERTIARIES
TERTIARY
TERTIATE
TERTIO
TERTON
TERTULIA
TERUAH
TERUNCIUS
TERUTERO
TERUTERU
TERVALENCE
TERVALENCY
TERVALENT
TERVARIANT
TERVE
TERVEE
TERZET
TERZETTO
TERZETTOS
TERZINA
TERZIO
TERZO
TESACK
TESCARIA
TESCHENITE
TESKERIA
TESSARA
TESSARACE
TESSARADECAD
TESSARAGLOT
TESSEL
TESSELLA
TESSELLAE
TESSELLAR
TESSELLATE
TESSELLATED
TESSELLATING
TESSELLATION
TESSERA
TESSERACT
TESSERAE
TESSERAL
TESSERARIAN
TESSERATOMIC
TESSERATOMY
TESSITURA
TESSULAR
TEST
TESTA
TESTABLE
TESTACEAN
TESTACEOLOGY
TESTACEOUS
TESTACY
TESTAE
TESTAMENT
TESTAMENTA
TESTAMENTAL
TESTAMENTARY
TESTAMENTATE
TESTAMENTUM
TESTAMUR
TESTAO
TESTAR
TESTATA
TESTATE
TESTATION
TESTATOR
TESTATORY
TESTATRICES
TESTATRIX
TESTATUM
TESTE
TESTED
TESTEE
TESTER
TESTES
TESTICLE
TESTICOND
TESTICULAR
TESTICULATE
TESTICULATED
TESTIER
TESTIERE
TESTIEST
TESTIFICATE
TESTIFICATOR
TESTIFIED
TESTIFIER
TESTIFY
TESTIFYING
TESTIMONIA
TESTIMONIAL
TESTIMONIES
TESTIMONIUM
TESTIMONY
TESTINESS
TESTING
TESTIS
TESTO
TESTON
TESTONE
TESTOON
TESTOR
TESTOSTERONE
TESTRIL
TESTS
TESTUDINAL
TESTUDINATE
TESTUDINEAL
TESTUDINEOUS
TESTUDINES
TESTUDINOUS
TESTUDO
TESTULE
TESTY
TESVINO
TETANIA
TETANIC
TETANICAL
TETANICALLY
TETANIFORM
TETANIGENOUS
TETANILLA
TETANINE
TETANISM
TETANIZATION
TETANIZE
TETANIZED
TETANIZING
TETANOID
TETANOLYSIN
TETANOMOTOR
TETANUS
TETANY
TETARD
TETARTOCONE
TETARTOCONID
TETARTOID
TETCH
TETCHIER
TETCHIEST
TETCHILY
TETCHINESS
TETCHY
TETE
TETEL
TETH
TETHELIN
TETHER
TETHERBALL
TETHERED
TETHERING
TETHERY
TETHYDAN
TETOTUM
TETRA
TETRAAMYLOSE
TETRABASIC
TETRABIBLOS
TETRABORATE
TETRABORIC
TETRABRACH
TETRABROMID
TETRABROMIDE
TETRACHLORID
TETRACHLORIDE
TETRACHLORO
TETRACHORD
TETRACHORDAL
TETRACHORDON
TETRACHORIC
TETRACID
TETRACOCCUS
TETRACOLIC
TETRACOLON
TETRACORAL
TETRACOSANE
TETRACT
TETRACTINAL
TETRACTINOSE
TETRACTYS
TETRACYCLIC
TETRACYCLINE
TETRAD
TETRADACTYL
TETRADACTYLE
TETRADACTYLY
TETRADARCHY
TETRADECANE
TETRADECYL
TETRADIC
TETRADRACHM
TETRADRACHMA
TETRADYMITE
TETRAETHYL
TETRAGAMY
TETRAGENOUS
TETRAGLOT
TETRAGLOTTIC
TETRAGON
TETRAGONAL
TETRAGONALLY
TETRAGONOUS
TETRAGRAM
TETRAGYN
TETRAGYNIAN
TETRAGYNOUS
TETRAHEDRA
TETRAHEDRAL
TETRAHEDRIC
TETRAHEDRITE
TETRAHEDROID
TETRAHEDRON
TETRAHEDRONS
TETRAHEXAHEDRON
TETRAHYDRATE
TETRAHYDRIC
TETRAHYDRID
TETRAHYDRIDE
TETRAHYDRO
TETRAHYDROXY
TETRAIODO
TETRAKETONE
TETRAKIS
TETRAKISAZO
TETRALEMMA
TETRALOGIC
TETRALOGIES
TETRALOGUE
TETRALOGY
TETRAMASTIA
TETRAMERAL
TETRAMERIC
TETRAMERISM
TETRAMEROUS
TETRAMETER
TETRAMETHYL
TETRAMINE
TETRAMORPH
TETRAMORPHIC
TETRANDER
TETRANDROUS
TETRANE
TETRANITRATE
TETRANITRO
TETRANT
TETRAODONT
TETRAONID
TETRAONINE
TETRAPHENOL
TETRAPHONY
TETRAPLA
TETRAPLEGIA
TETRAPLEURON
TETRAPLOID
TETRAPLOIDIC
TETRAPLOIDY
TETRAPLOUS
TETRAPOD
TETRAPODIC
TETRAPODOUS
TETRAPODY
TETRAPOLAR
TETRAPOLIS
TETRAPOLITAN
TETRAPOUS
TETRAPTERAN
TETRAPTERON
TETRAPTEROUS
TETRAPTOTE
TETRAPTYCH
TETRAPYLON
TETRAPYRAMID
TETRARCH
TETRARCHATE
TETRARCHIC
TETRARCHICAL
TETRARCHIES
TETRARCHY
TETRASACCHARIDE
TETRASEME
TETRASEMIC
TETRASKELE
TETRASKELION
TETRASPHERIC
TETRASPORE
TETRASPORIC
TETRASPOROUS
TETRASTER
TETRASTICH
TETRASTICHAL
TETRASTICHIC
TETRASTOON
TETRASTYLE
TETRASTYLIC
TETRASTYLOS
TETRASTYLOUS
TETRASULFID
TETRASULFIDE
TETRASULPHID
TETRATHEISM
TETRATHEITE
TETRATHIONIC
TETRATOMIC
TETRATONE
TETRAVALENCE
TETRAVALENCY
TETRAVALENT
TETRAXIAL
TETRAXILE
TETRAXON
TETRAZANE
TETRAZENE
TETRAZIN
TETRAZINE
TETRAZO
TETRAZOLE
TETRAZOLIUM
TETRAZOLYL

TETRAZONE
TETRAZOTIZE
TETREMIMERAL
TETRIC
TETRICAL
TETRICALNESS
TETRICITY
TETRICOUS
TETRIFOL
TETRIGID
TETRIODIDE
TETROBOL
TETROBOLON
TETRODE
TETROL
TETROLE
TETROLIC
TETRONIC
TETRONYMAL
TETROSE
TETROUS
TETROXALATE
TETROXID
TETROXIDE
TETRYL
TETTER
TETTERED
TETTERING
TETTEROUS
TETTERWORT
TETTERY
TETTISH
TETTIX
TETTY
TETUR
TEU
TEUCH
TEUCHIT
TEUCRIN
TEUGH
TEUGHLY
TEUGHNESS
TEUK
TEVEL
TEVISS
TEW
TEWART
TEWED
TEWEL
TEWER
TEWING
TEWIT
TEWKE
TEWLY
TEWSOME
TEWTAW
TEWTER
TEXAS
TEXGUINO
TEXT
TEXTARIAN
TEXTBOOK
TEXTIFEROUS
TEXTILE
TEXTILES
TEXTILIST
TEXTLET
TEXTMAN
TEXTORIAL
TEXTRINE
TEXTUAL
TEXTUALISM
TEXTUALIST
TEXTUALLY
TEXTUARIES
TEXTUARIST
TEXTUARY
TEXTURAL
TEXTURALLY
TEXTURE
TEXTURED
TEXTUS
TEYNE
TEZ
TEZKIRAH
THA
THACK
THACKER
THACKLESS
THACKOOR
THAE
THAG
THAIL
THAIRM
THAKUR
THAKURATE
THALAMI
THALAMIA
THALAMIC
THALAMITE
THALAMIUM
THALAMOCELE
THALAMOCOELE
THALAMUS
THALASSA
THALASSAL
THALASSIAN
THALASSIARCH
THALASSIC
THALASSICAL
THALASSINID
THALASSINOID
THALATTA
THALENITE
THALER
THALIACEAN
THALIDOMIDE
THALLI
THALLIC
THALLIFEROUS
THALLIFORM
THALLIN
THALLINE
THALLIOUS
THALLIUM
THALLOCHLORE
THALLODAL
THALLODIC
THALLOGEN
THALLOGENOUS
THALLOID
THALLOIDAL
THALLOME
THALLOPHYTE
THALLOPHYTIC
THALLOSE
THALLOUS
THALLUS
THALLUSES
THALPOSIS
THALPOTIC
THALTHAN
THALWEG
THAM
THAMAKAU
THAMENG
THAMIN
THAMNIUM
THAMNOPHILE
THAMNOPHILINE
THAMURIA
THAN
THANA
THANADAR
THANAGE
THANAH
THANATISM
THANATIST
THANATOID
THANATOLOGY
THANATOMETER
THANATOPSIS
THANATOSIS
THANATOTIC
THANATOUSIA
THANE
THANELAND
THANESS
THANK
THANKED
THANKEE
THANKER
THANKFUL
THANKFULLY
THANKFULNESS
THANKING
THANKLESS
THANKLESSLY
THANKS
THANKSGIVER
THANKSGIVING
THANKWORTHY
THANNADAR
THAPES
THAR
THARF
THARFCAKE
THARGINYAH
THARM
THAT
THATCH
THATCHED
THATCHER
THATCHING
THATCHWOOD
THATCHY
THATNESS
THAUGHT
THAUMASITE
THAUMATOGENY
THAUMATOLOGIES
THAUMATOLOGY
THAUMATROPE
THAUMATURGE
THAUMATURGI
THAUMATURGIA
THAUMATURGIC
THAUMATURGUS
THAUMATURGY
THAUMOSCOPIC
THAW
THAWED
THAWER
THAWIER
THAWIEST
THAWING
THAWY
THE
THEACEOUS
THEAK
THEAL
THEAM
THEANDRIC
THEANTHROPIC
THEANTHROPOS
THEANTHROPY
THEARCHIC
THEARCHIES
THEARCHY
THEASUM
THEAT
THEATER
THEATERGOER
THEATERGOING
THEATERS
THEATRAL
THEATRE
THEATREGOER
THEATREGOING
THEATRIC
THEATRICABLE
THEATRICAL
THEATRICALITY
THEATRICALS
THEATRICIAN
THEATRICISM
THEATRICIZE
THEATRICS
THEATRIZE
THEATROCRACY
THEATRON
THEAVE
THEB
THEBAIN
THEBAINE
THEBAISM
THECA
THECAE
THECAL
THECAPHORE
THECASPORAL
THECASPORE
THECASPORED
THECASPOROUS
THECATE
THECIA
THECITIS
THECIUM
THECLAN
THECODONT
THEDE
THEE
THEEDOM
THEEK
THEEKED
THEEKER
THEEKING
THEELIN
THEELOL
THEET
THEETSEE
THEEZAN
THEFT
THEFTBOTE
THEFTDOM
THEFTUOUS
THEFTUOUSLY
THEGETHER
THEGIDDER
THEGITHER
THEGN
THEGNDOM
THEGNHOOD
THEGNLAND
THEGNLIKE
THEGNLY
THEGNSHIP
THEGNWORTHY
THEI
THEIC
THEIFORM
THEIN
THEINE
THEIR
THEIRN
THEIRS
THEIRSELVES
THEISM
THEIST
THEISTIC
THEISTICAL
THELION
THELITIS
THELIUM
THELORRHAGIA
THELPHUSIAN
THELYBLAST
THELYBLASTIC
THELYOTOKOUS
THELYOTOKY
THEM
THEMA
THEMATA
THEMATIC
THEMATICAL
THEMATICALLY
THEMATIST
THEME
THEMED
THEMER
THEMING
THEMSELVES
THEN
THENABOUTS
THENADAYS
THENAGE
THENAL
THENAR
THENARDITE
THENCE
THENCEAFTER
THENCEFORTH
THENCEFROM
THENCEWARD
THENNESS
THEOBROMIN
THEOBROMINE
THEOCENTRIC
THEOCHRISTIC
THEOCRACIES
THEOCRACY
THEOCRASICAL
THEOCRASIES
THEOCRASY
THEOCRAT
THEOCRATIC
THEOCRATICAL
THEOCRATIST
THEODICEAN
THEODICIES
THEODICY
THEODIDACT
THEODOLITE
THEODOLITIC
THEODY
THEOGAMY
THEOGONAL
THEOGONIC
THEOGONICAL
THEOGONIES
THEOGONISM
THEOGONIST
THEOGONY
THEOKRASIA
THEOKTONIC
THEOKTONY
THEOLATROUS
THEOLATRY
THEOLOG
THEOLOGASTER
THEOLOGATE
THEOLOGEION
THEOLOGER
THEOLOGI
THEOLOGIAN

THEOLOGIC
THEOLOGICAL
THEOLOGICIAN
THEOLOGICS
THEOLOGIES
THEOLOGISE
THEOLOGISM
THEOLOGIST
THEOLOGIUM
THEOLOGIZE
THEOLOGIZED
THEOLOGIZER
THEOLOGIZING
THEOLOGUE
THEOLOGUS
THEOLOGY
THEOMACHIES
THEOMACHIST
THEOMACHY
THEOMAGIC
THEOMAGICAL
THEOMAGICS
THEOMAGY
THEOMANCY
THEOMANIA
THEOMANIAC
THEOMANTIC
THEOMASTIX
THEOMICRIST
THEOMORPHIC
THEOMORPHISM
THEOMORPHIZE
THEONOMY
THEOPANTISM
THEOPATHETIC
THEOPATHIC
THEOPATHIES
THEOPATHY
THEOPHAGIC
THEOPHAGITE
THEOPHAGOUS
THEOPHAGY
THEOPHANIA
THEOPHANIC
THEOPHANIES
THEOPHANISM
THEOPHANOUS
THEOPHANY
THEOPHILE
THEOPHOBIA
THEOPHORIC
THEOPHOROUS
THEOPHYLLIN
THEOPHYLLINE
THEOPNEUST
THEOPNEUSTED
THEOPNEUSTIC
THEOPNEUSTY
THEORBIST
THEORBO
THEORBOS
THEOREM
THEOREMATIC
THEOREMATIST
THEOREMIC
THEORETIC
THEORETICAL
THEORETICIAN
THEORETICS
THEORIA
THEORIAI
THEORIC
THEORICA
THEORICAL
THEORICALLY
THEORICIAN
THEORICON
THEORICS
THEORIES
THEORISE
THEORISM
THEORIST
THEORIZATION
THEORIZE
THEORIZED
THEORIZER
THEORIZING
THEORUM
THEORY
THEORYLESS
THEOSOPH
THEOSOPHEME
THEOSOPHER
THEOSOPHIC
THEOSOPHICAL
THEOSOPHIES
THEOSOPHISM
THEOSOPHIST
THEOSOPHY
THEOTECHNIC
THEOTECHNIST
THEOTECHNY
THEOTHERAPY
THEOW
THEOWDOM
THEOWMAN
THEOWMEN
THERALITE
THERAPEUSIS
THERAPEUTIC
THERAPEUTICS
THERAPEUTIST
THERAPIA
THERAPIES
THERAPIST
THERAPSID
THERAPY
THERAVADA
THERBLIG
THERE
THEREABOUT
THEREABOUTS
THEREABOVE
THEREACROSS
THEREAFTER
THEREAGAINST
THEREAMONG
THEREAMONGST
THEREANENT
THEREANENTS
THEREAROUND
THEREAS
THEREAT
THEREAWAY
THEREAWAYS
THEREBEFORE
THEREBEN
THEREBESIDE
THEREBIFORN
THEREBY
THEREFOR
THEREFORE
THEREFRO
THEREFROM
THEREIN
THEREINAFTER
THEREINTO
THERENESS
THEREOF
THEREOID
THEREOLOGIST
THEREOLOGY
THEREON
THEREONTO
THEREOUT
THEREOVER
THERERIGHT
THERESE
THERETHROUGH
THERETIL
THERETILL
THERETO
THERETOFORE
THERETOWARD
THEREUNDER
THEREUNTIL
THEREUNTO
THEREUP
THEREUPON
THEREVID
THEREWHILE
THEREWHILES
THEREWHILST
THEREWITH
THEREWITHAL
THEREWITHIN
THERF
THERIAC
THERIACA
THERIACAL
THERIAL
THERIATRICS
THERIDIID
THERIODONT
THERIOMANCY
THERIOMORPH
THERM
THERMAE
THERMAIC
THERMAL
THERMALGESIA
THERMALITY
THERMALLY
THERMANTIC
THERMATOLOGY
THERME
THERMEL
THERMIC
THERMICAL
THERMICALLY
THERMION
THERMIONIC
THERMIONICS
THERMISTOR
THERMIT
THERMITE
THERMOCHROIC
THERMOCHROSY
THERMOCLINE
THERMOCOUPLE
THERMOGEN
THERMOGENIC
THERMOGENOUS
THERMOGRAM
THERMOGRAPH
THERMOGRAPHY
THERMOLABILE
THERMOLOGY
THERMOLYSIS
THERMOLYTIC
THERMOLYZE
THERMOLYZED
THERMOLYZING
THERMOMETER
THERMOMETRIC
THERMOMETRY
THERMOMOTIVE
THERMOMOTOR
THERMONASTIC
THERMONASTY
THERMONOUS
THERMOPAIR
THERMOPHIL
THERMOPHILE
THERMOPHILIC
THERMOPHONE
THERMOPHORE
THERMOPILE
THERMOPLASTIC
THERMOPLEION
THERMOSCOPE
THERMOSCOPIC
THERMOSIPHON
THERMOSPHERE
THERMOSTABLE
THERMOSTAT
THERMOSTATIC
THERMOTACTIC
THERMOTANK
THERMOTAXIC
THERMOTAXIS
THERMOTIC
THERMOTICAL
THERMOTICS
THERMOTROPIC
THERMOTROPY
THERMOTYPE
THERMOTYPIC
THERMOTYPY
THERODONT
THEROID
THEROLOGIC
THEROLOGICAL
THEROLOGIST
THEROLOGY
THEROMORPH
THEROMORPHIA
THEROMORPHIC
THEROPOD
THEROPODAN
THEROPODOUS
THERSITEAN
THERSITICAL
THESAUR
THESAURI
THESAURUS
THESAURY
THESE
THESIAL
THESICLE
THESIS
THESMOTHETE
THESMOTHETES
THESOCYTE
THESTER
THESTREEN
THETA
THETCH
THETIC
THETICAL
THETICALLY
THETICS
THETIN
THETINE
THEURGIC
THEURGICAL
THEURGICALLY
THEURGIES
THEURGIST
THEURGY
THEVETIN
THEW
THEWED
THEWIER
THEWIEST
THEWLESS
THEWLIKE
THEWS
THEWY
THEY
THEYAOU
THIADIAZOLE
THIALDIN
THIALDINE
THIAMID
THIAMIDE
THIAMIN
THIAMINE
THIANTHRENE
THIASI
THIASITE
THIASOI
THIASOS
THIASOTE
THIASUS
THIAZIN
THIAZINE
THIAZOL
THIAZOLE
THIAZOLINE
THIBET
THIBLE
THICK
THICKE
THICKEN
THICKENED
THICKENER
THICKENING
THICKER
THICKEST
THICKET
THICKETED
THICKETY
THICKHEAD
THICKHEADED
THICKISH
THICKLEAF
THICKLIPS
THICKLY
THICKNESS
THICKSET
THICKSKIN
THICKSKULL
THICKSKULLED
THICKWIND
THICKWIT
THICKY
THIEF
THIEFCRAFT
THIEFDOM
THIEFLAND
THIEFLY
THIEFMAKER
THIEFMAKING
THIEFPROOF
THIEFTAKER
THIENONE
THIENYL
THIEVE
THIEVED
THIEVELESS
THIEVER
THIEVERIES
THIEVERY
THIEVES
THIEVING
THIEVISH
THIEVISHLY
THIEVISHNESS
THIG
THIGGER
THIGGING
THIGH
THIGHBONE
THIGHED

THIGHS
THIGHT
THIGHTNESS
THIGMOTACTIC
THIGMOTAXIS
THIGMOTROPIC
THIK
THILK
THILL
THILLER
THILLY
THIMBLE
THIMBLEBERRIES
THIMBLEBERRY
THIMBLED
THIMBLEFUL
THIMBLEFULS
THIMBLEMAKER
THIMBLEMAKING
THIMBLEMAN
THIMBLERIG
THIMBLERIGGED
THIMBLERIGGING
THIMBLES
THIMBLEWEED
THIN
THINDOWN
THINE
THING
THINGAL
THINGAMABOB
THINGAMAJIG
THINGISH
THINGLET
THINGMAN
THINGS
THINGUM
THINGUMABOB
THINGUMAJIG
THINGUMBOB
THINGUT
THINGY
THINK
THINKABLE
THINKABLY
THINKER
THINKING
THINKINGLY
THINLY
THINNED
THINNER
THINNESS
THINNEST
THINNING
THIO
THIOACETIC
THIOALDEHYDE
THIOAMID
THIOAMIDE
THIOARSENATE
THIOARSENIATE
THIOARSENITE
THIOCARBAMIC
THIOCARBONYL
THIOCRESOL
THIOCYANATE
THIOCYANIC
THIOCYANIDE
THIOCYANO
THIOCYANOGEN
THIOHYDRATE
THIOKETONE
THIOL
THIOLACETIC
THIONATE
THIONATION
THIONEINE
THIONIC
THIONIN
THIONINE
THIONITRITE
THIONYL
THIONYLAMINE
THIOPHEN
THIOPHENE
THIOPHENIC
THIOPHENOL
THIOPHOSGENE
THIOPHTHENE
THIOPYRAN
THIOSINAMINE
THIOSTANNIC
THIOSTANNITE
THIOSULFATE
THIOSULPHATE
THIOTOLENE
THIOTUNGSTIC
THIOUREA
THIOURETHAN
THIOXENE
THIOZONE
THIOZONID
THIOZONIDE
THIR
THIRD
THIRDBOROUGH
THIRDENDEAL
THIRDINGS
THIRDLING
THIRDLY
THIRDNESS
THIRDS
THIRDSMAN
THIRL
THIRLAGE
THIRLED
THIRLING
THIRST
THIRSTED
THIRSTER
THIRSTIER
THIRSTIEST
THIRSTILY
THIRSTINESS
THIRSTING
THIRSTINGLY
THIRSTLE
THIRSTY
THIRTEEN
THIRTEENER
THIRTEENTH
THIRTEENTHLY
THIRTIES
THIRTIETH
THIRTY
THIS
THISHOW
THISLIKE
THISNESS
THISSEN
THISTLE
THISTLEBIRD
THISTLED
THISTLEDOWN
THISTLY
THISWISE
THITHER
THITHERTO
THITHERWARD
THITHERWARDS
THITKA
THITSIOL
THIURAM
THIVEL
THIXLE
THIXOLABILE
THIXOTROPIC
THIXOTROPY
THLIPSIS
THO
THOA
THOB
THODE
THOFT
THOFTFELLOW
THOGHT
THOKE
THOKISH
THOLANCE
THOLE
THOLED
THOLEITE
THOLEMOD
THOLING
THOLOI
THOLOS
THOLUS
THOMAN
THOMASING
THOMISID
THOMIST
THOMSENOLITE
THOMSONITE
THON
THONDER
THONE
THONG
THONGED
THONGMAN
THONGS
THONGY
THOOID
THORACECTOMY
THORACES
THORACIC
THORACICAL
THORACIFORM
THORACOGRAPH
THORACOLYSIS
THORACOPAGUS
THORACOSCOPE
THORACOSCOPY
THORAL
THORAX
THORAXES
THORE
THORIA
THORIANITE
THORIATE
THORIC
THORIFEROUS
THORITE
THORIUM
THORN
THORNBACK
THORNBILL
THORNBUSH
THORNED
THORNEN
THORNIER
THORNIEST
THORNING
THORNLESS
THORNLET
THORNTAIL
THORNY
THORO
THOROGUMMITE
THORON
THOROUGH
THOROUGHBRED
THOROUGHFARE
THOROUGHFOOT
THOROUGHFOOTED
THOROUGHFOOTING
THOROUGHGOING
THOROUGHLY
THOROUGHNESS
THOROUGHPIN
THOROUGHSPED
THOROUGHSTEM
THOROUGHWAX
THOROUGHWORT
THORP
THORPE
THORTER
THORTVEITITE
THOSE
THOU
THOUGH
THOUGHT
THOUGHTED
THOUGHTFUL
THOUGHTFULLY
THOUGHTFULNESS
THOUGHTLESS
THOUGHTLESSLY
THOUGHTNESS
THOUGHTS
THOUGHTSICK
THOUGHTY
THOUSAND
THOUSANDFOLD
THOUSANDTH
THOWLESS
THRACK
THRAIL
THRAIN
THRALDOM
THRALL
THRALLBORN
THRALLDOM
THRAM
THRAMMLE
THRANG
THRANGITY
THRANITE
THRAP
THRAPPLE
THRASH
THRASHED
THRASHEL
THRASHER
THRASHERMAN
THRASHING
THRASONIC
THRASONICAL
THRAST
THRATCH
THRAVE
THRAVER
THRAW
THRAWART
THRAWARTLIKE
THRAWARTNESS
THRAWN
THRAWNLY
THRAWNNESS
THREAD
THREADBARE
THREADED
THREADEN
THREADER
THREADFIN
THREADFISH
THREADFISHES
THREADFLOWER
THREADFOOT
THREADIER
THREADIEST
THREADING
THREADLE
THREADLIKE
THREADMAKER
THREADMAKING
THREADS
THREADWAY
THREADWEED
THREADWORM
THREADY
THREAP
THREAPED
THREAPEN
THREAPER
THREAPING
THREAT
THREATEN
THREATENED
THREATENER
THREATENING
THREATENINGLY
THREAVE
THREE
THREEFOLD
THREELING
THREENESS
THREEP
THREEPED
THREEPENCE
THREEPENNY
THREEPING
THREES
THREESCORE
THREESOME
THREIP
THRENE
THRENETIC
THRENETICAL
THRENODE
THRENODIAL
THRENODIAN
THRENODIC
THRENODIES
THRENODIST
THRENODY
THRENOS
THREONINE
THREOSE
THREP
THREPE
THREPSOLOGY
THRESH
THRESHAL
THRESHED
THRESHEL
THRESHER
THRESHERMAN
THRESHING
THRESHOLD
THRESTLE
THREW
THRIBBLE
THRICE
THRICECOCK
THRID
THRIDACE
THRIDACIUM
THRIE
THRIFT
THRIFTBOX
THRIFTIER
THRIFTIEST
THRIFTILY
THRIFTINESS
THRIFTLESS

THRIFTY
THRILL
THRILLED
THRILLER
THRILLIER
THRILLIEST
THRILLING
THRILLINGLY
THRILLY
THRIMBLE
THRIMP
THRING
THRINGING
THRINTER
THRIOBOLY
THRIP
THRIPEL
THRIPID
THRIPPLE
THRIPS
THRIST
THRIVE
THRIVED
THRIVELESS
THRIVEN
THRIVER
THRIVING
THRIVINGLY
THRIVINGNESS
THRO
THROAT
THROATAL
THROATBAND
THROATBOLL
THROATED
THROATFUL
THROATIER
THROATIEST
THROATILY
THROATINESS
THROATING
THROATLASH
THROATLATCH
THROATLET
THROATROOT
THROATSTRAP
THROATWORT
THROATY
THROB
THROBBED
THROBBER
THROBBING
THROBBINGLY
THROBLESS
THROCK
THRODDEN
THRODDY
THROE
THROED
THROEING
THROM
THROMBI
THROMBIN
THROMBOCYST
THROMBOCYTE
THROMBOGEN
THROMBOGENIC
THROMBOID
THROMBOPENIA
THROMBOSE
THROMBOSED
THROMBOSES
THROMBOSING
THROMBOSIS
THROMBOTIC
THROMBUS
THRONAL
THRONE
THRONED
THRONELET
THRONES
THRONG
THRONGED
THRONGER
THRONGING
THRONING
THRONIZE
THROPE
THROPPLE
THROSTLE
THROTTLE
THROTTLED
THROTTLER
THROTTLING
THROTTLINGLY
THROUGH
THROUGHBEAR
THROUGHGANG
THROUGHGOING
THROUGHGROW
THROUGHLY
THROUGHOUT
THROUGHPUT
THROUGHWAY
THROVE
THROW
THROWAWAY
THROWBACK
THROWDOWN
THROWER
THROWING
THROWN
THROWOFF
THROWOUT
THROWST
THROWSTER
THRU
THRUM
THRUMBLE
THRUMMED
THRUMMER
THRUMMING
THRUMMY
THRUMWORT
THRUOUT
THRUSH
THRUSHEL
THRUSHER
THRUSHLIKE
THRUSHY
THRUST
THRUSTER
THRUSTING
THRUSTLE
THRUTCH
THRUTCHINGS
THRUWAY
THRYMSA
THUD
THUDDED
THUDDING
THUDDINGLY
THUG
THUGA
THUGGED
THUGGEE
THUGGERIES
THUGGERY
THUGGESS
THUGGING
THUGGISH
THUGGISM
THUJA
THUJENE
THUJONE
THUJYL
THULIA
THULIR
THULITE
THULIUM
THULUTH
THUMB
THUMBED
THUMBER
THUMBING
THUMBKIN
THUMBLE
THUMBLESS
THUMBLING
THUMBMARK
THUMBNAIL
THUMBNUT
THUMBPIECE
THUMBPRINT
THUMBROPE
THUMBSCREW
THUMBSTALL
THUMBSTRING
THUMBTACK
THUMBY
THUMP
THUMPED
THUMPER
THUMPING
THUMPINGLY
THUNBERGILENE
THUNDER
THUNDERBIRD
THUNDERBLAST
THUNDERBOLT
THUNDERBURST
THUNDERCLAP
THUNDERCLOUD
THUNDERCRACK
THUNDERED
THUNDERER
THUNDERFISH
THUNDERFISHES
THUNDERHEAD
THUNDERING
THUNDERINGLY
THUNDERLIGHT
THUNDEROUS
THUNDEROUSLY
THUNDERPEAL
THUNDERPLUMP
THUNDERPUMP
THUNDERSMITE
THUNDERSMITING
THUNDERSMOTE
THUNDERSQUALL
THUNDERSTONE
THUNDERSTORM
THUNDERSTROKE
THUNDERWOOD
THUNDERWORM
THUNDERWORT
THUNDERY
THUNDROUS
THUNGE
THUNK
THUOC
THUR
THURGI
THURIBLE
THURIBULER
THURIBULUM
THURIFER
THURIFEROUS
THURIFICATE
THURIFICATI
THURIFY
THURINGITE
THURL
THURLE
THURM
THURMUS
THURROCK
THURSE
THURST
THURT
THUS
THUSGATE
THUSLY
THUSWISE
THUTTER
THUYA
THWACK
THWACKED
THWACKER
THWACKING
THWACKINGLY
THWACKSTAVE
THWAITE
THWART
THWARTED
THWARTEOUS
THWARTER
THWARTING
THWARTINGLY
THWARTMAN
THWARTMEN
THWARTOVER
THWARTSAW
THWARTSHIP
THWARTSHIPS
THWITE
THWITTLE
THWORL
THY
THYINE
THYLACINE
THYLACITIS
THYMACETIN
THYME
THYMECTOMY
THYMELCOSIS
THYMELE
THYMELIC
THYMELICAL
THYMELICI
THYMENE
THYMETIC
THYMIAMA
THYMIC
THYMIER
THYMIEST
THYMIN
THYMINE
THYMIOSIS
THYMITIS
THYMOCYTE
THYMOGENIC
THYMOL
THYMOLATE
THYMOLIZE
THYMOMA
THYMOMATA
THYMOPATHY
THYMOPRIVIC
THYMOPSYCHE
THYMOQUINONE
THYMOTACTIC
THYMOTIC
THYMOTINIC
THYMS
THYMUS
THYMY
THYMYL
THYMYLIC
THYNNID
THYRATRON
THYREOID
THYRIDIA
THYRIDIAL
THYRIDIUM
THYROCARDIAC
THYROCELE
THYROCOLLOID
THYROGENIC
THYROGENOUS
THYROGLOSSAL
THYROHYAL
THYROHYOID
THYROID
THYROIDEA
THYROIDISM
THYROIDITIS
THYROIDLESS
THYROIDOTOMY
THYROLINGUAL
THYRONIN
THYRONINE
THYROPRIVAL
THYROPRIVIA
THYROPRIVIC
THYROPROTEIN
THYROSTRACAN
THYROTHERAPY
THYROTOMY
THYROTOXIC
THYROXIN
THYROXINE
THYROXINIC
THYRSE
THYRSI
THYRSOID
THYRSOIDAL
THYRSUS
THYSANOPTER
THYSANURAN
THYSANUROUS
THYSELF
THYSEN
TI
TIA
TIAL
TIANG
TIANGUE
TIAO
TIAR
TIARA
TIARELLA
TIB
TIBBIT
TIBBY
TIBERT
TIBET
TIBEY
TIBIA
TIBIAE
TIBIAL
TIBIALE
TIBIALIA
TIBIALIS
TIBIAS
TIBICEN
TIBIOFIBULA
TIBIOTARSAL
TIBIOTARSI
TIBIOTARSUS
TIBOURBOU
TIBURON
TIC
TICAL

TICCA
TICCHEN
TICE
TICEMENT
TICER
TICHEL
TICHODROME
TICHORRHINE
TICK
TICKBEAN
TICKBIRD
TICKED
TICKEN
TICKER
TICKET
TICKETED
TICKETER
TICKETING
TICKETMONGER
TICKEY
TICKIE
TICKING
TICKLE
TICKLEBACK
TICKLEBRAIN
TICKLED
TICKLELY
TICKLENBURG
TICKLENESS
TICKLER
TICKLESOME
TICKLEWEED
TICKLING
TICKLINGLY
TICKLISH
TICKLISHLY
TICKLISHNESS
TICKLY
TICKNEY
TICKSEED
TICKSEEDED
TICKTACK
TICKTACKER
TICKTACKTOE
TICKTACKTOO
TICKTICK
TICKTOCK
TICKWEED
TICKY
TICTACTOE
TICTIC
TICUL
TID
TIDAL
TIDBIT
TIDBITS
TIDDER
TIDDLE
TIDDLEDYWINKS
TIDDLER
TIDDLEY
TIDDLEYWINK
TIDDLING
TIDDLY
TIDDLYWINK
TIDDLYWINKER
TIDDLYWINKING
TIDDLYWINKS
TIDDY
TIDE
TIDECOACH
TIDED
TIDEFUL
TIDEHEAD
TIDELAND
TIDELESS
TIDELY
TIDEMAKER
TIDEMAKING
TIDEMARK
TIDERACE
TIDERIP
TIDES
TIDESMAN
TIDESURVEYOR
TIDEWAITER
TIDEWATER
TIDEWAY
TIDIED
TIDIER
TIDIES
TIDIEST
TIDIFE
TIDILY
TIDINESS
TIDING
TIDINGS
TIDIOSE
TIDLEY
TIDLING
TIDOLOGICAL
TIDOLOGY
TIDY
TIDYING
TIDYTIPS
TIE
TIEBACK
TIEBOY
TIED
TIEDOG
TIEGO
TIEING
TIEMANNITE
TIEN
TIENDA
TIENS
TIENTA
TIENTO
TIEPIN
TIER
TIERCE
TIERCERON
TIERED
TIERER
TIERRAS
TIERSMAN
TIES
TIETICK
TIEVINE
TIEWIG
TIFF
TIFFANIES
TIFFANY
TIFFANYITE
TIFFED
TIFFIE
TIFFIN
TIFFING
TIFFISH
TIFFLE
TIFFY
TIFINAGH
TIFLE
TIFT
TIFTER
TIG
TIGE
TIGELLA
TIGELLATE
TIGELLE
TIGELLUM
TIGELLUS
TIGER
TIGERBIRD
TIGEREYE
TIGERFLOWER
TIGERFOOT
TIGERISH
TIGERISHLY
TIGERISHNESS
TIGERISM
TIGERKIN
TIGERLY
TIGERNUT
TIGERS
TIGERWOOD
TIGGER
TIGH
TIGHT
TIGHTEN
TIGHTENED
TIGHTENER
TIGHTENING
TIGHTER
TIGHTEST
TIGHTFISTED
TIGHTISH
TIGHTLIER
TIGHTLIEST
TIGHTLIPPED
TIGHTLY
TIGHTNESS
TIGHTROPE
TIGHTS
TIGHTWAD
TIGHTWIRE
TIGLALDEHYDE
TIGLIC
TIGLINIC
TIGNON
TIGNUM
TIGRESS
TIGRINE
TIGRISH
TIGROID
TIGROLYSIS
TIGROLYTIC
TIGRONE
TIGTAG
TIKAL
TIKE
TIKI
TIKITIKI
TIKKA
TIKKER
TIKKUN
TIKLIN
TIKOLOSH
TIKOOR
TIKOR
TIKUG
TIKUR
TIL
TILAITE
TILAK
TILAKA
TILASITE
TILBURIES
TILBURY
TILDE
TILE
TILED
TILEFISH
TILEFISHES
TILER
TILERIES
TILEROOT
TILERY
TILES
TILESEED
TILESHERD
TILESTONE
TILETTE
TILIACEOUS
TILICETUM
TILIKUM
TILING
TILL
TILLABLE
TILLAGE
TILLANDSIA
TILLED
TILLER
TILLERED
TILLERING
TILLERMAN
TILLET
TILLEY
TILLICUM
TILLING
TILLITE
TILLMAN
TILLODONT
TILLOT
TILLY
TILMA
TILMUS
TILPAH
TILT
TILTBOARD
TILTED
TILTER
TILTH
TILTING
TILTUP
TILTURE
TILTY
TILTYARD
TILYER
TIMALIINE
TIMALINE
TIMAR
TIMARAU
TIMARIOT
TIMARRI
TIMAUA
TIMAWA
TIMAZITE
TIMBAL
TIMBALE
TIMBANG
TIMBE
TIMBER
TIMBERED
TIMBERER
TIMBERHEAD
TIMBERING
TIMBERJACK
TIMBERLAND
TIMBERLESS
TIMBERLIKE
TIMBERLING
TIMBERMAN
TIMBERMEN
TIMBERN
TIMBERS
TIMBERSOME
TIMBERTUNED
TIMBERWOOD
TIMBERWORK
TIMBERY
TIMBESTERE
TIMBO
TIMBRE
TIMBREL
TIMBRELED
TIMBRELER
TIMBRELLED
TIMBRELLER
TIME
TIMECARD
TIMED
TIMEFUL
TIMEKEEP
TIMEKEEPER
TIMEKEEPING
TIMELESS
TIMELESSLY
TIMELESSNESS
TIMELIER
TIMELIEST
TIMELILY
TIMELINESS
TIMELY
TIMENOGUY
TIMEOUS
TIMEOUSLY
TIMEPIECE
TIMEPLEASER
TIMER
TIMERAU
TIMERITY
TIMES
TIMESAVER
TIMESAVING
TIMESERVER
TIMESERVING
TIMETABLE
TIMETAKER
TIMETAKING
TIMEWORK
TIMEWORKER
TIMEWORN
TIMID
TIMIDER
TIMIDEST
TIMIDITY
TIMIDLY
TIMIDNESS
TIMIDOUS
TIMING
TIMISH
TIMIST
TIMMER
TIMOCRACIES
TIMOCRACY
TIMOCRATIC
TIMOCRATICAL
TIMON
TIMONEER
TIMOR
TIMOROSO
TIMOROUS
TIMOROUSLY
TIMOROUSNESS
TIMOTHY
TIMPANI
TIMPANIST
TIMPANO
TIMPANUM
TIN
TINA
TINAGE
TINAJA
TINAMINE
TINAMOU
TINAMPIPI
TINCAL
TINCHEL
TINCHILL
TINCLAD
TINCT
TINCTED
TINCTING
TINCTION

TINCTORIAL
TINCTORIALLY
TINCTURE
TINCTURED
TINCTURING
TIND
TINDAL
TINDALO
TINDER
TINDERBOX
TINDERED
TINDERISH
TINDERY
TINE
TINEA
TINEAL
TINEAN
TINED
TINEGRASS
TINEID
TINEINE
TINEMAN
TINEMEN
TINEOID
TINEOLA
TINES
TINETARE
TINETY
TINEWEED
TINFOIL
TING
TINGE
TINGED
TINGEING
TINGENT
TINGER
TINGI
TINGID
TINGING
TINGITID
TINGLASS
TINGLE
TINGLED
TINGLER
TINGLING
TINGLINGLY
TINGLISH
TINGLY
TINGTANG
TINGUAITE
TINGUAITIC
TINGUY
TINHORN
TINHOUSE
TINIER
TINIEST
TINING
TINK
TINKER
TINKERBIRD
TINKERED
TINKERER
TINKERING
TINKERLY
TINKERSHIRE
TINKERSHUE
TINKLE
TINKLED
TINKLER
TINKLING
TINKLINGLY
TINKLY
TINLET
TINMAN
TINMEN
TINNED
TINNEN
TINNER
TINNERY
TINNET
TINNIENT
TINNIER
TINNIEST
TINNIFIED
TINNILY
TINNINESS
TINNING
TINNITUS
TINNOCK
TINNY
TINOSA
TINSEL
TINSELED
TINSELING
TINSELLED
TINSELLING
TINSELLY
TINSELRY
TINSMAN
TINSMEN
TINSMITH
TINSMITHING
TINSMITHY
TINSTONE
TINSTUFF
TINSY
TINT
TINTA
TINTAGE
TINTAMAR
TINTAMARRE
TINTARRON
TINTED
TINTER
TINTERNELL
TINTIE
TINTING
TINTIST
TINTO
TINTOMETER
TINTOMETRIC
TINTOMETRY
TINTY
TINTYPE
TINTYPER
TINWALD
TINWARE
TINWORK
TINWORKER
TINWORKING
TINWORKS
TINY
TINZENITE
TIP
TIPBURN
TIPCART
TIPCAT
TIPE
TIPFUL
TIPHEAD
TIPI
TIPITI
TIPLE
TIPLET
TIPMAN
TIPMEN
TIPMOST
TIPOFF
TIPONI
TIPPABLE
TIPPED
TIPPEE
TIPPER
TIPPET
TIPPIER
TIPPIEST
TIPPING
TIPPLE
TIPPLED
TIPPLER
TIPPLING
TIPPY
TIPREE
TIPSIER
TIPSIEST
TIPSIFIER
TIPSIFY
TIPSILY
TIPSINESS
TIPSTAFF
TIPSTAFFS
TIPSTAVES
TIPSTER
TIPSTOCK
TIPSY
TIPTAIL
TIPTEERER
TIPTILT
TIPTOE
TIPTOED
TIPTOEING
TIPTOEINGLY
TIPTOES
TIPTOP
TIPTOPPER
TIPULID
TIPULOID
TIPUP
TIQUEUR
TIR
TIRADE
TIRAGE
TIRAILLEUR
TIRALEE
TIRASSE
TIRAZ
TIRE
TIRED
TIREDER
TIREDEST
TIREDLY
TIREDNESS
TIREHOUSE
TIRELESS
TIRELESSLY
TIRELESSNESS
TIREMAID
TIREMAN
TIREMEN
TIREMENT
TIRER
TIRES
TIRESMITH
TIRESOL
TIRESOME
TIRESOMELY
TIRESOMENESS
TIREWOMAN
TIREWOMEN
TIRIBA
TIRING
TIRL
TIRLING
TIRMA
TIRO
TIROCINIA
TIROCINIUM
TIROS
TIRR
TIRRACKE
TIRRALIRRA
TIRRET
TIRRIT
TIRRIVEE
TIRRIVIE
TIRRLIE
TIRRWIRR
TIRTHANKARA
TIRVE
TIRWIT
TIRY
TIS
TISANE
TISAR
TISSUAL
TISSUE
TISSUED
TISSUES
TISSUEY
TISSUING
TISSWOOD
TISWIN
TIT
TITANATE
TITANAUGITE
TITANIA
TITANIC
TITANIFEROUS
TITANITE
TITANITIC
TITANIUM
TITANOSAUR
TITANOTHERE
TITANOUS
TITANYL
TITAR
TITBIT
TITBITTY
TITE
TITER
TITFISH
TITHABLE
TITHAL
TITHE
TITHED
TITHER
TITHES
TITHING
TITHINGMAN
TITHINGMEN
TITHINGPENNY
TITHONIC
TITHONICITY
TITHONOMETER
TITHYMAL
TITI
TITIAN
TITIEN
TITILLABILITY
TITILLANT
TITILLATE
TITILLATED
TITILLATER
TITILLATING
TITILLATINGLY
TITILLATION
TITILLATIVE
TITILLATOR
TITILLATORY
TITIVATE
TITIVATION
TITIVATOR
TITIVIL
TITIVILLER
TITLARK
TITLE
TITLEBOARD
TITLED
TITLEHOLDER
TITLENE
TITLER
TITLING
TITLIST
TITMAL
TITMALL
TITMAN
TITMEN
TITMICE
TITMOUSE
TITOKI
TITRANT
TITRATABLE
TITRATE
TITRATED
TITRATING
TITRATION
TITRE
TITTER
TITTERATION
TITTERED
TITTEREL
TITTERER
TITTERING
TITTERINGLY
TITTERY
TITTIE
TITTIVATE
TITTIVATED
TITTIVATING
TITTIVATION
TITTIVATOR
TITTLE
TITTLEBAT
TITTLER
TITTLIN
TITTUP
TITTUPED
TITTUPING
TITTUPPED
TITTUPPING
TITTUPPY
TITTUPY
TITTY
TITTYMOUSE
TITUBANCY
TITUBANT
TITUBANTLY
TITUBATE
TITUBATION
TITULADO
TITULAR
TITULARIES
TITULARITY
TITULARLY
TITULARY
TITULE
TITULI
TITULUS
TIVER
TIVOLI
TIVY
TIZA
TIZEUR
TIZZIES
TIZZY
TJAELE
TJALK
TJANDI
TJANTING
TJENKAL
TJI
TJOSITE
TJURUNGA
TLAC
TLACO

TMEMA
TMEMATA
TMESIS
TO
TOA
TOAD
TOADBACK
TOADEAT
TOADEATER
TOADFISH
TOADFISHES
TOADFLAX
TOADFLOWER
TOADHEAD
TOADIED
TOADIER
TOADIES
TOADISH
TOADO
TOADPIPE
TOADPIPES
TOADROOT
TOADSTONE
TOADSTOOL
TOADY
TOADYING
TOADYISH
TOADYISM
TOAST
TOASTED
TOASTEE
TOASTER
TOASTINESS
TOASTING
TOASTMASTER
TOASTMASTERY
TOASTY
TOAT
TOATOA
TOBACCO
TOBACCOES
TOBACCOFIED
TOBACCOITE
TOBACCOMAN
TOBACCOMEN
TOBACCONING
TOBACCONIZE
TOBACCOROOT
TOBACCOS
TOBACCOSIM
TOBACCOY
TOBE
TOBER
TOBIES
TOBINE
TOBIRA
TOBOGGAN
TOBOGGANED
TOBOGGANER
TOBOGGANING
TOBOGGANIST
TOBY
TOBYMAN
TOBYMEN
TOCALOTE
TOCCATA
TOCCATINA
TOCHER
TOCK
TOCO
TOCOGENETIC
TOCOGONY
TOCOKININ
TOCOLOGICAL
TOCOLOGIST
TOCOLOGY
TOCOME
TOCOPHEROL
TOCORORO
TOCSIN
TOCUSSO
TOD
TODAY
TODAYISH
TODDER
TODDICK
TODDIES
TODDITE
TODDLE
TODDLED
TODDLER
TODDLING
TODDY
TODDYIZE
TODDYMAN
TODDYMEN
TODE
TODIES
TODLOWRIE
TODY
TOE
TOEBOARD
TOECAP
TOED
TOEHOLD
TOEING
TOELLITE
TOENAIL
TOEPLATE
TOETOE
TOEY
TOFF
TOFFEE
TOFFEEMAN
TOFFISH
TOFFY
TOFFYMAN
TOFFYMEN
TOFORE
TOFORN
TOFT
TOFTER
TOFTMAN
TOFTMEN
TOFU
TOG
TOGA
TOGAE
TOGAED
TOGAS
TOGATE
TOGATED
TOGE
TOGEMAN
TOGETHER
TOGETHERNESS
TOGGED
TOGGEL
TOGGERIES
TOGGERY
TOGGING
TOGGLE
TOGGLED
TOGGLER
TOGGLING
TOGLESS
TOGS
TOGT
TOGUE
TOHEROA
TOHI
TOHO
TOHUBOHU
TOHUNGA
TOI
TOIL
TOILE
TOILED
TOILER
TOILET
TOILETED
TOILETRIES
TOILETRY
TOILETTE
TOILETWARE
TOILFUL
TOILFULLY
TOILINET
TOILINETTE
TOILING
TOILINGLY
TOILSOME
TOILSOMELY
TOILSOMENESS
TOISE
TOISECH
TOISED
TOISING
TOISON
TOIST
TOIT
TOITISH
TOITOI
TOITY
TOKAY
TOKE
TOKEN
TOKENED
TOKENWORTH
TOKO
TOKOLOGY
TOKONOMA
TOKOPAT
TOKTOKJE
TOL
TOLA
TOLAN
TOLANE
TOLBOOTH
TOLD
TOLDERIA
TOLDO
TOLE
TOLED
TOLEDO
TOLERABILITY
TOLERABLE
TOLERABLY
TOLERANCE
TOLERANCY
TOLERANT
TOLERANTLY
TOLERATE
TOLERATED
TOLERATING
TOLERATION
TOLERATIVE
TOLERATOR
TOLERISM
TOLFRAEDIC
TOLGUACHA
TOLIDIN
TOLIDINE
TOLING
TOLIPANE
TOLITE
TOLKE
TOLL
TOLLABLE
TOLLAGE
TOLLBAR
TOLLBOOK
TOLLBOOTH
TOLLED
TOLLER
TOLLERY
TOLLGATE
TOLLGATHERER
TOLLHALL
TOLLHOUSE
TOLLHOUSES
TOLLIKER
TOLLING
TOLLKEEPER
TOLLMAN
TOLLMEN
TOLLON
TOLLS
TOLLWAY
TOLLY
TOLMEN
TOLPATCH
TOLPATCHERY
TOLSEL
TOLSESTER
TOLSEY
TOLT
TOLTER
TOLU
TOLUALDEHYDE
TOLUATE
TOLUENE
TOLUIC
TOLUID
TOLUIDE
TOLUIDIN
TOLUIDINE
TOLUIDO
TOLUNITRILE
TOLUOL
TOLUOLE
TOLUTATION
TOLUYL
TOLUYLENE
TOLYL
TOLYLENE
TOLYPEUTINE
TOLZEY
TOM
TOMAHAWK
TOMAHAWKED
TOMAHAWKER
TOMAHAWKING
TOMALLEY
TOMAN
TOMAND
TOMATILLO
TOMATO
TOMATOES
TOMB
TOMBAC
TOMBACK
TOMBAK
TOMBAL
TOMBE
TOMBED
TOMBIC
TOMBING
TOMBLET
TOMBOLA
TOMBOLO
TOMBOY
TOMBOYFUL
TOMBOYISH
TOMBOYISHLY
TOMBS
TOMBSTONE
TOMCAT
TOMCOD
TOME
TOMENT
TOMENTA
TOMENTOSE
TOMENTULOSE
TOMENTUM
TOMFOOL
TOMFOOLERIES
TOMFOOLERY
TOMFOOLISH
TOMIA
TOMIAL
TOMIN
TOMINES
TOMISH
TOMIUM
TOMJOHN
TOMJON
TOMKIN
TOMME
TOMMED
TOMMIES
TOMMING
TOMMY
TOMMYBAG
TOMMYCOD
TOMMYROT
TOMNODDY
TOMNORRY
TOMNOUP
TOMOGRAPHY
TOMOLO
TOMORN
TOMORROW
TOMORROWER
TOMORROWING
TOMORROWNESS
TOMOSIS
TOMPION
TOMPIPER
TOMRIG
TOMTATE
TOMTIT
TON
TONADA
TONAL
TONALAMATL
TONALIST
TONALITE
TONALITIES
TONALITIVE
TONALITY
TONALLY
TONALMATL
TONANT
TONDE
TONDI
TONDINO
TONDO
TONE
TONED
TONEDEAFNESS
TONEE
TONEL
TONELADA
TONELESS
TONELESSLY
TONELESSNESS
TONEME
TONER
TONES
TONETIC
TONETICALLY
TONETICIAN
TONETICS
TONETTE

TONG
TONGA
TONGED
TONGING
TONGKANG
TONGS
TONGSMAN
TONGSMEN
TONGUE
TONGUEBIRD
TONGUED
TONGUEFENCE
TONGUEFENCER
TONGUEFISH
TONGUEFISHES
TONGUEFUL
TONGUEFULS
TONGUELESS
TONGUELET
TONGUEMAN
TONGUEMEN
TONGUER
TONGUEY
TONGUING
TONGUY
TONIC
TONICAL
TONICALLY
TONICITY
TONICIZE
TONICKED
TONICKING
TONIER
TONIES
TONIEST
TONIFY
TONIGHT
TONING
TONISH
TONISHLY
TONISHNESS
TONITE
TONITRUONE
TONITRUOUS
TONJON
TONK
TONKA
TONLET
TONNAGE
TONNE
TONNEAU
TONNEAUS
TONNEAUX
TONNELLE
TONNER
TONNISH
TONNISHLY
TONNISHNESS
TONNLAND
TONOGRAM
TONOGRAPH
TONOLOGICAL
TONOLOGY
TONOMETRIC
TONOMETRY
TONOPHANT
TONOPLAST
TONOSCOPE
TONOTACTIC
TONOTAXIS
TONOUS
TONSBERGITE
TONSIL
TONSILAR
TONSILE
TONSILITIS
TONSILLAR
TONSILLARY
TONSILLITIC
TONSILLOLITH
TONSILLOTOMIES
TONSILLOTOMY
TONSOR
TONSORIAL
TONSURATE
TONSURE
TONSURED
TONSURING
TONTINE
TONTINER
TONUS
TONY
TONYHOOP
TOO
TOOART
TOODLE
TOOK
TOOL
TOOLACH
TOOLBOX
TOOLBUILDER
TOOLBUILDING
TOOLED
TOOLER
TOOLHOLDER
TOOLING
TOOLMAKER
TOOLMAKING
TOOLMAN
TOOLMARK
TOOLMARKING
TOOLMEN
TOOLPLATE
TOOLROOM
TOOLS
TOOLSI
TOOLSLIDE
TOOLSMITH
TOOLSTOCK
TOOLSTONE
TOOLSY
TOOM
TOOMLY
TOON
TOONWOOD
TOOP
TOORIE
TOOROCK
TOOROO
TOOSE
TOOSH
TOOSIE
TOOT
TOOTED
TOOTER
TOOTH
TOOTHACHE
TOOTHACHING
TOOTHACHY
TOOTHBILL
TOOTHBRUSH
TOOTHBRUSHY
TOOTHDRAWER
TOOTHDRAWING
TOOTHED
TOOTHER
TOOTHFLOWER
TOOTHFUL
TOOTHIER
TOOTHIEST
TOOTHILL
TOOTHING
TOOTHLESS
TOOTHLESSLY
TOOTHLET
TOOTHLETED
TOOTHPASTE
TOOTHPICK
TOOTHPLATE
TOOTHPOWDER
TOOTHPROOF
TOOTHSHELL
TOOTHSOME
TOOTHSOMELY
TOOTHSTICK
TOOTHWASH
TOOTHWORK
TOOTHWORT
TOOTHY
TOOTING
TOOTINGHOLE
TOOTLE
TOOTLED
TOOTLER
TOOTLING
TOOTLISH
TOOTMOOT
TOOTS
TOOTSIE
TOOTSIES
TOOTSY
TOOZLE
TOOZOO
TOP
TOPAESTHESIA
TOPARCH
TOPARCHIA
TOPARCHIAE
TOPARCHICAL
TOPARCHIES
TOPARCHY
TOPAS
TOPASS
TOPATO
TOPAU
TOPAZ
TOPAZES
TOPAZFELS
TOPAZINE
TOPAZITE
TOPAZOLITE
TOPAZY
TOPCAP
TOPCAST
TOPCOAT
TOPCOATING
TOPE
TOPECHEE
TOPECTOMIES
TOPECTOMY
TOPED
TOPEE
TOPEEWALLAH
TOPEK
TOPENG
TOPEPO
TOPER
TOPESTHESIA
TOPFILLED
TOPFLIGHT
TOPFUL
TOPFULL
TOPGALLANT
TOPH
TOPHACEOUS
TOPHAIKE
TOPHE
TOPHETIC
TOPHETICAL
TOPHI
TOPHUS
TOPI
TOPIA
TOPIARIA
TOPIARIAN
TOPIARIES
TOPIARIST
TOPIARY
TOPIC
TOPICAL
TOPICALITY
TOPICALLY
TOPINAMBOU
TOPING
TOPIS
TOPIWALA
TOPKICK
TOPKNOT
TOPKNOTTED
TOPLESS
TOPLESSNESS
TOPLIGHTED
TOPLINE
TOPLOFTICAL
TOPLOFTIER
TOPLOFTIEST
TOPLOFTILY
TOPLOFTINESS
TOPLOFTY
TOPMAKER
TOPMAN
TOPMAST
TOPMEN
TOPMINNOW
TOPMOST
TOPMOSTLY
TOPNET
TOPNOTCH
TOPNOTCHER
TOPO
TOPOALGIA
TOPODEME
TOPOGNOSIA
TOPOGNOSIS
TOPOGRAPH
TOPOGRAPHER
TOPOGRAPHIC
TOPOGRAPHICAL
TOPOGRAPHICS
TOPOGRAPHIES
TOPOGRAPHIST
TOPOGRAPHY
TOPOLATRY
TOPOLOGIC
TOPOLOGICAL
TOPOLOGY
TOPONARCOSIS
TOPONEURAL
TOPONEUROSIS
TOPONYM
TOPONYMAL
TOPONYMIC
TOPONYMICAL
TOPONYMICS
TOPONYMIES
TOPONYMY
TOPOPHOBIA
TOPOPHONE
TOPOPOLITAN
TOPOTACTIC
TOPOTAXIS
TOPOTYPE
TOPOTYPIC
TOPOTYPICAL
TOPPED
TOPPER
TOPPIECE
TOPPING
TOPPINGLY
TOPPINGNESS
TOPPLE
TOPPLED
TOPPLER
TOPPLING
TOPPLY
TOPPO
TOPPY
TOPRAIL
TOPROPE
TOPS
TOPSAIL
TOPSAILITE
TOPSIDE
TOPSMAN
TOPSMEN
TOPSOIL
TOPSTONE
TOPSWARM
TOPSYTURN
TOPT
TOPTAIL
TOPWORK
TOQUE
TOQUET
TOQUILLA
TOR
TORA
TORAH
TORAN
TORANA
TORBANITE
TORBANITIC
TORBERNITE
TORC
TORCEL
TORCH
TORCHBEARER
TORCHBEARING
TORCHER
TORCHERE
TORCHET
TORCHLIGHT
TORCHLIGHTED
TORCHLIKE
TORCHLIT
TORCHMAN
TORCHON
TORCHWOOD
TORCHWORT
TORCULAR
TORCULUS
TORDION
TORDRILLITE
TORE
TOREADOR
TORERO
TOREROS
TORET
TOREUTIC
TOREUTICS
TORFACEOUS
TORFEL
TORFLE
TORGOCH
TORI
TORIC
TORIES
TORII
TORIL
TORMA
TORMAE
TORMENT
TORMENTA
TORMENTATIVE
TORMENTED

TORMENTEDLY
TORMENTER
TORMENTIL
TORMENTILLA
TORMENTING
TORMENTINGLY
TORMENTIVE
TORMENTOR
TORMENTOUS
TORMENTRY
TORMENTUM
TORMINA
TORMINAL
TORMINOUS
TORMODONT
TORN
TORNADA
TORNADE
TORNADIC
TORNADO
TORNADOES
TORNADOS
TORNARIA
TORNARIAE
TORNARIAN
TORNESE
TORNESI
TORNILLA
TORNILLO
TORNOTE
TORNUS
TORO
TOROID
TOROIDAL
TOROLILLO
TORONJA
TOROROKOMBU
TOROS
TOROSE
TOROSITY
TOROTH
TOROTORO
TOROUS
TORP
TORPEDINEER
TORPEDINOUS
TORPEDO
TORPEDOED
TORPEDOER
TORPEDOES
TORPEDOING
TORPEDOIST
TORPEDOPLANE
TORPEDOS
TORPENT
TORPESCENCE
TORPESCENT
TORPEX
TORPID
TORPIDITIES
TORPIDITY
TORPIDLY
TORPIDNESS
TORPIDS
TORPIFIED
TORPIFY
TORPIFYING
TORPITUDE
TORPOR
TORPORIFIC
TORQUATE
TORQUATED
TORQUE
TORQUED
TORQUES
TORR
TORREFACTION
TORREFIED
TORREFY
TORREFYING
TORRENT
TORRENTFUL
TORRENTIAL
TORRENTIALLY
TORRENTINE
TORRENTUOUS
TORRET
TORRID
TORRIDITY
TORRIDLY
TORRIDNESS
TORRIFY
TORRONE
TORSADE
TORSALO
TORSE
TORSEL
TORSI
TORSIGRAPH
TORSILE
TORSIOGRAM
TORSIOGRAPH
TORSION
TORSIONAL
TORSIONALLY
TORSIONING
TORSIVE
TORSK
TORSKS
TORSO
TORSOCLUSION
TORSOS
TORT
TORTA
TORTAYS
TORTE
TORTEAU
TORTEAUS
TORTEAUX
TORTEN
TORTICOLLAR
TORTICOLLIS
TORTICONE
TORTIE
TORTIL
TORTILE
TORTILITY
TORTILLA
TORTILLAS
TORTILLE
TORTILLON
TORTIOUS
TORTIS
TORTIVE
TORTOISE
TORTOISES
TORTOISESHELL
TORTONI
TORTOR
TORTRICES
TORTRICID
TORTRICINE
TORTRICOID
TORTRIX
TORTUE
TORTULA
TORTULACEOUS
TORTUOSITIES
TORTUOSITY
TORTUOUS
TORTUOUSLY
TORTUOUSNESS
TORTURABLE
TORTURE
TORTURED
TORTUREDLY
TORTURER
TORTURING
TORTURINGLY
TORTUROUS
TORTUROUSLY
TORU
TORULA
TORULACEOUS
TORULAE
TORULI
TORULIFORM
TORULOID
TORULOSE
TORULOSIS
TORULOUS
TORULUS
TORUS
TORVID
TORVITY
TORVOUS
TORY
TORYHILLITE
TORYWEED
TOSAPHIST
TOSAPHOTH
TOSCA
TOSE
TOSH
TOSHAKHANA
TOSHER
TOSHERY
TOSHLY
TOSHNAIL
TOSHY
TOSIE
TOSS
TOSSED
TOSSER
TOSSICATED
TOSSING
TOSSINGLY
TOSSMENT
TOSSPOT
TOSSUP
TOSSUT
TOSSY
TOST
TOSTADO
TOSTAMENTE
TOSTAO
TOSTICATE
TOSTICATED
TOSTICATING
TOSTICATION
TOSTO
TOSTON
TOSY
TOSYL
TOT
TOTA
TOTAL
TOTALED
TOTALING
TOTALISATOR
TOTALITARIAN
TOTALITIES
TOTALITY
TOTALIZATION
TOTALIZATOR
TOTALIZE
TOTALIZED
TOTALIZER
TOTALIZING
TOTALLED
TOTALLING
TOTALLY
TOTANINE
TOTAQUINE
TOTARA
TOTE
TOTED
TOTELOAD
TOTEM
TOTEMIC
TOTEMICALLY
TOTEMISM
TOTEMIST
TOTEMISTIC
TOTEMIZATION
TOTER
TOTHER
TOTIENT
TOTING
TOTIPALMATE
TOTIPOTENCE
TOTIPOTENCY
TOTIPOTENT
TOTITIVE
TOTO
TOTOABA
TOTORA
TOTQUOT
TOTTED
TOTTER
TOTTERED
TOTTERER
TOTTERGRASS
TOTTERING
TOTTERINGLY
TOTTERISH
TOTTERY
TOTTING
TOTTLE
TOTTLISH
TOTTUM
TOTTY
TOTTYHEAD
TOTUAVA
TOTUM
TOTY
TOTYMAN
TOU
TOUART
TOUCAN
TOUCH
TOUCHABLE
TOUCHBACK
TOUCHBELL
TOUCHBOX
TOUCHDOWN
TOUCHE
TOUCHED
TOUCHEDNESS
TOUCHER
TOUCHHOLE
TOUCHIER
TOUCHIEST
TOUCHILY
TOUCHINESS
TOUCHING
TOUCHINGLY
TOUCHINGNESS
TOUCHLINE
TOUCHMARK
TOUCHOUS
TOUCHPAN
TOUCHPIECE
TOUCHSTONE
TOUCHUP
TOUCHWOOD
TOUCHY
TOUG
TOUGH
TOUGHEN
TOUGHENED
TOUGHENER
TOUGHENING
TOUGHER
TOUGHEST
TOUGHHEAD
TOUGHLY
TOUGHNESS
TOUGHRA
TOUGHT
TOUMNAH
TOUN
TOUP
TOUPEE
TOUPEED
TOUPET
TOUR
TOURACO
TOURBE
TOURBILLON
TOURED
TOURELLE
TOURER
TOURET
TOURETTE
TOURING
TOURISM
TOURIST
TOURISTIC
TOURISTICAL
TOURISTRY
TOURISTY
TOURMALIN
TOURMALINE
TOURMALINIC
TOURMALINIZE
TOURMALITE
TOURN
TOURNAI
TOURNAMENT
TOURNAMENTAL
TOURNASIN
TOURNAY
TOURNE
TOURNEE
TOURNEL
TOURNETTE
TOURNEUR
TOURNEY
TOURNEYED
TOURNEYER
TOURNEYING
TOURNEYS
TOURNIQUET
TOURNOIS
TOURNURE
TOURS
TOURT
TOURTE
TOUSCHE
TOUSE
TOUSEL
TOUSER
TOUSLE
TOUSLED
TOUSLING
TOUSLY
TOUST
TOUSTIE
TOUSY
TOUT
TOUTE
TOUTER
TOUZLE
TOVAR

TOVARIACEOUS
TOVARICH
TOVARISCH
TOVARISH
TOVE
TOVET
TOW
TOWAGE
TOWAI
TOWAN
TOWARD
TOWARDLINESS
TOWARDLY
TOWARDNESS
TOWARDS
TOWAWAY
TOWBOAT
TOWCOCK
TOWDIE
TOWED
TOWEL
TOWELED
TOWELETTE
TOWELING
TOWELLED
TOWELLING
TOWELRY
TOWER
TOWERED
TOWERING
TOWERINGLY
TOWERLET
TOWERLIKE
TOWERMAN
TOWERMEN
TOWERWORT
TOWERY
TOWGHT
TOWHEAD
TOWHEADED
TOWHEE
TOWING
TOWKAY
TOWLINE
TOWMAST
TOWMOND
TOWMONT
TOWN
TOWNED
TOWNEE
TOWNER
TOWNET
TOWNFARING
TOWNFOLK
TOWNFOLKS
TOWNGATE
TOWNHOUSE
TOWNIE
TOWNIES
TOWNIFIED
TOWNIFY
TOWNIFYING
TOWNINESS
TOWNISH
TOWNISHLY
TOWNISHNESS
TOWNIST
TOWNLAND
TOWNLET
TOWNLIKE
TOWNLING
TOWNLY
TOWNMAN
TOWNMEN
TOWNSBOY
TOWNSFELLOW
TOWNSHIP
TOWNSITE
TOWNSMAN
TOWNSMEN
TOWNSPEOPLE
TOWNSWOMAN
TOWNSWOMEN
TOWNWEAR
TOWNY
TOWPATH
TOWROPE
TOWSE
TOWSER
TOWSON
TOWSY
TOWT
TOWY
TOWZIE
TOX
TOXA
TOXAEMIA
TOXAEMIAS
TOXAEMIC
TOXALBUMIC
TOXALBUMIN
TOXALBUMOSE
TOXAMIN
TOXANAEMIA
TOXANEMIA
TOXEMIA
TOXEMIC
TOXIC
TOXICAL
TOXICALLY
TOXICANT
TOXICAROL
TOXICATE
TOXICATION
TOXICITIES
TOXICITY
TOXICOGENIC
TOXICOGNATH
TOXICOID
TOXICOLOGIC
TOXICOLOGIST
TOXICOLOGY
TOXICOMANIA
TOXICON
TOXICOPATHIC
TOXICOPATHY
TOXICOPHAGY
TOXICOPHIDIA
TOXICOSES
TOXICOSIS
TOXICUM
TOXIDERMIC
TOXIFER
TOXIFEROUS
TOXIFY
TOXIGENIC
TOXIN
TOXINAEMIA
TOXINE
TOXINEMIA
TOXINFECTION
TOXINOSIS
TOXIPHAGI
TOXIPHAGUS
TOXIPHOBIA
TOXIPHOBIAC
TOXIPHORIC
TOXITABELLAE
TOXITY
TOXODONT
TOXOGENESIS
TOXOGLOSSATE
TOXOID
TOXOLOGY
TOXOLYSIS
TOXON
TOXONE
TOXOPHIL
TOXOPHILE
TOXOPHILISM
TOXOPHILITE
TOXOPHILITIC
TOXOPHILOUS
TOXOPHILY
TOXOTAE
TOY
TOYED
TOYER
TOYFUL
TOYFULNESS
TOYING
TOYISH
TOYISHLY
TOYISHNESS
TOYLE
TOYMAN
TOYMEN
TOYO
TOYON
TOYOS
TOYSHOP
TOYSOME
TOYWORT
TOZE
TOZEE
TOZER
TOZIE
TRA
TRABACOLI
TRABACOLO
TRABACOLOS
TRABAL
TRABANT
TRABASCOLO
TRABEA
TRABEAE
TRABEATE
TRABEATED
TRABEATION
TRABECULA
TRABECULAE
TRABECULAR
TRABECULATE
TRABECULATED
TRABECULE
TRABES
TRABU
TRABUCH
TRABUCHO
TRABUCO
TRABUCOS
TRACASSERIE
TRACASSERIES
TRACE
TRACEABILITY
TRACEABLE
TRACEABLY
TRACED
TRACER
TRACERIED
TRACERIES
TRACERY
TRACHEA
TRACHEAE
TRACHEAL
TRACHEALGIA
TRACHEALIS
TRACHEAN
TRACHEARIAN
TRACHEARY
TRACHEAS
TRACHEATE
TRACHEATION
TRACHEID
TRACHEIDAL
TRACHEITIS
TRACHELAGRA
TRACHELATE
TRACHELISMUS
TRACHELITIS
TRACHELIUM
TRACHELOTOMY
TRACHENCHYMA
TRACHEOCELE
TRACHEOLAR
TRACHEOLE
TRACHEOPHONE
TRACHEOPHYTE
TRACHEOSCOPY
TRACHEOTOMIES
TRACHEOTOMY
TRACHINOID
TRACHITIS
TRACHLE
TRACHLED
TRACHLING
TRACHODONT
TRACHODONTID
TRACHOMA
TRACHOMATOUS
TRACHYANDESITE
TRACHYBASALT
TRACHYLINE
TRACHYPHONIA
TRACHYTE
TRACHYTIC
TRACHYTOID
TRACING
TRACK
TRACKABLE
TRACKAGE
TRACKBARROW
TRACKED
TRACKER
TRACKHOUND
TRACKING
TRACKLAYER
TRACKLESS
TRACKLESSLY
TRACKMAN
TRACKMASTER
TRACKMEN
TRACKPOT
TRACKSHIFTER
TRACKSICK
TRACKSIDE
TRACKWALKER
TRACKWAY
TRACT
TRACTABILITIES
TRACTABILITY
TRACTABLE
TRACTABLY
TRACTARIAN
TRACTATE
TRACTATION
TRACTATOR
TRACTELLATE
TRACTELLUM
TRACTIFEROUS
TRACTILE
TRACTILITY
TRACTION
TRACTIONAL
TRACTITIAN
TRACTIVE
TRACTOR
TRACTORATION
TRACTORISM
TRACTORIST
TRACTORIZE
TRACTRICES
TRACTRIX
TRACTUS
TRADAL
TRADE
TRADECRAFT
TRADED
TRADEFUL
TRADEMARK
TRADEMASTER
TRADER
TRADES
TRADESCANTIA
TRADESFOLK
TRADESMAN
TRADESMEN
TRADESPEOPLE
TRADESPERSON
TRADESWOMAN
TRADIMENT
TRADING
TRADITE
TRADITION
TRADITIONAL
TRADITIONARIES
TRADITIONARY
TRADITIONATE
TRADITIONER
TRADITIONIST
TRADITIONS
TRADITIVE
TRADITOR
TRADITORES
TRADUCE
TRADUCED
TRADUCENT
TRADUCER
TRADUCIAN
TRADUCIANISM
TRADUCIANIST
TRADUCIBLE
TRADUCING
TRADUCINGLY
TRADUCT
TRADUCTION
TRADY
TRAFFIC
TRAFFICABLE
TRAFFICKED
TRAFFICKER
TRAFFICKING
TRAFFICS
TRAFFICWAY
TRAG
TRAGACANTH
TRAGACANTHA
TRAGACANTHIN
TRAGICOLORED
TRAGICOMEDY
TRAGICOMIC
TRAGICOMICAL
TRAGION
TRAGOEDIA
TRAGOPAN
TRAGULE
TRAGUS
TRAH
TRAHEEN
TRAHISON
TRAIK
TRAIKY
TRAIL
TRAILBASTON
TRAILBLAZER

TRAILBLAZING
TRAILED
TRAILER
TRAILERY
TRAILING
TRAILINGLY
TRAILMAN
TRAILSMAN
TRAILSMEN
TRAILWAY
TRAILY
TRAIN
TRAINABLE
TRAINAGE
TRAINAGRAPH
TRAINANT
TRAINANTE
TRAINBAND
TRAINBEARER
TRAINBOLT
TRAINBOY
TRAINEAU
TRAINED
TRAINEE
TRAINEL
TRAINER
TRAINFUL
TRAINING
TRAINLOAD
TRAINMAN
TRAINMASTER
TRAINMEN
TRAINS
TRAINSTER
TRAINWAY
TRAINY
TRAIPSE
TRAIPSED
TRAIPSING
TRAIST
TRAIT
TRAITEUR
TRAITEURS
TRAITOR
TRAITOROUS
TRAITOROUSLY
TRAITORY
TRAITRESS
TRAITS
TRAJECT
TRAJECTED
TRAJECTILE
TRAJECTING
TRAJECTION
TRAJECTORIES
TRAJECTORY
TRAJET
TRALATITION
TRALATITIOUS
TRALIRA
TRAM
TRAMA
TRAMAL
TRAMCAR
TRAME
TRAMFUL
TRAMLINE
TRAMMED
TRAMMEL
TRAMMELED
TRAMMELER
TRAMMELHEAD
TRAMMELING
TRAMMELINGLY
TRAMMELLED
TRAMMELLER
TRAMMELLING
TRAMMER
TRAMMING
TRAMMON
TRAMONTANA
TRAMONTANE
TRAMP
TRAMPCOCK
TRAMPED
TRAMPER
TRAMPING
TRAMPLE
TRAMPLED
TRAMPLER
TRAMPLING
TRAMPOLIN
TRAMPOLINE
TRAMPOOSE
TRAMPOSO
TRAMPOT
TRAMPS
TRAMROAD
TRAMS
TRAMWAY
TRAMWAYMAN
TRAMWAYMEN
TRANCE
TRANCED
TRANCEDLY
TRANCHANT
TRANCHANTE
TRANCHE
TRANCHEFER
TRANCHET
TRANCHOIR
TRANCING
TRANEEN
TRANGAM
TRANI
TRANK
TRANKA
TRANKER
TRANKUM
TRANKY
TRANQUIL
TRANQUILER
TRANQUILEST
TRANQUILITY
TRANQUILIZE
TRANQUILIZER
TRANQUILIZING
TRANQUILLER
TRANQUILLEST
TRANQUILLISE
TRANQUILLITY
TRANQUILLIZE
TRANQUILLIZED
TRANQUILLO
TRANQUILLY
TRANQUILNESS
TRANS
TRANSACT
TRANSACTED
TRANSACTING
TRANSACTION
TRANSACTOR
TRANSALPINE
TRANSANNULAR
TRANSAPICAL
TRANSAUDIENT
TRANSBAIKAL
TRANSBOARD
TRANSBORDER
TRANSCALENCY
TRANSCALENT
TRANSCEIVER
TRANSCEND
TRANSCENDED
TRANSCENDENT
TRANSCENDENTAL
TRANSCENDING
TRANSCENSION
TRANSCOLOR
TRANSCREATE
TRANSCRIBBLE
TRANSCRIBE
TRANSCRIBED
TRANSCRIBER
TRANSCRIBING
TRANSCRIPT
TRANSCUR
TRANSCURRENT
TRANSDIALECT
TRANSDIURNAL
TRANSDUCER
TRANSDUCTION
TRANSECT
TRANSECTED
TRANSECTING
TRANSECTION
TRANSELEMENT
TRANSENNA
TRANSENNAE
TRANSEPT
TRANSEPTAL
TRANSEPTALLY
TRANSEUNT
TRANSFER
TRANSFERABLE
TRANSFERAL
TRANSFEREE
TRANSFERENCE
TRANSFERENT
TRANSFEROR
TRANSFERRAL
TRANSFERRED
TRANSFERRER
TRANSFERRING
TRANSFIGURE
TRANSFIGURED
TRANSFIGURING
TRANSFINITE
TRANSFIX
TRANSFIXED
TRANSFIXING
TRANSFIXION
TRANSFIXTURE
TRANSFLUENT
TRANSFLUX
TRANSFORM
TRANSFORMATION
TRANSFORMED
TRANSFORMER
TRANSFORMING
TRANSFORMISM
TRANSFORMIST
TRANSFUGE
TRANSFUSE
TRANSFUSED
TRANSFUSER
TRANSFUSING
TRANSFUSION
TRANSFUSIVE
TRANSGRESS
TRANSGRESSED
TRANSGRESSING
TRANSGRESSION
TRANSGRESSOR
TRANSHAPE
TRANSHIP
TRANSHIPMENT
TRANSHUMAN
TRANSHUMANCE
TRANSHUMANT
TRANSIENCE
TRANSIENCY
TRANSIENT
TRANSIENTLY
TRANSIGENCE
TRANSIGENT
TRANSILIAC
TRANSILIENCE
TRANSILIENCY
TRANSILIENT
TRANSIRE
TRANSISCHIAC
TRANSISTOR
TRANSIT
TRANSITABLE
TRANSITER
TRANSITION
TRANSITIONAL
TRANSITIVE
TRANSITIVELY
TRANSITIVISM
TRANSITIVITIES
TRANSITIVITY
TRANSITMAN
TRANSITMEN
TRANSITORILY
TRANSITORINESS
TRANSITORY
TRANSITUS
TRANSLADE
TRANSLATABLE
TRANSLATE
TRANSLATED
TRANSLATING
TRANSLATION
TRANSLATIVE
TRANSLATOR
TRANSLATORY
TRANSLAY
TRANSLEITHAN
TRANSLOCATE
TRANSLOCATED
TRANSLOCATING
TRANSLUCE
TRANSLUCENCE
TRANSLUCENCY
TRANSLUCENT
TRANSLUCID
TRANSLUNAR
TRANSLUNARY
TRANSMAKE
TRANSMARINE
TRANSMEDIAN
TRANSMEW
TRANSMIGRANT
TRANSMIGRATE
TRANSMIGRATED
TRANSMIGRATING
TRANSMIGRATION
TRANSMISSION
TRANSMISSIVE
TRANSMISSORY
TRANSMIT
TRANSMITTAL
TRANSMITTED
TRANSMITTER
TRANSMITTING
TRANSMOGRIFIED
TRANSMOGRIFY
TRANSMOGRIFYING
TRANSMONTANE
TRANSMUE
TRANSMUTATE
TRANSMUTATION
TRANSMUTE
TRANSMUTED
TRANSMUTER
TRANSMUTING
TRANSMUTUAL
TRANSNATURAL
TRANSNORMAL
TRANSOCEANIC
TRANSOM
TRANSOMED
TRANSONIC
TRANSPACIFIC
TRANSPADANE
TRANSPARENCE
TRANSPARENCIES
TRANSPARENCY
TRANSPARENT
TRANSPASS
TRANSPECIATE
TRANSPICUITY
TRANSPICUOUS
TRANSPIERCE
TRANSPIERCED
TRANSPIERCING
TRANSPIRE
TRANSPIRED
TRANSPIRING
TRANSPLACE
TRANSPLANT
TRANSPLANTED
TRANSPLANTER
TRANSPLANTING
TRANSPONDER
TRANSPONIBLE
TRANSPONTINE
TRANSPORT
TRANSPORTAL
TRANSPORTATION
TRANSPORTED
TRANSPORTER
TRANSPORTING
TRANSPORTIVE
TRANSPOSABLE
TRANSPOSE
TRANSPOSED
TRANSPOSER
TRANSPOSING
TRANSPOSITION
TRANSPOSITOR
TRANSPRINT
TRANSPROSE
TRANSPROSER
TRANSPYLORIC
TRANSRHENANE
TRANSSHAPE
TRANSSHAPED
TRANSSHAPING
TRANSSHIP
TRANSSHIPPED
TRANSSHIPPING
TRANSUBSTANTIATION
TRANSUDATE
TRANSUDATION
TRANSUDATIVE
TRANSUDATORY
TRANSUDE
TRANSUDED
TRANSUDING
TRANSUME
TRANSUMED
TRANSUMING
TRANSUMPT
TRANSUMPTION
TRANSUMPTIVE
TRANSURANIAN
TRANSURANIC
TRANSVAAL
TRANSVALUE
TRANSVALUED
TRANSVALUING
TRANSVASE

TRANSVECTANT
TRANSVECTION
TRANSVENOM
TRANSVERBATE
TRANSVERSAL
TRANSVERSALE
TRANSVERSAN
TRANSVERSARY
TRANSVERSE
TRANSVERSELY
TRANSVERSER
TRANSVERSION
TRANSVERSIVE
TRANSVERSUM
TRANSVERSUS
TRANSVERT
TRANSVERTER
TRANSVEST
TRANSVESTISM
TRANSVESTITE
TRANSWRITTEN
TRANT
TRANTER
TRANTLUM
TRANVIA
TRAP
TRAPAN
TRAPANNER
TRAPBALL
TRAPDOOR
TRAPES
TRAPEZE
TRAPEZIA
TRAPEZIAL
TRAPEZIAN
TRAPEZIFORM
TRAPEZING
TRAPEZIST
TRAPEZIUM
TRAPEZIUMS
TRAPEZIUS
TRAPEZOID
TRAPEZOIDAL
TRAPFALL
TRAPHOLE
TRAPICHE
TRAPIFEROUS
TRAPISH
TRAPLIGHT
TRAPPEAN
TRAPPED
TRAPPER
TRAPPING
TRAPPINGLY
TRAPPINGS
TRAPPIST
TRAPPOID
TRAPPOSE
TRAPPOUS
TRAPPY
TRAPROCK
TRAPS
TRAPSHOOT
TRAPSHOOTER
TRAPSHOOTING
TRAPSTICK
TRAPT
TRASH
TRASHED
TRASHERY
TRASHIER
TRASHIEST
TRASHIFY
TRASHILY
TRASHINESS
TRASHING
TRASHTRIE
TRASHY
TRASS
TRASY
TRATLER
TRATTLE
TRATTORIA
TRAUCHLE
TRAULISM
TRAUMA
TRAUMAS
TRAUMATA
TRAUMATIC
TRAUMATICIN
TRAUMATICINE
TRAUMATISM
TRAUMATIZE
TRAUMATOLOGY
TRAUMATOPNEA
TRAUMATOSIS
TRAUMATROPIC
TRAVADO
TRAVAIL
TRAVAILED
TRAVAILER
TRAVAILING
TRAVAILS
TRAVALE
TRAVALLY
TRAVATED
TRAVE
TRAVEL
TRAVELED
TRAVELER
TRAVELERS
TRAVELING
TRAVELLED
TRAVELLER
TRAVELLING
TRAVELOG
TRAVELOGUE
TRAVELOGUER
TRAVELS
TRAVERSABLE
TRAVERSAL
TRAVERSARY
TRAVERSE
TRAVERSED
TRAVERSER
TRAVERSING
TRAVERSION
TRAVERTIN
TRAVERTINE
TRAVEST
TRAVESTIED
TRAVESTIER
TRAVESTIES
TRAVESTY
TRAVESTYING
TRAVIS
TRAVISS
TRAVOIS
TRAVOISE
TRAVOISES
TRAVOY
TRAWL
TRAWLBOAT
TRAWLED
TRAWLER
TRAWLERMAN
TRAWLERMEN
TRAWLEY
TRAWLING
TRAWLNET
TRAY
TRAYNE
TREACHER
TREACHERIES
TREACHEROUS
TREACHERY
TREACLE
TREACLEWORT
TREACLINESS
TREACLY
TREAD
TREADBOARD
TREADER
TREADING
TREADLE
TREADLED
TREADLER
TREADLING
TREADMILL
TREADWHEEL
TREAGUE
TREASON
TREASONABLE
TREASONABLY
TREASONIST
TREASONOUS
TREASURABLE
TREASURE
TREASURED
TREASURER
TREASURIES
TREASURING
TREASUROUS
TREASURY
TREASURYSHIP
TREAT
TREATABLE
TREATABLY
TREATED
TREATEE
TREATER
TREATIES
TREATING
TREATISE
TREATISER
TREATMENT
TREATOR
TREATY
TREATYIST
TREATYITE
TREBLE
TREBLED
TREBLENESS
TREBLET
TREBLETREE
TREBLING
TREBLY
TREBUCHET
TREBUCKET
TRECENTIST
TRECENTO
TRECHMANNITE
TRECK
TRECKPOT
TRECKSCHUYT
TREDDLE
TREDECILE
TREDEFOWEL
TREDILLE
TREDRILLE
TREE
TREEBEARD
TREEBINE
TREED
TREEFISH
TREEFISHES
TREEHAIR
TREEING
TREELESS
TREELET
TREELIKE
TREELING
TREEMAKER
TREEMAKING
TREEMAN
TREEN
TREENAIL
TREES
TREESPEELER
TREETISE
TREETOP
TREEY
TREF
TREFA
TREFGORDD
TREFLE
TREFLEE
TREFOIL
TREFOILED
TREGET
TREGETOUR
TREHALA
TREHALASE
TREHALOSE
TREILLAGE
TREITOUR
TREITRE
TREK
TREKBOER
TREKKED
TREKKER
TREKKING
TREKOMETER
TREKPATH
TRELLIS
TRELLISED
TRELLISES
TRELLISING
TRELLISWORK
TREMATODE
TREMATOID
TREMBLE
TREMBLED
TREMBLEMENT
TREMBLER
TREMBLING
TREMBLINGLY
TREMBLY
TREMELINE
TREMELLIFORM
TREMELLOID
TREMELLOSE
TREMENDOUS
TREMENDOUSLY
TREMETOL
TREMEX
TREMIE
TREMOLANDO
TREMOLANT
TREMOLIST
TREMOLITE
TREMOLITIC
TREMOLO
TREMOLOS
TREMOLOSO
TREMOR
TREMPLIN
TREMULANDO
TREMULANT
TREMULATE
TREMULATION
TREMULENT
TREMULOUS
TREMULOUSLY
TREN
TRENAIL
TRENCH
TRENCHANCY
TRENCHANT
TRENCHANTLY
TRENCHED
TRENCHER
TRENCHERING
TRENCHERMAN
TRENCHERMEN
TRENCHES
TRENCHING
TRENCHLIKE
TRENCHMASTER
TRENCHMORE
TREND
TRENDED
TRENDEL
TRENDING
TRENDLE
TRENDY
TRENE
TRENTAL
TREPAN
TREPANATION
TREPANG
TREPANNED
TREPANNER
TREPANNING
TREPANNINGLY
TREPHINATION
TREPHINE
TREPHINED
TREPHINER
TREPHINING
TREPHONE
TREPID
TREPIDANCY
TREPIDANT
TREPIDATE
TREPIDATION
TREPIDATORY
TREPIDITY
TREPIDLY
TREPIDNESS
TREPONEME
TREPPE
TRES
TRESAIEL
TRESANCE
TRESCHE
TRESILLO
TRESIS
TRESPASS
TRESPASSAGE
TRESPASSED
TRESPASSER
TRESPASSING
TRESPASSORY
TRESS
TRESSED
TRESSILATE
TRESSILATION
TRESSON
TRESSOUR
TRESSURE
TRESSURED
TRESSY
TREST
TRESTLE
TRESTLETREE
TRESTLEWORK
TRESTLING
TRET
TRETIS
TREVALLY
TREVET
TREVIS
TREW
TREWAGE

TREWEL
TREWS
TREWSMAN
TREWSMEN
TREY
TRIABLE
TRIABLENESS
TRIACETATE
TRIACHENIUM
TRIACID
TRIACONTANE
TRIACONTER
TRIACT
TRIACTINAL
TRIACTINE
TRIAD
TRIADELPHOUS
TRIADIC
TRIADICAL
TRIADICALLY
TRIADISM
TRIADIST
TRIAENE
TRIAENOSE
TRIAGE
TRIAGONAL
TRIAKID
TRIAL
TRIALATE
TRIALISM
TRIALIST
TRIALITY
TRIALOGUE
TRIAMID
TRIAMIDE
TRIAMIN
TRIAMINE
TRIAMINO
TRIAMMONIUM
TRIAMORPH
TRIAMORPHOUS
TRIAMYLOSE
TRIANDER
TRIANDRIAN
TRIANDROUS
TRIANGLE
TRIANGLED
TRIANGLER
TRIANGULAR
TRIANGULARIS
TRIANGULARLY
TRIANGULATE
TRIANGULATED
TRIANGULATING
TRIANGULATOR
TRIANGULOID
TRIANNUAL
TRIANNULATE
TRIANON
TRIANTHOUS
TRIAPSIDAL
TRIARCH
TRIARCHATE
TRIARCHIES
TRIARCHY
TRIARIAN
TRIARII
TRIARY
TRIASTER
TRIATIC
TRIATOMIC
TRIATOMICITY
TRIAXAL
TRIAXIAL
TRIAXON
TRIAXONIAN
TRIAZANE
TRIAZIN
TRIAZINE
TRIAZO
TRIAZOLE
TRIBADE
TRIBADISM
TRIBADY
TRIBAL
TRIBALISM
TRIBALIST
TRIBALLY
TRIBASE
TRIBASIC
TRIBBLE
TRIBE
TRIBELESS
TRIBESMAN
TRIBESMEN
TRIBESPEOPLE
TRIBLET
TRIBOMETER
TRIBOROUGH
TRIBRACH
TRIBRACHIAL
TRIBRACHIC
TRIBRACTEATE
TRIBROMID
TRIBROMIDE
TRIBROMOETHANOL
TRIBUAL
TRIBUALLY
TRIBULAR
TRIBULATE
TRIBULATION
TRIBULOID
TRIBUNA
TRIBUNAL
TRIBUNARY
TRIBUNATE
TRIBUNE
TRIBUNESHIP
TRIBUNICIAL
TRIBUNICIAN
TRIBUNITIAL
TRIBUNITIAN
TRIBUNITIVE
TRIBUTABLE
TRIBUTARIES
TRIBUTARILY
TRIBUTARY
TRIBUTE
TRIBUTED
TRIBUTER
TRIBUTING
TRIBUTORIAN
TRICA
TRICAE
TRICALCIUM
TRICAR
TRICARBIMIDE
TRICARBON
TRICE
TRICED
TRICENARIES
TRICENARIUM
TRICENARY
TRICENNIAL
TRICEPHAL
TRICEPHALOUS
TRICEPHALUS
TRICEPS
TRICEPSES
TRICERATOPS
TRICERIA
TRICERION
TRICHAUXIS
TRICHECHINE
TRICHEVRON
TRICHI
TRICHIA
TRICHIASIS
TRICHINA
TRICHINAE
TRICHINAL
TRICHINIZE
TRICHINIZED
TRICHINIZING
TRICHINOPOLY
TRICHINOSIS
TRICHINOTIC
TRICHINOUS
TRICHION
TRICHITE
TRICHITIC
TRICHITIS
TRICHIURID
TRICHIUROID
TRICHLORID
TRICHLORIDE
TRICHLORO
TRICHOBLAST
TRICHOCLASIS
TRICHOCYST
TRICHOCYSTIC
TRICHODE
TRICHOGEN
TRICHOGENOUS
TRICHOGYNE
TRICHOGYNIAL
TRICHOGYNIC
TRICHOID
TRICHOLOGIST
TRICHOLOGY
TRICHOMA
TRICHOMATOSE
TRICHOME
TRICHOMIC
TRICHOMONAD
TRICHOMONIASIS
TRICHONOSIS
TRICHONOSUS
TRICHOPATHIC
TRICHOPATHY
TRICHOPHORE
TRICHOPHORIC
TRICHOPHYTE
TRICHOPHYTIC
TRICHOPORE
TRICHOPTER
TRICHOPTERA
TRICHOPTERAN
TRICHOPTERON
TRICHORD
TRICHOSIS
TRICHOTOMIC
TRICHOTOMIES
TRICHOTOMIST
TRICHOTOMIZE
TRICHOTOMOUS
TRICHROIC
TRICHROISM
TRICHROMAT
TRICHROMATE
TRICHROMATIC
TRICHROME
TRICHROMIC
TRICHRONOUS
TRICHURIASIS
TRICHY
TRICING
TRICINIUM
TRICIPITAL
TRICIRCULAR
TRICK
TRICKED
TRICKER
TRICKERIES
TRICKERY
TRICKIER
TRICKIEST
TRICKILY
TRICKINESS
TRICKING
TRICKINGLY
TRICKISH
TRICKISHLY
TRICKISHNESS
TRICKLE
TRICKLED
TRICKLESS
TRICKLET
TRICKLING
TRICKLINGLY
TRICKLY
TRICKMENT
TRICKS
TRICKSIER
TRICKSIEST
TRICKSINESS
TRICKSOME
TRICKSTER
TRICKSTERING
TRICKSY
TRICKTRACK
TRICKY
TRICLAD
TRICLINATE
TRICLINIA
TRICLINIARCH
TRICLINIARY
TRICLINIC
TRICLINIUM
TRICOCCOUS
TRICOLETTE
TRICOLIC
TRICOLON
TRICOLOR
TRICOLORED
TRICOLOUR
TRICON
TRICONCH
TRICONODONT
TRICONODONTY
TRICORN
TRICORNE
TRICORNERED
TRICORNUTE
TRICORPORAL
TRICORPORATE
TRICORYPHEAN
TRICOSANE
TRICOSANONE
TRICOSTATE
TRICOSYLIC
TRICOT
TRICOTEE
TRICOTINE
TRICOUNI
TRICRESOL
TRICROTIC
TRICROTISM
TRICROTOUS
TRICURVATE
TRICUSPID
TRICUSPIDAL
TRICUSPIDATE
TRICUSSATE
TRICYANIDE
TRICYCLE
TRICYCLED
TRICYCLENE
TRICYCLER
TRICYCLIC
TRICYCLING
TRICYCLIST
TRIDACTYL
TRIDAILY
TRIDDLER
TRIDECANE
TRIDECENE
TRIDECOIC
TRIDECYL
TRIDECYLENE
TRIDENT
TRIDENTAL
TRIDENTATE
TRIDENTATED
TRIDERMIC
TRIDIAPASON
TRIDIGITATE
TRIDIURNAL
TRIDOMINIUM
TRIDRACHM
TRIDUAN
TRIDUUM
TRIDYMITE
TRIDYNAMOUS
TRIECIOUS
TRIECIOUSLY
TRIED
TRIELAIDIN
TRIENE
TRIENNIA
TRIENNIAL
TRIENNIALITY
TRIENNIALLY
TRIENNIUM
TRIENNIUMS
TRIENS
TRIENTAL
TRIENTES
TRIER
TRIERARCH
TRIERARCHAL
TRIERARCHIES
TRIERARCHY
TRIES
TRIETERIC
TRIETERICS
TRIETHYL
TRIFACIAL
TRIFARIOUS
TRIFEROUS
TRIFID
TRIFISTULARY
TRIFLE
TRIFLED
TRIFLER
TRIFLES
TRIFLET
TRIFLING
TRIFLINGLY
TRIFLINGNESS
TRIFLORAL
TRIFLORATE
TRIFLOROUS
TRIFLUORIDE
TRIFOCAL
TRIFOIL
TRIFOLD
TRIFOLIATE
TRIFOLIATED
TRIFOLIOLATE
TRIFOLIOSIS
TRIFOLIUM
TRIFOLY
TRIFORIA
TRIFORIAL

TRIFORIUM
TRIFORM
TRIFORMED
TRIFORMITY
TRIFURCATE
TRIFURCATED
TRIFURCATION
TRIG
TRIGA
TRIGAMIST
TRIGAMOUS
TRIGAMY
TRIGEMINAL
TRIGEMINI
TRIGEMINOUS
TRIGEMINUS
TRIGENERIC
TRIGESIMAL
TRIGGED
TRIGGER
TRIGGERED
TRIGGERFISH
TRIGGERFISHES
TRIGGING
TRIGINTAL
TRIGLANDULAR
TRIGLID
TRIGLOT
TRIGLYPH
TRIGLYPHAL
TRIGLYPHED
TRIGLYPHIC
TRIGLYPHICAL
TRIGNESS
TRIGO
TRIGON
TRIGONAL
TRIGONALLY
TRIGONE
TRIGONELLIN
TRIGONELLINE
TRIGONEUTIC
TRIGONEUTISM
TRIGONIACEAN
TRIGONIC
TRIGONID
TRIGONITE
TRIGONITIS
TRIGONOID
TRIGONOMETER
TRIGONOMETRIES
TRIGONOMETRY
TRIGONON
TRIGONOTYPE
TRIGONOUS
TRIGRAM
TRIGRAMMATIC
TRIGRAPH
TRIGRAPHIC
TRIGYN
TRIGYNIAN
TRIGYNOUS
TRIHALID
TRIHALIDE
TRIHEDRA
TRIHEDRAL
TRIHEDRON
TRIHEDRONS
TRIHEMERAL
TRIHEMIMER
TRIHEMIMERAL
TRIHEMIMERIS
TRIHORAL
TRIHOURLY
TRIHYBRID
TRIHYDRATE
TRIHYDRATED
TRIHYDRIC
TRIHYDRIDE
TRIHYDROXY
TRIJUGATE
TRIJUGOUS
TRIKAYA
TRIKE
TRIKER
TRIKERIA
TRIKERION
TRIKETO
TRIKETONE
TRIKIR
TRILABE
TRILABIATE
TRILAMINAR
TRILATERAL
TRILATERALLY
TRILBIES
TRILEMMA
TRILINEAR
TRILINGUAL
TRILINGUAR
TRILINOLENIN
TRILITERAL
TRILITH
TRILITHIC
TRILITHON
TRILL
TRILLACHAN
TRILLADO
TRILLANDO
TRILLED
TRILLET
TRILLETTO
TRILLI
TRILLIACEOUS
TRILLIBUB
TRILLIIN
TRILLIL
TRILLING
TRILLION
TRILLIONAIRE
TRILLIONIZE
TRILLIONTH
TRILLIUM
TRILLO
TRILLOES
TRILOBAL
TRILOBATE
TRILOBATED
TRILOBATION
TRILOBE
TRILOBED
TRILOBITE
TRILOBITIC
TRILOCULAR
TRILOCULATE
TRILOGIC
TRILOGICAL
TRILOGIES
TRILOGIST
TRILOGY
TRILOPHODONT
TRILUMINAR
TRILUMINOUS
TRIM
TRIMACER
TRIMACULAR
TRIMACULATE
TRIMACULATED
TRIMASTIGATE
TRIME
TRIMELLIC
TRIMELLITIC
TRIMEMBRAL
TRIMENSUAL
TRIMER
TRIMERIC
TRIMERITE
TRIMEROUS
TRIMESIC
TRIMESITIC
TRIMESTER
TRIMESTRAL
TRIMESTRIAL
TRIMESYL
TRIMETALLIC
TRIMETALLISM
TRIMETER
TRIMETHOXY
TRIMETHYL
TRIMETHYLENE
TRIMETRIC
TRIMETRICAL
TRIMETROGON
TRIMLY
TRIMMED
TRIMMER
TRIMMERS
TRIMMEST
TRIMMING
TRIMNESS
TRIMOLECULAR
TRIMONTHLY
TRIMORIC
TRIMORPH
TRIMORPHIC
TRIMORPHISM
TRIMORPHOUS
TRIMSTONE
TRIMTRAM
TRIN
TRINAL
TRINALITY
TRINALIZE
TRINARY
TRINCHERA
TRINDLE
TRINE
TRINED
TRINELY
TRINEURAL
TRINGINE
TRINGLE
TRINGOID
TRINIDADO
TRINING
TRINITIES
TRINITRATE
TRINITRATION
TRINITRID
TRINITRIDE
TRINITRO
TRINITROTOLUENE
TRINITY
TRINK
TRINKERMAN
TRINKERMEN
TRINKET
TRINKETRIES
TRINKETRY
TRINKETY
TRINKLE
TRINKLET
TRINKUMS
TRINOCTIAL
TRINOCTILE
TRINODAL
TRINODE
TRINODINE
TRINOMIAL
TRINOMIALISM
TRINOMIALIST
TRINOMIALITY
TRINOMIALLY
TRINOPTICON
TRINQ
TRINTLE
TRINUCLEATE
TRINUNITY
TRIO
TRIOBOL
TRIOBOLON
TRIOCTILE
TRIODE
TRIODIA
TRIODION
TRIODONTOID
TRIOECIOUS
TRIOECIOUSLY
TRIOECISM
TRIOICOUS
TRIOLE
TRIOLEFIN
TRIOLEFINE
TRIOLET
TRIONFI
TRIONFO
TRIONYCHID
TRIONYCHOID
TRIONYM
TRIONYMAL
TRIOR
TRIORCHIS
TRIOS
TRIOSE
TRIOVULATE
TRIOXID
TRIOXIDE
TRIOZONID
TRIOZONIDE
TRIP
TRIPAL
TRIPALEOLATE
TRIPALMITATE
TRIPALMITIN
TRIPARA
TRIPART
TRIPARTED
TRIPARTEDLY
TRIPARTIBLE
TRIPARTIENT
TRIPARTITE
TRIPARTITELY
TRIPARTITION
TRIPASCHAL
TRIPE
TRIPEDAL
TRIPEL
TRIPEMAN
TRIPEMONGER
TRIPENNATE
TRIPENNY
TRIPERIES
TRIPERSONAL
TRIPERY
TRIPESHOP
TRIPESTONE
TRIPETALOID
TRIPETALOUS
TRIPEWIFE
TRIPEWOMAN
TRIPHAMMER
TRIPHANE
TRIPHASE
TRIPHENYL
TRIPHONY
TRIPHTHONG
TRIPHTHONGAL
TRIPHYLINE
TRIPHYLITE
TRIPHYLLOUS
TRIPINNATE
TRIPINNATED
TRIPINNATELY
TRIPLA
TRIPLANE
TRIPLASIAN
TRIPLASIC
TRIPLE
TRIPLEBACK
TRIPLED
TRIPLEFOLD
TRIPLEGIA
TRIPLET
TRIPLETAIL
TRIPLETREE
TRIPLEX
TRIPLEXITY
TRIPLICATE
TRIPLICATED
TRIPLICATELY
TRIPLICATING
TRIPLICATION
TRIPLICATIVE
TRIPLICATURE
TRIPLICE
TRIPLICITIES
TRIPLICITY
TRIPLING
TRIPLITE
TRIPLOID
TRIPLOIDIC
TRIPLOIDITE
TRIPLOIDY
TRIPLOPIA
TRIPLUM
TRIPLUMBIC
TRIPLY
TRIPOD
TRIPODAL
TRIPODIAL
TRIPODIAN
TRIPODIC
TRIPODIES
TRIPODY
TRIPOINTED
TRIPOLAR
TRIPOLI
TRIPOS
TRIPOSES
TRIPOT
TRIPOTAGE
TRIPOTER
TRIPPANT
TRIPPED
TRIPPER
TRIPPET
TRIPPING
TRIPPINGLY
TRIPPINGNESS
TRIPPLE
TRIPPLER
TRIPSILL
TRIPSIS
TRIPSOME
TRIPSOMELY
TRIPT
TRIPTANE
TRIPTEROUS
TRIPTOTE
TRIPTYCA
TRIPTYCH
TRIPTYQUE
TRIPUDIA
TRIPUDIAL
TRIPUDIANT

TRIPUDIARY
TRIPUDIATE
TRIPUDIATION
TRIPUDIST
TRIPUDIUM
TRIPY
TRIPYLAEAN
TRIPYLARIAN
TRIPYLEAN
TRIPYRENOUS
TRIQUET
TRIQUETRA
TRIQUETRAL
TRIQUETRIC
TRIQUETROUS
TRIQUETRUM
TRIQUINATE
TRIQUINOYL
TRIRADIAL
TRIRADIALLY
TRIRADIATE
TRIRADIATELY
TRIRADIATION
TRIREGNUM
TRIREME
TRISALT
TRISAZO
TRISECT
TRISECTED
TRISECTING
TRISECTION
TRISECTOR
TRISECTRIX
TRISEME
TRISEMIC
TRISEPALOUS
TRISEPTATE
TRISERIAL
TRISERIALLY
TRISERIATE
TRISERIATIM
TRISETOSE
TRISHA
TRISHNA
TRISKELE
TRISKELIA
TRISKELION
TRISMEGIST
TRISMEGISTIC
TRISMIC
TRISMUS
TRISOME
TRISPAST
TRISPASTON
TRISPERMOUS
TRISPORIC
TRISPOROUS
TRIST
TRISTACHYOUS
TRISTE
TRISTEARATE
TRISTESSE
TRISTEZA
TRISTFUL
TRISTFULLY
TRISTFULNESS
TRISTICH
TRISTICHIC
TRISTICHOUS
TRISTIGMATIC
TRISTILOQUY
TRISTISONOUS
TRISTIVE
TRISTYLOUS
TRISUL
TRISULA
TRISULC
TRISULCATE
TRISULCATED
TRISULFATE
TRISULFID
TRISULFIDE
TRISULFONE
TRISULFOXID
TRISULFOXIDE
TRISULPHATE
TRISULPHID
TRISULPHIDE
TRISULPHONE
TRISULPHONIC
TRISULPHOXID
TRISYLLABIC
TRISYLLABISM
TRISYLLABLE
TRITACTIC
TRITAGONIST
TRITANGENT
TRITANOPIA
TRITANOPSIA
TRITANOPTIC
TRITAPH
TRITE
TRITELY
TRITENESS
TRITERNATE
TRITERNATELY
TRITERPENE
TRITERPENOID
TRITHEISM
TRITHEIST
TRITHEISTIC
TRITHEITE
TRITHING
TRITHIONATES
TRITICAL
TRITICALITY
TRITICALLY
TRITICALNESS
TRITICEUM
TRITICIN
TRITICISM
TRITICOID
TRITICUM
TRITISH
TRITIUM
TRITOCONE
TRITOCONID
TRITOMITE
TRITON
TRITONE
TRITONOID
TRITONYMPH
TRITONYMPHAL
TRITOPATORES
TRITOR
TRITORAL
TRITOZOOID
TRITTICHAN
TRITUBERCULY
TRITURABLE
TRITURAL
TRITURATE
TRITURATED
TRITURATING
TRITURATION
TRITURATOR
TRITURATURE
TRITURIUM
TRIUMPH
TRIUMPHAL
TRIUMPHANCE
TRIUMPHANCY
TRIUMPHANT
TRIUMPHANTLY
TRIUMPHATOR
TRIUMPHED
TRIUMPHER
TRIUMPHING
TRIUMVIR
TRIUMVIRAL
TRIUMVIRATE
TRIUMVIRI
TRIUMVIRS
TRIUMVIRSHIP
TRIUNE
TRIUNGULIN
TRIUNITARIAN
TRIUNITIES
TRIUNITY
TRIURID
TRIVALENCE
TRIVALENCY
TRIVALENT
TRIVALVE
TRIVALVULAR
TRIVANT
TRIVARIANT
TRIVAT
TRIVERBIAL
TRIVET
TRIVIA
TRIVIAL
TRIVIALISM
TRIVIALIST
TRIVIALITIES
TRIVIALITY
TRIVIALIZE
TRIVIALLY
TRIVIALNESS
TRIVIRGA
TRIVIRGATE
TRIVIUM
TRIVOLTINE
TRIVVET
TRIWEEKLY
TRIZOIC
TRIZOMAL
TROAK
TROAT
TROBADOR
TROCA
TROCAR
TROCHA
TROCHAIC
TROCHAL
TROCHALOPOD
TROCHANTER
TROCHANTERIC
TROCHANTIN
TROCHANTINE
TROCHAR
TROCHATE
TROCHE
TROCHEAMETER
TROCHED
TROCHEE
TROCHEEIZE
TROCHEUS
TROCHID
TROCHIFEROUS
TROCHIFORM
TROCHIL
TROCHILI
TROCHILIC
TROCHILICS
TROCHILIDINE
TROCHILIDIST
TROCHILINE
TROCHILOS
TROCHILUS
TROCHING
TROCHISCI
TROCHISCUS
TROCHITE
TROCHITIC
TROCHLEA
TROCHLEAE
TROCHLEAR
TROCHLEARIS
TROCHLEARY
TROCHLEATE
TROCHLEIFORM
TROCHOID
TROCHOIDAL
TROCHOIDALLY
TROCHOIDES
TROCHOMETER
TROCHOPHORE
TROCHOSPHERE
TROCHOZOIC
TROCHOZOON
TROCK
TROCKERY
TROCO
TROCTOLITE
TROD
TRODDEN
TRODE
TROEGERITE
TROFFER
TROFT
TROG
TROGERITE
TROGGER
TROGGIN
TROGGS
TROGLODYTAL
TROGLODYTE
TROGLODYTIC
TROGON
TROGONOID
TROGS
TROGUE
TROIKA
TROIL
TROILITE
TROILUS
TROKE
TROKED
TROKER
TROKING
TROLAND
TROLL
TROLLED
TROLLEITE
TROLLER
TROLLEY
TROLLEYMAN
TROLLEYMEN
TROLLEYS
TROLLFLOWER
TROLLIES
TROLLIMOG
TROLLING
TROLLMAN
TROLLMEN
TROLLOL
TROLLOP
TROLLOPING
TROLLOPISH
TROLLOPS
TROLLOPY
TROLLY
TROLLYMAN
TROLLYMEN
TROMBA
TROMBASH
TROMBE
TROMBIDIASIS
TROMBONE
TROMBONIST
TROMBONY
TROMMEL
TROMOMETER
TROMOMETRIC
TROMOMETRY
TROMP
TROMPE
TROMPIL
TROMPILLO
TRON
TRONA
TRONADOR
TRONAGE
TRONC
TRONDHJEMITE
TRONE
TRONER
TRONK
TROODONT
TROOLIE
TROOLY
TROOP
TROOPED
TROOPER
TROOPFOWL
TROOPIAL
TROOPING
TROOPS
TROOPSHIP
TROOSHLACH
TROOSTITE
TROOZ
TROP
TROPACOCAINE
TROPAEOLA
TROPAEOLIN
TROPAEOLUM
TROPAEOLUMS
TROPAION
TROPAL
TROPARIA
TROPARION
TROPARY
TROPATE
TROPE
TROPEIC
TROPEIN
TROPEINE
TROPEOLIN
TROPER
TROPESIS
TROPHAEA
TROPHAEUM
TROPHALLAXIS
TROPHEDEMA
TROPHEMA
TROPHESIAL
TROPHESY
TROPHI
TROPHIC
TROPHICAL
TROPHICALLY
TROPHICITY
TROPHIED
TROPHIES
TROPHISM
TROPHOBIONT
TROPHOBIOSIS
TROPHOBIOTIC
TROPHOBLAST
TROPHOCYTE
TROPHODERM
TROPHODISC
TROPHOGENIC

TROPHOGENY
TROPHOLOGY
TROPHON
TROPHONEMA
TROPHOPATHY
TROPHOPHORE
TROPHOPHYTE
TROPHOPLASM
TROPHOPLAST
TROPHOSOMAL
TROPHOSOME
TROPHOSPERM
TROPHOSPHERE
TROPHOSPORE
TROPHOTAXIS
TROPHOTHYLAX
TROPHOTROPIC
TROPHOZOITE
TROPHOZOOID
TROPHY
TROPIC
TROPICAL
TROPICALITY
TROPICALIZE
TROPICALIZED
TROPICALIZING
TROPICALLY
TROPIDINE
TROPIN
TROPINE
TROPISM
TROPISMATIC
TROPIST
TROPISTIC
TROPOLOGIC
TROPOLOGICAL
TROPOLOGIES
TROPOLOGIZE
TROPOLOGIZED
TROPOLOGIZING
TROPOLOGY
TROPOMETER
TROPOPAUSE
TROPOPHIL
TROPOPHILOUS
TROPOPHYTE
TROPOPHYTIC
TROPOSPHERE
TROPOSPHERIC
TROPOYL
TROPPO
TROPTOMETER
TROPYL
TROSTERA
TROT
TROTCOZY
TROTH
TROTHED
TROTHING
TROTHLESS
TROTHPLIGHT
TROTLINE
TROTTED
TROTTER
TROTTERS
TROTTEUR
TROTTIE
TROTTING
TROTTLES
TROTTOIR
TROTTOIRED
TROTTY
TROTYL
TROUBADOR
TROUBADOUR
TROUBLE
TROUBLED
TROUBLEDLY
TROUBLEDNESS
TROUBLEMAKER
TROUBLER
TROUBLESHOOTER
TROUBLESOME
TROUBLESOMENESS
TROUBLING
TROUBLINGLY
TROUBLOUS
TROUBLOUSLY
TROUBLY
TROUGH
TROUGHING
TROUGHSTER
TROUGHWAY
TROUGHY
TROUNCE
TROUNCED
TROUNCER
TROUNCING
TROUPAND
TROUPE
TROUPED
TROUPER
TROUPIAL
TROUPING
TROUSE
TROUSER
TROUSERED
TROUSERETTES
TROUSERIAN
TROUSERING
TROUSERS
TROUSS
TROUSSE
TROUSSEAU
TROUSSEAUS
TROUSSEAUX
TROUT
TROUTER
TROUTLET
TROUTLING
TROUTY
TROUVAILLE
TROUVERE
TROUVEUR
TROVATORE
TROVE
TROVER
TROW
TROWABLE
TROWANE
TROWEL
TROWELBEAK
TROWELED
TROWELER
TROWELING
TROWELLED
TROWELLING
TROWELMAN
TROWIE
TROWING
TROWMAN
TROWSERS
TROWTH
TROY
TRUANCIES
TRUANCY
TRUANDISE
TRUANT
TRUANTISM
TRUANTLY
TRUANTNESS
TRUANTRY
TRUB
TRUBU
TRUCE
TRUCHA
TRUCHMAN
TRUCIAL
TRUCIDATION
TRUCK
TRUCKAGE
TRUCKED
TRUCKER
TRUCKING
TRUCKLE
TRUCKLED
TRUCKLER
TRUCKLING
TRUCKLINGLY
TRUCKMAN
TRUCKMASTER
TRUCKMEN
TRUCKS
TRUCKSTER
TRUCKWAY
TRUCULENCE
TRUCULENCY
TRUCULENT
TRUCULENTLY
TRUDDO
TRUDELLITE
TRUDGE
TRUDGED
TRUDGEN
TRUDGEON
TRUDGER
TRUDGING
TRUE
TRUEBORN
TRUEBRED
TRUED
TRUELOVE
TRUEMAN
TRUENESS
TRUEPENNY
TRUER
TRUEST
TRUEWOOD
TRUFF
TRUFFES
TRUFFLE
TRUFFLED
TRUFFLER
TRUG
TRUGMALLION
TRUING
TRUISM
TRUISMATIC
TRUISTIC
TRUISTICAL
TRULL
TRULLER
TRULLI
TRULLIZATION
TRULLO
TRULY
TRUMBASH
TRUMEAU
TRUMMEL
TRUMP
TRUMPED
TRUMPER
TRUMPERIES
TRUMPERINESS
TRUMPERY
TRUMPET
TRUMPETBUSH
TRUMPETED
TRUMPETER
TRUMPETING
TRUMPETRY
TRUMPETS
TRUMPETWEED
TRUMPETWOOD
TRUMPETY
TRUMPIE
TRUMPING
TRUMPS
TRUNCAGE
TRUNCAL
TRUNCATE
TRUNCATED
TRUNCATING
TRUNCATION
TRUNCATOR
TRUNCH
TRUNCHED
TRUNCHEON
TRUNCHEONED
TRUNCHEONER
TRUNCUS
TRUNDLE
TRUNDLED
TRUNDLEHEAD
TRUNDLER
TRUNDLESHOT
TRUNDLETAIL
TRUNDLING
TRUNK
TRUNKBACK
TRUNKED
TRUNKFISH
TRUNKFISHES
TRUNKING
TRUNKS
TRUNKWORK
TRUNNEL
TRUNNION
TRUNNIONED
TRUONG
TRUSH
TRUSION
TRUSS
TRUSSED
TRUSSELL
TRUSSER
TRUSSERY
TRUSSING
TRUSSWORK
TRUST
TRUSTBUSTER
TRUSTBUSTING
TRUSTED
TRUSTEE
TRUSTEED
TRUSTEEING
TRUSTEEISM
TRUSTEESHIP
TRUSTER
TRUSTFUL
TRUSTFULLY
TRUSTFULNESS
TRUSTIER
TRUSTIEST
TRUSTIFIED
TRUSTIFY
TRUSTIFYING
TRUSTING
TRUSTINGLY
TRUSTINGNESS
TRUSTLESS
TRUSTLESSLY
TRUSTMAN
TRUSTMEN
TRUSTWOMAN
TRUSTWORTHINESS
TRUSTWORTHY
TRUSTY
TRUTH
TRUTHABLE
TRUTHFUL
TRUTHFULLY
TRUTHFULNESS
TRUTHS
TRUTHSMAN
TRUTHTELLER
TRUTHTELLING
TRUTHY
TRUTINATE
TRUTINATION
TRUTINE
TRUTTACEOUS
TRUXILLIC
TRUXILLIN
TRUXILLINE
TRY
TRYE
TRYGON
TRYHOUSE
TRYING
TRYINGLY
TRYINGNESS
TRYMA
TRYMATA
TRYMS
TRYNE
TRYOUT
TRYP
TRYPA
TRYPANOLYSIN
TRYPANOSOMA
TRYPANOSOME
TRYPETID
TRYPIATE
TRYPOGRAPH
TRYPOGRAPHIC
TRYPSIN
TRYPSINIZE
TRYPSINOGEN
TRYPTASE
TRYPTIC
TRYPTONE
TRYPTONIZE
TRYPTOPHAN
TRYPTOPHANE
TRYSAIL
TRYST
TRYSTE
TRYSTED
TRYSTER
TRYSTING
TRYWORKS
TSADE
TSAMA
TSAMBA
TSANTSA
TSAR
TSARISM
TSARIST
TSATLEE
TSESSEBE
TSETSE
TSIA
TSINE
TSINGTAUITE
TSIOLOGY
TSITSITH
TSUBA
TSUBO
TSUKUPIN
TSUMEBITE
TSUN
TSUNAMI
TSUNGTU
TSWANA

TU
TUA
TUAN
TUANT
TUARN
TUART
TUATARA
TUATERA
TUATH
TUB
TUBA
TUBAE
TUBAGE
TUBAL
TUBAPHONE
TUBAR
TUBARON
TUBAS
TUBATE
TUBBA
TUBBABLE
TUBBAL
TUBBECK
TUBBED
TUBBER
TUBBIE
TUBBIER
TUBBIEST
TUBBING
TUBBISH
TUBBIST
TUBBOE
TUBBY
TUBE
TUBED
TUBEFORM
TUBEHEAD
TUBEHEARTED
TUBELET
TUBEMAN
TUBEMEN
TUBER
TUBERACEOUS
TUBERATION
TUBERCLE
TUBERCLED
TUBERCULA
TUBERCULAR
TUBERCULARLY
TUBERCULATE
TUBERCULATED
TUBERCULE
TUBERCULID
TUBERCULIDE
TUBERCULIN
TUBERCULINE
TUBERCULIZE
TUBERCULOID
TUBERCULOMA
TUBERCULOMAS
TUBERCULOMATA
TUBERCULOSED
TUBERCULOSIS
TUBERCULOUS
TUBERCULUM
TUBERIFEROUS
TUBERIFORM
TUBERIN
TUBERIZATION
TUBERIZE
TUBEROID
TUBEROSE
TUBEROSITIES
TUBEROSITY
TUBEROUS
TUBEROUSLY
TUBEROUSNESS
TUBFISH
TUBFISHES
TUBHUNTER
TUBICEN
TUBICINATE
TUBICINATION
TUBICOLAR
TUBICOLOUS
TUBICORN
TUBICORNOUS
TUBIFACIENT
TUBIFER
TUBIFEROUS
TUBIFEX
TUBIFLOROUS
TUBIFORM
TUBIG
TUBIK
TUBILINGUAL
TUBINARIAL
TUBINARINE
TUBING
TUBIPAROUS
TUBIPORE
TUBIPORID
TUBIPOROID
TUBIPOROUS
TUBMAN
TUBMEN
TUBOCURARINE
TUBORRHEA
TUBOTYMPANAL
TUBS
TUBSTER
TUBTAIL
TUBULAR
TUBULARITY
TUBULATE
TUBULATED
TUBULATING
TUBULATION
TUBULATOR
TUBULATURE
TUBULE
TUBULET
TUBULI
TUBULIFERAN
TUBULIFLORAL
TUBULIFORM
TUBULIPORE
TUBULIPORID
TUBULIPOROID
TUBULIZATION
TUBULOSE
TUBULOUS
TUBULOUSLY
TUBULOUSNESS
TUBULURE
TUBULUS
TUCAN
TUCANDERA
TUCHUN
TUCHUNATE
TUCHUNISM
TUCHUNIZE
TUCK
TUCKAHOE
TUCKED
TUCKER
TUCKERED
TUCKERING
TUCKET
TUCKING
TUCKNER
TUCKSHOP
TUCKTOO
TUCKY
TUCUM
TUCUMA
TUCUMAN
TUEBOR
TUEIRON
TUFA
TUFACEOUS
TUFAN
TUFF
TUFFACEOUS
TUFFET
TUFFING
TUFFOON
TUFT
TUFTAFFETA
TUFTED
TUFTER
TUFTHUNTER
TUFTHUNTING
TUFTING
TUFTS
TUFTY
TUG
TUGBOAT
TUGBOATMAN
TUGBOATMEN
TUGGED
TUGGER
TUGGERY
TUGGING
TUGGINGLY
TUGHRA
TUGUI
TUGURIA
TUGURIUM
TUI
TUILLE
TUILLETTE
TUILYIE
TUILZIE
TUINGA
TUISM
TUITION
TUITIONAL
TUITIONARY
TUITIVE
TUKE
TUKRA
TUKUTUKU
TULADI
TULARAEMIA
TULARE
TULAREMIA
TULASI
TULCAN
TULCE
TULCHAN
TULCHIN
TULE
TULIAC
TULIP
TULIPANT
TULIPFLOWER
TULIPI
TULIPIFEROUS
TULIPIST
TULIPOMANIA
TULIPOMANIAC
TULIPS
TULIPWOOD
TULIPY
TULISAN
TULISANES
TULK
TULLE
TULLIBEE
TULNIC
TULSI
TULWAR
TULWAUR
TULY
TUM
TUMAIN
TUMATAKURU
TUMB
TUMBAK
TUMBAKI
TUMBEK
TUMBEKI
TUMBLE
TUMBLEBUG
TUMBLED
TUMBLER
TUMBLEWEED
TUMBLING
TUMBLINGLY
TUMBLY
TUMBREL
TUMBRIL
TUMEFACIENT
TUMEFACTION
TUMEFIED
TUMEFY
TUMEFYING
TUMESCENCE
TUMESCENT
TUMFIE
TUMID
TUMIDITY
TUMIDLY
TUMIDNESS
TUMMALS
TUMMED
TUMMEL
TUMMELS
TUMMER
TUMMING
TUMMOCK
TUMMY
TUMOR
TUMORED
TUMORLIKE
TUMOROUS
TUMORS
TUMOUR
TUMOURED
TUMP
TUMPHY
TUMPLINE
TUMTUM
TUMULAR
TUMULARY
TUMULATE
TUMULATION
TUMULI
TUMULOSE
TUMULOSITY
TUMULOUS
TUMULT
TUMULTER
TUMULTUARIES
TUMULTUARILY
TUMULTUARY
TUMULTUOSO
TUMULTUOUS
TUMULTUOUSLY
TUMULUS
TUN
TUNA
TUNABLE
TUNABLENESS
TUNABLY
TUNAS
TUNBELLIED
TUNBELLY
TUNCA
TUND
TUNDATION
TUNDISH
TUNDRA
TUNDUN
TUNE
TUNED
TUNEFUL
TUNEFULLY
TUNEFULNESS
TUNELESS
TUNELESSLY
TUNELESSNESS
TUNER
TUNESMITH
TUNESOME
TUNG
TUNGAH
TUNGATE
TUNGO
TUNGSTATE
TUNGSTEN
TUNGSTENIC
TUNGSTENITE
TUNGSTIC
TUNGSTITE
TUNHOOF
TUNIC
TUNICA
TUNICAE
TUNICARY
TUNICATE
TUNICIN
TUNICKED
TUNICLE
TUNING
TUNK
TUNKET
TUNLAND
TUNMOOT
TUNNA
TUNNAGE
TUNNED
TUNNEL
TUNNELED
TUNNELER
TUNNELING
TUNNELITE
TUNNELLED
TUNNELLER
TUNNELLING
TUNNELLITE
TUNNELMAN
TUNNELMEN
TUNNER
TUNNERIES
TUNNERY
TUNNIES
TUNNING
TUNNLAND
TUNNY
TUNO
TUNS
TUNU
TUNY
TUP
TUPAIID
TUPAKIHI
TUPAN
TUPARA
TUPEK
TUPELO
TUPELOS
TUPIK
TUPMAN

TUPMEN
TUPPED
TUPPENCE
TUPPENY
TUPPING
TUPUNA
TUQUE
TUR
TURACIN
TURACOU
TURAKOO
TURANITE
TURANOSE
TURB
TURBAN
TURBANED
TURBANTO
TURBANTOP
TURBARIES
TURBARY
TURBEH
TURBELLARIAN
TURBESCENCY
TURBETH
TURBID
TURBIDIMETER
TURBIDIMETRY
TURBIDITY
TURBIDLY
TURBIDNESS
TURBINACEOUS
TURBINAGE
TURBINAL
TURBINATE
TURBINATED
TURBINATION
TURBINE
TURBINECTOMY
TURBINED
TURBINELLOID
TURBINER
TURBINIFORM
TURBINOID
TURBINOTOME
TURBINOTOMY
TURBIT
TURBITH
TURBITTEEN
TURBLE
TURBOCAR
TURBOFAN
TURBOJET
TURBOPROP
TURBOT
TURBOTS
TURBULENCE
TURBULENCY
TURBULENT
TURBULENTLY
TURCO
TURCOIS
TURCOPOLE
TURCOPOLIER
TURD
TURDIFORM
TURDINE
TURDOID
TUREEN
TURF
TURFED
TURFEN
TURFIER
TURFIEST
TURFINESS
TURFING
TURFITE
TURFMAN
TURFMEN
TURFS
TURFY
TURGENT
TURGENTLY
TURGESCE
TURGESCED
TURGESCENCE
TURGESCENCY
TURGESCENT
TURGESCENTLY
TURGESCING
TURGID
TURGIDITY
TURGIDLY
TURGIDNESS
TURGITE
TURGOID
TURGOR
TURGY
TURICATA
TURIO
TURION
TURJAITE
TURJITE
TURKEN
TURKESS
TURKEY
TURKEYBACK
TURKEYBERRY
TURKEYBUSH
TURKEYFOOT
TURKEYS
TURKIS
TURKLE
TURKOIS
TURLOUGH
TURM
TURMA
TURMALINE
TURMERIC
TURMET
TURMIT
TURMOIL
TURMOILER
TURMUT
TURN
TURNABLE
TURNABOUT
TURNAGAIN
TURNAROUND
TURNAWAY
TURNBACK
TURNBOUT
TURNBROACH
TURNBUCKLE
TURNCAP
TURNCOAT
TURNCOATISM
TURNCOCK
TURNDOWN
TURNDUN
TURNED
TURNEL
TURNER
TURNERACEOUS
TURNERIES
TURNERITE
TURNERY
TURNEY
TURNGATE
TURNHALL
TURNICINE
TURNING
TURNIP
TURNIPWEED
TURNIPWOOD
TURNIPY
TURNKEY
TURNKEYS
TURNOFF
TURNOR
TURNOUT
TURNOVER
TURNPIKE
TURNPIKER
TURNPIN
TURNPLATE
TURNPLOUGH
TURNPLOW
TURNPOKE
TURNROW
TURNS
TURNSCREW
TURNSHEET
TURNSKIN
TURNSOLE
TURNSPIT
TURNSTILE
TURNSTONE
TURNTABLE
TURNTAIL
TURNTALE
TURNUP
TURNVEREIN
TURNWAY
TURNWREST
TURNWRIST
TUROPHILE
TURP
TURPENTINE
TURPENTINED
TURPENTINIC
TURPENTINING
TURPENTINOUS
TURPENTINY
TURPETH
TURPETHIN
TURPID
TURPIDLY
TURPIFY
TURPITUDE
TURPS
TURQUET
TURQUOIS
TURQUOISE
TURQUOISES
TURR
TURREL
TURRELL
TURRET
TURRETED
TURRETING
TURRICAL
TURRICLE
TURRICULA
TURRICULAE
TURRICULAR
TURRICULATE
TURRICULATED
TURRIFEROUS
TURRIFORM
TURRIGEROUS
TURRILITE
TURRION
TURRITELLID
TURRITELLOID
TURRUM
TURSE
TURSIO
TURTLE
TURTLEBACK
TURTLEBLOOM
TURTLED
TURTLEDOM
TURTLEDOVE
TURTLEDOVED
TURTLEDOVING
TURTLEHEAD
TURTLEIZE
TURTLEPEG
TURTLER
TURTLES
TURTLESTONE
TURTLET
TURTLING
TURTOSA
TURTUR
TURURI
TURUS
TURVES
TURWAR
TUSCH
TUSCHE
TUSHE
TUSHED
TUSHER
TUSHERY
TUSHING
TUSK
TUSKAR
TUSKED
TUSKER
TUSKIER
TUSKIEST
TUSKING
TUSKLESS
TUSKY
TUSSAH
TUSSAL
TUSSAR
TUSSEH
TUSSER
TUSSICULAR
TUSSIS
TUSSIVE
TUSSLE
TUSSLED
TUSSLING
TUSSOCK
TUSSOCKED
TUSSOCKER
TUSSOCKY
TUSSORE
TUSSUCK
TUSSUR
TUT
TUTAMENT
TUTANIA
TUTBALL
TUTE
TUTEE
TUTEL
TUTELA
TUTELAE
TUTELAGE
TUTELAR
TUTELARIES
TUTELARY
TUTELE
TUTENAG
TUTENAGUE
TUTIN
TUTLER
TUTLY
TUTMAN
TUTMEN
TUTOIEMENT
TUTOR
TUTORAGE
TUTORED
TUTORER
TUTORESS
TUTORHOOD
TUTORIAL
TUTORIALLY
TUTORIATE
TUTORING
TUTORISM
TUTORIZATION
TUTORIZE
TUTORLY
TUTORSHIP
TUTORY
TUTOYER
TUTSAN
TUTSTER
TUTTA
TUTTE
TUTTED
TUTTI
TUTTIMAN
TUTTING
TUTTIS
TUTTO
TUTTY
TUTTYMAN
TUTU
TUTUH
TUTULUS
TUTWORK
TUUM
TUWI
TUX
TUXEDO
TUXEDOES
TUXEDOS
TUYERE
TUZ
TUZA
TUZZ
TWA
TWADDLE
TWADDLED
TWADDLEMENT
TWADDLER
TWADDLIER
TWADDLIEST
TWADDLING
TWADDLY
TWADDY
TWAG
TWAGGER
TWAIN
TWAITE
TWAL
TWALE
TWALPENNY
TWALT
TWANG
TWANGED
TWANGER
TWANGING
TWANGLE
TWANGLED
TWANGLER
TWANGLING
TWANGY
TWANK
TWANKER
TWANKING
TWANKINGLY
TWANKLE
TWANKY
TWARLY
TWASOME
TWAT
TWATCHEL

TWATTERLIGHT
TWATTLE
TWATTLED
TWATTLER
TWATTLING
TWAY
TWAYBLADE
TWAZZY
TWEAK
TWEAKED
TWEAKER
TWEAKING
TWEAKY
TWEE
TWEED
TWEEDED
TWEEDLE
TWEEDLED
TWEEDLEDEE
TWEEDLEDUM
TWEEDLING
TWEEDY
TWEEG
TWEEL
TWEEN
TWEENY
TWEER
TWEESE
TWEESH
TWEESHT
TWEEST
TWEET
TWEETER
TWEEZE
TWEEZED
TWEEZER
TWEEZERED
TWEEZERING
TWEEZERS
TWEEZING
TWEIL
TWELFTH
TWELL
TWELVE
TWELVEFOLD
TWELVEMO
TWELVEMONTH
TWELVEPENCE
TWELVEPENNY
TWELVESCORE
TWENTIES
TWENTIETH
TWENTY
TWENTYFOLD
TWENTYMO
TWERP
TWEYFOLD
TWIBIL
TWIBILL
TWIBILLED
TWICE
TWICER
TWICH
TWICHILD
TWICK
TWIDDLE
TWIDDLED
TWIDDLER
TWIDDLING
TWIDDLY
TWIER
TWIFALLOW
TWIFOIL
TWIFOLD
TWIG
TWIGGED
TWIGGEN
TWIGGER
TWIGGIER
TWIGGIEST
TWIGGING
TWIGGY
TWIGLESS
TWIGLET
TWIGS
TWIGWITHY
TWILIGHT
TWILIGHTY
TWILIT
TWILL
TWILLED
TWILLER
TWILLING
TWILLY
TWIN
TWINBERRIES
TWINBERRY
TWINBORN
TWIND
TWINDLE
TWINE
TWINEBUSH
TWINED
TWINER
TWINFLOWER
TWINFOLD
TWINGE
TWINGED
TWINGING
TWINGLE
TWINIGHT
TWINING
TWINK
TWINKLE
TWINKLED
TWINKLEDUM
TWINKLER
TWINKLES
TWINKLING
TWINKLINGLY
TWINKLY
TWINLEAF
TWINLING
TWINLY
TWINNED
TWINNER
TWINNING
TWINS
TWINSHIP
TWINSOMENESS
TWINT
TWINTER
TWINY
TWIRE
TWIRK
TWIRL
TWIRLED
TWIRLER
TWIRLIGIG
TWIRLING
TWIRLY
TWIRP
TWISCAR
TWISEL
TWIST
TWISTED
TWISTEDLY
TWISTER
TWISTHAND
TWISTICAL
TWISTING
TWISTINGLY
TWISTIWAYS
TWISTIWISE
TWISTLE
TWISTY
TWIT
TWITCH
TWITCHED
TWITCHEL
TWITCHELING
TWITCHER
TWITCHET
TWITCHETY
TWITCHFIRE
TWITCHING
TWITCHINGLY
TWITCHY
TWITE
TWITLARK
TWITTED
TWITTEN
TWITTER
TWITTERATION
TWITTERER
TWITTERING
TWITTERINGLY
TWITTERLY
TWITTERY
TWITTING
TWITTINGLY
TWITTLE
TWITTY
TWIXT
TWIZZLE
TWO
TWOES
TWOFER
TWOFOLD
TWOFOLDLY
TWOFOLDNESS
TWOLING
TWONESS
TWOPENCE
TWOPENNY
TWOS
TWOSOME
TWYER
TY
TYALL
TYAUVE
TYCHISM
TYCHITE
TYCHOPOTAMIC
TYCOON
TYCOONATE
TYDDEN
TYDDYN
TYDIE
TYE
TYEE
TYER
TYG
TYING
TYKE
TYKEN
TYKING
TYLARI
TYLARUS
TYLASTER
TYLE
TYLER
TYLI
TYLION
TYLOMA
TYLOPOD
TYLOPODOUS
TYLOSE
TYLOSES
TYLOSIS
TYLOSOID
TYLOSTERESIS
TYLOSTYLAR
TYLOSTYLE
TYLOSTYLOTE
TYLOSTYLUS
TYLOTATE
TYLOTE
TYLOTIC
TYLOTOXEA
TYLOTOXEATE
TYLUS
TYMBAL
TYMBALON
TYMP
TYMPAN
TYMPANA
TYMPANAL
TYMPANI
TYMPANIC
TYMPANIES
TYMPANING
TYMPANISM
TYMPANIST
TYMPANITES
TYMPANITIC
TYMPANITIS
TYMPANIZE
TYMPANO
TYMPANOHYAL
TYMPANOSIS
TYMPANOTOMY
TYMPANUM
TYMPANUMS
TYMPANY
TYND
TYPAL
TYPARCHICAL
TYPE
TYPECAST
TYPECASTING
TYPED
TYPEFACE
TYPEFACES
TYPEHOLDER
TYPER
TYPES
TYPESCRIPT
TYPESET
TYPESETTER
TYPESETTING
TYPEWRITE
TYPEWRITER
TYPEWRITING
TYPEWRITTEN
TYPEWROTE
TYPHAEMIA
TYPHEMIA
TYPHIA
TYPHIC
TYPHINIA
TYPHIZATION
TYPHLITIC
TYPHLITIS
TYPHLOLOGIES
TYPHLOLOGY
TYPHLON
TYPHLOPHILE
TYPHLOPID
TYPHLOSIS
TYPHLOSOLAR
TYPHLOSOLE
TYPHOAEMIA
TYPHOEMIA
TYPHOGENIC
TYPHOID
TYPHOIDAL
TYPHOIDIN
TYPHOIDLIKE
TYPHOLYSIN
TYPHOMALARIA
TYPHOMANIA
TYPHONIC
TYPHOON
TYPHOSE
TYPHOSIS
TYPHOTOXINE
TYPHOUS
TYPHUS
TYPIC
TYPICA
TYPICAL
TYPICALITY
TYPICALLY
TYPICALNESS
TYPICON
TYPICUM
TYPIFICATION
TYPIFIED
TYPIFIER
TYPIFY
TYPIFYING
TYPING
TYPIST
TYPO
TYPOBAR
TYPOCOSMY
TYPOGRAPHER
TYPOGRAPHIA
TYPOGRAPHIC
TYPOGRAPHIES
TYPOGRAPHIST
TYPOGRAPHY
TYPOLOGICAL
TYPOLOGIES
TYPOLOGIST
TYPOLOGY
TYPOMANIA
TYPOMETRY
TYPONYM
TYPONYMAL
TYPONYMIC
TYPONYMOUS
TYPOPHILE
TYPORAMA
TYPOS
TYPOTHETAE
TYPP
TYPTOLOGICAL
TYPTOLOGIST
TYPTOLOGY
TYPY
TYRAMIN
TYRAMINE
TYRANNESS
TYRANNIAL
TYRANNIC
TYRANNICAL
TYRANNICALLY
TYRANNICIDAL
TYRANNICIDE
TYRANNICLY
TYRANNIES
TYRANNINE
TYRANNIS
TYRANNISM
TYRANNIZE
TYRANNIZED
TYRANNIZER
TYRANNIZING
TYRANNOSAUR
TYRANNOUS
TYRANNOUSLY
TYRANNY
TYRANT

TYRASOLE
TYRE
TYREMESIS
TYRIASIS
TYRO
TYROGLYPHID
TYROLITE
TYROLOGY
TYROMA
TYROMANCY
TYROMAS
TYROMATA
TYROMATOUS
TYRONE
TYRONIC
TYRONISM
TYROS
TYROSINASE
TYROSINE
TYROSINURIA
TYROSYL
TYROTHRICIN
TYROTOXICON
TYROTOXINE
TYSONITE
TYSTE
TYSTIE
TYT
TYTE
TZAR
TZARDOM
TZARINA
TZEDAKAH
TZETZE
TZIGANE
TZIMMES
TZIRID
TZOLKIN
TZONTLE
TZUT
TZUTE

U

UAKARI
UALIS
UANG
UAYED
UBE
UBERANT
UBEROUS
UBEROUSLY
UBEROUSNESS
UBERTY
UBI
UBICATION
UBIETY
UBIQUARIAN
UBIQUE
UBIQUIOUS
UBIQUIT
UBIQUITARIAN
UBIQUITARIES
UBIQUITARY
UBIQUITOUS
UBIQUITOUSLY
UBIQUITY
UBUSSU
UCH
UCHE
UCKERS
UCKIA
UCUUBA
UDAD
UDAL
UDALER
UDALLER
UDALMAN
UDASI
UDDER
UDDERED
UDDERFUL
UDDERLESS
UDELL
UDGE
UDO
UDOMETER
UDOMETRIC
UDOMETRY
UDOMOGRAPH
UEBA
UFER
UG
UGGE
UGGLESOME
UGH
UGHTEN
UGLIER
UGLIEST
UGLIFICATION
UGLIFIED
UGLIFIER
UGLIFY
UGLIFYING
UGLILY
UGLINESS
UGLISOME
UGLY
UGRIANIZE
UGRUG
UGSOME
UHLAN
UHLLO
UHTENSANG
UHTSONG
UINAL
UINTAHITE
UINTAITE
UINTATHERE
UINTJIE
UIT
UITLANDER
UITSPAN
UJI
UKASE
UKE
UKIYO
UKIYOYE
UKU
UKULELE
ULA
ULAE
ULAMA
ULAN
ULATROPHIA
ULATROPHY
ULAULA
ULCER
ULCERATE
ULCERATED
ULCERATING
ULCERATION
ULCERATIVE
ULCERED
ULCEROUS
ULCEROUSLY
ULCEROUSNESS
ULCUS
ULCUSCLE
ULCUSCULE
ULE
ULEMA
ULERYTHEMA
ULETIC
ULEXINE
ULEXITE
ULIGINOSE
ULIGINOUS
ULITIS
ULL
ULLAGE
ULLAGED
ULLAGONE
ULLER
ULLING
ULLMANNITE
ULLUCO
ULLUCU
ULMACEOUS
ULME
ULMIC
ULMIN
ULMINIC
ULMO
ULNA
ULNAD
ULNAE
ULNAR
ULNARE
ULNARIA
ULNAS
ULNOCARPAL
ULNOCONDYLAR
ULNORADIAL
ULOBORID
ULOID
ULONCUS
ULOTRICHAN
ULOTRICHOUS
ULOTRICHY
ULPAN
ULRICHITE
ULSTER
ULSTERED
ULSTERETTE
ULSTERING
ULTERIOR
ULTERIORLY
ULTIMA
ULTIMACY
ULTIMATA
ULTIMATE
ULTIMATED
ULTIMATELY
ULTIMATENESS
ULTIMATING
ULTIMATION
ULTIMATUM
ULTIMATUMS
ULTIME
ULTIMITY
ULTIMO
ULTIMUM
ULTION
ULTRA
ULTRABASIC
ULTRABASITE
ULTRACIVIL
ULTRACOMPLEX
ULTRACONSERVATISM
ULTRACONSERVATIVE
ULTRACORDIAL
ULTRAFASHIONABLE
ULTRAFIDIAN
ULTRAFILTER
ULTRAGASEOUS
ULTRAGENTEEL
ULTRAGOOD
ULTRAGRAVE
ULTRAHEROIC
ULTRAISM
ULTRAIST
ULTRAISTIC
ULTRALENIENT
ULTRALIBERAL
ULTRALOGICAL
ULTRALOYAL
ULTRAMARINE
ULTRAMAXIMAL
ULTRAMINUTE
ULTRAMODERN
ULTRAMODEST
ULTRAMONTANE
ULTRAMONTANISM
ULTRAMOROSE
ULTRAMULISH
ULTRAMUNDANE
ULTRANICE
ULTRAOBSCURE
ULTRAORNATE
ULTRAPAPIST
ULTRAPERFECT
ULTRAPIOUS
ULTRAPOPISH
ULTRAPROUD
ULTRAPRUDENT
ULTRARADICAL
ULTRARAPID
ULTRARED
ULTRAREFINED
ULTRASELECT
ULTRASERVILE
ULTRASEVERE
ULTRASHREWD
ULTRASOLEMN
ULTRASONIC
ULTRASONICS
ULTRASPARTAN
ULTRASTELLAR
ULTRASTERILE
ULTRASTRICT
ULTRASUBTLE
ULTRATENSE
ULTRATRIVIAL
ULTRAUGLY
ULTRAURGENT
ULTRAVICIOUS
ULTRAVIOLENT
ULTRAVIOLET
ULTRAVIRUS
ULTRAVISIBLE
ULTRAWEALTHY
ULTRAWISE
ULTRAYOUNG
ULTRAZEALOUS
ULTRONEOUS
ULTRONEOUSLY
ULU
ULUA
ULUHI
ULULANT
ULULATE
ULULATED
ULULATING
ULULATION
ULULATIVE
ULULATORY
ULULU
ULUS
ULVACEOUS
ULYIE
ULZIE
UM
UMANGITE
UMBE
UMBECAST
UMBEL
UMBELAP
UMBELED
UMBELLA
UMBELLAR
UMBELLATE
UMBELLATED
UMBELLATELY
UMBELLED
UMBELLET
UMBELLIC
UMBELLIFER
UMBELLIFERONE
UMBELLIFORM
UMBELLOID
UMBELLULATE
UMBELLULE
UMBELWORT
UMBER
UMBERED
UMBERING
UMBERTY
UMBESET
UMBETHINK
UMBILIC
UMBILICAL
UMBILICALLY
UMBILICAR
UMBILICATE
UMBILICATED
UMBILICATION
UMBILICI
UMBILICIFORM
UMBILICUS
UMBILIFORM
UMBILROOT
UMBLES
UMBO
UMBOLATERAL
UMBONAL
UMBONATE
UMBONATED
UMBONATION
UMBONE
UMBONES
UMBONIAL
UMBONIC
UMBONULATE
UMBONULE
UMBRA
UMBRACLE
UMBRACULATE
UMBRACULUM
UMBRAE
UMBRAGE
UMBRAGEOUS
UMBRAGEOUSLY
UMBRAID
UMBRAL
UMBRALLY
UMBRANA
UMBRATE
UMBRATIC
UMBRATILE
UMBRE
UMBREL
UMBRELLA
UMBRELLAED
UMBRELLAWORT
UMBRET
UMBRETTE
UMBRIFEROUS
UMBRIL
UMBRINE
UMBROSE
UMBROSITY
UMBROUS
UME
UMEST
UMFAAN
UMGANG
UMIACK
UMIAK
UMIRI
UMLAND
UMLAUT
UMMAN
UMP
UMPIRAGE
UMPIRE
UMPIRED
UMPIRESHIP
UMPIRESS
UMPIRING
UMPLE
UMPTEEN
UMPTEENTH
UMPTEKITE
UMPTIETH
UMPTY
UMQUHILE
UMSET
UMSTROKE
UMU
UN
UNABASHED
UNABBREVIATED
UNABLE
UNABLENESS
UNABLY
UNABRIDGED
UNABSOLVABLE
UNACCENTED
UNACCEPTABLE
UNACCEPTED
UNACCOMPANIED
UNACCOUNTABLE

UNACCUSTOMED
UNACQUAINTED
UNACTION
UNACTIVE
UNACTIVELY
UNACTIVITY
UNACTUAL
UNACTUALITY
UNACTUALLY
UNADAPTABLE
UNADAPTABLY
UNADDITIONED
UNADDRESS
UNADEQUATE
UNADEQUATELY
UNADHERENCE
UNADHERENT
UNADHERENTLY
UNADORNED
UNADULTERATED
UNADVANCED
UNADVANCEDLY
UNADVANTAGEOUSLY
UNADVERTENCY
UNADVISABLE
UNADVISABLY
UNADVISED
UNADVISEDLY
UNAFFECTED
UNAFFECTEDLY
UNAFFIED
UNAFRAID
UNAGGRESSIVE
UNAGING
UNAGREEABLE
UNAIDED
UNAIMED
UNAKIN
UNAKITE
UNAL
UNALERT
UNALIENABLE
UNALIENABLY
UNALIKE
UNALIST
UNALLIED
UNALLIEDLY
UNALLOYED
UNALMSED
UNALTERABLE
UNALTERABLY
UNALTERED
UNAMBIGUOUS
UNAMBITION
UNAMBITIOUS
UNAMENABLE
UNAMENABLY
UNAMIABILITY
UNAMIABLE
UNAMIABLY
UNAMO
UNAMUSIVE
UNANCESTORED
UNANCESTRIED
UNANCHOR
UNANELED
UNANIMATE
UNANIMATED
UNANIMATEDLY
UNANIMATELY
UNANIME
UNANIMISM
UNANIMIST
UNANIMISTIC
UNANIMITER
UNANIMITY
UNANIMOUS
UNANIMOUSLY
UNANSWERABLE
UNANSWERABLY
UNANSWERED
UNAPPEALABLE
UNAPPEALABLY
UNAPPROACHABLE
UNAPPROVED
UNAPT
UNAPTLY
UNAPTNESS
UNARGUED
UNARK
UNARM
UNARMED
UNARMEDLY
UNARMEDNESS
UNARMORED
UNARMOURED
UNARRAY
UNARTED
UNARTFUL
UNARTFULLY
UNARTFULNESS
UNARTIFICIAL
UNARTISTIC
UNARTISTICAL
UNARY
UNASINOUS
UNASSAILABLE
UNASSAILABLY
UNASSENTED
UNASSISTED
UNASSOILED
UNASSUETUDE
UNASSUMED
UNASSUMING
UNASSUMINGLY
UNASSURED
UNASSUREDLY
UNATONABLE
UNATTACHED
UNATTAINABLE
UNATTAINTED
UNATTAINTEDLY
UNATTENDED
UNATTIRE
UNATTRACTIVE
UNAU
UNAUDIBLE
UNAUDIBLY
UNAUDIENCED
UNAUSPICIOUS
UNAUTHORIZE
UNAUTHORIZED
UNAUTORITIED
UNAVAILING
UNAVAILINGLY
UNAVOIDABLE
UNAVOIDABLY
UNAVOIDED
UNAVOWED
UNAWARE
UNAWARED
UNAWAREDLY
UNAWARENESS
UNAWARES
UNBACKED
UNBAG
UNBAIN
UNBAITED
UNBAIZED
UNBAKED
UNBALANCE
UNBALANCED
UNBALANCING
UNBALLAST
UNBALLASTED
UNBALLASTING
UNBANE
UNBANK
UNBANKED
UNBAPTIZED
UNBAR
UNBARBED
UNBARE
UNBARK
UNBARRED
UNBARREL
UNBARRING
UNBATED
UNBE
UNBEAR
UNBEARABLE
UNBEARABLY
UNBEARDED
UNBEARED
UNBEARING
UNBEAST
UNBEATEN
UNBEAVERED
UNBECOME
UNBECOMING
UNBECOMINGLY
UNBED
UNBEDDED
UNBEFIT
UNBEFITTING
UNBEFOOL
UNBEFRIEND
UNBEGET
UNBEGILT
UNBEGINNING
UNBEGOT
UNBEGOTTEN
UNBEGOTTENLY
UNBEGUILE
UNBEGUN
UNBEHOVING
UNBEING
UNBEJUGGLED
UNBEKNOWN
UNBEKNOWNST
UNBELIEF
UNBELIEFFUL
UNBELIEVABLE
UNBELIEVABLY
UNBELIEVE
UNBELIEVED
UNBELIEVER
UNBELIEVERS
UNBELIEVING
UNBELT
UNBEND
UNBENDED
UNBENDER
UNBENDING
UNBENDINGLY
UNBENT
UNBEREAVEN
UNBEREFT
UNBERUFEN
UNBESEEM
UNBESEEMING
UNBETHINK
UNBETHOUGHT
UNBETIDE
UNBEWARE
UNBEWILLED
UNBEWITCH
UNBIAS
UNBIASABLE
UNBIASED
UNBIASEDLY
UNBIASEDNESS
UNBIASING
UNBIASSABLE
UNBIASSED
UNBIASSEDLY
UNBIASSING
UNBID
UNBIDABLE
UNBIDDEN
UNBIGGED
UNBIND
UNBINDING
UNBIRDLY
UNBISHOP
UNBITTED
UNBITTING
UNBLAMABLE
UNBLAMABLY
UNBLEACHED
UNBLEMISHED
UNBLENCHED
UNBLESS
UNBLESSED
UNBLEST
UNBLISS
UNBLITHE
UNBLOCK
UNBLOCKED
UNBLOODED
UNBLOODILY
UNBLOODINESS
UNBLOODY
UNBLOOM
UNBLOWN
UNBLUSHING
UNBLUSHINGLY
UNBOAT
UNBODIED
UNBODILINESS
UNBODILY
UNBODKINED
UNBODY
UNBOLD
UNBOLDLY
UNBOLDNESS
UNBOLT
UNBOLTED
UNBOLTING
UNBONE
UNBONED
UNBONNET
UNBONNETED
UNBONNY
UNBOOKED
UNBOOT
UNBORN
UNBOSOM
UNBOSOMED
UNBOSOMER
UNBOSOMING
UNBOTTOMED
UNBOUGHT
UNBOUND
UNBOUNDED
UNBOUNDEDLY
UNBOUNDLESS
UNBOW
UNBOWABLE
UNBOWED
UNBOWEL
UNBOWELED
UNBOWELLED
UNBOWERED
UNBOWSOME
UNBOY
UNBRACE
UNBRACED
UNBRACING
UNBRAID
UNBRAINED
UNBRANDED
UNBREAKABLE
UNBREAST
UNBREATH
UNBREATHED
UNBRED
UNBREECH
UNBRENT
UNBREWED
UNBRICK
UNBRIDLE
UNBRIDLED
UNBRIDLEDLY
UNBROID
UNBROKE
UNBROKEN
UNBROKENLY
UNBROKENNESS
UNBRUTALIZE
UNBRUTE
UNBRUTIFY
UNBRUTIZE
UNBUCKLE
UNBUCKRAMED
UNBUDGEABLE
UNBUDGEABLY
UNBUILD
UNBUILDED
UNBUILDING
UNBUILT
UNBUNDLE
UNBUNG
UNBURDEN
UNBURDENMENT
UNBURIABLE
UNBURIAL
UNBURN
UNBURNISHED
UNBURNT
UNBURROW
UNBURTHEN
UNBURY
UNBUSH
UNBUSIED
UNBUSK
UNBUTTON
UNBUTTONED
UNBUXOM
UNBUXOMLY
UNC
UNCA
UNCAGE
UNCAGED
UNCALLED
UNCALLOW
UNCALLOWER
UNCALM
UNCAMP
UNCANDOR
UNCANDOUR
UNCANNILY
UNCANNINESS
UNCANNY
UNCANONIZE
UNCANONIZED
UNCANONIZING
UNCAP
UNCAPABLE
UNCAPABLY
UNCAPACITATE
UNCAPPED
UNCAPPER
UNCAPPING
UNCAREFUL

UNCAREFULLY
UNCARNATE
UNCART
UNCASE
UNCASTE
UNCASTLE
UNCASTRATED
UNCATE
UNCATHEDRALED
UNCAUGHT
UNCAUSED
UNCAUTELOUS
UNCAUTIOUS
UNCAUTIOUSLY
UNCE
UNCEASABLE
UNCEASING
UNCEASINGLY
UNCELLAR
UNCENTER
UNCENTRE
UNCENTURY
UNCEREMONIOUS
UNCEREMONIOUSLY
UNCERTAIN
UNCERTAINLY
UNCERTAINNESS
UNCERTAINTIES
UNCERTAINTY
UNCERTITUDE
UNCESSANT
UNCESSANTLY
UNCH
UNCHAIN
UNCHALLENGED
UNCHANCE
UNCHANCY
UNCHANGEABLE
UNCHANGEABLENESS
UNCHANGEABLY
UNCHANGING
UNCHARGE
UNCHARGED
UNCHARILY
UNCHARINESS
UNCHARITABLE
UNCHARITABLY
UNCHARITY
UNCHARM
UNCHARNEL
UNCHARTERED
UNCHARY
UNCHASTE
UNCHASTELY
UNCHASTENESS
UNCHASTITY
UNCHECK
UNCHECKED
UNCHEERFUL
UNCHEERFULLY
UNCHILD
UNCHILDISH
UNCHILDISHLY
UNCHRISOM
UNCHRIST
UNCHRISTEN
UNCHRISTENED
UNCHRISTIAN
UNCHURCH
UNCHURCHED
UNCI
UNCIA
UNCIAE
UNCIAL
UNCIALIZE
UNCIALLY
UNCIATIM
UNCIFORM
UNCINAL
UNCINARIASIS
UNCINARIATIC
UNCINATE
UNCINATED
UNCINI
UNCINUS
UNCIPHER
UNCIROSTRATE
UNCITY
UNCIVIL
UNCIVILIZED
UNCIVILLY
UNCLAD
UNCLAMP
UNCLASP
UNCLASSIFY
UNCLE
UNCLEAD
UNCLEAN
UNCLEANLILY
UNCLEANLY
UNCLEANNESS
UNCLEANSE
UNCLEAR
UNCLEARED
UNCLEARLY
UNCLEAVE
UNCLEMENT
UNCLEMENTLY
UNCLENCH
UNCLEVER
UNCLEVERLY
UNCLEW
UNCLIFY
UNCLINCH
UNCLING
UNCLOAK
UNCLOG
UNCLOISTER
UNCLOSE
UNCLOSED
UNCLOSING
UNCLOTHE
UNCLOTHED
UNCLOTHING
UNCLOUD
UNCLOUDED
UNCLUBABLE
UNCLUBBABLE
UNCLUBBY
UNCLUTCH
UNCO
UNCOACH
UNCOACTED
UNCOCK
UNCOFFER
UNCOFFLE
UNCOFT
UNCOGITABLE
UNCOGUIDISM
UNCOHERENT
UNCOHERENTLY
UNCOIF
UNCOIL
UNCOIN
UNCOINED
UNCOLIKE
UNCOLLECTED
UNCOLORED
UNCOLT
UNCOLY
UNCOMBED
UNCOMBINABLE
UNCOMBINABLY
UNCOMBINE
UNCOMBINED
UNCOME
UNCOMELIER
UNCOMELIEST
UNCOMELILY
UNCOMELY
UNCOMFORTABLE
UNCOMFORTABLY
UNCOMMERCIAL
UNCOMMITTED
UNCOMMIXED
UNCOMMODIOUS
UNCOMMON
UNCOMMONER
UNCOMMONEST
UNCOMMONLY
UNCOMMONNESS
UNCOMMUNICATIVE
UNCOMPACT
UNCOMPANIED
UNCOMPASSED
UNCOMPATIBLE
UNCOMPATIBLY
UNCOMPLIABLE
UNCOMPLICATED
UNCOMPLIMENTARY
UNCOMPOSED
UNCOMPOUND
UNCOMPOUNDED
UNCOMPREHEND
UNCOMPROMISING
UNCOMPT
UNCONCEALED
UNCONCEIVING
UNCONCERN
UNCONCERNED
UNCONCERNEDLY
UNCONCERNING
UNCONCLUDENT
UNCONCLUDING
UNCONCLUSIVE
UNCONCOCTED
UNCONDITED
UNCONDITIONAL
UNCONDITIONED
UNCONFINE
UNCONFINED
UNCONFIRMED
UNCONFORMIST
UNCONFORMITIES
UNCONFORMITY
UNCONGENIAL
UNCONNECTED
UNCONQUERED
UNCONQUEST
UNCONSCIOUS
UNCONSCIOUSLY
UNCONSECRATE
UNCONSENT
UNCONSIDERED
UNCONSISTENT
UNCONSONANCY
UNCONSONANT
UNCONSTANCY
UNCONSTANT
UNCONSTANTLY
UNCONSTRAINED
UNCONSTRAINT
UNCONSULT
UNCONTENT
UNCONTENTED
UNCONTROL
UNCONTROLLABLE
UNCONTROLLABLY
UNCONTROLLED
UNCONVENIENT
UNCONVENTIONAL
UNCONVERSING
UNCONVERSION
UNCONVERTED
UNCONVINCING
UNCOOKED
UNCORD
UNCORDED
UNCORDING
UNCORK
UNCORKER
UNCORKING
UNCORPORAL
UNCORRECTED
UNCORRIGIBLE
UNCORRUPT
UNCORRUPTION
UNCORVEN
UNCOS
UNCOST
UNCOUCH
UNCOUCHED
UNCOUCHING
UNCOUNTABLE
UNCOUNTABLY
UNCOUNTED
UNCOUPLE
UNCOUPLED
UNCOUPLER
UNCOUPLING
UNCOURSED
UNCOURTEOUS
UNCOUS
UNCOUTH
UNCOUTHLY
UNCOUTHNESS
UNCOUTHSOME
UNCOVENABLE
UNCOVER
UNCOVERABLE
UNCOVERED
UNCOVEREDLY
UNCOVERING
UNCOW
UNCOWL
UNCRAFTILY
UNCRAFTINESS
UNCRAFTY
UNCRAZED
UNCREATE
UNCREATED
UNCREATING
UNCREATION
UNCREDIBLE
UNCREDIT
UNCREDITABLE
UNCREDITABLY
UNCRINKLE
UNCRINKLED
UNCRINKLING
UNCRITICALLY
UNCRITICISM
UNCROOK
UNCROOKING
UNCROSS
UNCROWN
UNCROWNED
UNCROWNING
UNCRUDDED
UNCRUMPLE
UNCTION
UNCTIONAL
UNCTIONEER
UNCTIONLESS
UNCTIOUS
UNCTIOUSNESS
UNCTORIAN
UNCTUOSITY
UNCTUOUS
UNCTUOUSLY
UNCTUOUSNESS
UNCUBBED
UNCULAR
UNCULTED
UNCULTIVATED
UNCULTURE
UNCULTURED
UNCUMBER
UNCUMBERED
UNCUNNING
UNCUNNINGLY
UNCURABLE
UNCURABLY
UNCURB
UNCURBED
UNCURBING
UNCURED
UNCURL
UNCURLING
UNCURRENT
UNCURRENTLY
UNCURSE
UNCURTAIN
UNCURTAINED
UNCUS
UNCUSTOMED
UNCUT
UNCYA
UNDAMAGED
UNDAMPED
UNDANGERED
UNDARK
UNDARKENED
UNDASHED
UNDATE
UNDATED
UNDATEDNESS
UNDAUGHTERLY
UNDAUNTABLE
UNDAUNTED
UNDAUNTEDLY
UNDAZZLE
UNDE
UNDEADLY
UNDEAF
UNDEAN
UNDEAR
UNDECAGON
UNDECAYED
UNDECEIVABLE
UNDECEIVABLY
UNDECEIVE
UNDECEIVED
UNDECEIVER
UNDECEIVING
UNDECENCY
UNDECENNIAL
UNDECENT
UNDECENTLY
UNDECEPTION
UNDECIDE
UNDECIDED
UNDECIDEDLY
UNDECIDING
UNDECIMAL
UNDECIMAN
UNDECIMOLE
UNDECIPHER
UNDECIPHERED
UNDECISIVE
UNDECISIVELY
UNDECK
UNDECKED
UNDECLARE
UNDECLARED

UNDECLINABLE
UNDECOYED
UNDECREE
UNDECYL
UNDECYLENE
UNDECYLENIC
UNDECYLIC
UNDEE
UNDEEDED
UNDEEMED
UNDEEMOUS
UNDEEMOUSLY
UNDEEP
UNDEFEASIBLE
UNDEFECATED
UNDEFENDED
UNDEFENSIBLE
UNDEFILED
UNDEFINABLE
UNDEFINABLY
UNDEFINE
UNDEFINED
UNDEIFIED
UNDEIFY
UNDEIFYING
UNDELAYEDLY
UNDELIGHT
UNDELIVERABLE
UNDELIVERY
UNDELUDABLE
UNDEMONSTRATIVE
UNDENIABLE
UNDENIABLY
UNDEPENDABLE
UNDEPENDING
UNDEPRIVABLE
UNDER
UNDERACT
UNDERACTED
UNDERACTING
UNDERACTION
UNDERACTOR
UNDERAGE
UNDERAID
UNDERAIR
UNDERARM
UNDERARMING
UNDERBACK
UNDERBARRING
UNDERBEAR
UNDERBEARER
UNDERBEARING
UNDERBEING
UNDERBELLIES
UNDERBELLY
UNDERBID
UNDERBIDDER
UNDERBIDDING
UNDERBILL
UNDERBIND
UNDERBIT
UNDERBITTED
UNDERBITTEN
UNDERBOARD
UNDERBODICE
UNDERBODY
UNDERBORN
UNDERBOUGHT
UNDERBOWED
UNDERBOY
UNDERBRACED
UNDERBRED
UNDERBRIGHT
UNDERBRIM
UNDERBRUSH
UNDERBUILD
UNDERBURN
UNDERBURNED
UNDERBURNT
UNDERBURY
UNDERBUSH
UNDERBUTLER
UNDERBUY
UNDERBUYING
UNDERCANOPY
UNDERCARRIAGE
UNDERCARVED
UNDERCAST
UNDERCHARGE
UNDERCHARGED
UNDERCHARGING
UNDERCLASS
UNDERCLASSMAN
UNDERCLASSMEN
UNDERCLAY
UNDERCLIFF
UNDERCLOTHE
UNDERCLOTHES
UNDERCLUB
UNDERCOAT
UNDERCOATED
UNDERCOATING
UNDERCOLOR
UNDERCOLORED
UNDERCOOL
UNDERCOVER
UNDERCOVERT
UNDERCRAFT
UNDERCREEP
UNDERCREST
UNDERCROFT
UNDERCROP
UNDERCRUST
UNDERCURRENT
UNDERCUT
UNDERCUTTER
UNDERCUTTING
UNDERDEALER
UNDERDEALING
UNDERDECK
UNDERDEVELOPED
UNDERDID
UNDERDITCH
UNDERDO
UNDERDOER
UNDERDOG
UNDERDOING
UNDERDONE
UNDERDOSE
UNDERDRAG
UNDERDRAIN
UNDERDRAINER
UNDERDRAW
UNDERDRAWERS
UNDERDRAWN
UNDERDRESS
UNDERDRIVE
UNDEREARTH
UNDEREATEN
UNDEREDUCATED
UNDERENTER
UNDERER
UNDERESTIMATE
UNDERESTIMATED
UNDERESTIMATING
UNDEREXPOSE
UNDEREXPOSED
UNDEREXPOSING
UNDERFALL
UNDERFED
UNDERFEED
UNDERFEEDING
UNDERFEEL
UNDERFEET
UNDERFELLOW
UNDERFILL
UNDERFILLING
UNDERFIND
UNDERFIRE
UNDERFLEECE
UNDERFLOW
UNDERFO
UNDERFOLD
UNDERFONG
UNDERFOOT
UNDERFRAME
UNDERFRAMING
UNDERFREIGHT
UNDERFUR
UNDERFURROW
UNDERGAGE
UNDERGARMENT
UNDERGAUGE
UNDERGEAR
UNDERGIRD
UNDERGIRDED
UNDERGIRDER
UNDERGIRDING
UNDERGIRDLE
UNDERGIRT
UNDERGIRTH
UNDERGLAZE
UNDERGO
UNDERGOER
UNDERGOES
UNDERGOING
UNDERGONE
UNDERGOWN
UNDERGRADE
UNDERGRADUATE
UNDERGRADUETTE
UNDERGREEN
UNDERGROAN
UNDERGROPE
UNDERGROUND
UNDERGROVE
UNDERGROW
UNDERGROWN
UNDERGROWTH
UNDERHAND
UNDERHANDED
UNDERHANGING
UNDERHEAD
UNDERHEW
UNDERHIVE
UNDERHOLD
UNDERHOLE
UNDERHUNG
UNDERIVED
UNDERJAWED
UNDERKEEP
UNDERLAID
UNDERLAIN
UNDERLAP
UNDERLAY
UNDERLAYER
UNDERLAYING
UNDERLEAF
UNDERLEASE
UNDERLESSEE
UNDERLET
UNDERLETTER
UNDERLETTING
UNDERLEVEL
UNDERLEVER
UNDERLIE
UNDERLIER
UNDERLIFE
UNDERLINE
UNDERLINED
UNDERLINEN
UNDERLINER
UNDERLING
UNDERLINING
UNDERLIP
UNDERLIVE
UNDERLOAD
UNDERLOCK
UNDERLOOK
UNDERLOOKER
UNDERLOUT
UNDERLY
UNDERLYING
UNDERMAN
UNDERMANNED
UNDERMANNING
UNDERMASTED
UNDERMATCH
UNDERMATCHED
UNDERMEAL
UNDERMINE
UNDERMINED
UNDERMINER
UNDERMINING
UNDERMIRTH
UNDERMONEY
UNDERMOST
UNDERMUSLIN
UNDERN
UNDERNAM
UNDERNATURAL
UNDERNEATH
UNDERNESS
UNDERNIM
UNDERNOME
UNDERNOMEN
UNDERNOURISH
UNDERNSONG
UNDERNTIDE
UNDERNTIME
UNDERNUMEN
UNDERPAID
UNDERPAN
UNDERPANTS
UNDERPART
UNDERPASS
UNDERPASSION
UNDERPAY
UNDERPAYING
UNDERPICK
UNDERPICKED
UNDERPIN
UNDERPINNED
UNDERPINNER
UNDERPINNING
UNDERPITCH
UNDERPLANT
UNDERPLANTED
UNDERPLANTING
UNDERPLAY
UNDERPLOT
UNDERPLOTTER
UNDERPOLE
UNDERPOSE
UNDERPOWER
UNDERPRICE
UNDERPRINT
UNDERPROOF
UNDERPROP
UNDERPROPPED
UNDERPROPPER
UNDERPROPPING
UNDERPULL
UNDERPULLER
UNDERPUT
UNDERQUOTE
UNDERQUOTED
UNDERQUOTING
UNDERRAN
UNDERRATE
UNDERRATED
UNDERRATING
UNDERREACH
UNDERREAD
UNDERREAM
UNDERREAMER
UNDERRENT
UNDERRENTED
UNDERRIVER
UNDERROLL
UNDERROOF
UNDERROOT
UNDERRUN
UNDERRUNNING
UNDERSACRISTAN
UNDERSAIL
UNDERSAILED
UNDERSALLY
UNDERSAY
UNDERSCALE
UNDERSCORE
UNDERSCORED
UNDERSCORING
UNDERSCRIBER
UNDERSCRUB
UNDERSEA
UNDERSEAMAN
UNDERSEAS
UNDERSELL
UNDERSELLER
UNDERSELLING
UNDERSENSE
UNDERSERVE
UNDERSET
UNDERSETTER
UNDERSETTING
UNDERSETTLE
UNDERSEXED
UNDERSHAPEN
UNDERSHARP
UNDERSHERIFF
UNDERSHINING
UNDERSHIRT
UNDERSHOOT
UNDERSHOOTING
UNDERSHORE
UNDERSHOT
UNDERSHRUB
UNDERSHRUBBY
UNDERSHUT
UNDERSIDE
UNDERSIGN
UNDERSIGNED
UNDERSIGNER
UNDERSINGING
UNDERSIZE
UNDERSIZED
UNDERSKIRT
UNDERSLEEVE
UNDERSLOPE
UNDERSLUICE
UNDERSLUNG
UNDERSOIL
UNDERSOLD
UNDERSONG
UNDERSPARRED
UNDERSPEND
UNDERSPHERE
UNDERSPIN
UNDERSPORE
UNDERSPREAD
UNDERSPRING
UNDERSTAIRS
UNDERSTAND
UNDERSTANDED

UNDERSTANDER
UNDERSTANDING
UNDERSTATE
UNDERSTATED
UNDERSTATEMENT
UNDERSTATING
UNDERSTOCK
UNDERSTOOD
UNDERSTORY
UNDERSTRATA
UNDERSTRATUM
UNDERSTRATUMS
UNDERSTRIDE
UNDERSTRING
UNDERSTROKE
UNDERSTRUNG
UNDERSTUDIED
UNDERSTUDIES
UNDERSTUDY
UNDERSTUDYING
UNDERSURFACE
UNDERSWEAT
UNDERTAKE
UNDERTAKEN
UNDERTAKER
UNDERTAKING
UNDERTEACHER
UNDERTEAMED
UNDERTENANT
UNDERTHING
UNDERTHINK
UNDERTHRUST
UNDERTIME
UNDERTIMED
UNDERTINT
UNDERTONE
UNDERTONED
UNDERTOOK
UNDERTOW
UNDERTREAD
UNDERTREAT
UNDERTRICK
UNDERTRODDEN
UNDERTRUMP
UNDERTURF
UNDERTURN
UNDERTYPE
UNDERVALUE
UNDERVALUED
UNDERVALUER
UNDERVALUING
UNDERVEST
UNDERVOLTAGE
UNDERWAIST
UNDERWALK
UNDERWARD
UNDERWARP
UNDERWATCH
UNDERWATER
UNDERWAY
UNDERWEAR
UNDERWEIGH
UNDERWEIGHT
UNDERWENT
UNDERWING
UNDERWIT
UNDERWITTED
UNDERWOOD
UNDERWORK
UNDERWORKED
UNDERWORKER
UNDERWORKING
UNDERWORLD
UNDERWRIT
UNDERWRITE
UNDERWRITER
UNDERWRITING
UNDERWRITTEN
UNDERWROTE
UNDERWROUGHT
UNDESCRIPT
UNDESERT
UNDESERVE
UNDESERVED
UNDESERVER
UNDESIGNED
UNDESIGNING
UNDESIRABLE
UNDESIRABLY
UNDESIRE
UNDESIREDLY
UNDETERMINED
UNDEVELOPED
UNDEVIATING
UNDEVIATINGLY
UNDEVIL
UNDEVOTION
UNDID
UNDIES
UNDIFFERENCED
UNDIFFERENTIATED
UNDIG
UNDIGENOUS
UNDIGESTABLE
UNDIGESTED
UNDIGESTIBLE
UNDIGESTION
UNDIGHT
UNDIGHTED
UNDIGNE
UNDIGNIFIED
UNDIGNIFY
UNDILUTED
UNDIMINISHED
UNDIMMED
UNDINE
UNDINED
UNDIOCESED
UNDIRECT
UNDIRECTED
UNDIRECTLY
UNDISCERNING
UNDISCIPLINED
UNDISCLOSE
UNDISCLOSED
UNDISCOURSED
UNDISCREET
UNDISCREETLY
UNDISCRETION
UNDISCRIMINATING
UNDISGUISE
UNDISGUISED
UNDISMAY
UNDISMAYED
UNDISPENSED
UNDISPENSING
UNDISPLAY
UNDISPOSE
UNDISPOSED
UNDISPUTABLE
UNDISPUTABLY
UNDISPUTED
UNDISTINCT
UNDISTINCTLY
UNDISTINGUISHED
UNDISTORTED
UNDISTRESS
UNDISTURBED
UNDIVIDABLE
UNDIVIDABLY
UNDIVIDED
UNDIVIDEDLY
UNDIVIDUAL
UNDIVORCING
UNDO
UNDOCIBLE
UNDOCK
UNDOCTOR
UNDOER
UNDOG
UNDOGMATIC
UNDOING
UNDOMESTICATED
UNDONE
UNDOSE
UNDOUBLE
UNDOUBLED
UNDOUBLING
UNDOUBTABLE
UNDOUBTABLY
UNDOUBTED
UNDOUBTEDLY
UNDRAPE
UNDRAPED
UNDRAW
UNDRAWING
UNDRAWN
UNDREAMED
UNDREAMT
UNDRESS
UNDRESSED
UNDREST
UNDREW
UNDUE
UNDUKE
UNDULANT
UNDULAR
UNDULATANCE
UNDULATE
UNDULATED
UNDULATELY
UNDULATING
UNDULATION
UNDULATIVE
UNDULATORY
UNDULOID
UNDULOSE
UNDULOUS
UNDULY
UNDURE
UNDUST
UNDUSTED
UNDUTIFULNESS
UNDUTY
UNDWELT
UNDY
UNDYED
UNDYING
UNDYINGLY
UNDYINGNESS
UNE
UNEARED
UNEARNED
UNEARTH
UNEARTHED
UNEARTHING
UNEARTHLY
UNEASE
UNEASEFUL
UNEASEFULNESS
UNEASIER
UNEASIEST
UNEASILY
UNEASINESS
UNEASY
UNEATH
UNEATHS
UNEBRIATE
UNEDIBLE
UNEDIBLENESS
UNEDIBLY
UNEDITED
UNEDUCABLE
UNEDUCABLY
UNEDUCATE
UNEDUCATED
UNEFFABLE
UNEFFECTUAL
UNEGAL
UNEGALLY
UNEGALNESS
UNELEGANT
UNELEGANTLY
UNELIGIBLE
UNELIGIBLY
UNEMBELLISHED
UNEMBODIED
UNEMOTIONAL
UNEMOTIONALLY
UNEMOTIONED
UNEMPHATIC
UNEMPLOY
UNEMPLOYABLE
UNEMPLOYED
UNEMPLOYMENT
UNEMPT
UNENCUMBER
UNENCUMBERED
UNENDED
UNENDING
UNENDINGLY
UNENDLY
UNENGAGED
UNENGLISH
UNENJOYABLE
UNENLIGHTENED
UNENTANGLE
UNENTANGLER
UNENTERING
UNENTHUSIASTIC
UNENTRANCE
UNEPISCOPAL
UNEQUABLE
UNEQUABLY
UNEQUAL
UNEQUALED
UNEQUALITY
UNEQUALLED
UNEQUALLY
UNEQUIAXED
UNEQUITABLE
UNEQUITABLY
UNEQUIVOCAL
UNEQUIVOCALLY
UNERECT
UNERRABLE
UNERRABLY
UNERRING
UNERRINGLY
UNESCAPABLE
UNESCAPABLY
UNESSENCE
UNESSENTIAL
UNESTABLISH
UNESTIMABLE
UNETHIC
UNETHICAL
UNETHICALLY
UNEVEN
UNEVENLY
UNEVENNESS
UNEVENTFUL
UNEVENTFULLY
UNEVIDENT
UNEVITABLE
UNEVITABLY
UNEXACT
UNEXACTLY
UNEXACTNESS
UNEXAMPLED
UNEXCEPTIVE
UNEXCITED
UNEXCITING
UNEXCLUSIVE
UNEXCUSABLE
UNEXCUSABLY
UNEXPECT
UNEXPECTED
UNEXPECTEDLY
UNEXPEDIENT
UNEXPENDED
UNEXPENSIVE
UNEXPERIENCE
UNEXPERIENT
UNEXPERT
UNEXPERTLY
UNEXPIRED
UNEXPLAINED
UNEXPLICABLE
UNEXPLOITED
UNEXPOSED
UNEXPRESS
UNEXPRESSIVE
UNEXPURGATED
UNEXTRICABLE
UNEYED
UNFACE
UNFACT
UNFADABLE
UNFADED
UNFADING
UNFADINGLY
UNFAILABLE
UNFAILABLY
UNFAILING
UNFAILINGLY
UNFAIN
UNFAIR
UNFAIRLY
UNFAIRNESS
UNFAITH
UNFAITHFUL
UNFAITHFULLY
UNFALCATED
UNFALLIBLE
UNFALLIBLY
UNFALTERING
UNFAMILIAR
UNFAMILIARLY
UNFAMOUS
UNFARDLE
UNFASHION
UNFASHIONED
UNFAST
UNFASTEN
UNFATHERED
UNFATHOMABLE
UNFATHOMED
UNFAVORABLE
UNFAVORABLY
UNFAVOURABLE
UNFAVOURABLY
UNFEARY
UNFEASABLE
UNFEASABLY
UNFEASIBLE
UNFEASIBLY
UNFEASTLY
UNFEATHER
UNFEATURED
UNFEATY
UNFEEL
UNFEELABLE
UNFEELING
UNFEELINGLY

UNFEELINGNESS
UNFEIGNABLE
UNFEIGNABLY
UNFEIGNED
UNFEIGNEDLY
UNFEIGNING
UNFEIGNINGLY
UNFELE
UNFELICITOUS
UNFELLOWED
UNFERMENTED
UNFERTILE
UNFERTILITY
UNFESTIVAL
UNFETTER
UNFETTERED
UNFEUDALIZE
UNFEUED
UNFIGURED
UNFILIAL
UNFILIALLY
UNFILIALNESS
UNFILLABLE
UNFILLED
UNFILLETED
UNFINANCIAL
UNFINE
UNFINGERED
UNFINISH
UNFINISHED
UNFINISHEDLY
UNFIRED
UNFIRM
UNFIRMLY
UNFIRMNESS
UNFIT
UNFITLY
UNFITNESS
UNFITTED
UNFITTEN
UNFITTING
UNFITTY
UNFIX
UNFIXED
UNFLAG
UNFLAGGING
UNFLAGGINGLY
UNFLAME
UNFLAPPABLE
UNFLEDGED
UNFLEECE
UNFLESH
UNFLESHED
UNFLESHLY
UNFLESHY
UNFLEXIBLE
UNFLEXIBLY
UNFLINCHING
UNFLOWER
UNFLUSH
UNFOLD
UNFOLDED
UNFOLDEN
UNFOLDER
UNFOLDING
UNFOLDMENT
UNFOOL
UNFOOTED
UNFORBADE
UNFORCED
UNFORCEDLY
UNFORCEDNESS
UNFORESEE
UNFORESEEN
UNFORGIVER
UNFORGIVING
UNFORMAL
UNFORMALITY
UNFORMALLY
UNFORMALNESS
UNFORMED
UNFORTIFIED
UNFORTUNATE
UNFORTUNE
UNFOUND
UNFOUNDED
UNFOUNDEDLY
UNFOXED
UNFRAME
UNFRANGIBLE
UNFRANK
UNFRAUGHT
UNFREE
UNFREEDOM
UNFREELY
UNFREEMAN
UNFREENESS
UNFREQUENCY
UNFREQUENT
UNFREQUENTED
UNFREQUENTLY
UNFRET
UNFRIEND
UNFRIENDED
UNFRIENDING
UNFRIENDLY
UNFRIGHTED
UNFROCK
UNFROZEN
UNFRUCTIFY
UNFRUCTUOUS
UNFRUITFUL
UNFRUITFULLY
UNFULFIL
UNFULFILL
UNFULFILLMENT
UNFULFILMENT
UNFUMED
UNFUNDED
UNFUR
UNFURL
UNFURNISH
UNFURNISHED
UNFUSIBLE
UNFUSIBLY
UNGAIN
UNGAINLIKE
UNGAINLINESS
UNGAINLY
UNGAINNESS
UNGAITE
UNGALLANT
UNGALLANTLY
UNGARO
UNGEAR
UNGENDERED
UNGENEROUS
UNGENEROUSLY
UNGENIAL
UNGENIALITY
UNGENIALLY
UNGENIALNESS
UNGENITURED
UNGENTEEL
UNGENTEELY
UNGENTLE
UNGENTLEMAN
UNGENTLENESS
UNGENTLY
UNGET
UNGIFTED
UNGILD
UNGILL
UNGIRD
UNGIRDED
UNGIRT
UNGIRTH
UNGIVE
UNGKA
UNGLAZE
UNGLAZED
UNGLE
UNGLEE
UNGLORIOUS
UNGLORIOUSLY
UNGLORY
UNGLOSSY
UNGLOVE
UNGLUE
UNGNAW
UNGOD
UNGODLILY
UNGODLINESS
UNGODLY
UNGONE
UNGOOD
UNGOT
UNGOTTEN
UNGOVERNABLE
UNGOVERNABLY
UNGOWN
UNGRACE
UNGRACEFUL
UNGRACEFULLY
UNGRACIOUS
UNGRACIOUSLY
UNGRADED
UNGRAMMATIC
UNGRATEFUL
UNGRATEFULLY
UNGRAVE
UNGRAVELY
UNGREEABLE
UNGREEN
UNGRIPE
UNGROOMED
UNGROUNDED
UNGROUNDEDLY
UNGUAL
UNGUARD
UNGUARDED
UNGUARDEDLY
UNGUEAL
UNGUENT
UNGUENTARIA
UNGUENTARIAN
UNGUENTARIUM
UNGUENTARY
UNGUENTO
UNGUENTOUS
UNGUENTUM
UNGUES
UNGUICORN
UNGUICULATE
UNGUICULE
UNGUIFEROUS
UNGUIFORM
UNGUILED
UNGUILEFUL
UNGUILEFULLY
UNGUILTILY
UNGUILTINESS
UNGUILTLESS
UNGUILTY
UNGUINOUS
UNGUIROSTRAL
UNGUIS
UNGULA
UNGULAE
UNGULAR
UNGULATE
UNGULED
UNGULIGRADE
UNGULOUS
UNGUM
UNGUMMED
UNGYVE
UNGYVED
UNHABILE
UNHABIT
UNHAD
UNHAIR
UNHAIRER
UNHAIRING
UNHALE
UNHALLOW
UNHALLOWED
UNHALSED
UNHALTER
UNHAMPERED
UNHAND
UNHANDILY
UNHANDINESS
UNHANDSOME
UNHANDSOMELY
UNHANDY
UNHANG
UNHAP
UNHAPPIER
UNHAPPIEST
UNHAPPILY
UNHAPPINESS
UNHAPPY
UNHARBOR
UNHARBORED
UNHARBOUR
UNHARBOURED
UNHARD
UNHARDILY
UNHARDINESS
UNHARDY
UNHARMED
UNHARMONIOUS
UNHARNESS
UNHASP
UNHASTE
UNHAT
UNHATTED
UNHATTING
UNHEAD
UNHEADER
UNHEAL
UNHEALED
UNHEALTH
UNHEALTHFUL
UNHEALTHIER
UNHEALTHIEST
UNHEALTHILY
UNHEALTHSOME
UNHEALTHY
UNHEARD
UNHEARSE
UNHEART
UNHEARTEN
UNHEARTSOME
UNHEARTY
UNHEATED
UNHEAVEN
UNHEED
UNHEEDED
UNHEEDING
UNHEEDY
UNHEIRED
UNHELE
UNHELER
UNHELM
UNHELMET
UNHELP
UNHENDE
UNHENT
UNHEPPEN
UNHERD
UNHEROISM
UNHESITATING
UNHIDABLE
UNHIDABLY
UNHIDE
UNHIDEABLE
UNHIDEABLY
UNHINGE
UNHINGED
UNHINGING
UNHITCH
UNHIVE
UNHOARD
UNHOLD
UNHOLIER
UNHOLIEST
UNHOLILY
UNHOLINESS
UNHOLPEN
UNHOLY
UNHOME
UNHONEST
UNHONESTLY
UNHONESTY
UNHONORABLE
UNHONORABLY
UNHONOURABLE
UNHONOURABLY
UNHOOD
UNHOOK
UNHOOP
UNHOOPABLE
UNHOOPER
UNHOPE
UNHOPED
UNHOPEDLY
UNHOPEDNESS
UNHOPEFUL
UNHOPEFULLY
UNHOPPED
UNHORSE
UNHORSED
UNHORSING
UNHOSPITABLE
UNHOSPITABLY
UNHOSPITAL
UNHOUSE
UNHOUSED
UNHOUSELED
UNHUMAN
UNHURRIED
UNHURRIEDLY
UNHURT
UNHUSK
UNHUSKED
UNIAT
UNIATE
UNIAXIAL
UNIBIVALENT
UNIBLE
UNIC
UNICAMERAL
UNICELL
UNICELLATE
UNICELLED
UNICELLULAR
UNICHORD
UNICISM
UNICIST
UNICITY
UNICOLOR
UNICONSTANT
UNICORN

UNICORNIC
UNICOSTATE
UNICUM
UNICURSAL
UNICURSALITY
UNICURSALLY
UNICYCLE
UNICYCLIST
UNIDEAED
UNIDEAL
UNIDENTIFIED
UNIDEXTRAL
UNIDIRECT
UNIDLE
UNIDLENESS
UNIDLY
UNIE
UNIFACE
UNIFACED
UNIFACTORIAL
UNIFARIOUS
UNIFIABLE
UNIFIC
UNIFICATION
UNIFIED
UNIFIEDLY
UNIFIEDNESS
UNIFIER
UNIFILAR
UNIFLOROUS
UNIFLOW
UNIFOLIATE
UNIFOLIOLATE
UNIFORM
UNIFORMALIZE
UNIFORMALIZED
UNIFORMALIZING
UNIFORMED
UNIFORMIST
UNIFORMITIES
UNIFORMITY
UNIFORMIZE
UNIFORMLY
UNIFORMNESS
UNIFY
UNIFYING
UNIGENESIS
UNIGENETIC
UNIGENITAL
UNIGENITURE
UNIGENOUS
UNIGRAVIDA
UNIJUGATE
UNILATERAL
UNILATERALLY
UNILINGUAL
UNILITERAL
UNILOBE
UNILOCULAR
UNIMAGINABLE
UNIMAGINATIVE
UNIMANUAL
UNIMBATTLED
UNIMEDIAL
UNIMITABLE
UNIMITABLY
UNIMMERGIBLE
UNIMODAL
UNIMODALITY
UNIMPAIRED
UNIMPASSIONED
UNIMPEDED
UNIMPEDEDLY
UNIMPLICATE
UNIMPORTANCE
UNIMPORTANT
UNIMPRESSED
UNIMPRESSIVE
UNIMPROVABLE
UNIMPROVED
UNIMPROVEDLY
UNINCULCATED
UNINDEBTED
UNINDEBTEDLY
UNINDENTED
UNINFORMED
UNINGENIOUS
UNINGENUOUS
UNINGENUOUSLY
UNINHABITED
UNINHIBITED
UNINJURED
UNINOMINAL
UNINSPIRED
UNINSTRUCTED
UNINTELLIGENT
UNINTELLIGIBLE
UNINTENTIONAL
UNINTENTIONALLY
UNINTERESTED
UNINTERESTING
UNINTERMITTED
UNINTERMITTENT
UNINTERRUPTED
UNINTERRUPTEDLY
UNINTROITIVE
UNINVENTIVE
UNINVITE
UNINVITED
UNIOID
UNION
UNIONED
UNIONIC
UNIONID
UNIONIFORM
UNIONISM
UNIONIST
UNIONISTIC
UNIONIZATION
UNIONIZE
UNIONIZED
UNIONIZING
UNIONOID
UNIOVAL
UNIPARA
UNIPARENTAL
UNIPARIENT
UNIPAROUS
UNIPARTITE
UNIPED
UNIPERIODIC
UNIPERSONAL
UNIPETALOUS
UNIPLANAR
UNIPOLAR
UNIPOLARITY
UNIPOROUS
UNIPOTENCE
UNIPOTENT
UNIPULSE
UNIQUANTIC
UNIQUE
UNIQUELY
UNIQUENESS
UNIQUITY
UNIREME
UNISEPTATE
UNISEX
UNISEXED
UNISEXUAL
UNISEXUALITY
UNISEXUALLY
UNISON
UNISONAL
UNISONANT
UNISONO
UNISONOUS
UNISPARKER
UNISPIRAL
UNISTYLIST
UNIT
UNITABILITY
UNITABLE
UNITABLY
UNITAL
UNITARIAN
UNITARILY
UNITARINESS
UNITARISM
UNITARIST
UNITARY
UNITATION
UNITE
UNITEABLE
UNITEABLY
UNITED
UNITEDLY
UNITEDNESS
UNITELY
UNITEMIZED
UNITENESS
UNITER
UNITIES
UNITING
UNITION
UNITISM
UNITISTIC
UNITIVE
UNITIVELY
UNITIVENESS
UNITIZE
UNITRIVALENT
UNITROPE
UNITS
UNITUDE
UNITY
UNIVALENCE
UNIVALENCY
UNIVALENT
UNIVALID
UNIVALVE
UNIVALVED
UNIVALVULAR
UNIVARIANT
UNIVERSAL
UNIVERSALIA
UNIVERSALITIES
UNIVERSALITY
UNIVERSALIZE
UNIVERSALIZED
UNIVERSALIZING
UNIVERSALLY
UNIVERSE
UNIVERSEFUL
UNIVERSITAS
UNIVERSITIES
UNIVERSITIZE
UNIVERSITY
UNIVERSOLOGY
UNIVOCACY
UNIVOCAL
UNIVOCALLY
UNIVOCATION
UNIVOCITY
UNIVOLTINE
UNIVOROUS
UNJUDICIOUS
UNJUST
UNJUSTIFIED
UNJUSTLY
UNJUSTNESS
UNKAMED
UNKED
UNKEELED
UNKEMBED
UNKEMPT
UNKEMPTLY
UNKEMPTNESS
UNKEN
UNKEND
UNKENNED
UNKENNEL
UNKENNELED
UNKENNELING
UNKENNELLED
UNKENNELLING
UNKENNING
UNKENSOME
UNKENT
UNKEPT
UNKET
UNKID
UNKIND
UNKINDLILY
UNKINDLY
UNKINDNESS
UNKINDRED
UNKINDREDLY
UNKING
UNKINGER
UNKINGSHIP
UNKINK
UNKISS
UNKNIT
UNKNITTED
UNKNITTING
UNKNOW
UNKNOWABLE
UNKNOWABLY
UNKNOWING
UNKNOWINGLY
UNKNOWLEDGED
UNKNOWN
UNKNOWNLY
UNKNOWNNESS
UNKNOWNST
UNKO
UNLABORED
UNLABOURED
UNLACE
UNLACED
UNLACING
UNLADE
UNLADED
UNLADEN
UNLADIFIED
UNLADING
UNLADYFIED
UNLAID
UNLAND
UNLAP
UNLASH
UNLASHER
UNLATCH
UNLATINED
UNLAW
UNLAWED
UNLAWFUL
UNLAWFULLY
UNLAWFULNESS
UNLAY
UNLAYED
UNLAYING
UNLEAD
UNLEADED
UNLEARED
UNLEARN
UNLEARNED
UNLEARNEDLY
UNLEARNING
UNLEARNT
UNLEASH
UNLEAVE
UNLEAVENED
UNLEDE
UNLEEFUL
UNLEESOME
UNLEGITIMATE
UNLEISUM
UNLEISURED
UNLENGTH
UNLERED
UNLESS
UNLETTED
UNLETTERED
UNLETTEREDLY
UNLEVEL
UNLEWTY
UNLICKED
UNLID
UNLIEF
UNLIGHT
UNLIGHTED
UNLIGHTEDLY
UNLIGHTSOME
UNLIKE
UNLIKELIER
UNLIKELIEST
UNLIKELIHOOD
UNLIKELINESS
UNLIKELY
UNLIKEN
UNLIKENESS
UNLIKING
UNLIMB
UNLIMBER
UNLIME
UNLIMITABLE
UNLIMITABLY
UNLIMITED
UNLIMITEDLY
UNLINE
UNLINED
UNLINK
UNLINKED
UNLINKING
UNLIQUIDATED
UNLIQUORED
UNLIST
UNLISTED
UNLISTENED
UNLISTY
UNLIT
UNLITERAL
UNLITERALLY
UNLITTLE
UNLITURGICAL
UNLITURGIZE
UNLIVE
UNLIVED
UNLIVERY
UNLIVING
UNLOAD
UNLOADEN
UNLOADER
UNLOCATED
UNLOCK
UNLOCKER
UNLODGE
UNLOGIC
UNLOGICAL
UNLOGICALLY
UNLOOK
UNLOOKED
UNLOOSE

UNLOOSEN
UNLORD
UNLORDED
UNLORDLY
UNLOUKEN
UNLOUSY
UNLOVE
UNLOVED
UNLOVELIER
UNLOVELIEST
UNLOVELILY
UNLOVELINESS
UNLOVELY
UNLOVERLIKE
UNLOVERLY
UNLOVESOME
UNLOVING
UNLOVINGLY
UNLOVINGNESS
UNLUCK
UNLUCKFUL
UNLUCKIER
UNLUCKIEST
UNLUCKILY
UNLUCKINESS
UNLUCKLY
UNLUCKY
UNLUST
UNLUSTIE
UNLUSTIER
UNLUSTIEST
UNLUSTILY
UNLUSTINESS
UNLUSTY
UNLUTE
UNMACKLY
UNMADE
UNMAGISTRATE
UNMAIDEN
UNMAIL
UNMAILABLE
UNMAKE
UNMAKER
UNMAKING
UNMAN
UNMANACLE
UNMANAGEABLE
UNMANHOOD
UNMANIABLE
UNMANLIER
UNMANLIEST
UNMANLILY
UNMANLINESS
UNMANLY
UNMANNED
UNMANNERED
UNMANNEREDLY
UNMANNERLY
UNMANNING
UNMANTLE
UNMARKED
UNMARRIED
UNMARRY
UNMASK
UNMASKER
UNMASKING
UNMATCHED
UNMATURE
UNMATURELY
UNMATURENESS
UNMATURITY
UNMAZE
UNMEANING
UNMEANINGLY
UNMEANT
UNMEASURABLE
UNMEASURABLY
UNMEASURED
UNMEASUREDLY
UNMEASURELY
UNMECHANIC
UNMECHANICAL
UNMECHANIZE
UNMEDDLE
UNMEDULLATED
UNMEEDFUL
UNMEEDY
UNMEEK
UNMEEKLY
UNMEEKNESS
UNMEET
UNMEETLY
UNMEETNESS
UNMELODIOUS
UNMELT
UNMEMBER
UNMERCHANTABLE
UNMERCIABLE
UNMERCIABLY
UNMERCIED
UNMERCIFUL
UNMERCIFULLY
UNMERCILESS
UNMERITABLE
UNMESH
UNMETE
UNMETH
UNMETHODICAL
UNMEW
UNMIGHT
UNMIGHTY
UNMILD
UNMILDNESS
UNMILITARILY
UNMILITARY
UNMILLED
UNMIND
UNMINDED
UNMINDFUL
UNMINDFULLY
UNMINDING
UNMINGLE
UNMINGLEABLE
UNMINGLED
UNMIST
UNMISTAKABLE
UNMISTAKABLY
UNMITER
UNMITIGATED
UNMITRE
UNMIX
UNMIXED
UNMOBLE
UNMODERATE
UNMODERATELY
UNMODERNIZE
UNMODIFIED
UNMODULATED
UNMOLD
UNMOLEST
UNMOLESTED
UNMONEYED
UNMONOPOLIZE
UNMOOR
UNMOORED
UNMORAL
UNMORALIST
UNMORALITY
UNMORALIZED
UNMORALIZING
UNMORALLY
UNMORALNESS
UNMORRISED
UNMORTALIZE
UNMORTISE
UNMORTISED
UNMORTISING
UNMOTHERED
UNMOTIVED
UNMOULD
UNMOUNT
UNMOUNTED
UNMOVABILITY
UNMOVABLE
UNMOVABLETY
UNMOVABLY
UNMOVED
UNMOVEDLY
UNMOVING
UNMUDDLE
UNMUFFLE
UNMUFFLED
UNMUFFLING
UNMUSICAL
UNMUTABLE
UNMUZZLE
UNMYSTERY
UNNAIL
UNNAPKINED
UNNAPPED
UNNAPT
UNNATURAL
UNNATURALISM
UNNATURALIST
UNNATURALITY
UNNATURALIZE
UNNATURALLY
UNNATURE
UNNEALED
UNNEAR
UNNEATH
UNNECESSARY
UNNEEDED
UNNEIGHBORED
UNNEIGHBORLY
UNNERVE
UNNERVED
UNNERVING
UNNEST
UNNET
UNNETH
UNNETHE
UNNEWSED
UNNIMBED
UNNOBILITY
UNNOBLE
UNNOBLENESS
UNNOBLY
UNNOOKED
UNNOSE
UNNOTED
UNNOTICEABLE
UNNOTICEABLY
UNNOTICED
UNNOTIFY
UNNUMBERABLE
UNNUMBERABLY
UNNUMBERED
UNNUMERABLE
UNNUN
UNOBEDIENCE
UNOBEDIENT
UNOBEDIENTLY
UNOBJECTIONABLE
UNOBLIGING
UNOBLIGINGLY
UNOBSERVANCE
UNOBSERVANT
UNOBSERVED
UNOBSERVEDLY
UNOBSERVING
UNOBSTRUCTED
UNOBTAINABLE
UNOBTAINABLY
UNOBTRUSIVE
UNOCCUPIED
UNOCCUPIEDLY
UNODE
UNOFFENDED
UNOFFENDEDLY
UNOFFENDING
UNOFFENSIVE
UNOFFICIAL
UNOFFICIALLY
UNOFFICINAL
UNOFTEN
UNOIL
UNOLD
UNOPED
UNOPEN
UNOPENED
UNOPENLY
UNOPENNESS
UNOPERATIVE
UNOPERCULATE
UNOPPORTUNE
UNORDAINED
UNORDER
UNORDERED
UNORDERLY
UNORDINARILY
UNORDINARY
UNORDINATE
UNORDINATELY
UNORGANED
UNORGANIC
UNORGANICAL
UNORGANISED
UNORGANIZED
UNORIENTED
UNORIGINAL
UNORIGINATE
UNORIGINATED
UNORN
UNORTHODOX
UNORTHODOXLY
UNORTHODOXY
UNOSTENTATIOUS
UNOWED
UNOWN
UNOWNED
UNPACIFIED
UNPACIFIEDLY
UNPACK
UNPACKER
UNPAGED
UNPAID
UNPAINT
UNPAINTABLE
UNPAINTED
UNPAINTEDLY
UNPAIRED
UNPAISED
UNPALATABLE
UNPALE
UNPALPED
UNPANEL
UNPANNEL
UNPAPER
UNPARADISE
UNPARAGONED
UNPARALLELED
UNPARCH
UNPARDONABLE
UNPARDONABLY
UNPAREGAL
UNPARENTED
UNPARREL
UNPARROTED
UNPARTED
UNPARTIAL
UNPARTIALITY
UNPARTIALLY
UNPASSABLE
UNPASSABLY
UNPASSIONATE
UNPASTOR
UNPATHED
UNPATHWAYED
UNPATIENCE
UNPATIENT
UNPATIENTLY
UNPATRIOTIC
UNPATROLLED
UNPATRONIZED
UNPAVE
UNPAVED
UNPAWN
UNPAY
UNPEACE
UNPEDIGREED
UNPEEL
UNPEELED
UNPEERABLE
UNPEERED
UNPEG
UNPEN
UNPENITENT
UNPENITENTLY
UNPEOPLE
UNPEOPLED
UNPEOPLING
UNPERCEIVED
UNPERCH
UNPERFECT
UNPERFECTED
UNPERFECTION
UNPERFECTLY
UNPERFORATED
UNPERFORMING
UNPERISHABLE
UNPERISHABLY
UNPERMANENCY
UNPERMANENT
UNPERPLEX
UNPERSUASION
UNPERTURBED
UNPERVERT
UNPHRASABLE
UNPHRASED
UNPICK
UNPIECE
UNPIERCED
UNPILE
UNPILLED
UNPIN
UNPINION
UNPINKED
UNPINNED
UNPINNING
UNPITEOUS
UNPITEOUSLY
UNPITIED
UNPITIEDLY
UNPITIEDNESS
UNPITY
UNPITYING
UNPITYINGLY
UNPLACABLE
UNPLACABLY
UNPLACE
UNPLACED
UNPLAID
UNPLAIN
UNPLAINED

UNPLAINLY
UNPLAINNESS
UNPLAIT
UNPLANK
UNPLANNED
UNPLANNEDLY
UNPLANT
UNPLANTED
UNPLAT
UNPLAUSIVE
UNPLAYABLE
UNPLEASANT
UNPLEASANTLY
UNPLEASANTNESS
UNPLEASANTRIES
UNPLEASANTRY
UNPLEASED
UNPLEASING
UNPLEASINGLY
UNPLEASIVE
UNPLEASURE
UNPLEAT
UNPLEDGED
UNPLIGHT
UNPLOWED
UNPLUG
UNPLUMB
UNPLUMBED
UNPLUME
UNPOETIC
UNPOETICAL
UNPOETICALLY
UNPOISED
UNPOISON
UNPOLICED
UNPOLICIED
UNPOLISH
UNPOLISHED
UNPOLITE
UNPOLITELY
UNPOLITENESS
UNPOLITIC
UNPOLITICLY
UNPOLLED
UNPOLLUTED
UNPOLLUTEDLY
UNPOPE
UNPOPULAR
UNPOPULARITY
UNPOPULARIZE
UNPOPULARLY
UNPOPULATE
UNPOPULATED
UNPORTABLE
UNPORTUNATE
UNPORTUOUS
UNPOSSESS
UNPOSSIBLE
UNPOSSIBLY
UNPOWER
UNPOWERFUL
UNPRACTICAL
UNPRACTICED
UNPRACTISED
UNPRAISABLE
UNPRAISE
UNPRAY
UNPRAYABLE
UNPRAYED
UNPREACH
UNPREACHING
UNPREDICT
UNPREDICTABLE
UNPREGNABLE
UNPREJUDICE
UNPREJUDICED
UNPREMEDITATED
UNPREPARE
UNPREPARED
UNPREPAREDLY
UNPREPOSSESSING
UNPREST
UNPRETENDING
UNPRETENTIOUS
UNPREVENTED
UNPRICED
UNPRIEST
UNPRIME
UNPRINCE
UNPRINCIPLE
UNPRINCIPLED
UNPRINTABLE
UNPRINTABLY
UNPRISON
UNPRIVILEGED
UNPRIZABLE
UNPROBABLE
UNPROBABLY
UNPROCLAIMED
UNPROCREATE
UNPRODUCIBLE
UNPRODUCIBLY
UNPRODUCTIVE
UNPRODUCTIVENESS
UNPROFESSIONAL
UNPROFICIENT
UNPROFIT
UNPROFITABLE
UNPROFITABLY
UNPROFITED
UNPROGRESSIVE
UNPROMISE
UNPROMISING
UNPRONOUNCED
UNPROP
UNPROPER
UNPROPERLY
UNPROPERNESS
UNPROPERTIED
UNPROPICE
UNPROPITIOUS
UNPROPORTION
UNPROPRIETY
UNPROSELYTE
UNPROSPERITY
UNPROSPEROUS
UNPROTECTED
UNPROVABLE
UNPROVABLY
UNPROVIDE
UNPROVIDED
UNPROVIDEDLY
UNPROVIDENT
UNPROVISED
UNPROVISEDLY
UNPROVISION
UNPRUDENCE
UNPRUDENT
UNPRUDENTLY
UNPUBLISHED
UNPUCKER
UNPUFF
UNPULLED
UNPUNISHED
UNPUNISHEDLY
UNPUNISHING
UNPURE
UNPURED
UNPURELY
UNPURENESS
UNPURSE
UNPURVEYED
UNPUZZLE
UNQUAILED
UNQUALIFIED
UNQUALIFY
UNQUALITIED
UNQUALITY
UNQUANTIFIED
UNQUEEN
UNQUEME
UNQUEMELY
UNQUERT
UNQUESTIONABLE
UNQUESTIONED
UNQUESTIONING
UNQUICK
UNQUIESCENCE
UNQUIESCENT
UNQUIET
UNQUIETLY
UNQUIETNESS
UNQUIETOUS
UNQUIETUDE
UNQUIT
UNQUOD
UNQUOTE
UNRACED
UNRAKE
UNRAM
UNRANK
UNRATED
UNRATIFIED
UNRATTLED
UNRAVAGED
UNRAVEL
UNRAVELABLE
UNRAVELED
UNRAVELER
UNRAVELING
UNRAVELLABLE
UNRAVELLED
UNRAVELLER
UNRAVELLING
UNRAVELMENT
UNRAY
UNREAD
UNREADABLE
UNREADABLY
UNREADIER
UNREADIEST
UNREADILY
UNREADINESS
UNREADY
UNREAL
UNREALISM
UNREALIST
UNREALISTIC
UNREALITIES
UNREALITY
UNREALIZE
UNREALIZED
UNREALLY
UNREALNESS
UNREASON
UNREASONABLE
UNREASONABLENESS
UNREASONABLY
UNREASONED
UNREASONING
UNREAVE
UNREBUKABLE
UNREBUKABLY
UNREBUKEABLE
UNRECALLING
UNRECKLESS
UNRECOGNIZED
UNRECORDED
UNRECOVERABLE
UNRECOVERED
UNRECTIFIED
UNRECURING
UNRED
UNREDEEMED
UNREDUCT
UNREEL
UNREEVE
UNREEVED
UNREEVING
UNREFINE
UNREFINED
UNREFINEDLY
UNREFINEMENT
UNREFLECTING
UNREFLECTIVE
UNREGARD
UNREGENERACY
UNREGENERATE
UNREGENERATELY
UNREGISTERED
UNREGULAR
UNREGULATED
UNREHEARSED
UNREIN
UNRELATED
UNRELAXED
UNRELENTABLE
UNRELENTANCE
UNRELENTING
UNRELENTLESS
UNRELENTOR
UNRELEVANT
UNRELIABLE
UNRELIABLY
UNRELIANCE
UNRELIEVED
UNRELIGION
UNRELIGIOUS
UNREMEDIABLE
UNREMEMBER
UNREMITTING
UNREMOVED
UNREMUNERATIVE
UNRENOWNED
UNRENOWNEDLY
UNREPAIR
UNREPAIRABLE
UNREPENTABLE
UNREPENTANCE
UNREPLIABLE
UNREPLIABLY
UNREPORTED
UNREPORTEDLY
UNREPROVED
UNREPROVEDLY
UNREPUGNABLE
UNREPUTABLE
UNREQUEST
UNREQUITER
UNRESERVE
UNRESERVED
UNRESERVEDLY
UNRESERVEDNESS
UNRESISTABLE
UNRESISTABLY
UNRESISTANT
UNRESISTED
UNRESISTEDLY
UNRESISTIBLE
UNRESISTIBLY
UNRESISTING
UNRESOLUTE
UNRESOLVE
UNRESPECT
UNRESPECTIVE
UNRESPONSAL
UNRESPONSIVE
UNREST
UNRESTED
UNRESTING
UNRESTRAINED
UNRESTRAINT
UNRESTRICTED
UNRESTY
UNRETURNED
UNREVEALED
UNREVENUED
UNREVERENCE
UNREVEREND
UNREVERENDLY
UNREVERENT
UNREVERENTLY
UNREVOCABLE
UNREVOCABLY
UNREWARDED
UNRICHT
UNRID
UNRIDDLE
UNRIDDLED
UNRIDDLER
UNRIDDLING
UNRIDE
UNRIFLED
UNRIG
UNRIGGED
UNRIGGING
UNRIGHT
UNRIGHTEOUS
UNRIGHTEOUSNESS
UNRIGHTFUL
UNRIGHTFULLY
UNRIGHTLY
UNRIGHTWISE
UNRIND
UNRING
UNRINGED
UNRIP
UNRIPE
UNRIPELY
UNRIPENED
UNRIPENESS
UNRIPPED
UNRIPPING
UNRIVALED
UNRIVALEDLY
UNRIVALLED
UNRIVALLEDLY
UNRIVET
UNRO
UNROADED
UNROAST
UNROBE
UNROLL
UNROLLER
UNROLLMENT
UNROMANTIC
UNROMANTICAL
UNROOF
UNROOST
UNROOT
UNROPE
UNROUGH
UNROUND
UNROUT
UNROVE
UNROW
UNROYAL
UNROYALIST
UNROYALLY
UNROYALNESS
UNRUDE
UNRUEFULLY
UNRUFE
UNRUFFLE
UNRUFFLED

UNRULE
UNRULED
UNRULEDLY
UNRULEDNESS
UNRULEFUL
UNRULIER
UNRULIEST
UNRULILY
UNRULIMENT
UNRULINESS
UNRULY
UNRUMPLE
UNRUTH
UNSACK
UNSACRAMENT
UNSAD
UNSADDEN
UNSADDLE
UNSADDLED
UNSADDLING
UNSADNESS
UNSAFE
UNSAFELY
UNSAFENESS
UNSAFER
UNSAFEST
UNSAFETY
UNSAID
UNSAINT
UNSAINTLY
UNSAKED
UNSALABILITY
UNSALABLE
UNSALABLY
UNSALEABLE
UNSALEABLY
UNSAME
UNSAMPLED
UNSANCTIFIED
UNSANCTIFY
UNSANCTION
UNSANE
UNSANITARY
UNSANITATION
UNSASH
UNSATIABLE
UNSATIABLY
UNSATIATE
UNSATISFACTORY
UNSATISFY
UNSATISFYING
UNSATURABLE
UNSATURATED
UNSATURATION
UNSAUGHT
UNSAVOR
UNSAVORED
UNSAVORILY
UNSAVORINESS
UNSAVORLY
UNSAVORY
UNSAVOURED
UNSAVOURILY
UNSAVOURY
UNSAY
UNSAYING
UNSCALE
UNSCALED
UNSCALEDNESS
UNSCAPABLE
UNSCATHED
UNSCATHEDLY
UNSCENT
UNSCENTED
UNSCHOLAR
UNSCHOLARLY
UNSCHOOLED
UNSCHOOLEDLY
UNSCIENCE
UNSCIENCED
UNSCIENTIFIC
UNSCOTCH
UNSCOTTIFY
UNSCRAMBLE
UNSCRAMBLED
UNSCRAMBLING
UNSCRAPED
UNSCREEN
UNSCREW
UNSCRUPULOUS
UNSCRUTABLE
UNSEAL
UNSEALER
UNSEAM
UNSEARCHABLE
UNSEARCHABLY
UNSEASON
UNSEASONABLE
UNSEASONABLY
UNSEASONED
UNSEAT
UNSEATED
UNSEAWORTHY
UNSECONDED
UNSECRECY
UNSECRET
UNSECTARIAN
UNSECULARIZE
UNSECURE
UNSECURED
UNSECUREDLY
UNSECURELY
UNSECURENESS
UNSECURITY
UNSEE
UNSEEING
UNSEEL
UNSEELINESS
UNSEELY
UNSEEMING
UNSEEMINGLY
UNSEEMLIER
UNSEEMLIEST
UNSEEMLILY
UNSEEMLINESS
UNSEEMLY
UNSEEN
UNSEIZE
UNSEL
UNSELDOM
UNSELF
UNSELFISH
UNSELFISHLY
UNSELFNESS
UNSELINESS
UNSELTH
UNSELY
UNSEMINARED
UNSENSE
UNSENSED
UNSENSIBLE
UNSENSIBLY
UNSENSUALIZE
UNSENTENCED
UNSEPARABLE
UNSEPARABLY
UNSEPTATE
UNSEPTATED
UNSERRIED
UNSERVED
UNSERVICE
UNSET
UNSETTING
UNSETTLE
UNSETTLED
UNSEVEN
UNSEW
UNSEWERED
UNSEX
UNSEXED
UNSEXING
UNSHACKLE
UNSHACKLED
UNSHACKLING
UNSHADOW
UNSHAKABLE
UNSHAKABLY
UNSHAKEABLE
UNSHAKED
UNSHAKEN
UNSHAKENLY
UNSHAKENNESS
UNSHALE
UNSHAMEFUL
UNSHAMEFULLY
UNSHAPE
UNSHAPED
UNSHAPELY
UNSHAPEN
UNSHAPENLY
UNSHAPENNESS
UNSHARED
UNSHARPEN
UNSHAVE
UNSHAVED
UNSHAVEDLY
UNSHAVEDNESS
UNSHAVEN
UNSHAVENLY
UNSHAVENNESS
UNSHAWL
UNSHEAF
UNSHEATHE
UNSHEATHED
UNSHEATHING
UNSHED
UNSHEET
UNSHELL
UNSHELVE
UNSHENT
UNSHERIFF
UNSHEWED
UNSHIFTABLE
UNSHIFTINESS
UNSHIP
UNSHIPMENT
UNSHIPPED
UNSHIPPING
UNSHOD
UNSHOE
UNSHOOK
UNSHOP
UNSHORN
UNSHOT
UNSHOULDER
UNSHOUT
UNSHRINE
UNSHRINEMENT
UNSHRINK
UNSHROUD
UNSHRUBBED
UNSHUNNING
UNSHUT
UNSHUTTER
UNSIB
UNSICKER
UNSICKERLY
UNSICKERNESS
UNSICKLED
UNSIDED
UNSIEGE
UNSIGHT
UNSIGHTABLE
UNSIGHTED
UNSIGHTEDLY
UNSIGHTING
UNSIGHTLIER
UNSIGHTLIEST
UNSIGHTLY
UNSIGNABLE
UNSIGNED
UNSILENCED
UNSIMILAR
UNSIMILARLY
UNSIMPLICITY
UNSIN
UNSINCERE
UNSINCERELY
UNSINCERITY
UNSINEW
UNSING
UNSINGABLE
UNSISTER
UNSISTERLY
UNSISTING
UNSITTING
UNSITTINGLY
UNSIZED
UNSKAITHED
UNSKILFUL
UNSKILFULLY
UNSKILL
UNSKILLED
UNSKILLEDLY
UNSKILLFUL
UNSKILLFULLY
UNSKIMMED
UNSKIN
UNSKIRMISHED
UNSLAKED
UNSLATE
UNSLAVE
UNSLEEVE
UNSLEPT
UNSLING
UNSLINGING
UNSLIP
UNSLIT
UNSLOCKENED
UNSLOGH
UNSLOT
UNSLOTHFUL
UNSLOTHFULLY
UNSLUICE
UNSLUNG
UNSMART
UNSMARTLY
UNSMARTNESS
UNSMILING
UNSMOOTH
UNSMOTE
UNSNAP
UNSNAPPED
UNSNAPPING
UNSNARE
UNSNARL
UNSNECK
UNSOBER
UNSOBERLY
UNSOBERNESS
UNSOBRIETY
UNSOCIABLE
UNSOCIABLY
UNSOCIAL
UNSOCIALLY
UNSOCIALNESS
UNSOCKET
UNSODDEN
UNSOFT
UNSOIL
UNSOILED
UNSOLDER
UNSOLDIER
UNSOLDIERED
UNSOLDIERLY
UNSOLDIERY
UNSOLEMN
UNSOLEMNESS
UNSOLEMNIZE
UNSOLEMNLY
UNSOLICITED
UNSOLUBILITY
UNSOLUBLE
UNSOLVABLE
UNSOLVABLY
UNSOLVE
UNSOLVED
UNSOME
UNSON
UNSONCY
UNSONSIE
UNSONSY
UNSOOT
UNSOPHISTICATE
UNSOPHISTICATED
UNSORROWED
UNSORTED
UNSOUGHT
UNSOUL
UNSOUND
UNSOUNDLY
UNSOUNDNESS
UNSPAR
UNSPARABLE
UNSPARING
UNSPARINGLY
UNSPEAK
UNSPEAKABLE
UNSPEAKABLY
UNSPEAKING
UNSPECIFIED
UNSPED
UNSPEED
UNSPEEDFUL
UNSPELL
UNSPHERE
UNSPHERED
UNSPHERING
UNSPIABLE
UNSPIKE
UNSPILLABLE
UNSPIN
UNSPIRIT
UNSPIRITUAL
UNSPIT
UNSPLEENED
UNSPOIL
UNSPOILED
UNSPOILT
UNSPOKE
UNSPOKEN
UNSPOKENLY
UNSPORTSMANLIKE
UNSPOT
UNSPOTTED
UNSPOTTEDLY
UNSPOTTEN
UNSPREAD
UNSPRIGHTLY
UNSPRING
UNSPRUNG
UNSQUARE
UNSQUARED
UNSQUIRE
UNSTABILITY

UNSTABLE
UNSTABLED
UNSTABLENESS
UNSTABLY
UNSTACK
UNSTACKER
UNSTAID
UNSTAIDLY
UNSTAIDNESS
UNSTAIN
UNSTAINED
UNSTALKED
UNSTAR
UNSTARCH
UNSTATE
UNSTAYED
UNSTEADFAST
UNSTEADIER
UNSTEADIEST
UNSTEADILY
UNSTEADINESS
UNSTEADY
UNSTECK
UNSTEEK
UNSTEEL
UNSTEP
UNSTEPPED
UNSTEPPING
UNSTERILIZED
UNSTICK
UNSTIFFEN
UNSTILL
UNSTILLNESS
UNSTING
UNSTINTED
UNSTITCH
UNSTOCK
UNSTOIC
UNSTOICIZE
UNSTOKEN
UNSTONE
UNSTOP
UNSTOPPED
UNSTOPPER
UNSTOPPING
UNSTOPPLE
UNSTORE
UNSTORED
UNSTORIED
UNSTOW
UNSTOWED
UNSTRAIN
UNSTRAINED
UNSTRAND
UNSTRAP
UNSTRAPPED
UNSTRAPPING
UNSTRATIFIED
UNSTRENG
UNSTRENGTH
UNSTRENGTHEN
UNSTRESS
UNSTRESSED
UNSTRESSEDLY
UNSTRETCH
UNSTRIATED
UNSTRIDE
UNSTRIKE
UNSTRING
UNSTRINGING
UNSTRIP
UNSTRIPED
UNSTRONG
UNSTRUNG
UNSTUDIED
UNSTUFF
UNSTY
UNSTYLISH
UNSTYLISHLY
UNSUBDUED
UNSUBMISSION
UNSUBSTANTIAL
UNSUBTLE
UNSUBTLENESS
UNSUBTLETY
UNSUBTLY
UNSUCCESS
UNSUCCESSFUL
UNSUCCESSIVE
UNSUFFERABLE
UNSUFFERABLY
UNSUFFERED
UNSUFFICIENT
UNSUIT
UNSUITABLE
UNSUITABLENESS
UNSUITABLY
UNSUITED
UNSULLIED
UNSULLIEDLY
UNSUMMED
UNSUMMERED
UNSUNG
UNSUNNED
UNSUPERABLE
UNSUPERVISED
UNSUPPED
UNSUPPLIED
UNSUPPORTED
UNSURE
UNSURETY
UNSURMISED
UNSURPASSED
UNSUSPECT
UNSUSPECTED
UNSUSPECTING
UNSUSPICION
UNSUSPICIOUS
UNSWADDLE
UNSWATHE
UNSWATHED
UNSWATHING
UNSWEAR
UNSWEARING
UNSWEAT
UNSWEET
UNSWEETEN
UNSWEETLY
UNSWEETNESS
UNSWELL
UNSWERVING
UNSWERVINGLY
UNSWORE
UNSWORN
UNSYLLABIC
UNSYMMETRICAL
UNSYMMETRY
UNSYMPATHETIC
UNSYMPATHY
UNSYSTEMATIC
UNT
UNTACK
UNTACKLE
UNTACTFUL
UNTACTFULLY
UNTAINTED
UNTAKEN
UNTALENTED
UNTAMED
UNTAMEDLY
UNTAMEDNESS
UNTANGIBLE
UNTANGIBLY
UNTANGLE
UNTANGLED
UNTANGLING
UNTAP
UNTAPPICE
UNTAR
UNTASTE
UNTAUGHT
UNTAX
UNTEACH
UNTEACHABLE
UNTEACHABLY
UNTEACHING
UNTEAM
UNTECHNICAL
UNTEEM
UNTELL
UNTELLING
UNTEMPER
UNTEMPERANCE
UNTEMPERATE
UNTENABLE
UNTENABLY
UNTENANT
UNTENANTED
UNTENDED
UNTENDER
UNTENDERLY
UNTENIBLE
UNTENIBLY
UNTENT
UNTENTED
UNTENTY
UNTERMED
UNTERMINABLE
UNTERMINABLY
UNTERRED
UNTESTATE
UNTETHER
UNTEWED
UNTHANK
UNTHANKFUL
UNTHANKFULLY
UNTHATCH
UNTHAW
UNTHENDE
UNTHEWED
UNTHINK
UNTHINKABLE
UNTHINKABLY
UNTHINKER
UNTHINKING
UNTHINKINGLY
UNTHOLEABLE
UNTHOLEABLY
UNTHOUGHT
UNTHOUGHTED
UNTHOUGHTFUL
UNTHRALL
UNTHRASHED
UNTHREAD
UNTHRID
UNTHRIDDEN
UNTHRIFT
UNTHRIFTIER
UNTHRIFTIEST
UNTHRIFTILY
UNTHRIFTY
UNTHRIVE
UNTHRIVEN
UNTHRIVING
UNTHRIVINGLY
UNTHRONE
UNTIDIER
UNTIDIEST
UNTIDILY
UNTIDINESS
UNTIDY
UNTIE
UNTIED
UNTIGHT
UNTIGHTEN
UNTIGHTENED
UNTIGHTENING
UNTIGHTNESS
UNTIL
UNTILE
UNTILED
UNTILLED
UNTIME
UNTIMELESS
UNTIMELIER
UNTIMELIEST
UNTIMELINESS
UNTIMELY
UNTIMEOUS
UNTIMEOUSLY
UNTIMOUS
UNTIN
UNTINCT
UNTINE
UNTIRE
UNTIRING
UNTITLED
UNTO
UNTOGGLE
UNTOGGLER
UNTOILED
UNTOLD
UNTOLERABLE
UNTOLERABLY
UNTOLERATED
UNTOLLED
UNTOMB
UNTONALITY
UNTONE
UNTONGUE
UNTOOTH
UNTOP
UNTOPPED
UNTOUCH
UNTOUCHABLE
UNTOUCHABLY
UNTOUCHED
UNTOWARD
UNTOWARDLY
UNTOWARDNESS
UNTOWN
UNTRACE
UNTRACEABLE
UNTRACEABLY
UNTRACTABLE
UNTRACTABLY
UNTRACTED
UNTRADED
UNTRAINED
UNTRAINEDLY
UNTRAMMELED
UNTRAMMELLED
UNTRANCE
UNTRAVELED
UNTRAVELLED
UNTREAD
UNTREADING
UNTREASURE
UNTREATABLE
UNTREATABLY
UNTRENCHED
UNTREND
UNTRESSED
UNTRIED
UNTRIM
UNTRIMMED
UNTRIPE
UNTRIST
UNTRIUMPHED
UNTROD
UNTRODDEN
UNTROTH
UNTROUBLE
UNTROUBLED
UNTROUBLEDLY
UNTROWABLE
UNTROWED
UNTRUCED
UNTRUE
UNTRUENESS
UNTRUISM
UNTRULY
UNTRUNKED
UNTRUSS
UNTRUSSER
UNTRUST
UNTRUSTFUL
UNTRUSTWORTHINESS
UNTRUSTWORTHY
UNTRUSTY
UNTRUTH
UNTRUTHER
UNTRUTHFUL
UNTRUTHFULLY
UNTRUTHS
UNTUCK
UNTUCKERED
UNTUNE
UNTURF
UNTURN
UNTUTORED
UNTUTOREDLY
UNTWILLED
UNTWIND
UNTWINE
UNTWINED
UNTWINING
UNTWIRL
UNTWIST
UNTWISTED
UNTWITTEN
UNTYING
UNTZ
UNUNANIMITY
UNUNANIMOUS
UNUNIFORM
UNUNIFORMITY
UNUNIFORMLY
UNUNITABLE
UNUNITABLY
UNUNITED
UNUNIVERSITY
UNUPRIGHT
UNUPRIGHTLY
UNURED
UNUSABLE
UNUSABLY
UNUSAGE
UNUSE
UNUSED
UNUSEDNESS
UNUSUAL
UNUSUALITY
UNUSUALLY
UNUSUALNESS
UNUTTERABLE
UNUTTERABLY
UNUTTERED
UNVACCINATED
UNVALID
UNVALIDITY
UNVALIDLY
UNVALIDNESS
UNVALUABLE
UNVALUABLY

UNVALUE
UNVALUED
UNVARIABLE
UNVARIABLY
UNVARIED
UNVARIEDLY
UNVARNISHED
UNVARYING
UNVARYINGLY
UNVASSAL
UNVEIL
UNVEILED
UNVEILEDLY
UNVEILEDNESS
UNVEILER
UNVEILMENT
UNVENGED
UNVENOM
UNVENUED
UNVERACITY
UNVERBALIZED
UNVERIFIABLE
UNVERIFIABLY
UNVERIFIED
UNVERITY
UNVERSED
UNVERSEDLY
UNVERSEDNESS
UNVEST
UNVICAR
UNVINCIBLE
UNVINDICTIVE
UNVIOLATE
UNVIRGIN
UNVIRILITY
UNVIRTUE
UNVIRTUOUS
UNVIRTUOUSLY
UNVISIBLE
UNVISIBLY
UNVISOR
UNVITIATED
UNVITIATEDLY
UNVIZARD
UNVOCAL
UNVOICE
UNVOICED
UNVOICING
UNVOLUNTARY
UNVOTE
UNVOUCHED
UNVOUCHEDLY
UNVOWELED
UNVOWELLED
UNVULGARIZE
UNWAGED
UNWALKABLE
UNWALKING
UNWALLET
UNWALLOWED
UNWAN
UNWANDERED
UNWANTED
UNWARDED
UNWARE
UNWARELY
UNWARENESS
UNWARES
UNWARILY
UNWARINESS
UNWARLIKE
UNWARM
UNWARNED
UNWARNEDLY
UNWARNEDNESS
UNWARNING
UNWARNISHED
UNWARP
UNWARRANT
UNWARRANTED
UNWARRAYED
UNWARRED
UNWARREN
UNWARY
UNWASHED
UNWASHEN
UNWASTEFUL
UNWATER
UNWATERED
UNWAVERING
UNWAVERINGLY
UNWAX
UNWAYED
UNWEAKENED
UNWEAL
UNWEANED
UNWEAPON
UNWEARIABLE
UNWEARIABLY
UNWEARIED
UNWEARIEDLY
UNWEARILY
UNWEARINESS
UNWEARY
UNWEARYING
UNWEARYINGLY
UNWEATHERED
UNWEAVE
UNWEB
UNWED
UNWEDDED
UNWEDDEDLY
UNWEDDEDNESS
UNWEDGEABLE
UNWEEL
UNWEELNESS
UNWEETING
UNWEETINGLY
UNWEFT
UNWELCOME
UNWELCOMELY
UNWELDE
UNWELL
UNWELLNESS
UNWELTH
UNWEMMED
UNWEPT
UNWHETTED
UNWHIG
UNWHOLE
UNWHOLESOME
UNWIELD
UNWIELDIER
UNWIELDIEST
UNWIELDILY
UNWIELDINESS
UNWIELDLY
UNWIELDSOME
UNWIELDY
UNWIFED
UNWILD
UNWILIER
UNWILILY
UNWILINESS
UNWILL
UNWILLE
UNWILLED
UNWILLFUL
UNWILLFULLY
UNWILLING
UNWILLINGLY
UNWILLINGNESS
UNWILY
UNWIMPLE
UNWIN
UNWINCING
UNWINCINGLY
UNWIND
UNWINDING
UNWINDINGLY
UNWINK
UNWINKING
UNWINKINGLY
UNWINLY
UNWINTER
UNWIRE
UNWIRED
UNWISDOM
UNWISE
UNWISELY
UNWISENESS
UNWISH
UNWIST
UNWIT
UNWITCH
UNWITHHOLDEN
UNWITNESSED
UNWITTED
UNWITTILY
UNWITTING
UNWITTINGLY
UNWITTY
UNWIVED
UNWOMAN
UNWOMANLY
UNWONDER
UNWONT
UNWONTED
UNWONTEDLY
UNWONTEDNESS
UNWOODED
UNWOOF
UNWORDED
UNWORDY
UNWORK
UNWORKABLE
UNWORKABLY
UNWORKER
UNWORKMANLY
UNWORLD
UNWORLDLY
UNWORMED
UNWORN
UNWORRIED
UNWORRIEDLY
UNWORSHIP
UNWORTH
UNWORTHIER
UNWORTHIEST
UNWORTHILY
UNWORTHINESS
UNWORTHY
UNWOUND
UNWOUNDED
UNWRAP
UNWRAPPED
UNWRAPPER
UNWRAPPERED
UNWRAPPING
UNWREAKED
UNWREAKEN
UNWREATHE
UNWRENCH
UNWREST
UNWRINKLE
UNWRINKLED
UNWRINKLING
UNWRIT
UNWRITE
UNWRITTEN
UNWROKEN
UNWROUGHT
UNWRY
UNY
UNYEANED
UNYIELDING
UNYIELDINGLY
UNYOKE
UNYOKED
UNYOKING
UNYOLDEN
UNZE
UNZEN
UNZONED
UP
UPAITHRIC
UPALONG
UPANAYA
UPANAYANA
UPANISHADIC
UPAPURANA
UPARCHING
UPARNA
UPAS
UPBAND
UPBANK
UPBAR
UPBEAT
UPBRAID
UPBRAIDED
UPBRAIDER
UPBRAIDING
UPBRAIDINGLY
UPBRAST
UPBRAY
UPBREAK
UPBREATHE
UPBRING
UPBRINGING
UPBROUGHT
UPBROW
UPBUILD
UPBUILDER
UPBY
UPBYE
UPCARD
UPCAST
UPCHAMBER
UPCHAUNCE
UPCHEER
UPCHUCK
UPCLIMB
UPCLOSE
UPCLOSER
UPCOAST
UPCOME
UPCOMING
UPCOUNTRY
UPCUT
UPDATE
UPDATED
UPDATING
UPDIVE
UPDRAFT
UPDRAUGHT
UPDRESS
UPEND
UPERIZE
UPEYGAN
UPFEED
UPFINGERED
UPFOLD
UPGANG
UPGIVE
UPGO
UPGRADE
UPGRADED
UPGRADING
UPGRAVE
UPGROWTH
UPHALE
UPHAND
UPHEARTED
UPHEAVAL
UPHEAVALIST
UPHEAVE
UPHEAVED
UPHEAVING
UPHELD
UPHELYA
UPHER
UPHILL
UPHOLD
UPHOLDEN
UPHOLDER
UPHOLDING
UPHOLSTER
UPHOLSTERED
UPHOLSTERER
UPHOLSTERIES
UPHOLSTEROUS
UPHOLSTERY
UPHOVE
UPHROE
UPKEEP
UPLA
UPLAND
UPLANDER
UPLANDISH
UPLAY
UPLEAN
UPLEAP
UPLIFT
UPLIFTED
UPLIFTEDLY
UPLIFTEDNESS
UPLIFTER
UPLIFTING
UPLIFTINGLY
UPLIMBER
UPLONG
UPLOOK
UPLOOKER
UPLYING
UPMAKING
UPMOST
UPON
UPPBAD
UPPER
UPPERCLASSMAN
UPPERCLASSMEN
UPPERCUT
UPPERCUTTING
UPPERER
UPPERMORE
UPPERMOST
UPPERS
UPPERSTOCKS
UPPING
UPPISH
UPPISHLY
UPPISHNESS
UPPITY
UPPOWOC
UPRAISAL
UPRAISE
UPRAISED
UPRAISER
UPRAISING
UPRAUGHT
UPREAR
UPREARED
UPREARING
UPREST
UPRIGHT

UPRIGHTEOUS
UPRIGHTING
UPRIGHTLY
UPRIGHTMAN
UPRIGHTNESS
UPRISAL
UPRISE
UPRISEN
UPRISER
UPRISING
UPRIST
UPRIVER
UPROAR
UPROARER
UPROARIOUS
UPROARIOUSLY
UPROOT
UPROOTAL
UPROOTED
UPROOTER
UPROOTING
UPROSE
UPROUSE
UPROUSED
UPROUSING
UPSADDLE
UPSCUDDLE
UPSEDOUN
UPSEE
UPSEEK
UPSET
UPSETTAL
UPSETTED
UPSETTER
UPSETTING
UPSETTINGLY
UPSHOOT
UPSHOT
UPSIDE
UPSIDES
UPSIGHTED
UPSILON
UPSILONISM
UPSITTEN
UPSITTING
UPSKIP
UPSLIP
UPSPEAR
UPSPIN
UPSPRANG
UPSPRING
UPSPRINGING
UPSPRUNG
UPSTAGE
UPSTAGED
UPSTAGING
UPSTAIRS
UPSTAND
UPSTANDER
UPSTANDING
UPSTARE
UPSTART
UPSTATE
UPSTATER
UPSTAY
UPSTIR
UPSTRAIGHT
UPSTREAM
UPSTREET
UPSTRETCHED
UPSTROKE
UPSUN
UPSURGE
UPSURGED
UPSURGENCE
UPSURGING
UPSWARM
UPSWEEP
UPSWEEPING
UPSWELL
UPSWELLED
UPSWELLING
UPSWEPT
UPSWING
UPSWINGING
UPSWOLLEN
UPSWUNG
UPSY
UPTAKE
UPTAKER
UPTEAR
UPTHROW
UPTHRUST
UPTIGHT
UPTILL
UPTOWN
UPTOWNER
UPTRAIN
UPTREND
UPTRILL
UPTURN
UPTURNED
UPTURNING
UPUPOID
UPWARD
UPWARDLY
UPWARDS
UPWAY
UPWAYS
UPWIND
UPWITH
UR
URACHAL
URACHUS
URACIL
URAEMIA
URAEMIC
URAEUS
URAL
URALI
URALITE
URALITIC
URALITIZE
URALITIZED
URALITIZING
URAMIDO
URAMIL
URAMINO
URAN
URANALYSIS
URANATE
URANIC
URANIDIN
URANIDINE
URANIFEROUS
URANIN
URANINITE
URANION
URANISCUS
URANISM
URANIST
URANITE
URANITIC
URANIUM
URANOCIRCITE
URANOGRAPHER
URANOGRAPHIC
URANOGRAPHY
URANOLATRY
URANOLITE
URANOLOGICAL
URANOLOGY
URANOMETRIA
URANOMETRY
URANOPHANE
URANOPLASTIC
URANOPLASTY
URANOPLEGIA
URANORRHAPHY
URANOSCHISIS
URANOSCHISM
URANOSCOPE
URANOSCOPIA
URANOSCOPIC
URANOSCOPY
URANOSPINITE
URANOTHORITE
URANOTIL
URANOUS
URANYL
URANYLIC
URAO
URARE
URARI
URASE
URATAEMIA
URATE
URATEMIA
URATIC
URATOMA
URATOSIS
URATURIA
URAZIN
URAZINE
URAZOLE
URBACITY
URBAINITE
URBAN
URBANE
URBANELY
URBANENESS
URBANISM
URBANIST
URBANITE
URBANITIES
URBANITY
URBANIZATION
URBANIZE
URBANIZED
URBANIZING
URBARIAL
URBIC
URBICOLOUS
URBINATE
URBS
URCEI
URCEIFORM
URCEOLAR
URCEOLATE
URCEOLE
URCEOLI
URCEOLUS
URCEUS
URCHIN
URCHINESS
URCHINLY
URD
URDE
URDEE
URDY
URE
UREA
UREAL
UREAMETER
UREAMETRY
UREASE
URECHITIN
URECHITOXIN
UREDEMA
UREDINEAL
UREDINEOUS
UREDINIA
UREDINIAL
UREDINIUM
UREDINOID
UREDINOLOGY
UREDINOUS
UREDIUM
UREDO
UREDOSORUS
UREDOSPORE
UREDOSPORIC
UREDOSTAGE
UREIC
UREIDE
UREIDO
UREMIA
UREMIC
URENT
UREOMETER
UREOMETRY
URESIS
URETAL
URETER
URETERAL
URETERECTOMIES
URETERECTOMY
URETERIC
URETEROCELE
URETEROGRAM
URETEROGRAPH
URETEROLITH
URETEROLYSIS
URETEROSTOMA
URETEROSTOMY
URETEROTOMY
URETHAN
URETHANE
URETHRA
URETHRAE
URETHRAL
URETHRALGIA
URETHRAS
URETHRISM
URETHRITIC
URETHRITIS
URETHROCELE
URETHROGRAM
URETHROGRAPH
URETHROMETER
URETHROPHYMA
URETHROPLASTY
URETHRORRHEA
URETHROSCOPE
URETHROSCOPY
URETHROSPASM
URETHROSTOMY
URETHROTOME
URETHROTOMIC
URETHROTOMY
URETHYLAN
URETHYLANE
URETIC
UREYLENE
URF
URFIRNIS
URGE
URGED
URGEFUL
URGENCE
URGENCIES
URGENCY
URGENT
URGENTLY
URGER
URGING
URGINGLY
URHEEN
URIAL
URIC
URICOLYSIS
URICOLYTIC
URIDROSIS
URIN
URINAEMIA
URINAEMIC
URINAL
URINALIST
URINALYSIS
URINANT
URINARIES
URINARIUM
URINARY
URINATE
URINATED
URINATING
URINATION
URINATIVE
URINATOR
URINE
URINEMIA
URINEMIC
URINIFEROUS
URINIPAROUS
URINOGENITAL
URINOGENOUS
URINOLOGIST
URINOLOGY
URINOMANCY
URINOMETER
URINOMETRIC
URINOMETRY
URINOSCOPIC
URINOSCOPIES
URINOSCOPIST
URINOSCOPY
URINOSE
URINOUS
URINOUSNESS
URITE
URLAR
URLED
URLING
URLUCH
URMAN
URN
URNA
URNAL
URNFIELD
URNFLOWER
URNFUL
URNFULS
URNING
URNINGISM
UROBILIN
UROBILINEMIA
UROBILINOGEN
UROBILINURIA
UROCELE
UROCHLORALIC
UROCHORD
UROCHORDAL
UROCHORDATE
UROCHROME
UROCHROMOGEN
UROCHS
UROCYANOGEN
UROCYST
UROCYSTIC
UROCYSTITIS
URODAEUM
URODELAN
URODELE
URODELOUS
URODIALYSIS

URODYNIA
UROEDEMA
UROERYTHRIN
UROGASTER
UROGASTRIC
UROGENIC
UROGENITAL
UROGENOUS
UROGLAUCIN
UROGRAM
UROGRAPHY
UROHAEMATIN
UROHEMATIN
UROHYAL
UROLAGNIA
UROLITH
UROLITHIASIS
UROLITHIC
UROLITHOLOGY
UROLOGIC
UROLOGICAL
UROLOGIST
UROLOGY
UROLUTEIN
UROMANCY
UROMANTIA
UROMANTIST
UROMELANIN
UROMELUS
UROMERE
URONEPHROSIS
URONIC
UROPATAGIUM
UROPHAEIN
UROPHANIC
UROPHANOUS
UROPHEIN
UROPHTHISIS
UROPLANIA
UROPOD
UROPODAL
UROPODOUS
UROPOETIC
UROPOIESIS
UROPOIETIC
UROPORPHYRIN
UROPSILE
UROPTYSIS
UROPYGIAL
UROPYGIUM
UROPYLORIC
UROROSEIN
URORRHAGIA
URORRHEA
URORUBIN
UROSACRAL
UROSCHESIS
UROSCOPIC
UROSCOPIES
UROSCOPIST
UROSCOPY
UROSEPSIS
UROSIS
UROSOMATIC
UROSOME
UROSOMITE
UROSOMITIC
UROSTEALITH
UROSTEGAL
UROSTEGE
UROSTEGITE
UROSTEON
UROSTERNITE
UROSTHENE
UROSTHENIC
UROSTYLAR
UROSTYLE
UROTOXIC
UROTOXICITY
UROTOXIES
UROTOXIN
UROTOXY
UROX
UROXANATE
UROXANTHIN
UROXIN
URRHODIN
URRHODINIC
URSICIDAL
URSICIDE
URSIFORM
URSIGRAM
URSINE
URSOID
URSON
URSONE
URSUK
URTICACEOUS
URTICAL
URTICANT
URTICARIA
URTICARIAL
URTICARIOUS
URTICATE
URTICATED
URTICATING
URTICATION
URTICOSE
URTITE
URUBU
URUCA
URUCU
URUCUM
URUCURI
URUCURY
URUISG
URUNDAY
URUS
URUSHI
URUSHIOL
URUSHIYE
URVA
URVED
US
USABILITY
USABLE
USABLENESS
USABLY
USAGE
USAGER
USANCE
USANT
USAR
USARON
USATION
USAUNCE
USE
USEABLE
USED
USEDLY
USEDNESS
USEE
USEFUL
USEFULLISH
USEFULLY
USEFULNESS
USEHOLD
USELESS
USELESSLY
USELESSNESS
USER
USES
USHABTI
USHABTIU
USHER
USHERANCE
USHERED
USHERER
USHERETTE
USHERIAN
USHERING
USING
USINGS
USITATE
USITATIVE
USNEACEOUS
USNEOID
USQUABAE
USQUE
USQUEBAE
USQUEBAUGH
USSELF
USSELS
USSELVEN
USSINGITE
USTION
USTORIOUS
USTULATE
USTULATION
USUAL
USUALISM
USUALLY
USUALNESS
USUARY
USUCAPIENT
USUCAPION
USUCAPIONARY
USUCAPT
USUCAPTABLE
USUCAPTIBLE
USUFRUCT
USUFRUCTUARIES
USUFRUCTUARY
USURA
USURE
USURER
USURIES
USURIOUS
USURIOUSLY
USURIOUSNESS
USURP
USURPATION
USURPATIVE
USURPATIVELY
USURPATORY
USURPATURE
USURPED
USURPER
USURPING
USURPINGLY
USURY
USUS
UT
UTAC
UTAHITE
UTAI
UTAS
UTCH
UTCHY
UTENSIL
UTENSILE
UTENSILS
UTERALGIA
UTERECTOMY
UTERI
UTERINE
UTEROCELE
UTEROGRAM
UTEROGRAPHY
UTEROLITH
UTEROLOGY
UTEROMETER
UTEROPELVIC
UTEROPLASTY
UTEROSACRAL
UTEROSCOPE
UTEROTOMY
UTEROTONIC
UTEROTUBAL
UTEROVAGINAL
UTEROVENTRAL
UTEROVESICAL
UTERUS
UTIA
UTIBLE
UTICK
UTILE
UTILIDOR
UTILITARIAN
UTILITIES
UTILITY
UTILIZABLE
UTILIZATION
UTILIZE
UTILIZED
UTILIZER
UTILIZING
UTINAM
UTIS
UTLAGARY
UTMOST
UTOPIA
UTOPIAN
UTOPIANISM
UTOPIANIST
UTOPIAST
UTOPISM
UTOPIST
UTOPISTIC
UTOPOGRAPHER
UTRAQUIST
UTRAQUISTIC
UTRECHT
UTRICLE
UTRICULAR
UTRICULATE
UTRICULIFORM
UTRICULITIS
UTRICULOID
UTRICULOSE
UTRICULUS
UTRIFORM
UTRUBI
UTRUM
UTTER
UTTERABILITY
UTTERABLE
UTTERANCE
UTTERED
UTTERER
UTTEREST
UTTERING
UTTERLESS
UTTERLY
UTTERMOST
UTTERNESS
UTU
UTUM
UTURUNCU
UVA
UVAL
UVALA
UVALHA
UVANITE
UVAROVITE
UVATE
UVEA
UVEAL
UVEITIC
UVEITIS
UVEOUS
UVID
UVITIC
UVITO
UVULA
UVULAE
UVULAR
UVULARLY
UVULAS
UVULE
UVULITIS
UVULOPTOSIS
UVULOTOME
UVULOTOMIES
UVULOTOMY
UXORIAL
UXORIALITY
UXORIALLY
UXORICIDAL
UXORICIDE
UXORIOUS
UXORIOUSLY
UYEZD
UZAN
UZARIN
UZARON

V

VA
VAAD
VAAGMAER
VAAGMAR
VAALITE
VACANCE
VACANCIES
VACANCY
VACANT
VACANTIA
VACANTLY
VACATE
VACATED
VACATING
VACATION
VACATIONAL
VACATIONER
VACATIONIST
VACATUR
VACCARY
VACCICIDE
VACCIGENOUS
VACCINA
VACCINABLE
VACCINAL
VACCINATE
VACCINATED
VACCINATING
VACCINATION
VACCINATOR
VACCINATORY
VACCINE
VACCINEE
VACCINELLA
VACCINIA
VACCINIAL
VACCINIFER
VACCINIFORM
VACCINIOLA
VACCINIST
VACCINIZATION
VACHE
VACILLANCY
VACILLANT
VACILLATE
VACILLATED
VACILLATING
VACILLATION
VACILLATOR
VACILLATORY
VACOA
VACONA
VACOUA
VACOUF
VACUA
VACUAL
VACUATE
VACUATION
VACUEFY
VACUIST
VACUIT
VACUITIES
VACUITY
VACUO
VACUOLAR
VACUOLATED
VACUOLATION
VACUOLE
VACUOME
VACUOMETER
VACUOUS
VACUOUSLY
VACUUM
VACUUMIZE
VACUUMS
VADE
VADELECT
VADER
VADIMONIUM
VADIMONY
VADIUM
VADOSE
VADY
VAE
VAFROUS
VAG
VAGABOND
VAGABONDAGE
VAGABONDIA
VAGABONDISM
VAGABONDIZE
VAGABONDIZED
VAGABONDIZER
VAGABONDIZING
VAGABONDRY
VAGAL
VAGANCY
VAGANT
VAGARIAN
VAGARIES
VAGARIOUS
VAGARISH
VAGARISOME
VAGARIST
VAGARITY
VAGARY
VAGAS
VAGATION
VAGI
VAGIENT
VAGIFORM
VAGILE
VAGINA
VAGINAL
VAGINALITIS
VAGINANT
VAGINATE
VAGINECTOMY
VAGINERVOSE
VAGINICOLOUS
VAGINIFEROUS
VAGINISMUS
VAGINITIS
VAGINULA
VAGINULATE
VAGINULE
VAGITUS
VAGOGRAM
VAGOLYSIS
VAGOTOMIZE
VAGOTOMY
VAGOTONIA
VAGOTONIC
VAGOTONY
VAGOTROPIC
VAGOTROPISM
VAGOUS
VAGRANCE
VAGRANCY
VAGRANT
VAGRANTISM
VAGRANTIZE
VAGRANTLY
VAGRANTNESS
VAGRATE
VAGROM
VAGUE
VAGUELY
VAGUENESS
VAGUER
VAGUEST
VAGUITY
VAGULOUS
VAGUS
VAH
VAHINE
VAIL
VAILABLE
VAILE
VAIN
VAINER
VAINEST
VAINFUL
VAINGLORIOUS
VAINGLORY
VAINLY
VAIR
VAIRAGI
VAIRE
VAIREE
VAIVODE
VAJRA
VAJRASANA
VAKASS
VAKEEL
VAKIA
VAKIL
VAKKALIGA
VAKUF
VALANCE
VALANCED
VALANCHE
VALBELLITE
VALE
VALEDICTION
VALEDICTORIES
VALEDICTORY
VALENCE
VALENCIA
VALENCIANITE
VALENCIES
VALENCY
VALENT
VALENTINE
VALERAMID
VALERAMIDE
VALERATE
VALERIAN
VALERIANATE
VALERIANIC
VALERIC
VALERIN
VALERONE
VALERYL
VALERYLENE
VALET
VALETA
VALETED
VALETING
VALETRY
VALETUDE
VALETUDINARY
VALEUR
VALEW
VALEWE
VALGOID
VALGUS
VALI
VALIANCE
VALIANCY
VALIANT
VALIANTLY
VALIANTNESS
VALID
VALIDATE
VALIDATED
VALIDATING
VALIDATION
VALIDATORY
VALIDITY
VALIDOUS
VALINCH
VALINE
VALISE
VALISES
VALLA
VALLANCY
VALLAR
VALLARY
VALLATE
VALLATED
VALLATION
VALLECULA
VALLECULAR
VALLECULATE
VALLEVARITE
VALLEY
VALLEYS
VALLICULA
VALLICULAE
VALLICULAR
VALLIDOM
VALLIES
VALLIS
VALLUM
VALLUMS
VALONIA
VALONIACEOUS
VALOP
VALOR
VALORIZATION
VALORIZE
VALOROUS
VALOROUSLY
VALOROUSNESS
VALOUR
VALOUWE
VALSE
VALSOID
VALUABLE
VALUABLY
VALUATE
VALUATION
VALUATIONAL
VALUATOR
VALUE
VALUED
VALUELESS
VALUER
VALUES
VALUING
VALURE
VALUTA
VALVA
VALVAE
VALVAL
VALVAR
VALVATE
VALVE
VALVELESS
VALVELET
VALVEMAN
VALVEMEN
VALVIFEROUS
VALVIFORM
VALVOTOMY
VALVULA
VALVULAE
VALVULAR
VALVULATE
VALVULE
VALVULITIS
VALVULOTOME
VALVULOTOMY
VALYL
VALYLENE
VAMBRACE
VAMBRACED
VAMBRASH
VAMFONT
VAMMAZSA
VAMOOSE
VAMOS
VAMOSE
VAMP
VAMPED
VAMPER
VAMPEY
VAMPHORN
VAMPING
VAMPIRE
VAMPIRIC
VAMPIRISH
VAMPIRISM
VAMPIRIZE
VAMPLATE
VAMPYRE
VAMURE
VAN
VANADATE
VANADIATE
VANADIC
VANADINITE
VANADIOUS
VANADIUM
VANADOUS
VANADYL
VANCOURIER
VANDAL
VANDALISH
VANDALISM
VANDALISTIC
VANDALIZE
VANDELAS
VANE
VANED
VANESSIAN
VANFOSS
VANG
VANGEE
VANGELI
VANGLO
VANGLOE
VANGUARD
VANILLA
VANILLAL
VANILLAS
VANILLATE
VANILLE
VANILLERY
VANILLIC
VANILLIN
VANILLINE
VANILLISM
VANILLON
VANILLOYL
VANILLYL
VANISH
VANISHED
VANISHER
VANISHING
VANISHINGLY
VANISHMENT
VANITARIANISM
VANITIED

VANITIES
VANITORY
VANITOUS
VANITY
VANLAY
VANMAN
VANMEN
VANMOST
VANNED
VANNER
VANNERMAN
VANNERMEN
VANNET
VANNING
VANNUS
VANQUISH
VANQUISHED
VANQUISHER
VANQUISHING
VANS
VANSIRE
VANT
VANTAGE
VANTERIE
VANWARD
VAPID
VAPIDISM
VAPIDITY
VAPIDLY
VAPIDNESS
VAPOGRAPHY
VAPOR
VAPORABILITY
VAPORABLE
VAPORARIUM
VAPORATE
VAPORED
VAPORER
VAPORETTI
VAPORETTO
VAPORIFORM
VAPORIMETER
VAPORING
VAPORINGLY
VAPORISH
VAPORIZATION
VAPORIZE
VAPORIZER
VAPOROGRAPH
VAPOROSE
VAPOROSITY
VAPOROUS
VAPOROUSLY
VAPORS
VAPORY
VAPOUR
VAPOURABILITY
VAPOURABLE
VAPOURED
VAPOURER
VAPOURING
VAPOURINGLY
VAPOURISH
VAPOURIZE
VAPOURIZED
VAPOURIZER
VAPOURIZING
VAPOUROSE
VAPOUROUS
VAPOUROUSLY
VAPOURS
VAPOURY
VAPULATE
VAPULATION
VAPULATORY
VAQUERO
VAQUEROS
VAR
VARA
VARAN
VARAS
VARDAPET
VARDI
VARDY
VARE
VAREC
VARECH
VAREHEADED
VARELLA
VAREUSE
VARGE
VARGUENO
VARI
VARIA
VARIABILITY
VARIABLE
VARIABLENESS
VARIANCE
VARIANCY
VARIANT
VARIATE
VARIATED
VARIATING
VARIATION
VARIATIONAL
VARIATIONIST
VARIATIONS
VARIATIVE
VARIATIVELY
VARIATOR
VARICATED
VARICATION
VARICELLA
VARICELLAR
VARICELLATE
VARICELLATION
VARICELLOID
VARICELLOUS
VARICES
VARICIFORM
VARICOCELE
VARICOID
VARICOLORED
VARICOLOROUS
VARICOLOURED
VARICOSE
VARICOSED
VARICOSIS
VARICOSITIES
VARICOSITY
VARICOTOMY
VARICULA
VARIED
VARIEGATE
VARIEGATED
VARIEGATING
VARIEGATION
VARIEGATOR
VARIER
VARIETAL
VARIETAS
VARIETIES
VARIETIST
VARIETY
VARIFORM
VARIFORMED
VARIFORMITY
VARIFORMLY
VARIFY
VARIGRADATION
VARIOCOUPLER
VARIOLA
VARIOLAR
VARIOLATE
VARIOLATE
VARIOLATED
VARIOLATING
VARIOLATION
VARIOLE
VARIOLIC
VARIOLIFORM
VARIOLITE
VARIOLITIC
VARIOLOID
VARIOLOUS
VARIOMETER
VARIORUM
VARIOTINTED
VARIOUS
VARIOUSLY
VARIOUSNESS
VARISCITE
VARISSE
VARITYPE
VARITYPED
VARITYPING
VARITYPIST
VARIX
VARKAS
VARLET
VARLETAILLE
VARLETESS
VARLETRY
VARLETTO
VARMENT
VARMINT
VARNA
VARNASHRAMA
VARNISH
VARNISHED
VARNISHER
VARNISHING
VARNISHMENT
VARNISHY
VARNPLIKTIGE
VARNSINGITE
VARSHA
VARSITY
VARSOVIANA
VARSOVIENNE
VARTABED
VARUS
VARVE
VARVED
VARY
VARYING
VAS
VASA
VASAL
VASALLED
VASCON
VASCULA
VASCULAR
VASCULARITIES
VASCULARITY
VASCULARIZE
VASCULARIZED
VASCULARIZING
VASCULARLY
VASCULATED
VASCULATURE
VASCULIFEROUS
VASCULIFORM
VASCULITIS
VASCULOMOTOR
VASCULOSE
VASCULUM
VASE
VASECTOMIES
VASECTOMIZE
VASECTOMY
VASEFUL
VASHEGYITE
VASICENTRIC
VASICINE
VASIFEROUS
VASIFORM
VASO
VASOCORONA
VASODENTINE
VASODILATIN
VASODILATING
VASODILATION
VASODILATOR
VASOFACTIVE
VASOGANGLION
VASOLIGATION
VASOMOTION
VASOMOTOR
VASOPARESIS
VASOREFLEX
VASOSPASM
VASOTONIC
VASOTROPHIC
VASQUINE
VASSAL
VASSALAGE
VASSALED
VASSALESS
VASSALIC
VASSALING
VASSALISM
VASSALITY
VASSALIZE
VASSALIZED
VASSALIZING
VASSALLING
VASSALRY
VASSALS
VAST
VASTATE
VASTATION
VASTIDITY
VASTITIES
VASTITUDE
VASTITY
VASTLY
VASTNESS
VASTY
VASU
VAT
VATES
VATFUL
VATFULS
VATIC
VATICAL
VATICANAL
VATICANIC
VATICANICAL
VATICIDE
VATICINAL
VATICINANT
VATICINATE
VATICINATED
VATICINATING
VATICINATION
VATICINATOR
VATICINE
VATMAKER
VATMAKING
VATMAN
VATS
VATTED
VATTER
VATTING
VAU
VAUDEVILLE
VAUDEVILLIAN
VAUDEVILLIST
VAUDY
VAUGNERITE
VAULT
VAULTAGE
VAULTED
VAULTEDLY
VAULTER
VAULTING
VAULTY
VAUMURE
VAUNCE
VAUNT
VAUNTAGE
VAUNTED
VAUNTER
VAUNTERY
VAUNTFUL
VAUNTIE
VAUNTINESS
VAUNTING
VAUNTINGLY
VAUNTLAY
VAUNTMURE
VAUNTY
VAURIEN
VAUXITE
VAVASOR
VAVASORY
VAVASOUR
VAWARD
VAY
VAZA
VEADORE
VEAL
VEALER
VEALINESS
VEALSKIN
VEALY
VEAU
VECKE
VECTIGAL
VECTION
VECTIS
VECTOR
VECTORIAL
VECTORIALLY
VECTURE
VEDANA
VEDET
VEDETTE
VEDIKA
VEDRO
VEE
VEEN
VEER
VEERABLE
VEERIES
VEERING
VEERY
VEGA
VEGASITE
VEGECULTURE
VEGETABILITY
VEGETABLE
VEGETABLES
VEGETABLIZE
VEGETABLY
VEGETAL
VEGETALCULE
VEGETALITY
VEGETANT
VEGETARIAN
VEGETATE
VEGETATED
VEGETATING
VEGETATION

VEGETATIVE
VEGETE
VEGETENESS
VEGETISM
VEGETIVE
VEGETOUS
VEHEMENCE
VEHEMENCY
VEHEMENT
VEHEMENTLY
VEHICLE
VEHICLES
VEHICULAR
VEHICULARY
VEHICULATE
VEHICULATION
VEI
VEIGLE
VEIL
VEILED
VEILEDLY
VEILEDNESS
VEILER
VEILING
VEILLESS
VEILLEUSE
VEILY
VEIN
VEINAGE
VEINAL
VEINED
VEINER
VEINERY
VEINING
VEINLET
VEINOUS
VEINS
VEINSTONE
VEINULE
VEINULET
VEINY
VELA
VELAMEN
VELAMENTOUS
VELAMENTUM
VELAMINA
VELAR
VELARIC
VELARIUM
VELARIZE
VELARY
VELATE
VELATED
VELATION
VELATURA
VELD
VELDE
VELDMAN
VELDSCHOEN
VELDSCHOENEN
VELDSCHOENS
VELDT
VELDTSCHOEN
VELDTSMAN
VELIC
VELIFEROUS
VELIFORM
VELIGER
VELITATION
VELITES
VELL
VELLALA
VELLEITIES
VELLEITY
VELLICATE
VELLICATED
VELLICATING
VELLICATION
VELLICATIVE
VELLINCH
VELLINCHER
VELLON
VELLOSIN
VELLOSINE
VELLUM
VELLUMY
VELLUTE
VELO
VELOCE
VELOCIMAN
VELOCIMETER
VELOCIOUS
VELOCIOUSLY
VELOCIPEDAL
VELOCIPEDE
VELOCIPEDED
VELOCIPEDIC
VELOCIPEDING
VELOCITIES
VELOCITOUS
VELOCITY
VELODROME
VELOMETER
VELOUR
VELOURS
VELOUTE
VELOUTINE
VELT
VELTE
VELTFARE
VELUM
VELUMEN
VELUMINA
VELUNGE
VELURE
VELURED
VELURING
VELUTINOUS
VELVERET
VELVET
VELVETBREAST
VELVETED
VELVETEEN
VELVETEENED
VELVETINESS
VELVETING
VELVETLEAF
VELVETMAKER
VELVETMAKING
VELVETRY
VELVETSEED
VELVETWEED
VELVETWORK
VELVETY
VELYARDE
VENA
VENADA
VENAE
VENAL
VENALITIES
VENALITY
VENALIZATION
VENALIZE
VENANZITE
VENATIC
VENATICAL
VENATICALLY
VENATION
VENATIONAL
VENATOR
VENATORIAL
VENATORIOUS
VENATORY
VENCOLA
VEND
VENDACE
VENDAGE
VENDAVAL
VENDED
VENDEE
VENDER
VENDETTA
VENDETTAS
VENDETTIST
VENDEUSE
VENDIBILITIES
VENDIBILITY
VENDIBLE
VENDIBLENESS
VENDIBLY
VENDICATE
VENDING
VENDIS
VENDITATE
VENDITION
VENDITOR
VENDOR
VENDUE
VENE
VENEER
VENEERED
VENEERER
VENEERING
VENEERS
VENEFIC
VENEFICAL
VENEFICIOUS
VENENATE
VENENATION
VENENE
VENENIFEROUS
VENENIFIC
VENENOSE
VENENOSITY
VENENOUS
VENEPUNCTURE
VENERABILITY
VENERABLE
VENERABLY
VENERAL
VENERANCE
VENERANT
VENERATE
VENERATED
VENERATING
VENERATION
VENERATIVE
VENERATIVELY
VENERATOR
VENERE
VENEREAL
VENEREAN
VENERER
VENERIAL
VENERIAN
VENERIFORM
VENERO
VENEROS
VENERY
VENESECT
VENESECTION
VENESECTOR
VENESIA
VENEUR
VENEZOLANO
VENGEABLE
VENGEANCE
VENGEANCELY
VENGEANT
VENGEFUL
VENGEFULLY
VENGEOUSLY
VENGER
VENIABLE
VENIAL
VENIALITIES
VENIALITY
VENIALLY
VENIALNESS
VENIE
VENIN
VENIPLEX
VENIPUNCTURE
VENIRE
VENIREMAN
VENIREMEN
VENISE
VENISON
VENKISEN
VENLIN
VENNEL
VENNER
VENOM
VENOMED
VENOMER
VENOMIZE
VENOMOUS
VENOMOUSLY
VENOMSOME
VENOMY
VENOSAL
VENOSE
VENOSITY
VENOSTASIS
VENOUS
VENOUSLY
VENOUSNESS
VENT
VENTA
VENTAGE
VENTAIL
VENTANA
VENTED
VENTER
VENTHOLE
VENTIDUCT
VENTIFACT
VENTIL
VENTILABLE
VENTILAGIN
VENTILATE
VENTILATED
VENTILATING
VENTILATION
VENTILATIVE
VENTILATOR
VENTILATORY
VENTIN
VENTING
VENTOMETER
VENTOSE
VENTOSENESS
VENTOSITY
VENTOY
VENTPIECE
VENTRAD
VENTRAL
VENTRALLY
VENTRIC
VENTRICLE
VENTRICOSE
VENTRICOSITY
VENTRICULAR
VENTRICULI
VENTRICULUS
VENTRIDUCT
VENTRILOQUAL
VENTRILOQUE
VENTRILOQUIST
VENTRILOQUY
VENTRIMESAL
VENTRIMESON
VENTRINE
VENTRIPOTENT
VENTROMYEL
VENTROSITY
VENTS
VENTURE
VENTURED
VENTURER
VENTURESOME
VENTURESOMELY
VENTURI
VENTURINE
VENTURING
VENTUROUS
VENTUROUSLY
VENUE
VENULA
VENULAE
VENULAR
VENULE
VENULOSE
VENULOUS
VENUST
VENUSTY
VENVILLE
VENY
VER
VERA
VERACIOUS
VERACIOUSLY
VERACITIES
VERACITY
VERAMENT
VERANDA
VERANDAED
VERANDAH
VERANDAHED
VERASCOPE
VERATRAL
VERATRALBIN
VERATRALBINE
VERATRATE
VERATRIA
VERATRIC
VERATRIDIN
VERATRIDINE
VERATRIN
VERATRINA
VERATRINE
VERATRINIZE
VERATRINIZED
VERATRINIZING
VERATRIZED
VERATRIZING
VERATROL
VERATROLE
VERATROYL
VERATRYL
VERAY
VERB
VERBAL
VERBALISM
VERBALIST
VERBALITY
VERBALIZE
VERBALIZED
VERBALIZER
VERBALIZING
VERBARIAN
VERBARIUM
VERBASCO
VERBASCOSE
VERBATE

VERBATIM
VERBENA
VERBENACEOUS
VERBENALIKE
VERBENALIN
VERBENATE
VERBENATED
VERBENATING
VERBENE
VERBENONE
VERBERATE
VERBERATION
VERBERATIVE
VERBIAGE
VERBICIDE
VERBICULTURE
VERBID
VERBIFIED
VERBIFYING
VERBIGERATE
VERBIGERATED
VERBIGERATING
VERBILE
VERBOMANIAC
VERBOMOTOR
VERBOSE
VERBOSELY
VERBOSENESS
VERBOSITIES
VERBOSITY
VERBOTEN
VERBY
VERCHOC
VERD
VERDANCIES
VERDANCY
VERDANT
VERDEA
VERDELHO
VERDERER
VERDEROR
VERDET
VERDETTO
VERDICT
VERDIGRIS
VERDIGRISY
VERDIN
VERDITER
VERDOY
VERDUGO
VERDUN
VERDURE
VERDURED
VERDURER
VERDUROUS
VERECUND
VERECUNDITY
VERECUNDNESS
VEREDICT
VEREK
VERENDA
VERGE
VERGED
VERGENCE
VERGENCY
VERGENT
VERGENTNESS
VERGER
VERGERISM
VERGERY
VERGI
VERGIFORM
VERGING
VERGLAS
VERGOBRET
VERGOYNE
VERGUNNING
VERI
VERIDIC
VERIDICAL
VERIDICALITIES
VERIDICALITY
VERIDICALLY
VERIDICOUS
VERIDITY
VERIER
VERIEST
VERIFIABLE
VERIFIABLY
VERIFICATE
VERIFICATION
VERIFICATIVE
VERIFIED
VERIFIER
VERIFY
VERIFYING
VERILY
VERIMENT
VERIN
VERINE
VERISCOPE
VERISIMILAR
VERISIMILITY
VERISM
VERISMO
VERIST
VERISTIC
VERITABLE
VERITABLY
VERITAS
VERITE
VERITIES
VERITISM
VERITIST
VERITISTIC
VERITY
VERJUICE
VERMEIL
VERMENGING
VERMEOLOGIST
VERMEOLOGY
VERMETID
VERMIAN
VERMICELLI
VERMICEOUS
VERMICIDAL
VERMICIDE
VERMICIOUS
VERMICLE
VERMICULAR
VERMICULARLY
VERMICULATE
VERMICULATED
VERMICULATING
VERMICULATION
VERMICULE
VERMICULITE
VERMICULOSE
VERMICULOUS
VERMIFORM
VERMIFORMITY
VERMIFUGAL
VERMIFUGE
VERMIFUGOUS
VERMIGEROUS
VERMIGRADE
VERMIL
VERMILION
VERMILIONETTE
VERMILIONIZE
VERMILY
VERMIN
VERMINAL
VERMINATE
VERMINATION
VERMINER
VERMINLY
VERMINOSIS
VERMINOUS
VERMINOUSLY
VERMINY
VERMIPAROUS
VERMIS
VERMIVOROUS
VERMIX
VERMOREL
VERMOULU
VERMOULUE
VERMOUTH
VERNACCIA
VERNACLE
VERNACULAR
VERNACULARLY
VERNACULATE
VERNAGE
VERNAL
VERNALITY
VERNALIZE
VERNANT
VERNATION
VERNEUK
VERNEUKER
VERNEUKERY
VERNICLE
VERNICOSE
VERNIER
VERNILE
VERNILITY
VERNISSAGE
VERNITION
VERNIX
VERNONIN
VERONALISM
VERQUERE
VERRA
VERRAY
VERRE
VERREL
VERRELL
VERRICULATE
VERRICULATED
VERRICULE
VERRUCA
VERRUCAE
VERRUCANO
VERRUCATED
VERRUCOSE
VERRUCOSIS
VERRUCOSITIES
VERRUCOSITY
VERRUCOUS
VERRUCULOSE
VERRUGA
VERRUGAS
VERS
VERSABILITY
VERSABLE
VERSABLENESS
VERSAL
VERSANT
VERSATE
VERSATILE
VERSATILITIES
VERSATILITY
VERSATION
VERSATIVE
VERSE
VERSED
VERSEMAN
VERSEMANSHIP
VERSEMEN
VERSEMONGER
VERSER
VERSES
VERSET
VERSETTE
VERSEWRIGHT
VERSICLE
VERSICLER
VERSICOLOR
VERSICOLOUR
VERSICULAR
VERSICULE
VERSICULI
VERSICULUS
VERSIERA
VERSIFIABLE
VERSIFIASTER
VERSIFICATION
VERSIFICATOR
VERSIFIED
VERSIFIER
VERSIFORM
VERSIFY
VERSIFYING
VERSILOQUY
VERSION
VERSIONAL
VERSIONER
VERSIONIST
VERSIONIZE
VERSIPEL
VERSO
VERSOR
VERST
VERSTA
VERSTE
VERSUAL
VERSUS
VERSUTE
VERTEBRA
VERTEBRAE
VERTEBRAL
VERTEBRALESS
VERTEBRALLY
VERTEBRAS
VERTEBRATE
VERTEBRATED
VERTEBRATION
VERTEBRIFORM
VERTEP
VERTEX
VERTEXES
VERTIBILITY
VERTIBLE
VERTIBLENESS
VERTICAL
VERTICALED
VERTICALING
VERTICALISM
VERTICALITY
VERTICALLED
VERTICALLING
VERTICALLY
VERTICES
VERTICIL
VERTICILLARY
VERTICILLATE
VERTICILLI
VERTICILLUS
VERTICITY
VERTICOMENTAL
VERTIGINATE
VERTIGINES
VERTIGINOUS
VERTIGO
VERTIGOES
VERTILINEAR
VERTIMETER
VERTU
VERTUGAL
VERTY
VERULED
VERUMONTANUM
VERUTA
VERUTUM
VERVAIN
VERVE
VERVECEAN
VERVECINE
VERVEL
VERVELED
VERVELLE
VERVELLED
VERVENIA
VERVER
VERVET
VERVINE
VERY
VERZINI
VERZINO
VES
VESANIA
VESANIC
VESBITE
VESI
VESICA
VESICAE
VESICAL
VESICANT
VESICATE
VESICATED
VESICATING
VESICATION
VESICATORY
VESICLE
VESICOCELE
VESICOCLYSIS
VESICOTOMY
VESICULA
VESICULAE
VESICULAR
VESICULARLY
VESICULASE
VESICULATE
VESICULATED
VESICULATING
VESICULATION
VESICULE
VESICULOSE
VESICULOUS
VESICULUS
VESKIT
VESPACIDE
VESPAL
VESPER
VESPERAL
VESPERIAN
VESPERING
VESPERS
VESPERTIDE
VESPERTILIAN
VESPERTINAL
VESPERTINE
VESPETRO
VESPIARIES
VESPIARY
VESPID
VESPIFORM
VESPINE
VESPOID
VESSEL
VESSELED
VESSELLED
VESSELS

VESSES
VESSETS
VESSICNON
VESSIGNON
VEST
VESTAL
VESTED
VESTEE
VESTER
VESTIARIAN
VESTIARIES
VESTIARIUM
VESTIARY
VESTIBLE
VESTIBULA
VESTIBULAR
VESTIBULATE
VESTIBULE
VESTIBULED
VESTIBULING
VESTIBULUM
VESTIGE
VESTIGIA
VESTIGIAL
VESTIGIALLY
VESTIGIARY
VESTIGIUM
VESTIMENT
VESTIMENTAL
VESTING
VESTITURE
VESTLET
VESTMENT
VESTMENTAL
VESTMENTED
VESTRAL
VESTRICAL
VESTRIES
VESTRIFY
VESTRY
VESTRYMAN
VESTRYMANLY
VESTRYMEN
VESTUARY
VESTURAL
VESTURE
VESTURED
VESTURER
VESTURING
VESUVIAN
VESUVIANITE
VESUVIATE
VESUVIN
VESUVITE
VESZELYITE
VET
VETA
VETANDA
VETCH
VETCHIER
VETCHIEST
VETCHLING
VETCHY
VETERAN
VETERANIZE
VETERANS
VETERINARIAN
VETERINARIES
VETERINARY
VETITIVE
VETIVENE
VETIVENOL
VETIVER
VETO
VETOED
VETOER
VETOES
VETOING
VETOISM
VETOIST
VETOISTIC
VETOISTICAL
VETTED
VETTING
VETTURA
VETTURE
VETTURINO
VETUST
VETUSTY
VEUGLAIRE
VEUVE
VEX
VEXATION
VEXATIOUS
VEXATIOUSLY
VEXATORY
VEXED
VEXEDLY
VEXEDNESS
VEXER
VEXFUL
VEXIL
VEXILLA
VEXILLARIOUS
VEXILLARY
VEXILLATE
VEXILLATION
VEXILLUM
VEXING
VEYN
VIA
VIABILITY
VIABLE
VIADUCT
VIAE
VIAGE
VIAGGIATORY
VIAGRAM
VIAGRAPH
VIAJACA
VIAL
VIALED
VIALING
VIALLED
VIALLING
VIAMETER
VIAND
VIANDEN
VIANDER
VIANDRY
VIANDS
VIATIC
VIATICA
VIATICAL
VIATICALS
VIATICUM
VIATOR
VIATORES
VIATORIAL
VIATORIALLY
VIBES
VIBETOITE
VIBEX
VIBGYOR
VIBICES
VIBRACULA
VIBRACULAR
VIBRACULOID
VIBRACULUM
VIBRANCIES
VIBRANCY
VIBRANT
VIBRANTLY
VIBRAPHONE
VIBRATE
VIBRATED
VIBRATILE
VIBRATILITY
VIBRATING
VIBRATION
VIBRATIONAL
VIBRATIUNCLE
VIBRATIVE
VIBRATO
VIBRATOR
VIBRATORY
VIBRIOID
VIBRION
VIBRIONIC
VIBRISSA
VIBRISSAE
VIBRISSAL
VIBROGRAPH
VIBROMETER
VIBROMOTIVE
VIBROPHONE
VIBROSCOPE
VIBURNIC
VIBURNIN
VIC
VICAIRE
VICAR
VICARAGE
VICARATE
VICARESS
VICARIAL
VICARIAN
VICARIANISM
VICARIATE
VICARII
VICARIOUS
VICARIOUSLY
VICARIUS
VICARLY
VICARSHIP
VICE
VICECOMES
VICECOMITAL
VICECOMITES
VICED
VICEGERAL
VICEGERENCY
VICEGERENT
VICENARY
VICENNIAL
VICEREGAL
VICEREGALLY
VICEREINE
VICEROY
VICEROYAL
VICEROYALTY
VICETY
VICHY
VICHYSSOISE
VICI
VICIANIN
VICIANOSE
VICILIN
VICIN
VICINAGE
VICINAL
VICINE
VICING
VICINITIES
VICINITY
VICIOUS
VICIOUSLY
VICIOUSNESS
VICISSITOUS
VICISSITUDE
VICOITE
VICONTIEL
VICONTIELS
VICTIM
VICTIMIZABLE
VICTIMIZATION
VICTIMIZE
VICTIMIZED
VICTIMIZER
VICTIMIZING
VICTLESS
VICTOR
VICTORDOM
VICTORESS
VICTORFISH
VICTORFISHES
VICTORIATE
VICTORIATUS
VICTORIES
VICTORINE
VICTORIOUS
VICTORIOUSLY
VICTORIUM
VICTORY
VICTRESS
VICTRIX
VICTUAL
VICTUALAGE
VICTUALED
VICTUALER
VICTUALING
VICTUALLED
VICTUALLER
VICTUALLING
VICTUALS
VICTUS
VICUDA
VICUNA
VICUNAS
VICUS
VID
VIDAME
VIDAN
VIDDUI
VIDDUY
VIDE
VIDELICET
VIDENDA
VIDENDUM
VIDEO
VIDERUFF
VIDETTE
VIDETUR
VIDICON
VIDIMUS
VIDONIA
VIDRY
VIDUAGE
VIDUAL
VIDUALLY
VIDUATE
VIDUATED
VIDUATION
VIDUITY
VIDUOUS
VIDYA
VIE
VIED
VIEJA
VIELLE
VIER
VIERKLEUR
VIERLING
VIERTEL
VIEW
VIEWED
VIEWER
VIEWING
VIEWLESS
VIEWLESSLY
VIEWLY
VIEWPOINT
VIEWSTER
VIEWY
VIF
VIFDA
VIGA
VIGAS
VIGENTENNIAL
VIGESIMAL
VIGESIMATION
VIGGLE
VIGIA
VIGIL
VIGILANCE
VIGILANCY
VIGILANT
VIGILANTE
VIGILANTLY
VIGILATE
VIGILATION
VIGNERON
VIGNERONS
VIGNETTE
VIGNETTED
VIGNETTER
VIGNETTING
VIGNETTIST
VIGNIN
VIGOGNE
VIGONE
VIGONIA
VIGOR
VIGORISH
VIGORIST
VIGOROSO
VIGOROUS
VIGOROUSLY
VIGOROUSNESS
VIGOUR
VIHARA
VIHUELA
VIJAO
VIKING
VIKINGISM
VILA
VILAYET
VILD
VILDLY
VILDNESS
VILE
VILELY
VILENESS
VILER
VILEST
VILEYNS
VILIACO
VILIFICATION
VILIFIED
VILIFIER
VILIFY
VILIFYING
VILIPEND
VILIPENDED
VILIPENDER
VILIPENDING
VILIPENDIOUS
VILITIES
VILITY
VILL
VILLA
VILLACHE
VILLADOM
VILLAETTE
VILLAGE

VILLAGELET
VILLAGEOUS
VILLAGER
VILLAGERY
VILLAGET
VILLAGEY
VILLAGISM
VILLAIN
VILLAINESS
VILLAINIES
VILLAINIST
VILLAINOUS
VILLAINOUSLY
VILLAINY
VILLAKIN
VILLANAGE
VILLANCICO
VILLANELLA
VILLANELLE
VILLANETTE
VILLAR
VILLATE
VILLATIC
VILLAYET
VILLE
VILLEGIATURE
VILLEIN
VILLEINAGE
VILLEINHOLD
VILLENAGE
VILLI
VILLIAUMITE
VILLICUS
VILLIFORM
VILLITIS
VILLOID
VILLOSE
VILLOSITY
VILLOTA
VILLOTE
VILLOUS
VILLUS
VILY
VIM
VIMANA
VIMEN
VIMINA
VIMINAL
VIMINEOUS
VIMPA
VIN
VINA
VINACEOUS
VINAGE
VINAGRON
VINAIGRE
VINAIGRETTE
VINAIGRETTED
VINAIGRIER
VINAIGROUS
VINAL
VINASSE
VINATA
VINCENT
VINCETOXIN
VINCHUCA
VINCIBILITY
VINCIBLE
VINCIBLENESS
VINCIBLY
VINCULA
VINCULAR
VINCULATE
VINCULATION
VINCULUM
VINDEMIAL
VINDEMIATE
VINDEMIATION
VINDEMIATORY
VINDEX
VINDICABLE
VINDICABLY
VINDICATE
VINDICATED
VINDICATING
VINDICATION
VINDICATIVE
VINDICATOR
VINDICATORY
VINDICATRESS
VINDICES
VINDICT
VINDICTA
VINDICTIVE
VINDICTIVELY
VINE
VINEA
VINEAE
VINEAL
VINEATIC
VINED
VINEDRESSER
VINEGAR
VINEGARER
VINEGARETTE
VINEGARIST
VINEGARROON
VINEGARWEED
VINEGARY
VINEGROWER
VINEITY
VINELAND
VINELET
VINER
VINERIES
VINERY
VINESTALK
VINETTA
VINEW
VINEYARD
VINEYARDING
VINEYARDIST
VINEYARDS
VINGT
VINGTIEME
VINGTUN
VINHATICO
VINIA
VINIC
VINICULTURAL
VINICULTURE
VINIFERA
VINIFEROUS
VINIFICATION
VINIFICATOR
VINING
VINITOR
VINNY
VINO
VINOLENT
VINOLOGIST
VINOLOGY
VINOMETER
VINOSE
VINOSITY
VINOUS
VINOUSLY
VINOUSNESS
VINT
VINTA
VINTAGE
VINTAGER
VINTAGING
VINTEM
VINTENER
VINTLITE
VINTNER
VINTNERESS
VINTNERY
VINTRESS
VINTRY
VINUM
VINY
VINYL
VINYLENE
VINYLIC
VINYLIDENE
VINYON
VIOL
VIOLA
VIOLABILITY
VIOLABLE
VIOLABLENESS
VIOLABLY
VIOLACEOUS
VIOLACEOUSLY
VIOLAL
VIOLAN
VIOLAND
VIOLANIN
VIOLATE
VIOLATED
VIOLATER
VIOLATING
VIOLATION
VIOLATIONAL
VIOLATIVE
VIOLATOR
VIOLATURE
VIOLE
VIOLENCE
VIOLENT
VIOLENTLY
VIOLENTNESS
VIOLER
VIOLESCENT
VIOLET
VIOLETTE
VIOLETY
VIOLIN
VIOLINA
VIOLINE
VIOLINED
VIOLINETTE
VIOLINING
VIOLINIST
VIOLINISTIC
VIOLINO
VIOLIST
VIOLON
VIOLONCELLIST
VIOLONCELLO
VIOLONCELLOS
VIOLONE
VIOLOTTA
VIOLOUS
VIOLURIC
VIOSTEROL
VIPER
VIPERESS
VIPERFISH
VIPERFISHES
VIPERID
VIPERIFORM
VIPERINE
VIPEROID
VIPEROUS
VIPEROUSLY
VIPEROUSNESS
VIPERY
VIR
VIRAGIN
VIRAGINIAN
VIRAGINITY
VIRAGO
VIRAGOES
VIRAL
VIRASON
VIRE
VIRELAI
VIRELAY
VIREMENT
VIRENT
VIREO
VIREONINE
VIREOS
VIRES
VIRESCENCE
VIRESCENT
VIRGA
VIRGAL
VIRGATE
VIRGATER
VIRGATION
VIRGE
VIRGIN
VIRGINAL
VIRGINALIST
VIRGINALITY
VIRGINALLY
VIRGINEOUS
VIRGINHEAD
VIRGINITY
VIRGINIUM
VIRGINLY
VIRGULA
VIRGULAR
VIRGULATE
VIRGULE
VIRGULTUM
VIRIAL
VIRICIDE
VIRID
VIRIDARIA
VIRIDARIUM
VIRIDESCENCE
VIRIDESCENT
VIRIDIAN
VIRIDIGENOUS
VIRIDIN
VIRIDINE
VIRIDITE
VIRIDITY
VIRIFIC
VIRIFY
VIRILE
VIRILELY
VIRILENESS
VIRILESCENCE
VIRILIA
VIRILIFY
VIRILIOUSLY
VIRILISM
VIRILIST
VIRILITIES
VIRILITY
VIRIPOTENT
VIRITOOT
VIRITRATE
VIRL
VIROLE
VIROLED
VIROLOGIST
VIROLOGY
VIRON
VIROSE
VIROSES
VIROSIS
VIROUS
VIRTU
VIRTUAL
VIRTUALISM
VIRTUALIST
VIRTUALITY
VIRTUALLY
VIRTUE
VIRTUED
VIRTUEFY
VIRTUOSA
VIRTUOSE
VIRTUOSI
VIRTUOSIC
VIRTUOSITY
VIRTUOSO
VIRTUOSOS
VIRTUOUS
VIRTUOUSLY
VIRTUS
VIRTUTI
VIRTUTIS
VIRUCIDAL
VIRUCIDE
VIRUELA
VIRULENCE
VIRULENCY
VIRULENT
VIRULENTED
VIRULENTLY
VIRUS
VIS
VISA
VISAED
VISAGE
VISAGED
VISAGRAPH
VISAING
VISAMMIN
VISARD
VISARGA
VISCACHA
VISCERA
VISCERAL
VISCERATE
VISCERATED
VISCERATING
VISCERATION
VISCEROUS
VISCID
VISCIDITY
VISCIDIZE
VISCIDLY
VISCIDNESS
VISCIDULOUS
VISCIN
VISCOID
VISCOIDAL
VISCOMETER
VISCOMETRY
VISCONTAL
VISCONTIAL
VISCOSCOPE
VISCOSE
VISCOSIMETER
VISCOSITIES
VISCOSITY
VISCOUNT
VISCOUNTCIES
VISCOUNTCY
VISCOUNTESS
VISCOUNTY
VISCOUS
VISCOUSLY
VISCOUSNESS
VISCUS
VISE

VISED
VISEED
VISEING
VISEMENT
VISENOMY
VISIBILITIES
VISIBILITY
VISIBILIZE
VISIBLE
VISIBLENESS
VISIBLY
VISIE
VISIER
VISILE
VISING
VISION
VISIONAL
VISIONALLY
VISIONARILY
VISIONARY
VISIONED
VISIONER
VISIONIZE
VISIONS
VISIT
VISITA
VISITABLE
VISITADOR
VISITANT
VISITATION
VISITATIONAL
VISITATIVE
VISITATOR
VISITATORIAL
VISITE
VISITED
VISITING
VISITOR
VISITORIAL
VISITRESS
VISITS
VISIVE
VISNE
VISNEY
VISON
VISOR
VISORED
VISORING
VISORY
VISS
VISTA
VISTAED
VISTAL
VISTAMENTE
VISTO
VISUAL
VISUALIST
VISUALITIES
VISUALITY
VISUALIZE
VISUALIZED
VISUALIZER
VISUALIZING
VISUOMETER
VITA
VITAE
VITAGRAPH
VITAL
VITALISM
VITALIST
VITALISTIC
VITALITY
VITALIZATION
VITALIZE
VITALIZED
VITALIZER
VITALIZING
VITALIZINGLY
VITALLY
VITALNESS
VITALS
VITAMIN
VITAMINE
VITAMINIC
VITAMINIZE
VITAMINOLOGY
VITAMINS
VITAPATH
VITAPATHY
VITAPHONE
VITASCOPE
VITASCOPIC
VITASTI
VITATIVENESS
VITE
VITELLARIUM
VITELLARY
VITELLIN
VITELLINE
VITELLOSE
VITELLUS
VITERBITE
VITESSE
VITIABLE
VITIAL
VITIATE
VITIATED
VITIATING
VITIATION
VITIATOR
VITICETUM
VITICULTURE
VITICULTURIST
VITIFEROUS
VITILIGINOUS
VITILIGO
VITILITIGATE
VITIOSITIES
VITIOSITY
VITIUM
VITRAGE
VITRAIL
VITRAILED
VITRAILLIST
VITRAIN
VITRAUX
VITRE
VITREAL
VITREAN
VITRELLA
VITREMYTE
VITREOSITY
VITREOUS
VITREOUSLY
VITREOUSNESS
VITRESCENCE
VITRESCENCY
VITRESCENT
VITRESCIBLE
VITREUM
VITRIAL
VITRIC
VITRICS
VITRIFACTION
VITRIFACTURE
VITRIFIABLE
VITRIFICATE
VITRIFICATION
VITRIFIED
VITRIFORM
VITRIFY
VITRIFYING
VITRINE
VITRINOID
VITRIOL
VITRIOLATE
VITRIOLATED
VITRIOLATING
VITRIOLATION
VITRIOLED
VITRIOLIC
VITRIOLINE
VITRIOLING
VITRIOLIZE
VITRIOLIZED
VITRIOLIZING
VITRIOLLED
VITRIOLLING
VITRITE
VITRO
VITROBASALT
VITROPHYRE
VITROPHYRIC
VITROTYPE
VITROUS
VITRUM
VITRY
VITTA
VITTAE
VITTATE
VITTLE
VITTLES
VITULAR
VITULARY
VITULINE
VITUPER
VITUPERABLE
VITUPERATE
VITUPERATED
VITUPERATING
VITUPERATION
VITUPERATIVE
VITUPERATOR
VITUPERATORY
VITUPERY
VIUVA
VIVA
VIVACE
VIVACIOUS
VIVACIOUSLY
VIVACISSIMO
VIVACITIES
VIVACITY
VIVAMENTE
VIVANDIER
VIVANDIERE
VIVANT
VIVARIA
VIVARIES
VIVARIUM
VIVARIUMS
VIVARY
VIVAT
VIVAX
VIVDA
VIVE
VIVELY
VIVENCY
VIVER
VIVERRIFORM
VIVERRINE
VIVERS
VIVES
VIVEUR
VIVIANITE
VIVID
VIVIDER
VIVIDEST
VIVIDITY
VIVIDLY
VIVIDNESS
VIVIFIC
VIVIFICAL
VIVIFICANT
VIVIFICATE
VIVIFICATED
VIVIFICATING
VIVIFICATION
VIVIFICATIVE
VIVIFICATOR
VIVIFIED
VIVIFIER
VIVIFY
VIVIFYING
VIVIPARISM
VIVIPARITY
VIVIPAROUS
VIVIPARY
VIVIPERFUSE
VIVISECT
VIVISECTED
VIVISECTING
VIVISECTION
VIVISECTIVE
VIVISECTOR
VIVO
VIVRE
VIVRES
VIX
VIXEN
VIXENISH
VIXENISHLY
VIXENLY
VIZARD
VIZARDED
VIZARDING
VIZCACHA
VIZIER
VIZIERATE
VIZIERIAL
VIZIR
VIZIRATE
VIZIRIAL
VIZNOMY
VIZOR
VIZORED
VIZORING
VIZSLA
VIZY
VIZZY
VLEI
VLEY
VLOKA
VLY
VOAR
VOCABILITY
VOCABLE
VOCABLY
VOCABULAR
VOCABULARIAN
VOCABULARIED
VOCABULARIES
VOCABULARY
VOCABULATION
VOCABULIST
VOCAL
VOCALIC
VOCALION
VOCALISATION
VOCALISE
VOCALISM
VOCALIST
VOCALITY
VOCALIZATION
VOCALIZE
VOCALIZED
VOCALIZER
VOCALIZING
VOCALLER
VOCALLY
VOCALNESS
VOCATE
VOCATION
VOCATIONAL
VOCATIONALLY
VOCATIVE
VOCATIVELY
VOCE
VOCES
VOCI
VOCICULTURAL
VOCIFERANCE
VOCIFERANT
VOCIFERATE
VOCIFERATED
VOCIFERATING
VOCIFERATION
VOCIFERATIVE
VOCIFERATOR
VOCIFERIZE
VOCIFEROSITY
VOCIFEROUS
VOCIFEROUSLY
VOCIFICATION
VOCIMOTOR
VOCODER
VOCOID
VOCULAR
VOCULE
VODKA
VODUN
VOE
VOET
VOETGANGER
VOETSAK
VOEU
VOG
VOGER
VOGESITE
VOGIE
VOGLITE
VOGUE
VOGUISH
VOICE
VOICED
VOICEFUL
VOICEFULNESS
VOICELESS
VOICELESSLY
VOICER
VOICES
VOICING
VOID
VOIDABLE
VOIDANCE
VOIDED
VOIDEE
VOIDER
VOIDING
VOIDLY
VOIDNESS
VOIDS
VOILA
VOILE
VOILIER
VOISINAGE
VOITURE
VOITURETTE
VOITURIER
VOIVOD
VOIVODE
VOKIE
VOL
VOLA
VOLABLE

VOLACIOUS
VOLADOR
VOLAGE
VOLAILLE
VOLANT
VOLANTE
VOLANTLY
VOLAPIE
VOLAR
VOLARY
VOLATA
VOLATIC
VOLATILE
VOLATILELY
VOLATILENESS
VOLATILITIES
VOLATILITY
VOLATILIZATION
VOLATILIZE
VOLATILIZED
VOLATILIZER
VOLATILIZING
VOLATION
VOLATIONAL
VOLBORTHITE
VOLCANIAN
VOLCANIC
VOLCANICALLY
VOLCANICITY
VOLCANIST
VOLCANITE
VOLCANITY
VOLCANIZE
VOLCANIZED
VOLCANIZING
VOLCANO
VOLCANOES
VOLCANOLOGY
VOLCANOS
VOLE
VOLEE
VOLEMITE
VOLEMITOL
VOLENCY
VOLENT
VOLENTLY
VOLERIES
VOLERY
VOLET
VOLGE
VOLHYNITE
VOLITANT
VOLITATE
VOLITATION
VOLITATIONAL
VOLITIENCY
VOLITIENT
VOLITION
VOLITIONAL
VOLITIONARY
VOLITIONATE
VOLITIVE
VOLITORIAL
VOLK
VOLKSRAAD
VOLLENGE
VOLLEY
VOLLEYBALL
VOLLEYED
VOLLEYER
VOLLEYING
VOLLEYINGLY
VOLLEYS
VOLOST
VOLOW
VOLPLANE
VOLPLANIST
VOLSELLA
VOLT
VOLTA
VOLTAGE
VOLTAGRAPHY
VOLTAIC
VOLTAISM
VOLTAITE
VOLTAMETER
VOLTAMETRIC
VOLTAMMETER
VOLTAPLAST
VOLTATYPE
VOLTE
VOLTEADOR
VOLTEADORES
VOLTI
VOLTIGEUR
VOLTINISM
VOLTIVITY
VOLTIZE
VOLTMETER
VOLTO
VOLTZINE
VOLTZITE
VOLUBILITY
VOLUBLE
VOLUBLENESS
VOLUBLY
VOLUCRINE
VOLUME
VOLUMED
VOLUMEN
VOLUMETER
VOLUMETRIC
VOLUMETRY
VOLUMINA
VOLUMINAL
VOLUMINOSITY
VOLUMINOUS
VOLUMINOUSLY
VOLUMIST
VOLUMOMETER
VOLUNTARIATE
VOLUNTARIES
VOLUNTARILY
VOLUNTARIOUS
VOLUNTARISM
VOLUNTARIST
VOLUNTARITY
VOLUNTARY
VOLUNTARYISM
VOLUNTARYIST
VOLUNTATIVE
VOLUNTEER
VOLUNTEERED
VOLUNTEERING
VOLUNTEERLY
VOLUNTY
VOLUPER
VOLUPT
VOLUPTAS
VOLUPTUARIES
VOLUPTUARY
VOLUPTUATE
VOLUPTUOSITY
VOLUPTUOUS
VOLUPTUOUSNESS
VOLUPTY
VOLUTA
VOLUTAE
VOLUTATE
VOLUTATION
VOLUTE
VOLUTED
VOLUTIFORM
VOLUTIN
VOLUTION
VOLUTOID
VOLVA
VOLVATE
VOLVE
VOLVELL
VOLVELLE
VOLVENT
VOLVOCACEOUS
VOLVULUS
VOLYER
VOMBATID
VOME
VOMER
VOMERINE
VOMICA
VOMICIN
VOMICINE
VOMIT
VOMITED
VOMITER
VOMITING
VOMITINGLY
VOMITION
VOMITIVE
VOMITO
VOMITORIES
VOMITORY
VOMITURE
VOMITUS
VON
VONSENITE
VOODOO
VOODOOED
VOODOOING
VOODOOISM
VOODOOIST
VOODOOISTIC
VOOG
VOORHUIS
VOORTREKKER
VORACIOUS
VORACIOUSLY
VORACITY
VORAGE
VORAGINOUS
VORAGO
VORANT
VORAZ
VORHAND
VORLAGE
VORONDREO
VORPAL
VORTEX
VORTEXES
VORTICAL
VORTICALLY
VORTICEL
VORTICELLID
VORTICES
VORTICIFORM
VORTICISM
VORTICIST
VORTICITY
VORTICOSE
VORTICOSELY
VORTICULAR
VORTICULARLY
VORTIGINOUS
VOTA
VOTABLE
VOTAL
VOTALLY
VOTARESS
VOTARIES
VOTARIST
VOTARY
VOTATION
VOTE
VOTEABLE
VOTED
VOTEEN
VOTER
VOTES
VOTING
VOTIST
VOTIVE
VOTIVELY
VOTIVENESS
VOTOMETER
VOTRESS
VOUCH
VOUCHABLE
VOUCHED
VOUCHEE
VOUCHER
VOUCHING
VOUCHMENT
VOUCHSAFE
VOUCHSAFED
VOUCHSAFING
VOUGE
VOULGE
VOUR
VOUSSOIR
VOUST
VOUSTER
VOUSTY
VOW
VOWED
VOWEL
VOWELISM
VOWELIST
VOWELIZE
VOWELLIKE
VOWELLY
VOWELS
VOWELY
VOWER
VOWESS
VOWING
VOX
VOYAGE
VOYAGEABLE
VOYAGED
VOYAGER
VOYAGEUR
VOYAGING
VOYAL
VOYANCE
VOYEUR
VOYEURISM
VOYEUSE
VOYOL
VRAI
VRAIC
VRAICKER
VRAICKING
VRBAITE
VRIDDHI
VRILLE
VROCHT
VROTHER
VROUW
VUE
VUG
VUGG
VUGGY
VUGH
VUIDE
VULCANICITY
VULCANISM
VULCANIST
VULCANITE
VULCANIZATE
VULCANIZATION
VULCANIZE
VULCANIZED
VULCANIZER
VULCANIZING
VULCANO
VULCANOLOGY
VULGAR
VULGARE
VULGARER
VULGAREST
VULGARIAN
VULGARISM
VULGARIST
VULGARITIES
VULGARITY
VULGARIZATION
VULGARIZE
VULGARIZED
VULGARIZER
VULGARIZING
VULGARLY
VULGARNESS
VULGO
VULGUS
VULGUSES
VULN
VULNED
VULNERABILITY
VULNERABLE
VULNERABLY
VULNERAL
VULNERARY
VULNERATE
VULNERATIVE
VULNIFIC
VULNIFICAL
VULNOSE
VULPECULAR
VULPIC
VULPICIDAL
VULPICIDE
VULPICIDISM
VULPINE
VULPINIC
VULPINISM
VULPINITE
VULSELLA
VULSELLUM
VULSINITE
VULT
VULTURE
VULTURINE
VULTURISH
VULTURISM
VULTURN
VULTUROUS
VULVA
VULVAL
VULVAR
VULVATE
VULVIFORM
VULVITIS
VULVOCRURAL
VULVOUTERINE
VULVOVAGINAL
VULVOVAGINITIS
VUM
VYINGLY
VYT

W

WA
WAAG
WAAPA
WAB
WABAYO
WABBER
WABBLE
WABBLED
WABBLER
WABBLINESS
WABBLING
WABBLINGLY
WABBLY
WABBY
WABE
WABENO
WABI
WABRON
WABUR
WACADASH
WACAPOU
WACE
WACHNA
WACK
WACKE
WACKER
WACKIER
WACKIEST
WACKY
WAD
WADCUTTER
WADD
WADDED
WADDENT
WADDER
WADDIE
WADDIED
WADDIES
WADDING
WADDLE
WADDLED
WADDLER
WADDLESOME
WADDLING
WADDLY
WADDY
WADDYING
WADDYWOOD
WADE
WADED
WADER
WADGE
WADI
WADIES
WADING
WADINGLY
WADMAAL
WADMAKER
WADMAKING
WADMAL
WADMOL
WADMOLL
WADNA
WADSET
WADSETTED
WADSETTING
WADY
WAEFU
WAEFUL
WAEG
WAENESS
WAESUCK
WAESUCKS
WAF
WAFER
WAFERED
WAFERER
WAFERING
WAFERMAKER
WAFERWOMAN
WAFERWORK
WAFERY
WAFF
WAFFIE
WAFFLE
WAFFLIKE
WAFFLY
WAFFNESS
WAFT
WAFTAGE
WAFTED
WAFTER
WAFTING
WAFTURE
WAFTY
WAG
WAGANG
WAGATI
WAGBEARD
WAGE
WAGED
WAGELESS
WAGELING
WAGER
WAGERED
WAGERER
WAGERING
WAGES
WAGET
WAGEWORK
WAGEWORKER
WAGEWORKING
WAGGED
WAGGEL
WAGGER
WAGGERIES
WAGGERY
WAGGIE
WAGGING
WAGGISH
WAGGISHLY
WAGGISHNESS
WAGGLE
WAGGLED
WAGGLING
WAGGLINGLY
WAGGLY
WAGGON
WAGGONABLE
WAGGONAGE
WAGGONED
WAGGONER
WAGGONETTE
WAGGONING
WAGGONLOAD
WAGGONRY
WAGGONSMITH
WAGGONWAY
WAGGONWAYMAN
WAGGONWRIGHT
WAGGY
WAGH
WAGING
WAGNERITE
WAGON
WAGONABLE
WAGONAGE
WAGONED
WAGONER
WAGONETTE
WAGONING
WAGONLOAD
WAGONMAKER
WAGONMAKING
WAGONMAN
WAGONRY
WAGONSMITH
WAGONWAY
WAGONWAYMAN
WAGONWRIGHT
WAGSOME
WAGTAIL
WAGWAG
WAGWANTS
WAGWIT
WAH
WAHAHE
WAHCONDA
WAHINE
WAHOO
WAHWAH
WAIATA
WAIF
WAIK
WAIKLY
WAIKNESS
WAIL
WAILED
WAILER
WAILFUL
WAILFULLY
WAILING
WAILMENT
WAILSOME
WAILY
WAIN
WAINAGE
WAINBOTE
WAINER
WAINMAN
WAINMEN
WAINROPE
WAINSCOT
WAINSCOTED
WAINSCOTING
WAINSCOTTED
WAINSCOTTING
WAINWRIGHT
WAIPIRO
WAIR
WAIRCH
WAIRD
WAIREPO
WAIRSH
WAISE
WAIST
WAISTBAND
WAISTCLOTH
WAISTCOAT
WAISTCOATED
WAISTCOATEER
WAISTED
WAISTER
WAISTING
WAISTLESS
WAISTLINE
WAIT
WAITED
WAITER
WAITERAGE
WAITERING
WAITING
WAITINGLY
WAITRESS
WAITSMEN
WAIVATUA
WAIVE
WAIVED
WAIVER
WAIVERY
WAIVING
WAJANG
WAK
WAKA
WAKAN
WAKANDA
WAKE
WAKEA
WAKED
WAKEFUL
WAKEFULLY
WAKEFULNESS
WAKELESS
WAKEMAN
WAKEMEN
WAKEN
WAKENED
WAKENER
WAKENING
WAKER
WAKERIFE
WAKERIFENESS
WAKES
WAKETIME
WAKF
WAKIF
WAKIKI
WAKING
WAKINGLY
WAKIUP
WAKON
WAKONDA
WAKY
WAL
WALAHEE
WALD
WALDFLUTE
WALDGRAVE
WALDGRAVINE
WALDHORN
WALDMEISTER
WALE
WALED
WALEPIECE
WALER
WALI
WALING
WALK
WALKAWAY
WALKED
WALKENE
WALKER
WALKERS
WALKING
WALKIST
WALKMILL
WALKMILLER
WALKOUT
WALKOVER
WALKRIFE
WALKSMAN
WALKSMEN
WALKUP
WALKWAY
WALKYRIE
WALL
WALLA
WALLABA
WALLABIES
WALLABY
WALLAGO
WALLAH
WALLAROO
WALLBIRD
WALLBOARD
WALLED
WALLER
WALLET
WALLEYE
WALLEYED
WALLFLOWER
WALLHICK
WALLIE
WALLING
WALLOCH
WALLOON
WALLOP
WALLOPER
WALLOPING
WALLOW
WALLOWED
WALLOWER
WALLOWING
WALLOWISH
WALLOWISHLY
WALLPAPER
WALLPAPERING
WALLPIECE
WALLS
WALLWORT
WALLY
WALLYDRAG
WALLYDRAIGLE
WALM
WALNUT
WALPURGITE
WALRUS
WALRUSES
WALSH
WALSPERE
WALT
WALTER
WALTRON
WALTROT
WALTY
WALTZ
WALTZED
WALTZER
WALTZING
WALWE
WALY
WALYCOAT
WAMARA
WAMB
WAMBAIS
WAMBLE
WAMBLED
WAMBLINESS
WAMBLING
WAMBLINGLY
WAMBLY
WAME
WAMED
WAMEFOU
WAMEFU
WAMEFUL
WAMEL
WAMFLE
WAMMUS
WAMP
WAMPEE
WAMPISH
WAMPLE
WAMPUM
WAMPUMPEAG

WAMPUS
WAMUS
WAN
WANA
WANCHANCY
WAND
WANDE
WANDER
WANDERER
WANDERING
WANDERINGLY
WANDERLUST
WANDERLUSTER
WANDEROO
WANDERY
WANDERYEAR
WANDFLOWER
WANDLE
WANDOO
WANDOUGHT
WANDRETH
WANDSMAN
WANDY
WANE
WANED
WANELESS
WANEY
WANG
WANGA
WANGALA
WANGAN
WANGATEUR
WANGER
WANGHEE
WANGLE
WANGLED
WANGLER
WANGLING
WANGO
WANGRACE
WANGTOOTH
WANGUN
WANHAP
WANHAPPY
WANHOPE
WANHORN
WANIAND
WANIGAN
WANING
WANION
WANKAPIN
WANKLE
WANKLINESS
WANKLY
WANKY
WANLAS
WANLE
WANLY
WANMOL
WANNED
WANNER
WANNESS
WANNEST
WANNIGAN
WANNING
WANNY
WANREST
WANRESTFUL
WANRUFE
WANRULY
WANSHAPE
WANSITH
WANSOME
WANSONSY
WANT
WANTAGE
WANTED
WANTER
WANTFUL
WANTHILL
WANTHRIFT
WANTHRIVEN
WANTING
WANTINGLY
WANTINGNESS
WANTON
WANTONED
WANTONER
WANTONING
WANTONIZE
WANTONLY
WANTONNESS
WANTROKE
WANTRUST
WANTWIT
WANTY
WANWEIRD
WANWIT
WANWORDY
WANWORTH
WANY
WANZE
WAP
WAPACUT
WAPATA
WAPATOO
WAPED
WAPENTAKE
WAPIN
WAPITI
WAPITIS
WAPP
WAPPED
WAPPENED
WAPPENSCHAW
WAPPER
WAPPET
WAPPING
WAQF
WAR
WARABI
WARAL
WARATAH
WARBIRD
WARBITE
WARBLE
WARBLED
WARBLELIKE
WARBLER
WARBLERLIKE
WARBLET
WARBLING
WARBLINGLY
WARBLY
WARCH
WARCRAFT
WARD
WARDABLE
WARDAGE
WARDATOUR
WARDAY
WARDCORS
WARDED
WARDEN
WARDENCY
WARDENRIES
WARDENRY
WARDENSHIP
WARDER
WARDHOLDING
WARDIAN
WARDING
WARDITE
WARDMAID
WARDMAN
WARDMEN
WARDMOTE
WARDRESS
WARDROBE
WARDROBER
WARDROOM
WARDSHIP
WARDSMAID
WARDSMAN
WARDSWOMAN
WARDWITE
WARDWOMAN
WARDWOMEN
WARDWORD
WARE
WARED
WAREFUL
WAREHOU
WAREHOUSE
WAREHOUSED
WAREHOUSEMAN
WAREHOUSEMEN
WAREHOUSING
WARELESS
WARELY
WARENTMENT
WAREROOM
WARES
WARESHIP
WARF
WARFA
WARFARE
WARFARED
WARFARER
WARFARING
WARFUL
WARGUS
WARHEAD
WARI
WARIANCE
WARIANGLE
WARIED
WARIER
WARIEST
WARILY
WARIMENT
WARINE
WARINESS
WARINGIN
WARISH
WARISON
WARK
WARKAMOOWEE
WARKLOOM
WARKLUME
WARLIKE
WARLIKELY
WARLIKENESS
WARLING
WARLOCK
WARLOCKRY
WARLORD
WARLOW
WARLUCK
WARLY
WARM
WARMAKER
WARMAKING
WARMAN
WARMED
WARMEDLY
WARMEN
WARMER
WARMEST
WARMFUL
WARMHEARTED
WARMHOUSE
WARMING
WARMLY
WARMMESS
WARMONGER
WARMONGERING
WARMOUTH
WARMTH
WARMUP
WARMUS
WARN
WARNAGE
WARND
WARNED
WARNEL
WARNER
WARNING
WARNINGLY
WARNISH
WARNISON
WARNISS
WARNOTH
WARP
WARPAGE
WARPATH
WARPED
WARPER
WARPING
WARPLANE
WARPLE
WARPOWER
WARPROOF
WARRAGAL
WARRAMBOOL
WARRANDICE
WARRANT
WARRANTABLE
WARRANTABLY
WARRANTED
WARRANTEE
WARRANTER
WARRANTIES
WARRANTING
WARRANTISE
WARRANTIZE
WARRANTOR
WARRANTY
WARRAY
WARRE
WARRED
WARREE
WARREN
WARRENER
WARRER
WARRIGAL
WARRIN
WARRING
WARRIOR
WARRISH
WARROK
WARRYN
WARSAW
WARSHIP
WARSLE
WARSLED
WARSLER
WARSLING
WARSTLE
WARSTLER
WART
WARTED
WARTFLOWER
WARTH
WARTIER
WARTIEST
WARTIME
WARTLIKE
WARTWEED
WARTWORT
WARTY
WARTYBACK
WARVE
WARWARDS
WARWICKITE
WARWOLF
WARWORK
WARWORKER
WARWORN
WARY
WARYTREE
WAS
WASABI
WASE
WASEL
WASH
WASHABILITY
WASHABLE
WASHBASIN
WASHBASKET
WASHBOARD
WASHBOWL
WASHBREW
WASHCLOTH
WASHDAY
WASHDISH
WASHDOWN
WASHED
WASHER
WASHERIES
WASHERLESS
WASHERMAN
WASHERMEN
WASHERWIFE
WASHERWOMAN
WASHERWOMEN
WASHERY
WASHERYMAN
WASHERYMEN
WASHHAND
WASHHOUSE
WASHIER
WASHIEST
WASHIN
WASHINESS
WASHING
WASHINGS
WASHLAND
WASHLEATHER
WASHMAID
WASHMAN
WASHMEN
WASHOFF
WASHOUT
WASHPOT
WASHRAG
WASHROOM
WASHSHED
WASHSTAND
WASHTAIL
WASHTRAY
WASHTROUGH
WASHTUB
WASHWAY
WASHWOMAN
WASHWOMEN
WASHWORK
WASHY
WASP
WASPEN
WASPIER
WASPIEST
WASPISH
WASPISHLY
WASPISHNESS

WASPLING
WASPNESTING
WASPS
WASPY
WASSAIL
WASSAILED
WASSAILER
WASSAILING
WASSAILOUS
WASSIE
WAST
WASTABLE
WASTAGE
WASTE
WASTEBASKET
WASTED
WASTEFUL
WASTEFULLY
WASTEFULNESS
WASTEL
WASTELAND
WASTELBREAD
WASTELESS
WASTELOT
WASTELY
WASTEMAN
WASTEMEN
WASTEMENT
WASTENESS
WASTEPAPER
WASTER
WASTERFUL
WASTERIE
WASTERN
WASTERY
WASTETHRIFT
WASTEWAY
WASTEWEIR
WASTEWORD
WASTEYARD
WASTIER
WASTIEST
WASTINE
WASTING
WASTINGLY
WASTINGNESS
WASTME
WASTREL
WASTRIE
WASTRIFE
WASTRY
WASTY
WAT
WATAP
WATAPE
WATAPEH
WATCH
WATCHBAND
WATCHBILL
WATCHBOAT
WATCHCASE
WATCHCRY
WATCHDOG
WATCHED
WATCHER
WATCHERS
WATCHES
WATCHET
WATCHEYE
WATCHFREE
WATCHFUL
WATCHFULLY
WATCHFULNESS
WATCHGLASS
WATCHHOUSE
WATCHING
WATCHINGLY
WATCHKEEPER
WATCHLESS
WATCHMAKER
WATCHMAKING
WATCHMAN
WATCHMANLY
WATCHMATE
WATCHMEN
WATCHMENT
WATCHOUT
WATCHTOWER
WATCHWORD
WATCHWORK
WATE
WATER
WATERAGE
WATERBAILAGE
WATERBANK
WATERBEAR
WATERBELLY
WATERBLINK
WATERBLOOM
WATERBOARD
WATERBOK
WATERBORNE
WATERBOSH
WATERBOUND
WATERBRAIN
WATERBROO
WATERBROSE
WATERBUCK
WATERBUCKS
WATERBUSH
WATERCASTER
WATERCHAT
WATERCOLOR
WATERCOURSE
WATERCRAFT
WATERCRESS
WATERCUP
WATERDOE
WATERDROP
WATERED
WATERER
WATERFALL
WATERFINDER
WATERFLOOD
WATERFOWL
WATERFOWLS
WATERFREE
WATERFRONT
WATERGLASS
WATERHEAD
WATERHEAP
WATERHORSE
WATERIE
WATERILY
WATERINESS
WATERING
WATERINGLY
WATERINGMAN
WATERISH
WATERISHLY
WATERISHNESS
WATERLEAF
WATERLEAVE
WATERLESS
WATERLESSLY
WATERLINE
WATERLOG
WATERLOGGED
WATERLOGGER
WATERMAN
WATERMANSHIP
WATERMARK
WATERMARKED
WATERMASTER
WATERMELON
WATERMEN
WATERMONGER
WATERPIT
WATERPLANE
WATERPOT
WATERPOWER
WATERPROOF
WATERPROOFED
WATERPROOFER
WATERRUG
WATERSCAPE
WATERSHAKE
WATERSHED
WATERSHOOT
WATERSHUT
WATERSIDE
WATERSIDER
WATERSKIN
WATERSMEET
WATERSPOUT
WATERSTOUP
WATERTIGHT
WATERTIGHTAL
WATERWALL
WATERWAY
WATERWEED
WATERWHEEL
WATERWISE
WATERWOOD
WATERWORK
WATERWORKER
WATERWORKS
WATERWORM
WATERWORN
WATERWORT
WATERY
WATH
WATHE
WATHER
WATHSTEAD
WATO
WATT
WATTAGE
WATTAPE
WATTER
WATTEST
WATTIS
WATTLE
WATTLEBIRD
WATTLEBOY
WATTLED
WATTLES
WATTLESS
WATTLEWORK
WATTLING
WATTMAN
WATTMEN
WATTMETER
WAUBEEN
WAUBLE
WAUCH
WAUCHLE
WAUCHT
WAUF
WAUFF
WAUGH
WAUGHT
WAUGHY
WAUK
WAUKE
WAUKIT
WAUKRIFE
WAUL
WAUNS
WAUR
WAUREGAN
WAUVE
WAVABLE
WAVABLY
WAVE
WAVED
WAVELENGTH
WAVELESS
WAVELET
WAVELLITE
WAVEMARK
WAVEMENT
WAVEMETER
WAVEOFF
WAVER
WAVERED
WAVERER
WAVERING
WAVERINGLY
WAVERINGNESS
WAVEROUS
WAVERY
WAVESON
WAVEY
WAVEYS
WAVIER
WAVIES
WAVIEST
WAVILY
WAVINESS
WAVING
WAVINGLY
WAVY
WAW
WAWA
WAWAH
WAWASKEESH
WAWE
WAWL
WAX
WAXAND
WAXBERRIES
WAXBERRY
WAXBILL
WAXBIRD
WAXBUSH
WAXCHANDLER
WAXCHANDLERY
WAXCOMB
WAXED
WAXEN
WAXER
WAXES
WAXFLOWER
WAXHEARTED
WAXIER
WAXIEST
WAXINESS
WAXING
WAXINGLY
WAXMAKER
WAXMAKING
WAXMAN
WAXWEED
WAXWING
WAXWORK
WAXWORKER
WAXWORKING
WAXWORM
WAXY
WAY
WAYAKA
WAYANG
WAYBACK
WAYBERRY
WAYBILL
WAYBIRD
WAYBOOK
WAYBREAD
WAYBUNG
WAYER
WAYFARE
WAYFARER
WAYFARING
WAYFARINGLY
WAYFELLOW
WAYGANG
WAYGATE
WAYGOER
WAYGOING
WAYGONE
WAYGOOSE
WAYHOUSE
WAYING
WAYLAID
WAYLAY
WAYLAYER
WAYLAYING
WAYLEAVE
WAYMAKER
WAYMAN
WAYMARK
WAYMATE
WAYMEN
WAYMENT
WAYNE
WAYPOST
WAYS
WAYSIDE
WAYSIDER
WAYSLIDING
WAYTE
WAYTHORN
WAYWARD
WAYWARDEN
WAYWARDLY
WAYWARDNESS
WAYWISER
WAYWORN
WAYWORT
WAYZGOOSE
WAZIR
WAZIRATE
WAZIRSHIP
WE
WEA
WEAK
WEAKBRAINED
WEAKEN
WEAKENED
WEAKENER
WEAKENING
WEAKER
WEAKEST
WEAKFISH
WEAKFISHES
WEAKHANDED
WEAKHEARTED
WEAKISH
WEAKISHLY
WEAKISHNESS
WEAKLIER
WEAKLIEST
WEAKLINESS
WEAKLING
WEAKLY
WEAKMOUTHED
WEAKNESS
WEAKY
WEAL
WEALD
WEALDISH
WEALDSMAN
WEALDSMEN
WEALFUL

WEALSMAN
WEALSOME
WEALTH
WEALTHFUL
WEALTHFULLY
WEALTHIER
WEALTHIEST
WEALTHILY
WEALTHINESS
WEALTHMAKER
WEALTHMAKING
WEALTHMONGER
WEALTHY
WEAM
WEAN
WEANED
WEANEDNESS
WEANEL
WEANER
WEANIE
WEANING
WEANLING
WEANLY
WEANYER
WEAPON
WEAPONED
WEAPONEER
WEAPONLESS
WEAPONMAKER
WEAPONMAKING
WEAPONPROOF
WEAPONRY
WEAPONS
WEAR
WEARABILITY
WEARABLE
WEARED
WEARER
WEARIED
WEARIEDLY
WEARIEDNESS
WEARIER
WEARIEST
WEARIFUL
WEARIFULLY
WEARIFULNESS
WEARILESS
WEARILESSLY
WEARILY
WEARINESS
WEARING
WEARINGLY
WEARISH
WEARISHLY
WEARISHNESS
WEARISOME
WEARISOMELY
WEARISOMENESS
WEARY
WEARYING
WEARYINGLY
WEASAND
WEASEL
WEASELED
WEASELING
WEASELLY
WEASELS
WEASELSKIN
WEASELSNOUT
WEASER
WEASON
WEATHER
WEATHERBEATEN
WEATHERBOARD
WEATHERBREAK
WEATHERCAST
WEATHERCOCK
WEATHERCOCKY
WEATHERED
WEATHERER
WEATHERGLASS
WEATHERGLEAM
WEATHERHEAD
WEATHERING
WEATHERLY
WEATHERMAKER
WEATHERMAN
WEATHERMEN
WEATHERMOST
WEATHEROLOGY
WEATHERPROOF
WEATHERSICK
WEATHERTIGHT
WEATHERWORN
WEATHERY
WEATINGS
WEAVE
WEAVED
WEAVER
WEAVERBIRD
WEAVERESS
WEAVING
WEAZEN
WEAZENED
WEAZENY
WEB
WEBB
WEBBE
WEBBED
WEBBER
WEBBING
WEBBY
WEBELOS
WEBER
WEBEYE
WEBFEET
WEBFOOT
WEBMAKER
WEBMAKING
WEBSTER
WEBSTERITE
WEBWORK
WEBWORM
WECCHE
WECHT
WED
WEDANA
WEDBED
WEDBEDRIP
WEDDED
WEDDEDLY
WEDDEDNESS
WEDDEED
WEDDER
WEDDING
WEDDINGER
WEDE
WEDFEE
WEDGE
WEDGEBILL
WEDGED
WEDGER
WEDGIE
WEDGIER
WEDGIEST
WEDGING
WEDGWOOD
WEDGY
WEDLOCK
WEE
WEEBLE
WEED
WEEDA
WEEDAGE
WEEDED
WEEDER
WEEDERY
WEEDHOOK
WEEDIER
WEEDIEST
WEEDILY
WEEDINESS
WEEDING
WEEDLESS
WEEDS
WEEDY
WEEK
WEEKDAY
WEEKEND
WEEKENDER
WEEKLIES
WEEKLONG
WEEKLY
WEEKS
WEEKWAM
WEEL
WEELFARD
WEEM
WEEN
WEENIE
WEENIER
WEENIEST
WEENING
WEENONG
WEENSY
WEENT
WEENTY
WEENY
WEEP
WEEPER
WEEPERED
WEEPIER
WEEPIEST
WEEPING
WEEPLY
WEEPS
WEEPY
WEER
WEERISH
WEESHEE
WEESHY
WEEST
WEET
WEETBIRD
WEETLESS
WEETY
WEEVER
WEEVIL
WEEVILED
WEEVILLED
WEEVILLY
WEEVILY
WEEWAW
WEEWOW
WEEZE
WEEZLE
WEFT
WEFTAGE
WEFTED
WEFTWISE
WEFTY
WEGENERIAN
WEGOTISM
WEHRLITE
WEIBYEITE
WEICHSELWOOD
WEID
WEIGELA
WEIGELITE
WEIGH
WEIGHAGE
WEIGHBAR
WEIGHBAUK
WEIGHBRIDGE
WEIGHED
WEIGHER
WEIGHHOUSE
WEIGHIN
WEIGHING
WEIGHLOCK
WEIGHMAN
WEIGHMASTER
WEIGHMEN
WEIGHSHAFT
WEIGHT
WEIGHTCHASER
WEIGHTED
WEIGHTEDLY
WEIGHTEDNESS
WEIGHTER
WEIGHTIER
WEIGHTIEST
WEIGHTILY
WEIGHTINESS
WEIGHTING
WEIGHTLESS
WEIGHTLESSLY
WEIGHTOMETER
WEIGHTS
WEIGHTY
WEIHE
WEILANG
WEIN
WEIR
WEIRD
WEIRDFUL
WEIRDIE
WEIRDIES
WEIRDLESS
WEIRDLINESS
WEIRDLY
WEIRDNESS
WEIRDSOME
WEIRDWOMAN
WEIRDWOMEN
WEIRING
WEISBACHITE
WEISE
WEISSITE
WEIZE
WEJACK
WEKA
WEKAU
WEKEEN
WEKI
WEL
WELCH
WELCHER
WELCOME
WELCOMED
WELCOMELY
WELCOMENESS
WELCOMER
WELCOMING
WELCOMINGLY
WELD
WELDABILITY
WELDABLE
WELDED
WELDER
WELDING
WELE
WELFARE
WELFARING
WELI
WELK
WELKIN
WELL
WELLADAY
WELLAT
WELLAWAY
WELLBORN
WELLCURB
WELLED
WELLER
WELLHEAD
WELLHOLE
WELLING
WELLINGTON
WELLISH
WELLMAKER
WELLMAKING
WELLMAN
WELLMEN
WELLMOST
WELLNEAR
WELLQUEME
WELLRING
WELLS
WELLSIDE
WELLSITE
WELLSPRING
WELLSTEAD
WELLSTRAND
WELLY
WELLYARD
WELME
WELOO
WELS
WELSH
WELSHED
WELSHER
WELSHING
WELSIUM
WELSOM
WELT
WELTED
WELTER
WELTERED
WELTERING
WELTERWEIGHT
WELTING
WELY
WEM
WEME
WEMLESS
WEMMY
WEMOD
WEMODNESS
WEN
WENCH
WENCHED
WENCHEL
WENCHER
WENCHING
WEND
WENDE
WENDED
WENDIGO
WENDIGOS
WENDING
WENE
WENETH
WENLICHE
WENNEBERGITE
WENNISH
WENNY
WENRO
WENT
WENTLE
WENTLETRAP
WENZEL
WEPMAN
WEPMANKIN
WEPT

WER
WERD
WERE
WEREBEAR
WERECALF
WERED
WEREFOLK
WEREFOX
WEREGILD
WEREHYENA
WEREJAGUAR
WERELEOPARD
WERETIGER
WEREWALL
WEREWOLF
WEREWOLFISH
WEREWOLFISM
WEREWOLVES
WERF
WERGELD
WERGELT
WERGILD
WERI
WERING
WERK
WERMETHE
WERN
WERNARD
WERNE
WERNERITE
WEROOLE
WEROWANCE
WERP
WERSE
WERSH
WERSLETE
WERT
WERTE
WESKIT
WESSEL
WESSELTON
WEST
WESTAWAY
WESTBOUND
WESTE
WESTEN
WESTER
WESTERING
WESTERLIES
WESTERLINESS
WESTERLING
WESTERLY
WESTERN
WESTERNER
WESTERNISM
WESTERNIZE
WESTERNIZED
WESTERNIZING
WESTERNMOST
WESTERWARDS
WESTFALITE
WESTING
WESTLAN
WESTLAND
WESTLANDWAYS
WESTLINS
WESTME
WESTMELESS
WESTMOST
WESTNESS
WESTWARD
WESTWARDLY
WESTWARDS
WESTY
WET
WETA
WETBACK
WETBIRD
WETE
WETHE
WETHER
WETHERHOG
WETHERTEG
WETLANDS
WETLY
WETNESS
WETTABILITY
WETTABLE
WETTED
WETTER
WETTEST
WETTING
WETTISH
WEVE
WEVED
WEVET
WEY
WEYNE
WHA
WHAAP
WHABBY
WHACK
WHACKED
WHACKER
WHACKING
WHACKY
WHADDIE
WHALE
WHALEBACK
WHALEBIRD
WHALEBOAT
WHALEBONE
WHALEBONED
WHALED
WHALEHEAD
WHALELIKE
WHALEMAN
WHALEMEN
WHALER
WHALERIES
WHALEROAD
WHALERS
WHALERY
WHALES
WHALESHIP
WHALING
WHALISH
WHALL
WHALLY
WHALM
WHALY
WHAM
WHAMBLE
WHAME
WHAMMED
WHAMMIES
WHAMMING
WHAMMY
WHAMP
WHAMPLE
WHANG
WHANGAM
WHANGDOODLE
WHANGEE
WHANK
WHAP
WHAPPER
WHAPPET
WHAPPING
WHAPUKA
WHAPUKEE
WHAPUKU
WHAR
WHARE
WHARF
WHARFAGE
WHARFED
WHARFHEAD
WHARFHOLDER
WHARFIE
WHARFING
WHARFINGER
WHARFLAND
WHARFMAN
WHARFMASTER
WHARFMEN
WHARFRAE
WHARFS
WHARFSIDE
WHARL
WHARP
WHARROW
WHART
WHARVE
WHARVES
WHAT
WHATA
WHATABOUTS
WHATE
WHATEVER
WHATKIN
WHATLIKE
WHATMAN
WHATNESS
WHATNOT
WHATRECK
WHATSO
WHATSOEVER
WHATTEN
WHAU
WHAUP
WHAUVE
WHAWL
WHEAL
WHEALED
WHEALING
WHEALWORM
WHEAM
WHEAT
WHEATBIRD
WHEATEAR
WHEATEARED
WHEATEN
WHEATGRASS
WHEATGROWER
WHEATLAND
WHEATLIKE
WHEATWORM
WHEATY
WHEE
WHEEDLE
WHEEDLED
WHEEDLER
WHEEDLING
WHEEDLINGLY
WHEEL
WHEELAGE
WHEELBAND
WHEELBARROW
WHEELBASE
WHEELBIRD
WHEELBOX
WHEELCHAIR
WHEELED
WHEELER
WHEELERY
WHEELHOUSE
WHEELING
WHEELINGLY
WHEELLESS
WHEELMAKER
WHEELMAKING
WHEELMAN
WHEELMEN
WHEELRACE
WHEELROAD
WHEELS
WHEELSMAN
WHEELSMEN
WHEELSMITH
WHEELSPIN
WHEELWAY
WHEELWORK
WHEELWRIGHT
WHEELY
WHEEN
WHEENCAT
WHEEP
WHEEPLE
WHEEPLED
WHEEPLING
WHEERIKINS
WHEESHT
WHEETLE
WHEEZE
WHEEZED
WHEEZER
WHEEZIER
WHEEZIEST
WHEEZILY
WHEEZINESS
WHEEZING
WHEEZINGLY
WHEEZLE
WHEEZY
WHEFT
WHEKAU
WHEKI
WHELK
WHELKED
WHELKER
WHELKIER
WHELKIEST
WHELKY
WHELM
WHELMED
WHELMING
WHELP
WHELPED
WHELPING
WHELPLESS
WHELPLING
WHELVE
WHEMMEL
WHEMMLE
WHEN
WHENABOUTS
WHENAS
WHENCE
WHENCEFORTH
WHENCESOEVER
WHENCEVER
WHENEVER
WHENNESS
WHENSO
WHENSOEVER
WHENSOMEVER
WHERE
WHEREABOUT
WHEREABOUTS
WHEREAFTER
WHEREANENT
WHEREAS
WHEREASES
WHEREAT
WHEREAWAY
WHEREBY
WHEREFOR
WHEREFORE
WHEREFORTH
WHEREFROM
WHEREHENCE
WHEREIN
WHEREINTO
WHERENESS
WHEREOF
WHEREON
WHEREOUT
WHEREOVER
WHERESO
WHERESOEVER
WHERESOMEVER
WHERETHROUGH
WHERETILL
WHERETO
WHERETOEVER
WHEREUNDER
WHEREUNTIL
WHEREUNTO
WHEREUP
WHEREUPON
WHEREVER
WHEREWITH
WHEREWITHAL
WHERRET
WHERRIED
WHERRIES
WHERRIT
WHERRY
WHERRYING
WHERRYMAN
WHERVE
WHET
WHETHER
WHETILE
WHETROCK
WHETSTONE
WHETTED
WHETTER
WHETTING
WHEW
WHEWELLITE
WHEWER
WHEWL
WHEWT
WHEY
WHEYBEARD
WHEYBIRD
WHEYEY
WHEYEYNESS
WHEYFACE
WHEYFACED
WHEYISH
WHEYISNESS
WHEYNESS
WHEYWORM
WHEYWORMED
WHI
WHIBA
WHICH
WHICHEVER
WHICHSOEVER
WHICHWAY
WHICHWAYS
WHICK
WHICKER
WHID
WHIDAH
WHIFF
WHIFFED
WHIFFER
WHIFFET
WHIFFING
WHIFFLE
WHIFFLED

WHIFFLER
WHIFFLERIES
WHIFFLERY
WHIFFLETREE
WHIFFLING
WHIFFLINGLY
WHIFFY
WHIFT
WHIG
WHIGMALEERIE
WHIGMALEERY
WHIGMELEERIE
WHILE
WHILEAS
WHILEEN
WHILEND
WHILES
WHILEY
WHILIE
WHILK
WHILLABALLOO
WHILLALOO
WHILLILEW
WHILLY
WHILLYWHA
WHILOCK
WHILOM
WHILST
WHILTER
WHIM
WHIMBREL
WHIMLING
WHIMMED
WHIMMIER
WHIMMIEST
WHIMMING
WHIMMY
WHIMPER
WHIMPERED
WHIMPERER
WHIMPERING
WHIMPERINGLY
WHIMSEY
WHIMSEYS
WHIMSIC
WHIMSICAL
WHIMSICALITY
WHIMSICALLY
WHIMSIED
WHIMSIES
WHIMSY
WHIMWHAM
WHIN
WHINBERRIES
WHINBERRY
WHINCHACKER
WHINCHAT
WHINCHECK
WHINCOW
WHINDLE
WHINE
WHINED
WHINER
WHINESTONE
WHING
WHINGE
WHINGER
WHINING
WHININGLY
WHINNEL
WHINNER
WHINNIED
WHINNIES
WHINNOCK
WHINNY
WHINNYING
WHINSTONE
WHINY
WHINYARD
WHIP
WHIPBELLY
WHIPBIRD
WHIPCAT
WHIPCORD
WHIPCORDY
WHIPCRACK
WHIPCRACKER
WHIPCRAFT
WHIPGRAFT
WHIPJACK
WHIPKING
WHIPLASH
WHIPMAKER
WHIPMAKING
WHIPMAN
WHIPMANSHIP
WHIPMASTER
WHIPPA
WHIPPABLE
WHIPPAREE
WHIPPED
WHIPPER
WHIPPERGINNY
WHIPPERSNAPPER
WHIPPERTAIL
WHIPPET
WHIPPETER
WHIPPING
WHIPPINGLY
WHIPPLETREE
WHIPPOORWILL
WHIPPOST
WHIPPY
WHIPS
WHIPSAW
WHIPSAWED
WHIPSAWING
WHIPSAWN
WHIPSAWYER
WHIPSOCKET
WHIPSTAFF
WHIPSTALK
WHIPSTALL
WHIPSTER
WHIPSTICK
WHIPSTITCH
WHIPSTOCK
WHIPT
WHIPTAIL
WHIPTREE
WHIPWORM
WHIR
WHIRL
WHIRLABOUT
WHIRLBAT
WHIRLBLAST
WHIRLBONE
WHIRLBRAIN
WHIRLED
WHIRLER
WHIRLGIG
WHIRLICANE
WHIRLICOTE
WHIRLIGIG
WHIRLING
WHIRLPOOL
WHIRLPUFF
WHIRLS
WHIRLWIG
WHIRLWIND
WHIRLWINDISH
WHIRLWINDY
WHIRLY
WHIRLYBIRD
WHIRR
WHIRRED
WHIRREY
WHIRRICK
WHIRRIED
WHIRRING
WHIRRY
WHIRRYING
WHIRTLE
WHISH
WHISHT
WHISK
WHISKBROOM
WHISKED
WHISKER
WHISKERAGE
WHISKERANDO
WHISKERANDOS
WHISKERED
WHISKERER
WHISKERS
WHISKERY
WHISKET
WHISKEY
WHISKEYS
WHISKIED
WHISKIES
WHISKIFIED
WHISKIN
WHISKING
WHISKINGLY
WHISKY
WHISP
WHISPER
WHISPERATION
WHISPERED
WHISPERER
WHISPERING
WHISPERINGLY
WHISPEROUS
WHISPEROUSLY
WHISPERY
WHISS
WHIST
WHISTER
WHISTERPOOP
WHISTLE
WHISTLEBELLY
WHISTLED
WHISTLEFISH
WHISTLEFISHES
WHISTLER
WHISTLERISM
WHISTLEWING
WHISTLEWOOD
WHISTLING
WHISTLINGLY
WHIT
WHITBLOW
WHITE
WHITEBAIT
WHITEBARK
WHITEBEAM
WHITEBEARD
WHITEBELLY
WHITEBERRY
WHITEBILL
WHITEBLAZE
WHITEBLOW
WHITEBOY
WHITECAP
WHITECAPPER
WHITECOAT
WHITECOMB
WHITECORN
WHITECUP
WHITED
WHITEFACE
WHITEFEET
WHITEFISH
WHITEFISHER
WHITEFISHERY
WHITEFISHES
WHITEFLY
WHITEFOOT
WHITEFOOTISM
WHITEHANDED
WHITEHASS
WHITEHAWSE
WHITEHEAD
WHITEHEARTED
WHITELIKE
WHITELY
WHITEN
WHITENED
WHITENER
WHITENESS
WHITENING
WHITENOSE
WHITEOUT
WHITEPOT
WHITER
WHITEROOT
WHITERUMP
WHITES
WHITESARK
WHITESHANK
WHITESIDE
WHITESMITH
WHITEST
WHITESTONE
WHITESTRAITS
WHITETAIL
WHITETHORN
WHITETHROAT
WHITETIP
WHITETOP
WHITEVEIN
WHITEVEINS
WHITEWALL
WHITEWARE
WHITEWASH
WHITEWASHED
WHITEWASHER
WHITEWASHING
WHITEWEED
WHITEWING
WHITEWOOD
WHITEWORT
WHITEY
WHITHER
WHITHERWARD
WHITHERWARDS
WHITING
WHITINGS
WHITISH
WHITISHNESS
WHITLEATHER
WHITLING
WHITLOW
WHITLOWWORT
WHITNEY
WHITNEYITE
WHITRACK
WHITS
WHITSTER
WHITTAW
WHITTAWER
WHITTEN
WHITTER
WHITTERICK
WHITTLE
WHITTLED
WHITTLER
WHITTLING
WHITTLINGS
WHITTRET
WHITY
WHIZ
WHIZBANG
WHIZGIG
WHIZZ
WHIZZED
WHIZZER
WHIZZERMAN
WHIZZES
WHIZZING
WHIZZINGLY
WHIZZLE
WHO
WHOA
WHODUNIT
WHOEVER
WHOLE
WHOLEHEARTED
WHOLENESS
WHOLESALE
WHOLESALED
WHOLESALER
WHOLESALING
WHOLESOME
WHOLESOMELY
WHOLESOMER
WHOLESOMEST
WHOLEWISE
WHOLLY
WHOM
WHOMP
WHOMSO
WHOMSOEVER
WHON
WHONE
WHOO
WHOOF
WHOOP
WHOOPE
WHOOPED
WHOOPEE
WHOOPER
WHOOPING
WHOOPINGLY
WHOOSH
WHOOT
WHOP
WHOPPED
WHOPPER
WHOPPING
WHORAGE
WHORE
WHORED
WHOREDOM
WHOREHOUSE
WHOREMASTER
WHOREMASTERY
WHOREMONGER
WHOREMONGING
WHORESON
WHORING
WHORISH
WHORISHLY
WHORISHNESS
WHORL
WHORLE
WHORLED
WHORLFLOWER
WHORLY
WHORLYWORT
WHORRY
WHORT
WHORTLE
WHORTLEBERRY

WHOSE
WHOSESOEVER
WHOSO
WHOSOEVER
WHUD
WHUFF
WHUFFLE
WHULE
WHULTER
WHUMP
WHUP
WHURL
WHUSH
WHUTE
WHUTTER
WHUTTERING
WHY
WHYDAH
WHYEVER
WHYFOR
WHYO
WIBBLE
WICH
WICHTISITE
WICHTJE
WICK
WICKAWEE
WICKED
WICKEDLY
WICKEDNESS
WICKEN
WICKER
WICKERWARE
WICKERWORK
WICKERWORKED
WICKERWORKER
WICKET
WICKETKEEPER
WICKETS
WICKING
WICKIUP
WICKY
WICOPIES
WICOPY
WID
WIDBIN
WIDDERSHINS
WIDDIES
WIDDIFOW
WIDDLE
WIDDLED
WIDDLING
WIDDRIM
WIDDY
WIDE
WIDEGAB
WIDEGAP
WIDEHEARTED
WIDELY
WIDEMOUTHED
WIDEN
WIDENED
WIDENER
WIDENESS
WIDENING
WIDER
WIDERSHINS
WIDESPREAD
WIDESPREADLY
WIDEST
WIDEWHERE
WIDEWORK
WIDGE
WIDGEON
WIDGEONS
WIDGET
WIDOW
WIDOWED
WIDOWER
WIDOWERED
WIDOWERY
WIDOWHOOD
WIDOWLY
WIDOWMAN
WIDOWMEN
WIDOWY
WIDTH
WIDTHLESS
WIDTHWAY
WIDTHWAYS
WIDTHWISE
WIDU
WIEL
WIELARE
WIELD
WIELDED
WIELDER
WIELDING
WIELDY
WIENER
WIENERWURST
WIENIE
WIES
WIFE
WIFECARL
WIFED
WIFEHOOD
WIFELESS
WIFELESSNESS
WIFELIER
WIFELIEST
WIFELY
WIFETHING
WIFEWARD
WIFING
WIFLE
WIFT
WIG
WIGAN
WIGELING
WIGEON
WIGG
WIGGED
WIGGEN
WIGGER
WIGGERIES
WIGGERY
WIGGING
WIGGISM
WIGGLE
WIGGLER
WIGGLY
WIGGY
WIGHER
WIGHT
WIGHTLY
WIGHTNESS
WIGMAKER
WIGMAKING
WIGTAIL
WIGWAG
WIGWAGGED
WIGWAGGER
WIGWAGGING
WIGWAM
WIIKITE
WIKE
WIKEN
WIKING
WIKIUP
WIKIWIKI
WILCWEME
WILD
WILDBORE
WILDCAT
WILDCATS
WILDCATTED
WILDCATTER
WILDCATTING
WILDE
WILDEBEEST
WILDED
WILDER
WILDERED
WILDERING
WILDERMENT
WILDERN
WILDERNESS
WILDEST
WILDFIRE
WILDFLOWER
WILDFOWL
WILDFOWLS
WILDGRAVE
WILDING
WILDISH
WILDISHLY
WILDISHNESS
WILDLIFE
WILDLING
WILDLY
WILDNESS
WILDWIND
WILDWOOD
WILE
WILED
WILFUL
WILFULLY
WILFULNESS
WILGA
WILGERS
WILIER
WILIEST
WILILY
WILINESS
WILING
WILIWILI
WILK
WILKEITE
WILL
WILLABLE
WILLAWA
WILLE
WILLED
WILLEDNESS
WILLEMITE
WILLER
WILLES
WILLET
WILLETS
WILLEY
WILLFUL
WILLFULLY
WILLFULNESS
WILLIAMSITE
WILLICHE
WILLIED
WILLIER
WILLIES
WILLIEWAUCHT
WILLING
WILLINGHOOD
WILLINGLY
WILLINGNESS
WILLIWAW
WILLMAKER
WILLMAKING
WILLNESS
WILLOCK
WILLOW
WILLOWBITER
WILLOWED
WILLOWER
WILLOWISH
WILLOWLIKE
WILLOWWARE
WILLOWWEED
WILLOWWORM
WILLOWWORT
WILLOWY
WILLY
WILLYARD
WILLYART
WILLYER
WILLYING
WILN
WILNE
WILNING
WILRONE
WILROUN
WILSOME
WILSOMELY
WILSOMENESS
WILT
WILTED
WILTER
WILTING
WILY
WILYCOAT
WIM
WIMBLE
WIMBLED
WIMBLING
WIMICK
WIMLUNGE
WIMPLE
WIMPLED
WIMPLER
WIMPLING
WIN
WINARE
WINBROW
WINCE
WINCED
WINCER
WINCEY
WINCH
WINCHER
WINCHMAN
WINCHMEN
WINCING
WINCOPIPE
WIND
WINDABLE
WINDAGE
WINDAS
WINDBAG
WINDBAGGED
WINDBAGGERY
WINDBALL
WINDBERRY
WINDBIBBER
WINDBRACING
WINDBREAK
WINDBREAKER
WINDBROACH
WINDBURN
WINDBURNED
WINDBURNT
WINDCLOTHES
WINDCUFFER
WINDDOG
WINDED
WINDEDLY
WINDEDNESS
WINDEL
WINDER
WINDFALL
WINDFALLEN
WINDFANNER
WINDFIRM
WINDFISH
WINDFISHES
WINDFLAW
WINDFLOWER
WINDGALL
WINDGALLED
WINDHOLE
WINDHOVER
WINDIER
WINDIEST
WINDIGO
WINDIGOS
WINDILL
WINDILY
WINDINESS
WINDING
WINDINGLY
WINDINGNESS
WINDJAM
WINDJAMMER
WINDJAMMING
WINDLASS
WINDLASSED
WINDLASSER
WINDLASSING
WINDLE
WINDLES
WINDLESS
WINDLESTRAE
WINDLESTRAW
WINDLIN
WINDLING
WINDMILL
WINDMILLY
WINDORE
WINDOW
WINDOWED
WINDOWING
WINDOWLIKE
WINDOWMAKER
WINDOWMAKING
WINDOWMAN
WINDOWPANE
WINDOWPEEPER
WINDOWS
WINDOWSILL
WINDOWY
WINDPIPE
WINDPROOF
WINDRING
WINDROAD
WINDROOT
WINDROW
WINDROWED
WINDROWER
WINDROWING
WINDS
WINDSAIL
WINDSCREEN
WINDSHAKE
WINDSHIELD
WINDSHOCK
WINDSLAB
WINDSOCK
WINDSORITE
WINDSTORM
WINDSUCKER
WINDTIGHT
WINDUP
WINDWARD
WINDWARDLY
WINDWARDNESS
WINDWAY
WINDWAYWARD

WINDY
WINE
WINEBALL
WINEBERRIES
WINEBERRY
WINEBIBBER
WINEBIBBERY
WINEBIBBING
WINECONNER
WINED
WINEDRAF
WINEGLASS
WINEGLASSFUL
WINEGLASSFULS
WINEGROWER
WINEGROWING
WINEHOUSE
WINELIKE
WINEMAY
WINEPOT
WINEPRESS
WINEPRESSER
WINER
WINERIES
WINERY
WINES
WINESHOP
WINESKIN
WINESOP
WINETASTER
WINETREE
WINEVAT
WINEYARD
WINFREE
WING
WINGBACK
WINGBEAT
WINGBOW
WINGCUT
WINGDING
WINGED
WINGER
WINGFISH
WINGFISHES
WINGHANDED
WINGIER
WINGIEST
WINGING
WINGLE
WINGLESS
WINGLESSNESS
WINGLET
WINGLIKE
WINGMAN
WINGMANSHIP
WINGOVER
WINGPIECE
WINGPOST
WINGS
WINGSEED
WINGSPREAD
WINGSTEM
WINGY
WINIER
WINIEST
WINISH
WINK
WINKED
WINKEL
WINKELMAN
WINKER
WINKERED
WINKERS
WINKING
WINKINGLY
WINKLE
WINKLEHAWK
WINKLEHOLE
WINKLOT
WINLY
WINNA
WINNABLE
WINNARD
WINNEL
WINNER
WINNING
WINNINGLY
WINNINGNESS
WINNINISH
WINNLE
WINNOCK
WINNONISH
WINNOW
WINNOWED
WINNOWER
WINNOWING
WINOES
WINOS
WINSOME
WINSOMELY
WINSOMENESS
WINSOMER
WINSOMEST
WINSTER
WINTER
WINTERBERRY
WINTERBLOOM
WINTERBOURNE
WINTERDYKES
WINTERED
WINTERER
WINTERFEED
WINTERGREEN
WINTERHAIN
WINTERING
WINTERIZE
WINTERIZED
WINTERIZING
WINTERKILL
WINTERKILLED
WINTERLESS
WINTERLIKE
WINTERLINESS
WINTERLY
WINTERTIDE
WINTERTIME
WINTERWEED
WINTERY
WINTLE
WINTRIER
WINTRIEST
WINTRIFY
WINTRILY
WINTRINESS
WINTRY
WINY
WINZE
WINZEMAN
WINZEMEN
WIO
WIP
WIPE
WIPED
WIPER
WIPING
WIPPEN
WIR
WIRABLE
WIRBLE
WIRE
WIREBAR
WIREBIRD
WIRED
WIREDANCER
WIREDANCING
WIREDRAW
WIREDRAWER
WIREDRAWING
WIREDRAWN
WIREDREW
WIREGRASS
WIREHAIR
WIRELESS
WIRELESSLY
WIRELESSNESS
WIREMAKER
WIREMAKING
WIREMAN
WIREMEN
WIREMONGER
WIREPHOTO
WIREPULL
WIREPULLER
WIREPULLING
WIRER
WIRES
WIRESMITH
WIRESPUN
WIRESTITCHED
WIRETAIL
WIRETAP
WIRETAPPED
WIRETAPPER
WIRETAPPING
WIREWALKER
WIREWAY
WIREWEED
WIREWORK
WIREWORKER
WIREWORKING
WIREWORKS
WIREWORM
WIRIER
WIRIEST
WIRILY
WIRINESS
WIRING
WIRL
WIRLING
WIRR
WIRRA
WIRRAH
WIRRASTHRU
WIRTH
WIRY
WIS
WISDOM
WISE
WISEACRE
WISEACRED
WISECRACK
WISECRACKER
WISECRACKERY
WISEHEAD
WISEHEARTED
WISEHEIMER
WISELIER
WISELIEST
WISELIKE
WISELING
WISELY
WISEMAN
WISEN
WISENESS
WISENHEIMER
WISENT
WISER
WISEST
WISEWEED
WISEWOMAN
WISEWOMEN
WISH
WISHA
WISHBONE
WISHED
WISHEDLY
WISHER
WISHFUL
WISHFULLY
WISHFULNESS
WISHING
WISHINGLY
WISHLY
WISHMAY
WISHNESS
WISHT
WISHTONWISH
WISKET
WISKINKIE
WISKINKY
WISMUTH
WISP
WISPED
WISPIER
WISPIEST
WISPING
WISPISH
WISPY
WISS
WISSE
WISSEL
WISSHE
WISSING
WISSLE
WIST
WISTED
WISTENED
WISTER
WISTERIA
WISTFUL
WISTFULLY
WISTFULNESS
WISTING
WISTIT
WISTITI
WISTLESS
WISTLESSNESS
WISURE
WIT
WITAN
WITCH
WITCHBELLS
WITCHBROOM
WITCHCRAFT
WITCHED
WITCHEDLY
WITCHEN
WITCHERCULLY
WITCHERIES
WITCHERING
WITCHERY
WITCHET
WITCHETTY
WITCHGRASS
WITCHING
WITCHINGLY
WITCHLEAF
WITCHMAN
WITCHMONGER
WITCHUCK
WITCHWEED
WITCHWIFE
WITCHWOMAN
WITCHWOOD
WITCHWORK
WITCHY
WITCRAFT
WITE
WITELESS
WITENAGEMOT
WITENAGEMOTE
WITEPENNY
WITESS
WITFUL
WITH
WITHAL
WITHAM
WITHAMITE
WITHBEG
WITHCALL
WITHDRAUGHT
WITHDRAW
WITHDRAWAL
WITHDRAWER
WITHDRAWING
WITHDRAWMENT
WITHDRAWN
WITHDREW
WITHE
WITHED
WITHEN
WITHER
WITHERBAND
WITHERBLENCH
WITHERCRAFT
WITHERDEED
WITHERED
WITHEREDLY
WITHEREDNESS
WITHERER
WITHERING
WITHERINGLY
WITHERITE
WITHERLING
WITHERLY
WITHERNAM
WITHERS
WITHERSHINS
WITHERTIP
WITHERWEIGHT
WITHERY
WITHGANG
WITHGATE
WITHHELD
WITHHELE
WITHHIE
WITHHOLD
WITHHOLDAL
WITHHOLDEN
WITHHOLDER
WITHHOLDING
WITHHOLDMENT
WITHIES
WITHIN
WITHINDOORS
WITHINFORTH
WITHING
WITHINWARD
WITHINWARDS
WITHNAY
WITHNESS
WITHNIM
WITHOUT
WITHOUTDOORS
WITHOUTEN
WITHOUTFORTH
WITHOUTSIDE
WITHOUTWARDS
WITHSAVE
WITHSAW
WITHSAY
WITHSAYER
WITHSET
WITHSLIP
WITHSPAR

WITHSTAND
WITHSTANDER
WITHSTANDING
WITHSTAY
WITHSTOOD
WITHSTRAIN
WITHTAKE
WITHTEE
WITHTURN
WITHVINE
WITHY
WITHYPOT
WITHYWIND
WITIE
WITJAR
WITLESS
WITLESSLY
WITLESSNESS
WITLET
WITLING
WITLOOF
WITLOSEN
WITMONGER
WITNESS
WITNESSED
WITNESSER
WITNESSING
WITNEY
WITNEYER
WITS
WITSAFE
WITSHIP
WITTALL
WITTED
WITTEN
WITTER
WITTERING
WITTERLY
WITTERNESS
WITTICASTER
WITTICHENITE
WITTICISM
WITTICIZE
WITTIER
WITTIEST
WITTIFIED
WITTILY
WITTINESS
WITTING
WITTINGLY
WITTOL
WITTOME
WITTY
WITWALL
WITWANTON
WITWORD
WITWORM
WITZCHOURA
WIVE
WIVED
WIVER
WIVERN
WIVES
WIVING
WIWI
WIZ
WIZARD
WIZARDLY
WIZARDRY
WIZEN
WIZENED
WIZENEDNESS
WIZZEN
WLACH
WLAFF
WLANK
WLATE
WLATFUL
WLATSOME
WLECCHE
WLECH
WLENCH
WLITE
WLITY
WLO
WLOKA
WLONK
WLONKHEDE
WO
WOAD
WOADED
WOADER
WOADMAN
WOADWAXEN
WOALD
WOB
WOBBEGONG
WOBBLE
WOBBLED
WOBBLER
WOBBLIES
WOBBLINESS
WOBBLING
WOBBLINGLY
WOBBLY
WOBEGONE
WOBEGONENESS
WOBEGONISH
WOBSTER
WOCAS
WOCHEINITE
WOD
WODE
WODELEIE
WODGE
WODGY
WOE
WOEBEGONE
WOEBEGONISH
WOEFARE
WOEFUL
WOEFULLY
WOEFULNESS
WOEHLERITE
WOESOME
WOEVINE
WOEWORN
WOFFLER
WOFUL
WOFULLY
WOFULNESS
WOG
WOGE
WOGGLE
WOGH
WOGHE
WOGHNESS
WOGIET
WOHLAC
WOHLERITE
WOIBE
WOID
WOIDRE
WOIK
WOILIE
WOK
WOKAS
WOKE
WOKEN
WOKIE
WOKOWI
WOLD
WOLDES
WOLDSMAN
WOLDY
WOLE
WOLEAI
WOLF
WOLFACHITE
WOLFBERRIES
WOLFBERRY
WOLFED
WOLFEN
WOLFER
WOLFFISH
WOLFHOUND
WOLFING
WOLFISH
WOLFISHLY
WOLFISHNESS
WOLFKIN
WOLFLIKE
WOLFLING
WOLFRAM
WOLFRAMITE
WOLFRAMIUM
WOLFSBANE
WOLFSBERGITE
WOLFSKIN
WOLLASTONITE
WOLLOCK
WOLLOMAI
WOLVE
WOLVEBOON
WOLVER
WOLVERENE
WOLVERINE
WOLVERINES
WOLVES
WOMAN
WOMANBODIES
WOMANBODY
WOMANED
WOMANFOLK
WOMANFULLY
WOMANHEAD
WOMANHEARTED
WOMANHOOD
WOMANHOUSE
WOMANING
WOMANISH
WOMANISHLY
WOMANISM
WOMANIST
WOMANITY
WOMANIZE
WOMANIZED
WOMANIZER
WOMANIZING
WOMANKIND
WOMANLIER
WOMANLIEST
WOMANLIKE
WOMANLINESS
WOMANLY
WOMANMUCKLE
WOMANPOST
WOMB
WOMBAT
WOMBED
WOMBSIDE
WOMBSTONE
WOMBY
WOMEN
WOMENFOLK
WOMENFOLKS
WOMERA
WOMERAH
WOMMALA
WOMMERA
WOMMERAH
WOMP
WOMPLIT
WON
WOND
WONDE
WONDER
WONDERBERRY
WONDERDEED
WONDERED
WONDERER
WONDERFUL
WONDERFULLER
WONDERFULLY
WONDERING
WONDERINGLY
WONDERLAND
WONDERMENT
WONDERSMITH
WONDERSOME
WONDERWORK
WONDERWORTHY
WONDIE
WONDROUS
WONDROUSLY
WONDROUSNESS
WONE
WONG
WONGA
WONGAH
WONGSHY
WONGSKY
WONING
WONKIER
WONKIEST
WONKY
WONNA
WONNED
WONNER
WONNING
WONNOT
WONT
WONTED
WONTEDLY
WONTEDNESS
WONTING
WONTLESS
WOO
WOOABLE
WOOD
WOODBARK
WOODBIN
WOODBIND
WOODBINE
WOODBINED
WOODBLOCK
WOODBORER
WOODBOUND
WOODBUSH
WOODCARVER
WOODCARVING
WOODCHAT
WOODCHUCK
WOODCOCK
WOODCOCKIZE
WOODCOCKS
WOODCRACKER
WOODCRAFT
WOODCRAFTER
WOODCRAFTY
WOODCUT
WOODCUTTER
WOODCUTTING
WOODED
WOODEN
WOODENDITE
WOODENHEAD
WOODENHEADED
WOODENLY
WOODENNESS
WOODENWARE
WOODENWEARY
WOODFALL
WOODFISH
WOODGELD
WOODGRUB
WOODHACK
WOODHACKER
WOODHEN
WOODHEWER
WOODHOLE
WOODHORSE
WOODHOUSE
WOODHUNG
WOODIE
WOODIER
WOODIEST
WOODINE
WOODINESS
WOODING
WOODISH
WOODJOBBER
WOODKERN
WOODKNACKER
WOODLAND
WOODLANDER
WOODLARK
WOODLESS
WOODLIND
WOODLOCKED
WOODMAID
WOODMAN
WOODMANCRAFT
WOODMANSHIP
WOODMEN
WOODMONGER
WOODMOTE
WOODNESS
WOODNOTE
WOODPECK
WOODPECKER
WOODPECKERS
WOODPENNY
WOODPILE
WOODPRINT
WOODREED
WOODREEVE
WOODRICK
WOODRIME
WOODRIS
WOODROCK
WOODROW
WOODRUFF
WOODS
WOODSCREW
WOODSERE
WOODSHED
WOODSHIP
WOODSHOP
WOODSIDE
WOODSIER
WOODSIEST
WOODSILVER
WOODSKIN
WOODSMAN
WOODSMEN
WOODSPITE
WOODSTONE
WOODSY
WOODTURNER
WOODTURNING
WOODWALE
WOODWALL
WOODWARD
WOODWAX

WOODWAXEN
WOODWIND
WOODWINDS
WOODWISE
WOODWORK
WOODWORKER
WOODWORKING
WOODWORM
WOODWOSE
WOODY
WOODYARD
WOOED
WOOER
WOOF
WOOFED
WOOFELL
WOOFER
WOOFY
WOOHOO
WOOING
WOOINGLY
WOOL
WOOLD
WOOLDED
WOOLDER
WOOLDING
WOOLED
WOOLEN
WOOLENET
WOOLENETTE
WOOLENIZE
WOOLER
WOOLERT
WOOLFELL
WOOLGATHERER
WOOLGROWER
WOOLGROWING
WOOLHEAD
WOOLIE
WOOLLED
WOOLLEN
WOOLLENIZE
WOOLLENS
WOOLLIER
WOOLLIES
WOOLLIEST
WOOLLINESS
WOOLLY
WOOLLYHEAD
WOOLLYISH
WOOLMAN
WOOLMEN
WOOLPACK
WOOLPRESS
WOOLSACK
WOOLSEY
WOOLSHEARER
WOOLSHEARING
WOOLSHEARS
WOOLSHED
WOOLSKIN
WOOLSORTER
WOOLSORTING
WOOLSOWER
WOOLSTOCK
WOOLULOSE
WOOLWASHER
WOOLWEED
WOOLWHEEL
WOOLWINDER
WOOLWORK
WOOLWORKER
WOOLWORKING
WOOLY
WOOM
WOOMERA
WOOMERAH
WOOMERANG
WOON
WOONE
WOONS
WOORALI
WOORARI
WOOSH
WOOSTER
WOOT
WOOTZ
WOOZIER
WOOZIEST
WOOZILY
WOOZINESS
WOOZLE
WOOZY
WOP
WOPPISH
WOPS
WOPSE
WOPSY
WOPY
WORBLE
WORCESTER
WORD
WORDABLE
WORDABLY
WORDAGE
WORDBOOK
WORDBUILDING
WORDCRAFT
WORDED
WORDER
WORDIER
WORDIEST
WORDILY
WORDINESS
WORDING
WORDISH
WORDISHLY
WORDISHNESS
WORDLE
WORDLESS
WORDLESSLY
WORDLESSNESS
WORDLIER
WORDLORIST
WORDMAKER
WORDMAKING
WORDMAN
WORDMANSHIP
WORDMEN
WORDMONGER
WORDMONGERY
WORDNESS
WORDPLAY
WORDS
WORDSMAN
WORDSMANSHIP
WORDSMEN
WORDSMITH
WORDSPITE
WORDSTER
WORDY
WORE
WORK
WORKABILITY
WORKABLE
WORKABLENESS
WORKADAY
WORKAWAY
WORKBAG
WORKBASKET
WORKBENCH
WORKBOOK
WORKBOX
WORKBRITTLE
WORKDAY
WORKED
WORKER
WORKFELLOW
WORKFOLK
WORKFOLKS
WORKFUL
WORKGIRL
WORKHAND
WORKHORSE
WORKHOUSE
WORKHOUSED
WORKING
WORKINGLY
WORKINGMAN
WORKINGMEN
WORKINGWOMAN
WORKLESS
WORKLESSNESS
WORKLOAD
WORKLOOM
WORKMAN
WORKMANLIKE
WORKMANLY
WORKMANSHIP
WORKMASTER
WORKMEN
WORKOUT
WORKPEOPLE
WORKPIECE
WORKPLACE
WORKROOM
WORKS
WORKSHEET
WORKSHIP
WORKSHOP
WORKSOME
WORKSTAND
WORKTABLE
WORKTIME
WORKWAYS
WORKWISE
WORKWOMAN
WORKWOMANLY
WORKWOMEN
WORKY
WORKYARD
WORLD
WORLDAUGHT
WORLDED
WORLDISH
WORLDLIEST
WORLDLINESS
WORLDLING
WORLDLY
WORLDMAKER
WORLDMAKING
WORLDMAN
WORLDPROOF
WORLDQUAKE
WORLDS
WORLDWAY
WORLDWIDE
WORM
WORMED
WORMER
WORMHOLE
WORMHOLED
WORMIER
WORMIEST
WORMIL
WORMINESS
WORMING
WORMLIKE
WORMLING
WORMROOT
WORMS
WORMSEED
WORMWEED
WORMWOOD
WORMY
WORN
WORNNESS
WORRAL
WORREL
WORRIABLE
WORRICOW
WORRIECOW
WORRIED
WORRIEDLY
WORRIEDNESS
WORRIER
WORRIES
WORRIMENT
WORRISOME
WORRISOMELY
WORRIT
WORRITER
WORRY
WORRYING
WORRYINGLY
WORRYWART
WORSE
WORSEMENT
WORSEN
WORSENED
WORSENESS
WORSENING
WORSER
WORSET
WORSHIP
WORSHIPED
WORSHIPER
WORSHIPERS
WORSHIPFUL
WORSHIPFULLY
WORSHIPING
WORSHIPPED
WORSHIPPER
WORSHIPPING
WORST
WORSTED
WORSTING
WORSUM
WORT
WORTH
WORTHFUL
WORTHIER
WORTHIES
WORTHIEST
WORTHILY
WORTHINESS
WORTHING
WORTHLESS
WORTHLESSLY
WORTHLESSNESS
WORTHWHILE
WORTHY
WORTS
WORTWORM
WORY
WOSBIRD
WOSITH
WOSOME
WOST
WOT
WOTH
WOTLINK
WOTTE
WOU
WOUBIT
WOUGH
WOUHLECHE
WOULD
WOULDEST
WOULDING
WOULDST
WOUND
WOUNDED
WOUNDEDLY
WOUNDER
WOUNDILY
WOUNDING
WOUNDINGLY
WOUNDLESS
WOUNDLY
WOUNDS
WOUNDWORT
WOUNDWORTH
WOUNDY
WOURNIL
WOUSTOUR
WOVE
WOVEN
WOW
WOWENING
WOWER
WOWF
WOWL
WOWSER
WOWSERIAN
WOWSERISH
WOWSERISM
WOWSERY
WOWT
WOX
WOXE
WRABBE
WRABILL
WRACK
WRACKFUL
WRAGER
WRAGGLE
WRAIST
WRAITH
WRAITHE
WRAITHY
WRAKE
WRAKER
WRALL
WRAMP
WRANG
WRANGLE
WRANGLED
WRANGLER
WRANGLESOME
WRANGLING
WRANNOCK
WRANNY
WRAP
WRAPAROUND
WRAPLE
WRAPPAGE
WRAPPED
WRAPPER
WRAPPERER
WRAPPERING
WRAPPING
WRAPRASCAL
WRAPS
WRAPT
WRASE
WRASSE
WRAST
WRASTLE
WRASTLER
WRAT
WRATACK
WRATE
WRATH
WRATHFUL

WRATHFULLY
WRATHFULNESS
WRATHIER
WRATHIEST
WRATHILY
WRATHINESS
WRATHY
WRAW
WRAWL
WRAWLER
WRAXLE
WRAXLED
WRAXLING
WRAY
WRAYFUL
WREAK
WREAKED
WREAKER
WREAKFUL
WREAKING
WREAKLESS
WREATH
WREATHAGE
WREATHE
WREATHED
WREATHEN
WREATHER
WREATHING
WREATHMAKER
WREATHMAKING
WREATHS
WREATHWORK
WREATHWORT
WREATHY
WRECK
WRECKAGE
WRECKED
WRECKER
WRECKFISH
WRECKFISHES
WRECKFUL
WRECKING
WRECKY
WREIL
WRELE
WREN
WRENCH
WRENCHED
WRENCHER
WRENCHING
WRENCHINGLY
WRENLET
WRENTAIL
WREST
WRESTED
WRESTER
WRESTING
WRESTINGLY
WRESTLE
WRESTLED
WRESTLER
WRESTLING
WRETCH
WRETCHED
WRETCHEDLY
WRETCHEDNESS
WRETCHLESS
WRETCHLESSLY
WRETCHOCK
WRIBLE
WRICK
WRIDE
WRIED
WRIEL
WRIER
WRIEST
WRIG
WRIGGLE
WRIGGLED
WRIGGLER
WRIGGLESOME
WRIGGLING
WRIGGLY
WRIGHT
WRIGHTRY
WRIHTE
WRIMPLE
WRINE
WRING
WRINGBOLT
WRINGED
WRINGER
WRINGING
WRINGLE
WRINGSTAFF
WRINGSTAVES
WRINK
WRINKLE
WRINKLED
WRINKLEDY
WRINKLEFUL
WRINKLES
WRINKLET
WRINKLIER
WRINKLIEST
WRINKLING
WRINKLY
WRIST
WRISTBAND
WRISTBONE
WRISTED
WRISTER
WRISTFALL
WRISTIKIN
WRISTLET
WRISTLOCK
WRISTS
WRISTWATCH
WRISTWORK
WRIT
WRITABILITY
WRITABLE
WRITATION
WRITATIVE
WRITE
WRITEABLE
WRITEE
WRITER
WRITHE
WRITHED
WRITHEDLY
WRITHEDNESS
WRITHEN
WRITHENECK
WRITHER
WRITHING
WRITHINGLY
WRITHLED
WRITHY
WRITING
WRITINGER
WRITINGS
WRITTEN
WRITTER
WRIXLE
WRIZZLED
WRO
WROIK
WRONG
WRONGDOER
WRONGDOING
WRONGED
WRONGER
WRONGFUL
WRONGFULLY
WRONGFULNESS
WRONGHEAD
WRONGHEADED
WRONGHEARTED
WRONGING
WRONGLESS
WRONGLESSLY
WRONGLY
WRONGNESS
WRONGOUS
WRONGOUSLY
WRONGOUSNESS
WROOT
WROT
WROTE
WROTH
WROTHE
WROTHFUL
WROTHLY
WROTHSOME
WROUGHT
WROX
WRUNG
WRUNGNESS
WRY
WRYBILL
WRYER
WRYEST
WRYING
WRYLY
WRYMOUTH
WRYNECK
WRYNECKED
WRYNESS
WUD
WUDDIE
WUDGE
WUDU
WUGG
WULDER
WULFENITE
WUMMEL
WUN
WUND
WUNGEE
WUNNA
WUNTEE
WURD
WURLEY
WURLEYS
WURLIES
WURLY
WURP
WURRALUH
WURRUNG
WURRUP
WURRUS
WURST
WURTH
WURTZITE
WUSP
WUTHER
WUTHERING
WUYEN
WUZ
WUZU
WUZZER
WUZZLE
WUZZLED
WUZZLING
WY
WYCH
WYDE
WYE
WYES
WYF
WYLE
WYLED
WYLIECOAT
WYLING
WYLW
WYME
WYMOTE
WYN
WYND
WYNE
WYNKERNEL
WYNN
WYNRIS
WYPE
WYRE
WYROCK
WYROK
WYS
WYSTY
WYTHE

X

XALLE
XANTHALINE
XANTHAMID
XANTHAMIDE
XANTHANE
XANTHATE
XANTHATION
XANTHEIN
XANTHELASMA
XANTHENE
XANTHIC
XANTHID
XANTHIDE
XANTHIN
XANTHINE
XANTHINURIA
XANTHIONE
XANTHITE
XANTHIURIA
XANTHOCHROIA
XANTHOCHROID
XANTHOCONE
XANTHOCONITE
XANTHODERM
XANTHODERMA
XANTHOGEN
XANTHOGENATE
XANTHOGENIC
XANTHOMA
XANTHOMAS
XANTHOMATA
XANTHOMATOUS
XANTHOMETER
XANTHONE
XANTHOPHANE
XANTHOPHORE
XANTHOPHYL
XANTHOPHYLL
XANTHOPIA
XANTHOPSIA
XANTHOPSIN
XANTHOPTERIN
XANTHOSIS
XANTHOUS
XANTHOXENITE
XANTHOXYLIN
XANTHURIA
XANTHYDROL
XANTHYL
XARQUE
XAT
XEBEC
XEME
XENACANTHINE
XENAGOGUE
XENAGOGY
XENARTHRAL
XENARTHROUS
XENELASIA
XENELASY
XENIA
XENIAL
XENIAN
XENIUM
XENOBIOSIS
XENOBLAST
XENOCYST
XENODERM
XENODOCHIUM
XENODOCHY
XENOGAMOUS
XENOGAMY
XENOGENESIS
XENOGENOUS
XENOLITE
XENOLITH
XENOMANIA
XENOMORPHIC
XENON
XENOPARASITE
XENOPELTID
XENOPHOBE
XENOPHOBIA
XENOPHOBIC
XENOPHYA
XENOPODID
XENOPODOID
XENOPTERAN
XENOSAURID
XENOSAUROID
XENOTIME
XENYL
XENYLAMINE
XERAFIN
XERANSIS
XERANTIC
XERAPHIN
XERARCH
XERASIA
XERIC
XERIF
XERIFF
XERODERMA
XEROGRAPHER
XEROGRAPHIC
XEROGRAPHY
XEROMA
XEROMORPH
XEROMORPHIC
XEROMORPHOUS
XEROMORPHY
XEROMYRON
XERONATE
XERONIC
XEROPHAGY
XEROPHIL
XEROPHILE
XEROPHILOUS
XEROPHILY
XEROPHOBOUS
XEROPHYTE
XEROPHYTIC
XEROPHYTISM
XEROSERE
XEROSIS
XEROSTOMA
XEROTES
XEROTHERM
XEROTIC
XEROTRIPSIS
XEROX
XIBALBA
XIFOID
XIPHIIFORM
XIPHIOID
XIPHISTERNAL
XIPHISTERNUM
XIPHOCOSTAL
XIPHODYNIA
XIPHOID
XIPHOIDAL
XIPHOIDIAN
XIPHOPAGIC
XIPHOPAGOUS
XIPHOPAGUS
XIPHOSURAN
XIPHOSURE
XIPHOSUROUS
XIPHYDRIID
XOANA
XOANON
XUREL
XYLAN
XYLANTHRAX
XYLATE
XYLEM
XYLENE
XYLENOL
XYLENYL
XYLIC
XYLIDIN
XYLIDINE
XYLINDEIN
XYLITE
XYLITOL
XYLITONE
XYLOCARP
XYLOCARPOUS
XYLOCOPID
XYLOGEN
XYLOGLYPHY
XYLOGRAPH
XYLOGRAPHER
XYLOGRAPHIC
XYLOGRAPHY
XYLOID
XYLOIDIN
XYLOIDINE
XYLOL
XYLOLOGY
XYLOMA
XYLOMANCY
XYLOMAS
XYLOMATA
XYLOMETER
XYLON
XYLOPHAGAN
XYLOPHAGE
XYLOPHAGID
XYLOPHAGOUS
XYLOPHILOUS
XYLOPHONE
XYLOPHONIC
XYLOPHONIST
XYLOPLASTIC
XYLOPOLIST
XYLOQUINONE
XYLORCIN
XYLORCINOL
XYLOSE
XYLOSID
XYLOSIDE
XYLOSTROMA
XYLOSTROMATA
XYLOTILE
XYLOTOMIST
XYLOTOMOUS
XYLOTOMY
XYLOYL
XYLYL
XYLYLENE
XYRID
XYRIDACEOUS
XYST
XYSTA
XYSTER
XYSTUS

Y

YA
YABBER
YABBI
YABBIE
YABBLE
YABBY
YABOA
YABOO
YABU
YACAL
YACARE
YACATA
YACCA
YACH
YACHAN
YACHT
YACHTER
YACHTING
YACHTIST
YACHTMAN
YACHTSMAN
YACHTSMEN
YACHTY
YAD
YADAYIM
YADE
YAE
YAF
YAFE
YAFF
YAFFIL
YAFFLE
YAFFLER
YAGER
YAGUA
YAGUARUNDI
YAGUAS
YAGUAZA
YAH
YAHAN
YAHOO
YAHRZEIT
YAIR
YAIRD
YAJE
YAJEIN
YAJEINE
YAJENIN
YAJENINE
YAJNOPAVITA
YAK
YAKALO
YAKAMIK
YAKATTALO
YAKIN
YAKKA
YAKMAK
YAKS
YAKSA
YAKSHA
YAKSHI
YAL
YALD
YALI
YALLOCK
YAM
YAMAMAI
YAMASKITE
YAMEN
YAMILKE
YAMMADJI
YAMMER
YAMMERLY
YAMP
YAMPEE
YAMPH
YAMSHIK
YAMSTCHIK
YAN
YANACONA
YANCE
YANE
YANG
YANGGONA
YANGTAO
YANK
YANKED
YANKER
YANKING
YANKY
YANNAM
YANOLITE
YANQUI
YANTRA
YAP
YAPA
YAPNESS
YAPOCK
YAPOK
YAPON
YAPP
YAPPED
YAPPER
YAPPINESS
YAPPING
YAPPINGLY
YAPPISH
YAPPY
YAPSTER
YAQONA
YAR
YARAGE
YARAK
YARAY
YARB
YARD
YARDAGE
YARDANG
YARDARM
YARDBIRD
YARDED
YARDER
YARDGRASS
YARDING
YARDKEEP
YARDLAND
YARDMAN
YARDMASTER
YARDMEN
YARDS
YARDSMAN
YARDSTICK
YARDWAND
YARE
YARELY
YARETA
YARIYARI
YARK
YARKE
YARKEE
YARM
YARMULKE
YARN
YARNEN
YARNER
YARNS
YARNWINDLE
YAROVIZE
YARPHA
YARR
YARRAMAN
YARRAN
YARROW
YARRY
YARTHEN
YARWHELP
YARWHIP
YAS
YASHIRO
YASHMAC
YASHMAK
YAT
YATAGAN
YATAGHAN
YATALITE
YATCH
YATE
YATI
YATTER
YAUD
YAULD
YAUP
YAUPER
YAUPON
YAUTIA
YAVA
YAW
YAWD
YAWED
YAWING
YAWL
YAWLER
YAWMETER
YAWN
YAWNED
YAWNER
YAWNILY
YAWNINESS
YAWNING
YAWNINGLY
YAWNY
YAWP
YAWPER
YAWROOT
YAWS
YAWSHRUB
YAWWEED
YAWY
YAXCHE
YAY
YAYA
YCIE
YCLEPED
YCLEPT
YDRIADES
YE
YEA
YEAD
YEAGHE
YEAH
YEALING
YEAN
YEANED
YEANING
YEANLING
YEAR
YEARA
YEARBIRD
YEARBOOK
YEARDAY
YEARED
YEARLING
YEARLONG
YEARLY
YEARN
YEARNED
YEARNFUL
YEARNFULLY
YEARNFULNESS
YEARNING
YEARNINGLY
YEARNINGS
YEARNLING
YEAROCK
YEARS
YEAST
YEASTIER
YEASTIEST
YEASTING
YEASTY
YEAT
YED
YEDDA
YEDDE
YEDDING
YEDE
YEDER
YEDERLY
YEELIN
YEGG
YEGGMAN
YEGUITA
YEILD
YEKE
YELD
YELDE
YELDRIN
YELDRINE
YELDRING
YELDROCK
YELK
YELL
YELLED
YELLER
YELLING
YELLOCH
YELLOW
YELLOWBACK
YELLOWBARK
YELLOWBELLY
YELLOWBERRIES
YELLOWBERRY
YELLOWBILL
YELLOWBIRD
YELLOWER
YELLOWEST
YELLOWFIN
YELLOWFISH
YELLOWHAMMER
YELLOWHEAD
YELLOWISH
YELLOWLEGS
YELLOWLY
YELLOWMAN
YELLOWNESS
YELLOWROOT
YELLOWS
YELLOWSEED
YELLOWSHANK
YELLOWSHANKS
YELLOWSHINS
YELLOWTAIL
YELLOWTAILS
YELLOWTHROAT
YELLOWTOP
YELLOWWARE
YELLOWWEED
YELLOWWOOD
YELLOWWORT
YELLOWY
YELM
YELMER
YELP
YELPED
YELPER
YELPING
YELVER
YELWE
YEME
YEMELESS
YEMER
YEMING
YEMSCHIK
YEMSEL
YEN
YEND
YENI
YENITE
YENNED
YENNING
YENTNITE
YEOMAN
YEOMANLY
YEOMANRY
YEOMEN
YEORLING
YEOWOMAN
YEOWOMEN
YEP
YEPE
YEPELEIC
YEPELY
YEPHEDE
YEPLY
YER
YERBA
YERBAL
YERBALES
YERCUM
YERGA
YERK
YERN
YERNE
YERRA
YERTCHUK
YES
YESES
YESO
YESSO
YESTER
YESTERDAY
YESTEREVE
YESTEREVEN
YESTERMORN
YESTERN
YESTERNIGHT
YESTERNOON
YESTERWEEK
YESTERYEAR
YESTREEN
YET
YETAPA
YETER
YETH
YETHHOUNDS
YETI
YETLIN
YETLING
YETT
YETTE
YETTER
YETZER
YEUK
YEUKIENESS
YEUKY

YEW
YEWEN
YEWK
YEX
YEZ
YEZZY
YFACKS
YFERRE
YGOE
YGONE
YHTE
YIELD
YIELDANCE
YIELDED
YIELDER
YIELDING
YIELDINGLY
YIGH
YILL
YILT
YIN
YINCE
YIP
YIPE
YIPPIE
YIRD
YIRM
YIRMILIK
YIRN
YIRR
YIS
YISSE
YISSER
YISSING
YIT
YITE
YIVER
YIVERLY
YIVERNESS
YIZKOR
YLAHAYLL
YLE
YLEM
YLESPIL
YLICHE
YMAGE
YMMOTE
YMPET
YMPNE
YMUR
YNAMBU
YNGOODLY
YNKELL
YNPRIDID
YO
YOB
YOBI
YOCCO
YOCKEL
YOCKERNUT
YOD
YODEL
YODELED
YODELER
YODELING
YODELIST
YODELLED
YODELLER
YODELLING
YODH
YODLE
YODLED
YODLER
YOE
YOGA
YOGH
YOGHOURT
YOGHURT
YOGI
YOGIN
YOGISM
YOGIST
YOGOITE
YOGURT
YOHIMBI
YOHIMBIN
YOHIMBINE
YOHO
YOHOURT
YOICK
YOICKS
YOJAN
YOJANA
YOK
YOKAGE
YOKE
YOKEAGE
YOKED
YOKEFELLOW
YOKEL
YOKELESS
YOKELISH
YOKELRY
YOKEMATE
YOKEMATING
YOKER
YOKEWOOD
YOKING
YOKY
YOLDRING
YOLE
YOLK
YOLKED
YOLKIER
YOLKIEST
YOLKY
YOLL
YOLPE
YOM
YOMER
YON
YONCOPIN
YOND
YONDER
YONDWARD
YONGE
YONI
YONKER
YONSIDE
YOOP
YORA
YORE
YORETIME
YORK
YORKER
YORLIN
YOT
YOTACISM
YOTACIZE
YOTE
YOU
YOUDITH
YOUFF
YOUNG
YOUNGBERRIES
YOUNGBERRY
YOUNGER
YOUNGEST
YOUNGISH
YOUNGLET
YOUNGLING
YOUNGLY
YOUNGSTER
YOUNGTH
YOUNKER
YOUPON
YOUR
YOURN
YOURS
YOURSELF
YOURSELVES
YOURT
YOUSE
YOUSTIR
YOUT
YOUTH
YOUTHEN
YOUTHFUL
YOUTHFULLY
YOUTHFULNESS
YOUTHILY
YOUTHINESS
YOUTHLESS
YOUTHLIKE
YOUTHS
YOUTHSOME
YOUTHWORT
YOUTHY
YOUWARD
YOUWARDS
YOUZE
YOW
YOWDEN
YOWE
YOWIE
YOWL
YOWLED
YOWLER
YOWLEY
YOWLING
YOWT
YOX
YOY
YPERITE
YPSILIFORM
YPSILOID
YSOWNDIR
YTHE
YTTERBIA
YTTERBIC
YTTERBIUM
YTTRIA
YTTRIALITE
YTTRIC
YTTRIFEROUS
YTTRIUM
YTTROCERITE
YTTROCRASITE
YTTROGUMMITE
YTWYN
YUCA
YUCCA
YUCK
YUCKER
YUCKLE
YUFT
YUGADA
YUH
YUK
YUKKEL
YULAN
YULE
YULETIDE
YULOH
YUMMY
YUNGAN
YUNKER
YUPON
YURT
YURTA
YUS
YUSDRUM
YUTU
YUZLIK
YUZLUK
YWIS

Z

ZA
ZABAGLIONE
ZABETA
ZABRA
ZABTI
ZABURRO
ZAC
ZACATE
ZACATON
ZACHUN
ZAD
ZADDIK
ZADRUGA
ZAFFAR
ZAFFER
ZAFFIR
ZAFFRE
ZAFFREE
ZAG
ZAGGED
ZAGGING
ZAGUAN
ZAIBATSU
ZAIN
ZAK
ZAKAH
ZAKAT
ZAKUSKA
ZALAMBDODONT
ZAMAN
ZAMANG
ZAMARRA
ZAMARRO
ZAMBO
ZAMBOMBA
ZAMINDAR
ZAMINDARI
ZAMINDARY
ZAMORIN
ZAMORINE
ZAMOUSE
ZAMPOGNA
ZANANA
ZANDER
ZANDMOLE
ZANELLA
ZANIES
ZANJA
ZANJERO
ZANJON
ZANJONA
ZANT
ZANTE
ZANTHOXYLUM
ZANY
ZANYISH
ZANYISM
ZANZE
ZAPAS
ZAPATEADO
ZAPATERO
ZAPHARA
ZAPHRENTID
ZAPHRENTOID
ZAPOTE
ZAPTIAH
ZAPTIEH
ZAPUPE
ZAR
ZARAH
ZARATITE
ZAREBA
ZAREEBA
ZARF
ZARNEC
ZARNICH
ZARP
ZART
ZARZUELA
ZASTRUGA
ZASTRUGI
ZATI
ZATTARE
ZAX
ZAYAT
ZAYIN
ZEAL
ZEALED
ZEALOT
ZEALOTIC
ZEALOTICAL
ZEALOTISM
ZEALOTIST
ZEALOTRY
ZEALOUS
ZEALOUSLY
ZEALOUSNESS
ZEALOUSY
ZEAXANTHIN
ZEBEC
ZEBECK
ZEBRA
ZEBRAIC
ZEBRALIKE
ZEBRAS
ZEBRASS
ZEBRAWOOD
ZEBRINE
ZEBRINNIES
ZEBRINNY
ZEBROID
ZEBRULA
ZEBRULE
ZEBU
ZEBUB
ZEBURRO
ZEBUS
ZECCHINO
ZECHIN
ZED
ZEDOARY
ZEDS
ZEE
ZEEKOE
ZEES
ZEHNER
ZEIN
ZEINE
ZEISM
ZEIST
ZEL
ZELANT
ZELATOR
ZELATRICE
ZELATRIX
ZELOTYPIA
ZELOTYPIE
ZEME
ZEMEISM
ZEMI
ZEMIISM
ZEMINDAR
ZEMINDARI
ZEMMI
ZEMNI
ZEMSTVO
ZEMSTVOS
ZENANA
ZENDICIAN
ZENDIK
ZENDIKITE
ZENICK
ZENIK
ZENITH
ZENITHAL
ZENOCENTRIC
ZENOGRAPHIC
ZENOGRAPHY
ZENTNER
ZENU
ZENZIC
ZEOLITE
ZEOLITIC
ZEOLITIZE
ZEOLITIZED
ZEOLITIZING
ZEOSCOPE
ZEPHYR
ZEPHYREAN
ZEPHYRIAN
ZEPHYROUS
ZEPHYRUS
ZEPHYRY
ZEPP
ZEPPELIN
ZEQUIN
ZER
ZERDA
ZEREBA
ZERMAHBUB
ZERO
ZEROAXIAL
ZEROES
ZEROIZE
ZEROS
ZERUMBET
ZEST
ZESTED
ZESTFUL
ZESTING
ZESTY
ZETA
ZETACISM
ZETETIC
ZEUGITE
ZEUGLODONT
ZEUGMA
ZEUGMATIC
ZEUNERITE
ZHO
ZIAMET
ZIARA
ZIARAT
ZIBEB
ZIBELINE
ZIBELLINE
ZIBETH
ZIBETUM
ZIEGA
ZIEGER
ZIFFS
ZIG
ZIGANKA
ZIGGER
ZIGGURAT
ZIGZAG
ZIGZAGGEDLY
ZIGZAGGER
ZIGZAGGERY
ZIGZAGGY
ZIHAR
ZIIM
ZIKURAT
ZILLAH
ZIMARRA
ZIMB
ZIMBABWE
ZIMBALON
ZIMBI
ZIMENTWATER
ZIMME
ZIMMI
ZIMMIS
ZIMMY
ZIMOCCA
ZINC
ZINCALISM
ZINCATE
ZINCED
ZINCIC
ZINCID
ZINCIDE
ZINCIFEROUS
ZINCIFIED
ZINCIFY
ZINCIFYING
ZINCING
ZINCITE
ZINCKE
ZINCKED
ZINCKING
ZINCKY
ZINCO
ZINCOGRAPH
ZINCOGRAPHER
ZINCOGRAPHIC
ZINCOGRAPHY
ZINCOID
ZINCOLYSIS
ZINCOUS
ZINCUM
ZINCURET
ZINCY
ZINDIQ
ZINEB
ZINFANDEL
ZING
ZINGANA
ZINGANO
ZINGARA
ZINGARESCA
ZINGARI
ZINGARO
ZINGEL
ZINGERONE
ZINGIBERENE
ZINGIBEROL
ZINK
ZINKE
ZINKENITE
ZINKY
ZINNIA
ZINNWALDITE
ZINOBER
ZINSANG
ZIP
ZIPHIAN
ZIPHIOID
ZIPPER
ZIPPIER
ZIPPIEST
ZIPPING
ZIPPINGLY
ZIPPY
ZIRA
ZIRAI
ZIRAM
ZIRCITE
ZIRCON
ZIRCONATE
ZIRCONIA
ZIRCONIC
ZIRCONIUM
ZIRCONOID
ZIRCONYL
ZIRKELITE
ZIRKITE
ZITHER
ZITHERIST
ZITTERN
ZIZANY
ZIZEL
ZIZITH
ZIZZ
ZIZZLE
ZIZZLED
ZIZZLING
ZLOTY
ZLOTYS
ZNAK
ZO
ZOA
ZOACUM
ZOANTHID
ZOANTHODEME
ZOANTHODEMIC
ZOANTHOID
ZOANTHROPY
ZOARIA
ZOARIAL
ZOARIUM
ZOBO
ZOBTENITE
ZOBU
ZOCALO
ZOCCO
ZOCCOLO
ZODIAC
ZODIACAL
ZODIOPHILOUS
ZOEA
ZOEAFORM
ZOEAL
ZOEHEMERA
ZOETIC
ZOETROPE
ZOETROPIC
ZOGAN
ZOGO
ZOH
ZOIATRIA
ZOIC
ZOID
ZOIDOGAMOUS
ZOILUS
ZOISITE
ZOISITIZATION
ZOISM
ZOIST
ZOISTIC
ZOKOR
ZOLL
ZOLOTNIK
ZOMBI
ZOMBIE
ZOMBIES
ZOMBIISM
ZOMBIS
ZOMOTHERAPY
ZONA
ZONAE
ZONAESTHESIA
ZONAL
ZONALITY
ZONALLY

ZONAR
ZONARY
ZONATE
ZONATED
ZONATION
ZONDA
ZONE
ZONED
ZONELESS
ZONELET
ZONESTHESIA
ZONIC
ZONIFEROUS
ZONING
ZONITE
ZONITID
ZONNAR
ZONOCHLORITE
ZONOCILIATE
ZONOID
ZONOLIMNETIC
ZONOSKELETON
ZONULA
ZONULAR
ZONULE
ZONULET
ZONURE
ZONURID
ZONUROID
ZOO
ZOOBENTHOS
ZOOBLAST
ZOOCARP
ZOOCECIDIUM
ZOOCHEMY
ZOOCHORE
ZOOCULTURAL
ZOOCULTURE
ZOOCURRENT
ZOOCYST
ZOOCYTIAL
ZOOCYTIUM
ZOODENDRIUM
ZOODYNAMICS
ZOOECIA
ZOOECIAL
ZOOECIUM
ZOOERYTHRIN
ZOOFULVIN
ZOOGAMETE
ZOOGAMOUS
ZOOGAMY
ZOOGENE
ZOOGENOUS
ZOOGEOGRAPHY
ZOOGLER
ZOOGLOEA
ZOOGLOEAL
ZOOGLOEIC
ZOOGONIDIUM
ZOOGONOUS
ZOOGRAFT
ZOOGRAFTING
ZOOGRAPHER
ZOOGRAPHIC
ZOOGRAPHY
ZOOID
ZOOIDAL
ZOOLATER
ZOOLATRIES
ZOOLATROUS
ZOOLATRY
ZOOLITE
ZOOLITH
ZOOLITHIC
ZOOLITIC
ZOOLOGIC
ZOOLOGICAL
ZOOLOGIES
ZOOLOGIST
ZOOLOGIZE
ZOOLOGIZED
ZOOLOGIZING
ZOOLOGY
ZOOM
ZOOMAGNETIC
ZOOMAGNETISM
ZOOMANIA
ZOOMELANIN
ZOOMETRIC
ZOOMETRY
ZOOMIMETIC
ZOOMIMIC
ZOOMORPH
ZOOMORPHIC
ZOOMORPHISM
ZOOMORPHIZE
ZOOMORPHY
ZOON
ZOONAL
ZOONIC
ZOONIST
ZOONITE
ZOONITIC
ZOONOMY
ZOONOSES
ZOONOSIS
ZOONOSOLOGY
ZOONOTIC
ZOONS
ZOONULE
ZOOPANTHEON
ZOOPARASITE
ZOOPATHOLOGY
ZOOPERAL
ZOOPERIST
ZOOPERY
ZOOPHAGAN
ZOOPHAGOUS
ZOOPHARMACY
ZOOPHILE
ZOOPHILIA
ZOOPHILIC
ZOOPHILISM
ZOOPHILIST
ZOOPHILITE
ZOOPHILOUS
ZOOPHILY
ZOOPHOBIA
ZOOPHOBOUS
ZOOPHORI
ZOOPHORIC
ZOOPHORUS
ZOOPHYSICAL
ZOOPHYSICS
ZOOPHYTAL
ZOOPHYTE
ZOOPHYTIC
ZOOPHYTICAL
ZOOPHYTISH
ZOOPHYTOID
ZOOPHYTOLOGY
ZOOPLANKTON
ZOOPLASTIC
ZOOPLASTY
ZOOPRAXISCOPE
ZOOSCOPIC
ZOOSCOPY
ZOOSIS
ZOOSPERM
ZOOSPHERE
ZOOSPORANGE
ZOOSPORE
ZOOSPORIC
ZOOSPOROUS
ZOOTAXY
ZOOTECHNIC
ZOOTECHNY
ZOOTHECIA
ZOOTHECIAL
ZOOTHECIUM
ZOOTHEISM
ZOOTHEIST
ZOOTHEISTIC
ZOOTHERAPY
ZOOTHOME
ZOOTIC
ZOOTOMIC
ZOOTOMICAL
ZOOTOMIST
ZOOTOXIN
ZOOTROPHIC
ZOOTROPHY
ZOOTYPE
ZOOXANTHELLA
ZOOXANTHIN
ZOOZOO
ZOPE
ZOPILOTE
ZOPPA
ZOPPO
ZORGITE
ZORIL
ZORILLA
ZORILLE
ZORRA
ZORRILLO
ZORRO
ZORTZICO
ZOSTER
ZOSTERIFORM
ZOUNDS
ZOWIE
ZOYSIA
ZUCCARINO
ZUCCHETTO
ZUCCHINI
ZUCHE
ZUDDA
ZUFFOLO
ZUFOLO
ZUGZWANG
ZUISIN
ZULU
ZUMATIC
ZUMBOORUK
ZUNYITE
ZUPA
ZUPAN
ZUPANATE
ZUURVELDT
ZUZA
ZWANZIGER
ZWIEBACK
ZWITTER
ZWITTERION
ZYGA
ZYGADENIN
ZYGADENINE
ZYGAENID
ZYGAL
ZYGANTRUM
ZYGAPOPHYSIS
ZYGENID
ZYGION
ZYGITE
ZYGOBRANCH
ZYGODACTYL
ZYGODACTYLE
ZYGODACTYLIC
ZYGODONT
ZYGOLABIALIS
ZYGOMA
ZYGOMATA
ZYGOMATIC
ZYGOMATICUM
ZYGOMATICUS
ZYGOMORPHIC
ZYGOMORPHOUS
ZYGOMYCETE
ZYGOMYCETES
ZYGOMYCETOUS
ZYGON
ZYGONEURE
ZYGOPHORE
ZYGOPHORIC
ZYGOPHYCEOUS
ZYGOPHYTE
ZYGOPLEURAL
ZYGOPTERAN
ZYGOPTERID
ZYGOPTEROUS
ZYGOSE
ZYGOSIS
ZYGOSPERM
ZYGOSPHENAL
ZYGOSPHENE
ZYGOSPHERE
ZYGOSPORE
ZYGOSPORIC
ZYGOSTYLE
ZYGOTACTIC
ZYGOTAXIS
ZYGOTE
ZYGOTENE
ZYGOTOID
ZYGOUS
ZYGOZOOSPORE
ZYMASE
ZYME
ZYMIC
ZYMIN
ZYMITE
ZYMOGEN
ZYMOGENE
ZYMOGENESIS
ZYMOGENIC
ZYMOGENOUS
ZYMOID
ZYMOLOGIC
ZYMOLOGICAL
ZYMOLOGIST
ZYMOLOGY
ZYMOLYSIS
ZYMOLYTIC
ZYMOME
ZYMOMETER
ZYMOMIN
ZYMOPHORE
ZYMOPHORIC
ZYMOPLASTIC
ZYMOSCOPE
ZYMOSIMETER
ZYMOSIS
ZYMOSTEROL
ZYMOSTHENIC
ZYMOTECHNIC
ZYMOTECHNICS
ZYMOTIC
ZYMOTICALLY
ZYMURGY
ZYTHUM

PART II

High-Scoring Word Lists

Words Containing

High-Point Letters

J, Q, X and Z

High-Scoring Words Containing J

2-3 LETTER WORDS

ALPHABETICAL ORDER

AJI
AJO
DJO
HAJ
JA
JAB
JAD
JAG
JAK
JAM
JAN
JAP
JAR
JAW
JAY
JED
JEE
JEN
JES
JET
JEU
JEW
JIB
JIG
JIZ
JO
JOB
JOD
JOE
JOG
JOT
JOW
JOY
JUB
JUD
JUG
JUM
JUR
JUS
JUT
OJO
RAJ
SAJ
TAJ
TJI
UJI

POSITIONAL ORDER

JA
JAB
JAD
JAG
JAK
JAM
JAN
JAP
JAR
JAW
JAY
JED
JEE
JEN
JES
JET
JEU
JEW
JIB
JIG
JIZ
JO
JOB
JOD
JOE
JOG
JOT
JOW
JOY
JUB
JUD
JUG
JUM
JUR
JUS
JUT

AJI
AJO
DJO
OJO
TJI
UJI

HAJ
RAJ
SAJ
TAJ

SCORING ORDER

19
JIZ

14
JAK

13
HAJ
JAW
JAY
JEW
JOW
JOY

12
JAB
JAM
JAP
JIB
JOB
JUB
JUM

11
DJO
JAD
JAG
JED
JIG
JOD
JOG
JUD
JUG

10
AJI
AJO
JAN
JAR
JEE
JEN
JES
JET
JEU
JOE
JOT
JUR
JUS
JUT
OJO
RAJ
SAJ
TAJ
TJI

9
JA
JO

ALPHABETICAL LIST OF 4-LETTER WORDS

AJAR
AJAX
AJEE
AJOG
BAJU
BENJ
BIJA
CAJA
CAJI
CAJU
DJIN
DOJO
EJOO
FAJA
GAJO
GUNJ
HADJ
HAJE
HAJI
HAJJ
HOJA
IJMA
JACA
JACK
JACU
JADE
JADU
JADY
JAGG
JAGS
JAIL
JAKE
JAKO
JAMA

JAMB
JAMI
JANE
JANG
JANK
JANN
JAOB
JAPE
JARA
JARG
JARK
JARL
JASK
JASM
JASS
JATI
JATO
JAUD
JAUG
JAUK
JAUN
JAUP
JAVA
JAWS
JAWY
JAZZ
JEAN
JEEL
JEEP
JEER
JEEZ
JEFE
JEFF
JELL

JERK
JERL
JERM
JERT
JESS
JEST
JETE
JEUX
JHIL
JHOW
JHUM
JIBE
JIBI
JIFF
JILL
JILT
JIMP
JINA
JING
JINK
JINN
JINX
JIRD
JIRT
JITI
JIVA
JIVE
JOBE
JOBO
JOBS
JOCH
JOCK
JOCO

JOCU
JOES
JOEY
JOGI
JOHN
JOIN
JOKE
JOKY
JOLE
JOLI
JOLL
JOLT
JONG
JONK
JOOM
JOPY
JOSH
JOSS
JOTA
JOTI
JOUG
JOUK
JOVY
JOWL
JUBA
JUBE
JUBO
JUCK
JUDD
JUDO
JUEY
JUEZ
JUGA

JUJU
JUKE
JUMP
JUNE
JUNK
JUNT
JUPE
JURA
JURE
JURM
JURR
JURT
JURY
JUSI
JUST
JUTE
JYNX
KOJI
LIJA
LOJA
MAJA
MAJO
MOJO
MUNJ
PUJA
RAJA
REJA
ROJO
SOJA
SUJI
TAJO
TEJU
YAJE

POSITIONAL ORDER LIST OF 4-LETTER WORDS

JACA
JACK
JACU
JADE
JADU
JADY
JAGG
JAGS
JAIL
JAKE
JAKO
JAMA
JAMB
JAMI
JANE
JANG
JANK
JANN
JAOB
JAPE
JARA
JARG
JARK
JARL
JASK
JASM
JASS
JATI
JATO
JAUD
JAUG
JAUK
JAUN
JAUP
JAVA

JAWS
JAWY
JAZZ
JEAN
JEEL
JEEP
JEER
JEEZ
JEFE
JEFF
JELL
JERK
JERL
JERM
JERT
JESS
JEST
JETE
JEUX
JHIL
JHOW
JHUM
JIBE
JIBI
JIFF
JILL
JILT
JIMP
JINA
JING
JINK
JINN
JINX
JIRD

JIRT
JITI
JIVA
JIVE
JOBE
JOBO
JOBS
JOCH
JOCK
JOCO
JOCU
JOES
JOEY
JOGI
JOHN
JOIN
JOKE
JOKY
JOLE
JOLI
JOLL
JOLT
JONG
JONK
JOOM
JOPY
JOSH
JOSS
JOTA
JOTI
JOUG
JOUK
JOVY
JOWL

JUBA
JUBE
JUBO
JUCK
JUDD
JUDO
JUEY
JUEZ
JUGA
JUJU
JUKE
JUMP
JUNE
JUNK
JUNT
JUPE
JURA
JURE
JURM
JURR
JURT
JURY
JUSI
JUST
JUTE
JYNX

AJAR
AJAX
AJEE
AJOG
DJIN
EJOO
IJMA

BAJU
BIJA
CAJA
CAJI
CAJU
DOJO
FAJA
GAJO
HAJE
HAJI
HAJJ
HOJA
JUJU
KOJI
LIJA
LOJA
MAJA
MAJO
MOJO
PUJA
RAJA
REJA
ROJO
SOJA
SUJI
TAJO
TEJU
YAJE

BENJ
GUNJ
HADJ
HAJJ
MUNJ

SCORING ORDER LIST OF 4-LETTER WORDS

21
JYNX

20
JEEZ
JUEZ

19
JAZZ

18
AJAX
JEUX
JINX
JOKY

17
JACK
JAWY
JEFF
JHOW
JIFF
JOCK
JOVY
JUCK

16
JHUM
JOCH
JOPY

15
HADJ
JADY
JAKE
JAKO
JAMB
JANK
JARK
JASK
JAUK
JERK
JIMP
JINK
JOKE
JONK
JOUK
JUKE
JUMP
JUNK
KOJI

14
FAJA
HAJE
HAJI
HOJA
JAVA
JAWS
JEFE
JHIL
JIVA
JIVE
JOEY
JOHN
JOSH
JOWL
JUEY
JURY
YAJE

13
BAJU
BENJ
BIJA
CAJA
CAJI
CAJU
HAJJ
IJMA
JACA
JACU
JAGG
JAMA
JAMI
JAOB
JAPE
JASM
JAUP
JEEP
JERM
JIBE
JIBI
JOBE
JOBO
JOBS
JOCO
JOCU
JOOM
JUBA
JUBE
JUBO
JUDD
JUPE
JURM
MAJA
MAJO
MOJO
MUNJ
PUJA

12
AJOG
DJIN
DOJO
GAJO
GUNJ
JADE
JADU
JAGS
JANG
JARG
JAUD
JAUG
JING
JIRD
JOGI
JONG
JOUG
JUDO
JUGA

11
AJAR
AJEE
EJOO
JAIL
JANE
JANN
JARA
JARL
JASS
JATI
JATO
JAUN
JEAN
JEEL
JEER
JELL
JERL
JERT
JESS
JEST
JETE
JILL
JILT
JINA
JINN
JIRT
JITI
JOES
JOIN
JOLE
JOLI
JOLL
JOLT
JOSS
JOTA
JOTI
JUNE
JUNT
JURA
JURE
JURR
JURT
JUSI
JUST
JUTE
LIJA
LOJA
RAJA
REJA
ROJO
SOJA
SUJI
TAJO
TEJU

10
JUJU

ALPHABETICAL LIST OF 5-LETTER WORDS

ADJAB
ADJAG
AGUJA
AJAJA
AJARI
AJAVA
AJHAR
AJIVA
AJOUR
ANJAN
ARJAN
ARJUN
ATAJO
BADJU
BAJRA
BANJO
BEJAN
BEJEL
BENJY
BIJOU
BRUJO
CAJON
CAJOU
CAJUN
CHAJA
COOJA
DJATI
DJINN
DORJE
DUJAN
EJECT
EJIDO
ENJOY
FJALL
FJELD
FJORD
GANJA
GJOLL
GUIJO
GUNJA
HADJI
HAJIB
HAJJI
HODJA
IJMAA
INAJA
JABIA
JABOT
JACAL
JACKO
JACKS
JACKY
JADED
JADOO
JAELA
JAGAT
JAGER
JAGGY
JAGIR
JAGLA
JAGRA
JAGUA
JAKES
JAKEY
JAKOS
JALAP
JALEO
JALET
JALOP
JAMAH
JAMAN
JAMBA
JAMBE
JAMBO
JAMMY
JAMON
JANTU
JANTY
JANUA
JAOUR
JAPAN
JAPED
JAPER
JARDE
JARRA
JARRY
JASEY
JASPE
JATHA
JAUNE
JAUNT
JAUPS
JAVEL
JAVER
JAWAB
JAWED
JAZEL
JAZZY
JEANS
JEBAT
JEBEL
JEDGE
JEERS
JEERY
JEHAD
JEHUP
JELAB
JELLO
JELLY
JEMMY
JENNA
JENNY
JEREZ
JERIB
JERKS
JERKY
JERRY
JETEE
JETON
JETTO
JETTY
JEWEL
JEZIA
JHANA
JHEEL

JHOOL
JHOOM
JIBBA
JIBED
JIBER
JIBOA
JIFFY
JIGGY
JIGUA
JIHAD
JIMMY
JIMPY
JINGO
JINJA
JINKS
JINNI
JINNY
JIPPO
JIQUE
JIQUI
JIRGA
JIXIE
JIZYA
JNANA
JNANI
JOCKO
JOCKS
JOCUM
JODEL
JOINT
JOISE
JOIST
JOKED
JOKER
JOKEY
JOKUL
JOLIE
JOLLY
JOLTY
JOOLA
JORAM
JOREE
JORUM
JOSEF
JOSEY
JOSHI
JOSIE
JOSSA
JOSUP
JOTTY
JOUGH
JOUGS
JOULE
JOURS
JOUST
JOWAR
JOWEL
JOWER
JOWLY
JOWPY
JOYED
JUBBE
JUBUS
JUDEX
JUDGE
JUDKA
JUFTI
JUFTS
JUGAL
JUGER
JUGUM
JUICE
JUICY
JUISE
JUKES
JULEP
JULID
JULIO
JULOL
JUMBA
JUMBO
JUMBY
JUMMA
JUMPS
JUMPY
JUNCO
JUNDY
JUNKY
JUNTA
JUNTO
JUPES
JUPON
JURAL
JURAT
JUREL
JUROR
JUSTO
JUTES
JUTIA
JUTKA
JUTTY
JUVIA
JUXTA
KALIJ
KHAJA
KHOJA
KOPJE
LINJA
LINJE
MAJAS
MAJID
MAJOE
MAJOR
MAJOS
MOJOS
MUJER
MUJIK
NJAVE
OUIJA
PAJAK
POLJE
PONJA
POOJA
RAJAH
RAJAS
REJON
SAJOU
SAMAJ
SHOJI
SIJIL
SLOJD
SUJEE
TEJON
THUJA
TJALK
VAJRA
VIEJA
VIJAO
YOJAN
ZANJA

POSITIONAL ORDER LIST OF 5-LETTER WORDS

JABIA
JABOT
JACAL
JACKO
JACKS
JACKY
JADED
JADOO
JAELA
JAGAT
JAGER
JAGGY
JAGIR
JAGLA
JAGRA
JAGUA
JAKES
JAKEY
JAKOS
JALAP
JALEO
JALET
JALOP
JAMAH
JAMAN
JAMBA
JAMBE
JAMBO
JAMMY
JAMON
JANTU
JANTY
JANUA
JAOUR
JAPAN
JAPED
JAPER
JARDE
JARRA
JARRY
JASEY
JASPE
JATHA
JAUNE
JAUNT
JAUPS
JAVEL
JAVER
JAWAB
JAWED
JAZEL
JAZZY
JEANS
JEBAT
JEBEL
JEDGE
JEERS
JEERY
JEHAD
JEHUP
JELAB
JELLO
JELLY
JEMMY
JENNA
JENNY
JEREZ
JERIB
JERKS
JERKY
JERRY
JETEE
JETON
JETTO
JETTY
JEWEL
JEZIA
JHANA
JHEEL
JHOOL
JHOOM
JIBBA
JIBED
JIBER
JIBOA
JIFFY
JIGGY
JIGUA
JIHAD
JIMMY
JIMPY
JINGO
JINJA
JINKS
JINNI
JINNY
JIPPO
JIQUE
JIQUI
JIRGA
JIXIE
JIZYA
JNANA
JNANI
JOCKO
JOCKS
JOCUM
JODEL
JOINT
JOISE
JOIST
JOKED
JOKER
JOKEY
JOKUL
JOLIE
JOLLY
JOLTY
JOOLA
JORAM
JOREE
JORUM
JOSEF
JOSEY
JOSHI
JOSIE
JOSSA
JOSUP
JOTTY
JOUGH
JOUGS
JOULE
JOURS
JOUST
JOWAR
JOWEL
JOWER
JOWLY
JOWPY
JOYED
JUBBE
JUBUS
JUDEX
JUDGE
JUDKA
JUFTI
JUFTS
JUGAL
JUGER
JUGUM
JUICE
JUICY
JUISE
JUKES
JULEP
JULID
JULIO
JULOL
JUMBA
JUMBO
JUMBY
JUMMA
JUMPS
JUMPY
JUNCO
JUNDY
JUNKY
JUNTA
JUNTO
JUPES
JUPON
JURAL
JURAT
JUREL
JUROR
JUSTO
JUTES
JUTIA
JUTKA
JUTTY
JUVIA
JUXTA

AJAJA
AJARI
AJAVA
AJHAR
AJIVA
AJOUR
DJATI
DJINN
EJECT
EJIDO
FJALL
FJELD
FJORD
GJOLL
IJMAA
NJAVE
TJALK

ADJAB
ADJAG
ANJAN
ARJAN
ARJUN
BAJRA
BEJAN
BEJEL
BIJOU
CAJON
CAJOU
CAJUN
DUJAN
ENJOY

HAJIB
HAJJI
MAJAS
MAJID
MAJOE
MAJOR
MAJOS
MOJOS
MUJER
MUJIK
PAJAK
RAJAH

RAJAS
REJON
SAJOU
SIJIL
SUJEE
TEJON
VAJRA
VIJAO
YOJAN

AGUJA
AJAJA

ATAJO
BADJU
BANJO
BENJY
BRUJO
CHAJA
COOJA
DORJE
GANJA
GUIJO
GUNJA

HADJI
HAJJI
HODJA
INAJA
JINJA
KHAJA
KHOJA
KOPJE
LINJA
LINJE
OUIJA

POLJE
PONJA
POOJA
SHOJI
SLOJD
THUJA
VIEJA
ZANJA

KALIJ
SAMAJ

SCORING ORDER LIST OF 5-LETTER WORDS

24
JIZYA

23
JAZZY

21
JACKY
JAZEL
JEREZ
JEZIA
JIFFY
JIQUE
JIQUI
ZANJA

20
JOWPY
JUDEX

19
JAKEY
JAMMY
JEMMY
JERKY
JIMMY
JIMPY
JIXIE
JOKEY
JUMBY
JUMPY
JUNKY
JUXTA
KHAJA
KHOJA

18
JACKO
JACKS
JOCKO
JOCKS
JOWLY
KOPJE
MUJIK
PAJAK

17
BENJY
CHAJA
HAJIB
JAGGY
JAMAH
JAWAB
JEHUP
JHOOM
JIGGY
JOKED
JUDKA
JUICY

16
FJELD
FJORD
HADJI
HODJA
JAKES
JAKOS
JAMBA
JAMBE
JAMBO
JAWED
JEHAD
JERKS
JIBBA
JIHAD
JINKS
JIPPO
JOCUM
JOKER
JOKUL
JOUGH
JOYED
JUBBE
JUKES
JUMBA
JUMBO
JUMMA
JUMPS
JUNDY
JUTKA
KALIJ
TJALK

15
ADJAB
AJAVA
AJHAR
AJIVA
BADJU
ENJOY
FJALL
JANTY
JAPED
JARRY
JASEY
JATHA
JAVEL
JAVER
JEERY
JELLY
JENNY
JERRY
JETTY
JEWEL
JHANA
JHEEL
JHOOL
JIBED
JINNY
JOLLY
JOLTY
JOSEF
JOSEY
JOSHI
JOTTY
JOWAR
JOWEL
JOWER
JUFTI
JUFTS
JUGUM
JUTTY
JUVIA
MAJID
NJAVE
RAJAH
SHOJI
THUJA
VAJRA
VIEJA
VIJAO
YOJAN

14
ADJAG
BAJRA
BANJO
BEJAN
BEJEL
BIJOU
BRUJO
CAJON
CAJOU
CAJUN
COOJA
EJECT
HAJJI
IJMAA
JABIA
JABOT
JACAL
JADED
JALAP
JALOP
JAMAN
JAMON
JAPAN
JAPER
JASPE
JAUPS
JEBAT
JEBEL
JEDGE
JELAB
JERIB
JIBER
JIBOA
JORAM
JORUM
JOSUP
JUBUS
JUDGE
JUICE
JULEP
JUNCO
JUPES
JUPON
MAJAS
MAJOE
MAJOR
MAJOS
MOJOS
MUJER
POLJE
PONJA
POOJA
SAMAJ

13
AGUJA
DJATI
DJINN
DORJE
DUJAN
EJIDO
GANJA
GJOLL
GUIJO
GUNJA
JADOO
JAGAT
JAGER
JAGIR
JAGLA
JAGRA
JAGUA
JARDE
JIGUA
JINGO
JIRGA
JODEL
JOUGS
JUGAL
JUGER
JULID
SLOJD

12
AJARI
AJOUR
ANJAN
ARJAN
ARJUN
ATAJO
INAJA
JAELA
JALEO
JALET
JANTU
JANUA
JAOUR
JARRA
JAUNE
JAUNT
JEANS
JEERS
JELLO
JENNA
JETEE
JETON
JETTO
JINNI
JNANA
JNANI
JOINT
JOISE
JOIST
JOLIE
JOOLA
JOREE
JOSIE
JOSSA
JOULE
JOURS
JOUST
JUISE
JULIO
JULOL
JUNTA
JUNTO
JURAL
JURAT
JUREL
JUROR
JUSTO
JUTES
JUTIA
LINJA
LINJE
OUIJA
RAJAS
REJON
SAJOU
SIJIL
SUJEE
TEJON

11
AJAJA
JINJA

ALPHABETICAL LIST OF 6-LETTER WORDS

ABJECT
ABJURE
ACAJOU
ADJECT
ADJIGA
ADJOIN
ADJURE
ADJUST
AGUAJI
AGUJON
AJENJO
AJIMEZ
AJOINT
AJOURE
AJOWAN
ALFAJE
ALJAMA
ANTJAR
AVIJJA
BAJADA
BAJREE
BANJAK
BANJOS
BEJADE
BEJANT
BEJAPE
BEJUCO
BIJOUX
BOJITE
BOOJUM
CABUJA
CADJAN
CAJAVA
CAJETA
CAJOLE
CARAJO
CONJEE
CONJON
COROJO
CROJIK
CUNJAH
CUNJER
DEEJAY
DEJECT
DJEBEL
DJELFA
DJERIB
DJERSA
DJINNI
DONJON
EJECTA
EJIDAL
ELCAJA
ENJAIL
ENJAMB
ENJOIN
EVEJAR
FANJET
FINJAN
FREIJO
FYLGJA
GIDJEE
GOUJAT
GOUJON
GUNJAH
GURJAN
GURJUN
GYTTJA
HEJIRA
HIJACK
INJECT
INJURE
INJURY
INJUST
JABBED
JABBER
JABBLE
JABERS
JABIRU
JABOTS
JABULS
JACANA
JACARE
JACATE
JACENT
JACKAL
JACKED
JACKER
JACKET
JACOBY
JADDED
JADDER
JADERY
JADING
JADISH
JAEGER
JAGEER
JAGGAR
JAGGED
JAGGER
JAGHIR
JAGONG
JAGUAR
JAGUEY
JAILED
JAILER
JAILOR
JALAPA
JALKAR
JALOPY
JAMBEE
JAMBER
JAMBON
JAMBUL
JAMMED
JAMMER
JAMNUT
JAMOKE
JAMPAN
JANAPA
JANGAR
JANGLE
JANGLY
JANKER
JANNER
JANTEE
JAPERY
JAPING
JAPISH
JARABE
JARANA
JARBLE
JARBOT
JAREED
JARFLY
JARFUL
JARGON
JARINA
JARNUT
JAROOL
JARRAH
JARRED
JARRET
JARVEY
JASEYS
JASMIN
JASPER
JASPIS
JASSID
JATACO
JATOBA
JAUDIE
JAUNCE
JAUNER
JAUNTY
JAVALI
JAVVER
JAWING
JAYGEE
JAYPIE
JAYVEE
JAZZER
JEERED
JEERER
JEETEE
JEJUNA
JEJUNE
JELICK
JELLAB
JEMBLE
JENKIN
JENNET
JENOAR
JERBOA
JEREED
JERKED
JERKER
JERKIN
JERNIE
JERQUE
JERRID
JERSEY
JERVIA
JERVIN
JESSED
JESSUR
JESTED
JESTEE
JESTER
JETSAM
JETTED
JETTER
JETTON
JETTRU
JEWELS
JEWELY
JEWING
JEZAIL
JEZIAH
JHARAL
JIBBAH
JIBBED
JIBBEH
JIBBER
JIBING
JIBMAN
JIBMEN
JIBOYA
JICAMA
JICARA
JIFFLE
JIGGED
JIGGER
JIGGET
JIGGIT
JIGGLE
JIGGLY
JIGMAN
JIGMEN
JIGOTE
JIGSAW
JILLET
JILTED
JILTEE
JILTER
JIMJAM
JIMMER
JIMPLY
JIMSON
JINETE
JINGAL
JINGLE
JINGLY
JINKED
JINKER
JINKET
JINKLE
JINNEE
JINSHA
JIPPER
JIRBLE
JIRGAH
JITNEY
JITTER
JIZYAH
JIZZEN
JOBADE
JOBBED
JOBBER
JOBBLE
JOBMAN
JOBMEN
JOBSON
JOCANT
JOCKER
JOCKEY
JOCKOS
JOCOSE
JOCOTE
JOCUMA
JOCUND
JOGGED
JOGGER
JOGGLE
JOGGLY
JOHNIN
JOINED
JOINER
JOINTS
JOINTY
JOJOBA
JOKIER
JOKING
JOKISH
JOKIST
JOLLOP
JOLTED
JOLTER
JONDLA
JORDAN
JORDEN
JOROPO
JORRAM
JOSEPH
JOSHER
JOSKIN
JOSSER
JOSTLE
JOTISI
JOTTED
JOTTER
JOUNCE
JOUSTS
JOUTES
JOVIAL
JOWARI
JOWERY
JOWLER
JOWLOP
JOWSER
JOWTER
JOYANT
JOYFUL
JOYHOP
JOYING
JOYOUS
JUBARB
JUBATE
JUBBAH
JUBHAH
JUBILE
JUDDER
JUDGED
JUDGER
JUECES
JUFFER
JUGALE
JUGATE
JUGFUL
JUGGED
JUGGER
JUGGLE
JUGLAR
JUGULA
JUGUMS
JUICER
JUJUBE
JULOID
JULOLE
JUMART
JUMBIE
JUMBLE
JUMBLY
JUMBOS
JUMENT
JUMFRU
JUMPED
JUMPER
JUNCOS
JUNCUS
JUNDIE
JUNGLE
JUNGLI
JUNGLY
JUNIOR
JUNKER
JUNKET
JUNKIE
JUNTAS
JUNTOS
JUPATI
JURANT
JURARA
JURATA
JURIES
JURING
JURIST
JURORS
JUSLIK
JUSSAL
JUSSEL
JUSTEN
JUSTER
JUSTLE
JUSTLY
JUTTED
JUVENT
JUVITE
JUWISE
JUZAIL

KHAJUR
KHARAJ
KHOJAH
KONJAK
KURUNJ
LOGJAM
LUJULA
MAATJE
MAJOON
MANJAK
MANJEL
MASJID
MEISJE
MILJEE
MOONJA
MOUJIK
MUSJID
MUTSJE
MUZJIK
OBJECT
OBJURE
OREJON
OUTJUT
PAJAMA
PAJERO
PAJOCK
PAREJA
PINJRA
POOJAH
POPJOY
PRAJNA
PUNJUM
PYJAMA
RAKIJA
REJECT
REJOIN
REJOLT
SANJAK
SEJANT
SEJERO
SEJOIN
SEJOUR
SIJILL
SINJER
SJOMIL
SVARAJ
SWARAJ
TALAJE
TANJIB
TASAJO
TEJANO
THUJYL
TINAJA
TJAELE
TJANDI
TOMJON
TONJON
TRAJET
UNJUST
WAJANG
WEJACK
WITJAR
YAJEIN
YOJANA
ZANJON

POSITIONAL ORDER LIST OF 6-LETTER WORDS

JABBED
JABBER
JABBLE
JABERS
JABIRU
JABOTS
JABULS
JACANA
JACARE
JACATE
JACENT
JACKAL
JACKED
JACKER
JACKET
JACOBY
JADDED
JADDER
JADERY
JADING
JADISH
JAEGER
JAGEER
JAGGAR
JAGGED
JAGGER
JAGHIR
JAGONG
JAGUAR
JAGUEY
JAILED
JAILER
JAILOR
JALAPA
JALKAR
JALOPY
JAMBEE
JAMBER
JAMBON
JAMBUL
JAMMED
JAMMER
JAMNUT
JAMOKE
JAMPAN
JANAPA
JANGAR
JANGLE
JANGLY
JANKER
JANNER
JANTEE
JAPERY
JAPING
JAPISH
JARABE
JARANA
JARBLE
JARBOT
JAREED
JARFLY
JARFUL
JARGON
JARINA
JARNUT
JAROOL
JARRAH
JARRED
JARRET
JARVEY
JASEYS
JASMIN
JASPER
JASPIS
JASSID
JATACO
JATOBA
JAUDIE
JAUNCE
JAUNER
JAUNTY
JAVALI
JAVVER
JAWING
JAYGEE
JAYPIE
JAYVEE
JAZZER
JEERED
JEERER
JEETEE
JEJUNA
JEJUNE
JELICK
JELLAB
JEMBLE
JENKIN
JENNET
JENOAR
JERBOA
JEREED
JERKED
JERKER
JERKIN
JERNIE
JERQUE
JERRID
JERSEY
JERVIA
JERVIN
JESSED
JESSUR
JESTED
JESTEE
JESTER
JETSAM
JETTED
JETTER
JETTON
JETTRU
JEWELS
JEWELY
JEWING
JEZAIL
JEZIAH
JHARAL
JIBBAH
JIBBED
JIBBEH
JIBBER
JIBING
JIBMAN
JIBMEN
JIBOYA
JICAMA
JICARA
JIFFLE
JIGGED
JIGGER
JIGGET
JIGGIT
JIGGLE
JIGGLY
JIGMAN
JIGMEN
JIGOTE
JIGSAW
JILLET
JILTED
JILTEE
JILTER
JIMJAM
JIMJAM
JIMMER
JIMPLY
JIMSON
JINETE
JINGAL
JINGLE
JINGLY
JINKED
JINKER
JINKET
JINKLE
JINNEE
JINSHA
JIPPER
JIRBLE
JIRGAH
JITNEY
JITTER
JIZYAH
JIZZEN
JOBADE
JOBBED
JOBBER
JOBBLE
JOBMAN
JOBMEN
JOBSON
JOCANT
JOCKER
JOCKEY
JOCKOS
JOCOSE
JOCOTE
JOCUMA
JOCUND
JOGGED
JOGGER
JOGGLE
JOGGLY
JOHNIN
JOINED
JOINER
JOINTS
JOINTY
JOKIER
JOKING
JOKISH
JOKIST
JOLLOP
JOLTED
JOLTER
JONDLA
JORDAN
JORDEN
JOROPO
JORRAM
JOSEPH
JOSHER
JOSKIN
JOSSER
JOSTLE
JOTISI
JOTTED
JOTTER
JOUNCE
JOUSTS
JOUTES
JOVIAL
JOWARI
JOWERY
JOWLER
JOWLOP
JOWSER
JOWTER
JOYANT
JOYFUL
JOYHOP
JOYING
JOYOUS
JUBARB
JUBATE
JUBBAH
JUBHAH
JUBILE
JUDDER
JUDGED
JUDGER
JUECES
JUFFER
JUGALE
JUGATE
JUGFUL
JUGGED
JUGGER
JUGGLE
JUGLAR
JUGULA
JUGUMS
JUICER
JUJUBE
JULOID
JULOLE
JUMART
JUMBIE
JUMBLE
JUMBLY
JUMBOS
JUMENT
JUMFRU
JUMPED
JUMPER
JUNCOS
JUNCUS
JUNDIE
JUNGLE
JUNGLI
JUNGLY
JUNIOR
JUNKER
JUNKET
JUNKIE
JUNTAS
JUNTOS
JUPATI
JURANT
JURARA
JURATA
JURIES
JURING
JURIST
JURORS
JUSLIK

JUSSAL
JUSSEL
JUSTEN
JUSTER
JUSTLE
JUSTLY
JUTTED
JUVENT
JUVITE
JUWISE
JUZAIL

AJENJO
AJIMEZ
AJOINT
AJOURE
AJOWAN
DJEBEL
DJELFA
DJERIB
DJERSA
DJINNI
EJECTA
EJIDAL
SJOMIL
TJAELE
TJANDI

ABJECT
ABJURE
ADJECT
ADJIGA
ADJOIN
ADJURE
ADJUST
ALJAMA
BAJADA
BAJREE
BEJADE
BEJANT
BEJAPE
BEJUCO
BIJOUX
BOJITE
CAJAVA
CAJETA
CAJOLE
DEJECT
ENJAIL
ENJAMB
ENJOIN
HEJIRA
HIJACK
INJECT
INJURE
INJURY
INJUST
JEJUNA
JEJUNE
JUJUBE
LUJULA
MAJOON
OBJECT
OBJURE
PAJAMA
PAJERO
PAJOCK
PYJAMA
REJECT
REJOIN
REJOLT
SEJANT
SEJERO
SEJOIN
SEJOUR
SIJILL
TEJANO
UNJUST
WAJANG
WEJACK
YAJEIN
YOJANA

ACAJOU
AGUJON
ANTJAR
AVIJJA
BANJAK
BANJOS
BOOJUM
CROJIK
CADJAN
CONJEE
CONJON
CUNJAH
CUNJER
DEEJAY
DONJON
EVEJAR
FANJET
FINJAN
GIDJEE
GOUJAT
GOUJON
GUNJAH
GURJAN
GURJUN
KHAJUR
KHOJAH
KONJAK
LOGJAM
MANJAK
MANJEL
MASJID
MILJEE
MOUJIK
MUSJID
MUZJIK
OREJON
OUTJUT
PINJRA
POOJAH
POPJOY
PRAJNA
PUNJUM
SANJAK
SINJER
TANJIB
THUJYL
TOMJON
TONJON
TRAJET
WITJAR
ZANJON

AGUAJI
AJENJO
ALFAJE
AVIJJA
CABUJA
CARAJO
COROJO
ELCAJA
FREIJO
FYLGJA
GYTTJA
MAATJE
MEISJE
MOONJA
MUTSJE
PAREJA
RAKIJA
TALAJE
TASAJO
TINAJA

KHARAJ
KURUNJ
SVARAJ
SWARAJ

SCORING ORDER LIST OF 6-LETTER WORDS

28
JIZYAH
MUZJIK

25
JEZIAH

24
AJIMEZ

23
KHOJAH

22
BIJOUX
HIJACK
JERQUE
JEZAIL
JOCKEY
JUZAIL
WEJACK
ZANJON

21
JAZZER
JIZZEN
JOYHOP
JUBHAH
PAJOCK

20
FYLGJA
JACKED
JACOBY
JIBBAH
JIBBEH
JIMPLY
JOKISH
JUBBAH
JUMBLY
KHAJUR
KHARAJ
POPJOY
PYJAMA

19
BANJAK
CROJIK
JACKAL
JACKER
JACKET
JAMOKE
JARFLY
JARVEY
JAVVER
JAYVEE
JELICK
JEWELY
JIFFLE
JOCKER
JOCKOS
JOWERY
JOYFUL
JUFFER
MANJAK
MOUJIK
THUJYL

18
CAJAVA
CUNJAH
JABBED
JALOPY
JAMMED
JAPERY
JAPISH
JAYPIE
JERKED
JIBBED
JIBOYA
JIGGLY
JINKED
JOBBED
JOGGLY
JOKING
JOSEPH
JOWLOP
JUMFRU
JUMPED
POOJAH

17
ABJECT
BEJAPE
BEJUCO
BOOJUM
CABUJA
DEEJAY
DJELFA
ENJAMB
GUNJAH
GYTTJA
JABBER
JABBLE
JADERY
JADISH
JAGHIR
JAGUEY
JALKAR
JAMBEE
JAMBER
JAMBON
JAMBUL
JAMMER
JAMPAN
JANGLY
JANKER
JAWING
JAYGEE
JEMBLE
JENKIN
JERKER
JERKIN
JEWING
JIBBER
JIBMAN
JIBMEN
JICAMA
JIGSAW
JIMMER
JINGLY
JINKER
JINKET
JINKLE
JIPPER
JIRGAH
JOBBER
JOBBLE
JOBMAN
JOBMEN
JOCUMA
JOKIER
JOKIST
JOSKIN
JOYING
JUBARB
JUGFUL
JUMBIE
JUMBLE
JUMBOS
JUMPER
JUNGLY
JUNKER
JUNKET
JUNKIE
JUSLIK
KURUNJ
OBJECT
PAJAMA
PUNJUM
RAKIJA
SANJAK
WAJANG

16
ADJECT
AJOWAN
ALFAJE
BAJADA
BEJADE
CADJAN
DEJECT
DJEBEL
DJERIB
EVEJAR
FANJET
FINJAN
FREIJO
HEJIRA
INJURY
JADDED
JAGGED
JAPING
JARFUL
JARRAH
JASEYS
JAUNTY
JAVALI
JERSEY
JERVIA

JERVIN
JEWELS
JHARAL
JIBING
JIGGED
JIGMAN
JIGMEN
JIMJAM
JINSHA
JITNEY
JOBADE
JOCUND
JOGGED
JOINTY
JOSHER
JOVIAL
JOWARI
JOWLER
JOWSER
JOWTER
JOYANT
JOYOUS
JUDGED
JUGGED
JUGUMS
JUSTLY
JUVENT
JUVITE
JUWISE
KONJAK
LOGJAM
MASJID
MUSJID
SVARAJ
SWARAJ
WITJAR
YAJEIN
YOJANA

15

ABJURE
ACAJOU
ADJIGA
ALJAMA
AVIJJA
BAJREE
BANJOS
BEJANT
BOJITE
CAJETA
CAJOLE
CARAJO
CONJEE
CONJON
COROJO
CUNJER
EJECTA
ELCAJA
GIDJEE
INJECT
JABERS
JABIRU
JABOTS
JABULS
JACANA
JACARE
JACATE
JACENT
JADDER
JADING
JAGGAR
JAGGER
JAGONG
JALAPA
JAMNUT
JANAPA
JARABE
JARBLE
JARBOT
JASMIN
JASPER
JASPIS
JATACO
JATOBA
JAUNCE
JELLAB
JERBOA
JETSAM
JICARA
JIGGER
JIGGET
JIGGIT
JIGGLE
JIMSON
JIRBLE
JOBSON
JOCANT
JOCOSE
JOCOTE
JOGGER
JOGGLE
JOLLOP
JOROPO
JORRAM
JOUNCE
JUBATE
JUBILE
JUDDER
JUDGER
JUECES
JUGGER
JUGGLE
JUICER
JUMART
JUMENT
JUNCOS
JUNCUS
JUPATI
MAATJE
MAJOON
MANJEL
MEISJE
MILJEE
MOONJA
MUTSJE
OBJURE
PAJERO
PAREJA
PINJRA
PRAJNA
REJECT
SJOMIL
TANJIB
TOMJON

14

ADJOIN
ADJURE
ADJUST
AGUAJI
AGUJON
DJERSA
DJINNI
DONJON
EJIDAL
GOUJAT
GOUJON
GURJAN
GURJUN
JAEGER
JAGEER
JAGUAR
JAILED
JANGAR
JANGLE
JAREED
JARGON
JARRED
JASSID
JAUDIE
JEERED
JEREED
JERRID
JESSED
JESTED
JETTED
JIGOTE
JILTED
JINGAL
JINGLE
JOINED
JOJOBA
JOLTED
JONDLA
JORDAN
JORDEN
JOTTED
JUGALE
JUGATE
JUGLAR
JUGULA
JUJUBE
JULOID
JUNDIE
JUNGLE
JUNGLI
JURING
JUTTED
TJANDI

13

AJOINT
AJOURE
ANTJAR
ENJAIL
ENJOIN
INJURE
INJUST
JAILER
JAILOR
JANNER
JANTEE
JARANA
JARINA
JARNUT
JAROOL
JARRET
JAUNER
JEERER
JEETEE
JENNET
JENOAR
JERNIE
JESSUR
JESTEE
JESTER
JETTER
JETTON
JETTRU
JILLET
JILTEE
JILTER
JINETE
JINNEE
JITTER
JOINER
JOINTS
JOLTER
JOSSER
JOSTLE
JOTISI
JOTTER
JOUSTS
JOUTES
JULOLE
JUNIOR
JUNTAS
JUNTOS
JURANT
JURARA
JURATA
JURIES
JURIST
JURORS
JUSSAL
JUSSEL
JUSTEN
JUSTER
JUSTLE
LUJULA
OREJON
OUTJUT
REJOIN
REJOLT
SEJANT
SEJERO
SEJOIN
SEJOUR
SIJILL
SINJER
TALAJE
TASAJO
TEJANO
TINAJA
TJAELE
TONJON
TRAJET
UNJUST

12

AJENJO
JEJUNA
JEJUNE

ALPHABETICAL LIST OF 7-LETTER WORDS

ABADEJO
ABJOINT
ABJUDGE
ABJURED
ABJURER
ADJIGER
ADJOINT
ADJOURN
ADJOUST
ADJUDGE
ADJUNCT
ADJURED
ADJURER
ADJUROR
ADJUTOR
AJANGLE
AJITTER
AJIVIKA
ALFORJA
ALJAMIA
APAREJO
APOJOVE
ARVEJON
AZUELJO
BACKJAW
BAJOCCO
BAJOCHI
BAJOIRE
BANJARA
BANJOES
BANJORE
BASENJI
BEJESUS
BEJEWEL
BENJOIN
BIJASAL
BLIJVER
BRINJAL
CAJAPUT
CAJEPUT
CAJOLED
CAJOLER
CAJUELA
CAJUPUT
CATJANG
COJUROR
COMITJE
CONJECT
CONJOIN
CONJURE
CONJURY
DEJECTA
DEJEUNE
DISJECT
DISJOIN

DISJUNE
DJIBBAH
EJECTED
EJECTOR
EJULATE
EJURATE
ENJEWEL
ENJOYED
ENJOYER
FAUJDAR
FERIDJI
FERIJEE
FINDJAN
FJORDED
FOUJDAR
GALJOEN
GEITJIE
GIOJOSO
GJEDOST
GOTRAJA
GUAJIRA
HAJILIJ
HANDJAR
HIJINKS
IJOLITE
INJELLY
INJOINT
INJUNCT
INJURED
INJURER
INJURIA
JABBING
JABORIN
JABULES
JACALES
JACAMAR
JACAMIN
JACATOO
JACCHUS
JACINTH
JACKALS
JACKASH
JACKASS
JACKBOX
JACKBOY
JACKDAW
JACKEEN
JACKETY
JACKING
JACKLEG
JACKMAN
JACKMEN
JACKPOT
JACKROD
JACKSAW
JACKTAN
JACOBIN
JACOBUS
JACONET
JACTANT
JACTURE
JACUARU
JADDING
JADEDLY
JADEITE
JAGGARY
JAGGERY
JAGGIER
JAGGING
JAGHEER
JAGHIRE
JAGRATA
JAGUARS
JAILAGE
JALAPIC
JALAPIN
JALOPPY
JALOUSE
JAMBEAU
JAMBONE
JAMBOOL
JAMBOSA
JAMDANI
JAMMING
JAMPANI
JAMWOOD
JANAPAN
JANAPUM
JANDERS
JANGADA
JANGKAR
JANGLED
JANGLER
JANITOR
JANKERS
JANNOCK
JAPYGID
JAQUIMA
JARAGUA
JARBIRD
JARGOON
JARHEAD
JARKMAN
JARLESS
JARLITE
JARRING
JARVEYS
JASEYED
JASMINE
JASMONE
JASPERY
JASPOID
JAUNDER
JAUNTED
JAUNTIE
JAVELIN
JAVELOT
JAWBONE
JAWFALL
JAWFEET
JAWFISH
JAWFOOT
JAWHOLE
JAYHAWK
JAYPIET
JAYWALK
JAZERAN
JAZZBOW
JAZZIER
JAZZILY
JEALOUS
JECORAL
JECORIN
JEDCOCK
JEDDOCK
JEEPERS
JEEPNEY
JEERING
JEJUNAL
JEJUNUM
JELLICA
JELLICO
JELLIED
JELLIES
JELLIFY
JELLILY
JELLOID
JEMADAR
JEMIDAR
JEMMIES
JEMMILY
JENNIER
JENNIES
JEOFAIL
JEOPARD
JERICAN
JERKIER
JERKILY
JERKING
JERKISH
JERQUED
JERQUER
JERRIES
JERSEYS
JERVINA
JERVINE
JESSAMY
JESSANT
JESSING
JESTING
JETBEAD
JETPORT
JETTAGE
JETTEAU
JETTIED
JETTIES
JETTING
JETWARE
JEWBIRD
JEWBUSH
JEWELED
JEWELER
JEWELLY
JEWELRY
JEWFISH
JIBBING
JIBBOOM
JIBHEAD
JIBSTAY
JIFFIES
JIGGERS
JIGGETY
JIGGING
JIGGISH
JIGGLED
JIKUNGU
JILLING
JILLION
JILTING
JIMBANG
JIMJAMS
JIMMIED
JIMMIES
JINGALL
JINGLED
JINGLER
JINGLET
JINGOED
JINGOES
JINJILI
JINKING
JINNIES
JINRIKI
JINSING
JITNEUR
JITNEYS
JITTERS
JITTERY
JIVATMA
JOANNES
JOBARBE
JOBBERY
JOBBING
JOBBISH
JOBLESS
JOBSITE
JOCKEYS
JOCOQUE
JOCOQUI
JOCULAR
JOEBUSH
JOEWOOD
JOGGING
JOGGLED
JOGGLER
JOINANT
JOINDER
JOINERY
JOINING
JOINTED
JOINTER
JOINTLY
JOISTED
JOKELET
JOKIEST
JOLLIED
JOLLIER
JOLLIES
JOLLIFY
JOLLILY
JOLLITY
JOLTING
JONQUIL
JORNADA
JOSEITE
JOSTLED
JOSTLER
JOTTING
JOUBARB
JOUKERY
JOULEAN
JOUNCED
JOURNAL
JOURNEY
JOUSTER
JOYANCE
JOYANCY
JOYLEAF
JOYLESS
JOYRIDE
JOYSOME
JOYWEED
JUAMAVE
JUBILEE
JUBILUS
JUCHART
JUCKIES
JUDCOCK
JUDDOCK
JUDGING
JUDICES
JUGATED
JUGGING
JUGGINS
JUGGLED
JUGGLER
JUGHEAD
JUGLONE
JUGULAR
JUGULUM
JUICIER
JUICILY
JUJUIST
JUJITSU
JUJUISM
JUJUTSU
JUKEBOX
JULIDAN
JULIETT
JULOLIN
JUMBLED
JUMBLER
JUMBUCK
JUMELLE
JUMPERS
JUMPIER
JUMPING
JUMPOFF
JUNCITE
JUNCOUS
JUNCTLY
JUNGLED
JUNIATA
JUNIPER
JUNKING
JUNKMAN
JUNKMEN
JURALLY
JURATOR
JURIDIC
JURYMAN
JURYMEN
JUSSION
JUSSIVE
JUSSORY
JUSTICE
JUSTICO
JUSTIFY
JUSTLER
JUTTIES
JUTTING
JUVENAL
JYNGINE
KAJAWAH
KAJEPUT
KANDJAR
KANKREJ
KEDJAVE
KHANJAR
KHANJEE
KILADJA
KILLJOY
KORADJI
LOCKJAW
LONGJAW
MAHAJAN
MAHAJUN
MAHJONG
MAJAGUA
MAJESTY
MAJORAT
MANJACK
MANJEET
MOJARRA
MONTJOY
MUJERES
MUMJUMA
MUNJEET
MUNTJAC
MUNTJAK
NAARTJE
OBJECTS
OUTJAZZ
OUTJINX
OUTJUMP
OVERJOY
PAJAMAS
PARANJA
PERJINK
PERJURE
PERJURY
PINJANE
PIROJKI
PROJECT
PROPJET
PULAJAN
PULIJAN
PYJAMAS
REJOICE
REJONEO
REJOURN
REJUDGE
SAPAJOU
SATLIJK
SEJEANT

SEJUNCT
SJAMBOK
SJOMILA
SKIJORE
SKYJACK
SOJOURN

STANJEN
SUBJECT
SUBJOIN
TANJONG
THUJENE
THUJONE

TJENKAL
TJOSITE
TOMJOHN
TORONJA
TRAJECT

TURJITE
UINTJIE
VANJOHN
VIAJACA
WICHTJE

WINDJAM
YAJEINE
YAJENIN
ZANJERO
ZANJONA

POSITIONAL ORDER LIST OF 7-LETTER WORDS

JABBING
JABORIN
JABULES
JACALES
JACAMAR
JACAMIN
JACATOO
JACCHUS
JACINTH
JACKALS
JACKASH
JACKASS
JACKBOX
JACKBOY
JACKDAW
JACKEEN
JACKETY
JACKING
JACKLEG
JACKMAN
JACKMEN
JACKPOT
JACKROD
JACKSAW
JACKTAN
JACOBIN
JACOBUS
JACONET
JACTANT
JACTURE
JACUARU
JADDING
JADEDLY
JADEITE
JAGGARY
JAGGERY
JAGGIER
JAGGING
JAGHEER
JAGHIRE
JAGRATA
JAGUARS
JAILAGE
JALAPIC
JALAPIN
JALOPPY
JALOUSE
JAMBEAU
JAMBONE
JAMBOOL
JAMBOSA
JAMDANI
JAMMING
JAMPANI
JAMWOOD
JANAPAN
JANAPUM
JANDERS
JANGADA
JANGKAR
JANGLED
JANGLER
JANITOR
JANKERS
JANNOCK

JAPYGID
JAQUIMA
JARAGUA
JARBIRD
JARGOON
JARHEAD
JARKMAN
JARLESS
JARLITE
JARRING
JARVEYS
JASEYED
JASMINE
JASMONE
JASPERY
JASPOID
JAUNDER
JAUNTED
JAUNTIE
JAVELIN
JAVELOT
JAWBONE
JAWFALL
JAWFEET
JAWFISH
JAWFOOT
JAWHOLE
JAYHAWK
JAYPIET
JAYWALK
JAZERAN
JAZZBOW
JAZZIER
JAZZILY
JEALOUS
JECORAL
JECORIN
JEDCOCK
JEDDOCK
JEEPERS
JEEPNEY
JEERING
JEJUNAL
JEJUNUM
JELLICA
JELLICO
JELLIED
JELLIES
JELLIFY
JELLILY
JELLOID
JEMADAR
JEMIDAR
JEMMIES
JEMMILY
JENNIER
JENNIES
JEOFAIL
JEOPARD
JERICAN
JERKIER
JERKILY
JERKING
JERKISH
JERQUED

JERQUER
JERRIES
JERSEYS
JERVINA
JERVINE
JESSAMY
JESSANT
JESSING
JESTING
JETBEAD
JETPORT
JETTAGE
JETTEAU
JETTIED
JETTIES
JETTING
JETWARE
JEWBIRD
JEWBUSH
JEWELED
JEWELER
JEWELLY
JEWELRY
JEWFISH
JIBBING
JIBBOOM
JIBHEAD
JIBSTAY
JIFFIES
JIGGERS
JIGGETY
JIGGING
JIGGISH
JIGGLED
JIKUNGU
JILLING
JILLION
JILTING
JIMBANG
JIMJAMS
JIMMIED
JIMMIES
JINGALL
JINGLED
JINGLER
JINGLET
JINGOED
JINGOES
JINJILI
JINKING
JINNIES
JINRIKI
JINSING
JITNEUR
JITNEYS
JITTERS
JITTERY
JIVATMA
JOANNES
JOBARBE
JOBBERY
JOBBING
JOBBISH
JOBLESS
JOBSITE

JOCKEYS
JOCOQUE
JOCOQUI
JOCULAR
JOEBUSH
JOEWOOD
JOGGING
JOGGLED
JOGGLER
JOINANT
JOINDER
JOINERY
JOINING
JOINTED
JOINTER
JOINTLY
JOISTED
JOKELET
JOKIEST
JOLLIED
JOLLIER
JOLLIES
JOLLIFY
JOLLILY
JOLLITY
JOLTING
JONQUIL
JORNADA
JOSEITE
JOSTLED
JOSTLER
JOTTING
JOUBARB
JOUKERY
JOULEAN
JOUNCED
JOURNAL
JOURNEY
JOUSTER
JOYANCE
JOYANCY
JOYLEAF
JOYLESS
JOYRIDE
JOYSOME
JOYWEED
JUAMAVE
JUBILEE
JUBILUS
JUCHART
JUCKIES
JUDCOCK
JUDDOCK
JUDGING
JUDICES
JUGATED
JUGGING
JUGGINS
JUGGLED
JUGGLER
JUGHEAD
JUGLONE
JUGULAR
JUGULUM
JUICIER

JUICILY
JUJUIST
JUJITSU
JUJUISM
JUJUTSU
JUKEBOX
JULIDAN
JULIETT
JULOLIN
JUMBLED
JUMBLER
JUMBUCK
JUMELLE
JUMPERS
JUMPIER
JUMPING
JUMPOFF
JUNCITE
JUNCOUS
JUNCTLY
JUNGLED
JUNIATA
JUNIPER
JUNKING
JUNKMAN
JUNKMEN
JURALLY
JURATOR
JURIDIC
JURYMAN
JURYMEN
JUSSION
JUSSIVE
JUSSORY
JUSTICE
JUSTICO
JUSTIFY
JUSTLER
JUTTIES
JUTTING
JUVENAL
JYNGINE

AJANGLE
AJITTER
AJIVIKA
DJIBBAH
EJECTED
EJECTOR
EJULATE
EJURATE
FJORDED
GJEDOST
IJOLITE
SJAMBOK
SJOMILA
TJENKAL
TJOSITE

ABJOINT
ABJUDGE
ABJURED
ABJURER
ADJIGER
ADJOINT

ADJOURN
ADJOUST
ADJUDGE
ADJUNCT
ADJURED
ADJURER
ADJUROR
ADJUTOR
ALJAMIA
BAJOCCO
BAJOCHI
BAJOIRE
BEJESUS
BEJEWEL
BIJASAL
CAJAPUT
CAJEPUT
CAJOLED
CAJOLER
CAJUELA
CAJUPUT
COJUROR
DEJECTA
DEJEUNE
ENJEWEL
ENJOYED
ENJOYER
HAJILIJ
HIJINKS
INJELLY
INJOINT
INJUNCT
INJURED
INJURER
INJURIA
JEJUNAL
JEJUNUM
JUJUIST
JUJITSU
JUJUISM
JUJUTSU
KAJAWAH
KAJEPUT
MAJAGUA
MAJESTY
MAJORAT
MOJARRA
MUJERES
OBJECTS
PAJAMAS
PYJAMAS
REJOICE
REJONEO
REJOURN
REJUDGE
SEJEANT
SEJUNCT
SOJOURN
YAJEINE
YAJENIN

APOJOVE
BANJARA
BANJOES
BANJORE
BENJOIN
BLIJVER
CATJANG
CONJECT
CONJOIN
CONJURE
CONJURY
DISJECT
DISJOIN
DISJUNE
FAUJDAR
FOUJDAR
GALJOEN
GIOJOSO
GUAJIRA
JIMJAMS
JINJILI
KEDJAVE
MAHJONG
MANJACK
MANJEET
MUMJUMA
MUNJEET
OUTJAZZ
OUTJINX
OUTJUMP
PERJINK
PERJURE
PERJURY
PINJANE
PROJECT
SKIJORE
SKYJACK
SUBJECT
SUBJOIN
TANJONG
THUJENE
THUJONE
TOMJOHN
TRAJECT
TURJITE
VANJOHN
VIAJACA
ZANJERO
ZANJONA

ARVEJON
BACKJAW
BRINJAL
FERIJEE
FINDJAN
GEITJIE
HANDJAR
KANDJAR
KHANJAR
KHANJEE
KILLJOY
LOCKJAW
LONGJAW
MAHAJAN
MAHAJUN
MONTJOY
MUNTJAC
MUNTJAK
OVERJOY
PIROJKI
PROPJET
PULAJAN
PULIJAN
SAPAJOU
STANJEN
UINTJIE
WINDJAM

ABADEJO
ALFORJA
APAREJO
AZUELJO
BASENJI
COMITJE
FERIDJI
GOTRAJA
KILADJA
KORADJI
NAARTJE
PARANJA
SATLIJK
TORONJA
WICHTJE

HAJILIJ
KANKREJ

SCORING ORDER LIST OF 7-LETTER WORDS

29
JACKBOX

27
JAYHAWK
JAZZBOW
JUKEBOX

25
BACKJAW
JACKBOY
JAQUIMA
JAZZILY
JOCOQUE
JOCOQUI

24
JACKDAW
JAYWALK
JERQUED
JUMBUCK
JUMPOFF
KAJAWAH

23
AZUELJO
JACKASH
JACKETY
JACKSAW
JAWFISH
JAZERAN
JEDCOCK
JERQUER
JEWFISH
JOCKEYS
JONQUIL
JUDCOCK
LOCKJAW
ZANJERO
ZANJONA

22
DJIBBAH
JACKMAN
JACKMEN
JACKPOT
JAZZIER
JEDDOCK
JEWBUSH
JOYANCY
JUDDOCK
KEDJAVE
MANJACK
OUTJAZZ
SJAMBOK
SKYJACK
WICHTJE

21
AJIVIKA
BAJOCHI
HIJINKS
JACCHUS
JACKING
JACKLEG
JACKROD
JALOPPY
JAPYGID
JEMMILY
JERKILY
JERKISH
JOBBERY
JOBBISH
JOUKERY
JOYWEED
KHANJAR
KHANJEE
KILLJOY
OUTJINX
PYJAMAS

20
BAJOCCO
JACKALS
JACKASS
JACKEEN
JACKTAN
JAMWOOD
JANNOCK
JARKMAN
JARVEYS
JAWFALL
JAWFEET
JAWFOOT
JAWHOLE
JELLIFY
JEWBIRD
JEWELLY
JEWELRY
JIBBOOM
JIBHEAD
JIFFIES
JOLLIFY
JOYLEAF
JUCKIES
JUNKMAN
JUNKMEN
JUSTIFY
KAJEPUT
MAHJONG
MUNTJAK
OVERJOY
PERJINK
PIROJKI
VANJOHN
WINDJAM

19
APOJOVE
BEJEWEL
BLIJVER
CONJURY
FJORDED
JABBING
JACINTH
JADEDLY
JAGGARY
JAGGERY
JAMMING
JANGKAR
JASPERY
JAWBONE
JAYPIET
JEEPNEY
JERKING
JESSAMY
JIBBING
JIBSTAY
JIGGETY
JIGGISH
JIKUNGU
JIMBANG
JIMMIED
JINKING
JIVATMA
JOBBING
JOEBUSH
JOYANCE
JOYSOME
JUAMAVE
JUCHART
JUGHEAD
JUICILY
JUMBLED
JUMPING
JUNCTLY
JUNKING
JURYMAN
JURYMEN
KANDJAR
KILADJA
KORADJI
MAHAJAN
MAHAJUN
MAJESTY
MONTJOY
PERJURY
TOMJOHN
VIAJACA

18
ABJUDGE
CAJAPUT
CAJEPUT
CAJUPUT
COMITJE
CONJECT
ENJOYED
FAUJDAR
FERIDJI
FINDJAN
FOUJDAR
HANDJAR
JACAMAR
JACAMIN
JACOBIN
JACOBUS
JAGHEER
JAGHIRE
JALAPIC
JAMBEAU
JAMBONE
JAMBOOL
JAMBOSA
JAMPANI

JANAPUM
JANKERS
JARHEAD
JASEYED
JEMMIES
JERKIER
JEWELED
JIMMIES
JINRIKI
JOBARBE
JOEWOOD
JOKELET
JOKIEST
JOUBARB
JOYRIDE
JUMBLER
JUMPERS
JUMPIER
JYNGINE
LONGJAW
MUNTJAC
OBJECTS
OUTJUMP
PAJAMAS
PROJECT
PROPJET
SATLIJK
SKIJORE
SUBJECT
TJENKAL

17

ABADEJO
ABJURED
ADJUDGE
ADJUNCT
ALFORJA
ARVEJON
CAJOLED
CATJANG
DEJECTA
DISJECT
EJECTED
ENJEWEL
ENJOYER
FERIJEE
INJELLY
JADDING
JAGGING
JAMDANI
JARBIRD
JASPOID
JAVELIN
JAVELOT
JELLILY
JEMADAR
JEMIDAR
JEOFAIL
JEOPARD
JERSEYS
JERVINA
JERVINE
JETBEAD
JETWARE
JEWELER
JIGGING
JIGGLED
JIMJAMS
JITNEYS
JITTERY
JOGGING
JOGGLED
JOINERY
JOINTLY
JOLLILY
JOLLITY
JOUNCED
JOURNEY
JOYLESS
JUDGING
JUDICES
JUGGING
JUGGLED
JUGULUM
JURALLY
JURIDIC
JUSSIVE
JUSSORY
JUVENAL
KANKREJ
MAJAGUA
MUMJUMA
THUJENE
THUJONE
YAJEINE
YAJENIN

16

ABJOINT
ABJURER
ADJIGER
ADJURED
ALJAMIA
APAREJO
BAJOIRE
BANJARA
BANJOES
BANJORE
BASENJI
BEJESUS
BENJOIN
BIJASAL
BRINJAL
CAJOLER
CAJUELA
COJUROR
CONJOIN
CONJURE
EJECTOR
GJEDOST
HAJILIJ
INJUNCT
JABORIN
JABULES
JACALES
JACATOO
JACONET
JACTANT
JACTURE
JACUARU
JAGGIER
JALAPIN
JANAPAN
JANGADA
JANGLED
JASMINE
JASMONE
JECORAL
JECORIN
JEEPERS
JELLICA
JELLICO
JERICAN
JETPORT
JIGGERS
JINGLED
JINGOED
JOBLESS
JOBSITE
JOCULAR
JOGGLER
JUBILEE
JUBILUS
JUGATED
JUGGINS
JUGGLER
JUICIER
JUMELLE
JUNCITE
JUNCOUS
JUNGLED
JUNIPER
JUSTICE
JUSTICO
MAJORAT
MANJEET
MOJARRA
MUJERES
MUNJEET
PARANJA
PERJURE
PINJANE
PULAJAN
PULIJAN
REJOICE
REJUDGE
SAPAJOU
SEJUNCT
SJOMILA
SUBJOIN
TRAJECT

15

ADJOINT
ADJOURN
ADJOUST
ADJURER
ADJUROR
ADJUTOR
AJANGLE
DEJEUNE
DISJOIN
DISJUNE
GALJOEN
GEITJIE
GIOJOSO
GOTRAJA
GUAJIRA
INJURED
JADEITE
JAGRATA
JAGUARS
JAILAGE
JANDERS
JANGLER
JARAGUA
JARGOON
JARRING
JAUNDER
JAUNTED
JEERING
JEJUNUM
JELLIED
JELLOID
JESSING
JESTING
JETTAGE
JETTIED
JETTING
JILLING
JILTING
JINGALL
JINGLER
JINGLET
JINGOES
JINSING
JOINDER
JOINING
JOINTED
JOISTED
JOLLIED
JOLTING
JORNADA
JOSTLED
JOTTING
JUGLONE
JUGULAR
JUJUISM
JULIDAN
JUTTING
TANJONG

14

AJITTER
EJULATE
EJURATE
IJOLITE
INJOINT
INJURER
INJURIA
JALOUSE
JANITOR
JARLESS
JARLITE
JAUNTIE
JEALOUS
JELLIES
JENNIER
JENNIES
JERRIES
JESSANT
JETTEAU
JETTIES
JILLION
JINNIES
JITNEUR
JITTERS
JOANNES
JOINANT
JOINTER
JOLLIER
JOLLIES
JOSEITE
JOSTLER
JOULEAN
JOURNAL
JOUSTER
JULIETT
JULOLIN
JUNIATA
JURATOR
JUSSION
JUSTLER
JUTTIES
NAARTJE
REJONEO
REJOURN
SEJEANT
SOJOURN
STANJEN
TJOSITE
TORONJA
TURJITE
UINTJIE

13

JEJUNAL
JINJILI
JUJUIST
JUJITSU
JUJUTSU

ALPHABETICAL LIST OF 8-LETTER WORDS

ABJECTLY
ABJURING
ADJACENT
ADJOINED
ADJUDGED
ADJUDGER
ADJUGATE
ADJUMENT
ADJURING
ADJUSTED
ADJUSTER
ADJUSTOR
ADJUTAGE
ADJUTANT
ADJUTORY
ADJUTRIX
ADJUVANT
ADJUVATE
AJONJOLI
AJOURISE
AJUTMENT
ALJAMADO
ALJAMIAH
ALLELUJA
APAREJOS

BABAJAGA
BAJONADO
BAJULATE
BEJABERS
BEJUGGLE
BENJAMIN
BIAJAIBA
BIJUGATE
BIJUGOUS
BIJWONER
BLATJANG
BLUEJACK
BOBJEROM
BOOTJACK
BOSTANJI
BRINJAUL
BRUJERIA
BUCKJUMP
CAJOLERY
CAJOLING
CANAJONG
CARAJURA
CARCAJOU
COADJUST
COADJUTE
CONJOINT
CONJUGAL
CONJUNCT
CONJURED
CONJURER
CONJUROR
CRACKJAW
CUNJEVOI
DEJECTED
DEJERATE
DEJEUNER
DEMIJOHN
DEVARAJA
DISJEUNE
DISJOINT
DISJUNCT
DJAGOONG
DOORJAMB
EARJEWEL
EJECTING
EJECTION
EJECTIVE
EJICIENT
EMAJAGUA
ENJAMBED
ENJOINED
ENJOINER
ENJOYING
FERIDJEE
FLAPJACK
FLIPJACK
FORJUDGE
FOUJDARY
FRABJOUS
GALIONJI
GRANJENO
GUAJILLO
HAMINGJA
HIGHJACK
HIJACKER
HUAJILLO
IJUSSITE
INJECTED
INJECTOR
INJURIES
INJURING
INJUSTLY
JABBERED
JABBERER
JABORINE
JACCONET
JACCONOT
JACINTHE
JACITARA
JACKAROO
JACKBIRD
JACKBOOT
JACKEROO
JACKETED
JACKFISH
JACKHEAD
JACKPOTS
JACKROLL
JACKSHAY
JACKSHEA
JACKSTAY
JACKWEED
JACKWOOD
JACOBAEA
JACOLATT
JACOUNCE
JACQUARD
JACTANCE
JACTANCY
JACULATE
JADISHLY
JAGGEDLY
JAGGHERY
JAGGIEST
JAGIRDAR
JAILBIRD
JAILMATE
JAILYARD
JAKFRUIT
JALAPENO
JALLOPED
JALOPIES
JALOUSED
JALOUSIE
JALPAITE
JAMBEAUX
JAMBOLAN
JAMBOREE
JAMDANEE
JAMPANEE
JAMTLAND
JANGLING
JANICEPS
JANISARY
JANITRIX
JANIZARY
JAPANNED
JAPANNER
JAPERIES
JAPISHLY
JAPONICA
JAPYGOID
JAQUETTE
JARARACA
JARGONAL
JARGONED
JARGONEL
JARGONER
JARGONIC
JAROSITE
JAROVIZE
JASMINED
JASPERED
JASPONYX
JASPOPAL
JAUNDERS
JAUNDICE
JAUNTIER
JAUNTILY
JAUNTING
JAVELINA
JAWSMITH
JAZERANT
JAZZIEST
JEALOUSE
JEALOUSY
JECORIZE
JEJUNELY
JEJUNITY
JELERANG
JELLYING
JELOTONG
JELUTONG
JEOPARDY
JEREMIAD
JERKIEST
JERKINED
JERKSOME
JERMONAL
JEROBOAM
JERQUING
JERRICAN
JERRYISM
JERSEYED
JESTBOOK
JESTWORD
JETLINER
JETTISON
JEUNESSE
JEWELING
JEWELLED
JEWELLER
JEZEKITE
JIBBINGS
JIGGERED
JIGGERER
JIGGLING
JIMCRACK
JIMMYING
JIMPNESS
JIMSEDGE
JINGBANG
JINGLING
JINGOISH
JINGOISM
JINGOIST
JINNIYEH
JINSHANG
JIPIJAPA
JIRKINET
JITNEUSE
JIUJITSU
JIUJUTSU
JOBATION
JOBSMITH
JOCATORY
JOCKEYED
JOCOSELY
JOCOSITY
JOCTELEG
JOCUNDLY
JOCUNDRY
JODHPURS
JOGGLETY
JOGGLING
JOHANNES
JOHNBOAT
JOINERED
JOINHAND
JOINTAGE
JOINTING
JOINTIST
JOINTURE
JOISTING
JOKESOME
JOKESTER
JOKINGLY
JOLLIEST
JOLLITRY
JOLLOPED
JOLLYING
JOLTHEAD
JONGLERY
JONGLEUR
JOOKERIE
JORDANON
JOSEFITE
JOSTLING
JOTATION
JOTISARU
JOUNCING
JOURNEYS
JOUSTING
JOVIALLY
JOVIALTY
JOVILABE
JOYFULLY
JOYHOUSE
JOYOUSLY
JUBARTAS
JUBARTES
JUBEROUS
JUBILANT
JUBILATE
JUBILEAN
JUBILIST
JUBILIZE
JUDAIZER
JUDGMENT
JUDICATE
JUDICIAL
JUDICIUM
JUGATION
JUGGLERY
JUGGLING
JUGULATE
JUICIEST
JULIENNE
JULOLINE
JUMBLING
JUMBOISM
JUMPIEST
JUMPROCK
JUMPSEED
JUMPSOME
JUNCTION
JUNCTIVE
JUNCTURE
JUNEFISH
JUNGLIER
JUNKETED
JUNKETER
JUNKYARD
JURAMENT
JURATION
JURATIVE
JURATORY
JURISTIC
JUSSHELL
JUSTICED
JUSTICER
JUSTITIA
JUSTMENT
JUSTNESS
JUVENATE
JUVENILE
KABELJOU
KAJUGARU
KINKAJOU
KOMITAJI
KOMMETJE
KUJAWIAK
LONGJAWS
LUTJANID
MAHARAJA
MAHJONGG
MAJESTIC
MAJIDIEH
MAJOLICA
MAJOLIST
MAJORATE
MAJORITY
MAJORIZE
MARJORAM
MEDJIDIE
MEJORANA
MIJAKITE
MIJNHEER
MISJUDGE
MONTJOYE
MUJTAHID
NAUJAITE
NIGHTJAR
NONJUROR
OBJECTED
OBJECTEE
OBJECTOR
OVERJUMP
PAJAMAED
PEJERREY
PEJORATE
PEJORISM
PEJORIST
PEJORITY
PEJORITY
PERIJOVE
PERJURED
PERJURER
POPINJAY
PREJUDGE
PULSEJET
PYJAMAED
RAJBANSI
RAJOGUNA
READJUST
REJECTED
REJECTER
REJECTOR
REJOICED
REJOICER
REJOINED
REJOUNCE
SEDJADEH
SEJOINED
SEJUGATE
SEJUGOUS
SERJEANT
SKIJORER
SKIPJACK
SLAPJACK
SNAPJACK
SNIPJACK
SOURJACK
STICKJAW
SUBJOINT
SUBJUGAL
SUBJUNCT
SUCURUJU
TATMJOLK
TENDEJON
TJANTING
TJURUNGA
TOKTOKJE
TURBOJET
TURJAITE
UNJUSTLY
VERJUICE
YAJENINE
YAMMADJI

POSITIONAL ORDER LIST OF 8-LETTER WORDS

JABBERED
JABBERER
JABORINE
JACCONET
JACCONOT
JACINTHE
JACITARA
JACKAROO
JACKBIRD
JACKBOOT
JACKEROO
JACKETED
JACKFISH
JACKHEAD
JACKPOTS
JACKROLL
JACKSHAY
JACKSHEA
JACKSTAY
JACKWEED
JACKWOOD
JACOBAEA
JACOLATT
JACOUNCE
JACQUARD
JACTANCE
JACTANCY
JACULATE
JADISHLY
JAGGEDLY
JAGGHERY
JAGGIEST
JAGIRDAR
JAILBIRD
JAILMATE
JAILYARD
JAKFRUIT
JALAPENO
JALLOPED
JALOPIES
JALOUSED
JALOUSIE
JALPAITE
JAMBEAUX
JAMBOLAN
JAMBOREE
JAMDANEE
JAMPANEE
JAMTLAND
JANGLING
JANICEPS
JANISARY
JANITRIX
JANIZARY
JAPANNED
JAPANNER
JAPERIES
JAPISHLY
JAPONICA
JAPYGOID
JAQUETTE
JARARACA
JARGONAL
JARGONED
JARGONEL
JARGONER
JARGONIC
JAROSITE
JAROVIZE
JASMINED
JASPERED
JASPONYX
JASPOPAL
JAUNDERS

JAUNDICE
JAUNTIER
JAUNTILY
JAUNTING
JAVELINA
JAWSMITH
JAZERANT
JAZZIEST
JEALOUSE
JEALOUSY
JECORIZE
JEJUNELY
JEJUNITY
JELERANG
JELLYING
JELOTONG
JELUTONG
JEOPARDY
JEREMIAD
JERKIEST
JERKINED
JERKSOME
JERMONAL
JEROBOAM
JERQUING
JERRICAN
JERRYISM
JERSEYED
JESTBOOK
JESTWORD
JETLINER
JETTISON
JEUNESSE
JEWELING
JEWELLED
JEWELLER
JEZEKITE
JIBBINGS
JIGGERED
JIGGERER
JIGGLING
JIMCRACK
JIMMYING
JIMPNESS
JIMSEDGE
JINGBANG
JINGLING
JINGOISH
JINGOISM
JINGOIST
JINNIYEH
JINSHANG
JIPIJAPA
JIRKINET
JITNEUSE
JIUJITSU
JIUJUTSU
JOBATION
JOBSMITH
JOCATORY
JOCKEYED
JOCOSELY
JOCOSITY
JOCTELEG
JOCUNDLY
JOCUNDRY
JODHPURS
JOGGLETY
JOGGLING
JOHANNES
JOHNBOAT
JOINERED
JOINHAND
JOINTAGE

JOINTING
JOINTIST
JOINTURE
JOISTING
JOKESOME
JOKESTER
JOKINGLY
JOLLIEST
JOLLITRY
JOLLOPED
JOLLYING
JOLTHEAD
JONGLERY
JONGLEUR
JOOKERIE
JORDANON
JOSEFITE
JOSTLING
JOTATION
JOTISARU
JOUNCING
JOURNEYS
JOUSTING
JOVIALLY
JOVIALTY
JOVILABE
JOYFULLY
JOYHOUSE
JOYOUSLY
JUBARTAS
JUBARTES
JUBEROUS
JUBILANT
JUBILATE
JUBILEAN
JUBILIST
JUBILIZE
JUDAIZER
JUDGMENT
JUDICATE
JUDICIAL
JUDICIUM
JUGATION
JUGGLERY
JUGGLING
JUGULATE
JUICIEST
JULIENNE
JULOLINE
JUMBLING
JUMBOISM
JUMPIEST
JUMPROCK
JUMPSEED
JUMPSOME
JUNCTION
JUNCTIVE
JUNCTURE
JUNEFISH
JUNGLIER
JUNKETED
JUNKETER
JUNKYARD
JURAMENT
JURATION
JURATIVE
JURATORY
JURISTIC
JUSSHELL
JUSTICED
JUSTICER
JUSTITIA
JUSTMENT
JUSTNESS

JUVENATE
JUVENILE

AJONJOLI
AJONJOLI
AJOURISE
AJUTMENT
DJAGOONG
EJECTING
EJECTION
EJECTIVE
EJICIENT
IJUSSITE
TJANTING
TJURUNGA

ABJECTLY
ABJURING
ADJACENT
ADJOINED
ADJUDGED
ADJUDGER
ADJUGATE
ADJUMENT
ADJURING
ADJUSTED
ADJUSTER
ADJUSTOR
ADJUTAGE
ADJUTANT
ADJUTORY
ADJUTRIX
ADJUVANT
ADJUVATE
ALJAMADO
ALJAMIAH
BAJONADO
BAJULATE
BEJABERS
BEJUGGLE
BIJUGATE
BIJUGOUS
BIJWONER
CAJOLERY
CAJOLING
DEJECTED
DEJERATE
DEJEUNER
ENJAMBED
ENJOINED
ENJOINER
ENJOYING
HIJACKER
INJECTED
INJECTOR
INJURIES
INJURING
INJUSTLY
JEJUNELY
JEJUNITY
KAJUGARU
KUJAWIAK
MAJESTIC
MAJIDIEH
MAJOLICA
MAJOLIST
MAJORATE
MAJORITY
MAJORIZE
MEJORANA
MIJAKITE
MIJNHEER
MUJTAHID
OBJECTED

OBJECTEE
OBJECTOR
PAJAMAED
PEJERREY
PEJORATE
PEJORISM
PEJORIST
PEJORITY
PYJAMAED
RAJBANSI
RAJOGUNA
REJECTED
REJECTER
REJECTOR
REJOICED
REJOICER
REJOINED
REJOUNCE
SEJOINED
SEJUGATE
SEJUGOUS
UNJUSTLY
YAJENINE

BENJAMIN
BIAJAIBA
BOBJEROM
BRUJERIA
CONJOINT
CONJUGAL
CONJUNCT
CONJURED
CONJURER
CONJUROR
CUNJEVOI
DISJEUNE
DISJOINT
DISJUNCT
EARJEWEL
EMAJAGUA
FORJUDGE
FOUJDARY
GUAJILLO
HUAJILLO
JIUJITSU
JIUJUTSU
LUTJANID
MAHJONGG
MARJORAM
MEDJIDIE
MISJUDGE
NAUJAITE
NONJUROR
PERJURED
PERJURER
PREJUDGE
SEDJADEH
SERJEANT
SKIJORER
SUBJOINT
SUBJUGAL
SUBJUNCT
TURJAITE
VERJUICE

BABAJAGA
BLATJANG
BLUEJACK
BOOTJACK
BRINJAUL
BUCKJUMP
CANAJONG
CARAJURA
COADJUST

COADJUTE
DEMIJOHN
DOORJAMB
FLAPJACK
FLIPJACK
FRABJOUS
GRANJENO
HIGHJACK
JIPIJAPA
LONGJAWS
MONTJOYE
OVERJUMP
PERIJOVE
READJUST
SKIPJACK
SLAPJACK
SNAPJACK
SNIPJACK
SOURJACK
TATMJOLK

APAREJOS
CARCAJOU
CRACKJAW
FERIDJEE
KABELJOU
KINKAJOU
NIGHTJAR
POPINJAY
PULSEJET
STICKJAW
TENDEJON
TURBOJET

ALLELUJA
BOSTANJI
DEVARAJA
GALIONJI
HAMINGJA
KOMITAJI
KOMMETJE
MAHARAJA
SUCURUJU
TOKTOKJE
YAMMADJI

SCORING ORDER LIST OF 8-LETTER WORDS

28
HIGHJACK
JEZEKITE

27
BUCKJUMP
JACKFISH
JACKSHAY
JACQUARD
JANIZARY
JAROVIZE
JASPONYX

26
CRACKJAW
FLAPJACK
FLIPJACK
JAMBEAUX
JECORIZE
JUBILIZE
MAJORIZE

25
JACKHEAD
JACKWEED
JACKWOOD
JERQUING
JIMCRACK
JOCKEYED
JUDAIZER
JUMPROCK

24
HIJACKER
JACKBIRD
JACKSHEA
JACKSTAY
JAQUETTE
JAZERANT
JOYFULLY
STICKJAW

23
ADJUTRIX
BLUEJACK
BOOTJACK
JACKBOOT
JACKPOTS
JAGGHERY
JAPISHLY
JAWSMITH
JAZZIEST
JIMMYING
JOKINGLY
JUNKYARD
KOMMETJE
PYJAMAED
SLAPJACK
SNAPJACK
SNIPJACK
YAMMADJI

22
ABJECTLY
FOUJDARY
JACKETED
JACTANCY
JADISHLY
JAKFRUIT
JANITRIX
JAPYGOID
JOBSMITH
MAHJONGG
OVERJUMP
POPINJAY
SKIPJACK

21
BOBJEROM
DEMIJOHN
HAMINGJA
JACKAROO
JACKEROO
JACKROLL
JAGGEDLY
JEOPARDY
JERKSOME
JESTBOOK
JINNIYEH
JOCUNDLY
JOCUNDRY
JODHPURS
JOKESOME
JOVIALLY
JOVIALTY
JOYHOUSE
JOYOUSLY
JUMBOISM
JUMPSOME
JUNEFISH
KABELJOU
KOMITAJI
KUJAWIAK
MAJIDIEH
MIJAKITE
MUJTAHID
SOURJACK
TATMJOLK

20
ALJAMIAH
BABAJAGA
BIJWONER
CAJOLERY
CUNJEVOI
DOORJAMB
EJECTIVE
ENJAMBED
FORJUDGE
FRABJOUS
JABBERED
JACINTHE
JERKINED
JERRYISM
JIBBINGS
JOCATORY
JOCOSELY
JOCOSITY
JOGGLETY
JOHNBOAT
JOVILABE
JUDICIUM
JUGGLERY
JUMBLING
JUMPSEED
JUNCTIVE
JUNKETED
KAJUGARU
MAHARAJA
MAJORITY
MIJNHEER
MONTJOYE
OBJECTED
PAJAMAED
PEJERREY
PERIJOVE
SEDJADEH
VERJUICE

19
ADJUDGED
ADJUTORY
ADJUVANT
ADJUVATE
BEJABERS
BEJUGGLE
BENJAMIN
BIAJAIBA
CARCAJOU
CONJUNCT
DEJECTED
DEVARAJA
ENJOYING
FERIDJEE
JABBERER
JACCONET
JACCONOT
JACOBAEA
JACOUNCE
JACTANCE
JAILYARD
JAMBOLAN
JAMBOREE
JAMPANEE
JANICEPS
JAPONICA
JASPOPAL
JELLYING
JERKIEST
JEROBOAM
JERSEYED
JESTWORD
JEWELING
JEWELLED
JIMPNESS
JIMSEDGE
JINGBANG
JINGOISH
JINSHANG
JIRKINET
JOINHAND
JOKESTER
JOLLYING
JOLTHEAD
JONGLERY
JOOKERIE
JUDGMENT
JUMPIEST
JUNKETER
LONGJAWS
MAJESTIC
MAJOLICA
MARJORAM
MEDJIDIE
MISJUDGE
NIGHTJAR
OBJECTEE
OBJECTOR
PEJORISM
PREJUDGE
SKIJORER
SUBJUNCT

18
ABJURING
ADJACENT
ADJUDGER
ADJUMENT
ALJAMADO
BAJONADO
BIJUGATE
BIJUGOUS
BLATJANG
CAJOLING
CANAJONG
COADJUST
COADJUTE
CONJUGAL
CONJURED
DISJUNCT
DJAGOONG
EARJEWEL
EJECTING
EMAJAGUA
HUAJILLO
INJECTED
INJUSTLY
JAILBIRD
JALLOPED
JAMDANEE
JAMTLAND
JANISARY
JAPANNED
JARGONIC
JASMINED
JASPERED
JAUNDICE
JAUNTILY
JAVELINA
JEALOUSY
JEREMIAD
JEWELLER
JIGGERED
JIGGLING
JINGOISM
JIPIJAPA
JOCTELEG
JOGGLING
JOHANNES
JOLLITRY
JOLLOPED
JOSEFITE
JOUNCING
JOURNEYS
JUDICATE
JUDICIAL
JUGGLING
JURATIVE
JURATORY
JUSSHELL
JUSTICED
JUVENATE
JUVENILE
KINKAJOU
PERJURED
REJECTED
REJOICED
SUBJUGAL
TOKTOKJE
UNJUSTLY
YAJENINE

17
ADJOINED
ADJUGATE
ADJURING
ADJUSTED
ADJUTAGE
AJUTMENT
APAREJOS
BAJULATE
BOSTANJI
BRINJAUL
BRUJERIA
CARAJURA
CONJOINT
CONJURER
CONJUROR
EJECTION
EJICIENT
INJECTOR
JABORINE
JACITARA
JACOLATT
JACULATE
JAGGIEST
JAGIRDAR
JAILMATE
JALAPENO
JALOPIES

JALPAITE
JANGLING
JAPANNER
JAPERIES
JARARACA
JARGONED
JEJUNELY
JEJUNITY
JERMONAL
JERRICAN
JIGGERER
JINGLING
JOBATION
JUBARTAS
JUBARTES
JUBEROUS
JUBILANT
JUBILATE
JUBILEAN
JUBILIST
JUICIEST
JUNCTION
JUNCTURE
JURAMENT
JURISTIC
JUSTICER
JUSTMENT
MAJOLIST
MAJORATE
MEJORANA
PEJORATE
PEJORIST
PERJURER
PULSEJET
RAJBANSI
REJECTER
REJECTOR
REJOICER
REJOUNCE
SUBJOINT
SUCURUJU
TURBOJET

16

ADJUSTER
ADJUSTOR
ADJUTANT
DEJERATE
DEJEUNER
DISJEUNE
DISJOINT
ENJOINED
GALIONJI
GRANJENO
GUAJILLO
INJURING
JALOUSED
JARGONAL
JARGONEL
JARGONER
JAUNDERS
JAUNTING
JELERANG
JELOTONG
JELUTONG
JINGOIST
JOINERED
JOINTAGE
JOINTING
JOISTING
JONGLEUR
JORDANON
JOSTLING
JOUSTING
JUGATION
JUGULATE
JUNGLIER
LUTJANID
RAJOGUNA
READJUST
REJOINED
SEJOINED
SEJUGATE
SEJUGOUS
TENDEJON
TJANTING
TJURUNGA

15

AJOURISE
ALLELUJA
ENJOINER
IJUSSITE
INJURIES
JALOUSIE
JAROSITE
JAUNTIER
JEALOUSE
JETLINER
JETTISON
JEUNESSE
JITNEUSE
JOINTIST
JOINTURE
JOLLIEST
JOTATION
JOTISARU
JULIENNE
JULOLINE
JURATION
JUSTITIA
JUSTNESS
NAUJAITE
NONJUROR
SERJEANT
TURJAITE

14

AJONJOLI
JIUJITSU
JIUJUTSU

ALPHABETICAL LIST OF 9-LETTER WORDS

ABJECTION
ABJECTIVE
ADJACENCY
ADJECTION
ADJECTIVE
ADJOINING
ADJOURNAL
ADJUDGING
ADJUNCTLY
ADJUSTAGE
ADJUSTIVE
ADJUTANCY
ADJUTRICE
ALJAMIADO
ALJOFAINA
AMBERJACK
ANKLEJACK
APJOHNITE
APPLEJACK
APPLEJOHN
BACKJOINT
BANJORINE
BARAJILLO
BEJABBERS
BEJEWELED
BIJUGULAR
BLACKJACK
BLUEJOINT
BOOTJACKS
BRINJAREE
BRINJARRY
CAJUPUTOL
CISJURANE
COADJUTOR
CONJOINED
CONJOINER
CONJOBBLE
CONJUGACY
CONJUGANT
CONJUGATA
CONJUGATE
CONJUGIAL
CONJUGIUM
CONJURING
CROSSJACK
DEJECTILE
DEJECTION
DEJECTORY
DEJECTURE
DEMIJAMBE
DISJASKED
DISJASKIT
DISJECTED
DISJOINED
DJALMAITE
EJACULATE
EJECTMENT
ENJEOPARD
ENJOINDER
ENJOINING
ENJOYABLE
ENJOYABLY
ENJOYMENT
FAUJASITE
FOREJUDGE
FORJASKIT
FORJESKET
FORJUDGED
FORJUDGER
FOUJDARRY
FRAILEJON
GUEJARITE
INJECTING
INJECTION
INJUREDLY
INJURIOUS
INJUSTICE
INTERJECT
INTERJOIN
JABBERING
JABORANDI
JACARANDA
JACKEROOS
JACKETING
JACKFRUIT
JACKKNIFE
JACKLIGHT
JACKPLANE
JACKSCREW
JACKSHAFT
JACKSLAVE
JACKSMELT
JACKSMITH
JACKSNIPE
JACKSTOCK
JACKSTONE
JACKSTRAW
JACOBSITE
JACQUERIE
JACTATION
JACTITATE
JACULATED
JACULATOR
JACUTINGA
JADEDNESS
JAGHIRDAR
JAGUARETE
JAILERESS
JAILERING
JAILHOUSE
JAILORING
JALOUSIED
JALOUSING
JAMBALAYA
JAMBOLANA
JAMBSTONE
JAMROSADE
JANISSARY
JANITRESS
JAPACONIN
JAPANNERY
JAPANNING
JARGONING
JARGONISH
JARGONIST
JARGONIUM
JARGONIZE
JAROVIZED
JASPAGATE
JASPERITE
JASPERIZE
JASPEROID
JASPIDEAN
JASPILITE
JASPILYTE
JATAMANSI
JATROPHIC
JAUNDICED
JAUNTIEST
JAWBATION
JAWFALLEN
JAWFISHES
JAWFOOTED
JAYHAWKER
JAYWALKER
JAZZINESS
JEALOUSLY
JEERINGLY
JEJUNATOR
JEJUNITIS
JELLIFIED
JELLYBEAN
JELLYFISH
JELLYLEAF
JELLYLIKE
JEMMINESS
JENNERIZE
JENNETING
JEOPARDED
JEOPARDER
JEQUERITY
JEQUIRITY
JERKINESS
JERKWATER
JERMOONAL
JESSAKEED
JESSAMIES
JESSAMINE
JESTINGLY
JETTATORE
JETTATURA
JETTINESS
JETTYHEAD
JEWELLERY
JEWELLING
JEWELWEED
JEWFISHES
JIGAMAREE
JIGGERMAN
JIGGINESS
JIGGUMBOB
JILLFLIRT
JIMBERJAW
JIMMYWEED
JINGLEBOB
JINNESTAN
JINNIWINK
JINNYWINK
JITNEYMAN
JITTERBUG

JNANAYOGA
JOBBERIES
JOBHOLDER
JOBMASTER
JOBMONGER
JOCKEYING
JOCKEYISM
JOCKSTRAP
JOCKTELEG
JOCULARLY
JOCULATOR
JOCUNDITY
JOHANNITE
JOINERING
JOININGLY
JOINTEDLY
JOINTRESS
JOINTURED
JOINTWEED
JOINTWOOD
JOINTWORM
JOKESMITH
JOLLIFIED
JOLLIMENT
JOLLINESS
JOLLITIES
JOLLYHEAD
JOLTINESS
JONQUILLE
JORDANITE
JOURNALED
JOURNEYED
JOURNEYER
JOVIALIST
JOVIALITY
JOVIALIZE
JOYLESSLY
JOYPOPPER
JUBILANCE
JUBILANCY
JUBILATED
JUBILATIO
JUCUNDITY
JUDGEMENT
JUDGMATIC
JUDGMENTS
JUDICABLE
JUDICATOR
JUDICIARY
JUDICIOUS
JUGLANDIN
JUGULATED
JUICINESS
JULIENITE
JULOIDIAN
JULOLIDIN
JUMENTOUS
JUMILLITE
JUMPINESS
JUMPROCKS
JUNCIFORM
JUNECTOMY
JUNGLIEST
JUNIORATE
JUNIORITY
JUNKBOARD
JUNKERDOM
JUNKERISM
JUNKETING
JURAMENTA
JURIDICAL
JURUPAITE
JURYWOMAN
JUSTICIAL
JUSTICIAR
JUSTICIER
JUSTICIES
JUSTICING
JUSTIFIED
JUSTIFIER
JUSTMENTS
JUTTINGLY
JUVENILIA
JUVENTUDE
JUXTAPOSE
KILOJOULE
KOMITADJI
KOORAJONG
KURRAJONG
LUJAURITE
LUJAVRITE
MAHARAJAH
MAJESTIES
MAJORDOMO
MAJORETTE
MAJUSCULE
MARIJUANA
MATAJUELO
MEDJIDIEH
MISJUDGED
MISJUDGER
MUNJISTIN
NONINJURY
NONJURANT
NONJURING
NUTJOBBER
OBJECTIFY
OBJECTING
OBJECTION
OBJECTIVE
OBJECTIZE
OBJICIENT
OBJURGATE
OUTJOCKEY
OUTJUGGLE
OVERJUDGE
PEREJONET
PERJINKLY
PERJURIES
PERJURING
PREJACENT
PREJUDGED
PREJUDGER
PREJUDICE
PROJECTOR
QUILLAJIC
REDJACKET
REJECTAGE
REJECTING
REJECTION
REJECTIVE
REJOICING
REJOINDER
REJOINING
RETROJECT
SANJAKBEG
SEJUNCTLY
SEMIBEJAN
SERJEANCY
SERJEANTY
SKIJORING
SKIPJACKS
SMOKEJACK
SOJOURNED
SOJOURNER
SUBJACENT
SUBJECTED
SUBJOINED
SUBJUGATE
SURREJOIN
SWARAJISM
SWARAJIST
TASAJILLO
TRAJECTED
TRIJUGATE
TRIJUGOUS
UNIJUGATE
UNINJURED
VAJRASANA

POSITIONAL ORDER LIST OF 9-LETTER WORDS

JABBERING
JABORANDI
JACARANDA
JACKEROOS
JACKETING
JACKFRUIT
JACKKNIFE
JACKLIGHT
JACKPLANE
JACKSCREW
JACKSHAFT
JACKSLAVE
JACKSMELT
JACKSMITH
JACKSNIPE
JACKSTOCK
JACKSTONE
JACKSTRAW
JACOBSITE
JACQUERIE
JACTATION
JACTITATE
JACULATED
JACULATOR
JACUTINGA
JADEDNESS
JAGHIRDAR
JAGUARETE
JAILERESS
JAILERING
JAILHOUSE
JAILORING
JALOUSIED
JALOUSING
JAMBALAYA
JAMBOLANA
JAMBSTONE
JAMROSADE
JANISSARY
JANITRESS
JAPACONIN
JAPANNERY
JAPANNING
JARGONING
JARGONISH
JARGONIST
JARGONIUM
JARGONIZE
JAROVIZED
JASPAGATE
JASPERITE
JASPERIZE
JASPEROID
JASPIDEAN
JASPILITE
JASPILYTE
JATAMANSI
JATROPHIC
JAUNDICED
JAUNTIEST
JAWBATION
JAWFALLEN
JAWFISHES
JAWFOOTED
JAYHAWKER
JAYWALKER
JAZZINESS
JEALOUSLY
JEERINGLY
JEJUNATOR
JEJUNITIS
JELLIFIED
JELLYBEAN
JELLYFISH
JELLYLEAF
JELLYLIKE
JEMMINESS
JENNERIZE
JENNETING
JEOPARDED
JEOPARDER
JEQUERITY
JEQUIRITY
JERKINESS
JERKWATER
JERMOONAL
JESSAKEED
JESSAMIES
JESSAMINE
JESTINGLY
JETTATORE
JETTATURA
JETTINESS
JETTYHEAD
JEWELLERY
JEWELLING
JEWELWEED
JEWFISHES
JIGAMAREE
JIGGERMAN
JIGGINESS
JIGGUMBOB
JILLFLIRT
JIMBERJAW
JIMMYWEED
JINGLEBOB
JINNESTAN
JINNIWINK
JINNYWINK
JITNEYMAN
JITTERBUG
JNANAYOGA
JOBBERIES
JOBHOLDER
JOBMASTER
JOBMONGER
JOCKEYING
JOCKEYISM
JOCKSTRAP
JOCKTELEG
JOCULARLY
JOCULATOR
JOCUNDITY
JOHANNITE
JOINERING
JOININGLY
JOINTEDLY
JOINTRESS
JOINTURED
JOINTWEED
JOINTWOOD
JOINTWORM
JOKESMITH
JOLLIFIED
JOLLIMENT
JOLLINESS
JOLLITIES
JOLLYHEAD
JOLTINESS
JONQUILLE
JORDANITE
JOURNALED
JOURNEYED
JOURNEYER
JOVIALIST
JOVIALITY
JOVIALIZE
JOYLESSLY
JOYPOPPER
JUBILANCE
JUBILANCY
JUBILATED
JUBILATIO
JUCUNDITY
JUDGEMENT
JUDGMATIC
JUDGMENTS
JUDICABLE
JUDICATOR
JUDICIARY
JUDICIOUS
JUGLANDIN
JUGULATED
JUICINESS
JULIENITE
JULOIDIAN
JULOLIDIN
JUMENTOUS
JUMILLITE
JUMPINESS
JUMPROCKS
JUNCIFORM
JUNECTOMY
JUNGLIEST
JUNIORATE
JUNIORITY
JUNKBOARD
JUNKERDOM
JUNKERISM
JUNKETING
JURAMENTA
JURIDICAL
JURUPAITE
JURYWOMAN
JUSTICIAL
JUSTICIAR
JUSTICIER
JUSTICIES
JUSTICING
JUSTIFIED
JUSTIFIER
JUSTMENTS
JUTTINGLY
JUVENILIA
JUVENTUDE

JUXTAPOSE

DJALMAITE
EJACULATE
EJECTMENT

ABJECTION
ABJECTIVE
ADJACENCY
ADJECTION
ADJECTIVE
ADJOINING
ADJOURNAL
ADJUDGING
ADJUNCTLY
ADJUSTAGE
ADJUSTIVE
ADJUTANCY
ADJUTRICE
ALJAMIADO
ALJOFAINA
APJOHNITE
BEJABBERS
BEJEWELED
BIJUGULAR
CAJUPUTOL
DEJECTILE
DEJECTION
DEJECTORY
DEJECTURE
ENJEOPARD
ENJOINDER
ENJOINING
ENJOYABLE
ENJOYABLY
ENJOYMENT
INJECTING
INJECTION
INJUREDLY
INJURIOUS
INJUSTICE
JEJUNATOR
JEJUNITIS
LUJAURITE
LUJAVRITE
MAJESTIES
MAJORDOMO
MAJORETTE
MAJUSCULE
OBJECTIFY
OBJECTING
OBJECTION
OBJECTIVE
OBJECTIZE
OBJICIENT
OBJURGATE
REJECTAGE
REJECTING
REJECTION
REJECTIVE
REJOICING
REJOINDER
REJOINING
SEJUNCTLY
SOJOURNED
SOJOURNER
VAJRASANA

BANJORINE
CISJURANE
CONJOINED
CONJOINER
CONJOBBLE
CONJUGACY
CONJUGANT
CONJUGATA
CONJUGATE
CONJUGIAL
CONJUGIUM
CONJURING
DISJASKED
DISJASKIT
DISJECTED
DISJOINED
FAUJASITE
FORJASKIT
FORJESKET
FORJUDGED
FORJUDGER
FOUJDARRY
GUEJARITE
MEDJIDIEH
MISJUDGED
MISJUDGER
MUNJISTIN
NONJURANT
NONJURING
NUTJOBBER
OUTJOCKEY
OUTJUGGLE
PERJINKLY
PERJURIES
PERJURING
PREJACENT
PREJUDGED
PREJUDGER
PREJUDICE
PROJECTOR
REDJACKET
SANJAKBEG
SERJEANCY
SERJEANTY
SKIJORING
SUBJACENT
SUBJECTED
SUBJOINED
SUBJUGATE
TRAJECTED
TRIJUGATE
TRIJUGOUS
UNIJUGATE

BACKJOINT
BARAJILLO
BLUEJOINT
BOOTJACKS
BRINJAREE
BRINJARRY
COADJUTANT
COADJUTOR
DEMIJAMBE
FOREJUDGE
KILOJOULE
MARIJUANA
MATAJUELO
OVERJUDGE
PEREJONET
SKIPJACKS
TASAJILLO
UNINJURED

AMBERJACK
ANKLEJACK
APPLEJACK
APPLEJOHN
BLACKJACK
CROSSJACK
INTERJECT
INTERJOIN
KOORAJONG
KURRAJONG
NONINJURY
RETROJECT
SMOKEJACK
SURREJOIN
SWARAJISM
SWARAJIST

FRAILEJON
JIMBERJAW
MAHARAJAH
QUILLAJIC
SEMIBEJAN

KOMITADJI

SCORING ORDER LIST OF 9-LETTER WORDS

29
JAROVIZED
JAYHAWKER
OBJECTIZE

28
JACKSHAFT
JEQUERITY
JEQUIRITY
JOVIALIZE

27
JACKSCREW
JACKSMITH
JACQUERIE
JASPERIZE
JIMMYWEED
JOCKEYISM
QUILLAJIC

26
AMBERJACK
APPLEJACK
JACKLIGHT
JARGONIZE
JAYWALKER
JINNYWINK
JOCKEYING
JUMPROCKS
OBJECTIFY

25
BLACKJACK
JACKFRUIT
JACKSLAVE
JACKSTRAW
JAWFISHES
JELLYFISH
JENNERIZE
JEWFISHES
JOKESMITH
JONQUILLE
JUXTAPOSE
OUTJOCKEY
PERJINKLY

24
ADJACENCY
BACKJOINT
BOOTJACKS
CONJUGACY
CROSSJACK
ENJOYABLY
JACKKNIFE
JACKPLANE
JACKSMELT
JACKSNIPE
JAZZINESS
JIGGUMBOB
JOCKSTRAP
JURYWOMAN
MAHARAJAH

23
ABJECTIVE
APPLEJOHN
DEMIJAMBE
FORJASKIT
FORJESKET
FOUJDARRY
JACKETING
JACKSTOCK
JAMBALAYA
JATROPHIC
JAWFOOTED
JELLYLIKE
JERKWATER
JETTYHEAD
JEWELWEED
JINNIWINK
JOCKTELEG
JOLLYHEAD
JUBILANCY
JUNCIFORM
JUNECTOMY
JUNKBOARD
JUNKERDOM
KOMITADJI
MEDJIDIEH
OBJECTIVE
REDJACKET
SANJAKBEG
SKIPJACKS
SMOKEJACK

22
ADJECTIVE
ADJUNCTLY
ADJUTANCY
BEJEWELED
CONJOBBLE
DEJECTORY
DISJASKED
FORJUDGED
JACKEROOS
JACKSTONE
JAWFALLEN
JELLYLEAF
JEWELLERY
JIMBERJAW
JOBHOLDER
JOCUNDITY
JOVIALITY
JOYLESSLY
JOYPOPPER
JUCUNDITY
JUDGMATIC
JUDICIARY
JUNKERISM

21
ANKLEJACK
APJOHNITE
BRINJARRY
CONJUGIUM
DISJASKIT
ENJOYABLE
ENJOYMENT
FOREJUDGE
FORJUDGER
JABBERING
JAGHIRDAR
JAPANNERY
JASPILYTE
JAWBATION
JELLYBEAN
JESSAKEED
JINGLEBOB
JITNEYMAN
JOBMONGER
JOCULARLY
JOINTWORM
JUDICABLE
JUNKETING
KOORAJONG
KURRAJONG
MAJORDOMO
MISJUDGED
OBJECTING
OVERJUDGE
PREJUDGED
PREJUDICE
REJECTIVE
SEJUNCTLY
SERJEANCY
SKIJORING
SUBJECTED
SWARAJISM

20
ABJECTION
ADJUDGING
ADJUSTIVE
CAJUPUTOL
DISJECTED
EJECTMENT
INJUREDLY
JACOBSITE
JAMBOLANA
JAMBSTONE
JAPACONIN
JARGONISH
JAUNDICED
JEERINGLY
JELLIFIED
JEMMINESS
JEOPARDED
JERKINESS
JESTINGLY
JEWELLING
JIGGERMAN
JNANAYOGA
JOBBERIES
JOBMASTER
JOININGLY
JOINTEDLY
JOINTWEED
JOINTWOOD
JOLLIFIED
JOURNEYED

JUBILANCE
JUDGEMENT
JUDGMENTS
JUMPINESS
JUSTIFIED
JUTTINGLY
JUVENTUDE
KILOJOULE
MAJUSCULE
MISJUDGER
NUTJOBBER
OBJECTION
OBJICIENT
PREJACENT
PREJUDGER
PROJECTOR
SEMIBEJAN
SUBJACENT

19
ADJECTION
ADJUTRICE
ALJAMIADO
ALJOFAINA
BEJABBERS
BIJUGULAR
COADJUTOR
CONJOINED
CONJUGANT
CONJUGATA
CONJUGATE
CONJUGIAL
CONJURING
DEJECTILE
DEJECTION
DEJECTURE
DJALMAITE
ENJEOPARD
FAUJASITE
FRAILEJON
INJECTING
JABORANDI
JACARANDA
JACULATED
JACUTINGA
JAILHOUSE
JAMROSADE
JANISSARY
JAPANNING
JARGONIUM
JASPAGATE
JASPEROID
JASPIDEAN
JEALOUSLY
JEOPARDER
JIGAMAREE
JILLFLIRT
JITTERBUG
JOHANNITE
JOURNEYER
JOVIALIST
JUBILATED
JUDICATOR
JUDICIOUS
JUNIORITY
JURIDICAL
JUSTICING
JUSTIFIER
JUVENILIA
LUJAVRITE
NONINJURY
OBJURGATE
PERJURING
REJECTAGE
REJECTING
REJOICING
SERJEANTY
SUBJOINED
SUBJUGATE
SWARAJIST
TRAJECTED
VAJRASANA

18
ADJOINING
ADJUSTAGE
BANJORINE
BARAJILLO
BLUEJOINT
BRINJAREE
CISJURANE
CONJOINER
DISJOINED
EJACULATE
INJECTION
INJUSTICE
INTERJECT
JACTATION
JACTITATE
JACULATOR
JADEDNESS
JARGONING
JASPERITE
JASPILITE
JATAMANSI
JERMOONAL
JESSAMIES
JESSAMINE
JIGGINESS
JOCULATOR
JOLLIMENT
JUBILATIO
JUGLANDIN
JUGULATED
JUICINESS
JUMENTOUS
JUMILLITE
JURAMENTA
JURUPAITE
JUSTICIAL
JUSTICIAR
JUSTICIER
JUSTICIES
JUSTMENTS
MAJESTIES
MAJORETTE
MARIJUANA
MATAJUELO
MUNJISTIN
OUTJUGGLE
PEREJONET
PERJURIES
REJECTION
RETROJECT

17
ADJOURNAL
ENJOINDER
ENJOINING
GUEJARITE
JAGUARETE
JAILERING
JAILORING
JALOUSIED
JALOUSING
JARGONIST
JENNETING
JOINERING
JOINTURED
JORDANITE
JOURNALED
JULOIDIAN
JULOLIDIN
JUNGLIEST
NONJURING
REJOINDER
REJOINING
SOJOURNED
TRIJUGATE
TRIJUGOUS
UNIJUGATE
UNINJURED

16
INJURIOUS
INTERJOIN
JAILERESS
JANITRESS
JAUNTIEST
JETTATORE
JETTATURA
JETTINESS
JINNESTAN
JOINTRESS
JOLLINESS
JOLLITIES
JOLTINESS
JULIENITE
JUNIORATE
LUJAURITE
NONJURANT
SOJOURNER
SURREJOIN
TASAJILLO

15
JEJUNATOR
JEJUNITIS

ALPHABETICAL LIST OF 10-LETTER WORDS

ABJECTNESS
ABJUDICATE
ABJUNCTIVE
ABJURATION
ABJURATORY
ABJUREMENT
ADJACENTLY
ADJECTIVAL
ADJOINEDLY
ADJUDICATE
ADJUNCTION
ADJUNCTIVE
ADJURATION
ADJURATORY
ADJUSTABLE
ADJUSTMENT
ARROJADITE
BEJEWELING
BEJEWELLED
BIJOUTERIE
BLUEJACKET
BUTTERJAGS
CAJOLEMENT
CAJOLERIES
CAJOLINGLY
CAJUPUTENE
CAODJACENCY
CHAPARAJOS
CHAPAREJOS
CLAMJAMFRY
COADJACENT
COADJUMENT
COADJUTANT
COADJUTIVE
COADJUTRIX
COADJUVANT
CONJECTIVE
CONJECTURE
CONJOINING
CONJOINTLY
CONJUGABLE
CONJUGALLY
CONJUGATED
CONJUGATOR
CONJUNCTLY
CONJUNCTUR
CONJURATOR
CRACKAJACK
DEJECTEDLY
DIJUDICATE
DISJECTING
DISJECTION
DISJOINING
DISJOINTED
DISJOINTLY
DISJUNCTOR
EJACULATED
EJACULATOR
EJECTIVELY
EJECTIVITY
ENJAMBMENT
ENJEOPARDY
ENJOINMENT
EQUIJACENT
FIDEJUSSOR
FOREJUDGED
FOREJUDGER
FORJUDGING
FRABJOUSLY
HIGHJACKER
INCONJUNCT
INJUDICIAL
INJUNCTION
INJUNCTIVE
INTERJOIST
JABBERMENT
JABOTICABA
JACKANAPES
JACKASSERY
JACKFISHES
JACKHAMMER
JACKKNIVES
JACKSNIPES
JACTITATED
JACULATING
JACULATION
JACULATIVE
JACULATORY
JADISHNESS
JAGGEDNESS
JAGHEERDAR
JAGHIREDAR
JAGUARONDI
JAGUARUNDI
JAILKEEPER
JAMESONITE
JANITORIAL
JANIZARIES
JAPACONINE
JAPISHNESS
JARDINIERE
JARGONELLE
JARGONIZED
JAROVIZING
JASPACHATE
JASPERATED
JASPERIZED
JASPIDEOUS
JAUNDICING
JAUNTINESS
JAVELINEER
JAWBREAKER
JAWCRUSHER
JAYWALKING
JEALOUSIES
JEJUNENESS
JEJUNOTOMY
JELLIFYING
JENTACULAR
JEOPARDIED
JEOPARDING
JEOPARDIZE
JEOPARDOUS
JERRYBUILD
JERRYBUILT
JEWELHOUSE
JEWELSMITH
JIMPRICUTE
JINGLINGLY
JINGOISTIC
JINRICKSHA
JINRIKIMAN
JINRIKIMEN
JINRIKISHA
JNANAMARGA
JOAQUINITE
JOBBERNOWL
JOCOSENESS
JOCOSITIES
JOCULARITY

JOCULATORY
JOCUNDNESS
JOGGLEWORK
JOHNNYCAKE
JOINTURESS
JOINTURING
JOLLIFYING
JOLTERHEAD
JOLTHEADED
JOSTLEMENT
JOUISSANCE
JOULEMETER
JOURNALESE
JOURNALING
JOURNALISE
JOURNALISM
JOURNALIST
JOURNALIZE
JOURNALLED
JOURNEYING
JOURNEYMAN
JOURNEYMEN
JOVIALIZED
JOYFULNESS
JOYOUSNESS
JUBILANTLY
JUBILARIAN
JUBILATING
JUBILATION
JUBILATORY
JUDICATION
JUDICATIVE
JUDICATORY
JUDICATURE
JUDICIABLE
JUDICIALLY
JUDOPHOBIA
JUGGERNAUT
JUGGLEMENT
JUGGLERIES
JUGGLINGLY
JUGULATING
JUGULATION
JULOLIDINE
JUMBLEMENT
JUMPSCRAPE
JUNCACEOUS
JUNCTIONAL
JUNGLESIDE
JUNGLEWOOD
JUNKDEALER
JURAMENTAL
JURAMENTUM
JURATORIAL
JURIDICIAL
JURISTICAL
JUSTICIARY
JUSTIFYING
JUVENILELY
JUVENILIFY
JUVENILISM
JUVENILITY
JUXTAPOSED
JUXTAPOSIT
LUMBERJACK
MAJESTICAL
MAJESTIOUS
MAJORATION
MAJORITIES
MAJUSCULAE
MAJUSCULAR
MISJOINDER
MISJUDGING
NATTERJACK
NONABJURER
NONJOINDER
NONJURANCY
OBJECTABLE
OBJECTIONS
OBJECTIVAL
OBJECTIZED
OBJECTLESS
OBJURATION
OBJURGATED
OBJURGATOR
OTTAJANITE
OUTJOURNEY
PAJAHUELLO
PAJAROELLO
PANJANDRUM
PEJORATION
PEJORATIVE
PERJINKETY
PERJUREDLY
PERJURIOUS
POSTJACENT
PREADJUNCT
PREJUDGING
PREJUDICED
PROJACIENT
PROJECTILE
PROJECTING
PROJECTION
PROJECTIVE
PROJECTRIX
PROJECTURE
PROJICIENT
RATTLEJACK
READJUSTER
REJOICEFUL
REJONEADOR
REJUNCTION
REJUVENANT
REJUVENATE
REJUVENIZE
SEJUNCTION
SEJUNCTIVE
SERJEANTRY
SKIPJACKLY
SKYJACKING
SOJOURNING
SUBJACENCY
SUBJECTIFY
SUBJECTILE
SUBJECTING
SUBJECTION
SUBJECTIVE
SUBJICIBLE
SUBJOINDER
SUBJOINING
SUBJUGABLE
SUBJUGATED
SUBJUGATOR
SUBJUGULAR
SUPPLEJACK
SUPRAJURAL
TIMBERJACK
TRAJECTILE
TRAJECTING
TRAJECTION
TRAJECTORY
UNDERJAWED
UNJUSTNESS
WEREJAGUAR
WINDJAMMER
WOODJOBBER

POSITIONAL ORDER LIST OF 10-LETTER WORDS

JABBERMENT
JABOTICABA
JACKANAPES
JACKASSERY
JACKFISHES
JACKHAMMER
JACKKNIVES
JACKSNIPES
JACTITATED
JACULATING
JACULATION
JACULATIVE
JACULATORY
JADISHNESS
JAGGEDNESS
JAGHEERDAR
JAGHIREDAR
JAGUARONDI
JAGUARUNDI
JAILKEEPER
JAMESONITE
JANITORIAL
JANIZARIES
JAPACONINE
JAPISHNESS
JARDINIERE
JARGONELLE
JARGONIZED
JAROVIZING
JASPACHATE
JASPERATED
JASPERIZED
JASPIDEOUS
JAUNDICING
JAUNTINESS
JAVELINEER
JAWBREAKER
JAWCRUSHER
JAYWALKING
JEALOUSIES
JEJUNENESS
JEJUNOTOMY
JELLIFYING
JENTACULAR
JEOPARDIED
JEOPARDING
JEOPARDIZE
JEOPARDOUS
JERRYBUILD
JERRYBUILT
JEWELHOUSE
JEWELSMITH
JIMPRICUTE
JINGLINGLY
JINGOISTIC
JINRICKSHA
JINRIKIMAN
JINRIKIMEN
JINRIKISHA
JNANAMARGA
JOAQUINITE
JOBBERNOWL
JOCOSENESS
JOCOSITIES
JOCULARITY
JOCULATORY
JOCUNDNESS
JOGGLEWORK
JOHNNYCAKE
JOINTURESS
JOINTURING
JOLLIFYING
JOLTERHEAD
JOLTHEADED
JOSTLEMENT
JOUISSANCE
JOULEMETER
JOURNALESE
JOURNALING
JOURNALISE
JOURNALISM
JOURNALIST
JOURNALIZE
JOURNALLED
JOURNEYING
JOURNEYMAN
JOURNEYMEN
JOVIALIZED
JOYFULNESS
JOYOUSNESS
JUBILANTLY
JUBILARIAN
JUBILATING
JUBILATION
JUBILATORY
JUDICATION
JUDICATIVE
JUDICATORY
JUDICATURE
JUDICIABLE
JUDICIALLY
JUDOPHOBIA
JUGGERNAUT
JUGGLEMENT
JUGGLERIES
JUGGLINGLY
JUGULATING
JUGULATION
JULOLIDINE
JUMBLEMENT
JUMPSCRAPE
JUNCACEOUS
JUNCTIONAL
JUNGLESIDE
JUNGLEWOOD
JUNKDEALER
JURAMENTAL
JURAMENTUM
JURATORIAL
JURIDICIAL
JURISTICAL
JUSTICIARY
JUSTIFYING
JUVENILELY
JUVENILIFY
JUVENILISM
JUVENILITY
JUXTAPOSED
JUXTAPOSIT

EJACULATED
EJACULATOR
EJECTIVELY
EJECTIVITY

ABJECTNESS
ABJUDICATE
ABJUNCTIVE
ABJURATION
ABJURATORY
ABJUREMENT
ADJACENTLY
ADJECTIVAL
ADJOINEDLY
ADJUDICATE
ADJUNCTION
ADJUNCTIVE
ADJURATION
ADJURATORY
ADJUSTABLE
ADJUSTMENT
BEJEWELING
BEJEWELLED
BIJOUTERIE
CAJOLEMENT
CAJOLERIES
CAJOLINGLY
CAJUPUTENE
DEJECTEDLY
DIJUDICATE
ENJAMBMENT
ENJEOPARDY
ENJOINMENT
INJUDICIAL
INJUNCTION
INJUNCTIVE
JEJUNENESS
JEJUNOTOMY
MAJESTICAL
MAJESTIOUS
MAJORATION
MAJORITIES
MAJUSCULAE
MAJUSCULAR
OBJECTABLE
OBJECTIONS
OBJECTIVAL
OBJECTIZED
OBJECTLESS
OBJURATION
OBJURGATED
OBJURGATOR
PAJAHUELLO
PAJAROELLO
PEJORATION
PEJORATIVE
REJOICEFUL
REJONEADOR
REJUNCTION
REJUVENANT
REJUVENATE
REJUVENIZE
SEJUNCTION
SEJUNCTIVE
SOJOURNING
UNJUSTNESS

CONJECTIVE
CONJOINING
CONJOINTLY
CONJUGABLE
CONJUGALLY
CONJUGATED
CONJUGATOR
CONJUNCTLY

CONJUNCTUR
CONJURATOR
DISJECTING
DISJECTION
DISJOINING
DISJOINTED
DISJOINTLY
DISJUNCTOR
FORJUDGING
MISJOINDER
MISJUDGING
NONJOINDER
NONJURANCY
OUTJOURNEY
PANJANDRUM
PERJUREDLY
PERJURIOUS
PREJUDGING
PREJUDICED
PROJACIENT
PROJECTILE
PROJECTING
PROJECTION
PROJECTIVE
PROJECTRIX
PROJECTURE
PROJICIENT
SERJEANTRY
SKYJACKING
SUBJACENCY
SUBJECTIFY
SUBJECTILE
SUBJECTING
SUBJECTION
SUBJECTIVE
SUBJICIBLE
SUBJOINDER
SUBJOINING
SUBJUGABLE
SUBJUGATED
SUBJUGATOR
SUBJUGULAR
TRAJECTILE
TRAJECTING
TRAJECTION
TRAJECTORY

ARROJADITE
BLUEJACKET
CLAMJAMFRY
COADJACENT
COADJUMENT
COADJUTIVE
COADJUTRIX
COADJUVANT
EQUIJACENT
FIDEJUSSOR
FOREJUDGED
FOREJUDGER
FRABJOUSLY
HIGHJACKER
OTTAJANITE
POSTJACENT
READJUSTER
SKIPJACKLY
WEREJAGUAR
WINDJAMMER
WOODJOBBER
INCONJUNCT
INTERJOIST
NONABJURER
PREADJUNCT
SUPRAJURAL
UNDERJAWED

BUTTERJAGS
CRACKAJACK
LUMBERJACK
NATTERJACK
RATTLEJACK
SUPPLEJACK
TIMBERJACK

CHAPARAJOS
CHAPAREJOS

SCORING ORDER LIST OF 10-LETTER WORDS

31
OBJECTIZED

30
HIGHJACKER
JACKHAMMER
JAROVIZING
JOVIALIZED

29
CLAMJAMFRY
JACKFISHES
JASPERIZED
JEOPARDIZE
JOHNNYCAKE
REJUVENIZE

28
EQUIJACENT
JARGONIZED
JAYWALKING
PROJECTRIX

27
JUXTAPOSED
LUMBERJACK
SKIPJACKLY
SUBJECTIFY
SUPPLEJACK
TIMBERJACK

26
JACKASSERY
JANIZARIES
JAWBREAKER
JINRICKSHA
JOAQUINITE
JOGGLEWORK
JOURNALIZE
JUVENILIFY
JUXTAPOSIT
PERJINKETY
SKYJACKING
SUBJACENCY

25
BLUEJACKET
EJECTIVELY
EJECTIVITY
FRABJOUSLY
JACKANAPES
JACKKNIVES
JACKSNIPES
JAWCRUSHER
JEWELSMITH
JUDOPHOBIA
JUMPSCRAPE
WINDJAMMER
WOODJOBBER

24
ABJUNCTIVE
CHAPARAJOS
CHAPAREJOS
CONJECTIVE
CONJUNCTLY
DEJECTEDLY
JASPACHATE
JELLIFYING
JINRIKISHA
JOBBERNOWL
JOLLIFYING
JUSTIFYING
OBJECTIVAL
PROJECTIVE
SUBJECTIVE

23
ADJACENTLY
ADJECTIVAL
ADJUNCTIVE
BEJEWELING
BEJEWELLED
CAJOLINGLY
COADJUTIVE
COADJUVANT
CONJUGALLY
CRACKAJACK
ENJAMBMENT
ENJEOPARDY
FOREJUDGED
FORJUDGING
JABBERMENT
JABOTICABA
JAILKEEPER
JERRYBUILD
JEWELHOUSE
JIMPRICUTE
JINRIKIMAN
JINRIKIMEN
JOYFULNESS
JUDICATIVE
JUDICATORY
JUDICIALLY
JUGGLINGLY
JUMBLEMENT
JUVENILELY
JUVENILITY
NATTERJACK
OBJECTABLE
PERJUREDLY
PREJUDICED
RATTLEJACK
SUBJICIBLE

22
ABJUDICATE
ABJURATORY
ADJOINEDLY
COADJACENT
COADJUMENT
CONJOINTLY
CONJUGABLE
FOREJUDGER
INJUNCTIVE
JACULATIVE
JACULATORY
JAGHEERDAR
JAGHIREDAR
JAPISHNESS
JERRYBUILT
JINGLINGLY
JOCULARITY
JOCULATORY
JOLTHEADED
JOURNEYMAN
JOURNEYMEN
JUBILANTLY
JUBILATORY
JUDICIABLE
JUNGLEWOOD
JUNKDEALER
JUSTICIARY
JUVENILISM
MISJUDGING
NONJURANCY
PAJAHUELLO
PANJANDRUM
PEJORATIVE
PREADJUNCT
PREJUDGING
PROJECTING
REJOICEFUL
SEJUNCTIVE
SUBJECTING
SUBJUGABLE
TRAJECTORY
UNDERJAWED

21
ABJECTNESS
ABJUREMENT
ADJUDICATE
ADJURATORY
CAJOLEMENT
CAJUPUTENE
CONJECTURE
CONJUGATED
CONJUNCTUR
DIJUDICATE
DISJECTING
DISJOINTLY
FIDEJUSSOR
INCONJUNCT
JADISHNESS
JAPACONINE
JAUNDICING
JEJUNOTOMY
JEOPARDIED
JEOPARDING
JOLTERHEAD
JOURNEYING
JUGGLEMENT
JUNCACEOUS
JURAMENTUM
MAJESTICAL
MAJUSCULAE
MAJUSCULAR
OBJECTIONS
OBJECTLESS
OBJURGATED
POSTJACENT
PROJACIENT
PROJECTILE
PROJECTION
PROJECTURE
PROJICIENT
SUBJECTILE
SUBJECTION
SUBJUGATED
WEREJAGUAR

20
ADJUNCTION
ADJUSTABLE
ADJUSTMENT
BUTTERJAGS
COADJUTANT
CONJOINING
CONJUGATOR
DISJECTION
DISJUNCTOR
EJACULATED
INJUDICIAL
JACTITATED
JACULATING
JAGGEDNESS
JASPERATED
JASPIDEOUS
JAVELINEER
JEOPARDOUS
JINGOISTIC
JNANAMARGA
JOCUNDNESS
JOYOUSNESS
JUBILATING
JUDICATION
JUDICATURE
JURIDICIAL
MISJOINDER
OBJURGATOR
OUTJOURNEY
REJUVENANT
REJUVENATE
SERJEANTRY
SUBJOINDER
SUBJOINING
SUBJUGATOR
SUBJUGULAR
TRAJECTING

19
ABJURATION
BIJOUTERIE
CAJOLERIES
CONJURATOR
DISJOINING
DISJOINTED
EJACULATOR
ENJOINMENT
INJUNCTION
JACULATION
JAGUARONDI
JAGUARUNDI
JAMESONITE
JENTACULAR
JOCOSENESS
JOCOSITIES
JOSTLEMENT
JOUISSANCE

JOULEMETER
JOURNALISM
JUBILARIAN
JUBILATION
JUGGERNAUT
JUGGLERIES
JUGULATING
JUNCTIONAL
JUNGLESIDE
JURAMENTAL
JURISTICAL
MAJESTIOUS
MAJORATION
MAJORITIES
NONABJURER
OBJURATION
PAJAROELLO
PEJORATION
PERJURIOUS
REJUNCTION
SEJUNCTION
SUPRAJURAL
TRAJECTILE
TRAJECTION

18

ADJURATION
ARROJADITE
JARDINIERE
JARGONELLE
JOINTURING
JOURNALING
JOURNALLED
JUGULATION
JULOLIDINE
NONJOINDER
READJUSTER
REJONEADOR
SOJOURNING

17

INTERJOIST
JANITORIAL
JAUNTINESS
JEALOUSIES
JOINTURESS
JOURNALESE
JOURNALISE
JOURNALIST
JURATORIAL
OTTAJANITE
UNJUSTNESS

16

JEJUNENESS

ALPHABETICAL LIST OF WORDS OVER 10 LETTERS

ABJECTEDNESS
ABJUDICATION
ABJUDICATOR
ADJECTIONAL
ADJECTIVALLY
ADJECTIVELY
ADJOURNMENT
ADJUDICATED
ADJUDICATING
ADJUDICATION
ADJUDICATIVE
ADJUDICATOR
ADJUDICATURE
ADJUNCTIVELY
ADJUTANCIES
ADJUTANTSHIP
ADJUTORIOUS
BEJEWELLING
BENJAMINITE
BICONJUGATE
BRINJARRIES
CIRCUMJACENT
CLAMJAMFERY
CLAMJAMPHRIE
COADDJUVANCY
COADJACENCE
COADJACENTLY
COADJUTATOR
COADJUTEMENT
COADJUTRESS
COADJUTRICE
COADJUTRICES
CONJECTURAL
CONJECTURALLY
CONJECTURED
CONJECTURER
CONJECTURING
CONJOINTNESS
CONJUBILANT
CONJUGALITY
CONJUGATING
CONJUGATION
CONJUGATIVE
CONJUNCTION
CONJUNCTIVAE
CONJUNCTIVAL
CONJUNCTIVAS
CONJUNCTIVE
CONJUNCTIVELY
CONJUNCTURAL
CONJUNCTURE
CONJURATION
COPALJOCOTE
DEJECTEDNESS
DEJUNKERIZE
DIJUDICATION
DISJOINTEDLY
DISJOINTING
DISJOINTURE
DISJUNCTION
DISJUNCTIVE
DISJUNCTIVELY
DISJUNCTURE
EJACULATING
EJACULATION
EJACULATIVE
EJACULATORY
EJECTAMENTA
ENJAMBEMENT
ENJOYABLENESS
EXCONJUGANT
EXTRAJUDICIAL
FIDEJUSSION
FIDEJUSSORY
FOREJUDGING
GIMBALJAWED
GIMBERJAWED
GUANAJUATITE
IMPREJUDICE
INCONJOINABLE
INJUDICIALLY
INJUDICIOUS
INJUDICIOUSLY
INJUNCTIVELY
INJUREDNESS
INJURIOUSLY
INSUBJECTION
INTERJACENCE
INTERJACENT
INTERJECTED
INTERJECTING
INTERJECTION
INTERJECTOR
INTERJECTORY
INTERJUNCTION
INTROJECTION
JABBERINGLY
JACAMEROPINE
JACKPUDDING
JACTITATING
JACTITATION
JACULATORIAL
JACULIFEROUS
JAPACONITIN
JAPACONITINE
JARARACUSSU
JARGONIZING
JARGONNELLE
JAROVIZATION
JASMINEWOOD
JASPERIZING
JATEORHIZIN
JATEORHIZINE
JAUNDICEROOT
JAWBREAKING
JAWBREAKINGLY
JEALOUSNESS
JEFFERISITE
JEFFERSONITE
JEJUNOSTOMY
JELLIEDNESS
JELLIFICATION
JELLYFISHES
JEOPARDIOUS
JEOPARDIZED
JEOPARDIZING
JEOPARDOUSLY
JEOPARDYING
JEQUIRITIES
JERRYBUILDING
JESTINGSTOCK
JIMBERJAWED
JINGLEJANGLE
JNANASHAKTI
JNANENDRIYA
JOBLESSNESS
JOBMISTRESS
JOCOSERIOUS
JOCULARNESS
JOCUNDITIES
JOGTROTTISM
JOHNSTRUPITE
JOINTEDNESS
JOKESOMENESS
JOLLIFICATION
JOLTERHEADED
JOSEPHINITE
JOURNALISTIC
JOURNALIZED
JOURNALIZER
JOURNALIZING
JOURNALLING
JOURNEYCAKE
JOURNEYWOMAN
JOURNEYWOMEN
JOURNEYWORK
JOVIALISTIC
JOVIALIZING
JOVIALNESS
JOYLESSNESS
JUBILIZATION
JUDGMATICAL
JUDICATORIAL
JUDICATORIES
JUDICIALITY
JUDICIALIZE
JUDICIARIES
JUDICIARILY
JUDICIOUSLY
JUDICIOUSNESS
JURAMENTADO
JURAMENTALLY
JURIDICALLY
JURISCONSULT
JURISDICTION
JURISDICTIVE
JURISPRUDENCE
JURISPRUDENT
JURISTICALLY
JUSTAUCORPS
JUSTICEHOOD
JUSTICESHIP
JUSTICEWEED
JUSTICIABLE
JUSTIFIABLE
JUSTIFIABLY
JUSTIFICATION
JUSTIFICATIVE
JUSTIFICATOR
JUSTIFYINGLY
JUVENESCENCE
JUVENESCENT
JUVENILENESS
JUVENILITIES
JUXTAMARINE
JUXTAPOSING
JUXTAPOSITION
JUXTAPYLORIC
JUXTASPINAL
KATJEPIERING
KATZENJAMMER
KJELDAHLIZE
LEATHERJACKET
LUMBERJACKET
MAHARAJRANA
MAJESTICALLY
MALADJUSTED
MALADJUSTMENT
MISJUDGEMENT
MISJUDGINGLY
MISJUDGMENT
NATROJAROSITE
NONADJUSTIVE
NONDISJUNCT
NONJURANTISM
NONOBJECTIVE
OBJECTATION
OBJECTATIVE
OBJECTIFIED
OBJECTIFYING
OBJECTIONABLE
OBJECTIONABLY
OBJECTIONAL
OBJECTIONER
OBJECTIONIST
OBJECTIVATE
OBJECTIVATED
OBJECTIVATING
OBJECTIVATION
OBJECTIVELY
OBJECTIVENESS
OBJECTIVISM
OBJECTIVIST
OBJECTIVISTIC
OBJECTIVITY
OBJECTIVIZE
OBJECTIVIZED
OBJECTIVIZING
OBJECTIZATION
OBJECTIZING
OBJURGATING
OBJURGATION
OBJURGATIVE
OBJURGATIVELY
OBJURGATORILY
OBJURGATORY
OBJURGATRIX
PARIETOJUGAL
PAUCIJUGATE
PEJORATIVELY
PEREJONETTE
PERJINKITIES
PERJUREDNESS
PERJURIOUSLY
POSTADJUNCT
PREJUDGEMENT
PREJUDGMENT
PREJUDICATE
PREJUDICATOR
PREJUDICEDLY
PREJUDICIAL
PREJUDICING
PREJUDICIOUS
PROJECTEDLY
PROJECTINGLY
PROJECTIONAL
PROJECTIVITY
PROJICIENCE
PROJICIENTLY
READJUSTABLE
READJUSTMENT
REJECTAMENTA
REJOICEMENT
REJUVENATED
REJUVENATING
REJUVENATION
REJUVENATIVE
REJUVENATOR
REJUVENESCE
RETROJECTION
RETROJUGULAR
RUBIJERVINE
SEJUNCTIVELY
SEMIJUBILEE
SMOKEJUMPER
SOJOURNMENT
STEEPLEJACK
STOCKJOBBER
STOCKJOBBERY
STOCKJOBBING
STOCKJUDGING
STOLKJAERRE
STRAITJACKET
SUBJECTEDLY
SUBJECTEDNESS

SUBJECTIONAL
SUBJECTIVELY
SUBJECTIVISM
SUBJECTIVIST
SUBJECTIVITY
SUBJUGATING
SUBJUGATION
SUBJUNCTION
SUBJUNCTIVE
SUBJUNCTIVELY
SUBTERJACENT
SUPERJACENT
SURREJOINDER
THINGAMAJIG
THINGUMAJIG
TRAJECTORIES
TRONDHJEMITE
UNBEJUGGLED
UNJUDICIOUS
UNJUSTIFIED
UNPREJUDICE
UNPREJUDICED
WINDJAMMING
YAJNOPAVITA

POSITIONAL ORDER LIST OF WORDS OVER 10 LETTERS

JABBERINGLY
JACAMEROPINE
JACKPUDDING
JACTITATING
JACTITATION
JACULATORIAL
JACULIFEROUS
JAPACONITIN
JAPACONITINE
JARARACUSSU
JARGONIZING
JARGONNELLE
JAROVIZATION
JASMINEWOOD
JASPERIZING
JATEORHIZIN
JATEORHIZINE
JAUNDICEROOT
JAWBREAKING
JAWBREAKINGLY
JEALOUSNESS
JEFFERISITE
JEFFERSONITE
JEJUNOSTOMY
JELLIEDNESS
JELLIFICATION
JELLYFISHES
JEOPARDIOUS
JEOPARDIZED
JEOPARDIZING
JEOPARDOUSLY
JEOPARDYING
JEQUIRITIES
JERRYBUILDING
JESTINGSTOCK
JIMBERJAWED
JINGLEJANGLE
JNANASHAKTI
JNANENDRIYA
JOBLESSNESS
JOBMISTRESS
JOCOSERIOUS
JOCULARNESS
JOCUNDITIES
JOGTROTTISM
JOHNSTRUPITE
JOINTEDNESS
JOKESOMENESS
JOLLIFICATION
JOLTERHEADED
JOSEPHINITE
JOURNALISTIC
JOURNALIZED
JOURNALIZER
JOURNALIZING
JOURNALLING
JOURNEYCAKE
JOURNEYWOMAN
JOURNEYWOMEN
JOURNEYWORK
JOVIALISTIC
JOVIALIZING
JOVIALNESS
JOYLESSNESS
JUBILIZATION
JUDGMATICAL
JUDICATORIAL
JUDICATORIES
JUDICIALITY
JUDICIALIZE
JUDICIARIES
JUDICIARILY
JUDICIOUSLY
JUDICIOUSNESS
JURAMENTADO
JURAMENTALLY
JURIDICALLY
JURISCONSULT
JURISDICTION
JURISDICTIVE
JURISPRUDENCE
JURISPRUDENT
JURISTICALLY
JUSTAUCORPS
JUSTICEHOOD
JUSTICESHIP
JUSTICEWEED
JUSTICIABLE
JUSTIFIABLE
JUSTIFIABLY
JUSTIFICATION
JUSTIFICATIVE
JUSTIFICATOR
JUSTIFYINGLY
JUVENESCENCE
JUVENESCENT
JUVENILENESS
JUVENILITIES
JUXTAMARINE
JUXTAPOSING
JUXTAPOSITION
JUXTAPYLORIC
JUXTASPINAL

EJACULATING
EJACULATION
EJACULATIVE
EJACULATORY
EJECTAMENTA
EJEJUNOSTOMY
KJELDAHLIZE

ABJECTEDNESS
ABJUDICATION
ABJUDICATOR
ADJECTIONAL
ADJECTIVALLY
ADJECTIVELY
ADJOURNMENT
ADJUDICATED
ADJUDICATING
ADJUDICATION
ADJUDICATIVE
ADJUDICATOR
ADJUDICATURE
ADJUNCTIVELY
ADJUTANCIES
ADJUTANTSHIP
ADJUTORIUS
BEJEWELLING
DEJECTEDNESS
DEJUNKERIZE
DIJUDICATION
ENJAMBEMENT
ENJOYABLENESS
INJUDICIALLY
INJUDICIOUS
INJUDICIOUSLY
INJUNCTIVELY
INJUREDNESS
INJURIOUSLY
MAJESTICALLY
OBJECTATION
OBJECTATIVE
OBJECTIFIED
OBJECTIFYING
OBJECTIONABLE
OBJECTIONABLY
OBJECTIONAL
OBJECTIONER
OBJECTIONIST
OBJECTIVATE
OBJECTIVATED
OBJECTIVATING
OBJECTIVATION
OBJECTIVELY
OBJECTIVENESS
OBJECTIVISM
OBJECTIVIST
OBJECTIVISTIC
OBJECTIVITY
OBJECTIVIZE
OBJECTIVIZED
OBJECTIVIZING
OBJECTIZATION
OBJECTIZING
OBJURGATING
OBJURGATION
OBJURGATIVE
OBJURGATIVELY
OBJURGATORILY
OBJURGATORY
OBJURGATRIX
PEJORATIVELY
REJECTAMENTA
REJOICEMENT
REJUVENATED
REJUVENATING
REJUVENATION
REJUVENATIVE
REJUVENATOR
REJUVENESCE
SEJUNCTIVELY
SOJOURNMENT
UNJUDICIOUS
UNJUSTIFIED
YAJNOPAVITA

BENJAMINITE
CAODJACENCY
CONJECTURAL
CONJECTURALLY
CONJECTURE
CONJECTURED
CONJECTURER
CONJECTURING
CONJOINTNESS
CONJUBILANT
CONJUGALITY
CONJUGATING
CONJUGATION
CONJUGATIVE
CONJUNCTION
CONJUNCTIVAE
CONJUNCTIVAL
CONJUNCTIVAS
CONJUNCTIVE
CONJUNCTIVELY
CONJUNCTURAL
CONJUNCTURE
CONJURATION
DISJOINTEDLY
DISJOINTING
DISJOINTURE
DISJUNCTION
DISJUNCTIVE
DISJUNCTIVELY
DISJUNCTURE
KATJEPIERING
MISJUDGEMENT
MISJUDGINGLY
MISJUDGMENT
NONJURANTISM
PERJINKITIES
PERJUREDNESS
PERJURIOUSLY
PREJUDGEMENT
PREJUDGMENT
PREJUDICATE
PREJUDICATOR
PREJUDICEDLY
PREJUDICIAL
PREJUDICING
PREJUDICIOUS
PROJECTEDLY
PROJECTINGLY
PROJECTIONAL
PROJECTIVITY
PROJICIENCE
PROJICIENTLY
SUBJECTEDLY
SUBJECTEDNESS
SUBJECTIONAL
SUBJECTIVELY
SUBJECTIVISM
SUBJECTIVIST
SUBJECTIVITY
SUBJUGATING
SUBJUGATION
SUBJUNCTION
SUBJUNCTIVE
SUBJUNCTIVELY
TRAJECTORIES

BRINJARRIES
CLAMJAMFERY
CLAMJAMPHRIE
COADJACENCE
COADJACENTLY
COADJUTATOR
COADJUTEMENT
COADJUTRESS
COADJUTRICE
COADJUTRICES
FIDEJUSSION
FIDEJUSSORY
FOREJUDGING
PEREJONETTE
READJUSTABLE
READJUSTMENT
SEMIJUBILEE
UNBEJUGGLED

WINDJAMMING

BICONJUGATE
COADDJUVANCY
COPALJOCOTE
EXCONJUGANT
EXTRAJUDICIAL
GUANAJUATITE
IMPREJUDICE
INCONJOINABLE
INSUBJECTION
INTERJACENCE
INTERJACENT
INTERJECTED
INTERJECTING
INTERJECTION
INTERJECTOR
INTERJECTORY
INTERJUNCTION
INTROJECTION
MALADJUSTED
MALADJUSTMENT
NATROJAROSITE
NONADJUSTIVE
NONOBJECTIVE
PAUCIJUGATE
RETROJECTION
RETROJUGULAR
RUBIJERVINE
SMOKEJUMPER
STOCKJOBBER
STOCKJOBBERY
STOCKJOBBING
STOCKJUDGING
STOLKJAERRE
SUPERJACENT
SURREJOINDER
UNPREJUDICE
UNPREJUDICED

CIRCUMJACENT
GIMBALJAWED
GIMBERJAWED
JIMBERJAWED
JINGLEJANGLE
KATZENJAMMER
LUMBERJACKET
MAHARAJRANA
NONDISJUNCT
POSTADJUNCT
STRAITJACKET
SUBTERJACENT
TRONDHJEMITE

LEATHERJACKET
PARIETOJUGAL
STEEPLEJACK

THINGAMAJIG
THINGUMAJIG

SCORING ORDER LIST OF WORDS OVER 10 LETTERS

37
OBJECTIVIZING

36
KATZENJAMMER
OBJECTIVIZED

35
KJELDAHLIZE

34
OBJECTIVIZE

33
JAWBREAKINGLY
JUXTAPYLORIC
OBJECTIZATION

32
DEJUNKERIZE
JEOPARDIZING
OBJECTIZING
STOCKJOBBERY

31
COADDJUVANCY
JAROVIZATION
JATEORHIZINE
JEOPARDIZED
JOVIALIZING

30
CLAMJAMFERY
CLAMJAMPHRIE
CONJUNCTIVELY
EXTRAJUDICIAL
JASPERIZING
JATEORHIZIN
JUBILIZATION
JUDICIALIZE
OBJECTIFYING
STOCKJOBBING
SUBJUNCTIVELY

29
DISJUNCTIVELY
JACKPUDDING
JARGONIZING
JOURNALIZING
JUSTIFYINGLY
JUXTAPOSITION
LEATHERJACKET
LUMBERJACKET
OBJECTIONABLY
OBJECTIVISTIC
OBJURGATIVELY
PROJECTIVITY
SUBJECTIVELY
SUBJECTIVITY

28
ADJECTIVALLY
ADJUNCTIVELY
EXCONJUGANT
JAWBREAKING
JOURNALIZED
JOURNEYWORK
JUSTIFICATIVE
JUXTAPOSING
OBJECTIVATING
OBJECTIVELY
OBJECTIVITY
OBJURGATRIX
PREJUDICEDLY
SMOKEJUMPER
STOCKJOBBER
STOCKJUDGING
SUBJECTIVISM

27
ADJECTIVELY
COADJACENTLY
CONJECTURALLY
GIMBALJAWED
GIMBERJAWED
INJUNCTIVELY
JELLYFISHES
JEQUIRITIES
JERRYBUILDING
JOURNALIZER
JOURNEYCAKE
JOURNEYWOMAN
JOURNEYWOMEN
JUXTASPINAL
MISJUDGINGLY
OBJECTIVATED
OBJECTIVATION
OBJECTIVENESS
OBJECTIVISM
PEJORATIVELY
PROJECTINGLY
SEJUNCTIVELY
WINDJAMMING

26
ADJUDICATIVE
CONJUNCTIVAE
CONJUNCTIVAL
CONJUNCTIVAS
INJUDICIOUSLY
JABBERINGLY
JESTINGSTOCK
JUSTIFIABLY
JUVENESCENCE
KATJEPIERING
MAJESTICALLY
NONOBJECTIVE
OBJECTIFIED
OBJECTIONABLE
OBJURGATORILY
PROJECTEDLY
PROJICIENTLY
STEEPLEJACK
SUBJECTEDLY
SUBJECTIVIST
YAJNOPAVITA

25
ADJUTANTSHIP
CAODJACENCY
CONJUNCTIVE
ENJOYABLENESS
FIDEJUSSORY
IMPREJUDICE
INJUDICIALLY
JACAMEROPINE
JEFFERSONITE
JELLIFICATION
JEOPARDOUSLY
JEOPARDYING
JIMBERJAWED
JNANASHAKTI
JOKESOMENESS
JOLLIFICATION
JURISDICTIVE
JURISPRUDENCE
JUSTICESHIP
JUSTIFICATION
MALADJUSTMENT
MISJUDGEMENT
OBJECTATIVE
OBJECTIVATE
OBJECTIVIST
PERJINKITIES
PREJUDGEMENT
REJUVENATIVE
STRAITJACKET
SUBJECTEDNESS
SUBJUNCTIVE
THINGAMAJIG
THINGUMAJIG
TRONDHJEMITE
UNPREJUDICED

24
ABJECTEDNESS
ABJUDICATION
ADJUDICATING
BEJEWELLING
CIRCUMJACENT
COADJUTEMENT
COADJUTRICES
CONJECTURING
CONJUGALITY
CONJUGATIVE
COPALJOCOTE
DISJOINTEDLY
DISJUNCTIVE
ENJAMBEMENT
FOREJUDGING
INCONJOINABLE
INTERJECTORY
JACULIFEROUS
JASMINEWOOD
JEFFERISITE
JOHNSTRUPITE
JOLTERHEADED
JUDGMATICAL
JUDICIALITY
JUDICIARILY
JUDICIOUSLY
JURAMENTALLY
JURIDICALLY
JURISTICALLY
JUSTICEHOOD
JUSTICEWEED
JUSTIFICATOR
MISJUDGMENT
OBJURGATIVE
OBJURGATORY
PERJURIOUSLY
PREJUDGMENT
PREJUDICATOR
PREJUDICING
PREJUDICIOUS
PROJICIENCE

23
ABJUDICATOR
ADJUDICATED
ADJUDICATION
ADJUDICATURE
BICONJUGATE
COADJUTRICE
CONJECTURED
CONJUNCTURAL
DEJECTEDNESS
DIJUDICATION
EJACULATIVE
EJACULATORY
INSUBJECTION
INTERJACENCE
JAPACONITINE
JOSEPHINITE
JOVIALISTIC
JUDICIOUSNESS
JUSTIFIABLE
JUVENESCENT
MAHARAJRANA
NONADJUSTIVE
OBJECTIONIST
PAUCIJUGATE
POSTADJUNCT
PREJUDICATE
PREJUDICIAL
PROJECTIONAL
REJECTAMENTA
REJUVENATING
REJUVENESCE
RUBIJERVINE
SUBJECTIONAL
SUBTERJACENT
UNBEJUGGLED
UNPREJUDICE

22
ADJUDICATOR
BENJAMINITE
COADJACENCE
CONJECTURAL
CONJECTURER
CONJUBILANT
CONJUGATING
CONJUNCTION
CONJUNCTURE
EJECTAMENTA
FIDEJUSSION
INTERJECTING
INTERJUNCTION
JAPACONITIN
JAUNDICEROOT
JEJUNOSTOMY
JNANENDRIYA
JOBMISTRESS
JUDICATORIAL
JUDICATORIES
JURISDICTION
JURISPRUDENT
JUSTAUCORPS
JUSTICIABLE
JUVENILENESS
JUVENILITIES
MALADJUSTED
OBJECTATION
OBJECTIONAL
OBJECTIONER
OBJURGATING
PARIETOJUGAL
PERJUREDNESS
READJUSTABLE
READJUSTMENT
REJOICEMENT
REJUVENATED
REJUVENATION
SEMIJUBILEE
STOLKJAERRE
SUBJUGATING
SUBJUNCTION
SUPERJACENT
UNJUSTIFIED

21
ADJECTIONAL
ADJOURNMENT
ADJUTANCIES
COADJUTATOR
COADJUTRESS
CONJOINTNESS
CONJUGATION
DISJUNCTION
DISJUNCTURE
EJACULATING
INJUDICIOUS
INJURIOUSLY
INTERJECTED
INTERJECTION
INTROJECTION
JACTITATING
JACULATORIAL
JEOPARDIOUS
JOCUNDITIES
JOGTROTTISM
JOURNALISTIC
JOYLESSNESS
JUDICIARIES
JURAMENTADO
JURISCONSULT
NONDISJUNCT
NONJURANTISM
OBJURGATION
REJUVENATOR
RETROJECTION
SUBJUGATION
TRAJECTORIES
UNJUDICIOUS

20
BRINJARRIES
CONJURATION
DISJOINTING
EJACULATION
GUANAJUATITE
INTERJACENT
INTERJECTOR
JACTITATION
JARARACUSSU
JINGLEJANGLE
JOBLESSNESS
JOCOSERIOUS
JOCULARNESS
JOVIALNESS
NATROJAROSITE
PEREJONETTE
RETROJUGULAR
SOJOURNMENT
SURREJOINDER

19
ADJUTORIOUS
DISJOINTURE
INJUREDNESS
JARGONNELLE
JELLIEDNESS
JOINTEDNESS
JOURNALLING

18
JEALOUSNESS

High-Scoring Words Containing

Q

2-3 LETTER WORDS

ALPHABETICAL ORDER

QAT
QRI
QU
QUA
QUI
QUO
SUQ

POSITIONAL ORDER

QAT
QRI
QU
QUA
QUI
QUO
SUQ

SCORING ORDER

12
QAT
QRI
QUA
QUI
QUO
SUQ

11
QU

ALPHABETICAL LIST OF 4-LETTER WORDS

AQUA
AQUO
CINQ
OQUE
OQUI
QADI
QAID
QERI
QUAA
QUAB
QUAD
QUAG
QUAI
QUAN
QUAP
QUAR
QUAS
QUAT
QUAW
QUAX
QUAY
QUED
QUEE
QUEI
QUET
QUEY
QUIB
QUID
QUIM
QUIN
QUIP
QUIS
QUIT
QUIZ
QUOD
QUOG
QUOP
QUOT
QUOY
QUOZ
SHOQ
WAQF

POSITIONAL ORDER LIST OF 4-LETTER WORDS

QADI
QAID
QERI
QUAA
QUAB
QUAD
QUAG
QUAI
QUAN
QUAP
QUAR
QUAS
QUAT
QUAW
QUAX
QUAY
QUED
QUEE
QUEI
QUET
QUEY
QUIB
QUID
QUIM
QUIN
QUIP
QUIS
QUIT
QUIZ
QUOD
QUOG
QUOP
QUOT
QUOY
QUOZ

AQUA
AQUO
OQUE
OQUI

WAQF

CINQ
SHOQ

SCORING ORDER LIST OF 4-LETTER WORDS

22
QUIZ
QUOZ

20
QUAX

19
WAQF

16
QUAW
QUAY
QUEY
QUOY
SHOQ

15
CINQ
QUAB
QUAP
QUIB
QUIM
QUIP
QUOP

14
QADI
QAID
QUAD
QUAG
QUED
QUID
QUOD
QUOG

13
AQUA
AQUO
OQUE
OQUI
QERI
QUAA
QUAI
QUAN
QUAR
QUAS
QUAT
QUEE
QUEI
QUET
QUIN
QUIS
QUIT
QUOT

ALPHABETICAL LIST OF 5-LETTER WORDS

AQUAE
AQUAS
BEQAA
BULAQ
CEQUI
COQUE
EQUAL
EQUES
EQUID
EQUIP
FAQIH
JIQUE
JIQUI
MAQUI
MIQRA
NUQUE
OCQUE
PIQUE
QANEH
QASAB
QAZAQ
QIBLA
QINAH
QIYAS
QOBAR
QUACK
QUADE
QUAFF
QUAIL
QUAIR
QUAIS
QUAKE
QUAKY
QUALE
QUALM
QUANT
QUARE
QUARK
QUARL
QUART
QUASH
QUASI
QUASS
QUATE
QUAWK
QUEAK
QUEAL
QUEAN
QUECH
QUEDE
QUEED
QUEEL
QUEEN
QUEER
QUEET
QUELL
QUELT
QUEME
QUENA
QUENT
QUERL
QUERN
QUERY
QUEST
QUEUE
QUICA
QUICK
QUIET
QUIFF
QUILA
QUILE
QUILK
QUILL
QUILT
QUINA
QUINE
QUINK
QUINT
QUIPO
QUIPU
QUIRA
QUIRE
QUIRK
QUIRL
QUIRT
QUIST
QUITE
QUITS
QUOAD
QUOCK
QUOIN
QUOIT
QUONK
QUOTA
QUOTE
QUOTH
QUOTT
QUYTE
ROQUE
SEQUA
SQUAB
SQUAD
SQUAM
SQUAP
SQUAT

SQUAW
SQUEG
SQUET
SQUIB
SQUID
SQUIN
SQUIR
SQUIT
SQUIZ
SQUSH
TOQUE
TRINQ
TUQUE
USQUE

POSITIONAL ORDER LIST OF 5-LETTER WORDS

QANEH
QASAB
QAZAQ
QIBLA
QINAH
QIYAS
QOBAR
QUACK
QUADE
QUAFF
QUAIL
QUAIR
QUAIS
QUAKE
QUAKY
QUALE
QUALM
QUANT
QUARE
QUARK
QUARL
QUART
QUASH
QUASI
QUASS
QUATE
QUAWK
QUEAK
QUEAL
QUEAN
QUECH
QUEDE
QUEED
QUEEL
QUEEN
QUEER
QUEET
QUELL
QUELT
QUEME
QUENA
QUENT
QUERL
QUERN
QUERY
QUEST
QUEUE
QUICA
QUICK
QUIET
QUIFF
QUILA
QUILE
QUILK
QUILL
QUILT
QUINA
QUINE
QUINK
QUINT
QUIPO
QUIPU
QUIRA
QUIRE
QUIRK
QUIRL
QUIRT
QUIST
QUITE
QUITS
QUOAD
QUOCK
QUOIN
QUOIT
QUONK
QUOTA
QUOTE
QUOTH
QUOTT
QUYTE

AQUAE
AQUAS
EQUAL
EQUES
EQUID
EQUIP
SQUAB
SQUAD
SQUAM
SQUAP
SQUAT
SQUAW
SQUEG
SQUET
SQUIB
SQUID
SQUIN
SQUIR
SQUIT
SQUIZ
SQUSH

BEQAA
CEQUI
COQUE
FAQIH
JIQUE
JIQUI
MAQUI
MIQRA
NUQUE
OCQUE
PIQUE
ROQUE
SEQUA
TOQUE
TUQUE
USQUE

BULAQ
QAZAQ
TRINQ

SCORING ORDER LIST OF 5-LETTER WORDS

23
SQUIZ

22
QAZAQ

21
JIQUE
JIQUI
QUAKY
QUAWK

20
FAQIH
QUACK
QUAFF
QUICK
QUIFF
QUOCK

19
QUECH

18
QUAKE
QUARK
QUEAK
QUILK
QUINK
QUIRK
QUONK

17
QANEH
QINAH
QIYAS
QUASH
QUERY
QUOTH
QUYTE
SQUAW
SQUSH

16
BEQAA
BULAQ
CEQUI
COQUE
EQUIP
MAQUI
MIQRA
OCQUE
PIQUE
QASAB
QIBLA
QOBAR
QUALM
QUEME
QUICA
QUIPO
QUIPU
SQUAB
SQUAM
SQUAP
SQUIB

15
EQUID
QUADE
QUEDE
QUEED
QUOAD
SQUAD
SQUEG
SQUID

14
AQUAE
AQUAS
EQUAL
EQUES
NUQUE
QUAIL
QUAIR
QUAIS
QUALE
QUANT
QUARE
QUARL
QUART
QUASI
QUASS
QUATE
QUEAL
QUEAN
QUEEL
QUEEN
QUEER
QUEET
QUELL
QUELT
QUENA
QUENT
QUERL
QUERN
QUEST
QUEUE
QUIET
QUILA
QUILE
QUILL
QUILT
QUINA
QUINE
QUINT
QUIRA
QUIRE
QUIRL
QUIRT
QUIST
QUITE
QUITS
QUOIN
QUOIT
QUOTA
QUOTE
QUOTT
ROQUE
SEQUA
SQUAT
SQUET
SQUIN
SQUIR
SQUIT
TOQUE
TRINQ
TUQUE
USQUE

ALPHABETICAL LIST OF 6-LETTER WORDS

ACQUIT
AEQUOR
ANAQUA
AQUAGE
AQUATE
AQUILA
AQUOSE
ASQUAT
BANQUE
BARQUE
BASQUE
BISQUE
BOSQUE
BRIQUE
CAIQUE
CALQUE
CASQUE
CHEQUE
CINQUE
CIRQUE
CLAQUE
CLIQUE
CLIQUY
COQUET
COQUIN
EQUANT
EQUATE
EQUINE
EQUIPT
EQUITY
EQUOID
EVEQUE
EXEQUY
FAQUIR
JERQUE
LASQUE
LIQUET
LIQUID
LIQUOR
LOQUAT
MANQUE
MAQUIS
MARQUE
MASQUE
MOSQUE
NAIQUE
OPAQUE
PIQUED
PIQUET
PIQUIA
PIQURE
PLAQUE
PULQUE
QANTAR
QUACKY
QUADER
QUADLE
QUADRA
QUAERE
QUAGGA
QUAGGY
QUAHOG
QUAICH
QUAIFE
QUAIGH
QUAILY
QUAINT
QUAKED
QUAKER
QUALIA
QUALLY
QUALMY
QUANDY
QUANTA
QUARLE
QUARRY
QUARTA
QUARTE
QUARTO
QUARTZ
QUASAR
QUASHY
QUASKY
QUATCH
QUATRE
QUATTY
QUAVER
QUAYED
QUEACH
QUEASE
QUEASY
QUEDLY
QUEENS
QUEERY
QUEEST
QUEEVE
QUELCH
QUELME
QUENCH
QUENDA
QUERRE
QUESAL
QUETCH
QUETHE
QUEZAL
QUIAPO
QUIDAM
QUILES
QUILEZ
QUILLY
QUINAS
QUINCE
QUINCH
QUINET
QUINIA
QUINIC
QUININ
QUINOA
QUINOL
QUINON
QUINSE
QUINSY
QUINTA
QUINTE
QUINTO
QUINYL
QUINZE
QUIPPE
QUIPPU
QUIPPY
QUIPUS
QUIRED
QUIRKY
QUISBY
QUITCH
QUIVER
QUIZZY
QUOITS
QUOKKA
QUORUM
QUOTAS
QUOTED
QUOTEE
QUOTER
QUOTHA
QUOTUM
RAQUET
REQUIN
RISQUE
ROQUET
SACQUE
SAUQUI
SECQUE
SEQUEL
SEQUIN
SESQUI
SQUAIL
SQUALL
SQUAMA
SQUAME
SQUAMY
SQUARE
SQUARK
SQUARY
SQUASH
SQUAWK
SQUAWL
SQUDGE
SQUDGY
SQUEAK
SQUEAL
SQUEAM
SQUEEF
SQUEEL
SQUIDS
SQUILL
SQUINT
SQUIRE
SQUIRK
SQUIRL
SQUIRM
SQUIRR
SQUIRT
SQUISH
SQUISS
SQUSHY
SQUUSH
TAQIYA
TAQLID
TARIQA
TOQUET
TORQUE
UBIQUE
UNIQUE
UNQUIT
UNQUOD
XARQUE
YANQUI
YAQONA
ZEQUIN
ZINDIQ

POSITIONAL ORDER LIST OF 6-LETTER WORDS

QANTAR
QUACKY
QUADER
QUADLE
QUADRA
QUAERE
QUAGGA
QUAGGY
QUAHOG
QUAICH
QUAIFE
QUAIGH
QUAILY
QUAINT
QUAKED
QUAKER
QUALIA
QUALLY
QUALMY
QUANDY
QUANTA
QUARLE
QUARRY
QUARTA
QUARTE
QUARTO
QUARTZ
QUASAR
QUASHY
QUASKY
QUATCH
QUATRE
QUATTY
QUAVER
QUAYED
QUEACH
QUEASE
QUEASY
QUEDLY
QUEENS
QUEERY
QUEEST
QUEEVE
QUELCH
QUELME
QUENCH
QUENDA
QUERRE
QUESAL
QUETCH
QUETHE
QUEZAL
QUIAPO
QUIDAM
QUILES
QUILEZ
QUILLY
QUINAS
QUINCE
QUINCH
QUINET
QUINIA
QUINIC
QUININ
QUINOA
QUINOL
QUINON
QUINSE
QUINSY
QUINTA
QUINTE
QUINTO
QUINYL
QUINZE
QUIPPE
QUIPPU
QUIPPY
QUIPUS
QUIRED
QUIRKY
QUISBY
QUITCH
QUIZZY
QUIVER
QUOITS
QUOKKA
QUORUM
QUOTAS
QUOTED
QUOTEE
QUOTER
QUOTHA
QUOTUM

AQUAGE
AQUATE
AQUILA
AQUOSE
EQUANT
EQUATE
EQUINE
EQUIPT
EQUITY
EQUOID
SQUAIL
SQUALL
SQUAMA
SQUAME
SQUAMY
SQUARE
SQUARK
SQUARY
SQUASH
SQUAWK
SQUAWL
SQUDGE
SQUDGY
SQUEAK
SQUEAL
SQUEAM
SQUEEF
SQUEEL
SQUIDS
SQUILL
SQUINT
SQUIRE
SQUIRK
SQUIRL
SQUIRM
SQUIRR
SQUIRT
SQUISH
SQUISS
SQUSHY
SQUUSH

ACQUIT
AEQUOR
ASQUAT
COQUET
COQUIN
FAQUIR
LIQUET
LIQUID
LIQUOR
LOQUAT
MAQUIS
PIQUED
PIQUET
PIQUIA
PIQURE
RAQUET
REQUIN
ROQUET
SEQUEL
SEQUIN
TAQIYA
TAQLID
TOQUET
UNQUIT
UNQUOD
YAQONA
ZEQUIN
ANAQUA
BANQUE
BARQUE
BASQUE
BISQUE
BOSQUE
BRIQUE
CAIQUE
CALQUE
CASQUE
CHEQUE
CINQUE
CIRQUE
CLAQUE
CLIQUE
CLIQUY
EVEQUE
EXEQUY
JERQUE
LASQUE
MANQUE
MARQUE
MASQUE
MOSQUE
NAIQUE
OPAQUE
PLAQUE
PULQUE
RISQUE
SACQUE
SAUQUI
SECQUE
SESQUI
TORQUE
UBIQUE
UNIQUE
XARQUE
YANQUI

TARIQA

ZINDIQ

SCORING ORDER LIST OF 6-LETTER WORDS

26
QUIZZY

25
EXEQUY
ZINDIQ

24
QUACKY
QUARTZ
QUEZAL
QUILEZ
QUINZE
ZEQUIN

22
JERQUE
QUASKY
QUIPPY
QUIRKY
SQUAWK
XARQUE

21
QUASHY
SQUSHY

20
CHEQUE
CLIQUY
QUAGGY
QUAICH
QUAKED
QUALMY
QUATCH
QUEACH
QUELCH
QUENCH
QUETCH
QUINCH
QUISBY
QUITCH
SQUAMY
SQUDGY

19
QUAHOG
QUAIGH
QUAKER
QUANDY
QUAYED
QUEDLY
QUIPPE
QUIPPU
SQUARK
SQUEAK
SQUIRK

18
EQUITY
EVEQUE
FAQUIR
PIQUED
QUAIFE
QUAILY
QUALLY
QUARRY
QUATTY
QUAVER
QUEASY
QUEERY
QUEEVE
QUETHE
QUIDAM
QUILLY
QUINSY
QUINYL
QUIVER
QUOKKA
QUOTHA
SQUARY
SQUASH
SQUAWL
SQUEEF
SQUISH
SQUUSH
TAQIYA
YANQUI
YAQONA

17
ACQUIT
BANQUE
BARQUE
BASQUE
BISQUE
BOSQUE
BRIQUE
CAIQUE
CALQUE
CASQUE
CINQUE
CIRQUE
CLAQUE
CLIQUE
COQUET
COQUIN
EQUIPT
MANQUE
MAQUIS
MARQUE
MASQUE
MOSQUE
OPAQUE
PIQUET
PIQUIA
PIQURE
PLAQUE
PULQUE
QUAGGA
QUELME
QUIAPO
QUINCE
QUINIC
QUIPUS
QUORUM
QUOTUM
SACQUE
SECQUE
SQUAMA
SQUAME
SQUDGE
SQUEAM
SQUIRM
UBIQUE

16
AQUAGE
EQUOID
LIQUID
QUADER
QUADLE
QUADRA
QUENDA
QUIRED
QUOTED
SQUIDS
TAQLID
UNQUOD

15
AEQUOR
ANAQUA
AQUATE
AQUILA
AQUOSE
ASQUAT
EQUANT
EQUATE
EQUINE
LASQUE
LIQUET
LIQUOR
LOQUAT
NAIQUE
QANTAR
QUAERE
QUAINT
QUALIA
QUANTA
QUARLE
QUARTA
QUARTE
QUARTO
QUASAR
QUATRE
QUEASE
QUEENS
QUEEST
QUERRE
QUESAL
QUILES
QUINAS
QUINET
QUINIA
QUININ
QUINOA
QUINOL
QUINON
QUINSE
QUINTA
QUINTE
QUINTO
QUOITS
QUOTAS
QUOTEE
QUOTER
RAQUET
REQUIN
RISQUE
ROQUET
SAUQUI
SEQUEL
SEQUIN
SESQUI
SQUAIL
SQUALL
SQUARE
SQUEAL
SQUEEL
SQUILL
SQUINT
SQUIRE
SQUIRL
SQUIRR
SQUIRT
SQUISS
TARIQA
TOQUET
TORQUE
UNIQUE
UNQUIT

ALPHABETICAL LIST OF 7-LETTER WORDS

ACEQUIA
ACQUENT
ACQUEST
ACQUIRE
ACQUIST
ALFAQUI
ALIQUID
ALIQUOT
ALQUIER
ANQUERA
ANTIQUA
ANTIQUE
AQUABIB
AQUAFER
AQUARIA

AQUATIC
AQUAVIT
AQUEITY
AQUEOUS
AQUIFER
AQUIVER
ASQUARE
ASQUEAL
ASQUINT
ASQUIRM
BANQUET
BAROQUE
BASQUED
BATUQUE
BEQUEST
BEZIQUE
BOSQUET
BOUQUET
BRASQUE
BRIQUET
BRISQUE
BRUSQUE
CACIQUE
CASAQUE
CASQUED
CASQUET
CAWQUAW
CAZIQUE
CHALQUE
CHARQUI
CHEQUER
CLIQUED
COEQUAL
COMIQUE
CONQUER
COQUINA
COQUITA
COQUITO
COSAQUE
CROQUET
CROQUIS
CUMQUAT
DEQUEEN
ENQUIRE
ENQUIRY
EQUABLE
EQUABLY
EQUALED
EQUALLY
EQUATED
EQUATOR
EQUERRY
EQUILIN
EQUINAL
EQUINIA
EQUINOX
EQUINUS
EQUISON
EQUITES
EQUULEI
ESQUIRE
ESTOQUE
ETIQUET
EXQUIRE
FLASQUE
GRECQUE
INEQUAL
INQUEST
INQUIET
INQUIRE
INQUIRY
JAQUIMA
JERQUED
JERQUER
JOCOQUE
JOCOQUI
JONQUIL
KUMQUAT
LACQUER
LACQUEY
LAQUEAR
LAQUEUS
LIQUATE
LIQUEFY
LIQUEUR
LIQUIDS
LIQUIDY
LIQUIFY
LIQUORS
LIQUORY
LOQUENT
MACAQUE
MADOQUA
MANQUEE
MARQUEE
MARQUIS
MASQUER
MESQUIN
MEZQUIT
MUSQUAW
NAMAQUA
OBLIQUE
OBLOQUY
OBSEQUY
OPAQUED
OQUASSA
PARQUET
PASQUIL
PASQUIN
PATAQUE
PERIQUE
PICQUET
PIQUANT
PIQUERO
PIQUEUR
PIQUING
PURAQUE
QABBALA
QUABIRD
QUACHIL
QUACKED
QUACKLE
QUADDED
QUADDLE
QUADRAE
QUADRAL
QUADRAT
QUADREL
QUADRIC
QUADRIN
QUADRUM
QUAEDAM
QUAFFED
QUAFFER
QUAGGAS
QUAGGLE
QUAHAUG
QUAILED
QUAKIER
QUAKILY
QUAKING
QUALIFY
QUALITY
QUAMASH
QUANNET
QUANTIC
QUANTUM
QUARION
QUARLES
QUARRED
QUARREL
QUARTAN
QUARTER
QUARTET
QUARTIC
QUARTIN
QUARTOS
QUARTZY
QUASHED
QUASHEY
QUASSIA
QUASSIN
QUATERN
QUATERS
QUATRAL
QUATRIN
QUATTIE
QUATUOR
QUAVERY
QUAYAGE
QUAYING
QUEACHY
QUEASOM
QUEAZEN
QUEECHY
QUEENLY
QUEERER
QUEERLY
QUELITE
QUELLED
QUELLER
QUELLIO
QUEMADO
QUEMELY
QUERCIC
QUERCIN
QUERELA
QUERELE
QUERENT
QUERIDA
QUERIDO
QUERIED
QUERIER
QUERIES
QUERIST
QUERKEN
QUERNAL
QUESTED
QUESTER
QUESTOR
QUETSCH
QUETZAL
QUIBBLE
QUIBLET
QUICKED
QUICKEN
QUICKER
QUICKIE
QUICKLY
QUIDDER
QUIDDIT
QUIDDLE
QUIENAL
QUIESCE
QUIETED
QUIETEN
QUIETER
QUIETLY
QUIETUS
QUILATE
QUILKIN
QUILLAI
QUILLED
QUILLER
QUILLET
QUILLON
QUILTED
QUILTER
QUINARY
QUINATE
QUININA
QUININE
QUINITE
QUINNAT
QUINNET
QUINOID
QUINONE
QUINOYL
QUINTAD
QUINTAL
QUINTAN
QUINTET
QUINTIC
QUINTIN
QUINTON
QUINTUS
QUINYIE
QUIPPED
QUIPPER
QUIRCAL
QUIRING
QUIRKED
QUISCOS
QUITELY
QUITEVE
QUITTED
QUITTER
QUITTOR
QUIVERY
QUIZZED
QUIZZEE
QUIZZER
QUODDED
QUOINED
QUOITER
QUOMODO
QUONDAM
QUONIAM
QUORUMS
QUOTING
QUOTITY
RACQUET
RELIQUE
REQUEEN
REQUEST
REQUIEM
REQUINS
REQUIRE
REQUITE
RONQUIL
ROQUIST
RORQUAL
SEQUELA
SEQUENT
SEQUEST
SEQUOIA
SILIQUA
SILIQUE
SOSQUIL
SQUABBY
SQUACCO
SQUADDY
SQUADER
SQUAGGA
SQUAILS
SQUALID
SQUALLY
SQUALOR
SQUAMAE
SQUARED
SQUARER
SQUARES
SQUASHY
SQUATLY
SQUATTY
SQUAWKY
SQUEAKY
SQUEEGE
SQUEEZE
SQUEEZY
SQUELCH
SQUETEE
SQUIDGE
SQUIDGY
SQUIFFY
SQUILLA
SQUINCH
SQUINNY
SQUINTY
SQUIRED
SQUIRET
SQUIRTS
SQUIRTY
SQUISHY
SQUITCH
SQUUSHY
SURIQUE
TANQUAM
TANQUEN
TARIQAT
TEQUILA
TORQUED
TORQUES
TOTQUOT
TRIQUET
TURQUET
UBIQUIT
UNEQUAL
UNQUEEN
UNQUEME
UNQUERT
UNQUICK
UNQUIET
UNQUOTE
VAQUERO
VAQUITA

POSITIONAL ORDER LIST OF 7-LETTER WORDS

QABBALA
QUABIRD
QUACHIL
QUACKED
QUACKLE
QUADDED
QUADDLE
QUADRAE
QUADRAL
QUADRAT
QUADREL
QUADRIC
QUADRIN
QUADRUM
QUAEDAM

QUAFFED
QUAFFER
QUAGGAS
QUAGGLE
QUAHAUG
QUAILED
QUAKIER
QUAKILY
QUAKING
QUALIFY
QUALITY
QUAMASH
QUANNET
QUANTIC
QUANTUM
QUARION
QUARLES
QUARRED
QUARREL
QUARTAN
QUARTER
QUARTET
QUARTIC
QUARTIN
QUARTOS
QUARTZY
QUASHED
QUASHEY
QUASSIA
QUASSIN
QUATERN
QUATERS
QUATRAL
QUATRIN
QUATTIE
QUATUOR
QUAVERY
QUAYAGE
QUAYING
QUEACHY
QUEASOM
QUEAZEN
QUEECHY
QUEENLY
QUEERER
QUEERLY
QUELITE
QUELLED
QUELLER
QUELLIO
QUEMADO
QUEMELY
QUERCIC
QUERCIN
QUERELA
QUERELE
QUERENT
QUERIDA
QUERIDO
QUERIED
QUERIER
QUERIES
QUERIST
QUERKEN
QUERNAL
QUESTED
QUESTER
QUESTOR
QUETSCH
QUETZAL
QUIBBLE

QUIBLET
QUICKED
QUICKEN
QUICKER
QUICKIE
QUICKLY
QUIDDER
QUIDDIT
QUIDDLE
QUIENAL
QUIESCE
QUIETED
QUIETEN
QUIETER
QUIETLY
QUIETUS
QUILATE
QUILKIN
QUILLAI
QUILLED
QUILLER
QUILLET
QUILLON
QUILTED
QUILTER
QUINARY
QUINATE
QUININA
QUININE
QUINITE
QUINNAT
QUINNET
QUINOID
QUINONE
QUINOYL
QUINTAD
QUINTAL
QUINTAN
QUINTET
QUINTIC
QUINTIN
QUINTON
QUINTUS
QUINYIE
QUIPPED
QUIPPER
QUIRCAL
QUIRING
QUIRKED
QUISCOS
QUITELY
QUITEVE
QUITTED
QUITTER
QUITTOR
QUIVERY
QUIZZED
QUIZZEE
QUIZZER
QUODDED
QUOINED
QUOITER
QUOMODO
QUONDAM
QUONIAM
QUORUMS
QUOTING
QUOTITY

AQUABIB

AQUAFER
AQUARIA
AQUATIC
AQUAVIT
AQUEITY
AQUEOUS
AQUIFER
AQUIVER
EQUABLE
EQUABLY
EQUALED
EQUALLY
EQUATED
EQUATOR
EQUERRY
EQUILIN
EQUINAL
EQUINIA
EQUINOX
EQUINUS
EQUISON
EQUITES
EQUULEI
OQUASSA
SQUABBY
SQUACCO
SQUADDY
SQUADER
SQUAGGA
SQUAILS
SQUALID
SQUALLY
SQUALOR
SQUAMAE
SQUARED
SQUARER
SQUARES
SQUASHY
SQUATLY
SQUATTY
SQUAWKY
SQUEAKY
SQUEEGE
SQUEEZE
SQUEEZY
SQUELCH
SQUETEE
SQUIDGE
SQUIDGY
SQUIFFY
SQUILLA
SQUINCH
SQUINNY
SQUINTY
SQUIRED
SQUIRET
SQUIRTS
SQUIRTY
SQUISHY
SQUITCH
SQUUSHY

ACQUENT
ACQUEST
ACQUIRE
ACQUIST
ALQUIER
ANQUERA
ASQUARE
ASQUEAL

ASQUINT
ASQUIRM
BEQUEST
COQUINA
COQUITA
COQUITO
DEQUEEN
ENQUIRE
ENQUIRY
ESQUIRE
EXQUIRE
INQUEST
INQUIET
INQUIRE
INQUIRY
JAQUIMA
LAQUEAR
LAQUEUS
LIQUATE
LIQUEFY
LIQUEUR
LIQUIDS
LIQUIDY
LIQUIFY
LIQUORS
LIQUORY
LOQUENT
PIQUANT
PIQUERO
PIQUEUR
PIQUING
REQUEEN
REQUEST
REQUIEM
REQUINS
REQUIRE
REQUITE
ROQUIST
SEQUELA
SEQUENT
SEQUEST
SEQUOIA
TEQUILA
UNQUEEN
UNQUEME
UNQUERT
UNQUICK
UNQUIET
UNQUOTE
VAQUERO
VAQUITA

ACEQUIA
ALIQUID
ALIQUOT
BANQUET
BASQUED
BOSQUET
BOUQUET
BRIQUET
CASQUED
CASQUET
CAWQUAW
CHEQUER
CLIQUED
COEQUAL
CONQUER
CROQUET
CROQUIS
CUMQUAT

ETIQUET
INEQUAL
JERQUED
JERQUER
JONQUIL
KUMQUAT
LACQUER
LACQUEY
MANQUEE
MARQUEE
MARQUIS
MASQUER
MESQUIN
MEZQUIT
MUSQUAW
OPAQUED
PARQUET
PASQUIL
PASQUIN
PICQUET
RACQUET
RONQUIL
RORQUAL
SOSQUIL
TANQUAM
TANQUEN
TORQUED
TORQUES
TOTQUOT
TRIQUET
TURQUET
UBIQUIT
UNEQUAL

ALFAQUI
ANTIQUA
ANTIQUE
BAROQUE
BATUQUE
BEZIQUE
BRASQUE
BRISQUE
BRUSQUE
CACIQUE
CASAQUE
CAZIQUE
CHALQUE
CHARQUI
COMIQUE
COSAQUE
ESTOQUE
FLASQUE
GRECQUE
JOCOQUE
JOCOQUI
MACAQUE
MADOQUA
NAMAQUA
OBLIQUE
OBLOQUY
OBSEQUY
PATAQUE
PERIQUE
PURAQUE
RELIQUE
SILIQUA
SILIQUE
SURIQUE
TARIQAT

SCORING ORDER LIST OF 7-LETTER WORDS

28
QUARTZY
SQUEEZY

27
BEZIQUE
MEZQUIT

26
SQUAWKY

25
JAQUIMA
JOCOQUE
JOCOQUI
QUEAZEN
QUETZAL
QUICKLY
QUIZZED
SQUEEZE
SQUIFFY

24
CAWQUAW
JERQUED
QUEACHY
QUEECHY
QUIZZEE
QUIZZER

23
EQUINOX
EXQUIRE
JERQUER
JONQUIL
QUACKED
QUAFFED
QUAKILY
QUICKED
SQUABBY
SQUEAKY

22
KUMQUAT
LIQUEFY
LIQUIFY
QUACKLE
QUAFFER
QUALIFY
QUASHEY
QUAVERY
QUICKEN
QUICKER
QUICKIE
QUIVERY
SQUASHY
SQUISHY
SQUUSHY
UNQUICK

21
CHALQUE
CHARQUI
CHEQUER
EQUABLY
LACQUEY
MUSQUAW
OBLOQUY
OBSEQUY
QUACHIL
QUAKING
QUAMASH
QUEMELY
QUETSCH
QUIPPED
QUIRKED
SQUADDY
SQUELCH
SQUIDGY
SQUINCH
SQUITCH

20
AQUABIB
CACIQUE
COMIQUE
CUMQUAT
LIQUIDY
MACAQUE
PICQUET
QABBALA
QUAHAUG
QUAKIER
QUASHED
QUAYAGE
QUAYING
QUERCIC
QUERKEN
QUIBBLE
QUILKIN
QUIPPER
SQUACCO

19
ALFAQUI
AQUAFER
AQUAVIT
AQUEITY
AQUIFER
AQUIVER
BASQUED
CASQUED
CLIQUED
ENQUIRY
EQUALLY
EQUERRY
FLASQUE
GRECQUE
INQUIRY
LIQUORY
MADOQUA
OPAQUED
PIQUING
QUABIRD
QUADDED
QUADRIC
QUADRUM
QUAEDAM
QUALITY
QUEENLY
QUEERLY
QUEMADO
QUIETLY
QUINARY
QUINOYL
QUINYIE
QUITELY
QUITEVE
QUODDED
QUOMODO
QUONDAM
QUOTITY
SQUALLY
SQUATLY
SQUATTY
SQUINNY
SQUINTY
SQUIRTY
VAQUERO
VAQUITA

18
ACEQUIA
ACQUENT
ACQUEST
ACQUIRE
ACQUIST
AQUATIC
ASQUIRM
BANQUET
BAROQUE
BATUQUE
BEQUEST
BOSQUET
BOUQUET
BRASQUE
BRIQUET
BRISQUE
BRUSQUE
CASAQUE
CASQUET
COEQUAL
CONQUER
COQUINA
COQUITA
COQUITO
COSAQUE
CROQUET
CROQUIS
EQUABLE
LACQUER
MANQUEE
MARQUEE
MARQUIS
MASQUER
MESQUIN
NAMAQUA
OBLIQUE
PARQUET
PASQUIL
PASQUIN
PATAQUE
PERIQUE
PIQUANT
PIQUERO
PIQUEUR
PURAQUE
QUADDLE
QUAGGAS
QUAGGLE
QUANTIC
QUANTUM
QUARTIC
QUEASOM
QUERCIN
QUIBLET
QUIDDER
QUIDDIT
QUIDDLE
QUIESCE
QUINTIC
QUIRCAL
QUISCOS
QUONIAM
QUORUMS
RACQUET
REQUIEM
SQUAGGA
SQUAMAE
SQUIDGE
TANQUAM
UBIQUIT
UNQUEME

17
ALIQUID
DEQUEEN
EQUALED
EQUATED
LIQUIDS
QUADRAE
QUADRAL
QUADRAT
QUADREL
QUADRIN
QUAILED
QUARRED
QUELLED
QUERIDA
QUERIDO
QUERIED
QUESTED
QUIETED
QUILLED
QUILTED
QUINOID
QUINTAD
QUIRING
QUITTED
QUOINED
QUOTING
SQUADER
SQUALID
SQUARED
SQUEEGE
SQUIRED
TORQUED

16
ALIQUOT
ALQUIER
ANQUERA
ANTIQUA
ANTIQUE
AQUARIA
AQUEOUS
ASQUARE
ASQUEAL
ASQUINT
ENQUIRE
EQUATOR
EQUILIN
EQUINAL
EQUINIA
EQUINUS
EQUISON
EQUITES
EQUULEI
ESQUIRE
ESTOQUE
ETIQUET
INEQUAL
INQUEST
INQUIET
INQUIRE
LAQUEAR
LAQUEUS
LIQUATE
LIQUEUR
LIQUORS
LOQUENT
OQUASSA
QUANNET
QUARION
QUARLES
QUARREL
QUARTAN
QUARTER
QUARTET
QUARTIN
QUARTOS
QUASSIA
QUASSIN
QUATERN
QUATERS
QUATRAL
QUATRIN
QUATTIE
QUATUOR
QUEERER
QUELITE
QUELLER
QUELLIO
QUERELA
QUERELE
QUERENT
QUERIER
QUERIES
QUERIST
QUERNAL
QUESTER
QUESTOR
QUIENAL
QUIETEN
QUIETER
QUIETUS
QUILATE
QUILLAI
QUILLER
QUILLET
QUILLON
QUILTER
QUINATE
QUININA
QUININE
QUINITE
QUINNAT
QUINNET
QUINONE
QUINTAL
QUINTAN
QUINTET
QUINTIN
QUINTON
QUINTUS
QUITTER
QUITTOR
QUOITER
RELIQUE
REQUEEN
REQUEST
REQUINS
REQUIRE
REQUITE
RONQUIL
ROQUIST
RORQUAL
SEQUELA
SEQUENT
SEQUEST
SEQUOIA
SILIQUA
SILIQUE
SOSQUIL
SQUAILS
SQUALOR
SQUARER
SQUARES
SQUETEE
SQUILLA

SQUIRET
SQUIRTS
SURI**Q**UE
TAN**Q**UEN
TARI**Q**AT
TE**Q**UILA
TOR**Q**UES
TOT**Q**UOT
TRI**Q**UET
TUR**Q**UET
UNE**Q**UAL
UN**Q**UEEN
UN**Q**UERT
UN**Q**UIET
UN**Q**UOTE

ALPHABETICAL LIST OF 8-LETTER WORDS

AC**Q**UAINT
AC**Q**UIRED
AC**Q**UIRER
AC**Q**UITAL
ADE**Q**UACY
ADE**Q**UATE
ALAMI**Q**UI
ALFA**Q**UIN
ALI**Q**UANT
AL**Q**UEIRE
AL**Q**UIFOU
ANTI**Q**UED
ANTI**Q**UER
APPLI**Q**UE
A**Q**UACADE
A**Q**UALUNG
A**Q**UANAUT
A**Q**UARIAL
A**Q**UARIAN
A**Q**UARIST
A**Q**UARIUM
A**Q**UARTER
A**Q**UATICS
A**Q**UATILE
A**Q**UATINT
A**Q**UATION
A**Q**UATONE
A**Q**UEDUCT
A**Q**UIFORM
A**Q**UIFUGE
A**Q**UILEGE
A**Q**UILINE
A**Q**UILINO
A**Q**UOSITY
A**Q**UOTIZE
AR**Q**UEBUS
ASPI**Q**UEE
BARBE**Q**UE
BAR**Q**UEST
BAS**Q**UINE
BED**Q**UILT
BELDU**Q**UE
BE**Q**UEATH
BERLO**Q**UE
BI**Q**UARTZ
BORAS**Q**UE
BOUTI**Q**UE
BRAS**Q**UED
BRELO**Q**UE
BRO**Q**UERY
CALAN**Q**UE
CASA**Q**UIN
CHA**Q**UETA
CHE**Q**UEEN
CHE**Q**UERS
CHIC**Q**UED
CHIC**Q**UER
CHI**Q**UEST
CIN**Q**FOIL
CIN**Q**UAIN
CLA**Q**UEUR
CLINI**Q**UE
CLI**Q**UIER
CLI**Q**UING
CLI**Q**UISH
CLI**Q**UISM
COE**Q**UATE
COLLO**Q**UE
COLLO**Q**UY
CON**Q**UEST
CON**Q**UIAN
CO**Q**UETRY
CO**Q**UETTE
CO**Q**UILLE
CORSE**Q**UE
COT**Q**UEAN
CRITI**Q**UE
DAI**Q**UIRI
DETRA**Q**UE
DIS**Q**UIET
ELI**Q**UATE
ELO**Q**UENT
EMBUS**Q**UE
EN**Q**UIRER
E**Q**UACITY
E**Q**UAEVAL
E**Q**UALING
E**Q**UALISE
E**Q**UALIST
E**Q**UALITY
E**Q**UALIZE
E**Q**UALLED
E**Q**UATING
E**Q**UATION
E**Q**UATIVE
E**Q**UAIXED
E**Q**UIFORM
E**Q**UINATE
E**Q**UINITY
E**Q**UIPAGA
E**Q**UIPAGE
E**Q**UIPPED
E**Q**UIPPER
E**Q**UISETA
E**Q**UITANT
E**Q**UITIES
E**Q**UITIST
E**Q**UIVOKE
E**Q**UULEUS
ES**Q**UIRED
ES**Q**UISSE
EXE**Q**UIES
FABRI**Q**UE
FILIO**Q**UE
FRE**Q**UENT
HA**Q**UETON
HENE**Q**UEN
HUIS**Q**UIL
ICE**Q**UAKE
ILLI**Q**UID
INE**Q**UITY
INI**Q**UITY
IN**Q**UIRED
IN**Q**UIRER
IN**Q**UISIT
JAC**Q**UARD
JA**Q**UETTE
JER**Q**UING
LIME**Q**UAT
LIN**Q**UISH
LI**Q**UABLE
LI**Q**UAMEN
LI**Q**UATED
LI**Q**UESCE
LI**Q**UIDLY
LI**Q**UIDUS
LI**Q**UORED
LI**Q**UORER
LO**Q**UENCE
LO**Q**UENCY
LO**Q**UITUR
MA**Q**UETTE
MARO**Q**UIN
MAR**Q**UESS
MAR**Q**UISE
MAR**Q**UITO
MES**Q**UITA
MES**Q**UITE
MEZ**Q**UITE
MI**Q**UELET
MIS**Q**UOTE
MO**Q**UETTE
MOS**Q**UITO
MUS**Q**UASH
MYSTI**Q**UE
NASTALI**Q**
NON**Q**UOTA
OBLIC**Q**UE
OBLI**Q**UED
OBLI**Q**UUS
OPA**Q**UELY
OPA**Q**UING
OUT**Q**UEEN
OUT**Q**UOTE
PARA**Q**UET
PARO**Q**UET
PAURA**Q**UE
PERIO**Q**UE
PER**Q**UEER
PER**Q**UEIR
PER**Q**UEST
PHYSI**Q**UE
PI**Q**UABLE
PI**Q**UANCY
PI**Q**UETTE
PI**Q**UIERE
QABBALAH
QADARITE
QAIMA**Q**AM
QUACKERY
QUACKING
QUACKISH
QUACKISM
QUADRANS
QUADRANT
QUADRATE
QUADRIAD
QUADRIGA
QUADRINE
QUADROON
QUADRUAL
QUAESITA
QUAESTIO
QUAESTOR
QUAFFING
QUAGGIER
QUAGMIRE
QUAGMIRY
QUAILERY
QUAILING
QUAINTER
QUAINTLY
QUAKIEST
QUALMISH
QUALTAGH
QUANDANG
QUANDARY
QUANDONG
QUANTIFY
QUANTITY
QUANTIZE
QUANTONG
QUARANTY
QUARDEEL
QUARESMA
QUARRIED
QUARRIER
QUARRIES
QUARRION
QUARROME
QUARTANE
QUARTANO
QUARTAUT
QUARTERN
QUARTERS
QUARTILE
QUARTINE
QUARTOLE
QUARTZIC
QUASHING
QUASKIES
QUASSIIN
QUATENUS
QUATERON
QUATORZE
QUATRAIN
QUAVERED
QUAVERER
QUAVIVER
QUAYSIDE
QUEANISH
QUEASIER
QUEASILY
QUEBRADA
QUEBRITH
QUEDNESS
QUEDSHIP
QUEENCUP
QUEENING
QUEENITE
QUEENLET
QUEEREST
QUEERITY
QUELLING
QUELLUNG
QUEMEFUL
QUENCHED
QUENCHER
QUENELLE
QUENTISE
QUERCINE
QUERCITE
QUERELAE
QUERIDAS
QUERIDOS
QUERIMAN
QUERYING
QUESITED
QUESTEUR
QUESTING
QUESTION
QUESTMAN
QUESTMEN
QUEZALES
QUIA**Q**UIA
QUIBBLED
QUIBBLER
QUICKEST
QUICKING
QUICKSET
QUIDDANY
QUIDDITY
QUIDDLED
QUIDDLER
QUIDNUNC
QUIESCED
QUIETAGE
QUIETEST
QUIETING
QUIETISM
QUIETIST
QUIETIVE
QUIETUDE
QUILECES
QUILESES
QUILISMA
QUILLAIC
QUILLING
QUILLITY
QUILTING
QUINAMIN
QUINCUNX
QUINDENE
QUINELLA
QUINETUM
QUINIBLE
QUINICIN
QUINIDIN
QUINIELA
QUINITOL
QUINOGEN
QUINOLAS
QUINOLIN
QUINOLYL
QUINONIC

QUINONYL
QUINOVIN
QUINSIED
QUINTAIN
QUINTANT
QUINTARY
QUINTILE
QUINTOLE
QUIPPING
QUIPPISH
QUIPSOME
QUIPSTER
QUIRKIER
QUIRKING
QUIRKSEY
QUISLING
QUISTRON
QUITRENT
QUITTING
QUIVERED
QUIVERER
QUIXOTIC
QUIXOTRY
QUIZZERY
QUIZZIFY
QUIZZING
QUIZZISH
QUIZZISM
QUIZZITY
QUODDIES
QUODDING
QUODDITY
QUODLING
QUOILERS
QUOINING
QUOMINUS
QUONKING
QUOTABLE
QUOTABLY
QUOTIENT
QUOTIETY
RAMEQUIN
REMARQUE
REPIQUED
REPLIQUE
REQUIRED
REQUIRER
REQUITAL
REQUITED
REQUITER
ROQUETED
ROQUETTE
ROQUILLE
SAMBAQUI
SASANQUA
SEAQUAKE
SEQUACES
SEQUELAE
SEQUENCE
SEQUITUR
SHABEQUE
SOLIQUID
SQUABBED
SQUABBER
SQUABBLE
SQUABBLY
SQUACCOS
SQUADDED
SQUADROL
SQUADRON
SQUAILER
SQUALENE
SQUALLED
SQUALLER
SQUALOID
SQUAMATE
SQUAMIFY
SQUAMISH
SQUAMOID
SQUAMOSA
SQUAMOSE
SQUAMOUS
SQUAMULA
SQUAMULE
SQUANDER
SQUANTUM
SQUARELY
SQUARIER
SQUARING
SQUARISH
SQUARSON
SQUASHED
SQUASHER
SQUATTED
SQUATTER
SQUATTLE
SQUAWKED
SQUAWKER
SQUAWKIE
SQUEAKED
SQUEAKER
SQUEALED
SQUEALER
SQUEEGEE
SQUEEZED
SQUEEZER
SQUELCHY
SQUIBBED
SQUIBBER
SQUIDDED
SQUIDDER
SQUIDDLE
SQUIFFED
SQUIFFER
SQUIGGLE
SQUIGGLY
SQUILGEE
SQUILLID
SQUINACY
SQUINANT
SQUINTED
SQUINTER
SQUIRAGE
SQUIREEN
SQUIRELY
SQUIRESS
SQUIRING
SQUIRISH
SQUIRMED
SQUIRMER
SQUIRREL
SQUIRTED
SQUIRTER
SQUISHED
SQUITTER
SUNQUAKE
SURQUIDY
TEQUILLA
TORQUATE
TRANQUIL
TURQUOIS
UBIQUITY
UMQUHILE
UNIQUELY
UNIQUITY
UNSQUARE
UNSQUIRE
USQUABAE
USQUEBAE
VANQUISH
VAQUEROS
VASQUINE
VERQUERE

POSITIONAL ORDER LIST OF 8-LETTER WORDS

QABBALAH
QADARITE
QAIMAQAM
QUACKERY
QUACKING
QUACKISH
QUACKISM
QUADRANS
QUADRANT
QUADRATE
QUADRIAD
QUADRIGA
QUADRINE
QUADROON
QUADRUAL
QUAESITA
QUAESTIO
QUAESTOR
QUAFFING
QUAGGIER
QUAGMIRE
QUAGMIRY
QUAILERY
QUAILING
QUAINTER
QUAINTLY
QUAKIEST
QUALMISH
QUALTAGH
QUANDANG
QUANDARY
QUANDONG
QUANTIFY
QUANTITY
QUANTIZE
QUANTONG
QUARANTY
QUARDEEL
QUARESMA
QUARRIED
QUARRIER
QUARRIES
QUARRION
QUARROME
QUARTANE
QUARTANO
QUARTAUT
QUARTERN
QUARTERS
QUARTILE
QUARTINE
QUARTOLE
QUARTZIC
QUASHING
QUASKIES
QUASSIIN
QUATENUS
QUATERON
QUATORZE
QUATRAIN
QUAVERED
QUAVERER
QUAVIVER
QUAYSIDE
QUEANISH
QUEASIER
QUEASILY
QUEBRADA
QUEBRITH
QUEDNESS
QUEDSHIP
QUEENCUP
QUEENING
QUEENITE
QUEENLET
QUEEREST
QUEERITY
QUELLING
QUELLUNG
QUEMEFUL
QUENCHED
QUENCHER
QUENELLE
QUENTISE
QUERCINE
QUERCITE
QUERELAE
QUERIDAS
QUERIDOS
QUERIMAN
QUERYING
QUESITED
QUESTEUR
QUESTING
QUESTION
QUESTMAN
QUESTMEN
QUEZALES
QUIAQUIA
QUIBBLED
QUIBBLER
QUICKEST
QUICKING
QUICKSET
QUIDDANY
QUIDDITY
QUIDDLED
QUIDDLER
QUIDNUNC
QUIESCED
QUIETAGE
QUIETEST
QUIETING
QUIETISM
QUIETIST
QUIETIVE
QUIETUDE
QUILECES
QUILESES
QUILISMA
QUILLAIC
QUILLING
QUILLITY
QUILTING
QUINAMIN
QUINCUNX
QUINDENE
QUINELLA
QUINETUM
QUINIBLE
QUINICIN
QUINIDIN
QUINIELA
QUINITOL
QUINOGEN
QUINOLAS
QUINOLIN
QUINOLYL
QUINONIC
QUINONYL
QUINOVIN
QUINSIED
QUINTAIN
QUINTANT
QUINTARY
QUINTILE
QUINTOLE
QUIPPING
QUIPPISH
QUIPSOME
QUIPSTER
QUIRKIER
QUIRKING
QUIRKSEY
QUISLING
QUISTRON
QUITRENT
QUITTING
QUIVERED
QUIVERER
QUIXOTIC
QUIXOTRY
QUODDIES
QUIZZERY
QUIZZIFY
QUIZZING
QUIZZISH
QUIZZISM
QUIZZITY
QUODDING
QUODDITY
QUODLING
QUOILERS
QUOINING
QUOMINUS
QUONKING
QUOTABLE
QUOTABLY
QUOTIENT
QUOTIETY

AQUACADE
AQUALUNG
AQUANAUT
AQUARIAL
AQUARIAN
AQUARIST
AQUARIUM
AQUARTER
AQUATICS
AQUATILE
AQUATINT
AQUATION
AQUATONE
AQUEDUCT
AQUIFORM
AQUIFUGE
AQUILEGE
AQUILINE
AQUILINO

AQUOSITY
AQUOTIZE
EQUACITY
EQUAEVAL
EQUALING
EQUALISE
EQUALIST
EQUALITY
EQUALIZE
EQUALLED
EQUATING
EQUATION
EQUATIVE
EQUAIXED
EQUIFORM
EQUINATE
EQUINITY
EQUIPAGA
EQUIPAGE
EQUIPPED
EQUIPPER
EQUISETA
EQUITANT
EQUITIES
EQUITIST
EQUIVOKE
EQUULEUS
SQUABBED
SQUABBER
SQUABBLE
SQUABBLY
SQUACCOS
SQUADDED
SQUADROL
SQUADRON
SQUAILER
SQUALENE
SQUALLED
SQUALLER
SQUALOID
SQUAMATE
SQUAMIFY
SQUAMISH
SQUAMOID
SQUAMOSA
SQUAMOSE
SQUAMOUS
SQUAMULA
SQUAMULE
SQUANDER
SQUANTUM
SQUARELY
SQUARIER
SQUARING
SQUARISH
SQUARSON

SQUASHED
SQUASHER
SQUATTED
SQUATTER
SQUATTLE
SQUAWKED
SQUAWKER
SQUAWKIE
SQUEAKED
SQUEAKER
SQUEALED
SQUEALER
SQUEEGEE
SQUEEZED
SQUEEZER
SQUELCHY
SQUIBBED
SQUIBBER
SQUIDDED
SQUIDDER
SQUIDDLE
SQUIFFED
SQUIFFER
SQUIGGLE
SQUIGGLY
SQUILGEE
SQUILLID
SQUINACY
SQUINANT
SQUINTED
SQUINTER
SQUIRAGE
SQUIREEN
SQUIRELY
SQUIRESS
SQUIRING
SQUIRISH
SQUIRMED
SQUIRMER
SQUIRREL
SQUIRTED
SQUIRTER
SQUISHED
SQUITTER

ACQUAINT
ACQUIRED
ACQUIRER
ACQUITAL
ALQUEIRE
ALQUIFOU
ARQUEBUS
BEQUEATH
BIQUARTZ
COQUETRY

COQUETTE
COQUILLE
ENQUIRER
ESQUIRED
ESQUISSE
HAQUETON
INQUIRED
INQUIRER
INQUISIT
JAQUETTE
LIQUABLE
LIQUAMEN
LIQUATED
LIQUESCE
LIQUIDLY
LIQUIDUS
LIQUORED
LIQUORER
LOQUENCE
LOQUENCY
LOQUITUR
MAQUETTE
MIQUELET
MOQUETTE
PIQUABLE
PIQUANCY
PIQUETTE
PIQUIERE
REQUIRED
REQUIRER
REQUITAL
REQUITED
REQUITER
ROQUETED
ROQUETTE
ROQUILLE
SEQUACES
SEQUELAE
SEQUENCE
SEQUITUR
TEQUILLA
UMQUHILE
USQUABAE
USQUEBAE
VAQUEROS

ADEQUACY
ADEQUATE
ALIQUANT
BARQUEST
BASQUINE
BEDQUILT
BROQUERY
CHAQUETA
CHEQUEEN

CHEQUERS
CHIQUEST
CINQFOIL
CINQUAIN
CLAQUEUR
CLIQUIER
CLIQUING
CLIQUISH
CLIQUISM
COEQUATE
CONQUEST
CONQUIAN
COTQUEAN
DAIQUIRI
DISQUIET
ELIQUATE
ELOQUENT
EXEQUIES
FREQUENT
ICEQUAKE
INEQUITY
INIQUITY
JACQUARD
JERQUING
LINQUISH
MARQUESS
MARQUISE
MARQUITO
MESQUITA
MESQUITE
MEZQUITE
MISQUOTE
MOSQUITO
MUSQUASH
NONQUOTA
OPAQUELY
OPAQUING
OUTQUEEN
OUTQUOTE
PERQUEER
PERQUEIR
PERQUEST
SEAQUAKE
SUNQUAKE
SURQUIDY
TORQUATE
TURQUOIS
UBIQUITY
UNIQUELY
UNIQUITY
UNSQUARE
UNSQUIRE
VANQUISH
VASQUINE
VERQUERE

ALFAQUIN
ANTIQUED
ANTIQUER
ASPIQUEE
BRASQUED
CASAQUIN
CHICQUED
CHICQUER
HENEQUEN
HUISQUIL
ILLIQUID
LIMEQUAT
MAROQUIN
OBLIQUED
OBLIQUUS
PARAQUET
PAROQUET
QUIAQUIA
RAMEQUIN
REPIQUED
SOLIQUID
TRANQUIL

ALAMIQUI
APPLIQUE
BARBEQUE
BELDUQUE
BERLOQUE
BORASQUE
BOUTIQUE
BRELOQUE
CALANQUE
CLINIQUE
COLLOQUE
COLLOQUY
CORSEQUE
CRITIQUE
DETRAQUE
EMBUSQUE
FABRIQUE
FILIOQUE
MYSTIQUE
OBLICQUE
PAURAQUE
PERIOQUE
PHYSIQUE
QAIMAQAM
REMARQUE
REPLIQUE
SAMBAQUI
SASANQUA
SHABEQUE

NASTALIQ

SCORING ORDER LIST OF 8-LETTER WORDS

31
QUIZZIFY

28
BIQUARTZ
MEZQUITE
QUARTZIC
QUIZZERY
QUIZZISH
QUIZZITY

27
JACQUARD
QUIXOTRY
QUIZZISM
SQUEEZED

26
AQUOTIZE
EQUALIZE
QUACKERY
QUACKISH
QUANTIZE
QUATORZE
QUEZALES
QUINCUNX
QUIXOTIC
QUIZZING
SQUEEZER

25
CHICQUED
EQUAIXED
JERQUING
PHYSIQUE
QUACKISM
SQUAMIFY
SQUAWKED
SQUELCHY

24
CHICQUER
EQUIVOKE
EXEQUIES
JAQUETTE
PIQUANCY
QABBALAH
QUACKING
QUAFFING
QUICKING
QUIPPISH
QUIRKSEY
SQUABBLY
SQUAWKER
SQUAWKIE
SQUIFFED

23
ADEQUACY
ICEQUAKE
QUAGMIRY
QUANTIFY
QUAVIVER
QUEDSHIP
QUENCHED
QUICKEST
QUICKSET
SQUIFFER
VANQUISH

22
AQUIFORM
BEQUEATH
BROQUERY
CHAQUETA

CHEQUEEN
CHEQUERS
CHIQUEST
CINQFOIL
CLIQUISH
COLLOQUY
COQUETRY
EQUACITY
EQUIFORM
EQUIPPED
FABRIQUE
LOQUENCY
MUSQUASH
MYSTIQUE
OPAQUELY
QUALMISH
QUEBRITH
QUEMEFUL
QUENCHER
QUIBBLED
QUIDDANY
QUIDDITY
QUIPPING
QUIRKING
QUODDITY
QUONKING
QUOTABLY
SHABEQUE
SQUABBED
SQUAMISH
SQUEAKED
SQUIBBED
SQUIGGLY
SQUINACY
UBIQUITY
UMQUHILE

21

APPLIQUE
AQUIFUGE
BARBEQUE
CLIQUISM
EMBUSQUE
EQUIPPER
LIQUIDLY
OBLICQUE
PIQUABLE
QUAKIEST
QUALTAGH
QUANDARY
QUASHING
QUASKIES
QUAVERED
QUAYSIDE
QUEENCUP
QUERYING
QUIBBLER
QUIPSOME
QUIRKIER
QUIVERED
SAMBAQUI
SEAQUAKE
SQUABBER
SQUABBLE
SQUACCOS
SQUASHED
SQUEAKER
SQUIBBER
SQUISHED
SUNQUAKE
SURQUIDY

20

ACQUIRED
ALFAQUIN
ALQUIFOU
AQUACADE
AQUEDUCT
AQUOSITY
BEDQUILT
BELDUQUE
BRASQUED
CLIQUING
EQUAEVAL
EQUALITY
EQUATIVE
EQUINITY
EQUIPAGA
EQUIPAGE
FILIOQUE
FREQUENT
HAQUETON
HENEQUEN
HUISQUIL
INEQUITY
INIQUITY
LINQUISH
OBLIQUED
OPAQUING
QAIMAQAM
QUAGMIRE
QUAILERY
QUAINTLY
QUANTITY
QUARANTY
QUAVERER
QUEANISH
QUEASILY
QUEBRADA
QUEERITY
QUIDDLED
QUIDNUNC
QUIESCED
QUIETIVE
QUILLITY
QUINOLYL
QUINONYL
QUINOVIN
QUINTARY
QUIVERER
QUODDING
QUOTIETY
REPIQUED
SQUADDED
SQUAMOID
SQUARELY
SQUARISH
SQUASHER
SQUIDDED
SQUIRELY
SQUIRISH
SQUIRMED
UNIQUELY
UNIQUITY
VAQUEROS
VASQUINE
VERQUERE

19

ACQUAINT
ACQUIRER
ACQUITAL
ALAMIQUI
AQUARIUM
AQUATICS
ARQUEBUS
ASPIQUEE
BARQUEST
BASQUINE
BERLOQUE
BORASQUE
BOUTIQUE
BRELOQUE
CALANQUE
CASAQUIN
CINQUAIN
CLAQUEUR
CLINIQUE
CLIQUIER
COEQUATE
COLLOQUE
CONQUEST
CONQUIAN
COQUETTE
COQUILLE
CORSEQUE
COTQUEAN
CRITIQUE
LIMEQUAT
LIQUABLE
LIQUAMEN
LIQUESCE
LOQUENCE
MAQUETTE
MAROQUIN
MARQUESS
MARQUISE
MARQUITO
MESQUITA
MESQUITE
MIQUELET
MISQUOTE
MOQUETTE
MOSQUITO
OBLIQUUS
PARAQUET
PAROQUET
PAURAQUE
PERIOQUE
PERQUEER
PERQUEIR
PERQUEST
PIQUETTE
PIQUIERE
QUADRIAD
QUADRIGA
QUAGGIER
QUANDANG
QUANDONG
QUARESMA
QUARROME
QUERCINE
QUERCITE
QUERIMAN
QUESTMAN
QUESTMEN
QUIDDLER
QUIETISM
QUILECES
QUILISMA
QUILLAIC
QUINAMIN
QUINETUM
QUINIBLE
QUINICIN
QUINONIC
QUIPSTER
QUODDIES
QUODLING
QUOMINUS
QUOTABLE
RAMEQUIN
REMARQUE
REPLIQUE
SEQUACES
SEQUENCE
SQUAMATE
SQUAMOSA
SQUAMOSE
SQUAMOUS
SQUAMULA
SQUAMULE
SQUANTUM
SQUIDDER
SQUIDDLE
SQUIGGLE
SQUIRMER
USQUABAE

18

ADEQUATE
ANTIQUED
AQUALUNG
AQUILEGE
DAIQUIRI
DETRAQUE
DISQUIET
EQUALING
EQUALLED
EQUATING
ESQUIRED
ILLIQUID
INQUIRED
LIQUATED
LIQUIDUS
LIQUORED
QUADRANS
QUADRANT
QUADRATE
QUADRINE
QUADROON
QUADRUAL
QUAILING
QUANTONG
QUARDEEL
QUARRIED
QUEDNESS
QUEENING
QUELLING
QUELLUNG
QUERIDAS
QUERIDOS
QUESITED
QUESTING
QUIETAGE
QUIETING
QUIETUDE
QUILLING
QUILTING
QUINDENE
QUINIDIN
QUINOGEN
QUINSIED
QUISLING
QUITTING
QUOINING
REQUIRED
REQUITED
ROQUETED
SOLIQUID
SQUADROL
SQUADRON
SQUALLED
SQUALOID
SQUANDER
SQUARING
SQUATTED
SQUEALED
SQUEEGEE
SQUILGEE
SQUILLID
SQUINTED
SQUIRAGE
SQUIRING
SQUIRTED

17

ALIQUANT
ALQUEIRE
ANTIQUER
AQUANAUT
AQUARIAL
AQUARIAN
AQUARIST
AQUARTER
AQUATILE
AQUATINT
AQUATION
AQUATONE
AQUILINE
AQUILINO
ELIQUATE
ELOQUENT
ENQUIRER
EQUALISE
EQUALIST
EQUATION
EQUINATE
EQUISETA
EQUITANT
EQUITIES
EQUITIST
EQUULEUS
ESQUISSE
INQUIRER
INQUISIT
LIQUORER
LOQUITUR
NASTALIQ
NONQUOTA
OUTQUEEN
OUTQUOTE
QUAESITA
QUAESTIO
QUAESTOR
QUAINTER
QUARRIER
QUARRIES
QUARRION
QUARTANE
QUARTANO
QUARTAUT
QUARTERN
QUARTERS
QUARTILE
QUARTINE
QUARTOLE
QUASSIIN
QUATENUS
QUATERON
QUATRAIN
QUEASIER
QUEENITE
QUEENLET
QUEEREST
QUENELLE
QUENTISE
QUERELAE
QUESTEUR
QUESTION
QUIETEST
QUIETIST
QUILESES
QUINELLA
QUINIELA
QUINITOL
QUINOLAS
QUINOLIN
QUINTAIN
QUINTANT
QUINTILE
QUINTOLE
QUISTRON
QUITRENT
QUOILERS

QUOTIENT
REQUIRER
REQUITAL
REQUITER
ROQUETTE
ROQUILLE
SASANQUA
SEQUELAE
SEQUITUR
SQUAILER
SQUALENE
SQUALLER
SQUARIER
SQUARSON
SQUATTER
SQUATTLE
SQUEALER
SQUINANT
SQUINTER
SQUIREEN
SQUIRESS
SQUIRREL
SQUIRTER
SQUITTER
TEQUILLA
TORQUATE
TRANQUIL
TURQUOIS
UNSQUARE
UNSQUIRE

16
QUIAQUIA

ALPHABETICAL LIST OF 9-LETTER WORDS

ACQUEREUR
ACQUIESCE
ACQUIRING
ACQUISITA
ACQUISITE
ACQUITTAL
ACQUITTED
ACQUITTER
AEQUOREAL
ALAMBIQUE
ANGELIQUE
ANTILOQUY
ANTIQUARY
ANTIQUATE
ANTIQUELY
ANTIQUING
ANTIQUIST
ANTIQUITY
APPLIQUED
AQUAGREEN
AQUAMETER
AQUAPLANE
AQUARELLE
AQUARIIST
AQUARIUMS
AQUATICAL
AQUEOUSLY
AQUILEGIA
ARABESQUE
ARQUERITE
BALDAQUIN
BANQUETED
BANQUETER
BANQUETTE
BEQUIRTLE
BILBOQUET
BISQUETTE
BOURASQUE
BRASQUING
BRIQUETTE
BRODEQUIN
BRUSQUELY
BURLESQUE
CACIQUISM
CAIQUEJEE
CANNEQUIN
CARQUAISE
CASQUETEL
CASQUETTE
CHIBOUQUE
CHICQUING
CLINQUANT
CLIQUIEST
COEQUALLY
COEQUATED
COLOQUIES
CONQUEDLE
CONQUERED
CONQUEROR
COQUETOON
COQUETTED
CROQUETED
CROQUETTE
CUCKQUEAN
DELIQUIUM
DEMIPIQUE
DISQUISIT
DURAQUARA
ELIQUATED
ELOQUENCE
ENCHEQUER
EQUALIZED
EQUALIZER
EQUALLING
EQUALNESS
EQUERRIES
EQUIMODAL
EQUIMOLAR
EQUIPEDAL
EQUIPLUVE
EQUIPMENT
EQUIPOISE
EQUIPPING
EQUISETIC
EQUISETUM
EQUITABLE
EQUITABLY
EQUIVALVE
EQUIVOCAL
EQUIVOQUE
ESQUAMATE
ESQUIRING
ETIQUETTE
EXCHEQUER
EXEQUATUR
EXQUISITE
FANTASQUE
FOURQUINE
FREQUENCE
FREQUENCY
GRASSQUIT
GRIQUAITE
GROTESQUE
HALOESQUE
HARLEQUIN
HARQUEBUS
INEQUALLY
INQUIETLY
INQUILINE
INQUINATE
INQUIRENT
INQUIRIES
INQUIRING
INQUISITE
INSEQUENT
JACQUERIE
JEQUERITY
JEQUIRITY
JONQUILLE
LACQUERED
LACQUERER
LAQUEARIA
LIQUATING
LIQUATION
LIQUEFIED
LIQUEFIER
LIQUEURED
LIQUIDATE
LIQUIDITY
LIQUIDIZE
LIQUIFORM
LIQUORICE
LIQUORING
LIQUORISH
LIQUORIST
LONQUHARD
LOQUACITY
LOQUENTLY
MANNEQUIN
MARQUETRY
MARQUISAL
MISQUOTED
MISQUOTER
MONOCOQUE
MOSQUITAL
MOSQUITOS
OBLIQUATE
OBLIQUELY
OBLIQUING
OBLIQUITY
OBLOQUIAL
OBLOQUIES
OBSEQUENT
OBSEQUIAL
OBSEQUIES
OBSEQUITY
ODALISQUE
OVERQUELL
PALANQUIN
PARQUETED
PARQUETRY
PARROQUET
PASQUILER
PASQUILIC
PHYSIQUED
PICQUETER
PIQUANTLY
PLAQUETTE
PLASTIQUE
PROPINQUE
QUACKHOOD
QUACKSTER
QUADRABLE
QUADRATED
QUADRATIC
QUADRATUM
QUADRATUS
QUADRIFID
QUADRIGAE
QUADRILLE
QUADRIMUM
QUADRIVIA
QUADRUPED
QUADRUPLE
QUAESITUM
QUAGGIEST
QUAGMIRED
QUAILHEAD
QUAINTEST
QUAINTISE
QUAKETAIL
QUAKINESS
QUAKINGLY
QUALIFIED
QUALIFIER
QUALITIED
QUALITIES
QUANTICAL
QUANTIZED
QUANTULUM
QUARENDEN
QUARENDER
QUARRELED
QUARRYING
QUARRYMAN
QUARRYMEN
QUARTERED
QUARTERER
QUARTERLY
QUARTERON
QUARTETTE
QUARTINHO
QUARTZITE
QUARTZOID
QUARTZOSE
QUARTZOUS
QUATRAYLE
QUATREBLE
QUATRIBLE
QUATTRINI
QUATTRINO
QUAVERING
QUAVEROUS
QUAYSIDER
QUEACHIER
QUEASIEST
QUEBRACHO
QUEENCAKE
QUEENFISH
QUEENLIER
QUEENLIKE
QUEENROOT
QUEENWEED
QUEENWOOD
QUEERNESS
QUEERSOME
QUEINTISE
QUENCHING
QUERCETIC
QUERCETIN
QUERCETUM
QUERCITOL
QUERENCIA
QUERIMANS
QUERIMONY
QUERULENT
QUERULIST
QUERULITY
QUERULOUS
QUESITIVE
QUESTIONS
QUESTRIST
QUETENITE
QUIBBLING
QUICKBEAM
QUICKBORN
QUICKENED
QUICKENER
QUICKFOOT
QUICKLIME
QUICKNESS
QUICKSAND
QUICKSIDE
QUICKSTEP
QUICKWORK
QUIDDLING
QUIESCENT
QUIESCING
QUIETENER
QUIETLIKE
QUIETNESS
QUIETSOME
QUILLAJIC
QUILLBACK
QUILLETED
QUILLFISH
QUILLTAIL
QUILLWORK
QUILLWORT
QUINALDIC
QUINALDIN
QUINALDYL
QUINAMINE
QUINARIAN
QUINARIES
QUINARIUS
QUINDECAD
QUINDECIM
QUINICINE
QUINIDINE
QUININISM
QUININIZE
QUINISEXT
QUINOFORM
QUINOIDAL

QUINOIDIN
QUINOLINE
QUINOLOGY
QUINONIZE
QUINONOID
QUINOVATE
QUINOVOSE
QUINQUINA
QUINQUINO
QUINTETTE
QUINTETTO
QUINTFOIL
QUINTIPED
QUINTROON
QUINTUPLE
QUINZAINE
QUINZIEME
QUIREWISE
QUIRKIEST
QUIRKSOME
QUISQUOUS
QUISUTSCH
QUITANTIE
QUITCLAIM
QUITTANCE
QUIVERFUL
QUIVERING
QUIXOTISM
QUIXOTIZE
QUIZZICAL
QUODLIBET
QUOTATION
QUOTATIVE
QUOTELESS
QUOTIDIAN
QUOTINGLY
REACQUIRE
RELIQUARY
RELIQUIAE
RELIQUIAN
RELIQUISM
REPIQUING
REQUESTER
REQUIRING
REQUISITE
REQUITING
ROQUETING
SAMBAQUIS
SEMIQUOTE
SEQUACITY
SEQUELANT
SEQUENCER
SEQUESTER
SEQUESTRA
SILIQUOSE
SIMIESQUE
SOBRIQUET
SOLILOQUY
SQUABBASH
SQUABBIER
SQUABBING
SQUABBISH
SQUABBLED
SQUABBLER
SQUADDING
SQUADRATE
SQUADRISM
SQUADRONE
SQUALIDLY
SQUALLERY
SQUALLIER
SQUALLING
SQUAMATED
SQUAMELLA
SQUAMEOUS
SQUAMOSAL
SQUAMULAE
SQUAREAGE
SQUARECAP
SQUAREMAN
SQUAREMEN
SQUARROSE
SQUARROUS
SQUASHIER
SQUASHILY
SQUASHING
SQUATINID
SQUATMORE
SQUATNESS
SQUATTAGE
SQUATTIER
SQUATTILY
SQUATTING
SQUATTISH
SQUAWBUSH
SQUAWFISH
SQUAWKIER
SQUAWKING
SQUAWROOT
SQUAWWEED
SQUEAKERY
SQUEAKILY
SQUEAKING
SQUEALING
SQUEAMISH
SQUEEGEED
SQUEEZING
SQUELCHED
SQUELCHER
SQUELETTE
SQUIBBERY
SQUIBBING
SQUIBBISH
SQUIBSTER
SQUIDDING
SQUIDGIER
SQUIFFIER
SQUILGEED
SQUILGEER
SQUILLGEE
SQUILLIAN
SQUINANCE
SQUINTING
SQUIRALTY
SQUIRARCH
SQUIRMIER
SQUIRMING
SQUIRRELY
SQUIRTING
SQUIRTISH
SQUISHING
SUBAQUEAN
SUBSESQUI
SURQUEDRY
SURQUIDRY
TECHNIQUE
TORQUATED
TOTAQUINE
TRIPTYQUE
TRIQUETRA
TURQUOISE
UBIQUIOUS
UNEQUABLE
UNEQUABLY
UNEQUALED
UNEQUALLY
UNQUAILED
UNQUALIFY
UNQUALITY
UNQUEMELY
UNQUIETLY
UNREQUEST
UNSQUARED
UTRAQUIST
WELLQUEME

POSITIONAL ORDER LIST OF 9-LETTER WORDS

QUACKHOOD
QUACKSTER
QUADRABLE
QUADRATED
QUADRATIC
QUADRATUM
QUADRATUS
QUADRIFID
QUADRIGAE
QUADRILLE
QUADRIMUM
QUADRIVIA
QUADRUPED
QUADRUPLE
QUAESITUM
QUAGGIEST
QUAGMIRED
QUAILHEAD
QUAINTEST
QUAINTISE
QUAKETAIL
QUAKINESS
QUAKINGLY
QUALIFIED
QUALIFIER
QUALITIED
QUALITIES
QUANTICAL
QUANTIZED
QUANTULUM
QUARENDEN
QUARENDER
QUARRELED
QUARRYING
QUARRYMAN
QUARRYMEN
QUARTERED
QUARTERER
QUARTERLY
QUARTERON
QUARTETTE
QUARTINHO
QUARTZITE
QUARTZOID
QUARTZOSE
QUARTZOUS
QUATRAYLE
QUATREBLE
QUATRIBLE
QUATTRINI
QUATTRINO
QUAVERING
QUAVEROUS
QUAYSIDER
QUEACHIER
QUEASIEST
QUEBRACHO
QUEENCAKE
QUEENFISH
QUEENLIER
QUEENLIKE
QUEENROOT
QUEENWEED
QUEENWOOD
QUEERNESS
QUEERSOME
QUEINTISE
QUENCHING
QUERCETIC
QUERCETIN
QUERCETUM
QUERCITOL
QUERENCIA
QUERIMANS
QUERIMONY
QUERULENT
QUERULIST
QUERULITY
QUERULOUS
QUESITIVE
QUESTIONS
QUESTRIST
QUETENITE
QUIBBLING
QUICKBEAM
QUICKBORN
QUICKENED
QUICKENER
QUICKFOOT
QUICKLIME
QUICKNESS
QUICKSAND
QUICKSIDE
QUICKSTEP
QUICKWORK
QUIDDLING
QUIESCENT
QUIESCING
QUIETENER
QUIETLIKE
QUIETNESS
QUIETSOME
QUILLAJIC
QUILLBACK
QUILLETED
QUILLFISH
QUILLTAIL
QUILLWORK
QUILLWORT
QUINALDIC
QUINALDIN
QUINALDYL
QUINAMINE
QUINARIAN
QUINARIES
QUINARIUS
QUINDECAD
QUINDECIM
QUINICINE
QUINIDINE
QUININISM
QUININIZE
QUINISEXT
QUINOFORM
QUINOIDAL
QUINOIDIN
QUINOLINE
QUINOLOGY
QUINONIZE
QUINONOID
QUINOVATE
QUINOVOSE
QUINQUINA
QUINQUINO
QUINTETTE
QUINTETTO
QUINTFOIL
QUINTIPED
QUINTROON
QUINTUPLE
QUINZAINE
QUINZIEME
QUIREWISE
QUIRKIEST
QUIRKSOME
QUISQUOUS
QUISUTSCH
QUITANTIE
QUITCLAIM
QUITTANCE
QUIVERFUL
QUIVERING
QUIXOTISM
QUIXOTIZE
QUIZZICAL
QUODLIBET
QUOTATION
QUOTATIVE
QUOTELESS
QUOTIDIAN
QUOTINGLY

AQUAGREEN
AQUAMETER
AQUAPLANE
AQUARELLE
AQUARIIST
AQUARIUMS
AQUATICAL
AQUEOUSLY
AQUILEGIA
EQUALIZED
EQUALIZER
EQUALLING
EQUALNESS
EQUERRIES
EQUIMODAL
EQUIMOLAR
EQUIPEDAL
EQUIPLUVE
EQUIPMENT
EQUIPOISE
EQUIPPING
EQUISETIC
EQUISETUM
EQUITABLE
EQUITABLY
EQUIVALVE
EQUIVOCAL
EQUIVOQUE
SQUABBASH
SQUABBIER
SQUABBING
SQUABBISH
SQUABBLED
SQUABBLER
SQUADDING
SQUADRATE
SQUADRISM
SQUADRONE

SQUALIDLY
SQUALLERY
SQUALLIER
SQUALLING
SQUAMATED
SQUAMELLA
SQUAMEOUS
SQUAMOSAL
SQUAMULAE
SQUAREAGE
SQUARECAP
SQUAREMAN
SQUAREMEN
SQUARROSE
SQUARROUS
SQUASHIER
SQUASHILY
SQUASHING
SQUATINID
SQUATMORE
SQUATNESS
SQUATTAGE
SQUATTIER
SQUATTILY
SQUATTING
SQUATTISH
SQUAWBUSH
SQUAWFISH
SQUAWKIER
SQUAWKING
SQUAWROOT
SQUAWWEED
SQUEAKERY
SQUEAKILY
SQUEAKING
SQUEALING
SQUEAMISH
SQUEEGEED
SQUEEZING
SQUELCHED
SQUELCHER
SQUELETTE
SQUIBBERY
SQUIBBING
SQUIBBISH
SQUIBSTER
SQUIDDING
SQUIDGIER
SQUIFFIER
SQUILGEED
SQUILGEER
SQUILLGEE
SQUILLIAN
SQUINANCE
SQUINTING
SQUIRALTY
SQUIRARCH
SQUIRMIER
SQUIRMING
SQUIRRELY
SQUIRTING
SQUIRTISH

AC**Q**UEREUR
AC**Q**UIESCE
AC**Q**UIRING
AC**Q**UISITA
AC**Q**UISITE
AC**Q**UITTAL
AC**Q**UITTED
AC**Q**UITTER
AE**Q**UOREAL
AR**Q**UERITE
BE**Q**UIRTLE
CO**Q**UETOON
CO**Q**UETTED
ES**Q**UAMATE
ES**Q**UIRING
EX**Q**UISITE
IN**Q**UIETLY
IN**Q**UILINE
IN**Q**UINATE
IN**Q**UIRENT
IN**Q**UIRIES
IN**Q**UIRING
IN**Q**UISITE
JE**Q**UERITY
JE**Q**UIRITY
LA**Q**UEARIA
LI**Q**UATING
LI**Q**UATION
LI**Q**UEFIED
LI**Q**UEFIER
LI**Q**UEURED
LI**Q**UIDATE
LI**Q**UIDITY
LI**Q**UIDIZE
LI**Q**UIFORM
LI**Q**UORICE
LI**Q**UORING
LI**Q**UORISH
LI**Q**UORIST
LO**Q**UACITY
LO**Q**UENTLY
PI**Q**UANTLY
RE**Q**UESTER
RE**Q**UIRING
RE**Q**UISITE
RE**Q**UITING
RO**Q**UETING
SE**Q**UACITY
SE**Q**UELANT
SE**Q**UENCER
SE**Q**UESTER
SE**Q**UESTRA
UN**Q**UAILED
UN**Q**UALIFY
UN**Q**UALITY
UN**Q**UEMELY
UN**Q**UIETLY

BAN**Q**UETED
BAN**Q**UETER
BAN**Q**UETTE
BIS**Q**UETTE
BRI**Q**UETTE
CAI**Q**UEJEE
CAR**Q**UAISE
CAS**Q**UETEL
CAS**Q**UETTE
CLI**Q**UIEST
COE**Q**UALLY
COE**Q**UATED
CON**Q**UEDLE
CON**Q**UERED
CON**Q**UEROR
CRO**Q**UETED
CRO**Q**UETTE
DIS**Q**UISIT
ELI**Q**UATED
ELO**Q**UENCE
ETI**Q**UETTE
EXE**Q**UATUR
FRE**Q**UENCE
FRE**Q**UENCY
GRI**Q**UAITE
HAR**Q**UEBUS
INE**Q**UALLY
JAC**Q**UERIE
JON**Q**UILLE
LAC**Q**UERED
LAC**Q**UERER
LON**Q**UHARD
MAR**Q**UETRY
MAR**Q**UISAL
MIS**Q**UOTED
MIS**Q**UOTER
MOS**Q**UITAL
MOS**Q**UITOS
PAR**Q**UETED
PAR**Q**UETRY
PAS**Q**UILER
PAS**Q**UILIC
PIC**Q**UETER
PLA**Q**UETTE
SUR**Q**UEDRY
SUR**Q**UIDRY
TOR**Q**UATED
TRI**Q**UETRA
TUR**Q**UOISE
UBI**Q**UIOUS
UNE**Q**UABLE
UNE**Q**UABLY
UNE**Q**UALED
UNE**Q**UALLY
UNS**Q**UARED
VAN**Q**UISHER
VAN**Q**UISHED

ANTI**Q**UARY
ANTI**Q**UATE
ANTI**Q**UELY
ANTI**Q**UING
ANTI**Q**UIST
ANTI**Q**UITY
BRAS**Q**UING
BRUS**Q**UELY
CACI**Q**UISM
CHIC**Q**UING
CLIN**Q**UANT
COLO**Q**UIES
CUCK**Q**UEAN
DELI**Q**UIUM
DURA**Q**UARA
FOUR**Q**UINE
INSE**Q**UENT
OBLI**Q**UATE
OBLI**Q**UELY
OBLI**Q**UING
OBLI**Q**UITY
OBLO**Q**UIAL
OBLO**Q**UIES
OBSE**Q**UENT
OBSE**Q**UIAL
OBSE**Q**UIES
OBSE**Q**UITY
OVER**Q**UELL
QUIN**Q**UINA
QUIN**Q**UINO
QUIS**Q**UOUS
REAC**Q**UIRE
RELI**Q**UARY
RELI**Q**UIAE
RELI**Q**UIAN
RELI**Q**UISM
REPI**Q**UING
SEMI**Q**UOTE
SILI**Q**UOSE
SUBA**Q**UEAN
TOTA**Q**UINE
UNRE**Q**UEST
UTRA**Q**UIST
WELL**Q**UEME

APPLI**Q**UED
BALDA**Q**UIN
BILBO**Q**UET
BRODE**Q**UIN
CANNE**Q**UIN
ENCHE**Q**UER
EXCHE**Q**UER
GRASS**Q**UIT
HARLE**Q**UIN
MANNE**Q**UIN
PALAN**Q**UIN
PARRO**Q**UET
PHYSI**Q**UED
SAMBA**Q**UIS
SOBRI**Q**UET

ALAMBI**Q**UE
ANGELI**Q**UE
ANTILO**Q**UY
ARABES**Q**UE
BOURAS**Q**UE
BURLES**Q**UE
CHIBOU**Q**UE
DEMIPI**Q**UE
E**Q**UIVO**Q**UE
FANTAS**Q**UE
GROTES**Q**UE
HALOES**Q**UE
MONOCO**Q**UE
ODALIS**Q**UE
PLASTI**Q**UE
PROPIN**Q**UE
SIMIES**Q**UE
SOLILO**Q**UY
SUBSES**Q**UI
TECHNI**Q**UE
TRIPTY**Q**UE

SCORING ORDER LIST OF 9-LETTER WORDS

34
QUIXOTIZE

30
EXCHE**Q**UER

29
QUINZIEME

28
E**Q**UALIZED
JE**Q**UERITY
JE**Q**UIRITY
LI**Q**UIDIZE
QUACKHOOD
QUANTIZED
QUARTZOID
QUICKBEAM
QUIZZICAL
S**Q**UEEZING

27
CAI**Q**UEJEE
E**Q**UALIZER
JAC**Q**UERIE
PHYSI**Q**UED
QUARTZITE
QUARTZOSE
QUARTZOUS
QUICKFOOT
QUILLAJIC
QUININIZE
QUINONIZE
QUINZAINE
QUIXOTISM
S**Q**UAWFISH

26
CHIC**Q**UING
CUCK**Q**UEAN
FRE**Q**UENCY
QUAKINGLY
QUICKBORN
QUICKLIME
QUICKSTEP
QUICKWORK
QUILLBACK
S**Q**UAWBUSH
S**Q**UAWKING

25
CHIBOU**Q**UE
EXE**Q**UATUR
EX**Q**UISITE
JON**Q**UILLE
QUEBRACHO
QUICKENED
QUICKSAND
QUICKSIDE
QUILLWORK
QUINISEXT
S**Q**UABBASH
S**Q**UABBISH
S**Q**UAWKIER
S**Q**UAWWEED
S**Q**UEAKERY
S**Q**UEAKILY
S**Q**UIBBERY
S**Q**UIBBISH

24
CACI**Q**UISM
E**Q**UIVALVE
QUACKSTER
QUEENCAKE
QUEENFISH
QUENCHING
QUICKENER
QUICKNESS
QUILLFISH
QUIRKSOME
QUIVERFUL
S**Q**UASHILY
S**Q**UELCHED
S**Q**UIFFIER
UN**Q**UALIFY

23
APPLI**Q**UED
BRUS**Q**UELY
COE**Q**UALLY

DEMIPIQUE
ENCHEQUER
EQUIPLUVE
EQUIPPING
EQUITABLY
EQUIVOCAL
FREQUENCE
HARQUEBUS
LIQUIFORM
LOQUACITY
MARQUETRY
OBLIQUELY
OBLIQUITY
OBSEQUITY
PARQUETRY
PIQUANTLY
QUADRIFID
QUADRIMUM
QUARRYMAN
QUARRYMEN
QUEACHIER
QUERIMONY
QUIBBLING
QUINDECIM
QUINOFORM
QUISUTSCH
SEQUACITY
SQUABBING
SQUABBLED
SQUEAKING
SQUEAMISH
SQUELCHER
SQUIBBING
SQUIRARCH
TECHNIQUE
TRIPTYQUE
UNEQUABLY
UNQUEMELY
WELLQUEME

22

ACQUIESCE
ALAMBIQUE
BILBOQUET
EQUIPMENT
LIQUEFIED
LIQUIDITY
LONQUHARD
MONOCOQUE
PASQUILIC
PICQUETER
PROPINQUE
QUADRIVIA
QUADRUPED
QUAGMIRED
QUAILHEAD
QUAKETAIL
QUAKINESS
QUALIFIED
QUARRYING
QUAVERING
QUAYSIDER
QUEENLIKE
QUEENWEED
QUEENWOOD
QUERCETIC
QUERCETUM
QUIETLIKE
QUINALDYL
QUINDECAD
QUINOLOGY
QUIRKIEST
QUITCLAIM
QUIVERING
QUOTINGLY
SAMBAQUIS
SQUABBIER
SQUABBLER
SQUALIDLY
SQUARECAP
SQUASHING
SQUISHING
SURQUEDRY
SURQUIDRY

21

ACQUIRING
ACQUITTED
ANTILOQUY
ANTIQUARY
ANTIQUELY
ANTIQUITY
AQUEOUSLY
BALDAQUIN
BANQUETED
BRASQUING
BRODEQUIN
COEQUATED
CONQUEDLE
CONQUERED
COQUETTED
CROQUETED
DELIQUIUM
EQUIMODAL
EQUIPEDAL
FANTASQUE
FOURQUINE
HALOESQUE
HARLEQUIN
INEQUALLY
INQUIETLY
LACQUERED
LIQUEFIER
LIQUORISH
LOQUENTLY
MISQUOTED
OBLIQUING
OVERQUELL
PARQUETED
QUADRABLE
QUADRATIC
QUADRATUM
QUADRUPLE
QUALIFIER
QUARTERLY
QUARTINHO
QUATRAYLE
QUAVEROUS
QUERULITY
QUESITIVE
QUIDDLING
QUIESCING
QUILLWORT
QUINALDIC
QUINOVATE
QUINOVOSE
QUINTFOIL
QUINTIPED
QUIREWISE
QUODLIBET
QUOTATIVE
RELIQUARY
REPIQUING
SOLILOQUY
SQUADDING
SQUADRISM
SQUALLERY
SQUAMATED
SQUASHIER
SQUATTILY
SQUATTISH
SQUAWROOT
SQUIDDING
SQUIRALTY
SQUIRMING
SQUIRRELY
SQUIRTISH
UNEQUALLY
UNQUALITY
UNQUIETLY

20

ACQUEREUR
ACQUISITA
ACQUISITE
ACQUITTAL
ACQUITTER
AQUAMETER
AQUAPLANE
AQUARIUMS
AQUATICAL
ARABESQUE
BANQUETER
BANQUETTE
BEQUIRTLE
BISQUETTE
BOURASQUE
BRIQUETTE
BURLESQUE
CANNEQUIN
CARQUAISE
CASQUETEL
CASQUETTE
CLINQUANT
CLIQUIEST
COLOQUIES
CONQUEROR
COQUETOON
CROQUETTE
ELOQUENCE
EQUIMOLAR
EQUIPOISE
EQUISETIC
EQUISETUM
EQUITABLE
EQUIVOQUE
ESQUAMATE
LACQUERER
LIQUORICE
MANNEQUIN
MARQUISAL
MISQUOTER
MOSQUITAL
MOSQUITOS
OBLIQUATE
OBLOQUIAL
OBLOQUIES
OBSEQUENT
OBSEQUIAL
OBSEQUIES
PALANQUIN
PARROQUET
PASQUILER
PLAQUETTE
PLASTIQUE
QUADRATED
QUADRIGAE
QUAESITUM
QUAGGIEST
QUANTICAL
QUANTULUM
QUATREBLE
QUATRIBLE
QUEERSOME
QUERCETIN
QUERCITOL
QUERENCIA
QUERIMANS
QUIESCENT
QUIETSOME
QUINAMINE
QUINICINE
QUININISM
QUINTUPLE
QUITTANCE
REACQUIRE
RELIQUISM
SEMIQUOTE
SEQUENCER
SIMIESQUE
SOBRIQUET
SQUAMELLA
SQUAMEOUS
SQUAMOSAL
SQUAMULAE
SQUAREMAN
SQUAREMEN
SQUATMORE
SQUEEGEED
SQUIBSTER
SQUIDGIER
SQUILGEED
SQUINANCE
SQUIRMIER
SUBAQUEAN
SUBSESQUI
UBIQUIOUS
UNEQUABLE

19

ANGELIQUE
ANTIQUING
AQUAGREEN
AQUILEGIA
DISQUISIT
DURAQUARA
ELIQUATED
EQUALLING
ESQUIRING
GRASSQUIT
GRIQUAITE
GROTESQUE
INQUIRING
LIQUATING
LIQUEURED
LIQUIDATE
LIQUORING
ODALISQUE
QUADRATUS
QUADRILLE
QUALITIED
QUARENDEN
QUARENDER
QUARRELED
QUARTERED
QUILLETED
QUINALDIN
QUINIDINE
QUINOIDAL
QUINOIDIN
QUINONOID
QUOTIDIAN
REQUIRING
REQUITING
ROQUETING
SQUADRATE
SQUADRONE
SQUALLING
SQUAREAGE
SQUATINID
SQUATTAGE
SQUATTING
SQUEALING
SQUILGEER
SQUILLGEE
SQUINTING
SQUIRTING
TORQUATED
UNEQUALED
UNQUAILED
UNSQUARED

18

AEQUOREAL
ANTIQUATE
ANTIQUIST
AQUARELLE
AQUARIIST
ARQUERITE
EQUALNESS
EQUERRIES
ETIQUETTE
INQUILINE
INQUINATE
INQUIRENT
INQUIRIES
INQUISITE
INSEQUENT
LAQUEARIA
LIQUATION
LIQUORIST
QUAINTEST
QUAINTISE
QUALITIES
QUARTERER
QUARTERON
QUARTETTE
QUATTRINI
QUATTRINO
QUEASIEST
QUEENLIER
QUEENROOT
QUEERNESS
QUEINTISE
QUERULENT
QUERULIST
QUERULOUS
QUESTIONS
QUESTRIST
QUETENITE
QUIETENER
QUIETNESS
QUILLTAIL
QUINARIAN
QUINARIES
QUINARIUS
QUINOLINE
QUINTETTE
QUINTETTO
QUINTROON
QUITANTIE
QUOTATION
QUOTELESS
RELIQUIAE
RELIQUIAN
REQUESTER
REQUISITE
SEQUELANT
SEQUESTER
SEQUESTRA
SILIQUOSE
SQUALLIER
SQUARROSE
SQUARROUS
SQUATNESS
SQUATTIER
SQUELETTE
SQUILLIAN
TOTAQUINE
TRIQUETRA
TURQUOISE
UNREQUEST
UTRAQUIST

17

QUINQUINA
QUINQUINO
QUISQUOUS

ALPHABETICAL LIST OF 10-LETTER WORDS

ACEQUIADOR
ACQUAINTED
ACQUIESCED
ACQUIESCER
ACQUIRABLE
ACQUIRENDA
ACQUISIBLE
ACQUISITED
ACQUISITOR
ACQUISITUM
ACQUITMENT
ACQUITTING
ADEQUATELY
ADEQUATION
ADEQUATIVE
ALCORNOQUE
ANTIMASQUE
ANTIQUATED
ANTISQUAMA
APOQUININE
AQUAFORTIS
AQUAMARINE
AQUAPLANED
AQUASCUTUM
AQUATINTER
AQUAVALENT
AQUICOLOUS
AQUIFEROUS
AQUILAWOOD
AQUIPAROUS
ARBORESQUE
BANQUETEER
BANQUETING
BEQUEATHAL
BEQUEATHER
BIQUADRATE
BIQUINTILE
BLANQUETTE
BLANQUILLO
BLOTTESQUE
BROQUINEER
BRUSQUERIE
BURLESQUED
BURLESQUER
CATAFALQUE
CHAUTAUQUA
CHEQUERING
CHERQUERED
CHINQUAPIN
CHOUQUETTE
CIGARESQUE
CINQUEFOIL
CINQUEPACE
CLIQUISHLY
COEQUALITY
COEQUATION
COLLIQUATE
COLLOQUIAL
COLLOQUIST
COLLOQUIUM
COLLOQUIZE
CONQUERING
CONQUININE
CONSEQUENT
COQUELICOT
COQUELUCHE
COQUETRIES
COQUETTING
COQUETTISH
COQUIMBITE
CRAQUELURE
CROQUETING
DELINQUENT
DELIQUESCE
DEMIQUAVER
DESQUAMATE
DISQUALIFY
DISQUIETED
DISQUIETER
DISQUIETLY
DISQUISITE
DISQUIXOTE
DULCILOQUY
EARTHQUAKE
EARTHQUAVE
ELIQUATING
ELIQUATION
EQUABILITY
EQUALITIES
EQUALIZING
EQUANGULAR
EQUANIMITY
EQUANIMOUS
EQUATIONAL
EQUATOREAL
EQUATORIAL
EQUESTRIAN
EQUIFORMAL
EQUIJACENT
EQUILIBRIA
EQUIPARANT
EQUIPARATE
EQUIPOISED
EQUISETUMS
EQUISIGNAL
EQUISONANT
EQUITATION
EQUITATIVE
EQUIVALENT
EQUIVOCACY
EQUIVOCATE
EQUIVOROUS
EUMOLPIQUE
FOURSQUARE
FREQUENTED
FREQUENTER
FREQUENTLY
GRANDESQUE
HARLEQUINA
HARQUEBUSS
HEARTQUAKE
HUMORESQUE
ILLAQUEATE
ILLIQUIDLY
INADEQUACY
INADEQUATE
INELOQUENT
INEQUALITY
INEQUATION
INEQUITIES
INFREQUENT
INIQUITIES
INIQUITOUS
INQUESTUAL
INQUIETUDE
INQUINATED
INQUIRABLE
INQUIRENDO
INQUISITOR
JOAQUINITE
LACQUERING
LACQUERIST
LAMBREQUIN
LANSQUENET
LAQUEARIAN
LIQUEFYING
LIQUESCENT
LIQUEURING
LIQUIDABLE
LIQUIDATED
LIQUIDATOR
LIQUIDIZED
LIQUIDNESS
LOQUACIOUS
MAGNIFIQUE
MAQUAHUITL
MARQUISATE
MARQUISDOM
MARQUISESS
MARQUISINA
MASQUERADE
MEDRINAQUE
MISQUOTING
MOSQUITOES
MOSQUITOEY
MULTILOQUY
MUSQUASPEN
NOVANTIQUE
OBLOQUIOUS
OBSEQUENCE
OBSEQUIOUS
OPAQUENESS
OUTQUIBBLE
OXYQUINONE
PARCILOQUY
PARQUETING
PASQUILANT
PASQUILLER
PASQUILLIC
PASQUINADE
PAUCILOQUY
PENDELOQUE
PERQUADRAT
PERQUEERLY
PERQUISITE
PERRUQUIER
PLASMOQUIN
QUACKERIES
QUACKISHLY
QUADRANGLE
QUADRANTAL
QUADRATICS
QUADRATING
QUADRATRIX
QUADRATURE
QUADRENNIA
QUADRICEPS
QUADRICONE
QUADRIFORM
QUADRIGATE
QUADRILLED
QUADRILLES
QUADRILOGY
QUADRISECT
QUADRIVIAL
QUADRIVIUM
QUADRUMANE
QUADRUPLED
QUADRUPLET
QUADRUPLEX
QUAESTUARY
QUAILERIES
QUAINTANCE
QUAINTNESS
QUAKERBIRD
QUALIFYING
QUALIMETER
QUALMISHLY
QUANDARIES
QUANTIFIED
QUANTIFIER
QUANTITATE
QUANTITIED
QUANTITIES
QUANTITIVE
QUARANTINE
QUARENTENE
QUARRELING
QUARRELLED
QUARRELOUS
QUARTATION
QUARTERAGE
QUARTERING
QUARTERMAN
QUARTERMEN
QUARTERSAW
QUARTZITIC
QUASSATION
QUASSATIVE
QUATERNARY
QUATERNATE
QUATERNION
QUATERNITY
QUATORZAIN
QUATREFOIL
QUEACHIEST
QUEASINESS
QUEENCRAFT
QUEENLIEST
QUEENRIGHT
QUENCHABLE
QUENCHLESS
QUENSELITE
QUERCITRIN
QUERCITRON
QUERNSTONE
QUERYINGLY
QUESTHOUSE
QUESTIONED
QUESTIONEE
QUESTIONER
QUESTORIAL
QUICKENING
QUICKHATCH
QUICKSANDY
QUICKTHORN
QUICKWATER
QUIDDATIVE
QUIDDITIES
QUIESCENCE
QUIESCENCY
QUIETISTIC
QUINACRINE
QUINALDINE
QUINAMICIN
QUINAMIDIN
QUINAQUINA
QUINATOXIN
QUINAZOLIN
QUINAZOLYL
QUINCEWORT
QUINCUNXES
QUINDECIMA
QUINIRETIN
QUINIZARIN
QUINOIDINE
QUINOLINYL
QUINOMETRY
QUINONIMIN
QUINOPYRIN
QUINOXALIN
QUINOXALYL
QUINQUEVIR
QUINSYWORT
QUINTADENA
QUINTADENE
QUINTUPLED
QUINTUPLET
QUISQUEITE
QUIVERLEAF
QUIXOTICAL
QUOTENNIAL
QUOTIETIES
RADIOPAQUE
RELINQUENT
RELINQUISH
RELIQUAIRE
REQUIESCAT
REQUIRABLE
REQUISITOR
REQUITABLE
ROBOTESQUE
ROQUELAURE
SATYRESQUE
SEMICIRQUE
SEMIQUAVER
SEMISQUARE
SEQUACIOUS
SEQUENTIAL
SEQUESTRAL
SEQUESTRUM
SESQUINONA
SOMNILOQUY
SOUBRIQUET
SQUABASHER
SQUABBIEST
SQUABBLING
SQUADRONED
SQUALIDITY
SQUALIFORM
SQUALLIEST
SQUALODONT
SQUAMATINE
SQUAMATION
SQUAMELLAE
SQUAMIFORM
SQUAMOSELY
SQUAMOSITY
SQUAMOUSLY
SQUAMULATE
SQUAMULOSE
SQUANDERED
SQUANDERER
SQUAREFACE
SQUAREHEAD
SQUARENESS
SQUARETAIL
SQUARISHLY
SQUARSONRY
SQUASHIEST
SQUATAROLE
SQUATEROLE
SQUATINOID
SQUATTIEST
SQUAWBERRY
SQUAWKIEST
SQUEEZABLE
SQUEEZEMAN
SQUELCHIER
SQUELCHILY
SQUELCHING
SQUETEAGUE
SQUIBCRACK
SQUIDGIEST
SQUIFFIEST
SQUIGGLIER
SQUILLAGEE
SQUILLITIC
SQUIRARCHY
SQUIREARCH

SQUIRELING
SQUIRMIEST
STATEQUAKE
STATUESQUE
SUBAQUATIC
SUBAQUEOUS
SUBSEQUENT
TAUROESQUE
TERRAQUEAN
TOURNIQUET
TRANQUILER
TRANQUILLO
TRANQUILLY
TRIQUETRAL
TRIQUETRIC
TRIQUETRUM
TRIQUINATE
TRIQUINOYL
TURQUOISES
UBIQUARIAN
UBIQUITARY
UBIQUITOUS
UNADEQUATE
UNCONQUEST
UNDERQUOTE
UNEQUALITY
UNEQUALLED
UNEQUIAXED
UNFREQUENT
UNIQUANTIC
UNIQUENESS
UNLIQUORED
UNQUIETOUS
UNQUIETUDE
UNREQUITER
USQUEBAUGH
VANQUISHED
VANQUISHER
VERSILOQUY
WORLDQUAKE

POSITIONAL ORDER LIST OF 10-LETTER WORDS

QUACKERIES
QUACKISHLY
QUADRANGLE
QUADRANTAL
QUADRATICS
QUADRATING
QUADRATRIX
QUADRATURE
QUADRENNIA
QUADRICEPS
QUADRICONE
QUADRIFORM
QUADRIGATE
QUADRILLED
QUADRILLES
QUADRILOGY
QUADRISECT
QUADRIVIAL
QUADRIVIUM
QUADRUMANE
QUADRUPLED
QUADRUPLET
QUADRUPLEX
QUAESTUARY
QUAILERIES
QUAINTANCE
QUAINTNESS
QUAKERBIRD
QUALIFYING
QUALIMETER
QUALMISHLY
QUANDARIES
QUANTIFIED
QUANTIFIER
QUANTITATE
QUANTITIED
QUANTITIES
QUANTITIVE
QUARANTINE
QUARENTENE
QUARRELING
QUARRELLED
QUARRELOUS
QUARTATION
QUARTERAGE
QUARTERING
QUARTERMAN
QUARTERMEN
QUARTERSAW
QUARTZITIC
QUASSATION
QUASSATIVE
QUATERNARY
QUATERNATE
QUATERNION
QUATERNITY
QUATORZAIN
QUATREFOIL
QUEACHIEST
QUEASINESS
QUEENCRAFT
QUEENLIEST
QUEENRIGHT
QUENCHABLE
QUENCHLESS
QUENSELITE
QUERCITRIN
QUERCITRON
QUERNSTONE
QUERYINGLY
QUESTHOUSE
QUESTIONED
QUESTIONEE
QUESTIONER
QUESTORIAL
QUICKENING
QUICKHATCH
QUICKSANDY
QUICKTHORN
QUICKWATER
QUIDDATIVE
QUIDDITIES
QUIESCENCE
QUIESCENCY
QUIETISTIC
QUINACRINE
QUINALDINE
QUINAMICIN
QUINAMIDIN
QUINAQUINA
QUINATOXIN
QUINAZOLIN
QUINAZOLYL
QUINCEWORT
QUINCUNXES
QUINDECIMA
QUINIRETIN
QUINIZARIN
QUINOIDINE
QUINOLINYL
QUINOMETRY
QUINONIMIN
QUINOPYRIN
QUINOXALIN
QUINOXALYL
QUINQUEVIR
QUINSYWORT
QUINTADENA
QUINTADENE
QUINTUPLED
QUINTUPLET
QUISQUEITE
QUIVERLEAF
QUIXOTICAL
QUOTENNIAL
QUOTIETIES

AQUAFORTIS
AQUAMARINE
AQUAPLANED
AQUASCUTUM
AQUATINTER
AQUAVALENT
AQUICOLOUS
AQUIFEROUS
AQUILAWOOD
AQUIPAROUS
EQUABILITY
EQUALITIES
EQUALIZING
EQUANGULAR
EQUANIMITY
EQUANIMOUS
EQUATIONAL
EQUATOREAL
EQUATORIAL
EQUESTRIAN
EQUIFORMAL
EQUIJACENT
EQUILIBRIA
EQUIPARANT
EQUIPARATE
EQUIPOISED
EQUISETUMS
EQUISIGNAL
EQUISONANT
EQUITATION
EQUITATIVE
EQUIVALENT
EQUIVOCACY
EQUIVOCATE
EQUIVOROUS
SQUABASHER
SQUABBIEST
SQUABBLING
SQUADRONED
SQUALIDITY
SQUALIFORM
SQUALLIEST
SQUALODONT
SQUAMATINE
SQUAMATION
SQUAMELLAE
SQUAMIFORM
SQUAMOSELY
SQUAMOSITY
SQUAMOUSLY
SQUAMULATE
SQUAMULOSE
SQUANDERED
SQUANDERER
SQUAREFACE
SQUAREHEAD
SQUARENESS
SQUARETAIL
SQUARISHLY
SQUARSONRY
SQUASHIEST
SQUATAROLE
SQUATEROLE
SQUATINOID
SQUATTIEST
SQUAWBERRY
SQUAWKIEST
SQUEEZABLE
SQUEEZEMAN
SQUELCHIER
SQUELCHILY
SQUELCHING
SQUETEAGUE
SQUIBCRACK
SQUIDGIEST
SQUIFFIEST
SQUIGGLIER
SQUILLAGEE
SQUILLITIC
SQUIRARCHY
SQUIREARCH
SQUIRELING
SQUIRMIEST

ACQUAINTED
ACQUIESCED
ACQUIESCER
ACQUIRABLE
ACQUIRENDA
ACQUISIBLE
ACQUISITED
ACQUISITOR
ACQUISITUM
ACQUITMENT
ACQUITTING
BEQUEATHAL
BEQUEATHER
BIQUADRATE
BIQUINTILE
COQUELICOT
COQUELUCHE
COQUETRIES
COQUETTING
COQUETTISH
COQUIMBITE
INQUESTUAL
INQUIETUDE
INQUINATED
INQUIRABLE
INQUIRENDO
INQUISITOR
LAQUEARIAN
LIQUEFYING
LIQUESCENT
LIQUEURING
LIQUIDABLE
LIQUIDATED
LIQUIDATOR
LIQUIDIZED
LIQUIDNESS
LOQUACIOUS
MAQUAHUITL
REQUIESCAT
REQUIRABLE
REQUISITOR
REQUITABLE
ROQUELAURE
SEQUACIOUS
SEQUENTIAL
SEQUESTRAL
SEQUESTRUM
UNQUIETOUS
UNQUIETUDE
USQUEBAUGH
ACEQUIADOR
ADEQUATELY
ADEQUATION
ADEQUATIVE
APOQUININE
BANQUETEER
BANQUETING
BROQUINEER
CHEQUERING
CINQUEFOIL
CINQUEPACE
CLIQUISHLY
COEQUALITY
COEQUATION
CONQUERING
CONQUININE
CRAQUELURE
CROQUETING
DESQUAMATE
DISQUALIFY
DISQUIETED
DISQUIETER
DISQUIETLY
DISQUISITE
DISQUIXOTE
ELIQUATING
ELIQUATION
FREQUENTED
FREQUENTER
FREQUENTLY
HARQUEBUSS
INEQUALITY
INEQUATION
INEQUITIES
INIQUITIES
INIQUITOUS
JOAQUINITE
LACQUERING
LACQUERIST
MARQUISATE
MARQUISDOM
MARQUISESS
MARQUISINA
MASQUERADE
MISQUOTING
MOSQUITOES
MOSQUITOEY
MUSQUASPEN
OPAQUENESS
OUTQUIBBLE
OXYQUINONE
PARQUETING
PASQUILANT
PASQUILLER
PASQUILLIC
PASQUINADE
PERQUADRAT
PERQUEERLY
PERQUISITE
SESQUINONA
TRIQUETRAL
TRIQUETRIC
TRIQUETRUM

TRIQUINATE
TRIQUINOYL
TURQUOISES
UBIQUARIAN
UBIQUITARY
UBIQUITOUS
UNEQUALITY
UNEQUALLED
UNEQUIAXED
UNIQUANTIC
UNIQUENESS

ANTIQUATED
BLANQUETTE
BLANQUILLO
BRUSQUERIE
CHERQUERED
CHINQUAPIN
CHOUQUETTE
DELIQUESCE
DEMIQUAVER

ILLAQUEATE
ILLIQUIDLY
LANSQUENET
OBLOQUIOUS
OBSEQUENCE
OBSEQUIOUS
QUINQUEVIR
QUISQUEITE
RELIQUAIRE
SEMIQUAVER
SUBAQUATIC
SUBAQUEOUS
TRANQUILER
TRANQUILLO
TRANQUILLY
UNLIQUORED
UNREQUITER

ANTISQUAMA
COLLIQUATE
COLLOQUIAL

COLLOQUIST
COLLOQUIUM
COLLOQUIZE
CONSEQUENT
DELINQUENT
EARTHQUAKE
EARTHQUAVE
FOURSQUARE
HARLEQUINA
HEARTQUAKE
INADEQUACY
INADEQUATE
INELOQUENT
INFREQUENT
PERRUQUIER
QUINAQUINA
RELINQUENT
RELINQUISH
SEMISQUARE
STATEQUAKE

SUBSEQUENT
TERRAQUEAN
UNADEQUATE
UNCONQUEST
UNDERQUOTE
UNFREQUENT
WORLDQUAKE

BURLESQUED
BURLESQUER
LAMBREQUIN
PLASMOQUIN
SOUBRIQUET
TOURNIQUET

ALCORNOQUE
ANTIMASQUE
ARBORESQUE
BLOTTESQUE
CATAFALQUE

CHAUTAUQUA
CIGARESQUE
DULCILOQUY
EUMOLPIQUE
GRANDESQUE
HUMORESQUE
MAGNIFIQUE
MEDRINAQUE
MULTILOQUY
NOVANTIQUE
PARCILOQUY
PAUCILOQUY
PENDELOQUE
RADIOPAQUE
ROBOTESQUE
SATYRESQUE
SEMICIRQUE
SOMNILOQUY
STATUESQUE
TAUROESQUE

SCORING ORDER LIST OF 10-LETTER WORDS

33
QUICKHATCH

31
QUACKISHLY
QUINAZOLYL

30
LIQUIDIZED
QUARTZITIC
SQUEEZABLE
SQUEEZEMAN

29
EQUALIZING
EQUIVOCACY
OXYQUINONE
QUADRUPLEX
QUICKSANDY
QUINOXALYL
SQUIBCRACK

28
EQUIJACENT
QUATORZAIN
QUICKTHORN
QUICKWATER
QUINAZOLIN
QUINCUNXES
QUINIZARIN
QUIXOTICAL

27
CLIQUISHLY
DISQUIXOTE
QUADRATRIX
QUALMISHLY
SQUAWBERRY
SQUELCHILY
SQUILLAGEE
SQUIRARCHY
UNEQUIAXED
WORLDQUAKE

26
CHINQUAPIN
COQUELUCHE
DISQUALIFY
EARTHQUAKE
ELIQUATING
HEARTQUAKE
JOAQUINITE
LIQUEFYING
PARCILOQUY
PAUCILOQUY
QUAKERBIRD
QUALIFYING
QUENCHABLE
QUERYINGLY
QUICKENING
QUIESCENCY
QUINATOXIN
QUINOXALIN
SQUAMIFORM
SQUAWKIEST
VANQUISHED

25
CHEQUERING
CHERQUERED
CINQUEPACE
COQUIMBITE
DULCILOQUY
EARTHQUAVE
FREQUENTLY
INADEQUACY
MAGNIFIQUE
QUACKERIES
QUADRIFORM
QUADRIVIUM
QUINSYWORT
QUIVERLEAF
SQUARISHLY
SQUELCHING
SQUIFFIEST
USQUEBAUGH
VANQUISHER
VERSILOQUY

24
ACQUIESCED
BEQUEATHAL
BEQUEATHER
CATAFALQUE
CHAUTAUQUA
CHOUQUETTE
CINQUEFOIL
COEQUALITY
COQUETTISH
EQUABILITY
EQUANIMITY
EQUIFORMAL
EQUIVOCATE
HARQUEBUSS
HUMORESQUE
MAQUAHUITL
MARQUISDOM
MOSQUITOEY
MULTILOQUY
PERQUEERLY
QUADRICEPS
QUADRILOGY
QUEACHIEST
QUEENCRAFT
QUENCHLESS
QUIDDATIVE
QUINCEWORT
QUINDECIMA
QUINOMETRY
QUINOPYRIN
SEMIQUAVER
SOMNILOQUY
SQUABASHER
SQUABBLING
SQUALIFORM
SQUAMOSELY
SQUAMOSITY
SQUAMOUSLY
SQUAREFACE
SQUELCHIER
SQUIREARCH
UBIQUITARY

23
ACQUIESCER
ACQUIRABLE
ACQUISIBLE
ACQUISITUM
ACQUITMENT
ADEQUATELY
ADEQUATIVE
AQUASCUTUM
AQUILAWOOD
COLLOQUIUM
COQUELICOT
DISQUIETLY
EUMOLPIQUE
FREQUENTED
ILLIQUIDLY
LAMBREQUIN
MUSQUASPEN
OBSEQUENCE
OUTQUIBBLE
PASQUILLIC
PLASMOQUIN
QUADRIVIAL
QUADRUPLED
QUANTIFIED
QUEENRIGHT
QUIESCENCE
QUINAMICIN
SEMICIRQUE
SQUABBIEST
SQUALIDITY
SQUAREHEAD
STATEQUAKE
SUBAQUATIC
SUBSEQUENT

22
ACEQUIADOR
ACQUAINTED
ACQUIRENDA
ACQUISITED
ACQUITTING
AQUAFORTIS
AQUAPLANED
AQUAVALENT
AQUIFEROUS
BANQUETING
BIQUADRATE
BURLESQUED
CIGARESQUE
CONQUERING
COQUETTING
CROQUETING
DELIQUESCE
EQUIPOISED
EQUITATIVE
EQUIVALENT
EQUIVOROUS
FOURSQUARE
FREQUENTER
HARLEQUINA
INEQUALITY
INFREQUENT
LACQUERING
LIQUIDABLE
MASQUERADE
MEDRINAQUE
MISQUOTING
NOVANTIQUE
PARQUETING
PASQUINADE
PENDELOQUE
PERQUADRAT
QUADRATICS
QUADRICONE
QUADRISECT
QUADRUMANE
QUADRUPLET
QUAESTUARY
QUANTIFIER
QUANTITIVE
QUARTERSAW
QUASSATIVE
QUATERNARY
QUATERNITY
QUATREFOIL
QUESTHOUSE
QUINAMIDIN
QUINOLINYL
QUINTUPLED
RADIOPAQUE
SATYRESQUE
SQUARSONRY
SQUASHIEST
TRANQUILLY
TRIQUINOYL
UNEQUALITY
UNFREQUENT

21
ACQUISITOR
ALCORNOQUE
ANTIMASQUE
ANTISQUAMA
APOQUININE
AQUAMARINE
AQUICOLOUS
AQUIPAROUS
ARBORESQUE
BANQUETEER
BIQUINTILE
BLANQUETTE
BLANQUILLO
BLOTTESQUE
BROQUINEER
BRUSQUERIE
BURLESQUER

COEQUATION
COLLIQUATE
COLLOQUIAL
COLLOQUIST
CONQUININE
CONSEQUENT
COQUETRIES
CRAQUELURE
DISQUIETED
EQUANIMOUS
EQUIPARANT
EQUIPARATE
EQUISETUMS
GRANDESQUE
INQUIRABLE
LACQUERIST
LIQUESCENT
LIQUIDATED
LOQUACIOUS
MARQUISATE
MARQUISESS
MARQUISINA
MOSQUITOES
OBLOQUIOUS
OBSEQUIOUS
OPAQUENESS
PASQUILANT
PASQUILLER
PERQUISITE
PERRUQUIER
QUADRANGLE
QUADRATING
QUADRIGATE
QUADRILLED
QUAINTANCE
QUALIMETER
QUARTERMAN
QUARTERMEN
QUERCITRIN
QUERCITRON
QUIDDITIES
QUIETISTIC
QUINACRINE
QUINONIMIN
QUINQUEVIR
QUINTUPLET
REQUIESCAT
REQUIRABLE
REQUITABLE
ROBOTESQUE
SEMISQUARE
SEQUACIOUS
SEQUESTRUM
SOUBRIQUET
SQUADRONED
SQUAMATINE
SQUAMATION
SQUAMELLAE
SQUAMULATE
SQUAMULOSE
SQUANDERED
SQUIGGLIER
SQUILLITIC
SQUIRMIEST
TRIQUETRIC
TRIQUETRUM
UBIQUARIAN
UBIQUITOUS
UNCONQUEST
UNIQUANTIC

20

ADEQUATION
ANTIQUATED
DELINQUENT
DISQUIETER
DISQUISITE
EQUISIGNAL
INADEQUATE
INQUIETUDE
INQUINATED
INQUIRENDO
LIQUEURING
LIQUIDATOR
LIQUIDNESS
QUADRANTAL
QUADRATURE
QUADRENNIA
QUADRILLES
QUANDARIES
QUANTITIED
QUARRELING
QUARTERAGE
QUARTERING
QUESTIONED
QUINALDINE
QUINOIDINE
QUINTADENA
QUINTADENE
SQUALODONT
SQUANDERER
SQUATINOID
SQUETEAGUE
UNADEQUATE
UNDERQUOTE
UNEQUALLED
UNLIQUORED
UNQUIETUDE

19

AQUATINTER
ELIQUATION
EQUALITIES
EQUANGULAR
EQUATIONAL
EQUATOREAL
EQUATORIAL
EQUESTRIAN
EQUILIBRIA
EQUISONANT
EQUITATION
ILLAQUEATE
INELOQUENT
INEQUATION
INEQUITIES
INIQUITIES
INIQUITOUS
INQUESTUAL
INQUISITOR
LANSQUENET
LAQUEARIAN
QUAILERIES
QUAINTNESS
QUANTITATE
QUANTITIES
QUARANTINE
QUARENTENE
QUARRELOUS
QUARTATION
QUASSATION
QUATERNATE
QUATERNION
QUEASINESS
QUEENLIEST
QUENSELITE
QUERNSTONE
QUESTIONEE
QUESTIONER
QUESTORIAL
QUINIRETIN
QUOTENNIAL
QUOTIETIES
RELINQUENT
RELIQUAIRE
REQUISITOR
ROQUELAURE
SEQUENTIAL
SEQUESTRAL
SESQUINONA
SQUALLIEST
SQUARENESS
SQUARETAIL
SQUATAROLE
SQUATEROLE
SQUATTIEST
STATUESQUE
TAUROESQUE
TERRAQUEAN
TOURNIQUET
TRANQUILER
TRANQUILLO
TRIQUETRAL
TRIQUINATE
TURQUOISES
UNIQUENESS
UNQUIETOUS
UNREQUITER

18

QUINAQUINA
QUISQUEITE

ALPHABETICAL LIST OF WORDS OVER 10 LETTERS

ABSQUATULATE
ACQUAINTANCE
ACQUAINTANT
ACQUIESCENCE
ACQUIESCENT
ACQUIESCING
ACQUIREMENT
ACQUISITION
ACQUISITIVE
ACQUISITIVELY
ACQUITTANCE
ADEQUATENESS
ALTILOQUENCE
ALTILOQUENT
AMPHORILOQUY
ANTHRAQUINOL
ANTIMASQUER
ANTIQUARIAN
ANTIQUARIES
ANTIQUARISM
ANTIQUATING
ANTIQUATION
ANTIQUENESS
ANTIQUITIES
APPLIQUEING
AQUACULTURAL
AQUACULTURE
AQUAEMANALE
AQUAEMANALIA
AQUAFORTIST
AQUAPLANING
AQUAPUNCTURE
AQUARELLIST
AQUATICALLY
AQUATIVENESS
AQUEOGLACIAL
AQUEOIGNEOUS
AQUEOUSNESS
AQUICULTURAL
AQUICULTURE
AQUOTIZATION
ARABESQUELY
ARABESQUERIE
BANQUETEERING
BARBARESQUE
BARQUENTINE
BECQUERELITE
BIQUADRANTAL
BIQUADRATIC
BIQUARTERLY
BLOTTESQUELY
BOUDOIRESQUE
BOUQUETIERE
BOUQUINISTE
BREVILOQUENT
BRONCHILOQUY
BRUSQUENESS
BURLESQUELY
BURLESQUING
CHEQUERBOARD
CHEQUERWISE
CHEQUERWORK
CHIVALRESQUE
CHYMAQUEOUS
CINQUECENTO
CLIQUISHNESS
COEQUALNESS
COLLIQUATION
COLLIQUATIVE
COLLOQUIALLY
COLLOQUIZED
COLLOQUIZING
COLOQUINTIDA
CONQUERABLE
CONQUERINGLY
CONQUINAMINE
CONQUISTADOR
CONSEQUENCE
CONSEQUENTIAL
CONSEQUENTLY
CONTRAMARQUE
COQUECIGRUE
COQUETTISHLY
CROQUIGNOLE
DELINQUENCIES
DELINQUENCY
DELINQUENTLY
DELIQUESCED
DELIQUESCENT
DELIQUESCING
DENTILOQUIST
DESQUAMATED
DESQUAMATING
DESQUAMATION
DESQUAMATIVE
DESQUAMATORY
DISACQUAINT
DISCOTHEQUE
DISEQUALIZE
DISQUALIFIED
DISQUIETEDLY
DISQUIETING
DISQUIETUDE
DISQUIPARANT
DISQUISITED
DISQUISITING
DISQUISITION
DISQUISITIVE
DISQUISITOR
DISQUISITORY
DULCILOQUENT
DUROQUINONE
EARTHQUAKED
EARTHQUAKEN
EARTHQUAKING
ELOQUENTIAL
EQUABLENESS
EQUALITARIAN
EQUALIZATION
EQUANIMOUSLY
EQUATIONALLY
EQUATIONISM
EQUATIONIST
EQUATORIALLY
EQUESTRIENNE
EQUIDISTANCE
EQUIDISTANT
EQUIDISTANTLY
EQUIDIURNAL
EQUIFORMITY
EQUIGRANULAR
EQUILATERAL
EQUILIBRANT
EQUILIBRATE
EQUILIBRATED
EQUILIBRATING
EQUILIBRATING
EQUILIBRATION
EQUILIBRATIVE
EQUILIBRATOR
EQUILIBRATORY
EQUILIBRIAL
EQUILIBRIATE
EQUILIBRIOUS
EQUILIBRIST

EQUILIBRISTAT
EQUILIBRISTIC
EQUILIBRITY
EQUILIBRIUM
EQUILIBRIUMS
EQUILIBRIZE
EQUIMOLECULAR
EQUIMOMENTAL
EQUIMULTIPLE
EQUINANGULAR
EQUINOCTIAL
EQUINOCTIAL
EQUINOCTIALLY
EQUINOVARUS
EQUIPARATION
EQUIPARTILE
EQUIPARTITION
EQUIPOISING
EQUIPOISING
EQUIPOLLENCE
EQUIPOLLENCY
EQUIPOLLENT
EQUIPOLLENTLY
EQUIPONDERANT
EQUIPONDERATE
EQUIPOSTILE
EQUIPOTENTIAL
EQUIPROBABLE
EQUISETACEOUS
EQUISONANCE
EQUIVALENCE
EQUIVALENCED
EQUIVALENCY
EQUIVALENTLY
EQUIVOCALITY
EQUIVOCATED
EQUIVOCATING
EQUIVOCATION
EQUIVOCATOR
EQUIVOCATORY
EQUIVOLUMINAL
ESQUAMULOSE
ETIQUETTICAL
EXQUISITELY
EXQUISITENESS
EXQUISITISM
EXQUISITIVELY
FATILOQUENT
FOREQUARTER
FORMALESQUE
FOURSQUARELY
FREQUENCIES
FREQUENTABLE
FREQUENTAGE
FREQUENTATION
FREQUENTATIVE
FREQUENTING
FREQUENTNESS
GIGANTESQUE
GORGONESQUE
GRANDILOQUENT
GROTESQUELY
GROTESQUERIE
GROTESQUERY
HARLEQUINADE
HARLEQUINIC
HARLEQUINIZE
HEADQUARTER
HEADQUARTERS
HINDQUARTER
HINDQUARTERS
HYDROQUININE
HYDROQUINONE
ILLIQUATION
INADEQUATELY
INADEQUATION
INCONSEQUENCE

INCONSEQUENT
INELOQUENCE
INEQUALITIES
INEQUALNESS
INEQUITABLE
INEQUITABLY
INEQUIVALVE
INFREQUENCE
INFREQUENCY
INIQUITABLE
INIQUITOUSLY
INQUAINTANCE
INQUARTATION
INQUIETNESS
INQUILINISM
INQUILINITY
INQUILINOUS
INQUINATING
INQUINATION
INQUIRATION
INQUIRINGLY
INQUISITION
INQUISITIONAL
INQUISITIVE
INQUISITORIAL
INQUISITORY
ISOQUINOLINE
JEQUIRITIES
LACQUERWORK
LIQUEFACIENT
LIQUEFACTION
LIQUEFACTIVE
LIQUEFIABLE
LIQUESCENCE
LIQUESCENCY
LIQUIDAMBAR
LIQUIDAMBER
LIQUIDATING
LIQUIDATION
LIQUIDIZING
LIQUIDOGENIC
LIQUORISHLY
LIQUORISHNESS
LONGINQUITY
LOQUACIOUSLY
MAGNILOQUENT
MARQUETERIE
MARQUISETTE
MARQUISOTTE
MASQUERADED
MASQUERADER
MASQUERADING
MERIQUINONE
MERIQUINONIC
MILQUETOAST
MISQUOTATION
MONCHIQUITE
MOSQUITOBILL
MOUSQUETAIRE
MULTILOQUENT
MULTILOQUOUS
MUSQUASHROOT
MUSQUASHWEED
NATURALESQUE
NESQUEHONITE
OBLIQUATION
OBLIQUENESS
OBLIQUITIES
OBLIQUITOUS
OBSEQUIOUSLY
OMNILOQUENT
OSTEOPLAQUE
OUTQUESTION
OXYQUINOLINE
PALANQUINED
PALANQUINING
PARAQUADRATE

PASQUEFLOWER
PASQUILLANT
PASQUINADED
PASQUINADER
PASQUINADING
PAUCILOQUENT
PECTORILOQUE
PECTORILOQUY
PEREQUITATE
PERQUISITION
PERQUISITOR
PHENOQUINONE
PICTURESQUE
PIQUANTNESS
PLASMOQUINE
PLATERESQUE
POLYLOQUENT
PRECONQUEST
PREREQUISITE
PRETEREQUINE
PROPINQUANT
PROPINQUITY
PROPINQUOUS
PROQUAESTOR
PSEUDOAQUATIC
QUACKISHNESS
QUACKSALVER
QUADRAGESIMAL
QUADRANGLED
QUADRANGULAR
QUADRANGULED
QUADRANTILE
QUADRAPHONIC
QUADRATICAL
QUADRENNIAL
QUADRENNIUM
QUADRENNIUMS
QUADRICINIUM
QUADRICIPITAL
QUADRICYCLE
QUADRICYCLER
QUADRIENNIUM
QUADRIFILAR
QUADRIFOCAL
QUADRIFOLIUM
QUADRIFRONS
QUADRIGAMIST
QUADRIGATUS
QUADRIHYBRID
QUADRIJUGAL
QUADRILATERAL
QUADRILLING
QUADRILLION
QUADRINOMIAL
QUADRIPAROUS
QUADRIPLANAR
QUADRIURATE
QUADRIVALENT
QUADRIVIOUS
QUADRUMANAL
QUADRUMANOUS
QUADRUPEDAL
QUADRUPEDAN
QUADRUPEDANT
QUADRUPEDATE
QUADRUPEDOUS
QUADRUPLANE
QUADRUPLATE
QUADRUPLATOR
QUADRUPLING
QUAESTIONES
QUAESTORIAL
QUAESTORIAN
QUAESTORSHIP
QUALIFIABLE
QUALIFICATION
QUALIFICATOR

QUALIFIEDLY
QUALITATIVE
QUALMISHNESS
QUANTIFYING
QUANTIMETER
QUANTITATIVE
QUANTITIVELY
QUANTIVALENT
QUANTIZATION
QUANTIZING
QUANTOMETER
QUAQUAVERSAL
QUARANTINED
QUARANTINER
QUARANTINING
QUARRELLING
QUARRELLOUS
QUARRELOUSLY
QUARRELSOME
QUARRYSTONE
QUARTERBACK
QUARTERFOIL
QUARTERLAND
QUARTERLIES
QUARTERMASTER
QUARTERNIGHT
QUARTERNION
QUARTERPACE
QUARTERSAWED
QUARTERSAWING
QUARTERSAWN
QUARTERSTAFF
QUARTERSTAVES
QUARTIPAROUS
QUATERNARIES
QUATERNARIUS
QUATERNIONIC
QUATERNITIES
QUATERTENSES
QUATREFOILED
QUATTROCENTO
QUAVERINGLY
QUEBRACHITE
QUEBRACHITOL
QUEBRADILLA
QUEENFISHES
QUEENLINESS
QUEENSBERRIES
QUEENSBERRY
QUENCHLESSLY
QUERCITANNIN
QUERCIVOROUS
QUERIMONIES
QUERIMONIOUS
QUERULENTIAL
QUERULOSITY
QUERULOUSLY
QUESTIONABLE
QUESTIONABLY
QUESTIONARIES
QUESTIONARY
QUESTIONING
QUESTIONIST
QUESTIONLESS
QUESTIONNAIRE
QUESTMONGER
QUICKENANCE
QUICKENBEAM
QUICKSILVER
QUICKSILVERY
QUIDDITATIVE
QUIESCENTLY
QUIINACEOUS
QUILLFISHES
QUINALDINIC
QUINALDINIUM
QUINAMICINE

QUINAMIDINE
QUINANISOLE
QUINATOXINE
QUINAZOLINE
QUINCUNCIAL
QUINCUNXIAL
QUINDECAGON
QUINDECEMVIR
QUINDECEMVIRI
QUINDECIMVIR
QUINHYDRONE
QUINISEXTINE
QUINOIDATION
QUINOLINIUM
QUINOLOGIST
QUINONIMINE
QUINOXALINE
QUINQUENNIAD
QUINQUENNIA
QUINQUENNIAL
QUINQUENNIUM
QUINQUENNIUMS
QUINQUERTIUM
QUINQUEVIRS
QUINSYBERRIES
QUINSYBERRY
QUINTELEMENT
QUINTERNION
QUINTESSENCE
QUINTILLION
QUINTUPLING
QUINUCLIDINE
QUIPPISHNESS
QUIRITARIAN
QUIRQUINCHO
QUISLINGISM
QUISQUILIAN
QUISQUILIARY
QUISQUILIOUS
QUITCLAIMED
QUITCLAIMING
QUITTERBONE
QUIZZACIOUS
QUIZZATORIAL
QUIZZICALITY
QUIZZICALLY
QUODLIBETARY
QUODLIBETIC
QUOTABILITY
QUOTABLENESS
QUOTATIONAL
QUOTATIONIST
QUOTEWORTHY
QUOTIDIANLY
RELINQUISHED
RELINQUISHER
RELIQUARIES
REQUIESCENCE
REQUIREMENT
REQUISITELY
REQUISITION
REQUISITORY
REQUITATIVE
REQUITELESS
REQUITEMENT
RIBAUDEQUIN
SANCTILOQUENT
SCULPTURESQUE
SEMIANTIQUE
SEMIAQUATIC
SEMIQUARTILE
SEMIQUIETIST
SEQUACIOUSLY
SEQUENTIALITY
SEQUESTERED
SEQUESTERING
SEQUESTERMENT

SEQUESTRABLE
SEQUESTRANT
SEQUESTRATE
SEQUESTRATED
SEQUESTRATING
SEQUESTRATION
SEQUESTRATOR
SESQUIALTER
SESQUIALTERA
SESQUIALTERAL
SESQUINONAL
SESQUIOCTAVA
SESQUIPEDAL
SESQUIPLICATE
SESQUIQUARTA
SESQUIQUINTA
SESQUISEXTAL
SESQUITERPENE
SESQUITERTIA
SOLDATESQUE
SOLILOQUIES
SOLILOQUISE
SOLILOQUIST
SOLILOQUIZE
SOLILOQUIZED
SOLILOQUIZER
SOLILOQUIZING
SOMNILOQUENCE
SOMNILOQUENT
SOMNILOQUISM
SOMNILOQUIST
SOMNILOQUOUS
SQUABBLINGLY
SQUADRONING
SQUALIDNESS
SQUAMACEOUS
SQUAMELLATE
SQUAMIFEROUS
SQUAMIGEROUS
SQUAMOSENESS
SQUAMOUSNESS
SQUAMULATION
SQUANDERING
SQUANDERINGLY
SQUARROSELY
SQUARRULOSE
SQUASHBERRY
SQUASHINESS
SQUATTINESS
SQUATTOCRACY
SQUAWBERRIES
SQUAWFISHES
SQUAWFLOWER
SQUAWKINGLY
SQUEAKINESS
SQUEAKINGLY
SQUEAMISHLY
SQUEAMISHNESS
SQUEEGEEING
SQUEEZINGLY
SQUELCHIEST
SQUELCHINESS
SQUELCHINGLY
SQUIDGEREEN
SQUIGGLIEST
SQUILGEEING
SQUINTINGLY
SQUINTINGNESS
SQUIRARCHAL
SQUIREARCHAL
SQUIREARCHIES
SQUIREARCHY
SQUIRMINESS
SQUIRMINGLY
SQUIRRELFISH
SQUIRRELTAIL
SQUIRTINESS
SQUIRTINGLY
STATUESQUELY
STULTILOQUY
SUAVILOQUENT
SUBQUINTUPLE
SUBSEQUENCE
SUBSEQUENCY
SUBSEQUENTIAL
SUBSEQUENTLY
SYMPATHIQUE
TERLINQUAITE
TERRAQUEOUS
THUNDERSQUALL
THYMOQUINONE
TRANQUILEST
TRANQUILITY
TRANQUILIZE
TRANQUILIZER
TRANQUILIZING
TRANQUILLER
TRANQUILLEST
TRANQUILLISE
TRANQUILLITY
TRANQUILLIZE
TRANQUILLIZED
TRANQUILNESS
TRIQUETROUS
TRISTILOQUY
UBIQUITARIAN
UBIQUITARIES
UBIQUITOUSLY
UNACQUAINTED
UNADEQUATELY
UNCONQUERED
UNDERQUOTED
UNDERQUOTING
UNEQUITABLE
UNEQUITABLY
UNEQUIVOCAL
UNEQUIVOCALLY
UNFREQUENCY
UNFREQUENTED
UNFREQUENTLY
UNLIQUIDATED
UNQUALIFIED
UNQUALITIED
UNQUANTIFIED
UNQUESTIONED
UNQUESTIONING
UNQUIESCENCE
UNQUIESCENT
UNQUIETNESS
UTRAQUISTIC
VANQUISHING
VENTRILOQUAL
VENTRILOQUE
VENTRILOQUIST
VENTRILOQUY
XYLOQUINONE

POSITIONAL ORDER LIST OF WORDS OVER 10 LETTERS

QUACKISHNESS
QUACKSALVER
QUADRAGESIMAL
QUADRANGLED
QUADRANGULAR
QUADRANGULED
QUADRANTILE
QUADRAPHONIC
QUADRATICAL
QUADRENNIAL
QUADRENNIUM
QUADRENNIUMS
QUADRICINIUM
QUADRICIPITAL
QUADRICYCLE
QUADRICYCLER
QUADRIENNIUM
QUADRIFILAR
QUADRIFOCAL
QUADRIFOLIUM
QUADRIFRONS
QUADRIGAMIST
QUADRIGATUS
QUADRIHYBRID
QUADRIJUGAL
QUADRILATERAL
QUADRILLING
QUADRILLION
QUADRINOMIAL
QUADRIPAROUS
QUADRIPLANAR
QUADRIURATE
QUADRIVALENT
QUADRIVIOUS
QUADRUMANAL
QUADRUMANOUS
QUADRUPEDAL
QUADRUPEDAN
QUADRUPEDANT
QUADRUPEDATE
QUADRUPEDOUS
QUADRUPLANE
QUADRUPLATE
QUADRUPLATOR
QUADRUPLING
QUAESTIONES
QUAESTORIAL
QUAESTORIAN
QUAESTORSHIP
QUALIFIABLE
QUALIFICATION
QUALIFICATOR
QUALIFIEDLY
QUALITATIVE
QUALMISHNESS
QUANTIFYING
QUANTIMETER
QUANTITATIVE
QUANTITIVELY
QUANTIVALENT
QUANTIZATION
QUANTIZING
QUANTOMETER
QUAQUAVERSAL
QUARANTINED
QUARANTINER
QUARANTINING
QUARRELLING
QUARRELLOUS
QUARRELOUSLY
QUARRELSOME
QUARRYSTONE
QUARTERBACK
QUARTERFOIL
QUARTERLAND
QUARTERLIES
QUARTERMASTER
QUARTERNIGHT
QUARTERNION
QUARTERPACE
QUARTERSAWED
QUARTERSAWING
QUARTERSAWN
QUARTERSTAFF
QUARTERSTAVES
QUARTIPAROUS
QUATERNARIES
QUATERNARIUS
QUATERNIONIC
QUATERNITIES
QUATERTENSES
QUATREFOILED
QUATTROCENTO
QUAVERINGLY
QUEBRACHITE
QUEBRACHITOL
QUEBRADILLA
QUEENFISHES
QUEENLINESS
QUEENSBERRIES
QUEENSBERRY
QUENCHLESSLY
QUERCITANNIN
QUERCIVOROUS
QUERIMONIES
QUERIMONIOUS
QUERULENTIAL
QUERULOSITY
QUERULOUSLY
QUESTIONABLE
QUESTIONABLY
QUESTIONARIES
QUESTIONARY
QUESTIONING
QUESTIONIST
QUESTIONLESS
QUESTIONNAIRE
QUESTMONGER
QUICKENANCE
QUICKENBEAM
QUICKSILVER
QUICKSILVERY
QUIDDITATIVE
QUIESCENTLY
QUIINACEOUS
QUILLFISHES
QUINALDINIC
QUINALDINIUM
QUINAMICINE
QUINAMIDINE
QUINANISOLE
QUINATOXINE
QUINAZOLINE
QUINCUNCIAL
QUINCUNXIAL
QUINDECAGON
QUINDECEMVIR
QUINDECEMVIRI
QUINDECIMVIR
QUINHYDRONE
QUINISEXTINE
QUINOIDATION
QUINOLINIUM
QUINOLOGIST
QUINONIMINE
QUINOXALINE
QUINQUENNIA
QUINQUENNIAD
QUINQUENNIAL
QUINQUENNIUM
QUINQUENNIUMS
QUINQUERTIUM
QUINQUEVIRS
QUINSYBERRIES
QUINSYBERRY
QUINTELEMENT
QUINTERNION
QUINTESSENCE
QUINTILLION
QUINTUPLING
QUINUCLIDINE
QUIPPISHNESS
QUIRITARIAN
QUIRQUINCHO
QUISLINGISM
QUISQUILIAN
QUISQUILIARY
QUISQUILIOUS
QUITCLAIMED
QUITCLAIMING
QUITTERBONE
QUIZZACIOUS
QUIZZATORIAL
QUIZZICALITY
QUIZZICALLY
QUODLIBETARY
QUODLIBETIC
QUOTABILITY
QUOTABLENESS
QUOTATIONAL
QUOTATIONIST
QUOTEWORTHY
QUOTIDIANLY

AQUACULTURAL
AQUACULTURE
AQUAEMANALE
AQUAEMANALIA
AQUAFORTIST
AQUAPLANING
AQUAPUNCTURE
AQUARELLIST
AQUATICALLY
AQUATIVENESS
AQUEOGLACIAL
AQUEOIGNEOUS
AQUEOUSNESS
AQUICULTURAL
AQUICULTURE
AQUOTIZATION
EQUABLENESS
EQUALITARIAN
EQUALIZATION
EQUANIMOUSLY
EQUATIONALLY
EQUATIONISM
EQUATIONIST
EQUATORIALLY
EQUESTRIENNE
EQUIDISTANCE
EQUIDISTANT
EQUIDISTANTLY
EQUIDIURNAL
EQUIFORMITY
EQUIGRANULAR

EQUILATERAL
EQUILIBRANT
EQUILIBRATE
EQUILIBRATED
EQUILIBRATING
EQUILIBRATION
EQUILIBRATIVE
EQUILIBRATOR
EQUILIBRATORY
EQUILIBRIAL
EQUILIBRIATE
EQUILIBRIOUS
EQUILIBRIST
EQUILIBRISTAT
EQUILIBRISTIC
EQUILIBRITY
EQUILIBRIUM
EQUILIBRIUMS
EQUILIBRIZE
EQUIMOLECULAR
EQUIMOMENTAL
EQUIMULTIPLE
EQUINANGULAR
EQUINOCTIAL
EQUINOCTIAL
EQUINOCTIALLY
EQUINOVARUS
EQUIPARATION
EQUIPARTILE
EQUIPARTITION
EQUIPOISING
EQUIPOLLENCE
EQUIPOLLENCY
EQUIPOLLENT
EQUIPOLLENTLY
EQUIPONDERANT
EQUIPONDERAT
EQUIPOSTILE
EQUIPOTENTIAL
EQUIPROBABLE
EQUISETACEOUS
EQUISONANCE
EQUIVALENCE
EQUIVALENCED
EQUIVALENCY
EQUIVALENTLY
EQUIVOCALITY
EQUIVOCATED
EQUIVOCATING
EQUIVOCATION
EQUIVOCATOR
EQUIVOCATORY
EQUIVOLUMINAL
SQUABBLINGLY
SQUADRONING
SQUALIDNESS
SQUAMACEOUS
SQUAMELLATE
SQUAMIFEROUS
SQUAMIGEROUS
SQUAMOSENESS
SQUAMOUSNESS
SQUAMULATION
SQUANDERING
SQUANDERINGLY
SQUARROSELY
SQUARRULOSE
SQUASHBERRY
SQUASHINESS
SQUATTINESS
SQUATTOCRACY
SQUAWBERRIES
SQUAWFISHES
SQUAWFLOWER
SQUAWKINGLY
SQUEAKINESS
SQUEAKINGLY
SQUEAMISHLY
SQUEAMISHNESS
SQUEEGEEING
SQUEEZINGLY
SQUELCHIEST
SQUELCHINESS
SQUELCHINGLY
SQUIDGEREEN
SQUIGGLIEST
SQUILGEEING
SQUINTINGLY
SQUINTINGNESS
SQUIRARCHAL
SQUIREARCHAL
SQUIREARCHIES
SQUIREARCHY
SQUIRMINESS
SQUIRMINGLY
SQUIRRELFISH
SQUIRRELTAIL
SQUIRTINESS
SQUIRTINGLY

ACQUAINTANCE
ACQUAINTANT
ACQUIESCENCE
ACQUIESCENT
ACQUIESCING
ACQUIREMENT
ACQUISITION
ACQUISITIVE
ACQUISITIVELY
ACQUITTANCE
BIQUADRANTAL
BIQUADRATIC
BIQUARTERLY
COQUECIGRUE
COQUETTISHLY
ESQUAMULOSE
EXQUISITELY
EXQUISITENESS
EXQUISITISM
EXQUISITIVELY
INQUAINTANCE
INQUARTATION
INQUIETNESS
INQUILINISM
INQUILINITY
INQUILINOUS
INQUINATING
INQUINATION
INQUIRATION
INQUIRINGLY
INQUISITION
INQUISITIONAL
INQUISITIVE
INQUISITORIAL
INQUISITORY
JEQUIRITIES
LIQUEFACIENT
LIQUEFACTION
LIQUEFACTIVE
LIQUEFIABLE
LIQUESCENCE
LIQUESCENCY
LIQUIDAMBAR
LIQUIDAMBER
LIQUIDATING
LIQUIDATION
LIQUIDIZING
LIQUIDOGENIC
LIQUORISHLY
LIQUORISHNESS
LOQUACIOUSLY
PIQUANTNESS
REQUIESCENCE
REQUIREMENT
REQUISITELY
REQUISITION
REQUISITORY
REQUITATIVE
REQUITELESS
REQUITEMENT
SEQUACIOUSLY
SEQUENTIALITY
SEQUESTERED
SEQUESTERING
SEQUESTERMENT
SEQUESTRABLE
SEQUESTRANT
SEQUESTRATE
SEQUESTRATED
SEQUESTRATING
SEQUESTRATION
SEQUESTRATOR
UNQUALIFIED
UNQUALITIED
UNQUANTIFIED
UNQUESTIONED
UNQUESTIONING
UNQUIESCENCE
UNQUIESCENT
UNQUIETNESS

ABSQUATULATE
ADEQUATENESS
BANQUETEERING
BARQUENTINE
BECQUERELITE
BOUQUETIERE
BOUQUINISTE
CHEQUERBOARD
CHEQUERWISE
CHEQUERWORK
CINQUECENTO
CLIQUISHNESS
COEQUALNESS
CONQUERABLE
CONQUERINGLY
CONQUINAMINE
CONQUISTADOR
CONQUISTADORES
CROQUIGNOLE
DESQUAMATED
DESQUAMATING
DESQUAMATION
DESQUAMATIVE
DESQUAMATORY
DISQUALIFIED
DISQUIETEDLY
DISQUIETING
DISQUIETUDE
DISQUIPARANT
DISQUISITED
DISQUISITING
DISQUISITION
DISQUISITIVE
DISQUISITOR
DISQUISITORY
ELOQUENTIAL
ETIQUETTICAL
FREQUENCIES
FREQUENTABLE
FREQUENTAGE
FREQUENTATION
FREQUENTATIVE
FREQUENTING
FREQUENTNESS
INEQUALITIES
INEQUALNESS
INEQUITABLE
INEQUITABLY
INEQUIVALVE
INIQUITABLE
INIQUITOUSLY
ISOQUINOLINE
LACQUERWORK
MARQUETERIE
MARQUISETTE
MARQUISOTTE
MASQUERADED
MASQUERADER
MASQUERADING
MILQUETOAST
MISQUOTATION
MOSQUITOBILL
MUSQUASHROOT
MUSQUASHWEED
NESQUEHONITE
OUTQUESTION
OXYQUINOLINE
PASQUEFLOWER
PASQUILLANT
PASQUINADED
PASQUINADER
PASQUINADING
PERQUISITION
PERQUISITOR
PROQUAESTOR
QUAQUAVERSAL
SESQUIALTER
SESQUIALTERA
SESQUIALTERAL
SESQUINONAL
SESQUIOCTAVA
SESQUIPEDAL
SESQUIPLICATE
SESQUIQUARTA
SESQUIQUINTA
SESQUISEXTAL
SESQUITERPENE
SESQUITERTIA
SUBQUINTUPLE
TRIQUETROUS
UBIQUITARIAN
UBIQUITARIES
UBIQUITOUSLY
UNEQUITABLE
UNEQUITABLY
UNEQUIVOCAL
UNEQUIVOCALLY
VANQUISHING

ANTIQUARIAN
ANTIQUARIES
ANTIQUARISM
ANTIQUATING
ANTIQUATION
ANTIQUENESS
ANTIQUITIES
BRUSQUENESS
COLOQUINTIDA
DELIQUESCED
DELIQUESCENT
DELIQUESCING
DISEQUALIZE
DUROQUINONE
FOREQUARTER
HEADQUARTER
HEADQUARTERS
HINDQUARTER
HINDQUARTERS
ILLIQUATION
MERIQUINONE
MERIQUINONIC
MOUSQUETAIRE
OBLIQUATION
OBLIQUENESS
OBLIQUITIES
OBLIQUITOUS
OBSEQUIOUSLY
PARAQUADRATE
PEREQUITATE
QUINQUENNIA
QUINQUENNIAD
QUINQUENNIAL
QUINQUENNIUM
QUINQUENNIUMS
QUINQUERTIUM
QUINQUEVIRS
QUIRQUINCHO
QUISQUILIAN
QUISQUILIARY
QUISQUILIOUS
RELIQUARIES
SEMIQUARTILE
SEMIQUIETIST
TRANQUILEST
TRANQUILITY
TRANQUILIZE
TRANQUILIZER
TRANQUILIZING
TRANQUILLER
TRANQUILLEST
TRANQUILLISE
TRANQUILLITY
TRANQUILLIZE
TRANQUILLIZED
TRANQUILNESS
UNACQUAINTED
UNLIQUIDATED
UTRAQUISTIC
XYLOQUINONE

APPLIQUEING
CHYMAQUEOUS
COLLIQUATION
COLLIQUATIVE
COLLOQUIALLY
COLLOQUIZED
COLLOQUIZING
CONSEQUENCE
CONSEQUENTIAL
CONSEQUENTLY
DELINQUENCIES
DELINQUENCY
DELINQUENTLY
DISACQUAINT
EARTHQUAKED
EARTHQUAKEN
EARTHQUAKING
FOURSQUARELY
HARLEQUINADE
HARLEQUINIC
HARLEQUINIZE
HYDROQUININE
HYDROQUINONE
INADEQUATELY
INADEQUATION
INELOQUENCE
INFREQUENCE
INFREQUENCY
PALANQUINED
PALANQUINING
PHENOQUINONE
PREREQUISITE
RELINQUISHED
RELINQUISHER
SEMIAQUATIC
SUBSEQUENCE
SUBSEQUENCY
SUBSEQUENTIAL
SUBSEQUENTLY
TERRAQUEOUS
THYMOQUINONE
UNADEQUATELY
UNCONQUERED
UNDERQUOTED

UNDERQUOTING
UNFREQUENCY
UNFREQUENTED
UNFREQUENTLY

ALTILOQUENCE
ALTILOQUENT
ANTHRAQUINOL
ARABESQUELY
ARABESQUERIE
BURLESQUELY
BURLESQUING
FATILOQUENT
GROTESQUELY
GROTESQUERIE
GROTESQUERY
LONGINQUITY
MONCHIQUITE
OMNILOQUENT
PLASMOQUINE
POLYLOQUENT
PRECONQUEST
PROPINQUANT
PROPINQUITY
PROPINQUOUS
SESQUIQUARTA
SESQUIQUINTA
SOLILOQUIES
SOLILOQUISE
SOLILOQUIST
SOLILOQUIZE
SOLILOQUIZED
SOLILOQUIZER
SOLILOQUIZING
TERLINQUAITE
ANTIMASQUER
BLOTTESQUELY
BREVILOQUENT
DENTILOQUIST
DULCILOQUENT
INCONSEQUENCE
INCONSEQUENT
MAGNILOQUENT
MULTILOQUENT
MULTILOQUOUS
PAUCILOQUENT
PRETEREQUINE
PSEUDOAQUATIC
RIBAUDEQUIN
SOMNILOQUENCE
SOMNILOQUENT
SOMNILOQUISM
SOMNILOQUIST
SOMNILOQUOUS
STATUESQUELY
SUAVILOQUENT

BARBARESQUE
DISCOTHEQUE
FORMALESQUE
GIGANTESQUE
GORGONESQUE
GRANDILOQUENT
OSTEOPLAQUE
PICTURESQUE
PLATERESQUE
SANCTILOQUENT
SEMIANTIQUE
SOLDATESQUE
STULTILOQUY
SYMPATHIQUE
THUNDERSQUALL
TRISTILOQUY
VENTRILOQUAL
VENTRILOQUE
VENTRILOQUIST
VENTRILOQUY

AMPHORILOQUY
BOUDOIRESQUE
BRONCHILOQUY
CHIVALRESQUE
CONTRAMARQUE
NATURALESQUE
PECTORILOQUE
PECTORILOQUY

SCULPTURESQUE

SCORING ORDER LIST OF WORDS OVER 10 LETTERS

35
EXQUISITIVELY

34
QUIZZICALITY

33
HARLEQUINIZE
QUICKSILVERY
QUIZZICALLY
SQUEEZINGLY

32
CHEQUERWORK
SOLILOQUIZING
TRANQUILIZING

31
AMPHORILOQUY
BRONCHILOQUY
LIQUIDIZING
SOLILOQUIZED
SQUAWKINGLY

30
ACQUISITIVELY
AQUOTIZATION
CHYMAQUEOUS
DISEQUALIZE
EQUALIZATION
EXQUISITELY
MUSQUASHWEED
QUACKISHNESS
QUANTIZATION
QUICKENBEAM
QUINDECEMVIRI
QUIZZACIOUS
SOLILOQUIZER
SQUELCHINGLY
SYMPATHIQUE
TRANQUILIZER
TRANQUILLIZE
UNEQUIVOCALLY
XYLOQUINONE

29
CHEQUERBOARD
CHIVALRESQUE
COQUETTISHLY
EARTHQUAKING
EQUIVOCATORY
EXQUISITENESS
EXQUISITISM
LACQUERWORK
LIQUEFACTIVE
PASQUEFLOWER
QUACKSALVER
QUADRAPHONIC
QUADRICYCLER
QUADRIJUGAL
QUANTIZING
QUENCHLESSLY
QUICKSILVER
QUINAZOLINE
QUINCUNXIAL
QUINDECEMVIR
QUINDECIMVIR
QUIZZATORIAL
QUOTEWORTHY
SOLILOQUIZE
SQUABBLINGLY
SQUAWFISHES
SQUAWFLOWER
THYMOQUINONE
TRANQUILIZE

28
CHEQUERWISE
EARTHQUAKED
EQUIFORMITY
EQUIPOLLENCY
FREQUENTATIVE
HYDROQUININE
HYDROQUINONE
PECTORILOQUY
QUADRICYCLE
QUARTERBACK
QUEBRACHITOL
QUICKENANCE
QUINISEXTINE
QUINSYBERRY
QUIPPISHNESS
SESQUISEXTAL
SQUASHBERRY
SQUATTOCRACY
SQUEAKINGLY
SQUEAMISHLY
SQUIREARCHY
UNFREQUENCY

27
CONQUERINGLY
DESQUAMATIVE
DESQUAMATORY
EARTHQUAKEN
EQUILIBRATIVE
EQUILIBRATORY
EQUINOCTIALLY
EQUIPOLLENTLY
EQUIPROBABLE
EQUIVALENCED
EQUIVOCATING
EQUIVOLUMINAL
FOURSQUARELY
JEQUIRITIES
LIQUESCENCY
MONCHIQUITE
PROPINQUITY
PSEUDOAQUATIC
QUADRICIPITAL
QUADRIFOLIUM
QUALIFICATION
QUALIFIEDLY
QUANTIFYING
QUANTITIVELY
QUARTERSTAFF
QUAVERINGLY
QUEBRACHITE
QUINATOXINE
QUINHYDRONE
QUINOXALINE
QUINSYBERRIES
QUODLIBETARY
SQUANDERINGLY
SQUEAMISHNESS
SQUIREARCHIES
SQUIRRELFISH
SUBSEQUENCY
UNFREQUENTLY
VANQUISHING

26
BLOTTESQUELY
BREVILOQUENT
CLIQUISHNESS
COLLIQUATIVE
COLLOQUIALLY
CONSEQUENTLY
DELINQUENCY
DISCOTHEQUE
DISQUALIFIED
DISQUIETEDLY
EQUANIMOUSLY
EQUIDISTANTLY
EQUILIBRISTIC
EQUIMOLECULAR
EQUIVOCATED
EQUIVOCATION
FREQUENTABLE
LIQUEFACIENT
LIQUEFACTION
LIQUORISHLY
LOQUACIOUSLY
MUSQUASHROOT
OBSEQUIOUSLY
PHENOQUINONE
QUADRAGESIMAL
QUADRICINIUM
QUADRIFOCAL
QUAESTORSHIP
QUALIFICATOR
QUALMISHNESS
QUARTERSAWING
QUEENFISHES
QUERCIVOROUS
QUESTIONABLY
QUIDDITATIVE
QUILLFISHES
QUITCLAIMING
SCULPTURESQUE
SEQUACIOUSLY
SESQUIOCTAVA
SESQUIPLICATE
SOMNILOQUENCE
SQUAMIFEROUS
SQUAWBERRIES
SQUELCHINESS
SQUIREARCHAL
SQUIRMINGLY
SUBSEQUENTLY
THUNDERSQUALL
UBIQUITOUSLY
VENTRILOQUY

25
ACQUAINTANCE
ACQUIESCING
ACQUISITIVE
APPLIQUEING
AQUAPUNCTURE
AQUATICALLY
ARABESQUELY
BANQUETEERING
BECQUERELITE
BIQUADRATIC
BIQUARTERLY
BURLESQUELY
CONQUINAMINE
CONTRAMARQUE
COQUECIGRUE
DELINQUENCIES
DELINQUENTLY
DELIQUESCING
DESQUAMATING
DISQUISITIVE
DISQUISITORY
EQUILIBRITY
EQUILIBRIUMS
EQUIMOMENTAL
EQUIMULTIPLE
EQUIPOLLENCE
EQUIPONDERANT
EQUIVALENCE
EQUIVOCATOR
FORMALESQUE
FREQUENCIES
FREQUENTATION
HARLEQUINADE
HARLEQUINIC
HEADQUARTERS
HINDQUARTERS
LIQUEFIABLE
LIQUIDAMBAR
LIQUIDAMBER
LIQUIDOGENIC
LIQUORISHNESS
MASQUERADING
MERIQUINONIC
MOSQUITOBILL
PASQUINADING
PAUCILOQUENT
PECTORILOQUE
POLYLOQUENT
QUADRIGAMIST
QUADRIVALENT
QUADRUPEDANT
QUADRUPEDATE
QUADRUPEDOUS
QUALIFIABLE
QUARTERNIGHT
QUARTERSAWED
QUARTERSTAVES
QUATREFOILED
QUEENSBERRY
QUIESCENTLY
QUITCLAIMED
QUODLIBETIC
QUOTABILITY
RELINQUISHED
REQUIESCENCE
SEQUENTIALITY
SOMNILOQUISM
SQUELCHIEST
SQUIRARCHAL
SUBQUINTUPLE

UNADE**Q**UATELY
UNE**Q**UITABLY
UNE**Q**UIVOCAL
UNFRE**Q**UENTED
UN**Q**UANTIFIED
UN**Q**UIESCENCE
VENTRILO**Q**UIST

24

AC**Q**UIESCENCE
AC**Q**UIESCENT
AC**Q**UIREMENT
AC**Q**UITTANCE
ANTHRA**Q**UINOL
A**Q**UATIVENESS
A**Q**UEOGLACIAL
BARBARES**Q**UE
BI**Q**UADRANTAL
BOUDOIRES**Q**UE
CIN**Q**UECENTO
COLO**Q**UINTIDA
CON**Q**UERABLE
CON**Q**UISTADOR
CONSE**Q**UENCE
CONSE**Q**UENTIAL
DELI**Q**UESCED
DELI**Q**UESCENT
DES**Q**UAMATED
DES**Q**UAMATION
DIS**Q**UIPARANT
DULCILO**Q**UENT
E**Q**UATIONALLY
E**Q**UATORIALLY
E**Q**UIDISTANCE
E**Q**UILIBRATED
E**Q**UILIBRATION
E**Q**UILIBRISTAT
E**Q**UILIBRIUM
E**Q**UIPARTITION
E**Q**UIPONDERAT
E**Q**UIPOTENTIAL
E**Q**UISETACEOUS
FRE**Q**UENTAGE
FRE**Q**UENTING
FRE**Q**UENTNESS
GRANDILO**Q**UENT
GROTES**Q**UELY
GROTES**Q**UERY
HEAD**Q**UARTER
HIND**Q**UARTER
IN**Q**UIRINGLY
LI**Q**UESCENCE
LONGIN**Q**UITY
MAGNILO**Q**UENT
MAS**Q**UERADED
NES**Q**UEHONITE
PALAN**Q**UINING
PARA**Q**UADRATE
PAS**Q**UINADED
PICTURES**Q**UE
PLASMO**Q**UINE
PRECON**Q**UEST
PROPIN**Q**UANT
PROPIN**Q**UOUS
QUADRANGULED
QUADRENNIUMS
QUADRIENNIUM
QUADRIFILAR
QUADRIFRONS
QUADRINOMIAL
QUADRIPAROUS
QUADRIPLANAR
QUADRIVIOUS
QUADRUMANOUS
QUADRUPEDAL
QUADRUPEDAN
QUADRUPLATOR
QUADRUPLING
QUANTITATIVE
QUANTIVALENT
QUARRELOUSLY
QUARTERMASTER
QUARTERPACE
QUEENSBERRIES
QUINALDINIUM
QUINAMICINE
QUINCUNCIAL
QUINDECAGON
QUINUCLIDINE
QUIR**Q**UINCHO
QUOTIDIANLY
RELIN**Q**UISHER
SANCTILO**Q**UENT
SEMIA**Q**UATIC
SE**Q**UESTERMENT
SES**Q**UITERPENE
S**Q**UAMACEOUS
S**Q**UAMIGEROUS
S**Q**UEAKINESS
S**Q**UINTINGLY
S**Q**UIRTINGLY
STATUES**Q**UELY
SUAVILO**Q**UENT
SUBSE**Q**UENCE
SUBSE**Q**UENTIAL
TRAN**Q**UILLITY
UNAC**Q**UAINTED
UN**Q**UALIFIED
VENTRILO**Q**UAL

23

ABS**Q**UATULATE
ALTILO**Q**UENCE
A**Q**UACULTURAL
A**Q**UAEMANALIA
A**Q**UAFORTIST
A**Q**UAPLANING
A**Q**UICULTURAL
ARABES**Q**UERIE
BURLES**Q**UING
COLLI**Q**UATION
CRO**Q**UIGNOLE
DISAC**Q**UAINT
DIS**Q**UISITING
E**Q**UILIBRATOR
E**Q**UILIBRIATE
E**Q**UILIBRIOUS
E**Q**UINOVARUS
E**Q**UIPARATION
ETI**Q**UETTICAL
FATILO**Q**UENT
FORE**Q**UARTER
INELO**Q**UENCE
IN**Q**UISITIVE
IN**Q**UISITORY
MAS**Q**UERADER
MIS**Q**UOTATION
MOUS**Q**UETAIRE
MULTILO**Q**UENT
MULTILO**Q**UOUS
PALAN**Q**UINED
PAS**Q**UINADER
PER**Q**UISITION
PRERE**Q**UISITE
PRETERE**Q**UINE
QUADRANGLED
QUADRANGULAR
QUADRATICAL
QUADRENNIUM
QUADRILATERAL
QUADRUMANAL
QUADRUPLANE
QUADRUPLATE
QUALITATIVE
QUA**Q**UAVERSAL
QUARRYSTONE
QUARTERFOIL
QUARTERSAWN
QUARTIPAROUS
QUATERNIONIC
QUATTROCENTO
QUEBRADILLA
QUERCITANNIN
QUERIMONIOUS
QUERULOSITY
QUERULOUSLY
QUESTIONABLE
QUESTIONARY
QUESTMONGER
QUINALDINIC
QUINAMIDINE
QUIN**Q**UENNIUMS
QUINTELEMENT
QUINTESSENCE
QUINTUPLING
QUISLINGISM
QUIS**Q**UILIARY
QUOTABLENESS
RE**Q**UISITELY
RE**Q**UISITORY
RE**Q**UITATIVE
RIBAUDE**Q**UIN
SEMI**Q**UARTILE
SEMI**Q**UIETIST
SE**Q**UESTRABLE
SE**Q**UESTRATING
SES**Q**UIPEDAL
SOMNILO**Q**UENT
SOMNILO**Q**UIST
SOMNILO**Q**UOUS
S**Q**UAMOSENESS
S**Q**UAMOUSNESS
S**Q**UAMULATION
S**Q**UARROSELY
S**Q**UASHINESS
S**Q**UINTINGNESS
STULTILO**Q**UY
TRAN**Q**UILITY
TRISTILO**Q**UY
UBI**Q**UITARIAN
UBI**Q**UITARIES
UNCON**Q**UERED
UNDER**Q**UOTING
UNLI**Q**UIDATED
UN**Q**UESTIONING
VENTRILO**Q**UE

22

AC**Q**UAINTANT
AC**Q**UISITION
ADE**Q**UATENESS
ANTIMAS**Q**UER
ANTI**Q**UARISM
A**Q**UACULTURE
A**Q**UAEMANALE
A**Q**UEOIGNEOUS
A**Q**UICULTURE
BAR**Q**UENTINE
BOU**Q**UETIERE
BOU**Q**UINISTE
BRUS**Q**UENESS
COE**Q**UALNESS
DENTILO**Q**UIST
DIS**Q**UIETING
DIS**Q**UIETUDE
DIS**Q**UISITED
DIS**Q**UISITION
E**Q**UABLENESS
E**Q**UATIONISM
E**Q**UINANGULAR
E**Q**UIGRANULAR
E**Q**UILIBRANT
E**Q**UILIBRATE
E**Q**UILIBRIAL
E**Q**UILIBRIST
E**Q**UINOCTIAL
E**Q**UINOCTIAL
E**Q**UIPARTILE
E**Q**UIPOLLENT
E**Q**UIPOSTILE
E**Q**UISONANCE
ES**Q**UAMULOSE
GIGANTES**Q**UE
GORGONES**Q**UE
GROTES**Q**UERIE
LI**Q**UIDATING
MAR**Q**UETERIE
MAR**Q**UISETTE
MAR**Q**UISOTTE
MERI**Q**UINONE
MIL**Q**UETOAST
OBLI**Q**UATION
OBLI**Q**UENESS
OBLI**Q**UITIES
OBLI**Q**UITOUS
OMNILO**Q**UENT
OSTEOPLA**Q**UE
PAS**Q**UILLANT
PERE**Q**UITATE
PER**Q**UISITOR
PI**Q**UANTNESS
PLATERES**Q**UE
PRO**Q**UAESTOR
QUADRIGATUS
QUADRILLING
QUANTIMETER
QUANTOMETER
QUARANTINING
QUARRELSOME
QUERIMONIES
QUESTIONARIES
QUESTIONNAIRE
QUIINACEOUS
QUINOIDATION
QUINOLINIUM
QUINONIMINE
QUIN**Q**UENNIUM
QUIN**Q**UERTIUM
QUIN**Q**UEVIRS
QUITTERBONE
RE**Q**UIREMENT
RE**Q**UITEMENT
SEMIANTI**Q**UE
SE**Q**UESTERING
SE**Q**UESTRATED
SE**Q**UESTRATION
SES**Q**UIALTERAL
S**Q**UADRONING
S**Q**UAMELLATE
S**Q**UANDERING
S**Q**UEEGEEING
S**Q**UIDGEREEN
S**Q**UIGGLIEST
S**Q**UILGEEING
S**Q**UIRMINESS
UNDER**Q**UOTED
UNE**Q**UITABLE
UN**Q**UESTIONED
UN**Q**UIESCENT
UTRA**Q**UISTIC

21

ANTI**Q**UATING
DIS**Q**UISITOR
DURO**Q**UINONE
E**Q**UALITARIAN
E**Q**UESTRIENNE
E**Q**UIDISTANT
E**Q**UIDIURNAL
ISO**Q**UINOLINE
LI**Q**UIDATION
NATURALES**Q**UE
QUADRANTILE
QUADRENNIAL
QUADRILLION
QUADRIURATE
QUARANTINED
QUARRELLING
QUARTERLAND
QUATERNARIES
QUATERNARIUS
QUATERNITIES
QUATERTENSES
QUERULENTIAL
QUESTIONING
QUESTIONLESS
QUINOLOGIST
QUIN**Q**UENNIAD
QUOTATIONIST
SE**Q**UESTERED
SE**Q**UESTRATOR
SES**Q**UIALTERA
SOLDATES**Q**UE
SES**Q**UITERTIA
S**Q**UALIDNESS
S**Q**UIRRELTAIL
TERLIN**Q**UAITE
TRAN**Q**UILLEST
TRAN**Q**UILLISE
TRAN**Q**UILNESS
UN**Q**UALITIED

20

ALTILO**Q**UENT
ANTI**Q**UARIAN
ANTI**Q**UARIES
ANTI**Q**UATION
ANTI**Q**UENESS
ANTI**Q**UITIES
A**Q**UARELLIST
A**Q**UEOUSNESS
ELO**Q**UENTIAL
E**Q**UATIONIST
E**Q**UILATERAL
ILLI**Q**UATION
IN**Q**UIRATION
OUT**Q**UESTION
QUAESTIONES
QUAESTORIAL
QUAESTORIAN
QUARANTINER
QUARRELLOUS
QUARTERLIES
QUARTERNION
QUEENLINESS
QUESTIONIST
QUINANISOLE
QUIN**Q**UENNIAL
QUINTERNION
QUINTILLION
QUIRITARIAN
QUIS**Q**UILIOUS
QUOTATIONAL
RELI**Q**UARIES
RE**Q**UISITION
RE**Q**UITELESS
SE**Q**UESTRANT
SE**Q**UESTRATE
SES**Q**UIALTER
SES**Q**UI**Q**UARTA
SES**Q**UI**Q**UINTA
SES**Q**UINONAL
SOLILO**Q**UIES
SOLILO**Q**UISE
SOLILO**Q**UIST
S**Q**UATTINESS
S**Q**UIRTINESS
TERRA**Q**UEOUS
TRAN**Q**UILEST
TRAN**Q**UILLER
TRI**Q**UETROUS
UN**Q**UIETNESS

19

QUIN**Q**UENNIA
QUIS**Q**UILIAN

High-Scoring Words Containing

X

2-3 LETTER WORDS

ALPHABETICAL ORDER

ARX
AUX
AX
AXE
BOX
COX
DIX
DUX
EX
FAX
FIX
FOX
HEX
HOX
KEX
LAX
LEX
LOX
LUX
MAX
MIX
MUX
NIX
OX
OXO
OXY
PAX
PIX
POX
PYX
RAX
REX
RIX
ROX
RUX
SAX
SEX
SIX
SOX
TAX
TOX
TUX
VEX
VIX
VOX
WAX
WOX
XAT
YEX
YOX
ZAX

POSITIONAL ORDER

XAT

AX
AXE
EX
EXUL
OX
OXO
OXY

ARX
AUX
BOX
DIX
DUX
COX
FAX
FIX
FOX
HEX
HOX
KEX
LAX
LEX
LOX
LUX
MAX
MIX
MUX
NIX
PAX
PIX
POX
PYX
RAX
REX
RIX
ROX
RUX
SAX
SEX
SIX
SOX
TAX
TOX
TUX
VEX
VIX
VOX
WAX
WOX
YEX
YOX
ZAX

SCORING ORDER

19
ZAX

15
PYX

14
KEX

13
FAX
FIX
FOX
HEX
HOX
OXY
VEX
VIX
VOX
WAX
WOX
YEX
YOX

12
BOX
COX
MAX
MIX
MUX
PAX
PIX
POX

11
DIX
DUX

10
ARX
AUX
AXE
LAX
LEX
LOX
LUX
NIX
OXO
RAX
REX
RIX
ROX
RUX
SAX
SEX
SIX
SOX
TAX
TOX
TUX
XAT

9
AX
EX
OX

ALPHABETICAL LIST OF 4-LETTER WORDS

ABOX
APEX
AXAL
AXAN
AXED
AXEL
AXES
AXIL
AXIS
AXLE
AXON
BAXA
BOXY
CALX
CAXI
COAX
COIX
COXA
COXY
CRUX
DIXI
DIXY
DOUX
DOXY
EAUX
ELIX
ESOX
EXAM
EXEC
EXES
EXIT
EXON
EXUL
FAEX
FALX
FAUX
FIXT
FIXY
FLAX
FLEX
FLIX
FLUX
FOXY
GREX
HEXT
HOAX
IBEX
ILEX
JEUX
JINX
JYNX
KEXY
KREX
LANX
LUXE
LYNX
MAUX
MINX
MIXT
MIXY
MOXA
MYXA
MYXO
NEXT
NIXE
NIXY
NOIX
NOXA
OBEX
ONYX
ORYX
OXAN
OXEA
OXEN
OXER
OXID
OXIM
OXYL
PIXY
PLEX
POXY
PREX
PRIX
PROX
PUXY
QUAX
RIXY
ROUX
ROXY
SAEX
SEAX
SEXT
SEXY
SPEX
TAXI
TAXY
TEXT
TOXA
UROX
WAXY
WOXE
WROX
XEME
XYST

POSITIONAL ORDER LIST OF 4-LETTER WORDS

XEME
XYST

AXAL
AXAN
AXED
AXEL
AXES
AXIL
AXIS
AXLE
AXON
EXAM
EXEC
EXES
EXIT
EXON
OXAN
OXEA
OXEN
OXER
OXID
OXIM
OXYL

BAXA
BOXY
CAXI
COXA
COXY
DIXI
DIXY
DOXY
FIXT
FIXY
FOXY
HEXT
KEXY
LUXE
MIXT
MIXY
MOXA
MYXA
MYXO
NEXT
NIXE
NIXY
NOXA
PIXY
POXY
PUXY
RIXY
ROXY
SEXT
SEXY
TAXI
TAXY
TEXT
TOXA
WAXY
WOXE

ABOX
APEX
CALX
COAX
COIX
CRUX
DOUX
EAUX
ELIX
ESOX
FAEX
FALX
FAUX
FLAX
FLEX
FLIX
FLUX
GREX
HOAX
IBEX
ILEX
JEUX
JINX
JYNX
KREX
LANX
LYNX
MAUX
MINX
NOIX
OBEX
ONYX
ORYX
PLEX
PREX
PRIX
PROX
QUAX
ROUX
SAEX
SEAX
SPEX
UROX
WROX

SCORING ORDER LIST OF 4-LETTER WORDS

21
JYNX

20
QUAX

18
JEUX
JINX
KEXY

17
FIXY
FOXY
WAXY

16
BOXY
COXY
MIXY
MYXA
MYXO
PIXY
POXY
PUXY

15
DIXY
DOXY
KREX

14
FAEX
FALX
FAUX
FIXT
FLAX
FLEX
FLIX
FLUX
HEXT
HOAX
LYNX
NIXY
ONYX
ORYX
OXYL
RIXY
ROXY
SEXY
TAXY
WOXE
WROX
XYST

13
ABOX
APEX
BAXA
CALX
CAXI
COAX
COIX
COXA
CRUX
EXAM
EXEC
IBEX
MAUX
MINX
MIXT
MOXA
OBEX
OXIM
PLEX
PREX
PRIX
PROX
SPEX
XEME

12
AXED
DIXI
DOUX
GREX
OXID

11
AXAL
AXAN
AXEL
AXES
AXIL
AXIS

AXLE
AXON
EAUX
ELIX
ESOX
EXES
EXIT
EXON
EXUL
ILEX
LANX
LUXE
NEXT
NIXE
NOIX
NOXA
OXAN
OXEA
OXEN
OXER
ROUX
SAEX
SEAX
SEXT
TAXI
TEXT
TOXA
UROX

ALPHABETICAL LIST OF 5-LETTER WORDS

ADDAX
ADFIX
ADMIX
ADNEX
ADOXY
AFFIX
ALPAX
AMPYX
ANNEX
ATAXY
AUXIN
AXIAL
AXILE
AXINE
AXIOM
AXION
AXITE
AXLED
AXMAN
AXMEN
AXOID
AXONE
AZOXY
BERYX
BIXIN
BORAX
BOXEN
BOXER
BOXES
BOXTY
BRAXY
BUXOM
CAPAX
CAREX
CAXON
CHOUX
CIMEX
COAXY
CODEX
COXAE
COXAL
CYLIX
DEFIX
DESEX
DEVEX
DEWAX
DIOXY
DIXIE
DIXIT
DONAX
DOXIE
DRUXY
DURAX
DUXES
EMBOX
EPOXY
EXACT
EXALT
EXCEL
EXCUR
EXEAT
EXEDE
EXEEM
EXEME
EXERT
EXIDO
EXIES
EXILE
EXINE
EXIST
EXITE
EXLEX
EXODE
EXODY
EXORN
EXPEL
EXTER
EXTOL
EXTRA
EXTRE
EXUDE
EXULT
EXURB
EXUST
EXUTE
FAULX
FAXED
FIXED
FIXER
FLAXY
FOXED
FOXER
FOXES
GULIX
HELIX
HEXAD
HEXER
HEXIS
HEXYL
HUXEN
HYRAX
IMMIX
INDEX
INFIX
IXTLE
JIXIE
JUDEX
JUXTA
KYLIX
LARIX
LATEX
LAXER
LAXLY
LEXIA
LEXIC
LOXIA
LUXES
LUXUR
LUXUS
MALAX
MATAX
MAXIM
MIXED
MIXEN
MIXER
MIXUP
MONAX
MOXIE
MUREX
NEXAL
NEXUM
NEXUS
NIXEN
NIXES
NIXIE
NOXAE
NOXAL
NYXIS
OXANE
OXBOW
OXBOY
OXEYE
OXFLY
OXIDE
OXIDO
OXIME
OXLIP
OXMAN
OXMEN
OXTER
PANAX
PAUXI
PINAX
PIXIE
PODEX
PREXY
PROXY
PUMEX
PYREX
PYXIE
PYXIS
RADIX
RAMEX
REDUX
RELAX
REMEX
REXEN
SAXON
SEXED
SEXLY
SEXTO
SILEX
SIREX
SIXER
SIXMO
SIXTE
SIXTH
SIXTY
SOULX
STRIX
TAXED
TAXEL
TAXER
TAXES
TAXIS
TAXON
TAXOR
TELEX
TEXAS
TOXIC
TOXIN
TOXON
TWIXT
UNFIX
UNMIX
UNSEX
UNTAX
UNWAX
VARIX
VEXED
VEXER
VEXIL
VIBEX
VIVAX
VIXEN
WAXED
WAXEN
WAXER
WAXES
XALLE
XEBEC
XENIA
XENON
XENYL
XERIC
XERIF
XEROX
XOANA
XUREL
XYLAN
XYLEM
XYLIC
XYLON
XYLYL
XYRID
XYSTA

POSITIONAL ORDER LIST OF 5-LETTER WORDS

XALLE
XEBEC
XENIA
XENON
XENYL
XERIC
XERIF
XEROX
XOANA
XUREL
XYLAN
XYLEM
XYLIC
XYLON
XYLYL
XYRID
XYSTA

AXIAL
AXILE
AXINE
AXIOM
AXION
AXITE
AXLED
AXMAN
AXMEN
AXOID
AXONE
EXACT
EXALT
EXCEL
EXCUR
EXEAT
EXEDE
EXEEM
EXEME
EXERT
EXIDO
EXIES

EXILE
EXINE
EXIST
EXITE
EXLEX
EXODE
EXODY
EXORN
EXPEL
EXTER
EXTOL
EXTRA
EXTRE
EXUDE
EXULT
EXURB
EXUST
EXUTE
IXTLE
OXANE
OXBOW
OXBOY
OXEYE
OXFLY
OXIDE
OXIDO
OXIME
OXLIP
OXMAN
OXMEN
OXTER

AUXIN
BIXIN
BOXEN
BOXER
BOXES
BOXTY

BUXOM
CAXON
COXAE
COXAL
DIXIE
DIXIT
DOXIE
DUXES
FAXED
FIXED
FIXER
FOXED
FOXER
FOXES
HEXAD
HEXER
HEXIS
HEXYL
HUXEN
JIXIE
JUXTA
LAXER
LAXLY
LEXIA
LEXIC
LOXIA
LUXES
LUXUR
LUXUS
MAXIM
MIXED
MIXEN
MIXER
MIXUP
MOXIE
NEXAL
NEXUM
NEXUS

NIXEN
NIXES
NIXIE
NOXAE
NOXAL
NYXIS
PIXIE
PYXIE
PYXIS
REXEN
SAXON
SEXED
SEXLY
SEXTO
SIXER
SIXMO
SIXTE
SIXTH
SIXTY
TAXED
TAXEL
TAXER
TAXES
TAXIS
TAXON
TAXOR
TEXAS
TOXIC
TOXIN
TOXON
VEXED
VEXER
VEXIL
VIXEN
WAXED
WAXEN
WAXER
WAXES

ADOXY
ATAXY
AZOXY
BRAXY
COAXY
DIOXY
DRUXY
EPOXY
FLAXY
PAUXI
PREXY
PROXY
TWIXT

ADDAX
ADFIX
ADMIX
ADNEX
AFFIX
ALPAX
AMPYX
ANNEX
BERYX
BORAX
CAPAX
CAREX
CHOUX
CIMEX
CODEX
CYLIX
DEFIX
DESEX
DEVEX
DEWAX
DONAX
DURAX
EMBOX
FAULX

GULIX
HELIX
HYRAX
IMMIX
INDEX
INFIX
JUDEX
KYLIX
LARIX
LATEX
MALAX
MATAX
MONAX
MUREX
PANAX
PINAX
PODEX
PUMEX
PYREX
RADIX
RAMEX
REDUX
RELAX
REMEX
SILEX
SIREX
SOULX
STRIX
TELEX
UNFIX
UNMIX
UNSEX
UNTAX
UNWAX
VARIX
VIBEX
VIVAX
XEROX

SCORING ORDER LIST OF 5-LETTER WORDS

24
AZOXY

20
JUDEX

19
AMPYX
JIXIE
JUXTA
KYLIX

18
AFFIX
FLAXY
HEXYL
HYRAX
OXFLY
VIVAX
XYLYL

17
BERYX
BOXTY
BRAXY
CHOUX
COAXY
CYLIX
EPOXY
OXBOW
OXBOY
PREXY
PROXY
PYREX
PYXIE
PYXIS
VIBEX
XYLEM
XYLIC

16
ADFIX
ADOXY
BUXOM
CAPAX
CIMEX
DEFIX
DEVEX
DEWAX
DIOXY
DRUXY
EMBOX
EXODY
FAXED
FIXED
FOXED
HEXAD
IMMIX
MAXIM
MIXUP
PUMEX
VEXED
WAXED
XEBEC
XYRID

15
ADMIX
ATAXY
CODEX
FAULX
FIXER
FOXER
FOXES
HELIX
HEXER
HEXIS
HUXEN
INFIX
LAXLY
MIXED
NYXIS
OXEYE
PODEX
SEXLY
SIXTH
SIXTY
TWIXT
UNFIX
UNWAX
VARIX
VEXER
VEXIL
VIXEN
WAXEN
WAXER
WAXES
XENYL
XERIF
XYLAN
XYLON
XYSTA

14
ADDAX
ALPAX
AXIOM
AXMAN
AXMEN
BIXIN
BORAX
BOXEN
BOXER
BOXES
CAREX
CAXON
COXAE
COXAL
EXACT
EXCEL
EXCUR
EXEEM
EXEME
EXPEL
EXURB
LEXIC
MALAX
MATAX
MIXEN
MIXER
MONAX
MOXIE
MUREX
NEXUM
OXIME
OXLIP
OXMAN
OXMEN
PANAX
PAUXI
PINAX
PIXIE
RAMEX
REMEX
SIXMO
TOXIC
UNMIX
XERIC

13
ADNEX
AXLED
AXOID
DESEX
DIXIE
DIXIT
DONAX
DOXIE
DURAX
DUXES

EXEDE
EXIDO
EXODE
EXUDE
GULIX
INDEX
OXIDE
OXIDO
RADIX
REDUX
SEXED
TAXED

12
ANNEX
AUXIN
AXIAL
AXILE
AXINE
AXION
AXITE
AXONE
EXALT
EXEAT
EXERT
EXIES
EXILE
EXINE
EXIST
EXITE
EXORN
EXTER
EXTOL
EXTRA
EXTRE
EXULT
EXUST
EXUTE
IXTLE
LARIX
LATEX
LAXER
LEXIA
LOXIA
LUXES
LUXUR
LUXUS
NEXAL
NEXUS
NIXEN
NIXES
NIXIE
NOXAE
NOXAL
OXANE
OXTER
RELAX
REXEN
SAXON
SEXTO
SILEX
SIREX
SIXER
SIXTE
SOULX
STRIX
TAXEL
TAXER
TAXES
TAXIS
TAXON
TAXOR
TELEX
TEXAS
TOXIN
TOXON
UNSEX
UNTAX
XALLE
XENIA
XENON
XOANA
XUREL

11
EXLEX
XEROX

ALPHABETICAL LIST OF 6-LETTER WORDS

ADIEUX
ADMIXT
ADNEXA
AFFIXT
AFFLUX
ALEXIA
ALEXIN
ALKOXY
ALLOXY
AMIXIA
AMPLEX
ANAXON
ANNEXA
ANNEXE
ANOXIA
ANOXIC
APEXED
APEXES
AROXYL
ATAXIA
ATAXIC
ATWIXT
AUSPEX
AXEMAN
AXENIC
AXIATE
AXILLA
AXLIKE
AXONAL
AXSEED
AXTREE
AXUNGE
AXWEED
BADAXE
BAXTER
BIAXAL
BIFLEX
BIJOUX
BISEXT
BOLLIX
BOMBYX
BONXIE
BOXCAR
BOXING
BOXMAN
BOYAUX
BUTOXY
CALXES
CARANX
CARFAX
CAUDEX
CAXIRI
CERVIX
CIXIID
CLIMAX
COAXAL
COAXED
COAXER
COCCYX
COMMIX
CONFIX
CONNEX
CONVEX
CORDAX
CORTEX
COUXIA
COUXIO
COXIER
COXITE
CRUXES
DARNEX
DEFLEX
DEFLUX
DELUXE
DENTEX
DEXTER
DEXTRO
DIAXON
DIOXAN
DIPLEX
DIXAIN
DOXIES
DRUXEY
DUPLEX
EARWAX
EFFLUX
ELIXIR
EMPEXA
EUTAXY
EXACTA
EXALTE
EXAMEN
EXARCH
EXCAMB
EXCAVE
EXCEED
EXCELS
EXCEPT
EXCERN
EXCESS
EXCIDE
EXCISE
EXCITE
EXCOCT
EXCUSE
EXCUSS
EXCYST
EXEDRA
EXEMPT
EXEQUY
EXERCE
EXEUNT
EXHALE
EXHORT
EXHUME
EXILED
EXILER
EXILIC
EXITUS
EXODIC
EXODUS
EXOGEN
EXOLVE
EXOMIS
EXONER
EXOPOD
EXOTIC
EXPAND
EXPECT
EXPEDE
EXPEND
EXPERT
EXPIRE
EXPIRY
EXPLAT
EXPONE
EXPORT
EXPOSE
EXPUGN
EXSECT
EXSERT
EXTANT
EXTEND
EXTENT
EXTERN
EXTILL
EXTIMA
EXTIME
EXTINE
EXTIRP
EXTOLL
EXTORT
EXTUND
EXTURB
EXUDED
FIXAGE
FIXATE
FIXING
FIXITY
FIXURE
FLAXEN
FLEXED
FLEXOR
FLUXED
FLUXER
FORFEX
FORNIX
FOXERY
FOXIER
FOXILY
FOXING
FOXISH
FRAXIN
FRUTEX
GALAXY
HALLUX
HATBOX
HEXADE
HEXANE
HEXENE
HEXINE
HEXODE
HEXOIC
HEXONE
HEXOSE
HEXYNE
HOAXEE
HOAXER
HOTBOX
IBEXES
ICEBOX
ILEXES
IMBREX
IMMIXT
IMPLEX
INAXON
INFLEX
INFLUX
INTEXT
IODOXY
IXODIC
IXODID
KLAXON
KORDAX
LARNAX
LARYNX
LASTEX
LAXATE
LAXEST
LAXISM
LAXIST
LAXITY
LUMMOX
LUXATE
LUXIVE
LUXURY
LYNXES
LYXOSE
MASTAX
MATRIX
MAXIMA
MAXIXE
MENINX
MINXES
MIXING
MIXITE
MYSTAX
MYXOID
MYXOMA
NEXTLY
NOXIAL
ONYXES
ONYXIS
OPIFEX
OREXIS

OUTBOX
OUTFOX
OXALIC
OXALIS
OXALYL
OXAMIC
OXAZIN
OXBANE
OXBIRD
OXCART
OXEATE
OXEOTE
OXFORD
OXGALL
OXGANG
OXGATE
OXGOAD
OXHEAD
OXHEAL
OXHIDE
OXHOFT
OXHORN
OXLAND
OXLIKE
OXREIM
OXSHOE
OXSKIN
OXTAIL
OXWORT
OXYAZO
OXYGEN
OXYGON
OXYMEL
OXYOPY
PAPPOX
PATRIX
PAXWAX
PEGBOX
PERFIX
PERMIX
PEROXY
PHENIX
PICKAX
PINXIT
PIXIES
PLEXAL
PLEXOR
PLEXUS
POLEAX
POLLEX
PRAXIS
PRECOX
PREFIX
PROLIX
PROREX
PTYXIS
REFLEX
REFLUX
REXINE
RHEXIS
ROLLIX
SANDIX
SANDYX
SAXAUL
SCOLEX
SEXERN
SEXIER
SEXISM
SEXIST
SEXTAN
SEXTET
SEXTIC
SEXTON
SEXTRY
SEXTUR
SEXUAL
SIXAIN
SMILAX
SPADIX
SPHINX
STAXIS
STORAX
STUPEX
SUBFIX
SUFFIX
SURTAX
SYNTAX
SYRINX
TARBOX
TAXEME
TAXIED
TAXINE
TAXING
TAXITE
TAXMAN
TEABOX
TETTIX
TEXTUS
THIXLE
THORAX
TORPEX
TOXIFY
TOXINE
TOXITY
TOXOID
TOXONE
TREMEX
TUXEDO
UNISEX
UROXIN
VERMIX
VERNIX
VERTEX
VEXFUL
VEXING
VINDEX
VORTEX
WAXAND
WAXIER
WAXING
WAXMAN
WRAXLE
WRIXLE
XARQUE
XENIAL
XENIAN
XENIUM
XERIFF
XEROMA
XIFOID
XOANON
XYLATE
XYLENE
XYLITE
XYLOID
XYLOMA
XYLOSE
XYLOYL
XYSTER
XYSTUS
YAXCHE

POSITIONAL ORDER LIST OF 6-LETTER WORDS

XARQUE
XENIAL
XENIAN
XENIUM
XERIFF
XEROMA
XIFOID
XOANON
XYLATE
XYLENE
XYLITE
XYLOID
XYLOMA
XYLOSE
XYLOYL
XYSTER
XYSTUS

AXEMAN
AXENIC
AXIATE
AXILLA
AXLIKE
AXONAL
AXSEED
AXTREE
AXUNGE
AXWEED
EXACTA
EXALTE
EXAMEN
EXARCH
EXCAMB
EXCAVE
EXCEED
EXCELS
EXCEPT
EXCERN
EXCESS
EXCIDE
EXCISE
EXCITE
EXCOCT
EXCUSE
EXCUSS
EXCYST
EXEDRA
EXEMPT
EXEQUY
EXERCE
EXEUNT
EXHALE
EXHORT
EXHUME
EXILED
EXILER
EXILIC
EXITUS
EXODIC
EXODUS
EXOGEN
EXOLVE
EXOMIS
EXONER
EXOPOD
EXOTIC
EXPAND
EXPECT
EXPEDE
EXPEND
EXPERT
EXPIRE
EXPIRY
EXPLAT
EXPONE
EXPORT
EXPOSE
EXPUGN
EXSECT
EXSERT
EXTANT
EXTEND
EXTENT
EXTERN
EXTILL
EXTIMA
EXTIME
EXTINE
EXTIRP
EXTOLL
EXTORT
EXTUND
EXTURB
EXUDED
IXODIC
IXODID
OXALIC
OXALIS
OXALYL
OXAMIC
OXAZIN
OXBANE
OXBIRD
OXCART
OXEATE
OXEOTE
OXFORD
OXGALL
OXGANG
OXGATE
OXGOAD
OXHEAD
OXHEAL
OXHIDE
OXHOFT
OXHORN
OXLAND
OXLIKE
OXREIM
OXSHOE
OXSKIN
OXTAIL
OXWORT
OXYAZO
OXYGEN
OXYGON
OXYMEL
OXYOPY

BAXTER
BOXCAR
BOXING
BOXMAN
CAXIRI
CIXIID
COXIER
COXITE
DEXTER
DEXTRO
DIXAIN
DOXIES
FIXAGE
FIXATE
FIXING
FIXITY
FIXURE
FOXERY
FOXIER
FOXILY
FOXING
FOXISH
HEXADE
HEXANE
HEXENE
HEXINE
HEXODE
HEXOIC
HEXONE
HEXOSE
HEXYNE
LAXATE
LAXEST
LAXISM
LAXIST
LAXITY
LUXATE
LUXIVE
LUXURY
LYXOSE
MAXIMA
MAXIXE
MIXING
MIXITE
MYXOID
MYXOMA
NEXTLY
NOXIAL
PAXWAX
PIXIES
REXINE
SAXAUL
SEXERN
SEXIER
SEXISM
SEXIST
SEXTAN
SEXTET
SEXTIC
SEXTON
SEXTRY
SEXTUR
SEXUAL
SIXAIN
TAXEME
TAXIED
TAXINE
TAXING
TAXITE
TAXMAN
TEXTUS
TOXIFY
TOXINE
TOXITY
TOXOID
TOXONE

TUXEDO
VEXFUL
VEXING
WAXAND
WAXIER
WAXING
WAXMAN
YAXCHE

ALEXIA
ALEXIN
AMIXIA
ANAXON
ANOXIA
ANOXIC
APEXED
APEXES
AROXYL
ATAXIA
ATAXIC
BIAXAL
BONXIE
CALXES
COAXAL
COAXED
COAXER
COUXIA
COUXIO
CRUXES
DIAXON
DIOXAN
DRUXEY
ELIXIR
FLAXEN
FLEXED
FLEXOR
FLUXED
FLUXER
FRAXIN
HOAXEE
HOAXER
IBEXES
ILEXES
INAXON
KLAXON
LYNXES
MINXES
ONYXES
ONYXIS
OREXIS
PINXIT
PLEXAL
PLEXOR
PLEXUS
PRAXIS
PTYXIS
RHEXIS
STAXIS
THIXLE
UROXIN
WRAXLE
WRIXLE

ADMIXT
ADNEXA
AFFIXT
ALKOXY
ALLOXY
ANNEXA
ANNEXE
ATWIXT
BADAXE
BISEXT
BUTOXY
DELUXE
EMPEXA
EUTAXY
GALAXY
IMMIXT
INTEXT
IODOXY
MAXIXE
PEROXY

ADIEUX
AFFLUX
AMPLEX
AUSPEX
BIFLEX
BIJOUX
BOLLIX
BOMBYX
BOYAUX
CARANX
CARFAX
CAUDEX
CERVIX
CLIMAX
COCCYX
COMMIX
CONFIX
CONNEX
CONVEX
CORDAX
CORTEX
DARNEX
DEFLEX
DEFLUX
DENTEX
DIPLEX
DUPLEX
EARWAX
EFFLUX
FORFEX
FORNIX
FRUTEX
HALLUX
HATBOX
HOTBOX
ICEBOX
IMBREX
IMPLEX
INFLEX
INFLUX
KORDAX
LARNAX
LARYNX
LASTEX
LUMMOX
MASTAX
MATRIX
MENINX
MYSTAX
OPIFEX
OUTBOX
OUTFOX
PAPPOX
PATRIX
PAXWAX
PEGBOX
PERFIX
PERMIX
PHENIX
PICKAX
POLEAX
POLLEX
PRECOX
PREFIX
PROLIX
PROREX
REFLEX
REFLUX
ROLLIX
SANDIX
SANDYX
SCOLEX
SMILAX
SPADIX
SPHINX
STORAX
STUPEX
SUBFIX
SUFFIX
SURTAX
SYNTAX
SYRINX
TARBOX
TEABOX
TETTIX
THORAX
TORPEX
TREMEX
UNISEX
VERMIX
VERNIX
VERTEX
VINDEX
VORTEX

SCORING ORDER LIST OF 6-LETTER WORDS

25
EXEQUY
OXYAZO

22
BIJOUX
BOMBYX
OXAZIN
XARQUE

21
OXYOPY
PICKAX
YAXCHE

20
ALKOXY
MYXOMA

19
AFFIXT
AFFLUX
COCCYX
COMMIX
EFFLUX
EXCAMB
FIXITY
FORFEX
FOXERY
FOXILY
FOXISH
HEXYNE
MYXOID
OXHOFT
SUFFIX
TOXIFY
VEXFUL
XERIFF
XYLOYL

18
BIFLEX
BOYAUX
BUTOXY
CARFAX
CERVIX
CONFIX
CONVEX
EXARCH
EXCAVE
EXCYST
EXHUME
EXPIRY
HATBOX
HEXOIC
HOTBOX
KORDAX
MYSTAX
OPIFEX
OXYMEL
PEGBOX
PERFIX
PEROXY
PHENIX
PREFIX
PTYXIS
SPHINX
SUBFIX
VERMIX
WAXMAN
XYLOMA

17
AMPLEX
AXLIKE
AXWEED
BOXCAR
BOXMAN
CLIMAX
DEFLEX
DEFLUX
DRUXEY
EMPEXA
EXCEPT
EXCOCT
EXEMPT
EXPECT
FIXAGE
FIXING
FLEXED
FLUXED
FOXING
GALAXY
HEXADE
HEXODE
ICEBOX
IMBREX
IMMIXT
IMPLEX
IODOXY
KLAXON
LUMMOX
MAXIMA
OXAMIC
OXFORD
OXHEAD
OXHIDE
OXLIKE
OXSKIN
OXYGEN
OXYGON
PAXWAX
PERMIX
PRECOX
SANDYX
VEXING
VINDEX
WAXAND
WAXING
XIFOID
XYLOID

16
ADMIXT
ALLOXY
APEXED
AROXYL
ATWIXT
BADAXE
BOXING
CAUDEX
CIXIID
COAXED
CORDAX
DIPLEX
DUPLEX
EARWAX
EUTAXY
EXCEED
EXCIDE
EXHALE
EXHORT
EXODIC
EXOLVE
EXOPOD
EXPAND
EXPEDE
EXPEND
EXPUGN
FIXATE
FIXURE
FLAXEN
FLEXOR
FLUXER
FORNIX
FOXIER
FRAXIN
FRUTEX
HALLUX
HEXANE
HEXENE
HEXINE
HEXONE
HEXOSE
HOAXEE
HOAXER
INFLEX
INFLUX
IXODIC
LARYNX
LAXITY
LUXIVE
LUXURY
LYNXES
LYXOSE

MIXING
NEXTLY
ONYXES
ONYXIS
OUTFOX
OXALYL
OXBIRD
OXHEAL
OXHORN
OXSHOE
OXWORT
PAPPOX
REFLEX
REFLUX
RHEXIS
SEXTRY
SPADIX
SYNTAX
SYRINX
THIXLE
THORAX
TOXITY
VERNIX
VERTEX
VORTEX
WAXIER
WRAXLE
WRIXLE
XYLATE
XYLENE
XYLITE
XYLOSE
XYSTER
XYSTUS

15
AMIXIA
ANOXIC
APEXES
ATAXIC
AUSPEX
AXEMAN
AXENIC
BAXTER
BIAXAL
BISEXT
BOLLIX
BONXIE
CALXES
CARANX
CAXIRI
COAXAL
COAXER
CONNEX
CORTEX
COUXIA
COUXIO
COXIER
COXITE
CRUXES
EXACTA
EXAMEN
EXCELS
EXCERN
EXCESS
EXCISE
EXCITE
EXCUSE
EXCUSS
EXERCE
EXILIC
EXOMIS
EXOTIC
EXPERT
EXPIRE
EXPLAT
EXPONE
EXPORT
EXPOSE
EXSECT
EXTIMA
EXTIME
EXTIRP
EXTURB
EXUDED
IBEXES
IXODID
LAXISM
MASTAX
MATRIX
MENINX
MINXES
MIXITE
OUTBOX
OXALIC
OXBANE
OXCART
OXGANG
OXGOAD
OXREIM
PATRIX
PINXIT
PIXIES
PLEXAL
PLEXOR
PLEXUS
POLEAX
POLLEX
PRAXIS
PROLIX
PROREX
SCOLEX
SEXISM
SEXTIC
SMILAX
STUPEX
TARBOX
TAXEME
TAXMAN
TEABOX
TORPEX
TREMEX
XENIUM
XEROMA

14
ADIEUX
ADNEXA
AXSEED
AXUNGE
DARNEX
DELUXE
DENTEX
DEXTER
DEXTRO
DIAXON
DIOXAN
DIXAIN
DOXIES
EXEDRA
EXILED
EXODUS
EXOGEN
EXTEND
EXTUND
MAXIXE
OXGALL
OXGATE
OXLAND
SANDIX
TAXIED
TAXING
TOXOID
TUXEDO

13
ALEXIA
ALEXIN
ANAXON
ANNEXA
ANNEXE
ANOXIA
ATAXIA
AXIATE
AXILLA
AXONAL
AXTREE
ELIXIR
EXALTE
EXEUNT
EXILER
EXITUS
EXONER
EXSERT
EXTANT
EXTENT
EXTERN
EXTILL
EXTINE
EXTOLL
EXTORT
ILEXES
INAXON
INTEXT
LARNAX
LASTEX
LAXATE
LAXEST
LAXIST
LUXATE
NOXIAL
OREXIS
OXALIS
OXEATE
OXEOTE
OXTAIL
REXINE
ROLLIX
SAXAUL
SEXERN
SEXIER
SEXIST
SEXTAN
SEXTET
SEXTON
SEXTUR
SEXUAL
SIXAIN
STAXIS
STORAX
SURTAX
TAXINE
TAXITE
TETTIX
TEXTUS
TOXINE
TOXONE
UNISEX
UROXIN
XENIAL
XENIAN
XOANON

ALPHABETICAL LIST OF 7-LETTER WORDS

ABACAXI
ABAXIAL
ABAXILE
ABRASAX
ABRAXAS
ACRONYX
ADAXIAL
ADMIXED
ADNEXAL
ADNEXED
ADOXIES
AFFIXAL
AFFIXED
AFFIXER
AFFREUX
AGALAXY
AGNEAUX
ALEXINE
ALKOXID
ALKOXYL
ALLOXAN
AMPYXES
ANAXIAL
ANAXONE
ANNEXED
ANNEXER
ANOREXY
ANTAPEX
ANTEFIX
ANTHRAX
ANXIETY
ANXIOUS
APEXING
APOPLEX
APRAXIA
APTERYX
APYREXY
ARTIFEX
ARUSPEX
ASEXUAL
ASPHYXY
ATARAXY
ATAXITE
AURIFEX
AUXESIS
AUXETIC
AUXOTOX
AXIALLY
AXIFORM
AXILLAE
AXILLAR
AXINITE
AXMAKER
AXOGAMY
AXOLOTL
AXONEME
AXONOST
AXSTONE
AZOXINE
BANDBOX
BATEAUX
BAUXITE
BEESWAX
BENZOXY
BETWIXT
BIAXIAL
BIOTAXY
BISEXED
BISSEXT
BOSTRYX
BOXBUSH
BOXCARS
BOXFISH
BOXHAUL
BOXHEAD
BOXINGS
BOXLIKE
BOXROOM
BOXTREE
BOXWOOD
BOXWORK
BRAXIES
BREAKAX
BROADAX
BRUXISM
BUREAUX
BUTOXYL
BUXERRY
BUXOMLY
CACHEXY
CAKEBOX
CARAPAX
CAREFOX
CASEBOX
CASHBOX
CHOENIX
COALBOX
COAXIAL
COAXING
COEXIST

COLAUXE
COMMIXT
COMPLEX
CONFLUX
CONTEXT
COXALGY
COXCOMB
COXIEST
COXITIS
CURTAXE
CURTLAX
DEEDBOX
DEXTRAD
DEXTRAL
DEXTRAN
DEXTRIN
DIAXIAL
DIAXONE
DICEBOX
DIGOXIN
DIOXANE
DIOXIDE
DIOXIME
DUSTBOX
ELIXATE
EPAXIAL
EPOXIDE
EQUINOX
ESEXUAL
ETHOXYL
EUTAXIC
EUTAXIE
EUTEXIA
EXACTED
EXACTER
EXACTLY
EXACTOR
EXALATE
EXALTED
EXALTEE
EXALTER
EXAMINE
EXAMPLE
EXARATE
EXARCHY
EXASPER
EXCELSE
EXCERPT
EXCHEAT
EXCIDED
EXCIPLE
EXCISED
EXCISOR
EXCITED
EXCITER
EXCITON
EXCITOR
EXCLAIM
EXCLAVE
EXCLUDE
EXCRETA
EXCRETE
EXCUDIT
EXCURSE
EXCUSAL
EXCUSED
EXCUSER
EXECUTE
EXEDENT
EXEGETE
EXEMPLA
EXERGUE
EXERTED
EXESION
EXFLECT
EXHALED
EXHANCE
EXHAUST
EXHEDRA
EXHIBIT
EXHUMED
EXHUMER
EXIGENT
EXILIAN
EXILING
EXILITY
EXINITE
EXISTED
EXISTER
EXITIAL
EXITION
EXITURE
EXOCARP
EXOCONE
EXODERM
EXODIST
EXODIUM
EXOGAMY
EXOLETE
EXOMION
EXORATE
EXORMIA
EXOSMIC
EXOSTRA
EXOTISM
EXPANSE
EXPEDED
EXPENSE
EXPIATE
EXPIRED
EXPIREE
EXPIRER
EXPLAIN
EXPLANT
EXPLETE
EXPLODE
EXPLOIT
EXPLORE
EXPOSAL
EXPOSED
EXPOSER
EXPOSIT
EXPOUND
EXPREME
EXPRESS
EXPULSE
EXPUNGE
EXPURGE
EXQUIRE
EXRADIO
EXSCIND
EXSOLVE
EXSURGE
EXTANCY
EXTENSE
EXTERNA
EXTERNE
EXTINCT
EXTRACT
EXTREAT
EXTREME
EXTRUCT
EXTRUDE
EXUDATE
EXUDING
EXULATE
EXULTED
EXULTET
EXURBIA
EXUVIAE
EXUVIAL
FACTRIX
FEEDBOX
FIREBOX
FIXABLE
FIXATED
FIXATIF
FIXATOR
FIXEDLY
FIXINGS
FIXTURE
FLAXIER
FLAXMAN
FLEXILE
FLEXING
FLEXION
FLEXIVE
FLEXURA
FLEXURE
FLUMMOX
FLUXILE
FLUXING
FLUXION
FLUXIVE
FLUXURE
FOXBANE
FOXCHOP
FOXFEET
FOXFIRE
FOXFISH
FOXHOLE
FOXIEST
FOXLIKE
FOXSKIN
FOXTAIL
FOXTROT
GEARBOX
GEOTAXY
GITOXIN
GLOMMOX
GLYOXAL
GLYOXYL
GUAXIMA
HEADBOX
HELIXIN
HELLBOX
HEMIXIS
HEXACID
HEXADIC
HEXAGON
HEXAGYN
HEXAMER
HEXANAL
HEXAPED
HEXAPLA
HEXAPOD
HEXAXON
HEXEREI
HEXERIS
HEXITOL
HEXONIC
HEXOSAN
HEXYLIC
HOMODOX
INDEXED
INDEXER
INDEXES
INDOXYL
INEXACT
INEXIST
INFIXED
INFIXES
IXODIAN
JACKBOX
JUKEBOX
KICKXIA
KINEPOX
KLEENEX
LARIXIN
LATEXES
LAXNESS
LEXICAL
LEXICON
LOCKBOX
LOXOTIC
LUXATED
MAILBOX
MALAXED
MARTEXT
MARTRIX
MAXILLA
MAXIMAL
MAXIMED
MAXIMUM
MAXIMUS
MAXWELL
METHOXY
MEXICAL
MIXABLE
MIXHILL
MIXIBLE
MIXTION
MIXTURE
MONAXON
MUREXAN
MUREXES
MUREXID
MYOXINE
MYXEMIA
MYXOMAS
NARTHEX
NEXUSES
NOXIOUS
ORATRIX
OUTFLUX
OUTJINX
OVERTAX
OXALATE
OXALATO
OXAMATE
OXAMIDE
OXAZINE
OXAZOLE
OXBERRY
OXBITER
OXBLOOD
OXBRAKE
OXCHEEK
OXHEART
OXHOUSE
OXHUVUD
OXIDANT
OXIDASE
OXIDATE
OXIDISE
OXIDIZE
OXIMATE
OXONIUM
OXOZONE
OXYACID
OXYMORA
OXYNTIC
OXYOPIA
OXYPHIL
OXYTONE
OXYURID
PACKWAX
PANCHAX
PANMIXY
PARADOX
PARAXON
PAXILLA
PAXILLI
PAXIUBA
PEIXERE
PEMPHIX
PEROXYL
PERPLEX
PHALANX
PHARYNX
PHOENIX
PICKAXE
PILLBOX
PISTRIX
PLANXTY
PLAYBOX
PLEXURE
POLAXIS
POLEAXE
POSTBOX
POSTFIX
PRAECOX
PRETEXT
PREXIES
PRINCOX
PROPLEX
PROPOXY
PROTEXT
PROXENY
PROXIED
PROXIES
PROXIME
PROXIMO
PROXYSM
PYREXIA
PYREXIC
PYXIDES
RECTRIX
RELAXED
RELAXER
RELAXIN
RESEAUX
SALPINX
SALTBOX
SANDBOX
SAXHORN
SAXTUBA
SEEDBOX
SEXIEST
SEXLESS
SEXLIKE
SEXTAIN
SEXTANS
SEXTANT
SEXTERN
SEXTILE
SEXTOLE
SEXTUOR
SEXUALE
SEXUOUS
SIDEBOX
SIMPLEX
SINKBOX
SIXFOLD
SIXSOME
SIXTEEN
SIXTIES
SKEEZIX
SOAPBOX
SONOVOX
SPANDEX
SPITBOX
SUBOXID
SYNAXAR
SYNAXIS
TAXABLE
TAXABLY
TAXATOR
TAXIBUS
TAXICAB
TAXIMAN
TAXITIC
TAXPAID
TAXYING
TECTRIX

TELEVOX
TEXTILE
TEXTLET
TEXTMAN
TEXTUAL
TEXTURE
TOOLBOX
TORTRIX
TOXAMIN
TOXEMIA
TOXEMIC
TOXICAL
TOXICON
TOXICUM
TOXIFER

TOXOTAE
TRIAXAL
TRIAXON
TRIOXID
TRIPLEX
TUBIFEX
TUXEDOS
ULEXINE
ULEXITE
UNBUXOM
UNEXACT
UNFIXED
UNFOXED
UNSEXED

UROTOXY
UXORIAL
VAUXITE
VEXEDLY
VEXILLA
VICTRIX
VITRAUX
VIXENLY
WAXBILL
WAXBIRD
WAXBUSH
WAXCOMB
WAXIEST
WAXWEED

WAXWING
WAXWORK
WAXWORM
WEREFOX
WOODWAX
WORKBOX
WRAXLED
XANTHIC
XANTHID
XANTHIN
XANTHYL
XERAFIN
XERARCH
XERASIA

XERONIC
XEROSIS
XEROTES
XEROTIC
XIBALBA
XIPHOID
XYLENOL
XYLENYL
XYLIDIN
XYLITOL
XYLOGEN
XYLOMAS
XYLOSID
ZOOTAXY

POSITIONAL ORDER LIST OF 7-LETTER WORDS

XANTHIC
XANTHID
XANTHIN
XANTHYL
XERAFIN
XERARCH
XERASIA
XERONIC
XEROSIS
XEROTES
XEROTIC
XIBALBA
XIPHOID
XYLENOL
XYLENYL
XYLIDIN
XYLITOL
XYLOGEN
XYLOMAS
XYLOSID

AXIALLY
AXIFORM
AXILLAE
AXILLAR
AXINITE
AXMAKER
AXOGAMY
AXOLOTL
AXONEME
AXONOST
AXSTONE
EXACTED
EXACTER
EXACTLY
EXACTOR
EXALATE
EXALTED
EXALTEE
EXALTER
EXAMINE
EXAMPLE
EXARATE
EXARCHY
EXASPER
EXCELSE
EXCERPT
EXCHEAT
EXCIDED
EXCIPLE
EXCISED
EXCISOR
EXCITED
EXCITER
EXCITON
EXCITOR

EXCLAIM
EXCLAVE
EXCLUDE
EXCRETA
EXCRETE
EXCUDIT
EXCURSE
EXCUSAL
EXCUSED
EXCUSER
EXECUTE
EXEDENT
EXEGETE
EXEMPLA
EXERGUE
EXERTED
EXESION
EXFLECT
EXHALED
EXHANCE
EXHAUST
EXHEDRA
EXHIBIT
EXHUMED
EXHUMER
EXIGENT
EXILIAN
EXILING
EXILITY
EXINITE
EXISTED
EXISTER
EXITIAL
EXITION
EXITURE
EXOCARP
EXOCONE
EXODERM
EXODIST
EXODIUM
EXOGAMY
EXOLETE
EXOMION
EXORATE
EXORMIA
EXOSMIC
EXOSTRA
EXOTISM
EXPANSE
EXPEDED
EXPENSE
EXPIATE
EXPIRED
EXPIREE
EXPIRER
EXPLAIN

EXPLANT
EXPLETE
EXPLODE
EXPLOIT
EXPLORE
EXPOSAL
EXPOSED
EXPOSER
EXPOSIT
EXPOUND
EXPREME
EXPRESS
EXPULSE
EXPUNGE
EXPURGE
EXQUIRE
EXRADIO
EXSCIND
EXSOLVE
EXSURGE
EXTANCY
EXTENSE
EXTERNA
EXTERNE
EXTINCT
EXTRACT
EXTREAT
EXTREME
EXTRUCT
EXTRUDE
EXUDATE
EXUDING
EXULATE
EXULTED
EXULTET
EXURBIA
EXUVIAE
EXUVIAL
IXODIAN
OXALATE
OXALATO
OXAMATE
OXAMIDE
OXAZINE
OXAZOLE
OXBERRY
OXBITER
OXBLOOD
OXBRAKE
OXCHEEK
OXHEART
OXHOUSE
OXHUVUD
OXIDANT
OXIDASE
OXIDATE

OXIDISE
OXIDIZE
OXIMATE
OXONIUM
OXOZONE
OXYACID
OXYMORA
OXYNTIC
OXYOPIA
OXYPHIL
OXYSALT
OXYTONE
OXYURID
UXORIAL

ANXIETY
ANXIOUS
AUXESIS
AUXETIC
AUXOTOX
AUXOTOX
BOXBUSH
BOXCARS
BOXFISH
BOXHAUL
BOXHEAD
BOXINGS
BOXLIKE
BOXROOM
BOXTREE
BOXWOOD
BOXWORK
BUXERRY
BUXOMLY
COXALGY
COXCOMB
COXIEST
COXITIS
DEXTRAD
DEXTRAL
DEXTRAN
DEXTRIN
FIXABLE
FIXATED
FIXATIF
FIXATOR
FIXEDLY
FIXINGS
FIXTURE
FOXBANE
FOXCHOP
FOXFEET
FOXFIRE
FOXFISH
FOXHOLE
FOXIEST

FOXLIKE
FOXSKIN
FOXTAIL
FOXTROT
HEXACID
HEXADIC
HEXAGON
HEXAGYN
HEXAMER
HEXANAL
HEXAPED
HEXAPLA
HEXAPOD
HEXAXON
HEXEREI
HEXERIS
HEXITOL
HEXONIC
HEXOSAN
HEXYLIC
LAXNESS
LEXICAL
LEXICON
LOXOTIC
LUXATED
MAXILLA
MAXIMAL
MAXIMED
MAXIMUM
MAXIMUS
MAXWELL
MEXICAL
MIXABLE
MIXHILL
MIXIBLE
MIXTION
MIXTURE
MYXEMIA
MYXOMAS
NEXUSES
NOXIOUS
PAXILLA
PAXILLI
PAXIUBA
PYXIDES
SAXHORN
SAXTUBA
SEXIEST
SEXLESS
SEXLIKE
SEXTAIN
SEXTANS
SEXTANT
SEXTERN
SEXTILE
SEXTOLE

SEXTUOR
SEXUALE
SEXUOUS
SIXFOLD
SIXSOME
SIXTEEN
SIXTIES
TAXABLE
TAXABLY
TAXATOR
TAXIBUS
TAXICAB
TAXIMAN
TAXITIC
TAXPAID
TAXYING
TEXTILE
TEXTLET
TEXTMAN
TEXTUAL
TEXTURE
TOXAMIN
TOXEMIA
TOXEMIC
TOXICAL
TOXICON
TOXICUM
TOXIFER
TOXOTAE
TUXEDOS
VEXEDLY
VEXILLA
VIXENLY
WAXBILL
WAXBIRD
WAXBUSH
WAXCOMB
WAXIEST
WAXWEED
WAXWING
WAXWORK
WAXWORM

ABAXIAL
ABAXILE
ADAXIAL
ADOXIES
ALEXINE
ANAXIAL
ANAXONE
APEXING
ASEXUAL
ATAXITE
AZOXINE
BAUXITE
BIAXIAL
BRAXIES

BRUXISM
COAXIAL
COAXING
COEXIST
DIAXIAL
DIAXONE
DIOXANE
DIOXIDE
DIOXIME
ELIXATE
EPAXIAL
EPOXIDE
ESEXUAL
FLAXIER
FLAXMAN
FLEXILE
FLEXING
FLEXION
FLEXIVE
FLEXURA
FLEXURE
FLUXILE
FLUXING
FLUXION
FLUXIVE
FLUXURE
GUAXIMA
INEXACT
INEXIST
MYOXINE
PEIXERE
PLEXURE
PREXIES
PROXENY
PROXIED
PROXIES
PROXIME
PROXIMO
PROXYSM
ULEXINE
ULEXITE
UNEXACT
VAUXITE
WRAXLED

ABRAXAS
ADMIXED
ADNEXAL
ADNEXED
AFFIXAL
AFFIXED
AFFIXER
ALKOXID
ALKOXYL
ALLOXAN
AMPYXES
ANNEXED

ANNEXER
APRAXIA
BISEXED
BUTOXYL
DIGOXIN
ETHOXYL
EUTAXIC
EUTAXIE
EUTEXIA
GITOXIN
GLYOXAL
GLYOXYL
HELIXIN
HEMIXIS
HEXAXON
INDEXED
INDEXER
INDEXES
INDOXYL
INFIXED
INFIXES
KICKXIA
LARIXIN
LATEXES
MALAXED
MONAXON
MUREXAN
MUREXES
MUREXID
PARAXON
PEROXYL
PLANXTY
POLAXIS
PYREXIA
PYREXIC
RELAXED
RELAXER
RELAXIN
SUBOXID
SYNAXAR
SYNAXIS
TRIAXAL
TRIAXON
TRIOXID
UNBUXOM
UNFIXED
UNFOXED
UNSEXED

ABACAXI
AGALAXY
ANOREXY
APYREXY
ASPHYXY
ATARAXY
BENZOXY
BETWIXT

BIOTAXY
BISSEXT
CACHEXY
COLAUXE
COMMIXT
CONTEXT
CURTAXE
GEOTAXY
MARTEXT
METHOXY
PANMIXY
PICKAXE
POLEAXE
PRETEXT
PROPOXY
PROTEXT
UROTOXY
ZOOTAXY

ABRASAX
ACRONYX
AFFREUX
AGNEAUX
ANTAPEX
ANTEFIX
ANTHRAX
APOPLEX
APTERYX
ARTIFEX
ARUSPEX
AURIFEX
BANDBOX
BATEAUX
BEESWAX
BOSTRYX
BREAKAX
BROADAX
BUREAUX
CAKEBOX
CARAPAX
CAREFOX
CASEBOX
CASHBOX
CHOENIX
COALBOX
COMPLEX
CONFLUX
CURTLAX
DEEDBOX
DICEBOX
DUSTBOX
EQUINOX
FACTRIX
FEEDBOX
FIREBOX
FLUMMOX
GEARBOX

GLOMMOX
HEADBOX
HELLBOX
HOMODOX
JACKBOX
JUKEBOX
KINEPOX
KLEENEX
LOCKBOX
MAILBOX
MARTRIX
NARTHEX
ORATRIX
OUTFLUX
OUTJINX
OVERTAX
PACKWAX
PANCHAX
PARADOX
PEMPHIX
PERPLEX
PHALANX
PHARYNX
PHOENIX
PILLBOX
PISTRIX
PLAYBOX
POSTBOX
POSTFIX
PRAECOX
PRINCOX
PROPLEX
RECTRIX
RESEAUX
SALPINX
SALTBOX
SANDBOX
SEEDBOX
SIDEBOX
SIMPLEX
SINKBOX
SKEEZIX
SOAPBOX
SONOVOX
SPANDEX
SPITBOX
TECTRIX
TELEVOX
TOOLBOX
TORTRIX
TRIPLEX
TUBIFEX
VICTRIX
VITRAUX
WEREFOX
WOODWAX
WORKBOX

SCORING ORDER LIST OF 7-LETTER WORDS

29
JACKBOX

28
BENZOXY

27
JUKEBOX
SKEEZIX

26
ZOOTAXY

25
ASPHYXY
PACKWAX

24
CACHEXY
FOXCHOP
OXIDIZE
WAXWORK

23
AZOXINE
BOXWORK
EQUINOX
EXQUIRE
FOXFISH
OXAZINE
OXAZOLE
OXCHEEK
OXOZONE
PEMPHIX
WAXCOMB
WORKBOX

22
APYREXY
BOXFISH
CAKEBOX
COXCOMB
EXARCHY
HEXYLIC
LOCKBOX
METHOXY
OXYPHIL
PHARYNX
PICKAXE
WAXBUSH
WAXWORM

21
AFFIXED
ALKOXYL
AMPYXES
BOXBUSH
BUXOMLY
CASHBOX
FIXEDLY
FLUMMOX
FOXLIKE
FOXSKIN
GLYOXYL

HEXAGYN
MYXEMIA
MYXOMAS
OUTJINX
OXHUVUD
PANCHAX
PANMIXY
PLAYBOX
PROPOXY
PROXYSM
PYREXIC
VEXEDLY
WAXWEED
WAXWING
WOODWAX

20
AFFIXAL
AFFIXER
AFFREUX
AXMAKER
AXOGAMY
BOXHEAD
BOXLIKE
BOXWOOD
BREAKAX
COMMIXT
COMPLEX
COXALGY
ETHOXYL
EXHUMED
EXOGAMY
FEEDBOX
FIXATIF
FLEXIVE
FLUXIVE
FOXFEET
FOXFIRE
FOXHOLE
HEADBOX
HEXACID
HEXADIC
HEXAPED
HEXAPOD
HOMODOX
KINEPOX
OXBRAKE
OXYACID
PYXIDES
SINKBOX
VIXENLY
WAXBIRD
WEREFOX
XANTHYL
XIPHOID
XYLENYL

19
ACRONYX
ALKOXID
APTERYX
AXIFORM
BANDBOX
BEESWAX
BETWIXT
BIOTAXY
BOSTRYX
BOXHAUL
BUTOXYL
BUXERRY
CAREFOX
CHOENIX
CONFLUX
DICEBOX
EXACTLY
EXCHEAT
EXCLAVE
EXFLECT
EXHANCE
EXHIBIT
EXHUMER
EXTANCY
FACTRIX
FIREBOX
FIXABLE
FLAXMAN
FOXBANE
GLOMMOX
HELLBOX
HEMIXIS
HEXAMER
HEXAPLA
HEXONIC
KICKXIA
MAXIMED
MAXWELL
MIXHILL
MYOXINE
OXBERRY
OXYMORA
OXYNTIC
OXYOPIA
PEROXYL
PHALANX
PHOENIX
PLANXTY
POSTFIX
PROXENY
PYREXIA
TAXABLY
TUBIFEX
VICTRIX
WAXBILL
XANTHIC
XERARCH
XYLOMAS

18
ABACAXI
ADMIXED
AGALAXY
APOPLEX
BOXCARS
BOXROOM
BRUXISM
CARAPAX
CASEBOX
COALBOX
DEEDBOX
EXAMPLE
EXCERPT
EXCIDED
EXCIPLE
EXCLAIM
EXEMPLA
EXHALED
EXHEDRA
EXOCARP
EXOSMIC
EXPEDED
EXPREME
FIXATED
FIXINGS
FLEXING
FLUXING
GEOTAXY
GLYOXAL
HEXAGON
INDOXYL
INFIXED
KLEENEX
MAILBOX
MAXIMAL
MAXIMUS
MEXICAL
MIXABLE
MIXIBLE
OXYURID
PAXIUBA
PERPLEX
PILLBOX
POSTBOX
PRAECOX
PRINCOX
PROPLEX
PROXIME
PROXIMO
SEXLIKE
SIMPLEX
SIXFOLD
SOAPBOX
SPITBOX
TAXICAB
TAXYING
TOXEMIC
TOXICUM
UNBUXOM
UNFIXED
UNFOXED
WRAXLED
XANTHID
XIBALBA
XYLIDIN
XYLOGEN
XYLOSID

17
ANOREXY
ANTEFIX
ANTHRAX
ANXIETY
APEXING
ARTIFEX
ATARAXY
AURIFEX
AXIALLY
BISEXED
BOXINGS
BROADAX
COAXING
DIOXIME
DUSTBOX
EPOXIDE
EXACTED
EXCISED
EXCITED
EXCLUDE
EXCUDIT
EXCUSED
EXHAUST
EXILITY
EXODERM
EXODIUM
EXPIRED
EXPLODE
EXPOSED
EXPOUND
EXPUNGE
EXPURGE
EXSCIND
EXSOLVE
EXUVIAE
EXUVIAL
FIXATOR
FIXTURE
FLAXIER
FLEXILE
FLEXION
FLEXURA
FLEXURE
FLUXILE
FLUXION
FLUXURE
FOXIEST
FOXTAIL
FOXTROT
GEARBOX
GUAXIMA
HELIXIN
HEXANAL
HEXEREI
HEXERIS
HEXITOL
HEXOSAN
INFIXES
MALAXED
MAXIMUM
MUREXID
NARTHEX
OUTFLUX
OVERTAX
OXAMIDE
OXBLOOD
OXHEART
OXHOUSE
OXYTONE
PARADOX
PROXIED
SANDBOX
SAXHORN
SEEDBOX
SIDEBOX
SONOVOX
SPANDEX
SUBOXID
SYNAXAR
SYNAXIS
TAXPAID
TELEVOX
TOXIFER
UROTOXY
VAUXITE
VEXILLA
VITRAUX
WAXIEST
XANTHIN
XERAFIN
XYLENOL
XYLITOL

16
ABAXIAL
ABAXILE
ABRASAX
ABRAXAS
ADNEXED
ANTAPEX
APRAXIA
ARUSPEX
AUXETIC
AXONEME
BATEAUX
BAUXITE
BIAXIAL
BISSEXT
BOXTREE
BRAXIES
BUREAUX
COAXIAL
COEXIST
COLAUXE
CONTEXT
COXIEST
COXITIS
CURTAXE
CURTLAX
DEXTRAD
DIGOXIN
DIOXIDE
EPAXIAL
EUTAXIC
EXACTER
EXACTOR
EXAMINE
EXASPER
EXCELSE
EXCISOR
EXCITER
EXCITON
EXCITOR
EXCRETA
EXCRETE
EXCURSE
EXCUSAL
EXCUSER
EXECUTE
EXOCONE
EXOMION
EXORMIA
EXOTISM
EXPANSE
EXPENSE
EXPIATE
EXPIREE
EXPIRER
EXPLAIN
EXPLANT
EXPLETE
EXPLOIT
EXPLORE
EXPOSAL
EXPOSER
EXPOSIT
EXPRESS
EXPULSE
EXTINCT
EXTRACT
EXTREME
EXTRUCT
EXUDING
EXURBIA
HEXAXON
INDEXED
INEXACT
LEXICAL
LEXICON
LOXOTIC
MARTEXT
MARTRIX
MAXILLA
MIXTION
MIXTURE
MONAXON
MUREXAN
MUREXES
OXAMATE
OXBITER
OXIMATE
OXONIUM
PARAXON
PAXILLA
PAXILLI
PEIXERE
PISTRIX
PLEXURE
POLAXIS
POLEAXE
PRETEXT
PREXIES
PROTEXT
PROXIES
RECTRIX
SALPINX
SALTBOX
SAXTUBA

SIXSOME
TAXABLE
TAXIBUS
TAXIMAN
TAXITIC
TECTRIX
TEXTMAN
TOOLBOX
TOXAMIN
TOXEMIA
TOXICAL
TOXICON
TRIPLEX
UNEXACT
XERONIC
XEROTIC

15
ADAXIAL
ADNEXAL
ADOXIES
AGNEAUX
ANNEXED
DEXTRAL
DEXTRAN
DEXTRIN
DIAXIAL
DIAXONE
DIOXANE
EXALTED
EXEDENT
EXEGETE
EXERGUE
EXERTED
EXIGENT
EXILING
EXISTED
EXODIST
EXRADIO
EXSURGE
EXTRUDE
EXUDATE
EXULTED
GITOXIN
INDEXER
INDEXES
IXODIAN
LUXATED
OXIDANT
OXIDASE
OXIDATE
OXIDISE
RELAXED
TRIOXID
TUXEDOS
UNSEXED

14
ALEXINE
ALLOXAN
ANAXIAL
ANAXONE
ANNEXER
ANXIOUS
ASEXUAL
ATAXITE
AUXESIS
AXILLAE
AXILLAR
AXINITE
AXOLOTL
AXONOST
AXSTONE
ELIXATE
ESEXUAL
EUTAXIE
EUTEXIA
EXALATE
EXALTEE
EXALTER
EXARATE
EXESION
EXILIAN
EXINITE
EXISTER
EXITIAL
EXITION
EXITURE
EXOLETE
EXORATE
EXOSTRA
EXTENSE
EXTERNA
EXTERNE
EXTREAT
EXULATE
EXULTET
INEXIST
LARIXIN
LATEXES
LAXNESS
NEXUSES
NOXIOUS
ORATRIX
OXALATE
OXALATO
RELAXER
RELAXIN
RESEAUX
SEXIEST
SEXLESS
SEXTAIN
SEXTANS
SEXTANT
SEXTERN
SEXTILE
SEXTOLE
SEXTUOR
SEXUALE
SEXUOUS
SIXTEEN
SIXTIES
TAXATOR
TEXTILE
TEXTLET
TEXTUAL
TEXTURE
TORTRIX
TOXOTAE
TRIAXAL
TRIAXON
ULEXINE
ULEXITE
UXORIAL
XERASIA
XEROSIS
XEROTES

13
AUXOTOX

ALPHABETICAL LIST OF 8-LETTER WORDS

ACETOXIM
ACETOXYL
ACXOYATL
ADJUTRIX
ADMIXING
AFFIXING
AFFIXION
AGALAXIA
ALDOXIME
ALEXINIC
ALKOXIDE
AMIDOXYL
AMPLEXUS
ANATEXIS
ANATOXIN
ANAUXITE
ANNEXING
ANNEXION
ANNEXIVE
ANNEXURE
ANOREXIA
ANOXEMIA
ANOXEMIC
ANTEFIXA
ANTHELIX
APODIXIS
APOMIXIS
APOPLEXY
APOXESIS
APPENDIX
APPRAXIC
APYREXIA
ASPHYXIA
ATARAXIA
ATARAXIC
AUXILIAR
AUXILIUM
AUXIMONE
AUXOBODY
AUXOCYTE
AUXOLOGY
AVIATRIX
AXHAMMER
AXIALITY
AXIFUGAL
AXILEMMA
AXILLANT
AXILLARY
AXIOLITE
AXIOLOGY
AXLETREE
AXMAKING
AXMASTER
AXOFUGAL
AXOIDEAN
AXOLYSIS
AXOMETER
AXONEURE
AXOPETAL
AXOPHYTE
AXOPLASM
AXOSTYLE
BANDBOXY
BANDEAUX
BAROTAXY
BETWIXEN
BICONVEX
BILLYWIX
BINOXIDE
BISEXUAL
BIXBYITE
BOLLIXED
BOXBERRY
BOXBOARD
BOXTHORN
BREADBOX
BREAKAXE
BROADAXE
CACHEXIA
CACHEXIC
CACODOXY
CACOMIXL
CARBOXYL
CARNIFEX
CATHEXIS
CAUDEXES
CEROXYLE
CERVIXES
CHAFEWAX
CHAFFWAX
CHAPEAUX
CHATEAUX
CHRONAXY
CICATRIX
CLAVILUX
CLIMAXED
COEXTEND
COLOPEXY
COLTPIXY
COMMIXED
CONFIXED
CONNEXES
CONNEXUS
CONTUMAX
CONVEXED
CONVEXLY
COUTEAUX
COXALGIA
COXALGIC
COXBONES
COXCOMBY
COXSWAIN
CRESOXID
CRUCIFIX
DEFLEXED
DETOXIFY
DEXTRANE
DEXTRINE
DEXTROSE
DEXTROUS
DIAXONIC
DIPLEXER
DISANNEX
DIXENITE
DOXASTIC
DOXOLOGY
DUPLEXED
DUPLEXER
DUPLEXES
DUXELLES
DYSOREXY
DYSTAXIA
EFFLUXES
EPICALYX
EQUAIXED
ESSEXITE
ETHOXIDE
EUPRAXIA
EUTAXITE
EUXENITE
EXACTING
EXACTION
EXACTIVE
EXACUATE
EXALTATE
EXALTING
EXAMINED
EXAMINEE
EXAMINER
EXAMPLED
EXANTHEM
EXARCHAL
EXCALATE
EXCAMBER
EXCAVATE
EXCECATE
EXCEDENT
EXCEEDED
EXCELLED
EXCELSIN
EXCEPTED
EXCEPTER
EXCEPTIO
EXCERPTA
EXCHANGE
EXCIDING
EXCIPULE
EXCIRCLE
EXCISING
EXCISION
EXCITANT
EXCITATE
EXCITING
EXCITIVE
EXCITORY
EXCITRON
EXCLUDED
EXCLUDER
EXCRESCE
EXCRETAL
EXCRETED
EXCRETER
EXCRETES
EXCUBANT
EXCUDATE
EXCURSED
EXCURSUS
EXCURVED
EXCUSING
EXCUSIVE

EXCUSSED
EXCYSTED
EXECRATE
EXECUTED
EXECUTER
EXECUTOR
EXECUTRY
EXEGESES
EXEGESIS
EXEGETIC
EXEMPLAR
EXEMPLUM
EXEQUIAL
EXEQUIES
EXERCENT
EXERCISE
EXERESIS
EXERGUAL
EXERTING
EXERTION
EXERTIVE
EXFIGURE
EXHALANT
EXHALATE
EXHALING
EXHIBITS
EXHORTED
EXHORTER
EXHUMATE
EXHUMING
EXIGEANT
EXIGENCE
EXIGENCY
EXIGIBLE
EXIGUITY
EXIGUOUS
EXILARCH
EXIMIOUS
EXISTENT
EXISTING
EXITIOUS
EXOCLINE
EXOCOELE
EXODROMY
EXOGAMIC
EXOGENIC
EXOGRAPH
EXOLEMMA
EXOPHAGY
EXORABLE
EXORCISE
EXORCISM
EXORCIST
EXORCIZE
EXORDIAL
EXORDIUM
EXORDIZE
EXOSPERM
EXOSPORE
EXOSTOME
EXOSTRAE
EXOTERIC
EXOTHECA
EXOTOXIC
EXOTOXIN
EXPANDED
EXPANDER
EXPANSUM
EXPECTED
EXPECTER
EXPEDING
EXPEDITE
EXPELLED
EXPELLEE
EXPELLER
EXPENDED
EXPENDER
EXPENSES
EXPERTLY
EXPIABLE
EXPIATED
EXPIATOR
EXPILATE
EXPIRANT
EXPIRATE
EXPIRIES
EXPIRING
EXPLICIT
EXPLODED
EXPLODER
EXPLORED
EXPLORER
EXPONENT
EXPORTED
EXPORTER
EXPOSING
EXPOSURE
EXPULSER
EXPUNGED
EXPUNGER
EXRADIUS
EXRUPEAL
EXSCRIBE
EXSCRIPT
EXSECANT
EXSECTOR
EXSERTED
EXSHEATH
EXTENDED
EXTENDER
EXTENSOR
EXTENSUM
EXTERIOR
EXTERNAL
EXTERNAT
EXTERNUM
EXTISPEX
EXTOLLED
EXTOLLER
EXTORTED
EXTORTER
EXTRACTS
EXTRADOS
EXTRARED
EXTREMER
EXTREMES
EXTREMUM
EXTRORSE
EXTRUDED
EXTRUDER
EXTUBATE
EXTUSION
EXUDENCE
EXULTANT
EXULTING
EXUMBRAL
EXUNDATE
EXUVIATE
FABLIAUX
FIXATING
FIXATION
FIXATIVE
FIXATURE
FIXIDITY
FIXITIES
FLAXBIRD
FLAXBUSH
FLAXDROP
FLAXIEST
FLAXSEED
FLAXTAIL
FLAXWEED
FLAXWIFE
FLAXWORT
FLEXIBLE
FLEXIBLY
FLEXUOSE
FLEXUOUS
FLEXURAL
FLEXURED
FLUXIBLE
FLUXIBLY
FLUXROOT
FLUXWEED
FORNAXID
FOXBERRY
FOXGLOVE
FOXHOUND
FOXINESS
FRAXETIN
GALAXIAN
GALAXIAS
GENETRIX
GEOTAXIS
GLYOXIME
GREENWAX
HARUSPEX
HERITRIX
HEXAFOIL
HEXAFOOS
HEXAGLOT
HEXAGRAM
HEXAMINE
HEXAMMIN
HEXANDRY
HEXAPLAR
HEXAPODY
HEXARCHY
HEXASEME
HEXASTER
HEXYLENE
HOMAXIAL
HOMOTAXY
HORSEPOX
HYPAXIAL
INDEXING
INEXPERT
INFIXING
INFIXION
INFLEXED
INTERMIX
INTERREX
INTERSEX
INTERTEX
INTEXINE
JAMBEAUX
JANITRIX
JASPONYX
KETOXIME
LARYNXES
LAXATION
LAXATIVE
LEUCORYX
LIPOXENY
LITHOXYL
LIXIVIAL
LIXIVIUM
LOXOCOSM
LOXODONT
LOXOSOMA
LOXOTOMY
LUXATING
LUXATION
LUXURIES
LUXURIST
LUXURITY
MALAXAGE
MALAXATE
MALAXING
MANTEAUX
MASTAUXE
MATCHBOX
MATRIXES
MAXILLAE
MAXIMATE
MAXIMIST
MAXIMITE
MAXIMIZE
MAXIMUMS
MAZOPEXY
MEIOTAXY
MELAXUMA
MERETRIX
MEROXENE
METAXITE
METHOXYL
MILLILUX
MIREPOIX
MISOXENE
MISOXENY
MIXBLOOD
MIXERESS
MONAXIAL
MONOXIDE
MONOXYLA
MONOXYLE
MORCEAUX
MOROXITE
MORTREUX
MOUSSEUX
MUREXIDE
MYELAUXE
MYXAEMIA
MYXEDEMA
MYXINOID
MYXOCYTE
MYXOMATA
NEURAXIS
NEURAXON
NEXTNESS
NITROXYL
NIXTAMAL
NOSOTAXY
NOTAULIX
NOVATRIX
OCTUPLEX
OPOPANAX
ORTHODOX
OXALEMIA
OXALURIA
OXALURIC
OXAMIDIN
OXAMMITE
OXANILIC
OXHARROW
OXIDABLE
OXIDASIC
OXIDATED
OXIDATOR
OXIDIZED
OXIDIZER
OXPECKER
OXTONGUE
OXYAMINE
OXYAPHIA
OXYASTER
OXYBAPHA
OXYCRATE
OXYDIACT
OXYETHER
OXYETHYL
OXYGENIC
OXYGONAL
OXYMORON
OXYPHILE
OXYPHONY
OXYPHYTE
OXYRHINE
OXYSALT
OXYSTOME
OXYTOCIA
OXYTOCIC
OXYTOCIN
OXYUROUS
PAINTBOX
PANMIXIA
PARADOXY
PARALLAX
PARAXIAL
PAROXYSM
PAXILLAE
PAXILLAR
PAXILLUS
PEIXEREY
PEROXIDE
PHILODOX
PHORMINX
PLATEAUX
PLEXUSES
POLEAXER
POLYAXON
PONTIFEX
PREAXIAL
PRECIEUX
PREEXIST
PREFIXAL
PREFIXED
PREMIXED
PROLIXLY
PROTAXIS
PROTOXID
PROXENET
PROXENOS
PROXENUS
PROXIMAD
PROXIMAL
PROXYING
PYREXIAL
PYXIDATE
PYXIDIUM
QUINCUNX
QUIXOTIC
QUIXOTRY
REEXPORT
REFLEXED
REFLUXED
RELATRIX
RELAXANT
RELAXING
RETRAXIT
RIXATRIX
RIXDALER
RONDEAUX
ROULEAUX
SARDONYX
SAXATILE
SAXBOARD
SAXICOLE
SAXIFRAX
SAXONITE
SENATRIX
SEXANGLE
SEXENARY
SEXOLOGY
SEXTETTE
SEXTIPLY
SEXTOLET
SEXTUPLE
SEXTUPLY
SEXUALLY
SEXUPARA
SILEXITE
SILOXANE
SIXPENCE
SIXPENNY

SIXSCORE
SIXTIETH
SKATOXYL
SMALLPOX
SMOKEBOX
SNUFFBOX
SPHEXIDE
SPHINXES
SPINIFEX
SPINTEXT
SUBINDEX
SUBOXIDE
SUFFIXAL
SUFFIXED
SUPELLEX
SUPERFIX
SUPERSEX
SUPERTAX
SURTAXED
SWEATBOX
SWINEPOX
SYNAXARY
SYNTAXIS
SYNTEXIS
SYRINXES
TABLEAUX
TAXATION
TAXATIVE
TAXEATER
TAXEOPOD
TAXIARCH
TAXIAUTO
TAXINGLY
TAXODONT
TAXOLOGY
TAXONOMY
TAXPAYER
TEGUEXIN
TETRAXON
TETROXID
TEXGUINO
TEXTBOOK
TEXTILES
TEXTRINE
TEXTUARY
TEXTURAL
TEXTURED
THIOXENE
THORAXES
THYROXIN
TOADFLAX
TONNEAUX
TORTEAUX
TOUCHBOX
TOXAEMIA
TOXAEMIC
TOXICANT
TOXICATE
TOXICITY
TOXICOID
TOXODONT
TOXOLOGY
TOXOPHIL
TRACTRIX
TRANSFIX
TRIAXIAL
TRIOXIDE
TUXEDOES
UNEXPECT
UNEXPERT
UNIAXIAL
UNISEXED
UNSEXING
UROTOXIC
UROTOXIN
UXORIOUS
VENIPLEX
VERTEXES
VEXATION
VEXATORY
VEXILLUM
VIXENISH
VORTEXES
WAXBERRY
WAXINESS
WAXINGLY
WAXMAKER
WHEELBOX
WRAXLING
XANTHANE
XANTHATE
XANTHEIN
XANTHENE
XANTHIDE
XANTHINE
XANTHITE
XANTHOMA
XANTHONE
XANTHOUS
XENAGOGY
XENELASY
XENOCYST
XENODERM
XENOGAMY
XENOLITE
XENOLITH
XENOPHYA
XENOTIME
XERANSIS
XERANTIC
XERAPHIN
XERONATE
XEROPHIL
XEROSERE
XIPHIOID
XYLIDINE
XYLITONE
XYLOCARP
XYLOIDIN
XYLOLOGY
XYLOMATA
XYLORCIN
XYLOSIDE
XYLOTILE
XYLOTOMY
XYLYLENE
ZELATRIX
ZOOTOXIN

POSITIONAL ORDER LIST OF 8-LETTER WORDS

XANTHANE
XANTHATE
XANTHEIN
XANTHENE
XANTHIDE
XANTHINE
XANTHITE
XANTHOMA
XANTHONE
XANTHOUS
XENAGOGY
XENELASY
XENOCYST
XENODERM
XENOGAMY
XENOLITE
XENOLITH
XENOPHYA
XENOTIME
XERANSIS
XERANTIC
XERAPHIN
XERONATE
XEROPHIL
XEROSERE
XIPHIOID
XYLIDINE
XYLITONE
XYLOCARP
XYLOIDIN
XYLOLOGY
XYLOMATA
XYLORCIN
XYLOSIDE
XYLOTILE
XYLOTOMY
XYLYLENE

AXHAMMER
AXIALITY
AXIFUGAL
AXILEMMA
AXILLANT
AXILLARY
AXIOLITE
AXIOLOGY
AXLETREE
AXMAKING
AXMASTER
AXOFUGAL
AXOIDEAN
AXOLYSIS
AXOMETER
AXONEURE
AXOPETAL
AXOPHYTE
AXOPLASM
AXOSTYLE
EXACTING
EXACTION
EXACTIVE
EXACUATE
EXALTATE
EXALTING
EXAMINED
EXAMINEE
EXAMINER
EXAMPLED
EXANTHEM
EXARCHAL
EXCALATE
EXCAMBER
EXCAVATE
EXCECATE
EXCEDENT
EXCEEDED
EXCELLED
EXCELSIN
EXCEPTED
EXCEPTER
EXCEPTIO
EXCERPTA
EXCHANGE
EXCIDING
EXCIPULE
EXCIRCLE
EXCISING
EXCISION
EXCITANT
EXCITATE
EXCITING
EXCITIVE
EXCITORY
EXCITRON
EXCLUDED
EXCLUDER
EXCRESCE
EXCRETAL
EXCRETED
EXCRETER
EXCRETES
EXCUBANT
EXCUDATE
EXCURSED
EXCURSUS
EXCURVED
EXCUSING
EXCUSIVE
EXCUSSED
EXCYSTED
EXECRATE
EXECUTED
EXECUTER
EXECUTOR
EXECUTRY
EXEGESES
EXEGESIS
EXEGETIC
EXEMPLAR
EXEMPLUM
EXEQUIAL
EXEQUIES
EXERCENT
EXERCISE
EXERESIS
EXERGUAL
EXERTING
EXERTION
EXERTIVE
EXFIGURE
EXHALANT
EXHALATE
EXHALING
EXHIBITS
EXHORTED
EXHORTER
EXHUMATE
EXHUMING
EXIGEANT
EXIGENCE
EXIGENCY
EXIGIBLE
EXIGUITY
EXIGUOUS
EXILARCH
EXIMIOUS
EXISTENT
EXISTING
EXITIOUS
EXOCLINE
EXOCOELE
EXODROMY
EXOGAMIC
EXOGENIC
EXOGRAPH
EXOLEMMA
EXOPHAGY
EXORABLE
EXORCISE
EXORCISM
EXORCIST
EXORCIZE
EXORDIAL
EXORDIUM
EXORDIZE
EXOSPERM
EXOSPORE
EXOSTOME
EXOSTRAE
EXOTERIC
EXOTHECA
EXOTOXIC
EXOTOXIN
EXPANDED
EXPANDER
EXPANSUM
EXPECTED
EXPECTER
EXPEDING
EXPEDITE
EXPELLED
EXPELLEE
EXPELLER
EXPENDED
EXPENDER
EXPENSES
EXPERTLY
EXPIABLE
EXPIATED
EXPIATOR
EXPILATE
EXPIRANT
EXPIRATE
EXPIRIES
EXPIRING
EXPLICIT
EXPLODED
EXPLODER
EXPLORED
EXPLORER
EXPONENT
EXPORTED
EXPORTER
EXPOSING
EXPOSURE
EXPULSER
EXPUNGED
EXPUNGER
EXRADIUS
EXRUPEAL
EXSCRIBE
EXSCRIPT
EXSECANT
EXSECTOR
EXSERTED
EXSHEATH
EXTENDED
EXTENDER
EXTENSOR
EXTENSUM
EXTERIOR
EXTERNAL
EXTERNAT
EXTERNUM
EXTISPEX

EXTOLLED
EXTOLLER
EXTORTED
EXTORTER
EXTRACTS
EXTRADOS
EXTRARED
EXTREMER
EXTREMES
EXTREMUM
EXTRORSE
EXTRUDED
EXTRUDER
EXTUBATE
EXTUSION
EXUDENCE
EXULTANT
EXULTING
EXUMBRAL
EXUNDATE
EXUVIATE
OXALEMIA
OXALURIA
OXALURIC
OXAMIDIN
OXAMMITE
OXANILIC
OXHARROW
OXIDABLE
OXIDASIC
OXIDATED
OXIDATOR
OXIDIZED
OXIDIZER
OXPECKER
OXTONGUE
OXYAMINE
OXYAPHIA
OXYASTER
OXYBAPHA
OXYCRATE
OXYDIACT
OXYETHER
OXYETHYL
OXYGENIC
OXYGONAL
OXYMORON
OXYPHILE
OXYPHONY
OXYPHYTE
OXYRHINE
OXYSALT
OXYSTOME
OXYTOCIA
OXYTOCIC
OXYTOCIN
OXYUROUS
UXORIOUS

ACXOYATL
AUXILIAR
AUXILIUM
AUXIMONE
AUXOBODY
AUXOCYTE
AUXOLOGY
BIXBYITE
BOXBERRY
BOXBOARD
BOXTHORN
COXALGIA
COXALGIC
COXBONES
COXCOMBY
COXSWAIN
DEXTRANE
DEXTRINE
DEXTROSE
DEXTROUS
DIXENITE
DOXASTIC
DOXOLOGY
DUXELLES
EUXENITE
FIXATING
FIXATION
FIXATIVE
FIXATURE
FIXIDITY
FIXITIES
FOXBERRY
FOXGLOVE
FOXHOUND
FOXINESS
HEXAFOIL
HEXAFOOS
HEXAGLOT
HEXAGRAM
HEXAMINE
HEXAMMIN
HEXANDRY
HEXAPLAR
HEXAPODY
HEXARCHY
HEXASEME
HEXASTER
HEXYLENE
LAXATION
LAXATIVE
LIXIVIAL
LIXIVIUM
LOXOCOSM
LOXODONT
LOXOSOMA
LOXOTOMY
LUXATING
LUXATION
LUXURIES
LUXURIST
LUXURITY
MAXILLAE
MAXIMATE
MAXIMIST
MAXIMITE
MAXIMIZE
MAXIMUMS
MIXBLOOD
MIXERESS
MYXAEMIA
MYXEDEMA
MYXINOID
MYXOCYTE
MYXOMATA
NEXTNESS
NIXTAMAL
PAXILLAE
PAXILLAR
PAXILLUS
PYXIDATE
PYXIDIUM
RIXATRIX
RIXDALER
SAXATILE
SAXBOARD
SAXICOLE
SAXIFRAX
SAXONITE
SEXANGLE
SEXENARY
SEXOLOGY
SEXTETTE
SEXTIPLY
SEXTOLET
SEXTUPLE
SEXTUPLY
SEXUALLY
SEXUPARA
SIXPENCE
SIXPENNY
SIXSCORE
SIXTIETH
TAXATION
TAXATIVE
TAXEATER
TAXEOPOD
TAXIARCH
TAXIAUTO
TAXINGLY
TAXODONT
TAXOLOGY
TAXONOMY
TAXPAYER
TEXGUINO
TEXTBOOK
TEXTILES
TEXTRINE
TEXTUARY
TEXTURAL
TEXTURED
TOXAEMIA
TOXAEMIC
TOXICANT
TOXICATE
TOXICITY
TOXICOID
TOXODONT
TOXOLOGY
TOXOPHIL
TUXEDOES
VEXATION
VEXATORY
VEXILLUM
VIXENISH
WAXBERRY
WAXINESS
WAXINGLY
WAXMAKER

ALEXINIC
ANOXEMIA
ANOXEMIC
APOXESIS
COEXTEND
DIAXONIC
FLAXBIRD
FLAXBUSH
FLAXDROP
FLAXIEST
FLAXSEED
FLAXTAIL
FLAXWEED
FLAXWIFE
FLAXWORT
FLEXIBLE
FLEXIBLY
FLEXUOSE
FLEXUOUS
FLEXURAL
FLEXURED
FLUXIBLE
FLUXIBLY
FLUXROOT
FLUXWEED
FRAXETIN
INEXPERT
PEIXEREY
PLEXUSES
PROXENET
PROXENOS
PROXENUS
PROXIMAD
PROXIMAL
PROXYING
QUIXOTIC
QUIXOTRY
REEXPORT
UNEXPECT
UNEXPERT
WRAXLING

ADMIXING
AFFIXING
AFFIXION
ALDOXIME
ALKOXIDE
ANAUXITE
ANNEXING
ANNEXION
ANNEXIVE
ANNEXURE
BINOXIDE
BISEXUAL
CACOXENE
CEROXYLE
DETOXIFY
ESSEXITE
ETHOXIDE
EUTAXITE
GALAXIAN
GALAXIAS
GLYOXIME
HOMAXIAL
HYPAXIAL
INDEXING
INFIXING
INFIXION
INTEXINE
KETOXIME
LIPOXENY
MALAXAGE
MALAXATE
MALAXING
MELAXUMA
MEROXENE
METAXITE
MISOXENE
MISOXENY
MONAXIAL
MONOXIDE
MONOXYLA
MONOXYLE
MOROXITE
MUREXIDE
PARAXIAL
PAROXYSM
PEROXIDE
PREAXIAL
PREEXIST
PYREXIAL
RELAXANT
RELAXING
SILEXITE
SILOXANE
SPHEXIDE
SUBOXIDE
SYNAXARY
THIOXENE
TRIAXIAL
TRIOXIDE
UNIAXIAL
UNSEXING

ACETOXIM
ACETOXYL
AGALAXIA
AMIDOXYL
AMPLEXUS
ANATEXIS
ANATOXIN
ANOREXIA
APODIXIS
APOMIXIS
APPRAXIC
APYREXIA
ASPHYXIA
ATARAXIA
ATARAXIC
BETWIXEN
BOLLIXED
CACHEXIA
CACHEXIC
CARBOXYL
CATHEXIS
CAUDEXES
CERVIXES
CLIMAXED
COMMIXED
CONFIXED
CONNEXES
CONNEXUS
CONVEXED
CONVEXLY
CRESOXID
DEFLEXED
DIPLEXER
DUPLEXED
DUPLEXER
DUPLEXES
DYSTAXIA
EFFLUXES
EQUAIXED
EUPRAXIA
EXOTOXIC
EXOTOXIN
FORNAXID
GEOTAXIS
INFLEXED
LARYNXES
LITHOXYL
MATRIXES
METHOXYL
NEURAXIS
NEURAXON
NITROXYL
PANMIXIA
POLEAXER
POLYAXON
PREFIXAL
PREFIXED
PREMIXED
PROLIXLY
PROTAXIS
PROTOXID
REFLEXED
REFLUXED
RETRAXIT
SKATOXYL
SPHINXES
SUFFIXAL
SUFFIXED
SURTAXED
SYNTAXIS
SYNTEXIS
SYRINXES
TEGUEXIN
TETRAXON
TETROXID
THORAXES
THYROXIN
UNISEXED
UROTOXIC
UROTOXIN
VERTEXES
VORTEXES
ZOOTOXIN

ANTEFIXA
APOPLEXY
BANDBOXY
BAROTAXY
BREAKAXE
BROADAXE
CACODOXY
CACOMIXL
CHRONAXY
COLOPEXY
COLTPIXY
DYSOREXY
HOMOTAXY
MASTAUXE
MAZOPEXY
MEIOTAXY
MYELAUXE
NOSOTAXY
PARADOXY
SPINTEXT
ADJUTRIX
ANTHELIX
APPENDIX
AVIATRIX
BANDEAUX
BICONVEX
BILLYWIX
BREADBOX
CARNIFEX
CHAFEWAX
CHAFFWAX
CHAPEAUX
CHATEAUX
CICATRIX
CLAVILUX
CONTUMAX
COUTEAUX
CRUCIFIX
DISANNEX
EPICALYX
EXTISPEX
FABLIAUX
GENETRIX
GREENWAX
HARUSPEX
HERITRIX
HORSEPOX
INTERMIX
INTERREX
INTERSEX
INTERTEX
JAMBEAUX
JANITRIX
JASPONYX
LEUCORYX
MANTEAUX
MATCHBOX
MERETRIX
MILLILUX
MIREPOIX
MORCEAUX
MORTREUX
MOUSSEUX
NOTAULIX
NOVATRIX
OCTUPLEX
OPOPANAX
ORTHODOX
PAINTBOX
PARALLAX
PHILODOX
PHORMINX
PLATEAUX
PONTIFEX
PRECIEUX
QUINCUNX
RELATRIX
RIXATRIX
RONDEAUX
ROULEAUX
SARDONYX
SAXIFRAX
SENATRIX
SMALLPOX
SMOKEBOX
SNUFFBOX
SPINIFEX
SUBINDEX
SUPELLEX
SUPERFIX
SUPERSEX
SUPERTAX
SWEATBOX
SWINEPOX
TABLEAUX
TOADFLAX
TONNEAUX
TORTEAUX
TOUCHBOX
TRACTRIX
TRANSFIX
VENIPLEX
WHEELBOX
ZELATRIX

SCORING ORDER LIST OF 8-LETTER WORDS

31
MAZOPEXY

29
CHAFFWAX

28
MAXIMIZE

27
JASPONYX
QUIXOTRY

26
CHAFEWAX
COXCOMBY
EXORCIZE
HEXARCHY
JAMBEAUX
OXIDIZED
OXYPHONY
OXYPHYTE
QUINCUNX
QUIXOTIC

25
EQUAIXED
EXORDIZE
MYXOCYTE
OXIDIZER
OXYBAPHA

24
EXEQUIAL
EXEQUIES
EXOPHAGY
FLAXWIFE
HEXAPODY
MATCHBOX
OXYETHYL
WAXMAKER
ZELATRIX
ZOOTOXIN

23
ADJUTRIX
ASPHYXIA
AXOPHYTE
BANDBOXY
BILLYWIX
CACODOXY
CHRONAXY
CONVEXLY
FLAXBUSH
FLEXIBLY
FLUXIBLY
FOXBERRY
HOMOTAXY
HYPAXIAL
METHOXYL
MYXEDEMA
OXPECKER
OXYAPHIA
OXYPHILE
PYXIDIUM
SMOKEBOX
SNUFFBOX
WAXBERRY
WHEELBOX
XENOPHYA
XYLOTOMY

22
AFFIXING
APOPLEXY
AXHAMMER
AXMAKING
BICONVEX
BIXBYITE
BOXBERRY
CACHEXIA
CARBOXYL
CHAPEAUX
COLOPEXY
COLTPIXY
COMMIXED
CRUCIFIX
DETOXIFY
DYSOREXY
EPICALYX
FIXIDITY
FLAXWEED
FLUXWEED
FOXGLOVE
FOXHOUND
HEXAMMIN
HEXANDRY
JANITRIX
MYXAEMIA
MYXOMATA
OXYTOCIC
PAROXYSM
PHORMINX
SKATOXYL
SUFFIXED
TOUCHBOX
WAXINGLY
XYLOCARP
XYLOLOGY

21
AFFIXION
AMIDOXYL
APPRAXIC
AUXOBODY
BREAKAXE
CACHEXIC
CACOMIXL
CONFIXED
CONVEXED
EFFLUXES
EXCAMBER
EXCHANGE
EXCURVED
EXCYSTED
EXEMPLUM
EXHUMING
EXIGENCY
EXODROMY
EXOGRAPH
EXSHEATH
FIXATIVE
FLAXBIRD
FLAXDROP
FLAXWORT
GLYOXIME
HEXAFOIL
HEXAFOOS
HEXAGRAM
HEXYLENE
KETOXIME
LITHOXYL
MYXINOID
OXHARROW
OXYDIACT
OXYETHER
OXYGENIC
OXYRHINE
PARADOXY
PHILODOX
PREFIXED
PROXYING
PYXIDATE
SPHEXIDE
SUFFIXAL
SYNAXARY
TEXTBOOK
THYROXIN
VEXATORY
VIXENISH
XENOGAMY
XIPHIOID
XYLYLENE

20
ACETOXYL
ACXOYATL
ALKOXIDE
APPENDIX
APYREXIA
AUXOCYTE
BAROTAXY
BETWIXEN
BOXBOARD
BOXTHORN
BREADBOX
CARNIFEX
CATHEXIS
CEROXYLE
CERVIXES
CHATEAUX
CLAVILUX
CLIMAXED
COXALGIC
COXSWAIN
DEFLEXED
DOXOLOGY
EXACTIVE
EXAMPLED
EXANTHEM
EXARCHAL
EXCAVATE
EXCEPTED
EXCITIVE
EXCITORY
EXCUSIVE
EXECUTRY
EXHIBITS
EXHUMATE
EXILARCH
EXOGAMIC
EXOTHECA
EXPECTED
EXPERTLY
FABLIAUX
FLEXIBLE
FLUXIBLE
HARUSPEX
HEXAMINE
HEXAPLAR
HEXASEME
HOMAXIAL
HORSEPOX
LEUCORYX
LIPOXENY
LIXIVIUM
LOXOTOMY
MEIOTAXY
MISOXENY
MIXBLOOD
MONOXYLA
MONOXYLE
MYELAUXE
OXYAMINE
OXYCRATE
OXYMORON
OXYSTOME
OXYTOCIA
OXYTOCIN
PEIXEREY
POLYAXON
PONTIFEX
PREFIXAL
PREMIXED
PROLIXLY
PROXIMAD
PYREXIAL
SEXTIPLY
SEXTUPLY
SIXPENNY
SPHINXES
SPINIFEX
SUPERFIX
SWEATBOX
SWINEPOX
TAXIARCH
TAXONOMY
TAXPAYER
TOXICITY
TOXOPHIL

VENIPLEX
VEXILLUM
XANTHOMA
XENAGOGY
XENOCYST
XERAPHIN
XEROPHIL
XYLOMATA
XYLORCIN

19

ACETOXIM
ADMIXING
AMPLEXUS
ANOXEMIC
APOMIXIS
AUXOLOGY
AXIFUGAL
AXILEMMA
AXIOLOGY
AXOFUGAL
AXOPLASM
CACOXENE
CICATRIX
CONTUMAX
COXBONES
DUPLEXED
DYSTAXIA
ETHOXIDE
EXCECATE
EXCEEDED
EXCEPTER
EXCEPTIO
EXCERPTA
EXCIDING
EXCIPULE
EXCIRCLE
EXCLUDED
EXCRESCE
EXCUBANT
EXEMPLAR
EXFIGURE
EXHALING
EXHORTED
EXIGUITY
EXOLEMMA
EXORCISM
EXOSPERM
EXPANDED
EXPANSUM
EXPECTER
EXPEDING
EXPENDED
EXPIABLE
EXPLICIT
EXPLODED
EXPUNGED
EXSCRIBE
EXSCRIPT
EXTREMUM
EXUMBRAL
FIXATING
FLAXSEED
FLEXURED
FORNAXID
GREENWAX
HEXAGLOT
INFIXING
INFLEXED
LOXOCOSM
MAXIMATE
MAXIMIST
MAXIMITE
MELAXUMA
MIREPOIX
MORCEAUX
OCTUPLEX
OPOPANAX
ORTHODOX
OXAMMITE
OXYGONAL
PAINTBOX
PANMIXIA
PRECIEUX
PROXIMAL
REFLEXED
REFLUXED
SARDONYX
SEXOLOGY
SIXPENCE
SMALLPOX
TAXINGLY
TAXOLOGY
TOADFLAX
TOXAEMIC
TOXOLOGY
UNEXPECT
WRAXLING
XANTHIDE
XYLIDINE
XYLOIDIN
XYLOSIDE

18

ALDOXIME
ANNEXIVE
ANTEFIXA
ANTHELIX
APODIXIS
AVIATRIX
AXIALITY
AXILLARY
AXOLYSIS
AXOSTYLE
BANDEAUX
BINOXIDE
BOLLIXED
BROADAXE
CAUDEXES
COEXTEND
COXALGIA
CRESOXID
DIAXONIC
DIPLEXER
DOXASTIC
DUPLEXER
DUPLEXES
EXACTING
EXAMINED
EXCEDENT
EXCELLED
EXCISING
EXCITING
EXCLUDER
EXCRETED
EXCUDATE
EXCURSED
EXCUSING
EXCUSSED
EXECUTED
EXEGETIC
EXERTIVE
EXHALANT
EXHALATE
EXHORTER
EXIGENCE
EXIGIBLE
EXOGENIC
EXORDIUM
EXPANDER
EXPEDITE
EXPELLED
EXPENDER
EXPIATED
EXPIRING
EXPLODER
EXPLORED
EXPORTED
EXPOSING
EXPUNGER
EXUDENCE
EXUVIATE
FIXATION
FIXATURE
FIXITIES
FLAXIEST
FLAXTAIL
FLEXUOSE
FLEXUOUS
FLEXURAL
FLUXROOT
FOXINESS
FRAXETIN
HERITRIX
HEXASTER
INFIXION
LARYNXES
LAXATIVE
LIXIVIAL
LUXURITY
MALAXAGE
MALAXING
MAXIMUMS
MONOXIDE
MUREXIDE
NITROXYL
NOSOTAXY
NOVATRIX
OXAMIDIN
OXIDABLE
OXIDASIC
OXYASTER
OXYUROUS
PEROXIDE
PROTOXID
SAXBOARD
SEXENARY
SEXUALLY
SIXTIETH
SUBINDEX
SUBOXIDE
SYNTAXIS
SYNTEXIS
SYRINXES
TAXATIVE
TAXEOPOD
TEXTUARY
THIOXENE
THORAXES
TOXICOID
TRANSFIX
VERTEXES
VEXATION
VORTEXES
WAXINESS
XANTHANE
XANTHATE
XANTHEIN
XANTHENE
XANTHINE
XANTHITE
XANTHONE
XANTHOUS
XENELASY
XENODERM
XENOLITH
XYLITONE
XYLOTILE

17

ALEXINIC
ANOXEMIA
APOXESIS
ATARAXIC
AUXILIUM
AUXIMONE
AXMASTER
AXOMETER
AXOPETAL
BISEXUAL
CONNEXES
CONNEXUS
COUTEAUX
EUPRAXIA
EXACTION
EXACUATE
EXAMINEE
EXAMINER
EXCALATE
EXCELSIN
EXCISION
EXCITANT
EXCITATE
EXCITRON
EXCRETAL
EXCRETER
EXCRETES
EXCURSUS
EXECRATE
EXECUTER
EXECUTOR
EXERCENT
EXERCISE
EXIMIOUS
EXOCLINE
EXOCOELE
EXORABLE
EXORCISE
EXORCIST
EXOSPORE
EXOSTOME
EXOTERIC
EXPELLEE
EXPELLER
EXPENSES
EXPIATOR
EXPILATE
EXPIRANT
EXPIRATE
EXPIRIES
EXPLORER
EXPONENT
EXPORTER
EXPOSURE
EXPULSER
EXRUPEAL
EXSECANT
EXSECTOR
EXTENDED
EXTENSUM
EXTERNUM
EXTRACTS
EXTREMER
EXTREMES
EXTRUDED
EXTUBATE
INDEXING
INEXPERT
INTERMIX
LOXOSOMA
MALAXATE
MANTEAUX
MASTAUXE
MATRIXES
MAXILLAE
MERETRIX
MEROXENE
METAXITE
MILLILUX
MISOXENE
MIXERESS
MONAXIAL
MOROXITE
MORTREUX
MOUSSEUX
NIXTAMAL
OXALEMIA
OXALURIC
OXANILIC
OXIDATED
OXYSALT
PARALLAX
PARAXIAL
PAXILLAE
PAXILLAR
PAXILLUS
PLATEAUX
PLEXUSES
POLEAXER
PREAXIAL
PREEXIST
PROTAXIS
PROXENET
PROXENOS
PROXENUS
REEXPORT
SAXICOLE
SAXIFRAX
SEXTUPLE
SEXUPARA
SIXSCORE
SPINTEXT
SUPELLEX
SUPERSEX
SUPERTAX
TABLEAUX
TOXAEMIA
TOXICANT
TOXICATE
TRACTRIX
UNEXPERT
UROTOXIC
XENOTIME
XERANTIC

16

AGALAXIA
ANNEXING
AXOIDEAN
DEXTRANE
DEXTRINE
DEXTROSE
DEXTROUS
DISANNEX
DIXENITE
DUXELLES
EXALTING
EXEGESES
EXEGESIS
EXERGUAL
EXERTING
EXIGEANT
EXIGUOUS
EXISTING
EXORDIAL
EXOTOXIC
EXRADIUS
EXSERTED
EXTENDER
EXTISPEX
EXTOLLED

EXTORTED
EXTRADOS
EXTRARED
EXTRUDER
EXULTING
EXUNDATE
GALAXIAN
GALAXIAS
GENETRIX
GEOTAXIS
LOXODONT
LUXATING
OXIDATOR
OXTONGUE
RELAXING
RIXDALER
RONDEAUX
SEXANGLE
SURTAXED
TAXODONT
TEGUEXIN
TETROXID
TEXGUINO
TEXTURED
TOXODONT
TRIOXIDE
TUXEDOES
UNISEXED
UNSEXING

15

ANATEXIS
ANATOXIN
ANAUXITE
ANNEXION
ANNEXURE
ANOREXIA
ATARAXIA
AUXILIAR
AXILLANT
AXIOLITE
AXLETREE
AXONEURE
ESSEXITE
EUTAXITE
EUXENITE
EXALTATE
EXERESIS
EXERTION
EXISTENT
EXITIOUS
EXOSTRAE
EXTENSOR
EXTERIOR
EXTERNAL
EXTERNAT
EXTOLLER
EXTORTER
EXTRORSE
EXTUSION
EXULTANT
INTERREX
INTERSEX
INTERTEX
INTEXINE
LAXATION
LUXATION
LUXURIES
LUXURIST
NEURAXIS
NEURAXON
NEXTNESS
NOTAULIX
OXALURIA
RELATRIX
RELAXANT
RETRAXIT
RIXATRIX
ROULEAUX
SAXATILE
SAXONITE
SENATRIX
SEXTETTE
SEXTOLET
SILEXITE
SILOXANE
TAXATION
TAXEATER
TAXIAUTO
TETRAXON
TEXTILES
TEXTRINE
TEXTURAL
TONNEAUX
TORTEAUX
TRIAXIAL
UNIAXIAL
UROTOXIN
UXORIOUS
XENOLITE
XERANSIS
XERONATE
XEROSERE

14

EXOTOXIN

ALPHABETICAL LIST OF 9-LETTER WORDS

ABOIDEAUX
ACETOXIME
ADMIXTION
ADMIXTURE
ADNEXITIS
AEROTAXIS
AFFIXTURE
AFFLUXION
AGITATRIX
ALLOXANIC
ALLOXURIC
AMIDOXIME
AMPHIOXUS
AMYOTAXIA
ANAPTYXIS
ANNEXABLE
ANNEXMENT
ANOXAEMIA
ANOXAEMIC
ANTECOXAL
ANTEFIXAL
ANTEFIXES
ANTHOTAXY
ANTHROXAN
ANTIHELIX
ANXIETIES
ANXIETUDE
ANXIOUSLY
APOSTAXIS
APROSEXIA
APYREXIAL
ASEXUALLY
ASPHYXIAL
ASPHYXIED
ASSERTRIX
ATLOAXOID
AUTOTOXIC
AUTOTOXIN
AUXETICAL
AUXILIARY
AUXILIATE
AUXOBLAST
AUXOFLORE
AUXOFLUOR
AUXOGRAPH
AUXOMETER
AUXOSPORE
AUXOTONIC
AXBREAKER
AXEMASTER
AXILEMMAS
AXIOLITIC
AXIOMATIC
AXIOPISTY
AXLESMITH
AXMANSHIP
AXONEURON
AXOPODIUM
AZOXONIUM
BAROTAXIS
BAROXYTON
BASIFIXED
BAUXITITE
BIAXIALLY
BISECTRIX
BISEXUOUS
BIXACEOUS
BOISSEAUX
BOLLIXING
BOXHOLDER
BOXKEEPER
BOXWALLAH
BUTTERBOX
BUXACEOUS
BUXERRIES
BUXOMNESS
CACOMIXLE
CALCIPEXY
CANDLEBOX
CARBOXIDE
CARDIAUXE
CATALEXIS
CATAPLEXY
CAULOTAXY
CHEMOTAXY
CHRONAXIA
CHRONAXIE
CICUTOXIN
CLIMAXING
COAXATION
COAXIALLY
COAXINGLY
COLOPEXIA
COMMIXING
COMPLEXLY
COMPLEXUS
CONFIXING
CONNEXION
CONNEXITY
CONNEXIVA
CONNEXIVE
CONVEXITY
COXCOMBRY
COXODYNIA
CRESOXIDE
CYTOTAXIS
CYTOTOXIC
CYTOTOXIN
DECOMPLEX
DEFLEXING
DEFLEXION
DEFLEXURE
DEFLUXION
DENDRAXON
DEOXIDIZE
DEXTERITY
DEXTEROUS
DEXTRALLY
DEXTRORSE
DIAPLEXUS
DIAZEUXIS
DICTATRIX
DIGITOXIN
DIHYDROXY
DIMETHOXY
DIRECTRIX
DORSIFLEX
DRUXINESS
DUPLEXING
DUPLEXITY
ELIXATION
EMPHRAXIS
ENDOMIXIS
ENDOTOXIC
ENDOTOXIN
ENTERAUXE
ENTREDEUX
EPAXIALLY
EPIPLEXIS
EPISTAXIS
EPITOXOID
EPIZEUXIS
EUTAXITIC
EXACTABLE
EXACTMENT
EXACTNESS
EXADVERSO
EXAGITATE
EXAIRESIS
EXALTEDLY
EXAMINANT
EXAMINATE
EXAMINING
EXAMPLING
EXANIMATE
EXANTHEMA
EXANTLATE
EXARATION
EXARCHATE
EXARCHIST
EXCAMBION
EXCARNATE
EXCAUDATE
EXCAVATED
EXCAVATOR
EXCEEDING
EXCELENTE
EXCELLENT
EXCELLING
EXCELSIOR
EXCENTRAL
EXCENTRIC
EXCEPTANT
EXCEPTING
EXCEPTION
EXCEPTIVE
EXCERPTED
EXCERPTOR
EXCESSIVE
EXCESSMAN
EXCESSMEN
EXCHANGED
EXCHANGER
EXCHEQUER
EXCIPIENT
EXCIPULAR
EXCIPULUM
EXCISABLE
EXCISEMAN
EXCISEMEN
EXCITABLE
EXCITABLY
EXCITANCY
EXCITATOR
EXCITEDLY
EXCLAIMED
EXCLAIMER
EXCLUDING
EXCLUSION
EXCLUSIVE
EXCLUSORY
EXCOCTION
EXCORIATE
EXCREMENT
EXCRETING
EXCRETION
EXCRETIVE
EXCRETORY
EXCULPATE
EXCURRENT
EXCURSING
EXCURSION
EXCURSIVE
EXCURVATE
EXCUSABLE

EXCUSABLY
EXCUSATOR
EXCUSSING
EXECRABLE
EXECRABLY
EXECRATED
EXECRATOR
EXECUTANT
EXECUTING
EXECUTION
EXECUTIVE
EXECUTORY
EXECUTRIX
EXEGETICS
EXEGETIST
EXEMPLARY
EXEMPLIFY
EXEMPTILE
EXEMPTION
EXEMPTIVE
EXEQUATUR
EXERCISED
EXERCISER
EXERCISES
EXERCITOR
EXFODIATE
EXFOLIATE
EXHALABLE
EXHAUSTED
EXHAUSTER
EXHIBITED
EXHIBITOR
EXHORTING
EXHUMATED
EXHUMATOR
EXIGEANTE
EXIGENTER
EXIGENTLY
EXINANITE
EXISTENCE
EXOCARDIA
EXOCLINAL
EXOCOELAR
EXOCOELIC
EXOCOELOM
EXOCOELUM
EXOCULATE
EXOCYCLIC
EXODERMIS
EXODONTIA
EXODROMIC
EXOENZYME
EXOGAMOUS
EXOGENOUS
EXONERATE
EXONEURAL
EXOPATHIC
EXOPHORIA
EXOPHORIA
EXOPHORIC
EXOPODITE
EXORBITAL
EXORCISED
EXORCISER
EXORCIZED
EXORCIZER
EXORDIUMS
EXORGANIC
EXOSEPSIS
EXOSMOSIS
EXOSMOTIC
EXOSPHERE
EXOSPORAL
EXOSTOSED
EXOSTOSES
EXOSTOSIS
EXOSTOTIC
EXOTERICS
EXOTHECAL
EXOTICISM
EXOTICIST
EXOTICITY
EXOTROPIA
EXPALPATE
EXPANDING
EXPANSILE
EXPANSION
EXPANSIVE
EXPANSURE
EXPATIATE
EXPECTANT
EXPECTING
EXPECTIVE
EXPEDIATE
EXPEDIENT
EXPEDITED
EXPEDITER
EXPEDITOR
EXPELLANT
EXPELLENT
EXPELLING
EXPENDING
EXPENSIVE
EXPERIENT
EXPERTISE
EXPIATING
EXPIATION
EXPIATIST
EXPIATIVE
EXPIATORY
EXPILATOR
EXPIRATOR
EXPISCATE
EXPLAINED
EXPLAINER
EXPLANATE
EXPLEMENT
EXPLETIVE
EXPLETORY
EXPLICATE
EXPLODENT
EXPLODING
EXPLOITED
EXPLOITER
EXPLORING
EXPLOSION
EXPLOSIVE
EXPONENCE
EXPONENTS
EXPONIBLE
EXPORTING
EXPOSITOR
EXPOUNDED
EXPOUNDER
EXPRESSED
EXPRESSER
EXPRESSLY
EXPROBATE
EXPUITION
EXPULSION
EXPULSIVE
EXPULSORY
EXPUNGING
EXPURGATE
EXQUISITE
EXSCINDED
EXSECTILE
EXSECTION
EXSERTILE
EXSERTING
EXSERTION
EXSICCATE
EXSOMATIC
EXSPUTORY
EXSTROPHY
EXSUCCOUS
EXSUCTION
EXSURGENT
EXTEMPORE
EXTENDING
EXTENSILE
EXTENSION
EXTENSITY
EXTENSIVE
EXTENUATE
EXTERMINE
EXTERNATE
EXTERNIZE
EXTERNIZE
EXTINCTOR
EXTIRPATE
EXTISPICY
EXTOLLING
EXTOLMENT
EXTORSIVE
EXTORTING
EXTORTION
EXTORTIVE
EXTRABOLD
EXTRACTED
EXTRACTOR
EXTRADITE
EXTRALITE
EXTRALITY
EXTRANEAN
EXTRAVERT
EXTREMELY
EXTREMEST
EXTREMISM
EXTREMIST
EXTREMITY
EXTRICATE
EXTRINSIC
EXTRORSAL
EXTROVERT
EXTRUDING
EXTRUSILE
EXTRUSION
EXTRUSIVE
EXTRUSORY
EXUBERANT
EXUBERATE
EXUDATION
EXUDATIVE
EXUDATORY
EXULTANCY
EXULULATE
EXUVIABLE
EXUVIATED
FIXEDNESS
FLAMBEAUX
FLAXBOARD
FLAXWENCH
FLAXWOMAN
FLEXILITY
FLEXIONAL
FLUMMOXED
FLUXATION
FLUXILITY
FLUXIONAL
FLUXMETER
FOXTAILED
FUNDATRIX
GLYOXALIC
GLYOXYLIC
GONOCALYX
HEMIAUXIN
HEMOTOXIC
HEMOTOXIN
HEPTOXIDE
HETERODOX
HEXABASIC
HEXABIOSE
HEXACHORD
HEXACOLIC
HEXADECYL
HEXADIENE
HEXADIINE
HEXADIYNE
HEXAGONAL
HEXAHEDRA
HEXAMERAL
HEXAMERON
HEXAMETER
HEXAMMINE
HEXANDRIC
HEXAPLOID
HEXASEMIC
HEXASTICH
HEXASTIGM
HEXATHLON
HEXATOMIC
HOAXPROOF
HOMOTAXIS
HYDROXIDE
HYPOTAXIA
HYPOTAXIC
HYPOTAXIS
IMMIXTURE
IMPERMIXT
IMPOSTRIX
INCOMPLEX
INDEXICAL
INDOXYLIC
INEXACTLY
INEXPIATE
INEXPRESS
INFLEXION
INFLEXIVE
INFLUXION
INFLUXIVE
INMIXTURE
INNOXIOUS
INOXIDIZE
INTERAXAL
INTERAXIS
INTERMIXT
INTEXTINE
INTEXTURE
INTROFLEX
ISOXAZOLE
JUXTAPOSE
KATAPLEXY
KENOTOXIN
KOSOTOXIN
LATEXOSIS
LEPOTHRIX
LEUCOXENE
LEXICALIC
LIPOPEXIA
LITHOXYLE
LIXIVIATE
LIXIVIOUS
LOOMFIXER
LOXOCLASE
LOXODROME
LOXODROMY
LUXURIANT
LUXURIATE
LUXURIOUS
MALAXABLE
MALAXATOR
MALPRAXIS
MASTOPEXY
MAXILLARY
MAXIMALLY
MAXIMIZED
MAXIMIZER
MEDIATRIX
MEDIFIXED
MENOXENIA
MESAXONIC
MESOXALIC
MESOXALYL
METATAXIC
METATAXIS
METAXYLEM
MIXTIFORM
MONAXONIC
MONOXYLIC
MONOXYLON
MULTIPLEX
MYELOPLAX
MYXAMOEBA
MYXEDEMIC
MYXOEDEMA
MYXOINOMA
MYXOMYOMA
MYXOPODIA
MYXORRHEA
MYXOSPORE
MYXOTHECA
NEPHRAUXE
NEURATAXY
NEURAXONE
NOXIOUSLY
NULLIPLEX
OBNOXIETY
OBNOXIOUS
OBSTETRIX
OPERATRIX
ORTHODOXY
OVEREXERT
OVERSEXED
OVERTAXED
OXALAEMIA
OXALURATE
OXAMIDINE
OXANILATE
OXANILIDE
OXBERRIES
OXDIAZOLE
OXIDATING
OXIDATION
OXIDATIVE
OXIDIZING
OXIMATION
OXMANSHIP
OXYBENZYL
OXYDACTYL
OXYGENANT
OXYGENATE
OXYGENIUM
OXYGENIZE
OXYGENOUS
OXYGEUSIA
OXYGONIAL
OXYHALIDE
OXYHALOID
OXYHYDRIC
OXYIODIDE
OXYKETONE
OXYNEURIN
OXYPHENOL
OXYPHENYL
OXYPHILIC
OXYPHONIA
OXYPICRIC
OXYPURINE
OXYPYCNOS
OXYRHYNCH
OXYSULFID
OXYTOCOUS
OXYTOLUIC
OXYTONIZE

OXYTYLOTE
PANSEXUAL
PARADOXAL
PARADOXER
PARADOXIC
PARALEXIA
PARALEXIC
PARATAXIS
PARAXONIC
PAROREXIA
PAXILLARY
PAXILLATE
PAXILLOSE
PENTOXIDE
PEPPERBOX
PERIAXIAL
PEROXIDED
PEROXIDIC
PERPLEXED
PERPLEXER
PHALANXED
PHALANXES
PHARYNXES
PHENOXIDE
PHOENIXES
PHONOPLEX
PHOTOTAXY
PIXILATED
PLAINTEXT
PLEONEXIA
PLEXICOSE
PLEXIFORM
PLEXIGLAS
PLEXIPPUS
PLEXODONT
POLYAXONE
POLYOXIDE
POMPHOLIX
POMPHOLYX
POSTAXIAD
POSTAXIAL
POSTEXIST
POSTFIXED
PRAETEXTA
PRAXITHEA
PREATAXIC
PREEXILIC
PREFIXION
PREHALLUX
PREPOLLEX
PRESEXUAL
PRETEXTED
PROLIXITY
PROPLEXUS
PROSCOLEX
PROTAXIAL
PROTHORAX
PROTOXIDE
PROXENETE
PROXIMATE
PROXIMITY
PSEUDAXIS
PSEUDODOX
PYOTHORAX
PYREXICAL
PYRONYXIS
PYROTOXIN
PYROXENIC
PYROXYLIC
PYROXYLIN
QUINISEXT
QUIXOTISM
QUIXOTIZE
RATTLEBOX
RECTOPEXY
REEXAMINE
REFLEXISM
REFLEXIVE
RELAXABLE
RELAXEDLY
RETEXTURE
RETROFLEX
RHEOTAXIS
RHIZOTAXY
SAPOTOXIN
SAXCORNET
SAXOPHONE
SCHIZAXON
SCRAMASAX
SERVITRIX
SEXANGLED
SEXENNIAL
SEXENNIUM
SEXLESSLY
SEXOLOGIC
SEXTACTIC
SEXTANTAL
SEXTARIUS
SEXTIPARA
SEXTUPLED
SEXTUPLET
SEXUALISM
SEXUALIST
SEXUALITY
SEXUALIZE
SHADOWBOX
SIMPLEXED
SIXPENCES
SIXTEENER
SIXTEENMO
SIXTEENTH
SOAPBOXER
SPHINXIAN
SPHINXINE
SPLENAUXE
SPONDULIX
STRONGBOX
SUBCLIMAX
SUBCORTEX
SUBEXCITE
SUBLUXATE
SUFFIXING
SUFFIXION
SUFFRUTEX
SULFOXIDE
SULFOXISM
SULPHOXID
SUPERFLUX
SURTAXING
SUSOTOXIN
SUSSEXITE
SYNTAXIST
TARAXACUM
TAXACEOUS
TAXAMETER
TAXEATING
TAXEOPODY
TAXIDERMY
TAXIMETER
TAXIPLANE
TAXOMETER
TAXONOMER
TAXONOMIC
TAXPAYING
TESTATRIX
TETRAXILE
TETROXIDE
TEXTARIAN
TEXTILIST
TEXTORIAL
TEXTUALLY
THRIFTBOX
THYROXINE
TINDERBOX
TONOTAXIS
TOPOTAXIS
TOXAEMIAS
TOXANEMIA
TOXICALLY
TOXICAROL
TOXICOSES
TOXICOSIS
TOXIGENIC
TOXINEMIA
TOXINOSIS
TOXIPHAGI
TOXOLYSIS
TOXOPHILE
TOXOPHILY
TRANSFLUX
TRUXILLIC
TRUXILLIN
TYLOTOXEA
UNBUXOMLY
UNEXACTLY
UNEXCITED
UNEXPIRED
UNEXPOSED
UNEXPRESS
UNISEXUAL
UNPERPLEX
UNRELAXED
UROTOXIES
UROXANATE
UXORIALLY
UXORICIDE
VEXATIOUS
VEXEDNESS
VEXILLARY
VEXILLATE
WAXFLOWER
WAXMAKING
WAXWORKER
WOADWAXEN
WOODWAXEN
XANTHAMID
XANTHIONE
XANTHOGEN
XANTHOMAS
XANTHOPIA
XANTHOSIS
XANTHURIA
XENAGOGUE
XENELASIA
XENOBLAST
XENODOCHY
XENOMANIA
XENOPODID
XERODERMA
XEROMORPH
XEROMYRON
XEROPHAGY
XEROPHILE
XEROPHILY
XEROPHYTE
XEROSTOMA
XEROTHERM
XIPHOIDAL
XIPHOSURE
XYLINDEIN
XYLOCOPID
XYLOGRAPH
XYLOIDINE
XYLOMANCY
XYLOMETER
XYLOPHAGE
XYLOPHONE
ZEROAXIAL
ZYGOTAXIS

POSITIONAL ORDER LIST OF 9-LETTER WORDS

XANTHAMID
XANTHIONE
XANTHOGEN
XANTHOMAS
XANTHOPIA
XANTHOSIS
XANTHURIA
XENAGOGUE
XENELASIA
XENOBLAST
XENODOCHY
XENOMANIA
XENOPODID
XERODERMA
XEROMORPH
XEROMYRON
XEROPHAGY
XEROPHILE
XEROPHILY
XEROPHYTE
XEROSTOMA
XEROTHERM
XIPHOIDAL
XIPHOSURE
XYLINDEIN
XYLOCOPID
XYLOGRAPH
XYLOIDINE
XYLOMANCY
XYLOMETER
XYLOPHAGE
XYLOPHONE

AXBREAKER
AXEMASTER
AXILEMMAS
AXIOLITIC
AXIOMATIC
AXIOPISTY
AXLESMITH
AXMANSHIP
AXONEURON
AXOPODIUM
EXACTABLE
EXACTMENT
EXACTNESS
EXADVERSO
EXAGITATE
EXAIRESIS
EXALTEDLY
EXAMINANT
EXAMINATE
EXAMINING
EXAMPLING
EXANIMATE
EXANTHEMA
EXANTLATE
EXARATION
EXARCHATE
EXARCHIST
EXCAMBION
EXCARNATE
EXCAUDATE
EXCAVATED
EXCAVATOR
EXCEEDING
EXCELENTE
EXCELLENT
EXCELLING
EXCELSIOR
EXCENTRAL
EXCENTRIC
EXCEPTANT
EXCEPTING
EXCEPTION
EXCEPTIVE
EXCERPTED
EXCERPTOR
EXCESSIVE
EXCESSMAN
EXCESSMEN
EXCHANGED
EXCHANGER
EXCHEQUER
EXCIPIENT
EXCIPULAR
EXCIPULUM
EXCISABLE
EXCISEMAN
EXCISEMEN
EXCITABLE
EXCITABLY
EXCITANCY
EXCITATOR
EXCITEDLY
EXCLAIMED
EXCLAIMER
EXCLUDING
EXCLUSION
EXCLUSIVE
EXCLUSORY
EXCULPATE
EXCOCTION
EXCORIATE
EXCREMENT
EXCRETING
EXCRETION
EXCRETIVE
EXCRETORY
EXCURRENT
EXCURSING
EXCURSION
EXCURSIVE
EXCURVATE
EXCUSABLE
EXCUSABLY
EXCUSATOR
EXCUSSING
EXECRABLE
EXECRABLY
EXECRATED
EXECRATOR
EXECUTANT
EXECUTING
EXECUTION

EXECUTIVE
EXECUTORY
EXECUTRIX
EXEGETICS
EXEGETIST
EXEMPLARY
EXEMPLIFY
EXEMPTILE
EXEMPTION
EXEMPTIVE
EXEQUATUR
EXERCISED
EXERCISER
EXERCISES
EXERCITOR
EXFODIATE
EXFOLIATE
EXHALABLE
EXHAUSTED
EXHAUSTER
EXHIBITED
EXHIBITOR
EXHORTING
EXHUMATED
EXHUMATOR
EXIGEANTE
EXIGENTER
EXIGENTLY
EXINANITE
EXISTENCE
EXOCARDIA
EXOCLINAL
EXOCOELAR
EXOCOELIC
EXOCOELOM
EXOCOELUM
EXOCULATE
EXOCYCLIC
EXODERMIS
EXODONTIA
EXODROMIC
EXOENZYME
EXOGAMOUS
EXOGENOUS
EXONERATE
EXONEURAL
EXOPATHIC
EXOPHORIA
EXOPHORIC
EXOPODITE
EXORBITAL
EXORCISED
EXORCISER
EXORCIZED
EXORCIZER
EXORDIUMS
EXORGANIC
EXOSEPSIS
EXOSMOSIS
EXOSMOTIC
EXOSPHERE
EXOSPORAL
EXOSTOSED
EXOSTOSES
EXOSTOSIS
EXOSTOTIC
EXOTERICS
EXOTHECAL
EXOTICISM
EXOTICIST
EXOTICITY
EXOTROPIA
EXPALPATE
EXPANDING
EXPANSILE
EXPANSION
EXPANSIVE
EXPANSURE
EXPATIATE
EXPECTANT
EXPECTING
EXPECTIVE
EXPEDIATE
EXPEDIENT
EXPEDITED
EXPEDITER
EXPEDITOR
EXPELLANT
EXPELLENT
EXPELLING
EXPENDING
EXPENSIVE
EXPERIENT
EXPERTISE
EXPIATING
EXPIATION
EXPIATIST
EXPIATIVE
EXPIATORY
EXPILATOR
EXPIRATOR
EXPISCATE
EXPLAINED
EXPLAINER
EXPLANATE
EXPLEMENT
EXPLETIVE
EXPLETORY
EXPLICATE
EXPLODENT
EXPLODING
EXPLOITED
EXPLOITER
EXPLORING
EXPLOSION
EXPLOSIVE
EXPONENCE
EXPONENTS
EXPONIBLE
EXPORTING
EXPOSITOR
EXPOUNDED
EXPOUNDER
EXPRESSED
EXPRESSER
EXPRESSLY
EXPROBATE
EXPUITION
EXPULSION
EXPULSIVE
EXPULSORY
EXPUNGING
EXPURGATE
EXQUISITE
EXSCINDED
EXSECTILE
EXSECTION
EXSERTILE
EXSERTING
EXSERTION
EXSICCATE
EXSOMATIC
EXSPUTORY
EXSTROPHY
EXSUCCOUS
EXSUCTION
EXSURGENT
EXTEMPORE
EXTENDING
EXTENSILE
EXTENSION
EXTENSITY
EXTENSIVE
EXTENUATE
EXTERMINE
EXTERNATE
EXTERNIZE
EXTERNIZE
EXTINCTOR
EXTIRPATE
EXTISPICY
EXTOLLING
EXTOLMENT
EXTORSIVE
EXTORTING
EXTORTION
EXTORTIVE
EXTRABOLD
EXTRACTED
EXTRACTOR
EXTRADITE
EXTRALITE
EXTRALITY
EXTRANEAN
EXTRAVERT
EXTREMELY
EXTREMEST
EXTREMISM
EXTREMIST
EXTREMITY
EXTRICATE
EXTRINSIC
EXTRORSAL
EXTROVERT
EXTRUDING
EXTRUSILE
EXTRUSION
EXTRUSIVE
EXTRUSORY
EXUBERANT
EXUBERATE
EXUDATION
EXUDATIVE
EXUDATORY
EXULTANCY
EXULULATE
EXUVIABLE
EXUVIATED
OXALAEMIA
OXALURATE
OXAMIDINE
OXANILATE
OXANILIDE
OXBERRIES
OXDIAZOLE
OXIDATING
OXIDATION
OXIDATIVE
OXIDIZING
OXIMATION
OXMANSHIP
OXYBENZYL
OXYDACTYL
OXYGENANT
OXYGENATE
OXYGENIUM
OXYGENIZE
OXYGENOUS
OXYGEUSIA
OXYGONIAL
OXYHALIDE
OXYHALOID
OXYHYDRIC
OXYIODIDE
OXYKETONE
OXYNEURIN
OXYPHENOL
OXYPHENYL
OXYPHILIC
OXYPHONIA
OXYPICRIC
OXYPURINE
OXYPYCNOS
OXYRHYNCH
OXYSULFID
OXYTOCOUS
OXYTOLUIC
OXYTONIZE
OXYTYLOTE
UXORIALLY
UXORICIDE

ANXIETIES
ANXIETUDE
ANXIOUSLY
AUXETICAL
AUXILIARY
AUXILIATE
AUXOBLAST
AUXOFLORE
AUXOFLUOR
AUXOGRAPH
AUXOMETER
AUXOSPORE
AUXOTONIC
BIXACEOUS
BOXHOLDER
BOXKEEPER
BOXWALLAH
BUXACEOUS
BUXERRIES
BUXOMNESS
COXCOMBRY
COXODYNIA
DEXTERITY
DEXTEROUS
DEXTRALLY
DEXTRORSE
FIXEDNESS
FOXTAILED
HEXABASIC
HEXABIOSE
HEXACHORD
HEXACOLIC
HEXADECYL
HEXADIENE
HEXADIINE
HEXADIYNE
HEXAGONAL
HEXAHEDRA
HEXAMERAL
HEXAMERON
HEXAMETER
HEXAMMINE
HEXANDRIC
HEXAPLOID
HEXASEMIC
HEXASTICH
HEXASTIGM
HEXATHLON
HEXATOMIC
JUXTAPOSE
LEXICALIC
LIXIVIATE
LIXIVIOUS
LOXOCLASE
LOXODROME
LOXODROMY
LUXURIANT
LUXURIATE
LUXURIOUS
MAXILLARY
MAXIMALLY
MAXIMIZED
MAXIMIZER
MIXTIFORM
MYXAMOEBA
MYXEDEMIC
MYXOEDEMA
MYXOINOMA
MYXOMYOMA
MYXOPODIA
MYXORRHEA
MYXOSPORE
MYXOTHECA
NOXIOUSLY
PAXILLARY
PAXILLATE
PAXILLOSE
PIXILATED
SAXCORNET
SAXOPHONE
SEXANGLED
SEXENNIAL
SEXENNIUM
SEXLESSLY
SEXOLOGIC
SEXTACTIC
SEXTANTAL
SEXTARIUS
SEXTIPARA
SEXTUPLED
SEXTUPLET
SEXUALISM
SEXUALIST
SEXUALITY
SEXUALIZE
SIXPENCES
SIXTEENER
SIXTEENMO
SIXTEENTH
TAXACEOUS
TAXAMETER
TAXEATING
TAXEOPODY
TAXIDERMY
TAXIMETER
TAXIPLANE
TAXOMETER
TAXONOMER
TAXONOMIC
TAXPAYING
TEXTARIAN
TEXTILIST
TEXTORIAL
TEXTUALLY
TOXAEMIAS
TOXANEMIA
TOXICALLY
TOXICAROL
TOXICOSES
TOXICOSIS
TOXIGENIC
TOXINEMIA
TOXINOSIS
TOXIPHAGI
TOXOLYSIS
TOXOPHILE
TOXOPHILY
VEXATIOUS
VEXEDNESS
VEXILLARY
VEXILLATE
WAXFLOWER
WAXMAKING
WAXWORKER

ANOXAEMIA
ANOXAEMIC
ASEXUALLY
AZOXONIUM
BAUXITITE
BIAXIALLY
COAXATION
COAXIALLY

COAXINGLY
DEOXIDIZE
DRUXINESS
ELIXATION
EPAXIALLY
FLAXBOARD
FLAXWENCH
FLAXWOMAN
FLEXILITY
FLEXIONAL
FLUXATION
FLUXILITY
FLUXIONAL
FLUXMETER
HOAXPROOF
INEXACTLY
INEXPIATE
INEXPRESS
INOXIDIZE
ISOXAZOLE
PLEXICOSE
PLEXIFORM
PLEXIGLAS
PLEXIPPUS
PLEXODONT
PRAXITHEA
PROXENETE
PROXIMATE
PROXIMITY
QUIXOTISM
QUIXOTIZE
REEXAMINE
TRUXILLIC
TRUXILLIN
UNEXACTLY
UNEXCITED
UNEXPIRED
UNEXPOSED
UNEXPRESS
UROXANATE

ADMIXTION
ADMIXTURE
ADNEXITIS
AFFIXTURE
ALLOXANIC
ALLOXURIC
ANNEXABLE
ANNEXMENT
BAROXYTON
BISEXUOUS
EUTAXITIC
GLYOXALIC
GLYOXYLIC
IMMIXTURE
INDEXICAL
INDOXYLIC
INMIXTURE
INNOXIOUS
INTEXTINE
INTEXTURE
LATEXOSIS
MALAXABLE
MALAXATOR
MENOXENIA
MESAXONIC

MESOXALIC
MESOXALYL
METAXYLEM
MONAXONIC
MONOXYLIC
MONOXYLON
OBNOXIETY
OBNOXIOUS
PARAXONIC
PEROXIDED
PEROXIDIC
PREEXILIC
PYREXICAL
PYROXENIC
PYROXYLIC
PYROXYLIN
RELAXABLE
RELAXEDLY
RETEXTURE
SUBEXCITE
TARAXACUM
UNBUXOMLY

ACETOXIME
AFFLUXION
AMIDOXIME
APYREXIAL
ASPHYXIAL
ASPHYXIED
ATLOAXOID
BOLLIXING
CARBOXIDE
CLIMAXING
COMMIXING
CONFIXING
CONNEXION
CONNEXITY
CONNEXIVA
CONNEXIVE
CONVEXITY
CRESOXIDE
DEFLEXING
DEFLEXION
DEFLEXURE
DEFLUXION
DUPLEXING
DUPLEXITY
EPITOXOID
HEPTOXIDE
HYDROXIDE
INFLEXION
INFLEXIVE
INFLUXION
INFLUXIVE
LEUCOXENE
LITHOXYLE
NEURAXONE
OVEREXERT
PANSEXUAL
PENTOXIDE
PERIAXIAL
PHENOXIDE
POLYAXONE
POLYOXIDE
POSTAXIAD
POSTAXIAL

POSTEXIST
PREFIXION
PRESEXUAL
PRETEXTED
PROLIXITY
PROTAXIAL
PROTOXIDE
REFLEXISM
REFLEXIVE
SPHINXIAN
SPHINXINE
SUBLUXATE
SUFFIXING
SUFFIXION
SULFOXIDE
SULFOXISM
SURTAXING
SUSSEXITE
SYNTAXIST
TETRAXILE
TETROXIDE
THYROXINE
UNISEXUAL
UROTOXIES
ZEROAXIAL

AEROTAXIS
AMPHIOXUS
AMYOTAXIA
ANAPTYXIS
ANTECOXAL
ANTEFIXAL
ANTEFIXES
ANTHROXAN
APOSTAXIS
APROSEXIA
AUTOTOXIC
AUTOTOXIN
BAROTAXIS
BASIFIXED
CACOMIXLE
CATALEXIS
CHRONAXIA
CHRONAXIE
CICUTOXIN
COLOPEXIA
COMPLEXLY
COMPLEXUS
CYTOTAXIS
CYTOTOXIC
CYTOTOXIN
DENDRAXON
DIAPLEXUS
DIAZEUXIS
DIGITOXIN
EMPHRAXIS
ENDOMIXIS
ENDOTOXIC
ENDOTOXIN
EPIPLEXIS
EPISTAXIS
EPIZEUXIS
FLUMMOXED
HEMIAUXIN
HEMOTOXIC

HEMOTOXIN
HOMOTAXIS
HYPOTAXIA
HYPOTAXIC
HYPOTAXIS
INTERAXAL
INTERAXIS
KENOTOXIN
KOSOTOXIN
LIPOPEXIA
LOOMFIXER
MALPRAXIS
MEDIFIXED
METATAXIC
METATAXIS
OVERSEXED
OVERTAXED
PARADOXAL
PARADOXER
PARADOXIC
PARALEXIA
PARALEXIC
PARATAXIS
PAROREXIA
PERPLEXED
PERPLEXER
PHALANXED
PHALANXES
PHARYNXES
PHOENIXES
PLEONEXIA
POSTFIXED
PRAETEXTA
PREATAXIC
PROPLEXUS
PSEUDAXIS
PYRONYXIS
PYROTOXIN
RHEOTAXIS
SAPOTOXIN
SCHIZAXON
SIMPLEXED
SOAPBOXER
SULPHOXID
SUSOTOXIN
TONOTAXIS
TOPOTAXIS
TYLOTOXEA
UNRELAXED
WOADWAXEN
WOODWAXEN
ZYGOTAXIS

ANTHOTAXY
CALCIPEXY
CARDIAUXE
CATAPLEXY
CAULOTAXY
CHEMOTAXY
DIHYDROXY
DIMETHOXY
ENTERAUXE
IMPERMIXT
INTERMIXT
KATAPLEXY

MASTOPEXY
NEPHRAUXE
NEURATAXY
ORTHODOXY
PHOTOTAXY
PLAINTEXT
QUINISEXT
RECTOPEXY
RHIZOTAXY
SPLENAUXE

ABOIDEAUX
AGITATRIX
ANTIHELIX
ASSERTRIX
BISECTRIX
BOISSEAUX
BUTTERBOX
CANDLEBOX
DECOMPLEX
DICTATRIX
DIRECTRIX
DORSIFLEX
ENTREDEUX
EXECUTRIX
FLAMBEAUX
FUNDATRIX
GONOCALYX
HETERODOX
IMPOSTRIX
INCOMPLEX
INTROFLEX
LEPOTHRIX
MEDIATRIX
MULTIPLEX
MYELOPLAX
NULLIPLEX
OBSTETRIX
OPERATRIX
PEPPERBOX
PHONOPLEX
POMPHOLIX
POMPHOLYX
PREHALLUX
PREPOLLEX
PROSCOLEX
PROTHORAX
PSEUDODOX
PYOTHORAX
RATTLEBOX
RETROFLEX
SCRAMASAX
SERVITRIX
SHADOWBOX
SPONDULIX
STRONGBOX
SUBCLIMAX
SUBCORTEX
SUFFRUTEX
SUPERFLUX
TESTATRIX
THRIFTBOX
TINDERBOX
TRANSFLUX
UNPERPLEX

SCORING ORDER LIST OF 9-LETTER WORDS

34
QUIXOTIZE

33
OXYBENZYL

31
RHIZOTAXY

30
EXCHEQUER
EXOENZYME
MAXIMIZED
OXYRHYNCH
SCHIZAXON

29
MAXIMIZER
OXYGENIZE
ZYGOTAXIS

28
EXORCIZED
OXYHYDRIC
OXYTONIZE
POMPHOLYX

27
AZOXONIUM
COXCOMBRY
DEOXIDIZE
DIHYDROXY
DUPLEXITY
EPIZEUXIS
EXORCIZER
FLAXWENCH
OXIDIZING
OXYPHENYL
QUIXOTISM

26
CHEMOTAXY
DIAZEUXIS
EXEMPLIFY
HYPOTAXIC
INOXIDIZE
MYXEDEMIC
MYXOTHECA
OXDIAZOLE
OXYPHILIC
OXYPYCNOS
PYROXYLIC
WAXMAKING
WAXWORKER
XYLOMANCY

25
ASPHYXIED
CALCIPEXY
COMPLEXLY
DIMETHOXY
EXEQUATUR
EXQUISITE
EXTERNIZE
GLYOXYLIC
HEXACHORD
HEXADECYL
ISOXAZOLE
JUXTAPOSE
KATAPLEXY
MYXAMOEBA
MYXOMYOMA
OXYDACTYL
OXYPICRIC
POMPHOLIX
QUINISEXT
SEXUALIZE
SHADOWBOX
WAXFLOWER
XENODOCHY
XEROPHAGY
XYLOGRAPH
XYLOPHAGE
ZEROAXIAL

24
ASPHYXIAL
BOXKEEPER
BOXWALLAH
CONVEXITY
EXSTROPHY
FLAXWOMAN
FLUMMOXED
HEXASTICH
HOAXPROOF
HYDROXIDE
HYPOTAXIA
HYPOTAXIS
MYXOEDEMA
MYXOPODIA
MYXORRHEA
OXYPHENOL
OXYPHONIA
PHARYNXES
PHOTOTAXY
PYOTHORAX
PYRONYXIS
PYROXYLIN
THRIFTBOX
TOXOPHILY
XEROPHILY
XEROPHYTE
XYLOCOPID
XYLOPHONE

23
AMPHIOXUS
AXMANSHIP
CATAPLEXY
COMMIXING
CYTOTOXIC
DECOMPLEX
EMPHRAXIS
EXCEPTIVE
EXCHANGED
EXCITABLY
EXCITANCY
EXCUSABLY
EXECRABLY
EXEMPLARY
EXEMPTIVE
EXOPATHIC
EXOPHORIC
EXPECTIVE
EXTISPICY
FLAMBEAUX
HEMOTOXIC
HEXABASIC
HEXACOLIC
HEXADIYNE
HEXAHEDRA
HEXAMMINE
HEXASEMIC
HEXATOMIC
MASTOPEXY
MAXIMALLY
MEDIFIXED
METAXYLEM
MIXTIFORM
MONOXYLIC
MYELOPLAX
MYXOINOMA
MYXOSPORE
ORTHODOXY
OXMANSHIP
OXYHALIDE
OXYHALOID
OXYKETONE
OXYSULFID
PHONOPLEX
PLEXIFORM
PROXIMITY
PYREXICAL
PYROXENIC
RECTOPEXY
SUFFIXING
UNBUXOMLY
WOADWAXEN
WOODWAXEN
XEROMORPH

22
AFFIXTURE
AFFLUXION
ANTHOTAXY
AUXOGRAPH
AXBREAKER
BASIFIXED
BOXHOLDER
CACOMIXLE
COAXINGLY
COMPLEXUS
CONFIXING
COXODYNIA
EXCAMBION
EXCAVATED
EXCHANGER
EXCIPULUM
EXCITEDLY
EXHIBITED
EXHUMATED
EXOCYCLIC
FLAXBOARD
FLEXILITY
FLUXILITY
GLYOXALIC
GONOCALYX
HEPTOXIDE
HEXANDRIC
HEXAPLOID
HEXASTIGM
HEXATHLON
IMPERMIXT
INCOMPLEX
INDOXYLIC
INFLEXIVE
INFLUXIVE
LITHOXYLE
LOXODROMY
OXYGENIUM
OXYTYLOTE
PHALANXED
PHENOXIDE
POLYOXIDE
POSTFIXED
REFLEXIVE
SUBCLIMAX
SUFFIXION
SUFFRUTEX
SULPHOXID
TAXEOPODY
TAXIDERMY
TAXPAYING
THYROXINE
TOXIPHAGI
VEXILLARY
XANTHAMID
XIPHOIDAL

21
AMIDOXIME
AMYOTAXIA
ANAPTYXIS
APYREXIAL
AXIOPISTY
AXLESMITH
AXOPODIUM
BAROXYTON
BIAXIALLY
CANDLEBOX
CARBOXIDE
CAULOTAXY
CHRONAXIA
CHRONAXIE
CLIMAXING
COAXIALLY
CONNEXITY
CONNEXIVA
CONNEXIVE
CYTOTAXIS
CYTOTOXIN
DEFLEXING
EPAXIALLY
EXAMPLING
EXANTHEMA
EXARCHATE
EXARCHIST
EXCAVATOR
EXCEPTING
EXCERPTED
EXCESSIVE
EXCLAIMED
EXCLUSIVE
EXCLUSORY
EXCRETIVE
EXCRETORY
EXCURSIVE
EXCURVATE
EXECUTIVE
EXECUTORY
EXHALABLE
EXHIBITOR
EXHUMATOR
EXODROMIC
EXOSPHERE
EXOTHECAL
EXOTICITY
EXPANSIVE
EXPECTING
EXPENSIVE
EXPIATIVE
EXPIATORY
EXPLETIVE
EXPLETORY
EXPLOSIVE
EXPRESSLY
EXPULSIVE
EXPULSORY
EXSPUTORY
EXTREMELY
EXTREMITY
EXULTANCY
EXUVIABLE
FLUXMETER
HEMIAUXIN
HEMOTOXIN
HEXABIOSE
HEXAMERAL
HEXAMERON
HEXAMETER
HOMOTAXIS
INEXACTLY
LEPOTHRIX
LOOMFIXER
MAXILLARY
MESOXALYL
MONOXYLON
NEPHRAUXE
OBNOXIETY
OXYIODIDE
OXYPURINE
OXYTOCOUS
OXYTOLUIC
PARADOXIC
PAXILLARY
PEPPERBOX
PEROXIDIC
PERPLEXED
PHALANXES
PHOENIXES
POLYAXONE
PRAXITHEA
PREFIXION
PREHALLUX
PROLIXITY
PROTHORAX
PYROTOXIN
REFLEXISM
SAXOPHONE
SIMPLEXED
SPHINXIAN
SPHINXINE
SULFOXISM
SUPERFLUX
TOXICALLY
TOXOPHILE
UNEXACTLY
XANTHOMAS
XANTHOPIA
XEROMYRON
XEROPHILE
XEROTHERM
XIPHOSURE
XYLOMETER

20
ACETOXIME
ANOXAEMIC
AXILEMMAS
AXIOMATIC
BISECTRIX
BIXACEOUS
BUTTERBOX
BUXACEOUS
BUXOMNESS
CICUTOXIN
COLOPEXIA
DEFLEXION
DEFLEXURE
DEFLUXION
DEXTERITY
DEXTRALLY
DORSIFLEX
DUPLEXING
EPIPLEXIS
EXACTABLE
EXACTMENT
EXADVERSO
EXALTEDLY
EXCEEDING
EXCENTRIC
EXCEPTANT
EXCEPTION
EXCERPTOR
EXCESSMAN
EXCESSMEN
EXCIPIENT
EXCIPULAR
EXCISABLE
EXCISEMAN
EXCISEMEN
EXCITABLE
EXCLAIMER
EXCLUDING
EXCOCTION
EXCREMENT
EXCULPATE
EXCUSABLE
EXECRABLE
EXEMPTILE
EXEMPTION
EXFODIATE
EXHAUSTED
EXHORTING
EXIGENTLY
EXOCOELIC
EXOCOELOM
EXOCOELUM
EXOSMOTIC
EXOTICISM
EXPALPATE
EXPANDING
EXPECTANT
EXPEDITED
EXPENDING
EXPISCATE
EXPLEMENT
EXPLICATE
EXPLODING
EXPONENCE
EXPONIBLE
EXPOUNDED

EXPROBATE
EXPUNGING
EXSCINDED
EXSICCATE
EXSOMATIC
EXSUCCOUS
EXTEMPORE
EXTREMISM
EXUDATIVE
EXUDATORY
EXUVIATED
FIXEDNESS
FOXTAILED
FUNDATRIX
HETERODOX
HEXADIENE
HEXADIINE
HEXAGONAL
IMMIXTURE
IMPOSTRIX
KENOTOXIN
KOSOTOXIN
LEXICALIC
LIPOPEXIA
MALAXABLE
MALPRAXIS
MESAXONIC
MESOXALIC
METATAXIC
MONAXONIC
MULTIPLEX
OVERSEXED
OVERTAXED
OXIDATIVE
OXYGENANT
OXYGENATE
OXYGENOUS
OXYGEUSIA
OXYGONIAL
PARALEXIC
PARAXONIC
PEROXIDED
PERPLEXER
PLEXICOSE
PREATAXIC
PREEXILIC
PREPOLLEX
PROPLEXUS
PROSCOLEX
PROXIMATE
PSEUDODOX
RELAXEDLY
SCRAMASAX
SEXTACTIC
SIXPENCES
SOAPBOXER
SUBCORTEX
SUBEXCITE
SULFOXIDE
TARAXACUM
TAXONOMIC
UNPERPLEX
VEXEDNESS
XANTHOGEN
XENOPODID
XYLINDEIN
XYLOIDINE

19

ABOIDEAUX
ADMIXTION
ADMIXTURE
ANTEFIXAL
ANTEFIXES
ANTHROXAN
ANTIHELIX
ANXIOUSLY
ASEXUALLY
AUXILIARY
AUXOFLORE
AUXOFLUOR
BOLLIXING
CARDIAUXE
CRESOXIDE
DIAPLEXUS
DICTATRIX
DIRECTRIX
ENDOMIXIS
EPITOXOID
EXAMINING
EXCAUDATE
EXCELLING
EXCRETING
EXCURSING
EXCUSSING
EXECRATED
EXECUTING
EXEGETICS
EXERCISED
EXFOLIATE
EXHAUSTER
EXOCARDIA
EXODERMIS
EXOGAMOUS
EXOPODITE
EXORCISED
EXORDIUMS
EXORGANIC
EXPEDIATE
EXPEDIENT
EXPEDITER
EXPEDITOR
EXPELLING
EXPIATING
EXPLAINED
EXPLODENT
EXPLOITED
EXPLORING
EXPORTING
EXPOUNDER
EXPRESSED
EXPURGATE
EXTENSITY
EXTENSIVE
EXTORSIVE
EXTORTIVE
EXTRABOLD
EXTRACTED
EXTRALITY
EXTRAVERT
EXTROVERT
EXTRUSIVE
EXTRUSORY
FLEXIONAL
FLUXATION
FLUXIONAL
INDEXICAL
INFLEXION
INFLUXION
INTROFLEX
LIXIVIATE
LIXIVIOUS
LOXODROME
MEDIATRIX
NEURATAXY
NOXIOUSLY
OVEREXERT
OXAMIDINE
OXYNEURIN
PARADOXAL
PARADOXER
PENTOXIDE
PIXILATED
PLEXIGLAS
PLEXIPPUS
PLEXODONT
POSTAXIAD
PRETEXTED
PROTOXIDE
PSEUDAXIS
RETROFLEX
RHEOTAXIS
SERVITRIX
SEXLESSLY
SEXOLOGIC
SEXTUPLED
SEXUALITY
SIXTEENTH
SPONDULIX
STRONGBOX
SYNTAXIST
TEXTUALLY
TINDERBOX
TOXIGENIC
TOXOLYSIS
TRANSFLUX
TYLOTOXEA
UNEXCITED
UNEXPIRED
UNEXPOSED
UXORIALLY
UXORICIDE
VEXATIOUS
VEXILLATE
XANTHIONE
XANTHOSIS
XANTHURIA
XERODERMA

18

ALLOXANIC
ALLOXURIC
ANNEXABLE
ANNEXMENT
ANOXAEMIA
ANTECOXAL
APOSTAXIS
APROSEXIA
AUTOTOXIC
AUXETICAL
AUXOBLAST
AUXOMETER
AUXOSPORE
AUXOTONIC
AXEMASTER
AXIOLITIC
BAROTAXIS
BAUXITITE
BISEXUOUS
BOISSEAUX
BUXERRIES
CATALEXIS
COAXATION
CONNEXION
DENDRAXON
DIGITOXIN
EPISTAXIS
EUTAXITIC
EXACTNESS
EXAMINANT
EXAMINATE
EXANIMATE
EXCARNATE
EXCELENTE
EXCELLENT
EXCELSIOR
EXCENTRAL
EXCITATOR
EXCLUSION
EXCORIATE
EXCRETION
EXCURRENT
EXCURSION
EXCUSATOR
EXECRATOR
EXECUTANT
EXECUTION
EXERCISER
EXERCISES
EXERCITOR
EXISTENCE
EXOCLINAL
EXOCOELAR
EXOCULATE
EXORBITAL
EXORCISER
EXOSEPSIS
EXOSMOSIS
EXOSPORAL
EXOSTOTIC
EXOTERICS
EXOTICIST
EXOTROPIA
EXPANSILE
EXPANSION
EXPANSURE
EXPATIATE
EXPELLANT
EXPELLENT
EXPERIENT
EXPERTISE
EXPIATION
EXPIATIST
EXPILATOR
EXPIRATOR
EXPLAINER
EXPLANATE
EXPLOITER
EXPLOSION
EXPONENTS
EXPOSITOR
EXPRESSER
EXPUITION
EXPULSION
EXSECTILE
EXSECTION
EXSUCTION
EXTENDING
EXTERMINE
EXTINCTOR
EXTIRPATE
EXTOLMENT
EXTRACTOR
EXTREMEST
EXTREMIST
EXTRICATE
EXTRINSIC
EXTRUDING
EXUBERANT
EXUBERATE
INEXPIATE
INEXPRESS
INMIXTURE
INTERMIXT
LEUCOXENE
LOXOCLASE
MALAXATOR
MENOXENIA
METATAXIS
NULLIPLEX
OBNOXIOUS
OBSTETRIX
OPERATRIX
OXALAEMIA
OXBERRIES
OXIDATING
OXIMATION
PANSEXUAL
PARALEXIA
PARATAXIS
PAROREXIA
PAXILLATE
PAXILLOSE
PERIAXIAL
PLAINTEXT
PLEONEXIA
POSTAXIAL
POSTEXIST
PRAETEXTA
PRESEXUAL
PROTAXIAL
PROXENETE
RATTLEBOX
REEXAMINE
RELAXABLE
SAPOTOXIN
SAXCORNET
SEXANGLED
SEXENNIUM
SEXTIPARA
SEXTUPLET
SEXUALISM
SIXTEENMO
SPLENAUXE
SUBLUXATE
TAXACEOUS
TAXAMETER
TAXIMETER
TAXIPLANE
TAXOMETER
TAXONOMER
TOPOTAXIS
TOXAEMIAS
TOXANEMIA
TOXICAROL
TOXICOSES
TOXICOSIS
TOXINEMIA
TRUXILLIC
UNEXPRESS
XENAGOGUE
XENOBLAST
XENOMANIA
XEROSTOMA

17

ADNEXITIS
AGITATRIX
ANXIETUDE
ATLOAXOID
DEXTEROUS
DEXTRORSE
DRUXINESS
ENDOTOXIN
ENTREDEUX
EXAGITATE
EXECUTRIX
EXEGETIST
EXIGEANTE
EXIGENTER
EXODONTIA
EXOGENOUS
EXOSTOSED
EXSERTING
EXSURGENT
EXTOLLING
EXTORTING
EXTRADITE
EXUDATION
OXANILIDE
OXIDATION
SURTAXING
TAXEATING
TETROXIDE
UNRELAXED

16
AEROTAXIS
ANXIETIES
ASSERTRIX
AUTOTOXIN
AUXILIATE
AXONEURON
ELIXATION
ENTERAUXE
EXAIRESIS
EXARATION
EXINANITE
EXONERATE
EXONEURAL
EXOSTOSES
EXOSTOSIS
EXSERTILE
EXSERTION
EXTENSILE
EXTENSION
EXTENUATE
EXTERNATE
EXTORTION
EXTRALITE
EXTRANEAN
EXTRORSAL
EXTRUSILE
EXTRUSION
EXULULATE
INNOXIOUS
INTERAXAL
INTERAXIS
INTEXTINE
INTEXTURE
LATEXOSIS
LUXURIANT
LUXURIATE
LUXURIOUS
NEURAXONE
OXALURATE
OXANILATE
RETEXTURE
SEXENNIAL
SEXTANTAL
SEXTARIUS
SEXUALIST
SIXTEENER
SUSOTOXIN
SUSSEXITE
TESTATRIX
TETRAXILE
TEXTARIAN
TEXTILIST
TEXTORIAL
TONOTAXIS
TOXINOSIS
TRUXILLIN
UNISEXUAL
UROTOXIES
UROXANATE
XENELASIA

ALPHABETICAL LIST OF 10-LETTER WORDS

ACAROTOXIC
ACCUSATRIX
ACROATAXIA
ADIPOPEXIA
ADIPOPEXIS
ADNEXOPEXY
ADOXACEOUS
AFFIXATION
ALEXANDERS
ALEXITERIC
ALLOXANATE
ALLOXANTIN
AMAXOMANIA
AMBIDEXTER
AMBOSEXOUS
AMINOXYLOL
AMPHIMIXIS
ANEMOTAXIS
ANNEXATION
ANOXYSCOPE
ANTEFLEXED
ANTHOTAXIS
ANTICLIMAX
ANTIOXYGEN
ANTISPADIX
ANTITOXINE
APICIFIXED
APLOTAXENE
APPENDIXED
APPENDIXES
APPROXIMAL
ARSENOXIDE
ASEXUALITY
ASEXUALIZE
ASPHYXIANT
ASPHYXIATE
ATAXIAGRAM
ATAXINOMIC
ATAXONOMIC
AUTOXIDIZE
AUXANOGRAM
AUXANOLOGY
AUXILIARLY
AUXILIATOR
AUXOACTION
AUXOCARDIA
AUXOCHROME
AXEBREAKER
AXHAMMERED
AXILEMMATA
AXILLARIES
AXINOMANCY
AXIOLOGIST
AXIOMATIZE
AXONOMETRY
BIAXIALITY
BINOXALATE
BISEXUALLY
BISSEXTILE
BOBBYSOXER
BORDEREAUX
BOXBERRIES
BRACHYAXIS
CACODOXIAN
CACOXENITE
CARBOXYLIC
CARNIFEXES
CHAETOTAXY
CHALUMEAUX
CHATTERBOX
CHEMOTAXIS
CHRONAXIES
CICATRIXES
CIRCUMFLEX
COADJUTRIX
COEXISTENT
COLLOXYLIN
COLONOPEXY
COMMIXTION
COMMIXTURE
COMPLEXIFY
COMPLEXION
COMPLEXITY
CONNEXIVUM
CONTEXTUAL
CONTEXTURE
CONTRAPLEX
CONVEXEDLY
CONVEXNESS
COXCOMBESS
COXCOMICAL
COXOCERITE
COXOPODITE
CRIOSPHINX
CYCLOHEXYL
DEOXIDIZED
DEOXIDIZER
DERMATAUXE
DESOXALATE
DETOXICANT
DETOXICATE
DEXIOTROPE
DEXTERICAL
DEXTRALITY
DEXTRAURAL
DEXTRINASE
DEXTRINATE
DEXTRINIZE
DEXTRINOUS
DEXTROGYRE
DEXTRORSAL
DEXTROUSLY
DIASTATAXY
DIETOTOXIC
DIGITOXOSE
DISQUIXOTE
DISULFOXID
DORSIFIXED
DOXASTICON
DOXOGRAPHY
DOXOLOGIES
DOXOLOGIZE
DYSOXIDIZE
ECHOPRAXIA
ENDOTHORAX
ENTOMOTAXY
EPEXEGESIS
EPEXEGETIC
EPICALYXES
EPIPHARYNX
EPIPLOPEXY
ERGOTOXINE
ESONARTHEX
EUXANTHATE
EUXANTHONE
EXACERBATE
EXACTINGLY
EXACTITUDE
EXADVERSUM
EXAGGERATE
EXALTATION
EXALTATIVE
EXAMINABLE
EXAMINATOR
EXANTHEMAS
EXASPERATE
EXASPIDEAN
EXAUGURATE
EXCALATION
EXCALCEATE
EXCAVATING
EXCAVATION
EXCECATION
EXCELLENCE
EXCELLENCY
EXCEPTIOUS
EXCERPTING
EXCERPTION
EXCERPTIVE
EXCHANGING
EXCITATION
EXCITATIVE
EXCITATORY
EXCITEMENT
EXCITINGLY
EXCLAIMING
EXCOGITATE
EXCORIABLE
EXCORIATED
EXCORIATOR
EXCRESCENT
EXCRUCIATE
EXCUDERUNT
EXCULPABLE
EXCULPATED
EXCURVATED
EXCUSATIVE
EXCUSATORY
EXCYSTMENT
EXECRATING
EXECRATION
EXECRATIVE
EXECRATORY
EXECUTABLE
EXECUTANCY
EXECUTIONS
EXECUTRESS
EXEGETICAL
EXEMPLARIC
EXEMPTIBLE
EXENTERATE
EXERCISING
EXERCITANT
EXFOLIATED
EXHALATION
EXHALATORY
EXHAUSTING
EXHAUSTION
EXHAUSTIVE
EXHIBITANT
EXHIBITING
EXHIBITION
EXHIBITIVE
EXHIBITORY
EXHILARANT
EXHILARATE
EXHUMATING
EXHUMATION
EXHUMATORY
EXIGENCIES
EXIGUOUSLY
EXIMIOUSLY
EXINGUINAL
EXISTENTLY
EXOCARDIAC
EXOCARDIAL
EXOCENTRIC
EXOCHORION
EXOCOLITIS
EXOCULATED
EXOGASTRIC
EXOGENETIC
EXOMORPHIC
EXOMPHALOS
EXOMPHALUS
EXONARTHEX
EXONERATED
EXONERATOR
EXONERETUR
EXOPHAGOUS
EXOPODITIC
EXORBITANT
EXORBITATE
EXORCISING
EXORCISMAL
EXORCISORY
EXORCISTIC
EXORCIZING
EXORNATION
EXOSPHERIC
EXOSPORIUM
EXOSPOROUS
EXOTERICAL
EXOTHECATE
EXOTHECIUM
EXOTHERMAL
EXOTHERMIC
EXOTICALLY
EXOTICNESS
EXOTOSPORE
EXOTROPISM
EXPANDEDLY
EXPANSIBLE
EXPANSIBLY
EXPATIATED
EXPATIATER
EXPATIATOR
EXPATRIATE
EXPECTABLE
EXPECTANCE
EXPECTANCY
EXPEDIENCE
EXPEDIENCY
EXPEDIENTE
EXPEDITATE

EXPEDITELY
EXPEDITING
EXPEDITION
EXPELLABLE
EXPENDABLE
EXPENDITOR
EXPENSEFUL
EXPERIENCE
EXPERIMENT
EXPERTNESS
EXPILATION
EXPIRATION
EXPIRATORY
EXPISCATED
EXPISCATOR
EXPLAINING
EXPLANATOR
EXPLICABLE
EXPLICATED
EXPLICATOR
EXPLICITLY
EXPLOITAGE
EXPLOITING
EXPLOITIVE
EXPLOITURE
EXPLORATOR
EXPLOSIBLE
EXPLOSIVES
EXPORTABLE
EXPOSITION
EXPOSITIVE
EXPOSITORY
EXPOUNDING
EXPRESSAGE
EXPRESSING
EXPRESSIVE
EXPRESSMAN
EXPRESSWAY
EXPUGNABLE
EXPUNCTION
EXPURGATED
EXPURGATOR
EXSANGUINE
EXSCINDING
EXSIBILATE
EXSICCATAE
EXSICCATED
EXSILIENCY
EXSPUITION
EXSUFFLATE
EXTEMPORAL
EXTENDEDLY
EXTENDIBLE
EXTENSIBLE
EXTENUATED
EXTENUATOR
EXTERIORLY
EXTERNALLY
EXTINCTEUR
EXTINCTION
EXTINCTIVE
EXTINGUISH
EXTIRPATED
EXTIRPATOR
EXTISPICES
EXTOGENOUS
EXTOLLMENT
EXTOOLITIC
EXTRACTING
EXTRACTION
EXTRACTIVE
EXTRADITED
EXTRADOSED
EXTRADOTAL
EXTRAMURAL
EXTRANEITY
EXTRANEOUS
EXTRAPOLAR
EXTRASOLAR
EXTRATUBAL
EXTREMITAL
EXTRICABLE
EXTRICABLY
EXTRICATED
EXTROITIVE
EXTROPICAL
EXTRORSELY
EXTROSPECT
EXTUBATION
EXUBERANCE
EXUBERANCY
EXUBERATED
EXULCERATE
EXULTANTLY
EXULTATION
EXULTINGLY
EXUMBRELLA
EXUNDATION
EXURBANITE
EXUVIATING
EXUVIATION
EXZODIACAL
FLEXUOSITY
FLEXUOUSLY
FLUMMOXING
FLUXIONARY
FLUXIONIST
FOXBERRIES
FRAXINELLA
GASTROPEXY
GENERATRIX
GERONTOXON
GLYOXALASE
GLYOXALINE
GOOGOLPLEX
HELIOTAXIS
HEMOTHORAX
HETERODOXY
HEXABROMID
HEXACOSANE
HEXACTINAL
HEXACYCLIC
HEXADECANE
HEXAEMERIC
HEXAEMERON
HEXAGYNOUS
HEXAHEDRAL
HEXAHEDRON
HEXAHYDRIC
HEXAMERISM
HEXAMEROUS
HEXAMETRAL
HEXAMETRIC
HEXANDROUS
HEXANGULAR
HEXAPLARIC
HEXAPODIES
HEXARADIAL
HEXARCHIES
HEXASTICHY
HEXASTYLOS
HEXATRIOSE
HEXAVALENT
HEXPARTITE
HOLOPLEXIA
HOMOSEXUAL
HYDROTAXIS
HYPEROXIDE
HYPOPRAXIA
HYPOZEUXIS
IMPERATRIX
INDICATRIX
INEXERTION
INEXISTENT
INEXORABLE
INEXORABLY
INEXPECTED
INEXPERTLY
INEXPIABLE
INEXPIABLY
INEXPLICIT
INFLEXIBLE
INFLEXIBLY
INOXIDIZED
INSPECTRIX
INSPEXIMUS
INTERAXIAL
INTERMIXED
INTOXATION
INTOXICANT
INTOXICATE
JUXTAPOSED
JUXTAPOSIT
KERFLUMMOX
LACROIXITE
LACTOTOXIN
LAXATIVELY
LEUCOTOXIC
LEXICALITY
LEXICOLOGY
LEXICONIST
LEXICONIZE
LEXIGRAPHY
LEXIPHANIC
LIBERATRIX
LIENOTOXIN
LIPOMYXOMA
LIPOXENOUS
LIXIVIATED
LIXIVIATOR
LOXODROMIC
LUXURIANCE
LUXURIANCY
LUXURIATED
MALAXATION
MALAXERMAN
MALAXERMEN
MAXILLIPED
MAXIMATION
MAXIMISTIC
MAXIMIZING
MEDITHORAX
MENOSTAXIS
MESOTHORAX
MESOXALATE
METAGALAXY
METATHORAX
MIXILINEAL
MONAXONIAL
MONOXENOUS
MONOXYLOUS
MOXIEBERRY
MYDATOXINE
MYORRHEXIS
MYXADENOMA
MYXANGITIS
MYXOEDEMIC
MYXOGASTER
MYXOGLIOMA
MYXOLIPOMA
MYXOMATOUS
MYXOMYCETE
MYXOPODIUM
NECTOCALYX
NEPHROPEXY
NEURATAXIA
NEUROTOXIA
NEUROTOXIC
NEUROTOXIN
NOMINATRIX
NOMOPHYLAX
OXIDIZABLE
OLEOTHORAX
OMENTOPEXY
ONYCHAUXIS
OOPHORAUXE
OPTOMENINX
ORCHIOPEXY
OROPHARYNX
ORTHODOXAL
ORTHODOXLY
ORTHOPRAXY
OSCULATRIX
OVEREXPOSE
OVERTAXING
OXADIAZOLE
OXALACETIC
OXALURAMID
OXALYLUREA
OXAMETHANE
OXIDIMETRY
OXIDIZABLE
OXIDULATED
OXOZONIDES
OXYBLEPSIA
OXYBROMIDE
OXYBUTYRIA
OXYCALCIUM
OXYCAMPHOR
OXYCAPROIC
OXYCEPHALY
OXYCHLORIC
OXYCHLORID
OXYCYANIDE
OXYGENATED
OXYGENATOR
OXYGENIZED
OXYGENIZER
OXYHEMATIN
OXYHYDRATE
OXYMURIATE
OXYNEURINE
OXYNITRATE
OXYOPHITIC
OXYPHILOUS
OXYPROLINE
OXYQUINONE
OXYRHINOUS
OXYSTEARIC
OXYSULFIDE
OXYSULPHID
OXYTERPENE
OXYTOLUENE
OXYTONESIS
OXYTONICAL
OXYURIASIS
OXYURICIDE
OXYWELDING
PARADOXIAL
PARADOXIST
PARADOXURE
PARAPRAXIA
PARAPRAXES
PARAPRAXIS
PARAXIALLY
PAROXYSMAL
PAROXYSMIC
PAROXYTONE
PERIAXONAL
PERIPHRAXY
PERMIXABLE
PERMIXTION
PERMIXTIVE
PERMIXTURE
PEROXIDASE
PEROXIDING
PEROXIDIZE
PERPLEXING
PERPLEXITY
PETROSILEX
PETROXOLIN
PHILODOXER
PHLEBOPEXY
PHOENIXITY
PHOTOTAXIS
PHYLLOTAXY
PHYLLOXERA
PHYTOTOXIC
PHYTOTOXIN
PICROTOXIC
PICROTOXIN
PLEIOTAXIS
PLEXIGLASS
PLEXIMETER
PLEXIMETRY
PLURIAXIAL
PNEUMOPEXY
POLYMIXIID
POSTEXILIC
PRAEHALLUX
PRAXIOLOGY
PREAXIALLY
PREEXILIAN
PREFIXALLY
PREFIXEDLY
PREFIXTURE
PREFLEXION
PREMAXILLA
PROJECTRIX
PROLIXNESS
PROTEOPEXY
PROTOXYLEM
PROXICALLY
PYOSALPINX
PYRIDOXINE
PYROXENITE
PYROXYLINE
QUADRATRIX
QUADRUPLEX
QUINATOXIN
QUINCUNXES
QUINOXALIN
QUINOXALYL
QUIXOTICAL
RADIOTOXIC
REFLEXIBLE
RELAXATION
RELAXATIVE
RELAXATORY
RHIZOTAXIS
SAXICOLINE
SAXICOLOUS
SAXIGENOUS
SAXOPHONIC
SAXOTROMBA
SEPARATRIX
SEXAGENARY
SEXANGULAR
SEXDIGITAL
SEXOLOGIST
SEXPARTITE
SEXTENNIAL
SEXTILLION
SEXTIPOLAR
SEXTUPLING
SEXUPAROUS
SIMPLEXITY
SITOTOXISM
SNUFFBOXER
SOIXANTINE
SPECTATRIX
SPHINXLIKE
SPINTURNIX
SPLENOPEXY
STEREOTAXY

SUBAXILLAR
SUBMAXILLA
SUBMAXIMAL
SUFFIXMENT
SULFOXYLIC
SULPHOXIDE
SULPHOXISM
SUPEREXIST
SUPRACOXAL
SYNAXARION
SYNAXARIST
TAXABILITY
TAXATIONAL
TAXATIVELY
TAXIDERMAL
TAXIDERMIC
TAXONOMIST
TEXTUALISM
TEXTUALIST
TEXTUARIES
TEXTUARIST
TEXTURALLY
THEOMASTIX
THIXOTROPY
THYROTOXIC
TOXALBUMIC
TOXALBUMIN
TOXANAEMIA
TOXICATION
TOXICITIES
TOXICOLOGY
TOXIDERMIC
TOXIFEROUS
TOXINAEMIA
TOXIPHAGUS
TOXIPHOBIA
TOXIPHORIC
TRANSFIXED
TRIAXONIAN
TRICHAUXIS
TRIHYDROXY
TRIMETHOXY
TRIPLEXITY
TRISECTRIX
TROUSSEAUX
TRUXILLINE
TYROTOXINE
UNCOMMIXED
UNDERSEXED
UNEQUIAXED
UNEXAMPLED
UNEXCITING
UNEXPECTED
UNEXPENDED
UNEXPERTLY
UNFLEXIBLE
UNFLEXIBLY
UNIDEXTRAL
UNORTHODOX
UROXANTHIN
UXORIALITY
UXORICIDAL
UXORIOUSLY
VINCETOXIN
VIXENISHLY
WAXBERRIES
WAXHEARTED
WAXWORKING
XANTHALINE
XANTHAMIDE
XANTHATION
XANTHIURIA
XANTHOCONE
XANTHODERM
XANTHOMATA
XANTHOPHYL
XANTHOPSIA
XANTHOPSIN
XANTHYDROL
XENARTHRAL
XENOBIOSIS
XENOGAMOUS
XENOGENOUS
XENOPELTID
XENOPHOBIA
XENOPHOBIC
XENOPODOID
XENOPTERAN
XENOSAURID
XEROGRAPHY
XEROMORPHY
XEROPHYTIC
XIPHIIFORM
XIPHODYNIA
XIPHOIDIAN
XIPHOPAGIC
XIPHOPAGUS
XIPHOSURAN
XIPHYDRIID
XYLANTHRAX
XYLOGLYPHY
XYLOGRAPHY
XYLOPHAGAN
XYLOPHAGID
XYLOPHONIC
XYLOPOLIST
XYLORCINOL
XYLOSTROMA
XYLOTOMIST
XYLOTOMOUS
ZOOXANTHIN

POSITIONAL ORDER LIST OF 10-LETTER WORDS

XANTHALINE
XANTHAMIDE
XANTHATION
XANTHIURIA
XANTHOCONE
XANTHODERM
XANTHOMATA
XANTHOPHYL
XANTHOPSIA
XANTHOPSIN
XANTHYDROL
XENARTHRAL
XENOBIOSIS
XENOGAMOUS
XENOGENOUS
XENOPELTID
XENOPHOBIA
XENOPHOBIC
XENOPODOID
XENOPTERAN
XENOSAURID
XEROGRAPHY
XEROMORPHY
XEROPHYTIC
XIPHIIFORM
XIPHODYNIA
XIPHOIDIAN
XIPHOPAGIC
XIPHOPAGUS
XIPHOSURAN
XIPHYDRIID
XYLANTHRAX
XYLOGLYPHY
XYLOGRAPHY
XYLOPHAGAN
XYLOPHAGID
XYLOPHONIC
XYLOPOLIST
XYLORCINOL
XYLOSTROMA
XYLOTOMIST
XYLOTOMOUS

AXEBREAKER
AXHAMMERED
AXILEMMATA
AXILLARIES
AXINOMANCY
AXIOLOGIST
AXIOMATIZE
AXONOMETRY
EXACERBATE
EXACTINGLY
EXACTITUDE
EXADVERSUM
EXAGGERATE
EXALTATION
EXALTATIVE
EXAMINABLE
EXAMINATOR
EXANTHEMAS
EXASPERATE
EXASPIDEAN
EXAUGURATE
EXCALATION
EXCALCEATE
EXCAVATING
EXCAVATION
EXCECATION
EXCELLENCE
EXCELLENCY
EXCEPTIOUS
EXCERPTING
EXCERPTION
EXCERPTIVE
EXCHANGING
EXCITATION
EXCITATIVE
EXCITATORY
EXCITEMENT
EXCITINGLY
EXCLAIMING
EXCOGITATE
EXCORIABLE
EXCORIATED
EXCORIATOR
EXCRESCENT
EXCRUCIATE
EXCUDERUNT
EXCULPABLE
EXCULPATED
EXCURVATED
EXCUSATIVE
EXCUSATORY
EXCYSTMENT
EXECRATING
EXECRATION
EXECRATIVE
EXECRATORY
EXECUTABLE
EXECUTANCY
EXECUTIONS
EXECUTRESS
EXEGETICAL
EXEMPLARIC
EXEMPTIBLE
EXENTERATE
EXERCISING
EXERCITANT
EXFOLIATED
EXHALATION
EXHALATORY
EXHAUSTING
EXHAUSTION
EXHAUSTIVE
EXHIBITANT
EXHIBITING
EXHIBITION
EXHIBITIVE
EXHIBITORY
EXHILARANT
EXHILARATE
EXHUMATING
EXHUMATION
EXHUMATORY
EXIGENCIES
EXIGUOUSLY
EXIMIOUSLY
EXINGUINAL
EXISTENTLY
EXOCARDIAC
EXOCARDIAL
EXOCENTRIC
EXOCHORION
EXOCOLITIS
EXOCULATED
EXOGASTRIC
EXOGENETIC
EXOMORPHIC
EXOMPHALOS
EXOMPHALUS
EXONARTHEX
EXONERATED
EXONERATOR
EXONERETUR
EXOPHAGOUS
EXOPODITIC
EXORBITANT
EXORBITATE
EXORCISING
EXORCISMAL
EXORCISORY
EXORCISTIC
EXORCIZING
EXORNATION
EXOSPHERIC
EXOSPORIUM
EXOSPOROUS
EXOTERICAL
EXOTHECATE
EXOTHECIUM
EXOTHERMAL
EXOTHERMIC
EXOTICALLY
EXOTICNESS
EXOTOSPORE
EXOTROPISM
EXPANDEDLY
EXPANSIBLE
EXPANSIBLY
EXPATIATED
EXPATIATER
EXPATIATOR
EXPATRIATE
EXPECTABLE
EXPECTANCE
EXPECTANCY
EXPEDIENCE
EXPEDIENCY
EXPEDIENTE
EXPEDITATE
EXPEDITELY
EXPEDITING
EXPEDITION
EXPELLABLE
EXPENDABLE
EXPENDITOR
EXPENSEFUL
EXPERIENCE
EXPERIMENT
EXPERTNESS
EXPILATION
EXPIRATION
EXPIRATORY
EXPISCATED
EXPISCATOR
EXPLAINING
EXPLANATOR
EXPLICABLE
EXPLICATED
EXPLICATOR
EXPLICITLY
EXPLOITAGE
EXPLOITING
EXPLOITIVE
EXPLOITURE
EXPLORATOR
EXPLOSIBLE
EXPLOSIVES
EXPORTABLE
EXPOSITION
EXPOSITIVE
EXPOSITORY
EXPOUNDING
EXPRESSAGE
EXPRESSING
EXPRESSIVE
EXPRESSMAN
EXPRESSWAY
EXPUGNABLE
EXPUNCTION
EXPURGATED
EXPURGATOR
EXSANGUINE
EXSCINDING
EXSIBILATE
EXSICCATAE
EXSICCATED
EXSILIENCY
EXSPUITION
EXSUFFLATE
EXTEMPORAL
EXTENDEDLY
EXTENDIBLE
EXTENSIBLE
EXTENUATED
EXTENUATOR
EXTERIORLY
EXTERNALLY
EXTINCTEUR

EXTINCTION
EXTINCTIVE
EXTINGUISH
EXTIRPATED
EXTIRPATOR
EXTISPICES
EXTOGENOUS
EXTOLLMENT
EXTOOLITIC
EXTRACTING
EXTRACTION
EXTRACTIVE
EXTRADITED
EXTRADOSED
EXTRADOTAL
EXTRAMURAL
EXTRANEITY
EXTRANEOUS
EXTRAPOLAR
EXTRASOLAR
EXTRATUBAL
EXTREMITAL
EXTRICABLE
EXTRICABLY
EXTRICATED
EXTROITIVE
EXTROPICAL
EXTRORSELY
EXTROSPECT
EXTUBATION
EXUBERANCE
EXUBERANCY
EXUBERATED
EXULCERATE
EXULTANTLY
EXULTATION
EXULTINGLY
EXUMBRELLA
EXUNDATION
EXURBANITE
EXUVIATING
EXUVIATION
EXZODIACAL
OXIDIZABLE
OXADIAZOLE
OXALACETIC
OXALURAMID
OXALYLUREA
OXAMETHANE
OXIDIMETRY
OXIDIZABLE
OXIDULATED
OXOZONIDES
OXYBLEPSIA
OXYBROMIDE
OXYBUTYRIA
OXYCALCIUM
OXYCAMPHOR
OXYCAPROIC
OXYCEPHALY
OXYCHLORIC
OXYCHLORID
OXYCYANIDE
OXYGENATED
OXYGENATOR
OXYGENIZED
OXYGENIZER
OXYHEMATIN
OXYHYDRATE
OXYMURIATE
OXYNEURINE
OXYNITRATE
OXYOPHITIC
OXYPHILOUS
OXYPROLINE
OXYQUINONE
OXYRHINOUS

OXYSTEARIC
OXYSULFIDE
OXYSULPHID
OXYTERPENE
OXYTOLUENE
OXYTONESIS
OXYTONICAL
OXYURIASIS
OXYURICIDE
OXYWELDING
UXORIALITY
UXORICIDAL
UXORIOUSLY

AUXANOGRAM
AUXANOLOGY
AUXILIARLY
AUXILIATOR
AUXOACTION
AUXOCARDIA
AUXOCHROME
BOXBERRIES
COXCOMBESS
COXCOMICAL
COXOCERITE
COXOPODITE
DEXIOTROPE
DEXTERICAL
DEXTRALITY
DEXTRAURAL
DEXTRINASE
DEXTRINATE
DEXTRINIZE
DEXTRINOUS
DEXTROGYRE
DEXTRORSAL
DEXTROUSLY
DOXASTICON
DOXOGRAPHY
DOXOLOGIES
DOXOLOGIZE
EUXANTHATE
EUXANTHONE
FOXBERRIES
HEXABROMID
HEXACOSANE
HEXACTINAL
HEXACYCLIC
HEXADECANE
HEXAEMERIC
HEXAEMERON
HEXAGYNOUS
HEXAHEDRAL
HEXAHEDRON
HEXAHYDRIC
HEXAMERISM
HEXAMEROUS
HEXAMETRAL
HEXAMETRIC
HEXANDROUS
HEXANGULAR
HEXAPLARIC
HEXAPODIES
HEXARADIAL
HEXARCHIES
HEXASTICHY
HEXASTYLOS
HEXATRIOSE
HEXAVALENT
HEXPARTITE
JUXTAPOSED
JUXTAPOSIT
LAXATIVELY
LEXICALITY
LEXICOLOGY
LEXICONIST
LEXICONIZE

LEXIGRAPHY
LEXIPHANIC
LIXIVIATED
LIXIVIATOR
LOXODROMIC
LUXURIANCE
LUXURIANCY
LUXURIATED
MAXILLIPED
MAXIMATION
MAXIMISTIC
MAXIMIZING
MIXILINEAL
MOXIEBERRY
MYXADENOMA
MYXANGITIS
MYXOEDEMIC
MYXOGASTER
MYXOGLIOMA
MYXOLIPOMA
MYXOMATOUS
MYXOMYCETE
MYXOPODIUM
SAXICOLINE
SAXICOLOUS
SAXIGENOUS
SAXOPHONIC
SAXOTROMBA
SEXAGENARY
SEXANGULAR
SEXDIGITAL
SEXOLOGIST
SEXPARTITE
SEXTENNIAL
SEXTILLION
SEXTIPOLAR
SEXTUPLING
SEXUPAROUS
TAXABILITY
TAXATIONAL
TAXATIVELY
TAXIDERMAL
TAXIDERMIC
TAXONOMIST
TEXTUALISM
TEXTUALIST
TEXTUARIES
TEXTUARIST
TEXTURALLY
TOXALBUMIC
TOXALBUMIN
TOXANAEMIA
TOXICATION
TOXICITIES
TOXICOLOGY
TOXIDERMIC
TOXIFEROUS
TOXINAEMIA
TOXIPHAGUS
TOXIPHOBIA
TOXIPHORIC
VIXENISHLY
WAXBERRIES
WAXHEARTED
WAXWORKING

ADOXACEOUS
ALEXANDERS
ALEXITERIC
AMAXOMANIA
ANOXYSCOPE
ASEXUALITY
ASEXUALIZE
ATAXIAGRAM
ATAXINOMIC
ATAXONOMIC
BIAXIALITY

COEXISTENT
DEOXIDIZED
DEOXIDIZER
EPEXEGESIS
EPEXEGETIC
FLEXUOSITY
FLEXUOUSLY
FLUXIONARY
FLUXIONIST
FRAXINELLA
INEXERTION
INEXISTENT
INEXORABLE
INEXORABLY
INEXPECTED
INEXPERTLY
INEXPIABLE
INEXPIABLY
INEXPLICIT
INOXIDIZED
PLEXIGLASS
PLEXIMETER
PLEXIMETRY
PRAXIOLOGY
PROXICALLY
QUIXOTICAL
SOIXANTINE
THIXOTROPY
TRUXILLINE
UNEXAMPLED
UNEXCITING
UNEXPECTED
UNEXPENDED
UNEXPERTLY
UROXANTHIN
ZOOXANTHIN

AFFIXATION
ALLOXANATE
ALLOXANTIN
ANNEXATION
AUTOXIDIZE
BINOXALATE
BISEXUALLY
CACOXENITE
DESOXALATE
DETOXICANT
DETOXICATE
DYSOXIDIZE
GLYOXALASE
GLYOXALINE
INTOXATION
INTOXICANT
INTOXICATE
LIPOXENOUS
MALAXATION
MALAXERMAN
MALAXERMEN
MESOXALATE
MONAXONIAL
MONOXENOUS
MONOXYLOUS
PARAXIALLY
PAROXYSMAL
PAROXYSMIC
PAROXYTONE
PEROXIDASE
PEROXIDING
PEROXIDIZE
PREAXIALLY
PREEXILIAN
PYROXENITE
PYROXYLINE
RELAXATION
RELAXATIVE
RELAXATORY
SUBAXILLAR

SYNAXARION
SYNAXARIST
TRIAXONIAN

AMINOXYLOL
ANTIOXYGEN
APPROXIMAL
ASPHYXIANT
ASPHYXIATE
BISSEXTILE
CARBOXYLIC
COLLOXYLIN
COMMIXTION
COMMIXTURE
CONNEXIVUM
CONTEXTUAL
CONTEXTURE
CONVEXEDLY
CONVEXNESS
INFLEXIBLE
INFLEXIBLY
INSPEXIMUS
OVEREXPOSE
PERIAXONAL
PERMIXABLE
PERMIXTION
PERMIXTIVE
PERMIXTURE
PETROXOLIN
POSTEXILIC
PREFIXALLY
PREFIXEDLY
PREFIXTURE
PREMAXILLA
PROLIXNESS
PROTOXYLEM
QUINOXALIN
QUINOXALYL
REFLEXIBLE
SPHINXLIKE
SUBMAXILLA
SUBMAXIMAL
SUFFIXMENT
SULFOXYLIC
UNFLEXIBLE
UNFLEXIBLY
UNIDEXTRAL

AMBIDEXTER
AMBOSEXOUS
ANTITOXINE
APLOTAXENE
ARSENOXIDE
CACODOXIAN
CHRONAXIES
COMPLEXIFY
COMPLEXION
COMPLEXITY
DIGITOXOSE
DISQUIXOTE
ERGOTOXINE
FLUMMOXING
HOMOSEXUAL
HYPEROXIDE
INTERAXIAL
LACROIXITE
LIPOMYXOMA
MYDATOXINE
OVERTAXING
PARADOXIAL
PARADOXIST
PARADOXURE
PERPLEXING
PERPLEXITY
PHOENIXITY
PHYLLOXERA
PLURIAXIAL

POLYMIXIID
PREFLEXION
PYRIDOXINE
SIMPLEXITY
SITOTOXISM
SULPHOXIDE
SULPHOXISM
SUPEREXIST
TRIPLEXITY
TYROTOXINE

ACAROTOXIC
ACROATAXIA
ADIPOPEXIA
ADIPOPEXIS
AMPHIMIXIS
ANEMOTAXIS
ANTEFLEXED
ANTHOTAXIS
APICIFIXED
APPENDIXED
APPENDIXES
BOBBYSOXER
BRACHYAXIS
CARNIFEXES
CHEMOTAXIS
CICATRIXES
CYCLOHEXYL
DIETOTOXIC
DISULFOXID
DORSIFIXED
ECHOPRAXIA
EPICALYXES
GERONTOXON
HELIOTAXIS
HOLOPLEXIA
HYDROTAXIS
HYPOPRAXIA
HYPOZEUXIS
INTERMIXED
LACTOTOXIN
LEUCOTOXIC
LIENOTOXIN
MENOSTAXIS
MYORRHEXIS
NEURATAXIA
NEUROTOXIA
NEUROTOXIC
NEUROTOXIN
ONYCHAUXIS
ORTHODOXAL
ORTHODOXLY
PARAPRAXIA
PARAPRAXES
PARAPRAXIS
PHILODOXER
PHOTOTAXIS
PHYTOTOXIC
PHYTOTOXIN
PICROTOXIC
PICROTOXIN
PLEIOTAXIS
QUINATOXIN
QUINCUNXES
RADIOTOXIC
RHIZOTAXIS
SNUFFBOXER
SUPRACOXAL
THYROTOXIC
TRANSFIXED
TRICHAUXIS
UNCOMMIXED
UNDERSEXED
UNEQUIAXED
VINCETOXIN

ADNEXOPEXY
CHAETOTAXY
DERMATAUXE
DIASTATAXY
ENTOMOTAXY
EPIPLOPEXY
GASTROPEXY
HETERODOXY
METAGALAXY
NEPHROPEXY
OMENTOPEXY
OOPHORAUXE
ORCHIOPEXY
ORTHOPRAXY
PERIPHRAXY
PHLEBOPEXY
PHYLLOTAXY
PNEUMOPEXY
PROTEOPEXY
SPLENOPEXY
STEREOTAXY
TRIHYDROXY
TRIMETHOXY

ACCUSATRIX
ANTICLIMAX
ANTISPADIX
BORDEREAUX
CHALUMEAUX
CHATTERBOX
CIRCUMFLEX
COADJUTRIX
CONTRAPLEX
CRIOSPHINX
ENDOTHORAX
EPIPHARYNX
ESONARTHEX
EXONARTHEX
GENERATRIX
GOOGOLPLEX
HEMOTHORAX
IMPERATRIX
INDICATRIX
INSPECTRIX
KERFLUMMOX
LIBERATRIX
MEDITHORAX
MESOTHORAX
METATHORAX
NECTOCALYX
NOMINATRIX
NOMOPHYLAX
OLEOTHORAX
OPTOMENINX
OROPHARYNX
OSCULATRIX
PETROSILEX
PRAEHALLUX
PROJECTRIX
PYOSALPINX
QUADRATRIX
QUADRUPLEX
SEPARATRIX
SPECTATRIX
SPINTURNIX
THEOMASTIX
TRISECTRIX
TROUSSEAUX
UNORTHODOX
XYLANTHRAX

SCORING ORDER LIST OF 10-LETTER WORDS

34
HYPOZEUXIS

31
DYSOXIDIZE
MAXIMIZING
OXYGENIZED

30
CYCLOHEXYL
OXYCEPHALY
OXYGENIZER

29
COMPLEXIFY
DEOXIDIZED
EXORCIZING
EXZODIACAL
HEXAHYDRIC
MYXOMYCETE
OXIDIZABLE
OXYCAMPHOR
OXYQUINONE
PEROXIDIZE
PHLEBOPEXY
QUADRUPLEX
QUINOXALYL
RHIZOTAXIS
XYLOGRAPHY
ZOOXANTHIN

28
AXIOMATIZE
DEOXIDIZER
DOXOLOGIZE
HEXASTICHY
INOXIDIZED
KERFLUMMOX
LEXICONIZE
PHYLLOTAXY
PROJECTRIX
QUINCUNXES
QUIXOTICAL
WAXWORKING
XANTHOPHYL
XYLOGLYPHY

27
AUTOXIDIZE
BRACHYAXIS
DEXTRINIZE
DISQUIXOTE
DOXOGRAPHY
EPIPHARYNX
HYPOPRAXIA
JUXTAPOSED
MYXOEDEMIC
MYXOPODIUM
NEPHROPEXY
NOMOPHYLAX
ORCHIOPEXY
OXADIAZOLE
OXOZONIDES
OXYCHLORIC
OXYHYDRATE
OXYOPHITIC
PERIPHRAXY
PHYTOTOXIC
QUADRATRIX
TRIHYDROXY
UNEQUIAXED
XEROMORPHY
XEROPHYTIC
XIPHIIFORM
XIPHOPAGIC
XIPHYDRIID
XYLOPHAGID
XYLOPHONIC

26
AMPHIMIXIS
ASEXUALIZE
CARBOXYLIC
CIRCUMFLEX
COMPLEXITY
CONVEXEDLY
EXOMORPHIC
EXPECTANCY
HEXACYCLIC
HYPEROXIDE
JUXTAPOSIT
LEXIGRAPHY
LIPOMYXOMA
MYXOLIPOMA
OXYCALCIUM
OXYCAPROIC
OXYCHLORID
OXYCYANIDE
OXYSULPHID
PAROXYSMIC
PNEUMOPEXY
PREFIXEDLY
QUINATOXIN
QUINOXALIN
SPHINXLIKE
VIXENISHLY
XENOPHOBIC
XEROGRAPHY
XIPHODYNIA
XYLOPHAGAN

25
APICIFIXED
ASPHYXIANT
ASPHYXIATE
AXHAMMERED
CHAETOTAXY
COXCOMBESS
EXHIBITIVE
EXHIBITORY
EXHUMATORY
EXPEDIENCY
EXPRESSWAY
FLUMMOXING
HEMOTHORAX
HEXABROMID
HEXARCHIES
INFLEXIBLY
MYORRHEXIS
MYXADENOMA
MYXOGLIOMA
ONYCHAUXIS
OROPHARYNX
ORTHOPRAXY
OXYBROMIDE
OXYBUTYRIA
OXYHEMATIN
OXYPHILOUS
OXYWELDING
PHOENIXITY
PHYLLOXERA
PHYTOTOXIN
POLYMIXIID
PREFIXALLY
PYROXYLINE
SNUFFBOXER
SUFFIXMENT
SULFOXYLIC
THIXOTROPY
THYROTOXIC
TRIMETHOXY
UNFLEXIBLY
XIPHOPAGUS

24
ANOXYSCOPE
AUXOCHROME
AXINOMANCY
CHALUMEAUX
CHATTERBOX
CHEMOTAXIS
COLONOPEXY
CONNEXIVUM
CRIOSPHINX
ECHOPRAXIA
EPICALYXES
EXCELLENCY
EXCERPTIVE
EXCHANGING
EXCYSTMENT
EXECUTANCY
EXOMPHALOS
EXOMPHALUS
EXOSPHERIC
EXOTHECIUM
EXOTHERMIC
EXPANDEDLY
EXPANSIBLY
EXPLICITLY
EXTRICABLY
EXUBERANCY
HETERODOXY
HEXAEMERIC
HEXAGYNOUS
HEXAHEDRAL
HEXAHEDRON
HEXAMERISM
HEXAMETRIC
HEXAPLARIC
HYDROTAXIS
INEXPIABLY
LEXIPHANIC
MOXIEBERRY
MYXOMATOUS
NECTOCALYX
OMENTOPEXY
ORTHODOXLY
OXYBLEPSIA
OXYSULFIDE
PAROXYSMAL
PERMIXTIVE
PERPLEXITY
PLEXIMETRY
PROTEOPEXY
PROTOXYLEM

PROXICALLY
PYOSALPINX
SAXOPHONIC
SIMPLEXITY
SPLENOPEXY
SULPHOXISM
TOXIPHOBIA
TOXIPHORIC
UNCOMMIXED
WAXHEARTED
XANTHYDROL
XENOPHOBIA

23

AFFIXATION
APPENDIXED
APPROXIMAL
AXEBREAKER
BOBBYSOXER
COMMIXTION
COMMIXTURE
COMPLEXION
EPIPLOPEXY
EXACTINGLY
EXADVERSUM
EXCAVATING
EXCITINGLY
EXCULPABLE
EXCURVATED
EXEMPLARIC
EXEMPTIBLE
EXHALATORY
EXHAUSTIVE
EXHIBITING
EXHUMATING
EXOPHAGOUS
EXPECTABLE
EXPECTANCE
EXPEDITELY
EXPLICABLE
EXSUFFLATE
FLEXUOSITY
FLEXUOUSLY
FLUXIONARY
GASTROPEXY
HEXADECANE
HEXAPODIES
HEXASTYLOS
HEXAVALENT
LAXATIVELY
LEXICOLOGY
MAXIMISTIC
MEDITHORAX
METAGALAXY
MYDATOXINE
MYXANGITIS
MYXOGASTER
OXIDIMETRY
OXYRHINOUS
OXYURICIDE
PERMIXABLE
PHILODOXER
PICROTOXIC
PRAXIOLOGY
PYRIDOXINE
SUBMAXIMAL
SULPHOXIDE
TAXATIVELY
TOXALBUMIC
TOXICOLOGY
TOXIPHAGUS
XANTHAMIDE
XANTHODERM
XIPHOIDIAN

22

ADIPOPEXIA
ADIPOPEXIS
ADNEXOPEXY
AMBIDEXTER
AMINOXYLOL
APPENDIXES
AXONOMETRY
BIAXIALITY
BISEXUALLY
CACODOXIAN
CARNIFEXES
CHRONAXIES
COLLOXYLIN
CONVEXNESS
COXCOMICAL
COXOPODITE
DEXTROGYRE
DISULFOXID
DORSIFIXED
ENTOMOTAXY
EPEXEGETIC
EXANTHEMAS
EXCAVATION
EXCERPTING
EXCITATIVE
EXCITATORY
EXCLAIMING
EXCULPATED
EXCUSATIVE
EXCUSATORY
EXECRATIVE
EXECRATORY
EXHIBITANT
EXHIBITION
EXHUMATION
EXIMIOUSLY
EXOCARDIAC
EXOCHORION
EXOPODITIC
EXORCISORY
EXOTHECATE
EXOTHERMAL
EXOTICALLY
EXPEDIENCE
EXPENDABLE
EXPENSEFUL
EXPIRATORY
EXPISCATED
EXPLICATED
EXPLOITIVE
EXPLOSIVES
EXPOSITIVE
EXPOSITORY
EXPRESSIVE
EXPUGNABLE
EXSICCATED
EXSILIENCY
EXTENDEDLY
EXTINCTIVE
EXTRACTIVE
FOXBERRIES
HEXACOSANE
HEXACTINAL
HEXAEMERON
HEXAMEROUS
HEXAMETRAL
HEXPARTITE
HOLOPLEXIA
HOMOSEXUAL
INEXORABLY
INEXPECTED
INEXPERTLY
INFLEXIBLE
LEXICALITY
LOXODROMIC
LUXURIANCY
MAXILLIPED
MESOTHORAX
METATHORAX
MONOXYLOUS
OOPHORAUXE
OVEREXPOSE
OXAMETHANE
OXYGENATED
OXYMURIATE
OXYPROLINE
OXYSTEARIC
OXYTERPENE
OXYTONICAL
PARAXIALLY
PAROXYTONE
PERPLEXING
PHOTOTAXIS
PRAEHALLUX
PREAXIALLY
PREFIXTURE
PREFLEXION
PYROXENITE
REFLEXIBLE
TAXABILITY
TAXIDERMIC
THEOMASTIX
TOXIDERMIC
TRICHAUXIS
TRIPLEXITY
UNEXAMPLED
UNEXPECTED
UNEXPERTLY
UNFLEXIBLE
VINCETOXIN
WAXBERRIES
XANTHOCONE
XANTHOMATA
XANTHOPSIA
XANTHOPSIN
XIPHOSURAN
XYLANTHRAX
XYLOPOLIST
XYLORCINOL
XYLOSTROMA
XYLOTOMIST
XYLOTOMOUS

21

ACAROTOXIC
ACCUSATRIX
AMAXOMANIA
AMBOSEXOUS
ANTEFLEXED
ANTICLIMAX
ANTIOXYGEN
ATAXINOMIC
ATAXONOMIC
AUXANOLOGY
AXILEMMATA
BOXBERRIES
CACOXENITE
CICATRIXES
CONTRAPLEX
COXOCERITE
DEXTRALITY
DEXTROUSLY
DIASTATAXY
ENDOTHORAX
EXACERBATE
EXAMINABLE
EXCALCEATE
EXCECATION
EXCELLENCE
EXCEPTIOUS
EXCERPTION
EXCITEMENT
EXECUTABLE
EXFOLIATED
EXHAUSTING
EXIGUOUSLY
EXOCENTRIC
EXORCISMAL
EXORCISTIC
EXOSPORIUM
EXOTROPISM
EXPANSIBLE
EXPEDITING
EXPELLABLE
EXPERIENCE
EXPERIMENT
EXPISCATOR
EXPLICATOR
EXPLOSIBLE
EXPORTABLE
EXPOUNDING
EXPRESSMAN
EXPUNCTION
EXPURGATED
EXSCINDING
EXSICCATAE
EXTEMPORAL
EXTINGUISH
EXTISPICES
EXTRICABLE
EXTROPICAL
EXTROSPECT
EXUBERANCE
EXULTINGLY
EXUMBRELLA
EXUVIATING
GLYOXALASE
GLYOXALINE
GOOGOLPLEX
HEXANDROUS
HEXANGULAR
HEXARADIAL
IMPERATRIX
INEXPIABLE
INEXPLICIT
INSPECTRIX
INSPEXIMUS
LEUCOTOXIC
LIXIVIATED
MALAXERMAN
MALAXERMEN
MAXIMATION
OPTOMENINX
ORTHODOXAL
OVERTAXING
OXALACETIC
OXYGENATOR
PARAPRAXIA
PARAPRAXES
PARAPRAXIS
PERMIXTION
PERMIXTURE
PEROXIDING
PICROTOXIN
PLEXIMETER
POSTEXILIC
PREMAXILLA
SAXOTROMBA
SEXAGENARY
SPECTATRIX
SUBMAXILLA
SUPRACOXAL
TOXALBUMIN
TRANSFIXED
UNEXPENDED
UNORTHODOX
XENOPODOID

20

ADOXACEOUS
ANTHOTAXIS
ANTISPADIX
ASEXUALITY
ATAXIAGRAM
AUXANOGRAM
AUXILIARLY
AUXOCARDIA
BORDEREAUX
DERMATAUXE
DETOXICANT
DETOXICATE
DEXIOTROPE
DEXTERICAL
DIETOTOXIC
DOXASTICON
EPEXEGESIS
ESONARTHEX
EUXANTHATE
EUXANTHONE
EXACTITUDE
EXALTATIVE
EXASPIDEAN
EXCUDERUNT
EXECRATING
EXEGETICAL
EXERCISING
EXHALATION
EXHAUSTION
EXHILARANT
EXHILARATE
EXIGENCIES
EXISTENTLY
EXOCARDIAL
EXOCULATED
EXOGASTRIC
EXOGENETIC
EXORCISING
EXPATIATED
EXPEDIENTE
EXPEDITATE
EXPEDITION
EXPENDITOR
EXPLAINING
EXPLOITAGE
EXPLOITING
EXPRESSAGE
EXPRESSING
EXPURGATOR
EXTENDIBLE
EXTERIORLY
EXTERNALLY
EXTIRPATED
EXTRACTING
EXTRANEITY
EXTRICATED
EXTROITIVE
EXTRORSELY
EXUBERATED
EXULTANTLY
EXUVIATION
FLUXIONIST
FRAXINELLA
HELIOTAXIS
HEXATRIOSE
INDICATRIX
INTERMIXED
LIXIVIATOR
OLEOTHORAX
OXALURAMID
OXALYLUREA
OXYNEURINE
OXYNITRATE
OXYTOLUENE
OXYTONESIS
OXYURIASIS
PARADOXIAL
PARADOXIST
PARADOXURE
PEROXIDASE

PLEXIGLASS
RADIOTOXIC
RELAXATIVE
RELAXATORY
SEXTUPLING
STEREOTAXY
SYNAXARION
SYNAXARIST
TAXIDERMAL
TEXTURALLY
TOXIFEROUS
TYROTOXINE
UNEXCITING
UROXANTHIN
UXORIALITY
UXORICIDAL
UXORIOUSLY
XANTHALINE
XANTHATION
XANTHIURIA
XENARTHRAL
XENOGAMOUS
XENOPELTID

19

ACROATAXIA
ALEXITERIC
ANEMOTAXIS
APLOTAXENE
AUXOACTION
BINOXALATE
BISSEXTILE
COEXISTENT
CONTEXTUAL
CONTEXTURE
DIGITOXOSE
DOXOLOGIES
EXAGGERATE
EXAMINATOR
EXASPERATE
EXCALATION
EXCITATION
EXECRATION
EXECUTIONS
EXECUTRESS
EXERCITANT
EXOCOLITIS
EXONARTHEX
EXORBITANT
EXORBITATE
EXOSPOROUS
EXOTERICAL
EXOTICNESS
EXOTOSPORE
EXPATIATER
EXPATIATOR
EXPATRIATE
EXPERTNESS
EXPILATION
EXPIRATION
EXPLANATOR
EXPLOITURE
EXPLORATOR
EXPOSITION
EXSIBILATE
EXSPUITION
EXTENSIBLE
EXTINCTEUR
EXTINCTION
EXTIRPATOR
EXTOLLMENT
EXTOOLITIC
EXTRACTION
EXTRADITED
EXTRADOSED
EXTRAMURAL
EXTRAPOLAR
EXTRATUBAL
EXTREMITAL
EXTUBATION
EXULCERATE
EXURBANITE
INEXORABLE
INTOXICANT
INTOXICATE
LACROIXITE
LACTOTOXIN
LEXICONIST
LIBERATRIX
LIPOXENOUS
LUXURIANCE
MALAXATION
MENOSTAXIS
MESOXALATE
MIXILINEAL
MONAXONIAL
MONOXENOUS
NEUROTOXIC
NOMINATRIX
OSCULATRIX
OXIDULATED
PERIAXONAL
PETROSILEX
PETROXOLIN
PLEIOTAXIS
PLURIAXIAL
PREEXILIAN
PROLIXNESS
SAXICOLINE
SAXICOLOUS
SEPARATRIX
SEXDIGITAL
SEXPARTITE
SEXTIPOLAR
SEXUPAROUS
SITOTOXISM
SPINTURNIX
SUBAXILLAR
SUPEREXIST
TAXONOMIST
TEXTUALISM
TOXANAEMIA
TOXICATION
TOXICITIES
TOXINAEMIA
TRISECTRIX
UNDERSEXED
XENOBIOSIS
XENOPTERAN

18

ALEXANDERS
ARSENOXIDE
AXIOLOGIST
DESOXALATE
DEXTRAURAL
DEXTRINASE
DEXTRINATE
DEXTRINOUS
DEXTRORSAL
ERGOTOXINE
EXAUGURATE
EXINGUINAL
EXONERATED
EXSANGUINE
EXTENUATED
EXTOGENOUS
EXTRADOTAL
EXUNDATION
GENERATRIX
GERONTOXON
LUXURIATED
SAXIGENOUS
SEXANGULAR
SEXOLOGIST
UNIDEXTRAL
XENOGENOUS
XENOSAURID

17

ALLOXANATE
ALLOXANTIN
ANNEXATION
ANTITOXINE
AUXILIATOR
AXILLARIES
EXALTATION
EXENTERATE
EXONERATOR
EXONERETUR
EXORNATION
EXTENUATOR
EXTRANEOUS
EXTRASOLAR
EXULTATION
INEXERTION
INEXISTENT
INTERAXIAL
INTOXATION
LIENOTOXIN
NEURATAXIA
NEUROTOXIA
NEUROTOXIN
RELAXATION
SEXTENNIAL
SEXTILLION
SOIXANTINE
TAXATIONAL
TEXTUALIST
TEXTUARIES
TEXTUARIST
TRIAXONIAN
TROUSSEAUX
TRUXILLINE

ALPHABETICAL LIST OF WORDS OVER 10 LETTERS

ACROASPHYXIA
ACTINOPRAXIS
ADENOMYXOMA
ADMAXILLARY
ADOXOGRAPHY
ALEXANDRITE
ALEXIPHARMIC
ALEXIPYRETIC
AMBIDEXTERITY
AMBIDEXTRAL
AMBIDEXTROUS
AMIDOHEXOSE
AMPLEXATION
AMPLEXICAUL
AMYLODEXTRIN
ANAPHYLAXIS
ANDROSPHINX
ANGIOATAXIA
ANGIORRHEXIS
ANHYDROXIME
ANILIDOXIME
ANISALDOXIME
ANNEXATIONAL
ANNEXATIONIST
ANNEXIONIST
ANOXIDATIVE
ANOXYBIOSIS
ANOXYBIOTIC
ANTEFLEXION
ANTHEXIMETER
ANTHOXANTHIN
ANTHRAXOLITE
ANTHRAXYLON
ANTHROXANIC
ANTIOXIDANT
ANTIOXYGENIC
ANXIOUSNESS
AORTOMALAXIS
APHOTOTAXIS
APOPHYLAXIS
APOPLEXIOUS
APPENDIXING
APPROXIMATE
APPROXIMATED
APPROXIMATELY
APPROXIMATING
APPROXIMATION
APPROXIMATIVE
APPROXIMATOR
ARCHEOPTERYX
ARCHOSYRINX
ARTHROSYRINX
ASEXUALIZED
ASEXUALIZING
ASPHYXIATED
ASPHYXIATING
ASPHYXIATION
ASPHYXIATOR
ATAXAPHASIA
ATAXIAGRAPH
ATAXIAMETER
ATAXIAPHASIA
ATAXOPHEMIA
ATLANTOAXIAL
ATLOIDOAXOID
AUTOCRATRIX
AUTOTOXAEMIA
AUTOTOXEMIA
AUTOXIDATION
AUTOXIDATOR
AUXANOMETER
AUXETICALLY
AUXILIARIES
AUXILIATION
AUXILIATORY
AUXOAMYLASE
AUXOCHROMIC
AUXOCHROMISM
AUXOCHROMOUS
AUXOGRAPHIC
AUXOHORMONE
AXIOLOGICAL
AXIOMATICAL
AXISYMMETRIC
AXODENDRITE
AXONOLIPOUS
AXONOMETRIC
AXONOPHOROUS
AXOSPERMOUS
BACTERIOTOXIC
BANDBOXICAL
BENZALDOXIME
BIMAXILLARY
BISAXILLARY
BISEXUALISM
BISEXUALITY
CARBETHOXYL
CARBOLXYLOL
CARBOXYLASE
CARBOXYLATE
CARBOXYLATED
CARDIATAXIA
CARDIOTOXIC
CHALCEDONYX
CHARTOPHYLAX
CHEMIOTAXIC
CHEMIOTAXIS
CHEMOREFLEX
CHIROPRAXIS
CHYLOTHORAX
CIRCUMAXIAL
CIRCUMAXILE
CLITORIDAUXE
COEXISTENCE
COEXISTENCY
COEXTENSION
COEXTENSIVE
COLOPEXOTOMY
COLPORRHEXIS
COMPETITRIX
COMPLEXIONAL
COMPLEXIONARY
COMPLEXIONED
COMPLEXITIES
COMPLEXNESS
CONFLUXIBLE
CONNEXITIES
CONSOLATRIX
CONTEXTUALLY
CONTEXTURAL
CONTEXTURED
CONVEXEDNESS
CONVEXITIES
COSTOXIPHOID
COXARTHRITIS

COXCOMBICAL
COXOCERITIC
COXOFEMORAL
CREATOTOXISM
CRUCIFIXION
CYCLOHEXANE
CYCLOHEXANOL
CYCLOHEXENE
CYSTOMYXOMA
CYSTOSYRINX
CYTOPHARYNX
DECIMOSEXTO
DEOXIDIZING
DEOXYGENATE
DEOXYGENATED
DEOXYGENIZE
DESEXUALIZE
DESEXUALIZED
DETOXICATED
DETOXICATING
DETOXICATION
DETOXICATOR
DEXIOTROPIC
DEXIOTROPISM
DEXIOTROPOUS
DEXTEROUSLY
DEXTROCARDIA
DEXTROCULAR
DEXTROGYRATE
DEXTROSAZONE
DEXTROSURIA
DEXTROUSNESS
DIASTATAXIC
DICARBOXYLIC
DICATALEXIS
DIHEXAHEDRAL
DIHEXAHEDRON
DIRECTRIXES
DISOXYGENATE
DISPENSATRIX
DISULPHOXID
DISULPHOXIDE
DOPAOXIDASE
DORSIFLEXION
DORSIFLEXOR
DOXOGRAPHER
DOXOLOGICAL
DOXOLOGIZED
DOXOLOGIZING
DYSOXIDATION
ELECTROTAXIS
ENTEROPEXIA
ENTEROTOXEMIA
EPEXEGETICAL
ESOTHYROPEXY
EXACERBATED
EXACERBATING
EXACERBATION
EXACTINGNESS
EXACTIVENESS
EXAGGERATED
EXAGGERATING
EXAGGERATION
EXAGGERATIVE
EXAGGERATOR
EXAGGERATORY
EXALBUMINOSE
EXALBUMINOUS
EXALLOTRIOTE
EXALTEDNESS
EXAMINATION
EXAMINATIONAL
EXAMINATIVE
EXAMINATORY
EXANIMATION
EXANTHEMATIC
EXANTLATION
EXARTERITIS
EXARTICULATE
EXASPERATED
EXASPERATING
EXASPERATION
EXASPERATER
EXASPERATIVE
EXAUCTORATE
EXAUGURATION
EXAUTHORIZE
EXCALCARATE
EXCANDESCENT
EXCANTATION
EXCARNATION
EXCATHEDRAL
EXCAVATIONS
EXCEEDINGLY
EXCELLENCIES
EXCELLENTLY
EXCEPTIONAL
EXCEPTIONALLY
EXCEPTIONARY
EXCEPTIONER
EXCEPTIVELY
EXCERPTIBLE
EXCESSIVELY
EXCESSIVENESS
EXCHANGEABLE
EXCHANGEABLY
EXCIPULIFORM
EXCITABILITY
EXCITABLENESS
EXCITEDNESS
EXCITOMOTOR
EXCITOMOTORY
EXCLAMATION
EXCLAMATIONAL
EXCLAMATIVE
EXCLAMATIVELY
EXCLAMATORILY
EXCLAMATORY
EXCLUSIONARY
EXCLUSIONER
EXCLUSIONISM
EXCLUSIONIST
EXCLUSIVELY
EXCLUSIVENESS
EXCLUSIVISM
EXCLUSIVITY
EXCOGITABLE
EXCOGITATED
EXCOGITATING
EXCOGITATION
EXCOGITATIVE
EXCOGITATOR
EXCOMMUNICANT
EXCOMMUNICATE
EXCOMMUNION
EXCONJUGANT
EXCORIATING
EXCORIATION
EXCORTICATE
EXCORTICATED
EXCORTICATING
EXCORTICATION
EXCREMENTAL
EXCREMENTARY
EXCREMENTIVE
EXCRESCENCE
EXCRESCENCES
EXCRESCENCIES
EXCRESCENCY
EXCRESCENTIAL
EXCRETIONARY
EXCRIMINATE
EXCRUCIABLE
EXCRUCIATED
EXCRUCIATING
EXCRUCIATION
EXCRUCIATOR
EXCULPATING
EXCULPATION
EXCULPATIVE
EXCULPATORY
EXCURSIONAL
EXCURSIONARY
EXCURSIONER
EXCURSIONISM
EXCURSIONIST
EXCURSIONIZE
EXCURSIVELY
EXCURVATURE
EXCUSABILITY
EXCUSABLENESS
EXCYSTATION
EXECRABLENESS
EXECUTIONAL
EXECUTIONER
EXECUTIVELY
EXECUTIVENESS
EXECUTORIAL
EXECUTRICES
EXECUTRIXES
EXEGETICALLY
EXEMPLARILY
EXEMPLARINESS
EXEMPLARISM
EXEMPLARITY
EXEMPLIFIED
EXEMPLIFIER
EXEMPLIFYING
EXENCEPHALIA
EXENCEPHALIC
EXENCEPHALUS
EXENTERATED
EXENTERATING
EXENTERATION
EXERCISABLE
EXERCITATION
EXERCITORIAL
EXFIGURATION
EXFILTRATION
EXFLAGELLATE
EXFODIATION
EXFOLIATING
EXFOLIATION
EXFOLIATIVE
EXFOLIATORY
EXHAUSTEDLY
EXHAUSTEDNESS
EXHAUSTIBLE
EXHAUSTINGLY
EXHAUSTIVELY
EXHAUSTLESS
EXHAUSTLESSLY
EXHIBITIONAL
EXHIBITIONER
EXHIBITIONISM
EXHIBITIONIST
EXHIBITIVELY
EXHIBITORSHIP
EXHILARATED
EXHILARATING
EXHILARATION
EXHILARATIVE
EXHILARATOR
EXHILARATORY
EXHORTATIVE
EXHORTATIVELY
EXHORTATORY
EXIGUOUSNESS
EXILARCHATE
EXIMIOUSNESS
EXINANITION
EXISTENTIAL
EXISTENTIALLY
EXISTLESSNESS
EXOARTERITIS
EXOCCIPITAL
EXOCULATING
EXOGASTRITIS
EXOGENOUSLY
EXOGNATHION
EXOGNATHITE
EXOMETRITIS
EXOMOLOGESIS
EXOMORPHISM
EXOMPHALOUS
EXONERATING
EXONERATION
EXONERATIVE
EXOPERIDIUM
EXOPHTHALMIA
EXOPHTHALMIC
EXOPHTHALMOS
EXOPHTHALMUS
EXORABILITY
EXORABLENESS
EXORBITANCE
EXORBITANCY
EXORBITANTLY
EXORBITATION
EXORCISATION
EXORCISEMENT
EXORCISTICAL
EXORCIZATION
EXORCIZEMENT
EXOSKELETAL
EXOSKELETON
EXOSTRACISM
EXOSTRACIZE
EXOTERICALLY
EXOTERICISM
EXOTHERMOUS
EXOTICALNESS
EXPANDEDNESS
EXPANDINGLY
EXPANSIBILITY
EXPANSIONAL
EXPANSIONISM
EXPANSIONIST
EXPANSIVELY
EXPANSIVENESS
EXPANSIVITY
EXPATIATING
EXPATIATION
EXPATIATIVE
EXPATIATORY
EXPATRIATED
EXPATRIATING
EXPATRIATION
EXPECTANCIES
EXPECTANTLY
EXPECTATION
EXPECTATIVE
EXPECTORANT
EXPECTORATE
EXPECTORATED
EXPECTORATING
EXPECTORATION
EXPECTORATOR
EXPEDIENCIES
EXPEDIENTIAL
EXPEDIENTIST
EXPEDIENTLY
EXPEDITATED
EXPEDITATING
EXPEDITATION
EXPEDITENESS
EXPEDITIONARY
EXPEDITIONIST
EXPEDITIOUS
EXPEDITIOUSLY
EXPENDABILITY
EXPENDITRIX
EXPENDITURE
EXPENSILATION
EXPENSIVELY
EXPENSIVENESS
EXPENTHESIS
EXPERIENCED
EXPERIENCER
EXPERIENCES
EXPERIENCING
EXPERIENTIAL
EXPERIMENTAL
EXPERIMENTED
EXPERIMENTEE
EXPERIMENTER
EXPERIMENTING
EXPERIMENTIST
EXPERIMENTIZE
EXPERMENTIZED
EXPERIMENTLY
EXPIATIONAL
EXPIATORINESS
EXPISCATING
EXPISCATION
EXPISCATORY
EXPLAINABLE
EXPLANATION
EXPLANATIVE
EXPLANATIVELY
EXPLANATORILY
EXPLANATORY
EXPLANTATION
EXPLEMENTAL
EXPLETIVELY
EXPLETIVENESS
EXPLICATING
EXPLICATION
EXPLICATIVE
EXPLICATORY
EXPLICITNESS
EXPLOITABLE
EXPLOITATION
EXPLOITATIVE
EXPLORATION
EXPLORATIONAL
EXPLORATIVE
EXPLORATIVELY
EXPLORATORY
EXPLOREMENT
EXPLOSIBILITY
EXPLOSIONIST
EXPLOSIVELY
EXPLOSIVENESS
EXPONENTIAL
EXPONENTIALLY
EXPORTABILITY
EXPORTATION
EXPOSITIONAL
EXPOSITIONARY
EXPOSITIVELY
EXPOSITORIAL
EXPOSITORILY
EXPOSTULATE
EXPOSTULATED
EXPOSTULATING
EXPOSTULATION
EXPOSTULATIVE
EXPOSTULATOR
EXPOSTULATORY
EXPRESSIBLE
EXPRESSION
EXPRESSIONAL
EXPRESSIONISM
EXPRESSIONIST

EXPRESSIVELY
EXPRESSLESS
EXPROBRATORY
EXPROMISSION
EXPROPRIATE
EXPROPRIATED
EXPROPRIATING
EXPROPRIATION
EXPROPRIATOR
EXPULSATORY
EXPURGATING
EXPURGATION
EXPURGATIVE
EXPURGATORIAL
EXPURGATORY
EXQUISITELY
EXQUISITENESS
EXQUISITISM
EXQUISITIVELY
EXSANGUINATE
EXSANGUINOUS
EXSANGUIOUS
EXSCRIPTURAL
EXSCULPTATE
EXSCUTELLATE
EXSICCATING
EXSICCATION
EXSICCATIVE
EXSTIPULATE
EXSUFFLATION
EXSUFFLICATE
EXTEMPORALLY
EXTEMPORARY
EXTEMPORARILY
EXTEMPORIZE
EXTEMPORIZED
EXTEMPORIZER
EXTEMPORIZING
EXTENDEDNESS
EXTENDIBILITY
EXTENSIBILITY
EXTENSIMETER
EXTENSIONAL
EXTENSIONIST
EXTENSIVELY
EXTENSIVENESS
EXTENSOMETER
EXTENUATING
EXTENUATINGLY
EXTENUATION
EXTENUATIVE
EXTENUATORY
EXTERIORATE
EXTERIORATION
EXTERIORITY
EXTERIORIZE
EXTERIORIZED
EXTERIORIZING
EXTERIORNESS
EXTERMINATE
EXTERMINATED
EXTERMINATING
EXTERMINATION
EXTERMINATIVE
EXTERMINATOR
EXTERMINATORY
EXTERNALISM
EXTERNALIST
EXTERNALISTIC
EXTERNALITIES
EXTERNALITY
EXTERNALIZE
EXTERNATION
EXTERNIZATION
EXTEROCEPTIST
EXTEROCEPTIVE
EXTEROCEPTOR
EXTERRANEOUS
EXTERRESTRIAL
EXTERRITORIAL
EXTINGUISHED
EXTINGUISHER
EXTIRPATING
EXTIRPATION
EXTIRPATIVE
EXTIRPATORY
EXTISPICIOUS
EXTOLLATION
EXTORSIVELY
EXTORTIONARY
EXTORTIONATE
EXTORTIONER
EXTORTIONIST
EXTRABULBAR
EXTRACAPSULAR
EXTRACARPAL
EXTRACOSTAL
EXTRACTABLE
EXTRACTIBLE
EXTRACTIFORM
EXTRACYSTIC
EXTRADITABLE
EXTRADITING
EXTRADITION
EXTRADUCTION
EXTRAENTERIC
EXTRAFORMAL
EXTRAGALACTIC
EXTRAJUDICIAL
EXTRALATERAL
EXTRAMUNDANE
EXTRAMURALLY
EXTRANEOUSLY
EXTRAORDINARY
EXTRAPHYSICAL
EXTRAPOLATE
EXTRAPOLATED
EXTRAPOLATING
EXTRAPOLATION
EXTRAPOLATIVE
EXTRAPOLATOR
EXTRAREGULAR
EXTRARETINAL
EXTRASENSORY
EXTRASEROUS
EXTRASYSTOLE
EXTRATARSAL
EXTRATRIBAL
EXTRAUTERINE
EXTRAVAGANCE
EXTRAVAGANCY
EXTRAVAGANT
EXTRAVAGANTLY
EXTRAVAGANZA
EXTRAVAGATE
EXTRAVAGATED
EXTRAVAGATING
EXTRAVAGATION
EXTRAVAGINAL
EXTRAVASATE
EXTRAVASATED
EXTRAVASATING
EXTRAVASATION
EXTRAVASCULAR
EXTRAVERSION
EXTRAVIOLET
EXTREMENESS
EXTREMISTIC
EXTREMITIES
EXTRICATING
EXTRICATION
EXTRINSICAL
EXTRINSICALLY
EXTRINSICATE
EXTROSPECTION
EXTROSPECTIVE
EXTROVERSION
EXTROVERSIVE
EXTUMESCENCE
EXUBERANTLY
EXUBERANTNESS
EXUBERATING
EXUBERATION
EXULCERATED
EXULCERATING
EXULCERATION
EXULCERATIVE
EXULCERATORY
EXUMBRELLAR
EXUVIABILITY
FIBROMYXOMA
FLEXANIMOUS
FLEXIBILITY
FLEXIBLENESS
FLEXUOSITIES
FLEXUOUSNESS
FLUXIBILITY
FLUXIBLENESS
FLUXIONALLY
FORMALDOXIME
FORNICATRIX
FRICANDEAUX
FUCOXANTHIN
GALVANOTAXIS
GASTROTAXIS
GASTROXYNSIS
GENUFLEXION
GENUFLEXUOUS
GITOXIGENIN
GRIPPOTOXIN
GUBERNATRIX
HETERODOXIES
HETEROSEXUAL
HETEROTAXIA
HETEROTAXIC
HETEROTAXIS
HETEROXENOUS
HEXABROMIDE
HEXAGONALLY
HEXASTICHIC
HEXOBARBITAL
HOMOSEXUALITY
HYDROEXTRACT
HYDROTHORAX
HYPOPHARYNX
HYPOTOXICITY
HYPOXANTHINE
ICHTHYOTOXIN
IDEOPRAXIST
IMMUNOTOXIN
IMPROPRIATRIX
INDEXICALLY
INDEXTERITY
INEXACTITUDE
INEXACTNESS
INEXCUSABLE
INEXCUSABLY
INEXECUTION
INEXHAUSTIBLE
INEXHAUSTIVE
INEXISTENCE
INEXISTENCY
INEXPECTEDLY
INEXPEDIENCY
INEXPEDIENT
INEXPENSIVE
INEXPERIENCE
INEXPERIENCED
INEXPERTNESS
INEXPLICABLE
INEXPLICABLES
INEXPLICABLY
INEXPLICITLY
INEXPRESSIBLE
INEXPRESSIVE
INEXTENSIVE
INEXTIRPABLE
INEXTRICABLE
INEXTRICABLY
INFLEXIBILITY
INFLUXIONISM
INNOXIOUSLY
INOBNOXIOUS
INOXIDIZING
INTERMIXEDLY
INTERMIXING
INTERMIXTLY
INTERMIXTURE
INTERSEXUAL
INTERTEXTURE
INTERXYLARY
INTOXICABLE
INTOXICATED
INTOXICATING
INTOXICATION
INTOXICATIVE
INTOXICATOR
INTRAXYLARY
INTROFLEXION
IRREFLEXIVE
JUXTAMARINE
JUXTAPOSING
JUXTAPOSITION
JUXTAPYLORIC
JUXTASPINAL
KARYORRHEXIS
KERATONYXIS
LAURINOXYLON
LAXATIVENESS
LAXIFLOROUS
LAXIFOLIATE
LAXIFOLIOUS
LEGISLATRIX
LEXICOGRAPHY
LEXICOLOGIC
LEXICOLOGICAL
LEXICOLOGIST
LEXIGRAPHIC
LEXIGRAPHICAL
LIFERENTRIX
LITHANTHRAX
LITHOLAPAXY
LITHOXYLITE
LIXIVIATING
LIXIVIATION
LOXODOGRAPH
LOXODROMICS
LOXODROMISM
LUXULLIANITE
LUXURIANTLY
LUXURIANTNESS
LUXURIATING
LUXURIATION
LUXURIOUSLY
LUXURIOUSNESS
LYMPHOTOXIN
MAXILLARIES
MAXILLIFORM
MAXILLIPEDARY
MAXILLIPEDE
MAXILLOJUGAL
MAXILLOLABIAL
MAXIMIZATION
MERVEILLEUX
MESOAPPENDIX
MESOSALPINX
METAGALAXIES
METAVAUXITE
MICROTHORAX
MIXOBARBARIC
MIXOTROPHIC
MIXTILINEAR
MONILETHRIX
MORPHALLAXIS
MYELAPOPLEXY
MYELOPLAXES
MYTILOTOXINE
MYXADENITIS
MYXASTHENIA
MYXEDEMATOUS
MYXOBLASTOMA
MYXOCYSTOMA
MYXOFIBROMA
MYXOMATOSIS
MYXOMYCETOUS
MYXONEUROMA
MYXOSARCOMA
MYXOSPOROUS
NASOPHARYNX
NEGOTIATRIX
NEOORTHODOXY
NEPHROTOXIC
NEPHROTOXIN
NEUROPLEXUS
NONEXISTENCE
NONEXISTENT
NOXIOUSNESS
OBJURGATRIX
OBNOXIOUSLY
OBNOXIOUSNESS
ODONTEXESIS
ODONTOLOXIA
OOPHOROPEXY
ORCHIDOPEXY
OROPHARYNXES
ORTHODOXALLY
ORTHODOXIAN
ORTHODOXICAL
ORTHODOXIES
ORTHODOXISM
ORTHODOXIST
ORTHODOXNESS
OSCULATRIXES
OSTEOSTIXIS
OVEREXPOSED
OVEREXPOSING
OVEREXPOSURE
OVERTAXATION
OXALURAMIDE
OXIDABILITY
OXIDATIONAL
OXIDIMETRIC
OXYACANTHIN
OXYACANTHINE
OXYACANTHOUS
OXYACETYLENE
OXYALDEHYDE
OXYBERBERINE
OXYCARBONATE
OXYCELLULOSE
OXYCEPHALIC
OXYCEPHALISM
OXYCEPHALOUS
OXYCHLORATE
OXYCHLORIDE
OXYCHLORINE
OXYCHROMATIC
OXYCHROMATIN
OXYCINNAMIC
OXYCOPAIVIC
OXYCOUMARIN
OXYESTHESIA
OXYGENATING
OXYGENERATOR
OXYGENICITY

OXYGENIZABLE
OXYGENIZING
OXYGNATHOUS
OXYHAEMATIN
OXYHEXACTINE
OXYHEXASTER
OXYHYDROGEN
OXYLUCIFERIN
OXYMETHYLENE
OXYMURIATIC
OXYOSPHRESIA
OXYPETALOUS
OXYPHOSPHATE
OXYPHTHALIC
OXYPHYLLOUS
OXYPROPIONIC
OXYQUINOLINE
OXYRHYNCHID
OXYRHYNCHOUS
OXYRRHYNCHID
OXYSALICYLIC
OXYSTOMATOUS
OXYSULPHATE
OXYSULPHIDE
OXYTYLOTATE
PACHYMENINX
PANSEXUALISM
PANSEXUALIST
PANSEXUALITY
PANSEXUALIZE
PARADOXICAL
PARADOXICIAN
PARADOXIDIAN
PARADOXOLOGY
PARAVAUXITE
PAROXYSMALLY
PAROXYTONIC
PAXILLIFORM
PEPTOTOXINE
PERIAXILLARY
PERICOXITIS
PERPLEXEDLY
PERPLEXINGLY
PERPLEXITIES
PHENOXAZINE
PHILODOXICAL
PHLEBORRHEXIS
PHOTOSYNTAX
PHYLLOTAXIS
PHYLLOXERAN
PHYLLOXERIC
PILOTAXITIC
PLEXIMETRIC
PNEUMONOPEXY
PNEUMOTHORAX
PNEUMOTOXIN
POLYHYDROXY
POSTAXIALLY
POSTEXILIAN
POSTEXISTENT
POSTFLEXION
PRAEMAXILLA
PRAETAXATION
PRAXINOSCOPE
PREEXISTENCE
PREEXISTENT
PREFIXATION
PREMAXILLARY
PRETEXTUOUS
PROCATARXIS
PROCURATRIX
PROGENITRIX
PROLOCUTRIX
PROPHYLAXIS
PROTEOPEXIC
PROTEOPEXIS
PROTHORAXES
PROTOXIDIZE
PROTOXIDIZED
PROXENETISM
PROXIMATELY
PROXIMATION
PSEUDOCORTEX
PSEUDODOXAL
PSYCHOREFLEX
PSYCHOSEXUAL
PSYCHOTAXIS
PTEROTHORAX
PYOXANTHOSE
PYROXMANGITE
PYRRHULOXIA
QUINATOXINE
QUINCUNXIAL
QUINISEXTINE
QUINOXALINE
RADIOPRAXIS
REFLEXIONAL
REFLEXIVELY
REFLEXIVITY
REFLEXOLOGY
RELAXEDNESS
RETROFLEXED
RETROFLEXION
RETROXIPHOID
RHAMNOHEXOSE
RHAMNOHEXITE
RHINOPHARYNX
RHYOTAXITIC
SACROCOCCYX
SACROCOXITIS
SAXIFRAGANT
SAXIFRAGOUS
SAXOPHONIST
SCAPULOPEXY
SCEUOPHYLAX
SCILLITOXIN
SCLERONYXIS
SEMIFLEXIBLE
SEMISEXTILE
SESQUISEXTAL
SEXADECIMAL
SEXAGENARIAN
SEXAGESIMAL
SEXANGULARLY
SEXCENTENARY
SEXDIGITATE
SEXDIGITATED
SEXDIGITISM
SEXISYLLABLE
SEXLESSNESS
SEXOLOGICAL
SEXPLOITATION
SEXTILLIONTH
SEXTIPARTITE
SEXTUPLICATE
SEXTUPLICATED
SHIKIMOTOXIN
SIPHONOPLAX
SPASMOTOXIN
SPASMOTOXINE
SPECULATRIX
SPERMOTOXIN
SPLENOPEXIA
SPLENOPEXIS
SPLENOTOXIN
STAURAXONIA
STAURAXONIAL
STENOTHORAX
STEREOMATRIX
STEREOTAXIS
STIMULATRIX
STROPHOTAXIS
SUBAXILLARY
SUBLUXATION
SUBMAXILLAE
SUBMAXILLARY
SUBOXIDATION
SUBSEXTUPLE
SUFFIXATION
SULFOXYLATE
SULPHOXYLIC
SUPERFLEXION
SUPERMAXILLA
SUPERSEXUAL
SUPRAMAXILLA
SUPRAMAXIMAL
TAXABLENESS
TAXASPIDEAN
TAXEOPODOUS
TAXGATHERER
TAXGATHERING
TAXIDERMIST
TAXIDERMIZE
TAXIMETERED
TAXONOMICAL
TETRAHYDROXY
TETROXALATE
TEXTIFEROUS
THERMOTAXIC
THERMOTAXIS
THIGMOTAXIS
THIXOLABILE
THIXOTROPIC
THOROUGHWAX
TOXALBUMOSE
TOXICOGENIC
TOXICOGNATH
TOXICOLOGIC
TOXICOLOGIST
TOXICOMANIA
TOXICOPATHIC
TOXICOPATHY
TOXICOPHAGY
TOXICOPHIDIA
TOXINFECTION
TOXIPHOBIAC
TOXITABELLAE
TOXOGENESIS
TOXOGLOSSATE
TOXOPHILISM
TOXOPHILITIC
TOXOPHILOUS
TRANSFIXING
TRANSFIXION
TRANSFIXTURE
TRISULFOXID
TRISULPHOXID
TROPHALLAXIS
TROPHOTAXIS
TROPHOTHYLAX
TYLOTOXEATE
TYPHOTOXINE
TYROTOXICON
ULTRACOMPLEX
ULTRAMAXIMAL
UNDEREXPOSE
UNDEREXPOSED
UNDEREXPOSING
UNEXACTNESS
UNEXCEPTIVE
UNEXCLUSIVE
UNEXCUSABLE
UNEXCUSABLY
UNEXPECTEDLY
UNEXPEDIENT
UNEXPENSIVE
UNEXPERIENCE
UNEXPERIENT
UNEXPLAINED
UNEXPLICABLE
UNEXPLOITED
UNEXPRESSIVE
UNEXPURGATED
UNEXTRICABLE
UNISEXUALITY
UNISEXUALLY
UNORTHODOXLY
UNORTHODOXY
URECHITOXIN
UROTOXICITY
VASOREFLEX
VEXATIOUSLY
VEXILLARIOUS
VEXILLATION
WAXCHANDLER
WAXCHANDLERY
XANTHELASMA
XANTHINURIA
XANTHOCHROIA
XANTHOCHROID
XANTHOCONITE
XANTHODERMA
XANTHOGENATE
XANTHOGENIC
XANTHOMATOUS
XANTHOMETER
XANTHOPHANE
XANTHOPHORE
XANTHOPHYLL
XANTHOPTERIN
XANTHOXENITE
XANTHOXYLIN
XENACANTHINE
XENARTHROUS
XENODOCHIUM
XENOGENESIS
XENOMORPHIC
XENOPARASITE
XENOSAUROID
XENYLAMINE
XEROGRAPHER
XEROGRAPHIC
XEROMORPHIC
XEROMORPHOUS
XEROPHILOUS
XEROPHOBOUS
XEROPHYTISM
XEROTRIPSIS
XIPHISTERNAL
XIPHISTERNUM
XIPHOCOSTAL
XIPHOPAGOUS
XIPHOSUROUS
XYLOCARPOUS
XYLOGRAPHER
XYLOGRAPHIC
XYLOPHAGOUS
XYLOPHILOUS
XYLOPHONIST
XYLOPLASTIC
XYLOQUINONE
XYLOSTROMATA
XYRIDACEOUS
ZANTHOXYLUM
ZOOPRAXISCOPE
ZOOXANTHELLA

POSITIONAL ORDER LIST OF WORDS OVER 10 LETTERS

XANTHELASMA
XANTHINURIA
XANTHOCHROIA
XANTHOCHROID
XANTHOCONITE
XANTHODERMA
XANTHOGENATE
XANTHOGENIC
XANTHOMATOUS
XANTHOMETER
XANTHOPHANE
XANTHOPHORE
XANTHOPHYLL
XANTHOPTERIN
XANTHOXENITE
XANTHOXYLIN
XENACANTHINE
XENARTHROUS
XENODOCHIUM
XENOGENESIS
XENOMORPHIC
XENOPARASITE
XENOSAUROID
XENYLAMINE
XEROGRAPHER
XEROGRAPHIC
XEROMORPHIC
XEROMORPHOUS
XEROPHILOUS
XEROPHOBOUS
XEROPHYTISM
XEROTRIPSIS
XIPHISTERNAL
XIPHISTERNUM
XIPHOCOSTAL
XIPHOPAGOUS
XIPHOSUROUS
XYLOCARPOUS
XYLOGRAPHER
XYLOGRAPHIC
XYLOPHAGOUS
XYLOPHILOUS
XYLOPHONIST
XYLOPLASTIC
XYLOQUINONE
XYLOSTROMATA
XYRIDACEOUS

AXIOLOGICAL
AXIOMATICAL
AXISYMMETRIC
AXODENDRITE
AXONOLIPOUS
AXONOMETRIC
AXONOPHOROUS

AXOSPERMOUS
EXACERBATED
EXACERBATING
EXACERBATION
EXACTINGNESS
EXACTIVENESS
EXAGGERATED
EXAGGERATING
EXAGGERATION
EXAGGERATIVE
EXAGGERATOR
EXAGGERATORY
EXALBUMINOSE
EXALBUMINOUS
EXALLOTRIOTE
EXALTEDNESS
EXAMINATION
EXAMINATIONAL
EXAMINATIVE
EXAMINATORY
EXANIMATION
EXANTHEMATIC
EXARTERITIS
EXARTICULATE
EXASPERATED
EXASPERATER
EXASPERATING
EXASPERATION
EXASPERATIVE
EXAUCTORATE
EXAUGURATION
EXAUTHORIZE
EXCALCARATE
EXCANDESCENT
EXCANTATION
EXCARNATION
EXCATHEDRAL
EXCAVATIONS
EXCEEDINGLY
EXCELLENCIES
EXCELLENTLY
EXCEPTIONAL
EXCEPTIONALLY
EXCEPTIONARY
EXCEPTIONER
EXCEPTIVELY
EXCERPTIBLE
EXCESSIVELY
EXCESSIVENESS
EXCHANGEABLE
EXCHANGEABLY
EXCIPULIFORM
EXCITABILITY
EXCITABLENESS
EXCITEDNESS
EXCITOMOTOR
EXCITOMOTORY
EXCLAMATION
EXCLAMATIONAL
EXCLAMATIVE
EXCLAMATIVELY
EXCLAMATORILY
EXCLAMATORY
EXCLUSIONARY
EXCLUSIONER
EXCLUSIONISM
EXCLUSIONIST
EXCLUSIVELY
EXCLUSIVENESS
EXCLUSIVISM
EXCLUSIVITY
EXCOGITABLE
EXCOGITATED
EXCOGITATING
EXCOGITATION
EXCOGITATIVE
EXCOGITATOR
EXCOMMUNICANT
EXCOMMUNICATE
EXCOMMUNION
EXCONJUGANT
EXCORIATING
EXCORIATION
EXCORTICATE
EXCORTICATED
EXCORTICATING
EXCORTICATION
EXCREMENTAL
EXCREMENTARY
EXCREMENTIVE
EXCRESCENCE
EXCRESCENCES
EXCRESCENCIES
EXCRESCENCY
EXCRESCENTIAL
EXCRETIONARY
EXCRIMINATE
EXCRUCIABLE
EXCRUCIATED
EXCRUCIATING
EXCRUCIATION
EXCRUCIATOR
EXCULPATING
EXCULPATION
EXCULPATIVE
EXCULPATORY
EXCURSIONAL
EXCURSIONARY
EXCURSIONER
EXCURSIONISM
EXCURSIONIST
EXCURSIONIZE
EXCURSIVELY
EXCURVATURE
EXCUSABILITY
EXCUSABLENESS
EXCYSTATION
EXECRABLENESS
EXECUTIONAL
EXECUTIONER
EXECUTIVELY
EXECUTIVENESS
EXECUTORIAL
EXECUTRICES
EXECUTRIXES
EXEGETICALLY
EXEMPLARILY
EXEMPLARINESS
EXEMPLARISM
EXEMPLARITY
EXEMPLIFIED
EXEMPLIFIER
EXEMPLIFYING
EXENCEPHALIA
EXENCEPHALIC
EXENCEPHALUS
EXENTERATED
EXENTERATING
EXENTERATION
EXERCISABLE
EXERCITATION
EXERCITORIAL
EXFIGURATION
EXFILTRATION
EXFLAGELLATE
EXFODIATION
EXFOLIATING
EXFOLIATION
EXFOLIATIVE
EXFOLIATORY
EXHAUSTEDLY
EXHAUSTEDNESS
EXHAUSTIBLE
EXHAUSTINGLY
EXHAUSTIVELY
EXHAUSTLESS
EXHAUSTLESSLY
EXHIBITIONAL
EXHIBITIONER
EXHIBITIONISM
EXHIBITIONIST
EXHIBITIVELY
EXHIBITORSHIP
EXHILARATED
EXHILARATING
EXHILARATION
EXHILARATIVE
EXHILARATOR
EXHILARATORY
EXHORTATIVE
EXHORTATIVELY
EXHORTATORY
EXIGUOUSNESS
EXILARCHATE
EXIMIOUSNESS
EXINANITION
EXISTENTIAL
EXISTENTIALLY
EXISTLESSNESS
EXOARTERITIS
EXOCCIPITAL
EXOCULATING
EXOGASTRITIS
EXOGENOUSLY
EXOGNATHION
EXOGNATHITE
EXOMETRITIS
EXOMOLOGESIS
EXOMORPHISM
EXOMPHALOUS
EXONERATING
EXONERATION
EXONERATIVE
EXOPERIDIUM
EXOPHTHALMIA
EXOPHTHALMIC
EXOPHTHALMOS
EXOPHTHALMUS
EXORABILITY
EXORABLENESS
EXORBITANCE
EXORBITANCY
EXORBITANTLY
EXORBITATION
EXORCISATION
EXORCISEMENT
EXORCISTICAL
EXORCIZATION
EXORCIZEMENT
EXOSKELETAL
EXOSKELETON
EXOSTRACISM
EXOSTRACIZE
EXOTERICALLY
EXOTERICISM
EXOTHERMOUS
EXOTICALNESS
EXPANDEDNESS
EXPANDINGLY
EXPANSIBILITY
EXPANSIONAL
EXPANSIONISM
EXPANSIONIST
EXPANSIVELY
EXPANSIVENESS
EXPANSIVITY
EXPATIATING
EXPATIATION
EXPATIATIVE
EXPATIATORY
EXPATRIATED
EXPATRIATING
EXPATRIATION
EXPECTANCIES
EXPECTANTLY
EXPECTATION
EXPECTATIVE
EXPECTORANT
EXPECTORATE
EXPECTORATED
EXPECTORATING
EXPECTORATION
EXPECTORATOR
EXPEDIENCIES
EXPEDIENTIAL
EXPEDIENTIST
EXPEDIENTLY
EXPEDITATED
EXPEDITATING
EXPEDITATION
EXPEDITENESS
EXPEDITIONARY
EXPEDITIONIST
EXPEDITIOUS
EXPEDITIOUSLY
EXPENDABILITY
EXPENDITRIX
EXPENDITURE
EXPENSILATION
EXPENSIVELY
EXPENSIVENESS
EXPENTHESIS
EXPERIENCED
EXPERIENCER
EXPERIENCES
EXPERIENCING
EXPERIENTIAL
EXPERIMENTAL
EXPERIMENTED
EXPERIMENTEE
EXPERIMENTER
EXPERIMENTING
EXPERIMENTIST
EXPERIMENTIZE
EXPERMENTIZED
EXPERIMENTLY
EXPIATIONAL
EXPIATORINESS
EXPISCATING
EXPISCATION
EXPISCATORY
EXPLAINABLE
EXPLANATION
EXPLANATIVE
EXPLANATIVELY
EXPLANATORILY
EXPLANATORY
EXPLANTATION
EXPLEMENTAL
EXPLETIVELY
EXPLETIVENESS
EXPLICATING
EXPLICATION
EXPLICATIVE
EXPLICATORY
EXPLICITNESS
EXPLOITABLE
EXPLOITATION
EXPLOITATIVE
EXPLORATION
EXPLORATIONAL
EXPLORATIVE
EXPLORATIVELY
EXPLORATORY
EXPLOREMENT
EXPLOSIBILITY
EXPLOSIONIST
EXPLOSIVELY
EXPLOSIVENESS
EXPONENTIAL
EXPONENTIALLY
EXPORTABILITY
EXPORTATION
EXPOSITIONAL
EXPOSITIONARY
EXPOSITIVELY
EXPOSITORIAL
EXPOSITORILY
EXPOSTULATE
EXPOSTULATED
EXPOSTULATING
EXPOSTULATION
EXPOSTULATIVE
EXPOSTULATOR
EXPOSTULATORY
EXPRESSIBLE
EXPRESSION
EXPRESSIONAL
EXPRESSIONISM
EXPRESSIONIST
EXPRESSIVELY
EXPRESSLESS
EXPROBRATORY
EXPROMISSION
EXPROPRIATE
EXPROPRIATED
EXPROPRIATING
EXPROPRIATION
EXPROPRIATOR
EXPULSATORY
EXPURGATING
EXPURGATION
EXPURGATIVE
EXPURGATORIAL
EXPURGATORY
EXQUISITELY
EXQUISITENESS
EXQUISITISM
EXQUISITIVELY
EXSANGUINATE
EXSANGUINOUS
EXSANGUIOUS
EXSCRIPTURAL
EXSCULPTATE
EXSCUTELLATE
EXSICCATING
EXSICCATION
EXSICCATIVE
EXSTIPULATE
EXSUFFLATION
EXSUFFLICATE
EXTEMPORALLY
EXTEMPORARY
EXTEMPORARILY
EXTEMPORIZE
EXTEMPORIZED
EXTEMPORIZER
EXTEMPORIZING
EXTENDEDNESS
EXTENDIBILITY
EXTENSIBILITY
EXTENSIMETER
EXTENSIONAL
EXTENSIONIST
EXTENSIVELY
EXTENSIVENESS
EXTENSOMETER
EXTENUATING
EXTENUATINGLY
EXTENUATION
EXTENUATIVE
EXTENUATORY
EXTERIORATE
EXTERIORATION
EXTERIORITY

EXTERIORIZE
EXTERIORIZED
EXTERIORIZING
EXTERIORNESS
EXTERMINATE
EXTERMINATED
EXTERMINATING
EXTERMINATION
EXTERMINATIVE
EXTERMINATOR
EXTERMINATORY
EXTERNALISM
EXTERNALIST
EXTERNALISTIC
EXTERNALITIES
EXTERNALITY
EXTERNALIZE
EXTERNATION
EXTERNIZATION
EXTEROCEPTIST
EXTEROCEPTIVE
EXTEROCEPTOR
EXTERRANEOUS
EXTERRESTRIAL
EXTERRITORIAL
EXTINGUISHED
EXTINGUISHER
EXTIRPATING
EXTIRPATION
EXTIRPATIVE
EXTIRPATORY
EXTISPICIOUS
EXTOLLATION
EXTORSIVELY
EXTORTIONARY
EXTORTIONATE
EXTORTIONER
EXTORTIONIST
EXTRABULBAR
EXTRACAPSULAR
EXTRACARPAL
EXTRACOSTAL
EXTRACTABLE
EXTRACTIBLE
EXTRACTIFORM
EXTRACYSTIC
EXTRADITABLE
EXTRADITING
EXTRADITION
EXTRADUCTION
EXTRAENTERIC
EXTRAFORMAL
EXTRAGALACTIC
EXTRAJUDICIAL
EXTRALATERAL
EXTRAMUNDANE
EXTRAMURALLY
EXTRANEOUSLY
EXTRAORDINARY
EXTRAPHYSICAL
EXTRAPOLATE
EXTRAPOLATED
EXTRAPOLATING
EXTRAPOLATION
EXTRAPOLATIVE
EXTRAPOLATOR
EXTRAREGULAR
EXTRARETINAL
EXTRASENSORY
EXTRASEROUS
EXTRASYSTOLE
EXTRATARSAL
EXTRATRIBAL
EXTRAUTERINE
EXTRAVAGANCE
EXTRAVAGANCY
EXTRAVAGANT
EXTRAVAGANTLY
EXTRAVAGANZA
EXTRAVAGATE
EXTRAVAGATED
EXTRAVAGATING
EXTRAVAGATION
EXTRAVAGINAL
EXTRAVASATE
EXTRAVASATED
EXTRAVASATING
EXTRAVASATION
EXTRAVASCULAR
EXTRAVERSION
EXTRAVIOLET
EXTREMENESS
EXTREMISTIC
EXTREMITIES
EXTRICATING
EXTRICATION
EXTRINSICAL
EXTRINSICALLY
EXTRINSICATE
EXTROSPECTION
EXTROSPECTIVE
EXTROVERSION
EXTROVERSIVE
EXTUMESCENCE
EXUBERANTLY
EXUBERANTNESS
EXUBERATING
EXUBERATION
EXULCERATED
EXULCERATING
EXULCERATION
EXULCERATIVE
EXULCERATORY
EXUMBRELLAR
EXUVIABILITY
OXALURAMIDE
OXIDABILITY
OXIDATIONAL
OXIDIMETRIC
OXYACANTHIN
OXYACANTHINE
OXYACANTHOUS
OXYACETYLENE
OXYALDEHYDE
OXYBERBERINE
OXYCARBONATE
OXYCELLULOSE
OXYCEPHALIC
OXYCEPHALISM
OXYCEPHALOUS
OXYCHLORATE
OXYCHLORIDE
OXYCHLORINE
OXYCHROMATIC
OXYCHROMATIN
OXYCINNAMIC
OXYCOPAIVIC
OXYCOUMARIN
OXYESTHESIA
OXYGENATING
OXYGENERATOR
OXYGENICITY
OXYGENIZABLE
OXYGENIZING
OXYGNATHOUS
OXYHAEMATIN
OXYHEXACTINE
OXYHEXASTER
OXYHYDROGEN
OXYLUCIFERIN
OXYMETHYLENE
OXYMURIATIC
OXYOSPHRESIA
OXYPETALOUS
OXYPHOSPHATE
OXYPHTHALIC
OXYPHYLLOUS
OXYPROPIONIC
OXYQUINOLINE
OXYRHYNCHID
OXYRHYNCHOUS
OXYRRHYNCHID
OXYSALICYLIC
OXYSTOMATOUS
OXYSULPHATE
OXYSULPHIDE
OXYTYLOTATE

ANXIOUSNESS
AUXANOMETER
AUXETICALLY
AUXILIARIES
AUXILIATION
AUXILIATORY
AUXOAMYLASE
AUXOCHROMIC
AUXOCHROMISM
AUXOCHROMOUS
AUXOGRAPHIC
AUXOHORMONE
COXARTHRITIS
COXCOMBICAL
COXOCERITIC
COXOFEMORAL
DEXIOTROPIC
DEXIOTROPISM
DEXIOTROPOUS
DEXTEROUSLY
DEXTROCARDIA
DEXTROCULAR
DEXTROGYRATE
DEXTROSAZONE
DEXTROSURIA
DEXTROUSNESS
DOXOGRAPHER
DOXOLOGICAL
DOXOLOGIZED
DOXOLOGIZING
HEXABROMIDE
HEXAGONALLY
HEXASTICHIC
HEXOBARBITAL
JUXTAMARINE
JUXTAPOSING
JUXTAPOSITION
JUXTAPYLORIC
JUXTASPINAL
LAXATIVENESS
LAXIFLOROUS
LAXIFOLIATE
LAXIFOLIOUS
LEXICOGRAPHY
LEXICOLOGIC
LEXICOLOGICAL
LEXICOLOGIST
LEXIGRAPHIC
LEXIGRAPHICAL
LIXIVIATING
LIXIVIATION
LOXODOGRAPH
LOXODROMICS
LOXODROMISM
LUXULLIANITE
LUXURIANTLY
LUXURIANTNESS
LUXURIATING
LUXURIATION
LUXURIOUSLY
LUXURIOUSNESS
MAXILLARIES
MAXILLIFORM
MAXILLIPEDARY
MAXILLIPEDE
MAXILLOJUGAL
MAXILLOLABIAL
MAXIMIZATION
MIXOBARBARIC
MIXOTROPHIC
MIXTILINEAR
MYXADENITIS
MYXASTHENIA
MYXEDEMATOUS
MYXOBLASTOMA
MYXOCYSTOMA
MYXOFIBROMA
MYXOMATOSIS
MYXOMYCETOUS
MYXONEUROMA
MYXOSARCOMA
MYXOSPOROUS
NOXIOUSNESS
PAXILLIFORM
SAXIFRAGANT
SAXIFRAGOUS
SAXOPHONIST
SEXADECIMAL
SEXAGENARIAN
SEXAGESIMAL
SEXANGULARLY
SEXCENTENARY
SEXDIGITATE
SEXDIGITATED
SEXDIGITISM
SEXISYLLABLE
SEXLESSNESS
SEXOLOGICAL
SEXPLOITATION
SEXTILLIONTH
SEXTIPARTITE
SEXTUPLICATE
SEXTUPLICATED
TAXABLENESS
TAXASPIDEAN
TAXEOPODOUS
TAXGATHERER
TAXGATHERING
TAXIDERMIST
TAXIDERMIZE
TAXIMETERED
TAXONOMICAL
TEXTIFEROUS
TOXALBUMOSE
TOXICOGENIC
TOXICOGNATH
TOXICOLOGIC
TOXICOLOGIST
TOXICOMANIA
TOXICOPATHIC
TOXICOPATHY
TOXICOPHAGY
TOXICOPHIDIA
TOXINFECTION
TOXIPHOBIAC
TOXITABELLAE
TOXOGENESIS
TOXOGLOSSATE
TOXOPHILISM
TOXOPHILITIC
TOXOPHILOUS
VEXATIOUSLY
VEXILLARIOUS
VEXILLATION
WAXCHANDLER
WAXCHANDLERY

ADOXOGRAPHY
ALEXANDRITE
ALEXIPHARMIC
ALEXIPYRETIC
ANOXIDATIVE
ANOXYBIOSIS
ANOXYBIOTIC
ASEXUALIZED
ASEXUALIZING
ATAXAPHASIA
ATAXIAGRAPH
ATAXIAMETER
ATAXIAPHASIA
ATAXOPHEMIA
COEXISTENCE
COEXISTENCY
COEXTENSION
COEXTENSIVE
DEOXIDIZING
DEOXYGENATE
DEOXYGENATED
DEOXYGENIZE
EPEXEGETICAL
FLEXANIMOUS
FLEXIBILITY
FLEXIBLENESS
FLEXUOSITIES
FLEXUOUSNESS
FLUXIBILITY
FLUXIBLENESS
FLUXIONALLY
INEXACTITUDE
INEXACTNESS
INEXCUSABLE
INEXCUSABLY
INEXECUTION
INEXHAUSTIBLE
INEXHAUSTIVE
INEXISTENCE
INEXISTENCY
INEXPECTEDLY
INEXPEDIENCY
INEXPEDIENT
INEXPENSIVE
INEXPERIENCE
INEXPERIENCED
INEXPERTNESS
INEXPLICABLE
INEXPLICABLES
INEXPLICABLY
INEXPLICITLY
INEXPRESSIBLE
INEXPRESSIVE
INEXTENSIVE
INEXTIRPABLE
INEXTRICABLE
INEXTRICABLY
INOXIDIZING
PLEXIMETRIC
PRAXINOSCOPE
PROXENETISM
PROXIMATELY
PROXIMATION
PYOXANTHOSE
THIXOLABILE
THIXOTROPIC
UNEXACTNESS
UNEXCEPTIVE
UNEXCLUSIVE
UNEXCUSABLE
UNEXCUSABLY
UNEXPECTEDLY
UNEXPEDIENT
UNEXPENSIVE
UNEXPERIENCE
UNEXPERIENT
UNEXPLAINED
UNEXPLICABLE
UNEXPLOITED
UNEXPRESSIVE

UNEXPURGATED
UNEXTRICABLE
ZOOXANTHELLA

ADMAXILLARY
ANNEXATIONAL
ANNEXATIONIST
ANNEXIONIST
AUTOXIDATION
AUTOXIDATOR
BIMAXILLARY
BISAXILLARY
BISEXUALISM
BISEXUALITY
DESEXUALIZE
DESEXUALIZED
DETOXICATED
DETOXICATING
DETOXICATION
DETOXICATOR
DIHEXAHEDRAL
DIHEXAHEDRON
DISOXYGENATE
DYSOXIDATION
FUCOXANTHIN
GITOXIGENIN
HYPOXANTHINE
INDEXICALLY
INDEXTERITY
INNOXIOUSLY
INTOXICABLE
INTOXICATED
INTOXICATING
INTOXICATION
INTOXICATIVE
INTOXICATOR
NONEXISTENCE
NONEXISTENT
OBNOXIOUSLY
OBNOXIOUSNESS
PAROXYSMALLY
PAROXYTONIC
PREEXISTENCE
PREEXISTENT
PYROXMANGITE
RELAXEDNESS
SUBAXILLARY
SUBOXIDATION

AMPLEXATION
AMPLEXICAUL
ANTHEXIMETER
ANTHOXANTHIN
ANTIOXIDANT
ANTIOXYGENIC
APPROXIMATE
APPROXIMATED
APPROXIMATELY
APPROXIMATING
APPROXIMATION
APPROXIMATIVE
APPROXIMATOR
ASPHYXIATED
ASPHYXIATING
ASPHYXIATION
ASPHYXIATOR
CARBOXYLASE
CARBOXYLATE
CARBOXYLATED
CONNEXITIES
CONTEXTUALLY
CONTEXTURAL
CONTEXTURED
CONVEXEDNESS
CONVEXITIES
COSTOXIPHOID
DOPAOXIDASE
INFLEXIBILITY
INFLUXIONISM
INTERXYLARY
INTRAXYLARY
LITHOXYLITE
OVEREXPOSED
OVEREXPOSING
OVEREXPOSURE
OXYHEXACTINE
OXYHEXASTER
PANSEXUALISM
PANSEXUALIST
PANSEXUALITY
PANSEXUALIZE
PERIAXILLARY
PHENOXAZINE
POSTAXIALLY
POSTEXILIAN
POSTEXISTENT
PREFIXATION
PREMAXILLARY
PRETEXTUOUS
PROTOXIDIZE
PROTOXIDIZED
QUINOXALINE
REFLEXIONAL
REFLEXIVELY
REFLEXIVITY
REFLEXOLOGY
RETROXIPHOID
SUBLUXATION
SUBMAXILLAE
SUBMAXILLARY
SUBSEXTUPLE
SUFFIXATION
SULFOXYLATE
TETROXALATE
UNISEXUALITY
UNISEXUALLY
UROTOXICITY

AMBIDEXTERITY
AMBIDEXTRAL
AMBIDEXTROUS
ANTHRAXOLITE
ANTHRAXYLON
ANTHROXANIC
APOPLEXIOUS
AUTOTOXAEMIA
AUTOTOXEMIA
BANDBOXICAL
CARBOLXYLOL
COLOPEXOTOMY
COMPLEXIONAL
COMPLEXIONARY
COMPLEXIONED
COMPLEXITIES
COMPLEXNESS
CONFLUXIBLE
GASTROXYNSIS
HETEROXENOUS
HOMOSEXUALITY
HYDROEXTRACT
HYPOTOXICITY
INOBNOXIOUS
ODONTEXESIS
OVERTAXATION
PARADOXICAL
PARADOXICIAN
PARADOXIDIAN
PARADOXOLOGY
PERICOXITIS
PERPLEXEDLY
PERPLEXINGLY
PERPLEXITIES
PHYLLOXERAN
PHYLLOXERIC
PILOTAXITIC
PRAEMAXILLA
PRAETAXATION
RHYOTAXITIC
SEMISEXTILE
STAURAXONIA
STAURAXONIAL
SULPHOXYLIC
TYLOTOXEATE
TYROTOXICON
UNDEREXPOSE
UNDEREXPOSED
UNDEREXPOSING
XANTHOXENITE
XANTHOXYLIN
ZANTHOXYLUM
ZOOPRAXISCOPE

ADENOMYXOMA
AMIDOHEXOSE
AMYLODEXTRIN
ANHYDROXIME
ANILIDOXIME
ANTEFLEXION
APPENDIXING
CIRCUMAXIAL
CIRCUMAXILE
CRUCIFIXION
CYCLOHEXANE
CYCLOHEXANOL
CYCLOHEXENE
CYSTOMYXOMA
DICARBOXYLIC
FIBROMYXOMA
GENUFLEXION
GENUFLEXUOUS
IDEOPRAXIST
INTERMIXEDLY
INTERMIXING
INTERMIXTLY
INTERMIXTURE
INTERSEXUAL
INTERTEXTURE
IRREFLEXIVE
LAURINOXYLON
METAVAUXITE
ORTHODOXALLY
ORTHODOXIAN
ORTHODOXICAL
ORTHODOXIES
ORTHODOXISM
ORTHODOXIST
ORTHODOXNESS
PARAVAUXITE
PEPTOTOXINE
PHILODOXICAL
POSTFLEXION
QUINATOXINE
QUINCUNXIAL
QUINISEXTINE
SACROCOXITIS
SEMIFLEXIBLE
SUPERMAXILLA
SUPERSEXUAL
SUPRAMAXILLA
SUPRAMAXIMAL
TRANSFIXING
TRANSFIXION
TRANSFIXTURE
TYPHOTOXINE
ULTRAMAXIMAL

ANAPHYLAXIS
ANGIOATAXIA
ANISALDOXIME
APHOTOTAXIS
APOPHYLAXIS
ATLANTOAXIAL
ATLOIDOAXOID
BENZALDOXIME
CARBETHOXYL
CARDIATAXIA
CARDIOTOXIC
CHEMIOTAXIC
CHEMIOTAXIS
CHIROPRAXIS
COLONOPEXY
CREATOTOXISM
DECIMOSEXTO
DIASTATAXIC
DICATALEXIS
DIRECTRIXES
DISULPHOXID
DISULPHOXIDE
DORSIFLEXION
DORSIFLEXOR
ENTEROPEXIA
ENTEROTOXEMIA
EXECUTRIXES
FORMALDOXIME
GASTROTAXIS
GRIPPOTOXIN
HETERODOXIES
HETEROSEXUAL
HETEROTAXIA
HETEROTAXIC
HETEROTAXIS
IMMUNOTOXIN
INTROFLEXION
KERATONYXIS
LYMPHOTOXIN
METAGALAXIES
MYELOPLAXES
MYTILOTOXINE
NEPHROTOXIC
NEPHROTOXIN
NEUROPLEXUS
ODONTOLOXIA
OSTEOSTIXIS
PHYLLOTAXIS
PNEUMOTOXIN
PROCATARXIS
PROPHYLAXIS
PROTEOPEXIC
PROTEOPEXIS
PROTHORAXES
PSEUDODOXAL
PSYCHOSEXUAL
PSYCHOTAXIS
PYRRHULOXIA
RADIOPRAXIS
RETROFLEXED
RETROFLEXION
RHAMNOHEXOSE
RHAMNOHEXITE
SCILLITOXIN
SCLERONYXIS
SESQUISEXTAL
SPASMOTOXIN
SPASMOTOXINE
SPERMOTOXIN
SPLENOPEXIA
SPLENOPEXIS
SPLENOTOXIN
STEREOTAXIS
SUPERFLEXION
THERMOTAXIC
THERMOTAXIS
THIGMOTAXIS
TRISULFOXID
TROPHOTAXIS
URECHITOXIN

ACROASPHYXIA
ACTINOPRAXIS
ANGIORRHEXIS
AORTOMALAXIS
COLPORRHEXIS
ELECTROTAXIS
GALVANOTAXIS
ICHTHYOTOXIN
KARYORRHEXIS
LITHOLAPAXY
MORPHALLAXIS
OOPHOROPEXY
ORCHIDOPEXY
OROPHARYNXES
OSCULATRIXES
POLYHYDROXY
SCAPULOPEXY
SHIKIMOTOXIN
STROPHOTAXIS
TRISULPHOXID
TROPHALLAXIS
UNORTHODOXLY
UNORTHODOXY
VASOREFLEX

ANDROSPHINX
ARCHOSYRINX
AUTOCRATRIX
BACTERIOTOXIC
CHALCEDONYX
CHEMOREFLEX
CHYLOTHORAX
CLITORIDAUXE
COMPETITRIX
CONSOLATRIX
CYSTOSYRINX
CYTOPHARYNX
ESOTHYROPEXY
EXPENDITRIX
FORNICATRIX
FRICANDEAUX
GUBERNATRIX
HYDROTHORAX
HYPOPHARYNX
LEGISLATRIX
LIFERENTRIX
LITHANTHRAX
MERVEILLEUX
MESOSALPINX
MICROTHORAX
MONILETHRIX
MYELAPOPLEXY
NASOPHARYNX
NEGOTIATRIX
NEOORTHODOXY
OBJURGATRIX
PACHYMENINX
PHLEBORRHEXIS
PHOTOSYNTAX
PNEUMONOPEXY
PROCURATRIX
PROGENITRIX
PROLOCUTRIX
PTEROTHORAX
SACROCOCCYX
SCEUOPHYLAX
SIPHONOPLAX
SPECULATRIX
STENOTHORAX
STIMULATRIX
TETRAHYDROXY
THOROUGHWAX

ARCHEOPTERYX
ARTHROSYRINX
CHARTOPHYLAX
DISPENSATRIX
MESOAPPENDIX
PNEUMOTHORAX
PSEUDOCORTEX
PSYCHOREFLEX
RHINOPHARYNX
STEREOMATRIX
TROPHOTHYLAX
ULTRACOMPLEX
IMPROPRIATRIX

SCORING ORDER LIST OF WORDS OVER 10 LETTERS

35
EXQUISITIVELY
ZANTHOXYLUM
ZOOPRAXISCOPE

34
EXPERMENTIZED
EXTEMPORIZING
HYPOPHARYNX
OXYGENIZABLE
OXYRRHYNCHID

33
BENZALDOXIME
EXPERIMENTIZE
EXTEMPORIZED
JUXTAPYLORIC
OXYRHYNCHID
OXYRHYNCHOUS

32
CHARTOPHYLAX
DEOXYGENIZE
EXORCIZEMENT
EXTEMPORIZER
EXTRAVAGANZA
HYPOTOXICITY
MAXIMIZATION
OXYGENIZING
OXYPHOSPHATE
PHENOXAZINE
PROTOXIDIZED
PSYCHOREFLEX

31
CYTOPHARYNX
DOXOLOGIZING
EXOPHTHALMIC
EXTEMPORIZE
MYELAPOPLEXY
MYXOMYCETOUS
OXYCEPHALISM
OXYCHROMATIC
OXYPHTHALIC
OXYQUINOLINE
WAXCHANDLERY
ZOOXANTHELLA

30
CYSTOMYXOMA
DEOXIDIZING
DESEXUALIZED
DOXOLOGIZED
ESOTHYROPEXY
EXAUTHORIZE
EXCHANGEABLY
EXCLAMATIVELY
EXCURSIONIZE
EXEMPLIFYING
EXHIBITIVELY
EXHIBITORSHIP
EXORCIZATION
EXQUISITELY
EXTERIORIZING
EXTRAPHYSICAL
HYPOXANTHINE
ICHTHYOTOXIN
LEXICOGRAPHY
MYXOCYSTOMA
MYXOFIBROMA
OXYCEPHALIC
OXYCOPAIVIC
OXYMETHYLENE
PACHYMENINX
PANSEXUALIZE
PHLEBORRHEXIS
PROTOXIDIZE
RHINOPHARYNX
TAXIDERMIZE
TROPHOTHYLAX
XYLOQUINONE

29
ACROASPHYXIA
APPROXIMATELY
APPROXIMATIVE
ARCHEOPTERYX
ASEXUALIZING
CHALCEDONYX
CHYLOTHORAX
COMPLEXIONARY
CYCLOHEXANOL
DEXTROSAZONE
DICARBOXYLIC
EXHORTATIVELY
EXOPHTHALMIA
EXOPHTHALMOS
EXOPHTHALMUS
EXOSTRACIZE
EXQUISITENESS
EXQUISITISM
EXTERIORIZED
EXTERNIZATION
INOXIDIZING
JUXTAPOSITION
KARYORRHEXIS
MAXILLOJUGAL
ORCHIDOPEXY
OXYALDEHYDE
OXYCEPHALOUS
OXYCHROMATIN
OXYHYDROGEN
OXYPHYLLOUS
OXYSALICYLIC
PAROXYSMALLY
POLYHYDROXY
PSYCHOSEXUAL
QUINCUNXIAL
TETRAHYDROXY
TOXICOPHAGY
XANTHOPHYLL
XYLOGRAPHIC

28
ADOXOGRAPHY
ALEXIPHARMIC
AMBIDEXTERITY
APOPHYLAXIS
ASEXUALIZED
ASPHYXIATING
AUXOCHROMISM
AXISYMMETRIC
CARBETHOXYL
CHEMOREFLEX
COLOPEXOTOMY
CYCLOHEXANE
CYCLOHEXENE
DESEXUALIZE
EXCEPTIVELY
EXCIPULIFORM
EXCOMMUNICANT
EXCOMMUNICATE
EXCONJUGANT
EXENCEPHALIC
EXHAUSTIVELY
EXPENDABILITY
EXPLANATIVELY
EXPLORATIVELY
EXTRAVAGANCY
HEXASTICHIC
HOMOSEXUALITY
HYDROEXTRACT
HYDROTHORAX
INEXPLICABLY
INFLEXIBILITY
JUXTAPOSING
LEXIGRAPHICAL
LYMPHOTOXIN
MAXILLIPEDARY
MYXOBLASTOMA
OBJURGATRIX
OOPHOROPEXY
OXYPROPIONIC
PHYLLOXERIC
PNEUMONOPEXY
PROPHYLAXIS
PSYCHOTAXIS
QUINISEXTINE
SCEUOPHYLAX
SESQUISEXTAL
SHIKIMOTOXIN
SULPHOXYLIC
THOROUGHWAX
TOXICOPATHIC
TOXICOPATHY
XANTHOCHROID
XEROPHYTISM

27
ANHYDROXIME
APPROXIMATING
ASPHYXIATED
ASPHYXIATION
AUXOCHROMIC
CARBOXYLATED
CHEMIOTAXIC
COSTOXIPHOID
DIHEXAHEDRAL
DIHEXAHEDRON
EXCEPTIONALLY
EXCHANGEABLE
EXCLAMATORILY
EXHIBITIONISM
EXOMORPHISM
EXPANSIBILITY
EXPLOSIBILITY
EXPORTABILITY
EXPOSITIVELY
EXPRESSIVELY
EXSUFFLICATE
EXTEMPORARILY
EXTERIORIZE
EXTERNALIZE
EXTEROCEPTIVE
EXTRAVAGANTLY
EXTROSPECTIVE
EXUVIABILITY
FORMALDOXIME
INEXPECTEDLY
INEXPEDIENCY
JUXTASPINAL
MIXOBARBARIC
MIXOTROPHIC
MYXEDEMATOUS
MYXOSARCOMA
OROPHARYNXES
OXYACANTHINE
OXYACANTHOUS
OXYACETYLENE
OXYCHLORIDE
OXYCINNAMIC
OXYGENICITY
OXYLUCIFERIN
OXYOSPHRESIA
OXYSULPHIDE
PERPLEXINGLY
PHILODOXICAL
PYROXMANGITE
QUINATOXINE
QUINOXALINE
REFLEXIVELY
REFLEXIVITY
RHAMNOHEXOSE
RHAMNOHEXITE
SCAPULOPEXY
TOXICOPHIDIA
TOXIPHOBIAC
UNEXPECTEDLY
WAXCHANDLER
XANTHOCHROIA
XENOMORPHIC
XEROMORPHIC
XYLOGRAPHER
XYLOPHAGOUS

26
ADENOMYXOMA
ALEXIPYRETIC
ANAPHYLAXIS
APPROXIMATED
APPROXIMATION
ARCHOSYRINX
ASPHYXIATOR
AUXOCHROMOUS
AUXOGRAPHIC
BACTERIOTOXIC
COLPORRHEXIS
COMPLEXIONED
CYSTOSYRINX
DISULPHOXIDE
EXANTHEMATIC
EXCEPTIONARY
EXCESSIVELY
EXCITABILITY
EXCITOMOTORY
EXCLUSIVELY
EXCLUSIVITY
EXCREMENTARY
EXCREMENTIVE
EXCURSIVELY
EXCUSABILITY
EXECUTIVELY
EXEMPLIFIED
EXENCEPHALIA
EXENCEPHALUS
EXHAUSTINGLY
EXHAUSTLESSLY
EXPANSIVELY
EXPANSIVITY
EXPEDITIONARY
EXPEDITIOUSLY
EXPENSIVELY
EXPERIMENTLY
EXPLETIVELY
EXPLOSIVELY
EXPROBRATORY
EXTEMPORALLY
EXTENDIBILITY
EXTRACTIFORM
FLEXIBILITY
FLUXIBILITY
FUCOXANTHIN
HEXABROMIDE
HEXOBARBITAL
IMPROPRIATRIX
INEXPLICABLES
INEXPLICITLY
INEXTRICABLY
LEXIGRAPHIC
LITHOLAPAXY
MESOAPPENDIX
MORPHALLAXIS
MYXASTHENIA
NASOPHARYNX
NEOORTHODOXY
ORTHODOXALLY
OXYACANTHIN
OXYBERBERINE
OXYCARBONATE
OXYCHLORATE
OXYCHLORINE
OXYHAEMATIN
OXYHEXACTINE
OXYSULPHATE
PARADOXOLOGY
PERPLEXEDLY
PHOTOSYNTAX
PHYLLOTAXIS
PHYLLOXERAN
PNEUMOTHORAX
PREMAXILLARY
PYOXANTHOSE
PYRRHULOXIA
RHYOTAXITIC
SEMIFLEXIBLE
SUBMAXILLARY
TOXOPHILITIC
TYPHOTOXINE
UNORTHODOXLY
XANTHOPHANE
XANTHOPHORE
XENODOCHIUM
XEROGRAPHIC
XEROMORPHOUS
XIPHISTERNUM

XIPHOPAGOUS
XYLOPHILOUS
XYLOPHONIST

25

AMYLODEXTRIN
ANOXYBIOTIC
ANTHOXANTHIN
ANTIOXYGENIC
APPROXIMATOR
ARTHROSYRINX
ATAXOPHEMIA
BANDBOXICAL
BIMAXILLARY
CARBOLXYLOL
CARBOXYLASE
CARBOXYLATE
CHEMIOTAXIS
CHIROPRAXIS
COEXISTENCY
COMPLEXIONAL
COMPLEXITIES
CONFLUXIBLE
CONVEXEDNESS
COXCOMBICAL
COXOFEMORAL
CRUCIFIXION
DEOXYGENATED
DISULPHOXID
DOXOGRAPHER
EXCEEDINGLY
EXCESSIVENESS
EXCLAMATIVE
EXCLAMATORY
EXCLUSIVENESS
EXCLUSIVISM
EXCOGITATIVE
EXCORTICATING
EXCULPATIVE
EXCULPATORY
EXECUTIVENESS
EXEGETICALLY
EXEMPLARILY
EXEMPLARITY
EXEMPLIFIER
EXHAUSTEDLY
EXHIBITIONIST
EXHILARATIVE
EXHILARATORY
EXOMPHALOUS
EXORBITANCY
EXPANDINGLY
EXPANSIVENESS
EXPECTANCIES
EXPECTANTLY
EXPECTATIVE
EXPECTORATING
EXPENSIVENESS
EXPERIMENTING
EXPISCATORY
EXPLANATORILY
EXPLETIVENESS
EXPLICATIVE
EXPLICATORY
EXPLOSIVENESS
EXPONENTIALLY
EXPOSITIONARY
EXPOSTULATIVE
EXPOSTULATORY
EXPROPRIATING
EXSICCATIVE
EXSUFFLATION
EXTEMPORARY
EXTENSIBILITY
EXTERMINATIVE
EXTERMINATORY
EXTRACYSTIC
EXTRAGALACTIC
EXTRAPOLATIVE
EXTRAVAGANCE
EXTRAVAGATING
EXTRAVASCULAR
EXTRINSICALLY
EXTROVERSIVE
EXTUMESCENCE
HEXAGONALLY
INEXCUSABLY
INEXHAUSTIBLE
INEXHAUSTIVE
INEXPERIENCED
INEXPLICABLE
INTERMIXEDLY
KERATONYXIS
LEXICOLOGICAL
LOXODOGRAPH
MAXILLIFORM
MICROTHORAX
MYELOPLAXES
MYXOMATOSIS
MYXONEUROMA
MYXOSPOROUS
NEPHROTOXIC
ORTHODOXICAL
OVEREXPOSING
OXYCOUMARIN
OXYGNATHOUS
OXYMURIATIC
PAROXYTONIC
PAXILLIFORM
PRAXINOSCOPE
PROXIMATELY
REFLEXOLOGY
RETROXIPHOID
SEXTUPLICATED
SIPHONOPLAX
SUPRAMAXIMAL
THERMOTAXIC
THIXOTROPIC
TOXOPHILISM
TRISULPHOXID
ULTRACOMPLEX
UNEXCEPTIVE
UNEXCUSABLY
UNEXPLICABLE
UNORTHODOXY
XEROPHOBOUS
XIPHOCOSTAL
XYLOCARPOUS
XYLOPLASTIC

24

ADMAXILLARY
AMBIDEXTROUS
AMIDOHEXOSE
AMPLEXICAUL
ANDROSPHINX
ANTHEXIMETER
ANTHRAXYLON
APPENDIXING
APPROXIMATE
ATAXIAGRAPH
ATAXIAPHASIA
AXONOPHOROUS
CIRCUMAXIAL
CIRCUMAXILE
COMPETITRIX
COMPLEXNESS
CONTEXTUALLY
COXARTHRITIS
DEXIOTROPISM
DEXTROGYRATE
DISOXYGENATE
DYSOXIDATION
EPEXEGETICAL
EXACERBATING
EXACTIVENESS
EXAGGERATIVE
EXAGGERATORY
EXASPERATIVE
EXCANDESCENT
EXCATHEDRAL
EXCERPTIBLE
EXCITABLENESS
EXCLAMATIONAL
EXCLUSIONARY
EXCOMMUNION
EXCORTICATED
EXCORTICATION
EXCRESCENCY
EXCRESCENTIAL
EXCRETIONARY
EXCRUCIABLE
EXCRUCIATING
EXCURSIONARY
EXCUSABLENESS
EXECRABLENESS
EXEMPLARINESS
EXEMPLARISM
EXFOLIATIVE
EXFOLIATORY
EXHAUSTEDNESS
EXHIBITIONAL
EXHIBITIONER
EXHORTATIVE
EXHORTATORY
EXOCCIPITAL
EXORBITANTLY
EXOTERICALLY
EXPECTORATED
EXPECTORATION
EXPEDIENCIES
EXPEDIENTLY
EXPERIENCING
EXPERIMENTED
EXPERIMENTIST
EXPLOITATIVE
EXPOSITORILY
EXPRESSIONISM
EXPROPRIATED
EXPROPRIATION
EXPURGATIVE
EXPURGATORY
EXTENSIVELY
EXTENUATINGLY
EXTEROCEPTIST
EXTINGUISHED
EXTORSIVELY
EXTRACAPSULAR
EXTRAMURALLY
EXTRAORDINARY
EXTRAVAGATED
EXTRAVAGATION
EXTRAVASATING
EXTROSPECTION
EXULCERATIVE
EXULCERATORY
FLEXIBLENESS
FLUXIBLENESS
FLUXIONALLY
FRICANDEAUX
INDEXICALLY
INEXPRESSIBLE
INEXPRESSIVE
INFLUXIONISM
INTERXYLARY
INTOXICATIVE
INTRAXYLARY
IRREFLEXIVE
LITHANTHRAX
LITHOXYLITE
MAXILLOLABIAL
MYTILOTOXINE
MYXADENITIS
ORTHODOXISM
OVEREXPOSED
OVEREXPOSURE
OXIDABILITY
OXYCELLULOSE
OXYESTHESIA
OXYSTOMATOUS
OXYTYLOTATE
PANSEXUALITY
PARADOXICIAN
PERIAXILLARY
PLEXIMETRIC
PROTEOPEXIC
PSEUDOCORTEX
SEXCENTENARY
SEXISYLLABLE
STROPHOTAXIS
SUFFIXATION
SULFOXYLATE
SUPERFLEXION
TAXGATHERING
THIGMOTAXIS
TOXICOGNATH
TOXINFECTION
TROPHALLAXIS
UNDEREXPOSING
UNEXPRESSIVE
VEXATIOUSLY
XANTHOCONITE
XANTHODERMA
XANTHOGENIC
XANTHOMATOUS
XANTHOPTERIN
XENACANTHINE
XEROGRAPHER
XIPHISTERNAL
XYLOSTROMATA
XYRIDACEOUS

23

ACTINOPRAXIS
AMBIDEXTRAL
ANGIORRHEXIS
ANOXYBIOSIS
ANTHROXANIC
APHOTOTAXIS
ATAXAPHASIA
AUXETICALLY
AUXOAMYLASE
AUXOHORMONE
BISAXILLARY
BISEXUALITY
CARDIOTOXIC
COEXTENSIVE
CONVEXITIES
CREATOTOXISM
DECIMOSEXTO
DEOXYGENATE
DETOXICATING
DEXIOTROPIC
DEXTROCARDIA
DORSIFLEXION
EXACERBATED
EXACERBATION
EXALBUMINOSE
EXALBUMINOUS
EXAMINATIVE
EXAMINATORY
EXCAVATIONS
EXCELLENCIES
EXCELLENTLY
EXCLUSIONISM
EXCOGITABLE
EXCOGITATING
EXCRESCENCIES
EXCRUCIATED
EXCRUCIATION
EXCULPATING
EXCURSIONISM
EXCURVATURE
EXCYSTATION
EXFIGURATION
EXFLAGELLATE
EXHAUSTIBLE
EXHILARATING
EXILARCHATE
EXISTENTIALLY
EXOPERIDIUM
EXORABILITY
EXORCISEMENT
EXORCISTICAL
EXOTHERMOUS
EXPANDEDNESS
EXPANSIONISM
EXPATIATIVE
EXPATIATORY
EXPECTORATOR
EXPEDITATING
EXPEDITIONIST
EXPENTHESIS
EXPERIENCED
EXPERIMENTAL
EXPERIMENTEE
EXPERIMENTER
EXPISCATING
EXPLANATIVE
EXPLANATORY
EXPLICATING
EXPLICITNESS
EXPLORATIVE
EXPLORATORY
EXPOSTULATING
EXPROMISSION
EXPROPRIATOR
EXPULSATORY
EXPURGATORIAL
EXSCRIPTURAL
EXSICCATING
EXTENSIVENESS
EXTERMINATING
EXTEROCEPTOR
EXTINGUISHER
EXTIRPATIVE
EXTIRPATORY
EXTISPICIOUS
EXTRAFORMAL
EXTRAPOLATING
EXTRAVAGINAL
EXTRAVASATED
EXTRAVASATION
EXUBERANTLY
FLEXANIMOUS
FORNICATRIX
GALVANOTAXIS
GASTROXYNSIS
GENUFLEXUOUS
GRIPPOTOXIN
HETERODOXIES
HETEROTAXIC
INEXISTENCY
INEXPENSIVE
INEXPERIENCE
INEXTIRPABLE
INEXTRICABLE
INTERMIXTLY
LEXICOLOGIC
LOXODROMICS
LOXODROMISM
MAXILLIPEDE
MERVEILLEUX
METAVAUXITE
MONILETHRIX

NEPHROTOXIN
OBNOXIOUSLY
ORTHODOXNESS
OXIDIMETRIC
OXYGENATING
OXYGENERATOR
OXYHEXASTER
OXYPETALOUS
PANSEXUALISM
PARADOXICAL
PARADOXIDIAN
PARAVAUXITE
PERPLEXITIES
POSTAXIALLY
POSTFLEXION
PREEXISTENCE
PREFIXATION
PROTHORAXES
PTEROTHORAX
SACROCOCCYX
SACROCOXITIS
SAXOPHONIST
SCLERONYXIS
SEXADECIMAL
SEXANGULARLY
SEXTUPLICATE
SPASMOTOXINE
SUBAXILLARY
SUPERMAXILLA
SUPRAMAXILLA
THERMOTAXIS
THIXOLABILE
TOXICOGENIC
TOXICOLOGIC
TOXOPHILOUS
TROPHOTAXIS
TYROTOXICON
ULTRAMAXIMAL
UNDEREXPOSED
UNEXCLUSIVE
UNEXPENSIVE
UNEXPERIENCE
UNEXPURGATED
UNEXTRICABLE
URECHITOXIN
UROTOXICITY
VASOREFLEX
XANTHELASMA
XANTHOGENATE
XANTHOMETER
XANTHOXYLIN
XEROPHILOUS
XIPHOSUROUS

22

AMPLEXATION
ANISALDOXIME
ANOXIDATIVE
ANTHRAXOLITE
APOPLEXIOUS
AXIOMATICAL
AXONOMETRIC
AXOSPERMOUS
BISEXUALISM
CLITORIDAUXE
COEXISTENCE
DETOXICATED
DETOXICATION
DEXIOTROPOUS
DEXTEROUSLY
DISPENSATRIX
DOPAOXIDASE
DORSIFLEXOR
DOXOLOGICAL
EXACTINGNESS
EXAGGERATING
EXAMINATIONAL
EXASPERATING
EXCALCARATE
EXCEPTIONAL
EXCEPTIONER
EXCITOMOTOR
EXCLAMATION
EXCOGITATED
EXCOGITATION
EXCORTICATE
EXCREMENTAL
EXCRESCENCES
EXCRUCIATOR
EXCULPATION
EXECUTRICES
EXERCISABLE
EXFILTRATION
EXFODIATION
EXFOLIATING
EXHILARATED
EXHILARATION
EXOGENOUSLY
EXOGNATHION
EXOGNATHITE
EXOMOLOGESIS
EXORBITANCE
EXOSKELETAL
EXOSKELETON
EXOSTRACISM
EXOTERICISM
EXPATRIATING
EXPECTATION
EXPECTORANT
EXPECTORATE
EXPEDIENTIAL
EXPEDIENTIST
EXPEDITATED
EXPEDITATION
EXPEDITENESS
EXPENSILATION
EXPERIENCER
EXPERIENCES
EXPIATORINESS
EXPISCATION
EXPLAINABLE
EXPLEMENTAL
EXPLICATION
EXPLOITABLE
EXPLORATIONAL
EXPLOREMENT
EXPOSTULATED
EXPOSTULATION
EXPRESSIBLE
EXPRESSIONIST
EXPROPRIATE
EXPURGATING
EXSCULPTATE
EXSICCATION
EXTERMINATED
EXTERMINATION
EXTERNALISTIC
EXTORTIONARY
EXTRABULBAR
EXTRACARPAL
EXTRACTABLE
EXTRACTIBLE
EXTRADITABLE
EXTRADUCTION
EXTRAMUNDANE
EXTRANEOUSLY
EXTRAPOLATED
EXTRAPOLATION
EXTRASENSORY
EXTRASYSTOLE
EXTRAVAGANT
EXTRAVAGATE
EXTRAVERSION
EXTREMISTIC
EXTROVERSION
EXUBERANTNESS
EXULCERATING
EXUMBRELLAR
FLEXUOSITIES
FLEXUOUSNESS
GENUFLEXION
HETEROSEXUAL
HETEROXENOUS
INDEXTERITY
INEXACTITUDE
INEXCUSABLE
INTOXICABLE
INTOXICATING
INTROFLEXION
LAURINOXYLON
LAXATIVENESS
LEXICOLOGIST
LIXIVIATING
MESOSALPINX
METAGALAXIES
OBNOXIOUSNESS
ORTHODOXIAN
ORTHODOXIES
ORTHODOXIST
OVERTAXATION
PEPTOTOXINE
PERICOXITIS
PILOTAXITIC
PNEUMOTOXIN
PRAEMAXILLA
PROCATARXIS
PROCURATRIX
PROLOCUTRIX
PROTEOPEXIS
PROXENETISM
PROXIMATION
PSEUDODOXAL
RETROFLEXED
RETROFLEXION
SAXIFRAGANT
SAXIFRAGOUS
SEXDIGITATED
SEXDIGITISM
SEXPLOITATION
SEXTILLIONTH
SPASMOTOXIN
SPECULATRIX
SPERMOTOXIN
SPLENOPEXIA
SPLENOPEXIS
SUBMAXILLAE
SUBOXIDATION
SUBSEXTUPLE
TAXGATHERER
TAXONOMICAL
TOXALBUMOSE
TOXICOLOGIST
TOXICOMANIA
TRANSFIXING
TRANSFIXTURE
TRISULFOXID
UNEXCUSABLE
UNISEXUALITY
VEXILLARIOUS
XENYLAMINE

21

ANILIDOXIME
ANTEFLEXION
AORTOMALAXIS
ATLOIDOAXOID
AUTOTOXAEMIA
AUXILIATORY
AXIOLOGICAL
CARDIATAXIA
CONTEXTURED
COXOCERITIC
DETOXICATOR
DEXTROCULAR
DIASTATAXIC
DICATALEXIS
DIRECTRIXES
ELECTROTAXIS
EXAGGERATED
EXAGGERATION
EXARTICULATE
EXASPERATED
EXASPERATION
EXCITEDNESS
EXCLUSIONIST
EXCOGITATOR
EXCORIATING
EXCRESCENCE
EXCURSIONIST
EXERCITATION
EXERCITORIAL
EXFOLIATION
EXHAUSTLESS
EXHILARATOR
EXIMIOUSNESS
EXOCULATING
EXONERATIVE
EXORABLENESS
EXORBITATION
EXORCISATION
EXOTICALNESS
EXPANSIONIST
EXPATIATING
EXPATRIATED
EXPATRIATION
EXPEDITIOUS
EXPENDITURE
EXPERIENTIAL
EXPLANTATION
EXPLOITATION
EXPLOSIONIST
EXPOSITIONAL
EXPOSITORIAL
EXPOSTULATOR
EXPRESSIONAL
EXPURGATION
EXSCUTELLATE
EXTENDEDNESS
EXTENSIMETER
EXTENSOMETER
EXTENUATIVE
EXTENUATORY
EXTERIORITY
EXTERMINATOR
EXTERNALITY
EXTIRPATING
EXTRAENTERIC
EXTRAPOLATOR
EXTRAVASATE
EXTRAVIOLET
EXTRICATING
EXTRINSICATE
EXUBERATING
EXULCERATED
EXULCERATION
GUBERNATRIX
HETEROTAXIA
HETEROTAXIS
IDEOPRAXIST
INEXPEDIENT
INEXPERTNESS
INEXTENSIVE
INNOXIOUSLY
INTERMIXING
INTERMIXTURE
INTOXICATED
INTOXICATION
LAXIFLOROUS
LAXIFOLIATE
LAXIFOLIOUS
LIFERENTRIX
LIXIVIATION
LUXURIANTLY
LUXURIOUSLY
NONEXISTENCE
OSCULATRIXES
OXALURAMIDE
PANSEXUALIST
POSTEXISTENT
PRAETAXATION
PROGENITRIX
RADIOPRAXIS
REFLEXIONAL
SEXAGESIMAL
SEXOLOGICAL
SEXTIPARTITE
STENOTHORAX
STEREOMATRIX
TAXASPIDEAN
TAXEOPODOUS
TAXIDERMIST
TAXIMETERED
TEXTIFEROUS
TOXITABELLAE
TRANSFIXION
TYLOTOXEATE
UNDEREXPOSE
UNEXPEDIENT
UNEXPLAINED
UNEXPLOITED
UNISEXUALLY
VEXILLATION
XANTHINURIA
XANTHOXENITE
XENARTHROUS
XENOPARASITE

20

ANNEXATIONIST
ATAXIAMETER
AUTOCRATRIX
AUTOTOXEMIA
AUTOXIDATION
AUXANOMETER
AXODENDRITE
AXONOLIPOUS
COEXTENSION
CONNEXITIES
CONSOLATRIX
CONTEXTURAL
DEXTROUSNESS
ENTEROPEXIA
EXAGGERATOR
EXAMINATION
EXANIMATION
EXASPERATER
EXAUCTORATE
EXAUGURATION
EXCANTATION
EXCARNATION
EXCLUSIONER
EXCORIATION
EXCURSIONAL
EXCURSIONER
EXECUTIONAL
EXECUTIONER
EXECUTORIAL
EXENTERATING
EXIGUOUSNESS
EXISTLESSNESS
EXOGASTRITIS
EXOMETRITIS
EXPANSIONAL
EXPATIATION
EXPENDITRIX

EXPLANATION
EXPLORATION
EXPONENTIAL
EXPORTATION
EXPOSTULATE
EXPRESSLESS
EXSANGUINATE
EXSANGUINOUS
EXSTIPULATE
EXTERIORATION
EXTERMINATE
EXTERNALISM
EXTERNALITIES
EXTERRESTRIAL
EXTERRITORIAL
EXTIRPATION
EXTRACOSTAL
EXTRADITING
EXTRAPOLATE
EXTRAREGULAR
EXTRATRIBAL
EXTREMENESS
EXTREMITIES
EXTRICATION
EXTRINSICAL
EXUBERATION
GITOXIGENIN
INEXACTNESS
INEXECUTION
INEXISTENCE
INOBNOXIOUS
INTOXICATOR
LUXURIANTNESS
LUXURIOUSNESS
MAXILLARIES
MIXTILINEAR
NEUROPLEXUS
POSTEXILIAN
PREEXISTENT
PRETEXTUOUS
SCILLITOXIN
SEMISEXTILE
SEXAGENARIAN
SEXDIGITATE
SPLENOTOXIN
STIMULATRIX
SUBLUXATION
SUPERSEXUAL
TAXABLENESS
TOXOGLOSSATE
UNEXACTNESS
UNEXPERIENT
XEROTRIPSIS

19

ALEXANDRITE
ANGIOATAXIA
ANNEXATIONAL
ANTIOXIDANT
ATLANTOAXIAL
AUTOXIDATOR
DEXTROSURIA
EXALLOTRIOTE
EXALTEDNESS
EXECUTRIXES
EXENTERATED
EXENTERATION
EXOARTERITIS
EXONERATING
EXPIATIONA
EXPRESSION
EXSANGUIOUS
EXTENSIONIST
EXTENUATING
EXTERIORNESS
EXTERRANEOUS
EXTORTIONATE
EXTORTIONIST
EXTRADITION
EXTRALATERAL
EXTRARETINAL
EXTRAUTERINE
GASTROTAXIS
INTERTEXTURE
LEGISLATRIX
LUXULLIANITE
LUXURIATING
NEGOTIATRIX
ODONTEXESIS
ODONTOLOXIA
OXIDATIONAL
RELAXEDNESS
STAURAXONIAL
TOXOGENESIS
XENOGENESIS
XENOSAUROID

18

ANNEXIONIST
ANXIOUSNESS
AUXILIARIES
AUXILIATION
EXANTLATION
EXARTERITIS
EXINANITION
EXISTENTIAL
EXONERATION
EXTENSIONAL
EXTENUATION
EXTERIORATE
EXTERNALIST
EXTERNATION
EXTOLLATION
EXTORTIONER
EXTRASEROUS
EXTRATARSAL
INTERSEXUAL
LUXURIATION
NONEXISTENT
NOXIOUSNESS
OSTEOSTIXIS
SEXLESSNESS
STAURAXONIA
STEREOTAXIS
TETROXALATE

High-Scoring Words Containing

Z

2-3 LETTER WORDS

ALPHABETICAL ORDER

ADZ
AZO
BIZ
DZO
FEZ
FIZ
GAZ
GEZ
GUZ
HIZ
HUZ
JIZ
NIZ
POZ
SUZ
TEZ
TUZ
VIZ
WIZ
WUZ
YEZ
ZA
ZAC
ZAD
ZAG
ZAK
ZAR
ZAX
ZED
ZEE
ZEL
ZER
ZHO
ZIG
ZIP
ZO
ZOA
ZOH
ZOO

POSITIONAL ORDER

ZA
ZAC
ZAD
ZAG
ZAK
ZAR
ZAX
ZED
ZEE
ZEL
ZER
ZHO
ZIG
ZIP
ZO
ZOA
ZOH
ZOO

AZO
DZO

ADZ
BIZ
FEZ
FIZ
GAZ
GEZ
GUZ
HIZ
HUZ
JIZ
NIZ
POZ
SUZ
TEZ
TUZ
VIZ
WIZ
WUZ
YEZ

SCORING ORDER

19
JIZ
ZAX

16
ZAK

15
FEZ
FIZ
HIZ
HUZ
VIZ
WIZ
WUZ
YEZ
ZHO
ZOH

14
BIZ
POZ
ZAC
ZIP

13
ADZ
DZO
GAZ
GEZ
GUZ
ZAD
ZAG
ZED
ZIG

12
AZO
NIZ
SUZ
TEZ
TUZ
ZAR
ZEE
ZEL
ZER
ZOA
ZOO

11
ZA
ZO

ALPHABETICAL LIST OF 4-LETTER WORDS

ADZE
AZAM
AZAN
AZEW
AZON
AZYM
BATZ
BAZE
BIZE
BOZA
BOZO
BUZZ
CAZA
CAZY
CHEZ
COZE
COZY
CZAR
DAZE
DAZY
DOZE
DOZY
EZBA
FAZE
FIZZ
FOZE
FOZY
FRIZ
FUZE
FUZZ
GAZE
GAZI
GAZY
GIZZ
GUZE
HAYZ
HAZE
HAZY
HIZZ
HUZZ
IZAR
IZBA
IZLE
JAZZ
JEEZ
JUEZ
KAZI
KAZY
KNEZ
KOZO
LAZE
LAZO
LAZY
LEZA
LITZ
LIZA
LUTZ
MAZA
MAZE
MAZY
MOZO
MUZZ
NAZE
NAZI
NIZY
ONZA
OOZE
OOZY
OUZO
OYEZ
PIZE
PUTZ
QUIZ
QUOZ
RAZE
RAZZ
RITZ
SITZ
SIZE
SIZY
SIZZ
SUZU
SWIZ
TIZA
TOZE
TUZA
TUZZ
TZAR
TZUT
UNTZ
UNZE
UZAN
VAZA
VIZY
WHIZ
WUZU
ZAIN
ZANT
ZANY
ZARF
ZARP
ZART
ZATI
ZEAL
ZEBU
ZEDS
ZEES
ZEIN
ZEME
ZEMI
ZENU
ZEPP
ZERO
ZEST
ZETA
ZIIM
ZIMB
ZINC
ZING
ZINK
ZIRA
ZIZZ
ZNAK
ZOBO
ZOBU
ZOEA
ZOGO
ZOIC
ZOID
ZOLL
ZONA
ZONE
ZOOM
ZOON
ZOPE
ZULU
ZUPA
ZUZA
ZYME

POSITIONAL ORDER LIST OF 4-LETTER WORDS

ZAIN
ZANT
ZANY
ZARF
ZARP
ZART
ZATI
ZEAL
ZEBU
ZEDS
ZEES
ZEIN
ZEME
ZEMI
ZENU
ZEPP
ZERO
ZEST
ZETA
ZIIM
ZIMB
ZINC
ZING
ZINK
ZIRA
ZIZZ
ZNAK
ZOBO
ZOBU
ZOEA
ZOGO
ZOIC
ZOID
ZOLL
ZONA
ZONE
ZOOM
ZOON
ZOPE
ZULU
ZUPA
ZUZA
ZYGA
ZYME

AZAM
AZAN
AZEW
AZON
AZYM
CZAR
EZBA
IZAR
IZBA
IZLE
TZAR
TZUT
UZAN

ADZE
BAZE
BIZE
BOZA
BOZO
BUZZ
CAZA
CAZY
COZE
COZY
DAZE
DAZY
DOZE
DOZY
FAZE
FIZZ
FOZE
FOZY
FUZE
FUZZ
GAZE
GAZY
GIZZ
GUZE
HAZE
HAZY
HIZZ
HUZZ
JAZZ
KAZI
KAZY
KOZO
LAZE
LAZO
LAZY
LEZA
LIZA
MAZA
MAZE
MAZY
MOZO
MUZZ
NAZE
NAZI
NIZY
ONZA
OOZE
OOZY
OUZO
PIZE
RAZE
RAZZ
SIZE
SIZY
SIZZ
SUZU
TIZA
TOZE
TUZA
TUZZ
UNZE
VAZA
VIZY
WUZU
ZIZZ
ZUZA
BATZ
BUZZ
CHEZ
FIZZ
FRIZ
FUZZ
GIZZ
HAYZ
HIZZ
HUZZ
JAZZ
JEEZ
JUEZ
KNEZ
LITZ
LUTZ
MUZZ
OYEZ
PUTZ
QUIZ
QUOZ
RAZZ
RITZ
SITZ
SIZZ
SWIZ
TUZZ
UNTZ
WHIZ
ZIZZ

SCORING ORDER LIST OF 4-LETTER WORDS

22
QUIZ
QUOZ

20
JEEZ
JUEZ
KAZY

19
FOZY
HAYZ
HAZY
JAZZ
VIZY
WHIZ

18
AZYM
CAZY
CHEZ

COZY
MAZY
ZYME

17
DAZY
DOZY
GAZY
KAZI
KNEZ
KOZO
ZEPP
ZIMB
ZINK
ZNAK

16
AZEW
FAZE
FOZE
FRIZ
FUZE
HAZE
LAZY
NIZY
OOZY
OYEZ
SIZY
SWIZ
VAZA
WUZU
ZANY
ZARF

15
AZAM
BATZ
BAZE
BIZE
BOZA
BOZO
CAZA
COZE
CZAR
EZBA
FIZZ
FUZZ
HIZZ
HUZZ
IZBA
MAZA
MAZE
MOZO
PIZE
PUTZ
ZARP
ZEBU
ZEME
ZEMI
ZIIM
ZINC
ZOBO
ZOBU
ZOIC
ZOOM
ZOPE
ZUPA

14
ADZE
BUZZ
DAZE
DOZE
GAZE
GAZI
GUZE
MUZZ
ZEDS
ZING
ZOGO
ZOID

13
AZAN
AZON
GIZZ
IZAR
IZLE
LAZE
LAZO
LEZA
LITZ
LIZA
LUTZ
NAZE
NAZI
ONZA
OOZE
OUZO
RAZE
RITZ
SITZ
SIZE
SUZU
TIZA
TOZE
TUZA
TZAR
TZUT
UNTZ
UNZE
UZAN
ZAIN
ZANT
ZART
ZATI
ZEAL
ZEES
ZEIN
ZENU
ZERO
ZEST
ZETA
ZIRA
ZOEA
ZOLL
ZONA
ZONE
ZOON
ZULU

12
RAZZ
SIZZ
TUZZ
ZUZA

11
ZIZZ

ALPHABETICAL LIST OF 5-LETTER WORDS

ABAZE
ABUZZ
ADOZE
ADZER
ADZES
AGAZE
AIZLE
ALEZE
AMAZE
AMUZE
ARROZ
ARZUN
AZIDE
AZINE
AZLON
AZOCH
AZOFY
AZOIC
AZOLE
AZOTE
AZOTH
AZOXY
AZURE
AZURY
AZYME
BAIZA
BAIZE
BAZAR
BAZOO
BEZEL
BEZIL
BEZZO
BIZLE
BLAZE
BLAZY
BLITZ
BLIZZ
BONZA
BONZE
BORTZ
BOZAH
BOZAL
BOZZE
BRAZA
BRAZE
BRIZE
BRIZZ
BRUZZ
BUAZE
BUZZY
BWAZI
BYZEN
CAFIZ
CAHIZ
CHOZA
CLIZA
COLZA
COZED
COZEN
COZEY
COZIE
CRAZE
CRAZY
CROZE
DANZA
DARZI
DAZED
DIAZO
DIZEN
DIZZY
DOOZY
DOZED
DOZEN
DOZER
DROZE
ECIZE
ENZYM
ERIZO
FAIZE
FAZED
FEAZE
FEEZE
FELZE
FEZZY
FIZZY
FRAZE
FRIZE
FRIZZ
FROZE
FURZE
FURZY
FUZEE
FUZIL
FUZZY
GAIZE
GANZA
GAUZE
GAUZY
GAZED
GAZEL
GAZER
GAZET
GAZON
GAZOO
GAZOZ
GEYZE
GHAZI
GIZMO
GLAZE
GLAZY
GLOZE
GRAZE
GROSZ
GUAZA
HAFIZ
HAMZA
HAZAN
HAZEL
HAZEN
HAZER
HAZLE
HEAZY
HEEZE
HERTZ
HOOZE
HUZZA
HUZZY
IZARD
IZOTE
IZTLE
IZTLI
IZZAT
JAZEL
JAZZY
JEREZ
JEZIA
JIZYA
KAFIZ
KANZU
KAREZ
KAZAK
KAZOO
KNEZI
KNIAZ
KNYAZ
KONZE
KOUZA
KUDZU
LANAZ
LAZAR
LAZED
LAZZO
LEAZE
LOZEN
MAINZ
MAIZE
MATZO
MAZAR
MAZED
MAZER
MAZIC
MAZUT
METZE
MEZZA
MEZZO
MIMZY
MIRZA
MIZZY
MURZA
MUZZY
NAMAZ
NAZIM
NAZIR
NAZIS
NEEZE
NIZEY
OOZED
OOZEL
OUZEL
OWZEL

OZENA
OZONE
PEIZE
PEZZO
PIEZO
PIZZA
PLAZA
POIZE
PRIZE
QAZAQ
RAZEE
RAZED
RAZON
RAZOO
RAZOR
REZAI
RITZY
ROZUM
SABZI
SAZEN
SEIZE
SIZAR
SIZED
SIZER
SIZES
SMAZE
SNITZ
SOULZ
SOZIN
SPITZ
SQUIZ
SWIZZ
TAZIA
TAZZA
TEAZE
TENEZ
TERZO
TIRAZ
TIZZY
TOPAZ
TOZEE
TOZER
TOZIE
TROOZ
TZUTE
ULZIE
UNZEN
UYEZD
VIZIR
VIZOR
VIZZY
VORAZ
WALTZ
WANZE
WAZIR
WEEZE
WEIZE
WHIZZ
WINZE
WIZEN
WOOTZ
WOOZY
YEZZY
YOUZE
ZABRA
ZABTI
ZAKAH
ZAKAT
ZAMAN
ZAMBO
ZANJA
ZANTE
ZANZE
ZAPAS
ZARAH
ZAYAT
ZAYIN
ZEBEC
ZEBRA
ZEBUB
ZEBUS
ZEINE
ZEISM
ZEIST
ZEMMI
ZEMNI
ZENIK
ZERDA
ZEROS
ZESTY
ZIARA
ZIBEB
ZIEGA
ZIFFS
ZIHAR
ZIMBI
ZIMME
ZIMMI
ZIMMY
ZINCO
ZINCY
ZINEB
ZINKE
ZINKY
ZIPPY
ZIRAI
ZIRAM
ZIZEL
ZLOTY
ZOCCO
ZOEAL
ZOGAN
ZOISM
ZOIST
ZOKOR
ZOMBI
ZONAE
ZONAL
ZONAR
ZONDA
ZONED
ZONIC
ZOOID
ZOONS
ZOPPA
ZOPPO
ZORIL
ZORRA
ZORRO
ZOWIE
ZUCHE
ZUDDA
ZUPAN
ZYGAL
ZYGON
ZYMIC
ZYMIN

POSITIONAL ORDER LIST OF 5-LETTER WORDS

ZABRA
ZABTI
ZAKAH
ZAKAT
ZAMAN
ZAMBO
ZANJA
ZANTE
ZANZE
ZAPAS
ZARAH
ZAYAT
ZAYIN
ZEBEC
ZEBRA
ZEBUB
ZEBUS
ZEINE
ZEISM
ZEIST
ZEMMI
ZEMNI
ZENIK
ZERDA
ZEROS
ZESTY
ZIARA
ZIBEB
ZIEGA
ZIFFS
ZIHAR
ZIMBI
ZIMME
ZIMMI
ZIMMY
ZINCO
ZINCY
ZINEB
ZINKE
ZINKY
ZIPPY
ZIRAI
ZIRAM
ZIZEL
ZLOTY
ZOCCO
ZOEAL
ZOGAN
ZOISM
ZOIST
ZOKOR
ZOMBI
ZONAE
ZONAL
ZONAR
ZONDA
ZONED
ZONIC
ZOOID
ZOONS
ZOPPA
ZOPPO
ZORIL
ZORRA
ZORRO
ZOWIE
ZUCHE
ZUDDA
ZUPAN
ZYGAL
ZYGON
ZYMIC
ZYMIN

AZIDE
AZINE
AZLON
AZOCH
AZOFY
AZOIC
AZOLE
AZOTE
AZOTH
AZOXY
AZURE
AZURY
AZYME
IZARD
IZOTE
IZTLE
IZTLI
IZZAT
OZENA
OZONE
TZUTE

ADZER
ADZES
AIZLE
ARZUN
BAZAR
BAZOO
BEZEL
BEZIL
BEZZO
BIZLE
BOZAH
BOZAL
BOZZE
BUZZY
BYZEN
COZED
COZEN
COZEY
COZIE
DAZED
DIZEN
DIZZY
DOZED
DOZEN
DOZER
ENZYM
FAZED
FEZZY
FIZZY
FUZEE
FUZIL
FUZZY
GAZED
GAZEL
GAZER
GAZET
GAZI
GAZON
GAZOO
GAZOZ
GIZMO
HAZAN
HAZEL
HAZEN
HAZER
HAZLE
HUZZA
HUZZY
IZZAT
JAZEL
JAZZY
JEZIA
JIZYA
KAZAK
KAZOO
LAZAR
LAZED
LAZZO
LOZEN
MAZAR
MAZED
MAZER
MAZIC
MAZUT
MEZZA
MEZZO
MIZZY
MUZZY
NAZIM
NAZIR
NAZIS
NIZEY
OOZED
OOZEL
OUZEL
OWZEL
PEZZO
PIZZA
QAZAQ
RAZEE
RAZED
RAZON
RAZOO
RAZOR
REZAI
ROZUM
SAZEN
SIZAR
SIZED
SIZER
SIZES
SOZIN
TAZIA
TAZZA
TIZZY
TOZEE
TOZER
TOZIE
ULZIE
UNZEN
VIZIR
VIZOR
VIZZY
WAZIR
WIZEN
YEZZY
ZIZEL
ABAZE
ABUZZ
ADOZE
AGAZE
ALEZE
AMAZE
AMUZE
BAIZA
BAIZE
BEZZO
BLAZE
BLAZY

BLIZZ
BONZA
BONZE
BOZZE
BRAZA
BRAZE
BRIZE
BRIZZ
BRUZZ
BUAZE
BUZZY
BWAZI
CHOZA
CLIZA
COLZA
CRAZE
CRAZY
CROZE
DANZA
DARZI
DIAZO
DIZZY
DOOZY
DROZE
ECIZE
ERIZO
FAIZE
FEAZE
FEEZE
FELZE
FEZZY
FIZZY
FRAZE
FRIZE
FRIZZ
FROZE
FURZE
FURZY
FUZZY
GAIZE
GANZA
GAUZE
GAUZY
GEYZE
GHAZI
GLAZE
GLAZY
GLOZE
GRAZE
GUAZA
HAMZA
HEAZY
HEEZE
HOOZE
HUZZA
HUZZY
JAZZY
KANZU
KNEZI
KONZE
KOUZA
KUDZU
LAZZO
LEAZE
MAIZE
MATZO
METZE
MEZZA
MEZZO
MIMZY
MIRZA
MIZZY
MURZA
MUZZY
NEEZE
PEIZE
PEZZO
PIEZO
PIZZA
PLAZA
POIZE
PRIZE
RITZY
SABZI
SEIZE
SMAZE
SWIZZ
TAZZA
TEAZE
TERZO
TIZZY
UYEZD
VIZZY
WANZE
WEEZE
WEIZE
WHIZZ
WINZE
WOOZY
YEZZY
YOUZE
ZANZE

ABUZZ
ARROZ
BLITZ
BLIZZ
BORTZ
BRIZZ
BRUZZ
CAFIZ
CAHIZ
FRIZZ
GAZOZ
GROSZ
HAFIZ
HERTZ
JEREZ
KAFIZ
KAREZ
KNIAZ
KNYAZ
LANAZ
MAINZ
NAMAZ
SNITZ
SOULZ
SPITZ
SQUIZ
SWIZZ
TENEZ
TIRAZ
TOPAZ
TROOZ
VORAZ
WALTZ
WHIZZ
WOOTZ

SCORING ORDER LIST OF 5-LETTER WORDS

24
AZOXY
JIZYA

23
JAZZY
SQUIZ

22
QAZAQ

21
JAZEL
JEREZ
JEZIA
KAFIZ
KNYAZ
MIMZY
ZAKAH
ZANJA
ZIMMY
ZINKY
ZIPPY
ZYMIC

20
AZOFY
FURZY
HAFIZ
HEAZY
WOOZY
ZIFFS

19
AZOCH
AZYME
BLAZY
BOZAH
BWAZI
BYZEN
CAFIZ
CAHIZ
CHOZA
COZEY
CRAZY
ENZYM
FEZZY
FIZZY
FUZZY
HAMZA
HUZZY
KUDZU
VIZZY
WHIZZ
YEZZY
ZINCY
ZUCHE
ZYMIN

18
BUZZY
DOOZY
FAZED
GAUZY
GEYZE
GHAZI
GLAZY
KANZU
KAREZ
KAZOO
KNEZI
KNIAZ
KONZE
KOUZA
MAZIC
MIZZY
MUZZY
UYEZD
ZAKAT
ZAMBO
ZEBEC
ZEBUB
ZEMMI
ZENIK
ZIBEB
ZIMBI
ZIMME
ZIMMI
ZINKE
ZOCCO
ZOKOR
ZOMBI
ZOPPA
ZOPPO
ZYGAL
ZYGON

17
AZOTH
AZURY
COZED
DIZZY
FAIZE
FEAZE
FEEZE
FELZE
FRAZE
FRIZE
FROZE
FURZE
FUZEE
FUZIL
GIZMO
HAZAN
HAZEL
HAZEN
HAZER
HAZLE
HEEZE
HERTZ
HOOZE
KAZAK
MAZED
NIZEY
OWZEL
RITZY
VIZIR
VIZOR
VORAZ
WALTZ
WANZE
WAZIR
WEEZE
WEIZE
WINZE
WIZEN
WOOTZ
YOUZE
ZARAH
ZAYAT
ZAYIN
ZESTY
ZIHAR
ZLOTY
ZOWIE

16
ABAZE
AMAZE
AMUZE
AZOIC
BAIZA
BAIZE
BAZAR
BAZOO
BEZEL
BEZIL
BIZLE
BLAZE
BLITZ
BONZA
BONZE
BORTZ
BOZAL
BRAZA
BRAZE
BRIZE
BUAZE
CLIZA
COLZA
COZEN
COZIE
CRAZE
CROZE
DAZED
DOZED
ECIZE
FRIZZ
GAZED
HUZZA
MAINZ
MAIZE
MATZO
MAZAR
MAZER
MAZUT
METZE
MIRZA
MURZA
NAMAZ
NAZIM
PEIZE
PIEZO
PLAZA
POIZE
PRIZE
ROZUM
SABZI
SMAZE
SPITZ
SWIZZ
TIZZY
TOPAZ
ZABRA
ZABTI
ZAMAN
ZAPAS
ZEBRA
ZEBUS
ZEISM
ZEMNI
ZINCO
ZINEB
ZIRAM
ZOISM

ZONIC
ZUDDA
ZUPAN

15
ABUZZ
ADOZE
ADZER
ADZES
AGAZE
AZIDE
BEZZO
BLIZZ
BOZZE
BRIZZ
BRUZZ
DANZA
DARZI
DIAZO
DIZEN
DOZEN
DOZER
DROZE
GAIZE
GANZA
GAUZE
GAZEL
GAZER
GAZET
GAZON
GAZOO
GLAZE
GLOZE
GRAZE
GROSZ
GUAZA
IZARD
LAZED
MEZZA
MEZZO
OOZED
PEZZO
PIZZA
RAZED
SIZED
ZERDA
ZIEGA
ZOGAN
ZONDA
ZONED
ZOOID

14
AIZLE
ALEZE
ARROZ
ARZUN
AZINE
AZLON
AZOLE
AZOTE
AZURE
ERIZO
GAZOZ
IZOTE
IZTLE
IZTLI
LANAZ
LAZAR
LEAZE
LOZEN
NAZIR
NAZIS
NEEZE
OOZEL
OUZEL
OZENA
OZONE
RAZEE
RAZON
RAZOO
RAZOR
REZAI
SAZEN
SEIZE
SIZAR
SIZER
SIZES
SNITZ
SOULZ
SOZIN
TAZIA
TEAZE
TENEZ
TERZO
TIRAZ
TOZEE
TOZER
TOZIE
TROOZ
TZUTE
ULZIE
UNZEN
ZANTE
ZEINE
ZEIST
ZEROS
ZIARA
ZIRAI
ZOEAL
ZOIST
ZONAE
ZONAL
ZONAR
ZOONS
ZORIL
ZORRA
ZORRO

13
IZZAT
LAZZO
TAZZA
ZANZE

ALPHABETICAL LIST OF 6-LETTER WORDS

ABLAZE
ABRAZO
ACRAZE
AGAZED
AGNIZE
AJIMEZ
AKAZGA
ALAZOR
ALEZAN
ALTEZA
AMAZED
AMAZON
APOZEM
ASSIZE
ATAZIR
AVELOZ
AZALEA
AZILUT
AZIMIN
AZIOLA
AZONAL
AZONIC
AZOTEA
AZOTED
AZOTIC
AZOTIN
AZTECA
AZURED
AZYGOS
BAIZED
BANZAI
BATZEN
BAZAAR
BEDAZE
BEEZER
BENZAL
BENZIL
BENZIN
BENZOL
BENZYL
BEZANT
BEZOAR
BEZZLE
BLAZED
BLAZER
BLAZES
BLAZON
BLEEZE
BLEEZY
BLINTZ
BLOWZE
BLOWZY
BONNAZ
BONZER
BORIZE
BORZOI
BOZINE
BRAIZE
BRAZED
BRAZEN
BRAZER
BRAZIL
BREEZE
BREEZY
BRONZE
BRONZY
BROUZE
BRYNZA
BUDZAT
BUZANE
BUZZED
BUZZER
BUZZLE
BYZANT
CABEZA
CANZON
CAZIBI
CAZIMI
CENIZO
CEREZA
CHAZAN
CHINTZ
COROZO
CORYZA
COZIER
COZILY
COZING
CRAZED
CROZED
CROZER
CROZLE
CUNZIE
DANZON
DARZEE
DAZING
DAZZLE
DENIZE
DESIZE
DEUZAN
DEZINC
DIAZID
DIAZIN
DIZAIN
DIZDAR
DIZZEN
DONZEL
DOZENS
DOZENT
DOZIER
DOZILY
DOZING
DOZZLE
DRAZEL
DRAZIL
DURZEE
DZEREN
DZERIN
DZERON
ECZEMA
EGOIZE
ENDAZE
ENGAZE
ENTREZ
ENZYME
EOZOON
EPIZOA
ERSATZ
ETHIZE
FAZING
FEAZED
FEZZED
FEZZES
FIZGIG
FIZZED
FIZZER
FIZZLE
FLOOZY
FOOZLE
FRAZER
FRAZIL
FREEZE
FREEZY
FRENZY
FRIEZE
FRIEZY
FRIZEL
FRIZER
FRIZZY
FROUZE
FROUZY
FROWZE
FROWZY
FROZEN
FURZED
FUZZLE
GANZIE
GAZABO
GAZEBO
GAZING
GAZOOK
GEEZER
GHAZAL
GHAZEL
GIZZEN
GLAZED
GLAZEN
GLAZER
GLOZED
GLOZER
GOOZLE
GOZELL
GOZILL
GOZZAN
GRANZA
GRAZED
GROSZY
GROUZE
GROWZE
GROZER
GUZZLE
HALERZ
HALUTZ
HAMETZ
HAMZAH
HAZARD
HAZIER
HAZILY
HAZING
HAZZAN
HELZEL
HIZZIE
HOWITZ
HUZOOR
HUZZAH
IODIZE
IONIZE
IOTIZE
ITZEBU
IZAFAT
IZZARD

JAZZER
JEZAIL
JEZIAH
JIZYAH
JUZAIL
KHAZEN
KIBITZ
KOLKOZ
KORZEC
KRANTZ
KUDIZE
KUVASZ
KVUTZA
LANZON
LAZARY
LAZIER
LAZILY
LAZING
LAZULE
LAZULI
LIZARD
LIZARY
MAHZOR
MAIZER
MAMZER
MANZIL
MARKAZ
MATZOH
MATZOS
MATZOT
MAZAME
MAZARD
MAZIER
MAZILY
MAZING
MAZUCA
MAZUMA
MEZCAL
MEZUZA
MEZZOS
MIZZEN
MIZZLE
MIZZLY
MOUZAH
MOZING
MUZHIK
MUZJIK
MUZZLE
MYZONT
NAZARD
NAZIFY
NOZZLE
NUZZER
NUZZLE
OBRIZE
OKRUZI
OOZIER
OOZILY
OOZING
OOZOID
OUYEZD
OXAZIN
OZAENA
OZOENA
OZONED
OZONER
OZONIC
OZONID
PALETZ
PANZER
PAPIZE
PHIZOG
PIAZIN
PIAZZA
PIZZLE
PRIZED
PRIZER
PRIZES
PUSZTA
PUZZLE
QUARTZ
QUEZAL
QUILEZ
QUINZE
QUIZZY
RAZEED
RAZING
RAZOUR
RAZZIA
RAZZLY
REBOZO
RESIZE
RIZZAR
RIZZER
RIZZLE
RIZZOM
SCAZON
SCHANZ
SCORZA
SCRAZE
SCRUZE
SEIZED
SEIZER
SEIZIN
SEIZOR
SHINZA
SINZER
SIZIER
SIZING
SIZZLE
SLEAZY
SLEEZY
SLEPEZ
SMALTZ
SNAZZY
SNEEZE
SNEEZY
SNOOZE
SNOOZY
SOZZLE
SOZZLY
SPELTZ
SPRITZ
STANZA
STANZE
STANZO
SUIVEZ
SYZYGY
TAFWIZ
TARZAN
TAZEEA
TEAZEL
TEAZLE
TENZON
TERFEZ
TERZET
TERZIO
TIZEUR
TOLZEY
TOOZLE
TOOZOO
TOPAZY
TOUZLE
TOWZIE
TRIAZO
TWAZZY
TWEEZE
TZETZE
TZIRID
UNMAZE
URAZIN
UZARIN
UZARON
VIZARD
VIZIER
VIZSLA
WEAZEN
WEEZLE
WENZEL
WHEEZE
WHEEZY
WIZARD
WIZZEN
WOOZLE
WUZZER
WUZZLE
YETZER
YIZKOR
YUZLIK
YUZLUK
ZABETA
ZACATE
ZACHUN
ZADDIK
ZAFFAR
ZAFFER
ZAFFIR
ZAFFRE
ZAGGED
ZAGUAN
ZAMANG
ZANANA
ZANDER
ZANIES
ZANJON
ZAPOTE
ZAPUPE
ZAREBA
ZARNEC
ZEALED
ZEALOT
ZEBECK
ZEBRAS
ZECHIN
ZEEKOE
ZEHNER
ZELANT
ZENANA
ZENDIK
ZENICK
ZENITH
ZENZIC
ZEPHYR
ZEQUIN
ZEREBA
ZEROES
ZESTED
ZEUGMA
ZIAMET
ZIARAT
ZIBETH
ZIEGER
ZIGGER
ZIGZAG
ZILLAH
ZIMMIS
ZINCED
ZINCIC
ZINCID
ZINCKE
ZINCKY
ZINCUM
ZINDIQ
ZINGEL
ZINNIA
ZIPPER
ZIRCON
ZITHER
ZIZANY
ZIZITH
ZIZZLE
ZLOTYS
ZOACUM
ZOARIA
ZOCALO
ZODIAC
ZOETIC
ZOILUS
ZOMBIE
ZOMBIS
ZONARY
ZONATE
ZONING
ZONITE
ZONNAR
ZONOID
ZONULA
ZONULE
ZONURE
ZOONAL
ZOONIC
ZOOSIS
ZOOTIC
ZOOZOO
ZOSTER
ZOUNDS
ZOYSIA
ZUFOLO
ZUISIN
ZYGION
ZYGITE
ZYGOMA
ZYGOSE
ZYGOTE
ZYGOUS
ZYMASE
ZYMITE
ZYMOID
ZYMOME
ZYTHUM

POSITIONAL ORDER LIST OF 6-LETTER WORDS

ZABETA
ZACATE
ZACHUN
ZADDIK
ZAFFAR
ZAFFER
ZAFFIR
ZAFFRE
ZAGGED
ZAGUAN
ZAMANG
ZANANA
ZANDER
ZANIES
ZANJON
ZAPOTE
ZAPUPE
ZAREBA
ZARNEC
ZEALED
ZEALOT
ZEBECK
ZEBRAS
ZECHIN
ZEEKOE
ZEHNER
ZELANT
ZENANA
ZENDIK
ZENICK
ZENITH
ZENZIC
ZEPHYR
ZEQUIN
ZEREBA
ZEROES
ZESTED
ZEUGMA
ZIAMET
ZIARAT
ZIBETH
ZIEGER
ZIGGER
ZIGZAG
ZILLAH
ZIMMIS
ZINCED
ZINCIC
ZINCID
ZINCKE
ZINCKY
ZINCUM
ZINDIQ
ZINGEL
ZINNIA
ZIPPER
ZIRCON
ZITHER
ZIZANY
ZIZITH
ZIZZLE
ZLOTYS
ZOACUM
ZOARIA
ZOCALO
ZODIAC
ZOETIC
ZOILUS
ZOMBIE
ZOMBIS
ZONARY
ZONATE
ZONING
ZONITE
ZONNAR
ZONOID
ZONULA
ZONULE
ZONURE
ZOONAL

ZOONIC
ZOOSIS
ZOOTIC
ZOOZOO
ZOSTER
ZOUNDS
ZOYSIA
ZUFOLO
ZUISIN
ZYGION
ZYGITE
ZYGOMA
ZYGOSE
ZYGOTE
ZYGOUS
ZYMASE
ZYMITE
ZYMOID
ZYMOME
ZYTHUM

AZALEA
AZILUT
AZIMIN
AZIOLA
AZONAL
AZONIC
AZOTEA
AZOTED
AZOTIC
AZOTIN
AZTECA
AZURED
AZYGOS
DZEREN
DZERIN
DZERON
IZAFAT
IZZARD
OZAENA
OZOENA
OZONED
OZONER
OZONIC
OZONID
TZETZE
TZIRID
UZARIN
UZARON

BAZAAR
BEZANT
BEZOAR
BEZZLE
BOZINE
BUZANE
BUZZED
BUZZER
BUZZLE
BYZANT
CAZIBI
CAZIMI
COZIER
COZILY
COZING
DAZING
DAZZLE
DEZINC
DIZAIN
DIZDAR
DIZZEN
DOZENS
DOZENT
DOZIER
DOZILY
DOZING
DOZZLE

ECZEMA
ENZYME
EOZOON
FAZING
FEZZED
FEZZES
FIZGIG
FIZZED
FIZZER
FIZZLE
FUZZLE
GAZABO
GAZEBO
GAZING
GAZOOK
GIZZEN
GOZELL
GOZILL
GOZZAN
GUZZLE
HAZARD
HAZIER
HAZILY
HAZING
HAZZAN
HIZZIE
HUZOOR
HUZZAH
ITZEBU
IZZARD
JAZZER
JEZAIL
JEZIAH
JIZYAH
JUZAIL
LAZARY
LAZIER
LAZILY
LAZING
LAZULE
LAZULI
LIZARD
LIZARY
MAZAME
MAZARD
MAZIER
MAZILY
MAZING
MAZUCA
MAZUMA
MEZCAL
MEZUZA
MEZZOS
MIZZEN
MIZZLE
MIZZLY
MOZING
MUZHIK
MUZJIK
MUZZLE
MYZONT
NAZARD
NAZIFY
NOZZLE
NUZZER
NUZZLE
OOZIER
OOZILY
OOZING
OOZOID
PIZZLE
PUZZLE
RAZEED
RAZING
RAZOUR
RAZZIA
RAZZLY

RIZZAR
RIZZER
RIZZLE
RIZZOM
SIZIER
SIZING
SIZZLE
SOZZLE
SOZZLY
SYZYGY
TAZEEA
TIZEUR
VIZARD
VIZIER
VIZSLA
WIZARD
WIZZEN
WUZZER
WUZZLE
YIZKOR
YUZLIK
YUZLUK
ZIZANY
ZIZITH
ZIZZLE

AGAZED
AKAZGA
ALAZOR
ALEZAN
AMAZED
AMAZON
APOZEM
ATAZIR
BAIZED
BANZAI
BATZEN
BEEZER
BENZAL
BENZIL
BENZIN
BENZOL
BENZYL
BEZZLE
BLAZED
BLAZER
BLAZES
BLAZON
BONZER
BORZOI
BRAZED
BRAZEN
BRAZER
BRAZIL
BUDZAT
BUZZED
BUZZER
BUZZLE
CANZON
CHAZAN
CRAZED
CROZED
CROZER
CROZLE
CUNZIE
DANZON
DARZEE
DAZZLE
DEUZAN
DIAZID
DIAZIN
DIZZEN
DONZEL
DOZZLE
DRAZEL
DRAZIL
DURZEE

EPIZOA
FEAZED
FEZZED
FEZZES
FIZZED
FIZZER
FIZZLE
FOOZLE
FRAZER
FRAZIL
FRIZEL
FRIZER
FRIZZY
FROZEN
FURZED
FUZZLE
GANZIE
GEEZER
GHAZAL
GHAZEL
GIZZEN
GLAZED
GLAZEN
GLAZER
GLOZED
GLOZER
GOOZLE
GOZZAN
GRAZED
GROZER
GUZZLE
HAMZAH
HAZZAN
HELZEL
HIZZIE
HUZZAH
JAZZER
KHAZEN
KORZEC
LANZON
MAHZOR
MAIZER
MAMZER
MANZIL
MATZOH
MATZOS
MATZOT
MEZZOS
MIZZEN
MIZZLE
MIZZLY
MOUZAH
MUZZLE
NOZZLE
NUZZER
NUZZLE
OXAZIN
PANZER
PHIZOG
PIAZIN
PIAZZA
PIZZLE
PRIZED
PRIZER
PRIZES
PUSZTA
PUZZLE
QUEZAL
QUIZZY
RAZZIA
RAZZLY
RIZZAR
RIZZER
RIZZLE
RIZZOM
SCAZON
SEIZED

SEIZER
SEIZIN
SEIZOR
SINZER
SIZZLE
SNAZZY
SOZZLE
SOZZLY
TARZAN
TEAZEL
TEAZLE
TENZON
TERZET
TERZIO
TOLZEY
TOOZLE
TOOZOO
TOUZLE
TOWZIE
TWAZZY
URAZIN
WEAZEN
WEEZLE
WENZEL
WIZZEN
WOOZLE
WUZZER
WUZZLE
YETZER
ZENZIC
ZIGZAG
ZIZZLE
ZOOZOO

ABLAZE
ABRAZO
ACRAZE
AGNIZE
ALTEZA
ASSIZE
BEDAZE
BLEEZE
BLEEZY
BLOWZE
BLOWZY
BORIZE
BRAIZE
BREEZE
BREEZY
BRONZE
BRONZY
BROUZE
BRYNZA
CABEZA
CENIZO
CEREZA
COROZO
CORYZA
DENIZE
DESIZE
EGOIZE
ENDAZE
ENGAZE
ETHIZE
FLOOZY
FREEZE
FREEZY
FRENZY
FRIEZE
FRIEZY
FRIZZY
FROUZE
FROUZY
FROWZE
FROWZY
GRANZA
GROSZY

GROUZE
GROWZE
IODIZE
IONIZE
IOTIZE
KUDIZE
KVUTZA
MEZUZA
OBRIZE
OKRUZI
OUYEZD
PAPIZE
PIAZZA
QUINZE
QUIZZY
REBOZO
RESIZE
SCORZA
SCRAZE
SCRUZE
SHINZA
SLEAZY
SLEEZY
SNAZZY
SNEEZE
SNEEZY
SNOOZE
SNOOZY
STANZA
STANZE
STANZO
TOPAZY
TRIAZO
TWAZZY
TWEEZE
TZETZE
UNMAZE
WHEEZE
WHEEZY

AJIMEZ

AVELOZ
BLINTZ
BONNAZ
CHINTZ
ENTREZ
ERSATZ
HALERZ
HALUTZ
HAMETZ
HOWITZ
KIBITZ
KOLKOZ
KRANTZ
KUVASZ
MARKAZ
PALETZ
QUARTZ
QUILEZ
SCHANZ
SLEPEZ
SMALTZ
SPELTZ
SPRITZ
SUIVEZ
TAFWIZ
TERFEZ

SCORING ORDER LIST OF 6-LETTER WORDS

28
JIZYAH
MUZJIK

26
QUIZZY

25
JEZIAH
ZINDIQ

24
AJIMEZ
FROWZY
MUZHIK
QUARTZ
QUEZAL
QUILEZ
QUINZE
WHEEZY
ZEQUIN
ZINCKY

23
BLOWZY
HAMZAH
ZEBECK
ZEPHYR
ZYTHUM

22
JEZAIL
JUZAIL
KHAZEN
KUVASZ
KVUTZA
OXAZIN
YIZKOR
YUZLIK
YUZLUK
ZANJON
ZYMOME

21
FLOOZY
FREEZY
FRENZY
FRIEZY
FROUZY
FROWZE
HAZILY
HOWITZ
JAZZER
KIBITZ
KORZEC
MARKAZ
NAZIFY
PHIZOG
SYZYGY
TAFWIZ
WHEEZE
ZADDIK
ZAFFAR
ZAFFER
ZAFFIR
ZAFFRE
ZENICK
ZINCKE
ZYGOMA
ZYMOID

20
AKAZGA
BENZYL
BLEEZY
BLOWZE
BREEZY
BRONZY
BRYNZA
BYZANT
CHAZAN
CHINTZ
CORYZA
COZILY
ENZYME
FIZGIG
FRIZZY
GAZOOK
HAMETZ
HUZZAH
KUDIZE
MAHZOR
MATZOH
MAZILY
MOUZAH
MYZONT
SCHANZ
TOPAZY
TWAZZY
ZACHUN
ZECHIN
ZENDIK
ZIBETH
ZYMASE
ZYMITE

19
APOZEM
AZYGOS
CABEZA
CAZIBI
CAZIMI
DOZILY
ECZEMA
FAZING
FEAZED
FURZED
GHAZAL
GHAZEL
GROSZY
GROWZE
HAZARD
HAZING
KRANTZ
MAMZER
MAZAME
MAZUCA
MAZUMA
MEZCAL
MIZZLY
OKRUZI
OUYEZD
PAPIZE
VIZARD
WIZARD
ZAPUPE
ZEEKOE
ZIMMIS
ZINCIC
ZINCUM
ZIPPER
ZOACUM
ZOMBIE
ZOMBIS
ZYGION
ZYGITE
ZYGOSE
ZYGOTE
ZYGOUS

18
AMAZED
AVELOZ
BAIZED
BEDAZE
BLAZED
BRAZED
BUDZAT
COZING
CRAZED
CROZED
DEZINC
ETHIZE
FEZZED
FIZZED
FOOZLE
FRAZER
FRAZIL
FREEZE
FRIEZE
FRIZEL
FRIZER
FROZEN
GAZABO
GAZEBO
HALERZ
HALUTZ
HAZIER
HELZEL
HUZOOR
IZAFAT
KOLKOZ
LAZARY
LAZILY
LIZARY
MAZARD
MAZING
MOZING
OOZILY
OOZING
PRIZED
SHINZA
SLEAZY
SLEEZY
SNEEZY
SNOOZY
SUIVEZ
TERFEZ
TOLZEY
TOWZIE
TWEEZE
VIZIER
VIZSLA
WEAZEN
WEEZLE
WENZEL
WOOZLE
YETZER
ZAGGED
ZAMANG
ZEHNER
ZENITH
ZEUGMA
ZILLAH
ZINCED
ZINCID
ZITHER
ZLOTYS
ZODIAC
ZONARY
ZOYSIA
ZUFOLO

17
ABLAZE
ABRAZO
ACRAZE
AGAZED
AMAZON
AZIMIN
AZONIC
AZOTIC
AZTECA
BANZAI
BATZEN
BAZAAR
BEEZER
BENZAL
BENZIL
BENZIN
BENZOL
BEZANT
BEZOAR
BLAZER
BLAZES
BLAZON
BLEEZE
BLINTZ
BONNAZ
BONZER
BORIZE
BORZOI
BOZINE
BRAIZE
BRAZEN
BRAZER
BRAZIL
BREEZE
BRONZE
BROUZE
BUZANE
BUZZED
CANZON
CENIZO
CEREZA
COROZO
COZIER
CROZER
CROZLE
CUNZIE
DAZING
DIAZID
DIZDAR
DOZING
EPIZOA
FEZZES
FIZZER
FIZZLE
FUZZLE
GAZING
GLAZED
GLOZED
GRAZED
HAZZAN
HIZZIE
ITZEBU
MAIZER
MANZIL
MATZOS
MATZOT

MAZIER
OBRIZE
OZONIC
PALETZ
PANZER
PIAZIN
PRIZER
PRIZES
PUSZTA
RAZZLY
REBOZO
SCAZON
SCORZA
SCRAZE
SCRUZE
SLEPEZ
SMALTZ
SNAZZY
SOZZLY
SPELTZ
SPRITZ
UNMAZE
WIZZEN
WUZZER
WUZZLE
ZABETA
ZACATE
ZAPOTE
ZAREBA
ZARNEC
ZEBRAS
ZEREBA
ZIAMET
ZIGGER
ZIRCON
ZIZANY
ZIZITH
ZOCALO
ZOETIC
ZOONIC
ZOOTIC

16

AGNIZE
AZOTED
AZURED
BEZZLE
BUZZER
BUZZLE
DANZON
DARZEE
DENIZE
DESIZE
DEUZAN
DIAZIN
DIZAIN
DONZEL
DOZENS
DOZENT
DOZIER
DRAZEL
DRAZIL
DURZEE
DZEREN
DZERIN
DZERON
EGOIZE
ENDAZE
ENGAZE
GANZIE
GEEZER
GLAZEN
GLAZER
GLOZER
GOOZLE
GOZELL
GOZILL
GRANZA
GROUZE
GROZER
IODIZE
LAZING
LIZARD
MEZUZA
MEZZOS
MIZZEN
MIZZLE
MUZZLE
NAZARD
OOZOID
OZONED
OZONID
PIAZZA
PIZZLE
PUZZLE
RAZEED
RAZING
RIZZOM
SEIZED
SIZING
TZIRID
ZAGUAN
ZANDER
ZEALED
ZENZIC
ZESTED
ZIEGER
ZIGZAG
ZINGEL
ZONING
ZONOID
ZOUNDS

15

ALAZOR
ALEZAN
ALTEZA
ASSIZE
ATAZIR
AZALEA
AZILUT
AZIOLA
AZONAL
AZOTEA
AZOTIN
DAZZLE
DIZZEN
DOZZLE
ENTREZ
EOZOON
ERSATZ
GIZZEN
GOZZAN
GUZZLE
IONIZE
IOTIZE
IZZARD
LANZON
LAZIER
LAZULE
LAZULI
OOZIER
OZAENA
OZOENA
OZONER
RAZOUR
RESIZE
SEIZER
SEIZIN
SEIZOR
SINZER
SIZIER
SNEEZE
SNOOZE
STANZA
STANZE
STANZO
TARZAN
TAZEEA
TEAZEL
TEAZLE
TENZON
TERZET
TERZIO
TIZEUR
TOOZLE
TOOZOO
TOUZLE
TRIAZO
URAZIN
UZARIN
UZARON
ZANANA
ZANIES
ZEALOT
ZELANT
ZENANA
ZEROES
ZIARAT
ZINNIA
ZOARIA
ZOILUS
ZONATE
ZONITE
ZONNAR
ZONULA
ZONULE
ZONURE
ZOONAL
ZOOSIS
ZOSTER
ZUISIN

14

NOZZLE
NUZZER
NUZZLE
RAZZIA
RIZZAR
RIZZER
RIZZLE
SIZZLE
SOZZLE
TZETZE
ZOOZOO

13

ZIZZLE

ALPHABETICAL LIST OF 7-LETTER WORDS

ABBOZZO
ABLEEZE
ACIDIZE
ADAZZLE
ADONIZE
AGATIZE
AGENIZE
AGNIZED
AGONIZE
AKAZGIN
ALCAZAR
ALECIZE
ALFEREZ
ALGAZEL
ALIZARI
ALTEZZA
ALVELOZ
AMAZING
ANALYZE
ANIMIZE
ANODIZE
APOZEMA
APPRIZE
ARIENZO
ARMSIZE
ASSEIZE
ASSIZED
ASSIZER
ASSIZES
ATHEIZE
ATOMIZE
AZAFRAN
AZAFRIN
AZAROLE
AZELAIC
AZELATE
AZIMENE
AZIMINE
AZIMINO
AZIMUTH
AZOFIER
AZONIUM
AZOPHEN
AZORITE
AZOTATE
AZOTINE
AZOTITE
AZOTOUS
AZOXINE
AZUELJO
AZULENE
AZULITE
AZUMBRE
AZUREAN
AZURINE
AZURITE
AZUROUS
AZYGOTE
AZYGOUS
AZYMITE
AZYMOUS
BAIZING
BAPTIZE
BAZOOKA
BAZZITE
BEDIZEN
BEMAZED
BENZEIN
BENZENE
BENZINE
BENZOIC
BENZOIN
BENZOLE
BENZOXY
BENZOYL
BEZANTE
BEZANTY
BEZETTA
BEZETTE
BEZIQUE
BEZZANT
BEZZLED
BIOZONE
BIZARRE
BLAZING
BLINTZE
BLOWZED
BONANZA
BONZERY
BONZIAN
BOOZING
BORAZON
BRAZERA
BRAZIER
BRAZING
BREEZED
BRITZKA
BROMIZE
BRONZED
BRONZEN
BRONZER
BROWZER
BRULZIE
BUDZART
BUMBAZE
BUZZARD
BUZZIER
BUZZIES
BUZZING
BUZZWIG
CABEZON
CACHAZA
CADENZA
CALZADA
CANEZOU

CANZONA
CANZONE
CANZONI
CAPATAZ
CAPSIZE
CARRIZO
CAZIQUE
CHALAZA
CHALAZE
CHAZZAN
CHEMIZO
CHINTZE
CHINTZY
CHIZZEL
CITIZEN
COALIZE
COCUIZA
COGNIZE
COROZOS
COZENER
COZIEST
CRAZIER
CRAZIES
CRAZILY
CRAZING
CRITIZE
CRIZZLE
CRIZZEL
CROZIER
CROZING
CROZZLE
CROZZLY
CRUZADO
CYANIZE
CYCLIZE
CZARDOM
CZARINA
CZARISH
CZARISM
CZARIST
CZIGANY
DAMOZEL
DAZEDLY
DAZZLED
DAZZLED
DAZZLER
DEGLAZE
DENIZEN
DIALYZE
DIARIZE
DIAZIDE
DIAZINE
DIAZOIC
DIAZOLE
DIAZOMA
DIZAINE
DIZENED
DIZZARD
DIZZIED
DIZZIER
DIZZILY
DOCKIZE
DOZENED
DOZENER
DOZENTH
DOZIEST
DOZZLED
DRIZZLE
DRIZZLY
DUALIZE
DUREZZA
EBONIZE
ECHOIZE
ECTOZOA
EGOTIZE
ELEGIZE
EMBLAZE
EMERIZE
EMPRIZE
ENOLIZE
ENTOZOA
EPIZOAL
EPIZOAN
EPIZOIC
EPIZOON
FAHLERZ
FANZINE
FAZENDA
FEAZING
FILAZER
FILMIZE
FIZZIER
FIZZING
FIZZLED
FOOZLED
FOOZLER
FRAZZLE
FREEZER
FRIEZED
FRIEZER
FRISZKA
FRIZADO
FRIZZES
FRIZZED
FRIZZEN
FRIZZER
FRIZZLE
FRIZZLY
FURZERY
FUZZIER
FUZZILY
GALLIZE
GARNETZ
GAUZIER
GAUZILY
GAZABOS
GAZEBOS
GAZELLE
GAZETTE
GENIZAH
GEZERAH
GHAWAZI
GHAZIES
GHIZITE
GIZZARD
GIZZERN
GLAIZIE
GLAZIER
GLAZILY
GLAZING
GLOZING
GODDIZE
GONZALO
GOZZARD
GRAZIER
GRAZING
GRIZARD
GRIZZLE
GRIZZLY
GROTZEN
GROZART
GRUNZIE
GUANIZE
GUAZUTI
GUEREZA
GUZERAT
GUZZLED
GUZZLER
HAMOTZI
HAZANUT
HAZELED
HAZELLY
HAZIEST
HOATZIN
HORIZON
HUARIZO
HUMBUZZ
HUTZPAH
HUZZARD
IAMBIZE
IDOLIZE
IMBLAZE
INDAZOL
IODIZED
IODIZER
IONIZER
IOTIZED
IRIDIZE
IRONIZE
ITEMIZE
JAZERAN
JAZZBOW
JAZZIER
JAZZILY
KIBBUTZ
KLEZMER
KOLKHOZ
KREUZER
KUNZITE
KVUTZAH
KWAZOKU
KYANIZE
LAICIZE
LAZARET
LAZARLY
LAZIEST
LAZYBED
LIONIZE
LOZENGE
LOZENGY
MAGHZEN
MAKHZAN
MAKHZEN
MANZANA
MATANZA
MATZOON
MATZOTH
MAZDOOR
MAZEDLY
MAZEFUL
MAZIEST
MAZURKA
MAZZARD
MESTIZA
MESTIZO
METREZA
MEZQUIT
MEZUZAH
MINOIZE
MISMAZE
MITZVAH
MIZMAZE
MIZRACH
MIZZLED
MONOAZO
MOZETTA
MUZOONA
MUZZIER
MUZZLED
MUZZLER
NIZAMAT
NIZAMUT
NOUNIZE
NOZZLER
NUZZLED
OBELIZE
ODORIZE
ODYLIZE
ONYMIZE
OOZIEST
OPALIZE
ORGANZA
OSAZONE
OUTBUZZ
OUTGAZE
OUTJAZZ
OUTRAZE
OUTSIZE
OUTZANY
OVALIZE
OXAZINE
OXAZOLE
OXIDIZE
OXOZONE
OZONATE
OZONIDE
OZONIFY
OZONIZE
OZONOUS
OZOTYPE
PALAZZI
PALAZZO
PAZAREE
PECTIZE
PEPTIZE
PETZITE
POETIZE
PONZITE
PRENZIE
PRETZEL
PREZONE
PRIZERY
PRIZING
PUZZLED
PUZZLER
PYRAZIN
QUARTZY
QUEAZEN
QUETZAL
QUIZZED
QUIZZEE
QUIZZER
RANTIZE
RAZZING
REALIZE
RESEIZE
RESIZED
RESIZER
RETZIAN
RHIZINE
RHIZOID
RHIZOMA
RHIZOME
RHIZOTE
RIBZUBA
RITZIER
ROMANZA
SAZERAC
SCHERZI
SCHERZO
SCHIZZO
SCHMALZ
SCHMELZ
SCHNITZ
SCHWARZ
SEIZING
SEIZURE
SELTZER
SEROZEM
SHEGETZ
SHIZOKU
SIZABLE
SIZABLY
SIZEINE
SIZEMAN
SIZIEST
SIZINGS
SIZZARD
SIZZING
SIZZLED
SIZZLER
SKEEZIX
SNEEZED
SNEEZER
SNOOZED
SNOOZER
SNOOZLE
SNOZZLE
SNUZZLE
SOVENEZ
SOVKHOZ
SOZOLIC
SOZZLED
SPATZLE
SPITZER
SPULZIE
SQUEEZE
SQUEEZY
STANZAS
STATIZE
STYLIZE
SUBZONE
SURSIZE
SWIZZLE
SYZYGAL
SYZYGIA
TAILZEE
TAILZIE
TERZINA
TETRAZO
THEEZAN
THIAZIN
THIAZOL
TIZZIES
TOPAZES
TRAPEZE
TRIAZIN
TRISAZO
TRIZOIC
TUILZIE
TWEEZED
TWEEZER
TWIZZLE
TZARDOM
TZARINA
TZIGANE
TZIMMES
TZOLKIN
TZONTLE
UNGLAZE
UNITIZE
UNSEIZE
UNSIZED
UNZONED
UPERIZE
URAZINE
URAZOLE
UTILIZE
VERZINI
VERZINO
VIZNOMY
VIZORED
VOLTIZE
WALTZED
WALTZER
WEAZENY
WHEEZED
WHEEZER
WHEEZLE
WHIZGIG

WHIZZED
WHIZZER
WHIZZES
WHIZZLE
WIZENED
WOOZIER
WOOZILY
WUZZLED
YAGUAZA
ZABURRO
ZACATON
ZADRUGA
ZAFFREE
ZAGGING
ZAKUSKA
ZAMARRA
ZAMARRO
ZAMORIN
ZAMOUSE
ZANELLA
ZANJERO
ZANJONA
ZANYISH
ZANYISM
ZAPHARA
ZAPTIAH
ZAPTIEH
ZAREEBA
ZARNICH
ZATTARE
ZEALOUS
ZEBRAIC
ZEBRINE
ZEBROID
ZEBRULE
ZEBURRO
ZEDOARY
ZELATOR
ZEMEISM
ZEMIISM
ZEMSTVO
ZENTNER
ZEOLITE
ZEPHYRY
ZEROIZE
ZESTFUL
ZESTING
ZETETIC
ZEUGITE
ZIBETUM
ZIGANKA
ZIKURAT
ZIMARRA
ZIMOCCA
ZINCATE
ZINCIDE
ZINCIFY
ZINCING
ZINCITE
ZINCKED
ZINCOID
ZINCOUS
ZINGANA
ZINGANO
ZINGARA
ZINGARI
ZINGARO
ZINOBER
ZINSANG
ZIPHIAN
ZIPPIER
ZIPPING
ZIRCITE
ZIRKITE
ZITTERN
ZIZZLED
ZOARIAL
ZOARIUM
ZOCCOLO
ZOISITE
ZOISTIC
ZOMBIES
ZONALLY
ZONATED
ZONELET
ZONITID
ZONULAR
ZONULET
ZONURID
ZOOCARP
ZOOCYST
ZOOECIA
ZOOGAMY
ZOOGENE
ZOOGLER
ZOOIDAL
ZOOLITE
ZOOLITH
ZOOLOGY
ZOONIST
ZOONITE
ZOONOMY
ZOONULE
ZOOPERY
ZOOTAXY
ZOOTYPE
ZORGITE
ZORILLA
ZORILLE
ZUFFOLO
ZUMATIC
ZUNYITE
ZWITTER
ZYGENID
ZYGOSIS
ZYMOGEN
ZYMOMIN
ZYMOSIS
ZYMOTIC
ZYMURGY

POSITIONAL ORDER LIST OF 7-LETTER WORDS

ZABURRO
ZACATON
ZADRUGA
ZAFFREE
ZAGGING
ZAKUSKA
ZAMARRA
ZAMARRO
ZAMORIN
ZAMOUSE
ZANELLA
ZANJERO
ZANJONA
ZANYISH
ZANYISM
ZAPHARA
ZAPTIAH
ZAPTIEH
ZAREEBA
ZARNICH
ZATTARE
ZEALOUS
ZEBRAIC
ZEBRINE
ZEBROID
ZEBRULE
ZEBURRO
ZEDOARY
ZELATOR
ZEMEISM
ZEMIISM
ZEMSTVO
ZENTNER
ZEOLITE
ZEPHYRY
ZEROIZE
ZESTFUL
ZESTING
ZETETIC
ZEUGITE
ZIBETUM
ZIGANKA
ZIKURAT
ZIMARRA
ZIMOCCA
ZINCATE
ZINCIDE
ZINCIFY
ZINCING
ZINCITE
ZINCKED
ZINCOID
ZINCOUS
ZINGANA
ZINGANO
ZINGARA
ZINGARI
ZINGARO
ZINOBER
ZINSANG
ZIPHIAN
ZIPPIER
ZIPPING
ZIRCITE
ZIRKITE
ZITTERN
ZIZZLED
ZOARIAL
ZOARIUM
ZOCCOLO
ZOISITE
ZOISTIC
ZOMBIES
ZONALLY
ZONATED
ZONELET
ZONITID
ZONULAR
ZONULET
ZONURID
ZOOCARP
ZOOCYST
ZOOECIA
ZOOGAMY
ZOOGENE
ZOOGLER
ZOOIDAL
ZOOLITE
ZOOLITH
ZOOLOGY
ZOONIST
ZOONITE
ZOONOMY
ZOONULE
ZOOPERY
ZOOTAXY
ZOOTYPE
ZORGITE
ZORILLA
ZORILLE
ZUFFOLO
ZUMATIC
ZUNYITE
ZWITTER
ZYGENID
ZYGOSIS
ZYMOGEN
ZYMOMIN
ZYMOSIS
ZYMOTIC
ZYMURGY

AZAFRAN
AZAFRIN
AZAROLE
AZELAIC
AZELATE
AZIMENE
AZIMINE
AZIMINO
AZIMUTH
AZOFIER
AZONIUM
AZOPHEN
AZORITE
AZOTATE
AZOTINE
AZOTITE
AZOTOUS
AZOXINE
AZUELJO
AZULENE
AZULITE
AZUMBRE
AZUREAN
AZURINE
AZURITE
AZUROUS
AZYGOTE
AZYGOUS
AZYMITE
AZYMOUS
CZARDOM
CZARINA
CZARISH
CZARISM
CZARIST
CZIGANY
OZONATE
OZONIDE
OZONIFY
OZONIZE
OZONOUS
OZOTYPE
TZARDOM
TZARINA
TZIGANE
TZIMMES
TZOLKIN
TZONTLE

BAZOOKA
BAZZITE
BEZANTE
BEZANTY
BEZETTA
BEZETTE
BEZIQUE
BEZZANT
BEZZLED
BIZARRE
BUZZARD
BUZZIER
BUZZIES
BUZZING
BUZZWIG
COZENER
COZIEST
DAZEDLY
DAZZLED
DAZZLER
DIZAINE
DIZENED
DIZZARD
DIZZIED
DIZZIER
DIZZILY
DOZENED
DOZENER
DOZENTH
DOZIEST
DOZZLED
FAZENDA
FIZZIER
FIZZING
FIZZLED
FUZZIER
FUZZILY
GAZABOS
GAZEBOS
GAZELLE
GAZETTE
GEZERAH
GIZZARD
GIZZERN
GOZZARD
GUZERAT
GUZZLED
GUZZLER
HAZANUT
HAZELED
HAZELLY
HAZIEST
HUZZARD
JAZERAN
JAZZBOW
JAZZIER
JAZZILY
LAZARET
LAZARLY
LAZIEST
LAZYBED
LOZENGE
LOZENGY
MAZDOOR
MAZEDLY
MAZEFUL
MAZIEST
MAZURKA
MAZZARD

MEZQUIT
MEZUZAH
MIZMAZE
MIZRACH
MIZZLED
MOZETTA
MUZOONA
MUZZIER
MUZZLED
MUZZLER
NIZAMAT
NIZAMUT
NOZZLER
NUZZLED
OOZIEST
PAZAREE
PUZZLED
PUZZLER
RAZZING
SAZERAC
SIZABLE
SIZABLY
SIZEINE
SIZEMAN
SIZIEST
SIZINGS
SIZZARD
SIZZING
SIZZLED
SIZZLER
SOZOLIC
SOZZLED
SYZYGAL
SYZYGIA
TIZZIES
UNZONED
VIZNOMY
VIZORED
WIZENED
WUZZLED
ZIZZLED

ADAZZLE
AKAZGIN
ALIZARI
AMAZING
APOZEMA
BAIZING
BAZZITE
BENZEIN
BENZENE
BENZINE
BENZOIC
BENZOIN
BENZOLE
BENZOXY
BENZOYL
BEZZANT
BEZZLED
BIOZONE
BLAZING
BONZERY
BONZIAN
BOOZING
BRAZERA
BRAZIER
BRAZING
BUDZART
BUZZARD
BUZZIER
BUZZIES
BUZZING
BUZZWIG
CALZADA
CANZONA
CANZONE
CANZONI

CHAZZAN
CHIZZEL
CRAZIER
CRAZIES
CRAZILY
CRAZING
CRIZZLE
CRIZZEL
CROZIER
CROZING
CROZZLE
CROZZLY
CRUZADO
DAZZLED
DAZZLER
DIAZIDE
DIAZINE
DIAZOIC
DIAZOLE
DIAZOMA
DIZZARD
DIZZIED
DIZZIER
DIZZILY
DOZZLED
DRIZZLE
DRIZZLY
EPIZOAL
EPIZOAN
EPIZOIC
EPIZOON
FANZINE
FEAZING
FIZZIER
FIZZING
FIZZLED
FOOZLED
FOOZLER
FRAZZLE
FRIZADO
FRIZZES
FRIZZED
FRIZZEN
FRIZZER
FRIZZLE
FRIZZLY
FURZERY
FUZZIER
FUZZILY
GAUZIER
GAUZILY
GHAZIES
GHIZITE
GIZZARD
GIZZERN
GLAZIER
GLAZILY
GLAZING
GLOZING
GONZALO
GOZZARD
GRAZIER
GRAZING
GRIZARD
GRIZZLE
GRIZZLY
GROZART
GUAZUTI
GUZZLED
GUZZLER
HUTZPAH
HUZZARD
JAZZBOW
JAZZIER
JAZZILY
KLEZMER
KUNZITE

KWAZOKU
MANZANA
MATZOON
MATZOTH
MAZZARD
MITZVAH
MIZZLED
MUZZIER
MUZZLED
MUZZLER
NOZZLER
NUZZLED
OSAZONE
OUTZANY
OXAZINE
OXAZOLE
OXOZONE
PETZITE
PONZITE
PREZONE
PRIZERY
PRIZING
PUZZLED
PUZZLER
QUIZZED
QUIZZEE
QUIZZER
RAZZING
RETZIAN
RHIZINE
RHIZOID
RHIZOMA
RHIZOME
RHIZOTE
RIBZUBA
RITZIER
SEIZURE
SHIZOKU
SIZZARD
SIZZING
SIZZLED
SIZZLER
SNOZZLE
SNUZZLE
SOZZLED
SUBZONE
SWIZZLE
TERZINA
TIZZIES
TRIZOIC
TWIZZLE
URAZINE
URAZOLE
VERZINI
VERZINO
WEAZENY
WHIZGIG
WHIZZED
WHIZZER
WHIZZES
WHIZZLE
WOOZIER
WOOZILY
WUZZLED
ZIZZLED

ABBOZZO
ADAZZLE
AGNIZED
ALCAZAR
ALGAZEL
ALTEZZA
ASSIZED
ASSIZER
ASSIZES
BEDIZEN
BEMAZED

BLOWZED
BORAZON
BREEZED
BRITZKA
BRONZED
BRONZEN
BRONZER
BROWZER
BRULZIE
CABEZON
CANEZOU
CHAZZAN
CHIZZEL
CITIZEN
COROZOS
CRIZZLE
CRIZZEL
CROZZLE
CROZZLY
DAMOZEL
DENIZEN
DRIZZLE
DRIZZLY
DUREZZA
ECTOZOA
ENTOZOA
FILAZER
FRAZZLE
FREEZER
FRIEZED
FRIEZER
FRISZKA
FRIZZES
FRIZZED
FRIZZEN
FRIZZER
FRIZZLE
FRIZZLY
GENIZAH
GLAIZIE
GRIZZLE
GRIZZLY
GROTZEN
GRUNZIE
HOATZIN
HORIZON
INDAZOL
IODIZED
IODIZER
IONIZER
IOTIZED
KREUZER
KVUTZAH
MAGHZEN
MAKHZAN
MAKHZEN
MEZUZAH
PALAZZI
PALAZZO
PRENZIE
PRETZEL
PYRAZIN
QUEAZEN
QUETZAL
QUIZZED
QUIZZEE
QUIZZER
RESIZED
RESIZER
SCHIZZO
SELTZER
SEROZEM
SKEEZIX
SNEEZED
SNEEZER
SNOOZED
SNOOZER

SNOOZLE
SNOZZLE
SNUZZLE
SPATZLE
SPITZER
SPULZIE
STANZAS
SWIZZLE
TAILZEE
TAILZIE
THEEZAN
THIAZIN
THIAZOL
TOPAZES
TRIAZIN
TUILZIE
TWEEZED
TWEEZER
TWIZZLE
UNSIZED
WALTZED
WALTZER
WHEEZED
WHEEZER
WHEEZLE
WHIZZED
WHIZZER
WHIZZES
WHIZZLE

ABBOZZO
ABLEEZE
ACIDIZE
ADONIZE
AGATIZE
AGENIZE
AGONIZE
ALECIZE
ALTEZZA
ANALYZE
ANIMIZE
ANODIZE
APPRIZE
ARIENZO
ARMSIZE
ASSEIZE
ATHEIZE
ATOMIZE
BAPTIZE
BLINTZE
BONANZA
BROMIZE
BUMBAZE
CACHAZA
CAPSIZE
CARRIZO
CHALAZA
CHALAZE
CHEMIZO
CHINTZE
CHINTZY
COALIZE
COCUIZA
COGNIZE
CRITIZE
CYANIZE
CYCLIZE
DEGLAZE
DIALYZE
DIARIZE
DOCKIZE
DUALIZE
DUREZZA
EBONIZE
ECHOIZE
EGOTIZE
ELEGIZE

EMBLAZE
EMERIZE
EMPRIZE
ENOLIZE
FILMIZE
GALLIZE
GHAWAZI
GODDIZE
GUANIZE
GUEREZA
HAMOTZI
HUARIZO
HUMBUZZ
IAMBIZE
IDOLIZE
IMBLAZE
IRIDIZE
IRONIZE
ITEMIZE
KYANIZE
LAICIZE
LIONIZE
MATANZA
MESTIZA
MESTIZO
METREZA
MINOIZE
MISMAZE
MIZMAZE
MONOAZO
NOUNIZE
OBELIZE
ODORIZE
ODYLIZE
ONYMIZE
OPALIZE
ORGANZA
OUTBUZZ
OUTGAZE
OUTJAZZ
OUTRAZE
OUTSIZE
OVALIZE
OXIDIZE
OZONIZE
PALAZZI
PALAZZO
PECTIZE
PEPTIZE
POETIZE
QUARTZY
RANTIZE
REALIZE
RESEIZE
ROMANZA
SCHERZI
SCHERZO
SCHIZZO
SQUEEZE
SQUEEZY
STATIZE
STYLIZE
SURSIZE
TETRAZO
TRAPEZE
TRISAZO
UNGLAZE
UNITIZE
UNSEIZE
UPERIZE
UTILIZE
VOLTIZE
YAGUAZA
ZEROIZE
ALFEREZ
ALVELOZ
CAPATAZ
FAHLERZ
GARNETZ
HUMBUZZ
KIBBUTZ
KOLKHOZ
OUTBUZZ
OUTJAZZ
SCHMALZ
SCHMELZ
SCHNITZ
SCHWARZ
SHEGETZ
SOVENEZ
SOVKHOZ

SCORING ORDER LIST OF 7-LETTER WORDS

28
BENZOXY
QUARTZY
SQUEEZY

27
BEZIQUE
JAZZBOW
MEZQUIT
SKEEZIX
ZEPHYRY

26
KVUTZAH
SOVKHOZ
ZOOTAXY

25
JAZZILY
MAKHZAN
MAKHZEN
QUEAZEN
QUETZAL
QUIZZED
SQUEEZE
ZYMURGY

24
CHINTZY
HUTZPAH
KIBBUTZ
MITZVAH
OXIDIZE
QUIZZEE
QUIZZER
SCHWARZ
VIZNOMY
WHIZGIG
ZINCIFY

23
AZOXINE
AZUELJO
CACHAZA
CHEMIZO
CYCLIZE
DOCKIZE
FRISZKA
GHAWAZI
JAZERAN
KYANIZE
MIZRACH
OXAZINE
OXAZOLE
OXOZONE
SCHMALZ
SCHMELZ
SHIZOKU
SYZYGAL
SYZYGIA
WHEEZED
ZANJERO
ZANJONA
ZINCKED
ZYMOMIN
ZYMOTIC

22
BAZOOKA
BLOWZED
BRITZKA
BUMBAZE
CZIGANY
FAHLERZ
FURZERY
HAZELLY
HUMBUZZ
JAZZIER
KLEZMER
KOLKHOZ
KWAZOKU
LAZYBED
MAGHZEN
MAZEDLY
MAZURKA
OUTJAZZ
OZONIFY
WEAZENY
WHEEZER
WHEEZLE
WHIZZED
WOOZILY
ZAFFREE
ZANYISH
ZIMOCCA
ZOOGAMY
ZUFFOLO
ZYMOGEN

21
AKAZGIN
AZIMUTH
AZOPHEN
AZYMITE
AZYMOUS
BEMAZED
BENZOYL
BEZANTY
BONZERY
BROWZER
BUZZWIG
CHALAZA
CHALAZE
CHINTZE
CRAZILY
CYANIZE
CZARDOM
CZARISH
DAZEDLY
ECHOIZE
FILMIZE
FRIZZLY
FUZZILY
HAMOTZI
MATZOTH
MAZEFUL
ONYMIZE
OZOTYPE
PRIZERY
PYRAZIN
RHIZOMA
RHIZOME
SCHERZI
SCHERZO
SCHNITZ
SIZABLY
WHIZZER
WHIZZES
WHIZZLE
ZANYISM
ZAPHARA
ZAPTIAH
ZAPTIEH
ZARNICH
ZEMSTVO
ZIGANKA
ZIPHIAN
ZIPPING
ZOOCYST
ZOONOMY
ZOOPERY
ZOOTYPE
ZYGENID
ZYMOSIS

20
APOZEMA
APPRIZE
AZUMBRE
AZYGOTE
AZYGOUS
BAPTIZE
BENZOIC
BROMIZE
CABEZON
CAPATAZ
CAPSIZE
COCUIZA
COZENAGE
CROZZLY
CZARISM
DIALYZE
DOZENTH
EMBLAZE
EMPRIZE
EPIZOIC
FAZENDA
FEAZING
FOOZLED
FRIEZED
FRIZADO
GAUZILY
GENIZAH
GEZERAH
GHAZIES
GHIZITE
GLAZILY
HAZELED
IAMBIZE
IMBLAZE
KREUZER
KUNZITE
LOZENGY
MEZUZAH
MISMAZE
ODYLIZE
PECTIZE
PEPTIZE
RHIZOID
RIBZUBA
SCHIZZO
SHEGETZ
TWEEZED
TZIMMES
TZOLKIN
VIZORED
WALTZED
WIZENED
YAGUAZA
ZEBRAIC
ZEDOARY
ZEMEISM
ZEMIISM
ZIBETUM
ZIKURAT
ZIPPIER
ZIRKITE
ZOCCOLO
ZOMBIES
ZOOCARP
ZOOLOGY
ZUMATIC
ZYGOSIS

19
ABBOZZO
ACIDIZE
ALFEREZ
ALVELOZ
AMAZING
ANALYZE
ATHEIZE
AZAFRAN
AZAFRIN
AZOFIER
BAIZING
BEDIZEN
BLAZING
BOOZING
BRAZING
BREEZED
BRONZED
BUDZART
CADENZA
CALZADA
COGNIZE
CRAZING
CROZING
CRUZADO
DAMOZEL
DIAZOIC
DIAZOMA
DIZZILY
DRIZZLY
FANZINE
FILAZER
FIZZING
FIZZLED
FOOZLER
FREEZER
FRIEZER
FRIZZED
GAZABOS
GAZEBOS
GODDIZE

GRIZZLY
HAZANUT
HAZIEST
HOATZIN
HORIZON
HUARIZO
HUZZARD
LAZARLY
MAZDOOR
MIZMAZE
OUTZANY
OVALIZE
PRIZING
RHIZINE
RHIZOTE
SOVENEZ
STYLIZE
THEEZAN
THIAZIN
THIAZOL
TWEEZER
TZARDOM
VERZINI
VERZINO
VOLTIZE
WALTZER
WOOZIER
WUZZLED
ZAGGING
ZAKUSKA
ZEBROID
ZESTFUL
ZINCIDE
ZINCING
ZINCOID
ZONALLY
ZOOLITH
ZUNYITE
ZWITTER

18
ABLEEZE
AGNIZED
ALCAZAR
ALECIZE
ANIMIZE
ARMSIZE
ATOMIZE
AZELAIC
AZIMENE
AZIMINE
AZIMINO
AZONIUM
BENZEIN
BENZENE
BENZINE
BENZOIN
BENZOLE
BEZANTE
BEZETTA
BEZETTE
BEZZLED
BIOZONE
BIZARRE
BLINTZE
BONANZA
BONZIAN
BORAZON
BRAZERA
BRAZIER
BRONZEN
BRONZER
BRULZIE
BUZZARD
BUZZING

CANEZOU
CANZONA
CANZONE
CANZONI
CARRIZO
CITIZEN
COALIZE
COROZOS
COZENER
COZIEST
CRAZIER
CRAZIES
CRITIZE
CROZIER
CZARINA
CZARIST
DEGLAZE
DIAZIDE
DIZENED
DOZENED
EBONIZE
ECTOZOA
EMERIZE
EPIZOAL
EPIZOAN
EPIZOON
FIZZIER
FRAZZLE
FRIZZES
FRIZZEN
FRIZZER
FRIZZLE
FUZZIER
GLAZING
GLOZING
GRAZING
GRIZARD
IODIZED
ITEMIZE
LAICIZE
MANZANA
MATANZA
MATZOON
MAZIEST
MAZZARD
MESTIZA
MESTIZO
METREZA
MINOIZE
MIZZLED
MONOAZO
MOZETTA
MUZOONA
MUZZLED
NIZAMAT
NIZAMUT
OBELIZE
OPALIZE
PAZAREE
PETZITE
POETIZE
PONZITE
PRENZIE
PRETZEL
PREZONE
PUZZLED
ROMANZA
SAZERAC
SEROZEM
SIZABLE
SIZEMAN
SOZOLIC
SPATZLE
SPITZER
SPULZIE

SUBZONE
SWIZZLE
TOPAZES
TRAPEZE
TRIZOIC
TWIZZLE
UPERIZE
ZABURRO
ZACATON
ZADRUGA
ZAMARRA
ZAMARRO
ZAMORIN
ZAMOUSE
ZAREEBA
ZEBRINE
ZEBRULE
ZEBURRO
ZETETIC
ZIMARRA
ZINCATE
ZINCITE
ZINCOUS
ZINOBER
ZIRCITE
ZOARIUM
ZOISTIC
ZOOECIA

17
ADONIZE
AGATIZE
AGENIZE
AGONIZE
ALGAZEL
ANODIZE
ASSIZED
BAZZITE
BEZZANT
BUZZIER
BUZZIES
CRIZZLE
CRIZZEL
CROZZLE
DAZZLED
DENIZEN
DIARIZE
DIAZINE
DIAZOLE
DIZAINE
DIZZARD
DIZZIED
DOZENER
DOZIEST
DOZZLED
DUALIZE
EGOTIZE
ELEGIZE
GALLIZE
GARNETZ
GAUZIER
GAZELLE
GAZETTE
GIZZARD
GLAIZIE
GLAZIER
GONZALO
GOZZARD
GRAZIER
GROTZEN
GROZART
GRUNZIE
GUANIZE
GUAZUTI
GUEREZA

GUZERAT
GUZZLED
IDOLIZE
INDAZOL
IODIZER
IOTIZED
IRIDIZE
LOZENGE
MUZZIER
MUZZLER
ODORIZE
ORGANZA
OUTBUZZ
OUTGAZE
OZONIDE
PALAZZI
PALAZZO
PUZZLER
RESIZED
SEIZING
SIZINGS
SNEEZED
SNOOZED
TZIGANE
UNGLAZE
UNSIZED
UNZONED
ZESTING
ZEUGITE
ZINGANA
ZINGANO
ZINGARA
ZINGARI
ZINGARO
ZINSANG
ZONATED
ZONITID
ZONURID
ZOOGENE
ZOOGLER
ZOOIDAL
ZORGITE

16
ADAZZLE
ALIZARI
ARIENZO
ASSEIZE
ASSIZER
ASSIZES
AZAROLE
AZELATE
AZORITE
AZOTATE
AZOTINE
AZOTITE
AZOTOUS
AZULENE
AZULITE
AZUREAN
AZURINE
AZURITE
AZUROUS
DAZZLER
DIZZIER
DRIZZLE
DUREZZA
ENOLIZE
ENTOZOA
GIZZERN
GRIZZLE
GUZZLER
IONIZER
IRONIZE
LAZARET

LAZIEST
LIONIZE
NOUNIZE
NUZZLED
OOZIEST
OSAZONE
OUTRAZE
OUTSIZE
OZONATE
OZONOUS
RANTIZE
RAZZING
REALIZE
RESEIZE
RESIZER
RETZIAN
RITZIER
SEIZURE
SELTZER
SIZEINE
SIZIEST
SIZZARD
SIZZING
SIZZLED
SNEEZER
SNOOZER
SNOOZLE
SOZZLED
STANZAS
STATIZE
SURSIZE
TAILZEE
TAILZIE
TERZINA
TETRAZO
TRIAZIN
TRISAZO
TUILZIE
TZARINA
TZONTLE
UNITIZE
UNSEIZE
URAZINE
URAZOLE
UTILIZE
ZANELLA
ZATTARE
ZEALOUS
ZELATOR
ZENTNER
ZEOLITE
ZITTERN
ZOARIAL
ZOISITE
ZONELET
ZONULAR
ZONULET
ZOOLITE
ZOONIST
ZOONITE
ZOONULE
ZORILLA
ZORILLE

15
ALTEZZA
NOZZLER
OZONIZE
SIZZLER
SNOZZLE
SNUZZLE
TIZZIES
ZEROIZE
ZIZZLED

ALPHABETICAL LIST OF 8-LETTER WORDS

ACTIVIZE
ADONIZED
AGATIZED
AGNIZING
AGONIZED
AGONIZER
AKAZGINE
ALBIZZIA
ALBRONZE
ALCAZABA
ALCAZAVA
ALDOLIZE
ALGUAZIL
ALIZARIN
ALKALIZE
ALKYLIZE
ALMUERZO
AMAZEFUL
AMINOAZO
AMORTIZE
ANALGIZE
ANALYZED
ANALYZER
ANGELIZE
ANNALIZE
ANODIZED
ANTICIZE
ANTIZOEA
APHETIZE
APHORIZE
APPETIZE
APPRIZAL
APPRIZER
APRENDIZ
ARANZADA
ARBORIZE
ARCHAIZE
ARMOZEEN
ARMOZINE
ARRHIZAL
ASSIZING
ASTATIZE
ATHEIZER
ATHETIZE
ATMOLYZE
ATOMIZED
ATOMIZER
ATTICIZE
AUTOLYZE
AVESTRUZ
AVIANIZE
AZOBLACK
AZOGREEN
AZOHUMIC
AZOIMIDE
AZOTEMIA
AZOTIZED
AZOTURIA
BACONIZE
BAETZNER
BAKELIZE
BAPTIZED
BAPTIZEE
BAPTIZER
BAROMETZ
BARTIZAN
BARUKHZY
BEDAZZLE
BENZENYL
BENZIDIN
BENZILIC
BENZOATE
BENZOBIS
BENZYLIC
BEZANTEE
BEZONIAN
BEZZLING
BIBENZYL
BIGAMIZE
BIQUARTZ
BIZZARRO
BLAZONED
BLAZONER
BLAZONRY
BLIZZARD
BLOWZIER
BLOWZING
BOMBAZET
BOTANIZE
BRACOZZO
BRAGOZZO
BOZZETTO
BRAZENED
BRAZENLY
BRAZIERY
BREEZIER
BREEZING
BREEZILY
BRITZSKA
BROMIZER
BRONZIFY
BRONZING
BRONZINE
BRONZITE
BROOZLED
BRUNIZEM
BRYOZOAN
BRYOZOON
BRYOZOUM
BULLDOZE
BUZZIEST
CACOZEAL
CACOZYME
CALABAZA
CALABOZO
CALORIZE
CALZOONS
CANALIZE
CANONIZE
CANZONET
CAPONIZE
CAPSIZAL
CAPSIZED
CARBAZIC
CARBAZIN
CARROZZA
CATALYZE
CATZERIE
CHALAZAE
CHALAZAL
CHALAZAS
CHINTZES
CHUTZPAH
CINEMIZE
CIVILIZE
COALIZED
COENZYME
COGNIZED
COGNIZEE
COGNIZER
COGNIZOR
COLONIZE
COMPRIZE
CORONIZE
COZENAGE
COZENING
COZINESS
CRAZEDLY
CRAZIEST
CRAZYCAT
CREOLIZE
CRUELIZE
CRUZEIRO
CURARIZE
CUTINIZE
CYANIZED
CYTOZOIC
CYTOZOON
CYTOZYME
CZAREVNA
CZARITZA
DANDYIZE
DAZZLING
DECATIZE
DEGLAZED
DEIONIZE
DEMONIZE
DENAZIFY
DENIZATE
DEPUTIZE
DETONIZE
DEVILIZE
DIALYZED
DIALYZER
DIAZOATE
DIAZOTIC
DIBENZYL
DIGITIZE
DISDIAZO
DISPRIZE
DISSEIZE
DIVINIZE
DIZENING
DIZZIEST
DIZZYING
DONZELLA
DOUZAINE
DOUZEPER
DOZINESS
DRIZZLED
DUALIZED
DUELLIZE
DYNAMIZE
EBONIZED
ECHOIZED
ECTOZOAN
ECTOZOIC
EGOTIZED
ELEGIZED
EMBEZZLE
EMBLAZED
EMBLAZER
EMBLAZON
EMBOLIZE
EMBRONZE
ENERGIZE
ENFRENZY
ENTOZOAL
ENTOZOAN
ENTOZOIC
ENTOZOON
ENZOOTIC
EOZOONAL
EPIZOOTY
EQUALIZE
ERGOTIZE
ERZAHLER
ESTERIZE
ETERNIZE
ETHERIZE
ETHICIZE
ETIOLIZE
EULOGIZE
EUPHUIZE
EXORCIZE
EXORDIZE
FABULIZE
FARADIZE
FATALIZE
FEAZINGS
FEMINIZE
FIBERIZE
FIGURIZE
FILMIZED
FINALIZE
FIZZIEST
FIZZLING
FLOOZIES
FLUIDIZE
FOCALIZE
FOOZLING
FORMAZAN
FORMAZYL
FORUMIZE
FOZINESS
FRAZZLED
FREEZING
FRENZIED
FRENZIES
FRENZILY
FRIEZING
FRIZETTE
FRIZZIER
FRIZZILY
FRIZZING
FRIZZLED
FRIZZLER
FROWZIER
FROWZILY
FROWZLED
FROZENLY
FUELIZER
FURZETOP
FUZZBALL
FUZZIEST
FUZZTAIL
GARBANZO
GARVANZO
GAUZIEST
GAZABOES
GAZEBOES
GAZELESS
GAZELLES
GAZEMENT
GAZETTAL
GAZETTED
GAZINGLY
GAZOGENE
GAZPACHO
GAZZETTA
GHAWAZEE
GIANTIZE
GIZZENED
GLAZIERS
GLAZIERY
GLAZIEST
GOYAZITE
GRANDEZA
GRAZIERY
GRAZIOSO
GRIZZLED
GRIZZLER
GUZZLING
GWERZIOU
HALAZONE
HALUTZIM
HAZARDER
HAZARDRY
HAZELNUT
HAZINESS
HAZNADAR
HAZZANUT
HEMOZOON
HEPATIZE
HEREZELD
HERTZIAN
HETERIZE
HOACTZIN
HOLOZOIC
HOMILIZE
HOWITZER
HUMANIZE
HUMORIZE
HYDRAZIN
HYLOZOIC
HYPOZOAN
HYPOZOIC
IDEALIZE
IDIOZOME
IDOLIZED
IDOLIZER
IMIDAZOL
IMMUNIZE
INDAZOLE
INDENIZE
INFAMIZE
INSULIZE
IODIZING
IOTIZING
IRIDIZED
ISOZOOID
ITEMIZED
ITEMIZER
JANIZARY
JAROVIZE
JAZERANT
JAZZIEST
JECORIZE
JEZEKITE
JUBILIZE
JUDAIZER
KAMIKAZE
KATALYZE
KETONIZE
KEVUTZAH
KIBITZER
KREUTZER
LABILIZE
LACONIZE
LAICIZED
LAICIZER
LATINIZE
LAZAROLE
LAZARONE
LAZAROUS
LAZINESS
LAZULITE
LAZURITE
LAZYBACK
LAZYBIRD
LAZYBONE
LAZYLEGS
LEGALIZE
LHERZITE
LINENIZE
LIONIZED
LIONIZER
LOCALIZE
LOGICIZE
LOZENGED

LOZENGER
LUNATIZE
MACARIZE
MAGADIZE
MAGAZINE
MAGAZINY
MAJORIZE
MALGUZAR
MARKAZES
MARZIPAN
MATEZITE
MAXIMIZE
MAZAGRAN
MAZALGIA
MAZARINE
MAZINESS
MAZOPEXY
MAZOURKA
MEDALIZE
MELANIZE
MELODIZE
MEMORIZE
MESOZOAN
MESTIZOS
METALIZE
METAZOAL
METAZOAN
METAZOEA
METAZOIC
METAZOON
METRAZOL
MEZEREON
MEZEREUM
MEZQUITE
MEZUZAHS
MEZUZOTH
MICASIZE
MICROZOA
MINIMIZE
MISPRIZE
MITZVAHS
MITZVOTH
MIZZLING
MOBILIZE
MODALIZE
MODELIZE
MODULIZE
MONAZITE
MONETIZE
MONODIZE
MONOZOAN
MONOZOIC
MORALIZE
MOTORIZE
MOUZOUNA
MOZEMIZE
MUSTAFUZ
MUZZIEST
MUZZLING
NAKEDIZE
NAMAZLIK
NASALIZE
NATURIZE
NAZIFIED
NEBULIZE
NICOTIZE
NIZAMATE
NODULIZE
NOTARIZE
NOVELIZE
NUZZLING
OBELIZED
OOLOGIZE
OOZINESS
OPALIZED
OPSONIZE
OPTIMIZE
ORANGIZE
ORGANIZE
ORMUZINE
ORYZANIN
ORYZENIN
OSMAZOME
OUTBLAZE
OUTSIZED
OVERGAZE
OVERSIZE
OXIDIZED
OXIDIZER
OZARKITE
OZOBROME
OZONIZED
OZONIZER
PAEANIZE
PAGANIZE
PALATIZE
PANZOISM
PANZOOTY
PAPALIZE
PARALYZE
PARTIZAN
PATINIZE
PAVONIZE
PECTIZED
PELORIZE
PENALIZE
PEPTIZED
PEPTIZER
PEREZONE
PETUNTZE
PEZANTIC
PEZIZOID
PHENAZIN
PIAZZAED
PIAZZIAN
PIZZERIA
POETIZED
POETIZER
POLARIZE
POLEMIZE
POLICIZE
POLITIZE
POLYZOAN
POLYZOIC
POLYZOON
PREZONAL
PRIZABLE
PRIZEMAN
PRIZEMEN
PROTOZOA
PTYALIZE
PUPILIZE
PUZZLING
PYRAZINE
PYRAZOLE
PYRITIZE
QUANTIZE
QUARTZIC
QUATORZE
QUEZALES
QUIZZERY
QUIZZIFY
QUIZZING
QUIZZISH
QUIZZISM
QUIZZITY
RAADZAAL
RACEMIZE
RADZIMIR
RAMBOOZE
RAZBOOCH
RAZEEING
RAZORMAN
REALIZED
REALIZER
REGALIZE
REGULIZE
RENDZINA
RENOVIZE
RESEIZER
RESINIZE
RESIZING
RETINIZE
RHIZOBIA
RHIZOGEN
RHIZOIDAL
RHIZOMIC
RHIZOPOD
RHIZOTIC
RIBAZUBA
RITZIEST
RIVALIZE
RIZIFORM
RIZZOMED
ROBOTIZE
ROYALIZE
RUMBOOZE
RURALIZE
SALINIZE
SANITIZE
SARRAZIN
SATANIZE
SATINIZE
SATIRIZE
SAVAGIZE
SCHERZOS
SCHIZOID
SCHIZONT
SCHIZTIC
SCHMALTZ
SCHMALZY
SCHMOOZE
SEIZABLE
SERENIZE
SEVERIZE
SFORZATO
SHAATNEZ
SHAHZADA
SIEROZEM
SILICIZE
SIMILIZE
SIMONIZE
SIMULIZE
SINAPIZE
SIRENIZE
SITZMARK
SIZEABLE
SIZINESS
SIZYGIUM
SIZZLING
SMORZATO
SNEEZING
SNOOZING
SOBERIZE
SOLARIZE
SOLECIZE
SOLONETZ
SONORIZE
SORORIZE
SPITZKOP
SPRITZER
SPUILZIE
SQUEEZED
SQUEEZER
STANITZA
STANZAED
STANZAIC
STARGAZE
STOLZITE
STYLIZED
STYLIZER
SUBERIZE
SUBSIZAR
SUBZONAL
SUZERAIN
SWIZZLER
SYNERIZE
SYZYGIAL
SYZYGIES
SYZYGIUM
SZLACHTA
SZOPELKA
TAILZIED
TEMPLIZE
TERRAZZO
TERZETTO
TETANIZE
TETRAZIN
TEZKIRAH
THEORIZE
THIAZINE
THIAZOLE
THIOZONE
THRONIZE
TIMAZITE
TODDYIZE
TONICIZE
TOPAZINE
TOPAZITE
TOTALIZE
TRAPEZIA
TRIAZANE
TRIAZINE
TRIAZOLE
TRISTEZA
TRIZOMAL
TROTCOZY
TUBERIZE
TUTORIZE
TWEEZERS
TWEEZING
TZEDAKAH
UNBAIZED
UNCRAZED
UNDAZZLE
UNFROZEN
UNGLAZED
UNIONIZE
UNMUZZLE
UNPUZZLE
UNVIZARD
URBANIZE
VALORIZE
VAMMAZSA
VAPORIZE
VELARIZE
VENALIZE
VENOMIZE
VITALIZE
VIZARDED
VIZCACHA
VIZIRATE
VIZIRIAL
VIZORING
VOCALIZE
VOLTZINE
VOLTZITE
VOWELIZE
UTILIZED
UTILIZER
WALTZING
WAZIRATE
WEAZENED
WHEEZIER
WHEEZILY
WHEEZING
WHIZBANG
WHIZZING
WINZEMAN
WINZEMEN
WIZARDLY
WIZARDRY
WOOZIEST
WRIZZLED
WOMANIZE
WURTZITE
WUZZLING
YAHRZEIT
YAROVIZE
YOTACIZE
ZAIBATSU
ZAMBOMBA
ZAMINDAR
ZAMORINE
ZAMPOGNA
ZANDMOLE
ZAPATERO
ZARATITE
ZARZUELA
ZASTRUGA
ZASTRUGI
ZEALOTIC
ZEALOTRY
ZEALOUSY
ZEBRINNY
ZECCHINO
ZELATRIX
ZEMINDAR
ZEMSTVOS
ZENITHAL
ZEOLITIC
ZEOSCOPE
ZEPHYRUS
ZEPPELIN
ZERUMBET
ZETACISM
ZIBELINE
ZIGGURAT
ZIGZAGGY
ZIMBABWE
ZIMBALON
ZINCKING
ZINCURET
ZIPHIOID
ZIPPIEST
ZIRCONIA
ZIRCONIC
ZIRCONYL
ZIZZLING
ZOANTHID
ZODIACAL
ZOEAFORM
ZOETROPE
ZOIATRIA
ZOLOTNIK
ZOMBIISM
ZONALITY
ZONATION
ZONELESS
ZONUROID
ZOOBLAST
ZOOCHEMY
ZOOCHORE
ZOOECIAL
ZOOECIUM
ZOOGLOEA
ZOOGRAFT
ZOOLATER
ZOOLATRY
ZOOLITIC
ZOOLOGIC
ZOOMANIA
ZOOMETRY
ZOOMIMIC
ZOOMORPH

ZOONITIC
ZOONOSES
ZOONOSIS
ZOONOTIC
ZOOPERAL
ZOOPHILE
ZOOPHILY
ZOOPHORI
ZOOPHYTE
ZOOSCOPY
ZOOSPORE
ZOOTHOME
ZOOTOMIC
ZOOTOXIN
ZOPILOTE
ZORRILLO
ZORTZICO
ZUCCHINI
ZUGZWANG
ZUPANATE
ZWIEBACK
ZYGAENID
ZYGODONT
ZYGOMATA
ZYGOTENE
ZYGOTOID
ZYMOGENE
ZYMOLOGY

POSITIONAL ORDER LIST OF 8-LETTER WORDS

ZAIBATSU
ZAMBOMBA
ZAMINDAR
ZAMORINE
ZAMPOGNA
ZANDMOLE
ZAPATERO
ZARATITE
ZARZUELA
ZASTRUGA
ZASTRUGI
ZEALOTIC
ZEALOTRY
ZEALOUSY
ZEBRINNY
ZECCHINO
ZELATRIX
ZEMINDAR
ZEMSTVOS
ZENITHAL
ZEOLITIC
ZEOSCOPE
ZEPHYRUS
ZEPPELIN
ZERUMBET
ZETACISM
ZIBELINE
ZIGGURAT
ZIGZAGGY
ZIMBABWE
ZIMBALON
ZINCKING
ZINCURET
ZIPHIOID
ZIPPIEST
ZIRCONIA
ZIRCONIC
ZIRCONYL
ZIZZLING
ZOANTHID
ZODIACAL
ZOEAFORM
ZOETROPE
ZOIATRIA
ZOLOTNIK
ZOMBIISM
ZONALITY
ZONATION
ZONELESS
ZONUROID
ZOOBLAST
ZOOCHEMY
ZOOCHORE
ZOOECIAL
ZOOECIUM
ZOOGLOEA
ZOOGRAFT
ZOOLATER
ZOOLATRY
ZOOLITIC
ZOOLOGIC
ZOOMANIA
ZOOMETRY
ZOOMIMIC
ZOOMORPH
ZOONITIC
ZOONOSES
ZOONOSIS
ZOONOTIC
ZOOPERAL
ZOOPHILE
ZOOPHILY
ZOOPHORI
ZOOPHYTE
ZOOSCOPY
ZOOSPERM
ZOOSPORE
ZOOTHOME
ZOOTOMIC
ZOOTOXIN
ZOPILOTE
ZORRILLO
ZORTZICO
ZUCCHINI
ZUGZWANG
ZUPANATE
ZWIEBACK
ZYGAENID
ZYGODONT
ZYGOMATA
ZYGOTENE
ZYGOTOID
ZYMOGENE
ZYMOLOGY

AZOBLACK
AZOGREEN
AZOHUMIC
AZOIMIDE
AZOTEMIA
AZOTIZED
AZOTURIA
CZAREVNA
CZARITZA
OZARKITE
OZOBROME
OZONIZED
OZONIZER
SZLACHTA
SZOPELKA
TZEDAKAH

BEZANTEE
BEZONIAN
BEZZLING
BIZZARRO
BOZZETTO
BUZZIEST
CAZIQUE
COZENAGE
COZENING
COZINESS
DAZZLING
DIZENING
DIZZIEST
DIZZYING
DOZINESS
ENZOOTIC
EOZOONAL
ERZAHLER
FIZZIEST
FIZZLING
FOZINESS
FUZZBALL
FUZZIEST
FUZZTAIL
GAZABOES
GAZEBOES
GAZELESS
GAZELLES
GAZEMENT
GAZETTAL
GAZETTED
GAZINGLY
GAZOGENE
GAZPACHO
GAZZETTA
GIZZENED
GUZZLING
HAZARDER
HAZARDRY
HAZELNUT
HAZINESS
HAZNADAR
HAZZANUT
JAZERANT
JAZZIEST
JEZEKITE
LAZAROLE
LAZARONE
LAZAROUS
LAZINESS
LAZULITE
LAZURITE
LAZYBACK
LAZYBIRD
LAZYBONE
LAZYLEGS
LOZENGED
LOZENGER
MAZAGRAN
MAZALGIA
MAZARINE
MAZINESS
MAZOPEXY
MAZOURKA
MEZEREON
MEZEREUM
MEZQUITE
MEZUZAHS
MEZUZOTH
MIZZLING
MOZEMIZE
MOZEMIZE
MUZZIEST
MUZZLING
NAZIFIED
NIZAMATE
NUZZLING
OOZINESS
PEZANTIC
PEZIZOID
PIZZERIA
PUZZLING
RAZBOOCH
RAZEEING
RAZORMAN
RIZIFORM
RIZZOMED
SIZEABLE
SIZINESS
SIZYGIUM
SIZZLING
SUZERAIN
SYZYGIAL
SYZYGIES
SYZYGIUM
TEZKIRAH
VIZARDED
VIZCACHA
VIZIRATE
VIZIRIAL
VIZORING
WAZIRATE
WIZARDLY
WIZARDRY
WUZZLING
ZIZZLING
ZYZYPHUS

AKAZGINE
ALIZARIN
AMAZEFUL
BENZENYL
BENZIDIN
BENZILIC
BENZOATE
BENZOBIS
BENZYLIC
BEZZLING
BIZZARRO
BLAZONED
BLAZONER
BLAZONRY
BLIZZARD
BOZZETTO
BRAZENED
BRAZENLY
BRAZIERY
BUZZIEST
CALZOONS
CANZONET
CATZERIE
CRAZEDLY
CRAZIEST
CRAZYCAT
CRUZEIRO
DAZZLING
DIAZOATE
DIAZOTIC
DIZZIEST
DIZZYING
DONZELLA
DOUZAINE
DOUZEPER
DRIZZLED
EPIZOOTY
FEAZINGS
FIZZIEST
FIZZLING
FOOZLING
FRAZZLED
FRIZETTE
FRIZZIER
FRIZZILY
FRIZZING
FRIZZLED
FRIZZLER
FROZENLY
FURZETOP
FUZZBALL
FUZZIEST
FUZZTAIL
GAUZIEST
GAZZETTA
GIZZENED
GLAZIERS
GLAZIERY
GLAZIEST
GRAZIERY
GRAZIOSO
GRIZZLED
GRIZZLER
GUZZLING
HAZZANUT
ISOZOOID
JAZZIEST
MARZIPAN
MITZVAHS
MITZVOTH
MIZZLING
MOUZOUNA
MUZZIEST
MUZZLING
NUZZLING
ORYZANIN
ORYZENIN
PANZOISM
PANZOOTY
PIAZZAED
PIAZZIAN
PIZZERIA
PREZONAL
PRIZABLE
PRIZEMAN
PRIZEMEN
PUZZLING
QUEZALES
QUIZZERY
QUIZZIFY
QUIZZING
QUIZZISH
QUIZZISM
QUIZZITY
RADZIMIR
RHIZOBIA
RHIZOGEN
RHIZOIDAL
RHIZOMIC
RHIZOPOD
RHIZOTIC
RITZIEST
RIZZOMED
SEIZABLE
SITZMARK

SIZZLING
SUBZONAL
SWIZZLER
TERZETTO
TRIZOMAL
WEAZENED
WHIZBANG
WHIZZING
WINZEMAN
WINZEMEN
WOOZIEST
WRIZZLED
WUZZLING
ZARZUELA
ZIGZAGGY
ZIZZLING
ZUGZWANG

AGNIZING
ALBIZZIA
ALCAZABA
ALCAZAVA
ANTIZOEA
ARANZADA
ARMOZEEN
ARMOZINE
ASSIZING
BAETZNER
BEDAZZLE
BLIZZARD
BLOWZIER
BLOWZING
BREEZIER
BREEZING
BREEZILY
BRITZSKA
BRONZIFY
BRONZING
BRONZINE
BRONZITE
BROOZLED
BRYOZOAN
BRYOZOON
BRYOZOUM
CACOZEAL
CACOZYME
CHUTZPAH
COENZYME
CYTOZOIC
CYTOZOON
CYTOZYME
DENAZIFY
DENIZATE
DRIZZLED
ECTOZOAN
ECTOZOIC
EMBEZZLE
ENTOZOAL
ENTOZOAN
ENTOZOIC
ENTOZOON
FLOOZIES
FRAZZLED
FREEZING
FRENZIED
FRENZIES
FRENZILY
FRIEZING
FRIZZIER
FRIZZILY
FRIZZING
FRIZZLED
FRIZZLER
FROWZIER
FROWZILY
FROWZLED
GOYAZITE
GRIZZLED
GRIZZLER
GWERZIOU
HALAZONE
HEMOZOON
HEREZELD
HERTZIAN
HOLOZOIC
HYLOZOIC
HYPOZOAN
HYPOZOIC
IDIOZOME
INDAZOLE
IODIZING
IOTIZING
JANIZARY
LHERZITE
MAGAZINE
MAGAZINY
MATEZITE
MESOZOAN
METAZOAL
METAZOAN
METAZOEA
METAZOIC
METAZOON
MEZUZAHS
MEZUZOTH
MONAZITE
MONOZOAN
MONOZOIC
NAMAZLIK
ORMUZINE
OSMAZOME
PEREZONE
PEZIZOID
PIAZZAED
PIAZZIAN
POLYZOAN
POLYZOIC
POLYZOON
PYRAZINE
PYRAZOLE
QUIZZERY
QUIZZIFY
QUIZZING
QUIZZISH
QUIZZISM
QUIZZITY
RAADZAAL
RENDZINA
RESIZING
RIBAZUBA
SCHIZOID
SCHIZONT
SCHIZTIC
SFORZATO
SHAHZADA
SMORZATO
SNEEZING
SNOOZING
SPITZKOP
STANZAED
STANZAIC
STOLZITE
SWIZZLER
TAILZIED
THIAZINE
THIAZOLE
THIOZONE
TIMAZITE
TOPAZINE
TOPAZITE
TRIAZANE
TRIAZINE
TRIAZOLE
TWEEZERS
TWEEZING
UNDAZZLE
UNMUZZLE
UNPUZZLE
UNVIZARD
VOLTZINE
VOLTZITE
WALTZING
WHEEZIER
WHEEZILY
WHEEZING
WHIZZING
WRIZZLED
WURTZITE
YAHRZEIT
ZORTZICO

ADONIZED
AGATIZED
AGONIZED
AGONIZER
ALBIZZIA
ALGUAZIL
ANALYZED
ANALYZER
ANODIZED
APPRIZAL
APPRIZER
ARRHIZAL
ATHEIZER
ATOMIZED
ATOMIZER
AZOTIZED
BAPTIZED
BAPTIZEE
BAPTIZER
BARTIZAN
BEDAZZLE
BIBENZYL
BOMBAZET
BRACOZZO
BRAGOZZO
BROMIZER
BRUNIZEM
CADENZA
CAPSIZAL
CARBAZIC
CARBAZIN
CARROZZA
CHALAZAE
CHALAZAL
CHALAZAS
CHINTZES
COALIZED
COGNIZED
COGNIZEE
COGNIZER
COGNIZOR
CYANIZED
DEGLAZED
DIALYZED
DIALYZER
DIBENZYL
DUALIZED
EBONIZED
ECHOIZED
EGOTIZED
ELEGIZED
EMBEZZLE
EMBLAZED
EMBLAZER
EMBLAZON
FILMIZED
FORMAZAN
FORMAZYL
FUELIZER
GHAWAZEE
HALUTZIM
HOACTZIN
HOWITZER
HYDRAZIN
IDOLIZED
IDOLIZER
IMIDAZOL
IRIDIZED
ITEMIZED
ITEMIZER
JUDAIZER
KEVUTZAH
KIBITZER
KREUTZER
LAICIZED
LAICIZER
LIONIZED
LIONIZER
MALGUZAR
MARKAZES
MESTIZOS
METRAZOL
MICROZOA
OBELIZED
OPALIZED
OUTSIZED
OXIDIZED
OXIDIZER
OZONIZED
OZONIZER
PARTIZAN
PECTIZED
PEPTIZED
PEPTIZER
PHENAZIN
POETIZED
POETIZER
PROTOZOA
QUARTZIC
REALIZED
REALIZER
RESEIZER
SARRAZIN
SCHERZOS
SIEROZEM
SPRITZER
SPUILZIE
SQUEEZED
SQUEEZER
STYLIZED
STYLIZER
SUBSIZAR
TERRAZZO
TETRAZIN
TRAPEZIA
UNBAIZED
UNCRAZED
UNDAZZLE
UNFROZEN
UNGLAZED
UNMUZZLE
UNPUZZLE
UTILIZED
UTILIZER
VAMMAZSA

ACTIVIZE
ALBRONZE
ALDOLIZE
ALKALIZE
ALKYLIZE
ALMUERZO
AMINOAZO
AMORTIZE
ANALGIZE
ANGELIZE
ANNALIZE
ANTICIZE
APHETIZE
APHORIZE
APPETIZE
ARBORIZE
ARCHAIZE
ASTATIZE
ATHETIZE
ATMOLYZE
ATTICIZE
AUTOLYZE
AVIANIZE
BACONIZE
BAKELIZE
BARUKHZY
BIGAMIZE
BOTANIZE
BRACOZZO
BRAGOZZO
BULLDOZE
CALABAZA
CALABOZO
CALORIZE
CANALIZE
CANONIZE
CAPONIZE
CARROZZA
CATALYZE
CINEMIZE
CIVILIZE
COLONIZE
COMPRIZE
CORONIZE
CREOLIZE
CRUELIZE
CURARIZE
CUTINIZE
CZARITZA
DANDYIZE
DECATIZE
DEIONIZE
DEMONIZE
DEPUTIZE
DETONIZE
DEVILIZE
DIGITIZE
DISDIAZO
DISPRIZE
DISSEIZE
DIVINIZE
DUELLIZE
DYNAMIZE
EMBOLIZE
EMBRONZE
ENERGIZE
ENFRENZY
EQUALIZE
ERGOTIZE
ESTERIZE
ETERNIZE
ETHERIZE
ETHICIZE
ETIOLIZE
EULOGIZE
EUPHUIZE
EXORCIZE
EXORDIZE
FABULIZE
FARADIZE
FATALIZE
FEMINIZE
FIBERIZE
FIGURIZE
FINALIZE
FLUIDIZE
FOCALIZE
FORUMIZE

GARBANZO
GARVANZO
GIANTIZE
GRANDEZA
HEPATIZE
HETERIZE
HOMILIZE
HUMANIZE
HUMORIZE
IDEALIZE
IMMUNIZE
INDENIZE
INFAMIZE
INSULIZE
JAROVIZE
JECORIZE
JUBILIZE
KAMIKAZE
KATALYZE
KETONIZE
LABILIZE
LACONIZE
LATINIZE
LEGALIZE
LINENIZE
LOCALIZE
LOGICIZE
LUNATIZE
MACARIZE
MAGADIZE
MAJORIZE
MAXIMIZE
MEDALIZE
MELANIZE
MELODIZE
MEMORIZE
METALIZE
MICASIZE
MINIMIZE
MISPRIZE
MOBILIZE
MODALIZE
MODELIZE
MODULIZE
MONETIZE
MONODIZE
MORALIZE
MOTORIZE
NAKEDIZE
NASALIZE
NATURIZE
NEBULIZE
NICOTIZE
NODULIZE
NOTARIZE
NOVELIZE
OOLOGIZE
OPSONIZE
OPTIMIZE
ORANGIZE
ORGANIZE
OUTBLAZE
OVERGAZE
OVERSIZE
PAEANIZE
PAGANIZE
PALATIZE
PAPALIZE
PARALYZE
PATINIZE
PAVONIZE
PELORIZE
PENALIZE
PETUNTZE
POLARIZE
POLEMIZE
POLICIZE
POLITIZE
PTYALIZE
PUPILIZE
PYRITIZE
QUANTIZE
QUATORZE
RACEMIZE
RAMBOOZE
REGALIZE
REGULIZE
RENOVIZE
RESINIZE
RETINIZE
RIVALIZE
ROBOTIZE
ROYALIZE
RUMBOOZE
RURALIZE
SALINIZE
SANITIZE
SATANIZE
SATINIZE
SATIRIZE
SAVAGIZE
SCHMALZY
SCHMOOZE
SERENIZE
SEVERIZE
SILICIZE
SIMILIZE
SIMONIZE
SIMULIZE
SINAPIZE
SIRENIZE
SOBERIZE
SOLARIZE
SOLECIZE
SONORIZE
SORORIZE
STANITZA
STARGAZE
SUBERIZE
SYNERIZE
TEMPLIZE
TERRAZZO
TETANIZE
THEORIZE
THRONIZE
TODDYIZE
TONICIZE
TOTALIZE
TRISTEZA
TROTCOZY
TUBERIZE
TUTORIZE
UNIONIZE
URBANIZE
VALORIZE
VAPORIZE
VELARIZE
VENALIZE
VENOMIZE
VITALIZE
VOCALIZE
VOWELIZE
WOMANIZE
YAROVIZE
YOTACIZE

APRENDIZ
AVESTRUZ
BAROMETZ
BIQUARTZ
MUSTAFUZ
SCHMALTZ
SHAATNEZ
SOLONETZ

SCORING ORDER LIST OF 8-LETTER WORDS

31
MAZOPEXY
QUIZZIFY

29
BARUKHZY

28
BIQUARTZ
JEZEKITE
LAZYBACK
MAXIMIZE
MEZQUITE
QUARTZIC
QUIZZERY
QUIZZISH
QUIZZITY
ZWIEBACK

27
CHUTZPAH
CYTOZYME
HYPOZOIC
JANIZARY
JAROVIZE
KEVUTZAH
QUIZZISM
SCHMALZY
SQUEEZED
VIZCACHA
ZOOCHEMY

26
CACOZYME
EQUALIZE
EXORCIZE
FROWZILY
JECORIZE
JUBILIZE
MAJORIZE
OXIDIZED
QUANTIZE
QUATORZE
QUEZALES
QUIZZING
SQUEEZER
SYZYGIUM
WHEEZILY
WHIZBANG
ZIMBABWE
ZYMOLOGY

25
AZOBLACK
BRONZIFY
EXORDIZE
FORMAZYL
GAZPACHO
HYLOZOIC
HYPOZOAN
JUDAIZER
MITZVAHS
MITZVOTH
OXIDIZER
SPITZKOP
TZEDAKAH
ZAMBOMBA
ZEPHYRUS
ZOOPHILY
ZOOPHYTE

24
ALKYLIZE
AZOHUMIC
BENZYLIC
BIBENZYL
BRYOZOUM
COENZYME
CRAZYCAT
CYTOZOIC
DENAZIFY
FROWZLED
GHAWAZEE
HAZARDRY
HYDRAZIN
JAZERANT
KATALYZE
POLYZOIC
RAZBOOCH
RHIZOMIC
SCHIZTIC
SCHMALTZ
SCHMOOZE
SHAHZADA
SYZYGIAL
SYZYGIES
TEZKIRAH
VAMMAZSA
WHEEZING
WIZARDLY
WIZARDRY
ZECCHINO
ZELATRIX
ZINCKING
ZOOMORPH
ZOOSCOPY
ZOOTOXIN
ZUCCHINI

23
BAKELIZE
BLOWZING
BOMBAZET
BRITZSKA
CARBAZIC
CARBAZIDE
COMPRIZE
CRAZEDLY
CYANIZED
DIBENZYL
DYNAMIZE
ECHOIZED
ENFRENZY
FILMIZED
FRENZILY
FROWZIER
FROZENLY
HOWITZER
JAZZIEST
KIBITZER
LAZYBIRD
MAGAZINY
MARKAZES
MAZOURKA
NAMAZLIK
RHIZOPOD
SCHIZOID
SITZMARK
SIZYGIUM
SZOPELKA
VOWELIZE
WHEEZIER
WHIZZING
YAHRZEIT
YAROVIZE
ZIPHIOID
ZOMBIISM
ZOOMIMIC
ZYGOMATA
ZYMOGENE

22
ACTIVIZE
AKAZGINE
ALCAZAVA
AMAZEFUL
APHETIZE
APHORIZE
ARCHAIZE
ATMOLYZE
BAPTIZED
BENZENYL
BIGAMIZE
BLAZONRY
BLOWZIER
BRAZENLY
BRAZIERY
BREEZILY
BRYOZOAN
BRYOZOON
CAPSIZED
CATALYZE
CHALAZAE
CHALAZAL
CHALAZAS
CHINTZES
CIVILIZE
CYTOZOON
CZAREVNA
DANDYIZE
DIALYZED
EMBLAZED
EPIZOOTY
ETHICIZE
EUPHUIZE
FABULIZE
FEMINIZE
FIBERIZE
FOCALIZE
FORMAZAN
FORUMIZE
FRIZZILY
FURZETOP
GAZINGLY
HALUTZIM
HEMOZOON
HEPATIZE
HOACTZIN
HOLOZOIC
HOMILIZE

HUMANIZE
HUMORIZE
INFAMIZE
KAMIKAZE
LAZYBONE
MUSTAFUZ
NAKEDIZE
PANZOOTY
PARALYZE
PAVONIZE
PECTIZED
PEPTIZED
PHENAZIN
POLYZOAN
POLYZOON
PTYALIZE
PYRAZINE
PYRAZOLE
PYRITIZE
RHIZOBIA
RHIZOIDAL
RHIZOTIC
RIZIFORM
SCHERZOS
SCHIZONT
SZLACHTA
TODDYIZE
TROTCOZY
VAPORIZE
VENOMIZE
VIZARDED
VOCALIZE
WINZEMAN
WINZEMEN
WOMANIZE
YOTACIZE
ZAMPOGNA
ZEBRINNY
ZEMSTVOS
ZIGZAGGY
ZIRCONYL
ZOEAFORM
ZOOCHORE
ZOOMETRY
ZOOPHILE
ZOOPHORI
ZOOTHOME
ZYGAENID
ZYGODONT
ZYGOTOID

21

ALCAZABA
ALKALIZE
ANALYZED
APPETIZE
APPRIZAL
APPRIZER
BACONIZE
BAPTIZEE
BAPTIZER
BAROMETZ
BENZILIC
BENZOBIS
BROMIZER
BRUNIZEM
CACOZEAL
CALABAZA
CALABOZO
CAPONIZE
CAPSIZAL
CARBAZIN
CINEMIZE
COGNIZED
DEVILIZE
DIALYZER
DIVINIZE
DIZZYING
ECTOZOIC
EMBLAZER
EMBLAZON
EMBOLIZE
EMBRONZE
FARADIZE
FEAZINGS
FIGURIZE
FLUIDIZE
FOOZLING
FREEZING
FRENZIED
FRIEZING
FUZZBALL
GARVANZO
GLAZIERY
GOYAZITE
GRAZIERY
GWERZIOU
HAZARDER
HAZNADAR
HEREZELD
IMMUNIZE
KETONIZE
KREUTZER
LAZYLEGS
MACARIZE
MAGADIZE
MARZIPAN
MEMORIZE
METAZOIC
MEZEREUM
MEZUZAHS
MEZUZOTH
MICASIZE
MICROZOA
MINIMIZE
MISPRIZE
MOBILIZE
MONOZOIC
NAZIFIED
OPTIMIZE
OSMAZOME
OVERGAZE
OZARKITE
OZOBROME
PANZOISM
PAPALIZE
PEPTIZER
PEZANTIC
POLEMIZE
POLICIZE
PRIZABLE
PRIZEMAN
PRIZEMEN
PUPILIZE
RACEMIZE
RAMBOOZE
RHIZOGEN
RIBAZUBA
RUMBOOZE
SAVAGIZE
STYLIZED
TEMPLIZE
TWEEZING
UNVIZARD
VIZORING
WALTZING
WEAZENED
ZEOSCOPE
ZEPPELIN
ZERUMBET
ZETACISM
ZIMBALON
ZIPPIEST
ZIRCONIC
ZOANTHID
ZOLOTNIK
ZOOECIUM
ZOOGRAFT
ZOOTOMIC
ZUGZWANG
ZYGOTENE

20

ANALYZER
APRENDIZ
ARRHIZAL
ATHEIZER
ATHETIZE
ATOMIZED
AUTOLYZE
AVESTRUZ
AVIANIZE
AZOIMIDE
BENZIDIN
BLAZONED
BRACOZZO
BRAZENED
BREEZING
BRONZING
BROOZLED
BULLDOZE
COALIZED
COGNIZEE
COGNIZER
COGNIZOR
COZENING
DECATIZE
DEGLAZED
DEMONIZE
DEPUTIZE
DIAZOTIC
DISPRIZE
DOUZEPER
EBONIZED
EMBEZZLE
ERZAHLER
ETHERIZE
FATALIZE
FINALIZE
FIZZLING
FLOOZIES
FOZINESS
FRAZZLED
FRENZIES
FRIZETTE
FRIZZING
FRIZZLED
FUELIZER
GARBANZO
GAZABOES
GAZEBOES
GAZEMENT
HALAZONE
HAZELNUT
HAZINESS
HERTZIAN
HETERIZE
IDIOZOME
IMIDAZOL
ITEMIZED
LAICIZED
LHERZITE
LOGICIZE
MAGAZINE
MALGUZAR
MAZAGRAN
MAZALGIA
MEDALIZE
MELODIZE
MODALIZE
MODELIZE
MODULIZE
MONODIZE
MOZEMIZE
NOVELIZE
OBELIZED
OPALIZED
ORYZANIN
ORYZENIN
OVERSIZE
PAGANIZE
POETIZED
RADZIMIR
RENOVIZE
RIVALIZE
ROYALIZE
SEVERIZE
SFORZATO
SHAATNEZ
STYLIZER
SYNERIZE
THEORIZE
THIAZINE
THIAZOLE
THIOZONE
THRONIZE
TWEEZERS
UNBAIZED
UNCRAZED
UNFROZEN
VALORIZE
VELARIZE
VENALIZE
VITALIZE
VIZIRATE
VIZIRIAL
VOLTZINE
VOLTZITE
WAZIRATE
WOOZIEST
WRIZZLED
WURTZITE
WUZZLING
ZAMINDAR
ZANDMOLE
ZEALOTRY
ZEALOUSY
ZEMINDAR
ZENITHAL
ZODIACAL
ZONALITY
ZOOLATRY
ZOOLOGIC

19

ADONIZED
AGATIZED
AGNIZING
AGONIZED
ALBRONZE
ALMUERZO
AMINOAZO
AMORTIZE
ANODIZED
ANTICIZE
ARBORIZE
ARMOZEEN
ARMOZINE
ATOMIZER
ATTICIZE
AZOTEMIA
BAETZNER
BARTIZAN
BEDAZZLE
BENZOATE
BEZANTEE
BEZONIAN
BEZZLING
BLAZONER
BLIZZARD
BOTANIZE
BRAGOZZO
BREEZIER
BRONZINE
BRONZITE
CALORIZE
CALZOONS
CANALIZE
CANONIZE
CANZONET
CATZERIE
COLONIZE
CORONIZE
COZINESS
CRAZIEST
CREOLIZE
CRUELIZE
CRUZEIRO
CURARIZE
CUTINIZE
DIGITIZE
DISDIAZO
DIZENING
DUALIZED
ECTOZOAN
EGOTIZED
ELEGIZED
ENTOZOIC
ENZOOTIC
FIZZIEST
FRIZZIER
FRIZZLER
FUZZIEST
FUZZTAIL
GAZETTED
GAZOGENE
GRANDEZA
HAZZANUT
IDOLIZED
IODIZING
IRIDIZED
ITEMIZER
LABILIZE
LACONIZE
LAICIZER
LOCALIZE
LOZENGED
MATEZITE
MAZARINE
MAZINESS
MELANIZE
MESOZOAN
MESTIZOS
METALIZE
METAZOAL
METAZOAN
METAZOEA
METAZOON
METRAZOL
MEZEREON
MIZZLING
MONAZITE
MONETIZE
MONOZOAN
MORALIZE
MOTORIZE
MOUZOUNA
MUZZLING
NEBULIZE
NICOTIZE
NIZAMATE
OPSONIZE
ORMUZINE
OUTBLAZE
PAEANIZE

PALATIZE
PARTIZAN
PATINIZE
PELORIZE
PENALIZE
PEREZONE
PETUNTZE
PEZIZOID
PIAZZAED
POETIZER
POLARIZE
POLITIZE
PREZONAL
PROTOZOA
PUZZLING
RAZORMAN
RIZZOMED
ROBOTIZE
SEIZABLE
SIEROZEM
SILICIZE
SIMILIZE
SIMONIZE
SIMULIZE
SINAPIZE
SIZEABLE
SMORZATO
SOBERIZE
SOLECIZE
SPRITZER
SPUILZIE
STANZAIC
SUBERIZE
SUBSIZAR
SUBZONAL
SWIZZLER
TIMAZITE
TONICIZE
TOPAZINE
TOPAZITE
TRAPEZIA
TRIZOMAL
TUBERIZE
UNGLAZED
URBANIZE
ZAIBATSU
ZAMORINE
ZAPATERO
ZEALOTIC
ZEOLITIC
ZIBELINE
ZIGGURAT
ZINCURET
ZIRCONIA
ZOETROPE
ZOOBLAST
ZOOECIAL
ZOOLITIC
ZOOMANIA
ZOONITIC
ZOONOTIC
ZOOPERAL
ZOOSPORE
ZOPILOTE
ZUPANATE

18
AGONIZER
ALBIZZIA
ALDOLIZE
ALGUAZIL
ANALGIZE
ANGELIZE
ARANZADA
ASSIZING
AZOGREEN
BIZZARRO
BUZZIEST
CZARITZA
DAZZLING
DEIONIZE
DENIZATE
DETONIZE
DIAZOATE
DISSEIZE
DONZELLA
DOUZAINE
DOZINESS
DRIZZLED
DUELLIZE
ENERGIZE
ERGOTIZE
EULOGIZE
GAUZIEST
GAZELESS
GAZELLES
GAZETTAL
GIANTIZE
GIZZENED
GLAZIERS
GLAZIEST
GRAZIOSO
GRIZZLED
GUZZLING
IDEALIZE
IDOLIZER
INDAZOLE
INDENIZE
IOTIZING
ISOZOOID
LEGALIZE
LIONIZED
LOZENGER
MUZZIEST
NODULIZE
OOLOGIZE
ORANGIZE
ORGANIZE
OUTSIZED
PIAZZIAN
PIZZERIA
RAADZAAL
RAZEEING
REALIZED
REALIZER
REGALIZE
REGULIZE
RENDZINA
RESIZING
SNEEZING
SNOOZING
STANZAED
STARGAZE
TAILZIED
UNMUZZLE
UNPUZZLE
UTILIZED
ZASTRUGA
ZASTRUGI
ZONUROID
ZOOGLOEA
ZORTZICO

17
ALIZARIN
ANNALIZE
ANTIZOEA
ASTATIZE
AZOTIZED
AZOTURIA
DIZZIEST
ENTOZOAL
ENTOZOAN
ENTOZOON
EOZOONAL
ESTERIZE
ETERNIZE
ETIOLIZE
GAZZETTA
GRIZZLER
INSULIZE
LATINIZE
LAZAROLE
LAZARONE
LAZAROUS
LAZINESS
LAZULITE
LAZURITE
LINENIZE
LIONIZER
LUNATIZE
NASALIZE
NATURIZE
NOTARIZE
NUZZLING
OOZINESS
OZONIZED
RESEIZER
RESINIZE
RETINIZE
RITZIEST
RURALIZE
SALINIZE
SANITIZE
SARRAZIN
SATANIZE
SATINIZE
SATIRIZE
SERENIZE
SIRENIZE
SIZINESS
SIZZLING
SOLARIZE
SOLONETZ
SONORIZE
SORORIZE
STANITZA
STOLZITE
SUZERAIN
TERZETTO
TETANIZE
TETRAZIN
TOTALIZE
TRIAZANE
TRIAZINE
TRIAZOLE
TRISTEZA
TUTORIZE
UNDAZZLE
UNIONIZE
UTILIZER
ZARATITE
ZOIATRIA
ZONATION
ZONELESS
ZOOLATER
ZOONOSES
ZOONOSIS
ZORRILLO

16
OZONIZER
TERRAZZO
ZARZUELA
ZIZZLING

ALPHABETICAL LIST OF 9-LETTER WORDS

ABURABOZU
ACADEMIZE
ACETALIZE
ACETONIZE
ACETYLIZE
ACTIONIZE
ACTUALIZE
ADONIZING
ADVERTIZE
AGATIZING
AGONIZING
AGROMYZID
ALCARRAZA
ALCHEMIZE
ALDOLIZED
ALIZARATE
ALIZARINE
ALKALIZER
ALLOZOOID
ALTERNIZE
ALUMETIZE
ALUMINIZE
AMAZEMENT
AMAZONITE
AMORTIZED
ANABOLIZE
ANALOGIZE
ANALYZING
ANARCHIZE
ANATOMIZE
ANGELIZED
ANGLICIZE
ANHYDRIZE
ANIMALIZE
ANNUALIZE
ANODIZING
ANTHOZOAN
ANTHOZOIC
ANTHOZOON
APHIDOZER
APHORIZED
APHORIZER
APHRIZITE
APOLOGIZE
APPETIZED
APPETIZER
APPRIZING
ARBORIZED
ARCHAIZED
ARCHAIZER
ARCHIZOIC
ARCTICIZE
ARIZONITE
AROMATIZE
ARRHIZOUS
ARZRUNITE
ASSOILZIE
ASTATIZED
ASTATIZER
ATHETIZED
ATMOLYZER
ATOMIZING
ATTICIZED
AUTHORIZE
AUTOZOOID
AVIZANDUM
AZALEAMUM
AZEDARACH
AZEOTROPE
AZEOTROPY
AZIETHANE
AZIMUTHAL
AZLACTONE
AZOBENZIL
AZOBENZOL
AZOCYCLIC
AZOFORMIC
AZOLITMIN
AZOPHENOL
AZOPHENYL
AZOTIZING
AZOXONIUM
BACTERIZE
BALKANIZE
BALSAMIZE
BALZARINE
BAMBOOZLE
BANTAMIZE
BAPTIZING
BARBARIZE
BEAVERIZE
BEDAZZLED
BEDIZENED
BEDLAMIZE
BENZAMIDE
BENZAMIDO
BENZENOID
BENZIDINE
BENZIDINO
BENZOATED
BENZOLATE
BENZOLINE
BENZOLIZE
BERGINIZE
BEZESTEEN

BEZOARDIC
BILHARZIC
BIOLOGIZE
BIZARDITE
BIZARRELY
BLAZONING
BLIZZARDY
BLOWZIEST
BOMBAZINE
BOOZINESS
BOTANIZED
BOTANIZER
BRAZENING
BRAZILEIN
BRAZILITE
BREEZEWAY
BREEZIEST
BRUTALIZE
BULLDOZED
BULLDOZER
BURKUNDAZ
BURTONIZE
BUZZARDLY
BUZZGLOAK
CALORIZER
CANALIZED
CANONIZED
CANONIZER
CAPONIZER
CAPRIZANT
CAPSIZING
CARBAZIDE
CARBAZINE
CARBAZOLE
CARBOLIZE
CARBONIZE
CARBURIZE
CARNALIZE
CARTELIZE
CATALYZED
CATALYZER
CATECHIZE
CATHARIZE
CAUPONIZE
CAUTERIZE
CEREBRIZE
CHABAZITE
CHALAZIAN
CHALAZION
CHALAZIUM
CHEMOLYZE
CHERNOZEM
CHINTZIER
CHORIZONT
CHRYSAZIN
CHRYSAZOL
CICATRIZE
CITIZENLY
CITIZENRY
CITRONIZE
CIVILIZEE
CIVILIZED
CIVILIZER
CLAVELIZE
CLIMATIZE
COALIZING
COCAINIZE
COELOZOIC
COGNIZANT
COGNIZING
COLAZIONE
COLONIZED
COLONIZER
COMMUNIZE
COMPRIZAL
COMPRIZED
COPPERIZE
COPROZOIC
COSMOZOIC
COTTONIZE
COURTEZAN
CRAZINESS
CRAZYWEED
CREOLEIZE
CREOLIZED
CRITICIZE
CURARIZED
CUTINIZED
CYANIZING
CZARINIAN
CZARISTIC
DAZEDNESS
DECADENZA
DECATIZER
DEEPFROZE
DEFERRIZE
DEGLAZING
DEMONIZED
DENITRIZE
DENTALIZE
DEODORIZE
DEOXIDIZE
DEOZONIZE
DEPUTIZED
DESPOTIZE
DEVILIZED
DEZINCIFY
DEZINKIFY
DIABOLIZE
DIALOGIZE
DIALYZATE
DIALYZING
DIAZEUTIC
DIAZEUXIS
DIAZOAMIN
DIAZONIUM
DIAZOTATE
DIAZOTIZE
DIAZOTYPE
DIBENZOYL
DIESELIZE
DIETZEITE
DIGITIZED
DIGITIZER
DISPRIZED
DISSEIZED
DISSEIZEE
DISSEIZOR
DIVINIZED
DIZENMENT
DIZYGOTIC
DIZZARDLY
DIZZINESS
DOCTORIZE
DOGMATIZE
DOUZEPERS
DRAGONIZE
DRAMATIZE
DRIZZLING
DUALIZING
DUCTILIZE
DUNZIEKTE
DZIGGETAI
EBONIZING
ECHOIZING
ECONOMIZE
ECPHORIZE
ECTOENZYM
EGOTIZING
EKPHORIZE
ELECTRIZE
ELEGIZING
ELENCHIZE
EMBEZZLED
EMBEZZLER
EMBLAZING
EMBLEMIZE
EMPHASIZE
ENDENIZEN
ENERGIZED
ENERGIZER
ENZYMATIC
ENZYMOSIS
ENZYMOTIC
EPILOGIZE
EPIPOLIZE
EPITOMIZE
EPIZEUXIS
EPIZOOTIC
EQUALIZED
EQUALIZER
ERGOTIZED
ESOTERIZE
ETERNIZED
ETHERIZED
ETHERIZER
ETHICIZED
EULOGIZED
EULOGIZER
EUPHEMIZE
EUPHONIZE
EUPHUIZED
EVAPORIZE
EXOENZYME
EXORCIZED
EXORCIZER
FACTORIZE
FACULTIZE
FANTASIZE
FARADIZED
FARADIZER
FAUCALIZE
FECUNDIZE
FERTILIZE
FETICHIZE
FEUDALIZE
FIBERIZER
FILMIZING
FINALIZED
FISCALIZE
FISTULIZE
FIZELYITE
FLORIZINE
FLUIDIZED
FOCALIZED
FOREPRIZE
FORMALIZE
FORMULIZE
FORTHGAZE
FOSSILIZE
FRAZZLING
FREEZABLE
FRENZYING
FRIVOLIZE
FRIZZIEST
FRIZZLING
FROWZIEST
FURZECHAT
FUZZINESS
GALLINAZO
GALVANIZE
GARDENIZE
GAUZELIKE
GAUZEWING
GAUZINESS
GAZEHOUND
GAZETTEER
GAZETTING
GENIALIZE
GENTILIZE
GEOLOGIZE
GERMANIZE
GIGANTIZE
GLAMORIZE
GLAZEWORK
GLAZINESS
GLUTINIZE
GLYCERIZE
GONOZOOID
GORGONIZE
GOSPELIZE
GRANITIZE
GRANULIZE
GRAZINGLY
GRIZZLIER
GRIZZLIES
GRIZZLING
GUACONIZE
HAMLETIZE
HAPHAZARD
HARMONIZE
HAZARDOUS
HELIOZOAN
HERALDIZE
HERBALIZE
HERBARIZE
HERBORIZE
HISTORIZE
HUMANIZER
HUMOURIZE
HYALINIZE
HYBRIDIZE
HYDRAZINE
HYDRAZOIC
HYDRAZONE
HYDROLYZE
HYDROZOAL
HYDROZOAŇ
HYDROZOIC
HYDROZOON
HYGIENIZE
HYLOZOISM
HYLOZOIST
HYPNOTIZE
HYPOCRIZE
IDEALIZED
IDEALIZER
IDOLIZING
IMIDAZOLE
IMMUNIZED
INFAMIZED
INFLUENZA
INOXIDIZE
IONIZABLE
IRIDIZING
ISOMERIZE
ISONIAZID
ISOXAZOLE
ITALICIZE
ITEMIZING
IZVOZCHIK
JARGONIZE
JAROVIZED
JASPERIZE
JAZZINESS
JENNERIZE
JOVIALIZE
KAOLINIZE
KEVAZINGO
KEVUTZOTH
KIBBUTZIM
KRANTZITE
LABIALIZE
LACONIZED
LACONIZER
LACTONIZE
LADRONIZE
LAICIZING
LAMZIEKTE
LAZARETTE
LAZARETTO
LAZULITIC
LAZYBONES
LAZYBOOTS
LAZZARONE
LAZZARONI
LEGALIZED
LICHENIZE
LIGNITIZE
LINEARIZE
LINENIZER
LIONIZING
LIQUIDIZE
LITURGIZE
LOCALIZED
LOCALIZER
MACARIZED
MAGAZINED
MAGAZINER
MAGNETIZE
MAINPRIZE
MAIZEBIRD
MALGUZARI
MAMMONIZE
MANGANIZE
MANGONIZE
MANNERIZE
MANZANITA
MARBELIZE
MARBLEIZE
MARMARIZE
MARRANIZE
MARTYRIZE
MATRONIZE
MAXIMIZED
MAXIMIZER
MAZEDNESS
MAZODYNIA
MAZOLYSIS
MAZOLYTIC
MECHANIZE
MEDIALIZE
MEDIATIZE
MEDIUMIZE
MEGAZOOID
MELODIZED
MELODIZER
MEMORIZED
MEMORIZER
MENDOZITE
MENSALIZE
MERCERIZE
MERCURIZE
MESMERIZE
MESTIZOES
METALIZED
METALLIZE
METEORIZE
METHODIZE
METRICIZE
MEZCALINE
MEZZANINE
MEZZOTINT
MICROZOAL
MICROZOAN
MICROZOIC
MICROZONE
MICROZOON
MICROZYMA
MICROZYME
MINIMIZED
MINIMIZER
MISPRIZED
MISPRIZER
MIZENMAST

MIZZONITE
MNEMONIZE
MOBILIZED
MODERNIZE
MONACHIZE
MONETIZED
MONZONITE
MORALIZED
MORALIZER
MORGANIZE
MORSELIZE
MORTALIZE
MOTORIZED
MULLENIZE
MUTUALIZE
MYCORHIZA
MYSTERIZE
MYTHICIZE
NARCOTIZE
NASALIZED
NAZIFYING
NEBULIZED
NEBULIZER
NECROTIZE
NECTARIZE
NEOLOGIZE
NEOTERIZE
NEUMATIZE
NICKELIZE
NITRIDIZE
NODULIZED
NORMALIZE
NOTARIZED
NOVELIZED
OBELIZING
OBJECTIZE
ONIONIZED
OPALIZING
OPERATIZE
OPTIMIZED
ORATORIZE
ORGANIZED
ORGANIZER
ORGANZINE
ORIENTIZE
ORYZANINE
OSTRACIZE
OUTBRAZEN
OUTDAZZLE
OVERGLAZE
OVERGRAZE
OVERPRIZE
OVERSIZED
OXDIAZOLE
OXIDIZING
OXYBENZYL
OXYGENIZE
OXYTONIZE
OZOCERITE
OZONATION
OZONIZING
OZOSTOMIA
PAEANIZED
PAGANIZED
PAGANIZER
PALLADIZE
PALLETIZE
PAMPERIZE
PANDERIZE
PANZOOTIA
PANZOOTIC
PAPALIZER
PARALYZED
PARALYZER
PASTORIZE
PATRIZATE
PATRONIZE
PAUPERIZE
PAVONAZZO
PECTIZING
PEDANTIZE
PEGMATIZE
PENALIZED
PEOPLEIZE
PEPTIZING
PEPTONIZE
PERHAZARD
PERSONIZE
PESSIMIZE
PETROLIZE
PEZOGRAPH
PHENAZINE
PHENAZONE
PHENOLIZE
PHILOZOIC
PHLORIZIN
PHONETIZE
PHYTOZOAN
PHYTOZOON
PIAZZETTA
PICTURIZE
PILLORIZE
PIZZICATO
PLATINIZE
PLURALIZE
POETICIZE
POETIZING
POLARIZED
POLARIZER
POLICIZER
POLYZOARY
POLYZOISM
POLYZONAL
POLYZOOID
POLZENITE
POSTERIZE
POSTURIZE
POTENTIZE
POWDERIZE
POZZOLANA
PRECONIZE
PREIOTIZE
PRELATIZE
PRELUDIZE
PRESTEZZA
PRIZEABLE
PROFANIZE
PROLOGIZE
PROPOLIZE
PROTOZOAL
PROTOZOAN
PROTOZOEA
PROTOZOIC
PROTOZOON
PROZYMITE
PRYTANIZE
PTYALIZED
PUBLICIZE
PULVERIZE
PUPILLIZE
PUPPETIZE
PURPURIZE
PUZZLEDLY
PUZZLEMAN
PYRAZOLYL
PYTHONIZE
QUANTIZED
QUARTZITE
QUARTZOID
QUARTZOSE
QUARTZOUS
QUININIZE
QUINONIZE
QUINZAINE
QUINZIEME
QUIZZICAL
RABBINIZE
RACEMIZED
RACIALIZE
RADIALIZE
RADIUMIZE
RANDOMIZE
RAPTURIZE
RAZORBACK
RAZORBILL
RAZOREDGE
RAZZBERRY
REALIZING
REBAPTIZE
RECOGNIZE
RESEIZURE
RHETORIZE
RHEUMATIZ
RHIZINOUS
RHIZOBIUM
RHIZOCARP
RHIZOCAUL
RHIZOCORM
RHIZOTAXY
RHIZOTOMI
RHIZOTOMY
RHODIZITE
RHYTHMIZE
ROUTINIZE
RUBBERIZE
RUBRICIZE
RURALIZED
RUSTICIZE
SANITIZED
SAPROZOIC
SATIRIZED
SATIRIZER
SATURNIZE
SCAZONTIC
SCENARIZE
SCHIZAXON
SCHIZOPOD
SCHNAUZER
SCHNITZEL
SCHNOZZLE
SCIENTIZE
SCLERIZED
SENSITIZE
SERIALIZE
SERMONIZE
SEXUALIZE
SFORZANDO
SHAHZADAH
SIGNALIZE
SILVERIZE
SISTERIZE
SIZARSHIP
SLIVOVITZ
SMORZANDO
SOCIALIZE
SOLARIZED
SOLECIZED
SOLECIZER
SOLEMNIZE
SOLMIZATE
SOLVOLYZE
SONNETIZE
SORBITIZE
SOVIETIZE
SPIRALIZE
SPIRITIZE
SPONDAIZE
SPOROZOAL
SPOROZOAN
SPOROZOIC
SPOROZOID
SPOROZOON
SQUEEZING
STABILIZE
STARGAZED
STARGAZER
STERILIZE
STRAMAZON
STYLIZING
SUBERIZED
SUBSIDIZE
SULCALIZE
SULFATIZE
SULFAZIDE
SULFURIZE
SULPHAZID
SULTANIZE
SUMMARIZE
SURGERIZE
SURPRIZAL
SYLLABIZE
SYLLOGIZE
SYMBOLIZE
SYNCOPIZE
SYNERGIZE
SYNEZISIS
SYNIZESIS
SYNOECIZE
SYNOPSIZE
SYNTONIZE
SYPHILIZE
SYSTEMIZE
SYZYGETIC
TANDEMIZE
TANTALIZE
TARIFFIZE
TARTARIZE
TARTRAZIN
TAVERNIZE
TELEOZOIC
TELEOZOON
TELLURIZE
TEMPORIZE
TENDERIZE
TERMINIZE
TERRORIZE
TERZETTOS
TETANIZED
TETRAZANE
TETRAZENE
TETRAZINE
TETRAZOLE
TETRAZONE
THEATRIZE
THEORIZED
THEORIZER
THIOZONID
THYMOLIZE
TINZENITE
TOPAZFELS
TOTALIZED
TOTALIZER
TRAPEZIAL
TRAPEZIAN
TRAPEZING
TRAPEZIST
TRAPEZIUM
TRAPEZIUS
TRAPEZOID
TRINALIZE
TRIOZONID
TUCHUNIZE
TURTLEIZE
TWEEZERED
TYMPANIZE
TYRANNIZE
UGRIANIZE
UNBRUTIZE
UNCIALIZE
UNDERSIZE
UNIONIZED
UNREALIZE
URALITIZE
URBANIZED
UTILIZING
VACUUMIZE
VAMPIRIZE
VANDALIZE
VAPORIZER
VAPOURIZE
VASSALIZE
VERBALIZE
VERNALIZE
VICTIMIZE
VISCIDIZE
VISIONIZE
VISUALIZE
VITALIZED
VITALIZER
VIZARDING
VIZIERATE
VIZIERIAL
VOCALIZED
VOCALIZER
VOLCANIZE
VULCANIZE
VULGARIZE
WANTONIZE
WAYZGOOSE
WAZIRSHIP
WHEEZIEST
WINTERIZE
WITTICIZE
WOMANIZED
WOMANIZER
WOOLENIZE
WOOZINESS
ZAMINDARI
ZAMINDARY
ZAPATEADO
ZEALOTISM
ZEALOTIST
ZEALOUSLY
ZEBRALIKE
ZEBRAWOOD
ZELATRICE
ZELOTYPIA
ZELOTYPIE
ZEMINDARI
ZENDICIAN
ZENDIKITE
ZEOLITIZE
ZEPHYREAN
ZEPHYRIAN
ZEPHYROUS
ZERMAHBUB
ZEROAXIAL
ZEUGMATIC
ZEUNERITE
ZIBELLINE
ZINCALISM
ZINCIFIED
ZINFANDEL
ZINGERONE
ZINKENITE
ZIPPINGLY
ZIRCONATE
ZIRCONIUM
ZIRCONOID
ZIRKELITE
ZITHERIST
ZOANTHOID
ZOBTENITE
ZOEHEMERA
ZOETROPIC

ZOOCYTIAL
ZOOCYTIUM
ZOOFULVIN
ZOOGAMETE
ZOOGAMOUS
ZOOGENOUS
ZOOGLOEAL
ZOOGLOEIC
ZOOGONOUS
ZOOGRAPHY
ZOOLITHIC
ZOOLOGIES

ZOOLOGIST
ZOOLOGIZE
ZOOMETRIC
ZOOMORPHY
ZOOPERIST
ZOOPHAGAN
ZOOPHILIA
ZOOPHILIC
ZOOPHOBIA
ZOOPHORIC
ZOOPHORUS
ZOOPHYTAL

ZOOPHYTIC
ZOOPLASTY
ZOOSCOPIC
ZOOSPHERE
ZOOSPORIC
ZOOTECHNY
ZOOTHECIA
ZOOTHEISM
ZOOTHEIST
ZOOTOMIST
ZOOTROPHY

ZUCCARINO
ZUCCHETTO
ZUMBOORUK
ZUURVELDT
ZWANZIGER
ZYGADENIN
ZYGANTRUM
ZYGOMATIC
ZYGONEURE
ZYGOPHORE
ZYGOPHYTE

ZYGOSPERM
ZYGOSPORE
ZYGOSTYLE
ZYGOTAXIS
ZYMOGENIC
ZYMOLOGIC
ZYMOLYSIS
ZYMOLYTIC
ZYMOMETER
ZYMOPHORE
ZYMOSCOPE

POSITIONAL ORDER LIST OF 9-LETTER WORDS

ZAMINDARI
ZAMINDARY
ZAPATEADO
ZEALOTISM
ZEALOTIST
ZEALOUSLY
ZEBRALIKE
ZEBRAWOOD
ZELATRICE
ZELOTYPIA
ZELOTYPIE
ZEMINDARI
ZENDICIAN
ZENDIKITE
ZEOLITIZE
ZEPHYREAN
ZEPHYRIAN
ZEPHYROUS
ZERMAHBUB
ZEROAXIAL
ZEUGMATIC
ZEUNERITE
ZIBELLINE
ZINCALISM
ZINCIFIED
ZINFANDEL
ZINGERONE
ZINKENITE
ZIPPINGLY
ZIRCONATE
ZIRCONIUM
ZIRCONOID
ZIRKELITE
ZITHERIST
ZOANTHOID
ZOBTENITE
ZOEHEMERA
ZOETROPIC
ZOOCYTIAL
ZOOCYTIUM
ZOOFULVIN
ZOOGAMETE
ZOOGAMOUS
ZOOGENOUS
ZOOGLOEAL
ZOOGLOEIC
ZOOGONOUS
ZOOGRAPHY
ZOOLITHIC
ZOOLOGIES
ZOOLOGIST
ZOOLOGIZE
ZOOMETRIC
ZOOMORPHY
ZOOPERIST
ZOOPHAGAN
ZOOPHILIA
ZOOPHILIC
ZOOPHOBIA

ZOOPHORIC
ZOOPHORUS
ZOOPHYTAL
ZOOPHYTIC
ZOOPLASTY
ZOOSCOPIC
ZOOSPHERE
ZOOSPORIC
ZOOTECHNY
ZOOTHECIA
ZOOTHEISM
ZOOTHEIST
ZOOTOMIST
ZOOTROPHY
ZUCCARINO
ZUCCHETTO
ZUMBOORUK
ZUURVELDT
ZWANZIGER
ZYGADENIN
ZYGANTRUM
ZYGOMATIC
ZYGONEURE
ZYGOPHORE
ZYGOPHYTE
ZYGOSPERM
ZYGOSPORE
ZYGOSTYLE
ZYGOTAXIS
ZYMOGENIC
ZYMOLOGIC
ZYMOLYSIS
ZYMOLYTIC
ZYMOMETER
ZYMOPHORE
ZYMOSCOPE

AZALEAMUM
AZEDARACH
AZEOTROPE
AZEOTROPY
AZIETHANE
AZIMUTHAL
AZLACTONE
AZOBENZIL
AZOBENZOL
AZOCYCLIC
AZOFORMIC
AZOLITMIN
AZOPHENOL
AZOPHENYL
AZOTIZING
AZOXONIUM
CZARINIAN
CZARISTIC
DZIGGETAI
IZVOZCHIK
OZOCERITE
OZONATION

OZONIZING
OZOSTOMIA

ARZRUNITE
BEZESTEEN
BEZOARDIC
BIZARDITE
BIZARRELY
BUZZARDLY
BUZZGLOAK
DAZEDNESS
DEZINCIFY
DEZINKIFY
DIZENMENT
DIZYGOTIC
DIZZARDLY
DIZZINESS
ENZYMATIC
ENZYMOSIS
ENZYMOTIC
FIZELYITE
FUZZINESS
GAZEHOUND
GAZETTEER
GAZETTING
HAZARDOUS
JAZZINESS
LAZARETTE
LAZARETTO
LAZULITIC
LAZYBONES
LAZYBOOTS
LAZZARONE
LAZZARONI
MAZEDNESS
MAZODYNIA
MAZOLYSIS
MAZOLYTIC
MEZCALINE
MEZZANINE
MEZZOTINT
MIZENMAST
MIZZONITE
NAZIFYING
PEZOGRAPH
PIZZICATO
POZZOLANA
PUZZLEDLY
PUZZLEMAN
RAZORBACK
RAZORBILL
RAZOREDGE
RAZZBERRY
SIZARSHIP
SYZYGETIC
VIZARDING
VIZIERATE
VIZIERIAL
WAZIRSHIP

ALIZARATE
ALIZARINE
AMAZEMENT
AMAZONITE
ARIZONITE
AVIZANDUM
BALZARINE
BENZAMIDE
BENZAMIDO
BENZENOID
BENZIDINE
BENZIDINO
BENZOATED
BENZOLATE
BENZOLINE
BENZOLIZE
BLAZONING
BLIZZARDY
BOOZINESS
BRAZENING
BRAZILEIN
BRAZILITE
BUZZARDLY
BUZZGLOAK
CRAZINESS
CRAZYWEED
DIAZEUTIC
DIAZEUXIS
DIAZOAMIN
DIAZONIUM
DIAZOTATE
DIAZOTIZE
DIAZOTYPE
DIZZARDLY
DIZZINESS
DOUZEPERS
DRIZZLING
DUNZIEKTE
EPIZEUXIS
EPIZOOTIC
FRAZZLING
FRIZZIEST
FRIZZLING
FURZECHAT
FUZZINESS
GAUZELIKE
GAUZEWING
GAUZINESS
GLAZEWORK
GLAZINESS
GRAZINGLY
GRIZZLIER
GRIZZLIES
GRIZZLING
JAZZINESS
LAMZIEKTE
LAZZARONE
LAZZARONI
MAIZEBIRD

MANZANITA
MEZZANINE
MEZZOTINT
MIZZONITE
MONZONITE
ORYZANINE
PANZOOTIA
PANZOOTIC
PIAZZETTA
PIZZICATO
POLZENITE
POZZOLANA
PRIZEABLE
PROZYMITE
PUZZLEDLY
PUZZLEMAN
QUIZZICAL
RAZZBERRY
RHIZINOUS
RHIZOBIUM
RHIZOCARP
RHIZOCAUL
RHIZOCORM
RHIZOTAXY
RHIZOTOMI
RHIZOTOMY
SCAZONTIC
TERZETTOS
TINZENITE
WAYZGOOSE
WOOZINESS

ALLOZOOID
AUTOZOOID
BEDAZZLED
BEDIZENED
BLIZZARDY
BLOWZIEST
BREEZEWAY
BREEZIEST
CITIZENLY
CITIZENRY
COLAZIONE
DIETZEITE
DRIZZLING
EMBEZZLED
EMBEZZLER
FRAZZLING
FREEZABLE
FRENZYING
FRIZZIEST
FRIZZLING
FROWZIEST
GONOZOOID
GRIZZLIER
GRIZZLIES
GRIZZLING
HYLOZOISM
HYLOZOIST

IONIZABLE
IZVOZCHIK
KEVAZINGO
MAGAZINED
MAGAZINER
MEGAZOOID
PIAZZETTA
POLYZOARY
POLYZOISM
POLYZONAL
POLYZOOID
PYRAZOLYL
QUINZAINE
QUINZIEME
QUIZZICAL
SCHIZAXON
SCHIZOPOD
SFORZANDO
SHAHZADAH
SMORZANDO
SYNEZISIS
SYNIZESIS
THIOZONID
TOPAZFELS
TRIOZONID
TWEEZERED
WHEEZIEST
ZWANZIGER

ADONIZING
AGATIZING
AGONIZING
ANALYZING
ANODIZING
ANTHOZOAN
ANTHOZOIC
ANTHOZOON
APHRIZITE
APPRIZING
ARCHIZOIC
ARRHIZOUS
ATOMIZING
AZOTIZING
BAPTIZING
BEDAZZLED
BOMBAZINE
CAPRIZANT
CAPSIZED
CAPSIZING
CARBAZIDE
CARBAZINE
CARBAZOLE
CHABAZITE
CHALAZIAN
CHALAZION
CHALAZIUM
CHINTZIER
CHORIZONT
COALIZING
COELOZOIC
COGNIZANT
COGNIZING
COPROZOIC
COSMOZOIC
CYANIZING
DEGLAZING
DIALYZATE
DIALYZING
DIBENZOYL
DUALIZING
EBONIZING
ECHOIZING
EGOTIZING
ELEGIZING
EMBEZZLED
EMBEZZLER
EMBLAZING

EXOENZYME
FILMIZING
FLORIZINE
HAPHAZARD
HELIOZOAN
HYDRAZINE
HYDRAZOIC
HYDRAZONE
HYDROZOAL
HYDROZOAN
HYDROZOIC
HYDROZOON
IDOLIZING
IMIDAZOLE
IRIDIZING
ISOXAZOLE
ITEMIZING
KEVUTZOTH
KRANTZITE
LAICIZING
LIONIZING
MALGUZARI
MENDOZITE
MESTIZOES
MICROZOAL
MICROZOAN
MICROZOIC
MICROZONE
MICROZOON
MICROZYMA
MICROZYME
OBELIZING
OPALIZING
ORGANZINE
OUTDAZZLE
OXDIAZOLE
OXIDIZING
OZONIZING
PATRIZATE
PECTIZING
PEPTIZING
PERHAZARD
PHENAZINE
PHENAZONE
PHILOZOIC
PHYTOZOAN
PHYTOZOON
POETIZING
PROTOZOAL
PROTOZOAN
PROTOZOEA
PROTOZOIC
PROTOZOON
QUARTZITE
QUARTZOID
QUARTZOSE
QUARTZOUS
REALIZING
RESEIZURE
RHODIZITE
SAPROZOIC
SCHNOZZLE
SOLMIZATE
SPOROZOAL
SPOROZOAN
SPOROZOIC
SPOROZOID
SPOROZOON
SQUEEZING
STYLIZING
SULFAZIDE
TELEOZOIC
TELEOZOON
TETRAZANE
TETRAZENE
TETRAZINE
TETRAZOLE

TETRAZONE
TRAPEZIAL
TRAPEZIAN
TRAPEZING
TRAPEZIST
TRAPEZIUM
TRAPEZIUS
TRAPEZOID
UTILIZING

AGROMYZID
ALDOLIZED
ALKALIZER
AMORTIZED
ANGELIZED
APHIDOZER
APHORIZED
APHORIZER
APPETIZED
APPETIZER
ARBORIZED
ARCHAIZED
ARCHAIZER
ASSOILZIE
ASTATIZED
ASTATIZER
ATHETIZED
ATMOLYZER
ATTICIZED
AZOBENZIL
AZOBENZOL
BAMBOOZLE
BILHARZIC
BOTANIZED
BOTANIZER
BULLDOZED
BULLDOZER
CALORIZER
CANALIZED
CANONIZED
CANONIZER
CAPONIZER
CATALYZED
CATALYZER
CHERNOZEM
CHRYSAZIN
CHRYSAZOL
CIVILIZEE
CIVILIZED
CIVILIZER
COLONIZED
COLONIZER
COMPRIZAL
COMPRIZED
COURTEZAN
CREOLIZED
CURARIZED
CUTINIZED
DECATIZER
DEMONIZED
DEPUTIZED
DEVILIZED
DIGITIZED
DIGITIZER
DISPRIZED
DISSEIZED
DISSEIZEE
DISSEIZOR
DIVINIZED
ECTOENZYM
ENDENIZEN
ENERGIZED
ENERGIZER
EQUALIZED
EQUALIZER
ERGOTIZED
ETERNIZED

ETHERIZED
ETHERIZER
ETHICIZED
EULOGIZED
EULOGIZER
EUPHUIZED
EXORCIZED
EXORCIZER
FARADIZED
FARADIZER
FIBERIZER
FINALIZED
FLUIDIZED
FOCALIZED
HUMANIZER
IDEALIZED
IDEALIZER
IMMUNIZED
INFAMIZED
ISONIAZID
JAROVIZED
KIBBUTZIM
LACONIZED
LACONIZER
LEGALIZED
LINENIZER
LOCALIZED
LOCALIZER
MACARIZED
MAXIMIZED
MAXIMIZER
MELODIZED
MELODIZER
MEMORIZER
METALIZED
MINIMIZED
MINIMIZER
MISPRIZED
MISPRIZER
MOBILIZED
MONETIZED
MORALIZED
MORALIZER
MOTORIZED
NASALIZED
NEBULIZED
NEBULIZER
NODULIZED
NOTARIZED
NOVELIZED
ONIONIZED
OPTIMIZED
ORGANIZED
ORGANIZER
OUTBRAZEN
OUTDAZZLE
OVERSIZED
OXYBENZYL
PAEANIZED
PAGANIZED
PAGANIZER
PAPALIZER
PARALYZED
PARALYZER
PAVONAZZO
PENALIZED
PHLORIZIN
POLARIZED
POLARIZER
POLICIZER
PRESTEZZA
PTYALIZED
QUANTIZED
RACEMIZED
RURALIZED
SANITIZED
SATIRIZED

SATIRIZER
SCHNAUZER
SCHNITZEL
SCHNOZZLE
SCLERIZED
SOLARIZED
SOLECIZED
SOLECIZER
STARGAZED
STARGAZER
STRAMAZON
SUBERIZED
SULPHAZID
SURPRIZAL
TARTRAZIN
TETANIZED
THEORIZED
THEORIZER
TOTALIZED
TOTALIZER
UNIONIZED
URBANIZED
VAPORIZER
VITALIZED
VITALIZER
VOCALIZED
VOCALIZER
WOMANIZED
WOMANIZER

ABURABOZU
ACADEMIZE
ACETALIZE
ACETONIZE
ACETYLIZE
ACTIONIZE
ACTUALIZE
ADVERTIZE
ALCARRAZA
ALCHEMIZE
ALTERNIZE
ALUMETIZE
ALUMINIZE
ANABOLIZE
ANALOGIZE
ANARCHIZE
ANATOMIZE
ANGLICIZE
ANHYDRIZE
ANIMALIZE
ANNUALIZE
APOLOGIZE
ARCTICIZE
AROMATIZE
AUTHORIZE
BACTERIZE
BALKANIZE
BALSAMIZE
BANTAMIZE
BARBARIZE
BEAVERIZE
BEDLAMIZE
BERGINIZE
BIOLOGIZE
BRUTALIZE
BURTONIZE
CARBOLIZE
CARBONIZE
CARBURIZE
CARNALIZE
CARTELIZE
CATECHIZE
CATHARIZE
CAUPONIZE
CAUTERIZE
CEREBRIZE
CHEMOLYZE

CICATRIZE
CITRONIZE
CLAVELIZE
CLIMATIZE
COCAINIZE
COMMUNIZE
COPPERIZE
COTTONIZE
CREOLEIZE
CRITICIZE
DECADENZA
DEEPFROZE
DEFERRIZE
DENITRIZE
DENTALIZE
DEODORIZE
DEOXIDIZE
DEOZONIZE
DESPOTIZE
DIABOLIZE
DIALOGIZE
DIAZOTIZE
DIESELIZE
DOCTORIZE
DOGMATIZE
DRAGONIZE
DRAMATIZE
DUCTILIZE
ECONOMIZE
ECPHORIZE
EKPHORIZE
ELECTRIZE
ELENCHIZE
EMBLEMIZE
EMPHASIZE
EPILOGIZE
EPIPOLIZE
EPITOMIZE
ESOTERIZE
EUPHEMIZE
EUPHONIZE
EVAPORIZE
FACTORIZE
FACULTIZE
FANTASIZE
FAUCALIZE
FECUNDIZE
FERTILIZE
FETICHIZE
FEUDALIZE
FISCALIZE
FISTULIZE
FOREPRIZE
FORMALIZE
FORMULIZE
FORTHGAZE
FOSSILIZE
FRIVOLIZE
GALLINAZO
GALVANIZE
GARDENIZE

GENIALIZE
GENTILIZE
GEOLOGIZE
GERMANIZE
GIGANTIZE
GLAMORIZE
GLUTINIZE
GLYCERIZE
GORGONIZE
GOSPELIZE
GRANITIZE
GRANULIZE
GUACONIZE
HAMLETIZE
HARMONIZE
HERALDIZE
HERBALIZE
HERBARIZE
HERBORIZE
HISTORIZE
HUMOURIZE
HYALINIZE
HYBRIDIZE
HYDROLYZE
HYGIENIZE
HYPNOTIZE
HYPOCRIZE
INFLUENZA
INOXIDIZE
ISOMERIZE
ITALICIZE
JARGONIZE
JASPERIZE
JENNERIZE
JOVIALIZE
KAOLINIZE
LABIALIZE
LACTONIZE
LADRONIZE
LICHENIZE
LIGNITIZE
LINEARIZE
LIQUIDIZE
LITURGIZE
MAGNETIZE
MAINPRIZE
MAMMONIZE
MANGANIZE
MANGONIZE
MANNERIZE
MARBELIZE
MARBLEIZE
MARMARIZE
MARRANIZE
MARTYRIZE
MATRONIZE
MECHANIZE
MEDIALIZE
MEDIATIZE
MEDIUMIZE

MEMORIZED
MENSALIZE
MERCERIZE
MERCURIZE
MESMERIZE
METALLIZE
METEORIZE
METHODIZE
METRICIZE
MNEMONIZE
MODERNIZE
MONACHIZE
MORGANIZE
MORSELIZE
MORTALIZE
MULLENIZE
MUTUALIZE
MYCORHIZA
MYSTERIZE
MYTHICIZE
NARCOTIZE
NECROTIZE
NECTARIZE
NEOLOGIZE
NEOTERIZE
NEUMATIZE
NICKELIZE
NITRIDIZE
NORMALIZE
OBJECTIZE
OPERATIZE
ORATORIZE
ORIENTIZE
OSTRACIZE
OVERGLAZE
OVERGRAZE
OVERPRIZE
OXYGENIZE
OXYTONIZE
PALLADIZE
PALLETIZE
PAMPERIZE
PANDERIZE
PASTORIZE
PATRONIZE
PAUPERIZE
PAVONAZZO
PEDANTIZE
PEGMATIZE
PEOPLEIZE
PEPTONIZE
PERSONIZE
PESSIMIZE
PETROLIZE
PHENOLIZE
PHONETIZE
PICTURIZE
PILLORIZE
PLATINIZE
PLURALIZE

POETICIZE
POSTERIZE
POSTURIZE
POTENTIZE
POWDERIZE
PRECONIZE
PREIOTIZE
PRELATIZE
PRELUDIZE
PRESTEZZA
PROFANIZE
PROLOGIZE
PROPOLIZE
PRYTANIZE
PUBLICIZE
PULVERIZE
PUPILLIZE
PUPPETIZE
PURPURIZE
PYTHONIZE
QUININIZE
QUINONIZE
RABBINIZE
RACIALIZE
RADIALIZE
RADIUMIZE
RANDOMIZE
RAPTURIZE
REBAPTIZE
RECOGNIZE
RHETORIZE
RHYTHMIZE
ROUTINIZE
RUBBERIZE
RUBRICIZE
RUSTICIZE
SATURNIZE
SCENARIZE
SCIENTIZE
SENSITIZE
SERIALIZE
SERMONIZE
SEXUALIZE
SIGNALIZE
SILVERIZE
SISTERIZE
SOCIALIZE
SOLEMNIZE
SOLVOLYZE
SONNETIZE
SORBITIZE
SOVIETIZE
SPIRALIZE
SPIRITIZE
SPONDAIZE
STABILIZE
STERILIZE
SUBSIDIZE
SULCALIZE
SULFATIZE

SULFURIZE
SULTANIZE
SUMMARIZE
SURGERIZE
SYLLABIZE
SYLLOGIZE
SYMBOLIZE
SYNCOPIZE
SYNERGIZE
SYNOECIZE
SYNOPSIZE
SYNTONIZE
SYPHILIZE
SYSTEMIZE
TANDEMIZE
TANTALIZE
TARIFFIZE
TARTARIZE
TAVERNIZE
TELLURIZE
TEMPORIZE
TENDERIZE
TERMINIZE
TERRORIZE
THEATRIZE
THYMOLIZE
TRINALIZE
TUCHUNIZE
TURTLEIZE
TYMPANIZE
TYRANNIZE
UGRIANIZE
UNBRUTIZE
UNCIALIZE
UNDERSIZE
UNREALIZE
URALITIZE
VACUUMIZE
VAMPIRIZE
VANDALIZE
VAPOURIZE
VASSALIZE
VERBALIZE
VERNALIZE
VICTIMIZE
VISCIDIZE
VISIONIZE
VISUALIZE
VOLCANIZE
VULCANIZE
VULGARIZE
WANTONIZE
WINTERIZE
WITTICIZE
WOOLENIZE
ZOOLOGIZE

BURKUNDAZ
RHEUMATIZ
SLIVOVITZ

SCORING ORDER LIST OF 9-LETTER WORDS

33
OXYBENZYL

31
RHIZOTAXY

30
EXOENZYME
MAXIMIZED
SCHIZAXON
ZYGOPHYTE
ZYGOTAXIS

29
DEZINKIFY
IZVOZCHIK
JAROVIZED
MAXIMIZER
OBJECTIZE
OXYGENIZE
QUINZIEME

28
CHEMOLYZE
EQUALIZED
EXORCIZED
HYDROLYZE
HYPOCRIZE
JOVIALIZE
KEVUTZOTH
KIBBUTZIM
LIQUIDIZE
MYCORHIZA
MYTHICIZE
OXYTONIZE
QUANTIZED
QUARTZOID
QUIZZICAL
SQUEEZING
ZOOMORPHY
ZOOPHYTIC
ZYMOLYTIC
ZYMOPHORE

27
AZOXONIUM
CRAZYWEED
DEOXIDIZE
DEZINCIFY
EKPHORIZE

EPIZEUXIS
EQUALIZER
EXORCIZER
HAPHAZARD
HYBRIDIZE
HYDRAZOIC
HYDROZOIC
JASPERIZE
MICROZYMA
MICROZYME
OXIDIZING
QUARTZITE
QUARTZOSE
QUARTZOUS
QUININIZE
QUINONIZE
QUINZAINE
SYZYGETIC
ZERMAHBUB
ZOOGRAPHY
ZYGOPHORE
ZYMOSCOPE

26

AZOPHENYL
BREEZEWAY
CHRYSAZIN
CHRYSAZOL
DIAZEUXIS
FETICHIZE
FURZECHAT
GLAZEWORK
HYLOZOISM
HYPNOTIZE
INOXIDIZE
JARGONIZE
KEVAZINGO
OXDIAZOLE
PEZOGRAPH
PHYTOZOAN
PHYTOZOON
POLYZOARY
PYRAZOLYL
PYTHONIZE
RAZORBACK
RHIZOTOMY
SCHIZOPOD
SYPHILIZE
THYMOLIZE
WAZIRSHIP
ZEPHYREAN
ZEPHYRIAN
ZEPHYROUS
ZIPPINGLY
ZOOPHYTAL
ZOOTECHNY
ZOOTROPHY
ZUMBOORUK
ZYGOMATIC
ZYGOSPERM
ZYMOGENIC
ZYMOLOGIC
ZYMOLYSIS

25

AGROMYZID
ALCHEMIZE
ANHYDRIZE
ARCHIZOIC
AZOFORMIC
BILHARZIC
BURKUNDAZ
CATECHIZE
CHABAZITE
CHALAZIUM
CHERNOZEM
COMPRIZED
DIZYGOTIC
ECPHORIZE
ECTOENZYM
EMPHASIZE
ENZYMATIC
ENZYMOTIC
EUPHEMIZE
FORTHGAZE
FRENZYING
HYDRAZINE
HYDRAZONE
HYDROZOAL
HYDROZOAN
HYDROZOID
HYDROZOON
HYGIENIZE
ISOXAZOLE
JENNERIZE
MAZOLYTIC
MECHANIZE
MONACHIZE
NAZIFYING
PHILOZOIC
POLYZOISM
PROZYMITE
RHIZOBIUM
RHIZOCARP
RHIZOCORM
SEXUALIZE
SYMBOLIZE
SYNCOPIZE
TYMPANIZE
VACUUMIZE
VAMPIRIZE
VICTIMIZE
WAYZGOOSE
ZEROAXIAL
ZOOCYTIUM
ZOOPHILIC
ZOOPHOBIA
ZOOPHORIC
ZUCCHETTO
ZYGOSTYLE
ZYMOMETER

24

APHIDOZER
APHORIZED
ARCHAIZED
AVIZANDUM
AZEDARACH
AZOCYCLIC
BALKANIZE
BAMBOOZLE
BOMBAZINE
BUZZGLOAK
CATALYZED
CIVILIZED
COMMUNIZE
COMPRIZAL
COPPERIZE
COPROZOIC
COSMOZOIC
CYANIZING
DEEPFROZE
DIAZOTYPE
DIBENZOYL
ECHOIZING
EMBLEMIZE
ETHICIZED
EUPHUIZED
FECUNDIZE
FILMIZING
FIZELYITE
FOCALIZED
FRIVOLIZE
FROWZIEST
GLYCERIZE
HYALINIZE
HYLOZOIST
INFAMIZED
JAZZINESS
LAMZIEKTE
MAZODYNIA
METHODIZE
MICROZOIC
NICKELIZE
PAMPERIZE
PARALYZED
PERHAZARD
POLYZOOID
POWDERIZE
PTYALIZED
PUBLICIZE
SHAHZADAH
SLIVOVITZ
SOLVOLYZE
SULPHAZID
TARIFFIZE
VISCIDIZE
VOCALIZED
WHEEZIEST
WOMANIZED
ZAMINDARY
ZEBRALIKE
ZEBRAWOOD
ZINCIFIED
ZOOFULVIN
ZOOPHAGAN
ZOOSCOPIC
ZYGANTRUM
ZYGOSPORE

23

ACADEMIZE
ACETYLIZE
ANARCHIZE
ANTHOZOIC
APHORIZER
APHRIZITE
APPETIZED
APPRIZING
ARCHAIZER
ATMOLYZER
AZEOTROPY
AZIMUTHAL
AZOPHENOL
BAPTIZING
BEAVERIZE
BEDLAMIZE
BENZAMIDE
BENZAMIDO
BEZOARDIC
BIZARRELY
BLIZZARDY
BLOWZIEST
BUZZARDLY
CAPSIZING
CATALYZER
CATHARIZE
CHALAZIAN
CHALAZION
CHINTZIER
CHORIZONT
CITIZENLY
CITIZENRY
CIVILIZEE
CIVILIZER
CLAVELIZE
FACTORIZE
DEVILIZED
DIALYZING
DIVINIZED
DUNZIEKTE
ELENCHIZE
EMBLAZING
ENZYMOSIS
EUPHONIZE
EVAPORIZE
FACULTIZE
FARADIZED
FAUCALIZE
FIBERIZER
FISCALIZE
FLUIDIZED
FOREPRIZE
FORMALIZE
FORMULIZE
FREEZABLE
GAUZELIKE
GAUZEWING
GAZEHOUND
GRAZINGLY
GRIZZLIER
HAMLETIZE
HARMONIZE
HERBALIZE
HERBARIZE
HERBORIZE
HUMANIZER
HUMOURIZE
IMMUNIZED
LAZYBONES
LAZYBOOTS
LICHENIZE
MACARIZED
MAIZEBIRD
MARTYRIZE
MAZOLYSIS
MEDIUMIZE
MEMORIZED
MINIMIZED
MISPRIZED
MOBILIZED
MYSTERIZE
OPTIMIZED
OVERPRIZE
PARALYZER
PECTIZING
PEGMATIZE
PEPTIZING
PHENAZINE
PHENAZONE
PHENOLIZE
PHLORIZIN
PHONETIZE
POLYZONAL
PROFANIZE
PRYTANIZE
PULVERIZE
PUZZLEDLY
RACEMIZED
RHEUMATIZ
RHIZOCAUL
RHIZOTOMI
SCHNAUZER
SCHNITZEL
SIZARSHIP
SYLLABIZE
SYNOECIZE
SYNOPSIZE
SYSTEMIZE
TOPAZFELS
TUCHUNIZE
VAPORIZER
VAPOURIZE
VERBALIZE
VIZARDING
VOCALIZER
VOLCANIZE
VULCANIZE
WITTICIZE
WOMANIZER
ZELOTYPIA
ZELOTYPIE
ZENDIKITE
ZEUGMATIC
ZOEHEMERA
ZOOCYTIAL
ZOOLITHIC
ZOOPHILIA
ZOOPHORUS
ZOOPLASTY
ZOOSPHERE
ZOOTHECIA
ZOOTHEISM
ZYGADENIN

22

ABURABOZU
ADVERTIZE
ALKALIZER
AMAZEMENT
ANALYZING
APPETIZER
ARCTICIZE
ATHETIZED
AZALEAMUM
BACTERIZE
BALSAMIZE
BANTAMIZE
BARBARIZE
BEDIZENED
BULLDOZED
CAPONIZER
CAPRIZANT
CARBAZINE
CARBAZOLE
CARBOLIZE
CARBONIZE
CARBURIZE
CAUPONIZE
CEREBRIZE
CICATRIZE
CLIMATIZE
COCAINIZE
COELOZOIC
COGNIZING
CRITICIZE
CZARISTIC
DECADENZA
DEFERRIZE
DEMONIZED
DEPUTIZED
DIALYZATE
DISPRIZED
DIZZARDLY
DOGMATIZE
ECONOMIZE
EMBEZZLED
EPIPOLIZE
EPITOMIZE
EPIZOOTIC
ETHERIZED
FARADIZER
FEUDALIZE
FINALIZED
GALVANIZE
HAZARDOUS
HERALDIZE
KAOLINIZE
KRANTZITE
MAGAZINED
MAINPRIZE
MARBELIZE
MARBLEIZE
MARMARIZE
MEGAZOOID
MELODIZED

MEMORIZER
MERCERIZE
MERCURIZE
MESMERIZE
METRICIZE
MEZCALINE
MICROZOAL
MICROZOAN
MICROZONE
MICROZOON
MINIMIZER
MISPRIZER
MIZENMAST
MNEMONIZE
NOVELIZED
OVERGLAZE
OVERGRAZE
OVERSIZED
PAGANIZED
PANZOOTIC
PAPALIZER
PAUPERIZE
PAVONAZZO
PEOPLEIZE
PEPTONIZE
PESSIMIZE
POETICIZE
POLICIZER
PRECONIZE
PRIZEABLE
PROPOLIZE
PROTOZOIC
PUPILLIZE
PURPURIZE
RABBINIZE
RAZZBERRY
REBAPTIZE
RHODIZITE
RUBBERIZE
RUBRICIZE
SAPROZOIC
SCAZONTIC
SCHNOZZLE
SFORZANDO
SPOROZOIC
STYLIZING
SULFAZIDE
SUMMARIZE
SYLLOGIZE
SYNERGIZE
TEMPORIZE
THEORIZED
THIOZONID
TRAPEZIUM
TWEEZERED
VANDALIZE
VITALIZED
VULGARIZE
ZINCALISM
ZINFANDEL
ZINKENITE
ZIRCONIUM
ZIRKELITE
ZOANTHOID
ZOETROPIC
ZOOMETRIC
ZOOSPORIC
ZUCCARINO
ZUURVELDT
ZYGONEURE

21

AMORTIZED
ANGLICIZE
ANTHOZOAN
ANTHOZOON
APOLOGIZE
ARBORIZED
ARRHIZOUS
ATOMIZING
ATTICIZED
AUTHORIZE
AZIETHANE
BEDAZZLED
BENZENOID
BENZIDINE
BENZIDINO
BENZOATED
BERGINIZE
BIOLOGIZE
BIZARDITE
BLAZONING
BOTANIZED
BRAZENING
BULLDOZER
CANALIZED
CANONIZED
COALIZING
COGNIZANT
COLONIZED
CREOLIZED
CURARIZED
CUTINIZED
DECATIZER
DEGLAZING
DESPOTIZE
DIABOLIZE
DIAZEUTIC
DIAZOAMIN
DIÀZONIUM
DIGITIZED
DIZENMENT
DOCTORIZE
DOUZEPERS
DRAMATIZE
DUCTILIZE
DZIGGETAI
EBONIZING
EMBEZZLER
EPILOGIZE
ETHERIZER
FANTASIZE
FERTILIZE
FISTULIZE
FLORIZINE
FOSSILIZE
FRAZZLING
FRIZZLING
GERMANIZE
GLAMORIZE
GOSPELIZE
GUACONIZE
HELIOZOAN
HISTORIZE
IMIDAZOLE
INFLUENZA
ITEMIZING
LACONIZED
LAICIZING
LOCALIZED
MAGAZINER
MAGNETIZE
MALGUZARI
MAMMONIZE
MANGANIZE
MANGONIZE
MAZEDNESS
MEDIALIZE
MEDIATIZE
MELODIZER
MENDOZITE
METALIZED
MODERNIZE
MONETIZED
MORALIZED
MORGANIZE
MOTORIZED
NEBULIZED
OBELIZING
OPALIZING
ORYZANINE
PAEANIZED
PAGANIZER
PALLADIZE
PANDERIZE
PEDANTIZE
PENALIZED
PIZZICATO
POETIZING
POLARIZED
PRELUDIZE
PROLOGIZE
PUPPETIZE
PUZZLEMAN
RADIUMIZE
RANDOMIZE
RECOGNIZE
RHETORIZE
RHIZINOUS
SCLERIZED
SILVERIZE
SMORZANDO
SOLECIZED
SOVIETIZE
SPONDAIZE
SPOROZOID
SUBERIZED
SUBSIDIZE
SULFATIZE
SULFURIZE
SYNEZISIS
SYNIZESIS
SYNTONIZE
TANDEMIZE
TAVERNIZE
THEATRIZE
THEORIZER
TRAPEZING
TRAPEZOID
TYRANNIZE
URBANIZED
VASSALIZE
VERNALIZE
VISIONIZE
VISUALIZE
VITALIZER
VIZIERATE
VIZIERIAL
WANTONIZE
WINTERIZE
WOOLENIZE
WOOZINESS
ZAMINDARI
ZAPATEADO
ZEALOUSLY
ZEMINDARI
ZENDICIAN
ZIRCONOID
ZITHERIST
ZOOGAMETE
ZOOGAMOUS
ZOOGLOEIC
ZOOTHEIST
ZWANZIGER

20

ACETALIZE
ACETONIZE
ACTIONIZE
ACTUALIZE
ADONIZING
AGATIZING
AGONIZING
ALCARRAZA
ALDOLIZED
ALUMETIZE
ALUMINIZE
AMAZONITE
ANABOLIZE
ANATOMIZE
ANGELIZED
ANIMALIZE
ANODIZING
AROMATIZE
AZEOTROPE
AZLACTONE
AZOLITMIN
BALZARINE
BENZOLATE
BENZOLINE
BEZESTEEN
BOOZINESS
BOTANIZER
BRAZILEIN
BRAZILITE
BRUTALIZE
BURTONIZE
CALORIZER
CANONIZER
CARNALIZE
CARTELIZE
CAUTERIZE
CITRONIZE
COLAZIONE
COLONIZER
COTTONIZE
COURTEZAN
CRAZINESS
CREOLEIZE
CZARINIAN
DAZEDNESS
DEODORIZE
DIALOGIZE
DIGITIZER
DISSEIZED
DRAGONIZE
DUALIZING
EGOTIZING
ELECTRIZE
ELEGIZING
ENERGIZED
ERGOTIZED
EULOGIZED
FRIZZIEST
FUZZINESS
GARDENIZE
GAZETTING
GEOLOGIZE
GIGANTIZE
GONOZOOID
GORGONIZE
IDEALIZED
IDOLIZING
IONIZABLE
IRIDIZING
ISOMERIZE
ITALICIZE
LABIALIZE
LACONIZER
LACTONIZE
LAZULITIC
LEGALIZED
LOCALIZER
MANNERIZE
MANZANITA
MARRANIZE
MATRONIZE
MENSALIZE
MESTIZOES
METALLIZE
METEORIZE
MONZONITE
MORALIZER
MORSELIZE
MORTALIZE
MULLENIZE
MUTUALIZE
NARCOTIZE
NEBULIZER
NECROTIZE
NECTARIZE
NEUMATIZE
NODULIZED
NORMALIZE
OPERATIZE
ORGANIZED
OSTRACIZE
OUTBRAZEN
OZOCERITE
OZOSTOMIA
PALLETIZE
PANZOOTIA
PASTORIZE
PATRIZATE
PATRONIZE
PERSONIZE
PETROLIZE
PILLORIZE
PLATINIZE
PLURALIZE
POLARIZER
POLZENITE
POSTERIZE
POSTURIZE
POTENTIZE
PREIOTIZE
PRELATIZE
PROTOZOAL
PROTOZOAN
PROTOZOEA
PROTOZOON
RACIALIZE
RAPTURIZE
RAZORBILL
RAZOREDGE
RUSTICIZE
SCENARIZE
SCIENTIZE
SERMONIZE
SOCIALIZE
SOLECIZER
SOLEMNIZE
SOLMIZATE
SORBITIZE
SPIRALIZE
SPIRITIZE
SPOROZOAL
SPOROZOAN
SPOROZOON
STABILIZE
STARGAZED
STRAMAZON
SULCALIZE
SURPRIZAL
TELEOZOIC
TERMINIZE
TRAPEZIAL
TRAPEZIAN
TRAPEZIST
TRAPEZIUS
UNBRUTIZE
UNCIALIZE
ZEALOTISM
ZELATRICE
ZIBELLINE

ZIRLONATE
ZOOPERIST
ZOOTOMIST

19

ALLOZOOID
ANALOGIZE
ASTATIZED
AUTOZOOID
AZOBENZIL
AZOBENZOL
BENZOLIZE
DENITRIZE
DENTALIZE
DIAZOTATE
DIESELIZE
DIETZEITE
DISSEIZOR
DRIZZLING
ENDENIZEN
ENERGIZER
ETERNIZED
EULOGIZER
GALLINAZO
GAUZINESS
GAZETTEER
GENIALIZE
GENTILIZE
GLAZINESS
GLUTINIZE
GRANITIZE
GRANULIZE
GRIZZLING
IDEALIZER
ISONIAZID
LADRONIZE
LIGNITIZE
LIONIZING
LITURGIZE
MEZZANINE
MEZZOTINT
MIZZONITE
NASALIZED
NEOLOGIZE
NITRIDIZE
NOTARIZED
ONIONIZED
ORGANIZER
ORGANZINE
PIAZZETTA
POZZOLANA
PRESTEZZA
RADIALIZE
REALIZING
RURALIZED
SANITIZED
SATIRIZED
SIGNALIZE
SOLARIZED
STARGAZER
SURGERIZE
TENDERIZE
TETANIZED
TOTALIZED
TRIOZONID
UNDERSIZE
UNIONIZED
UTILIZING
ZINGERONE
ZOOGENOUS
ZOOGLOEAL
ZOOGONOUS
ZOOLOGIES
ZOOLOGIST

18

ALIZARATE
ALIZARINE
ALTERNIZE
ANNUALIZE
ARIZONITE
ARZRUNITE
ASSOILZIE
ASTATIZER
AZOTIZING
DEOZONIZE
DIAZOTIZE
DIZZINESS
ESOTERIZE
GRIZZLIES
LAZARETTE
LAZARETTO
LINEARIZE
LINENIZER
NEOTERIZE
ORATORIZE
ORIENTIZE
OUTDAZZLE
OZONATION
OZONIZING
RESEIZURE
ROUTINIZE
SATIRIZER
SATURNIZE
SENSITIZE
SERIALIZE
SISTERIZE
SONNETIZE
STERILIZE
SULTANIZE
TANTALIZE
TARTARIZE
TARTRAZIN
TELEOZOON
TELLURIZE
TERRORIZE
TERZETTOS
TETRAZANE
TETRAZENE
TETRAZINE
TETRAZOLE
TETRAZONE
TINZENITE
TOTALIZER
TRINALIZE
TURTLEIZE
UNREALIZE
URALITIZE
ZEALOTIST
ZEUNERITE
ZOOLOGIZE

17

LAZZARONE
LAZZARONI
ZEOLITIZE

ALPHABETICAL LIST OF 10-LETTER WORDS

ACADEMIZED
ACETYLIZER
ACTINOZOAL
ACTINOZOAN
ACTIONIZED
ACTUALIZED
ADRENALIZE
ADULTERIZE
AGGRANDIZE
AGLAOZONIA
AIZOACEOUS
AKHUNDZADA
ALBUMENIZE
ALBUMINIZE
ALCALIZATE
ALCHEMIZED
ALCOHOLIZE
ALDOLIZING
ALGEBRAIZE
ALKALINIZE
ALKALIZATE
ALLEGORIZE
ALLOCHEZIA
ALTAZIMUTH
ALUMINIZED
AMALGAMIZE
AMIDRAZONE
AMMONOLYZE
AMORTIZING
ANABIBAZON
ANALOGIZED
ANALYZABLE
ANATHEMIZE
ANATOMIZED
ANATOMIZER
ANAZOTURIA
ANGELICIZE
ANGELIZING
ANGLICIZED
ANGULARIZE
ANIMALIZED
ANTAGONIZE
ANTHOZOOID
ANTIFREEZE
APHORIZING
APOLOGIZED
APOLOGIZER
APOSTATIZE
APOSTOLIZE
APOZEMICAL
APPETIZING
ARBORIZING
ARCHAIZING
ARCTICIZED
AROMATIZED
AROMATIZER
ARSENICIZE
ARTHROZOAN
ARTHROZOIC
ASEPTICIZE
ASEXUALIZE
ASSIZEMENT
ASTATIZING
ASYZYGETIC
ATHETIZING
ATROPINIZE
ATTICIZING
AUTHORIZED
AUTHORIZER
AUTOLYZATE
AUTOMATIZE
AUTONOMIZE
AUTOTOMIZE
AUTOXIDIZE
AXIOMATIZE
AZEOTROPIC
AZOBENZENE
AZOBENZOIC
AZOCORINTH
AZOCYANIDE
AZOGALLEIN
AZOMETHINE
AZOPHENINE
AZOPROTEIN
AZOTENESIS
AZOTOLUENE
AZOTOMETER
AZOTORRHEA
AZOVERNINE
AZTHIONIUM
AZYGOSPERM
AZYGOSPORE
BACTERIZED
BALKANIZED
BAMBOOZLED
BAMBOOZLER
BANTINGIZE
BARBARIZED
BARTIZANED
BASTARDIZE
BEBIZATION
BEDAZZLING
BEDIZENING
BENZEDRINE
BENZOCAINE
BENZOPYRAN
BENZOYLATE
BERZELIITE
BESTIALIZE
BILHARZIAL
BITUMINIZE
BIZARRERIE
BLAZONMENT
BLIZZARDLY
BOBIZATION
BOLSHEVIZE
BOMBAZETTE
BOTANIZING
BOUCHERIZE
BOURBONIZE
BOWDLERIZE
BRAZENFACE
BRAZENNESS
BRAZILETTE
BRAZILWOOD
BREEZINESS
BRONZEWING
BRONZITITE
BRUTALIZED
BULLDOZING
BURGLARIZE
BURNETTIZE
CALZONERAS
CANALIZING
CANONIZANT
CANONIZING
CAPITALIZE
CARAMELIZE
CARBAZYLIC
CARBOLIZED
CARBONIZED
CARBONIZER
CARBURIZED
CARBURIZER
CARNALIZED
CASTORIZED
CATABOLIZE
CATALYZING
CATECHIZED
CATECHIZER
CATEGORIZE
CATHARIZED
CAUSTICIZE
CAUTERIZED
CENTRALIZE
CHALAZOGAM
CHANNELIZE
CHATTELIZE
CHERVONETZ
CHIMPANZEE
CHINTZIEST
CHITINIZED
CHLORALIZE
CHLORAZIDE
CHLORIDIZE
CHLORITIZE
CHLORODIZE
CHRIZONTAL
CHROMATIZE
CHROMICIZE
CICATRIZED
CICATRIZER
CICERONIZE
CINCHONIZE
CITIZENESS
CITIZENISM
CITIZENIZE
CIVILIZING
CLASSICIZE
COAZERVATE
COCAINIZED
COCKNEYIZE
COGNIZABLE
COGNIZABLY
COGNIZANCE
COLEORHIZA
COLLOQUIZE
COLONIZING
COMMUNIZED
COMPRIZING

CONCERTIZE
CONCRETIZE
COSMOZOANS
COSMOZOISM
COZENINGLY
CRAZEDNESS
CREOLIZING
CRITICIZED
CRITICIZER
CROFTERIZE
CRYPTOZOIC
CUCKOLDIZE
CURARIZING
CUTINIZING
CUTIZATION
CYTOZYMASE
CZAREVITCH
DANDIZETTE
DASTARDIZE
DAZZLINGLY
DEALKALIZE
DECIMALIZE
DECIVILIZE
DECOLORIZE
DEEPFREEZE
DEEPFROZEN
DEFEMINIZE
DEFERRIZED
DEFINITIZE
DEHEMATIZE
DEHEPATIZE
DEHUMANIZE
DELEGALIZE
DELIMITIZE
DELOCALIZE
DELUMINIZE
DEMOBILIZE
DEMONIZING
DEMORALIZE
DENATURIZE
DENAZIFIED
DENIZATION
DENIZENIZE
DEODORIZED
DEODORIZER
DEOXIDIZED
DEOXIDIZER
DEOZONIZER
DEPETALIZE
DEPOLARIZE
DEPRIORIZE
DEPUTIZING
DERESINIZE
DEVILIZING
DEVIRILIZE
DEVITALIZE
DEVOCALIZE
DEXTRINIZE
DEZYMOTIZE
DIABOLIZED
DIALOGIZED
DIALYZABLE
DIALYZATOR
DIAMONDIZE
DIAZOAMINE
DIAZOIMIDE
DIAZOTIZED
DIGITALIZE
DIGITIZING
DIPLOIDIZE
DIPOLARIZE
DISASINIZE
DISPRIZING
DISREALIZE
DISSEIZURE
DIVINIZING
DOCTRINIZE
DOGGRELIZE
DOGMATIZED
DOGMATIZER
DOLOMITIZE
DOUZAINIER
DOXOLOGIZE
DRAMATIZED
DRAMATIZER
DUCTILIZED
DYSOXIDIZE
ECONOMIZED
ECONOMIZER
ECTOENZYME
ECZEMATOID
ECZEMATOUS
EFFEMINIZE
ELASTICIZE
ELECTRIZED
ELECTRIZER
EMBEZZLING
EMBLAZONED
EMBLAZONER
EMBLAZONRY
EMBLEMIZED
EMOTIONIZE
EMPATHIZED
EMPHASIZED
EMPHATHIZE
ENDOENZYME
ENERGIZING
ENGRANDIZE
ENIGMATIZE
ENOLIZABLE
ENTHRONIZE
ENZYMOLOGY
EPILOGIZED
EPIRHIZOUS
EPISCOPIZE
EPISTOLIZE
EPITAPHIZE
EPITHELIZE
EPITOMIZED
EPITOMIZER
EQUALIZING
ERGOTIZING
ESTERIZING
ETERNALIZE
ETERNIZING
ETHERIZING
ETHICIZING
EUHEMERIZE
EULOGIZING
EUPHEMIZED
EUPHEMIZER
EUPHONIZED
EUPHUIZING
EUPOLYZOAN
EURYZYGOUS
EVANGELIZE
EXORCIZING
EXZODIACAL
FACKELTANZ
FACTORIZED
FANATICIZE
FANTASIZED
FARCIALIZE
FASCISTIZE
FASHIONIZE
FAZENDEIRO
FEDERALIZE
FERTILIZED
FERTILIZER
FERTILIZIN
FEUDALIZED
FICTIONIZE
FINALIZING
FISCALIZED
FLUIDIZING
FOCALIZING
FORMALIZED
FORMULIZED
FORMULIZER
FOSSILIZED
FRATERNIZE
FRENZIEDLY
FRIVOLIZED
FRIZZINESS
FROWZINESS
FROZENNESS
GALLICIZER
GALVANIZED
GALVANIZER
GAZANGABIN
GELATINIZE
GENERALIZE
GEOLOGIZED
GEOMETRIZE
GLAMORIZED
GLOTTALIZE
GLUTTONIZE
GNATHONIZE
GOLANDAUZE
GOLUNDAUZE
GORGONIZED
GRANGERIZE
GRAPHITIZE
GRIZZLIEST
GRIZZLYMAN
HARMONIZER
HEMATOZOON
HERETICIZE
HOMOGENIZE
HOMOLOGIZE
HOMOZYGOTE
HOMOZYGOUS
HORIZONTAL
HYBRIDIZER
HYDRAZOATE
HYDRORHIZA
HYPNOIDIZE
HYPOZEUGMA
HYPOZEUXIS
ICHTHYIZED
IDEALIZING
IDOLATRIZE
ILLEGALIZE
IMIDAZOLYL
IMMOBILIZE
INFAMIZING
INFAMONIZE
INFLUENZAL
INFLUENZIC
INGRANDIZE
INKHORNIZE
INOXIDIZED
INTERMEZZI
INTERMEZZO
INTERZONAL
INTHRONIZE
IODIZATION
IONIZATION
IOTIZATION
ITALICIZED
JANIZARIES
JARGONIZED
JAROVIZING
JASPERIZED
JEOPARDIZE
JOURNALIZE
JOVIALIZED
KAMAREZITE
KATABOLIZE
KERATINIZE
LABIALIZED
LACONIZING
LATERALIZE
LATIBULIZE
LAZARETTOS
LEGALIZING
LEGITIMIZE
LETHARGIZE
LEXICONIZE
LIBERALIZE
LINGUALIZE
LIONIZABLE
LIQUIDIZED
LITERALIZE
LIZARDTAIL
LOCALIZING
LOGICALIZE
MACADAMIZE
MACARIZING
MAGAZINAGE
MAGAZINING
MAGAZINISM
MAGAZINIST
MAGNETIZED
MAGNETIZER
MAHOGANIZE
MAINPRIZER
MALLEINIZE
MANZANILLA
MANZANILLO
MARBLEIZED
MARBLEIZER
MARMARIZED
MARTIALIZE
MARTYRIZED
MARTYRIZER
MATRONIZED
MAXIMIZING
MAZAPILITE
MAZOPATHIA
MAZOPATHIC
MECHANIZER
MEDIATIZED
MELEZITASE
MELEZITOSE
MELODIZING
MEMORIZING
MERCERIZED
MERCERIZER
MERCURIZED
MEROTOMIZE
MESMERIZED
MESMERIZEE
MESMERIZER
METABOLIZE
METALIZING
METHODIZED
METHODIZER
MEZZOGRAPH
MEZZOTINTO
MICROZOARY
MICROZOOID
MILITARIZE
MILLIONIZE
MINERALIZE
MINIMIZING
MIRACULIZE
MISBAPTIZE
MISPRIZING
MIZZENMAST
MNEMONIZED
MOBILIZING
MODERNIZED
MODERNIZER
MONARCHIZE
MONETIZING
MONGRELIZE
MONOLOGIZE
MONONYMIZE
MONOPOLIZE
MONOTONIZE
MONZONITIC
MORALIZING
MORPHINIZE
MORTALIZED
MOTORIZING
MOZZARELLA
MUSICALIZE
MUTUALIZED
MUZZLEWOOD
MYCETOZOAN
MYCETOZOON
MYCOLOGIZE
MYCORHIZAL
MYCORRHIZA
MYECTOMIZE
MYTHICIZED
MYTHICIZER
MYZOSTOMID
NANIZATION
NARCOTIZED
NASALIZING
NATURALIZE
NEBULARIZE
NEBULIZING
NEOLOGIZED
NESSLERIZE
NEUTRALIZE
NICOTINIZE
NONCITIZEN
NORMALIZED
NORMALIZER
NOTARIZING
NOTHINGIZE
NOTORHIZAL
NOVELIZING
OBITUARIZE
OBJECTIZED
ONTOLOGIZE
ORGANIZING
ORGANZINED
ORIGANIZED
OSTRACIZED
OSTRACIZER
OVERFRIEZE
OVERGLAZED
OVERPRIZED
OVERPRIZER
OXADIAZOLE
OXIDIZABLE
OXOZONIDES
OXYGENIZED
OXYGENIZER
OZONOMETER
OZONOMETRY
OZONOSCOPE
PAEANIZING
PAGANIZING
PALATALIZE
PALLETIZED
PANEGYRIZE
PARABOLIZE
PARAGOGIZE
PARALOGIZE
PARALYZANT
PARALYZING
PARASITIZE
PARAZONIUM
PARENESIZE
PARONYMIZE
PASSEMEZZO
PASTEURIZE
PATRONIZED
PATRONIZER
PATTERNIZE

PAUPERIZED
PEASANTIZE
PECTIZABLE
PENALIZING
PEPTIZABLE
PEPTONIZED
PEPTONIZER
PERIPATIZE
PERITOMIZE
PERIZONIUM
PEROXIDIZE
PETROLIZED
PEZIZIFORM
PHANTASIZE
PHANTOMIZE
PHILIPPIZE
PHILOZOIST
PHLORHIZIN
PHLORIDZIN
PHLYZACIUM
PICRORHIZA
PIEZOMETER
PIEZOMETRY
PIGMENTIZE
PILEORHIZA
PILEORHIZE
PILGRIMIZE
PIPERAZINE
PLAGIARIZE
PLASMOLYZE
PLASTICIZE
PLATINIZED
PLURALIZED
PLURALIZER
PNEUMATIZE
POLARIZING
POLITICIZE
POLYGAMIZE
POLYMERIZE
POLYTHEIZE
POLYZOARIA
POPULARIZE
POSITIVIZE
POSTURIZED
POULARDIZE
POWDERIZER
POZZOLANIC
POZZUOLANA
PRAGMATIZE
PRECOGNIZE
PRECONIZED
PRECONIZER
PREDAZZITE
PRESSURIZE
PRISMATIZE
PRIZEFIGHT
PRIZETAKER
PROBLEMIZE
PROCTORIZE
PROLOGUIZE
PROPHETIZE
PROVERBIZE
PSALMODIZE
PTYALIZING
PUBLICIZED
PULVERIZED
PULVERIZER
PUZZLEHEAD
PUZZLEMENT
PUZZLEPATE
PUZZLINGLY
PYRAZOLINE
PYRAZOLONE
PYRIDAZINE
PYRIDINIZE
QUINAZOLIN
QUINAZOLYL
QUINIZARIN
QUARTZITIC
QUATORZAIN
RACEMIZING
RADICALIZE
RAMFEEZLED
RANDOMIZED
RAZORMAKER
RAZORSTROP
REALIZABLE
REBAPTIZER
RECOGNIZEE
RECOGNIZED
RECOGNIZER
RECOGNIZOR
REDISSEIZE
REGULARIZE
REJUVENIZE
REMONETIZE
RENDEZVOUS
REORGANIZE
REVALORIZE
REVITALIZE
REZBANYITE
RHAPSODIZE
RHEUMATIZE
RHIZOGENIC
RHIZOMATIC
RHIZOMELIC
RHIZOMORPH
RHIZONEURE
RHIZOPHORE
RHIZOPHYTE
RHIZOPLAST
RHIZOPODAL
RHIZOPODAN
RHIZOSTOME
RHIZOTAXIS
RHODIZONIC
ROUTINIZED
RUBBERIZED
RUFFIANIZE
RURALIZING
SACCHARIZE
SALICYLIZE
SAPIENTIZE
SATIRIZING
SCANDALIZE
SCEPTICIZE
SCHEDULIZE
SCHEMATIZE
SCHEMOZZLE
SCHERZANDO
SCHIZOCARP
SCHIZOGAMY
SCHIZOGONY
SCHIZOLITE
SCORBUTIZE
SCRUTINIZE
SCYPHOZOAN
SECTIONIZE
SECULARIZE
SELTZOGENE
SEMINARIZE
SENSITIZED
SENSITIZER
SENSUALIZE
SERIALIZED
SERMONIZED
SERMONIZER
SERPENTIZE
SEVERALIZE
SFORZANDOS
SHERARDIZE
SIGNALIZED
SILICIDIZE
SILICONIZE
SIMPLICIZE
SIZZLINGLY
SKEPTICIZE
SLEAZINESS
SLENDERIZE
SNEEZEWEED
SNEEZEWOOD
SNEEZEWORT
SOCIALIZED
SOCIALIZER
SOLARIZING
SOLECIZING
SOLEMNIZED
SOLEMNIZER
SOLIDARIZE
SOLUBILIZE
SOLVOLYZED
SOPHRONIZE
SOVIETIZED
SPATIALIZE
SPECIALIZE
SPERMATIZE
SPHETERIZE
SPIRANTIZE
SPITZFLUTE
SPOROZOITE
SPOROZOOID
SQUEEZABLE
SQUEEZEMAN
STABILIZED
STABILIZER
STANZAICAL
STARGAZING
STERILIZED
STERILIZER
STIGMATIZE
STRATEGIZE
STYFZIEKTE
STYLOPIZED
SUBERINIZE
SUBERIZING
SUBSIDIZED
SUBSIDIZER
SUBTILIZED
SUBTILIZER
SULFATIZED
SULFURIZED
SULPHATIZE
SULPHAZIDE
SULPHIDIZE
SULPHURIZE
SUMMARIZED
SUMMARIZER
SUZERAINTY
SYLLABIZED
SYLLOGIZED
SYLLOGIZER
SYMBOLIZED
SYMBOLIZER
SYMMETRIZE
SYMPATHIZE
SYMPHONIZE
SYMPHYTIZE
SYNCRETIZE
SYNONYMIZE
SYNTHESIZE
SYNTHETIZE
SYNTONIZED
SYNTONIZER
SYPHILIZED
SYSTEMIZED
SYSTEMIZER
TABULARIZE
TANTALIZED
TANTALIZER
TARLTONIZE
TARTARIZED
TARTRAZINE
TAUTOZONAL
TELFORDIZE
TELLURIZED
TEMPORIZED
TEMPORIZER
TENDERIZED
TENDERIZER
TENOTOMIZE
TEPONAZTLI
TERRORIZED
TERRORIZER
TETANIZING
TETRAZOLYL
THEOLOGIZE
THEORIZING
THERMOLYZE
THIAZOLINE
THIOZONIDE
TOPAZOLITE
TOTALIZING
TRACTORIZE
TRAPEZIUMS
TRAUMATIZE
TRICHINIZE
TRIOZONIDE
TRITOZOOID
TRIVIALIZE
TROCHEEIZE
TROCHOZOIC
TROCHOZOON
TRYPSINIZE
TRYPTONIZE
TWEEZERING
TYRANNIZED
TYRANNIZER
WARRANTIZE
UNBAPTIZED
UNCANONIZE
UNDERGLAZE
UNDERSIZED
UNIFORMIZE
UNIONIZING
UNITEMIZED
UNPRIZABLE
UNREALIZED
UNSTOICIZE
URALITIZED
URBANIZING
UTILIZABLE
VAGOTOMIZE
VAGRANTIZE
VAPOURIZED
VAPOURIZER
VASSALIZED
VENEZOLANO
VERATRIZED
VERBALIZED
VERBALIZER
VERSIONIZE
VESZELYITE
VETERANIZE
VICTIMIZED
VICTIMIZER
VISIBILIZE
VISUALIZED
VISUALIZER
VITALIZING
VITAMINIZE
VITRIOLIZE
VOCALIZING
VOCIFERIZE
VOLATILIZE
VOLCANIZED
VULCANIZED
VULCANIZER
VULGARIZED
VULGARIZER
WESTERNIZE
WHEEZINESS
WHEEZINGLY
WHITEBLAZE
WHIZZERMAN
WHIZZINGLY
WINTERIZED
WITZCHOURA
WOMANIZING
WOOLLENIZE
ZABAGLIONE
ZAPHRENTID
ZEALOTICAL
ZEBRINNIES
ZENOGRAPHY
ZEOLITIZED
ZEUGLODONT
ZIGZAGGERY
ZINCIFYING
ZINCOGRAPH
ZINCOLYSIS
ZINGARESCA
ZINGIBEROL
ZOANTHROPY
ZONIFEROUS
ZOOBENTHOS
ZOOCULTURE
ZOOCURRENT
ZOOGRAPHER
ZOOGRAPHIC
ZOOLATRIES
ZOOLATROUS
ZOOLOGICAL
ZOOLOGIZED
ZOOMELANIN
ZOOMIMETIC
ZOOMORPHIC
ZOOPHAGOUS
ZOOPHILISM
ZOOPHILIST
ZOOPHILITE
ZOOPHILOUS
ZOOPHOBOUS
ZOOPHYSICS
ZOOPHYTISH
ZOOPHYTOID
ZOOPLASTIC
ZOOSPOROUS
ZOOTECHNIC
ZOOTHECIAL
ZOOTHECIUM
ZOOTHERAPY
ZOOTOMICAL
ZOOTROPHIC
ZOOXANTHIN
ZWITTERION
ZYGADENINE
ZYGOBRANCH
ZYGODACTYL
ZYGOMYCETE
ZYGOPHORIC
ZYGOSPHENE
ZYGOSPHERE
ZYGOSPORIC
ZYGOTACTIC
ZYMOGENOUS
ZYMOLOGIST
ZYMOPHORIC
ZYMOSTEROL

POSITIONAL ORDER LIST OF 10-LETTER WORDS

ZABAGLIONE
ZAPHRENTID
ZEALOTICAL
ZEBRINNIES
ZENOGRAPHY
ZEOLITIZED
ZEUGLODONT
ZIGZAGGERY
ZINCIFYING
ZINCOGRAPH
ZINCOLYSIS
ZINGARESCA
ZINGIBEROL
ZOANTHROPY
ZONIFEROUS
ZOOBENTHOS
ZOOCULTURE
ZOOCURRENT
ZOOGRAPHER
ZOOGRAPHIC
ZOOLATRIES
ZOOLATROUS
ZOOLOGICAL
ZOOLOGIZED
ZOOMELANIN
ZOOMIMETIC
ZOOMORPHIC
ZOOPHAGOUS
ZOOPHILISM
ZOOPHILIST
ZOOPHILITE
ZOOPHILOUS
ZOOPHOBOUS
ZOOPHYSICS
ZOOPHYTISH
ZOOPHYTOID
ZOOPLASTIC
ZOOSPOROUS
ZOOTECHNIC
ZOOTHECIAL
ZOOTHECIUM
ZOOTHERAPY
ZOOTOMICAL
ZOOTROPHIC
ZOOXANTHIN
ZWITTERION
ZYGADENINE
ZYGOBRANCH
ZYGODACTYL
ZYGOMYCETE
ZYGOPHORIC
ZYGOSPHENE
ZYGOSPHERE
ZYGOSPORIC
ZYGOTACTIC
ZYMOGENOUS
ZYMOLOGIST
ZYMOPHORIC
ZYMOSTEROL

AZEOTROPIC
AZOBENZENE
AZOBENZOIC
AZOCORINTH
AZOCYANIDE
AZOGALLEIN
AZOMETHINE
AZOPHENINE
AZOPROTEIN
AZOTENESIS
AZOTOLUENE
AZOTOMETER
AZOTORRHEA
AZOVERNINE
AZTHIONIUM
AZYGOSPERM
AZYGOSPORE
CZAREVITCH
OZONOMETER
OZONOMETRY
OZONOSCOPE

AIZOACEOUS
BIZARRERIE
COZENINGLY
DAZZLINGLY
DEZYMOTIZE
ECZEMATOID
ECZEMATOUS
ENZYMOLOGY
EXZODIACAL
FAZENDEIRO
GAZANGABIN
LAZARETTOS
LIZARDTAIL
MAZAPILITE
MAZOPATHIA
MAZOPATHIC
MEZZOGRAPH
MEZZOTINTO
MIZZENMAST
MOZZARELLA
MUZZLEWOOD
MYZOSTOMID
PEZIZIFORM
POZZOLANIC
POZZUOLANA
PUZZLEHEAD
PUZZLEMENT
PUZZLEPATE
PUZZLINGLY
RAZORMAKER
RAZORSTROP
REZBANYITE
SIZZLINGLY
SUZERAINTY

ANAZOTURIA
APOZEMICAL
ASYZYGETIC
BENZEDRINE
BENZOCAINE
BENZOPYRAN
BENZOYLATE
BERZELIITE
BLAZONMENT
BLIZZARDLY
BRAZENFACE
BRAZENNESS
BRAZILETTE
BRAZILWOOD
CALZONERAS
COAZERVATE
CRAZEDNESS
DAZZLINGLY
DEOZONIZER
DIAZOAMINE
DIAZOIMIDE
DIAZOTIZED
DOUZAINIER
FRIZZINESS
FROZENNESS
GRIZZLIEST
GRIZZLYMAN
MANZANILLA
MANZANILLO
MEZZOGRAPH
MEZZOTINTO
MIZZENMAST
MONZONITIC
MOZZARELLA
MUZZLEWOOD
OXOZONIDES
PIEZOMETER
PIEZOMETRY
POZZOLANIC
POZZUOLANA
PRIZEFIGHT
PRIZETAKER
PUZZLEHEAD
PUZZLEMENT
PUZZLEPATE
PUZZLINGLY
RHIZOGENIC
RHIZOMATIC
RHIZOMELIC
RHIZOMORPH
RHIZONEURE
RHIZOPHORE
RHIZOPHYTE
RHIZOPLAST
RHIZOPODAL
RHIZOPODAN
RHIZOSTOME
RHIZOTAXIS
SIZZLINGLY
VESZELYITE
WHIZZERMAN
WHIZZINGLY
WITZCHOURA
ZIGZAGGERY

ALTAZIMUTH
ASSIZEMENT
BEBIZATION
BEDAZZLING
BEDIZENING
BLIZZARDLY
BOBIZATION
BREEZINESS
BRONZEWING
BRONZITITE
CHRIZONTAL
CITIZENESS
CITIZENISM
CITIZENIZE
CUTIZATION
CYTOZYMASE
DENAZIFIED
DENIZATION
DENIZENIZE
EMBEZZLING
EURYZYGOUS
FRENZIEDLY
FRIZZINESS
FROWZINESS
GRIZZLIEST
GRIZZLYMAN
HOMOZYGOTE
HOMOZYGOUS
HORIZONTAL
HYPOZEUGMA
HYPOZEUXIS
IODIZATION
IONIZATION
IOTIZATION
JANIZARIES
MAGAZINAGE
MAGAZINING
MAGAZINISM
MAGAZINIST
MELEZITASE
MELEZITOSE
NANIZATION
PARAZONIUM
PERIZONIUM
PEZIZIFORM
PHLYZACIUM
POLYZOARIA
PYRAZOLINE
PYRAZOLONE
SCHIZOCARP
SCHIZOGAMY
SCHIZOGONY
SCHIZOLITE
SELTZOGENE
SFORZANDOS
SLEAZINESS
SNEEZEWEED
SNEEZEWOOD
SNEEZEWORT
SPITZFLUTE
STANZAICAL
STYFZIEKTE
THIAZOLINE
THIOZONIDE
TOPAZOLITE
TRIOZONIDE
TWEEZERING
VENEZOLANO
WHEEZINESS
WHEEZINGLY
WHIZZERMAN
WHIZZINGLY

AGLAOZONIA
ANALYZABLE
ANTHOZOOID
BARTIZANED
BEDAZZLING
BOMBAZETTE
CARBAZYLIC
CHALAZOGAM
CHINTZIEST
COGNIZABLE
COGNIZABLY
COGNIZANCE
COSMOZOANS
COSMOZOISM
DANDIZETTE
DIALYZABLE
DIALYZATOR
EMBEZZLING
EMBLAZONED
EMBLAZONER
EMBLAZONRY
ENOLIZABLE
HYDRAZOATE
IMIDAZOLYL
INTERZONAL
LIONIZABLE
MICROZOARY
MICROZOOID
ORGANZINED
OXIDIZABLE
PECTIZABLE
PEPTIZABLE
PHILOZOIST
PREDAZZITE
QUARTZITIC
QUINAZOLIN
QUINAZOLYL
QUINIZARIN
REALIZABLE
RENDEZVOUS
RHODIZONIC
SCHERZANDO
SPOROZOITE
SPOROZOOID
SQUEEZABLE
SQUEEZEMAN
TAUTOZONAL
TETRAZOLYL
TRAPEZIUMS
TRITOZOOID
UNPRIZABLE
UTILIZABLE

ACTINOZOAL
ACTINOZOAN
AKHUNDZADA
ALCALIZATE
ALDOLIZING
ALKALIZATE
AMIDRAZONE
AMORTIZING
ANGELIZING
APHORIZING
APPETIZING
ARBORIZING
ARCHAIZING
ARTHROZOAN
ARTHROZOIC
ASTATIZING
ATHETIZING
ATTICIZING
AUTOLYZATE
AZOBENZENE
AZOBENZOIC
BAMBOOZLED
BAMBOOZLER
BILHARZIAL
BOTANIZING
BULLDOZING
CANALIZING
CANONIZANT
CANONIZING
CATALYZING
CHLORAZIDE
CIVILIZING
COLONIZING
COMPRIZING
CREOLIZING
CRYPTOZOIC
CURARIZING
CUTINIZING
DEMONIZING
DEPUTIZING
DEVILIZING
DIGITIZING
DISPRIZING
DISSEIZURE
DIVINIZING
ECTOENZYME
ENDOENZYME
ENERGIZING
EPIRHIZOUS
EQUALIZING
ERGOTIZING
ESTERIZING
ETERNIZING
ETHERIZING
ETHICIZING
EULOGIZING
EUPHUIZING
EUPOLYZOAN
EXORCIZING
FINALIZING
FLUIDIZING
FOCALIZING

HEMATOZOON
IDEALIZING
INFAMIZING
JAROVIZING
KAMAREZITE
LACONIZING
LEGALIZING
LOCALIZING
MACARIZING
MAXIMIZING
MELODIZING
MEMORIZING
METALIZING
MINIMIZING
MISPRIZING
MOBILIZING
MONETIZING
MORALIZING
MOTORIZING
MYCETOZOAN
MYCETOZOON
NASALIZING
NEBULIZING
NOTARIZING
NOVELIZING
ORGANIZING
OXADIAZOLE
PAEANIZING
PAGANIZING
PARALYZANT
PARALYZING
PENALIZING
PIPERAZINE
POLARIZING
PREDAZZITE
PTYALIZING
PYRIDAZINE
QUATORZAIN
RACEMIZING
RAMFEEZLED
RURALIZING
SATIRIZING
SCHEMOZZLE
SCYPHOZOAN
SOLARIZING
SOLECIZING
STARGAZING
SUBERIZING
SULPHAZIDE
TARTRAZINE
TEPONAZTLI
TETANIZING
THEORIZING
TOTALIZING
TROCHOZOIC
TROCHOZOON
UNIONIZING
URBANIZING
VITALIZING
VOCALIZING

ACADEMIZED
ACETYLIZER
ACTIONIZED
ACTUALIZED
ALCHEMIZED
ALLOCHEZIA
ALUMINIZED
ANABIBAZON
ANALOGIZED
ANGLICIZED
ANIMALIZED
APOLOGIZED
APOLOGIZER
ARCTICIZED
AROMATIZED
AROMATIZER
AUTHORIZED
AUTHORIZER
BACTERIZED
BALKANIZED
BARBARIZED
BRUTALIZED
CARBOLIZED
CARBONIZED
CARBONIZER
CARBURIZED
CARBURIZER
CARNALIZED
CASTORIZED
CATECHIZED
CATECHIZER
CATHARIZED
CAUTERIZED
CHIMPANZEE
CHITINIZED
CICATRIZED
CICATRIZER
COCAINIZED
COMMUNIZED
CRITICIZED
CRITICIZER
DEEPFROZEN
DEFERRIZED
DEODORIZED
DEODORIZER
DEOXIDIZED
DEOXIDIZER
DEOZONIZER
DIABOLIZED
DIALOGIZED
DIAZOTIZED
DOGMATIZED
DOGMATIZER
DRAMATIZED
DRAMATIZER
DUCTILIZED
ECONOMIZED
ECONOMIZER
ELECTRIZED
ELECTRIZER
EMBLEMIZED
EMPATHIZED
EMPHASIZED
EPILOGIZED
EPITOMIZED
EPITOMIZER
EUPHEMIZED
EUPHEMIZER
EUPHONIZED
FACTORIZING
FANTASIZED
FERTILIZED
FERTILIZER
FERTILIZIN
FEUDALIZED
FISCALIZED
FORMALIZED
FORMULIZED
FORMULIZER
FOSSILIZED
FRIVOLIZED
GALLICIZER
GALVANIZED
GALVANIZER
GEOLOGIZED
GLAMORIZED
GORGONIZED
HARMONIZER
HYBRIDIZER
ICHTHYIZED
INFLUENZAL
INFLUENZIC
INOXIDIZED
INTERMEZZI
INTERMEZZO
ITALICIZED
JARGONIZED
JASPERIZED
JOVIALIZED
LABIALIZED
LIQUIDIZED
MAGNETIZED
MAGNETIZER
MAINPRIZER
MARBLEIZED
MARBLEIZER
MARMARIZED
MARTYRIZED
MARTYRIZER
MATRONIZED
MECHANIZER
MEDIATIZED
MERCERIZED
MERCERIZER
MERCURIZED
MESMERIZED
MESMERIZEE
MESMERIZER
METHODIZED
METHODIZER
MNEMONIZED
MODERNIZED
MODERNIZER
MORTALIZED
MUTUALIZED
MYCORHIZAL
MYTHICIZED
MYTHICIZER
NARCOTIZED
NEOLOGIZED
NONCITIZEN
NORMALIZED
NORMALIZER
NOTORHIZAL
OBJECTIZED
ORIGANIZED
OSTRACIZED
OSTRACIZER
OVERGLAZED
OVERPRIZED
OVERPRIZER
OXYGENIZED
OXYGENIZER
PALLETIZED
PASSEMEZZO
PATRONIZED
PATRONIZER
PAUPERIZED
PEPTONIZED
PEPTONIZER
PETROLIZED
PHLORHIZIN
PHLORIDZIN
PLATINIZED
PLURALIZED
PLURALIZER
POSTURIZED
POWDERIZER
PRECONIZED
PRECONIZER
PUBLICIZED
PULVERIZED
PULVERIZER
RANDOMIZED
REBAPTIZER
RECOGNIZEE
RECOGNIZED
RECOGNIZER
RECOGNIZOR
ROUTINIZED
RUBBERIZED
SCHEMOZZLE
SENSITIZED
SENSITIZER
SERIALIZED
SERMONIZED
SERMONIZER
SIGNALIZED
SOCIALIZED
SOCIALIZER
SOLEMNIZED
SOLEMNIZER
SOLVOLYZED
SOVIETIZED
STABILIZED
STABILIZER
STERILIZED
STERILIZER
STYLOPIZED
SUBSIDIZED
SUBSIDIZER
SUBTILIZED
SUBTILIZER
SULFATIZED
SULFURIZED
SUMMARIZED
SUMMARIZER
SYLLABIZED
SYLLOGIZED
SYLLOGIZER
SYMBOLIZED
SYMBOLIZER
SYNTONIZED
SYNTONIZER
SYPHILIZED
SYSTEMIZED
SYSTEMIZER
TANTALIZED
TANTALIZER
TARTARIZED
TELLURIZED
TEMPORIZED
TEMPORIZER
TENDERIZED
TENDERIZER
TERRORIZED
TERRORIZER
TYRANNIZED
TYRANNIZER
UNBAPTIZED
UNDERSIZED
UNITEMIZED
UNREALIZED
URALITIZED
VAPOURIZED
VAPOURIZER
VASSALIZED
VERATRIZED
VERBALIZED
VERBALIZER
VICTIMIZED
VICTIMIZER
VISUALIZED
VISUALIZER
VOLCANIZED
VULCANIZED
VULCANIZER
VULGARIZED
VULGARIZER
WINTERIZED
ZOOLOGIZED

ADRENALIZE
ADULTERIZE
AGGRANDIZE
ALBUMENIZE
ALBUMINIZE
ALCOHOLIZE
ALGEBRAIZE
ALKALINIZE
ALLEGORIZE
AMALGAMIZE
AMMONOLYZE
ANATHEMIZE
ANGELICIZE
ANGULARIZE
ANTAGONIZE
ANTIFREEZE
APOSTATIZE
APOSTOLIZE
ARSENICIZE
ASEPTICIZE
ASEXUALIZE
ATROPINIZE
AUTOMATIZE
AUTONOMIZE
AUTOTOMIZE
AUTOXIDIZE
AXIOMATIZE
BANTINGIZE
BASTARDIZE
BESTIALIZE
BITUMINIZE
BOLSHEVIZE
BOUCHERIZE
BOURBONIZE
BOWDLERIZE
BURGLARIZE
BURNETTIZE
CAPITALIZE
CARAMELIZE
CATABOLIZE
CATEGORIZE
CAUSTICIZE
CENTRALIZE
CHANNELIZE
CHATTELIZE
CHLORALIZE
CHLORIDIZE
CHLORITIZE
CHLORODIZE
CHROMATIZE
CHROMICIZE
CICERONIZE
CINCHONIZE
CITIZENIZE
CLASSICIZE
COCKNEYIZE
COLEORHIZA
COLLOQUIZE
CONCERTIZE
CROFTERIZE
CUCKOLDIZE
DASTARDIZE
DEALKALIZE
DECIMALIZE
DECIVILIZE
DECOLORIZE
DEEPFREEZE
DEFEMINIZE
DEFINITIZE
DEHEMATIZE
DEHEPATIZE
DEHUMANIZE
DELEGALIZE
DELIMITIZE
DELOCALIZE
DELUMINIZE
DEMOBILIZE
DEMORALIZE
DENATURIZE
DENIZENIZE
DEPETALIZE
DEPOLARIZE

DEPRIORIZE
DERESINIZE
DEVIRILIZE
DEVITALIZE
DEVOCALIZE
DEXTRINIZE
DEZYMOTIZE
DIAMONDIZE
DIGITALIZE
DIPLOIDIZE
DIPOLARIZE
DISASINIZE
DISREALIZE
DOCTRINIZE
DOGGRELIZE
DOLOMITIZE
DOXOLOGIZE
DYSOXIDIZE
EFFEMINIZE
ELASTICIZE
EMOTIONIZE
EMPHATHIZE
ENGRANDIZE
ENIGMATIZE
ENTHRONIZE
EPISCOPIZE
EPISTOLIZE
EPITAPHIZE
EPITHELIZE
ETERNALIZE
EUHEMERIZE
EVANGELIZE
FANATICIZE
FARCIALIZE
FASCISTIZE
FASHIONIZE
FEDERALIZE
FICTIONIZE
FRATERNIZE
GELATINIZE
GENERALIZE
GEOMETRIZE
GLOTTALIZE
GLUTTONIZE
GNATHONIZE
GOLANDAUZE
GOLUNDAUZE
GORMANDIZE
GRANGERIZE
GRAPHITIZE
HERETICIZE
HOMOGENIZE
HOMOLOGIZE
HYDRORHIZA
HYPNOIDIZE
IDOLATRIZE
ILLEGALIZE
IMMOBILIZE
INFAMONIZE
INGRANDIZE
INKHORNIZE
INTERMEZZI
INTERMEZZO
INTHRONIZE
JEOPARDIZE
JOURNALIZE
KATABOLIZE
KERATINIZE
LATERALIZE
LATIBULIZE
LEGITIMIZE
LETHARGIZE
LEXICONIZE
LIBERALIZE
LINGUALIZE
LITERALIZE
LOGICALIZE
MACADAMIZE
MAHOGANIZE
MALLEINIZE
MARTIALIZE
MEROTOMIZE
METABOLIZE
MILITARIZE
MILLIONIZE
MINERALIZE
MIRACULIZE
MISBAPTIZE
MONARCHIZE
MONGRELIZE
MONOLOGIZE
MONONYMIZE
MONOPOLIZE
MONOTONIZE
MORPHINIZE
MUSICALIZE
MYCOLOGIZE
MYCORRHIZA
MYECTOMIZE
NATURALIZE
NEBULARIZE
NESSLERIZE
NEUTRALIZE
NICOTINIZE
NOTHINGIZE
OBITUARIZE
ONTOLOGIZE
OVERFRIEZE
PALATALIZE
PANEGYRIZE
PARABOLIZE
PARAGOGIZE
PARALOGIZE
PARASITIZE
PARENESIZE
PARONYMIZE
PASSEMEZZO
PASTEURIZE
PATTERNIZE
PEASANTIZE
PERIPATIZE
PERITOMIZE
PEROXIDIZE
PHANTASIZE
PHANTOMIZE
PHILIPPIZE
PICRORHIZA
PIGMENTIZE
PILEORHIZA
PILEORHIZE
PILGRIMIZE
PLAGIARIZE
PLASMOLYZE
PLASTICIZE
PNEUMATIZE
POLITICIZE
POLYGAMIZE
POLYMERIZE
POLYTHEIZE
POPULARIZE
POSITIVIZE
POULARDIZE
PRAGMATIZE
PRECOGNIZE
PRESSURIZE
PRISMATIZE
PROBLEMIZE
PROCTORIZE
PROLOGUIZE
PROPHETIZE
PROVERBIZE
PSALMODIZE
PYRIDINIZE
RADICALIZE
REDISSEIZE
REGULARIZE
REJUVENIZE
REMONETIZE
REORGANIZE
REVALORIZE
REVITALIZE
RHAPSODIZE
RHEUMATIZE
RUFFIANIZE
SACCHARIZE
SALICYLIZE
SAPIENTIZE
SCANDALIZE
SCEPTICIZE
SCHEDULIZE
SCHEMATIZE
SCORBUTIZE
SCRUTINIZE
SECTIONIZE
SECULARIZE
SEMINARIZE
SENSUALIZE
SERPENTIZE
SEVERALIZE
SHERARDIZE
SILICIDIZE
SILICONIZE
SIMPLICIZE
SKEPTICIZE
SLENDERIZE
SOLIDARIZE
SOLUBILIZE
SOPHRONIZE
SPATIALIZE
SPECIALIZE
SPERMATIZE
SPHETERIZE
SPIRANTIZE
STIGMATIZE
STRATEGIZE
SUBERINIZE
SULPHATIZE
SULPHIDIZE
SULPHURIZE
SYMMETRIZE
SYMPATHIZE
SYMPHONIZE
SYMPHYTIZE
SYNCRETIZE
SYNONYMIZE
SYNTHESIZE
SYNTHETIZE
TABULARIZE
TARLTONIZE
TELFORDIZE
TENOTOMIZE
THEOLOGIZE
THERMOLYZE
TRACTORIZE
TRAUMATIZE
TRICHINIZE
TRIVIALIZE
TROCHEEIZE
TRYPSINIZE
TRYPTONIZE
UNCANONIZE
UNDERGLAZE
UNIFORMIZE
UNSTOICIZE
VAGOTOMIZE
VAGRANTIZE
VERSIONIZE
VETERANIZE
VISIBILIZE
VITAMINIZE
VITRIOLIZE
VOCIFERIZE
VOLATILIZE
WARRANTIZE
WESTERNIZE
WHITEBLAZE
WOOLLENIZE

CHERVONETZ
FACKELTANZ

SCORING ORDER LIST OF 10-LETTER WORDS

34
HYPOZEUXIS

32
SYMPHYTIZE

31
DYSOXIDIZE
ICHTHYIZED
MAXIMIZING
OBJECTIZED
OXYGENIZED
PHLYZACIUM
QUINAZOLYL
ZYMOPHORIC

30
COCKNEYIZE
HYPOZEUGMA
JAROVIZING
JOVIALIZED
LIQUIDIZED
MYTHICIZED
OXYGENIZER
QUARTZITIC
RHIZOPHYTE
SCHIZOGAMY
SQUEEZABLE
SQUEEZEMAN
ZOOPHYTISH
ZYGOBRANCH
ZYGOMYCETE
ZYGOPHORIC

29
CYTOZYMASE
CZAREVITCH
DEOXIDIZED
EMPHATHIZE
EQUALIZING
EXORCIZING
EXZODIACAL
HYDRORHIZA
JASPERIZED
JEOPARDIZE
MYCORHIZAL
MYCORRHIZA
MYTHICIZER
OXIDIZABLE
PEROXIDIZE
REJUVENIZE
RHIZOMORPH
RHIZOTAXIS
SCYPHOZOAN
STYFZIEKTE
SYMPATHIZE
SYMPHONIZE
WHEEZINGLY
ZOOPHYSICS
ZOOXANTHIN
ZYGODACTYL

28
AKHUNDZADA
ASYZYGETIC
AXIOMATIZE
CARBAZYLIC
CHIMPANZEE
CHROMICIZE
CRYPTOZOIC
CUCKOLDIZE
DEOXIDIZER
DOXOLOGIZE
ENZYMOLOGY
FACKELTANZ
HOMOZYGOTE
HOMOZYGOUS
HYBRIDIZER
HYPNOIDIZE
INOXIDIZED
JARGONIZED
LEXICONIZE
MAZOPATHIC
MYECTOMIZE
PRIZEFIGHT
QUATORZAIN
QUINAZOLIN
QUINIZARIN
SCHIZOCARP
SCHIZOGONY
SYPHILIZED
WHIZZINGLY
ZENOGRAPHY
ZINCIFYING
ZOOMORPHIC
ZOOPHYTOID
ZYGOSPHENE
ZYGOSPHERE

27
ALCHEMIZED
AUTOXIDIZE
AZYGOSPERM
BOLSHEVIZE
CATECHIZED
CHALAZOGAM
CHERVONETZ
COGNIZABLY
DEXTRINIZE
EFFEMINIZE
EMPATHIZED
EMPHASIZED
EUPHEMIZED
MYCOLOGIZE
MYZOSTOMID

OXADIAZOLE
OXOZONIDES
PHLORHIZIN
POLYGAMIZE
POLYTHEIZE
RHIZOPHORE
SKEPTICIZE
SYMBOLIZED
SYNONYMIZE
THERMOLYZE
VICTIMIZED
VOCIFERIZE
WHITEBLAZE
WITZCHOURA
ZINCOGRAPH
ZOANTHROPY
ZOOGRAPHIC
ZOOTHERAPY
ZYGOSPORIC
ZYGOTACTIC

26

AMMONOLYZE
ASEXUALIZE
BALKANIZED
BAMBOOZLED
BENZOPYRAN
BOUCHERIZE
BRAZENFACE
CATECHIZER
CHROMATIZE
CINCHONIZE
COMMUNIZED
COMPRIZING
ECTOENZYME
EMBLAZONRY
EMBLEMIZED
EPITAPHIZE
EUPHEMIZER
EURYZYGOUS
FRENZIEDLY
FRIVOLIZED
HYDRAZOATE
INKHORNIZE
JANIZARIES
JOURNALIZE
MACADAMIZE
MAZOPATHIA
MECHANIZER
METHODIZED
MEZZOGRAPH
MICROZOARY
MONARCHIZE
MONONYMIZE
MORPHINIZE
MYCETOZOAN
MYCETOZOON
PARONYMIZE
PHANTOMIZE
PICRORHIZA
PIEZOMETRY
PLASMOLYZE
POLYMERIZE
PROPHETIZE
PROVERBIZE
PUBLICIZED
RHIZOMATIC
RHIZOMELIC
SACCHARIZE
SCHEMATIZE
SOLVOLYZED
SYMBOLIZER
SYMMETRIZE
TANTALIZED
TROCHOZOIC
VICTIMIZER
WHIZZERMAN

ZOOPHILISM
ZOOPHOBOUS
ZOOTECHNIC
ZOOTHECIUM
ZOOTROPHIC

25

ACADEMIZED
APHORIZING
APOZEMICAL
ARCHAIZING
AZOCYANIDE
AZYGOSPORE
BAMBOOZLER
BOMBAZETTE
BOWDLERIZE
BRAZILWOOD
BRONZEWING
CATALYZING
CATHARIZED
CHITINIZED
CHLORAZIDE
CHLORIDIZE
CHLORODIZE
CIVILIZING
COSMOZOISM
COZENINGLY
DECIVILIZE
DEEPFREEZE
DEEPFROZEN
DEFEMINIZE
DEHEMATIZE
DEHEPATIZE
DEHUMANIZE
DEVOCALIZE
DIALYZABLE
ENDOENZYME
EPISCOPIZE
ETHICIZING
EUPHONIZED
EUPHUIZING
FACTORIZED
FASHIONIZE
FISCALIZED
FOCALIZING
FORMALIZED
FORMULIZED
FROWZINESS
GRAPHITIZE
HOMOGENIZE
HOMOLOGIZE
IMIDAZOLYL
IMMOBILIZE
INFAMIZING
KAMAREZITE
KATABOLIZE
MAHOGANIZE
MARTYRIZED
METHODIZER
MISBAPTIZE
OVERFRIEZE
OVERPRIZED
PANEGYRIZE
PARALYZING
PECTIZABLE
PEPTIZABLE
PEZIZIFORM
PHILIPPIZE
PHLORIDZIN
POWDERIZER
PRIZETAKER
PROBLEMIZE
PTYALIZING
PULVERIZED
PYRIDAZINE
PYRIDINIZE
RAMFEEZLED

RAZORMAKER
RHAPSODIZE
RHIZOGENIC
RHIZOPODAL
RHIZOPODAN
RHODIZONIC
RUFFIANIZE
SCEPTICIZE
SCHEDULIZE
SCHEMOZZLE
SCHERZANDO
SIMPLICIZE
STYLOPIZED
SULPHAZIDE
SULPHIDIZE
SYLLABIZED
SYNTHESIZE
SYNTHETIZE
SYSTEMIZED
VAGOTOMIZE
VAPOURIZED
VERBALIZED
VESZELYITE
VOCALIZING
VOLCANIZED
VULCANIZED
WHEEZINESS
WOMANIZING
ZAPHRENTID
ZOOGRAPHER
ZOOMIMETIC
ZOOPHAGOUS
ZYMOGENOUS
ZYMOLOGIST

24

ACETYLIZER
ALCOHOLIZE
ALLOCHEZIA
ALTAZIMUTH
AMALGAMIZE
ANALYZABLE
ANATHEMIZE
APPETIZING
ARCTICIZED
ARTHROZOIC
AZOCORINTH
AZOMETHINE
AZOPHENINE
AZTHIONIUM
BACTERIZED
BARBARIZED
BENZOYLATE
BILHARZIAL
BLIZZARDLY
CARBOLIZED
CARBONIZED
CARBURIZED
CHANNELIZE
CHATTELIZE
CHINTZIEST
CHLORALIZE
CHLORITIZE
CHRIZONTAL
CICATRIZED
COAZERVATE
COCAINIZED
COGNIZABLE
COGNIZANCE
COLEORHIZA
CRITICIZED
CROFTERIZE
DEALKALIZE
DECIMALIZE
DEFERRIZED
DEMOBILIZE
DENAZIFIED

DEVILIZING
DEZYMOTIZE
DIVINIZING
DOGMATIZED
ECONOMIZED
ECZEMATOID
EMBLAZONED
EPIRHIZOUS
EPITHELIZE
EPITOMIZED
EUHEMERIZE
EUPOLYZOAN
FANATICIZE
FARCIALIZE
FASCISTIZE
FEUDALIZED
FICTIONIZE
FLUIDIZING
FORMULIZER
GALVANIZED
GRIZZLYMAN
HARMONIZER
HEMATOZOON
HERETICIZE
INFAMONIZE
INFLUENZIC
MACARIZING
MAGAZINISM
MARBLEIZED
MARMARIZED
MARTYRIZER
MEMORIZING
MERCERIZED
MERCURIZED
MESMERIZED
MICROZOOID
MINIMIZING
MISPRIZING
MNEMONIZED
MOBILIZING
MUZZLEWOOD
OVERGLAZED
OVERPRIZER
OZONOMETRY
PARALYZANT
PAUPERIZED
PEPTONIZED
PHANTASIZE
PHILOZOIST
PIGMENTIZE
PILEORHIZA
PILEORHIZE
PILGRIMIZE
POLYZOARIA
POSITIVIZE
PRAGMATIZE
PRECOGNIZE
PRECONIZED
PSALMODIZE
PULVERIZER
PUZZLEHEAD
PUZZLINGLY
PYRAZOLINE
PYRAZOLONE
RACEMIZING
REZBANYITE
RHEUMATIZE
RHIZOPLAST
RHIZOSTOME
RUBBERIZED
SALICYLIZE
SCHIZOLITE
SOPHRONIZE
SPHETERIZE
SPITZFLUTE
SULPHATIZE
SULPHURIZE

SUMMARIZED
SYLLOGIZED
SYNCRETIZE
SYSTEMIZER
TEMPORIZED
TRICHINIZE
TROCHEEIZE
TROCHOZOON
TRYPSINIZE
TRYPTONIZE
UNBAPTIZED
UNIFORMIZE
VAPOURIZER
VERBALIZER
VISIBILIZE
VITAMINIZE
VULCANIZER
VULGARIZED
ZIGZAGGERY
ZINCOLYSIS
ZOOBENTHOS
ZOOPHILIST
ZOOPHILITE
ZOOPHILOUS
ZOOTHECIAL
ZYGADENINE
ZYMOSTEROL

23

ALBUMENIZE
ALBUMINIZE
ALKALINIZE
ALKALIZATE
ANABIBAZON
ANGLICIZED
ANTHOZOOID
APOLOGIZED
ASEPTICIZE
ATHETIZING
AUTHORIZED
AZEOTROPIC
BEBIZATION
BEDIZENING
BENZOCAINE
BITUMINIZE
BLAZONMENT
BOBIZATION
BOURBONIZE
BULLDOZING
CAPITALIZE
CARAMELIZE
CARBONIZER
CARBURIZER
CATABOLIZE
CAUSTICIZE
CICATRIZER
CICERONIZE
CITIZENISM
CLASSICIZE
CONCERTIZE
CONCRETIZE
COSMOZOANS
CRITICIZER
DAZZLINGLY
DEFINITIZE
DEMONIZING
DEPUTIZING
DEVIRILIZE
DEVITALIZE
DIABOLIZED
DIALYZATOR
DIAMONDIZE
DIAZOIMIDE
DIPLOIDIZE
DISPRIZING
DOGMATIZER
DRAMATIZED

DUCTILIZED
ECONOMIZER
ECZEMATOUS
EMBEZZLING
EMBLAZONER
EPILOGIZED
EPITOMIZER
ETHERIZING
EVANGELIZE
FANTASIZED
FAZENDEIRO
FEDERALIZE
FERTILIZED
FINALIZING
FOSSILIZED
GALVANIZER
GAZANGABIN
GLAMORIZED
GNATHONIZE
GORMANDIZE
KERATINIZE
LETHARGIZE
MAGAZINAGE
MAGAZINING
MAGNETIZED
MAINPRIZER
MARBLEIZER
MAZAPILITE
MEDIATIZED
MELODIZING
MERCERIZER
MEROTOMIZE
MESMERIZEE
MESMERIZER
METABOLIZE
MIRACULIZE
MODERNIZED
MONOPOLIZE
MONZONITIC
MUSICALIZE
NOTHINGIZE
NOVELIZING
OZONOSCOPE
PAGANIZING
PARABOLIZE
PARAGOGIZE
PARAZONIUM
PEPTONIZER
PERIPATIZE
PERITOMIZE
PERIZONIUM
PIEZOMETER
PIPERAZINE
PLASTICIZE
PNEUMATIZE
POLITICIZE
POPULARIZE
PRECONIZER
PRISMATIZE
PROCTORIZE
RANDOMIZED
REBAPTIZER
RECOGNIZED
RENDEZVOUS
SCORBUTIZE
SFORZANDOS
SHERARDIZE
SNEEZEWEED
SNEEZEWOOD
SOVIETIZED
SPECIALIZE
SPERMATIZE
SUBSIDIZED
SULFATIZED
SULFURIZED
SUMMARIZER
SYLLOGIZER
SYNTONIZED
TELFORDIZE
TEMPORIZER
THEOLOGIZE
THEORIZING
THIOZONIDE
TRAPEZIUMS
TWEEZERING
TYRANNIZED
UNPRIZABLE
VAGRANTIZE
VASSALIZED
VERATRIZED
VISUALIZED
VITALIZING
VULGARIZER
WINTERIZED
ZOOPLASTIC
ZOOTOMICAL

22

ACTIONIZED
ACTUALIZED
AGGRANDIZE
ALGEBRAIZE
ALUMINIZED
AMIDRAZONE
AMORTIZING
ANATOMIZED
ANGELICIZE
ANIMALIZED
ANTIFREEZE
APOLOGIZER
ARBORIZING
AROMATIZED
ARTHROZOAN
ATTICIZING
AUTHORIZER
AUTOLYZATE
AZOBENZOIC
AZOTORRHEA
AZOVERNINE
BANTINGIZE
BARTIZANED
BASTARDIZE
BEDAZZLING
BENZEDRINE
BOTANIZING
BRUTALIZED
BURGLARIZE
CANALIZING
CANONIZING
CARNALIZED
CASTORIZED
CATEGORIZE
CAUTERIZED
COLONIZING
CRAZEDNESS
CREOLIZING
CURARIZING
CUTINIZING
DECOLORIZE
DELIMITIZE
DELOCALIZE
DELUMINIZE
DEMORALIZE
DEODORIZED
DEPETALIZE
DEPOLARIZE
DEPRIORIZE
DIALOGIZED
DIAZOAMINE
DIGITIZING
DIPOLARIZE
DOCTRINIZE
DOGGRELIZE
DOLOMITIZE
DRAMATIZER
ELECTRIZED
ENIGMATIZE
ENTHRONIZE
FERTILIZER
FERTILIZIN
FRATERNIZE
FROZENNESS
GALLICIZER
GEOLOGIZED
GEOMETRIZE
GORGONIZED
HORIZONTAL
INFLUENZAL
INTHRONIZE
ITALICIZED
LABIALIZED
LACONIZING
LEGITIMIZE
LOCALIZING
LOGICALIZE
MAGAZINIST
MAGNETIZER
MATRONIZED
METALIZING
MIZZÈNMAST
MODERNIZER
MONETIZING
MONGRELIZE
MONOLOGIZE
MORALIZING
MORTALIZED
MOTORIZING
MUTUALIZED
NARCOTIZED
NEBULIZING
NORMALIZED
NOTORHIZAL
OSTRACIZED
PAEANIZING
PALLETIZED
PARALOGIZE
PASSEMEZZO
PATRONIZED
PENALIZING
PETROLIZED
PLAGIARIZE
PLATINIZED
PLURALIZED
POLARIZING
POSTURIZED
POULARDIZE
POZZOLANIC
PROLOGUIZE
PUZZLEMENT
PUZZLEPATE
RADICALIZE
RECOGNIZEE
RECOGNIZER
RECOGNIZOR
REVALORIZE
REVITALIZE
RHIZONEURE
SCANDALIZE
SERMONIZED
SEVERALIZE
SILICIDIZE
SIZZLINGLY
SNEEZEWORT
SOCIALIZED
SOLECIZING
SOLEMNIZED
SPOROZOOID
STABILIZED
STIGMATIZE
SUBERIZING
SUBSIDIZER
SUBTILIZED
SUZERAINTY
SYNTONIZER
TETRAZOLYL
THIAZOLINE
TRIVIALIZE
TYRANNIZER
UNITEMIZED
URBANIZING
VENEZOLANO
VERSIONIZE
VETERANIZE
VISUALIZER
VITRIOLIZE
VOLATILIZE
WARRANTIZE
WESTERNIZE
WOOLLENIZE
ZABAGLIONE
ZINGARESCA
ZINGIBEROL
ZONIFEROUS
ZOOLOGICAL
ZWITTERION

21

ACTINOZOAL
ACTINOZOAN
AIZOACEOUS
ALCALIZATE
ALDOLIZING
ANALOGIZED
ANATOMIZER
ANGELIZING
APOSTATIZE
APOSTOLIZE
AROMATIZER
ARSENICIZE
ASSIZEMENT
ATROPINIZE
AUTOMATIZE
AUTONOMIZE
AUTOTOMIZE
AZOPROTEIN
AZOTOMETER
BERZELIITE
BESTIALIZE
BIZARRERIE
BRAZENNESS
BRAZILETTE
BREEZINESS
BRONZITITE
BURNETTIZE
CALZONERAS
CANONIZANT
CENTRALIZE
CITIZENESS
CUTIZATION
DASTARDIZE
DELEGALIZE
DEODORIZER
DIGITALIZE
ELASTICIZE
ELECTRIZER
EMOTIONIZE
ENERGIZING
ENGRANDIZE
ENOLIZABLE
EPISTOLIZE
ERGOTIZING
EULOGIZING
FRIZZINESS
GOLANDAUZE
GOLUNDAUZE
GRANGERIZE
IDEALIZING
INGRANDIZE
LATIBULIZE
LEGALIZING
LIBERALIZE
LIONIZABLE
MALLEINIZE
MANZANILLA
MANZANILLO
MARTIALIZE
MELEZITASE
MELEZITOSE
MILITARIZE
MILLIONIZE
MINERALIZE
MONOTONIZE
NEBULARIZE
NEOLOGIZED
NICOTINIZE
NONCITIZEN
NORMALIZER
OBITUARIZE
ORGANIZING
ORGANZINED
ORIGANIZED
OSTRACIZER
OZONOMETER
PALATALIZE
PARASITIZE
PARENESIZE
PASTEURIZE
PATRONIZER
PATTERNIZE
PEASANTIZE
PLURALIZER
PREDAZZITE
PRESSURIZE
RAZORSTROP
REALIZABLE
REMONETIZE
SAPIENTIZE
SCRUTINIZE
SECTIONIZE
SECULARIZE
SEMINARIZE
SERMONIZER
SERPENTIZE
SIGNALIZED
SILICONIZE
SOCIALIZER
SOLEMNIZER
SOLUBILIZE
SPATIALIZE
SPIRANTIZE
SPOROZOITE
STABILIZER
STANZAICAL
STARGAZING
SUBERINIZE
SUBTILIZER
TABULARIZE
TENDERIZED
TENOTOMIZE
TEPONAZTLI
TOPAZOLITE
TRACTORIZE
TRAUMATIZE
UNCANONIZE
UNDERGLAZE
UNDERSIZED
UTILIZABLE
ZEALOTICAL
ZEBRINNIES
ZEUGLODONT
ZOOCULTURE
ZOOCURRENT
ZOOMELANIN
ZOOSPOROUS

20

ADRENALIZE
ADULTERIZE
AGLAOZONIA
ALLEGORIZE
ANGULARIZE
ANTAGONIZE
ASTATIZING
AZOBENZENE
AZOGALLEIN
CITIZENIZE
DENATURIZE
DENIZATION
DERESINIZE
DIAZOTIZED
DISASINIZE
DISREALIZE
DISSEIZURE
DOUZAINIER
ESTERIZING
ETERNIZING
GELATINIZE
GENERALIZE
GLOTTALIZE
GLUTTONIZE
IDOLATRIZE
ILLEGALIZE
INTERMEZZI
INTERMEZZO
IODIZATION
LINGUALIZE
LIZARDTAIL
MEZZOTINTO
MOZZARELLA
NASALIZING
NOTARIZING
ONTOLOGIZE
POZZUOLANA
REDISSEIZE
REGULARIZE
REORGANIZE
ROUTINIZED
RURALIZING
SATIRIZING
SELTZOGENE
SENSITIZED
SERIALIZED
SLENDERIZE
SOLARIZING
SOLIDARIZE
STERILIZED
STRATEGIZE
TARTARIZED
TELLURIZED
TENDERIZER
TERRORIZED
TETANIZING
TOTALIZING
TRIOZONIDE
TRITOZOOID
UNIONIZING
UNREALIZED
URALITIZED
ZOOLOGIZED

19

ANAZOTURIA
AZOTENESIS
AZOTOLUENE
DENIZENIZE
DEOZONIZER
ETERNALIZE
GRIZZLIEST
INTERZONAL
IONIZATION
IOTIZATION
LATERALIZE
LAZARETTOS
LITERALIZE
NANIZATION
NATURALIZE
NESSLERIZE
NEUTRALIZE
SENSITIZER
SENSUALIZE
SLEAZINESS
STERILIZER
TANTALIZER
TARLTONIZE
TARTRAZINE
TAUTOZONAL
TERRORIZER
UGRIANIZE
ZEOLITIZED
ZOOLATRIES
ZOOLATROUS

ALPHABETICAL LIST OF WORDS OVER 10 LETTERS

ABASTARDIZE
ABNORMALIZE
ABOLITIONIZE
ACADEMIZING
ACCLIMATIZE
ACCLIMATIZED
ACCLIMATIZER
ACCLIMATIZING
ACCULTURIZE
ACCUSTOMIZE
ACCUSTOMIZED
ACCUSTOMIZING
ACETOBENZOIC
ACETONIZATION
ACETYLIZABLE
ACETYLIZATION
ACHROMATIZE
ACHROMATIZED
ACTIONIZING
ACTUALIZATION
ACTUALIZING
ADENIZATION
ADVERBIALIZE
ADVERTIZEMENT
ADVERTIZING
AESTHETICIZE
AGGUTINIZE
AGGRANDIZED
AGGRANDIZER
AGGRANDIZING
AGRARIANIZE
ALBITIZATION
ALBUMENIZED
ALBUMENIZER
ALBUMENIZING
ALBUMINIZED
ALBUMINIZING
ALCHEMIZING
ALCOHOLIZED
ALCOHOLIZING
ALDOLIZATION
ALGEBRAIZED
ALGEBRIZATION
ALGEBRAIZING
ALKALINIZED
ALKALINIZING
ALKALIZABLE
ALKALIZATION
ALLEGORIZED
ALLEGORIZER
ALLEGORIZING
ALLOTROPIZE
ALPHABETIZE
ALPHABETIZED
ALPHABETIZER
ALPHABETIZING
ALUMINIZING
AMMONIZATION
AMORTIZABLE
AMORTIZATION
AMORTIZEMENT
ANABAPTIZED
ANABAPTIZING
ANACEPHALIZE
ANACHRONIZE
ANAESTHETIZE
ANAESTHETIZED
ANAESTHETIZER
ANALOGIZING
ANALYZATION
ANATHEMATIZE
ANATOMIZING
ANESTHETIZE
ANESTHETIZER
ANGIOSTOMIZE
ANGLICIZING
ANHYDRIDIZE
ANIMALIZATION
ANIMALIZING
ANTAGONIZED
ANTAGONIZER
ANTAGONIZING
ANTHEROZOID
ANTHEROZOOID
ANTHOLOGIZE
ANTHOLOGIZED
ANTHOLOGIZING
ANTHROPOZOIC
ANTIFREEZING
ANTIPATHIZE
ANTISEPTICIZE
ANTITHESIZE
APAESTHETIZE
APESTHETIZE
APOLOGIZING
APOSTATIZED
APOSTATIZING
APOSTROPHIZE
APOTHEOSIZE
APOTHEOSIZED
APPETIZINGLY
APPRIZEMENT
ARBORIZATION
ARCTICIZING
ARITHMETIZE
AROMATIZING
ARSENIZATION
ARTERIALIZE
ARTERIALIZED
ASBESTINIZE
ASCIDIOZOOID
ASEPTICIZED
ASEPTICIZING
ASEXUALIZED
ASEXUALIZING
ASPHETERIZE
ASTIGMATIZER
ASTROLOGIZE
ASTRONOMIZE
ATMOLYZATION
ATOMIZATION
ATTITUDINIZE
AUTHORIZATION
AUTHORIZING
AUTOCATALYZE
AZADIRACHTA
AZEOTROPISM
AZIMETHYLENE
AZIMUTHALLY
AZOCOCHINEAL
AZOCORALLINE
AZODIPHENYL
AZOERYTHRIN
AZOFICATION
AZOOSPERMIA
AZOPARAFFIN
AZOPHENETOLE
AZOPHENYLENE
AZOPHOSPHIN
AZOPHOSPHORE
AZOSULPHINE
AZOSULPHONIC
AZOTETRAZOLE
AZOTHIONIUM
AZOTOBACTER
AZOTORRHOEA
AZYGOMATOUS
BACCHANALIZE
BACHELORIZE
BACTERIOLYZE
BACTERIZING
BALKANIZING
BAMBOOZLEMENT
BAMBOOZLING
BAPTIZEMENT
BARBARIZING
BASTARDIZED
BASTARDIZING
BATTOLOGIZE
BEDAZZLINGLY
BEDIZENMENT
BENZALDEHYDE
BENZALDOXIME
BENZINDULINE
BENZOHYDROL
BENZOINATED
BENZONITRILE
BENZONITROL
BENZOPHENONE
BENZOYLATION
BENZYLAMINE
BERGINIZATION
BERZELIANITE
BESSEMERIZE
BESSEMERIZED
BESSEMERIZING
BESTIALIZED
BESTIALIZING
BILHARZIASIS
BILHARZIOSIS
BIOGRAPHIZE
BISTETRAZOLE
BISTRIAZOLE
BITUMINIZED
BIVOCALIZED
BIZARRENESS
BIZYGOMATIC
BLIZZARDOUS
BOLSHEVIZED
BOLSHEVIZING
BOWDLERIZED
BOWDLERIZING
BRAZENFACED
BROMIZATION
BROMOBENZENE
BROMOIODIZED
BRONZESMITH
BRUTALIZING
BURGLARIZED
BURGLARIZING
BURKUNDAUZE
BURNETTIZED
BURNETTIZING
BURTONIZATION
BUZZERPHONE
CACOPHONIZE
CACOZEALOUS
CALABAZILLA
CANALIZATION
CANNIBALIZE
CANNIBALIZED
CANNIBALIZING
CANONIZATION
CANTHARIDIZE
CAPERCAILZIE
CAPITALIZED
CAPITALIZING
CARAMELIZED
CARAMELIZING
CARBOAZOTINE
CARBOLIZING
CARBONIZING
CARBURIZING
CARNALIZING
CATABIBAZON
CATABOLIZED
CATABOLIZING
CATALEPTIZE
CATALOGUIZE
CATALYZATOR

CATECHIZATION
CATECHIZING
CATEGORIZED
CATEGORIZING
CATHARIZING
CATHETERIZE
CATHETERIZED
CATHOLICIZE
CATHOLICIZED
CATHOLICIZING
CAUSTICIZED
CAUSTICIZER
CAUSTICIZING
CAUTERIZATION
CAUTERIZING
CELESTIALIZE
CELESTIALIZED
CENOZOOLOGY
CENTRALIZED
CENTRALIZER
CENTRALIZING
CHALAZOGAMIC
CHALAZOGAMY
CHALAZOIDITE
CHAMELEONIZE
CHAMPAGNIZE
CHAMPAGNIZED
CHAMPAGNIZING
CHANNELIZED
CHANNELIZING
CHARACTERIZE
CHARACTERIZED
CHARACTERIZER
CHEERFULIZE
CHEMICALIZE
CHITINIZATION
CHLAMYDOZOAN
CHLORALIZED
CHLORALIZING
CHLORIDIZED
CHLORIDIZING
CHLORODIZED
CHLORODIZING
CHORIAMBIZE
CHORIZATION
CHORIZONTES
CHORIZONTIC
CHORIZONTIST
CHROMICIZING
CHRONOLOGIZE
CHRONOLOGIZED
CICATRIZANT
CICATRIZATE
CICATRIZING
CINCHONIZED
CINCHONIZING
CIRCULARIZE
CIRCULARIZED
CIRCULARIZING
CITIZENIZED
CITIZENIZING
CITIZENRIES
CITIZENSHIP
CIVILIZABLE
CIVILIZATION
CIVILIZATORY
CLASSICIZED
CLASSICIZING
COAZERVATION
COCAINIZING
COLLECTIVIZE
COLLECTIVIZED
COLLODIONIZE
COLLOQUIZED
COLLOQUIZING
COLONIZATION
COMMEMORIZE
COMMEMORIZED
COMMEMORIZING
COMMERCIALIZE
COMMUNALIZE
COMMUNALIZED
COMMUNALIZER
COMMUNIZATION
COMMUNIZING
COMPANIONIZE
COMPANIONIZED
CONCERTIZED
CONCERTIZER
CONCERTIZING
CONCRETIZED
CONCRETIZING
CONSERVATIZE
CONSONANTIZE
CONTEMPORIZE
CONTEMPORIZED
COPOLYMERIZE
COPOLYMERIZED
COPPERIZATION
CORPOREALIZE
COSMOGONIZE
CREOLIZATION
CRITICIZABLE
CRITICIZING
CRYPTOZONATE
CRYPTOZYGOUS
CRYSTALLIZE
CRYSTALLIZED
CRYSTALLIZER
CRYSTALLIZING
CURARIZATION
CUTICULARIZE
CUTINIZATION
CYCLIZATION
DACTYLOZOOID
DAMENIZATION
DEBENZOLIZE
DECAFFEINIZE
DECARBONIZE
DECARBONIZED
DECARBONIZER
DECARBURIZE
DECARBURIZED
DECENTRALIZE
DECEREBRIZE
DECHORALIZE
DECICERONIZE
DECIMALIZED
DECIMALIZING
DECOLORIZED
DECOLORIZER
DECOLORIZING
DECOLOURIZE
DEEPFREEZED
DEEPFREEZING
DEFERRIZING
DEFIBRINIZE
DEFINITIZED
DEFINITIZING
DEHUMANIZED
DEHUMANIZING
DEHYPNOTIZE
DEHYPNOTIZED
DEJUNKERIZE
DELIMITIZED
DELIMITIZING
DELOCALIZED
DELOCALIZING
DEMAGNETIZE
DEMAGNETIZED
DEMAGNETIZER
DEMANGANIZE
DEMENTHOLIZE
DEMEPHITIZE
DEMICIVILIZED
DEMILITARIZE
DEMILITARIZED
DEMINERALIZE
DEMOBILIZED
DEMOBILIZING
DEMOCRATIZE
DEMOCRATIZED
DEMONETIZED
DEMONETIZING
DEMORALIZED
DEMORALIZER
DEMORALIZING
DEMUTIZATION
DENATURALIZE
DENATURIZER
DENAZIFYING
DENICOTINIZE
DENIZENATION
DEODORIZING
DEOXIDIZING
DEOXYGENIZE
DEPAUPERIZE
DEPAUPERIZED
DEPERSONIZE
DEPIGMENTIZE
DEPOLARIZED
DEPOLARIZER
DEPOLARIZING
DEPOLYMERIZE
DERACIALIZE
DERATIZATION
DERMATOZOON
DESACRALIZE
DESCLOIZITE
DESENSITIZE
DESENSITIZER
DESEXUALIZE
DESEXUALIZED
DESILICONIZE
DESILVERIZE
DESILVERIZER
DESTERILIZE
DESTINEZITE
DESULFURIZE
DESULFURIZED
DESULFURIZER
DESULPHURIZE
DESYNONYMIZE
DETRIBALIZE
DEUTEROZOOID
DEVITALIZED
DEVITALIZING
DEVITAMINIZE
DEVOCALIZED
DEVOCALIZING
DEVULGARIZE
DEXTROSAZONE
DEZINCATION
DEZINCIFIED
DEZINCIFYING
DIABOLIZING
DIAGONALIZE
DIALECTALIZE
DIALECTICIZE
DIALOGIZING
DIALYZATION
DIAMONDIZED
DIAMONDIZING
DIAZENTITHAL
DIAZOBENZENE
DIAZOMETHANE
DIAZOTIZING
DICHOTOMIZE
DICHOTOMIZED
DIEZEUGMENON
DIMERIZATION
DIPHTHONGIZE
DIPHTHONGIZED
DIPHYOZOOID
DIPLOMATIZE
DIPLOMATIZED
DISCANONIZE
DISCANONIZED
DISEQUALIZE
DISGOSPELIZE
DISHARMONIZE
DISORGANIZE
DISORGANIZED
DISORGANIZER
DISPAUPERIZE
DISSEIZORESS
DISSOCIALIZE
DISSYLLABIZE
DIVINIZATION
DOCKIZATION
DOCTRINIZED
DOCTRINIZING
DOCUMENTIZE
DOGGERELIZE
DOGGERELIZER
DOGGERELIZING
DOGMATIZING
DOMESTICIZE
DOMESTICIZED
DOXOLOGIZED
DOXOLOGIZING
DRAMATIZATION
DRAMATIZING
DUALIZATION
DUCTILIZING
DYNAMIZATION
ECONOMIZATION
ECONOMIZING
ECZEMATOSIS
EDITORIALIZE
EDITORIALIZED
EFFECTUALIZE
EFFEMINATIZE
EFFEMINIZED
EFFEMINIZING
ELASTICIZER
ELECTRALIZE
ELECTRICALIZE
ELECTRICIZE
ELECTRIZING
ELECTROLYZE
ELECTROLYZED
ELECTROLYZER
ELECTROLYZING
ELECTROTONIZE
EMBEZZLEMENT
EMBLEMATICIZE
EMBLEMATIZE
EMBLEMATIZED
EMBLEMATIZING
EMBLEMIZING
EMOTIONALIZE
EMOTIONALIZED
EMPATHIZING
EMPHASIZING
EMULSIONIZE
ENCARNALIZE
ENCARNALIZED
ENCARNALIZING
ENCYCLOPEDIZE
ENHYPOSTATIZE
ENIGMATIZED
ENIGMATIZING
ENOLIZATION
ENSORCELIZE
ENSORCERIZE
ENTHRONIZED
ENTHRONIZING
ENTOMOLOGIZE
ENTOMOLOGIZED
ENTOZOOLOGY
ENZYMICALLY
ENZYMOLYSIS
ENZYMOLYTIC
EPENTHESIZE
EPIDOTIZATION
EPIGRAMMATIZE
EPILOGIZING
EPISCOPIZED
EPISCOPIZING
EPISTOLIZABLE
EPITHALAMIZE
EPITOMIZATION
EPITOMIZING
EPIZOOTIOLOGY
EQUALIZATION
EQUILIBRIZE
ERGOTIZATION
ERYTHROZYME
ESTERIZATION
ETERNIZATION
ETHEREALIZE
ETHEREALIZED
ETHEREALIZING
ETHERIZATION
ETHNOZOOLOGY
ETYMOLOGIZE
ETYMOLOGIZED
ETYMOLOGIZING
EUCHARISTIZE
EUCHARISTIZED
EUDAEMONIZE
EUHEMERIZED
EUHEMERIZING
EULOGIZATION
EUPHEMIZING
EUPHONIZING
EVANGELIZED
EVANGELIZER
EVANGELIZING
EVENTUALIZE
EVOLUTIONIZE
EXAUTHORIZE
EXCURSIONIZE
EXORCIZATION
EXORCIZEMENT
EXOSTRACIZE
EXPERIMENTIZE
EXPERMENTIZED
EXTEMPORIZE
EXTEMPORIZED
EXTEMPORIZER
EXTEMPORIZING
EXTERIORIZE
EXTERIORIZED
EXTERIORIZING
EXTERNALIZE
EXTERNIZATION
EXTRAVAGANZA
FACSIMILIZE
FACTORIZATION
FACTORIZING
FAMILIARIZE
FAMILIARIZED
FAMILIARIZER
FAMILIARIZING
FANATICIZED
FANATICIZING
FANTASIZING
FARADIZATION
FASCISTICIZE
FEDERALIZED
FEDERALIZING
FEMINIZATION
FERTILIZABLE

FERTILIZATION
FERTILIZING
FEUDALIZATION
FEUDALIZING
FICTIONALIZED
FICTIONIZED
FICTIONIZING
FISCALIZATION
FISCALIZING
FLAMBOYANTIZE
FLUIDIZATION
FOCALIZATION
FORMALIZATION
FORMALIZING
FORMULARIZE
FORMULARIZED
FORMULARIZING
FORMULIZATION
FORMULIZING
FOSSILIZATION
FOSSILIZING
FRACTIONALIZE
FRACTIONIZE
FRACTIONIZING
FRATERNIZED
FRATERNIZER
FRATERNIZING
FRICTIONIZE
FRICTIONIZED
FRICTIONIZING
FRIVOLIZING
FUNCTIONIZE
FUROMONAZOLE
GABERLUNZIE
GALVANIZATION
GALVANIZING
GASTEROZOOID
GASTROZOOID
GAZETTEERAGE
GAZINGSTOCK
GELATINIZED
GELATINIZER
GELATINIZING
GENEALOGIZE
GENEALOGIZER
GENERALIZABLE
GENERALIZED
GENERALIZER
GEOGRAPHIZE
GEOGRAPHIZED
GEOLOGIZING
GEOMETRICIZE
GEOMETRIZED
GEOMETRIZING
GLAMORIZING
GLUCOSAZONE
GLUTTONIZED
GLUTTONIZING
GLYCERINIZE
GLYCYRRHIZIN
GORMANDIZER
GRAMMATICIZE
GRANULITIZE
GRAPHITIZED
GUTTURALIZE
GUTTURALIZING
GYNECOMAZIA
GYROHORIZON
HAPHAZARDLY
HAPHAZARDNESS
HARLEQUINIZE
HARMONIZING
HARZBURGITE
HAZARDOUSLY
HAZARDOUSNESS
HETEROZYGOTE
HETEROZYGOUS
HIERARCHIZE
HOMOGENIZER
HOPPERDOZER
HORIZOMETER
HORIZONTALITY
HORIZONTALIZE
HORIZONTALLY
HORIZONTICAL
HOSPITALIZE
HURRICANIZE
HYBRIDIZABLE
HYBRIDIZATION
HYDROBENZOIN
HYDROGENIZE
HYDROLYZATE
HYDRORHIZAL
HYDROZINCITE
HYPERBOLIZE
HYPERBOLIZED
HYPOSTATIZE
ICHTHYIZATION
IDEALIZATION
IDOLATRIZED
IDOLATRIZER
IDOLATRIZING
IDOLIZATION
ILLEGALIZED
ILLEGALIZING
IMBASTARDIZE
IMMATERIALIZE
IMMETHODIZE
IMMOBILIZED
IMMOBILIZING
IMMORTALIZE
IMMORTALIZED
IMMORTALIZER
IMMORTALIZING
IMPACTIONIZE
IMPATRONIZE
IMPERIALIZE
IMPERIALIZED
IMPERIALIZING
IMPERSONALIZE
IMPROBABILIZE
INDIVIDUALIZE
INDOCTRINIZE
INFORMALIZE
INOXIDIZING
INTELLIGIZE
INTERMEZZOS
INTERNALIZE
INTHRONIZATE
IODOBENZENE
IRIDIZATION
IRREALIZABLE
IRREGULARIZE
ISOCHRONIZE
ISOCHRONIZED
ISOCHRONIZING
ITALICIZING
ITEMIZATION
JARGONIZING
JAROVIZATION
JASPERIZING
JATEORHIZIN
JATEORHIZINE
JEOPARDIZED
JEOPARDIZING
JOURNALIZED
JOURNALIZER
JOURNALIZING
JOVIALIZING
JUBILIZATION
JUDICIALIZE
KATZENJAMMER
KETONIZATION
KJELDAHLIZE
KYANIZATION
LABIALIZING
LABILIZATION
LAICIZATION
LALAPALOOZA
LALLAPALOOZA
LAPAROTOMIZE
LATERALIZED
LATERALIZING
LATERIZATION
LEGALIZATION
LEGITIMATIZE
LEGITIMATIZED
LEGITIMIZED
LEGITIMIZING
LETHARGIZED
LETHARGIZING
LIBERALIZED
LIBERALIZER
LIBERALIZING
LICHENIZATION
LIEDERKRANZ
LINEARIZATION
LIONIZATION
LIQUIDIZING
LITERALIZED
LITERALIZER
LITERALIZING
LITHOTOMIZE
LOCALIZABLE
LOCALIZATION
LOGOMACHIZE
LORENZENITE
MACADAMIZED
MACADAMIZER
MACADAMIZING
MAGAZINABLE
MAGNETIZABLE
MAGNETIZATION
MAGNETIZING
MALLEABLEIZE
MALLEABLEIZED
MALLEABLIZE
MAMMONIZATION
MANORIALIZE
MARBLEIZING
MARGINALIZE
MARMARIZING
MARSUPIALIZE
MARTYRIZING
MATERIALIZE
MATERIALIZED
MATERIALIZER
MATERIALIZING
MATERNALIZE
MATHEMATIZE
MATRONIZING
MAXIMIZATION
MECHANALIZE
MECHANIZATION
MEDIATIZING
MEGAZOOSPORE
MEIZOSEISMAL
MEIZOSEISMIC
MELANCHOLIZE
MELODRAMATIZE
MEMORANDIZE
MEMORIALIZE
MEMORIALIZED
MEMORIALIZER
MEMORIALIZING
MEMORIZATION
MERCERIZING
MERCHANDIZE
MERCURIALIZE
MERCURIZING
MERMITHIZED
MERORGANIZE
MESMERIZATION
MESMERIZING
METABOLIZED
METABOLIZING
METALIZATION
METALLIZATION
METAMERIZED
METAMORPHIZE
METAPHONIZE
METASTASIZE
METASTASIZED
METHODIZING
MEZZOTINTED
MEZZOTINTER
MEZZOTINTING
MICASIZATION
MICROSCOPIZE
MICROZOARIA
MICROZOARIAN
MICROZYMIAN
MIGNIARDIZE
MILITARIZED
MILITARIZING
MINERALIZED
MINERALIZER
MINERALIZING
MINERALOGIZE
MINIATURIZE
MINIATURIZED
MINIMIZATION
MISCOGNIZANT
MISEMPHASIZE
MISSIONARIZE
MISSIONIZER
MITHRIDATIZE
MIZZENTOPMAN
MIZZENTOPMEN
MNEMONIZING
MOBILIZATION
MODERNIZATION
MODERNIZING
MONARCHIZED
MONARCHIZER
MONARCHIZING
MONETIZATION
MONOCHORDIZE
MONOLOGIZED
MONOLOGIZING
MONOPOLIZED
MONOPOLIZER
MONOPOLIZING
MONOZYGOTIC
MONZODIORITE
MONZOGABBRO
MORALIZATION
MORTALIZING
MOTORIZATION
MUNICIPALIZE
MUNICIPALIZED
MUSCOVITIZE
MUSCOVITIZED
MUSCULARIZE
MUTUALIZING
MUZZLELOADER
MUZZLELOADING
MYCORRHIZAL
MYCORRHIZIC
MYOSYNIZESIS
MYTHICIZING
MYTHOLOGIZE
MYTHOLOGIZED
MYTHOLOGIZER
MYTHOLOGIZING
MYTHOPOETIZE
MYZOSTOMIDAN
MYZOSTOMOUS
NAPHTHALIZE
NARCOTIZING
NASALIZATION
NATIONALIZE
NATIONALIZED
NATIONALIZER
NATIONALIZING
NATURALIZED
NATURALIZER
NATURALIZING
NAZIFICATION
NEBULIZATION
NEMATOZOOID
NEOLOGIZING
NEOPAGANIZE
NESSLERIZED
NEUROLOGIZE
NEUROTOMIZE
NEUTRALIZED
NEUTRALIZER
NEUTRALIZING
NEWSMAGAZINE
NIGHTINGALIZE
NITRIDIZATION
NITROBENZENE
NITROGENIZE
NITROGENIZED
NITROGENIZING
NIVELLIZATION
NODULIZING
NONENTITIZE
NONPARTIZAN
NORMALIZATION
NORMALIZING
NOTARIZATION
NOVELIZATION
NUPTIALIZE
OBJECTIVIZE
OBJECTIVIZED
OBJECTIVIZING
OBJECTIZATION
OBJECTIZING
OBLIVIONIZE
ODYLIZATION
OFFICIALIZE
OLIGARCHIZE
OLIGORHIZOUS
OPSONIZATION
OPTIMIZATION
OPTIMIZING
OPTIONALIZE
ORGANIZABLE
ORGANIZATION
ORGANIZATORY
ORGANZINING
ORIENTALIZE
ORIENTALIZED
ORIENTALIZING
ORYZIVOROUS
OSMAZOMATIC
OSMAZOMATOUS
OSTRACIZATION
OSTRACIZING
OUTTYRANNIZE
OVALIZATION
OVARIOTOMIZE
OVERGLAZING
OVERPRIZING
OVERZEALOUS
OXYGENIZABLE
OXYGENIZING
OZONIFEROUS
OZONIZATION
OZONOSCOPIC
OZONOSPHERE
OZONOSPHERIC
PAGANIZATION

PALATIZATION
PALEOZOOLOGY
PALLADIUMIZE
PALLETIZING
PAMPHLETIZE
PANCREATIZE
PANEGYRICIZE
PANEGYRIZED
PANEGYRIZER
PANEGYRIZING
PANSEXUALIZE
PANTHEONIZE
PAPALIZATION
PARABOLIZED
PARABOLIZER
PARABOLIZING
PARAENESIZE
PARALYZATION
PARCHMENTIZE
PARENTHESIZE
PASTEURIZED
PASTEURIZER
PASTEURIZING
PASTORALIZE
PATERNALIZE
PATRIZATION
PATRONIZING
PAUPERIZING
PECTIZATION
PECULIARIZE
PECULIARIZED
PELORIZATION
PEMMICANIZE
PENALIZATION
PENTAMETRIZE
PEPTIZATION
PEPTONIZING
PERFECTIVIZE
PERMORALIZE
PERSONALIZE
PERSONALIZED
PETROLIZING
PEZIZACEOUS
PEZIZAEFORM
PHAGOCYTIZE
PHANEROZOIC
PHANTOMIZER
PHENMIAZINE
PHENOXAZINE
PHILIPPICIZE
PHILIPPIZER
PHILOLOGIZE
PHILOSOPHIZE
PHILOZOONIST
PHLEBOTOMIZE
PHLYZACIOUS
PHONETICIZE
PHONETIZATION
PHOSPHATIZE
PHOSPHATIZED
PHOSPHORIZE
PHRENOLOGIZE
PHYLACTERIZE
PHYLLOZOOID
PHYSIOLOGIZE
PHYTOBEZOAR
PICRORHIZIN
PIEZOMETRIC
PLAGIARIZED
PLAGIARIZER
PLAGIARIZING
PLASTICIZED
PLASTICIZER
PLASTICIZING
PLATINIZING
PLEBEIANIZE
PLEBEIANIZED
PLURALIZING
PNEUMATIZED
POETIZATION
POLARIZABLE
POLARIZATION
POLITICALIZE
POLITICIZED
POLITICIZER
POLITICIZING
POLITZERIZE
POLYCHROMIZE
POLYZOARIAL
POLYZOARIUM
POPULARIZED
POPULARIZER
POPULARIZING
PORCELAINIZE
PORCELLANIZE
POSTURIZING
POTENTIALIZE
POZZUOLANIC
PRACTICALIZE
PRACTICALIZED
PRAGMATIZER
PREACHERIZE
PRESERVATIZE
PRESSURIZED
PRESSURIZING
PRIZEFIGHTER
PRIZEHOLDER
PROBABILIZE
PROBLEMATIZE
PRODIGALIZE
PROLETARIZE
PROLOGUIZER
PROPAGANDIZE
PROSELYTIZE
PROSELYTIZED
PROSELYTIZER
PROTOCITIZEN
PROTOCOLIZE
PROTOXIDIZE
PROTOXIDIZED
PROTOZOEAN
PROTOZOIASIS
PROTOZOONAL
PSYCHIATRIZE
PSYCHOLOGIZE
PUBLICIZING
PULVERIZATE
PULVERIZATOR
PULVERIZING
PUZZLEATION
PUZZLEDNESS
PUZZLEHEADED
PUZZLEPATED
PUZZLINGNESS
PYRRODIAZOLE
QUANTIZATION
QUIZZICALITY
QUIZZICALLY
QUIZZACIOUS
QUIZZATORIAL
RACEMIZATION
RACIALIZATION
RADIALIZATION
RADIUMIZATION
RANDOMIZING
RATIONALIZE
RATIONALIZED
RATIONALIZER
RAZORMAKING
RAZZBERRIES
REACTUALIZE
REALISTICIZE
REALIZATION
REBAPTIZATION
RECAPITALIZE
RECAPITALIZED
RECARBONIZE
RECARBONIZER
RECARBURIZE
RECARBURIZER
RECIPROCALIZE
RECOGNIZABLE
RECOGNIZABLY
RECOGNIZANCE
RECOGNIZANT
RECOGNIZING
RECRYSTALLIZE
REFORESTIZE
REGIONALIZE
REGULARIZED
REGULARIZER
REHARMONIZE
RELIGIONIZE
REORGANIZED
REORGANIZER
REORGANIZING
RESTERILIZE
REVITALIZED
REVITALIZER
REVITALIZING
RHAPSODIZED
RHAPSODIZING
RHIZANTHOUS
RHIZOCARPIC
RHIZOCARPOUS
RHIZOCAULUS
RHIZODERMIS
RHIZOGENETIC
RHIZOGENOUS
RHIZOMATOUS
RHIZOMORPHIC
RHIZOPHAGOUS
RHIZOPHILOUS
RHIZOPODIST
RHIZOPODOUS
RHIZOSTOMOUS
RHYTHMICIZE
RHYTHMIZABLE
RINFORZANDO
ROBOTIZATION
ROENTGENIZE
ROMANTICIZE
ROTARIANIZE
ROUTINIZING
ROYALIZATION
RUBBERIZING
RURALIZATION
SACCHARIZED
SACCHARIZING
SACRAMENTIZE
SAILORIZING
SANCTUARIZE
SARCOPHAGIZE
SATIRIZABLE
SCANDALIZED
SCANDALIZING
SCENARIZING
SCEPTICIZED
SCEPTICIZING
SCHILLERIZE
SCHILLERIZED
SCHILLERIZING
SCHISMATIZE
SCHISMATIZED
SCHISMATIZING
SCHIZOCARPIC
SCHIZOCHROAL
SCHIZOCOELE
SCHIZODINIC
SCHIZOGENESIS
SCHIZOGENETIC
SCHIZOGENIC
SCHIZOGENOUS
SCHIZOGNATH
SCHIZOGONIC
SCHIZOIDISM
SCHIZOMYCETE
SCHIZOMYCETES
SCHIZOPELMOUS
SCHIZOPHASIA
SCHIZOPHRENE
SCHIZOPHRENIA
SCHIZOPHYTE
SCHIZOPODAL
SCHIZOPODOUS
SCHIZORHINAL
SCHIZOSPORE
SCHIZOSTELE
SCHIZOSTELIC
SCHIZOSTELY
SCHIZOTHECAL
SCHIZOTHYME
SCHIZOTHYMIA
SCHIZOTHYMIC
SCHIZOTRICHIA
SCLEROTIZED
SCRUTINIZED
SCRUTINIZER
SCRUTINIZING
SECTARIANIZE
SECTARIANIZED
SECTIONALIZE
SECTIONALIZED
SECULARIZED
SECULARIZING
SEMICIVILIZED
SEMPITERNIZE
SENSIBILIZE
SENSITIZATION
SENSITIZING
SENSUALIZED
SENSUALIZING
SEPTICIZATION
SERIALIZATION
SERIALIZING
SERMONIZING
SERPENTINIZE
SHERARDIZED
SHERARDIZING
SHERBETZIDE
SIDEREALIZE
SIGNALIZING
SIMULACRIZE
SINGULARIZE
SINGULARIZED
SINGULARIZING
SIPHONOZOOID
SIZABLENESS
SKELETONIZE
SKELETONIZED
SKELETONIZER
SKELETONIZING
SKEPTICIZED
SKEPTICIZING
SLENDERIZED
SLENDERIZING
SLUGGARDIZE
SOCIALIZATION
SOCIALIZING
SOLARIZATION
SOLEMNIZATION
SOLEMNIZING
SOLIDARIZED
SOLIDARIZING
SOLILOQUIZE
SOLILOQUIZED
SOLILOQUIZER
SOLILOQUIZING
SOLITUDINIZE
SOLITUDINIZED
SOLMIZATION
SOLVOLYZING
SOMNAMBULIZE
SOPHRONIZED
SOPHRONIZING
SOUTHERNIZE
SOVEREIGNIZE
SOVIETIZATION
SOVIETIZING
SPECIALIZED
SPECIALIZER
SPECIALIZING
SPECIFICIZE
SPECIMENIZE
SPECIMENIZED
SPERMATOZOA
SPERMATOZOAL
SPERMATOZOAN
SPERMATOZOIC
SPERMATOZOID
SPERMATOZOON
SPHEROIDIZE
SPHERULITIZE
SPIRALIZATION
SPIRITUALIZE
SPIRITUALIZED
SPIRITUALIZER
SPITZENBERG
SPITZENBURG
SPLENIZATION
SPONDYLIZEMA
SQUEEZINGLY
STABILIZATION
STABILIZATOR
STABILIZING
STALLIONIZE
STALWARTIZE
STANDARDIZE
STANDARDIZED
STANDARDIZER
STANDARDIZING
STANZAICALLY
STATISTICIZE
STERILIZATION
STERILIZING
STIGMATIZED
STIGMATIZER
STIGMATIZING
STRUCTURALIZE
STRYCHNINIZE
STYLIZATION
SUBERIZATION
SUBSIDIZATION
SUBSIDIZING
SUBSTANTIVIZE
SUBSTANTIZE
SUBTILIZATION
SUBTILIZING
SUBURBANIZE
SUBVITALIZED
SULCALIZATION
SULFADIAZINE
SULFATIZING
SULFOBENZIDE
SULFOBENZOIC
SULFURIZING
SULPHATIZED
SULPHATIZING
SULPHAZOTIZE
SULPHOBENZID
SULPHURIZED
SULPHURIZING
SUMMARIZATION
SUMMARIZING
SYCOPHANTIZE

SYLLABIZING
SYLLOGIZING
SYMBOLIZATION
SYMBOLIZING
SYMMETRIZED
SYMMETRIZING
SYMPATHIZED
SYMPATHIZER
SYMPATHIZING
SYMPHONIZED
SYMPHONIZING
SYMPTOMATIZE
SYNCHRONIZE
SYNCHRONIZED
SYNCHRONIZER
SYNCHRONIZING
SYNCRETIZED
SYNCRETIZING
SYNDICALIZE
SYNONYMIZED
SYNONYMIZING
SYNTHESIZED
SYNTHESIZER
SYNTHESIZING
SYNTHETIZER
SYNTONIZING
SYPHILIZING
SYSTEMATIZE
SYSTEMATIZED
SYSTEMATIZER
SYSTEMATIZING
SYSTEMIZATION
SYSTEMIZING
SZAIBELYITE
TABULARIZED
TABULARIZING
TANTALIZING
TARANTARIZE
TARTARIZING
TARTRAZINIC
TAUTOLOGIZE
TAUTOLOGIZED
TAUTOLOGIZER
TAXIDERMIZE
TCHERVONETZ
TECHNICALIZE
TEETOTUMIZE
TELEPATHIZE
TELFORDIZED
TELFORDIZING
TELLURIZING
TEMPORALIZE
TEMPORIZING
TENDERIZING
TENEMENTIZE
TERRORIZING
TETANIZATION
TETRAKISAZO
TETRAZOLIUM
TETRAZOTIZE
THEATRICIZE
THEOLOGIZED
THEOLOGIZER
THEOLOGIZING
THEOMORPHIZE
THEORIZATION
THERMOLYZED
THERMOLYZING
THIADIAZOLE
TOBACCONIZE
TOTALIZATION
TOTALIZATOR
TOTEMIZATION
TOURMALINIZE
TRAILBLAZER
TRAILBLAZING
TRANQUILIZE
TRANQUILIZER
TRANQUILIZING
TRANQUILLIZE
TRANQUILLIZED
TRAPEZIFORM
TRAPEZOIDAL
TRICHINIZED
TRICHINIZING
TRICHOTOMIZE
TRILLIONIZE
TROPHOZOITE
TROPHOZOOID
TROPICALIZE
TROPICALIZED
TROPICALIZING
TROPOLOGIZE
TROPOLOGIZED
TROPOLOGIZING
TRULLIZATION
TUBERCULIZE
TUBERIZATION
TUBULIZATION
TUTORIZATION
TYPHIZATION
TYRANNIZING
ULTRAZEALOUS
UNAUTHORIZE
UNAUTHORIZED
UNBRUTALIZE
UNCANONIZED
UNCANONIZING
UNCIVILIZED
UNFEUDALIZE
UNIFORMALIZE
UNIFORMALIZED
UNIONIZATION
UNIVERSALIZED
UNIVERSITIZE
UNLITURGIZE
UNMECHANIZE
UNMODERNIZE
UNMORALIZED
UNMORALIZING
UNMORTALIZE
UNNATURALIZE
UNORGANIZED
UNPATRONIZED
UNPOPULARIZE
UNRECOGNIZED
UNSECULARIZE
UNSOLEMNIZE
UNSTERILIZED
UNVERBALIZED
UNVULGARIZE
URALITIZING
URBANIZATION
UTILIZATION
VACCINIZATION
VAGABONDIZE
VAGABONDIZED
VAGABONDIZER
VAGABONDIZING
VALORIZATION
VAPORIZATION
VAPOURIZING
VASCULARIZE
VASCULARIZED
VASCULARIZING
VASECTOMIZE
VASSALIZING
VEGETABLIZE
VENALIZATION
VERATRINIZE
VERATRINIZED
VERATRINIZING
VERATRIZING
VERBALIZING
VERMILIONIZE
VICTIMIZABLE
VICTIMIZATION
VICTIMIZING
VISUALIZING
VITALIZATION
VITALIZINGLY
VITRIOLIZED
VITRIOLIZING
VOCALIZATION
VOLATILIZED
VOLATILIZER
VOLATILIZING
VOLCANIZING
VULCANIZATE
VULCANIZATION
VULCANIZING
VULGARIZATION
VULGARIZING
WESTERNIZED
WESTERNIZING
WINTERIZING
WIZENEDNESS
WOODCOCKIZE
ZANTHOXYLUM
ZAPHRENTOID
ZEALOUSNESS
ZENOCENTRIC
ZENOGRAPHIC
ZEOLITIZING
ZIGZAGGEDLY
ZIMENTWATER
ZINCIFEROUS
ZINCOGRAPHER
ZINCOGRAPHIC
ZINCOGRAPHY
ZINGIBERENE
ZINNWALDITE
ZOANTHODEME
ZOANTHODEMIC
ZODIOPHILOUS
ZOIDOGAMOUS
ZOISITIZATION
ZOMOTHERAPY
ZONAESTHESIA
ZONESTHESIA
ZONOCHLORITE
ZONOCILIATE
ZONOLIMNETIC
ZONOSKELETON
ZOOCECIDIUM
ZOOCULTURAL
ZOODENDRIUM
ZOODYNAMICS
ZOOERYTHRIN
ZOOGEOGRAPHY
ZOOGONIDIUM
ZOOGRAFTING
ZOOLOGIZING
ZOOMAGNETIC
ZOOMAGNETISM
ZOOMORPHISM
ZOOMORPHIZE
ZOONOSOLOGY
ZOOPANTHEON
ZOOPARASITE
ZOOPATHOLOGY
ZOOPHARMACY
ZOOPHYSICAL
ZOOPHYTICAL
ZOOPHYTOLOGY
ZOOPLANKTON
ZOOPRAXISCOPE
ZOOSPORANGE
ZOOTHEISTIC
ZOOXANTHELLA
ZOSTERIFORM
ZYGAPOPHYSIS
ZYGODACTYLE
ZYGODACTYLIC
ZYGOLABIALIS
ZYGOMATICUM
ZYGOMATICUS
ZYGOMORPHIC
ZYGOMORPHOUS
ZYGOMYCETES
ZYGOMYCETOUS
ZYGOPHYCEOUS
ZYGOPLEURAL
ZYGOPTERAN
ZYGOPTERID
ZYGOPTEROUS
ZYGOSPHENAL
ZYMOGENESIS
ZYMOLOGICAL
ZYMOPLASTIC
ZYMOSIMETER
ZYMOSTHENIC
ZYMOTECHNIC
ZYMOTECHNICS
ZYMOTICALLY

POSITIONAL ORDER LIST OF WORDS OVER 10 LETTERS

ZANTHOXYLUM
ZAPHRENTOID
ZEALOUSNESS
ZENOCENTRIC
ZENOGRAPHIC
ZEOLITIZING
ZIGZAGGEDLY
ZIMENTWATER
ZINCIFEROUS
ZINCOGRAPHER
ZINCOGRAPHIC
ZINCOGRAPHY
ZINGIBERENE
ZINNWALDITE
ZOANTHODEME
ZOANTHODEMIC
ZODIOPHILOUS
ZOIDOGAMOUS
ZOISITIZATION
ZOMOTHERAPY
ZONAESTHESIA
ZONESTHESIA
ZONOCHLORITE
ZONOCILIATE
ZONOLIMNETIC
ZONOSKELETON
ZOOCECIDIUM
ZOOCULTURAL
ZOODENDRIUM
ZOODYNAMICS
ZOOERYTHRIN
ZOOGEOGRAPHY
ZOOGONIDIUM
ZOOGRAFTING
ZOOLOGIZING
ZOOMAGNETIC
ZOOMAGNETISM
ZOOMORPHISM
ZOOMORPHIZE
ZOONOSOLOGY
ZOOPANTHEON
ZOOPARASITE
ZOOPATHOLOGY
ZOOPHARMACY
ZOOPHYSICAL
ZOOPHYTICAL
ZOOPHYTOLOGY
ZOOPLANKTON
ZOOPRAXISCOPE
ZOOSPORANGE
ZOOTHEISTIC
ZOOXANTHELLA
ZOSTERIFORM
ZYGAPOPHYSIS
ZYGODACTYLE
ZYGODACTYLIC
ZYGOLABIALIS
ZYGOMATICUM
ZYGOMATICUS
ZYGOMORPHIC
ZYGOMORPHOUS
ZYGOMYCETES
ZYGOMYCETOUS
ZYGOPHYCEOUS
ZYGOPLEURAL
ZYGOPTERAN
ZYGOPTERID
ZYGOPTEROUS
ZYGOSPHENAL
ZYMOGENESIS
ZYMOLOGICAL
ZYMOPLASTIC
ZYMOSIMETER
ZYMOSTHENIC
ZYMOTECHNIC
ZYMOTECHNICS
ZYMOTICALLY

AZADIRACHTA
AZEOTROPISM
AZIMETHYLENE
AZIMUTHALLY
AZOCOCHINEAL
AZOCORALLINE
AZODIPHENYL
AZOERYTHRIN
AZOFICATION
AZOOSPERMIA
AZOPARAFFIN
AZOPHENETOLE
AZOPHENYLENE
AZOPHOSPHIN
AZOPHOSPHORE
AZOSULPHINE
AZOSULPHONIC
AZOTETRAZOLE
AZOTHIONIUM
AZOTOBACTER
AZOTORRHOEA
AZYGOMATOUS

OZONIFEROUS
OZONIZATION
OZONOSCOPIC
OZONOSPHERE
OZONOSPHERIC
SZAIBELYITE

BIZARRENESS
BIZYGOMATIC
BUZZERPHONE
DEZINCATION
DEZINCIFIED
DEZINCIFYING
ECZEMATOSIS
ENZYMICALLY
ENZYMOLYSIS
ENZYMOLYTIC
GAZETTEERAGE
GAZINGSTOCK
HAZARDOUSLY
HAZARDOUSNESS
MEZZOTINTED
MEZZOTINTER
MEZZOTINTING
MIZZENTOPMAN
MIZZENTOPMEN
MUZZLELOADER
MUZZLELOADING
MYZOSTOMIDAN
MYZOSTOMOUS
NAZIFICATION
PEZIZACEOUS
PEZIZAEFORM
POZZUOLANIC
PUZZLEATION
PUZZLEDNESS
PUZZLEHEADED
PUZZLEPATED
PUZZLINGNESS
RAZORMAKING
RAZZBERRIES
SIZABLENESS
WIZENEDNESS

BENZALDEHYDE
BENZALDOXIME
BENZINDULINE
BENZOHYDROL
BENZOINATED
BENZONITRILE
BENZONITROL
BENZOPHENONE
BENZOYLATION
BENZYLAMINE
BERZELIANITE
BLIZZARDOUS
BRAZENFACED
BUZZERPHONE
COAZERVATION
DIAZENTITHAL
DIAZOBENZENE
DIAZOMETHANE
DIAZOTIZING
DIEZEUGMENON
EPIZOOTIOLOGY
HARZBURGITE
KATZENJAMMER
MEIZOSEISMAL
MEIZOSEISMIC
MEZZOTINTED
MEZZOTINTER
MEZZOTINTING
MIZZENTOPMAN
MIZZENTOPMEN
MONZODIORITE
MONZOGABBRO
MUZZLELOADER

MUZZLELOADING
ORYZIVOROUS
PIEZOMETRIC
POZZUOLANIC
PRIZEFIGHTER
PRIZEHOLDER
PUZZLEATION
PUZZLEDNESS
PUZZLEHEADED
PUZZLEPATED
PUZZLINGNESS
QUIZZACIOUS
QUIZZATORIAL
QUIZZICALITY
QUIZZICALLY
RAZZBERRIES
RHIZANTHOUS
RHIZOCARPIC
RHIZOCARPOUS
RHIZOCAULUS
RHIZODERMIS
RHIZOGENETIC
RHIZOGENOUS
RHIZOMATOUS
RHIZOMORPHIC
RHIZOPHAGOUS
RHIZOPHILOUS
RHIZOPODIST
RHIZOPODOUS
RHIZOSTOMOUS
ZIGZAGGEDLY

BEDAZZLINGLY
BEDIZENMENT
BLIZZARDOUS
BRONZESMITH
CACOZEALOUS
CENOZOOLOGY
CITIZENIZED
CITIZENIZING
CITIZENRIES
CITIZENSHIP
DENAZIFYING
DENIZENATION
EMBEZZLEMENT
ENTOZOOLOGY
HORIZOMETER
HORIZONTALITY
HORIZONTALIZE
HORIZONTALLY
HORIZONTICAL
MAGAZINABLE
MEGAZOOSPORE
MONOZYGOTIC
OSMAZOMATIC
OSMAZOMATOUS
OVERZEALOUS
PEZIZACEOUS
PEZIZAEFORM
PHLYZACIOUS
POLYZOARIAL
POLYZOARIUM
QUIZZACIOUS
QUIZZATORIAL
QUIZZICALITY
QUIZZICALLY
SCHIZOCARPIC
SCHIZOCHROAL
SCHIZOCOELE
SCHIZODINIC
SCHIZOGENESIS
SCHIZOGENETIC
SCHIZOGENIC
SCHIZOGENOUS
SCHIZOGNATH
SCHIZOGONIC
SCHIZOIDISM

SCHIZOMYCETE
SCHIZOMYCETES
SCHIZOPELMOUS
SCHIZOPHASIA
SCHIZOPHRENE
SCHIZOPHRENIA
SCHIZOPHYTE
SCHIZOPODAL
SCHIZOPODOUS
SCHIZORHINAL
SCHIZOSPORE
SCHIZOSTELE
SCHIZOSTELIC
SCHIZOSTELY
SCHIZOTHECAL
SCHIZOTHYME
SCHIZOTHYMIA
SCHIZOTHYMIC
SCHIZOTRICHIA
SPITZENBERG
SPITZENBURG
STANZAICALLY

ADENIZATION
ANALYZATION
APPRIZEMENT
ATOMIZATION
BAPTIZEMENT
BEDAZZLINGLY
BROMIZATION
CHALAZOGAMIC
CHALAZOGAMY
CHALAZOIDITE
CHORIZATION
CHORIZONTES
CHORIZONTIC
CHORIZONTIST
CYCLIZATION
DEBENZOLIZE
DIALYZATION
DOCKIZATION
DUALIZATION
EMBEZZLEMENT
ENOLIZATION
ETHNOZOOLOGY
HAPHAZARDLY
HAPHAZARDNESS
HYDROZINCITE
IDOLIZATION
IRIDIZATION
ITEMIZATION
KYANIZATION
LAICIZATION
LIONIZATION
LORENZENITE
MICROZOARIA
MICROZOARIAN
MICROZYMIAN
ODYLIZATION
ORGANZINING
OVALIZATION
OZONIZATION
PALEOZOOLOGY
PATRIZATION
PECTIZATION
PEPTIZATION
PHILOZOONIST
POETIZATION
PROTOZOEAN
PROTOZOIASIS
PROTOZOONAL
QUINAZOLINE
QUINAZOLINE
REALIZATION
SOLMIZATION
SQUEEZINGLY
STYLIZATION

TETRAZOLIUM
TETRAZOTIZE
TRAPEZIFORM
TRAPEZOIDAL
TYPHIZATION
ULTRAZEALOUS
UTILIZATION

ALBITIZATION
ALDOLIZATION
ALKALIZABLE
ALKALIZATION
AMMONIZATION
AMORTIZABLE
AMORTIZATION
AMORTIZEMENT
APPETIZINGLY
ARBORIZATION
ARSENIZATION
ATMOLYZATION
BAMBOOZLEMENT
BAMBOOZLING
BILHARZIASIS
BILHARZIOSIS
CALABAZILLA
CANALIZATION
CANONIZATION
CARBOAZOTINE
CATALYZATOR
CIVILIZABLE
CIVILIZATION
CIVILIZATORY
COLONIZATION
CREOLIZATION
CRYPTOZONATE
CRYPTOZYGOUS
CURARIZATION
CUTINIZATION
DAMENIZATION
DEMUTIZATION
DERATIZATION
DIMERIZATION
DIPHYOZOOID
DISSEIZORESS
DIVINIZATION
DYNAMIZATION
EQUALIZATION
ERGOTIZATION
ESTERIZATION
ETERNIZATION
ETHERIZATION
EULOGIZATION
EXORCIZATION
EXORCIZEMENT
FARADIZATION
FEMINIZATION
FLUIDIZATION
FOCALIZATION
GASTROZOOID
HETEROZYGOTE
HETEROZYGOUS
IDEALIZATION
JAROVIZATION
JUBILIZATION
KETONIZATION
LABILIZATION
LATERIZATION
LEGALIZATION
LOCALIZABLE
LOCALIZATION
MAXIMIZATION
MEMORIZATION
METALIZATION
MICASIZATION
MINIMIZATION
MOBILIZATION
MONETIZATION

MORALIZATION
MOTORIZATION
NASALIZATION
NEBULIZATION
NEMATOZOOID
NODULIZING
NOTARIZATION
NOVELIZATION
OPSONIZATION
OPTIMIZATION
OPTIMIZING
ORGANIZABLE
ORGANIZATION
ORGANIZATORY
PAGANIZATION
PALATIZATION
PAPALIZATION
PARALYZATION
PELORIZATION
PENALIZATION
PHYLLOZOOID
POLARIZABLE
POLARIZATION
QUANTIZATION
QUANTIZING
QUANTIZING
RACEMIZATION
RINFORZANDO
ROBOTIZATION
ROYALIZATION
RURALIZATION
SATIRIZABLE
SOLARIZATION
SPLENIZATION
SUBERIZATION
TARTRAZINIC
TETANIZATION
THEORIZATION
TOTALIZATION
TOTALIZATOR
TOTEMIZATION
TROPHOZOITE
TROPHOZOOID
TRULLIZATION
TUBERIZATION
TUBULIZATION
TUTORIZATION
UNIONIZATION
URBANIZATION
VALORIZATION
VAPORIZATION
VENALIZATION
VITALIZATION
VITALIZINGLY
VOCALIZATION

ACADEMIZING
ACETONIZATION
ACETYLIZABLE
ACETYLIZATION
ACTIONIZING
ACTUALIZATION
ACTUALIZING
ADVERTIZEMENT
ADVERTIZING
ALCHEMIZING
ALGEBRIZATION
ALUMINIZING
ANALOGIZING
ANATOMIZING
ANGLICIZING
ANIMALIZATION
ANIMALIZING
ANTHEROZOID
ANTHEROZOOID
APOLOGIZING
ARCTICIZING

AROMATIZING
ASCIDIOZOOID
AUTHORIZATION
AUTHORIZING
BACTERIZING
BALKANIZING
BARBARIZING
BERGINIZATION
BISTRIAZOLE
BRUTALIZING
BURTONIZATION
CARBOLIZING
CARBONIZING
CARBURIZING
CARNALIZING
CATECHIZATION
CATECHIZING
CATHARIZING
CAUTERIZATION
CAUTERIZING
CHITINIZATION
CICATRIZANT
CICATRIZATE
CICATRIZING
COCAINIZING
COMMUNIZATION
COMMUNIZING
COPPERIZATION
CRITICIZABLE
CRITICIZING
DACTYLOZOOID
DEFERRIZING
DEODORIZING
DEOXIDIZING
DERMATOZOON
DESCLOIZITE
DESTINEZITE
DEUTEROZOOID
DIABOLIZING
DIALOGIZING
DIAZOTIZING
DOGMATIZING
DRAMATIZATION
DRAMATIZING
DUCTILIZING
ECONOMIZATION
ECONOMIZING
ELECTRIZING
EMBLEMIZING
EMPATHIZING
EMPHASIZING
EPIDOTIZATION
EPILOGIZING
EPITOMIZATION
EPITOMIZING
ERYTHROZYME
EUPHEMIZING
EUPHONIZING
EXTERNIZATION
FACTORIZATION
FANTASIZING
FERTILIZABLE
FERTILIZATION
FERTILIZING
FEUDALIZATION
FEUDALIZING
FISCALIZATION
FISCALIZING
FORMALIZATION
FORMALIZING
FORMULIZATION
FORMULIZING
FOSSILIZATION
FOSSILIZING
FRIVOLIZING
GALVANIZATION
GALVANIZING

GASTEROZOOID
GEOLOGIZING
GLAMORIZING
GLUCOSAZONE
HARMONIZING
HYBRIDIZABLE
HYBRIDIZATION
HYDROLYZATE
ICHTHYIZATION
INOXIDIZING
INTERMEZZOS
IODOBENZENE
IRREALIZABLE
ITALICIZING
JARGONIZING
JASPERIZING
JOVIALIZING
LABIALIZING
LICHENIZATION
LINEARIZATION
LIQUIDIZING
MAGNETIZABLE
MAGNETIZATION
MAGNETIZING
MAMMONIZATION
MARBLEIZING
MARMARIZING
MARTYRIZING
MATRONIZING
MECHANIZATION
MEDIATIZING
MERCERIZING
MERCURIZING
MESMERIZATION
MESMERIZING
METALLIZATION
METHODIZING
MNEMONIZING
MODERNIZATION
MODERNIZING
MORTALIZING
MUTUALIZING
MYOSYNIZESIS
MYTHICIZING
NARCOTIZING
NEOLOGIZING
NITRIDIZATION
NIVELLIZATION
NORMALIZATION
NORMALIZING
OBJECTIZATION
OBJECTIZING
OSTRACIZATION
OSTRACIZING
OVERGLAZING
OVERPRIZING
OXYGENIZABLE
OXYGENIZING
PALLETIZING
PATRONIZING
PAUPERIZING
PEPTONIZING
PETROLIZING
PHANEROZOIC
PHENMIAZINE
PHENOXAZINE
PHONETIZATION
PHYTOBEZOAR
PLATINIZING
PLURALIZING
POSTURIZING
PUBLICIZING
PULVERIZATE
PULVERIZATOR
PULVERIZING
RACIALIZATION
RADIALIZATION

RADIUMIZATION
RANDOMIZING
REBAPTIZATION
RECOGNIZABLE
RECOGNIZABLY
RECOGNIZANCE
RECOGNIZANT
RECOGNIZING
RHYTHMIZABLE
ROUTINIZING
RUBBERIZING
SAILORIZING
SCENARIZING
SENSITIZATION
SENSITIZING
SEPTICIZATION
SERIALIZATION
SERIALIZING
SERMONIZING
SHERBETZIDE
SIGNALIZING
SIPHONOZOOID
SOCIALIZATION
SOCIALIZING
SOLEMNIZATION
SOLEMNIZING
SOLVOLYZING
SOVIETIZATION
SOVIETIZING
SPIRALIZATION
STABILIZATION
STABILIZATOR
STABILIZING
STERILIZATION
STERILIZING
SUBSIDIZATION
SUBSIDIZING
SUBTILIZATION
SUBTILIZING
SULCALIZATION
SULFATIZING
SULFURIZING
SUMMARIZATION
SUMMARIZING
SYLLABIZING
SYLLOGIZING
SYMBOLIZATION
SYMBOLIZING
SYNTONIZING
SYPHILIZING
SYSTEMIZATION
SYSTEMIZING
TANTALIZING
TARTARIZING
TELLURIZING
TEMPORIZING
TENDERIZING
TERRORIZING
THIADIAZOLE
TYRANNIZING
URALITIZING
VACCINIZATION
VAPOURIZING
VASSALIZING
VERATRIZING
VERBALIZING
VICTIMIZABLE
VICTIMIZATION
VICTIMIZING
VISUALIZING
VOLCANIZING
VULCANIZATE
VULCANIZATION
VULCANIZING
VULGARIZATION
VULGARIZING
WINTERIZING

ZEOLITIZING
ZOISITIZATION
ZOOLOGIZING

ACETOBENZOIC
AGGUTINIZE
AGGRANDIZED
AGGRANDIZER
AGGRANDIZING
ALBUMENIZED
ALBUMENIZER
ALBUMENIZING
ALBUMINIZED
ALBUMINIZING
ALCOHOLIZED
ALCOHOLIZING
ALGEBRAIZED
ALKALINIZED
ALKALINIZING
ALLEGORIZED
ALLEGORIZER
ALLEGORIZING
ANABAPTIZED
ANABAPTIZING
ANTAGONIZED
ANTAGONIZER
ANTAGONIZING
ANTHROPOZOIC
ANTIFREEZING
APOSTATIZED
APOSTATIZING
ASEPTICIZED
ASEPTICIZING
ASEXUALIZED
ASEXUALIZING
AZOTETRAZOLE
BASTARDIZED
BASTARDIZING
BESTIALIZED
BESTIALIZING
BISTETRAZOLE
BITUMINIZED
BIVOCALIZED
BOLSHEVIZED
BOLSHEVIZING
BOWDLERIZED
BOWDLERIZING
BROMOBENZENE
BURGLARIZED
BURGLARIZING
BURNETTIZED
BURNETTIZING
CAPITALIZED
CAPITALIZING
CARAMELIZED
CARAMELIZING
CATABIBAZON
CATABOLIZED
CATABOLIZING
CATEGORIZED
CATEGORIZING
CAUSTICIZED
CAUSTICIZER
CAUSTICIZING
CENTRALIZED
CENTRALIZER
CENTRALIZING
CHANNELIZED
CHANNELIZING
CHLAMYDOZOAN
CHLORALIZED
CHLORALIZING
CHLORIDIZED
CHLORIDIZING
CHLORODIZED
CHLORODIZING
CHROMICIZING

CINCHONIZED
CINCHONIZING
CITIZENIZED
CITIZENIZING
CLASSICIZED
CLASSICIZING
COLLOQUIZED
COLLOQUIZING
CONCERTIZED
CONCERTIZER
CONCERTIZING
CONCRETIZE
CONCRETIZED
CONCRETIZING
DECIMALIZED
DECIMALIZING
DECOLORIZED
DECOLORIZER
DECOLORIZING
DEEPFREEZED
DEEPFREEZING
DEFINITIZED
DEFINITIZING
DEHUMANIZED
DEHUMANIZING
DELIMITIZED
DELIMITIZING
DELOCALIZED
DELOCALIZING
DEMOBILIZED
DEMOBILIZING
DEMONETIZED
DEMONETIZING
DEMORALIZED
DEMORALIZER
DEMORALIZING
DENATURIZER
DEPOLARIZED
DEPOLARIZER
DEPOLARIZING
DEVITALIZED
DEVITALIZING
DEVOCALIZED
DEVOCALIZING
DEXTROSAZONE
DIAMONDIZED
DIAMONDIZING
DIAZOBENZENE
DOCTRINIZED
DOCTRINIZING
DOXOLOGIZED
DOXOLOGIZING
EFFEMINIZED
EFFEMINIZING
ELASTICIZER
ENIGMATIZED
ENIGMATIZING
ENTHRONIZED
ENTHRONIZING
EPISCOPIZED
EPISCOPIZING
EPISTOLIZABLE
EUHEMERIZED
EUHEMERIZING
EVANGELIZED
EVANGELIZER
EVANGELIZING
FANATICIZED
FANATICIZING
FEDERALIZED
FEDERALIZING
FICTIONIZED
FICTIONIZING
FRATERNIZED
FRATERNIZER
FRATERNIZING
FUROMONAZOLE

GABERLUNZIE
GELATINIZED
GELATINIZER
GELATINIZING
GENERALIZABLE
GENERALIZED
GENERALIZER
GEOMETRIZED
GEOMETRIZING
GLUTTONIZED
GLUTTONIZING
GORMANDIZER
GRAPHITIZED
GYNECOMAZIA
GYROHORIZON
HOMOGENIZER
HOPPERDOZER
HYDROBENZOIN
HYDRORHIZAL
IDOLATRIZED
IDOLATRIZER
IDOLATRIZING
ILLEGALIZED
ILLEGALIZING
IMMOBILIZED
IMMOBILIZING
INTERMEZZOS
INTHRONIZATE
JATEORHIZIN
JATEORHIZINE
JEOPARDIZED
JEOPARDIZING
JOURNALIZED
JOURNALIZER
JOURNALIZING
LATERALIZED
LATERALIZING
LEGITIMIZED
LEGITIMIZING
LETHARGIZED
LETHARGIZING
LIBERALIZED
LIBERALIZER
LIBERALIZING
LITERALIZED
LITERALIZER
LITERALIZING
MACADAMIZED
MACADAMIZER
MACADAMIZING
MERMITHIZED
METABOLIZED
METABOLIZING
METAMERIZED
MILITARIZED
MILITARIZING
MINERALIZED
MINERALIZER
MINERALIZING
MISCOGNIZANT
MISSIONIZER
MONARCHIZED
MONARCHIZER
MONARCHIZING
MONOLOGIZED
MONOLOGIZING
MONOPOLIZED
MONOPOLIZER
MONOPOLIZING
MYCORRHIZAL
MYCORRHIZIC
NATURALIZED
NATURALIZER
NATURALIZING
NESSLERIZED
NEUTRALIZED
NEUTRALIZER
NEUTRALIZING
NEWSMAGAZINE
NITROBENZENE
NONPARTIZAN
NUPTIALIZE
OLIGORHIZOUS
PANEGYRIZED
PANEGYRIZER
PANEGYRIZING
PARABOLIZED
PARABOLIZER
PARABOLIZING
PASTEURIZED
PASTEURIZER
PASTEURIZING
PHANTOMIZER
PHILIPPIZER
PICRORHIZIN
PLAGIARIZED
PLAGIARIZER
PLAGIARIZING
PLASTICIZED
PLASTICIZER
PLASTICIZING
PNEUMATIZED
POLITICIZED
POLITICIZER
POLITICIZING
POPULARIZED
POPULARIZER
POPULARIZING
PRAGMATIZER
PRESSURIZED
PRESSURIZING
PROLOGUIZER
PYRRODIAZOLE
REGULARIZED
REGULARIZER
REORGANIZED
REORGANIZER
REORGANIZING
REVITALIZED
REVITALIZER
REVITALIZING
RHAPSODIZED
RHAPSODIZING
SACCHARIZED
SACCHARIZING
SCANDALIZED
SCANDALIZING
SCEPTICIZED
SCEPTICIZING
SCLEROTIZED
SCRUTINIZED
SCRUTINIZER
SCRUTINIZING
SECULARIZED
SECULARIZING
SENSUALIZED
SENSUALIZING
SHERARDIZED
SHERARDIZING
SKEPTICIZED
SKEPTICIZING
SLENDERIZED
SLENDERIZING
SOLIDARIZED
SOLIDARIZING
SOPHRONIZED
SOPHRONIZING
SPECIALIZED
SPECIALIZER
SPECIALIZING
SPERMATOZOA
SPERMATOZOAL
SPERMATOZOAN
SPERMATOZOIC
SPERMATOZOID
SPERMATOZOON
SPONDYLIZEMA
STIGMATIZED
STIGMATIZER
STIGMATIZING
SULFADIAZINE
SULFOBENZIDE
SULFOBENZOIC
SULPHATIZED
SULPHATIZING
SULPHURIZED
SULPHURIZING
SYMMETRIZED
SYMMETRIZING
SYMPATHIZED
SYMPATHIZER
SYMPATHIZING
SYMPHONIZED
SYMPHONIZING
SYNCRETIZED
SYNCRETIZING
SYNONYMIZED
SYNONYMIZING
SYNTHESIZED
SYNTHESIZER
SYNTHESIZING
SYNTHETIZER
TABULARIZED
TABULARIZING
TELFORDIZED
TELFORDIZING
THEOLOGIZED
THEOLOGIZER
THEOLOGIZING
THERMOLYZED
THERMOLYZING
TRAILBLAZER
TRAILBLAZING
TRICHINIZED
TRICHINIZING
UNCANONIZED
UNCANONIZING
UNCIVILIZED
UNMORALIZED
UNMORALIZING
UNORGANIZED
VITRIOLIZED
VITRIOLIZING
VOLATILIZED
VOLATILIZER
VOLATILIZING
WESTERNIZED
WESTERNIZING

ABASTARDIZE
ABNORMALIZE
ACCLIMATIZE
ACCLIMATIZED
ACCLIMATIZER
ACCLIMATIZING
ACCULTURIZE
ACCUSTOMIZE
ACCUSTOMIZED
ACCUSTOMIZING
ACHROMATIZE
ACHROMATIZED
AGRARIANIZE
ALGEBRAIZING
ALLOTROPIZE
ALPHABETIZE
ALPHABETIZED
ALPHABETIZER
ALPHABETIZING
ANACHRONIZE
ANESTHETIZE
ANESTHETIZER
ANHYDRIDIZE
ANTHOLOGIZE
ANTHOLOGIZED
ANTHOLOGIZING
ANTIPATHIZE
ANTITHESIZE
APESTHETIZE
APOTHEOSIZE
APOTHEOSIZED
ARITHMETIZE
ARTERIALIZE
ARTERIALIZED
ASBESTINIZE
ASPHETERIZE
ASTIGMATIZER
ASTROLOGIZE
ASTRONOMIZE
BACHELORIZE
BATTOLOGIZE
BESSEMERIZE
BESSEMERIZED
BESSEMERIZING
BIOGRAPHIZE
BROMOIODIZED
BURKUNDAUZE
CACOPHONIZE
CANNIBALIZE
CANNIBALIZED
CANNIBALIZING
CAPERCAILZIE
CATALEPTIZE
CATALOGUIZE
CATHETERIZE
CATHETERIZED
CATHOLICIZE
CATHOLICIZED
CATHOLICIZING
CHAMPAGNIZE
CHAMPAGNIZED
CHAMPAGNIZING
CHEERFULIZE
CHEMICALIZE
CHORIAMBIZE
CIRCULARIZE
CIRCULARIZED
CIRCULARIZING
COMMEMORIZE
COMMEMORIZED
COMMEMORIZING
COMMUNALIZE
COMMUNALIZED
COMMUNALIZER
COSMOGONIZE
CRYSTALLIZE
CRYSTALLIZED
CRYSTALLIZER
CRYSTALLIZING
DEBENZOLIZE
DECARBONIZE
DECARBONIZED
DECARBONIZER
DECARBURIZE
DECARBURIZED
DECEREBRIZE
DECHORALIZE
DECOLOURIZE
DEFIBRINIZE
DEHYPNOTIZE
DEHYPNOTIZED
DEJUNKERIZE
DEMAGNETIZE
DEMAGNETIZED
DEMAGNETIZER
DEMANGANIZE
DEMEPHITIZE
DEMOCRATIZE
DEMOCRATIZED
DEOXYGENIZE
DEPAUPERIZE
DEPAUPERIZED
DEPERSONIZE
DERACIALIZE
DESACRALIZE
DESENSITIZE
DESENSITIZER
DESEXUALIZE
DESEXUALIZED
DESILVERIZE
DESILVERIZER
DESTERILIZE
DESULFURIZE
DESULFURIZED
DESULFURIZER
DETRIBALIZE
DEVULGARIZE
DIAGONALIZE
DICHOTOMIZE
DICHOTOMIZED
DIPLOMATIZE
DIPLOMATIZED
DISCANONIZE
DISCANONIZED
DISEQUALIZE
DISORGANIZE
DISORGANIZED
DISORGANIZER
DOCUMENTIZE
DOGGERELIZE
DOGGERELIZER
DOGGERELIZING
DOMESTICIZE
DOMESTICIZED
ELECTRALIZE
ELECTRICIZE
ELECTROLYZE
ELECTROLYZED
ELECTROLYZER
ELECTROLYZING
EMBLEMATIZE
EMBLEMATIZED
EMBLEMATIZING
EMULSIONIZE
ENCARNALIZE
ENCARNALIZED
ENCARNALIZING
ENSORCELIZE
ENSORCERIZE
EPENTHESIZE
EQUILIBRIZE
ETHEREALIZE
ETHEREALIZED
ETHEREALIZING
ETYMOLOGIZE
ETYMOLOGIZED
ETYMOLOGIZING
EUDAEMONIZE
EVENTUALIZE
EXAUTHORIZE
EXOSTRACIZE
EXTEMPORIZE
EXTEMPORIZED
EXTEMPORIZER
EXTEMPORIZING
EXTERIORIZE
EXTERIORIZED
EXTERIORIZING
EXTERNALIZE
FACSIMILIZE
FAMILIARIZE
FAMILIARIZED
FAMILIARIZER
FAMILIARIZING
FORMULARIZE
FORMULARIZED

FORMULARIZING
FRACTIONIZATIO
FRACTIONIZE
FRACTIONIZING
FRICTIONIZE
FRICTIONIZED
FRICTIONIZING
FUNCTIONIZE
GENEALOGIZE
GENEALOGIZER
GEOGRAPHIZE
GEOGRAPHIZED
GLYCERINIZE
GLYCYRRHIZIN
GRANULITIZE
GUTTURALIZE
GUTTURALIZING
HIERARCHIZE
HOSPITALIZE
HURRICANIZE
HYDROGENIZE
HYPERBOLIZE
HYPERBOLIZED
HYPOSTATIZE
IMMETHODIZE
IMMORTALIZE
IMMORTALIZED
IMMORTALIZER
IMMORTALIZING
IMPATRONIZE
IMPERIALIZE
IMPERIALIZED
IMPERIALIZING
INFORMALIZE
INTELLIGIZE
INTERNALIZE
ISOCHRONIZE
ISOCHRONIZED
ISOCHRONIZING
JUDICIALIZE
KJELDAHLIZE
LALAPALOOZA
LITHOTOMIZE
LOGOMACHIZE
MALLEABLIZE
MANORIALIZE
MARGINALIZE
MATERIALIZE
MATERIALIZED
MATERIALIZER
MATERIALIZING
MATERNALIZE
MATHEMATIZE
MECHANALIZE
MEMORANDIZE
MEMORIALIZE
MEMORIALIZED
MEMORIALIZER
MEMORIALIZING
MERCHANDIZE
MERORGANIZE
METAPHONIZE
METASTASIZE
METASTASIZED
MIGNIARDIZE
MINIATURIZE
MINIATURIZED
MUSCOVITIZE
MUSCOVITIZED
MUSCULARIZE
MYTHOLOGIZE
MYTHOLOGIZED
MYTHOLOGIZER
MYTHOLOGIZING
NAPHTHALIZE
NATIONALIZE
NATIONALIZED
NATIONALIZER
NATIONALIZING
NEOPAGANIZE
NEUROLOGIZE
NEUROTOMIZE
NITROGENIZE
NITROGENIZED
NITROGENIZING
NONENTITIZE
OBJECTIVIZE
OBJECTIVIZED
OBJECTIVIZING
OBLIVIONIZE
OFFICIALIZE
OLIGARCHIZE
OPTIONALIZE
ORIENTALIZE
ORIENTALIZED
ORIENTALIZING
PAMPHLETIZE
PANCREATIZE
PANTHEONIZE
PARAENESIZE
PASTORALIZE
PATERNALIZE
PECULIARIZE
PECULIARIZED
PEMMICANIZE
PERMORALIZE
PERSONALIZE
PERSONALIZED
PHAGOCYTIZE
PHILOLOGIZE
PHONETICIZE
PHOSPHATIZE
PHOSPHATIZED
PHOSPHORIZE
PLEBEIANIZE
PLEBEIANIZED
POLITZERIZE
PREACHERIZE
PROBABILIZE
PRODIGALIZE
PROLETARIZE
PROSELYTIZE
PROSELYTIZED
PROSELYTIZER
PROTOCITIZEN
PROTOCOLIZE
PROTOXIDIZE
PROTOXIDIZED
RATIONALIZE
RATIONALIZED
RATIONALIZER
REACTUALIZE
RECARBONIZE
RECARBONIZER
RECARBURIZE
RECARBURIZER
REFORESTIZE
REGIONALIZE
REHARMONIZE
RELIGIONIZE
RESTERILIZE
RHYTHMICIZE
ROENTGENIZE
ROMANTICIZE
ROTARIANIZE
SANCTUARIZE
SCHILLERIZE
SCHILLERIZED
SCHILLERIZING
SCHISMATIZE
SCHISMATIZED
SCHISMATIZING
SENSIBILIZE
SIDEREALIZE
SIMULACRIZE
SINGULARIZE
SINGULARIZED
SINGULARIZING
SKELETONIZE
SKELETONIZED
SKELETONIZER
SKELETONIZING
SLUGGARDIZE
SOLILOQUIZE
SOLILOQUIZED
SOLILOQUIZER
SOLILOQUIZING
SOUTHERNIZE
SPECIFICIZE
SPECIMENIZE
SPECIMENIZED
SPHEROIDIZE
STALLIONIZE
STALWARTIZE
STANDARDIZE
STANDARDIZED
STANDARDIZER
STANDARDIZING
SUBSTANTIZE
SUBURBANIZE
SUBVITALIZED
SULPHOBENZID
SYNCHRONIZE
SYNCHRONIZED
SYNCHRONIZER
SYNCHRONIZING
SYNDICALIZE
SYSTEMATIZE
SYSTEMATIZED
SYSTEMATIZER
SYSTEMATIZING
TARANTARIZE
TAUTOLOGIZE
TAUTOLOGIZED
TAUTOLOGIZER
TAXIDERMIZE
TEETOTUMIZE
TELEPATHIZE
TEMPORALIZE
TENEMENTIZE
TETRAKISAZO
TETRAZOTIZE
THEATRICIZE
TOBACCONIZE
TRANQUILIZE
TRANQUILIZER
TRANQUILIZING
TRILLIONIZE
TROPICALIZE
TROPICALIZED
TROPICALIZING
TROPOLOGIZE
TROPOLOGIZED
TROPOLOGIZING
TUBERCULIZE
UNAUTHORIZE
UNAUTHORIZED
UNBRUTALIZE
UNFEUDALIZE
UNLITURGIZE
UNMECHANIZE
UNMODERNIZE
UNMORTALIZE
UNPATRONIZED
UNRECOGNIZED
UNSOLEMNIZE
UNSTERILIZED
UNVERBALIZED
UNVULGARIZE
VAGABONDIZE
VAGABONDIZED
VAGABONDIZER
VAGABONDIZING
VASCULARIZE
VASCULARIZED
VASCULARIZING
VASECTOMIZE
VEGETABLIZE
VERATRINIZE
VERATRINIZED
VERATRINIZING
WOODCOCKIZE
ZOOMORPHIZE

ABOLITIONIZE
ADVERBIALIZE
AESTHETICIZE
ANACEPHALIZE
ANAESTHETIZE
ANAESTHETIZED
ANAESTHETIZER
ANATHEMATIZE
ANGIOSTOMIZE
APAESTHETIZE
APOSTROPHIZE
ATTITUDINIZE
AUTOCATALYZE
BACCHANALIZE
BACTERIOLYZE
CANTHARIDIZE
CELESTIALIZE
CELESTIALIZED
CHAMELEONIZE
CHARACTERIZE
CHARACTERIZED
CHARACTERIZER
CHRONOLOGIZE
CHRONOLOGIZED
COLLECTIVIZE
COLLECTIVIZED
COLLODIONIZE
COMPANIONIZE
COMPANIONIZED
CONSERVATIZE
CONSONANTIZE
CONTEMPORIZE
CONTEMPORIZED
COPOLYMERIZE
COPOLYMERIZED
CORPOREALIZE
CUTICULARIZE
DECAFFEINIZE
DECENTRALIZE
DECICERONIZE
DEMENTHOLIZE
DEMICIVILIZED
DEMILITARIZE
DEMILITARIZED
DEMINERALIZE
DENATURALIZE
DENICOTINIZE
DEPIGMENTIZE
DEPOLYMERIZE
DESILICONIZE
DESULPHURIZE
DESYNONYMIZE
DEVITAMINIZE
DIALECTALIZE
DIALECTICIZE
DIPHTHONGIZE
DIPHTHONGIZED
DISGOSPELIZE
DISHARMONIZE
DISPAUPERIZE
DISSOCIALIZE
DISSYLLABIZE
EDITORIALIZE
EDITORIALIZED
EFFECTUALIZE
EFFEMINATIZE
EMOTIONALIZE
EMOTIONALIZED
ENTOMOLOGIZE
ENTOMOLOGIZED
EPITHALAMIZE
EUCHARISTIZE
EUCHARISTIZED
EVOLUTIONIZE
EXCURSIONIZE
EXPERMENTIZED
EXTRAVAGANZA
FASCISTICIZE
FICTIONALIZED
GEOMETRICIZE
GRAMMATICIZE
HARLEQUINIZE
IMBASTARDIZE
IMPACTIONIZE
INDOCTRINIZE
IRREGULARIZE
LALLAPALOOZA
LAPAROTOMIZE
LEGITIMATIZE
LEGITIMATIZED
LIEDERKRANZ
MALLEABLEIZE
MALLEABLEIZED
MARSUPIALIZE
MELANCHOLIZE
MERCURIALIZE
METAMORPHIZE
MICROSCOPIZE
MINERALOGIZE
MISEMPHASIZE
MISSIONARIZE
MITHRIDATIZE
MONOCHORDIZE
MUNICIPALIZE
MUNICIPALIZED
MYTHOPOETIZE
OUTTYRANNIZE
OVARIOTOMIZE
PALLADIUMIZE
PANEGYRICIZE
PANSEXUALIZE
PARCHMENTIZE
PARENTHESIZE
PENTAMETRIZE
PERFECTIVIZE
PHILIPPICIZE
PHILOSOPHIZE
PHLEBOTOMIZE
PHRENOLOGIZE
PHYLACTERIZE
PHYSIOLOGIZE
POLITICALIZE
POLYCHROMIZE
PORCELAINIZE
PORCELLANIZE
POTENTIALIZE
PRACTICALIZE
PRACTICALIZED
PRESERVATIZE
PROBLEMATIZE
PROPAGANDIZE
PSYCHIATRIZE
PSYCHOLOGIZE
REALISTICIZE
RECAPITALIZE
RECAPITALIZED
SACRAMENTIZE
SARCOPHAGIZE
SECTARIANIZE
SECTARIANIZED
SECTIONALIZE

SECTIONALIZED
SEMICIVILIZED
SEMPITERNIZE
SERPENTINIZE
SOLITUDINIZE
SOLITUDINIZED
SOMNAMBULIZE
SOVEREIGNIZE
SPHERULITIZE
SPIRITUALIZE
SPIRITUALIZED
SPIRITUALIZER
STATISTICIZE
STRYCHNINIZE
SULPHAZOTIZE
SULPHAZOTIZE
SYCOPHANTIZE
SYMPTOMATIZE
TCHERVONETZ
TECHNICALIZE
THEOMORPHIZE
TOURMALINIZE
TRANQUILLIZE
TRANQUILLIZED
TRICHOTOMIZE
UNIFORMALIZE
UNIFORMALIZED
UNIVERSALIZED
UNIVERSITIZE
UNNATURALIZE
UNPOPULARIZE
UNSECULARIZE
VERMILIONIZE
ANTISEPTICIZE
COMMERCIALIZE.
ELECTRICALIZE
ELECTROTONIZE
EMBLEMATICIZE
ENCYCLOPEDIZE
ENHYPOSTATIZE
EPIGRAMMATIZE
EXPERIMENTIZE
FLAMBOYANTIZE
FRACTIONALIZE
HORIZONTALIZE
IMMATERIALIZE
IMPERSONALIZE
IMPROBABILIZE
INDIVIDUALIZE
MELODRAMATIZE
NIGHTINGALIZE
RECIPROCALIZE
RECRYSTALLIZE
STRUCTURALIZE
SUBSTANTIVIZE

SCORING ORDER LIST OF WORDS OVER 10 LETTERS

37
OBJECTIVIZING

36
KATZENJAMMER
OBJECTIVIZED
SCHIZOTHYMIC

35
KJELDAHLIZE
ZANTHOXYLUM
ZOOPRAXISCOPE
ZYGAPOPHYSIS
ZYGOPHYCEOUS

34
EXPERMENTIZED
EXTEMPORIZING
OBJECTIVIZE
OXYGENIZABLE
QUIZZICALITY
RHYTHMIZABLE
SCHIZOMYCETES
SCHIZOTHYMIA

33
BENZALDOXIME
CHAMPAGNIZING
DIPHTHONGIZED
EXPERIMENTIZE
EXTEMPORIZED
GLYCYRRHIZIN
HARLEQUINIZE
ICHTHYIZATION
OBJECTIZATION
POLYCHROMIZE
QUIZZICALLY
RHIZOMORPHIC
SCHIZOMYCETE
SCHIZOPHYTE
SCHIZOTHYME
SQUEEZINGLY
ZOOPHYTOLOGY
ZYGODACTYLIC
ZYGOMORPHIC
ZYMOTECHNICS

32
CHAMPAGNIZED
CHLAMYDOZOAN
COPOLYMERIZED
CRYPTOZYGOUS
DEJUNKERIZE
DEOXYGENIZE
ENCYCLOPEDIZE
EXORCIZEMENT
EXTEMPORIZER
EXTRAVAGANZA
FLAMBOYANTIZE
HAPHAZARDLY
HYBRIDIZABLE
HYPERBOLIZED
JEOPARDIZING
MAXIMIZATION
MYCORRHIZIC
MYTHOLOGIZING
OBJECTIZING
OXYGENIZING
PHENOXAZINE
PHOSPHATIZED
PROTOXIDIZED
PSYCHOLOGIZE
SCHIZOPHRENIA
SCHIZOTRICHIA
SOLILOQUIZING
SYMPATHIZING
SYMPHONIZING
TRANQUILIZING
TRANQUILLIZED
WOODCOCKIZE
ZOOPHARMACY
ZYGOMORPHOUS
ZYGOMYCETOUS
ZYMOTECHNIC

31
AZOPHOSPHORE
BENZALDEHYDE
CHALAZOGAMIC
CHALAZOGAMY
CHROMICIZING
DEHYPNOTIZED
DEMICIVILIZED
DEZINCIFYING
DIPHTHONGIZE
DOXOLOGIZING
EQUILIBRIZE
ERYTHROZYME
EXTEMPORIZE
HAPHAZARDNESS
HYBRIDIZATION
JAROVIZATION
JATEORHIZINE
JEOPARDIZED
JOVIALIZING
LIQUIDIZING
MYTHICIZING
MYTHOLOGIZED
MYTHOPOETIZE
PERFECTIVIZE
PHAGOCYTIZE
PHILOSOPHIZE
PHYLACTERIZE
PSYCHIATRIZE
SCHIZOCHROAL
SCHIZOPELMOUS
SCHIZOPHASIA
SCHIZOPHRENE
SCHIZOTHECAL
SOLILOQUIZED
SYCOPHANTIZE
SYMPATHIZED
SYMPHONIZED
SYNCHRONIZING
THEOMORPHIZE
ZINCOGRAPHIC
ZINCOGRAPHY
ZOOGEOGRAPHY
ZOOXANTHELLA
ZYGOMYCETES

30
ALPHABETIZING
AZOPHOSPHIN
BACCHANALIZE
BAMBOOZLEMENT
BIZYGOMATIC
BOLSHEVIZING
CATHOLICIZING
CHAMPAGNIZE
CHARACTERIZED
COLLECTIVIZED
COMMERCIALIZE
COPOLYMERIZE
DECAFFEINIZE
DEOXIDIZING
DESEXUALIZED
DESYNONYMIZE
DICHOTOMIZED
DIPHYOZOOID
DISEQUALIZE
DOXOLOGIZED
EFFEMINIZING
EMBLEMATICIZE
ENHYPOSTATIZE
ENZYMICALLY
ENZYMOLYTIC
EQUALIZATION
EXAUTHORIZE
EXCURSIONIZE
EXORCIZATION
EXTERIORIZING
HYDROBENZOIN
HYDROLYZATE
HYDRORHIZAL
HYDROZINCITE
HYPERBOLIZE
IMPROBABILIZE
JASPERIZING
JATEORHIZIN
JUBILIZATION
JUDICIALIZE
METAMORPHIZE
MISEMPHASIZE
MYCORRHIZAL
MYTHOLOGIZER
PANSEXUALIZE
PARCHMENTIZE
PHLEBOTOMIZE
PHLYZACIOUS
PHOSPHATIZE
PHOSPHORIZE
PHYSIOLOGIZE
PHYTOBEZOAR
PRIZEFIGHTER
PROTOXIDIZE
QUANTIZATION
QUIZZACIOUS
RHIZOPHAGOUS
SCHISMATIZING
SCHIZOGENETIC
SEMICIVILIZED
SKEPTICIZING
SOLILOQUIZER
SYMPATHIZER
SYMPTOMATIZE
SYNCHRONIZED
SYNONYMIZING
TAXIDERMIZE
THERMOLYZING
TRANQUILIZER
TRANQUILLIZE
VAGABONDIZING
VICTIMIZABLE
ZOMOTHERAPY
ZOOPATHOLOGY
ZOOPHYSICAL
ZOOPHYTICAL
ZYGODACTYLE
ZYGOMATICUM
ZYMOSTHENIC
ZYMOTICALLY

29
ACCLIMATIZING
ACCUSTOMIZING
ACHROMATIZED
ALPHABETIZED
APPETIZINGLY
ASEXUALIZING
AZIMETHYLENE
AZODIPHENYL
AZOPHENYLENE
BENZOHYDROL
BOLSHEVIZED
CACOPHONIZE
CATECHIZATION
CATHOLICIZED
CHARACTERIZER
CHEMICALIZE
CHORIAMBIZE
CHRONOLOGIZED
CINCHONIZING
CIVILIZATORY
COMPANIONIZED
CONTEMPORIZED
DEHYPNOTIZE
DEPOLYMERIZE
DEXTROSAZONE
EFFECTUALIZE
EFFEMINATIZE
EFFEMINIZED
EMBLEMATIZING
EPIGRAMMATIZE
ETYMOLOGIZING
EXOSTRACIZE
EXTERIORIZED
EXTERNIZATION
GEOGRAPHIZED
INOXIDIZING
JARGONIZING
JOURNALIZING
MACADAMIZING
MECHANIZATION
MICROSCOPIZE
MICROZYMIAN
MONARCHIZING
MONOCHORDIZE
MUNICIPALIZED
MUSCOVITIZED
MYOSYNIZESIS
MYTHOLOGIZE
MYZOSTOMIDAN
PAMPHLETIZE
PANEGYRICIZE
PHILIPPICIZE
PHYLLOZOOID
PRACTICALIZED
QUANTIZING
QUINAZOLINE
QUIZZATORIAL
RECOGNIZABLY
RHIZOCARPIC
RHIZOPHILOUS
SACCHARIZING
SARCOPHAGIZE
SCHISMATIZED
SCHIZOCARPIC
SCHIZOGNATH
SCHIZOPODOUS
SCHIZORHINAL
SKEPTICIZED
SOLILOQUIZE
SPECIFICIZE
SPONDYLIZEMA
STRYCHNINIZE
SULPHOBENZID
SYMBOLIZATION
SYMMETRIZING
SYNCHRONIZER
SYNONYMIZED
SYPHILIZING
THERMOLYZED
TRANQUILIZE
VACCINIZATION
VAGABONDIZED
VICTIMIZATION
ZINCOGRAPHER
ZOANTHODEMIC
ZOOMORPHISM

ZYGOSPHENAL
ZYMOPLASTIC

28
ACCLIMATIZED
ACCUSTOMIZED
ACETYLIZABLE
ADVERTIZEMENT
ALCHEMIZING
ALPHABETIZER
ANACEPHALIZE
ANHYDRIDIZE
ANTHROPOZOIC
APOSTROPHIZE
ASEXUALIZED
AZIMUTHALLY
AZOCOCHINEAL
AZOPARAFFIN
AZOSULPHONIC
BACTERIOLYZE
BENZOPHENONE
BIOGRAPHIZE
BIVOCALIZED
BOWDLERIZING
BRAZENFACED
CATECHIZING
CHAMELEONIZE
CHARACTERIZE
CHEERFULIZE
CHLORIDIZING
CHLORODIZING
CINCHONIZED
COLLECTIVIZE
COMMEMORIZING
COMMUNALIZED
COMMUNIZATION
COPPERIZATION
CRYPTOZONATE
CRYSTALLIZING
DACTYLOZOOID
DEEPFREEZING
DEHUMANIZING
DEMEPHITIZE
DESEXUALIZE
DEVOCALIZING
DICHOTOMIZE
ELECTROLYZING
EMBLEMATIZED
EMPATHIZING
EMPHASIZING
ENZYMOLYSIS
EPISCOPIZING
EPITHALAMIZE
EPIZOOTIOLOGY
ETHNOZOOLOGY
ETYMOLOGIZED
EUCHARISTIZED
EUPHEMIZING
FAMILIARIZING
FASCISTICIZE
FICTIONALIZED
FORMULARIZING
FRACTIONIZING
FRICTIONIZING
GAZINGSTOCK
GRAMMATICIZE
GYNECOMAZIA
HETEROZYGOTE
HETEROZYGOUS
HIERARCHIZE
HOPPERDOZER
HORIZONTALITY
HYDROGENIZE
HYPOSTATIZE
IMMETHODIZE
IMMOBILIZING
ISOCHRONIZING
JOURNALIZED
LOGOMACHIZE
MACADAMIZED
MELANCHOLIZE
MERCHANDIZE
MERMITHIZED
MONARCHIZED
MONOZYGOTIC
NAPHTHALIZE
OFFICIALIZE
OZONOSPHERIC
PANEGYRIZING
PEMMICANIZE
RECIPROCALIZE
RHAPSODIZING
RHIZOCARPOUS
SACCHARIZED
SCEPTICIZING
SCHILLERIZING
SCHIZODINIC
SCHIZOGENESIS
SCHIZOGENIC
SCHIZOGONIC
SCHIZOIDISM
SCHIZOPODAL
SCHIZOSTELIC
SCHIZOSTELY
SPECIMENIZED
SULFOBENZOIC
SYMBOLIZING
SYMMETRIZED
SYNCHRONIZE
SYNTHESIZING
SYSTEMATIZING
TCHERVONETZ
TECHNICALIZE
TRICHOTOMIZE
TYPHIZATION
UNIFORMALIZED
VAGABONDIZER
VASCULARIZING
VICTIMIZING
VITALIZINGLY
ZENOGRAPHIC
ZOODYNAMICS
ZYGOMATICUS
ZYMOLOGICAL

27
ACCLIMATIZER
ACETOBENZOIC
ACETYLIZATION
ACHROMATIZE
ADVERBIALIZE
ALCOHOLIZING
ALPHABETIZE
ANTHOLOGIZING
APOTHEOSIZED
BACHELORIZE
BALKANIZING
BAMBOOZLING
BEDAZZLINGLY
BENZYLAMINE
BESSEMERIZING
BOWDLERIZED
BROMOBENZENE
BROMOIODIZED
BRONZESMITH
BURKUNDAUZE
CANNIBALIZING
CANTHARIDIZE
CAPERCAILZIE
CATHETERIZED
CATHOLICIZE
CHALAZOIDITE
CHANNELIZING
CHITINIZATION
CHLORALIZING
CHLORIDIZED
CHLORODIZED
CHORIZONTIC
CHRONOLOGIZE
CIRCULARIZING
CITIZENSHIP
CIVILIZABLE
COMMEMORIZED
COMMUNALIZER
COMMUNIZING
COMPANIONIZE
CONTEMPORIZE
CRITICIZABLE
CRYSTALLIZED
CYCLIZATION
DECARBONIZED
DECARBURIZED
DECIMALIZING
DEEPFREEZED
DEHUMANIZED
DEMENTHOLIZE
DEMOBILIZING
DEMOCRATIZED
DEPAUPERIZED
DEPIGMENTIZE
DESULPHURIZE
DEVITAMINIZE
DEVOCALIZED
DEZINCIFIED
DIAZOMETHANE
DIPLOMATIZED
DISHARMONIZE
DISSYLLABIZE
DOCKIZATION
DOMESTICIZED
DYNAMIZATION
ELECTROLYZED
EMBLEMIZING
EPISCOPIZED
EUHEMERIZING
EXTERIORIZE
EXTERNALIZE
FACSIMILIZE
FACTORIZATION
FAMILIARIZED
FANATICIZING
FICTIONIZING
FISCALIZATION
FORMALIZATION
FORMULARIZED
FORMULIZATION
FRACTIONALIZE
FRICTIONIZED
FRIVOLIZING
GEOGRAPHIZE
GRAPHITIZED
GYROHORIZON
HAZARDOUSLY
HORIZONTALLY
IMMOBILIZED
IMMORTALIZING
IMPACTIONIZE
IMPERIALIZING
INDIVIDUALIZE
ISOCHRONIZED
JOURNALIZER
KYANIZATION
LICHENIZATION
MACADAMIZER
MALLEABLEIZED
MATHEMATIZE
MECHANALIZE
MEIZOSEISMIC
MELODRAMATIZE
MEMORIALIZING
METAPHONIZE
METHODIZING
MITHRIDATIZE
MONARCHIZER
MONZOGABBRO
MUNICIPALIZE
MUSCOVITIZE
MYZOSTOMOUS
NEWSMAGAZINE
NIGHTINGALIZE
PALEOZOOLOGY
PANEGYRIZED
PHANEROZOIC
PHANTOMIZER
PHENMIAZINE
PHONETICIZE
PHONETIZATION
PHRENOLOGIZE
PICRORHIZIN
POLYZOARIUM
PRACTICALIZE
PREACHERIZE
PROBLEMATIZE
PROPAGANDIZE
PROSELYTIZED
PUBLICIZING
PUZZLEHEADED
PYRRODIAZOLE
RAZORMAKING
RECAPITALIZED
RECRYSTALLIZE
RHAPSODIZED
RHIZOGENETIC
SCEPTICIZED
SCHILLERIZED
SCHISMATIZE
SCHIZOCOELE
SCHIZOGENOUS
SCHIZOSPORE
SIPHONOZOOID
SKELETONIZING
SOLVOLYZING
SOMNAMBULIZE
SOPHRONIZING
SPERMATOZOIC
SUBSTANTIVIZE
SUBVITALIZED
SULFOBENZIDE
SULPHATIZING
SULPHURIZING
SYNCRETIZING
SYNTHESIZED
SYSTEMATIZED
SYSTEMIZATION
TRAPEZIFORM
TRICHINIZING
TROPICALIZING
UNMECHANIZE
UNVERBALIZED
VAGABONDIZE
VASCULARIZED
VASECTOMIZE
VULCANIZATION
ZODIOPHILOUS
ZOOCECIDIUM
ZYGOLABIALIS
ZYMOSIMETER

26
ACADEMIZING
ACCLIMATIZE
ACCUSTOMIZE
AESTHETICIZE
ALBUMENIZING
ALBUMINIZING
ALCOHOLIZED
ALKALINIZING
ALKALIZABLE
ANABAPTIZING
ANAESTHETIZED
ANATHEMATIZE
ANTHOLOGIZED
ANTISEPTICIZE
APAESTHETIZE
APPRIZEMENT
ASEPTICIZING
ATMOLYZATION
AUTOCATALYZE
AZADIRACHTA
AZOERYTHRIN
AZOPHENETOLE
AZYGOMATOUS
BAPTIZEMENT
BENZOYLATION
BESSEMERIZED
BILHARZIASIS
BILHARZIOSIS
BUZZERPHONE
CANNIBALIZED
CAPITALIZING
CARAMELIZING
CATABIBAZON
CATABOLIZING
CATHARIZING
CAUSTICIZING
CENOZOOLOGY
CHANNELIZED
CHLORALIZED
CHORIZONTIST
CIRCULARIZED
CIVILIZATION
CLASSICIZING
COAZERVATION
COMMUNALIZE
CONCERTIZING
CONCRETIZING
CONSERVATIZE
CRYSTALLIZER
DECARBONIZER
DECHORALIZE
DECICERONIZE
DECIMALIZED
DEFIBRINIZE
DEFINITIZING
DEMAGNETIZED
DEMILITARIZED
DEMOBILIZED
DESULFURIZED
DEVITALIZING
DIALECTICIZE
DIAMONDIZING
DISPAUPERIZE
DOGGERELIZING
ECONOMIZATION
ELECTROLYZER
EMBEZZLEMENT
EMBLEMATIZE
ENTOMOLOGIZED
EPISTOLIZABLE
EPITOMIZATION
ETHEREALIZING
ETYMOLOGIZE
EUCHARISTIZE
EUHEMERIZED
EUPHONIZING
EVANGELIZING
FACTORIZING
FAMILIARIZER
FANATICIZED
FEDERALIZING
FEMINIZATION
FERTILIZABLE
FEUDALIZATION
FICTIONIZED
FISCALIZING

FOCALIZATION
FORMALIZING
FORMULIZING
FUROMONAZOLE
GALVANIZATION
GEOMETRICIZE
GLYCERINIZE
HARMONIZING
HARZBURGITE
HAZARDOUSNESS
HOMOGENIZER
HORIZONTICAL
IMBASTARDIZE
IMMATERIALIZE
IMMORTALIZED
IMPERIALIZED
IMPERSONALIZE
LEGITIMATIZED
LETHARGIZING
MAGNETIZABLE
MARTYRIZING
MEGAZOOSPORE
MEMORIALIZED
MESMERIZATION
METABOLIZING
MISCOGNIZANT
MIZZENTOPMAN
MIZZENTOPMEN
MONOPOLIZING
NAZIFICATION
OLIGARCHIZE
ORYZIVOROUS
OSMAZOMATIC
OVARIOTOMIZE
OVERPRIZING
OZONOSCOPIC
PALLADIUMIZE
PANEGYRIZER
PARABOLIZING
PARALYZATION
PARENTHESIZE
PECULIARIZED
PEZIZAEFORM
PHILIPPIZER
PHILOLOGIZE
PHILOZOONIST
PIEZOMETRIC
PLASTICIZING
PLEBEIANIZED
POLITICIZING
POPULARIZING
PRESERVATIZE
PRIZEHOLDER
PROBABILIZE
PROSELYTIZER
PULVERIZATOR
PULVERIZING
REBAPTIZATION
RECOGNIZABLE
RECOGNIZANCE
RHIZANTHOUS
RHIZODERMIS
RHIZOPODIST
RHIZOPODOUS
RHIZOSTOMOUS
SEPTICIZATION
SHERARDIZING
SHERBETZIDE
SKELETONIZED
SOPHRONIZED
SPECIALIZING
SPECIMENIZE
SPERMATOZOID
SPHEROIDIZE
SPHERULITIZE
STANZAICALLY
SULPHATIZED
SULPHURIZED
SUMMARIZATION
SYLLABIZING
SYNCRETIZED
SYNDICALIZE
SYNTHESIZER
SYNTHETIZER
SYSTEMATIZER
SYSTEMIZING
TELFORDIZING
THEOLOGIZING
TOBACCONIZE
TRICHINIZED
TROPHOZOOID
TROPICALIZED
TROPOLOGIZING
UNCIVILIZED
UNIFORMALIZE
UNIVERSALIZED
VAPORIZATION
VAPOURIZING
VEGETABLIZE
VERATRINIZING
VERBALIZING
VERMILIONIZE
VOCALIZATION
VOLCANIZING
VULCANIZING
VULGARIZATION
ZAPHRENTOID
ZIGZAGGEDLY
ZOANTHODEME
ZONOCHLORITE
ZOOERYTHRIN
ZOOMAGNETISM
ZOOMORPHIZE
ZOOPLANKTON
ZYGOPLEURAL
ZYGOPTERID
ZYGOPTEROUS
ZYMOGENESIS

25

ADVERTIZING
AGGRANDIZING
ALBUMENIZED
ALBUMINIZED
ALGEBRIZATION
ALKALINIZED
ALKALIZATION
AMMONIZATION
AMORTIZEMENT
ANABAPTIZED
ANACHRONIZE
ANAESTHETIZER
ANTHEROZOOID
ANTIFREEZING
ANTIPATHIZE
APESTHETIZE
APOTHEOSIZE
ARCTICIZING
ARITHMETIZE
ASCIDIOZOOID
ASEPTICIZED
ASPHETERIZE
AUTHORIZATION
AZOFICATION
AZOSULPHINE
AZOTHIONIUM
BACTERIZING
BARBARIZING
BASTARDIZING
BEDIZENMENT
BERGINIZATION
BITUMINIZED
BURGLARIZING
CAPITALIZED
CARAMELIZED
CARBOAZOTINE
CARBOLIZING
CARBONIZING
CARBURIZING
CATABOLIZED
CATALYZATOR
CATEGORIZING
CATHETERIZE
CAUSTICIZED
CELESTIALIZED
CHORIZATION
CHORIZONTES
CICATRIZING
CLASSICIZED
COCAINIZING
COMMEMORIZE
CONCERTIZED
CONCRETIZED
CORPOREALIZE
COSMOGONIZE
CRITICIZING
CRYSTALLIZE
CUTICULARIZE
DECARBONIZE
DECARBURIZE
DECEREBRIZE
DECOLORIZING
DEFERRIZING
DEFINITIZED
DELIMITIZING
DELOCALIZING
DEMAGNETIZER
DEMOCRATIZE
DEMORALIZING
DEPAUPERIZE
DEPOLARIZING
DESILVERIZER
DESULFURIZER
DEVITALIZED
DEVULGARIZE
DIAMONDIZED
DIAZENTITHAL
DIEZEUGMENON
DIPLOMATIZE
DISCANONIZED
DISGOSPELIZE
DIVINIZATION
DOCTRINIZING
DOCUMENTIZE
DOGMATIZING
DOMESTICIZE
DRAMATIZATION
ECONOMIZING
ELECTROLYZE
EMOTIONALIZED
ENCARNALIZING
ENIGMATIZING
ENTHRONIZING
EPENTHESIZE
EPIDOTIZATION
EPITOMIZING
ETHEREALIZED
EVANGELIZED
FAMILIARIZE
FARADIZATION
FEDERALIZED
FERTILIZATION
FEUDALIZING
FLUIDIZATION
FORMULARIZE
FOSSILIZATION
FRACTIONIZE
FRATERNIZING
FRICTIONIZE
FUNCTIONIZE
GALVANIZING
GENERALIZABLE
GEOMETRIZING
HORIZOMETER
HOSPITALIZE
HURRICANIZE
IMMORTALIZER
INFORMALIZE
ISOCHRONIZE
KETONIZATION
LAPAROTOMIZE
LEGITIMIZING
LETHARGIZED
LIEDERKRANZ
LITHOTOMIZE
MAGAZINABLE
MAGNETIZATION
MALLEABLEIZE
MAMMONIZATION
MARBLEIZING
MARMARIZING
MARSUPIALIZE
MATERIALIZING
MEIZOSEISMAL
MEMORANDIZE
MEMORIALIZER
MEMORIZATION
MERCERIZING
MERCURIALIZE
MERCURIZING
MESMERIZING
METABOLIZED
METAMERIZED
MICASIZATION
MICROZOARIAN
MINIMIZATION
MNEMONIZING
MOBILIZATION
MODERNIZATION
MONOLOGIZING
MONOPOLIZED
MUZZLELOADING
NIVELLIZATION
OBLIVIONIZE
OLIGORHIZOUS
OPTIMIZATION
ORGANIZATORY
OSMAZOMATOUS
OVERGLAZING
OZONOSPHERE
PANTHEONIZE
PAPALIZATION
PARABOLIZED
PAUPERIZING
PENTAMETRIZE
PEPTONIZING
PLAGIARIZING
PLASTICIZED
PNEUMATIZED
POLITICALIZE
POLITICIZED
POLYZOARIAL
POPULARIZED
PORCELAINIZE
PORCELANIZE
PRAGMATIZER
PROSELYTIZE
PROTOCITIZEN
PULVERIZATE
RACEMIZATION
RADIUMIZATION
RECAPITALIZE
RECARBONIZER
RECARBURIZER
REHARMONIZE
REVITALIZING
RHIZOCAULUS
RHIZOMATOUS
RUBBERIZING
SACRAMENTIZE
SCANDALIZING
SCHILLERIZE
SCHIZOSTELE
SECTARIANIZED
SECTIONALIZED
SEMPITERNIZE
SHERARDIZED
SKELETONIZER
SOVEREIGNIZE
SOVIETIZATION
SPECIALIZED
SPERMATOZOAL
SPERMATOZOAN
SPERMATOZOON
SPIRITUALIZED
SPITZENBERG
SPITZENBURG
STANDARDIZING
STIGMATIZING
SUBSIDIZATION
SULFADIAZINE
SULPHAZOTIZE
SUMMARIZING
SYLLOGIZING
SYSTEMATIZE
SZAIBELYITE
TELEPATHIZE
TELFORDIZED
TEMPORIZING
THEATRICIZE
THEOLOGIZED
TROPHOZOITE
TROPOLOGIZED
UNAUTHORIZED
UNPOPULARIZE
UNRECOGNIZED
VASCULARIZE
VERATRINIZED
VITRIOLIZING
VOLATILIZING
VULCANIZATE
VULGARIZING
WESTERNIZING
ZIMENTWATER
ZINCIFEROUS
ZONOLIMNETIC
ZONOSKELETON
ZOOGRAFTING
ZOOMAGNETIC
ZOOPANTHEON
ZOOTHEISTIC
ZOSTERIFORM
ZYGOPTERAN

24

ABNORMALIZE
ACCULTURIZE
ACETONIZATION
ACTUALIZATION
AGGRANDIZED
ALBUMENIZER
ALGEBRAIZED
AMORTIZABLE
ANAESTHETIZE
ANESTHETIZER
ANGIOSTOMIZE
ANGLICIZING
ANIMALIZATION
ANTHEROZOID
ANTHOLOGIZE
APOLOGIZING
APOSTATIZING
ASTIGMATIZER
AUTHORIZING
AZEOTROPISM

AZOOSPERMIA
AZOTOBACTER
BASTARDIZED
BENZINDULINE
BESSEMERIZE
BESTIALIZING
BROMIZATION
BURGLARIZED
BURNETTIZING
BURTONIZATION
CACOZEALOUS
CALABAZILLA
CANNIBALIZE
CATALEPTIZE
CATEGORIZED
CAUSTICIZER
CAUTERIZATION
CENTRALIZING
CICATRIZANT
CICATRIZATE
CIRCULARIZE
COLLODIONIZE
CONCERTIZER
DAMENIZATION
DECENTRALIZE
DECOLORIZED
DELIMITIZED
DELOCALIZED
DEMAGNETIZE
DEMANGANIZE
DEMILITARIZE
DEMINERALIZE
DEMONETIZED
DEMORALIZED
DENICOTINIZE
DEPOLARIZED
DESILICONIZE
DESILVERIZE
DESULFURIZE
DIABOLIZING
DIALECTALIZE
DIALYZATION
DIMERIZATION
DISORGANIZED
DISSOCIALIZE
DOCTRINIZED
DOGGERELIZER
DRAMATIZING
DUCTILIZING
ECZEMATOSIS
EDITORIALIZED
ELECTRICIZE
ELECTROTONIZE
ENCARNALIZED
ENIGMATIZED
ENTHRONIZED
ENTOMOLOGIZE
ENTOZOOLOGY
EPILOGIZING
ETHERIZATION
EVANGELIZER
EVOLUTIONIZE
FANTASIZING
FERTILIZING
FOSSILIZING
FRATERNIZED
GEOMETRIZED
GLAMORIZING
GORMANDIZER
GUTTURALIZING
HORIZONTALIZE
IMMORTALIZE
IMPATRONIZE
IMPERIALIZE
INDOCTRINIZE
INTHRONIZATE
LEGITIMATIZE
LEGITIMIZED
LIBERALIZING
LOCALIZABLE
MAGNETIZING
MALLEABLIZE
MATERIALIZED
MEDIATIZING
MEMORIALIZE
METALLIZATION
METASTASIZED
MICROZOARIA
MIGNIARDIZE
MILITARIZING
MINERALIZING
MINERALOGIZE
MINIATURIZED
MODERNIZING
MONOLOGIZED
MONOPOLIZER
MONZODIORITE
MUSCULARIZE
NITROGENIZING
NORMALIZATION
NOVELIZATION
ODYLIZATION
OPTIMIZING
OSTRACIZATION
OUTTYRANNIZE
PAGANIZATION
PANCREATIZE
PARABOLIZER
PASTEURIZING
PECTIZATION
PECULIARIZE
PEPTIZATION
PERMORALIZE
PERSONALIZED
PLAGIARIZED
PLASTICIZER
PLEBEIANIZE
POLARIZABLE
POLITICIZER
POPULARIZER
PRESSURIZING
PRODIGALIZE
PROTOCOLIZE
PUZZLEPATED
RACIALIZATION
RANDOMIZING
RECARBONIZE
RECARBURIZE
RECOGNIZING
REVITALIZED
RHIZOGENOUS
RINFORZANDO
ROMANTICIZE
ROYALIZATION
SCANDALIZED
SCRUTINIZING
SECULARIZING
SIMULACRIZE
SINGULARIZING
SKELETONIZE
SOCIALIZATION
SOLEMNIZATION
SOLITUDINIZED
SOVIETIZING
SPECIALIZER
SPERMATOZOA
SPIRALIZATION
SPIRITUALIZER
STABILIZATION
STANDARDIZED
STIGMATIZED
STRUCTURALIZE
SUBSIDIZING
SUBTILIZATION
SUBURBANIZE
SULCALIZATION
SULFATIZING
SULFURIZING
SYNTONIZING
TABULARIZING
TEMPORALIZE
TETRAKISAZO
THEOLOGIZER
THEORIZATION
THIADIAZOLE
TRAILBLAZING
TROPICALIZE
TUBERCULIZE
TYRANNIZING
UNCANONIZING
UNFEUDALIZE
UNIVERSITIZE
UNMORALIZING
UNPATRONIZED
UNVULGARIZE
VALORIZATION
VASSALIZING
VENALIZATION
VERATRIZING
VISUALIZING
VITALIZATION
VITRIOLIZED
VOLATILIZED
WESTERNIZED
WINTERIZING
WIZENEDNESS
ZENOCENTRIC
ZINNWALDITE
ZOIDOGAMOUS
ZONAESTHESIA
ZOODENDRIUM
ZOOGONIDIUM

23

ABASTARDIZE
ABOLITIONIZE
ACTIONIZING
ACTUALIZING
AGGRANDIZER
ALBITIZATION
ALLEGORIZING
ALUMINIZING
AMORTIZATION
ANALYZATION
ANATOMIZING
ANESTHETIZE
ANIMALIZING
ANTAGONIZING
ANTITHESIZE
APOSTATIZED
ARBORIZATION
AROMATIZING
AZOCORALLINE
AZOTORRHOEA
BATTOLOGIZE
BENZOINATED
BENZONITRILE
BERZELIANITE
BESTIALIZED
BISTETRAZOLE
BRUTALIZING
BURNETTIZED
CANALIZATION
CANONIZATION
CARNALIZING
CATALOGUIZE
CAUTERIZING
CELESTIALIZE
CENTRALIZED
CITIZENIZING
COLONIZATION
CONSONANTIZE
CREOLIZATION
CURARIZATION
CUTINIZATION
DECOLORIZER
DECOLOURIZE
DEMONTETIZE
DEMORALIZER
DENAZIFYING
DEODORIZING
DEPERSONIZE
DEPOLARIZER
DERACIALIZE
DERMATOZOON
DESACRALIZE
DESCLOIZITE
DETRIBALIZE
DEUTEROZOOID
DEZINCATION
DIALOGIZING
DIAZOBENZENE
DISCANONIZE
DISORGANIZER
DOGGERELIZE
ELECTRIZING
EMOTIONALIZE
ETHEREALIZE
EUDAEMONIZE
EVENTUALIZE
FRATERNIZER
GABERLUNZIE
GASTEROZOOID
GAZETTEERAGE
GELATINIZING
GENEALOGIZER
GEOLOGIZING
GLUCOSAZONE
GLUTTONIZING
IDOLATRIZING
ILLEGALIZING
IODOBENZENE
IRREALIZABLE
ITALICIZING
LABIALIZING
LABILIZATION
LALLAPALOOZA
LIBERALIZED
LOCALIZATION
MARGINALIZE
MATERIALIZER
MATRONIZING
MERORGANIZE
METALIZATION
MEZZOTINTING
MILITARIZED
MINERALIZED
MISSIONARIZE
MONETIZATION
MORALIZATION
MORTALIZING
MOTORIZATION
MUTUALIZING
MUZZLELOADER
NARCOTIZING
NATIONALIZING
NEBULIZATION
NEMATOZOOID
NEOPAGANIZE
NITRIDIZATION
NITROBENZENE
NITROGENIZED
NORMALIZING
OPSONIZATION
ORGANIZABLE
ORIENTALIZING
OSTRACIZING
OVALIZATION
OVERZEALOUS
OZONIFEROUS
PALATIZATION
PALLETIZING
PASTEURIZED
PATRONIZING
PELORIZATION
PENALIZATION
PETROLIZING
PEZIZACEOUS
PLAGIARIZER
PLATINIZING
PLURALIZING
POLARIZATION
POSTURIZING
POTENTIALIZE
POZZUOLANIC
PRESSURIZED
PROLOGUIZER
PROTOZOIASIS
PUZZLINGNESS
RADIALIZATION
REALISTICIZE
RECOGNIZANT
REFORESTIZE
REORGANIZING
REVITALIZER
RHYTHMICIZE
ROBOTIZATION
SCENARIZING
SCLEROTIZED
SCRUTINIZED
SECTARIANIZE
SECTIONALIZE
SECULARIZED
SERMONIZING
SERPENTINIZE
SINGULARIZED
SLENDERIZING
SLUGGARDIZE
SOCIALIZING
SOLEMNIZING
SOLIDARIZING
SOUTHERNIZE
SPIRITUALIZE
SPLENIZATION
STABILIZATOR
STABILIZING
STALWARTIZE
STANDARDIZER
STATISTICIZE
STIGMATIZER
STYLIZATION
SUBERIZATION
SUBTILIZING
TABULARIZED
TAUTOLOGIZED
TOTEMIZATION
TOURMALINIZE
TRAPEZOIDAL
TROPOLOGIZE
TUBERIZATION
TUBULIZATION
UNAUTHORIZE
UNCANONIZED
UNMODERNIZE
UNMORALIZED
UNSECULARIZE
URBANIZATION
VERATRINIZE
VOLATILIZER
ZINGIBERENE
ZONESTHESIA
ZOOSPORANGE

22

ALDOLIZATION

ALLEGORIZED
ALLOTROPIZE
ANALOGIZING
ANTAGONIZED
ARTERIALIZED
ASBESTINIZE
ASTRONOMIZE
ATOMIZATION
ATTITUDINIZE
BENZONITROL
BISTRIAZOLE
BIZARRENESS
BLIZZARDOUS
CENTRALIZER
CITIZENIZED
CITIZENRIES
DEBENZOLIZE
DENATURALIZE
DENIZENATION
DERATIZATION
DESENSITIZER
DIAGONALIZE
DISORGANIZE
DISSEIZORESS
EDITORIALIZE
ELASTICIZER
ELECTRALIZE
ELECTRICALIZE
EMULSIONIZE
ENCARNALIZE
ENSORCELIZE
ENSORCERIZE
ERGOTIZATION
EULOGIZATION
GASTROZOOID
GELATINIZED
GENEALOGIZE
GENERALIZED
GLUTTONIZED
IDEALIZATION
IDOLATRIZED
ILLEGALIZED
IRREGULARIZE
ITEMIZATION
LAICIZATION
LALAPALOOZA
LATERALIZING
LEGALIZATION
LIBERALIZER
LINEARIZATION
LITERALIZING
MANORIALIZE
MATERIALIZE
MATERNALIZE
METASTASIZE
MEZZOTINTED
MINERALIZER
MINIATURIZE
MISSIONIZER
NATIONALIZED
NATURALIZING
NEOLOGIZING
NEUROTOMIZE
NEUTRALIZING
NONPARTIZAN
OPTIONALIZE
ORGANIZATION
ORGANZINING
ORIENTALIZED
PARAENESIZE
PASTEURIZER
PASTORALIZE
PATERNALIZE
PATRIZATION
PERSONALIZE
POETIZATION
PROLETARIZE
PROTOZOONAL
PUZZLEDNESS
RATIONALIZED
REACTUALIZE
REGULARIZED
REORGANIZED
SANCTUARIZE
SATIRIZABLE
SCRUTINIZER
SENSIBILIZE
SENSITIZATION
SENSUALIZING
SERIALIZATION
SIGNALIZING
SIZABLENESS
SLENDERIZED
SOLIDARIZED
SOLITUDINIZE
SOLMIZATION
STANDARDIZE
STERILIZATION
SUBSTANTIZE
TARTRAZINIC
TAUTOLOGIZER
TEETOTUMIZE
TENDERIZING
TENEMENTIZE
TETRAZOLIUM
TRAILBLAZER
UNBRUTALIZE
UNMORTALIZE
UNORGANIZED
UNSOLEMNIZE
UNSTERILIZED
ZONOCILIATE
ZOOCULTURAL
ZOOPARASITE

21

ADENIZATION
AGGUTINIZE
AGRARIANIZE
ALLEGORIZER
ANTAGONIZER
ARSENIZATION
ASTROLOGIZE
DENATURIZER
DESENSITIZE
DESTERILIZE
DESTINEZITE
DIAZOTIZING
DUALIZATION
ESTERIZATION
ETERNIZATION
GELATINIZER
GENERALIZER
GRANULITIZE
GUTTURALIZE
IDOLATRIZER
IDOLIZATION
INTELLIGIZE
INTERMEZZOS
IRIDIZATION
LATERALIZED
LATERIZATION
LITERALIZED
MEZZOTINTER
NASALIZATION
NATIONALIZER
NATURALIZED
NESSLERIZED
NEUROLOGIZE
NEUTRALIZED
NITROGENIZE
NODULIZING
NOTARIZATION
NUPTIALIZE
POLITZERIZE
PROTOZOEAN
PUZZLEATION
RATIONALIZER
RAZZBERRIES
REGIONALIZE
REGULARIZER
RELIGIONIZE
REORGANIZER
ROENTGENIZE
ROUTINIZING
RURALIZATION
SAILORIZING
SENSITIZING
SENSUALIZED
SERIALIZING
SIDEREALIZE
SINGULARIZE
SOLARIZATION
STERILIZING
TANTALIZING
TARTARIZING
TAUTOLOGIZE
TELLURIZING
TERRORIZING
TETANIZATION
TOTALIZATION
TRULLIZATION
TUTORIZATION
ULTRAZEALOUS
UNIONIZATION
UNLITURGIZE
UNNATURALIZE
URALITIZING
ZOISITIZATION
ZOOLOGIZING

20

ARTERIALIZE
AZOTETRAZOLE
ENOLIZATION
INTERNALIZE
LIONIZATION
LITERALIZER
LORENZENITE
NATIONALIZE
NATURALIZER
NEUTRALIZER
NONENTITIZE
ORIENTALIZE
RATIONALIZE
REALIZATION
RESTERILIZE
ROTARIANIZE
STALLIONIZE
TARANTARIZE
TOTALIZATOR
TRILLIONIZE
UTILIZATION
ZEALOUSNESS
ZEOLITIZING

19

OZONIZATION
TETRAZOTIZE

About the Authors

TOM PULLIAM has more than thirty years' experience in the field of words, word usage, games, and contests. This interest has encompassed solving, constructing, and writing on these subjects, although always as an avocation.

For practically all his business life Mr. Pulliam has been engaged in the area of training and management development. In this specialized field he has held key positions with a number of nationally known firms, and has served as a management consultant for a period of years. Today he serves as Manager of Training and Development for Wilson Foods Corporation in Oklahoma City, Oklahoma.

Pulliam has a particular interest in logology. In early years he constructed crossword puzzles for several newspapers and was a frequent contributor to collected volumes of *Double-Crostics.* His name is well known in American contesting circles. He has written a number of articles for *Word Ways: The Journal of Recreational Linguistics,* several of which have been reprinted in academic journals. Most recently, he acted as co-editor of *The New York Times Crossword Puzzle Dictionary.*

Mr. Pulliam lives in Edmond, Oklahoma.

GORTON CARRUTH, a founding member of The Hudson Group, a publishing cooperative, and formerly editor-in-chief of Funk & Wagnalls, has twenty-five years of experience in publishing dictionaries and other word books. He began his publishing career as Editor of Reference Books for the Thomas Y. Crowell Company; later he was an executive editor of McGraw-Hill Book Company.

He is author of *The Encyclopedia of American Facts and Dates* and the forthcoming *Facts on File Encyclopedia of World Dates and Events.* He is a co-author of the *Oxford American Dictionary* and of *The Oxford Illustrated Literary Guide to the United States.* Mr. Carruth lives in Pleasantville, New York.

STUDENTS FIRST!

1st In Customer Satisfaction

ACCOUNTING PRINCIPLES, 6/E puts students first by giving you everything you need to master the principles of accounting!

Included with this text is an ***INTERACTIVE CD*** packed with a learning styles assessment, an accounting cycle tutorial, self-tests with invidualized feedback, demonstration problems complete with action plans and solutions, key term matching exercises, professional profiles, a database of annual reports, and much more. All of this is designed to help you get the best grade you can in the course... and to get the best job you can get when you graduate!

THIS CD HELPS YOU SUCCEED BY TEACHING YOU...

... HOW TO STUDY

Everybody learns in different ways. Understanding how you learn best will help you get **the best possible grade you can from this — or any other — course.**

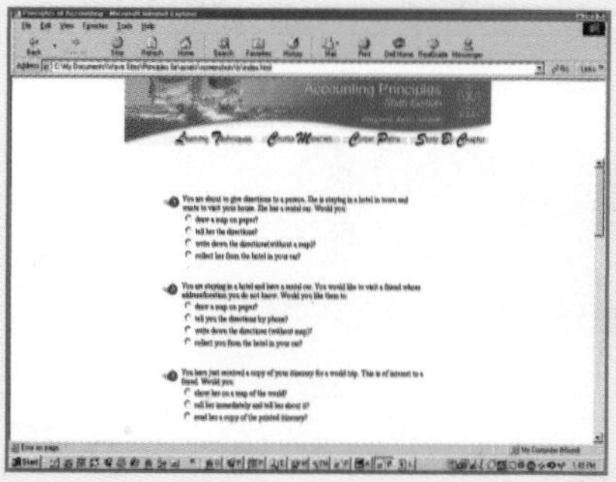

You can discover how you learn best by taking the *Interactive Learning Styles Quiz* on the Interactive CD. Once you know how you learn best, you can pinpoint the study aids in the text that will help you learn the material based on your learning style (the CD includes an *Interactive Study Skills Chart* to help you do this). Then let the *Navigator* show you how to use the study aids in the text most effectively.

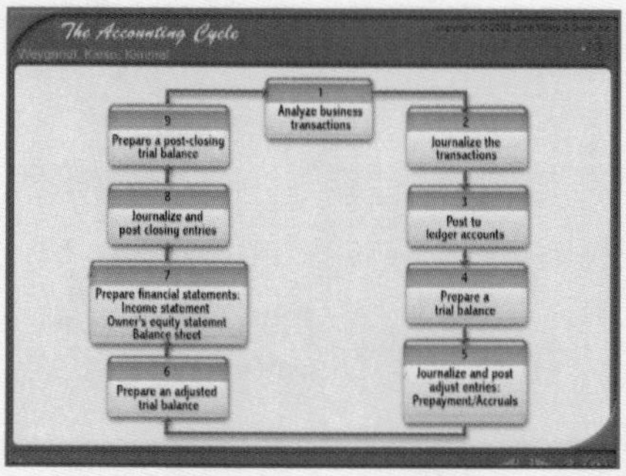

... WHAT TO STUDY

► **Master the Accounting Cycle**– the key to your success in Principles Of Accounting– with the help of the *Accounting Cycle Tutorial*

► Use the Self-Test feature for each chapter to take **interactive practice tests**

► **Improve your problem solving skills** with *Demonstration Problems with Action Plans.*

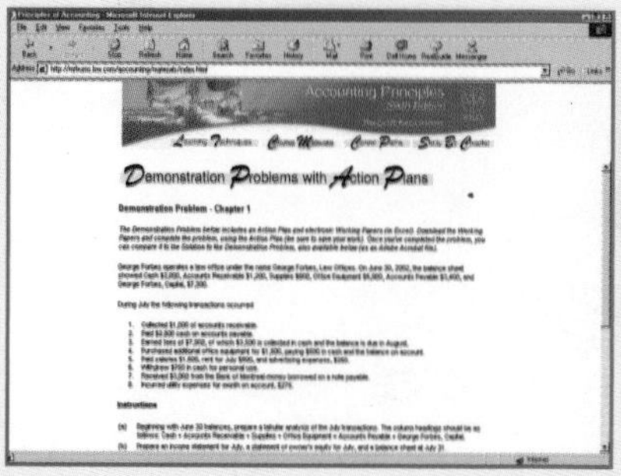

► **Expand your skills and apply your knowledge** with the *Writing Handbook, Surviving the Group Project, Database of Real Companies,* and *Real-World Cases* sections.

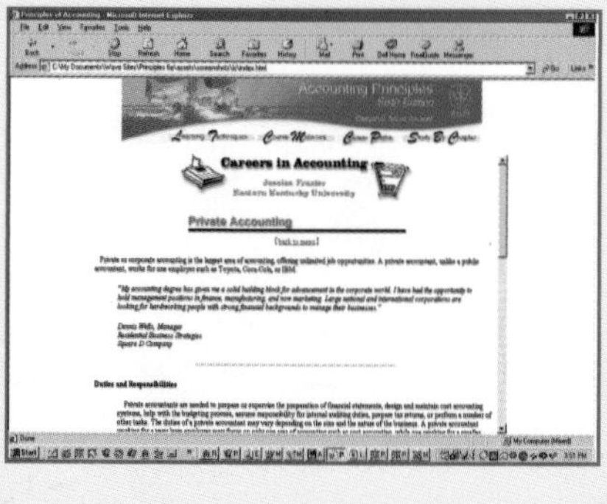

... WHY YOU STUDY!

When you succeed in this course, you've taken the first step on your way to a successful career. **This CD gets you started on your career by helping you:**

► Gain insight into *Why Accounting Is Important*

► Explore the opportunities available to you in *Careers in Accounting*

► Meet business professionals in the *Professional Profiles* section

6th EDITION

Accounting Principles

Jerry J. Weygandt *PhD, CPA*
Arthur Andersen Alumni Professor of Accounting
University of Wisconsin
Madison, Wisconsin

Donald E. Kieso *PhD, CPA*
KPMG Peat Marwick
Emeritus Professor of Accountancy
Northern Illinois University
DeKalb, Illinois

Paul D. Kimmel *PhD, CPA*
Associate Professor of Accounting
University of Wisconsin—Milwaukee
Milwaukee, Wisconsin

JOHN WILEY & SONS, INC.

NEW YORK • CHICHESTER • WEINHEIM • BRISBANE • TORONTO • SINGAPORE

Dedicated to
our mothers-in-law,
Maxyne Stottrup, Mathilda Reichenbacher, Rhojeanne Thompson,
and their daughters,
Enid, Donna, and Merlynn.

Special Dedication to
Walter G. Kell
Scholar-athlete, husband, father, teacher, author, gentleman, and friend

EXECUTIVE EDITOR *Brent Gordon*
SENIOR DEVELOPMENT EDITOR *Nancy Perry*
ASSOCIATE EDITOR *Cynthia Taylor*
SENIOR MARKETING MANAGER *Clancy Marshall*
PRODUCTION SERVICES MANAGER *Jeanine Furino*
NEW MEDIA EDITOR *David Kear*
PRODUCTION COORDINATOR *Elm Street Publishing Services, Inc.*
ART DIRECTOR *Dawn L. Stanley*
TEXT DESIGNER *Sheree Goodman*
COVER DESIGNER *Dawn L. Stanley*
PHOTO EDITOR *Sara Wight*
PHOTO RESEARCHER *Elyse Rieder*
ILLUSTRATION EDITOR *Sandra Rigby*
ART STUDIO *Precision Graphics*
COVER PHOTO © *James Bareham/Stone*

This book was set in Times Ten by York Graphic Services and printed and bound by Von Hoffmann Press. The cover was printed by Von Hoffmann Press.

Recognizing the importance of preserving what has been written, it is a policy of John Wiley & Sons, Inc. to have books of enduring value published in the United States printed on acid-free paper, and we exert our best efforts to that end.

The paper in this book was manufactured by a mill whose forest management programs include sustained yield harvesting of its timberlands. Sustained yield harvesting principles ensure that the number of trees cut each year does not exceed the amount of new growth.

We are grateful for permission to use the following material: The Lands' End logo throughout the text and the Lands' End 2000 Annual Report in Appendix A. Lands' End is a registered trademark of Lands' End Direct Merchants, Inc. Used with permission. The Abercrombie & Fitch 2000 Annual Report in Appendix B: Printed with permission of Abercrombie & Fitch Co.

ISBN 0-471-38228-0

Printed in the United States of America

10 9 8 7 6 5 4 3 2 1

STUDENT OWNER'S MANUAL

STUDENT TO STUDENT

Greetings!

Congratulations on your decision to take on one of the most challenging and satisfying courses offered . . . Accounting. As your semester progresses, I am sure that you will have a very good understanding of the accounting field and all that it involves. To help you through your class, here are some tips that I used to achieve academic success:

- Read ahead! Before going over a chapter in the classroom, take the time to read over the chapter so that while the professor is introducing the material you will already have an understanding of the objectives. Start with the *Concepts for Review*, the *Feature Story*, the *Study Objectives*, and the *Preview*; they will help you focus on the main points of the chapter. Then, as you read the chapter and follow the examples, you will be able to comprehend the material by yourself.
- Review! Once your instructor has presented the chapter material in class, be sure to re-read the chapter, concentrating on any areas that seem confusing. Look at the *Study Objectives* in the margins again and do the *Before You Go On* exercises to check whether you have understood and learned the material in each section. Look closely at the *Demonstration Problems* and answer the *Self-Study Questions* at the end of the chapter.
- Do the homework! I cannot over-stress the importance of doing the problems. The problems at the end of each chapter are the best way to gauge your understanding of the chapter material. If you can answer the problems in the chapter with confidence, you will be confident with the material.
- Use a highlighter! This textbook belongs to you, and if you are planning a career in business you will want to keep this book for reference material. Highlighting any material you feel is important in the chapter, or any material you are struggling with, will help you concentrate on those areas when you come back to the chapter review.
- Stay current! Accounting is a course where you build a foundation, and subsequent lessons stand on that foundation. Do not allow yourself to fall behind. Staying current with the lessons being taught in class is a crucial key to success in the course.

I hope that you will find these tips helpful and that your experience in accounting will be as rewarding as my own.

I wish you success,

Robert H. McNamara

Robert H. McNamara
Suffolk County Community College

HOW TO USE THE STUDY AIDS IN THIS BOOK

THE RECORDING PROCESS

THE NAVIGATOR ✓

- Understand *Concepts for Review* ❑
- Read *Feature Story* ❑
- Scan *Study Objectives* ❑
- Read *Preview* ❑
- Read text and answer *Before You Go On* *p. 49* ❑ *p. 52* ❑ *p. 62* ❑ *p. 66* ❑
- Work *Demonstration Problem* ❑
- Review *Summary of Study Objectives* ❑
- Answer *Self-Study Questions* ❑
- Complete *Assignments* ❑

The Navigator is a learning system designed to guide you through each chapter and help you succeed in learning the material. It consists of (1) a checklist at the beginning of the chapter, which outlines text features and study skills you will need, and (2) a series of check boxes that prompt you to use the learning aids in the chapter and set priorities as you study.

The **Feature Story** helps you picture how the chapter topic relates to the real world of accounting and business. Throughout the chapter, references to the Feature Story will help you put new ideas in context, organize them, and remember them. The problem called **A Look Back at Our Feature Story** toward the end of the chapter helps you pull together the ideas learned in the chapter. Many Feature Stories end with the **URL** of the company cited in the story.

CONCEPTS FOR REVIEW

Before studying this chapter, you should know or, if necessary, review:

a. What are assets, liabilities, owner's capital, owner's drawings, revenues, and expenses. (Ch. 1, pp. 13–14)

b. Why assets equal liabilities plus owner's equity. (Ch. 1, p. 12)

c. What transactions are and how they affect the basic accounting equation. (Ch. 1, pp. 15–20)

THE NAVIGATOR

Concepts for Review, listed at the beginning of each chapter, are the accounting concepts you learned in previous chapters that you will need to know in order to understand the topics you are about to learn. Page references are provided if you need to review before reading the chapter.

FEATURE STORY

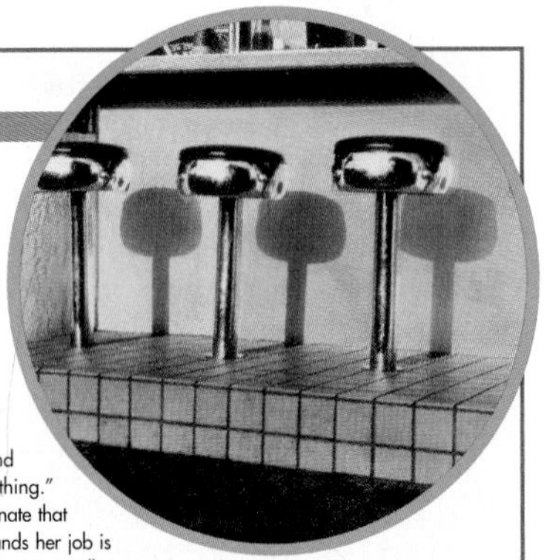

No Such Thing As a Perfect World

When she got a job doing the accounting for **Forster's Restaurants**, Tanis Anderson had almost finished her business administration degree at Simon Fraser University. But even after Tanis completed her degree requirements, her education still continued—this time, in the real world.

Tanis's responsibilities include paying the bills, tracking food and labor costs, and managing the payroll for **The Mug and Musket**, a popular destination restaurant in Surrey, British Columbia. "My title is Director of Finance," she laughs, "but really that means I take care of whatever needs doing!"

The use of judgment is a big part of the job. As Tanis says, "I learned all the fundamentals in my business classes, but school prepares you for a perfect world, and there is no such thing."

She feels fortunate that her boss understands her job is a learning experience as well as a responsibility. "Sometimes he's let me do something he knew perfectly well was a mistake so I can learn something through experience," she admits.

To help others gain the benefits of her real-world learning, Tanis is always happy to help students in the area who want to use Forster's as the subject of a project or report. "It's the least I can do," she says.

THE NAVIGATOR

Study Objectives at the beginning of each chapter give you a framework for learning the specific concepts and procedures covered in the chapter. Each study objective reappears in the margin at the point where the concept is discussed. Finally, you can review all the study objectives in the **Summary** at the end of the chapter.

STUDY OBJECTIVES

After studying this chapter, you should be able to:

1. Explain what an account is and how it helps in the recording process.
2. Define debits and credits and explain how they are used to record business transactions.
3. Identify the basic steps in the recording process.
4. Explain what a journal is and how it helps in the recording process.
5. Explain what a ledger is and how it helps in the recording process.
6. Explain what posting is and how it helps in the recording process.
7. Prepare a trial balance and explain its purposes.

THE NAVIGATOR

The **Preview** begins by linking the Feature Story with the major topics of the chapter. It is followed by a graphic outline of major topics and subtopics that will be discussed. This narrative and visual preview gives you a mental framework upon which to arrange the new information you are learning.

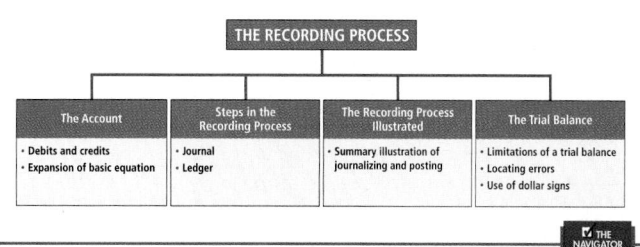

PREVIEW OF CHAPTER 2

In Chapter 1, we analyzed business transactions in terms of the accounting equation. The cumulative effects of these transactions were presented in tabular form. Imagine a restaurant and gift shop such as **The Mug and Musket** using the same tabular format as Softbyte to keep track of every one of its transactions. In a single day, this restaurant and gift shop engages in hundreds of business transactions. To record each transaction this way would be impractical, expensive, and unnecessary. Instead, a set of procedures and records are used to keep track of transaction data more easily.

This chapter introduces and illustrates these basic procedures and records. The content and organization of Chapter 2 are as follows.

THE RECORDING PROCESS

- **The Account**
  - Debits and credits
  - Expansion of basic equation
- **Steps in the Recording Process**
  - Journal
  - Ledger
- **The Recording Process Illustrated**
  - Summary illustration of journalizing and posting
- **The Trial Balance**
  - Limitations of a trial balance
  - Locating errors
  - Use of dollar signs

THE NAVIGATOR

A **CD** icon at various places throughout the book refers you to the CD that came with your textbook. On the CD, you will find *further discussion and examples*, an *Accounting Cycle Tutorial*, additional *Demonstration Problems*, *Self-Tests*, and *Key Term Matching Activities* to help you study, and additional *real-world cases*.

STUDY OBJECTIVE 1

Explain what an account is and how it helps in the recording process.

Accounting Cycle Tutorial—The Recording Process

THE ACCOUNT

An **account** is an individual accounting record of increases and decreases in a specific asset, liability, or owner's equity item. For example, Softbyte (the company discussed in Chapter 1) would have separate accounts for Cash, Accounts Receivable, Accounts Payable, Service Revenue, Salaries Expense, and so on. In its simplest form, an account consists of three parts: (1) the title of the account, (2) a left or debit side, and (3) a right or credit side. Because the alignment of these parts of an account resembles the letter T, it is referred to as a **T account**. The basic form of an account is shown in Illustration 2-1.

Illustration 2-1

Basic form of account

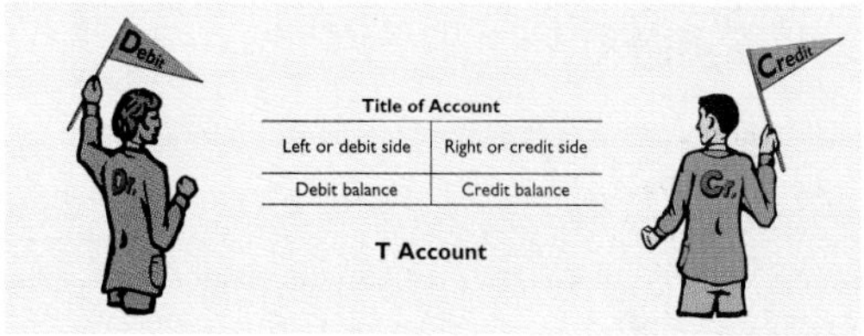

Steps in the Recording Process 53

THE LEDGER

The entire group of accounts maintained by a company is called the **ledger**. The ledger keeps in one place all the information about changes in specific account balances.

Companies may use various kinds of ledgers, but every company has a general ledger. A **general ledger** contains all the assets, liabilities, and owner's equity accounts, as shown in Illustration 2-15. A business can use a looseleaf binder or card file for the ledger. Each account is kept on a separate sheet or card. Whenever we use the term ledger in this textbook without a modifying adjective, we mean the general ledger.

STUDY OBJECTIVE 5

Explain what a ledger is and how it helps in the recording process.

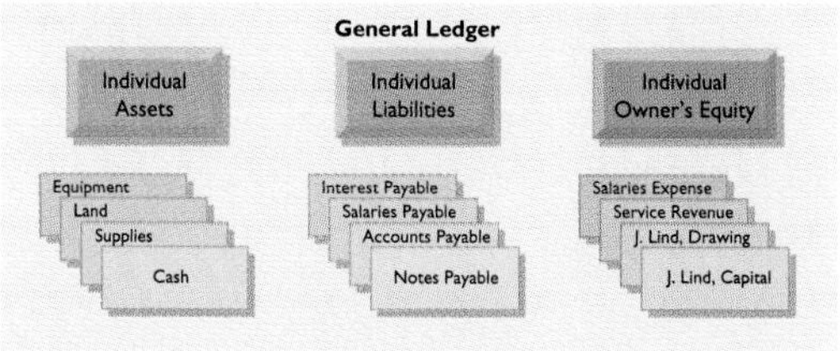

Illustration 2-15

The general ledger

The ledger should be arranged in the order in which accounts are presented in the financial statements, beginning with the balance sheet accounts. First in order are the asset accounts, followed by liability accounts, owner's capital, owner's drawing, revenues, and expenses. Each account is numbered for easier identification.

The ledger provides management with the balances in various accounts. For example, the Cash account shows the amount of cash that is available to meet current obligations. Amounts due from customers can be found by examining Accounts Receivable, and amounts owed to creditors can be found by examining Accounts Payable.

Study Objectives reappear in the margins at the point where the topic is discussed. End-of-chapter assignments are keyed to study objectives.

Color illustrations visually reinforce important concepts and therefore often contain material that may appear on exams.

Accounting in Action boxes give you more glimpses into the real world of business. These high-interest boxes are classified by three types of issues—business, ethics, and international—each identified by its own icon. New in this edition, **e-Business Insights** describe how e-business technology is expanding the services provided by accountants.

62 CHAPTER 2 The Recording Process

ACCOUNTING IN ACTION *e*-Business Insight

E-business is having a tremendous impact on how companies share information within the company, and with people outside the company, such as suppliers, creditors, and investors. A new type of software, Extensible Markup Language (XML), is enabling the creation of a universal way to exchange data. An organization called XBRL.org is using XML to develop an internationally accepted framework called the Extensible Business Reporting Model (XBRL). The organization is comprised of representatives from industry, accounting firms, investment houses, bankers, regulators, and others. The goal of this organization is to establish a framework that "the global business information supply chain will use to create, exchange, and analyze financial reporting information including, but not limited to, regulatory filings such as annual and quarterly financial statements, general ledger information, and audit schedules."

Before You Go On sections follow each key topic. ***Review It*** questions prompt you to stop and review the key points you have just studied. If you cannot answer these questions, you should go back and read the section again.

Review It questions marked with the Lands' End icon ask you to find information in Lands' End's 2000 Annual Report, which is packaged with this text and excerpted in Appendix A at the end of the text.

Brief ***Do It*** exercises ask you to put your newly acquired knowledge to work. They outline an ***Action Plan*** necessary to complete the exercise, and the accompanying ***Solution*** helps you see how the problem should be solved. (The ***Do It*** exercises are keyed to similar homework exercises.)

Accounts Receivable 371

BEFORE YOU GO ON...

▶ *REVIEW IT*

1. What is the primary criticism of the direct write-off method?
2. Explain the difference between the percentage of sales and the percentage of receivables methods.
3. Lands' End has a generous customer return policy. What accounting treatment does Lands' End use for customer returns? (*Hint:* Review Lands' End's notes.) The answer to this question is provided on page 396.

LANDS' END

▶ *DO IT*

Brule Co. has been in business 5 years. The ledger at the end of the current year shows: Accounts Receivable $30,000, Sales $180,000, and Allowance for Doubtful Accounts with a debit balance of $2,000. Bad debts are estimated to be 10% of receivables. Prepare the entry to adjust the Allowance for Doubtful Accounts.

ACTION PLAN

- Report receivables at their cash (net) realizable value.
- Estimate the amount the company does not expect to collect.
- Consider the existing balance in the allowance account when using the percentage of receivables basis.

SOLUTION

The following entry should be made to bring the balance in the Allowance for Doubtful Accounts up to a balance of $3,000 (0.1 × $30,000):

Bad Debts Expense	5,000	
Allowance for Doubtful Accounts		5,000
(To record estimate of uncollectible accounts)		

Related exercise material: BE9-3, BE9-4, BE9-5, BE9-6, BE9-7, E9-2, E9-3, and E9-4.

THE NAVIGATOR

Infographics, a special type of illustration, pictorially link concepts to the real world and provide visual reminders of key concepts.

50 CHAPTER 2 The Recording Process

The Recording Process
JOURNAL
LEDGER
Analyze each transaction
Enter transaction in a journal
Transfer journal information to ledger accounts

Illustration 2-12
The recording process

The basic steps in the recording process occur repeatedly. The analysis of transactions was illustrated in Chapter 1. Further examples will be given in this and later chapters. The other steps in the recording process are explained in the next sections.

Technology in Action examples show how computer technology is used in accounting and business.

Technology in Action boxes show how computers are used by accountants and by users of accounting information.

TECHNOLOGY IN ACTION

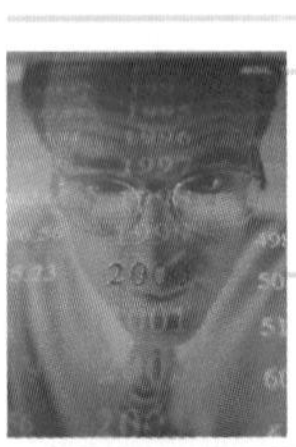

Computerized and manual accounting systems basically parallel one another. Most of the procedures are handled by electronic circuitry in computerized systems. They seem to occur invisibly. But, to fully comprehend how computerized systems operate, you need to understand manual approaches for processing accounting data.

Key Terms and concepts are printed in blue where they are first explained in the text, and they are defined again in the end-of-chapter glossary.

THE JOURNAL

STUDY OBJECTIVE 4

Explain what a journal is and how it helps in the recording process.

Transactions are initially recorded in chronological order in a **journal** before being transferred to the accounts. Thus, the journal is referred to as the book of original entry. For each transaction the journal shows the debit and credit effects on specific accounts. Companies may use various kinds of journals, but every company has the most basic form of journal, a **general journal**. Typically, a general journal has spaces for dates, account titles and explanations, references, and two amount columns. Whenever we use the term journal in this textbook without a revenues. In fact, an accrued expense on the books of one company is an accrued revenue to another company. For example, the $200 accrual of fees by Pioneer is an accrued expense to the client that received the service.

Adjustments for accrued expenses are needed for two purposes: (1) to record the obligations that exist at the balance sheet date, and (2) to recognize the expenses that apply to the current accounting period. Prior to adjustment, both liabilities and expenses are understated. Thus, **the adjusting entry for accrued expenses results in a debit (increase) to an expense account and a credit (increase) to a liability account.**

ACCRUED INTEREST. Pioneer Advertising Agency signed a $5,000, 3-month note payable on October 1. The note requires interest at an annual rate of 12%. The amount of the interest accumulation is determined by three factors: (1) the face value of the note, (2) the interest rate, which is always expressed as an annual rate, and (3) the length of time the note is outstanding. In this instance, the total interest due on the $5,000 note at its due date 3 months hence is $150 ($5,000 × 12% × 3/12), or $50 for one month. The formula for computing interest and its application to Pioneer Advertising Agency for the month of October[2] are shown in Illustration 3-12. Note that the time period is expressed as a fraction of a year.

HELPFUL HINT
Interest is a cost of borrowing money that accumulates with the passage of time.

Helpful Hints in the margins are like having an instructor with you as you read. They further clarify concepts being discussed.

Illustration 3-12
Formula for computing interest

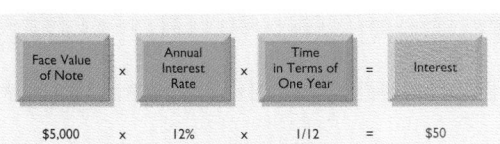

Face Value of Note	×	Annual Interest Rate	×	Time in Terms of One Year	=	Interest
$5,000	×	12%	×	1/12	=	$50

The accrued expense adjusting entry at October 31 is:

Oct. 31	Interest Expense	50	
	Interest Payable		50
	(To record interest on notes payable)		

A = L + OE
+50 −50

Accounting equation analyses have been inserted in the margin next to key journal entries. They help you understand the impact of an accounting transaction on the financial statements.

After this adjusting entry is posted, the accounts show:

Illustration 3-13
Interest accounts after adjustment

Interest Expense		Interest Payable	
10/31 Adj. 50			10/31 Adj. 50

Interest Expense shows the interest charges for the month. The amount of interest owed at the statement date is shown in Interest Payable. It will not be paid until the note comes due at the end of 3 months. The Interest Payable account is used instead of crediting (increasing) Notes Payable. The reason for using the two accounts is to disclose the two types of obligations (interest and principal) in the accounts and statements. **If this adjusting entry is not made, liabilities and interest**

Financial statements appear throughout the book. Those from real companies are identified by a logo or related photo. Often, numbers or categories are highlighted in colored type to draw your attention to key information.

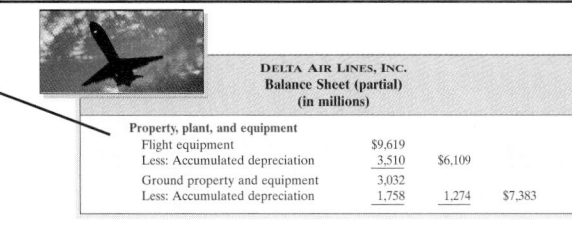

Illustration 4-20
Property, plant, and equipment section

DELTA AIR LINES, INC.
Balance Sheet (partial)
(in millions)

Property, plant, and equipment			
Flight equipment	$9,619		
Less: Accumulated depreciation	3,510	$6,109	
Ground property and equipment	3,032		
Less: Accumulated depreciation	1,758	1,274	$7,383

Intangible Assets

Intangible assets are noncurrent resources that do not have physical substance. They are recorded at cost, and this cost is expensed over the useful life of the intangible asset. Intangible assets include patents, copyrights, and trademarks or

For example, **Lands' End** reported in its 2000 Annual Report a beginning inventory of $219,686,000, and cost of goods sold for the year ended January 28, 2000, of $727,291,000. The inventory turnover formula and computation for Lands' End are shown below.

Illustration 6-28
Inventory turnover formula and computation for **Lands' End**

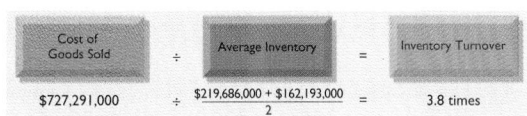

Cost of Goods Sold	÷	Average Inventory	=	Inventory Turnover
$727,291,000	÷	($219,686,000 + $162,193,000) / 2	=	3.8 times

A variant of the inventory turnover ratio is the **average days to sell inventory**. For example, the inventory turnover for Lands' End of 3.8 times divided into 365 is approximately 96 days. This is the approximate age of the inventory.

There are typical levels of inventory in every industry. Companies that are able to keep their inventory at lower levels and higher turnovers and still satisfy customer needs are the most successful.

One technique for determining the meaning of the information on financial statements is **ratio analysis**. Throughout this text, you will analyze key financial ratios using data from Lands' End's financial statements. (Also, Chapter 19 addresses the topic of financial statement analysis in detail.)

The last **Before You Go On** exercise takes you back for a critical look at the chapter-opening Feature Story.

BEFORE YOU GO ON...

REVIEW IT

1. What is a trial balance and what is its primary purpose?
2. How is a trial balance prepared?
3. What are the limitations of a trial balance?

A LOOK BACK AT OUR FEATURE STORY

Refer back to the Feature Story about **The Mug and Musket** at the beginning of the chapter, and answer the following questions.

1. What accounting entries would Tanis likely make to record (a) the receipt of cash from a customer in payment of their bill, (b) payment of a utility bill, and (c) payment of wages for the waiters?
2. How did Tanis's job as Director of Finance help in her studies as she finished her business administration degree?

SOLUTION

1. Tanis would likely make the following entries.
   (a) Cash
   Food Sales Revenue
   (Receipt of payment for food services)
   (b) Utility Expense
   Cash
   (Payment of electric bill)
   (c) Salaries (or Wages) Expense
   Cash
   (Paid waiters' wages)
2. As a result of her accounting position, Tanis was able to relate the subject matter as well as much of the assignment material in her business courses to a real-world context. From her job, she knew how bills were paid, how supplies were determined, how employees were hired, managed, evaluated, and paid.

THE NAVIGATOR

Demonstration Problem 67

DEMONSTRATION PROBLEM

Bob Sample opened the Campus Laundromat on September 1, 2002. During the first month of operations the following transactions occurred.

Sept. 1 Invested $20,000 cash in the business.
2 Paid $1,000 cash for store rent for the month of September.
3 Purchased washers and dryers for $25,000, paying $10,000 in cash and signing a $15,000, 6-month, 12% note payable.
4 Paid $1,200 for one-year accident insurance policy.
10 Received bill from the *Daily News* for advertising the opening of the laundromat $200.
20 Withdrew $700 cash for personal use.
30 Determined that cash receipts for laundry services for the month were $6,200.

Additional Demonstration Problem

The chart of accounts for the company is the same as in Pioneer Advertising Agency except for the following: No. 154 Laundry Equipment and No. 610 Advertising Expense.

Instructions

(a) Journalize the September transactions. (Use J1 for the journal page number.)
(b) Open ledger accounts and post the September transactions.
(c) Prepare a trial balance at September 30, 2002.

SOLUTION TO DEMONSTRATION PROBLEM

(a) GENERAL JOURNAL **J1**

Date	Account Titles and Explanation	Ref.	Debit	Credit
2002				
Sept. 1	Cash	101	20,000	
	Bob Sample, Capital	301		20,000
	(Owner's investment of cash in business)			
2	Rent Expense	729	1,000	
	Cash	101		1,000
	(Paid September rent)			
3	Laundry Equipment	154	25,000	
	Cash	101		10,000
	Notes Payable	200		15,000
	(Purchased laundry equipment for cash and 6-month, 12% note payable)			
4	Prepaid Insurance	130	1,200	
	Cash	101		1,200
	(Paid one-year insurance policy)			
10	Advertising Expense	610	200	
	Accounts Payable	201		200
	(Received bill from *Daily News* for advertising)			
20	Bob Sample, Drawing	306	700	
	Cash	101		700
	(Withdrew cash for personal use)			
30	Cash	101	6,200	
	Service Revenue	400		6,200
	(Received cash for services provided)			

ACTION PLAN

- Make separate journal entries for each transaction.
- In journalizing, make sure debits equal credits.
- In journalizing, use specific account titles taken from the chart of accounts.
- Provide appropriate description of journal entry.
- Arrange ledger in statement order, beginning with the balance sheet accounts.
- Post in chronological order.
- Use numbers in the reference column to indicate the amount has been posted.
- In the trial balance, list accounts in the order in which they appear in the ledger.
- List debit balances in the left column, and credit balances in the right column.

Demonstration Problems review the chapter material. These sample problems provide you with ***Action Plans*** that list the strategies needed to solve the problem and with ***Solutions***. The *CD icon* tells you there is an additional demonstration problem you can work through on the CD that came with your textbook.

The **Summary of Study Objectives** relates the study objectives to the key points in the chapter. It gives you another opportunity to review as well as to see how all the key topics within the chapter are related.

The **Glossary** defines all the terms and concepts introduced in the chapter. Page references help you find any terms you need to study further. The *CD icon* tells you that there is a Key Term Matching Activity on the CD that came with your textbook that will help you master the material.

SUMMARY OF STUDY OBJECTIVES

1. ***Explain what an account is and how it helps in the recording process.*** An account is a record of increases and decreases in specific asset, liability, and owner's equity items.

2. ***Define debits and credits and explain how they are used to record business transactions.*** The terms debit and credit are synonymous with left and right. Assets, drawings, and expenses are increased by debits and decreased by credits. Liabilities, owner's capital, and revenues are increased by credits and decreased by debits.

3. ***Identify the basic steps in the recording process.*** The basic steps in the recording process are: (a) analyze each transaction in terms of its effects on the accounts, (b) enter the transaction information in a journal, (c) transfer the journal information to the appropriate accounts in the ledger.

4. ***Explain what a journal is and how it helps in the recording process.*** The initial accounting record of a transaction is entered in a journal before the data are entered in the accounts. A journal (a) discloses in one place the complete effects of a transaction, (b) provides a chronological record of transactions, and (c) prevents or locates errors because the debit and credit amounts for each entry can be readily compared.

5. ***Explain what a ledger is and how it helps in the recording process.*** The entire group of accounts maintained by a company is referred to as the ledger. The ledger keeps in one place all the information about changes in specific account balances.

6. ***Explain what posting is and how it helps in the recording process.*** Posting is the procedure of transferring journal entries to the ledger accounts. This phase of the recording process accumulates the effects of journalized transactions in the individual accounts.

7. ***Prepare a trial balance and explain its purposes.*** A trial balance is a list of accounts and their balances at a given time. Its primary purpose is to prove the equality of debits and credits after posting. A trial balance also uncovers errors in journalizing and posting and is useful in preparing financial statements.

THE NAVIGATOR

Key Term Matching Activity

GLOSSARY

Account A record of increases and decreases in specific asset, liability, or owner's equity items. (p. 44).

Chart of accounts A list of accounts and the account numbers that identify their location in the ledger. (p. 56).

Compound entry A journal entry that involves three or more accounts. (p. 52).

Credit The right side of an account. (p. 45).

Debit The left side of an account. (p. 45).

Double-entry system A system that records in appropriate accounts the dual effect of each transaction. (p. 45).

General journal The most basic form of journal. (p. 50).

General ledger A ledger that contains all asset, liability, and owner's equity accounts. (p. 53).

Journal An accounting record in which transactions are initially recorded in chronological order. (p. 50).

Journalizing The entering of transaction data in the journal. (p. 50).

Ledger The entire group of accounts maintained by a company. (p. 53).

Posting The procedure of transferring journal entries to the ledger accounts. (p. 54).

Simple entry A journal entry that involves only two accounts. (p. 51).

T account The basic form of an account. (p. 44).

Three-column form of account A form with columns for debit, credit, and balance amounts in an account. (p. 54).

Trial balance A list of accounts and their balances at a given time. (p. 64).

Chapter 2 Self-Test

SELF-STUDY QUESTIONS

Answers are at the end of the chapter.

(SO 1) **1.** Which of the following statements about an account is true?
a. In its simplest form, an account consists of two parts.
b. An account is an individual accounting record of increases and decreases in specific asset, liability, and owner's equity items.
c. There are separate accounts for specific assets and liabilities but only one account for owner's equity items.
d. The left side of an account is the credit or decrease side.

(SO 2) **2.** Debits:
a. increase both assets and liabilities.
b. decrease both assets and liabilities.
c. increase assets and decrease liabilities.
d. decrease assets and increase liabilities.

(SO 2) **3.** A revenue account:
a. is increased by debits.
b. is decreased by credits.
c. has a normal balance of a debit.
d. is increased by credits.

Self-Study Questions are a practice test, keyed to Study Objectives, that gives you an opportunity to check your knowledge of important topics. Answers appear on the last page of the chapter. The *CD icon* tells you that there is an additional Self-Test on the CD that came with your textbook to help you master the material.

(SO 2) **4.** Accounts that normally have debit balances are:
a. assets, expenses, and revenues.
b. assets, expenses, and owner's capital.
c. assets, liabilities, and owner's drawings.
d. assets, owner's drawings, and expenses.

(SO 3) **5.** Which of the following is *not* part of the recording process?
a. Analyzing transactions.
b. Preparing a trial balance.
c. Entering transactions in a journal.
d. Posting transactions.

(SO 4) **6.** Which of the following statements about a journal is false?
a. It is not a book of original entry.
b. It provides a chronological record of transactions.
c. It helps to locate errors because the debit and credit amounts for each entry can be readily compared.
d. It discloses in one place the complete effect of a transaction.

(SO 5) **7.** A ledger:
a. contains only asset and liability accounts.
b. should show accounts in alphabetical order.
c. is a collection of the entire group of accounts maintained by a company.
d. is a book of original entry.

8. Posting:
a. norma
b. transf
c. is an
d. transf

9. A trial b
a. is a lis
b. proves
transa
c. will n
d. proves

10. A trial b
a. a corr
b. the pu
plies
c. a $100
Drawi
d. a $450
ited t
and c

QUESTIONS

1. Describe the parts of a T account.

2. "The terms *debit* and *credit* mean increase and decrease, respectively." Do you agree? Explain.

3. José Amaro, a fellow student, contends that the double-entry system means each transaction must be recorded twice. Is José correct? Explain.

4. Teresa Alvarez, a beginning accounting student, believes debit balances are favorable and credit balances are unfavorable. Is Teresa correct? Discuss.

5. State the rules of debit and credit as applied to (a) asset accounts, (b) liability accounts, and (c) the owner's equity accounts (revenue, expenses, owner's drawing, and owner's capital).

6. What is the normal balance for each of the following accounts? (a) Accounts Receivable. (b) Cash. (c) Owner's Drawing. (d) Accounts Payable. (e) Service Revenue. (f) Salaries Expense. (g) Owner's Capital.

7. Indicate whether each of the following accounts is an asset, a liability, or an owner's equity account and whether it has a normal debit or credit balance: (a) Accounts Receivable, (b) Accounts Payable, (c) Equipment, (d) Owner's Drawing, (e) Supplies.

8. For the following transactions, indicate the account debited and the account credited.
(a) Supplies are purchased on account.
(b) Cash is received on signing a note payable.
(c) Employees are paid salaries in cash.

9. Indicate whether the following accounts generally will have (a) debit entries only, (b) credit entries only, or (c) both debit and credit entries.

(1) Cash. (4) Accounts Payable.
(2) Accounts Receivable. (5) Salaries Expense.
(3) Owner's Drawing. (6) Service Revenue.

10. What are the basic steps in the recording process?

11. What are the advantages of using a journal in the recording process?

12. (a) When entering a transaction in the journal, should the debit or credit be written first?
(b) Which should be indented, the debit or credit?

13. Describe a compound entry, and provide an example.

14. (a) Should business transaction debits and credits be recorded directly in the ledger accounts?
(b) What are the advantages of first recording transactions in the journal and then posting to the ledger?

15. The account number is entered as the last step in posting the amounts from the journal to the ledger. What is the advantage of this step?

16. Journalize the following business transactions.
(a) Doris Wang invests $9,000 cash in the business.
(b) Insurance of $800 is paid for the year.
(c) Supplies of $1,500 are purchased on account.
(d) Cash of $7,500 is received for services rendered.

17. (a) What is a ledger?
(b) What is a chart of accounts and why is it important?

18. What is a trial balance and what are its purposes?

19. Kap Shin is confused about how accounting information flows through the accounting system. He believes the flow of information is as follows.
(a) Debits and credits posted to the ledger.
(b) Business transaction occurs.

Questions allow you to explain your understanding of concepts and relationships covered in the chapter.

(c) Information entered in the journal.
(d) Financial statements are prepared.
(e) Trial balance is prepared.
Is Kap correct? If not, indicate to Kap the proper flow of the information.

20. Two students are discussing the use of a trial balance. They wonder whether the following errors, each considered separately, would prevent the trial balance from balancing.
(a) The bookkeeper debited Cash for $600 and credited Wages Expense for $600 for payment of wages.
(b) Cash collected on account was debited to Cash for $900 and Service Revenue was credited for $90.
What would you tell them?

BRIEF EXERCISES

BE2-1 For each of the following accounts indicate the effects of (a) a debit and (b) a credit on the accounts and (c) the normal balance of the account.

Indicate debit and credit effects and normal balance. (SO 2)

1. Accounts Payable.
2. Advertising Expense.
3. Service Revenue.
4. Accounts Receivable.
5. B. C. Jardine, Capital.
6. B. C. Jardine, Drawing.

BE2-2 Transactions for the H. J. Oslo Company for the month of June are presented below. Identify the accounts to be debited and credited for each transaction.

Identify accounts to be debited and credited. (SO 2)

June 1 H. J. Oslo invests $3,000 cash in a small welding business of which he is the sole proprietor.
2 Purchases equipment on account for $900.
3 $500 cash is paid to landlord for June rent.
12 Bills J. Kronsnoble $300 for welding work done on account.

BE2-3 Using the data in BE2-2, journalize the transactions. (You may omit explanations.)

Journalize transactions. (SO 4)

BE2-4 Tage Shumway, a fellow student, is unclear about the basic steps in the recording process. Identify and briefly explain the steps in the order in which they occur.

Identify and explain steps in recording process. (SO 3)

BE2-5 J. A. Norris has the following transactions during August of the current year. Indicate (a) the effect on the accounting equation and (b) the debit-credit analysis illustrated on pages 57–61 of the text.

Indicate basic and debit-credit analysis. (SO 4)

Aug. 1 Opens an office as a financial advisor, investing $6,000 in cash.
4 Pays insurance in advance for 6 months, $1,800 cash.
16 Receives $800 from clients for services rendered.
27 Pays secretary $500 salary.

BE2-6 Using the data in BE2-5, journalize the transactions. (You may omit explanations.)

Journalize transactions. (SO 4)

BE2-7 Selected transactions for the Gonzales Company are presented in journal form below. Post the transactions to T accounts. Make one T account for each item and determine each account's ending balance.

Post journal entries to T accounts. (SO 6)

J1

Date	Account Titles and Explanation	Ref.	Debit	Credit
May 5	Accounts Receivable		5,000	
	Service Revenue			5,000
	(Billed for services provided)			
12	Cash		2,400	
	Accounts Receivable			2,400
	(Received cash in payment of account)			
15	Cash		2,000	
	Service Revenue			2,000
	(Received cash for services provided)			

Brief Exercises help you focus on one Study Objective at a time and thus help you build confidence in your basic skills and knowledge. A pencil icon in any of the end-of-chapter materials marks an exercise or problem that will help you practice business writing skills. (Keyed to Study Objectives.)

al entries for the Gonzales Company are presented in BE2-7. Post the
tandard form of account.

er balances given below, prepare a trial balance for the P. J. Carland
002. List the accounts in the order shown on page 65 of the text. All ac-
mal.
$7,000, Cash $6,800, P. J. Carland, Capital $20,000, P. J. Carland, Draw-
$17,000, Service Revenue $6,000, Accounts Receivable $3,000, Salaries
ent Expense $1,000.

nced bookkeeper prepared the following trial balance. Prepare a correct
all account balances are normal.

GOMEZ COMPANY
Trial Balance
December 31, 2002

	Debit	Credit
Cash	$18,800	
Prepaid Insurance		$ 3,500
Accounts Payable		3,000
Unearned Revenue	4,200	
P. Gomez, Capital		15,000
P. Gomez, Drawing		4,500
Service Revenue		25,600
Salaries Expense	18,600	
Rent Expense		2,400
	$41,600	$54,000

Exercises, which are more difficult than Brief Exercises, help you continue to build confidence in your ability to use the material learned in the chapter. (Keyed to Study Objectives.)

EXERCISES

Identify debits, credits, and normal balances. (SO 2)

E2-1 Selected transactions for A. Mane, an interior decorator, in her first month of business, are as follows.

Jan. 2 Invested $10,000 cash in business.
3 Purchased used car for $4,000 cash for use in business.
9 Purchased supplies on account for $500.
11 Billed customers $1,800 for services performed.
16 Paid $200 cash for advertising start of business.
20 Received $700 cash from customers billed on January 11.
23 Paid creditor $300 cash on account.
28 Withdrew $1,000 cash for personal use of owner.

Instructions
For each transaction indicate the following.

(a) The basic type of account debited and credited (asset, liability, owner's equity).
(b) The specific account debited and credited (cash, rent expense, service revenue, etc.).
(c) Whether the specific account is increased or decreased.
(d) The normal balance of the specific account.

Use the following format, in which the January 2 transaction is given as an example.

	Account Debited				Account Credited			
Date	(a) Basic Type	(b) Specific Account	(c) Effect	(d) Normal Balance	(a) Basic Type	(b) Specific Account	(c) Effect	(d) Normal Balance
Jan. 2	Asset	Cash	Increase	Debit	Owner's Equity	A. Mane, Capital	Increase	Credit

Accounts Receivable	$ 8,642	Prepaid Insurance	$ 1,968
Accounts Payable	8,396	Repair Expense	961
Cash	?	Service Revenue	10,610
Delivery Equipment	49,360	I. M. Tardy, Drawing	700
Gas and Oil Expense	758	I. M. Tardy, Capital	44,636
Insurance Expense	523	Salaries Expense	4,428
Notes Payable	21,450	Salaries Payable	815

Instructions

Prepare a trial balance with the accounts arranged as illustrated in the chapter and fill in the missing amount for Cash.

PROBLEMS: SET A

Journalize a series of transactions.
(SO 2, 4)

P2-1A Frontier Park was started on April 1 by C. J. Sanculi. The following selected events and transactions occurred during April.

Apr. 1 Sanculi invested $40,000 cash in the business.
4 Purchased land costing $30,000 for cash.
8 Incurred advertising expense of $1,800 on account.
11 Paid salaries to employees $1,500.
12 Hired park manager at a salary of $4,000 per month, effective May 1.

Each **Problem** helps you pull together and apply several concepts from the chapter. Two sets of **Problems—A** and **B**—are keyed to the same Study Objectives and provide additional opportunities to apply concepts learned in the chapter.

General Ledger Problems, identified by an icon, are selected problems that can be solved using the *General Ledger Software* package.

Problems marked with the **Peachtree** icon can be worked using *Peachtree Complete® Accounting to Accompany Accounting Principles, Sixth Edition.* A separate student workbook that includes the newly released software is available for purchase.

78 CHAPTER 2 **The Recording Process**

Trial balance totals $26,630

Instructions

Prepare a correct trial balance. Note: The chart of accounts includes the following: T. Santos, Drawing, and Supplies. (*Hint:* It helps to prepare the correct journal entry for the transaction described and compare it to the mistake made.)

Journalize transactions, post, and prepare a trial balance.
(SO 2, 4, 6, 7)

P2-5A The Lake Theater is owned by Avtar Sandhu. All facilities were completed on March 31. At this time, the ledger showed: No. 101 Cash $6,000; No. 140 Land $10,000; No. 145 Buildings (concession stand, projection room, ticket booth, and screen) $8,000; No. 157 Equipment $6,000; No. 201 Accounts Payable $2,000; No. 275 Mortgage Payable $8,000; and No. 301 Avtar Sandhu, Capital $20,000. During April, the following events and transactions occurred.

Apr. 2 Paid film rental of $800 on first movie.
3 Ordered two additional films at $500 each.
9 Received $1,800 cash from admissions.
10 Made $2,000 payment on mortgage and $1,000 on accounts payable.
11 Lake Theater contracted with R. Thoms Company to operate the concession stand. Thoms is to pay 17% of gross concession receipts (payable monthly) for the right to operate the concession stand.
12 Paid advertising expenses $300.
20 Received one of the films ordered on April 3 and was billed $500. The film will be shown in April.
25 Received $4,200 cash from admissions.
29 Paid salaries $1,600.
30 Received statement from R. Thoms showing gross concession receipts of $1,000 and the balance due to The Lake Theater of $170 ($1,000 × 17%) for April. Thoms paid one-half of the balance due and will remit the remainder on May 5.
30 Prepaid $900 rental on special film to be run in May.

In addition to the accounts identified above, the chart of accounts shows: No. 112 Accounts Receivable, No. 136 Prepaid Rentals, No. 405 Admission Revenue, No. 406 Concession Revenue, No. 610 Advertising Expense, No. 632 Film Rental Expense, and No. 726 Salaries Expense.

Instructions

Trial balance totals $33,670

(a) Enter the beginning balances in the ledger as of April 1. Insert a check mark (✓) in the reference column of the ledger for the beginning balance.
(b) Journalize the April transactions.
(c) Post the April journal entries to the ledger. Assume that all entries are posted from page 1 of the journal.
(d) Prepare a trial balance on April 30, 2002.

Marginal **check figures** provide a key number part way through your problem solution, to help you know you're on the right track with your work.

PROBLEMS: SET B

Journalize a series of transactions.
(SO 2, 4)

P2-1B Surepar Miniature Golf and Driving Range was opened on March 1 by Jane McInnes. The following selected events and transactions occurred during March:

Mar. 1 Invested $50,000 cash in the business.
3 Purchased Lee's Golf Land for $38,000 cash. The price consists of land $23,000, building $9,000, and equipment $6,000. (Make one compound entry.)
5 Advertised the opening of the driving range and miniature golf course, paying

Spreadsheet Problems, identified by an icon, are selected problems that can be solved using the spreadsheet software *Solving Accounting Principles Problems Using Excel and Lotus 1-2-3 for Windows.*

80 CHAPTER 2 **The Recording Process**

Prepare a correct trial balance.
(SO 7)

P2-4B The trial balance of Thom Wargo Co. shown below does not balance.

THOM WARGO CO.
Trial Balance
June 30, 2002

	Debit	Credit
Cash		$ 3,840
Accounts Receivable	$ 3,231	
Supplies	800	
Equipment	3,000	
Accounts Payable		2,666
Unearned Revenue	2,200	
T. Wargo, Capital		9,000
T. Wargo, Drawing	800	
Service Revenue		2,380
Salaries Expense	3,400	
Office Expense	910	
	$14,341	$17,886

Each of the listed accounts has a normal balance per the general ledger. An examination of the ledger and journal reveals the following errors.

1. Cash received from a customer on account was debited for $570, and Accounts Receivable was credited for the same amount. The actual collection was for $750.
2. The purchase of a typewriter on account for $340 was recorded as a debit to Supplies for $340 and a credit to Accounts Payable for $340.
3. Services were performed on account for a client for $890. Accounts Receivable was debited for $890, and Service Revenue was credited for $89.

25 Billed customers $3,000 for cleaning services.
31 Paid gas and oil for month on truck $200.
31 Withdrew $900 cash for personal use.

The chart of accounts for Terry's Window Washing contains the following accounts: No. 101 Cash, No. 112 Accounts Receivable, No. 128 Cleaning Supplies, No. 130 Prepaid Insurance, No. 157 Equipment, No. 158 Accumulated Depreciation—Equipment, No. 201 Accounts Payable, No. 212 Salaries Payable, No. 301 Terry Duffy, Capital, No. 306 Terry Duffy, Drawing, No. 350 Income Summary, No. 400 Service Revenue, No. 633 Gas & Oil Expense, No. 634 Cleaning Supplies Expense, No. 711 Depreciation Expense, No. 722 Insurance Expense, No. 726 Salaries Expense.

Instructions

(a) Journalize and post the July transactions. Use page J1 for the journal and the three-column form of account.

(b) Prepare a trial balance at July 31 on a work sheet.

(c) Enter the following adjustments on the work sheet and complete the work sheet.
  (1) Services provided but unbilled and uncollected at July 31 were $1,100.
  (2) Depreciation on equipment for the month was $200.
  (3) One-twelfth of the insurance expired.
  (4) An inventory count shows $600 of cleaning supplies on hand at July 31.
  (5) Accrued but unpaid employee salaries were $400.

(d) Prepare the income statement and owner's equity statement for July and a classified balance sheet at July 31.

(e) Journalize and post adjusting entries. Use page J2 for the journal.

(f) Journalize and post closing entries and complete the closing process. Use page J3 for the journal.

(g) Prepare a post-closing trial balance at July 31.

(b) Trial balance $16,900
(c) Adjusted trial balance $18,600
(d) Net income $4,200; Total assets $15,100
(g) Post-closing trial balance $15,300

In selected chapters, a **Comprehensive Problem** follows the A and B Problem sets. The Comprehensive Problem pulls together and uses topics you have learned over several chapters.

COMPREHENSIVE PROBLEM: CHAPTERS 2 TO 4

Bill Murphy opened Bill's Window Washing on July 1, 2002. During July, the following transactions were completed.

July 1 Invested $10,000 cash in the business.
1 Purchased a used truck for $8,000, paying $3,000 cash and the balance on account.
3 Purchased cleaning supplies for $800 on account.
5 Paid $2,400 on a one-year insurance policy, effective July 1.
12 Billed customers $3,500 for cleaning services.
18 Paid $1,000 of amount owed on truck, and $400 of amount owed on cleaning supplies.
20 Paid $1,600 for employee salaries.
21 Collected $1,400 from customer billed on July 12.

Broadening Your Perspective 81

31 Received statement from M. Brewer showing gross receipts from concessions of $8,000 and the balance due to Sabo Theater of $1,200 ($8,000 × 15%) for March. Brewer paid one-half the balance due and will remit the remainder on April 5.
31 Received $15,000 cash from admissions.

In addition to the accounts identified above, the chart of accounts includes: No. 112 Accounts Receivable, No. 405 Admission Revenue, No. 406 Concession Revenue, No. 610 Advertising Expense, No. 632 Film Rental Expense, and No. 726 Salaries Expense.

Instructions

(a) Enter the beginning balances in the ledger. Insert a check mark (✓) in the reference column of the ledger for the beginning balance.

(b) Journalize the March transactions.

(c) Post the March journal entries to the ledger. Assume that all entries are posted from page 1 of the journal.

(d) Prepare a trial balance on March 31, 2002.

Trial balance totals $118,900

The **Broadening Your Perspective** section helps you pull together various concepts covered in the chapter and apply them to real-world business decisions.

BROADENING YOUR PERSPECTIVE

FINANCIAL REPORTING AND ANALYSIS

FINANCIAL REPORTING PROBLEM: Lands' End, Inc.

BYP2-1 The financial statements of **Lands' End, Inc.** are presented in Appendix A. The notes accompanying the statements contain the following selected accounts, stated in thousands of dollars.

Accounts Payable	$ 74,510	Income Taxes Payable	$ 10,255
Accounts Receivable	17,753	Interest Expense	1,890
Property, Plant, and Equipment	283,139	Inventory	162,193

Instructions

(a) Answer the following questions.
  (1) What is the increase and decrease side for each account?
  (2) What is the normal balance for each account?

(b) Identify the probable other account in the transaction and the effect on that account when:
  (1) Accounts Receivable is decreased.
  (2) Accounts Payable is decreased.
  (3) Inventory is increased.

(c) Identify the other account(s) that ordinarily would be involved when:
  (1) Interest Expense is increased.
  (2) Property, Plant, and Equipment is increased.

The **Financial Reporting Problem** directs you to study various aspects of the financial statements in Lands' End's 2000 Annual Report, which is packaged with the text and excerpted in Appendix A at the end of the text.

COMPARATIVE ANALYSIS PROBLEM: Lands' End vs. Abercrombie & Fitch

BYP2-2 **Lands' End's** financial statements are presented in Appendix A. **Abercrombie & Fitch's** financial statements are presented in Appendix B.

Instructions

(a) Based on the information contained in the financial statements, determine the normal balance of the listed accounts for each company.

Lands' End	Abercrombie & Fitch
1. Inventory	1. Accounts Receivable
2. Property, Plant, and Equipment	2. Cash and Equivalents
3. Accounts Payable	3. Cost of Goods Sold
4. Interest Expense	4. Sales (revenue)

A **Comparative Analysis Problem** offers the opportunity to compare and contrast the financial reporting of Lands' End with that of a competitor, Abercrombie & Fitch, whose financial statements are excerpted in Appendix B.

INTERPRETING FINANCIAL STATEMENTS: A Global Focus

BYP2-3 **Doman Industries Ltd.**, whose products are sold in 30 countries worldwide, is an integrated Canadian forest products company.

Doman sells the majority of its lumber products in the United States and a significant amount of its pulp products in Asia. Doman also has loans from other countries. For example, on June 18, 1999, the Company borrowed US$160 million at an annual interest rate of 12%. Doman must repay this loan, and interest, in U.S. dollars.

One of the challenges global companies face is to make themselves attractive to investors from other countries. This is difficult to do when different accounting rules in different countries blur the real impact of earnings. For example, in 1998 Doman reported a loss of $2.3 million, using Canadian accounting rules. Had it reported under U.S. accounting rules, its loss would have been $12.1 million.

Many companies that want to be more easily compared with U.S. and other global competitors have switched to U.S. accounting principles. **Canadian National Railway**, **Corel**, **Cott**, **Inco**, and the **Thomson Corporation** are but a few examples of large Canadian companies whose financial statements are now presented in U.S. dollars, which adhere to U.S. GAAP, or are reconciled to U.S. GAAP.

Instructions

(a) Identify advantages and disadvantages that companies should consider when switching to U.S. reporting standards.

(b) Suppose you wish to compare Doman Industries to a U.S.-based competitor. Do you believe the use of country-specific accounting policies would hinder your comparison? If so, explain how.

(c) Suppose you wish to compare Doman Industries to a Canadian-based competitior. If the companies chose to apply generally acceptable Canadian accounting policies differently, how could this affect your comparison of their financial results?

(d) Do you see any significant distinction between comparing statements prepared using generally accepted accounting principles of different countries and comparing statements prepared using generally accepted accounting principles of the same country (e.g., U.S.) but that apply the principles differently?

Interpreting Financial Statements: A Global Focus asks you to apply concepts presented in the chapter to specific situations faced by actual foreign companies.

EXPLORING THE WEB

BYP2-4 Much information about specific companies is available on the World Wide Web. Such information includes basic descriptions of the company's location, activities, industry, financial health, and financial performance.

Address: biz.yahoo.com/i *(or go to www.wiley.com/college/weygandt)*

Steps:

1. Type in a company name, or use index to find company name.
2. Choose **Profile**. Perform instructions (a)–(c) below.
3. Click on the company's specific industry to identify competitors. Perform instructions

Exploring the Web exercises guide you to Internet sites where you can find and analyze information related to the chapter topic. The Internet sites referred to in the Exploring the Web exercises can be accessed directly, or by going through the textbook's Web site at **www.wiley.com/college/weygandt**. At the book's Web site you also can find many other valuable resources and activities, such as additional Internet exercises, Interactive Quizzing, and PowerPoint slides.

The **Group Decision Cases** require teams of students to evaluate a manager's decision or choose from among alternative courses of action. They help prepare you for the business world by giving you practice in solving problems with colleagues.

GROUP DECISION CASE

BYP2-5 Lucy Lars operates Lucy Lars Riding Academy. The academy's primary sources of revenue are riding fees and lesson fees, which are paid on a cash basis. Lucy also boards horses for owners, who are billed monthly for boarding fees. In a few cases, boarders pay in advance of expected use. For its revenue transactions, the academy maintains the following accounts: No. 1 Cash, No. 5 Boarding Accounts Receivable, No. 27 Unearned Boarding Revenue, No. 51 Riding Revenue, No. 52 Lesson Revenue, and No. 53 Boarding Revenue.

The academy owns 10 horses, a stable, a riding corral, riding equipment, and office equipment. These assets are accounted for in accounts No. 11 Horses, No. 12 Building, No. 13 Riding Corral, No. 14 Riding Equipment, and No. 15 Office Equipment.

For its expenses, the academy maintains the following accounts: No. 6 Hay and Feed Supplies, No. 7 Prepaid Insurance, No. 21 Accounts Payable, No. 60 Salaries Expense, No. 61 Advertising Expense, No. 62 Utilities Expense, No. 63 Veterinary Expense, No. 64 Hay and Feed Expense, and No. 65 Insurance Expense.

Communication Activities help you build business communication skills by asking you to engage in real-world business situations using writing, speaking, or presentation skills.

COMMUNICATION ACTIVITY

BYP2-6 Merlynn's Maid Company offers home cleaning service. Two recurring transactions for the company are billing customers for services rendered and paying employee salaries. For example, on March 15, bills totaling $6,000 were sent to customers and $2,000 was paid in salaries to employees.

Instructions

Write a memo to your instructor that explains and illustrates the steps in the recording process for each of the March 15 transactions. Use the format illustrated in the text under the heading, "The Recording Process Illustrated" (p. 57).

Through the **Ethics Cases**, you will reflect on typical ethical dilemmas, learn how to analyze such situations, and decide on an appropriate course of action.

ETHICS CASE

BYP2-7 Megan Menard is the assistant chief accountant at Hokey Company, a manufacturer of computer chips and cellular phones. The company presently has total sales of $20 million. It is the end of the first quarter. Megan is hurriedly trying to prepare a general ledger trial balance so that quarterly financial statements can be prepared and released to management and the regulatory agencies. The total credits on the trial balance exceed the debits by $1,000. In order to meet the 4 p.m. deadline, Megan decides to force the debits and credits into balance by adding the amount of the difference to the Equipment account. She chose Equipment because it is one of the larger account balances; percentage-wise, it will be the least misstated. Megan "plugs" the difference! She believes that the difference will not affect anyone's decisions. She wishes that she had another few days to find the error but realizes that the financial statements are already late.

Instructions

(a) Who are the stakeholders in this situation?
(b) What are the ethical issues involved in this case?
(c) What are Megan's alternatives?

Answers to Self-Study Questions provide feedback on your understanding of concepts.

Answers to Self-Study Questions

1. b 2. c 3. d 4. d 5. b 6. a 7. c 8. d 9. a 10. c

Answers to *Review It* Questions based on the Lands' End financial statements provide feedback to your search for information in the Lands' End Annual Report.

Answer to Lands' End Review It Question 4, p. 49

Cash—debit; Accounts Payable—credit; Interest Expense—debit.

After you complete your homework assignments, it's a good idea to go back to **The Navigator** checklist at the start of the chapter to see if you have used all the study aids of the chapter.

Remember to go back to the Navigator box on the chapter-opening page and check off your completed work.

HOW DO I LEARN BEST?

This questionnaire aims to find out something about your preferences for the way you work with information. You will have a preferred learning style and one part of that learning style is your preference for the intake and the output of ideas and information.

Circle the letter of the answer that best explains your preference. Circle more than one if a single answer does not match your perception. Leave blank any question that does not apply.

1. You are about to give directions to a person who is standing with you. She is staying in a hotel in town and wants to visit your house later. She has a rental car. Would you
   a. draw a map on paper?
   b. tell her the directions?
   c. write down the directions (without a map)?
   d. pick her up at the hotel in your car?
2. You are not sure whether a word should be spelled "dependent" or "dependant." Do you
   c. look it up in the dictionary?
   a. see the word in your mind and choose by the way it looks?
   b. sound it out in your mind?
   d. write both versions down on paper and choose one?
3. You have just received a copy of your itinerary for a world trip. This is of interest to a friend. Would you
   b. call her immediately and tell her about it?
   c. send her a copy of the printed itinerary?
   a. show her on a map of the world?
   d. share what you plan to do at each place you visit?
4. You are going to cook something as a special treat for your family. Do you
   d. cook something familiar without the need for instructions?
   a. thumb through the cookbook looking for ideas from the pictures?
   c. refer to a specific cookbook where there is a good recipe?
5. A group of tourists has been assigned to you to find out about wildlife reserves or parks. Would you
   d. drive them to a wildlife reserve or park?
   a. show them slides and photographs?
   c. give them pamphlets or a book on wildlife reserves or parks?
   b. give them a talk on wildlife reserves or parks?
6. You are about to purchase a new CD player. Other than price, what would most influence your decision?
   b. The salesperson telling you what you want to know.
   c. Reading the details about it.
   d. Playing with the controls and listening to it.
   a. Its fashionable and upscale appearance.
7. Recall a time in your life when you learned how to do something like playing a new board game. Try to avoid choosing a very physical skill, e.g., riding a bike. How did you learn best? By
   a. visual clues — pictures, diagrams, charts?
   c. written instructions?
   b. listening to somebody explaining it?
   d. doing it or trying it?
8. You have an eye problem. Would you prefer that the doctor
   b. tell you what is wrong?
   a. show you a diagram of what is wrong?
   d. use a model to show what is wrong?
9. You are about to learn to use a new program on a computer. Would you
   d. sit down at the keyboard and begin to experiment with the program's features?
   c. read the manual that comes with the program?
   b. call a friend and ask questions about it?
10. You are staying in a hotel and have a rental car. You would like to visit friends whose address/location you do not know. Would you like them to
    a. draw you a map on paper?
    b. tell you the directions?
    c. write down the directions (without a map)?
    d. pick you up at the hotel in their car?
11. Apart from price, what would most influence your decision to buy a particular book?
    d. You have used a copy before.
    b. A friend talking about it.
    c. Quickly reading parts of it.
    a. The appealing way it looks.
12. A new movie has arrived in town. What would most influence your decision to go (or not go)?
    b. You heard a radio review about it.
    c. You read a review about it.
    a. You saw a preview of it.
13. Do you prefer a lecturer or teacher who likes to use
    c. a textbook, handouts, readings?
    a. flow diagrams, charts, graphs?
    d. field trips, labs, practical sessions?
    b. discussion, guest speakers?

	a.	b.	c.	d.
Count your choices:	❑	❑	❑	❑
	V	A	R	K

Now match the letter or letters you have recorded most to the same letter or letters in the Learning Styles Chart. You may have more than one learning style preference—many people do. Next to each letter in the chart are suggestions that will refer you to different learning aids throughout this text.

LEARNING STYLES CHART

V VISUAL

INTAKE: TO TAKE IN THE INFORMATION	TO MAKE A STUDY PACKAGE	TEXT FEATURES THAT MAY HELP YOU THE MOST	OUTPUT: TO DO WELL ON EXAMS
• Pay close attention to charts, drawings, and handouts your instructor uses. • Underline. • Use different colors. • Use symbols, flow charts, graphs, different arrangements on the page, white space.	Convert your lecture notes into "page pictures." To do this: • Use the "Intake" strategies. • Reconstruct images in different ways. • Redraw pages from memory. • Replace words with symbols and initials. • Look at your pages.	**The Navigator** **Feature Story** **Preview** **Infographics/Illustrations** **Photos** **Accounting in Action** **Accounting Equation Analyses** **Key Terms in blue** **Words in bold** **Demonstration Problem/Action Plan** **Questions/Exercises/Problems** **Financial Reporting Problem** **Comparative Analysis Problem** **Interpreting Financial Statements** **Exploring the Web**	• Recall your "page pictures." • Draw diagrams where appropriate. • Practice turning your visuals back into words.

A AURAL

INTAKE: TO TAKE IN THE INFORMATION	TO MAKE A STUDY PACKAGE	TEXT FEATURES THAT MAY HELP YOU THE MOST	OUTPUT: TO DO WELL ON EXAMS
• Attend lectures and tutorials. • Discuss topics with students and instructors. • Explain new ideas to other people. • Use a tape recorder. • Leave spaces in your lecture notes for later recall. • Describe overheads, pictures, and visuals to somebody who was not in class.	You may take poor notes because you prefer to listen. Therefore: • Expand your notes by talking with others and with information from your textbook. • Tape record summarized notes and listen. • Read summarized notes out loud. • Explain your notes to another "aural" person.	**Preview** **Infographics/Illustrations** **Accounting in Action** **Review It/Do It/Action Plan** **Summary of Study Objectives** **Glossary** **Demonstration Problem/Action Plan** **Self-Study Questions** **Questions/Exercises/Problems** **Financial Reporting Problem** **Comparative Analysis Problem** **Exploring the Web** **Group Decision Case** **Communication Activity** **Ethics Case**	• Talk with the instructor. • Spend time in quiet places recalling the ideas. • Practice writing answers to old exam questions. • Say your answers out loud.

R READING/WRITING

INTAKE: TO TAKE IN THE INFORMATION	TO MAKE A STUDY PACKAGE	TEXT FEATURES THAT MAY HELP YOU THE MOST	OUTPUT: TO DO WELL ON EXAMS
• Use lists and headings. • Use dictionaries, glossaries, and definitions. • Read handouts, textbooks, and supplementary library readings. • Use lecture notes.	• Write out words again and again. • Reread notes silently. • Rewrite ideas and principles into other words. • Turn charts, diagrams, and other illustrations into statements.	**The Navigator** **Feature Story** **Study Objectives** **Preview** **Review It/Do It/Action Plan** **Summary of Study Objectives** **Glossary** **Self-Study Questions** **Questions/Exercises/Problems** **Writing Problems** **Financial Reporting Problem** **Comparative Analysis Problem** **Interpreting Financial Statements: Global Focus** **Exploring the Web** **Group Decision Case** **Communication Activity**	• Write exam answers. • Practice with multiple-choice questions. • Write paragraphs, beginnings and endings. • Write your lists in outline form. • Arrange your words into hierarchies and points.

K KINESTHETIC

INTAKE: TO TAKE IN THE INFORMATION	TO MAKE A STUDY PACKAGE	TEXT FEATURES THAT MAY HELP YOU THE MOST	OUTPUT: TO DO WELL ON EXAMS
• Use all your senses. • Go to labs, take field trips. • Listen to real-life examples. • Pay attention to applications. • Use hands-on approaches. • Use trial-and-error methods.	You may take poor notes because topics do not seem concrete or relevant. Therefore: • Put examples in your summaries. • Use case studies and applications to help with principles and abstract concepts. • Talk about your notes with another "kinesthetic" person. • Use pictures and photographs that illustrate an idea.	**The Navigator** **Feature Story** **Preview** **Infographics/Illustrations** **Review It/Do It/Action Plan** **Summary of Study Objectives** **Demonstration Problem/Action Plan** **Self-Study Questions** **Questions/Exercises/Problems** **Financial Reporting Problem** **Comparative Analysis Problem** **Interpreting Financial Statements: Global Focus** **Exploring the Web** **Group Decision Case** **Communication Activity**	• Write practice answers. • Role-play the exam situation.

For all learning styles: Be sure to use the CD to enhance your understanding of the concepts and procedures of the text. In particular, use the **Study Skills Tips**, **Interactive Navigator**, **Accounting Cycle Tutorial**, **Additional Demonstration Problems**, **Interactive Self-Tests**, and **Key Term Matching Activities.**

SPECIAL STUDENT SUPPLEMENTS THAT HELP YOU GET THE BEST GRADE YOU CAN

The Accounting Principles Web Site at http://www.wiley.com/college/weygandt

This resource and learning tool serves as a launching pad for you to numerous activities, resources, and related sites. On the Web site, you'll find Exploring the Web activities, Internet Exercises, Interactive Quizzing, Learning Styles Assessment, and more. In addition, there are links to companies discussed in the text and items available for downloading such as the PowerPoint Presentations.

NEW Accounting Principles, Interactive Learning Edition

The Interactive Learning Edition (ILE) combines the full text with interactive learning tools to accommodate various learning styles. This dynamic *ebook* offers an active approach to learning that enables you to do things like take detailed notes in the program's text, highlight important information as you read the text, consult a hypertext glossary by simply rolling over key words in the text, search the text, and view additional media such as animations and videos.

Working Papers Volume I: Chapters 1–13 and Volume II: Chapters 14–27

Working Papers are partially completed accounting forms for all end-of-chapter exercises, problems, and cases. A convenient resource for organizing and completing homework assignments, the Working Papers demonstrate how to correctly set up solution formats and are tied directly to textbook assignments.

NEW Electronic Working Papers

Available on a CD-ROM, these Excel-formatted, partially completed accounting forms can be used for end-of-chapter exercises, problems, and cases.

Problem-Solving Survival Guide Volume I: Chapters 1–13 and Volume II: Chapters 14–27

The Problem-Solving Survival Guide tutorial is designed to improve your success rate in solving accounting principles homework assignments and exam questions. The Problem-Solving Survival Guide also provides additional insight and tips on how to study accounting. Each chapter includes an overview of key chapter topics and a review of chapter study objectives; purpose statements for each question, case, or exercise and a direct link to study objectives; and tips to alert you to common pitfalls and misconceptions, as well as reminders of concepts and principles to help solve problems. A selection of multiple-choice exercises and cases representative of common exam questions or homework assignments enhance your proficiency, and detailed solutions and explanations assist you in the approach, setup, and completion of problems.

This new edition also features an online companion powered by WILEY eGrade. This online version includes all of the wonderful resources and tips for solving accounting principles homework assignments and exam questions as the print version, within an interactive Web environment. It provides you with immediate scoring and individualized feedback on your work. The ***eGrade* Student Learning Guide**, automatically bundled with the Problem-Solving Survival Guide, helps you in getting started with the *eGrade* Online Assessment System.

Student Study Guide Volume I: Chapters 1–13 and Volume II: Chapters 14–27

The Student Study Guide is a comprehensive review of accounting and a powerful tool for you to use in the classroom, guiding you through chapter content, tied to study objectives, and providing resources for use during lectures. This is an excellent resource when preparing for exams.

Each chapter of the Student Study Guide includes study objectives and a chapter review consisting of 20 to 30 key points; a demonstration problem linked to study objectives in the textbook; and additional opportunities for you to practice your knowledge and skills through true/false, multiple-choice, and matching questions related to key terms and exercises linked to study objectives. Solutions to the exercises explain the hows and whys so you get immediate feedback.

NEW A Reader's Guide to Accounting Principles: Strategies for Successful Reading and Supplemental Glossary

With this guide, you will learn reading strategies that will increase your comprehension, help you remember information better, and make your experience reading *Accounting Principles* more successful.

Business Extra Web Site at http://www.wiley.com/college/businessextra

The Business Extra Web site gives you instant access to a wealth of current articles dealing with all aspects of financial and managerial accounting. The articles are organized by topic, and discussion questions follow each article. The Business Extra password card is available for purchase.

NEW WSJ.com at http://www.wiley.com/college/wsjseries

Get "street smart" using *The Wall Street Journal*! WSJ.com contains articles and activities that put you at the cutting edge of today's business world. *The Journal* offers essential tools for business success, including resources for research and advice on career development. The WSJ.com password card is available for purchase.

Practice Sets

Practice sets expose you to a real-world simulation of maintaining a complete set of accounting records for a business. You'll find that practice sets reinforce the concepts and procedures learned in each chapter of the textbook. They also show you how concepts and procedures are brought together to generate the accounting information that is essential in assessing the financial position and operating results of a company. The practice sets available are:

- Campus Cycle Shop
- Heritage Home Furniture
- University Bookstore, Inc.
- *NEW* Custom Party Associates

General Ledger Software

The General Ledger Software program allows you to solve selected end-of-chapter text problems, which are identified by an icon in the margin of the text, using a computerized accounting system. The software allows you to complete the Campus Cycle Shop, Heritage Home Furniture, University Bookstore, Inc., and Custom Party Associates practice sets on a computer.

NEW Peachtree Complete® Accounting Problems and Software

Peachtree

The Peachtree Complete® Accounting Problems are selected problems denoted by the Peachtree logo that can be solved using *Peachtree Complete® Accounting to Accompany Accounting Principles, Sixth Edition.* A separate student workbook that includes the newly released software is available.

Solving Accounting Principles Problems Using Excel and Lotus 1-2-3

These electronic spreadsheet templates (available in either Excel or Lotus) allow you to complete selected end-of-chapter exercises and problems, identified by an icon in the margin of the text. The manuals, which include the disks, guide you step-by-step from an introduction to computers and Excel or Lotus, to completing preprogrammed spreadsheets, to designing your own spreadsheets.

ACKNOWLEDGMENTS

During the course of the development of *Accounting Principles*, Sixth Edition, the authors benefited greatly from feedback from numerous instructors and students of accounting principles courses throughout the country, including many users of the Fifth Edition of the text. Their criticism, constructive suggestions, and innovative ideas helped focus the revision on the needs of the students. We are indebted to the contributions of the following accounting professionals.

Reviewers and Focus Group Participants for Prior Editions of Accounting Principles

Hector Agostini, Middlesex Community College; Linda Alderson, Cabrillo College; Marilyn Allan, Central Michigan University; Walter Allen, North Virginia Community College; Melody Ashenfelter, Southwestern Oklahoma State University; Peter Barton, University of Wisconsin-Whitewater; Abdul Baten, North Virginia Community College; Don Baynham, Eastfield College; Janet Becker, University of Pittsburgh-Johnstown; Steven Becker, University of Wisconsin-Platteville; Harold Bland, Roosevelt University; Dennis Bolen, Augustana College; Lana Bone, West Valley College; Nancy Boyd, Middle Tennessee State University; Eugene Braun, North Virginia Community College; Russell Breslaur, Chabot College; William Brooks, Southwestern Oklahoma State University; Virginia Brunell, Diablo Valley College; Jim Bryant, Catonsville Community College; Terry Bullock, College of DuPage; Ashley Burrowes, California State University-Bakersfield; Madeline Carlin, University of Pittsburgh; Lloyd Carroll, Borough of Manhattan Community College; Janet Cassagio, Nassau Community College; Randy Castello, West Valley College; Ed Castelloe, Lincoln Land Community College; Barbara Chiapetta, Nassau Community College; Joan Cook, Milwaukee Area Technical College; John Corradetti, Joliet Junior College; Sharon Cotton, Schoolcraft College; Carolyn Craig, Shepherd College; Mark Dawson, Indiana University of Pennsylvania; Michael Deda, Fairleigh Dickinson University; Irene Douma, Montclair State College; Charles Downing, Massasoit Community College; Roger DuFresne, Northern Essex Community College; Dean Eiteman, Indiana University of Pennsylvania; David Erlich, Queens College; Cecelia Fewox, Trident Technical College; Carl Fisher, Foothills College; Michael Foland, Belleville Area College; Jeannie Folk, College of DuPage; Mary Kathryn Gardner, Johnson & Wales University; Angelo Gazzola, University of Wisconsin-Fox Valley; Robert Giacoletti, Eastern Kentucky University; Debra Goorbin, Westchester Community College; Ed Gordon, Triton College; W. Michael Gough, DeAnza College; Janet Grange, Chicago State University; Don Green, State University of New York-Farmingdale; Gloria Halpern, Montgomery College; Margie Hamilton, Lewis & Clark Community College; Clo Hampton, West Valley College; Ken Hardy, Catonsville Community College; Patricia Harrison, University of New Orleans; John Hartwick, Bucks County Community College; Nabil Hassan, Wright State University; Alene Helling, Stark Technical College; Keith Hendrick, Wallace State College; Thomas Hofmeister, Northwestern Business School; Lou Jacoby, Saginaw Valley State University; Joe Kederabek, Baldwin-Wallace College; Janice Kelley, St. Louis Community College; Robert Kirsch, Bowling Green State University; Shirly Kleiner, Johnson County Community College; Carol Klinger, Queens College; Jeanette Klosterman, Hutchinson Community College; Roann Kopel, Eastern Illinois University; John Lannen, Salem State College; Doug Larson, Salem State College; Kathy Larson, Middlesex Community College; Larry Larson, Triton College; Robyn Lawrence, University of Scranton; Bruce Leauby, LaSalle University; Marcella Lecky, University of Southwestern Louisiana; Henri LeClerc, Suffolk Community College; Paul Lisowski, Edinboro University; Garry Lym, Golden Gate University; Johnnie Mapp, Norfolk State University; Mary Maury, St. John's University; Jean McKenzie, Fergus Falls Community College; Noel McKeon, Florida Community College-Jacksonville; Greg Mostyn, Mission College; Rhonda Mulkonen, University of South Dakota; Deborah Niemer, Oakland Community College-Royal Oak; Betty Nolen, Floyd Junior College; Cletus O'Drobinak, South Suburban College; Lynn Mazzola Paluska, Nassau Community College; Deanne Pannell, Pellissippi State Technical College; Sandra Penn, Wayne State University; Wayne Pfingsten, Belleville Area College; Rose Marie Pilcher, Abilene Christian University; Beverly Piper, Ashland University; Paul Polachek, Loyola University of Chicago; Kay Poston, Arizona State University-West Campus; Charles Reilly, Suffolk Community College; Bill Reynolds, St. Charles Community College; James Rosa, Queensborough Community College; Victoria Rymer, University of Maryland; Stephen Schaefer, Contra Costa College; Nancy Sheridan, Bucks County Community College; Barry Smith, DeAnza College; Jerome Spallino, Westmoreland Community College; Melvin Stinnett, Oklahoma Christian University; John Sullivan, North Shore Community College; Carolyn Strikler, Ohlone College; Lynda Thompson, Massasoit Community College; Cynthia Tomes, Des Moines Area Community College-Urban Campus; Karen Ulbrich, Parkland College; DuWayne Wacker, University of North Dakota; Janis Waivio, Delta College; Daniel Ward, Southwest Louisiana State University; Michael Watters, New Mexico State University; John Wells, Triton College; Robert Wernagel, College of the Mainland; Kathleen Wessman, Montgomery College; Chris Widmer, Tidewater Community College; Steven Wong, San Jose City College.

Reviewers and Focus Group Participants for Accounting Principles, *Sixth Edition*

Victoria Beard, University of North Dakota; Ken Couvillion, San Joaquin Delta College; Linda Dening, Jefferson Community College; Albert Fisher, Community College of Southern Nevada; George Gardner, Bemidji State University; Marc Giullian, University of Louisiana-Lafayette; Kathy Horton, College of DuPage; Margaret Hoskins, Henderson State University; Inam Hussain, Purdue University; Sharon Johnson, Kansas City Community College; J. Suzanne King, University of Charleston; Terry Kubichan, Old Dominion University; Melanie Mackey, Ocean County College; Jamie O'Brien, South Dakota State University; Shelly Ota, Leeward Community College; Peter J. Poznanski, Cleveland State University; David Ravetch, University of California-Los Angeles; Paul J. Shinal, Cayuga Community College; Beverly Terry, Central Piedmont Community College.

Student Reviewers for Prior Editions of Accounting Principles*—Schools*

Appalachian State University, College of Lake County, Hofstra University, Massasoit Community College, Nassau Community College, North Carolina A & M University, Ocean County Community College, Ohlone State College, Phoenix College, Providence College, Queensborough Community College, University of Maine-Bangor, University of Scranton, University of Southwestern Louisiana, University of Texas-San Antonio, Wake Forest Technical College.

Student Reviewers for Accounting Principles, *Sixth Edition*

Special thanks go to Kathy Horton and the students of the *College of DuPage* and to Alphonse J. Ruggiero and the students of *Suffolk County Community College.*

Reviewers of Supplements for Prior Editions of Accounting Principles

Jim Benedum, Milwaukee Area Technical College; Joan Cook, Milwaukee Area Technical College; Gaspare Di-Lorenzo, Gloucester County College; David Erlach, Queens College; Mark Holtzman, Hofstra University; Phil Kishimori, Leeward Community College; Lynn Koshiyama, University of Alaska-Anchorage; Laura Ruff, Milwaukee Area Technical College; Nathan Saltzberg, Milwaukee Area Technical College; Anita Singer, Kings College; Daniel Small, Jay Sargeant Reynolds Community College; David Zaumeyer, Rutgers University.

General Ledger Software Advisory Board

Denise Bloom, Upper Iowa University; Kevin Dooley, Kapiolani Community College; Peter Doran, North Shore Community College; Jeannie Folk, College of DuPage; Carolyn Harris, University of Texas-San Antonio; Molly Linksz, Anne Arundel Community College; Shelly Ota, Leeward Community College; Patricia A. Robinson, Johnson & Wales University; Robert R. Rovegno, Suffolk Community College; Alphonse J. Ruggiero, Suffolk Community College; Karen Russom, North Harris Community College; Lynda Thompson, Massasoit Community College; Anne Tippitt, Tarrant County Junior College-South Campus.

Special Thanks

Special thanks to Barbara Trenholm, University of New Brunswich, for her insights, and a very special thank you to Ann Torbert for her outstanding editorial efforts and other contributions that raised the quality of this book.

We also sincerely appreciate the work of the supplement authors for the Sixth Edition: Marianne Bradford, Bryant College; Mel Coe, DeVry Institute of Technology—Atlanta; Joan Cook, Milwaukee Area Technical College; Denise M. English, Boise State University; Larry Falcetto, Emporia State University; Patricia Fedje, Minot State University; Sarah L. Frank, University of West Florida; Jessica Frazier, Eastern Kentucky University; Candace Humphrey, Northeast Iowa Community College; Marilyn Hunt, University of Central Florida; Doug Kieso, University of California—Irvine; David R. Koeppen, Boise State University; Gary Lubin, Merck; Sally Nelson, Northeast Iowa Community College; Rex A. Schildhouse, University of Phoenix—San Diego Campus; David Schwinghamer, Collège Ahuntsic, Montreal; Dick Wasson, Southwestern College.

We also thank those who have assured the accuracy of our supplements: Jack Borke, University of Wisconsin-Platteville; Denise M. English, Boise State University; Marc Giullian, University of Louisiana—Lafayette; Jennifer Laudermilch, Coopers & Lybrand; David R. Koeppen, Boise State University; Laura Ruff, Milwaukee Area Technical College—West; Alice Sineath, Forsyth Technical College; Teresa Speck, St. Mary's University; Chris Tomas, Northeast Iowa Community College; Beth M. Woods, CPA.

In addition, special recognition goes to Ivan Pagan of the University of Wisconsin-Madison and Jo Koehn of Central Missouri State University for their work in applying Bloom's Taxonomy; to Karen Huffman of Palomar College for her assessment of the text's pedagogy and suggestions on how to increase its helpfulness to students; to Gary R. Morrison of Wayne State University for his review of the instructional design; to Nancy Galli of Palomar College for her work on learning styles; and to Wayne Higley of Buena Vista University for his technical proofing.

We also thank the editorial, marketing, production, design, and illustration staff of John Wiley & Sons. The following individuals were particularly helpful: Brent Gordon, Nancy Perry, David Kear, Susan Elbe, Joe Heider, Clancy Marshall, Cynthia Taylor, Summer Macey, Robert Meador, Steve Kazlauskas, Alida Setford, Jeanine Furino, Dawn Stanley, Madelyn Lesure, Sandra Rigby, Sara Wight, Mary Ann Benson, Alison Bamert, Sarah Warfield, Lenore Belton, Jaime Perea, and Marsheela Evans. In addition, a note of gratitude to Ginger Yarrow, Barb Lange, and Jennifer Wood of Elm Street Publishing Services and Jackie Henry of York Graphic Services for their help on this project.

Finally, our thanks for the support provided by Will Pesce, President and Chief Executive Officer, and Bonnie Lieberman, Senior Vice-President of the College Division. Suggestions and comments from users—instructors and students alike—will be appreciated.

Jerry J. Weygandt
Donald E. Kieso
Paul D. Kimmel

BRIEF CONTENTS

DETAILED CONTENTS

ABOUT THE AUTHORS

Jerry J. Weygandt, PhD, CPA, is Arthur Andersen Alumni Professor of Accounting at the University of Wisconsin — Madison. He holds a Ph.D. in accounting from the University of Illinois. Articles by Professor Weygandt have appeared in the *Accounting Review, Journal of Accounting Research, Accounting Horizons, Journal of Accountancy*, and other academic and professional journals. These articles have examined such financial reporting issues as accounting for price-level adjustments, pensions, convertible securities, stock option contracts, and interim reports. Professor Weygandt is author of other accounting and financial reporting books and is a member of the American Accounting Association, the American Institute of Certified Public Accountants, and the Wisconsin Society of Certified Public Accountants. He has served on numerous committees of the American Accounting Association and as a member of the editorial board of the *Accounting Review*; he also has served as President and Secretary-Treasurer of the American Accounting Association. In addition, he has been actively involved with the American Institute of Certified Public Accountants and has been a member of the Accounting Standards Executive Committee (AcSEC) of that organization. He has served on the FASB task force that examined the reporting issues related to accounting for income taxes and is presently a trustee of the Financial Accounting Foundation. Professor Weygandt has received the Chancellor's Award for Excellence in Teaching and the Beta Gamma Sigma Dean's Teaching Award. He is on the board of directors of M & I Bank of Southern Wisconsin and the Dean Foundation. He is the recipient of the Wisconsin Institute of CPA's Outstanding Educator's Award and the Lifetime Achievement Award. In 2001 he received the American Accounting Association's Outstanding Accounting Educator Award.

Donald E. Kieso, PhD, CPA, received his bachelor's degree from Aurora University and his doctorate in accounting from the University of Illinois. He has served as chairman of the Department of Accountancy and is currently the KPMG Peat Marwick Emeritus Professor of Accountancy at Northern Illinois University. He has public accounting experience with Price Waterhouse & Co. (San Francisco and Chicago) and Arthur Andersen & Co. (Chicago) and research experience with the Research Division of the American Institute of Certified Public Accountants (New York). He has done postdoctorate work as a Visiting Scholar at the University of California at Berkeley and is a recipient of NIU's Teaching Excellence Award and four Golden Apple Teaching Awards. Professor Kieso is the author of other accounting and business books and is a member of the American Accounting Association, the American Institute of Certified Public Accountants, and the Illinois CPA Society. He has served as a member of the Board of Directors of the Illinois CPA Society, the AACSB's Accounting Accreditation Committees, the State of Illinois Comptroller's Commission, as Secretary-Treasurer of the Federation of Schools of Accountancy, and as Secretary-Treasurer of the American Accounting Association. Professor Kieso is currently serving on the Board of Trustees and Executive Committee of Aurora University, as a member of the Board of Directors of Castle BancGroup Inc., and as Treasurer and Director of Valley West Community Hospital. From 1989 to 1993 he served as a charter member of the national Accounting Education Change Commission. In 1988 he received the Outstanding Accounting Educator Award from the Illinois CPA Society, in 1992 he received the FSA's Joseph A. Silvoso Award of Merit and the NIU Foundation's Humanitarian Award for Service to Higher Education, in 1995 he received a Distinguished Service Award from the Illinois CPA Society, and in 2000 he was awarded the Community Citizen of the Year Award by Rotary International.

Paul D. Kimmel, PhD, CPA, received his bachelor's degree from the University of Minnesota and his doctorate in accounting from the University of Wisconsin. He is an Associate Professor at the University of Wisconsin — Milwaukee, and has public accounting experience with Deloitte & Touche (Minneapolis). He was the recipient of the UWM School of Business Advisory Council Teaching Award, the Reggie Taite Excellence in Teaching Award, and a three-time winner of the Outstanding Teaching Assistant Award at the University of Wisconsin. He is also a recipient of the Elijah Watts Sells Award for Honorary Distinction for his results on the CPA exam. He is a member of the American Accounting Association and has published articles in *Accounting Review, Accounting Horizons, Issues in Accounting Education, Journal of Accounting Education*, as well as other journals. His research interests include accounting for financial instruments and innovation in accounting education. He has published papers and given numerous talks on incorporating critical thinking into accounting education, and helped prepare a catalog of critical thinking resources for the Federated Schools of Accountancy.

ACCOUNTING IN ACTION

1

THE NAVIGATOR ✓

- Understand *Concepts for Review* ❑
- Read *Feature Story* ❑
- Scan *Study Objectives* ❑
- Read *Preview* ❑
- Read text and answer *Before You Go On* *p.* 9 ❑ *p.* 14 ❑ *p.* 21 ❑ *p.* 25 ❑
- Work *Demonstration Problem* ❑
- Review *Summary of Study Objectives* ❑
- Answer *Self-Study Questions* ❑
- Complete *Assignments* ❑

The Navigator is a learning system designed to prompt you to use the learning aids in the chapter and set priorities as you study.

CONCEPTS FOR REVIEW

Before studying this chapter, you should know or, if necessary, review:

a. How to use the study aids in this book. (Student Owner's Manual, pages iv-xiii)

b. How you learn best. (Student Owner's Manual, pages xiv–xvi)

c. The nature of the special student supplements that accompany this textbook. (Student Owner's Manual, pages xvii–xviii)

Concepts for Review highlight concepts from your earlier reading that you need to understand before starting the new chapter.

THE NAVIGATOR

The Feature Story helps you picture how the chapter topic relates to the real world of accounting and business. You will find references to the story throughout the chapter and in the exercise set toward the end of the chapter.

FEATURE STORY

Things Rarely Go the Way You Plan

As the Scottish poet Robert Burns said, "The best laid schemes o' mice an' men gang aft a'gley." Or, in plain English, things rarely go the way you plan. Take, for example, the life of Gary Comer. Gary wanted to start a company, he liked to sail, and he knew how to write ad copy for catalogs. So in 1963 Gary founded a company that sold sailing gear by catalog. Until 1975 the company, located in Chicago, was primarily a struggling sailing-gear company. That year, 28 pages of its 30-page catalog were devoted to sailing. Only two years later a shift had begun. By then, 13 pages of its 40-page catalog were devoted to clothing.

In the nearly 40 years since the company was founded, much has changed: The company no longer sells sailing gear, it is no longer headquartered in Chicago, and Gary no longer writes his own ad copy. Instead, the copy for the 260 million catalogs that his company distributes annually is written by some of the 7,200 people Gary now employs.

His company, **Lands' End, Inc.**, still relies on catalogs to generate most of its $1 billion in annual sales. In the future the company wants to be able to sell its goods throughout the world, and to do so using retail stores, catalogs, or the Internet—whatever it takes to get the goods out the door and onto the customers' backs.

Although things do not always go as planned, *lack* of planning is often a recipe for disaster. Lands' End did not become one of the largest mail-order companies in the world without careful planning. Its managers are constantly working to increase revenues and minimize costs. Careful consideration must be given to many types of decisions: what new products to sell and which to discontinue, how to finance current operations and expansion, where to locate, and whether to buy or rent properties.

The information needed for these decisions is provided by the company's accounting system. In addition, the company must report its results to the investors and creditors who provide it with the funds it needs to operate. A company communicates its past performance and its plans for the future in its annual report. A copy of the Lands' End, Inc. 2000 Annual Report accompanies this text. In this book you will learn how the accounting information in the annual report was determined, and how to use such information to make business decisions of all sorts.

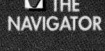

THE NAVIGATOR

www.landsend.com

STUDY OBJECTIVES

After studying this chapter, you should be able to:

Study Objectives give you a framework for learning the specific concepts covered in the chapter.

1. Explain what accounting is.
2. Identify the users and uses of accounting.
3. Understand why ethics is a fundamental business concept.
4. Explain the meaning of generally accepted accounting principles and the cost principle.
5. Explain the meaning of the monetary unit assumption and the economic entity assumption.
6. State the basic accounting equation, and explain the meaning of assets, liabilities, and owner's equity.
7. Analyze the effects of business transactions on the basic accounting equation.
8. Understand what the four financial statements are and how they are prepared.

THE NAVIGATOR

PREVIEW OF CHAPTER 1

The opening story about **Lands' End, Inc.** highlights the importance of having good financial information to make effective business decisions. Whatever one's pursuits or occupation, the need for financial information is inescapable. You cannot earn a living, spend money, buy on credit, make an investment, or pay taxes without receiving, using, or dispensing financial information. Good decision making depends on good information.

The purpose of this chapter is to show you that accounting is the system used to provide useful financial information. The content and organization of Chapter 1 are as follows.

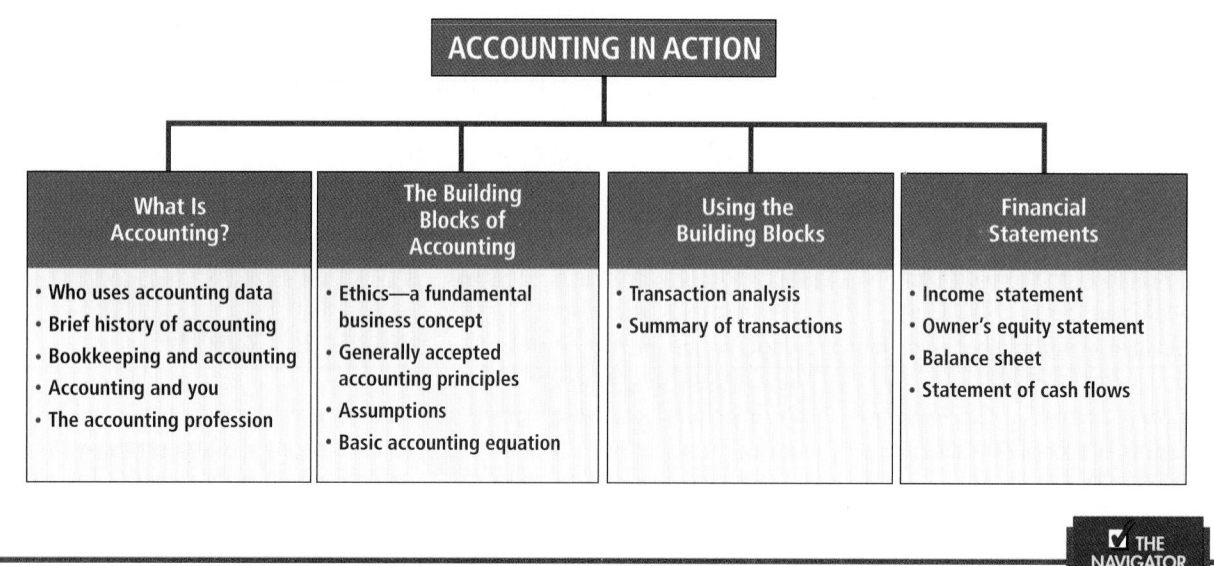

ACCOUNTING IN ACTION

- **What Is Accounting?**
  - Who uses accounting data
  - Brief history of accounting
  - Bookkeeping and accounting
  - Accounting and you
  - The accounting profession
- **The Building Blocks of Accounting**
  - Ethics—a fundamental business concept
  - Generally accepted accounting principles
  - Assumptions
  - Basic accounting equation
- **Using the Building Blocks**
  - Transaction analysis
  - Summary of transactions
- **Financial Statements**
  - Income statement
  - Owner's equity statement
  - Balance sheet
  - Statement of cash flows

THE NAVIGATOR

The **Preview** describes and outlines the major topics and subtopics you will see in the chapter.

WHAT IS ACCOUNTING?

STUDY OBJECTIVE 1

Explain what accounting is.

Essential terms are printed in blue when they first appear, and are defined in the end-of-chapter glossary.

Accounting is an information system that **identifies**, **records**, and **communicates** the economic events of an organization to interested users. Let's take a closer look at these three activities.

1. **Identifying** economic events involves selecting the **economic activities relevant to a particular organization**. The sale of goods by **Lands' End**, the providing of services by **Sprint**, the payment of wages by **Ford Motor Company**, and the collection of ticket and broadcast money and the payment of expenses by major league sports teams are examples of economic events.
2. Once identified, economic events are **recorded** to provide a history of the organization's financial activities. Recording consists of keeping a **systematic, chronological diary of events**, measured in dollars and cents. In recording, economic events are also classified and summarized.
3. The identifying and recording activities are of little use unless the information is **communicated** to interested users. Financial information is communicated through **accounting reports**, the most common of which are called **financial statements**. To make the reported financial information meaningful, accountants report the recorded data in a standardized way. Information resulting

from similar transactions is accumulated and totaled. For example, all sales transactions of **Lands' End** are accumulated over a certain period of time and reported as one amount in the company's financial statements. Such data are said to be reported **in the aggregate**. By presenting the recorded data in the aggregate, the accounting process simplifies a multitude of transactions and makes a series of activities understandable and meaningful.

References throughout the chapter tie the accounting concepts you are learning to the story that opened the chapter.

A vital element in communicating economic events is the accountant's ability to **analyze** and **interpret** the reported information. Analysis involves the use of ratios, percentages, graphs, and charts to highlight significant financial trends and relationships. Interpretation involves **explaining the uses, meaning, and limitations of reported data**. Appendix A of this textbook illustrates the financial statements and accompanying notes and graphs from **Lands' End, Inc.**; Appendix B illustrates the financial statements of **Abercrombie & Fitch Co.** We refer to these statements at various places throughout the text. At this point, they probably strike you as complex and confusing. By the end of this course, you'll be surprised at your ability to understand and interpret them.

In summary, the accounting process may be summarized as follows.

Illustration 1-1

Accounting process

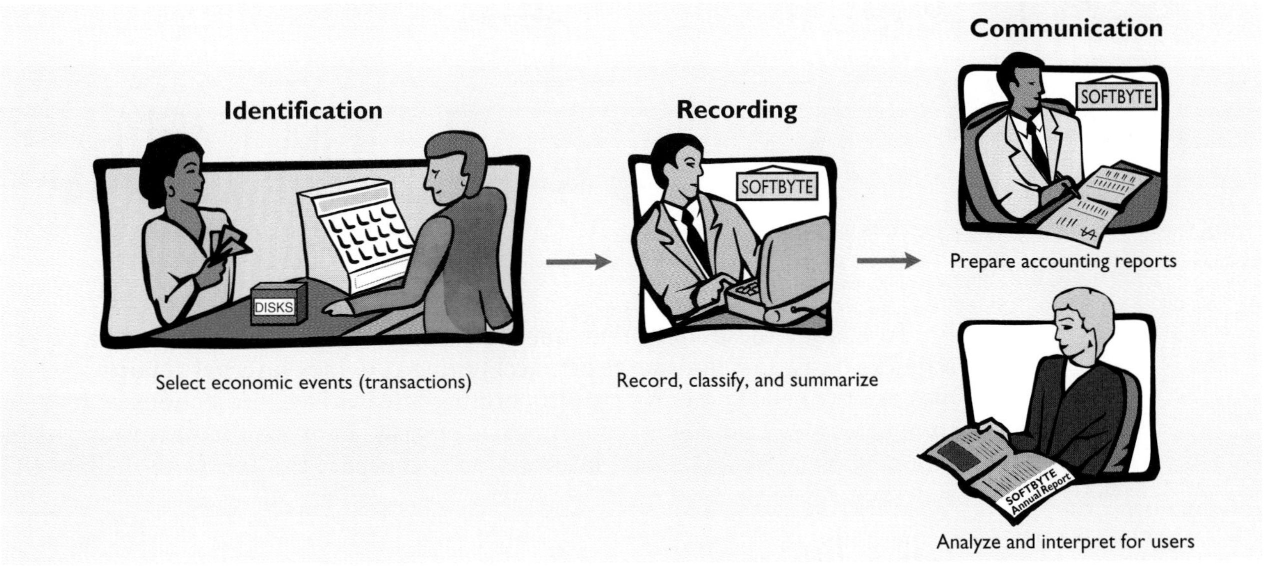

Accounting should consider the needs of the users of financial information. Therefore, you should know who these users are and something about their needs for information.

WHO USES ACCOUNTING DATA

STUDY OBJECTIVE 2

Identify the users and uses of accounting.

Because it communicates financial information, accounting is often called "the language of business." The information that a user of financial information needs depends upon the kinds of decisions the user makes. The differences in the decisions divide the users of financial information into two broad groups: internal users and external users.

Internal Users

Internal users of accounting information are managers who plan, organize, and run a business. These include **marketing managers**, **production supervisors**, **finance directors**, **and company officers**. In running a business, managers must answer many important questions, as shown in Illustration 1-2.

Illustration 1-2
Questions asked by internal users

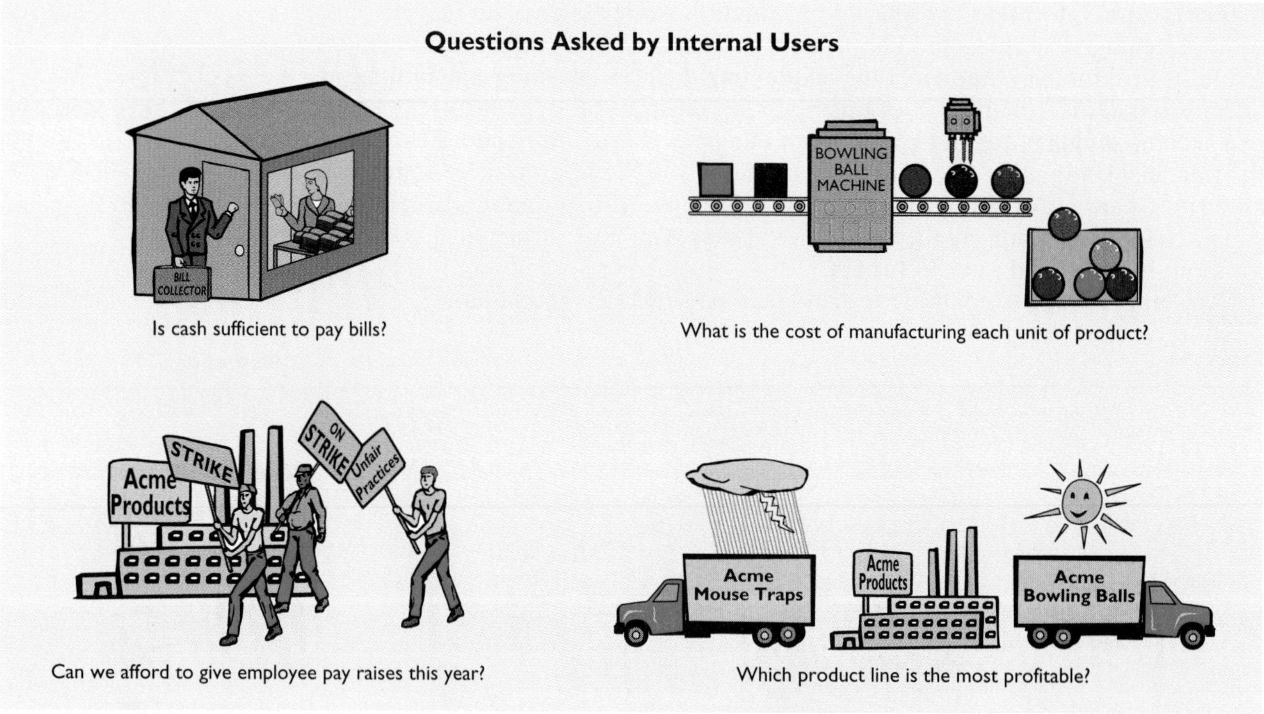

To answer these and other questions, users need detailed information on a timely basis. For internal users, accounting provides **internal reports**. Examples are financial comparisons of operating alternatives, projections of income from new sales campaigns, and forecasts of cash needs for the next year. In addition, summarized financial information is presented in the form of financial statements.

External Users

There are several types of **external users** of accounting information. **Investors** (owners) use accounting information to make decisions to buy, hold, or sell stock. **Creditors** such as suppliers and bankers use accounting information to evaluate the risks of granting credit or lending money. Some questions that may be asked by investors and creditors about a company are shown in Illustration 1-3.

HELPFUL HINT
The IRS requires businesses to retain records that can be audited. Also, the Foreign Corrupt Practices Act requires public companies to keep records.

The information needs and questions of other external users vary considerably. **Taxing authorities**, such as the Internal Revenue Service, want to know whether the company complies with the tax laws. **Regulatory agencies**, such as the Securities and Exchange Commission and the Federal Trade Commission, want to know whether the company is operating within prescribed rules. **Customers** are interested in whether a company will continue to honor product warranties and support its product lines. **Labor unions** want to know whether the owners can pay increased wages and benefits. **Economic planners** use accounting information to forecast economic activity.

Illustration 1-3

Questions asked by external users

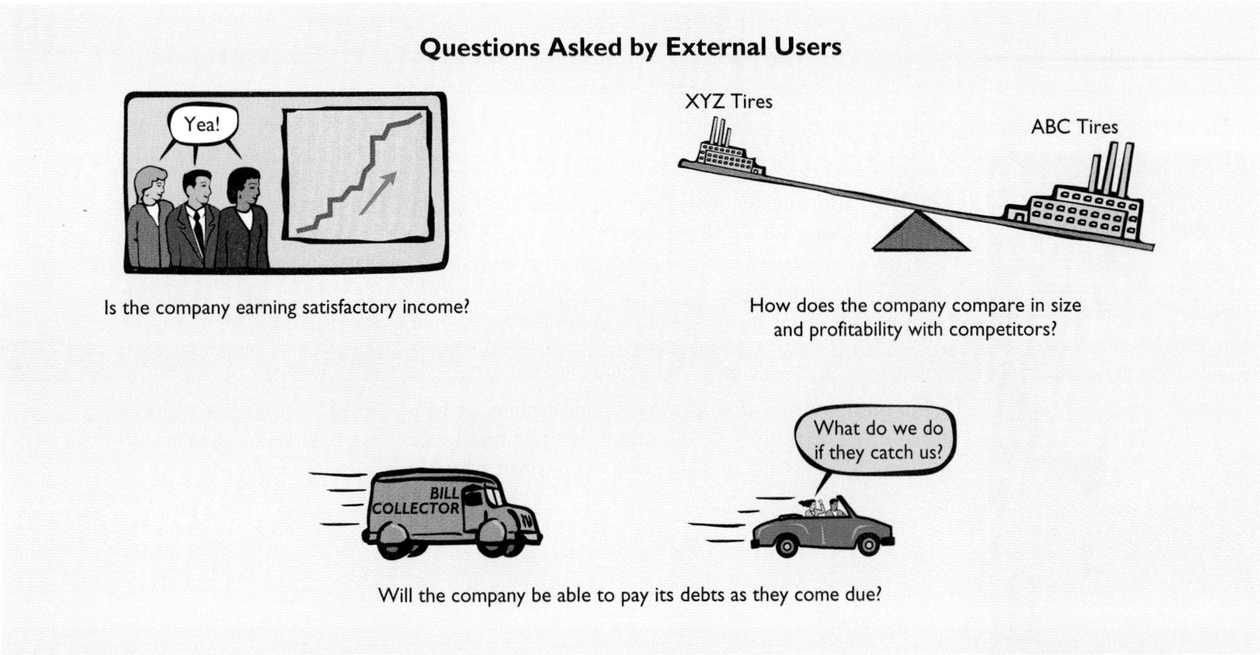
Questions Asked by External Users
Yea!
Is the company earning satisfactory income?
XYZ Tires
ABC Tires
How does the company compare in size and profitability with competitors?
What do we do if they catch us?
BILL COLLECTOR
Will the company be able to pay its debts as they come due?

ACCOUNTING IN ACTION *International Insight*

When the chief engineer of **Irkutsk Energo**, a public utility in Moscow, addressed a gathering of international investors, he provided them with all kinds of financial information about the company. The reason: Russians are learning that corporate openness lures much-needed foreign investment. But foreign investors have been reluctant to invest because Russian firms have been secretive (and sometimes deceptive) about their financial affairs. Now, however, things may change because firms such as Irkutsk Energo have enjoyed stock price surges after providing candid accounting information. In short, good accounting information may help Russia solve some of its economic problems.

SOURCE: The Wall Street Journal, June 9, 1995, p. A-6.

Accounting in Action examples illustrate important and interesting accounting situations in business.

BRIEF HISTORY OF ACCOUNTING

The **origins of accounting** are generally attributed to the work of Luca Pacioli, an Italian Renaissance mathematician. Pacioli was a close friend and tutor to Leonardo da Vinci and a contemporary of Christopher Columbus. In his text *Summa de Arithmetica, Geometria, Proportione et Proportionalite,* Pacioli described a system to ensure that financial information was recorded efficiently and accurately.

With the advent of the **industrial age** in the nineteenth century and, later, the emergence of large corporations, a separation of the owners from the managers of businesses took place. As a result, the need to report the financial status of the enterprise became more important, to ensure that managers acted in accord with owners' wishes. Also, transactions between businesses became more complex, making necessary improved approaches for reporting financial information.

Our economy has now evolved into a post-industrial age—**the information age**—in which many "products" are information services. The computer has been the driver of the information age.

E Business Insight examples show how e-business technology has expanded the services provided by accountants.

ACCOUNTING IN ACTION e Business Insight

E-business involves much more than simply selling goods over the Internet. According to Lou Gerstner, **IBM's** CEO, "e-business is all about cycle time, speed, globalization, enhanced productivity, reaching new customers, and sharing knowledge across institutions for competitive advantage." Many accountants are involved in designing and implementing computer systems, including systems for e-business. In fact, in recent years e-business consulting has been one of the largest areas of growth for large accounting firms. Many accountants choose to communicate their computer expertise to potential customers by gaining professional certification. Certification is accomplished by taking professional exams, such as those provided by the Institute for Certification of Computing Professionals *(www.aitp.org).*

DISTINGUISHING BETWEEN BOOKKEEPING AND ACCOUNTING

Many individuals mistakenly consider bookkeeping and accounting to be the same. This confusion is understandable because the accounting process **includes the bookkeeping function**. However, accounting also includes much more. **Bookkeeping usually involves only the recording of economic events**. It is therefore just one part of the accounting process. In total, **accounting involves the entire process of identifying, recording, and communicating economic events**.

Accounting may be further divided into financial accounting and managerial accounting. **Financial accounting** is the field of accounting that provides economic and financial information for investors, creditors, and other external users. **Managerial accounting** provides economic and financial information for managers and other internal users. Financial accounting is covered in Chapters 1–19 of this text. Managerial accounting is discussed in Chapters 20–27.

ACCOUNTING AND YOU

One question frequently asked by students of accounting is, "How will the study of accounting help me?" It should help you a great deal, because a working knowledge of accounting is desirable for virtually every field of endeavor. Some examples of how accounting is used in other careers include:

General management: Imagine running **General Motors**, a major hospital, a school, a **McDonald's** franchise, a bike shop. All general managers need to understand accounting data in order to make wise business decisions.

Marketing: A marketing specialist develops strategies to help the sales force be successful. But making a sale is meaningless unless it is a profitable sale. Marketing people must be sensitive to costs and benefits, which accounting helps them quantify and understand.

Finance: Do you want to be a banker, an investment analyst, a stock broker? These fields rely heavily on accounting. In all of them you will regularly examine and analyze financial statements. In fact, it is difficult to get a good job in a finance function without two or three courses in accounting.

Real estate: The most prevalent career in real estate is that of a broker, a person who sells real estate. Because a third party—the bank—is almost always involved in financing a real estate transaction, brokers must understand the numbers involved: Can the buyer afford to make the payments to the bank? Does the cash flow from an industrial property justify the purchase price? What are the tax benefits of the purchase?

Accounting is useful even for occupations you might think completely unrelated. If you become a doctor, a lawyer, a social worker, a teacher, an engineer, an architect, or an entrepreneur—you name it—a working knowledge of accounting is relevant. You will need to understand financial reports in any enterprise you are associated with.

THE ACCOUNTING PROFESSION

What would you do if you join the accounting profession? You probably would work in one of three major fields—public accounting, private accounting, or not-for-profit accounting.

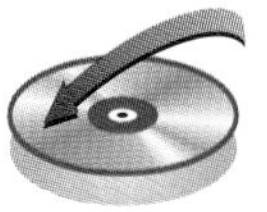

Careers in Accounting

This **CD icon** informs you of additional resources available on the CD that came with your text.

Public Accounting

In **public accounting**, you would offer expert service to the general public in much the same way that a doctor serves patients and a lawyer serves clients. A major portion of public accounting involves **auditing**. In this area, a certified public accountant (CPA) examines the financial statements of companies and expresses an opinion as to the fairness of presentation. When the presentation is fair, users consider the statements to be **reliable**. For example, **Lands' End** investors would demand audited financial statements before extending it financing.

Taxation is another major area of public accounting. The work performed by tax specialists includes tax advice and planning, preparing tax returns, and representing clients before governmental agencies such as the Internal Revenue Service.

A third area in public accounting is **management consulting**. It ranges from the installing of basic accounting systems to helping companies determine whether they should use the space shuttle for high-tech research and development projects.

Private Accounting

Instead of working in public accounting, you might choose to be an employee of a business enterprise. In **private (or managerial) accounting**, you would be involved in one of the following activities.

1. **General accounting**—recording daily transactions and preparing financial statements and related information.
2. **Cost accounting**—determining the cost of producing specific products.
3. **Budgeting**—assisting management in quantifying goals concerning revenues, costs of goods sold, and operating expenses.
4. **Accounting information systems**—designing both manual and computerized data processing systems.
5. **Tax accounting**—preparing tax returns and doing tax planning for the company.
6. **Internal auditing**—reviewing the company's operations to see if they comply with management policies and evaluating the efficiency of operations.

You can see that within a specific company, private accountants perform as wide a variety of duties as the public accountant.

Illustration 1-4 presents the general career paths in public and private accounting.

Illustration 1-4

Career paths in public and private accounting

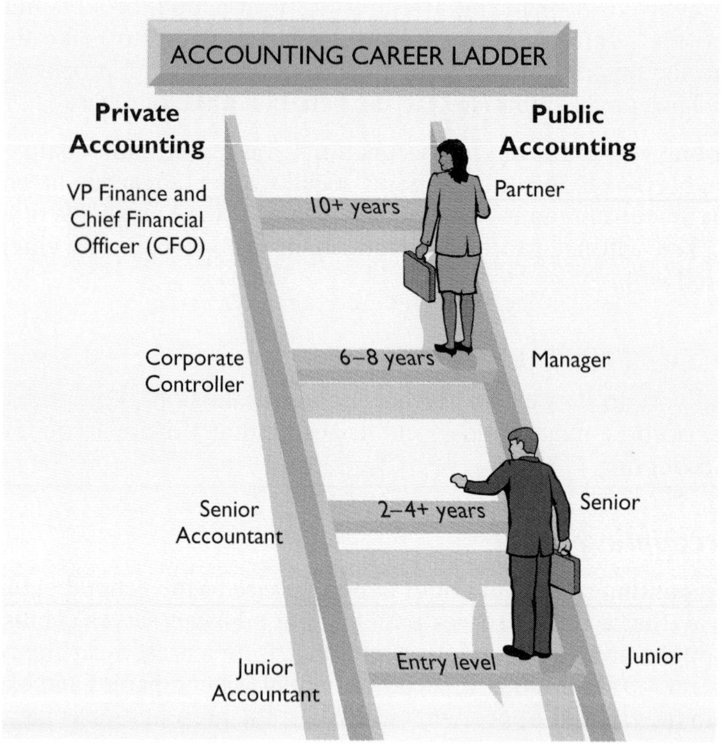

Not-for-Profit Accounting

Like businesses that exist to make a profit, not-for-profit organizations also need sound financial reporting and control. Donors to such organizations as the **United Way**, the **Ford Foundation**, and the **Red Cross** want information about how well the organization has met its financial objectives and whether continued support is justified. Hospitals, colleges, and universities must make decisions about allocating funds. Local, state, and federal governmental units provide financial information to legislators, citizens, employees, and creditors. At the federal level, the largest employers of accountants are the **Internal Revenue Service**, the **General Accounting Office**, the **Federal Bureau of Investigation**, and the **Securities and Exchange Commission**.

ACCOUNTING IN ACTION *Business Insight*

Help Wanted: Forensic CPAs

Tom Taylor's job at the **FBI** has changed. He used to pack a .357 magnum; now he wields a No. 2 pencil and a notebook computer. Taylor, age 37, for two years an FBI agent, is a forensic accountant, somebody who sniffs through company books to ferret out white-collar crime. Demand for this service has surged in the past few years. In one recent year, a recruiter for San Diego's **Robert Half International**, a headhunting firm, had requests for more than 1,000 such snoops.

Qualifications: a CPA with FBI, IRS, or similar government experience. Interestingly, despite its macho image, the FBI has long hired mostly accountants and lawyers as agents.

BEFORE YOU GO ON...

REVIEW IT

1. What is accounting?
2. Who uses accounting information?
3. What is the difference between bookkeeping and accounting?
4. How can you use your accounting knowledge?
5. If you join the accounting profession, in what three major fields do you have a choice of a job?
6. What types of services are provided by public accountants?
7. What activities might you be involved in if you work in private accounting?
8. Name five not-for-profit organizations.

THE NAVIGATOR

Before You Go On questions at the end of major text sections offer an opportunity to stop and reexamine the key points you have studied.

THE BUILDING BLOCKS OF ACCOUNTING

Every profession develops a body of theory consisting of principles, assumptions, and standards. Accounting is no exception. Just as a doctor follows certain standards in treating a patient's illness, an accountant follows certain standards in reporting financial information. For these standards to work, a fundamental business concept is followed—ethical behavior.

ETHICS—A FUNDAMENTAL BUSINESS CONCEPT

STUDY OBJECTIVE 3

Understand why ethics is a fundamental business concept.

Wherever you make your career—whether in accounting, marketing, management, finance, government, or elsewhere—your actions will affect other people and organizations. The standards of conduct by which one's actions are judged as right or wrong, honest or dishonest, fair or not fair, are **ethics**. Imagine trying to carry on a business or invest money if you could not depend on the individuals you deal with to be honest. If managers, customers, investors, co-workers, and creditors all consistently lied, effective communication and economic activity would be impossible. Information would have no credibility.

Fortunately most individuals in business are ethical. Their actions are both legal and responsible, and they consider the organization's interests in their decision making. However, sometimes public officials and business executives act unethically. For example, a former chief of the finance committee of the **House of Representatives** was indicted for possible illegal behavior; **Sears** was accused of widespread customer overcharging on car repairs; **Woolworth Corp.** executives were dismissed because they reported false income numbers. As one business leader noted: "We are all embarrassed by the events that make *The Wall Street Journal* read like the *Police Gazette.*"

To sensitize you to ethical situations and to give you practice at solving ethical dilemmas, we have included in the book three types of ethics materials: (1) marginal notes that provide helpful hints for developing ethical sensitivity, (2) Ethics in Accounting boxes that highlight ethics situations and issues, and (3) at the end of the chapter, an ethics case simulating a business situation. In the process of analyzing these ethics cases and your own ethical experiences, you should apply the three steps outlined in Illustration 1-5.

Illustration 1-5

Steps in analyzing ethics cases

Solving an Ethical Dilemma

1. Recognize an ethical situation and the ethical issues involved.

Use your personal ethics to identify ethical situations and issues. Some businesses and professional organizations provide written codes of ethics for guidance in some business situations.

2. Identify and analyze the principal elements in the situation.

Identify the *stakeholders*—persons or groups who may be harmed or benefited. Ask the question: What are the responsibilities and obligations of the parties involved?

3. Identify the alternatives, and weigh the impact of each alternative on various stakeholders.

Select the most ethical alternative, considering all the consequences. Sometimes there will be one right answer. Other situations involve more than one right solution; these situations require an evaluation of each and a selection of the best alternative.

GENERALLY ACCEPTED ACCOUNTING PRINCIPLES

STUDY OBJECTIVE 4

Explain the meaning of generally accepted accounting principles and the cost principle.

The accounting profession has developed standards that are generally accepted and universally practiced. This common set of standards is called **generally accepted accounting principles (GAAP)**. These standards indicate how to report economic events.

Two organizations are primarily responsible for establishing generally accepted accounting principles. The first is the **Financial Accounting Standards Board (FASB)**. This private organization establishes broad reporting standards of general applicability as well as specific accounting rules. The second standards-setting group is the **Securities and Exchange Commission (SEC)**. The SEC is a governmental agency that requires companies to file financial reports following generally accepted accounting principles. In situations where no principles exist, the SEC often mandates that certain guidelines be used. In general, the FASB and the SEC work hand in hand to assure that timely and useful accounting principles are developed.

INTERNATIONAL NOTE

The standards-setting processes in Canada, Mexico, and the United States are similar in most respects. All three have relatively open deliberations on new rules, and they support efforts to follow international standards. The use of similar accounting principles within North America has implications for the success of the North American Free Trade Agreement (NAFTA).

One important principle is the **cost principle**, which states that assets should be recorded at their cost. **Cost is the value exchanged at the time something is acquired.** If you buy a house today, the cost is the amount you pay for it, say $200,000. If you sell the house in two years for $230,000, the sales price is its **market value**—the value determined by the market for homes at that time. At the time of acquisition, cost and fair market value are the same. In subsequent periods, cost and fair market value may vary, **but the cost amount continues to be used in the accounting records.**

To see the importance of the cost principle, consider the following example. At one time, **Greyhound Corporation** had 128 bus stations nationwide that cost approximately $200 million. The current market value of the stations is now close to $1 billion. But, until the bus stations are actually sold, estimates of their market values are subjective—they are informed estimates. So, under the cost principle, the bus stations are recorded and reported at $200 million, not $1 billion.

ALTERNATIVE TERMINOLOGY

The cost principle is often referred to as the *historical cost principle*.

As the Greyhound example indicates, cost has an important advantage over other valuations: Cost is **reliable**. The values exchanged at the time something is acquired generally can be **objectively measured** and can be **verified**. Critics argue that cost is often not relevant and that market values provide more useful information. Despite this shortcoming, cost continues to be used in the financial statements because of its reliability.

ASSUMPTIONS

STUDY OBJECTIVE 5

Explain the meaning of the monetary unit assumption and the economic entity assumption.

In developing generally accepted accounting principles, certain basic assumptions are made. These assumptions provide a foundation for the accounting process.

Two main assumptions are the **monetary unit assumption** and the **economic entity assumption**.

Monetary Unit Assumption

The **monetary unit assumption** requires that only transaction data that can be expressed in terms of money be included in the accounting records. This assumption enables accounting to quantify (measure) economic events. The monetary unit assumption is vital to applying the cost principle discussed earlier. This assumption does prevent some relevant information from being included in the accounting records. For example, the health of the owner, the quality of service, and the morale of employees would not be included because they cannot be quantified in terms of money.

An important part of the monetary unit assumption is the added assumption that the unit of measure remains sufficiently constant over time. However, the assumption of a stable monetary unit has been challenged because of the significant decline in the purchasing power of the dollar. For example, what used to cost $1.00 in 1960 costs over $4.00 in 2001. In such situations, adding, subtracting, or comparing 1960 dollars with 2001 dollars is highly questionable. The profession has recognized this problem and encourages companies to disclose the effects of changing prices.

Economic Entity Assumption

An economic entity can be any organization or unit in society. It may be a business enterprise (such as **General Electric Company**), a governmental unit (the state of Ohio), a municipality (Seattle), a school district (St. Louis District 48), or a church (Southern Baptist). The **economic entity assumption** requires that the activities of the entity be kept separate and distinct from the activities of its owner and all other economic entities. To illustrate, Sally Rider, owner of Sally's Boutique, should keep her personal living costs separate from the expenses of the Boutique. **Lands' End, L.L. Bean,** and **Eddie Bauer** are segregated into separate economic entities for accounting purposes.

ACCOUNTING IN ACTION *Ethics Insight*

A violation of the economic entity assumption contributed to the resignation by the chief executive of **W. R. Grace and Company**. Investors were angered to learn that company funds were used for personal medical care, a Manhattan apartment, and a personal chef for the company's chief. Funds were also used to support a hotel interest owned by the chief executive's son.

We will generally discuss the economic entity assumption in relation to a business enterprise, which may be organized as a proprietorship, partnership, or corporation.

PROPRIETORSHIP. A business owned by one person is generally a **proprietorship**. The owner is often the manager/operator of the business. Small service-type businesses (plumbing companies, beauty salons, and auto repair shops), farms, and small retail stores (antique shops, clothing stores, and used-book stores) are often sole proprietorships. **Usually only a relatively small amount of money (capital) is necessary to start in business as a proprietorship. The owner**

> **HELPFUL HINT**
> Approximately 70% of U. S. companies are proprietorships; however, they account for only 6.5% of gross revenues. Corporations, on the other hand, are approximately 19% of all companies, but account for 90% of the revenues. Obviously, proprietorships, though numerous, tend to be small.

(proprietor) receives any profits, suffers any losses, and is personally liable for all debts of the business. There is no legal distinction between the business as an economic unit and the owner, but the accounting records of the business activities are kept separate from the personal records and activities of the owner.

PARTNERSHIP. A business owned by two or more persons associated as partners is a **partnership**. In most respects a partnership is like a proprietorship except that more than one owner is involved. Typically a partnership agreement (written or oral) sets forth such terms as initial investment, duties of each partner, division of net income (or net loss), and settlement to be made upon death or withdrawal of a partner. Each partner generally has unlimited personal liability for the debts of the partnership. **Like a proprietorship, for accounting purposes the partnership affairs must be kept separate from the personal activities of the partners.** Partnerships are often used to organize retail and service-type businesses, including professional practices (lawyers, doctors, architects, and certified public accountants).

CORPORATION. A business organized as a separate legal entity under state corporation law and having ownership divided into transferable shares of stock is a **corporation**. The holders of the shares (stockholders) **enjoy limited liability**; that is, they are not personally liable for the debts of the corporate entity. Stockholders **may transfer all or part of their shares to other investors at any time** (i.e., sell their shares). The ease with which ownership can change adds to the attractiveness of investing in a corporation. Because ownership can be transferred without dissolving the corporation, the corporation **enjoys an unlimited life**.

Although the combined number of proprietorships and partnerships in the United States is more than four times the number of corporations, the revenue produced by corporations is nine times greater. Most of the largest enterprises in the United States—for example, **Exxon Mobil**, **General Motors**, **Wal-Mart**, **Citigroup**, and **Lands' End, Inc.**—are corporations.

BASIC ACCOUNTING EQUATION

STUDY OBJECTIVE 6

State the basic accounting equation, and explain the meaning of assets, liabilities, and owner's equity.

Accounting Cycle Tutorial—Analyzing Business Transactions

Other essential building blocks of accounting are the categories into which economic events are classified. The two basic elements of a business are what it owns and what it owes. **Assets** are the resources owned by a business. For example, Lands' End's competitor **Abercrombie & Fitch** has total assets of approximately $458 million. Liabilities and owner's equity are the rights or claims against these resources. Thus, a company such as Abercrombie & Fitch that has $458 million of assets also has $458 million of claims against those assets. Claims of those to whom money is owed (creditors) are called **liabilities**. Claims of owners are called **owner's equity**. For example, Abercrombie & Fitch has liabilities of $147 million and owners' equity of $311 million. This relationship of assets, liabilities, and owner's equity can be expressed as an equation as follows.

Illustration 1-6

The basic accounting equation

Assets = Liabilities + Owner's Equity

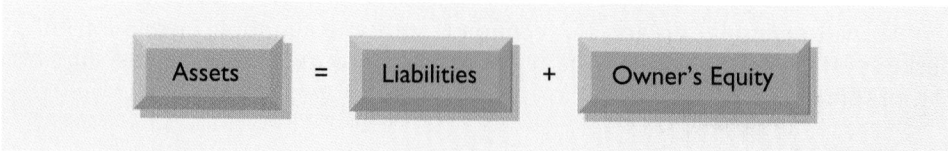

This relationship is referred to as the **basic accounting equation**. Assets must equal the sum of liabilities and owner's equity. Because creditors' claims must be paid before ownership claims if a business is liquidated, liabilities are shown before owner's equity in the basic accounting equation.

The accounting equation applies to all **economic entities** regardless of size, nature of business, or form of business organization. It applies to a small proprietorship such as a corner grocery store as well as to a giant corporation such as **Kellogg** or **General Mills**. The equation provides the **underlying framework** for recording and summarizing the economic events of a business enterprise.

Let's look in more detail at the categories in the basic accounting equation.

HELPFUL HINT
In some places we use the term *owner's equity* and in others we use *owners' equity*. *Owner's* refers to one owner (the case with a sole proprietorship), and *owners'* refers to multiple owners (the case with partnerships or corporations).

Assets

As noted above, **assets** are resources owned by a business. They are used in carrying out such activities as production, consumption, and exchange. The common characteristic possessed by all assets is the capacity to provide future services or benefits. In a business enterprise, that service potential or future economic benefit eventually results in cash inflows (receipts) to the enterprise.

For example, the enterprise Campus Pizza owns a delivery truck that provides economic benefits from its use in delivering pizzas. Other assets of Campus Pizza are tables, chairs, jukebox, cash register, oven, mugs and silverware, and, of course, cash.

Liabilities

Liabilities are claims against assets. That is, **liabilities are existing debts and obligations**. For example, businesses of all sizes usually borrow money and purchase merchandise on credit. Campus Pizza, for instance, purchases cheese, sausage, flour, and beverages on credit from suppliers. These obligations are called **accounts payable**. Campus Pizza also has a **note payable** to First National Bank for the money borrowed to purchase the delivery truck. Campus Pizza may also have **wages payable** to employees and **sales and real estate taxes payable** to the local government. All of these persons or entities to whom Campus Pizza owes money are its **creditors**.

Most claims of creditors attach to the entity's **total** assets rather than to the specific assets provided by the creditor. Creditors may legally force the liquidation of a business that does not pay its debts. In that case, the law requires that creditor claims be paid before ownership claims.

Owner's Equity

The ownership claim on total assets is known as **owner's equity**. It is equal to total assets minus total liabilities. Here is why: The assets of a business are supplied or claimed by either creditors or owners. To find out what belongs to owners, we subtract the creditors' claims (the liabilities) from assets. The remainder is the owner's claim on the assets—the owner's equity. Since the claims of creditors must be paid before ownership claims, owner's equity is often referred to as **residual equity**.

INCREASES IN OWNER'S EQUITY. In a proprietorship, owner's equity is increased by owner's investments and revenues.

Investments by Owner. **Investments by owner** are the assets the owner puts into the business. These investments increase owner's equity.

Revenues. **Revenues** are the **gross increase in owner's equity resulting from business activities entered into for the purpose of earning income**. Generally, revenues result from the sale of merchandise, the performance of services, the rental of property, and the lending of money.

Revenues usually result in an increase in an asset. They may arise from different sources and are identified by various names depending on the nature of the business. Campus Pizza, for instance, has two categories of sales revenues—pizza sales and beverage sales. Common sources of revenue are: sales, fees, services, commissions, interest, dividends, royalties, and rent.

DECREASES IN OWNER'S EQUITY. In a proprietorship, owner's equity is decreased by owner's drawings and expenses.

Drawings. An owner may withdraw cash or other assets for personal use. These withdrawals could be recorded as a direct decrease of owner's equity. However, it is generally considered preferable to use a separate classification called **drawings** to determine the total withdrawals for each accounting period. **Drawings decrease owner's equity.**

Expenses. **Expenses** are the cost of assets consumed or services used in the process of earning revenue. They are **decreases in owner's equity that result from operating the business**. Expenses represent actual or expected cash outflows (payments). Like revenues, expenses take many forms and are identified by various names depending on the type of asset consumed or service used. For example, Campus Pizza recognizes the following expenses: cost of ingredients (meat, flour, cheese, tomato paste, mushrooms, etc.); cost of beverages; wages expense; utility expense (electric, gas, and water expense); telephone expense; delivery expense (gasoline, repairs, licenses, etc.); supplies expense (napkins, detergents, aprons, etc.); rent expense; interest expense; and property tax expense.

In summary, owner's equity is increased by an owner's investments and by revenues from business operations. In contrast, owner's equity is decreased by an owner's withdrawals of assets and by expenses. These relationships are shown in Illustration 1-7. **Net income** results when revenues exceed expenses. A **net loss** occurs when expenses exceed revenues.

Illustration 1-7

Increases and decreases in owner's equity

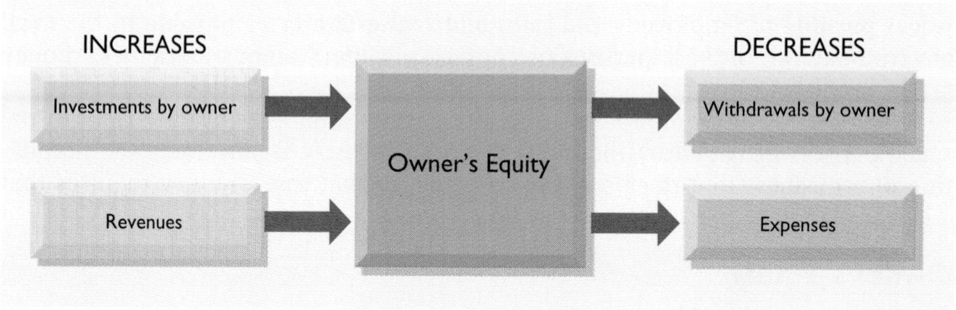

BEFORE YOU GO ON...

Review It questions marked with this icon require that you use Lands' End's 2000 Annual Report.

REVIEW IT

1. Why is ethics a fundamental business concept?
2. What are generally accepted accounting principles? Give an example.
3. Explain the monetary unit and the economic entity assumptions.
4. The accounting equation is: Assets = Liabilities + Owner's Equity. Replacing the words in that equation with dollar amounts, what is **Lands' End's** accounting equation at January 28, 2000? (*Hint:* Owner's equity is equivalent to stockholders' equity. The answer to this question is provided on page 41.)
5. What are assets, liabilities, and owner's equity?

DO IT

Classify the following items as investment by owner (I), owner's drawings (D), revenues (R), or expenses (E). Then indicate whether the following items increase or decrease owner's equity: (1) rent expense, (2) service revenue, (3) drawings, and (4) salaries expense.

ACTION PLAN

- Review the rules for changes in owner's equity: Investments and revenues increase owner's equity. Expenses and drawings decrease owner's equity.
- Understand the sources of revenue: the sale of merchandise, performance of services, rental of property, and lending of money.

- Understand what causes expenses: the consumption of assets or services.
- Recognize that drawings are withdrawals of cash or other assets from the business for personal use.

SOLUTION

1. Rent expense is classified as an expense (E); it decreases owner's equity.
2. Service revenue is classified as revenue (R); it increases owner's equity.
3. Drawings is classified as owner's drawings (D); it decreases owner's equity.
4. Salaries expense is classified as an expense (E); it decreases owner's equity.

Related exercise material: BE1-1, BE1-2, BE1-3, BE1-4, BE1-5, BE1-6, BE1-7, BE1-9, E1-1, E1-2, E1-3, E1-4, E1-6, and E1-7.

THE NAVIGATOR

USING THE BUILDING BLOCKS

STUDY OBJECTIVE 7

Analyze the effects of business transactions on the basic accounting equation.

Transactions (often referred to as business transactions) are the economic events of an enterprise that are recorded. Transactions may be identified as external or internal. **External transactions involve economic events between the company and some outside enterprise.** For example, Campus Pizza's purchase of cooking equipment from a supplier, payment of monthly rent to the landlord, and sale of pizzas to customers are external transactions. **Internal transactions are economic events that occur entirely within one company.** The use of cooking and cleaning supplies illustrates internal transactions for Campus Pizza.

A company may carry on many activities that do not in themselves represent business transactions. Hiring employees, answering the telephone, talking with customers, and placing orders for merchandise are examples. Some of these activities, however, may lead to business transactions: Employees will earn wages, and merchandise will be delivered by suppliers. Each event must be analyzed to find out if it has an effect on the components of the basic accounting equation. If it does, it will be recorded in the accounting process. Illustration 1-8 demonstrates the transaction identification process.

Illustration 1-8

Transaction identification process

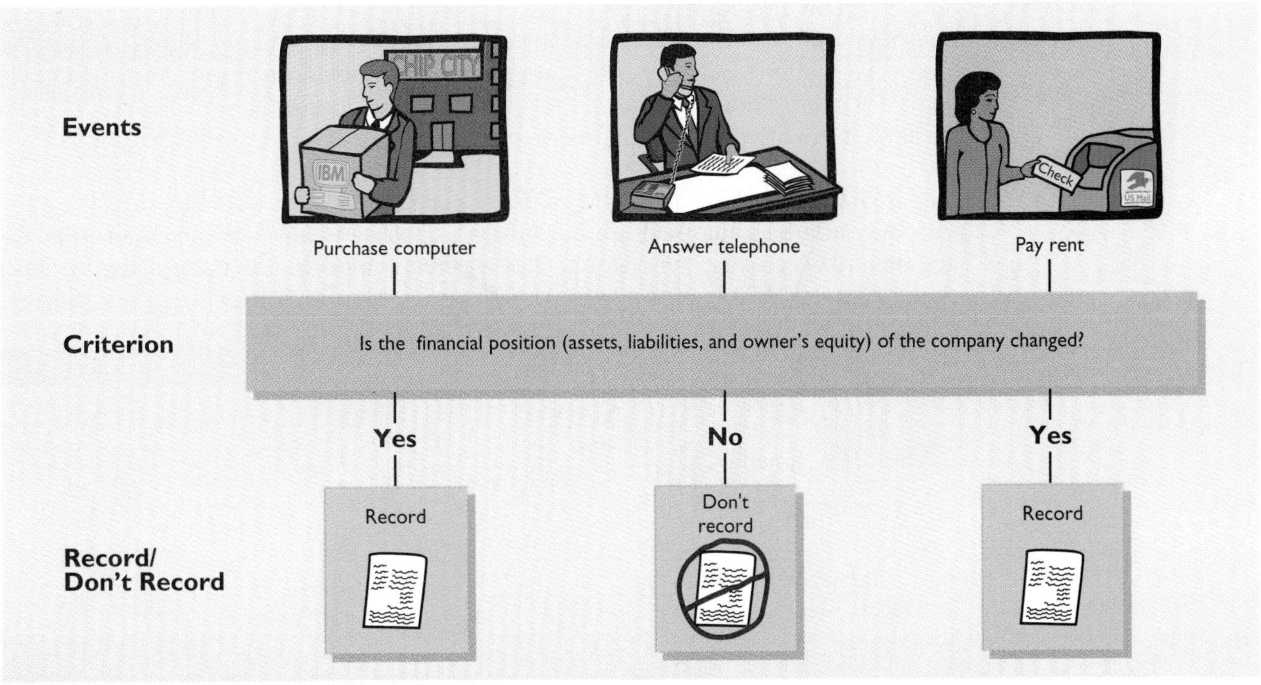

The equality of the basic equation must be preserved. Therefore, each transaction must have a dual effect on the equation. For example, if an asset is increased, there must be a corresponding:

1. Decrease in another asset, or
2. Increase in a specific liability, or
3. Increase in owner's equity.

It follows that two or more items could be affected when an asset is increased. For example, as one asset is increased $10,000, another asset could decrease $6,000 and a specific liability could increase $4,000. Any change in a liability or ownership claim is subject to similar analysis.

TRANSACTION ANALYSIS

The following examples are business transactions for a computer programming business during its first month of operations. You will want to study these transactions until you are sure you understand them. They are not difficult, but they are important to your success in this course. The ability to analyze transactions in terms of the basic accounting equation is essential for an understanding of accounting.

TRANSACTION (1). INVESTMENT BY OWNER. Ray Neal decides to open a computer programming service which he names Softbyte. On September 1, 2002, he invests $15,000 cash in the business. This transaction results in an equal increase in assets and owner's equity. The asset Cash increases $15,000, as does the owner's equity, identified as R. Neal, Capital. The effect of this transaction on the basic equation is:

	Assets	=	**Liabilities**	+	**Owner's Equity**	
	Cash	=			R. Neal, Capital	
(1)	**+$15,000**	=			**+$15,000**	**Investment**

Observe that the equality of the basic equation has been maintained. Note also that the source of the increase in owner's equity (Investment) is indicated. Why does this matter? Because investments by the owner do not represent revenues, and they are excluded in determining net income. Therefore it is necessary to make clear that the increase is an investment rather than revenue from operations.

TRANSACTION (2). PURCHASE OF EQUIPMENT FOR CASH. Softbyte purchases computer equipment for $7,000 cash. This transaction results in an equal increase and decrease in total assets, though the composition of assets changes: Cash is decreased $7,000, and the asset Equipment is increased $7,000. The specific effect of this transaction and the cumulative effect of the first two transactions are:

		Assets		=	**Liabilities**	+	**Owner's Equity**
		Cash	Equipment	=			R. Neal, Capital
	Old Bal.	$15,000					$15,000
(2)		**−7,000**	**+$7,000**				
	New Bal.	$ 8,000	$7,000	=			$15,000
		$15,000					

Observe that total assets are still $15,000, and Neal's equity also remains at $15,000, the amount of his original investment.

TRANSACTION (3). PURCHASE OF SUPPLIES ON CREDIT. Softbyte purchases for $1,600 from Acme Supply Company computer paper and other supplies expected to last several months. Acme agrees to allow Softbyte to pay this bill next month, in October. This transaction is referred to as a purchase on account or a credit purchase. Assets are increased because of the expected future benefits of using the paper and supplies, and liabilities are increased by the amount due Acme Company. The asset Supplies is increased $1,600, and the liability Accounts Payable is increased by the same amount. The effect on the equation is:

		Assets					=	Liabilities	+	Owner's Equity
		Cash	+	Supplies	+	Equipment	=	Accounts Payable	+	R. Neal, Capital
	Old. Bal.	$8,000				$7,000				$15,000
(3)				+$1,600				+$1,600		
	New Bal.	$8,000	+	$1,600	+	$7,000	=	$1,600	+	$15,000
				$16,600					$16,600	

Total assets are now $16,600. This total is matched by a $1,600 creditor's claim and a $15,000 ownership claim.

TRANSACTION (4). SERVICES PROVIDED FOR CASH. Softbyte receives $1,200 cash from customers for programming services it has provided. This transaction represents Softbyte's principal revenue-producing activity. Recall that **revenue increases owner's equity**. In this transaction, Cash is increased $1,200, and R. Neal, Capital is increased $1,200. The new balances in the equation are:

		Assets					=	Liabilities	+	Owner's Equity	
		Cash	+	Supplies	+	Equipment	=	Accounts Payable	+	R. Neal, Capital	
	Old Bal.	$8,000		$1,600		$7,000		$1,600		$15,000	
(4)		+1,200								+1,200	**Service Revenue**
	New Bal.	$9,200	+	$1,600	+	$7,000	=	$1,600	+	$16,200	
				$17,800					$17,800		

The two sides of the equation balance at $17,800. The source of the increase in owner's equity is indicated as Service Revenue. Service revenue is included in determining Softbyte's net income.

TRANSACTION (5). PURCHASE OF ADVERTISING ON CREDIT. Softbyte receives a bill for $250 from the *Daily News* for advertising but postpones payment of the bill until a later date. This transaction results in an increase in liabilities and a decrease in owner's equity. The specific items involved are Accounts Payable and R. Neal, Capital. The effect on the equation is:

		Assets			=	Liabilities	+	Owner's Equity	
		Cash	+ Supplies	+ Equipment	=	Accounts Payable	+	R. Neal, Capital	
	Old Bal.	$9,200	$1,600	$7,000		$1,600		$16,200	
(5)						**+250**		**−250**	**Advertising Expense**
	New Bal.	$9,200	+ $1,600	+ $7,000	=	$1,850	+	$15,950	
			$17,800				$17,800		

The two sides of the equation still balance at $17,800. Owner's equity is decreased when the expense is incurred, and the specific cause of the decrease (advertising expense) is noted. Expenses do not have to be paid in cash at the time they are incurred. When payment is made at a later date, the liability Accounts Payable will be decreased and the asset Cash will be decreased [see Transaction (8)]. The cost of advertising is considered an expense, as opposed to an asset, because the benefits have been used. This expense is included in determining net income.

TRANSACTION (6). SERVICES PROVIDED FOR CASH AND CREDIT. Softbyte provides $3,500 of programming services for customers. Cash of $1,500 is received from customers, and the balance of $2,000 is billed on account. This transaction results in an equal increase in assets and owner's equity. Three specific items are affected: Cash is increased $1,500; Accounts Receivable is increased $2,000; and R. Neal, Capital is increased $3,500. The new balances are as follows.

		Assets				=	Liabilities	+	Owner's Equity	
		Cash	+ Accounts Receivable	+ Supplies	+ Equipment	=	Accounts Payable	+	R. Neal, Capital	
	Old Bal.	$9,200		$1,600	$7,000		$1,850		$15,950	
(6)		**+1,500**	**+$2,000**						**+3,500**	**Service Revenue**
	New Bal.	$10,700	+ $2,000	+ $1,600	+ $7,000	=	$1,850	+	$19,450	
			$21,300					$21,300		

Why increase owner's equity $3,500 when only $1,500 has been collected? Because the inflow of assets resulting from the earning of revenues does not have to be in the form of cash. Remember that owner's equity is increased when revenues are earned; in Softbyte's case revenues are earned when the service is provided. When collections on account are received later, Cash will be increased and Accounts Receivable will be decreased [see Transaction (9)].

TRANSACTION (7). PAYMENT OF EXPENSES. Expenses paid in cash for September are store rent $600, salaries of employees $900, and utilities $200. These payments result in an equal decrease in assets and owner's equity. Cash is decreased $1,700, and R. Neal, Capital is decreased by the same amount. The effect of these payments on the equation is:

		Assets				=	Liabilities	+	Owner's Equity	
		Cash	+ Accounts Receivable	+ Supplies	+ Equipment	=	Accounts Payable	+	R. Neal, Capital	
	Old Bal.	$10,700	$2,000	$1,600	$7,000		$1,850		$19,450	
(7)		**−1,700**							**−600**	**Rent Expense**
									−900	**Salaries Expense**
									−200	**Utilities Expense**
	New Bal.	$ 9,000 +	$2,000 +	$1,600 +	$7,000	=	$1,850	+	$17,750	
			$19,600				$19,600			

The two sides of the equation now balance at $19,600. Three lines are required in the analysis to indicate the different types of expenses that have been incurred.

TRANSACTION (8). PAYMENT OF ACCOUNTS PAYABLE. Softbyte pays its $250 *Daily News* advertising bill in cash. Remember that the bill was previously recorded [in Transaction (5)] as an increase in Accounts Payable and a decrease in owner's equity. This payment "on account" decreases the asset Cash by $250 and also decreases the liability Accounts Payable by $250. The effect of this transaction on the equation is:

		Assets				=	Liabilities	+	Owner's Equity
		Cash	+ Accounts Receivable	+ Supplies	+ Equipment	=	Accounts Payable	+	R. Neal, Capital
	Old Bal.	$9,000	$2,000	$1,600	$7,000		$1,850		$17,750
(8)		**−250**					**−250**		
	New Bal.	$8,750 +	$2,000 +	$1,600 +	$7,000	=	$1,600	+	$17,750
			$19,350				$19,350		

Observe that the payment of a liability related to an expense that has previously been recorded does not affect owner's equity. The expense was recorded in Transaction (5) and should not be recorded again.

TRANSACTION (9). RECEIPT OF CASH ON ACCOUNT. The sum of $600 in cash is received from customers who have previously been billed for services [in Transaction (6)]. This transaction does not change total assets, but it changes the composition of those assets. Cash is increased $600 and Accounts Receivable is decreased $600. The new balances are:

		Assets				=	Liabilities	+	Owner's Equity
		Cash	+ Accounts Receivable	+ Supplies	+ Equipment	=	Accounts Payable	+	R. Neal, Capital
	Old Bal.	$8,750	$2,000	$1,600	$7,000		$1,600		$17,750
(9)		**+600**	**−600**						
	New Bal.	$9,350 +	$1,400 +	$1,600 +	$7,000	=	$1,600	+	$17,750
			$19,350				$19,350		

Note that a collection on account for services previously billed and recorded does not affect owner's equity. Revenue was already recorded in Transaction (6) and should not be recorded again.

TRANSACTION (10). WITHDRAWAL OF CASH BY OWNER. Ray Neal withdraws $1,300 in cash from the business for his personal use. This transaction results in an equal decrease in assets and owner's equity. Both Cash and R. Neal, Capital are decreased $1,300, as shown below.

	Assets							=	**Liabilities**	+	**Owner's Equity**	
	Cash	+	Accounts Receivable	+	Supplies	+	Equipment	=	Accounts Payable	+	R. Neal, Capital	
Old Bal.	$9,350		$1,400		$1,600		$7,000		$1,600		$17,750	
(10)	**−1,300**										**−1,300**	**Drawings**
New Bal.	$8,050	+	$1,400	+	$1,600	+	$7,000	=	$1,600	+	$16,450	
			$18,050								$18,050	

Observe that the effect of a cash withdrawal by the owner is the opposite of the effect of an investment by the owner. **Owner's drawings are not expenses.** Like owner's investment, they are excluded in determining net income.

SUMMARY OF TRANSACTIONS

The September transactions of Softbyte are summarized in Illustration 1-9. The transaction number, the specific effects of the transaction, and the balances after each transaction are indicated. The illustration demonstrates some significant facts listed on the next page.

Illustration 1-9

Tabular summary of Softbyte transactions

	Assets							=	**Liabilities**	+	**Owner's Equity**	
Transaction	Cash	+	Accounts Receivable	+	Supplies	+	Equipment	=	Accounts Payable	+	R. Neal, Capital	
(1)	+$15,000										+$15,000	**Investment**
(2)	−7,000						+$7,000					
	8,000					+	7,000	=			15,000	
(3)					+$1,600				+$1,600			
	8,000			+	1,600	+	7,000	=	1,600	+	15,000	
(4)	+1,200										+1,200	**Service Revenue**
	9,200			+	1,600	+	7,000	=	1,600	+	16,200	
(5)									+250		−250	**Advertising Expense**
	9,200			+	1,600	+	7,000	=	1,850	+	15,950	
(6)	+1,500		+$2,000								+3,500	**Service Revenue**
	10,700	+	2,000	+	1,600	+	7,000	=	1,850	+	19,450	
(7)	−1,700										−600	**Rent Expense**
											−900	**Salaries Expense**
											−200	**Utilities Expense**
	9,000	+	2,000	+	1,600	+	7,000	=	1,850	+	17,750	
(8)	−250								−250			
	8,750	+	2,000	+	1,600	+	7,000	=	1,600	+	17,750	
(9)	+600		−600									
	9,350	+	1,400	+	1,600	+	7,000	=	1,600	+	17,750	
(10)	−1,300										−1,300	**Drawings**
	$ 8,050	+	$1,400	+	$1,600	+	$7,000	=	$1,600	+	$16,450	
			$18,050						$18,050			

1. Each transaction must be analyzed in terms of its effect on:
   (a) the three components of the basic accounting equation.
   (b) specific types (kinds) of items within each component.
2. The two sides of the equation must always be equal.
3. The causes of each change in the owner's claim on assets must be indicated in the owner's equity column.

There! You made it through transaction analysis. If you feel a bit shaky on any of the transactions, it might be a good idea at this point to get up, take a short break, and come back again for a 10- to 15-minute review of the transactions, to make sure you understand them before you go on to the next section.

BEFORE YOU GO ON . . .

REVIEW IT

1. What is an example of an external transaction? What is an example of an internal transaction?
2. If an asset increases, what are the three possible effects on the basic accounting equation?

DO IT

A tabular analysis of the transactions made by Roberta Mendez & Co., a certified public accounting firm, for the month of August is shown below. Each increase and decrease in owner's equity is explained.

	Assets			=	**Liabilities**	+	**Owner's Equity**	
	Cash	+	**Office Equipment**	=	**Accounts Payable**	+	**R. Mendez, Capital**	
1.	+$25,000						+25,000	Investment
2.			+7,000		+7,000			
3.	+8,000						+8,000	Service Revenue
4.	−850						−850	Rent Expense

Describe each transaction that occurred for the month.

ACTION PLAN

- Analyze the tabular analysis to determine the nature and effect of each transaction.
- Keep the accounting equation always in balance.
- Remember that a change in an asset will require a change in another asset, a liability, or in owner's equity.

SOLUTION

1. The owner invested $25,000 of cash in the business.
2. The company purchased $7,000 of office equipment on credit.
3. The company received $8,000 of cash in exchange for services performed.
4. The company paid $850 for this month's rent.

Related exercise material: BE1-4, BE1-5, BE1-6, BE1-7, E1-2, E1-3, E1-4, E1-6, and E1-7.

THE NAVIGATOR

FINANCIAL STATEMENTS

STUDY OBJECTIVE 8

Understand what the four financial statements are and how they are prepared.

After transactions are identified, recorded, and summarized, four financial statements are prepared from the summarized accounting data:

1. An **income statement** presents the revenues and expenses and resulting net income or net loss for a specific period of time.
2. An **owner's equity statement** summarizes the changes in owner's equity for a specific period of time.
3. A **balance sheet** reports the assets, liabilities, and owner's equity at a specific date.
4. A **statement of cash flows** summarizes information about the cash inflows (receipts) and outflows (payments) for a specific period of time.

Each statement provides management, owners, and other interested parties with relevant financial data.

HELPFUL HINT

The income statement, owner's equity statement, and statement of cash flows are all for a *period* of time, whereas the balance sheet is for a *point* in time.

The financial statements of Softbyte are shown in Illustration 1-10. The statements are interrelated: **(1) Net income of $2,750 shown on the income statement is added to the beginning balance of owner's capital in the owner's equity statement. (2) Owner's capital of $16,450 at the end of the reporting period shown in the owner's equity statement is reported on the balance sheet. (3) Cash of $8,050 on the balance sheet is reported on the statement of cash flows.**

Also, every set of financial statements is accompanied by explanatory notes and supporting schedules that are an integral part of the statements. Examples of these notes and schedules are illustrated in later chapters of this textbook.

Be sure to carefully examine the format and content of each statement. The essential features of each are briefly described in the following sections.

INCOME STATEMENT

ALTERNATIVE TERMINOLOGY

The income statement is sometimes referred to as the *statement of operations*, *earnings statement*, or *profit and loss statement*.

Softbyte's income statement reports the revenues and expenses for a specific period of time (in this case, "For the Month Ended September 30, 2002"). Its income statement is prepared from the data appearing in the owner's equity column of Illustration 1-9.

On the income statement, revenues are listed first, followed by expenses. Finally net income (or net loss) is determined. Although practice varies, we have chosen in our illustrations and homework solutions to list expenses in order of magnitude. Alternative formats for the income statement will be considered in later chapters.

Note that investment and withdrawal transactions between the owner and the business are not included in the measurement of net income. For example, the withdrawal by Ray Neal of cash from Softbyte was not regarded as a business expense, as explained earlier.

OWNER'S EQUITY STATEMENT

Softbyte's owner's equity statement reports the changes in owner's equity for a specific period of time. The time period is the same as that covered by the income statement. Data for the preparation of the owner's equity statement are obtained from the owner's equity column of the tabular summary (Illustration 1-9) and from the income statement. The beginning owner's equity amount is shown on the first line of the statement. Then, the owner's investments, net income, and the owner's drawings are identified. The information in this statement indicates the reasons why owner's equity has increased or decreased during the period.

Illustration 1-10

Financial statements and their interrelationships

SOFTBYTE
Income Statement
For the Month Ended September 30, 2002

Revenues		
Service revenue		$4,700
Expenses		
Salaries expense	$900	
Rent expense	600	
Advertising expense	250	
Utilities expense	200	
Total expenses		1,950
Net income		**$2,750** ①

SOFTBYTE
Owner's Equity Statement
For the Month Ended September 30, 2002

R. Neal, Capital, September 1		$ –0–
Add: Investments	$15,000	
Net income	**2,750**	17,750
		17,750
Less: Drawings		1,300
R. Neal, Capital, September 30		**$16,450** ②

SOFTBYTE
Balance Sheet
September 30, 2002

Assets

Cash ③	**$ 8,050**
Accounts receivable	1,400
Supplies	1,600
Equipment	7,000
Total assets	$18,050

Liabilities and Owner's Equity

Liabilities	
Accounts payable	$ 1,600
Owner's equity	
R. Neal, Capital	**16,450**
Total liabilities and owner's equity	$18,050

SOFTBYTE
Statement of Cash Flows
For the Month Ended September 30, 2002

Cash flows from operating activities		
Cash receipts from revenues		$3,300
Cash payments for expenses		(1,950)
Net cash provided by operating activities		1,350
Cash flows from investing activities		
Purchase of equipment		(7,000)
Cash flows from financing activities		
Investments by owner	$15,000	
Drawings by owner	(1,300)	13,700
Net increase in cash		8,050
Cash at the beginning of the period		0
Cash at the end of the period		**$8,050**

HELPFUL HINT
The heading of each statement identifies the company, the type of statement, and the specific date or time period covered by the statement.

HELPFUL HINT
Note that final sums are double-underlined, and negative amounts are presented in parentheses.

HELPFUL HINT
Net income is computed first and is needed to determine the ending balance in owner's equity. The ending balance in owner's equity is needed in preparing the balance sheet. The cash shown on the balance sheet is needed in preparing the statement of cash flows.

What if Softbyte reported a net loss in its first month? Let's assume that during the month of September 2002, Softbyte lost $10,000. The presentation in the owner's equity statement of a net loss appears in Illustration 1-11.

Illustration 1-11

Presentation of net loss

SOFTBYTE
Owner's Equity Statement
For the Month Ended September 30, 2002

R. Neal, Capital, September 1		$ –0–
Add: Investments		15,000
		15,000
Less: Drawings	$ 1,300	
Net loss	**10,000**	11,300
R. Neal, Capital, September 30		$ 3,700

Any additional investments are reported as investments in the owner's equity statement.

BALANCE SHEET

Softbyte's balance sheet reports the assets, liabilities, and owner's equity at a specific date (in this case, September 30, 2002). The balance sheet is prepared from the column headings and the month-end data shown in the last line of the tabular summary (Illustration 1-9). Observe that the assets are listed at the top, followed by liabilities and owner's equity. Total assets must equal total liabilities and owner's equity. In the Softbyte balance sheet, only one liability, accounts payable, is reported. In most cases, there will be more than one liability. When two or more liabilities are involved, a customary way of listing is as follows.

Illustration 1-12

Presentation of liabilities

Liabilities	
Notes payable	$10,000
Accounts payable	63,000
Salaries payable	18,000
Total liabilities	$91,000

The balance sheet is like a snapshot of the company's financial condition at a specific moment in time (usually the month-end or year-end).

ACCOUNTING IN ACTION *Business Insight*

Why do companies choose the particular year-ends that they do? Not every company uses December 31 as the accounting year-end. Many companies choose to end their accounting year when inventory or operations are at a low. This is advantageous because compiling accounting information requires much time and effort by managers, so they would rather do it when they aren't as busy operating the business. Also, inventory is easier and less costly to count when it is low. Some companies whose year-ends differ from December 31 are **Delta Air Lines**, June 30; **Walt Disney Productions**, September 30; **Kmart Corp.**, January 31; and **Dunkin' Donuts Inc.**, October 31.

STATEMENT OF CASH FLOWS

Softbyte's statement of cash flows provides information on the cash receipts and payments for a specific period of time. The statement of cash flows reports (1) the cash effects of a company's operations during a period, (2) its investing transactions, (3) its financing transactions, (4) the net increase or decrease in cash during the period, and (5) the cash amount at the end of the period.

Reporting the sources, uses, and net increase or decrease in cash is useful because investors, creditors, and others want to know what is happening to a company's most liquid resource. The statement of cash flows, therefore, provides answers to the following simple but important questions.

1. Where did the cash come from during the period?
2. What was the cash used for during the period?
3. What was the change in the cash balance during the period?

Softbyte's statement of cash flows is provided in Illustration 1-10.

As shown in the statement, cash increased $8,050 during the period. Net cash flow provided from operating activities increased cash $1,350. Cash flow from investing transactions decreased cash $7,000. And cash flow from financing transactions increased cash $13,700. At this time, you need not be concerned with how these amounts are determined. Chapter 18 will examine the statement of cash flows in detail.

HELPFUL HINT
Investing activities pertain to investments made by the company, not investments made by the owner.

BEFORE YOU GO ON...

REVIEW IT

1. What are the income statement, statement of owner's equity, balance sheet, and statement of cash flows?
2. How are the financial statements interrelated?

A LOOK BACK AT OUR FEATURE STORY

Refer back to the Feature Story about **Lands' End** at the beginning of the chapter, and answer the following questions.

1. If you were interested in investing in Lands' End, what would the balance sheet and income statement tell you?
2. Would you request audited financial statements? Explain.
3. Will the financial statements show the market value of the company? Explain.

SOLUTION

1. The balance sheet reports the assets, liabilities, and owner's equity of the company. The income statement presents the revenues and expenses and resulting net income (or net loss) for a specific period of time. The balance sheet is like a snapshot of the company's financial condition at a point in time. The income statement indicates the profitability of the company. Also, the sources of the company's revenues and its expenses are provided in the income statement.
2. You should request **audited** financial statements—statements that a CPA has examined and expressed an opinion as to the fairness of presentation. You should not make decisions without having audited financial statements.
3. The financial statements will not show the market value of the company. One important principle of accounting is the cost principle, which states that assets should be recorded at cost. Cost has an important advantage over other valuations: it is reliable.

THE NAVIGATOR

LANDS' END DIRECT MERCHANTS

A Look Back exercises refer to the chapter-opening Feature Story. These exercises help you analyze that real-world situation in terms of the accounting topic of the chapter.

Additional Demonstration Problem

Demonstration Problems are a final review of the chapter. The **Action Plan** gives tips about how to approach the problem, and the **solution** demonstrates both the form and content of complete answers.

DEMONSTRATION PROBLEM

Mary Malone opens her own law office on July 1, 2002. During the first month of operations, the following transactions occurred.

1. Invested $10,000 in cash in the law practice.
2. Paid $800 for July rent on office space.
3. Purchased office equipment on account $3,000.
4. Provided legal services to clients for cash $1,500.
5. Borrowed $700 cash from a bank on a note payable.
6. Performed legal services for client on account $2,000.
7. Paid monthly expenses: salaries $500, utilities $300, and telephone $100.

Instructions

(a) Prepare a tabular summary of the transactions.

(b) Prepare the income statement, owner's equity statement, and balance sheet at July 31 for Mary Malone, Attorney at Law.

ACTION PLAN

- Remember that assets must equal liabilities and owner's equity after each transaction.
- Investments and revenues increase owner's equity.
- Expenses decrease owner's equity.
- The income statement shows revenues and expenses for a period of time.
- The owner's equity statement shows the changes in owner's equity for a period of time.
- The balance sheet reports assets, liabilities, and owner's equity at a specific date.

SOLUTION TO DEMONSTRATION PROBLEM

(a)

	Assets					=	Liabilities			+	Owner's Equity	
Transaction	Cash	+	Accounts Receivable	+	Equipment	=	Notes Payable	+	Accounts Payable	+	Mary Malone, Capital	
(1)	+$10,000										+$10,000	Investment
(2)	−800										−800	Rent Expense
	9,200					=					9,200	
(3)					+$3,000				+$3,000			
	9,200			+	3,000	=			3,000	+	9,200	
(4)	+1,500										+1,500	Service Revenue
	10,700			+	3,000	=			3,000	+	10,700	
(5)	+700						+$700					
	11,400			+	3,000	=	700	+	3,000	+	10,700	
(6)			+$2,000								+2,000	Service Revenue
	11,400	+	2,000	+	3,000	=	700	+	3,000	+	12,700	
(7)	−900										−500	Salaries Expense
											−300	Utilities Expense
											−100	Telephone Expense
	$10,500	+	$2,000	+	$3,000	=	$700	+	$3,000	+	$11,800	

(b)

MARY MALONE
Attorney at Law
Income Statement
For the Month Ended July 31, 2002

Revenues		
Service revenue		$3,500
Expenses		
Rent expense	$800	
Salaries expense	500	
Utilities expense	300	
Telephone expense	100	
Total expenses		1,700
Net income		$1,800

MARY MALONE
Attorney at Law
Owner's Equity Statement
For the Month Ended July 31, 2002

Mary Malone, Capital, July 1		$ -0-
Add: Investments	$10,000	
Net income	1,800	11,800
Mary Malone, Capital, July 31		$11,800

MARY MALONE
Attorney at Law
Balance Sheet
July 31, 2002

Assets	
Cash	$10,500
Accounts receivable	2,000
Equipment	3,000
Total assets	$15,500
Liabilities and Owner's Equity	
Liabilities	
Notes payable	$ 700
Accounts payable	3,000
Total liabilities	3,700
Owner's equity	
Mary Malone, Capital	11,800
Total liabilities and owner's equity	$15,500

This would be a good time to return to the **Student Owner's Manual** at the beginning of the book (or look at it for the first time if you skipped it before) to read about the various types of assignment materials that appear at the end of each chapter. Knowing the purpose of the different assignments will help you appreciate what each contributes to your accounting skills and competencies.

THE NAVIGATOR

SUMMARY OF STUDY OBJECTIVES

1. ***Explain what accounting is.*** Accounting is an information system that identifies, records, and communicates the economic events of an organization to interested users.

2. ***Identify the users and uses of accounting.*** The major users and uses of accounting are: (a) Management uses accounting information in planning, controlling, and evaluating business operations. (b) Investors (owners) decide whether to buy, hold, or sell their financial interests on the basis of accounting data. (c) Creditors (suppliers and bankers) evaluate the risks of granting credit or lending money on the basis of accounting information. Other groups that use accounting information are taxing authorities, regulatory agencies, customers, labor unions, and economic planners.

3. ***Understand why ethics is a fundamental business concept.*** Ethics are the standards of conduct by which actions are judged as right or wrong. If you cannot depend on the honesty of the individuals you deal with, effective communication and economic activity would be impossible, and information would have no credibility.

4. ***Explain the meaning of generally accepted accounting principles and the cost principle.*** Generally accepted accounting principles are a common set of standards used by accountants. The cost principle states that assets should be recorded at their cost.

5. ***Explain the meaning of the monetary unit assumption and the economic entity assumption.*** The monetary unit assumption requires that only transaction data capable of being expressed in terms of money be included in the accounting records. The economic entity assumption requires that the activities of each economic entity be kept separate from the activities of its owner and other economic entities.

6. ***State the basic accounting equation, and explain the meaning of assets, liabilities, and owner's equity.*** The basic accounting equation is:

Assets = Liabilities + Owner's Equity

Assets are resources owned by a business. Liabilities are creditorship claims on total assets. Owner's equity is the ownership claim on total assets.

7. ***Analyze the effects of business transactions on the basic accounting equation.*** Each business transaction must have a dual effect on the accounting equation. For example, if an individual asset is increased, there must be a corresponding (1) decrease in another asset, or (2) increase in a specific liability, or (3) increase in owner's equity.

8. ***Understand what the four financial statements are and how they are prepared.*** An income statement presents the revenues and expenses of a company for a specified period of time. An owner's equity statement summarizes the changes in owner's equity that have occurred for a specific period of time. A balance sheet reports the assets, liabilities, and owner's equity of a business at a specific date. A statement of cash flows summarizes information about the cash inflows (receipts) and outflows (payments) for a specific period of time.

THE NAVIGATOR

Key Term Matching Activity

GLOSSARY

Accounting The information system that identifies, records, and communicates the economic events of an organization to interested users. (p. 2).

Assets Resources owned by a business. (p. 13).

Auditing The examination of financial statements by a certified public accountant in order to express an opinion as to the fairness of presentation. (p. 7).

Balance sheet A financial statement that reports the assets, liabilities, and owner's equity at a specific date. (p. 22).

Basic accounting equation Assets = Liabilities + Owner's Equity. (p. 12).

Bookkeeping A part of accounting that involves only the recording of economic events. (p. 6).

Corporation A business organized as a separate legal entity under state corporation law, having ownership divided into transferable shares of stock. (p. 12).

Cost principle An accounting principle that states that assets should be recorded at their cost. (p. 10).

Drawings Withdrawal of cash or other assets from an unincorporated business for the personal use of the owner(s). (p. 14).

Economic entity assumption An assumption that requires that the activities of the entity be kept separate and distinct from the activities of its owner and all other economic entities. (p. 11).

Ethics The standards of conduct by which one's actions are judged as right or wrong, honest or dishonest, fair or not fair. (p. 9).

Expenses The cost of assets consumed or services used in the process of earning revenue. (p. 14).

Financial accounting The field of accounting that provides economic and financial information for investors, creditors, and other external users. (p. 6).

Financial Accounting Standards Board (FASB) A private organization that establishes generally accepted accounting principles. (p. 10).

Generally accepted accounting principles (GAAP) Common standards that indicate how to report economic events. (p. 10).

Income statement A financial statement that presents the revenues and expenses and resulting net income or net loss of a company for a specific period of time. (p. 22).

Investments by owner The assets put into the business by the owner. (p. 13).

Liabilities Creditorship claims on total assets. (p. 13).

Management consulting An area of public accounting that involves financial planning and control and the development of accounting and computer systems. (p. 7).

Managerial accounting The field of accounting that provides economic and financial information for managers and other internal users. (p. 6)

Monetary unit assumption An assumption stating that only transaction data that can be expressed in terms of money be included in the accounting records. (p. 11).

Net income The amount by which revenues exceed expenses. (p. 14).

Net loss The amount by which expenses exceed revenues. (p. 14).

Owner's equity The ownership claim on total assets. (p. 13).

Owner's equity statement A financial statement that summarizes the changes in owner's equity for a specific period of time. (p. 22).

Partnership An association of two or more persons to carry on as co-owners of a business for profit. (p. 12).

Private (or managerial) accounting An area of accounting within a company that involves such activities as cost accounting, budgeting, and accounting information systems. (p. 7).

Proprietorship A business owned by one person. (p. 11).

Public accounting An area of accounting in which the accountant offers expert service to the general public. (p. 7).

Revenues The gross increase in owner's equity resulting from business activities entered into for the purpose of earning income. (p. 13).

Securities and Exchange Commission (SEC) A governmental agency that requires companies to file financial reports in accordance with generally accepted accounting principles. (p. 10).

Statement of cash flows A financial statement that summarizes information about the cash inflows (receipts) and cash outflows (payments) for a specific period of time. (p. 22).

Taxation An area of public accounting that involves tax advice, tax planning, and preparing tax returns. (p. 7).

Transactions The economic events of an enterprise that are recorded by accountants. (p. 15).

Chapter 1 Self-Test

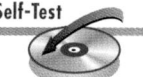

SELF-STUDY QUESTIONS

Answers are at the end of the chapter.

(SO 1) 1. Which of the following is *not* a step in the accounting process?
a. identification. c. recording.
b. verification. d. communication.

(SO 2) 2. Which of the following statements about users of accounting information is *incorrect*?
a. Management is an internal user.
b. Taxing authorities are external users.
c. Present creditors are external users.
d. Regulatory authorities are internal users.

(SO 2) 3. Services provided by a public accountant include:
a. auditing, taxation, and management consulting.
b. auditing, budgeting, and management consulting.
c. auditing, budgeting, and cost accounting.
d. internal auditing, budgeting, and management consulting.

(SO 4) 4. The cost principle states that:
a. assets should be initially recorded at cost and adjusted when the market value changes.
b. activities of an entity are to be kept separate and distinct from its owner.
c. assets should be recorded at their cost.
d. only transaction data capable of being expressed in terms of money be included in the accounting records.

(SO 5) 5. Which of the following statements about basic assumptions is *incorrect*?
a. Basic assumptions are the same as accounting principles.
b. The economic entity assumption states that there should be a particular unit of accountability.
c. The monetary unit assumption enables accounting to measure economic events.
d. An important part of the monetary unit assumption is the stable monetary unit assumption.

6. Net income will result during a time period when: (SO 6)
a. assets exceed liabilities.
b. assets exceed revenues.
c. expenses exceed revenues.
d. revenues exceed expenses.

7. Performing services on account will have the following effects on the components of the basic accounting equation: (SO 7)
a. increase assets and decrease owner's equity.
b. increase assets and increase owner's equity.
c. increase assets and increase liabilities.
d. increase liabilities and increase owner's equity.

8. As of December 31, 2002, Stoneland Company has assets of $3,500 and owner's equity of $2,000. What are the liabilities for Stoneland Company as of December 31, 2002? (SO 7)
a. $1,500. b. $1,000. c. $2,500. d. $2,000.

9. On the last day of the period, Genesis Company buys a $900 machine on credit. This transaction will affect the: (SO 8)
a. income statement only.
b. balance sheet only.
c. income statement and owner's equity statement only.
d. income statement, owner's equity statement, and balance sheet.

10. The financial statement that reports assets, liabilities, and owner's equity is the: (SO 8)
a. income statement.
b. owner's equity statement.
c. balance sheet.
d. statement of cash flow.

THE NAVIGATOR

QUESTIONS

1. "Accounting is ingrained in our society and it is vital to our economic system." Do you agree? Explain.
2. Identify and describe the steps in the accounting process.
3. (a) Who are internal users of accounting data?(b) How does accounting provide relevant data to these users?
4. What uses of financial accounting information are made by (a) investors and (b) creditors?
5. "Bookkeeping and accounting are the same." Do you agree? Explain.
6. John Alcorn Travel Agency purchased land for $85,000 cash on December 10, 2002. At December 31, 2002, the land's value has increased to $93,000. What amount should be reported for land on John Alcorn's balance sheet at December 31, 2002? Explain.
7. What is the monetary unit assumption? What impact does inflation have on the monetary unit assumption?
8. What is the economic entity assumption?
9. What are the three basic forms of business organizations for profit-oriented enterprises?
10. Kathy Mendoza is the owner of a successful printing shop. Recently her business has been increasing, and Kathy has been thinking about changing the organization of her business from a proprietorship to a corporation. Discuss some of the advantages Kathy would enjoy if she were to incorporate her business.
11. What is the basic accounting equation?
12. (a) Define the terms assets, liabilities, and owner's equity. (b) What items affect owner's equity?

13. Which of the following items are liabilities of Design Jewelry Stores?
(a) Cash.
(b) Accounts payable.
(c) Drawings.
(d) Accounts receivable.
(e) Supplies.
(f) Equipment.
(g) Salaries payable.
(h) Service revenue.
(i) Rent expense.

14. Can a business enter into a transaction in which only the left side of the basic accounting equation is affected? If so, give an example.

15. Are the following events recorded in the accounting records? Explain your answer in each case.
(a) The owner of the company dies.
(b) Supplies are purchased on account.
(c) An employee is fired.
(d) The owner of the business withdraws cash from the business for personal use.

16. Indicate how the following business transactions affect the basic accounting equation.
(a) Paid cash for janitorial services.
(b) Purchased equipment for cash.
(c) Invested cash in the business.
(d) Paid accounts payable in full.

17. Listed below are some items found in the financial statements of Alberto Rivera Co. Indicate in which financial statement(s) the following items would appear.
(a) Service revenue.
(b) Equipment.
(c) Advertising expense.
(d) Accounts receivable.
(e) Alberto Rivera, Capital.
(f) Wages payable.

18. In February 2002, Joe Kirby invested an additional $10,000 in his business, Kirby's Pharmacy, which is organized as a proprietorship. Kirby's accountant, Lance Jones, recorded this receipt as an increase in cash and revenues. Is this treatment appropriate? Why or why not?

19. "A company's net income appears directly on the income statement and the owner's equity statement, and it is included indirectly in the company's balance sheet." Do you agree? Explain.

20. King Enterprises had a capital balance of $168,000 at the beginning of the period. At the end of the accounting period, the capital balance was $198,000.
(a) Assuming no additional investment or withdrawals during the period, what is the net income for the period?
(b) Assuming an additional investment of $13,000 but no withdrawals during the period, what is the net income for the period?

21. Summarized operations for Kaustav Sen Co. for the month of July are as follows.

Revenues earned: for cash $35,000; on account $70,000.

Expenses incurred: for cash $26,000; on account $40,000.

Indicate for Kaustav Sen Co. (a) the total revenues, (b) the total expenses, and (c) net income for the month of July.

BRIEF EXERCISES

Use basic accounting equation. (SO 6)

BE1-1 Presented below is the basic accounting equation. Determine the missing amounts.

	Assets	=	Liabilities	+	Owner's Equity
(a)	$80,000		$50,000		?
(b)	?		$45,000		$70,000
(c)	$94,000		?		$62,000

Use basic accounting equation. (SO 6)

BE1-2 Given the accounting equation, answer each of the following questions.

(a) The liabilities of Weber Company are $100,000 and the owner's equity is $252,000. What is the amount of Weber Company's total assets?

(b) The total assets of Kafka Company are $170,000 and its owner's equity is $80,000. What is the amount of its total liabilities?

(c) The total assets of Motzek Co. are $600,000 and its liabilities are equal to one half of its total assets. What is the amount of Motzek Co.'s owner's equity?

Use basic accounting equation. (SO 6)

BE1-3 At the beginning of the year, Gilles Company had total assets of $820,000 and total liabilities of $500,000. Answer the following questions.

(a) If total assets increased $150,000 during the year and total liabilities decreased $80,000, what is the amount of owner's equity at the end of the year?

(b) During the year, total liabilities increased $100,000 and owner's equity decreased $70,000. What is the amount of total assets at the end of the year?

(c) If total assets decreased $90,000 and owner's equity increased $120,000 during the year, what is the amount of total liabilities at the end of the year?

Determine effect of transactions on basic accounting equation. (SO 7)

BE1-4 Presented below are three business transactions. On a sheet of paper, list the letters (a), (b), (c) with columns for assets, liabilities, and owner's equity. For each column, indicate whether the transactions increased (+), decreased (−), or had no effect (NE) on assets, liabilities, and owner's equity.

(a) Purchased supplies on account.
(b) Received cash for providing a service.
(c) Paid expenses in cash.

BE1-5 Follow the same format as BE1-4 above. Determine the effect on assets, liabilities, and owner's equity of the following three transactions.

Determine effect of transactions on basic accounting equation.
(SO 7)

(a) Invested cash in the business.
(b) Withdrawal of cash by owner.
(c) Received cash from a customer who had previously been billed for services provided.

BE1-6 Classify each of the following items as owner's drawing (D), revenue (R), or expense (E).

Determine effect of transactions on owner's equity.
(SO 7)

____**(a)** Advertising expense	____**(e)** Farve, Drawing
____**(b)** Commission revenue	____**(f)** Rent revenue
____**(c)** Insurance expense	____**(g)** Utilities expense
____**(d)** Salaries expense	

BE1-7 Presented below are three transactions. Mark each transaction as affecting owner's investment (I), owner's drawings (D), revenue (R), expense (E), or not affecting owner's equity (NOE).

Determine effect of transactions on owner's equity.
(SO 7)

____**(a)** Received cash for services performed
____**(b)** Paid cash to purchase equipment
____**(c)** Paid employee salaries.

BE1-8 In alphabetical order below are balance sheet items for Cheng Company at December 31, 2002. Kim Cheng is the owner of Cheng Company. Prepare a balance sheet, following the format of Illustration 1-10.

Prepare a balance sheet.
(SO 8)

Accounts payable	$80,000
Accounts receivable	$72,500
Cash	$39,000
Kim Cheng, Capital	$31,500

BE1-9 Indicate whether each of the following items is an asset (A), liability (L), or part of owner's equity (OE).

Identify assets, liabilities, and owner's equity.
(SO 6)

____**(a)** Accounts receivable	____ **(d)** Office supplies
____**(b)** Salaries payable	____ **(e)** Owner's investment
____**(c)** Equipment	____ **(f)** Notes payable

BE1-10 Indicate whether the following items would appear on the income statement (IS), balance sheet (BS), or owner's equity statement (OE).

Determine where items appear on financial statements.
(SO 8)

____**(a)** Notes payable	____ **(d)** Cash
____**(b)** Advertising expense	____ **(e)** Service revenue
____**(c)** H. Bruns, Capital	

EXERCISES

E1-1 Robbins Cleaners has the following balance sheet items.

Classify accounts as assets, liabilities, and owner's equity.
(SO 6)

Accounts payable	Accounts receivable
Cash	Notes payable
Cleaning equipment	Salaries payable
Cleaning supplies	J. Robbins, Capital

Instructions

Classify each item as an asset, liability, or owner's equity.

E1-2 Selected transactions for Green Acres Lawn Care Company are listed below.

Analyze the effect of transactions.
(SO 6, 7)

1. Made cash investment to start business.
2. Paid monthly rent.

3. Purchased equipment on account.
4. Billed customers for services performed.
5. Withdrew cash for owner's personal use.
6. Received cash from customers billed in (4).
7. Incurred advertising expense on account.
8. Purchased additional equipment for cash.
9. Received cash from customers when service was performed.

Instructions

List the numbers of the above transactions and describe the effect of each transaction on assets, liabilities, and owner's equity. For example, the first answer is: (1) Increase in assets and increase in owner's equity.

Analyze the effect of transactions on assets, liabilities, and owner's equity.
(SO 6, 7)

E1-3 Kidman Computer Timeshare Company entered into the following transactions during May 2002.

1. Purchased computer terminals for $21,500 from Digital Equipment on account.
2. Paid $4,000 cash for May rent on storage space.
3. Received $15,000 cash from customers for contracts billed in April.
4. Provided computer services to Fisher Construction Company for $3,000 cash.
5. Paid Northern States Power Co. $11,000 cash for energy usage in May.
6. Kidman invested an additional $32,000 in the business.
7. Paid Digital Equipment for the terminals purchased in (1) above.
8. Incurred advertising expense for May of $1,200 on account.

Instructions

Indicate with the appropriate letter whether each of the transactions above results in:

(a) an increase in assets and a decrease in assets.
(b) an increase in assets and an increase in owner's equity.
(c) an increase in assets and an increase in liabilities.
(d) a decrease in assets and a decrease in owner's equity.
(e) a decrease in assets and a decrease in liabilities.
(f) an increase in liabilities and a decrease in owner's equity.
(g) an increase in owner's equity and a decrease in liabilities.

Analyze transactions and compute net income.
(SO 7)

E1-4 An analysis of the transactions made by Roberta Mendez & Co., a certified public accounting firm, for the month of August is shown below. Each increase and decrease in owner's equity is explained.

	Cash	+ Accounts Receivable	+ Supplies	+ Office Equipment	= Accounts Payable	+ Owner's Equity R. Mendez, Capital	
1.	+$12,000					+$12,000	Investment
2.	−2,000			+$5,000	+$3,000		
3.	−750		+$750				
4.	+2,600	+$3,700				+6,300	Service Revenue
5.	−1,500				−1,500		
6.	−2,000					−2,000	Drawings
7.	−650					−650	Rent Expense
8.	+450	−450					
9.	−2,900					−2,900	Salaries Expense
10.					+500	−500	Utilities Expense

Instructions

(a) Describe each transaction that occurred for the month.
(b) Determine how much owner's equity increased for the month.
(c) Compute the amount of net income for the month.

Prepare an income statement and owner's equity statement.
(SO 8)

E1-5 An analysis of transactions for Roberta Mendez & Co. was presented in E1-4.

Instructions

Prepare an income statement and an owner's equity statement for August and a balance sheet at August 31, 2002.

Determine net income (or loss).
(SO 7)

E1-6 The Padre Company had the following assets and liabilities on the dates indicated.

December 31	Total Assets	Total Liabilities
2002	$400,000	$250,000
2003	$460,000	$305,000
2004	$590,000	$400,000

Padre began business on January 1, 2002, with an investment of $100,000.

Instructions

From an analysis of the change in owner's equity during the year, compute the net income (or loss) for:

(a) 2002, assuming Padre's drawings were $15,000 for the year.
(b) 2003, assuming Padre made an additional investment of $50,000 and had no drawings in 2003.
(c) 2004, assuming Padre made an additional investment of $15,000 and had drawings of $20,000 in 2004.

Analyze financial statements items.
(SO 6, 7)

E1-7 Two items are omitted from each of the following summaries of balance sheet and income statement data for two proprietorships for the year 2002, Neve Campbell and Maxim Enterprises.

	Neve Campbell	Maxim Enterprises
Beginning of year:		
Total assets	$ 97,000	$129,000
Total liabilities	80,000	(c)
Total owner's equity	(a)	95,000
End of year:		
Total assets	160,000	180,000
Total liabilities	120,000	50,000
Total owner's equity	40,000	130,000
Changes during year in owner's equity:		
Additional investment	(b)	25,000
Drawings	24,000	(d)
Total revenues	215,000	100,000
Total expenses	175,000	85,000

Instructions

Determine the missing amounts.

Prepare income statement and owner's equity statement.
(SO 8)

E1-8 The following information relates to Stanley Tucci Co. for the year 2002.

Stanley Tucci, Capital, January 1, 2002	$ 48,000	Advertising expense	$ 1,800
Stanley Tucci, Drawing during 2002	5,000	Rent expense	10,400
Service revenue	57,500	Utilities expense	3,100
Salaries expense	28,000		

Instructions

After analyzing the data, prepare an income statement and an owner's equity statement for the year ending December 31, 2002.

Correct an incorrectly prepared balance sheet.
(SO 8)

E1-9 Glenn Close is the bookkeeper for Amaro Company. Glenn has been trying to get the balance sheet of Amaro Company to balance. Amaro's balance sheet is as follows.

AMARO COMPANY
Balance Sheet
December 31, 2002

Assets		Liabilities	
Cash	$20,500	Accounts payable	$20,000
Supplies	8,000	Accounts receivable	(8,500)
Equipment	46,000	Amaro, Capital	67,500
Amaro, Drawing	4,500		
Total assets	$79,000	Total liabilities and owner's equity	$79,000

Instructions
Prepare a correct balance sheet.

Compute net income and prepare a balance sheet.
(SO 8)

E1-10 Kap Shin is the sole owner of Bear Park, a public camping ground near the Lake Mead National Recreation Area. Kap has compiled the following financial information as of December 31, 2002.

Revenues during 2002—camping fees	$160,000	Market value of equipment	$140,000
Revenues during 2002—general store	47,000	Notes payable	60,000
Accounts payable	11,000	Expenses during 2002	150,000
Cash on hand	20,000	Supplies on hand	2,500
Original cost of equipment	115,500		

Instructions
(a) Determine Kap Shin's net income from Bear Park for 2002.
(b) Prepare a balance sheet for Bear Park as of December 31, 2002.

Prepare an income statement.
(SO 8)

E1-11 Presented below is financial information related to the 2002 operations of Hockenberry Cruise Company.

Maintenance expense	$ 77,000
Property tax expense (on dock facilities)	10,000
Salaries expense	142,000
Advertising expense	3,500
Ticket revenue	325,000

Instructions
Prepare the 2002 income statement for Hockenberry Cruise Company.

Prepare an owner's equity statement.
(SO 8)

E1-12 Presented below is information related to the sole proprietorship of Mark Garland, attorney.

Legal service revenue—2002	$360,000
Total expenses—2002	211,000
Assets, January 1, 2002	85,000
Liabilities, January 1, 2002	62,000
Assets, December 31, 2002	168,000
Liabilities, December 31, 2002	70,000
Drawings—2002	?

Instructions
Prepare the 2002 owner's equity statement for Mark Garland's legal practice.

PROBLEMS: SET A

Analyze transactions and compute net income.
(SO 6, 7)

P1-1A Affleck's Repair Shop was started on May 1 by B. Affleck. A summary of May transactions is presented below.

1. Invested $10,000 cash to start the repair shop.
2. Purchased equipment for $5,000 cash.
3. Paid $400 cash for May office rent.
4. Paid $500 cash for supplies.
5. Incurred $250 of advertising costs in the *Beacon News* on account.
6. Received $4,100 in cash from customers for repair service.
7. Withdrew $500 cash for personal use.
8. Paid part-time employee salaries $1,000.
9. Paid utility bills $140.
10. Provided repair service on account to customers $850.
11. Collected cash of $120 for services billed in transaction (10).

Instructions

(a) Ending capital $12,660

(a) Prepare a tabular analysis of the transactions, using the following column headings: Cash, Accounts Receivable, Supplies, Equipment, Accounts Payable, and B. Affleck, Capital. Revenue is called Service Revenue.

(b) From an analysis of the column B. Affleck, Capital, compute the net income or net loss for May.

(b) Net income $3,160

P1-2A Judi Dench opened a veterinary business in Nashville, Tennessee, on August 1. On August 31, the balance sheet showed Cash $9,000, Accounts Receivable $1,700, Supplies $600, Office Equipment $6,000, Accounts Payable $3,600, and J. Dench, Capital $13,700. During September the following transactions occurred.

Analyze transactions and prepare income statement and owner's equity statement.
(SO 6, 7, 8)

1. Paid $2,900 cash on accounts payable.
2. Collected $1,300 of accounts receivable.
3. Purchased additional office equipment for $2,100, paying $800 in cash and the balance on account.
4. Earned revenue of $6,300, of which $2,500 is paid in cash and the balance is due in October.
5. Withdrew $600 cash for personal use.
6. Paid salaries $700, rent for September $900, and advertising expense $300.
7. Incurred utility expenses for month on account $170.
8. Received $7,000 from Capital Bank—money borrowed on a note payable.

Instructions

(a) Prepare a tabular analysis of the September transactions beginning with August 31 balances. The column headings should be as follows: Cash + Accounts Receivable + Supplies + Office Equipment = Notes Payable + Accounts Payable + J. Dench, Capital.

(a) Ending capital $17,330

(b) Prepare an income statement for September, an owner's equity statement for September, and a balance sheet at September 30.

(b) Net income $4,230
Total assets $26,500

P1-3A On May 1, Dennis Chambers started Skyline Flying School, a company that provides flying lessons, by investing $45,000 cash in the business. Following are the assets and liabilities of the company on May 31, 2002, and the revenues and expenses for the month of May.

Prepare income statement, owner's equity statement, and balance sheet.
(SO 8)

Cash	$ 6,500	Notes Payable	$30,000
Accounts Receivable	7,200	Rent Expense	1,200
Equipment	64,000	Repair Expense	400
Lesson Revenue	8,600	Fuel Expense	2,500
Advertising Expense	500	Insurance Expense	400
		Accounts Payable	800

Dennis Chambers made no additional investment in May, but he withdrew $1,700 in cash for personal use.

Instructions

(a) Prepare an income statement and owner's equity statement for the month of May and a balance sheet at May 31.

(b) Prepare an income statement and owner's equity statement for May assuming the following data are not included above: (1) $900 of revenue was earned and billed but not collected at May 31, and (2) $3,300 of fuel expense was incurred but not paid.

(a) Net income $3,600
Owner's equity $46,900
Total assets $77,700
(b) Net income $1,200
Owner's equity $44,500

P1-4A Ron Salem started his own delivery service, Salem Deliveries, on June 1, 2002. The following transactions occurred during the month of June.

Analyze transactions and prepare financial statements.
(SO 7, 8)

June 1 Ron invested $10,000 cash in the business.
2 Purchased a used van for deliveries for $10,000. Ron paid $2,000 cash and signed a note payable for the remaining balance.
3 Paid $500 for office rent for the month.
5 Performed $1,400 of services on account.
9 Withdrew $200 cash for personal use.
12 Purchased supplies for $150 on account.
15 Received a cash payment of $750 for services provided on June 5.
17 Purchased gasoline for $100 on account.
20 Received a cash payment of $1,500 for services provided.
23 Made a cash payment of $500 on the note payable.
26 Paid $250 for utilities.
29 Paid for the gasoline purchased on account on June 17.
30 Paid $500 for employee salaries.

Instructions

(a) Ending capital $11,350

(a) Show the effects of the previous transactions on the accounting equation using the following format.

	Assets					Liabilities		Owner's Equity
Date	**Cash** +	**Accounts Receivable** +	**Supplies** +	**Delivery Van**	=	**Notes Payable** +	**Accounts Payable** +	**R. Salem, Capital**

Include explanations for any changes in the R. Salem, Capital account in your analysis.

(b) Net income $1,550
(c) Cash $8,200

(b) Prepare an income statement for the month of June.
(c) Prepare a balance sheet at June 30, 2002.

Determine financial statement amounts and prepare owner's equity statements.
(SO 7, 8)

P1-5A Financial statement information about four different companies is as follows.

	Zarle Company	Wasicsko Company	McCain Company	Russe Company
January 1, 2002				
Assets	$ 84,000	$110,000	(g)	$170,000
Liabilities	50,000	(d)	75,000	(j)
Owner's equity	(a)	60,000	50,000	90,000
December 31, 2002				
Assets	(b)	147,000	200,000	(k)
Liabilities	55,000	65,000	(h)	80,000
Owner's equity	58,000	(e)	130,000	180,000
Owner's equity changes in year				
Additional investment	(c)	15,000	10,000	15,000
Drawings	25,000	(f)	14,000	20,000
Total revenues	350,000	420,000	(i)	520,000
Total expenses	320,000	385,000	342,000	(1)

Instructions

(a) Determine the missing amounts.
(b) Prepare the owner's equity statement for Wasicsko Company.
(c) Write a memorandum explaining the sequence for preparing financial statements and the interrelationship of the owner's equity statement to the income statement and balance sheet.

PROBLEMS: SET B

Analyze transactions and compute net income.
(SO 6, 7)

P1-1B On April 1, Dolly Parton established Matrix Travel Agency. The following transactions were completed during the month.

1. Invested $10,000 cash to start the agency.
2. Paid $400 cash for April office rent.
3. Purchased office equipment for $2,500 cash.
4. Incurred $300 of advertising costs in the *Chicago Tribune,* on account.
5. Paid $600 cash for office supplies.
6. Earned $9,500 for services rendered: $1,000 cash is received from customers, and the balance of $8,500 is billed to customers on account.
7. Withdrew $200 cash for personal use.
8. Paid *Chicago Tribune* amount due in transaction (4).
9. Paid employees' salaries $2,200.
10. Received $8,000 in cash from customers who have previously been billed in transaction (6).

Instructions

(a) Ending capital $16,400

(a) Prepare a tabular analysis of the transactions using the following column headings: Cash, Accounts Receivable, Supplies, Office Equipment, Accounts Payable, and Dolly Parton, Capital.

(b) From an analysis of the column Dolly Parton, Capital, compute the net income or net loss for April.

(b) Net income $6,600

P1-2B Michelle Pfeiffer opened a law office, Michelle Pfeiffer, Attorney at Law, on July 1, 2002. On July 31, the balance sheet showed Cash $4,000, Accounts Receivable $1,500, Supplies $500, Office Equipment $5,000, Accounts Payable $4,200, and Michelle Pfeiffer, Capital $6,800. During August the following transactions occurred.

Analyze transactions and prepare income statement and owner's equity statement.
(SO 6, 7, 8)

1. Collected $1,400 of accounts receivable.
2. Paid $2,700 cash on accounts payable.
3. Earned revenue of $7,500 of which $3,000 is collected in cash and the balance is due in September.
4. Purchased additional office equipment for $1,000, paying $400 in cash and the balance on account.
5. Paid salaries $2,500, rent for August $900, and advertising expenses $350.
6. Withdrew $550 in cash for personal use.
7. Received $2,000 from Standard Federal Bank—money borrowed on a note payable.
8. Incurred utility expenses for month on account $250.

Instructions

(a) Prepare a tabular analysis of the August transactions beginning with July 31 balances. The column headings should be as follows: Cash + Accounts Receivable + Supplies + Office Equipment = Notes Payable + Accounts Payable + Michelle Pfeiffer, Capital.

(a) Ending capital $9,750

(b) Prepare an income statement for August, an owner's equity statement for August, and a balance sheet at August 31.

(b) Net income $3,500
Total assets $14,100

P1-3B On June 1, Cindy Crawford started Divine Cosmetics Co., a company that provides individual skin care treatment, by investing $26,200 cash in the business. Following are the assets and liabilities of the company at June 30 and the revenues and expenses for the month of June.

Prepare income statement, owner's equity statement, and balance sheet.
(SO 8)

Cash	$12,000	Notes Payable	$13,000
Accounts Receivable	4,000	Accounts Payable	1,200
Service Revenue	7,500	Supplies Expense	1,600
Cosmetic Supplies	2,000	Gas and Oil Expense	800
Advertising Expense	500	Utilities Expense	300
Equipment	25,000		

Cindy made no additional investment in June, but withdrew $1,700 in cash for personal use during the month.

Instructions

(a) Prepare an income statement and owner's equity statement for the month of June and a balance sheet at June 30, 2002.

(b) Prepare an income statement and owner's equity statement for June assuming the following data are not included above: (1) $800 of revenue was earned and billed but not collected at June 30, and (2) $100 of gas and oil expense was incurred but not paid.

(a) Net income $4,300
Owner's equity $28,800
Total assets $43,000
(b) Net income $5,000
Owner's equity $29,500

P1-4B Julie Spengel started her own consulting firm, Spengel Consulting, on May 1, 2002. The following transactions occurred during the month of May.

Analyze transactions and prepare financial statements.
(SO 7, 8)

May 1 Spengel invested $8,000 cash in the business.
2 Paid $800 for office rent for the month.
3 Purchased $500 of supplies on account.
5 Paid $50 to advertise in the *County News*.
9 Received $1,000 cash for services provided.
12 Withdrew $700 cash for personal use.
15 Performed $3,300 of services on account.
17 Paid $2,500 for employee salaries.
20 Paid for the supplies purchased on account on May 3.
23 Received a cash payment of $2,000 for services provided on account on May 15.
26 Borrowed $5,000 from the bank on a note payable.
29 Purchased office equipment for $2,400 on account.
30 Paid $150 for utilities.

Instructions

(a) Ending capital $8,100

(a) Show the effects of the previous transactions on the accounting equation using the following format.

	Assets					Liabilities			Owner's Equity
Date	**Cash** +	**Accounts Receivable** +	**Supplies** +	**Office Equipment**	=	**Notes Payable** +	**Accounts Payable**	+	**J. Spengel, Capital**

Include explanations for any changes in the J. Spengel, Capital account in your analysis.

(b) Net income $800
(c) Cash $11,300

(b) Prepare an income statement for the month of May.

(c) Prepare a balance sheet at May 31, 2002.

Determine financial statement amounts and prepare owner's equity statements.
(SO 7, 8)

P1-5B Financial statement information about four different companies is as follows.

	Yanni Company	Selara Company	Candlebox Company	Winans Company
January 1, 2002				
Assets	$ 75,000	$90,000	(g)	$150,000
Liabilities	50,000	(d)	75,000	(j)
Owner's equity	(a)	60,000	54,000	90,000
December 31, 2002				
Assets	(b)	117,000	180,000	(k)
Liabilities	55,000	62,000	(h)	80,000
Owner's equity	45,000	(e)	110,000	140,000
Owner's equity changes in year				
Additional investment	(c)	8,000	10,000	15,000
Drawings	10,000	(f)	12,000	10,000
Total revenues	350,000	400,000	(i)	500,000
Total expenses	335,000	385,000	360,000	(l)

Instructions

(a) Determine the missing amounts. (*Hint:* For example, to solve for (a), Assets − Liabilities = Owner's equity = $25,000.)

(b) Prepare the owner's equity statement for Yanni Company.

(c) Write a memorandum explaining the sequence for preparing financial statements and the interrelationship of the owner's equity statement to the income statement and balance sheet.

BROADENING YOUR PERSPECTIVE

FINANCIAL REPORTING AND ANALYSIS

FINANCIAL REPORTING PROBLEM: Lands' End, Inc.

BYP1-1 The actual financial statements of **Lands' End**, as presented in the company's 2000 Annual Report, are contained in Appendix A (at the back of the textbook).

Instructions

Refer to Lands' End's financial statements and answer the following questions.

(a) What were Lands' End's total assets at January 28, 2000? At January 29, 1999?

(b) How much cash (and cash equivalents) did Land's End have on January 28, 2000?

(c) What amount of accounts payable did Lands' End report on January 28, 2000? On January 29, 1999?
(d) What were Lands' End's net sales in 1998? In 1999? In 2000?
(e) What is the amount of the change in Lands' End's net income from 1999 to 2000?

COMPARATIVE ANALYSIS PROBLEM: Lands' End vs. Abercrombie & Fitch

BYP1-2 **Lands' End's** financial statements are presented in Appendix A. **Abercrombie & Fitch's** financial statements are presented in Appendix B.

Instructions

(a) Based on the information contained in these financial statements, determine the following for each company.
  (1) Total assets at January 28, 2000, for Lands' End and at January 29, 2000, for Abercrombie & Fitch.
  (2) Accounts (notes) receivable, net at January 28, 2000, for Lands' End and at January 29, 2000, for Abercrombie & Fitch.
  (3) Net sales for year ended in 2000.
  (4) Net income for year ended in 2000.
(b) What conclusions concerning the two companies can be drawn from these data?

INTERPRETING FINANCIAL STATEMENTS: A Global Focus

BYP1-3 Today companies must compete in a global economy. **Nestlé**, a Swiss company, is the largest food company in the world. If you were interested in broadening your investment portfolio, you might consider investing in Nestlé. However, investing in international companies can pose some additional challenges. Consider the following excerpts from the notes to Nestlé's financial statements.

NESTLÉ
Notes to the Financial Statements (partial)

(a) The Group accounts comply with International Accounting Standards (IAS) issued by the International Accounting Standards Committee (IASC) and with the Standards Interpretations issued by the Standards Interpretation Committee of the IASC (SIC).
(b) The accounts have been prepared under the historical cost convention and on an accrual basis. All significant consolidated companies have a 31st December accounting year end. All disclosures required by the 4th and 7th European Union company law directives are provided.
(c) On consolidation, assets and liabilities of Group companies denominated in foreign currencies are translated into Swiss francs at year-end rates. Income and expense items are translated into Swiss francs at the annual average rates of exchange or, where known or determinable, at the rate on the date of the transaction for significant items.

Instructions
Discuss the implications of each of these items in terms of the effect it might have (positive or negative) on your ability to compare Nestlé to a U.S. food company such as Tootsie Roll or Hershey Foods. (*Hint:* In preparing your answer review the discussion of principles and assumptions in financial reporting on pages 10 and 11.)

EXPLORING THE WEB

BYP1-4 This exercise will familiarize you with skill requirements, job descriptions, and salaries for accounting careers.

Address: **www.cob.ohio-state.edu/dept/fin/jobs/account.htm *(or go to www.wiley.com/college/weygandt)***

Instructions
Go to the site shown above. Answer the following questions.

(a) What are the three broad areas of accounting (from "Skills and Requirements")?
(b) List eight skills required in accounting.
(c) How do the three accounting areas differ in terms of these eight required skills?
(d) Explain one of the key job functions in accounting.
(e) Based on the *Smart Money* survey, what is the salary range for a junior staff accountant with Deloitte & Touche?

CRITICAL THINKING

GROUP DECISION CASE

BYP1-5 Jill and Mark Illster, local golf stars, opened the Chip-Shot Driving Range on March 1, 2002, by investing $10,000 of their cash savings in the business. A caddy shack was constructed for cash at a cost of $4,000, and $800 was spent on golf balls and golf clubs. The Illsters leased five acres of land at a cost of $1,000 per month and paid the first month's rent. During the first month, advertising costs totaled $750, of which $150 was unpaid at March 31, and $400 was paid to members of the high-school golf team for retrieving golf balls. All revenues from customers were deposited in the company's bank account. On March 15, Jill and Mark withdrew a total of $800 in cash for personal living expenses. A $100 utility bill was received on March 31 but was not paid. On March 31, the balance in the company's bank account was $7,550.

Jill and Mark thought they had a pretty good first month of operations. But, their estimates of profitability ranged from a loss of $2,450 to net income of $2,100.

Instructions
With the class divided into groups, answer the following.

(a) How could the Illsters have concluded that the business operated at a loss of $2,450? Was this a valid basis on which to determine net income?
(b) How could the Illsters have concluded that the business operated at a net income of $2,100? (*Hint:* Prepare a balance sheet at March 31.) Was this a valid basis on which to determine net income?
(c) Without preparing an income statement, determine the actual net income for March.
(d) What was the revenue earned in March?

COMMUNICATION ACTIVITY

BYP1-6 Sarah Rankin, the bookkeeper for New York Company, has been trying to get the balance sheet to balance. The company's balance sheet is as follows.

NEW YORK COMPANY
Balance Sheet
For the Month Ended December 31, 2002

Assets		**Liabilities**	
Equipment	$20,500	Thompson, Capital	$23,000
Cash	9,000	Accounts receivable	(6,000)
Supplies	2,000	Thompson, Drawing	(2,000)
Accounts payable	(6,000)	Notes payable	10,500
	$25,500		$25,500

Instructions
Explain to Sarah Rankin in a memo why the original balance sheet is incorrect, and what should be done to correct it.

ETHICS CASE

BYP1-7 After numerous campus interviews, Warren Filler, a senior at Great Northern College, received two office interview invitations from the Baltimore offices of two large firms.

Both firms offered to cover his out-of-pocket expenses (travel, hotel, and meals). He scheduled the interviews for both firms on the same day, one in the morning and one in the afternoon. At the conclusion of each interview, he submitted to both firms his total out-of-pocket expenses for the trip to Baltimore: mileage $70 (280 miles at $0.25), hotel $130, meals $36, parking and tolls $18, for a total of $254. He believes this approach is appropriate. If he had made two trips, his cost would have been two times $254. He is also certain that neither firm knew he had visited the other on that same trip. Within ten days Warren received two checks in the mail, each in the amount of $254.

Instructions

(a) Who are the stakeholders (affected parties) in this situation?
(b) What are the ethical issues in this case?
(c) What would you do in this situation?

Answers to Self-Study Questions

1. b **2.** d **3.** a **4.** c **5.** a **6.** d **7.** b **8.** a **9.** b **10.** c

Answer to Lands' End Review It Question 4, p. 14

Lands' End's accounting equation is:

Assets	=	Liabilities	+	Owner's (Stockholders') Equity
$456,196,000	=	$159,989,000	+	$296,207,000

LANDS' END DIRECT MERCHANTS

Remember to go back to the Navigator box on the chapter-opening page and check off your completed work.

THE RECORDING PROCESS

2

THE NAVIGATOR ✓

- Understand *Concepts for Review* ❑
- Read *Feature Story* ❑
- Scan *Study Objectives* ❑
- Read *Preview* ❑
- Read text and answer *Before You Go On*
  p. 49 ❑ *p.* 52 ❑ *p.* 62 ❑ *p.* 66 ❑
- Work *Demonstration Problem* ❑
- Review *Summary of Study Objectives* ❑
- Answer *Self-Study Questions* ❑
- Complete *Assignments* ❑

CONCEPTS FOR REVIEW

Before studying this chapter, you should know or, if necessary, review:

a. What are assets, liabilities, owner's capital, owner's drawings, revenues, and expenses. (Ch. 1, pp. 13–14)

b. Why assets equal liabilities plus owner's equity. (Ch. 1, p. 12)

c. What transactions are and how they affect the basic accounting equation. (Ch. 1, pp. 15–20)

☑ THE NAVIGATOR

FEATURE STORY

No Such Thing As a Perfect World

When she got a job doing the accounting for **Forster's Restaurants**, Tanis Anderson had almost finished her business administration degree at Simon Fraser University. But even after Tanis completed her degree requirements, her education still continued—this time, in the real world.

Tanis's responsibilities include paying the bills, tracking food and labor costs, and managing the payroll for **The Mug and Musket**, a popular destination restaurant in Surrey, British Columbia. "My title is Director of Finance," she laughs, "but really that means I take care of whatever needs doing!"

The use of judgment is a big part of the job. As Tanis says, "I learned all the fundamentals in my business classes, but school prepares you for a perfect world, and there is no such thing."

She feels fortunate that her boss understands her job is a learning experience as well as a responsibility. "Sometimes he's let me do something he knew perfectly well was a mistake so I can learn something through experience," she admits.

To help others gain the benefits of her real-world learning, Tanis is always happy to help students in the area who want to use Forster's as the subject of a project or report. "It's the least I can do," she says.

☑ THE NAVIGATOR

STUDY OBJECTIVES

After studying this chapter, you should be able to:

1. Explain what an account is and how it helps in the recording process.
2. Define debits and credits and explain how they are used to record business transactions.
3. Identify the basic steps in the recording process.
4. Explain what a journal is and how it helps in the recording process.
5. Explain what a ledger is and how it helps in the recording process.
6. Explain what posting is and how it helps in the recording process.
7. Prepare a trial balance and explain its purposes.

☑ THE NAVIGATOR

PREVIEW OF CHAPTER 2

In Chapter 1, we analyzed business transactions in terms of the accounting equation. The cumulative effects of these transactions were presented in tabular form. Imagine a restaurant and gift shop such as **The Mug and Musket** using the same tabular format as Softbyte to keep track of every one of its transactions. In a single day, this restaurant and gift shop engages in hundreds of business transactions. To record each transaction this way would be impractical, expensive, and unnecessary. Instead, a set of procedures and records are used to keep track of transaction data more easily.

This chapter introduces and illustrates these basic procedures and records. The content and organization of Chapter 2 are as follows.

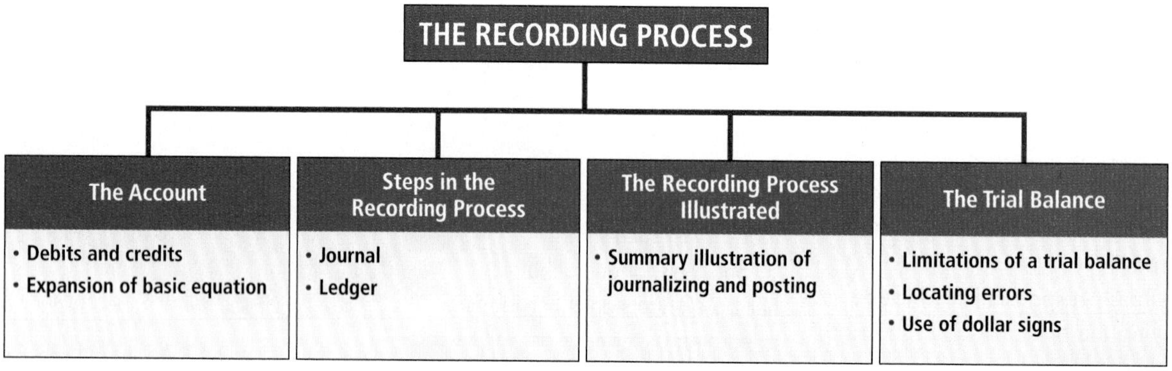

THE NAVIGATOR

STUDY OBJECTIVE 1

Explain what an account is and how it helps in the recording process.

Accounting Cycle Tutorial—Recording Business Transactions

THE ACCOUNT

An **account** is an individual accounting record of increases and decreases in a specific asset, liability, or owner's equity item. For example, Softbyte (the company discussed in Chapter 1) would have separate accounts for Cash, Accounts Receivable, Accounts Payable, Service Revenue, Salaries Expense, and so on. In its simplest form, an account consists of three parts: (1) the title of the account, (2) a left or debit side, and (3) a right or credit side. Because the alignment of these parts of an account resembles the letter T, it is referred to as a **T account**. The basic form of an account is shown in Illustration 2-1.

Illustration 2-1

Basic form of account

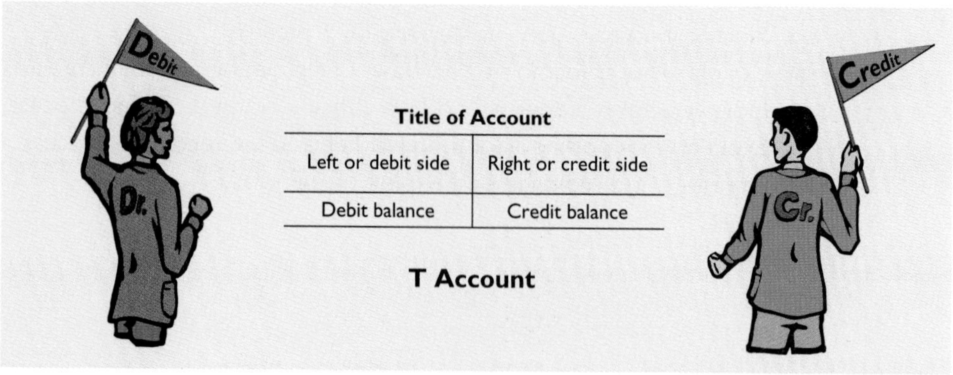

The T account is a standard shorthand in accounting that helps make clear the effects of transactions on individual accounts. We will use it often throughout this book to explain basic accounting relationships. (Note that when we are referring to a specific account, we capitalize its name.)

DEBITS AND CREDITS

STUDY OBJECTIVE 2

Define debits and credits and explain how they are used to record business transactions.

The term **debit** means left, and **credit** means right. They are commonly abbreviated as Dr. for debit and Cr. for credit.[1] These terms are directional signals: They indicate which side of a T account a number will be recorded on. Entering an amount on the left side of an account is called **debiting** the account; making an entry on the right side is **crediting** the account.

The procedure of having debits on the left and credits on the right is an accounting custom, or rule (like the custom of driving on the right-hand side of the road in the United States). **This rule applies to all accounts.** When the totals of the two sides are compared, an account will have a **debit balance** if the total of the debit amounts exceeds the credits. An account will have a **credit balance** if the credit amounts exceed the debits.

The recording of debits and credits in an account is shown in Illustration 2-2 for the cash transactions of Softbyte. The data are taken from the cash column of the tabular summary in Illustration 1-9.

Illustration 2-2

Tabular summary compared to account form

Tabular Summary

Cash
$15,000
−7,000
1,200
1,500
−1,700
−250
600
−1,300
$ 8,050

Account Form

Cash			
(Debits)	15,000	(Credits)	7,000
	1,200		1,700
	1,500		250
	600		1,300
Balance (Debit)	8,050		

HELPFUL HINT
At this point, don't think about increases and decreases in relation to debits and credits. As you'll soon learn, the effects of debits and credits depend on the type of account involved.

In the tabular summary every positive item represents a receipt of cash; every negative amount represents a payment of cash. Notice that in the account form the increases in cash are recorded as debits, and the decreases in cash are recorded as credits. Having increases on one side and decreases on the other helps in determining the total of each side of the account as well as the overall balance in the account. The account balance, a debit of $8,050, indicates that Softbyte has had $8,050 more increases than decreases in cash.

Debit and Credit Procedure

HELPFUL HINT
Debits must equal credits for each transaction.

In Chapter 1 you learned the effect of a transaction on the basic accounting equation. Remember that each transaction must affect two or more accounts to keep the basic accounting equation in balance. In other words, for each transaction debits must equal credits in the accounts. The equality of debits and credits provides the basis for the **double-entry system** of recording transactions.

Under the double-entry system the dual (two-sided) effect of each transaction is recorded in appropriate accounts. This universally used system provides a logical method for recording transactions. It also offers a means of proving the

[1]These terms and their abbreviations come from the Latin words *debere* (Dr.) and *credere* (Cr.).

accuracy of the recorded amounts. If every transaction is recorded with equal debits and credits, then the sum of all the debits to the accounts must equal the sum of all the credits.

The double-entry system for determining the equality of the accounting equation is much more efficient than the plus/minus procedure used in Chapter 1. There, it was necessary after each transaction to compare total assets with total liabilities and owner's equity to determine the equality of the two sides of the accounting equation.

ASSETS AND LIABILITIES. We know that both sides of the basic equation (Assets = Liabilities + Owner's equity) must be equal. It follows that increases and decreases in assets and liabilities must be recorded opposite from each other. In Illustration 2-2, increases in cash—an asset—were entered on the left side, and decreases in cash were entered on the right side. Therefore, increases in liabilities must be entered on the right or credit side, and decreases in liabilities must be entered on the left or debit side. The effects that debits and credits have on assets and liabilities are summarized as follows.

Illustration 2-3

Debit and credit effects—assets and liabilities

Debits	Credits
Increase assets	Decrease assets
Decrease liabilities	Increase liabilities

HELPFUL HINT
The normal balance for an account is always the same as the increase side.

Debits to a specific asset account should exceed the credits to that account. Credits to a liability account should exceed debits to that account. The **normal balance** of an account is on the side where an increase in the account is recorded. Thus, asset accounts normally show debit balances, and liability accounts normally show credit balances. The normal balances can be diagrammed as follows.

Illustration 2-4

Normal balances—assets and liabilities

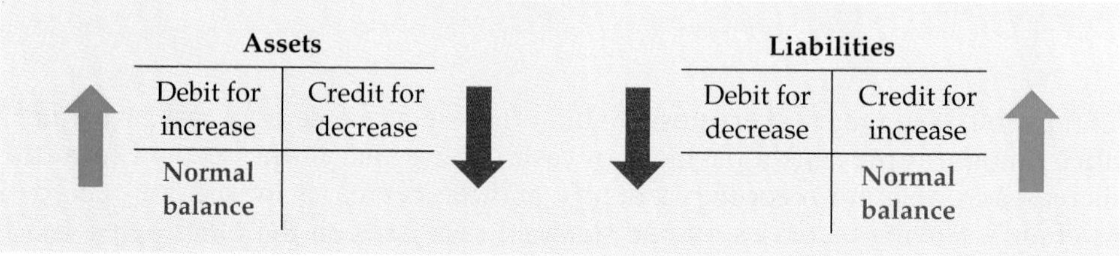

Knowing the normal balance in an account may help you trace errors. For example, a credit balance in an asset account such as Land or a debit balance in a liability account such as Wages Payable would indicate recording errors. Occasionally, an abnormal balance may be correct. The Cash account, for example, will have a credit balance when a company has overdrawn its bank balance (i.e., written a "bad" check).

OWNER'S EQUITY. As indicated in Chapter 1, owner's equity is increased by owner's investments and by revenues. It is decreased by owner's drawings and by expenses. In a double-entry system, accounts are kept for each of these types of transactions, as explained below.

Owner's Capital. Investments by owners are credited to the Owner's Capital account. Credits increase this account and debits decrease it. For example, when cash is invested in the business, Cash is debited (increased) and Owner's Capital is credited (increased). When the owner's investment in the business is reduced, Owner's Capital is debited (decreased).

The rules of debit and credit for the Owner's Capital account are stated as follows.

Debits	Credits
Decrease Owner's Capital	Increase Owner's Capital

Illustration 2-5

Debit and credit effects—Owner's Capital

The normal balance in this account can be diagrammed as follows.

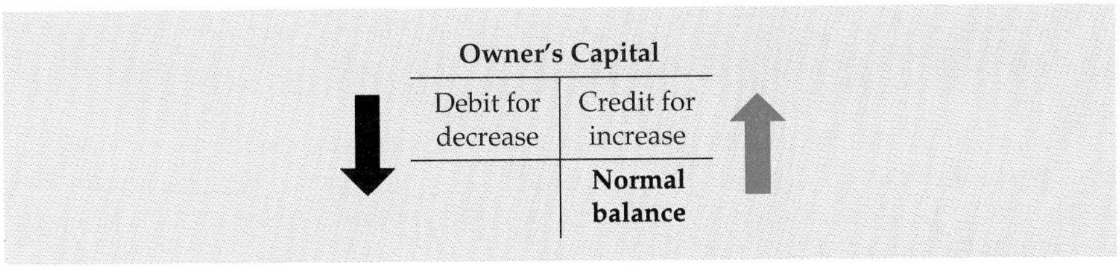

Illustration 2-6

Normal balance—Owner's Capital

Owner's Drawing. An owner may withdraw cash or other assets for personal use. Withdrawals could be debited directly to Owner's Capital to indicate a decrease in owner's equity. However, it is preferable to establish a separate account, called the Owner's Drawing account. This separate account makes it easier to determine total withdrawals for each accounting period. **The drawing account decreases owner's equity. It is not an income statement account like revenues and expenses.** Owner's Drawing is increased by debits and decreased by credits. Normally, the drawing account will have a debit balance.

The rules of debit and credit for the drawing account are stated as follows.

Debits	Credits
Increase Owner's Drawing	Decrease Owner's Drawing

Illustration 2-7

Debit and credit effects—Owner's Drawing

The normal balance can be diagrammed as follows.

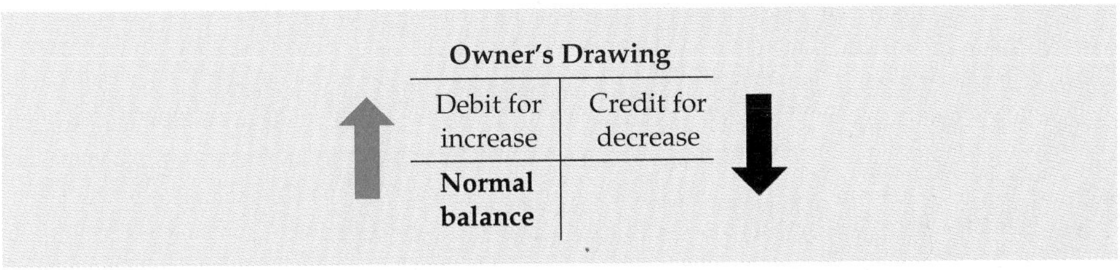

Illustration 2-8

Normal balance—Owner's Drawing

Revenues and Expenses. Remember that the ultimate purpose of earning revenues is to benefit the owner(s) of the business. When revenues are earned, owner's equity is increased. Therefore, **the effect of debits and credits on revenue accounts is the same as their effect on Owner's Capital**. Revenue accounts are increased by credits and decreased by debits.

> **HELPFUL HINT**
> Because revenues increase owner's equity, a revenue account has the same debit and credit rules as does the Owner's Capital account. Conversely, expenses have the opposite effect.

Expenses have the opposite effect: expenses decrease owner's equity. Since expenses are the negative factor in computing net income, and revenues are the positive factor, it is logical that the increase and decrease sides of expense accounts should be the reverse of revenue accounts. Thus, expense accounts are increased by debits and decreased by credits.

The effect of debits and credits on revenues and expenses can be stated as follows.

Illustration 2-9

Debit and credit effects—revenues and expenses

Debits	Credits
Decrease revenues	Increase revenues
Increase expenses	Decrease expenses

Credits to revenue accounts should exceed debits, and debits to expense accounts should exceed credits. Thus, revenue accounts normally show credit balances and expense accounts normally show debit balances. The normal balances can be diagrammed as follows.

Illustration 2-10

Normal balances—revenues and expenses

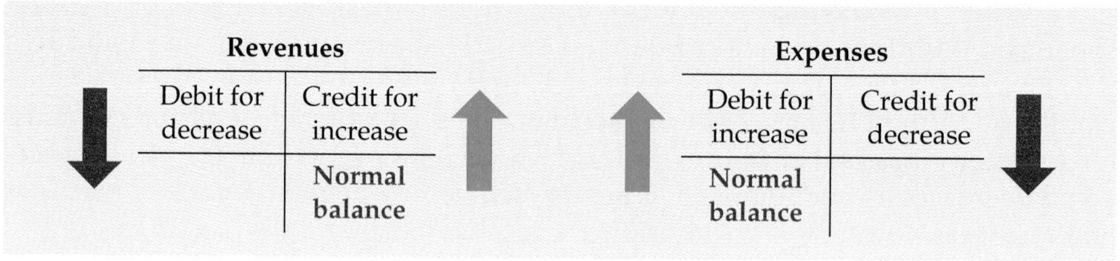

EXPANSION OF BASIC EQUATION

You have already learned the basic accounting equation. Illustration 2-11 expands this equation to show the accounts that comprise owner's equity. In addition, the debit/credit rules and effects on each type of account are illustrated. Study this diagram carefully. It will help you understand the fundamentals of the double-entry system. Like the basic equation, the expanded basic equation must be in balance (total debits equal total credits).

Illustration 2-11

Expanded basic equation and debit/credit rules and effects

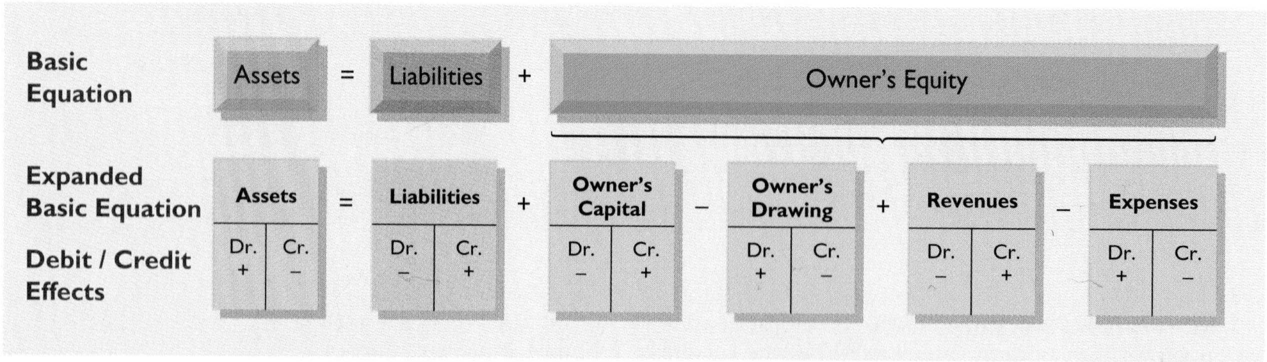

BEFORE YOU GO ON...

REVIEW IT

1. What do the terms debit and credit mean?
2. What are the debit and credit effects on assets, liabilities, and owner's capital?
3. What are the debit and credit effects on revenues, expenses, and owner's drawing?
4. What are the normal balances for **Lands' End's** Cash, Accounts Payable, and Interest Expense accounts? The answers to this question are provided on page 84.

LANDS' END DIRECT MERCHANTS

DO IT

Kate Browne has just rented space in a shopping mall in which she will open a beauty salon, to be called "Hair It Is." Long before opening day and before purchasing equipment, hiring employees, and remodeling the space, Kate has been advised to set up a double-entry set of accounting records in which to record all of her business transactions.

Identify the balance sheet accounts that Kate will likely need to record the transactions needed to open her business. Indicate whether the normal balance of each account is a debit or a credit.

ACTION PLAN

- Determine the types of accounts needed: Kate will need asset accounts for each different type of asset she invests in the business, and liability accounts for any debts she incurs.
- Understand the types of owner's equity accounts: Only Owner's Capital will be needed when Kate begins the business. Other owner's equity accounts will be needed later.

SOLUTION: Kate would likely need the following accounts in which to record the transactions necessary to ready her beauty salon for opening day: Cash (debit balance); Equipment (debit balance); Supplies (debit balance); Accounts Payable (credit balance); if she borrows money, Notes payable (credit balance); K. Browne, Capital (credit balance).

Related exercise material: BE2-1, BE2-2, E2-1, E2-3, and E2-10.

THE NAVIGATOR

STEPS IN THE RECORDING PROCESS

STUDY OBJECTIVE 3

Identify the basic steps in the recording process.

In practically every business, the basic steps in the recording process are:

1. Analyze each transaction for its effects on the accounts.
2. Enter the transaction information in a journal (book of original entry).
3. Transfer the journal information to the appropriate accounts in the ledger (book of accounts).

Although it is possible to enter transaction information directly into the accounts without using a journal or ledger, few businesses do so.

The sequence of events in the recording process begins with the transaction. Evidence of the transaction is provided by a **business document**, such as a sales slip, a check, a bill, or a cash register tape. This evidence is analyzed to determine the effects of the transaction on specific accounts. The transaction is then entered in the journal. Finally, the journal entry is transferred to the designated accounts in the ledger. The sequence of events in the recording process is shown in Illustration 2-12.

The Recording Process
JOURNAL
JOURNAL
LEDGER
Analyze each transaction
Enter transaction in a journal
Transfer journal information to ledger accounts

Illustration 2-12

The recording process

The basic steps in the recording process occur repeatedly. The analysis of transactions was illustrated in Chapter 1. Further examples will be given in this and later chapters. The other steps in the recording process are explained in the next sections.

Technology in Action examples show how computer technology is used in accounting and business.

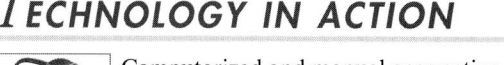

TECHNOLOGY IN ACTION

Computerized and manual accounting systems basically parallel one another. Most of the procedures are handled by electronic circuitry in computerized systems. They seem to occur invisibly. But, to fully comprehend how computerized systems operate, you need to understand manual approaches for processing accounting data.

THE JOURNAL

STUDY OBJECTIVE 4

Explain what a journal is and how it helps in the recording process.

Transactions are initially recorded in chronological order in a **journal** before being transferred to the accounts. Thus, the journal is referred to as the book of original entry. For each transaction the journal shows the debit and credit effects on specific accounts. Companies may use various kinds of journals, but every company has the most basic form of journal, a **general journal**. Typically, a general journal has spaces for dates, account titles and explanations, references, and two amount columns. Whenever we use the term journal in this textbook without a modifying adjective, we mean the general journal.

The journal makes several significant contributions to the recording process:

1. It discloses in one place the complete effects of a transaction.
2. It provides a chronological record of transactions.
3. It helps to prevent or locate errors because the debit and credit amounts for each entry can be readily compared.

Journalizing

Entering transaction data in the journal is known as **journalizing**. Separate journal entries are made for each transaction. A complete entry consists of: (1) the date of the transaction, (2) the accounts and amounts to be debited and credited, and (3) a brief explanation of the transaction.

Illustration 2-13 shows the technique of journalizing, using the first two transactions of Softbyte. These transactions were: September 1, Ray Neal invested $15,000 cash in the business, and computer equipment was purchased for $7,000 cash. The numbered J1 indicates that these two entries are recorded on the first page of the journal.

Illustration 2-13
Technique of journalizing

GENERAL JOURNAL				J1
Date	**Account Titles and Explanation**	**Ref.**	**Debit**	**Credit**
2002				
Sept. 1	Cash		15,000	
	R. Neal, Capital			15,000
	(Owner's investment of cash in business)			
1	Computer Equipment		7,000	
	Cash			7,000
	(Purchase of equipment for cash)			

The standard form and content of journal entries are as follows.

1. The date of the transaction is entered in the Date column. The date recorded should include the year, month, and day of the transaction.
2. The debit account title (that is, the account to be debited) is entered first at the extreme left margin of the column headed "Account Titles and Explanation," and the amount of the debit is recorded in the Debit column.
3. The credit account title (that is, the account to be credited) is indented and entered on the next line in the column headed "Account Titles and Explanation," and the amount of the credit is recorded in the Credit column.
4. A brief explanation of the transaction is given on the line below the credit account title.
5. A space is left between journal entries. The blank space separates individual journal entries and makes the entire journal easier to read.
6. The column titled Ref. (which stands for reference) is left blank when the journal entry is made. This column is used later when the journal entries are transferred to the ledger accounts. At that time, the ledger account number is placed in the Reference column to indicate where the amount in the journal entry was transferred.

It is important to use correct and specific account titles in journalizing. Since most accounts appear later in the financial statements, wrong account titles lead to incorrect financial statements. Some flexibility exists initially in selecting account titles. The main criterion is that each title must appropriately describe the content of the account. For example, the account title used for the cost of delivery trucks may be Delivery Equipment, Delivery Trucks, or Trucks. Once a company chooses the specific title to use, all later transactions involving the account should be recorded under that account title.[2]

If an entry involves only two accounts, one debit and one credit, it is considered a **simple entry**. Some transactions, however, require more than two accounts

[2] In homework problems, when specific account titles are given, they should be used. When account titles are not given, you may select account titles that identify the nature and content of each account. The account titles used in journalizing should not contain explanations such as Cash Paid or Cash Received.

in journalizing. When three or more accounts are required in one journal entry, the entry is referred to as a **compound entry**. To illustrate, assume that on July 1, Butler Company purchases a delivery truck costing $14,000 by paying $8,000 cash and the balance on account (to be paid later). The compound entry is as follows.

Illustration 2-14

Compound journal entry

GENERAL JOURNAL **J1**

Date	Account Titles and Explanation	Ref.	Debit	Credit
2002				
July 1	Delivery Equipment		14,000	
	Cash			8,000
	Accounts Payable			6,000
	(Purchased truck for cash with balance on account)			

HELPFUL HINT
Assume you find this compound entry:

Wages Expense	700	
Cash		1,200
Advert. Expense	400	
(Paid cash for wages and advertising)		

Is the entry correct? No. It is incorrect in form because both debits should be listed before the credit. It is incorrect in content because the debit amounts do not equal the credit amount.

In a compound entry, the total debit and credit amounts must be equal. Also, the standard format requires that all debits be listed before the credits.

BEFORE YOU GO ON...

REVIEW IT

1. What is the sequence of the steps in the recording process?
2. What contribution does the journal make to the recording process?
3. What is the standard form and content of a journal entry made in the general journal?

DO IT

In establishing her beauty salon, Hair It Is, Kate Browne engaged in the following activities:

1. Opened a bank account in the name of Hair It Is and deposited $20,000 of her own money in this account as her initial investment.
2. Purchased equipment on account (to be paid in 30 days) for a total cost of $4,800.
3. Interviewed three persons for the position of beautician.

In what form (type of record) should Kate record these three activities? Prepare the entries to record the transactions.

ACTION PLAN

- Understand which activities need to be recorded and which do not. Any that have economic effects should be recorded in a journal.
- Analyze the effects of transactions on asset, liability, and owner's equity accounts.

SOLUTION: Each transaction that is recorded is entered in the general journal. The three activities would be recorded as follows.

1. Cash	20,000	
K. Browne, Capital		20,000
(Owner's investment of cash in business)		
2. Equipment	4,800	
Accounts Payable		4,800
(Purchase of equipment on account)		
3. No entry because no transaction has occurred.		

Related exercise material: BE2-3, BE2-5, BE2-6, E2-2, E2-4, E2-6, E2-7, and E2-8.

THE NAVIGATOR

THE LEDGER

STUDY OBJECTIVE 5

Explain what a ledger is and how it helps in the recording process.

The entire group of accounts maintained by a company is called the **ledger**. The ledger keeps in one place all the information about changes in specific account balances.

Companies may use various kinds of ledgers, but every company has a general ledger. A **general ledger** contains all the assets, liabilities, and owner's equity accounts, as shown in Illustration 2-15. A business can use a looseleaf binder or card file for the ledger. Each account is kept on a separate sheet or card. Whenever we use the term ledger in this textbook without a modifying adjective, we mean the general ledger.

Illustration 2-15

The general ledger

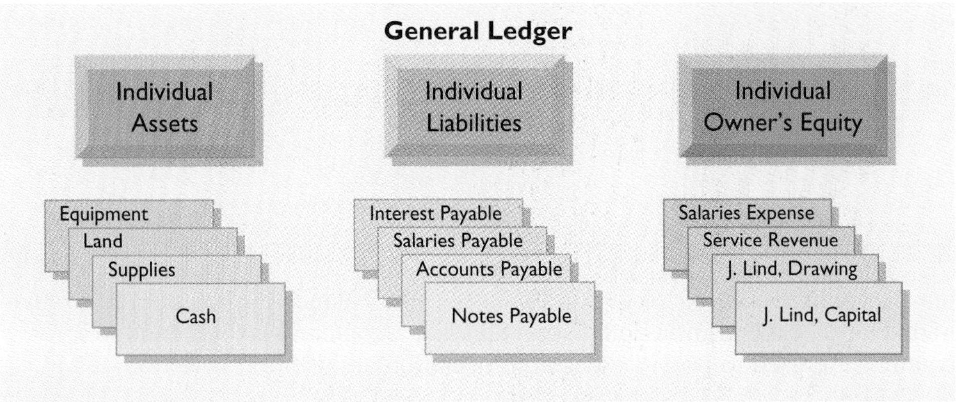

The ledger should be arranged in the order in which accounts are presented in the financial statements, beginning with the balance sheet accounts. First in order are the asset accounts, followed by liability accounts, owner's capital, owner's drawing, revenues, and expenses. Each account is numbered for easier identification.

The ledger provides management with the balances in various accounts. For example, the Cash account shows the amount of cash that is available to meet current obligations. Amounts due from customers can be found by examining Accounts Receivable, and amounts owed to creditors can be found by examining Accounts Payable.

ACCOUNTING IN ACTION *Business Insight*

In his autobiography Sam Walton described the double-entry accounting system he began the **Wal-Mart** empire with: "We kept a little pigeonhole on the wall for the cash receipts and paperwork of each [Wal-Mart] store. I had a blue binder ledger book for each store. When we added a store, we added a pigeonhole. We did this at least up to twenty stores. Then once a month, the bookkeeper and I would enter the merchandise, enter the sales, enter the cash, and balance it."

SOURCE: Sam Walton, *Made in America* (New York: Doubleday, 1992), p. 53.

Standard Form of Account

The simple T-account form used in accounting textbooks is often very useful for illustration purposes. However, in practice, the account forms used in ledgers are much more structured. A widely used form is shown in Illustration 2-16, using assumed data from a cash account.

Illustration 2-16

Three-column form of account

CASH — No. 101

Date	Explanation	Ref.	Debit	Credit	Balance
2002					
June 1			25,000		25,000
2				8,000	17,000
3			4,200		21,200
9			7,500		28,700
17				11,700	17,000
20				250	16,750
30				7,300	9,450

This form is often called the **three-column form of account** because it has three money columns—debit, credit, and balance. The balance in the account is determined after each transaction. Note that the explanation space and reference columns are used to provide special information about the transaction.

Posting

STUDY OBJECTIVE 6

Explain what posting is and how it helps in the recording process.

The procedure of transferring journal entries to the ledger accounts is called **posting**. Posting involves the following steps.

1. In the ledger, enter in the appropriate columns of the account(s) debited the date, journal page, and debit amount shown in the journal.
2. In the reference column of the journal, write the account number to which the debit amount was posted.
3. In the ledger, enter in the appropriate columns of the account(s) credited the date, journal page, and credit amount shown in the journal.
4. In the reference column of the journal, write the account number to which the credit amount was posted.

These four steps are diagrammed in Illustration 2-17 (on page 55) using the first journal entry of Softbyte. The boxed numbers indicate the sequence of the steps.

Posting should be performed in chronological order. That is, all the debits and credits of one journal entry should be posted before proceeding to the next journal entry. Postings should be made on a timely basis to ensure that the ledger is up to date.[3]

HELPFUL HINT
How can one tell whether all postings have been completed? Answer: Scan the reference column of the journal to see whether there are any blanks opposite account titles. If there are no blanks, all postings have been made.

The reference column **in the journal** serves several purposes. The numbers in this column indicate the entries that have been posted. After the last entry has been posted, this column should be scanned to see that all postings have been made.

The reference column **of a ledger** account indicates the journal page from which the transaction was posted. The explanation space of the ledger account is used infrequently because an explanation already appears in the journal. It generally is used only when detailed analysis of account activity is required.

[3] In homework problems, it will be permissible to journalize all transactions before posting any of the journal entries.

Illustration 2-17

Posting a journal entry

GENERAL JOURNAL J1

Date	Account Titles and Explanation	Ref.	Debit	Credit
2002				
Sept. 1	Cash	101	15,000	
	R. Neal, Capital	306		15,000
	(Owner's investment of cash in business)			

GENERAL LEDGER

Cash No.101

Date	Explanation	Ref.	Debit	Credit	Balance
2002					
Sept. 1		J1	15,000		15,000

R. Neal, Capital No.306

Date	Explanation	Ref.	Debit	Credit	Balance
2002					
Sept. 1		J1		15,000	15,000

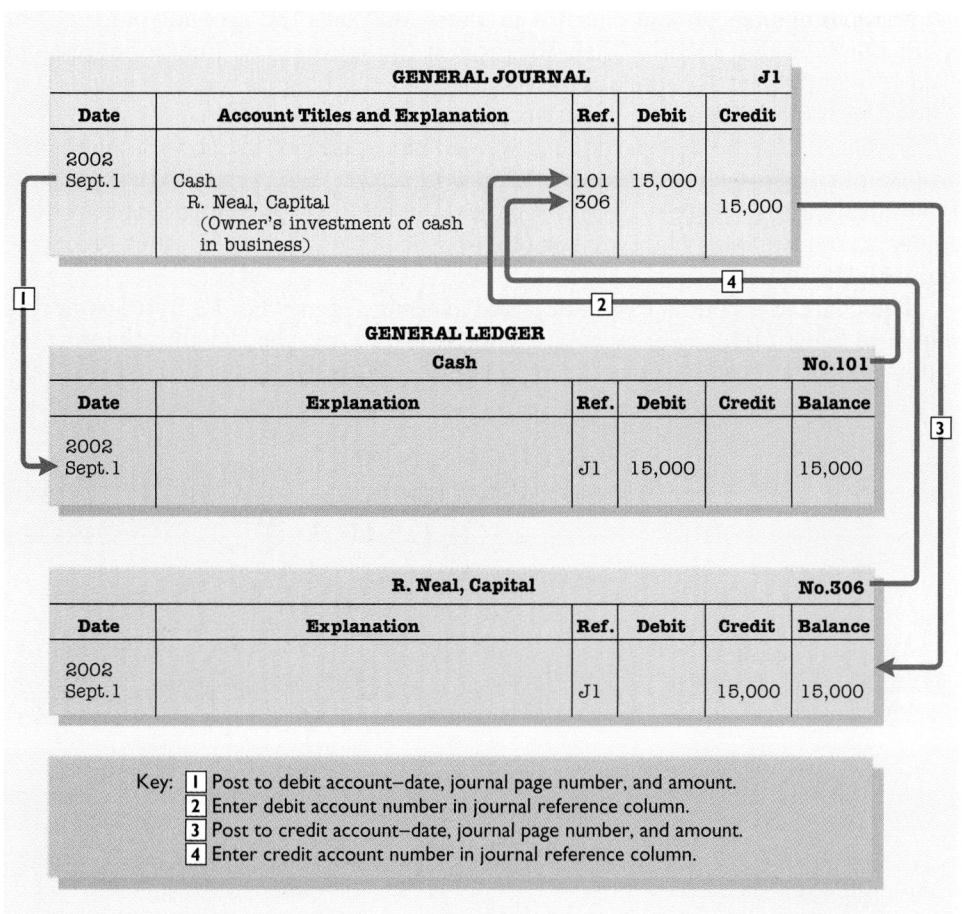

Key:
1 Post to debit account–date, journal page number, and amount.
2 Enter debit account number in journal reference column.
3 Post to credit account–date, journal page number, and amount.
4 Enter credit account number in journal reference column.

TECHNOLOGY IN ACTION

Determining what to record is the most critical (and for most businesses the most expensive) point in the accounting process. In computerized systems, after this phase is completed, the input and all further processing just boil down to merging files and generating reports. Programmers and management information system types with good accounting backgrounds (such as they should gain from a good principles textbook) are better able to develop effective computerized systems.

Chart of Accounts

The number and type of accounts used differ for each enterprise. The number of accounts depends on the amount of detail desired by management. For example, the management of one company may want one account for all types of utility expense. Another may keep separate expense accounts for each type of utility, such as gas, electricity, and water. Similarly, a single proprietorship like Softbyte will have fewer accounts than a corporate giant like **Ford Motor Company**. Softbyte may be able to manage and report its activities in twenty to thirty accounts, while Ford requires thousands of accounts to keep track of its worldwide activities.

Most companies have a **chart of accounts** that lists the accounts and the account numbers that identify their location in the ledger. The numbering system used to identify the accounts usually starts with the balance sheet accounts and follows with the income statement accounts.

In this and the next two chapters, we will be explaining the accounting for the proprietorship Pioneer Advertising Agency (a service enterprise). Accounts 101–199 indicate asset accounts; 200–299 indicate liabilities; 301–350 indicate owner's equity accounts; 400–499, revenues; 601–799, expenses; 800–899, other revenues; and 900–999, other expenses.

The chart of accounts for Pioneer Advertising Agency (C. R. Byrd, owner) is shown in Illustration 2-18. Accounts shown in red are used in this chapter; accounts shown in black are explained in later chapters.

Illustration 2-18

Chart of accounts

CHART OF ACCOUNTS
Pioneer Advertising Agency

Assets	Owner's Equity
101 Cash	**301 C. R. Byrd, Capital**
112 Accounts Receivable	**306 C. R. Byrd, Drawing**
126 Advertising Supplies	350 Income Summary
130 Prepaid Insurance	
157 Office Equipment	**Revenues**
158 Accumulated Depreciation—Office Equipment	**400 Service Revenue**
Liabilities	**Expenses**
200 Notes Payable	631 Advertising Supplies Expense
201 Accounts Payable	711 Depreciation Expense
209 Unearned Revenue	722 Insurance Expense
212 Salaries Payable	**726 Salaries Expense**
230 Interest Payable	**729 Rent Expense**
	905 Interest Expense

You will notice that there are gaps in the numbering system of the chart of accounts for Pioneer Advertising. Gaps are left to permit the insertion of new accounts as needed during the life of the business.

THE RECORDING PROCESS ILLUSTRATED

Illustrations 2-19 through 2-28 show the basic steps in the recording process, using the October transactions of the Pioneer Advertising Agency. Its accounting period is a month. A basic analysis and a debit-credit analysis precede the journalizing and posting of each transaction. For simplicity, the T-account form is used in the illustrations instead of the standard account form.

Study the transaction analyses in Illustrations 2-19 through 2-28 carefully. **The purpose of transaction analysis is first to identify the type of account involved, and then to determine whether a debit or a credit to the account is required.** You should always perform this type of analysis before preparing a journal entry. Doing so will help you understand the journal entries discussed in this chapter as well as more complex journal entries to be described in later chapters.

Keep in mind that every journal entry affects one or more of the following items: assets, liabilities, owner's capital, owner's drawing, revenues, or expenses. By becoming skilled at transaction analysis, you will be able to recognize quickly the impact of any transaction on these six items.

Illustration 2-19

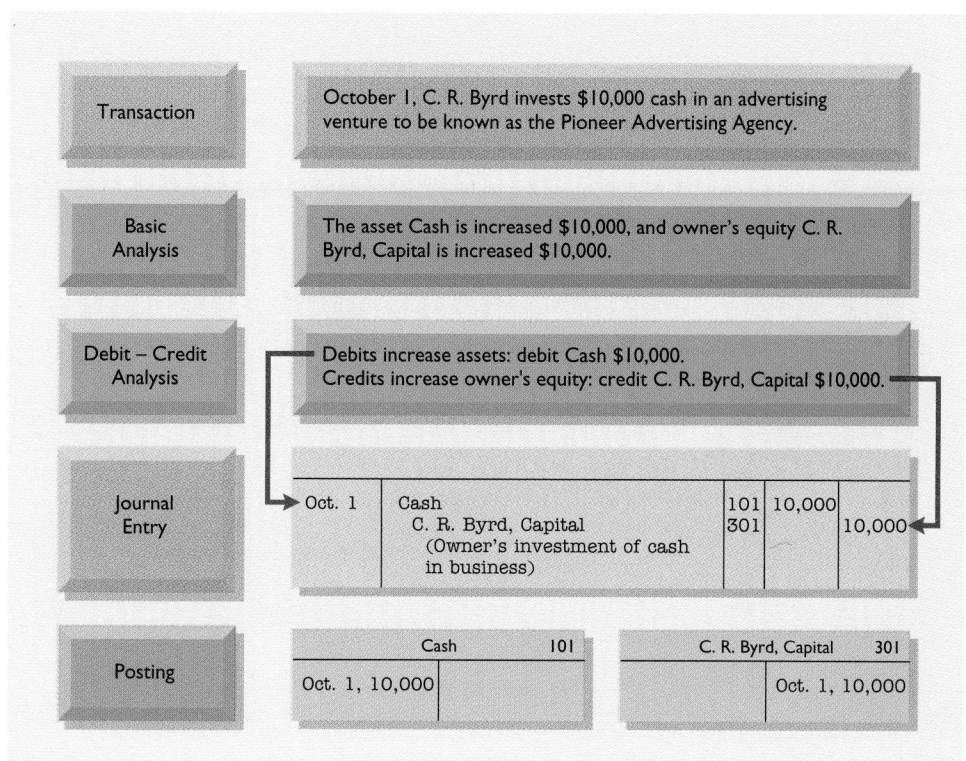

Investment of cash by owner

Transaction	October 1, C. R. Byrd invests $10,000 cash in an advertising venture to be known as the Pioneer Advertising Agency.
Basic Analysis	The asset Cash is increased $10,000, and owner's equity C. R. Byrd, Capital is increased $10,000.
Debit – Credit Analysis	Debits increase assets: debit Cash $10,000. Credits increase owner's equity: credit C. R. Byrd, Capital $10,000.

Journal Entry

Oct. 1	Cash	101	10,000	
	C. R. Byrd, Capital	301		10,000
	(Owner's investment of cash in business)			

Posting

Cash	101
Oct. 1, 10,000	

C. R. Byrd, Capital	301
	Oct. 1, 10,000

HELPFUL HINT

To correctly record a transaction, you must carefully analyze the event and translate that analysis into debit and credit language.
First: Determine what type of account is involved.
Second: Determine what items increased or decreased and by how much.
Third: Translate the increases and decreases into debits and credits.

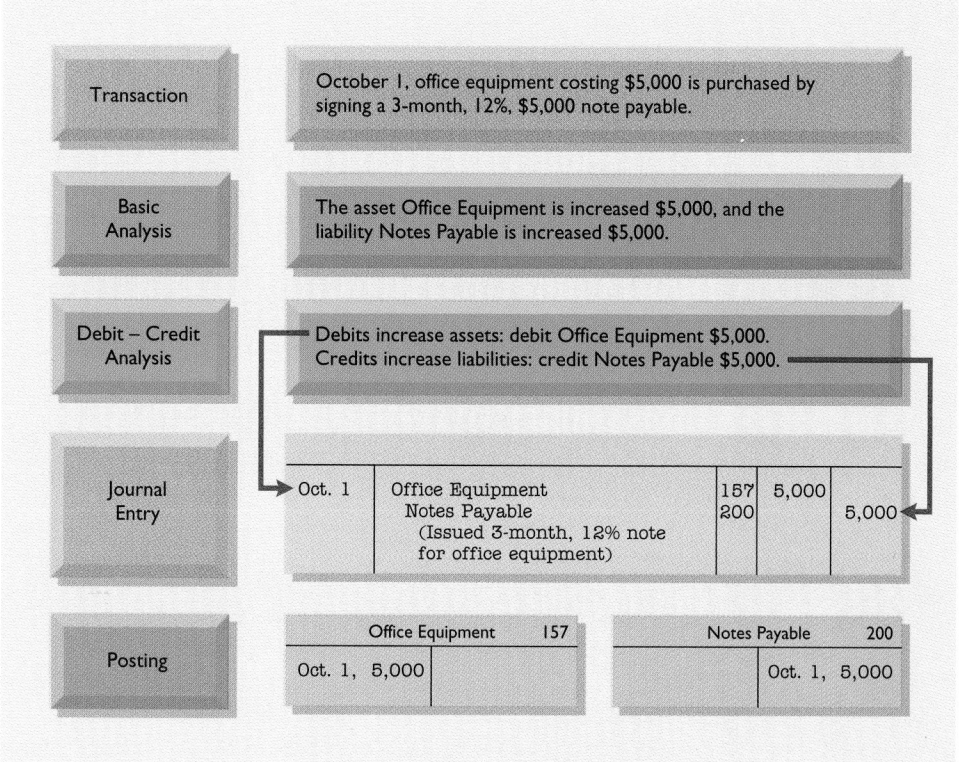

Illustration 2-20

Purchase of office equipment

Transaction	October 1, office equipment costing $5,000 is purchased by signing a 3-month, 12%, $5,000 note payable.
Basic Analysis	The asset Office Equipment is increased $5,000, and the liability Notes Payable is increased $5,000.
Debit – Credit Analysis	Debits increase assets: debit Office Equipment $5,000. Credits increase liabilities: credit Notes Payable $5,000.

Journal Entry

Oct. 1	Office Equipment	157	5,000	
	Notes Payable	200		5,000
	(Issued 3-month, 12% note for office equipment)			

Posting

Office Equipment	157
Oct. 1, 5,000	

Notes Payable	200
	Oct. 1, 5,000

Illustration 2-21

Receipt of cash for future service

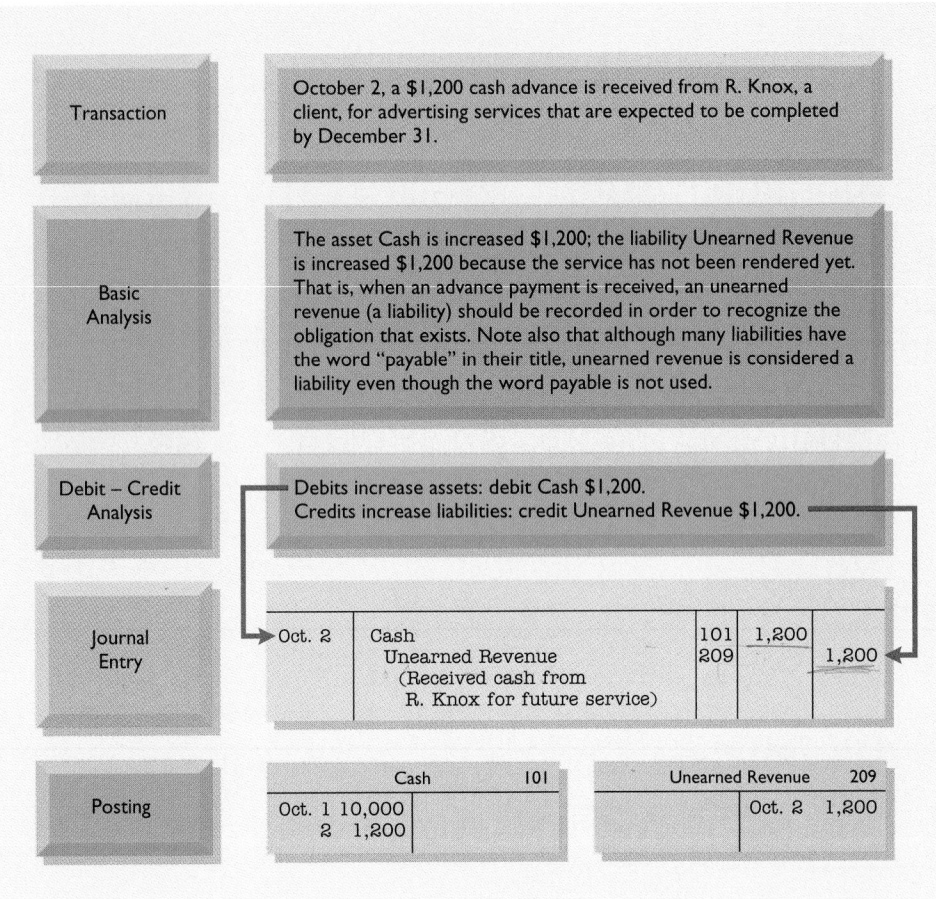

Transaction

October 2, a $1,200 cash advance is received from R. Knox, a client, for advertising services that are expected to be completed by December 31.

Basic Analysis

The asset Cash is increased $1,200; the liability Unearned Revenue is increased $1,200 because the service has not been rendered yet. That is, when an advance payment is received, an unearned revenue (a liability) should be recorded in order to recognize the obligation that exists. Note also that although many liabilities have the word "payable" in their title, unearned revenue is considered a liability even though the word payable is not used.

HELPFUL HINT

When the revenue is earned, the Unearned Revenue account is debited (decreased), and a revenue account is credited (increased).

Debit – Credit Analysis

Debits increase assets: debit Cash $1,200.
Credits increase liabilities: credit Unearned Revenue $1,200.

Journal Entry

Oct. 2	Cash	101	1,200	
	Unearned Revenue	209		1,200
	(Received cash from R. Knox for future service)			

Posting

Cash	101
Oct. 1 10,000 2 1,200	

Unearned Revenue	209
	Oct. 2 1,200

Illustration 2-22

Payment of monthly rent

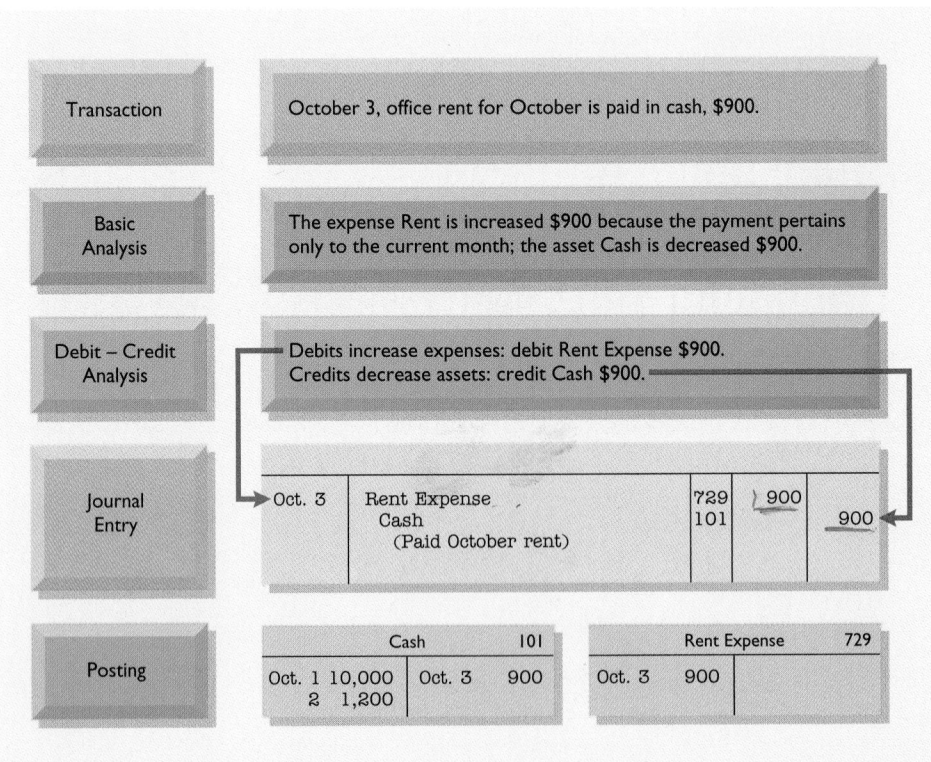

Transaction

October 3, office rent for October is paid in cash, $900.

Basic Analysis

The expense Rent is increased $900 because the payment pertains only to the current month; the asset Cash is decreased $900.

Debit – Credit Analysis

Debits increase expenses: debit Rent Expense $900.
Credits decrease assets: credit Cash $900.

Journal Entry

Oct. 3	Rent Expense	729	900	
	Cash	101		900
	(Paid October rent)			

Posting

Cash	101
Oct. 1 10,000 2 1,200	Oct. 3 900

Rent Expense	729
Oct. 3 900	

Illustration 2-23

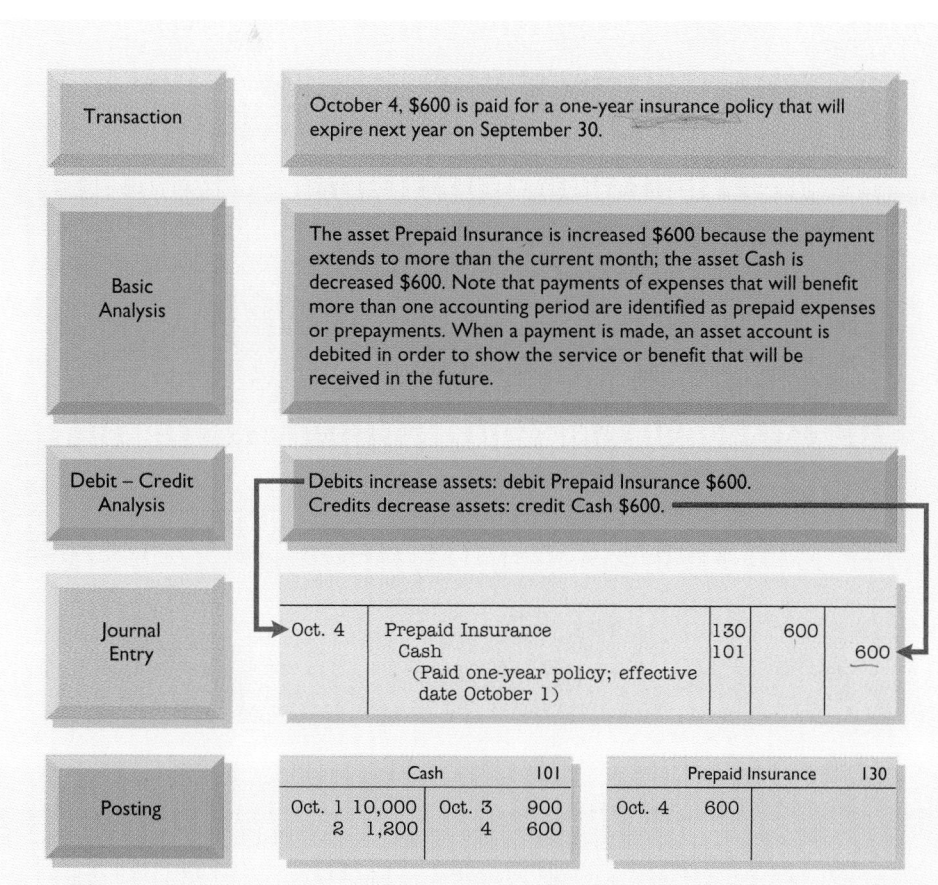

Payment for insurance

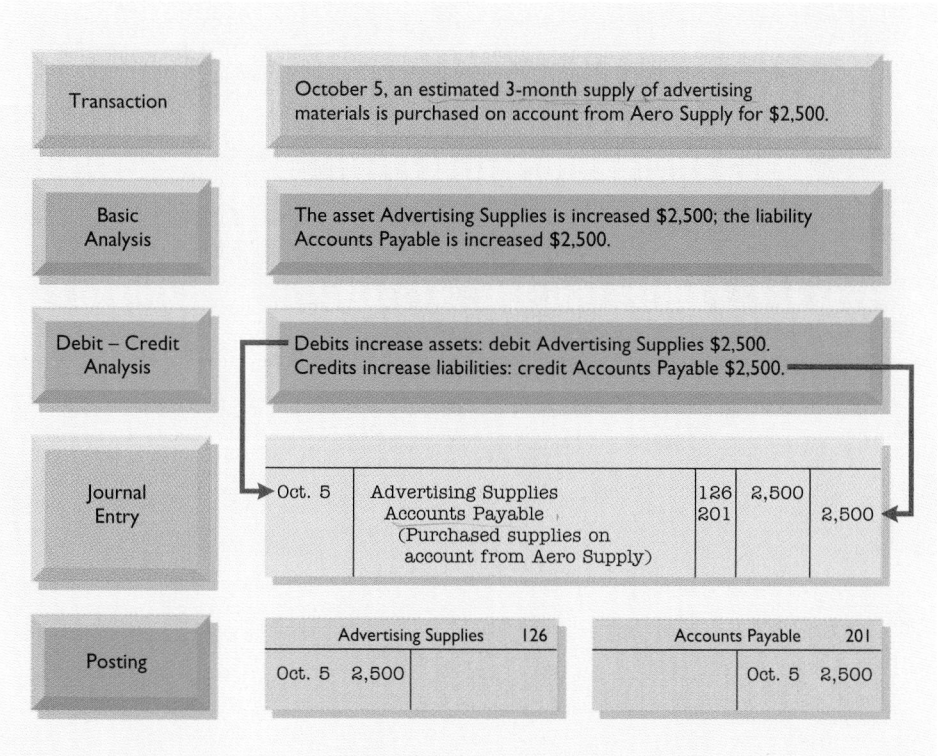

Transaction

October 4, $600 is paid for a one-year insurance policy that will expire next year on September 30.

Basic Analysis

The asset Prepaid Insurance is increased $600 because the payment extends to more than the current month; the asset Cash is decreased $600. Note that payments of expenses that will benefit more than one accounting period are identified as prepaid expenses or prepayments. When a payment is made, an asset account is debited in order to show the service or benefit that will be received in the future.

Debit – Credit Analysis

Debits increase assets: debit Prepaid Insurance $600.
Credits decrease assets: credit Cash $600.

Journal Entry

Oct. 4	Prepaid Insurance	130	600	
	Cash	101		600
	(Paid one-year policy; effective date October 1)			

Posting

Cash	101
Oct. 1 10,000	Oct. 3 900
2 1,200	4 600

Prepaid Insurance	130
Oct. 4 600	

Illustration 2-24

Purchase of supplies on credit

Transaction

October 5, an estimated 3-month supply of advertising materials is purchased on account from Aero Supply for $2,500.

Basic Analysis

The asset Advertising Supplies is increased $2,500; the liability Accounts Payable is increased $2,500.

Debit – Credit Analysis

Debits increase assets: debit Advertising Supplies $2,500.
Credits increase liabilities: credit Accounts Payable $2,500.

Journal Entry

Oct. 5	Advertising Supplies	126	2,500	
	Accounts Payable	201		2,500
	(Purchased supplies on account from Aero Supply)			

Posting

Advertising Supplies	126
Oct. 5 2,500	

Accounts Payable	201
	Oct. 5 2,500

Illustration 2-25

Hiring of employees

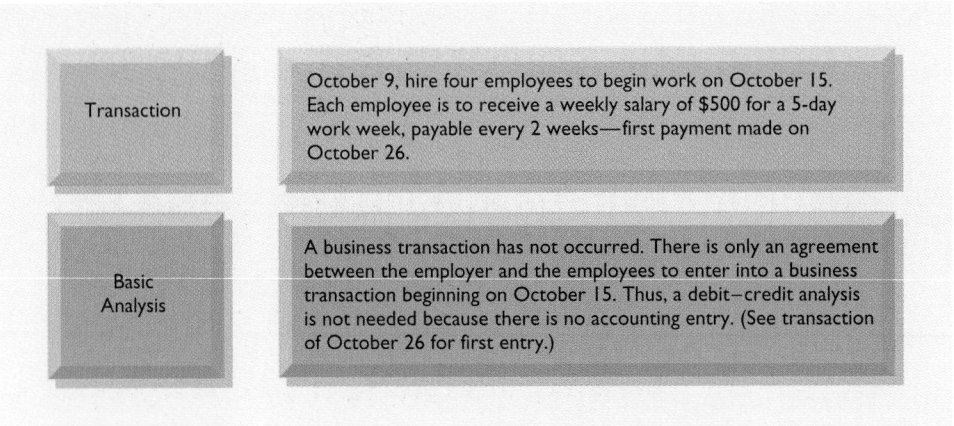

Transaction	October 9, hire four employees to begin work on October 15. Each employee is to receive a weekly salary of $500 for a 5-day work week, payable every 2 weeks—first payment made on October 26.
Basic Analysis	A business transaction has not occurred. There is only an agreement between the employer and the employees to enter into a business transaction beginning on October 15. Thus, a debit–credit analysis is not needed because there is no accounting entry. (See transaction of October 26 for first entry.)

Illustration 2-26

Withdrawal of cash by owner

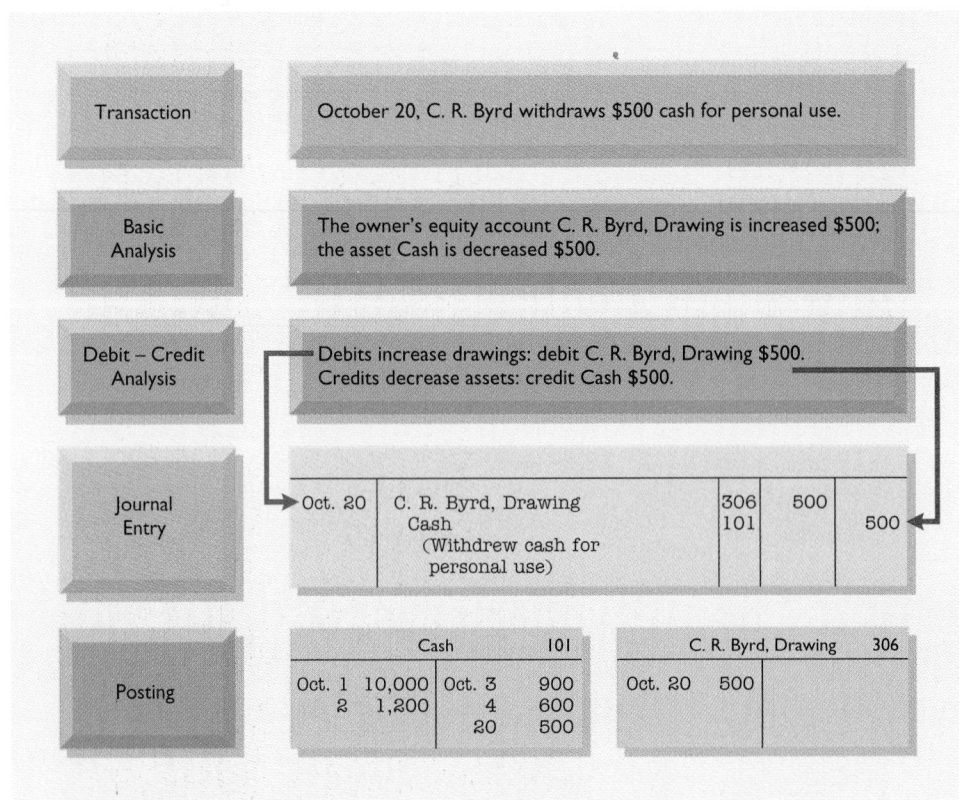

Transaction	October 20, C. R. Byrd withdraws $500 cash for personal use.
Basic Analysis	The owner's equity account C. R. Byrd, Drawing is increased $500; the asset Cash is decreased $500.
Debit – Credit Analysis	Debits increase drawings: debit C. R. Byrd, Drawing $500. Credits decrease assets: credit Cash $500.

Journal Entry

Oct. 20	C. R. Byrd, Drawing	306	500	
	Cash	101		500
	(Withdrew cash for personal use)			

Posting

Cash			101
Oct. 1	10,000	Oct. 3	900
2	1,200	4	600
		20	500

C. R. Byrd, Drawing		306
Oct. 20	500	

Illustration 2-27

Payment of salaries

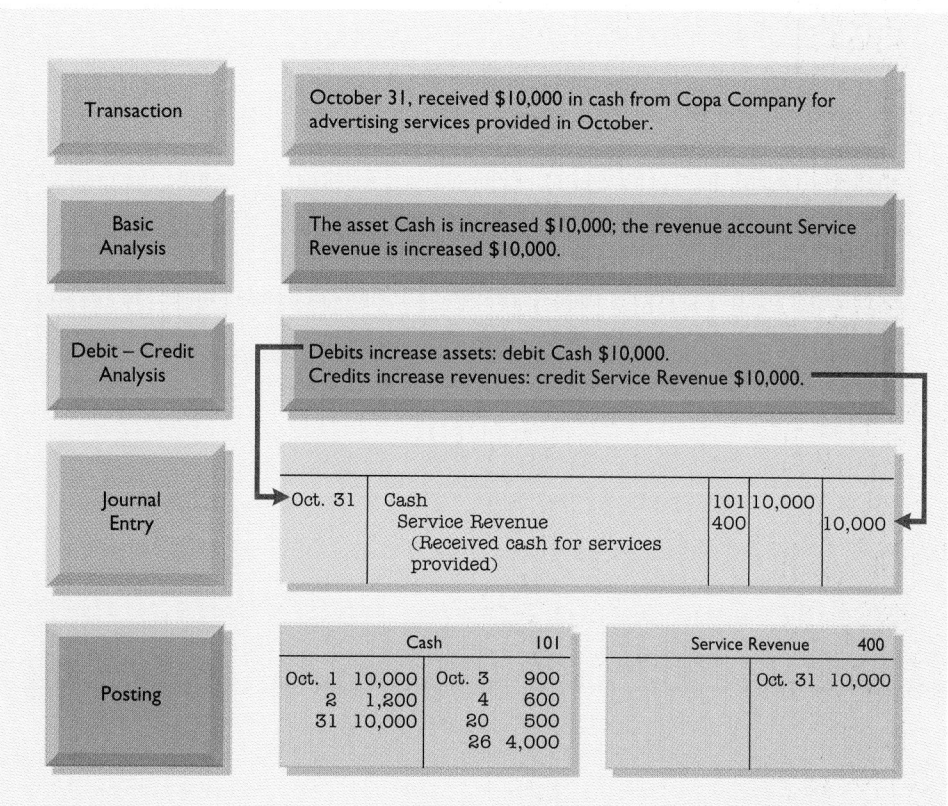

Transaction	October 26, employee salaries of $4,000 are owed and paid in cash. (See October 9 transaction.)
Basic Analysis	The expense account Salaries Expense is increased $4,000; the asset Cash is decreased $4,000.
Debit – Credit Analysis	Debits increase expenses: debit Salaries Expense $4,000. Credits decrease assets: credit Cash $4,000.

Journal Entry

Oct. 26	Salaries Expense	726	4,000	
	Cash	101		4,000
	(Paid salaries to date)			

Posting

Cash			101
Oct. 1	10,000	Oct. 3	900
2	1,200	4	600
		20	500
		26	4,000

Salaries Expense			726
Oct. 26	4,000		

Illustration 2-28

Receipt of cash for services provided

Transaction	October 31, received $10,000 in cash from Copa Company for advertising services provided in October.
Basic Analysis	The asset Cash is increased $10,000; the revenue account Service Revenue is increased $10,000.
Debit – Credit Analysis	Debits increase assets: debit Cash $10,000. Credits increase revenues: credit Service Revenue $10,000.

Journal Entry

Oct. 31	Cash	101	10,000	
	Service Revenue	400		10,000
	(Received cash for services provided)			

Posting

Cash			101
Oct. 1	10,000	Oct. 3	900
2	1,200	4	600
31	10,000	20	500
		26	4,000

Service Revenue			400
		Oct. 31	10,000

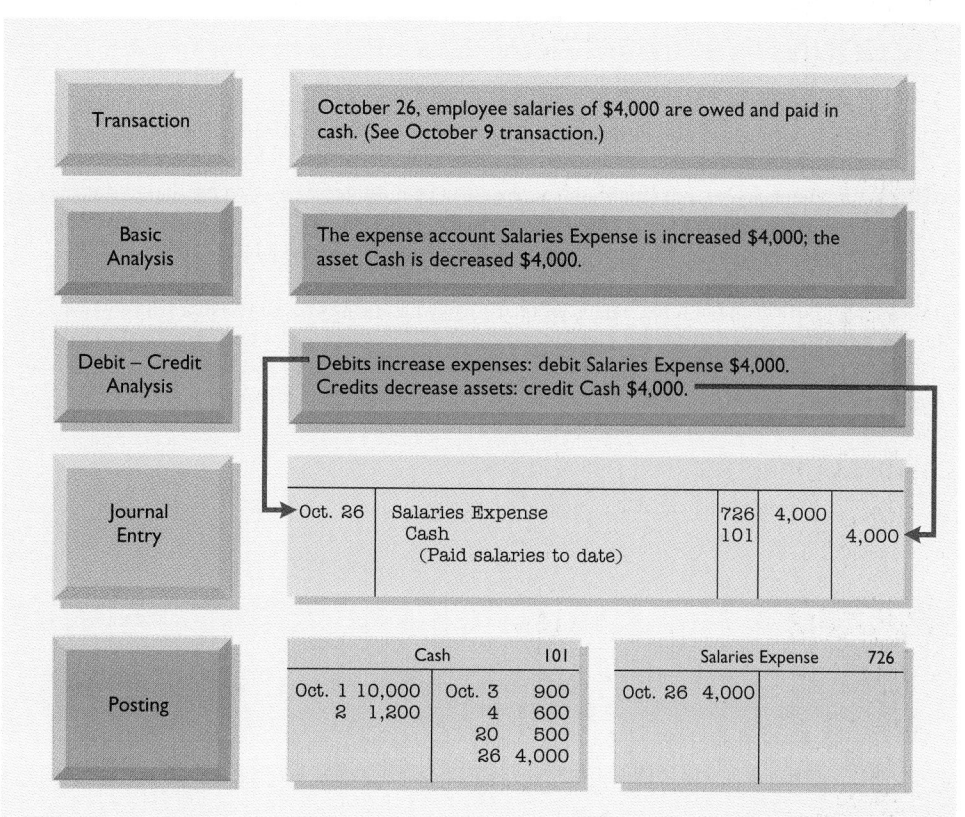

ACCOUNTING IN ACTION e Business Insight

E-business is having a tremendous impact on how companies share information within the company, and with people outside the company, such as suppliers, creditors, and investors. A new type of software, Extensible Markup Language (XML), is enabling the creation of a universal way to exchange data.

An organization called XBRL.org is using XML to develop an internationally accepted framework called the Extensible Business Reporting Model (XBRL). The organization is comprised of representatives from industry, accounting firms, investment houses, bankers, regulators, and others. The goal of this organization is to establish a framework that "the global business information supply chain will use to create, exchange, and analyze financial reporting information including, but not limited to, regulatory filings such as annual and quarterly financial statements, general ledger information, and audit schedules."

SOURCE: www.XBRL.org.

BEFORE YOU GO ON...

▶ *REVIEW IT*

1. How does journalizing differ from posting?
2. What is the purpose of (a) the ledger and (b) a chart of accounts?

▶ *DO IT*

Kate Brown recorded the following transactions in a general journal during the month of March.

Cash	2,280	
Service Revenue		2,280
Wages Expense	400	
Cash		400
Utilities Expense	92	
Cash		92

Post these entries to the Cash account of the general ledger to determine the ending balance in cash. The beginning balance in cash on March 1 was $600.

ACTION PLAN

- Recall that posting involves transferring the journalized debits and credits to specific accounts in the ledger.
- Determine the ending balance by netting the total debits and credits.

SOLUTION

Cash

3/1	600	400
	2,280	92
3/31 Bal.	2,388	

Related exercise material: BE2-7, BE2-8, E2-2, E2-5, and E2-8.

THE NAVIGATOR

SUMMARY ILLUSTRATION OF JOURNALIZING AND POSTING

The journal for Pioneer Advertising Agency for October is shown in Illustration 2-29. The ledger is shown in Illustration 2-30, on page 64, with all balances in color.

Illustration 2-29

General journal entries

GENERAL JOURNAL				Page J1
Date	**Account Titles and Explanation**	**Ref.**	**Debit**	**Credit**
2002				
Oct. 1	Cash	101	10,000	
	C. R. Byrd, Capital	301		10,000
	(Owner's investment of cash in business)			
1	Office Equipment	157	5,000	
	Notes Payable	200		5,000
	(Issued 30-month, 12% note for office equipment)			
2	Cash	101	1,200	
	Unearned Revenue	209		1,200
	(Received cash for future services)			
3	Rent Expense	729	900	
	Cash	101		900
	(Paid October rent)			
4	Prepaid Insurance	130	600	
	Cash	101		600
	(Paid one-year policy; effective date October 1)			
5	Advertising Supplies	126	2,500	
	Accounts Payable	201		2,500
	(Purchased supplies on account from Aero Supply)			
20	C. R. Byrd, Drawing	306	500	
	Cash	101		500
	(Withdrew cash for personal use)			
26	Salaries Expense	726	4,000	
	Cash	101		4,000
	(Paid salaries to date)			
31	Cash	101	10,000	
	Service Revenue	400		10,000
	(Received cash for services provided)			

GENERAL LEDGER

Cash **No. 101**

Date	Explanation	Ref.	Debit	Credit	Balance
2002					
Oct. 1		J1	10,000		10,000
2		J1	1,200		11,200
3		J1		900	10,300
4		J1		600	9,700
20		J1		500	9,200
26		J1		4,000	5,200
31		J1	10,000		**15,200**

Advertising Supplies **No. 126**

Date	Explanation	Ref.	Debit	Credit	Balance
2002					
Oct. 5		J1	2,500		**2,500**

Prepaid Insurance **No. 130**

Date	Explanation	Ref.	Debit	Credit	Balance
2002					
Oct. 4		J1	600		**600**

Office Equipment **No. 157**

Date	Explanation	Ref.	Debit	Credit	Balance
2002					
Oct. 1		J1	5,000		**5,000**

Notes Payable **No. 200**

Date	Explanation	Ref.	Debit	Credit	Balance
2002					
Oct. 1		J1		5,000	**5,000**

Accounts Payable **No. 201**

Date	Explanation	Ref.	Debit	Credit	Balance
2002					
Oct. 5		J1		2,500	**2,500**

Unearned Revenue **No. 209**

Date	Explanation	Ref.	Debit	Credit	Balance
2002					
Oct. 2		J1		1,200	**1,200**

C. R. Byrd, Capital **No. 301**

Date	Explanation	Ref.	Debit	Credit	Balance
2002					
Oct. 1		J1		10,000	**10,000**

C. R. Byrd, Drawing **No. 306**

Date	Explanation	Ref.	Debit	Credit	Balance
2002					
Oct. 20		J1	500		**500**

Service Revenue **No. 400**

Date	Explanation	Ref.	Debit	Credit	Balance
2002					
Oct. 31		J1		10,000	**10,000**

Salaries Expense **No. 726**

Date	Explanation	Ref.	Debit	Credit	Balance
2002					
Oct. 26		J1	4,000		**4,000**

Rent Expense **No. 729**

Date	Explanation	Ref.	Debit	Credit	Balance
2002					
Oct. 3		J1	900		**900**

Illustration 2-30

General ledger

THE TRIAL BALANCE

STUDY OBJECTIVE 7

Prepare a trial balance and explain its purposes.

HELPFUL HINT

A trial balance is so named because it is a test to see if the sum of the debit balances equals the sum of the credit balances.

A **trial balance** is a list of accounts and their balances at a given time. Customarily, a trial balance is prepared at the end of an accounting period. The accounts are listed in the order in which they appear in the ledger; debit balances are listed in the left column and credit balances in the right column.

The primary purpose of a trial balance is to prove (check) that the debits equal the credits after posting. In other words, the sum of the debit account balances in the trial balance should equal the sum of the credit account balances. **If the debits and credits do not agree, the trial balance can be used to uncover errors in journalizing and posting. In addition, it is useful in the preparation of financial statements,** as will be explained in the next two chapters.

The steps for preparing a trial balance are:

1. List the account titles and their balances.
2. Total the debit and credit columns.
3. Prove the equality of the two columns.

The trial balance prepared from Pioneer Advertising's ledger is shown below.

Illustration 2-31
A trial balance

PIONEER ADVERTISING AGENCY
Trial Balance
October 31, 2002

	Debit	Credit
Cash	$15,200	
Advertising Supplies	2,500	
Prepaid Insurance	600	
Office Equipment	5,000	
Notes Payable		$ 5,000
Accounts Payable		2,500
Unearned Revenue		1,200
C. R. Byrd, Capital		10,000
C. R. Byrd, Drawing	500	
Service Revenue		10,000
Salaries Expense	4,000	
Rent Expense	900	
	$28,700	**$28,700**

HELPFUL HINT
To sum a column of figures is sometimes referred to as *to foot* the column. The column is then said to be *footed*.

Note that the total debits ($28,700) equal the total credits ($28,700). Account numbers are sometimes shown to the left of the account titles in the trial balance.

A trial balance is a necessary checkpoint for uncovering certain types of errors before you proceed to other steps in the accounting process. For example, if only the debit portion of a journal entry has been posted, the trial balance would bring this error to light.

LIMITATIONS OF A TRIAL BALANCE

A trial balance does not guarantee freedom from recording errors, however. **It does not prove that all transactions have been recorded or that the ledger is correct**. Numerous errors may exist even though the trial balance columns agree. For example, the trial balance may balance even when (1) a transaction is not journalized, (2) a correct journal entry is not posted, (3) a journal entry is posted twice, (4) incorrect accounts are used in journalizing or posting, or (5) offsetting errors are made in recording the amount of a transaction. In other words, as long as equal debits and credits are posted, even to the wrong account or in the wrong amount, the total debits will equal the total credits.

LOCATING ERRORS

The procedure for preparing a trial balance is relatively simple. However, if the trial balance does not balance, locating an error in a manual system can be time-consuming, tedious, and frustrating. Errors generally result from mathematical mistakes, incorrect postings, or simply transcribing data incorrectly.

What do you do if you are faced with a trial balance that does not balance? First determine the amount of the difference between the two columns of the trial balance. After this amount is known, the following steps are often helpful:

ETHICS NOTE
Auditors are required to differentiate *errors* from *irregularities* when evaluating the accounting system. An error is the result of an unintentional mistake; as such, it is neither ethical nor unethical. An irregularity, on the other hand, is an intentional misstatement, which is viewed as unethical.

1. If the error is $1, $10, $100, or $1,000, re-add the trial balance columns and recompute the account balances.
2. If the error is divisible by 2, scan the trial balance to see whether a balance equal to half the error has been entered in the wrong column.

3. If the error is divisible by 9, retrace the account balances on the trial balance to see whether they are incorrectly copied from the ledger. For example, if a balance was $12 and it was listed as $21, a $9 error has been made. Reversing the order of numbers is called a transposition error.
4. If the error is not divisible by 2 or 9 (for example, $365), scan the ledger to see whether an account balance of $365 has been omitted from the trial balance, and scan the journal to see whether a $365 posting has been omitted.

TECHNOLOGY IN ACTION

In a computerized system, the trial balance is often only one column (no debit or credit columns), and the accounts have plus and minus signs associated with them. The final balance therefore is zero. Any errors that develop in a computerized system will undoubtedly involve the initial recording rather than some error in the posting or preparation of a trial balance.

USE OF DOLLAR SIGNS

Note that dollar signs do not appear in the journals or ledgers. Dollar signs are usually used only in the trial balance and the financial statements. Generally, a dollar sign is shown only for the first item in the column and for the total of that column. A single line is placed under the column of figures to be added or subtracted; the total amount is double underlined to indicate the final sum.

BEFORE YOU GO ON...

REVIEW IT

1. What is a trial balance and what is its primary purpose?
2. How is a trial balance prepared?
3. What are the limitations of a trial balance?

A LOOK BACK AT OUR FEATURE STORY

Refer back to the Feature Story about **The Mug and Musket** at the beginning of the chapter, and answer the following questions.

1. What accounting entries would Tanis likely make to record (a) the receipt of cash from a customer in payment of their bill, (b) payment of a utility bill, and (c) payment of wages for the waiters?
2. How did Tanis's job as Director of Finance help in her studies as she finished her business administration degree?

SOLUTION

1. Tanis would likely make the following entries.
   (a) Cash
   Food Sales Revenue
   (Receipt of payment for food services)
   (b) Utility Expense
   Cash
   (Payment of electric bill)
   (c) Salaries (or Wages) Expense
   Cash
   (Paid waiters' wages)
2. As a result of her accounting position, Tanis was able to relate the subject matter as well as much of the assignment material in her business courses to a real-world context. From her job, she knew how bills were paid, how supplies were determined, how employees were hired, managed, evaluated, and paid.

THE NAVIGATOR

DEMONSTRATION PROBLEM

Additional Demonstration Problem

Bob Sample opened the Campus Laundromat on September 1, 2002. During the first month of operations the following transactions occurred.

Sept. 1 Invested $20,000 cash in the business.
2 Paid $1,000 cash for store rent for the month of September.
3 Purchased washers and dryers for $25,000, paying $10,000 in cash and signing a $15,000, 6-month, 12% note payable.
4 Paid $1,200 for one-year accident insurance policy.
10 Received bill from the *Daily News* for advertising the opening of the laundromat $200.
20 Withdrew $700 cash for personal use.
30 Determined that cash receipts for laundry services for the month were $6,200.

The chart of accounts for the company is the same as in Pioneer Advertising Agency except for the following: No. 154 Laundry Equipment and No. 610 Advertising Expense.

Instructions

(a) Journalize the September transactions. (Use J1 for the journal page number.)
(b) Open ledger accounts and post the September transactions.
(c) Prepare a trial balance at September 30, 2002.

SOLUTION TO DEMONSTRATION PROBLEM

(a) GENERAL JOURNAL **J1**

Date	Account Titles and Explanation	Ref.	Debit	Credit
2002				
Sept. 1	Cash	101	20,000	
	Bob Sample, Capital	301		20,000
	(Owner's investment of cash in business)			
2	Rent Expense	729	1,000	
	Cash	101		1,000
	(Paid September rent)			
3	Laundry Equipment	154	25,000	
	Cash	101		10,000
	Notes Payable	200		15,000
	(Purchased laundry equipment for cash and 6-month, 12% note payable)			
4	Prepaid Insurance	130	1,200	
	Cash	101		1,200
	(Paid one-year insurance policy)			
10	Advertising Expense	610	200	
	Accounts Payable	201		200
	(Received bill from *Daily News* for advertising)			
20	Bob Sample, Drawing	306	700	
	Cash	101		700
	(Withdrew cash for personal use)			
30	Cash	101	6,200	
	Service Revenue	400		6,200
	(Received cash for services provided)			

ACTION PLAN

- Make separate journal entries for each transaction.
- In journalizing, make sure debits equal credits.
- In journalizing, use specific account titles taken from the chart of accounts.
- Provide appropriate description of journal entry.
- Arrange ledger in statement order, beginning with the balance sheet accounts.
- Post in chronological order.
- Use numbers in the reference column to indicate the amount has been posted.
- In the trial balance, list accounts in the order in which they appear in the ledger.
- List debit balances in the left column, and credit balances in the right column.

(b)

GENERAL LEDGER

Cash **No. 101**

Date	Explanation	Ref.	Debit	Credit	Balance
2002					
Sept. 1		J1	20,000		20,000
2		J1		1,000	19,000
3		J1		10,000	9,000
4		J1		1,200	7,800
20		J1		700	7,100
30		J1	6,200		13,300

Prepaid Insurance **No. 130**

Date	Explanation	Ref.	Debit	Credit	Balance
2002					
Sept. 4		J1	1,200		1,200

Laundry Equipment **No. 154**

Date	Explanation	Ref.	Debit	Credit	Balance
2002					
Sept. 3		J1	25,000		25,000

Notes Payable **No. 200**

Date	Explanation	Ref.	Debit	Credit	Balance
2002					
Sept. 3		J1		15,000	15,000

Accounts Payable **No. 201**

Date	Explanation	Ref.	Debit	Credit	Balance
2002					
Sept. 10		J1		200	200

Bob Sample, Capital **No. 301**

Date	Explanation	Ref.	Debit	Credit	Balance
2002					
Sept. 1		J1		20,000	20,000

Bob Sample, Drawing **No. 306**

Date	Explanation	Ref.	Debit	Credit	Balance
2002					
Sept. 20		J1	700		700

Service Revenue **No. 400**

Date	Explanation	Ref.	Debit	Credit	Balance
2002					
Sept. 30		J1		6,200	6,200

Advertising Expense **No. 610**

Date	Explanation	Ref.	Debit	Credit	Balance
2002					
Sept. 10		J1	200		200

Rent Expense **No. 729**

Date	Explanation	Ref.	Debit	Credit	Balance
2002					
Sept. 2		J1	1,000		1,000

(c)

CAMPUS LAUNDROMAT
Trial Balance
September 30, 2002

	Debit	Credit
Cash	$13,300	
Prepaid Insurance	1,200	
Laundry Equipment	25,000	
Notes Payable		$15,000
Accounts Payable		200
Bob Sample, Capital		20,000
Bob Sample, Drawing	700	
Service Revenue		6,200
Advertising Expense	200	
Rent Expense	1,000	
	$41,400	$41,400

THE NAVIGATOR

SUMMARY OF STUDY OBJECTIVES

1. *Explain what an account is and how it helps in the recording process.* An account is a record of increases and decreases in specific asset, liability, and owner's equity items.

2. *Define debits and credits and explain how they are used to record business transactions.* The terms debit and credit are synonymous with left and right. Assets, drawings, and expenses are increased by debits and decreased by credits. Liabilities, owner's capital, and revenues are increased by credits and decreased by debits.

3. *Identify the basic steps in the recording process.* The basic steps in the recording process are: (a) analyze each transaction in terms of its effects on the accounts, (b) enter the transaction information in a journal, (c) transfer the journal information to the appropriate accounts in the ledger.

4. *Explain what a journal is and how it helps in the recording process.* The initial accounting record of a transaction is entered in a journal before the data are entered in the accounts. A journal (a) discloses in one place the complete effects of a transaction, (b) provides a chronological record of transactions, and (c) prevents or locates errors because the debit and credit amounts for each entry can be readily compared.

5. *Explain what a ledger is and how it helps in the recording process.* The entire group of accounts maintained by a company is referred to as the ledger. The ledger keeps in one place all the information about changes in specific account balances.

6. *Explain what posting is and how it helps in the recording process.* Posting is the procedure of transferring journal entries to the ledger accounts. This phase of the recording process accumulates the effects of journalized transactions in the individual accounts.

7. *Prepare a trial balance and explain its purposes.* A trial balance is a list of accounts and their balances at a given time. Its primary purpose is to prove the equality of debits and credits after posting. A trial balance also uncovers errors in journalizing and posting and is useful in preparing financial statements.

THE NAVIGATOR

Key Term Matching Activity

GLOSSARY

Account A record of increases and decreases in specific asset, liability, or owner's equity items. (p. 44).

Chart of accounts A list of accounts and the account numbers that identify their location in the ledger. (p. 56).

Compound entry A journal entry that involves three or more accounts. (p. 52).

Credit The right side of an account. (p. 45).

Debit The left side of an account. (p. 45).

Double-entry system A system that records in appropriate accounts the dual effect of each transaction. (p. 45).

General journal The most basic form of journal. (p. 50).

General ledger A ledger that contains all asset, liability, and owner's equity accounts. (p. 53).

Journal An accounting record in which transactions are initially recorded in chronological order. (p. 50).

Journalizing The entering of transaction data in the journal. (p. 50).

Ledger The entire group of accounts maintained by a company. (p. 53).

Posting The procedure of transferring journal entries to the ledger accounts. (p. 54).

Simple entry A journal entry that involves only two accounts. (p. 51).

T account The basic form of an account. (p. 44).

Three-column form of account A form with columns for debit, credit, and balance amounts in an account. (p. 54).

Trial balance A list of accounts and their balances at a given time. (p. 64).

Chapter 2 Self-Test

SELF-STUDY QUESTIONS

Answers are at the end of the chapter.

(SO 1) **1.** Which of the following statements about an account is true?
   a. In its simplest form, an account consists of two parts.
   b. An account is an individual accounting record of increases and decreases in specific asset, liability, and owner's equity items.
   c. There are separate accounts for specific assets and liabilities but only one account for owner's equity items.
   d. The left side of an account is the credit or decrease side.

2. Debits: (SO 2)
   a. increase both assets and liabilities.
   b. decrease both assets and liabilities.
   c. increase assets and decrease liabilities.
   d. decrease assets and increase liabilities.

3. A revenue account: (SO 2)
   a. is increased by debits.
   b. is decreased by credits.
   c. has a normal balance of a debit.
   d. is increased by credits.

(SO 2) **4.** Accounts that normally have debit balances are:
a. assets, expenses, and revenues.
b. assets, expenses, and owner's capital.
c. assets, liabilities, and owner's drawings.
d. assets, owner's drawings, and expenses.

(SO 3) **5.** Which of the following is *not* part of the recording process?
a. Analyzing transactions.
b. Preparing a trial balance.
c. Entering transactions in a journal.
d. Posting transactions.

(SO 4) **6.** Which of the following statements about a journal is false?
a. It is not a book of original entry.
b. It provides a chronological record of transactions.
c. It helps to locate errors because the debit and credit amounts for each entry can be readily compared.
d. It discloses in one place the complete effect of a transaction.

(SO 5) **7.** A ledger:
a. contains only asset and liability accounts.
b. should show accounts in alphabetical order.
c. is a collection of the entire group of accounts maintained by a company.
d. is a book of original entry.

8. Posting: (SO 6)
a. normally occurs before journalizing.
b. transfers ledger transaction data to the journal.
c. is an optional step in the recording process.
d. transfers journal entries to ledger accounts.

9. A trial balance: (SO 7)
a. is a list of accounts with their balances at a given time.
b. proves the mathematical accuracy of journalized transactions.
c. will not balance if a correct journal entry is posted twice.
d. proves that all transactions have been recorded.

10. A trial balance will not balance if: (SO 7)
a. a correct journal entry is posted twice.
b. the purchase of supplies on account is debited to Supplies and credited to Cash.
c. a $100 cash drawing by the owner is debited to Owner's Drawing for $1,000 and credited to Cash for $100.
d. a $450 payment on account is debited to Accounts Payable for $45 and credited to Cash for $45.

THE NAVIGATOR

QUESTIONS

1. Describe the parts of a T account.

2. "The terms *debit* and *credit* mean increase and decrease, respectively." Do you agree? Explain.

3. José Amaro, a fellow student, contends that the double-entry system means each transaction must be recorded twice. Is José correct? Explain.

4. Teresa Alvarez, a beginning accounting student, believes debit balances are favorable and credit balances are unfavorable. Is Teresa correct? Discuss.

5. State the rules of debit and credit as applied to (a) asset accounts, (b) liability accounts, and (c) the owner's equity accounts (revenue, expenses, owner's drawing, and owner's capital).

6. What is the normal balance for each of the following accounts? (a) Accounts Receivable. (b) Cash. (c) Owner's Drawing. (d) Accounts Payable. (e) Service Revenue. (f) Salaries Expense. (g) Owner's Capital.

7. Indicate whether each of the following accounts is an asset, a liability, or an owner's equity account and whether it has a normal debit or credit balance: (a) Accounts Receivable, (b) Accounts Payable, (c) Equipment, (d) Owner's Drawing, (e) Supplies.

8. For the following transactions, indicate the account debited and the account credited.
(a) Supplies are purchased on account.
(b) Cash is received on signing a note payable.
(c) Employees are paid salaries in cash.

9. Indicate whether the following accounts generally will have (a) debit entries only, (b) credit entries only, or (c) both debit and credit entries.
(1) Cash.
(2) Accounts Receivable.
(3) Owner's Drawing.
(4) Accounts Payable.
(5) Salaries Expense.
(6) Service Revenue.

10. What are the basic steps in the recording process?

11. What are the advantages of using a journal in the recording process?

12. (a) When entering a transaction in the journal, should the debit or credit be written first?
(b) Which should be indented, the debit or credit?

13. Describe a compound entry, and provide an example.

14. (a) Should business transaction debits and credits be recorded directly in the ledger accounts?
(b) What are the advantages of first recording transactions in the journal and then posting to the ledger?

15. The account number is entered as the last step in posting the amounts from the journal to the ledger. What is the advantage of this step?

16. Journalize the following business transactions.
(a) Doris Wang invests $9,000 cash in the business.
(b) Insurance of $800 is paid for the year.
(c) Supplies of $1,500 are purchased on account.
(d) Cash of $7,500 is received for services rendered.

17. (a) What is a ledger?
(b) What is a chart of accounts and why is it important?

18. What is a trial balance and what are its purposes?

19. Kap Shin is confused about how accounting information flows through the accounting system. He believes the flow of information is as follows.
(a) Debits and credits posted to the ledger.
(b) Business transaction occurs.

(c) Information entered in the journal.
(d) Financial statements are prepared.
(e) Trial balance is prepared.
Is Kap correct? If not, indicate to Kap the proper flow of the information.

20. Two students are discussing the use of a trial balance. They wonder whether the following errors, each considered separately, would prevent the trial balance from balancing.
(a) The bookkeeper debited Cash for $600 and credited Wages Expense for $600 for payment of wages.
(b) Cash collected on account was debited to Cash for $900 and Service Revenue was credited for $90.
What would you tell them?

BRIEF EXERCISES

Indicate debit and credit effects and normal balance.
(SO 2)

BE2-1 For each of the following accounts indicate the effects of (a) a debit and (b) a credit on the accounts and (c) the normal balance of the account.

1. Accounts Payable.
2. Advertising Expense.
3. Service Revenue.
4. Accounts Receivable.
5. B. C. Jardine, Capital.
6. B. C. Jardine, Drawing.

Identify accounts to be debited and credited.
(SO 2)

BE2-2 Transactions for the H. J. Oslo Company for the month of June are presented below. Identify the accounts to be debited and credited for each transaction.

June 1 H. J. Oslo invests $3,000 cash in a small welding business of which he is the sole proprietor.
2 Purchases equipment on account for $900.
3 $500 cash is paid to landlord for June rent.
12 Bills J. Kronsnoble $300 for welding work done on account.

Journalize transactions.
(SO 4)

BE2-3 Using the data in BE2-2, journalize the transactions. (You may omit explanations.)

Identify and explain steps in recording process.
(SO 3)

BE2-4 Tage Shumway, a fellow student, is unclear about the basic steps in the recording process. Identify and briefly explain the steps in the order in which they occur.

Indicate basic and debit-credit analysis.
(SO 4)

BE2-5 J. A. Norris has the following transactions during August of the current year. Indicate (a) the effect on the accounting equation and (b) the debit-credit analysis illustrated on pages 57–61 of the text.

Aug. 1 Opens an office as a financial advisor, investing $6,000 in cash.
4 Pays insurance in advance for 6 months, $1,800 cash.
16 Receives $800 from clients for services rendered.
27 Pays secretary $500 salary.

Journalize transactions.
(SO 4)

BE2-6 Using the data in BE2-5, journalize the transactions. (You may omit explanations.)

Post journal entries to T accounts.
(SO 6)

BE2-7 Selected transactions for the Gonzales Company are presented in journal form below. Post the transactions to T accounts. Make one T account for each item and determine each account's ending balance.

J1

Date	Account Titles and Explanation	Ref.	Debit	Credit
May 5	Accounts Receivable		5,000	
	Service Revenue			5,000
	(Billed for services provided)			
12	Cash		2,400	
	Accounts Receivable			2,400
	(Received cash in payment of account)			
15	Cash		2,000	
	Service Revenue			2,000
	(Received cash for services provided)			

Post journal entries to standard form of account.
(SO 6)

BE2-8 Selected journal entries for the Gonzales Company are presented in BE2-7. Post the transactions using the standard form of account.

Prepare a trial balance.
(SO 7)

BE2-9 From the ledger balances given below, prepare a trial balance for the P. J. Carland Company at June 30, 2002. List the accounts in the order shown on page 65 of the text. All account balances are normal.

Accounts Payable $7,000, Cash $6,800, P. J. Carland, Capital $20,000, P. J. Carland, Drawing $1,200, Equipment $17,000, Service Revenue $6,000, Accounts Receivable $3,000, Salaries Expense $4,000, and Rent Expense $1,000.

Prepare a correct trial balance.
(SO 7)

BE2-10 An inexperienced bookkeeper prepared the following trial balance. Prepare a correct trial balance, assuming all account balances are normal.

GOMEZ COMPANY
Trial Balance
December 31, 2002

	Debit	Credit
Cash	$18,800	
Prepaid Insurance		$ 3,500
Accounts Payable		3,000
Unearned Revenue	4,200	
P. Gomez, Capital		15,000
P. Gomez, Drawing		4,500
Service Revenue		25,600
Salaries Expense	18,600	
Rent Expense		2,400
	$41,600	$54,000

EXERCISES

Identify debits, credits, and normal balances.
(SO 2)

E2-1 Selected transactions for A. Mane, an interior decorator, in her first month of business, are as follows.

Jan. 2 Invested $10,000 cash in business.
3 Purchased used car for $4,000 cash for use in business.
9 Purchased supplies on account for $500.
11 Billed customers $1,800 for services performed.
16 Paid $200 cash for advertising start of business.
20 Received $700 cash from customers billed on January 11.
23 Paid creditor $300 cash on account.
28 Withdrew $1,000 cash for personal use of owner.

Instructions

For each transaction indicate the following.

(a) The basic type of account debited and credited (asset, liability, owner's equity).
(b) The specific account debited and credited (cash, rent expense, service revenue, etc.).
(c) Whether the specific account is increased or decreased.
(d) The normal balance of the specific account.

Use the following format, in which the January 2 transaction is given as an example.

	Account Debited				Account Credited			
Date	**(a) Basic Type**	**(b) Specific Account**	**(c) Effect**	**(d) Normal Balance**	**(a) Basic Type**	**(b) Specific Account**	**(c) Effect**	**(d) Normal Balance**
Jan. 2	Asset	Cash	Increase	Debit	Owner's Equity	A. Mane, Capital	Increase	Credit

Journalize transactions and post using standard account form. (SO 4)

E2-2 Data for A. Mane, interior decorator, are presented in E2-1.

Instructions
Journalize the transactions using journal page J1. (You may omit explanations.)

Analyze transactions and determine their effect on accounts. (SO 2)

E2-3 Presented below is information related to Marx Real Estate Agency.

Oct. 1 Lynn Marx begins business as a real estate agent with a cash investment of $10,000.
2 Hires an administrative assistant.
3 Purchases office furniture for $1,900, on account.
6 Sells a house and lot for B. Rollins; bills B. Rollins $3,200 for realty services provided.
27 Pays $700 on the balance related to the transaction of October 3.
30 Pays the administrative assistant $1,500 in salary for October.

Instructions
Prepare the debit-credit analysis for each transaction as illustrated on pages 57–61.

Journalize transactions. (SO 4)

E2-4 Transaction data for Marx Real Estate Agency are presented in E2-3.

Instructions
Journalize the transactions. (You may omit explanations.)

Post journal entries and prepare a trial balance. (SO 6, 7)

E2-5 Selected transactions from the journal of J. L. Kang, investment broker, are presented below.

Date	Account Titles and Explanation	Ref.	Debit	Credit
Aug. 1	Cash		2,000	
	J. L Kang, Capital			2,000
	(Owner's investment of cash in business)			
10	Cash		2,400	
	Service Revenue			2,400
	(Received cash for services provided)			
12	Office Equipment		4,000	
	Cash			1,000
	Notes Payable			3,000
	(Purchased office equipment for cash and notes payable)			
25	Accounts Receivable		1,600	
	Service Revenue			1,600
	(Billed for services provided)			
31	Cash		900	
	Accounts Receivable			900
	(Receipt of cash on account)			

Instructions
(a) Post the transactions to T accounts.
(b) Prepare a trial balance at August 31, 2002.

Journalize transactions from account data and prepare a trial balance. (SO 4, 7)

E2-6 The T accounts on the next page summarize the ledger of Kim Landscaping Company at the end of the first month of operations.

Cash — No. 101

4/1	5,000	4/15	600
4/12	900	4/25	1,500
4/29	400		
4/30	800		

Accounts Receivable — No. 112

4/7	3,200	4/29	400

Supplies — No. 126

4/4	1,800		

Accounts Payable — No. 201

4/25	1,500	4/4	1,800

Unearned Revenue — No. 205

		4/30	800

J. Kim, Capital — No. 301

		4/1	5,000

Service Revenue — No. 400

		4/7	3,200
		4/12	900

Salaries Expense — No. 726

4/15	600		

Instructions

(a) Prepare the complete general journal (including explanations) from which the postings to Cash were made.

(b) Prepare a trial balance at April 30, 2002.

Journalize transactions from account data and prepare a trial balance.
(SO 4, 7)

E2-7 Presented below is the ledger for Holly Co.

Cash — No. 101

10/1	6,000	10/4	400
10/10	650	10/12	1,500
10/10	5,000	10/15	250
10/20	500	10/30	300
10/25	2,000	10/31	500

Accounts Receivable — No. 112

10/6	800	10/20	500
10/20	940		

Supplies — No. 126

10/4	400		

Furniture — No. 149

10/3	2,000		

Notes Payable — No. 200

		10/10	5,000

Accounts Payable — No. 201

10/12	1,500	10/3	2,000

Holly, Capital — No. 301

		10/1	6,000
		10/25	2,000

Holly, Drawing — No. 306

10/30	300		

Service Revenue — No. 407

		10/6	800
		10/10	650
		10/20	940

Store Wages Expense — No. 628

10/31	500		

Rent Expense — No. 729

10/15	250		

Instructions

(a) Reproduce the journal entries for the transactions that occurred on October 1, 10, and 20, and provide explanations for each.

(b) Determine the October 31 balance for each of the accounts above, and prepare a trial balance at October 31, 2002.

E2-8 Selected transactions for Craig Stevenson Company during its first month in business are presented below.

Prepare journal entries and post using standard account form.
(SO 4, 6)

Sept. 1 Invested $10,000 cash in the business.
5 Purchased equipment for $10,000 paying $5,000 in cash and the balance on account.
25 Paid $3,000 cash on balance owed for equipment.
30 Withdrew $500 cash for personal use.

Stevenson's chart of accounts shows: No. 101 Cash, No. 157 Equipment, No. 201 Accounts Payable, No. 301 Craig Stevenson, Capital, No. 306 Craig Stevenson, Drawing.

Instructions

(a) Journalize the transactions on page J1 of the journal.
(b) Post the transactions using the standard account form.

E2-9 The bookkeeper for John Castle's Equipment Repair made a number of errors in journalizing and posting, as described below.

Analyze errors and their effects on trial balance.
(SO 7)

1. A credit posting of $400 to Accounts Receivable was omitted.
2. A debit posting of $750 for Prepaid Insurance was debited to Insurance Expense.
3. A collection on account of $100 was journalized and posted as a debit to Cash $100 and a credit to Service Revenue $100.
4. A credit posting of $300 to Property Taxes Payable was made twice.
5. A cash purchase of supplies for $250 was journalized and posted as a debit to Supplies $25 and a credit to Cash $25.
6. A debit of $485 to Advertising Expense was posted as $458.

Instructions

For each error:

(a) Indicate whether the trial balance will balance.
(b) If the trial balance will not balance, indicate the amount of the difference.
(c) Indicate the trial balance column that will have the larger total.

Consider each error separately. Use the following form, in which error (1) is given as an example.

Error	(a) In Balance	(b) Difference	(c) Larger Column
(1)	No	$400	debit

E2-10 The accounts in the ledger of Tardy Delivery Service contain the following balances on July 31, 2002.

Prepare a trial balance
(SO 2, 7)

Accounts Receivable	$ 8,642	Prepaid Insurance	$ 1,968
Accounts Payable	8,396	Repair Expense	961
Cash	?	Service Revenue	10,610
Delivery Equipment	49,360	I. M. Tardy, Drawing	700
Gas and Oil Expense	758	I. M. Tardy, Capital	44,636
Insurance Expense	523	Salaries Expense	4,428
Notes Payable	21,450	Salaries Payable	815

Instructions

Prepare a trial balance with the accounts arranged as illustrated in the chapter and fill in the missing amount for Cash.

PROBLEMS: SET A

P2-1A Frontier Park was started on April 1 by C. J. Sanculi. The following selected events and transactions occurred during April.

Journalize a series of transactions.
(SO 2, 4)

Peachtree

Apr. 1 Sanculi invested $40,000 cash in the business.
4 Purchased land costing $30,000 for cash.
8 Incurred advertising expense of $1,800 on account.
11 Paid salaries to employees $1,500.
12 Hired park manager at a salary of $4,000 per month, effective May 1.

13 Paid $1,500 cash for a one-year insurance policy.
17 Withdrew $600 cash for personal use.
20 Received $5,700 in cash for admission fees.
25 Sold 100 coupon books for $25 each. Each book contains 10 coupons that entitle the holder to one admission to the park.
30 Received $5,900 in cash admission fees.
30 Paid $900 on account for advertising incurred on April 8.

Sanculi uses the following accounts: Cash; Prepaid Insurance; Land; Accounts Payable; Unearned Admission Revenue; C. J. Sanculi, Capital; C. J. Sanculi, Drawing; Admission Revenue; Advertising Expense; and Salaries Expense.

Instructions
Journalize the April transactions.

Journalize transactions, post, and prepare a trial balance.
(SO 2, 4, 6, 7)

P2-2A Iva Holz is a licensed CPA. During the first month of operations of her business, the following events and transactions occurred.

May 1 Holz invested $30,000 cash.
2 Hired a secretary-receptionist at a salary of $1,000 per month.
3 Purchased $1,500 of supplies on account from Read Supply Company.
7 Paid office rent of $900 cash for the month.
11 Completed a tax assignment and billed client $1,100 for services rendered.
12 Received $3,500 advance on a management consulting engagement.
17 Received cash of $1,200 for services completed for H. Arnold Co.
31 Paid secretary-receptionist $1,000 salary for the month.
31 Paid 40% of balance due Read Supply Company.

Iva uses the following chart of accounts: No. 101 Cash, No. 112 Accounts Receivable, No. 126 Supplies, No. 201 Accounts Payable, No. 205 Unearned Revenue, No. 301 Iva Holz, Capital, No. 400 Service Revenue, No. 726 Salaries Expense, and No. 729 Rent Expense.

Instructions

Trial balance totals $36,700

(a) Journalize the transactions.
(b) Post to the ledger accounts.
(c) Prepare a trial balance on May 31, 2002.

Journalize and post transactions, prepare a trial balance, and determine elements of financial statements.
(SO 2, 4, 6, 7)

P2-3A Leo Mataruka owns and manages a computer repair service, which had the following trial balance on December 31, 2001 (the end of its fiscal year).

BYTE REPAIR SERVICE
Trial Balance
December 31, 2001

Cash	$ 8,000	
Accounts Receivable	15,000	
Parts Inventory	13,000	
Prepaid Rent	3,000	
Shop Equipment	21,000	
Accounts Payable		$19,000
Leo Mataruka, Capital		41,000
	$ 60,000	$60,000

Summarized transactions for January 2002 were as follows.

1. Advertising costs, paid in cash, $1,000.
2. Additional repair parts inventory acquired on account $3,000.
3. Miscellaneous expenses, paid in cash, $2,000.
4. Cash collected from customers on account $13,000.
5. Cash paid to creditors on account $15,000.

6. Repair parts used during January $4,000. (*Hint:* Debit this to Repair Parts Expense.)
7. Repair services performed during January: for cash $4,000; on account $9,000.
8. Wages for January, paid in cash, $3,000.
9. Rent expense for January recorded. However, no cash was paid out for rent during January. A rent payment had been made for 3 months, in advance, on December 1, 2001, in the amount of $4,500.
10. Leo's drawings during January were $2,000.

Instructions

(a) Explain why the December 31, 2001, balance in the Prepaid Rent account is $3,000. (Refer to the Trial Balance and item (9) above.)
(b) Open T accounts for each of the accounts listed in the trial balance, and enter the opening balances for 2002.
(c) Prepare journal entries to record each of the January transactions.
(d) Post the journal entries to the accounts in the ledger. (Add accounts as needed.)
(e) Prepare a trial balance as of January 31, 2002.
(f) Determine the total assets as of January 31, 2002. (It is not necessary to prepare a balance sheet. Simply list the relevant amounts from the trial balance and calculate the total.)
(g) Determine the net income or loss for the month of January 2002. (It is not necessary to prepare an income statement. Simply list the relevant amounts from the trial balance, and calculate the amount of the net income or loss.)

Trial balance totals $61,000

P2-4A The trial balance of the Santos Company shown below does not balance.

Prepare a correct trial balance.
(SO 7)

SANTOS COMPANY
Trial Balance
May 31, 2002

	Debit	Credit
Cash	$ 3,850	
Accounts Receivable		$ 2,750
Prepaid Insurance	700	
Equipment	12,000	
Accounts Payable		4,500
Property Taxes Payable	560	
T. Santos, Capital		11,700
Service Revenue	8,690	
Salaries Expense	4,200	
Advertising Expense		1,100
Property Tax Expense	800	
	$30,800	$20,050

Your review of the ledger reveals that each account has a normal balance. You also discover the following errors.

1. The totals of the debit sides of Prepaid Insurance, Accounts Payable, and Property Tax Expense were each understated $100.
2. Transposition errors were made in Accounts Receivable and Service Revenue. Based on postings made, the correct balances were $2,570 and $8,960, respectively.
3. A debit posting to Salaries Expense of $200 was omitted.
4. A $700 cash drawing by the owner was debited to T. Santos, Capital for $700 and credited to Cash for $700.
5. A $520 purchase of supplies on account was debited to Equipment for $520 and credited to Cash for $520.
6. A cash payment of $450 for advertising was debited to Advertising Expense for $45 and credited to Cash for $45.
7. A collection from a customer for $210 was debited to Cash for $210 and credited to Accounts Payable for $210.

Instructions

Trial balance totals $26,630

Prepare a correct trial balance. Note: The chart of accounts includes the following: T. Santos, Drawing, and Supplies. (*Hint:* It helps to prepare the correct journal entry for the transaction described and compare it to the mistake made.)

Journalize transactions, post, and prepare a trial balance.
(SO 2, 4, 6, 7)

Peachtree

P2-5A The Lake Theater is owned by Avtar Sandhu. All facilities were completed on March 31. At this time, the ledger showed: No. 101 Cash $6,000; No. 140 Land $10,000; No. 145 Buildings (concession stand, projection room, ticket booth, and screen) $8,000; No. 157 Equipment $6,000; No. 201 Accounts Payable $2,000; No. 275 Mortgage Payable $8,000; and No. 301 Avtar Sandhu, Capital $20,000. During April, the following events and transactions occurred.

Apr. 2 Paid film rental of $800 on first movie.
3 Ordered two additional films at $500 each.
9 Received $1,800 cash from admissions.
10 Made $2,000 payment on mortgage and $1,000 on accounts payable.
11 Lake Theater contracted with R. Thoms Company to operate the concession stand. Thoms is to pay 17% of gross concession receipts (payable monthly) for the right to operate the concession stand.
12 Paid advertising expenses $300.
20 Received one of the films ordered on April 3 and was billed $500. The film will be shown in April.
25 Received $4,200 cash from admissions.
29 Paid salaries $1,600.
30 Received statement from R. Thoms showing gross concession receipts of $1,000 and the balance due to The Lake Theater of $170 ($1,000 × 17%) for April. Thoms paid one-half of the balance due and will remit the remainder on May 5.
30 Prepaid $900 rental on special film to be run in May.

In addition to the accounts identified above, the chart of accounts shows: No. 112 Accounts Receivable, No. 136 Prepaid Rentals, No. 405 Admission Revenue, No. 406 Concession Revenue, No. 610 Advertising Expense, No. 632 Film Rental Expense, and No. 726 Salaries Expense.

Instructions

Trial balance totals $33,670

(a) Enter the beginning balances in the ledger as of April 1. Insert a check mark (✓) in the reference column of the ledger for the beginning balance.
(b) Journalize the April transactions.
(c) Post the April journal entries to the ledger. Assume that all entries are posted from page 1 of the journal.
(d) Prepare a trial balance on April 30, 2002.

PROBLEMS: SET B

Journalize a series of transactions.
(SO 2, 4)

P2-1B Surepar Miniature Golf and Driving Range was opened on March 1 by Jane McInnes. The following selected events and transactions occurred during March:

Mar. 1 Invested $50,000 cash in the business.
3 Purchased Lee's Golf Land for $38,000 cash. The price consists of land $23,000, building $9,000, and equipment $6,000. (Make one compound entry.)
5 Advertised the opening of the driving range and miniature golf course, paying advertising expenses of $1,600.
6 Paid cash $1,480 for a one-year insurance policy.
10 Purchased golf clubs and other equipment for $2,600 from Palmer Company payable in 30 days.
18 Received $800 in cash for golf fees earned.
19 Sold 100 coupon books for $15 each. Each book contains 10 coupons that enable the holder to one round of miniature golf or to hit one bucket of golf balls.
25 Withdrew $500 cash for personal use.
30 Paid salaries of $600.
30 Paid Palmer Company in full.
31 Received $500 cash for fees earned.

Jane McInnes uses the following accounts: Cash; Prepaid Insurance; Land; Buildings; Equipment; Accounts Payable; Unearned Revenue; Jane McInnes, Capital; Jane McInnes, Drawing; Golf Revenue; Advertising Expense; and Salaries Expense.

Instructions

Journalize the March transactions.

Journalize transactions, post, and prepare a trial balance.
(SO 2, 4, 6, 7)

P2-2B Patricia Perez is a licensed architect. During the first month of the operation of her business, the following events and transactions occurred.

April	1	Invested $20,000 cash.
	1	Hired a secretary-receptionist at a salary of $300 per week payable monthly.
	2	Paid office rent for the month $800.
	3	Purchased architectural supplies on account from Halo Company $1,500.
	10	Completed blueprints on a carport and billed client $900 for services.
	11	Received $500 cash advance from R. Welk for the design of a new home.
	20	Received $1,500 cash for services completed and delivered to P. Donahue.
	30	Paid secretary-receptionist for the month $1,500.
	30	Paid $600 to Halo Company on account.

Patricia uses the following chart of accounts: No. 101 Cash, No. 112 Accounts Receivable, No. 126 Supplies, No. 201 Accounts Payable, No. 205 Unearned Revenue, No. 301 Patricia Perez, Capital, No. 400 Service Revenue, No. 726 Salaries Expense, and No. 729 Rent Expense.

Instructions

(a) Journalize the transactions.
(b) Post to the ledger accounts.
(c) Prepare a trial balance on April 30, 2002.

Trial balance totals $23,800

Journalize transactions, post, and prepare a trial balance and financial statements.
(SO 2, 4, 6, 7)

P2-3B Bablad Brokerage Services was formed on May 1, 2002. The following transactions took place during the first month.

Transactions on May 1:

1. Jacob Bablad invested $120,000 cash in the company, as its sole owner.
2. Hired two employees to work in the warehouse. They will each be paid a salary of $2,000 per month.
3. Signed a 2-year rental agreement on a warehouse; paid $48,000 cash in advance for the first year. (*Hint:* The portion of the cost related to May 2002 is an expense for this month.)
4. Purchased furniture and equipment costing $70,000. A cash payment of $20,000 was made immediately; the remainder will be paid in 6 months.
5. Paid $3,000 cash for a one-year insurance policy on the furniture and equipment. (*Hint:* The portion of the cost related to May 2002 is an expense for this month.)

Transactions during the remainder of the month:

6. Purchased basic office supplies for $1,000 cash.
7. Purchased more office supplies for $2,000 on account.
8. Total revenues earned were $30,000—$10,000 cash and $20,000 on account.
9. Paid $800 to suppliers on account.
10. Collected $5,000 from customers on account.
11. Received utility bills in the amount of $400, to be paid next month.
12. Paid the monthly salaries of the two employees, totalling $4,000.

Instructions

(a) Prepare journal entries to record each of the events listed.
(b) Post the journal entries to T accounts.
(c) Prepare a trial balance as of May 31, 2002.
(d) Prepare an income statement and a statement of owner's equity for Bablad Brokerage Services for the month ended May 31, 2002, and a balance sheet as of May 31, 2002.

Trial balance totals $201,600

Prepare a correct trial balance.
(SO 7)

P2-4B The trial balance of Thom Wargo Co. shown below does not balance.

THOM WARGO CO.
Trial Balance
June 30, 2002

	Debit	Credit
Cash		$ 3,840
Accounts Receivable	$ 3,231	
Supplies	800	
Equipment	3,000	
Accounts Payable		2,666
Unearned Revenue	2,200	
T. Wargo, Capital		9,000
T. Wargo, Drawing	800	
Service Revenue		2,380
Salaries Expense	3,400	
Office Expense	910	
	$14,341	$17,886

Each of the listed accounts has a normal balance per the general ledger. An examination of the ledger and journal reveals the following errors.

1. Cash received from a customer on account was debited for $570, and Accounts Receivable was credited for the same amount. The actual collection was for $750.
2. The purchase of a typewriter on account for $340 was recorded as a debit to Supplies for $340 and a credit to Accounts Payable for $340.
3. Services were performed on account for a client for $890. Accounts Receivable was debited for $890, and Service Revenue was credited for $89.
4. A debit posting to Salaries Expense of $600 was omitted.
5. A payment on account for $206 was credited to Cash for $206 and credited to Accounts Payable for $260.
6. The withdrawal of $500 cash for Wargo's personal use was debited to Salaries Expense for $500 and credited to Cash for $500.

Instructions

Prepare a correct trial balance. (*Hint:* It helps to prepare the correct journal entry for the transaction described and compare it to the mistake made.)

Trial balance totals $16,581

Journalize transactions, post, and prepare a trial balance.
(SO 2, 4, 6, 7)

P2-5B The Sabo Theater, owned by Adam Sabo, will begin operations in March. The Sabo will be unique in that it will show only triple features of sequential theme movies. As of February 28, the ledger of Sabo showed: No. 101 Cash $16,000; No. 140 Land $42,000; No. 145 Buildings (concession stand, projection room, ticket booth, and screen) $18,000; No. 157 Equipment $16,000; No. 201 Accounts Payable $12,000; and No. 301 A. Sabo, Capital $80,000. During the month of March the following events and transactions occurred.

Mar. 2 Acquired the three *Star Wars* movies (*Star Wars, The Empire Strikes Back,* and *The Return of the Jedi*) to be shown for the first 3 weeks of March. The film rental was $9,000; $3,000 was paid in cash and $6,000 will be paid on March 10.
3 Ordered the first three *Star Trek* movies to be shown the last 10 days of March. It will cost $300 per night.
9 Received $6,500 cash from admissions.
10 Paid balance due on *Star Wars* movies rental and $3,000 on February 28 accounts payable.
11 Sabo Theater contracted with M. Brewer Company to operate the concession stand. Brewer is to pay 15% of gross concession receipts (payable monthly) for the right to operate the concession stand.
12 Paid advertising expenses $800.
20 Received $7,200 cash from admissions.
20 Received the *Star Trek* movies and paid the rental fee of $3,000.
31 Paid salaries of $4,800.

31 Received statement from M. Brewer showing gross receipts from concessions of $8,000 and the balance due to Sabo Theater of $1,200 ($8,000 × 15%) for March. Brewer paid one-half the balance due and will remit the remainder on April 5.

31 Received $15,000 cash from admissions.

In addition to the accounts identified above, the chart of accounts includes: No. 112 Accounts Receivable, No. 405 Admission Revenue, No. 406 Concession Revenue, No. 610 Advertising Expense, No. 632 Film Rental Expense, and No. 726 Salaries Expense.

Instructions

(a) Enter the beginning balances in the ledger. Insert a check mark (✓) in the reference column of the ledger for the beginning balance.
(b) Journalize the March transactions.
(c) Post the March journal entries to the ledger. Assume that all entries are posted from page 1 of the journal.
(d) Prepare a trial balance on March 31, 2002.

Trial balance totals $118,900

BROADENING YOUR PERSPECTIVE

FINANCIAL REPORTING AND ANALYSIS

FINANCIAL REPORTING PROBLEM: Lands' End, Inc.

BYP2-1 The financial statements of **Lands' End, Inc.** are presented in Appendix A. The notes accompanying the statements contain the following selected accounts, stated in thousands of dollars.

Accounts Payable	$ 74,510	Income Taxes Payable	$ 10,255
Accounts Receivable	17,753	Interest Expense	1,890
Property, Plant, and Equipment	283,139	Inventory	162,193

Instructions

(a) Answer the following questions.
  (1) What is the increase and decrease side for each account?
  (2) What is the normal balance for each account?

(b) Identify the probable other account in the transaction and the effect on that account when:
  (1) Accounts Receivable is decreased.
  (2) Accounts Payable is decreased.
  (3) Inventory is increased.

(c) Identify the other account(s) that ordinarily would be involved when:
  (1) Interest Expense is increased.
  (2) Property, Plant, and Equipment is increased.

COMPARATIVE ANALYSIS PROBLEM: Lands' End vs. Abercrombie & Fitch

BYP2-2 **Lands' End's** financial statements are presented in Appendix A. **Abercrombie & Fitch's** financial statements are presented in Appendix B.

Instructions

(a) Based on the information contained in the financial statements, determine the normal balance of the listed accounts for each company.

Lands' End	Abercrombie & Fitch
1. Inventory	1. Accounts Receivable
2. Property, Plant, and Equipment	2. Cash and Equivalents
3. Accounts Payable	3. Cost of Goods Sold
4. Interest Expense	4. Sales (revenue)

(b) Identify the other account ordinarily involved when:

(1) Accounts Receivable is increased.
(2) Accrued Payroll is decreased.
(3) Property, Plant, and Equipment is increased.
(4) Interest Expense is increased.

INTERPRETING FINANCIAL STATEMENTS: A Global Focus

BYP2-3 **Doman Industries Ltd.**, whose products are sold in 30 countries worldwide, is an integrated Canadian forest products company.

Doman sells the majority of its lumber products in the United States and a significant amount of its pulp products in Asia. Doman also has loans from other countries. For example, on June 18, 1999, the Company borrowed US$160 million at an annual interest rate of 12%. Doman must repay this loan, and interest, in U.S. dollars.

One of the challenges global companies face is to make themselves attractive to investors from other countries. This is difficult to do when different accounting rules in different countries blur the real impact of earnings. For example, in 1998 Doman reported a loss of $2.3 million, using Canadian accounting rules. Had it reported under U.S. accounting rules, its loss would have been $12.1 million.

Many companies that want to be more easily compared with U.S. and other global competitors have switched to U.S. accounting principles. **Canadian National Railway**, **Corel**, **Cott**, **Inco**, and the **Thomson Corporation** are but a few examples of large Canadian companies whose financial statements are now presented in U.S. dollars, which adhere to U.S. GAAP, or are reconciled to U.S. GAAP.

Instructions

(a) Identify advantages and disadvantages that companies should consider when switching to U.S. reporting standards.
(b) Suppose you wish to compare Doman Industries to a U.S.-based competitor. Do you believe the use of country-specific accounting policies would hinder your comparison? If so, explain how.
(c) Suppose you wish to compare Doman Industries to a Canadian-based competitior. If the companies chose to apply generally acceptable Canadian accounting policies differently, how could this affect your comparison of their financial results?
(d) Do you see any significant distinction between comparing statements prepared using generally accepted accounting principles of different countries and comparing statements prepared using generally accepted accounting principles of the same country (e.g., U.S.) but that apply the principles differently?

EXPLORING THE WEB

www.wiley.com/college/weygandt

BYP2-4 Much information about specific companies is available on the World Wide Web. Such information includes basic descriptions of the company's location, activities, industry, financial health, and financial performance.

Address:* biz.yahoo.com/i *(or go to* www.wiley.com/college/weygandt*)

Steps:

1. Type in a company name, or use index to find company name.
2. Choose **Profile**. Perform instructions (a)–(c) below.
3. Click on the company's specific industry to identify competitors. Perform instructions (d)–(g) below.

Instructions

Answer the following questions.

(a) What is the company's industry?
(b) What was the company's total sales?
(c) What was the company's net income?
(d) What are the names of four of the company's competitors?
(e) Choose one of these competitors.
(f) What is this competitor's name? What were its sales? What was its net income?
(g) Which of these two companies is larger by size of sales? Which one reported higher net income?

CRITICAL THINKING

GROUP DECISION CASE

BYP2-5 Lucy Lars operates Lucy Lars Riding Academy. The academy's primary sources of revenue are riding fees and lesson fees, which are paid on a cash basis. Lucy also boards horses for owners, who are billed monthly for boarding fees. In a few cases, boarders pay in advance of expected use. For its revenue transactions, the academy maintains the following accounts: No. 1 Cash, No. 5 Boarding Accounts Receivable, No. 27 Unearned Boarding Revenue, No. 51 Riding Revenue, No. 52 Lesson Revenue, and No. 53 Boarding Revenue.

The academy owns 10 horses, a stable, a riding corral, riding equipment, and office equipment. These assets are accounted for in accounts No. 11 Horses, No. 12 Building, No. 13 Riding Corral, No. 14 Riding Equipment, and No. 15 Office Equipment.

For its expenses, the academy maintains the following accounts: No. 6 Hay and Feed Supplies, No. 7 Prepaid Insurance, No. 21 Accounts Payable, No. 60 Salaries Expense, No. 61 Advertising Expense, No. 62 Utilities Expense, No. 63 Veterinary Expense, No. 64 Hay and Feed Expense, and No. 65 Insurance Expense.

Lucy makes periodic withdrawals of cash for personal living expenses. To record Lucy's equity in the business and her drawings, two accounts are maintained: No. 50 Lucy Lars, Capital, and No. 51 Lucy Lars, Drawing.

During the first month of operations an inexperienced bookkeeper was employed. Lucy Lars asks you to review the following eight entries of the 50 entries made during the month. In each case, the explanation for the entry is correct.

May	1	Cash	18,000	
		Lucy Lars, Capital		18,000
		(Invested $18,000 cash in business)		
	5	Cash	250	
		Riding Revenue		250
		(Received $250 cash for lessons provided)		
	7	Cash	500	
		Boarding Revenue		500
		(Received $500 for boarding of horses beginning June 1)		
	14	Riding Equipment	80	
		Cash		800
		(Purchased desk and other office equipment for $800 cash)		
	15	Salaries Expense	400	
		Cash		400
		(Issued check to Lucy Lars for personal use)		
	20	Cash	148	
		Riding Revenue		184
		(Received $184 cash for riding fees)		
	30	Veterinary Expense	75	
		Accounts Payable		75
		(Received bill of $75 from veterinarian for services rendered)		
	31	Hay and Feed Expense	1,700	
		Cash		1,700
		(Purchased an estimated 2 months' supply of feed and hay for $1,700 on account)		

Instructions

With the class divided into groups, answer the following.

(a) Identify each journal entry that is correct. For each journal entry that is incorrect, prepare the entry that should have been made by the bookkeeper.
(b) Which of the incorrect entries would prevent the trial balance from balancing?
(c) What was the correct net income for May, assuming the bookkeeper reported net income of $4,500 after posting all 50 entries?
(d) What was the correct cash balance at May 31, assuming the bookkeeper reported a balance of $12,475 after posting all 50 entries (and the only errors occurred in the items listed above)?

COMMUNICATION ACTIVITY

BYP2-6 Merlynn's Maid Company offers home cleaning service. Two recurring transactions for the company are billing customers for services rendered and paying employee salaries. For example, on March 15, bills totaling $6,000 were sent to customers and $2,000 was paid in salaries to employees.

Instructions

Write a memo to your instructor that explains and illustrates the steps in the recording process for each of the March 15 transactions. Use the format illustrated in the text under the heading, "The Recording Process Illustrated" (p. 57).

ETHICS CASE

BYP2-7 Megan Menard is the assistant chief accountant at Hokey Company, a manufacturer of computer chips and cellular phones. The company presently has total sales of $20 million. It is the end of the first quarter. Megan is hurriedly trying to prepare a general ledger trial balance so that quarterly financial statements can be prepared and released to management and the regulatory agencies. The total credits on the trial balance exceed the debits by $1,000. In order to meet the 4 p.m. deadline, Megan decides to force the debits and credits into balance by adding the amount of the difference to the Equipment account. She chose Equipment because it is one of the larger account balances; percentage-wise, it will be the least misstated. Megan "plugs" the difference! She believes that the difference will not affect anyone's decisions. She wishes that she had another few days to find the error but realizes that the financial statements are already late.

Instructions

(a) Who are the stakeholders in this situation?
(b) What are the ethical issues involved in this case?
(c) What are Megan's alternatives?

Answers to Self-Study Questions

1. b **2.** c **3.** d **4.** d **5.** b **6.** a **7.** c **8.** d **9.** a **10.** c

LANDS' END DIRECT MERCHANTS

Answer to Lands' End Review It Question 4, p. 49

Cash—debit; Accounts Payable—credit; Interest Expense—debit.

Remember to go back to the Navigator box on the chapter-opening page and check off your completed work.

3

ADJUSTING THE ACCOUNTS

THE NAVIGATOR ✓

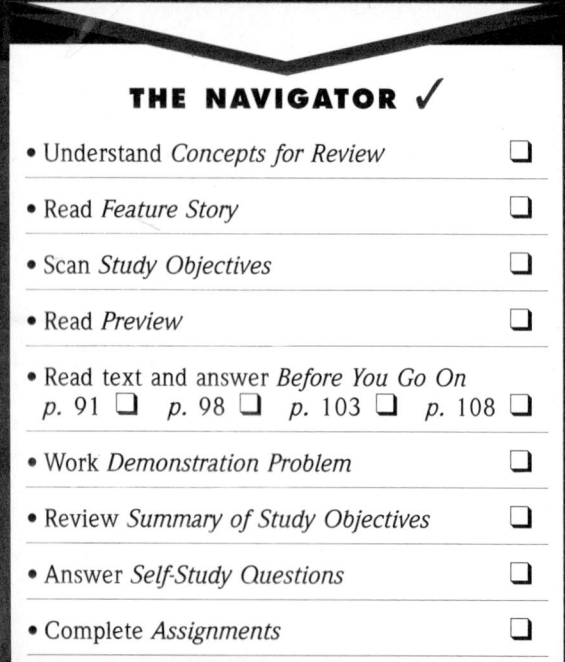

- Understand *Concepts for Review* ❑
- Read *Feature Story* ❑
- Scan *Study Objectives* ❑
- Read *Preview* ❑
- Read text and answer *Before You Go On* *p.* 91 ❑ *p.* 98 ❑ *p.* 103 ❑ *p.* 108 ❑
- Work *Demonstration Problem* ❑
- Review *Summary of Study Objectives* ❑
- Answer *Self-Study Questions* ❑
- Complete *Assignments* ❑

CONCEPTS FOR REVIEW

Before studying this chapter, you should know or, if necessary, review:

a. What a double-entry system is. (Ch. 2, p. 45)

b. How to increase or decrease assets, liabilities, and owner's equity using debit and credit procedures. (Ch. 2, pp. 45–48)

c. How to journalize a transaction. (Ch. 2, pp. 50–52)

d. How to post a transaction. (Ch. 2, pp. 54–56)

e. How to prepare a trial balance. (Ch. 2, pp. 64–66)

☑ THE NAVIGATOR

FEATURE STORY

Timing Is Everything

In Chapter 1 you learned a neat little formula: Net income = Revenues − Expenses. And in Chapter 2 you learned some nice, orderly rules for recording corporate revenue and expense transactions. Guess what? Things are not really that nice and neat. In fact, it is often difficult to determine in what time period some revenues and expenses should be reported. And, in measuring net income, timing is everything.

There are rules that give guidance on these issues. But occasionally these rules are overlooked, misinterpreted, or even intentionally ignored. Consider the following examples.

- **McKesson HBOC**, one of the largest prescription drug distributors, restated its first-quarter, 1999, earnings because $26.2 million included in healthcare software sales weren't final and should not have been recorded. This negative surprise caused McKesson's share price to plummet 48 percent overnight, from $65.75 to $34.50, wiping out $9 billion in the market value of its stock.
- **Cambridge Biotech Corp.**, which develops vaccines and diagnostic tests for humans and animals, said that it reported revenue from transactions that "don't appear to be bona fide."
- **Media Vision Technology Inc.**, a maker of sound and animation equipment for computers, was accused of operating a "phantom" warehouse to hide inventory for returned products already recorded as sales.
- **Penguin USA**, a book publisher, said that it understated expenses in a number of years because it failed to report expenses for discounts given to customers for paying early.

In each case, accrual accounting concepts were violated. That is, revenues or expenses were not recorded in the proper period, which had a substantial impact on reported income. Their timing was off!

THE NAVIGATOR

STUDY OBJECTIVES

After studying this chapter, you should be able to:

1. Explain the time period assumption.
2. Explain the accrual basis of accounting.
3. Explain why adjusting entries are needed.
4. Identify the major types of adjusting entries.
5. Prepare adjusting entries for prepayments.
6. Prepare adjusting entries for accruals.
7. Describe the nature and purpose of an adjusted trial balance.

THE NAVIGATOR

PREVIEW OF CHAPTER 3

In Chapter 2 we examined the recording process through the preparation of the trial balance. Before we will be ready to prepare financial statements from the trial balance, additional steps need to be taken. The timing mismatch between revenues and expenses of the four companies mentioned in our Feature Story illustrates the types of situations that make these additional steps necessary. For example, long-lived assets purchased or constructed in prior accounting years are being used to produce goods and provide services in the current year. What portion of these assets' costs, if any, should be recognized as an expense of the current period? Before financial statements can be prepared, this and other questions relating to the recognition of revenues and expenses must be answered. With the answers in hand, we can then adjust the relevant account balances.

The content and organization of Chapter 3 are as follows.

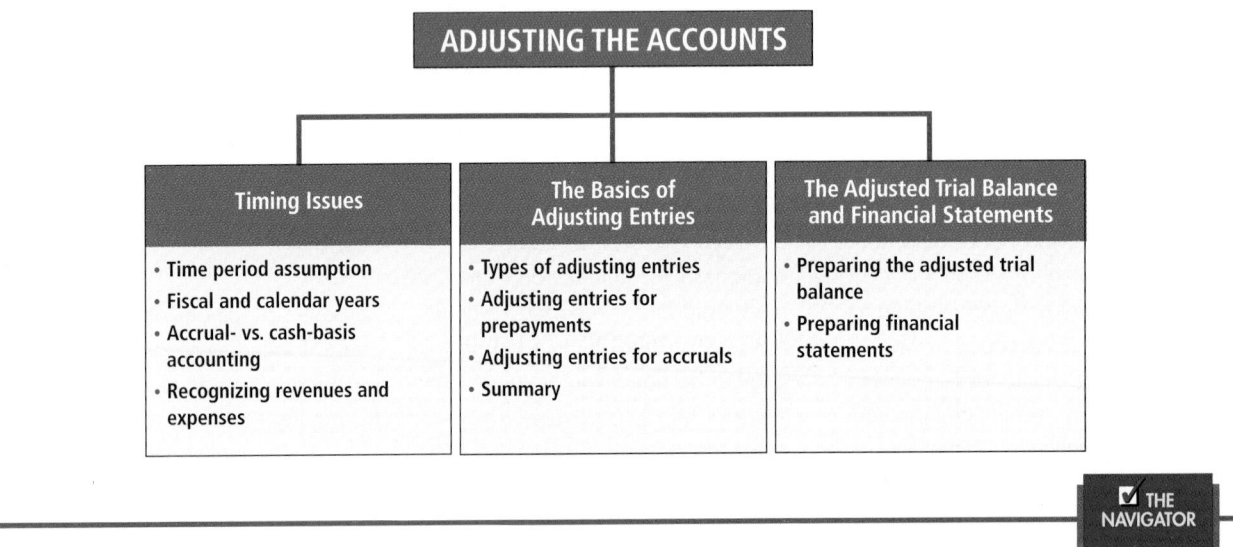

ADJUSTING THE ACCOUNTS

Timing Issues	The Basics of Adjusting Entries	The Adjusted Trial Balance and Financial Statements
• Time period assumption • Fiscal and calendar years • Accrual- vs. cash-basis accounting • Recognizing revenues and expenses	• Types of adjusting entries • Adjusting entries for prepayments • Adjusting entries for accruals • Summary	• Preparing the adjusted trial balance • Preparing financial statements

THE NAVIGATOR

TIMING ISSUES

STUDY OBJECTIVE 1

Explain the time period assumption.

No adjustments would be necessary if we could wait to prepare financial statements until a company ended its operations. At that point, we could easily determine its final balance sheet and the amount of lifetime income it earned. The following anecdote illustrates one way to compute lifetime income.

> A grocery store owner from the old country kept his accounts payable on a spindle, accounts receivable on a note pad, and cash in a cigar box. His daughter, having just passed the CPA exam, chided the father: "I don't understand how you can run your business this way. How do you know what your profits are?"
>
> "Well," the father replied, "when I got off the boat 40 years ago, I had nothing but the pants I was wearing. Today your brother is a doctor, your sister is a college professor, and you are a CPA. Your mother and I have a nice car, a well-furnished house, and a lake home. We have a good business, and everything is paid for. So, you add all that together, subtract the pants, and there's your profit."

SELECTING AN ACCOUNTING TIME PERIOD

Although the old grocer may be correct in his evaluation, it is impractical to wait so long for the results of operations. All entities, from the corner grocery, to a global company like **Kellogg**, to your college or university, find it desirable and necessary to report the results of their activities more frequently. For example, management usually wants monthly financial statements, and the Internal Revenue Service requires all businesses to file annual tax returns. Therefore, **accountants divide the economic life of a business into artificial time periods**. This convenient assumption is referred to as the **time period assumption**.

Many business transactions affect more than one of these arbitrary time periods. For example, Farmer Brown's milking machine bought in 1998 and the airplanes purchased by **Delta Air Lines** five years ago are still in use today. Therefore we must determine the relevance of each business transaction to specific accounting periods. Doing so may involve subjective judgments and estimates.

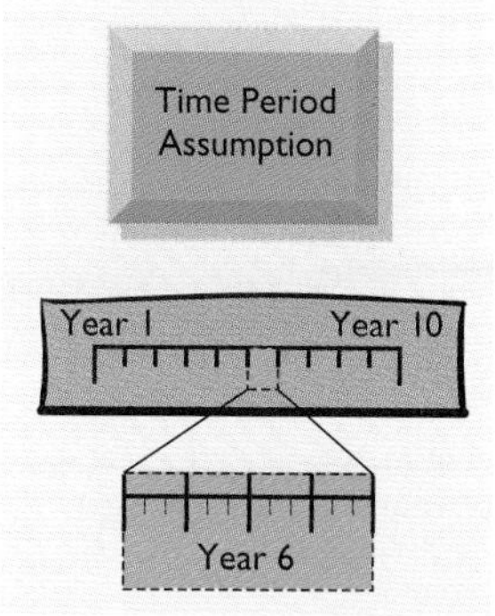

ALTERNATIVE TERMINOLOGY
The time period assumption is also called the *periodicity assumption.*

FISCAL AND CALENDAR YEARS

Both small and large companies prepare financial statements periodically in order to assess their financial condition and results of operations. **Accounting time periods are generally a month, a quarter, or a year.** Monthly and quarterly time periods are called **interim periods**. Most large companies are required to prepare both quarterly and annual financial statements.

An accounting time period that is one year in length is referred to as a **fiscal year**. A fiscal year usually begins with the first day of a month and ends twelve months later on the last day of a month. The accounting period used by most businesses coincides with the **calendar year** (January 1 to December 31). Companies whose fiscal year differs from the calendar year include **Delta Air Lines**, June 30; **Walt Disney Productions**, September 30; and **Kmart Corp.**, January 31. Sometimes a company's year-end will vary from year to year. For example, **Lands' End's** fiscal year ends on the Friday closest to January 31, which was January 29 in 1999 and January 28 in 2000.

ACCRUAL- VS. CASH-BASIS ACCOUNTING

STUDY OBJECTIVE 2
Explain the accrual basis of accounting.

What you will learn in this chapter is **accrual-basis accounting**. Under the accrual basis, transactions that change a company's financial statements are recorded **in the periods in which the events occur**. For example, using the accrual basis to determine net income means recognizing revenues when earned (rather than when the cash is received). It also means recognizing expenses when incurred (rather than when paid). Information presented on an accrual basis reveals relationships likely to be important in predicting future results. Under accrual accounting, revenues are recognized when services are performed, so trends in revenues are thus more meaningful for decision-making.

An alternative to the accrual basis is the cash basis. Under **cash-basis accounting**, revenue is recorded when cash is received, and an expense is recorded when cash is paid. The cash basis often leads to misleading financial statements. It fails to record revenue that has been earned but for which the cash has not been received. Also, expenses are not matched with earned revenues. **Cash-basis accounting is not in accordance with generally accepted accounting principles (GAAP).**

INTERNATIONAL NOTE
Although different accounting standards are often used in other major industrialized countries, accrual-basis accounting is followed by all these countries.

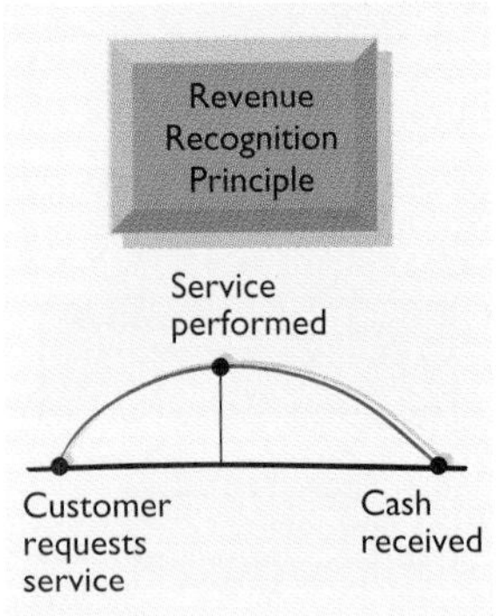

Most companies use accrual-basis accounting. Individuals and some small companies use cash-basis accounting. The cash basis is justified for small businesses because they often have few receivables and payables. Accountants are sometimes asked to convert cash-basis records to the accrual basis. As you might expect, extensive adjusting entries are required for this task.

RECOGNIZING REVENUES AND EXPENSES

Determining the amount of revenues and expenses to be reported in a given accounting period can be difficult. To help in this task, accountants have developed two principles as part of generally accepted accounting principles (GAAP): the revenue recognition principle and the matching principle.

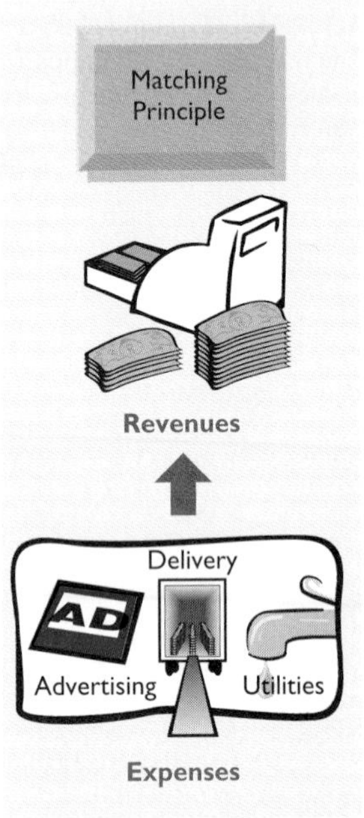

The **revenue recognition principle** dictates that revenue be recognized in the accounting period in which it is earned. **In a service enterprise, revenue is considered to be earned at the time the service is performed.** To illustrate, assume that a dry cleaning business cleans clothing on June 30 but customers do not claim and pay for their clothes until the first week of July. Under the revenue recognition principle, revenue is earned in June when the service is performed, rather than in July when the cash is received. At June 30, the dry cleaner would report a receivable on its balance sheet and revenue in its income statement for the service performed.

Accountants follow the approach of "let expenses follow revenues." That is, expense recognition is tied to revenue recognition. In the preceding example, this principle means that the salary expense incurred in performing the cleaning service on June 30 should be reported in the income statement for the same period in which the service revenue is recognized. The critical issue in expense recognition is when the expense makes its contribution to revenue. This may or may not be the same period in which the expense is paid. If the salary incurred on June 30 is not paid until July, the dry cleaner would report salaries payable on its June 30 balance sheet. The practice of expense recognition is referred to as the **matching principle** because it dictates that efforts (expenses) be matched with accomplishments (revenues).

ACCOUNTING IN ACTION *Business Insight*

Suppose you are a filmmaker like George Lucas and spend $11 million to produce a film such as *Star Wars*. Over what period should the cost be expensed? It should be expensed over the economic life of the film. But what is its economic life? The filmmaker must estimate how much revenue will be earned from box office sales, video sales, television, and games and toys—a period that could be less than a year or more than 20 years, as is the case for Twentieth Century Fox's *Star Wars*. Originally released in 1977, and rereleased in 1997, domestic revenues total nearly $500 million for *Star Wars* and continue to grow. This situation demonstrates the difficulty of properly matching expenses to revenues.

SOURCE: Star Trek Newsletter, 22.

Once the economic life of a business has been divided into artificial time periods, the revenue recognition and matching principles can be applied. This one assumption and two principles thus provide guidelines as to when revenues and expenses should be reported. These relationships are shown in Illustration 3-1.

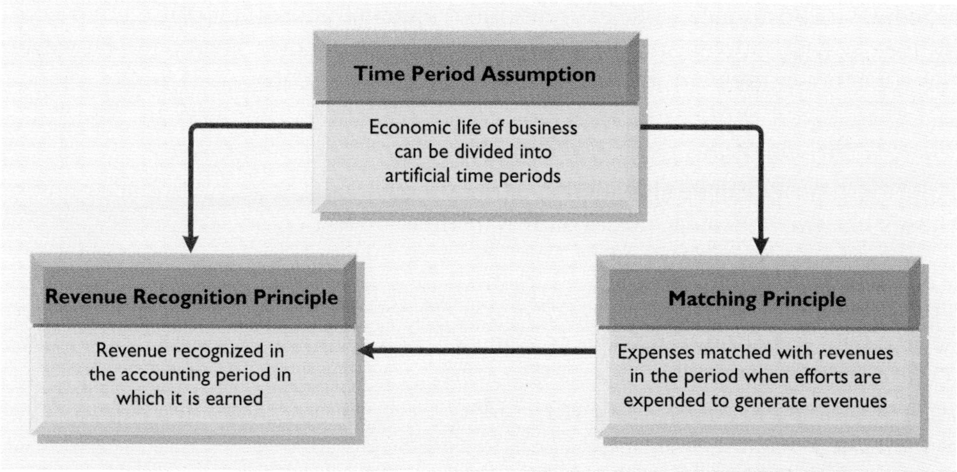

Illustration 3-1
GAAP relationships in revenue and expense recognition

BEFORE YOU GO ON...

REVIEW IT

1. What is the relevance of the time period assumption to accounting?
2. What are the revenue recognition and matching principles?

THE NAVIGATOR

THE BASICS OF ADJUSTING ENTRIES

STUDY OBJECTIVE 3
Explain why adjusting entries are needed.

In order for revenues to be recorded in the period in which they are earned, and for expenses to be recognized in the period in which they are incurred, adjusting entries are made at the end of the accounting period. In short, **adjusting entries are needed to ensure that the revenue recognition and matching principles are followed**.

Adjusting entries make it possible to report on the balance sheet the appropriate assets, liabilities, and owner's equity at the statement date and to report on the income statement the proper net income (or loss) for the period. However, the trial balance—the first pulling together of the transaction data—may not contain up-to-date and complete data. This is true for the following reasons.

1. Some events are not journalized daily because it is inexpedient to do so. Examples are the consumption of supplies and the earning of wages by employees.
2. Some costs are not journalized during the accounting period because they expire with the passage of time rather than through recurring daily transactions. Examples are equipment deterioration, and rent and insurance.
3. Some items may be unrecorded. An example is a utility service bill that will not be received until the next accounting period.

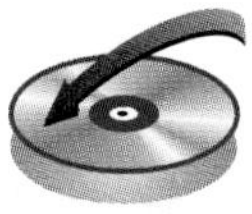

Accounting Cycle Tutorial—Making Adjusting Entries

Adjusting entries are required every time financial statements are prepared. The starting point is an analysis of each account in the trial balance to determine whether it is complete and up-to-date. The analysis requires a thorough understanding of the company's operations and the interrelationship of accounts. Preparing adjusting entries is often an involved process. The company may need to make inventory counts of supplies and repair parts. It may need to prepare supporting

HELPFUL HINT
Adjusting entries are needed to enable financial statements to be in conformity with GAAP.

schedules of insurance policies, rental agreements, and other contractual commitments. Adjustments are often prepared after the balance sheet date. However, the adjusting entries are dated as of the balance sheet date.

STUDY OBJECTIVE 4

Identify the major types of adjusting entries.

TYPES OF ADJUSTING ENTRIES

Adjusting entries can be classified as either prepayments or accruals. Each of these classes has two subcategories as shown in Illustration 3-2.

Illustration 3-2

Categories of adjusting entries

Prepayments

1. **Prepaid Expenses.** Expenses paid in cash and recorded as assets before they are used or consumed.
2. **Unearned Revenues.** Cash received and recorded as liabilities before revenue is earned.

Accruals

1. **Accrued Revenues.** Revenues earned but not yet received in cash or recorded.
2. **Accrued Expenses.** Expenses incurred but not yet paid in cash or recorded.

Specific examples and explanations of each type of adjustment are given on the following pages. Each example is based on the October 31 trial balance of Pioneer Advertising Agency, from Chapter 2, reproduced in Illustration 3-3.

Illustration 3-3

Trial balance

PIONEER ADVERTISING AGENCY
Trial Balance
October 31, 2002

	Debit	Credit
Cash	$15,200	
Advertising Supplies	2,500	
Prepaid Insurance	600	
Office Equipment	5,000	
Notes Payable		$ 5,000
Accounts Payable		2,500
Unearned Revenue		1,200
C. R. Byrd, Capital		10,000
C. R. Byrd, Drawing	500	
Service Revenue		10,000
Salaries Expense	4,000	
Rent Expense	900	
	$28,700	$28,700

We assume that Pioneer Advertising uses an accounting period of one month. Thus, monthly adjusting entries will be made. The entries will be dated October 31.

STUDY OBJECTIVE 5

Prepare adjusting entries for prepayments.

ADJUSTING ENTRIES FOR PREPAYMENTS

As indicated earlier, prepayments are either prepaid expenses or unearned revenues. Adjusting entries for prepayments are required to record the portion of the prepayment that represents the **expense incurred or the revenue earned** in the current accounting period.

If an adjustment is needed for prepayments, the asset and liability are overstated and the related expense and revenue are understated before the adjustment. For example, in the trial balance, the balance in the asset Advertising Supplies shows only supplies purchased. This balance is overstated; a related expense account, Advertising Supplies Expense, is understated because the cost of supplies used has not been recognized. Thus the adjusting entry for prepayments will **decrease a balance sheet account** (Advertising Supplies) and **increase an income statement account** (Advertising Supplies Expense). The effects of adjusting entries for prepayments are graphically depicted in Illustration 3-4.

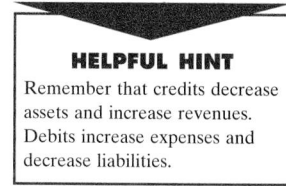

HELPFUL HINT
Remember that credits decrease assets and increase revenues. Debits increase expenses and decrease liabilities.

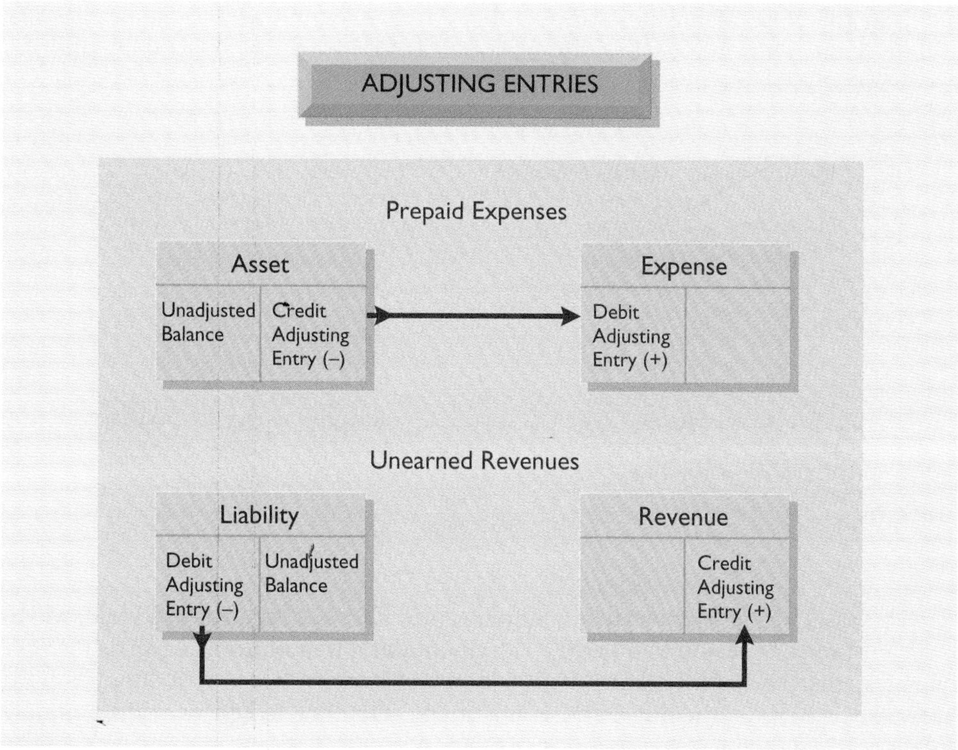

Illustration 3-4
Adjusting entries for prepayments

Prepaid Expenses

As stated on page 92, expenses paid in cash and recorded as assets before they are used or consumed are called **prepaid expenses**. When a cost is prepaid, an asset account is debited to show the service or benefit that will be received in the future. Prepayments often occur in regard to insurance, supplies, advertising, and rent. In addition, prepayments are made when buildings and equipment are purchased.

Prepaid expenses expire either with the passage of time (e.g., rent and insurance) or through use and consumption (e.g., supplies). The expiration of these costs does not require daily journal entries, which would be unnecessary and impractical. Instead, it is customary to postpone recognizing cost expirations until financial statements are prepared. At each statement date, adjusting entries are made for two purposes: (1) to record the expenses that apply to the current accounting period, and (2) to show the unexpired costs in the asset accounts.

Prior to adjustment, assets are overstated and expenses are understated. **Thus, the prepaid expense adjusting entry results in a debit (increase) to an expense account and a credit (decrease) to an asset account.**

SUPPLIES. Businesses use various types of supplies. For example, a CPA firm will have **office supplies** such as stationery, envelopes, and accounting paper. An advertising firm will have **advertising supplies** such as graph paper, video film, and poster paper. Supplies are generally debited to an asset account when they are acquired. In the course of operations, supplies are depleted, but recognition of supplies used is deferred until the adjustment process. At that point, a physical inventory (count) of supplies is taken. The difference between the balance in the Supplies (asset) account and the cost of supplies on hand represents the supplies used (expense) for the period.

Pioneer Advertising Agency purchased advertising supplies costing $2,500 on October 5. A debit (increase) was made to the asset Advertising Supplies. This account shows a balance of $2,500 in the October 31 trial balance. An inventory count at the close of business on October 31 reveals that $1,000 of supplies are still on hand. Thus, the cost of supplies used is $1,500 ($2,500 − $1,000), and the following adjusting entry is made.

Equation analyses summarize the effects of the transaction on the accounting equation.

Oct. 31	Advertising Supplies Expense	1,500	
	Advertising Supplies		1,500
	(To record supplies used)		

Equation Analysis

A	=	L	+	OE
−1,500				−1,500

After the adjusting entry is posted, the two supplies accounts show:

Illustration 3-5

Supplies accounts after adjustment

Advertising Supplies				**Advertising Supplies Expense**	
10/5	2,500	10/31 **Adj.**	**1,500**	10/31 **Adj.**	**1,500**
10/31 Bal.	1,000				

The asset account Advertising Supplies now shows a balance of $1,000, which is the cost of supplies on hand at the statement date. In addition, Advertising Supplies Expense shows a balance of $1,500, which equals the cost of supplies used in October. **If the adjusting entry is not made, October expenses will be understated and net income overstated by $1,500. Also, both assets and owner's equity will be overstated by $1,500 on the October 31 balance sheet.**

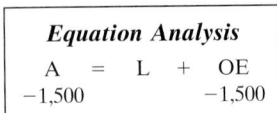

ACCOUNTING IN ACTION *Business Insight*

The costs of product advertising are sometimes considered prepayments. As a manager for **Procter & Gamble** noted, "If we run a long ad campaign for soap and bleach, we sometimes report the costs as prepayments if we think we'll receive sales benefits from the campaign down the road." Presently it is a judgment call whether these costs should be prepayments or expenses in the current period. It is difficult to develop guidelines consistent with the matching principle because situations vary widely across companies. Outlays for advertising can be substantial. Recent big advertising spenders: **Sears, Roebuck and Co.** spent $1.28 billion, **Nike** $978 million, and **McDonald's** $503 million.

INSURANCE. Most companies have fire and theft insurance on merchandise and equipment, personal liability insurance for accidents suffered by customers, and automobile insurance on company cars and trucks. The cost of insurance protection is determined by the payment of insurance premiums. The minimum term of coverage is usually one year, but three- to five-year terms are available and offer lower annual premiums. Insurance premiums normally are charged to the asset account Prepaid Insurance when paid. At the financial statement date it is necessary to debit (increase) Insurance Expense and credit (decrease) Prepaid Insurance for the cost that has expired during the period.

On October 4, Pioneer Advertising Agency paid $600 for a one-year fire insurance policy. The effective date of coverage was October 1. The premium was charged to Prepaid Insurance when it was paid, and this account shows a balance of $600 in the October 31 trial balance. Analysis reveals that $50 ($600 ÷ 12) of insurance expires each month. Thus, the following adjusting entry is made.

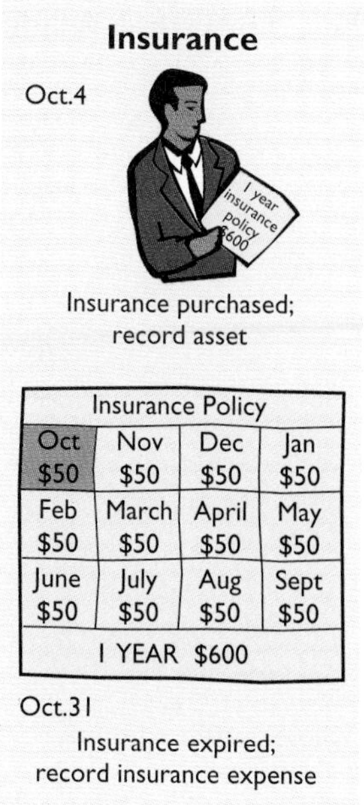

Insurance
Oct.4
1 year insurance policy $600
Insurance purchased; record asset
Insurance Policy
Oct $50
Nov $50
Dec $50
Jan $50
Feb $50
March $50
April $50
May $50
June $50
July $50
Aug $50
Sept $50
1 YEAR $600
Oct.31
Insurance expired; record insurance expense

Oct. 31	Insurance Expense	50	
	Prepaid Insurance		50
	(To record insurance expired)		

After the adjusting entry is posted, the accounts show:

Prepaid Insurance				Insurance Expense		
10/4	600	10/31 **Adj.**	**50**	10/31 **Adj.**	**50**	
10/31 Bal.	550					

Illustration 3-6

Insurance accounts after adjustment

The asset Prepaid Insurance shows a balance of $550. This amount represents the unexpired cost for the remaining eleven months of coverage. The $50 balance in Insurance Expense is equal to the insurance cost that has expired in October. **If this adjustment is not made, October expenses will be understated by $50 and net income overstated by $50. Also, both assets and owner's equity will be overstated by $50 on the October 31 balance sheet.**

DEPRECIATION. A business enterprise typically owns productive facilities such as buildings, equipment, and vehicles. Because these assets provide service for a number of years, each is recorded as an asset, rather than an expense, in the year it is acquired. As explained in Chapter 1, such assets are recorded at cost, as required by the cost principle. The term of service is referred to as the **useful life**.

According to the matching principle, a portion of the cost of a long-lived asset should be reported as an expense during each period of the asset's useful life. **Depreciation** is the allocation of the cost of an asset to expense over its useful life in a rational and systematic manner.

Depreciation
Oct.1
Office equipment purchased; record asset
Office Equipment
Oct $40
Nov $40
Dec $40
Jan $40
Feb $40
March $40
April $40
May $40
June $40
July $40
Aug $40
Sept $40
Depreciation = $480/year
Oct.31
Depreciation recognized; record depreciation expense

Need for Depreciation Adjustment. From an accounting standpoint, acquiring productive facilities is viewed essentially as a long-term prepayment for services. The need for periodic adjusting entries for depreciation is, therefore, the same as that for other prepaid expenses: to recognize the cost that has expired (expense) during the period and to report the unexpired cost (asset) at the end of the period.

At the time an asset is acquired, its useful life cannot be known with certainty. The asset may be useful for a longer or shorter time than expected, depending on such factors as actual use, deterioration due to the elements or obsolescence. Thus, you should recognize that **depreciation is an estimate** rather than a factual measurement of the cost that has expired. A common procedure in computing depreciation expense is to divide the cost of the asset by its useful life. For example, if cost is $10,000 and useful life is expected to be 10 years, annual depreciation is $1,000.[1]

[1] Additional consideration is given to computing depreciation expense in Chapter 10.

For Pioneer Advertising, depreciation on the office equipment is estimated to be $480 a year, or $40 per month. Accordingly, depreciation for October is recognized by the following adjusting entry.

A	=	L	+	OE
−40				−40

Oct. 31	Depreciation Expense	40	
	Accumulated Depreciation—Office Equipment		40
	(To record monthly depreciation)		

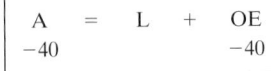

After the adjusting entry is posted, the accounts show:

Illustration 3-7

Accounts after adjustment for depreciation

Office Equipment

10/1	5,000	

Accumulated Depreciation—Office Equipment

	10/31 **Adj.**	**40**

Depreciation Expense

10/31 **Adj.**	**40**	

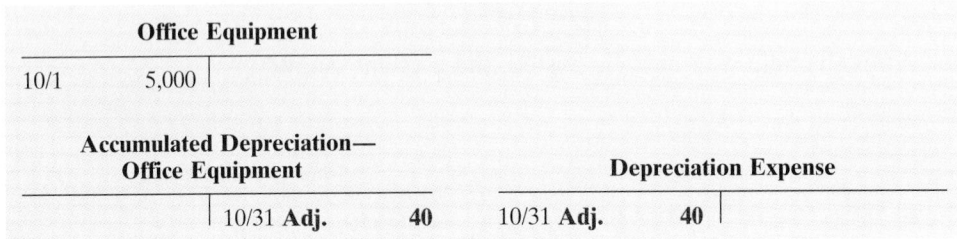

The balance in the accumulated depreciation account will increase $40 each month. After journalizing and posting the adjusting entry at November 30, the balance will be $80; at December 31, $120; and so on.

HELPFUL HINT
All contra accounts have increases, decreases, and normal balances opposite to the account to which they relate.

Statement Presentation. Accumulated Depreciation—Office Equipment is a contra asset account. A **contra asset account** is one that is offset against an asset account on the balance sheet. This accumulated depreciation account appears just after Office Equipment on the balance sheet. Its normal balance is a credit. An alternative would be to credit (decrease) Office Equipment directly for the depreciation each month. But use of the contra account provides disclosure of **both the original cost** of the equipment **and the total cost that has expired to date**. In the balance sheet, Accumulated Depreciation—Office Equipment is deducted from the related asset account as follows.

Illustration 3-8

Balance sheet presentation of accumulated depreciation

Office equipment	$5,000	
Less: Accumulated depreciation—office equipment	40	**$4,960**

ALTERNATIVE TERMINOLOGY
Book value is sometimes referred to as *carrying value* or *unexpired cost*.

The difference between the cost of any depreciable asset and its related accumulated depreciation is referred to as the **book value** of that asset. In Illustration 3-8, the book value of the equipment at the balance sheet date is $4,960. You should realize that the book value is generally different from the market value (the price at which the asset could be sold in the marketplace). The reason the two are different is that depreciation is a means of cost allocation, not a matter of valuation.

Depreciation expense also identifies that portion of the asset's cost that has expired in October. As in the case of other prepaid adjustments, the omission of this adjusting entry would cause total assets, total owner's equity, and net income to be overstated and depreciation expense to be understated.

If the company owns additional equipment, such as delivery or store equipment, or if it has buildings, depreciation expense is recorded on each of those items. Related accumulated depreciation accounts also are established, such as: Accumulated Depreciation—Delivery Equipment; Accumulated Depreciation—Store Equipment; and Accumulated Depreciation—Buildings.

Unearned Revenues

As stated on page 92, cash received and recorded as liabilities before revenue is earned is called **unearned revenues**. Such items as rent, magazine subscriptions, and customer deposits for future service may result in unearned revenues. Airlines such as **United**, **American**, and **Delta** treat receipts from the sale of tickets as unearned revenue until the flight service is provided. Similarly, college tuition received prior to the start of a semester is considered unearned revenue. Unearned revenues are the opposite of prepaid expenses. Indeed, unearned revenue on the books of one company is likely to be a prepayment on the books of the company that has made the advance payment. For example, if identical accounting periods are assumed, a landlord will have unearned rent revenue when a tenant has prepaid rent.

Unearned Revenues

Oct.2

Thank you in advance for your work
I will finish by Dec. 31
$1,200

Cash is received in advance; liability is recorded

Oct.31

Service is provided; revenue is recorded

When the payment is received for services to be provided in a future accounting period, an unearned revenue account (a liability) should be credited (increased) to recognize the obligation that exists. Later, unearned revenues are earned by providing service to a customer. It may not be practical to make daily journal entries as the revenue is earned. In such cases, recognition of earned revenue is delayed until the end of the period. Then an adjusting entry is made to record the revenue that has been earned and to show the liability that remains. In the typical case, liabilities are overstated and revenues are understated prior to adjustment. Thus, **the adjusting entry for unearned revenues results in a debit (decrease) to a liability account and a credit (increase) to a revenue account.**

Pioneer Advertising Agency received $1,200 on October 2 from R. Knox for advertising services expected to be completed by December 31. The payment was credited to Unearned Revenue; this account shows a balance of $1,200 in the October 31 trial balance. Analysis reveals that $400 of those fees was earned in October. The following adjusting entry is made.

ALTERNATIVE TERMINOLOGY
Unearned revenue is sometimes referred to as *deferred revenue.*

Oct. 31	Unearned Revenue	400	
	Service Revenue		400
	(To record revenue for services provided)		

A	=	L	+	OE
		−400		+400

After the adjusting entry is posted, the accounts show:

Unearned Revenue

10/31 **Adj.**	**400**	10/2	1,200
		10/31 Bal.	800

Service Revenue

		10/31 Bal.	10,000
		31 **Adj.**	**400**

Illustration 3-9
Revenue accounts after prepayments adjustment

The liability Unearned Revenue now shows a balance of $800. This amount represents the remaining prepaid advertising services to be performed in the future. At the same time, Service Revenue shows total revenue of $10,400 earned in October. **If this adjustment is not made, revenues and net income would be understated by $400 in the income statement. Also, liabilities would be overstated and owner's equity would be understated by $400 on the October 31 balance sheet.**

ACCOUNTING IN ACTION e Business Insight

Many early dot-com investors focused almost entirely on revenue growth instead of net income. Many early dot-com companies earned most of their revenue from selling advertising space on their Web sites. To boost reported revenue, some sites began swapping ad space. Company A would put an ad for its Web site on company B's Web site, and company B would put an ad for its Web site on company A's Web site. No money ever changed hands, but each company recorded revenue (for the value of the space that it gave up on its site) and expense (for the value of its ad that it placed on the other company's site). This practice did little to boost net income and resulted in no additional cash inflow—but it did boost *reported* revenue. This practice was quickly put to an end because accountants felt that it did not meet the criteria of the revenue recognition principle.

BEFORE YOU GO ON...

REVIEW IT

1. What are the four types of adjusting entries?
2. What is the effect on assets, owner's equity, expenses, and net income if a prepaid expense adjusting entry is not made?
3. What is the effect on liabilities, owner's equity, revenues, and net income if an unearned revenue adjusting entry is not made?
4. Using the Eleven-Year Consolidated Financial Summary of **Lands' End's** financial statements, what was the amount of depreciation and amortization expense for 2000 and for 1999? The answer to this question is provided on page 131.

DO IT

The ledger of Hammond, Inc. on March 31, 2002, includes the following selected accounts before adjusting entries.

	Debit	Credit
Prepaid Insurance	3,600	
Office Supplies	2,800	
Office Equipment	25,000	
Accumulated Depreciation—Office Equipment		5,000
Unearned Revenue		9,200

An analysis of the accounts shows the following.

1. Insurance expires at the rate of $100 per month.
2. Supplies on hand total $800.
3. The office equipment depreciates $200 a month.
4. One-half of the unearned revenue was earned in March.

Prepare the adjusting entries for the month of March.

ACTION PLAN

- Make adjusting entries at the end of the period for revenues earned and expenses incurred in the period.
- Don't forget to make adjusting entries for prepayments. Failure to adjust for prepayments leads to overstatement of the asset or liability and related understatement of the expense or revenue.

SOLUTION

1. Insurance Expense	100	
Prepaid Insurance		100
(To record insurance expired)		

2. Office Supplies Expense	2,000	
Office Supplies		2,000
(To record supplies used)		
3. Depreciation Expense	200	
Accumulated Depreciation—Office Equipment		200
(To record monthly depreciation)		
4. Unearned Revenue	4,600	
Service Revenue		4,600
(To record revenue for services provided)		

Related exercise material: BE3-3, BE3-4, BE3-5, BE3-6, E3-2, E3-3, E3-4, E3-5, E3-6, E3-7, E3-8, and E3-9.

THE NAVIGATOR

ADJUSTING ENTRIES FOR ACCRUALS

STUDY OBJECTIVE 6

Prepare adjusting entries for accruals.

The second category of adjusting entries is **accruals**. Adjusting entries for accruals are required to record revenues earned and expenses incurred in the current accounting period that have not been recognized through daily entries.

An accrual adjustment is needed when various accounts are understated: the revenue account and the related asset account, and/or the expense account and the related liability account. Thus, the adjusting entry for accruals will **increase both a balance sheet and an income statement account**. Adjusting entries for accruals are graphically depicted in Illustration 3-10.

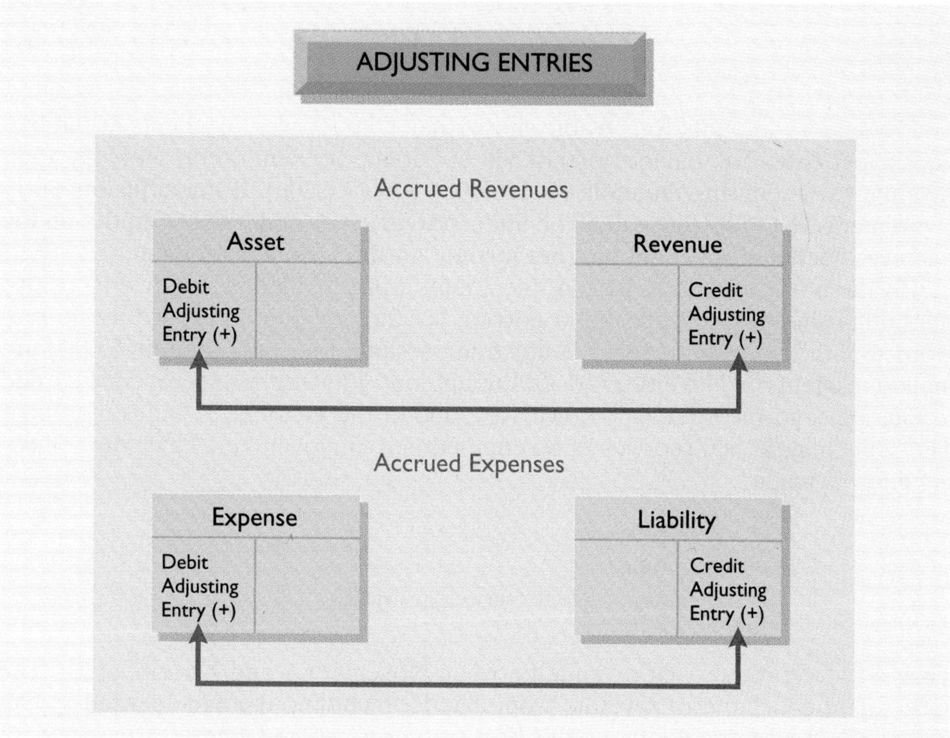

Illustration 3-10

Adjusting entries for accruals

Rent expence —— +x
Rent payable

Accrued Revenues

As explained on page 92, revenues earned but not yet received in cash or recorded at the statement date are **accrued revenues**. Accrued revenues may accumulate (accrue) with the passing of time, as in the case of interest revenue and rent

Accrued Revenues

Oct.31

Revenue and receivable are recorded for unbilled services

Nov.

Cash is received; receivable is reduced

revenue. Or they may result from services that have been performed but neither billed nor collected, as in the case of commissions and fees. The former are unrecorded because the earning of interest and rent does not involve daily transactions. The latter may be unrecorded because only a portion of the total service has been provided.

An adjusting entry is required for two purposes: (1) to show the receivable that exists at the balance sheet date, and (2) to record the revenue that has been earned during the period. Prior to adjustment both assets and revenues are understated. Thus, **an adjusting entry for accrued revenues results in a debit (increase) to an asset account and a credit (increase) to a revenue account.**

In October Pioneer Advertising Agency earned $200 for advertising services that were not billed to clients before October 31. Because these services have not been billed, they have not been recorded. The following adjusting entry is made.

A	=	L	+	OE
+200				+200

Oct. 31	Accounts Receivable	200	
	Service Revenue		200
	(To record revenue for services provided)		

After the adjusting entry is posted, the accounts show:

Illustration 3-11

Receivable and revenue accounts after accrual adjustment

Accounts Receivable			Service Revenue	
10/31 Adj.	200		10/31	10,000
			31	400
			31 Adj.	200
			10/31 Bal.	10,600

The asset Accounts Receivable shows that $200 is owed by clients at the balance sheet date. The balance of $10,600 in Service Revenue represents the total revenue earned during the month ($10,000 + $400 + $200). **If the adjusting entry is not made, the following will all be understated: assets and owner's equity on the balance sheet, and revenues and net income on the income statement.**

ALTERNATIVE TERMINOLOGY
Accrued revenues are also called *accrued receivables*.

In the next accounting period, the clients will be billed. The entry to record the billing should recognize that a portion has already been recorded in the previous month's adjusting entry. To illustrate, assume that bills totaling $3,000 are mailed to clients on November 10. Of this amount, $200 represents revenue earned in October and recorded as Service Revenue in the October 31 adjusting entry. The remaining $2,800 represents revenue earned in November. Thus, the following entry is made.

A	=	L	+	OE
+2,800				+2,800

Nov. 10	Accounts Receivable	2,800	
	Service Revenue		2,800
	(To record revenue for services provided)		

This entry records service revenue between November 1 and November 10. The subsequent collection of revenue from clients (including the $200 earned in October) will be recorded with a debit (increase) to Cash and a credit (decrease) to Accounts Receivable.

Accrued Expenses

ALTERNATIVE TERMINOLOGY
Accrued expenses are also called *accrued liabilities*.

As indicated on page 92, expenses incurred but not yet paid or recorded at the statement date are called **accrued expenses**. Interest, rent, taxes, and salaries can be accrued expenses. Accrued expenses result from the same causes as accrued revenues. In fact, an accrued expense on the books of one company is an accrued revenue to another company. For example, the $200 accrual of fees by Pioneer is an accrued expense to the client that received the service.

Adjustments for accrued expenses are needed for two purposes: (1) to record the obligations that exist at the balance sheet date, and (2) to recognize the expenses that apply to the current accounting period. Prior to adjustment, both liabilities and expenses are understated. Thus, **the adjusting entry for accrued expenses results in a debit (increase) to an expense account and a credit (increase) to a liability account.**

ACCRUED INTEREST. Pioneer Advertising Agency signed a $5,000, 3-month note payable on October 1. The note requires interest at an annual rate of 12%. The amount of the interest accumulation is determined by three factors: (1) the face value of the note, (2) the interest rate, which is always expressed as an annual rate, and (3) the length of time the note is outstanding. In this instance, the total interest due on the $5,000 note at its due date 3 months hence is $150 ($5,000 × 12% × 3/12), or $50 for one month. The formula for computing interest and its application to Pioneer Advertising Agency for the month of October[2] are shown in Illustration 3-12. Note that the time period is expressed as a fraction of a year.

HELPFUL HINT
Interest is a cost of borrowing money that accumulates with the passage of time.

Illustration 3-12
Formula for computing interest

Face Value of Note	×	Annual Interest Rate	×	Time in Terms of One Year	=	Interest
$5,000	×	12%	×	1/12	=	$50

The accrued expense adjusting entry at October 31 is:

Oct. 31	Interest Expense	50	
	Interest Payable		50
	(To record interest on notes payable)		

A	=	L	+	OE
		+50		−50

After this adjusting entry is posted, the accounts show:

Illustration 3-13
Interest accounts after adjustment

Interest Expense		Interest Payable	
10/31 Adj. 50			10/31 Adj. 50

Interest Expense shows the interest charges for the month. The amount of interest owed at the statement date is shown in Interest Payable. It will not be paid until the note comes due at the end of 3 months. The Interest Payable account is used instead of crediting (increasing) Notes Payable. The reason for using the two accounts is to disclose the two types of obligations (interest and principal) in the accounts and statements. **If this adjusting entry is not made, liabilities and interest expense will be understated, and net income and owner's equity will be overstated.**

ACCRUED SALARIES. Some types of expenses are paid for after the services have been performed. Examples are employee salaries and commissions. At

[2]The computation of interest will be considered in more depth in later chapters.

Pioneer Advertising, salaries were last paid on October 26; the next payday is November 9. As shown in the calendar in Illustration 3-14, three working days remain in October (October 29–31).

Illustration 3-14

Calendar showing Pioneer's pay periods

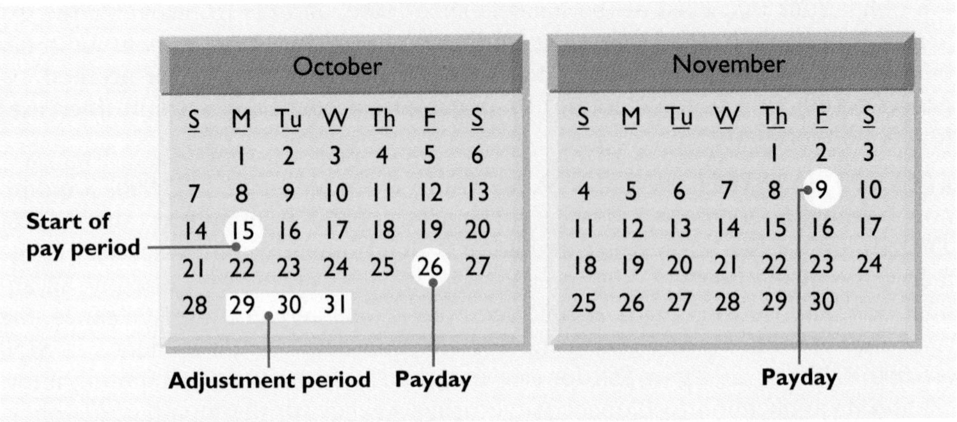

At October 31, the salaries for the last three days of the month represent an accrued expense and a related liability. The employees receive total salaries of $2,000 for a five-day work week, or $400 per day. Thus, accrued salaries at October 31 are $1,200 ($400 × 3). The adjusting entry is:

A	=	L	+	OE
		+1,200		−1,200

Oct. 31	Salaries Expense	1,200	
	Salaries Payable		1,200
	(To record accrued salaries)		

After this adjusting entry is posted, the accounts show:

Illustration 3-15

Salary accounts after adjustment

Salaries Expense			Salaries Payable	
10/26	4,000			10/31 **Adj.** **1,200**
31 **Adj.**	**1,200**			
10/31 Bal.	5,200			

After this adjustment, the balance in Salaries Expense of $5,200 (13 days × $400) is the actual salary expense for October. (The employees started work on October 15.) The balance in Salaries Payable of $1,200 is the amount of the liability for salaries owed as of October 31. **If the $1,200 adjustment for salaries is not recorded, Pioneer's expenses will be understated $1,200, and its liabilities will be understated $1,200.**

At Pioneer Advertising, salaries are payable every two weeks. The next payday is November 9, when total salaries of $4,000 will again be paid. The payment will consist of $1,200 of salaries payable at October 31 plus $2,800 of salaries expense for November (seven working days as shown in the November calendar × $400). Therefore, the following entry is made on November 9.

A	=	L	+	OE
−4,000		−1,200		−2,800

Nov. 9	Salaries Payable	1,200	
	Salaries Expense	2,800	
	Cash		4,000
	(To record November 9 payroll)		

This entry does two things: (1) It eliminates the liability for Salaries Payable that was recorded in the October 31 adjusting entry. (2) It records the proper amount of Salaries Expense for the period between November 1 and November 9.

TECHNOLOGY IN ACTION

In many computer systems, the adjusting process is handled like any other transaction, with the accountant inputting the adjustment at the time required. The main difference between adjusting entries and regular transactions is that with adjusting entries, one part of the computer system may perform the required calculation for such items as depreciation or interest and then "feed" these figures to the journalizing process.

Such systems are also able to display information before and after changes were made. Management may be interested in such information to highlight the impact that adjustments have on the various accounts and financial statements.

BEFORE YOU GO ON...

REVIEW IT

1. If an accrued revenue adjusting entry is not made, what is the effect on assets, owner's equity, revenues, and net income?
2. If an accrued expense adjusting entry is not made, what is the effect on liabilities, owner's equity, and interest expense?

DO IT

Calvin and Hobbs are the new owners of Micro Computer Services. At the end of August 2002, their first month of ownership, Calvin and Hobbs are trying to prepare monthly financial statements. They have the following information for the month.

1. At August 31, Calvin and Hobbs owed employees $800 in salaries that will be paid on September 1.
2. On August 1, Calvin and Hobbs borrowed $30,000 from a local bank on a 15-year mortgage. The annual interest rate is 10%.
3. Service revenue unrecorded in August totaled $1,100.

Prepare the adjusting entries needed at August 31, 2002.

ACTION PLAN

- Make adjusting entries at the end of the period for revenues earned and expenses incurred in the period.
- Don't forget to make adjusting entries for accruals. Adjusting entries for accruals will increase both a balance sheet and an income statement account.

SOLUTION

1. Salaries Expense	800	
Salaries Payable		800
(To record accrued salaries)		
2. Interest Expense	250	
Interest Payable		250
(To record interest)		
($30,000 × 10% × 1/12 = $250)		
3. Accounts Receivable	1,100	
Service Revenue		1,100
(To record revenue for services provided)		

Related exercise material: BE3-7, E3-2, E3-3, E3-4, E3-5, E3-6, E3-7, E3-8, and E3-9.

THE NAVIGATOR

SUMMARY OF BASIC RELATIONSHIPS

The four basic types of adjusting entries are summarized in Illustration 3-16. Take some time to study and analyze the adjusting entries shown in the summary. Be sure to note that **each adjusting entry affects one balance sheet account and one income statement account.**

Illustration 3-16

Summary of adjusting entries

Type of Adjustment	Reason for Adjustment	Accounts before Adjustment	Adjusting Entry
1. Prepaid expenses	Prepaid expenses originally recorded in asset accounts have been used.	Assets overstated Expenses understated	Dr. Expenses Cr. Assets
2. Unearned revenues	Unearned revenues initially recorded in liability accounts have been earned.	Liabilities overstated Revenues understated	Dr. Liabilities Cr. Revenues
3. Accrued revenues	Revenues have been earned but not yet received in cash or recorded.	Assets understated Revenues understated	Dr. Assets Cr. Revenues
4. Accrued expenses	Expenses have been incurred but not yet paid in cash or recorded.	Expenses understated Liabilities understated	Dr. Expenses Cr. Liabilities

The journalizing and posting of adjusting entries for Pioneer Advertising Agency on October 31 are shown in Illustrations 3-17 and 3-18. All adjustments are identified in the ledger by the reference J2 because they have been journalized on page 2 of the general journal. A center caption entitled "Adjusting Entries" may be inserted between the last transaction entry and the first adjusting entry to identify these entries. When reviewing the general ledger in Illustration 3-18, note that the adjustments are highlighted in color.

Illustration 3-17

General journal showing adjusting entries

HELPFUL HINT

(1) Adjusting entries should not involve debits or credits to cash.
(2) Evaluate whether the adjustment makes sense. For example, an adjustment to recognize supplies used should increase supplies expense.
(3) Double-check all computations.

GENERAL JOURNAL — J2

Date	Account Titles and Explanation	Ref.	Debit	Credit
2002	Adjusting Entries			
Oct. 31	Advertising Supplies Expense	631	1,500	
	Advertising Supplies	126		1,500
	(To record supplies used)			
31	Insurance Expense	722	50	
	Prepaid Insurance	130		50
	(To record insurance expired)			
31	Depreciation Expense	711	40	
	Accumulated Depreciation—Office Equipment	158		40
	(To record monthly depreciation)			
31	Unearned Revenue	209	400	
	Service Revenue	400		400
	(To record revenue for services provided)			
31	Accounts Receivable	112	200	
	Service Revenue	400		200
	(To record revenue for services provided)			
31	Interest Expense	905	50	
	Interest Payable	230		50
	(To record interest on notes payable)			
31	Salaries Expense	726	1,200	
	Salaries Payable	212		1,200
	(To record accrued salaries)			

GENERAL LEDGER

Cash — No. 101

Date	Explanation	Ref.	Debit	Credit	Balance
2002					
Oct. 1		J1	10,000		10,000
2		J1	1,200		11,200
3		J1		900	10,300
4		J1		600	9,700
20		J1		500	9,200
26		J1		4,000	5,200
31		J1	10,000		15,200

Accounts Receivable — No. 112

Date	Explanation	Ref.	Debit	Credit	Balance
2002					
Oct. 31	**Adj. entry**	**J2**	**200**		**200**

Advertising Supplies — No. 126

Date	Explanation	Ref.	Debit	Credit	Balance
2002					
Oct. 5		J1	2,500		2,500
31	**Adj. entry**	**J2**		**1,500**	**1,000**

Prepaid Insurance — No. 130

Date	Explanation	Ref.	Debit	Credit	Balance
2002					
Oct. 4		J1	600		600
31	**Adj. entry**	**J2**		**50**	**550**

Office Equipment — No. 157

Date	Explanation	Ref.	Debit	Credit	Balance
2002					
Oct. 1		J1	5,000		5,000

Accumulated Depreciation—Office Equipment — No. 158

Date	Explanation	Ref.	Debit	Credit	Balance
2002					
Oct. 31	**Adj. entry**	**J2**		**40**	**40**

Notes Payable — No. 200

Date	Explanation	Ref.	Debit	Credit	Balance
2002					
Oct. 1		J1		5,000	5,000

Accounts Payable — No. 201

Date	Explanation	Ref.	Debit	Credit	Balance
2002					
Oct. 5		J1		2,500	2,500

Unearned Revenue — No. 209

Date	Explanation	Ref.	Debit	Credit	Balance
2002					
Oct. 2		J1		1,200	
31	**Adj. entry**	**J2**	**400**		**800**

Salaries Payable — No. 212

Date	Explanation	Ref.	Debit	Credit	Balance
2002					
Oct. 31	**Adj. entry**	**J2**		**1,200**	**1,200**

Interest Payable — No. 230

Date	Explanation	Ref.	Debit	Credit	Balance
2002					
Oct. 31	**Adj. entry**	**J2**		**50**	**50**

C. R. Byrd, Capital — No. 301

Date	Explanation	Ref.	Debit	Credit	Balance
2002					
Oct. 1		J1		10,000	10,000

C. R. Byrd, Drawing — No. 306

Date	Explanation	Ref.	Debit	Credit	Balance
2002					
Oct. 20		J1	500		500

Service Revenue — No. 400

Date	Explanation	Ref.	Debit	Credit	Balance
2002					
Oct. 31		J1		10,000	10,000
31	**Adj. entry**	**J2**		**400**	**10,400**
31	**Adj. entry**	**J2**		**200**	**10,600**

Advertising Supplies Expense — No. 631

Date	Explanation	Ref.	Debit	Credit	Balance
2002					
Oct. 31	**Adj. entry**	**J2**	**1,500**		**1,500**

Depreciation Expense — No. 711

Date	Explanation	Ref.	Debit	Credit	Balance
2002					
Oct. 31	**Adj. entry**	**J2**	**40**		**40**

Insurance Expense — No. 722

Date	Explanation	Ref.	Debit	Credit	Balance
2002					
Oct. 31	**Adj. entry**	**J2**	**50**		**50**

Salaries Expense — No. 726

Date	Explanation	Ref.	Debit	Credit	Balance
2002					
Oct. 26		J1	4,000		4,000
31	**Adj. entry**	**J2**	**1,200**		**5,200**

Rent Expense — No. 729

Date	Explanation	Ref.	Debit	Credit	Balance
2002					
Oct. 3		J1	900		900

Interest Expense — No. 905

Date	Explanation	Ref.	Debit	Credit	Balance
2002					
Oct. 31	**Adj. entry**	**J2**	**50**		**50**

Illustration 3-18

General ledger after adjustment

STUDY OBJECTIVE 7

Describe the nature and purpose of an adjusted trial balance.

THE ADJUSTED TRIAL BALANCE AND FINANCIAL STATEMENTS

After all adjusting entries have been journalized and posted, another trial balance is prepared from the ledger accounts. This is called an **adjusted trial balance**. Its purpose is to **prove the equality** of the total debit balances and the total credit balances in the ledger after all adjustments have been made. The accounts in the adjusted trial balance contain all data that are needed for the preparation of financial statements.

PREPARING THE ADJUSTED TRIAL BALANCE

The adjusted trial balance for Pioneer Advertising Agency is presented in Illustration 3-19. It has been prepared from the ledger accounts in Illustration 3-18. The amounts affected by the adjusting entries are highlighted in color. Compare these amounts to those in the unadjusted trial balance in Illustration 3-3 on page 92.

Illustration 3-19

Adjusted trial balance

PIONEER ADVERTISING AGENCY
Adjusted Trial Balance
October 31, 2002

	Dr.	Cr.
Cash	$15,200	
Accounts Receivable	200	
Advertising Supplies	1,000	
Prepaid Insurance	550	
Office Equipment	5,000	
Accumulated Depreciation—Office Equipment		$ 40
Notes Payable		5,000
Accounts Payable		2,500
Unearned Revenue		800
Salaries Payable		1,200
Interest Payable		50
C. R. Byrd, Capital		10,000
C. R. Byrd, Drawing	500	
Service Revenue		10,600
Salaries Expense	5,200	
Advertising Supplies Expense	1,500	
Rent Expense	900	
Insurance Expense	50	
Interest Expense	50	
Depreciation Expense	40	
	$30,190	$30,190

PREPARING FINANCIAL STATEMENTS

Financial statements can be prepared directly from the adjusted trial balance. Illustrations 3-20 and 3-21 show the interrelationships of data in the adjusted trial balance and the financial statements.

As shown in Illustration 3-20, the income statement is first prepared from the revenue and expense accounts. The owner's equity statement is derived from the owner's capital and drawing accounts and the net income (or net loss) from the income statement. As shown in Illustration 3-21, the balance sheet is then prepared from the asset and liability accounts and the ending owner's capital balance as reported in the owner's equity statement.

Illustration 3-20

Preparation of the income statement and owner's equity statement from the adjusted trial balance

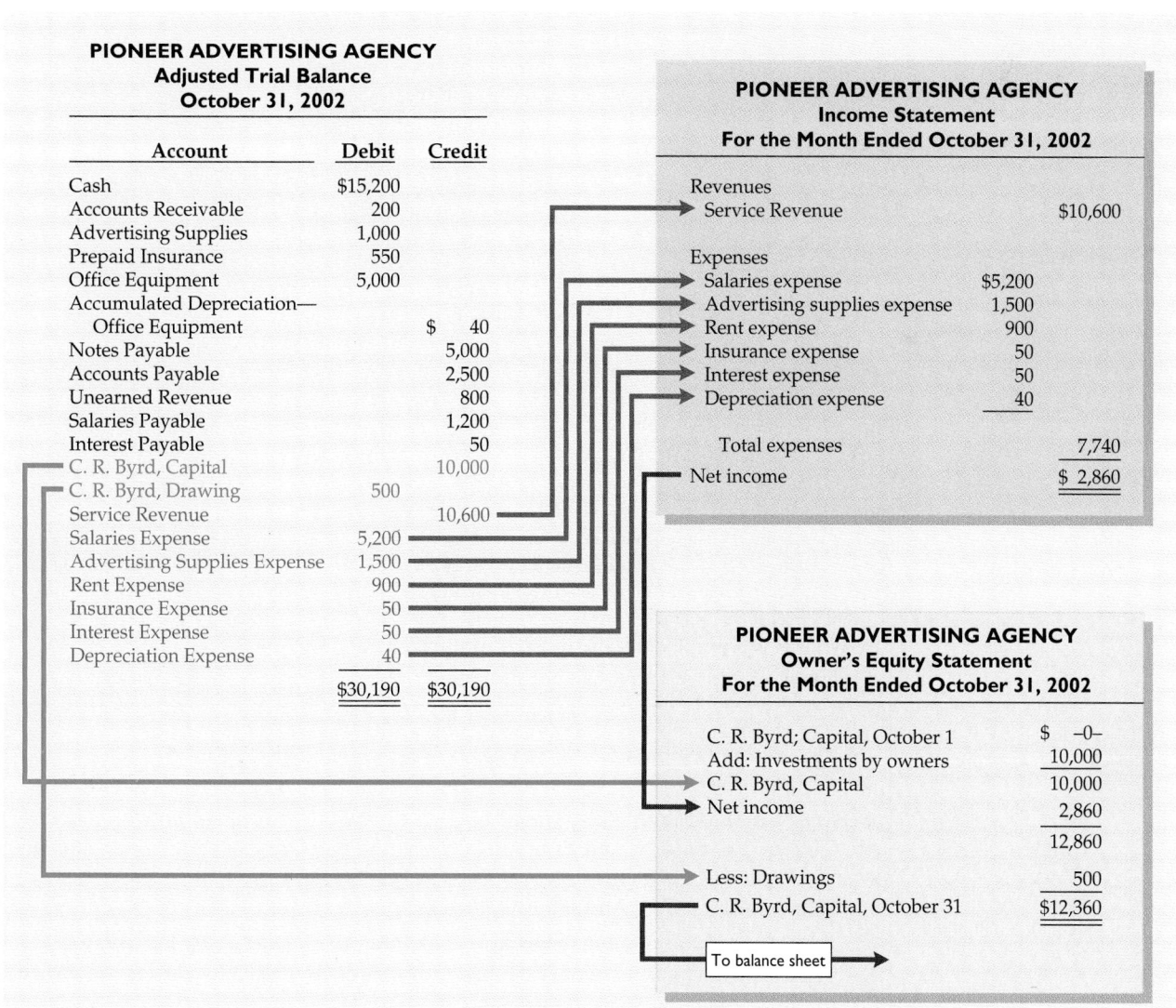

PIONEER ADVERTISING AGENCY
Adjusted Trial Balance
October 31, 2002

Account	Debit	Credit
Cash	$15,200	
Accounts Receivable	200	
Advertising Supplies	1,000	
Prepaid Insurance	550	
Office Equipment	5,000	
Accumulated Depreciation—Office Equipment		$ 40
Notes Payable		5,000
Accounts Payable		2,500
Unearned Revenue		800
Salaries Payable		1,200
Interest Payable		50
C. R. Byrd, Capital		10,000
C. R. Byrd, Drawing	500	
Service Revenue		10,600
Salaries Expense	5,200	
Advertising Supplies Expense	1,500	
Rent Expense	900	
Insurance Expense	50	
Interest Expense	50	
Depreciation Expense	40	
	$30,190	$30,190

PIONEER ADVERTISING AGENCY
Income Statement
For the Month Ended October 31, 2002

Revenues		
Service Revenue		$10,600
Expenses		
Salaries expense	$5,200	
Advertising supplies expense	1,500	
Rent expense	900	
Insurance expense	50	
Interest expense	50	
Depreciation expense	40	
Total expenses		7,740
Net income		$ 2,860

PIONEER ADVERTISING AGENCY
Owner's Equity Statement
For the Month Ended October 31, 2002

C. R. Byrd; Capital, October 1	$ -0-
Add: Investments by owners	10,000
C. R. Byrd, Capital	10,000
Net income	2,860
	12,860
Less: Drawings	500
C. R. Byrd, Capital, October 31	$12,360

To balance sheet

Illustration 3-21

Preparation of the balance sheet from the adjusted trial balance

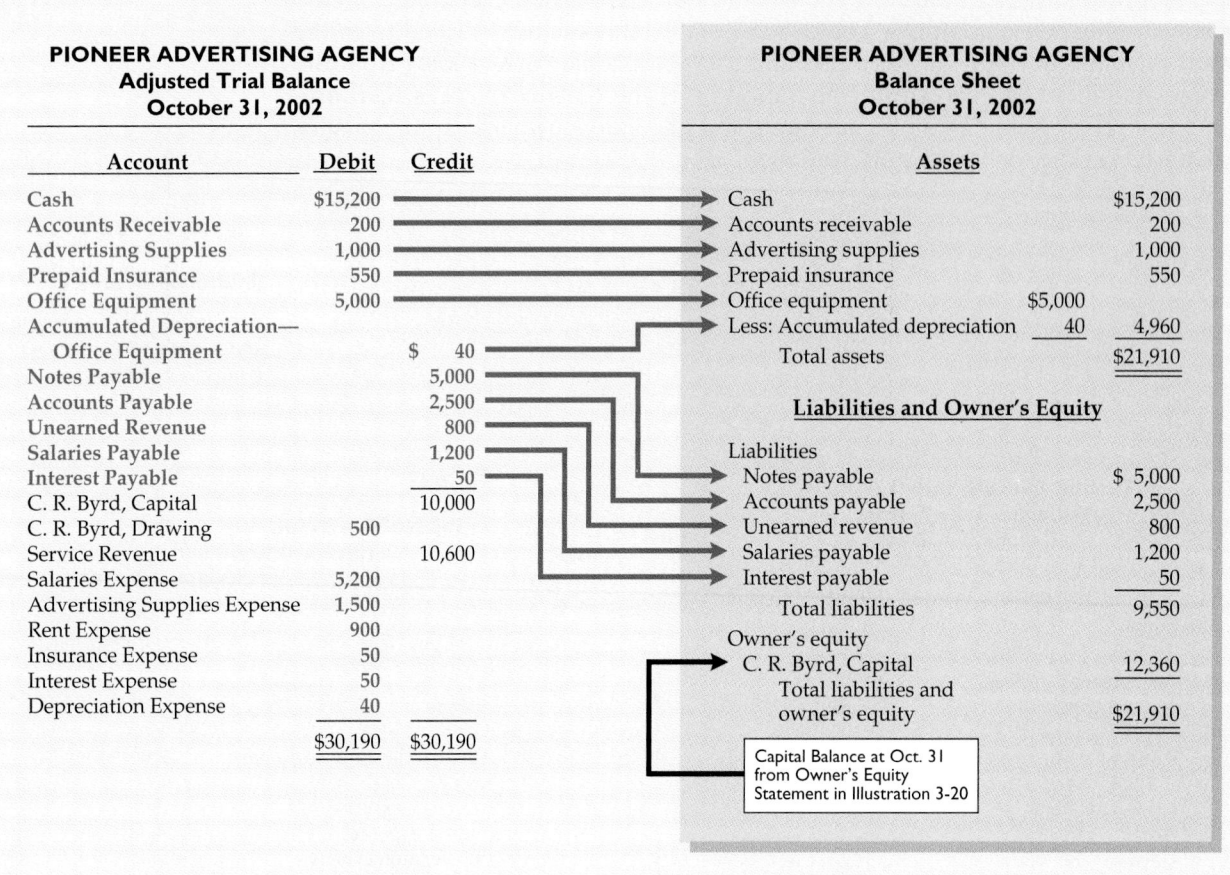

PIONEER ADVERTISING AGENCY
Adjusted Trial Balance
October 31, 2002

Account	Debit	Credit
Cash	$15,200	
Accounts Receivable	200	
Advertising Supplies	1,000	
Prepaid Insurance	550	
Office Equipment	5,000	
Accumulated Depreciation—Office Equipment		$ 40
Notes Payable		5,000
Accounts Payable		2,500
Unearned Revenue		800
Salaries Payable		1,200
Interest Payable		50
C. R. Byrd, Capital		10,000
C. R. Byrd, Drawing	500	
Service Revenue		10,600
Salaries Expense	5,200	
Advertising Supplies Expense	1,500	
Rent Expense	900	
Insurance Expense	50	
Interest Expense	50	
Depreciation Expense	40	
	$30,190	$30,190

PIONEER ADVERTISING AGENCY
Balance Sheet
October 31, 2002

Assets		
Cash		$15,200
Accounts receivable		200
Advertising supplies		1,000
Prepaid insurance		550
Office equipment	$5,000	
Less: Accumulated depreciation	40	4,960
Total assets		$21,910
Liabilities and Owner's Equity		
Liabilities		
Notes payable		$ 5,000
Accounts payable		2,500
Unearned revenue		800
Salaries payable		1,200
Interest payable		50
Total liabilities		9,550
Owner's equity		
C. R. Byrd, Capital		12,360
Total liabilities and owner's equity		$21,910

Capital Balance at Oct. 31 from Owner's Equity Statement in Illustration 3-20

BEFORE YOU GO ON...

REVIEW IT

1. What is the purpose of an adjusted trial balance?
2. How is an adjusted trial balance prepared?

A LOOK BACK AT OUR FEATURE STORY

Refer back to the Feature Story about **McKesson HBOC**, **Cambridge Biotech**, **Media Vision Technology**, and **Penguin USA** at the beginning of the chapter, and answer the following questions.

1. What are the purposes of adjusting entries?
2. What do these four companies have in common relative to accrual accounting?
3. What adjusting entries should be made for long-lived productive assets purchased by these four companies in prior years?
4. What other types of adjusting entries do you believe these companies might make?

SOLUTION

1. Adjusting entries are necessary to make the financial statements complete and accurate. Adjusting entries are made to record revenues in the period in which they are earned and to recognize expenses in the period in which they are incurred. Therefore, adjustments ensure that the revenue recognition and matching principles are followed.
2. Each of the companies misstated net income by either overstating revenues (sales) or understating expenses. They failed to properly **time** the reporting of revenues or expenses.
3. The purchase and use of long-lived assets in the production of revenue requires the systematic allocation of their cost over their useful lives by recording depreciation expense periodically.
4. (a) Accrued expenses: rent, salaries, utilities, interest, taxes.
   (b) Accrued revenues: interest earned, rent, commissions, fees.
   (c) Prepaid expenses: insurance, rent, supplies, advertising.
   (d) Unearned revenues: rent, subscriptions, customer deposits, and prepayments.

THE NAVIGATOR

DEMONSTRATION PROBLEM

Terry Thomas opens the Green Thumb Lawn Care Company on April 1. At April 30, the trial balance shows the following balances for selected accounts.

Prepaid Insurance	$ 3,600
Equipment	28,000
Notes Payable	20,000
Unearned Revenue	4,200
Service Revenue	1,800

Additional Demonstration Problem

Analysis reveals the following additional data.

1. Prepaid insurance is the cost of a 2-year insurance policy, effective April 1.
2. Depreciation on the equipment is $500 per month.
3. The note payable is dated April 1. It is a 6-month, 12% note.
4. Seven customers paid for the company's 6 months' lawn service package of $600 beginning in April. These customers were serviced in April.
5. Lawn services provided other customers but not billed at April 30 totaled $1,500.

Instructions

Prepare the adjusting entries for the month of April. Show computations.

SOLUTION TO DEMONSTRATION PROBLEM

GENERAL JOURNAL **J1**

Date	Account Titles and Explanation	Ref.	Debit	Credit
	Adjusting Entries			
Apr. 30	Insurance Expense		150	
	Prepaid Insurance			150
	(To record insurance expired:			
	$3,600 ÷ 24 = $150 per month)			
30	Depreciation Expense		500	
	Accumulated Depreciation—Equipment			500
	(To record monthly depreciation)			

ACTION PLAN

- Note that adjustments are being made for one month.
- Make computations carefully.
- Select account titles carefully.
- Make sure debits are made first and credits are indented.
- Check that debits equal credits for each entry.

30	Interest Expense		200	
	Interest Payable			200
	(To record interest on notes payable: $\$20,000 \times 12\% \times 1/12 = \$200$)			
30	Unearned Revenue		700	
	Service Revenue			700
	(To record service revenue: $\$600 \div 6 = \$100$; $\$100$ per month $\times 7 = \$700$)			
30	Accounts Receivable		1,500	
	Service Revenue			1,500
	(To record revenue for services provided)			

THE NAVIGATOR

SUMMARY OF STUDY OBJECTIVES

1. ***Explain the time period assumption.*** The time period assumption assumes that the economic life of a business can be divided into artificial time periods.

2. ***Explain the accrual basis of accounting.*** Accrual-basis accounting means that events that change a company's financial statements are recorded in the periods in which the events occur, rather than in the periods in which the company receives or pays cash.

3. ***Explain why adjusting entries are needed.*** Adjusting entries are made at the end of an accounting period. They ensure that revenues are recorded in the period in which they are earned and that expenses are recognized in the period in which they are incurred.

4. ***Identify the major types of adjusting entries.*** The major types of adjusting entries are prepaid expenses, unearned revenues, accrued revenues, and accrued expenses.

5. ***Prepare adjusting entries for prepayments.*** Prepayments are either prepaid expenses or unearned revenues. Adjusting entries for prepayments are required at the statement date to record the portion of the prepayment that represents the expense incurred or the revenue earned in the current accounting period.

6. ***Prepare adjusting entries for accruals.*** Accruals are either accrued revenues or accrued expenses. Adjusting entries for accruals are required to record revenues earned and expenses incurred in the current accounting period that have not been recognized through daily entries.

7. ***Describe the nature and purpose of an adjusted trial balance.*** An adjusted trial balance shows the balances of all accounts, including those that have been adjusted, at the end of an accounting period. Its purpose is to show the effects of all financial events that have occurred during the accounting period.

THE NAVIGATOR

Key Term Matching Activity

GLOSSARY

Accrual-basis accounting Accounting basis in which transactions that change a company's financial statements are recorded in the periods in which the events occur. (p. 89).

Accrued expenses Expenses incurred but not yet paid in cash or recorded. (p. 100).

Accrued revenues Revenues earned but not yet received in cash or recorded. (p. 99).

Adjusted trial balance A list of accounts and their balances after all adjustments have been made. (p. 106).

Adjusting entries Entries made at the end of an accounting period to ensure that the revenue recognition and matching principles are followed. (p. 91).

Book value The difference between the cost of a depreciable asset and its related accumulated depreciation. (p. 96).

Calendar year An accounting period that extends from January 1 to December 31. (p. 89).

Cash-basis accounting Accounting basis in which revenue is recorded when cash is received and an expense is recorded when cash is paid. (p. 89).

Contra asset account An account that is offset against an asset account on the balance sheet. (p. 96).

Depreciation The allocation of the cost of an asset to expense over its useful life in a rational and systematic manner. (p. 95).

Fiscal year An accounting period that is one year in length. (p. 89).

Interim periods Monthly or quarterly accounting time periods. (p. 89).

Matching principle The principle that efforts (expenses) be matched with accomplishments (revenues). (p. 90).

Prepaid expenses Expenses paid in cash and recorded as assets before they are used or consumed. (p. 93).

Revenue recognition principle The principle that revenue be recognized in the accounting period in which it is earned. (p. 90).

Time period assumption An assumption that the economic life of a business can be divided into artificial time periods. (p. 89).

Unearned revenues Cash received and recorded as liabilities before revenue is earned. (p. 97).

Useful life The length of service of a productive facility. (p. 95).

APPENDIX *Alternative Treatment of Prepaid Expenses and Unearned Revenues*

STUDY OBJECTIVE 8

Prepare adjusting entries for the alternative treatment of prepayments.

In our discussion of adjusting entries for prepaid expenses and unearned revenues, we illustrated transactions for which the initial entries were made to balance sheet accounts. In the case of prepaid expenses, the prepayment was debited to an asset account. In the case of unearned revenue, the cash received was credited to a liability account. Some businesses use an alternative treatment: (1) At the time an expense is prepaid, it is debited to an expense account. (2) At the time of a receipt for future services, it is credited to a revenue account. The circumstances that justify such entries and the different adjusting entries that may be required are described below. The alternative treatment of prepaid expenses and unearned revenues has the same effect on the financial statements as the procedures described in the chapter.

PREPAID EXPENSES

Prepaid expenses become expired costs either through the passage of time (e.g., insurance) or through consumption (e.g., advertising supplies). If, at the time of purchase, the company expects to consume the supplies before the next financial statement date, **it may be more convenient initially to debit (increase) an expense account rather than an asset account.**

Assume that Pioneer Advertising expects that all of the supplies purchased on October 5 will be used before the end of the month. A debit of $2,500 to Advertising Supplies Expense (rather than to the asset account Advertising Supplies) on October 5 will eliminate the need for an adjusting entry on October 31, if all the supplies are used. At October 31, the Advertising Supplies Expense account will show a balance of $2,500, which is the cost of supplies used between October 5 and October 31.

But what if the company does not use all the supplies, and an inventory of $1,000 of advertising supplies remains on October 31? Obviously, an adjusting entry is needed. Prior to adjustment, the expense account Advertising Supplies Expense is overstated $1,000, and the asset account Advertising Supplies is understated $1,000. Thus the following adjusting entry is made.

Oct. 31	Advertising Supplies	1,000	
	Advertising Supplies Expense		1,000
	(To record supplies inventory)		

A	=	L	+	OE
+1,000				+1,000

After posting the adjusting entry, the accounts show:

Illustration 3A-1

Prepaid expenses accounts after adjustment

Advertising Supplies			
10/31 **Adj.**	**1,000**		

Advertising Supplies Expense			
10/5	2,500	10/31 **Adj.**	**1,000**
10/31 **Bal.**	**1,500**		

After adjustment, the asset account Advertising Supplies shows a balance of $1,000, which is equal to the cost of supplies on hand at October 31. In addition, Advertising Supplies Expense shows a balance of $1,500, which is equal to the cost of supplies used between October 5 and October 31. If the adjusting entry is not made, expenses will be overstated and net income will be understated by $1,000 in the October income statement. Also, both assets and owner's equity will be understated by $1,000 on the October 31 balance sheet.

A comparison of the entries and accounts for advertising supplies is shown in Illustration 3A-2.

Illustration 3A-2

Adjustment approaches—a comparison

Prepayment Initially Debited to Asset Account (per chapter)				Prepayment Initially Debited to Expense Account (per appendix)			
Oct. 5	Advertising Supplies	2,500		Oct. 5	Advertising Supplies Expense	2,500	
	Accounts Payable		2,500		Accounts Payable		2,500
Oct. 31	Advertising Supplies Expense	1,500		Oct. 31	Advertising Supplies	1,000	
	Advertising Supplies		1,500		Advertising Supplies Expense		1,000

After posting the entries, the accounts appear as follows.

Illustration 3A-3

Comparison of accounts

(per chapter)
Advertising Supplies

10/5	2,500	10/31 **Adj.**	**1,500**
10/31 **Bal.**	**1,000**		

Advertising Supplies Expense

10/31 **Adj.**	**1,500**		

(per appendix)
Advertising Supplies

10/31 **Adj.**	**1,000**		

Advertising Supplies Expense

10/5	2,500	10/31 **Adj.**	**1,000**
10/31 **Bal.**	**1,500**		

Note that the account balances under each alternative are the same at October 31: Advertising Supplies $1,000, and Advertising Supplies Expense $1,500.

UNEARNED REVENUES

Unearned revenues become earned either through the passage of time (e.g., unearned rent) or through providing the service (e.g., unearned fees). Similar to the case for prepaid expenses, a revenue account may be credited (increased) when cash is received for future services.

To illustrate, assume that Pioneer Advertising received $1,200 for future services on October 2. The services were expected to be performed before October 31.[3] In such a case, Service Revenue is credited. If revenue is in fact earned before October 31, no adjustment is needed.

[3]This example focuses only on the alternative treatment of unearned revenues. In the interest of simplicity, the entries to Service Revenue pertaining to the immediate earning of revenue ($10,000) and the adjusting entry for accrued revenue ($200) have been ignored.

However, if at the statement date $800 of the services have not been performed, an adjusting entry is required. The revenue account Service Revenue is overstated $800, and the liability account Unearned Revenue is understated $800. Thus, the following adjusting entry is made.

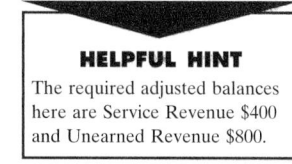

HELPFUL HINT
The required adjusted balances here are Service Revenue $400 and Unearned Revenue $800.

Oct. 31	Service Revenue	800	
	Unearned Revenue		800
	(To record unearned revenue)		

A	=	L	+	OE
		+800		−800

After posting the adjusting entry, the accounts show:

Illustration 3A-4
Unearned revenue accounts after adjustment

Unearned Revenue

Debit		Credit	
		10/31 **Adj.**	**800**

Service Revenue

Debit		Credit	
10/31 **Adj.**	**800**	10/2	1,200
		10/31 **Bal.**	**400**

The liability account Unearned Revenue shows a balance of $800. This is equal to the services that will be provided in the future. In addition, the balance in Service Revenue equals the services provided in October. If the adjusting entry is not made, both revenues and net income will be overstated by $800 in the October income statement. Also, liabilities will be understated by $800, and owner's equity will be overstated by $800 on the October 31 balance sheet.

A comparison of the entries and accounts for service revenue earned and unearned is shown in Illustration 3A-5.

Illustration 3A-5
Adjustment approaches—a comparison

Unearned Revenue Initially Credited to Liability Account (per chapter)				**Unearned Revenue Initially Credited to Revenue Account (per appendix)**			
Oct. 2	Cash	1,200		Oct. 2	Cash	1,200	
	Unearned Revenue		1,200		Service Revenue		1,200
Oct. 31	Unearned Revenue	400		Oct. 31	Service Revenue	800	
	Service Revenue		400		Unearned Revenue		800

After posting the entries, the accounts appear as follows.

Illustration 3A-6
Comparison of accounts

(per chapter) Unearned Revenue

Debit		Credit	
10/31 **Adj.**	**400**	10/2	1,200
		10/31 **Bal.**	**800**

(per appendix) Unearned Revenue

Debit		Credit	
		10/31 **Adj.**	**800**

(per chapter) Service Revenue

Debit		Credit	
		10/31 **Adj.**	**400**

(per appendix) Service Revenue

Debit		Credit	
10/31 **Adj.**	**800**	10/2	1,200
		10/31 **Bal.**	**400**

Note that the balances in the accounts are the same under the two alternatives: Unearned Revenue $800, and Service Revenue $400.

SUMMARY OF ADDITIONAL ADJUSTMENT RELATIONSHIPS

The use of alternative adjusting entries requires additions to the summary of basic relationships presented earlier in Illustration 3-16. The additions are shown in color in Illustration 3A-7.

Alternative adjusting entries **do not apply** to accrued revenues and accrued expenses because **no entries occur before these types of adjusting entries are made.** Therefore, the entries in Illustration 3-16 for these two types of adjustments remain unchanged.

Illustration 3A-7

Summary of basic relationships for prepayments

Type of Adjustment	Reason for Adjustment	Account Balances before Adjustment	Adjusting Entry
1. Prepaid expenses	(a) Prepaid expenses initially recorded in asset accounts have been used.	Assets overstated Expenses understated	Dr. Expenses Cr. Assets
	(b) Prepaid expenses initially recorded in expense accounts have not been used.	**Assets understated Expenses overstated**	**Dr. Assets Cr. Expenses**
2. Unearned revenues	(a) Unearned revenues initially recorded in liability accounts have been earned.	Liabilities overstated Revenues understated	Dr. Liabilities Cr. Revenues
	(b) Unearned revenues initially recorded in revenue accounts have not been earned.	**Liabilities understated Revenues overstated**	**Dr. Revenues Cr. Liabilities**

SUMMARY OF STUDY OBJECTIVE FOR APPENDIX

8. *Prepare adjusting entries for the alternative treatment of prepayments.* Prepayments may be initially debited to an expense account. Unearned revenues may be credited to a revenue account. At the end of the period, these accounts may be overstated. The adjusting entries for prepaid expenses are a debit to an asset account and a credit to an expense account. Adjusting entries for unearned revenues are a debit to a revenue account and a credit to a liability account.

***Note:** All asterisked Questions, Exercises, and Problems relate to material in the appendix to the chapter.

Chapter 3 Self-Test

SELF-STUDY QUESTIONS

Answers are at the end of the chapter.

(SO 1) **1.** The time period assumption states that:
a. revenue should be recognized in the accounting period in which it is earned.
b. expenses should be matched with revenues.
c. the economic life of a business can be divided into artificial time periods.
d. the fiscal year should correspond with the calendar year.

(SO 2) **2.** The principle dictating that efforts (expenses) be matched with accomplishments (revenues) is the:
a. matching principle.
b. cost principle.
c. periodicity principle.
d. revenue recognition principle.

3. One of the following statements about the accrual basis of accounting is *false*. That statement is: (SO 2)
a. Events that change a company's financial statements are recorded in the periods in which the events occur.
b. Revenue is recognized in the period in which it is earned.
c. This basis is in accord with generally accepted accounting principles.
d. Revenue is recorded only when cash is received, and expense is recorded only when cash is paid.

(SO 3) 4. Adjusting entries are made to ensure that:
   a. expenses are recognized in the period in which they are incurred.
   b. revenues are recorded in the period in which they are earned.
   c. balance sheet and income statement accounts have correct balances at the end of an accounting period.
   d. all of the above.

(SO 4) 5. Each of the following is a major type (or category) of adjusting entries *except:*
   a. prepaid expenses.
   b. accrued revenues.
   c. accrued expenses.
   d. earned revenues.

(SO 5) 6. The trial balance shows Supplies $1,350 and Supplies Expense $0. If $600 of supplies are on hand at the end of the period, the adjusting entry is:

a. Supplies	600	
Supplies Expense		600
b. Supplies	750	
Supplies Expense		750
c. Supplies Expense	750	
Supplies		750
d. Supplies Expense	600	
Supplies		600

(SO 5) 7. Adjustments for unearned revenues:
   a. decrease liabilities and increase revenues.
   b. have an assets and revenues account relationship.
   c. increase assets and increase revenues.
   d. decrease revenues and decrease assets.

(SO 6) 8. Adjustments for accrued revenues:
   a. have a liabilities and revenues account relationship.
   b. have an assets and revenues account relationship.
   c. decrease assets and revenues.
   d. decrease liabilities and increase revenues.

9. Kathy Siska earned a salary of $400 for the last week of September. She will be paid on October 1. The adjusting entry for Kathy's employer at September 30 is: (SO 6)
   a. No entry is required.

b. Salaries Expense	400	
Salaries Payable		400
c. Salaries Expense	400	
Cash		400
d. Salaries Payable	400	
Cash		400

10. Which of the following statements is *incorrect* concerning the adjusted trial balance? (SO 7)
   a. An adjusted trial balance proves the equality of the total debit balances and the total credit balances in the ledger after all adjustments are made.
   b. The adjusted trial balance provides the primary basis for the preparation of financial statements.
   c. The adjusted trial balance lists the account balances segregated by assets and liabilities.
   d. The adjusted trial balance is prepared after the adjusting entries have been journalized and posted.

*11. The trial balance shows Supplies $0 and Supplies Expense $1,500. If $800 of supplies are on hand at the end of the period, the adjusting entry is: (SO 8)
   a. Debit Supplies $800 and credit Supplies Expense $800.
   b. Debit Supplies Expense $800 and credit Supplies $800.
   c. Debit Supplies $700 and credit Supplies Expense $700.
   d. Debit Supplies Expense $700 and credit Supplies $700.

☑ THE NAVIGATOR

QUESTIONS

1. (a) How does the time period assumption affect an accountant's analysis of business transactions?
   (b) Explain the terms *fiscal year, calendar year,* and *interim periods.*
2. State two generally accepted accounting principles that relate to adjusting the accounts.
3. Bon Barone, a lawyer, accepts a legal engagement in March, performs the work in April, and is paid in May. If Barone's law firm prepares monthly financial statements, when should it recognize revenue from this engagement? Why?
4. Why do accrual-basis financial statements provide more useful information than cash-basis statements?
5. In completing the engagement in (3) above, Barone incurs $4,500 of expenses in March, which are paid in April. How much expense should be deducted from revenues in the month the revenue is recognized? Why?
6. "Adjusting entries are required by the cost principle of accounting." Do you agree? Explain.
7. Why may a trial balance not contain up-to-date and complete financial information?
8. Distinguish between the two categories of adjusting entries, and identify the types of adjustments applicable to each category.
9. What is the debit/credit effect of a prepaid expense adjusting entry?
10. "Depreciation is a valuation process that results in the reporting of the fair market value of the asset." Do you agree? Explain.
11. Explain the differences between depreciation expense and accumulated depreciation.
12. Shen Company purchased equipment for $15,000. By the current balance sheet date, $7,000 had been depreciated. Indicate the balance sheet presentation of the data.
13. What is the debit/credit effect of an unearned revenue adjusting entry?
14. A company fails to recognize revenue earned but not yet received. Which of the following accounts are involved

in the adjusting entry: (a) asset, (b) liability, (c) revenue, or (d) expense? For the accounts selected, indicate whether they would be debited or credited in the entry.

15. A company fails to recognize an expense incurred but not paid. Indicate which of the following accounts is debited and which is credited in the adjusting entry: (a) asset, (b) liability, (c) revenue, or (d) expense.

16. A company makes an accrued revenue adjusting entry for $800 and an accrued expense adjusting entry for $600. How much was net income understated prior to these entries? Explain.

17. On January 9, a company pays $5,000 for salaries, of which $2,000 was reported as Salaries Payable on December 31. Give the entry to record the payment.

18. For each of the following items before adjustment, indicate the type of adjusting entry (prepaid expense, unearned revenue, accrued revenue, and accrued expense) that is needed to correct the misstatement. If an item could result in more than one type of adjusting entry, indicate each of the types.
(a) Assets are understated.
(b) Liabilities are overstated.
(c) Liabilities are understated.
(d) Expenses are understated.
(e) Assets are overstated.
(f) Revenue is understated.

19. One-half of the adjusting entry is given below. Indicate the account title for the other half of the entry.
(a) Salaries Expense is debited.
(b) Depreciation Expense is debited.
(c) Interest Payable is credited.
(d) Supplies is credited.
(e) Accounts Receivable is debited.
(f) Unearned Service Revenue is debited.

20. "An adjusting entry may affect more than one balance sheet or income statement account." Do you agree? Why or why not?

21. Why is it possible to prepare financial statements directly from an adjusted trial balance?

*22. The Alpha Company debits Supplies Expense for all purchases of supplies and credits Rent Revenue for all advanced rentals. For each type of adjustment, give the adjusting entry.

BRIEF EXERCISES

Indicate why adjusting entries are needed.
(SO 3)

BE3-1 The ledger of Hilo Company includes the following accounts. Explain why each account may require adjustment.
(a) Prepaid Insurance
(b) Depreciation Expense
(c) Unearnd Revenue
(d) Interest Payable

Identify the major types of adjusting entries.
(SO 4)

BE3-2 Riko Company accumulates the following adjustment data at December 31. Indicate **(a)** the type of adjustment (prepaid expense, accrued revenues and so on), and **(b)** the accounts before adjustment (overstated or understated).
1. Supplies of $100 are on hand.
2. Services provided but unbilled total $900.
3. Interest of $200 has accumulated on a note payable.
4. Rent collected in advance totaling $800 has been earned.

Prepare adjusting entry for supplies.
(SO 5)

BE3-3 Sain Advertising Company's trial balance at December 31 shows Advertising Supplies $8,700 and Advertising Supplies Expense $0. On December 31, there are $1,700 of supplies on hand. Prepare the adjusting entry at December 31, and using T accounts, enter the balances in the accounts, post the adjusting entry, and indicate the adjusted balance in each account.

Prepare adjusting entries for depreciation.
(SO 5)

BE3-4 At the end of its first year, the trial balance of Shuey Company shows Equipment $25,000 and zero balances in Accumulated Depreciation—Equipment and Depreciation Expense. Depreciation for the year is estimated to be $5,000. Prepare the adjusting entry for depreciation at December 31, post the adjustments to T accounts, and indicate the balance sheet presentation of the equipment at December 31.

Prepare adjusting entries for prepaid expense.
(SO 5)

BE3-5 On July 1, 2002, Cheng Co. pays $15,000 to Wanzo Insurance Co. for a 3-year insurance contract. Both companies have fiscal years ending December 31. For Cheng Co., journalize and post the entry on July 1 and the adjusting entry on December 31.

Prepare adjusting entry for unearned revenue.
(SO 5)

BE3-6 Using the data in BE3-5, journalize and post the entry on July 1 and the adjusting entry on December 31 for Wanzo Insurance Co. Wanzo uses the accounts Unearned Insurance Revenue and Insurance Revenue.

BE3-7 The bookkeeper for Rosenberg Company asks you to prepare the following accrued adjusting entries at December 31.

Prepare adjusting entries for accruals. (SO 6)

1. Interest on notes payable of $300 is accrued.
2. Services provided but unbilled total $1,250.
3. Salaries earned by employees of $900 have not been recorded.

Use the following account titles: Service Revenue, Accounts Receivable, Interest Expense, Interest Payable, Salaries Expense, and Salaries Payable.

BE3-8 The trial balance of Hoi Company includes the following balance sheet accounts. Identify the accounts that require adjustment. For each account that requires adjustment, indicate **(a)** the type of adjusting entry (prepaid expenses, unearned revenues, accrued revenues, and accrued expenses) and **(b)** the related account in the adjusting entry.

Analyze accounts in an adjusted trial balance. (SO 7)

Accounts Receivable	Interest Payable
Prepaid Insurance	Unearned Service Revenue
Accumulated Depreciation—Equipment	

BE3-9 The adjusted trial balance of Lumas Company at December 31, 2002, includes the following accounts: S. Lumas, Capital $15,600; S. Lumas, Drawing $6,000; Service Revenue $38,400; Salaries Expense $13,000; Insurance Expense $2,000; Rent Expense $4,000; Supplies Expense $1,500; and Depreciation Expense $1,300 Prepare an income statement for the year.

Prepare an income statement from an adjusted trial balance. (SO 7)

BE3-10 Partial adjusted trial balance data for Lumas Company is presented in BE3-9. The balance in S. Lumas, Capital is the balance as of January 1. Prepare an owner's equity statement for the year assuming net income is $16,600 for the year.

Prepare an owner's equity statement from an adjusted trial balance. (SO 7)

***BE3-11** Lam Company records all prepayments in income statement accounts. At April 30, the trial balance shows Supplies Expense $2,800, Service Revenue $9,200, and zero balances in related balance sheet accounts. Prepare the adjusting entries at April 30 assuming **(a)** $1,000 of supplies on hand and **(b)** $800 of service revenue should be reported as unearned.

Prepare adjusting entries under alternative treatment of prepayments. (SO 8)

EXERCISES

E3-1 On numerous occasions, proposals have surfaced to put the federal government on the accrual basis of accounting. This is no small issue. If this basis were used, it would mean that billions in unrecorded liabilities would have to be booked, and the federal deficit would increase substantially.

Distinguish between cash and accrual basis of accounting. (SO 2)

Instructions

(a) What is the difference between accrual-basis accounting and cash-basis accounting?
(b) Why would politicians prefer the cash basis over the accrual basis?
(c) Write a letter to your senator explaining why the federal government should adopt the accrual basis of accounting.

E3-2 Jawson Company accumulates the following adjustment data at December 31.

Identify types of adjustments and account relationships. (SO 4, 5, 6)

1. Services provided but unbilled total $750.
2. Store supplies of $300 have been used.
3. Utility expenses of $225 are unpaid.
4. Unearned revenue of $260 has been earned.
5. Salaries of $900 are unpaid.
6. Prepaid insurance totaling $350 has expired.

Instructions

For each of the above items indicate the following.

(a) The type of adjustment (prepaid expense, unearned revenue, accrued revenue, or accrued expense).
(b) The accounts before adjustment (overstatement or understatement).

E3-3 The ledger of Easy Rental Agency on March 31 of the current year includes the following selected accounts before adjusting entries have been prepared.

Prepare adjusting entries from selected account data. (SO 5, 6, 7)

	Debit	Credit
Prepaid Insurance	$ 3,600	
Supplies	2,800	
Equipment	25,000	
Accumulated Depreciation—Equipment		$ 8,400
Notes Payable		20,000
Unearned Rent		9,900
Rent Revenue		60,000
Interest Expense	–0–	
Wage Expense	14,000	

An analysis of the accounts shows the following.

1. The equipment depreciates $250 per month.
2. One-third of the unearned rent was earned during the quarter.
3. Interest of $500 is accrued on the notes payable.
4. Supplies on hand total $650.
5. Insurance expires at the rate of $300 per month.

Instructions

Prepare the adjusting entries at March 31, assuming that adjusting entries are made quarterly. Additional accounts are: Depreciation Expense, Insurance Expense, Interest Payable, and Supplies Expense.

Prepare adjusting entries.
(SO 5, 6, 7)

E3-4 Karen Tong, D.D.S., opened a dental practice on January 1, 2002. During the first month of operations the following transactions occurred.

1. Performed services for patients who had dental plan insurance. At January 31, $875 of such services was earned but not yet billed to the insurance companies.
2. Utility expenses incurred but not paid prior to January 31 totaled $520.
3. Purchased dental equipment on January 1 for $80,000, paying $20,000 in cash and signing a $60,000, 3-year note payable. The equipment depreciates $400 per month. Interest is $500 per month.
4. Purchased a one-year malpractice insurance policy on January 1 for $12,000.
5. Purchased $1,600 of dental supplies. On January 31, determined that $700 of supplies were on hand.

Instructions

Prepare the adjusting entries on January 31. Account titles are: Accumulated Depreciation—Dental Equipment, Depreciation Expense, Service Revenue, Accounts Receivable, Insurance Expense, Interest Expense, Interest Payable, Prepaid Insurance, Supplies, Supplies Expense, Utilities Expense, and Utilities Payable.

Prepare adjusting entries.
(SO 5, 6, 7)

E3-5 The trial balance for Pioneer Advertising Agency is shown in Illustration 3-3, p. 92. In lieu of the adjusting entries shown in the text at October 31, assume the following adjustment data.

1. Advertising supplies on hand at October 31 total $1,100.
2. Expired insurance for the month is $100.
3. Depreciation for the month is $50.
4. Unearned revenue in October totals $600.
5. Services provided but unbilled at October 31 are $300.
6. Interest accrued at October 31 is $70.
7. Accrued salaries at October 31 are $1,400.

Instructions

Prepare the adjusting entries for the items above.

Prepare correct income statement
(SO 2, 5, 6, 7)

E3-6 The income statement of Weller Co. for the month of July shows net income of $1,400 based on Service Revenue $5,500, Wages Expense $2,300, Supplies Expense $1,200, and Utilities Expense $600. In reviewing the statement, you discover the following.

1. Insurance expired during July of $400 was omitted.
2. Supplies expense includes $500 of supplies that are still on hand at July 31.
3. Depreciation on equipment of $150 was omitted.

4. Accrued but unpaid wages at July 31 of $300 were not included.
5. Services provided but unrecorded totaled $1,100.

Instructions

Prepare a correct income statement for July.

E3-7 A partial adjusted trial balance of Cordero Company at January 31, 2002, shows the following.

Analyze adjusted data.
(SO 4, 5, 6, 7)

CORDERO COMPANY
Adjusted Trial Balance
January 31, 2002

	Debit	Credit
Supplies	$ 850	
Prepaid Insurance	2,400	
Salaries Payable		$ 800
Unearned Revenue		750
Supplies Expense	950	
Insurance Expense	400	
Salaries Expense	1,800	
Service Revenue		2,000

Instructions

Answer the following questions, assuming the year begins January 1.

(a) If the amount in Supplies Expense is the January 31 adjusting entry, and $850 of supplies was purchased in January, what was the balance in Supplies on January 1?
(b) If the amount in Insurance Expense is the January 31 adjusting entry, and the original insurance premium was for one year, what was the total premium and when was the policy purchased?
(c) If $2,500 of salaries was paid in January, what was the balance in Salaries Payable at December 31, 2001?
(d) If $1,600 was received in January for services performed in January, what was the balance in Unearned Revenue at December 31, 2001?

E3-8 Selected accounts of Felipe Company are shown below.

Journalize basic transactions and adjusting entries.
(SO 5, 6, 7)

Supplies Expense

7/31	700		

Supplies

7/1 Bal.	1,100	7/31	700
7/10	200		

Salaries Payable

		7/31	1,200

Accounts Receivable

7/31	500		

Unearned Revenue

7/31	900	7/1 Bal.	1,500
		7/20	750

Salaries Expense

7/15	1,200		
7/31	1,200		

Service Revenue

		7/14	3,000
		7/31	900
		7/31	500

Instructions

After analyzing the accounts, journalize **(a)** the July transactions and **(b)** the adjusting entries that were made on July 31. (*Hint:* July transactions were for cash.)

E3-9 The trial balances before and after adjustment for Tang Company at the end of its fiscal year are presented below.

Prepare adjusting entries from analysis of trial balances.
(SO 5, 6, 7)

TANG COMPANY
Trial Balance
August 31, 2001

	Before Adjustment		After Adjustment	
	Dr.	**Cr.**	**Dr.**	**Cr.**
Cash	$10,400		$10,400	
Accounts Receivable	8,800		9,500	
Office Supplies	2,300		700	
Prepaid Insurance	4,000		2,500	
Office Equipment	14,000		14,000	
Accumulated Depreciation—Office Equipment		$ 3,600		$ 4,800
Accounts Payable		5,800		5,800
Salaries Payable		–0–		1,100
Unearned Rent		1,500		600
T. Tang, Capital		15,600		15,600
Service Revenue		34,000		34,700
Rent Revenue		11,000		11,900
Salaries Expense	17,000		18,100	
Office Supplies Expense	–0–		1,600	
Rent Expense	15,000		15,000	
Insurance Expense	–0–		1,500	
Depreciation Expense	–0–		1,200	
	$71,500	$71,500	$74,500	$74,500

Instructions

Prepare the adjusting entries that were made.

Prepare financial statements from adjusted trial balance. (SO 5, 6, 7)

E3-10 The adjusted trial balance for Tang Company is given in E3-9.

Instructions

Prepare the income and owner's equity statements for the year and the balance sheet at August 31.

Record transactions on accrual basis; convert revenue to cash receipts. (SO 5, 6)

E3-11 The following data are taken from the comparative balance sheets of Breakers Billiards Club, which prepares its financial statements using the accrual basis of accounting.

December 31	**2002**	**2001**
Fees receivable from members	$12,000	$ 9,000
Unearned fees revenue	17,000	22,000

Fees are billed to members based upon their use of the club's facilities. Unearned fees arise from the sale of gift certificates, which members can apply to their future use of club facilities. The 2002 income statement for the club showed that fees revenue of $153,000 was earned during the year.

Instructions

(*Hint:* You will probably find it helpful to use T accounts to analyze this data.)

(a) Prepare journal entries for each of the following events that took place during 2002.

(1) Fees receivable from 2001 were all collected.

(2) Gift certificates outstanding at the end of 2001 were all redeemed.

(3) An additional $30,000 worth of gift certificates were sold during 2002. A portion of these were used by the recipients during the year; the remainder were still outstanding at the end of 2002.

(4) Fees for 2002 were billed to members.

(5) Fees receivable for 2002 (i.e., those billed in item [4] above) were partially collected.

(b) Determine the amount of cash received by the club, with respect to fees, during 2002.

*E3-12 At Devereaux Company, prepayments are debited to expense when paid, and unearned revenues are credited to revenue when received. During January of the current year, the following transactions occurred.

Journalize transactions and adjusting entries using appendix.
(SO 8)

Jan.	2	Paid $1,800 for fire insurance protection for the year.
	10	Paid $1,700 for supplies.
	15	Received $5,100 for services to be performed in the future.

On January 31, it is determined that $1,500 of the services fees have been earned and that there are $800 of supplies on hand.

Instructions

(a) Journalize and post the January transactions. (Use T accounts.)
(b) Journalize and post the adjusting entries at January 31.
(c) Determine the ending balance in each of the accounts.

PROBLEMS: SET A

P3-1A Han Solo started his own consulting firm, Solo Company, on June 1, 2002. The trial balance at June 30 is as follows.

Prepare adjusting entries, post to ledger accounts, and prepare adjusted trial balance.
(SO 5, 6, 7)

SOLO COMPANY
Trial Balance
June 30, 2002

Account Number		Debit	Credit
100	Cash	$ 7,750	
110	Accounts Receivable	6,000	
120	Prepaid Insurance	2,400	
130	Supplies	2,000	
135	Office Equipment	15,000	
200	Accounts Payable		$ 4,500
230	Unearned Service Revenue		4,000
300	H. Solo, Capital		21,750
400	Service Revenue		7,900
510	Salaries Expense	4,000	
520	Rent Expense	1,000	
		$38,150	$38,150

In addition to those accounts listed on the trial balance, the chart of accounts for Solo Company also contains the following accounts and account numbers: No. 136 Accumulated Depreciation—Office Equipment, No. 210 Utilities Payable, No. 220 Salaries Payable, No. 530 Depreciation Expense, No. 540 Insurance Expense, No. 550 Utilities Expense, and No. 560 Supplies Expense.

Other data:

1. Supplies on hand at June 30 are $1,300.
2. A utility bill for $150 has not been recorded and will not be paid until next month.
3. The insurance policy is for a year.
4. $2,500 of unearned service revenue has been earned at the end of the month.
5. Salaries of $1,500 are accrued at June 30.
6. The office equipment has a 5-year life with no salvage value. It is being depreciated at $250 per month for 60 months.
7. Invoices representing $3,000 of services performed during the month have not been recorded as of June 30.

Instructions

(a) Prepare the adjusting entries for the month of June. Use J3 as the page number for your journal.

(b) Post the adjusting entries to the ledger accounts. Enter the totals from the trial balance as beginning account balances and place a check mark in the posting reference column.

(c) Prepare an adjusted trial balance at June 30, 2002.

Prepare adjusting entries, adjusted trial balance, and financial statements.
(SO 5, 6, 7)

Peachtree

P3-2A Muddy River Resort opened for business on June 1 with eight air-conditioned units. Its trial balance before adjustment on August 31 is as follows.

MUDDY RIVER RESORT
Trial Balance
August 31, 2002

Account Number		Debit	Credit
101	Cash	$ 19,600	
126	Supplies	3,300	
130	Prepaid Insurance	6,000	
140	Land	25,000	
143	Cottages	125,000	
149	Furniture	26,000	
201	Accounts Payable		$ 6,500
208	Unearned Rent		7,400
275	Mortgage Payable		80,000
301	P. Javorek, Capital		100,000
306	P. Javorek, Drawing	5,000	
429	Rent Revenue		80,000
622	Repair Expense	3,600	
726	Salaries Expense	51,000	
732	Utilities Expense	9,400	
		$273,900	$273,900

In addition to those accounts listed on the trial balance, the chart of accounts for Muddy River Resort also contains the following accounts and account numbers: No. 112 Accounts Receivable, No. 144 Accumulated Depreciation—Cottages, No. 150 Accumulated Depreciation—Furniture, No. 212 Salaries Payable, No. 230 Interest Payable, No. 620 Depreciation Expense—Cottages, No. 621 Depreciation Expense—Furniture, No. 631 Supplies Expense, No. 718 Interest Expense, and No. 722 Insurance Expense.

Other data:

1. Insurance expires at the rate of $400 per month.
2. A count on August 31 shows $900 of supplies on hand.
3. Annual depreciation is $4,800 on cottages and $2,400 on furniture.
4. Unearned rent of $5,100 was earned prior to August 31.
5. Salaries of $400 were unpaid at August 31.
6. Rentals of $800 were due from tenants at August 31. (Use Accounts Receivable.)
7. The mortgage interest rate is 12% per year. (The mortgage was taken out on August 1.)

Instructions

(a) Journalize the adjusting entries on August 31 for the 3-month period June 1–August 31.

(b) Prepare a ledger using the three-column form of account. Enter the trial balance amounts and post the adjusting entries. (Use J1 as the posting reference.)

(c) Prepare an adjusted trial balance on August 31.

(d) Prepare an income statement and an owner's equity statement for the 3 months ending August 31 and a balance sheet as of August 31.

(c) Adj. trial balance $277,700
(d) Net income $15,300
Ending capital balance $110,300
Total assets $200,300

Prepare adjusting entries and financial statements.
(SO 5, 6, 7)

P3-3A Grant Advertising Agency was founded by Thomas Grant in January of 1998. Presented on the next page are both the adjusted and unadjusted trial balances as of December 31, 2002.

GRANT ADVERTISING AGENCY
Trial Balance
December 31, 2002

	Unadjusted		Adjusted	
	Dr.	**Cr.**	**Dr.**	**Cr.**
Cash	$ 11,000		$ 11,000	
Accounts Receivable	20,000		21,500	
Art Supplies	8,600		5,000	
Prepaid Insurance	3,350		2,500	
Printing Equipment	60,000		60,000	
Accumulated Depreciation		$ 28,000		$ 35,000
Accounts Payable		5,000		5,000
Interest Payable		–0–		150
Notes Payable		5,000		5,000
Unearned Advertising Fees		7,200		5,600
Salaries Payable		–0–		1,300
T. Grant, Capital		25,500		25,500
T. Grant, Drawing	12,000		12,000	
Advertising Revenue		58,600		61,700
Salaries Expense	10,000		11,300	
Insurance Expense			850	
Interest Expense	350		500	
Depreciation Expense			7,000	
Art Supplies Expense			3,600	
Rent Expense	4,000		4,000	
	$129,300	$129,300	$139,250	$139,250

Instructions

(a) Journalize the annual adjusting entries that were made.

(b) Prepare an income statement and a statement of owner's equity for the year ending December 31, 2002, and a balance sheet at December 31.

(b) Net income $34,450
Ending capital $47,950
Total assets $65,000

(c) Answer the following questions.

(1) If the note has been outstanding 6 months, what is the annual interest rate on that note?

(2) If the company paid $13,500 in salaries in 2002, what was the balance in Salaries Payable on December 31, 2001?

(c) (1) 6%
(2) $3,500

P3-4A A review of the ledger of Greenberg Company at December 31, 2002, produces the following data pertaining to the preparation of annual adjusting entries.

Preparing adjusting entries.
(SO 5, 6)

1. Salaries Payable $0. There are eight salaried employees. Salaries are paid every Friday for the current week. Five employees receive a salary of $750 each per week, and three employees earn $500 each per week. December 31 is a Tuesday. Employees do not work weekends. All employees worked the last 2 days of December.

1. Salaries expense $2,100

2. Unearned Rent $324,000. The company began subleasing office space in its new building on November 1. At December 31, the company had the following rental contracts that are paid in full for the entire term of the lease.

2. Rent revenue $74,000

Date	Term (in months)	Monthly Rent	Number of Leases
Nov. 1	6	$4,000	5
Dec. 1	6	$8,500	4

3. Prepaid Advertising $13,200. This balance consists of payments on two advertising contracts. The contracts provide for monthly advertising in two trade magazines. The terms of the contracts are as follows.

3. Advertising expense $4,900

Contract	Date	Amount	Number of Magazine Issue
A650	May 1	$6,000	12
B974	Oct. 1	7,200	24

The first advertisement runs in the month in which the contract is signed.

4. Interest expense $7,000

4. Notes Payable $100,000. This balance consists of a note for one year at an annual interest rate of 12%, dated June 1.

Instructions

Prepare the adjusting entries at December 31, 2002. (Show all computations.)

Journalize transactions and follow through accounting cycle to preparation of financial statements.
(SO 5, 6, 7)

Peachtree

P3-5A On September 1, 2002, the account balances of Rijo Equipment Repair were as follows.

No.	Debits		No.	Credits	
101	Cash	$ 4,880	154	Accumulated Depreciation	$ 1,500
112	Accounts Receivable	3,520	201	Accounts Payable	3,400
126	Supplies	2,000	209	Unearned Service Revenue	1,400
153	Store Equipment	15,000	212	Salaries Payable	500
			301	J. Rijo, Capital	18,600
		$25,400			$25,400

During September the following summary transactions were completed.

Sept. 8 Paid $1,100 for salaries due employees, of which $600 is for September.
10 Received $1,200 cash from customers on account.
12 Received $3,400 cash for services performed in September.
15 Purchased store equipment on account $3,000.
17 Purchased supplies on account $1,500.
20 Paid creditors $4,500 on account.
22 Paid September rent $500.
25 Paid salaries $1,050.
27 Performed services on account and billed customers for services rendered $700.
29 Received $650 from customers for future service.

Adjustment data consist of:

1. Supplies on hand $1,700.
2. Accrued salaries payable $400.
3. Depreciation is $200 per month.
4. Unearned service revenue of $1,450 is earned.

Instructions

(a) Enter the September 1 balances in the ledger accounts.
(b) Journalize the September transactions.
(c) Post to the ledger accounts. Use J1 for the posting reference. Use the following accounts: No. 407 Service Revenue, No. 615 Depreciation Expense, No. 631 Supplies Expense, No. 726 Salaries Expense, and No. 729 Rent Expense.
(d) Prepare a trial balance at September 30.
(e) Journalize and post adjusting entries.
(f) Prepare an adjusted trial balance.
(g) Prepare an income statement and an owner's equity statement for September and a balance sheet at September 30.

(d) Trial balance $29,650
(f) Adj. trial balance $30,250
(g) Net income $1,000
Ending capital $19,600
Total assets $24,000

Prepare adjusting entries, adjusted trial balance, and financial statements using appendix.
(SO 5, 6, 7, 8)

***P3-6A** Global Graphics Company was organized on January 1, 2002, by Jill Jay. At the end of the first 6 months of operations, the trial balance contained the following accounts.

Debits		Credits	
Cash	$ 9,500	Notes Payable	$ 17,000
Accounts Receivable	14,000	Accounts Payable	9,000
Equipment	45,000	Jill Jay, Capital	25,000
Insurance Expense	1,800	Graphic Revenue	52,100
Salaries Expense	30,000	Consulting Revenue	6,000
Supplies Expense	3,700		
Advertising Expense	1,900		
Rent Expense	1,500		
Utilities Expense	1,700		
	$109,100		$109,100

Analysis reveals the following additional data.

1. The $3,700 balance in Supplies Expense represents supplies purchased in January. At June 30, $1,300 of supplies was on hand.
2. The note payable was issued on February 1. It is a 12%, 6-month note.
3. The balance in Insurance Expense is the premium on a one-year policy, dated March 1, 2002.
4. Consulting fees are credited to revenue when received. At June 30, consulting fees of $1,100 are unearned.
5. Graphic revenue earned but unbilled at June 30 totals $2,000.
6. Depreciation is $2,000 per year.

Instructions

(a) Journalize the adjusting entries at June 30. (Assume adjustments are recorded every 6 months.)

(b) Prepare an adjusted trial balance.

(c) Prepare an income statement and owner's equity statement for the 6 months ended June 30 and a balance sheet at June 30.

(b) Adj. trial balance $112,950
(c) Net income $19,050
Ending capital $44,050
Total assets $72,000

PROBLEMS: SET B

P3-1B Julie Brown started her own consulting firm, Astromech Consulting, on May 1, 2002. The trial balance at May 31 is as follows.

Prepare adjusting entries, post to ledger accounts, and prepare an adjusted trial balance. (SO 5, 6, 7)

ASTROMECH CONSULTING
Trial Balance
May 31, 2002

Account Number		Debit	Credit
101	Cash	$ 6,500	
110	Accounts Receivable	4,000	
120	Prepaid Insurance	3,600	
130	Supplies	1,500	
135	Office Furniture	12,000	
200	Accounts Payable		$ 3,500
230	Unearned Service Revenue		3,000
300	J. Brown, Capital		19,100
400	Service Revenue		6,000
510	Salaries Expense	3,000	
520	Rent Expense	1,000	
		$31,600	$31,600

In addition to those accounts listed on the trial balance, the chart of accounts for Astromech Consulting also contains the following accounts and account numbers: No. 136 Accumulated Depreciation—Office Furniture, No. 210 Travel Payable, No. 220 Salaries Payable, No. 530 Depreciation Expense, No. 540 Insurance Expense, No. 550 Travel Expense, and No. 560 Supplies Expense.

Other data:

1. $500 of supplies have been used during the month.
2. Travel expense incurred but not paid on May 31, 2001, $200.
3. The insurance policy is for 2 years.
4. $1,000 of the balance in the unearned service revenue account remains unearned at the end of the month.
5. May 31 is a Wednesday, and employees are paid on Fridays. Astromech Consulting has two employees, who are paid $500 each for a 5-day work week.
6. The office furniture has a 5-year life with no salvage value. It is being depreciated at $200 per month for 60 months.
7. Invoices representing $2,000 of services performed during the month have not been recorded as of May 31.

Instructions

(a) Prepare the adjusting entries for the month of May. Use J4 as the page number for your journal.
(b) Post the adjusting entries to the ledger accounts. Enter the totals from the trial balance as beginning account balances and place a check mark in the posting reference column.
(c) Prepare an adjusted trial balance at May 31, 2002.

Prepare adjusting entries, adjusted trial balance, and financial statements.
(SO 5, 6, 7)

P3-2B The Roach Motel opened for business on May 1, 2002. Its trial balance before adjustment on May 31 is as follows.

ROACH MOTEL
Trial Balance
May 31, 2002

Account Number		Debit	Credit
101	Cash	$ 2,500	
126	Supplies	1,900	
130	Prepaid Insurance	2,400	
140	Land	15,000	
141	Lodge	70,000	
149	Furniture	16,800	
201	Accounts Payable		$ 5,300
208	Unearned Rent		3,600
275	Mortgage Payable		35,000
301	Sara Sutton, Capital		60,000
429	Rent Revenue		9,200
610	Advertising Expense	500	
726	Salaries Expense	3,000	
732	Utilities Expense	1,000	
		$113,100	$113,100

In addition to those accounts listed on the trial balance, the chart of accounts for Roach Motel also contains the following accounts and account numbers: No. 142 Accumulated Depreciation—Lodge, No. 150 Accumulated Depreciation—Furniture, No. 212 Salaries Payable, No. 230 Interest Payable, No. 619 Depreciation Expense—Lodge, No. 621 Depreciation Expense—Furniture, No. 631 Supplies Expense, No. 718 Interest Expense, and No. 722 Insurance Expense.

Other data:

1. Insurance expires at the rate of $200 per month.
2. A count of supplies shows $900 of unused supplies on May 31.
3. Annual depreciation is $3,600 on the lodge and $3,000 on furniture.

4. The mortgage interest rate is 12%. (The mortgage was taken out on May 1.)
5. Unearned rent of $1,500 has been earned.
6. Salaries of $300 are accrued and unpaid at May 31.

Instructions

(a) Journalize the adjusting entries on May 31.
(b) Prepare a ledger using the three-column form of account. Enter the trial balance amounts and post the adjusting entries. (Use J1 as the posting reference.)
(c) Prepare an adjusted trial balance on May 31.
(d) Prepare an income statement and an owner's equity statement for the month of May and a balance sheet at May 31.

(c) Adj. trial balance $114,300
(d) Net income $3,800
Ending capital balance $63,800
Total assets $106,850

P3-3B Otaki Co. was organized on July 1, 2002. Quarterly financial statements are prepared. The unadjusted and adjusted trial balances as of September 30 are shown below.

Prepare adjusting entries and financial statements.
(SO 5, 6, 7)

OTAKI CO.
Trial Balance
September 30, 2002

	Unadjusted		Adjusted	
	Dr.	Cr.	Dr.	Cr.
Cash	$ 6,700		$ 6,700	
Accounts Receivable	400		1,100	
Prepaid Rent	1,500		900	
Supplies	1,200		1,000	
Equipment	15,000		15,000	
Accumulated Depreciation—Equipment				$ 350
Notes Payable		$ 5,000		5,000
Accounts Payable		1,510		1,510
Salaries Payable				400
Interest Payable				50
Unearned Rent		900		500
Yosuke Otaki, Capital		14,000		14,000
Yosuke Otaki, Drawing	600		600	
Commission Revenue		14,000		14,700
Rent Revenue		400		800
Salaries Expense	9,000		9,400	
Rent Expense	900		1,500	
Depreciation Expense			350	
Supplies Expense			200	
Utilities Expense	510		510	
Interest Expense			50	
	$35,810	$35,810	$37,310	$37,310

Instructions

(a) Journalize the adjusting entries that were made.
(b) Prepare an income statement and an owner's equity statement for the 3 months ending September 30 and a balance sheet at September 30.
(c) If the note bears interest at 12%, how many months has it been outstanding?

(b) Net income $3,490
Ending capital $16,890
Total assets $24,350

P3-4B A review of the ledger of Zieger Company at December 31, 2002, produces the following data pertaining to the preparation of annual adjusting entries.

Prepare adjusting entries
(SO 5, 6)

1. Prepaid Insurance $12,300. The company has separate insurance policies on its buildings and its motor vehicles. Policy B4564 on the building was purchased on July 1, 2001, for $9,000. The policy has a term of 3 years. Policy A2958 on the vehicles was purchased on January 1, 2002, for $4,800. This policy has a term of 2 years.

1. Insurance expense $5,400

2. Unearned Subscriptions $49,000. The company began selling magazine subscriptions in 2002 on an annual basis. The selling price of a subscription is $50. A review of subscription contracts reveals the following.

2. Subscription revenue $7,000

Subscription Date	Number of Subscriptions
October 1	200
November 1	300
December 1	480
	980

3. Interest expense $1,600

4. Salaries expense $3,240

3. Notes Payable $40,000. This balance consists of a note for 6 months at an annual interest rate of 12%, dated September 1.
4. Salaries Payable $0. There are eight salaried employees. Salaries are paid every Friday for the current week. Five employees receive a salary of $600 each per week, and three employees earn $800 each per week. December 31 is a Wednesday. Employees do not work weekends. All employees worked the last 3 days of December.

Instructions

Prepare the adjusting entries at December 31, 2002.

Journalize transactions and follow through accounting cycle to preparation of financial statements.
(SO 5, 6, 7)

P3-5B On November 1, 2002, the account balances of Thao Equipment Repair were as follows.

No.	Debits		No.	Credits	
101	Cash	$ 2,790	154	Accumulated Depreciation	$ 500
112	Accounts Receivable	2,510	201	Accounts Payable	2,100
126	Supplies	2,000	209	Unearned Service Revenue	1,400
153	Store Equipment	10,000	212	Salaries Payable	500
			301	P. Thao, Capital	12,800
		$17,300			$17,300

During November the following summary transactions were completed.

Nov. 8 Paid $1,100 for salaries due employees, of which $600 is for November.
10 Received $1,200 cash from customers on account.
12 Received $1,400 cash for services performed in November.
15 Purchased store equipment on account $3,000.
17 Purchased supplies on account $1,500.
20 Paid creditors on account $2,500.
22 Paid November rent $300.
25 Paid salaries $1,000.
27 Performed services on account and billed customers for services rendered $900.
29 Received $550 from customers for future service.

Adjustment data consist of:

1. Supplies on hand $1,600.
2. Accrued salaries payable $500.
3. Depreciation for the month is $120.
4. Unearned service revenue of $1,250 is earned.

Instructions

(a) Enter the November 1 balances in the ledger accounts.
(b) Journalize the November transactions.
(c) Post to the ledger accounts. Use J1 for the posting reference. Use the following accounts: No. 407 Service Revenue, No. 615 Depreciation Expense, No. 631 Supplies Expense, No. 726 Salaries Expense, and No. 729 Rent Expense.
(d) Prepare a trial balance at November 30.
(e) Journalize and post adjusting entries.
(f) Prepare an adjusted trial balance.
(g) Prepare an income statement and an owner's equity statement for November and a balance sheet at November 30.

(d) Trial balance $21,650
(f) Adj. trial balance $22,270
(g) Net loss $870; Ending capital $11,930; Total assets $17,230

BROADENING YOUR PERSPECTIVE

FINANCIAL REPORTING AND ANALYSIS

FINANCIAL REPORTING PROBLEM: Lands' End, Inc.

BYP3-1 The financial statements of **Lands' End** are presented in Appendix A at the end of this textbook.

Instructions

(a) Using the consolidated financial statements and related information, identify items that may result in adjusting entries for prepayments.

(b) Using the consolidated financial statements and related information, identify items that may result in adjusting entries for accruals.

(c) Using the Eleven-Year Consolidated Financial Summary, what has been the trend since 1990 for depreciation and amortization expense?

COMPARATIVE ANALYSIS PROBLEM: Lands' End vs. Abercrombie & Fitch

BYP3-2 **Lands' End's** financial statements are presented in Appendix A. **Abercrombie & Fitch's** financial statements are presented in Appendix B.

Instructions

Based on information contained in these financial statements, determine the following for each company.

(a) Net increase (decrease) in property, plant, and equipment (net) from 1999 to 2000.

(b) Increase (decrease) in selling, general, and administrative expenses from 1999 to 2000.

(c) Increase (decrease) in accounts payable from 1999 to 2000.

(d) Increase (decrease) in net income from 1999 to 2000.

(e) Increase (decrease) in cash and cash equivalents from 1999 to 2000.

INTERPRETING FINANCIAL STATEMENTS: A Global Focus

BYP3-3 **Hoescht Marion Roussel (HMR)** is one of the world's largest research-based pharmaceutical companies. It is headquartered in Frankfurt, Germany. It conducts research in Germany, France, and the United States. Its financial statements are based on the International Accounting Standards of the International Accounting Standards Committee.

Instructions

Answer each of the following questions.

(a) The statement of cash flows reports interest paid during 1998 of $344 million, while the income statement reports interest expense of $721 million. What might explain this difference? Give an example of the journal entry that you would expect to see that would cause this difference (ignore amounts).

(b) Among its liabilities, the company reports provisions for litigation and environmental protection. What types of litigation and environmental protection costs might this company incur? What are the possible points in time that litigation costs might be expensed? At what point do you think these costs should be expensed on the income statement in order to provide proper matching of revenues and expenses? What challenges to matching does litigation present?

(c) The notes to the company's financial statements state that the company records revenues "at the time of shipment of products or performance of services." Is this consistent with the revenue recognition practices described in this chapter? What considerations might you want to take into account in determining whether this is the appropriate approach to recognize revenues?

EXPLORING THE WEB

BYP3-4 A wealth of accounting-related information is available via the Internet. For example the Rutgers Accounting Web offers access to a great variety of sources.

Address: www.rutgers.edu/accounting/raw ***(or go to www.wiley.com/college/weygandt)***

Steps: Click on **Accounting Resources**, or click on **RAW's Features**. (*Note:* Once on this page, you may have to click on the **text only** box to access the available information.)

Instructions

(a) List the categories of information available through the **Accounting Resources** page.
(b) Select any one of these categories and briefly describe the types of information available.

CRITICAL THINKING

GROUP DECISION CASE

BYP3-5 The Happy Travel Court was organized on April 1, 2001, by Nancy Fox. Nancy is a good manager but a poor accountant. From the trial balance prepared by a part-time bookkeeper, Nancy prepared the following income statement for the quarter that ended March 31, 2002.

HAPPY TRAVEL COURT
Income Statement
For the Quarter Ended March 31, 2002

Revenues		
Travel court rental revenue		$95,000
Operating expenses		
Advertising	$ 5,200	
Wages	29,800	
Utilities	900	
Depreciation	800	
Repairs	4,000	
Total operating expenses		40,700
Net income		$54,300

Nancy knew that something was wrong with the statement because net income had never exceeded $20,000 in any one quarter. Knowing that you are an experienced accountant, she asks you to review the income statement and other data.

You first look at the trial balance. In addition to the account balances reported above in the income statement, the ledger contains the following additional selected balances at March 31, 2002.

Supplies	$ 5,200
Prepaid Insurance	7,200
Notes Payable	12,000

You then make inquiries and discover the following.

1. Travel court rental fees include advanced rentals for summer month occupancy $30,000.
2. There were $1,300 of supplies on hand at March 31.
3. Prepaid insurance resulted from the payment of a one-year policy on January 1, 2002.
4. The mail on April 1, 2002, brought the following bills: advertising for week of March 24, $110; repairs made March 10, $260; and utilities, $180.
5. There are four employees, who receive wages totaling $350 per day. At March 31, 2 days' wages have been incurred but not paid.
6. The note payable is a 3-month, 10% note dated January 1, 2002.

Instructions

With the class divided into groups, answer the following.

(a) Prepare a correct income statement for the quarter ended March 31, 2002.

(b) Explain to Nancy the generally accepted accounting principles that she did not recognize in preparing her income statement and their effect on her results.

COMMUNICATION ACTIVITY

BYP3-6 In reviewing the accounts of Marylee Co. at the end of the year, you discover that adjusting entries have not been made.

Instructions

Write a memo to Mary Lee Virgil, the owner of Marylee Co., that explains the following: the nature and purpose of adjusting entries, why adjusting entries are needed, and the types of adjusting entries that may be made.

ETHICS CASE

BYP3-7 Die Hard Company is a pesticide manufacturer. Its sales declined greatly this year due to the passage of legislation outlawing the sale of several of Die Hard's chemical pesticides. In the coming year, Die Hard will have environmentally safe and competitive chemicals to replace these discontinued products. Sales in the next year are expected to greatly exceed any prior year's. The decline in sales and profits appears to be a one-year aberration. But even so, the company president fears a large dip in the current year's profits. He believes that such a dip could cause a significant drop in the market price of Die Hard's stock and make the company a takeover target.

To avoid this possibility, the company president calls in Becky Freeman, controller, to discuss this period's year-end adjusting entries. He urges her to accrue every possible revenue and to defer as many expenses as possible. He says to Becky, "We need the revenues this year, and next year can easily absorb expenses deferred from this year. We can't let our stock price be hammered down!" Becky didn't get around to recording the adjusting entries until January 17, but she dated the entries December 31 as if they were recorded then. Becky also made every effort to comply with the president's request.

Instructions

(a) Who are the stakeholders in this situation?

(b) What are the ethical considerations of (1) the president's request and (2) Becky's dating the adjusting entries December 31?

(c) Can Becky accrue revenues and defer expenses and still be ethical?

Answers to Self-Study Questions

1. c **2.** a **3.** d **4.** d **5.** d **6.** c **7.** a **8.** b **9.** b **10.** c **11.** a

Answer to Lands' End Review It Question 4, p. 98

LANDS' END DIRECT MERCHANTS

2000 depreciation and amortization expense is $20.7 million; 1999 depreciation and amortization expense is $18.7 million.

Remember to go back to the Navigator box on the chapter-opening page and check off your completed work.

COMPLETION OF THE ACCOUNTING CYCLE

4

THE NAVIGATOR ✓

- Understand *Concepts for Review* ❑
- Read *Feature Story* ❑
- Scan *Study Objectives* ❑
- Read *Preview* ❑
- Read text and answer *Before You Go On* *p.* 140 ❑ *p.* 150 ❑ *p.* 156 ❑
- Work *Demonstration Problem* ❑
- Review *Summary of Study Objectives* ❑
- Answer *Self-Study Questions* ❑
- Complete *Assignments* ❑

CONCEPTS FOR REVIEW

Before studying this chapter, you should know or, if necessary, review:

a. How to apply the revenue recognition and matching principles. (Ch. 3, pp. 90–91)

b. How to make adjusting entries. (Ch. 3, pp. 91–103)

c. How to prepare an adjusted trial balance. (Ch. 3, p. 106)

d. How to prepare a balance sheet, income statement, and owner's equity statement. (Ch. 3, pp. 107–108)

☑ THE NAVIGATOR

FEATURE STORY

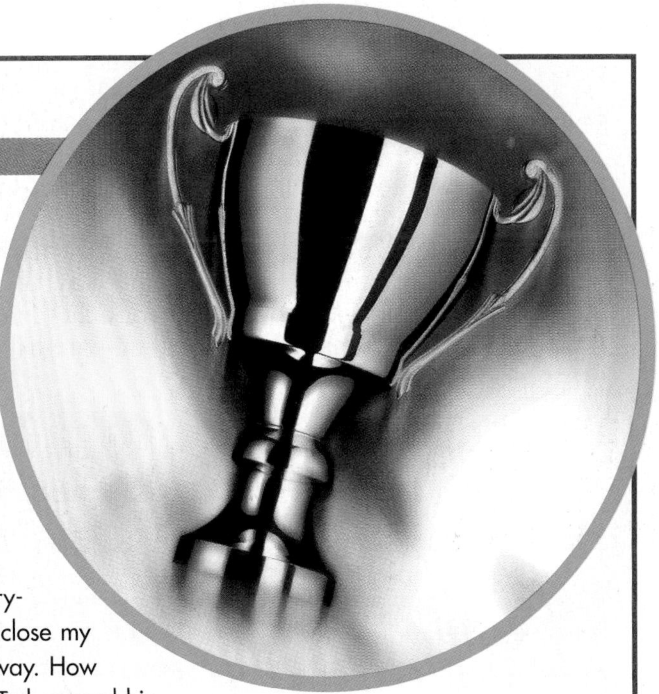

Everyone Likes to Win

When Ted Castle was a hockey coach at the University of Vermont, his players were self-motivated by their desire to win. Hockey was a game you either won or lost. But at **Rhino Foods, Inc.**, a specialty-bakery-foods company he founded in Burlington, Vermont, he discovered that manufacturing-line workers were not so self-motivated. Ted thought, what if he turned the food-making business into a game, with rules, strategies, and trophies?

Ted knew that in a game knowing the score is all-important. He felt that only if the employees know the score—know exactly how the business is doing daily, weekly, monthly—could he turn food-making into a game. But Rhino is a closely held, family-owned business, and its financial statements and profits were confidential. Should Ted open Rhino's books to the employees?

A consultant he was working with put Ted's concerns in perspective. The consultant said, "Imagine you're playing touch football. You play for an hour or two, and the whole time I'm sitting there with a book, keeping score. All of a sudden I blow the whistle, and I say, 'OK, that's it. Everybody go home.' I close my book and walk away. How would you feel?" Ted opened his books and revealed the financial statements to his employees.

The next step was to teach employees the rules and strategies of how to win at making food. The first lesson: "Your opponent at Rhino is expenses. You must cut and control expenses." Ted and his staff distilled those lessons into daily scorecards (production reports and income statements) that keep Rhino's employees up-to-date on the game. At noon each day, Ted posts the previous day's results at the entrance to the production room. Everyone checks whether they made or lost money on what they produced the day before. And it's not just an academic exercise; there's a bonus check for each employee at the end of every four-week "game" that meets profitability guidelines. Everyone can be a winner!

Rhino has flourished since the first game, three years ago. Employment has nearly tripled to 58, while both revenues and profits have grown by about 600 percent.

☑ THE NAVIGATOR

STUDY OBJECTIVES

After studying this chapter, you should be able to:

1. Prepare a work sheet.
2. Explain the process of closing the books.
3. Describe the content and purpose of a post-closing trial balance.
4. State the required steps in the accounting cycle.
5. Explain the approaches to preparing correcting entries.
6. Identify the sections of a classified balance sheet.

☑ THE NAVIGATOR

PREVIEW OF CHAPTER 4

As was true at **Rhino Foods, Inc.** financial statements can help employees understand what is happening in the business. In Chapter 3, we prepared financial statements directly from the adjusted trial balance. However, with so many details involved in the end-of-period accounting procedures, it is easy to make errors. Locating and correcting errors can cost much time and effort. One way to minimize errors in the records and to simplify the end-of-period procedures is to use a work sheet.

In this chapter we will explain the role of the work sheet in accounting as well as the remaining steps in the accounting cycle, most especially, the closing process, again using Pioneer Advertising Agency as an example. Then we will consider (1) correcting entries and (2) classified balance sheets. The content and organization of Chapter 4 are as follows.

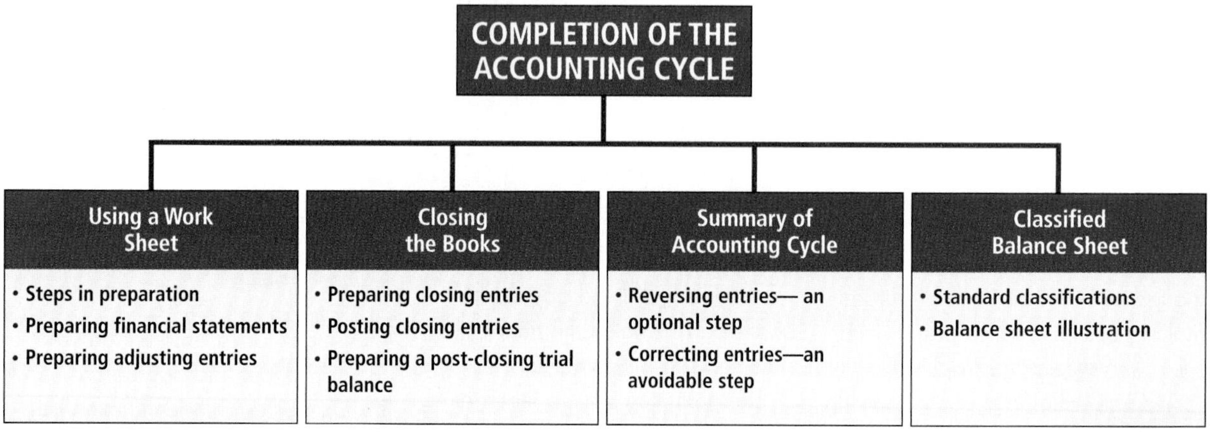

THE NAVIGATOR

USING A WORK SHEET

STUDY OBJECTIVE 1

Prepare a work sheet.

A **work sheet** is a multiple-column form that may be used in the adjustment process and in preparing financial statements. As its name suggests, the work sheet is a working tool. **A work sheet is not a permanent accounting record**; it is neither a journal nor a part of the general ledger. The work sheet is merely a device used to make it easier to prepare adjusting entries and the financial statements. In small companies with relatively few accounts and adjustments, a work sheet may not be needed. In large companies with numerous accounts and many adjustments, it is almost indispensable.

The basic form of a work sheet and the procedure (five steps) for preparing it are shown in Illustration 4-1. Each step must be performed in the prescribed sequence.

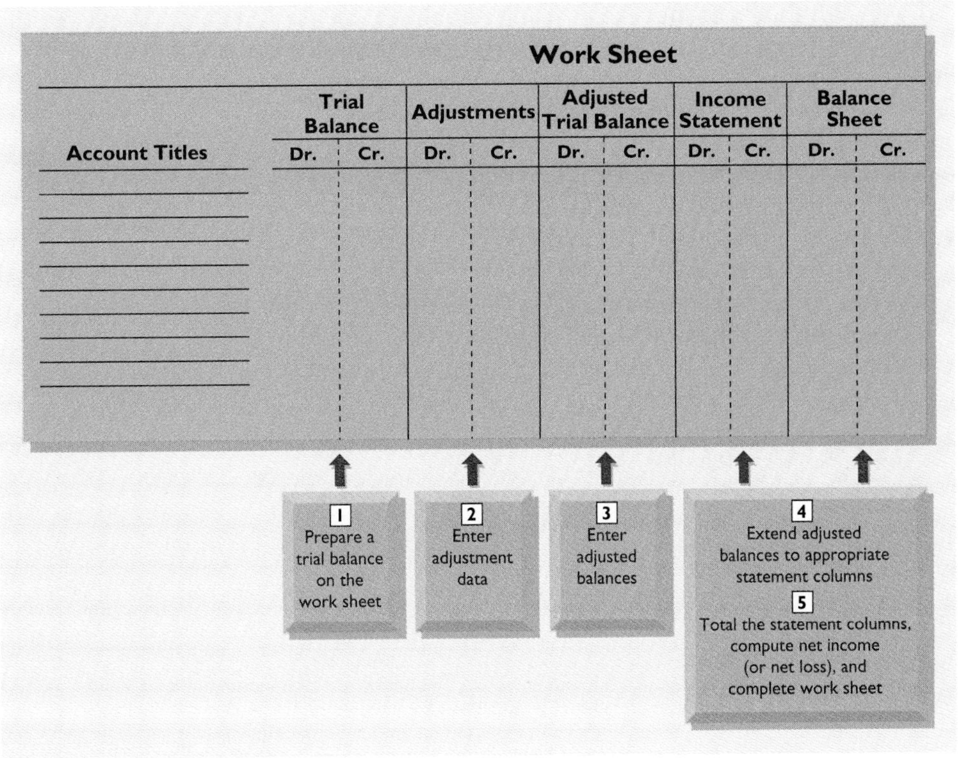

Work Sheet
Account Titles
Trial Balance
Adjustments
Adjusted Trial Balance
Income Statement
Balance Sheet
Dr. Cr. Dr. Cr. Dr. Cr. Dr. Cr. Dr. Cr.
1 Prepare a trial balance on the work sheet
2 Enter adjustment data
3 Enter adjusted balances
4 Extend adjusted balances to appropriate statement columns
5 Total the statement columns, compute net income (or net loss), and complete work sheet

Illustration 4-1

Form and procedure for a work sheet

The use of a work sheet is optional. When one is used, financial statements are prepared from the work sheet. The adjustments are entered in the work sheet columns and are then journalized and posted after the financial statements have been prepared. Thus, management and other interested parties can receive the financial statements at an earlier date when a work sheet is used.

STEPS IN PREPARING A WORK SHEET

We will use the October 31 trial balance and adjustment data of Pioneer Advertising in Chapter 3 to illustrate the preparation of a work sheet. Each step of the process is described below and demonstrated in Illustrations 4-2 and 4-3A, B, C, and D following page 138.

STEP 1. PREPARE A TRIAL BALANCE ON THE WORK SHEET. All ledger accounts with balances are entered in the account title space. Debit and credit amounts from the ledger are entered in the trial balance columns. The work sheet trial balance for Pioneer Advertising Agency is shown in Illustration 4-2.

STEP 2. ENTER THE ADJUSTMENTS IN THE ADJUSTMENTS COLUMNS. **Turn over the first transparency, Illustration 4-3A.** When a work sheet is used, all adjustments are entered in the adjustments columns. In entering the adjustments, applicable trial balance accounts should be used. If additional accounts are needed, they are inserted on the lines immediately below the trial balance totals. Each adjustment is indexed and keyed; this practice facilitates the journalizing of the adjusting entry in the general journal. **The adjustments are not journalized until after the work sheet is completed and the financial statements have been prepared.**

The adjustments for Pioneer Advertising Agency are the same as the adjustments illustrated on page 104. They are keyed in the adjustments columns of the work sheet as follows.

(a) An additional account Advertising Supplies Expense is debited $1,500 for the cost of supplies used, and Advertising Supplies is credited $1,500.
(b) An additional account Insurance Expense is debited $50 for the insurance that has expired, and Prepaid Insurance is credited $50.
(c) Two additional depreciation accounts are needed. Depreciation Expense is debited $40 for the month's depreciation, and Accumulated Depreciation—Office Equipment is credited $40.
(d) Unearned Revenue is debited $400 for services provided, and Service Revenue is credited $400.
(e) An additional account Accounts Receivable is debited $200 for services provided but not billed, and Service Revenue is credited $200.
(f) Two additional accounts relating to interest are needed. Interest Expense is debited $50 for accrued interest, and Interest Payable is credited $50.
(g) Salaries Expense is debited $1,200 for accrued salaries, and an additional account Salaries Payable is credited $1,200.

Note in the illustration that after all the adjustments have been entered, the adjustments columns are totaled and the equality of the column totals is proved.

STEP 3. ENTER ADJUSTED BALANCES IN THE ADJUSTED TRIAL BALANCE COLUMNS. **Turn over the second transparency, Illustration 4-3B.** The adjusted balance of an account is obtained by combining the amounts entered in the first four columns of the work sheet for each account. For example, the Prepaid Insurance account in the trial balance columns has a $600 debit balance and a $50 credit in the adjustments columns. The result is a $550 debit balance recorded in the adjusted trial balance columns. **For each account on the work sheet, the amount in the adjusted trial balance columns is the account balance that will appear in the ledger after the adjusting entries have been journalized and posted.** The balances in these columns are the same as those in the adjusted trial balance in Illustration 3-19 (page 106).

After all account balances have been entered in the adjusted trial balance columns, the columns are totaled and their equality is proved. The agreement of the column totals facilitates the completion of the work sheet. If these columns are not in agreement, the financial statement columns will not balance and the financial statements will be incorrect.

HELPFUL HINT
Every adjusted trial balance amount must be extended to one of the four statement columns. Debit amounts go to debit columns and credit amounts go to credit columns.

STEP 4. EXTEND ADJUSTED TRIAL BALANCE AMOUNTS TO APPROPRIATE FINANCIAL STATEMENT COLUMNS. **Turn over the third transparency, Illustration 4-3C.** The fourth step is to extend adjusted trial balance amounts to the income statement and balance sheet columns of the work sheet. Balance sheet accounts are entered in the appropriate balance sheet debit and credit columns. For instance, Cash is entered in the balance sheet debit column, and Notes Payable is entered in the credit column. Accumulated Depreciation is extended to the balance sheet credit column. The reason is that accumulated depreciation is a contra-asset account with a credit balance.

Because the work sheet does not have columns for the owner's equity statement, the balance in owner's capital is extended to the balance sheet credit column. In addition, the balance in owner's drawing is extended to the balance sheet debit column because it is an owner's equity account with a debit balance.

The expense and revenue accounts such as Salaries Expense and Service Revenue are entered in the appropriate income statement columns.

All of these extensions are shown in Illustration 4-3C.

STEP 5. TOTAL THE STATEMENT COLUMNS, COMPUTE THE NET INCOME (OR NET LOSS), AND COMPLETE THE WORK SHEET. **Turn over the fourth transparency, Illustration 4-3D.** Each of the financial statement columns must be totaled. The net income or loss for the period is then found by computing the difference between the totals of the two income statement columns. If total credits exceed total debits, net income has resulted. In such a case, as shown in Illustration 4-3D, the words "Net Income" are inserted in the account titles space. The amount then is entered in the income statement debit column and the balance sheet credit column. **The debit amount balances the income statement columns, and the credit amount balances the balance sheet columns.** In addition, the credit in the balance sheet column indicates the increase in owner's equity resulting from net income.

If, instead, total debits in the income statement columns exceed total credits, a net loss has occurred. The amount of the net loss is entered in the income statement credit column and the balance sheet debit column.

After the net income or net loss has been entered, new column totals are determined. The totals shown in the debit and credit income statement columns will match. The totals shown in the debit and credit balance sheet columns will also match. If either the income statement columns or the balance sheet columns are not equal after the net income or net loss has been entered, an error has been made in the work sheet. The completed work sheet for Pioneer Advertising Agency is shown in Illustration 4-3D.

HELPFUL HINT
All pairs of columns must balance for a work sheet to be complete.

TECHNOLOGY IN ACTION

The work sheet can be computerized using an electronic spreadsheet program. The Excel supplement for this textbook is one of the most popular versions of such spreadsheet packages. With a program like Excel, you can produce any type of work sheet (accounting or otherwise) that you could produce with paper and pencil on a columnar pad. The tremendous advantage of an electronic work sheet over the paper-and-pencil version is the ability to change selected data easily. When data are changed, the computer updates the balance of your computations instantly. More specific applications of electronic spreadsheets will be noted as we proceed.

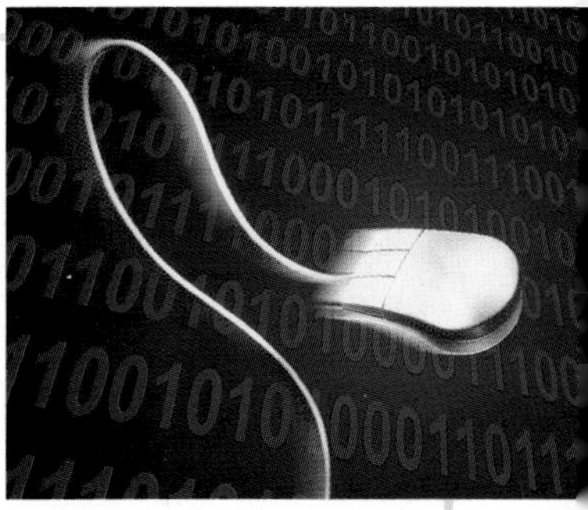

PREPARING FINANCIAL STATEMENTS FROM A WORK SHEET

After a work sheet has been completed, all the data that are required for the preparation of financial statements are at hand. The income statement is prepared from the income statement columns. The balance sheet and owner's equity statement are prepared from the balance sheet columns. The financial statements prepared from the work sheet for Pioneer Advertising Agency are shown in Illustration 4-4. At this point, adjusting entries have not been journalized and posted. Therefore, the ledger does not support all financial statement amounts.

Accounting Cycle Tutorial—Preparing Financial Statements and Closing the Books

The amount shown for owner's capital on the work sheet is the account balance **before considering drawings and net income (or loss).** When there have been no additional investments of capital by the owner during the period, this amount is the balance at the beginning of the period.

Using a work sheet, financial statements can be prepared before adjusting entries are journalized and posted. **However, the completed work sheet is not a substitute for formal financial statements.** Data in the financial statement columns of the work sheet are not properly arranged for statement purposes. Also, as noted above, the financial statement presentation for some accounts differs from their statement columns on the work sheet. **A work sheet is essentially a working tool of the accountant; it is not distributed to management and other parties.**

(**Note:** Text continues on page 139, following acetate overlays.)

Illustration 4-2

Preparing a trial balance

PIONEER ADVERTISING AGENCY
Work Sheet
For the Month Ended October 31, 2002

Account Titles	Trial Balance Dr.	Trial Balance Cr.	Adjustments Dr.	Adjustments Cr.	Adjusted Trial Balance Dr.	Adjusted Trial Balance Cr.	Income Statement Dr.	Income Statement Cr.	Balance Sheet Dr.	Balance Sheet Cr.
Cash	15,200									
Advertising Supplies	2,500									
Prepaid Insurance	600									
Office Equipment	5,000									
Notes Payable		5,000								
Accounts Payable		2,500								
Unearned Revenue		1,200								
C. R. Byrd, Capital		10,000								
C. R. Byrd, Drawing	500									
Service Revenue		10,000								
Salaries Expense	4,000									
Rent Expense	900									
Totals	28,700	28,700								

Include all accounts with balances from ledger.

Trial balance amounts are taken directly from ledger accounts.

Illustration 4-3A

Entering the adjustments in the adjustments columns

Add additional accounts as needed to complete the adjustments:

(a) Supplies Used.
(b) Insurance Expired.
(c) Depreciation Expensed.
(d) Service Revenue Earned.
(e) Service Revenue Accrued.
(f) Interest Accrued.
(g) Salaries Accrued.

Enter adjustment amounts in appropriate columns, and use letters to cross-reference the debit and credit adjustments.

Total adjustments columns and check for equality.

Illustration 4-3C

Extending the adjusted trial balance amounts to appropriate financial statement columns

Extend all revenue and expense account balances to the income statement columns.
Extend all asset and liability account balances, as well as owner's capital and drawing account balances, to the balance sheet columns.

Illustration

Computing
net loss and
work sheet

Illustration

Computing
net loss and
work sheet

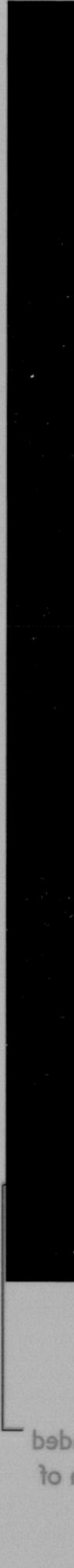

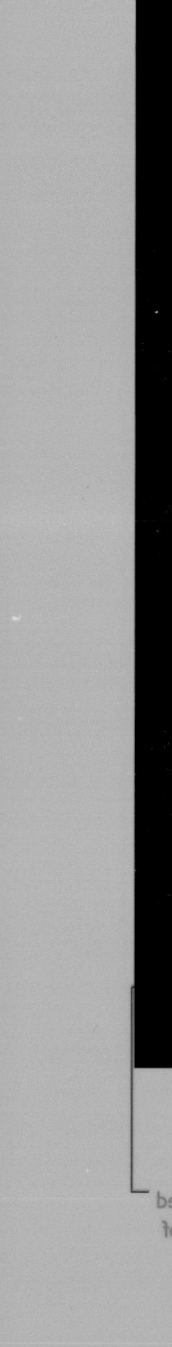

tended
umn of
t
ss
ed
mn.)

Illustration 4-4

Financial statements from a work sheet

PIONEER ADVERTISING AGENCY
Income Statement
For the Month Ended October 31, 2002

Revenues		
Service revenue		$10,600
Expenses		
Salaries expense	$5,200	
Advertising supplies expense	1,500	
Rent expense	900	
Insurance expense	50	
Interest expense	50	
Depreciation expense	40	
Total expenses		7,740
Net income		$ 2,860

PIONEER ADVERTISING AGENCY
Owner's Equity Statement
For the Month Ended October 31, 2002

C. R. Byrd, Capital, October 1		$ -0-
Add: Investments	$10,000	
Net income	2,860	12,860
		12,860
Less: Drawings		500
C. R. Byrd, Capital, October 31		$12,360

PIONEER ADVERTISING AGENCY
Balance Sheet
October 31, 2002

Assets		
Cash		$15,200
Accounts receivable		200
Advertising supplies		1,000
Prepaid insurance		550
Office equipment	$5,000	
Less: Accumulated depreciation	40	4,960
Total assets		$21,910
Liabilities and Owner's Equity		
Liabilities		
Notes payable		$ 5,000
Accounts payable		2,500
Interest payable		50
Unearned revenue		800
Salaries payable		1,200
Total liabilities		9,550
Owner's equity		
C. R. Byrd, Capital		12,360
Total liabilities and owner's equity		$21,910

PREPARING ADJUSTING ENTRIES FROM A WORK SHEET

A work sheet is not a journal, and it cannot be used as a basis for posting to ledger accounts. To adjust the accounts, it is necessary to journalize the adjustments and post them to the ledger. **The adjusting entries are prepared from the adjustments columns of the work sheet.** The reference letters in the adjustments columns and the explanations of the adjustments at the bottom of the work sheet help identify the adjusting entries. However, writing the explanation to the adjustments at the bottom of the work sheet is not required. As indicated previously, the journalizing and posting of adjusting entries **follows** the preparation of financial statements when a work sheet is used. The adjusting entries on October 31 for Pioneer Advertising Agency are the same as those shown in Illustration 3-17 (page 104).

BEFORE YOU GO ON...

REVIEW IT

1. What are the five steps in preparing a work sheet?
2. How is net income or net loss shown in a work sheet?
3. How does a work sheet relate to preparing financial statements and adjusting entries?

DO IT

Susan Elbe is preparing a work sheet. Explain to Susan how the following adjusted trial balance accounts should be extended to the financial statement columns of the work sheet: Cash; Accumulated Depreciation; Accounts Payable; Julie Kerr, Drawing; Service Revenue; and Salaries Expense.

ACTION PLAN

- Extend asset balances to the balance sheet debit column. Extend liability balances to the balance sheet credit column. Extend accumulated depreciation to the balance sheet credit column.
- Extend the drawing account to the balance sheet debit column.
- Extend expenses to the income statement debit column.
- Extend revenue accounts to the income statement credit column.

SOLUTION

Income statement debit column—Salaries Expense
Income statement credit column—Service Revenue
Balance sheet debit column—Cash; Julie Kerr, Drawing
Balance sheet credit column—Accumulated Depreciation; Accounts Payable

As indicated in the Technology in Action box on page 137, the work sheet is an ideal application for electronic spreadsheet software like Microsoft Excel and LOTUS 1–2–3.

Related exercise material: BE4-1, BE4-2, BE4-3, E4-1, E4-2, E4-4, and E4-5.

THE NAVIGATOR

CLOSING THE BOOKS

STUDY OBJECTIVE 2

Explain the process of closing the books.

At the end of the accounting period, the accounts are made ready for the next period. This is called **closing the books**. In closing the books, it is necessary to distinguish between temporary and permanent accounts. **Temporary** or **nominal accounts** relate only to a given accounting period. They include all income statement accounts and owner's drawing. All temporary accounts are closed. In contrast, **permanent** or **real accounts** relate to one or more future accounting periods. They consist of all balance sheet accounts, including owner's capital. Permanent accounts are not closed. Instead, their balances are carried forward into the next accounting period. Illustration 4-5 identifies the accounts in each category.

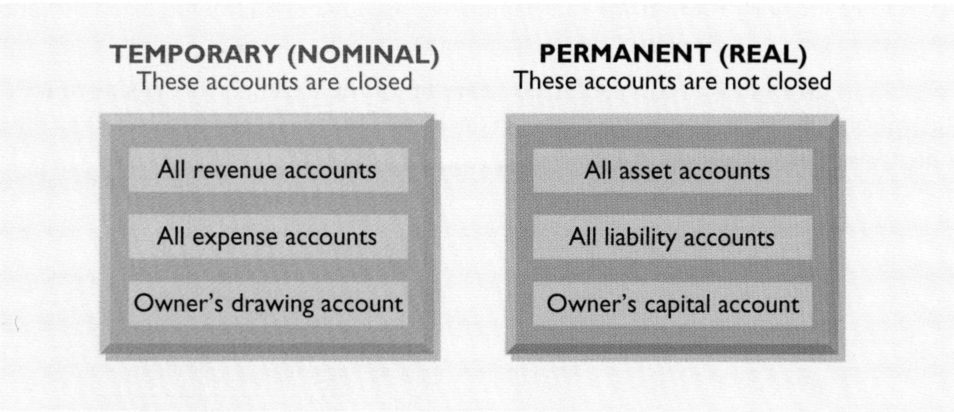

TEMPORARY (NOMINAL)
These accounts are closed
All revenue accounts
All expense accounts
Owner's drawing account
PERMANENT (REAL)
These accounts are not closed
All asset accounts
All liability accounts
Owner's capital account

Illustration 4-5
Temporary versus permanent accounts

HELPFUL HINT
A contra asset account, such as accumulated depreciation, is a permanent account also.

PREPARING CLOSING ENTRIES

At the end of the accounting period, the temporary account balances are transferred to the permanent owner's equity account, owner's capital, through the preparation of closing entries.[1] Closing entries formally recognize in the ledger the transfer of net income (or net loss) and owner's drawing to owner's capital. The results of these entries are shown in the owner's equity statement. **These entries also produce a zero balance in each temporary account. These accounts are then ready to accumulate data in the next accounting period separate from the data of prior periods.** Permanent accounts are not closed.

Journalizing and posting closing entries is a required step in the accounting cycle. (See Illustration 4-12 on page 148.) This step is performed after financial statements have been prepared. In contrast to the steps in the cycle that you have already studied, closing entries are generally journalized and posted **only at the end of a company's annual accounting period**. This practice facilitates the preparation of annual financial statements because all temporary accounts will contain data for the entire year.

In preparing closing entries, each income statement account could be closed directly to owner's capital. However, to do so would result in excessive detail in the permanent owner's capital account. Instead, the revenue and expense accounts are closed to another temporary account, Income Summary; only the net income or net loss is transferred from this account to owner's capital.

Closing entries are journalized in the general journal. A center caption entitled Closing Entries, inserted in the journal between the last adjusting entry and the first closing entry, identifies these entries. Then the closing entries are posted to the ledger accounts.

Closing entries may be prepared directly from the adjusted balances in the ledger, from the income statement and balance sheet columns of the work sheet, or from the income and owner's equity statements. Separate closing entries could be prepared for each nominal account, but the following four entries accomplish the desired result more efficiently:

1. Debit each revenue account for its balance, and credit Income Summary for total revenues.
2. Debit Income Summary for total expenses, and credit each expense account for its balance.
3. Debit Income Summary and credit Owner's Capital for the amount of net income.

---
[1] Closing entries for a partnership and for a corporation are explained in Chapters 13 and 14, respectively.

HELPFUL HINT
Owner's Drawing is closed directly to Capital and *not* to Income Summary because Owner's Drawing is not an expense.

4. Debit Owner's Capital for the balance in the Owner's Drawing account, and credit Owner's Drawing for the same amount.

The four entries are referenced in the diagram of the closing process shown in Illustration 4-6 and in the journal entries in Illustration 4-7. The posting of closing entries is shown in Illustration 4-8.

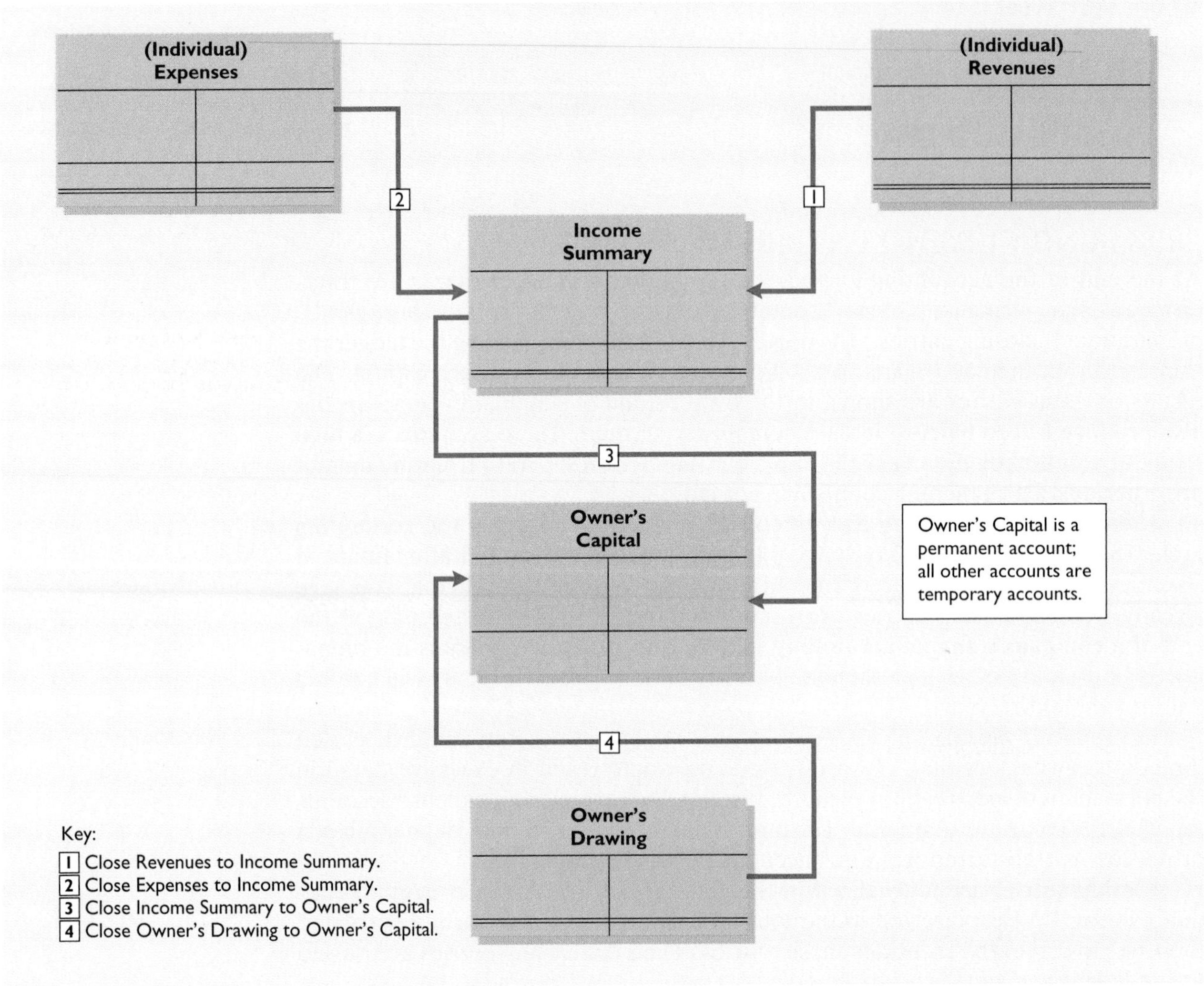
(Individual) Expenses
(Individual) Revenues
Income Summary
Owner's Capital
Owner's Drawing
1
2
3
4
Owner's Capital is a permanent account; all other accounts are temporary accounts.
Key:
1 Close Revenues to Income Summary.
2 Close Expenses to Income Summary.
3 Close Income Summary to Owner's Capital.
4 Close Owner's Drawing to Owner's Capital.

Illustration 4-6
Diagram of closing process—proprietorship

If there were a net loss because expenses exceeded revenues, entry 3 in Illustration 4-6 would be reversed: Credit Income Summary and debit Owner's Capital.

ACCOUNTING IN ACTION *Business Insight*

Until Sam Walton had opened twenty Wal-Mart stores, he used what he called the "ESP method" of closing the books. ESP was a pretty basic method: If the books didn't balance, Walton calculated the amount by which they were off and entered that amount under the heading ESP—which stood for "Error Some Place." As Walton noted, "It really sped things along when it came time to close those books."

SOURCE: Sam Walton, *Made in America* (New York: Doubleday Publishing Company, 1992), p. 53.

Closing Entries Illustrated

In practice, closing entries are generally prepared only at the end of the annual accounting period. However, to illustrate the journalizing and posting of closing entries, we will assume that Pioneer Advertising Agency closes its books monthly. The closing entries at October 31 are shown in Illustration 4-7.

Illustration 4-7

Closing entries journalized

GENERAL JOURNAL J3

Date	Account Titles and Explanation	Ref.	Debit	Credit
	Closing Entries			
	(1)			
2002				
Oct. 31	Service Revenue	400	10,600	
	Income Summary	350		10,600
	(To close revenue account)			
	(2)			
31	Income Summary	350	7,740	
	Advertising Supplies Expense	631		1,500
	Depreciation Expense	711		40
	Insurance Expense	722		50
	Salaries Expense	726		5,200
	Rent Expense	729		900
	Interest Expense	905		50
	(To close expense accounts)			
	(3)			
31	Income Summary	350	2,860	
	C. R. Byrd, Capital	301		2,860
	(To close net income to capital)			
	(4)			
31	C. R. Byrd, Capital	301	500	
	C. R. Byrd, Drawing	306		500
	(To close drawings to capital)			

HELPFUL HINT
Income Summary is a very descriptive title: total revenues are closed to Income Summary; total expenses are closed to Income Summary; and the balance in the Income Summary is a net income or net loss.

Note that the amounts for Income Summary in entries (1) and (2) are the totals of the income statement credit and debit columns, respectively, in the work sheet.

A couple of cautions in preparing closing entries: (1) Avoid unintentionally doubling the revenue and expense balances rather than zeroing them. (2) Do not close owner's drawing through the Income Summary account. **Owner's drawing is not an expense, and it is not a factor in determining net income.**

POSTING CLOSING ENTRIES

The posting of the closing entries and the ruling of the accounts are shown in Illustration 4-8. Note that all temporary accounts have zero balances after posting the closing entries. In addition, you should realize that the balance in owner's capital (C. R. Byrd, Capital) represents the total equity of the owner at the end of the accounting period. This balance is shown on the balance sheet and is the ending capital reported on the owner's equity statement, as shown in Illustration 4-4 on page 139. **The Income Summary account is used only in closing**. No entries are journalized and posted to this account during the year.

As part of the closing process, the **temporary accounts** (revenues, expenses, and owner's drawing) in T-account form are totaled, balanced, and double-ruled as shown in Illustration 4-8. The **permanent accounts** (assets, liabilities, and owner's capital) are not closed: A single rule is drawn beneath the current period entries, and the account balance carried forward to the next period is entered below the single rule. (For example, see C. R. Byrd, Capital.)

HELPFUL HINT
The balance in Income Summary before it is closed must equal the net income or net loss for the period.

Illustration 4-8

Posting of closing entries

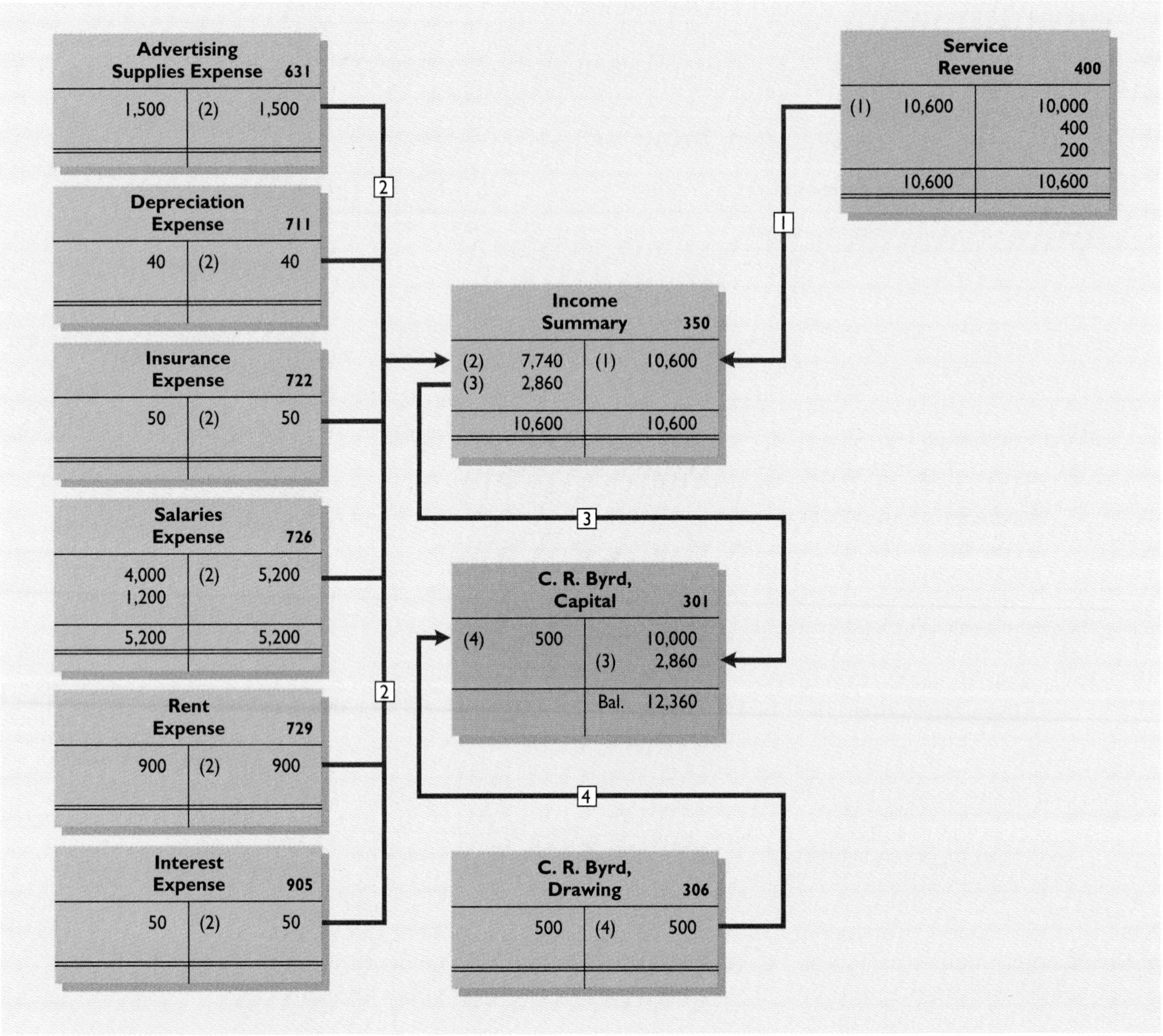

ACCOUNTING IN ACTION *Business Insight*

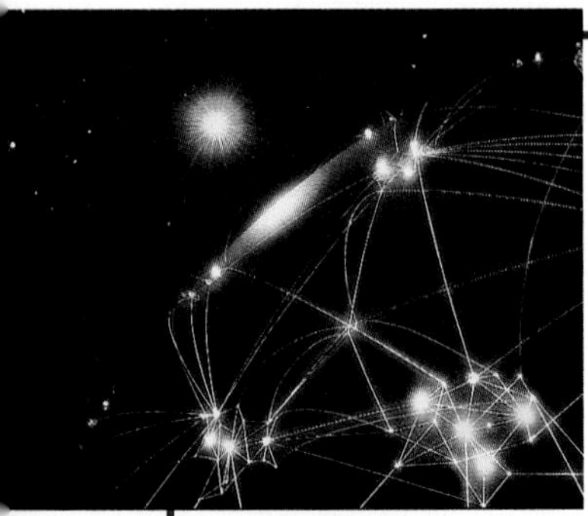

Technology has dramatically changed the accounting process. When Larry Carter became chief financial officer of **Cisco Systems**, closing the quarterly accounts would take up to ten days. Within four years he got it down to two days and halved the cost of finance, to 1 percent of sales. Now he is aiming to be able to do a "virtual close"—closing within a day on any day in the quarter.

This is not just showing off. Knowing exactly where you are all of the time, says Mr. Carter, allows you to respond faster than your competitors. But it also means that the 600 people who used to spend 10 days a quarter tracking transactions can now be more usefully employed on things such as mining data for business intelligence.

SOURCE: Excerpted from "Business and the Internet," *The Economist*, June 26, 1999, p. 12.

PREPARING A POST-CLOSING TRIAL BALANCE

STUDY OBJECTIVE 3

Describe the content and purpose of a post-closing trial balance.

After all closing entries have been journalized and posted, another trial balance, called a **post-closing trial balance**, is prepared from the ledger. The post-closing trial balance lists permanent accounts and their balances after closing entries have been journalized and posted. **The purpose of this trial balance is to prove the equality of the permanent account balances that are carried forward into the next accounting period.** Since all temporary accounts will have zero balances, **the post-closing trial balance will contain only permanent—balance sheet—accounts.**

The procedure for preparing a post-closing trial balance again consists entirely of listing the accounts and their balances. The post-closing trial balance for Pioneer Advertising Agency is shown in Illustration 4-9. These balances are the same as those reported in the company's balance sheet in Illustration 4-4.

Illustration 4-9

Post-closing trial balance

PIONEER ADVERTISING AGENCY
Post-Closing Trial Balance
October 31, 2002

	Debit	Credit
Cash	$15,200	
Accounts Receivable	200	
Advertising Supplies	1,000	
Prepaid Insurance	550	
Office Equipment	5,000	
Accumulated Depreciation—Office Equipment		$ 40
Notes Payable		5,000
Accounts Payable		2,500
Unearned Revenue		800
Salaries Payable		1,200
Interest Payable		50
C. R. Byrd, Capital		12,360
	$21,950	**$21,950**

HELPFUL HINT

Will total debits in a post-closing trial balance equal total assets on the balance sheet? Answer: No. Accumulated depreciation is deducted from assets on the balance sheet but added to the credit balance total in a post-closing trial balance.

The post-closing trial balance is prepared from the permanent accounts in the ledger. The permanent accounts of Pioneer Advertising are shown in the general ledger in Illustration 4-10 on page 146. Remember that the balance of each permanent account is computed after every posting. Therefore, no additional work on these accounts is needed as part of the closing process.

A post-closing trial balance provides evidence that the journalizing and posting of closing entries have been properly completed. It also shows that the accounting equation is in balance at the end of the accounting period. However, like the trial balance, it does not prove that all transactions have been recorded or that the ledger is correct. For example, the post-closing trial balance will balance if a transaction is not journalized and posted or if a transaction is journalized and posted twice.

The remaining accounts in the general ledger are temporary accounts (shown in Illustration 4-11 on page 147). After the closing entries are correctly posted, each temporary account has a zero balance. These accounts are double-ruled to finalize the closing process.

(Permanent Accounts Only)

GENERAL LEDGER

Cash — No. 101

Date	Explanation	Ref.	Debit	Credit	Balance
2002					
Oct. 1		J1	10,000		10,000
2		J1	1,200		11,200
3		J1		900	10,300
4		J1		600	9,700
20		J1		500	9,200
26		J1		4,000	5,200
31		J1	10,000		**15,200**

Accounts Receivable — No. 112

Date	Explanation	Ref.	Debit	Credit	Balance
2002					
Oct. 31	Adj. entry	J2	**200**		**200**

Advertising Supplies — No. 126

Date	Explanation	Ref.	Debit	Credit	Balance
2002					
Oct. 5		J1	2,500		2,500
31	Adj. entry	J2		**1,500**	**1,000**

Prepaid Insurance — No. 130

Date	Explanation	Ref.	Debit	Credit	Balance
2002					
Oct. 4		J1	600		600
31	Adj. entry	J2		**50**	**550**

Office Equipment — No. 157

Date	Explanation	Ref.	Debit	Credit	Balance
2002					
Oct. 1		J1	5,000		**5,000**

Accumulated Depreciation—Office Equipment — No. 158

Date	Explanation	Ref.	Debit	Credit	Balance
2002					
Oct. 31	Adj. entry	J2		**40**	**40**

Notes Payable — No. 200

Date	Explanation	Ref.	Debit	Credit	Balance
2002					
Oct. 1		J1		5,000	**5,000**

Accounts Payable — No. 201

Date	Explanation	Ref.	Debit	Credit	Balance
2002					
Oct. 5		J1		2,500	**2,500**

Unearned Revenue — No. 209

Date	Explanation	Ref.	Debit	Credit	Balance
2002					
Oct. 2		J1		1,200	1,200
31	Adj. entry	J2	400		**800**

Salaries Payable — No. 212

Date	Explanation	Ref.	Debit	Credit	Balance
2002					
Oct. 31	Adj. entry	J2		**1,200**	**1,200**

Interest Payable — No. 230

Date	Explanation	Ref.	Debit	Credit	Balance
2002					
Oct. 31	Adj. entry	J2		**50**	**50**

C. R. Byrd, Capital — No. 301

Date	Explanation	Ref.	Debit	Credit	Balance
2002					
Oct. 1		J1		10,000	10,000
31	**Closing entry**	**J3**		**2,860**	**12,860**
31	**Closing entry**	**J3**	**500**		**12,360**

Note: The permanent accounts for Pioneer Advertising Agency are shown here; the temporary accounts are shown in Illustration 4-11. Both permanent and temporary accounts are part of the general ledger; they are segregated here to aid in learning.

Illustration 4-10

General ledger, permanent accounts

SUMMARY OF THE ACCOUNTING CYCLE

STUDY OBJECTIVE 4

State the required steps in the accounting cycle.

The steps in the accounting cycle are shown in Illustration 4-12 on page 148. From the graphic you can see that the cycle begins with the analysis of business transactions and ends with the preparation of a post-closing trial balance. The steps in the cycle are performed in sequence and are repeated in each accounting period.

(Temporary Accounts Only)

GENERAL LEDGER

C. R. Byrd, Drawing — No. 306

Date	Explanation	Ref.	Debit	Credit	Balance
2002					
Oct. 20		J1	500		500
31	**Closing entry**	**J3**		**500**	**-0-**

Income Summary — No. 350

Date	Explanation	Ref.	Debit	Credit	Balance
2002					
Oct. 31	**Closing entry**	**J3**		**10,600**	**10,600**
31	**Closing entry**	**J3**	**7,740**		**2,860**
31	**Closing entry**	**J3**	**2,860**		**-0-**

Service Revenue — No. 400

Date	Explanation	Ref.	Debit	Credit	Balance
2002					
Oct. 31		J1		10,000	10,000
31	Adj. entry	J2		**400**	10,400
31	Adj. entry	J2		**200**	10,600
31	**Closing entry**	**J3**	**10,600**		**-0-**

Advertising Supplies Expense — No. 631

Date	Explanation	Ref.	Debit	Credit	Balance
2002					
Oct. 31	Adj. entry	J2	**1,500**		1,500
31	**Closing entry**	**J3**		**1,500**	**-0-**

Depreciation Expense — No. 711

Date	Explanation	Ref.	Debit	Credit	Balance
2002					
Oct. 31	Adj. entry	J2	**40**		40
31	**Closing entry**	**J3**		**40**	**-0-**

Insurance Expense — No. 722

Date	Explanation	Ref.	Debit	Credit	Balance
2002					
Oct. 31	Adj. entry	J2	**50**		50
31	**Closing entry**	**J3**		**50**	**-0-**

Salaries Expense — No. 726

Date	Explanation	Ref.	Debit	Credit	Balance
2002					
Oct. 26		J1	4,000		4,000
31	Adj. entry	J2	**1,200**		5,200
31	**Closing entry**	**J3**		**5,200**	**-0-**

Rent Expense — No. 729

Date	Explanation	Ref.	Debit	Credit	Balance
2002					
Oct. 3		J1	900		900
31	**Closing entry**	**J3**		**900**	**-0-**

Interest Expense — No. 905

Date	Explanation	Ref.	Debit	Credit	Balance
2002					
Oct. 31	Adj. entry	J2	**50**		50
31	**Closing entry**	**J3**		**50**	**-0-**

Note: The temporary accounts for Pioneer Advertising Agency are shown here; the permanent accounts are shown in Illustration 4-10. Both permanent and temporary accounts are part of the general ledger; they are segregated here to aid in learning.

Illustration 4-11

General ledger, temporary accounts

Steps 1–3 may occur daily during the accounting period, as explained in Chapter 2. Steps 4–7 are performed on a periodic basis, such as monthly, quarterly, or annually. Steps 8 and 9, closing entries, and a post-closing trial balance, are usually prepared only at the end of a company's **annual** accounting period.

There are also two optional steps in the accounting cycle. As you have seen, a work sheet may be used in preparing adjusting entries and financial statements. In addition, reversing entries may be used as explained below.

REVERSING ENTRIES—AN OPTIONAL STEP

Some accountants prefer to reverse certain adjusting entries at the beginning of a new accounting period. A **reversing entry** is made at the beginning of the next accounting period. It is the exact opposite of the adjusting entry made in the previous period. **The preparation of reversing entries is an optional bookkeeping procedure that is not a required step in the accounting cycle.** Accordingly, we have chosen to cover this topic in an appendix at the end of the chapter.

Illustration 4-12

Steps in the accounting cycle

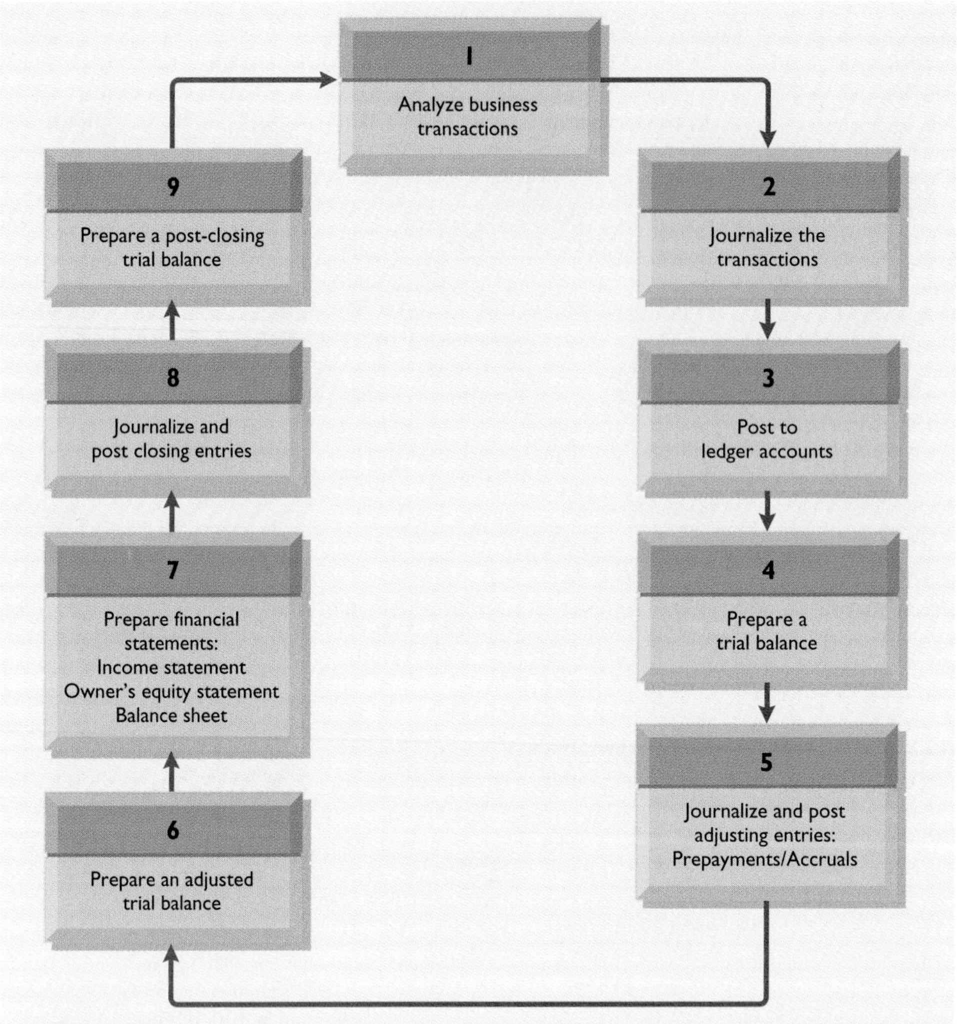

Optional steps: If a work sheet is prepared, steps 4, 5, and 6 are incorporated in the work sheet. If reversing entries are prepared, they occur between steps 9 and 1 as discussed on page 147.

CORRECTING ENTRIES—AN AVOIDABLE STEP

STUDY OBJECTIVE 5

Explain the approaches to preparing correcting entries.

Unfortunately, errors may occur in the recording process. Errors should be corrected **as soon as they are discovered** by journalizing and posting **correcting entries**. If the accounting records are free of errors, no correcting entries are necessary.

You should recognize several differences between correcting entries and adjusting entries. First, adjusting entries are an integral part of the accounting cycle. Correcting entries, on the other hand, are unnecessary if the records are free of errors. Second, **adjustments are journalized and posted only at the end of an accounting period. In contrast, correcting entries are made whenever an error is discovered.** Finally, adjusting entries always affect at least one balance sheet account and one income statement account. In contrast, correcting entries may involve any combination of accounts in need of correction. **Correcting entries must be posted before closing entries.**

To determine the correcting entry, it is useful to compare the incorrect entry with the correct entry. Doing so helps identify the accounts and amounts that should—and should not—be corrected. After comparison, a correcting entry is made to correct the accounts. This approach is illustrated in the following two cases.

ETHICS NOTE

Citigroup once reported a correcting entry reducing reported revenue by $23 million, while firing 11 employees. Company officials did not specify why the employees had apparently intentionally inflated the revenue figures, although it was noted that their bonuses were tied to their unit's performance.

CASE 1. On May 10, a $50 cash collection on account from a customer is journalized and posted as a debit to Cash $50 and a credit to Service Revenue $50. The error is discovered on May 20, when the customer pays the remaining balance in full.

Illustration 4-13
Comparison of entries

Incorrect Entry (May 10)			**Correct Entry (May 10)**		
Cash	50		Cash	50	
Service Revenue		50	Accounts Receivable		50

A comparison of the incorrect entry with the correct entry reveals that the debit to Cash $50 is correct. However, the $50 credit to Service Revenue should have been credited to Accounts Receivable. As a result, both Service Revenue and Accounts Receivable are overstated in the ledger. The following correcting entry is required.

Illustration 4-14
Correcting entry

Correcting Entry

May 20	Service Revenue	50	
	Accounts Receivable		50
	(To correct entry of May 10)		

A	=	L	+	OE
−50				−50

CASE 2. On May 18, office equipment costing $450 is purchased on account. The transaction is journalized and posted as a debit to Delivery Equipment $45 and a credit to Accounts Payable $45. The error is discovered on June 3, when the monthly statement for May is received from the creditor.

Illustration 4-15
Comparison of entries

Incorrect Entry (May 18)			**Correct Entry (May 18)**		
Delivery Equipment	45		Office Equipment	450	
Accounts Payable		45	Accounts Payable		450

A comparison of the two entries shows that three accounts are incorrect. Delivery Equipment is overstated $45; Office Equipment is understated $450; and Accounts Payable is understated $405. The correcting entry is:

Illustration 4-16
Correcting entry

Correcting Entry

June 3	Office Equipment	450	
	Delivery Equipment		45
	Accounts Payable		405
	(To correct entry of May 18)		

A	=	L	+	OE
+450				
−45		+405		

Instead of preparing a correcting entry, **it is possible to reverse the incorrect entry and then prepare the correct entry**. This approach will result in more entries and postings than a correcting entry, but it will accomplish the desired result.

ACCOUNTING IN ACTION *Business Insight*

Yale Express, a short-haul trucking firm, turned over much of its cargo to local truckers for delivery completion. Yale collected the entire delivery charge and, when billed by the local trucker, sent payment for the final phase to the local trucker. Yale used a cutoff period of 20 days into the next accounting period in making its adjusting entries for accrued liabilities. That is, it waited 20 days to receive the local truckers' bills to determine the amount of the unpaid but incurred delivery charges as of the balance sheet date.

On the other hand, **Republic Carloading**, a nationwide, long-distance freight forwarder, frequently did not receive transportation bills from truckers to whom it passed on cargo until months after the year-end. In making its year-end adjusting entries, Republic waited for months in order to include all of these outstanding transportation bills.

When Yale Express merged with Republic Carloading, Yale's vice president employed the 20-day cutoff procedure for both firms. As a result, millions of dollars of Republic's accrued transportation bills went unrecorded. When the erroneous procedure was detected and correcting entries were made, these and other errors changed a reported profit of $1.14 million into a loss of $1.88 million!

BEFORE YOU GO ON...

REVIEW IT

1. How do permanent accounts differ from temporary accounts?
2. What four different types of entries are required in closing the books?
3. What is the content and purpose of a post-closing trial balance?
4. What are the required and optional steps in the accounting cycle?

DO IT

The work sheet for Hancock Company shows the following in the financial statement columns: R. Hancock, Drawing $15,000, R. Hancock, Capital $42,000, and net income $18,000. Prepare the closing entries at December 31 that affect owner's capital.

ACTION PLAN

- Remember to make closing entries in the correct sequence.
- Make the first two entries to close revenues and expenses.
- Make the third entry to close net income to owner's capital.
- Make the final entry to close owner's drawing to owner's capital.

SOLUTION

Dec. 31	Income Summary	18,000	
	R. Hancock, Capital		18,000
	(To close net income to capital)		
Dec. 31	R. Hancock, Capital	15,000	
	R. Hancock, Drawing		15,000
	(To close drawings to capital)		

Related exercise material: BE4-4, BE4-5, BE4-6, BE4-8, E4-3, E4-6, E4-8, and E4-9.

THE NAVIGATOR

CLASSIFIED BALANCE SHEET

STUDY OBJECTIVE 6

Identify the sections of a classified balance sheet.

The financial statements illustrated up to this point were purposely kept simple. We classified items as assets, liabilities, and owner's equity in the balance sheet, and as revenues and expenses in the income statement. **Financial statements, however, become more useful to management, creditors, and potential investors when the elements are classified into significant subgroups.** In the remainder of this chapter we will introduce you to the primary balance sheet classifications. The classified income statement will be presented in Chapter 5. The classified financial statements are what Ted Castle, owner of **Rhino Foods, Inc.,** gave to his employees to understand what was happening in the business.

STANDARD CLASSIFICATIONS

A classified balance sheet usually contains these standard classifications:

Illustration 4-17

Standard balance sheet classifications

Assets	Liabilities and Owner's Equity
Current assets	Current liabilities
Long-term investments	Long-term liabilities
Property, plant, and equipment	Owner's (Stockholders') equity
Intangible assets	

These sections help the financial statement user determine such matters as (1) the availability of assets to meet debts as they come due and (2) the claims of short- and long-term creditors on total assets. A classified balance sheet also makes it easier to compare companies in the same industry, such as **GM**, **Ford**, and **DaimlerChrysler** in the automobile industry. Each of the sections is explained below.

A complete set of specimen financial statements for **Lands' End, Inc.** is shown in Appendix A at the back of the book.

Current Assets

Current assets are cash and other resources that are reasonably expected to be realized in cash or sold or consumed in the business within one year of the balance sheet date or the company's operating cycle, whichever is longer. For example, accounts receivable are current assets because they will be realized in cash through collection within one year. A prepayment such as supplies is a current asset because of its expected use or consumption in the business within one year.

The operating cycle of a company is the average time that is required to go from cash to cash in producing revenues. The term "cycle" suggests a circular flow, which in this case, starts and ends with cash. For example, in municipal transit companies, the operating cycle would tend to be short since services are provided entirely on a cash basis. On the other hand, the operating cycle in manufacturing companies is longer: they purchase goods and materials, manufacture and sell products, bill customers, and collect cash. This is a cash to cash cycle that may extend for several months. Most companies have operating cycles of less than one year. More will be said about operating cycles in later chapters.

INTERNATIONAL NOTE

Other countries use a different format for the balance sheet. In Great Britain, for example, property, plant, and equipment are reported first on the balance sheet; assets and liabilities are netted and grouped into net current and net total assets.

In a service enterprise, it is customary to recognize four types of current assets: (1) cash, (2) short-term investments such as U.S. government bonds,

(3) receivables (notes receivable, accounts receivable, and interest receivable), and (4) prepaid expenses (insurance and supplies). **These items are listed in the order of liquidity.** That is, they are listed in the order in which they are expected to be converted into cash. This arrangement is illustrated below in the presentation of **UAL, Inc. (United Airlines).**

Illustration 4-18

Current assets section

UNITED AIRLINES

UAL, INC, (UNITED AIRLINES)
Balance Sheet (partial)
(in millions)

Current assets	
Cash	$ 310
Short-term investments	379
Receivables	1,284
Aircraft fuel, spare parts, and supplies	340
Prepaid expenses	368
Other current assets	254
Total current assets	$2,935

A company's current assets are important in assessing the company's short-term debt-paying ability, as explained later in the chapter.

Long-Term Investments

HELPFUL HINT
Long-term investments are investments *made by* the business—not investments by the owner *in* the business. Investments by the owner in the business are reported as part of owner's (stockholders') equity (see p. 155).

Like current assets, **long-term investments** are resources that can be realized in cash. However, the conversion into cash is not expected within one year or the operating cycle, whichever is longer. In addition, long-term investments are not intended for use or consumption within the business. This category, often just called "investments," normally includes stocks and bonds of other corporations. **Deluxe Corporation** reported the following in its balance sheet.

Illustration 4-19

Long-term investments section

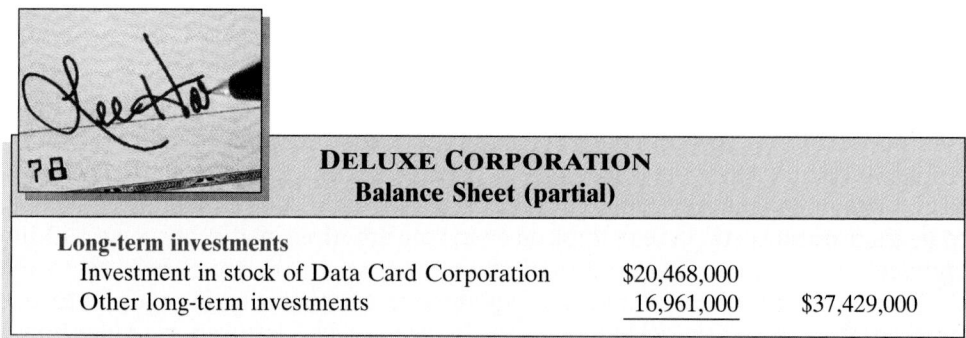

DELUXE CORPORATION
Balance Sheet (partial)

Long-term investments		
Investment in stock of Data Card Corporation	$20,468,000	
Other long-term investments	16,961,000	$37,429,000

Property, Plant, and Equipment

ALTERNATIVE TERMINOLOGY
Property, plant, and equipment are sometimes referred to as *plant assets* or *fixed assets*.

Property, plant, and equipment are tangible resources of a relatively permanent nature that are used in the business and not intended for sale. This category includes land, buildings, machinery and equipment, delivery equipment, and furniture and fixtures. Assets subject to depreciation should be reported at cost less accumulated depreciation. This practice is illustrated in the following presentation of **Delta Air Lines**.

Illustration 4-20

Property, plant, and equipment section

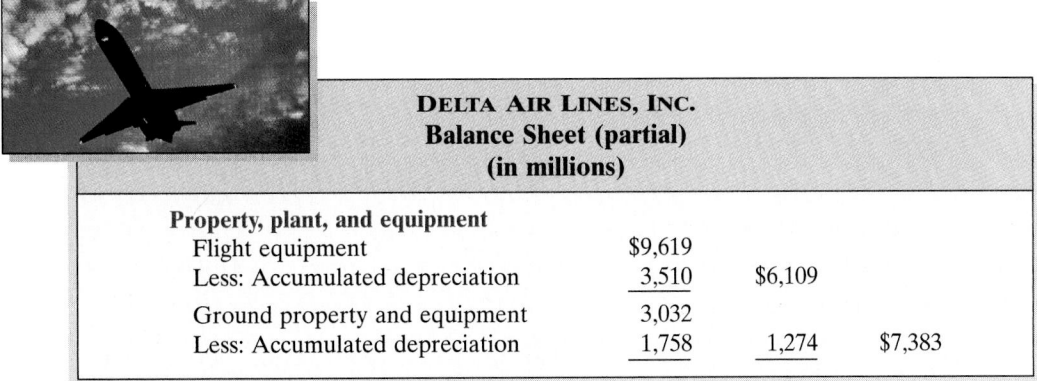

DELTA AIR LINES, INC.
Balance Sheet (partial)
(in millions)

Property, plant, and equipment			
Flight equipment	$9,619		
Less: Accumulated depreciation	3,510	$6,109	
Ground property and equipment	3,032		
Less: Accumulated depreciation	1,758	1,274	$7,383

Intangible Assets

Intangible assets are noncurrent resources that do not have physical substance. They are recorded at cost, and this cost is expensed over the useful life of the intangible asset. Intangible assets include patents, copyrights, and trademarks or trade names that give the holder **exclusive right** of use for a specified period of time. Their value to a company is generally derived from the rights or privileges granted by governmental authority.

In its balance sheet, **Brunswick Corporation** reported the following.

Illustration 4-21

Intangible assets section

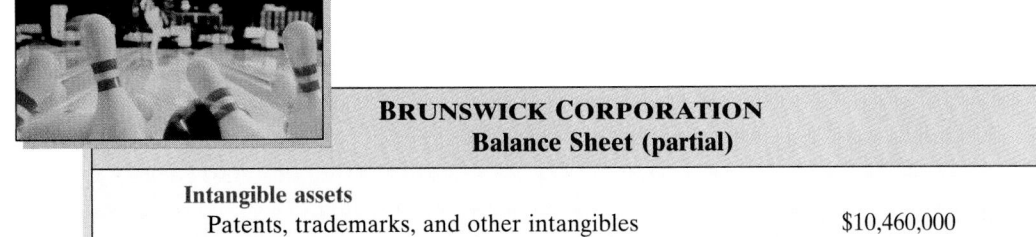

BRUNSWICK CORPORATION
Balance Sheet (partial)

Intangible assets	
Patents, trademarks, and other intangibles	$10,460,000

Current Liabilities

Listed first in the liabilities and owner's equity section of the balance sheet are current liabilities. **Current liabilities** are obligations that are reasonably expected to be paid from existing current assets or through the creation of other current liabilities. As in the case of current assets, the time period for payment is one year or the operating cycle, whichever is longer. Current liabilities include (1) debts related to the operating cycle, such as accounts payable and wages and salaries payable, and (2) other short-term debts, such as bank loans payable, interest payable, taxes payable, and current maturities of long-term obligations (payments to be made within the next year on long-term obligations).

The arrangement of items within the current liabilities section has evolved through custom rather than from a prescribed rule. Notes payable is usually listed first, followed by accounts payable. Other items are then listed in any order. The current liabilities section adapted from the balance sheet of **UAL, Inc. (United Airlines)** is as follows.

Illustration 4-22

Current liabilities section

UNITED AIRLINES

UAL, INC. (UNITED AIRLINES)
Balance Sheet (partial)
(in thousands)

Current liabilities	
Notes payable	$ 297,518
Accounts payable	382,967
Current maturities of long-term obligations	81,525
Unearned ticket revenue	432,979
Salaries and wages payable	435,622
Taxes payable	80,390
Other current liabilities	240,652
Total current liabilities	$1,951,653

Users of financial statements look closely at the relationship between current assets and current liabilities. This relationship is important in evaluating a company's **liquidity**—its ability to pay obligations that are expected to become due within the next year or operating cycle. When current assets exceed current liabilities at the balance sheet date, the likelihood for paying the liabilities is favorable. When the reverse is true, short-term creditors may not be paid, and the company may ultimately be forced into bankruptcy.

Long-Term Liabilities

ALTERNATIVE TERMINOLOGY
Long-term liabilities are also called *long-term debt* or *noncurrent liabilities.*

Obligations expected to be paid after one year or an operating cycle, whichever is longer, are classified as **long-term liabilities**. Liabilities in this category include bonds payable, mortgages payable, long-term notes payable, lease liabilities, and obligations under employee pension plans. Many companies report long-term debt maturing after one year as a single amount in the balance sheet. They then show the details of the debt in the notes that accompany the financial statements. Others list the various sources of long-term liabilities. In its balance sheet, **Consolidated Freightways, Inc.** reported the following.

CONSOLIDATED FREIGHTWAYS

CONSOLIDATED FREIGHTWAYS, INC.
Balance Sheet (partial)
(in thousands)

Long-term liabilities	
Bank notes payable	$10,000
Mortgage payable	2,900
Bonds payable	53,422
Other long-term debt	9,597
Total long-term liabilities	$75,919

Illustration 4-23

Long-term liabilities section

Owner's Equity

The content of the owner's equity section varies with the form of business organization. In a proprietorship, there is one capital account. In a partnership, there is a capital account for each partner. For a corporation, owners' equity is divided into two accounts—Capital Stock and Retained Earnings. Investments of assets in the business by the stockholders are recorded by debiting an asset account and crediting the Capital Stock account. Income retained for use in the business is recorded in the Retained Earnings account. The Capital Stock and Retained Earnings accounts are combined and reported as **stockholders' equity** on the balance sheet. (We'll learn more about these corporation accounts in later chapters.)

In its balance sheet, **Dell Computer Corporation** recently reported its owners' (stockholders') equity section as follows.

DELL COMPUTER CORPORATION
($ in thousands)

Stockholders' equity	
Common stock, 2,543,000,000 shares	$1,781,000
Retained earnings	540,000
Total stockholders' equity	$2,321,000

Illustration 4-24

Stockholders' equity section

CLASSIFIED BALANCE SHEET, ILLUSTRATED

An unclassified, report form balance sheet of Pioneer Advertising Agency was presented in Illustration 3-21 on page 108. Using the same adjusted trial balance accounts at October 31, 2002, we can prepare the classified balance sheet shown in Illustration 4-25. For illustrative purposes, assume that $1,000 of the notes payable is due currently and $4,000 is long-term.

The balance sheet is most often presented in **report form**, with assets listed above liabilities and owner's equity. The balance sheet may also be presented in **account form**: the assets section is placed on the left and the liabilities and owner's equity sections on the right, as shown in Illustration 4-25.

PIONEER ADVERTISING AGENCY
Balance Sheet
October 31, 2002

Assets			Liabilities and Owner's Equity	
Current assets			Current liabilities	
Cash		$15,200	Notes payable	$1,000
Accounts receivable		200	Accounts payable	2,500
Advertising supplies		1,000	Unearned revenue	800
Prepaid insurance		550	Salaries payable	1,200
Total current assets		16,950	Interest payable	50
			Total current liabilities	5,550
Property, plant, and equipment			Long-term liabilites	
Office equipment	$5,000		Notes payable	4,000
Less: Accumulated depreciation	40	4,960		
Total assets		$21,910	Total liabilities	9,550
			Owner's equity	
			C. R. Byrd, Capital	12,360
			Total liabilities and owner's equity	$21,910

Illustration 4-25

Classified balance sheet in account form

Another, more complete example of a classified balance sheet is presented in report form in Illustration 4-26.

Illustration 4-26

Classified balance sheet in report form

FRANKLIN CORPORATION
Balance Sheet
October 31, 2002

Assets			
Current assets			
Cash		$ 6,600	
Short-term investments		2,000	
Accounts receivable		7,000	
Inventories		4,000	
Supplies		2,100	
Prepaid insurance		400	
Total current assets			$22,100
Long-term investments			
Investment in stock of Walters Corp.			7,200
Property, plant, and equipment			
Land		10,000	
Office equipment	$ 24,000		
Less: Accumulated depreciation	5,000	19,000	29,000
Intangible assets			
Patents			3,100
Total assets			$61,400
Liabilities and Owner's Equity			
Current liabilities			
Notes payable		$11,000	
Accounts payable		2,100	
Unearned revenue		900	
Salaries payable		1,600	
Interest payable		450	
Total current liabilities			$16,050
Long-term liabilities			
Notes payable		1,300	
Mortgage payable		10,000	
Total long-term liabilities			11,300
Total liabilities			27,350
Owner's equity			
B. Franklin, Capital			34,050
Total liabilities and owner's equity			$61,400

BEFORE YOU GO ON...

REVIEW IT

1. What are the major sections in a classified balance sheet?
2. Using the **Lands' End, Inc.** annual report, determine its current liabilities at January 28, 2000, and January 29, 1999. Were current liabilities higher or lower than current assets in these two years? The answer to this question is provided on page 180.
3. What is the difference between the report form and the account form of the classified balance sheet?

A LOOK BACK AT OUR FEATURE STORY

Refer back to the Feature Story about **Rhino Foods, Inc.** at the beginning of the chapter, and answer the following questions.

1. What is the lesson of the Rhino Foods story and Ted Castle's innovations?
2. How did Rhino's employees' knowledge of financial statements, especially production reports and the income statement, contribute to their effectiveness as employees?

SOLUTION

1. If you give employees equity in the company and provide them with the training and the information to understand the financial consequences of their decisions and actions, they will act more responsibly and make a greater contribution to the sales and income of the company. In other words, they begin to think like owners.
2. By understanding the income statement, they now recognize the impact of revenues and expenses in arriving at net income—as well as how productivity and expenses affect their bonuses.

☑ THE NAVIGATOR

DEMONSTRATION PROBLEM

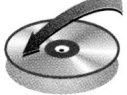

Additional Demonstration Problem

At the end of its first month of operations, Watson Answering Service has the following unadjusted trial balance.

WATSON ANSWERING SERVICE
August 31, 2002
Trial Balance

	Debit	Credit
Cash	$ 5,400	
Accounts Receivable	2,800	
Prepaid Insurance	2,400	
Supplies	1,300	
Equipment	60,000	
Notes Payable		$40,000
Accounts Payable		2,400
Ray Watson, Capital		30,000
Ray Watson, Drawing	1,000	
Service Revenue		4,900
Salaries Expense	3,200	
Utilities Expense	800	
Advertising Expense	400	
	$77,300	$77,300

Other data consist of the following:

1. Insurance expires at the rate of $200 per month.
2. There are $1,000 of supplies on hand at August 31.
3. Monthly depreciation on the equipment is $900.
4. Interest of $500 on the notes payable has accrued during August.

Instructions

(a) Prepare a work sheet.

(b) Prepare a classified balance sheet assuming $35,000 of the notes payable are long-term.

(c) Journalize the closing entries.

ACTION PLAN

- In completing the work sheet, be sure to (a) key the adjustments, (b) start at the top of the adjusted trial balance columns and extend adjusted balances to the correct statement columns, and (c) enter net income (or net loss) in the proper columns.
- In preparing a classified balance sheet, know the contents of each of the sections.
- In journalizing closing entries, remember that there are only four entries and that owner's drawing is closed to owner's capital.

SOLUTION TO DEMONSTRATION PROBLEM

(a)

WATSON ANSWERING SERVICE
Work Sheet
For the Month Ended August 31, 2002

	Trial Balance		Adjustments		Adjusted Trial Balance		Income Statement		Balance Sheet	
Account Titles	**Dr.**	**Cr.**	**Dr.**	**Cr.**	**Dr.**	**Cr.**	**Dr.**	**Cr.**	**Dr.**	**Cr.**
Cash	5,400				5,400				5,400	
Accounts Receivable	2,800				2,800				2,800	
Prepaid Insurance	2,400			(a) 200	2,200				2,200	
Supplies	1,300			(b) 300	1,000				1,000	
Equipment	60,000				60,000				60,000	
Notes Payable		40,000				40,000				40,000
Accounts Payable		2,400				2,400				2,400
Ray Watson, Capital		30,000				30,000				30,000
Ray Watson, Drawing	1,000				1,000				1,000	
Service Revenue		4,900				4,900		4,900		
Salaries Expense	3,200				3,200		3,200			
Utilities Expense	800				800		800			
Advertising Expense	400				400		400			
Totals	77,300	77,300								
Insurance Expense			(a) 200		200		200			
Supplies Expense			(b) 300		300		300			
Depreciation Expense			(c) 900		900		900			
Accumulated Depreciation—Equipment				(c) 900		900				900
Interest Expense			(d) 500		500		500			
Interest Payable				(d) 500		500				500
Totals			1,900	1,900	78,700	78,700	6,300	4,900	72,400	73,800
Net Loss								1,400	1,400	
Totals							6,300	6,300	73,800	73,800

Explanation: (a) Insurance expired, (b) Supplies used, (c) Depreciation expensed, (d) Interest accrued.

(b)

WATSON ANSWERING SERVICE
Balance Sheet
August 31, 2002

Assets

Current assets		
Cash		$ 5,400
Accounts receivable		2,800
Prepaid insurance		2,200
Supplies		1,000
Total current assets		11,400
Property, plant, and equipment		
Equipment	$60,000	
Less: Accumulated depreciation—equipment	900	59,100
Total assets		$70,500

Liabilities and Owner's Equity

Current liabilities		
Notes payable	$ 5,000	
Accounts payable	2,400	
Interest payable	500	
Total current liabilities	7,900	
Long-term liabilities		
Notes payable	35,000	
Total liabilities	42,900	
Owner's equity		
Ray Watson, Capital	27,600*	
Total liabilities and owner's equity	$70,500	

*Ray Watson, Capital, $30,000 less drawings $1,000 and net loss $1,400.

(c)

Date	Account	Debit	Credit
Aug. 31	Service Revenue	4,900	
	Income Summary		4,900
	(To close revenue account)		
31	Income Summary	6,300	
	Salaries Expense		3,200
	Depreciation Expense		900
	Utilities Expense		800
	Interest Expense		500
	Advertising Expense		400
	Supplies Expense		300
	Insurance Expense		200
	(To close expense accounts)		
31	Ray Watson, Capital	1,400	
	Income Summary		1,400
	(To close net loss to capital)		
31	Ray Watson, Capital	1,000	
	Ray Watson, Drawing		1,000
	(To close drawings to capital)		

THE NAVIGATOR

SUMMARY OF STUDY OBJECTIVES

1. *Prepare a work sheet.* The steps in preparing a work sheet are: (a) prepare a trial balance on the work sheet, (b) enter the adjustments in the adjustments columns, (c) enter adjusted balances in the adjusted trial balance columns, (d) extend adjusted trial balance amounts to appropriate financial statement columns, and (e) total the statement columns, compute net income (or net loss), and complete the work sheet.

2. *Explain the process of closing the books.* Closing the books occurs at the end of an accounting period. The process is to journalize and post closing entries and then rule and balance all accounts. In closing the books, separate entries are made to close revenues and expenses to Income Summary, Income Summary to Owner's Capital, and Owner's Drawings to Owner's Capital. Only temporary accounts are closed.

3. *Describe the content and purpose of a post-closing trial balance.* A post-closing trial balance contains the balances in permanent accounts that are carried forward to the next accounting period. The purpose of this trial balance is to prove the equality of these balances.

4. *State the required steps in the accounting cycle.* The required steps in the accounting cycle are: (a) analyze business transactions, (b) journalize the transactions, (c) post to ledger accounts, (d) prepare a trial balance, (e) journalize and post adjusting entries, (f) prepare an adjusted trial balance, (g) prepare financial statements, (h) journalize and post closing entries, and (i) prepare a post-closing trial balance.

5. *Explain the approaches to preparing correcting entries.* One approach for determining the correcting entry is to compare the incorrect entry with the correct entry. After comparison, a correcting entry is made to correct the accounts. An alternative to a correcting entry is to reverse the incorrect entry and then prepare the correct entry.

6. ***Identify the sections of a classified balance sheet.*** In a classified balance sheet, assets are classified as current assets; long-term investments; property, plant, and equipment; and intangibles. Liabilities are classified as either current or long-term. There is also an owner's equity section, which varies with the form of business organization.

THE NAVIGATOR

Key Term Matching Activity

GLOSSARY

Classified balance sheet A balance sheet that contains a number of standard classifications or sections. (p. 151).

Closing entries Entries made at the end of an accounting period to transfer the balances of temporary accounts to a permanent owner's equity account, Owner's Capital. (p. 141).

Correcting entries Entries to correct errors made in recording transactions. (p. 148).

Current assets Cash and other resources that are reasonably expected to be realized in cash or sold or consumed in the business within one year or the operating cycle, whichever is longer. (p. 151).

Current liabilities Obligations reasonably expected to be paid from existing current assets or through the creation of other current liabilities within the next year or operating cycle, whichever is longer. (p. 153).

Income Summary A temporary account used in closing revenue and expense accounts. (p. 141).

Intangible assets Noncurrent resources that do not have physical substance. (p. 153).

Liquidity The ability of a company to pay obligations that are expected to become due within the next year or operating cycle. (p. 154).

Long-term investments Resources not expected to be realized in cash within the next year or operating cycle. (p. 152).

Long-term liabilities Obligations expected to be paid after one year. (p. 154).

Operating cycle The average time required to go from cash to cash in producing revenues. (p. 151).

Permanent (real) accounts Balance sheet accounts whose balances are carried forward to the next accounting period. (p. 140).

Post-closing trial balance A list of permanent accounts and their balances after closing entries have been journalized and posted. (p. 145).

Property, plant, and equipment Assets of a relatively permanent nature that are being used in the business and not intended for sale. (p. 152).

Reversing entry An entry made at the beginning of the next accounting period that is the exact opposite of the adjusting entry made in the previous period. (p. 147).

Stockholders' equity The ownership claim of shareholders on total assets. It is to a corporation what owner's equity is to a proprietorship. (p. 155).

Temporary (nominal) accounts Revenue, expense, and drawing accounts whose balances are transferred to owner's capital at the end of an accounting period. (p. 140).

Work sheet A multiple-column form that may be used in the adjustment process and in preparing financial statements. (p. 134).

APPENDIX *Reversing Entries*

STUDY OBJECTIVE 7

Prepare reversing entries.

After the financial statements are prepared and the books are closed, it is often helpful to reverse some of the adjusting entries before recording the regular transactions of the next period. Such entries are called reversing entries. **A reversing entry is made at the beginning of the next accounting period and is the exact opposite of the adjusting entry made in the previous period.** The recording of reversing entries is an **optional** step in the accounting cycle.

The purpose of reversing entries is to simplify the recording of a subsequent transaction related to an adjusting entry. In Chapter 3, you may recall, the payment of salaries after an adjusting entry resulted in two debits: one to Salaries Payable and the other to Salaries Expense. With reversing entries, the entire subsequent payment can be debited to Salaries Expense. **The use of reversing entries does not change the amounts reported in the financial statements. What it does is simplify the recording of subsequent transactions.**

ILLUSTRATION OF REVERSING ENTRIES

Reversing entries are most often used to reverse two types of adjusting entries: accrued revenues and accrued expenses. They are seldom made for prepaid expenses and unearned revenues. To illustrate the optional use of reversing entries for accrued expenses, we will use the salaries expense transactions for Pioneer Advertising Agency. The transaction and adjustment data are as follows.

1. October 26 (initial salary entry): $4,000 of salaries earned between October 15 and October 26 are paid.
2. October 31 (adjusting entry): Salaries earned between October 29 and October 31 are $1,200. These will be paid in the November 9 payroll.
3. November 9 (subsequent salary entry): Salaries paid are $4,000. Of this amount, $1,200 applied to accrued wages payable and $2,800 was earned between November 1 and November 9.

The comparative entries with and without reversing entries are shown in Illustration 4A-1.

Illustration 4A-1

Comparative entries—not reversing vs. reversing

When Reversing Entries Are Not Used (per chapter)				When Reversing Entries Are Used (per appendix)			
	Initial Salary Entry				**Initial Salary Entry**		
Oct. 26	Salaries Expense	4,000		**Oct. 26**	**Salaries Expense**	**4,000**	
	Cash		4,000		**Cash**		**4,000**
	Adjusting Entry				Adjusting Entry		
Oct. 31	Salaries Expense	1,200		**Oct. 31**	**Salaries Expense**	**1,200**	
	Salaries Payable		1,200		**Salaries Payable**		**1,200**
	Closing Entry				Closing Entry		
Oct. 31	Income Summary	5,200		**Oct. 31**	**Income Summary**	**5,200**	
	Salaries Expense		5,200		**Salaries Expense**		**5,200**
	Reversing Entry				Reversing Entry		
Nov. 1	No reversing entry is made.			**Nov. 1**	**Salaries Payable**	**1,200**	
					Salaries Expense		**1,200**
	Subsequent Salary Entry				Subsequent Salary Entry		
Nov. 9	Salaries Payable	1,200		**Nov. 9**	**Salaries Expense**	**4,000**	
	Salaries Expense	2,800			**Cash**		**4,000**
	Cash		4,000				

The first three entries are the same whether or not reversing entries are used. The last two entries are different. The November 1 **reversing entry** eliminates the $1,200 balance in Salaries Payable that was created by the October 31 adjusting entry. The reversing entry also creates a $1,200 credit balance in the Salaries Expense account. As you know, it is unusual for an expense account to have a credit balance. The balance is correct in this instance, though, because it anticipates that the entire amount of the first salary payment in the new accounting period will be debited to Salaries Expense. This debit will eliminate the credit balance, and the resulting debit balance in the expense account will equal the salaries expense incurred in the new accounting period ($2,800 in this example).

TECHNOLOGY IN ACTION

Using reversing entries in a computerized accounting system is more efficient than in a manual system. The reversing entry saves writing a program to locate the amount accrued from the preceding period and making the more complicated entry in the current period. That is, the computer does not have to be programmed to determine whether any accrued items exist.

When reversing entries are made, all cash payments of expenses can be debited to the expense account. This means that on November 9 (and every payday) Salaries Expense can be debited for the amount paid without regard to any accrued salaries payable. Being able to make the same entry each time simplifies the recording process: Subsequent transactions can be recorded as if the related adjusting entry had never been made.

The posting of the entries with reversing entries is shown in Illustration 4A-2.

Illustration 4A-2

Postings with reversing entries

Salaries Expense

10/26 Paid	4,000	10/31 Closing	5,200
31 Adjusting	1,200		
	5,200		5,200
11/9 Paid	4,000	**11/1 Reversing**	**1,200**

Salaries Payable

11/1 Reversing	**1,200**	10/31 Adjusting	1,200

Reversing entries may also be made for accrued revenue adjusting entries. For Pioneer Advertising, the adjusting entry was: Accounts Receivable (Dr.) $200 and Service Revenue (Cr.) $200. Thus, the reversing entry on November 1 is:

A	=	L	+	OE
−200				−200

Nov. 1	Service Revenue	200	
	Accounts Receivable		200
	(To reverse October 31 adjusting entry)		

When the accrued fees are collected, Cash is debited and Service Revenue is credited.

SUMMARY OF STUDY OBJECTIVE FOR APPENDIX

7. *Prepare reversing entries.* Reversing entries are the opposite of the adjusting entries made in the preceding period. They are made at the beginning of a new accounting period to simplify the recording of later transactions related to the adjusting entries. In most cases, only accrued adjusting entries are reversed.

***Note:** All asterisked Questions, Exercises, and Problems relate to material in the appendix to the chapter.

Chapter 4 Self-Test

SELF-STUDY QUESTIONS

Answers are at the end of the chapter.

(SO 1) **1.** Which of the following statements is *incorrect* concerning the work sheet?
   a. The work sheet is essentially a working tool of the accountant.
   b. The work sheet is distributed to management and other interested parties.
   c. The work sheet cannot be used as a basis for posting to ledger accounts.
   d. Financial statements can be prepared directly from the work sheet before journalizing and posting the adjusting entries.

2. In a work sheet, net income is entered in the following columns: (SO 1)

a. income statement (Dr) and balance sheet (Dr).
b. income statement (Cr) and balance sheet (Dr).
c. income statement (Dr) and balance sheet (Cr).
d. income statement (Cr) and balance sheet (Cr).

(SO 2) 3. An account that will have a zero balance after closing entries have been journalized and posted is:
a. Service Revenue.
b. Advertising Supplies.
c. Prepaid Insurance.
d. Accumulated Depreciation.

(SO 2) 4. When a net loss has occurred, Income Summary is:
a. debited and Owner's Capital is credited.
b. credited and Owner's Capital is debited.
c. debited and Owner's Drawing is credited.
d. credited and Owner's Drawing is debited.

(SO 2) 5. The closing process involves separate entries to close (1) expenses, (2) drawings, (3) revenues, and (4) income summary. The correct sequencing of the entries is:
a. (4), (3), (2), (1)
b. (1), (2), (3), (4)
c. (3), (1), (4), (2)
d. (3), (2), (1), (4)

(SO 3) 6. Which types of accounts will appear in the post-closing trial balance?
a. Permanent (real) accounts.
b. Temporary (nominal) accounts.
c. Accounts shown in the income statement columns of a work sheet.
d. None of the above.

(SO 4) 7. All of the following are required steps in the accounting cycle *except*:
a. journalizing and posting closing entries.
b. preparing financial statements.
c. journalizing the transactions.
d. preparing a work sheet.

8. Cash of $100 received at the time the service was provided was journalized and posted as a debit to Cash $100 and a credit to Accounts Receivable $100. Assuming the incorrect entry is not reversed, the correcting entry is: (SO 5)
a. debit Service Revenue $100 and credit Accounts Receivable $100.
b. debit Accounts Receivable $100 and credit Service Revenue $100.
c. debit Cash $100 and credit Service Revenue $100.
d. debit Accounts Receivable $100 and credit Cash $100.

9. In a classified balance sheet, assets are usually classified using the following categories: (SO 6)
a. current assets; long-term assets; property, plant, and equipment; and intangible assets.
b. current assets; long-term investments; property, plant, and equipment; and other assets.
c. current assets; long-term investments; tangible assets; and intangible assets.
d. current assets; long-term investments; property, plant, and equipment; and intangible assets.

10. Current assets are listed: (SO 6)
a. by liquidity.
b. by importance.
c. by longevity.
d. alphabetically.

*11. On December 31, Regis Company correctly made an adjusting entry to recognize $2,000 of accrued salaries payable. On January 8 of the next year, total salaries of $3,400 were paid. Assuming the correct reversing entry was made on January 1, the entry on January 8 will result in a credit to Cash $3,400 and the following debit(s): (SO 7)
a. Salaries Payable $1,400, and Salaries Expense $2,000.
b. Salaries Payable $2,000 and Salaries Expense $1,400.
c. Salaries Expense $3,400.
d. Salaries Payable $3,400.

THE NAVIGATOR

QUESTIONS

1. "A work sheet is a permanent accounting record and its use is required in the accounting cycle." Do you agree? Explain.
2. Explain the purpose of the work sheet.
3. What is the relationship, if any, between the amount shown in the adjusted trial balance column for an account and that account's ledger balance?
4. If a company's revenues are $125,000 and its expenses are $113,000, in which financial statement columns of the work sheet will the net income of $12,000 appear? When expenses exceed revenues, in which columns will the difference appear?
5. Why is it necessary to prepare formal financial statements if all of the data are in the statement columns of the work sheet?
6. Identify the account(s) debited and credited in each of the four closing entries, assuming the company has net income for the year.
7. Describe the nature of the Income Summary account and identify the types of summary data that may be posted to this account.
8. What are the content and purpose of a post-closing trial balance?
9. Which of the following accounts would not appear in the post-closing trial balance? Interest Payable; Equipment; Depreciation Expense; Kathy Ho, Drawing; Unearned Revenue; Accumulated Depreciation—Equipment; and Service Revenue.
10. Distinguish between a reversing entry and an adjusting entry. Are reversing entries required?

11. Indicate, in the sequence in which they are made, the three required steps in the accounting cycle that involve journalizing.
12. Identify, in the sequence in which they are prepared, the three trial balances that are often used to report financial information about a company.
13. How do correcting entries differ from adjusting entries?
14. What standard classifications are used in preparing a classified balance sheet?
15. What is meant by the term "operating cycle?"
16. Define current assets. What basis is used for arranging individual items within the current assets section?
17. Distinguish between long-term investments and property, plant, and equipment.
18. How do current liabilities differ from long-term liabilities?
19. (a) What is the term used to describe the owner's equity section of a corporation? (b) Identify the two owner's equity accounts in a corporation and indicate the purpose of each.
20. How does a report form balance sheet differ from an account form balance sheet?
*21. Clearwater Company prepares reversing entries. If the adjusting entry for interest payable is reversed, what type of an account balance, if any, will there be in Interest Payable and Interest Expense after the reversing entry is posted?
*22. At December 31, accrued salaries payable totaled $4,500. On January 10, total salaries of $8,000 are paid. (a) Assume that reversing entries are made at January 1. Give the January 10 entry, and indicate the Salaries Expense account balance after the entry is posted. (b) Repeat part (a) assuming reversing entries are not made.

BRIEF EXERCISES

List the steps in preparing a work sheet.
(SO 1)

BE4-1 The steps in using a work sheet are presented in random order below. List the steps in the proper order by placing numbers 1–5 in the blank spaces.

(a) ____ Prepare a trial balance on the work sheet.
(b) ____ Enter adjusted balances.
(c) ____ Extend adjusted balances to appropriate statement columns.
(d) ____ Total the statement columns, compute net income (loss), and complete the work sheet.
(e) ____ Enter adjustment data.

Prepare partial work sheet.
(SO 1)

BE4-2 The ledger of Giovanni Company includes the following unadjusted balances: Prepaid Insurance $4,000, Service Revenue $58,000, and Salaries Expense $25,000. Adjusting entries are required for **(a)** expired insurance $1,200; **(b)** services provided $900, but unbilled and uncollected; and **(c)** accrued salaries payable $800. Enter the unadjusted balances and adjustments into a work sheet and complete the work sheet for all accounts. *Note:* You will need to add the following accounts: Accounts Receivable, Salaries Payable, and Insurance Expense.

Identify work sheet columns for selected accounts.
(SO 1)

BE4-3 The following selected accounts appear in the adjusted trial balance columns of the work sheet for Gordon Company: Accumulated Depreciation; Depreciation Expense; B. Gordon, Capital; B. Gordon, Drawing; Service Revenue; Supplies; and Accounts Payable. Indicate the financial statement column (income statement Dr., balance sheet Cr., etc.) to which each balance should be extended.

Prepare closing entries from ledger balances.
(SO 2)

BE4-4 The ledger of Benson Company contains the following balances: D. Benson, Capital $30,000; D. Benson, Drawing $2,000; Service Revenue $50,000; Salaries Expense $26,000; and Supplies Expense $4,000. Prepare the closing entries at December 31.

Post closing entries; rule and balance T accounts.
(SO 2)

BE4-5 Using the data in BE4-4, enter the balances in T accounts, post the closing entries, and rule and balance the accounts.

Journalize and post closing entries using the three-column form of account.
(SO 2)

BE4-6 The income statement for Edgebrook Golf Club for the month ending July 31 shows Green Fee Revenue $14,000, Salaries Expense $8,200, Maintenance Expense $2,500, and Net Income $3,300. Prepare the entries to close the revenue and expense accounts. Post the entries to the revenue and expense accounts, and complete the closing process for these accounts using the three-column form of account.

Identify post-closing trial balance accounts.
(SO 3)

BE4-7 Using the data in BE4-3, identify the accounts that would be included in a post-closing trial balance.

List the required steps in the accounting cycle in sequence.
(SO 4)

BE4-8 The steps in the accounting cycle are listed in random order below. List the steps in proper sequence, assuming no work sheet is prepared, by placing numbers 1–9 in the blank spaces.

(a) ____ Prepare a trial balance.
(b) ____ Journalize the transactions.

(c) ____ Journalize and post closing entries.
(d) ____ Prepare financial statements.
(e) ____ Journalize and post adjusting entries.
(f) ____ Post to ledger accounts.
(g) ____ Prepare a post-closing trial balance.
(h) ____ Prepare an adjusted trial balance.
(i) ____ Analyze business transactions.

BE4-9 At Piccola Company, the following errors were discovered after the transactions had been journalized and posted. Prepare the correcting entries.

Prepare correcting entries. (SO 5)

1. A collection on account from a customer for $780 was recorded as a debit to Cash $780 and a credit to Service Revenue $780.
2. The purchase of store supplies on account for $1,730 was recorded as a debit to Store Supplies $1,370 and a credit to Accounts Payable $1,370.

BE4-10 The balance sheet debit column of the work sheet for Salsa Company includes the following accounts: Accounts Receivable $12,500; Prepaid Insurance $3,600; Cash $18,400; Supplies $5,200, and Marketable Securities $8,200. Prepare the current assets section of the balance sheet, listing the accounts in proper sequence.

Prepare the current assets section of a balance sheet. (SO 6)

***BE4-11** At October 31, Orlaida Company made an accrued expense adjusting entry of $800 for salaries. Prepare the reversing entry on November 1, and indicate the balances in Salaries Payable and Salaries Expense after posting the reversing entry.

Prepare reversing entries. (SO 7)

EXERCISES

E4-1 The adjusted trial balance columns of the work sheet for Jose Tortilla Company are as follows.

Complete work sheet. (SO 1)

JOSE TORTILLA COMPANY
Work Sheet (partial)
For the Month Ended April 30, 2002

Account Titles	Adjusted Trial Balance Dr.	Adjusted Trial Balance Cr.	Income Statement Dr.	Income Statement Cr.	Balance Sheet Dr.	Balance Sheet Cr.
Cash	15,052					
Accounts Receivable	7,840					
Prepaid Rent	2,280					
Equipment	23,050					
Accumulated Depreciation		4,921				
Notes Payable		5,700				
Accounts Payable		5,972				
J. Tortilla, Capital		33,960				
J. Tortilla, Drawing	3,650					
Service Revenue		12,590				
Salaries Expense	9,840					
Rent Expense	760					
Depreciation Expense	671					
Interest Expense	57					
Interest Payable		57				
Totals	63,200	63,200				

Instructions

Complete the work sheet.

Prepare financial statements from work sheet.
(SO 1, 6)

E4-2 Work sheet data for Jose Tortilla Company are presented in E4-1. The owner did not make any additional investments in the business in April.

Instructions

Prepare an income statement, an owner's equity statement, and a classified balance sheet.

Journalize and post closing entries and prepare a post-closing trial balance.
(SO 2, 3)

E4-3 Work sheet data for the Jose Tortilla Company are presented in E4-1.

Instructions

(a) Journalize the closing entries at April 30.
(b) Post the closing entries to Income Summary and J. Tortilla, Capital. Use T accounts.
(c) Prepare a post-closing trial balance at April 30.

Prepare adjusting entries from a work sheet and extend balances to work sheet columns.
(SO 1)

E4-4 The adjustments columns of the work sheet for Gilberto Company are shown below.

	Adjustments	
Account Titles	**Debit**	**Credit**
Accounts Receivable	600	
Prepaid Insurance		400
Accumulated Depreciation		1,000
Salaries Payable		500
Service Revenue		600
Salaries Expense	500	
Insurance Expense	400	
Depreciation Expense	1,000	
	2,500	2,500

Instructions

(a) Prepare the adjusting entries.
(b) Assuming the adjusted trial balance amount for each account is normal, indicate the financial statement column to which each balance should be extended.

Derive adjusting entries from work sheet data.
(SO 1)

E4-5 Selected work sheet data for Karen Allman Company are presented below.

Account Titles	**Trial Balance**		**Adjusted Trial Balance**	
	Dr.	**Cr.**	**Dr.**	**Cr.**
Accounts Receivable	?		34,000	
Prepaid Insurance	26,000		18,000	
Supplies	9,000		?	
Accumulated Depreciation		12,000		?
Salaries Payable		?		6,000
Service Revenue		88,000		95,000
Insurance Expense			?	
Depreciation Expense			10,000	
Supplies Expense			4,000	
Salaries Expense	?		49,000	

Instructions

(a) Fill in the missing amounts.
(b) Prepare the adjusting entries that were made.

E4-6 The adjusted trial balance of Mozart Company at the end of its fiscal year is:

Journalize and post closing entries and prepare a post-closing trial balance.
(SO 2, 3)

MOZART COMPANY
Adjusted Trial Balance
July 31, 2002

No.	Account Titles	Debits	Credits
101	Cash	$ 14,940	
112	Accounts Receivable	8,780	
157	Equipment	15,900	
167	Accumulated Depreciation		$ 5,400
201	Accounts Payable		4,220
208	Unearned Rent Revenue		1,800
301	W.A. Mozart, Capital		45,200
306	W.A. Mozart, Drawing	14,000	
404	Commission Revenue		65,100
429	Rent Revenue		6,500
711	Depreciation Expense	4,000	
720	Salaries Expense	55,700	
732	Utilities Expense	14,900	
		$128,220	$128,220

Instructions

(a) Prepare the closing entries using page J15.

(b) Post to W.A. Mozart, Capital and No. 350 Income Summary accounts. (Use the three-column form.)

(c) Prepare a post-closing trial balance at July 31.

E4-7 The adjusted trial balance for Mozart Company is presented in E4-6.

Prepare financial statements.
(SO 6)

Instructions

(a) Prepare an income statement and an owner's equity statement for the year. Mozart did not make any capital investments during the year.

(b) Prepare a classified balance sheet at July 31.

E4-8 Selected accounts for Eden Salon are presented below. All June 30 postings are from closing entries.

Prepare closing entries and an owner's equity statement.
(SO 2)

Salaries Expense

6/10	3,200	6/30	8,800
6/28	5,600		

Service Revenue

6/30	15,600	6/15	7,200
		6/24	8,400

Barbara Eden, Capital

6/30	2,500	6/1	12,000
		6/30	2,300
		Bal.	11,800

Supplies Expense

6/12	800	6/30	1,500
6/24	700		

Rent Expense

6/1	3,000	6/30	3,000

Barbara Eden, Drawing

6/13	1,000	6/30	2,500
6/25	1,500		

Instructions

(a) Prepare the closing entries that were made.

(b) Post the closing entries to Income Summary.

Prepare correcting entries.
(SO 5)

Acc. Payable

E4-9 Lipizzan Company has an inexperienced accountant. During the first 2 weeks on the job, the accountant made the following errors in journalizing transactions. All entries were posted as made.

1. A payment on account of $830 to a creditor was debited to Accounts Payable $380 and credited to Cash $380.
2. The purchase of supplies on account for $600 was debited to Equipment $60 and credited to Accounts Payable $60.
3. A $400 withdrawal of cash for T. Lipizzan's personal use was debited to Salaries Expense $400 and credited to Cash $400.

Instructions

Prepare the correcting entries.

Prepare a classified balance sheet.
(SO 6)

E4-10 The adjusted trial balance for Bristol Bowling Alley at December 31, 2002, contains the following accounts.

Debits		Credits	
Building	$128,800	Amy Bristol, Capital	$115,000
Accounts Receivable	14,520	Accumulated Depreciation—Building	45,600
Prepaid Insurance	4,680	Accounts Payable	13,480
Cash	20,840	Mortgage Payable	93,600
Equipment	62,400	Accumulated Depreciation—Equipment	18,720
Land	61,200	Interest Payable	2,600
Insurance Expense	780	Bowling Revenues	14,180
Depreciation Expense	7,360		$303,180
Interest Expense	2,600		
	$303,180		

Instructions

(a) Prepare a classified balance sheet; assume that $13,600 of the mortgage payable will be paid in 2003.

(b) Comment on the liquidity of the company.

Prepare closing and reversing entries.
(SO 2, 4, 7)

***E4-11** On December 31, the adjusted trial balance of Becky Employment Agency shows the following selected data.

Accounts Receivable	$24,000	Commission Revenue	$92,000
Interest Expense	7,800	Interest Payable	2,000

Analysis shows that adjusting entries were made to (1) accrue $5,000 of commission revenue and (2) accrue $2,000 interest expense.

Instructions

(a) Prepare the closing entries for the temporary accounts at December 31.

(b) Prepare the reversing entries on January 1.

(c) Post the entries in (a) and (b). Rule and balance the accounts. (Use T accounts.)

(d) Prepare the entries to record (1) the collection of the accrued commissions on January 10 and (2) the payment of all interest due ($2,700) on January 15.

(e) Post the entries in (d) to the temporary accounts.

PROBLEMS: SET A

Prepare work sheet, financial statements, and adjusting and closing entries.
(SO 1, 2, 3, 6)

P4-1A Darth Vader began operations as a private investigator on January 1, 2002. The trial balance columns of the work sheet for Darth Vader P.I. at March 31 are as follows.

DARTH VADER P.I.
Work Sheet
For the Quarter Ended March 31, 2002

	Trial Balance	
Account Titles	**Dr.**	**Cr.**
Cash	11,400	
Accounts Receivable	5,620	
Supplies	1,050	
Prepaid Insurance	2,400	
Equipment	30,000	
Notes Payable		10,000
Accounts Payable		12,350
D. Vader, Capital		20,000
D. Vader, Drawing	600	
Service Revenue		13,620
Salaries Expense	2,200	
Travel Expense	1,300	
Rent Expense	1,200	
Miscellaneous Expense	200	
	55,970	55,970

Other data:

1. Supplies on hand total $750.
2. Depreciation is $500 per quarter.
3. Interest accrued on 6-month note payable, issued January 1, $300.
4. Insurance expires at the rate of $150 per month.
5. Services provided but unbilled at March 31 total $750.

Instructions

(a) Enter the trial balance on a work sheet and complete the work sheet.
(b) Prepare an income statement and owner's equity statement for the quarter and a classified balance sheet at March 31. D. Vader did not make any additional investments in the business during the quarter ended March 31, 2002.
(c) Journalize the adjusting entries from the adjustments columns of the work sheet.
(d) Journalize the closing entries from the financial statement columns of the work sheet.

(a) Adjusted trial balance $57,520
(b) Net income $7,920
Total assets $49,970

Complete work sheet; prepare financial statements, closing entries, and post-closing trial balance.
(SO 1, 2, 3, 6)

P4-2A The adjusted trial balance columns of the work sheet for Shmi Skywalker Company is as follows.

SHMI SKYWALKER COMPANY
Work Sheet
For the Year Ended December 31, 2002

		Adjusted Trial Balance	
Account No.	**Account Titles**	**Dr.**	**Cr.**
101	Cash	20,800	
112	Accounts Receivable	15,400	
126	Supplies	2,300	
130	Prepaid Insurance	4,800	
151	Office Equipment	44,000	
152	Accumulated Depreciation—Office Equipment		18,000
200	Notes Payable		20,000
201	Accounts Payable		8,000

Account No.	Account Titles	Adjusted Trial Balance Dr.	Cr.
212	Salaries Payable		3,000
230	Interest Payable		1,000
301	S. Skywalker, Capital		36,000
306	S. Skywalker, Drawing	12,000	
400	Service Revenue		79,000
610	Advertising Expense	12,000	
631	Supplies Expense	3,700	
711	Depreciation Expense	6,000	
722	Insurance Expense	4,000	
726	Salaries Expense	39,000	
905	Interest Expense	1,000	
	Totals	165,000	165,000

(a) Net income $13,300
(b) Current assets $43,300
Current liabilities $22,000

(e) Post-closing trial balance $87,300

Instructions

(a) Complete the work sheet by extending the balances to the financial statement columns.

(b) Prepare an income statement, owner's equity statement, and a classified balance sheet. $10,000 of the notes payable become due in 2003. S. Skywalker did not make any additional investments in the business during 2002.

(c) Prepare the closing entries. Use J14 for the journal page.

(d) Post the closing entries. Use the three-column form of account. Income Summary is No. 350.

(e) Prepare a post-closing trial balance.

Prepare financial statements, closing entries, and post-closing trial balance.
(SO 1, 2, 3, 6)

P4-3A The completed financial statement columns of the work sheet for Panaka Company are shown below.

PANAKA COMPANY
Work Sheet
For the Year Ended December 31, 2002

Account No.	Account Titles	Income Statement Dr.	Cr.	Balance Sheet Dr.	Cr.
101	Cash			10,200	
112	Accounts Receivable			7,500	
130	Prepaid Insurance			1,800	
157	Equipment			28,000	
167	Accumulated Depreciation				8,600
201	Accounts Payable				12,000
212	Salaries Payable				3,000
301	O. Panaka, Capital				34,000
306	O. Panaka, Drawing			7,200	
400	Service Revenue		44,000		
622	Repair Expense	3,200			
711	Depreciation Expense	2,800			
722	Insurance Expense	1,200			
726	Salaries Expense	36,000			
732	Utilities Expense	3,700			
	Totals	46,900	44,000	54,700	57,600
	Net Loss		2,900	2,900	
		46,900	46,900	57,600	57,600

(a) Net loss $2,900
Ending capital $23,900
Total assets $38,900

Instructions

(a) Prepare an income statement, owner's equity statement, and a classified balance sheet. O. Panaka made an additional investment in the business of $4,000 during 2002.

(b) Prepare the closing entries.

(c) Post the closing entries and rule and balance the accounts. Use T accounts. Income Summary is No. 350.
(d) Prepare a post-closing trial balance.

(d) Post-closing trial balance $47,500

P4-4A Wookie Amusement Park has a fiscal year ending on September 30. Selected data from the September 30 work sheet are presented below.

Complete work sheet; prepare classified balance sheet, entries, and post-closing trial balance.
(SO 1, 2, 3, 6)

WOOKIE AMUSEMENT PARK
Work Sheet
For the Year Ended September 30, 2002

	Trial Balance		Adjusted Trial Balance	
	Dr.	**Cr.**	**Dr.**	**Cr.**
Cash	41,400		41,400	
Supplies	18,600		1,200	
Prepaid Insurance	31,900		3,900	
Land	80,000		80,000	
Equipment	120,000		120,000	
Accumulated Depreciation		36,200		43,000
Accounts Payable		14,600		14,600
Unearned Admissions Revenue		3,700		1,700
Mortgage Payable		50,000		50,000
I.M. Wookie, Capital		109,700		109,700
I.M. Wookie, Drawing	14,000		14,000	
Admissions Revenue		277,500		279,500
Salaries Expense	105,000		105,000	
Repair Expense	30,500		30,500	
Advertising Expense	9,400		9,400	
Utilities Expense	16,900		16,900	
Property Taxes Expense	18,000		21,000	
Interest Expense	6,000		12,000	
Totals	491,700	491,700		
Insurance Expense			28,000	
Supplies Expense			17,400	
Interest Payable				6,000
Depreciation Expense			6,800	
Property Taxes Payable				3,000
Totals			507,500	507,500

Instructions

(a) Prepare a complete work sheet.
(b) Prepare a classified balance sheet. (*Note:* $10,000 of the mortgage payable is due for payment in the next fiscal year.)
(c) Journalize the adjusting entries using the work sheet as a basis.
(d) Journalize the closing entries using the work sheet as a basis.
(e) Prepare a post-closing trial balance.

(a) Net income $32,500
(b) Total current assets $46,500
(e) Post-closing trial balance $246,500

P4-5A Ewok-Ackbar opened Ewok's Carpet Cleaners on March 1. During March, the following transactions were completed.

Complete all steps in accounting cycle.
(SO 1, 2, 3, 4, 6)

Peachtree

Mar.	1	Invested $10,000 cash in the business.
	1	Purchased used truck for $6,000, paying $4,000 cash and the balance on account.
	3	Purchased cleaning supplies for $1,200 on account.
	5	Paid $1,800 cash on one-year insurance policy effective March 1.
	14	Billed customers $2,800 for cleaning services.
	18	Paid $1,500 cash on amount owed on truck and $500 on amount owed on cleaning supplies.
	20	Paid $1,500 cash for employee salaries.
	21	Collected $1,600 cash from customers billed on March 14.

28 Billed customers $2,500 for cleaning services.
31 Paid gas and oil for month on truck $200.
31 Withdrew $700 cash for personal use.

The chart of accounts for Ewok's Carpet Cleaners contains the following accounts: No. 101 Cash, No. 112 Accounts Receivable, No. 128 Cleaning Supplies, No. 130 Prepaid Insurance, No. 157 Equipment, No. 158 Accumulated Depreciation—Equipment, No. 201 Accounts Payable, No. 212 Salaries Payable, No. 301 A. Ewok, Capital, No. 306, A. Ewok, Drawing, No. 350 Income Summary, No. 400 Service Revenue, No. 633 Gas & Oil Expense, No. 634 Cleaning Supplies Expense, No. 711 Depreciation Expense, No. 722 Insurance Expense, No. 726 Salaries Expense.

Instructions

(a) Journalize and post the March transactions. Use page J1 for the journal and the three-column form of account.

(b) Trial balance $16,500

(b) Prepare a trial balance at March 31 on a work sheet.

(c) Adjusted trial balance $17,850

(c) Enter the following adjustments on the work sheet and complete the work sheet.
  (1) Earned but unbilled revenue at March 31 was $600.
  (2) Depreciation on equipment for the month was $250.
  (3) One-twelfth of the insurance expired.
  (4) An inventory count shows $400 of cleaning supplies on hand at March 31.
  (5) Accrued but unpaid employee salaries were $500.

(d) Net income $2,500
Total assets $13,500

(d) Prepare the income statement and owner's equity statement for March and a classified balance sheet at March 31.

(e) Journalize and post adjusting entries. Use page J2 for the journal.

(f) Journalize and post closing entries and complete the closing process. Use page J3 for the journal.

(g) Post-closing trial balance $13,750

(g) Prepare a post-closing trial balance at March 31.

Analyze errors and prepare correcting entries.
(SO 5)

P4-6A Bob Thebeau, CPA, was retained by Doneright TV Repair to prepare financial statements for April 2002. Thebeau accumulated all the ledger balances per Doneright's records and found the following.

DONERIGHT TV REPAIR
Trial Balance
April 30, 2002

	Debit	Credit
Cash	$ 4,100	
Accounts Receivable	3,200	
Supplies	800	
Equipment	10,600	
Accumulated Depreciation		$ 1,350
Accounts Payable		2,100
Salaries Payable		500
Unearned Revenue		890
B. Thebeau, Capital		12,900
Service Revenue		5,450
Salaries Expense	3,300	
Advertising Expense	400	
Miscellaneous Expense	290	
Depreciation Expense	500	
	$23,190	$23,190

Bob Thebeau reviewed the records and found the following errors.

1. Cash received from a customer on account was recorded as $950 instead of $590.
2. A payment of $30 for advertising expense was entered as a debit to Miscellaneous Expense $30 and a credit to Cash $30.

3. The first salary payment this month was for $1,900, which included $500 of salaries payable on March 31. The payment was recorded as a debit to Salaries Expense $1,900 and a credit to Cash $1,900. (No reversing entries were made on April 1.)
4. The purchase on account of a typewriter costing $340 was recorded as a debit to Supplies and a credit to Accounts Payable for $340.
5. A cash payment of repair expense on equipment for $86 was recorded as a debit to Equipment $68 and a credit to Cash $68.

Instructions

(a) Prepare an analysis of each error showing (1) the incorrect entry, (2) the correct entry, and (3) the correcting entry. Items 4 and 5 occurred on April 30, 2002.

(b) Prepare a correct trial balance.

Trial balance $22,690

PROBLEMS: SET B

Prepare a work sheet, financial statements, and adjusting and closing entries.
(SO 1, 2, 3, 6)

P4-1B The trial balance columns of the work sheet for Phantom Roofing at March 31, 2002, are as follows.

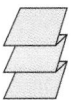

PHANTOM ROOFING
Work Sheet
For the Month Ended March 31, 2002

	Trial Balance	
Account Titles	**Dr.**	**Cr.**
Cash	2,500	
Accounts Receivable	1,600	
Roofing Supplies	1,100	
Equipment	6,000	
Accumulated Depreciation—Equipment		1,200
Accounts Payable		1,100
Unearned Revenue		300
Z. Phantom, Capital		7,000
Z. Phantom, Drawing	600	
Service Revenue		3,000
Salaries Expense	700	
Miscellaneous Expense	100	
	12,600	12,600

Other data:

1. A physical count reveals only $220 of roofing supplies on hand.
2. Depreciation for March is $200.
3. Unearned revenue amounted to $200 after adjustment on March 31.
4. Accrued salaries are $400.

Instructions

(a) Enter the trial balance on a work sheet and complete the work sheet.

(b) Prepare an income statement and owner's equity statement for the month of March and a classified balance sheet at March 31. Z. Phantom did not make any additional investments in the business in March.

(c) Journalize the adjusting entries from the adjustments columns of the work sheet.

(d) Journalize the closing entries from the financial statement columns of the work sheet.

(a) Adjusted trial balance $13,200
(b) Net income $820
Total assets $8,920

Complete work sheet; prepare financial statements, closing entries, and post-closing trial balance.
(SO 1, 2, 3, 6)

P4-2B The adjusted trial balance columns of the work sheet for Boss Nass Company, owned by Boss Nass, are as follows.

BOSS NASS COMPANY
Work Sheet
For the Year Ended December 31, 2002

Account No.	Account Titles	Adjusted Trial Balance Dr.	Adjusted Trial Balance Cr.
101	Cash	13,600	
112	Accounts Receivable	15,400	
126	Supplies	1,500	
130	Prepaid Insurance	2,800	
151	Office Equipment	34,000	
152	Accumulated Depreciation—Office Equipment		8,000
200	Notes Payable		16,000
201	Accounts Payable		6,000
212	Salaries Payable		3,000
230	Interest Payable		500
301	Boss Nass, Capital		25,000
306	Boss Nass, Drawing	10,000	
400	Service Revenue		88,000
610	Advertising Expense	12,000	
631	Supplies Expense	5,700	
711	Depreciation Expense	4,000	
722	Insurance Expense	5,000	
726	Salaries Expense	42,000	
905	Interest Expense	500	
	Totals	146,500	146,500

(a) Net income $18,800
(b) Current assets $33,300; Current liabilities $19,500

Instructions

(a) Complete the work sheet by extending the balances to the financial statement columns.
(b) Prepare an income statement, owner's equity statement, and a classified balance sheet. (*Note:* $10,000 of the notes payable become due in 2003.) Boss Nass did not make any additional investments in the business during the year.
(c) Prepare the closing entries. Use J14 for the journal page.
(d) Post the closing entries. Use the three-column form of account. Income Summary is No. 350.
(e) Prepare a post-closing trial balance.

(e) Post-closing trial balance $67,300

Prepare financial statements, closing entries, and post-closing trial balance.
(SO 1, 2, 3, 6)

P4-3B The completed financial statement columns of the work sheet for Nute Gunray Company are shown below.

NUTE GUNRAY COMPANY
Work Sheet
For the Year Ended December 31, 2002

Account No.	Account Titles	Income Statement Dr.	Income Statement Cr.	Balance Sheet Dr.	Balance Sheet Cr.
101	Cash			16,600	
112	Accounts Receivable			13,500	
130	Prepaid Insurance			3,500	
157	Equipment			26,000	
167	Accumulated Depreciation				5,600
201	Accounts Payable				11,300
212	Salaries Payable				3,000
301	Nute Gunray, Capital				36,000
306	Nute Gunray, Drawing			12,000	
400	Service Revenue		59,000		
622	Repair Expense	1,800			
711	Depreciation Expense	2,600			

Account No.	Account Titles	Income Statement Dr.	Income Statement Cr.	Balance Sheet Dr.	Balance Sheet Cr.
722	Insurance Expense	2,200			
726	Salaries Expense	35,000			
732	Utilities Expense	1,700			
	Totals	43,300	59,000	71,600	55,900
	Net Income	15,700			15,700
		59,000	59,000	71,600	71,600

Instructions

(a) Prepare an income statement, owner's equity statement, and a classified balance sheet.

(b) Prepare the closing entries. Nute did not make any additional investments during the year.

(c) Post the closing entries and rule and balance the accounts. Use T accounts. Income Summary is No. 350.

(d) Prepare a post-closing trial balance.

(a) Ending capital $39,700; Total current assets $33,600

(d) Post-closing trial balance $59,600

P4-4B Rebecca Sherrick Management Services began business on January 1, 2002, with a capital investment of $120,000. The company manages condominiums for owners (Service Revenue) and rents space in its own office building (Rent Revenue). The trial balance and adjusted trial balance columns of the work sheet at the end of the first year are as follows.

Complete work sheet; prepare classified balance sheet, entries, and post-closing trial balance. (SO 1, 2, 3, 6)

REBECCA SHERRICK MANAGEMENT SERVICES
Work Sheet
For the Year Ended December 31, 2002

Account Titles	Trial Balance Dr.	Trial Balance Cr.	Adjusted Trial Balance Dr.	Adjusted Trial Balance Cr.
Cash	14,500		14,500	
Accounts Receivable	23,600		23,600	
Prepaid Insurance	3,100		1,600	
Land	56,000		56,000	
Building	106,000		106,000	
Equipment	48,000		48,000	
Accounts Payable		10,400		10,400
Unearned Rent Revenue		5,000		1,800
Mortgage Payable		100,000		100,000
R. Sherrick, Capital		120,000		120,000
R. Sherrick, Drawing	20,000		20,000	
Service Revenue		75,600		75,600
Rent Revenue		23,000		26,200
Salaries Expense	30,000		30,000	
Advertising Expense	17,000		17,000	
Utilities Expense	15,800		15,800	
Totals	334,000	334,000		
Insurance Expense			1,500	
Depreciation Expense—Building			2,500	
Accumulated Depreciation—Building				2,500
Depreciation Expense—Equipment			3,900	
Accumulated Depreciation—Equipment				3,900
Interest Expense			10,000	
Interest Payable				10,000
Totals			350,400	350,400

Instructions

(a) Prepare a complete work sheet.

(b) Prepare a classified balance sheet. (*Note:* $10,000 of the mortgage payable is due for payment next year.)

(a) Net income $21,100

(b) Total current assets $39,700

(e) Post-closing trial balance $249,700

(c) Journalize the adjusting entries.
(d) Journalize the closing entries.
(e) Prepare a post-closing trial balance.

Complete all steps in accounting cycle.
(SO 1, 2, 3, 4, 6)

P4-5B Terry Duffy opened Terry's Window Washing on July 1, 2002. During July the following transactions were completed.

July	1	Duffy invested $9,000 cash in the business.
	1	Purchased used truck for $6,000, paying $3,000 cash and the balance on account.
	3	Purchased cleaning supplies for $900 on account.
	5	Paid $1,200 cash on one-year insurance policy effective July 1.
	12	Billed customers $2,500 for cleaning services.
	18	Paid $1,000 cash on amount owed on truck and $500 on amount owed on cleaning supplies.
	20	Paid $1,200 cash for employee salaries.
	21	Collected $1,400 cash from customers billed on July 12.
	25	Billed customers $3,000 for cleaning services.
	31	Paid gas and oil for month on truck $200.
	31	Withdrew $900 cash for personal use.

The chart of accounts for Terry's Window Washing contains the following accounts: No. 101 Cash, No. 112 Accounts Receivable, No. 128 Cleaning Supplies, No. 130 Prepaid Insurance, No. 157 Equipment, No. 158 Accumulated Depreciation—Equipment, No. 201 Accounts Payable, No. 212 Salaries Payable, No. 301 Terry Duffy, Capital, No. 306 Terry Duffy, Drawing, No. 350 Income Summary, No. 400 Service Revenue, No. 633 Gas & Oil Expense, No. 634 Cleaning Supplies Expense, No. 711 Depreciation Expense, No. 722 Insurance Expense, No. 726 Salaries Expense.

Instructions

(a) Journalize and post the July transactions. Use page J1 for the journal and the three-column form of account.

(b) Trial balance $16,900
(c) Adjusted trial balance $18,600

(b) Prepare a trial balance at July 31 on a work sheet.
(c) Enter the following adjustments on the work sheet and complete the work sheet.
  (1) Services provided but unbilled and uncollected at July 31 were $1,100.
  (2) Depreciation on equipment for the month was $200.
  (3) One-twelfth of the insurance expired.
  (4) An inventory count shows $600 of cleaning supplies on hand at July 31.
  (5) Accrued but unpaid employee salaries were $400.

(d) Net income $4,200; Total assets $15,100

(d) Prepare the income statement and owner's equity statement for July and a classified balance sheet at July 31.
(e) Journalize and post adjusting entries. Use page J2 for the journal.
(f) Journalize and post closing entries and complete the closing process. Use page J3 for the journal.

(g) Post-closing trial balance $15,300

(g) Prepare a post-closing trial balance at July 31.

COMPREHENSIVE PROBLEM: CHAPTERS 2 TO 4

Bill Murphy opened Bill's Window Washing on July 1, 2002. During July, the following transactions were completed.

July	1	Invested $10,000 cash in the business.
	1	Purchased a used truck for $8,000, paying $3,000 cash and the balance on account.
	3	Purchased cleaning supplies for $800 on account.
	5	Paid $2,400 on a one-year insurance policy, effective July 1.
	12	Billed customers $3,500 for cleaning services.
	18	Paid $1,000 of amount owed on truck, and $400 of amount owed on cleaning supplies.
	20	Paid $1,600 for employee salaries.
	21	Collected $1,400 from customer billed on July 12.

25 Billed customers $2,500 for cleaning services.
31 Paid gas and oil for the month on the truck, $300.
31 Withdrew $400 cash for personal use.

The chart of accounts for Bill's Window Washing contains the following accounts: No. 101 Cash, No. 112 Accounts Receivable, No. 128 Cleaning Supplies, No. 130 Prepaid Insurance, No. 157 Equipment, No. 158 Accumulated Depreciation—Equipment, No. 201 Accounts Payable, No. 212 Salaries Payable, No. 301, Bill Murphy, Capital, No. 306 Bill Murphy, Drawing, No. 350 Income Summary, No. 400 Service Revenue, No. 633 Gas & Oil Expense, No. 634 Cleaning Supplies Expense, No. 711 Depreciation Expense, No. 722 Insurance Expense, No. 726 Salaries Expense.

Instructions

(a) Journalize and post the July transactions. Use page J1 for the journal.
(b) Prepare a trial balance at July 31 on a work sheet. (b) T/B totals $20,400
(c) Enter the following adjustments on the work sheet, and complete the work sheet.
  (1) Earned but unbilled fees at July 31 were $1,300.
  (2) Depreciation on equipment for the month was $200.
  (3) One-twelfth of the insurance expired.
  (4) An inventory count shows $200 of cleaning supplies on hand at July 31.
  (5) Accrued but unpaid employee salaries were $300.
(d) Prepare the income statement and statement of owner's equity for July, and a classified balance sheet at July 31, 2002. (d) NI $4,100 T/A $18,400
(e) Journalize and post the adjusting entries. Use page J2 for the journal.
(f) Journalize and post the closing entries, and complete the closing process. Use page J3 for the journal.
(g) Prepare a post-closing trial balance at July 31. (g) T/B totals $18,600

BROADENING YOUR PERSPECTIVE

FINANCIAL REPORTING AND ANALYSIS

FINANCIAL REPORTING PROBLEM: Lands' End, Inc.

BYP4-1 The financial statements of **Lands' End, Inc.** are presented in Appendix A at the end of this textbook.

Instructions

Answer the following questions using the Consolidated Balance Sheet and the Notes to Consolidated Financial Statements section.

(a) What were Lands' End's total current assets at January 28, 2000 and January 29, 1999?
(b) Are assets that Lands' End's included under current assets listed in proper order? Explain.
(c) How are Lands' End's assets classified?
(d) What are "cash equivalents"?
(e) What were Lands' End's total current liabilities at January 28, 2000 and January 29, 1999?

COMPARATIVE ANALYSIS PROBLEM: Lands' End vs. Abercrombie & Fitch

BYP4-2 **Lands' End's** financial statements are presented in Appendix A. **Abercrombie & Fitch's** financial statements are presented in Appendix B.

Instructions

(a) Based on the information contained in these financial statements, determine each of the following for Lands' End at January 28, 2000, and for Abercrombie & Fitch at January 29, 2000.
  (1) Total current assets.
  (2) Net amount of property, plant, and equipment (land, buildings, and equipment).
  (3) Total current liabilities.
  (4) Total stockholders' (shareholders') equity.
(b) What conclusions concerning the companies' respective financial positions can be drawn from these data?

INTERPRETING FINANCIAL STATEMENTS: A Global Focus

BYP4-3 **Mo och Comsjo AB (MoDo)** is one of Europe's largest forest products companies. It has production facilities in Sweden, France, and Great Britain. Its headquarters is in Stockholm, Sweden. Its statements are presented in conformity with the standards issued by the Swedish Standards Board. Its financial statements are presented to be harmonized (that is, to have minimal difference in methods) with member countries of the European Union. The balance sheet on the next page was taken from a recent annual report.

Instructions

List all differences that you notice between MoDo's balance sheet presentation (format and terminology) and the presentation of U.S. companies shown in the chapter. For differences in terminology, list the corresponding terminology used by U.S. companies.

EXPLORING THE WEB

BYP4-4 Numerous companies have established home pages on the Internet, e.g., **Boston Beer Company (www.samadams.com), Ford Motor Company (www.ford.com),** and **Kodak (www.kodak.com).** You may have noticed company Internet addresses in television commercials or magazine advertisements.

Instructions

Examine the home pages of any two companies and answer the following questions.

(a) What type of information is available?
(b) Is any accounting-related information presented?
(c) Would you describe the home page as informative, promotional, or both? Why?

CRITICAL THINKING

GROUP DECISION CASE

BYP4-5 Everclean Janitorial Service was started 2 years ago by Bonnie Harris. Because business has been exceptionally good, Bonnie decided on July 1, 2002, to expand operations by acquiring an additional truck and hiring two more assistants. To finance the expansion, Bonnie obtained on July 1, 2002, a $25,000, 10% bank loan, payable $10,000 on July 1, 2003, and the balance on July 1, 2004. The terms of the loan require the borrower to have $10,000 more current assets than current liabilities at December 31, 2002. If these terms are not met, the bank loan will be refinanced at 15% interest. At December 31, 2002, the accountant for Everclean Janitorial Service Inc. prepared the following balance sheet.

EVERCLEAN JANITORIAL SERVICE
Balance Sheet
December 31, 2002

Assets		Liabilities and Owner's Equity	
Current assets		Current liabilities	
Cash	$ 6,500	Notes payable	$10,000
Accounts receivable	9,000	Accounts payable	2,500
Janitorial supplies	5,200	Total current liabilities	12,500
Prepaid insurance	4,800	Long-term liability	
Total current assets	25,500	Notes payable	15,000
Property, plant, and equipment		Total liabilities	27,500
Cleaning equipment (net)	22,000	Owner's equity	
Delivery trucks (net)	34,000	Bonnie Harris, capital	54,000
Total property, plant, and equipment	56,000		
Total assets	$81,500	Total liabilities and owner's equity	$81,500

Bonnie presented the balance sheet to the bank's loan office on January 2, 2003, confident that the company had met the terms of the loan. The loan officer was not impressed. She said,

MoDo

MODO
Consolidated Balance Sheet
at December 31
(Swedish kronor, in millions)

	1998	1997
Assets		
Fixed assets		
Intangible assets		
Goodwill, leases and similar rights	32	69
Tangible assets		
Forest land	4,585	4,560
Buildings, other land and land installations	2,565	2,049
Machinery and equipment	13,216	12,814
Fixed plants under construction and advance payments	341	128
	20,707	19,551
Financial assets		
Shares and participations		
Associate companies	89	129
Other shares and participations	59	48
Other long-term receivables	44	49
	192	226
	20,931	19,846
Current assets		
Inventories, etc.	3,648	3,620
Current receivables	4,614	4,600
Short-term placements	780	1,189
Cash in bank	461	447
	9,503	9,856
	30,434	29,702
Equity and Liabilities		
Equity		
Restricted equity		
Share capital	4,443	4,443
Restricted reserves	7,819	5,985
Non-restricted equity		
Non-restricted reserves	3,611	4,513
Profit for the year	2,504	1,434
	18,377	16,375
Minority interests	5	5
Provisions		
Interest-bearing		
Pension provisions	135	1,544
Interest-free		
Tax provisions	3,228	3,815
Other provisions	240	239
	3,603	5,598
Liabilities		
Financial liabilities	4,249	3,961
Operating liabilities	4,200	3,763
	8,449	7,724
	30,434	29,702
Pledged assets	445	481
Contingent liabilities	233	182

"We need financial statements audited by a CPA." A CPA was hired and immediately realized that the balance sheet had been prepared from a trial balance and not from an adjusted trial balance. The adjustment data at the balance sheet date consisted of the following.

(1) Earned but unbilled janitorial services were $5,000.
(2) Janitorial supplies on hand were $2,500.
(3) Prepaid insurance was a 3-year policy dated January 1, 2002.
(4) December expenses incurred but unpaid at December 31, $300.
(5) Interest on the bank loan was not recorded.
(6) The amounts for property, plant, and equipment presented in the balance sheet were reported net of accumulated depreciation (cost less accumulated depreciation). These amounts were $4,000 for cleaning equipment and $5,000 for delivery trucks as of January 1, 2002. Depreciation for 2000 was $2,000 for cleaning equipment and $5,000 for delivery trucks.

Instructions

With the class divided into groups, answer the following.

(a) Prepare a correct balance sheet.
(b) Were the terms of the bank loan met? Explain.

COMMUNICATION ACTIVITY

BYP4-6 The accounting cycle is important in understanding the accounting process.

Instructions

Write a memo to your instructor that lists the steps of the accounting cycle in the order in which they should be completed. Complete your memo with a paragraph that explains the optional steps in the cycle.

ETHICS CASE

BYP4-7 As the controller of TellTale Perfume Company, you discover a misstatement that overstated net income in the prior year's financial statements. The misleading financial statements appear in the company's annual report which was issued to banks and other creditors less than a month ago. After much thought about the consequences of telling the president, Eddie Lieman, about this misstatement, you gather your courage to inform him. Eddie says, "Hey! What they don't know won't hurt them. But, just so we set the record straight, we'll adjust this year's financial statements for last year's misstatement. We can absorb that misstatement better in this year than in last year anyway! Just don't make such a mistake again."

Instructions

(a) Who are the stakeholders in this situation?
(b) What are the ethical issues in this situation?
(c) What would you do as a controller in this situation?

Answers to Self-Study Questions

1. b **2.** c **3.** a **4.** b **5.** c **6.** a **7.** d **8.** b **9.** d **10.** a **11.** c

LANDS' END DIRECT MERCHANTS

Answers to Lands' End Review It Question 2, p. 156

Current liabilities in 2000 were $150,872,000. Current liabilities in 1999 were $205,283,000. In both 2000 and 1999, current liabilities were less than current assets.

Remember to go back to the Navigator box on the chapter-opening page and check off your completed work.

ACCOUNTING FOR MERCHANDISING OPERATIONS

5

THE NAVIGATOR ✓

- Understand *Concepts for Review* ❑
- Read *Feature Story* ❑
- Scan *Study Objectives* ❑
- Read *Preview* ❑
- Read text and answer *Before You Go On* *p.* 191 ❑ *p.* 194 ❑ *p.* 197 ❑ *p.* 202 ❑
- Work *Demonstration Problem* ❑
- Review *Summary of Study Objectives* ❑
- Answer *Self-Study Questions* ❑
- Complete *Assignments* ❑

CONCEPTS FOR REVIEW

Before studying this chapter, you should know or, if necessary, review:

a. How to close revenue, expense, and drawing accounts. (Ch. 4, pp. 140–144)

b. The steps in the accounting cycle. (Ch. 4, pp. 146–148)

THE NAVIGATOR

FEATURE STORY

Selling Dollars for 85 Cents

For most of the last decade **Wal-Mart** has set the rules of the retail game. Entrepreneur Scott Blum, CEO of **Buy.com**, has a different game plan. He is selling consumer products at or below cost. Buy.com is trying to create an outlet synonymous with low prices—in the hope of becoming the leading e-commerce portal on the Internet. He plans to make up the losses from sales by selling advertising on the company's Web site.

As if the idea of selling below cost weren't unusual enough, Blum has added another twist to merchandising: He doesn't want to handle inventory. So he has wholesalers and distributors ship the products directly to his Web site customers.

Buy.com's slogan, "The lowest prices on earth," may be the most eye-catching sales pitch ever. The company is ruthlessly committed to being the price leader—even if it means losing money on every sale. Its own computers search competitors' Web sites to make sure that Buy.com has the lowest prices on the Internet.

The amount of available capital (cash) is the natural limit to a business model in which money is lost on every sale. During the 3-month period ended June 30, 2000, Buy.com still had not generated a net positive cash flow, and it reported a net loss of $32.8 million. At June 30, 2000, the company had $140 million in cash, so even if it loses money on each sale, Buy.com should be able to run for a while.

Consider the implications if Buy.com is successful. Buy.com's success could change the very way wholesalers and distributors view their businesses. Its success may have an impact on all kinds of retailers—starting with Buy.com itself. If Buy.com proves that the ad space on a product order form—its Web site—is almost as valuable as the product being ordered, another virtual reseller is sure to enter the market with even lower prices. In addition, Wal-Mart is also experimenting with Internet retailing.

Of course, there is one big winner if Buy.com succeeds: you. It has never been a better time to be a customer.

Source: J. William Gurley, "Buy.com May Fail, But If It Succeeds, Retailing May Never Be the Same," *Fortune*, January 11, 1999, pp. 150–152.

THE NAVIGATOR

www.buy.com

STUDY OBJECTIVES

After studying this chapter, you should be able to:

1. Identify the differences between a service enterprise and a merchandiser.
2. Explain the entries for purchases under a perpetual inventory system.
3. Explain the entries for sales revenues under a perpetual inventory system.
4. Explain the steps in the accounting cycle for a merchandiser.
5. Distinguish between a multiple-step and a single-step income statement.
6. Explain the computation and importance of gross profit.

THE NAVIGATOR

PREVIEW OF CHAPTER 5

As indicated in the Feature Story, **Buy.com** is an unusual merchandiser because it does not have its own inventory. Like traditional merchandisers such as Wal-Mart, though, it generates revenues by selling goods to customers rather than performing services. Merchandisers that purchase and sell directly to consumers—such as **Kmart**, **Safeway**, and **Toys "R" Us**—are called **retailers**. In contrast, merchandisers that sell to retailers are known as **wholesalers**. For example, retailer **Walgreens** might buy goods from wholesaler **McKesson HBOC**; **Office Depot** might buy office supplies from wholesaler **United Stationers**.

The steps in the accounting cycle for a merchandiser are the same as the steps for a service enterprise. But merchandisers use additional accounts and entries that are required in recording merchandising transactions.

The content and organization of Chapter 5 are as follows.

ACCOUNTING FOR MERCHANDISING OPERATIONS

- **Merchandising Operations**
  - Operating cycles
  - Inventory systems
- **Recording Purchases of Merchandise**
  - Purchase returns and allowances
  - Freight costs
  - Purchase discounts
- **Recording Sales of Merchandise**
  - Sales returns and allowances
  - Sales discounts
- **Completing the Accounting Cycle**
  - Adjusting entries
  - Closing entries
  - Summary of entries
- **Forms of Financial Statements**
  - Multiple-step income statement
  - Single-step income statement
  - Classified balance sheet

THE NAVIGATOR

MERCHANDISING OPERATIONS

STUDY OBJECTIVE 1

Identify the differences between a service enterprise and a merchandiser.

Measuring net income for a merchandiser is conceptually the same as for a service enterprise. That is, net income (or loss) results from the matching of expenses with revenues. For a merchandiser, the primary source of revenues is the sale of merchandise. This revenue source is often referred to as **sales revenue** or **sales**. Unlike expenses for a service company, expenses for a merchandiser are divided into two categories: (1) the cost of goods sold and (2) operating expenses.

The **cost of goods sold** is the total cost of merchandise sold during the period. This expense is directly related to the revenue recognized from the sale of the goods. Sales revenue less cost of goods sold is called **gross profit** on sales. For example, when a calculator costing $15 is sold for $25, the gross profit is $10. Merchandisers report gross profit on sales in the income statement.

After gross profit is calculated, operating expenses are deducted to determine net income (or net loss). **Operating expenses** are expenses incurred in the process of earning sales revenue. Examples of operating expenses are sales salaries, advertising expense, and insurance expense. The operating expenses of a merchandiser include many of the expenses found in a service company.

The income measurement process for a merchandiser is diagrammed in Illustration 5-1. The items in the three blue boxes are peculiar to a merchandiser. They are not used by a service company.

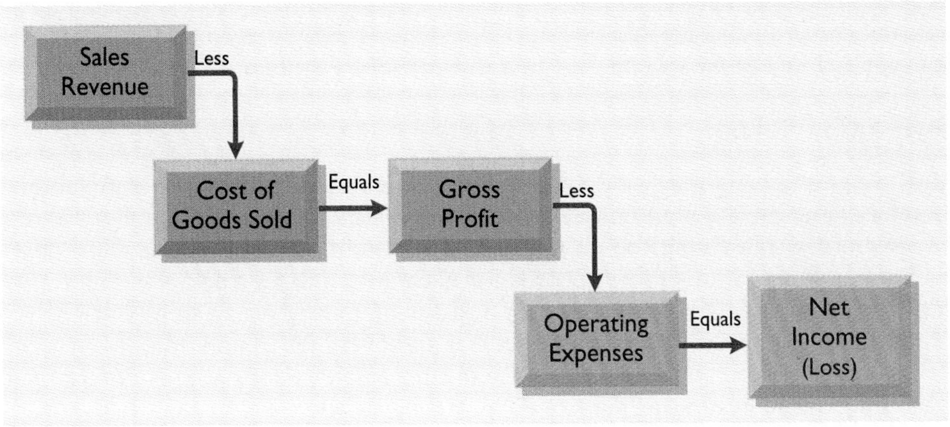

Illustration 5-1
Income measurement process for a merchandiser

OPERATING CYCLES

The operating cycle of a merchandiser differs from that of a service company, as shown in Illustration 5-2. The operating cycle of a merchandiser ordinarily is longer than that of a service company. The purchase of merchandise inventory

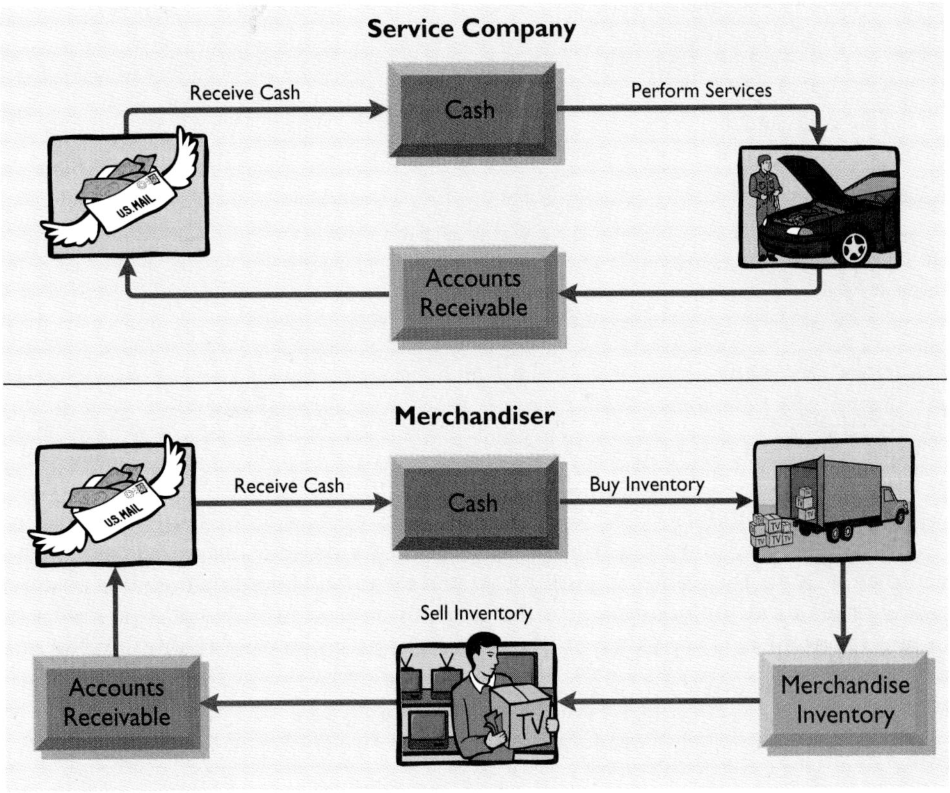

Illustration 5-2
Operating cycles for a service company and a merchandiser

and its eventual sale lengthen the cycle. Note that the added asset account for a merchandising company is an **inventory** account. It is usually entitled Merchandise Inventory. Merchandise inventory is reported as a current asset on the balance sheet.

INVENTORY SYSTEMS

A merchandiser keeps track of its inventory to determine what is available for sale and what has been sold. One of two systems is used to account for inventory: a **perpetual inventory system** or a **periodic inventory system**.

Perpetual System

In a **perpetual inventory system**, detailed records of the cost of each inventory purchase and sale are maintained. This system continuously—perpetually—shows the inventory that should be on hand for every item. For example, a **Ford** dealership has separate inventory records for each automobile, truck, and van on its lot. With the use of bar codes and optical scanners, a grocery store can keep a daily running record of every box of cereal and every jar of jelly that it buys and sells. Under a perpetual inventory system, the cost of goods sold is **determined each time a sale occurs**.

HELPFUL HINT
For control purposes a physical inventory count is taken under the perpetual system, even though it is not needed to determine cost of goods sold.

TECHNOLOGY IN ACTION

What's in a bar code? First, the bar code usually doesn't contain descriptive data (just as your Social Security number or car's license plate number doesn't have anything about your name or where you live). For example, the bar codes found on food items at grocery stores don't contain the price or description of the food item. Instead, the bar code has a 12-digit "product number" in it. When read by a bar code reader and transmitted to the computer, the computer finds the disk file item record(s) associated with that item number. In the disk file is the price, vendor name, quantity on-hand, description, and so on. The computer does a "price lookup" by reading the bar code, and then it creates a register of the items and adds the price to the subtotal of the groceries sold. It also subtracts the quantity from the "on-hand" total.

SOURCE: Excerpted from *A Bar Code Primer*, © 1997 Worth Data.

Periodic System

In a **periodic inventory system**, detailed inventory records of the goods on hand are not kept throughout the period. The cost of goods sold is **determined only at the end of the accounting period**—that is, periodically. At that time, a physical inventory count is taken to determine the cost of goods on hand (Merchandise Inventory). To determine the cost of goods sold under a periodic inventory system, the following steps are necessary: (1) Determine the cost of goods on hand at the beginning of the accounting period. (2) Add to it the cost of goods purchased. (3) Subtract the cost of goods on hand at the end of the accounting period.

Illustration 5-3 graphically compares the sequence of activities and the timing of the cost of goods sold computation under the two inventory systems.

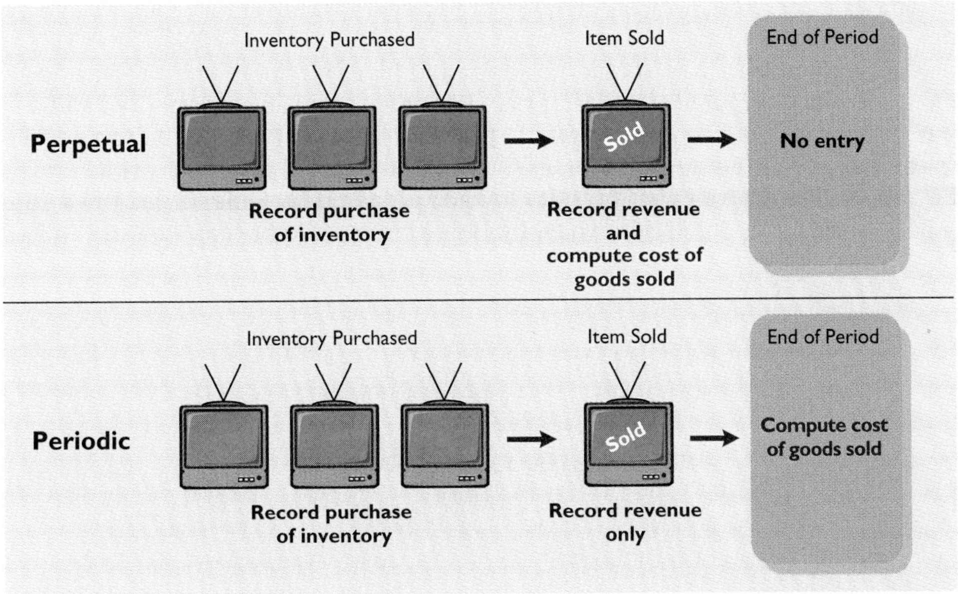

Illustration 5-3
Comparing periodic and perpetual inventory systems

Additional Considerations

Perpetual systems have traditionally been used by companies that sell merchandise with high unit values. Examples are automobiles, furniture, and major home appliances. The widespread use of computers and electronic scanners now enables many more companies to install perpetual inventory systems. The perpetual inventory system is so named because the accounting records continuously—perpetually—show the quantity and cost of the inventory that should be on hand at any time.

A perpetual inventory system provides better control over inventories than a periodic system. The inventory records show the quantities that should be on hand. So, the goods can be counted at any time to see whether the amount of goods actually on hand agrees with the inventory records. Any shortages uncovered can be investigated immediately. A perpetual inventory system does require additional clerical work and additional cost to maintain the subsidiary records. But a computerized system can minimize this cost. Much of **Wal-Mart's** success is attributed to its sophisticated perpetual inventory system. When snowboard maker **Morrow Snowboards Inc.** issued shares of stock to the public for the first time, some investors expressed reluctance to invest in Morrow. They were concerned about a number of accounting control problems. To reduce investor concerns, Morrow implemented a perpetual inventory system to improve its control over inventory.

Because the perpetual inventory system is growing in popularity and use, we illustrate it in this chapter. The periodic system, still widely used, is described in the next chapter.

RECORDING PURCHASES OF MERCHANDISE

STUDY OBJECTIVE 2
Explain the entries for purchases under a perpetual inventory system.

Purchases of inventory may be made for cash or on account (credit). Purchases are normally recorded when the goods are received from the seller. Every purchase should be supported by business documents that provide written evidence of the transaction. Each cash purchase should be supported by a canceled check or a cash register receipt indicating the items purchased and amounts paid. Cash purchases are recorded by an increase in Merchandise Inventory and a decrease in Cash.

Each credit purchase should be supported by a **purchase invoice**. This document indicates the total purchase price and other relevant information. But the purchaser does not prepare a separate purchase invoice. Instead, the copy of the sales invoice sent by the seller is used by the buyer as a purchase invoice. In Illustration 5-4, for example, the sales invoice prepared by Sellers Electronix (the seller) is used as a purchase invoice by Beyer Video (the buyer).

Illustration 5-4

Sales invoice used as purchase invoice by Beyer Video

INVOICE NO. 731

SELLERS ELECTRONIX
27 CIRCLE DRIVE
HARDING, MICHIGAN 48281

SOLD TO
Firm Name Beyer Video
Attention of James Hoover, Purchasing Agent
Address 125 Main Street
Chelsea (City) Illinois (State) 60915 (Zip)

Date 5/4/02	Salesperson Malone	Terms 2/10, n/30	Freight Paid by Buyer	
Catalog No.	**Description**	**Quantity**	**Price**	**Amount**
X572Y9820	Printed Circuit Board-prototype	1	2,300	$2,300
A2547Z45	Production Model Circuits	5	300	1,500
IMPORTANT: ALL RETURNS MUST BE MADE WITHIN 10 DAYS			**TOTAL**	$3,800

HELPFUL HINT
To better understand the contents of this invoice, identify these items:
1. Seller
2. Invoice date
3. Purchaser
4. Salesperson
5. Credit terms
6. Freight terms
7. Goods sold: catalog number, description, quantity, price per unit
8. Total invoice amount

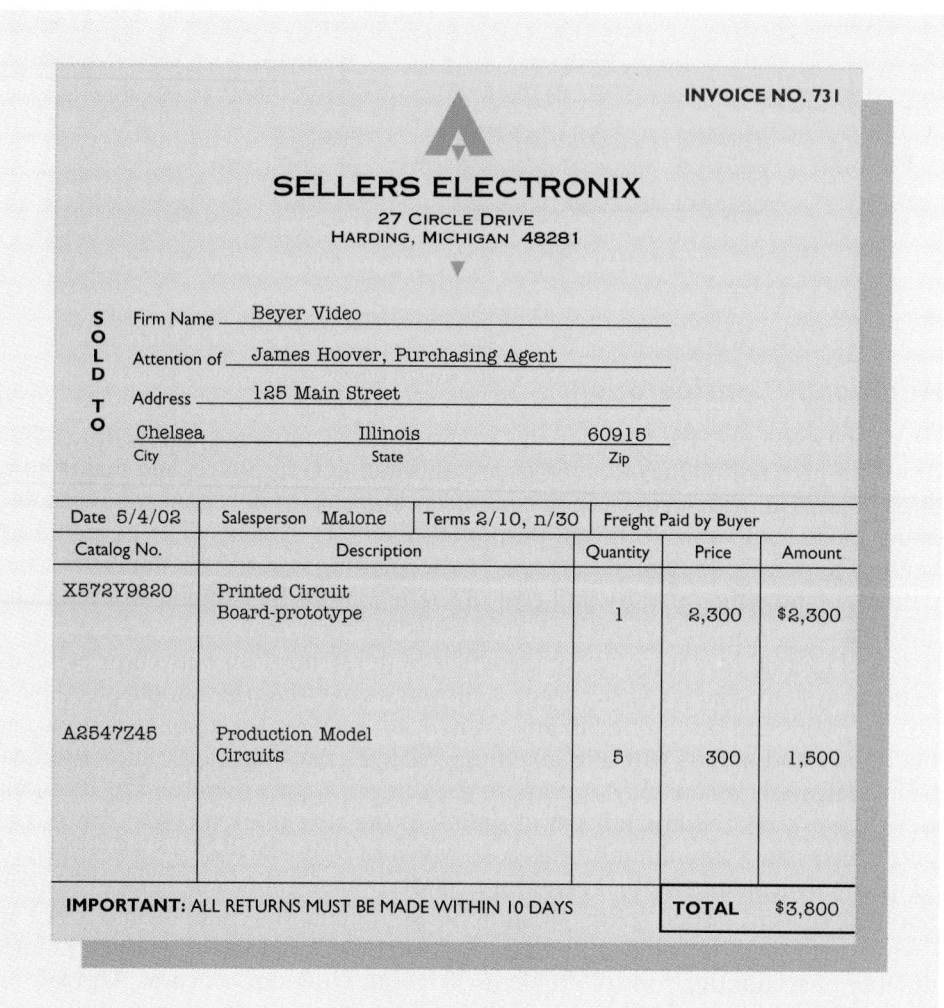

The associated entry for Beyer Video for the invoice from Sellers Electronix is:

A	=	L	+	OE
+3,800		+3,800		

May 4	Merchandise Inventory	3,800	
	Accounts Payable		3,800
	(To record goods purchased on account from Sellers Electronix)		

Under the perpetual inventory system, purchases of merchandise for sale are recorded in the Merchandise Inventory account. Thus, a retailer of general merchandise such as **Wal-Mart** would debit Merchandise Inventory for clothing, sporting goods, and anything else purchased for resale to customers.

Not all purchases are debited to Merchandise Inventory, however. Purchases of assets acquired for use and not for resale (such as supplies, equipment, and similar items) are recorded as increases to specific asset accounts rather than to Merchandise Inventory. Wal-Mart would increase Supplies to record the purchase of materials used to make shelf signs or for cash register receipt paper.

PURCHASE RETURNS AND ALLOWANCES

A purchaser may be dissatisfied with the merchandise received. The goods may be damaged or defective, of inferior quality, or perhaps they do not meet the purchaser's specifications. In such cases, the purchaser may return the goods to the seller. The purchaser is granted credit if the sale was made on credit, or a cash refund if the purchase was for cash. This transaction is known as a **purchase return**. Or the purchaser may choose to keep the merchandise if the seller is willing to grant an allowance (deduction) from the purchase price. This transaction is known as a **purchase allowance**.

Assume that Beyer Video returned goods costing $300 to Sellers Electronix on May 8. The entry by Beyer Video for the returned merchandise is:

May 8	Accounts Payable	300	
	Merchandise Inventory		300
	(To record return of goods received from Sellers Electronix)		

A	=	L	+	OE
−300		−300		

Beyer Video increased Merchandise Inventory when the goods were received. So, Beyer Video decreases Merchandise Inventory when it returns the goods or when it is granted an allowance.

FREIGHT COSTS

The sales agreement should indicate whether the seller or the buyer is to pay the cost of transporting the goods to the buyer's place of business. When a common carrier such as a railroad, trucking company, or airline is used, the transportation company prepares a freight bill (often called a bill of lading) in accordance with the sales agreement. Freight terms are expressed as either **FOB shipping point** or **FOB destination**. The letters FOB mean **free on board**. Thus, **FOB shipping point** means that goods are placed free on board the carrier by the seller, and the buyer pays the freight costs. Conversely, **FOB destination** means that the goods are placed free on board to the buyer's place of business, and the seller pays the freight. For example, the sales invoice in Illustration 5-4 on page 188 indicates that the buyer (Beyer Video) pays the freight charges.

HELPFUL HINT
Freight terms may be stated by location. A Chicago seller may use "FOB Chicago" for FOB shipping point and the buyer's city for FOB destination.

When the purchaser directly incurs the freight costs, the account Merchandise Inventory is debited. For example, if upon delivery of the goods on May 6, Beyer Video pays Acme Freight Company $150 for freight charges, the entry on Beyer Video's books is:

May 6	Merchandise Inventory	150	
	Cash		150
	(To record payment of freight on goods purchased)		

A	=	L	+	OE
+150				
−150				

In contrast, **freight costs incurred by the seller on outgoing merchandise are an operating expense to the seller**. These costs increase an expense account titled Freight-out or Delivery Expense. If the freight terms on the invoice in Illustration

5-4 had required that Sellers Electronix pay the $150 freight charges, the entry by Sellers Electronix would have been:

A	=	L	+	OE
−150				−150

May 4	Freight-out (or Delivery Expense)	150	
	Cash		150
	(To record payment of freight on goods sold)		

When the freight charges are paid by the seller, the seller will usually establish a higher invoice price for the goods to cover the expense of shipping.

ACCOUNTING IN ACTION e Business Insight

It can cost a lot to convert from traditional business to e-commerce. For example, when **Borders**, the second largest seller of books, went online, it had to build an entirely new $15 million distribution center. The reason? It previously shipped large orders of books to its stores. Instead, it now has to distribute tiny orders to individual customers. The distribution costs of online sales can be suprisingly high—as much as 15 percent of sales.

PURCHASE DISCOUNTS

The credit terms of a purchase on account may permit the buyer to claim a cash discount for prompt payment. The buyer calls this cash discount a **purchase discount**. This incentive offers advantages to both parties: The purchaser saves money, and the seller is able to shorten the operating cycle by converting the accounts receivable into cash earlier.

The **credit terms** specify the amount of the cash discount and time period during which it is offered. They also indicate the length of time in which the purchaser is expected to pay the full invoice price. In the sales invoice in Illustration 5-4, credit terms are 2/10, n/30. This is read "two-ten, net thirty." It means that a 2 percent cash discount may be taken on the invoice price, less ("net of") any returns or allowances, if payment is made within 10 days of the invoice date (the **discount period**). If payment is not made in that time, the invoice price, less any returns or allowances, is due 30 days from the invoice date. Or, the discount period may extend to a specified number of days after the month in which the sale occurs. For example, 1/10 EOM (end of month) means that a 1 percent discount is available if the invoice is paid within the first 10 days of the next month.

HELPFUL HINT
The term *net* in "net 30" means the remaining amount due after subtracting any sales returns and allowances and partial payments.

The seller may elect not to offer a cash discount for prompt payment. In that case, credit terms will specify only the maximum time period for paying the balance due. For example, the time period may be stated as n/30, n/60, or n/10 EOM. These mean, respectively, that the net amount must be paid in 30 days, 60 days, or within the first 10 days of the next month.

When an invoice is paid within the discount period, the amount of the discount decreases Merchandise Inventory. Inventory is recorded at its cost and, by paying within the discount period, the merchandiser has reduced its cost. To illustrate, assume Beyer Video pays the balance due of $3,500 (gross invoice price of $3,800 less purchase returns and allowances of $300) on May 14, the last day of the discount period. The cash discount is $70 ($3,500 × 2%), and the amount of cash paid by Beyer Video is $3,430 ($3,500 − $70). The entry to record the May 14 payment by Beyer Video is:

May 14	Accounts Payable	3,500	
	Cash		3,430
	Merchandise Inventory		70
	(To record payment within discount period)		

A	=	L	+	OE
−3,430		−3,500		
−70				

If Beyer Video failed to take the discount and instead made full payment on June 3, Beyer Video's entry would be:

June 3	Accounts Payable	3,500	
	Cash		3,500
	(To record payment with no discount taken)		

A	=	L	+	OE
−3,500		−3,500		

ACCOUNTING IN ACTION *Business Insight*

In the 1990s, **Sears** wielded its retail clout by telling its suppliers that, rather than pay its obligations in the standard 30-day period, it would now pay in 60 days. This practice is often adopted by firms that are experiencing a shortage of cash. A Sears spokesperson insisted, however, that Sears did not have cash problems. Rather, it was simply utilizing "vendor-financed inventory methods to improve its return on investment." Supplier trade groups were outspoken critics of Sears's policy. They suggested that consumers would be the ultimate victims, because the financing costs would eventually be passed on to them.

A merchandiser usually should take all available discounts. Passing up the discount may be viewed as **paying interest** for use of the money. For example, if Beyer Video passed up the discount, it would be like paying an interest rate of 2 percent for the use of $3,500 for 20 days. This is the equivalent of an annual interest rate of approximately 36.5 percent (2% × 365/20). Obviously, it would be better for Beyer Video to borrow at prevailing bank interest rates of 8 percent to 12 percent than to lose the discount.

HELPFUL HINT
So as not to miss purchase discounts, unpaid invoices should be filed by due dates. This procedure helps the purchaser remember the discount date, prevents early payment of bills, and maximizes the time that cash can be used for other purposes.

BEFORE YOU GO ON...

REVIEW IT

1. How does the measurement of net income in a merchandising company differ from that in a service enterprise?
2. In what ways is a perpetual inventory system different from a periodic system?
3. Under the perpetual inventory system, what entries are made to record purchases, purchase returns and allowances, purchase discounts, and freight costs?

THE NAVIGATOR

RECORDING SALES OF MERCHANDISE

STUDY OBJECTIVE 3
Explain the entries for sales revenues under a perpetual inventory system.

Sales revenues, like service revenues, are recorded when earned. This is done in accord with the revenue recognition principle. Typically, sales revenues are earned when the goods are transferred from the seller to the buyer. At this point the sales transaction is completed, and the sales price has been established.

Sales may be made on credit or for cash. Every sales transaction should be supported by a **business document** that provides written evidence of the sale. **Cash register tapes** provide evidence of cash sales. A **sales invoice**, like the one that was shown in Illustration 5-4 (page 188), provides support for a credit sale. The original copy of the invoice goes to the customer. A copy is kept by the seller for use in recording the sale. The invoice shows the date of sale, customer name, total sales price, and other relevant information.

Two entries are made for each sale. The first entry records the sale: Cash (or Accounts Receivable, if a credit sale) is increased by a debit, and Sales is increased by a credit at the selling (invoice) price of the goods. The second entry records the cost of the merchandise sold: Cost of Goods Sold is increased by a debit, and Merchandise Inventory is decreased by a credit for the cost of those goods. As a result, the Merchandise Inventory account will show at all times the amount of inventory that should be on hand.

To illustrate a credit sales transaction, Sellers Electronix's sale of $3,800 on May 4 to Beyer Video (see Illustration 5-4, page 188) is recorded as follows. (Assume the merchandise cost Sellers Electronix $2,400.)

A	=	L	+	OE
+3,800				+3,800

A	=	L	+	OE
−2,400				−2,400

May 4	Accounts Receivable	3,800	
	Sales		3,800
	(To record credit sale to Beyer Video per invoice #731)		
4	Cost of Goods Sold	2,400	
	Merchandise Inventory		2,400
	(To record cost of merchandise sold on invoice #731 to Beyer Video)		

HELPFUL HINT
The Sales account is credited only for sales of goods held for resale. Sales of assets not held for resale (such as equipment or land) are credited directly to the asset account.

For internal decision-making purposes, merchandisers may use more than one sales account. For example, Sellers Electronix may keep separate sales accounts for its TV sets, videocassette recorders, and microwave ovens. By using separate sales accounts for major product lines, company management can monitor sales trends more closely and respond more strategically to changes in sales patterns. For example, if TV sales are increasing while microwave oven sales are decreasing, the company could reevaluate its advertising and pricing policies on each of these items.

However, on its income statement presented to outside investors, a merchandiser would normally provide only a single sales figure—the sum of all of its individual sales accounts. This is done for two reasons. First, providing detail on individual sales accounts would add length to the income statement. Second, companies do not want their competitors to know the details of their operating results.

SALES RETURNS AND ALLOWANCES

HELPFUL HINT
If the customer is sent cash, then credit Cash rather than Accounts Receivable.

We now look at the "flipside" of purchase returns and allowances, which are **sales returns and allowances** recorded on the books of the seller. Sellers Electronix's entries to record credit for returned goods involve two entries: (1) The first is an increase in Sales Returns and Allowances and a decrease in Accounts Receivable at the $300 selling price. (2) The second is an increase in Merchandise Inventory (assume a $140 cost) and a decrease in Cost of Goods Sold. The entries are as follows.

May 8	Sales Returns and Allowances	300		
	Accounts Receivable		300	
	(To record credit granted to Beyer Video for returned goods)			

A	=	L	+	OE
−300				−300

8	Merchandise Inventory	140	
	Cost of Goods Sold		140
	(To record cost of goods returned)		

A	=	L	+	OE
+140				+140

If goods are returned because they are damaged or defective, then the entry to Merchandise Inventory and Cost of Goods Sold should be for the estimated value of the returned goods, rather than their cost. For example, if the goods returned to Sellers Electronix were defective and had a scrap value of $50, Merchandise Inventory would be debited for $50, and Cost of Goods Sold would be credited for $50.

Sales Returns and Allowances is a **contra revenue account** to Sales. The normal balance of Sales Returns and Allowances is a debit. A contra account is used, instead of debiting Sales, to disclose in the accounts the amount of sales returns and allowances. This information is important to management. Excessive returns and allowances suggest inferior merchandise, inefficiencies in filling orders, errors in billing customers, and mistakes in delivery or shipment of goods. Also, a debit recorded directly to Sales could distort comparisons between total sales in different accounting periods.

HELPFUL HINT
Remember that the increases, decreases, and normal balances of contra accounts are the opposite of the accounts to which they correspond.

ACCOUNTING IN ACTION *Business Insight*

Returned goods can represent 15 percent of total sales volume. Most companies do a poor job of dealing with returned goods, often destroying perfectly good merchandise. A new piece of software developed by cosmetic company **Estee Lauder** may change this. When boxes of Estee Lauder lipstick and other products arrive back from a retailer, each barcode is scanned, and each item's expiration date and condition are determined. It is then either scrapped or sorted for resale to employees, in "seconds" stores, or in developing countries. The system paid for its $1.5 million development cost in 9 months because it enabled the company to resell two-and-a-half times as many items, at less than half the cost of the old system.

SOURCE: "Cash from Trash," *The Economist,* February 6, 1999.

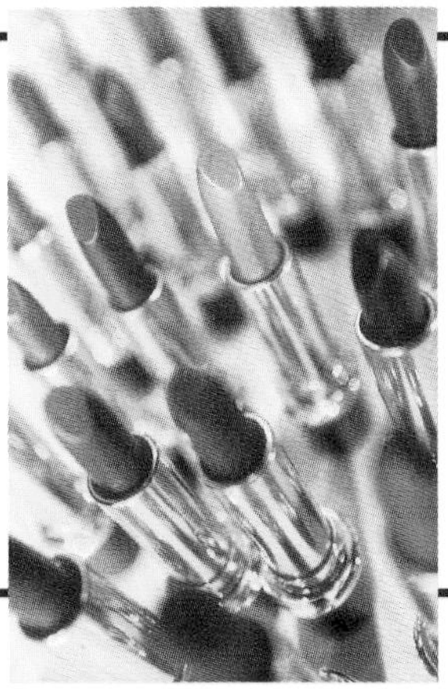

SALES DISCOUNTS

As mentioned in our discussion of purchase transactions, the seller may offer the customer a cash discount for the prompt payment of the balance due. From the seller's point of view, this is called a **sales discount**. Like a purchase discount, a sales discount is based on the invoice price less returns and allowances, if any. The Sales Discounts account is debited for discounts that are taken. The entry by Sellers Electronix to record the cash receipt on May 14 from Beyer Video within the discount period is:

May 14	Cash	3,430	
	Sales Discounts	70	
	Accounts Receivable		3,500
	(To record collection within 2/10, n/30 discount period from Beyer Video)		

A	=	L	+	OE
+3,430				−70
−3,500				

Like Sales Returns and Allowances, Sales Discounts is a **contra revenue account** to Sales. Its normal balance is a debit. This account is used, instead of debiting Sales, to disclose cash discounts taken by customers. If the discount is not taken, Sellers Electronix debits Cash for $3,500 and credits Accounts Receivable for the same amount at the date of collection.

BEFORE YOU GO ON...

REVIEW IT

1. Under a perpetual inventory system, what are the two entries that must be recorded at the time of each sale?
2. Why is it important to use the Sales Returns and Allowances account, rather than simply reducing the Sales account, when goods are returned?

DO IT

On September 5, De La Hoya Company buys merchandise on account from Junot Diaz Company. The selling price of the goods is $1,500, and the cost to Diaz Company was $800. On September 8 defective goods with a selling price of $200 and a scrap value of $80 are returned. Record the transaction on the books of both companies.

ACTION PLAN

- Purchaser: Record purchases of inventory at its cost and directly reduce the Merchandise Inventory account for returned goods.
- Seller: Record both the sale and the cost of goods sold at the time of the sale. Record returns in a contra account, Sales Returns and Allowances.

SOLUTION

De La Hoya Company

Sept. 5	Merchandise Inventory	1,500	
	Accounts Payable		1,500
	(To record goods purchased on account)		
8	Accounts Payable	200	
	Merchandise Inventory		200
	(To record return of defective goods)		

Junot Diaz Company

Sept. 5	Accounts Receivable	1,500	
	Sales		1,500
	(To record credit sale)		
5	Cost of Goods Sold	800	
	Merchandise Inventory		800
	(To record cost of goods sold on account)		
8	Sales Returns and Allowances	200	
	Accounts Receivable		200
	(To record credit granted for receipt of returned goods)		
8	Merchandise Inventory	80	
	Cost of Goods Sold		80
	(To record scrap value of goods returned)		

Related exercise material: BE5-1, BE5-2, BE5-3, BE5-4, E5-1, E5-2, E5-3, and E5-4.

THE NAVIGATOR

COMPLETING THE ACCOUNTING CYCLE

Up to this point, we have illustrated the basic entries in recording transactions relating to purchases and sales in a perpetual inventory system. Now we consider the remaining steps in the accounting cycle for a merchandiser. Each of the required steps described in Chapter 4 for a service company applies to a merchandising company. Use of a worksheet by a merchandiser (an optional step) is shown in the appendix to this chapter.

STUDY OBJECTIVE 4

Explain the steps in the accounting cycle for a merchandiser.

ADJUSTING ENTRIES

A merchandiser generally has the same types of adjusting entries as a service company. But a merchandiser using a perpetual system will require one additional adjustment to make the records agree with the actual inventory on hand. Here's why: At the end of each period, a merchandiser using a perpetual system will take a physical count of its goods on hand for control purposes. A company's unadjusted balance in Merchandise Inventory will usually not agree with the actual amount of inventory on hand at year-end. The perpetual inventory records may be incorrect due to a variety of causes such as recording errors, theft, or waste. As a result, the perpetual records need adjustment to ensure that the recorded inventory amount agrees with the actual inventory on hand. **This involves adjusting Merchandise Inventory and Cost of Goods Sold.**

For example, suppose that the records of Sellers Electronix report an unadjusted balance in Merchandise Inventory of $40,500. Through a physical count, the company determines that its actual merchandise inventory on hand at year-end is $40,000. The adjusting entry would be to debit Cost of Goods Sold for $500 and to credit Merchandise Inventory for $500.

HELPFUL HINT

The steps required to determine the actual inventory on hand are discussed in Chapter 6.

CLOSING ENTRIES

For a merchandiser, like a service enterprise, all accounts that affect the determination of net income are closed to Income Summary. In journalizing, all temporary accounts with debit balances are credited, and all temporary accounts with credit balances are debited, as shown below for Sellers Electronix. Cost of goods sold is a new account that must be closed to Income Summary.

Dec. 31	Sales	480,000	
	Income Summary		480,000
	(To close income statement accounts with credit balances)		
31	Income Summary	450,000	
	Sales Returns and Allowances		12,000
	Sales Discounts		8,000
	Cost of Goods Sold		316,000
	Store Salaries Expense		45,000
	Rent Expense		19,000
	Freight-out		7,000
	Advertising Expense		16,000
	Utilities Expense		17,000
	Depreciation Expense		8,000
	Insurance Expense		2,000
	(To close income statement accounts with debit balances)		

HELPFUL HINT

The easiest way to prepare the first two closing entries is to identify the temporary accounts by their balances and then prepare one entry for the credits and one for the debits.

31	Income Summary	30,000	
	R.A. Lamb, Capital		30,000
	(To close net income to capital)		
31	R.A. Lamb, Capital	15,000	
	R.A. Lamb, Drawing		15,000
	(To close drawings to capital)		

After the closing entries are posted, all temporary accounts have zero balances. In addition, R.A. Lamb, Capital has a credit balance of $98,000: beginning balance + net income − drawings ($83,000 + $30,000 − $15,000).

SUMMARY OF MERCHANDISING ENTRIES

The entries for the merchandising accounts using a perpetual inventory system are summarized in Illustration 5-5.

Illustration 5-5

Daily recurring and adjusting and closing entries

	Transactions	Daily Recurring Entries	Dr.	Cr.
Sales Transactions	Selling merchandise to customers.	Cash or Accounts Receivable	XX	
		Sales		XX
		Cost of Goods Sold	XX	
		Merchandise Inventory		XX
	Granting sales returns or allowances to customers.	Sales Returns and Allowances	XX	
		Cash or Accounts Receivable		XX
		Merchandise Inventory	XX	
		Cost of Goods Sold		XX
	Paying freight costs on sales; FOB destination.	Freight-out	XX	
		Cash		XX
	Receiving payment from customers within discount period.	Cash	XX	
		Sales Discounts	XX	
		Accounts Receivable		XX
Purchase Transactions	Purchasing merchandise for resale.	Merchandise Inventory	XX	
		Cash or Accounts Payable		XX
	Paying freight costs on merchandise purchased; FOB shipping point.	Merchandise Inventory	XX	
		Cash		XX
	Receiving purchase returns or allowances from suppliers.	Cash or Accounts Payable	XX	
		Merchandise Inventory		XX
	Paying suppliers within discount period.	Accounts Payable	XX	
		Merchandise Inventory		XX
		Cash		XX

Events	Adjusting and Closing Entries		
Adjust because book amount is higher than the inventory amount determined to be on hand.	Cost of Goods Sold	XX	
	Merchandise Inventory		XX
Closing temporary accounts with credit balances.	Sales	XX	
	Income Summary		XX
Closing temporary accounts with debit balances.	Income Summary	XX	
	Sales Returns and Allowances		XX
	Sales Discounts		XX
	Cost of Goods Sold		XX
	Freight-out		XX
	Expenses		XX

BEFORE YOU GO ON...

REVIEW IT

1. Why is an adjustment to the Merchandise Inventory account usually needed?
2. What merchandising account(s) will appear in the post-closing trial balance?

DO IT

The trial balance of Revere Clothing Company at December 31 shows Merchandise Inventory $25,000, Sales $162,400, Sales Returns and Allowances $4,800, Sales Discounts $3,600, Cost of Goods Sold $110,000, Rental Revenue $6,000, Freight-out $1,800, Rent Expense $8,800, and Salaries and Wages Expense $22,000. Prepare the closing entries for the above accounts.

ACTION PLAN

- Close all temporary accounts with credit balances to Income Summary by debiting these accounts.
- Close all temporary accounts with debit balances to Income Summary by crediting these accounts.

SOLUTION: The two closing entries are:

Dec. 31	Sales	162,400	
	Rental Revenue	6,000	
	Income Summary		168,400
	(To close accounts with credit balances)		
Dec. 31	Income Summary	151,000	
	Cost of Goods Sold		110,000
	Sales Returns and Allowances		4,800
	Sales Discounts		3,600
	Freight-out		1,800
	Rent Expense		8,800
	Salaries and Wages Expense		22,000
	(To close accounts with debit balances)		

Related exercise material: BE5-7, E5-5, and E5-6.

THE NAVIGATOR

FORMS OF FINANCIAL STATEMENTS

STUDY OBJECTIVE 5

Distinguish between a multiple-step and a single-step income statement.

Two forms of the income statement are widely used by merchandisers. Also, merchandisers use the classified balance sheet, introduced in Chapter 4. The use of these financial statements by merchandisers is explained below.

MULTIPLE-STEP INCOME STATEMENT

The **multiple-step income statement** is so named because it shows the steps in determining net income (or net loss). It shows two main steps: (1) Cost of goods sold is subtracted from net sales, to determine gross profit. (2) Operating expenses are deducted from gross profit, to determine net income. These steps relate to the company's principal operating activities. A multiple-step statement also distinguishes between **operating** and **non-operating activities**. This distinction provides users with more information about a company's income performance. The statement also highlights intermediate components of income and shows subgroupings of expenses.

Income Statement Presentation of Sales

The multiple-step income statement begins by presenting sales revenue. As contra revenue accounts, sales returns and allowances, and sales discounts are deducted from sales to arrive at **net sales**. The sales revenues section for Sellers Electronix, using assumed data, is as follows.

Illustration 5-6

Computation of net sales

SELLERS ELECTRONIX Income Statement (partial)		
Sales revenues		
Sales		$480,000
Less: Sales returns and allowances	$12,000	
Sales discounts	8,000	20,000
Net sales		**$460,000**

This presentation discloses the key aspects of the company's principal revenue-producing activities.

Gross Profit

STUDY OBJECTIVE 6

Explain the computation and importance of gross profit.

From Illustration 5-1, you learned that cost of goods sold is deducted from sales revenue to determine **gross profit**. Sales revenue used for this computation is **net sales**. On the basis of the sales data presented in Illustration 5-6 (net sales of $460,000) and the cost of goods sold under the perpetual inventory system (assume $316,000), the gross profit for Sellers Electronix is $144,000, computed as follows.

Illustration 5-7

Computation of gross profit

Net sales	$460,000
Cost of goods sold	316,000
Gross profit	**$144,000**

A company's gross profit may also be expressed as a percentage. This is done by dividing the amount of gross profit by net sales. For Sellers Electronix the **gross profit rate** is 31.3 percent, computed as follows.

Illustration 5-8

Gross profit rate formula and computation

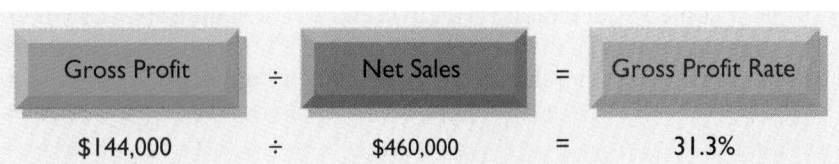

Gross Profit	÷	Net Sales	=	Gross Profit Rate
$144,000	÷	$460,000	=	31.3%

The gross profit rate is generally considered to be more useful than the gross profit amount. The rate expresses a more meaningful (qualitative) relationship between net sales and gross profit. For example, a gross profit of $1,000,000 may be impressive. But, if it is the result of a gross profit rate of only 7 percent, it is not so impressive. The gross profit rate tells how many cents of each sales dollar go to gross profit.

Gross profit represents the **merchandising profit** of a company. It is not a measure of the overall profitability, because operating expenses have not been deducted. But the amount and trend of gross profit is closely watched by management and other interested parties. They compare current gross profit with amounts reported in past periods. They also compare the company's gross profit rate with rates of competitors and with industry averages. Such comparisons provide information about the effectiveness of a company's purchasing function and the soundness of its pricing policies.

Operating Expenses and Net Income

Operating expenses are the third component in measuring net income for a merchandiser. As indicated earlier, these expenses are similar in merchandising and service enterprises. At Sellers Electronix, operating expenses were $114,000. The firm's net income is determined by subtracting operating expenses from gross profit. Thus, net income is $30,000, as shown below.

Gross profit	$144,000
Operating expenses	114,000
Net income	$ 30,000

Illustration 5-9

Operating expenses in computing net income

The net income amount is the "bottom line" of a company's income statement.

Nonoperating Activities

Nonoperating activities consist of (1) revenues and expenses from auxiliary operations and (2) gains and losses that are unrelated to the company's operations. The results of nonoperating activities are shown in two sections: "**Other revenues and gains**" and "**Other expenses and losses.**" For a merchandiser, these sections will typically include the following items.

Nonoperating Activities

Other revenues and gains	Other expenses and losses
Interest revenue from notes receivable and marketable securities	Interest expense on notes and loans payable
Dividend revenue from investments in capital stock	Casualty losses from recurring causes such as vandalism and accidents
Rent revenue from subleasing a portion of the store	Loss from the sale or abandonment of property, plant, and equipment
Gain from the sale of property, plant, and equipment	Loss from strikes by employees and suppliers

Illustration 5-10

Items reported in nonoperating sections

The nonoperating activities are reported in the income statement immediately after the company's primary operating activities. These sections are shown in Illustration 5-11, using assumed data for Sellers Electronix.

Illustration 5-11

Multiple-step income statement—nonoperating sections and subgroupings of operating expenses

HELPFUL HINT

Financial statements prepared for external users (such as investors and creditors) are far less detailed than those prepared for internal use. For example, Lands' End's income statement (in Appendix A) provides considerably less detail than the income statement in Illustration 5-11.

SELLERS ELECTRONIX
Income Statement
For the Year Ended December 31, 2002

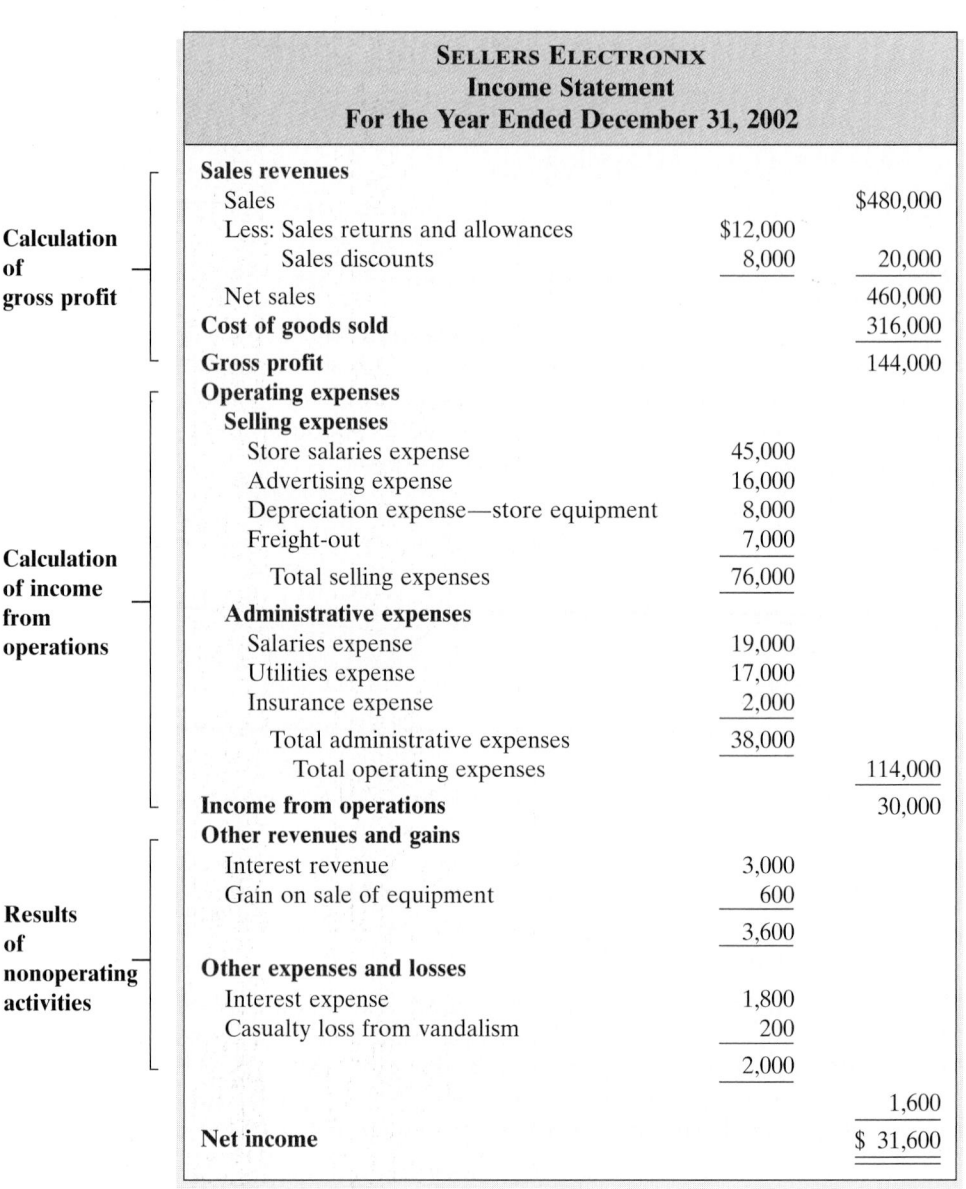

Calculation of gross profit	**Sales revenues**		
	Sales		$480,000
	Less: Sales returns and allowances	$12,000	
	Sales discounts	8,000	20,000
	Net sales		460,000
	Cost of goods sold		316,000
	Gross profit		144,000
Calculation of income from operations	**Operating expenses**		
	Selling expenses		
	Store salaries expense	45,000	
	Advertising expense	16,000	
	Depreciation expense—store equipment	8,000	
	Freight-out	7,000	
	Total selling expenses	76,000	
	Administrative expenses		
	Salaries expense	19,000	
	Utilities expense	17,000	
	Insurance expense	2,000	
	Total administrative expenses	38,000	
	Total operating expenses		114,000
	Income from operations		30,000
Results of nonoperating activities	**Other revenues and gains**		
	Interest revenue	3,000	
	Gain on sale of equipment	600	
		3,600	
	Other expenses and losses		
	Interest expense	1,800	
	Casualty loss from vandalism	200	
		2,000	
			1,600
	Net income		$ 31,600

HELPFUL HINT

Operating income relates to the sale of primary goods in the ordinary course of business.

When the two nonoperating sections are included, the label "**Income from operations**" (or Operating income) precedes them. It clearly identifies the results of the company's normal operations. Income from operations is determined by subtracting cost of goods sold and operating expenses from net sales.

In the nonoperating activities sections, items are generally reported at the net amount. Thus, if a company received a $2,500 insurance settlement on vandalism losses of $2,700, the loss is reported at $200. Note, too, that the results of the two nonoperating sections are netted. The difference is added to or subtracted from income from operations to determine net income. It is not uncommon for companies to combine these two nonoperating sections into a single "Other revenues and expenses" section.

ACCOUNTING IN ACTION *Business Insight*

During a recent quarter, the earnings of computer chip maker **Intel** shot up 79 percent. But enthusiasm about the huge jump was dampened by the fact that some analysts questioned the earnings figure. The analysts were concerned because included in the ordinary earnings figure were a variety of special items and "one-time" gains from sales of investments. The analysts would prefer that these items were reported separately, under "Other revenues and expenses." In evaluating the company, some analysts simply ignore the investment gains.

Subgrouping of Operating Expenses

In larger companies, operating expenses are often subdivided into selling expenses and administrative expenses, as illustrated in Illustration 5-11. **Selling expenses** are those associated with making sales. They include expenses for sales promotion as well as expenses of completing the sale, such as delivery and shipping. **Administrative expenses** (sometimes called general expenses) relate to general operating activities such as personnel management, accounting, and store security.

When subgroupings are made, some expenses may have to be prorated (e.g., 70% to selling and 30% to administrative expenses). For example, if a store building is used for both selling and general functions, building expenses such as depreciation, utilities, and property taxes will need to be allocated.

Any reasonable classification of expenses that serves to inform those who use the statement is satisfactory. The present tendency in statements prepared for management's internal use is to present in considerable detail expense data grouped along lines of responsibility.

ETHICS NOTE

At the end of a celebratory lunch the employees of a sales department each gave the manager $10, and he paid the bill with his charge card. During the next week you notice that the manager reported the full amount of the lunch bill on his expense report (and requested reimbursement). When this question was posed to the CEO of Intel, he suggested that an appropriate action would be to report the problem anonymously to the internal audit staff for investigation. What would you do? Does it make a difference if the company is large or small?

SINGLE-STEP INCOME STATEMENT

Another income statement format is the **single-step income statement**. The statement is so named because only one step, subtracting total expenses from total revenues, is required in determining net income (or net loss).

In a single-step statement, all data are classified under two categories: (1) revenues and (2) expenses. The **revenues** category includes both operating revenues and other revenues and gains. The **expenses** category includes cost of goods sold, operating expenses, and other expenses and losses. A condensed single-step statement for Sellers Electronix is shown in Illustration 5-12.

Illustration 5-12

Single-step income statement

SELLERS ELECTRONIX
Income Statement
For the Year Ended December 31, 2002

Revenues		
Net sales		$460,000
Interest revenue		3,000
Gain on sale of equipment		600
Total revenues		463,600
Expenses		
Cost of goods sold	$316,000	
Selling expenses	76,000	
Administrative expenses	38,000	
Interest expense	1,800	
Casualty loss from vandalism	200	
Total expenses		432,000
Net income		$ 31,600

There are two primary reasons for using the single-step format: (1) A company does not realize any type of profit or income until total revenues exceed total expenses, so it makes sense to divide the statement into these two categories. (2) The format is simpler and easier to read than the multiple-step format. But for homework problems, the single-step format should be used only when it is specifically requested.

CLASSIFIED BALANCE SHEET

HELPFUL HINT
Merchandise inventory is a current asset because it is expected to be sold within one year or the operating cycle, whichever is longer.

In the balance sheet, merchandise inventory is reported as a current asset immediately below accounts receivable. Recall from Chapter 4 that items are listed under current assets in their order of liquidity. Merchandise inventory is less liquid than accounts receivable because the goods must first be sold and then collection must be made from the customer. Illustration 5-13 presents the assets section of a classified balance sheet for Sellers Electronix.

Illustration 5-13

Assets section of a classified balance sheet (partial)

SELLERS ELECTRONIX
Balance Sheet (partial)
December 31, 2002

Assets		
Current assets		
Cash		$ 9,500
Accounts receivable		16,100
Merchandise inventory		**40,000**
Prepaid insurance		1,800
Total current assets		67,400
Property, plant, and equipment		
Store equipment	$80,000	
Less: Accumulated depreciation—store equipment	24,000	56,000
Total assets		$123,400

HELPFUL HINT
The $40,000 is the cost of the inventory on hand, not its expected selling price.

BEFORE YOU GO ON...

REVIEW IT

1. Determine **Lands' End's** gross profit rate for 2000 and 1999. Indicate whether it increased or decreased from 1999 to 2000. The answer to this question is provided on page 221.
2. What are nonoperating activities, and how are they reported in the income statement?
3. How does a single-step income statement differ from a multiple-step income statement?

A LOOK BACK AT OUR FEATURE STORY

Refer back to the Feature Story about **Buy.com** at the beginning of the chapter, and answer the following questions.

1. What is the business of Buy.com? What makes it attractive to consumers?
2. How much inventory does Buy.com carry?
3. How does Buy.com's operating cycle differ from those of other retailers because of its unique merchandising system?

4. In what way might Buy.com's unique method of merchandising affect the general ledger accounts used?
5. How does Buy.com expect to sell products below cost and still remain in business long term?

SOLUTION

1. Buy.com is a Web retailer that sells and delivers goods directly from wholesalers to consumers. Buy.com's slogan is, "The lowest prices on earth." The company is committed to being the price leader—even if it means losing money on every sale.
2. Buy.com has no inventory. It is a *virtual* corporation that advertises on a Web site and places orders with wholesalers who deliver direct to customers from whom Buy.com has taken orders.
3. Buy.com's operating cycle is more like that of a service company than a merchandiser because it carries no inventory. Therefore, the operating cycle is abbreviated—cash to accounts receivable to cash.
4. Buy.com's general ledger will contain no Merchandise Inventory account and may or may not contain the following accounts: Freight-in, Freight-out, Purchase Returns and Allowances, Sales Returns and Allowances, Purchase Discounts, and Sales Discounts. The use of these accounts depends on the agreement Buy.com has with it suppliers (the wholesalers and distributors who deliver direct to customers) and with its customers.
5. Buy.com is trying to create a brand synonymous with low price. If it becomes the leading e-commerce portal, its site becomes valuable ad space. Buy.com hopes to make up its deficit through advertising revenues.

THE NAVIGATOR

DEMONSTRATION PROBLEM

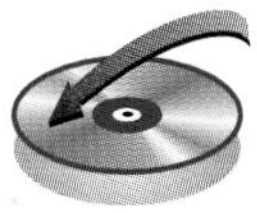

Additional Demonstration Problem

The adjusted trial balance columns of the work sheet for the year ended December 31, 2002, for Dykstra Company are as follows.

Debit		Credit	
Cash	14,500	Accumulated Depreciation	18,000
Accounts Receivable	11,100	Notes Payable	25,000
Merchandise Inventory	29,000	Accounts Payable	10,600
Prepaid Insurance	2,500	Gene Dykstra, Capital	81,000
Store Equipment	95,000	Sales	536,800
Gene Dykstra, Drawing	12,000	Interest Revenue	2,500
Sales Returns and Allowances	6,700		673,900
Sales Discounts	5,000		
Cost of Goods Sold	363,400		
Freight-out	7,600		
Advertising Expense	12,000		
Store Salaries Expense	56,000		
Utilities Expense	18,000		
Rent Expense	24,000		
Depreciation Expense	9,000		
Insurance Expense	4,500		
Interest Expense	3,600		
	673,900		

Instructions

Prepare an income statement assuming Dykstra Company does not use subgroupings for operating expenses.

ACTION PLAN

- Remember that the key components of the income statement are net sales, cost of goods sold, gross profit, total operating expenses, and net income (loss). Report these components in the right-hand column of the income statement.
- Put nonoperating items after income from operations.

THE NAVIGATOR

SOLUTION TO DEMONSTRATION PROBLEM

Dykstra Company
Income Statement
For the Year Ended December 31, 2002

Sales revenues		
Sales		$536,800
Less: Sales returns and allowances	$6,700	
Sales discounts	5,000	11,700
Net sales		525,100
Cost of goods sold		363,400
Gross profit		161,700
Operating expenses		
Store salaries expense	56,000	
Rent expense	24,000	
Utilities expense	18,000	
Advertising expense	12,000	
Depreciation expense	9,000	
Freight-out	7,600	
Insurance expense	4,500	
Total operating expenses		131,100
Income from operations		30,600
Other revenues and gains		
Interest revenue	2,500	
Other expenses and losses		
Interest expense	3,600	1,100
Net income		$ 29,500

SUMMARY OF STUDY OBJECTIVES

1. *Identify the differences between a service enterprise and a merchandiser.* Because of inventory, a merchandiser has sales revenue, cost of goods sold, and gross profit. To account for inventory, a merchandiser must choose between a perpetual inventory system and a periodic inventory system.

2. *Explain the entries for purchases under a perpetual inventory system.* The Merchandise Inventory account is debited for all purchases of merchandise, freight-in, and other costs, and it is credited for purchase discounts and purchase returns and allowances.

3. *Explain the entries for sales revenues under a perpetual inventory system.* When inventory is sold, Accounts Receivable (or Cash) is debited, and Sales is credited for the **selling price** of the merchandise. At the same time, Cost of Goods Sold is debited, and Merchandise Inventory is credited for the **cost** of the inventory items sold.

4. *Explain the steps in the accounting cycle for a merchandiser.* Each of the required steps in the accounting cycle for a service enterprise applies to a merchandiser. A work sheet is again an optional step. Under a perpetual inventory system, the Merchandise Inventory account must be adjusted to agree with the physical count.

5. *Distinguish between a multiple-step and a single-step income statement.* A multiple-step income statement shows numerous steps in determining net income, including nonoperating activities sections. In a single-step income statement all data are classified under two categories, revenues or expenses, and net income is determined by one step.

6. *Explain the computation and importance of gross profit.* Gross profit is computed by subtracting cost of goods sold from net sales. Gross profit represents the merchandising profit of a company. The amount and trend of gross profit are closely watched by management and other interested parties.

THE NAVIGATOR

Key Term Matching Activity

GLOSSARY

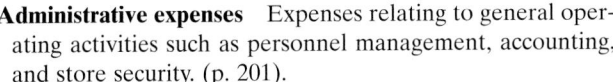

Administrative expenses Expenses relating to general operating activities such as personnel management, accounting, and store security. (p. 201).

Contra revenue account An account that is offset against a revenue account on the income statement. (p. 193).

Cost of goods sold The total cost of merchandise sold during the period. (p. 184).

FOB destination Freight terms indicating that the goods will be placed free on board at the buyer's place of business, and the seller pays the freight costs. (p. 189).

FOB shipping point Freight terms indicating that goods are placed free on board the carrier by the seller, and the buyer pays the freight costs. (p. 189).

Gross profit The excess of net sales over the cost of goods sold. (p. 184).

Income from operations Income from a company's principal operating activity; determined by subtracting cost of goods sold and operating expenses from net sales. (p. 200).

Multiple-step income statement An income statement that shows numerous steps in determining net income (or net loss). (p. 197).

Net sales Sales less sales returns and allowances and sales discounts. (p. 198).

Operating expenses Expenses incurred in the process of earning sales revenues that are deducted from gross profit in the income statement. (p. 184).

Other expenses and losses A nonoperating activities section of the income statement that shows expenses from auxiliary operations and losses unrelated to the company's operations. (p. 199).

Other revenues and gains A nonoperating activities section of the income statement that shows revenues from auxiliary operations and gains unrelated to the company's operations. (p. 199).

Periodic inventory system An inventory system in which detailed records are not maintained throughout the accounting period and the cost of goods sold is determined only at the end of an accounting period. (p. 186).

Perpetual inventory system An inventory system in which the cost of each inventory item is maintained throughout the accounting period and detailed records continuously show the inventory that should be on hand. (p. 186).

Purchase discount A cash discount claimed by a buyer for prompt payment of a balance due. (p. 190).

Purchase invoice A document that supports each credit purchase. (p. 188).

Sales discount A reduction given by a seller for prompt payment of a credit sale. (p. 193).

Sales invoice A document that supports each credit sale. (p. 192).

Sales revenue (sales) Primary source of revenue in a merchandising company. (p. 184).

Selling expenses Expenses associated with making sales. (p. 201).

Single-step income statement An income statement that shows only one step in determining net income (or net loss). (p. 201).

APPENDIX *Work Sheet for a Merchandiser*

USING A WORK SHEET

STUDY OBJECTIVE 7

Prepare a work sheet for a merchandiser.

As indicated in Chapter 4, a work sheet enables financial statements to be prepared before the adjusting entries are journalized and posted. The steps in preparing a work sheet for a merchandiser are the same as they are for a service enterprise (see page 135). The work sheet for Sellers Electronix is shown in Illustration 5A-1 (on page 206). The unique accounts for a merchandiser using a perpetual inventory system are shown in capital letters in red.

TRIAL BALANCE COLUMNS

Data for the trial balance are obtained from the ledger balances of Sellers Electronix at December 31. The amount shown for Merchandise Inventory, $40,500, is the year-end inventory amount from the perpetual inventory system.

Illustration 5A-1

Work sheet for merchandiser

SELLERS ELECTRONIX
Work Sheet
For the Year Ended December 31, 2002

	Trial Balance		Adjustments		Adjusted Trial Balance		Income Statement		Balance Sheet	
	Dr.	Cr.	Dr.	Cr.	Dr.	Cr.	Dr.	Cr.	Dr.	Cr.
Cash	9,500				9,500				9,500	
Accounts Receivable	16,100				16,100				16,100	
MERCHANDISE INVENTORY	**40,500**			(a) 500	**40,000**				**40,000**	
Prepaid Insurance	3,800			(b) 2,000	1,800				1,800	
Store Equipment	80,000				80,000				80,000	
Accumulated Depreciation		16,000		(c) 8,000		24,000				24,000
Accounts Payable		20,400				20,400				20,400
R.A. Lamb, Capital		83,000				83,000				83,000
R.A. Lamb, Drawing	15,000				15,000				15,000	
SALES		**480,000**				**480,000**		**480,000**		
SALES RETURNS AND ALLOWANCES	**12,000**				**12,000**		**12,000**			
SALES DISCOUNTS	**8,000**				**8,000**		**8,000**			
COST OF GOODS SOLD	**315,500**		(a) 500		**316,000**		**316,000**			
Freight-out	7,000				7,000		7,000			
Advertising Expense	16,000				16,000		16,000			
Rent Expense	19,000				19,000		19,000			
Store Salaries Expense	40,000		(d) 5,000		45,000		45,000			
Utilities Expense	17,000				17,000		17,000			
Totals	599,400	599,400								
Insurance Expense			(b) 2,000		2,000		2,000			
Depreciation Expense			(c) 8,000		8,000		8,000			
Salaries Payable				(d) 5,000		5,000				5,000
Totals			15,000	15,000	612,400	612,400	450,000	480,000	162,400	132,400
Net Income							30,000			30,000
Totals							480,000	480,000	162,400	162,400

Key: (a) Adjustment to inventory on hand, (b) Insurance expired, (c) Depreciation expense, (d) Salaries accrued.

ADJUSTMENTS COLUMNS

A merchandiser generally has the same types of adjustments as a service company. As you see in the work sheet, adjustments (b), (c), and (d) are for insurance, depreciation, and salaries. These adjustments were also required for Pioneer Advertising Agency, as illustrated in Chapters 3 and 4. Adjustment (a) was required to adjust the perpetual inventory carrying amount to the actual count.

After all adjustments data are entered on the work sheet, the equality of the adjustments column totals is established. The balances in all accounts are then extended to the adjusted trial balance columns.

ADJUSTED TRIAL BALANCE

The adjusted trial balance shows the balance of all accounts after adjustment at the end of the accounting period.

INCOME STATEMENT COLUMNS

The accounts and balances that affect the income statement are transferred from the adjusted trial balance columns to the income statement columns. For Sellers Electronix, Sales of $480,000 is shown in the credit column. The contra revenue accounts Sales Returns and Allowances $12,000 and Sales Discounts $8,000 are shown in the debit column. The difference of $460,000 is the net sales shown on the income statement (Illustration 5-11).

Finally, all the credits in the income statement column should be totaled and compared to the total of the debits in the income statement column. If the credits exceed the debits, the company has net income. In Sellers Electronix's case there was net income of $30,000. If the debits exceed the credits, the company would report a net loss.

BALANCE SHEET COLUMNS

The major difference between the balance sheets of a service company and a merchandiser is inventory. For Sellers Electronix, the ending inventory amount of $40,000 is shown in the balance sheet debit column. The information to prepare the owner's equity statement is also found in these columns. That is, the capital account of R. A. Lamb is $83,000. The drawings for R. A. Lamb are $15,000. Net income results when the total of the debit column exceeds the total of the credit column in the balance sheet columns. A net loss results when the total of the credits exceeds the total of the debit balances.

SUMMARY OF STUDY OBJECTIVE

7. ***Prepare a work sheet for a merchandiser.*** The steps in preparing a work sheet for a merchandiser are the same as they are for a service company. The unique accounts for a merchandiser are Merchandise Inventory, Sales, Sales Returns and Allowances, Sales Discounts, and Cost of Goods Sold.

Note: All **asterisked** Questions, Exercises, and Problems relate to material in the appendix to the chapter.

Chapter 5 Self-Test

SELF-STUDY QUESTIONS

Answers are at the end of the chapter.

(SO 1) **1.** Gross profit will result if:
a. operating expenses are less than net income.
b. sales revenues are greater than operating expenses.
c. sales revenues are greater than cost of goods sold.
d. operating expenses are greater than cost of goods sold.

(SO 2) **2.** Under a perpetual inventory system, when goods are purchased for resale by a company:
a. purchases on account are debited to Merchandise Inventory.
b. purchases on account are debited to Purchases.
c. purchase returns are debited to Purchase Returns and Allowances.
d. freight costs are debited to Freight-out.

(SO 3) **3.** The sales accounts that normally have a debit balance are:
a. Sales Discounts.
b. Sales Returns and Allowances.
c. both (a) and (b).
d. neither (a) nor (b).

4. A credit sale of $750 is made on June 13, terms 2/10, net/30. A return of $50 is granted on June 16. The amount received as payment in full on June 23 is: (SO 3)
a. $700.
b. $686.
c. $685.
d. $650.

5. Which of the following accounts will normally appear in the ledger of a merchandising company that uses a perpetual inventory system? (SO 3)
a. Purchases.
b. Freight-in.
c. Cost of Goods Sold.
d. Purchase Discounts.

(SO 5) **6.** The multiple-step income statement for a merchandiser shows each of the following features *except*:
a. gross profit.
b. cost of goods sold.
c. a sales revenue section.
d. investing activities section.

(SO 6) **7.** If sales revenues are $400,000, cost of goods sold is $310,000, and operating expenses are $60,000, the gross profit is:
a. $30,000.
b. $90,000.
c. $340,000.
d. $400,000.

(SO 5) **8.** In a single-step income statement:
a. gross profit is reported.
b. cost of goods sold is not reported.
c. sales revenues and "other revenues and gains" are reported in the revenues section of the income statement.
d. operating income is separately reported.

9. Which of the following appears on both a single-step and a multiple-step income statement? (SO 5)
a. sales.
b. gross profit.
c. income from operations.
d. cost of goods sold.

***10.** In a work sheet, Merchandise Inventory is shown in the following columns: (SO 7)
a. Adjusted trial balance debit and balance sheet debit.
b. Income statement debit and balance sheet debit.
c. Income statement credit and balance sheet debit.
d. Income statement credit and adjusted trial balance debit.

THE NAVIGATOR

QUESTIONS

1. (a) "The steps in the accounting cycle for a merchandising company are different from the accounting cycle for a service enterprise." Do you agree or disagree? (b) Is the measurement of net income for a merchandiser conceptually the same as for a service enterprise? Explain.
2. Why is the normal operating cycle for a merchandiser likely to be longer than for a service company?
3. (a) How do the components of revenues and expenses differ between a merchandiser and a service enterprise? (b) Explain the income measurement process in a merchandising company.
4. How does income measurement differ between a merchandiser and a service company?
5. When is cost of goods sold determined in a perpetual inventory system?
6. Distinguish between FOB shipping point and FOB destination. Identify the freight terms that will result in a debit to Merchandise Inventory by the purchaser and a debit to Freight-out by the seller.
7. Explain the meaning of the credit terms 2/10, n/30.
8. Goods costing $2,000 are purchased on account on July 15 with credit terms of 2/10, n/30. On July 18 a $200 credit memo is received from the supplier for damaged goods. Give the journal entry on July 24 to record payment of the balance due within the discount period using a perpetual inventory system.
9. Joan Hollins believes revenues from credit sales may be earned before they are collected in cash. Do you agree? Explain.
10. (a) What is the primary source document for recording (1) cash sales, (2) credit sales, and (3) sales returns and allowances? (b) Using XXs for amounts, give the journal entry for each of the transactions in part (a).
11. A credit sale is made on July 10 for $900, terms 2/10, n/30. On July 12, $100 of goods are returned for credit. Give the journal entry on July 19 to record the receipt of the balance due within the discount period.
12. Explain why the Merchandise Inventory account will usually require adjustment at year-end.
13. Prepare the closing entries for the Sales account, assuming a balance of $200,000 and the Cost of Goods Sold account with a $130,000 balance.
14. What merchandising account(s) will appear in the post-closing trial balance?
15. Frank Voris Co. has sales revenue of $115,000, cost of goods sold of $70,000, and operating expenses of $20,000. What is its gross profit?
16. Elizabeth Sherrick Company reports net sales of $800,000, gross profit of $570,000, and net income of $200,000. What are its operating expenses?
17. Identify the distinguishing features of an income statement for a merchandising company.
18. Identify the sections of a multiple-step income statement that relate to (a) operating activities, and (b) nonoperating activities.
19. Distinguish between the types of functional groupings of operating expenses. What problem is created by these groupings?
20. How does the single-step form of income statement differ from the multiple-step form?

*21. Indicate the columns of the work sheet in which (a) merchandise inventory and (b) cost of goods sold will be shown.

BRIEF EXERCISES

BE5-1 Presented below are the components in Sang Nam Company's income statement. Determine the missing amounts.

Compute missing amounts in determining net income. (SO 1)

	Sales	Cost of Goods Sold	Gross Profit	Operating Expenses	Net Income
(a)	$75,000	?	$31,500	?	$10,800
(b)	$108,000	$70,000	?	?	$29,500
(c)	?	$71,900	$99,600	$39,500	?

BE5-2 Keo Company buys merchandise on account from Cesar Company. The selling price of the goods is $800, and the cost of the goods is $560. Both companies use perpetual inventory systems. Journalize the transaction on the books of both companies.

Journalize perpetual inventory entries. (SO 2, 3)

BE5-3 Prepare the journal entries to record the following transactions on Rowen Company's books using a perpetual inventory system.

Journalize sales transactions. (SO 3)

(a) On March 2, Rowen Company sold $800,000 of merchandise to Mosquera Company, terms 2/10, n/30. The cost of the merchandise sold was $580,000.

(b) On March 6, Mosquera Company returned $120,000 of the merchandise purchased on March 2 because it was defective. The cost of the returned merchandise was $90,000.

(c) On March 12, Rowen Company received the balance due from Mosquera Company.

BE5-4 From the information in BE5-3, prepare the journal entries to record these transactions on Mosquera Company's books under a perpetual inventory system.

Journalize purchase transactions. (SO 2)

BE5-5 Rafeul Huda Company provides the following information for the month ended October 31, 2002: Sales on credit $280,000, cash sales $100,000 sales discounts $11,000, sales returns and allowances $20,000. Prepare the sales revenues section of the income statement based on this information.

Prepare sales revenues section of income statement. (SO 3)

BE5-6 At year-end the perpetual inventory records of Kren Company showed merchandise inventory of $98,000. The company determined, however, that its actual inventory on hand was $97,100. Record the necessary adjusting entry.

Prepare adjusting entry for merchandise inventory. (SO 4)

BE5-7 Prasad Company has the following merchandise account balances: Sales $180,000, Sales Discounts $2,000, Cost of Goods Sold $105,000, and Merchandise Inventory $40,000. Prepare the entries to record the closing of these items to Income Summary.

Prepare closing entries for merchandise accounts. (SO 4)

BE5-8 Explain where each of the following items would appear on (1) a multiple-step income statement, and on (2) a single-step income statement: **(a)** gain on sale of equipment, **(b)** casualty loss from vandalism, and **(c)** cost of goods sold.

Contrast presentation in multiple-step and single-step income statements. (SO 5)

BE5-9 Assume Cajon Company has the following account balances: Sales $500,000, Sales Returns and Allowances $15,000, Cost of Goods Sold $350,000, Selling Expenses $70,000, and Administrative Expenses $40,000. Compute the following: **(a)** net sales, **(b)** gross profit, and **(c)** income from operations.

Compute net sales, gross profit, and income from operations. (SO 3, 5, 6)

***BE5-10** Presented below is the format of the work sheet presented in the chapter.

Identify work sheet columns for selected accounts. (SO 7)

Trial Balance		Adjustments		Adjusted Trial Balance		Income Statement		Balance Sheet	
Dr.	Cr.	Dr.	Cr.	Dr.	Cr.	Dr.	Cr.	Dr.	Cr.

Indicate where the following items will appear on the work sheet: **(a)** Cash, **(b)** Merchandise Inventory, **(c)** Sales, **(d)** Cost of goods sold.

Example:
Cash: Trial balance debit column; Adjusted trial balance debit column; and Balance sheet debit column.

EXERCISES

Journalize purchases transactions. (SO 2)

E5-1 Information related to Munoz Co. is presented below.

1. On April 5, purchased merchandise from Freeman Company for $17,000 terms 2/10, net/30, FOB shipping point.
2. On April 6 paid freight costs of $900 on merchandise purchased from Freeman.
3. On April 7, purchased equipment on account for $26,000.
4. On April 8, returned damaged merchandise to Freeman Company and was granted a $3,000 allowance.
5. On April 15 paid the amount due to Freeman Company in full.

Instructions

(a) Prepare the journal entries to record these transactions on the books of Munoz Co. under a perpetual inventory system.

(b) Assume that Munoz Co. paid the balance due to Freeman Company on May 4 instead of April 15. Prepare the journal entry to record this payment.

Journalize perpetual inventory entries. (SO 2, 3)

E5-2 On September 1, Roth Office Supply had an inventory of 30 pocket calculators at a cost of $20 each. The company uses a perpetual inventory system. During September, the following transactions occurred.

Sept. 6 Purchased 80 calculators at $19 each from Lanza Co. for cash.
9 Paid freight of $80 on calculators purchased from Lanza Co.
10 Returned 2 calculators to Lanza Co. for $40 credit (including freight) because they did not meet specifications.
12 Sold 26 calculators costing $20 (including freight) for $31 each to Really Big Book Store, terms n/30.
14 Granted credit of $31 to Really Big Book Store for the return of one calculator that was not ordered.
20 Sold 30 calculators costing $20 for $31 each to Mallik Card Shop, terms n/30.

Instructions

Journalize the September transactions.

Prepare purchase and sale entries and closing entries. (SO 2, 3)

E5-3 On June 10, Kogan Company purchased $6,000 of merchandise from R. Rego Company FOB shipping point, terms 2/10, n/30. Kogan pays the freight costs of $300 on June 11. Damaged goods totaling $400 are returned to R. Rego for credit on June 12. The scrap value of these goods is $200. On June 19, Kogan pays R. Rego Company in full, less the purchase discount. Both companies use a perpetual inventory system.

Instructions

(a) Prepare separate entries for each transaction on the books of Kogan Company.

(b) Prepare separate entries for each transaction for Rego Company. The merchandise purchased by Kogan on June 10 had cost Rego $3,000.

Journalize sales transactions. (SO 3)

E5-4 Presented below are transactions related to R. Garg Company.

1. On December 3, R. Garg Company sold $480,000 of merchandise to G. Wallace Co., terms 2/10, n/30, FOB shipping point. The cost of the merchandise sold was $320,000.
2. On December 8, G. Wallace Co. was granted an allowance of $25,000 for merchandise purchased on December 3.
3. On December 13, R. Garg Company received the balance due from G. Wallace Co.

Instructions

(a) Prepare the journal entries to record these transactions on the books of R. Garg Company using a perpetual inventory system.

(b) Assume that R. Garg Company received the balance due from G. Wallace Co. on January 2 of the following year instead of December 13. Prepare the journal entry to record the receipt of payment on January 2.

Prepare sales revenues section and closing entries. (SO 3, 4, 5)

E5-5 The adjusted trial balance of Dimitry Company shows the following data pertaining to sales at the end of its fiscal year October 31, 2002: Sales $800,000, Freight-out $12,000, Sales Returns and Allowances $25,000, and Sales Discounts $15,000.

Instructions

(a) Prepare the sales revenues section of the income statement.

(b) Prepare separate closing entries for (1) sales, and (2) the contra accounts to sales.

Prepare adjusting and closing entries. (SO 4)

E5-6 Presented is information related to Croce Co. for the month of January 2002.

Ending inventory per perpetual records	$ 21,600	Salary expense	$ 61,000
Ending inventory actually on hand	21,200	Sales discounts	8,000
Cost of goods sold	208,000	Sales returns and allowances	13,000
Freight-out	7,000	Sales	350,000
Insurance expense	12,000		
Rent expense	20,000		

Instructions

(a) Prepare the necessary adjusting entry for inventory.

(b) Prepare the necessary closing entries.

Prepare multiple-step and single-step income statements. (SO 5)

E5-7 In its income statement for the year ended December 31, 2002, Berman Company reported the following condensed data.

Administrative expenses	$ 435,000	Selling expenses	$ 490,000
Cost of goods sold	1,289,000	Loss on sale of equipment	10,000
Interest expense	70,000	Net sales	2,350,000
Interest revenue	45,000		

Instructions

(a) Prepare a multiple-step income statement.

(b) Prepare a single-step income statement.

Prepare correcting entries for sales and purchases. (SO 2, 3)

E5-8 An inexperienced accountant for Chinchilla Company made the following errors in recording merchandising transactions.

1. A $175 refund to a customer for faulty merchandise was debited to Sales $175 and credited to Cash $175.
2. A $200 credit purchase of supplies was debited to Merchandise Inventory $200 and credited to Cash $200.
3. An $80 sales discount was debited to Sales.
4. A cash payment of $30 for freight on merchandise purchases was debited to Freight-out $300 and credited to Cash $300.

Instructions

Prepare separate correcting entries for each error, assuming that the incorrect entry is not reversed. (Omit explanations.)

Compute missing amounts. (SO 5, 6)

E5-9 Presented below is financial information for two different companies.

	Amoruso Company	Tamburri Company
Sales	$90,000	(d)
Sales returns	(a)	$ 5,000
Net sales	83,000	95,000
Cost of goods sold	56,000	(e)
Gross profit	(b)	38,000
Operating expenses	15,000	(f)
Net income	(c)	15,000

Instructions

Determine the missing amounts.

Complete work sheet.
(SO 7)

*E5-10 Presented below are selected accounts for Garland Company as reported in the work sheet at the end of May 2002.

Accounts	Adjusted Trial Balance		Income Statement		Balance Sheet	
	Dr.	Cr.	Dr.	Cr.	Dr.	Cr.
Cash	9,000					
Merchandise Inventory	80,000					
Sales		450,000				
Sales Returns and Allowances	10,000					
Sales Discounts	7,000					
Cost of Goods Sold	250,000					

Instructions

Complete the work sheet by extending amounts reported in the adjusted trial balance to the appropriate columns in the work sheet. Do not total individual columns.

PROBLEMS: SET A

Journalize purchase and sales transactions under a perpetual inventory system.
(SO 2, 3)

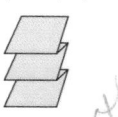

P5-1A Travel Warehouse distributes suitcases to retail stores and extends credit terms of 1/10, n/30 to all of its customers. At the end of July, Travel's inventory consisted of 40 suitcases purchased at $30 each. During the month of July the following merchandising transactions occurred.

July 1 Purchased 50 suitcases on account for $30 each from Suitcase Manufacturers, FOB destination, terms 1/15, n/30. The appropriate party also made a cash payment of $100 for freight on this date.
3 Sold 40 suitcases on account to Luggage World for $50 each.
9 Paid Suitcase Manufacturers in full.
12 Received payment in full from Luggage World.
17 Sold 30 suitcases on account to The Travel Spot for $50 each.
18 Purchased 60 suitcases on account for $1,700 from Vacation Manufacturers, FOB shipping point, terms 2/10, n/30. The appropriate party also made a cash payment of $100 for freight on this date.
20 Received $300 credit (including freight) for 10 suitcases returned to Vacation Manufacturers.
21 Received payment in full from The Travel Spot.
22 Sold 40 suitcases on account to Vacations-Are-Us for $50 each.
30 Paid Vacation Manufacturers in full.
31 Granted Vacations-Are-Us $250 credit for 5 suitcases returned costing $150.

Travel Warehouse's chart of accounts includes the following: No. 101 Cash, No. 112 Accounts Receivable, No. 120 Merchandise Inventory, No. 201 Accounts Payable, No. 401 Sales, No. 412 Sales Returns and Allowances, No. 414 Sales Discounts, No. 505 Cost of Goods Sold.

Instructions

Journalize the transactions for the month of July for Travel Warehouse using a perpetual inventory system.

Journalize, post, and prepare a partial income statement.
(SO 2, 3, 5, 6)

P5-2A Hubbs Distributing Company completed the following merchandising transactions in the month of April. At the beginning of April, the ledger of Hubbs showed Cash of $9,000 and M. Hubbs, Capital of $9,000.

Apr. 2 Purchased merchandise on account from Leshner Supply Co. $5,900, terms 2/10, n/30.
4 Sold merchandise on account $5,200, FOB destination, terms 2/10, n/30. The cost of the merchandise sold was $4,100.
5 Paid $200 freight on April 4 sale.
6 Received credit from Leshner Supply Co. for merchandise returned $300.
11 Paid Leshner Supply Co. in full, less discount.
13 Received collections in full, less discounts, from customers billed on April 4.
14 Purchased merchandise for cash $4,400.
16 Received refund from supplier on cash purchase of April 14, $500.
18 Purchased merchandise from Testa Distributors $4,200, FOB shipping point, terms 2/10, n/30.
20 Paid freight on April 18 purchase $100.
23 Sold merchandise for cash $6,400. The merchandise sold had a cost of $5,120.
26 Purchased merchandise for cash $2,300.
27 Paid Testa Distributors in full, less discount.
29 Made refunds to cash customers for defective merchandise $90. The returned merchandise had a scrap value of $30.
30 Sold merchandise on account $3,700, terms n/30. The cost of the merchandise sold was $3,000.

Hubbs Company's chart of accounts includes the following: No. 101 Cash, No. 112 Accounts Receivable, No. 120 Merchandise Inventory, No. 201 Accounts Payable, No. 301 M. Hubbs, Capital, No. 401 Sales, No. 412 Sales Returns and Allowances, No. 414 Sales Discounts, No. 505 Cost of Goods Sold, and No. 644 Freight-out.

Instructions

(a) Journalize the transactions using a perpetual inventory system.
(b) Enter the beginning cash and capital balances, and post the transactions. (Use J1 for the journal reference.)
(c) Prepare the income statement through gross profit for the month of April 2002.

(c) Gross profit $2,916

Prepare financial statements and adjusting and closing entries.
(SO 4, 5)

P5-3A Gitler Department Store is located near the Village shopping mall. At the end of the company's fiscal year on December 31, 2002, the following accounts appeared in two of its trial balances.

	Unadjusted	**Adjusted**		**Unadjusted**	**Adjusted**
Accounts Payable	$ 79,300	$ 79,300	Interest Payable		$ 8,000
Accounts Receivable	50,300	50,300	Interest Revenue	$ 4,000	4,000
Accumulated Depr.—Building	42,100	52,500	Merchandise Inventory	75,000	75,000
Accumulated Depr.—Equipment	29,600	42,900	Mortgage Payable	80,000	80,000
Building	190,000	190,000	Office Salaries Expense	32,000	32,000
Cash	23,000	23,000	Prepaid Insurance	9,600	2,400
L. Gitler, Capital	176,600	176,600	Property Taxes Expense		4,800
Cost of Goods Sold	412,700	412,700	Property Taxes Payable		4,800
Depr. Expense—Building		10,400	Sales Salaries Expense	76,000	76,000
Depr. Expense—Equipment		13,300	Sales	628,000	628,000
L. Gitler, Drawing	28,000	28,000	Sales Commissions Expense	11,000	15,500
Equipment	110,000	110,000	Sales Commissions Payable		4,500
Insurance Expense		7,200	Sales Returns and Allowances	8,000	8,000
Interest Expense	3,000	11,000	Utilities Expense	11,000	11,000

Analysis reveals the following additional data.

1. Insurance expense and utilities expense are 60% selling and 40% administrative.
2. $20,000 of the mortgage payable is due for payment next year.
3. Depreciation on the building and property tax expense are administrative expenses; depreciation on the equipment is a selling expense.

Instructions

(a) Net income $30,100
Capital $178,700
Total assets $355,300

(a) Prepare a multiple-step income statement, an owner's equity statement, and a classified balance sheet.
(b) Journalize the adjusting entries that were made.
(c) Journalize the closing entries that are necessary.

Journalize, post, and prepare a trial balance.
(SO 2, 3, 4)

Peachtree

P5-4A Mike Young, a former professional tennis star, operates Mike's Tennis Shop at the Jackson Lake Resort. At the beginning of the current season, the ledger of Mike's Tennis Shop showed Cash $2,500, Merchandise Inventory $1,700, and M. Young, Capital $4,200. The following transactions were completed during April.

Apr. 4 Purchased racquets and balls from Sampras Co. $640, FOB shipping point, terms 3/10, n/30.
6 Paid freight on purchase from Sampras Co. $40.
8 Sold merchandise to members $1,150, terms n/30. The merchandise sold had a cost of $750.
10 Received credit of $40 from Sampras Co. for a damaged racquet that was returned.
11 Purchased tennis shoes from Alan Sports for cash, $300.
13 Paid Sampras Co. in full.
14 Purchased tennis shirts and shorts from Tiger's Sportswear $700, FOB shipping point, terms 2/10, n/60.
15 Received cash refund of $50 from Alan Sports for damaged merchandise that was returned.
17 Paid freight on Tiger's Sportswear purchase $30.
18 Sold merchandise to members $800, terms n/30. The cost of the merchandise sold was $530.
20 Received $500 in cash from members in settlement of their accounts.
21 Paid Tiger's Sportswear in full.
27 Granted an allowance of $30 to members for tennis clothing that did not fit properly.
30 Received cash payments on account from members, $675.

The chart of accounts for the tennis shop includes the following: No. 101 Cash, No. 112 Accounts Receivable, No. 120 Merchandise Inventory, No. 201 Accounts Payable, No. 301 M. Young, Capital, No. 401 Sales, No. 412 Sales Returns and Allowances, No. 505 Cost of Goods Sold.

Instructions

(a) Journalize the April transactions using a perpetual inventory system.
(b) Enter the beginning balances in the ledger accounts and post the April transactions. (Use J1 for the journal reference.)

(c) Total debits $6,150

(c) Prepare a trial balance on April 30, 2002.

Complete accounting cycle beginning with a work sheet.
(SO 4, 5, 6, 7)

***P5-5A** The trial balance of Brennan Fashion Center contained the following accounts at November 30, the end of the company's fiscal year.

BRENNAN FASHION CENTER
Trial Balance
November 30, 2002

	Debit	Credit
Cash	$ 28,700	
Accounts Receivable	33,700	
Merchandise Inventory	45,000	
Store Supplies	5,500	
Store Equipment	85,000	
Accumulated Depreciation—Store Equipment		$ 18,000
Delivery Equipment	48,000	
Accumulated Depreciation—Delivery Equipment		6,000
Notes Payable		51,000
Accounts Payable		48,500
C. Brennan, Capital		110,000
C. Brennan, Drawing	12,000	
Sales		759,200
Sales Returns and Allowances	4,200	
Cost of Goods Sold	497,400	
Salaries Expense	140,000	
Advertising Expense	26,400	
Utilities Expense	14,000	
Repair Expense	12,100	
Delivery Expense	16,700	
Rent Expense	24,000	
Totals	$992,700	$992,700

Adjustment data:

1. Store supplies on hand totaled $3,500.
2. Depreciation is $9,000 on the store equipment and $7,000 on the delivery equipment.
3. Interest of $11,000 is accrued on notes payable at November 30.
4. Merchandise inventory actually on hand is $44,400.

Other data:

1. Salaries expense is 70% selling and 30% administrative.
2. Rent expense and utilities expense are 80% selling and 20% administrative.
3. $30,000 of notes payable are due for payment next year.
4. Repair expense is 100% administrative.

Instructions

(a) Enter the trial balance on a work sheet, and complete the work sheet.
(b) Prepare a multiple-step income statement and owner's equity statement for the year and a classified balance sheet as of November 30, 2002.
(c) Journalize the adjusting entries.
(d) Journalize the closing entries.
(e) Prepare a post-closing trial balance.

(a) Adj. trial balance $1,019,700
Net loss $5,200
(b) Gross profit $257,000
Total assets $203,300

PROBLEMS: SET B

P5-1B Dazzle Book Warehouse distributes hardback books to retail stores and extends credit terms of 2/10, n/30 to all of its customers. At the end of May, Dazzle's inventory consisted of 240 books purchased at $1,200. During the month of June the following merchandising transactions occurred.

Journalize purchase and sale transactions under a perpetual inventory system.
(SO 2, 3)

June 1 Purchased 130 books on account for $5 each from Reader's World Publishers, FOB destination, terms 1/10, n/30. The appropriate party also made a cash payment of $50 for the freight on this date.
3 Sold 140 books on account to the Book Nook for $10 each.
6 Received $50 credit for 10 books returned to Reader's World Publishers.
9 Paid Reader's World Publishers in full, less discount.
15 Received payment in full from the Book Nook.
17 Sold 120 books on account to Read-A-Lot Bookstore for $10 each.
20 Purchased 120 books on account for $5 each from Read More Publishers, FOB destination, terms 2/15, n/30. The appropriate party also made a cash payment of $50 for the freight on this date.
24 Received payment in full from Read-A-Lot Bookstore.
26 Paid Read More Publishers in full, less discount.
28 Sold 110 books on account to Readers Bookstore for $10 each.
30 Granted Readers Bookstore $150 credit for 15 books returned costing $75.

Dazzle Book Warehouse's chart of accounts includes the following: No. 101 Cash, No. 112 Accounts Receivable, No. 120 Merchandise Inventory, No. 201 Accounts Payable, No. 401 Sales, No. 412 Sales Returns and Allowances, No. 414 Sales Discounts, No. 505 Cost of Goods Sold.

Instructions
Journalize the transactions for the month of June for Dazzle Book Warehouse using a perpetual inventory system.

Journalize, post, and prepare partial income statement.
(SO 2, 3, 5, 6)

P5-2B Eagle Hardware Store completed the following merchandising transactions in the month of May. At the beginning of May, the ledger of Eagle showed Cash of $5,000 and J. Eagle, Capital of $5,000.

May 1 Purchased merchandise on account from Lathrop Wholesale Supply $6,000, terms 2/10, n/30.
2 Sold merchandise on account $4,700, terms 2/10, n/30. The cost of the merchandise sold was $3,100.
5 Received credit from Lathrop Wholesale Supply for merchandise returned $200.
9 Received collections in full, less discounts, from customers billed on sales of $4,500 on May 2.
10 Paid Lathrop Wholesale Supply in full, less discount.
11 Purchased supplies for cash $900.
12 Purchased merchandise for cash $2,400.
15 Received refund for poor quality merchandise from supplier on cash purchase $230.
17 Purchased merchandise from Kumar Distributors $1,900, FOB shipping point, terms 2/10, n/30.
19 Paid freight on May 17 purchase $250.
24 Sold merchandise for cash $6,200. The merchandise sold had a cost of $4,340.
25 Purchased merchandise from Tsai Inc. $1,000, FOB destination, terms 2/10, n/30.
27 Paid Kumar Distributors in full, less discount.
29 Made refunds to cash customers for defective merchandise $100. The returned merchandise had a scrap value of $20.
31 Sold merchandise on account $1,600, terms n/30. The cost of the merchandise sold was $1,120.

Eagle Hardware's chart of accounts includes the following: No. 101 Cash, No. 112 Accounts Receivable, No. 120 Merchandise Inventory, No. 126 Supplies, No. 201 Accounts Payable, No. 301 J. Eagle, Capital, No. 401 Sales, No. 412 Sales Returns and Allowances, No. 414 Sales Discounts, No. 505 Cost of Goods Sold.

Instructions

(a) Journalize the transactions using a perpetual inventory system.

(b) Enter the beginning cash and capital balances and post the transactions. (Use J1 for the journal reference.)

(c) Prepare an income statement through gross profit for the month of May 2002.

(c) Gross profit $3,770

P5-3B Forcina Department Store is located in midtown Metropolis. During the past several years, net income has been declining because of suburban shopping centers. At the end of the company's fiscal year on November 30, 2002, the following accounts appeared in two of its trial balances.

Prepare financial statements and adjusting and closing entries.
(SO 4, 5)

	Unadjusted	Adjusted		Unadjusted	Adjusted
Accounts Payable	$ 47,310	$ 47,310	Interest Revenue	$ 5,000	$ 5,000
Accounts Receivable	11,770	11,770	Merchandise Inventory	36,200	36,200
Accumulated Depr.—Delivery Equip.	15,680	19,680	Notes Payable	46,000	46,000
Accumulated Depr.—Store Equip.	32,300	41,800	Prepaid Insurance	13,500	4,500
Cash	8,000	8,000	Property Tax Expense		3,500
N. Forcina, Capital	84,200	84,200	Property Taxes Payable		3,500
Cost of Goods Sold	633,220	633,220	Rent Expense	19,000	19,000
Delivery Expense	8,200	8,200	Salaries Expense	120,000	120,000
Delivery Equipment	57,000	57,000	Sales	850,000	850,000
Depr. Expense—Delivery Equip.		4,000	Sales Commissions Expense	8,000	12,750
Depr. Expense—Store Equip.		9,500	Sales Commissions Payable		4,750
N. Forcina, Drawing	12,000	12,000	Sales Returns and Allowances	10,000	10,000
Insurance Expense		9,000	Store Equip.	125,000	125,000
Interest Expense	8,000	8,000	Utilities Expense	10,600	10,600

Analysis reveals the following additional data.

1. Salaries expense is 70% selling and 30% administrative.
2. Insurance expense is 50% selling and 50% administrative.
3. Rent expense, utilities expense, and property tax expense are administrative expenses.
4. Notes payable are due in 2005.

Instructions

(a) Prepare a multiple-step income statement, an owner's equity statement, and a classified balance sheet.

(b) Journalize the adjusting entries that were made.

(c) Journalize the closing entries that are necessary.

(a) Net income $7,230
Capital $79,430
Total assets $180,990

P5-4B Gregory Scott, a former professional golf star, operates Greg's Pro Shop at Bay Golf Course. At the beginning of the current season on April 1, the ledger of Greg's Pro Shop showed Cash $2,500, Merchandise Inventory $3,500, and G. Scott, Capital $6,000. The following transactions were completed during April.

Journalize, post, and prepare a trial balance.
(SO 2, 3, 4)

Apr. 5 Purchased golf bags, clubs, and balls on account from Hardy Co. $1,600, FOB shipping point, terms 2/10, n/60.
7 Paid freight on Hardy purchase $80.
9 Received credit from Hardy Co. for merchandise returned $100.
10 Sold merchandise on account to members $1,100, terms n/30. The merchandise sold had a cost of $730.
12 Purchased golf shoes, sweaters, and other accessories on account from Titleist Sportswear $660, terms 1/10, n/30.
14 Paid Hardy Co. in full, less discount.
17 Received credit from Titleist Sportswear for merchandise returned $60.
20 Made sales on account to members $700, terms n/30. The cost of the merchandise sold was $490, less discount.
21 Paid Titleist Sportswear in full.
27 Granted an allowance to members for clothing that did not fit properly $30.
30 Received payments on account from members $1,200.

The chart of accounts for the pro shop includes the following: No. 101 Cash, No. 112 Accounts Receivable, No. 120 Merchandise Inventory, No. 201 Accounts Payable, No. 301 G. Scott, Capital, No. 401 Sales, No. 412 Sales Returns and Allowances, No. 505 Cost of Goods Sold.

Instructions

(a) Journalize the April transactions using a perpetual inventory system.
(b) Enter the beginning balances in the ledger accounts and post the April transactions. (Use J1 for the journal reference.)
(c) Prepare a trial balance on April 30, 2002.

(c) Total debits $7,800

Complete accounting cycle beginning with a work sheet.
(SO 4, 5, 6, 7)

***P5-5B** The trial balance of Graham Wholesale Company contained the following accounts at December 31, the end of the company's fiscal year.

GRAHAM WHOLESALE COMPANY
Trial Balance
December 31, 2002

	Debit	Credit
Cash	$ 25,400	
Accounts Receivable	37,600	
Merchandise Inventory	90,000	
Land	92,000	
Buildings	197,000	
Accumulated Depreciation—Buildings		$ 54,000
Equipment	83,500	
Accumulated Depreciation—Equipment		42,400
Notes Payable		50,000
Accounts Payable		37,500
M. Graham, Capital		267,800
M. Graham, Drawing	10,000	
Sales		904,100
Sales Discounts	4,600	
Cost of Goods Sold	709,900	
Salaries Expense	69,800	
Utilities Expense	19,400	
Repair Expense	5,900	
Gas and Oil Expense	7,200	
Insurance Expense	3,500	
Totals	$1,355,800	$1,355,800

Adjustment data:

1. Depreciation is $10,000 on buildings and $9,000 on equipment. (Both are administrative expenses.)
2. Interest of $7,000 is due and unpaid on notes payable at December 31.
3. Merchandise inventory actually on hand is $89,200.

Other data:

1. Salaries are 80% selling and 20% administrative.
2. Utilities expense, repair expense, and insurance expense are 100% administrative.
3. $15,000 of the notes payable are payable next year.
4. Gas and oil expense is a selling expense.

Instructions

(a) Enter the trial balance on a work sheet, and complete the work sheet.
(b) Prepare a multiple-step income statement and owner's equity statement for the year, and a classified balance sheet at December 31, 2002.
(c) Journalize the adjusting entries.
(d) Journalize the closing entries.
(e) Prepare a post-closing trial balance.

(a) Adj. trial balance total $1,381,800
Net income $57,000
(b) Gross profit $188,800
Total assets $409,300
(e) Total debits $524,700

BROADENING YOUR PERSPECTIVE

FINANCIAL REPORTING AND ANALYSIS

FINANCIAL REPORTING PROBLEM: Lands' End, Inc.

BYP5-1 The financial statements of **Lands' End, Inc.** are presented in Appendix A at the end of this textbook.

Instructions
Answer the following questions using the Consolidated Statement of Earnings.

(a) What was the percentage change in (1) sales and in (2) net income from 1998 to 1999 and from 1999 to 2000?
(b) What was the company's gross profit rate in 1998, 1999, and 2000?
(c) What was the company's percentage of net income to net sales in 1998, 1999, and 2000? Comment on any trend in this percentage.

COMPARATIVE ANALYSIS PROBLEM: Lands' End vs. Abercrombie & Fitch

BYP5-2 **Lands' End's** financial statements are presented in Appendix A. **Abercrombie & Fitch's** financial statements are presented in Appendix B.

Instructions
(a) Based on the information contained in these financial statements, determine each of the following for each company.
(1) Gross profit for 2000.
(2) Gross profit rate for 2000.
(3) Operating income for 2000.
(4) Percent change in operating income from 1999 to 2000.

(b) What conclusions concerning the relative profitability of the two companies can be drawn from these data?

INTERPRETING FINANCIAL STATEMENTS: A Global Focus

BYP5-3 In August 1999 it was announced that two giant French retailers, **Carrefour SA** and **Promodes SA**, would merge. A headline in *The Wall Street Journal* blared, "French Retailers Create New Wal-Mart Rival." While **Wal-Mart's** total sales would still exceed those of the combined company, Wal-Mart's international sales are far less than those of the combined company. This is a serious concern for Wal-Mart, since its primary opportunity for future growth lies outside of the United States.

Below are basic financial data for the combined corporation (in French francs) and Wal-Mart (in U.S. dollars). Even though their results are presented in different currencies, by employing ratios we can make some basic comparisons.

	Carrefour/ Promodes (in billions)	Wal-Mart (in billions)
Sales	Fr 298.0	$137.6
Cost of goods sold	274.0	108.7
Operating expenses	9.6	22.4
Net income	5.5	4.4
Total assets	155.0	50.0
Average total assets	140.4	47.7
Current assets	63.5	21.1
Current liabilities	85.8	16.8
Total liabilities	114.2	28.9

Instructions
Compare the two companies by answering the following.

(a) Calculate the gross profit rate for each of the companies, and discuss their relative abilities to control cost of goods sold.

(b) Calculate the operating expense to sales ratio (operating expenses ÷ sales), and discuss the companies' relative abilities to control operating expenses.
(c) What concerns might you have in relying on this comparison?

EXPLORING THE WEB

BYP5-4 No financial decision maker should ever rely solely on the financial information reported in the annual report to make decisions. It is important to keep abreast of financial news. This activity demonstrates how to search for financial news on the Web.

Address: **biz.yahoo.com/i** *(or go to **www.wiley.com/college/weygandt**)*

Steps:

1. Type in either Lands' End or Abercrombie & Fitch.
2. Choose **News**.
3. Select an article that sounds interesting to you.

Instructions

(a) What was the source of the article? (For example, Reuters, Businesswire, PR Newswire.)
(b) Pretend that you are a personal financial planner and that one of your clients owns stock in the company. Write a brief memo to your client, summarizing the article and explaining the implications of the article for their investment.

CRITICAL THINKING

GROUP DECISION CASE

BYP5-5 Three years ago, Kathy Webb and her brother-in-law John Utley opened FedCo Department Store. For the first two years, business was good, but the following condensed income results for 2001 were disappointing.

FEDCO DEPARTMENT STORE
Income Statement
For the Year Ended December 31, 2001

Net sales		$700,000
Cost of goods sold		546,000
Gross profit		154,000
Operating expenses		
Selling expenses	$100,000	
Administrative expenses	25,000	125,000
Net income		$ 29,000

Kathy believes the problem lies in the relatively low gross profit rate (gross profit divided by net sales) of 22%. John believes the problem is that operating expenses are too high.

Kathy thinks the gross profit rate can be improved by making both of the following changes:

1. Increase average selling prices by 17%. This increase is expected to lower sales volume so that total sales will increase only 6%.
2. Buy merchandise in larger quantities and take all purchase discounts. These changes are expected to increase the gross profit rate by 3%.

Kathy does not anticipate that these changes will have any effect on operating expenses.

John thinks expenses can be cut by making both of the following changes.

1. Cut 2001 sales salaries of $60,000 in half and give sales personnel a commission of 2% of net sales.
2. Reduce store deliveries to one day per week rather than twice a week; this change will reduce 2001 delivery expenses of $30,000 by 40%.

John feels that these changes will not have any effect on net sales.

Kathy and John come to you for help in deciding the best way to improve net income.

Instructions

With the class divided into groups, answer the following.

(a) Prepare a condensed income statement for 2002 assuming (1) Kathy's changes are implemented and (2) John's ideas are adopted.
(b) What is your recommendation to Kathy and John?
(c) Prepare a condensed income statement for 2002 assuming both sets of proposed changes are made.

COMMUNICATION ACTIVITY

BYP5-6 The following situation is in chronological order.

1. Dexter decides to buy a surfboard.
2. He calls Surfing USA Co. to inquire about their surfboards.
3. Two days later he requests Surfing USA Co. to make him a surfboard.
4. Three days later, Surfing USA Co. sends him a purchase order to fill out.
5. He sends back the purchase order.
6. Surfing USA Co. receives the completed purchase order.
7. Surfing USA Co. completes the surfboard.
8. Dexter picks up the surfboard.
9. Surfing USA Co. bills Dexter.
10. Surfing USA Co. receives payment from Dexter.

Instructions
In a memo to the president of Surfing USA Co., explain the following.
(a) When should Surfing USA Co. record the sale?
(b) Suppose that with his purchase order, Dexter is required to make a down payment. Would that change your answer?

ETHICS CASE

BYP5-7 Rita Pelzer was just hired as the assistant treasurer of Yorkshire Store. The company is a specialty chain store with nine retail stores concentrated in one metropolitan area. Among other things, the payment of all invoices is centralized in one of the departments Rita will manage. Her primary responsibility is to maintain the company's high credit rating by paying all bills when due and to take advantage of all cash discounts.

Jamie Caterino, the former assistant treasurer who has been promoted to treasurer, is training Rita in her new duties. He instructs Rita that she is to continue the practice of preparing all checks "net of discount" and dating the checks the last day of the discount period. "But," Jamie continues, "we always hold the checks at least 4 days beyond the discount period before mailing them. That way we get another 4 days of interest on our money. Most of our creditors need our business and don't complain. And, if they scream about our missing the discount period, we blame it on the mail room or the post office. We've only lost one discount out of every hundred we take that way. I think everybody does it. By the way, welcome to our team!"

Instructions
(a) What are the ethical considerations in this case?
(b) Who are the stakeholders that are harmed or benefitted in this situation?
(c) Should Rita continue the practice started by Jamie? Does she have any choice?

Answers to Self-Study Questions

1. c 2. a 3. c 4. b 5. c 6. d 7. b 8. c 9. d 10. a

Answer to *Lands' End* Review It Question 1, p. 202

For Lands' End, the 2000 gross profit rate is 44.9% ($593 ÷ $1,320). The 1999 gross profit rate was 45% ($617 ÷ $1,371). The rate therefore decreased by 0.1% from 1999 to 2000. All this information was provided in Lands' End's management discussion and analysis section. It also could be computed from the income statement presented.

Remember to go back to the Navigator box on the chapter-opening page and check off your completed work.

INVENTORIES

6

THE NAVIGATOR ✓

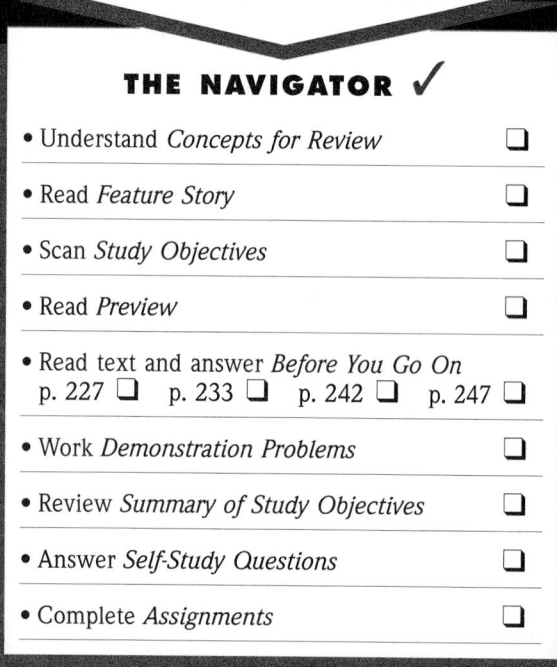

- Understand *Concepts for Review* ❑
- Read *Feature Story* ❑
- Scan *Study Objectives* ❑
- Read *Preview* ❑
- Read text and answer *Before You Go On* p. 227 ❑ p. 233 ❑ p. 242 ❑ p. 247 ❑
- Work *Demonstration Problems* ❑
- Review *Summary of Study Objectives* ❑
- Answer *Self-Study Questions* ❑
- Complete *Assignments* ❑

CONCEPTS FOR REVIEW

Before studying this chapter, you should know or, if necessary, review:

a. The cost principle (Ch. 1, p. 10) and matching principle of accounting. (Ch. 3, p. 90)

b. How to record purchases, sales, and cost of goods sold under a perpetual inventory system. (Ch. 5, pp. 187–194)

c. How to prepare financial statements for a merchandiser. (Ch. 5, pp. 197–202)

THE NAVIGATOR

FEATURE STORY

Taking Stock—from Backpacks to Bicycles

Backpacks and jackets sporting the jagged peaks of the **Mountain Equipment Co-op (MEC)** logo are a familiar sight on hiking trails and campuses. Sales of these popular items help the Vancouver-based co-op to finance its primary goal: to provide members with products and services for wilderness recreational activities at a reasonable cost.

MEC has five retail stores across Canada and a huge market in catalogue sales around the world. It ships everything from climbing ropes, kayaks, and bike helmets to destinations as far away as Japan and South America.

Keeping financial track of the flow of these items is a responsibility of Fara Jumani, a member of the inventory costing group at MEC and a part-time college student. "We have tens of thousands of items in inventory, and we are adding new ones all the time," says Ms. Jumani. "Because we make a lot of our own clothing goods, we also have a lot of in-house inventory—fabric and supplies that will be used to make products."

MEC tracks the cost of its inventory using the average cost of the various items in inventory, weighted by the number purchased at each different unit cost. (This procedure is called the weighted average cost method.) "Because costs tend to fluctuate," explains Ms. Jumani, "that method best captures our overall costs."

Unlike most retail operations, MEC is not out to make a profit. As a co-op, it exists to serve its members. "But we have to stay fiscally healthy to do that," points out Ms. Jumani. "If we go bankrupt, we won't be serving anyone." Accounting for inventory—from backpacks to bicycles—is an important part of MEC's fiscal fitness routine.

THE NAVIGATOR

STUDY OBJECTIVES

After studying this chapter, you should be able to:

1. Describe the steps in determining inventory quantities.
2. Prepare the entries for purchases and sales of inventory under a periodic inventory system.
3. Determine cost of goods sold under a periodic inventory system.
4. Identify the unique features of the income statement for a merchandiser using a periodic inventory system.
5. Explain the basis of accounting for inventories, and describe the inventory cost flow methods.
6. Explain the financial statement and tax effects of each of the inventory cost flow methods.
7. Explain the lower of cost or market basis of accounting for inventories.
8. Indicate the effects of inventory errors on the financial statements.
9. Compute and interpret inventory turnover.

THE NAVIGATOR

PREVIEW OF CHAPTER 6

As indicated in the opening story about **Mountain Equipment Co-op**, careful accounting for inventory is necessary to stay in business. In this chapter we will explain the methods used in determining the cost of inventory on hand at the balance sheet date. We also will discuss differences in perpetual and periodic inventory systems, and the effects of inventory errors on a company's financial statements.

The content and organization of Chapter 6 are as follows.

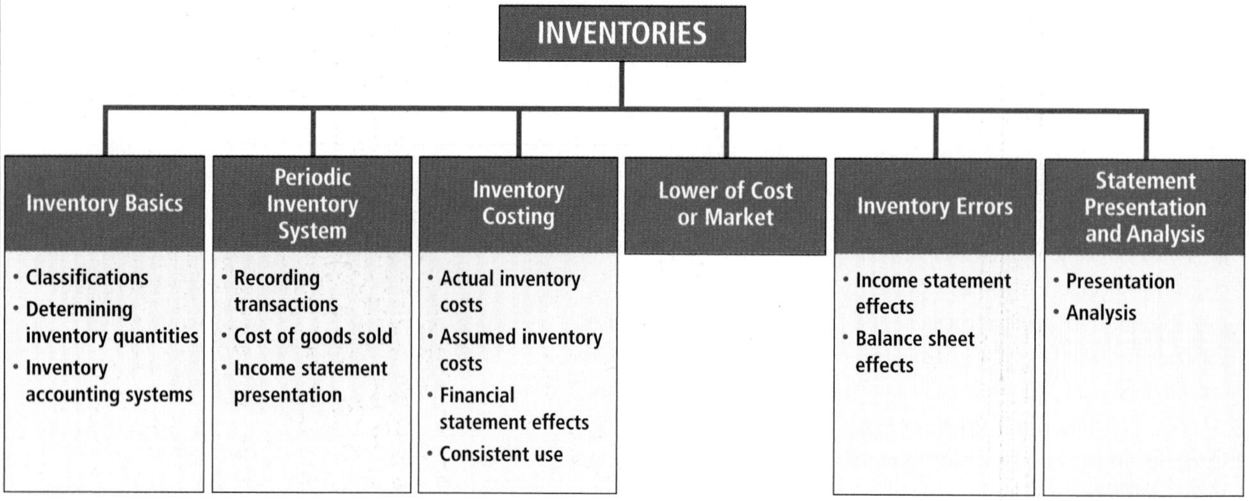

THE NAVIGATOR

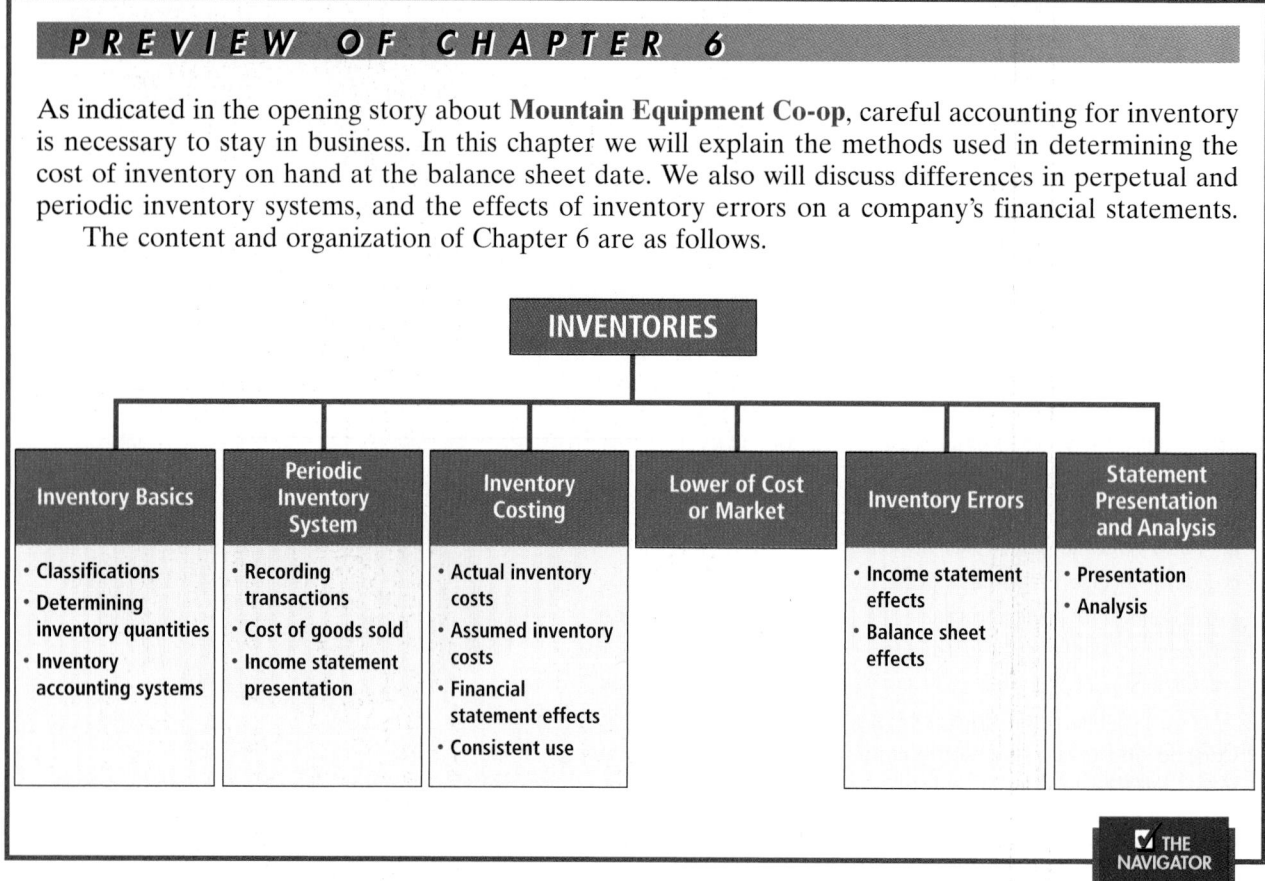

INVENTORY BASICS

In our economy, inventories are an important barometer of business activity. The U.S. Commerce Department publishes monthly inventory data for retailers, wholesalers, and manufacturers. The amount of inventories and the time required to sell the goods on hand are two closely watched indicators. During downturns in the economy, there is an initial buildup of inventories, as it takes longer to sell existing quantities. Inventories generally decrease with an upturn in business activity. A delicate balance must be maintained between too little inventory and too much. A company with too little inventory to meet demand will have dissatisfied customers and sales personnel. One with too much inventory will be burdened with unnecessary carrying costs.

Inventories affect both the balance sheet and the income statement. In the **balance sheet** of merchandising companies, inventory is frequently the most significant current asset. Of course, its amount and relative importance can vary, even for companies in the same industry. For example, **Wal-Mart** reported inventory of $17 billion, representing 81% of total current assets. For the same period, **J.C. Penney Company** reported $6 billion of inventory, representing 54% of total current assets. In the **income statement**, inventory is vital in determining the results of operations for a particular period. Also, gross profit (net sales less cost of goods sold) is closely watched by management, owners, and other interested parties (as explained in Chapter 5).

CLASSIFYING INVENTORY

How a company classifies its inventory depends on whether the firm is a merchandiser or a manufacturer. A **merchandiser's** inventory consists of many different items. For example, in a grocery store, canned goods, dairy products, meats, and produce are just a few of the inventory items on hand. These items have two common characteristics: (1) They are owned by the company, and (2) they are in a form ready for sale in the ordinary course of business. Only one inventory classification, **merchandise inventory**, is needed to describe the many different items that make up the total inventory.

A **manufacturer's** inventories are also owned by the company, but some goods may not yet be ready for sale. As a result, inventory is usually classified into three categories: finished goods, work in process, and raw materials. For example, **General Motors** classifies vehicles completed and ready for sale as **finished goods**. The vehicles in various stages of production are classified as **work in process**. The steel, glass, upholstery, and other components that are on hand waiting to be used in production are **raw materials**.

The accounting principles and concepts discussed in this chapter apply to inventory classifications of both merchandising and manufacturing companies. In this chapter we will focus on merchandise inventory.

HELPFUL HINT
Regardless of the classification, all inventories are reported under current assets on the balance sheet.

DETERMINING INVENTORY QUANTITIES

STUDY OBJECTIVE 1
Describe the steps in determining inventory quantities.

Many businesses take a physical inventory count on the last day of the year. Businesses using the periodic inventory system must make such a count to determine the inventory on hand at the balance sheet date and to compute cost of goods sold. Even businesses using a perpetual inventory system must take a physical inventory at some time during the year.

Determining inventory quantities consists of two steps: (1) taking a physical inventory of goods on hand, and (2) determining the ownership of goods.

Taking a Physical Inventory

Taking a physical inventory involves actually counting, weighing, or measuring each kind of inventory on hand. In many companies, taking an inventory is a formidable task. Retailers such as **Kmart**, **Home Depot**, or your favorite music store have thousands of different inventory items. An inventory count is generally more accurate when goods are not being sold or received during the counting. So, companies often "take inventory" when the business is closed or when business is slow. Many retailers, for example, close early on a chosen day in January—after the holiday sales and returns—to count inventory.

To minimize errors in taking the inventory, a company should adhere to **internal control** principles and practices that safeguard inventory:

1. The counting should be done by employees who do not have custodial responsibility for the inventory.
2. Each counter should establish the authenticity of each inventory item. For example, does each box contain a 25-inch television set? Does each storage tank contain gasoline?
3. There should be a second count by another employee.
4. Prenumbered inventory tags should be used. All inventory tags should be accounted for.
5. At the end of the count, a designated supervisor should check that all inventory items are tagged and that no items have more than one tag.

After the physical inventory is taken, the quantity of each kind of inventory is listed on **inventory summary sheets**. To ensure accuracy, the listing should be verified by a second employee. Later, unit costs will be applied to the quantities in order to determine a total cost of the inventory—which is the topic of later sections.[1]

ACCOUNTING IN ACTION *Business Insight*

Failure to observe the foregoing internal control procedures contributed to the Great Salad Oil Swindle. In this case, management intentionally overstated its salad oil inventory, which was stored in large holding tanks. Three procedures contributed to overstating the oil inventory: (1) Water added to the bottom of the holding tanks caused the oil to float to the top. Inventory-taking crews who viewed the holding tanks from the top observed only salad oil. In fact, as much as 37 out of 40 feet of many of the holding tanks contained water. (2) The company's inventory records listed more holding tanks than it actually had. The company repainted numbers on the tanks after inventory crews examined them, so the crews counted the same tanks twice. (3) Underground pipes pumped oil from one holding tank to another during the inventory taking. Therefore, the same salad oil was counted more than once. Although the salad oil swindle was unusual, it demonstrates the complexities involved in assuring that inventory is properly counted.

Determining Ownership of Goods

Before we can begin to calculate the cost of inventory, we need to consider the ownership of goods. Specifically, we need to be sure that we have not included in the inventory any goods that do not belong to the company.

GOODS IN TRANSIT. Goods are considered **in transit** when they are in the hands of a public carrier (such as a railroad, trucking, or airline company) at the statement date. Goods in transit should be included in the inventory of the party that has legal title to the goods. Legal title is determined by the terms of sale, as shown in Illustration 6-1 and described below.

1. **FOB (free on board) shipping point:** Ownership of the goods passes to the buyer when the public carrier accepts the goods from the seller.
2. **FOB destination:** Legal title to the goods remains with the seller until the goods reach the buyer.

Illustration 6-1

Terms of sale

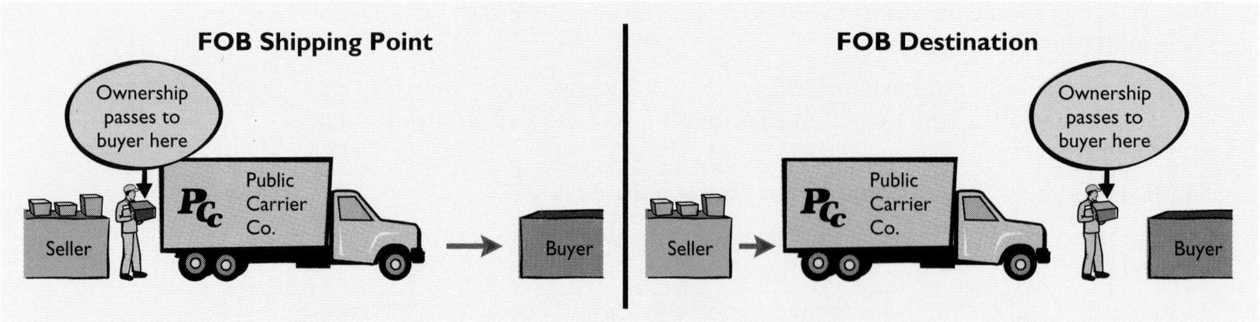

[1] To estimate the cost of inventory when a physical inventory cannot be taken (the inventory is destroyed) or when it is inconvenient (during interim periods), estimating methods are applied. These methods (gross profit method and retail inventory method) are discussed in Appendix 6B.

Inventory quantities may be seriously miscounted if goods in transit at the statement date are ignored. Assume that Hargrove Company has 20,000 units of inventory on hand on December 31. It also has the following goods in transit: (1) **sales** of 1,500 units shipped December 31 FOB destination, and (2) **purchases** of 2,500 units shipped FOB shipping point by the seller on December 31. Hargrove has legal title to both the units sold and the units purchased. If units in transit are ignored, inventory quantities would be understated by 4,000 units (1,500 + 2,500).

TECHNOLOGY IN ACTION

Many companies have invested large amounts of time and money in automated inventory systems. One of the most sophisticated is **Federal Express's** Digitally Assisted Dispatch System (DADS). It uses hand-held "SuperTrackers" to transmit data about the packages and documents to the firm's computer system. Based on bar codes, the system allows the firm to know where any package is at any time to prevent losses and to fulfill the firm's delivery commitments. More recently, FedEx's software enables customers to track shipments on their own PCs.

CONSIGNED GOODS. In some lines of business, it is customary to acquire merchandise on consignment. Under such an arrangement, the holder of the goods (the *consignee*) does not own the goods. Ownership remains with the shipper of the goods (the *consignor*) until the goods are actually sold to a customer. Because **consigned goods** are not owned by the consignee, they should not be included in the consignee's physical inventory count. But, the consignor should include merchandise held by the consignee as part of its inventory.

INVENTORY ACCOUNTING SYSTEMS

One of two basic systems of accounting for inventories may be used: **(1) the perpetual inventory system,** or **(2) the periodic inventory system**. Chapter 5 discussed and illustrated the perpetual inventory system. This chapter discusses and illustrates the periodic inventory system. Appendix 6A compares the periodic inventory system with the perpetual inventory system. Appendix 6C continues coverage of the perpetual inventory system.

Some businesses find it either unnecessary or uneconomical to invest in a computerized perpetual inventory system. As illustrated in Chapter 5, a perpetual inventory system keeps track of inventory in number of units **and** in dollar costs per unit. Many small merchandising business managers still feel that a perpetual inventory system costs more than it is worth. These managers can control merchandise and manage day-to-day operations either without detailed inventory records or with a perpetual **units only** inventory system.

BEFORE YOU GO ON...

▶ *REVIEW IT*

1. What steps are involved in determining inventory quantities?
2. How is ownership determined for goods in transit at the balance sheet date?
3. Who has title to consigned goods?

▶ *DO IT*

Hasbeen Company completed its inventory count. It arrived at a total inventory value of $200,000. You have been informed of the information listed below. Discuss how this information affects the reported cost of inventory.

1. Goods held on consignment for Falls Co., costing $15,000, were included in the inventory.
2. Purchased goods of $10,000 which were in transit (terms: FOB shipping point) were not included in the count.
3. Sold inventory with a cost of $12,000 which was in transit (terms: FOB shipping point) was not included in the count.

ACTION PLAN

- Apply the rules of ownership to goods held on consignment.
- Apply the rules of ownership to goods in transit FOB shipping point.

SOLUTION

The goods of $15,000 held on consignment should be deducted from the inventory count. The goods of $10,000 purchased FOB shipping point should be added to the inventory count. Sold goods of $12,000 which were in transit FOB shipping point should not be included in the ending inventory. Thus, inventory should be carried at $195,000.

Related exercise material: BE6-4, E6-1, and E6-4.

THE NAVIGATOR

PERIODIC INVENTORY SYSTEM

STUDY OBJECTIVE 2

Prepare the entries for purchases and sales of inventory under a periodic inventory system.

In a **periodic inventory system**, revenues from the sale of merchandise are recorded when sales are made, in the same way as in a perpetual system. But, no attempt is made on the date of sale to record the cost of the merchandise sold. Instead, a physical inventory count is taken at the end of the period. This count determines (1) the cost of the merchandise on hand and (2) the cost of the goods sold during the period. There is another key difference: Under a periodic system, purchases of merchandise are recorded in a Purchases account rather than a Merchandise Inventory account. Also, under a periodic system, it is customary to record the following in separate accounts: purchase returns and allowances, purchase discounts, and freight-in on purchases. That way, accumulated amounts for each are known.

RECORDING TRANSACTIONS

To illustrate the recording of merchandise transactions under a periodic inventory system, we will use the purchase/sale transactions between Sellers Electronix and Beyer Video discussed in Chapter 5.

RECORDING PURCHASES OF MERCHANDISE

HELPFUL HINT

Be careful not to fall into the trap of debiting purchases of equipment or supplies to Purchases.

On the basis of the sales invoice (Illustration 5-4 shown on page 188) and receipt of the merchandise ordered from Sellers Electronix, Beyer Video records the $3,800 purchase as follows.

A	=	L	+	OE
		+3,800		−3,800

May 4	Purchases	3,800	
	Accounts Payable		3,800
	(To record goods purchased on account, terms 2/10, n/30)		

Purchases is a temporary account whose normal balance is a debit.

Purchase Returns and Allowances

Some of the merchandise received from Sellers Electronix is inoperable. Beyer Video returns $300 worth of the goods and prepares the following entry to recognize the purchase return.

May 8	Accounts Payable	300	
	Purchase Returns and Allowances		300
	(To record return of inoperable goods purchased from Sellers Electronix)		

A	=	L	+	OE
		−300		+300

Purchase Returns and Allowances is a temporary account whose normal balance is a credit.

Freight Costs

When the purchaser directly incurs the freight costs, the account Freight-in is debited. For example, upon delivery of the goods on May 6, Beyer pays Acme Freight Company $150 for freight charges on its purchase from Sellers Electronix. The entry on Beyer's books is:

May 9	Freight-in	150	
	Cash		150
	(To record payment of freight, terms FOB shipping point)		

A	=	L	+	OE
−150				−150

Like Purchases, Freight-in is a temporary account whose normal balance is a debit. **Freight-in is part of cost of goods purchased**. In accordance with the cost principle, cost of goods purchased should include any freight charges necessary to bring the goods to the purchaser. Freight costs are not subject to a purchase discount. Purchase discounts apply only on the invoice cost of the merchandise.

ALTERNATIVE TERMINOLOGY
Freight-in is frequently called *transportation-in*.

Purchase Discounts

On May 14 Beyer Video pays the balance due on account to Sellers Electronix. Beyer takes the 2% cash discount allowed by Sellers for payment within 10 days. The payment and discount are recorded by Beyer Video as follows.

May 14	Accounts Payable	3,500	
	Purchase Discounts		70
	Cash		3,430
	(To record payment to Sellers Electronix within the discount period)		

A	=	L	+	OE
−3,430		−3,500		+70

Purchase Discounts is a temporary account whose normal balance is a credit.

RECORDING SALES OF MERCHANDISE

The sale of $3,800 of merchandise to Beyer Video on May 4 (sales invoice No. 731, Illustration 5-4 on page 188) is recorded by Sellers Electronix as follows.

May 4	Accounts Receivable	3,800	
	Sales		3,800
	(To record credit sales per invoice #731 to Beyer Video)		

A	=	L	+	OE
+3,800				+3,800

Sales Returns and Allowances

Based on the receipt of returned goods from Beyer Video on May 8, Sellers Electronix records the $300 sales return as follows.

A	=	L	+	OE
−300				−300

May 8	Sales Returns and Allowances	300	
	Accounts Receivable		300
	(To record return of goods from Beyer Video)		

Sales Discounts

On May 15, Sellers Electronix receives payment of $3,430 on account from Beyer Video. Sellers honors the 2% cash discount and records the payment of Beyer's account receivable in full as follows.

A	=	L	+	OE
+3,430				−70
−3,500				

May 15	Cash	3,430	
	Sales Discounts	70	
	Accounts Receivable		3,500
	(To record collection from Beyer Video within 2/10, n/30 discount period)		

COMPARISON OF ENTRIES—PERPETUAL VS. PERIODIC

For purposes of comparison, the periodic inventory system entries above are shown in Illustration 6A-1 (in Appendix 6A on page 250) next to those from Chapter 5 (pages 188–193) under the perpetual inventory system for both Sellers Electronix and Beyer Video.

COST OF GOODS SOLD

STUDY OBJECTIVE 3

Determine cost of goods sold under a periodic inventory system.

As the entries above indicate, under a periodic inventory system a running account of the changes in inventory is not recorded as either purchases or sales transactions occur. Neither the daily amount of merchandise on hand is known nor is the cost of goods sold. **To determine the cost of goods sold under a periodic inventory system**, three steps are required: (1) Record purchases of merchandise (as shown above). (2) Determine the cost of goods purchased. (3) Determine the cost of goods on hand at the beginning and end of the accounting period. The cost of goods on hand must be determined by a physical inventory count and application of the cost to the items counted in the inventory. In this section, we look in more detail at this process.

DETERMINING COST OF GOODS PURCHASED

Earlier in this chapter we used four accounts to record the purchase of inventory under a periodic inventory system. These accounts are:

Illustration 6-2

Normal balances: cost of goods purchased accounts

Account	Normal Balance
Purchases	Debit
Purchase Returns and Allowances	Credit
Purchase Discounts	Credit
Freight-in	Debit

All of these accounts are **temporary accounts**. They are used to determine the cost of goods sold, which is an expense disclosed on the income statement. Therefore, the balances in these accounts must be reduced to zero at the end of each accounting period. Information about cost of goods sold can then be accumulated for the next accounting period.

The procedure for determining the cost of goods purchased is as follows.

1. The accounts with credit balances (Purchase Returns and Allowances, Purchase Discounts) are subtracted from Purchases. The result is **net purchases**.
2. Freight-in is then added to net purchases. The result is **cost of goods purchased**.

To illustrate, assume that Sellers Electronix shows the following balances for the accounts above: Purchases $325,000; Purchase Returns and Allowances $10,400; Purchase Discounts $6,800; and Freight-in $12,200. Net purchases is $307,800, and cost of goods purchased is $320,000, as computed in Illustration 6-3.

Purchases		$325,000
(1) Less: Purchase returns and allowances	$10,400	
Purchase discounts	6,800	17,200
Net purchases		**307,800**
(2) Add: Freight-in		12,200
Cost of goods purchased		**$320,000**

Illustration 6-3

Computation of net purchases and cost of goods purchased

Determining Cost of Goods on Hand

To **determine the cost of inventory on hand, Sellers Electronix must take a physical inventory**. Taking a physical inventory involves:

1. Counting the units on hand for each item of inventory.
2. Applying unit costs to the total units on hand for each item.
3. Totaling the costs for each item of inventory, to determine the total cost of goods on hand.

A physical inventory should be taken at or near the balance sheet date.

The account Merchandise Inventory is used to record the cost of inventory on hand at the balance sheet date. This amount becomes the beginning inventory for the next accounting period. For Sellers Electronix, the balance in Merchandise Inventory at December 31, 2001, is $36,000. This amount is also the January 1, 2002, balance in Merchandise Inventory. During the year, **no entries are made to Merchandise Inventory**. At the end of the year, entries are made to eliminate the beginning inventory and to record the ending inventory. We will assume that Sellers Electronix's ending inventory on December 31, 2002, is $40,000.

Computing Cost of Goods Sold

We have now reached the point where we can compute cost of goods sold. Doing so involves two steps:

1. Add the cost of goods purchased to the cost of goods on hand at the beginning of the period (beginning inventory). The result is the **cost of goods available for sale**.
2. Subtract the cost of goods on hand at the end of the period (ending inventory) from the cost of goods available for sale. The result is the **cost of goods sold**.

ALTERNATIVE TERMINOLOGY
Some use the term *cost of sales* instead of *cost of goods sold*.

For Sellers Electronix the cost of goods available for sale is $356,000, and the cost of goods sold is $316,000, as shown below.

Illustration 6-4

Computation of cost of goods available for sale and cost of goods sold

	Beginning inventory	$ 36,000
(1)	Add: Cost of goods purchased	320,000
	Cost of goods available for sale	**356,000**
(2)	Less: Ending inventory	40,000
	Cost of goods sold	**$316,000**

Gross profit, operating expenses, and net income are computed and reported in a periodic inventory system in the same manner as under a perpetual inventory system, as shown in Illustration 6-5. (See also Chapter 5, Illustration 5-11, page 200).

Illustration 6-5

Income statement for a merchandiser using a periodic inventory system

SELLERS ELECTRONIX
Income Statement
For the Year Ended December 31, 2002

Sales revenue				
Sales				$480,000
Less: Sales returns and allowances			$ 12,000	
Sales discounts			8,000	20,000
Net sales				460,000
Cost of goods sold				
Inventory, January 1			**36,000**	
Purchases		**$325,000**		
Less: Purchase returns and allowances	**$10,400**			
Purchase discounts	**6,800**	**17,200**		
Net purchases		**307,800**		
Add: Freight-in		**12,200**		
Cost of goods purchased			**320,000**	
Cost of goods available for sale			**356,000**	
Inventory, December 31			**40,000**	
Cost of goods sold				**316,000**
Gross profit				144,000
Operating expenses				
Store salaries expense			45,000	
Rent expense			19,000	
Utilities expense			17,000	
Advertising expense			16,000	
Depreciation expense—store equipment			8,000	
Freight-out			7,000	
Insurance expense			2,000	
Total operating expenses				114,000
Net income				$ 30,000

HELPFUL HINT
The far right column identifies the major subdivisions of the income statement. The next column identifies the primary items comprising cost of goods sold of $316,000 and operating expenses of $114,000; in addition, contra revenue items of $20,000 are reported. The third column explains cost of goods purchased of $320,000. The fourth column reports contra purchase items of $17,200.

Chapter 6 — Completing the Accounting Cycle, Periodic Inventory System

STUDY OBJECTIVE 4

Identify the unique features of the income statement for a merchandiser using a periodic inventory system.

INCOME STATEMENT PRESENTATION

The income statement for merchandisers under a periodic inventory system contains three features not found in the income statement of a service enterprise.

These features are: (1) a sales revenue section, (2) a cost of goods sold section, and (3) gross profit. These same three features appear for a merchandiser under a perpetual inventory system. But, under a periodic inventory system, the cost of goods sold section generally will contain more detail. Using assumed data for specific operating expenses, the income statement for Sellers Electronix using a periodic inventory system is shown in Illustration 6-5. Whether the periodic or the perpetual inventory system is used, merchandise inventory is reported at the same amount in the current assets section.

ALTERNATIVE TERMINOLOGY
Gross profit is sometimes referred to as *merchandising profit* or *gross margin*.

BEFORE YOU GO ON...

REVIEW IT

1. Name two basic systems of accounting for inventory.
2. Identify the three steps in determining cost of goods sold.
3. What accounts are used in determining the cost of goods purchased?
4. What is included in cost of goods available for sale?

DO IT

Aerosmith Company's accounting records show the following at year-end: Purchase Discounts $3,400; Freight-in $6,100; Sales $240,000; Purchases $162,500; Beginning Inventory $18,000; Ending Inventory $20,000; Sales Discounts $10,000; Purchase Returns $5,200; and Operating Expenses $57,000. Compute the following amounts for Aerosmith Company: net sales, cost of goods purchased, cost of goods sold, gross profit, and net income.

ACTION PLAN

- Understand the relationships of the cost components in measuring net income for a merchandising company.
- Compute net sales.
- Compute cost of goods purchased.
- Compute cost of goods sold.
- Compute gross profit.
- Compute net income.

SOLUTION

Net sales: $240,000 – $10,000 = $230,000.
Cost of goods purchased: $162,500 – $5,200 – $3,400 + $6,100 = $160,000.
Cost of goods sold: $18,000 + $160,000 – $20,000 = $158,000.
Gross profit: $230,000 – $158,000 = $72,000.
Net income: $72,000 – $57,000 = $15,000.

Related exercise material: BE6-2, BE6-3, E6-2, and E6-3.

THE NAVIGATOR

INVENTORY COSTING UNDER A PERIODIC INVENTORY SYSTEM

STUDY OBJECTIVE 5
Explain the basis of accounting for inventories, and describe the inventory cost flow methods.

All expenditures needed to acquire goods and to make them ready for sale are included as inventoriable costs. **Inventoriable costs** may be regarded as a pool of costs that consists of two elements: (1) the cost of the beginning inventory and (2) the cost of goods purchased during the year. The sum of these two equals the cost of goods available for sale.

Conceptually, the costs of the purchasing, receiving, and warehousing departments (whose efforts make the goods available for sale) should also be included in inventoriable costs. But, there are practical difficulties in allocating these costs to inventory. So these costs are generally accounted for as **operating expenses** in the period in which they are incurred.

Inventoriable costs are allocated either to ending inventory or to cost of goods sold. Under a periodic inventory system, the allocation is made at the end of the accounting period. First, the costs for the ending inventory are determined. Next, the cost of the ending inventory is subtracted from the cost of goods available for sale, to determine the cost of goods sold.

HELPFUL HINT
Under a perpetual inventory system, described in Chapter 5, the allocation of costs is recognized continuously as purchases and sales are made.

To illustrate, assume that General Suppliers has a cost of goods available for sale of $120,000. This amount is based on a beginning inventory of $20,000 and cost of goods purchased of $100,000. The physical inventory indicates that 5,000 units are on hand. The costs applicable to the units are $3.00 per unit. The allocation of the pool of costs is shown in Illustration 6-6. As shown, the $120,000 of goods available for sale are allocated $15,000 to ending inventory (5,000 × $3.00) and $105,000 to cost of goods sold.

Illustration 6-6

Allocation (matching) of pool of costs

Pool of Costs

Cost of Goods Available for Sale

Beginning inventory	$ 20,000
Cost of goods purchased	100,000
Cost of goods available for sale	**$120,000**

Step 1 — **Ending Inventory**

Units	Unit Cost	Total Cost
5,000	$3.00	**$15,000**

Step 2 — **Cost of Goods Sold**

Cost of goods available for sale	$120,000
Less: Ending inventory	15,000
Cost of goods sold	**$105,000**

USING ACTUAL PHYSICAL FLOW COSTING—SPECIFIC IDENTIFICATION

Costing of the inventory is complicated because specific items of inventory on hand may have been purchased at different prices. For example, a company may experience several increases in the cost of identical goods within a given year. Or, unit costs may decline. Under such circumstances, how should different unit costs be allocated between the ending inventory and cost of goods sold?

One answer is to use specific identification of the units purchased. This method tracks the **actual physical flow** of the goods. **Each item of inventory is marked, tagged, or coded with its "specific" unit cost.** At the end of the year the specific costs of items still in inventory make up the total cost of the ending inventory. Assume, for example, that Southland Music Company purchases three 46-inch television sets at costs of $700, $750, and $800, respectively. During the year, two sets are sold at $1,200 each. At December 31, the $750 set is still on hand. The ending inventory is $750, and the cost of goods sold is $1,500 ($700 + $800). This is shown graphically in Illustration 6-7.

HELPFUL HINT
What gross profit will Southland Music report? Answer: $900 (Sales $2,400 − CGS $1,500).

Specific identification is possible when a company sells a limited variety of high-unit-cost items that can be clearly identified from purchase through sale. Examples are automobile dealerships (cars, trucks, and vans), music stores (pianos and organs), and antique shops (tables and cabinets).

Illustration 6-7

Specific identification method

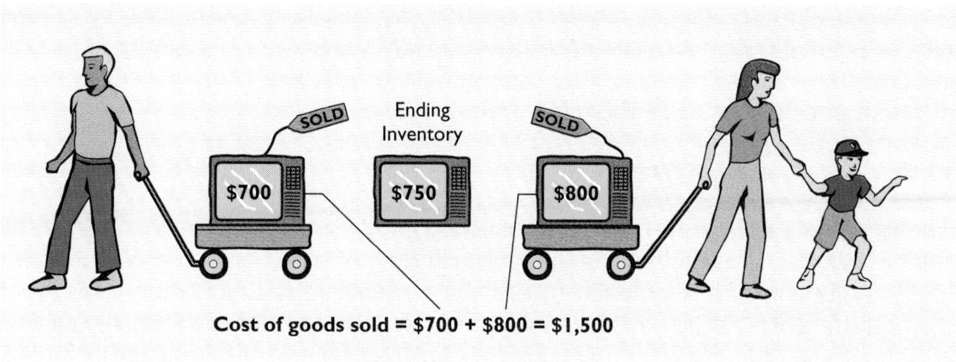

But what if we cannot specifically identify particular inventory items? For example, drug, grocery, and hardware stores sell thousands of relatively low-unit-cost items of inventory. These are often indistinguishable from one another. It may be impossible or impractical to track each item's cost. In that case (as the next section will show), we must make assumptions about which units were sold.

The general rule is this: When feasible, specific identification is the ideal method of allocating cost of goods available for sale. It reports ending inventory at actual cost and matches the actual cost of goods sold against sales revenue.

However, specific identification may enable management to manipulate net income. To see how, assume that a music store has three identical Steinway grand pianos, purchased at different costs. When selling one piano, management could maximize net income by selecting the piano with the lowest cost to match against revenues. Or, it could minimize net income (and lower its taxes) by selecting the highest-cost piano.

HELPFUL HINT

A major disadvantage of the specific identification method is that management may be able to manipulate net income through specific identification of items sold.

USING ASSUMED COST FLOW METHODS—FIFO, LIFO, AND AVERAGE COST

Because specific identification is often impractical, other cost flow methods are allowed. These assume flows of costs that may be unrelated to the physical flow of goods. For this reason we call them **assumed cost flow methods** or **cost flow assumptions**. They are:

1. First-in, first-out (FIFO).
2. Last-in, first-out (LIFO).
3. Average cost.

To illustrate these three inventory cost flow methods, we will assume that Bow Valley Electronics uses a **periodic inventory system**. The information shown in Illustration 6-8 relates to its Z202 Astro Condenser.

INTERNATIONAL NOTE

A survey of accounting standards in 21 major industrial countries found that all three methods were permissible. In Ireland and the U.K., LIFO is permitted only in extreme circumstances.

Illustration 6-8

Inventoriable units and costs for Bow Valley Electronics

BOW VALLEY ELECTRONICS
Z202 Astro Condensers

Date	Explanation	Units	Unit Cost	Total Cost
1/1	Beginning inventory	100	$10	$ 1,000
4/15	Purchase	200	11	2,200
8/24	Purchase	300	12	3,600
11/27	Purchase	400	13	5,200
	Total	1,000		$12,000

During the year, 550 units were sold, and 450 units are on hand at 12/31.

There is no accounting requirement that the cost flow assumption be consistent with the physical movement of the goods. Management selects the appropriate cost flow method. Even in the same industry, different companies may reach different conclusions as to the most appropriate method.

First-in, First-out (FIFO)

The **FIFO method** assumes that the **earliest goods** purchased are the first to be sold. FIFO often parallels the actual physical flow of merchandise because it generally is good business practice to sell the earliest units first. Under the FIFO method, the **costs** of the earliest goods purchased are the first to be recognized as cost of goods sold. (Note that this does not necessarily mean that the earliest units *are* sold first, but that the costs of the earliest units are recognized first. In a bin of picture hangers at the hardware store, for example, no one really knows, nor would it matter, which hangers are sold first.) The allocation of the cost of goods available for sale at Bow Valley Electronics under FIFO is shown in Illustrations 6-9 and 6-10.

Illustration 6-9

Allocation of costs — FIFO method

Pool of Costs

Cost of Goods Available for Sale

Date	Explanation	Units	Unit Cost	Total Cost
1/1	Beginning inventory	100	$10	$ 1,000
4/15	Purchase	200	11	2,200
8/24	Purchase	300	12	3,600
11/27	Purchase	400	13	5,200
	Total	1,000		$12,000

Step 1

Ending Inventory

Date	Units	Unit Cost	Total Cost
11/27	400	$13	$5,200
8/24	50	12	600
Total	450		$5,800

Step 2

Cost of Goods Sold

Cost of goods available for sale	$12,000
Less: Ending inventory	5,800
Cost of goods sold	$ 6,200

HELPFUL HINT

Note the sequencing of the allocation: (1) Compute ending inventory. (2) Determine cost of goods sold.

Illustration 6-10

FIFO—First costs in are first costs out in computing cost of goods sold

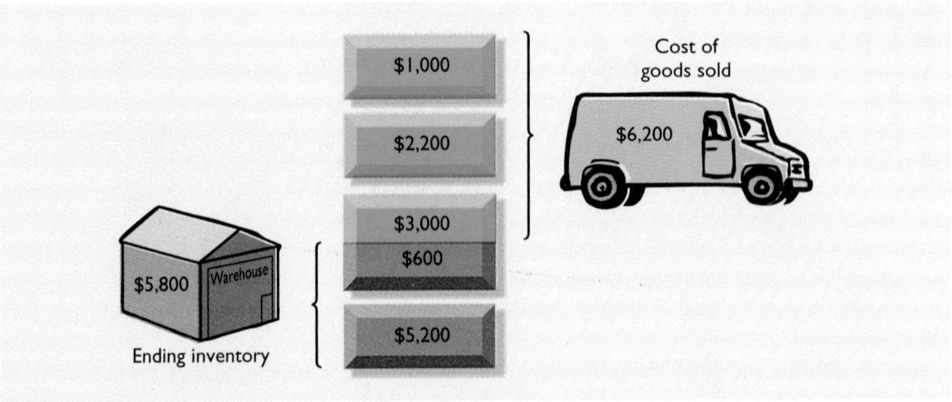

Note that the ending inventory is based on the latest units purchased. That is, **under FIFO, the cost of the ending inventory is found by taking the unit cost of the most recent purchase and working backward until all units of inventory are costed.**

We can verify the accuracy of the cost of goods sold by recognizing that the **first units acquired are the first units sold**. The computations for the 550 units sold are shown in Illustration 6-11.

Illustration 6-11

Proof of cost of goods sold

Date	Units		Unit Cost		Total Cost
1/1	100	×	$10	=	$1,000
4/15	200	×	11	=	2,200
8/24	250	×	12	=	3,000
Total	550				**$6,200**

Last-in, First-out (LIFO)

The **LIFO method** assumes that the **latest goods** purchased are the first to be sold. LIFO seldom coincides with the actual physical flow of inventory. Only for goods in piles, such as hay, coal, or produce at the grocery store would LIFO match the physical flow of inventory. Under the LIFO method, the **costs** of the latest goods purchased are the first to be assigned to cost of goods sold. The allocation of the cost of goods available for sale at Bow Valley Electronics under LIFO is shown in Illustration 6-12.

Illustration 6-12

Allocation of costs—LIFO method

Pool of Costs

Cost of Goods Available for Sale

Date	Explanation	Units	Unit Cost	Total Cost
1/1	Beginning inventory	100	$10	$ 1,000
4/15	Purchase	200	11	2,200
8/24	Purchase	300	12	3,600
11/27	Purchase	400	13	5,200
	Total	1,000		**$12,000**

Step 1

Ending Inventory

Date	Units	Unit Cost	Total Cost
1/1	100	$10	$1,000
4/15	200	11	2,200
8/24	150	12	1,800
Total	450		**$5,000**

Step 2

Cost of Goods Sold

Cost of goods available for sale	$12,000
Less: Ending inventory	5,000
Cost of goods sold	**$ 7,000**

HELPFUL HINT

The costs allocated to ending inventory ($5,000) plus the costs allocated to CGS ($7,000) must equal CGAS ($12,000).

Illustration 6-13 graphically displays the LIFO cost flow.

Under the LIFO method, **the cost of the ending inventory is found by taking the unit cost of the oldest goods and working forward until all units of inventory are costed.** As a result, the first costs assigned to ending inventory are the costs of the beginning inventory. Proof of the costs allocated to cost of goods sold is shown in Illustration 6-14.

Illustration 6-13

LIFO—Last costs in are first costs out in computing cost of goods sold

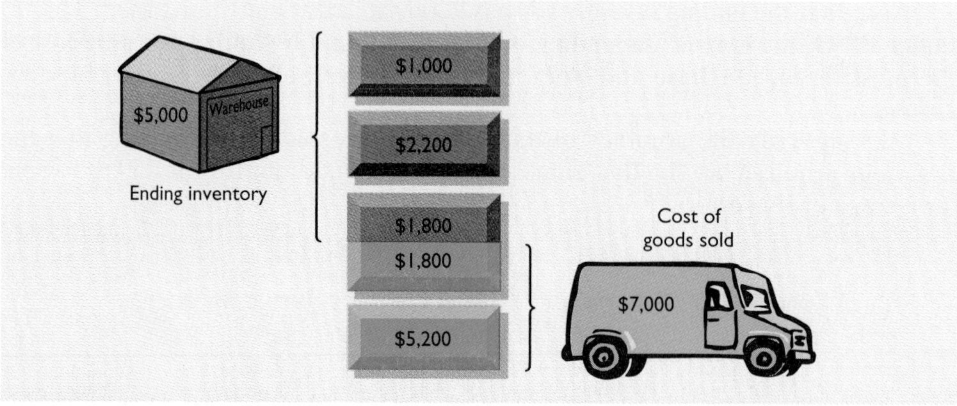

Illustration 6-14

Proof of cost of goods sold

Date	Units		Unit Cost		Total Cost
11/27	400	×	$13	=	$5,200
8/24	150	×	12	=	1,800
Total	550				**$7,000**

Under a periodic inventory system, **all goods purchased during the period are assumed to be available for the first sale, regardless of the date of purchase**.

Average Cost

The **average cost method** assumes that the goods available for sale have the same (average) cost per unit. Generally such goods are identical. Under this method, the cost of goods available for sale is allocated on the basis of the **weighted-average unit cost**. The formula and a sample computation of the weighted-average unit cost are as follows.

Illustration 6-15

Formula for weighted-average unit cost

Cost of Goods Available for Sale	÷	Total Units Available for Sale	=	Weighted-Average Unit Cost
$12,000	÷	1,000	=	$12.00

The weighted-average unit cost is then applied to the units on hand. This computation determines the cost of the ending inventory. The allocation of the cost of goods available for sale at Bow Valley Electronics using average cost is shown in Illustrations 6-16 and 6-17.

To verify the cost of goods sold data in Illustration 6-16, multiply the units sold by the weighted-average unit cost (550 × $12 = $6,600). Note that this method does not use the average of the **unit costs**. That average is $11.50 ($10 + $11 + $12 + $13 = $46; $46 ÷ 4). Instead, the average cost method uses the average **weighted** by the quantities purchased at each unit cost.

Illustration 6-16

Allocation of costs—average cost method

Pool of Costs
Cost of Goods Available for Sale

Date	Explanation	Units	Unit Cost	Total Cost
1/1	Beginning inventory	100	$10	$ 1,000
4/15	Purchase	200	11	2,200
8/24	Purchase	300	12	3,600
11/27	Purchase	400	13	5,200
	Total	1,000		**$12,000**

Step 1
Ending Inventory

$12,000	÷	1,000	=	$12.00
Units		**Unit Cost**		**Total Cost**
450	×	$12.00	=	**$5,400**

Step 2
Cost of Goods Sold

Cost of goods available for sale	$12,000
Less: Ending inventory	5,400
Cost of goods sold	**$ 6,600**

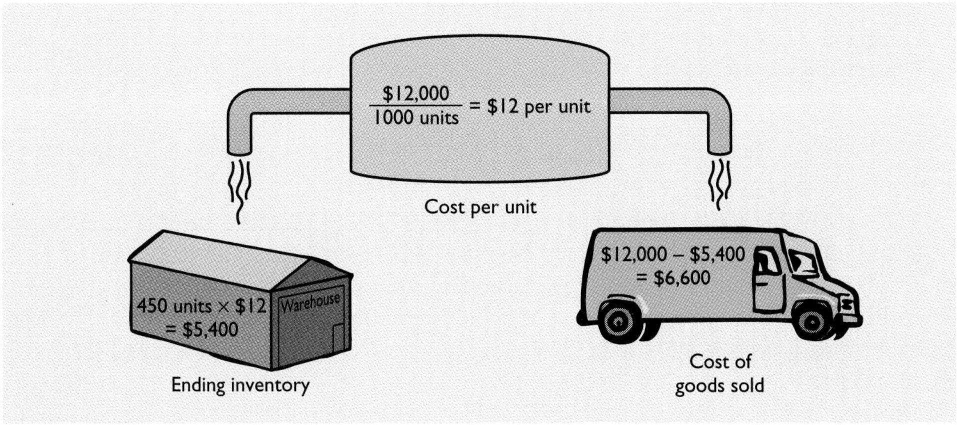

Illustration 6-17

Average cost—the average cost of the goods available for sale during the period is the cost used to compute cost of goods sold

FINANCIAL STATEMENT EFFECTS OF COST FLOW METHODS

Each of the three cost flow methods is acceptable. For example, **Black and Decker Manufacturing Company** and **Wendy's International** currently use the FIFO method. **Campbell Soup Company**, **Kroger Co.**, and **Walgreen Drugs** use LIFO. **Bristol-Myers-Squibb Co.** and **Motorola, Inc.** use the average cost method. A company may also use more than one cost flow method at the same time. **Del Monte Corporation** uses LIFO for domestic inventories and FIFO for foreign inventories. Illustration 6-18 shows the use of the three methods in the 600 largest U.S. companies. Companies adopt different inventory cost flow methods for various reasons. Usually, one of the following factors is involved:

1. Income statement effects.
2. Balance sheet effects.
3. Tax effects.

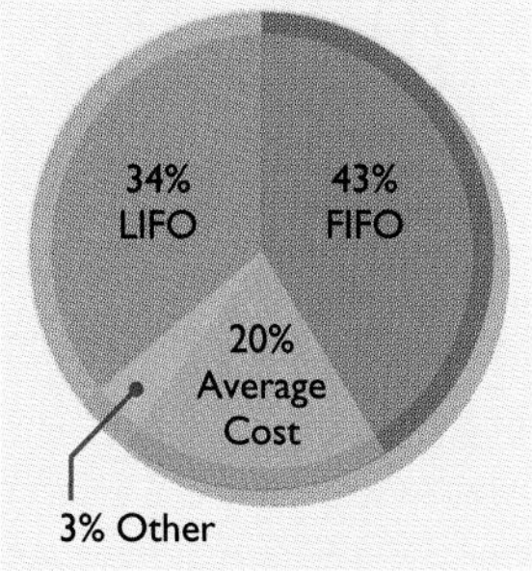

Illustration 6-18

Use of cost flow methods in major U.S. companies

STUDY OBJECTIVE 6

Explain the financial statement and tax effects of each of the inventory cost flow methods.

Income Statement Effects

To understand why companies might choose a particular cost flow method, let's compare their effects on the financial statements of Bow Valley Electronics. The condensed income statements in Illustration 6–19 assume that Bow Valley sold its 550 units for $11,500, and its operating expenses were $2,000. Its income tax rate is 30%.

Illustration 6-19

Comparative effects of cost flow methods

BOW VALLEY ELECTRONICS
Condensed Income Statements

	FIFO	LIFO	Average Cost
Sales	$11,500	$11,500	$11,500
Beginning inventory	1,000	1,000	1,000
Purchases	11,000	11,000	11,000
Cost of goods available for sale	12,000	12,000	12,000
Ending inventory	**5,800**	**5,000**	**5,400**
Cost of goods sold	6,200	7,000	6,600
Gross profit	5,300	4,500	4,900
Operating expenses	2,000	2,000	2,000
Income before income taxes[2]	3,300	2,500	2,900
Income tax expense (30%)	990	750	870
Net income	**$ 2,310**	**$ 1,750**	**$ 2,030**

The cost of goods available for sale ($12,000) is the same under each of the three inventory cost flow methods. But the ending inventory is different in each method, and this difference affects cost of goods sold. Each dollar of difference in ending inventory therefore results in a corresponding dollar difference in income before income taxes. For Bow Valley, there is an $800 difference between FIFO and LIFO.

In a period of rising prices, FIFO produces a higher net income. This happens because the expenses matched against revenues are the lower unit costs of the first units purchased. In a period of rising prices (as is the case here), FIFO reports the highest net income ($2,310) and LIFO the lowest ($1,750); average cost falls in the middle ($2,030). To management, higher net income is an advantage: It causes external users to view the company more favorably. Also, if management bonuses are based on net income, FIFO will provide the basis for higher bonuses.

HELPFUL HINT

If prices are falling, the results from the use of FIFO and LIFO are reversed: FIFO will report the lowest net income and LIFO the highest.

Some argue that the use of LIFO in a period of rising prices enables the company to avoid reporting **paper or phantom profit** as economic gain. To illustrate, assume that Kralik Company buys 200 XR492s at $20 per unit on January 10. It buys 200 more on December 31 at $24 each. During the year, it sells 200 units at $30 each. The results under FIFO and LIFO are shown in Illustration 6-20.

Illustration 6-20

Income statement effects compared

	FIFO	LIFO
Sales (200 × $30)	$6,000	$6,000
Cost of goods sold	**4,000 (200 × $20)**	**4,800 (200 × $24)**
Gross profit	$2,000	$1,200

[2] It is assumed that Bow Valley is a corporation, and corporations are required to pay income taxes.

Under LIFO, the company has recovered the current replacement cost ($4,800) of the units sold. The gross profit in economic terms under LIFO is real. Under FIFO, the company has recovered only the January 10 cost ($4,000). To replace the units sold, it must reinvest $800 (200 × $4) of the gross profit. Thus, $800 of the gross profit under FIFO is phantom, or illusory. As a result, reported net income under FIFO is also overstated in real terms.

Balance Sheet Effects

A major advantage of FIFO is that in a period of rising prices, the costs allocated to ending inventory will be close to their current cost. For Bow Valley, for example, 400 of the 450 units in the ending inventory are costed at the November 27 unit cost of $13.

A major shortcoming of LIFO is that in a period of rising prices, the costs allocated to ending inventory may be understated in terms of current cost. This is true for Bow Valley: The cost of the ending inventory includes the $10 unit cost of the beginning inventory. The understatement becomes even greater if the inventory includes goods purchased in one or more prior accounting periods.

Tax Effects

We have seen that both inventory on the balance sheet and net income on the income statement are higher when FIFO is used in a period of rising prices. Why, then, would a company use LIFO? The reason is that LIFO results in the lowest income taxes during times of rising prices. The lower net income reported by LIFO translates to a lower tax liability. For example, at Bow Valley Electronics, income taxes are $750 under LIFO, compared to $990 under FIFO. The tax saving of $240 makes more cash available for use in the business.

ACCOUNTING IN ACTION *Business Insight*

Most small firms use the FIFO method. But fears of rising prices often cause firms to switch to LIFO. For example, **Chicago Heights Steel Co.** boosted cash "by 5% to 10% by lowering income taxes" when it switched to LIFO. Electronic games distributor **Atlas Distributing Inc.** considered a switch "because the costs of our games, made in Japan, are rising 15% a year," said Joseph Serpico, treasurer. When inflation heats up, the number of companies choosing LIFO rises dramatically.

USING INVENTORY COST FLOW METHODS CONSISTENTLY

Whatever cost flow method a company chooses, it should be used consistently from one period to another. Consistent application makes financial statements more comparable over successive time periods. In contrast, using FIFO in one year and LIFO in the next would make it difficult to compare the net incomes of the two years.

Although consistent application is preferred, a company *may* change its method of inventory costing. Such a change and its effects on net income should be disclosed in the financial statements. A typical disclosure is shown in Illustration 6-21, using information from recent financial statements of **Quaker Oats Company**.

Illustration 6-21

Disclosure of change in cost flow method

QUAKER OATS COMPANY
Notes to the Financial Statements

Note 1 Effective July 1, the Company adopted the LIFO cost flow assumption for valuing the majority of U.S. Grocery Products inventories. The Company believes that the use of the LIFO method better matches current costs with current revenues. The effect of this change on the current year was to decrease net income by $16.0 million.

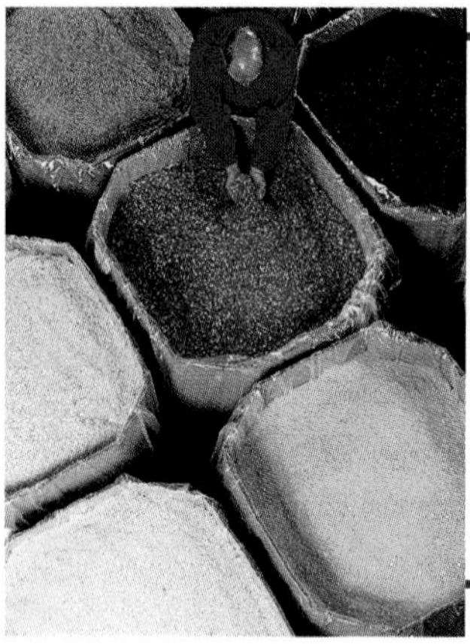

ACCOUNTING IN ACTION *International Insight*

U.S. companies typically choose between LIFO and FIFO. Many choose LIFO because it reduces inventory profits and taxes. However, the international community recently considered rules that would ban LIFO entirely and force companies to use FIFO. This proposal was defeated, but the issue will not go away.

The issue is sensitive. As John Wulff, controller for **Union Carbide** noted, "We were in support of the international effort up until the proposal to eliminate LIFO." Wulff says that if Union Carbide had been suddenly forced to switch from LIFO to FIFO, its reported $632 million pretax income would have jumped by $300 million. That would have increased Carbide's income tax bill by as much as $120 million. Given this, do you believe that accounting principles and rules should be the same around the world?

BEFORE YOU GO ON...

REVIEW IT

1. How do the cost and matching principles apply to inventoriable costs?
2. How are the three assumed cost flow methods applied in allocating inventoriable costs?
3. What factors should be considered by management in selecting an inventory cost flow method?
4. Which inventory cost flow method produces (a) the highest net income in a period of rising prices, and (b) the lowest income taxes?
5. What amount is reported by **Lands' End** in its 2000 Annual Report as inventories at January 28, 2000? Which inventory cost flow method does Lands' End use? The answer to this question is provided on p. 273.

DO IT

The accounting records of Shumway Ag Implement show the following data.

Beginning inventory	4,000 units at $3
Purchases	6,000 units at $4
Sales	5,000 units at $12

Determine the cost of goods sold during the period under a periodic inventory system using (a) the FIFO method, (b) the LIFO method, and (c) the average cost method.

ACTION PLAN

- Understand the periodic inventory system.
- Compute the cost of goods sold under the periodic inventory system using the FIFO cost flow method.

- Compute the cost of goods sold under the periodic inventory system using the LIFO cost flow method.
- Compute the cost of goods sold under the periodic inventory system using the average cost method.

SOLUTION

(a) FIFO: (4,000 @ \$3) + (1,000 @ \$4) = \$12,000 + \$4,000 = \$16,000.
(b) LIFO: 5,000 @ \$4 = \$20,000.
(c) Average cost: [(4,000 @ \$3) + (6,000 @ \$4)] ÷ \$10,000 = (\$12,000 + \$24,000) ÷ 10,000 = \$3.60 per unit; 5,000 @ \$3.60 = \$18,000.

Related exercise material: BE6-6, BE6-7, E6-5, E6-6, and E6-7.

THE NAVIGATOR

VALUING INVENTORY AT THE LOWER OF COST OR MARKET (LCM)

STUDY OBJECTIVE 7

Explain the lower of cost or market basis of accounting for inventories.

Inventory values sometimes fall due to changes in technology or in fashion. When the value of inventory is lower than its cost, the inventory is written down to its market value. This is done by valuing the inventory at the **lower of cost or market (LCM)** in the period in which the decline occurs. LCM is an example of the **conservatism** constraint: When choosing among alternatives, the best choice is the method that is least likely to overstate assets and net income.

Under the LCM basis, "market" is defined as **current replacement cost**, not selling price. For a merchandiser, "market" is the cost of purchasing the same goods at the present time from the usual suppliers in the usual quantities.

Assume that Len's TV has the following lines of merchandise with costs and market values as indicated. LCM produces the following result.

Illustration 6-22

Computation of lower of cost or market

	Cost	Market	Lower of Cost or Market
Television sets			
Consoles	\$ 60,000	\$ 55,000	\$ 55,000
Portables	45,000	52,000	45,000
Total	105,000	107,000	
Video equipment			
Recorders	48,000	45,000	45,000
Movies	15,000	14,000	14,000
Total	63,000	59,000	
Total inventory	\$168,000	\$166,000	**\$159,000**

The amount entered in the final column is the lower of the cost or market amount for **each item**. LCM is applied to the items in inventory after one of the costing methods (specific identification, FIFO, LIFO, or average cost) has been applied to determine cost.

INVENTORY ERRORS

STUDY OBJECTIVE 8

Indicate the effects of inventory errors on the financial statements.

Unfortunately, errors occasionally occur in taking or costing inventory. Some errors are caused by counting or pricing the inventory incorrectly. Others occur because of improper recognition of the transfer of legal title to goods in transit. When errors occur, they affect both the income statement and the balance sheet.

INCOME STATEMENT EFFECTS

Remember that both the beginning and ending inventories are used to determine cost of goods sold in a periodic system. The ending inventory of one period automatically becomes the beginning inventory of the next period. Inventory errors thus affect the determination of cost of goods sold and net income.

The effects on cost of goods sold can be determined by using the following formula. First enter the incorrect data in the formula. Then substitute the correct data, and find the difference between the two CGS amounts.

Illustration 6-23

Formula for cost of goods sold

Beginning Inventory + Cost of Goods Purchased − Ending Inventory = Cost of Goods Sold

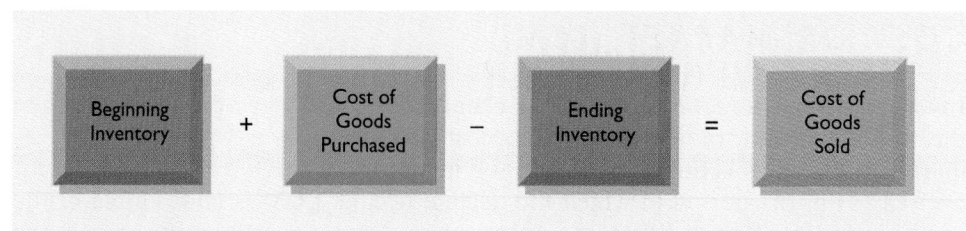

If beginning inventory is understated, cost of goods sold will be understated. If ending inventory is understated, cost of goods sold will be overstated. The effects of inventory errors on the current year's income statement are shown in Illustration 6-24.

Illustration 6-24

Effects of inventory errors on current year's income statement

Inventory Error	Cost of Goods Sold	Net Income
Beginning inventory understated	Understated	Overstated
Beginning inventory overstated	Overstated	Understated
Ending inventory understated	Overstated	Understated
Ending inventory overstated	Understated	Overstated

ETHICS NOTE

Inventory fraud includes pricing inventory at amounts in excess of their actual value, or claiming to have inventory when no inventory exists. Inventory fraud is usually done to overstate ending inventory, which understates cost of goods sold and creates higher income.

An error in ending inventory in the current period will have a **reverse effect on net income of the next period**. This is shown in Illustration 6-25 on the next page. Note that understating ending inventory in 2002 understates beginning inventory in 2003 and overstates net income in 2003.

Over the two years, total net income is correct. The errors offset one another. Notice that for 2002 and 2003 total income using incorrect data is $35,000 ($22,000 + $13,000). This is the same as the total income of $35,000 ($25,000 + $10,000) using correct data. Also note in this example that an error in the beginning inventory does not result in a corresponding error in the ending inventory. The correctness of the ending inventory depends entirely on the accuracy of taking and costing the inventory at the balance sheet date.

Condensed Income Statement

	2002				2003			
	Incorrect		Correct		Incorrect		Correct	
Sales		$80,000		$80,000		$90,000		$90,000
Beginning inventory	$20,000		$20,000		**$12,000**		**$15,000**	
Cost of goods purchased	40,000		40,000		68,000		68,000	
Cost of goods available for sale	60,000		60,000		80,000		83,000	
Ending inventory	**12,000**		**15,000**		23,000		23,000	
Cost of goods sold		48,000		45,000		57,000		60,000
Gross profit		32,000		35,000		33,000		30,000
Operating expenses		10,000		10,000		20,000		20,000
Net income		$22,000		$25,000		$13,000		$10,000

($3,000) Net income understated — **$3,000** Net income overstated

Total income for 2 years correct

Illustration 6-25

Effects of inventory errors on two years' income statements

BALANCE SHEET EFFECTS

The effect of ending-inventory errors on the balance sheet can be determined by the basic accounting equation: Assets = Liabilities + Owner's equity. Errors in the ending inventory have the following effects on these components.

Illustration 6-26

Ending inventory error—balance sheet effects

Ending Inventory Error	Assets	Liabilities	Owner's Equity
Overstated	Overstated	None	Overstated
Understated	Understated	None	Understated

The effect of an error in ending inventory on the next period was shown in Illustration 6-25. If the error is not corrected, total net income for the two periods would be correct. Thus, total owner's equity reported on the balance sheet at the end of the next period will also be correct.

STATEMENT PRESENTATION AND ANALYSIS

PRESENTATION

As indicated in Chapter 5, inventory is classified as a current asset after receivables in the balance sheet. In a multiple-step income statement, cost of goods sold is subtracted from sales. There also should be disclosure of (1) the major inventory classifications, (2) the basis of accounting (cost, or lower of cost or market), and (3) the costing method (FIFO, LIFO, or average).

Lands' End, for example, in its January 28, 2000, balance sheet reported inventory of $162,193,000 under current assets. The accompanying notes to the financial statements, as shown in Illustration 6-27, disclosed the following information.

Illustration 6-27

Inventory disclosures by **Lands' End**

LANDS' END DIRECT MERCHANTS

LANDS' END, INC.
Notes to the Financial Statements

Note 1. Summary of significant accounting policies

Inventory

Inventory, primarily merchandise held for resale, is stated at last-in, first-out (LIFO) cost, which is lower than market.

As indicated in this brief note, Lands' End values its inventories at the lower of cost or market using the LIFO method.

ANALYSIS

The amount of inventory carried by a company has significant economic consequences. And inventory management is a double-edged sword that requires constant attention. On the one hand, management wants to have a great variety and quantity on hand so that customers have a wide selection and items are always in stock. But such a policy may incur high carrying costs (e.g., investment, storage, insurance, obsolescence, and damage). On the other hand, low inventory levels lead to stockouts and lost sales.

Common ratios used to manage and evaluate inventory levels are inventory turnover and a related measure, average days to sell the inventory.

STUDY OBJECTIVE 9

Compute and interpret inventory turnover.

Inventory turnover measures the number of times on average the inventory is sold during the period. Its purpose is to measure the liquidity of the inventory. The inventory turnover is computed by dividing cost of goods sold by the average inventory during the period. Unless seasonal factors are significant, average inventory can be computed from the beginning and ending inventory balances. For example, **Lands' End** reported in its 2000 Annual Report a beginning inventory of $219,686,000, and cost of goods sold for the year ended January 28, 2000, of $727,291,000. The inventory turnover formula and computation for Lands' End are shown below.

Illustration 6-28

Inventory turnover formula and computation for **Lands' End**

LANDS' END DIRECT MERCHANTS

$$\text{Cost of Goods Sold} \div \text{Average Inventory} = \text{Inventory Turnover}$$

$$\$727{,}291{,}000 \div \frac{\$219{,}686{,}000 + \$162{,}193{,}000}{2} = 3.8 \text{ times}$$

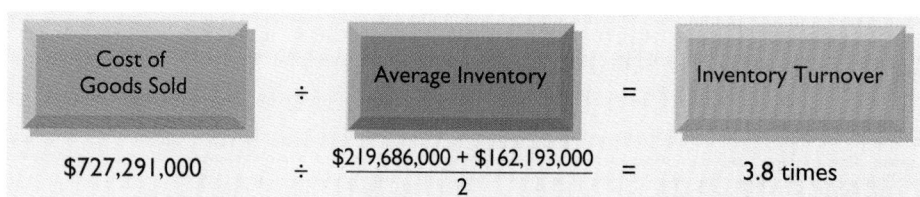

A variant of the inventory turnover ratio is the **average days to sell inventory**. For example, the inventory turnover for Lands' End of 3.8 times divided into 365 is approximately 96 days. This is the approximate age of the inventory.

There are typical levels of inventory in every industry. Companies that are able to keep their inventory at lower levels and higher turnovers and still satisfy customer needs are the most successful.

BEFORE YOU GO ON...

REVIEW IT

1. Why is it appropriate to report inventories at the lower of cost or market?
2. How do inventory errors affect financial statements?
3. What does inventory turnover reveal?

A LOOK BACK AT OUR FEATURE STORY

Refer back to the Feature Story concerning **Mountain Equipment Co-op (MEC)** at the beginning of the chapter, and answer the following questions.

1. Why does MEC use the weighted average cost flow method to determine inventory?
2. Should MEC consider changing from the periodic weighted average cost method to a perpetual inventory system to track inventory costs? List the advantages and disadvantages of such a change.

SOLUTION

1. MEC uses the weighted average cost flow method because of fluctuations in costs of these inventory items.
2. MEC would find a perpetual inventory method useful to monitor its large number of inventory items. This is important with catalogue sales. When customers call to place an order, MEC would know immediately whether the item is in stock. Also, large fluctuations in the cost of each inventory item could be tracked to ensure that selling prices are adjusted where necessary to recover cost and any desired markup. A disadvantage of the perpetual inventory method would be the need for more recordkeeping than under the current periodic inventory method. Scanners and new computing equipment might also be required. Also, full disclosure would have to be made in the notes to the financial statements in the year of the change.

THE NAVIGATOR

DEMONSTRATION PROBLEM 1

Additional Demonstration Problem

Gerald D. Englehart Company has the following inventory, purchases, and sales data for the month of March.

Inventory:	March 1	200 units @ $4.00	$ 800
Purchases:			
	March 10	500 units @ $4.50	2,250
	March 20	400 units @ $4.75	1,900
	March 30	300 units @ $5.00	1,500
Sales:			
	March 15	500 units	
	March 25	400 units	

The physical inventory count on March 31 shows 500 units on hand.

Instructions

Under a **periodic inventory system**, determine the cost of inventory on hand at March 31 and the cost of goods sold for March under the (a) first-in, first-out (FIFO) method, (b) last-in, first-out (LIFO) method, and (c) average cost method.

ACTION PLAN

- Compute the cost of inventory under the periodic FIFO method by allocating to the units on hand the **latest costs**.
- Compute the cost of inventory under the periodic LIFO method by allocating to the units on hand the **earliest costs**.
- Compute the cost of inventory under the periodic average cost method by allocating to the units on hand a **weighted-average cost**.

THE NAVIGATOR

SOLUTION TO DEMONSTRATION PROBLEM 1

The cost of goods available for sale is $6,450, as follows.

Inventory:		200 units @ $4.00	$ 800
Purchases:			
	March 10	500 units @ $4.50	2,250
	March 20	400 units @ $4.75	1,900
	March 30	300 units @ $5.00	1,500
Total cost of goods available for sale			$6,450

Under a **periodic inventory system**, the cost of goods sold under each cost flow method is as follows.

FIFO Method

Ending inventory:

Date	Units	Unit Cost	Total Cost	
March 30	300	$5.00	$1,500	
March 20	200	4.75	950	$2,450

Cost of goods sold: $6,450 − $2,450 = $4,000

LIFO Method

Ending inventory:

Date	Units	Unit Cost	Total Cost	
March 1	200	$4.00	$ 800	
March 10	300	4.50	1,350	$2,150

Cost of goods sold: $6,450 − $2,150 = $4,300

Weighted-Average Cost Method

Weighted-average unit cost: $6,450 ÷ 1,400 = $4.607

Ending inventory: 500 × $4.607 = $2,303.50

Cost of goods sold: $6,450 − $2,303.50 = $4,146.50

SUMMARY OF STUDY OBJECTIVES

1. ***Describe the steps in determining inventory quantities.*** The steps in determining inventory quantities are (1) taking a physical inventory of goods on hand and (2) determining the ownership of goods in transit.

2. ***Prepare the entries for purchases and sales of inventory under a periodic inventory system.*** In recording purchases, entries are required for (a) cash and credit purchases, (b) purchase returns and allowances, (c) purchase discounts, and (d) freight costs. In recording sales, entries are required for (a) cash and credit sales, (b) sales returns and allowances, and (c) sales discounts.

d.

3. ***Determine cost of goods sold under a periodic inventory system.*** The steps in determining cost of goods sold are (a) record the purchases of merchandise, (b) determine the cost of goods purchased, and (c) determine the cost of goods on hand at the beginning and end of the accounting period.

+ beg. inv.
Purchases.
− end inv
COGS

4. ***Identify the unique features of the income statement for a merchandiser using a periodic inventory system.*** The income statement for a merchandiser contains three sections: sales revenue, cost of goods sold, and operating expenses. The cost of goods sold section under a periodic inventory system generally reports beginning and ending inventory, cost of goods purchased, and cost of goods available for sale.

5. ***Explain the basis of accounting for inventories, and describe the inventory cost flow methods.*** The primary basis of accounting for inventories is cost. Cost includes all expenditures necessary to acquire goods and to make them ready for sale. Inventoriable costs include (1) the cost of beginning inventory and (2) the cost of goods purchased. The inventory cost flow methods are: specific identification, FIFO, LIFO, and average cost.

beg Inv
+ Purch
COGAS

6. ***Explain the financial statement and tax effects of each of the inventory cost flow methods.*** The cost of goods available for sale may be allocated to cost of goods sold and ending inventory by specific identification or by a method based on an assumed cost flow. These methods have different effects on financial statements during periods of changing prices. When prices are rising, FIFO results in lower cost of goods sold and higher net income than the average cost and the LIFO methods. LIFO results in the lowest income taxes (because of lower net income). In the balance sheet, FIFO results in an ending inventory that is closest to current value. The inventory under LIFO is the farthest from current value.

7. ***Explain the lower of cost or market basis of accounting for inventories.*** The lower of cost or market (LCM) basis is used when the current replacement cost (market) is less than cost. Under LCM, the loss is recognized in the period in which the price decline occurs.

8. ***Indicate the effects of inventory errors on the financial statements.*** In the income statement of the current year: (a) An error in beginning inventory will have a reverse effect on net income (overstatement of inventory results in understatement of net income); and (b) an error in ending inventory will have a similar effect on net income (overstatement of inventory results in overstatement of net income). If ending inventory errors are not corrected in the next period, their effect on net income for that period is reversed, and total net income for the two years will be correct. In the balance sheet, ending inventory errors will have the same effect on total assets and total stockholders' equity and no effect on liabilities.

9. ***Compute and interpret inventory turnover.*** Inventory turnover is calculated as cost of goods sold divided by average inventory. It can be converted to average days in inventory by dividing 365 days by the inventory turnover ratio. A higher turnover or lower average days in inventory suggests that management is trying to keep inventory levels low relative to sales.

THE NAVIGATOR

Key Term Matching Activity

GLOSSARY

Average cost method Inventory costing method that assumes that the goods available for sale have the same (average) cost per unit; generally the goods are identical. (p. 238).

Consigned goods Goods shipped by a consignor, who retains ownership, to another party called the consignee. (p. 227).

Cost of goods available for sale The sum of the beginning merchandise inventory plus the cost of goods purchased. (p. 231).

Cost of goods purchased The sum of net purchases plus freight-in. (p. 231).

Cost of goods sold The total cost of merchandise sold during the period, determined by subtracting ending inventory from the cost of goods available for sale. (p. 231).

Current replacement cost The amount that would be paid at the present time to acquire an identical item. (p. 243).

First-in, first-out (FIFO) method Inventory costing method that assumes that the costs of the earliest goods acquired are the first to be recognized as cost of goods sold. (p. 236).

Inventoriable costs The pool of costs that consists of two elements: (1) the cost of the beginning inventory and (2) the cost of goods purchased during the period. (p. 233).

Inventory turnover A measure of the number of times on average the inventory is sold during the period; computed by dividing cost of goods sold by the average inventory during the period. (p. 246).

Last-in, first-out (LIFO) method Inventory costing method that assumes that the costs of the latest units purchased are the first to be allocated to cost of goods sold. (p. 237).

Lower of cost or market (LCM) basis Method of valuing inventory that recognizes the decline in the value when the current purchase price (market) is less than cost. (p. 243).

Net purchases Purchases less purchase returns and allowances and purchase discounts. (p. 231).

Periodic inventory system An inventory system in which inventoriable costs are allocated to ending inventory and cost of goods sold at the end of the period. Cost of goods sold is computed at the end of the period by subtracting the ending inventory (costs are assigned based on a physical count of items on hand) from the cost of goods available for sale. (p. 228).

Specific identification method An actual, physical flow inventory costing method in which items still in inventory are specifically costed to arrive at the total cost of the ending inventory. (p. 234).

APPENDIX 6A *Comparison of Entries—Perpetual vs. Periodic*

The periodic inventory system entries shown in this chapter are reproduced in the righthand column of Illustration 6A-1 on the next page. (They are printed in red.) In the middle column (printed in blue) are the entries from Chapter 5 (pages 188–193) for the perpetual inventory system for both Sellers Electronix and Beyer Video. Having these entries side-by-side should help you compare the differences. The entries that are different in the two inventory systems are highlighted.

Illustration 6A-1

Comparison of journal entries under perpetual and periodic inventory systems

ENTRIES ON BEYER VIDEO'S BOOKS

Transaction	Perpetual Inventory System			Periodic Inventory System		
May 4 Purchase of merchandise on credit.	Merchandise Inventory	3,800		Purchases	3,800	
	Accounts Payable		3,800	Accounts Payable		3,800
May 8 Purchase returns and allowances.	Accounts Payable	300		Accounts Payable	300	
	Merchandise Inventory		300	Purchase Returns and Allowances		300
May 9 Freight costs on purchase.	Merchandise Inventory	150		Freight-in	150	
	Cash		150	Cash		150
May 14 Payment on account with a discount.	Accounts Payable	3,500		Accounts Payable	3,500	
	Cash		3,430	Cash		3,430
	Merchandise Inventory		70	Purchase Discounts		70

ENTRIES ON SELLERS ELECTRONIX'S BOOKS

Transaction	Perpetual Inventory System			Periodic Inventory System		
May 4 Sale of merchandise on credit.	Accounts Receivable	3,800		Accounts Receivable	3,800	
	Sales		3,800	Sales		3,800
	Cost of Goods Sold	2,400		No entry for cost of goods sold		
	Merchandise Inventory		2,400			
May 8 Return of merchandise sold.	Sales Returns and Allowances	300		Sales Returns and Allowances	300	
	Accounts Receivable		300	Accounts Receivable		300
	Merchandise Inventory	140		No entry		
	Cost of Goods Sold		140			
May 15 Cash received on account with a discount.	Cash	3,430		Cash	3,430	
	Sales Discounts	70		Sales Discounts	70	
	Accounts Receivable		3,500	Accounts Receivable		3,500

APPENDIX 6B *Estimating Inventories*

STUDY OBJECTIVE 10

Describe the two methods of estimating inventories.

We assumed in the chapter that a company would be able to physically count its inventory. But what if it cannot? What if the inventory were destroyed by fire, for example? In that case, we would use an estimate.

Two circumstances explain why inventories are sometimes estimated. First, management may want monthly or quarterly financial statements, but a physical inventory is taken only annually. Second, a casualty such as fire, flood, or earthquake may make it impossible to take a physical inventory. The need for estimating inventories is associated primarily with a periodic inventory system because of the absence of detailed inventory records.

There are two widely used methods of estimating inventories: (1) the gross profit method and (2) the retail inventory method.

GROSS PROFIT METHOD

The **gross profit method** estimates the cost of ending inventory by applying a gross profit rate to net sales. It is used in preparing monthly financial statements under a periodic system. This method is relatively simple but effective. It will detect large errors. Accountants, auditors, and managers frequently use the gross profit method to test the reasonableness of the ending inventory amount.

To use this method, a company needs to know its net sales, cost of goods available for sale, and gross profit rate. With the gross profit rate, the company can estimate its gross profit for the period. The formulas for using the gross profit method are given in Illustration 6B-1.

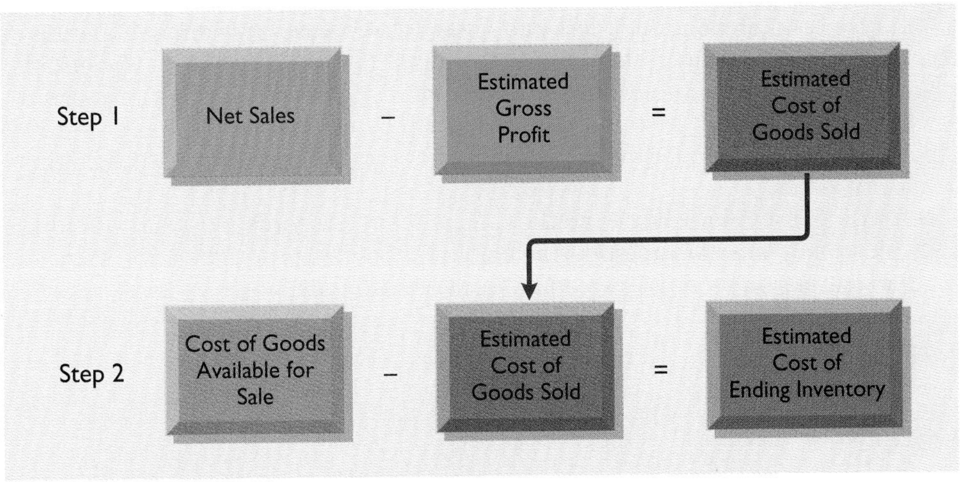

Illustration 6B-1

Gross profit method formulas

To illustrate, assume that Williams Company wishes to prepare an income statement for the month of January. Its records show net sales $200,000, beginning inventory $40,000, and cost of goods purchased $120,000. In the preceding year, the company realized a 30% gross profit rate. It expects to earn the same rate this year. Given these facts and assumptions, the estimated cost of the ending inventory at January 31 can be computed under the gross profit method as follows.

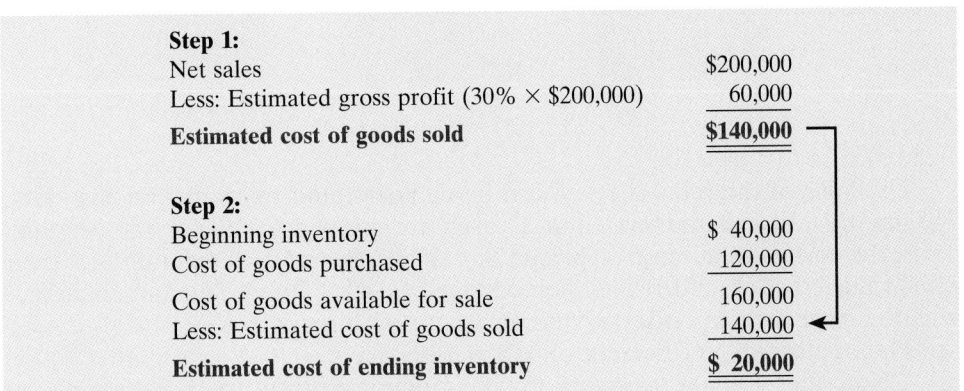

Illustration 6B-2

Example of gross profit method

Step 1:	
Net sales	$200,000
Less: Estimated gross profit (30% × $200,000)	60,000
Estimated cost of goods sold	**$140,000**
Step 2:	
Beginning inventory	$ 40,000
Cost of goods purchased	120,000
Cost of goods available for sale	160,000
Less: Estimated cost of goods sold	140,000
Estimated cost of ending inventory	**$ 20,000**

The gross profit method is based on the assumption that the gross profit rate will remain constant. But it may not remain constant, because of a change in merchandising policies or in market conditions. In such cases, the rate should be adjusted to reflect current operating conditions. In some cases, a more accurate estimate can be obtained by applying this method on a department or product-line basis.

The gross profit method should not be used in preparing a company's financial statements at the end of the year. These statements should be based on a physical inventory count.

RETAIL INVENTORY METHOD

A retail store such as **Kmart**, **Ace Hardware**, or **Wal-Mart** has thousands of different types of merchandise at low unit costs. In such cases it is difficult and time-consuming to apply unit costs to inventory quantities. An alternative is to use the **retail inventory method** to estimate the cost of inventory. In most retail concerns, a relationship between cost and sales price can be established. The cost-to-retail percentage is then applied to the ending inventory at retail prices to determine inventory at cost.

To use the retail inventory method, a company's records must show both the cost and retail value of the goods available for sale. The formulas for using the retail inventory method are presented in Illustration 6B-3.

Illustration 6B-3

Retail inventory method formulas

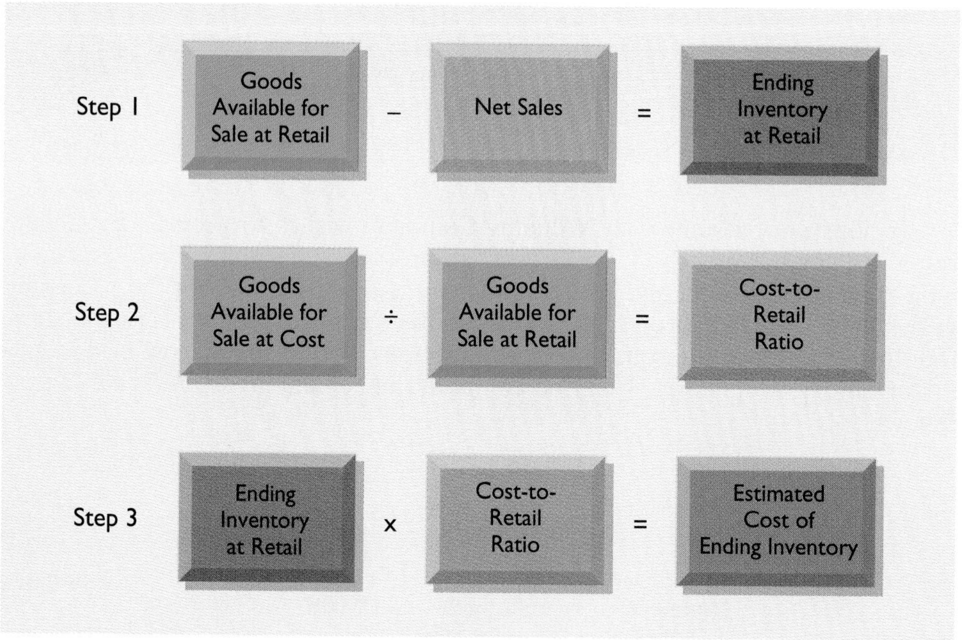

The logic of the retail method can be demonstrated by using unit-cost data. Assume that 10 units purchased at \$7 each are marked to sell for \$10 per unit. Thus, the cost-to-retail ratio is 70% (\$70 ÷ \$100). If 4 units remain unsold, their retail value is \$40 (4 × \$10), and their cost is \$28 (\$40 × 70%). This amount agrees with the total cost of goods on hand on a per unit basis (4 × \$7).

The application of the retail method for Lacy Co. is shown in Illustration 6B-4. Note that it is not necessary to take a physical inventory to determine the estimated cost of goods on hand at any given time.

Illustration 6B-4

Example of retail inventory method

		At Cost	At Retail
	Beginning inventory	$14,000	$ 21,500
	Goods purchased	61,000	78,500
	Goods available for sale	$75,000	100,000
	Net sales		70,000
(1)	**Ending inventory at retail**		**$ 30,000**
(2)	**Cost-to-retail ratio = ($75,000 ÷ $100,000) = 75%**		
(3)	**Estimated cost of ending inventory = ($30,000 × 75%)**	**$22,500**	

The retail inventory method also facilitates taking a physical inventory at the end of the year. The goods on hand can be valued at the prices marked on the merchandise. The cost-to-retail ratio is then applied to the goods on hand at retail to determine the ending inventory at cost.

The major disadvantage of the retail method is that it is an averaging technique. It may produce an incorrect inventory valuation if the mix of the ending inventory is not representative of the mix in the goods available for sale. Assume, for example, that the cost-to-retail ratio of 75% for Lacy Co. consists of equal proportions of inventory items that have cost-to-retail ratios of 70%, 75%, and 80%. If the ending inventory contains only items with a 70% ratio, an incorrect inventory cost will result. This problem can be minimized by applying the retail method on a department or product-line basis.

HELPFUL HINT

In determining inventory at retail, selling prices on the units are used. Tracing actual unit costs to invoices is unnecessary.

SUMMARY OF STUDY OBJECTIVE FOR APPENDIX 6B

10. *Describe the two methods of estimating inventories.* The two methods of estimating inventories are the gross profit method and the retail inventory method. Under the gross profit method, a gross profit rate is applied to net sales to determine estimated cost of goods sold. Estimated cost of goods sold is then subtracted from cost of goods available for sale to determine the estimated cost of the ending inventory.

Under the retail inventory method, a cost-to-retail ratio is computed by dividing the cost of goods available for sale by the retail value of the goods available for sale. This ratio is then applied to the ending inventory at retail to determine the estimated cost of the ending inventory.

GLOSSARY FOR APPENDIX 6B

Gross profit method A method for estimating the cost of the ending inventory by applying a gross profit rate to net sales. (p. 251).

Retail inventory method A method used to estimate the cost of the ending inventory by applying a cost-to-retail ratio to the ending inventory at retail. (p. 252).

APPENDIX 6C *INVENTORY COST FLOW METHODS IN PERPETUAL INVENTORY SYSTEMS*

STUDY OBJECTIVE 11

Apply the inventory cost flow methods to perpetual inventory records.

Each of the inventory cost flow methods described in the chapter for a periodic inventory system can be used in a perpetual inventory system. To illustrate the application of the three assumed cost flow methods (FIFO, LIFO, and average cost), we will use the data shown below and in this chapter for Bow Valley Electronics' product Z202 Astro Condenser.

Illustration 6C-1

Inventoriable units and costs

BOW VALLEY ELECTRONICS
Z202 Astro Condensers

Date	Explanation	Units	Unit Cost	Total Cost	Balance in Units
1/1	Beginning inventory	100	$10	$ 1,000	100
4/15	Purchases	200	11	2,200	300
8/24	Purchases	300	12	3,600	600
9/10	Sales	550			50
11/27	Purchases	400	13	5,200	450
				$12,000	

FIRST-IN, FIRST-OUT (FIFO)

Under FIFO, the cost of the earliest goods on hand prior to each sale is charged to cost of goods sold. The cost of goods sold on September 10 consists of the units on hand January 1 and the units purchased April 15 and August 24. The inventory on a FIFO method perpetual system is shown in Illustration 6C-2.

Illustration 6C-2

Perpetual system—FIFO

Date	Purchases	Sales	Balance
January 1			(100 @ $10) $1,000
April 15	(200 @ $11) $2,200		(100 @ $10) (200 @ $11) } $3,200
August 24	(300 @ $12) $3,600		(100 @ $10) (200 @ $11) (300 @ $12) } $6,800
September 10		(100 @ $10) (200 @ $11) (250 @ $12) **$6,200**	(50 @ $12) $ 600
November 27	(400 @ $13) $5,200		(50 @ $12) (400 @ $13) } **$5,800**

The ending inventory in this situation is $5,800. The cost of goods sold is $6,200 [(100 @ $10) + (200 @ $11) + (250 @ $12)].

The results under FIFO in a perpetual system are the **same as in a periodic system**. See Illustration 6-9 on page 236. There, similarly, the ending inventory is $5,800 and cost of goods sold is $6,200. Regardless of the system, the first costs in are the costs assigned to cost of goods sold.

LAST-IN, FIRST-OUT (LIFO)

Under the LIFO method using a perpetual system, the cost of the most recent purchase prior to sale is allocated to the units sold. The cost of the goods sold on September 10 consists of all the units from the August 24 and April 15 purchases and 50 of the units in beginning inventory. The ending inventory on a LIFO method is computed in Illustration 6C-3.

Illustration 6C-3

Perpetual system—LIFO

Date	Purchases	Sales	Balance
January 1			(100 @ $10) $1,000
April 15	(200 @ $11) $2,200		(100 @ $10) (200 @ $11) } $3,200
August 24	(300 @ $12) $3,600		(100 @ $10) (200 @ $11) (300 @ $12) } $6,800
September 10		(300 @ $12) (200 @ $11) (50 @ $10) **$6,300**	(50 @ $10) $ 500
November 27	(400 @ $13) $5,200		(50 @ $10) (400 @ $13) } **$5,700**

The use of LIFO in a perpetual system will usually produce cost allocations that differ from using LIFO in a periodic system. In a perpetual system, the latest units incurred **prior to each sale** are allocated to cost of goods sold. In contrast, in a periodic system, the latest units incurred **during the period** are allocated to cost of goods sold. Thus, when a purchase is made after the last sale, the LIFO periodic system will apply this purchase to the previous sale. See Illustration 6-14 on page 238. There, the proof shows the 400 units @ $13 purchased on November 27 applied to the sale of 550 units on September 10. As shown above under the LIFO perpetual system, the 400 units @ $13 purchased on November 27 are all applied to the ending inventory.

The ending inventory in this LIFO perpetual example is $5,700 and cost of goods sold is $6,300. Compare these amounts to the LIFO periodic illustration where the ending inventory is $5,000 and cost of goods sold is $7,000.

AVERAGE COST

The average cost method in a perpetual inventory system is called the **moving-average method.** Under this method a new average is computed **after each purchase.** The average cost is computed by dividing the cost of goods available for sale by the units on hand. The average cost is then applied to: (1) the units sold, to determine the cost of goods sold, and (2) the remaining units on hand, to determine the ending inventory amount. The application of the average cost method by Bow Valley Electronics is shown in Illustration 6C-4.

Illustration 6C-4

Perpetual system—average cost method

Date	Purchases	Sales	Balance
January 1			(100 @ $10) $1,000
April 15	(200 @ $11) $2,200		(300 @ $10.667) $3,200
August 24	(300 @ $12) $3,600		(600 @ $11.333) $6,800
September 10		(550 @ $11.333) **($6,233)**	(50 @ $11.333) $ 567
November 27	(400 @ $13) $5,200		(450 @ $12.816) **$5,767**

As indicated above, **a new average is computed each time a purchase is made.** On April 15, after 200 units are purchased for $2,200, a total of 300 units costing $3,200 ($1,000 + $2,200) are on hand. The average unit cost is $10.667 ($3,200 ÷ 300). On August 24, after 300 units are purchased for $3,600, a total of 600 units costing $6,800 ($1,000 + $2,200 + $3,600) are on hand at an average cost per unit of $11.333 ($6,800 ÷ 600). This unit cost of $11.333 is used in costing sales until another purchase is made, when a new unit cost is computed. Thus, the unit cost of the 550 units sold on September 10 is $11.333, and the total cost of goods sold is $6,233. On November 27, following the purchase of 400 units for $5,200, there are 450 units on hand costing $5,767 ($567 + $5,200), with a new average cost of $12.816 ($5,767 ÷ 450).

Compare this moving-average cost under the perpetual inventory system to Illustration 6-16 on page 239 showing the weighted-average method under a periodic inventory system.

DEMONSTRATION PROBLEM 2

Additional Demonstration Problem

Demonstration Problem 1 on pages 247–248 showed cost of goods sold computations under a periodic inventory system. Now let's assume that Gerald D. Englehart Company uses a perpetual inventory system. The company has the same inventory, purchases, and sales data for the month of March as shown earlier.

Inventory:	March 1	200 units @ $4.00	$ 800
Purchases:	March 10	500 units @ $4.50	2,250
	March 20	400 units @ $4.75	1,900
	March 30	300 units @ $5.00	1,500
Sales:	March 15	500 units	
	March 25	400 units	

The physical inventory count on March 31 shows 500 units on hand.

Instructions

Under a **perpetual inventory system**, determine the cost of inventory on hand at March 31 and the cost of goods sold for March under the (a) first-in, first-out (FIFO) method, (b) last-in, first-out (LIFO) method, and (c) average cost method.

SOLUTION TO DEMONSTRATION PROBLEM 2

The cost of goods available for sale is $6,450, as follows.

Inventory:		200 units @ $4.00	$ 800
Purchases:	March 10	500 units @ $4.50	2,250
	March 20	400 units @ $4.75	1,900
	March 30	300 units @ $5.00	1,500
Total cost of goods available for sale			$6,450

Under a **perpetual inventory system**, the cost of goods sold under each cost flow method is as follows.

FIFO Method

Date	Purchases		Sales	Balance	
March 1				(200 @ $4.00)	$ 800
March 10	(500 @ $4.50)	$2,250		(200 @ $4.00) (500 @ $4.50)	$3,050
March 15			(200 @ $4.00) (300 @ $4.50) $2,150	(200 @ $4.50)	$ 900
March 20	(400 @ $4.75)	$1,900		(200 @ $4.50) (400 @ $4.75)	$2,800
March 25			(200 @ $4.50) (200 @ $4.75) $1,850	(200 @ $4.75)	$ 950
March 30	(300 @ $5.00)	$1,500		(200 @ $4.75) (300 @ $5.00)	$2,450
Ending inventory,		$2,450	Cost of goods sold: $6,450 − $2,450 =		$4,000

ACTION PLAN

- Compute the cost of goods sold under the perpetual FIFO method by allocating to the goods sold the **earliest** cost of goods purchased.
- Compute the cost of goods sold under the perpetual LIFO method by allocating to the goods sold the **latest** cost of goods purchased.
- Compute the cost of goods sold under the perpetual average cost method by allocating to the goods sold a **moving-average** cost.

LIFO Method

Date	Purchases		Sales		Balance	
March 1					(200 @ $4.00)	$ 800
March 10	(500 @ $4.50)	$2,250			(200 @ $4.00) (500 @ $4.50)	$3,050
March 15			(500 @ $4.50)	$2,250	(200 @ $4.00)	$ 800
March 20	(400 @ $4.75)	$1,900			(200 @ $4.00) (400 @ $4.75)	$2,700
March 25			(400 @ $4.75)	$1,900	(200 @ $4.00)	$ 800
March 30	(300 @ $5.00)	$1,500			(200 @ $4.00) (300 @ $5.00)	$2,300

Ending inventory, $2,300 Cost of goods sold: $6,450 − $2,300 = $4,150

Moving-Average Cost Method

Date	Purchases		Sales		Balance	
March 1					(200 @ $ 4.00)	$ 800
March 10	(500 @ $4.50)	$2,250			(700 @ $4.357)	$3,050
March 15			(500 @ $4.357)	$2,179	(200 @ $4.357)	$ 871
March 20	(400 @ $4.75)	$1,900			(600 @ $4.618)	$2,771
March 25			(400 @ $4.618)	$1,847	(200 @ $4.618)	$ 924
March 30	(300 @ $5.00)	$1,500			(500 @ $4.848)	$2,424

Ending inventory, $2,424 Cost of goods sold: $6,450 − $2,424 = $4,026

THE NAVIGATOR

SUMMARY OF STUDY OBJECTIVE FOR APPENDIX 6C

11. *Apply the inventory cost flow methods to perpetual inventory records.* Under FIFO, the cost of the earliest goods on hand prior to each sale is charged to cost of goods sold. Under LIFO, the cost of the most recent purchase prior to sale is charged to cost of goods sold. Under the average cost method, a new average cost is computed after each purchase.

***Note:** All **asterisked** Questions, Exercises, and Problems relate to material in the appendixes to the chapter.

Chapter 6 Self-Test

SELF-STUDY QUESTIONS

Answers are at the end of the chapter.

(SO 1) **1.** Which of the following should *not* be included in the physical inventory of a company?
a. Goods held on consignment from another company.
b. Goods shipped on consignment to another company.
c. Goods in transit from another company shipped FOB shipping point.
d. None of the above.

(SO 2) **2.** When goods are purchased for resale by a company using a periodic inventory system:
a. purchases on account are debited to Merchandise Inventory.
b. purchases on account are debited to Purchases.
c. purchase returns are debited to Purchase Returns and Allowances.
d. freight costs are debited to Purchases.

3. In determining cost of goods sold: (SO 3)
a. purchase discounts are deducted from net purchases.
b. freight-out is added to net purchases.
c. purchase returns and allowances are deducted from net purchases.
d. freight-in is added to net purchases.

4. If beginning inventory is $60,000, cost of goods purchased is $380,000, and ending inventory is $50,000, cost of goods sold is: (SO 3)
a. $390,000. c. $330,000.
b. $370,000. d. $420,000.

5. Inventoriable costs consist of two elements: beginning inventory and (SO 5)
a. ending inventory.
b. cost of goods purchased.
c. cost of goods sold.
d. cost of goods available for sale.

(SO 5) **6.** Bullwinkle Company has the following:

	Units	Unit Cost
Inventory, Jan. 1	8,000	$11
Purchase, June 19	13,000	12
Purchase, Nov. 8	5,000	13

If 9,000 units are on hand at December 31, the cost of the ending inventory under FIFO is:
a. $99,000. c. $113,000.
b. $108,000. d. $117,000.

(SO 5) **7.** Using the data in (6) above, the cost of the ending inventory under LIFO is:
a. $113,000. c. $99,000.
b. $108,000. d. $100,000.

(SO 6) **8.** In periods of rising prices, LIFO will produce:
a. higher net income than FIFO.
b. the same net income as FIFO.
c. lower net income than FIFO.
d. higher net income than average costing.

(SO 6) **9.** Factors that affect the selection of an inventory costing method do *not* include:
a. tax effects.
b. balance sheet effects.
c. income statement effects.
d. perpetual vs. periodic inventory system.

(SO 7) **10.** The lower of cost or market basis may be applied to:
a. categories of inventories.
b. individual items of inventories.
c. total inventory.
d. all of the above.

(SO 8) **11.** Titan A.E. Company's ending inventory is understated $4,000. The effects of this error on the current year's cost of goods sold and net income, respectively, are:
a. understated, overstated.
b. overstated, understated.
c. overstated, overstated.
d. understated, understated.

12. Which of these would cause the inventory turnover ratio to increase the most? (SO 9)
a. Increasing the amount of inventory on hand.
b. Keeping the amount of inventory on hand constant but increasing sales.
c. Keeping the amount of inventory on hand constant but decreasing sales.
d. Decreasing the amount of inventory on hand and increasing sales.

***13.** Butterfly Company has sales of $150,000 and cost of goods available for sale of $135,000. If the gross profit rate is 30%, the estimated cost of the ending inventory under the gross profit method is: (SO 10)
a. $15,000.
b. $30,000.
c. $45,000.
d. $75,000.

***14.** In a perpetual inventory system, (SO 10)
a. LIFO cost of goods sold will be the same as in a periodic inventory system.
b. average costs are based entirely on unit cost averages.
c. a new average is computed under the average cost method after each sale.
d. FIFO cost of goods sold will be the same as in a periodic inventory system.

THE NAVIGATOR

QUESTIONS

1. Goods costing $2,000 are purchased on account on July 15 with credit terms of 2/10, n/30. On July 18 a $200 credit memo is received from the supplier for damaged goods. Give the journal entry on July 24 to record payment of the balance due within the discount period.
2. Identify the accounts that are added to or deducted from Purchases to determine the cost of goods purchased. For each account, indicate (a) whether it is added or deducted and (b) its normal balance.
3. In the following separate mini cases, using a periodic inventory system, identify the item(s) designated by letter.
   (a) Purchases − X − Y = Net purchases.
   (b) Cost of goods purchased − Net purchases = X.
   (c) Beginning inventory + X = Cost of goods available for sale.
   (d) Cost of goods available for sale − Cost of goods sold = X.
4. "The key to successful business operations is effective inventory management." Do you agree? Explain.
5. An item must possess two characteristics to be classified as inventory by a merchandiser. What are these two characteristics?
6. Your friend Tom Wetzel has been hired to help take the physical inventory in Kikujiro Hardware Store. Explain to Tom Wetzel what this job will entail.
7. (a) Janine Company ships merchandise to Laura Company on December 30. The merchandise reaches the buyer on January 6. Indicate the terms of sale that will result in the goods being included in (1) Janine's December 31 inventory, and (2) Laura's December 31 inventory.
   (b) Under what circumstances should Janine Company include consigned goods in its inventory?
8. Brim Hat Shop received a shipment of hats for which it paid the wholesaler $2,940. The price of the hats was $3,000 but Brim was given a $60 cash discount and required to pay freight charges of $80. In addition, Brim

paid $130 to cover the travel expenses of an employee who negotiated the purchase of the hats. What amount will Brim record for inventory? Why?

9. What is the primary basis of accounting for inventories? What is the major objective in accounting for inventories? What accounting principles are involved here?

10. Identify the distinguishing features of an income statement for a merchandiser.

11. Roger Holloway believes that the allocation of inventoriable costs should be based on the actual physical flow of the goods. Explain to Roger why this may be both impractical and inappropriate.

12. What is a major advantage and a major disadvantage of the specific identification method of inventory costing?

13. "The selection of an inventory cost flow method is a decision made by accountants." Do you agree? Explain. Once a method has been selected, what accounting requirement applies?

14. Which assumed inventory cost flow method:
(a) usually parallels the actual physical flow of merchandise?
(b) assumes that goods available for sale during an accounting period are identical?
(c) assumes that the latest units purchased are the first to be sold?

15. In a period of rising prices, the inventory reported in Terry Duffy Company's balance sheet is close to the current cost of the inventory. Greg Hanson Company's inventory is considerably below its current cost. Identify the inventory cost flow method being used by each company. Which company has probably been reporting the higher gross profit?

16. Char Lewis Company has been using the FIFO cost flow method during a prolonged period of rising prices. During the same time period, Char Lewis has been paying out all of its net income as dividends. What adverse effects may result from this policy?

17. Bob Thebeau is studying for the next accounting midterm examination. What should Bob know about (a) departing from the cost basis of accounting for inventories and (b) the meaning of "market" in the lower of cost or market method?

18. Henning Music Center has 5 CD players on hand at the balance sheet date. Each cost $400. The current replacement cost is $320 per unit. Under the lower of cost or market basis of accounting for inventories, what value should be reported for the CD players on the balance sheet? Why?

19. What methods may be used under the lower of cost or market basis of accounting for inventories? Which method will produce the lowest inventory value?

20. Hitachi Company discovers in 2002 that its ending inventory at December 31, 2001, was $5,000 understated. What effect will this error have on (a) 2001 net income, (b) 2002 net income, and (c) the combined net income for the 2 years?

21. Maureen & Nathan Company's balance sheet shows Inventories $162,800. What additional disclosures should be made?

22. Under what circumstances might inventory turnover be too high? That is, what possible negative consequences might occur?

***23.** When is it necessary to estimate inventories?

***24.** Both the gross profit method and the retail inventory method are based on averages. For each method, indicate the average used, how it is determined, and how it is applied.

***25.** Jana Kingston Company has net sales of $400,000 and cost of goods available for sale of $300,000. If the gross profit rate is 30%, what is the estimated cost of the ending inventory? Show computations.

***26.** Cavanaugh Shoe Shop had goods available for sale in 2002 with a retail price of $120,000. The cost of these goods was $84,000. If sales during the period were $100,000, what is the ending inventory at cost using the retail inventory method?

***27.** "When perpetual inventory records are kept, the results under the FIFO and LIFO methods are the same as they would be in a periodic inventory system." Do you agree? Explain.

***28.** How does the average cost method of inventory costing differ between a perpetual inventory system and a periodic inventory system?

BRIEF EXERCISES

BE6-1 Prepare the journal entries to record the following transactions on IMAX Company's books using a periodic inventory system.

Journalize purchases transactions.
(SO 2)

(a) On March 2, IMAX Company purchased $700,000 of merchandise from Sing Tao Company, terms 2/10, n/30.
(b) On March 6, IMAX Company returned $130,000 of the merchandise purchased on March 2 because it was defective.
(c) On March 12, IMAX Company paid the balance due to Sing Tao Company.

Compute net purchases and cost of goods purchased.
(SO 3)

BE6-2 Assume that Mephisto Company uses a periodic inventory system and has the following account balances: Purchases $480,000, Purchase Returns and Allowances $11,000, Purchase Discounts $8,000, and Freight-in $16,000. Determine (a) net purchases and (b) cost of goods purchased.

Compute cost of goods sold and gross profit.
(SO 3)

BE6-3 Assume the same information as in BE6-2, and also that Mephisto Company has beginning inventory of $60,000, ending inventory of $90,000, and net sales of $620,000. Determine the amounts to be reported for cost of goods sold and gross profit.

Identify items to be included in taking a physical inventory.
(SO 1)

BE6-4 Fantasia Press Company identifies the following items for possible inclusion in the taking of a physical inventory. Indicate whether each item should be included or excluded from the inventory taking.

(a) Goods shipped on consignment by Fantasia Press to another company.
(b) Goods in transit from a supplier shipped FOB destination.
(c) Goods sold but being held for customer pickup.
(d) Goods held on consignment from another company.

Identify the components of inventoriable costs.
(SO 5)

BE6-5 The ledger of Shinhan Company includes the following items: **(a)** Freight-in, **(b)** Purchase Returns and Allowances, **(c)** Purchases, **(d)** Sales Discounts, **(e)** Purchase Discounts. Identify which items are included in inventoriable costs.

Compute ending inventory using FIFO and LIFO.
(SO 5)

BE6-6 In its first month of operations, Manion Company made three purchases of merchandise in the following sequence: (1) 300 units at $6, (2) 400 units at $7, and (3) 300 units at $8. Assuming there are 450 units on hand, compute the cost of the ending inventory under the **(a)** FIFO method and **(b)** LIFO method. Manion uses a periodic inventory system.

Compute the ending inventory using average costs.
(SO 5)

BE6-7 Data for Manion Company are presented in BE6-6. Compute the cost of the ending inventory under the average cost method, assuming there are 450 units on hand.

Determine the LCM valuation using inventory categories.
(SO 7)

BE6-8 Svenska Appliance Center accumulates the following cost and market data at December 31.

Inventory Categories	Cost Data	Market Data
Cameras	$12,000	$11,200
Camcorders	9,000	9,700
VCRs	14,000	12,800

Compute the lower of cost or market valuation using categories.

Compute inventory turnover and days in inventory.
(SO 9)

BE6-9 At December 31, 2002, the following information was available for B. Sherrick Company: ending inventory $80,000, beginning inventory $60,000, cost of goods sold $280,000, and sales revenue $380,000. Calculate inventory turnover and days in inventory for B. Sherrick Company.

Determine correct income statement amounts.
(SO 8)

BE6-10 Rome Company reports net income of $90,000 in 2002. However, ending inventory was understated $5,000. What is the correct net income for 2002? What effect, if any, will this error have on total assets as reported in the balance sheet at December 31, 2002?

Apply the gross profit method.
(SO 10)

***BE6-11** At May 31, Denmark Company has net sales of $350,000 and cost of goods available for sale of $230,000. Compute the estimated cost of the ending inventory, assuming the gross profit rate is 40%.

Apply the retail inventory method.
(SO 10)

***BE6-12** On June 30, Irish Fabrics has the following data pertaining to the retail inventory method: Goods available for sale: at cost $35,000, at retail $50,000; net sales $40,000, and ending inventory at retail $10,000. Compute the estimated cost of the ending inventory using the retail inventory method.

Apply cost flow methods to records.
(SO 11)

***BE6-13** Dodi's Department Store uses a perpetual inventory system. Data for product E2-D2 include the following purchases.

Date	Number of Units	Unit Price
May 7	50	$10
July 28	30	15

On June 1 Dodi's sold 30 units, and on August 27, 35 more units. Prepare the perpetual inventory card for the above transactions using (1) FIFO, (2) LIFO, and (3) average cost.

EXERCISES

E6-1 Presented below is the following information related to Argentina Co.

Journalize purchases transactions. (SO 2)

1. On April 5, purchased merchandise from Chile Company for $15,000, terms 2/10, net/30, FOB shipping point.
2. On April 6, paid freight costs of $800 on merchandise purchased from Chile.
3. On April 7, purchased equipment on account from Wayne Higley Mfg. Co. for $26,000.
4. On April 8, returned damaged merchandise to Chile Company and was granted a $3,000 allowance.
5. On April 15, paid the amount due to Chile Company in full.

Instructions

(a) Prepare the journal entries to record these transactions on the books of Argentina Co. using a periodic inventory system.

(b) Assume that Argentina Co. paid the balance due to Chile Company on May 4 instead of April 15. Prepare the journal entry to record this payment.

E6-2 The trial balance of Peru Company at the end of its fiscal year, August 31, 2002, includes the following accounts: Merchandise Inventory $17,200, Purchases $145,400, Sales $190,000, Freight-in $4,000, Sales Returns and Allowances $3,000, Freight-out $1,000, and Purchase Returns and Allowances $2,000. The ending (August 31, 2002) merchandise inventory is $25,000.

Prepare cost of goods sold section. (SO 3)

Instructions

Prepare a cost of goods sold section for the year ending August 31 (periodic inventory).

E6-3 Presented is information related to Bolivia Co. for the month of January 2002.

Prepare an income statement. (SO 4)

Freight-in	$ 10,000	Rent expense	$ 19,000
Freight-out	5,000	Salary expense	61,000
Insurance expense	12,000	Sales discounts	8,000
Purchases	220,000	Sales returns and allowances	13,000
Purchase discounts	3,000	Sales	325,000
Purchase returns and allowances	6,000		

Beginning merchandise inventory was $42,000. Ending inventory was $63,000.

Instructions

Prepare an income statement using the format presented on page 232. Operating expenses should not be segregated into selling and administrative expenses.

E6-4 Rockford Bank and Trust is considering giving Canada Company a loan. Before doing so, they decide that further discussions with Canada's accountant may be desirable. One area of particular concern is the inventory account, which has a year-end balance of $297,000. Discussions with the accountant reveal the following.

Determine the correct inventory amount. (SO 1)

1. Canada sold goods costing $38,000 to Cineplex Company, FOB shipping point, on December 28. The goods are not expected to arrive at Cineplex until January 12. The goods were not included in the physical inventory because they were not in the warehouse.
2. The physical count of the inventory did not include goods costing $95,000 that were shipped to Canada FOB destination on December 27 and were still in transit at year-end.
3. Canada received goods costing $20,000 on January 2. The goods were shipped FOB shipping point on December 26 by Gladiator Co. The goods were not included in the physical count.
4. Canada sold goods costing $40,000 to Rochelle Co., FOB destination, on December 30. The goods were received at Rochelle on January 8. They were not included in Canada's physical inventory.
5. Canada received goods costing $44,000 on January 2 that were shipped FOB destination on December 29. The shipment was a rush order that was supposed to arrive December 31. This purchase was included in the ending inventory of $297,000.

Instructions

Determine the correct inventory amount on December 31.

E6-5 Spain Co. uses a periodic inventory system. Its records show the following for the month of May, in which 70 units were sold.

Compute inventory and cost of goods sold using FIFO and LIFO. (SO 5)

		Units	Unit Cost	Total Cost
May 1	Inventory	30	$ 8	$240
15	Purchases	25	10	250
24	Purchases	35	13	455
	Totals	90		$945

Instructions

Compute the ending inventory at May 31 using the FIFO and LIFO methods. Prove the amount allocated to cost of goods sold under each method.

Compute inventory and cost of goods sold using FIFO and LIFO.
(SO 5, 6)

E6-6 In June, Naperville Company reports the following for the month of June.

		Units	Unit Cost	Total Cost
June 1	Inventory	200	$5	$1,000
12	Purchases	300	6	1,800
23	Purchases	500	7	3,500
30	Inventory	150		

Instructions

(a) Compute the cost of the ending inventory and the cost of goods sold under (1) FIFO and (2) LIFO.
(b) Which costing method gives the higher ending inventory? Why?
(c) Which method results in the higher cost of goods sold? Why?

Compute inventory and cost of goods sold using average costs.
(SO 5, 6)

E6-7 Inventory data for Naperville Company are presented in E6-6.

Instructions

(a) Compute the cost of the ending inventory and the cost of goods sold using the average cost method.
(b) Will the results in (a) be higher or lower than the results under (1) FIFO and (2) LIFO?
(c) Why is the average unit cost not $6?

Determine ending inventory under lower of cost or market inventory method.
(SO 7)

E6-8 Oriental Camera Shop uses the lower of cost or market basis for its inventory. The following data are available at December 31.

Item	Units	Unit Cost	Market
Cameras:			
Minolta	5	$170	$160
Canon	6	150	152
Light Meters:			
Vivitar	12	125	110
Kodak	11	115	135

Instructions

Determine the amount of the ending inventory by applying the lower of cost or market basis to **(a)** individual items, **(b)** inventory categories, and **(c)** the total inventory.

Determine effects of inventory errors.
(SO 8)

E6-9 Iqbal Hardware reported cost of goods sold as follows.

	2002	2003
Beginning inventory	$ 20,000	$ 30,000
Cost of goods purchased	150,000	175,000
Cost of goods available for sale	170,000	205,000
Ending inventory	30,000	35,000
Cost of goods sold	$140,000	$170,000

Iqbal made two errors: (1) 2002 ending inventory was overstated $5,000, and (2) 2003 ending inventory was understated $4,000.

Instructions

Compute the correct cost of goods sold for each year.

Prepare correct income statements.
(SO 8)

E6-10 Finlandia Watch Company reported the following income statement data for a 2-year period.

	2002	2003
Sales	$210,000	$250,000
Cost of goods sold		
Beginning inventory	32,000	40,000
Cost of goods purchased	173,000	202,000
Cost of goods available for sale	205,000	242,000
Ending inventory	40,000	52,000
Cost of goods sold	165,000	190,000
Gross profit	$ 45,000	$ 60,000

Finlandia uses a periodic inventory system. The inventories at January 1, 2002, and December 31, 2003, are correct. However, the ending inventory at December 31, 2002, was overstated $3,000.

Instructions

(a) Prepare correct income statement data for the 2 years.
(b) What is the cumulative effect of the inventory error on total gross profit for the 2 years?
(c) Explain in a letter to the president of Finlandia Company what has happened—i.e., the nature of the error and its effect on the financial statements.

E6-11 This information is available for Wideangle Lens Corporation for 2000, 2001, and 2002.

Compute inventory turnover, days in inventory, and gross profit rate.
(SO 9, 10)

	2000	2001	2002
Beginning inventory	$ 200,000	$ 300,000	$ 400,000
Ending inventory	300,000	400,000	500,000
Cost of goods sold	850,000	1,120,000	1,200,000
Sales	1,200,000	1,600,000	1,900,000

Instructions

Calculate inventory turnover, days in inventory, and gross profit rate (from Chapter 5) for Wideangle Lens Corporation for 2000, 2001, 2002. Comment on any trends.

***E6-12** The inventory of Odeon Company was destroyed by fire on March 1. From an examination of the accounting records, the following data for the first 2 months of the year are obtained: Sales $51,000, Sales Returns and Allowances $1,000, Purchases $28,200, Freight-in $1,200, and Purchase Returns and Allowances $1,400.

Determine merchandise lost using the gross profit method of estimating inventory.
(SO 10)

Instructions

Determine the merchandise lost by fire, assuming:

(a) A beginning inventory of $25,000 and a gross profit rate of 30% on net sales.
(b) A beginning inventory of $30,000 and a gross profit rate of 25% on net sales.

***E6-13** Gucci Shoe Store uses the retail inventory method for its two departments, Women's Shoes and Men's Shoes. The following information for each department is obtained.

Determine ending inventory at cost using retail method.
(SO 10)

Item	Women's Department	Men's Department
Beginning inventory at cost	$ 32,000	$ 46,450
Cost of goods purchased at cost	148,000	137,300
Net sales	177,000	185,000
Beginning inventory at retail	45,000	60,000
Cost of goods purchased at retail	182,000	185,000

Instructions

Compute the estimated cost of the ending inventory for each department under the retail inventory method.

***E6-14** Alpine Appliance uses a perpetual inventory system. For its flat-screen television sets, the January 1 inventory was 4 sets at $600 each. On January 10, Alpine purchased 6 units at $640 each. The company sold 2 units on January 8 and 5 units on January 15.

Apply cost flow methods to perpetual records.
(SO 11)

Instructions

Compute the ending inventory under (1) FIFO, (2) LIFO, and (3) average cost.

PROBLEMS: SET A

Journalize, post, and prepare a trial balance and partial income statement.
(SO 2, 3, 4)

P6-1A Vanessa Williams, a professional tennis star, operates VW's Tennis Shop at the Florida Lake Resort. At the beginning of the current season, the ledger of VW's Tennis Shop showed Cash $2,500, Merchandise Inventory $1,700, and Capital $4,200. The following transactions were completed during April.

Apr. 4 Purchased racquets and balls from Daddy Co. $840 FOB shipping point, terms 3/10, n/30.
6 Paid freight on Daddy Co. purchase $40.
8 Sold merchandise to members $900, terms n/30.
10 Received credit of $40 from Daddy Co. for a damaged racquet that was returned.
11 Purchased tennis shoes from Niki Sports for cash $300.
13 Paid Daddy Co. in full.
14 Purchased tennis shirts and shorts from Martina's Sportswear $900, FOB shipping point, terms 2/10, n/60.
15 Received cash refund of $50 from Niki Sports for damaged merchandise that was returned.
17 Paid freight on Martina's Sportswear purchase $30.
18 Sold merchandise to members $800, terms n/30.
20 Received $500 in cash from members in settlement of their accounts.
21 Paid Martina's Sportswear in full.
27 Granted credit of $30 to members for tennis clothing that did not fit.
30 Sold merchandise to members $900, terms n/30.
30 Received cash payments on account from members $500.

The chart of accounts for the tennis shop includes the following: No. 101 Cash, No. 112 Accounts Receivable, No. 120 Merchandise Inventory, No. 201 Accounts Payable, No. 301 Capital, No. 401 Sales, No. 412 Sales Returns and Allowances, No. 510 Purchases, No. 512 Purchase Returns and Allowances, No. 514 Purchase Discounts, No. 516 Freight-in.

Instructions

(a) Journalize the April transactions using a periodic inventory system.
(b) Enter the beginning balances in the ledger accounts and post the April transactions. (Use J1 for the journal reference.)
(c) Prepare a trial balance on April 30, 2002.
(d) Prepare an income statement through gross profit, assuming merchandise inventory on hand at April 30 is $1,800.

(c) Total debits $6,932
(d) Gross profit $692

Prepare an income statement.
(SO 3, 4)

P6-2A Anna Mossity Department Store is located near the Village shopping mall. At the end of the company's fiscal year on December 31, 2002, the following accounts appeared in its adjusted trial balance.

Accounts Payable	$ 89,300
Accounts Receivable	50,300
Accumulated Depreciation—Building	52,500
Accumulated Depreciation—Equipment	42,900
Building	190,000
Cash	23,000
Depreciation Expense—Building	10,400
Depreciation Expense—Equipment	13,300
Equipment	110,000
Freight-in	3,600
Insurance Expense	7,200
Merchandise Inventory	40,500
Mortgage Payable	80,000
Office Salaries Expense	32,000
Prepaid Insurance	2,400
Property Taxes Payable	4,300
Purchases	482,000

Purchase Discounts	12,000
Purchase Returns and Allowances	6,400
Sales Salaries Expense	74,000
Sales	658,000
Sales Commissions Expense	14,500
Sales Commissions Payable	4,000
Sales Returns and Allowances	8,000
A. Mossity, Capital	177,600
A. Mossity, Drawing	28,000
Property Taxes Expense	4,800
Utilities Expense	11,000

Analysis reveals the following additional data.

1. Merchandise inventory on December 31, 2002, is $75,000.
2. Insurance expense and utilities expense are 60% selling and 40% administrative.
3. Depreciation on the building and property tax expense are administrative expenses; depreciation on the equipment is a selling expense.

Instructions

Prepare an income statement for the year ended December 31, 2002.

Net income $50,100

P6-3A Scott Company had a beginning inventory of 400 units of Product E2-D2 at a cost of $8.00 per unit. During the year, purchases were:

Determine cost of goods sold and ending inventory, using FIFO, LIFO, and average cost.
(SO 5, 6)

Feb. 20	700 units at $9.00	Aug. 12	300 units at $11.00
May 5	500 units at $10.00	Dec. 8	100 units at $12.00

Scott Company uses a periodic inventory system. Sales totaled 1,500 units.

Instructions

(a) Determine the cost of goods available for sale.
(b) Determine (1) the ending inventory, and (2) the cost of goods sold under each of the assumed cost flow methods (FIFO, LIFO, and average). Prove the accuracy of the cost of goods sold under the FIFO and LIFO methods.
(c) Which cost flow method results in (1) the lowest inventory amount for the balance sheet, and (2) the lowest cost of goods sold for the income statement?

P6-4A The management of Aurora Co. is reevaluating the appropriateness of using its present inventory cost flow method, which is average cost. They request your help in determining the results of operations for 2002 if either the FIFO method or the LIFO method had been used. For 2002, the accounting records show the following data.

Compute ending inventory, prepare income statements, and answer questions using FIFO and LIFO.
(SO 5, 6)

Inventories		Purchases and Sales	
Beginning (15,000 units)	$34,000	Total net sales (225,000 units)	$865,000
Ending (20,000 units)		Total cost of goods purchased (230,000 units)	591,500

Purchases were made quarterly as follows.

Quarter	Units	Unit Cost	Total Cost
1	60,000	$2.40	$144,000
2	50,000	2.50	125,000
3	50,000	2.60	130,000
4	70,000	2.75	192,500
	230,000		$591,500

Operating expenses were $147,000, and the company's income tax rate is 32%.

Instructions

(a) Prepare comparative condensed income statements for 2002 under FIFO and LIFO. (Show computations of ending inventory.)

(a) Net income
FIFO $100,300
LIFO $94,180

(b) (4) $2,880

(b) Answer the following questions for management in the form of a business letter.

(1) Which cost flow method (FIFO or LIFO) produces the more meaningful inventory amount for the balance sheet? Why?

(2) Which cost flow method (FIFO or LIFO) produces the more meaningful net income? Why?

(3) Which cost flow method (FIFO or LIFO) is more likely to approximate actual physical flow of the goods? Why?

(4) How much additional cash will be available for management under LIFO than under FIFO? Why?

(5) Will gross profit under the average cost method be higher or lower than (a) FIFO and (b) LIFO? (*Note:* It is not necessary to quantify your answer.)

Estimate inventory loss using gross profit method.
(SO 10)

***P6-5A** Wayne E. Weather Company lost 80% of its inventory in a fire on March 25, 2002. The accounting records showed the following gross profit data for February and March.

	February	**March (to 3/25)**
Net sales	$300,000	$260,000
Net purchases	200,800	191,000
Freight-in	2,900	4,000
Beginning inventory	16,500	25,200
Ending inventory	25,200	?

Wayne E. Weather Company is fully insured for fire losses but must prepare a report for the insurance company.

Instructions

(a) Compute the gross profit rate for the month of February.

(b) Using the gross profit rate for February, determine both the estimated total inventory and inventory lost in the fire in March.

Compute ending inventory and cost of inventory lost using retail method.
(SO 10)

***P6-6A** Korean Department Store uses the retail inventory method to estimate its monthly ending inventories. The following information is available for two of its departments at August 31, 2002.

	Sporting Goods		**Jewelry and Cosmetics**	
	Cost	**Retail**	**Cost**	**Retail**
Net sales		$1,010,000		$1,150,000
Purchases	$670,000	1,066,000	$733,000	1,158,000
Purchase returns	(26,000)	(40,000)	(12,000)	(20,000)
Purchase discounts	(15,360)	—	(9,440)	—
Freight-in	6,000	—	8,000	—
Beginning inventory	47,360	74,000	36,440	62,000

At December 31, Korean Department Store takes a physical inventory at retail. The actual retail values of the inventories in each department are Sporting Goods $85,000, and Jewelry and Cosmetics $54,000.

Instructions

(a) Determine the estimated cost of the ending inventory for each department on **August 31**, 2002, using the retail inventory method.

(b) Compute the ending inventory at cost for each department at **December 31**, assuming the cost-to-retail ratios are 60% for Sporting Goods and 65% for Jewelry and Cosmetics.

Determine ending inventory under a perpetual inventory system.
(SO 11)

***P6-7A** Reliable Appliance Mart begins operations on May 1. It uses a perpetual inventory system. During May the company had the following purchases and sales for its Model 25 Sureshot camera.

Date	Purchases Units	Purchases Unit Cost	Sales Units
May 1	7	$150	
4			5
8	8	$170	
12			5
15	5	$180	
20			4
25			2

Instructions

(a) Determine the ending inventory under a perpetual inventory system using (1) FIFO, (2) average cost, and (3) LIFO.

(b) Which costing method produces (1) the highest ending inventory valuation and (2) the lowest ending inventory valuation?

(a) FIFO $720
Average $692
LIFO $640

PROBLEMS: SET B

Journalize, post, and prepare trial balance and partial income statement.
(SO 2, 3, 4)

P6-1B Nicklaus Bear, a former professional golf star, operates Nick's Pro Shop at Bay Golf Course. At the beginning of the current season on April 1, 2002, the ledger of Nick's Pro Shop showed Cash $3,000, Merchandise Inventory $3,500, and Capital $6,500. The following transactions were completed during April.

Apr. 5 Purchased golf bags, clubs, and balls on account from Balata Co. $1,900, FOB shipping point, terms 2/10, n/60.
7 Paid freight on Balata purchase $80.
9 Received credit from Balata Co. for merchandise returned $100.
10 Sold merchandise on account to members $900, terms n/30.
12 Purchased golf shoes, sweaters, and other accessories on account from Westphal Sportswear $860, terms 1/10, n/30.
14 Paid Balata Co. in full.
17 Received credit from Westphal Sportswear for merchandise returned $60.
20 Made sales on account to members $700, terms n/30.
21 Paid Westphal Sportswear in full.
27 Granted credit to members for clothing that did not fit $30.
30 Made cash sales $600.
30 Received payments on account from members $1,100.

The chart of accounts for the pro shop includes the following: No. 101 Cash, No. 112 Accounts Receivable, No. 120 Merchandise Inventory, No. 201 Accounts Payable, No. 301 Capital, No. 401 Sales, No. 412 Sales Returns and Allowances, No. 510 Purchases, No. 512 Purchase Returns and Allowances, No. 514 Purchase Discounts, No. 516 Freight-in.

Instructions

(a) Journalize the April transactions using a periodic inventory system.

(b) Enter the beginning balances in the ledger accounts and post the April transactions. (Use J1 for the journal reference.)

(c) Prepare a trial balance on April 30, 2002.

(d) Prepare an income statement through gross profit, assuming merchandise inventory on hand at April 30 is $4,200.

(c) Total debits $8,904
(d) Gross profit $234

Prepare an income statement.
(SO 3, 4)

P6-2B Bedazzle Department Store is located in midtown Metropolis. During the past several years, net income has been declining because of suburban shopping centers. At the end of the company's fiscal year on November 30, 2002, the following accounts appeared in its adjusted trial balance.

Accounts Payable	$ 35,310
Accounts Receivable	11,770
Accumulated Depreciation—Delivery Equipment	19,680
Accumulated Depreciation—Store Equipment	41,800
Cash	8,000
Delivery Expense	8,200
Delivery Equipment	57,000
Depreciation Expense—Delivery Equipment	4,000
Depreciation Expense—Store Equipment	9,500
Freight-in	5,060
B. Dazzle, Capital	87,200
B. Dazzle, Drawing	12,000
Insurance Expense	9,000
Merchandise Inventory	34,360
Notes Payable	46,000
Prepaid Insurance	4,500
Property Tax Expense	3,500
Purchases	650,000
Purchase Discounts	7,000
Purchase Returns and Allowances	3,000
Rent Expense	19,000
Salaries Expense	150,000
Sales	910,000
Sales Commissions Expense	12,000
Sales Commissions Payable	8,000
Sales Returns and Allowances	10,000
Store Equipment	125,000
Property Taxes Payable	3,500
Utilities Expense	10,600

Analysis reveals the following additional data.

1. Salaries expense is 70% selling and 30% administrative.
2. Insurance expense is 50% selling and 50% administrative.
3. Merchandise inventory at November 30, 2002, is $36,200.
4. Rent expense, utilities expense, and property tax expense are administrative expenses.

Instructions

Net income $30,980

Prepare an income statement for the year ended November 30, 2002.

Determine cost of goods sold and ending inventory, using FIFO, LIFO, and average cost with analysis.
(SO 5, 6)

P6-3B John Lewis Company had a beginning inventory on January 1 of 100 units of Product WD-44 at a cost of $20 per unit. During the year, the following purchases were made.

Mar. 15	300 units at $24	Sept. 4	300 units at $28
July 20	200 units at $25	Dec. 2	100 units at $30

750 units were sold. John Lewis Company uses a periodic inventory system.

Instructions

(a) Determine the cost of goods available for sale.

(b) Determine (1) the ending inventory, and (2) the cost of goods sold under each of the assumed cost flow methods (FIFO, LIFO, and average cost). Prove the accuracy of the cost of goods sold under the FIFO and LIFO methods.

(c) Which cost flow method results in (1) the highest inventory amount for the balance sheet, and (2) the highest cost of goods sold for the income statement?

Compute ending inventory, prepare income statements, and answer questions using FIFO and LIFO.
(SO 5, 6)

P6-4B The management of Congo Co. asks your help in determining the comparative effects of the FIFO and LIFO inventory cost flow methods. For 2002, the accounting records show the following data.

Inventory, January 1 (10,000 units)	$ 35,000
Cost of 110,000 units purchased	478,000
Selling price of 95,000 units sold	665,000
Operating expenses	120,000

Units purchased consisted of 40,000 units at $4.20 on May 10; 50,000 units at $4.40 on August 15; and 20,000 units at $4.50 on November 20. Income taxes are 28%.

Instructions

(a) Prepare comparative condensed income statements for 2002 under FIFO and LIFO. (Show computations of ending inventory.)

(b) Answer the following questions for management in the form of a business letter.

(1) Which inventory cost flow method produces the most meaningful inventory amount for the balance sheet? Why?

(2) Which inventory cost flow method produces the most meaningful net income? Why?

(3) Which inventory cost flow method is most likely to approximate actual physical flow of the goods? Why?

(4) How much additional cash will be available for management under LIFO than under FIFO? Why?

(5) How much of the gross profit under FIFO is illusory in comparison with the gross profit under LIFO?

(a) Net income
FIFO $103,680
LIFO $93,600
(b) (5) $14,000

***P6-5B** Dutch Company lost all of its inventory in a fire on December 26, 2002. The accounting records showed the following gross profit data for November and December.

Compute gross profit rate and inventory loss using gross profit method.
(SO 10)

	November	December (to 12/26)
Net sales	$500,000	$400,000
Beginning inventory	22,100	31,100
Purchases	314,975	236,000
Purchase returns and allowances	11,800	5,000
Purchase discounts	8,577	6,000
Freight-in	4,402	3,700
Ending inventory	31,100	?

Dutch is fully insured for fire losses but must prepare a report for the insurance company.

Instructions

(a) Compute the gross profit rate for November.

(b) Using the gross profit rate for November, determine the estimated cost of the inventory lost in the fire.

***P6-6B** Enlighten Book Store uses the retail inventory method to estimate its monthly ending inventories. The following information is available for two of its departments at October 31, 2002.

Compute ending inventory using retail method.
(SO 10)

	Hardcovers		Paperbacks	
	Cost	Retail	Cost	Retail
Beginning inventory	$ 260,000	$ 400,000	$ 65,000	$ 90,000
Purchases	1,180,000	1,800,000	266,000	380,000
Freight-in	5,000		2,000	
Purchase discounts	15,000		4,000	
Net sales		1,820,000		368,000

At December 31, Enlighten takes a physical inventory at retail. The actual retail values of the inventories in each department are Hardcovers $400,000 and Paperbacks $95,000.

Instructions

(a) Determine the estimated cost of the ending inventory for each department at **October 31**, 2002, using the retail inventory method.

(b) Compute the ending inventory at cost for each department at **December 31**, assuming the cost-to-retail ratios for the year are 65% for hardcovers and 70% for paperbacks.

***P6-7B** Angelina Jolie Co. began operations on July 1. It uses a perpetual inventory system. During July the company had the following purchases and sales.

Determine ending inventory under a perpetual inventory system.
(SO 11)

	Purchases		
Date	Units	Unit Cost	Sales Units
July 1	5	$ 90	
July 6			3
July 11	4	$ 99	
July 14			3
July 21	3	$106	
July 27			3

Instructions

(a) Determine the ending inventory under a perpetual inventory system using (1) FIFO, (2) average cost, and (3) LIFO.
(b) Which costing method produces the highest ending inventory valuation?

BROADENING YOUR PERSPECTIVE

FINANCIAL REPORTING AND ANALYSIS

FINANCIAL REPORTING PROBLEM: Lands' End, Inc.

BYP6-1 The notes that accompany a company's financial statements provide informative details that would clutter the amounts and descriptions presented in the statements. Refer to the financial statements of **Lands' End, Inc**. and the Notes to Consolidated Financial Statements in Appendix A.

Instructions

Answer the following questions. Complete the requirements in millions of dollars, as shown in Lands' End's annual report.

(a) What did Lands' End report for the amount of inventories in its Consolidated Balance Sheet at January 28, 2000? At January 29, 1999?
(b) Compute the dollar amount of change and the percentage change in inventories between 1999 and 2000. Compute inventory as a percentage of current assets at January 28, 2000.
(c) How does Lands' End value its inventories? Which inventory cost flow method does Lands' End use?
(d) What is the cost of sales (cost of goods sold) reported by Lands' End for 2000, 1999, and 1998? Compute the percentage of cost of sales to net sales in 2000.

COMPARATIVE ANALYSIS PROBLEM: Lands' End vs. Abercrombie & Fitch

BYP6-2 **Lands' End's** financial statements are presented in Appendix A. **Abercrombie & Fitch's** financial statements are presented in Appendix B.

Instructions

(a) Based on the information contained in these financial statements, compute the following 2000 ratios for each company.
 (1) Inventory turnover ratio
 (2) Average days to sell inventory
(b) What conclusions concerning the management of the inventory can be drawn from these data?

INTERPRETING FINANCIAL STATEMENTS: A Global Focus

BYP6-3 **Fuji Photo Film Company** is a Japanese manufacturer of photographic products. Its U.S. counterpart, and arch rival, is **Eastman Kodak**. Together the two dominate the global market for film. The following information was extracted from the financial statements of the two companies.

FUJIFILM

FUJI PHOTO FILM
Notes to the Financial Statements

Summary of significant accounting policies
The Company and its domestic subsidiaries maintain their records and prepare their financial statements in accordance with accounting practices generally accepted in Japan. . . . Certain reclassifications and adjustments, including those relating to tax effects of temporary differences and the accrual of certain expenses, have been incorporated in the accompanying consolidated financial statements to conform with accounting principles generally accepted in the United States.

Inventories
Inventories are valued at the lower of cost or market, cost being determined generally by the moving-average method, except that the cost of the principal raw materials is determined by the last-in, first-out method.

Note 6. Inventories
Inventories at March 31, 1998 and 1997, consisted of the following:

	(millions of yen)		(thousands of U.S. dollars)
	1998	1997	1998
Finished goods	¥135,795	¥123,010	$1,028,750
Work in process	51,001	48,867	386,371
Raw materials and supplies	55,525	46,959	420,644
	¥242,321	¥218,836	$1,835,765

Kodak

EASTMAN KODAK COMPANY
Notes to the Financial Statements

Inventories
Inventories are valued at cost, which is not in excess of market. The cost of most inventories in the U.S. is determined by the "last-in, first-out" (LIFO) method.

Note 3. Inventories

	(in millions)	
	1998	1997
At FIFO or average cost (approximates current cost)		
Finished goods	$ 907	$ 788
Work in process	569	538
Raw materials and supplies	439	460
	1,915	1,786
LIFO reserve	(491)	(534)
Total at LIFO	$1,424	$1,252

Inventories valued on the LIFO method are approximately 57% and 56% of total inventories in 1998 and 1997, respectively.

Additional information:

	Fuji Photo Film (yen)	Eastman Kodak (dollars)
1998 Cost of goods sold (millions)	735,953	7,293

Instructions
Answer each of the following questions.

(a) Why do you suppose that Fuji makes adjustments to its accounts so that they conform with U.S. accounting principles when it reports its results?
(b) What are the 1998 inventory turnover ratios and average days in inventory of the two companies (use inventory at FIFO, that is, before the LIFO reserve).
(c) What are the 1998 inventory turnover and average days in inventory of the two companies, adjusting for the LIFO reserve, if given? Do you encounter any problems when making this comparison?
(d) Calculate as a percentage of total inventory the portion that each of the components of 1998 inventory (raw materials, work in process, and finished goods) represents. Comment on your findings. (Use FIFO for Kodak.)

EXPLORING THE WEB

BYP6-4 A company's annual report usually will identify the inventory method used. Knowing that, you can analyze the effects of the inventory method on the income statement and balance sheet.

Address: www.cisco.com *(or go to www.wiley.com/college/weygandt)*

Steps:

1. From Cisco System's homepage, choose **Investor Relations.**
2. Choose **Annual Reports.**
3. Choose **2000 Annual Report.**
4. Choose **Online Report.**
5. Choose **Financial.**

Instructions
Answer the following questions based on the 2000 Annual Report.

(a) At Cisco's fiscal year-end, what was the net inventory on the balance sheet?
(b) How has this changed from the previous fiscal year-end?
(c) How much of the inventory was finished goods?
(d) What inventory method does Cisco use?

CRITICAL THINKING

GROUP DECISION CASE

BYP6-5 On April 10, 2001, fire damaged the office and warehouse of Gibson Company. Most of the accounting records were destroyed, but the following account balances were determined as of March 31, 2001: Merchandise Inventory, January 1, 2001, $80,000; Sales (January 1–March 31, 2001), $180,000; Purchases (January 1–March 31, 2001) $94,000.

The company's fiscal year ends on December 31. It uses a periodic inventory system.

From an analysis of the April bank statement, you discover cancelled checks of $4,200 for cash purchases during the period April 1–10. Deposits during the same period totaled $18,500. Of that amount, 60% were collections on accounts receivable, and the balance was cash sales.

Correspondence with the company's principal suppliers revealed $12,400 of purchases on account from April 1 to April 10. Of that amount, $1,800 was for merchandise in transit on April 10 that was shipped FOB destination.

Correspondence with the company's principal customers produced acknowledgments of credit sales totaling $28,000 from April 1 to April 10. It was estimated that $4,600 of credit sales will never be acknowledged or recovered from customers.

Gibson Company reached an agreement with the insurance company that its fire-loss claim should be based on the average of the gross profit rates for the preceding 2 years. The financial statements for 1999 and 2000 showed the following data.

	2000	1999
Net sales	$600,000	$480,000
Cost of goods purchased	416,000	356,000
Beginning inventory	60,000	40,000
Ending inventory	80,000	60,000

Inventory with a cost of $19,000 was salvaged from the fire.

Instructions

With the class divided into groups, answer the following.

(a) Determine the balances in (1) Sales and (2) Purchases at April 10.

***(b)** Determine the average profit rate for the years 1999 and 2000. (*Hint:* Find the gross profit rate for each year and divide the sum by 2.)

***(c)** Determine the inventory loss as a result of the fire, using the gross profit method.

COMMUNICATION ACTIVITY

BYP6-6 You are the controller of Small Toys Inc. Andy Manion, the president, recently mentioned to you that he found an error in the 2001 financial statements which he believes has corrected itself. He determined, in discussions with the Purchasing Department, that 2001 ending inventory was overstated by $1 million. Andy says that the 2002 ending inventory is correct. Thus he assumes that 2002 income is correct. Andy says to you, "What happened has happened—there's no point in worrying about it anymore."

Instructions

You conclude that Andy is incorrect. Write a brief, tactful memo to Andy, clarifying the situation.

ETHICS CASE

BYP6-7 J.K. Leask Wholesale Corp. uses the LIFO method of inventory costing. In the current year, profit at J.K. Leask is running unusually high. The corporate tax rate is also high this year, but it is scheduled to decline significantly next year. In an effort to lower the current year's net income and to take advantage of the changing income tax rate, the president of J.K. Leask Wholesale instructs the plant accountant to recommend to the purchasing department a large purchase of inventory for delivery 3 days before the end of the year. The price of the inventory to be purchased has doubled during the year, and the purchase will represent a major portion of the ending inventory value.

Instructions

(a) What is the effect of this transaction on this year's and next year's income statement and income tax expense? Why?

(b) If J.K. Leask Wholesale had been using the FIFO method of inventory costing, would the president give the same directive?

(c) Should the plant accountant order the inventory purchase to lower income? What are the ethical implications of this order?

Answers to Self-Study Questions

1. a **2.** b **3.** d **4.** a **5.** b **6.** c **7.** d **8.** c **9.** d **10.** d
11. b **12.** d ***13.** b ***14.** d

Answer to Lands' End Review It Question 5, p. 242

Lands' End reported inventories of $162,193,000 at January 28, 2000. Lands' End reports in "Note 1—Summary of significant accounting policies" that it uses the last-in, first-out (LIFO) cost method in applying product costs to inventories and cost of goods sold.

Remember to go back to the Navigator box on the chapter-opening page and check off your completed work.

7

ACCOUNTING INFORMATION SYSTEMS

THE NAVIGATOR ✓

- Understand *Concepts for Review* ❑
- Read *Feature Story* ❑
- Scan *Study Objectives* ❑
- Read *Preview* ❑
- Read text and answer *Before You Go On* *p.* 281 ❑ *p.* 294 ❑
- Work *Demonstration Problem* ❑
- Review *Summary of Study Objectives* ❑
- Answer *Self-Study Questions* ❑
- Complete *Assignments* ❑

CONCEPTS FOR REVIEW

Before studying this chapter, you should know or, if necessary, review:

a. How to perform each of the steps in the accounting cycle. (Ch. 4, pp. 146–150)

b. How to record transactions for a merchandiser. (Ch. 5, pp. 184–197)

c. How to prepare financial statements for a merchandiser. (Ch. 5, pp. 197–202)

☑ THE NAVIGATOR

FEATURE STORY

Accidents Happen

How organized are you financially? Take a short quiz.

- Is your wallet jammed full of gas station receipts from places you don't remember ever going?
- Is your wallet such a mess that it is often faster to fish for money in the crack of your car seat than to dig around in your wallet?
- Have you ever been tempted to burn down your house so you don't have to look for the receipts and records that you need to fill out your tax returns?

If you think it is hard to keep track of the many transactions that make up *your* life, imagine what it is like for a major corporation like **Fidelity Investments**. As the largest mutual fund management firm in the world, Fidelity manages more than $400 billion of investments. Millions of individuals have the bulk of their life savings invested in mutual funds. If you had your savings invested at Fidelity, you might be just slightly displeased if, when you called to find out your balance, the representative said, "You know, I kind of remember someone with a name like yours sending us some money—now what did we do with that?"

To ensure the accuracy of your balance and the security of your funds, Fidelity Investments, like all other companies large and small, relies on a sophisticated accounting information system. That's not to say that Fidelity or anybody else is error-free. In fact, if you've ever really messed up your checkbook register, you may take some comfort from one accountant's mistake at Fidelity Investments. The accountant failed to include a minus sign while doing a calculation, making what was actually a $1.3 billion loss look like a $1.3 billion gain! Fortunately, like most accounting errors, it was detected before any real harm was done.

No one expects that kind of mistake at a firm like Fidelity, which has sophisticated computer systems and top investment managers. In explaining the mistake to shareholders, a spokesperson wrote: "Some people have asked how, in this age of technology, such a mistake could be made. While many of our processes are computerized, accounting systems are complex and dictate that some steps must be handled manually by our managers and accountants, and people can make mistakes."

THE NAVIGATOR

www.fidelity.com

STUDY OBJECTIVES

After studying this chapter, you should be able to:

1. Identify the basic principles of accounting information systems.
2. Explain the major phases in the development of an accounting system.
3. Describe the nature and purpose of a subsidiary ledger.
4. Explain how special journals are used in journalizing.
5. Indicate how a multi-column journal is posted.

THE NAVIGATOR

PREVIEW OF CHAPTER 7

As you see from the Feature Story, a reliable information system is a necessity for any company. Whether you use pen, pencil, or computers in maintaining accounting records, certain principles and procedures apply. The purpose of this chapter is to explain and illustrate these features.

The content and organization of Chapter 7 are as follows.

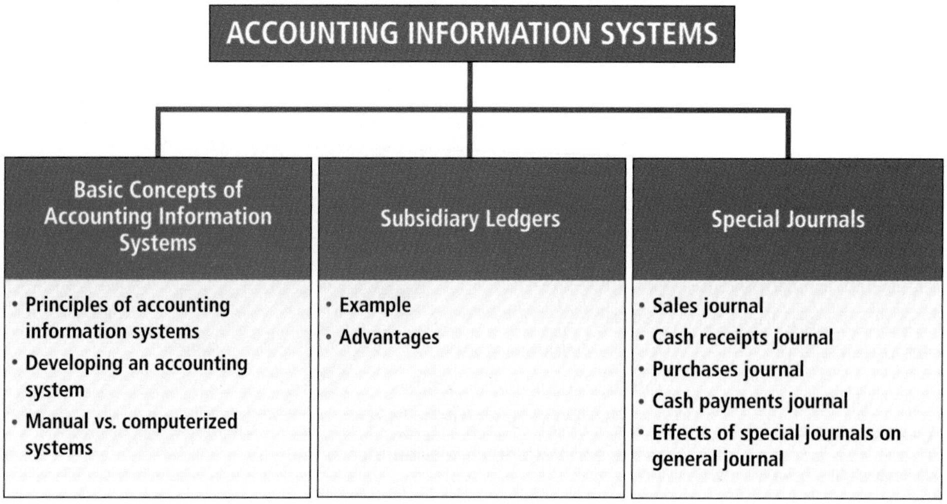

BASIC CONCEPTS OF ACCOUNTING INFORMATION SYSTEMS

The system that collects and processes transaction data and disseminates financial information to interested parties is known as the **accounting information system**. It includes each of the steps in the accounting cycle that you have studied in earlier chapters. It also includes the documents that provide evidence of the transactions and events, and the records, trial balances, work sheets, and financial statements that result. An accounting information system may be either manual or electronic (computerized).

In this chapter, we explore the basic concepts that underlie accounting information systems, which from here on we will often refer to simply as **accounting systems**.

PRINCIPLES OF ACCOUNTING INFORMATION SYSTEMS

STUDY OBJECTIVE 1

Identify the basic principles of accounting information systems.

Efficient and effective accounting information systems are based on certain basic principles. These principles are: (1) cost effectiveness, (2) usefulness, and (3) flexibility, as described in Illustration 7-1. If the accounting system is cost effective, provides useful output, and has the flexibility to meet future needs, it can contribute to both individual and organizational goals.

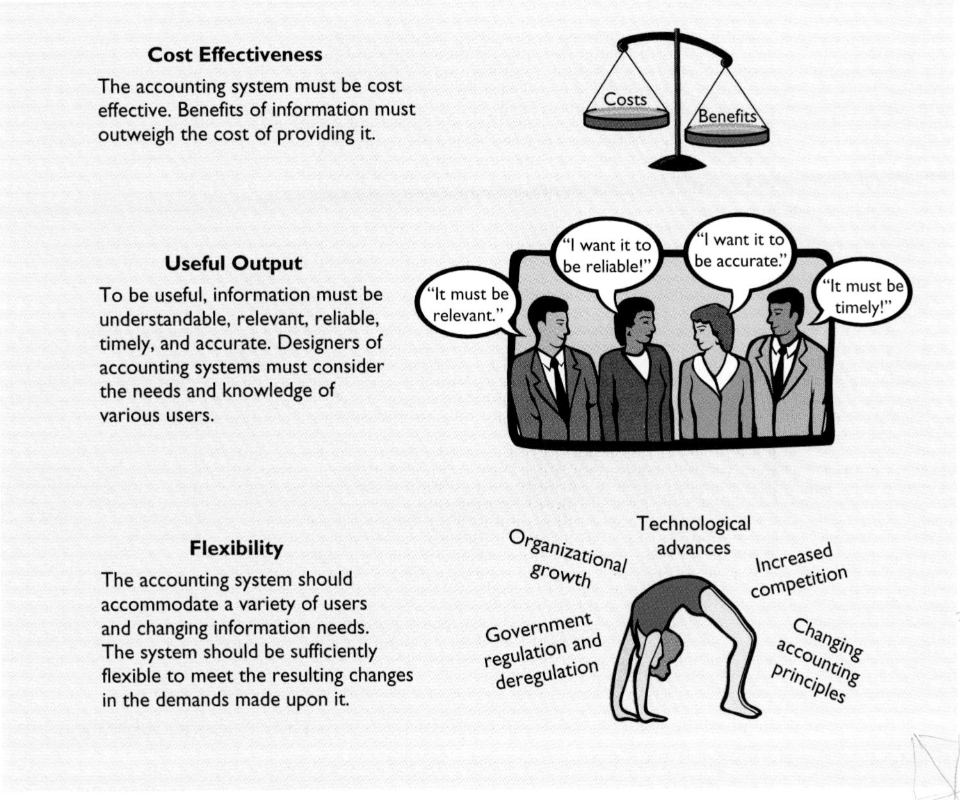
Cost Effectiveness
The accounting system must be cost effective. Benefits of information must outweigh the cost of providing it.
Costs
Benefits
Useful Output
To be useful, information must be understandable, relevant, reliable, timely, and accurate. Designers of accounting systems must consider the needs and knowledge of various users.
"It must be relevant."
"I want it to be reliable!"
"I want it to be accurate."
"It must be timely!"
Flexibility
The accounting system should accommodate a variety of users and changing information needs. The system should be sufficiently flexible to meet the resulting changes in the demands made upon it.
Organizational growth
Technological advances
Increased competition
Government regulation and deregulation
Changing accounting principles

Illustration 7-1

Principles of an efficient and effective accounting information system

DEVELOPING AN ACCOUNTING SYSTEM

STUDY OBJECTIVE 2

Explain the major phases in the development of an accounting system.

Good accounting systems do not just happen. They are carefully planned, designed, installed, managed, and refined. Generally, an accounting system is developed in the following four phases.

1. **Analysis.** The starting point is to determine the information needs of internal and external users. The system analyst then identifies the sources of the needed information and the records and procedures for collecting and reporting the data. If an existing system is being analyzed, its strengths and weaknesses must be identified.
2. **Design.** A new system must be built from the ground up: forms and documents designed, methods and procedures selected, job descriptions prepared, controls integrated, reports formatted, and equipment selected. Redesigning an existing system may involve only minor changes or a complete overhaul.
3. **Implementation.** Implementation of new or revised systems requires that documents, procedures, and processing equipment be installed and made operational. Also, personnel must be trained and closely supervised through a start-up period.
4. **Follow-up.** After the system is up and running, it must be monitored for weaknesses or breakdowns. Also, its effectiveness must be compared to design and organizational objectives. Changes in design or implementation may be necessary.

Illustration 7-2 highlights the relationship of these four phases in the life cycle of the accounting system.

Illustration 7-2

Phases in the development of an accounting system

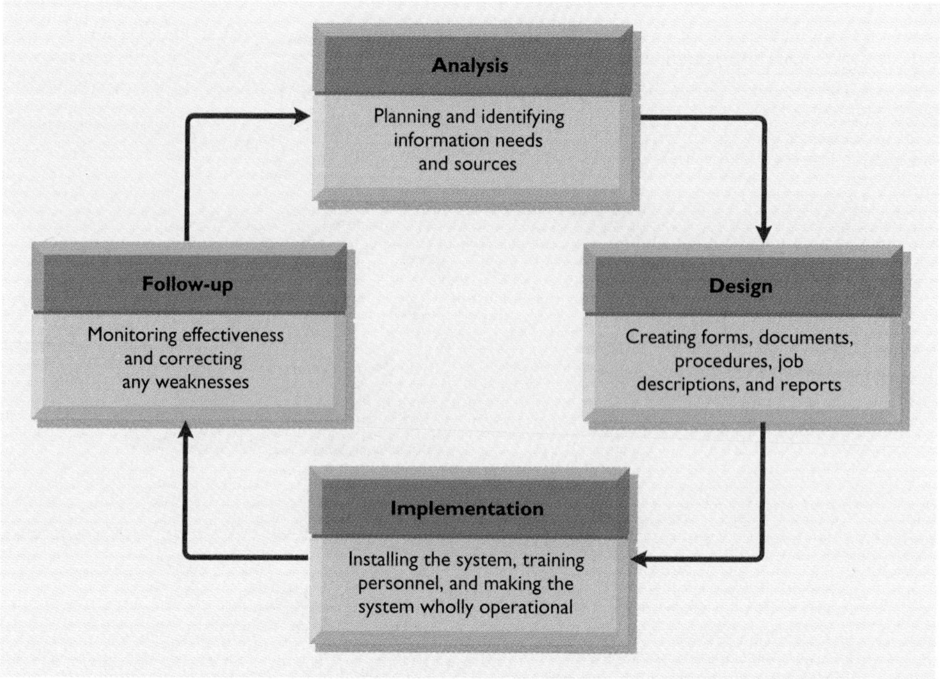

These phases represent the life cycle of an accounting system. They suggest that few systems remain the same forever. As experience and knowledge are obtained, and as technological and organizational changes occur, the accounting system may also have to grow and change.

The accounting system represented in the first six chapters is satisfactory in a company where the volume of transactions is extremely low. However, in most companies, it is necessary to add additional ledgers and journals to the accounting system to record transaction data efficiently.

MANUAL VS. COMPUTERIZED SYSTEMS

In a **manual accounting system**, each of the steps in the accounting cycle is performed by hand. For example, each accounting transaction is entered manually in the journal; each is posted manually to the ledger. Other manual computations must be made to obtain ledger account balances and to prepare a trial balance and financial statements.

In a computerized accounting system, there are programs for performing the steps in the accounting cycle, such as journalizing, posting, and preparing a trial balance. In addition, there is software for business functions such as billing customers, preparing the payroll, and budgeting.

ACCOUNTING IN ACTION e Business Insight

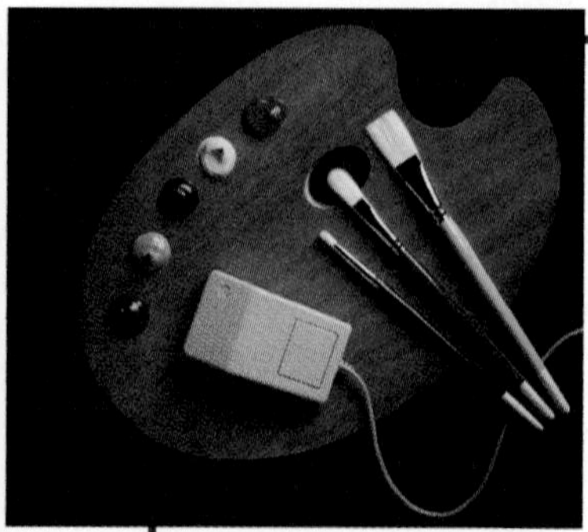

Accounting software companies have recognized the tremendous opportunities that result from making the accounting system an integral part of a comprehensive e-business package. For example, **Great Plains** recently published a story about an online art gallery called Art.com that uses two Great Plains e-business packages, eEnterprise™ and e.Commerce™ to meet the information needs of every aspect of its business. eEnterprise provides financial, distribution, purchasing, and manufacturing applications. e.Commerce provides real-time product information and on-the-fly customer data collection, reducing the need for order-desk staff because the customer keys in the order. This feature eliminates data re-entry errors.

SOURCE: www.greatplains.com/ebusiness

You might be wondering, "Why cover manual accounting systems if the real world uses computerized systems?" First, small businesses still abound. Most of them begin operations with manual accounting systems and convert to computerized systems as the business grows. Second, to understand what computerized accounting systems do, you need to understand how manual accounting systems work.

SUBSIDIARY LEDGERS

STUDY OBJECTIVE 3

Describe the nature and purpose of a subsidiary ledger.

Imagine a business that has several thousand charge (credit) customers and shows the transactions with these customers in only one general ledger account—Accounts Receivable. It would be virtually impossible to determine the balance owed by an individual customer at any specific time. Similarly, the amount payable to one creditor would be difficult to locate quickly from a single Accounts Payable account in the general ledger.

Instead, companies use subsidiary ledgers to keep track of individual balances. A **subsidiary ledger** is a group of accounts with a common characteristic (for example, all accounts receivable). The subsidiary ledger frees the general ledger from the details of individual balances. A subsidiary ledger is an addition to, and an expansion of, the general ledger.

Two common subsidiary ledgers are:

1. The **accounts receivable** (or **customers'**) **subsidiary ledger**, which collects transaction data of individual customers.
2. The **accounts payable** (or **creditors'**) **subsidiary ledger**, which collects transaction data of individual creditors.

In each of these subsidiary ledgers, individual accounts are usually arranged in alphabetical order.

The detailed data from a subsidiary ledger are summarized in a general ledger account. For example, the detailed data from the accounts receivable subsidiary ledger are summarized in Accounts Receivable in the general ledger. The general ledger account that summarizes subsidiary ledger data is called a **control account**. An overview of the relationship of subsidiary ledgers to the general ledger is shown in Illustration 7-3. The general ledger control accounts and subsidiary ledger accounts are shown in green color. Note that cash and owner's capital in this illustration are not control accounts because there are no subsidiary ledger accounts related to these accounts.

Illustration 7-3

Relationship of general ledger and subsidiary ledgers

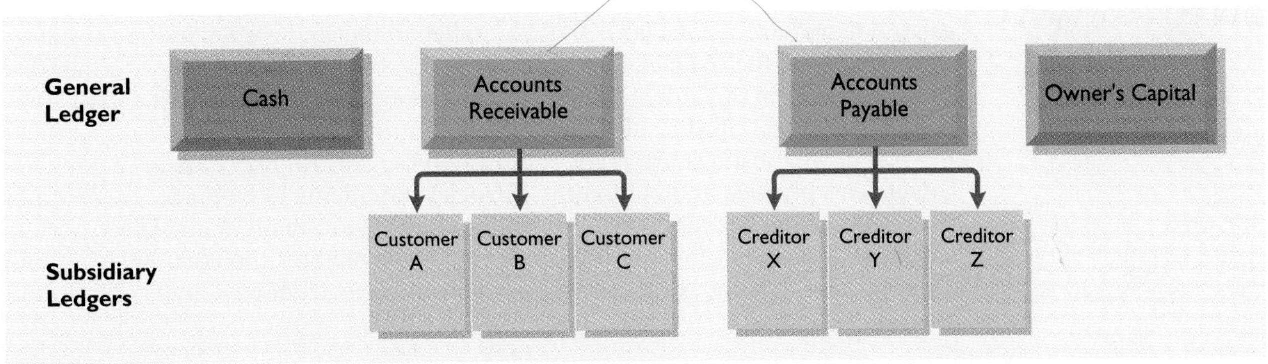

Each general ledger control account balance must equal the composite balance of the individual accounts in the related subsidiary ledger at the end of an accounting period. For example, the balance in Accounts Payable in Illustration 7-3 must equal the total of the subsidiary balances of Creditors X + Y + Z.

EXAMPLE

An example of a control account and subsidiary ledger for Larson Enterprises is provided in Illustration 7-4. (The explanation column in these accounts is not shown in this and subsequent illustrations due to space considerations.)

Illustration 7-4

Relationship between general and subsidiary ledgers

ACCOUNTS RECEIVABLE SUBSIDIARY LEDGER

Aaron Co.

Date	Ref.	Debit	Credit	Balance
2002				
Jan 10		6,000		6,000
19			4,000	**2,000**

Branden Inc.

Date	Ref.	Debit	Credit	Balance
2002				
Jan 12		3,000		3,000
21			3,000	------

Caron Co.

Date	Ref.	Debit	Credit	Balance
2002				
Jan 20		3,000		3,000
29			1,000	**2,000**

GENERAL LEDGER

Accounts Receivable **No. 112**

Date	Ref.	Debit	Credit	Balance
2002				
Jan 31		12,000		12,000
31			8,000	**4,000**

The subsidiary ledger is separate from the general ledger.

Accounts Receivable is a control account.

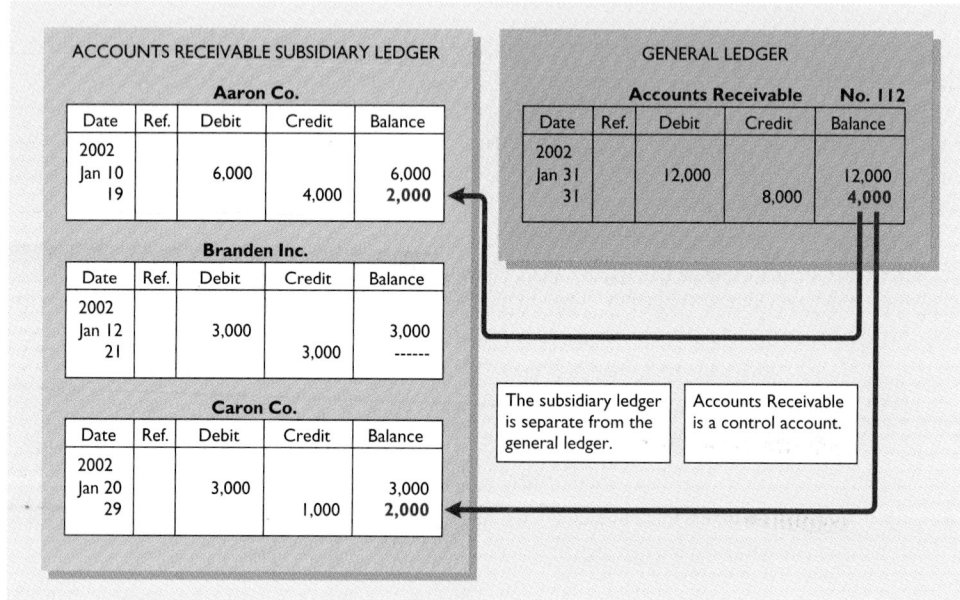

The example is based on the transactions listed below.

Illustration 7-5

Sales and collection transactions

Credit Sales			Collections on Account		
Jan. 10	Aaron Co.	$ 6,000	Jan. 19	Aaron Co.	$ 4,000
12	Branden Inc.	3,000	21	Branden Inc.	3,000
20	Caron Co.	3,000	29	Caron Co.	1,000
		$12,000			$ 8,000

The total debits ($12,000) and credits ($8,000) in Accounts Receivable in the general ledger are reconcilable to the detailed debits and credits in the subsidiary accounts. Also, the balance of $4,000 in the control account agrees with the total of the balances in the individual accounts (Aaron Co. $2,000 + Branden Inc. $0 + Caron Co. $2,000) in the subsidiary ledger.

As shown, postings are made monthly to the control accounts in the general ledger. This practice allows monthly financial statements to be prepared. Postings to the individual accounts in the subsidiary ledger are made daily. Daily posting ensures that account information is current. This enables the company to monitor credit limits, bill customers, and answer inquiries from customers about their account balances.

ADVANTAGES OF SUBSIDIARY LEDGERS

Subsidiary ledgers have several advantages. They:

1. **Show transactions affecting one customer or one creditor in a single account,** thus providing up-to-date information on specific account balances.
2. **Free the general ledger of excessive details.** As a result, a trial balance of the general ledger does not contain vast numbers of individual account balances.
3. **Help locate errors in individual accounts** by reducing the number of accounts in one ledger and by using control accounts.
4. **Make possible a division of labor** in posting. One employee can post to the general ledger while someone else posts to the subsidiary ledgers.

TECHNOLOGY IN ACTION

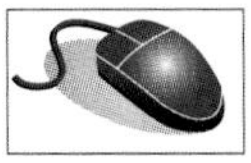

Rather than relying on customer or creditor names in a subsidiary ledger, a computerized system expands the account number of the control account in a pre-specified manner. For example, if Accounts Receivable was numbered 10010, the first account in the accounts receivable subsidiary ledger might be numbered 10010-0001. Most systems allow inquiries about specific accounts in the subsidiary ledger (by account number) or about the control account. With the latter, the system would automatically total all the subsidiary accounts whenever an inquiry to the control account was made.

BEFORE YOU GO ON...

▶ *REVIEW IT*

1. What basic principles are followed in designing and developing an effective accounting information system?
2. What are the major phases in the development of an accounting information system?
3. What is a subsidiary ledger, and what purpose does it serve?

▶ *DO IT*

Presented below is information related to Sims Company for its first month of operations. Determine the balances that appear in the accounts payable subsidiary ledger. What Accounts Payable balance appears in the general ledger at the end of January?

Credit Purchases			Cash Paid		
Jan. 5	Devon Co.	$11,000	Jan. 9	Devon Co.	$7,000
11	Shelby Co.	7,000	14	Shelby Co.	2,000
22	Taylor Co.	14,000	27	Taylor Co.	9,000

ACTION PLAN

- Subtract cash paid from credit purchases to determine the balances in the accounts payable subsidiary ledger.
- Sum the individual balances to determine the Accounts Payable balance.

SOLUTION

Subsidiary ledger balances: Devon Co. $4,000 ($11,000 − $7,000); Shelby Co. $5,000 ($7,000 − $2,000); Taylor Co. $5,000 ($14,000 − $9,000). General ledger Accounts Payable balance: $14,000 ($4,000 + $5,000 + $5,000).

Related exercise material: BE7-3, BE7-4, E7-1, E7-2, E7-3, E7-4, E7-5, and E7-9.

THE NAVIGATOR

SPECIAL JOURNALS

STUDY OBJECTIVE 4

Explain how special journals are used in journalizing.

So far you have learned to journalize transactions in a two-column general journal and post each entry to the general ledger. This procedure is satisfactory in only the very smallest companies. To expedite journalizing and posting, most companies use special journals **in addition to the general journal.**

A **special journal** is used to record similar types of transactions. Examples would be all sales of merchandise on account, or all cash receipts. What special journals a company uses depends largely on the types of transactions that occur frequently. Most merchandising enterprises use the journals shown in Illustration 7-6 to record transactions daily.

Illustration 7-6

Use of special journals and the general journal

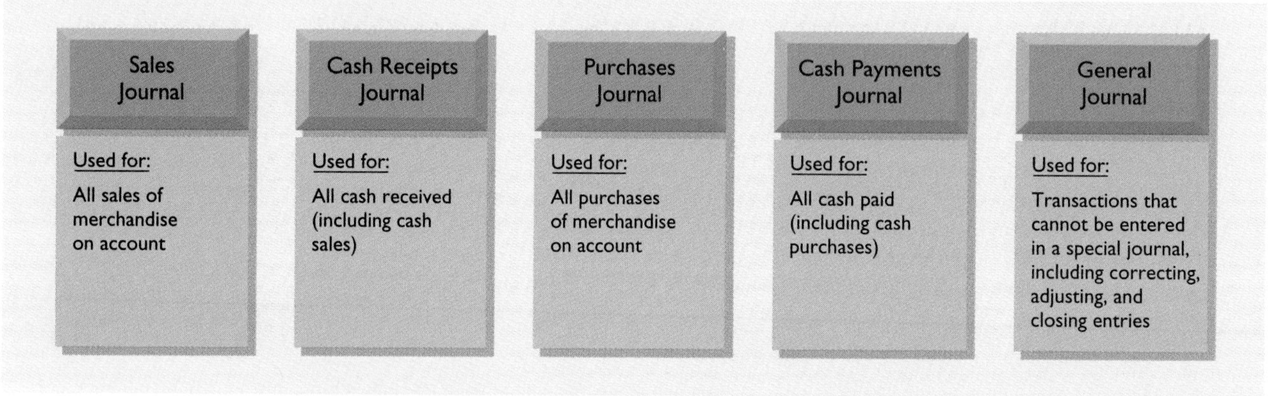

If a transaction cannot be recorded in a special journal, it is recorded in the general journal. For example, if you had special journals only for the four types of transactions listed above, purchase returns and allowances would be recorded in the general journal. So would sales returns and allowances. Similarly, **correcting, adjusting, and closing entries are recorded in the general journal.** Other types of special journals may sometimes be used in some situations. For example, when sales returns and allowances are frequent, special journals may be used to record these transactions.

Special journals **permit greater division of labor** because several people can record entries in different journals at the same time. For example, one employee may journalize all cash receipts, and another may journalize all credit sales. Also, the use of special journals **reduces the time needed to complete the posting process.** With special journals, some accounts may be posted monthly, instead of daily, as will be illustrated later in the chapter.

SALES JOURNAL

The **sales journal** is used to record sales of merchandise on account. Cash sales of merchandise are entered in the cash receipts journal. Credit sales of assets other than merchandise are entered in the general journal.

Journalizing Credit Sales

Karns Wholesale Supply uses a **perpetual inventory** system. Under this system, each entry in the sales journal results in one entry **at selling price** and another entry at cost—a debit to Accounts Receivable (a control account) and a credit of equal amount to Sales. The entry **at cost** is a debit to Cost of Goods Sold and a credit of equal amount to Merchandise Inventory (a control account). A sales journal with two amount columns can show on only one line a sales transaction at both selling price and cost. The two-column sales journal of Karns Wholesale Supply is shown in Illustration 7-7, using assumed credit sales transactions (for sales invoices 101–107).

HELPFUL HINT

Postings are also made daily to individual ledger accounts in the inventory subsidiary ledger to maintain a perpetual inventory.

Karns Wholesale Supply
SALES JOURNAL **S1**

Date	Account Debited	Invoice No.	Ref.	Accts. Receivable Dr. Sales Cr.	Cost of Goods Sold Dr. Merchandise Inventory Cr.
2002					
May 3	Abbot Sisters	101		10,600	6,360
7	Babson Co.	102		11,350	7,370
14	Carson Bros.	103		7,800	5,070
19	Deli Co.	104		9,300	6,510
21	Abbot Sisters	105		15,400	10,780
24	Deli Co.	106		21,210	15,900
27	Babson Co.	107		14,570	10,200
				90,230	62,190

Illustration 7-7

Journalizing the sales journal—perpetual inventory system

The reference (Ref.) column is not used in journalizing. It is used in posting the sales journal, as explained in the next section. Also, note that, unlike the general journal, an explanation is not required for each entry in a special journal. Finally, note that each invoice is prenumbered to ensure that all invoices are journalized.

Posting the Sales Journal

Postings from the sales journal are made **daily to the individual accounts receivable** in the subsidiary ledger. Posting **to the general ledger** is made **monthly**. Illustration 7-8 (on page 284) shows both the daily and monthly postings.

A check mark (✓) is inserted in the reference posting column to indicate that the daily posting to the customer's account has been made. A check mark (✓) is used in this illustration because the subsidiary ledger accounts are not numbered. At the end of the month, the column totals of the sales journal are posted to the general ledger. Here, the column totals are a debit of $90,230 to Accounts Receivable (account No. 112), a credit of $90,230 to Sales (account No. 401), a debit of $62,190 to Cost of Goods Sold (account No. 505), and a credit of $62,190 to Merchandise Inventory (account No. 120). Insertion of the account numbers below the column total indicates that the postings have been made. In both the general ledger and subsidiary ledger accounts, the reference **S1** indicates that the posting came from page 1 of the sales journal.

Proving the Ledgers

The next step is to "prove" the ledgers. To do so, we must determine two things: (1) The total of the general ledger debit balances must equal the total of the general ledger credit balances. (2) The sum of the subsidiary ledger balances must equal the balance in the control account. The proof of the postings from the sales journal to the general and subsidiary ledger is shown in Illustration 7-9 (on page 285).

Advantages of the Sales Journal

The use of a special journal to record sales on account has a number of advantages. First, the one-line entry for each sales transaction **saves time**. In the sales journal, it is not necessary to write out the four account titles for each transaction. Second, only totals, rather than individual entries, are posted to the general ledger. This **saves posting time and reduces the possibilities of errors in posting**. Finally, **a division of labor results**, because one individual can take responsibility for the sales journal.

Illustration 7-8

Posting the sales journal

Karns Wholesale Supply
SALES JOURNAL

S1

Date	Account Debited	Invoice No.	Ref.	Accts. Receivable Dr. Sales Cr.	Cost of Goods Sold Dr. Merchandise Inventory Cr.
2002					
May 3	Abbot Sisters	101	√	10,600	6,360
7	Babson Co.	102	√	11,350	7,370
14	Carson Bros.	103	√	7,800	5,070
19	Deli Co.	104	√	9,300	6,510
21	Abbot Sisters	105	√	15,400	10,780
24	Deli Co.	106	√	21,210	15,900
27	Babson Co.	107	√	14,570	10,200
				90,230	62,190
				(112) / (401)	(505) / (120)

Totals are posted at the end of the accounting period to the general ledger.

Individual amounts are posted daily to the subsidiary ledger.

ACCOUNTS RECEIVABLE SUBSIDIARY LEDGER

Abbot Sisters

Date	Ref.	Debit	Credit	Balance
2002				
May 3	S1	10,600		10,600
21	S1	15,400		26,000

Babson Co.

Date	Ref.	Debit	Credit	Balance
2002				
May 7	S1	11,350		11,350
27	S1	14,570		25,920

Carson Bros.

Date	Ref.	Debit	Credit	Balance
2002				
May 14	S1	7,800		7,800

Deli Co.

Date	Ref.	Debit	Credit	Balance
2002				
May 19	S1	9,300		9,300
24	S1	21,210		30,510

GENERAL LEDGER

Accounts Receivable **No. 112**

Date	Ref.	Debit	Credit	Balance
2002				
May 31	S1	90,230		90,230

Merchandise Inventory **No. 120**

Date	Ref.	Debit	Credit	Balance
2002				
May 31	S1		62,190	62,190[1]

Sales **No. 401**

Date	Ref.	Debit	Credit	Balance
2002				
May 31	S1		90,230	90,230

Cost of Goods Sold **No. 505**

Date	Ref.	Debit	Credit	Balance
2002				
May 31	S1	62,190		62,190

The subsidiary ledger is separate from the general ledger.

Accounts Receivable is a control account.

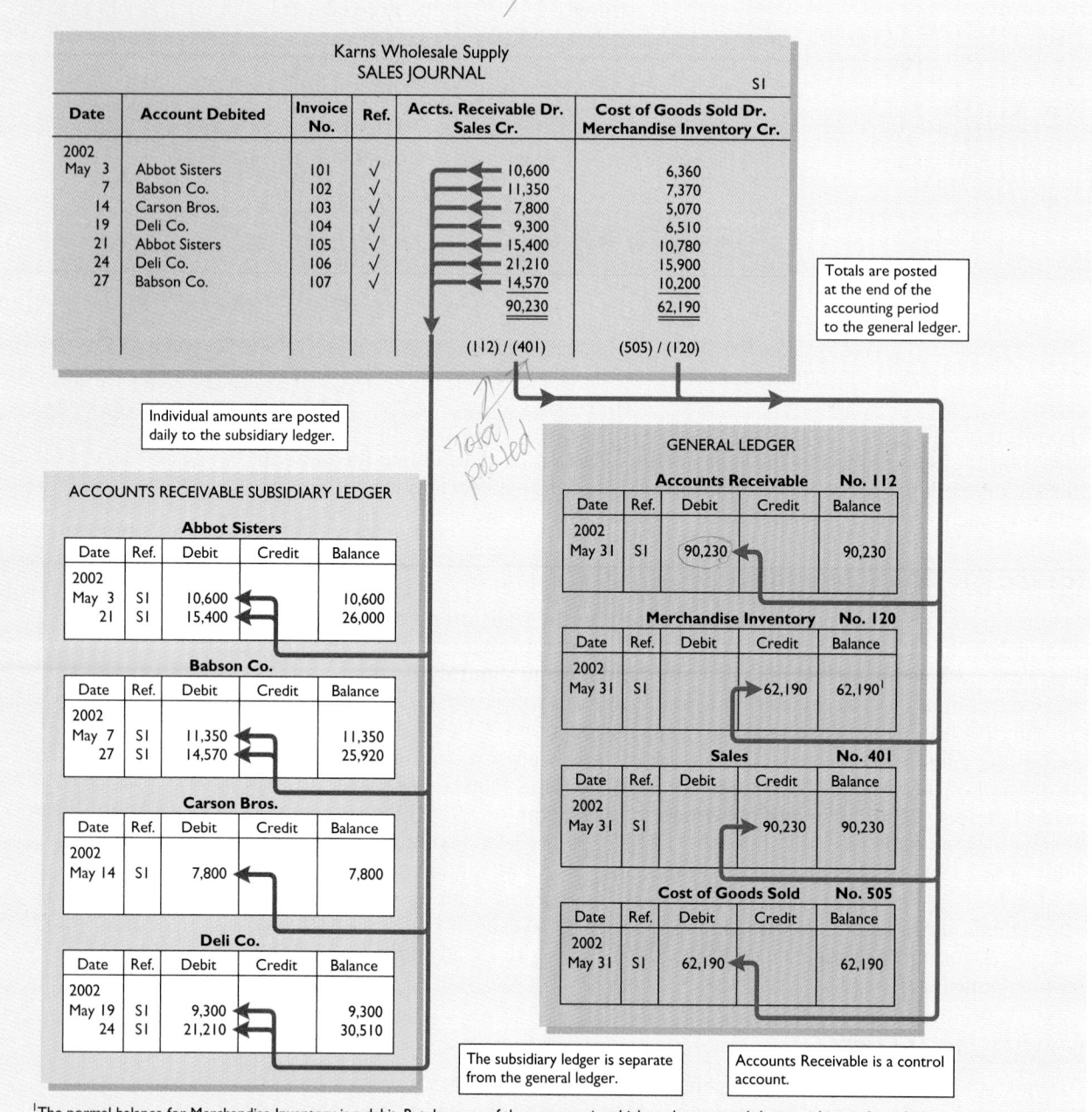

[1]The normal balance for Merchandise Inventory is a debit. But, because of the sequence in which we have posted the special journals, with the sales journals first, the credits to Merchandise Inventory are posted before the debits. This posting sequence explains the credit balance, in Merchandise Inventory, which exists only until the other journals are posted.

CASH RECEIPTS JOURNAL

All receipts of cash are recorded in the **cash receipts journal**. The most common types of cash receipts are cash sales of merchandise and collections of accounts receivable. Many other possibilities exist, such as receipt of money from bank loans and cash proceeds from disposal of equipment. A one- or two-column cash receipts journal would not have space enough for all possible cash receipt transactions. Therefore, a multiple-column cash receipts journal is used.

Illustration 7-9

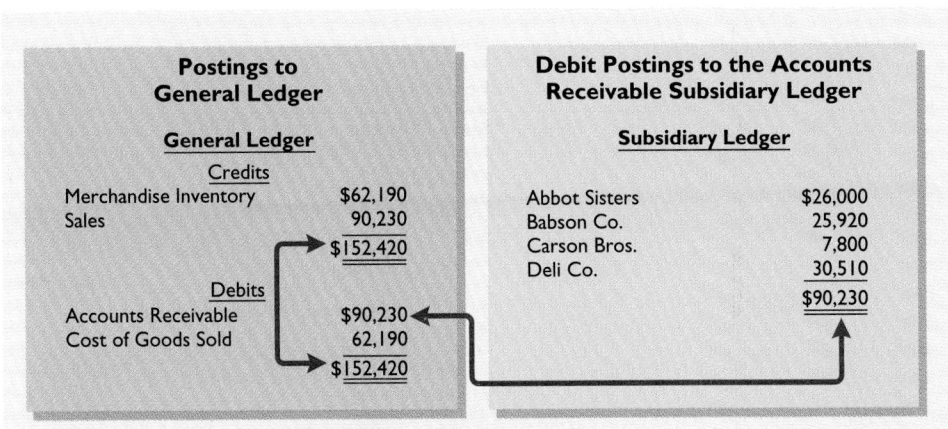

Proving the equality of the postings from the sales journal

Postings to General Ledger

General Ledger

Credits	
Merchandise Inventory	$62,190
Sales	90,230
	$152,420

Debits	
Accounts Receivable	$90,230
Cost of Goods Sold	62,190
	$152,420

Debit Postings to the Accounts Receivable Subsidiary Ledger

Subsidiary Ledger

Abbot Sisters	$26,000
Babson Co.	25,920
Carson Bros.	7,800
Deli Co.	30,510
	$90,230

Generally, a cash receipts journal includes the following columns: debit columns for cash and sales discounts; and credit columns for accounts receivable, sales, and "other" accounts. The Other Accounts category is used when the cash receipt does not involve a cash sale or a collection of accounts receivable. Under a perpetual inventory system, each sales entry is accompanied by another entry that debits Cost of Goods Sold and credits Merchandise Inventory for the cost of the merchandise sold. This entry may be recorded separately. A six-column cash receipts journal is shown in Illustration 7-10 (on page 286).

Additional credit columns may be used if they significantly reduce postings to a specific account. For example, a loan company, such as **Household International**, receives thousands of cash collections from customers. A significant saving in posting would result from using separate credit columns for Loans Receivable and Interest Revenue, rather than using the Other Accounts credit column. In contrast, a retailer that has only one interest collection a month would not find it useful to have a separate column for Interest Revenue.

Journalizing Cash Receipts Transactions

To illustrate the journalizing of cash receipts transactions, we will continue with the May transactions of Karns Wholesale Supply. Collections from customers relate to the entries recorded in the sales journal in Illustration 7-7. The entries in the cash receipts journal are based on the following cash receipts.

May 1 D. A. Karns makes an investment of $5,000 in the business.
7 Cash sales of merchandise total $1,900 (cost, $1,240).
10 A check for $10,388 is received from Abbot Sisters in payment of invoice No. 101 for $10,600 less a 2% discount.
12 Cash sales of merchandise total $2,600 (cost, $1,690).
17 A check for $11,123 is received from Babson Co. in payment of invoice No. 102 for $11,350 less a 2% discount.
22 Cash is received by signing a note for $6,000.
23 A check for $7,644 is received from Carson Bros. in full for invoice No. 103 for $7,800 less a 2% discount.
28 A check for $9,114 is received from Deli Co. in full for invoice No. 104 for $9,300 less a 2% discount.

Further information about the columns in the cash receipts journal (see Illustration 7-10) is listed on page 287.

Illustration 7-10

Journalizing and posting the cash receipts journal

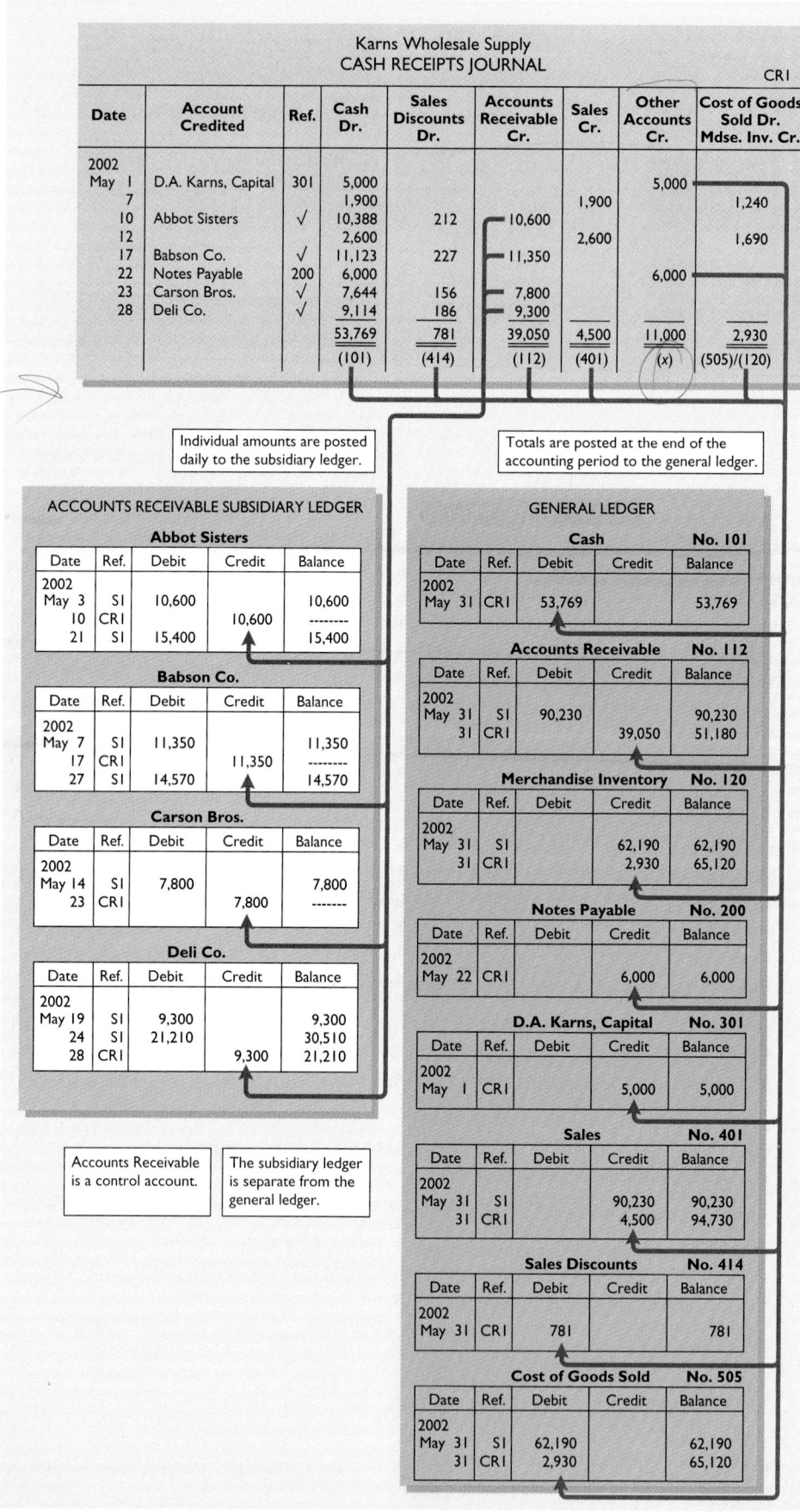

Karns Wholesale Supply
CASH RECEIPTS JOURNAL

CR1

Date	Account Credited	Ref.	Cash Dr.	Sales Discounts Dr.	Accounts Receivable Cr.	Sales Cr.	Other Accounts Cr.	Cost of Goods Sold Dr. Mdse. Inv. Cr.
2002								
May 1	D.A. Karns, Capital	301	5,000				5,000	
7			1,900			1,900		1,240
10	Abbot Sisters	√	10,388	212	10,600			
12			2,600			2,600		1,690
17	Babson Co.	√	11,123	227	11,350			
22	Notes Payable	200	6,000				6,000	
23	Carson Bros.	√	7,644	156	7,800			
28	Deli Co.	√	9,114	186	9,300			
			53,769	781	39,050	4,500	11,000	2,930
			(101)	(414)	(112)	(401)	(x)	(505)/(120)

Individual amounts are posted daily to the subsidiary ledger.

Totals are posted at the end of the accounting period to the general ledger.

ACCOUNTS RECEIVABLE SUBSIDIARY LEDGER

Abbot Sisters

Date	Ref.	Debit	Credit	Balance
2002				
May 3	S1	10,600		10,600
10	CR1		10,600	--------
21	S1	15,400		15,400

Babson Co.

Date	Ref.	Debit	Credit	Balance
2002				
May 7	S1	11,350		11,350
17	CR1		11,350	--------
27	S1	14,570		14,570

Carson Bros.

Date	Ref.	Debit	Credit	Balance
2002				
May 14	S1	7,800		7,800
23	CR1		7,800	-------

Deli Co.

Date	Ref.	Debit	Credit	Balance
2002				
May 19	S1	9,300		9,300
24	S1	21,210		30,510
28	CR1		9,300	21,210

Accounts Receivable is a control account.

The subsidiary ledger is separate from the general ledger.

GENERAL LEDGER

Cash **No. 101**

Date	Ref.	Debit	Credit	Balance
2002				
May 31	CR1	53,769		53,769

Accounts Receivable **No. 112**

Date	Ref.	Debit	Credit	Balance
2002				
May 31	S1	90,230		90,230
31	CR1		39,050	51,180

Merchandise Inventory **No. 120**

Date	Ref.	Debit	Credit	Balance
2002				
May 31	S1		62,190	62,190
31	CR1		2,930	65,120

Notes Payable **No. 200**

Date	Ref.	Debit	Credit	Balance
2002				
May 22	CR1		6,000	6,000

D.A. Karns, Capital **No. 301**

Date	Ref.	Debit	Credit	Balance
2002				
May 1	CR1		5,000	5,000

Sales **No. 401**

Date	Ref.	Debit	Credit	Balance
2002				
May 31	S1		90,230	90,230
31	CR1		4,500	94,730

Sales Discounts **No. 414**

Date	Ref.	Debit	Credit	Balance
2002				
May 31	CR1	781		781

Cost of Goods Sold **No. 505**

Date	Ref.	Debit	Credit	Balance
2002				
May 31	S1	62,190		62,190
31	CR1	2,930		65,120

Debit Columns:

1. **Cash.** The amount of cash actually received in each transaction is entered in this column. The column total indicates the total cash receipts for the month.
2. **Sales Discounts.** Karns includes a Sales Discounts column in its cash receipts journal. By doing so, it is not necessary to enter sales discount items in the general journal. As a result, the collection of an account receivable within the discount period is expressed on one line in the appropriate columns of the cash receipts journal.

Credit Columns:

3. **Accounts Receivable.** The Accounts Receivable column is used to record cash collections on account. The amount entered here is the amount to be credited to the individual customer's account.
4. **Sales.** The Sales column records all cash sales of merchandise. Cash sales of other assets (plant assets, for example) are not reported in this column.
5. **Other Accounts.** The Other Accounts column is used whenever the credit is other than to Accounts Receivable or Sales. For example, in the first entry, $5,000 is entered as a credit to D. A. Karns, Capital. This column is often referred to as the **sundry accounts column.**

HELPFUL HINT

When is an account title entered in the "Account Credited" column of the cash receipts journal?
Answer: A *subsidiary ledger* title is entered there whenever the entry involves a collection of accounts receivable. A *general ledger* account title is entered there whenever the entry involves an account that is not the subject of a special column (and an amount must be entered in the Other Accounts column). No account title is entered there if neither of the foregoing applies.

Debit and Credit Column:

6. **Cost of Goods Sold and Merchandise Inventory.** This column records debits to Cost of Goods Sold and credits to Merchandise Inventory.

In a multi-column journal, generally only one line is needed for each entry. Debit and credit amounts for each line must be equal. When the collection from Abbot Sisters on May 10 is journalized, for example, three amounts are indicated. Note also that the Account Credited column is used to identify both general ledger and subsidiary ledger account titles. General ledger accounts are illustrated in the May 1 and May 22 entries. A subsidiary account is illustrated in the May 10 entry for the collection from Abbot Sisters.

When the journalizing of a multi-column journal has been completed, the amount columns are totaled, and the totals are compared to prove the equality of debits and credits. The proof of the equality of Karns's cash receipts journal is as follows.

Illustration 7-11

Proving the equality of the cash receipts journal

Debits	
Cash	$53,769
Sales Discounts	781
Cost of Goods Sold	2,930
	$57,480

Credits	
Accounts Receivable	$39,050
Sales	4,500
Other Accounts	11,000
Merchandise Inventory	2,930
	$57,480

Totaling the columns of a journal and proving the equality of the totals is called **footing** and **cross-footing** a journal.

Posting the Cash Receipts Journal

Posting a multi-column journal involves the following steps.

STUDY OBJECTIVE 5

Indicate how a multi-column journal is posted.

1. All column totals except for the Other Accounts total are posted **once at the end of the month** to the account title(s) specified in the column heading (such as Cash or Accounts Receivable). Account numbers are entered below the column totals to show that they have been posted. Cash is posted to account No. 101, accounts receivable to account No. 112, merchandise inventory to account No. 120, sales to account No. 401, sales discounts to account No. 414, and cost of goods sold to account No. 505.
2. The **individual amounts comprising the Other Accounts total are posted separately** to the general ledger accounts specified in the Account Credited column. See, for example, the credit posting to D. A. Karns, Capital. The total amount of this column is not posted. The symbol (X) is inserted below the total to this column to indicate that the amount has not been posted.
3. The individual amounts in a column, posted in total to a control account (Accounts Receivable, in this case), are posted **daily to the subsidiary ledger** account specified in the Account Credited column. See, for example, the credit posting of $10,600 to Abbot Sisters.

The symbol **CR** is used in both the subsidiary and general ledgers to identify postings from the cash receipts journal.

Proving the Ledgers

After posting of the cash receipts journal is completed, it is necessary to prove the ledgers. As shown in Illustration 7-12, the general ledger totals are in agreement. Also, the sum of the subsidary ledger balances equals the control account balance.

Illustration 7-12

Proving the ledgers after posting the sales and the cash receipts journals

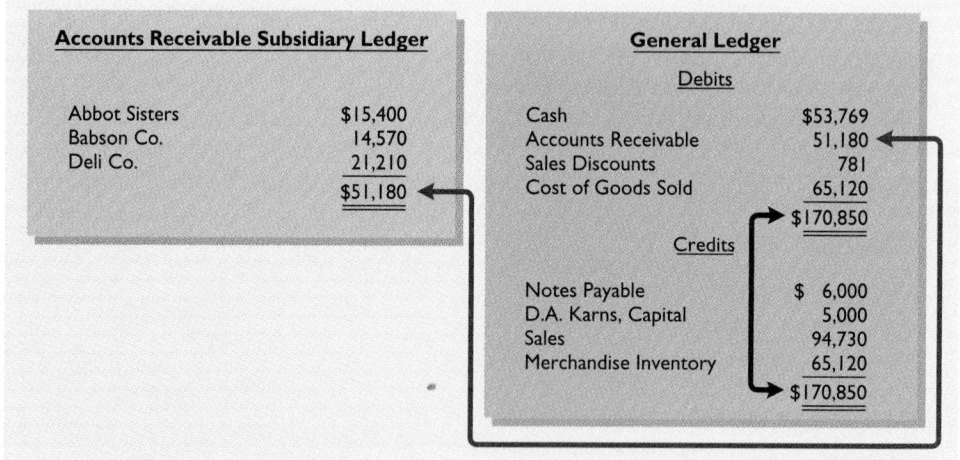

Accounts Receivable Subsidiary Ledger

Abbot Sisters	$15,400
Babson Co.	14,570
Deli Co.	21,210
	$51,180

General Ledger

Debits	
Cash	$53,769
Accounts Receivable	51,180
Sales Discounts	781
Cost of Goods Sold	65,120
	$170,850

Credits	
Notes Payable	$ 6,000
D.A. Karns, Capital	5,000
Sales	94,730
Merchandise Inventory	65,120
	$170,850

PURCHASES JOURNAL

All purchases of merchandise on account are recorded in the **purchases journal**. Each entry in this journal results in a debit to Merchandise Inventory and a credit to Accounts Payable. When a one-column purchases journal is used (as in Illustration 6-13), other types of purchases on account and cash purchases cannot be journalized in it. For example, credit purchases of equipment or supplies must be recorded in the general journal. Likewise, all cash purchases are entered in the cash payments journal. As illustrated later, where credit purchases for items other than merchandise are numerous, the purchases journal is often expanded to a multi-column format. The purchases journal for Karns Wholesale Supply is shown in Illustration 7-13.

Illustration 7-13

Journalizing and posting the purchases journal

Karns Wholesale Supply
PURCHASES JOURNAL   P1

Date	Account Credited	Terms	Ref.	Merchandise Inventory Dr. Accounts Payable Cr.
2002				
May 6	Jasper Manufacturing Inc.	2/10, n/30	✓	11,000
10	Eaton and Howe Inc.	3/10, n/30	✓	7,200
14	Fabor and Son	1/10, n/30	✓	6,900
19	Jasper Manufacturing Inc.	2/10, n/30	✓	17,500
26	Fabor and Son	1/10, n/30	✓	8,700
29	Eaton and Howe Inc.	3/10, n/30	✓	12,600
				63,900
				(120)/(201)

Individual amounts are posted daily to the subsidiary ledger.

Totals are posted at the end of the accounting period to the general ledger.

ACCOUNTS PAYABLE SUBSIDIARY LEDGER

Eaton and Howe Inc.

Date	Ref.	Debit	Credit	Balance
2002				
May 10	P1		7,200	7,200
29	P1		12,600	19,800

Fabor and Son

Date	Ref.	Debit	Credit	Balance
2002				
May 14	P1		6,900	6,900
26	P1		8,700	15,600

Jasper Manufacturing Inc.

Date	Ref.	Debit	Credit	Balance
2002				
May 6	P1		11,000	11,000
19	P1		17,500	28,500

GENERAL LEDGER

Merchandise Inventory No. 120

Date	Ref.	Debit	Credit	Balance
2002				
May 31	S1		62,190	62,190
31	CR1		2,930	65,120
31	P1	63,900		1,220

Accounts Payable No. 201

Date	Ref.	Debit	Credit	Balance
2002				
May 31	P1		63,900	63,900

The subsidiary ledger is separate from the general ledger.

Accounts Payable is a control account.

HELPFUL HINT

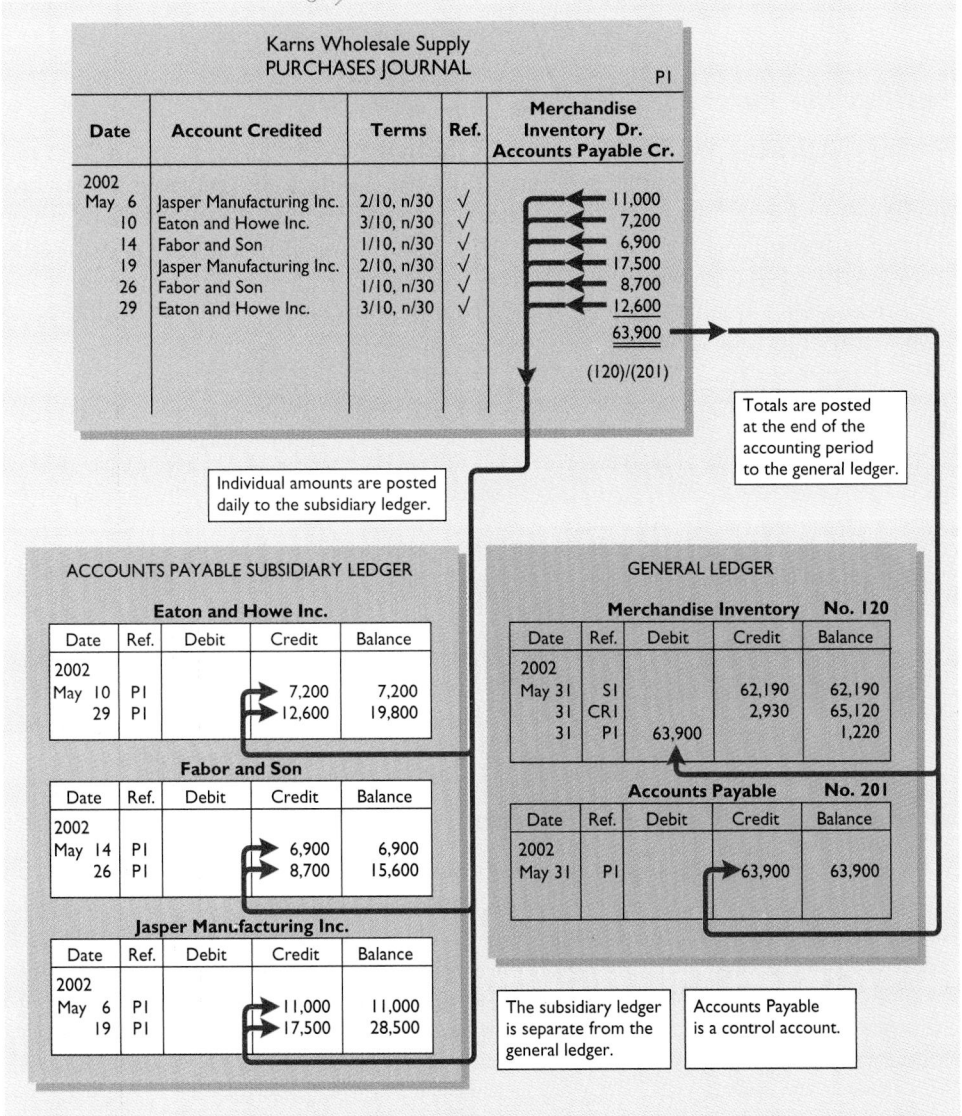

A single-column purchases journal needs only to be footed to prove the equality of debits and credits.

Journalizing Credit Purchases of Merchandise

Entries in the purchases journal are made from purchase invoices. The journalizing procedure is similar to that for a sales journal. In contrast to the sales journal, the purchases journal may not have an invoice number column, because invoices received from different suppliers will not be in numerical sequence. To assure that all purchase invoices are recorded, some companies consecutively number each invoice upon receipt and then use an internal document number column in the purchases journal.

The entries for Karns Wholesale Supply are based on the following assumed credit purchases.

Illustration 7-14

Credit purchases transactions

Date	Supplier	Amount
5/6	Jasper Manufacturing Inc.	$11,000
5/10	Eaton and Howe Inc.	7,200
5/14	Fabor and Son	6,900
5/19	Jasper Manufacturing Inc.	17,500
5/26	Fabor and Son	8,700
5/29	Eaton and Howe Inc.	12,600

HELPFUL HINT
Postings to subsidiary ledger accounts are done daily because it is often necessary to know a current balance for the subsidiary accounts.

Posting the Purchases Journal

The procedures for posting the purchases journal are similar to those for the sales journal. In this case, postings are made **daily** to the **accounts payable ledger** and **monthly** to Merchandise Inventory and Accounts Payable in the general ledger. In both ledgers, P1 is used in the reference column to show that the postings are from page 1 of the purchases journal.

Proof of the equality of the postings from the purchases journal to both ledgers is shown by the following.

Illustration 7-15

Proving the equality of the purchases journal

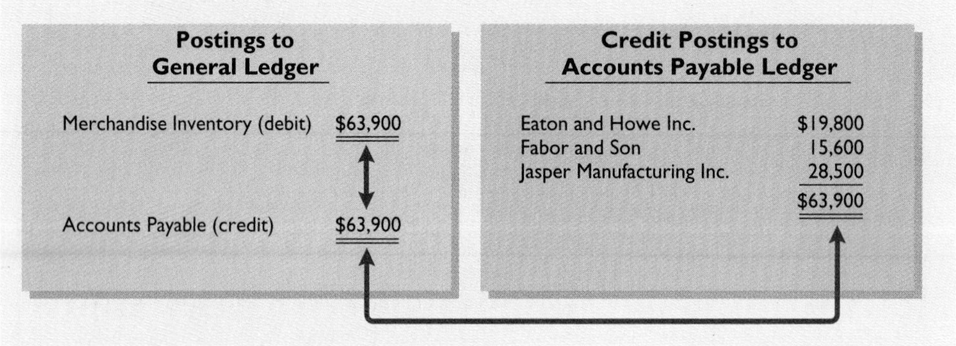

Postings to General Ledger
Merchandise Inventory (debit) $63,900
Accounts Payable (credit) $63,900
Credit Postings to Accounts Payable Ledger
Eaton and Howe Inc. $19,800
Fabor and Son 15,600
Jasper Manufacturing Inc. 28,500
$63,900

HELPFUL HINT
A multiple-column purchases journal must be footed and cross-footed to prove the equality of debits and credits.

Expanding the Purchases Journal

Some companies expand the purchases journal to include all types of purchases on account. Instead of one column for merchandise inventory and accounts payable, they use a multiple-column format. The multi-column format usually includes a credit column for accounts payable and debit columns for purchases of merchandise, of office supplies, of store supplies, and other accounts. Illustration 7-16 is an example of a multi-column purchases journal for Hanover Co. The posting procedures are similar to those illustrated earlier for posting the cash receipts journal.

Illustration 7-16

Columnar purchases journal

Hanover Co.
PURCHASES JOURNAL **P1**

Date	Account Credited	Ref.	Accounts Payable Cr.	Merchandise Inventory Dr.	Office Supplies Dr.	Store Supplies Dr.	Other Accounts Dr. Account	Ref.	Amount
2002									
June 1	Signe Audio	✓	2,000		2,000				
3	Wright Co.	✓	1,500	1,500					
5	Orange Tree Co.	✓	2,600				Equipment	157	2,600
30	Sue's Business Forms	✓	800			800			
			56,600	43,000	7,500	1,200			4,900

CASH PAYMENTS JOURNAL

All disbursements of cash are entered in a **cash payments journal**. Entries are made from prenumbered checks. Because cash payments are made for various purposes, the cash payments journal has multiple columns. A four-column journal is shown in Illustration 7-17.

ALTERNATIVE TERMINOLOGY
The cash payments journal is sometimes called the *cash disbursements journal.*

Illustration 7-17

Journalizing and posting the cash payments journal

Karns Wholesale Supply
CASH PAYMENTS JOURNAL
CP1

Date	Ck. No.	Account Debited	Ref.	Other Accounts Dr.	Accounts Payable Dr.	Merchandise Inventory Cr.	Cash Cr.
2002							
May 1	101	Prepaid Insurance	130	1,200			1,200
3	102	Mdse. Inventory	120	100			100
8	103	Mdse. Inventory	120	4,400			4,400
10	104	Jasper Manuf. Inc.	√		11,000	220	10,780
19	105	Eaton & Howe Inc.	√		7,200	216	6,984
23	106	Fabor and Son	√		6,900	69	6,831
28	107	Jasper Manuf. Inc.	√		17,500	350	17,150
30	108	D.A. Karns, Drawing	306	500			500
				6,200	42,600	855	47,945
				(x)	(201)	(120)	(101)

Individual amounts are posted daily to the subsidiary ledger.

Totals are posted at the end of the accounting period to the general ledger.

ACCOUNTS PAYABLE SUBSIDIARY LEDGER

Eaton and Howe Inc.

Date	Ref.	Debit	Credit	Balance
2002				
May 10	P1		7,200	7,200
19	CP1	7,200		-------
29	P1		12,600	12,600

Fabor and Son

Date	Ref.	Debit	Credit	Balance
2002				
May 14	P1		6,900	6,900
23	CP1	6,900		-------
26	P1		8,700	8,700

Jasper Manufacturing Inc.

Date	Ref.	Debit	Credit	Balance
2002				
May 6	P1		11,000	11,000
10	CP1	11,000		--------
19	P1		17,500	17,500
28	CP1	17,500		--------

Accounts Payable is a control account.

The subsidiary ledger is separate from the general ledger.

GENERAL LEDGER

Cash No. 101

Date	Ref.	Debit	Credit	Balance
2002				
May 31	CR1	53,769		53,769
31	CP1		47,945	5,824

Merchandise Inventory No. 120

Date	Ref.	Debit	Credit	Balance
2002				
May 3	CP1	100		100
8	CP1	4,400		4,500
31	S1		62,190	57,690
31	CR1		2,930	60,620
31	P1	63,900		3,280
31	CP1		855	2,425

Prepaid Insurance No. 130

Date	Ref.	Debit	Credit	Balance
2002				
May 1	CP1	1,200		1,200

Accounts Payable No. 201

Date	Ref.	Debit	Credit	Balance
2002				
May 31	P1		63,900	63,900
31	CP1	42,600		21,300

D.A. Karns, Drawing No. 306

Date	Ref.	Debit	Credit	Balance
2002				
May 30	CP1	500		500

Journalizing Cash Payments Transactions

The procedures for journalizing transactions in this journal are similar to those described earlier for the cash receipts journal. Each transaction is entered on one line, and for each line there must be equal debit and credit amounts. The entries in the cash payments journal in Illustration 7-17 are based on the following transactions for Karns Wholesale Supply.

May	1	Check No. 101 for $1,200 issued for the annual premium on a fire insurance policy.
	3	Check No. 102 for $100 issued in payment of freight when terms were FOB shipping point.
	8	Check No. 103 for $4,400 issued for the purchase of merchandise.
	10	Check No. 104 for $10,780 sent to Jasper Manufacturing Inc. in payment of May 6 invoice for $11,000 less a 2% discount.
	19	Check No. 105 for $6,984 mailed to Eaton and Howe Inc. in payment of May 10 invoice for $7,200 less a 3% discount.
	23	Check No. 106 for $6,831 sent to Fabor and Son in payment of May 14 invoice for $6,900 less a 1% discount.
	28	Check No. 107 for $17,150 sent to Jasper Manufacturing Inc. in payment of May 19 invoice for $17,500 less a 2% discount.
	30	Check No. 108 for $500 issued to D. A. Karns as a cash withdrawal for personal use.

Note that whenever an amount is entered in the Other Accounts column, a specific general ledger account must be identified in the Account Debited column. The entries for checks No. 101, 102, and 103 illustrate this situation. Similarly, a subsidiary account must be identified in the Account Debited column whenever an amount is entered in the Accounts Payable column. See, for example, the entry for check No. 104.

After the cash payments journal has been journalized, the columns are totaled. The totals are then balanced to prove the equality of debits and credits.

Posting the Cash Payments Journal

The procedures for posting the cash payments journal are similar to those for the cash receipts journal. The amounts recorded in the Accounts Payable column are posted individually to the subsidiary ledger and in total to the control account. Merchandise Inventory and Cash are posted only in total at the end of the month. Transactions in the Other Accounts column are posted individually to the appropriate account(s) affected. No totals are posted for this column.

The posting of the cash payments journal is shown in Illustration 7-17. Note that the symbol **CP** is used as the posting reference. After postings are completed, the equality of the debit and credit balances in the general ledger should be determined. In addition, the control account balances should agree with the subsidiary ledger total balance. The agreement of these balances is shown in Illustration 7-18.

EFFECTS OF SPECIAL JOURNALS ON GENERAL JOURNAL

Special journals for sales, purchases, and cash substantially reduce the number of entries that are made in the general journal. **Only transactions that cannot be entered in a special journal are recorded in the general journal.** For example, the general journal may be used to record such transactions as granting of credit to a customer for a sales return or allowance, granting of credit from a supplier for purchases returned, acceptance of a note receivable from a customer, and pur-

Illustration 7-18

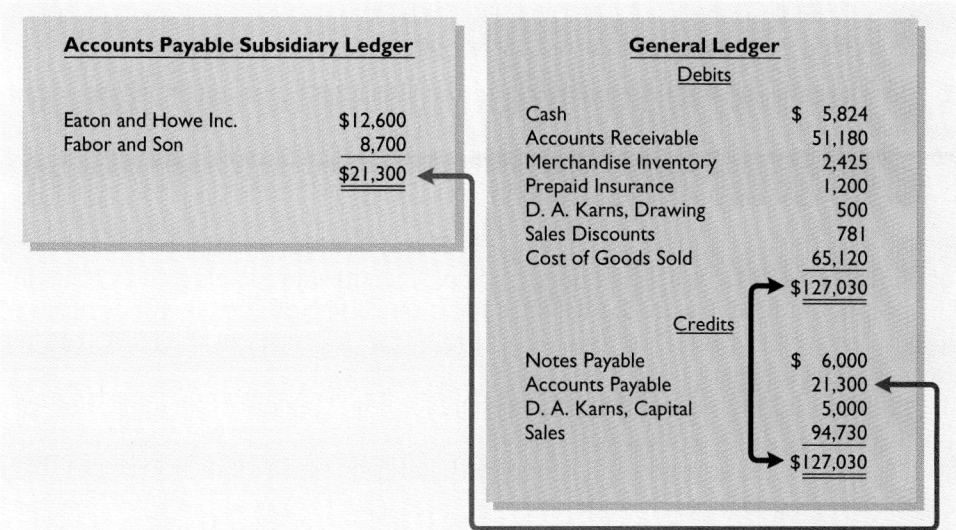

Proving the ledgers after postings from the sales, cash receipts, purchases, and cash payments journals

Accounts Payable Subsidiary Ledger

Eaton and Howe Inc.	$12,600
Fabor and Son	8,700
	$21,300

General Ledger

Debits	
Cash	$ 5,824
Accounts Receivable	51,180
Merchandise Inventory	2,425
Prepaid Insurance	1,200
D. A. Karns, Drawing	500
Sales Discounts	781
Cost of Goods Sold	65,120
	$127,030
Credits	
Notes Payable	$ 6,000
Accounts Payable	21,300
D. A. Karns, Capital	5,000
Sales	94,730
	$127,030

chase of equipment by issuing a note payable. Also, correcting, adjusting, and closing entries are made in the general journal.

The general journal has columns for date, account title and explanation, reference, and debit and credit amounts. When control and subsidiary accounts are not involved, the procedures for journalizing and posting of transactions are the

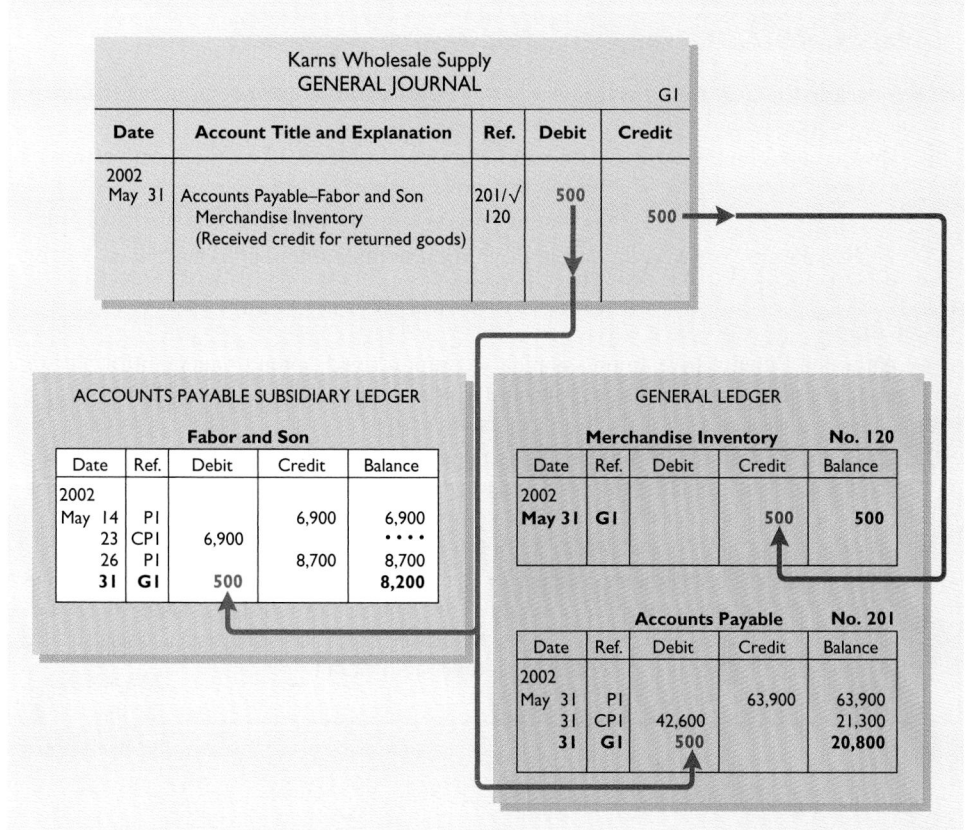

Illustration 7-19

Journalizing and posting the general journal

Karns Wholesale Supply
GENERAL JOURNAL
G1

Date	Account Title and Explanation	Ref.	Debit	Credit
2002				
May 31	Accounts Payable–Fabor and Son	201/√	500	
	Merchandise Inventory	120		500
	(Received credit for returned goods)			

ACCOUNTS PAYABLE SUBSIDIARY LEDGER

Fabor and Son

Date	Ref.	Debit	Credit	Balance
2002				
May 14	P1		6,900	6,900
23	CP1	6,900		• • • •
26	P1		8,700	8,700
31	**G1**	500		**8,200**

GENERAL LEDGER

Merchandise Inventory **No. 120**

Date	Ref.	Debit	Credit	Balance
2002				
May 31	**G1**		500	**500**

Accounts Payable **No. 201**

Date	Ref.	Debit	Credit	Balance
2002				
May 31	P1		63,900	63,900
31	CP1	42,600		21,300
31	**G1**	500		**20,800**

same as those described in earlier chapters. When control and subsidiary accounts are involved, two changes from the earlier procedures are required:

1. In **journalizing**, both the control and the subsidiary accounts must be identified.
2. In **posting**, there must be a **dual posting**: once to the control account and once to the subsidiary account.

To illustrate, assume that on May 31, Karns Wholesale Supply returns $500 of merchandise for credit to Fabor and Son. The entry in the general journal and the posting of the entry are shown in Illustration 7-19. Note that if cash is received instead of credit granted on this return, then the transaction is recorded in the cash receipts journal.

Observe in the journal that two accounts are indicated for the debit, and two postings ("201/✓") are indicated in the reference column. One amount is posted to the control account and the other to the creditor's account in the subsidiary ledger.

BEFORE YOU GO ON...

REVIEW IT

1. What types of special journals are frequently used to record transactions? Why are special journals used?
2. Explain how transactions recorded in the sales journal and the cash receipts journal are posted.
3. Indicate the types of transactions that are recorded in the general journal when special journals are used.

A LOOK BACK AT OUR FEATURE STORY

Refer back to the Feature Story about **Fidelity Investments** at the beginning of the chapter, and answer the following questions.

1. How could a highly sophisticated and computerized firm like Fidelity Investments make an embarrassing $1.3 billion accounting error?
2. Is it likely that in the future some businesses will continue to use manual systems?
3. The balance of your account at Fidelity Investments is found in its subsidiary ledger. Why do companies use subsidiary ledgers?

SOLUTION

1. Although Fidelity Investments is highly computerized, some financial information, like the computation of some gains and losses, is generated manually. When people perform such tasks, they occasionally make errors.
2. While the percentage of businesses using manual systems will likely decline, it will probably always make sense for certain businesses to use manual systems. For many start-up businesses, or businesses with few transactions, the advantages of installing a computerized system do not appear to outweigh the costs.
3. Advantages of a subsidiary ledger for a company like Fidelity are: (1) It shows transactions for one customer or creditor in a single account. (2) It frees the general ledger of excessive detail. (3) It helps locate errors in individual accounts. And (4) in manual systems it provides for a division of labor.

THE NAVIGATOR

DEMONSTRATION PROBLEM

Additional Demonstration Problem

Celine Dion Company uses a six-column cash receipts journal with the following columns: Cash (Dr.), Sales Discounts (Dr.), Accounts Receivable (Cr.), Sales (Cr.), Other Accounts (Cr.), and Cost of Goods Sold (Dr.) and Merchandise Inventory (Cr.). Cash receipts transactions for the month of July 2002 are as follows.

July 3 Cash sales total $5,800 (cost, $3,480).
5 A check for $6,370 is received from Jeltz Company in payment of an invoice dated June 26 for $6,500, terms 2/10, n/30.
9 An additional investment of $5,000 in cash is made in the business by Celine Dion, the proprietor.
10 Cash sales total $12,519 (cost, $7,511).
12 A check for $7,275 is received from R. Eliot & Co. in payment of a $7,500 invoice dated July 3, terms 3/10, n/30.
15 A customer advance of $700 cash is received for future sales.
20 Cash sales total $15,472 (cost, $9,283).
22 A check for $5,880 is received from Beck Company in payment of $6,000 invoice dated July 13, terms 2/10, n/30.
29 Cash sales total $17,660 (cost, $10,596).
31 Cash of $200 is received on interest earned for July.

Instructions

(a) Journalize the transactions in the cash receipts journal.
(b) Contrast the posting of the Accounts Receivable and Other Accounts columns.

ACTION PLAN

- Record all cash receipts in the cash receipts journal.
- The "account credited" indicates items posted individually to the subsidiary ledger or general ledger.
- Record cash sales in the cash receipts journal—not in the sales journal.
- The total debits must equal the total credits.

SOLUTION TO DEMONSTRATION PROBLEM

(a)

Celine Dion Company
CASH RECEIPTS JOURNAL **CR1**

Date	Account Credited	Ref.	Cash Dr.	Sales Discounts Dr.	Accounts Receivable Cr.	Sales Cr.	Other Accounts Cr.	Cost of Goods Sold Dr. Mdse. Inv. Cr.
2002								
7/3			5,800			5,800		3,480
5	Jeltz Company		6,370	130	6,500			
9	Celine Dion, Capital		5,000				5,000	
10			12,519			12,519		7,511
12	R. Eliot & Co.		7,275	225	7,500			
15	Unearned Revenues		700				700	
20			15,472			15,472		9,283
22	Beck Company		5,880	120	6,000			
29			17,660			17,660		10,596
31	Interest Revenue		200				200	
			76,876	475	20,000	51,451	5,900	30,870

(b) The Accounts Receivable column is posted as a credit to Accounts Receivable. The individual amounts are credited to the customers' accounts identified in the Account Credited column, which are maintained in the accounts receivable subsidiary ledger.

The amounts in the Other Accounts column are only posted individually. They are credited to the account titles identified in the Account Credited column.

THE NAVIGATOR

SUMMARY OF STUDY OBJECTIVES

1. *Identify the basic principles of accounting information systems.* The basic principles in developing an accounting information system are cost effectiveness, useful output, and flexibility.

2. *Explain the major phases in the development of an accounting system.* The major phases in the development of an accounting system are analysis, design, implementation, and follow-up.

3. *Describe the nature and purpose of a subsidiary ledger.* A subsidiary ledger is a group of accounts with a common characteristic. It facilitates the recording process by freeing the general ledger from details of individual balances.

4. *Explain how special journals are used in journalizing.* A special journal is used to group similar types of transactions. In a special journal, generally only one line is used to record a complete transaction.

5. *Indicate how a multi-column journal is posted.* In posting a multi-column journal:

(a) All column totals except for the Other Accounts column are posted once at the end of the month to the account title specified in the column heading.

(b) The total of the Other Accounts column is not posted. Instead, the individual amounts comprising the total are posted separately to the general ledger accounts specified in the Account Credited column.

(c) The individual amounts in a column posted in total to a control account are posted daily to the subsidiary ledger accounts specified in the Account Credited column.

THE NAVIGATOR

Key Term Matching Activity

GLOSSARY

Accounting information system A system that collects and processes transaction data, and disseminates financial information to interested parties. (p. 276).

Accounts payable (creditors') subsidiary ledger A subsidiary ledger that contains accounts of individual creditors. (p. 279).

Accounts receivable (customers') subsidiary ledger A subsidiary ledger that contains individual customer accounts. (p. 279).

Cash payments journal A special journal used to record all cash paid. (p. 291).

Cash receipts journal A special journal used to record all cash received. (p. 284).

Control account An account in the general ledger that controls a subsidiary ledger. (p. 279).

Manual accounting system A system in which each of the steps in the accounting cycle is performed by hand. (p. 278).

Purchases journal A special journal used to record all purchases of merchandise on account. (p. 288).

Sales journal A special journal used to record all sales of merchandise on account. (p. 282).

Special journal A journal that is used to record similar types of transactions, such as all credit sales. (p. 282).

Subsidiary ledger A group of accounts with a common characteristic. (p. 279).

Chapter 7 Self-Test

SELF-STUDY QUESTIONS

Answers are at the end of the chapter.

(SO 1) **1.** The basic principles of an accounting information system include all of the following *except*:
a. cost effectiveness.
b. flexibility.
c. useful output.
d. periodicity.

(SO 2) **2.** Which of the following is *not* a major phase in the development of an accounting information system?
a. Design.
b. Responsiveness.
c. Implementation.
d. Follow-up.

(SO 3) **3.** Which of the following is *incorrect* concerning subsidiary ledgers?
a. The purchases ledger is a common subsidiary ledger for creditor accounts.
b. The accounts receivable ledger is a subsidiary ledger.
c. A subsidiary ledger is a group of accounts with a common characteristic.
d. An advantage of the subsidiary ledger is that it permits a division of labor in posting.

4. A sales journal will be used for: (SO 4)

	Credit Sales	Cash Sales	Sales Discounts
a.	no	yes	yes
b.	yes	no	yes
c.	yes	no	no
d.	yes	yes	no

5. Which of the following statements is correct? (SO 5)
a. The sales discount column is included in the cash receipts journal.

b. The purchases journal records all purchases of merchandise whether for cash or on account.
c. The cash receipts journal records sales on account.
d. Merchandise returned by the buyer is recorded by the seller in the purchases journal.

(SO 5) **6.** Which of the following is *incorrect* concerning the posting of the cash receipts journal?
a. The total of the Other Accounts column is not posted.
b. All column totals except the total for the Other Accounts column are posted once at the end of the month to the account title(s) specified in the column heading.
c. The totals of all columns are posted daily to the accounts specified in the column heading.
d. The individual amounts in a column posted in total to a control account are posted daily to the subsidiary ledger account specified in the Account Credited column.

(SO 5) **7.** Postings from the purchases journal to the subsidiary ledger are generally made:
a. yearly.
b. monthly.
c. weekly.
d. daily.

8. Which statement is *incorrect* regarding the general journal? (SO 4)
a. Only transactions that cannot be entered in a special journal are recorded in the general journal.
b. Dual postings are always required in the general journal.
c. The general journal may be used to record acceptance of a note receivable in payment of an account receivable.
d. Correcting, adjusting, and closing entries are made in the general journal.

9. When special journals are used: (SO 4)
a. all purchase transactions are recorded in the purchases journal.
b. all cash received, except from cash sales, is recorded in the cash receipts journal.
c. all cash disbursements are recorded in the cash payments journal.
d. a general journal is not necessary.

10. If a customer returns goods for credit, an entry is normally made in the: (SO 4)
a. cash payments journal.
b. sales journal.
c. general journal.
d. cash receipts journal.

☑ THE NAVIGATOR

QUESTIONS

1. (a) What is an accounting information system? (b) "An accounting information system applies only to a manual system." Do you agree? Explain.

2. Certain principles should be followed in the development of an accounting information system. Identify and explain each of the principles.

3. Hawkeye Company might change its accounting system for accounts receivable billing. At present, the procedure is performed manually by three clerks. A consultant has recommended that a new computer and related software be purchased for $1,000,000. What basic principle of designing and developing an effective accounting system might be violated by this proposal?

4. There are four phases in the life cycle of an accounting system. Identify and briefly explain each phase.

5. What are the advantages of using subsidiary ledgers?

6. (a) When are postings normally made to (1) the subsidiary accounts and (2) the general ledger control accounts? (b) Describe the relationship between a control account and a subsidiary ledger.

7. Identify and explain the four specific journals discussed in the chapter. List an advantage of using each of these journals rather than using only a general journal.

8. A. Mega Company uses special journals. A sale made on account to K. Hansen for $435 was recorded in a sales journal. A few days later, K. Hansen returns $70 worth of merchandise for credit. Where should A. Mega Company record the sales return? Why?

9. A $500 purchase of merchandise on account from Julia Company was properly recorded in the purchases journal. When posted, however, the amount recorded in the subsidiary ledger was $50. How might this error be discovered?

10. Why would special journals used in different businesses not be identical in format? Can you think of a business that would maintain a cash receipts journal but not include a column for accounts receivable?

11. The cash and the accounts receivable columns in the cash receipts journal were mistakenly overadded by $4,000 at the end of the month. (a) Will the customers' ledger agree with the Accounts Receivable control account? (b) Assuming no other errors, will the trial balance totals be equal?

12. One column total of a special journal is posted at month-end to only two general ledger accounts. One of these two accounts is Accounts Receivable. What is the name of this special journal? What is the other general ledger account to which that same month-end total is posted?

13. In what journal would the following transactions be recorded? (Assume that a two-column sales journal and a single-column purchases journal are used.)
(a) Recording of depreciation expense for the year.
(b) Credit given to a customer for merchandise purchased on credit and returned.
(c) Sales of merchandise for cash.
(d) Sales of merchandise on account.

(e) Collection of cash on account from a customer.
(f) Purchase of office supplies on account.

14. In what journal would the following transactions be recorded? (Assume that a two-column sales journal and a single-column purchases journal are used.)
(a) Cash received from signing a note payable.
(b) Investment of cash by the owner of the business.
(c) Closing of the expense accounts at the end of the year.
(d) Purchase of merchandise on account.
(e) Credit received for merchandise purchased and returned to supplier.
(f) Payment of cash on account due a supplier.

15. What transactions might be included in a multiple-column purchases journal that would not be included in a single-column purchases journal?

16. Give an example of a transaction in the general journal that causes an entry to be posted twice (i.e., to two accounts), one in the general ledger, the other in the subsidiary ledger. Does this affect the debit/credit equality of the general ledger?

17. Give some examples of appropriate general journal transactions for an organization using special journals.

BRIEF EXERCISES

Identify basic principles of accounting information system development.
(SO 1)

BE7-1 Indicate whether each of the following statements is true or false.

1. When designing an accounting system, we need to think about the needs and knowledge of both the top management and various other users.
2. When the environment changes as a result of technological advances, increased competition, or government regulation, an accounting system does not have to be sufficiently flexible to meet the changes in order to save money.
3. In developing an accounting system, cost is relevant. The system must be cost-effective. That is, the benefits obtained from the information disseminated must outweigh the cost of providing it.

Identify major phases in accounting system development.
(SO 2)

BE7-2 The development of an accounting system involves four phases: analysis, design, implementation, and follow-up. Identify the statement that best describes each of these four phases.

1. Determining internal and external information needs, identifying information sources and the needs for controls, and studying alternatives.
2. Evaluation and monitoring of effectiveness and efficiency, and correction of weaknesses, implementation, and design.
3. Creation of forms and documents, selection of procedures, and preparation of job descriptions.
4. Implementing new or revised documents, procedures, reports, and processing equipment; hiring and training personnel through a start-up or transition period.

Identify subsidiary ledger balances.
(SO 3)

BE7-3 Presented below is information related to Bradley Company for its first month of operations. Identify the balançes that appear in the accounts receivable subsidiary ledger and the accounts receivable balance that appears in the general ledger at the end of January.

Credit Sales			Cash Collections		
Jan. 7	Avon Co.	$8,000	Jan. 17	Avon Co.	$7,000
15	Barto Co.	6,000	24	Barto Co.	5,000
23	Cecil Co.	9,000	29	Cecil Co.	9,000

Identify subsidiary ledger accounts.
(SO 3)

BE7-4 Identify in what ledger (general or subsidiary) each of the following accounts is shown.

1. Rent Expense
2. Accounts Receivable—Olsen
3. Notes Payable
4. Accounts Payable—Kerns

Identify special journals.
(SO 4)

BE7-5 Identify the journal in which each of the following transaction is recorded.

1. Cash sales
2. Owner withdrawal of cash
3. Cash purchase of land
4. Credit sales
5. Purchase of merchandise on account
6. Receipt of cash for services performed

Identify entries to cash receipts journal.
(SO 4)

BE7-6 Indicate whether each of the following debits and credits is included in the cash receipts journal. (Use "Yes" or "No" to answer this question.)

1. Debit to Sales
2. Credit to Merchandise Inventory
3. Credit to Accounts Receivable
4. Debit to Accounts Payable

BE7-7 Steering Computer Components Inc. uses a multi-column cash receipts journal. Indicate which column(s) is/are posted only in total, only daily, or both in total and daily.

Indicate postings to cash receipts journal. (SO 5)

1. Accounts Receivable
2. Sales Discounts
3. Cash
4. Other Accounts

BE7-8 Cohen Co. uses special journals and a general journal. Identify the journal in which each of the following transactions is recorded.

Identify transactions for special journals. (SO 4)

(a) Purchased equipment on account.
(b) Purchased merchandise on account.
(c) Paid utility expense in cash.
(d) Sold merchandise on account.

BE7-9 Identify the special journal(s) in which the following column headings appear.

Identify transactions for special journals. (SO 4)

1. Sales Discounts Dr.
2. Accounts Receivable Cr.
3. Cash Dr.
4. Sales Cr.
5. Merchandise Inventory Dr.

EXERCISES

E7-1 Yan Company uses both special journals and a general journal as described in this chapter. On June 30, after all monthly postings had been completed, the Accounts Receivable control account in the general ledger had a debit balance of $350,000; the Accounts Payable control account had a credit balance of $87,000.

Determine control account balances, and explain posting of special journals. (SO 3, 5)

The July transactions recorded in the special journals are summarized below. No entries affecting accounts receivable and accounts payable were recorded in the general journal for July.

Sales journal	Total sales $161,400
Purchases journal	Total purchases $54,360
Cash receipts journal	Accounts receivable column total $141,000
Cash payments journal	Accounts payable column total $47,500

Instructions

(a) What is the balance of the Accounts Receivable control account after the monthly postings on July 31?
(b) What is the balance of the Accounts Payable control account after the monthly postings on July 31?
(c) To what account(s) is the column total of $161,400 in the sales journal posted?
(d) To what account(s) is the accounts receivable column total of $144,000 in the cash receipts journal posted?

E7-2 Presented below is the subsidiary accounts receivable account of Warren Moyer.

Explain postings to subsidiary ledger. (SO 3)

Date	Ref.	Debit	Credit	Balance
2002				
Sept. 2	S31	61,000		61,000
9	G4		14,000	47,000
27	CR8		47,000	—

Instructions

Write a memo that explains each transaction.

E7-3 On September 1 the balance of the Accounts Receivable control account in the general ledger of Odesto Company was $11,960. The customers' subsidiary ledger contained account balances as follows: Edmonds $2,440, Park $2,640, Roemer $2,060, Schulz $4,820. At the end of September the various journals contained the following information.

Post various journals to control and subsidiary accounts. (SO 3, 5)

Sales journal: Sales to Schulz $800; to Edmonds $1,350; to Henry $1,030; to Roemer $1,100.

Cash receipts journal: Cash received from Roemer $1,310; from Schulz $2,300; from Henry $410; from Park $1,800; from Edmonds $1,240.

General journal: An allowance is granted to Schulz $220.

Instructions

(a) Set up control and subsidiary accounts and enter the beginning balances. Do not construct the journals.
(b) Post the various journals. Post the items as individual items or as totals, whichever would be the appropriate procedure. (No sales discounts given.)
(c) Prepare a list of customers and prove the agreement of the controlling account with the subsidiary ledger at September 30, 2002.

Record transactions in sales and purchases journal.
(SO 3, 4)

E7-4 Hurley Company uses special journals and a general journal. The following transactions occurred during September 2002.

Sept. 2 Sold merchandise on account to S. Rusch, invoice no. 101, $480, terms n/30. The cost of the merchandise sold was $300.
10 Purchased merchandise on account from L. Dayne $600, terms 2/10, n/30.
12 Purchased office equipment on account from B. Piazza $6,500.
21 Sold merchandise on account to L. Perez, invoice no. 102 for $800, terms 2/10, n/30. The cost of the merchandise sold was $480.
25 Purchased merchandise on account from F. Sage $900, terms n/30.
27 Sold merchandise to M. Deitrich for $700 cash. The cost of the merchandise sold was $420.

Instructions

(a) Draw a sales journal (see Illustration 7-8) and a single-column purchase journal (see Illustration 7-13). (Use page 1 for each journal.)
(b) Record the transaction(s) for September that should be journalized in the sales journal and the purchases journal.

Record transactions in cash receipts and cash payments journal.
(SO 3, 4)

E7-5 Pena Co. uses special journals and a general journal. The following transactions occurred during May 2002.

May 1 R. Pena invested $60,000 cash in the business.
2 Sold merchandise to J. Simon for $6,000 cash. The cost of the merchandise sold was $4,200.
3 Purchased merchandise for $9,000 from L. M. Farr using check no. 101.
14 Paid salary to S. Little $700 by issuing check no. 102.
16 Sold merchandise on account to B. Jones for $900, terms n/30. The cost of the merchandise sold was $630.
22 A check of $9,000 is received from R. Dusto in full for invoice 101; no discount given.

Instructions

(a) Draw a multiple-column cash receipts journal (see Illustration 7-10) and a multiple-column cash payments journal (see Illustration 7-17). (Use page 1 for each journal.)
(b) Record the transaction(s) for May that should be journalized in the cash receipts journal and cash payments journal.

Explain journalizing in cash journals.
(SO 4)

E7-6 Abbott Company uses the columnar cash journals illustrated in the textbook. In April, the following selected cash transactions occurred.

A) cash receit/ disbursments

b) just say which column

1. Made a refund to a customer for the return of damaged goods.
2. Received collection from customer within the 3% discount period.
3. Purchased merchandise for cash.
4. Paid a creditor within the 3% discount period.
5. Received collection from customer after the 3% discount period had expired.
6. Paid freight on merchandise purchased.
7. Paid cash for office equipment.
8. Received cash refund from supplier for merchandise returned.
9. Withdrew cash for personal use of owner.
10. Made cash sales.

Instructions

Indicate **(a)** the journal, and **(b)** the columns in the journal that should be used in recording each transaction.

Journalize transactions in general journal and post.
(SO 3, 4)

E7-7 Santiago Company has the following selected transactions during March.

Mar.	2	Purchased equipment costing $6,000 from Briggs Company on account.
	5	Received credit memorandum for $300 from Sanchez Company for merchandise damaged in shipment to Santiago.
	7	Issued a credit memorandum for $400 to Sparks Company for merchandise the customer returned. The returned merchandise had a cost of $260.

Santiago Company uses a one-column purchases journal, a sales journal, the columnar cash journals used in the text, and a general journal.

Instructions

(a) Journalize the transactions in the general journal.
(b) In a brief memo to the president of Santiago Company, explain the postings to the control and subsidiary accounts.

Indicate journalizing in special journals.
(SO 4)

E7-8 Below are some typical transactions incurred by Heide Company.

1. Payment of creditors on account.
2. Return of merchandise sold for credit.
3. Collection on account from customers.
4. Sale of land for cash.
5. Sale of merchandise on account.
6. Sale of merchandise for cash.
7. Received credit for merchandise purchased on credit.
8. Sales discount taken on goods sold.
9. Payment of employee wages.
10. Income summary closed to owner's capital.
11. Depreciation on building.
12. Purchase of office supplies for cash.
13. Purchase of merchandise on account.

Instructions

For each transaction, indicate whether it would normally be recorded in a cash receipts journal, cash payments journal, sales journal, single-column purchases journal, or general journal.

Explain posting to control account and subsidiary ledger.
(SO 3, 5)

E7-9 The general ledger of Williams Company contained the following Accounts Payable control account (in T-account form). Also shown is the related subsidiary ledger.

GENERAL LEDGER

Accounts Payable

Feb. 15	General journal	1,400	Feb. 1	Balance	26,025
28	?	?	5	General journal	265
			11	General journal	550
			28	Purchases	13,900
			Feb. 28	Balance	9,840

ACCOUNTS PAYABLE LEDGER

Sealy

	Feb. 28 Bal. 4,600

Gates

	Feb. 28 Bal. 2,000

Wolcott

	Feb. 28 Bal. ?

Instructions

(a) Indicate the missing posting reference and amount in the control account, and the missing ending balance in the subsidiary ledger.
(b) Indicate the amounts in the control account that were dual-posted (i.e., posted to the control account and the subsidiary accounts).

Prepare purchases and general journals.
(SO 3, 4)

E7-10 Selected accounts from the ledgers of Juan Perez Company at July 31 showed the following.

GENERAL LEDGER

Store Equipment No. 153

Date	Explanation	Ref.	Debit	Credit	Balance
July 1		G1	3,600		3,600

Accounts Payable No. 201

Date	Explanation	Ref.	Debit	Credit	Balance
July 1		G1		3,600	3,600
15		G1		400	4,000
18		G1	100		3,900
25		G1	200		3,700
31		P1		8,700	12,400

Merchandise Inventory No. 120

Date	Explanation	Ref.	Debit	Credit	Balance
July 15		G1	400		400
18		G1		100	300
25		G1		200	100
31		P1	8,400		8,500

ACCOUNTS PAYABLE LEDGER

Alou Equipment Co.

Date	Explanation	Ref.	Debit	Credit	Balance
July 1		G1		3,600	3,600

Dunlap Co.

Date	Explanation	Ref.	Debit	Credit	Balance
July 14		P1		1,100	1,100
25		G1	200		900

Benton Co.

Date	Explanation	Ref.	Debit	Credit	Balance
July 3		P1		2,000	2,000
20		P1		700	2,700

Emerick Co.

Date	Explanation	Ref.	Debit	Credit	Balance
July 12		P1		500	500
21		P1		600	1,100

Comerica Materials

Date	Explanation	Ref.	Debit	Credit	Balance
July 17		P1		1,400	1,400
18		G1	100		1,300
29		P1		2,100	3,400

Galant Transit

Date	Explanation	Ref.	Debit	Credit	Balance
July 15		G1		400	400

Instructions

From the data prepare:

(a) the single-column purchases journal for July.
(b) the general journal entries for July.

Determine correct posting amount to control account.
(SO 5)

E7-11 Valdez Products uses both special journals and a general journal as described in this chapter. Valdez also posts customers' accounts in the accounts receivable subsidiary ledger. The postings for the most recent month are included in the subsidiary T accounts below.

Ellie

Bal.	340	250
	200	

Rambo

Bal.	150	150
	290	

Panos

Bal.	–0–	145
	145	

Tenant

Bal.	120	120
	190	
	170	

Instructions

Determine the correct amount of the end-of-month posting from the sales journal to the Accounts Receivable control account.

PROBLEMS: SET A

Journalize transactions in cash receipts journal; post to control account and subsidiary ledger.
(SO 3, 4, 5)

Peachtree

P7-1A Lemon Company's chart of accounts includes the following selected accounts.

101 Cash	401 Sales
112 Accounts Receivable	414 Sales Discounts
120 Merchandise Inventory	505 Cost of Goods Sold
301 F. Lemon, Capital	

On April 1 the accounts receivable ledger of Lemon Company showed the following balances: Horner $1,550, Harris $1,200, Northeast Co. $2,900, and Smith $1,700. The April transactions involving the receipt of cash were as follows.

Apr. 1 The owner, F. Lemon, invested additional cash in the business $6,000.
4 Received check for payment of account from Smith less 2% cash discount.
5 Received check for $620 in payment of invoice no. 307 from Northeast Co.
8 Made cash sales of merchandise totaling $7,245. The cost of the merchandise sold was $4,347.
10 Received check for $800 in payment of invoice no. 309 from Horner.
11 Received cash refund from a supplier for damaged merchandise $550.
23 Received check for $1,500 in payment of invoice no. 310 from Northeast Co.
29 Received check for payment of account from Harris.

Instructions

(a) Journalize the transactions above in a six-column cash receipts journal with columns for Cash Dr., Sales Discounts Dr., Accounts Receivable Cr., Sales Cr., Other Accounts Cr., and Cost of Goods Sold Dr./Merchandise Inventory Cr. Foot and crossfoot the journal.

(a) Balancing totals $19,615

(b) Insert the beginning balances in the Accounts Receivable control and subsidiary accounts, and post the April transactions to these accounts.

(c) Prove the agreement of the control account and subsidiary account balances.

(c) Accounts Receivable $1,530

Journalize transactions in cash payments journal; post to control account and subsidiary ledgers.
(SO 3, 4, 5)

P7-2A Simpson Company's chart of accounts includes the following selected accounts.

101 Cash	201 Accounts Payable
120 Merchandise Inventory	306 L. Simpson, Drawing
130 Prepaid Insurance	505 Cost of Goods Sold
157 Equipment	

On October 1 the accounts payable ledger of Simpson Company showed the following balances: Hester Company $1,700, Milo Co. $2,500, Ontario Co. $1,400, and Pagan Company $3,700. The October transactions involving the payment of cash were as follows.

Oct. 1 Purchased merchandise, check no. 63, $700.
3 Purchased equipment, check no. 64, $800.
5 Paid Hester Company balance due of $1,700, less 2% discount, check no. 65, $1,666.
10 Purchased merchandise, check no. 66, $2,250.
15 Paid Ontario Co. balance due of $1,400, check no. 67.
16 L. Simpson, the owner, pays his personal insurance premium of $400, check no. 68.
19 Paid Milo Co. in full for invoice no. 610, $1,400 less 2% cash discount, check no. 69, $1,372.
29 Paid Pagan Company in full for invoice no. 264, $2,600, check no. 70.

Instructions

(a) Balancing totals $11,250

(c) Accounts Payable $2,200

(a) Journalize the transactions above in a four-column cash payments journal with columns for Other Accounts Dr., Accounts Payable Dr., Merchandise Inventory Cr., and Cash Cr. Foot and crossfoot the journal.

(b) Insert the beginning balances in the Accounts Payable control and subsidiary accounts, and post the October transactions to these accounts.

(c) Prove the agreement of the control account and the subsidiary account balances.

Journalize transactions in multi-column purchases journal; post to the general and subsidiary ledgers.
(SO 3, 4, 5)

Peachtree

P7-3A The chart of accounts of Hernandez Company includes the following selected accounts.

112 Accounts Receivable	401 Sales
120 Merchandise Inventory	412 Sales Returns and Allowances
126 Supplies	505 Cost of Goods Sold
157 Equipment	610 Advertising Expense
201 Accounts Payable	

In July the following selected transactions were completed. All purchases and sales were on account. The cost of all merchandise sold was 70% of the sales price.

July	1	Purchased merchandise from Denton Company $7,000.
	2	Received freight bill from Johnson Shipping on Denton purchase $400.
	3	Made sales to Lyons Company $1,300, and to Franklin Bros. $1,900.
	5	Purchased merchandise from Grant Company $3,200.
	8	Received credit on merchandise returned to Grant Company $300.
	13	Purchased store supplies from Brent Supply $720.
	15	Purchased merchandise from Denton Company $3,600 and from Ruiz Company $2,900.
	16	Made sales to Martin Company $3,450 and to Franklin Bros. $1,570.
	18	Received bill for advertising from Marlin Advertisements $600.
	21	Sales were made to Lyons Company $310 and to Randee Company $2,300.
	22	Granted allowance to Lyons Company for merchandise damaged in shipment $40.
	24	Purchased merchandise from Grant Company $3,000.
	26	Purchased equipment from Brent Supply $600.
	28	Received freight bill from Johnson Shipping on Grant purchase of July 24, $380.
	30	Sales were made to Martin Company $4,900.

Instructions

(a) Purchases journal—Accounts Payable $22,400
Sales journal $15,730

(c) Accounts Receivable $15,690
Accounts Payable $22,100

(a) Journalize the transactions above in a purchases journal, a sales journal, and a general journal. The purchases journal should have the following column headings: Date, Account Credited (Debited), Ref., Other Accounts Dr., and Merchandise Inventory Dr./Accounts Payable Cr.

(b) Post to both the general and subsidiary ledger accounts. (Assume that all accounts have zero beginning balances.)

(c) Prove the agreement of the control and subsidiary accounts.

Journalize transactions in special journals.
(SO 3, 4, 5)

P7-4A Selected accounts from the chart of accounts of Clark Company are shown below.

101 Cash	401 Sales
112 Accounts Receivable	412 Sales Returns and Allowances
120 Merchandise Inventory	414 Sales Discounts
126 Supplies	505 Cost of Goods Sold
157 Equipment	726 Salaries Expense
201 Accounts Payable	

The cost of all merchandise sold was 60% of the sales price. During January, Clark completed the following transactions.

Jan.	3	Purchased merchandise on account from Bell Co. $10,000.
	4	Purchased supplies for cash $80.
	4	Sold merchandise on account to Gilbert $7,250, invoice no. 371, terms 1/10, n/30.
	5	Issued a debit memorandum to Bell Co. and returned $300 worth of damaged goods.
	6	Made cash sales for the week totaling $3,150.
	8	Purchased merchandise on account from Law Co. $4,500.
	9	Sold merchandise on account to Mays Corp. $5,800, invoice no. 372, terms 1/10, n/30.
	11	Purchased merchandise on account from Hoble Co. $3,700.
	13	Paid in full Bell Co. on account less a 2% discount.
	13	Made cash sales for the week totaling $5,340.
	15	Received payment from Mays Corp. for invoice no. 372.
	15	Paid semi-monthly salaries of $14,300 to employees.
	17	Received payment from Gilbert for invoice no. 371.
	17	Sold merchandise on account to Amber Co. $1,200, invoice no. 373, terms 1/10, n/30.
	19	Purchased equipment on account from Johnson Corp. $5,500.
	20	Cash sales for the week totaled $3,200.
	20	Paid in full Law Co. on account less a 2% discount.
	23	Purchased merchandise on account from Bell Co. $7,800.
	24	Purchased merchandise on account from Levine Corp. $4,690.
	27	Made cash sales for the week totaling $3,730.
	30	Received payment from Amber Co. for invoice no. 373.
	31	Paid semi-monthly salaries of $13,200 to employees.
	31	Sold merchandise on account to Gilbert $9,330, invoice no. 374, terms 1/10, n/30.

Clark Company uses the following journals.

1. Sales journal.
2. Single-column purchases journal.
3. Cash receipts journal with columns for Cash Dr., Sales Discounts Dr., Accounts Receivable Cr., Sales Cr., Other Accounts Cr., and Cost of Goods Sold Dr./Merchandise Inventory Cr.
4. Cash payments journal with columns for Other Accounts Dr., Accounts Payable Dr., Merchandise Inventory Cr., and Cash Cr.
5. General journal.

Instructions

Using the selected accounts provided:

(a) Record the January transactions in the appropriate journal noted.
(b) Foot and crossfoot all special journals.
(c) Show how postings would be made by placing ledger account numbers and checkmarks as needed in the journals. (Actual posting to ledger accounts is not required.)

(a) Sales journal $23,580
Purchases journal $30,690
Cash receipts journal balancing total $29,670
Cash payments journal balancing total $41,780

P7-5A Presented below are the purchases and cash payments journals for Collins Co. for its first month of operations.

Journalize in sales and cash receipts journals; post; prepare a trial balance; prove control to subsidiary; prepare adjusting entries; prepare an adjusted trial balance.
(SO 3, 4, 5)

Peachtree

PURCHASES JOURNAL **P1**

Date		Account Credited	Ref.	Merchandise Inventory Dr. Accounts Payable Cr.
July	4	J. Dixon		6,800
	5	W. Engel		7,500
	11	R. Gamble		3,920
	13	M. Hill		15,300
	20	D. Jacob		8,800
				42,320

CASH PAYMENTS JOURNAL **CP1**

Date	Account Debited	Ref.	Other Accounts Dr.	Accounts Payable Dr.	Merchandise Inventory Cr.	Cash Cr.
July 4	Store Supplies		600			600
10	W. Engel			7,500	75	7,425
11	Prepaid Rent		6,000			6,000
15	J. Dixon			6,800		6,800
19	Collins, Drawing		2,500			2,500
21	M. Hill			15,300	153	15,147
			9,100	29,600	228	38,472

In addition, the following transactions have not been journalized for July. The cost of all merchandise sold was 65% of the sales price.

July 1 The founder, R. Collins, invests $80,000 in cash.
6 Sell merchandise on account to Hardy Co. $5,400 terms 1/10, n/30.
7 Make cash sales totaling $4,000.
8 Sell merchandise on account to D. Wasburn $3,600, terms 1/10, n/30.
10 Sell merchandise on account to L. Lemansky $4,900, terms 1/10, n/30.
13 Receive payment in full from D. Wasburn.
16 Receive payment in full from L. Lemansky.
20 Receive payment in full from Hardy Co.
21 Sell merchandise on account to S. Kane $4,000, terms 1/10, n/30.
29 Returned damaged goods to J. Dixon and received cash refund of $450.

Instructions

(a) Open the following accounts in the general ledger.

101 Cash
112 Accounts Receivable
120 Merchandise Inventory
127 Store Supplies
131 Prepaid Rent
201 Accounts Payable
301 Collins, Capital
306 Collins, Drawing
401 Sales
414 Sales Discounts
505 Cost of Goods Sold
631 Supplies Expense
729 Rent Expense

(b) Sales journal total $17,900
Cash receipts journal balancing totals $98,350

(b) Journalize the transactions that have not been journalized in the sales journal, the cash receipts journal (see Illustration 7-10), and the general journal.

(c) Post to the accounts receivable and accounts payable subsidiary ledgers. Follow the sequence of transactions as shown in the problem.

(d) Post the individual entries and totals to the general ledger.

(e) Totals $114,620
(f) Accounts Receivable $4,000
Accounts Payable $12,720

(e) Prepare a trial balance at July 31, 2002.

(f) Determine whether the subsidiary ledgers agree with the control accounts in the general ledger.

(g) The following adjustments at the end of July are necessary.
(1) A count of supplies indicates that $140 is still on hand.
(2) Recognize rent expense for July, $500.
Prepare the necessary entries in the general journal. Post the entries to the general ledger.

(h) Totals $114,620

(h) Prepare an adjusted trial balance at July 31, 2002.

P7-6A The post-closing trial balance for Alomar Co. is as follows.

Journalize in special journals; post; prepare a trial balance.
(SO 3, 4, 5)

ALOMAR CO.
Post-Closing Trial Balance
December 31, 2002

	Debit	Credit
Cash	$ 41,500	
Accounts Receivable	15,000	
Notes Receivable	45,000	
Merchandise Inventory	23,000	
Equipment	6,450	
Accumulated Depreciation—Equipment		$ 1,500
Accounts Payable		43,000
S. Alomar, Capital		86,450
	$130,950	$130,950

The subsidiary ledgers contain the following information: (1) accounts receivable—R. Barton $2,500, B. Cole $7,500, S. Devine $5,000; (2) accounts payable—S. Field $10,000, R. Grilson $18,000, and D. Harms $15,000. The cost of all merchandise sold was 65% of the sales price.

The transactions for January 2003 are as follows.

Jan. 3 Sell merchandise to B. Senton $4,000, terms 2/10, n/30.
5 Purchase merchandise from S. Warren $2,500, terms 2/10, n/30.
7 Receive a check from S. Devine $3,500.
11 Pay freight on merchandise purchased $300.
12 Pay rent of $1,000 for January.
13 Receive payment in full from B. Senton.
14 Post all entries to the subsidiary ledgers. Issue a credit memo to acknowledge receipt of damaged merchandise of $700 returned by R. Barton.
15 Send D. Harms a check for $14,850 in full payment of account, discount $150.
17 Purchase merchandise from D. Lapeska $1,600, terms 2/10, n/30.
18 Pay sales salaries of $2,800 and office salaries $1,500.
20 Give R. Grilson a 60-day note for $18,000 in full payment of account payable.
23 Total cash sales amount to $8,600.
24 Post all entries to the subsidiary ledgers. Sell merchandise on account to B. Cole $7,700, terms 1/10, n/30.
27 Send S. Warren a check for $950.
29 Receive payment on a note of $40,000 from S. Lava.
30 Return merchandise of $500 to D. Lapeska for credit. Post all journals to the subsidiary ledger.

Instructions

(a) Open general and subsidiary ledger accounts for the following.

101 Cash	301 S. Alomar, Capital
112 Accounts Receivable	401 Sales
115 Notes Receivable	412 Sales Returns and Allowances
120 Merchandise Inventory	414 Sales Discounts
157 Equipment	505 Cost of Goods Sold
158 Accumulated Depreciation—Equipment	726 Sales Salaries Expense
200 Notes Payable	727 Office Salaries Expense
201 Accounts Payable	729 Rent Expense

(b) Record the January transactions in a sales journal, a single-column purchases journal, a cash receipts journal (see Illustration 7-10), a cash payments journal (see Illustration 7-17), and a general journal.

(c) Post the appropriate amounts to the general ledger.

(d) Prepare a trial balance at January 31, 2003.

(e) Determine whether the subsidiary ledgers agree with controlling accounts in the general ledger.

(b) Sales journal $11,700
Purchases journal $4,100
Cash receipts journal (balancing) $56,100
Cash payments journal (balancing) $21,550
(d) Totals $138,900
(e) Accounts Receivable $18,500
Accounts Payable $12,650

PROBLEMS: SET B

Journalize transactions in cash receipts journal; post to control account and subsidiary ledger.
(SO 3, 4, 5)

P7-1B Kimball Company's chart of accounts includes the following selected accounts.

101 Cash	401 Sales
112 Accounts Receivable	414 Sales Discounts
120 Merchandise Inventory	505 Cost of Goods Sold
301 J. Kimball, Capital	

On June 1 the accounts receivable ledger of Kimball Company showed the following balances: Block & Son $3,500, Field Co. $1,900, Green Bros. $1,600, and Mastin Co. $1,000. The June transactions involving the receipt of cash were as follows.

June	1	The owner, J. Kimball, invested additional cash in the business $10,000.
	3	Received check in full from Mastin Co. less 2% cash discount.
	6	Received check in full from Field Co. less 2% cash discount.
	7	Made cash sales of merchandise totaling $6,135. The cost of the merchandise sold was $4,090.
	9	Received check in full from Block & Son less 2% cash discount.
	11	Received cash refund from a supplier for damaged merchandise $200.
	15	Made cash sales of merchandise totaling $5,250. The cost of the merchandise sold was $3,500.
	20	Received check in full from Green Bros. $1,600.

Instructions

(a) Balancing totals $29,585

(a) Journalize the transactions above in a six-column cash receipts journal with columns for Cash Dr., Sales Discounts Dr., Accounts Receivable Cr., Sales Cr., Other Accounts Cr., and Cost of Goods Sold Dr./Merchandise Inventory Cr. Foot and crossfoot the journal.

(b) Insert the beginning balances in the Accounts Receivable control and subsidiary accounts, and post the June transactions to these accounts.

(c) Accounts Receivable $0

(c) Prove the agreement of the control account and subsidiary account balances.

Journalize transactions in cash payments journal; post to the general and subsidiary ledgers.
(SO 3, 4, 5)

P7-2B Creek Company's chart of accounts includes the following selected accounts.

101 Cash	157 Equipment
120 Merchandise Inventory	201 Accounts Payable
130 Prepaid Insurance	306 V. Creek, Drawing

On November 1 the accounts payable ledger of Creek Company showed the following balances: R. Huff & Co. $4,500, G. Paul $2,350, R. Snyder $1,000, and Waldo Bros. $1,900. The November transactions involving the payment of cash were as follows.

Nov.	1	Purchased merchandise, check no. 11, $900.
	3	Purchased store equipment, check no. 12, $1,700.
	5	Paid Waldo Bros. balance due of $1,900, less 1% discount, check no. 13, $1,881.
	11	Purchased merchandise, check no. 14, $2,000.
	15	Paid R. Snyder balance due of $1,000, less 3% discount, check no. 15, $970.
	16	V. Creek, the owner, withdrew $500 cash for own use, check no. 16.
	19	Paid G. Paul in full for invoice no. 1245, $1,300 less 2% discount, check no. 17, $1,274.
	25	Paid premium due on one-year insurance policy, check no. 18, $3,000.
	30	Paid R. Huff & Co. in full for invoice no. 832, $2,500, check no. 19.

Instructions

(a) Balancing totals $14,800

(a) Journalize the transactions above in a four-column cash payments journal with columns for Other Accounts Dr., Accounts Payable Dr., Merchandise Inventory Cr., and Cash Cr. Foot and crossfoot the journal.

(b) Insert the beginning balances in the Accounts Payable control and subsidiary accounts, and post the November transactions to these accounts.

(c) Accounts Payable $3,050

(c) Prove the agreement of the control account and the subsidiary account balances.

Journalize transactions in multi-column purchases journal; post to the general and subsidiary ledgers.
(SO 3, 4, 5)

P7-3B The chart of accounts of Virginia Company includes the following selected accounts.

112 Accounts Receivable	401 Sales
120 Merchandise Inventory	412 Sales Returns and Allowances
126 Supplies	505 Cost of Goods Sold
157 Equipment	610 Advertising Expense
201 Accounts Payable	

In May the following selected transactions were completed. All purchases and sales were on account except as indicated. The cost of all merchandise sold was 70% of the sales price.

May 2 Purchased merchandise from Vons Company $9,500.
3 Received freight bill from Acme Freight on Vons purchase $400.
5 Sales were made to Penner Company $1,750, Hendrix Bros. $2,700, and Nelles Company $1,500.
8 Purchased merchandise from Golden Company $8,000 and Dorn Company $8,700.
10 Received credit on merchandise returned to Dorn Company $500.
15 Purchased supplies from Engle Supply $900.
16 Purchased merchandise from Vons Company $4,500, and Golden Company $6,000.
17 Returned supplies to Engle Supply, receiving credit $100. (*Hint:* Credit Supplies.)
18 Received freight bills on May 16 purchases from Acme Freight $500.
20 Returned merchandise to Vons Company receiving credit $300.
23 Made sales to Hendrix Bros. $2,400 and to Nelles Company $2,200.
25 Received bill for advertising from Ball Advertising $900.
26 Granted allowance to Nelles Company for merchandise damaged in shipment $200.
28 Purchased equipment from Engle Supply $250.

Instructions

(a) Journalize the transactions above in a purchases journal, a sales journal, and a general journal. The purchases journal should have the following column headings: Date, Accounts Credited (Debited), Ref., Other Accounts Dr., and Merchandise Inventory Dr./Accounts Payable Cr.

(a) Purchases journal—Accounts Payable Cr. $39,650
Sales journal total $10,550

(b) Post to both the general and subsidiary ledger accounts. (Assume that all accounts have zero beginning balances.)

(c) Prove the agreement of the control and subsidiary accounts.

(c) Accounts Receivable $10,350
Accounts Payable $38,750

Journalize transactions in special journals.
(SO 3, 4, 5)

P7-4B Selected accounts from the chart of accounts of Ramos Company are shown below.

101 Cash	201 Accounts Payable
112 Accounts Receivable	401 Sales
120 Merchandise Inventory	414 Sales Discounts
126 Supplies	505 Cost of Goods Sold
140 Land	610 Advertising Expense
145 Buildings	

The cost of all merchandise sold was 60% of the sales price. During October, Ramos Company completed the following transactions.

Oct. 2 Purchased merchandise on account from Mason Company $18,500.
4 Sold merchandise on account to Parker Co. $9,000. Invoice no. 204, terms 2/10, n/30.
5 Purchased supplies for cash $80.
7 Made cash sales for the week totaling $9,160.
9 Paid in full the amount owed Mason Company less a 2% discount.
10 Purchased merchandise on account from Quinn Corp. $4,200.
12 Received payment from Parker Co. for invoice no. 204.
13 Issued a debit memorandum to Quinn Corp. and returned $250 worth of damaged goods.
14 Made cash sales for the week totaling $8,180.
16 Sold a parcel of land for $27,000 cash, the land's book value.

17 Sold merchandise on account to L. Boyton & Co. $5,350, invoice no. 205, terms 2/10, n/30.
18 Purchased merchandise for cash $2,125.
21 Made cash sales for the week totaling $8,465.
23 Paid in full the amount owed Quinn Corp. for the goods kept (no discount).
25 Purchased supplies on account from Frey Co. $260.
25 Sold merchandise on account to Green Corp. $5,220, invoice no. 206, terms 2/10, n/30.
25 Received payment from L. Boyton & Co. for invoice no. 205.
26 Purchased for cash a small parcel of land and a building on the land to use as a storage facility. The total cost of $35,000 was allocated $21,000 to the land and $14,000 to the building.
27 Purchased merchandise on account from Schmid Co. $8,500.
28 Made cash sales for the week totaling $8,540.
30 Purchased merchandise on account from Mason Company $14,000.
30 Paid advertising bill for the month from the *Gazette*, $400.
30 Sold merchandise on account to L. Boyton & Co. $4,600, invoice no. 207, terms 2/10, n/30.

(b) Sales journal $24,170
Purchases journal $45,200
Cash receipts journal, Cash debit $75,408
Cash payments journal, Cash credit $59,685

Ramos Company uses the following journals.

1. Sales journal.
2. Single-column purchases journal.
3. Cash receipts journal with columns for Cash Dr., Sales Discounts Dr., Accounts Receivable Cr., Sales Cr., Other Accounts Cr., and Cost of Goods Sold Dr./Merchandise Inventory Cr.
4. Cash payments journal with columns for Other Accounts Dr., Accounts Payable Dr., Merchandise Inventory Cr., and Cash Cr.
5. General journal.

Instructions

Using the selected accounts provided:

(a) Record the October transactions in the appropriate journals.
(b) Foot and crossfoot all special journals.
(c) Show how postings would be made by placing ledger account numbers and check marks as needed in the journals. (Actual posting to ledger accounts is not required.)

Journalize in purchase and cash payments journals; post; prepare a trial balance; prove control to subsidiary; prepare adjusting entries; prepare an adjusted trial balance.
(SO 3, 4, 5)

P7-5B Presented below are the sales and cash receipts journals for Toko Co. for its first month of operations.

SALES JOURNAL **S1**

Date	Account Debited	Ref.	Accounts Receivable Dr. Sales Cr.	Cost of Goods Sold Dr. Merchandise Inventory Cr.
Feb. 3	D. Adams		5,500	3,630
9	P. Babcock		6,500	4,290
12	D. Chambers		8,000	5,280
26	K. Dawson		6,000	3,960
			26,000	17,160

CASH RECEIPTS JOURNAL **CR1**

Date	Account Credited	Ref.	Cash Dr.	Sales Discounts Dr.	Accounts Receivable Cr.	Sales Cr.	Other Accounts Cr.	Cost of Goods Sold Dr. Merchandise Inventory Cr.
Feb. 1	J. Toko, Capital		30,000				30,000	
2			6,500			6,500		4,290
13	D. Adams		5,445	55	5,500			
18	Merchandise Inventory		150				150	
26	P. Babcock		6,500		6,500			
			48,595	55	12,000	6,500	30,150	4,290

In addition, the following transactions have not been journalized for February 2002.

Feb. 2 Purchased merchandise on account from S. Healy for $4,000, terms 1/10, n/30.
7 Purchased merchandise on account from L. Held for $30,000, terms 1/10, n/30.
9 Paid cash of $1,000 for purchase of supplies.
12 Paid $3,960 to S. Healy in payment for $4,000 invoice, less 1% discount.
15 Purchased equipment for $8,000 cash.
16 Purchased merchandise on account from R. Landly $2,400, terms 2/10, n/30.
17 Paid $29,700 to L. Held in payment of $30,000 invoice, less 1% discount.
20 Withdrew cash of $1,100 from business for personal use.
21 Purchased merchandise on account from J. Able for $6,500, terms 1/10, n/30.
28 Paid $2,400 to R. Landly in payment of $2,400 invoice.

Instructions

(a) Open the following accounts in the general ledger.

101 Cash	301 J. Toko, Capital
112 Accounts Receivable	306 J. Toko, Drawing
120 Merchandise Inventory	401 Sales
126 Supplies	414 Sales Discounts
157 Equipment	505 Cost of Goods Sold
158 Accumulated Depreciation—Equipment	631 Supplies Expense
201 Accounts Payable	711 Depreciation Expense

(b) Journalize the transactions that have not been journalized in a one-column purchases journal and the cash payments journal (see Illustration 7-17).

(b) Purchases journal total $42,900
Cash payments journal Cash, Cr. $46,160

(c) Post to the accounts receivable and accounts payable subsidiary ledgers. Follow the sequence of transactions as shown in the problem.

(d) Post the individual entries and totals to the general ledger.

(e) Prepare a trial balance at February 28, 2002.

(e) Totals $69,000

(f) Determine that the subsidiary ledgers agree with the control accounts in the general ledger.

(f) Accounts Receivable $14,000
Accounts Payable $6,500

(g) The following adjustments at the end of February are necessary.
(1) A count of supplies indicates that $300 is still on hand.
(2) Depreciation on equipment for February is $200.
Prepare the adjusting entries and then post the adjusting entries to the general ledger.

(h) Prepare an adjusted trial balance at February 28, 2002.

(h) Totals $69,200

COMPREHENSIVE PROBLEM: CHAPTERS 3 TO 7

Hunt Company has the following opening account balances in its general and subsidiary ledgers on January 1. All accounts have normal debit and credit balances.

General Ledger

Account Number	Account Title	January 1 Opening Balance
101	Cash	$35,750
112	Accounts Receivable	13,000
115	Notes Receivable	39,000
120	Merchandise Inventory	18,000
125	Office Supplies	1,000
130	Prepaid Insurance	2,000
157	Equipment	6,450
158	Accumulated Depreciation	1,500
201	Accounts Payable	35,000
301	S. Hunt, Capital	78,700

Accounts Receivable Subsidiary Ledger

Customer	January 1 Opening Balance
R. Dansig	$1,500
B. Jaggar	7,500
S. Lowell	4,000

Accounts Payable Subsidiary Ledger

Creditor	January 1 Opening Balance
S. Lee	$ 9,000
R. Mannon	15,000
D. Nordin	11,000

Jan. 3 Sell merchandise on credit to B. Sargent $3,100, invoice no. 510, and J. Eaton $1,800, invoice no. 511.
5 Purchase merchandise from S. Walden $3,000 and D. Landell $2,200.
7 Receive checks for $4,000 from S. Lowell and $2,000 from B. Jaggar.
8 Pay freight on merchandise purchased $180.
9 Send checks to S. Lee for $9,000 and D. Nordin for $11,000.
9 Issue credit memo for $300 to J. Eaton for merchandise returned.
10 Summary cash sales total $15,500.
11 Sell merchandise on credit to R. Dansig for $1,300, invoice no. 512, and to S. Lowell $900, invoice no. 513.
Post all entries to the subsidiary ledgers.
12 Pay rent of $1,000 for January.
13 Receive payment in full from B. Sargent and J. Eaton.
15 Withdraw $800 cash by S. Hunt for personal use.
16 Purchase merchandise from D. Nordin for $15,000, from S. Lee for $14,200, and from S. Walden for $1,500.
17 Pay $400 cash for office supplies.
18 Return $200 of merchandise to S. Lee and receive credit.
20 Summary cash sales total $17,500.
21 Issue $15,000 note to R. Mannon in payment of balance due.
21 Receive payment in full from S. Lowell.
Post all entries to the subsidiary ledgers.
22 Sell merchandise on credit to B. Sargent for $1,700, invoice no. 514, and to R. Dansig for $800, invoice no. 515.
23 Send checks to D. Nordin and S. Lee in full payment.
25 Sell merchandise on credit to B. Jaggar for $3,500, invoice no. 516, and to J. Eaton for $6,100, invoice no. 517.
27 Purchase merchandise from D. Nordin for $14,500, from D. Landell for $1,200, and from S. Walden for $2,800.
28 Pay $200 cash for office supplies.
31 Summary cash sales total $21,300.
31 Pay sales salaries of $4,300 and office salaries of $2,600.

Instructions

(a) Record the January transactions in the appropriate journal—sales, purchases, cash receipts, cash payments, and general.

(b) Post the journals to the general and subsidiary ledgers. New accounts should be added and numbered in an orderly fashion as needed.

(c) Prepare a trial balance at January 31, 2002, using a work sheet. Complete the work sheet using the following additional information.

(1) Office supplies at January 31 total $500.
(2) Insurance coverage expires on October 31, 2002.
(3) Annual depreciation on the equipment is $1,500.
(4) Interest of $30 has accrued on the note payable.
(5) Merchandise inventory at January 31 is $16,000.

(d) Prepare a multiple-step income statement and a statement of owner's equity for January and a classified balance sheet at the end of January.

(e) Prepare and post the adjusting and closing entries.

(f) Prepare a post-closing trial balance, and determine whether the subsidiary ledgers agree with the control accounts in the general ledger.

BROADENING YOUR PERSPECTIVE

FINANCIAL REPORTING AND ANALYSIS

FINANCIAL REPORTING PROBLEM—MINI PRACTICE SET

BYP7-1 (The working papers that accompany this textbook are needed in order to work this mini practice set.)

Cheng Co. uses both an accounts receivable and an accounts payable subsidiary ledger. Balances related to both the general ledger and the subsidiary ledger for Cheng are indicated in the working papers. Presented below are a series of transactions for Cheng Co. for the month of January. Credit sales terms are 2/10, n/30. The cost of all merchandise sold was 60% of the sales price.

Jan. 3 Sell merchandise on credit to B. Sanchez $3,200, invoice no. 510, and to J. Egan $1,800, invoice no. 511.
5 Purchase merchandise from S. Whitfield $3,000 and D. Land $2,200, terms n/30.
7 Receive checks from S. Levin $4,000 and B. Jiminez $2,000 after discount period has lapsed.
8 Pay freight on merchandise purchased $180.
9 Send checks to S. Jin for $9,000 less 2% cash discount, and to D. Northcutt for $11,000 less 1% cash discount.
9 Issue credit memo for $300 to J. Egan for merchandise returned.
10 Summary daily cash sales total $15,500.
11 Sell merchandise on credit to R. Danforth $1,300, invoice no. 512, and to S. Levin $900, invoice no. 513.
12 Pay rent of $1,000 for January.
13 Receive payment in full from B. Sanchez and J. Egan less cash discounts.
15 Withdraw $800 cash by M. Cheng for personal use.
15 Post all entries to the subsidiary ledgers.
16 Purchase merchandise from D. Northcutt $16,000, terms 1/10, n/30; S. Jin $14,200, terms 2/10, n/30; and S. Whitfield $1,500, terms n/30.
17 Pay $400 cash for office supplies.
18 Return $200 of merchandise to S. Jin and receive credit.
20 Summary daily cash sales total $17,500.
21 Issue $15,000 note to R. Manual in payment of balance due.
21 Receive payment in full from S. Levin less cash discount.
22 Sell merchandise on credit to B. Sanchez $2,700, invoice no. 514, and to R. Danforth $800, invoice no. 515.
22 Post all entries to the subsidiary ledger.
23 Send checks to D. Northcutt and S. Jin in full payment less cash discounts.
25 Sell merchandise on credit to B. Jiminez $3,500, invoice no. 516, and to J. Egan $6,100, invoice no. 517.
27 Purchase merchandise from D. Northcutt $14,500, terms 1/10, n/30; D. Land $1,200, terms n/30; and S. Whitfield $4,800, terms n/30.
27 Post all entries to the subsidiary ledger.
28 Pay $200 cash for office supplies.
31 Summary daily cash sales total $21,300.
31 Pay sales salaries $4,300 and office salaries $2,600.

Instructions

(a) Record the January transactions in a sales journal, a single-column purchases journal, a cash receipts journal as shown on page 286, a cash payments journal as shown on page 291, and a two-column general journal.

(b) Post the journals to the general ledger.

(c) Prepare a trial balance at January 31, 2002, in the trial balance columns of the work sheet. Complete the work sheet using the following additional information.

(1) Office supplies at January 31 total $500.
(2) Insurance coverage expires on October 31, 2002.
(3) Annual depreciation on the equipment is $1,500.
(4) Interest of $60 has accrued on the note payable.

(d) Prepare a multiple-step income statement and an owner's equity statement for January and a classified balance sheet at the end of January.
(e) Prepare and post adjusting and closing entries.
(f) Prepare a post-closing trial balance, and determine whether the subsidiary ledgers agree with the control accounts in the general ledger.

EXPLORING THE WEB

BYP7-2 **Great Plains' Accounting** is one of the leading accounting software packages. Information related to this package is found at its Web site.

Address: **www.greatplains.com/accounting/productinfo.asp** *(or go to www.wiley.com/college/weygandt)*

Steps:
1. Go to the site shown above.
2. Choose **General Ledger**. Perform instruction (a) below.
3. Choose **Accounts Payable**. Perform instruction (b) below.

Instructions

(a) What are three key features of the general ledger module highlighted by the company?
(b) What are three key features of the payables management module highlighted by the company?

CRITICAL THINKING

GROUP DECISION CASE

BYP7-3 Ehlert & Ramos is a wholesaler of small appliances and parts. Ehlert & Ramos is operated by two owners, Bill Ehlert and Denise Ramos. In addition, the company has one employee, a repair specialist, who is on a fixed salary. Revenues are earned through the sale of appliances to retailers (approximately 75% of total revenues), appliance parts to do-it-yourselfers (10%), and the repair of appliances brought to the store (15%). Appliance sales are made on both a credit and cash basis. Customers are billed on prenumbered sales invoices. Credit terms are always net/30 days. All parts sales and repair work are cash only.

Merchandise is purchased on account from the manufacturers of both the appliances and the parts. Practically all suppliers offer cash discounts for prompt payments, and it is company policy to take all discounts. Most cash payments are made by check. Checks are most frequently issued to suppliers, to trucking companies for freight on merchandise purchases, and to newspapers, radio, and TV stations for advertising. All advertising bills are paid as received. Bill and Denise each make a monthly drawing in cash for personal living expenses. The salaried repairman is paid twice monthly. Ehlert & Ramos currently has a manual accounting system.

Instructions
With the class divided into groups, answer the following.

(a) Identify the special journals that Ehlert & Ramos should have in its manual system. List the column headings appropriate for each of the special journals.
(b) What control and subsidiary accounts should be included in Ehlert & Ramos's manual system? Why?

COMMUNICATION ACTIVITY

BYP7-4 Sue Marsh, a classmate, has a part-time bookkeeping job. She is concerned about the inefficiencies in journalizing and posting transactions. Raul Hindi is the owner of the company where Sue works. In response to numerous complaints from Sue and others, Raul hired two additional bookkeepers a month ago. However, the inefficiencies have continued at an even higher rate. The accounting information system for the company has only a general journal and a general ledger. Raul refuses to install an electronic accounting system.

Instructions

Now that Sue is an expert in manual accounting information systems, she decides to send a letter to Raul Hindi explaining (1) why the additional personnel did not help and (2) what changes should be made to improve the efficiency of the accounting department. Write the letter that you think Sue should send.

ETHICS CASE

BYP7-5 Tyler Products Company operates three divisions, each with its own manufacturing plant and marketing/sales force. The corporate headquarters and central accounting office are in Tyler, and the plants are in Freeport, Rockport, and Bayport, all within 50 miles of Tyler. Corporate management treats each division as an independent profit center and encourages competition among them. They each have similar but different product lines. As a competitive incentive, bonuses are awarded each year to the employees of the fastest growing and most profitable division.

Don Henke is the manager of Tyler's centralized computer accounting operation that keyboards the sales transactions and maintains the accounts receivable for all three divisions. Don came up in the accounting ranks from the Bayport division where his wife, several relatives, and many friends still work.

As sales documents are keyboarded into the computer, the originating division is identified by code. Most sales documents (95%) are coded, but some (5%) are not coded or are coded incorrectly. As the manager, Don has instructed the keyboard operators to assign the Bayport code to all uncoded and incorrectly coded sales documents. This is done he says, "in order to expedite processing and to keep the computer files current since they are updated daily." All receivables and cash collections for all three divisions are handled by Tyler as one subsidiary accounts receivable ledger.

Instructions

(a) Who are the stakeholders in this situation?
(b) What are the ethical issues in this case?
(c) How might the system be improved to prevent this situation?

Answers to Self-Study Questions

1. d **2.** b **3.** a **4.** c **5.** a **6.** c **7.** d **8.** b **9.** c **10.** c

Remember to go back to the Navigator box on the chapter-opening page and check off your completed work.

INTERNAL CONTROL AND CASH

8

THE NAVIGATOR ✓

- Understand *Concepts for Review* ❑
- Read *Feature Story* ❑
- Scan *Study Objectives* ❑
- Read *Preview* ❑
- Read text and answer *Before You Go On* *p.* 324 ❑ *p.* 332 ❑ *p.* 340 ❑ *p.* 341 ❑
- Work *Demonstration Problem* ❑
- Review *Summary of Study Objectives* ❑
- Answer *Self-Study Questions* ❑
- Complete *Assignments* ❑

CONCEPTS FOR REVIEW

Before studying this chapter, you should know or, if necessary, review:

a. How cash transactions are recorded. (Ch. 2, pp. 54–63)

b. How cash is classified on a balance sheet. (Ch. 4, pp. 155–156)

c. The role ethics plays in proper financial reporting. (Ch.1, pp. 9–10)

THE NAVIGATOR

FEATURE STORY

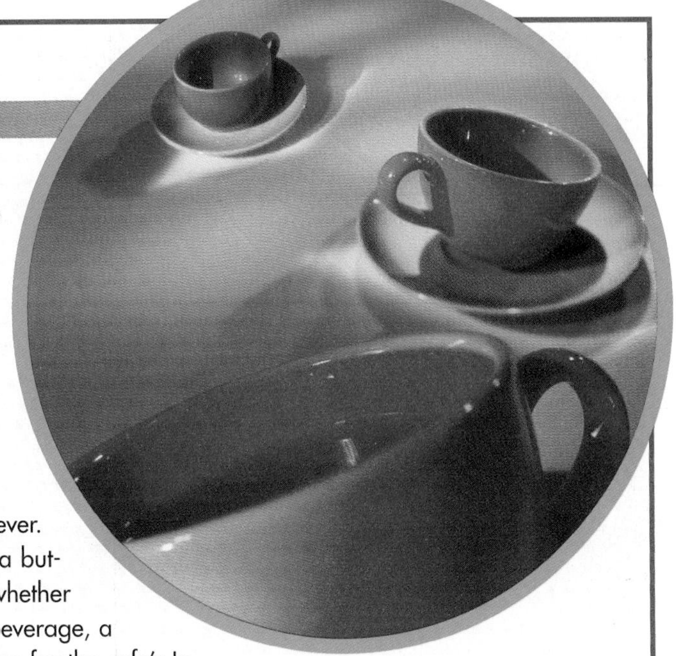

Minding the Money in Moose Jaw

If you're ever looking for a cappuccino in Moose Jaw, Saskatchewan, stop by **Stephanie's Gourmet Coffee and More**, located on Main Street. Staff there serve, on average, 646 cups of coffee a day—including both regular and specialty coffees—not to mention soups, Italian sandwiches, and a wide assortment of gourmet cheesecakes.

"We've got high school students who come here, and students from the community college," says owner/manager Stephanie Mintenko, who has run the place since opening it in 1995. "We have customers who are retired, and others who are working people and have only 30 minutes for lunch. We have to be pretty quick."

That means that the cashiers have to be efficient. Like most businesses where purchases are low-cost and high-volume, cash control has to be simple.

"We have an electronic cash register, but it's not the fancy new kind where you just punch in the item," explains Ms. Mintenko. "You have to punch in the prices." The machine does keep track of sales in several categories, however. Cashiers punch a button to indicate whether each item is a beverage, a meal, or a charge for the cafe's Internet connections. All transactions are recorded on an internal tape in the machine; the customer receives a receipt only upon request.

There is only one cash register. "Up to three of us might operate it on any given shift, including myself," says Ms. Mintenko.

She and her staff do two "cashouts" each day—one with the shift change at 5:00, and one when the shop closes at 10:00. The cash in the register drawer is counted. That amount, minus the cash change carried forward (the float), should match the shift total on the register tape. If there's a discrepancy, they do another count. Then, if necessary, "we go through the whole tape to find the mistake," she explains. "It usually turns out to be someone who punched in $18 instead of $1.80, or something like that."

Ms. Mintenko sends all the cash tapes and float totals to a bookkeeper, who double checks everything and provides regular reports. "We try to keep the accounting simple, so we can concentrate on making great coffee and food."

THE NAVIGATOR

STUDY OBJECTIVES

After studying this chapter, you should be able to:

1. Define internal control.
2. Identify the principles of internal control.
3. Explain the applications of internal control principles to cash receipts.
4. Explain the applications of internal control principles to cash disbursements.
5. Describe the operation of a petty cash fund.
6. Indicate the control features of a bank account.
7. Prepare a bank reconciliation.
8. Explain the reporting of cash.

THE NAVIGATOR

PREVIEW OF CHAPTER 8

As the story about recording cash sales at **Stephanie's Gourmet Coffee and More** indicates, control of cash is important. Controls are also needed to safeguard other types of assets. For example, Stephanie's undoubtedly has controls to prevent the theft of food and supplies, and controls to prevent the theft of silverware and dishes from its kitchen.

In this chapter, we explain the essential features of an internal control system and then describe how those controls apply to cash. The applications include some controls with which you may be already familiar. Toward the end of the chapter, we describe the use of a bank and explain how cash is reported on the balance sheet.

The content and organization of Chapter 8 are as follows.

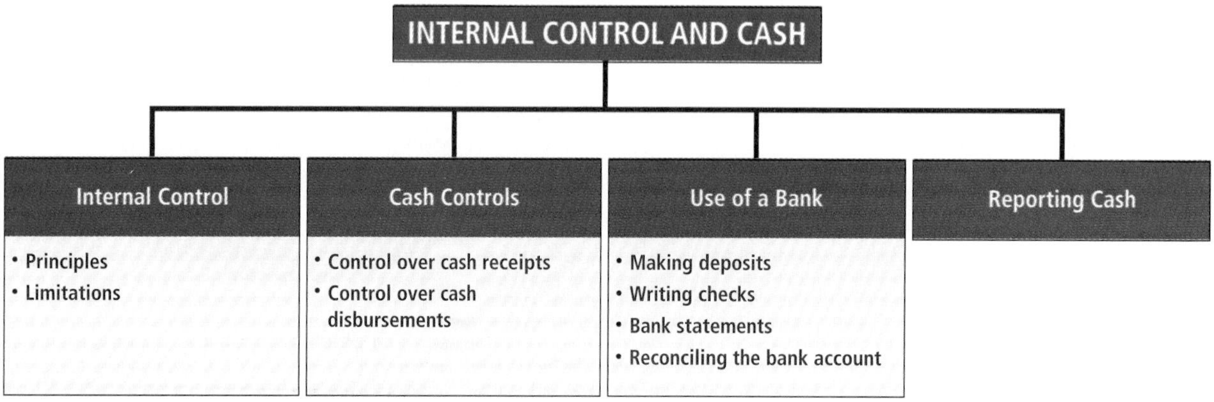

THE NAVIGATOR

INTERNAL CONTROL

STUDY OBJECTIVE 1

Define internal control.

Could there be dishonest employees where you work? Unfortunately, the answer sometimes is Yes. For example, the financial press recently reported the following.

> A bookkeeper in a small company diverted $750,000 of bill payments to a personal bank account over a 3-year period.
>
> A shipping clerk with 28 years of service shipped $125,000 of merchandise to himself.
>
> A computer operator embezzled $21 million from **Wells Fargo Bank** over a 2-year period.
>
> A church treasurer "borrowed" $150,000 of church funds to finance a friend's business dealings.

These situations emphasize the need for a good system of internal control.

Internal control consists of the plan of organization and all the related methods and measures adopted within a business to:

1. **Safeguard its assets** from employee theft, robbery, and unauthorized use.
2. **Enhance the accuracy and reliability of its accounting records.** This is done by reducing the risk of **errors** (unintentional mistakes) and **irregularities** (intentional mistakes and misrepresentations) in the accounting process.

The Foreign Corrupt Practices Act of 1977 requires all major U.S. corporations to maintain an adequate system of internal control. Companies that fail to comply are subject to fines, and company officers may be imprisoned. Also, the National Commission on Fraudulent Financial Reporting concluded that all companies whose stock is publicly traded should maintain internal controls that can provide reasonable assurance that fraudulent financial reporting will be prevented or subject to early detection.[1]

INTERNATIONAL NOTE

U.S. companies also adopt model business codes that guide their international operations to provide for a safe and healthy workplace, avoid child and forced labor, abstain from bribes, and follow sound environmental practices.

TECHNOLOGY IN ACTION

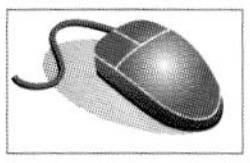

Good internal control must be designed into computerized systems. The starting point is usually flow charts that graphically depict each component of a firm's operations. The assembled flow charts serve as the basis for writing detailed programs. An example of flow charting is given in this chapter (see Illustration 8-6). When attempts to automate or improve accounting systems fail, it is often due to the absence of such well-documented procedures.

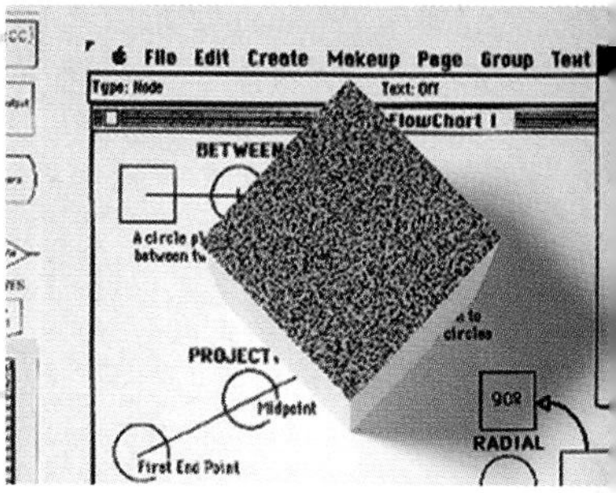

PRINCIPLES OF INTERNAL CONTROL

STUDY OBJECTIVE 2

Identify the principles of internal control.

To safeguard its assets and enhance the accuracy and reliability of its accounting records, a company follows specific control principles. Of course, internal control measures vary with the size and nature of the business and with management's control philosophy. The six principles listed in Illustration 8-1 apply to most enterprises. Each principle is explained in the following sections.

Illustration 8-1

Principles of internal control

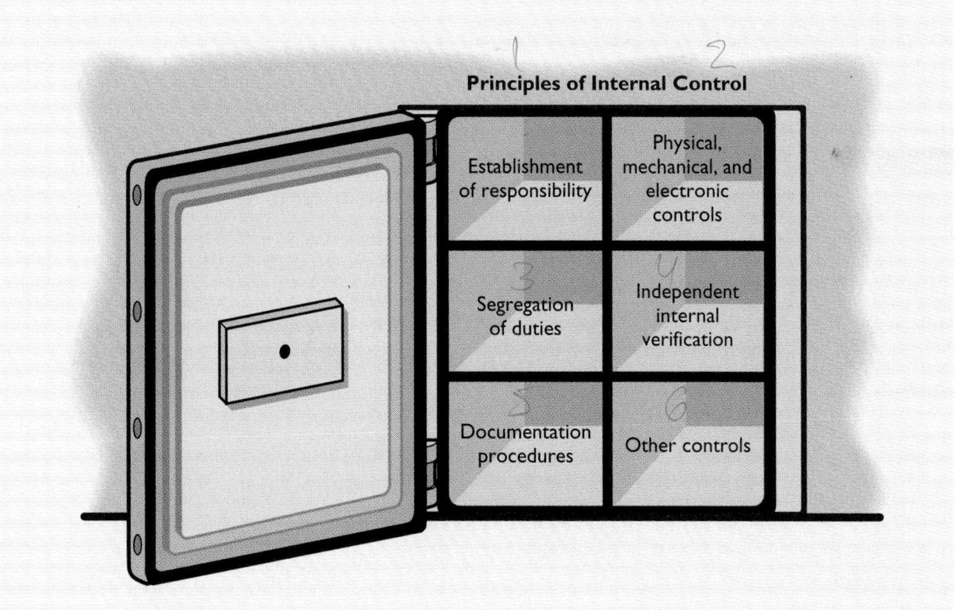

[1] Report of the National Commission on Fraudulent Financial Reporting, October 1987, p. 11.

It's your shift now. I'm turning in my cash drawer and heading home.
Transfer of cash drawers

Establishment of Responsibility

An essential characteristic of internal control is the assignment of responsibility to specific employees. **Control is most effective when only one person is responsible for a given task.** To illustrate, assume that the cash on hand at the end of the day in a **Safeway** supermarket is $10 short of the cash rung up on the cash register. If only one person has operated the register, responsibility for the shortage can be assessed quickly. If two or more individuals have worked the register, it may be impossible to determine who is responsible for the error unless each person is assigned a separate cash drawer and register key. The principle of establishing responsibility does not appear to be strictly applied by **Stephanie's** (in the Feature Story) since three people operate the cash register on any given shift. To identify any shortages quickly at Stephanie's, two cashouts are performed each day.

Establishing responsibility includes the authorization and approval of transactions. For example, the vice president of sales should have the authority to establish policies for making credit sales. The policies ordinarily will require written credit department approval of credit sales.

Segregation of Duties

Segregation of duties (also called separation of functions or division of work) is indispensable in a system of internal control. There are two common applications of this principle:

1. Related activities should be assigned to different individuals.
2. Establishing the accountability (keeping the records) for an asset should be separate from the physical custody of that asset.

The rationale for segregation of duties is this: **The work of one employee should, without a duplication of effort, provide a reliable basis for evaluating the work of another employee.**

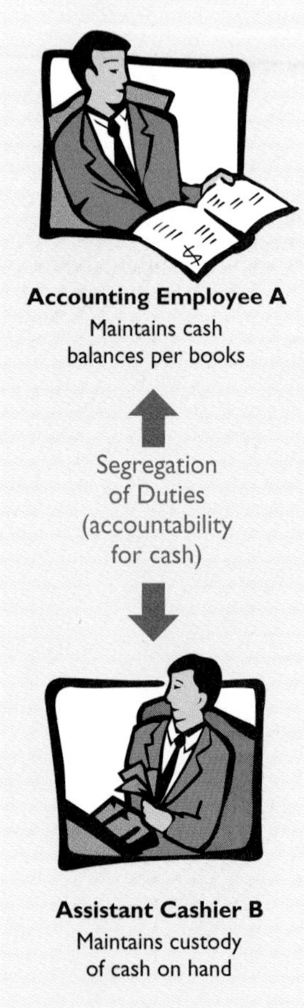
Accounting Employee A
Maintains cash balances per books
Segregation of Duties (accountability for cash)
Assistant Cashier B
Maintains custody of cash on hand

RELATED ACTIVITIES. Related activities that should be assigned to different individuals arise in both purchasing and selling. **When one individual is responsible for all of the related activities, the potential for errors and irregularities is increased.** Related purchasing activities include ordering merchandise, receiving the goods, and paying (or authorizing payment) for the merchandise. In purchasing, for example, orders could be placed with friends or with suppliers who give kickbacks. Or, only a cursory count and inspection could be made upon receiving the goods, which could lead to errors and poor-quality merchandise. Payment might be authorized without a careful review of the invoice. Even worse, fictitious invoices might be approved for payment. When the ordering, receiving, and paying are assigned to different individuals, the risk of such abuses is minimized.

Similarly, related sales activities should be assigned to different individuals. Related selling activities include making a sale, shipping (or delivering) the goods to the customer, billing the customer, and receiving payment. When one person handles related sales transactions, a salesperson could make sales at unauthorized prices to increase sales commissions; a shipping clerk could ship goods to himself; a billing clerk could understate the amount billed for sales made to friends and relatives. These abuses are reduced by dividing the sales tasks: the salespersons make the sale; the shipping department ships the goods on the basis of the sales order; and the billing department prepares the sales invoice after comparing the sales order with the report of goods shipped.

ACCOUNTABILITY FOR ASSETS. To provide a valid basis of accountability for an asset, the accountant should have neither physical custody of the asset nor access to it. Likewise, the custodian of the asset should not maintain or have access to the accounting records. **When one employee maintains the record of the asset that should be on hand, and a different employee has physical custody of the asset, the custodian of the asset is not likely to convert the asset to personal use.** The separation of accounting responsibility from the custody of assets is especially important for cash and inventories because these assets are very vulnerable to unauthorized use or misappropriation.

ACCOUNTING IN ACTION *International Insight*

Sumitomo Corporation announced a huge loss, $1.8 billion, due to a single copper trader. Some blamed Sumitomo's poor internal control on Japanese culture because it encourages group harmony over confrontation. For example, good controls require that both parties to a copper trade send a confirmation slip to management to verify the trade. In Japan, the counterparty to the trade often sends the confirmation slip to the trader, who then forwards it to management. Thus, it is possible for the trader to change the confirmation slip. An unethical trader could create fictitious trades to hide losses for an extended period of time or to conceal trades that are larger than allowed limits.

SOURCE: Sheryl Wudunn, "Big New Loss Makes Japan Look Inward," *New York Times,* June 17, 1996, p. D1.

Documentation Procedures

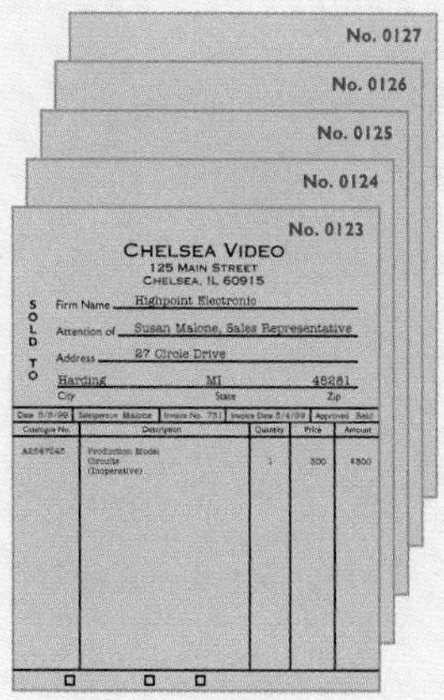

Prenumbered invoices

Documents provide evidence that transactions and events have occurred. At **Stephanie's Gourmet Coffee and More**, the cash register tape was the restaurant's documentation for the sale and the amount of cash received. Similarly, the shipping document indicates that the goods have been shipped, and the sales invoice indicates that the customer has been billed for the goods. By adding signatures (or initials) to the documents, the individual(s) responsible for the transaction or event can be identified. Documentation of transactions should be made when the transaction occurs. Documentation of events, such as those leading to adjusting entries, is generally developed when the adjustments are made.

Several procedures should be established for documents. First, whenever possible, **documents should be prenumbered, and all documents should be accounted for**. Prenumbering helps to prevent a transaction from being recorded more than once. It also helps to prevent the transactions from not being recorded. Second, documents that are **source documents for accounting entries should be promptly forwarded to the accounting department. This control measure helps to ensure timely recording of the transaction** and contributes directly to the accuracy and reliability of the accounting records.

HELPFUL HINT
An important corollary to prenumbering is that voided documents be kept until all documents are accounted for.

Physical, Mechanical, and Electronic Controls

Use of physical, mechanical, and electronic controls is essential. Physical controls relate primarily to the safeguarding of assets. Mechanical and electronic controls also safeguard assets; some enhance the accuracy and reliability of the accounting records. Examples of these controls are shown in Illustration 8-2.

Illustration 8-2

Physical, mechanical, and electronic controls

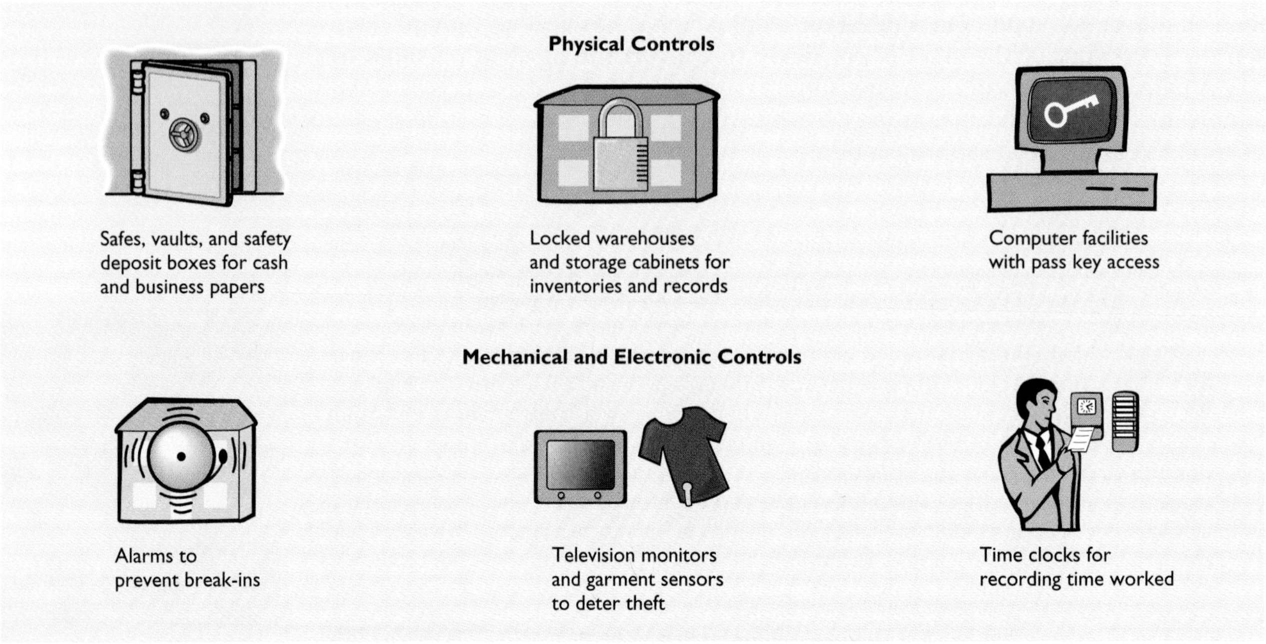
Physical Controls
Safes, vaults, and safety deposit boxes for cash and business papers
Locked warehouses and storage cabinets for inventories and records
Computer facilities with pass key access
Mechanical and Electronic Controls
Alarms to prevent break-ins
Television monitors and garment sensors to deter theft
Time clocks for recording time worked

ACCOUNTING IN ACTION *Business Insight*

John Patterson, a young Ohio merchant, couldn't understand why his retail business didn't show a profit. There were lots of customers, but the money just seemed to disappear. Patterson suspected pilferage and sloppy bookkeeping by store clerks. Frustrated, he placed an order with a Dayton, Ohio, company for two rudimentary cash registers. A year later, Patterson's store was in the black.

"What is a good thing for this little store is a good thing for every retail store in the world," he observed. A few months later, in 1884, John Patterson and his brother, Frank, bought the tiny cash register maker for $6,500. The word around Dayton was that the Patterson boys got stung.

In the following 37 years, John Patterson built **National Cash Register Co.** into a corporate giant. Patterson died in 1922, the year in which NCR sold its two millionth cash register.

SOURCE: The Wall Street Journal, January 28, 1989.

Independent Internal Verification

Most internal control systems provide for **independent internal verification**. This principle involves the review, comparison, and reconciliation of data prepared by other employees. To obtain maximum benefit from independent internal verification:

1. The verification should be made periodically or on a surprise basis.
2. The verification should be done by someone who is independent of the employee responsible for the information.
3. Discrepancies and exceptions should be reported to a management level that can take appropriate corrective action.

Independent internal verification is especially useful in comparing recorded accountability with existing assets. The reconciliation of the cash register tape with the cash in the register at **Stephanie's Gourmet Coffee and More** is an example of this internal control principle. Another common example is the reconciliation by an independent person of the cash balance per books with the cash balance per bank. The relationship between this principle and the segregation of duties principle is shown graphically in Illustration 8-3.

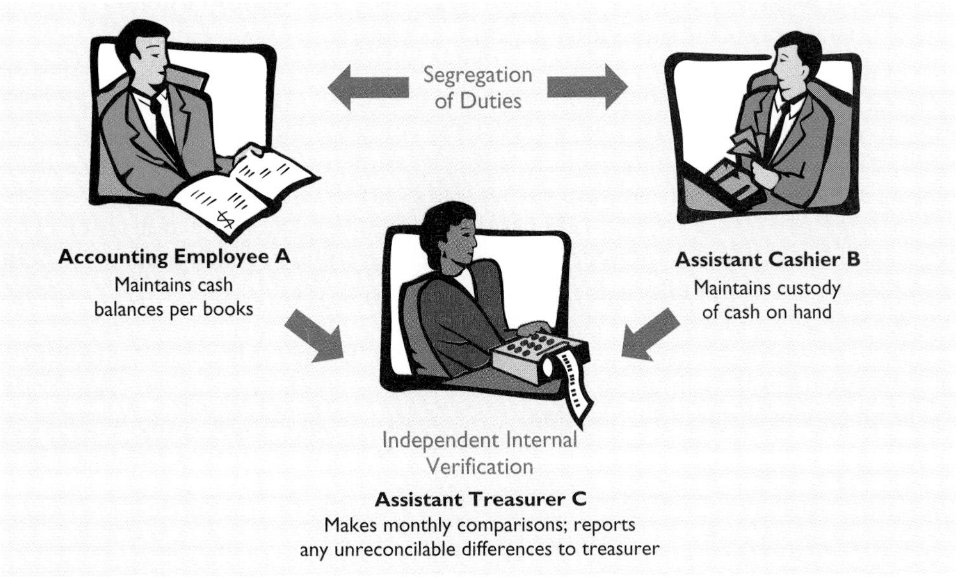

Illustration 8-3

Comparison of segregation of duties principle with independent internal verification principle

In large companies, independent internal verification is often assigned to internal auditors. **Internal auditors** are company employees who evaluate on a continuous basis the effectiveness of the company's system of internal control. They periodically review the activities of departments and individuals to determine whether prescribed internal controls are being followed. They also recommend improvements when needed. The importance of this function is illustrated by the number of internal auditors employed by companies.

Other Controls

Other control measures include the following.

1. **Bonding of employees who handle cash.** Bonding involves obtaining insurance protection against misappropriation of assets by dishonest employees. This measure contributes to the safeguarding of cash in two ways: First, the insurance company carefully screens all individuals before adding them to the policy and may reject risky applicants. Second, bonded employees know that the insurance company will vigorously prosecute all offenders.
2. **Rotating employees' duties and requiring employees to take vacations.** These measures are designed to deter employees from attempting any thefts since they will not be able to permanently conceal their improper actions. Many bank embezzlements, for example, have been discovered when the perpetrator was on vacation or assigned to a new position.

If I take a vacation
they will know that
I've been stealing.

LIMITATIONS OF INTERNAL CONTROL

A company's system of internal control is generally designed to provide **reasonable assurance** that assets are properly safeguarded and that the accounting records

HELPFUL HINT
Controls may vary with the risk level of the activity. For example, management may consider cash to be high risk and maintaining inventories in the stock room as low risk. Thus management would have stricter controls for cash.

are reliable. **The concept of reasonable assurance rests on the premise that the costs of establishing control procedures should not exceed their expected benefit.** To illustrate, consider shoplifting losses in retail stores. Such losses could be eliminated by having a security guard stop and search customers as they leave the store. But, store managers have concluded that the negative effects of adopting such a procedure cannot be justified. Instead, stores have attempted to "control" shoplifting losses by less costly procedures such as: (1) posting signs saying, "We reserve the right to inspect all packages," and "All shoplifters will be prosecuted," (2) using hidden TV cameras and store detectives to monitor customer activity, and (3) using sensoring equipment at exits.

The **human element** is an important factor in every system of internal control. A good system can become ineffective as a result of employee fatigue, carelessness, or indifference. For example, a receiving clerk may not bother to count goods received or may just "fudge" the counts. Occasionally, two or more individuals may work together to get around prescribed controls. Such **collusion** can significantly impair the effectiveness of a system, eliminating the protection offered by segregation of duties. If a supervisor and a cashier collaborate to understate cash receipts, the system of internal control may be negated (at least in the short run). No system of internal control is perfect.

The size of the business also may impose limitations on internal control. In a small company, for example, it may be difficult to segregate duties or to provide for independent internal verification.

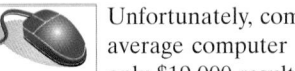

TECHNOLOGY IN ACTION

Unfortunately, computer-related frauds have become a major concern. The average computer fraud loss is $650,000, compared with an average loss of only $19,000 resulting from other types of white-collar crime.

Computer fraud can be perpetrated almost invisibly and done with electronic speed. Psychologically, stealing with impersonal computer tools can seem far less criminal to some people. Therefore, the moral threshold to commit computer fraud is lower than fraud involving person-to-person contact.

Preventing and detecting computer fraud represents a major challenge. One of the best ways for a company to minimize the likelihood of computer fraud is to have a good system of internal control that allows the benefits of computerization to be gained without opening the possibility for rampant fraud.

BEFORE YOU GO ON...

REVIEW IT

1. What are the two primary objectives of internal control?
2. Identify and describe the principles of internal control.
3. What are the limitations of internal control?

DO IT

Li Song owns a small retail store. Li wants to establish good internal control procedures but is confused about the difference between segregation of duties and independent internal verification. Explain the differences to Li.

ACTION PLAN

- Understand and explain the differences between (1) segregation of duties and (2) independent internal verification.

SOLUTION: Segregation of duties involves assigning responsibility so that the work of one employee evaluates the work of another employee. Segregation of duties occurs daily in executing and recording transactions. In contrast, independent internal verification involves reviewing, comparing, and reconciling data prepared by one or several employees. Independent internal verification occurs after the fact, as in the case of reconciling cash register totals at the end of the day with cash on hand.

Related exercise material: BE8-1, BE8-2, and E8-1.

THE NAVIGATOR

CASH CONTROLS

Just as cash is the beginning of a company's operating cycle, it is also usually the starting point for a company's system of internal control. Cash is the one asset that is readily convertible into any other type of asset. It is easily concealed and transported, and it is highly desired. Because of these characteristics, **cash is the asset most susceptible to improper diversion and use**. Moreover, because of the large volume of cash transactions, numerous errors may occur in executing and recording them. To safeguard cash and to ensure the accuracy of the accounting records for cash, effective internal control over cash is imperative.

Cash consists of coins, currency (paper money), checks, money orders, and money on hand or on deposit in a bank or similar depository. The general rule is that if the bank will accept it for deposit, it is cash. Items such as postage stamps and postdated checks (checks payable in the future) are not cash. Stamps are a prepaid expense; the postdated checks are accounts receivable. In the following sections we explain the application of internal control principles to cash receipts and cash disbursements.

INTERNATIONAL NOTE

Other countries also have control problems. For example, a judge in France has issued a 36-page "book" detailing many of the scams that are widespread, such as kickbacks in public-works contracts, the skimming of development aid money to Africa, and bribes on arms sales.

INTERNAL CONTROL OVER CASH RECEIPTS

Cash receipts come from a variety of sources: cash sales; collections on account from customers; the receipt of interest, rent, and dividends; investments by owners; bank loans; and proceeds from the sale of noncurrent assets. Illustration 8-4 shows how the internal control principles explained earlier apply to cash receipts transactions.

As might be expected, companies vary considerably in how they apply these principles. To illustrate internal control over cash receipts, we will examine control measures for a retail store with both over-the-counter and mail receipts.

STUDY OBJECTIVE 3

Explain the applications of internal control principles to cash receipts.

Over-the-Counter Receipts

Control of over-the-counter receipts in retail businesses is centered on cash registers that are visible to customers. In supermarkets and in variety stores such as **Kmart**, cash registers are placed in check-out lines near the exit. In stores such as **Sears, Roebuck & Co.** and **J. C. Penney**, each department has its own cash register. A cash sale is "rung up" on a cash register **with the amount clearly visible to the customer**. This measure prevents the cashier from ringing up a lower amount and pocketing the difference. The customer receives an itemized cash register receipt slip and is expected to count the change received. A cash register tape is locked into the register until removed by a supervisor or manager. This tape accumulates the daily transactions and totals. When the tape is removed, the supervisor compares the total with the amount of cash in the register. The tape should show all registered receipts accounted for. The supervisor's findings are reported on a cash count sheet which is signed by both the cashier and supervisor. The cash count sheet used by Alrite Food Mart is shown in Illustration 8-5.

Illustration 8-4

Application of internal control principles to cash receipts

Internal Control over Cash Receipts

Establishment of Responsibility

Only designated personnel are authorized to handle cash receipts (cashiers)

Physical, Mechanical, and Electronic Controls

Store cash in safes and bank vaults; limit access to storage areas; use cash registers

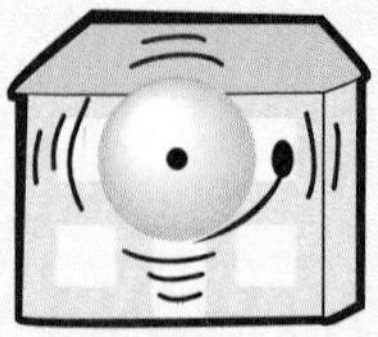

Segregation of Duties

Different individuals receive cash, record cash receipts, and hold the cash

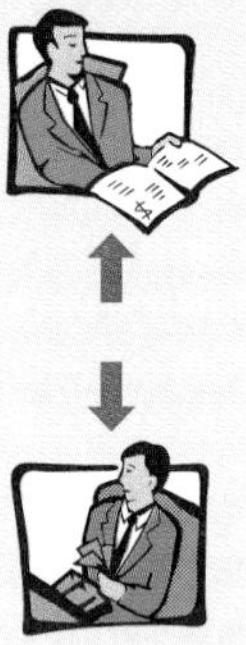

Independent Internal Verification

Supervisors count cash receipts daily; treasurer compares total receipts to bank deposits daily

Documentation Procedures

Use remittance advice (mail receipts), cash register tapes, and deposit slips

Other Controls

Bond personnel who handle cash; require employees to take vacations; deposit all cash in bank daily

Illustration 8-5

Cash count sheet

Store No. 8	Date March 8, 2002
1. Opening cash balance	$ 50.00
2. Cash sales per tape (attached)	6,956.20
3. Total cash to be accounted for	7,006.20
4. Cash on hand (see list)	6,996.10
5. Cash (short) or over	$ (10.10)
6. Ending cash balance	$ 50.00
7. Cash for deposit (Line 4 – Line 6)	$6,946.10
Cashier J. Cruse	Supervisor M. Braun

The count sheets, register tapes, and cash are then given to the head cashier. This individual prepares a daily cash summary showing the total cash received and the amount from each source, such as cash sales and collections on account. The head cashier sends one copy of the summary to the accounting department for entry into the cash receipts journal. The other copy goes to the treasurer's office for later comparison with the daily bank deposit.

Next, the head cashier prepares a deposit slip (see Illustration 8-9 on page 333) and makes the bank deposit. The total amount deposited should be equal to the total receipts on the daily cash summary. This will ensure that all receipts have been placed in the custody of the bank. In accepting the bank deposit, the bank stamps (authenticates) the duplicate deposit slip and sends it to the company treasurer, who makes the comparison with the daily cash summary.

These measures for cash sales are graphically presented in Illustration 8-6. The activities of the sales department are shown separately from those of the cashier's department to indicate the segregation of duties in handling cash.

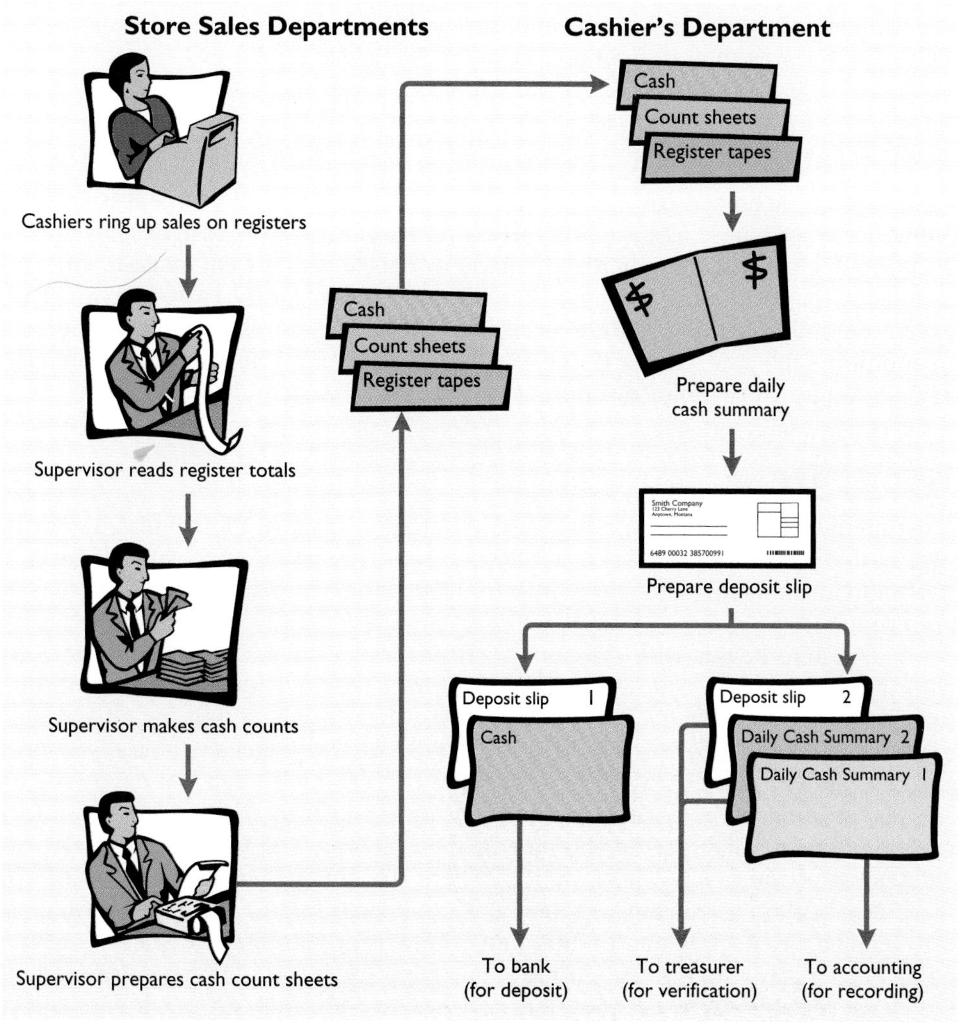

Illustration 8-6
Executing over-the-counter cash sales

HELPFUL HINT
Flowcharts such as this one enhance the understanding of the flow of documents, the processing steps, and the internal control procedures.

Mail Receipts

As an individual customer, you may be more familiar with over-the-counter receipts than with mail receipts. However, mail receipts resulting from billings and credit sales are by far the most common way cash is received by businesses. Think, for example, of the number of checks received through the mail daily by a national retailer such as **Lands' End** or **Abercrombie & Fitch**.

All mail receipts should be opened in the presence of two mail clerks. These receipts are generally in the form of checks or money orders. They frequently are accompanied by a remittance advice stating the purpose of the check (sometimes attached to the check, but often a part of the bill that the customer tears off and returns). Each check should be promptly endorsed "For Deposit Only" by use of a company stamp. This **restrictive endorsement** reduces the likelihood that the check will be diverted to personal use. Banks will not give an individual any cash under this type of endorsement.

A list of the checks received each day should be prepared in duplicate. This list shows the name of the issuer of the check, the purpose of the payment, and the amount of the check. Each mail clerk should sign the list to establish responsibility for the data. The original copy of the list, along with the checks and remittance advices, are then sent to the cashier's department. There they are added to over-the-counter receipts (if any) in preparing the daily cash summary and in making the daily bank deposit. Also, a copy of the list is sent to the treasurer's office for comparison with the total mail receipts shown on the daily cash summary. This copy ensures that all mail receipts have been included.

INTERNAL CONTROL OVER CASH DISBURSEMENTS

STUDY OBJECTIVE 4

Explain the applications of internal control principles to cash disbursements.

Cash may be disbursed for a variety of reasons, such as to pay expenses and liabilities, or to purchase assets. **Generally, internal control over cash disbursements is more effective when payments are made by check, rather than by cash.** One exception is **for incidental amounts that are paid out of petty cash.**[2] Payment by check generally occurs only after specified control procedures have been followed. In addition, the "paid" check provides proof of payment. Illustration 8-7 (on page 329) shows how principles of internal control apply to cash disbursements.

Voucher System

Most medium and large companies use vouchers as part of their internal control over cash disbursements. A **voucher system** is a network of approvals by authorized individuals acting independently to ensure that all disbursements by check are proper.

The system begins with the authorization to incur a cost or expense. It ends with the issuance of a check for the liability incurred. A **voucher** is an authorization form prepared for each expenditure. Vouchers are required for all types of cash disbursements except those from petty cash. The voucher generally is prepared in the accounts payable department.

The starting point in preparing a voucher is to fill in the appropriate information about the liability on the face of the voucher. The vendor's invoice provides most of the needed information. Then, the voucher must be recorded (in the journal called a **voucher register**) and filed according to the date on which it is to be paid. A check is sent on that date, the voucher is stamped "paid," and the paid voucher is sent to the accounting department for recording (in a journal called the **check register**). A voucher system involves two journal entries, similar to any accounts payable transaction, one to issue the voucher and a second to pay the voucher.

[2] The operation of a petty cash fund is explained on pages 330–332.

Illustration 8-7

Application of internal control principles to cash disbursements

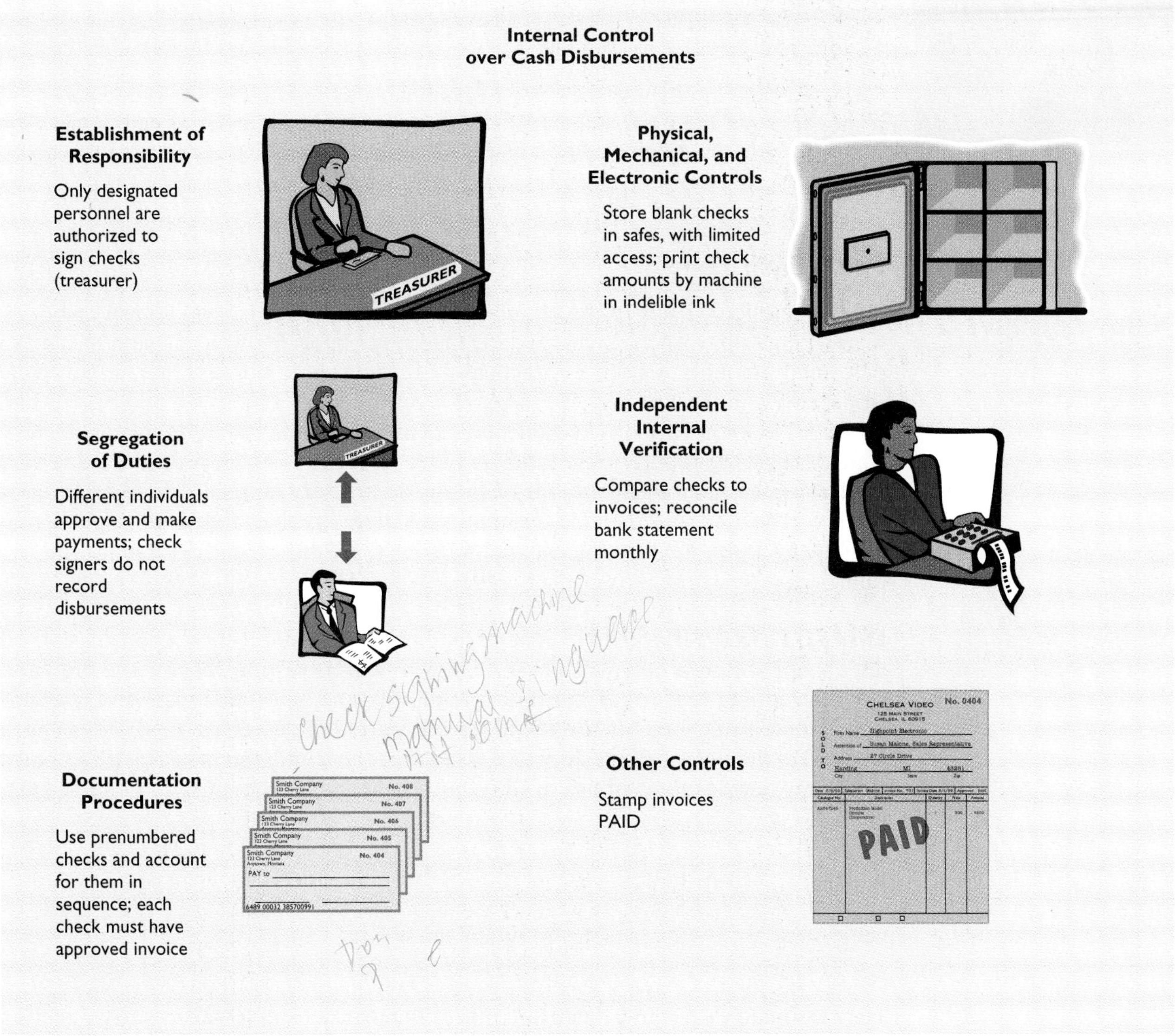
Internal Control over Cash Disbursements
Establishment of Responsibility
Only designated personnel are authorized to sign checks (treasurer)
TREASURER
Physical, Mechanical, and Electronic Controls
Store blank checks in safes, with limited access; print check amounts by machine in indelible ink
Segregation of Duties
Different individuals approve and make payments; check signers do not record disbursements
TREASURER
Independent Internal Verification
Compare checks to invoices; reconcile bank statement monthly
Documentation Procedures
Use prenumbered checks and account for them in sequence; each check must have approved invoice
Smith Company
No. 408
No. 407
No. 406
No. 405
No. 404
PAY to
Other Controls
Stamp invoices PAID
CHELSEA VIDEO
No. 0404
PAID

Electronic Funds Transfer (EFT) System

To account for and control cash is an expensive and time-consuming process. It was estimated recently that the cost to process a check through a bank system ranges from $0.55 to $1.00 and is increasing. It is not surprising that new approaches are being developed to transfer funds among parties without the use of paper (deposit tickets, checks, etc.). Such a procedure is called **electronic funds transfer (EFT)**. This disbursement system uses wire, telephone, telegraph, or computer to transfer cash from one location to another. Use of EFT is quite common. For example, the authors receive no formal payroll checks from their universities, which instead send magnetic tapes to the appropriate banks for deposit. Regular payments such as those for house, car, and utilities are frequently made by EFT.

TECHNOLOGY IN ACTION

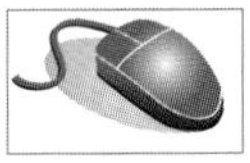

The development of EFT will continue. Already it is estimated that over 80 percent of the total volume of bank transactions in the United States is performed using EFT. The computer technology is available to create a "checkless" society. The only major barriers appear to be the individual's concern for privacy and protection and certain legislative constraints. Numerous safeguards have been built into EFT systems and are continuing to improve. However, the possibility of errors and fraud still exists because only a limited number of individuals are involved in the transfers, which may prevent appropriate segregation of duties.

Petty Cash Fund

STUDY OBJECTIVE 5

Describe the operation of a petty cash fund.

As you learned earlier in the chapter, better internal control over cash disbursements is possible when payments are made by check. However, using checks to pay small amounts is both impractical and a nuisance. For instance, a company would not want to write checks to pay for postage due, employee lunches, or taxi fares. A common way of handling such payments, while maintaining satisfactory control, is to use a petty cash fund. A **petty cash fund** is a cash fund used to pay relatively small amounts but still maintain satisfactory control. The operation of a petty cash fund, often called an **imprest system**, involves three steps: (1) establishing the fund, (2) making payments from the fund, and (3) replenishing the fund.[3]

ESTABLISHING THE FUND. Two essential steps in establishing a petty cash fund are (1) appointing a petty cash custodian who will be responsible for the fund and (2) determining the size of the fund. Ordinarily, the amount is expected to cover anticipated disbursements for a 3- to 4-week period. To establish the fund, a check payable to the petty cash custodian is issued for the stipulated amount. If the Laird Company decides to establish a $100 fund on March 1, the entry in general journal form is:

A	=	L	+	OE
+100				
−100				

Mar. 1	Petty Cash	100	
	Cash		100
	(To establish a petty cash fund)		

The custodian cashes the check and places the proceeds in a locked petty cash box or drawer. Most petty cash funds are established on a fixed-amount basis. No additional entries will be made to the Petty Cash account unless management changes the stipulated amount of the fund. For example, if Laird Company decides on July 1 to increase the size of the fund to $250, it would debit Petty Cash $150 and credit Cash $150.

MAKING PAYMENTS FROM THE FUND. The custodian of the petty cash fund has the authority to make payments from the fund that conform to prescribed management policies. Usually, management limits the size of expenditures that may be made. Likewise, it may not permit use of the fund for certain types of transactions (such as making short-term loans to employees). Each payment from the fund must be documented on a prenumbered petty cash receipt (or petty cash voucher), as shown in Illustration 8-8. Note that the signatures of both the custo-

[3]The term "imprest" means an advance of money for a designated purpose.

Illustration 8-8

Petty cash receipt

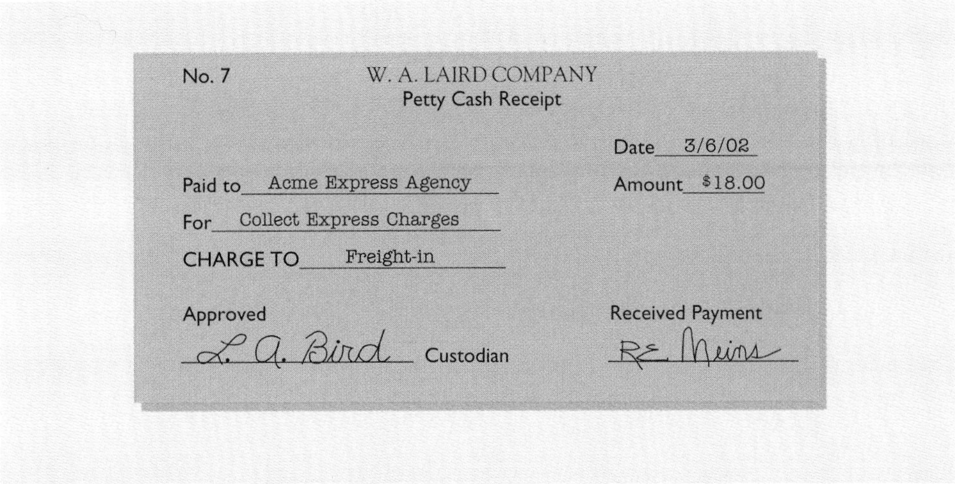
No. 7 W. A. LAIRD COMPANY
Petty Cash Receipt

Date 3/6/02

Paid to Acme Express Agency Amount $18.00

For Collect Express Charges

CHARGE TO Freight-in

Approved Received Payment

L. A. Bird Custodian R. E. Meins

dian and the person receiving payment are required on the receipt. If other supporting documents such as a freight bill or invoice are available, they should be attached to the petty cash receipt.

The receipts are kept in the petty cash box until the fund runs low and needs to be replenished. The sum of the petty cash receipts and money in the fund should equal the established total at all times. Surprise counts can be made at any time by an independent person, such as an internal auditor, to determine whether the fund is being maintained intact.

No accounting entry is made to record a payment at the time it is made from petty cash. It is considered unnecessary to do so. Instead, the accounting effects of each payment are recognized when the fund is replenished.

REPLENISHING THE FUND. When the money in the petty cash fund reaches a minimum level, the fund is replenished. The request for reimbursement is initiated by the petty cash custodian. This individual prepares a schedule (or summary) of the payments that have been made and sends the schedule, supported by petty cash receipts and other documentation, to the treasurer's office. The receipts and supporting documents are examined in the treasurer's office to verify that they were proper payments from the fund. The treasurer then approves the request and a check is prepared to restore the fund to its established amount. At the same time, all supporting documentation is stamped "paid" so that it cannot be submitted again for payment.

To illustrate, assume that on March 15 the petty cash custodian requests a check for $87. The fund contains $13 cash and petty cash receipts for postage $44, freight-out $38, and miscellaneous expenses $5. The general journal entry to record the check is:

Mar. 15	Postage Expense	44	
	Freight-out	38	
	Miscellaneous Expense	5	
	Cash		87
	(To replenish petty cash fund)		

A	=	L	+	OE
−87				−44
				−38
				−5

Note that the Petty Cash account is not affected by the reimbursement entry. Replenishment changes the composition of the fund by replacing the petty cash receipts with cash. It does not change the balance in the fund.

HELPFUL HINT
Cash over and short situations result from mathematical errors or from failure to keep accurate records.

It may be necessary in replenishing a petty cash fund to recognize a cash shortage or overage. This results when the cash plus receipts in the petty cash box do not equal the established amount of the petty cash fund. To illustrate, assume in the example on the preceding page that the custodian had only $12 in cash in the fund plus the receipts as listed. The request for reimbursement would, therefore, have been for $88. The following entry would be made:

A	=	L	+	OE
−88				−44
				−38
				−5
				−1

Mar. 15	Postage Expense	44	
	Freight-out	38	
	Miscellaneous Expense	5	
	Cash Over and Short	1	
	Cash		88
	(To replenish petty cash fund)		

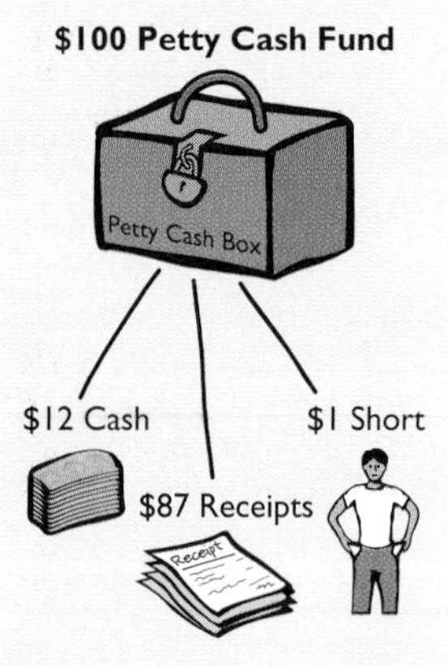

If the custodian had $14 in cash, the reimbursement request would have been for $86 and Cash Over and Short would have been credited for $1 (overage). A debit balance in Cash Over and Short is reported in the income statement as miscellaneous expense. A credit balance in the account is reported as miscellaneous revenue. Cash Over and Short is closed to Income Summary at the end of the year.

A petty cash fund should be replenished at the end of the accounting period regardless of the cash in the fund. Replenishment at this time is necessary in order to recognize the effects of the petty cash payments on the financial statements.

Internal control over a petty cash fund is strengthened by (1) having a supervisor make surprise counts of the fund to ascertain whether the paid vouchers and fund cash equal the imprest amount and (2) canceling or mutilating the paid vouchers so they cannot be resubmitted for reimbursement.

BEFORE YOU GO ON...

REVIEW IT

1. How do the principles of internal control apply to cash receipts?
2. How do the principles of internal control apply to cash disbursements?
3. When are entries required in a petty cash system?

DO IT

L. R. Cortez is concerned about the control over cash receipts in his fast-food restaurant, Big Cheese. The restaurant has two cash registers. At no time do more than two employees take customer orders and ring up sales. Work shifts for employees range from 4 to 8 hours. Cortez asks your help in installing a good system of internal control over cash receipts.

ACTION PLAN

- Differentiate among the internal control principles of (1) establishing responsibility, (2) using electronic controls, and (3) independent internal verification.
- Design an effective system of internal control over cash receipts.

SOLUTION: Cortez should assign a cash register to each employee at the start of each work shift, with register totals set at zero. Each employee should be instructed to use only the assigned register and to ring up all sales. At the end of each work shift, Cortez or a supervisor/manager should total the register and make a cash count to see whether all cash is accounted for.

Related exercise material: BE8-3, BE8-4, BE8-5, E8-2, E8-3, E8-4, and E8-5.

THE NAVIGATOR

USE OF A BANK

STUDY OBJECTIVE 6

Indicate the control features of a bank account.

The use of a bank contributes significantly to good internal control over cash. A company can safeguard its cash by using a bank as a depository and as a clearing house for checks received and checks written. Use of a bank minimizes the amount of currency that must be kept on hand. Also, the use of a bank facilitates the control of cash because it creates a double record of all bank transactions—one by the business and the other by the bank. The asset account Cash maintained by the depositor is the reciprocal of the bank's liability account for each depositor. It should be possible to **reconcile these accounts** (make them agree) at any time.

Opening a bank checking account is a relatively simple procedure. Typically, the bank makes a credit check on the new customer and the depositor is required to sign a **signature card**. The card contains the signatures of each person authorized to sign checks on the account. The signature card is used by bank employees to validate signatures on the checks.

Soon after an account is opened, the bank provides the depositor with serially numbered checks and deposit slips imprinted with the depositor's name and address. Each check and deposit slip is imprinted with both a bank and a depositor identification number. This number, printed in magnetic ink, permits computer processing of transactions.

Many companies have more than one bank account. For efficiency of operations and better control, national retailers like **Wal-Mart** and **Kmart** may have regional bank accounts. A company such as **Intel** with more than 70,000 employees may have a payroll bank account, as well as one or more general bank accounts. Also, a company may maintain several bank accounts in order to have more than one source for short-term loans when needed.

MAKING BANK DEPOSITS

Bank deposits should be made by an authorized employee, such as the head cashier. Each deposit must be documented by a deposit slip (ticket), as shown in Illustration 8-9.

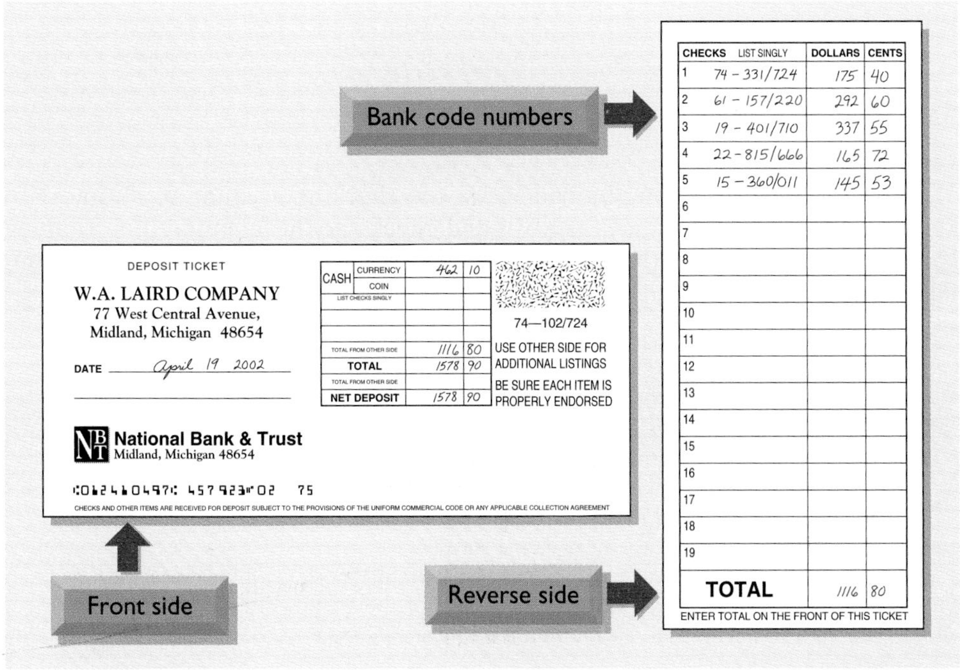
DEPOSIT TICKET

W.A. LAIRD COMPANY
77 West Central Avenue,
Midland, Michigan 48654

DATE April 19 2002

CASH			
	CURRENCY	462	10
	COIN		
LIST CHECKS SINGLY			
TOTAL FROM OTHER SIDE		1116	80
TOTAL		1578	90
TOTAL FROM OTHER SIDE			
NET DEPOSIT		1578	90

74—102/724

USE OTHER SIDE FOR ADDITIONAL LISTINGS

BE SURE EACH ITEM IS PROPERLY ENDORSED

National Bank & Trust
Midland, Michigan 48654

CHECKS AND OTHER ITEMS ARE RECEIVED FOR DEPOSIT SUBJECT TO THE PROVISIONS OF THE UNIFORM COMMERCIAL CODE OR ANY APPLICABLE COLLECTION AGREEMENT

CHECKS LIST SINGLY		DOLLARS	CENTS
1	74-331/724	175	40
2	61-157/220	292	60
3	19-401/710	337	55
4	22-815/666	165	72
5	15-360/011	145	53
6			
7			
8			
9			
10			
11			
12			
13			
14			
15			
16			
17			
18			
19			
TOTAL		1116	80

ENTER TOTAL ON THE FRONT OF THIS TICKET

Illustration 8-9
Deposit slip

Deposit slips are prepared in duplicate. The original is retained by the bank; the duplicate, machine-stamped by the bank to establish its authenticity, is retained by the depositor.

WRITING CHECKS

A **check** is a written order signed by the depositor directing the bank to pay a specified sum of money to a designated recipient. There are three parties to a check: (1) the **maker** (or drawer) who issues the check; (2) the **bank** (or payer) on which the check is drawn; and (3) the **payee** to whom the check is payable. A check is a **negotiable instrument** that can be transferred to another party by endorsement. Each check should be accompanied by an explanation of its purposes. In many businesses, this is done by a remittance advice attached to the check, as shown in Illustration 8-10.

Illustration 8-10

Check with remittance advice

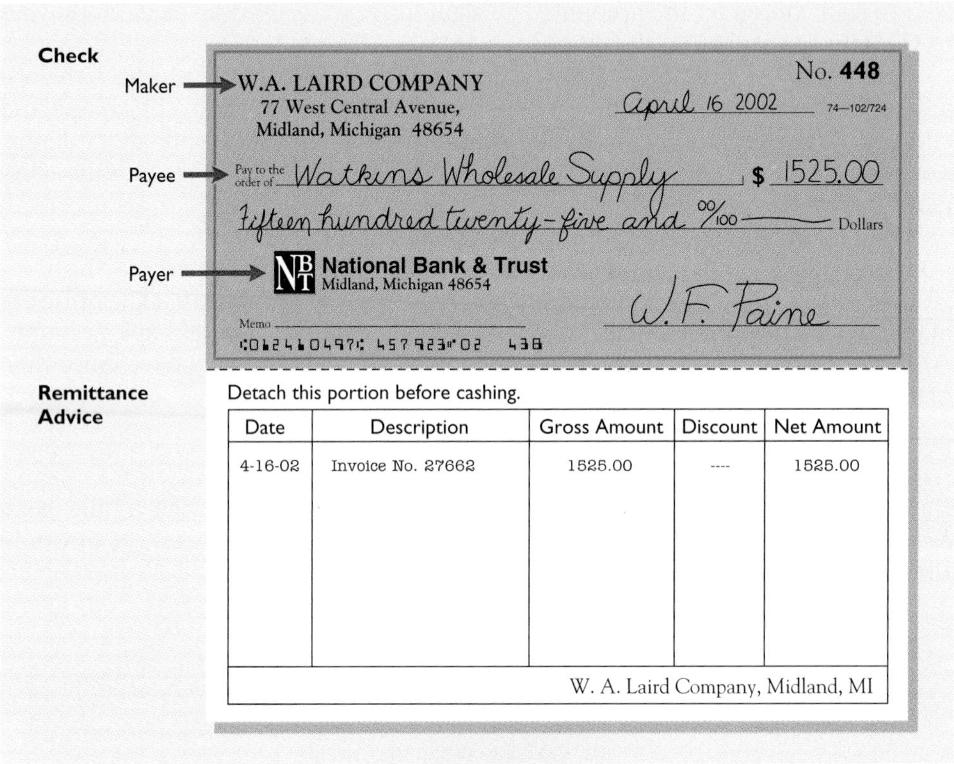

Date	Description	Gross Amount	Discount	Net Amount
4-16-02	Invoice No. 27662	1525.00	----	1525.00

W. A. Laird Company, Midland, MI

It is important to know the balance in the checking account at all times. To keep the balance current, each deposit and check should be entered on running balance memorandum forms provided by the bank or on the check stubs contained in the checkbook.

ACCOUNTING IN ACTION e Business Insight

Cash is virtually obsolete. We use debit cards and credit cards to pay for most of our purchases. But debit cards are usable only at specified locations, and credit cards are cumbersome for small transactions. They are no good for transferring cash between individuals or to small companies that don't want to pay credit card fees. Digital cash is the next online wave.

There are many digital-cash companies. One of the most flexible appears to be **PayPal.com.** PayPal has become popular with users of the auction site **eBay**, because it allows them to transfer funds to each other as easily as sending e-mail.

SOURCE: Mathew Ingram, "Will Digital Cash Work This Time?" *The Globe and Mail,* March 18, 2000, p. N4.

BANK STATEMENTS

Each month, the depositor receives a bank statement from the bank. A **bank statement** shows the depositor's bank transactions and balances. A typical statement is presented in Illustration 8-11. It shows (1) checks paid and other debits that reduce the balance in the depositor's account, (2) deposits and other credits that increase the balance in the depositor's account, and (3) the account balance after each day's transactions.

> **HELPFUL HINT**
> Essentially, the bank statement is a copy of the bank's records sent to the customer for periodic review.

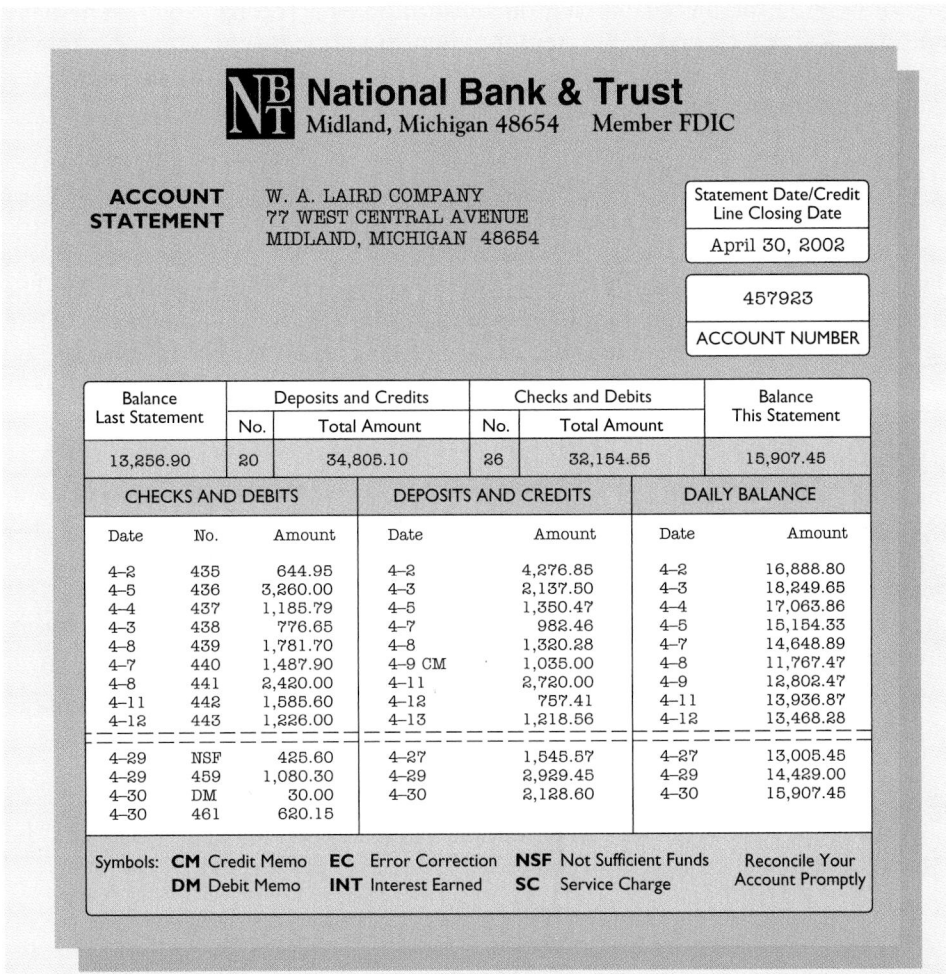

Illustration 8-11

Bank statement

National Bank & Trust
Midland, Michigan 48654 Member FDIC

ACCOUNT STATEMENT

W. A. LAIRD COMPANY
77 WEST CENTRAL AVENUE
MIDLAND, MICHIGAN 48654

Statement Date/Credit Line Closing Date
April 30, 2002

457923
ACCOUNT NUMBER

Balance Last Statement	Deposits and Credits		Checks and Debits		Balance This Statement
	No.	Total Amount	No.	Total Amount	
13,256.90	20	34,805.10	26	32,154.55	15,907.45

CHECKS AND DEBITS			DEPOSITS AND CREDITS		DAILY BALANCE	
Date	No.	Amount	Date	Amount	Date	Amount
4-2	435	644.95	4-2	4,276.85	4-2	16,888.80
4-5	436	3,260.00	4-3	2,137.50	4-3	18,249.65
4-4	437	1,185.79	4-5	1,350.47	4-4	17,063.86
4-3	438	776.65	4-7	982.46	4-5	15,154.33
4-8	439	1,781.70	4-8	1,320.28	4-7	14,648.89
4-7	440	1,487.90	4-9 CM	1,035.00	4-8	11,767.47
4-8	441	2,420.00	4-11	2,720.00	4-9	12,802.47
4-11	442	1,585.60	4-12	757.41	4-11	13,936.87
4-12	443	1,226.00	4-13	1,218.56	4-12	13,468.28
4-29	NSF	425.60	4-27	1,545.57	4-27	13,005.45
4-29	459	1,080.30	4-29	2,929.45	4-29	14,429.00
4-30	DM	30.00	4-30	2,128.60	4-30	15,907.45
4-30	461	620.15				

Symbols: **CM** Credit Memo **EC** Error Correction **NSF** Not Sufficient Funds
DM Debit Memo **INT** Interest Earned **SC** Service Charge

Reconcile Your Account Promptly

> **HELPFUL HINT**
> Every deposit received by the bank is *credited* to the customer's account. The reverse occurs when the bank "pays" a check issued by a company on its checking account balance: Payment reduces the bank's liability. Thus it is *debited* to the customer's account with the bank.

All "paid" checks are listed in numerical sequence on the bank statement along with the date the check was paid and its amount. Upon paying a check, the bank stamps the check "paid"; a paid check is sometimes referred to as a **canceled** check. Most banks offer depositors the option of receiving "paid" checks with their bank statements. For those who decline, the bank keeps a record of each check on microfilm.

The bank also includes on the bank statement memoranda explaining other debits and credits made by the bank to the depositor's account.

Debit Memorandum

Banks charge a monthly fee for their services. Often the fee is charged only when the average monthly balance in a checking account falls below a specified amount.

The fee, called a **bank service charge**, is identified on the bank statement by a code symbol such as SC. A debit memorandum explaining the charge is included with the bank statement and noted on the statement. Separate debit memoranda may also be issued for other bank services such as the cost of printing checks, issuing traveler's checks, and wiring funds to other locations. The symbol DM is often used for such charges.

A debit memorandum is also used by the bank when a deposited check from a customer "bounces" because of insufficient funds. In such a case, the check is marked **NSF** (not sufficient funds) by the customer's bank and is returned to the depositor's bank. The bank then debits the depositor's account, as shown by the symbol NSF on the bank statement in Illustration 8-11 (on page 335). The bank sends the NSF check and debit memorandum to the depositor as notification of the charge. The NSF check creates an account receivable for the depositor and reduces cash in the bank account.

Credit Memorandum

A depositor may ask the bank to collect its notes receivable. In such a case, the bank will credit the depositor's account for the cash proceeds of the note. This is illustrated on the W. A. Laird Company bank statement by the symbol CM. The bank will issue a credit memorandum which is sent with the statement to explain the entry. Many banks also offer interest on checking accounts. The interest earned may be indicated on the bank statement by the symbol CM or INT.

RECONCILING THE BANK ACCOUNT

STUDY OBJECTIVE 7

Prepare a bank reconciliation.

The bank and the depositor maintain independent records of the depositor's checking account. If you've never had a checking account, you might assume that the respective balances will always agree. In fact, the two balances are seldom the same at any given time. It is therefore necessary to make the balance per books agree with the balance per bank—a process called **reconciling the bank account**. The lack of agreement between the two balances is due to:

1. **Time lags** that prevent one of the parties from recording the transaction in the same period.
2. **Errors** by either party in recording transactions.

Time lags occur frequently. For example, several days may elapse between the time a check is mailed to a payee and the date the check is paid by the bank.

ACCOUNTING IN ACTION *Ethics Insight*

Some firms have used time lags to their advantage. For example, **E. F. Hutton** managers at one time overdrew their accounts by astronomical amounts—on some days the overdrafts totaled $1 billion. These overdrafts created interest-free loans that the company could invest. The loans lasted as long as it took for the covering checks to be collected. Although not technically illegal at the time, Hutton's actions were wrong because it did not have the bank's permission to do so. The discovery of this practice led to E. F. Hutton's demise.

Similarly, when the depositor uses the bank's night depository to make its deposits, there will be a difference of at least one day between the time the receipts are recorded by the depositor and the time they are recorded by the bank. A time lag also occurs whenever the bank mails a debit or credit memorandum to the depositor.

Also, errors sometimes occur. The incidence of errors depends on the effectiveness of the internal controls of the depositor and the bank. Bank errors are infrequent. However, either party could inadvertently record a $450 check as $45 or $540. In addition, the bank might mistakenly charge a check drawn by C. D. Berg to the account of C. D. Burg.

Reconciliation Procedure

To obtain maximum benefit from a bank reconciliation, the reconciliation should be prepared by an employee who has no other responsibilities pertaining to cash. When the internal control principle of independent internal verification is not followed in preparing the reconciliation, cash embezzlements may go unnoticed. For example, a cashier who prepares the reconciliation can embezzle cash and conceal the embezzlement by misstating the reconciliation. Thus, the bank accounts would reconcile, and the embezzlement would not be detected.

In reconciling the bank account, it is customary to reconcile the balance per books and balance per bank to their adjusted (correct or true) cash balances. The reconciliation schedule is divided into two sections. The starting point in preparing the reconciliation is to enter the balance per bank statement and balance per books on the schedule. Adjustments are then made to each section, as shown in Illustration 8-12. The steps listed on the next page should reveal all the reconciling items that cause the difference between the two balances.

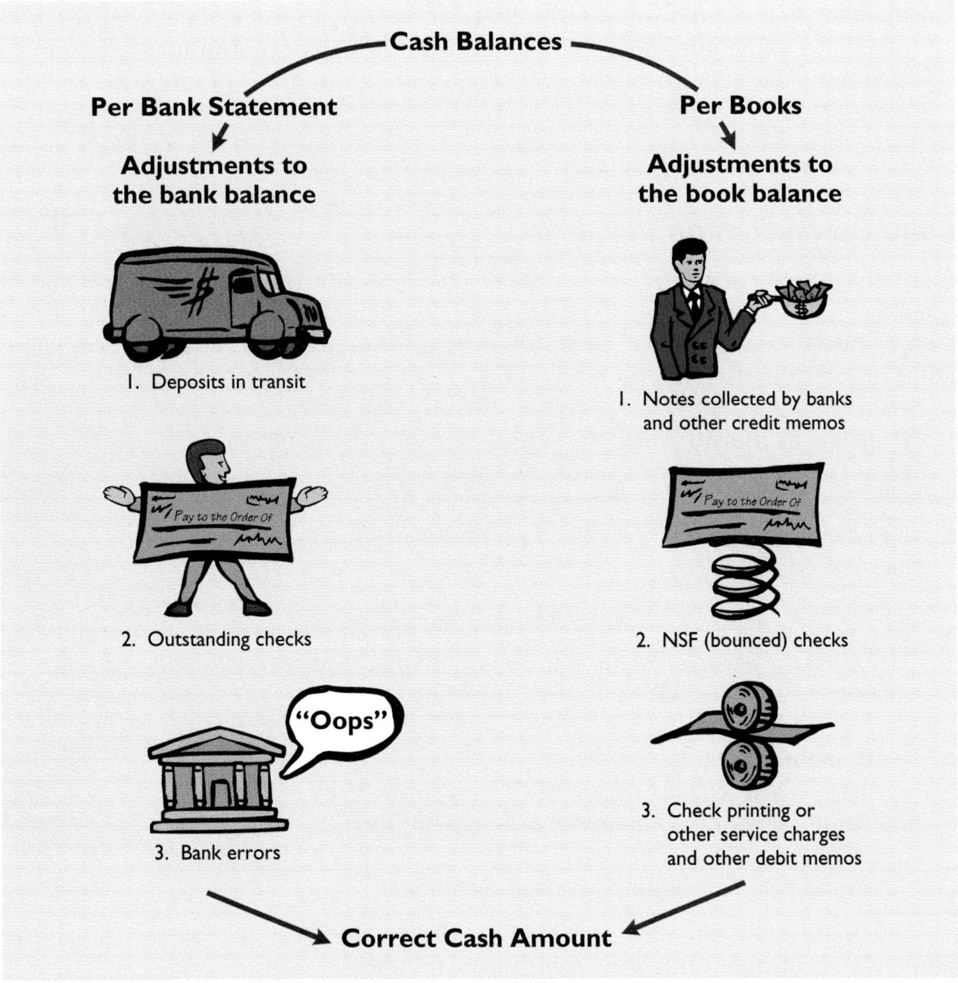

Illustration 8-12

Bank reconciliation procedures

Steps in the Reconciliation Procedure

1. **Deposits in transit.** Compare the individual deposits on the bank statement with deposits in transit from the preceding bank reconciliation and with the deposits per company records or duplicate deposit slips. Deposits recorded by the depositor that have not been recorded by the bank represent **deposits in transit**. They are added to the balance per bank.

> **HELPFUL HINT**
> Deposits in transit and outstanding checks are reconciling items because of time lags.

2. **Outstanding checks.** Compare the paid checks shown on the bank statement or the paid checks returned with the bank statement with (a) checks outstanding from the preceding bank reconciliation, and (b) checks issued by the company as recorded in the cash payments journal. Issued checks recorded by the company that have not been paid by the bank represent **outstanding checks**. They are deducted from the balance per the bank.

3. **Errors.** Note any **errors** discovered in the foregoing steps. List them in the appropriate section of the reconciliation schedule. For example, if a paid check correctly written by the company for $195 was mistakenly recorded by the company for $159, the error of $36 is deducted from the balance per books. All errors made by the depositor are reconciling items in determining the adjusted cash balance per books. In contrast, all errors made by the bank are reconciling items in determining the adjusted cash balance per the bank.

4. **Bank memoranda.** Trace **bank memoranda** to the depositor's records. Any unrecorded memoranda should be listed in the appropriate section of the reconciliation schedule. For example, a $5 debit memorandum for bank service charges is deducted from the balance per books, and $32 of interest earned is added to the balance per books.

Bank Reconciliation Illustrated

The bank statement for Laird Company was shown in Illustration 8-11. It shows a balance per bank of $15,907.45 on April 30, 2002. On this date the balance of cash per books is $11,589.45. From the foregoing steps, the following reconciling items are determined.

1. **Deposits in transit:** April 30 deposit (received by bank on May 1).	$2,201.40
2. **Outstanding checks:** No. 453, $3,000.00; no. 457, $1,401.30; no. 460, $1,502.70.	5,904.00
3. **Errors:** Check no. 443 was correctly written by Laird for $1,226.00 and was correctly paid by the bank. However, it was recorded for $1,262.00 by Laird Company.	36.00
4. **Bank memoranda:**	
a. Debit—NSF check from J. R. Baron for $425.60	425.60
b. Debit—Printing company checks charge $30.00	30.00
c. Credit—Collection of note receivable for $1,000 plus interest earned $50, less bank collection fee $15.00	1,035.00

> **HELPFUL HINT**
> Note in the bank statement that checks no. 459 and 461 have been paid but check no. 460 is not listed. Thus, this check is outstanding. If a complete bank statement were provided, checks no. 453 and 457 would also not be listed. The amounts for these three checks are obtained from the company's cash payments records.

The bank reconciliation is shown in Illustration 8-13.

Illustration 8-13

Bank reconciliation

W. A. LAIRD COMPANY Bank Reconciliation April 30, 2002		
Cash balance per bank statement		$15,907.45
Add: Deposits in transit		2,201.40
		18,108.85
Less: Outstanding checks		
No. 453	$3,000.00	
No. 457	1,401.30	
No. 460	1,502.70	5,904.00
Adjusted cash balance per bank		**$12,204.85**
Cash balance per books		$11,589.45
Add: Collection of note receivable $1,000, plus interest earned $50, less collection fee $15	$1,035.00	
Error in recording check no. 443	36.00	1,071.00
		12,660.45
Less: NSF check	425.60	
Bank service charge	30.00	455.60
Adjusted cash balance per books		**$12,204.85**

ALTERNATIVE TERMINOLOGY
The terms *adjusted balance, true cash balance,* and *correct cash balance* may be used interchangeably.

Entries from Bank Reconciliation

Each reconciling item in determining the **adjusted cash balance per books** should be recorded by the depositor. **If these items are not journalized and posted, the Cash account will not show the correct balance.** The entries for W. A. Laird Company on April 30 are as follows.

HELPFUL HINT
The entries that follow are adjusting entries. In prior chapters, Cash was an account that did not require adjustment. That was a simplifying assumption for learning purposes, because a bank reconciliation had not been explained.

COLLECTION OF NOTE RECEIVABLE. This entry involves four accounts. Assuming that the interest of $50 has not been accrued and the collection fee is charged to Miscellaneous Expense, the entry is:

Apr. 30	Cash	1,035.00	
	Miscellaneous Expense	15.00	
	Notes Receivable		1,000.00
	Interest Revenue		50.00
	(To record collection of notes receivable by bank)		

A	=	L	+	OE
+1,035				−15
−1,000				+50

BOOK ERROR. The cash disbursements journal shows that check no. 443 was a payment on account to Andrea Company, a supplier. The correcting entry is:

Apr. 30	Cash	36.00	
	Accounts Payable—Andrea Company		36.00
	(To correct error in recording check no. 443)		

A	=	L	+	OE
+36		+36		

NSF CHECK. As indicated earlier, an NSF check becomes an account receivable to the depositor. The entry is:

Apr. 30	Accounts Receivable—J. R. Baron	425.60	
	Cash		425.60
	(To record NSF check)		

A	=	L	+	OE
+425.60				
−425.60				

BANK SERVICE CHARGES. Check printing charges (DM) and other bank service charges (SC) are debited to Miscellaneous Expense. They are usually nominal in amount. The entry is:

A	=	L	+	OE
−30				−30

Apr. 30	Miscellaneous Expense	30.00	
	Cash		30.00
	(To record charge for printing company checks)		

The foregoing four entries could also be combined into one compound entry.

After the entries are posted, the cash account will show the following.

Illustration 8-14

Adjusted balance in cash account

Cash

Apr. 30 Bal.	11,589.45	Apr. 30	425.60
30	1,035.00	30	30.00
30	36.00		
Apr. 30 Bal.	**12,204.85**		

The adjusted cash balance in the ledger should agree with the adjusted cash balance per books in the bank reconciliation in Illustration 8-13.

What entries does the bank make? If any bank errors are discovered in preparing the reconciliation, the bank should be notified. It then can make the necessary corrections on its records. The bank does not make any entries for deposits in transit or outstanding checks. Only when these items reach the bank will the bank record these items.

BEFORE YOU GO ON...

REVIEW IT

1. Why is it necessary to reconcile a bank account?
2. What steps are involved in the reconciliation procedure?
3. What information is included in a bank reconciliation?

DO IT

Sally Kist owns Linen Kist Fabrics. Sally asks you to explain how the following reconciling items should be treated in reconciling the bank account: (1) a debit memorandum for an NSF check, (2) a credit memorandum for a note collected by the bank, (3) outstanding checks, and (4) a deposit in transit.

ACTION PLAN

- Understand the purpose of a bank reconciliation.
- Identify time lags and explain how they cause reconciling items.

SOLUTION: In reconciling the bank account, the reconciling items are treated as follows.

NSF check: Deducted from balance per books.
Collection of note: Added to balance per books.
Outstanding checks: Deducted from balance per bank.
Deposit in transit: Added to balance per bank.

Related exercise material: BE8-6, BE8-7, BE8-8, BE8-9, BE8-10, E8-6, E8-7, E8-8, E8-9, and E8-10.

THE NAVIGATOR

REPORTING CASH

STUDY OBJECTIVE 8

Explain the reporting of cash.

Cash on hand, cash in banks, and petty cash are often combined and reported simply as **Cash**. Because it is the most liquid asset owned by a company, cash is listed first in the current assets section of the balance sheet. Some companies use the term "Cash and cash equivalents" in reporting cash, as illustrated by the following.

Illustration 8-15

Presentation of cash and cash equivalents

EASTMAN KODAK COMPANY
Balance Sheets (partial)

	1999	1998
Current assets (in millions)		
Cash and cash equivalents	$373	$457

Cash equivalents are highly liquid investments that can be converted into a specific amount of cash. They typically have maturities of three months or less when purchased. They include money market funds, money market savings certificates, bank certificates of deposit, and U.S. Treasury bills and notes.

A company may have cash that is restricted for a special purpose. An example is a payroll bank account for paying salaries and wages. Another would be a plant expansion cash fund for financing new construction. If the restricted cash is expected to be used **within the next year**, the amount should be reported as a current asset. When the restricted funds will not be used in that time, they should be reported as a noncurrent asset. Since a payroll bank account will be used as early as the next payday, it is reported as a current asset. In contrast, unless the new construction will begin within the next year, plant expansion fund cash is classified as a noncurrent asset (long-term investment).

In making loans to depositors, banks commonly require borrowers to maintain minimum cash balances. These minimum balances, called **compensating balances**, provide the bank with support for the loans. They are a restriction on the use of cash that may affect a company's liquidity. Thus, compensating balances should be disclosed in the financial statements.

BEFORE YOU GO ON...

REVIEW IT

1. What is generally reported as cash on a company's balance sheet?
2. What is meant by cash equivalents and compensating balances?
3. At what amount does **Lands' End** report cash and cash equivalents in its 2000 consolidated balance sheet? The answer to this question is provided on page 359.

A LOOK BACK AT OUR FEATURE STORY

Refer back to the Feature Story about **Stephanie's Gourmet Coffee and More** café at the beginning of the chapter, and answer the following questions.

1. Does Stephanie Mintenko have a valid basis for establishing responsibility for overages or shortages? Why or why not?
2. What internal control principles are applicable to reconciling the cash register tape and the amount of cash in the cash drawer at the end of each shift?
3. What internal control principle is violated by not printing a receipt for each customer who purchases beverages, a meal, or uses the café's computers?
4. Do you think cashiers are, or should be, bonded (insured against misappropriation of assets)?
5. What adjusting entry would the bookkeeper likely make to record a cash shortage of $5?

SOLUTION

1. Establishing responsibility for overages or shortages occurs twice a day: at the end of the 5:00 pm shift, and at closing. This procedure provides a valid basis for evaluation only if one person worked an assigned register since the last reconciliation. Since up to three people work a single register during a shift, there is no valid basis for establishing who is responsible for any overage or shortage.
2. Internal control principles are: (a) Authorization—not applicable since cashiers are not assigned to a specific cash register for their shift. (b) Segregation of duties—cashiers (other than the owner/manager) are not involved in performing the reconciliation. (c) Documentation—the cash register tape provides the documentation for total receipts for the shift. (d) Safeguard assets—an electronic cash register is used with an internal tape whose access presumably is restricted. (e) Independent verification—a bookkeeper, in addition to Stephanie Mintenko, performs the reconciliation regularly.
3. The principle of documentation procedures is involved. If a customer making a purchase sees that a sale isn't rung up or if the customer doesn't request a receipt, there is a possibility that the transaction has not been recorded. But the internal control does not reside in the receipt itself. The control is forcing the cashier to ring up each sale so that a receipt is produced. Each receipt is recorded on an internal cash register tape. At the end of the day, the tape is used in determining overages or shortages.
4. It is doubtful that Stephanie's café would bond part-time employees. From the employer's standpoint, bonding is protection against major embezzlements by dishonest employees. The risk of this occurring in a small café, with the active participation of the owner/manager, is relatively low.
5. Cash Over and Short (miscellaneous expense account) and Cash:

Cash Over and Short (miscellaneous expense account)	5	
Cash		5

THE NAVIGATOR

DEMONSTRATION PROBLEM

Additional Demonstration Problem

Trillo Company's bank statement for May 2002 shows the following data.

Balance 5/1	$12,650	Balance 5/31	$14,280
Debit memorandum:		Credit memorandum:	
NSF check	$175	Collection of note receivable	$505

The cash balance per books at May 31 is $13,319. Your review of the data reveals the following.

1. The NSF check was from Hup Co., a customer.
2. The note collected by the bank was a $500, 3-month, 12% note. The bank charged a $10 collection fee. No interest has been accrued.
3. Outstanding checks at May 31 total $2,410.
4. Deposits in transit at May 31 total $1,752.
5. A Trillo Company check for $352 dated May 10 cleared the bank on May 25. This check, which was a payment on account, was journalized for $325.

Instructions

(a) Prepare a bank reconciliation at May 31.
(b) Journalize the entries required by the reconciliation.

SOLUTION TO DEMONSTRATION PROBLEM

(a)

TRILLO COMPANY
Bank Reconciliation
May 31, 2002

Cash balance per bank statement		$14,280
Add: Deposits in transit		1,752
		16,032
Less: Outstanding checks		2,410
Adjusted cash balance per bank		$13,622
Cash balance per books		$13,319
Add: Collection of note receivable $500, plus $15 interest, less collection fee $10		505
		13,824
Less: NSF check	$175	
Error in recording check	27	202
Adjusted cash balance per books		$13,622

(b)

May 31	Cash	505	
	Miscellaneous Expense	10	
	Notes Receivable		500
	Interest Revenue		15
	(To record collection of note by bank)		
31	Accounts Receivable—Hup Co.	175	
	Cash		175
	(To record NSF check from Hup Co.)		
31	Accounts Payable	27	
	Cash		27
	(To correct error in recording check)		

ACTION PLAN

- Follow the four steps in the reconciliation procedure. (p. 338).
- Work carefully to minimize mathematical errors in the reconciliation.
- Prepare adjusting entries from reconciling items per books.
- Make sure the cash ledger balance after posting the reconciling entries agrees with the adjusted cash balance per books.

THE NAVIGATOR

SUMMARY OF STUDY OBJECTIVES

1. *Define internal control.* Internal control is the plan of organization and related methods and procedures adopted within a business to safeguard its assets and to enhance the accuracy and reliability of its accounting records.

2. *Identify the principles of internal control.* The principles of internal control are: establishment of responsibility; segregation of duties; documentation procedures; physical, mechanical, and electronic controls; independent internal verification; and other controls.

3. *Explain the applications of internal control principles to cash receipts.* Internal controls over cash receipts include: (a) designating only personnel such as cashiers to handle cash; (b) assigning the duties of receiving cash, recording cash, and custody of cash to different individuals; (c) obtaining remittance advices for mail receipts, cash register tapes for over-the-counter receipts, and deposit slips for bank deposits; (d) using company safes and bank vaults to store cash with access limited to authorized personnel, and using cash registers in executing over-the-counter receipts; (e) making independent daily counts of register receipts and daily comparisons of total receipts with total deposits; and (f) bonding personnel that handle cash and requiring them to take vacations.

4. *Explain the applications of internal control principles to cash disbursements.* Internal controls over cash disbursements include: (a) having only specified individuals such as the treasurer authorized to sign checks; (b) assigning the duties of approving items for payment, paying the items, and recording the payment to different individuals; (c) using prenumbered checks and accounting for all checks, with each check supported by an approved invoice; (d) storing blank checks in a safe or vault with access restricted to authorized personnel, and using a checkwriter to imprint amounts on checks; (e) comparing each check with the approved invoice before issuing the check, and making monthly reconciliations of bank and book balances; and (f) after payment, stamping each approved invoice "paid."

5. *Describe the operation of a petty cash fund.* In operating a petty cash fund, it is necessary to establish the fund, make payments from the fund, and replenish the fund.

6. *Indicate the control features of a bank account.* A bank account contributes to good internal control by providing physical controls for the storage of cash. It minimizes the amount of currency that must be kept on hand, and it creates a double record of a depositor's bank transactions.

7. *Prepare a bank reconciliation.* It is customary to reconcile the balance per books and balance per bank to their adjusted balances. The steps in determining the reconciling items are to ascertain deposits in transit, outstanding checks, errors by the depositor or the bank, and unrecorded bank memoranda.

8. *Explain the reporting of cash.* Cash is listed first in the current assets section of the balance sheet. In some cases, cash is reported together with cash equivalents. Cash restricted for a special purpose is reported separately as a current asset or as a noncurrent asset, depending on when the cash is expected to be used.

THE NAVIGATOR

Key Term Matching Activity

GLOSSARY

Bank service charge A fee charged by a bank for the use of its services. (p. 336).

Bank statement A statement received monthly from the bank that shows the depositor's bank transactions and balances. (p. 335).

Cash Resources that consist of coins, currency, checks, money orders, and money on hand or on deposit in a bank or similar depository. (p. 325).

Cash equivalents Highly liquid investments, with maturities of three months or less when purchased, that can be converted to a specific amount of cash. (p. 341).

Check A written order signed by the depositor directing the bank to pay a specified sum of money to a designated recipient. (p. 334).

Compensating balances Minimum cash balances required by a bank in support of bank loans. (p. 341).

Deposits in transit Deposits recorded by the depositor that have not been recorded by the bank. (p. 338).

Electronic funds transfer (EFT) A disbursement system that uses wire, telephone, telegraph, or computer to transfer cash from one location to another. (p. 329).

Internal auditors Company employees who evaluate on a continuous basis the effectiveness of the company's system of internal control. (p. 323).

Internal control The plan of organization and all the related methods and measures adopted within a business to safeguard its assets and enhance the accuracy and reliability of its accounting records. (p. 318).

NSF check A check that is not paid by a bank because of insufficient funds in a customer's bank account. (p. 336).

Outstanding checks Checks issued and recorded by a company that have not been paid by the bank. (p. 338).

Petty cash fund A cash fund used to pay relatively small amounts. (p. 330).

Voucher An authorization form prepared for each payment by check in a voucher system. (p. 328).

Voucher system A network of approvals by authorized individuals acting independently to ensure that all disbursements by check are proper. (p. 328).

Chapter 8 Self-Test

SELF-STUDY QUESTIONS

Answers are at the end of the chapter.

(SO 1) **1.** Internal control is used in a business to enhance the accuracy and reliability of its accounting records and to:
a. safeguard its assets.
b. prevent fraud.
c. produce correct financial statements.
d. deter employee dishonesty.

(SO 2) **2.** The principles of internal control do not include:
a. establishment of responsibility.
b. documentation procedures.
c. management responsibility.
d. independent internal verification.

(SO 2) **3.** Physical controls do *not* include:
a. safes and vaults to store cash.
b. independent bank reconciliations.
c. locked warehouses for inventories.
d. bank safety deposit boxes for important papers.

(SO 3) **4.** Which of the following items in a cash drawer at November 30 is *not* cash?
a. Money orders.
b. Coins and currency.
c. A customer check dated December 1.
d. A customer check dated November 28.

(SO 3) **5.** Permitting only designated personnel to handle cash receipts is an application of the principle of:
a. segregation of duties.
b. establishment of responsibility.
c. independent check.
d. other controls.

(SO 4) **6.** The use of prenumbered checks in disbursing cash is an application of the principle of:
a. establishment of responsibility.
b. segregation of duties.
c. physical, mechanical, and electronic controls.
d. documentation procedures.

7. A check is written to replenish a $100 petty cash fund (SO 5)
when the fund contains receipts of $94 and $3 in cash. In recording the check,
a. Cash Over and Short should be debited for $3.
b. Petty Cash should be debited for $94.
c. Cash should be credited for $94.
d. Petty Cash should be credited for $3.

8. The control features of a bank account do *not* include: (SO 6)
a. having bank auditors verify the correctness of the bank balance per books.
b. minimizing the amount of cash that must be kept on hand.
c. providing a double record of all bank transactions.
d. safeguarding cash by using a bank as a depository.

9. In a bank reconciliation, deposits in transit are: (SO 7)
a. deducted from the book balance.
b. added to the book balance.
c. added to the bank balance.
d. deducted from the bank balance.

10. The reconciling item in a bank reconciliation that will (SO 7)
result in an adjusting entry by the depositor is:
a. outstanding checks.
b. deposit in transit.
c. a bank error.
d. bank service charges.

11. The statement that correctly describes the reporting of (SO 8)
cash is:
a. Cash cannot be combined with cash equivalents.
b. Restricted cash funds may be combined with Cash.
c. Cash is listed first in the current assets section.
d. Restricted cash funds cannot be reported as a current asset.

THE NAVIGATOR

QUESTIONS

1. "Internal control is concerned only with enhancing the accuracy of the accounting records." Do you agree? Explain.

2. What principles of internal control apply to most business enterprises?

3. At the corner grocery store, all sales clerks make change out of one cash register drawer. Is this a violation of internal control? Why?

4. Roger Holloway is reviewing the principle of segregation of duties. What are the two common applications of this principle?

5. How do documentation procedures contribute to good internal control?

6. What internal control objectives are met by physical, mechanical, and electronic controls?

7. (a) Explain the control principle of independent internal verification. (b) What practices are important in applying this principle?

8. The management of Borke Company asks you, as the company accountant, to explain (a) the concept of reasonable assurance in internal control and (b) the importance of the human factor in internal control.

9. Fred's Fertilizer Co. owns the following assets at the balance sheet date.

Cash in bank savings account	$ 6,000
Cash on hand	850
Cash refund due from the IRS	1,000
Checking account balance	12,000
Postdated checks	500

What amount should be reported as cash in the balance sheet?

10. What principle(s) of internal control is (are) involved in making daily cash counts of over-the-counter receipts?

11. Motown Department Stores has just installed new electronic cash registers in its stores. How do cash registers improve internal control over cash receipts?

12. At West Side Wholesale Company, two mail clerks open all mail receipts. How does this strengthen internal control?

13. "To have maximum effective internal control over cash disbursements, all payments should be made by check." Is this true? Explain.

14. Mary Miller Company's internal controls over cash disbursements provide for the treasurer to sign checks imprinted by a checkwriter after comparing the check with the approved invoice. Identify the internal control principles that are present in these controls.

15. How do the principles of (a) physical, mechanical, and electronic controls and (b) other controls apply to cash disbursements?

16. (a) What is a voucher system? (b) What principles of internal control apply to a voucher system?

17. What is the essential feature of an electronic funds transfer (EFT) procedure?

18. (a) Identify the three activities that pertain to a petty cash fund, and indicate an internal control principle that is applicable to each activity. (b) When are journal entries required in the operation of a petty cash fund?

19. "The use of a bank contributes significantly to good internal control over cash." Is this true? Why or why not?

20. Jana Kingston is confused about the lack of agreement between the cash balance per books and the balance per the bank. Explain the causes for the lack of agreement to Jana, and give an example of each cause.

21. What are the four steps involved in finding differences between the balance per books and balance per bank?

22. Candy Mowinski asks your help concerning an NSF check. Explain to Candy (a) what an NSF check is, (b) how it is treated in a bank reconciliation, and (c) whether it will require an adjusting entry per bank.

23. (a) "Cash equivalents are the same as cash." Do you agree? Explain. (b) How should restricted cash funds be reported on the balance sheet?

BRIEF EXERCISES

Explain the importance of internal control.
(SO 1)

BE8-1 Sandy Alcorn is the new owner of Galaxy Parking. She has heard about internal control but is not clear about its importance for her business. Explain to Sandy the two purposes of internal control and give her one application of each purpose for Galaxy Parking.

Identify internal control principles.
(SO 2)

BE8-2 The internal control procedures in Energy Company provide that:

(a) Employees who have physical custody of assets do not have access to the accounting records.

(b) Each month the assets on hand are compared to the accounting records by an internal auditor.

(c) A prenumbered shipping document is prepared for each shipment of goods to customers.

Identify the principles of internal control that are being followed.

Identify the internal control principles applicable to cash receipts.
(SO 3)

BE8-3 Endrun Company has the following internal control procedures over cash receipts. Identify the internal control principle that is applicable to each procedure.

1. All over-the-counter receipts are registered on cash registers.
2. All cashiers are bonded.
3. Daily cash counts are made by cashier department supervisors.
4. The duties of receiving cash, recording cash, and custody of cash are assigned to different individuals.
5. Only cashiers may operate cash registers.

Identify the internal control principle applicable to cash disbursements.
(SO 4)

BE8-4 Oswego Company has the following internal control procedures over cash disbursements. Identify the internal control principle that is applicable to each procedure.

1. Company checks are prenumbered.
2. The bank statement is reconciled monthly by an internal auditor.
3. Blank checks are stored in a safe in the treasurer's office.
4. Only the treasurer or assistant treasurer may sign checks.
5. Check signers are not allowed to record cash disbursement transactions.

BE8-5 On March 20, Elgin's petty cash fund of $100 is replenished when the fund contains $11 in cash and receipts for postage $52, freight-out $26, and travel expense $10. Prepare the journal entry to record the replenishment of the petty cash fund.

Prepare entry to replenish a petty cash fund.
(SO 5)

BE8-6 John Gleason is uncertain about the control features of a bank account. Explain the control benefits of **(a)** a signature card, **(b)** a check, and **(c)** a bank statement.

Identify the control features of a bank account.
(SO 6)

BE8-7 The following reconciling items are applicable to the bank reconciliation for St. Charles Company: (1) outstanding checks, (2) bank debit memorandum for service charge, (3) bank credit memorandum for collecting a note for the depositor, (4) deposit in transit. Indicate how each item should be shown on a bank reconciliation.

Indicate location of reconciling items in a bank reconciliation.
(SO 7)

BE8-8 Using the data in BE8-7, indicate **(a)** the items that will result in an adjustment to the depositor's records and **(b)** why the other items do not require adjustment.

Identify reconciling items that require adjusting entries.
(SO 7)

BE8-9 At July 31, Batavia Company has the following bank information: cash balance per bank $7,420, outstanding checks $762, deposits in transit $1,700, and a bank service charge $20. Determine the adjusted cash balance per bank at July 31.

Prepare partial bank reconciliation.
(SO 7)

BE8-10 At August 31, Eola Company has a cash balance per books of $9,200 and the following additional data from the bank statement: charge for printing Eola Company checks $35, interest earned on checking account balance $40, and outstanding checks $800. Determine the adjusted cash balance per books at August 31.

Prepare partial bank reconciliation.
(SO 7)

BE8-11 Naperville Company has the following cash balances: Cash in Bank $15,742, Payroll Bank Account $6,000, and Plant Expansion Fund Cash $25,000. Explain how each balance should be reported on the balance sheet.

Explain the statement presentation of cash balances.
(SO 8)

EXERCISES

E8-1 Jackie Bennett is the owner of Bennett's Pizza. Bennett's is operated strictly on a carry-out basis. Customers pick up their orders at a counter where a clerk exchanges the pizza for cash. While at the counter, the customer can see other employees making the pizzas and the large ovens in which the pizzas are baked.

Identify the principles of internal control.
(SO 2)

Instructions

Identify the six principles of internal control and give an example of each principle that you might observe when picking up your pizza. (*Note:* It may not be possible to observe all the principles.)

E8-2 The following control procedures are used at Sheridan Company for over-the-counter cash receipts.

Identify internal control weaknesses over cash receipts and suggest improvements.
(SO 2, 3)

1. To minimize the risk of robbery, cash in excess of $100 is stored in an unlocked attaché case in the stock room until it is deposited in the bank.
2. All over-the-counter receipts are registered by three clerks who use a cash register with a single cash drawer.
3. The company accountant makes the bank deposit and then records the day's receipts.
4. At the end of each day, the total receipts are counted by the cashier on duty and reconciled to the cash register total.
5. Cashiers are experienced; they are not bonded.

Instructions

(a) For each procedure, explain the weakness in internal control, and identify the control principle that is violated.

(b) For each weakness, suggest a change in procedure that will result in good internal control.

E8-3 The following control procedures are used in Erin's Boutique Shoppe for cash disbursements.

Identify internal control weaknesses over cash disbursements and suggest improvements.
(SO 2, 4)

1. The company accountant prepares the bank reconciliation and reports any discrepancies to the owner.
2. The store manager personally approves all payments before signing and issuing checks.
3. Each week, Erin leaves 100 company checks in an unmarked envelope on a shelf behind the cash register.
4. After payment, bills are filed in a paid invoice folder.
5. The company checks are unnumbered.

Instructions

(a) For each procedure, explain the weakness in internal control, and identify the internal control principle that is violated.

(b) For each weakness, suggest a change in the procedure that will result in good internal control.

Identify internal control weaknesses for cash disbursements and suggest improvements.
(SO 4)

E8-4 At Elburn Company, checks are not prenumbered because both the puchasing agent and the treasurer are authorized to issue checks. Each signer has access to unissued checks kept in an unlocked file cabinet. The purchasing agent pays all bills pertaining to goods purchased for resale. Prior to payment, the purchasing agent determines that the goods have been received and verifies the mathematical accuracy of the vendor's invoice. After payment, the invoice is filed by vendor, and the purchasing agent records the payment in the cash disbursements journal. The treasurer pays all other bills following approval by authorized employees. After payment, the treasurer stamps all bills PAID, files them by payment date, and records the checks in the cash disbursements journal. Elburn Company maintains one checking account that is reconciled by the treasurer.

Instructions

(a) List the weaknesses in internal control over cash disbursements.

(b) Write a memo to the company treasurer indicating your recommendations for improvement.

Prepare journal entries for a petty cash fund.
(SO 5)

E8-5 Leland Company uses an imprest petty cash system. The fund was established on March 1 with a balance of $100. During March the following petty cash receipts were found in the petty cash box.

Date	Receipt No.	For	Amount
3/5	1	Stamp Inventory	$35
7	2	Freight-out	19
9	3	Miscellaneous Expense	12
11	4	Travel Expense	24
14	5	Miscellaneous Expense	5

The fund was replenished on March 15 when the fund contained $4 in cash. On March 20, the amount in the fund was increased to $150.

Instructions

Journalize the entries in March that pertain to the operation of the petty cash fund.

Prepare bank reconciliation and adjusting entries.
(SO 7)

E8-6 Cindy Crawford is unable to reconcile the bank balance at January 31. Cindy's reconciliation is as follows.

Cash balance per bank	$3,660.20
Add: NSF check	630.00
Less: Bank service charge	25.00
Adjusted balance per bank	$4,265.20
Cash balance per books	$3,875.20
Less: Deposits in transit	490.00
Add: Outstanding checks	930.00
Adjusted balance per books	$4,315.20

Instructions

(a) Prepare a correct bank reconciliation.

(b) Journalize the entries required by the reconciliation.

Determine outstanding checks.
(SO 7)

E8-7 On April 30, the bank reconciliation of Hinckley Company shows three outstanding checks: no. 254, $650, no. 255, $720, and no. 257, $410. The May bank statement and the May cash payments journal show the following.

Bank Statement

Checks Paid

Date	Check No.	Amount
5/4	254	650
5/2	257	410
5/17	258	159
5/12	259	275
5/20	261	500
5/29	263	480
5/30	262	750

Cash Payments Journal

Checks Issued

Date	Check No.	Amount
5/2	258	159
5/5	259	275
5/10	260	925
5/15	261	500
5/22	262	750
5/24	263	480
5/29	264	560

Instructions

Using step 2 in the reconciliation procedure, list the outstanding checks at May 31.

Prepare bank reconciliation and adjusting entries.
(SO 7)

E8-8 The following information pertains to Cody Video Company.

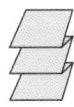

1. Cash balance per bank, July 31, $7,263.
2. July bank service charge not recorded by the depositor $15.
3. Cash balance per books, July 31, $7,190.
4. Deposits in transit, July 31, $1,500.
5. Bank collected $800 note for Cody in July, plus interest $36, less fee $20. The collection has not been recorded by Cody, and no interest has been accrued.
6. Outstanding checks, July 31, $772.

Instructions

(a) Prepare a bank reconciliation at July 31.
(b) Journalize the adjusting entries at July 31 on the books of Cody Video Company.

Prepare bank reconciliation and adjusting entries.
(SO 7)

E8-9 The information below relates to the Cash account in the ledger of Newark Company.

Balance September 1—$17,150; Cash deposited—$64,000.
Balance September 30—$17,404; Checks written—$63,746.

The September bank statement shows a balance of $16,422 on September 30 and the following memoranda.

Credits		**Debits**	
Collection of $1,500 note plus interest $30	$1,530	NSF check: J.E. Hoover	$410
Interest earned on checking account	$45	Safety deposit box rent	$30

At September 30, deposits in transit were $4,500, and outstanding checks totaled $2,383.

Instructions

(a) Prepare the bank reconciliation at September 30.
(b) Prepare the adjusting entries at September 30, assuming (1) the NSF check was from a customer on account, and (2) no interest had been accrued on the note.

Compute deposits in transit and outstanding checks for two bank reconciliations.
(SO 7)

E8-10 The cash records of Ottawa Company show the following four situations.

1. The June 30 bank reconciliation indicated that deposits in transit total $950. During July the general ledger account Cash shows deposits of $15,750, but the bank statement indicates that only $15,600 in deposits were received during the month.
2. The June 30 bank reconciliation also reported outstanding checks of $920. During the month of July, Ottawa Company books show that $17,200 of checks were issued. The bank statement showed that $16,400 of checks cleared the bank in July.
3. In September, deposits per the bank statement totaled $26,700, deposits per books were $25,400, and deposits in transit at September 30 were $2,600.
4. In September, cash disbursements per books were $23,700, checks clearing the bank were $24,000, and outstanding checks at September 30 were $2,100.

There were no bank debit or credit memoranda. No errors were made by either the bank or Ottawa Company.

Instructions

Answer the following questions.

(a) In situation (1), what were the deposits in transit at July 31?
(b) In situation (2), what were the outstanding checks at July 31?
(c) In situation (3), what were the deposits in transit at August 31?
(d) In situation (4), what were the outstanding checks at August 31?

PROBLEMS: SET A

Identify internal control principles over cash disbursements.
(SO 2, 4)

P8-1A Mexican Office Supply Company recently changed its system of internal control over cash disbursements. The system includes the following features.

Instead of being unnumbered and manually prepared, all checks must now be prenumbered and written by using the new checkwriter purchased by the company. Before a check can be issued, each invoice must have the approval of Norma Hanson, the purchasing agent, and John Countryman, the receiving department supervisor. Checks must be signed by either Linda Anderson, the treasurer, or Bob Skabo, the assistant treasurer. Before signing a check, the signer is expected to compare the amount of the check with the amount on the invoice.

After signing a check, the signer stamps the invoice PAID and inserts within the stamp, the date, check number, and amount of the check. The "paid" invoice is then sent to the accounting department for recording.

Blank checks are stored in a safe in the treasurer's office. The combination to the safe is known only by the treasurer and assistant treasurer. Each month, the bank statement is reconciled with the bank balance per books by the assistant chief accountant.

Instructions

Identify the internal control principles and their application to cash disbursements of Mexican Office Supply Company.

Journalize and post petty cash fund transactions.
(SO 5)

Peachtree

P8-2A Maple Park Company maintains a petty cash fund for small expenditures. The following transactions occurred over a 2-month period.

July	1	Established petty cash fund by writing a check on Cortland Bank for $200.
	15	Replenished the petty cash fund by writing a check for $197.00. On this date the fund consisted of $3.00 in cash and the following petty cash receipts: freight-out $94.00, postage expense $42.40, entertainment expense $46.60, and miscellaneous expense $11.90.
	31	Replenished the petty cash fund by writing a check for $192.00. At this date, the fund consisted of $8.00 in cash and the following petty cash receipts: freight-out $82.10, charitable contributions expense $40.00, postage expense $27.80, and miscellaneous expense $42.10.
Aug.	15	Replenished the petty cash fund by writing a check for $187.00. On this date, the fund consisted of $13.00 in cash and the following petty cash receipts: freight-out $74.60, entertainment expense $43.00, postage expense $33.00, and miscellaneous expense $37.00.
	16	Increased the amount of the petty cash fund to $300 by writing a check for $100.
	31	Replenished petty cash fund by writing a check for $284.00. On this date, the fund consisted of $16 in cash and the following petty cash receipts: postage expense $140.00, travel expense $95.60, and freight-out $46.40.

Instructions

(a) July 15, Cash short $2.10
(b) Aug. 31 balance $300

(a) Journalize the petty cash transactions.
(b) Post to the Petty Cash account.
(c) What internal control features exist in a petty cash fund?

Prepare a bank reconciliation and adjusting entries.
(SO 7)

P8-3A On May 31, 2002, Sosa Company had a cash balance per books of $6,781.50. The bank statement from Sandwich Community Bank on that date showed a balance of $6,804.60. A comparison of the statement with the cash account revealed the following facts.

1. The statement included a debit memo of $40 for the printing of additional company checks.
2. Cash sales of $836.15 on May 12 were deposited in the bank. The cash receipts journal entry and the deposit slip were incorrectly made for $846.15. The bank credited Sosa Company for the correct amount.
3. Outstanding checks at May 31 totaled $276.25. Deposits in transit were $1,936.15.
4. On May 18, the company issued check No. 1181 for $685 to Kap Shin, on account. The check, which cleared the bank in May, was incorrectly journalized and posted by Sosa Company for $658.
5. A $3,000 note receivable was collected by the bank for Sosa Company on May 31 plus $80 interest. The bank charged a collection fee of $20. No interest has been accrued on the note.
6. Included with the cancelled checks was a check issued by Tacamoto Company to Yee Chow for $600 that was incorrectly charged to Sosa Company by the bank.
7. On May 31, the bank statement showed an NSF charge of $700 for a check issued by John Lewis, a customer, to Sosa Company on account.

Instructions

(a) Prepare the bank reconciliation at May 31, 2002.
(b) Prepare the necessary adjusting entries for Sosa Company at May 31, 2002.

(a) Adjusted cash balance per bank $9,064.50

P8-4A The bank portion of the bank reconciliation for Hilo Company at November 30, 2002, was as follows.

Prepare a bank reconciliation and adjusting entries from detailed data.
(SO 7)

HILO COMPANY
Bank Reconciliation
November 30, 2002

Cash balance per bank			$14,367.90
Add: Deposits in transit			2,530.20
			16,898.10
Less: Outstanding checks			
	Check Number	Check Amount	
	3451	$2,260.40	
	3470	720.10	
	3471	844.50	
	3472	1,426.80	
	3474	1,050.00	6,301.80
Adjusted cash balance per bank			$10,596.30

The adjusted cash balance per bank agreed with the cash balance per books at November 30.
The December bank statement showed the following checks and deposits.

Bank Statement

Checks			Deposits	
Date	**Number**	**Amount**	**Date**	**Amount**
12-1	3451	$ 2,260.40	12-1	$ 2,530.20
12-2	3471	844.50	12-4	1,211.60
12-7	3472	1,426.80	12-8	2,365.10
12-4	3475	1,640.70	12-16	2,672.70
12-8	3476	1,300.00	12-21	2,945.00
12-10	3477	2,130.00	12-26	2,567.30
12-15	3479	3,080.00	12-29	2,836.00
12-27	3480	600.00	12-30	1,025.00
12-30	3482	475.50	Total	$18,152.90
12-29	3483	1,140.00		
12-31	3485	540.80		
	Total	$15,438.70		

The cash records per books for December showed the following.

Cash Payments Journal

Date	Number	Amount	Date	Number	Amount
12-1	3475	$1,640.70	12-20	3482	$ 475.50
12-2	3476	1,300.00	12-22	3483	1,140.00
12-2	3477	2,130.00	12-23	3484	832.00
12-4	3478	538.20	12-24	3485	450.80
12-8	3479	3,080.00	12-30	3486	1,889.50
12-10	3480	600.00	Total		$14,884.10
12-17	3481	807.40			

Cash Receipts Journal

Date	Amount
12-3	$ 1,211.60
12-7	2,365.10
12-15	2,672.70
12-20	2,954.00
12-25	2,567.30
12-28	2,836.00
12-30	1,025.00
12-31	1,190.40
Total	$16,822.10

The bank statement contained two memoranda:

1. A credit of $3,645 for the collection of a $3,500 note for Hilo Company plus interest of $160 and less a collection fee of $15.00. Hilo Company has not accrued any interest on the note.
2. A debit of $547.10 for an NSF check written by D. Lu, a customer. At December 31, the check had not been redeposited in the bank.

At December 31 the cash balance per books was $12,534.30, and the cash balance per the bank statement was $20,180.00. The bank did not make any errors, but two errors were made by Hilo Company.

Instructions

(a) Adjusted balance per books $15,533.20

(a) Using the four steps in the reconciliation procedure, prepare a bank reconciliation at December 31.

(b) Prepare the adjusting entries based on the reconciliation. (*Hint*: The correction of any errors pertaining to recording checks should be made to Accounts Payable. The correction of any errors relating to recording cash receipts should be made to Accounts Receivable.)

Prepare a bank reconciliation and adjusting entries.
(SO 7)

Peachtree

P8-5A Videosoft Company maintains a checking account at the Intelex Bank. At July 31, selected data from the ledger balance and the bank statement are as follows.

	Cash in Bank	
	Per Books	**Per Bank**
Balance, July 1	$17,600	$18,800
July receipts	82,000	
July credits		80,470
July disbursements	76,900	
July debits		74,740
Balance, July 31	$22,700	$24,530

Analysis of the bank data reveals that the credits consist of $79,000 of July deposits and a credit memorandum of $1,470 for the collection of a $1,400 note plus interest revenue of $70. The July debits per bank consist of checks cleared $74,700 and a debit memorandum of $40 for printing additional company checks.

You also discover the following errors involving July checks: (1) A check for $230 to a creditor on account that cleared the bank in July was journalized and posted as $320. (2) A salary check to an employee for $255 was recorded by the bank for $155.

The June 30 bank reconciliation contained only two reconciling items: deposits in transit $5,000 and outstanding checks of $6,200.

Instructions

(a) Adjusted balance per books $24,220

(a) Prepare a bank reconciliation at July 31.

(b) Journalize the adjusting entries to be made by Videosoft Company at July 31, 2002. Assume that the interest on the note has been accrued.

Identify internal control weaknesses in cash receipts and cash disbursements.
(SO 2, 3, 4, 5, 6)

P8-6A Cedar Grove Middle School wants to raise money for a new sound system for its auditorium. The primary fund-raising event is a dance at which the famous disc jockey Obnoxious Al will play classic and not-so-classic dance tunes. Roger DeMaster, the music and theater instructor, has been given the responsibility for coordinating the fund-raising efforts. This is Roger's first experience with fund-raising. He decides to put the eighth-grade choir in charge of the event; he will be a relatively passive observer.

Roger had 500 unnumbered tickets printed for the dance. He left the tickets in a box on his desk and told the choir students to take as many tickets as they thought they could sell for \$5 each. In order to ensure that no extra tickets would be floating around, he told them to dispose of any unsold tickets. When the students received payment for the tickets, they were to bring the cash back to Roger, and he would put it in a locked box in his desk drawer.

Some of the students were responsible for decorating the gymnasium for the dance. Roger gave each of them a key to the money box and told them that if they took money out to purchase materials, they should put a note in the box saying how much they took and what it was used for. After 2 weeks the money box appeared to be getting full, so Roger asked Steve Stevens to count the money, prepare a deposit slip, and deposit the money in a bank account Roger had opened.

The day of the dance, Roger wrote a check from the account to pay the DJ. Obnoxious Al, however, said that he accepted only cash and did not give receipts. So Roger took \$200 out of the cash box and gave it to Al. At the dance Roger had Sara Billings working at the entrance to the gymnasium, collecting tickets from students and selling tickets to those who had not prepurchased them. Roger estimated that 400 students attended the dance.

The following day Roger closed out the bank account, which had \$250 in it, and gave that amount plus the \$180 in the cash box to Principal Skinner. Principal Skinner seemed surprised that, after generating roughly \$2,000 in sales, the dance netted only \$430 in cash. Roger did not know how to respond.

Instructions

Identify as many internal control weaknesses as you can in this scenario, and suggest how each could be addressed.

PROBLEMS: SET B

Identify internal control weaknesses over cash receipts.
(SO 2, 3)

P8-1B Sycamore Theater is located in the Sycamore Mall. A cashier's booth is located near the entrance to the theater. Two cashiers are employed. One works from 1–5 P.M., the other from 5–9 P.M. Each cashier is bonded. The cashiers receive cash from customers and operate a machine that ejects serially numbered tickets. The rolls of tickets are inserted and locked into the machine by the theater manager at the beginning of each cashier's shift.

After purchasing a ticket, the customer takes the ticket to an usher stationed at the entrance of the theater lobby some 60 feet from the cashier's booth. The usher tears the ticket in half, admits the customer, and returns the ticket stub to the customer. The other half of the ticket is dropped into a locked box by the usher.

At the end of each cashier's shift, the theater manager removes the ticket rolls from the machine and makes a cash count. The cash count sheet is initialed by the cashier. At the end of the day, the manager deposits the receipts in total in a bank night deposit vault located in the mall. The manager also sends copies of the deposit slip and the initialed cash count sheets to the theater company treasurer for verification and to the company's accounting department. Receipts from the first shift are stored in a safe located in the manager's office.

Instructions

(a) Identify the internal control principles and their application to the cash receipts transactions of the Sycamore Theater.

(b) If the usher and cashier decide to collaborate to misappropriate cash, what actions might they take?

Journalize and post petty cash fund transactions.
(SO 5)

P8-2B DeKalb Company maintains a petty cash fund for small expenditures. The following transactions occurred over a 2-month period.

July 1 Established petty cash fund by writing a check on Corner Bank for $200.
15 Replenished the petty cash fund by writing a check for $196.30. On this date the fund consisted of $3.70 in cash and the following petty cash receipts: freight-out $94.00, postage expense $42.40, entertainment expense $46.60, and miscellaneous expense $10.70.
31 Replenished the petty cash fund by writing a check for $192.00. At this date, the fund consisted of $8.00 in cash and the following petty cash receipts: freight-out $82.10, charitable contributions expense $30.00, postage expense $47.80, and miscellaneous expense $32.10.
Aug. 15 Replenished the petty cash fund by writing a check for $188.00. On this date, the fund consisted of $12.00 in cash and the following petty cash receipts: freight-out $74.40, entertainment expense $43.00, postage expense $33.00, and miscellaneous expense $38.00.
16 Increased the amount of the petty cash fund to $300 by writing a check for $100.
31 Replenished petty cash fund by writing a check for $283.00. On this date, the fund consisted of $17 in cash and the following petty cash receipts: postage expense $145.00, entertainment expense $90.60, and freight-out $45.40.

Instructions

(a) July 15 Cash short $2.60
(b) Aug. 31 balance $300

(a) Journalize the petty cash transactions.
(b) Post to the Petty Cash account.
(c) What internal control features exist in a petty cash fund?

Prepare a bank reconciliation and adjusting entries.
(SO 7)

P8-3B Agricultural Genetics Company of Emporia, Kansas, spreads herbicides and applies liquid fertilizer for local farmers. On May 31, 2002, the company's cash account per its general ledger showed the following balance.

CASH **No. 101**

Date	Explanation	Ref.	Debit	Credit	Balance
May 31	Balance				6,781.50

The bank statement from Emporia State Bank on that date showed the following balance.

EMPORIA STATE BANK

Checks and Debits	Deposits and Credits	Daily Balance
XXX	XXX	5/31 6,804.60

A comparison of the details on the bank statement with the details in the cash account revealed the following facts.

1. The statement included a debit memo of $40 for the printing of additional company checks.
2. Cash sales of $836.15 on May 12 were deposited in the bank. The cash receipts journal entry and the deposit slip were incorrectly made for $846.15. The bank credited Agricultural Genetics Company for the correct amount.
3. Outstanding checks at May 31 totaled $276.25, and deposits in transit were $936.15.
4. On May 18, the company issued check no. 1181 for $685 to L. Kingston, on account. The check, which cleared the bank in May, was incorrectly journalized and posted by Agricultural Genetics Company for $658.
5. A $2,000 note receivable was collected by the bank for Agricultural Genetics Company on May 31 plus $80 interest. The bank charged a collection fee of $20. No interest has been accrued on the note.
6. Included with the cancelled checks was a check issued by Teller Company to Larry Falcetto for $600 that was incorrectly charged to Agricultural Genetics Company by the bank.
7. On May 31, the bank statement showed an NSF charge of $700 for a check issued by Pete Dell, a customer, to Agricultural Genetics Company on account.

Instructions

(a) Adj. cash bal. $8,064.50

(a) Prepare the bank reconciliation at May 31, 2002.
(b) Prepare the necessary adjusting entries for Agricultural Genetics Company at May 31, 2002.

P8-4B The bank portion of the bank reconciliation for Rochelle Company at October 31, 2002 was as follows.

Prepare a bank reconciliation and adjusting entries from detailed data.
(SO 7)

ROCHELLE COMPANY
Bank Reconciliation
October 31, 2002

Cash balance per bank			$12,367.90
Add: Deposits in transit			1,530.20
			13,898.10
Less: Outstanding checks			
	Check Number	Check Amount	
	2451	$1,260.40	
	2470	720.10	
	2471	844.50	
	2472	426.80	
	2474	1,050.00	4,301.80
Adjusted cash balance per bank			$ 9,596.30

The adjusted cash balance per bank agreed with the cash balance per books at October 31.
The November bank statement showed the following checks and deposits:

Bank Statement

Checks			Deposits	
Date	**Number**	**Amount**	**Date**	**Amount**
11-1	2470	$ 720.10	11-1	$ 1,530.20
11-2	2471	844.50	11-4	1,211.60
11-5	2474	1,050.00	11-8	990.10
11-4	2475	1,640.70	11-13	2,575.00
11-8	2476	2,830.00	11-18	1,472.70
11-10	2477	600.00	11-21	2,945.00
11-15	2479	1,750.00	11-25	2,567.30
11-18	2480	1,330.00	11-28	1,650.00
11-27	2481	695.40	11-30	1,186.00
11-30	2483	575.50	Total	$16,127.90
11-29	2486	900.00		
	Total	$12,936.20		

The cash records per books for November showed the following.

Cash Payments Journal

Date	Number	Amount	Date	Number	Amount
11-1	2475	$1,640.70	11-20	2483	$ 575.50
11-2	2476	2,830.00	11-22	2484	829.50
11-2	2477	600.00	11-23	2485	974.80
11-4	2478	538.20	11-24	2486	900.00
11-8	2479	1,570.00	11-29	2487	398.00
11-10	2480	1,330.00	11-30	2488	1,200.00
11-15	2481	695.40	Total		$14,694.10
11-18	2482	612.00			

Cash Receipts Journal

Date	Amount
11-3	$ 1,211.60
11-7	990.10
11-12	2,575.00
11-17	1,472.70
11-20	2,954.00
11-24	2,567.30
11-27	1,650.00
11-29	1,186.00
11-30	1,225.00
Total	$15,831.70

The bank statement contained two bank memoranda:

1. A credit of $1,505.00 for the collection of a $1,400 note for Rochelle Company plus interest of $120 and less a collection fee of $15. Rochelle Company has not accrued any interest on the note.
2. A debit for the printing of additional company checks $50.00.

At November 30, the cash balance per books was $10,733.90, and the cash balance per the bank statement was $17,014.60. The bank did not make any errors, but two errors were made by Rochelle Company.

Instructions

(a) Adjusted cash balance per bank $11,999.90

(a) Using the four steps in the reconciliation procedure described on page 338, prepare a bank reconciliation at November 30.

(b) Prepare the adjusting entries based on the reconciliation. (*Hint*: The correction of any errors pertaining to recording checks should be made to Accounts Payable. The correction of any errors relating to recording cash receipts should be made to Accounts Receivable).

Prepare a bank reconciliation and adjusting entries. (SO 7)

P8-5B Bettendorf Company's bank statement from Last National Bank at August 31, 2002, shows the following information.

Balance, August 1	$17,400	Bank credit memoranda:	
August deposits	72,000	Collection of note	
Checks cleared in August	69,660	receivable plus $90	
Balance, August 31	24,850	interest	$5,090
		Interest earned	45
		Bank debit memorandum:	
		Safety deposit box rent	25

A summary of the Cash account in the ledger for August shows: Balance, August 1, $16,900; receipts $77,000; disbursements $73,570; and balance, August 31, $20,330. Analysis reveals that the only reconciling items on the July 31 bank reconciliation were a deposit in transit for $4,000 and outstanding checks of $4,500. The deposit in transit was the first deposit recorded by the bank in August. In addition, you determine that there were two errors involving company checks drawn in August: (1) A check for $400 to a creditor on account that cleared the bank in August was journalized and posted for $420. (2) A salary check to an employee for $275 was recorded by the bank for $285.

Instructions

(a) Adjusted balance per books $25,460

(a) Prepare a bank reconciliation at August 31.

(b) Journalize the adjusting entries to be made by Bettendorf Company at August 31. Assume the interest on the note has been accrued by the company.

Prepare comprehensive bank reconciliation with theft and internal control deficiencies. (SO 2, 3, 4, 7)

P8-6B Gigantic Company is a very profitable small business. It has not, however, given much consideration to internal control. For example, in an attempt to keep clerical and office expenses to a minimum, the company has combined the jobs of cashier and bookkeeper. As a result, Jake Stickyfingers handles all cash receipts, keeps the accounting records, and prepares the monthly bank reconciliations.

The balance per the bank statement on October 31, 2002, was $18,280. Outstanding checks were: no. 62 for $326.75, no. 183 for $150, no. 284 for $253.25, no. 862 for $190.71, no. 863 for $226.80, and no. 864 for $165.28. Included with the statement was a credit memorandum of $300 indicating the collection of a note receivable for Gigantic Company by the bank on October 25. This memorandum has not been recorded by Gigantic Company.

The company's ledger showed one cash account with a balance of $21,892.72. The balance included undeposited cash on hand. Because of the lack of internal controls, Stickyfingers took for personal use all of the undeposited receipts in excess of $3,795.51. He then prepared the following bank reconciliation in an effort to conceal his theft of cash.

BANK RECONCILIATION

Cash balance per books, October 31		$21,892.72
Add: Outstanding checks		
No. 862	$190.71	
No. 863	226.80	
No. 864	165.28	482.79
		22,375.51
Less: Undeposited receipts		3,795.51
Unadjusted balance per bank, October 31		18,580.00
Less: Bank credit memorandum		300.00
Cash balance per bank statement, October 31		$18,280.00

Instructions

(a) Prepare a correct bank reconciliation. (*Hint*: Deduct the amount of the theft from the adjusted balance per books.)

(a) Adjusted balance per books $20,762.72

(b) Indicate the three ways that Stickyfingers attempted to conceal the theft and the dollar amount pertaining to each method.

(c) What principles of internal control were violated in this case?

BROADENING YOUR PERSPECTIVE

FINANCIAL REPORTING AND ANALYSIS

FINANCIAL REPORTING PROBLEM: Lands' End, Inc.

BYP8-1 The financial statements of **Lands' End, Inc.** are presented in Appendix A at the end of this textbook.

LANDS' END DIRECT MERCHANTS

Instructions

(a) What comments, if any, are made about cash in the report of the independent auditors?

(b) What data about cash and cash equivalents are shown in the consolidated balance sheet (statement of financial condition)?

(c) What activities are identified in the consolidated statement of cash flows as being responsible for the changes in cash during the year ended January 28, 2000?

(d) In management's letter that assumes "Responsibility for Consolidated Financial Statements," what does Lands' End's management say about internal control? (See page 31 of its 2000 Annual Report.)

COMPARATIVE ANALYSIS PROBLEM: Lands' End vs. Abercrombie & Fitch

BYP8-2 **Lands' End's** financial statements are presented in Appendix A. **Abercrombie & Fitch's** financial statements are presented in Appendix B.

LANDS' END DIRECT MERCHANTS

Instructions

(a) Based on the information contained in these financial statements, determine each of the following for each company:

(1) Cash and cash equivalents balance at January 28, 2000, for Lands' End and at January 29, 2000, for Abercrombie & Fitch.

(2) Increase (decrease) in cash and cash equivalents from 1999 to 2000.

(3) Cash provided by operating activities during the year ended January 2000 (from Statement of Cash Flows).

(b) What conclusions concerning the management of cash can be drawn from these data?

INTERPRETING FINANCIAL STATEMENTS: A Global Focus

BYP8-3 The July 10, 2000, issue of *The Wall Street Journal* includes an article by Michael M. Phillips entitled "U.S., Major Allies to Urge Bank Scrutiny of 15 Nations' Money-Laundering Curbs."

Instructions
Read the article and answer the following questions.

(a) Countries around the world have worked to improve capital mobility (the ease with which funds can flow from one country to another). What is the potential "dark side" to international capital mobility?
(b) What countries were named in the warning?
(c) What possible actions might be taken against countries on the list?

EXPLORING THE WEB

BYP8-4 All organizations should have systems of internal control. Universities are no exception. This site discusses the basics of internal control in a university setting.

Address: **www.bc.edu/bc_org/fvp/ia/ic/intro.html** ***(or go to www.wiley.com/college/weygandt)***

Steps: Go the site shown above.

Instructions
The front page of this site provides links to pages that answer six critical questions. Use these links to answer the following questions.

(a) In a university setting who has responsibility for evaluating the adequacy of the system of internal control?
(b) What do reconciliations ensure in the university setting? Who should review the reconciliation?
(c) What are some examples of physical controls?
(d) What are two ways to accomplish inventory counts?

CRITICAL THINKING

GROUP DECISION CASE

BYP8-5 The board of trustees of a local church is concerned about the internal accounting controls for the offering collections made at weekly services. The trustees ask you to serve on a three-person audit team with the internal auditor of a local college and a CPA who has just joined the church.

At a meeting of the audit team and the board of trustees you learn the following.

1. The church's board of trustees has delegated responsibility for the financial management and audit of the financial records to the finance committee. This group prepares the annual budget and approves major disbursements. It is not involved in collections or record keeping. No audit has been made in recent years because the same trusted employee has kept church records and served as financial secretary for 15 years. The church does not carry any fidelity insurance.
2. The collection at the weekly service is taken by a team of ushers who volunteer to serve one month. The ushers take the collection plates to a basement office at the rear of the church. They hand their plates to the head usher and return to the church service. After all plates have been turned in, the head usher counts the cash received. The head usher then places the cash in the church safe along with a notation of the amount counted. The head usher volunteers to serve for 3 months.
3. The next morning the financial secretary opens the safe and recounts the collection. The secretary withholds \$150–\$200 in cash, depending on the cash expenditures expected for the week, and deposits the remainder of the collections in the bank. To facilitate the deposit, church members who contribute by check are asked to make their checks payable to "Cash."
4. Each month, the financial secretary reconciles the bank statement and submits a copy of the reconciliation to the board of trustees. The reconciliations have rarely contained any bank errors and have never shown any errors per books.

Instructions

With the class divided into groups, answer the following.

(a) Indicate the weaknesses in internal accounting control over the handling of collections.

(b) List the improvements in internal control procedures that you plan to make at the next meeting of the audit team for (1) the ushers, (2) the head usher, (3) the financial secretary, and (4) the finance committee.

(c) What church policies should be changed to improve internal control?

COMMUNICATION ACTIVITY

BYP8-6 As a new auditor for the CPA firm of Kennedy, Maison, and Davis you have been assigned to review the internal controls over mail cash receipts of Emerik Company. Your review reveals the following: Checks are promptly endorsed "For Deposit Only," but no list of the checks is prepared by the person opening the mail. The mail is opened either by the cashier or by the employee who maintains the accounts receivable records. Mail receipts are deposited in the bank weekly by the cashier.

Instructions

Write a letter to L. S. Croix, owner of the Emerik Company, explaining the weaknesses in internal control and your recommendations for improving the system.

ETHICS CASE

BYP8-7 You are the assistant controller in charge of general ledger accounting at Bad Water Bottling Company. Your company has a large loan from an insurance company. The loan agreement requires that the company's cash account balance be maintained at $200,000 or more, as reported monthly.

At June 30 the cash balance is $80,000, which you report to Marais Thompson, the financial vice president. Marais excitedly instructs you to keep the cash receipts book open for one additional day for purposes of the June 30 report to the insurance company. Marais says, "If we don't get that cash balance over $200,000, we'll default on our loan agreement. They could close us down, put us all out of our jobs!" Marais continues, "I talked to Grochum Distributors (one of Bad Water's largest customers) this morning. They said they sent us a check for $150,000 yesterday. We should receive it tomorrow. If we include just that one check in our cash balance, we'll be in the clear. It's in the mail!"

Instructions

(a) Who will suffer negative effects if you do not comply with Marais Thompson's instructions? Who will suffer if you do comply?

(b) What are the ethical considerations in this case?

(c) What alternatives do you have?

Answers to Self-Study Questions

1. a **2.** c **3.** b **4.** c **5.** b **6.** d **7.** a **8.** a **9.** c **10.** d **11.** c

Answer to Lands' End Review It Question 3, p. 341

Lands' End reports cash and cash equivalents on its balance sheet for 2000 of $76.4 million.

LANDS' END DIRECT MERCHANTS

Remember to go back to the Navigator box on the chapter-opening page and check off your completed work.

ACCOUNTING FOR RECEIVABLES

9

THE NAVIGATOR ✓

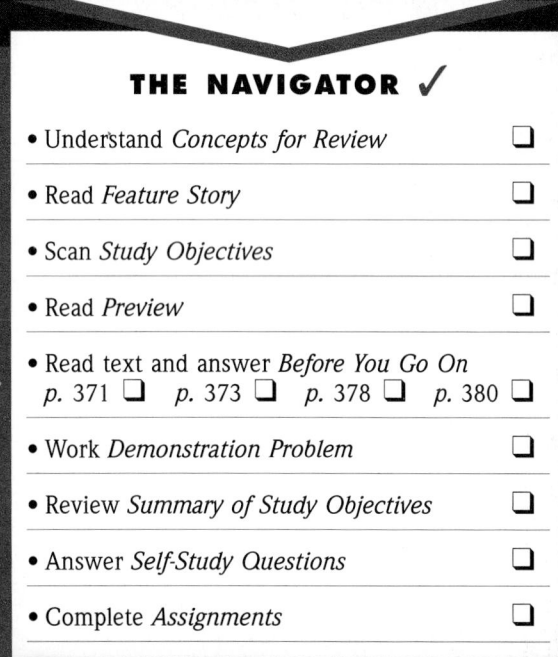

- Understand *Concepts for Review* ❑
- Read *Feature Story* ❑
- Scan *Study Objectives* ❑
- Read *Preview* ❑
- Read text and answer *Before You Go On* *p.* 371 ❑ *p.* 373 ❑ *p.* 378 ❑ *p.* 380 ❑
- Work *Demonstration Problem* ❑
- Review *Summary of Study Objectives* ❑
- Answer *Self-Study Questions* ❑
- Complete *Assignments* ❑

CONCEPTS FOR REVIEW

Before studying this chapter, you should know or, if necessary, review:

a. How to record sales transactions. (Ch. 5, pp. 191–194)

b. Why adjusting entries are made. (Ch. 3, pp. 91–92)

c. How to compute interest. (Ch. 3, p. 101)

☑ THE NAVIGATOR

FEATURE STORY

How Do You Spell Relief?

Fred Tarter believes that in every problem lies an opportunity—and sometimes that opportunity can mean a big profit. For example, today fewer people pay cash for their prescriptions. Instead, pharmacies bill a customer's health plan for some or all of the prescription's cost. As a result, pharmacies must spend a lot of time and energy collecting cash from these health plans. This procedure is a headache for pharmacies because there are 4,500 different health plans in the United States. Also, it often leaves pharmacies with too many receivables and not enough cash. Their suppliers want to be paid within 15 days, but their receivables are outstanding for 30 and often 60 days.

Enter Fred Tarter. Having recently sold his advertising agency, Fred had some spare time and money on his hands. While reading a pharmacy trade journal, he learned of the pharmacies' headache. To Fred this problem spelled opportunity.

Fred found out that 56,000 pharmacies are connected by computer to a claims-processing business. Fred's idea was this: Using this network, he would purchase pharmacy receivables, charging a fee of 1.4–2 percent. Pharmacies would be willing to pay this fee because they would get their cash sooner and would be spared the headache of having to collect the accounts. Fred would then use the receivables as backing to raise new money so he could buy more receivables.

Based on this idea, Fred started a company called the **Pharmacy Fund**. Over 500 small pharmacies sell their receivables to his company. By means of a computer link with each pharmacy, the Pharmacy Fund buys the receivables at the end of each day and credits the pharmacy's account immediately. Rather than having to wait weeks to receive its cash from insurance companies, the pharmacy gets its cash the same day as the sale. The Pharmacy Fund's customers say that this has solved their cash-flow problems. It also has reduced their overhead costs and allowed them to automate their billing and record-keeping.

Fred Tarter has already identified his next opportunity—a target some would say is a "natural" for him: dentistry receivables. (Get it? Tarter—dentistry. We'll stick to accounting jokes from now on!)

THE NAVIGATOR

STUDY OBJECTIVES

After studying this chapter, you should be able to:

1. Identify the different types of receivables.
2. Explain how accounts receivable are recognized in the accounts.
3. Distinguish between the methods and bases used to value accounts receivable.
4. Describe the entries to record the disposition of accounts receivable.
5. Compute the maturity date of and interest on notes receivable.
6. Explain how notes receivable are recognized in the accounts.
7. Describe how notes receivable are valued.
8. Describe the entries to record the disposition of notes receivable.
9. Explain the statement presentation and analysis of receivables.

THE NAVIGATOR

PREVIEW OF CHAPTER 9

As indicated in the Feature Story, receivables are a significant asset on the books of many pharmacies. Receivables are significant to companies in other industries as well, because a significant portion of sales are done on credit in the United States. As a consequence, companies must pay close attention to their receivables and manage them carefully. In this chapter you will learn what journal entries companies make when products are sold, when cash is collected from those sales, and when accounts that cannot be collected are written off.

The content and organization of the chapter are as follows.

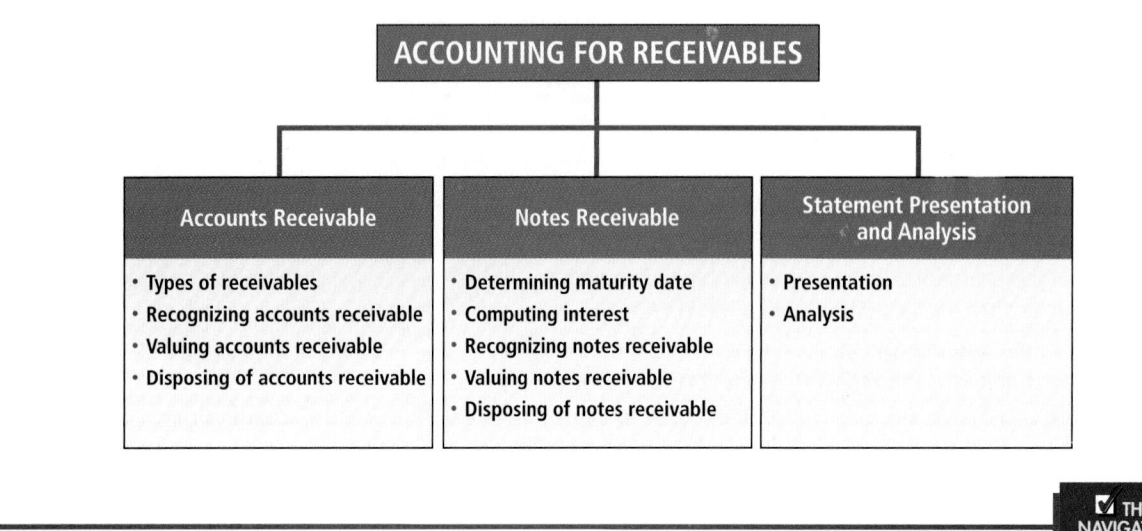

ACCOUNTING FOR RECEIVABLES

Accounts Receivable	Notes Receivable	Statement Presentation and Analysis
• Types of receivables	• Determining maturity date	• Presentation
• Recognizing accounts receivable	• Computing interest	• Analysis
• Valuing accounts receivable	• Recognizing notes receivable	
• Disposing of accounts receivable	• Valuing notes receivable	
	• Disposing of notes receivable	

ACCOUNTS RECEIVABLE

TYPES OF RECEIVABLES

STUDY OBJECTIVE 1

Identify the different types of receivables.

The term "receivables" refers to amounts due from individuals and other companies. They are claims that are expected to be collected in cash. Receivables are frequently classified as (1) accounts, (2) notes, and (3) other.

Accounts receivable are amounts owed by customers on account. They result from the sale of goods and services. These receivables generally are expected to be collected within 30 to 60 days. They are the most significant type of claim held by a company.

Notes receivable are claims for which formal instruments of credit are issued as proof of the debt. A note receivable normally extends for time periods of 60–90 days or longer and requires the debtor to pay interest. Notes and accounts receivable that result from sales transactions are often called **trade receivables**.

Other receivables include nontrade receivables. Examples are interest receivable, loans to company officers, advances to employees, and income taxes refundable. These are unusual. Therefore they are generally classified and reported as separate items in the balance sheet.

ETHICS NOTE

Receivables from employees and officers of a company are reported in the financial statements. The reason: Sometimes those assets are valued inappropriately or are not based on an "arm's length" transaction.

Three primary accounting issues are associated with accounts receivable.

1. **Recognizing** accounts receivable.
2. **Valuing** accounts receivable.
3. **Disposing of** accounts receivable.

RECOGNIZING ACCOUNTS RECEIVABLE

STUDY OBJECTIVE 2

Explain how accounts receivable are recognized in the accounts.

Recognizing accounts receivable is relatively straightforward. In Chapter 5 we saw how accounts receivable are affected by the sale of merchandise. To illustrate, assume that Jordache Co. on July 1, 2002, sells merchandise on account to Polo Company for $1,000 terms 2/10, n/30. On July 5, Polo returns merchandise worth $100 to Jordache Co. On July 11, Jordache receives payment from Polo Company for the balance due. The journal entries to record these transactions on the books of Jordache Co. are as follows.

July 1	Accounts Receivable—Polo Company	1,000	
	Sales		1,000
	(To record sales on account)		
July 5	Sales Returns and Allowances	100	
	Accounts Receivable—Polo Company		100
	(To record merchandise returned)		
July 11	Cash ($900 − $18)	882	
	Sales Discounts ($900 × .02)	18	
	Accounts Receivable—Polo Company		900
	(To record collection of accounts receivable)		

A	=	L	+	OE
+1,000				+1,000

A	=	L	+	OE
−100				−100

A	=	L	+	OE
+882				−18
−900				

The opportunity to receive a cash discount usually occurs when a manufacturer sells to a wholesaler or a wholesaler sells to a retailer. A discount is given in these situations either to encourage prompt payment or for competitive reasons.

Retailers rarely grant cash discounts to customers. We would be surprised if you ever received a cash discount in purchasing goods from any well-known retailer, such as **Sears**, **Kmart**, or **Wal-Mart**. In fact, when you use a retailer's credit card (Sears, for example), instead of giving a discount, the retailer charges interest on the balance due if not paid within a specified period (usually 25–30 days).

HELPFUL HINT

The preceding entries are the same as those described in Chapter 5. For simplicity, inventory and cost of goods sold are omitted from this set of journal entries and from end-of-chapter material.

To illustrate, assume that you use your **J. C. Penney Co.** credit card to purchase an outfit with a sales price of $300. J. C. Penney will make the following entry at the date of sale.

Accounts Receivable	300	
Sales		300
(To record sale of merchandise)		

A	=	L	+	OE
+300				+300

J. C. Penney will send you a monthly statement of this transaction and any others that have occurred during the month. If you do not pay in full within 30 days, J. C. Penney adds an interest (financing) charge to the balance due. Although interest rates vary by region and over time, a common rate for retailers is 18% per year (1.5% per month).

When financing charges are added, the seller recognizes interest revenue. Assuming that you owe $300 at the end of the month, and J. C. Penney charges 1.5%

per month on the balance due, the adjusting entry to record interest revenue of $4.50 ($300 × 1.5%) is as follows.

A	=	L	+	OE
+4.50				+4.50

Accounts Receivable	4.50	
Interest Revenue		4.50
(To record interest on amount due)		

Interest revenue is often substantial for many retailers.

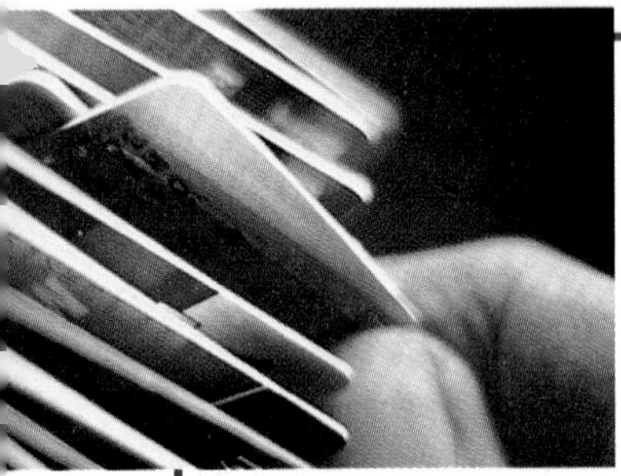

ACCOUNTING IN ACTION *Business Insight*

Interest rates on most credit cards are quite high, averaging 18.8 percent. As a result, consumers often look for companies that charge lower rates. Be careful—some companies offer lower interest rates but have eliminated the standard 25-day grace period before finance charges are incurred. Other companies encourage consumers to get more in debt by advertising that only a $1 minimum payment is due on a $1,000 account balance. The less you pay off, the more interest they earn! One bank markets a credit card that allows cardholders to skip a payment twice a year. However, the outstanding balance continues to incur interest. Other credit card companies calculate finance charges initially on two-month, rather than one-month, averages, a practice which often translates into higher interest charges. In short, read the fine print.

VALUING ACCOUNTS RECEIVABLE

STUDY OBJECTIVE 3

Distinguish between the methods and bases used to value accounts receivable.

Once receivables are recorded in the accounts, the next question is: How should receivables be reported in the financial statements? They are reported on the balance sheet as an asset. But determining the **amount** to report is sometimes difficult because some receivables will become uncollectible.

Each customer must satisfy the credit requirements of the seller before the credit sale is approved. Inevitably, though, some accounts receivable become uncollectible. For example, one of your customers may not be able to pay because of a decline in sales due to a downturn in the economy. Similarly, individuals may be laid off from their jobs or be faced with unexpected hospital bills. Credit losses are recorded as debits to **Bad Debts Expense** (or Uncollectible Accounts Expense). Such losses are considered a normal and necessary risk of doing business on a credit basis.

Two methods are used in accounting for uncollectible accounts: (1) the direct write-off method and (2) the allowance method. These methods are explained in the following sections.

Direct Write-off Method for Uncollectible Accounts

Under the **direct write-off method**, when a particular account is determined to be uncollectible, the loss is charged to Bad Debts Expense. Assume, for example, that Warden Co. writes off M. E. Doran's $200 balance as uncollectible on December 12. The entry is:

A	=	L	+	OE
−200				−200

Dec. 12	Bad Debts Expense	200	
	Accounts Receivable—M. E. Doran		200
	(To record write-off of M. E. Doran account)		

When this method is used, bad debts expense will show only **actual losses** from uncollectibles. Accounts receivable will be reported at its gross amount.

Although this method is simple, its use can reduce the usefulness of both the income statement and balance sheet. Consider the following example. Assume that in 2002, Quick Buck Computer Company decided it could increase its revenues by offering computers to college students without requiring any money down and with no credit-approval process. On campuses across the country it distributed 1,000,000 computers with a selling price of $800 each. This increased Quick Buck's revenues and receivables by $800,000,000. The promotion was a huge success! The 2002 balance sheet and income statement looked great. Unfortunately, during 2003, nearly 40 percent of the college student customers defaulted on their loans. This made the 2003 income statement and balance sheet look terrible. Illustration 9-1 shows the effect of these events on the financial statements if the direct write-off method is used.

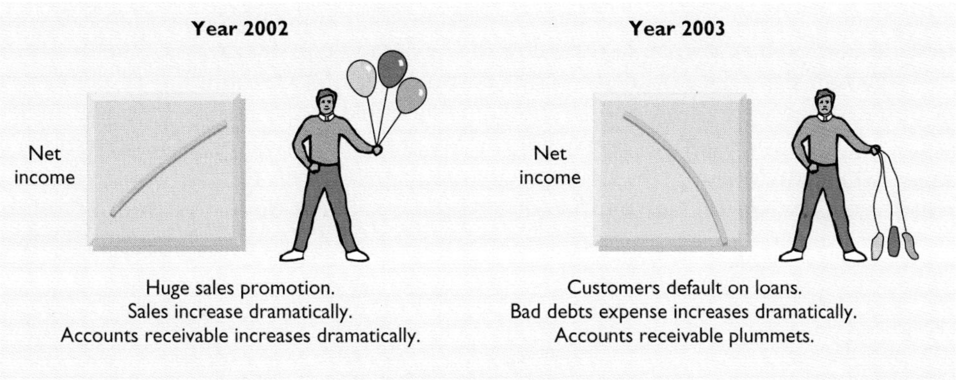

Year 2002
Net income
Huge sales promotion.
Sales increase dramatically.
Accounts receivable increases dramatically.
Year 2003
Net income
Customers default on loans.
Bad debts expense increases dramatically.
Accounts receivable plummets.

Illustration 9-1
Effects of direct write-off method

Under the direct write-off method, bad debts expense is often recorded in a period different from the period in which the revenue was recorded. No attempt is made to match bad debts expense to sales revenues in the income statement. Nor does the direct write-off method show accounts receivable in the balance sheet at the amount actually expected to be received. **Consequently, unless bad debts losses are insignificant, the direct write-off method is not acceptable for financial reporting purposes.**

Allowance Method for Uncollectible Accounts

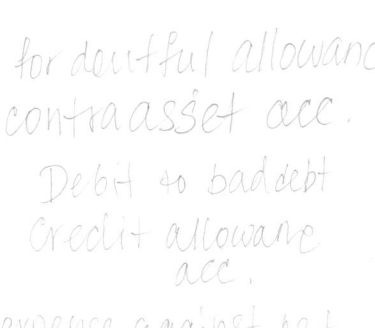

The **allowance method** of accounting for bad debts involves estimating uncollectible accounts at the end of each period. This provides better matching on the income statement and ensures that receivables are stated at their cash (net) realizable value on the balance sheet. **Cash (net) realizable value** is the net amount expected to be received in cash. It excludes amounts that the company estimates it will not collect. Receivables are therefore reduced by estimated uncollectible receivables in the balance sheet through use of this method.

The allowance method is required for financial reporting purposes when bad debts are material in amount. It has three essential features:

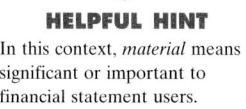

> **HELPFUL HINT**
> In this context, *material* means significant or important to financial statement users.

1. Uncollectible accounts receivable are **estimated**. This estimate is treated as an expense and is **matched against sales** in the same accounting period in which the sales occurred.
2. Estimated uncollectibles are debited to Bad Debts Expense and are credited to Allowance for Doubtful Accounts (a contra asset account) through an adjusting entry at the end of each period.

3. When a specific account is written off, actual uncollectibles are debited to Allowance for Doubtful Accounts and credited to Accounts Receivable.

RECORDING ESTIMATED UNCOLLECTIBLES. To illustrate the allowance method, assume that Hampson Furniture has credit sales of $1,200,000 in 2002. Of this amount, $200,000 remains uncollected at December 31. The credit manager estimates that $12,000 of these sales will be uncollectible. The adjusting entry to record the estimated uncollectibles is:

A	=	L	+	OE
−12,000				−12,000

Dec. 31	Bad Debts Expense	12,000	
	Allowance for Doubtful Accounts		12,000
	(To record estimate of uncollectible accounts)		

Bad Debts Expense is reported in the income statement as an operating expense (usually as a selling expense). Thus, the estimated uncollectibles are matched with sales in 2002. The expense is recorded in the same year the sales are made.

Allowance for Doubtful Accounts shows the estimated amount of claims on customers that are expected to become uncollectible in the future. This contra account is used instead of a direct credit to Accounts Receivable because we do not know which customers will not pay. The credit balance in the allowance account will absorb the specific write-offs when they occur. It is deducted from accounts receivable in the current assets section of the balance sheet as shown in Illustration 9-2.

Illustration 9-2

Presentation of allowance for doubtful accounts

HAMPSON FURNITURE
Balance Sheet (partial)

Current assets		
Cash		$ 14,800
Accounts receivable	**$200,000**	
Less: Allowance for doubtful accounts	**12,000**	**188,000**
Merchandise inventory		310,000
Prepaid expense		25,000
Total current assets		$537,800

INTERNATIONAL NOTE

The Finance Ministry in Japan recently noted that financial institutions should make better disclosure of bad loans. This disclosure would help depositors pick healthy banks.

The amount of $188,000 in Illustration 9-2 represents the expected **cash realizable value** of the accounts receivable at the statement date. **Allowance for Doubtful Accounts is not closed at the end of the fiscal year.**

RECORDING THE WRITE-OFF OF AN UNCOLLECTIBLE ACCOUNT. Companies use various methods of collecting past-due accounts, such as letters, calls, and legal action. When all means of collecting a past-due account have been exhausted and collection appears impossible, the account should be written off. In the credit card industry, for example, it is standard practice to write off accounts that are 210 days past due. To prevent premature or unauthorized write-offs, each write-off should be formally approved in writing by management. To maintain good internal control, authorization to write off accounts should not be given to someone who also has daily responsibilities related to cash or receivables.

To illustrate a receivables write-off, assume that the vice-president of finance of Hampson Furniture authorizes a write-off of the $500 balance owed by R. A. Ware on March 1, 2003. The entry to record the write-off is:

Mar. 1	Allowance for Doubtful Accounts	500	
	Accounts Receivable—R. A. Ware		500
	(Write-off of R. A. Ware account)		

A	=	L	+	OE
+500				
−500				

Bad Debts Expense is not increased when the write-off occurs. **Under the allowance method, every bad debt write-off is debited to the allowance account rather than to Bad Debts Expense.** A debit to Bad Debts Expense would be incorrect because the expense has already been recognized when the adjusting entry was made for estimated bad debts. Instead, the entry to record the write-off of an uncollectible account reduces both Accounts Receivable and the Allowance for Doubtful Accounts. After posting, the general ledger accounts will appear as in Illustration 9-3.

Illustration 9-3

General ledger balances after write-off

Accounts Receivable		Allowance for Doubtful Accounts	
Jan. 1 Bal. 200,000	Mar. 1 **500**	Mar. 1 **500**	Jan. 1 Bal. 12,000
Mar. 1 Bal. 199,500			Mar. 1 Bal. 11,500

A write-off affects only balance sheet accounts. The write-off of the account reduces both Accounts Receivable and Allowance for Doubtful Accounts. Cash realizable value in the balance sheet, therefore, remains the same, as shown in Illustration 9-4.

Illustration 9-4

Cash realizable value comparison

	Before Write-off	After Write-off
Accounts receivable	$200,000	$199,500
Allowance for doubtful accounts	12,000	11,500
Cash realizable value	**$188,000**	**$188,000**

RECOVERY OF AN UNCOLLECTIBLE ACCOUNT. Occasionally, a company collects from a customer after the account has been written off. Two entries are required to record the recovery of a bad debt: (1) The entry made in writing off the account is reversed to reinstate the customer's account. (2) The collection is journalized in the usual manner.

To illustrate, assume that on July 1, R. A. Ware pays the $500 amount that had been written off on March 1. These are the entries:

(1)

July 1	Accounts Receivable—R. A. Ware	500	
	Allowance for Doubtful Accounts		500
	(To reverse write-off of R. A. Ware account)		

A	=	L	+	OE
+500				
−500				

(2)

July 1	Cash	500	
	Accounts Receivable—R. A. Ware		500
	(To record collection from R. A. Ware)		

A	=	L	+	OE
+500				
−500				

Note that the recovery of a bad debt, like the write-off of a bad debt, affects only balance sheet accounts. The net effect of the two entries above is a debit to Cash and a credit to Allowance for Doubtful Accounts for $500. Accounts Receivable is debited and the Allowance for Doubtful Accounts is credited in entry (1) for two reasons: First, the company made an error in judgment when it wrote

HELPFUL HINT

Like the write-off, a recovery does not involve the income statement.

off the account receivable. Second, after R. A. Ware did pay, Accounts Receivable in the general ledger and Ware's account in the subsidiary ledger should show the collection for possible future credit purposes.

BASES USED FOR ALLOWANCE METHOD. To simplify the preceding explanation, we assumed we knew the amount of the expected uncollectibles. In "real life," companies must estimate that amount if they use the allowance method. Two bases are used to determine this amount: **(1) percentage of sales,** and **(2) percentage of receivables**. Both bases are generally accepted. The choice is a management decision. It depends on the relative emphasis that management wishes to give to expenses and revenues on the one hand or to cash realizable value of the accounts receivable on the other. The choice is whether to emphasize income statement or balance sheet relationships. Illustration 9-5 compares the two bases.

Illustration 9-5

Comparison of bases for estimating uncollectibles

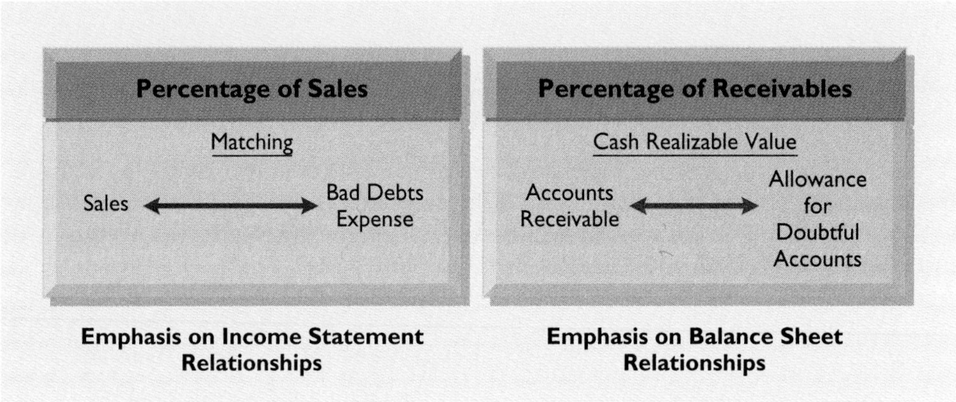

The percentage of sales basis results in a better matching of expenses with revenues—an income statement viewpoint. The percentage of receivables basis produces the better estimate of cash realizable value—a balance sheet viewpoint. Under both bases, it is necessary to determine the company's past experience with bad debt losses.

Percentage of Sales. In the **percentage of sales basis**, management estimates what percentage of credit sales will be uncollectible. This percentage is based on past experience and anticipated credit policy.

The percentage is applied to either total credit sales or net credit sales of the current year. To illustrate, assume that Gonzalez Company elects to use the percentage of sales basis. It concludes that 1 percent of net credit sales will become uncollectible. If net credit sales for 2002 are $800,000, the estimated bad debts expense is $8,000 (1% × $800,000). The adjusting entry is:

A	=	L	+	OE
−8,000				−8,000

Dec. 31	Bad Debts Expense	8,000	
	Allowance for Doubtful Accounts		8,000
	(To record estimated bad debts for year)		

After the adjusting entry is posted, assuming the allowance account already has a credit balance of $1,723, the accounts of Gonzalez Company will show:

Illustration 9-6

Bad debts accounts after posting

Bad Debts Expense			
Dec. 31 Adj.	**8,000**		

Allowance for Doubtful Accounts			
		Jan. 1 Bal.	1,723
		Dec. 31 Adj.	**8,000**
		Dec. 31 Bal.	9,723

3 Receivable

This basis of estimating uncollectibles emphasizes the matching of expenses with revenues. As a result, Bad Debts Expense will show a direct percentage relationship to the sales base on which it is computed. **When the adjusting entry is made, the existing balance in Allowance for Doubtful Accounts is disregarded.** The adjusted balance in this account should be a reasonable approximation of the realizable value of the receivables. If actual write-offs differ significantly from the amount estimated, the percentage for future years should be modified.

Other
Interes R.

Percentage of Receivables. Under the **percentage of receivables basis**, management estimates what percentage of receivables will result in losses from uncollectible accounts. An **aging schedule** is prepared, in which customer balances are classified by the length of time they have been unpaid. Because of its emphasis on time, the analysis is often called **aging the accounts receivable**.

ACCOUNTING IN ACTION e Business Insight

Companies that provide services and bill on a per hour basis often must spend considerable time preparing detailed bills that specify the billable activities performed. A new company, **TimeBills.com**, has an online product that reduces the amount of time it takes to prepare a bill, while increasing the information provided to the customer. To use the service, you create an electronic record that lists the type of project, customer name, project dates, and billing rate. By clicking on the "timer" function, you can automatically track time spent on a particular project as the work is being performed. TimeBills.com will either mail or e-mail invoices to customers, and keep track of collections, including providing an aging schedule.

After the accounts are aged, the expected bad debt losses are determined. This is done by applying percentages based on past experience to the totals in each category. The longer a receivable is past due, the less likely it is to be collected. So, the estimated percentage of uncollectible debts increases as the number of days past due increases. An aging schedule for Dart Company is shown in Illustration 9-7. Note the increasing percentages from 2 to 40 percent.

Illustration 9-7
Aging schedule

			Number of Days Past Due			
Customer	**Total**	**Not Yet Due**	**1–30**	**31–60**	**61–90**	**Over 90**
T. E. Adert	$ 600		$ 300		$ 200	$ 100
R. C. Bortz	300	$ 300				
B. A. Carl	450		200	$ 250		
O. L. Diker	700	500			200	
T. O. Ebbet	600			300		300
Others	36,950	26,200	5,200	2,450	1,600	1,500
	$39,600	$27,000	$5,700	$3,000	$2,000	$1,900
Estimated Percentage Uncollectible		2%	4%	10%	20%	40%
Total Estimated Bad Debts	**$ 2,228**	$ 540	$ 228	$ 300	$ 400	$ 760

HELPFUL HINT
The higher percentages are used for the older categories because the longer an account is past due, the less likely it is to be collected.

Total estimated bad debts for Dart Company ($2,228) represent the amount of existing customer claims expected to become uncollectible in the future. This amount represents the **required balance** in Allowance for Doubtful Accounts at the balance sheet date. **The amount of the bad debt adjusting entry is the difference between the required balance and the existing balance in the allowance account.** If the trial balance shows Allowance for Doubtful Accounts with a credit balance of $528, an adjusting entry for $1,700 ($2,228 − $528) is necessary, as shown below.

A	=	L	+	OE
−1,700				−1,700

Date	Account	Debit	Credit
Dec. 31	Bad Debts Expense	1,700	
	Allowance for Doubtful Accounts		1,700
	(To adjust allowance account to total estimated uncollectibles)		

After the adjusting entry is posted, the accounts of the Dart Company will show:

Illustration 9-8

Bad debts accounts after posting

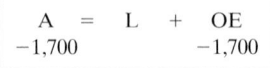

Bad Debts Expense		Allowance for Doubtful Accounts	
Dec. 31 Adj. **1,700**			Bal. 528
			Dec. 31 Adj. **1,700**
			Bal. 2,228

Occasionally the allowance account will have a **debit balance** prior to adjustment. This occurs when write-offs during the year have exceeded previous provisions for bad debts. In such a case **the debit balance is added to the required balance** when the adjusting entry is made. Thus, if there had been a $500 debit balance in the allowance account before adjustment, the adjusting entry would have been for $2,728 ($2,228 + $500) to arrive at a credit balance of $2,228.

The percentage of receivables method will normally result in the better approximation of cash realizable value. But it will not result in the better matching of expenses with revenues if some customers' accounts are more than one year past due. In such a case, bad debts expense for the current period would include amounts related to the sales of a prior year.

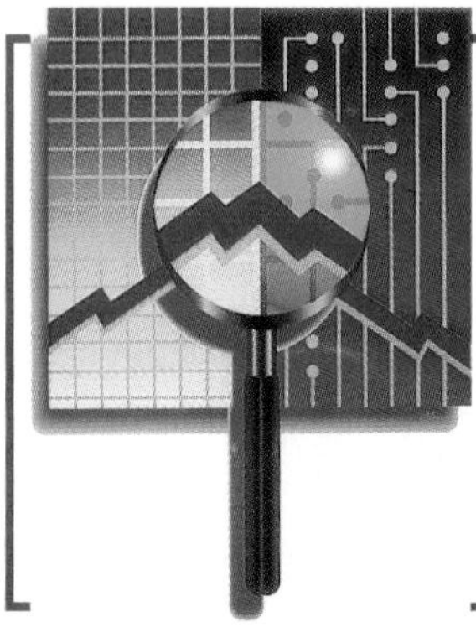

ACCOUNTING IN ACTION *Business Insight*

Nearly half of the goods sold by **Sears, Roebuck & Co.** are purchased with a Sears credit card. This means that how Sears accounts for its uncollectible accounts can have a very significant effect on Sears's net income. In one quarter in a recent year Sears reduced its bad debts expense by 61 percent compared to the same quarter in the previous year. In so doing, Sears was able to report earnings that slightly exceeded analysts' forecasts. Some analysts expressed concern that, because the number of delinquent accounts receivable had actually increased, Sears should probably have *increased* its bad debts expense, rather than reduced it. While Sears management defended its actions, analysts appeared to be unimpressed, and Sears's stock price declined on the news.

Acc Receivable = Trade

BEFORE YOU GO ON...

▶ *REVIEW IT*

1. What is the primary criticism of the direct write-off method?
2. Explain the difference between the percentage of sales and the percentage of receivables methods.
3. **Lands' End** has a generous customer return policy. What accounting treatment does Lands' End use for customer returns? (*Hint:* Review Lands' End's notes.) The answer to this question is provided on page 396.

LANDS' END DIRECT MERCHANTS

▶ *DO IT*

Brule Co. has been in business 5 years. The ledger at the end of the current year shows: Accounts Receivable $30,000, Sales $180,000, and Allowance for Doubtful Accounts with a debit balance of $2,000. Bad debts are estimated to be 10% of receivables. Prepare the entry to adjust the Allowance for Doubtful Accounts.

ACTION PLAN

- Report receivables at their cash (net) realizable value.
- Estimate the amount the company does not expect to collect.
- Consider the existing balance in the allowance account when using the percentage of receivables basis.

SOLUTION

The following entry should be made to bring the balance in the Allowance for Doubtful Accounts up to a balance of $3,000 (0.1 × $30,000):

Bad Debts Expense	5,000	
Allowance for Doubtful Accounts		5,000
(To record estimate of uncollectible accounts)		

Related exercise material: BE9-3, BE9-4, BE9-5, BE9-6, BE9-7, E9-2, E9-3, and E9-4.

THE NAVIGATOR

DISPOSING OF ACCOUNTS RECEIVABLE

STUDY OBJECTIVE 4

Describe the entries to record the disposition of accounts receivable.

In the normal course of events, accounts receivable are collected in cash and removed from the books. However, as credit sales and receivables have grown in significance, their "normal course of events" has changed. Companies now frequently sell their receivables to another company for cash, thereby shortening the cash-to-cash operating cycle.

Receivables are sold for two major reasons. First, **receivables may be sold because they may be the only reasonable source of cash**. When money is tight, companies may not be able to borrow money in the usual credit markets. Or, if money is available, the cost of borrowing may be prohibitive.

A second reason for selling receivables is that **billing and collection are often time consuming and costly**. It is often easier for a retailer to sell the receivable to another party with expertise in billing and collection matters. Credit card companies such as **MasterCard**, **VISA**, **American Express**, and **Diners Club** specialize in billing and collecting accounts receivable.

HELPFUL HINT

Two common expressions apply here:

1. Time is money. That is, waiting for the normal collection process costs money.
2. A bird in the hand is worth two in the bush. That is, getting cash now is better than getting it later.

Sale of Receivables

A common sale of receivables is a sale to a factor. A **factor** is a finance company or bank that buys receivables from businesses and then collects the payments directly from the customers. Factoring is a multibillion dollar business. For example, **Sears, Roebuck and Co.** recently sold $14.8 billion of customer accounts receivable to a factor.

Factoring arrangements vary widely. Typically the factor charges a commission to the company that is selling the receivables. This fee ranges from 1–3 percent of the amount of receivables purchased. To illustrate, assume that Hendredon Furniture factors $600,000 of receivables to Federal Factors. Federal Factors assesses a service charge of 2 percent of the amount of receivables sold. The journal entry to record the sale by Hendredon Furniture is as follows.

A	=	L	+	OE
+588,000				−12,000
−600,000				

Cash	588,000	
Service Charge Expense (2% × $600,000)	12,000	
Accounts Receivable		600,000
(To record the sale of accounts receivable)		

If the company often sells its receivables, the service charge expense (such as that incurred by Hendredon) is recorded as selling expense. If receivables are sold infrequently, this amount may be reported in the "other expenses and losses" section of the income statement.

Credit Card Sales

HELPFUL HINT
By accepting credit cards such as VISA, a retailer can increase its sales while reducing its bad debts expense.

One billion credit cards were estimated to be in use recently—more than three credit cards for every man, woman, and child in this country. Companies such as VISA, MasterCard, Discover, American Express, and Diners Club offer national credit cards. Three parties are involved when national credit cards are used in making retail sales: (1) the credit card issuer, who is independent of the retailer, (2) the retailer, and (3) the customer. A retailer's acceptance of a national credit card is another form of selling (factoring) the receivable.

The major advantages of these national credit cards to the retailer are shown in Illustration 9–9. In exchange for these advantages, the retailer pays the credit card issuer a fee of 2–6 percent of the invoice price for its services.

Illustration 9-9

Advantages of credit cards to the retailer

CASH SALES: VISA AND MASTERCARD. Sales resulting from the use of **VISA** and **MasterCard** are considered cash sales by the retailer. These cards are issued by banks. Upon receipt of credit card sales slips from a retailer, the bank immediately adds the amount to the seller's bank balance, deducting a fee of 2–4 percent of the credit card sales slips for this service. These credit card sales slips are recorded in the same manner as checks deposited from a cash sale.

To illustrate, Anita Ferreri purchases $1,000 of compact discs for her restaurant from Karen Kerr Music Co., using her VISA First Bank Card. The service fee that First Bank charges is 3 percent. The entry to record this transaction by Karen Kerr Music is as follows.

	Debit	Credit
Cash	970	
Service Charge Expense	30	
Sales		1,000
(To record VISA credit card sales)		

A	=	L	+	OE
+970				−30
				+1,000

CREDIT SALES: AMERICAN EXPRESS AND DINERS CLUB. Sales using **American Express** and **Diners Club** cards are reported as credit sales, not cash sales. Conversion into cash does not occur until these companies remit the net amount to the seller. To illustrate, assume that Four Seasons restaurant accepts an American Express card for a $300 bill. The entry for the sale by Four Seasons, assuming a 5 percent service fee, is:

	Debit	Credit
Accounts Receivable—American Express	285	
Service Charge Expense	15	
Sales		300
(To record American Express credit card sales)		

A	=	L	+	OE
+285				−15
				+300

American Express will subsequently pay the restaurant $285. The restaurant will record this payment as follows.

	Debit	Credit
Cash	285	
Accounts Receivable—American Express		285
(To record redemption of credit card billings)		

A	=	L	+	OE
+285				
−285				

Service Charge Expense is reported by the restaurant as a selling expense in the income statement.

BEFORE YOU GO ON...

REVIEW IT

1. Why do companies sell their receivables?
2. What is the journal entry when a company sells its receivables to a factor?
3. How are sales using a VISA or MasterCard reported? Is a sale using an American Express card recorded differently? Explain.

DO IT

Peter M. Dell Wholesalers Co. has been expanding faster than it can raise capital. According to its local banker, the company has reached its debt ceiling. Dell's customers are slow in paying (60–90 days), but its suppliers (creditors) are demanding 30-day payment. Dell has a cash flow problem.

Dell needs $120,000 in cash to safely cover next Friday's employee payroll. Its balance of outstanding receivables totals $750,000. What might Dell do to alleviate this cash crunch? Record the entry that Dell would make when it raises the needed cash.

ACTION PLAN

- To speed up the collection of cash, sell receivables to a factor.

- Calculate service charge expense as a percentage of the factored receivables.

SOLUTION: Assuming that Dell Co. factors $125,000 of its accounts receivable at a 1% service charge, the following entry would be made.

Cash	123,750	
Service Charge Expense	1,250	
Accounts Receivable		125,000
(To record sale of receivables to factor)		

Related exercise material: BE9–10 and E9–5.

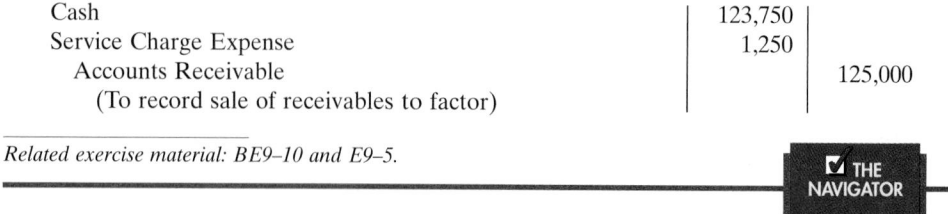

THE NAVIGATOR

NOTES RECEIVABLE

Credit may also be granted in exchange for a promissory note. A **promissory note** is a written promise to pay a specified amount of money on demand or at a definite time. Promissory notes may be used (1) when individuals and companies lend or borrow money; (2) when the amount of the transaction and the credit period exceed normal limits; or (3) in settlement of accounts receivable.

In a promissory note, the party making the promise to pay is called the **maker**. The party to whom payment is to be made is called the **payee**. The payee may be specifically identified by name or may be designated simply as the bearer of the note. In the note shown in Illustration 9-10, Brent Company is the maker, Wilma Company is the payee. To Wilma Company, the promissory note is a note receivable; to Brent Company, it is a note payable.

Illustration 9-10

Promissory note

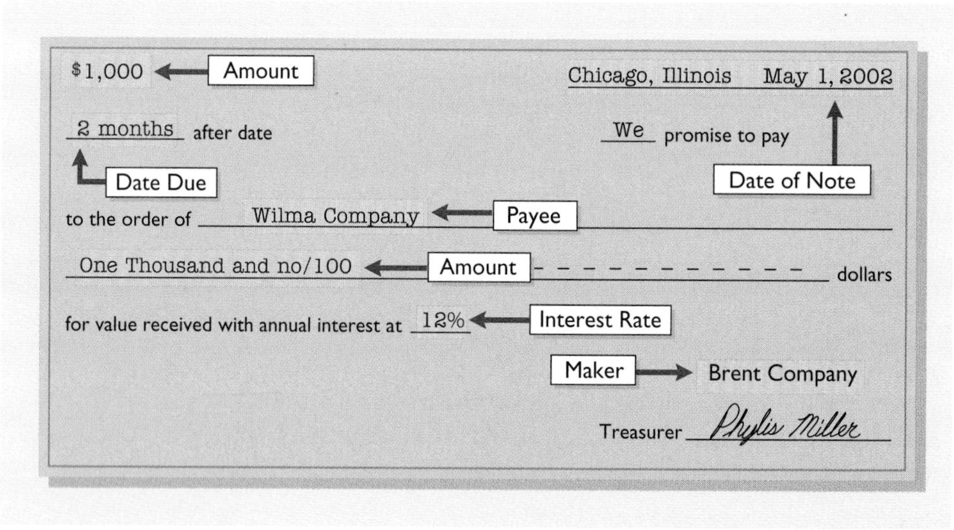

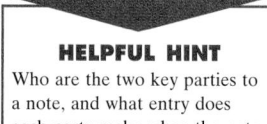

HELPFUL HINT
Who are the two key parties to a note, and what entry does each party make when the note is issued?
Answer:
1. The maker, Brent Company, credits Notes Payable.
2. The payee, Wilma Company, debits Notes Receivable.

Notes receivable give the payee a stronger legal claim to assets than accounts receivable. Like accounts receivable, notes receivable can be readily sold to another party. Promissory notes are negotiable instruments (as are checks), which means that they can be transferred to another party by endorsement.

Notes receivable are frequently accepted from customers who need to extend the payment of an account receivable. They are often required from high-risk customers. In some industries (such as the pleasure boat industry), all credit sales are supported by notes. The majority of notes originate from loans. The basic issues in accounting for notes receivable are the same as those for accounts receivable:

1. **Recognizing** notes receivable.
2. **Valuing** notes receivable.
3. **Disposing of** notes receivable.

On the following pages, we will look at these issues. Before we do, we need to consider two issues that did not apply to accounts receivable: maturity date and computing interest.

DETERMINING THE MATURITY DATE

STUDY OBJECTIVE 5

Compute the maturity date of and interest on notes receivable.

When the life of a note is expressed in terms of months, the due date when it matures is found by counting the months from the date of issue. For example, the maturity date of a three-month note dated May 1 is August 1. A note drawn on the last day of a month matures on the last day of a subsequent month. That is, a July 31 note due in two months matures on September 30. When the due date is stated in terms of days, you need to count the exact number of days to determine the maturity date. In counting, **the date the note is issued is omitted but the due date is included**. For example, the maturity date of a 60-day note dated July 17 is September 15, computed as follows.

Illustration 9-11

Computation of maturity date

Term of note		60 days
July (31 − 17)	14	
August	31	45
Maturity date: September		**15**

The due date (maturity date) of a promissory note may be stated in one of three ways, as shown in Illustration 9-12.

Illustration 9-12

Maturity date of different notes

COMPUTING INTEREST

As indicated in Chapter 3, the basic formula for computing interest on an interest-bearing note is:

Illustration 9-13

Formula for computing interest

Face Value of Note × Annual Interest Rate × Time in Terms of One Year = Interest

HELPFUL HINT

The interest rate specified is the *annual* rate.

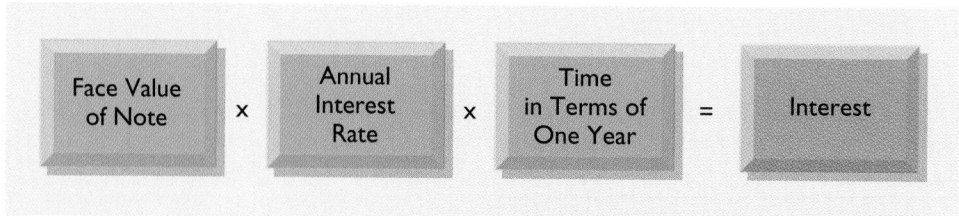

The interest rate specified in a note is an **annual** rate of interest. The time factor in the formula above expresses the fraction of a year that the note is outstanding. When the maturity date is stated in days, the time factor is often the number of days divided by 360. When the due date is stated in months, the time factor is the number of months divided by 12. Computation of interest for various time periods is shown in Illustration 9-14.

Illustration 9-14

Computation of interest

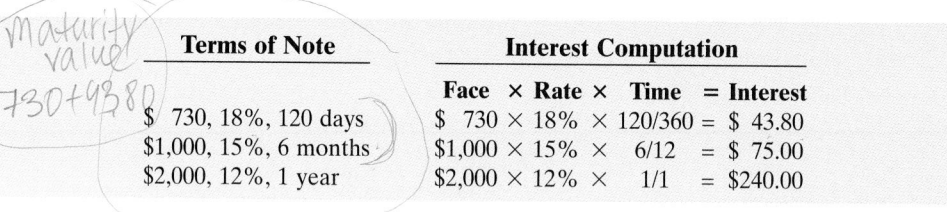

Terms of Note	Interest Computation
	Face × Rate × Time = Interest
$ 730, 18%, 120 days	$ 730 × 18% × 120/360 = $ 43.80
$1,000, 15%, 6 months	$1,000 × 15% × 6/12 = $ 75.00
$2,000, 12%, 1 year	$2,000 × 12% × 1/1 = $240.00

There are many different ways to calculate interest. The computation above assumed 360 days for the length of the year. Many financial institutions use 365 days. It is more profitable to use 360 days; the holder of the note receives more interest than if 365 days are used. For homework problems, assume 360 days.

RECOGNIZING NOTES RECEIVABLE

STUDY OBJECTIVE 6

Explain how notes receivable are recognized in the accounts.

To illustrate the basic entry for notes receivable, we will use the $1,000, 2-month, 12% promissory note on page 374. Assuming that the note was written to settle an open account, the entry for the receipt of the note by Wilma Company is:

May 1	Notes Receivable	1,000	
	Accounts Receivable—Brent Company		1,000
	(To record acceptance of Brent Company note)		

A	=	L	+	OE
+1,000				
−1,000				

Observe that the note receivable is recorded at its **face value**, the value shown on the face of the note. No interest revenue is reported when the note is accepted because the revenue recognition principle does not recognize revenue until earned. Interest is earned (accrued) as time passes.

If a note is exchanged for cash, the entry is a debit to Notes Receivable and a credit to Cash in the amount of the loan.

VALUING NOTES RECEIVABLE

STUDY OBJECTIVE 7

Describe how notes receivable are valued.

Valuing short-term notes receivable is the same as valuing accounts receivable. Like accounts receivable, short-term notes receivable are reported at their **cash (net) realizable value**. The notes receivable allowance account is Allowance for Doubtful Accounts. The estimations involved in determining cash realizable value and in recording bad debts expense and related allowance are similar.

ACCOUNTING IN ACTION *International Insight*

Long-term receivables do pose additional estimation problems. For example, banks that loaned money to developing countries have often found it difficult to collect on those receivables. At one time, banks were owed $1.3 trillion by developing countries. (A trillion is a lot of money—-enough to give every man, woman, and child in the world $250 each.) Banks made these loans for various reasons: (1) to provide stability to these governments and increase trade, (2) in the belief that governments would never default on payment, and (3) with the desire to increase banks' income by lending. Determining the proper allowance is understandably difficult for these types of long-term receivables.

DISPOSING OF NOTES RECEIVABLE

STUDY OBJECTIVE 8

Describe the entries to record the disposition of notes receivable.

Notes may be held to their maturity date, at which time the face value plus accrued interest is due. Sometimes the maker of the note defaults and an adjustment to the accounts must be made. At other times the holder of the note speeds up the conversion to cash by selling the note. The entries for honoring and dishonoring notes are illustrated below.

Honor of Notes Receivable

A note is **honored** when it is paid in full at its maturity date. For an interest-bearing note, the amount due at maturity is the face value of the note plus interest for the length of time specified on the note.

To illustrate, assume that Betty Co. lends Wayne Higley Inc. $10,000 on June 1, accepting a 4-month, 9% interest note. Interest will be $300 ($10,000 × 9% × 4/12). The amount due, the maturity value, will be $10,300. To obtain payment, Betty Co. (the payee) must present the note either to Wayne Higley Inc. (the maker) or to the maker's duly appointed agent, such as a bank. Assuming that Betty Co. presents the note to Wayne Higley Inc. on the maturity date, the entry by Betty Co. to record the collection is:

Oct. 1	Cash	10,300	
	Notes Receivable		10,000
	Interest Revenue		300
	(To record collection of Higley Inc. note)		

A	=	L	+	OE
+10,300				+300
−10,000				

If Betty Co. prepares financial statements as of September 30, it would be necessary to accrue interest. In this case, the adjusting entry by Betty Co. would be to record 4 months' interest ($300), as shown below.

Sept. 30	Interest Receivable	300	
	Interest Revenue		300
	(To accrue 4 months' interest)		

A	=	L	+	OE
+300				+300

When interest has been accrued, at maturity it is necessary to credit Interest Receivable. The entry by Betty Co. to record the honoring of the Wayne Higley Inc. note on October 1 is:

Oct. 1	Cash	10,300	
	Notes Receivable		10,000
	Interest Receivable		300
	(To record collection of note at maturity)		

A	=	L	+	OE
+10,300				
−10,000				
−300				

In this case, Interest Receivable is credited because the receivable was established in the adjusting entry.

Dishonor of Notes Receivable

A **dishonored note** is a note that is not paid in full at maturity. A dishonored note receivable is no longer negotiable. However, the payee still has a claim against the maker of the note. Therefore the Notes Receivable account is usually transferred to an Account Receivable.

To illustrate, assume that Wayne Higley Inc. on October 1 indicates that it cannot pay at the present time. The entry to record the dishonor of the note depends on whether eventual collection is expected. If Betty Co. expects eventual collection, the amount due (face value and interest) on the note is debited to Accounts Receivable. Betty Co. would make the following entry at the time the note is dishonored (assuming no previous accrual of interest).

A	=	L	+	OE
+10,300				+300
−10,000				

Oct. 1	Accounts Receivable—Wayne Higley Inc.	10,300	
	Notes Receivable		10,000
	Interest Revenue		300
	(To record the dishonor of Higley Inc. note)		

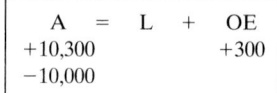

If there is no hope of collection, the face value of the note would be written off by debiting the Allowance for Doubtful Accounts. No interest revenue would be recorded because collection will not occur.

Sale of Notes Receivable

The accounting for the sales of notes receivable is recorded similarly to the sale of accounts receivable. The accounting entries for the sale of notes receivable are left for a more advanced course.

BEFORE YOU GO ON...

REVIEW IT

1. What is the basic formula for computing interest?
2. At what value are notes receivable reported on the balance sheet?
3. Explain the difference between honoring and dishonoring a note receivable.

DO IT

Gambit Stores accepts from Leonard Co. a $3,400, 90-day, 12% note dated May 10 in settlement of Leonard's overdue account. What is the maturity date of the note? What is the entry made by Gambit at the maturity date, assuming Leonard pays the note and interest in full at that time?

ACTION PLAN

- Count the exact number of days to determine the maturity date. Omit the date the note is issued, but include the due date.
- Determine whether interest was accrued. The entry here assumes that no interest has been previously accrued on this note.

SOLUTION: The maturity date is August 8, computed as follows.

Term of note:		90 days
May (31 − 10)	21	
June	30	
July	31	82
Maturity date: August		8

The interest payable at maturity date is $102, computed as follows.

Face	×	Rate	×	Time	=	Interest
$3,400	×	12%	×	90/360	=	$102

The entry recorded by Gambit Stores at the maturity date is:

Cash	3,502	
Notes Receivable		3,400
Interest Revenue		102
(To record collection of Leonard note)		

Related exercise material: BE9-8, BE9-9, E9-8, E9-9, and E9-10.

THE NAVIGATOR

ACCOUNTING IN ACTION *Business Insight*

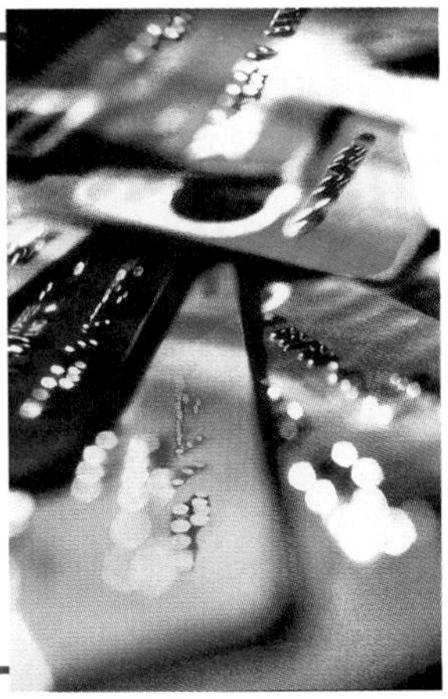

Give the man credit. Like most of us, John Galbreath receives piles of unsolicited, "preapproved" credit card applications in the mail. Galbreath doesn't just toss them out, though. He filled out a credit card application on which he stated he was 97 years old and had no income, no telephone, and no Social Security number. In a space inviting him to let the credit card company pay off his other credit card balances, Galbreath said he owed money to the Mafia.

Back came a credit card and a letter welcoming John to the fold with a $1,500 credit limit. Galbreath had requested the card under a false name, John C. Reath, an alias under which he had received two other credit cards—earning exemplary credit. John C. Reath might be a senior citizen with no means, but it seems he paid his bills on time.

SOURCE: "Forbes Informer," edited by Kate Bohner Lewis, *Forbes*, August 14, 1995, p. 19. Reprinted by permission of FORBES Magazine © Forbes Inc., 1995.

STATEMENT PRESENTATION AND ANALYSIS

PRESENTATION

STUDY OBJECTIVE 9

Explain the statement presentation and analysis of receivables.

Each of the major types of receivables should be identified in the balance sheet or in the notes to the financial statements. Short-term receivables are reported in the current assets section of the balance sheet, below short-term investments. Short-term investments appear before receivables, because short-term investments are more liquid (nearer to cash). Both the gross amount of receivables and the allowance for doubtful accounts should be reported.

In a multiple-step income statement, bad debts expense and service charge expense are reported as selling expenses in the operating expenses section. Interest revenue is shown under "other revenues and gains" in the nonoperating activities section of the income statement.

ANALYSIS

Financial ratios are frequently computed to evaluate the liquidity of a company's accounts receivable. The **accounts receivable turnover ratio** is used to assess the liquidity of the receivables. This ratio measures the number of times, on average, accounts receivable are collected during the period. It is computed by dividing net credit sales (net sales less cash sales) by the average net accounts receivable during the year. Unless seasonal factors are significant, average net accounts receivable outstanding can be computed from the beginning and ending balances of net accounts receivable.

For example, in 2000 **Lands' End** had net sales of $1,319.8 million for the year. It had a beginning net accounts receivable balance of $21.1 million and an ending net accounts receivable balance of $17.8 million. Assuming that Lands' End's sales were all on credit, its accounts receivable turnover ratio is computed as follows.

Illustration 9-15

Accounts receivable turnover ratio and computation

LANDS' END DIRECT MERCHANTS

Net Credit Sales	÷	Average Net Accounts Receivable	=	Accounts Receivable Turnover
$1,319.8	÷	$\frac{\$21.1 + \$17.8}{2}$	=	68 times

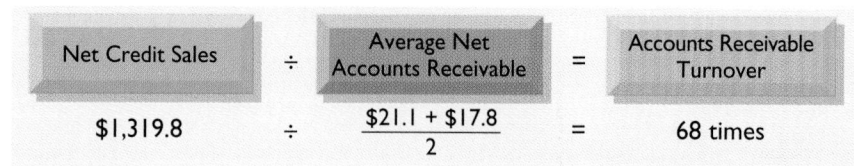

The result indicates an accounts receivable turnover ratio of 68 times per year. The higher the turnover ratio the more liquid the company's receivables.

A variant of the accounts receivable turnover ratio that makes the liquidity even more evident is the conversion of it into an **average collection period** in terms of days. This is done by dividing the turnover ratio into 365 days. For example, Lands' End's turnover of 68 times is divided into 365 days, as follows, to obtain approximately 5.4 days.

Illustration 9-16

Average collection period for receivables formula and computation

LANDS' END DIRECT MERCHANTS

Days in Year	÷	Accounts Receivable Turnover	=	Average Collection Period in Days
365 days	÷	68 times	=	5.4 days

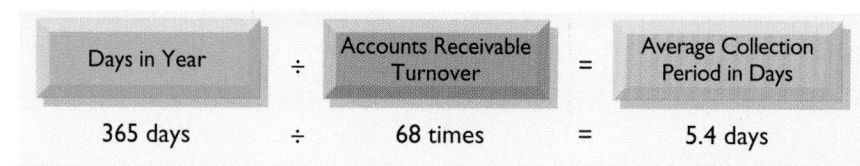

This means that it takes Lands' End about 5.4 days to collect its accounts receivable.

The average collection period is frequently used to assess the effectiveness of a company's credit and collection policies. The general rule is that the collection period should not greatly exceed the credit term period (i.e., the time allowed for payment).[1]

BEFORE YOU GO ON...

REVIEW IT

1. Explain where accounts and notes receivable are reported on the balance sheet.
2. Where are bad debts expense, service charge expense, and interest revenue reported on the multiple-step income statement?

A LOOK BACK AT OUR FEATURE STORY

Refer back to the Feature Story about Fred Tarter's **Pharmacy Fund** at the beginning of the chapter, and answer the following questions.

1. Why has the pharmacy business moved from a cash-based business to a receivables-based business?
2. What is the economic motivation for pharmacies to sell their receivables?
3. What is the economic motivation for the Pharmacy Fund to purchase the receivables?

SOLUTION

1. Due to the proliferation of health plans (of which there are more than 4,500 in the U.S.), pharmacists now deal with many small receivables from third-party payers instead of cash payments from customers.

[1] One factor that may distort this liquidity analysis is that Lands' End's sales number includes many cash sales. Therefore, the receivables turnover ratio would be high, and the days to collect receivables would be low.

2. Pharmacists must wait between 30 and 60 days to receive their receivables. Selling the receivables provides cash within 24 hours and relieves pharmacists of collection responsibilities. (It is estimated that credit losses equal 3 percent of the $40 billion of prescriptions purchased through health care plans.)
3. The Pharmacy Fund maintains credit files on health plan sponsors. Thus, it can minimize credit losses. The fund receives a 1.4–2 percent fee on receivables purchased. As the volume of business expands, it is expected that this fee will cover expenses and provide a profit.

THE NAVIGATOR

DEMONSTRATION PROBLEM

Additional Demonstration Problem

The following selected transactions relate to Falcetto Company.

Mar. 1	Sold $20,000 of merchandise to Potter Company, terms 2/10, n/30.
11	Received payment in full from Potter Company for balance due.
12	Accepted Juno Company's $20,000, 6-month, 12% note for balance due.
13	Made Falcetto Company credit card sales for $13,200.
15	Made American Express credit sales totaling $6,700. A 5% service fee is charged by American Express.
30	Received payment in full from American Express Company.
Apr. 11	Sold accounts receivable of $8,000 to Harcot Factor. Harcot Factor assesses a service charge of 2% of the amount of receivables sold.
13	Received collections of $8,200 on Falcetto Company credit card sales and added finance charges of 1.5% to the remaining balances.
May 10	Wrote off as uncollectible $16,000 of accounts receivable. Falcetto uses the percentage of sales basis to estimate bad debts.
June 30	Credit sales for the first 6 months total $2,000,000. The bad debt percentage is 1% of credit sales. At June 30, the balance in the allowance account is $3,500.
July 16	One of the accounts receivable written off in May was from J. Simon, who pays the amount due, $4,000, in full.

Instructions

Prepare the journal entries for the transactions.

SOLUTION TO DEMONSTRATION PROBLEM

Mar. 1	Accounts Receivable–Potter	20,000	
	Sales		20,000
	(To record sales on account)		
Mar. 11	Cash	19,600	
	Sales Discounts (2% × $20,000)	400	
	Accounts Receivable—Potter		20,000
	(To record collection of accounts receivable)		
Mar. 12	Notes Receivable	20,000	
	Accounts Receivable—Juno		20,000
	(To record acceptance of Juno Company note)		
Mar. 13	Accounts Receivable	13,200	
	Sales		13,200
	(To record company credit card sales)		
Mar. 15	Accounts Receivable—American Express	6,365	
	Service Charge Expense (5% × $6,700)	335	
	Sales		6,700
	(To record credit card sales)		

ACTION PLAN

- Generally, record accounts receivable at invoice price.
- Recognize that sales returns and allowances and cash discounts reduce the amount received on accounts receivable.
- Record a service charge expense on the seller's books when accounts receivable are sold.
- Prepare an adjusting entry for bad debts expense.
- Ignore any balance in the allowance account under the percentage of sales basis. Recognize the balance in the allowance account under the percentage of receivables basis.
- Record write-offs of accounts receivable only in balance sheet accounts.

Mar. 30	Cash	6,365	
	Accounts Receivable—American Express		6,365
	(To record redemption of credit card billings)		
Apr. 11	Cash	7,840	
	Service Charge Expense (2% × $8,000)	160	
	Accounts Receivable		8,000
	(To record sale of receivables to factor)		
Apr. 13	Cash	8,200	
	Accounts Receivable		8,200
	(To record collection of accounts receivable)		
	Accounts Receivable [($13,200 − $8,200) × 1.5%]	75	
	Interest Revenue		75
	(To record interest on amount due)		
May 10	Allowance for Doubtful Accounts	16,000	
	Accounts Receivable		16,000
	(To record write-off of accounts receivable)		
June 30	Bad Debts Expense ($2,000,000 × 1%)	20,000	
	Allowance for Doubtful Accounts		20,000
	(To record estimate of uncollectible accounts)		
July 16	Accounts Receivable—J. Simon	4,000	
	Allowance for Doubtful Accounts		4,000
	(To reverse write-off of accounts receivable)		
	Cash	4,000	
	Accounts Receivable—J. Simon		4,000
	(To record collection of accounts receivable)		

THE NAVIGATOR

SUMMARY OF STUDY OBJECTIVES

1. *Identify the different types of receivables.* Receivables are frequently classified as (1) accounts, (2) notes, and (3) other. Accounts receivable are amounts owed by customers on account. Notes receivable are claims for which formal instruments of credit are issued as proof of the debt. Other receivables include nontrade receivables such as interest receivable, loans to company officers, advances to employees, and income taxes refundable.

2. *Explain how accounts receivable are recognized in the accounts.* Accounts receivable are recorded at invoice price. They are reduced by Sales Returns and Allowances. Cash discounts reduce the amount received on accounts receivable. When interest is charged on a past due receivable, this interest is added to the accounts receivable balance and is recognized as interest revenue.

3. *Distinguish between the methods and bases used to value accounts receivable.* There are two methods of accounting for uncollectible accounts: (1) the allowance method and (2) the direct write-off method. Either the percentage of sales or the percentage of receivables basis may be used to estimate uncollectible accounts using the allowance method. The percentage of sales basis emphasizes the matching principle. The percentage of receivables basis emphasizes the cash realizable value of the accounts receivable. An aging schedule is often used with this basis.

4. *Describe the entries to record the disposition of accounts receivable.* When an account receivable is collected, Accounts Receivable is credited. When an account receivable is sold, a service charge expense is charged which reduces the amount collected.

5. *Compute the maturity date of and interest on notes receivable.* The maturity date of a note must be computed unless the due date is specified or the note is payable on demand. For a note stated in months, the maturity date is found by counting the months from the date of issue. For a note stated in days, the number of days is counted, omitting the issue date and counting the due date. The formula for computing interest is face value × interest rate × time.

6. *Explain how notes receivable are recognized in the accounts.* Notes receivable are recorded at face value. In some cases, it is necessary to accrue interest prior to maturity. In this case, Interest Receivable is debited and Interest Revenue is credited.

7. *Describe how notes receivable are valued.* Like accounts receivable, notes receivable are reported at their cash (net) realizable value. The notes receivable allowance account is the Allowance for Doubtful Accounts. The computation and estimations involved in valuing notes receivable at cash realizable value, and in recording the proper amount of bad debts expense and related allowance are similar to those for accounts receivable.

8. *Describe the entries to record the disposition of notes receivable.* Notes can be held to maturity. At that time the face value plus accrued interest is due, and the note is removed from the accounts. In many cases, the holder of the note speeds up the conversion by selling the receivable to another party. In some situations, the maker of the note dishonors the note (defaults), and the note is written off.

9. *Explain the statement presentation and analysis of receivables.* Each major type of receivable should be identified in the balance sheet or in the notes to the financial statements. Short-term receivables are considered current assets. The gross amount of receivables and the allowance for doubtful accounts should be reported. Bad debts and service charge expenses are reported in the multiple-step income statement as operating (selling) expenses; interest revenue is shown as other revenues and gains in the nonoperating activities section of the statement. Accounts receivable may be evaluated for liquidity by computing a turnover ratio and an average collection period.

THE NAVIGATOR

Key Term Matching Activity

GLOSSARY

Accounts receivable turnover ratio A measure of the liquidity of accounts receivable; computed by dividing net credit sales by average net accounts receivable. (p. 379).

Aging of accounts receivable The analysis of customer balances by the length of time they have been unpaid. (p. 369).

Allowance method A method of accounting for bad debts that involves estimating uncollectible accounts at the end of each period. (p. 365).

Average collection period The average amount of time that a receivable is outstanding; calculated by dividing 365 days by the receivables turnover ratio. (p. 380).

Bad Debts Expense An expense account to record uncollectible receivables. (p. 364).

Cash (net) realizable value The net amount expected to be received in cash. (p. 365).

Direct write-off method A method of accounting for bad debts that involves expensing accounts at the time they are determined to be uncollectible. (p. 364).

Dishonored note A note that is not paid in full at maturity. (p. 378).

Factor A finance company or bank that buys receivables from businesses and then collects the payments directly from the customers. (p. 371).

Maker The party in a promissory note who is making the promise to pay. (p. 374).

Payee The party to whom payment of a promissory note is to be made. (p. 374).

Percentage of receivables basis Management establishes a percentage relationship between the amount of receivables and the expected losses from uncollectible accounts. (p. 369).

Percentage of sales basis Management establishes a percentage relationship between the amount of credit sales and expected losses from uncollectible accounts. (p. 368).

Promissory note A written promise to pay a specified amount of money on demand or at a definite time. (p. 374).

Trade receivables Notes and accounts receivable that result from sales transactions. (p. 362).

Chapter 9 Self-Test

SELF-STUDY QUESTIONS

Answers are at the end of the chapter.

(SO 2) **1.** Remmers Company on June 15 sells merchandise on account to Tucci Co. for $1,000, terms 2/10, n/30. On June 20, Tucci Co. returns merchandise worth $300 to Remmers Company. On June 24, payment is received from Tucci Co. for the balance due. What is the amount of cash received?
a. $700.
b. $680.
c. $686.
d. None of the above.

(SO 3) **2.** Which of the following approaches for bad debts is best described as a balance sheet method?
a. Percentage of receivables basis.
b. Direct write-off method.
c. Percentage of sales basis.
d. Both a and b.

(SO 3) **3.** Net sales for the month are $800,000, and bad debts are expected to be 1.5% of net sales. The company uses the percentage of sales basis. If the Allowance for Doubtful Accounts has a credit balance of $15,000 before adjustment, what is the balance after adjustment?
a. $15,000.
b. $27,000.
c. $23,000.
d. $31,000.

4. In 2002, Roland Carlson Company had net credit sales of $750,000. On January 1, 2002, Allowance for Doubtful Accounts had a credit balance of $18,000. During 2002, $30,000 of uncollectible accounts receivable were written off. Past experience indicates that 3% of net credit sales become uncollectible. What should be the adjusted balance of Allowance for Doubtful Accounts at December 31, 2002? (SO 3)
a. $10,050.
b. $10,500.
c. $22,500.
d. $40,500.

(SO 3) **5.** An analysis and aging of the accounts receivable of Machiavelli Company at December 31 reveals the following data.

Accounts receivable	$800,000
Allowance for doubtful accounts per books before adjustment	50,000
Amounts expected to become uncollectible	65,000

The cash realizable value of the accounts receivable at December 31, after adjustment, is:

a. $685,000.
b. $750,000.
c. $800,000.
d. $735,000.

(SO 6) **6.** One of the following statements about promissory notes is incorrect. The *incorrect* statement is:

a. The party making the promise to pay is called the maker.
b. The party to whom payment is to be made is called the payee.
c. A promissory note is not a negotiable instrument.
d. A promissory note is more liquid than an account receivable.

(SO 4) **7.** Which of the following statements about VISA credit card sales is *incorrect*?

a. The credit card issuer makes the credit investigation of the customer.
b. The retailer is not involved in the collection process.
c. Two parties are involved.
d. The retailer receives cash more quickly than it would from individual customers on account.

(SO 4) **8.** Morgan Retailers accepted $50,000 of Citibank VISA credit card charges for merchandise sold on July 1. Citibank charges 4% for its credit card use. The entry to record this transaction by Morgan Retailers will include a credit to Sales of $50,000 and a debit(s) to:

a. Cash	$48,000
and Service Charge Expense	2,000
b. Accounts Receivable	$48,000
and Service Charge Expense	$2,000
c. Cash	$50,000
d. Accounts Receivable	$50,000

9. Bickner Co. accepts a $1,000, 3-month, 12% promissory note in settlement of an account with Streisand Co. The entry to record this transaction is as follows. (SO 6)

a. Notes Receivable	1,030	
Accounts Receivable		1,030
b. Notes Receivable	1,000	
Accounts Receivable		1,000
c. Notes Receivable	1,000	
Sales		1,000
d. Notes Receivable	1,020	
Accounts Receivable		1,020

10. Schlicht Co. holds Osgrove Inc.'s $10,000, 120-day, 9% note. The entry made by Schlicht Co. when the note is collected, assuming no interest has been previously accrued, is: (SO 8)

a. Cash	10,300	
Notes Receivable		10,300
b. Cash	10,000	
Notes Receivable		10,000
c. Accounts Receivable	10,300	
Notes Receivable		10,000
Interest Revenue		300
d. Cash	10,300	
Notes Receivable		10,000
Interest Revenue		300

THE NAVIGATOR

QUESTIONS

1. What is the difference between an account receivable and a note receivable?
2. What are some common types of receivables other than accounts receivable and notes receivable?
3. Texaco Oil Company issues its own credit cards. Assume that Texaco charges you $40 on an unpaid balance. Prepare the journal entry that Texaco makes to record this revenue.
4. What are the essential features of the allowance method of accounting for bad debts?
5. Soo Eng cannot understand why cash realizable value does not decrease when an uncollectible account is written off under the allowance method. Clarify this point for Soo Eng.
6. Distinguish between the two bases that may be used in estimating uncollectible accounts.
7. Hersee Company has a credit balance of $3,500 in Allowance for Doubtful Accounts. The estimated bad debts expense under the percentage of sales basis is $4,100. The total estimated uncollectibles under the percentage of receivables basis is $5,800. Prepare the adjusting entry under each basis.
8. How are bad debts accounted for under the direct write-off method? What are the disadvantages of this method?
9. Hope Company accepts both its own credit cards and national credit cards. What are the advantages of accepting both types of cards?
10. An article recently appeared in *The Wall Street Journal* indicating that companies are selling their receivables at a record rate. Why are companies selling their receivables?
11. Eastern Textiles decides to sell $800,000 of its accounts receivable to First Factors Inc. First Factors assesses a

service charge of 2% of the amount of receivables sold. Prepare the journal entry that Eastern Textiles makes to record this sale.

12. Your roommate is uncertain about the advantages of a promissory note. Compare the advantages of a note receivable with those of an account receivable.

13. How may the maturity date of a promissory note be stated?

14. Indicate the maturity date of each of the following promissory notes:

Date of Note	Terms
(a) March 13	one year after date of note
(b) May 4	3 months after date
(c) June 20	30 days after date
(d) July 1	60 days after date

15. Compute the missing amounts for each of the following notes.

	Principal	Annual Interest Rate	Time	Total Interest
(a)	?	9%	120 days	$ 450
(b)	$30,000	10%	3 years	?
(c)	$60,000	?	5 months	$3,000
(d)	$50,000	11%	?	$1,375

16. In determining interest revenue, some financial institutions use 365 days per year and others use 360 days. Why might a financial institution use 360 days?

17. May Company dishonors a note at maturity. What actions by May may occur with the dishonoring of the note?

18. **General Motors Corporation** has accounts receivable and notes receivable. How should the receivables be reported on the balance sheet?

19. The accounts receivable turnover ratio is 8.25, and average net receivables during the period are $300,000. What is the amount of net credit sales for the period?

BRIEF EXERCISES

Identify different types of receivables. (SO 1)

BE9-1 Presented below are three receivables transactions. Indicate whether these receivables are reported as accounts receivable, notes receivable, or other receivables on a balance sheet.

(a) Sold merchandise on account for $70,000 to a customer.
(b) Received a promissory note of $57,000 for services performed.
(c) Advanced $10,000 to an employee.

Record basic accounts receivable transactions. (SO 2)

BE9-2 Record the following transactions on the books of Essex Co.

(a) On July 1, Essex Co. sold merchandise on account to Harrard Inc. for $16,000, terms 2/10, n/30.
(b) On July 8, Harrard Inc. returned merchandise worth $3,800 to Essex Co.
(c) On July 11, Harrard Inc. paid for the merchandise.

Prepare entries for allowance method and classifications. (SO 3, 9)

BE9-3 During its first year of operations, Jose Company had credit sales of $3,000,000; $600,000 remained uncollected at year-end. The credit manager estimates that $36,000 of these receivables will become uncollectible.

(a) Prepare the journal entry to record the estimated uncollectibles.
(b) Prepare the current assets section of the balance sheet for Jose Company. Assume that in addition to the receivables it has cash of $90,000, merchandise inventory of $130,000, and prepaid expenses of $13,000.

Prepare entries for write-off; determine cash realizable value. (SO 3)

BE9-4 At the end of 2002, Searcy Co. has accounts receivable of $700,000 and an allowance for doubtful accounts of $54,000. On January 24, 2003, the company learns that its receivable from Hunt Inc. is not collectible, and management authorizes a write-off of $7,000.

(a) Prepare the journal entry to record the write-off.
(b) What is the cash realizable value of the accounts receivable (1) before the write-off and (2) after the write-off?

Prepare entries for collection of bad debts write-off. (SO 3)

BE9-5 Assume the same information as BE9-4. On March 4, 2003, Searcy Co. receives payment of $7,000 in full from Hunt Inc. Prepare the journal entries to record this transaction.

Prepare entry using percentage of sales method. (SO 3)

BE9-6 Massey Co. elects to use the percentage of sales basis in 2002 to record bad debts expense. It estimates that 2% of net credit sales will become uncollectible. Sales are $800,000 for 2002, sales returns and allowances are $40,000, and the allowance for doubtful accounts has a credit balance of $12,000. Prepare the adjusting entry to record bad debts expense in 2002.

Prepare entry using percentage of receivables method.
(SO 3)

BE9-7 St. Pierre Co. uses the percentage of accounts receivable basis to record bad debts expense. It estimates that 2% of accounts receivable will become uncollectible. Accounts receivable are $400,000 at the end of the year, and the allowance for doubtful accounts has a credit balance of $3,000.

(a) Prepare the adjusting journal entry to record bad debts expense for the year.
(b) If the allowance for doubtful accounts had a debit balance of $800 instead of a credit balance of $3,000, determine the amount to be reported for bad debts expense.

Compute interest and determine maturity dates on notes.
(SO 5)

BE9-8 Compute interest and find the maturity date for the following notes.

	Date of Note	Principal	Interest Rate (%)	Terms
(a)	June 10	$100,000	9%	60 days
(b)	July 14	$ 50,000	$7\frac{1}{2}$%	90 days
(c)	April 27	$ 12,000	8%	75 days

Determine maturity dates and compute interest and rates on notes.
(SO 5)

BE9-9 Presented below are data on three promissory notes. Determine the missing amounts.

	Date of Note	Terms	Maturity Date	Principal	Annual Interest Rate	Total Interest
(a)	April 1	60 days	?	$900,000	9%	?
(b)	July 2	30 days	?	90,000	?	$600
(c)	March 7	6 months	?	120,000	12%	?

Prepare entries to dispose of accounts receivable.
(SO 4)

BE9-10 Presented below are two independent transactions.

(a) Raja Restaurant accepted a VISA card in payment of a $200 lunch bill. The bank charges a 3% fee. What entry should Raja make?
(b) Wendy Company sold its accounts receivable of $80,000. What entry should Wendy make, given a service charge of 3% on the amount of receivables sold?

Prepare entry for notes receivable exchanged for account receivable.
(SO 6)

BE9-11 On January 10, 2002, Opal Co. sold merchandise on account to Fernando Alvarez for $12,000, n/30. On February 9, Fernando Alvarez gave Opal Co. a 10% promissory note in settlement of this account. Prepare the journal entry to record the sale and the settlement of the account receivable.

Compute ratios to analyze receivables.
(SO 9)

BE9-12 The financial statements of **Minnesota Mining and Manufacturing Company (3M)** report net sales of $15.0 billion. Accounts receivable are $2.5 billion at the beginning of the year and $2.8 billion at the end of the year. Compute 3M's receivables turnover ratio. Compute 3M's average collection period for accounts receivable in days.

EXERCISES

Journalize entries for recognizing accounts receivable.
(SO 2)

E9-1 Presented below are two independent situations.

(a) On January 6, Whitney Co. sells merchandise on account to Julio, Inc. for $5,000, terms 2/10, n/30. On January 16, Julio, Inc. pays the amount due. Prepare the entries on Whitney's books to record the sale and related collection.
(b) On January 10, Sue Ernesto uses her Oregon Co. credit card to purchase merchandise from Oregon Co. for $11,000. On February 10, Ernesto is billed for the amount due of $11,000. On February 12, Ernesto pays $6,000 on the balance due. On March 10, Ernesto is billed for the amount due, including interest at 2% per month on the unpaid balance as of February 12. Prepare the entries on Oregon Co.'s books related to the transactions that occurred on January 10, February 12, and March 10.

Journalize entries to record allowance for doubtful accounts using two different bases.
(SO 3)

E9-2 The ledger of Salizar Company at the end of the current year shows Accounts Receivable $110,000, Sales $840,000, and Sales Returns and Allowances $40,000.

Instructions

(a) If Allowance for Doubtful Accounts has a credit balance of $2,500 in the trial balance, journalize the adjusting entry at December 31, assuming bad debts are expected to be (1) 1% of net sales, and (2) 10% of accounts receivable.
(b) If Allowance for Doubtful Accounts has a debit balance of $500 in the trial balance, journalize the adjusting entry at December 31, assuming bad debts are expected to be (1) 0.75% of net sales and (2) 6% of accounts receivable.

E9-3 Patillo Company has accounts receivable of $97,500 at March 31. An analysis of the accounts shows the following.

Determine bad debts expense; prepare the adjusting entry for bad debts expense. (SO 3)

Month of Sale	Balance, March 31
March	$65,000
February	17,600
January	8,500
Prior to January	6,400
	$97,500

Credit terms are 2/10, n/30. At March 31, Allowance for Doubtful Accounts has a credit balance of $1,600 prior to adjustment. The company uses the percentage of receivables basis for estimating uncollectible accounts. The company's estimate of bad debts is as follows.

Age of Accounts	Estimated Percentage Uncollectible
1–30 days past due	2.0%
30–60 days past due	5.0%
60–90 days past due	30.0%
Over 90 days	50.0%

Instructions

(a) Determine the total estimated uncollectibles.

(b) Prepare the adjusting entry at March 31 to record bad debts expense.

E9-4 On December 31, 2002, Garcia Co. estimates that 2% of its net sales of $400,000 will become uncollectible. The company records this amount as an addition to Allowance for Doubtful Accounts. On May 11, 2003, Garcia Co. determined that Ray William's account was uncollectible and wrote off $1,100. On June 12, 2003, William paid the amount previously written off.

Journalize percentage of sales basis, write-off, recovery. (SO 3)

Instructions

Prepare the journal entries on December 31, 2002, May 11, 2003, and June 12, 2003.

E9-5 Presented below are two independent situations.

Journalize entries for the sale of accounts receivable. (SO 4)

(a) On March 3, Lisa Ceja Appliances sells $700,000 of its receivables to Horatio Factors Inc. Horatio Factors assesses a finance charge of 3% of the amount of receivables sold. Prepare the entry on Lisa Ceja Appliances' books to record the sale of the receivables.

(b) On May 10, Worthy Company sold merchandise for $4,000 and accepted the customer's Firstar Bank MasterCard. At the end of the day, the Firstar Bank MasterCard receipts were deposited in the company's bank account. Firstar Bank charges a 4% service charge for credit card sales. Prepare the entry on Worthy Company's books to record the sale of merchandise.

E9-6 Presented below are two independent situations.

Journalize entries for credit card sales. (SO 4)

(a) On April 2, Sue Moat uses her J. C. Penney Company credit card to purchase merchandise from a J.C. Penney store for $1,300. On May 1, Moat is billed for the $1,300 amount due. Moat pays $700 on the balance due on May 3. On June 1, Moat receives a bill for the amount due, including interest at 1.0% per month on the unpaid balance as of May 3. Prepare the entries on J. C. Penney Co.'s books related to the transactions that occurred on April 2, May 3, and June 1.

(b) On July 4, Healy's Restaurant accepts an American Express card for a $300 dinner bill. American Express charges a 4% service fee. On July 10, American Express pays Healy $288. Prepare the entries on Healy's books related to the transactions.

E9-7 Satter Stores accepts both its own and national credit cards. During the year the following selected summary transactions occurred.

Journalize credit card sales, and indicate the statement presentation of financing charges and service charge expense. (SO 4)

Jan. 15 Made Satter credit card sales totaling $15,000. (There were no balances prior to January 15.)

20 Made American Express credit card sales (service charge fee 5%) totaling $4,500.

30	Received payment in full from American Express less a 5% service charge.
Feb. 10	Collected $12,000 on Satter credit card sales.
15	Added finance charges of 1.5% to Satter credit card balance.

Instructions

(a) Journalize the transactions for Satter Stores.
(b) Indicate the statement presentation of the financing charges and the credit card service expense for Satter Stores.

Journalize entries for notes receivable transactions.
(SO 5, 6)

E9-8 Gore Supply Co. has the following transactions related to notes receivable during the last 2 months of the year.

Nov. 1	Loaned $18,000 cash to Sally Morgan on a 1-year, 10% note.
Dec. 11	Sold goods to Sue Adams, Inc., receiving a $6,000, 90-day, 12% note.
16	Received a $4,000, 6-month, 12% note on account from Prentice Berge.
31	Accrued interest revenue on all notes receivable.

Instructions

Journalize the transactions for Gore Supply Co.

Journalize entries for notes receivable.
(SO 5, 6)

E9-9 Record the following transactions for Icke Co. in the general journal.

2002

May 1	Received a $10,500, 1-year, 10% note on account from Paul Warfield
Dec. 31	Accrued interest on the Warfield note.
Dec. 31	Closed the interest revenue account.

2003

May 1	Received principal plus interest on the Warfield note. (No interest has been accrued in 2003.)

Journalize entries for dishonor of notes receivable.
(SO 5, 8)

E9-10 On May 2, Chung Company lends $7,000 to Ann Johnson, Inc., issuing a 6-month, 10% note. At the maturity date, November 2, Johnson indicates that it cannot pay.

Instructions

(a) Prepare the entry to record the dishonor of the note, assuming that Chung Company expects collection will occur.
(b) Prepare the entry to record the dishonor of the note, assuming that Chung Company does not expect collection in the future.

Determine missing amounts related to sales and accounts receivable.
(SO 2, 4, 9)

E9-11 The following information pertains to Moosa Merchandising Company.

Merchandise inventory at end of year	$33,000
Accounts receivable at beginning of year	24,000
Cash sales made during the year	15,000
Gross profit on sales	27,000
Accounts receivable written off during the year	1,000
Purchases made during the year	60,000
Accounts receivable collected during the year	78,000
Merchandise inventory at beginning of year	36,000

Instructions

(a) Calculate the amount of credit sales made during the year. (*Hint:* You will need to use income statement relationships—introduced in Chapter 5—in order to determine this.)
(b) Calculate the balance of accounts receivable at the end of the year.

PROBLEMS: SET A

Prepare journal entries related to bad debts expense.
(SO 2, 3, 4)

P9-1A At December 31, 2002, Cellular Ten Co. reported the following information on its balance sheet.

Accounts receivable	$960,000
Less: Allowance for doubtful accounts	70,000

During 2003, the company had the following transactions related to receivables.

1.	Sales on account	$3,300,000
2.	Sales returns and allowances	50,000
3.	Collections of accounts receivable	2,800,000
4.	Write-offs of accounts receivable deemed uncollectible	90,000
5.	Recovery of bad debts previously written off as uncollectible	25,000

Instructions

(a) Prepare the journal entries to record each of these five transactions. Assume that no cash discounts were taken on the collections of accounts receivable.

(b) Enter the January 1, 2003, balances in Accounts Receivable and Allowance for Doubtful Accounts, post the entries to the two accounts (use T accounts), and determine the balances.

(b) Accounts receivable $1,320,000
ADA $5,000

(c) Prepare the journal entry to record bad debts expense for 2003, assuming that an aging of accounts receivable indicates that expected bad debts are $125,000.

(c) Bad debts expense $120,000

(d) Compute the accounts receivable turnover ratio for 2003.

P9-2A Information related to Holland Company for 2002 is summarized below.

Compute bad debts amounts.
(SO 3)

Total credit sales	$2,100,000
Accounts receivable at December 31	840,000
Bad debts written off	38,000

Instructions

(a) What amount of bad debts expense will Holland Company report if it uses the direct write-off method of accounting for bad debts?

(b) Assume that Holland Company estimates its bad debts expense to be 3% of credit sales. What amount of bad debts expense will Holland record if it has an Allowance for Doubtful Accounts credit balance of $4,000?

(c) Assume that Holland Company estimates its bad debts expense based on 6% of accounts receivable. What amount of bad debts expense will Holland record if it has an Allowance for Doubtful Accounts credit balance of $3,000?

(d) Assume the same facts as in (c), except that there is a $3,000 debit balance in Allowance for Doubtful Accounts. What amount of bad debts expense will Holland record?

(e) What is the weakness of the direct write-off method of reporting bad debts expense?

P9-3A Presented below is an aging schedule for Sandy Grifton Company.

Journalize entries to record transactions related to bad debts.
(SO 2, 3)

Customer	Total	Not Yet Due	Number of Days Past Due 1–30	31–60	61–90	Over 90
Anita	$ 22,000		$10,000	$12,000		
Barry	40,000	$ 40,000				
Chagnon	57,000	16,000	6,000		$35,000	
David	34,000					$34,000
Others	132,000	96,000	16,000	14,000		6,000
	$285,000	$152,000	$32,000	$26,000	$35,000	$40,000
Estimated Percentage Uncollectible		4%	7%	13%	25%	50%
Total Estimated Bad Debts	$ 40,450	$ 6,080	$ 2,240	$ 3,380	$ 8,750	$20,000

At December 31, 2002, the unadjusted balance in Allowance for Doubtful Accounts is a credit of $12,000.

Instructions

(a) Journalize and post the adjusting entry for bad debts at December 31, 2002.

(a) Bad debts expense $28,450

(b) Journalize and post to the allowance account the following events and transactions in the year 2003.

(1) On March 31, a $1,000 customer balance originating in 2002 is judged uncollectible.
(2) On May 31, a check for $1,000 is received from the customer whose account was written off as uncollectible on March 31.

(c) Bad debts expense $31,100

(c) Journalize the adjusting entry for bad debts on December 31, 2003, assuming that the unadjusted balance in Allowance for Doubtful Accounts is a debit of $800 and the aging schedule indicates that total estimated bad debts will be $30,300.

Journalize entries to record transactions related to bad debts.
(SO 3)

P9-4A At December 31, 2002, the trial balance of Lexington Company contained the following amounts before adjustment.

	Debits	Credits
Accounts Receivable	$400,000	
Allowance for Doubtful Accounts		$ 800
Sales		930,000

Instructions

(a) Based on the information given, which method of accounting for bad debts is Lexington Company using—the direct write-off method or the allowance method? How can you tell?

(b) (2) $9,300

(b) Prepare the adjusting entry at December 31, 2002, for bad debts expense under each of the following independent assumptions.
(1) An aging schedule indicates that $11,750 of accounts receivable will be uncollectible.
(2) The company estimates that 1% of sales will be uncollectible.

(c) Repeat part (b) assuming that instead of a credit balance there is an $800 debit balance in Allowance for Doubtful Accounts.

(d) During the next month, January 2003, a $5,000 account receivable is written off as uncollectible. Prepare the journal entry to record the write-off.

(e) Repeat part (d) assuming that Lexington uses the direct write-off method instead of the allowance method in accounting for uncollectible accounts receivable.

(f) What type of account is the Allowance for Doubtful Accounts? How does it affect how accounts receivable is reported on the balance sheet at the end of the accounting period?

Prepare entries for various notes receivable transactions.
(SO 2, 4, 5, 8, 9)

Peachtree

P9-5A Melanie Griffith Company closes its books monthly. On September 30, selected ledger account balances are:

Notes Receivable	$28,000
Interest Receivable	$ 216

Notes Receivable include the following.

Date	Maker	Face	Term	Interest
Aug. 16	Foran Inc.	$ 8,000	60 days	12%
Aug. 25	Drexler Co.	8,000	60 days	12%
Sept. 30	Sego Corp.	12,000	6 months	9%

Interest is computed using a 360-day year. During October, the following transactions were completed.

Oct. 7 Made sales of $6,900 on Melanie Griffith credit cards.
12 Made sales of $750 on MasterCard credit cards. The credit card service charge is 4%.
15 Added $485 to Melanie Griffith customer balance for finance charges on unpaid balances.
15 Received payment in full from Foran Inc. on the amount due.
24 Received notice that Drexler note has been dishonored. (Assume that Drexler is expected to pay in the future.)

Instructions

(a) Journalize the October transactions and the October 31 adjusting entry for accrued interest receivable.

(b) Enter the balances at October 1 in the receivable accounts. Post the entries to all of the receivable accounts.

(c) Show the balance sheet presentation of the receivable accounts at October 31.

(b) Accounts receivable $15,545
(c) Total receivables $27,635

Prepare entries for various receivable transactions.
(SO 2, 4, 5, 6, 7, 8)

P9-6A On January 1, 2002, John Diego Company had Accounts Receivable $146,000, Notes Receivable $15,000, and Allowance for Doubtful Accounts $13,200. The note receivable is from Trudy Borke Company. It is a 4-month, 12% note dated December 31, 2001. John Diego Company prepares financial statements annually. During the year the following selected transactions occurred.

Jan.	5	Sold $18,000 of merchandise to Jones Company, terms n/15.
	20	Accepted Jones Company's $18,000, 3-month, 9% note for balance due.
Feb.	18	Sold $8,000 of merchandise to Swan Company and accepted Swan's $8,000, 6-month, 10% note for the amount due.
Apr.	20	Collected Jones Company note in full.
	30	Received payment in full from Trudy Borke Company on the amount due.
May	25	Accepted Avita Inc.'s $6,000, 3-month, 8% note in settlement of a past-due balance on account.
Aug.	18	Received payment in full from Swan Company on note due.
	25	The Avita Inc. note was dishonored. Avita Inc. is not bankrupt; future payment is anticipated.
Sept.	1	Sold $12,000 of merchandise to Jose Trevino Company and accepted a $12,000, 6-month, 10% note for the amount due.

Instructions

Journalize the transactions.

PROBLEMS: SET B

Prepare journal entries related to bad debts expense.
(SO 2, 3, 4)

P9-1B At December 31, 2002, Murlow Imports reported the following information on its balance sheet.

Accounts receivable	$1,000,000
Less: Allowance for doubtful accounts	60,000

During 2003, the company had the following transactions related to receivables.

1. Sales on account	$2,700,000
2. Sales returns and allowances	40,000
3. Collections of accounts receivable	2,300,000
4. Write-offs of accounts receivable deemed uncollectible	65,000
5. Recovery of bad debts previously written off as uncollectible	25,000

Instructions

(a) Prepare the journal entries to record each of these five transactions. Assume that no cash discounts were taken on the collections of accounts receivable.

(b) Enter the January 1, 2003, balances in Accounts Receivable and Allowance for Doubtful Accounts. Post the entries to the two accounts (use T accounts), and determine the balances.

(c) Prepare the journal entry to record bad debts expense for 2003, assuming that an aging of accounts receivable indicates that estimated bad debts are $95,000.

(d) Compute the accounts receivable turnover ratio for the year 2003.

(b) Accounts receivable $1,295,000
ADA $20,000
(c) Bad debts expense $75,000

Compute bad debts amounts.
(SO 3)

P9-2B Information related to Cain Company for 2002 is summarized below.

Total credit sales	$1,600,000
Accounts receivable at December 31	640,000
Bad debts written off	26,000

Instructions

(a) What amount of bad debts expense will Cain Company report if it uses the direct write-off method of accounting for bad debts?

(b) Assume that Cain Company decides to estimate its bad debts expense to be 3% of credit sales. What amount of bad debts expense will Cain record if Allowance for Doubtful Accounts has a credit balance of $3,000?

(c) Assume that Cain Company decides to estimate its bad debts expense based on 5% of accounts receivable. What amount of bad debts expense will Cain Company record if Allowance for Doubtful Accounts has a credit balance of $4,000?

(d) Assume the same facts as in (c), except that there is a $2,000 debit balance in Allowance for Doubtful Accounts. What amount of bad debts expense will Cain record?

(e) What is the weakness of the direct write-off method of reporting bad debts expense?

Journalize entries to record transactions related to bad debts.
(SO 2, 3)

P9-3B This is an aging schedule for Timban Company.

Customer	Total	Not Yet Due	Number of Days Past Due 1–30	31–60	61–90	Over 90
Aber	$ 20,000		$ 9,000	$11,000		
Bohr	30,000	$ 30,000				
Case	50,000	15,000	5,000		$30,000	
Datz	38,000					$38,000
Others	126,000	92,000	15,000	13,000		6,000
	$264,000	$137,000	$29,000	$24,000	$30,000	$44,000
Estimated Percentage Uncollectible		3%	6%	12%	24%	50%
Total Estimated Bad Debts	$ 37,930	$ 4,110	$ 1,740	$ 2,880	$ 7,200	$22,000

At December 31, 2002, the unadjusted balance in Allowance for Doubtful Accounts is a credit of $10,000.

Instructions

(a) Bad debts expense $27,930

(a) Journalize and post the adjusting entry for bad debts at December 31, 2002.

(b) Journalize and post to the allowance account the following events and transactions in the year 2003.

(1) March 1, an $1,100 customer balance originating in 2002 is judged uncollectible.

(2) May 1, a check for $1,100 is received from the customer whose account was written off as uncollectible on March 1.

(c) Bad debts expense $30,300

(c) Journalize the adjusting entry for bad debts on December 31, 2003. Assume that the unadjusted balance in Allowance for Doubtful Accounts is a debit of $1,200, and the aging schedule indicates that total estimated bad debts will be $29,100.

Journalize entries to record transactions related to bad debts.
(SO 3)

P9-4B At December 31, 2002, the trial balance of Mario Tizani Company contained the following amounts before adjustment.

	Debits	Credits
Accounts Receivable	$350,000	
Allowance for Doubtful Accounts		$ 1,300
Sales		860,000

Instructions

(a) (2) $17,200

(a) Prepare the adjusting entry at December 31, 2002, to record bad debts expense under each of the following independent assumptions.

(1) An aging schedule indicates that $16,750 of accounts receivable will be uncollectible.

(2) The company estimates that 2% of sales will be uncollectible.

(b) Repeat part (a) assuming that instead of a credit balance, there is a $1,300 debit balance in Allowance for Doubtful Accounts.

(c) During the next month, January 2003, a $4,500 account receivable is written off as uncollectible. Prepare the journal entry to record the write-off.
(d) Repeat part (c) assuming that Mario Tizani Company uses the direct write-off method instead of the allowance method in accounting for uncollectible accounts receivable.
(e) What are the advantages of using the allowance method in accounting for uncollectible accounts as compared to the direct write-off method?

Prepare entries for various notes receivable transactions.
(SO 2, 4, 5, 8, 9)

P9-5B John Gleason Co. closes its books monthly. On June 30, selected ledger account balances are:

Notes Receivable	$31,000
Interest Receivable	$ 245

Notes Receivable include the following.

Date	Maker	Face	Term	Interest
May 21	Alder Inc.	$ 6,000	60 days	12%
May 25	Dorn Co.	15,000	60 days	11%
June 30	MJH Corp.	10,000	6 months	9%

During July, the following transactions were completed.

July 5 Made sales of $6,200 on John Gleason Co. credit cards.
14 Made sales of $700 on VISA credit cards. The credit card service charge is 3%.
16 Added $440 to John Gleason Co. credit card customer balances for finance charges on unpaid balances.
20 Received payment in full from Alder Inc. on the amount due.
25 Received notice that Dorn Co. note has been dishonored. (Assume that Dorn Co. is expected to pay in the future.)

Instructions

(a) Journalize the July transactions and the July 31 adjusting entry for accrued interest receivable. (Interest is computed using 360 days.)
(b) Enter the balances at July 1 in the receivable accounts. Post the entries to all of the receivable accounts.
(c) Show the balance sheet presentation of the receivable accounts at July 31.

(b) Accounts receivable $21,915
(c) Total receivables $31,990

Prepare entries for various receivables transactions.
(SO 2, 4, 5, 6, 7, 8)

P9-6B On January 1, 2002, Case Western Company had Accounts Receivable $54,200 and Allowance for Doubtful Accounts $4,700. Case Western Company prepares financial statements annually. During the year the following selected transactions occurred.

Jan. 5 Sold $7,000 of merchandise to Garth Brooks Company, terms n/30.
Feb. 2 Accepted a $7,000, 4-month, 12% promissory note from Garth Brooks Company for balance due.
12 Sold $7,800 of merchandise to Gage Company and accepted Gage's $7,800, 2-month, 10% note for the balance due.
26 Sold $4,000 of merchandise to Mathias Co., terms n/10.
Apr. 5 Accepted a $4,000, 3-month, 8% note from Mathias Co. for balance due.
12 Collected Gage Company note in full.
June 2 Collected Garth Brooks Company note in full.
July 5 Mathias Co. dishonors its note of April 5. It is expected that Mathias will eventually pay the amount owed.
15 Sold $5,000 of merchandise to Tritt Co. and accepted Tritt's $5,000, 3-month, 12% note for the amount due.
Oct. 15 Tritt Co.'s note was dishonored. Tritt Co. is bankrupt, and there is no hope of future settlement.

Instructions

Journalize the transactions.

BROADENING YOUR PERSPECTIVE

FINANCIAL REPORTING AND ANALYSIS

FINANCIAL REPORTING PROBLEM: SCH Company

BYP9-1 SCH Company sells office equipment and supplies to many organizations in the city and surrounding area on contract terms of 2/10, n/30. In the past, over 75% of the credit customers have taken advantage of the discount by paying within 10 days of the invoice date.

The number of customers taking the full 30 days to pay has increased within the last year. Current indications are that less than 60% of the customers are now taking the discount. Bad debts as a percentage of gross credit sales have risen from the 1.5% provided in past years to about 4% in the current year.

The company's Finance Committee has requested more information on the collections of accounts receivable. The controller responded to this request with the report reproduced below.

SCH COMPANY
Accounts Receivable Collections
May 31, 2002

The fact that some credit accounts will prove uncollectible is normal. Annual bad debts write-offs have been 1.5% of gross credit sales over the past 5 years. During the last fiscal year, this percentage increased to slightly less than 4%. The current Accounts Receivable balance is $1,400,000. The condition of this balance in terms of age and probability of collection is as follows.

Proportion of Total	Age Categories	Probability of Collection
60%	not yet due	98%
22%	less than 30 days past due	95½%
9%	30 to 60 days past due	94%
5%	61 to 120 days past due	91%
2½%	121 to 180 days past due	75%
1½%	over 180 days past due	30%

The Allowance for Doubtful Accounts had a credit balance of $29,500 on June 1, 2001. SCH has provided for a monthly bad debts expense accrual during the current fiscal year based on the assumption that 4% of gross credit sales will be uncollectible. Total gross credit sales for the 2001–02 fiscal year amounted to $2,800,000. Write-offs of bad accounts during the year totaled $96,000.

Instructions

(a) Prepare an accounts receivable aging schedule for SCH Company using the age categories identified in the controller's report to the Finance Committee showing the following.
  (1) The amount of accounts receivable outstanding for each age category and in total.
  (2) The estimated amount that is uncollectible for each category and in total.

(b) Compute the amount of the year-end adjustment necessary to bring Allowance for Doubtful Accounts to the balance indicated by the age analysis. Then prepare the necessary journal entry to adjust the accounting records.

(c) In a recessionary environment with tight credit and high interest rates:
  (1) Identify steps SCH Company might consider to improve the accounts receivable situation.
  (2) Then evaluate each step identified in terms of the risks and costs involved.

COMPARATIVE ANALYSIS PROBLEM: Lands' End vs. Abercrombie & Fitch

BYP9-2 **Lands' End's** financial statements are presented in Appendix A. **Abercrombie & Fitch's** financial statements are presented in Appendix B.

Instructions

(a) Based on the information contained in these financial statements, compute the following 2000 ratios for each company. (Assume all sales are credit sales.)
  (1) Accounts receivable turnover ratio.
  (2) Average collection period for receivables.

(b) What conclusions concerning the management of accounts receivable can be drawn from these data?

INTERPRETING FINANCIAL STATEMENTS: A Global Focus

BYP9-3 **Art World Industries, Inc.** was incorporated in 1986 in Delaware, and is located in Los Angeles. The company prints, publishes, and sells limited-edition graphics and reproductive prints in the wholesale market.

The company's balance sheet at the end of a recent year showed an allowance for doubtful accounts of $175,477. The allowance was set up against certain Japanese accounts receivable that average more than one year in age. The Japanese acknowledge the amount due, but with the slow economy in Japan lack the resources to pay at this time.

Instructions

(a) Which method of accounting for uncollectible accounts does Art World Industries use?

(b) Explain the difference between the direct write-off and percentage of receivables methods. Based on Art World's disclosure above, what important factor would you have to consider in arriving at appropriate percentages to apply for the percentage of receivables method?

(c) What are the implications for a company's receivables management of selling its products internationally?

EXPLORING THE WEB

BYP9-4 ***Purpose:*** The Security Exchange Act of 1934 requires any firm that is listed on one of the national exchanges to file annual reports (form 10-K), financial statements, and quarterly reports (form 10-Q) with the SEC. This exercise demonstrates how to search and access available SEC filings through the Internet.

Address: **biz.yahoo.com/i** ***(or go to www.wiley.com/college/weygandt)***

Steps:

1. Type in a company's name, or use index to find a company name.
2. Choose **Profile**.
3. Choose **Raw SEC Filings**.

Instructions

Answer the following questions.

(a) Which SEC filings were available for the company you selected?

(b) In the company's quarterly report (SEC form 10-Q), what was one key point discussed in the "Management's Discussion and Analysis of Results of Operations and Financial Condition"?

(c) What was the net income for the period selected?

CRITICAL THINKING

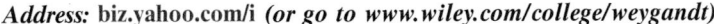

GROUP DECISION CASE

BYP9-5 Johanna and Jake Berkvom own Campus Fashions. From its inception Campus Fashions has sold merchandise on either a cash or credit basis, but no credit cards have been accepted. During the past several months, the Berkvoms have begun to question their sales policies. First, they have lost some sales because of refusing to accept credit cards. Second, representatives of two metropolitan banks have been persuasive in almost convincing them to accept their national credit cards. One bank, City National Bank, has stated that (1) its credit card fee is 4%, and (2) it pays the retailer 96 cents on each $1 of sales within 3 days of receiving the credit card billings.

The Berkvoms decide that they should determine the cost of carrying their own credit sales. From the accounting records of the past 3 years they accumulate the following data.

	2002	2001	2000
Net credit sales	$500,000	$600,000	$400,000
Collection agency fees for slow-paying customers	2,450	2,500	2,400
Salary of part-time accounts receivable clerk	3,800	3,800	3,800

Credit and collection expenses as a percentage of net credit sales are: uncollectible accounts 1.6%, billing and mailing costs 0.5%, and credit investigation fee on new customers 0.15%.

Johanna and Jake also determine that the average accounts receivable balance outstanding during the year is 5% of net credit sales. The Berkvoms estimate that they could earn an average of 10% annually on cash invested in other business opportunities.

Instructions

With the class divided into groups, answer the following.

(a) Prepare a table showing, for each year, total credit and collection expenses in dollars and as a percentage of net credit sales.

(b) Determine the net credit and collection expense in dollars and as a percentage of sales after considering the revenue not earned from other investment opportunities. (*Note:* The income lost on the cash held by the bank for 3 days is considered to be immaterial.)

(c) Discuss both the financial and nonfinancial factors that are relevant to the decision.

COMMUNICATION ACTIVITY

BYP9-6 Jackie Henning, a friend of yours, overheard a discussion at work about changes her employer wants to make in accounting for uncollectible accounts. Jackie knows little about accounting, and she asks you to help make sense of what she heard. Specifically, she asks you to explain the differences between the percentage of sales, percentage of receivables, and the direct write-off methods for uncollectible accounts.

Instructions

In a letter of one page (or less), explain to Jackie the three methods of accounting for uncollectibles. Be sure to discuss differences among these methods.

ETHICS CASE

BYP 9-7 The controller of Shirt Co. believes that the yearly allowance for doubtful accounts for Shirt Co. should be 2% of net credit sales. The president of Shirt Co., nervous that the stockholders might expect the company to sustain its 10% growth rate, suggests that the controller increase the allowance for doubtful accounts to 4%. The president thinks that the lower net income, which reflects a 6% growth rate, will be a more sustainable rate for Shirt Co.

Instructions

(a) Who are the stakeholders in this case?

(b) Does the president's request pose an ethical dilemma for the controller?

(c) Should the controller be concerned with Shirt Co.'s growth rate in estimating the allowance? Explain your answer.

Answers to Self-Study Questions

1. c **2.** a **3.** b **4.** b **5.** d **6.** c **7.** c **8.** a **9.** b **10.** d

LANDS' END DIRECT MERCHANTS

Answer to Lands' End Review It Question 3, p. 371

At the time of sale, the company provides a reserve equal to the gross profit on projected merchandise returns, based on its prior return experience.

Remember to go back to the Navigator box on the chapter-opening page and check off your completed work.

PLANT ASSETS, NATURAL RESOURCES, AND INTANGIBLE ASSETS

10

THE NAVIGATOR ✓

- Understand *Concepts for Review* ❑
- Read *Feature Story* ❑
- Scan *Study Objectives* ❑
- Read *Preview* ❑
- Read text and answer *Before You Go On* *p.* 403 ❑ *p.* 411 ❑ *p.* 417 ❑ *p.* 424 ❑
- Work *Demonstration Problems* ❑
- Review *Summary of Study Objectives* ❑
- Answer *Self-Study Questions* ❑
- Complete *Assignments* ❑

CONCEPTS FOR REVIEW

Before studying this chapter, you should know or, if necessary, review:

a. The time period assumption. (Ch. 3, p. 89)

b. The cost principle (Ch. 1, p. 10) and the matching principle. (Ch. 3, pp. 90–91)

c. What is depreciation? (Ch. 3, p. 95)

d. How to make adjustments for depreciation. (Ch. 3, pp. 95–97)

THE NAVIGATOR

FEATURE STORY

How Much Must I Pay for a Ride to the Beach?

It's spring break. Your plane has landed, you've finally found your bags, and you're dying to hit the beach—but first you need a "vehicular unit" to get you there. As you turn away from baggage claim you see a long row of rental agency booths. Many are names you are familiar with—Hertz, Avis, and Budget. But a booth at the far end catches your eye—**Rent-A-Wreck**. Now there's a company making a clear statement!

Any company that relies on equipment to generate revenues must make decisions about what kind of equipment to buy, how long to keep it, and how vigorously to maintain it. Rent-A-Wreck has decided to rent used rather than new cars and trucks. It rents these vehicles across the United States, Europe, and Asia. While the big-name agencies push vehicles with that "new car smell," Rent-A-Wreck competes on price. The message is simple: Rent a used car and save some cash. It's not a message that appeals to everyone. If you're a marketing executive wanting to impress a big client, you probably don't want to pull up in a Rent-A-Wreck car. But if you want to get from point A to point B for the minimum cash per mile, then they are playing your tune. The company's message seems to be getting across to the right clientele. Revenues have increased from $29.9 million in 1996 to $51.7 million in 2000.

When you rent a car from Rent-A-Wreck, you are renting from an independent business person who has paid a "franchise fee" for the right to use the Rent-A-Wreck name. In order to gain a franchise, he or she must meet financial and other criteria, and must agree to run the rental agency according to rules prescribed by Rent-A-Wreck. Some of these rules require that each franchise maintain its cars in a reasonable fashion. This ensures that, though you might not be flying down Daytona Beach's Atlantic Avenue in a Mercedes convertible, you can be reasonably assured that you won't be calling a tow-truck.

☑ THE NAVIGATOR

www.rent-a-wreck.com

STUDY OBJECTIVES

After studying this chapter, you should be able to:

1. Describe the application of the cost principle to plant assets.
2. Explain the concept of depreciation.
3. Compute periodic depreciation using different methods.
4. Describe the procedure for revising periodic depreciation.
5. Distinguish between revenue and capital expenditures, and explain the entries for these expenditures.
6. Explain how to account for the disposal of a plant asset through retirement, sale, or exchange.
7. Compute periodic depletion of natural resources.
8. Contrast the accounting for intangible assets with the accounting for plant assets.
9. Indicate how plant assets, natural resources, and intangible assets are reported and analyzed.

☑ THE NAVIGATOR

PREVIEW OF CHAPTER 10

The accounting for long-term assets has important implications for a company's reported results. In this chapter, we explain the application of the cost principle of accounting to property, plant, and equipment, such as **Rent-A-Wreck** vehicles, as well as to natural resources and intangible assets such as the "Rent-A-Wreck" trademark. We also describe the methods that may be used to allocate an asset's cost over its useful life. In addition, the accounting for expenditures incurred during the useful life of assets, such as the cost of replacing tires and brake pads on rental cars, is discussed.

The content and organization of Chapter 10 are as follows.

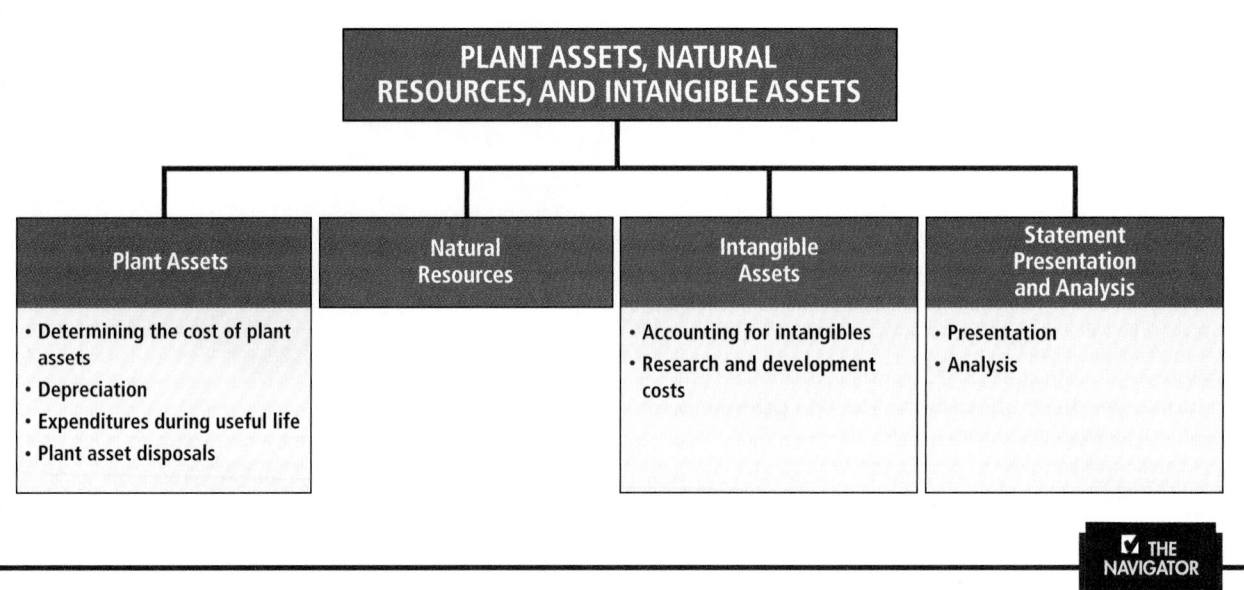

PLANT ASSETS, NATURAL RESOURCES, AND INTANGIBLE ASSETS

- **Plant Assets**
  - Determining the cost of plant assets
  - Depreciation
  - Expenditures during useful life
  - Plant asset disposals
- **Natural Resources**
- **Intangible Assets**
  - Accounting for intangibles
  - Research and development costs
- **Statement Presentation and Analysis**
  - Presentation
  - Analysis

THE NAVIGATOR

SECTION 1 *Plant Assets*

Plant assets are tangible resources that are used in the operations of a business and are not intended for sale to customers. They are also called **property, plant, and equipment**; **plant and equipment**; or **fixed assets**. These assets are generally long-lived. They are expected to provide services to the company for a number of years. Except for land, plant assets decline in service potential over their useful lives. Many companies have substantial investments in plant assets. Illustration 10-1 shows the percentages of plant assets in relation to total assets of companies in a number of industries.

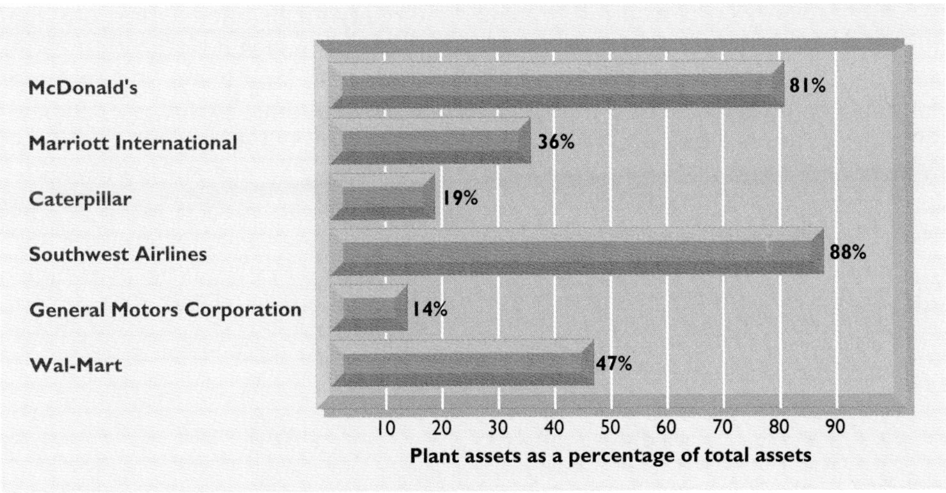

Illustration 10-1

Percentages of plant assets in relation to total assets

Plant assets are often subdivided into four classes:

1. **Land**, such as a building site.
2. **Land improvements**, such as driveways, parking lots, fences, and underground sprinkler systems.
3. **Buildings**, such as stores, offices, factories, and warehouses.
4. **Equipment**, such as store check-out counters, cash registers, coolers, office furniture, factory machinery, and delivery equipment.

Like the purchase of a home by an individual, the acquisition of plant assets is an important decision for a business. It is also important for a business to (1) keep assets in good operating condition, (2) replace worn-out or outdated assets, and (3) expand its productive resources as needed. The decline of rail travel in the United States can be traced in part to the failure of railroad companies to meet the first two conditions. The growth of U.S. air travel is due in part to airlines having generally met these conditions.

DETERMINING THE COST OF PLANT ASSETS

STUDY OBJECTIVE 1

Describe the application of the cost principle to plant assets.

Plant assets are recorded **at cost** in accordance with the **cost principle** of accounting. Thus the vehicles at **Rent-A-Wreck** are recorded at cost. Cost consists of **all expenditures necessary to acquire the asset and make it ready for its intended use**. For example, the cost of factory machinery includes the purchase price, freight costs paid by the purchaser, and installation costs. Once cost is established, it becomes the basis of accounting for the plant asset over its useful life. Current market or replacement values are not used after acquisition.

The application of the cost principle to each of the major classes of plant assets is explained in the following sections.

INTERNATIONAL NOTE

The United Kingdom (UK) is more flexible than the U.S. about asset valuation. Most companies in the UK make revaluations to fair value when they believe fair value is more relevant. Other countries that permit revaluations are Switzerland and the Netherlands.

LAND

The cost of land includes the cash purchase price plus other related costs. These costs might include closing costs such as title and attorney's fees, real estate brokers' commissions, and accrued property taxes and other liens on the land assumed by the purchaser. For example, if the cash price is $50,000 and the purchaser agrees to pay accrued taxes of $5,000, the cost of the land is $55,000.

HELPFUL HINT
Management's intended use is important in applying the cost principle.

All necessary costs incurred to make land **ready for its intended use** are debited to the Land account. For vacant land, these costs include expenditures for clearing, draining, filling, and grading. Sometimes the land has a building on it that must be removed before construction of a new building. In this case, all demolition and removal costs, less any proceeds from salvaged materials, are debited to the Land account. To illustrate, assume that Hayes Manufacturing Company acquires land for $100,000. An old warehouse on the property is razed at a net cost of $6,000 ($7,500 in costs less $1,500 proceeds from salvaged materials). Other expenditures are the attorney's fee, $1,000, and the real estate broker's commission, $8,000. The cost of the land is $115,000, computed as follows.

Illustration 10-2
Computation of cost of land

Land	
Cash price of property	$100,000
Net removal cost of warehouse	6,000
Attorney's fee	1,000
Real estate broker's commission	8,000
Cost of land	**$115,000**

In recording the acquisition, Land is debited for $115,000 and Cash is credited for $115,000.

LAND IMPROVEMENTS

The cost of land improvements includes all expenditures needed to make the improvements ready for their intended use. For example, the cost of a new company parking lot will include the amount paid for paving, fencing, and lighting. Thus, these costs are debited to Land Improvements. Because these improvements have limited useful lives and their maintenance and replacement are the responsibility of the company, **they are depreciated over their useful lives**.

BUILDINGS

All necessary costs related to the purchase or construction of a building are debited to the Buildings account. When a building is purchased, such costs include the purchase price, closing costs (attorney's fees, title insurance, etc.) and broker's commission. Costs to make the building ready for its intended use include expenditures for remodeling and replacing or repairing the roof, floors, electrical wiring, and plumbing.

When a new building is constructed, cost consists of the contract price plus payments for architects' fees, building permits, and excavation costs. Also, interest costs incurred to finance the project are included when a significant period of time is required to get the building ready for use. These interest costs are considered as necessary as materials and labor. The inclusion of interest costs is **limited to the construction period**, however. When construction has been completed, subsequent interest payments on funds borrowed to finance the construction are debited to Interest Expense.

HELPFUL HINT
Two criteria apply in determining cost here: (1) the frequency of the cost—one-time or recurring, and (2) the benefit period—life of asset or one year.

EQUIPMENT

The cost of equipment, such as **Rent-A-Wreck** vehicles, consists of the **cash purchase price plus certain related costs**. These costs include **sales taxes, freight charges, and insurance during transit paid by the purchaser**. They also include **expenditures required in assembling, installing, and testing the unit**. However, motor vehicle licenses and accident insurance on company trucks and cars are not included in the cost of equipment. They are treated as expenses as they are incurred. They represent annual recurring expenditures and do not benefit future periods.

To illustrate, assume Merten Company purchases factory machinery at a cash price of $50,000. Related expenditures consist of sales taxes $3,000, insurance during shipping $500, and installation and testing $1,000. The cost of the factory machinery is $54,500, computed as follows.

Illustration 10-3

Computation of cost of factory machinery

Factory Machinery	
Cash price	$50,000
Sales taxes	3,000
Insurance during shipping	500
Installation and testing	1,000
Cost of factory machinery	**$54,500**

The summary entry to record the purchase and related expenditures is:

Factory Machinery	54,500	
Cash		54,500
(To record purchase of factory machine)		

A	=	L	+	OE
+54,500				
−54,500				

For another example, assume that Lenard Company purchases a delivery truck at a cash price of $22,000. Related expenditures consist of sales taxes $1,320, painting and lettering $500, motor vehicle license $80, and a 3-year accident insurance policy $1,600. The cost of the delivery truck is $23,820, computed as follows.

Illustration 10-4

Computation of cost of delivery truck

Delivery Truck	
Cash price	$22,000
Sales taxes	1,320
Painting and lettering	500
Cost of delivery truck	**$23,820**

The motor vehicle license is expensed when incurred; the insurance policy is a prepaid asset. The summary entry to record the purchase of the truck and related expenditures is:

Delivery Truck	23,820	
License Expense	80	
Prepaid Insurance	1,600	
Cash		25,500
(To record purchase of delivery truck and related expenditures)		

A	=	L	+	OE
+23,820				−80
+1,600				
−25,500				

BEFORE YOU GO ON...

REVIEW IT

1. What are plant assets? What are the major classes of plant assets? How is the cost principle applied to accounting for plant assets?
2. What classifications and amounts does **Lands' End** report on its balance sheet under the heading "Property, plant and equipment, at cost"? The answer to this question is provided on p. 443.

LANDS' END DIRECT MERCHANTS

DO IT

Assume that a delivery truck is purchased for $15,000 cash, plus sales taxes of $900 and delivery costs to the dealer of $500. The buyer also pays $200 for painting and lettering, $600 for an annual insurance policy, and $80 for a motor vehicle license. Explain how each of these costs would be accounted for.

ACTION PLAN

- Identify expenditures made in order to get delivery equipment ready for its intended use.
- Expense operating costs incurred during the useful life of the equipment.

SOLUTION: The first four payments ($15,000, $900, $500, and $200) are considered to be expenditures necessary to make the truck ready for its intended use. Thus, the cost of the truck is $16,600. The payments for insurance and the license are considered to be operating expenses incurred during the useful life of the asset.

Related exercise material: BE10-1, BE10-2, E10-1, and E10-2.

THE NAVIGATOR

DEPRECIATION

STUDY OBJECTIVE 2

Explain the concept of depreciation.

As explained in Chapter 3, **depreciation is the allocation of the cost of a plant asset to expense over its useful (service) life in a rational and systematic manner.** Cost allocation provides for the proper matching of expenses with revenues in accordance with the matching principle (see Illustration 10-5).

Illustration 10-5

Depreciation as an allocation concept

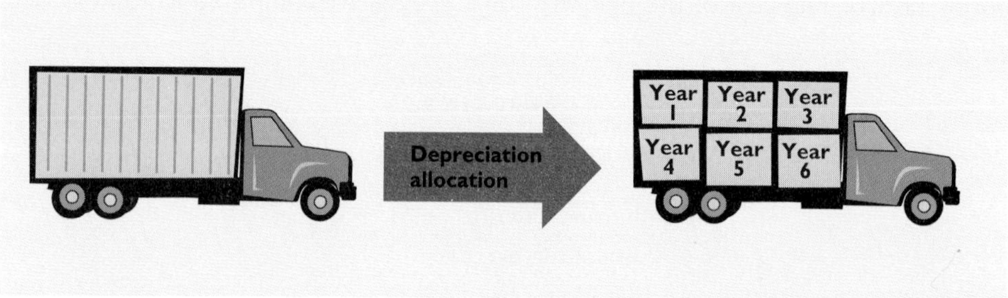

HELPFUL HINT
Remember that depreciation is the allocation of cost over the useful life of an asset. It is not a measure of value.

HELPFUL HINT
Land does not depreciate because it does not wear out.

Depreciation is a process of cost allocation, not a process of asset valuation. The change in an asset's market value is not measured during ownership because plant assets are not held for resale. So, the **book value** (cost less accumulated depreciation) of a plant asset may be quite different from its market value.

Depreciation applies to three classes of plant assets: land improvements, buildings, and equipment. Each asset in these classes is considered to be a **depreciable asset**. Why? Because the usefulness to the company and revenue-producing ability of each asset will decline over the asset's useful life. Depreciation does not apply to land because its usefulness and revenue-producing ability generally remain intact over time. In fact, in many cases, the usefulness of land is greater over time because of the scarcity of good land sites. Thus, **land is not a depreciable asset**.

During a depreciable asset's useful life its revenue-producing ability will decline because of **wear and tear**. A delivery truck that has been driven 100,000 miles will be less useful to a company than one driven only 800 miles. Trucks and planes exposed to snow and salt will deteriorate faster than equipment that is not exposed to these elements.

Revenue-producing ability may also decline because of **obsolescence**. Obsolescence is the process of becoming out of date before the asset physically wears out. Major airlines were re-routed from Chicago's Midway Airport to Chicago-

O'Hare International Airport because Midway's runways were too short for jumbo jets, for example.

It is important to understand that **recognizing depreciation on an asset does not result in an accumulation of cash for replacement of the asset**. The balance in Accumulated Depreciation represents the total cost that has been charged to expense. It is not a cash fund.

FACTORS IN COMPUTING DEPRECIATION

Three factors affect the computation of depreciation:

1. **Cost.** Issues affecting the cost of a depreciable asset were explained earlier in this chapter. Recall that plant assets are recorded at cost, in accordance with the cost principle.
2. **Useful life.** **Useful life** is an estimate of the expected productive life, also called service life, of the asset. Useful life may be expressed in terms of time, units of activity (such as machine hours), or units of output. Useful life is an estimate. In making the estimate, management considers such factors as the intended use of the asset, its expected repair and maintenance, and its vulnerability to obsolescence. Past experience with similar assets is often helpful in deciding on expected useful life. We might reasonably expect the estimated useful life used by **Rent-A-Wreck** to differ from that used by **Avis**.
3. **Salvage value.** **Salvage value** is an estimate of the asset's value at the end of its useful life. This value may be based on the asset's worth as scrap or on its expected trade-in value. Like useful life, salvage value is an estimate. In making the estimate, management considers how it plans to dispose of the asset and its experience with similar assets.

ALTERNATIVE TERMINOLOGY
Another term sometimes used for salvage value is *residual value*.

Illustration 10-6 summarizes the three factors used in computing depreciation.

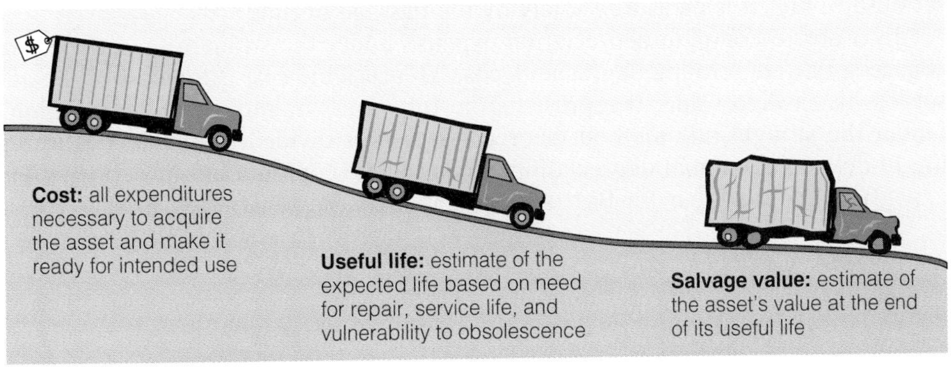

$
Cost: all expenditures necessary to acquire the asset and make it ready for intended use
Useful life: estimate of the expected life based on need for repair, service life, and vulnerability to obsolescence
Salvage value: estimate of the asset's value at the end of its useful life

Illustration 10-6

Three factors in computing depreciation

HELPFUL HINT
Depreciation expense is reported on the income statement, and accumulated depreciation is reported as a deduction from plant assets on the balance sheet.

ACCOUNTING IN ACTION *Business Insight*

Willamette Industries, Inc., of Portland, Oregon, said in March 1999 that it would change its accounting estimates relating to depreciation of certain assets, beginning with the first quarter of 1999. The vertically integrated forest products company said the changes were due to advances in technology that have increased the service life on its equipment an extra five years. Willamette expected the accounting changes to increase its 1999 full-year earnings by about $57 milion, or $0.52 a share. Its 1998 earnings were $89 million, or $0.80 a share. Imagine a 65 percent improvement in earnings per share from a mere change in the estimated life of equipment!

DEPRECIATION METHODS

STUDY OBJECTIVE 3

Compute periodic depreciation using different methods.

Depreciation is generally computed using one of the following methods:

1. Straight-line
2. Units-of-activity
3. Declining-balance

Each method is acceptable under generally accepted accounting principles. Management selects the method(s) it believes to be appropriate. The objective is to select the method that best measures an asset's contribution to revenue over its useful life. Once a method is chosen, it should be applied consistently over the useful life of the asset. Consistency enhances the comparability of financial statements.

We will compare the three depreciation methods using the following data for a small delivery truck purchased by Barb's Florists on January 1, 2002.

Illustration 10-7

Delivery truck data

Cost	$13,000
Expected salvage value	$ 1,000
Estimated useful life in years	5
Estimated useful life in miles	100,000

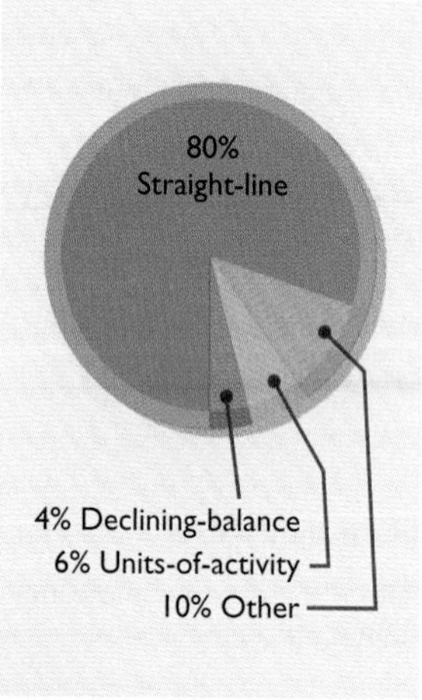

Illustration 10-8

Use of depreciation methods in 600 large U.S. companies

Depreciation affects the balance sheet through accumulated depreciation and the income statement through depreciation expense. Illustration 10-8 (in the margin) shows the use of the different depreciation methods in 600 of the largest companies in the United States.

Straight-Line

Under the **straight-line method**, depreciation is the same for each year of the asset's useful life. It is measured solely by the passage of time.

In order to compute depreciation expense under the straight-line method, it is necessary to determine depreciable cost. **Depreciable cost** is the cost of the asset less its salvage value. It represents the total amount subject to depreciation. Under the straight-line method, depreciable cost is divided by the asset's useful life to determine annual depreciation expense. The computation of depreciation expense in the first year for Barb's Florists is shown in Illustration 10-9.

Illustration 10-9

Formula for straight-line method

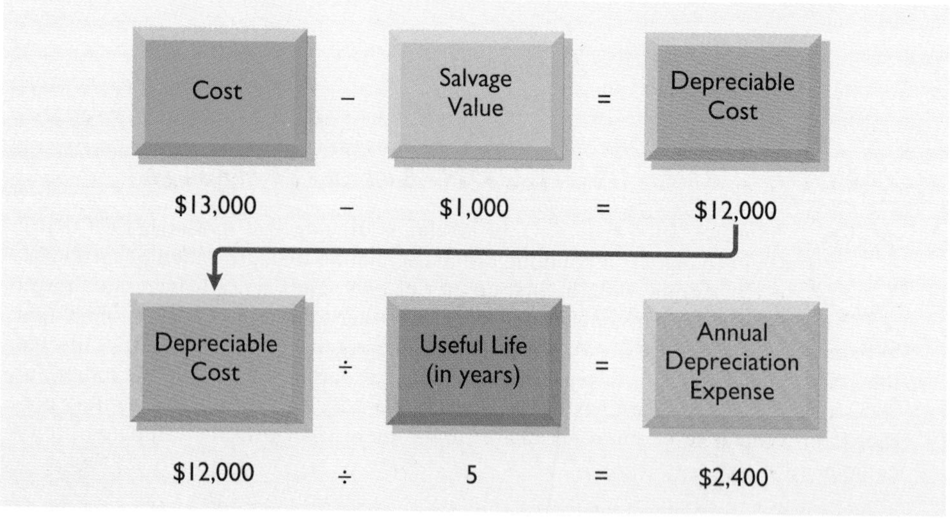

Alternatively, we also can compute an **annual rate of depreciation**. In this case, the rate is 20% (100% ÷ 5 years). When an annual straight-line rate is used, the percentage rate is applied to the depreciable cost of the asset. The use of an annual rate is shown in the following **depreciation schedule**.

Illustration 10-10

Straight-line depreciation schedule

BARB'S FLORISTS

	Computation					End of Year	
Year	**Depreciable Cost**	×	**Depreciation Rate**	=	**Annual Depreciation Expense**	**Accumulated Depreciation**	**Book Value**
2002	$12,000		20%		**$2,400**	$ 2,400	$10,600*
2003	12,000		20		**2,400**	4,800	8,200
2004	12,000		20		**2,400**	7,200	5,800
2005	12,000		20		**2,400**	9,600	3,400
2006	12,000		20		**2,400**	12,000	**1,000**

*($13,000 − $2,400).

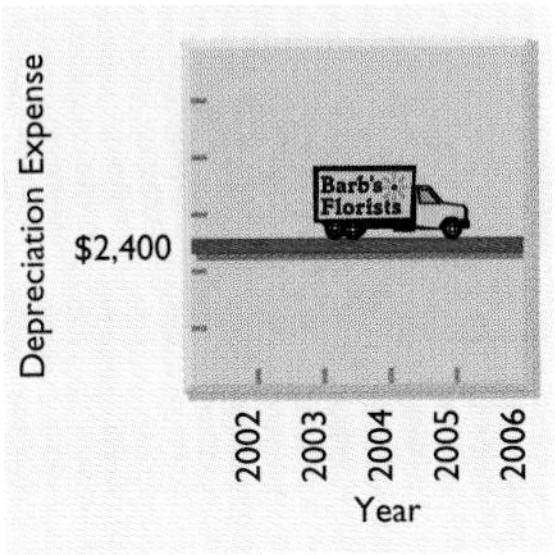

Note that the depreciation expense of $2,400 is the same each year. The book value at the end of the useful life is equal to the estimated $1,000 salvage value.

What happens when an asset is purchased **during** the year, rather than on January 1, as in our example? In that case, it is necessary to **prorate the annual depreciation** on a time basis. If Barb's Florists had purchased the delivery truck on April 1, 2002, the depreciation for 2002 would be $1,800 ($12,000 × 20% × 9/12 of a year).

The straight-line method predominates in practice. Such large companies as **Campbell Soup**, **Marriott Corporation**, and **General Mills** use the straight-line method. It is simple to apply, and it matches expenses with revenues when the use of the asset is reasonably uniform throughout the service life. In the Feature Story, for simplicity **Rent-A-Wreck** is probably using the straight-line method of depreciation for its vehicles.

Units-of-Activity

Under the **units-of-activity method**, useful life is expressed in terms of the total units of production or use expected from the asset, rather than as a time period. The units-of-activity method is ideally suited to factory machinery. Production can be measured in units of output or in machine hours. This method can also be used for such assets as delivery equipment (miles driven) and airplanes (hours in use). The units-of-activity method is generally not suitable for buildings or furniture, because depreciation for these assets is more a function of time than of use.

ALTERNATIVE TERMINOLOGY
Another term often used is the *units-of-production method*.

To use this method, the total units of activity for the entire useful life are estimated, and these units are divided into depreciable cost. The resulting number represents the depreciation cost per unit. The depreciation cost per unit is then applied to the units of activity during the year to determine the annual depreciation expense.

To illustrate, assume that Barb's Florists' delivery truck is driven 15,000 miles in the first year. The computation of depreciation expense in the first year is:

HELPFUL HINT
Under any method, depreciation stops when the asset's book value equals expected salvage value.

Illustration 10-11

Formula for units-of-activity method

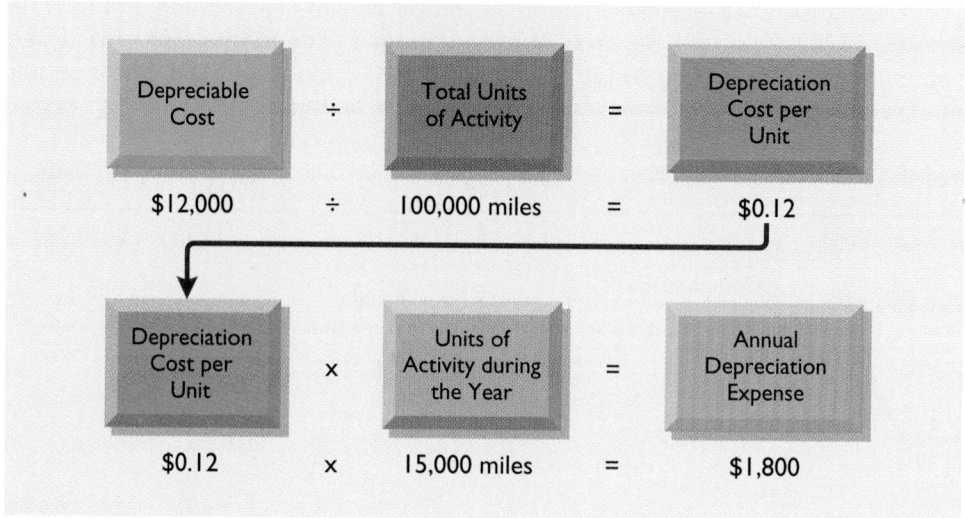

Depreciable Cost	÷	Total Units of Activity	=	Depreciation Cost per Unit
$12,000	÷	100,000 miles	=	$0.12

Depreciation Cost per Unit	x	Units of Activity during the Year	=	Annual Depreciation Expense
$0.12	x	15,000 miles	=	$1,800

The units-of-activity depreciation schedule, using assumed mileage, is as follows.

Illustration 10-12

Units-of-activity depreciation schedule

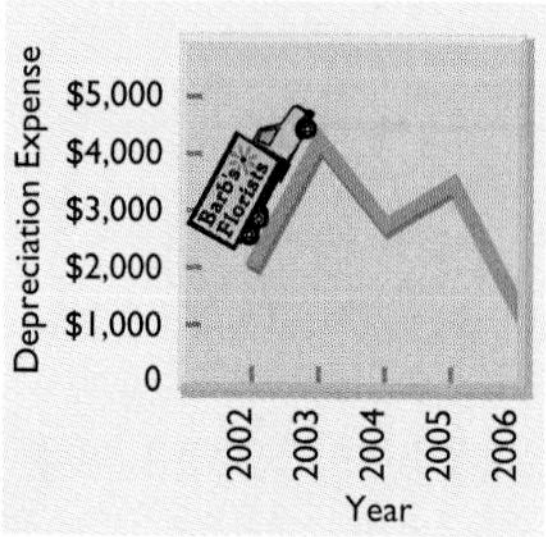

Barb's Florists

	Computation					End of Year	
Year	Units of Activity	×	Depreciation Cost/Unit	=	Annual Depreciation Expense	Accumulated Depreciation	Book Value
2002	15,000		$0.12		**$1,800**	$ 1,800	$11,200*
2003	30,000		0.12		**3,600**	5,400	7,600
2004	20,000		0.12		**2,400**	7,800	5,200
2005	25,000		0.12		**3,000**	10,800	2,200
2006	10,000		0.12		**1,200**	12,000	**1,000**

*($13,000 − $1,800).

This method is easy to apply when assets are purchased during the year. In such a case, the productivity of the asset for the partial year is used in computing the depreciation.

The units-of-activity method is not nearly as popular as the straight-line method (see Illustration 10-8), primarily because it is often difficult to make a reasonable estimate of total activity. However, this method is used by some very large companies, such as **Chevron Oil** and **Boise Cascade Corporation** (a forestry company). When the productivity of an asset varies significantly from one period to another, the units-of-activity method results in the best matching of expenses with revenues.

Declining-Balance

The **declining-balance method** produces a decreasing annual depreciation expense over the asset's useful life. The method is so named because the periodic depreciation is based on a **declining book value** (cost less accumulated depreciation) of the asset. Annual depreciation expense is computed by multiplying the book value at the beginning of the year by the declining-balance depreciation rate. **The depreciation rate remains constant from year to year, but the book value to which the rate is applied declines each year.**

HELPFUL HINT

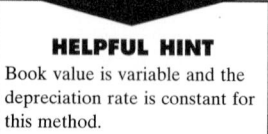

Book value is variable and the depreciation rate is constant for this method.

Book value at the beginning of the first year is the cost of the asset. This is so because the balance in accumulated depreciation at the beginning of the asset's useful life is zero. In subsequent years, book value is the difference between cost and accumulated depreciation to date. Unlike the other depreciation methods, the declining-balance method does not use depreciable cost. That is, **salvage value is ignored in determining the amount to which the declining-balance rate is applied.** Salvage value, however, does limit the total depreciation that can be taken. Depreciation stops when the asset's book value equals expected salvage value.

A common declining-balance rate is double the straight-line rate. As a result, the method is often referred to as the **double-declining-balance method**. If Barb's Florists uses the double-declining-balance method, the depreciation rate is 40% (2 × the straight-line rate of 20%). The computation of depreciation for the first year on the delivery truck is:

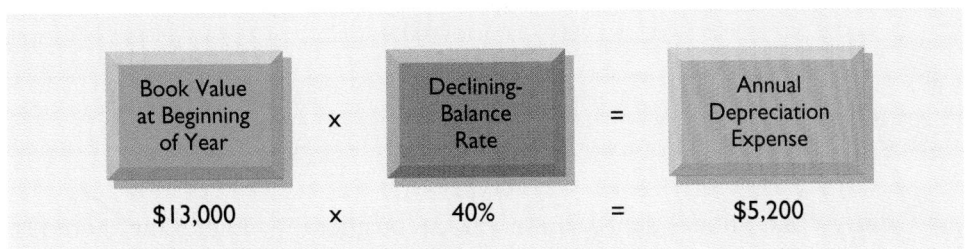

Illustration 10-13

Formula for declining-balance method

Book Value at Beginning of Year	×	Declining-Balance Rate	=	Annual Depreciation Expense
$13,000	×	40%	=	$5,200

The depreciation schedule under this method is as follows.

Illustration 10-14

Double-declining-balance depreciation schedule

BARB'S FLORISTS

	Computation					End of Year	
Year	Book Value Beginning of Year	×	Depreciation Rate	=	Annual Depreciation Expense	Accumulated Depreciation	Book Value
2002	$13,000		40%		**$5,200**	$ 5,200	$7,800
2003	7,800		40		**3,120**	8,320	4,680
2004	4,680		40		**1,872**	10,192	2,808
2005	2,808		40		**1,123**	11,315	1,685
2006	1,685		40		**685***	12,000	**1,000**

*Computation of $674 ($1,685 × 40%) is adjusted to $685 in order for book value to equal salvage value.

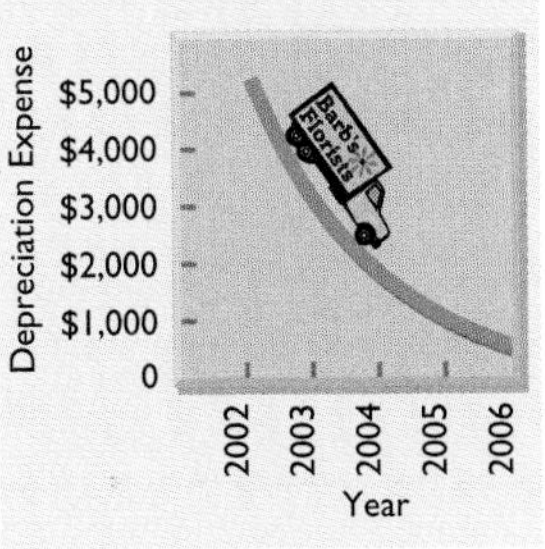

You can see that the delivery equipment is 69% depreciated ($8,320 ÷ $12,000) at the end of the second year. Under the straight-line method it would be depreciated 40% ($4,800 ÷ $12,000) at that time. Because the declining-balance method produces higher depreciation expense in the early years than in the later years, it is considered an **accelerated-depreciation method**. The declining-balance method is compatible with the matching principle. The higher depreciation expense in early years is matched with the higher benefits received in these years. On the other hand, lower depreciation expense is recognized in later years when the asset's contribution to revenue is less. Also, some assets lose usefulness rapidly because of obsolescence. In these cases, the declining-balance method provides a more appropriate depreciation amount.

HELPFUL HINT

The method to be used for an asset that is expected to be more productive in the first half of its useful life is the declining-balance method.

When an asset is purchased during the year, the first year's declining-balance depreciation must be prorated on a time basis. For example, if Barb's Florists had purchased the truck on April 1, 2002, depreciation for 2002 would become $3,900

(\$13,000 × 40% × 9/12). The book value at the beginning of 2003 is then \$9,100 (\$13,000 − \$3,900), and the 2003 depreciation is \$3,640 (\$9,100 × 40%). Subsequent computations would follow from those amounts.

Comparison of Methods

A comparison of annual and total depreciation expense under each of the three methods is shown for Barb's Florists in Illustration 10-15.

Illustration 10-15

Comparison of depreciation methods

Year	Straight-Line	Units-of-Activity	Declining-Balance
2002	\$ 2,400	\$ 1,800	\$ 5,200
2003	2,400	3,600	3,120
2004	2,400	2,400	1,872
2005	2,400	3,000	1,123
2006	2,400	1,200	685
	\$12,000	**\$12,000**	**\$12,000**

Observe that annual depreciation varies considerably among the methods. But total depreciation is the same for the 5-year period under all three methods. Each method is acceptable in accounting, because each recognizes the decline in service potential of the asset in a rational and systematic manner. The depreciation expense pattern under each method is presented graphically in Illustration 10-16.

Illustration 10-16

Patterns of depreciation

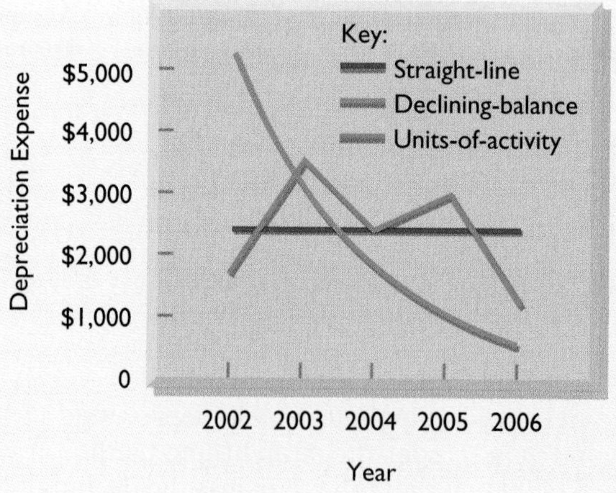

DEPRECIATION AND INCOME TAXES

The Internal Revenue Service (IRS) allows corporate taxpayers to deduct depreciation expense when they compute taxable income. However, the IRS does not require the taxpayer to use the same depreciation method on the tax return that is used in preparing financial statements. Many corporations use straight-line in their financial statements to maximize net income. At the same time, they use a special accelerated-depreciation method on their tax returns to minimize their income taxes. Taxpayers must use on their tax returns either the straight-line method or a special accelerated-depreciation method called the **Modified Accelerated Cost Recovery System** (MACRS).

TECHNOLOGY IN ACTION

Software packages to account for plant assets exist for both large and small computer systems. Even the least sophisticated packages can maintain a control and subsidiary ledger for plant assets and make the necessary depreciation computations and adjusting entries. Many packages also maintain separate depreciation schedules for both financial statement and income tax purposes, with reconciliations made for any differences.

REVISING PERIODIC DEPRECIATION

STUDY OBJECTIVE 4

Describe the procedure for revising periodic depreciation.

Depreciation is one example of the use of estimation in the accounting process. Annual depreciation expense should be reviewed periodically by management. If wear and tear or obsolescence indicate that annual depreciation estimates are inadequate or excessive, a change should be made.

When a change in an estimate is required, the change is made in **current and future years**. It is not made retroactively **to prior periods**. Thus, there is no correction of previously recorded depreciation expense. Instead, depreciation expense for current and future years is revised. The rationale is that continual restatement of prior periods would adversely affect confidence in financial statements.

To determine the new annual depreciation expense, we first compute the asset's depreciable cost at the time of the revision. We then allocate the revised depreciable cost to the remaining useful life. To illustrate, assume that Barb's Florists decides on January 1, 2005, to extend the useful life of the truck one year because of its excellent condition. The company has used the straight-line method to depreciate the asset to date, and book value is $5,800 ($13,000 − $7,200). The new annual depreciation is $1,600, computed as follows.

Illustration 10-17

Revised depreciation computation

Book value, 1/1/05	$5,800	
Less: Salvage value	1,000	
Depreciable cost	$4,800	
Remaining useful life	3 years	(2005–2007)
Revised annual depreciation ($4,800 ÷ 3)	**$1,600**	

Barb's Florists makes no entry for the change in estimate. On December 31, 2005, during the preparation of adjusting entries, it would record depreciation expense of $1,600. Significant changes in estimates must be described in the financial statements.

HELPFUL HINT
Use a step-by-step approach: (1) determine new depreciable cost; (2) divide by remaining useful life.

BEFORE YOU GO ON...

REVIEW IT

1. What is the relationship, if any, of depreciation to (a) cost allocation, (b) asset valuation, and (c) cash accumulation?
2. Explain the factors that affect the computation of depreciation.

3. What are the formulas for computing annual depreciation under each of the depreciation methods?
4. How do the methods differ in terms of their effects on annual depreciation over the useful life of the asset?
5. Are revisions of periodic depreciation made to prior periods? Explain.

▶ *DO IT*

On January 1, 2002, Iron Mountain Ski Corporation purchased a new snow-grooming machine for \$50,000. The machine is estimated to have a 10-year life with a \$2,000 salvage value. What journal entry would Iron Mountain Ski Corporation make at December 31, 2002, if it uses the straight-line method of depreciation?

ACTION PLAN

- Calculate depreciable cost (Cost − Salvage value).
- Divide the depreciable cost by the estimated useful life.

SOLUTION

$$\text{Depreciation expense} = \frac{\text{Cost} - \text{Salvage value}}{\text{Useful life}} = \frac{\$50{,}000 - \$2{,}000}{10} = \$4{,}800$$

The entry to record the first year's depreciation would be:

Dec. 31	Depreciation Expense	4,800	
	Accumulated Depreciation		4,800
	(To record annual depreciation on snow-grooming machine)		

Related exercise material: BE10-3, BE10-4, BE10-5, BE10-6, E10-3, and E10-4.

THE NAVIGATOR

EXPENDITURES DURING USEFUL LIFE

STUDY OBJECTIVE 5

Distinguish between revenue and capital expenditures, and explain the entries for these expenditures.

During the useful life of a plant asset a company may incur costs for ordinary repairs, additions, or improvements. **Ordinary repairs** are expenditures to maintain the operating efficiency and productive life of the unit. They usually are fairly small amounts that occur frequently. Motor tune-ups and oil changes, the painting of buildings, and the replacing of worn-out gears on machinery are examples. Such repairs are debited to Repair (or Maintenance) Expense as they are incurred. Because they are immediately charged as an expense against revenues, these costs are often referred to as **revenue expenditures**.

Additions and improvements are costs incurred to increase the operating efficiency, productive capacity, or useful life of a plant asset. They are usually material in amount and occur infrequently. Additions and improvements increase the company's investment in productive facilities and are generally debited to the plant asset affected. They are often referred to as **capital expenditures**. Most major U.S. corporations disclose annual capital expenditures. In a recent year, both **IBM** and **General Motors** reported capital expenditures slightly in excess of \$6 billion.

PLANT ASSET DISPOSALS

STUDY OBJECTIVE 6

Explain how to account for the disposal of a plant asset through retirement, sale, or exchange.

Plant assets may be disposed of in three ways—retirement, sale, or exchange—as shown in Illustration 10-18. Whatever the method, at the time of disposal it is necessary to determine the book value of the plant asset. As noted earlier, book value is the difference between the cost of a plant asset and the accumulated depreciation to date.

Piper Co.
Lowy Co.
Ford Trucks
+ $
Lowy Co.
Retirement
Equipment is scrapped or discarded.
Sale
Equipment is sold to another party.
Exchange
Existing equipment is traded for new equipment.

Illustration 10-18

Methods of plant asset disposal

At the time of disposal, depreciation for the fraction of the year to the date of disposal must be recorded. The book value is then eliminated by debiting (decreasing) Accumulated Depreciation for the total depreciation to date and crediting (decreasing) the asset account for the cost of the asset. In this section we will examine the accounting for each of the three methods of plant asset disposal.

RETIREMENT OF PLANT ASSETS

To illustrate the retirement of plant assets, assume that Hobart Enterprises retires its computer printers, which cost $32,000. The accumulated depreciation on these printers is $32,000. The equipment, therefore, is fully depreciated (zero book value). The entry to record this retirement is as follows.

Accumulated Depreciation—Printing Equipment	32,000	
Printing Equipment		32,000
(To record retirement of fully depreciated equipment)		

A	=	L	+	OE
+32,000				
−32,000				

What happens if a fully depreciated plant asset is still useful to the company? In this case, the asset and its accumulated depreciation continue to be reported on the balance sheet without further depreciation adjustment until the asset is retired. Reporting the asset and related accumulated depreciation on the balance sheet informs the financial statement reader that the asset is still in use. However, once an asset is fully depreciated, even if it is still being used, no additional depreciation should be taken. In no situation can the accumulated depreciation on a plant asset exceed its cost.

If a plant asset is retired before it is fully depreciated, and no scrap or salvage value is received, a loss on disposal occurs. For example, assume that Sunset Company discards delivery equipment that cost $18,000 and has accumulated depreciation of $14,000. The entry is as follows.

HELPFUL HINT
When a plant asset is disposed of, all amounts related to the asset must be removed from the accounts. This includes the original cost in the asset account and the total depreciation to date in the accumulated depreciation account.

Accumulated Depreciation—Delivery Equipment	14,000	
Loss on Disposal	4,000	
Delivery Equipment		18,000
(To record retirement of delivery equipment at a loss)		

A	=	L	+	OE
+14,000				−4,000
−18,000				

The loss on disposal is reported in the "other expenses and losses" section of the income statement.

SALE OF PLANT ASSETS

In a disposal by sale, the book value of the asset is compared with the proceeds received from the sale. **If the proceeds of the sale exceed the book value of the plant asset, a gain on disposal occurs. If the proceeds of the sale are less than the book value of the plant asset sold, a loss on disposal occurs.**

Only by coincidence will the book value and the fair market value of the asset be the same when the asset is sold. Gains and losses on sales of plant assets are therefore quite common. For example, **Delta Airlines** reported a $94,343,000 gain on the sale of five **Boeing** B-727-200 aircraft and five **Lockheed** L-1011-1 aircraft.

Gain on Disposal

To illustrate a gain, assume that on July 1, 2002, Wright Company sells office furniture for $16,000 cash. The office furniture originally cost $60,000. As of January 1, 2002, it had accumulated depreciation of $41,000. Depreciation for the first 6 months of 2002 is $8,000. The entry to record depreciation expense and update accumulated depreciation to July 1 is as follows.

A	=	L	+	OE
−8,000				−8,000

July 1	Depreciation Expense	8,000	
	Accumulated Depreciation—Office Furniture		8,000
	(To record depreciation expense for the first 6 months of 2002)		

After the accumulated depreciation balance is updated, a gain on disposal of $5,000 is computed:

Illustration 10-19

Computation of gain on disposal

Cost of office furniture	$60,000
Less: Accumulated depreciation ($41,000 + $8,000)	49,000
Book value at date of disposal	11,000
Proceeds from sale	16,000
Gain on disposal	**$ 5,000**

The entry to record the sale and the gain on disposal is as follows.

A	=	L	+	OE
+16,000				+5,000
+49,000				
−60,000				

July 1	Cash	16,000	
	Accumulated Depreciation—Office Furniture	49,000	
	Office Furniture		60,000
	Gain on Disposal		5,000
	(To record sale of office furniture at a gain)		

The gain on disposal is reported in the "other revenues and gains" section of the income statement.

Loss on Disposal

Assume that instead of selling the office furniture for $16,000, Wright sells it for $9,000. In this case, a loss of $2,000 is computed:

Illustration 10-20

Computation of loss on disposal

Cost of office furniture	$60,000
Less: Accumulated depreciation	49,000
Book value at date of disposal	11,000
Proceeds from sale	9,000
Loss on disposal	**$ 2,000**

The entry to record the sale and the loss on disposal is as follows.

July 1	Cash	9,000	
	Accumulated Depreciation—Office Furniture	49,000	
	Loss on Disposal	2,000	
	Office Furniture		60,000
	(To record sale of office furniture at a loss)		

A	=	L	+	OE
+9,000				−2,000
+49,000				
−60,000				

The loss on disposal is reported in the "other expenses and losses" section of the income statement.

EXCHANGE OF PLANT ASSETS

Plant assets may also be disposed of through exchange. Exchanges can be for either similar or dissimilar assets. Because exchanges of similar assets are more common, they are discussed here. An exchange of similar assets occurs, for example, when old office furniture is exchanged for new office furniture. In an exchange of similar assets, the new asset performs the **same function** as the old asset.

In exchanges of similar plant assets, it is necessary to determine two things: (1) the cost of the asset acquired, and (2) the gain or loss on the asset given up. Because a noncash asset is given up in the exchange, cost is the **cash equivalent price** paid. That is, cost is the fair market value of the asset given up plus the cash paid. The gain or loss on disposal is the **difference between the fair market value and the book value of the asset given up**. These determinations are explained and illustrated below.

HELPFUL HINT
A building costing $200,000 was destroyed by fire. At the date of the fire, accumulated depreciation was $150,000. Insurance proceeds were $325,000. Prepare the entry to record the insurance proceeds and disposition of building. Answer: Debit Cash $325,000; debit Accumulated Depreciation $150,000; credit Building $200,000; and credit Gain on Disposal $275,000.

Loss Treatment

A loss on the exchange of similar assets is recognized immediately. To illustrate, assume that Roland Company exchanged old office equipment for new office equipment. The book value of the old equipment is $26,000 (cost $70,000 less accumulated depreciation $44,000). Its fair market value is $10,000, and cash of $81,000 is paid. The cost of the new office equipment, $91,000, is computed as follows.

Illustration 10-21
Computation of cost of new office equipment

Fair market value of old office equipment	$10,000
Cash	81,000
Cost of new office equipment	**$91,000**

A loss on disposal of $16,000 on this exchange is incurred. The reason is that the book value is greater than the fair market value of the asset given up. The computation is as follows.

Illustration 10-22
Computation of loss on disposal

Book value of old office equipment ($70,000 − $44,000)	$26,000
Fair market value of old office equipment	10,000
Loss on disposal	**$16,000**

In recording an exchange at a loss, three steps are required: (1) Eliminate the book value of the asset given up, (2) record the cost of the asset acquired, and (3) recognize the loss on disposal. The entry for Roland Company is as follows.

A	=	L	+	OE
+91,000				−16,000
+44,000				
−70,000				
−81,000				

Office Equipment (new)	91,000	
Accumulated Depreciation—Office Equipment (old)	44,000	
Loss on Disposal	16,000	
Office Equipment (old)		70,000
Cash		81,000
(To record exchange of old office equipment for similar new equipment)		

Gain Treatment

A gain on the exchange of similar assets is not recognized immediately but, instead, is deferred. This is done by reducing the cost basis of the new asset. In determining the cost of the new asset, compute the **cost before deferral of the gain** and then the **cost after deferral of the gain.**

HELPFUL HINT
Why aren't gains on the exchange of similar assets recognized? Because the earnings process is not considered completed. To be conservative, however, losses are recognized.

To illustrate, assume that Mark's Express Delivery decides to exchange its old delivery equipment plus cash of $3,000 for new delivery equipment. The book value of the old delivery equipment is $12,000 (cost $40,000 less accumulated depreciation $28,000). The fair market value of the old delivery equipment is $19,000.

The cost of the new asset (before deferral of the gain) is the **fair market value of the old asset exchanged plus any cash (or other consideration given up)**. The cost of the new delivery equipment (before deferral of the gain) is $22,000, computed as follows.

Illustration 10-23
Cost of new equipment (before deferral of gain)

Fair market value of old delivery equipment	$19,000
Cash	3,000
Cost of new delivery equipment (before deferral of gain)	**$22,000**

A gain results when the fair market value is greater than the book value of the asset given up. For Mark's Express, there is a gain of $7,000, computed as follows, on the disposal.

Illustration 10-24
Computation of gain on disposal

Fair market value of old delivery equipment	$19,000
Book value of old delivery equipment ($40,000 − $28,000)	12,000
Gain on disposal	**$ 7,000**

The $7,000 gain on disposal is then offset against the $22,000 cost of the new delivery equipment. The result is a $15,000 cost of the new delivery equipment, after deferral of the gain, as shown in Illustration 10-25.

Illustration 10-25
Cost of new equipment (after deferral of gain)

Cost of new delivery equipment (before deferral of gain)	$22,000
Less: Gain on disposal	7,000
Cost of new delivery equipment (after deferral of gain)	**$15,000**

The entry to record the exchange is as follows.

Delivery Equipment (new)	15,000	
Accumulated Depreciation—Delivery Equipment (old)	28,000	
Delivery Equipment (old)		40,000
Cash		3,000
(To record exchange of old delivery equipment for similar new delivery equipment)		

A	=	L	+	OE
+15,000				
+28,000				
−40,000				
−3,000				

This entry does not eliminate the gain; it just postpones or defers it to future periods. The deferred gain of $7,000 reduces the $22,000 cost to $15,000. As a result, net income in future periods increases because depreciation expense on the newly acquired delivery equipment is less by $7,000.

Summarizing, the rules for accounting for exchanges of similar assets are as follows.

Illustration 10-26

Accounting rules for plant asset exchanges

Type of Event	Recognition
Loss	Recognize immediately by debiting Loss on Disposal
Gain	Defer and reduce cost of new asset

BEFORE YOU GO ON...

REVIEW IT

1. How does a capital expenditure differ from a revenue expenditure?
2. What is the proper accounting for the retirement and sale of plant assets?
3. What is the proper accounting for the exchange of similar plant assets?

DO IT

Overland Trucking has an old truck that cost $30,000. The truck has accumulated depreciation of $16,000 and a fair value of $17,000. Overland has a choice of either selling the truck for $17,000 cash or exchanging the old truck and $3,000 cash for a new truck. What is the entry that Overland Trucking would record under each option?

ACTION PLAN

- Compare the asset's book value and fair value to determine whether a gain or loss has occurred.
- Defer gains on the exchange of similar assets by reducing the recorded value of the new asset.

SOLUTION

Sale of truck for cash:

Cash	17,000	
Accumulated Depreciation—Truck (old)	16,000	
Truck (old)		30,000
Gain on Disposal [$17,000 − ($30,000 − $16,000)]		3,000
(To record sale of truck at a gain)		

Exchange of old truck and cash for new truck:

Truck (new)	17,000*	
Accumulated Depreciation—Truck (old)	16,000	
Truck (old)		30,000
Cash		3,000
(To record exchange of old truck for similar new truck)		
*($20,000 − $3,000)		

If the old truck is exchanged for the new truck, the $3,000 gain is deferred, and the recorded cost of the new truck is reduced by $3,000.

Related exercise material: BE10-8, BE10-9, BE10-10, BE10-11, E10-6, E10-7, E10-8, and E10-9.

THE NAVIGATOR

SECTION 2 *Natural Resources*

HELPFUL HINT
On a balance sheet, natural resources may be described more specifically as timberlands, mineral deposits, oil reserves, and so on.

Natural resources consist of standing timber and underground deposits of oil, gas, and minerals. These long-lived productive assets have two distinguishing characteristics: (1) They are physically extracted in operations (such as mining, cutting, or pumping), and (2) they are replaceable only by an act of nature. The acquisition cost of a natural resource is the price needed to acquire the resource and prepare it for its intended use. For an already discovered resource, such as an existing coal mine, cost is the price paid for the property.

STUDY OBJECTIVE 7
Compute periodic depletion of natural resources.

The allocation of the cost of natural resources to expense in a rational and systematic manner over the resource's useful life is called **depletion**. **The units-of-activity method** (learned earlier in the chapter) **is generally used to compute depletion.** The reason it is used is that **depletion generally is a function of the units extracted during the year.**

Under the units-of-activity method, the total cost of the natural resource minus salvage value is divided by the number of units estimated to be in the resource. The result is a depletion cost per unit of product. The depletion cost per unit is then multiplied by the number of units extracted and sold. The result is the annual depletion expense. The formula is as follows.

Illustration 10-27
Formula to compute depletion expense

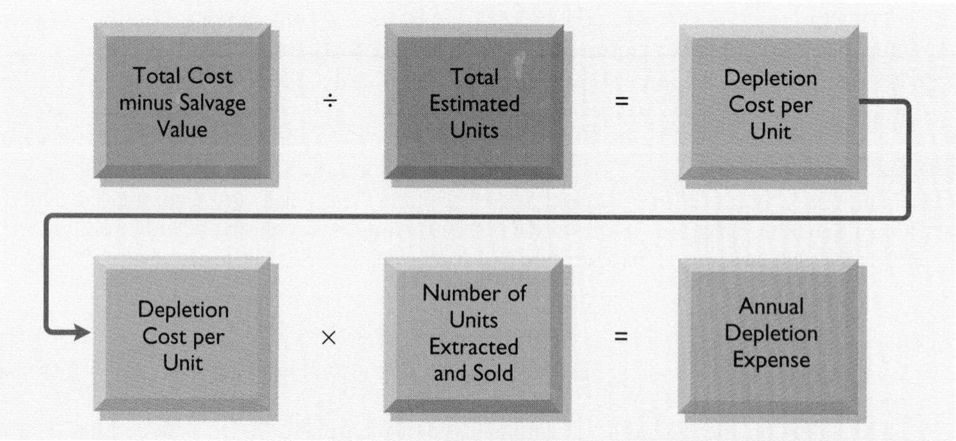

HELPFUL HINT
This computation for depletion is similar to the computation for depreciation using the units-of-activity method of depreciation.

To illustrate, assume that Lane Coal Company invests $5 million in a mine estimated to have 10 million tons of coal and no salvage value. In the first year, 800,000 tons of coal are extracted and sold. Using the formulas above, the computations are as follows:

$5,000,000 ÷ 10,000,000 = $0.50 depletion cost per ton

$0.50 × 800,000 = $400,000 annual depletion expense

The entry to record depletion expense for the first year of operation is as follows.

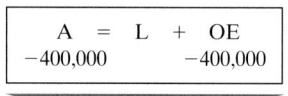

A	=	L	+	OE
−400,000				−400,000

Dec. 31	Depletion Expense	400,000	
	Accumulated Depletion		400,000
	(To record depletion expense on coal deposits)		

HELPFUL HINT
Natural resources are generally reported as part of "property, plant, and equipment" on the balance sheet.

The account Depletion Expense is reported as a part of the cost of producing the product. Accumulated Depletion is a contra asset account similar to accumulated depreciation. It is deducted from the cost of the natural resource in the balance sheet, as shown in Illustration 10-28.

Illustration 10-28

Statement presentation of accumulated depletion

LANE COAL COMPANY Balance Sheet (partial)		
Coal mine	$5,000,000	
Less: Accumulated depletion	**400,000**	$4,600,000

However, in many companies an Accumulated Depletion account is not used. In such cases, the amount of depletion is credited directly to the natural resources account.

Sometimes, natural resources extracted in one accounting period will not be sold until a later period. In this case, depletion is not expensed until the resource is sold. The amount not sold is reported in the current assets section as inventory.

SECTION 3 *Intangible Assets*

Intangible assets are rights, privileges, and competitive advantages that result from the ownership of long-lived assets that do not possess physical substance. Evidence of intangibles may exist in the form of contracts or licenses. Intangibles may arise from:

1. Government grants, such as patents, copyrights, and trademarks.
2. Acquisition of another business, in which the purchase price includes a payment for the company's favorable attributes (called goodwill).
3. Private monopolistic arrangements arising from contractual agreements, such as franchises and leases.

Some widely known intangibles are the patents of **Polaroid**, the franchises of **McDonald's**, the trade name of Col. Sander's **Kentucky Fried Chicken**, and the trademark **Rent-A-Wreck** in the Feature Story.

ACCOUNTING FOR INTANGIBLE ASSETS

STUDY OBJECTIVE 8

Contrast the accounting for intangible assets with the accounting for plant assets.

In general, accounting for intangible assets parallels the accounting for plant assets. That is, **intangible assets are recorded at cost**, and this cost is expensed **over the useful life of the intangible asset in a rational and systematic manner**. At disposal, the book value of the intangible asset is eliminated, and a gain or loss, if any, is recorded.

There are several differences between accounting for intangible assets and accounting for plant assets. First, the term used to describe the allocation of the cost of an intangible asset to expense is **amortization**, rather than depreciation. Also, to record amortization of an intangible, an amortization expense is debited and the specific intangible asset is credited (rather than crediting a contra account). An alternative is to credit an accumulated amortization account, similar to accumulated depreciation.

There is also a difference in determining cost. For plant assets, cost includes both the purchase price of the asset and the costs incurred in designing and constructing the asset. In contrast, cost for an intangible asset includes only the purchase price. Any costs incurred in developing an intangible asset are expensed as incurred.

A final difference is that **the amortization period of an intangible asset cannot be longer than 40 years**. Even if the useful life of an intangible asset is 60 years, it must be written off over 40 years. If the useful life is less than 40 years, the useful life is used. This rule ensures that all intangibles, especially those with indeterminable lives, will be written off in a reasonable period of time.

Intangible assets are typically amortized on a straight-line basis. The widespread use of this method adds comparability in accounting for intangible assets.

PATENTS

A **patent** is an exclusive right issued by the U.S. Patent Office that enables the recipient to manufacture, sell, or otherwise control an invention for a period of 20 years from the date of the grant. A patent is nonrenewable. But the legal life of a patent may be extended by obtaining new patents for improvements or other changes in the basic design.

The initial cost of a patent is the cash or cash equivalent price paid to acquire the patent. The saying, "A patent is only as good as the money you're prepared to spend defending it" is very true. Many patents are subject to some type of litigation. For example, **Polaroid** won a patent infringement suit against **Eastman Kodak** in protecting its patent on instant cameras. Legal costs an owner incurs in successfully defending a patent in an infringement suit are considered necessary to establish the validity of the patent. **They are added to the Patent account and amortized over the remaining life of the patent**.

The cost of a patent should be amortized over its 20-year legal life or its useful life, whichever is shorter. Obsolescence and inadequacy should be considered in determining useful life. These factors may cause a patent to become economically ineffective before the end of its legal life.

To illustrate the computation of patent expense, assume that National Labs purchases a patent at a cost of $60,000. If the useful life of the patent is 8 years, the annual amortization expense is $7,500 ($60,000 ÷ 8). The entry to record the annual amortization is:

A	=	L	+	OE
−7,500				−7,500

Dec. 31	Amortization Expense—Patents	7,500	
	Patents		7,500
	(To record patent amortization)		

Amortization Expense—Patents is classified as an **operating expense** in the income statement.

COPYRIGHTS

Copyrights are grants from the federal government, giving the owner the exclusive right to reproduce and sell an artistic or published work. Copyrights extend for the life of the creator plus 50 years. The cost of a copyright is the **cost of acquiring and defending it**. The cost may be only the $10 fee paid to the U.S. Copyright Office. Or it may amount to a great deal more if a copyright infringement suit is involved.

Similar to other intangible assets, the maximum write-off is 40 years. The useful life of a copyright generally is significantly shorter than its legal life, though. Therefore, copyrights usually are amortized over a relatively short period of time.

TRADEMARKS AND TRADE NAMES

A **trademark** or **trade name** is a word, phrase, jingle, or symbol that identifies a particular enterprise or product. Trade names like Wheaties, Game Boy, Sunkist, Kleenex, Windows, Coca-Cola, Big Mac, and Jeep create immediate product identification. They also generally enhance the sale of the product. The creator or original user may obtain exclusive legal right to the trademark or trade name by registering it with the U.S. Patent Office. Such registration provides 20 years' protection. The registration may be renewed indefinitely as long as the trademark or trade name is in use.

If the trademark or trade name is **purchased** by the company that will sell the product, its cost is the purchase price. If the trademark or trade name is **developed** by the company itself, the cost includes attorney's fees, registration fees, design costs, successful legal defense costs, and other expenditures directly related to securing it.

As with other intangibles, the cost of trademarks and trade names must be amortized over the shorter of 40 years or the useful life. Because of the uncertainty involved in estimating the useful life, the cost is frequently amortized over a much shorter period.

FRANCHISES AND LICENSES

When you drive down the street in your RAV4 purchased from a **Toyota** dealer, fill up your tank at the corner **Shell** station, eat lunch at **Taco Bell**, or rent a car from **Rent-A-Wreck**, you are dealing with franchises. A **franchise** is a contractual arrangement under which the franchisor grants the franchisee the right to sell certain products, render specific services, or use certain trademarks or trade names. The franchise is usually restricted to a designated geographical area.

Another type of franchise is that entered into between a governmental body (commonly municipalities) and a business enterprise. This franchise permits the enterprise to use public property in performing its services. Examples are the use of city streets for a bus line or taxi service, use of public land for telephone and electric lines, and the use of airwaves for radio or TV broadcasting. Such operating rights are referred to as **licenses**.

When costs can be identified with the acquisition of a franchise or license, an intangible asset should be recognized. Franchises and licenses may be granted for a definite period of time, an indefinite period, or perpetual. The cost of a limited-life franchise (or license) should be amortized over the useful life. If the life is indefinite or perpetual, the cost may be amortized over a reasonable period not to exceed 40 years. Annual payments made under a franchise agreement are recorded as **operating expenses** in the period in which they are incurred.

ETHICS NOTE

A pharmaceutical company was growing rapidly by buying unwanted drug licensing rights. These licensing rights, reported as intangible assets, represented over 70% of the company's total assets. The company experienced a 50% drop in value when the market realized the rights were being amortized over 40 years. If a more reasonable life had been used to amortize the rights, the company's reported profits would, instead, have been huge losses.

ACCOUNTING IN ACTION *Business Insight*

King World's most valuable asset is the right to license television shows such as "Wheel of Fortune," "Jeopardy," "The Oprah Winfrey Show," and "Inside Edition." Almost 88 percent of its $683.8 million in 1998 came from the fees associated with the rights to licenses on these intangible assets.

GOODWILL

Usually, the largest intangible asset that appears on a company's balance sheet is goodwill. **Goodwill** is the value of all favorable attributes that relate to a business enterprise. These include exceptional management, desirable location, good customer relations, skilled employees, high-quality products, and harmonious relations with labor unions. Some view goodwill as expected earnings in excess of normal earnings. Goodwill is therefore unusual: Unlike other assets such as investments and plant assets, which can be sold individually in the marketplace, goodwill can be identified only with the business as a whole.

HELPFUL HINT
Goodwill is recorded only when it has been purchased along with tangible and identifiable intangible assets of a business.

If goodwill can be identified only with the business as a whole, how can it be determined? One could try to put a dollar value on the factors listed above (exceptional management, desirable location, and so on), but the results would be very subjective. Such subjective valuations would not contribute to the reliability of financial statements. **Therefore, goodwill is recorded only when there is a transaction that involves the purchase of an entire business. In that case, goodwill is the excess of cost over the fair market value of the net assets (assets less liabilities) acquired.**

In recording the purchase of a business, the net assets are debited at their fair market values, cash is credited for the purchase price, and goodwill is debited for the difference. Subsequently, goodwill is written off over its useful life, not to exceed 40 years. The amortization entry generally results in a debit to Amortization Expense—Goodwill and a credit to Goodwill. Goodwill is reported in the balance sheet under intangible assets.

ACCOUNTING IN ACTION *International Insight*

Does the amortization requirement for goodwill create a disadvantage for U.S. companies? British companies do not have to amortize goodwill against earnings. Rather, they bypass the income statement completely and charge goodwill directly to stockholders' equity. For example, **Pillsbury** was purchased by **Grand Met**, a British firm. Many complained that U.S. companies were reluctant to bid for Pillsbury because it would mean that they would have to record a large amount of goodwill, which would substantially depress income in the future.

What can or should be done when accounting practices are different among countries and perhaps give one country a competitive edge?

RESEARCH AND DEVELOPMENT COSTS

HELPFUL HINT
Research and development (R&D) costs are not intangible assets. But because they may lead to patents and copyrights, we discuss them in this section.

Research and development costs are expenditures that may lead to patents, copyrights, new processes, and new products. Many companies spend considerable sums of money on research and development (R&D). For example, in a recent year **IBM** spent over $2.5 billion on R&D, an amount greater than the total expenditure budget of some state governments.

Research and development costs present accounting problems. For one thing, it is sometimes difficult to assign the costs to specific projects. Also, there are uncertainties in identifying the extent and timing of future benefits. As a result, R&D costs are **usually recorded as an expense when incurred**, whether the research and development is successful or not.

To illustrate, assume that Laser Scanner Company spent $3 million on research and development. This expenditure resulted in the development of two highly successful patents. The R&D costs, however, cannot be included in the cost of the patent. Rather, they are recorded as an expense when incurred.

Many disagree with this accounting approach. They argue that expensing R&D costs leads to understated assets and net income. Others, however, argue that capitalizing these costs will lead to highly speculative assets on the balance sheet. It is difficult to determine who is right. The controversy illustrates how difficult it is to establish proper guidelines for financial reporting.

STATEMENT PRESENTATION AND ANALYSIS

PRESENTATION

STUDY OBJECTIVE 9

Indicate how plant assets, natural resources, and intangible assets are reported and analyzed.

Usually plant assets and natural resources are combined under "property, plant, and equipment" in the balance sheet. Intangibles are shown separately under intangible assets. The balances of the major classes of assets, such as land, buildings, and equipment, and accumulated depreciation by major classes or in total should be disclosed in the balance sheet or notes. In addition, the depreciation and amortization methods that were used should be described. Finally, the amount of depreciation and amortization expense for the period should be disclosed.

The financial statement presentation of property, plant, and equipment and intangibles by **Lands' End** in its 2000 balance sheet is shown in Illustration 10-29.

Illustration 10-29

Lands' End's presentation of property, plant, and equipment, and intangible assets

LANDS' END, INC.
Balance Sheet (partial)
(in thousands)

	January 28, 2000	January 29, 1999
Property, plant and equipment, at cost		
Land and buildings	$102,776	$102,018
Fixtures and equipment	175,910	154,663
Leasehold improvements	4,453	5,475
Total property, plant and equipment	283,139	262,156
Less: Accumulated depreciation and amortization	117,317	101,570
Property, plant and equipment, net	165,822	160,586
Intangibles, net	966	1,030

The notes to Lands' End's financial statements present greater details, namely, that the intangibles section contains goodwill and trademarks.

Another comprehensive presentation of property, plant, and equipment, excerpted from the balance sheet of **Owens-Illinois**, is shown in Illustration 10-30.

Illustration 10-30

Owens-Illinois' presentation of property, plant, and equipment, and intangible assets

OWENS-ILLINOIS, INC.
Balance Sheet (partial)
(in millions)

Property, plant, and equipment			
Timberlands, at cost, less accumulated depletion		$ 95.4	
Buildings and equipment, at cost	$2,207.1		
Less: Accumulated depreciation	1,229.0	978.1	
Total property, plant, and equipment			$1,073.5
Intangibles			
Patents			410.0
Total			$1,483.5

The notes to the financial statements of Owens-Illinois identify the major classes of property, plant, and equipment. They also indicate that depreciation is by the straight-line method, depletion is by the units-of-activity method, and amortization is by the straight-line method.

ANALYSIS

We can analyze how efficiently a company uses its assets to generate sales. The **asset turnover ratio** analyzes the productivity of a company's assets. It is computed by dividing net sales by average total assets for the period, as shown in the formula in Illustration 10-31. The computation is for **Lands' End**. Its net sales for 2000 were $1,320 million; its total ending assets were $456 million, and beginning assets also were $456 million.

Illustration 10-31

Asset turnover formula and computation

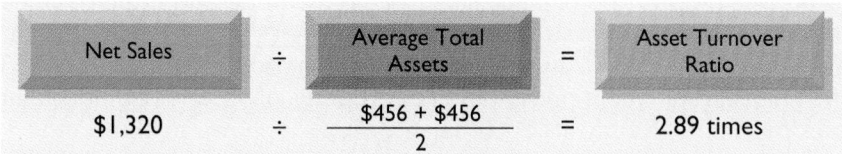

Net Sales	÷	Average Total Assets	=	Asset Turnover Ratio
$1,320	÷	($456 + $456) / 2	=	2.89 times

This ratio shows the dollars of sales produced for each dollar invested in average total assets. Each dollar invested in assets produced $2.89 in sales for Lands' End. If a company is using its assets efficiently, each dollar of assets will create a high amount of sales. This ratio varies greatly among different industries—from those that are asset intensive (utilities) to those that are not (services).

BEFORE YOU GO ON...

REVIEW IT

1. How is depletion expense computed?
2. What are the main differences between accounting for intangible assets and for plant assets?
3. Identify the major types of intangibles and the proper accounting for them.
4. Explain the accounting for research and development costs.
5. What ratio may be computed to analyze property, plant, and equipment?

A LOOK BACK AT OUR FEATURE STORY

Refer back to the Feature Story about **Rent-A-Wreck** at the beginning of the chapter, and answer the following questions.

1. Why should Rent-A-Wreck depreciate its vehicles?
2. How could Rent-A-Wreck have an asset with a zero book value but a substantial market value?
3. Give some examples of intangibles other than a trademark that you might find on your college campus.
4. Give some examples of company or product trademarks or trade names. Are trade names and trademarks reported on a company's balance sheet? Explain.

SOLUTION

1. Rent-A-Wreck depreciates its vehicles in order to allocate the cost of the vehicles to the periods in which they are used.
2. An asset can have a zero book value if it has no salvage value and it is fully depreciated—that is, if it has been used for a period longer than its expected life. Because depreciation is used to allocate cost rather than to reflect actual value, it is not at all unlikely that an asset could have a low or zero book value, but a positive market value.

3. Examples of other intangibles that might be found on a college campus are franchise of a bookstore chain or a fast-food outlet, license to operate a radio station, patents developed by professors, and a permit to operate a bus service.
4. Typical company or product trade names are:
   Clothes—Gap, Gitano, Dockers, Calvin Klein, Chaus, Guess.
   Perfume—Passion, Ruffles, Chanel No. 5, Diamonds.
   Cars—TransAm, Nova, Prelude, Cherokee, Outback.
   Shoes—Nike, Florsheim, L.A. Gear, Adidas.
   Breakfast cereals—Cheerios, Wheaties, Frosted Mini-Wheats, Rice Krispies.

Trade names and trademarks are reported on a balance sheet if there is a cost attached to them. If the trade name or trademark has been purchased, the cost is the purchase price. If it has been developed by the enterprise, the cost includes attorney's fees, registration fees, design costs, successful legal defense costs, and other expenditures directly related to securing the trade name or trademark.

THE NAVIGATOR

DEMONSTRATION PROBLEM 1

DuPage Company purchases a factory machine at a cost of $18,000 on January 1, 2002. The machine is expected to have a salvage value of $2,000 at the end of its 4-year useful life.

During its useful life, the machine is expected to be used 160,000 hours. Actual annual hourly use was: 2002, 40,000; 2003, 60,000; 2004, 35,000; and 2005, 25,000.

Additional Demonstration Problem

Instructions

Prepare depreciation schedules for the following methods: (a) the straight-line, (b) units-of-activity, and (c) declining-balance using double the straight-line rate.

SOLUTION TO DEMONSTRATION PROBLEM 1

(a)

Straight-Line Method

	Computation				Annual	End of Year	
Year	Depreciable Cost	×	Depreciation Rate	=	Depreciation Expense	Accumulated Depreciation	Book Value
2002	$16,000		25%		$4,000	$ 4,000	$14,000*
2003	16,000		25%		4,000	8,000	10,000
2004	16,000		25%		4,000	12,000	6,000
2005	16,000		25%		4,000	16,000	2,000

*$18,000 – $4,000.

(b)

Units-of-Activity Method

	Computation				Annual	End of Year	
Year	Units of Activity	×	Depreciation Cost/Unit	=	Depreciation Expense	Accumulated Depreciation	Book Value
2002	40,000		$0.10		$4,000	$ 4,000	$14,000
2003	60,000		0.10		6,000	10,000	8,000
2004	35,000		0.10		3,500	13,500	4,500
2005	25,000		0.10		2,500	16,000	2,000

ACTION PLAN

- Under the straight-line method, apply the depreciation rate to depreciable cost.
- Under the units-of-activity method, compute the depreciation cost per unit by dividing depreciable cost by total units of activity.
- Under the declining-balance method, apply the depreciation rate to **book value** at the beginning of the year.

(c)

Declining-Balance Method

	Computation					End of Year	
Year	Book Value Beginning of Year	×	Depreciation Rate	=	Annual Depreciation Expense	Accumulated Depreciation	Book Value
2002	$18,000		50%		$9,000	$ 9,000	$9,000
2003	9,000		50%		4,500	13,500	4,500
2004	4,500		50%		2,250	15,750	2,250
2005	2,250		50%		250*	16,000	2,000

*Adjusted to $250 because ending book value should not be less than expected salvage value.

THE NAVIGATOR

DEMONSTRATION PROBLEM 2

Additional Demonstration Problem

On January 1, 2000, Skyline Limousine Co. purchased a limo at an acquisition cost of $28,000. The vehicle has been depreciated by the straight-line method using a 4-year service life and a $4,000 salvage value. The company's fiscal year ends on December 31.

Instructions

Prepare the journal entry or entries to record the disposal of the limousine assuming that it was:

(a) Retired and scrapped with no salvage value on January 1, 2004.
(b) Sold for $5,000 on July 1, 2003.
(c) Traded in on a new limousine on January 1, 2003. The fair market value of the old vehicle was $9,000, and $22,000 was paid in cash.
(d) Traded in on a new limousine on January 1, 2003. The fair market value of the old vehicle was $11,000, and $2,000 was paid in cash.

SOLUTION TO DEMONSTRATION PROBLEM 2

ACTION PLAN

- At the time of disposal, determine the book value of the asset.
- Recognize any gain or loss from disposal of the asset.
- Remove the book value of the asset from the records by debiting Accumulated Depreciation for the total depreciation to date of disposal and crediting the asset account for the cost of the asset.

(a)	1/1/04	Accumulated Depreciation—Limousine	24,000	
		Loss on Disposal	4,000	
		Limousine		28,000
		(To record retirement of limousine)		
(b)	7/1/03	Depreciation Expense	3,000	
		Accumulated Depreciation—Limousine		3,000
		(To record depreciation to date of disposal)		
		Cash	5,000	
		Accumulated Depreciation—Limousine	21,000	
		Loss on Disposal	2,000	
		Limousine		28,000
		(To record sale of limousine)		
(c)	1/1/03	Limousine (new)	31,000	
		Accumulated Depreciation—Limousine (old)	18,000	
		Loss on Disposal	1,000	
		Limousine (old)		28,000
		Cash		22,000
		(To record exchange of limousines)		
(d)	1/1/03	Limousine (new)*	12,000	
		Accumulated Depreciation—Limousine (old)	18,000	
		Limousine (old)		28,000
		Cash		2,000
		(To record exchange of limousines)		
		*($11,000 + $2,000 − $1,000)		

THE NAVIGATOR

SUMMARY OF STUDY OBJECTIVES

1. *Describe the application of the cost principle to plant assets.* The cost of plant assets includes all expenditures necessary to acquire the asset and make it ready for its intended use. Cost is measured by the cash or cash equivalent price paid.

2. *Explain the concept of depreciation.* Depreciation is the allocation of the cost of a plant asset to expense over its useful (service) life in a rational and systematic manner. Depreciation is not a process of valuation. Nor is it a process that results in an accumulation of cash. Depreciation is caused by wear and tear or by obsolescence.

3. *Compute periodic depreciation using different methods.* There are three depreciation methods:

Method	Effect on Annual Depreciation	Formula
Straight-line	Constant amount	Depreciable cost ÷ Useful life (in years)
Units-of-activity	Varying amount	Depreciation cost per unit × Units of activity during the year
Declining-balance	Decreasing amount	Book value at beginning of year × Declining-balance rate

4. *Describe the procedure for revising periodic depreciation.* Revisions of periodic depreciation are made in present and future periods, not retroactively. The new annual depreciation is found by dividing the depreciable cost at the time of the revision by the remaining useful life.

5. *Distinguish between revenue and capital expenditures, and explain the entries for these expenditures.* Revenue expenditures are incurred to maintain the operating efficiency and expected productive life of the asset. These expenditures are debited to Repair Expense as incurred. Capital expenditures increase the operating efficiency, productive capacity, or expected useful life of the asset. These expenditures are generally debited to the plant asset affected.

6. *Explain how to account for the disposal of a plant asset through retirement, sale, or exchange.* The accounting for disposal of a plant asset through retirement or sale is as follows:

(a) Eliminate the book value of the plant asset at the date of disposal.
(b) Record cash proceeds, if any.
(c) Account for the difference between the book value and the cash proceeds as a gain or loss on disposal.

In accounting for exchanges of similar assets:

(a) Eliminate the book value of the old asset at the date of the exchange.
(b) Record the acquisition cost of the new asset.
(c) Account for the loss or gain, if any, on the old asset:
  (1) If a loss, recognize it immediately.
  (2) If a gain, defer and reduce the cost of the new asset.

7. *Compute periodic depletion of natural resources.* Compute depletion cost per unit by dividing the total cost of the natural resource minus salvage value by the number of units estimated to be in the resource. Then multiply the depletion cost per unit by the number of units extracted and sold.

8. *Contrast the accounting for intangible assets with the accounting for plant assets.* The accounting for intangible assets and plant assets is much the same. One difference is that the term used to describe the write-off of an intangible asset is amortization, rather than depreciation. Also, the amortization of an intangible asset cannot be longer than 40 years. The straight-line method is normally used for amortizing intangible assets.

9. *Indicate how plant assets, natural resources, and intangible assets are reported and analyzed.* Usually plant assets and natural resources are combined under property, plant, and equipment; intangibles are shown separately under intangible assets. Either within the balance sheet or in the notes, the balances of the major classes of assets, such as land, buildings, and equipment, and accumulated depreciation by major classes or in total, should be disclosed. Also, the depreciation and amortization methods used should be described, and the amount of depreciation and amortization expense for the period should be disclosed. The asset turnover ratio measures the productivity of a company's assets in generating sales.

THE NAVIGATOR

Key Term Matching Activity

GLOSSARY

Accelerated-depreciation method Depreciation method that produces higher depreciation expense in the early years than in the later years. (p. 409).

Additions and improvements Costs incurred to increase the operating efficiency, productive capacity, or useful life of a plant asset. (p. 412).

Amortization The allocation of the cost of an intangible asset to expense over its useful life in a systematic and rational manner. (p. 419).

Asset turnover ratio A measure of how efficiently a company uses its assets to generate sales; calculated as net sales divided by average total assets. (p. 424).

Capital expenditures Expenditures that increase the company's investment in productive facilities. (p. 412).

Copyright Exclusive grant from the federal government that allows the owner to reproduce and sell an artistic or published work. (p. 420).

Declining-balance method Depreciation method that applies a constant rate to the declining book value of the asset and produces a decreasing annual depreciation expense over the useful life of the asset. (p. 408).

Depletion The allocation of the cost of a natural resource to expense in a rational and systematic manner over the resource's useful life. (p. 418).

Depreciable cost The cost of a plant asset less its salvage value. (p. 406).

Franchise (license) A contractual arrangement under which the franchisor grants the franchisee the right to sell certain products, render specific services, or use certain trademarks or trade names, usually within a designated geographical area. (p. 421).

Goodwill The value of all favorable attributes that relate to a business enterprise. (p. 421).

Intangible assets Rights, privileges, and competitive advantages that result from the ownership of long-lived assets that do not possess physical substance. (p. 419).

Licenses Operating rights to use public property, granted to a business enterprise by a governmental agency. (p. 421).

Natural resources Assets that consist of standing timber and underground deposits of oil, gas, or minerals. (p. 418).

Ordinary repairs Expenditures to maintain the operating efficiency and productive life of the unit. (p. 412).

Patent An exclusive right issued by the U.S. Patent Office that enables the recipient to manufacture, sell, or otherwise control an invention for a period of 20 years from the date of the grant. (p. 420).

Plant assets Tangible resources that are used in the operations of the business and are not intended for sale to customers. (p. 400).

Research and development (R&D) costs Expenditures that may lead to patents, copyrights, new processes, or new products. (p. 422).

Revenue expenditures Expenditures that are immediately charged against revenues as an expense. (p. 412).

Salvage value An estimate of an asset's value at the end of its useful life. (p. 405).

Straight-line method Depreciation method in which periodic depreciation is the same for each year of the asset's useful life. (p. 406).

Trademark (trade name) A word, phrase, jingle, or symbol that identifies a particular enterprise or product. (p. 420).

Units-of-activity method Depreciation method in which useful life is expressed in terms of the total units of production or use expected from an asset. (p. 407).

Useful life An estimate of the expected productive life, also called service life, of an asset. (p. 405).

Chapter 10 Self-Test

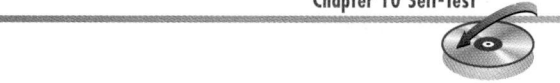

SELF-STUDY QUESTIONS

Answers are at the end of the chapter.

(SO 1) **1.** Erin Danielle Company purchased equipment and incurred the following costs.

Cash price	$24,000
Sales taxes	1,200
Insurance during transit	200
Installation and testing	400
Total costs	$25,800

What amount should be recorded as the cost of the equipment?

a. $24,000.
b. $25,200.
c. $25,400.
d. $25,800.

(SO 2) **2.** Depreciation is a process of:

a. valuation.
b. cost allocation.
c. cash accumulation.
d. appraisal.

(SO 3) **3.** Micah Bartlett Company purchased equipment on January 1, 2001, at a total invoice cost of $400,000. The equipment has an estimated salvage value of $10,000 and an estimated useful life of 5 years. The amount of accumulated depreciation at December 31, 2002, if the straight-line method of depreciation is used, is:

a. $80,000.
b. $160,000.
c. $78,000.
d. $156,000.

4. Ann Torbert purchased a truck for $11,000 on January 1, 2001. The truck will have an estimated salvage value of $1,000 at the end of 5 years. Using the units-of-activity method, the balance in accumulated depreciation at December 31, 2002, can be computed by the following formula: (SO 3)

a. ($11,000 ÷ Total estimated activity) × Units of activity for 2002.
b. ($10,000 ÷ Total estimated activity) × Units of activity for 2002.
c. ($11,000 ÷ Total estimated activity) × Units of activity for 2001 and 2002.
d. ($10,000 ÷ Total estimated activity) × Units of activity for 2001 and 2002.

5. When there is a change in estimated depreciation: (SO 4)

a. previous depreciation should be corrected.
b. current and future years' depreciation should be revised.
c. only future years' depreciation should be revised.
d. None of the above.

6. Additions to plant assets are: (SO 5)

a. revenue expenditures.
b. debited to a Repair Expense account.
c. debited to a Purchases account.
d. capital expenditures.

7. Schopenhauer Company exchanged an old machine, with a book value of $39,000 and a fair market value of $35,000, and paid $10,000 cash for a similar new machine. At what amount should the machine acquired in the exchange be recorded on Schopenhauer's books? (SO 6)

a. $45,000.
b. $46,000.
c. $49,000.
d. $50,000.

(SO 6) 8. In exchanges of similar assets:
a. neither gains nor losses are recognized immediately.
b. gains, but not losses, are recognized immediately.
c. losses, but not gains, are recognized immediately.
d. both gains and losses are recognized immediately.

(SO 7) 9. Maggie Sharrer Company expects to extract 20 million tons of coal from a mine that cost $12 million. If no salvage value is expected, and 2 million tons are mined and sold in the first year, the entry to record depletion will include a:
a. debit to Accumulated Depletion of $2,000,000.
b. credit to Depletion Expense of $1,200,000.
c. debit to Depletion Expense of $1,200,000.
d. credit to Accumulated Depletion of $2,000,000.

(SO 8, 9) 10. Martha Beyerlein Company incurred $150,000 of research and development costs in its laboratory to develop a patent granted on January 2, 2002. On July 31, 2002, Beyerlein paid $35,000 for legal fees in a successful defense of the patent. The total amount debited to Patents through July 31, 2002, should be:
a. $150,000.
b. $35,000.
c. $185,000.
d. some other amount.

11. Indicate which of the following statements is *true*. (SO 9)
a. Since intangible assets lack physical substance, they need be disclosed only in the notes to the financial statements.
b. Goodwill should be reported as a contra-account in the owner's equity section.
c. Totals of major classes of assets can be shown in the balance sheet, with asset details disclosed in the notes to the financial statements.
d. Intangible assets are typically combined with plant assets and natural resources and shown in the property, plant, and equipment section.

THE NAVIGATOR

QUESTIONS

1. Joe Barone is uncertain about the applicability of the cost principle to plant assets. Explain the principle to Joe.
2. What are some examples of land improvements?
3. Sam-Ho Company acquires the land and building owned by Corrs Company. What types of costs may be incurred to make the asset ready for its intended use if Sam-Ho Company wants to use (a) only the land, and (b) both the land and the building?
4. In a recent newspaper release, the president of Smashing Pumpkins Company asserted that something has to be done about depreciation. The president said, "Depreciation does not come close to accumulating the cash needed to replace the asset at the end of its useful life." What is your response to the president?
5. Thomas is studying for the next accounting examination. He asks your help on two questions: (a) What is salvage value? (b) Is salvage value used in determining depreciable cost under each depreciation method? Answer Thomas's questions.
6. Contrast the straight-line method and the units-of-activity method as to (a) useful life, and (b) the pattern of periodic depreciation over useful life.
7. Contrast the effects of the three depreciation methods on annual depreciation expense.
8. In the fourth year of an asset's 5-year useful life, the company decides that the asset will have a 6-year service life. How should the revision of depreciation be recorded? Why?
9. Distinguish between revenue expenditures and capital expenditures during useful life.
10. How is a gain or loss on the sale of a plant asset computed?
11. Lopez Corporation owns a machine that is fully depreciated but is still being used. How should Lopez account for this asset and report it in the financial statements?
12. When similar assets are exchanged, how is the gain or loss on disposal computed?
13. Lim Refrigeration Company trades in an old machine on a new model when the fair market value of the old machine is greater than its book value. Should Lim recognize a gain on disposal? If the fair market value of the old machine is less than its book value, should Lim recognize a loss on disposal?
14. Moon Company experienced a gain on disposal when exchanging similar machines. In accordance with generally accepted accounting principles, the gain was not recognized. How will Moon's future financial statements be affected by not recognizing the gain?
15. What are natural resources, and what are their distinguishing characteristics?
16. Explain what depletion is and how it is computed.
17. What are the similarities and differences between the terms depreciation, depletion, and amortization?
18. Guen Company hires an accounting intern who says that intangible assets should always be amortized over their legal lives. Is the intern correct? Explain.
19. Goodwill has been defined as the value of all favorable attributes that relate to a business enterprise. What types of attributes could result in goodwill?
20. Clint Eastwood, a business major, is working on a case problem for one of his classes. In the case problem, the company needs to raise cash to market a new product it developed. Jack Gleason, an engineering major, takes one look at the company's balance sheet and says, "This company has an awful lot of goodwill. Why don't you recommend that they sell some of it to raise cash?" How should Clint respond to Jack?
21. Under what conditions is goodwill recorded?

22. Often research and development costs provide companies with benefits that last a number of years. (For example, these costs can lead to the development of a patent that will increase the company's income for many years.) However, generally accepted accounting principles require that such costs be recorded as an expense when incurred. Why?

23. **McDonald's Corporation** reports total average assets of $14.5 billion and net sales of $9.8 billion. What is the company's asset turnover ratio?

24. Overheu Corporation and Orlow Corporation operate in the same industry. Overheu uses the straight-line method to account for depreciation; Orlow uses an accelerated method. Explain what complications might arise in trying to compare the results of these two companies.

25. Lucille Corporation uses straight-line depreciation for financial reporting purposes but an accelerated method for tax purposes. Is it acceptable to use different methods for the two purposes? What is Lucille's motivation for doing this?

26. You are comparing two companies in the same industry. You have determined that Wow Corp. depreciates its plant assets over a 40-year life, whereas Wooster Corp. depreciates its plant assets over a 20-year life. Discuss the implications this has for comparing the results of the two companies.

27. Pizner Company is doing significant work to revitalize its warehouses. It is not sure whether it should capitalize these costs or expense them. What are the implications for current-year net income and future net income of expensing versus capitalizing these costs?

BRIEF EXERCISES

Determine the cost of land. (SO 1)

BE10-1 The following expenditures were incurred by Gene Shumway Company in purchasing land: cash price $50,000, accrued taxes $3,000, attorneys' fees $2,500, real estate broker's commission $2,000, and clearing and grading $3,500. What is the cost of the land?

Determine the cost of a truck. (SO 1)

BE10-2 Shirley Basler Company incurs the following expenditures in purchasing a truck: cash price $25,000, accident insurance $2,000, sales taxes $900, motor vehicle license $100, and painting and lettering $400. What is the cost of the truck?

Compute straight-line depreciation. (SO 3)

BE10-3 Graig Mabasa Company acquires a delivery truck at a cost of $30,000. The truck is expected to have a salvage value of $2,000 at the end of its 4-year useful life. Compute annual depreciation for the first and second years using the straight-line method.

Compute depreciation and evaluate treatment. (SO 3)

BE10-4 Olympic Company purchased land and a building on January 1, 2002. Management's best estimate of the value of the land was $100,000 and of the building $200,000. But management told the accounting department to record the land at $220,000 and the building at $80,000. The building is being depreciated on a straight-line basis over 20 years with no salvage value. Why do you suppose management requested this accounting treatment? Is it ethical?

Compute declining-balance depreciation. (SO 3)

BE10-5 Depreciation information for Graig Mabasa Company is given in BE10-3. Assuming the declining-balance depreciation rate is double the straight-line rate, compute annual depreciation for the first and second years under the declining-balance method.

Compute depreciation using the units-of-activity method. (SO 3)

BE10-6 Jerry Englehart Taxi Service uses the units-of-activity method in computing depreciation on its taxicabs. Each cab is expected to be driven 150,000 miles. Taxi no. 10 cost $36,500 and is expected to have a salvage value of $500. Taxi no. 10 is driven 30,000 miles in year 1 and 20,000 miles in year 2. Compute the depreciation for each year.

Compute revised depreciation. (SO 4)

BE10-7 On January 1, 2002, the Jose Villaluz Company ledger shows Equipment $32,000 and Accumulated Depreciation $9,000. The depreciation resulted from using the straight-line method with a useful life of 10 years and salvage value of $2,000. On this date, the company concludes that the equipment has a remaining useful life of only 5 years with the same salvage value. Compute the revised annual depreciation.

Prepare entries for disposal by retirement. (SO 6)

BE10-8 Prepare journal entries to record the following.

(a) Ruiz Company retires its delivery equipment, which cost $41,000. Accumulated depreciation is also $41,000 on this delivery equipment. No salvage value is received.

(b) Assume the same information as (a), except that accumulated depreciation for Ruiz Company is $39,000, instead of $41,000.

Prepare entries for disposal by sale. (SO 6)

BE10-9 Welch Company sells office equipment on September 30, 2002, for $20,000 cash. The office equipment originally cost $72,000 and as of January 1, 2002, had accumulated depreciation of $42,000. Depreciation for the first 9 months of 2002 is $6,000. Prepare the journal entries to **(a)** update depreciation to September 30, 2002, and **(b)** record the sale of the equipment.

BE10-10 Concord Company exchanges old delivery equipment for similar new delivery equipment. The book value of the old delivery equipment is $31,000 (cost $61,000 less accumulated depreciation $30,000). Its fair market value is $21,000, and cash of $5,000 is paid. Prepare the entry to record the exchange.

Prepare entry for disposal by exchange.
(SO 6)

BE10-11 Assume the same information as BE10-10, except that the fair market value of the old delivery equipment is $40,000. Prepare the entry to record the exchange.

Prepare entry for disposal by exchange.
(SO 6)

BE10-12 Cuono Mining Co. purchased for $7 million a mine that is estimated to have 28 million tons of ore and no salvage value. In the first year, 4 million tons of ore are extracted and sold.

Prepare depletion expense entry and balance sheet presentation for natural resources.
(SO 7)

(a) Prepare the journal entry to record depletion expense for the first year.
(b) Show how this mine is reported on the balance sheet at the end of the first year.

BE10-13 Popper Company purchases a patent for $180,000 on January 2, 2002. Its estimated useful life is 10 years.

Prepare patent expense entry and balance sheet presentation for intangibles.
(SO 8)

(a) Prepare the journal entry to record patent expense for the first year.
(b) Show how this patent is reported on the balance sheet at the end of the first year.

BE10-14 Information related to plant assets, natural resources, and intangibles at the end of 2002 for Joker Company is as follows: buildings $900,000; accumulated depreciation—buildings $650,000; goodwill $410,000; coal mine $300,000; accumulated depletion—coal mine $108,000. Prepare a partial balance sheet of Joker Company for these items.

Classify long-lived assets on balance sheet.
(SO 9)

BE10-15 In its 1998 annual report **McDonald's Corporation** reported beginning total assets of $18.2 billion; ending total assets of $19.8 billion; property, plant, and equipment (at cost) of $20.1 billion; and net sales of $12.4 billion. Compute McDonald's asset turnover ratio.

Analyze long-lived assets.
(SO 9)

EXERCISES

E10-1 The following expenditures relating to plant assets were made by John Kosinski Company during the first 2 months of 2002.

Determine cost of plant acquisitions.
(SO 1)

1. Paid $5,000 of accrued taxes at time plant site was acquired.
2. Paid $200 insurance to cover possible accident loss on new factory machinery while the machinery was in transit.
3. Paid $850 sales taxes on new delivery truck.
4. Paid $17,500 for parking lots and driveways on new plant site.
5. Paid $250 to have company name and advertising slogan painted on new delivery truck.
6. Paid $8,000 for installation of new factory machinery.
7. Paid $900 for one-year accident insurance policy on new delivery truck.
8. Paid $75 motor vehicle license fee on the new truck.

Instructions

(a) Explain the application of the cost principle in determining the acquisition cost of plant assets.
(b) List the numbers of the foregoing transactions, and opposite each indicate the account title to which each expenditure should be debited.

E10-2 On March 1, 2002, Roy Orbis Company acquired real estate on which it planned to construct a small office building. The company paid $80,000 in cash. An old warehouse on the property was razed at a cost of $6,600; the salvaged materials were sold for $1,700. Additional expenditures before construction began included $1,100 attorney's fee for work concerning the land purchase, $4,000 real estate broker's fee, $7,800 architect's fee, and $14,000 to put in driveways and a parking lot.

Determine acquisition costs on land.
(SO 1)

Instructions

(a) Determine the amount to be reported as the cost of the land.
(b) For each cost not used in part (a), indicate the account to be debited.

Compute depreciation under units-of-activity method.
(SO 3)

E10-3 Always-Late Bus Lines uses the units-of-activity method in depreciating its buses. One bus was purchased on January 1, 2002, at a cost of $128,000. Over its 4-year useful life, the bus is expected to be driven 100,000 miles. Salvage value is expected to be $8,000.

Instructions

(a) Compute the depreciation cost per unit.
(b) Prepare a depreciation schedule assuming actual mileage was: 2002, 26,000; 2003, 32,000; 2004, 25,000; and 2005, 17,000.

Determine depreciation for partial periods.
(SO 3)

E10-4 Elvis Costello Company purchased a new machine on October 1, 2002, at a cost of $89,000. The company estimated that the machine will have a salvage value of $12,000. The machine is expected to be used for 70,000 working hours during its 5-year life.

Instructions

Compute the depreciation expense under the following methods for the year indicated.
(a) Straight-line for 2002.
(b) Units-of-activity for 2002, assuming machine usage was 1,700 hours.
(c) Declining-balance using double the straight-line rate for 2002 and 2003.

Compute revised annual depreciation.
(SO 3, 4)

E10-5 Lindy Rig, the new controller of Bellingham Company, has reviewed the expected useful lives and salvage values of selected depreciable assets at the beginning of 2002. Her findings are as follows.

Type of Asset	Date Acquired	Cost	Accumulated Depreciation 1/1/02	Useful Life in Years		Salvage Value	
				Old	**Proposed**	**Old**	**Proposed**
Building	1/1/96	$800,000	$114,000	40	50	$40,000	$70,000
Warehouse	1/1/99	100,000	11,400	25	20	5,000	3,600

All assets are depreciated by the straight-line method. Bellingham Company uses a calendar year in preparing annual financial statements. After discussion, management has agreed to accept Lindy's proposed changes.

Instructions

(a) Compute the revised annual depreciation on each asset in 2002. (Show computations.)
(b) Prepare the entry (or entries) to record depreciation on the building in 2002.

Journalize entries for disposal of plant assets.
(SO 6)

E10-6 Presented below are selected transactions at Beck Company for 2002.

Jan. 1 Retired a piece of machinery that was purchased on January 1, 1992. The machine cost $62,000 on that date. It had a useful life of 10 years with no salvage value.

June 30 Sold a computer that was purchased on January 1, 1999. The computer cost $35,000. It had a useful life of 7 years with no salvage value. The computer was sold for $22,000.

Dec. 31 Discarded a delivery truck that was purchased on January 1, 1998. The truck cost $30,000. It was depreciated based on a 6-year useful life with a $3,000 salvage value.

5yrs
30,000-3,000 / 6 Depr/yr. X 5 = Acc. 27000

Instructions

Journalize all entries required on the above dates, including entries to update depreciation, where applicable, on assets disposed of. Beck Company uses straight-line depreciation. (Assume depreciation is up to date as of December 31, 2001.)

Journalize entries for exchange of similar assets.
(SO 6)

E10-7 Presented below are two independent transactions.

1. Noyes Co. exchanged old trucks (cost $64,000 less $22,000 accumulated depreciation) plus cash of $17,000 for new trucks. The old trucks had a fair market value of $40,000.
2. Salzer Inc. trades its used machine (cost $10,000 less $5,000 accumulated depreciation) for a new machine. In addition to exchanging the old machine (which had a fair market value of $9,000), Salzer also paid cash of $2,000.

Instructions

(a) Prepare the entry to record the exchange of similar assets by Noyes Co.
(b) Prepare the entry to record the exchange of similar assets by Salzer Inc.

Journalize entries for the exchange of similar plant assets.
(SO 6)

E10-8 Mueller Company exchanges similar equipment with Logan Company. Also Sun Company exchanges similar equipment with Moon Company. The following information pertains to these two exchanges.

	Mueller Co.	Sun Co.
Equipment (cost)	$28,000	$22,000
Accumulated depreciation	21,000	5,000
Fair market value of equipment	12,000	13,000
Cash paid	2,000	–0–

Instructions
Prepare the journal entries to record the exchange on the books of Mueller Company and Sun Company.

Journalize entries for the exchange of similar plant assets.
(SO 6)

E10-9 Abner's Delivery Company and Wainwrights' Express Delivery exchanged similar delivery trucks on January 1, 2002. Abner's truck cost $20,000. It has accumulated depreciation of $13,000 and a fair market value of $4,000. Wainwrights' truck cost $10,000. It has accumulated depreciation of $8,000 and a fair market value of $4,000.

Instructions
(a) Journalize the exchange for Abner's Delivery Company.
(b) Journalize the exchange for Wainwright's Express Delivery.

Journalize entries for natural resources depletion.
(SO 7)

E10-10 On July 1, 2002, Phillips Inc. invested $320,000 in a mine estimated to have 800,000 tons of ore of uniform grade. During the last 6 months of 2002, 100,000 tons of ore were mined and sold.

Instructions

(a) Prepare the journal entry to record depletion expense.
(b) Assume that the 100,000 tons of ore were mined, but only 80,000 units were sold. How are the costs applicable to the 20,000 unsold units reported?

Prepare adjusting entries for amortization.
(SO 8)

E10-11 The following are selected 2002 transactions of Graf Corporation.

Jan. 1	Purchased a small company and recorded goodwill of $180,000. The goodwill has a useful life of 55 years.
May 1	Purchased for $45,000 a patent with an estimated useful life of 5 years and a legal life of 20 years.

Instructions
Prepare all adjusting entries at December 31 to record amortization required by the events above.

Prepare entries to set up appropriate accounts for different intangibles; amortize intangible assets.
(SO 8)

E10-12 Collins Company, organized in 2002, has the following transactions related to intangible assets.

1/2/02	Purchased patent (7-year life)	$490,000
4/1/02	Goodwill purchased (indefinite life)	360,000
7/1/02	10-year franchise; expiration date 7/1/2012	420,000
9/1/02	Research and development costs	185,000

Instructions
Prepare the necessary entries to record these intangibles. All costs incurred were for cash. Make the entries as of December 31, 2002, recording any necessary amortization and reflecting all balances accurately as of that date.

Calculate asset turnover ratio.
(SO 9)

E10-13 During 2001 Onyinke Corporation reported net sales of $3,500,000 and net income of $1,500,000. Its balance sheet reported total assets of $1,400,000.

Instructions
Calculate the asset turnover ratio.

PROBLEMS: SET A

Determine acquisition costs of land and building.
(SO 1)

P10-1A Mendoza Company was organized on January 1. During the first year of operations, the following plant asset expenditures and receipts were recorded in random order.

Debits

1. Cost of filling and grading the land	$ 4,000
2. Full payment to building contractor	700,000
3. Real estate taxes on land paid for the current year	5,000
4. Cost of real estate purchased as a plant site (land $100,000 and building $45,000)	145,000
5. Excavation costs for new building	20,000
6. Architect's fees on building plans	10,000
7. Accrued real estate taxes paid at time of purchase of real estate	2,000
8. Cost of parking lots and driveways	14,000
9. Cost of demolishing building to make land suitable for construction of new building	15,000
	$915,000

Credits

10. Proceeds from salvage of demolished building	$ 3,500

Totals
Land $162,500
Building $730,000

Instructions

Analyze the foregoing transactions using the following column headings. Insert the number of each transaction in the Item space, and insert the amounts in the appropriate columns. For amounts entered in the Other Accounts column, also indicate the account titles.

Item	Land	Building	Other Accounts

Compute depreciation under different methods.
(SO 3)

P10-2A In recent years, Waterfront Transportation purchased three used buses. Because of frequent turnover in the accounting department, a different accountant selected the depreciation method for each bus, and various methods were selected. Information concerning the buses is summarized below.

Bus	Acquired	Cost	Salvage Value	Useful Life in Years	Depreciation Method
1	1/1/00	$ 86,000	$ 6,000	4	Straight-line
2	1/1/00	140,000	10,000	5	Declining-balance
3	1/1/01	80,000	8,000	5	Units-of-activity

For the declining-balance method, the company uses the double-declining rate. For the units-of-activity method, total miles are expected to be 120,000. Actual miles of use in the first 3 years were: 2001, 24,000; 2002, 34,000; and 2003, 30,000.

Instructions

(a) Compute the amount of accumulated depreciation on each bus at December 31, 2002.
(b) If bus no. 2 was purchased on April 1 instead of January 1, what is the depreciation expense for this bus in (1) 2000 and (2) 2001?

Compute depreciation under different methods.
(SO 3)

P10-3A On January 1, 2002, Khan Company purchased the following two machines for use in its production process.

Machine A: The cash price of this machine was $30,000. Related expenditures included: sales tax $1,500, shipping costs $150, insurance during shipping $80, installation and testing costs $70, and $100 of oil and lubricants to be used with the machinery during its first year of operations. Khan estimates that the useful life of the machine is 5 years with a $5,000 salvage value remaining at the end of that time period. Assume that the straight-line method of depreciation is used.

Machine B: The recorded cost of this machine was $60,000. Khan estimates that the useful life of the machine is 4 years with a $5,000 salvage value remaining at the end of that time period.

Instructions

(a) Prepare the following for Machine A.

(1) The journal entry to record its purchase on January 1, 2002.

(2) The journal entry to record annual depreciation at December 31, 2002.

(b) Calculate the amount of depreciation expense that Khan should record for machine B each year of its useful life under the following assumptions.

(1) Khan uses the straight-line method of depreciation.

(2) Khan uses the declining-balance method. The rate used is twice the straight-line rate.

(3) Khan uses the units-of-activity method and estimates that the useful life of the machine is 125,000 units. Actual usage is as follows: 2002, 45,000 units; 2003, 35,000 units; 2004, 25,000 units; 2005, 20,000 units.

(c) Which method used to calculate depreciation on machine B reports the highest amount of depreciation expense in year 1 (2002)? The highest amount in year 4 (2005)? The highest total amount over the 4-year period?

Calculate revisions to depreciation expense.
(SO 3, 4)

P10-4A At the beginning of 2000, Duncan Company acquired equipment costing $60,000. It was estimated that this equipment would have a useful life of 6 years and a residual value of $6,000 at that time. The straight-line method of depreciation was considered the most appropriate to use with this type of equipment. Depreciation is to be recorded at the end of each year.

During 2002 (the third year of the equipment's life), the company's engineers reconsidered their expectations, and estimated that the equipment's useful life would probably be 7 years (in total) instead of 6 years. The estimated residual value was not changed at that time. However, during 2005 the estimated residual value was reduced to $4,400.

Instructions

Indicate how much depreciation expense should be recorded each year for this equipment, by completing the following table.

Year	Depreciation Expense	Accumulated Depreciation
2000		
2001		
2002		
2003		
2004		
2005		
2006		

Journalize a series of equipment transactions related to purchase, sale, retirement, and depreciation.
(SO 6, 9)

P10-5A At December 31, 2002, Santa Fe Company reported the following as plant assets.

Land		$ 4,000,000
Buildings	$28,500,000	
Less: Accumulated depreciation—buildings	12,100,000	16,400,000
Equipment	48,000,000	
Less: Accumulated depreciation—equipment	5,000,000	43,000,000
Total plant assets		$63,400,000

During 2003, the following selected cash transactions occurred.

April 1	Purchased land for $2,630,000.
May 1	Sold equipment that cost $570,000 when purchased on January 1, 1999. The equipment was sold for $350,000.
June 1	Sold land purchased on June 1, 1993, for $1,800,000. The land cost $200,000.
July 1	Purchased equipment for $2,000,000.
Dec. 31	Retired equipment that cost $500,000 when purchased on December 31, 1993. No salvage value was received.

Instructions

(a) Journalize the above transactions. The company uses straight-line depreciation for buildings and equipment. The buildings are estimated to have a 50-year life and no salvage value. The equipment is estimated to have a 10-year useful life and no salvage value. Update depreciation on assets disposed of at the time of sale or retirement.

(b) Record adjusting entries for depreciation for 2003.

(c) Prepare the plant assets section of Santa Fe's balance sheet at December 31, 2003.

(b) Depreciation Expense—building $570,000; equipment $4,793,000
(c) Total plant assets $62,075,000

Record disposals.
(SO 6)

P10-6A Elliot Co. has office furniture that cost $75,000 and that has been depreciated $48,000. Record the disposal under the following assumptions.

(a) It was scrapped as having no value.
(b) It was sold for $21,000.
(c) It was sold for $61,000.
(d) It was exchanged for similar office furniture. The old office furniture has a fair market value of $46,000, and $8,000 was paid.
(e) It was exchanged for similar office furniture. The old office furniture has a fair market value of $25,000, and $29,000 was paid.

Prepare entries to record transactions related to acquisition and amortization of intangibles; prepare the intangible assets section.
(SO 8, 9)

P10-7A The intangible assets section of Toribio Company at December 31, 2002, is presented below.

Patent ($70,000 cost less $7,000 amortization)	$63,000
Copyright ($48,000 cost less $19,200 amortization)	28,800
Total	$91,800

The patent was acquired in January 2002 and has a useful life of 10 years. The copyright was acquired in January 1999 and also has a useful life of 10 years. The following cash transactions may have affected intangible assets during 2000.

Jan. 2	Paid $27,000 legal costs to successfully defend the patent against infringement by another company.
Jan.–June	Developed a new product, incurring $140,000 in research and development costs. A patent was granted for the product on July 1. Its useful life is equal to its legal life.
Sept. 1	Paid $80,000 to an extremely large defensive lineman to appear in commercials advertising the company's products. The commercials will air in September and October.
Oct. 1	Acquired a copyright for $120,000. The copyright has a useful life of 50 years.

(b) Amortization Expense—Patents $10,000
Amortization Expense—Copyrights $5,550
(c) Total intangible assets $223,250

Instructions

(a) Prepare journal entries to record the transactions above.
(b) Prepare journal entries to record the 2003 amortization expense.
(c) Prepare the intangible assets section of the balance sheet at December 31, 2003.

Prepare entries to correct for errors made in recording and amortizing intangible assets.
(SO 8)

P10-8A Due to rapid turnover in the accounting department, a number of transactions involving intangible assets were improperly recorded by the Henry Company in 2002.

1. Henry developed a new manufacturing process, incurring research and development costs of $186,900. The company also purchased a patent for $39,100. In early January, Henry capitalized $226,000 as the cost of the patents. Patent amortization expense of $11,300 was recorded based on a 20-year useful life.
2. On July 1, 2002, Henry purchased a small company and as a result acquired goodwill of $92,000. Henry recorded a half-year's amortization in 2002, based on a 50-year life ($920 amortization).

1. R&D $186,900
2. Amortization Expense—Goodwill $230

Instructions

Prepare all journal entries necessary to correct any errors made during 2002. Assume the books have not yet been closed for 2002.

Calculate and comment on asset turnover ratio.
(SO 9)

P10-9A Samone Company and Baxter Corporation, two corporations of roughly the same size, are both involved in the manufacture of in-line skates. Each company depreciates its plant assets using the straight-line approach. An investigation of their financial statements reveals the following information.

	Samone Co.	Baxter Corp.
Net income	$ 700,000	$1,000,000
Sales	1,400,000	1,300,000
Total assets	2,500,000	2,000,000
Plant assets	1,800,000	1,000,000

Instructions

(a) For each company, calculate the asset turnover ratio.
(b) Based on your calculations in part (a), comment on the relative effectiveness of the two companies in using their assets to generate sales and produce net income.

PROBLEMS: SET B

Determine acquisition costs of land and building.
(SO 1)

P10-1B Leno Company was organized on January 1. During the first year of operations, the following plant asset expenditures and receipts were recorded in random order.

Debits

1. Accrued real estate taxes paid at time of purchase of real estate	$ 2,000
2. Real estate taxes on land paid for the current year	3,000
3. Full payment to building contractor	600,000
4. Excavation costs for new building	20,000
5. Cost of real estate purchased as a plant site (land $100,000 and building $25,000)	125,000
6. Cost of parking lots and driveways	15,000
7. Architect's fees on building plans	10,000
8. Installation cost of fences around property	4,000
9. Cost of demolishing building to make land suitable for construction of new building	13,000
	$792,000

Credit

10. Proceeds from salvage of demolished building	$ 2,500

Instructions

Analyze the foregoing tranactions using the following column headings. Insert the number of each transaction in the Item space, and insert the amounts in the appropriate columns. For amounts entered in the Other Accounts column, also indicate the account title.

Item	Land	Building	Other Accounts

Totals
Land $137,500
Building $630,000

Compute depreciation under different methods.
(SO 3)

P10-2B In recent years, Letterman Company purchased three machines. Because of heavy turnover in the accounting department, a different accountant was in charge of selecting the depreciation method for each machine, and various methods were selected. Information concerning the machines is summarized below.

Machine	Acquired	Cost	Salvage Value	Useful Life in Years	Depreciation Method
1	1/1/99	$96,000	$ 6,000	10	Straight-line
2	1/1/00	60,000	10,000	8	Declining-balance
3	11/1/02	66,000	6,000	6	Units-of-activity

For the declining-balance method, the company uses the double-declining rate. For the units-of-activity method, total machine hours are expected to be 24,000. Actual hours of use in the first 3 years were: 2002, 1,000; 2003, 4,500; and 2004, 5,000.

Instructions

(a) Compute the amount of accumulated depreciation on each machine at December 31, 2002.
(b) If machine 2 had been purchased on April 1 instead of January 1, what would be the depreciation expense for this machine in (1) 2000 and (2) 2001?

Compute depreciation under different methods.
(SO 3)

P10-3B On January 1, 2002, Gaudinez Company purchased the following two machines for use in its production process.

Machine A: The cash price of this machine was $35,000. Related expenditures included: sales tax $1,800, shipping costs $175, insurance during shipping $75, installation and testing costs $50, and $90 of oil and lubricants to be used with the machinery during its first year of operation. Gaudinez estimates that the useful life of the machine is 4 years with a $5,000 salvage value remaining at the end of that time period.

Machine B: The recorded cost of this machine was $80,000. Gaudinez estimates that the useful life of the machine is 4 years with a $5,000 salvage value remaining at the end of that time period.

Instructions

(a) Prepare the following for Machine A.

(a) (2) $8,025

(1) The journal entry to record its purchase on January 1, 2002.
(2) The journal entry to record annual depreciation at December 31, 2002, assuming the straight-line method of depreciation is used.

(b) Calculate the amount of depreciation expense that Gaudinez should record for machine B each year of its useful life under the following assumption.
(1) Gaudinez uses the straight-line method of depreciation.
(2) Gaudinez uses the declining-balance method. The rate used is twice the straight-line rate.
(3) Gaudinez uses the units-of-activity method and estimates the useful life of the machine is 25,000 units. Actual usage is as follows: 2002, 6,500 units; 2003, 7,500 units; 2004, 6,000 units; 2005, 5,000 units.

(c) Which method used to calculate depreciation on machine B reports the lowest amount of depreciation expense in year 1 (2002)? The lowest amount in year 4 (2005)? The lowest total amount over the 4-year period?

Calculate revisions to depreciation expense.
(SO 3, 4)

P10-4B At the beginning of 2000, Boenes Company acquired equipment costing $40,000. It was estimated that this equipment would have a useful life of 6 years and a residual value of $4,000 at that time. The straight-line method of depreciation was considered the most appropriate to use with this type of equipment. Depreciation is to be recorded at the end of each year.

During 2002 (the third year of the equipment's life), the company's engineers reconsidered their expectations, and estimated that the equipment's useful life would probably be 7 years (in total) instead of 6 years. The estimated residual value was not changed at that time. However, during 2005 the estimated residual value was reduced to $2,400.

Instructions

Indicate how much depreciation expense should be recorded for this equipment each year by completing the following table.

Year	Depreciation Expense	Accumulated Depreciation
2000		
2001		
2002		
2003		
2004		
2005		
2006		

2006 depreciation expense, $5,600

Journalize a series of equipment transactions related to purchase, sale, retirement, and depreciation.
(SO 6, 9)

P10-5B At December 31, 2002, Hamsmith Company reported the following as plant assets.

Land		$ 3,000,000
Buildings	$26,500,000	
Less: Accumulated depreciation—buildings	12,100,000	14,400,000
Equipment	40,000,000	
Less: Accumulated depreciation—equipment	5,000,000	35,000,000
Total plant assets		$52,400,000

During 2003, the following selected cash transactions occurred.

April 1	Purchased land for $2,200,000.
May 1	Sold equipment that cost $540,000 when purchased on January 1, 1999. The equipment was sold for $360,000.
June 1	Sold land purchased on June 1, 1993, for $1,800,000. The land cost $500,000.
July 1	Purchased equipment for $1,400,000.
Dec. 31	Retired equipment that cost $500,000 when purchased on December 31, 1993. No salvage value was received.

Instructions

(a) Journalize the above transactions. Hamsmith uses straight-line depreciation for buildings and equipment. The buildings are estimated to have a 50-year useful life and no salvage value. The equipment is estimated to have a 10-year useful life and no salvage value. Update depreciation on assets disposed of at the time of sale or retirement.
(b) Record adjusting entries for depreciation for 2003.
(c) Prepare the plant assets section of Hamsmith's balance sheet at December 31, 2003.

(b) Depreciation Expense—Building $530,000; Equipment $3,966,000
(c) Total plant assets $50,630,000

Record disposals.
(SO 6)

P10-6B Express Co. has delivery equipment that cost $45,000 and that has been depreciated $20,000. Record the disposal under the following assumptions.

(a) It was scrapped as having no value.
(b) It was sold for $31,000.
(c) It was sold for $18,000.
(d) It was exchanged for similar delivery equipment. The old delivery equipment has a fair market value of $12,000, and $32,000 was paid.
(e) It was exchanged for similar delivery equipment. The old delivery equipment has a fair market value of $35,000, and $9,000 was paid.

Prepare entries to record transactions related to acquisition and amortization of intangibles; prepare the intangible assets section.
(SO 8, 9)

P10-7B The intangible assets section of Zevon Company at December 31, 2002, is presented below.

Patent ($60,000 cost less $6,000 amortization)	$54,000
Copyright ($36,000 cost less $14,400 amortization)	21,600
Total	$75,600

The patent was acquired in January 2002 and has a useful life of 10 years. The copyright was acquired in January 1999 and also has a useful life of 10 years. The following cash transactions may have affected intangible assets during 2003.

Jan. 2	Paid $27,000 legal costs to successfully defend the patent against infringement by another company.
Jan.–June	Developed a new product, incurring $140,000 in research and development costs. A patent was granted for the product on July 1. Its useful life is equal to its legal life.
Sept. 1	Paid $60,000 to a quarterback to appear in commercials advertising the company's products. The commercials will air in September and October.
Oct. 1	Acquired a copyright for $40,000. The copyright has a useful life of 50 years.

Instructions

(a) Prepare journal entries to record the transactions above.
(b) Prepare journal entries to record the 2003 amortization expense for intangible assets.
(c) Prepare the intangible assets section of the balance sheet at December 31, 2003.
(d) Prepare the note to the financials on Zevon's intangibles as of December 31, 2003.

(b) Amortization Expense—Patents $9,000; Amortization Expense—Copyrights $3,850
(c) Total intangible assets, $129,750

Prepare entries to correct errors made in recording and amortizing intangible assets.
(SO 8)

P10-8B Due to rapid turnover in the accounting department, a number of transactions involving intangible assets were improperly recorded by Lee Company in 2002.

1. Lee developed a new manufacturing process, incurring research and development costs of $85,000. The company also purchased a patent for $37,000. In early January, Lee capitalized $122,000 as the cost of the patents. Patent amortization expense of $6,100 was recorded based on a 20-year useful life.
2. On July 1, 2002, Lee purchased a small company and as a result acquired goodwill of $80,000. Lee recorded a half-year's amortization in 2002, based on a 50-year life ($800 amortization).

Instructions

Prepare all journal entries necessary to correct any errors made during 2002. Assume the books have not yet been closed for 2002.

R&D $85,000
Amortization Expense—Goodwill $200

Calculate and comment on asset turnover ratio.
(SO 9)

P10-9B Croix Corporation and Marais Corporation, two corporations of roughly the same size, are both involved in the manufacture of canoes and sea kayaks. Each company depreciates its plant assets using the straight-line approach. An investigation of their financial statements reveals the following information.

	Croix Corp.	Marais Corp.
Net income	$ 400,000	$ 600,000
Sales	1,600,000	1,350,000
Total assets	2,000,000	1,500,000
Plant assets	1,500,000	800,000

Instructions

(a) Croix Corp. .80 times

(a) For each company, calculate the asset turnover ratio.
(b) Based on your calculations in part (a), comment on the relative effectiveness of the two companies in using their assets to generate sales and produce net income.

BROADENING YOUR PERSPECTIVE

FINANCIAL REPORTING AND ANALYSIS

FINANCIAL REPORTING AND ANALYSIS: Lands' End, Inc.

BYP10-1 The financial statements and the Notes to Consolidated Financial Statements of **Lands' End, Inc.** are presented in Appendix A.

Instructions

Refer to Lands' End's financial statements and answer the following questions.

(a) What was the total cost and book value of property, plant, and equipment at January 28, 2000?
(b) What method or methods of depreciation are used by the company for financial reporting purposes?
(c) What was the amount of depreciation and amortization expense for each of the three years 1998–2000?
(d) Using the statement of cash flows, what is the amount of additions to properties (capital additions) in 2000 and 1999?
(e) Where does the company disclose its intangible assets, and what types of intangibles did it have at January 28, 2000?

COMPARATIVE ANALYSIS PROBLEM: Lands' End vs. Abercrombie & Fitch

BYP10-2 **Lands' End's** financial statements are presented in Appendix A. **Abercrombie & Fitch's** financial statements are presented in Appendix B.

Instructions

(a) Compute the asset turnover ratio for each company for 2000.
(b) What conclusions concerning the efficiency of assets can be drawn from these data?

INTERPRETING FINANCIAL STATEMENTS: A Global Focus

BYP10-3 As noted in the chapter, the accounting for goodwill differs in countries around the world. The following discussion of a change in goodwill accounting practices was taken from the notes to the financial statements of **J Sainsbury Plc**, one of the world's leading retailers. Headquartered in the United Kingdom, it serves 15 million customers a week.

J Sainsbury plc

J SAINSBURY PLC
Notes to the Financial Statements

Accounting Policies

Goodwill arising in connection with the acquisition of shares in subsidiaries and associated undertakings is calculated as the excess of the purchase price over the fair value of the net tangible assets acquired. In prior years goodwill has been deducted from reserves in the period of acquisition. FRS 10 is applicable in the currect financial year, and in accordance with the standard acquired goodwill is now shown as an asset on the Group's Balance Sheet. As permitted by FRS 10, goodwill written off to reserves in prior periods has not been restated as an asset.

Goodwill is treated as having an indefinite economic life where it is considered that the acquired business has strong customer loyalty built up over a long period of time, based on advantageous store locations and a commitment to maintain the marketing advantage of the retail brand. The carrying value of the goodwill will be reviewed annually for impairment and adjusted to its recoverable amount if required. Where goodwill is considered to have a finite life, amortisation will be applied over that period.

For amounts stated as goodwill which are considered to have indefinite life, no amortisation is charged to the Profit and Loss Account.

Instructions

(a) How does the initial determination and recording of goodwill compare with that in the United States? That is, is goodwill initially recorded in the same circumstances, and is the calculation of the initial amount the same in both the United Kingdom and the United States?

(b) Prior to adoption of the new accounting standard (FRS 10), how did the company account for goodwill? What were the implications for the income statement?

(c) Under the new accounting standard, how does the company account for its goodwill? Is it possible, under the new standard, for a company to avoid charging goodwill amortization to net income?

(d) In what ways is the new standard similar to U.S. standards, and in what ways is it different?

EXPLORING THE WEB

BYP10-4 A company's annual report identifies the amount of its plant assets and the depreciation method used.

Address: **www.reportgallery.com** *(or go to www.wiley.com/college/weygandt)*

Steps:

1. From Report Gallery Homepage, choose **Library of Annual Reports**.
2. Select a particular company.
3. Choose **Annual Report**.
4. Follow instructions below.

Instructions

(a) What is the name of the company?
(b) At fiscal year-end, what is the net amount of its plant assets?
(c) What is the accumulated depreciation?
(d) Which method of depreciation does the company use?

CRITICAL THINKING

GROUP DECISION CASE

BYP10-5 Fresno Company and Auburn Company are two proprietorships that are similar in many respects. One difference is that Fresno Company uses the straight-line method and Auburn

Company uses the declining-balance method at double the straight-line rate. On January 2, 2000, both companies acquired the following depreciable assets.

Asset	Cost	Salvage Value	Useful Life
Building	$320,000	$20,000	50 years
Equipment	110,000	10,000	10 years

Including the appropriate depreciation charges, annual net income for the companies in the years 2000, 2001, and 2002 and total income for the 3 years were as follows.

	2000	2001	2002	Total
Fresno Company	$84,000	$88,400	$90,000	$262,400
Auburn Company	68,000	76,000	85,000	229,000

At December 31, 2002, the balance sheets of the two companies are similar except that Auburn Company has more cash than Fresno Company.

Mary Flaherty is interested in buying one of the companies. She comes to you for advice.

Instructions

With the class divided into groups, answer the following.

(a) Determine the annual and total depreciation recorded by each company during the 3 years.
(b) Assuming that Auburn Company also uses the straight-line method of depreciation instead of the declining-balance method as in (a), prepare comparative income data for the 3 years.
(c) Which company should Mary Flaherty buy? Why?

COMMUNICATION ACTIVITY

BYP10-6 The following was published with the financial statements to **American Exploration Company**.

AMERICAN EXPLORATION COMPANY
Notes to the Financial Statements

Property, Plant, and Equipment—The Company accounts for its oil and gas exploration and production activities using the successful efforts method of accounting. Under this method, acquisition costs for proved and unproved properties are capitalized when incurred.... The costs of drilling exploratory wells are capitalized pending determination of whether each well has discovered proved reserves. If proved reserves are not discovered, such drilling costs are charged to expense.... Depletion of the cost of producing oil and gas properties is computed on the units-of-activity method.

Instructions

Write a brief memo to your instructor discussing American Exploration Company's note regarding property, plant, and equipment. Your memo should address what is meant by the "successful efforts method" and "units-of-activity method."

ETHICS CASE

BYP10-7 Finney Container Company is suffering declining sales of its principal product, nonbiodegradeable plastic cartons. The president, Philip Shapeero, instructs his controller, Sharon Fetters, to lengthen asset lives to reduce depreciation expense. A processing line of automated plastic extruding equipment, purchased for $2.7 million in January 2002, was originally estimated to have a useful life of 8 years and a salvage value of $300,000. Depreciation has been recorded for 2 years on that basis. Philip wants the estimated life changed to 12 years total, and the straight-line method continued. Sharon is hesitant to make the change, believing it is unethical to increase net income in this manner. Philip says, "Hey, the life is only an estimate, and I've heard that our competition uses a 12-year life on their production equipment."

Instructions

(a) Who are the stakeholders in this situation?

(b) Is the change in asset life unethical, or is it simply a good business practice by an astute president?

(c) What is the effect of Philip Shapeero's proposed change on income before taxes in the year of change?

Answers to Self-Study Questions

1. d **2.** b **3.** d **4.** d **5.** b **6.** d **7.** a **8.** c **9.** c **10.** b **11.** c

Answer to Lands' End Review It Question 2, p. 403

LANDS' END DIRECT MERCHANTS

Lands' End reports the following categories and amounts under the heading "Property, plant and equipment, at cost": Land and buildings $102,776,000; Fixtures and equipment $175,910,000; and Leasehold improvements $4,453,000.

Remember to go back to the Navigator box on the chapter-opening page and check off your completed work.

CURRENT LIABILITIES AND PAYROLL ACCOUNTING

11

THE NAVIGATOR ✓

- Understand *Concepts for Review* ❑
- Read *Feature Story* ❑
- Scan *Study Objectives* ❑
- Read *Preview* ❑
- Read text and answer *Before You Go On* *p.* 453 ❑ *p.* 463 ❑ *p.* 467 ❑ *p.* 469 ❑
- Work *Demonstration Problem* ❑
- Review *Summary of Study Objectives* ❑
- Answer *Self-Study Questions* ❑
- Complete *Assignments* ❑

CONCEPTS FOR REVIEW

Before studying this chapter, you should know or, if necessary, review:

a. The importance of liquidity in evaluating the financial position of a company. (Ch. 4, p. 154)

b. How to make adjusting entries related to unearned revenue (Ch. 3, pp. 97–98) and accrued expenses. (Ch. 3, pp. 101–103)

c. The principles of internal control. (Ch. 8, p. 319)

☑ THE NAVIGATOR

FEATURE STORY

Financing His Dreams

What would you do if you had a great idea for a new product, but couldn't come up with the cash to get the business off the ground? Small businesses often can't attract investors, nor can they obtain traditional debt financing through bank loans or bond issuances. Instead, they often resort to unusual, and costly, forms of nontraditional financing.

Such was the case for Wilbert Murdock. Murdock grew up in a New York housing project, and always had great ambitions. This ambitious spirit led him into some business ventures that failed: a medical diagnostic tool, a device to eliminate carpal-tunnel syndrome, custom sneakers, and a device to keep people from falling asleep while driving.

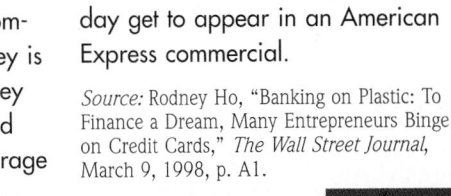

His latest idea was computerized golf clubs that analyze a golfer's swing and provide immediate feedback. Murdock saw great potential in the idea: Many golfers are willing to shell out considerable sums of money for devices that might improve their game. But Murdock had no cash to develop his product, and banks and other lenders had shied away. Rather than give up, Murdock resorted to credit cards—in a big way. He quickly owed $25,000 to credit card companies.

While funding a business with credit cards might sound unusual, it isn't. A recent study found that one-third of businesses with fewer than 20 employees financed at least part of their operations with credit cards. As Murdock explained, credit cards are an appealing way to finance a start-up because "credit-card companies don't care how the money is spent." But they do care how they are paid. And so Murdock faced high interest charges and a barrage of credit card collection letters.

Murdock's debt forced him to sacrifice nearly everything in order to keep his business afloat. His car stopped running, he barely has enough money to buy food, and he lives and works out of a dimly lit apartment in his mother's basement. Through it all he tries to maintain a positive spirit, joking that, if he becomes successful, he might some day get to appear in an American Express commercial.

Source: Rodney Ho, "Banking on Plastic: To Finance a Dream, Many Entrepreneurs Binge on Credit Cards," *The Wall Street Journal*, March 9, 1998, p. A1.

☑ THE NAVIGATOR

STUDY OBJECTIVES

After studying this chapter, you should be able to:

1. Explain a current liability, and identify the major types of current liabilities.
2. Describe the accounting for notes payable.
3. Explain the accounting for other current liabilities.
4. Explain the financial statement presentation and analysis of current liabilities.
5. Describe the accounting and disclosure requirements for contingent liabilities.
6. Discuss the objectives of internal control for payroll.
7. Compute and record the payroll for a pay period.
8. Describe and record employer payroll taxes.
9. Identify additional fringe benefits associated with employee compensation.

☑ THE NAVIGATOR

PREVIEW OF CHAPTER 11

Inventor-entrepreneur Wilbert Murdock, as you can tell from the Feature Story, has had to use multiple credit cards to finance his business ventures. Murdock's credit card debts would be classified as *current liabilities* because they are due every month. Yet by making minimal payments and paying high interest each month, Murdock uses this credit source long-term. Some credit card balances remain outstanding for years as they accumulate interest.

In Chapter 4, we defined liabilities as creditors' claims on total assets and as existing debts and obligations. These claims, debts, and obligations must be settled or paid at some time **in the future** by the transfer of assets or services. The future date on which they are due or payable (maturity date) is a significant feature of liabilities. This "future date" feature gives rise to two basic classifications of liabilities: (1) current liabilities and (2) long-term liabilities. We will explain current liabilities, along with payroll accounting, in this chapter. We will explain long-term liabilities in Chapter 16.

The content and organization of Chapter 11 are as follows.

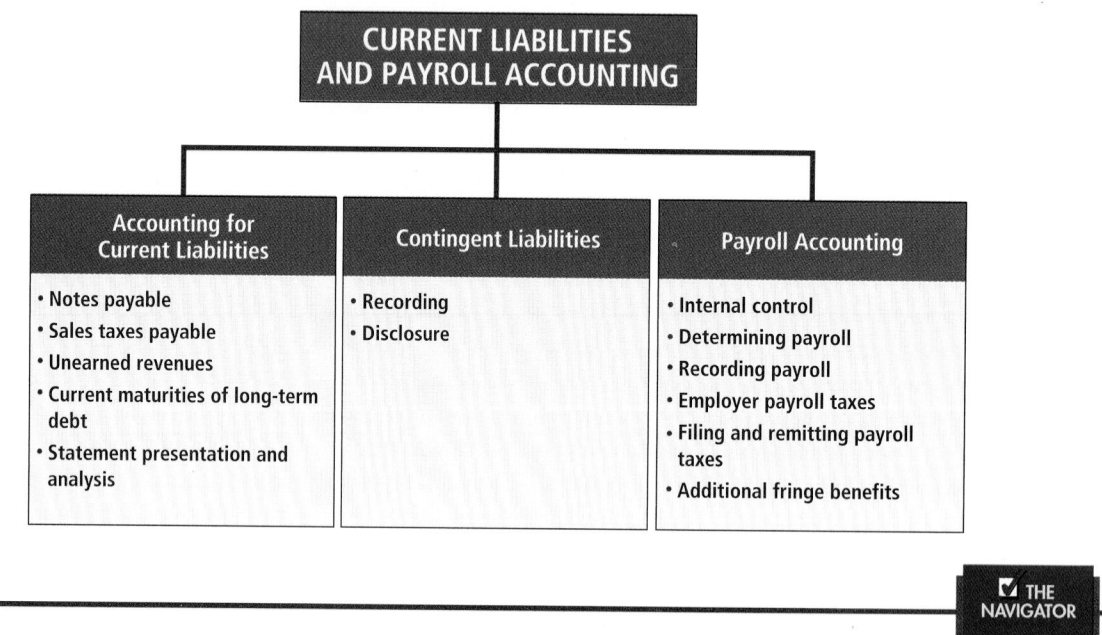

CURRENT LIABILITIES AND PAYROLL ACCOUNTING

- **Accounting for Current Liabilities**
  - Notes payable
  - Sales taxes payable
  - Unearned revenues
  - Current maturities of long-term debt
  - Statement presentation and analysis
- **Contingent Liabilities**
  - Recording
  - Disclosure
- **Payroll Accounting**
  - Internal control
  - Determining payroll
  - Recording payroll
  - Employer payroll taxes
  - Filing and remitting payroll taxes
  - Additional fringe benefits

THE NAVIGATOR

ACCOUNTING FOR CURRENT LIABILITIES

STUDY OBJECTIVE 1

Explain a current liability, and identify the major types of current liabilities.

As explained in Chapter 4, a **current liability** is a debt with two key features: (1) It can reasonably be expected to be paid from existing current assets or through the creation of other current liabilities. And (2) it will be paid within one year or the operating cycle, whichever is longer. Debts that do not meet **both criteria** are classified as long-term liabilities. Most companies pay current liabilities within one year out of current assets, rather than by creating other liabilities.

Companies must carefully monitor the relationship of current liabilities to current assets. This relationship is critical in evaluating a company's short-term debt-paying ability. A company that has more current liabilities than current assets is usually the subject of some concern because the company may not be able to meet its current obligations when they become due.

HELPFUL HINT

The current liabilities section of the balance sheet gives creditors a good idea of what obligations are coming due.

Current liabilities include notes payable, accounts payable, and unearned revenues. They also include accrued liabilities such as taxes, salaries and wages, and interest payable. The entries for accounts payable and adjusting entries for some current liabilities have been explained in previous chapters. Other types of current liabilities that are often encountered are discussed in the following sections.

NOTES PAYABLE

STUDY OBJECTIVE 2

Describe the accounting for notes payable.

Obligations in the form of written promissory notes are recorded as **notes payable**. Notes payable are often used instead of accounts payable. Doing so gives the lender formal proof of the obligation in case legal remedies are needed to collect the debt. Notes payable usually require the borrower to pay interest and frequently are issued to meet short-term financing needs.

Notes are issued for varying periods. **Those due for payment within one year of the balance sheet date are usually classified as current liabilities.** Most notes are interest bearing.

To illustrate the accounting for notes payable, assume that First National Bank agrees to lend $100,000 on March 1, 2002, if Cole Williams Co. signs a $100,000, 12%, 4-month note. With an interest-bearing promissory note, the amount of assets received upon issuance of the note generally equals the note's face value. Cole Williams Co. therefore will receive $100,000 cash and will make the following journal entry.

Mar. 1	Cash	100,000	
	Notes Payable		100,000
	(To record issuance of 12%, 4-month note to First National Bank)		

A	=	L	+	OE
+100,000		+100,000		

Interest accrues over the life of the note and must be recorded periodically. If Cole Williams Co. prepares financial statements semiannually, an adjusting entry is required at June 30 to recognize interest expense and interest payable of $4,000 ($100,000 × 12% × 4/12). The formula for computing interest and its application to Cole Williams Co.'s note are shown in Illustration 11-1.

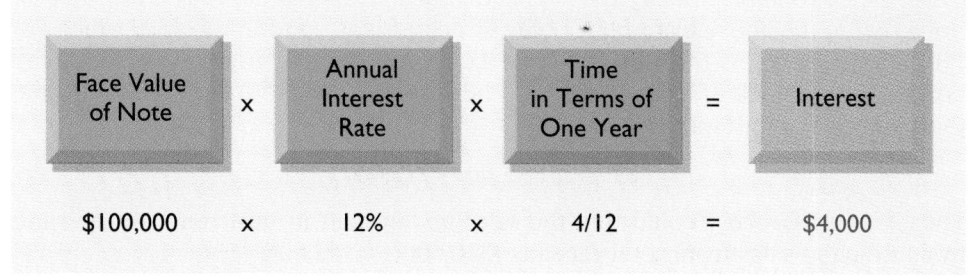

Face Value of Note	×	Annual Interest Rate	×	Time in Terms of One Year	=	Interest
$100,000	×	12%	×	4/12	=	$4,000

Illustration 11-1

Formula for computing interest

The adjusting entry is:

June 30	Interest Expense	4,000	
	Interest Payable		4,000
	(To accrue interest for 4 months on First National Bank note)		

A	=	L	+	OE
		+4,000		−4,000

In the June 30 financial statements, the current liabilities section of the balance sheet will show notes payable $100,000 and interest payable $4,000. In addition, interest expense of $4,000 will be reported under "other expenses and losses" in the income statement. If Cole Williams Co. prepared financial statements monthly, the adjusting entry at the end of each month would have been $1,000 ($100,000 × 12% × 1/12).

At maturity (July 1, 2002), Cole Williams Co. must pay the face value of the note ($100,000) plus $4,000 interest ($100,000 × 12% × 4/12). The entry to record payment of the note and accrued interest is as follows.

July 1	Notes Payable	100,000	
	Interest Payable	4,000	
	Cash		104,000
	(To record payment of First National Bank interest-bearing note and accrued interest at maturity)		

SALES TAXES PAYABLE

STUDY OBJECTIVE 3

Explain the accounting for other current liabilities.

As a consumer, you know that many of the products you purchase at retail stores are subject to sales taxes. The tax is expressed as a stated percentage of the sales price. The retailer collects the tax from the customer when the sale occurs. Periodically (usually monthly), the retailer remits the collections to the state's department of revenue.

Under most state sales tax laws, the amount of the sale and the amount of the sales tax collected must be rung up separately on the cash register. (Gasoline sales are a major exception.) The cash register readings are then used to credit Sales and Sales Taxes Payable. For example, if the March 25 cash register reading for Cooley Grocery shows sales of $10,000 and sales taxes of $600 (sales tax rate of 6%), the entry is:

A	=	L	+	OE
+10,600		+600		+10,000

Mar. 25	Cash	10,600	
	Sales		10,000
	Sales Taxes Payable		600
	(To record daily sales and sales taxes)		

When the taxes are remitted to the taxing agency, Sales Taxes Payable is debited and Cash is credited. The company does not report sales taxes as an expense. It simply forwards to the government the amount paid by the customers. Thus, Cooley Grocery serves only as a **collection agent** for the taxing authority.

When sales taxes are not rung up separately on the cash register, they must be extracted from the total receipts. To determine the amount of sales in such cases, divide total receipts by 100% plus the sales tax percentage. To illustrate, assume that in the above example Cooley Grocery rings up total receipts, which are $10,600. The receipts from the sales are equal to the sales price (100%) plus the tax percentage (6% of sales), or 1.06 times the sales total. We can compute the sales amount as follows.

$$\$10,600 \div 1.06 = \$10,000$$

Thus, Cooley Grocery could find the sales tax amount it must remit to the state by subtracting sales from total receipts ($10,600 − $10,000).

HELPFUL HINT

Alternatively, Cooley could find the tax by multiplying sales by the sales tax rate ($10,000 × 6%).

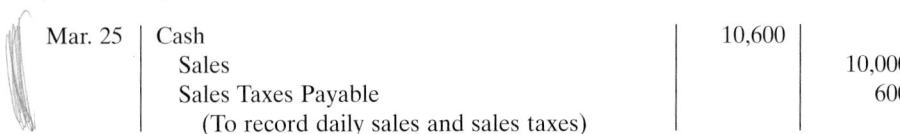

ACCOUNTING IN ACTION e Business Insight

If you buy a book at a bookstore, you pay sales tax. If you buy the same book over the Internet, you don't pay a sales tax (in most cases). This is one reason why e-commerce, as it has come to be called, is growing exponentially and why "dot-com" businesses like **Amazon.com** have become so popular. A recent study suggested that Internet sales would fall by 30 percent if sales tax were applied. Partly as a result of this study, the Clinton administration and Congress agreed to a three-year moratorium on Internet taxation. Most people in Washington expect that after the moratorium runs out in 2001, some kind of sales tax will be imposed on e-commerce. The idea is that by then the e-commerce model will have "matured" and can serve as a veritable gold mine for federal, state, and local taxation.

SOURCE: John Ellis. "The Tax Consequences of Commerce on the Internet," *Boston Globe*, April 10, 1999, p. A23.

UNEARNED REVENUES

A magazine publisher, such as **Sports Illustrated**, receives a customer's check when magazines are ordered. An airline company, such as **American Airlines**, receives cash when it sells tickets for future flights. Through these transactions, both companies have incurred unearned revenues—revenues that are received before goods are delivered or services are rendered. How do companies account for unearned revenues?

1. When the advance payment is received, Cash is debited, and a current liability account identifying the source of the unearned revenue is credited.
2. When the revenue is earned, the Unearned Revenue account is debited, and an earned revenue account is credited.

To illustrate, assume that Superior University sells 10,000 season football tickets at $50 each for its five-game home schedule. The entry for the sale of season tickets is:

Aug. 6	Cash	500,000	
	Unearned Football Ticket Revenue		500,000
	(To record sale of 10,000 season tickets)		

A	=	L	+	OE
+500,000		+500,000		

As each game is completed, the following entry is made:

Sept. 7	Unearned Football Ticket Revenue	100,000	
	Football Ticket Revenue		100,000
	(To record football ticket revenues earned)		

A	=	L	+	OE
		−100,000		+100,000

Any balance in an unearned revenue account (in Unearned Football Ticket Revenue, for example) is reported as a current liability in the balance sheet. As revenue is earned, a transfer from unearned revenue to earned revenue occurs. Unearned revenue is material for some companies: In the airline industry, for example, tickets sold for future flights represent almost 50% of total current liabilities. At **United Air Lines**, unearned ticket revenue is the largest current liability, recently amounting to over $1 billion.

Illustration 11-2 shows specific unearned and earned revenue accounts used in selected types of businesses.

Illustration 11-2

Unearned and earned revenue accounts

Type of Business	Account Title: Unearned Revenue	Account Title: Earned Revenue
Airline	Unearned Passenger Ticket Revenue	Passenger Revenue
Magazine publisher	Unearned Subscription Revenue	Subscription Revenue
Hotel	Unearned Rental Revenue	Rental Revenue
Insurance company	Unearned Premium Revenue	Premium Revenue

CURRENT MATURITIES OF LONG-TERM DEBT

Companies often have a portion of long-term debt that comes due in the current year. That amount would be considered a current liability. For example, assume that Wendy Construction issues a 5-year interest-bearing $25,000 note on January 1, 2002. Each January 1, starting January 1, 2003, $5,000 of the note is due to be paid. When financial statements are prepared on December 31, 2002, $5,000 should be reported as a current liability. The remaining $20,000 on the note would be reported as a long-term liability. Current maturities of long-term debt are often termed **long-term debt due within one year**.

It is not necessary to prepare an adjusting entry to recognize the current maturity of long-term debt. The proper statement classification of each balance sheet account is recognized when the balance sheet is prepared.

STATEMENT PRESENTATION AND ANALYSIS

STUDY OBJECTIVE 4

Explain the financial statement presentation and analysis of current liabilities.

Presentation

As indicated in Chapter 4, current liabilities are the first category under liabilities on the balance sheet. Each of the principal types of current liabilities is listed separately. In addition, the terms of notes payable and other key information about the individual items are disclosed in the notes to the financial statements.

Current liabilities are seldom listed in the order of maturity. The reason is that varying maturity dates may exist for specific obligations such as notes payable. A more common method of presenting current liabilities is to list them by **order of magnitude**, with the largest ones first. Or, many companies, as a matter of custom, show notes payable and accounts payable first, regardless of amount. The following adapted excerpt from the balance sheet of **Lands' End, Inc.** illustrates its order of presentation.

Illustration 11-3

Balance sheet presentation of current liabilities

LANDS' END DIRECT MERCHANTS

LANDS' END, INC.
Balance Sheet
January 28, 2000
(in millions)

Assets	
Current assets	$289.4
Property, plant and equipment (net)	165.8
Intangibles, net	1.0
Total assets	$456.2
Liabilities and Stockholders' Equity	
Current liabilities	
Lines of credit	**$ 11.7**
Accounts payable	**74.5**
Reserve for returns	**7.9**
Accrued liabilities	**43.8**
Accrued profit sharing	**2.7**
Income taxes payable	**10.3**
Total current liabilities	**150.9**
Noncurrent liabilities	9.1
Total liabilities	160.0
Shareholders' equity	296.2
Total liabilities and stockholders' equity	$456.2

HELPFUL HINT

For another example of a current liabilities section, refer to the **Abercrombie & Fitch** balance sheet in Appendix B.

Analysis

Use of current and noncurrent classifications makes it possible to analyze a company's liquidity. **Liquidity** refers to the ability to pay maturing obligations and meet unexpected needs for cash. The relationship of current assets to current liabilities is critical in analyzing liquidity. This relationship can be expressed as a dollar amount (called working capital) and as a ratio (called the current ratio).

The excess of current assets over current liabilities is **working capital**. The formula for the computation of Lands' End's working capital is shown in Illustration 11-4 (dollar amounts in millions).

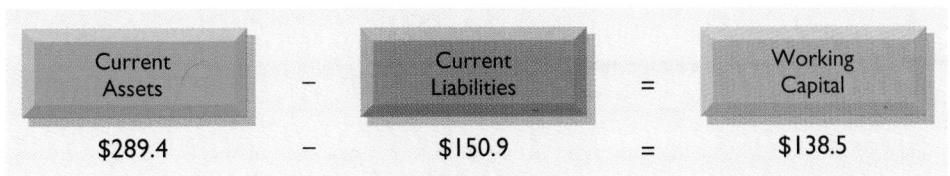

Current Assets	−	Current Liabilities	=	Working Capital
$289.4	−	$150.9	=	$138.5

Illustration 11-4

Working capital formula and computation

As an absolute dollar amount, working capital is limited in its informational value. For example, $1 million of working capital may be far more than needed for a small company but be inadequate for a large corporation. And, $1 million of working capital may be adequate for a company at one time but be inadequate at another time.

The **current ratio** permits us to compare the liquidity of different sized companies and of a single company at different times. The current ratio is current assets divided by current liabilities. The formula for this ratio is illustrated below, along with its computation using Lands' End's current asset and current liability data (dollar amounts in millions).

Current Assets	÷	Current Liabilities	=	Current Ratio
$289.4	÷	$150.9	=	1.9:1

Illustration 11-5

Current ratio formula and computation

Historically, a ratio of 2:1 was considered to be the standard for a good credit rating. In recent years, however, many healthy companies have maintained ratios well below 2:1. Lands' End's ratio of 1.9:1 is comparable to the standard of 2:1.

CONTINGENT LIABILITIES

STUDY OBJECTIVE 5

Describe the accounting and disclosure requirements for contingent liabilities.

With notes payable, interest payable, accounts payable, and sales taxes payable, we know that an obligation to make payment exists. But suppose that your company is involved in a dispute with the Internal Revenue Service (IRS) over the amount of its income tax liability. Should you report the disputed amount as a liability on the balance sheet? Or suppose your company is involved in a lawsuit which, if you lose, might result in bankruptcy. How should this major contingency be reported? The answers to these questions are difficult, because these liabilities are dependent—contingent—upon some future event. In other words, a **contingent liability** is a potential liability that may become an actual liability in the future.

How should contingent liabilities be reported? Guidelines have been adopted that help resolve these problems. The guidelines require that:

1. If the contingency is **probable** (if it is likely to occur) **and** the amount can be **reasonably estimated**, the liability should be recorded in the accounts.
2. If the contingency is only **reasonably possible** (if it could happen), then it need be disclosed only in the notes that accompany the financial statements.
3. If the contingency is **remote** (if it is unlikely to occur), it need not be recorded or disclosed.

HELPFUL HINT

Another example of a contingency is toxic waste cleanup costs. Some companies expect that insurance will cover these costs, but insurance companies are arguing that general liability policies were never meant to cover this type of situation.

ACCOUNTING IN ACTION *Business Insight*

Contingent liabilities abound in the real world. Consider the following: **Manville Corp.** filed for bankruptcy when it was hit by billions of dollars in asbestos product-liability claims. Companies having multiple toxic waste sites are faced with cleanup costs that average $10 to $30 million and can reach as high as $500 million depending on the type of waste. For life and health insurance companies and their stockholders, the cost of AIDS is like an iceberg: Everyone wonders how big it really is and what damage it might do in the future; according to the U.S. Centers for Disease Control treatment costs could be $8 billion to $16 billion. And frequent-flyer programs are so popular that airlines at one time owed participants more than 3 million round-trip domestic tickets. That's enough to fly at least 5.4 billion miles—free for the passengers, but at what future cost to the airlines?

RECORDING A CONTINGENT LIABILITY

INTERNATIONAL NOTE

International accounting standards basically use criteria similar to those in the U.S. in determining how to account for contingencies.

Product warranties are an example of a contingent liability that should be recorded in the accounts. Warranty contracts result in future costs that may be incurred in replacing defective units or repairing malfunctioning units. Generally, a manufacturer, such as **Black & Decker**, knows that some warranty costs will be incurred. From prior experience with the product, the company usually can reasonably estimate the anticipated cost of servicing (honoring) the warranty.

The accounting for warranty costs is based on the matching principle. **The estimated cost of honoring product warranty contracts should be recognized as an expense in the period in which the sale occurs.** To illustrate, assume that in 2002 Denson Manufacturing Company sells 10,000 washers and dryers at an average price of $600 each. The selling price includes a one-year warranty on parts. It is expected that 500 units (5%) will be defective and that warranty repair costs will average $80 per unit. In 2002, warranty contracts are honored on 300 units at a total cost of $24,000.

At December 31, it is necessary to accrue the estimated warranty costs on the 2002 sales. The computation is as follows.

Illustration 11-6

Computation of estimated product warranty liability

Number of units sold	10,000
Estimated rate of defective units	× 5%
Total estimated defective units	500
Average warranty repair cost	× $80
Estimated product warranty liability	**$40,000**

The adjusting entry, therefore, is:

A = L + OE
+40,000 −40,000

Dec. 31	Warranty Expense	40,000	
	Estimated Warranty Liability		40,000
	(To accrue estimated warranty costs)		

The entry to record those repair costs incurred in 2002 to honor warranty contracts on 2002 sales is shown below.

A = L + OE
−24,000 −24,000

Jan. 1–Dec. 31	Estimated Warranty Liability	24,000	
	Repair Parts		24,000
	(To record honoring of 300 warranty contracts on 2002 sales)		

Warranty expense of $40,000 is reported under selling expenses in the income statement. Estimated warranty liability of $16,000 ($40,000 − $24,000) is classified as a current liability on the balance sheet.

In the following year, all expenses incurred in honoring warranty contracts on 2002 sales should be debited to Estimated Warranty Liability. To illustrate, assume that 20 defective units are replaced in January 2003, at an average cost of $80 in parts and labor. The summary entry for the month of January 2003 is:

Jan. 31	Estimated Warranty Liability	1,600	
	Repair Parts		1,600
	(To record honoring of 20 warranty contracts on 2002 sales)		

A	=	L	+	OE
−1,600		−1,600		

DISCLOSURE OF CONTINGENT LIABILITIES

When it is probable that a contingent liability will be incurred but the amount cannot be reasonably estimated, or when the contingent liability is only reasonably possible, only disclosure of the contingency is required. Examples of contingencies that may require disclosure are pending or threatened lawsuits and assessment of additional income taxes pending an IRS audit of the tax return.

The disclosure should identify the nature of the item and, if known, the amount of the contingency and the expected outcome of the future event. Disclosure is usually accomplished through a note to the financial statements, as illustrated by the following.

Illustration 11-7

Disclosure of contingent liability

USAIR
Notes to the Financial Statements

Legal Proceedings
The Company and various subsidiaries have been named as defendants in various suits and proceedings which involve, among other things, environmental concerns about noise and air pollution and employment matters. These suits and proceedings are in various stages of litigation, and the status of the law with respect to several of the issues involved is unsettled. For these reasons the outcome of these suits and proceedings is difficult to predict. In the Company's opinion, however, the disposition of these matters is not likely to have a material adverse effect on its financial condition.

BEFORE YOU GO ON...

REVIEW IT

1. What are the two criteria for classifying a debt as a current liability?
2. Identify three liabilities classified as current by **Lands' End**. The answer to this question is provided on page 485.
3. What entries are made for an interest-bearing note payable?
4. How are sales taxes recorded by a retailer? Identify three unearned revenues.
5. How may the liquidity of a company be analyzed?
6. What are the accounting guidelines for contingent liabilities?

LANDS' END DIRECT MERCHANTS

DO IT

You and several classmates are studying for the next accounting examination. They ask you to answer the following questions: (1) How is the sales tax amount determined when the cash register total includes sales taxes? (2) When should a contingency be recorded in the accounts?

ACTION PLAN

- Remove the sales tax from the total sales.
- Identify the criteria for recording and disclosing contingent liabilities.

SOLUTION

(1) First, divide the total proceeds by 100% plus the sales tax percentage to find the sales amount. Second, subtract the sales amount from the total proceeds to determine the sales taxes.

(2) A contingency should be recorded when it is *probable* that a liability will be incurred *and* the amount can be *reasonably* estimated.

Related exercise material: BE11-3, BE11-4, BE11-5, E11-2, E11-3, E11-4, and E11-5.

THE NAVIGATOR

PAYROLL ACCOUNTING

Payroll and related fringe benefits often make up a large percentage of current liabilities. Employee compensation is often the most significant expense that a company incurs. For example, **General Motors** recently reported total employees of 516,000 and labor costs of $31.3 billion. Add to labor costs such fringe benefits as health insurance, life insurance, disability insurance, and so on, and you can see why proper accounting and control of payroll are so important.

Payroll accounting involves more than paying employees' wages. Companies are required by law to maintain payroll records for each employee, file and pay payroll taxes, and comply with numerous state and federal tax laws related to employee compensation. Accounting for payroll has become much more complex due to these regulations.

The term "payroll" pertains to both salaries and wages. Managerial, administrative, and sales personnel are generally paid **salaries**. Salaries are often expressed in terms of a specified amount per month or per year rather than an hourly rate. For example, the faculty and administrative personnel at the college or university you are attending are paid salaries. In contrast, store clerks, factory employees, and manual laborers are normally paid **wages**. Wages are based on a rate per hour or on a piecework basis (such as per unit of product). Frequently, the terms "salaries" and "wages" are used interchangeably.

The term "payroll" does not apply to payments made for services of professionals such as certified public accountants, attorneys, and architects. Such professionals are independent contractors rather than salaried employees. Payments to them are called **fees**, rather than salaries or wages. This distinction is important because government regulations relating to the payment and reporting of payroll taxes apply only to employees.

INTERNAL CONTROL

STUDY OBJECTIVE 6

Discuss the objectives of internal control for payroll.

Internal control was introduced in Chapter 8. As applied to payrolls, the objectives of internal control are (1) to safeguard company assets against unauthorized payments of payrolls, and (2) to ensure the accuracy and reliability of the accounting records pertaining to payrolls.

Irregularities often result if internal control is lax. Overstating hours, using unauthorized pay rates, adding fictitious employees to the payroll, continuing terminated employees on the payroll, and distributing duplicate payroll checks are all methods of stealing from a company. Moreover, inaccurate records will result in incorrect paychecks, financial statements, and payroll tax returns.

TECHNOLOGY IN ACTION

A Senate hearing revealed that the U.S. Army spent $8 million on unauthorized pay, including payments to deserters and "ghost" soldiers. The underlying cause was a computer system so lax that it was possible to create new pay records and destroy old ones without leaving an audit trail.

Payroll activities involve four functions: hiring employees, timekeeping, preparing the payroll, and paying the payroll. For effective internal control, these four functions should be assigned to different departments or individuals. To illustrate these functions, we will examine the case of Academy Company and one of its employees, Michael Jordan.

Hiring Employees

The human resources (personnel) department is responsible for posting job openings, screening and interviewing applicants, and hiring employees. From a control standpoint, this department provides significant documentation and authorization. When an employee is hired, the human resources department prepares an authorization form. The one used by Academy Company for Michael Jordan is shown in Illustration 11-8.

Hiring Employees

Human Resources department documents and authorizes employment.

The authorization form is sent to the payroll department, where it is used to place the new employee on the payroll. A chief concern of the human resources department is ensuring the accuracy of this form. The reason is quite simple: one of the most common types of payroll frauds is adding fictitious employees to the payroll.

The human resources department is also responsible for authorizing changes in employment status. Specifically, they must authorize (1) changes in pay rates

Illustration 11-8

Authorization form prepared by the human resources department

ACADEMY COMPANY

Employee Name: Jordan, (LAST) Michael (FIRST) (MI) Starting Date: 9/01/98

Classification: Skilled-Level 10 Social Security No.: 329-36-9547

Department: Shipping Division: Entertainment

NEW HIRE	Classification: Clerk — Salary Grade: Level 10 — Trans. from Temp. ☐ Rate $: 10.00 per: hour — Bonus: N/A — Non-exempt ☒ Exempt ☐
RATE CHANGE	New Rate $: 12.00 — Effective Date: 9/1/00 Present Rate $: 10.00 Merit ☒ Promotion ☐ Decrease ☐ Other ____ Previous Increase Date: None — Amount $ ____ per ____ Type ____
SEPARATION	Resignation ☐ Discharge ☐ Retirement ☐ Reason ____ Leave of absence ☐ From ____ to ____ Type ____ Last Day Worked ____
APPROVALS	BEW (BRANCH OR DEPT. MANAGER) — 9/1/00 (DATE) — EMW (DIVISION V.P.) — 9-1-00 (DATE) James E. Speer (PERSONNEL DEPARTMENT)

Timekeeping

Supervisors monitor hours worked through time cards and time reports.

and (2) terminations of employment. Every authorization should be in writing, and a copy of the change in status should be sent to the payroll department. Notice in Illustration 11-8 that Jordan received a pay increase of $2 per hour.

Timekeeping

Another area in which internal control is important is timekeeping. Hourly employees are usually required to record time worked by "punching" a time clock. Times of arrival and departure are automatically recorded by the employee by inserting a time card into the clock. Michael Jordan's time card is shown in Illustration 11-9.

Illustration 11-9

Time card

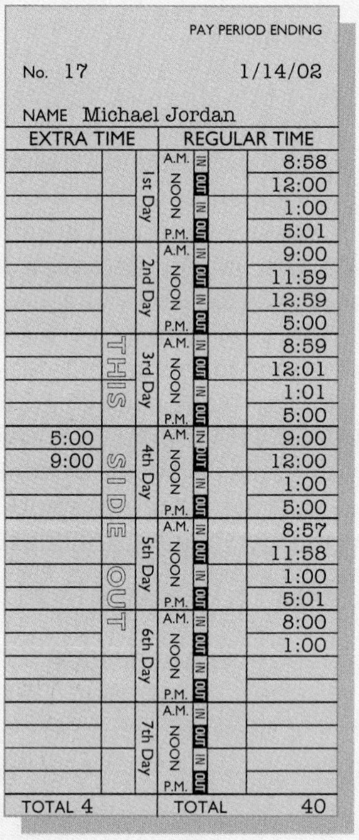

PAY PERIOD ENDING

No. 17 1/14/02

NAME Michael Jordan

Day	Extra Time In	Extra Time Out	A.M. In	Noon Out	Noon In	P.M. Out
1st Day			8:58	12:00	1:00	5:01
2nd Day			9:00	11:59	12:59	5:00
3rd Day			8:59	12:01	1:01	5:00
4th Day	5:00	9:00	9:00	12:00	1:00	5:00
5th Day			8:57	11:58	1:00	5:01
6th Day			8:00	1:00		
7th Day						
TOTAL	4		TOTAL			40

THIS SIDE OUT

In large companies, time clock procedures are often monitored by a supervisor or security guard to make sure an employee punches only one card. At the end of the pay period, each employee's supervisor approves the hours shown by signing the time card. When overtime hours are involved, approval by a supervisor is usually mandatory. This guards against unauthorized overtime. The approved time cards are then sent to the payroll department. For salaried employees, a manually prepared weekly or monthly time report kept by a supervisor may be used to record time worked.

Preparing the Payroll

Two (or more) employees verify payroll amounts; supervisor approves.

Preparing the Payroll

The payroll is prepared in the payroll department on the basis of two inputs: (1) human resources department authorizations and (2) approved time cards. Numerous calculations are involved in determining gross wages and payroll deductions. Therefore, a second payroll department employee, working independently, verifies all calculated amounts, and a payroll department supervisor then approves the payroll. The payroll department is also responsible for preparing (but not signing) payroll checks, maintaining payroll records, and preparing payroll tax returns.

Paying the Payroll

The payroll is paid by the treasurer's department. **Payment by check minimizes the risk of loss from theft, and the endorsed check provides proof of payment.** For good internal control, payroll checks should be prenumbered, and all checks should be accounted for. All checks must be signed by the treasurer (or a designated agent). Distribution of the payroll checks to employees should be controlled by the treasurer's department. Checks may be distributed by the treasurer or paymaster.

Occasionally the payroll is paid in currency. In such cases it is customary to have a second person count the cash in each pay envelope. The paymaster should obtain a signed receipt from the employee upon payment. If alleged discrepancies arise, adequate safeguards have been established to protect each party involved.

Paying the Payroll

Treasurer signs and distributes checks.

DETERMINING THE PAYROLL

Determining the payroll involves computing three amounts: (1) gross earnings, (2) payroll deductions, and (3) net pay.

STUDY OBJECTIVE 7

Compute and record the payroll for a pay period.

Gross Earnings

Gross earnings is the total compensation earned by an employee. It consists of wages or salaries, plus any bonuses and commissions.

Total **wages** for an employee are determined by multiplying the hours worked by the hourly rate of pay. In addition to the hourly pay rate, most companies are required by law to pay hourly workers a minimum of $1\frac{1}{2}$ times the regular hourly rate for overtime work in excess of 8 hours per day or 40 hours per week. In addition, many employers pay overtime rates for work done at night, on weekends, and on holidays.

Michael Jordan's time card shows that he worked 44 hours for the weekly pay period ending January 14. The computation of his gross earnings (total wages) is as follows.

HELPFUL HINT

The law that governs pay rates is the Federal Fair Labor Standards Act. It applies to all companies involved in interstate commerce.

Type of Pay	Hours	×	Rate	=	Gross Earnings
Regular	40	×	$12.00	=	$480.00
Overtime	4	×	18.00	=	72.00
Total wages					**$552.00**

Illustration 11-10

Computation of total wages

This computation assumes that Jordan receives $1\frac{1}{2}$ times his regular hourly rate ($12.00 × 1.5) for his overtime hours. Union contracts often require that overtime rates be as much as twice the regular rates.

The **salary** for an employee is generally based on a monthly or yearly rate. These rates are then prorated to the payroll periods used by the company. Most executive and administrative positions are salaried. Federal law does not require overtime pay for employees in such positions.

Many companies have **bonus** agreements for management personnel and other employees. A recent survey found that over 94% of the largest U.S. manufacturing companies offer annual bonuses to their key executives. Bonus arrangements may be based on such factors as increased sales or net income. Bonuses may be paid in cash and/or by granting executives and employees the opportunity to acquire shares of company stock at favorable prices (called stock option plans).

ETHICS NOTE

Bonuses often reward outstanding individual performance; but successful corporations also need considerable teamwork. A challenge is to motivate individuals while preventing an unethical employee from taking another's idea for his or her own advantage.

Payroll Deductions

As anyone who has received a paycheck knows, gross earnings are usually very different from the amount actually received. The difference is due to **payroll deductions**. Such deductions do not result in payroll tax expense to the employer.

The employer is merely a collection agent, and subsequently transfers the amounts deducted to the government and designated recipients. Payroll deductions may be mandatory or voluntary. Mandatory deductions are required by law and consist of FICA taxes and income taxes. Voluntary deductions are at the option of the employee. Illustration 11-11 summarizes the types of payroll deductions.

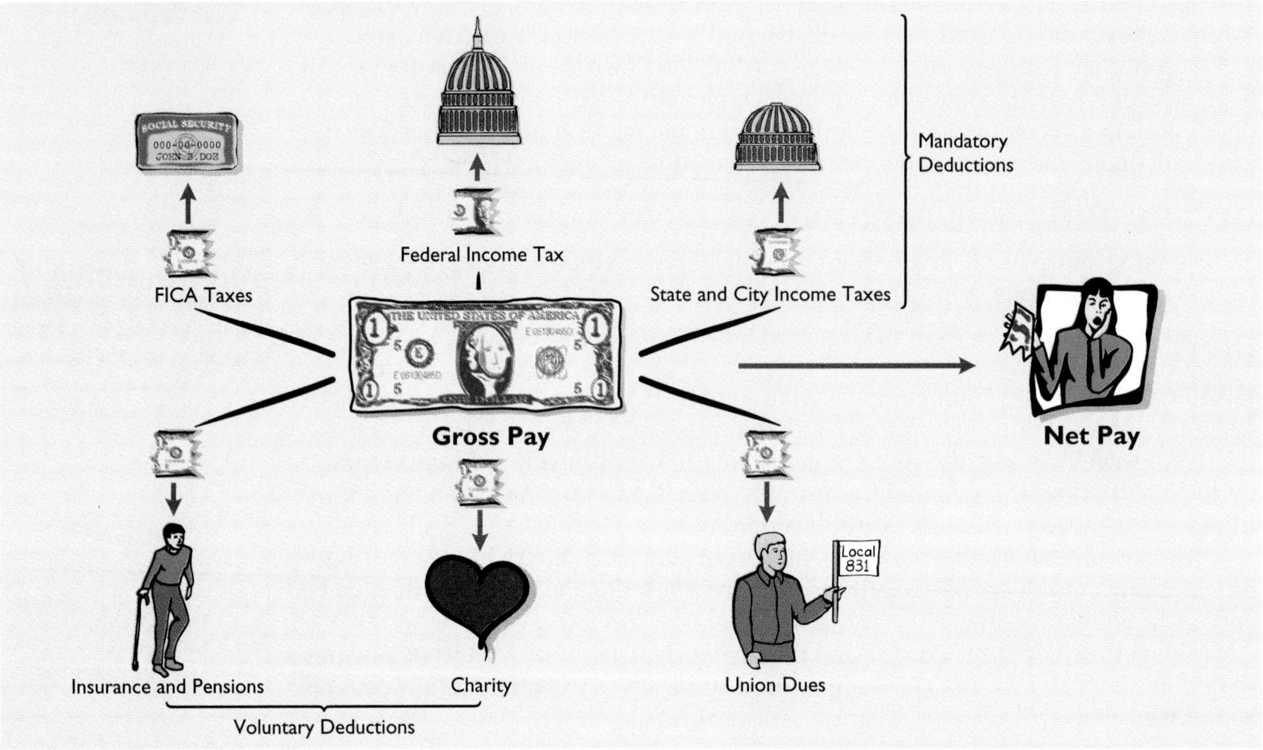

Illustration 11-11
Payroll deductions

FICA TAXES. In 1937 Congress enacted the Federal Insurance Contribution Act (FICA). **FICA taxes are designed to provide workers with supplemental retirement, employment disability, and medical benefits.** In 1965, benefits were expanded to include Medicare for individuals over 65 years of age. The benefits are financed by a tax levied on employees' earnings. FICA taxes are commonly referred to as **Social Security taxes**.

The tax rate and the tax base for FICA taxes are set by Congress. When FICA taxes were first imposed, the rate was 1% on the first $3,000 of gross earnings, or a maximum of $30 per year. The rate and base have changed dramatically since that time! In 2000, the rate was 7.65% (6.2% Social Security plus 1.45% Medicare) on the first $80,400 of gross earnings for each employee.[1] For purpose of illustration in this chapter, we will assume a rate of 8% on the first $65,000 of gross earnings, or a maximum of $5,200. Using the 8% rate, the FICA withholding for Jordan for the weekly pay period ending January 14 is $44.16 ($552 × 8%).

INCOME TAXES. Under the U.S. pay-as-you-go system of federal income taxes, employers are required to withhold income taxes from employees each pay period. The amount to be withheld is determined by three variables: (1) the employee's gross earnings; (2) the number of allowances claimed by the employee; and (3) the length of the pay period. The number of allowances claimed typically includes the employee, his or her spouse, and other dependents. **To indicate to**

[1]The Medicare provision also includes a tax of 1.45% on gross earnings in excess of $80,400. In the interest of simplification, we ignore this 1.45% charge in our end-of-chapter assignment material. We assume zero FICA withholdings on gross earnings above $65,000.

the Internal Revenue Service the number of allowances claimed, the employee must complete an Employee's Withholding Allowance Certificate (Form W-4). As shown in Illustration 11-12, Michael Jordan claims two allowances on his W-4.

Withholding tables furnished by the Internal Revenue Service indicate the

Illustration 11-12

W-4 form

Form **W-4** — Department of the Treasury, Internal Revenue Service

Employee's Withholding Allowance Certificate

► For Privacy Act and Paperwork Reduction Act Notice, see page 2.

OMB No. 1545-0010 — **2001**

1 Type or print your first name and middle initial: Michael — Last name: Jordan — 2 Your social security number: 329-36-9547

Home address (number and street or rural route): 2345 Mifflin Ave. — 3 ☐ Single ☒ Married ☐ Married, but withhold at higher Single rate.

Note: *If married, but legally separated, or spouse is a nonresident alien, check the Single box.*

City or town, State, and ZIP code: Hampton, MI 48292 — 4 If your last name differs from that on your social security card, check here and call 1-800-772-1213 for a new card . . . . . ► ☐

5 Total number of allowances you are claiming (from line H above or from the worksheet on page 2 if they apply) . . . 5 | 2

6 Additional amount, if any, you want withheld from each paycheck . . . . 6 | $

7 I claim exemption from withholding for 2001, and I certify that I meet BOTH of the following conditions for exemption:

- Last year I had a right to a refund of ALL Federal income tax withheld because I had NO tax liability AND
- This year I expect a refund of ALL Federal income tax withheld because I expect to have NO tax liability.

If you meet both conditions, enter "Exempt" here . . . . ► 7

Under penalties of perjury, I certify that I am entitled to the number of withholding allowances claimed on this certificate or entitled to claim exempt status.

Employee's signature ► *Michael Jordan* — Date ► September 1, 2001

8 Employer's name and address (Employer: Complete 8 and 10 only if sending to the IRS) — 9 Office code (optional) — 10 Employer identification number

Cat. No. 102200

amount of income tax to be withheld. Withholding amounts are based on gross wages and the number of allowances claimed. Separate tables are provided for weekly, biweekly, semimonthly, and monthly pay periods. The withholding tax table for Michael Jordan (assuming he earns $552 per week) is shown in Illustration 11-13. For a weekly salary of $552 with two allowances, the income tax to be withheld is $49.

Most states (and some cities) also require **employers** to withhold income taxes

Illustration 11-13

Withholding tax table

MARRIED Persons — **WEEKLY** Payroll Period

(For Wages Paid in 2002)

If the wages are –		And the number of withholding allowances claimed is –										
At least	But less than	0	1	2	3	4	5	6	7	8	9	10
		The amount of income tax to be withheld is –										
490	**500**	56	48	40	32	24	17	9	1	0	0	0
500	**510**	57	49	42	34	26	18	10	3	0	0	0
510	**520**	59	51	43	35	27	20	12	4	0	0	0
520	**530**	60	52	45	37	29	21	13	6	0	0	0
530	**540**	62	54	46	38	30	23	15	7	0	0	0
540	**550**	63	55	48	40	32	24	16	9	1	0	0
550	**560**	65	57	**49**	41	33	26	18	10	2	0	0
560	**570**	66	58	51	43	35	27	19	12	4	0	0
570	**580**	68	60	52	44	36	29	21	13	5	0	0
580	**590**	69	61	54	46	38	30	22	15	7	0	0
590	**600**	71	63	55	47	39	32	24	16	8	1	0
600	**610**	72	64	57	49	41	33	25	18	10	2	0
610	**620**	74	66	58	50	42	35	27	19	11	4	0
620	**630**	75	67	60	52	44	36	28	21	13	5	0
630	**640**	77	69	61	53	45	38	30	22	14	7	0
640	**650**	78	70	63	55	47	39	31	24	16	8	0
650	**660**	80	72	64	56	48	41	33	25	17	10	2
660	**670**	81	73	66	58	50	42	34	27	19	11	3
670	**680**	83	75	67	59	51	44	36	28	20	13	5
680	**690**	84	76	69	61	53	45	37	30	22	14	6

from employees' earnings. As a rule, the amounts withheld are a percentage (specified in the state revenue code) of the amount withheld for the federal income tax. Or they may be a specified percentage of the employee's earnings. For the sake of simplicity, we have assumed that Jordan's wages are subject to state income taxes of 2%, or \$11.04 (2% × \$552) per week.

There is no limit on the amount of gross earnings subject to income tax withholdings. In fact, the higher the earnings, the higher the amount of taxes withheld.

OTHER DEDUCTIONS. Employees may voluntarily authorize withholdings for charitable, retirement, and other purposes. All voluntary deductions from gross earnings should be authorized in writing by the employee. The authorization(s) may be made individually or as part of a group plan. Deductions for charitable organizations, such as the United Fund, or for financial arrangements, such as U.S. savings bonds and repayment of loans from company credit unions, are made individually. Deductions for union dues, health and life insurance, and pension plans are often made on a group basis. We will assume that Jordan has weekly voluntary deductions of \$10 for the United Fund and \$5 for union dues.

Net Pay

ALTERNATIVE TERMINOLOGY
Net pay is also called *take-home pay*.

Net pay is determined by subtracting payroll deductions from gross earnings. For Michael Jordan, net pay for the pay period is \$432.80, computed as follows. Assuming that Michael Jordan's wages for each week during the year are \$552,

Illustration 11-14

Computation of net pay

Gross earnings		\$552.00
Payroll deductions:		
FICA taxes	\$44.16	
Federal income taxes	49.00	
State income taxes	11.04	
United Fund	10.00	
Union dues	5.00	119.20
Net pay		**\$432.80**

total wages for the year are \$28,704 (52 × \$552). Thus, all of Jordan's wages are subject to FICA tax during the year. Let's assume that Jordan's department head earns \$1,350 per week, or \$70,200 for the year. Since only the first \$65,000 is subject to FICA taxes, the maximum FICA withholdings on the department head's earnings would be \$5,200 (\$65,000 × 8%).

RECORDING THE PAYROLL

Recording the payroll involves maintaining payroll department records, recognizing payroll expenses and liabilities, and recording payment of the payroll.

Maintaining Payroll Department Records

To comply with state and federal laws, an employer must keep a cumulative record of each employee's gross earnings, deductions, and net pay during the year. The record that provides this information is the **employee earnings record**. Michael

Illustration 11-15

Employee earnings record

ACADEMY COMPANY
Employee Earnings Record
For the Year 2002

Name	Michael Jordan	**Address**	2345 Mifflin Ave.
Social Security Number	329-36-9547		Hampton, Michigan 48292
Date of Birth	December 24, 1962	**Telephone**	555-238-9051
Date Employed	September 1, 1998	**Date Employment Ended**	
Sex	Male	**Exemptions**	2
Single		**Married**	x

2002 Period Ending	Total Hours	Gross Earnings Regular	Overtime	Total	Cumulative	Deductions FICA	Fed. Inc. Tax	State Inc. Tax	United Fund	Union Dues	Total	Payment Net Amount	Check No.
1/7	42	480.00	36.00	516.00	516.00	41.28	43.00	10.32	10.00	5.00	109.60	406.40	974
1/14	**44**	**480.00**	**72.00**	**552.00**	**1,068.00**	**44.16**	**49.00**	**11.04**	**10.00**	**5.00**	**119.20**	**432.80**	**1028**
1/21	43	480.00	54.00	534.00	1,602.00	42.72	46.00	10.68	10.00	5.00	114.40	419.60	1077
1/28	42	480.00	36.00	516.00	2,118.00	41.28	43.00	10.32	10.00	5.00	109.60	406.40	1133
Jan. Total		1,920.00	198.00	2,118.00		169.44	181.00	42.36	40.00	20.00	452.80	1,665.20	

Jordan's employee earnings record is shown in Illustration 11-15.

A separate earnings record is kept for each employee. It is updated after each pay period. The cumulative payroll data on the earnings record are used by the employer to: (1) determine when an employee has earned the maximum earnings subject to FICA taxes, (2) file state and federal payroll tax returns (as explained later in the chapter), and (3) provide each employee with a statement of gross earnings and tax withholdings for the year. Illustration 11-19 on page 466 shows this statement.

In addition to employee earnings records, many companies find it useful to prepare a **payroll register**. This record accumulates the gross earnings, deductions, and net pay by employee for each pay period. It provides the documentation for preparing a paycheck for each employee. Academy Company's payroll register is presented in Illustration 11-16. It shows the data for Michael Jordan in the wages section. In this example, Academy Company's total weekly payroll is $17,210, as shown in the gross earnings column.

Note that this record is a listing of each employee's payroll data for the pay period. In some companies, a payroll register is a journal or book of original entry. Postings are made from it directly to ledger accounts. In other companies, the payroll register is a memorandum record that provides the data for a general journal entry and subsequent posting to the ledger accounts. At Academy Company, the latter procedure is followed.

Illustration 11-16

Payroll register

ACADEMY COMPANY
Payroll Register
For the Week Ending January 14, 2002

		Earnings			Deductions						Paid		Accounts Debited	
Employee	**Total Hours**	**Regular**	**Over-time**	**Gross**	**FICA**	**Federal Income Tax**	**State Income Tax**	**United Fund**	**Union Dues**	**Total**	**Net Pay**	**Check No.**	**Office Salaries Expense**	**Wages Expense**
Office Salaries														
Arnold, Patricia	40	580.00		580.00	46.40	61.00	11.60	15.00		134.00	446.00	998	580.00	
Canton, Matthew	40	590.00		590.00	47.20	63.00	11.80	20.00		142.00	448.00	999	590.00	
Mueller, William	40	530.00		530.00	42.40	54.00	10.60	11.00		118.00	412.0	1000	530.00	
Subtotal		5,200.00		5,200.00	416.00	1,090.00	104.00	120.00		1,730.00	3,470.00		5,200.00	
Wages														
Bennett, Robin	42	480.00	36.00	516.00	41.28	43.00	10.32	18.00	5.00	117.60	398.40	1025		516.00
Jordan, Michael	**44**	**480.00**	**72.00**	**552.00**	**44.16**	**49.00**	**11.04**	**10.00**	**5.00**	**119.20**	**432.80**	**1028**		**552.00**
Milroy, Lee	43	480.00	54.00	534.00	42.72	46.00	10.68	10.00	5.00	114.40	419.60	1029		534.00
Subtotal		11,000.00	1,010.00	12,010.00	960.80	2,400.00	240.20	301.50	115.00	4,017.50	7,992.50			12,010.00
Total		16,200.00	1,010.00	17,210.00	1,376.80	3,490.00	344.20	421.50	115.00	5,747.50	11,462.50		5,200.00	12,010.00

Recognizing Payroll Expenses and Liabilities

From the payroll register in Illustration 11-16, a journal entry is made to record the payroll. For the week ending January 14 the entry is:

Jan. 14	Office Salaries Expense	5,200.00	
	Wages Expense	12,010.00	
	FICA Taxes Payable		1,376.80
	Federal Income Taxes Payable		3,490.00
	State Income Taxes Payable		344.20
	United Fund Payable		421.50
	Union Dues Payable		115.00
	Salaries and Wages Payable		11,462.50
	(To record payroll for the week ending January 14)		

A	=	L	+	OE
		+1,376.80		−5,200.00
		+3,490.00		−12,010.00
		+344.20		
		+421.50		
		+115.00		
		+11,462.50		

Specific liability accounts are credited for the mandatory and voluntary deductions made during the pay period. In the example, debits to Office Salaries and Wages Expense are used for gross earnings because office workers are on a salary and other employees are paid on an hourly rate. In other companies, there may be debits to other accounts such as Store Salaries or Sales Salaries. The amount credited to Salaries and Wages Payable is the sum of the individual checks the employees will receive.

Recording Payment of the Payroll

Payment by check is made either from the employer's regular bank account or a payroll bank account. Each paycheck is usually accompanied by a detachable **statement of earnings** document. This shows the employee's gross earnings, payroll deductions, and net pay for the period and for the year-to-date. The Academy Company uses its regular bank account for payroll checks. The paycheck and statement of earnings for Michael Jordan are shown in Illustration 11-17.

Illustration 11-17

Paycheck and statement of earnings

AC

ACADEMY COMPANY
19 Center St.
Hampton, MI 48291

No. 1028

January 14, 2002 62—1113/610

Pay to the order of Michael Jordan $ 432.80

Four Hundred Thirty-two and 80/100 Dollars

City Bank & Trust
P.O. Box 3000
Hampton, MI 48291

For Payroll

Randall E. Barnes

003244771" 7 6 0

DETACH AND RETAIN THIS PORTION FOR YOUR RECORDS

NAME	SOC. SEC. NO.	EMPL. NUMBER	NO. EXEMP	PAY PERIOD ENDING
Michael Jordan	329-36-9547		2	1/14/02

REG. HRS.	O.T. HRS.	OTH. HRS. (1)	OTH. HRS. (2)	REG. EARNINGS	O.T. EARNINGS	OTH. EARNINGS (1)	OTH. EARNINGS (2)	GROSS
40	4			480.00	72.00			$552.00

FED. W/H TAX	FICA	STATE TAX	LOCAL TAX	OTHER DEDUCTIONS (1)	(2)	(3)	(4)	NET PAY
49.00	44.16	11.04		10.00	5.00			432.80

YEAR TO DATE

FED. W/H TAX	FICA	STATE TAX	LOCAL TAX	OTHER DEDUCTIONS (1)	(2)	(3)	(4)	NET PAY
92.00	85.44	21.36		20.00	10.00			$839.20

HELPFUL HINT

Do any of the income tax liabilities result in payroll tax expense for the employer? Answer: No. The employer is acting only as a collection agent for the government.

Following payment of the payroll, the check numbers are entered in the payroll register. The entry to record payment of the payroll for Academy Company is as follows.

Jan. 14	Salaries and Wages Payable	11,462.50	
	Cash		11,462.50
	(To record payment of payroll)		

A	=	L	+	OE
−11,462.50		−11,462.50		

When currency is used in payment, one check is prepared for the payroll's total amount of net pay. This check is then cashed, and the coins and currency are inserted in individual pay envelopes for disbursement to individual employees.

TECHNOLOGY IN ACTION

In addition to supplying the entry to record the payroll, the output for a computerized payroll system would include (1) payroll checks, (2) a payroll check register sorted by check and department, and (3) updated employee earnings records. Those employee records become the source for monthly, quarterly, and annual reporting of wages to taxing agencies.

BEFORE YOU GO ON...

REVIEW IT

1. Identify two internal control procedures that apply to each payroll function.
2. What are the primary sources of gross earnings?
3. What payroll deductions are (a) mandatory and (b) voluntary?
4. What account titles are used in recording a payroll, assuming only mandatory payroll deductions are involved?

DO IT

Your cousin Stan is establishing a house-cleaning business and will have a number of employees working for him. He is aware that documentation procedures are an important part of internal control. But he is confused about the difference between an employee earnings record and a payroll register. He asks you to explain the principal differences, because he wants to be sure that he sets up the proper payroll procedures.

ACTION PLAN

- Determine the earnings and deductions data that must be recorded and reported for each employee.
- Design a record that will accumulate earnings and deductions data and will serve as a basis for journal entries to be prepared and posted to the general ledger accounts.
- Explain the difference between the employee earnings record and the payroll register.

SOLUTION: An employee earnings record is kept for *each* employee. It shows gross earnings, payroll deductions, and net pay for each pay period. It provides cumulative payroll data for that employee. In contrast, a payroll register is a listing of *all* employees' gross earnings, payroll deductions, and net pay for each pay period. It is the documentation for preparing paychecks and for recording the payroll. Of course, Stan will need to keep both documents.

Related exercise material: BE11-7, BE11-8, BE11-9, E11-8, E11-9, E11-10, and E11-11.

THE NAVIGATOR

EMPLOYER PAYROLL TAXES

STUDY OBJECTIVE 8

Describe and record employer payroll taxes.

Payroll tax expense for businesses results from three taxes **levied on employers** by governmental agencies. These taxes are: (1) FICA, (2) federal unemployment tax, and (3) state unemployment tax. These taxes plus such items as paid vacations and pensions are collectively referred to as **fringe benefits**. As indicated earlier, the cost of fringe benefits in many companies is substantial.

FICA Taxes

We have seen that each employee must pay FICA taxes. An employer must match each employee's FICA contribution. The matching contribution results in **payroll tax expense** to the employer. The employer's tax is subject to the same rate and maximum earnings applicable to the employee. The account, FICA Taxes Payable, is used for both the employee's and the employer's FICA contributions. For the January 14 payroll, Academy Company's FICA tax contribution is $1,376.80 ($17,210.00 × 8%).

Federal Unemployment Taxes

HELPFUL HINT

FICA taxes are paid by both the employer and employee. Federal unemployment taxes and (in most states) the state unemployment taxes are borne entirely by the employer.

The Federal Unemployment Tax Act (FUTA) is another feature of the federal Social Security program. **Federal unemployment taxes** provide benefits for a limited period of time to employees who lose their jobs through no fault of their own. Under provisions of the Act, the employer is required to pay a tax of 6.2% on the first $7,000 of gross wages paid to each employee during a calendar year. The law allows the employer a maximum credit of 5.4% on the federal rate for contributions to state unemployment taxes. Because of this provision, state unemployment tax laws generally provide for a 5.4% rate. The effective federal unemployment tax rate thus becomes 0.8% (6.2% − 5.4%). This tax is borne **entirely by the employer**. There is no deduction or withholding from employees.

The account Federal Unemployment Taxes Payable is used to recognize this liability. The federal unemployment tax for Academy Company for the January 14 payroll is $137.68 ($17,210.00 × 0.8%).

State Unemployment Taxes

All states have unemployment compensation programs under state unemployment tax acts (SUTA). Like federal unemployment taxes, **state unemployment taxes** provide benefits to employees who lose their jobs. These taxes are levied on employers.[2] The basic rate is usually 5.4% on the first $7,000 of wages paid to an employee during the year. The basic rate is adjusted according to the employer's experience rating: Companies with a history of unstable employment may pay more than the basic rate. Companies with a history of stable employment may pay less than 5.4%. Regardless of the rate paid, the credit on the federal unemployment tax is still 5.4%.

The account State Unemployment Taxes Payable is used for this liability. The state unemployment tax for Academy Company for the January 14 payroll is $929.34 ($17,210.00 × 5.4%).

Illustration 11-18 summarizes the types of employer payroll taxes.

Illustration 11-18

Employer payroll taxes

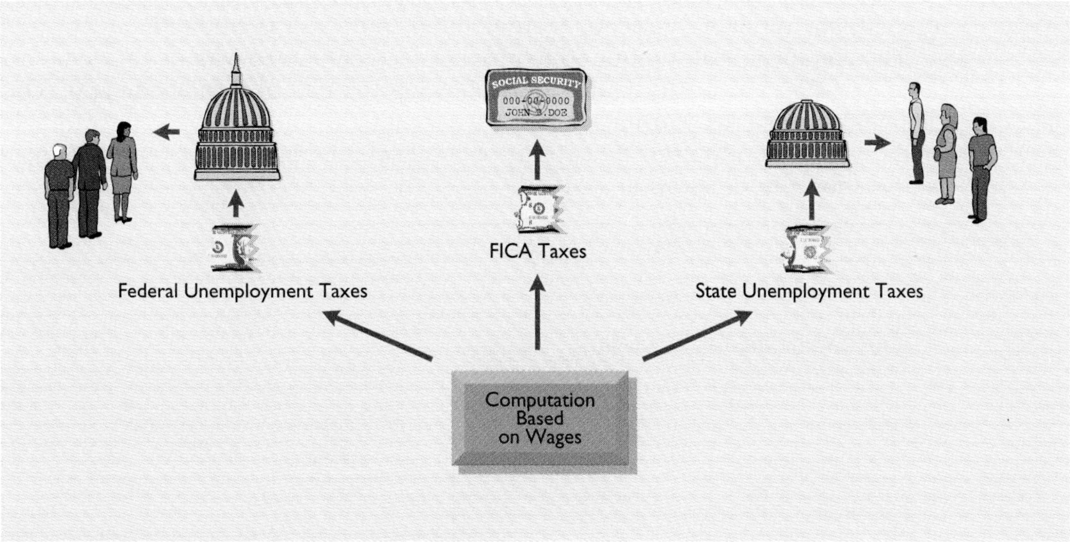

Recording Employer Payroll Taxes

Employer payroll taxes are usually recorded at the same time the payroll is journalized. The entire amount of gross pay ($17,210.00) shown in the payroll register in Illustration 11-16 is subject to each of the three taxes mentioned above. Accordingly, the entry to record the payroll tax expense associated with the January 14 payroll is:

Jan. 14	Payroll Tax Expense	2,443.82	
	FICA Taxes Payable		1,376.80
	Federal Unemployment Taxes Payable		137.68
	State Unemployment Taxes Payable		929.34
	(To record employer's payroll taxes on January 14 payroll)		

A	=	L	+	OE
		+1,376.80		−2,443.82
		+137.68		
		+929.34		

[2]In a few states, the employee is also required to make a contribution. In this textbook, including the homework, we will assume that the tax is only on the employer.

Separate liability accounts are used instead of a single credit to Payroll Taxes Payable. Why? Because these liabilities are payable to different taxing authorities at different dates. The liability accounts are classified in the balance sheet as current liabilities since they will be paid within the next year. Payroll Tax Expense is classified on the income statement as an operating expense.

FILING AND REMITTING PAYROLL TAXES

Preparation of payroll tax returns is the responsibility of the payroll department. Payment of the taxes is made by the treasurer's department. Much of the information for the returns is obtained from employee earnings records.

For purposes of reporting and remitting to the IRS, FICA taxes and federal income taxes that were withheld are combined. **The taxes must be reported quarterly**, no later than one month following the close of each quarter. The remitting requirements depend on the amount of taxes withheld and the length of the pay period. Remittances are made through deposits in either a Federal Reserve bank or an authorized commercial bank.

Federal unemployment taxes are generally filed and remitted **annually** on or before January 31 of the subsequent year. Earlier payments are required when the tax exceeds a specified amount. State unemployment taxes usually must be filed and paid by the **end of the month following each quarter**. When payroll taxes are paid, payroll liability accounts are debited, and Cash is credited.

The employer is also required to provide each employee with a **Wage and Tax Statement (Form W-2)** by January 31 following the end of a calendar year. This statement shows gross earnings, FICA taxes withheld, and income taxes withheld for the year. The required W-2 form for Michael Jordan, using assumed annual data, is shown in Illustration 11-19.

Illustration 11-19

W-2 form

Form **W-2 Wage and Tax Statement** Calendar Year **2002**

1 Control number

OMB No. 1545-0008

2 Employer's name, address and ZIP code Academy Company 19 Center St. Hampton, MI 48291		3 Employer's identification number 36-2167852	4 Employer's State number
		5 Stat. employee ☐ Deceased ☐ Legal rep. ☐ 942 emp. ☐ Subtotal ☐ Void ☐	
		6 Allocated tips	7 Advance EIC payment
8 Employee's social security number 329-36-9547	9 Federal income tax withheld $2,248.00	10 Wages, tips, other compensation $26,300.00	11 Social security tax withheld $2,104.00
12 Employee's name, address, and ZIP code Michael Jordan 2345 Mifflin Ave. Hampton, MI 48292		13 Social security wages $26,300.00	14 Social security tips
		16	
		17 State income tax $526.00 · 18 State wages, tips, etc.	19 Name of State Michigan
		20 Local income tax · 21 Local wages, tips, etc.	22 Name of locality

The employer must send a copy of each employee's Wage and Tax Statement (Form W-2) to the Social Security Administration. This agency subsequently furnishes the Internal Revenue Service with the income data required.

BEFORE YOU GO ON...

REVIEW IT

1. What payroll taxes are levied on employers?
2. What accounts are involved in accruing employer payroll taxes?

DO IT

In January, the payroll supervisor determines that gross earnings in Halo Company are $70,000. All earnings are subject to 8% FICA taxes, 5.4% state unemployment taxes, and 0.8% federal unemployment taxes. You are asked to record the employer's payroll taxes.

ACTION PLAN

- Compute the employer's payroll taxes on the period's gross earnings.
- Identify the expense account(s) to be debited.
- Identify the liability account(s) to be credited.

SOLUTION: The entry to record the employer's payroll taxes is:

Payroll Tax Expense	9,940	
FICA Taxes Payable ($70,000 × 8%)		5,600
Federal Unemployment Taxes Payable ($70,000 × 0.8%)		560
State Unemployment Taxes Payable ($70,000 × 5.4%)		3,780
(To record employer's payroll taxes on January payroll)		

Related exercise material: BE11-10, E11-10, and E11-12.

THE NAVIGATOR

ADDITIONAL FRINGE BENEFITS

STUDY OBJECTIVE 9

Identify additional fringe benefits associated with employee compensation.

In addition to the three payroll tax fringe benefits, employers incur other substantial fringe benefit costs. Two of the most important are paid absences and postretirement benefits.

Paid Absences

Employees often are given rights to receive compensation for absences when certain conditions of employment are met. The compensation may be for paid vacations, sick pay benefits, and paid holidays. When the payment for such absences is **probable** and the amount can be **reasonably estimated**, a liability should be accrued for paid future absences. When the amount cannot be reasonably estimated, the potential liability should be disclosed. Ordinarily, vacation pay is the only paid absence that is accrued. The other types of paid absences are only disclosed.[3]

To illustrate, assume that Academy Company employees are entitled to one day's vacation for each month worked. If 30 employees earn an average of $110 per day in a given month, the accrual for vacation benefits in one month is $3,300. The liability is recognized at the end of the month by the following adjusting entry.

Jan. 31	Vacation Benefits Expense	3,300	
	Vacation Benefits Payable		3,300
	(To accrue vacation benefits expense)		

A	=	L	+	OE
		+3,300		−3,300

This accrual is required by the matching principle. Vacation Benefits Expense is reported as an operating expense in the income statement, and Vacation Benefits Payable is reported as a current liability in the balance sheet.

[3] The typical U.S. company provides an average of 12 days of paid vacations for its employees, at an average cost of 5% of gross earnings.

Later, when vacation benefits are paid, Vacation Benefits Payable is debited and Cash is credited. For example, if the above benefits for 10 employees are paid in July, the entry is:

A	=	L	+	OE
−1,100		−1,100		

July 31	Vacation Benefits Payable	1,100	
	Cash		1,100
	(To record payment of vacation benefits)		

The magnitude of unpaid absences has gained employers' attention. Consider the case of an assistant superintendent of schools who worked for 20 years and rarely took a vacation or sick day. A month or so before she retired, the school district discovered that she was due nearly $30,000 in accrued benefits. Yet the liability had never been accrued.

Postretirement Benefits

Postretirement benefits are benefits provided by employers to retired employees for (1) health care and life insurance and (2) pensions. For many years the accounting for postretirement benefits was on a cash basis. Now, both types of postretirement benefits are accounted for on the accrual basis.

POSTRETIREMENT HEALTH CARE AND LIFE INSURANCE BENEFITS. Providing medical and related health care benefits for retirees was at one time an inexpensive and highly effective way of generating employee goodwill. This practice has now turned into one of corporate America's most worrisome financial problems. Runaway medical costs, early retirement, and increased longevity are sending the liability for retiree health plans through the roof.

Many companies began offering retiree health care coverage in the form of Medicare supplements in the 1960s. Almost all plans operated on a pay-as-you-go basis. The companies simply paid for the bills as they came in, rather than setting aside funds to meet the cost of future benefits. These plans were accounted for on the cash basis. But, the FASB concluded that shareholders and creditors should know the amount of the employer's obligations. As a result, employers must now use the **accrual basis** in accounting for postretirement health care and life insurance benefits.

ACCOUNTING IN ACTION *Business Insight*

The battle over fringe benefits has increased as benefits outpace wages and salaries. Growing faster than pay, benefits equaled 38% of wages and salaries in a recent year. While vacations and other forms of paid leave still take the biggest bite of the benefits pie, medical costs are the fastest-growing item.

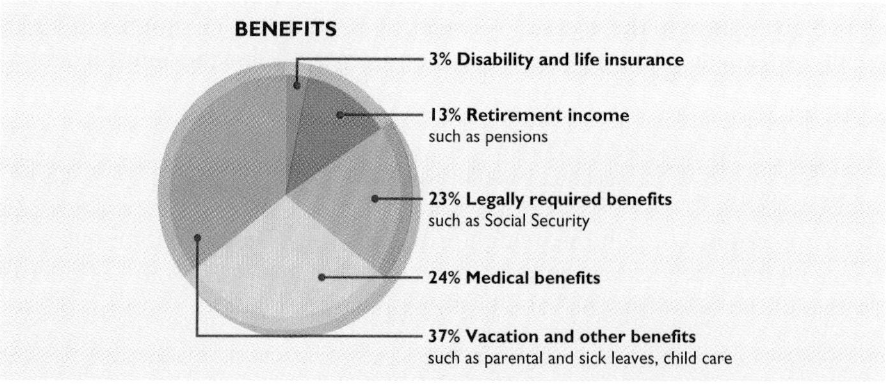

PENSION PLANS. A **pension plan** is an agreement whereby an employer provides benefits (payments) to employees after they retire. Over 50 million workers currently participate in pension plans in the United States. The need for good accounting for pension plans becomes apparent when one appreciates the size of existing pension funds. Most pension plans are subject to the provisions of ERISA (Employee Retirement Income Security Act), a law enacted to curb abuses in the administration and funding of such plans.

> **HELPFUL HINT**
> With more than $4 trillion in assets overall, both public and private pension funds comprise over one-fifth of the total financial assets in the United States today—and these amounts are growing.

Three parties are generally involved in a pension plan. The **employer** (company) sponsors the pension plan. The **plan administrator** receives the contributions from the employer, invests the pension assets, and makes the benefit payments to the **pension recipients** (retired employees). Illustration 11-20 indicates the flow of cash among the three parties involved in a pension plan.

Illustration 11-20

Parties in a pension plan

An employer-financed pension is part of the employees' compensation. ERISA establishes the minimum contribution that a company must make each year toward employee pensions. The company records the pension costs as an expense while the employees are working because that is when the company receives benefits from the employees' services. Generally the pension expense is reported as an operating expense in the company's income statement.

Frequently, the amount contributed by the company to the pension plan is different from the amount of the pension expense. A **liability** is recognized when the pension expense to date is **more than** the company's contributions to date. An **asset** is recognized when the pension expense to date is **less than** the company's contributions to date. Further consideration of the accounting for pension plans is left for more advanced courses.

BEFORE YOU GO ON...

REVIEW IT

1. What accounts are involved in accruing and paying vacation benefits?
2. What basis should be used in accounting for postretirement benefits?

A LOOK BACK AT OUR FEATURE STORY

Refer back to the Feature Story about Wilbert Murdock at the beginning of the chapter, and answer the following questions.

1. Why do entrepreneurs like Wilbert Murdock and other small businesses have difficulty obtaining traditional debt financing?
2. What type of financing did Wilbert Murdock resort to, as did one-third of businesses with fewer than 20 employees? Why is Murdock's method of financing at all appealing?
3. What are the disadvantages of using credit cards as a means of debt financing?

SOLUTION

1. Traditional debt financing is generally not available to entrepreneurs and other small businesses because bank loans and bond issuances require established credit ratings, earnings records, positive cash flow, and collateral—none of which are usually possessed by new, emerging small businesses.
2. Wilbert Murdock resorted to using credit cards to finance his business ventures. Credit cards are appealing because they are readily available (new card applications appear in mailboxes weekly) and because credit card companies don't monitor how the money is spent.
3. Credit card financing is generally expensive, with interest ranging between 14% and 21% (except for special introductory offers, which are temporary in nature), and the amounts per individual credit card are generally small ($2,000–$10,000).

THE NAVIGATOR

DEMONSTRATION PROBLEM

Additional Demonstration Problem

Indiana Jones Company had the following selected transactions.

Feb. 1 Signs a $50,000, 6-month, 9%-interest-bearing note payable to CitiBank and receives $50,000 in cash.

10 Cash register sales total $43,200, which includes an 8% sales tax.

28 The payroll for the month consists of Sales Salaries $32,000 and Office Salaries $18,000. All wages are subject to 8% FICA taxes. A total of $8,900 federal income taxes are withheld. The salaries are paid on March 1.

28 The following adjustment data are developed.

1. Interest expense of $375 has been incurred on the note.
2. Employer payroll taxes include 8% FICA taxes, a 5.4% state unemployment tax, and a 0.8% federal unemployment tax.
3. Some sales were made under warranty. Of the units sold under warranty, 350 are expected to become defective. Repair costs are estimated to be $40 per unit.

Instructions

(a) Journalize the February transactions.
(b) Journalize the adjusting entries at February 28.

ACTION PLAN

- To determine sales, divide the cash register total by 100% plus the sales tax percentage.
- Base payroll taxes on gross earnings.
- Expense warranty costs in the period in which the sale occurs.

SOLUTION TO DEMONSTRATION PROBLEM

(a) Feb. 1	Cash	50,000	
	Notes Payable		50,000
	(Issued 6-month, 9%-interest-bearing note to CitiBank)		
10	Cash	43,200	
	Sales ($43,200 ÷ 1.08)		40,000
	Sales Taxes Payable ($40,000 × 8%)		3,200
	(To record sales and sales taxes payable)		
28	Sales Salaries Expense	32,000	
	Office Salaries Expense	18,000	
	FICA Taxes Payable (8% × $50,000)		4,000
	Federal Income Taxes Payable		8,900
	Salaries Payable		37,100
	(To record February salaries)		
(b) Feb. 28	Interest Expense	375	
	Interest Payable		375
	(To record accrued interest for February)		

28	Payroll Tax Expense	7,100	
	FICA Taxes Payable		4,000
	Federal Unemployment Taxes Payable (0.8% × $50,000)		400
	State Unemployment Taxes Payable (5.4% × $50,000)		2,700
	(To record employer's payroll taxes on February payroll)		
28	Warranty Expense (350 × $40)	14,000	
	Estimated Warranty Liability		14,000
	(To record estimated product warranty liability)		

THE NAVIGATOR

SUMMARY OF STUDY OBJECTIVES

1. *Explain a current liability, and identify the major types of current liabilities.* A current liability is a debt that can reasonably be expected to be paid (1) from existing current assets or through the creation of other current liabilities, and (2) within one year or the operating cycle, whichever is longer. The major types of current liabilities are notes payable, accounts payable, sales taxes payable, unearned revenues, and accrued liabilities such as taxes, salaries and wages, and interest payable.

2. *Describe the accounting for notes payable.* When a promissory note is interest-bearing, the amount of assets received upon the issuance of the note is generally equal to the face value of the note. Interest expense is accrued over the life of the note. At maturity, the amount paid is equal to the face value of the note plus accrued interest.

3. *Explain the accounting for other current liabilities.* Sales taxes payable are recorded at the time the related sales occur. The company serves as a collection agent for the taxing authority. Sales taxes are not an expense to the company. Unearned revenues are initially recorded in an unearned revenue account. As the revenue is earned, a transfer from unearned revenue to earned revenue occurs. The current maturities of long-term debt are reported as a current liability in the balance sheet.

4. *Explain the financial statement presentation and analysis of current liabilities.* The nature and amount of each current liability should be reported in the balance sheet or in schedules in the notes accompanying the statements. The liquidity of a company may be analyzed by computing working capital and the current ratio.

5. *Describe the accounting and disclosure requirements for contingent liabilities.* If the contingency is probable (likely to occur) and the amount is reasonably estimable, the liability should be recorded in the accounts. If the contingency is only reasonably possible (it could happen), then it should be disclosed only in the notes to the financial statements. If the possibility that the contingency will happen is remote (unlikely to occur), it need not be recorded or disclosed.

6. *Discuss the objectives of internal control for payroll.* The objectives of internal control for payroll are (1) to safeguard company assets against unauthorized payments of payrolls, and (2) to ensure the accuracy of the accounting records pertaining to payrolls.

7. *Compute and record the payroll for a pay period.* The computation of the payroll involves gross earnings, payroll deductions, and net pay. In recording the payroll, salaries (or wages) expense is debited for gross earnings, individual tax and other liability accounts are credited for payroll deductions, and salaries (wages) payable is credited for net pay. When the payroll is paid, Salaries and Wages Payable is debited, and Cash is credited.

8. *Describe and record employer payroll taxes.* Employer payroll taxes consist of FICA, federal unemployment taxes, and state unemployment taxes. The taxes are usually accrued at the time the payroll is recorded by debiting Payroll Tax Expense and crediting separate liability accounts for each type of tax.

9. *Identify additional fringe benefits associated with employee compensation.* Additional fringe benefits associated with wages are paid absences (paid vacations, sick pay benefits, and paid holidays), and postretirement benefits (health care and life insurance and pensions). Both types of benefits should be accounted for on the accrual basis.

THE NAVIGATOR

Key Term Matching Activity

GLOSSARY

Bonus Compensation to management and other personnel, based on factors such as increased sales or the amount of net income. (p. 457).

Contingent liability A potential liability that may become an actual liability in the future. (p. 451).

Current ratio A measure of a company's liquidity; computed as current assets divided by current liabilities. (p. 451).

Employee earnings record A cumulative record of each employee's gross earnings, deductions, and net pay during the year. (p. 461).

Employee's Withholding Allowance Certificate (Form W-4) An Internal Revenue Service form on which the employee indicates the number of allowances claimed for withholding federal income taxes. (p. 459).

Federal unemployment taxes Taxes imposed on the employer by the federal government that provide benefits for a limited time period to employees who lose their jobs through no fault of their own. (p. 464).

FICA taxes Taxes designed to provide workers with supplemental retirement, employment disability, and medical benefits. (p. 458).

Gross earnings Total compensation earned by an employee. (p. 457).

Net pay Gross earnings less payroll deductions. (p. 460).

Notes payable Obligations in the form of written promissory notes. (p. 447).

Payroll deductions Deductions from gross earnings to determine the amount of a paycheck. (p. 457).

Payroll register A payroll record that accumulates the gross earnings, deductions, and net pay by employee for each pay period. (p. 461).

Pension plan An agreement whereby an employer provides benefits to employees after they retire. (p. 469).

Postretirement benefits Payments by employers to retired employees for health care, life insurance, and pensions. (p. 468).

Salaries Employee pay based on a fixed amount rather than an hourly rate. (p. 454).

Statement of earnings A document attached to a paycheck that indicates the employee's gross earnings, payroll deductions, and net pay. (p. 462).

State unemployment taxes Taxes imposed on the employer by states that provide benefits to employees who lose their jobs. (p. 465).

Wage and Tax Statement (Form W-2) A form showing gross earnings, FICA taxes withheld, and income taxes withheld, prepared annually by an employer for each employee. (p. 466).

Wages Amounts paid to employees based on a rate per hour or on a piece-work basis. (p. 454).

Working capital A measure of a company's liquidity; computed as current assets minus current liabilities. (p. 450).

Chapter 11 Self-Test

SELF-STUDY QUESTIONS

Answers are at the end of the chapter.

(SO 1) **1.** The time period for classifying a liability as current is one year or the operating cycle, whichever is:
a. longer.
b. shorter.
c. probable.
d. possible.

(SO 1) **2.** To be classified as a current liability, a debt must be expected to be paid:
a. out of existing current assets.
b. by creating other current liabilities.
c. within 2 years.
d. both (a) and (b).

(SO 2) **3.** Maggie Sharrer Company borrows $88,500 on September 1, 2002, from Sandwich State Bank by signing an $88,500, 12%, one-year note. What is the accrued interest at December 31, 2002?
a. $2,655.
b. $3,540.
c. $4,425.
d. $10,620.

(SO 3) **4.** Rhodes Company has total proceeds from sales of $4,515. If the proceeds include sales taxes of 5%, the amount to be credited to Sales is:
a. $4,000.
b. $4,300.
c. $4,289.25.
d. No correct answer given.

(SO 4) **5.** Working capital is calculated as:
a. current assets minus current liabilities.
b. total assets minus total liabilities.
c. long-term liabilities minus current liabilities.
d. both (b) and (c).

(SO 5) **6.** A contingent liability should be recorded in the accounts when:
a. it is probable the contingency will happen, but the amount cannot be reasonably estimated.
b. it is reasonably possible the contingency will happen, and the amount can be reasonably estimated.
c. it is probable the contingency will happen, and the amount can be reasonably estimated.
d. it is reasonably possible the contingency will happen, but the amount cannot be reasonably estimated.

7. At December 31, Hanes Company prepares an adjusting entry for a product warranty contract. Which of the following accounts is/are included in the entry? (SO 5)
a. Miscellaneous Expense.
b. Estimated Warranty Liability.
c. Repair Parts/Wages Payable.
d. Both (a) and (b).

8. The department that should pay the payroll is the: (SO 6)
a. timekeeping department.
b. human resources department.
c. payroll department.
d. treasurer's department.

9. J. Barr earns $14 per hour for a 40-hour week and $21 per hour for any overtime work. If Barr works 45 hours in a week, gross earnings are: (SO 7)
a. $560.
b. $630.
c. $650.
d. $665.

10. Employer payroll taxes do not include: (SO 8)
a. federal unemployment taxes.
b. state unemployment taxes.
c. federal income taxes.
d. FICA taxes.

11. Which of the following is *not* an additional fringe benefit? (SO 9)
a. Postretirement pensions.
b. Paid absences.
c. Paid vacations.
d. Salaries.

THE NAVIGATOR

QUESTIONS

1. Jeff Baumgartner believes a current liability is a debt that can be expected to be paid in one year. Is Jeff correct? Explain.
2. Mesa Verde Company obtains $25,000 in cash by signing a 9%, 6-month, $25,000 note payable to First Bank on July 1. Mesa Verde's fiscal year ends on September 30. What information should be reported for the note payable in the annual financial statements?
3. (a) Your roommate says, "Sales taxes are reported as an expense in the income statement." Do you agree? Explain.
   (b) Planet Hollywood has cash proceeds from sales of $10,400. This amount includes $400 of sales taxes. Give the entry to record the proceeds.
4. Aurora University sold 10,000 season football tickets at $80 each for its five-game home schedule. What entries should be made (a) when the tickets were sold, and (b) after each game?
5. What is liquidity? What are two measures of liquidity?
6. What is a contingent liability? Give an example of a contingent liability that is usually recorded in the accounts.
7. Under what circumstances is a contingent liability disclosed only in the notes to the financial statements? Under what circumstances is a contingent liability not recorded in the accounts nor disclosed in the notes to the financial statements?
8. You are a newly hired accountant with Spartan Company. On your first day, the controller asks you to identify the main internal control objectives related to payroll accounting. How would you respond?
9. What are the four functions associated with payroll activities?
10. What is the difference between gross pay and net pay? Which amount should a company record as wages or salaries expense?
11. Which payroll tax is levied on both employers and employees?
12. Are the federal and state income taxes withheld from employee paychecks a payroll tax expense for the employer? Explain your answer.
13. What do the following acronyms stand for: FICA, FUTA, and SUTA?
14. What information is shown in a W-4 statement? In a W-2 statement?
15. Distinguish between the two types of payroll deductions and give examples of each.
16. What are the primary uses of the employee earnings record?
17. (a) Identify the three types of employer payroll taxes.
    (b) How are tax liability accounts and payroll tax expense classified in the financial statements?
18. Identify three additional types of fringe benefits associated with employees' compensation.
19. Often during job interviews, the candidate asks the potential employer about the firm's paid absences policy. What are paid absences? How are they accounted for?
20. What are two types of postretirement benefits? During what years does the FASB advocate expensing the employer's costs of these postretirement benefits?
21. What basis of accounting for the employer's cost of postretirement health care and life insurance benefits has been used by most companies, and what basis does the FASB now require? Explain the basic difference between these methods in accounting for postretirement benefit costs.
22. Identify the three parties in a pension plan. What role does each party have in the plan?

BRIEF EXERCISES

Identify whether obligations are current liabilities.
(SO 1)

BE11-1 Compagna Company has the following obligations at December 31: (a) a note payable for $100,000 due in 2 years, (b) a 10-year mortgage payable of $400,000 payable in ten $40,000 annual payments, (c) interest payable of $15,000 on the mortgage, and (d) accounts payable of $60,000. For each obligation, indicate whether it should be classified as a current liability. (Assume an operating cycle of less than one year.)

Prepare entries for an interest-bearing note payable.
(SO 2)

BE11-2 Borke Company borrows $90,000 on July 1 from the bank by signing a $90,000, 10%, one-year note payable.

(a) Prepare the journal entry to record the proceeds of the note.
(b) Prepare the journal entry to record accrued interest at December 31, assuming adjusting entries are made only at the end of the year.

Compute and record sales taxes payable.
(SO 3)

BE11-3 Brotcke Auto Supply does not segregate sales and sales taxes at the time of sale. The register total for March 16 is $11,970. All sales are subject to a 5% sales tax. Compute sales taxes payable, and make the entry to record sales taxes payable and sales.

Prepare entries for unearned revenues.
(SO 3)

BE11-4 Illinois State University sells 4,000 season basketball tickets at $96 each for its 12-game home schedule. Give the entry to record (a) the sale of the season tickets and (b) the revenue earned by playing the first home game.

Analyze liquidity.
(SO 4)

BE11-5 **Yahoo! Inc.'s** 1998 financial statements contain the following selected data (in thousands).

Current assets	$467,239
Total assets	621,884
Current liabilities	79,983
Total liabilities	85,674

Compute the following ratios.

(a) Working capital.
(b) Current ratio.

Prepare adjusting entry for warranty costs.
(SO 5)

BE11-6 On December 1, Gonzalez Company introduces a new product that includes a one-year warranty on parts. In December, 1,000 units are sold. Management believes that 5% of the units will be defective and that the average warranty costs will be $75 per unit. Prepare the adjusting entry at December 31 to accrue the estimated warranty cost.

Identify payroll functions.
(SO 6)

BE11-7 Gutierrez Company has the following payroll procedures.

(a) Supervisor approves overtime work.
(b) The human resources department prepares hiring authorization forms for new hires.
(c) A second payroll department employee verifies payroll calculations.
(d) The treasurer's department pays employees.

Identify the payroll function to which each procedure pertains.

Compute gross earnings and net pay.
(SO 7)

BE11-8 Becky Sherrick's regular hourly wage rate is $14, and she receives an hourly rate of $21 for work in excess of 40 hours. During a January pay period, Becky works 45 hours. Becky's federal income tax withholding is $95, and she has no voluntary deductions. Compute Becky Sherrick's gross earnings and net pay for the pay period.

Record a payroll and the payment of wages.
(SO 7)

BE11-9 Data for Becky Sherrick are presented in BE11-8. Prepare the journal entries to record **(a)** Becky's pay for the period and **(b)** the payment of Becky's wages. Use January 15 for the end of the pay period and the payment date.

Record employer payroll taxes.
(SO 8)

BE11-10 In January, gross earnings in Bri Company totaled $70,000. All earnings are subject to 8% FICA taxes, 5.4% state unemployment taxes, and 0.8% federal unemployment taxes. Prepare the entry to record January payroll tax expense.

Record estimated vacation benefits.
(SO 9)

BE11-11 At Sublette.com Company employees are entitled to one day's vacation for each month worked. In January, 50 employees worked the full month. Record the vacation pay liability for January assuming the average daily pay for each employee is $150.

EXERCISES

Prepare entries for interest-bearing notes.
(SO 2)

E11-1 On June 1, Eddy Microchip Company borrows $70,000 from First Bank on a 6-month, $70,000, 12% note.

Instructions

(a) Prepare the entry on June 1.
(b) Prepare the adjusting entry on June 30.
(c) Prepare the entry at maturity (December 1), assuming monthly adjusting entries have been made through November 30.
(d) What was the total financing cost (interest expense)?

Journalize sales and related taxes.
(SO 3)

E11-2 In providing accounting services to small businesses, you encounter the following situations pertaining to cash sales.

1. Valarie Flynn Company rings up sales and sales taxes separately on its cash register. On April 10, the register totals are sales $25,000 and sales taxes $1,500.
2. Fleury Company does not segregate sales and sales taxes. Its register total for April 15 is $18,404, which includes a 7% sales tax.

Instructions

Prepare the entry to record the sales transactions and related taxes for each client.

Journalize unearned subscription revenue.
(SO 3)

E11-3 Etheredge Company publishes a monthly sports magazine, *Fishing Preview*. Subscriptions to the magazine cost $30 per year. During November 2002, Etheredge sells 8,000 subscriptions beginning with the December issue. Etheredge prepares financial statements quarterly and recognizes subscription revenue earned at the end of the quarter. The company uses the accounts Unearned Subscriptions and Subscription Revenue.

Instructions

(a) Prepare the entry in November for the receipt of the subscriptions.

(b) Prepare the adjusting entry at December 31, 2002, to record subscription revenue earned in December 2002.

(c) Prepare the adjusting entry at March 31, 2003, to record subscription revenue earned in the first quarter of 2003.

Record estimated liability and expense for warranties.
(SO 5)

E11-4 Zareena Company sells automatic can openers under a 75-day warranty for defective merchandise. Based on past experience, Zareena estimates that 4% of the units sold will become defective during the warranty period. Management estimates that the average cost of replacing or repairing a defective unit is $15. The units sold and units defective that occurred during the last 2 months of 2002 are as follows.

Month	Units Sold	Units Defective Prior to December 31
November	30,000	700
December	32,000	500

Instructions

(a) Determine the estimated warranty liability at December 31 for the units sold in November and December.

(b) Prepare the journal entries to record the estimated liability for warranties and the costs incurred in honoring 1,200 warranty claims. (Assume actual costs of $18,000.)

(c) Give the entry to record the honoring of 550 warranty contracts in January at an average cost of $15.

Prepare the current liability section of the balance sheet.
(SO 1, 2, 3, 4, 5)

E11-5 Leask Online Company has the following liability accounts after posting adjusting entries: Accounts Payable $66,000, Unearned Ticket Revenue $24,000, Estimated Warranty Liability $18,000, Interest Payable $8,000, Mortgage Payable $120,000, Notes Payable $80,000, and Sales Taxes Payable $10,000. Assume the company's operating cycle is less than 1 year, ticket revenue will be earned within 1 year, warranty costs are expected to be incurred within 1 year, and the notes mature in 3 years.

Instructions

(a) Prepare the current liabilities section of the balance sheet, assuming $30,000 of the mortgage is payable next year.

(b) Comment on Leask Online Company's liquidity, assuming total current assets are $300,000.

Calculate liquidity ratios.
(SO 4)

E11-6 **Kroger Co.'s** 2000 financial statements contained the following selected data (in millions).

Current assets	$ 5,531	Accounts receivable	$622
Total assets	17,966	Interest expense	652
Current liabilities	5,728	Income taxes	491
Total liabilities	15,283	Net income	628
Cash	281		

Instructions

Compute these values:

(a) Working capital.

(b) Current ratio.

Calculate current ratio and working capital before and after paying accounts payable.
(SO 4)

E11-7 The following financial data were reported by **Polaroid Corporation** for 1998 and 1999 ($ in millions).

Polaroid

POLAROID CORPORATION
Balance Sheets (partial)

	1998	1999
Current assets		
Cash and cash equivalents	$ 105.0	$ 92.0
Accounts receivable, net	459.6	489.7
Inventories	533.3	395.6
Prepaid expenses and other assets	195.5	139.6
Total current assets	$1,293.4	$1,116.9
Current liabilities	$ 933.0	$ 750.2

Instructions

(a) Calculate the current ratio and working capital for Polaroid for 1998 and 1999.

(b) Suppose that at the end of 1999 Polaroid management used $85 million cash to pay off $85 million of accounts payable. How would its current ratio and working capital have changed?

Compute net pay and record pay for one employee. (SO 7)

E11-8 Linda O'Neill's regular hourly wage rate is $16.00, and she receives a wage of $1\frac{1}{2}$ times the regular hourly rate for work in excess of 40 hours. During a March weekly pay period Linda worked 42 hours. Her gross earnings prior to the current week were $19,000. Linda is married and claims three withholding allowances. Her only voluntary deduction is for group hospitalization insurance at $15.00 per week.

Instructions

(a) Compute the following amounts for Linda's wages for the current week.

- **(1)** Gross earnings.
- **(2)** FICA taxes. (Assume an 8% rate on maximum of $65,000.)
- **(3)** Federal income taxes withheld. (Use the withholding table in the text, page 459.)
- **(4)** State income taxes withheld. (Assume a 2.0% rate.)
- **(5)** Net pay.

(b) Record Linda's pay, assuming she is an office computer operator.

Compute maximum FICA deductions. (SO 7)

E11-9 Employee earnings records for Borelias Company reveal the following gross earnings for four employees through the pay period of December 15.

C. Mull	$62,500	D. Chambers	$64,300
L. Church	$64,600	T. Olejnik	$65,000

For the pay period ending December 31, each employee's gross earnings is $2,000. The FICA tax rate is 8% on gross earnings of $65,000.

Instructions

Compute the FICA withholdings that should be made for each employee for the December 31 pay period. (Show computations.)

Prepare payroll register and record payroll and payroll tax expense. (SO 7, 8)

E11-10 Martinez Company has the following data for the weekly payroll ending January 31.

	Hours							Federal	
Employee	**M**	**T**	**W**	**T**	**F**	**S**	**Hourly Rate**	**Income Tax Withholding**	**Health Insurance**
M. Miller	8	8	9	8	10	3	$10	$34	$10
E. Neupert	8	8	8	8	8	2	12	37	15
K. Mann	9	10	8	8	9	0	13	58	15

Employees are paid $1\frac{1}{2}$ times the regular hourly rate for all hours worked in excess of 40 hours per week. FICA taxes are 8% on the first $65,000 of gross earnings. Martinez Company is subject to 5.4% state unemployment taxes and 0.8% federal unemployment taxes on the first $7,000 of gross earnings.

Instructions

(a) Prepare the payroll register for the weekly payroll.

(b) Prepare the journal entries to record the payroll and Martinez's payroll tax expense.

E11-11 Selected data from a February payroll register for Andrew Manion Company are presented below. Some amounts are intentionally omitted.

Compute missing payroll amounts and record payroll.
(SO 7)

Gross earnings:		State income taxes	$ (3)
Regular	$8,900	Union dues	100
Overtime	(1)		
Total	(2)	Total deductions	(4)
Deductions:		Net pay	$ 7,660
FICA taxes	$ 800	Accounts debited:	
Federal income taxes	1,140	Warehouse wages	(5)
		Store wages	$ 4,000

FICA taxes are 8%. State income taxes are 3% of gross earnings.

Instructions

(a) Fill in the missing amounts.

(b) Journalize the February payroll and the payment of the payroll.

E11-12 According to a payroll register summary of Parolini Company, the amount of employees' gross pay in December was $800,000, of which $70,000 was not subject to FICA tax and $760,000 was not subject to state and federal unemployment taxes.

Determine employer's payroll taxes; record payroll tax expense.
(SO 8)

Instructions

(a) Determine the employer's payroll tax expense for the month, using the following rates: FICA 8%, state unemployment 5.4%, federal unemployment 0.8%.

(b) Prepare the journal entry to record December payroll tax expense.

E11-13 Sawdey Company has two fringe benefit plans for its employees:

Prepare adjusting entries for fringe benefits.
(SO 9)

1. It grants employees 2 days' vacation for each month worked. Ten employees worked the entire month of March at an average daily wage of $100 per employee.
2. In its pension plan the company recognizes 10% of gross earnings as an expense. Gross earnings in March were $40,000. No contribution has been made to the pension fund.

Instructions

Prepare the adjusting entries at March 31.

PROBLEMS: SET A

P11-1A On January 1, 2002, the ledger of Twyla Company contains the following liability accounts.

Prepare current liability entries, adjusting entries, and current liabilities section.
(SO 1, 2, 3, 4, 5)

Accounts Payable	$52,000
Sales Taxes Payable	7,700
Unearned Service Revenue	16,000

During January the following selected transactions occurred.

Jan. 5 Sold merchandise for cash totaling $16,632, which includes 8% sales taxes.
12 Provided services for customers who had made advance payments of $10,000. (Credit Service Revenue.)
14 Paid state revenue department for sales taxes collected in December 2001 ($7,700).
20 Sold 500 units of a new product on credit at $50 per unit, plus 8% sales tax. This new product is subject to a 1-year warranty.
21 Borrowed $18,000 from UCLA Bank on a 3-month, 10%, $18,000 note.
25 Sold merchandise for cash totaling $11,340, which includes 8% sales taxes.

Instructions

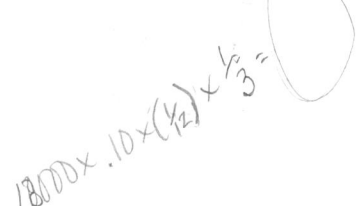

(a) Journalize the January transactions.

(b) Journalize the adjusting entries at January 31 for (1) the outstanding notes payable, and (2) estimated warranty liability, assuming warranty costs are expected to equal 7% of sales of the new product. (*Hint:* Use one-third of a month for the UCLA Bank note.)

(c) Current liability total $81,872

(c) Prepare the current liabilities section of the balance sheet at January 31, 2002. Assume no change in accounts payable.

Prepare payroll register and payroll entries.
(SO 7, 8)

P11-2A Happy Hardware has four employees who are paid on an hourly basis plus time-and-a half for all hours worked in excess of 40 a week. Payroll data for the week ended March 15, 2002, are presented below.

Employee	Hours Worked	Hourly Rate	Federal Income Tax Withholdings	United Fund
Joe McKane	40	$14.00	$?	$5.00
Mary Miller	42	13.00	?	5.00
Andy Manion	44	13.00	60	8.00
Kim Cheng	46	13.00	51	5.00

McKane and Miller are married. They claim 0 and 4 withholding allowances, respectively. The following tax rates are applicable: FICA 8%, state income taxes 3%, state unemployment taxes 5.4%, and federal unemployment 0.8%. The first three employees are sales clerks (store wages expense). The fourth employee performs administrative duties (office wages expense).

Instructions

(a) Net pay $1,862.06; Store wages expense $1,717

(b) Payroll tax expense $334.27

(d) Cash paid $586.64

(a) Prepare a payroll register for the weekly payroll. (Use the wage-bracket withholding table in the text for federal income tax withholdings.)
(b) Journalize the payroll on March 15, 2002, and the accrual of employer payroll taxes.
(c) Journalize the payment of the payroll on March 16, 2002.
(d) Journalize the deposit in a Federal Reserve bank on March 31, 2002, of the FICA and federal income taxes payable to the government.

Identify internal control weaknesses and make recommendations for improvement.
(SO 6)

P11-3A Selected payroll procedures of Palmcopiolet Company are described below.

1. Department managers interview applicants and on the basis of the interview either hire or reject the applicants. When an applicant is hired, the applicant fills out a W-4 form (Employer's Withholding Exemption Certificate). One copy of the form is sent to the human resources department, and one copy is sent to the payroll department as notice that the individual has been hired. On the copy of the W-4 sent to payroll, the managers manually indicate the hourly pay rate for the new hire.
2. The payroll checks are manually signed by the chief accountant and given to the department managers for distribution to employees in their department. The managers are responsible for seeing that any absent employees receive their checks.
3. There are two clerks in the payroll department. The payroll is divided alphabetically; one clerk has employees A to L and the other has employees M to Z. Each clerk computes the gross earnings, deductions, and net pay for employees in the section and posts the data to the employee earning records.

Instructions

(a) Indicate the weaknesses in internal control.
(b) For each weakness, describe the control procedures that will provide effective internal control. Use the following format for your answer:

(a) Weaknesses **(b) Recommended Procedures**

Journalize payroll transactions and adjusting entries.
(SO 7, 8, 9)

Peachtree

P11-4A The following payroll liability accounts are included in the ledger of Nam Viet Company on January 1, 2002.

FICA Taxes Payable	$ 760.00
Federal Income Taxes Payable	1,004.60
State Income Taxes Payable	108.95
Federal Unemployment Taxes Payable	288.95
State Unemployment Taxes Payable	1,954.40
Union Dues Payable	870.00
U.S. Savings Bonds Payable	360.00

In January, the following transactions occurred.

Jan.	10	Sent check for $870.00 to union treasurer for union dues.
	12	Deposited check for $1,764.60 in Federal Reserve bank for FICA taxes and federal income taxes withheld.
	15	Purchased U.S. Savings Bonds for employees by writing check for $360.00.
	17	Paid state income taxes withheld from employees.
	20	Paid federal and state unemployment taxes.
	31	Completed monthly payroll register, which shows office salaries $14,600, store wages $28,400, FICA taxes withheld $3,440, federal income taxes payable $1,684, state income taxes payable $360, union dues payable $400, United Fund contributions payable $1,888, and net pay $35,228.
	31	Prepared payroll checks for the net pay and distributed checks to employees.

At January 31, the company also makes the following accrued adjustments pertaining to employee compensation.

1. Employer payroll taxes: FICA taxes 8%, federal unemployment taxes 0.8%, and state unemployment taxes 5.4%.
2. Vacation pay: 6% of gross earnings.

Instructions

(a) Journalize the January transactions.

(b) Journalize the adjustments pertaining to employee compensation at January 31.

(b) Payroll tax expense $6,106.00; Vacation benefits expense $2,580

Prepare entries for payroll and payroll taxes; prepare W-2 data.
(SO 7, 8, 9)

P11-5A For the year ended December 31, 2002, Malaysia Electrical Repair Company reports the following summary payroll data.

Gross earnings:	
Administrative salaries	$180,000
Electricians' wages	470,000
Total	$650,000
Deductions:	
FICA taxes	$ 45,200
Federal income taxes withheld	188,000
State income taxes withheld (2.6%)	16,900
United Fund contributions payable	32,500
Hospital insurance premiums	20,300
Total	$302,900

Malaysia Company's payroll taxes are: FICA 8%, state unemployment 2.5% (due to a stable employment record), and 0.8% federal unemployment. Gross earnings subject to FICA taxes total $565,000, and unemployment taxes total $145,000.

Instructions

(a) Prepare a summary journal entry at December 31 for the full year's payroll.

(b) Journalize the adjusting entry at December 31 to record the employer's payroll taxes.

(c) The W-2 Wage and Tax Statement requires the following dollar data.

(a) Wages payable $347,100
(b) Payroll tax expense $49,985

Wages, Tips, Other Compensation	Federal Income Tax Withheld	State Income Tax Withheld	FICA Wages	FICA Tax Withheld

Complete the required data for the following employees.

Employee	Gross Earnings	Federal Income Tax Withheld
Anna Makarov	$59,000	$28,500
Sharon Livingston	28,000	10,800

Journalize and post note transactions; show balance sheet presentation.
(SO 2)

P11-6A The following are selected transactions of Cosky Company. Cosky prepares financial statements *quarterly*.

Jan.	2	Purchased merchandise on account from Alicea Company, $15,000, terms 2/10, n/30.
Feb.	1	Issued a 10%, 2-month, $15,000 note to Alicea in payment of account.

Mar. 31	Accrued interest for 2 months on Alicea note.
Apr. 1	Paid face value and interest on Alicea note.
July 1	Purchased equipment from Vincent Equipment paying $11,000 in cash and signing a 10%, 3-month, $25,000 note.
Sept. 30	Accrued interest for 3 months on Vincent note.
Oct. 1	Paid face value and interest on Vincent note.
Dec. 1	Borrowed $20,000 from the Otago Bank by issuing a 3-month, 12%-interest-bearing note with a face value of $20,000.
Dec. 31	Recognized interest expense for 1 month on Otago Bank note.

Instructions

(a) Prepare journal entries for the above transactions and events.
(b) Post to the accounts Notes Payable, Interest Payable, and Interest Expense.
(c) Show the balance sheet presentation of notes payable at December 31.
(d) $1,075
(d) What is total interest expense for the year?

PROBLEMS: SET B

Prepare current liability entries, adjusting entries, and current liabilities section.
(SO 1, 2, 3, 4, 5)

P11-1B On January 1, 2002, the ledger of Malaga Software Company contains the following liability accounts.

Accounts Payable	$42,500
Sales Taxes Payable	5,800
Unearned Service Revenue	15,000

During January the following selected transactions occurred.

Jan. 1	Borrowed $15,000 in cash from Amsterdam Bank on a 4-month, 12%, $15,000 note.
5	Sold merchandise for cash totaling $7,800, which includes 4% sales taxes.
12	Provided services for customers who had made advance payments of $9,000. (Credit Service Revenue.)
14	Paid state treasurer's department for sales taxes collected in December 2001, $5,800.
20	Sold 500 units of a new product on credit at $52 per unit, plus 4% sales tax. This new product is subject to a 1-year warranty.
25	Sold merchandise for cash totaling $11,440, which includes 4% sales taxes.

Instructions

(a) Journalize the January transactions.
(b) Journalize the adjusting entries at January 31 for (1) the outstanding notes payable, and (2) estimated warranty liability, assuming warranty costs are expected to equal 8% of sales of the new product.
(c) Current liability total $67,510
(c) Prepare the current liabilities section of the balance sheet at January 31, 2002. Assume no change in accounts payable.

Prepare payroll register and payroll entries.
(SO 7, 8)

P11-2B Paris Drug Store has four employees who are paid on an hourly basis plus time-and-a-half for all hours worked in excess of 40 a week. Payroll data for the week ended February 15, 2002, are presented below.

Employees	Hours Worked	Hourly Rate	Federal Income Tax Withholdings	United Fund
L. Scott	39	$13.00	$?	$-0-
S. Stahl	42	12.00	?	5.00
M. Rasheed	44	12.00	61	7.50
L. Quick	46	12.00	49	5.00

Scott and Stahl are married. They claim 2 and 4 withholding allowances, respectively. The following tax rates are applicable: FICA 8%, state income taxes 3%, state unemployment taxes 5.4%, and federal unemployment 0.8%. The first three employees are sales clerks (store wages expense). The fourth employee performs administrative duties (office wages expense).

Instructions

(a) Prepare a payroll register for the weekly payroll. (Use the wage-bracket withholding table in the text for federal income tax withholdings.)

(b) Journalize the payroll on February 15, 2002, and the accrual of employer payroll taxes.

(c) Journalize the payment of the payroll on February 16, 2002.

(d) Journalize the deposit in a Federal Reserve bank on February 28, 2002, of the FICA and federal income taxes payable to the government.

(a) Net pay $1,728.57; Store wages expense $1,575.00
(b) Payroll tax expense $307.14
(d) Cash paid $525.08

Identify internal control weaknesses and make recommendations for improvement.
(SO 6)

P11-3B The payroll procedures used by three different companies are described below.

1. In Ecom Company each employee is required to mark on a clock card the hours worked. At the end of each pay period, the employee must have this clock card approved by the department manager. The approved card is then given to the payroll department by the employee. Subsequently, the treasurer's department pays the employee by check.
2. In Yerkes Computer Company clock cards and time clocks are used. At the end of each pay period, the department manager initials the cards, indicates the rates of pay, and sends them to payroll. A payroll register is prepared from the cards by the payroll department. Cash equal to the total net pay in each department is given to the department manager, who pays the employees in cash.
3. In Min Wu Company employees are required to record hours worked by "punching" clock cards in a time clock. At the end of each pay period, the clock cards are collected by the department manager. The manager prepares a payroll register in duplicate and forwards the original to payroll. In payroll, the summaries are checked for mathematical accuracy, and a payroll supervisor pays each employee by check.

Instructions

(a) Indicate the weakness(es) in internal control in each company.

(b) For each weakness, describe the control procedure(s) that will provide effective internal control. Use the following format for your answer:

(a) Weaknesses	(b) Recommended Procedures

Journalize payroll transactions and adjusting entries.
(SO 7, 8, 9)

P11-4B The following payroll liability accounts are included in the ledger of Nathan Microscanner Company on January 1, 2002.

FICA Taxes Payable	$ 662.20
Federal Income Taxes Payable	1,054.60
State Income Taxes Payable	102.15
Federal Unemployment Taxes Payable	2,400.00
State Unemployment Taxes Payable	1,954.40
Union Dues Payable	250.00
U.S. Savings Bonds Payable	350.00

In January, the following transactions occurred.

Jan. 10	Sent check for $250.00 to union treasurer for union dues.
12	Deposited check for $1,716.80 in Federal Reserve bank for FICA taxes and federal income taxes withheld.
15	Purchased U.S. Savings Bonds for employees by writing check for $350.00.
17	Paid state income taxes withheld from employees.
20	Paid federal and state unemployment taxes.
31	Completed monthly payroll register, which shows office salaries $14,600, store wages $27,400, FICA taxes withheld $3,360, federal income taxes payable $1,654, state income taxes payable $360, union dues payable $400, United Fund contributions payable $1,688, and net pay $34,538.
31	Prepared payroll checks for the net pay and distributed checks to employees.

At January 31, the company also makes the following accruals pertaining to employee compensation.

1. Employer payroll taxes: FICA taxes 8%, state unemployment taxes 5.4%, and federal unemployment taxes 0.8%.
2. Vacation pay: 5% of gross earnings.

(b) Payroll tax expense $5,964.00; Vacation benefits expense $2,100

Instructions

(a) Journalize the January transactions.

(b) Journalize the adjustments pertaining to employee compensation at January 31.

Prepare entries for payroll and payroll taxes; prepare W-2 data.
(SO 7, 8, 9)

P11-5B For the year ended December 31, 2002, R. Westphal Company reports the following summary payroll data.

Gross earnings:	
Administrative salaries	$180,000
Electricians' wages	370,000
Total	$550,000
Deductions:	
FICA taxes	$ 38,800
Federal income taxes withheld	168,000
State income taxes withheld (2.6%)	14,300
United Fund contributions payable	27,500
Hospital insurance premiums	17,200
Total	265,800

R. Westphal Company's payroll taxes are: FICA 8%, state unemployment 2.5% (due to a stable employment record), and 0.8% federal unemployment. Gross earnings subject to FICA taxes total $485,000, and unemployment taxes total $120,000.

(a) Wages Payable $284,200
(b) Payroll tax expense $42,760

Instructions

(a) Prepare a summary journal entry at December 31 for the full year's payroll.

(b) Journalize the adjusting entry at December 31 to record the employer's payroll taxes.

(c) The W-2 Wage and Tax Statement requires the following dollar data.

Wages, Tips, Other Compensation	Federal Income Tax Withheld	State Income Tax Withheld	FICA Wages	FICA Tax Withheld

Complete the required data for the following employees.

Employee	Gross Earnings	Federal Income Tax Withheld
R. Cheng	$60,000	$27,500
K. McNeil	25,000	10,200

BROADENING YOUR PERSPECTIVE

FINANCIAL REPORTING AND ANALYSIS

FINANCIAL REPORTING PROBLEM: Lands' End, Inc.

LANDS' END DIRECT MERCHANTS

BYP11-1 The financial statements of **Lands' End, Inc.** and the Notes to Consolidated Financial Statements appear in Appendix A.

Instructions

Refer to Lands' End's financial statements and answer the following questions about current and contingent liabilities and payroll costs.

(a) What were Lands' End's total current liabilities at January 28, 2000? What was the increase/decrease in Lands' End's total current liabilities from the prior year?

(b) What is the nature (composition) of the "Reserve for returns" at January 28, 2000? (See Lands' End's Note 1 for a discussion of "Reserve for losses on customer returns.")

(c) What were the components of total current liabilities on January 28, 2000 (other than "Reserve for returns" already discussed in (b) above)?

COMPARATIVE ANALYSIS PROBLEM: Lands' End vs. Abercrombie & Fitch

BYP11-2 **Lands' End's** financial statements are presented in Appendix A. **Abercrombie & Fitch's** financial statements are presented in Appendix B.

Instructions

(a) At January 28, 2000, what was Lands' End's largest current liability account? What were its total current liabilities? At January 29, 2000, what was Abercrombie & Fitch's largest current liability account? What were its total current liabilities?

(b) Based on information contained in those financial statements, compute the following 2000 values for each company.

(1) Working capital.

(2) Current ratio.

(c) What conclusions concerning the relative liquidity of these companies can be drawn from these data?

INTERPRETING FINANCIAL STATEMENTS: A Global Focus

BYP11-3 Many multinational companies find it beneficial to have their shares listed on stock exchanges in foreign countries. In order to do this, they must comply with the securities laws of those countries. Some of these laws relate to the form of financial disclosure the company must provide, including disclosures related to contingent liabilities. This exercise investigates the **Tokyo Stock Exchange**, the largest stock exchange in Japan.

Address: **www.tse.or.jp/eindex.html** ***(or go to www.wiley.com/college/weygandt)***

Steps:

1. Choose **K-square**. Answer questions (a) and (b).
2. Choose **Investor Info**.
3. Choose **Listing guide for foreign corporations**.
4. Choose **Disclosure after listing**. Answer questions (c) and (d).

Instructions

Answer the following questions.

(a) When was the first stock exchange opened in Japan? How many exchanges does Japan have today?

(b) What event caused trading to stop for a period of time in Japan?

(c) What are four examples of decisions by corporations that must be disclosed at the time of their occurrence?

(d) What are four examples of "occurrence of material fact" that must be disclosed at the time of their occurrence?

EXPLORING THE WEB

BYP11-4 The Internal Revenue Service provides considerable information over the Internet. The following demonstrates how useful one of its sites is in answering payroll tax questions faced by employers.

Address: **www.irs.ustreas.gov/prod/forms_pubs/index.html**
(or go to www.wiley.com/college/weygandt)

Steps:

1. Go to the site shown above.
2. Choose **Publications Online**.
3. Choose **Circular E, Employer's Tax Guide**.

Instructions

Answer each of the following questions.

(a) How does the government define "employees"?

(b) What are the special rules for Social Security and Medicare regarding children who are employed by their parents?

(c) How can an employee obtain a Social Security card if he or she doesn't have one?
(d) Must employees report to their employer tips received from customers? If so, what is the process?
(e) Where should the employer deposit Social Security taxes withheld or contributed?

CRITICAL THINKING

GROUP DECISION CASE

BYP11-5 Kishwaukee Processing Company provides word-processing services for business clients and students in a university community. The work for business clients is fairly steady throughout the year. The work for students peaks significantly in December and May as a result of term papers, research project reports, and dissertations.

Two years ago, the company attempted to meet the peak demand by hiring part-time help. However, this led to numerous errors and considerable customer dissatisfaction. A year ago, the company hired four experienced employees on a permanent basis instead of using part-time help. This proved to be much better in terms of productivity and customer satisfaction. But, it has caused an increase in annual payroll costs and a significant decline in annual net income.

Recently, Valarie Flynn, a sales representative of Harrington Services Inc., has made a proposal to the company. Under her plan, Harrington Services will provide up to four experienced workers at a daily rate of $110 per person for an 8-hour workday. Harrington workers are not available on an hourly basis. Kishwaukee Processing would have to pay only the daily rate for the workers used.

The owner of Kishwaukee Processing, Martha Bell, asks you, as the company's accountant, to prepare a report on the expenses that are pertinent to the decision. If the Harrington plan is adopted, Martha will terminate the employment of two permanent employees and will keep two permanent employees. At the moment, each employee earns an annual income of $30,000. Kishwaukee Processing pays 8% FICA taxes, 0.8% federal unemployment taxes, and 5.4% state unemployment taxes. The unemployment taxes apply to only the first $7,000 of gross earnings. In addition, Kishwaukee Processing pays $40 per month for each employee for medical and dental insurance.

Martha indicates that if the Harrington Services plan is accepted, her needs for workers will be as follows.

Months	Number	Working Days per Month
January–March	2	20
April–May	3	25
June–October	2	18
November–December	3	23

Instructions
With the class divided into groups, answer the following.

(a) Prepare a report showing the comparative payroll expense of continuing to employ permanent workers compared to adopting the Harrington Services Inc. plan.
(b) What other factors should Martha consider before finalizing her decision?

COMMUNICATION ACTIVITY

BYP11-6 Emil Korenewych, president of the Low Cloud Company, has recently hired a number of additional employees. He recognizes that additional payroll taxes will be due as a result of this hiring, and that the company will serve as the collection agent for other taxes.

Instructions
In a memorandum to Emil Korenewych, explain each of the taxes, and identify the taxes that result in payroll tax expense to Low Cloud Company.

ETHICS CASE

BYP11-7 Harry Smith owns and manages Harry's Restaurant, a 24-hour restaurant near the city's medical complex. Harry employs 9 full-time employees and 16 part-time employees. He pays all of the full-time employees by check, the amounts of which are determined by Harry's public accountant, Pam Web. Harry pays all of his part-time employees in currency. He computes their wages and withdraws the cash directly from his cash register.

Pam has repeatedly urged Harry to pay all employees by check. But as Harry has told his competitor and friend, Steve Hill, who owns the Greasy Diner, "First of all, my part-time employees prefer the currency over a check, and secondly I don't withhold or pay any taxes or workmen's compensation insurance on those wages because they go totally unrecorded and unnoticed."

Instructions

(a) Who are the stakeholders in this situation?
(b) What are the legal and ethical considerations regarding Harry's handling of his payroll?
(c) Pam Web is aware of Harry's payment of the part-time payroll in currency. What are her ethical responsibilities in this case?
(d) What internal control principle is violated in this payroll process?

Answers to Self-Study Questions

1. a **2.** d **3.** b **4.** b **5.** a **6.** c **7.** b **8.** d **9.** d **10.** c **11.** d

Answer to Lands' End Review It Question 2, p. 453

LANDS' END DIRECT MERCHANTS

Under the heading of current liabilities, Lands' End has listed lines of credit, accounts payable, reserve for returns, accrued liabilities, accrued profit sharing, and income taxes payable.

Remember to go back to the Navigator box on the chapter-opening page and check off your completed work.

12

ACCOUNTING PRINCIPLES

THE NAVIGATOR ✓

- Understand *Concepts for Review* ❑
- Read *Feature Story* ❑
- Scan *Study Objectives* ❑
- Read *Preview* ❑
- Read text and answer *Before You Go On* *p.* 492 ❑ *p.* 503 ❑
- Work *Demonstration Problems* ❑
- Review *Summary of Study Objectives* ❑
- Answer *Self-Study Questions* ❑
- Complete *Assignments* ❑

CONCEPTS FOR REVIEW

Before studying this chapter, you should know or, if necessary, review:

a. The two organizations primarily responsible for setting accounting standards. (Ch. 1, p. 10)

b. The monetary unit assumption, the economic entity assumption, and the time period assumption. (Chs. 1 and 3, pp. 11 and 89)

c. The cost principle, the revenue recognition principle, and the matching principle. (Chs. 1 and 3, pp. 10 and 90–91)

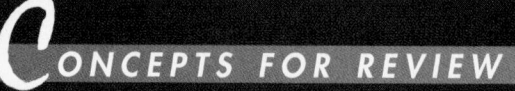

☑ THE NAVIGATOR

FEATURE STORY

Certainly Worth Investigating!

It is often difficult to determine in what period some revenues and expenses should be reported. There are rules that give guidance, but occasionally these rules are overlooked, misinterpreted, or even intentionally ignored. Consider the following examples.

- **Policy Management Systems**, which makes insurance software, said that it reported some sales before contracts were signed or products delivered.
- **Sunbeam Corporation**, while under the control of the (in)famous "Chainsaw" Al Dunlap, prematurely booked revenues and recorded overly large restructuring charges. Ultimately the company was forced to restate its net income figures, and Mr. Dunlap lost his job.
- **Rent-Way Inc.**, which owns a large chain of rent-to-own stores, saw its share price plummet from \$23.44 down to \$5 within a week after it disclosed what the company termed "fictitious" accounting entries on its books. These entries included improper accounting for fixed-asset write-offs, and understating the amount of damaged or missing merchandise.

Often in cases such as these, the company's shareholders sue the company because of the decline in the stock price due to the disclosure of the misinformation. In light of this eventuality, why might management want to report revenues or expenses in the wrong period? Company managers are under intense pressure to report higher earnings every year. If actual performance falls short of expectations, management might be tempted to bend the rules.

One analyst suggests that investors and auditors should be suspicious of sharp increases in monthly sales at the end of each quarter or big jumps in fourth-quarter sales. Such events don't always mean management is cheating, but they are certainly worth investigating.

THE NAVIGATOR

STUDY OBJECTIVES

After studying this chapter, you should be able to:

1. Explain the meaning of generally accepted accounting principles and identify the key items of the conceptual framework.
2. Describe the basic objectives of financial reporting.
3. Discuss the qualitative characteristics of accounting information and elements of financial statements.
4. Identify the basic assumptions used by accountants.
5. Identify the basic principles of accounting.
6. Identify the two constraints in accounting.
7. Explain the accounting principles used in international operations.

THE NAVIGATOR

PREVIEW OF CHAPTER 12

As indicated in the Feature Story, it is important that general guidelines be available to resolve accounting issues. Without these basic guidelines, each enterprise would have to develop its own set of accounting practices. If this happened, we would have to become familiar with every company's peculiar accounting and reporting rules in order to understand their financial statements. It would be difficult, if not impossible, to compare the financial statements of different companies. This chapter explores the basic accounting principles that are followed in developing specific accounting guidelines.

The content and organization of Chapter 12 are as follows.

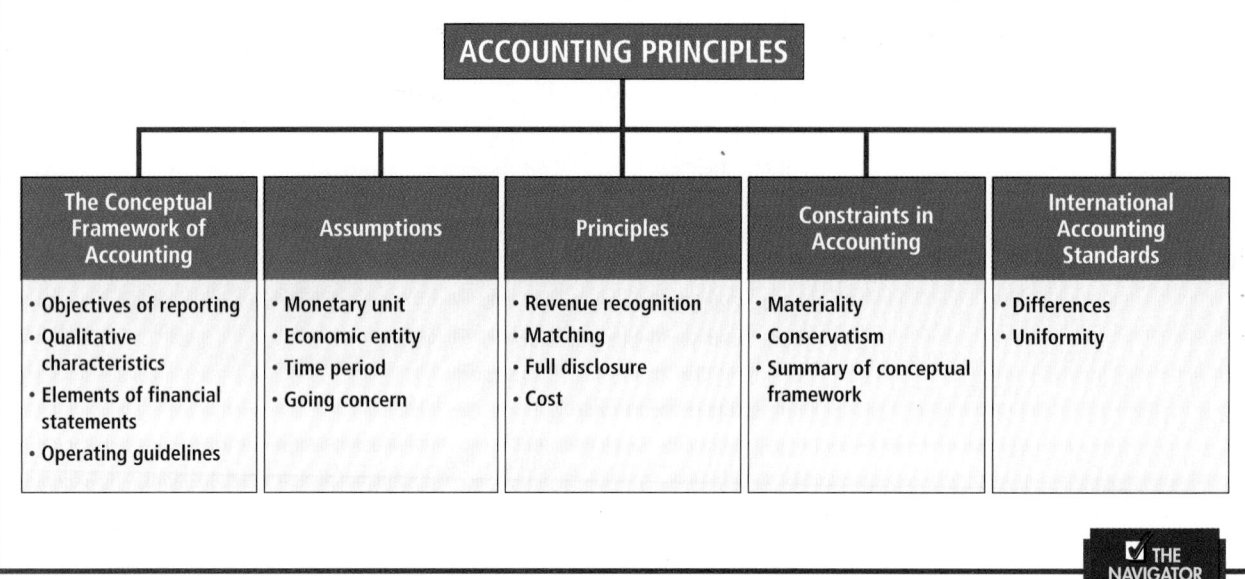

ACCOUNTING PRINCIPLES

The Conceptual Framework of Accounting	Assumptions	Principles	Constraints in Accounting	International Accounting Standards
• Objectives of reporting • Qualitative characteristics • Elements of financial statements • Operating guidelines	• Monetary unit • Economic entity • Time period • Going concern	• Revenue recognition • Matching • Full disclosure • Cost	• Materiality • Conservatism • Summary of conceptual framework	• Differences • Uniformity

THE NAVIGATOR

THE CONCEPTUAL FRAMEWORK OF ACCOUNTING

STUDY OBJECTIVE 1

Explain the meaning of generally accepted accounting principles and identify the key items of the conceptual framework.

What you have learned up to this point in the book is a process that leads to the preparation of financial reports about a company. These are the company's financial statements. This area of accounting is called **financial accounting**. The accounting profession has established a set of standards and rules that are recognized as a general guide for financial reporting. This recognized set of standards is called **generally accepted accounting principles (GAAP)**. "Generally accepted" means that these principles must have "substantial authoritative support." Such support usually comes from two standard-setting bodies: the Financial Accounting Standards Board (FASB) and the Securities and Exchange Commission (SEC).[1]

Since the early 1970s the business and governmental communities have given the FASB the responsibility for developing accounting principles in this country.

[1]The SEC is an agency of the U.S. government that was established in 1933 to administer laws and regulations relating to the exchange of securities and the publication of financial information by U.S. businesses. The agency has the authority to mandate generally accepted accounting principles for companies under its jurisdiction. However, throughout its history, the SEC has been willing to accept the principles set forth by the FASB and similar bodies.

This is an ongoing process; accounting principles change to reflect changes in the business environment and in the needs of users of accounting information.

Prior to the establishment of the FASB, accounting principles were developed on a problem-by-problem basis. Rule-making bodies developed accounting rules and methods to solve specific problems. Critics charged that the problem-by-problem approach led over time to inconsistent rules and practices. No clearly developed conceptual framework of accounting existed to refer to in solving new problems.

In response to these criticisms, the FASB developed a **conceptual framework**. It serves as the basis for resolving accounting and reporting problems. The FASB spent considerable time and effort on this project. The Board views its conceptual framework as ". . . a constitution, a coherent system of interrelated objectives and fundamentals."[2]

The FASB's conceptual framework consists of the following four items:

1. Objectives of financial reporting.
2. Qualitative characteristics of accounting information.
3. Elements of financial statements.
4. Operating guidelines (assumptions, principles, and constraints).

We will discuss these items on the following pages.

HELPFUL HINT
Accounting principles are affected by economic and political conditions which change over time. As a result, accounting principles are not cut into stone like the periodic table in chemistry or a formula in math.

ACCOUNTING IN ACTION *International Insight*

You should recognize that different political and cultural influences affect the accounting that occurs in foreign countries. For example, in Sweden, accounting is considered an instrument to be used to shape fiscal policy. In Europe generally, more emphasis is given to social reporting (more information on employment statistics, health of workers, and so on) than it is in the United States. European labor organizations are strong and demand that type of information from management.

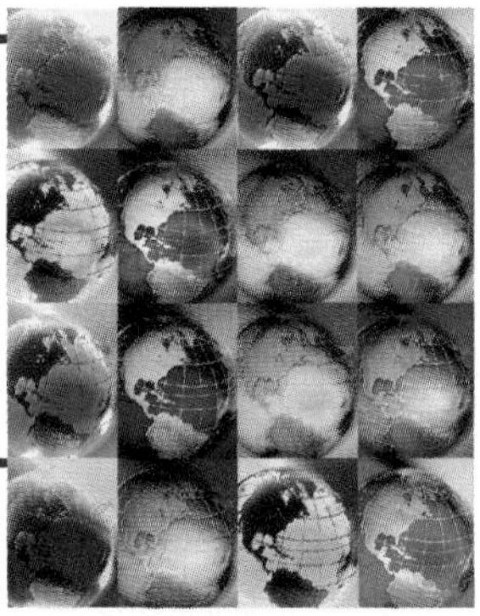

OBJECTIVES OF FINANCIAL REPORTING

STUDY OBJECTIVE 2
Describe the basic objectives of financial reporting.

The FASB began to work on the conceptual framework by looking at the objectives of financial reporting. Determining these objectives required answers to such basic questions as: Who uses financial statements? Why? What information do they need? How knowledgeable about business and accounting are financial statement users? How should financial information be reported so that it is best understood?

In answering these questions, the FASB concluded that the objectives of financial reporting are to provide information that:

1. Is useful to those making investment and credit decisions.
2. Is helpful in assessing future cash flows.
3. Identifies the economic resources (assets), the claims to those resources (liabilities), and the changes in those resources and claims.

The FASB then undertook to describe the characteristics that make accounting information useful.

[2]"Conceptual Framework for Financial Accounting and Reporting: Elements of Financial Statements and Their Measurement," *FASB Discussion Memorandum* (Stamford, Conn.: 1976), p. 1.

QUALITATIVE CHARACTERISTICS OF ACCOUNTING INFORMATION

STUDY OBJECTIVE 3

Discuss the qualitative characteristics of accounting information and elements of financial statements.

How does a company like **Microsoft** decide on the amount of financial information to disclose? In what format should its financial information be presented? How should assets, liabilities, revenues, and expenses be measured? The FASB concluded that the overriding criterion for such accounting choices is **decision usefulness**. The accounting practice selected should be the one that generates the most useful financial information for making a decision. To be useful, information should possess the following qualitative characteristics: relevance, reliability, comparability, and consistency.

Relevance

Accounting information has **relevance** if it makes a difference in a decision. Relevant information has either predictive or feedback value or both. **Predictive value** helps users forecast future events. For example, when **ExxonMobil** issues financial statements, the information in them is considered relevant because it provides a basis for predicting future earnings. **Feedback value** confirms or corrects prior expectations. When ExxonMobil issues financial statements, it confirms or corrects prior expectations about the financial health of the company.

HELPFUL HINT
What makes accounting information relevant? Answer: Relevant accounting information provides feedback, serves as a basis for predictions, and is timely (current).

In addition, accounting information has relevance if it is **timely**. It must be available to decision makers before it loses its capacity to influence decisions. If ExxonMobil reported its financial information only every five years, the information would be of limited use in decision-making.

Reliability

Reliability of information means that the information is free of error and bias. In short, it can be depended on. To be reliable, accounting information must be **verifiable**: We must be able to prove that it is free of error and bias. It also must be a **faithful representation** of what it purports to be: It must be factual. If **Sears, Roebuck's** income statement reports sales of \$100 billion when it had sales of \$51 billion, then the statement is not a faithful representation. Finally, accounting information must be **neutral**: It cannot be selected, prepared, or presented to favor one set of interested users over another. To ensure reliability, certified public accountants audit financial statements.

HELPFUL HINT
What makes accounting information reliable? Answer: Reliable accounting information is free of error and bias, is factual, verifiable, and neutral.

Comparability

Accounting information about an enterprise is most useful when it can be compared with accounting information about other enterprises. **Comparability** results when different companies use the same accounting principles. For example, **Lands' End**, **L. L. Bean**, and **The Limited** all use the cost principle in reporting plant assets on the balance sheet. Also, each company uses the revenue recognition and matching principles in determining its net income.

Conceptually, comparability should also extend to the methods used by companies in complying with an accounting principle. Accounting methods include the FIFO and LIFO methods of inventory costing, and various depreciation methods. At this point, comparability of methods is not required, even for companies in the same industry. Thus, **Ford**, **General Motors**, and **DaimlerChrysler** may use different inventory costing and depreciation methods in their financial statements. The only accounting requirement is that each company **must disclose** the accounting methods used. From the disclosures, the external user can determine whether the financial information is comparable.

Consistency

Consistency means that a company uses the same accounting principles and methods from year to year. If a company selects FIFO as the inventory costing method in the first year of operations, it is expected to use FIFO in succeeding years. When financial information has been reported on a consistent basis, the financial statements permit meaningful analysis of trends within a company.

A company *can* change to a new method of accounting. To do so, management must justify that the new method results in more meaningful financial information. In the year in which the change occurs, the change must be disclosed in the notes to the financial statements. Such disclosure makes users of the financial statements aware of the lack of consistency.

ACCOUNTING IN ACTION *Business Insight*

There is a classic story that professors often tell students about a company looking for an accountant. The company approached the first accountant and asked: "What do you believe our net income will be this year?" The accountant said "4 million dollars." The company asked the second accountant the same question, and the answer was "What would you like it to be?" Guess who got the job?

The reason we tell the story here is that, because accounting principles offer flexibility, it is important that a consistent treatment be provided from period to period. Otherwise it would be very difficult to interpret financial statements. Perhaps *no* alternative methods should be permitted in accounting. What do you think?

The qualitative characteristics of accounting information are summarized in Illustration 12-1.

Illustration 12-1
Qualitative characteristics of accounting information

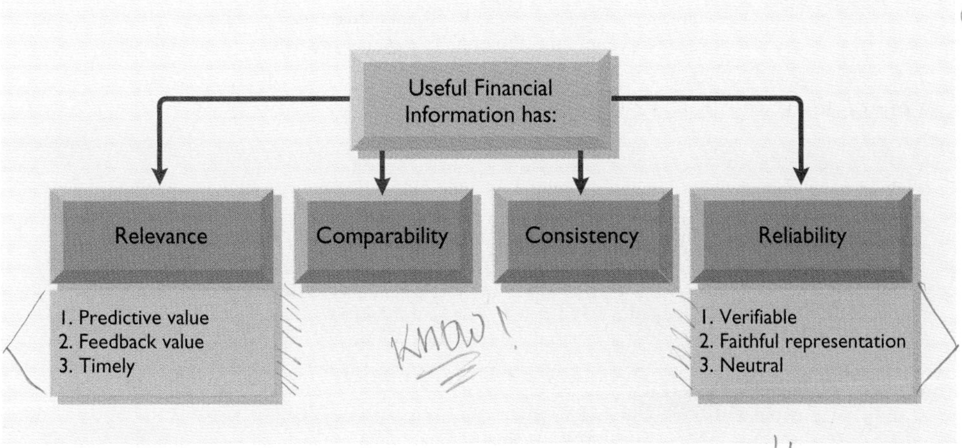

ELEMENTS OF FINANCIAL STATEMENTS

An important part of the accounting conceptual framework is a set of definitions that describe the basic terms used in accounting. The FASB refers to this set of definitions as the **elements of financial statements**. They include such terms as assets, liabilities, equity, revenues, and expenses.

Because these elements are so important, it is crucial that they be precisely defined and universally applied. Finding the appropriate definition for many of these elements is not easy. For example, should the value of a company's employees be reported as an asset on a balance sheet? Should the death of the company's president be reported as a loss? A good set of definitions should provide answers to these types of questions. Because you have already encountered most of these definitions in earlier chapters, they are not repeated here.

OPERATING GUIDELINES

The objectives of financial reporting, the qualitative characteristics of accounting information, and the elements of financial statements are very broad. Because practicing accountants must solve practical problems, more detailed guidelines are needed. In its conceptual framework, the FASB recognized the need for operating guidelines. We classify these guidelines as assumptions, principles, and constraints. These guidelines are well-established and accepted in accounting.

Assumptions provide a foundation for the accounting process. **Principles** are specific rules that indicate how economic events should be reported in the accounting process. **Constraints** on the accounting process allow for a relaxation of the principles under certain circumstances. Illustration 12-2 provides a roadmap of the operating guidelines of accounting. These guidelines (some of which you know from earlier chapters) are discussed in more detail in the following sections.

Illustration 12-2
The operating guidelines of accounting

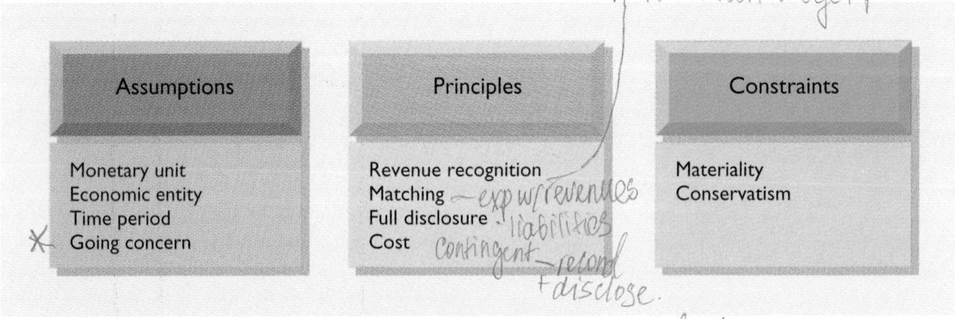

BEFORE YOU GO ON...

► *REVIEW IT*

1. What are generally accepted accounting principles?
2. What is stated about generally accepted accounting principles in the Report of Independent Public Accountants for **Lands' End**? The answer to this question appears on page 517.
3. What are the basic objectives of financial information?
4. What are the qualitative characteristics that make accounting information useful? Identify two elements of the financial statements.

THE NAVIGATOR

ASSUMPTIONS

STUDY OBJECTIVE 4
Identify the basic assumptions used by accountants.

As noted above, assumptions provide a foundation for the accounting process. You already know three of the major assumptions—the monetary unit, economic entity, and time period assumptions. The fourth is the going concern assumption.

MONETARY UNIT ASSUMPTION

The **monetary unit assumption** states that only transaction data that can be expressed in terms of money be included in the accounting records. For example, the value of a company president is not reported in a company's financial records because it cannot be expressed easily in dollars.

An important corollary to the monetary unit assumption is the assumption that the unit of measure remains relatively constant over time. This point will be discussed in more detail later in this chapter.

ECONOMIC ENTITY ASSUMPTION

The **economic entity assumption** states that the activities of the entity be kept separate and distinct from the activities of the owner and of all other economic entities. For example, it is assumed that the activities of **IBM** can be distinguished from those of other computer companies such as **Apple**, **Compaq**, and **Hewlett-Packard**.

INTERNATIONAL NOTE

In an action that sent shock waves through the French business community, the CEO of Alcatel-Alsthom was taken into custody for an apparent violation of the economic entity assumption. Allegedly, the executive improperly used company funds to install an expensive security system in his home.

TIME PERIOD ASSUMPTION

The **time period assumption** states that the economic life of a business can be divided into artificial time periods. Thus, it is assumed that the activities of business enterprises such as **General Electric**, **America Online**, **ExxonMobil**, or any enterprise can be subdivided into months, quarters, or a year for meaningful financial reporting purposes.

GOING CONCERN ASSUMPTION

The **going concern assumption** assumes that the enterprise will continue in operation long enough to carry out its existing objectives. In spite of numerous business failures, companies have a fairly high continuance rate. It has proved useful to adopt a going concern assumption for accounting purposes.

The accounting implications of this assumption are critical. If a going concern assumption is not used, then plant assets should be stated at their liquidation value (selling price less cost of disposal)—not at their cost. In that case, depreciation and amortization of these assets would not be needed. Each period, these assets would simply be reported at their liquidation value. Also, without this assumption, the current–noncurrent classification of assets and liabilities would not matter. Labeling anything as long-term would be difficult to justify.

Acceptance of the going concern assumption gives credibility to the cost principle. Only when liquidation appears imminent is the going concern assumption inapplicable. In that case, assets would be better stated at liquidation value than at cost.

These basic accounting assumptions are illustrated graphically in Illustration 12-3 on the next page.

HELPFUL HINT

(1) Which accounting assumption assumes that an enterprise will remain in business long enough to recover the cost of its assets? (2) Which accounting assumption is justification for the cost principle?
Answers: (1) and (2) Going concern assumption.

PRINCIPLES

STUDY OBJECTIVE 5

Identify the basic principles of accounting.

On the basis of the fundamental assumptions of accounting, the accounting profession has developed principles that dictate how economic events should be recorded and reported. In earlier chapters we discussed the cost principle (Chapter 1) and the revenue recognition and matching principles (Chapter 3). Here we now examine a number of reporting issues related to these principles. In addition, we introduce another principle, the full disclosure principle.

Illustration 12-3

Assumptions used in accounting

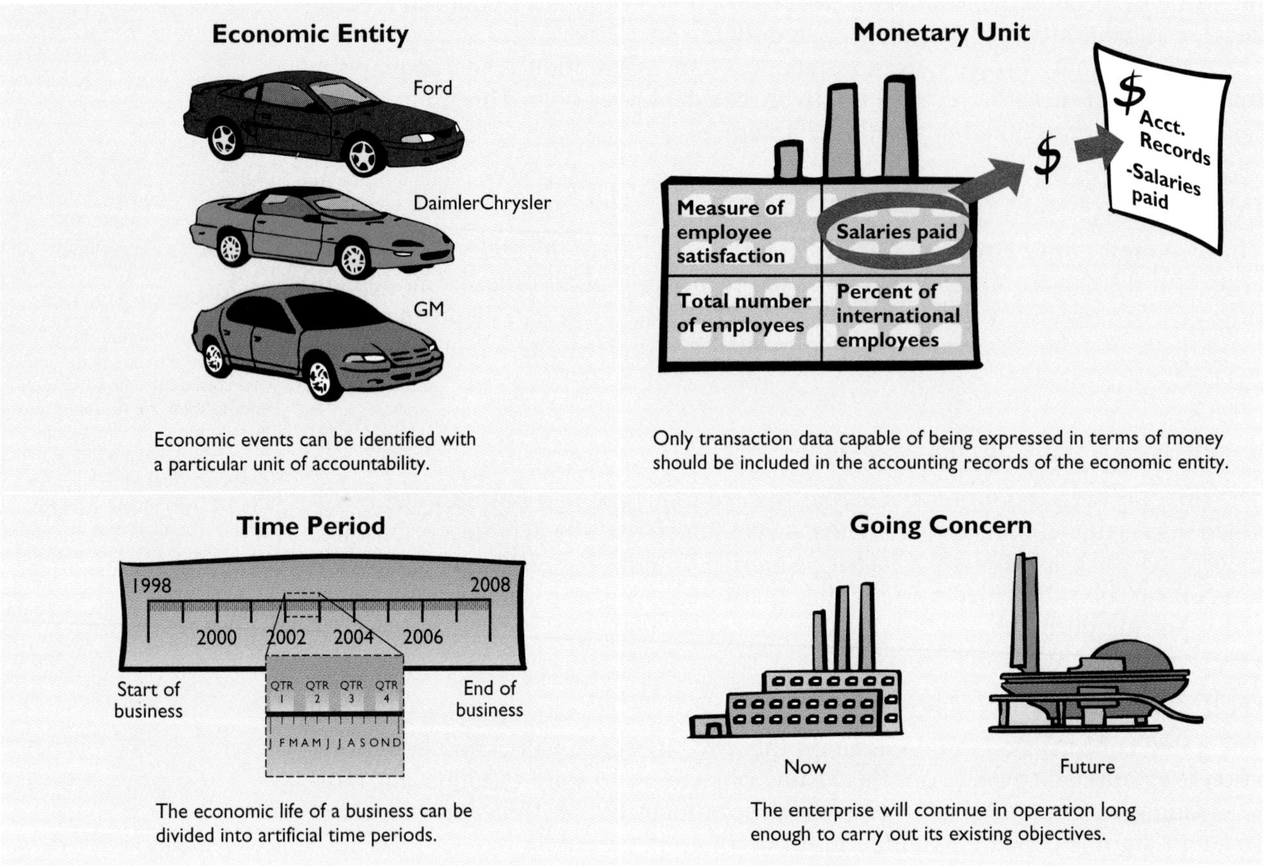
Economic Entity
Ford
DaimlerChrysler
GM
Economic events can be identified with a particular unit of accountability.
Monetary Unit
Measure of employee satisfaction
Salaries paid
Total number of employees
Percent of international employees
$
$ Acct. Records -Salaries paid
Only transaction data capable of being expressed in terms of money should be included in the accounting records of the economic entity.
Time Period
1998
2008
2000
2002
2004
2006
Start of business
End of business
QTR 1 QTR 2 QTR 3 QTR 4
J F M A M J J A S O N D
The economic life of a business can be divided into artificial time periods.
Going Concern
Now
Future
The enterprise will continue in operation long enough to carry out its existing objectives.

REVENUE RECOGNITION PRINCIPLE

> **HELPFUL HINT**
> Revenue should be recognized in the accounting period in which it is earned. This may not be the period in which the related cash is received. In a retail establishment, the point of sale is often the critical point in the process of earning revenue.

The **revenue recognition principle** dictates that revenue should be recognized in the accounting period in which it is earned. But applying this general principle in practice can be difficult. For example, some companies improperly recognize revenue on goods that have not been shipped to customers. Similarly, until recently, financial institutions immediately recorded a large portion of their fees for granting a loan as revenue rather than spreading those fees over the life of the loan.

When a sale is involved, revenue is recognized at the point of sale. This **sales basis** involves an exchange transaction between the seller and buyer. The sales price is an objective measure of the amount of revenue realized. However, there are two exceptions to the sales basis for revenue recognition that have become generally accepted. They are the percentage-of-completion method and the installment method.

Percentage-of-Completion Method

In long-term construction contracts, revenue recognition is usually required before the contract is completed. For example, assume that Warrior Construction Co. had a contract to build a dam for the U.S. Department of the Interior for $400 million. Construction is estimated to take 3 years (starting in 2000) at a cost of

$360 million. If Warrior applies the point-of-sale basis, it will report no revenues and no profit in the first two years. In 2002, when completion and sale take place, Warrior will report $400 million in revenues, costs of $360 million, and the entire profit of $40 million. Was Warrior really producing no revenues and earning no profit in 2000 and 2001? Obviously not. Instead, the earning process can be considered substantially completed at various stages. Therefore revenue should be recognized as construction progresses.

In recognizing revenue, Warrior can apply the **percentage-of-completion method**. This method recognizes revenue on a long-term project on the basis of reasonable estimates of progress toward completion. Progress toward completion is measured by comparing the costs incurred in a year to the total estimated costs for the entire project. That percentage is multiplied by the total revenue for the project. The result is then recognized as revenue for the period. The formulas for this method are as follows.

HELPFUL HINT

For long-term construction contracts, it is appropriate to use the percentage-of-completion method of revenue recognition. The critical event in the earning process is making progress toward completion. The ultimate sale and selling price are assured by the contract.

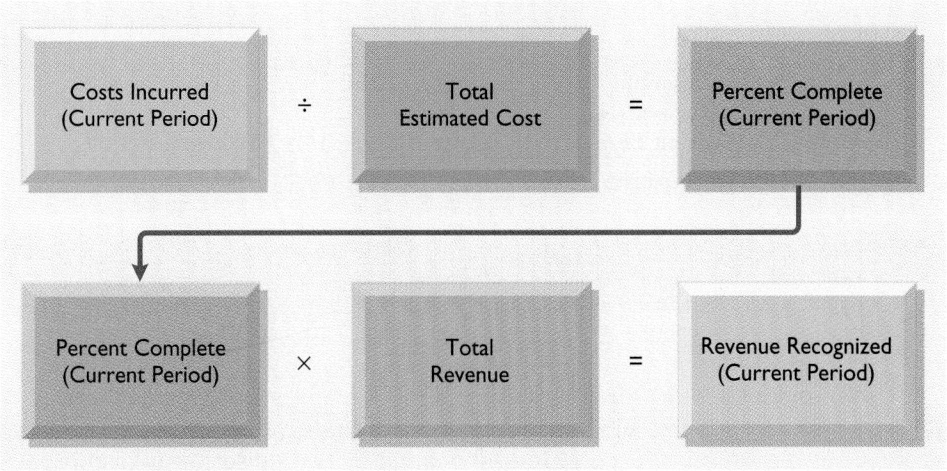

Illustration 12-4

Formula to recognize revenue in the percentage-of-completion method

The costs incurred in the current period are then subtracted from the revenue recognized during the current period to arrive at the gross profit for the current period. This formula is shown in Illustration 12-5.

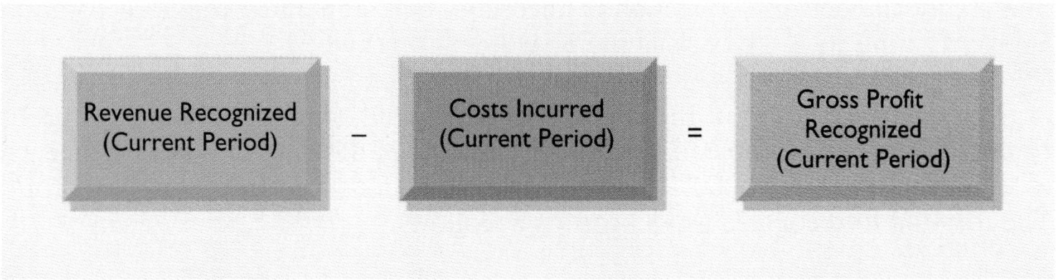

Illustration 12-5

Formula to compute gross profit in current period

Let's look at an illustration of the percentage-of-completion method. Assume that Warrior Construction Co. incurs costs of $54 million in 2000, $180 million in 2001, and $126 million in 2002 on the dam project. The portion of the $400 million of revenue recognized in each of the three years is shown in Illustration 12-6.

Year	Costs Incurred (Current Period)	÷	Total Estimated Cost	=	Percent Complete (Current Period)	×	Total Revenue	=	Revenue Recognized (Current Period)
2000	$ 54,000,000		$360,000,000		15%		$400,000,000		**$ 60,000,000**
2001	180,000,000		360,000,000		50%		400,000,000		**200,000,000**
2002	126,000,000		Balance required to complete the contract						**140,000,000**
Totals	$360,000,000								**$400,000,000**

Illustration 12-6

Revenue recognized—percentage-of-completion method

No estimate is made of the percentage of work completed during the final period. In the final period, all remaining revenue is recognized. In this example, the company's cost estimates have been very accurate. The costs incurred in the third year were 35% of the total estimated cost ($126,000 ÷ $360,000).

The gross profit recognized each period is as follows.

Illustration 12-7

Gross profit recognized—percentage-of-completion method

Year	Revenue Recognized (Current Period)	−	Actual Cost Incurred (Current Period)	=	Gross Profit Recognized (Current Period)
2000	$ 60,000,000		$ 54,000,000		**$ 6,000,000**
2001	200,000,000		180,000,000		**20,000,000**
2002	140,000,000		126,000,000		**14,000,000**
Totals	$400,000,000		$360,000,000		**$40,000,000**

Use of the percentage-of-completion method involves some subjectivity. As a result, errors are possible in determining the amount of revenue recognized and gross profit recognized. Yet to wait until completion would seriously distort each period's financial statements. Naturally, **if it is not possible to obtain dependable estimates of costs and progress, then the revenue should be recognized at the completion date** and not by the percentage-of-completion method.

Installment Method

Another basis for revenue recognition is the receipt of cash. The **cash basis** is generally used only when it is difficult to determine the revenue amount at the time of a credit sale because collection is uncertain. One popular revenue recognition approach using the cash basis is the **installment method**.

Under the installment method, each cash collection from a customer consists of (1) a partial recovery of the cost of the goods sold, and (2) partial gross profit from the sale. For example, if the gross profit rate at the date of sale is 40%, each receipt of cash consists of 60% recovery of cost of goods sold and 40% gross profit. The formula to recognize gross profit is as follows.

Illustration 12-8

Gross profit formula—installment method

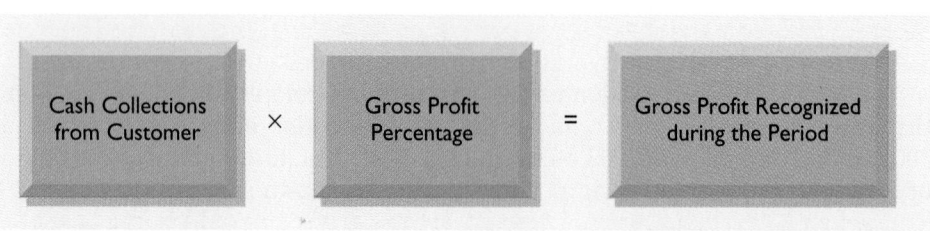

Cash Collections from Customer	×	Gross Profit Percentage	=	Gross Profit Recognized during the Period

To illustrate, assume that an Iowa farm machinery dealer in the first year of operations had installment sales of $600,000. Its cost of goods sold on installment was $420,000. Total gross profit is therefore $180,000 ($600,000 − $420,000), and the gross profit percentage is 30% ($180,000 ÷ $600,000). Collections on the installment sales were as follows: first year $280,000 (down payment plus monthly payments), second year $200,000, and third year $120,000. The computation of gross profit recognized is shown in Illustration 12-9. (Interest charges are ignored in this illustration.)

Illustration 12-9

Gross profit recognized—installment method

Year	Cash Collected	×	Gross Profit Percentage	=	Gross Profit Recognized
2000	$280,000		30%		**$ 84,000**
2001	200,000		30%		**60,000**
2002	120,000		30%		**36,000**
Total	$600,000				**$180,000**

Under the installment method of accounting, gross profit is therefore recognized **in the period in which the cash is collected.**

As indicated earlier, the installment method is used when there is risk of not collecting an account receivable. In that case, the sale itself is not sufficient evidence for revenue to be recognized.

ACCOUNTING IN ACTION *Business Insight*

Datapoint Corp. encouraged its customers to load up with large shipments at the end of the year. This strategy allowed Datapoint to report these shipments as revenues, even though payment hadn't been collected. Unfortunately, some of the customers either went broke or quit before paying for the equipment received. The company had to record substantial bad debts or in some cases reverse previously recorded sales. If Datapoint had used the installment method, this revenue would not have been reported. As a result, revenue recognition practices that are cash-basis oriented, such as the installment method, are becoming more acceptable as it becomes difficult to tell when a sale is a sale.

MATCHING PRINCIPLE (EXPENSE RECOGNITION)

Expense recognition is traditionally tied to revenue recognition: "Let the expense follow the revenue." As you learned in Chapter 3, this practice is referred to as the **matching principle**. It dictates that expenses be matched with revenues in the period in which efforts are made to generate revenues. Expenses are not recognized when cash is paid, or when the work is performed, or when the product is produced. Rather, they are recognized when the labor (service) or the product actually makes its contribution to revenue.

But, it is sometimes difficult to determine the accounting period in which the expense contributed to revenues. Several approaches have therefore been devised for matching expenses and revenues on the income statement.

To understand these approaches, you need to understand the nature of expenses. Costs are the source of expenses. Costs that will generate revenues only in the current accounting period are expensed immediately. They are reported as **operating expenses** in the income statement. Examples include costs for advertising, sales salaries, and repairs. These expenses are often called **expired costs**.

HELPFUL HINT
Costs become expenses when they are charged against revenue.

Costs that will generate revenues in future accounting periods are recognized as assets. Examples include merchandise inventory, prepaid expenses, and plant assets. These costs represent **unexpired costs**. Unexpired costs become expenses in two ways:

1. **Cost of goods sold.** Costs carried as merchandise inventory become expenses when the inventory is sold. They are expensed as cost of goods sold in the period when the sale occurs. Thus, there is a direct matching of expenses with revenues.
2. **Operating expenses.** Other unexpired costs become operating expenses through use or consumption (as in the case of store supplies) or through the passage of time (as in the case of prepaid insurance). The costs of plant assets and other long-lived resources are expensed through rational and systematic allocation methods—periodic depreciation or amortization. Operating expenses contribute to the revenues for the period, but their association with revenues is less direct than for cost of goods sold.

These points about expense recognition are illustrated in Illustration 12-10.

ETHICS NOTE

Many appear to do it, but few like to discuss it: It's earnings management, and it's a clear violation of the revenue recognition and matching principles. Banks sometimes time the sale of investments or the expensing of bad debts to accomplish earnings objectives. Prominent companies have been accused of matching one-time gains with one-time charge-offs so that current-period earnings are not so high that they can't be surpassed next period.

Illustration 12-10

Expense recognition pattern

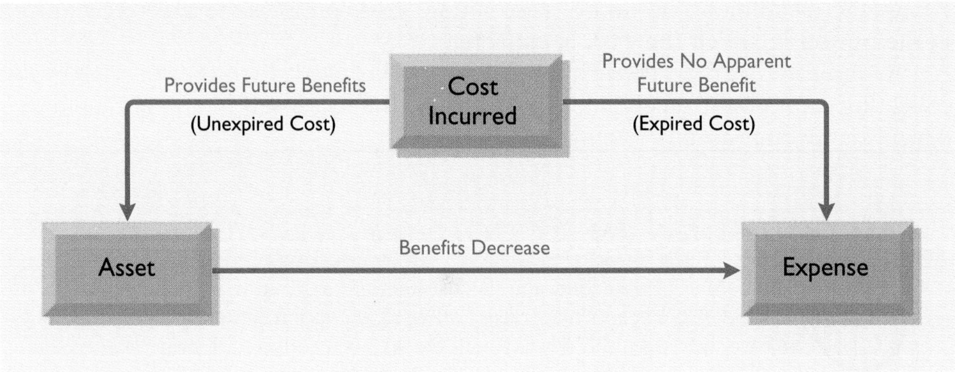

ACCOUNTING IN ACTION *Business Insight*

Implementing expense recognition guidelines can be difficult. Consider, for example, **Harold's Club** (a gambling casino) in Reno, Nevada. How should it report expenses related to the payoff of its progressive slot machines? Progressive slot machines, which generally have no ceiling on their jackpots, provide a lucky winner with all the money that many losers had previously put in. Payoffs tend to be huge, but infrequent. At Harold's, the progressive slots pay off on average every 4½ months.

The basic accounting question is: Can Harold's deduct the millions of dollars sitting in its progressive slot machines from the revenue recognized at the end of the accounting period? One might argue that no, you cannot deduct the money until the "winning handle pull." However, a winning handle pull might not occur for many months or even years. Although an estimate would have to be used, the better answer is to match these costs with the revenue recognized, assuming that an average 4½ months' payout is well documented. Obviously, the matching principle can be difficult to apply in practice.

FULL DISCLOSURE PRINCIPLE

The **full disclosure principle** requires that circumstances and events that make a difference to financial statement users be disclosed. For example, most accountants would agree that **Manville Corporation** should have disclosed the 52,000 asbestos liability suits (totaling $2 billion) pending against it. Interested parties would want to be made aware of this contingent loss. Similarly, it is generally agreed that companies should disclose the major provisions of employee pension plans and long-term lease contracts.

Compliance with the full disclosure principle occurs through the data in the financial statements and the information in the notes that accompany the statements. The first note in most cases is a **summary of significant accounting policies**. It includes, among others, the methods used for inventory costing, depreciation of plant assets, and amortization of intangible assets.

Deciding how much disclosure is enough can be difficult. Accountants could disclose every financial event that occurs and every contingency that exists. But the benefits of providing additional information in some cases may be less than the costs of doing so. Many companies complain of an accounting standards overload. They also object to requirements that force them to disclose confidential information. Determining where to draw the line on disclosure is not easy.

One thing is certain: financial statements were much simpler years ago. In 1930, **General Electric** had no notes to its financial statements. Today it has over 20 pages of notes! Why this change? A major reason is that the objectives of financial statements have changed. In the past, information was generally presented on what the business had done. Today, the objectives of financial reporting are more future-oriented. The goal is to provide information that makes it possible to predict the amounts, timing, and uncertainty of future cash flows.

ACCOUNTING IN ACTION e Business Insight

Some accountants are reconsidering the current means of financial reporting. They propose a database concept of financial reporting. In such a system, all the information from transactions would be stored in a computerized database to be accessed by various user groups. The main benefit of such a system is the ability to tailor the information requested to the needs of each user.

What makes this idea controversial? Discussion currently revolves around access and aggregation issues. Questions abound: "Who should be allowed to make inquiries of the system?" "What is the lowest/smallest level of information to be provided?" "Will such a system necessarily improve on the current means of disclosure?" Such questions must be answered before database financial accounting can be implemented on a large scale.

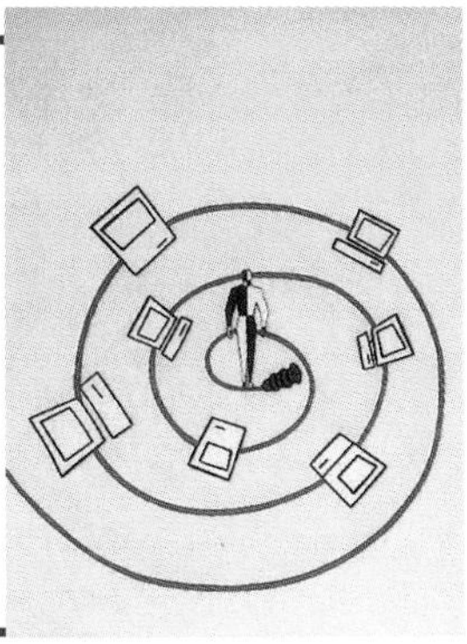

COST PRINCIPLE

As you know, the **cost principle** dictates that assets be recorded at their cost. Cost is used because it is both relevant and reliable. Cost is **relevant** because it represents the price paid, the assets sacrificed, or the commitment made at date of acquisition. Cost is **reliable** because it is objectively measurable, factual, and verifiable. It is the result of an exchange transaction. Cost is the basis used in preparing financial statements.

The cost principle, however, has come under criticism. Some criticize it as irrelevant. After acquisition, the argument goes, the cost of an asset is not equivalent to market value or current value. Also, as the purchasing power of the dollar changes, so does the meaning associated with the dollar used as the basis of measurement. Consider the classic story about the individual who went to sleep and woke up 10 years later. Hurrying to a telephone, he called his broker and asked what his formerly modest stock portfolio was worth. He was told that he was a multi-millionaire. His **General Motors** stock was worth $5 million, and his **Microsoft** stock was up to $10 million. Elated, he was about to inquire about his

> **HELPFUL HINT**
> Are you a winner or loser when you hold cash in a period of inflation? Answer: A loser, because the value of the cash declines as inflation climbs.

other holdings, when the telephone operator cut in with "Your time is up. Please deposit $100,000 for the next three minutes."[3]

Despite the inevitability of changing prices due to inflation, the accounting profession still follows the stable monetary unit assumption in preparing the primary financial statements. While admitting that some changes in prices do occur, the profession believes the unit of measure—the dollar—has remained sufficiently constant over time to provide meaningful financial information. Sometimes, the **disclosure of price-level adjusted data is in the form of supplemental information** that accompanies the financial statements.

The basic principles of accounting are summarized in Illustration 12-11.

Illustration 12-11

Basic principles used in accounting

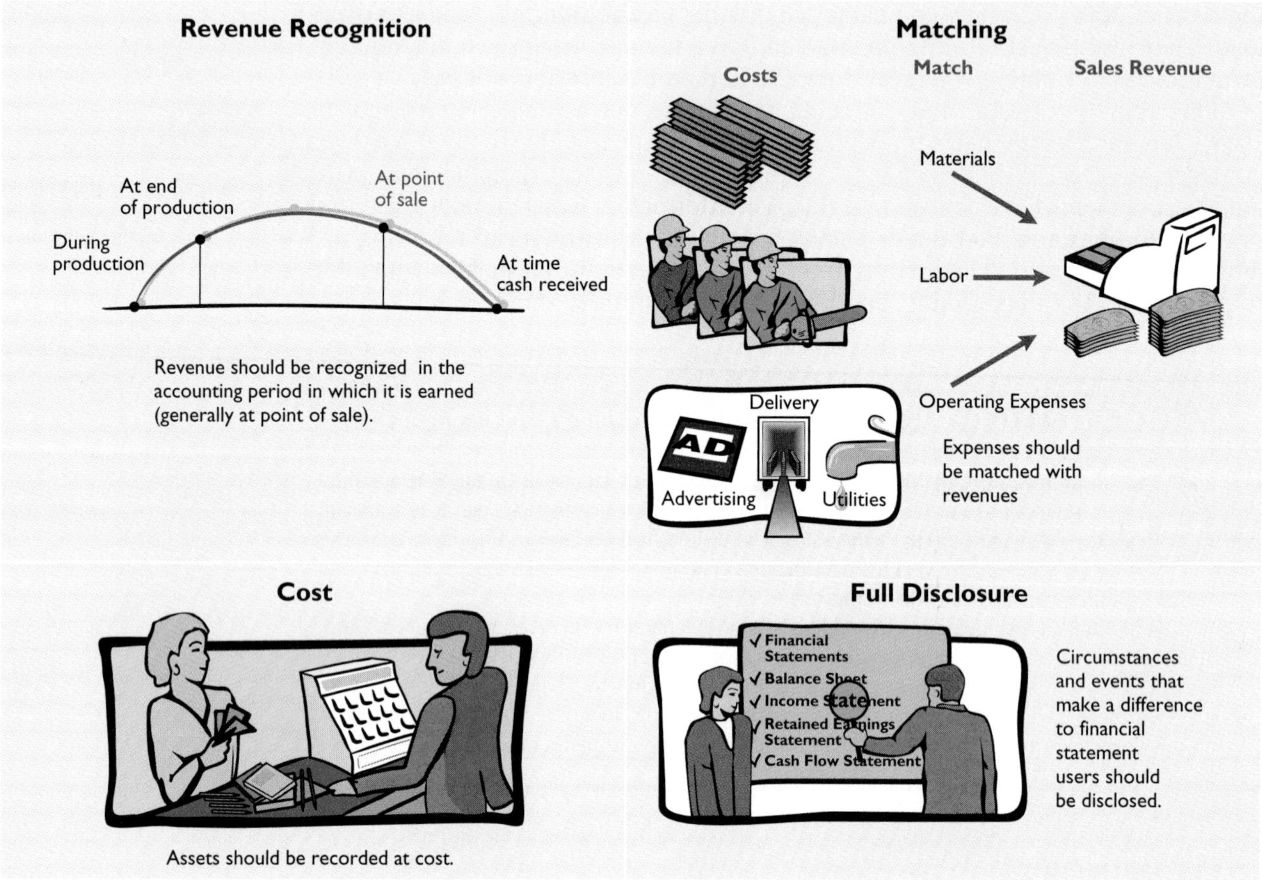
Revenue Recognition
At end of production
At point of sale
During production
At time cash received
Revenue should be recognized in the accounting period in which it is earned (generally at point of sale).
Matching
Costs
Match
Sales Revenue
Materials
Labor
Delivery
AD
Advertising
Utilities
Operating Expenses
Expenses should be matched with revenues
Cost
Assets should be recorded at cost.
Full Disclosure
√ Financial Statements
√ Balance Sheet
√ Income Statement
√ Retained Earnings Statement
√ Cash Flow Statement
Circumstances and events that make a difference to financial statement users should be disclosed.

CONSTRAINTS IN ACCOUNTING

STUDY OBJECTIVE 6

Identify the two constraints in accounting.

Constraints permit a company to modify generally accepted accounting principles without reducing the usefulness of the reported information. The constraints are materiality and conservatism.

MATERIALITY

Materiality relates to an item's impact on a firm's overall financial condition and operations. An item is **material** when it is likely to influence the decision of a reasonably prudent investor or creditor. It is immaterial if its inclusion or omission

[3]Adapted from *Barron's*, January 28, 1980, p. 27.

has no impact on a decision maker. In short, if the item does not make a difference in decision making, GAAP does not have to be followed. To determine the materiality of an amount, the accountant usually compares it with such items as total assets, total liabilities, and net income.

To illustrate how the materiality constraint is applied, assume that Rodriguez Co. purchases a number of low-cost plant assets, such as wastepaper baskets. Although the proper accounting would appear to be to depreciate these wastepaper baskets over their useful life, they are usually expensed immediately. This practice is justified because these costs are considered immaterial. Establishing depreciation schedules for these assets is costly and time-consuming and will not make a material difference on total assets and net income. Another application of the materiality constraint would be the expensing of small tools. Some companies expense any plant assets under a specified dollar amount.

CONSERVATISM

The **conservatism** constraint dictates that when in doubt, choose the method that will be least likely to overstate assets and income. It does **not** mean **understating** assets or income. Conservatism provides a reasonable guide in difficult situations: Do not overstate assets and income.

> **HELPFUL HINT**
> In other words, if two methods are otherwise equally appropriate, choose the one that will least likely overstate assets and income.

A common application of the conservatism constraint is the use of the lower of cost or market method for inventories. As indicated in Chapter 6, inventories are reported at market value if market value is below cost. This practice results in a higher cost of goods sold and lower net income. In addition, inventory on the balance sheet is stated at a lower amount.

Other examples of conservatism in accounting are the use of the LIFO method for inventory valuation when prices are rising and the use of accelerated depreciation methods for plant assets. Both these methods result in lower asset carrying values and lower net income than alternative methods.

The two constraints in accounting are graphically depicted in Illustration 12-12.

Illustration 12-12
Constraints in accounting

Materiality
Conservatism
Assets
Income
For small amounts, GAAP does not have to be followed.
When in doubt, choose the solution that will be least likely to overstate assets and income.

SUMMARY OF CONCEPTUAL FRAMEWORK

As we have seen, the conceptual framework for developing sound reporting practices starts with a set of objectives for financial reporting. It follows with the description of qualities that make information useful. In addition, elements of financial statements are defined. More detailed operating guidelines are then provided. These guidelines take the form of assumptions and principles.

The conceptual framework also recognizes that constraints exist on the reporting environment. The conceptual framework is illustrated graphically in Illustration 12-13.

Illustration 12-13

Conceptual framework

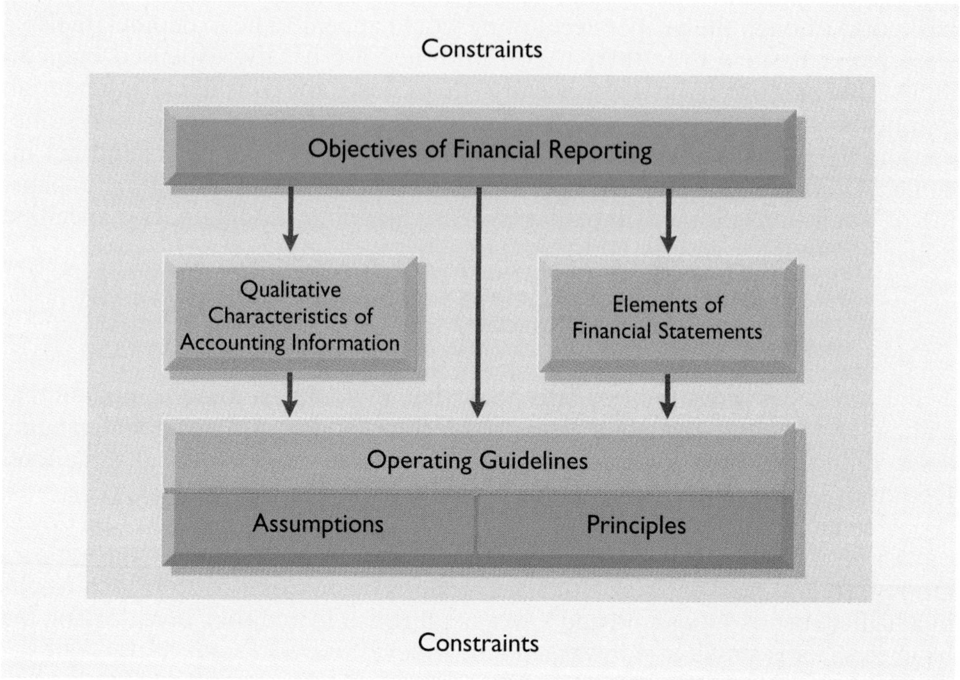

INTERNATIONAL ACCOUNTING STANDARDS

STUDY OBJECTIVE 7

Explain the accounting principles used in international operations.

World markets are becoming increasingly intertwined. Foreigners use American computers, eat American breakfast cereals, read American magazines, listen to American rock music, watch American movies and TV shows, and drink American soda. Americans drive Japanese cars, wear Italian shoes and Scottish woolens, drink Brazilian coffee and Indian tea, eat Swiss chocolate bars, sit on Danish furniture, and use Arabian oil. The variety and volume of exported and imported goods indicates the extensive involvement of U.S. business in international trade. Many U.S. companies consider the world their market.

Firms that conduct operations in more than one country through subsidiaries, divisions, or branches in foreign countries are referred to as **multinational corporations**. The accounting for such corporations is complicated because foreign currencies are involved. These international transactions must be translated into U.S. dollars.

DIFFERENCES IN STANDARDS

In the new global economy many investment and credit decisions require the analysis of foreign financial statements. Unfortunately, accounting standards are not uniform from country to country. This lack of uniformity results from differences in legal systems, in processes for developing accounting standards, in governmental requirements, and in economic environments.

ACCOUNTING IN ACTION *International Insight*

Research and development costs are an example of different international accounting standards. Compare how four countries account for research and development (R&D):

Country	Accounting Treatment
United States	Expenditures are expensed.
United Kingdom	Certain expenditures may be capitalized.
Germany	Expenditures are expensed.
Japan	Expenditures may be capitalized and amortized over 5 years.

Thus, an R&D expenditure of $100 million is charged totally to expense in the current period in the United States and Germany. This same expense could range from zero to $100 million in the United Kingdom and from $20 million to $100 million in Japan!

Do you believe that accounting principles should be comparable across countries?

UNIFORMITY IN STANDARDS

Efforts to obtain uniformity in international accounting practices are taking place. In 1973 the **International Accounting Standards Committee (IASC)** was formed by agreement of accounting organizations in the United States, the United Kingdom, Canada, Australia, France, Germany, Japan, Mexico, and the Netherlands. Its purpose is to formulate international accounting standards and to promote their acceptance worldwide.

To date, numerous standards have been issued for IASC members to introduce to their respective countries. But, the IASC has no enforcement powers, so these standards are by no means universally applied. They are, though, generally followed by the multinational companies that are audited by international public accounting firms. The foundation has been laid for progress toward greater uniformity in international accounting.

BEFORE YOU GO ON...

REVIEW IT

1. What are the monetary unit assumption, the economic entity assumption, the time period assumption, and the going concern assumption?
2. What are the revenue recognition principle, the matching principle, the full disclosure principle, and the cost principle?
3. What are the materiality constraint and the conservatism constraint?
4. What is the purpose of the International Accounting Standards Committee?

A LOOK BACK AT OUR FEATURE STORY

Refer back to the Feature Story at the beginning of the chapter, and answer the following questions.

1. **Policy Management Systems Corp.** produces insurance software. It reported some sales before contracts were signed or products delivered. Is the concept of revenue recognition violated in this situation? Explain.

2. **Sunbeam Corporation** prematurely booked revenues and recorded overly large restructuring charges.

SOLUTION

1. The revenue recognition principle dictates that revenue should be recognized in the accounting period in which it is earned. Revenue is generally recognized at the point of sale. Policy Management violated the revenue recognition principle because the sale had not yet occurred.
2. Many companies feel intense pressure to report higher earnings every year. If actual performance falls short of expectations, management might be tempted to bend the rules to prevent its stock price from falling. Although high-tech firms are particularly susceptible to earnings declines, many companies attempt to manage their net income from period to period, as Sunbeam Corporation appears to have done.

THE NAVIGATOR

DEMONSTRATION PROBLEM 1

Additional Demonstration Problem

Carver Construction Company is under contract to build a condominium at a contract price of $2,000,000. The building will take 18 months to complete at an estimated cost of $1,400,000. Construction began in November 2001, and was finished in April 2003. Actual construction costs incurred in each year were: 2001, $140,000; 2002, $910,000; and 2003, $350,000.

Instructions

Compute the gross profit to be recognized in each year.

ACTION PLAN

- Determine percent complete by dividing costs incurred by total estimated costs.
- Find revenue recognized by multiplying percent complete by contract price.
- Calculate gross profit: revenue recognized less actual costs incurred.
- Under percentage-of-completion method, recognize revenue as the construction occurs. (Revenue is viewed as a series of sales.)

THE NAVIGATOR

SOLUTION TO DEMONSTRATION PROBLEM 1

Year	Costs Incurred (Current Period)	÷	Total Estimated Cost	=	Percent Complete (Current Period)	×	Total Revenue	=	Revenue Recognized (Current Period)
2001	$ 140,000		$1,400,000		10%		$2,000,000		$ 200,000
2002	910,000		1,400,000		65%		2,000,000		1,300,000
2003	350,000		Balance to complete contract						500,000
	$1,400,000								$2,000,000

Year	Revenue Recognized (Current Period)	–	Actual Costs Incurred (Current Period)	=	Gross Profit Recognized (Current Period)
2001	$ 200,000		$ 140,000		$ 60,000
2002	1,300,000		910,000		390,000
2003	500,000		350,000		150,000
	$2,000,000		$1,400,000		$600,000

DEMONSTRATION PROBLEM 2

Additional Demonstration Problem

Valdes Inc. uses the installment method in accounting for its sales. In 2000, its first year of operations, it had installment sales of $900,000 and a cost of goods sold on installments of $600,000. The collections on installment sales were as follows: 2000, $330,000; 2001, $420,000; and 2002, $150,000.

Instructions

Compute the amount of gross profit to be recognized each year.

SOLUTION TO DEMONSTRATION PROBLEM 2

Year	Cash Collected	×	Gross Profit Percentage*	=	Gross Profit Recognized
2000	$330,000		33⅓%		$110,000
2001	420,000		33⅓%		140,000
2002	150,000		33⅓%		50,000
	$900,000				$300,000

*$900,000 − $600,000 = $300,000; $300,000 ÷ $900,000 = 33⅓%

ACTION PLAN

- Use the installment method when cash collection is uncertain.
- Always find gross profit percentage.
- Recognize gross profit each period by multiplying cash collected times gross profit percentage.

THE NAVIGATOR

SUMMARY OF STUDY OBJECTIVES

1. *Explain the meaning of generally accepted accounting principles and identify the key items of the conceptual framework.* Generally accepted accounting principles are a set of rules and practices that are recognized as a general guide for financial reporting purposes. Generally accepted means that these principles must have "substantial authoritative support." The key items of the conceptual framework are: (1) objectives of financial reporting; (2) qualitative characteristics of accounting information; (3) elements of financial statements; and (4) operating guidelines (assumptions, principles, and constraints).

2. *Describe the basic objectives of financial reporting.* The basic objectives of financial reporting are to provide information that is (1) useful to those making investment and credit decisions; (2) helpful in assessing future cash flows; and (3) helpful in identifying economic resources (assets), the claims to those resources (liabilities), and the changes in those resources and claims.

3. *Discuss the qualitative characteristics of accounting information and elements of financial statements.* To be judged useful, information should possess the following qualitative characteristics: relevance, reliability, comparability, and consistency. The elements of financial statements are a set of definitions that can be used to describe the basic terms used in accounting.

4. *Identify the basic assumptions used by accountants.* The major assumptions are: monetary unit, economic entity, time period, and going concern.

5. *Identify the basic principles of accounting.* The major principles are revenue recognition, matching, full disclosure, and cost.

6. *Identify the two constraints in accounting.* The major constraints are materiality and conservatism.

7. *Explain the accounting principles used in international operations.* There are few recognized worldwide accounting standards. The International Accounting Standards Committee (IASC) is working to obtain conformity in international accounting practices.

THE NAVIGATOR

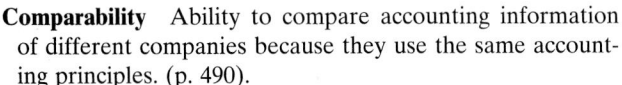

Key Term Matching Activity

GLOSSARY

Comparability Ability to compare accounting information of different companies because they use the same accounting principles. (p. 490).

Conceptual framework A coherent system of interrelated objectives and fundamentals that can lead to consistent standards. (p. 489).

Conservatism The constraint of choosing an accounting method, when in doubt, that will least likely overstate assets and net income. (p. 501).

Consistency Use of the same accounting principles and methods from year to year within a company. (p. 491).

Cost principle The principle that assets should be recorded at their historical cost. (p. 499).

Economic entity assumption The assumption that the activities of an economic entity be kept separate from the activities of the owner and of all other entities. (p. 493).

Elements of financial statements Definitions of basic terms used in accounting. (p. 491).

Full disclosure principle The principle that circumstances and events that make a difference to financial statement users should be disclosed. (p. 498).

Generally accepted accounting principles (GAAP) A set of rules and practices, having substantial authoritative support, that are recognized as a general guide for financial reporting purposes. (p. 488).

Going concern assumption The assumption that the enterprise will continue in operation long enough to carry out its existing objectives and commitments. (p. 493).

Installment method A method of recognizing revenue using the cash basis; each cash collection consists of a partial recovery of cost of goods sold and partial gross profit from the sale. (p. 496).

International Accounting Standards Committee (IASC) An accounting organization whose purpose is to formulate and publish international accounting standards and to promote their acceptance worldwide. (p. 503).

Matching principle The principle that expenses should be matched with revenues in the period when efforts are expended to generate revenues. (p. 497).

Materiality The constraint of determining if an item is important enough to likely influence the decision of a reasonably prudent investor or creditor. (p. 500).

Monetary unit assumption The assumption that only transaction data capable of being expressed in monetary terms should be included in accounting records. (p. 493).

Percentage-of-completion method A method of recognizing revenue and income on a construction project on the basis of costs incurred during the period to the total estimated costs for the entire project. (p. 495).

Relevance The quality of information that indicates the information makes a difference in a decision. (p. 490).

Reliability The quality of information that gives assurance that information is free of error and bias. (p. 490).

Revenue recognition principle The principle that revenue should be recognized in the accounting period in which it is earned (generally at the point of sale). (p. 494).

Time period assumption The assumption that the economic life of a business can be divided into artificial time periods. (p. 493).

Chapter 12 Self-Test

SELF-STUDY QUESTIONS

Answers are at the end of the chapter.

(SO 1) 1. Generally accepted accounting principles are:
a. a set of standards and rules that are recognized as a general guide for financial reporting.
b. usually established by the Internal Revenue Service.
c. the guidelines used to resolve ethical dilemmas.
d. fundamental truths that can be derived from the laws of nature.

(SO 2) 2. Which of the following is *not* an objective of financial reporting?
a. Provide information that is useful in investment and credit decisions.
b. Provide information about economic resources, claims to those resources, and changes in them.
c. Provide information that is useful in assessing future cash flows.
d. Provide information on the liquidation value of a business.

(SO 3) 3. The primary criterion by which accounting information can be judged is:
a. consistency.
b. predictive value.
c. decision-usefulness.
d. comparability.

(SO 3) 4. Verifiability is an ingredient of:

	Reliability	Relevance
a.	Yes	Yes
b.	No	No
c.	Yes	No
d.	No	Yes

(SO 4, 5, 6) 5. Valuing assets at their liquidation value rather than their cost is *inconsistent* with the:
a. time period assumption.
b. matching principle.
c. going concern assumption.
d. materiality constraint.

(SO 5) 6. Gonzalez's Construction Company began a long-term construction contract on January 1, 2002. The contract is expected to be completed in 2003 at a total cost of $20,000,000. Gonzalez's revenue for the project is $24,000,000. Gonzalez incurred contract costs of $4,000,000 in 2002. What gross profit should be recognized in 2002?
a. $800,000.
b. $1,000,000.
c. $2,000,000.
d. $4,000,000.

7. Dunlop Company had installment sales of $1,000,000 in its first year of operations. The cost of goods sold on installment was $650,000. Dunlop collected a total of $500,000 on the installment sales. Using the installment method, how much gross profit should be recognized in the first year? (SO 5)
a. $140,000.
b. $175,000.
c. $350,000.
d. $500,000.

8. The full disclosure principle dictates that: (SO 5)
a. financial statements should disclose all assets at their cost.
b. financial statements should disclose only those events that can be measured in dollars.
c. financial statements should disclose all events and circumstances that would matter to users of financial statements.
d. financial statements should not be relied on unless an auditor has expressed an unqualified opinion on them.

9. The accounting constraint that means that when in doubt the accountant should choose the method that will be least likely to overstate assets and income is called: (SO 6)
a. the matching principle.
b. materiality.
c. conservatism.
d. the monetary unit assumption.

10. The organization that issues international accounting standards is the: (SO 7)
a. Financial Accounting Standards Board.
b. International Accounting Standards Committee.
c. International Auditing Standards Committee.
d. None of the above.

THE NAVIGATOR

QUESTIONS

1. (a) What are generally accepted accounting principles (GAAP)? (b) What bodies provide authoritative support for GAAP?
2. What elements comprise the FASB's conceptual framework?
3. (a) What are the objectives of financial reporting? (b) Identify the qualitative characteristics of accounting information.
4. Mark McGwire, the president of Cardinal Company, is pleased. Cardinal substantially increased its net income in 2002 while keeping its unit inventory relatively the same. Sammy Sosa, chief accountant, cautions McGwire that since Cardinal changed from the LIFO to the FIFO method of inventory valuation, there is a consistency problem. It would be difficult to determine if Cardinal is better off. Is Sosa correct? Why or why not?
5. What is the distinction between comparability and consistency?
6. Why is it necessary for accountants to assume that an economic entity will remain a going concern?
7. When should revenue be recognized? Why has the date of sale been chosen as the point at which to recognize the revenue resulting from the entire producing and selling process?
8. Goodwin Construction Company has a $210 million contract to build a bridge. Its total estimated cost for the project is $170 million. Costs incurred in the first year of the project were $34 million. Goodwin appropriately uses the percentage-of-completion method. How much revenue and gross profit should Goodwin recognize in the first year of the project?
9. Merchandise with a cost of $80,000 was sold during the year for $100,000. Cash collected for the year amounted to $45,000. How much gross profit should be recognized during the year if the company uses the installment method?
10. Distinguish between expired costs and unexpired costs.
11. (a) Where does the accountant disclose information about an entity's financial position, operations, and cash flows? (b) The full disclosure principle recognizes that the nature and amount of information included in financial reports reflect a series of judgmental trade-offs. What are the objectives of these trade-offs?
12. Mark Lofton is the president of Mystery Books. He has no accounting background. Lofton cannot understand why current cost is not used as the basis for accounting measurement and reporting. Explain what basis is used and why.
13. Describe the two constraints inherent in the presentation of accounting information.
14. Your roommate believes that international accounting standards are uniform throughout the world. Is your roommate correct? Explain.
15. What organization establishes international accounting standards?

BRIEF EXERCISES

Identify generally accepted accounting principles. (SO 1)

BE12-1 Indicate whether each of the following statements is true or false.

(a) ____ "Generally accepted" means that these principles must have "substantial authoritative support."

(b) ____ GAAP is a set of rules and practices established by the accounting profession to serve as a general guide for financial reporting purposes.

(c) ____ Substantial authoritative support for GAAP usually comes from two standard-setting bodies: the FASB and the IRS.

Identify items included in conceptual framework. (SO 1)

BE12-2 Indicate which of the following items is(are) included in the FASB's conceptual framework. (Use "Yes" or "No" to answer this question.)

(a) ____ Qualitative characteristics of accounting information.

(b) ____ Analysis of financial statement ratios.

(c) ____ Objectives of financial reporting.

Identify objectives of financial reporting. (SO 2)

BE12-3 According to the FASB's conceptual framework, which of the following are objectives of financial reporting? (Use "Yes" or "No" to answer this question.)

(a) ____ Provide information that identifies the economic resources (assets), the claims to those resources (liabilities), and the changes in those resources and claims.

(b) ____ Provide information that is helpful in assessing past cash flows and stock prices.

(c) ____ Provide information that is useful to those making investment and credit decisions.

Identify qualitative characteristics. (SO 3)

BE12-4 Presented on page 508 is a chart of the qualitative characteristics of accounting information. Fill in the blanks from (a) to (e).

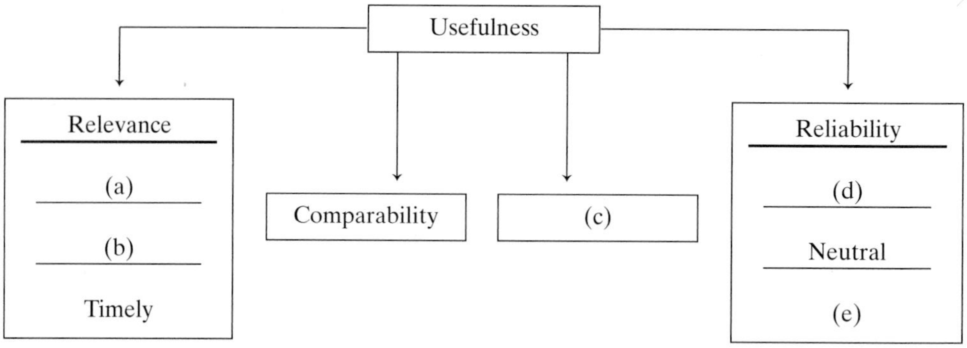

Identify qualitative characteristics.
(SO 3)

BE12-5 Given the *qualitative characteristics* of accounting established by the FASB's conceptual framework, complete each of the following statements.

(a) ____ is the quality of information that gives assurance that it is free of error and bias; it can be depended on.
(b) ____ means using the same accounting principles and methods from year to year within a company.
(c) For information to be ____, it should have predictive or feedback value, and it must be presented on a timely basis.

Identify qualitative characteristics.
(SO 3)

BE12-6 Presented below is a set of qualitative characteristics of accounting information.

1. Predictive value   **3.** Verifiable
2. Neutral   **4.** Timely

Match these qualitative characteristics to the following statements, using numbers 1 through 4.

(a) ____Accounting information should help users make predictions about the outcome of past, present, and future events.
(b) ____Accounting information cannot be selected, prepared, or presented to favor one set of interested users over another.
(c) ____Accounting information must be proved to be free of error and bias.
(d) ____Accounting information must be available to decision makers before it loses its capacity to influence their decisions.

Identify operating guidelines.
(SO 4, 5, 6)

BE12-7 Presented below are four concepts discussed in this chapter.

1. Time period assumption   **3.** Full disclosure principle
2. Cost principle   **4.** Conservatism

Match these concepts to the following accounting practices. Each number can be used only once.

(a) ____Recording inventory at its purchase price.
(b) ____Using notes and supplementary schedules in the financial statements.
(c) ____Preparing financial statements on an annual basis.
(d) ____Using the lower of cost or market method for inventory valuation.

Compute revenue—percentage-of-completion.
(SO 5)

BE12-8 Yoon Construction Company is under contract to build a commercial building at a price of $3,800,000. Construction began in January 2001 and was finished in December 2003. Total estimated construction costs are $2,800,000. Actual construction costs incurred in each year were: 2001, $560,000; 2002, $1,820,000; 2003, $420,000. Compute the revenue to be recognized in each year using the percentage-of-completion method.

Compute gross profit—installment method.
(SO 5)

BE12-9 Padillio Co. uses the installment method to determine its net income. In 2002, its first year of operations, it had installment sales of $800,000 and a cost of goods sold of $480,000. The collections on installment sales were as follows: 2002, $360,000; 2003, $440,000. Determine the gross profit recognized for 2002 and 2003.

Identify the constraints that have been violated.
(SO 6)

BE12-10 Alomar Company uses the following accounting practices.

(a) Small tools are recorded as plant assets and depreciated.
(b) Inventory is reported at cost when market value is lower.
(c) The income statement shows paper clips expense of $10.
(d) Revenue on installment sales is recognized at the time of sale.

Indicate the accounting constraint, if any, that has been violated by each practice.

EXERCISES

E12-1 A number of accounting reporting situations are described below.

Identify the assumption, principle, or constraint that has been violated.
(SO 4, 5, 6)

1. Person Company is in its fifth year of operation and has yet to issue financial statements. (Do not use full disclosure principle.)
2. Nevin Company has inventory on hand that cost $400,000. Nevin reports inventory on its balance sheet at its current market value of $425,000.
3. Sue Jackson, president of Always Music Company, bought a computer for her personal use. She paid for the computer by using company funds and debited the "computers" account.
4. Boone Company recognizes revenue at the end of the production cycle, but before sale. The price of the product, as well as the amount that can be sold, is not certain.
5. In preparing its financial statements, Rupe Company omitted information concerning its method of accounting for inventories.
6. Larkin Company uses the direct write-off method of accounting for uncollectible accounts.
7. Brantley Hospital Supply Corporation reports only current assets and current liabilities on its balance sheet. Property, plant, and equipment are reported as current assets. Bonds payable are reported as current liabilities. Liquidation of the company is unlikely.

Instructions

For each of the above, list the assumption, principle, or constraint that has been violated, if any. List only one term for each case.

E12-2 Presented below are some business transactions that occurred during 2002 for Cleveland Co.

Identify the assumption, principle, or constraint that has been violated; prepare correct entries.
(SO 4, 5, 6)

1. An account receivable has been deemed to be a bad debt. The following entry was made.

Allowance for Doubtful Accounts	10,000	
Accounts Receivable		10,000

2. The president of Cleveland Co., Ben Williams, purchased a truck for personal use and charged it to his expense account. The following entry was made.

Travel Expense	18,000	
Cash		18,000

3. An electric pencil sharpener costing $40 is being depreciated over 5 years. The following entry was made.

Depreciation Expense—Pencil Sharpener	8	
Accumulated Depreciation—Pencil Sharpener		8

4. Equipment worth $80,000 was acquired at a cost of $60,000 from a company that had water damage in a flood. The following entry was made.

Equipment	80,000	
Cash		60,000
Gain		20,000

5. Merchandise inventory with a cost of $208,000 is reported at its market value of $260,000. The following entry was made.

Merchandise Inventory	52,000	
Gain		52,000

Instructions

In each of the situations above, identify the assumption, principle, or constraint that has been violated, if any. Discuss the appropriateness of the journal entries, and give the correct journal entry, if necessary.

E12-3 Presented below are the assumptions, principles, and constraints discussed in this chapter:

Identify accounting assumptions, principles, and constraints.
(SO 4, 5, 6)

1. Economic entity assumption
2. Going concern assumption
3. Monetary unit assumption
4. Time period assumption
5. Cost principle
6. Matching principle
7. Full disclosure principle
8. Revenue recognition principle
9. Materiality
10. Conservatism

Instructions

Identify by number the accounting assumption, principle, or constraint that describes each situation below. Do not use a number more than once.

(a) Requires recognition of expenses in the same period as related revenues.
(b) Indicates that market value changes subsequent to purchase are not recorded in the accounts.
(c) Is the rationale for why plant assets are not reported at liquidation value. (Do not use historical cost principle.)
(d) Indicates that personal and business record keeping should be separately maintained.
(e) Ensures that all relevant financial information is reported.
(f) Assumes that the dollar is the "measuring stick" used to report on financial performance.
(g) Requires that the operational guidelines be followed for all significant items.
(h) Separates financial information into time periods for reporting purposes.

Determine the amount of revenue to be recognized.
(SO 5)

E12-4 Consider the following transactions of Hacking Group Company for 2002.

1. Leased office space to Easley Supplies for a 1-year period beginning September 1. The rent of $18,000 was paid in advance.
2. Sold a 6-month insurance policy to Orosco Corporation for $8,000 on March 1.
3. Received a sales order for merchandise costing $9,000 and a sales price of $12,000 on December 28 from Warren Company. The goods were shipped FOB shipping point on December 31. Warren received them on January 3, 2003.
4. Signed a long-term contract to construct a building at a total price of $1,800,000. Total estimated cost of construction is $1,200,000. During 2002, the company incurred $300,000 of costs and collected $330,000 in cash. The percentage-of-completion method is used to recognize revenue.
5. Had merchandise inventory on hand at year-end that amounted to $160,000. Hacking Group expects to sell the inventory in 2003 for $190,000.

Instructions

For each item above, indicate the amount of revenue Hacking Group should recognize in calendar year 2002. Explain.

Determine gross profit for construction projects.
(SO 5)

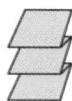

E12-5 Ortiz Construction Company currently has one long-term construction project. The project has a contract price of $120,000,000, with total estimated costs of $100,000,000. Ortiz appropriately uses the percentage-of-completion method. After 2 years of construction, the following costs have been accumulated.

Actual cost incurred, Year 1	$30,000,000
Total estimated cost remaining after Year 1	70,000,000
Actual cost incurred, Year 2	50,000,000
Total estimated cost remaining after Year 2	20,000,000

Instructions

Determine the gross profit for each of the first 2 years of the construction contract.

Determine gross profit using installment sales and point-of-sale bases.
(SO 5)

E12-6 Buford Company sold equipment for $300,000 in 2001. Collections on the sale were as follows: 2001, $70,000; 2002, $190,000; 2003, $40,000. Buford's cost of goods sold is typically 60% of sales.

Instructions

(a) Determine Buford's gross profit for 2001, 2002, and 2003, assuming that Buford recognizes revenue under the installment method.
(b) Determine Buford's gross profit for 2001, 2002, and 2003, assuming that Buford recognizes revenue under the point-of-sale basis.

PROBLEMS: SET A

Analyze transactions to identify accounting principle or assumption violated, and prepare correct entries.
(SO 4, 5)

P12-1A Jeter and Yu are accountants for Landmark Printers. They disagree over the following transactions that occurred during the year.

1. Land costing $41,000 was appraised at $49,000. Jeter suggests the following journal entry.

Land	8,000	
Gain on Appreciation of Land		8,000

2. Landmark bought equipment for $40,000, including installation costs. The equipment has a useful life of 5 years. Landmark depreciates equipment using the straight-line method. "Since the equipment as installed into our system cannot be removed without considerable damage, it will have no resale value. Therefore, it should not be depreciated, but instead should be expensed immediately," argues Jeter. "Besides, it lowers net income."
3. Depreciation for the year was $26,000. Since net income is expected to be lower this year, Jeter suggests deferring depreciation to a year when there is more net income.
4. Landmark purchased equipment at a fire sale for $20,000. The equipment was worth $26,000. Jeter believes that the following entry should be made.

Equipment	26,000	
Cash		20,000
Gain		6,000

5. Jeter suggests that Landmark should carry equipment on the balance sheet at its liquidation value, which is $20,000 less than its cost.
6. Landmark rented office space for 1 year starting October 1, 2002. The total amount of $20,000 was paid in advance. Jeter believes that the following entry should be made on October 1.

Rent Expense	20,000	
Cash		20,000

Yu disagrees with Jeter on each of the situations above.

Instructions

For each transaction, indicate why Yu disagrees. Identify the accounting principle or assumption that Jeter would be violating if his suggestions were used. Prepare the correct journal entry for each transaction, if any.

Determine the appropriateness of journal entries in terms of generally accepted accounting principles or assumptions.
(SO 4, 5)

P12-2A Presented below are a number of business transactions that occurred during the current year for Delgado, Inc.

1. Because the general level of prices increased during the current year, Delgado, Inc. determined that there was a $40,000 understatement of depreciation expense on its equipment and decided to record it in its accounts. The following entry was made.

Depreciation Expense	40,000	
Accumulated Depreciation		40,000

2. Because of a "flood sale," equipment obviously worth $300,000 was acquired at a cost of $240,000. The following entry was made.

Equipment	300,000	
Cash		240,000
Gain on Purchase of Equipment		60,000

3. An order for $60,000 has been received from a customer for products on hand. This order is to be shipped on January 9 next year. The following entry was made.

Accounts Receivable	60,000	
Sales		60,000

4. Land was purchased on April 30 for $200,000. This amount was entered in the Land account. On December 31, the land would have cost $230,000, so the following entry was made.

Land	30,000	
Gain on Land		30,000

5. The president of Delgado, Inc. used his expense account to purchase a pre-owned Mercedes-Benz E420 solely for personal use. The following entry was made.

Miscellaneous Expense	54,000	
Cash		54,000

Instructions

In each situation, discuss the appropriateness of the journal entries in terms of generally accepted accounting principles.

Recognize gross profit using the percentage-of-completion method.
(SO 5)

P12-3A Cruz Construction Company is involved in a long-term construction contract to build a shopping center with a total estimated cost of $20 million, and a contract price of $26 million. Additional information follows.

	Shopping Center	
	Cash Collections	Actual Costs Incurred
2001	$ 4,500,000	$3,000,000
2002	10,000,000	9,000,000
2003	7,000,000	5,000,000
2004	4,500,000	3,000,000

The project was completed in 2004, and all cash collections related to the contract have been received.

Instructions

Prepare a schedule to determine the gross profit for each year for the long-term construction contract, using the percentage-of-completion method.

Recognize gross profit using the installment method.
(SO 5)

P12-4A Bunill sold to Lee Management Company condominiums it had constructed. The sales price was $6 million. Bunill's cost to construct the condominiums was $3.9 million. Bunill appropriately uses the installment method. Additional information follows.

	Cash Collected
2001	$ 900,000
2002	3,800,000
2003	1,300,000

Instructions

(a) Prepare a schedule to determine the gross profit for each year using the installment method.
(b) Repeat (a) assuming construction costs were $4.2 million.

Identify accounting assumptions, principles, and constraints.
(SO 4, 5, 6)

P12-5A Presented below are assumptions, principles, and constraints.

1. Economic entity assumption	**6.** Revenue recognition principle
2. Going concern assumption	**7.** Matching principle
3. Monetary unit assumption	**8.** Cost principle
4. Time period assumption	**9.** Materiality
5. Full disclosure principle	**10.** Conservatism

Instructions

Identify by number the accounting assumption, principle, or constraint that describes each situation below. Do not use a number more than once.

(a) All important information related to inventories is presented in the financial statements or in the footnotes.
(b) Assets are not stated at their liquidation value. (Do not use the cost principle.)
(c) The death of the president is not recorded in the accounts.
(d) Pencil sharpeners are expensed when purchased.
(e) An allowance for doubtful accounts is established. (Do not use conservatism.)
(f) Each entity is kept as a unit distinct from its owner or owners.
(g) Reporting must be done at defined intervals.
(h) Revenue is recorded at the point of sale.
(i) When in doubt, it is better to understate rather than overstate net income.

PROBLEMS: SET B

Analyze transactions to identify accounting principle or assumption violated, and prepare correct entries.
(SO 4, 5)

P12-1B Dye and Zaur are accountants for Desktop Computers. They disagree over the following transactions that occurred during the calendar year 2002.

1. Dye suggests that equipment should be reported on the balance sheet at its liquidation value, which is $15,000 less than its cost.

2. Desktop bought a custom-made piece of equipment for $24,000. This equipment has a useful life of 6 years. Desktop depreciates equipment using the straight-line method. "Since the equipment is custom-made, it will have no resale value. Therefore, it shouldn't be depreciated but instead should be expensed immediately," argues Dye. "Besides, it provides for lower net income."
3. Depreciation for the year was $18,000. Since net income is expected to be lower this year, Dye suggests deferring depreciation to a year when there is more net income.
4. Land costing $60,000 was appraised at $90,000. Dye suggests the following journal entry.

Land	30,000	
Gain on Appreciation of Land		30,000

5. Desktop purchased equipment for $30,000 at a going-out-of-business sale. The equipment was worth $45,000. Dye believes that the following entry should be made.

Equipment	45,000	
Cash		30,000
Gain		15,000

Zaur disagrees with Dye on each of the above situations.

Instructions

For each transaction, indicate why Zaur disagrees. Identify the accounting principle or assumption that Dye would be violating if his suggestions were used. Prepare the correct journal entry for each transaction, if any.

Determine the appropriateness of journal entries in terms of generally accepted accounting principles or assumptions.
(SO 4, 5)

P12-2B Presented below are a number of business transactions that occurred during the current year for Chavez, Inc.

1. Because the general level of prices increased during the current year, Chavez, Inc. determined that there was a $10,000 understatement of depreciation expense on its equipment and decided to record it in its accounts. The following entry was made.

Depreciation Expense	10,000	
Accumulated Depreciation		10,000

2. Because of a "flood sale," equipment obviously worth $250,000 was acquired at a cost of $150,000. The following entry was made.

Equipment	250,000	
Cash		150,000
Gain on Purchase of Equipment		100,000

3. The president of Chavez, Inc. used his expense account to purchase a new Saab 9000 solely for personal use. The following entry was made.

Miscellaneous Expense	34,000	
Cash		34,000

4. An order for $30,000 has been received from a customer for products on hand. This order is to be shipped on January 9 next year. The following entry was made.

Accounts Receivable	30,000	
Sales		30,000

5. Materials were purchased on March 31 for $65,000. This amount was entered in the Inventory account. On December 31, the materials would have cost $85,000, so the following entry was made.

Inventory	20,000	
Gain on Inventories		20,000

Instructions

In each situation, discuss the appropriateness of the journal entries in terms of generally accepted accounting principles.

Recognize gross profit using percentage-of-completion.
(SO 5)

P12-3B Wallace Construction Company is involved in a long-term construction contract to build an office building. The estimated cost is $30 million, and the contract price is $36 million. Additional information follows.

	Office Building	
	Cash Collections	Actual Costs Incurred
2001	$ 6,000,000	$ 4,500,000
2002	8,000,000	6,000,000
2003	12,500,000	12,000,000
2004	9,500,000	7,500,000

The project is completed in 2004, and all cash to be received from the contract has been received.

Instructions

Prepare a schedule to determine the gross profit in each year for the long-term construction contract using the percentage-of-completion method.

Recognize gross profit using the installment method.
(SO 5)

P12-4B Coomer Construction sold to Walker Management Company apartments it had constructed. The sales price was $2.5 million. Coomer's cost to construct the apartments was $1.4 million. Coomer appropriately uses the installment method. Additional information follows.

	Cash Collected
2001	$ 800,000
2002	1,200,000
2003	500,000

(a) Determine the gross profit for each year using the installment method.
(b) Repeat (a) assuming the construction costs were $1.5 million.

Identify accounting assumptions, principles, and constraints.
(SO 4, 5, 6)

P12-5B Presented below are the assumptions, principles, and constraints used in this chapter.

1. Economic entity assumption	**6.** Revenue recognition principle
2. Going concern assumption	**7.** Matching principle
3. Monetary unit assumption	**8.** Cost principle
4. Time period assumption	**9.** Materiality
5. Full disclosure principle	**10.** Conservatism

Identify by number the accounting assumption, principle, or constraint that describes each situation below. Do not use a number more than once.

(a) Repair tools are expensed when purchased. These repair tools have a useful life of more than one accounting period. (Do not use conservatism.)
(b) Expenses should be allocated to revenues in proper period.
(c) The dollar is the measuring stick used to report financial information.
(d) Financial information is separated into time periods for reporting purposes.
(e) Market value changes subsequent to purchase are not recorded in the accounts. (Do not use the revenue recognition principle.)
(f) Personal and business record keeping should be separately maintained.
(g) All relevant financial information should be reported.
(h) Lower of cost or market is used to value inventories.

COMPREHENSIVE PROBLEM: CHAPTERS 9 TO 12

Nahas Company and Nordlund Company are competing businesses. Both began operations 6 years ago and are quite similar in most respects. The current balance sheet data for the two companies are as follows.

	Nahas Company	Nordlund Company
Cash	$ 50,300	$ 48,400
Accounts receivable	309,700	312,500
Allowance for doubtful accounts	(13,600)	-0-
Merchandise inventory	463,900	520,200
Plant and equipment	245,300	257,300
Accumulated depreciation, plant and equipment	(107,650)	(189,850)
Total assets	$947,950	$948,550
Current liabilities	$440,200	$436,500
Long-term liabilities	78,000	80,000
Total liabilities	518,200	516,500
Owner's equity	429,750	432,050
Total liabilities and owner's equity	$947,950	$948,550

You have been engaged as a consultant to conduct a review of the two companies. Your goal is to determine which of them is in the stronger financial position.

Your review of their financial statements quickly reveals that the two companies have not followed the same accounting practices. The differences and your conclusions regarding them are summarized below.

1. Nahas Company has used the allowance method of accounting for bad debts. A review shows that the amount of its write-offs each year has been quite close to the allowances that have been provided. It therefore seems reasonable to have confidence in its current estimate of bad debts.

   Nordlund Company has used the direct write-off method for bad debts, and it has been somewhat slow to write off its uncollectible accounts. Based upon an aging analysis and review of its accounts receivable, it is estimated that $24,000 of its existing accounts will probably prove to be uncollectible.

2. Nahas Company has determined the cost of its merchandise inventory on a LIFO basis. The result is that its inventory appears on the balance sheet at an amount that is below its current replacement cost. Based upon a detailed physical examination of its merchandise on hand, the current replacement cost of its inventory is estimated at $517,000.

   Nordlund Company has used the FIFO method of valuing its merchandise inventory. Its ending inventory appears on the balance sheet at an amount that quite closely approximates its current replacement cost.

3. Nahas Company estimated a useful life of 12 years and a salvage value of $30,000 for its plant and equipment. It has been depreciating them on a straight-line basis.

   Nordlund Company has the same type of plant and equipment. However, it estimated a useful life of 10 years and a salvage value of $10,000. It has been depreciating its plant and equipment using the double-declining-balance method.

   Based upon engineering studies of these types of plant and equipment, you conclude that Nordlund's estimates and method for calculating depreciation are the more appropriate.

4. Among its current liabilities, Nahas has included the portions of long-term liabilities that become due within the next year. Nordlund has not done so.

   You find that $20,000 of Nordlund's $80,000 of long-term liabilities are due to be repaid in the current year.

Instructions

(a) Revise the balance sheets presented above so that the data are comparable and reflect the current financial position for each of the two companies.

(b) Prepare a brief report to your client stating your conclusions.

(a) Total assets:
Nahas $847,604
Nordlund $924,550

BROADENING YOUR PERSPECTIVE

FINANCIAL REPORTING AND ANALYSIS

FINANCIAL REPORTING PROBLEM

BYP12-1 Becky Bishop successfully completed her first accounting course during the spring semester. She is now working as a management trainee for First Arizona Bank during the summer. One of her fellow management trainees, Lance Jones, is taking the same accounting course this summer and has been having a "lot of trouble." On the second exam, for example, Lance became confused about inventory valuation methods. He completely missed all the points on a problem involving LIFO and FIFO.

Lance's instructor recently indicated that the third exam will probably have a number of essay questions dealing with accounting principle issues. Lance is quite concerned about the third exam for two reasons. First, he has never taken an accounting exam in which essay answers were required. Second, Lance feels he must do well on this exam to get an acceptable grade in the course.

Lance has asked Becky to help him prepare for the next exam. She agrees, and suggests that Lance develop a set of possible questions on the accounting principles material that they might discuss.

Instructions

Answer the following questions that were developed by Lance.

(a) What is a conceptual framework?
(b) Why is there a need for a conceptual framework?
(c) What are the objectives of financial reporting?
(d) If you had to explain generally accepted accounting principles to a nonaccountant, what essential characteristics would you include in your explanation?
(e) What are the qualitative characteristics of accounting? Explain each one.
(f) Identify the basic assumptions used in accounting.
(g) What are two major constraints involved in financial reporting? Explain both of them.

EXPLORING THE WEB

BYP12-2 The **Financial Accounting Standards Board (FASB)** is a private organization established to improve accounting standards and financial reporting. The FASB conducts extensive research before issuing a "Statement of Financial Accounting Standards," which represents an authoritative expression of generally accepted accounting principles.

Address: **www.rutgers.edu/accounting/raw** ***(or go to www.wiley.com/college/weygandt)***

Steps:

1. Choose **FASB**.
2. Choose **FASB Facts**.

Instructions

Answer the following questions.

(a) What is the mission of the FASB?
(b) How are topics added to the FASB technical agenda?
(c) What characteristics make the FASB's procedures an "open" decision-making process?

CRITICAL THINKING

GROUP DECISION CASE

BYP12-3 Margo Industries has two operating divisions—Talley Construction Division and Shumway Securities Division. Each division maintains its own accounting system and method of revenue recognition.

Talley Construction Division

During the fiscal year ended November 30, 2002, Talley Construction Division had one construction project in process. A $30,000,000 contract for construction of a civic center was granted on June 19, 2002, and construction began on August 1, 2002. Estimated costs of completion at the contract date were $26,000,000 over a 2-year time period from the date of the contract. On November 30, 2002, construction costs of $9,000,000 had been incurred. The construction costs to complete the remainder of the project were reviewed on November 30, 2002, and were estimated to amount to only $16,000,000 because of an expected decline in raw materials costs. Revenue recognition is based upon a percentage-of-completion method.

Shumway Securities Division

Shumway Securities Division works through manufacturers' agents in various cities. Orders for alarm systems and down payments are forwarded from agents, and the division ships the goods f.o.b. factory directly to customers (usually police departments and security guard companies). Customers are billed directly for the balance due plus actual shipping costs. The firm received orders for $6,000,000 of goods during the fiscal year ended November 30, 2002. Down payments of $600,000 were received and goods with a selling price of $5,500,000 were billed and shipped. Actual freight costs of $100,000 were also billed. Commissions of 10% on product price are paid manufacturing agents after goods are shipped to customers. Such goods are covered under warranty for 90 days after shipment, and warranty returns have been about 1% of sales. Revenue is recognized at the point of sale by this division.

Instructions

With the class divided into groups, answer the following.

(a) There are a variety of methods of revenue recognition. Define and describe each of the following methods of revenue recognition, and indicate whether each is in accordance with generally accepted accounting principles.
 (1) Point of sale.
 (2) Percentage-of-completion.
 (3) Installment contract.

(b) Compute the revenue to be recognized in fiscal year 2002 for both operating divisions of Margo Industries in accordance with generally accepted accounting principles.

ETHICS CASE

BYP12-4 When the Financial Accounting Standards Board issues new standards, the required implementation date is usually 12 months or more from the date of issuance, with early implementation encouraged. Sarah Lane, accountant at Mintur Corporation, discusses with her financial vice president the need for early implementation of a recently issued standard that would result in a much fairer presentation of the company's financial condition and earnings. When the financial vice president determines that early implementation of the standard will adversely affect reported net income for the year, he strongly discourages Sarah from implementing the standard until it is required.

Instructions

(a) Who are the stakeholders in this situation?

(b) What, if any, are the ethical considerations in this situation?

(c) What does Sarah have to gain by advocating early implementation? Who might be affected by the decision against early implementation?

Answers to Self-Study Questions

1. a **2.** d **3.** c **4.** c **5.** c **6.** a **7.** b **8.** c **9.** c **10.** b

Answer to Lands' End Review It Question 2, p. 492

The Report of Independent Public Accountants indicates that Lands' End's financial statements (balance sheet, income statement, shareholders' equity, and cash flows) are presented fairly, in accordance with generally accepted accounting principles.

Remember to go back to the Navigator box on the chapter-opening page and check off your completed work.

13

ACCOUNTING FOR PARTNERSHIPS

THE NAVIGATOR ✓

- Understand *Concepts for Review* ❑
- Read *Feature Story* ❑
- Scan *Study Objectives* ❑
- Read *Preview* ❑
- Read text and answer *Before You Go On*
  p. 524 ❑ *p.* 530 ❑ *p.* 538 ❑ *p.* 543 ❑
- Work *Demonstration Problem* ❑
- Review *Summary of Study Objectives* ❑
- Answer *Self-Study Questions* ❑
- Complete *Assignments* ❑

CONCEPTS FOR REVIEW

Before studying this chapter, you should know or, if necessary, review:

a. The cost principle of accounting. (Ch. 1, p. 10)

b. The owner's equity statement. (Ch. 1, pp. 22–24)

c. How to make closing entries and prepare the post-closing trial balance. (Ch. 4, pp. 140–145)

d. The steps in the accounting cycle. (Ch. 4, p. 148)

e. The format of classified financial statements. (Ch. 4, pp. 151–156)

☑ THE NAVIGATOR

FEATURE STORY

From Trials to the Top Ten

In 1990 Cliff Chenfield and Craig Balsam gave up the razors, ties, and six-figure salaries they had become accustomed to as New York lawyers. Instead, they set up a partnership, **Razor & Tie Music**, in Cliff's living room. Ten years later the label is the only record company in the country that has achieved success by selling music both on television and in the stores. Razor & Tie's entertaining and effective TV commercials have yielded unprecedented sales for multi-artist music compilations. At the same time, its hot young retail label has been behind some of the most recent original, progressive releases.

Razor & Tie's first TV release, *Those Fabulous '70s* (100,000 copies sold), was followed by *Disco Fever* (over 300,000 sold). These albums generated so much publicity that partners Cliff and Craig were guests on dozens of TV interview shows.

After restoring the respectability of the oft-maligned 1970s, the partners forged into the musical '80s with the same zeal that elicited success with their first releases. In July 1993, Razor & Tie released *Totally '80s*, a collection of Top-10 singles from the 1980s that has sold over 450,000 units since its release. Featuring the tag line, "The greatest hits from the decade when communism died and music videos were born," *Totally '80s* was the best-selling direct-response album in the country in 1993.

In 1995, Razor & Tie broke into the contemporary music world with *Living In The '90s*, the most successful record in the history of the company. Featuring a number of songs that were still recurrent hits on the radio at the time the package initially aired, *Living In The '90s* was a blockbuster. It received Gold certification in less than nine months and rewrote the rules on direct-response albums. For the first time, contemporary music was available through an album offered only through direct-response spots.

How has Razor & Tie carved out its sizable piece of the market? Through the complementary talents of the two partners. Their imagination and savvy, along with exciting new releases planned for the coming years, ensure Razor & Tie such continued growth that the partnership form of organization may be challenged to its limits.

www.razorandtie.com

☑ THE NAVIGATOR

STUDY OBJECTIVES

After studying this chapter, you should be able to:

1. Identify the characteristics of the partnership form of business organization.
2. Explain the accounting entries for the formation of a partnership.
3. Identify the bases for dividing net income or net loss.
4. Describe the form and content of partnership financial statements.
5. Explain the effects of the entries when a new partner is admitted.
6. Describe the effects of the entries when a partner withdraws from the firm.
7. Explain the effects of the entries to record the liquidation of a partnership.

☑ THE NAVIGATOR

PREVIEW OF CHAPTER 13

It is not surprising that when Cliff Chenfield and Craig Balsam began **Razor & Tie**, they decided to use the partnership form of organization. Both saw the need for hands-on control of their product and its promotion. In this chapter, we will discuss reasons why the partnership form of organization is often selected. We also will explain the major issues in accounting for partnerships.

The content and organization of Chapter 13 are as follows.

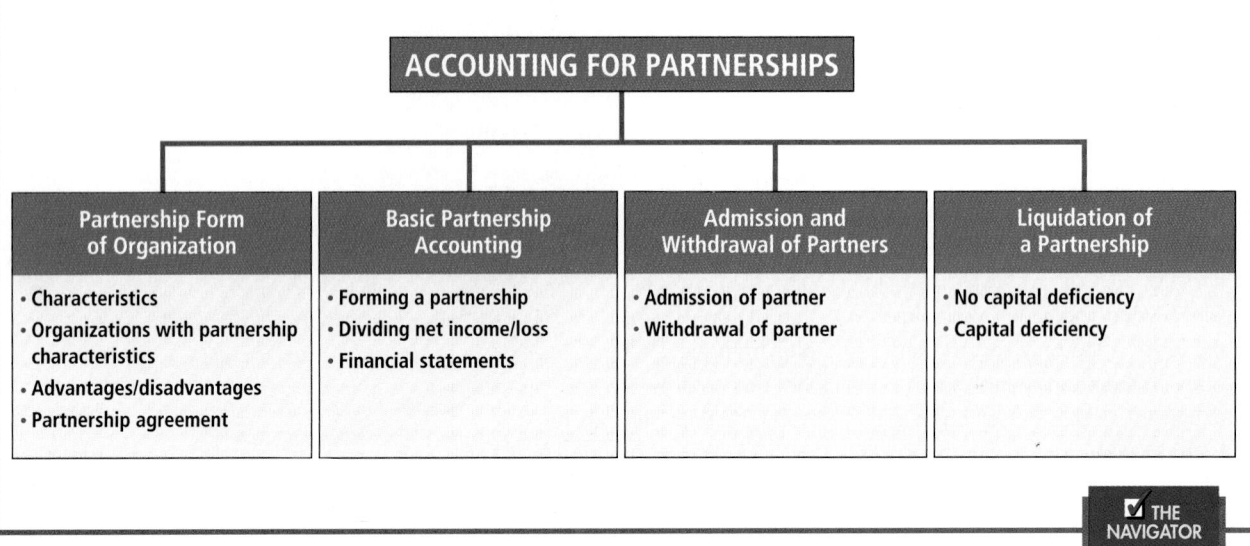

ACCOUNTING FOR PARTNERSHIPS

Partnership Form of Organization	Basic Partnership Accounting	Admission and Withdrawal of Partners	Liquidation of a Partnership
• Characteristics • Organizations with partnership characteristics • Advantages/disadvantages • Partnership agreement	• Forming a partnership • Dividing net income/loss • Financial statements	• Admission of partner • Withdrawal of partner	• No capital deficiency • Capital deficiency

THE NAVIGATOR

PARTNERSHIP FORM OF ORGANIZATION

The Uniform Partnership Act provides the basic rules for the formation and operation of partnerships in more than 90 percent of the states. This act defines a **partnership** as an association of two or more persons to carry on as co-owners of a business for profit. Partnerships are common in retail establishments and in small manufacturing companies. Also, accountants, lawyers, and doctors find it desirable to form partnerships with other professionals in their field. Professional partnerships vary in size from a medical partnership of 3 to 5 doctors, to 150 to 200 partners in a large law firm, to more than 2,000 partners in an international accounting firm.

CHARACTERISTICS OF PARTNERSHIPS

STUDY OBJECTIVE 1

Identify the characteristics of the partnership form of business organization.

Partnerships are fairly easy to form. They can be formed simply by a verbal agreement or, more formally, by putting in writing the rights and obligations of the partners. Partners who have not put their agreement in writing sometimes have found that the characteristics of partnerships can lead to later difficulties. The principal characteristics of the partnership form of business organization are shown in Illustration 13-1 and explained in the following sections.

Illustration 13-1
Partnership characteristics

Association of Individuals

The voluntary association of two or more individuals in a partnership may be based on as simple an act as a handshake. However, it is preferable to state the agreement in writing. Under the Uniform Partnership Act, a partnership is a legal entity for certain purposes. For instance, property (land, buildings, equipment) can be owned in the name of the partnership, and the firm can sue or be sued. **A partnership also is an accounting entity for financial reporting purposes.** Thus, the purely personal assets, liabilities, and transactions of the partners are excluded from the accounting records of the partnership, just as they are in a proprietorship.

The net income of a partnership is not taxed as a separate entity. But, a partnership must file an information tax return showing partnership net income and each partner's share of that net income. Each partner's share is taxable at personal tax rates, regardless of the amount of net income withdrawn from the business during the year.

Mutual Agency

Mutual agency means that each partner acts on behalf of the partnership when engaging in partnership business. The act of any partner is binding on all other partners. This is true even when partners act beyond the scope of their authority, so long as the act appears to be appropriate for the partnership. For example, a partner of a grocery store who purchases a delivery truck creates a binding contract in the name of the partnership, even if the partnership agreement denies this authority. On the other hand, if a partner in a law firm purchased a snowmobile for the partnership, such an act would not be binding on the partnership. The purchase is clearly outside the scope of partnership business.

HELPFUL HINT
Because of mutual agency, an individual should be extremely cautious in selecting partners.

Limited Life

A partnership does not have unlimited life. It may be ended voluntarily at any time through the acceptance of a new partner or the withdrawal of a partner. A partnership may be ended involuntarily by the death or incapacity of a partner. Thus the life of a partnership is indefinite. **Partnership dissolution** occurs whenever a partner withdraws or a new partner is admitted. Dissolution of a partnership does not necessarily mean that the business ends. If the continuing partners agree, operations can continue without interruption by forming a new partnership.

Unlimited Liability

Each partner is **personally and individually liable** for all partnership liabilities. Creditors' claims attach first to partnership assets. If these are insufficient, the claims then attach to the personal resources of any partner, irrespective of that partner's equity in the partnership. Because each partner is responsible for all the debts of the partnership, each partner is said to have **unlimited liability**.

ACCOUNTING IN ACTION ***Business Insight***

The prestigious New York law firm of **Kaye, Scholer, Fierman, Hays, & Handler**, accused of withholding damaging information during a federal investigation of its client **Lincoln Savings & Loan**, settled out of court for $41 million. The firm's liability insurance covered only $25 million of the total. Its 109 partners had to pay the remaining $16 million out of their own pockets.

In a recent year, court damage awards in malpractice suits against U.S. accountants and attorneys was close to $1 billion.

Co-Ownership of Property

Partnership assets are owned jointly by the partners. If the partnership is dissolved, the assets do not legally revert to the original contributor. Each partner has a claim on total assets equal to the balance in his or her respective capital account. This claim does not attach to specific assets that an individual partner contributed to the firm. Similarly, if a partner invests a building in the partnership valued at $100,000 and the building is later sold at a gain of $20,000, that partner does not personally receive the entire gain.

Partnership net income (or net loss) is also co-owned. **If the partnership contract does not specify to the contrary, all net income or net loss is shared equally by the partners.** As you will see later, though, partners may agree to unequal sharing of net income or net loss.

ORGANIZATIONS WITH PARTNERSHIP CHARACTERISTICS

With surprising speed, states are creating special forms of business organizations that have partnership characteristics. These new organizations are being adopted by many small companies. These special forms are: limited partnerships, limited liability partnerships, limited liability companies, and "S" corporations.

Limited Partnerships

In a **limited partnership**, one or more partners have **unlimited liability** and one or more partners have **limited liability** for the debts of the firm. Those with unlimited liability are called **general partners**. Those with limited liability are called **limited partners**. Limited partners are responsible for the debts of the partnership up to the limit of their investment in the firm. This organization is identified in its name with the words "Limited Partnership," or "Ltd.," or "LP." For the privilege of limited liability, the limited partner usually accepts less compensation than a general partner and exercises less influence in the affairs of the firm.

Limited Liability Partnership

Most states allow professionals such as lawyers, doctors, and accountants to form a **limited liability partnership** or "LLP." The LLP is designed to protect innocent partners from malpractice or negligence claims resulting from the acts of another partner. LLPs generally carry large insurance policies in case the partnership is guilty of malpractice.

Limited Liability Companies

A new, hybrid form of business organization with certain features like a corporation and others like a limited partnership is the **limited liability company**, or "LLC" (or "LC"). An LLC usually has a limited life. The owners, called **members**, have limited liability like owners of a corporation. Whereas limited partners do not actively participate in the management of a limited partnership (LP), the members of a limited liability company (LLC) can assume an active management role. For income tax purposes, the IRS usually classifies an LLC as a partnership.

"S" Corporations

An **"S" corporation** is a corporation that is taxed in the same way that a partnership is taxed. To qualify as an "S" corporation, the company must have 75 or fewer stockholders, all of whom must be citizens or residents of the United States. The advantage of an "S" corporation (also called a Sub-Chapter "S" corporation) is that, like a partnership and unlike a corporation, it does not pay income taxes.

ADVANTAGES AND DISADVANTAGES OF PARTNERSHIPS

Why do people choose partnerships? One major advantage of a partnership is that the **skills and resources of two or more individuals can be combined**. For example, a large public accounting firm such as **Ernst & Young** must have expertise in auditing, taxation, and management consulting. In addition, a partnership is **easily formed and is relatively free from governmental regulations and restrictions**. A partnership does not have to contend with the "red tape" that a corporation must face. Also, decisions can be made quickly on substantive matters affecting the firm; there is no board of directors that must be consulted.

On the other hand, partnerships also have some major disadvantages: **mutual agency**, **limited life**, and **unlimited liability**. Unlimited liability is particularly troublesome. Many individuals fear they may lose not only their initial investment but also their personal assets, if those assets are needed to pay partnership creditors. As a result, partnerships often find it difficult to obtain large amounts of investment capital. That is one reason why the largest business enterprises in the United States are corporations, not partnerships.

The advantages and disadvantages of the partnership form of business organization are summarized in Illustration 13-2.

Illustration 13-2

Advantages and disadvantages of a partnership

Advantages	Disadvantages
Combining skills and resources of two or more individuals	Mutual agency
Ease of formation	Limited life
Freedom from governmental regulations and restrictions	Unlimited liability
Ease of decision making	

THE PARTNERSHIP AGREEMENT

ETHICS NOTE

A well-developed partnership agreement reduces ethical conflict among partners. It specifies in clear and concise language the process by which ethical and legal problems will be resolved. This issue is especially significant when the partnership experiences financial distress.

Ideally, the agreement of two or more individuals to form a partnership should be expressed in writing. This written contract is often called the **partnership agreement** or **articles of co-partnership**. The partnership agreement contains such basic information as the name and principal location of the firm, the purpose of the business, and date of inception. In addition, relationships among the partners should be specified, such as:

1. Names and capital contributions of partners.
2. Rights and duties of partners.
3. Basis for sharing net income or net loss.
4. Provision for withdrawals of assets.
5. Procedures for submitting disputes to arbitration.
6. Procedures for the withdrawal or addition of a partner.
7. Rights and duties of surviving partners in the event of a partner's death.

We cannot overemphasize the importance of a written contract. The agreement should be drawn with care and should attempt to anticipate all possible situations, contingencies, and disagreements. The help of a lawyer is highly desirable in preparing the agreement.

ACCOUNTING IN ACTION e Business Insight

Accounting firms generally use the limited liability (LLP) form. As a consequence, they do not have publicly traded shares of stock. During the dot-com stock market craze of the late 1990s, this proved to be somewhat of a disadvantage for partnerships. The reason: Many dot-com firms lured top high-tech employees to their companies by offering shares of stock. As dot-com stock prices soared, many of these people became very rich—at least for a while. However, when many of these same dot-com companies started to falter and fail, their stock prices plummeted, and they laid off many employees.

BEFORE YOU GO ON...

REVIEW IT

1. What are the distinguishing characteristics of a partnership?
2. What are the principal advantages and disadvantages of a partnership? Why is Land's End, Inc. not a partnership? The answer to this question is provided on page 556.
3. What are the major items in a partnership agreement?

THE NAVIGATOR

BASIC PARTNERSHIP ACCOUNTING

We now turn to the basic accounting for partnerships. The major accounting issues relate to forming the partnership, dividing income or loss, and preparing financial statements.

STUDY OBJECTIVE 2

Explain the accounting entries for the formation of a partnership.

FORMING A PARTNERSHIP

Each partner's initial investment in a partnership is entered in the partnership records. These investments should be recorded at the **fair market value of the assets at the date of their transfer to the partnership**. The values assigned must be agreed to by all of the partners.

To illustrate, assume that A. Rolfe and T. Shea combine their proprietorships to start a partnership named U.S. Software. The firm will specialize in developing financial modeling software packages. Rolfe and Shea have the following assets prior to the formation of the partnership.

Illustration 13-3

Book and market values of assets invested

	Book Value		Market Value	
	A. Rolfe	**T. Shea**	**A. Rolfe**	**T. Shea**
Cash	$ 8,000	$ 9,000	**$ 8,000**	**$ 9,000**
Office equipment	5,000		**4,000**	
Accumulated depreciation	(2,000)			
Accounts receivable		4,000		**4,000**
Allowance for doubtful accounts		(700)		**(1,000)**
	$11,000	$12,300	**$12,000**	**$12,000**

The entries to record the investments are:

Investment of A. Rolfe

Cash	8,000	
Office Equipment	4,000	
A. Rolfe, Capital		12,000
(To record investment of Rolfe)		

A	=	L	+	OE
+8,000				+12,000
+4,000				

Investment of T. Shea

Cash	9,000	
Accounts Receivable	4,000	
Allowance for Doubtful Accounts		1,000
T. Shea, Capital		12,000
(To record investment of Shea)		

A	=	L	+	OE
+9,000				+12,000
+4,000				
−1,000				

Note that neither the original cost of the office equipment ($5,000) nor its book value ($5,000 − $2,000) is recorded by the partnership. The equipment is recorded at its fair market value, $4,000. Because the equipment has not been used by the partnership, there is no accumulated depreciation.

In contrast, the gross claims on customers ($4,000) are carried forward to the partnership. The allowance for doubtful accounts is adjusted to $1,000 to arrive at a cash (net) realizable value of $3,000. A partnership may start with an allowance for doubtful accounts because it will continue to collect existing accounts receivable, some of which are expected to be uncollectible. In addition, this procedure maintains the control and subsidiary relationship between Accounts Receivable and the accounts receivable subsidiary ledger.

After the partnership has been formed, the accounting for transactions is similar to any other type of business organization. For example, all transactions with outside parties, such as the purchase or sale of merchandise inventory and the payment or receipt of cash, should be recorded the same for a partnership as for a proprietorship.

The steps in the accounting cycle described in Chapter 4 for a proprietorship also apply to a partnership. For example, the partnership prepares a trial balance and journalizes and posts adjusting entries. A work sheet may be used. There are minor differences in journalizing and posting closing entries and in preparing financial statements, as explained in the following sections. The differences occur because there is more than one owner.

DIVIDING NET INCOME OR NET LOSS

Partnership net income or net loss is shared equally unless the partnership contract indicates otherwise. The same basis of division usually applies to both net income and net loss. It is customary to refer to this basis as the **income ratio**, the

income and loss ratio, or the **profit and loss (P&L) ratio**. Because of its wide acceptance, we will use the term **income ratio** to identify the basis for dividing net income and net loss. A partner's share of net income or net loss is recognized in the accounts through closing entries.

Closing Entries

As in the case of a proprietorship, four entries are required in preparing closing entries for a partnership. The entries are:

1. Debit each revenue account for its balance, and credit Income Summary for total revenues.
2. Debit Income Summary for total expenses, and credit each expense account for its balance.
3. Debit Income Summary for its balance, and credit each partner's capital account for his or her share of net income. Or, credit Income Summary, and debit each partner's capital account for his or her share of net loss.
4. Debit each partner's capital account for the balance in that partner's drawing account, and credit each partner's drawing account for the same amount.

The first two entries are the same as in a proprietorship. The last two entries are different because (1) there are two or more owners' capital and drawing accounts, and (2) it is necessary to divide net income (or net loss) among the partners.

To illustrate the last two closing entries, assume that AB Company has net income of $32,000 for 2002. The partners, L. Arbor and D. Barnett, share net income and net loss equally. Drawings for the year were Arbor $8,000 and Barnett $6,000. The last two closing entries are:

Illustration 13-4

Closing net income and drawing accounts

Dec. 31	Income Summary	32,000	
	L. Arbor, Capital ($32,000 × 50%)		16,000
	D. Barnett, Capital ($32,000 × 50%)		16,000
	(To transfer net income to partners' capital accounts)		
31	L. Arbor, Capital	8,000	
	D. Barnett, Capital	6,000	
	L. Arbor, Drawing		8,000
	D. Barnett, Drawing		6,000
	(To close drawing accounts to capital accounts)		

Assume that the beginning capital balance is $47,000 for Arbor and $36,000 for Barnett. The capital and drawing accounts will show the following after posting the closing entries.

Illustration 13-5

Partners' capital and drawing accounts after closing

L. Arbor, Capital

Debit		Credit	
12/31 **Clos.**	**8,000**	1/1 Bal.	47,000
		12/31 **Clos.**	**16,000**
		12/31 Bal.	55,000

D. Barnett, Capital

Debit		Credit	
12/31 **Clos.**	**6,000**	1/1 Bal.	36,000
		12/31 **Clos.**	**16,000**
		12/31 Bal.	46,000

L. Arbor, Drawing

Debit		Credit	
12/31 Bal.	8,000	12/31 **Clos.**	**8,000**

D. Barnett, Drawing

Debit		Credit	
12/31 Bal.	6,000	12/31 **Clos.**	**6,000**

Draw. — Dr.
Capital — credit!

As in a proprietorship, the partners' capital accounts are permanent accounts; their drawing accounts are temporary accounts. Normally, the capital accounts will have credit balances and the drawing accounts will have debit balances. Drawing accounts are debited when partners withdraw cash or other assets from the partnership for personal use.

Income Ratios

STUDY OBJECTIVE 3

Identify the bases for dividing net income or net loss.

As noted earlier, the partnership agreement should specify the basis for sharing net income or net loss. The following are typical income ratios.

1. A fixed ratio, expressed as a proportion (6:4), a percentage (70% and 30%), or a fraction (2/3 and 1/3).
2. A ratio based either on capital balances at the beginning of the year or on average capital balances during the year.
3. Salaries to partners and the remainder on a fixed ratio.
4. Interest on partners' capital balances and the remainder on a fixed ratio.
5. Salaries to partners, interest on partners' capital, and the remainder on a fixed ratio.

The objective is to settle on a basis that will equitably reflect the partners' capital investment and service to the partnership.

A fixed ratio is easy to apply, and it may be an equitable basis in some circumstances. Assume, for example, that Hughes and Lane are partners. Each contributes the same amount of capital, but Hughes expects to work full-time in the partnership and Lane expects to work only half-time. Accordingly, the partners agree to a fixed ratio of 2/3 to Hughes and 1/3 to Lane.

HELPFUL HINT

Use one relationship for all; that is, proportion—3:1 percentage—75% and 25% fraction— 3/4 and 1/4

A ratio based on capital balances may be appropriate when the funds invested in the partnership are considered the critical factor. Capital ratios may also be equitable when a manager is hired to run the business and the partners do not plan to take an active role in daily operations.

The three remaining ratios (items 3, 4, and 5) give specific recognition to differences among partners. These ratios provide salary allowances for time worked and interest allowances for capital invested. Then, any remaining net income or net loss is allocated on a fixed ratio. Some caution needs to be exercised in working with these types of income ratios. These ratios pertain exclusively to **the computations that are required in dividing net income or net loss** among the partners.

Salaries to partners and interest on partners' capital are not expenses of the partnership. Therefore, these items do not enter into the matching of expenses with revenues and the determination of net income or net loss. For a partnership, as for other entities, salaries expense pertains to the cost of services performed by employees. Likewise, interest expense relates to the cost of borrowing from creditors. But partners, as owners, are not considered either **employees** or **creditors**. Therefore, when the income ratio includes a salary allowance for partners, some partnership agreements permit the partner to make monthly withdrawals of cash based on their "salary." Such withdrawals are debited to the partner's drawing account.

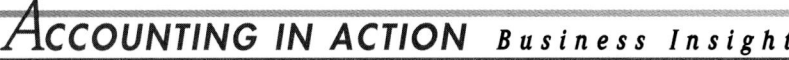

ACCOUNTING IN ACTION *Business Insight*

Partners in professional firms can make substantial incomes. In one international public accounting firm, the average earnings of all partners in a recent year was over $600,000. Note, though, that the compensation of partners in most large partnerships differs in both form and substance from the compensation of a corporate executive. Partners are not guaranteed an annual salary. Compensation depends entirely on each year's operating results. Also, substantial investment is required of each partner. This capital is at risk for the partner's entire career—often 25–30 years—without an established return. Upon leaving, it is repayable without adjustment for inflation or appreciation in value.

Salaries, Interest, and Remainder on a Fixed Ratio

Under income ratio (5) in the list above, the provisions for salaries and interest must be applied **before** the remainder is allocated on the specified fixed ratio. **This is true even if the provisions exceed net income. It is also true even if the partnership has suffered a net loss for the year.** Detailed information concerning the division of net income or net loss should be shown below net income on the income statement.

To illustrate this income ratio, assume that Sara King and Ray Lee are copartners in the Kingslee Company. The partnership agreement provides for: (1) salary allowances of $8,400 to King and $6,000 to Lee, (2) interest allowances of 10% on capital balances at the beginning of the year, and (3) the remainder equally. Capital balances on January 1 were King $28,000, and Lee $24,000. In 2002, partnership net income is $22,000. The division of net income is as follows.

Illustration 13-6

Income statement with division of net income

KINGSLEE COMPANY
Income Statement (partial)
For the Year Ended December 31, 2002

Sales			$200,000
Net income			$ 22,000

Division of Net Income

	Sara King	Ray Lee	Total
Salary allowance	$ 8,400	$6,000	$14,400
Interest allowance on partners' capital			
Sara King ($28,000 × 10%)	2,800		
Ray Lee ($24,000 × 10%)		2,400	
Total interest allowance			5,200
Total salaries and interest	11,200	8,400	19,600
Remaining income, $2,400 ($22,000 − $19,600)			
Sara King ($2,400 × 50%)	1,200		
Ray Lee ($2,400 × 50%)		1,200	
Total remainder			2,400
Total division of net income	**$12,400**	**$9,600**	**$22,000**

The entry to record the division of net income is:

Dec. 31	Income Summary	22,000	
	Sara King, Capital		12,400
	Ray Lee, Capital		9,600
	(To close net income to partners' capital)		

A	=	L	+	OE
				−22,000
				+12,400
				+9,600

Now let's look at a situation in which the salary and interest allowances exceed net income. Assume that Kingslee Company's net income is only $18,000. In this case, the salary and interest allowances will create a deficiency of $1,600 ($19,600 − $18,000). The computations of the allowances are the same as those in the preceding example. Beginning with total salaries and interest, we complete the division of net income as follows.

Illustration 13-7

Division of net income—income deficiency

	Sara King	Ray Lee	Total
Total salaries and interest	$11,200	$8,400	$19,600
Remaining deficiency ($1,600)			
($18,000 − $19,600)			
Sara King ($1,600 × 50%)	(800)		
Ray Lee ($1,600 × 50%)		(800)	
Total remainder			(1,600)
Total division	**$10,400**	**$7,600**	**$18,000**

PARTNERSHIP FINANCIAL STATEMENTS

STUDY OBJECTIVE 4

Describe the form and content of partnership financial statements.

The financial statements of a partnership are similar to those of a proprietorship. The differences are due to the number of owners involved. The income statement for a partnership is identical to the income statement for a proprietorship except for the division of net income, as shown earlier.

The owners' equity statement for a partnership is called the **partners' capital statement**. Its function is to explain the changes in each partner's capital account and in total partnership capital during the year. The partners' capital statement for Kingslee Company is shown below. It is based on the division of $22,000 of net income in Illustration 13-6. The statement includes assumed data for the additional investment and drawings.

Illustration 13-8

Partners' capital statement

KINGSLEE COMPANY
Partners' Capital Statement
For the Year Ended December 31, 2002

	Sara King	Ray Lee	Total
Capital, January 1	$28,000	$24,000	$52,000
Add: Additional investment	2,000		2,000
Net income	12,400	9,600	22,000
	42,400	33,600	76,000
Less: Drawings	7,000	5,000	12,000
Capital, December 31	**$35,400**	**$28,600**	**$64,000**

HELPFUL HINT

As in a proprietorship, partners' capital may change due to (1) additional investment, (2) drawings, and (3) net income or net loss.

The partners' capital statement is prepared from the income statement and the partners' capital and drawing accounts.

The balance sheet for a partnership is the same as for a proprietorship except for the owner's equity section. In a partnership, the capital balances of each partner are shown in the balance sheet. The owners' equity section for Kingslee Company would show the following.

Illustration 13-9

Owners' equity section of a partnership balance sheet

KINGSLEE COMPANY
Balance Sheet (partial)
December 31, 2002

Total liabilities (assumed amount)		$115,000
Owners' equity		
Sara King, Capital	$35,400	
Ray Lee, Capital	28,600	
Total owners' equity		64,000
Total liabilities and owners' equity		$179,000

BEFORE YOU GO ON...

REVIEW IT

1. How should a partner's initial investment of assets be valued?
2. What are the closing entries for a partnership?
3. What income ratios may be used in a partnership?
4. How do partnership financial statements differ from proprietorship financial statements?

DO IT

LeeMay Company reports net income of $57,000. The partnership agreement provides for salaries of $15,000 to L. Lee and $12,000 to R. May. The remainder is to be shared on a 60:40 basis (60% to Lee). L. Lee asks your help to divide the net income between the partners and to prepare the closing entry.

ACTION PLAN

- Compute net income exclusive of any salaries to partners and interest on partners' capital.
- Deduct salaries to partners from net income.
- Apply the partners' income ratios to the remaining net income.
- Prepare the closing entry distributing net income or net loss among the partners' capital accounts.

SOLUTION: The division of net income is as follows.

	L. Lee	R. May	Total
Salary allowance	$15,000	$12,000	$27,000
Remaining income ($57,000 − $27,000)			
L. Lee (60% × $30,000)	18,000		
R. May (40% × $30,000)		12,000	
Total remaining income			30,000
Total division of net income	$33,000	$24,000	$57,000

The closing entry for net income therefore is:

Income Summary	57,000	
L. Lee, Capital		33,000
R. May, Capital		24,000
(To close net income to partners' capital accounts)		

Related exercise material: BE13-3, BE13-4, BE13-5, and E13-2.

THE NAVIGATOR

ADMISSION AND WITHDRAWAL OF PARTNERS

We have seen how the basic accounting for a partnership works. We now look at how to account for a common occurrence in partnerships—the addition or withdrawal of a partner.

ADMISSION OF A PARTNER

STUDY OBJECTIVE 5

Explain the effects of the entries when a new partner is admitted.

The admission of a new partner results in the **legal dissolution of the existing partnership** and **the beginning of a new one**. From an economic standpoint, the admission of a new partner (or partners) may be of minor significance in the continuity of the business. For example, in large public accounting or law firms, partners are admitted annually without any change in operating policies. **To recognize the economic effects, it is necessary only to open a capital account for each new partner.** In the entries illustrated below, we assume that the accounting records of the predecessor firm will continue to be used by the new partnership.

A new partner may be admitted either by (1) purchasing the interest of an existing partner or (2) investing assets in the partnership, as shown in Illustration 13-10. The former affects only the capital accounts of the partners who are parties to the transaction. The latter increases both net assets and total capital of the partnership.

Illustration 13-10

Procedures in adding partners

Purchase of a Partner's Interest

The **admission** of a partner **by purchase of an interest** is a personal transaction between one or more existing partners and the new partner. Each party acts as an individual separate from the partnership entity. The price paid is negotiated by the individuals involved. It may be equal to or different from the capital equity acquired. The purchase price passes directly from the new partner to the partners who are giving up part or all of their ownership claims.

HELPFUL HINT

In a purchase of an interest, the partnership is **not** a participant in the transaction. No cash is contributed to the partnership.

Any money or other consideration exchanged is the personal property of the participants and **not** the property of the partnership. Upon purchase of an interest, the new partner acquires each selling partner's capital interest and income ratio.

Accounting for the purchase of an interest is straightforward. In the partnership records, only the realignment of partners' capital is recorded. **Each partner's capital account is debited for the ownership claims that have been relinquished, and the new partner's capital account is credited with the capital equity purchased.** Total assets, total liabilities, and total capital remain unchanged, as do all individual asset and liability accounts.

To illustrate, assume that L. Carson agrees to pay $10,000 each to C. Ames and D. Barker for $33\frac{1}{3}\%$ (one-third) of their interest in the Ames–Barker partnership. At the time of the admission of Carson, each partner has a $30,000 capital balance. Both partners, therefore, give up $10,000 of their capital equity. The entry to record the admission of Carson is:

C. Ames, Capital	10,000	
D. Barker, Capital	10,000	
L. Carson, Capital		20,000
(To record admission of Carson by purchase)		

Illustration 13-11

Ledger balances after purchase of a partner's interest

The effect of this transaction on net assets and partners' capital is shown below.

Net Assets		C. Ames, Capital		D. Barker, Capital		L. Carson, Capital	
60,000		**10,000**	30,000	**10,000**	30,000		**20,000**
			Bal. 20,000		Bal. 20,000		

Note that net assets remain unchanged at $60,000, and each partner has a $20,000 capital balance. Ames and Barker continue as partners in the firm, but the capital interest of each has changed. The cash paid by Carson goes directly to the individual partners and not to the partnership.

Regardless of the amount paid by Carson for the one-third interest, the entry above would be exactly the same. If Carson pays $12,000 each to Ames and Barker for $33\frac{1}{3}\%$ of the partnership, the foregoing entry is still made.

Investment of Assets in a Partnership

The admission of a partner by an investment of assets is a transaction between the new partner and the partnership. Often referred to simply as **admission by investment**, the transaction **increases both the net assets and total capital of the partnership**. Assume that instead of purchasing an interest, Carson invests $30,000 in cash in the Ames–Barker partnership for a $33\frac{1}{3}\%$ capital interest. In such a case, the entry is:

Cash	30,000	
L. Carson, Capital		30,000
(To record admission of Carson by investment)		

Illustration 13-12

Ledger balances after investment of assets

The effects of this transaction on the partnership accounts would be:

Net Assets		C. Ames, Capital		D. Barker, Capital		L. Carson, Capital	
60,000			30,000		30,000		**30,000**
30,000							
Bal. 90,000							

Note that both net assets and total capital have increased by $30,000.

Remember that Carson's one-third capital interest might not result in a one-third income ratio. Carson's income ratio should be specified in the new partnership agreement, and it may or may not be equal to the one-third capital interest.

The different effects of the purchase of an interest and admission by investment are shown in the comparison of the net assets and capital balances in Illustration 13-13.

Illustration 13-13

Comparison of purchase of an interest and admission by investment

Purchase of an Interest		**Admission by Investment**	
Net Assets	**$60,000**	**Net Assets**	**$90,000**
Capital		Capital	
C. Ames	$20,000	C. Ames	$30,000
D. Barker	20,000	D. Barker	30,000
L. Carson	20,000	L. Carson	30,000
Total capital	**$60,000**	**Total capital**	**$90,000**

When an interest is purchased, the total net assets and total capital of the partnership do not change. When a partner is admitted by investment, both the total net assets and the total capital change.

In the case of admission by investment, further complications occur when the new partner's investment differs from the capital equity acquired. When those amounts are not the same, the difference is considered a bonus either to (1) the existing (old) partners or (2) the new partner.

BONUS TO OLD PARTNERS. For both personal and business reasons, the existing partners may be unwilling to admit a new partner without receiving a bonus. In an established firm, existing partners may insist on a bonus as compensation for the work they have put into the company over the years. Two accounting factors underlie the business reason: First, total partners' capital equals the **book value** of the recorded net assets of the partnership. When the new partner is admitted, the fair market values of assets such as land and buildings may be higher than their book values. The bonus will help make up the difference between fair market value and book value. Second, when the partnership has been profitable, goodwill may exist. But, the goodwill will not be recorded or included in total partners' capital. In such cases the new partner is usually willing to pay the bonus to become a partner.

A bonus to old partners results when the new partner's investment in the firm is greater than the capital credit on the date of admittance. The bonus results in **an increase in the capital balances of the old partners. It is allocated to them on the basis of their income ratios before the admission of the new partner.**

To illustrate, assume that the Bart–Cohen partnership, owned by Sam Bart and Tom Cohen, has total capital of $120,000. Lea Eden acquires a 25% ownership (capital) interest in the partnership by making a cash investment of $80,000. The procedure for determining Eden's capital credit and the bonus to the old partners is as follows.

1. **Determine the total capital of the new partnership:** Add the new partner's investment to the total capital of the old partnership. In this case the total capital of the new firm is $200,000, computed as follows.

Total capital of existing partnership	$120,000
Investment by new partner, Eden	80,000
Total capital of new partnership	$200,000

2. **Determine the new partner's capital credit:** Multiply the total capital of the new partnership by the new partner's ownership interest. Eden's capital credit is $50,000 ($200,000 × 25%).
3. **Determine the amount of bonus:** Subtract the new partner's capital credit from the new partner's investment. The bonus in this case is $30,000 ($80,000 – $50,000).
4. **Allocate the bonus to the old partners on the basis of their income ratios:** Assuming the ratios are Bart 60%, and Cohen 40%, the allocation is: Bart $18,000 ($30,000 × 60%) and Cohen $12,000 ($30,000 × 40%).

The entry to record the admission of Eden is:

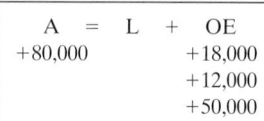

A	=	L	+	OE
+80,000				+18,000
				+12,000
				+50,000

Cash	80,000	
Sam Bart, Capital		18,000
Tom Cohen, Capital		12,000
Lea Eden, Capital		50,000
(To record admission of Eden and bonus to old partners)		

BONUS TO NEW PARTNER. A bonus to a new partner results when the new partner's investment in the firm is less than his or her capital credit. This may occur when the new partner possesses resources or special attributes that are desired by the partnership. For example, the new partner may be able to supply cash that is urgently needed for expansion or to meet maturing debts. Or the new partner may be a recognized expert or authority in a relevant field. Thus, an engineering firm may be willing to give a renowned engineer a bonus to join the firm. The partners of a restaurant may offer a bonus to a sports celebrity in order to add the athlete's name to the partnership. A bonus to a new partner may also result when recorded book values on the partnership books are higher than their market values.

A bonus to a new partner results in a **decrease in the capital balances of the old partners. The amount of the decrease for each partner is based on their income ratios before the admission of the new partner.** To illustrate, assume that Lea Eden invests $20,000 in cash for a 25% ownership interest in the Bart–Cohen partnership. Using the four procedures described in the preceding section, the computations for Eden's capital credit and the bonus are as follows.

Illustration 13-14

Computation of capital credit and bonus to new partner

1. Total capital of Bart–Cohen partnership		$120,000
Investment by new partner, Eden		20,000
Total capital of new partnership		$140,000
2. **Eden's capital credit** (25% × $140,000)		**$ 35,000**
3. **Bonus to Eden** ($35,000 – $20,000)		**$ 15,000**
4. Allocation of bonus to old partners:		
Bart ($15,000 × 60%)	$9,000	
Cohen ($15,000 × 40%)	6,000	$ 15,000

The entry to record the admission of Eden is as follows:

A	=	L	+	OE
+20,000				−9,000
				−6,000
				+35,000

Cash	20,000	
Sam Bart, Capital	9,000	
Tom Cohen, Capital	6,000	
Lea Eden, Capital		35,000
(To record Eden's admission and bonus)		

WITHDRAWAL OF A PARTNER

STUDY OBJECTIVE 6

Describe the effects of the entries when a partner withdraws from the firm.

Now let's look at the opposite situation—the withdrawal of a partner. A partner may withdraw from a partnership **voluntarily**, by selling his or her equity in the firm. Or he or she may withdraw **involuntarily**, by reaching mandatory retirement age or by dying. The withdrawal of a partner, like the admission of a partner, legally dissolves the partnership. The legal effects may be recognized by dissolving the firm. However, it is customary to record only the economic effects of the partner's withdrawal, while the firm continues to operate and reorganizes itself legally.

As indicated earlier, the partnership agreement should specify the terms of withdrawal. The withdrawal of a partner may be accomplished by (1) payment from partners' personal assets or (2) payment from partnership assets, as shown in Illustration 13-15. The former affects only the partners' capital accounts. The latter decreases total net assets and total capital of the partnership.

Illustration 13-15

Procedures in partnership withdrawal

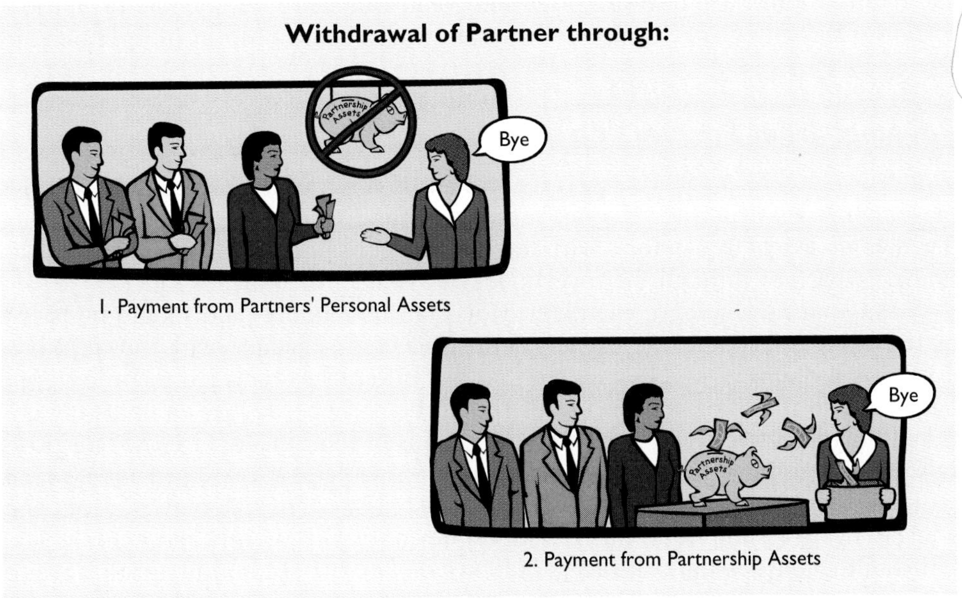

Payment from Partners' Personal Assets

Withdrawal by payment from partners' personal assets is a personal transaction between the partners. **It is the direct opposite of admitting a new partner who purchases a partner's interest.** Payment to the retiring partner is made directly from the remaining partners' personal assets. **Partnership assets are not involved in any way, and total capital does not change.** The effect on the partnership is limited to a realignment of the partners' capital balances.

To illustrate, assume that Anne Morz, Mary Nead, and Jill Odom have capital balances of $25,000, $15,000, and $10,000, respectively. Morz and Nead agree to buy out Odom's interest. Each of them agrees to pay Odom $8,000 in exchange for one-half of Odom's total interest of $10,000. The entry to record the withdrawal is:

Jill Odom, Capital	10,000	
Anne Morz, Capital		5,000
Mary Nead, Capital		5,000
(To record purchase of Odom's interest)		

A	=	L	+	OE
				−10,000
				+5,000
				+5,000

The effect of this entry on the partnership accounts is shown below.

Net Assets		Anne Morz, Capital		Mary Nead, Capital		Jill Odom, Capital	
50,000			25,000		15,000	**10,000**	10,000
			5,000		**5,000**		Bal. –0–
			Bal. 30,000		Bal. 20,000		

Illustration 13-16

Ledger balances after payment from partners' personal assets

Note that net assets and total capital remain the same at $50,000.

What about the $16,000 paid to Odom? You've probably noted that it is not recorded. Odom's capital is debited only for $10,000, not for the $16,000 that she received. Similarly, both Morz and Nead credit their capital accounts for only $5,000, not for the $8,000 they each paid.

After Odom's withdrawal, Morz and Nead will share net income or net loss equally unless they specifically indicate another income ratio in the partnership agreement.

Payment from Partnership Assets

Withdrawal by payment from partnership assets is a transaction that involves the partnership. **Both partnership net assets and total capital are decreased.** Using partnership assets to pay for a withdrawing partner's interest is the **reverse** of admitting a partner through the investment of assets in the partnership.

Many partnership agreements provide that the amount paid should be based on the fair market value of the assets at the time of the partner's withdrawal. When this basis is required, some maintain that any differences between recorded asset balances and their fair market values should be (1) recorded by an adjusting entry and (2) allocated to all partners on the basis of their income ratios. This position has serious flaws. Recording the revaluations violates the cost principle, which requires that assets be stated at original cost. It also is a departure from the going-concern assumption, which assumes the entity will continue indefinitely. The terms of the partnership contract should not dictate the accounting for this event.

In accounting for a withdrawal by payment from partnership assets, asset revaluations should not be recorded. Any difference between the amount paid and the withdrawing partner's capital balance should be considered a bonus to the retiring partner or a bonus to the remaining partners.

BONUS TO RETIRING PARTNER. A bonus may be paid to a retiring partner when:

1. The fair market value of partnership assets is more than their book value,
2. There is unrecorded goodwill resulting from the partnership's superior earnings record, or
3. The remaining partners are anxious to remove the partner from the firm.

The bonus is deducted from the remaining partners' capital balances on the basis of their income ratios at the time of the withdrawal.

To illustrate, assume that the following capital balances exist in the RST partnership: Fred Roman $50,000, Dee Sand $30,000, and Betty Terk $20,000. The partners share income in the ratio of 3:2:1, respectively. Terk retires from the partnership and receives a cash payment of $25,000 from the firm. The procedure for determining the bonus to the retiring partner and the allocation of the bonus to the remaining partners is as follows.

1. **Determine the amount of the bonus:** Subtract the retiring partner's capital balance from the cash paid by the partnership. The bonus in this case is $5,000 ($25,000 − $20,000).
2. **Allocate the bonus to the remaining partners on the basis of their income ratios:** The ratios of Roman and Sand are 3:2. Thus, the allocation of the $5,000 bonus is: Roman $3,000 ($5,000 × 3/5) and Sand $2,000 ($5,000 × 2/5).

The entry to record the withdrawal of Terk is:

Betty Terk, Capital	20,000	
Fred Roman, Capital	3,000	
Dee Sand, Capital	2,000	
Cash		25,000
(To record withdrawal of and bonus to Terk)		

A	=	L	+	OE
−25,000				−20,000
				−3,000
				−2,000

The remaining partners, Roman and Sand, will recover the bonus given to Terk as the undervalued assets are sold or used.

HELPFUL HINT
Compare this entry to the one at the top of page 534.

BONUS TO REMAINING PARTNERS. The retiring partner may give a bonus to the remaining partners when:

1. Recorded assets are overvalued,
2. The partnership has a poor earnings record, or
3. The partner is anxious to leave the partnership.

In such cases, the cash paid to the retiring partner will be less than the retiring partner's capital balance. **The bonus is allocated (credited) to the capital accounts of the remaining partners on the basis of their income ratios.**

To illustrate, assume (instead of the example above) that Terk is paid only $16,000 for her $20,000 equity when she withdraws from the partnership. In that case:

1. The bonus to remaining partners is $4,000 ($20,000 − $16,000).
2. The allocation of the $4,000 bonus is: Roman $2,400 ($4,000 × 3/5) and Sand $1,600 ($4,000 × 2/5).

The entry to record the withdrawal is:

Betty Terk, Capital	20,000	
Fred Roman, Capital		2,400
Dee Sand, Capital		1,600
Cash		16,000
(To record withdrawal of Terk and bonus to remaining partners)		

A	=	L	+	OE
−16,000				−20,000
				+2,400
				+1,600

Note that if Sand had withdrawn from the partnership, any bonus would be divided between Roman and Terk on the basis of their income ratio, which is 3:1 or 75% and 25%.

HELPFUL HINT
Compare this entry to the one at the top of page 534.

Death of a Partner

The death of a partner dissolves the partnership. But provision generally is made for the surviving partners to continue operations. When a partner dies, it usually is necessary to determine the partner's equity at the date of death. This is done by (1) determining the net income or loss for the year to date, (2) closing the books, and (3) preparing financial statements. The partnership agreement may also require an independent audit of the financial statements and a revaluation of assets by an appraisal firm.

The surviving partners may agree to purchase the deceased partner's equity from their personal assets. Or it may use partnership assets to settle with the deceased partner's estate. In both instances, the entries to record the withdrawal of the partner are similar to those presented earlier.

To facilitate payment from partnership assets, some partnerships obtain life insurance policies on each partner. The partnership is named as the beneficiary. The proceeds from the insurance policy on the deceased partner are then used to settle with the estate.

BEFORE YOU GO ON...

REVIEW IT

1. How does the accounting for admission by purchase of an interest differ from admission by investing assets in the partnership?
2. Contrast the accounting effects of the withdrawal of a partner by payment from (a) personal assets and (b) partnership assets.

DO IT

Curly, Moe, and Larry have a partnership. Each partner has a $40,000 balance in his capital account. Record journal entries for each of the independent events listed below.

1. Curly, Moe, and Larry agree to admit Stan as a new one-quarter-interest partner. Stan pays $10,000 in cash directly to each partner.
2. Curly, Moe, and Larry agree to admit Stan as a new one-quarter-interest partner. Stan contributes $40,000 into the partnership.
3. Curly and Moe agree to let Larry withdraw from the partnership; $30,000 of partnership cash is distributed to Larry. Curly and Moe share income and losses equally.
4. Curly and Moe agree to let Larry withdraw from the partnership. Each pays Larry $25,000 out of his personal assets. Curly and Moe share income and losses equally.

ACTION PLAN

- Recognize that the admission (withdrawal) by purchase (sale) of a partnership interest is a personal transaction between one or more existing partners and the new (withdrawing) partner.
- Recognize that the admission (withdrawal) by investment (distribution) of partnership assets is a transaction between the new (withdrawing) partner and the partnership.

SOLUTION

1.	Curly, Capital	10,000	
	Moe, Capital	10,000	
	Larry, Capital	10,000	
	Stan, Capital		30,000
	(To record admission of Stan by purchase)		
2.	Cash	40,000	
	Stan, Capital		40,000
	(To record admission of Stan by investment)		
3.	Larry, Capital	40,000	
	Cash		30,000
	Curly, Capital		5,000
	Moe, Capital		5,000
	(To record withdrawal of Larry and bonus to remaining partners)		

4. Larry, Capital	40,000	
Curly, Capital		20,000
Moe, Capital		20,000
(To record purchase of Larry's interest)		

Related exercise material: BE13-6, BE13-7, BE13-8, BE13-9, E13-4, E13-5, E13-6, and E13-7.

THE NAVIGATOR

LIQUIDATION OF A PARTNERSHIP

STUDY OBJECTIVE 7

Explain the effects of the entries to record the liquidation of a partnership.

The liquidation of a partnership terminates the business. It involves selling the assets of the firm, paying liabilities, and distributing any remaining assets to the partners. Liquidation may result from the sale of the business by mutual agreement of the partners, from the death of a partner, or from bankruptcy. In contrast to partnership dissolution, partnership liquidation ends both the legal and economic life of the entity.

From an accounting standpoint, liquidation should be preceded by completing the accounting cycle for the final operating period. This includes preparing adjusting entries and financial statements. It also involves preparing closing entries and a post-closing trial balance. Thus, only balance sheet accounts should be open as the liquidation process begins.

In liquidation, the sale of noncash assets for cash is called **realization**. Any difference between book value and the cash proceeds is called the **gain or loss on realization**. To liquidate a partnership, it is necessary to:

1. Sell noncash assets for cash and recognize a gain or loss on realization.
2. Allocate gain/loss on realization to the partners based on their income ratios.
3. Pay partnership liabilities in cash.
4. Distribute remaining cash to partners on the basis of their **capital balances**.

Each of the steps must be performed in sequence. Creditors must be paid **before** partners receive any cash distributions. Each step also must be recorded by an accounting entry.

When a partnership is liquidated, all partners may have credit balances in their capital accounts. This situation is called no capital deficiency. Or, at least one partner's capital account may have a debit balance. This situation is termed a capital deficiency. To illustrate each of these conditions, assume that the Ace Company is liquidated when its ledger shows the following assets, liabilities, and owners' equity accounts.

Illustration 13-17
Account balances prior to liquidation

Assets		Liabilities and Owners' Equity	
Cash	$ 5,000	Notes payable	$15,000
Accounts receivable	15,000	Accounts payable	16,000
Inventory	18,000	R. Arnet, Capital	15,000
Equipment	35,000	P. Carey, Capital	17,800
Accum. depr.—equipment	(8,000)	W. Eaton, Capital	1,200
	$65,000		$65,000

NO CAPITAL DEFICIENCY

The partners of Ace Company agree to liquidate the partnership on the following terms: (1) The noncash assets of the partnership will be sold to Jackson Enterprises for $75,000 cash. And (2) the partnership will pay its partnership liabilities. The income ratios of the partners are 3:2:1, respectively. The steps in the liquidation process are as follows.

1. The noncash assets (accounts receivable, inventory, and equipment) are sold for $75,000. The book value of these assets is $60,000 ($15,000 + $18,000 + $35,000 − $8,000). Thus a gain of $15,000 is realized on the sale. The entry is:

A	= L	+ OE
+75,000		+15,000
+8,000		
−15,000		
−18,000		
−35,000		

(1)

Cash	75,000	
Accumulated Depreciation–Equipment	8,000	
Accounts Receivable		15,000
Inventory		18,000
Equipment		35,000
Gain on Realization		15,000
(To record realization of noncash assets)		

2. The gain on realization of $15,000 is allocated to the partners on their income ratios, which are 3:2:1. The entry is:

A	= L	+ OE
		−15,000
		+7,500
		+5,000
		+2,500

(2)

Gain on Realization	15,000	
R. Arnet, Capital ($15,000 × 3/6)		7,500
P. Carey, Capital ($15,000 × 2/6)		5,000
W. Eaton, Capital ($15,000 × 1/6)		2,500
(To allocate gain to partners' capital accounts)		

3. Partnership liabilities consist of Notes Payable $15,000 and Accounts Payable $16,000. Creditors are paid in full by a cash payment of $31,000. The entry is:

A	= L	+ OE
−31,000	−15,000	
	−16,000	

(3)

Notes Payable	15,000	
Accounts Payable	16,000	
Cash		31,000
(To record payment of partnership liabilities)		

4. The remaining cash is distributed to the partners on the basis of **their capital balances**. After the entries in the first three steps are posted, all partnership accounts, including Gain on Realization, will have zero balances except for four accounts: Cash $49,000; R. Arnet, Capital $22,500; P. Carey, Capital $22,800; and W. Eaton, Capital $3,700, as shown below.

Illustration 13-18

Ledger balances before distribution of cash

Cash

Debit	Credit
Bal. 5,000	(3) 31,000
(1) 75,000	
Bal. 49,000	

R. Arnet, Capital

Debit	Credit
	Bal. 15,000
	(2) 7,500
	Bal. 22,500

P. Carey, Capital

Debit	Credit
	Bal. 17,800
	(2) 5,000
	Bal. 22,800

W. Eaton, Capital

Debit	Credit
	Bal. 1,200
	(2) 2,500
	Bal. 3,700

The entry to record the distribution of cash is as follows.

A	= L	+ OE
−49,000		−22,500
		−22,800
		−3,700

(4)

R. Arnet, Capital	22,500	
P. Carey, Capital	22,800	
W. Eaton, Capital	3,700	
Cash		49,000
(To record distribution of cash to partners)		

HELPFUL HINT
Zero balances after posting is a quick proof of the accuracy of the cash distribution entry.

After this entry is posted, all partnership accounts will have zero balances.

A word of caution: **Cash should not be distributed to partners on the basis of their income-sharing ratios.** On this basis, Arnet would receive three-sixths, or $24,500, which would produce an erroneous debit balance of $2,000. The income ratio is the proper basis for allocating net income or loss. **It is not a proper basis for making the final distribution of cash to the partners.**

Schedule of Cash Payments

Some accountants prepare a cash payments schedule to determine the distribution of cash to the partners in the liquidation of a partnership. The **schedule of cash payments** is organized around the basic accounting equation. The schedule for the Ace Company is shown in Illustration 13-19. The numbers in parentheses refer to the four required steps in the liquidation of a partnership. They also identify the accounting entries that must be made. The cash payments schedule is especially useful when the liquidation process extends over a period of time.

ALTERNATIVE TERMINOLOGY
The schedule of cash payments is sometimes called a *safe cash payments schedule.*

Illustration 13-19

Schedule of cash payments, no capital deficiency

ACE COMPANY
Schedule of Cash Payments

Item		Cash	+	Noncash Assets	=	Liabilities	+	R. Arnet Capital	+	P. Carey Capital	+	W. Eaton Capital
Balances before liquidation		5,000	+	60,000	=	31,000	+	15,000	+	17,800	+	1,200
Sales of noncash assets and allocation of gain	(1)&(2)	75,000	+	(60,000)	=			7,500	+	5,000	+	2,500
New balances		80,000	+	–0–	=	31,000	+	22,500	+	22,800	+	3,700
Pay liabilities	(3)	(31,000)			=	(31,000)						
New balances		49,000	+	–0–	=	–0–	+	22,500	+	22,800	+	3,700
Cash distribution to partners	(4)	(49,000)			=			(22,500)	+	(22,800)	+	(3,700)
Final balances		–0–		–0–		–0–		–0–		–0–		–0–

CAPITAL DEFICIENCY

A capital deficiency may be caused by recurring net losses, excessive drawings, or losses from realization suffered during liquidation. To illustrate, assume that Ace Company is on the brink of bankruptcy. The partners decide to liquidate by having a "going-out-of-business" sale. Merchandise is sold at substantial discounts, and the equipment is sold at auction. Cash proceeds from these sales and collections from customers total only $42,000. Thus, the loss from liquidation is $18,000 ($60,000 – $42,000). The steps in the liquidation process are as follows.

1. The entry for the realization of noncash assets is:

(1)

	Debit	Credit
Cash	42,000	
Accumulated Depreciation—Equipment	8,000	
Loss on Realization	18,000	
Accounts Receivable		15,000
Inventory		18,000
Equipment		35,000
(To record realization of noncash assets)		

A	=	L	+	OE
+42,000				−18,000
+8,000				
−15,000				
−18,000				
−35,000				

2. The loss on realization is allocated to the partners on the basis of their income ratios. The entry is:

(2)

	Debit	Credit
R. Arnet, Capital ($18,000 × 3/6)	9,000	
P. Carey, Capital ($18,000 × 2/6)	6,000	
W. Eaton, Capital ($18,000 × 1/6)	3,000	
Loss on Realization		18,000
(To allocate loss on realization to partners)		

A	=	L	+	OE
				−9,000
				−6,000
				−3,000
				+18,000

3. Partnership liabilities are paid. This entry is the same as in the previous example.

A	=	L	+	OE
−31,000		−15,000		
		−16,000		

(3)

Notes Payable	15,000	
Accounts Payable	16,000	
Cash		31,000
(To record payment of partnership liabilities)		

4. After posting the three entries, two accounts will have debit balances—Cash $16,000, and W. Eaton, Capital $1,800. Two accounts will have credit balances—R. Arnet, Capital $6,000, and P. Carey, Capital $11,800. All four accounts are shown below.

Illustration 13-20

Ledger balances before distribution of cash

Cash		R. Arnet, Capital		P. Carey, Capital		W. Eaton, Capital	
Bal. 5,000	(3) 31,000	(2) 9,000	Bal. 15,000	(2) 6,000	Bal. 17,800	(2) 3,000	Bal. 1,200
(1) 42,000			**Bal. 6,000**		**Bal. 11,800**	**Bal. 1,800**	
Bal. 16,000							

Eaton has a capital deficiency of $1,800, and so owes the partnership $1,800. Arnet and Carey have a legally enforceable claim for that amount against Eaton's personal assets. The distribution of cash is still made on the basis of capital balances. But the amount will vary depending on how Eaton's deficiency is settled. Two alternatives are presented below.

Payment of Deficiency

If the partner with the capital deficiency pays the amount owed the partnership, the deficiency is eliminated. To illustrate, assume that Eaton pays $1,800 to the partnership. The entry is:

A	=	L	+	OE
+1,800				+1,800

(a)

Cash	1,800	
W. Eaton, Capital		1,800
(To record payment of capital deficiency by Eaton)		

After posting this entry, account balances are as follows.

Cash		R. Arnet, Capital		P. Carey, Capital		W. Eaton, Capital	
Bal. 5,000	(3) 31,000	(2) 9,000	Bal. 15,000	(2) 6,000	Bal. 17,800	(2) 3,000	Bal. 1,200
(1) 42,000			**Bal. 6,000**		**Bal. 11,800**		(a) 1,800
(a) 1,800							**Bal. -0-**
Bal. 17,800							

Illustration 13-21

Ledger balances after paying capital deficiency

The cash balance of $17,800 is now equal to the credit balances in the capital accounts (Arnet $6,000 + Carey $11,800). Cash now is distributed on the basis of these balances. The entry is:

A	=	L	+	OE
−17,800				−6,000
				−11,800

R. Arnet, Capital	6,000	
P. Carey, Capital	11,800	
Cash		17,800
(To record distribution of cash to the partners)		

After this entry is posted, all accounts will have zero balances.

Nonpayment of Deficiency

If a partner with a capital deficiency is unable to pay the amount owed to the partnership, the partners with credit balances must absorb the loss. The loss is allocated on the basis of the income ratios that exist between the partners with credit balances.

For example, the income ratios of Arnet and Carey are 3:2, or 3/5 and 2/5, respectively. Thus, the following entry would be made to remove Eaton's capital deficiency.

(a)

R. Arnet, Capital ($1,800 × 3/5)	1,080	
P. Carey, Capital ($1,800 × 2/5)	720	
W. Eaton, Capital		1,800
(To record write-off of capital deficiency)		

A	=	L	+	OE
				−1,080
				−720
				+1,800

After posting this entry, the cash and capital accounts will have the following balances.

Illustration 13-22

Ledger balances after nonpayment of capital deficiency

Cash				**R. Arnet, Capital**				**P. Carey, Capital**				**W. Eaton, Capital**			
Bal.	5,000	(3)	31,000	(2)	9,000	Bal.	15,000	(2)	6,000	Bal.	17,800	(2)	3,000	Bal.	1,200
(1)	42,000			(a)	1,080			(a)	720					(a)	1,800
Bal.	**16,000**					**Bal.**	**4,920**			**Bal.**	**11,080**			**Bal.**	**-0-**

The cash balance of $16,000 now equals the sum of the credit balances in the capital accounts (Arnet $4,920 + Carey $11,080). The entry to record the distribution of cash is:

R. Arnet, Capital	4,920	
P. Carey, Capital	11,080	
Cash		16,000
(To record distribution of cash to the partners)		

A	=	L	+	OE
−16,000				−4,920
				−11,080

After this entry is posted, all accounts will have zero balances.

BEFORE YOU GO ON...

REVIEW IT

1. What are the steps in liquidating a partnership?
2. What basis is used in making the final distribution of cash to the partners?

A LOOK BACK AT OUR FEATURE STORY

Refer back to the Feature Story about **Razor & Tie Music** at the beginning of the chapter, and answer the following questions.

1. Speculate as to why Razor & Tie selected the partnership form of organization for its business.
2. What might be some of the major items written into the partnership agreement for Razor & Tie?
3. How is net income or loss divided if the partnership is silent regarding the percentage allocation?

SOLUTION

1. Cliff Chenfield and Craig Balsam may have chosen to form a partnership, rather than a corporation, for a number of reasons. First, the partnership is much quicker and easier to form, with little of the red tape a corporation faces. Second, the partnership form has distinct tax advantages relative to a corporation. Third, since the two partners knew each other well, they may have had fewer concerns about the risk of unlimited liabilities that might be incurred by the other partner.
2. The partnership agreement of Razor & Tie should specify the capital contributed by both partners, and the basis for sharing income and losses and for withdrawing funds. Also, it might specify mechanisms for resolving disputes, adding or removing a partner, or what to do in the event of the death of one of the partners. A well-written partnership agreement can significantly reduce conflicts as the firm grows.
3. In this case, income and losses are shared equally.

THE NAVIGATOR

DEMONSTRATION PROBLEM

Additional Demonstration Problem

On January 1, 2002, the capital balances in Hollingsworth Company are Lois Holly $26,000, and Jim Worth $24,000. In 2002 the partnership reports net income of $30,000. The income ratio provides for salary allowances of $12,000 for Holly and $10,000 to Worth and the remainder equally. Neither partner had any drawings in 2002.

Assume that the following independent transactions occur on January 1, 2003.

1. Donna Reichenbacher purchases one-half of Holly's capital interest for $25,000.
2. Marsha Mears is admitted with a 25% capital interest by a cash investment of $40,000.
3. Stan Wells is admitted with a 35% capital interest by a cash investment of $40,000.

Instructions

(a) Prepare a schedule showing the distribution of net income in 2002.

(b) Journalize the division of 2002 net income to the partners.

(c) Journalize each of the independent transactions that occurred on January 1, 2003.

SOLUTION TO DEMONSTRATION PROBLEM

ACTION PLAN

- Compute the net income of the partnership.
- Allocate the partners' salaries.
- Divide the remaining net income among the partners, applying the income/loss ratio.
- Journalize the division of net income in a closing entry.
- Recognize the admission by purchase of a partnership interest as a personal transaction between an existing partner and the new partner.
- Recognize the admission by investment of partnership assets as a transaction between the new partner and the partnership.

(a) Net income $30,000

Division of Net Income

	Lois Holly	Jim Worth	Total
Salary allowance	$12,000	$10,000	$22,000
Remaining income $8,000 ($30,000 − $22,000)			
Lois Holly ($8,000 × 50%)	4,000		
Jim Worth ($8,000 × 50%)		4,000	
Total remainder			8,000
Total division of net income	$16,000	$14,000	$30,000

(b)

12/31/02	Income Summary	30,000	
	Lois Holly, Capital		16,000
	Jim Worth, Capital		14,000
	(To close net income to partners' capital)		

(c)

(1)

1/1/03	Lois Holly, Capital [($26,000 + $16,000) × ½]	21,000	
	Donna Reichenbacher, Capital		21,000
	(To record purchase of one-half of Holly's interest)		

(2)

1/1/03	Cash	40,000	
	Lois Holly, Capital		5,000
	Jim Worth, Capital		5,000
	Marsha Mears, Capital		30,000
	(To record admission of Mears and bonus to old partners)		

Total capital after investment: $120,000 (Holly, $42,000, Worth $38,000, Mears investment $40,000)		
Mears' capital credit (25% × $120,000)		$30,000
Bonus to old partners ($40,000 − $30,000)		$10,000
Allocation of bonus:		
Holly ($10,000 × 50%)	$ 5,000	
Worth ($10,000 × 50%)	5,000	$10,000

(3)

1/1/03	Cash	40,000	
	Lois Holly, Capital	1,000	
	Jim Worth, Capital	1,000	
	Stan Wells, Capital		42,000
	(To record Wells's admission and bonus)		

Wells's capital credit (35% × $120,000)		$42,000
Bonus to Wells ($42,000 − $40,000)		$ 2,000
Allocation of bonus:		
Holly ($2,000 × 50%)	$1,000	
Worth ($2,000 × 50%)	1,000	$ 2,000

THE NAVIGATOR

SUMMARY OF STUDY OBJECTIVES

1. *Identify the characteristics of the partnership form of business organization*. The principal characteristics of a partnership are: (a) association of individuals, (b) mutual agency, (c) limited life, (d) unlimited liability, and (e) co-ownership of property.

2. *Explain the accounting entries for the formation of a partnership*. When a partnership is formed, each partner's initial investment should be recorded at the fair market value of the assets at the date of their transfer to the partnership.

3. *Identify the bases for dividing net income or net loss*. Net income or net loss is divided on the basis of the income ratio, which may be (a) a fixed ratio, (b) a ratio based on beginning or average capital balances, (c) salaries to partners and the remainder on a fixed ratio, (d) interest on partners' capital and the remainder on a fixed ratio, and (e) salaries to partners, interest on partners' capital, and the remainder on a fixed ratio.

4. *Describe the form and content of partnership financial statements*. The financial statements of a partnership are similar to those of a proprietorship. The principal differences are: (a) the division of net income is shown on the income statement, (b) the owners' equity statement is called a partners' capital statement, and (c) each partner's capital is reported on the balance sheet.

5. *Explain the effects of the entries when a new partner is admitted*. The entry to record the admittance of a new partner by purchase of a partner's interest affects only partners' capital accounts. The entries to record the admittance by investment of assets in the partnership (a) increase both net assets and total capital and (b) may result in recognition of a bonus to either the old partners or the new partner.

6. *Describe the effects of the entries when a partner withdraws from the firm*. The entry to record a withdrawal from the firm when payment is made from partners' personal assets affects only partners' capital accounts. The entry to record a withdrawal when payment is made from partnership assets (a) decreases net assets and total capital and (b) may result in recognizing a bonus either to the retiring partner or the remaining partners.

7. *Explain the effects of the entries to record the liquidation of a partnership*. When a partnership is liquidated, it is necessary to record the (a) sale of noncash assets, (b) allocation of the gain or loss on realization, (c) payment of partnership liabilities, and (d) distribution of cash to the partners on the basis of their capital balances.

THE NAVIGATOR

Key Term Matching Activity

GLOSSARY

Admission by investment Admission of a partner by investing assets in the partnership, causing both partnership net assets and total capital to increase. (p. 532).

Admission by purchase of an interest Admission of a partner in a personal transaction between one or more existing partners and the new partner; does not change total partnership assets or total capital. (p. 531).

Capital deficiency A debit balance in a partner's capital account after allocation of gain or loss. (p. 539).

General partner A partner who has unlimited liability for the debts of the firm. (p. 522).

Income ratio The basis for dividing net income and net loss in a partnership. (p. 526).

Limited liability company A form of business organization, usually classified as a partnership and usually with limited life, in which partners, who are called *members*, have limited liability. (p. 523).

Limited liability partnership A partnership of professionals in which partners are given limited liability and the public is protected from malpractice by insurance carried by the partnership. (p. 523).

Limited partner A partner who has limited liability for the debts of the firm. (p. 522).

Limited partnership A partnership in which one or more general partners have unlimited liability and one or more partners have limited liability for the obligations of the firm. (p. 522).

No capital deficiency All partners have credit balances after allocation of gain or loss. (p. 539).

Partners' capital statement The owners' equity statement for a partnership which shows the changes in each partner's capital balance and in total partnership capital during the year. (p. 529).

Partnership An association of two or more persons to carry on as co-owners of a business for profit. (p. 520).

Partnership agreement A written contract expressing the voluntary agreement of two or more individuals in a partnership. (p. 524).

Partnership dissolution A change in partners due to withdrawal or admission, which does not necessarily terminate the business. (p. 521).

Partnership liquidation An event that ends both the legal and economic life of a partnership. (p. 539).

"S" corporation Corporation, with 75 or fewer stockholders, that is taxed like a partnership. (p. 523).

Schedule of cash payments A schedule showing the distribution of cash to the partners in a partnership liquidation. (p. 541).

Withdrawal by payment from partners' personal assets Withdrawal of a partner in a personal transaction between partners; does not change total partnership assets or total capital. (p. 535).

Withdrawal by payment from partnership assets Withdrawal of a partner in a transaction involving the partnership, causing both partnership net assets and total capital to decrease. (p. 536).

Chapter 13 Self-Test

SELF-STUDY QUESTIONS

Answers are at the end of the chapter.

(SO 1) **1.** Which of the following is *not* a characteristic of a partnership?
a. Taxable entity
b. Co-ownership of property
c. Mutual agency
d. Limited life

(SO 1) **2.** The advantages of a partnership do *not* include:
a. ease of formation.
b. unlimited liability.
c. freedom from government regulation.
d. ease of decision making.

(SO 2) **3.** Upon formation of a partnership, each partner's initial investment of assets should be recorded at their:
a. book values.
b. cost.
c. market values.
d. appraised values.

(SO 3) **4.** The NBC Company reports net income of $60,000. If partners N, B, and C have an income ratio of 50%, 30%, and 20%, respectively, C's share of the net income is:
a. $30,000.
b. $12,000.
c. $18,000.
d. No correct answer is given.

5. Using the data in (4) above, what is B's share of net income if the percentages are applicable after each partner receives a $10,000 salary allowance? (SO 3)
a. $12,000
b. $20,000
c. $19,000
d. $21,000

6. Which of the following statements about partnership financial statements is true? (SO 4)
a. Details of the distribution of net income are shown in the owners' equity statement.
b. The distribution of net income is shown on the balance sheet.
c. Only the total of all partner capital balances is shown in the balance sheet.
d. The owners' equity statement is called the partners' capital statement.

7. Maria Taxco purchases 50% of Louie Lime's capital interest in the K & L partnership for $22,000. If the capital balance of Kim Kanary and Louie Lime are $40,000 (SO 5)

and $30,000, respectively, Taxco's capital balance following the purchase is:
a. $22,000.
b. $35,000.
c. $20,000.
d. $15,000.

(SO 5) 8. Capital balances in the DEA partnership are Don Capital $60,000, Ed Capital $50,000, and Amy Capital $40,000, and income ratios are 5:3:2, respectively. The DEAR partnership is formed by admitting Ray to the firm with a cash investment of $60,000 for a 25% capital interest. The bonus to be credited to Amy Capital in admitting Ray is:
a. $10,000.
b. $7,500.
c. $3,750.
d. $1,500.

(SO 6) 9. Capital balances in the TERM partnership are Terry Capital $50,000, Enid Capital $40,000, Rob Capital $30,000, and Mary Capital $20,000, and income ratios are 4:3:2:1, respectively. Mary withdraws from the firm following payment of $29,000 in cash from the partnership. Enid's capital balance after recording the withdrawal of Mary is:
a. $36,000.
b. $37,000.
c. $38,000.
d. $40,000.

10. In the liquidation of a partnership it is necessary to (1) distribute cash to the partners, (2) sell noncash assets, (3) allocate any gain or loss on realization to the partners, and (4) pay liabilities. These steps should be performed in the following order: (SO 7)
a. (2), (3), (4), (1).
b. (2), (3), (1), (4).
c. (3), (2), (1), (4).
d. (3), (2), (4), (1).

THE NAVIGATOR

QUESTIONS

1. The characteristics of a partnership include the following: (a) association of individuals, (b) limited life, and (c) co-ownership of property. Explain each of these terms.
2. Vera Cruz is confused about the partnership characteristics of (a) mutual agency and (b) unlimited liability. Explain these two characteristics for Vera.
3. Swen Varberg and Egor Karlstad are considering a business venture. They ask you to explain the advantages and disadvantages of the partnership form of organization.
4. Ginny Brown and Dorothy Fleming form a partnership. Brown contributes land with a book value of $50,000 and a fair market value of $75,000. Brown also contributes equipment with a book value of $52,000 and a fair market value of $57,000. The partnership assumes a $20,000 mortgage on the land. What should be the balance in Brown's capital account upon formation of the partnership?
5. Roy Orbison, S. Innis, and David Bowie have a partnership called Depeche Mode. A dispute has arisen among the partners. Orbison has invested twice as much in assets as the other two partners, and he believes net income and net losses should be shared in accordance with the capital ratios. The partnership agreement does not specify the division of profits and losses. How will net income and net loss be divided?
6. Leon Redbone and Elvis Costello are discussing how income and losses should be divided in a partnership they plan to form. What factors should be considered in determining the division of net income or net loss?
7. Doreen Shaffer and Quincy Jones have partnership capital balances of $40,000 and $80,000, respectively. The partnership agreement indicates that net income or net loss should be shared equally. If net income for the partnership is $24,000, how should the net income be divided?
8. Robben Ford and Gregg Allman share net income and net loss equally. (a) Which account(s) is (are) debited and credited to record the division of net income between the partners? (b) If Robben Ford withdraws $30,000 in cash for personal use in lieu of salary, which account is debited and which is credited?
9. Partners Reba McEntire and B. Zander are provided salary allowances of $30,000 and $25,000, respectively. They divide the remainder of the partnership income in a ratio of 60:40. If partnership net income is $50,000, how much is allocated to McEntire and Zander?
10. Are the financial statements of a partnership similar to those of a proprietorship? Discuss.
11. Patty Loveless decides to pay $50,000 for a one-third interest in an existing partnership. What effect does this transaction have on partnership net assets?
12. Billy Joel decides to invest $25,000 in a new partnership for a one-sixth capital interest. How much do the partnership's net assets increase? Does Joel also acquire a one-sixth income ratio through this investment?
13. Pia Zadora purchases for $72,000 Cole's interest in the Morgan-Cole partnership. Assuming that Cole has a $63,000 capital balance in the partnership, what journal entry is made by the partnership to record this transaction?
14. Won Jang has a $37,000 capital balance in a partnership. She sells her interest to Carla Cardosa for $45,000 cash. What entry is made by the partnership for this transaction?
15. Natalie Cole retires from the partnership of Suarez, Tanks, and Cole. She receives $89,000 of partnership assets in settlement of her capital balance of $77,000. Assuming that the income-sharing ratios are 5:3:2, respectively, how much of Cole's bonus is debited to Tanks' capital account?

16. Your roommate argues that partnership assets should be revalued in situations like those in question 15. Why is this generally not done?

17. How is a deceased partner's equity determined?

18. How does the liquidation of a partnership differ from the dissolution of a partnership?

19. Phil Collins and Herb Alpert are discussing the liquidation of a partnership. Phil maintains that all cash should be distributed to partners on the basis of their income ratios. Is he correct? Explain.

20. In continuing their discussion, Herb says that even in the case of a capital deficiency, all cash should still be distributed on the basis of capital balances. Is Herb correct? Explain.

21. Erin, Cole, and Morgan have income ratios of 5:3:2 and capital balances of $34,000, $31,000, and $28,000, respectively. Noncash assets are sold at a gain. After creditors are paid, $119,000 of cash is available for distribution to the partners. How much cash should be paid to Cole?

22. Before the final distribution of cash, account balances are: Cash $25,000; B. Springsteen, Capital $19,000 (Cr.); L. Hamilton, Capital $12,000 (Cr.); and T. Zaret, Capital $6,000 (Dr.). Zaret is unable to pay any of the capital deficiency. If the income-sharing ratios are 5:3:2, respectively, how much cash should be paid to L. Hamilton?

BRIEF EXERCISES

Journalize entries in forming a partnership.
(SO 2)

BE13-1 Britney Spears and Pablo Cruise decide to organize the ALL-Star partnership. Britney Spears invests $15,000 cash, and Cruise contributes $10,000 cash and equipment having a book value of $3,500. Prepare the entry to record Cruise's investment in the partnership, assuming the equipment has a fair market value of $7,000

Prepare portion of opening balance sheet for partnership.
(SO 2)

BE13-2 H. Tylo and R. Moss decide to merge their proprietorships into a partnership called Tylomoss Company. The balance sheet of Moss Co. shows:

Accounts receivable	$16,000	
Less: Allowance for doubtful accounts	1,200	$14,800
Equipment	20,000	
Less: Accumulated depreciation	8,000	12,000

The partners agree that the net realizable value of the receivables is $12,500 and that the fair market value of the equipment is $10,000. Indicate how the four accounts should appear in the opening balance sheet of the partnership.

Journalize the division of net income using fixed income ratios.
(SO 3)

BE13-3 Led Zeppelin Co. reports net income of $70,000. The income ratios are Led 60% and Zeppelin 40%. Indicate the division of net income to each partner, and prepare the entry to distribute the net income.

Compute division of net income with a salary allowance and fixed ratios.
(SO 3)

BE13-4 MET Co. reports net income of $65,000. Partner salary allowances are Moses $20,000, Evelyn $5,000, and Tom $5,000. Indicate the division of net income to each partner, assuming the income ratio is 50:30:20, respectively.

Show division of net income when allowances exceed net income.
(SO 3)

BE13-5 Bill&Til Co. reports net income of $24,000. Interest allowances are Bill $6,000 and Til $5,000; salary allowances are Bill $15,000 and Til $10,000; the remainder is shared equally. Show the distribution of income on the income statement.

Journalize admission by purchase of an interest.
(SO 5)

BE13-6 In Kansas Co. capital balances are: Ali $30,000, Babson $25,000, and Curtis $22,000. The partners share income equally. Daniel is admitted to the firm by purchasing one-half of Curtis's interest for $14,000. Journalize the admission of Daniel to the partnership.

Journalize admission by investment.
(SO 5)

BE13-7 In Nebraska Co., capital balances are Evelynn $40,000 and Zane $30,000. The partners share income equally. Kerns is admitted to the firm with a 45% interest by an investment of cash of $42,000. Journalize the admission of Kerns.

Journalize withdrawal paid by personal assets.
(SO 6)

BE13-8 Capital balances in DEB Co. are Ditka $40,000, Elbert $30,000, and Bob $30,000. Ditka and Elbert each agree to pay Bob $12,000 from their personal assets. Ditka and Elbert each receive 50% of Bob's equity. The partners share income equally. Journalize the withdrawal of Bob.

Journalize withdrawal paid by partnership assets.
(SO 6)

BE13-9 Data pertaining to DEB Co. are presented in BE13-8. Instead of payment from personal assets, assume that Bob receives $32,000 from partnership assets in withdrawing from the firm. Journalize the withdrawal of Bob.

Journalize final cash distribution in liquidation.
(SO 7)

BE13-10 After liquidating noncash assets and paying creditors, account balances in the Missouri Co. are Cash $21,000, A Capital (Cr.) $9,000, R Capital (Cr.) $7,000, and B Capital (Cr.) $5,000. The partners share income equally. Journalize the final distribution of cash to the partners.

EXERCISES

Journalize entry for formation of a partnership. (SO 2)

E13-1 Frank Voris has owned and operated a proprietorship for several years. On January 1, he decides to terminate this business and become a partner in the firm of Payne and Voris. Voris's investment in the partnership consists of $15,000 in cash, and the following assets of the proprietorship: accounts receivable $14,000 less allowance for doubtful accounts of $2,000, and equipment $20,000 less accumulated depreciation of $4,000. It is agreed that the allowance for doubtful accounts should be $3,000 for the partnership. The fair market value of the equipment is $17,500.

Instructions

Journalize Voris's admission to the firm of Payne and Voris.

Prepare schedule showing distribution of net income and closing entry. (SO 3)

E13-2 B. Manilow and O. Newton have capital balances on January 1 of $50,000 and $40,000, respectively. The partnership income-sharing agreement provides for (1) annual salaries of $20,000 for Manilow and $12,000 for Newton, (2) interest at 10% on beginning capital balances, and (3) remaining income or loss to be shared 70% by Manilow and 30% by Newton.

Instructions

(a) Prepare a schedule showing the distribution of net income, assuming net income is (1) $55,000 and (2) $30,000.

(b) Journalize the allocation of net income in each of the situations above.

Prepare partners' capital statement and partial balance sheet. (SO 4)

E13-3 In Fleetwood Mac Co., beginning capital balances on January 1, 2002, are Ken Tucki $20,000 and Chris Cross $18,000. During the year, drawings were Tucki $8,000 and Cross $3,000. Net income was $32,000, and the partners share income equally.

Instructions

(a) Prepare the partners' capital statement for the year.

(b) Prepare the owners' equity section of the balance sheet at December 31, 2002.

Journalize admission of a new partner by purchase of an interest. (SO 5)

E13-4 T. Halo, K. Rose, and J. Lamp share income on a 5:3:2 basis. They have capital balances of $32,000, $26,000, and $18,000, respectively, when Dave Matthews is admitted to the partnership.

Instructions

Prepare the journal entry to record the admission of Dave Matthews under each of the following assumptions.

(a) Purchase of 50% of Halo's equity for $19,000.

(b) Purchase of 50% of Rose's equity for $10,000.

(c) Purchase of $33\frac{1}{3}$% of Lamp's equity for $9,000.

Journalize admission of a new partner by investment. (SO 5)

E13-5 Joe Keho and Mike McLain share income on a 6:4 basis. They have capital balances of $90,000 and $70,000, respectively, when Liz Hurley is admitted to the partnership.

Instructions

Prepare the journal entry to record the admission of Liz Hurley under each of the following assumptions.

(a) Investment of $100,000 cash for a 30% ownership interest with bonuses to the existing partners.

(b) Investment of $36,000 cash for a 30% ownership interest with a bonus to the new partner.

Journalize withdrawal of a partner with payment from partners' personal assets. (SO 6)

E13-6 Mary Toshiba, Vera Miles, and Barb Eden have capital balances of $50,000, $40,000, and $25,000, respectively. Their income ratios are 5:3:2. Eden withdraws from the partnership under each of the following independent conditions.

1. Toshiba and Miles agree to purchase Eden's equity by paying $15,000 each from their personal assets. Each purchaser receives 50% of Eden's equity.
2. Miles agrees to purchase all of Eden's equity by paying $22,000 cash from her personal assets.
3. Toshiba agrees to purchase all of Eden's equity by paying $26,000 cash from her personal assets.

Instructions

Journalize the withdrawal of Eden under each of the assumptions above.

Journalize withdrawal of a partner with payment from partnership assets. (SO 6)

E13-7 Dale Nagel, Rocky Rim, and Todd Rundgren have capital balances of $95,000, $75,000, and $60,000, respectively. They share income or loss on a 5:3:2 basis. Rim withdraws from the partnership under each of the following conditions.

1. Rim is paid $85,500 in cash from partnership assets, and a bonus is granted to the retiring partner.
2. Rim is paid $68,000 in cash from partnership assets, and bonuses are granted to the remaining partners.

Instructions
Journalize the withdrawal of Rim under each of the assumptions above.

Prepare cash distribution schedule.
(SO 7)

E13-8 The Pips Company at December 31 has cash $20,000, noncash assets $100,000, liabilities $55,000, and the following capital balances: Agnes $45,000 and Mildred $20,000. The firm is liquidated, and $120,000 in cash is received for the noncash assets. Agnes and Mildred income ratios are 55% and 45%, respectively.

Instructions
Prepare a cash distribution schedule.

Journalize transactions in a liquidation.
(SO 7)

E13-9 Data for The Pips partnership are presented in E13-8.

Instructions
Prepare the entries to record:

(a) The sale of noncash assets.
(b) The allocation of the gain or loss on liquidation to the partners.
(c) Payment of creditors.
(d) Distribution of cash to the partners.

Journalize transactions with a capital deficiency.
(SO 7)

E13-10 Prior to the distribution of cash to the partners, the accounts in the MEL Company are: Cash $30,000, Maureen Capital (Cr.) $18,000, Ellen Capital (Cr.) $14,000, and Lou Capital (Dr.) $2000. The income ratios are 5:3:2, respectively.

Instructions
(a) Prepare the entry to record (1) Lou's payment of $2,000 in cash to the partnership and (2) the distribution of cash to the partners with credit balances.
(b) Prepare the entry to record (1) the absorption of Lou's capital deficiency by the other partners and (2) the distribution of cash to the partners with credit balances.

PROBLEMS: SET A

Prepare entries for formation of a partnership and a balance sheet.
(SO 2, 4)

Peachtree

P13-1A The post-closing trial balances of two proprietorships on January 1, 2002, are presented below.

	Mel Company		Gibson Company	
	Dr.	**Cr.**	**Dr.**	**Cr.**
Cash	$ 14,000		$ 13,000	
Accounts receivable	17,500		26,000	
Allowance for doubtful accounts		$ 3,000		$ 4,400
Merchandise inventory	26,500		18,400	
Equipment	45,000		28,000	
Accumulated depreciation—equipment		24,000		12,000
Notes payable		20,000		15,000
Accounts payable		20,000		31,000
Mel, Capital		36,000		
Gibson, Capital				23,000
	$103,000	$103,000	$ 85,400	$85,400

Mel and Gibson decide to form a partnership, Mel Gibson Company, with the following agreed upon valuations for noncash assets.

	Mel Company	Gibson Company
Accounts receivable	$17,500	$26,000
Allowance for doubtful accounts	4,500	4,000
Merchandise inventory	30,000	20,000
Equipment	25,000	18,000

All cash will be transferred to the partnership, and the partnership will assume all the liabilities of the two proprietorships. Further, it is agreed that Mel will invest $3,000 in cash, and Gibson will invest $18,000 in cash.

Instructions

(a) Prepare separate journal entries to record the transfer of each proprietorship's assets and liabilities to the partnership.

(b) Journalize the additional cash investment by each partner.

(c) Prepare a balance sheet for the partnership on January 1, 2002.

(a) Mel, Capital $42,000
Gibson, Capital $27,000

(c) Total assets $176,000

P13-2A At the end of its first year of operations on December 31, 2002, MTC Company's accounts show the following.

Journalize divisions of net income and prepare a partners' capital statement.
(SO 3, 4)

Partner	Drawings	Capital
Teena Marie	$23,000	$48,000
Robin Tower	14,000	30,000
George Clinton	10,000	25,000

The capital balance represents each partner's initial capital investment. Therefore, net income or net loss for 2002 has not been closed to the partners' capital accounts.

Instructions

(a) Journalize the entry to record the division of net income for the year 2002 under each of the following independent assumptions.

(1) Net income is $28,000. Income is shared 6:3:1.

(2) Net income is $34,000. Marie and Tower are given salary allowances of $18,000 and $10,000, respectively. The remainder is shared equally.

(3) Net income is $22,000. Each partner is allowed interest of 10% on beginning capital balances. Marie is given a $15,000 salary allowance. The remainder is shared equally.

(b) Prepare a schedule showing the division of net income under assumption (3) above.

(c) Prepare a partners' capital statement for the year under assumption (3) above.

(a) (1) Marie $16,800
(2) Marie $20,000
(3) Marie $18,700

(c) Marie $43,700

P13-3A At April 30, partners' capital balances in NTW Company are: A. Nolan $62,000, T. Tritt $36,000, and T. Wuhan $12,000. The income sharing ratios are 5:4:1, respectively. On May 1, the NTWO Company is formed by admitting M. Otton to the firm as a partner.

Journalize admission of a partner under different assumptions.
(SO 5)

Instructions

(a) Journalize the admission of Otton under each of the following independent assumptions.

(1) Otton purchases 50% of Wuhan's ownership interest by paying Wuhan $16,000 in cash.

(2) Otton purchases $33\frac{1}{3}$% of Tritt's ownership interest by paying Tritt $15,000 in cash.

(3) Otton invests $70,000 for a 30% ownership interest, and bonuses are given to the old partners.

(4) Otton invests $40,000 for a 30% ownership interest, which includes a bonus to the new partner.

(b) Tritt's capital balance is $30,000 after admitting Otton to the partnership by investment. If Tritt's ownership interest is 20% of total partnership capital, what were (1) Otton's cash investment and (2) the bonus to the new partner?

(a) (1) Otton, Capital $6,000
(2) Otton $12,000
(3) Otton $54,000
(4) Otton $45,000

P13-4A On December 31, the capital balances and income ratios in BAG Company are as follows.

Journalize withdrawal of a partner under different assumptions.
(SO 6)

Partner	Capital Balance	Income Ratio
Lois Hamilton	$60,000	50%
Mary McGovern	40,000	30%
Donna Guehler	34,000	20%

Instructions

(a) Journalize the withdrawal of Guehler under each of the following assumptions.

(1) Each of the continuing partners agrees to pay $18,000 in cash from personal funds to purchase Guehler's ownership equity. Each receives 50% of Guehler's equity.

(2) McGovern agrees to purchase Guehler's ownership interest for $30,000 cash.

(a) (1) McGovern, Capital $17,000
(2) McGovern, Capital $34,000

(3) Bonus $4,000

(3) Guehler is paid $38,000 from partnership assets, which includes a bonus to the retiring partner.

(4) Bonus $6,000

(4) Guehler is paid $28,000 from partnership assets, and bonuses to the remaining partners are recognized.

(b) If McGovern's capital balance after Guehler's withdrawal is $43,000 what were (1) the total bonus to the remaining partners and (2) the cash paid by the partnership to Guehler?

Prepare entries with a capital deficiency in liquidation of a partnership.
(SO 7)

P13-5A The partners in Wilkowski Company decide to liquidate the firm when the balance sheet shows the following.

WILKOWSKI COMPANY
Balance Sheet
May 31, 2002

Assets		Liabilities and Owners' Equity	
Cash	$ 27,500	Notes payable	$ 13,500
Accounts receivable	25,000	Accounts payable	27,000
Allowance for doubtful accounts	(1,000)	Wages payable	3,800
Merchandise inventory	34,500	S. Wilkowski, Capital	36,000
Equipment	21,000	J. Harkins, Capital	20,000
Accumulated depreciation—equipment	(5,500)	Mick Jagger, Capital	1,200
Total	$101,500	Total	$101,500

The partners share income and loss 5:3:2. During the process of liquidation, the following transactions were completed in the following sequence.

1. A total of $53,000 was received from converting noncash assets into cash.
2. Liabilities were paid in full.
3. Mick Jagger paid his capital deficiency.
4. Cash was paid to the partners with credit balances.

Instructions

(a) Prepare the entries to record the transactions.
(b) Post to the cash and capital accounts.
(c) Assume that Jagger is unable to pay the capital deficiency.
   (1) Prepare the entry to allocate Jagger's debit balance to Wilkowski and Harkins.
   (2) Prepare the entry to record the final distribution of cash.

PROBLEMS: SET B

Prepare entries for formation of a partnership and a balance sheet.
(SO 2, 4)

P13-1B The post-closing trial balances of two proprietorships on January 1, 2002, are presented below.

	Randy Company		Travis Company	
	Dr.	Cr.	Dr.	Cr.
Cash	$ 7,500		$ 6,000	
Accounts receivable	15,000		23,000	
Allowance for doubtful accounts		$ 2,500		$ 4,000
Merchandise inventory	28,000		17,000	
Equipment	52,000		30,000	
Accumulated depreciation—equipment		24,000		13,000
Notes payable		20,000		
Accounts payable		25,000		37,000
Randy, Capital		31,000		
Travis, Capital				22,000
	$102,500	$102,500	$76,000	$76,000

Randy and Travis decide to form a partnership, Randy Travis Company, with the following agreed upon valuations for noncash assets.

	Randy Company	Travis Company
Accounts receivable	$15,000	$23,000
Allowance for doubtful accounts	3,500	5,000
Merchandise inventory	32,000	21,000
Equipment	31,000	18,000

All cash will be transferred to the partnership, and the partnership will assume all the liabilities of the two proprietorships. Further, it is agreed that Randy will invest $3,000 in cash, and Travis will invest $14,000 in cash.

Instructions

(a) Prepare separate journal entries to record the transfer of each proprietorship's assets and liabilities to the partnership.

(a) Randy, Capital $37,000
Travis, Capital $26,000

(b) Journalize the additional cash investment by each partner.

(c) Prepare a balance sheet for the partnership on January 1, 2002.

(c) Total assets $162,000

P13-2B At the end of its first year of operations on December 31, 2002, the KMC Company's accounts show the following.

Journalize divisions of net income and prepare a partners' capital statement.
(SO 3, 4)

Partner	Drawings	Capital
Jana Kingston	$12,000	$33,000
Mary Mio	9,000	20,000
Kim Casey	6,000	10,000

The capital balance represents each partner's initial capital investment. Therefore, net income or net loss for 2002 has not been closed to the partners' capital accounts.

Instructions

(a) Journalize the entry to record the division of net income for 2002 under each of the following independent assumptions.

(a) (1) Kingston $16,300
(2) Kingston $16,000
(3) Kingston $19,600

(1) Net income is $32,600. Income is shared 5:3:2.

(2) Net income is $30,000. Kingston and Mio are given salary allowances of $13,000 and $8,000, respectively. The remainder is shared equally.

(3) Net income is $25,200. Each partner is allowed interest of 10% on beginning capital balances. Kingston is given a $15,000 salary allowance. The remainder is shared equally.

(b) Prepare a schedule showing the division of net income under assumption (3) above.

(c) Prepare a partner's capital statement for the year under assumption (3) above.

(c) Kingston $40,600

P13-3B At April 30, partners' capital balances in ELM Company are: V. Easi $49,000, K. Lester $24,000, and W. Matt $22,000. The income-sharing ratios are 5:3:2, respectively. On May 1, the ELMO Company is formed by admitting N. Ortiz to the firm as a partner.

Journalize admission of a partner under different assumptions.
(SO 5)

Instructions

(a) Journalize the admission of Ortiz under each of the following independent assumptions.

(a) (1) Ortiz, Capital $11,000
(2) Ortiz $12,000
(3) Ortiz $52,000
(4) Ortiz $18,750

(1) Ortiz purchases 50% of Matt's ownership interest by paying Matt $9,000 in cash.

(2) Ortiz purchases 50% of Lester's ownership interest by paying Lester $16,000 in cash.

(3) Ortiz invests $35,000 cash in the partnership for a 40% ownership interest that includes a bonus to the new partner.

(4) Ortiz invests $30,000 in the partnership for a 15% ownership interest, and bonuses are given to the old partners.

(b) Matt's capital balance is $24,000 after admitting Ortiz to the partnership by investment. If Matt's ownership interest is 15% of total partnership capital, what were (1) Ortiz's cash investment and (2) the total bonus to the old partners?

P13-4B On December 31, the capital balances and income ratios in the Blue Man Company are as follows.

Journalize withdrawal of a partner under different assumptions.
(SO 6)

Partner	Capital Balance	Income Ratio
Pat Schoen	$70,000	60%
Natalie Striegl	30,000	30
Malou Nelson	21,500	10

(a) (1) Striegl, Capital $10,750
(2) Striegl, Capital $21,500
(3) Bonus $7,500
(4) Bonus $4,500

Instructions

(a) Journalize the withdrawal of Nelson under each of the following independent assumptions.

(1) Each of the remaining partners agrees to pay $12,000 in cash from personal funds to purchase Nelson's ownership equity. Each receives 50% of Nelson's equity.

(2) Striegl agrees to purchase Nelson's ownership interest for $18,000 in cash.

(3) From partnership assets, Nelson is paid $29,000, which includes a bonus to the retiring partner.

(4) Nelson is paid $17,000 from partnership assets. Bonuses to the remaining partners are recognized.

(b) If Striegl's capital balance after Nelson's withdrawal is $33,000, what were (1) the total bonus to the remaining partners and (2) the cash paid by the partnership to Nelson?

Prepare entries and schedule of cash payments in liquidation of a partnership
(SO 7)

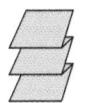

P13-5B The partners in Holiday Company decide to liquidate the firm when the balance sheet shows the following.

HOLIDAY COMPANY
Balance Sheet
April 30, 2002

Assets		**Liabilities and Owners' Equity**	
Cash	$24,000	Notes payable	$14,000
Accounts receivable	19,000	Accounts payable	24,000
Allowance for doubtful accounts	(1,000)	Wages payable	2,000
Merchandise inventory	30,000	Gert Robson, Capital	25,000
Equipment	17,000	Dottie Olson, Capital	12,800
Accumulated depreciation—equipment	(8,000)	Debbie Bailey, Capital	3,200
Total	$81,000	Total	$81,000

The partners share income and loss 5:3:2. During the process of liquidation, the transactions below were completed in the following sequence.

1. A total of $48,000 was received from converting noncash assets into cash.
2. Liabilities were paid in full.
3. Cash was paid to the partners with credit balances.

Instructions

(a) Prepare a cash distribution schedule.

(b) Prepare the entries to record the transactions.

(c) Post to the cash and capital accounts.

BROADENING YOUR PERSPECTIVE

FINANCIAL REPORTING AND ANALYSIS

EXPLORING THE WEB

BYP13-1 This exercise is an introduction to the Big Five Accounting firms, all of which are partnerships.

Addresses:

Arthur Andersen	**www.arthurandersen.com/**
Deloitte & Touche	**www.dttus.com/**
Ernst & Young	**www.ey.com/**
KPMG Peat Marwick	**www.us.kpmg.com/**
PricewaterhouseCoopers	**www.pw.com/**

(or go to www.wiley.com/college/weygandt)

Steps:

1. Select a firm that is of interest to you.
2. Go to the firm's homepage.

Instructions

(a) Name two services provided by the firm.
(b) What is the firm's total annual revenue?
(c) How many clients does it service?
(d) How many people are employed by the firm?
(e) How many partners are there in the firm?

CRITICAL THINKING

GROUP DECISION CASE

BYP13-2 Doug Stahl and Joy Sommers, two professionals in the finance area, have worked for Pimpernel Leasing for a number of years. Pimpernel Leasing is a company that leases high-tech medical equipment to hospitals. Doug and Joy have decided that, with their financial expertise, they might start their own company to provide consulting services to individuals interested in leasing equipment. One form of organization they are considering is a partnership.

If they start a partnership, each individual plans to contribute $50,000 in cash. In addition, Doug has a used IBM microcomputer that originally cost $3,700, which he intends to invest in the partnership. The computer has a present market value of $1,500.

Although both Doug and Joy are financial wizards, they do not know a great deal about how a partnership operates. As a result, they have come to you for advice.

Instructions

With the class divided into groups, answer the following.

(a) What are the major disadvantages of starting a partnership?
(b) What type of document is needed for a partnership, and what should this document contain?
(c) Both Doug and Joy plan to work full-time in the new partnership. They believe that net income or net loss should be shared equally. However, they are wondering how they can provide compensation to Doug Stahl for his additional investment of the microcomputer. What would you tell them?
(d) Doug is not sure how the computer equipment should be reported on his tax return. What would you tell him?
(e) As indicated above, Doug and Joy have worked together for a number of years. Doug's skills complement Joy's and vice versa. If one of them dies, it will be very difficult for the other to maintain the business, not to mention the difficulty of paying the deceased partner's estate for his or her partnership interest. What would you advise them to do?

COMMUNICATION ACTIVITY

BYP13-3 You are an expert in the field of forming partnerships. George Clooney and Enid Halsingborg want to establish a partnership to start "Enid's Pasta Shop," and they are going to meet with you to discuss their plans. Prior to the meeting you will send them a memo discussing the issues they need to consider before their visit.

Instructions

Write a memo in good form to be sent to Clooney and Halsingborg.

ETHICS CASE

BYP13-4 Morgan and Erin operate a beauty salon as partners who share profits and losses equally. The success of their business has exceeded their expectations; the salon is operating quite profitably. Erin is anxious to maximize profits and schedules appointments from 8 a.m. to 6 p.m. daily, even sacrificing some lunch hours to accommodate regular customers. Morgan schedules her appointments from 9 a.m. to 5 p.m. and takes long lunch hours. Morgan regularly makes significantly larger withdrawals of cash than Erin does, but, she says, "Erin, you needn't worry, I never make a withdrawal without you knowing about it, so it is properly recorded in my drawing account and charged against my capital at the end of the year." Morgan's withdrawals to date are double Erin's.

Instructions

(a) Who are the stakeholders in this situation?
(b) Identify the problems with Morgan's actions and discuss the ethical considerations of her actions.
(c) How might the partnership agreement be revised to accommodate the differences in Morgan's and Erin's work and withdrawal habits?

Answers to Self-Study Questions

1. a **2.** b **3.** c **4.** b **5.** c **6.** d **7.** d **8.** d **9.** b **10.** a

Answer to Lands' End Review It Question 2, p. 524

LANDS' END DIRECT MERCHANTS

Mutual agency, limited life, unlimited liability, and co-ownership of property are major characteristics of a partnership. As a company like Lands' End becomes very large, it becomes difficult to remain as a partnership because of these factors. Unlimited liability is particularly troublesome because owners may lose not only their initial investment but also their personal assets, if those assets are needed to pay partnership creditors.

Remember to go back to the Navigator box on the chapter-opening page and check off your completed work.

CORPORATIONS: ORGANIZATION AND CAPITAL STOCK TRANSACTIONS

14

THE NAVIGATOR ✓

- Understand *Concepts for Review* ❑
- Read *Feature Story* ❑
- Scan *Study Objectives* ❑
- Read *Preview* ❑
- Read text and answer *Before You Go On* *p.* 566 ❑ *p.* 570 ❑ *p.* 573 ❑ *p.* 577 ❑ *p.* 584 ❑
- Work *Demonstration Problem* ❑
- Review *Summary of Study Objectives* ❑
- Answer *Self-Study Questions* ❑
- Complete *Assignments* ❑

CONCEPTS FOR REVIEW

Before studying this chapter, you should know or, if necessary, review:

a. The content of the owner's equity section of the balance sheet for a proprietorship (Ch. 1, pp. 22–24, Ch. 4, pp. 154–156) and for a partnership. (Ch. 13, pp. 531–532)

b. How to prepare closing entries for a proprietorship (Ch. 4, pp. 140–144) and for a partnership. (Ch. 13, pp. 528–529)

✓ THE NAVIGATOR

Feature Story

"Have You Driven a Ford Lately?"

A company that has produced such renowned successes as the Model T and the Mustang, and such a dismal failure as the Edsel, would have some interesting tales to tell. Henry Ford was a defiant visionary from the day **Ford Motor Company** was formed in 1903. His goal from day one was to design a car he could mass-produce and sell at a price that was affordable to the masses. In short order he accomplished this goal. By 1920, 60 percent of all vehicles on U.S. roads were Fords.

Henry Ford was intolerant of anything that stood between him and success. In the early years Ford had issued shares to the public in order to finance the company's exponential growth. In 1916 he decided to retain funds to finance expansion, rather than pay funds out to stockholders in the form of a dividend. The shareholders sued. Henry Ford's reaction was swift and direct: If the shareholders didn't see things his way, he would get rid of them. In 1919 the Ford family purchased 100 percent of the outstanding shares of Ford, eliminating any outside "interference." It was over 35 years before shares were again issued to the public.

Ford Motor Company has continued to evolve and grow over the years into one of the largest international corporations. Today there are nearly a billion shares of publicly traded Ford stock outstanding, and the president and chief executive of the company is not a member of the Ford family. But the Ford family still retains a significant stake in Ford Motor Company. In a move Henry Ford might have supported, top management recently decided to centralize decision making—that is, to have more key decisions made by top management, rather than by division managers. And, reminiscent of Henry Ford's most famous car, the company is attempting to make a "global car"—a mass-produced car that can be sold around the world with only minor changes.

☑ THE NAVIGATOR

www.ford.com

Study Objectives

After studying this chapter, you should be able to:

1. Identify the major characteristics of a corporation.
2. Differentiate between paid-in capital and retained earnings.
3. Record the issuance of common stock.
4. Explain the accounting for treasury stock.
5. Differentiate preferred stock from common stock.
6. Prepare a stockholders' equity section.
7. Compute book value per share.

☑ THE NAVIGATOR

PREVIEW OF CHAPTER 14

Corporations like **Ford Motor Company** have substantial resources. In fact, the corporation is the dominant form of business organization in the United States in terms of dollar volume of sales and earnings, and number of employees. All of the 500 largest companies in the United States are corporations. In this chapter we will explain the essential features of a corporation and the accounting for a corporation's capital stock transactions. In Chapter 15 we will look at other issues related to accounting for corporations.

The content and organization of Chapter 14 are as follows.

CORPORATIONS: ORGANIZATION AND CAPITAL STOCK TRANSACTIONS

The Corporate Form of Organization	Accounting for Common Stock Issues	Accounting for Treasury Stock	Preferred Stock	Statement Presentation and Analysis
• Characteristics • Formation • Stockholder rights • Stock issue considerations • Corporate capital	• Issuing par value stock • Issuing no-par stock • Issuing stock for services or noncash assets	• Purchase of treasury stock • Disposal of treasury stock	• Dividend preferences • Liquidation preference • Convertible preferred • Callable preferred	• Presentation • Analysis—Book value per share

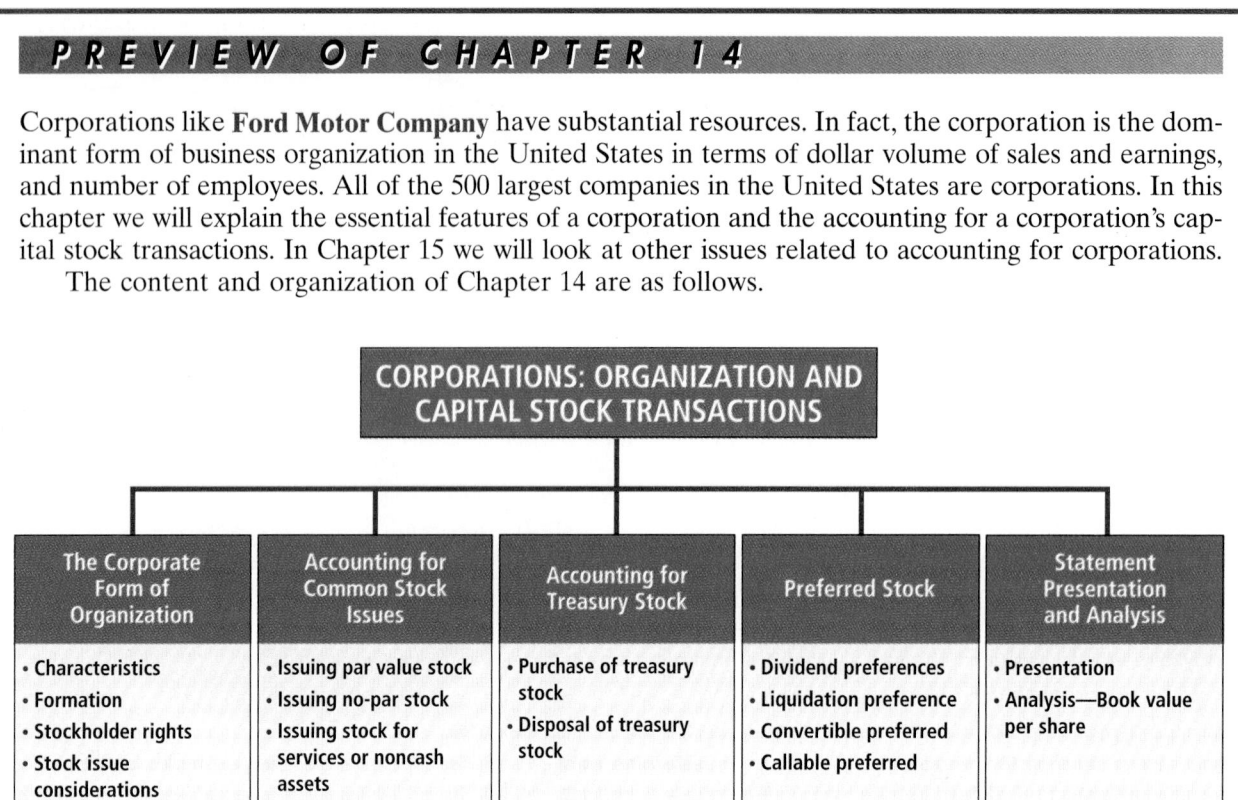

THE NAVIGATOR

THE CORPORATE FORM OF ORGANIZATION

In 1819, Chief Justice John Marshall defined a corporation as "an artificial being, invisible, intangible, and existing only in contemplation of law." This definition is the foundation for the prevailing legal interpretation that a corporation is an **entity separate and distinct from its owners**.

A corporation is created by law, and its continued existence depends upon the statutes of the state in which it is incorporated. As a legal entity, a corporation has most of the rights and privileges of a person. The major exceptions relate to privileges that only a living person can exercise, such as the right to vote or to hold public office. A corporation is subject to the same duties and responsibilities as a person. For example, it must abide by the laws and it must pay taxes.

Corporations may be classified in a variety of ways. Two common bases are by purpose and by ownership. A corporation may be organized for the purpose of making a **profit**, or it may be **nonprofit**. Corporations for profit include such well-known companies as **McDonald's**, **General Motors**, **Lands' End**, and **Apple Computer**. Nonprofit corporations are organized for charitable, medical, or educational purposes. Examples are the **Salvation Army**, the **American Cancer Society**, and the **Ford Foundation**.

Classification by **ownership** distinguishes between publicly held and privately held corporations. A publicly held corporation may have thousands of stockholders. Its stock is regularly traded on a national securities exchange such as the

New York Stock Exchange. Most of the largest U.S. corporations are publicly held. Examples of publicly held corporations are **Intel**, **IBM**, **Caterpillar Inc.**, and **General Electric**. In contrast, a **privately held corporation**, often referred to as a closely held corporation, usually has only a few stockholders, and does not offer its stock for sale to the general public. Privately held companies are generally much smaller than publicly held companies, although some notable exceptions exist. **Cargill Inc.**, a private corporation that trades in grain and other commodities, is one of the largest companies in the United States.

CHARACTERISTICS OF A CORPORATION

STUDY OBJECTIVE 1

Identify the major characteristics of a corporation.

A number of characteristics distinguish a corporation from proprietorships and partnerships. The most important of these characteristics are explained below.

Separate Legal Existence

As an entity separate and distinct from its owners, the corporation acts under its own name rather than in the name of its stockholders. **Ford Motor Company** may buy, own, and sell property. It may borrow money, and may enter into legally binding contracts in its own name. It may also sue or be sued, and it pays its own taxes.

Remember that in a partnership the acts of the owners (partners) bind the partnership. In contrast, the acts of its owners (stockholders) do not bind the corporation unless such owners are duly appointed agents of the corporation. For example, if you owned shares of Ford Motor Company stock, you would not have the right to purchase automobile parts for the company unless you were appointed as an agent of the corporation.

Legal existence separate from owners

Limited Liability of Stockholders

Since a corporation is a separate legal entity, creditors have recourse only to corporate assets to satisfy their claims. The liability of stockholders is normally limited to their investment in the corporation. Creditors have no legal claim on the personal assets of the owners unless fraud has occurred. Even in the event of bankruptcy, stockholders' losses are generally limited to their capital investment in the corporation.

Limited liability of stockholders

Transferable Ownership Rights

Ownership of a corporation is held in shares of capital stock. These are transferable units. Stockholders may dispose of part or all of their interest in a corporation simply by selling their stock. Remember that the transfer of an ownership interest in a partnership requires the consent of each owner. In contrast, the transfer of stock is entirely at the discretion of the stockholder. It does not require the approval of either the corporation or other stockholders.

The transfer of ownership rights between stockholders normally has no effect on the operating activities of the corporation. Nor does it affect the corporation's assets, liabilities, and total ownership equity. The transfer of these ownership rights is a transaction between individual owners. The enterprise does not participate in such transfers after it issues the capital stock.

Transferable ownership rights

Ability to Acquire Capital

It is relatively easy for a corporation to obtain capital through the issuance of stock. Buying stock in a corporation is often attractive to an investor because a stockholder has limited liability and shares of stock are readily transferable. Also, numerous individuals can become stockholders by investing small amounts of money. In sum, the ability of a successful corporation to obtain capital is virtually unlimited.

Ability to acquire capital

Continuous Life

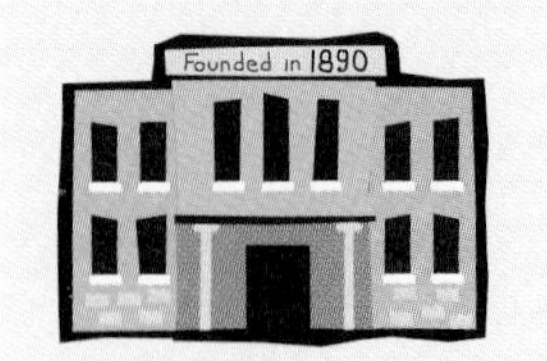

Continuous life

The life of a corporation is stated in its charter. The life may be perpetual or it may be limited to a specific number of years. If it is limited, the life can be extended through renewal of the charter. Since a corporation is a separate legal entity, its continuance as a going concern is not affected by the withdrawal, death, or incapacity of a stockholder, employee, or officer. As a result, a successful enterprise can have a continuous and perpetual life.

Corporation Management

As in **Ford Motor Company**, stockholders legally own the corporation. But they manage the corporation indirectly through a board of directors they elect. The board, in turn, formulates the operating policies for the company. The board also selects officers, such as a president and one or more vice presidents, to execute policy and to perform daily management functions.

A typical organization chart showing the delegation of responsibility is shown in Illustration 14-1.

Illustration 14-1

Corporation organization chart

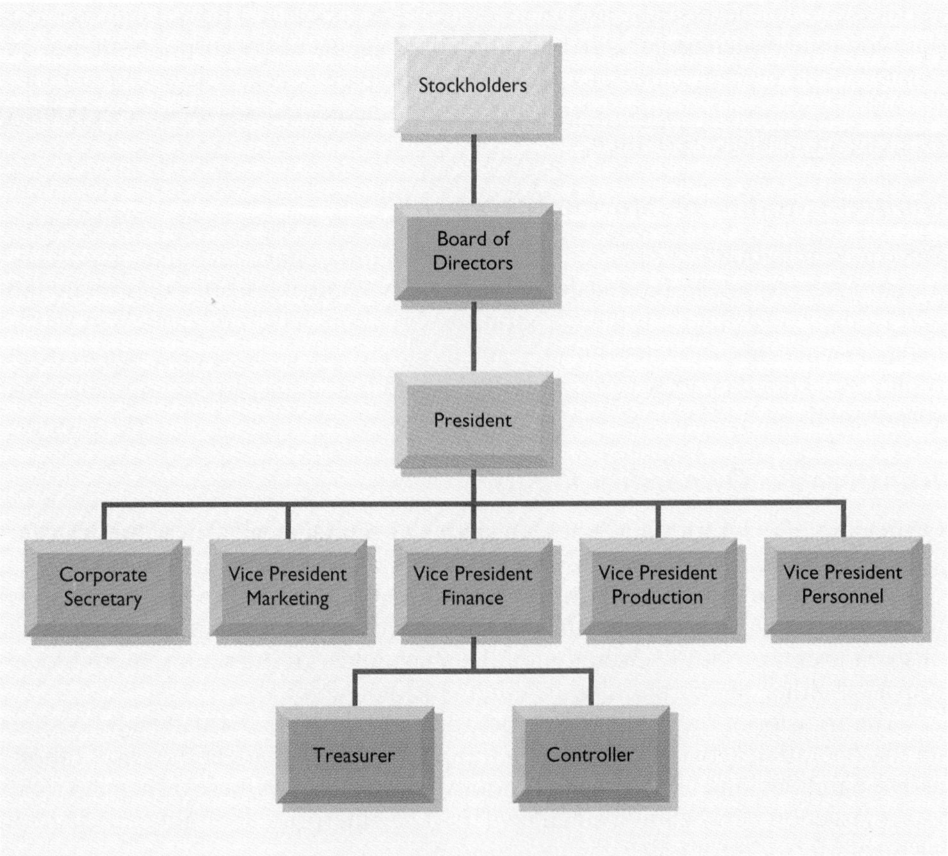

ETHICS NOTE

Managers who are not owners are often compensated based upon the performance of the firm. They thus may be tempted to exaggerate firm performance by inflating income figures.

The **president** is the chief executive officer. This individual has direct responsibility for managing the business. As the organization chart shows, the president delegates responsibility to other officers. The chief accounting officer is the **controller**. The controller's responsibilities include (1) maintaining the accounting records, (2) maintaining an adequate system of internal control, and (3) preparing financial statements, tax returns, and internal reports. The **treasurer** has custody of the corporation's funds and is responsible for maintaining the company's cash position.

The organizational structure of a corporation enables a company to hire professional managers to run the business. On the other hand, the separation of ownership and management prevents owners from having an active role in managing the company, which some owners like to have.

ACCOUNTING IN ACTION e Business Insight

When a group of investors in a company is unhappy with a company's performance, it sometimes tries to elect new members to the board of directors at the company's annual stockholder meeting. This is referred to as a proxy fight. Usually these efforts fail because it has been very expensive to get in contact with all of the company's shareholders to try to convince them to vote for your group of nominees.

But the Internet has changed that, says James Heard, chief executive of **Proxy Monitor**, a New York firm that consults institutional shareholders on how to vote on corporate governance issues. "Increasingly the Internet is being used as a tool of communication among shareholders to pressure managements," he said. One recent case involved an effort by a shareholder at **Luby's** to get four new people elected to that company's board of directors. He attracted considerable support from other Luby's shareholders by posting messages on a **Yahoo!** message board.

SOURCE: Aaron Elstein, "Online Grousing Over Luby's Escalates to Proxy Solicitation," *The Wall Street Journal*, October 25, 2000.

Government Regulations

A corporation is subject to numerous state and federal regulations. State laws usually prescribe the requirements for issuing stock, the distributions of earnings permitted to stockholders, and the effects of retiring stock. Federal securities laws govern the sale of capital stock to the general public. Also, most publicly held corporations are required to make extensive disclosure of their financial affairs to the Securities and Exchange Commission through quarterly and annual reports. In addition, when a corporate stock is traded on organized securities exchanges, the corporation must comply with the reporting requirements of these exchanges. Government regulations are designed to protect the owners of the corporation. Such protection is needed because most stockholders do not participate in the day-to-day management of the company.

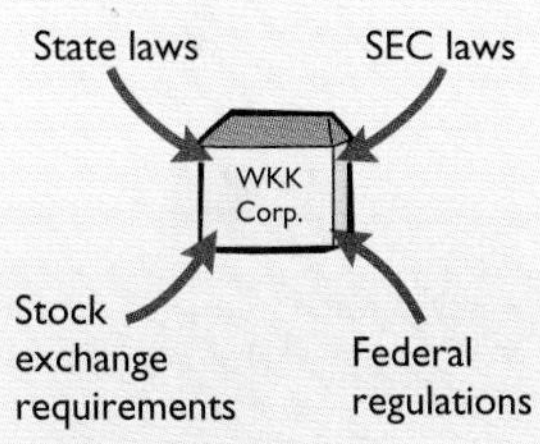

Goverment regulations

Additional Taxes

Neither proprietorships nor partnerships pay income taxes. The owner's share of earnings from these organizations is reported on his or her personal income tax return. Taxes are then paid by the individual on this amount. Corporations, on the other hand, must pay federal and state income taxes as a separate legal entity. These taxes are substantial: They can amount to more than 40 percent of taxable income.

Additional taxes

In addition, stockholders are required to pay taxes on cash dividends (pro rata distributions of net income). Thus, many argue that corporate income is **taxed twice (double taxation)**, once at the corporate level, and again at the individual level.

From the foregoing, we can identify the following advantages and disadvantages of a corporation compared to a proprietorship and partnership.

Illustration 14-2

Advantages and disadvantages of a corporation

Advantages	Disadvantages
Separate legal existence	Corporation management—separation of ownership and management
Limited liability of stockholders	Government regulations
Transferable ownership rights	Additional taxes
Ability to acquire capital	
Continuous life	
Corporation management—professional managers	

FORMING A CORPORATION

The initial step in forming a corporation is to file an application with the Secretary of State in the state in which incorporation is desired. The application contains such information as: (1) the name and purpose of the proposed corporation; (2) amounts, kinds, and number of shares of capital stock to be authorized; (3) the names of the incorporators; and (4) the shares of stock to which each has subscribed.

ALTERNATIVE TERMINOLOGY
The charter is often referred to as the *articles of incorporation*.

After the application is approved, a **charter** is granted. The charter may be an approved copy of the application form or it may be a separate document containing the same basic data. The issuance of the charter creates the corporation. Upon receipt of the charter, the corporation develops its by-laws. The **by-laws** establish the internal rules and procedures for conducting the affairs of the corporation. They also indicate the powers of the stockholders, directors, and officers of the enterprise.[1]

Regardless of the number of states in which a corporation has operating divisions, it is incorporated in only one state. It is to the company's advantage to incorporate in a state whose laws are favorable to the corporate form of business organization. **General Motors**, for example, is incorporated in Delaware, whereas **QUALCOMM** is a New Jersey corporation. Many corporations choose to incorporate in states with rules favorable to existing management. For example, **Gulf Oil** at one time changed its state of incorporation to Delaware to thwart possible unfriendly takeovers. There, certain defensive tactics against takeovers can be approved by the board of directors alone, without a vote by shareholders.

ACCOUNTING IN ACTION *Business Insight*

It is not necessary for a corporation to have an office in the state in which it incorporates. In fact, more than 50 percent of the Fortune 500 corporations are incorporated in Delaware. A primary reason is the Delaware courts' longstanding "business judgment rule." The rule provides that as long as directors exercise "due care" in the interests of stockholders, their actions will not be second-guessed by the courts. The rule has enabled directors to reject hostile takeover offers and to spurn takeovers simply because they did not want to sell the company. However, new interpretations are emerging. In a recent case, the state court ruled for a company that made a hostile takeover bid. On appeal, the Delaware Supreme Court ruled for the directors but gave the following guideline to the state courts: "Was the board's response reasonable in the light of the threat posed?"

[1]Following approval by two-thirds of the stockholders, the by-laws become binding upon all stockholders, directors, and officers. Legally, a corporation is regulated first by the laws of the state, second by its charter, and third by its by-laws. Care must be exercised to ensure that the provisions of the by-laws are not in conflict with either state laws or the charter.

Corporations engaged in interstate commerce must also obtain a license from each state in which they do business. The license subjects the corporation's operating activities to the corporation laws of the state.

Costs incurred in the formation of a corporation are called **organization costs**. These costs include legal and state fees, and promotional expenditures involved in the organization of the business. **Organization costs are expensed as incurred.** To determine the amount and timing of future benefits is so difficult that a conservative approach of expensing these costs immediately is followed.

> **INTERNATIONAL NOTE**
>
> U.S. corporations are identified by *Inc.*, which stands for Incorporated. In Italy the letters used are *SpA* (Societa per Azioni); in Sweden *AB* (Aktiebolag); in France *SA* (Sociedad Anonima); and in the Netherlands *NV* (Naamloze Vennootschap).
>
> In the United Kingdom public limited corporations are identified by *PLC*, and private corporations are denoted by *LTD*. The parallel designations in Germany are *AG* for public corporations and *GmbH* for private corporations.

OWNERSHIP RIGHTS OF STOCKHOLDERS

When chartered, the corporation may begin selling ownership rights in the form of shares of stock. When a corporation has only one class of stock, it is identified as **common stock**. Each share of common stock gives the stockholder the ownership rights pictured in Illustration 14-3. The ownership rights of a share of stock are stated in the articles of incorporation or in the by-laws.

Illustration 14-3

Ownership rights of stockholders

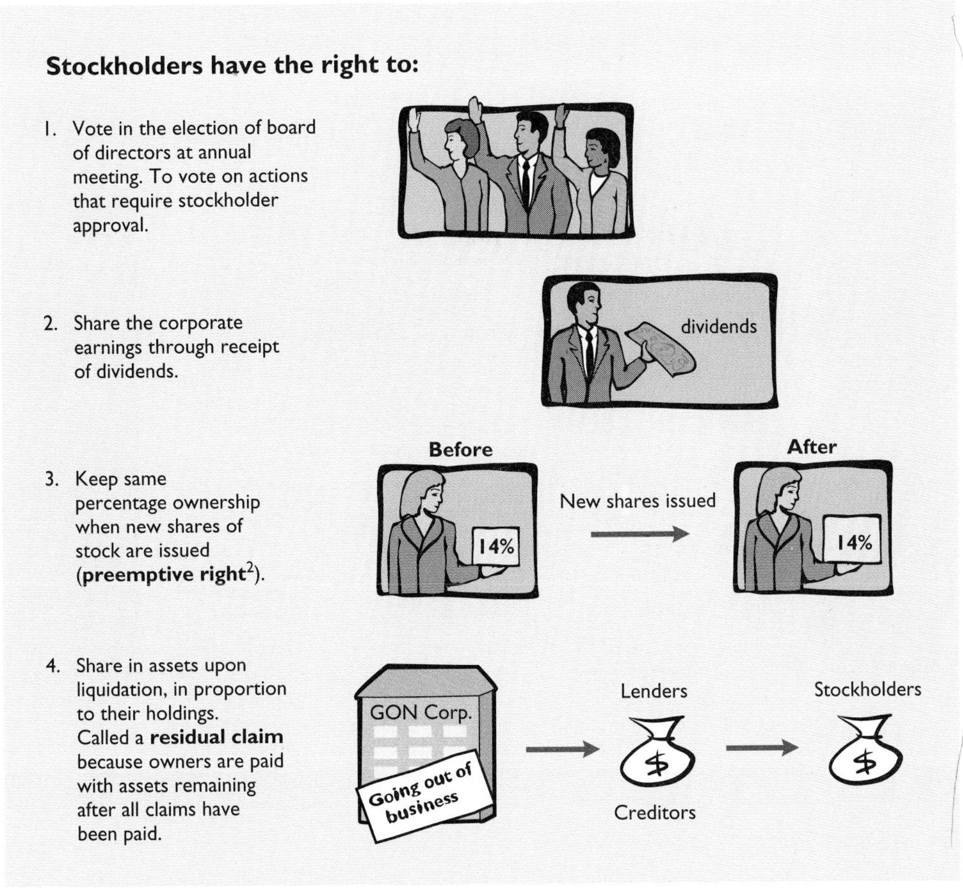
Stockholders have the right to:
1. Vote in the election of board of directors at annual meeting. To vote on actions that require stockholder approval.
2. Share the corporate earnings through receipt of dividends.
dividends
3. Keep same percentage ownership when new shares of stock are issued (preemptive right²).
Before
14%
New shares issued
After
14%
4. Share in assets upon liquidation, in proportion to their holdings. Called a residual claim because owners are paid with assets remaining after all claims have been paid.
GON Corp.
Going out of business
Lenders
Creditors
Stockholders

[2] A number of companies have eliminated the preemptive right, because they believe it makes an unnecessary and cumbersome demand on management. For example, by stockholder approval, **IBM** has dropped its preemptive right for stockholders.

ACCOUNTING IN ACTION *International Insight*

In Japan, stockholders are considered to be far less important to a corporation than employees, customers, and suppliers. There, stockholders are rarely asked to vote on an issue, and the notion of bending corporate policy to favor stockholders borders on the heretical. This attitude toward stockholders appears to be slowly changing, however, as influential Japanese are advocating listening to investors, raising the extremely low dividends paid by Japanese corporations, and improving disclosure of financial information.

Proof of stock ownership is evidenced by a form known as a **stock certificate**. As shown in Illustration 14-4, the face of the certificate shows the name of the corporation, the stockholder's name, the class and special features of the stock, the number of shares owned, and the signatures of duly authorized corporate officials. Certificates are prenumbered to facilitate accountability. They may be issued for any quantity of shares.

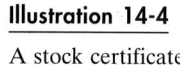

Illustration 14-4

A stock certificate

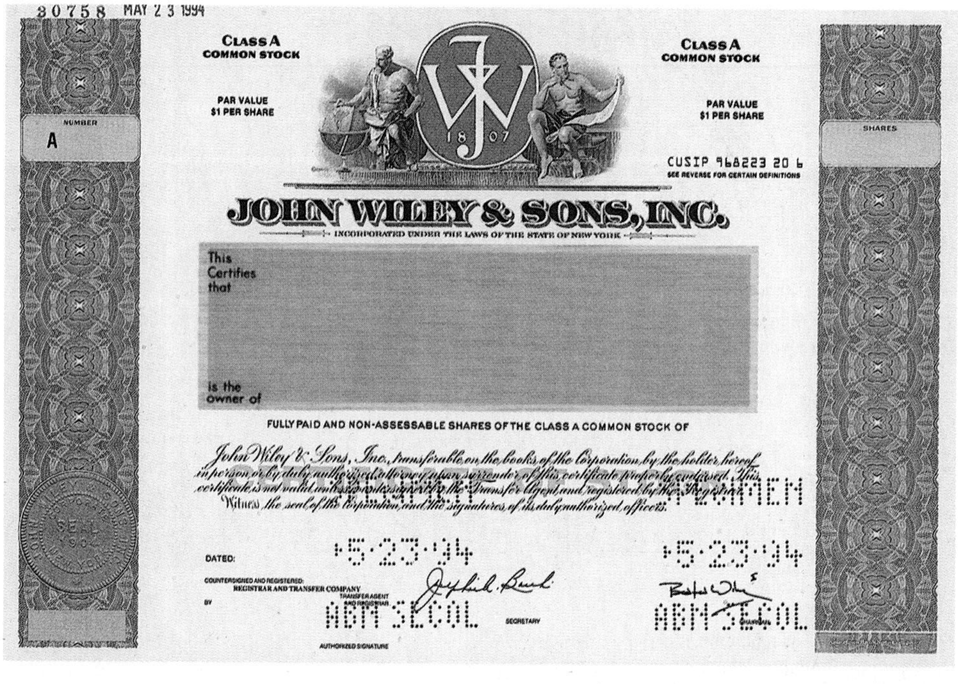

BEFORE YOU GO ON...

REVIEW IT

1. What are the advantages and disadvantages of a corporation compared to a proprietorship and a partnership?
2. Identify the principal steps in forming a corporation.
3. What rights are inherent in owning a share of stock in a corporation?

THE NAVIGATOR

STOCK ISSUE CONSIDERATIONS

In considering the issuance of stock, a corporation must resolve a number of basic questions: How many shares should be authorized for sale? How should the stock be issued? At what price should the shares be issued? What value should be assigned to the stock? These questions are answered in the following sections.

> **INTERNATIONAL NOTE**
>
> U.S. and U.K. corporations raise most of their capital through millions of outside shareholders and bondholders. In contrast, companies in Germany, France, and Japan acquire financing from large banks or other institutions. In the latter environment, shareholders are less important, and external reporting and auditing receive less emphasis.

Authorized Stock

The amount of stock that a corporation is **authorized** to sell is indicated in its charter. The total amount of **authorized stock** at the time of incorporation normally anticipates both initial and subsequent capital needs. As a result, the number of shares authorized generally exceeds the number initially sold. If all authorized stock is sold, a corporation must obtain consent of the state to amend its charter before it can issue additional shares.

The authorization of capital stock does not result in a formal accounting entry. This event has no immediate effect on either corporate assets or stockholders' equity. But, disclosure of the number of authorized shares is often reported in the stockholders' equity section. It is then simple to determine the number of unissued shares that can be issued without amending the charter: subtract the total shares issued from the total authorized. For example, if Advanced Micro was authorized to sell 100,000 shares of common stock and issued 80,000 shares, 20,000 shares would remain unissued.

Issuance of Stock

A corporation can issue common stock **directly** to investors. Or it can issue the stock **indirectly** through an investment banking firm (brokerage house) that specializes in bringing securities to the attention of prospective investors. Direct issue is typical in closely held companies. Indirect issue is customary for a publicly held corporation.

In an indirect issue, the investment banking firm may agree to **underwrite** the entire stock issue. In this arrangement, the investment banker buys the stock from the corporation at a stipulated price and resells the shares to investors. The corporation thus avoids any risk of being unable to sell the shares. Also, it obtains immediate use of the cash received from the underwriter. The investment banking firm, in turn, assumes the risk of reselling the shares in return for an underwriting fee.[3] For example, **Kolff Medical**, maker of the Jarvik artificial heart, used an underwriter to help it issue common stock to the public. The underwriter charged a 6.6 percent underwriting fee on Kolff Medical's approximately $20 million public offering.

Indirect Issuance

How does a corporation set the price for a new issue of stock? Among the factors to be considered are (1) the company's anticipated future earnings, (2) its expected dividend rate per share, (3) its current financial position, (4) the current state of the economy, and (5) the current state of the securities market. The calculation can be complex and is properly the subject of a finance course.

Market Value of Stock

The stock of publicly held companies is traded on organized exchanges. The dollar prices per share are established by the interaction between buyers and sellers.

[3]Alternatively, the investment banking firm may agree only to enter into a **best efforts** contract with the corporation. In such cases, the banker agrees to sell as many shares as possible at a specified price. The corporation bears the risk of unsold stock. Under a best efforts arrangement, the banking firm is paid a fee or commission for its services.

In general, the prices set by the marketplace tend to follow the trend of a company's earnings and dividends. But, factors beyond a company's control, such as an oil embargo, changes in interest rates, and the outcome of a presidential election, may cause day-to-day fluctuations in market prices.

ACCOUNTING IN ACTION *Business Insight*

The volume of trading on national and international exchanges is heavy. Shares in excess of 800 million are often traded daily on the New York Stock Exchange alone. For each listed stock, the financial press reports the total volume of stock traded for a given day, the high and low price for the day (now in decimals), the closing market price, and the net change for the day. A recent listing for **Lands' End** is shown below.

Stock	Volume	High	Low	Close	Net Change
LandsEnd	3478	28^{38}	26^{63}	26^{94}	-1^{19}

These numbers indicate that Lands' End's trading volume was 347,800 shares. The high, low, and closing prices for that date were \$28.38, \$26.63, and \$26.94, respectively. The net change for the day was a decrease of \$1.19 per share.

The trading of capital stock on securities exchanges involves the transfer of **already issued shares** from an existing stockholder to another investor. These transactions have no impact on a corporation's stockholders' equity.

TECHNOLOGY IN ACTION

Giant, publicly held corporations could not exist without the organized stock markets, and the stock markets could not exist without massive computerization. Not too many years ago, the NYSE "ticker" would run behind, or trading would even be halted, when sales exceeded 30 million shares or so. Now, with sales sometimes in excess of 800 million shares, the NYSE and its companion exchanges throughout the country operate efficiently with computer technology. Technology has also made possible extended trading hours. An investor in New York can trade electronically at 3:30 A.M., which is the time in New York when the London Stock Exchange opens. Some predict that 24-hour trading is not far off.

Par and No-Par Value Stocks

Par value stock is capital stock that has been assigned a value per share in the corporate charter. The par value may be any amount selected by the corporation. Generally, the par value is quite low, because states often levy a tax on the corporation based on par value. For example, **Eastman Kodak** has a par of \$2.50, **Ford Motor Company** has a \$1 par, **PepsiCo** has a $1\frac{2}{3}$ cents par, and **America Online** has a 1 cent par.

Par value does not indicate the worth or market value of the stock. **IBM** has a par value of \$1.25, but its recent market price was \$120 per share. **Par**

value has legal significance. It represents the legal capital per share that must be retained in the business for the protection of corporate creditors. That amount is not available for withdrawal by stockholders. Thus, most states require the corporation to sell its shares at par or above.

No-par value stock is capital stock that has not been assigned a value in the corporate charter. It is often issued because some confusion still exists concerning par value and fair market value. If shares are not assigned a par value, the questionable use of par value as a basis for fair market value never arises. The major disadvantage of no-par value stock is that some states levy a high tax on such shares.

No-par value stock is quite common today. For example, **Procter & Gamble** and **North American Van Lines** both have no-par stock. In many states the board of directors is permitted to assign a stated value to the no-par shares. This value becomes the legal capital per share. The stated value of no-par stock may be changed at any time by action of the directors. Stated value, like par value, does not indicate the market value of the stock. When there is no assigned stated value, the entire proceeds received upon issuance of the stock is considered to be legal capital.

The relationship of par and no-par value to legal capital is shown below.

Illustration 14-5

Relationship of par and no-par value stock to legal capital

Stock		Legal Capital per Share
Par value	→	Par value
No-par value with stated value	→	Stated value
No-par value without stated value	→	Entire proceeds

CORPORATE CAPITAL

STUDY OBJECTIVE 2

Differentiate between paid-in capital and retained earnings.

Owners' equity is identified as **stockholders' equity**, **shareholders' equity**, or **corporate capital**. The stockholders' equity section of a corporation's balance sheet consists of: (1) paid-in (contributed) capital and (2) retained earnings (earned capital). The distinction between paid-in capital and retained earnings is important from both a legal and a financial point of view. Legally, distributions of earnings (dividends) can be declared out of retained earnings in all states, but in many states they cannot be declared out of paid-in capital. Financially, management, stockholders, and others look to earnings for the continued existence and growth of the corporation.

Paid-in Capital

Paid-in capital is the total amount of cash and other assets paid in to the corporation by stockholders in exchange for capital stock. As noted earlier, when a corporation has only one class of stock, it is identified as **common stock**.

Retained Earnings

Retained earnings is net income that is retained in a corporation. Net income is recorded in Retained Earnings by a closing entry in which Income Summary is debited and Retained Earnings is credited. For example, assuming that net income for Delta Robotics in its first year of operations is $130,000, the closing entry is:

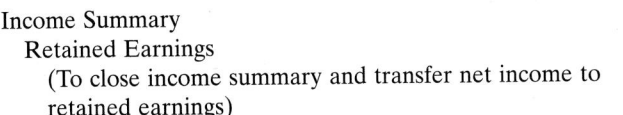

	Debit	Credit
Income Summary	130,000	
Retained Earnings		130,000
(To close income summary and transfer net income to retained earnings)		

A	=	L	+	SE
				−130,000
				+130,000

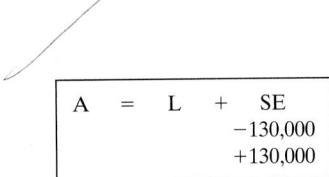

If Delta Robotics has a balance of $800,000 in common stock at the end of its first year, its stockholders' equity section is as follows.

Illustration 14-6

Stockholders' equity section

DELTA ROBOTICS Balance Sheet (partial)		
Stockholders' equity		
Paid-in-capital		
Common stock	$800,000	
Retained earnings	130,000	
Total stockholders' equity		$930,000

The following illustration compares the owners' equity (stockholders' equity) accounts reported on a balance sheet for a proprietorship, a partnership, and a corporation.

Illustration 14-7

Comparison of owners' equity accounts

Proprietorship	Partnership	Corporation
Able, Capital — Normal bal. (credit)	**Able, Capital** — Normal bal. (credit)	**Common Stock** — Normal bal. (credit)
	Baker, Capital — Normal bal. (credit)	**Retained Earnings** — Normal bal. (credit)

BEFORE YOU GO ON...

REVIEW IT

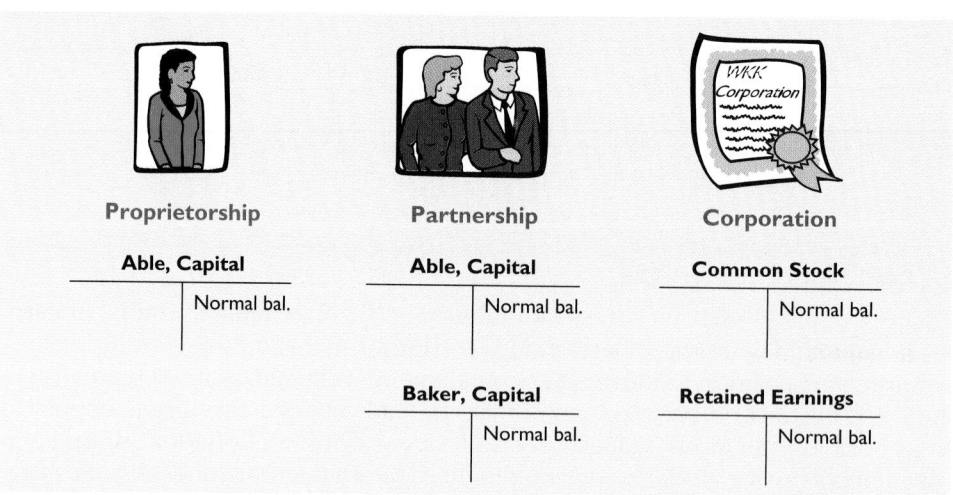

1. Of what significance to a corporation is the amount of authorized stock?
2. What alternative approaches may a corporation use in issuing stock?
3. Distinguish between par value and fair market value.

DO IT

At the end of its first year of operation, Doral Corporation has $750,000 of common stock and net income of $122,000. Prepare (a) the closing entry for net income and (b) the stockholders' equity section at year-end.

ACTION PLAN

- Record net income in Retained Earnings by a closing entry in which Income Summary is debited and Retained Earnings is credited.
- In the stockholders' equity section, show (1) paid-in capital and (2) retained earnings.

SOLUTION

(a) Income Summary	122,000	
Retained Earnings		122,000
(To close income summary and transfer net income to retained earnings)		

(b) Stockholders' equity		
Paid-in capital		
Common stock	$750,000	
Retained earnings	122,000	
Total stockholders' equity		$872,000

Related exercise material: BE14-2, BE14-8, E14-5, and E14-9.

THE NAVIGATOR

ACCOUNTING FOR COMMON STOCK ISSUES

STUDY OBJECTIVE 3

Record the issuance of common stock.

Let's now look at how to account for issues of common stock. The primary objectives in accounting for the issuance of common stock are: (1) to identify the specific sources of paid-in capital and (2) to maintain the distinction between paid-in capital and retained earnings. **The issuance of common stock affects only paid-in capital accounts.**

ISSUING PAR VALUE COMMON STOCK FOR CASH

As discussed earlier, par value does not indicate a stock's market value. Therefore, the cash proceeds from issuing par value stock may be equal to, greater than, or less than par value. When the issuance of common stock for cash is recorded, the par value of the shares is credited to Common Stock. The portion of the proceeds that is above or below par value is recorded in a separate paid-in capital account.

To illustrate, assume that Hydro-Slide, Inc. issues 1,000 shares of $1 par value common stock at par for cash. The entry to record this transaction is:

Cash	1,000	
Common Stock		1,000
(To record issuance of 1,000 shares of $1 par common stock at par)		

A	=	L	+	SE
+1,000				+1,000

ALTERNATIVE TERMINOLOGY

Paid-in Capital in Excess of Par is also called *Premium on Stock.*

If Hydro-Slide issues an additional 1,000 shares of the $1 par value common stock for cash at $5 per share, the entry is:

Cash	5,000	
Common Stock		1,000
Paid-in Capital in Excess of Par Value		4,000
(To record issuance of 1,000 shares of common stock in excess of par)		

A	=	L	+	SE
+5,000				+1,000
				+4,000

The total paid-in capital from these two transactions is $6,000, and the legal capital is $2,000. If Hydro-Slide, Inc. has retained earnings of $27,000, the stockholders' equity section is shown in Illustration 14-8.

Illustration 14-8

Stockholders' equity—paid-in capital in excess of par value

HYDRO-SLIDE, INC.
Balance Sheet (partial)

Stockholders' equity	
Paid-in-capital	
Common stock	$ 2,000
Paid-in capital in excess of par value	**4,000**
Total paid-in capital	6,000
Retained earnings	27,000
Total stockholders' equity	$33,000

When stock is issued for less than par value, the account Paid-in Capital in Excess of Par Value is debited, if a credit balance exists in this account. If a credit balance does not exist, then the amount less than par is debited to Retained Earnings. This situation occurs only rarely: The sale of common stock below par value is not permitted in most states, because stockholders may be held personally liable for the difference between the price paid upon original sale and par value.

ISSUING NO-PAR COMMON STOCK FOR CASH

When no-par common stock has a stated value, the entries are similar to those illustrated for par value stock. The stated value represents legal capital. Therefore it is credited to Common Stock. Also, when the selling price of no-par stock exceeds stated value, the excess is credited to Paid-in Capital in Excess of Stated Value. For example, assume that instead of $1 par value stock, Hydro-Slide, Inc. has $5 stated value no-par stock and the company issues 5,000 shares at $8 per share for cash. The entry is:

A	=	L	+	SE
+40,000				+25,000
				+15,000

Cash	40,000	
Common Stock		25,000
Paid-in Capital in Excess of Stated Value		15,000
(To record issue of 5,000 shares of $5 stated value no-par stock)		

Paid-in Capital in Excess of Stated Value is reported as part of paid-in capital in the stockholders' equity section.

What happens when no-par stock does not have a stated value? In that case, the entire proceeds from the issue become legal capital and are credited to Common Stock. Thus, if Hydro-Slide does not assign a stated value to its no-par stock, the issuance of the 5,000 shares at $8 per share for cash is recorded as follows.

A	=	L	+	SE
+40,000				+40,000

Cash	40,000	
Common Stock		40,000
(To record issue of 5,000 shares of no-par stock)		

The amount of legal capital for Hydro-Slide stock with a $5 stated value is $25,000. Without a stated value, it is $40,000.

ISSUING COMMON STOCK FOR SERVICES OR NONCASH ASSETS

Stock may also be issued for services (compensation to attorneys or consultants) or for noncash assets (land, buildings, and equipment). In such cases, what cost should be recognized in the exchange transaction? To comply with the **cost prin-**

ciple, in a noncash transaction **cost is the cash equivalent price**. Thus, **cost is either the fair market value of the consideration given up, or the fair market value of the consideration received**, whichever is more clearly determinable.

To illustrate, assume that attorneys have helped Jordan Company incorporate. They have billed the company $5,000 for their services. They agree to accept 4,000 shares of $1 par value common stock in payment of their bill. At the time of the exchange, there is no established market price for the stock. In this case, the market value of the consideration received, $5,000, is more clearly evident. Accordingly, the entry is:

Organization Expense	5,000	
Common Stock		4,000
Paid-in Capital in Excess of Par Value		1,000
(To record issuance of 4,000 shares of $1 par value stock to attorneys)		

A	=	L	+	SE
				−5,000
				+4,000
				+1,000

As explained on page 565, organization costs are expensed as incurred.

In contrast, assume that Athletic Research Inc. is an existing publicly held corporation. Its $5 par value stock is actively traded at $8 per share. The company issues 10,000 shares of stock to acquire land recently advertised for sale at $90,000. The most clearly evident value in this noncash transaction is the market price of the consideration given, $80,000. The transaction is recorded as follows.

Land	80,000	
Common Stock		50,000
Paid-in Capital in Excess of Par Value		30,000
(To record issuance of 10,000 shares of $5 par value stock for land)		

A	=	L	+	SE
+80,000				+50,000
				+30,000

As illustrated in these examples, **the par value of the stock is never a factor in determining the cost of the assets received**. This is also true of the stated value of no-par stock.

BEFORE YOU GO ON...

REVIEW IT

1. Explain the accounting for par and no-par common stock issued for cash.
2. Explain the accounting for the issuance of stock for services or noncash assets.
3. What is the par or stated value per share of **Lands' End's** common stock? How many shares has Lands' End issued at January 28, 2000? The answers to these questions are provided on page 598.

LANDS' END DIRECT MERCHANTS

DO IT

Cayman Corporation begins operations on March 1 by issuing 100,000 shares of $10 par value common stock for cash at $12 per share. On March 15 it issues 5,000 shares of common stock to attorneys in settlement of their bill of $50,000 for organization costs. Journalize the issuance of the shares, assuming the stock is not publicly traded.

ACTION PLAN

- In issuing shares for cash, credit Common Stock for par value per share.
- Credit any additional proceeds in excess of par value to a separate paid-in capital account.
- When stock is issued for services, use the cash equivalent price.
- For the cash equivalent price use either the fair market value of what is given up or the fair market value of what is received, whichever is more clearly determinable.

SOLUTION

Mar. 1	Cash	1,200,000	
	Common Stock		1,000,000
	Paid-in Capital in Excess of Par Value		200,000
	(To record issuance of 100,000 shares at $12 per share)		
Mar. 15	Organization Expense	50,000	
	Common Stock		50,000
	(To record issuance of 5,000 shares for attorneys' fees)		

Related exercise material: BE14-3, BE14-4, BE14-5, E14-1, E14-2, E14-3, E14-7, and E14-8.

THE NAVIGATOR

ACCOUNTING FOR TREASURY STOCK

STUDY OBJECTIVE 4

Explain the accounting for treasury stock.

Treasury stock is a corporation's own stock that has been issued, fully paid for, and reacquired by the corporation but not retired. A corporation may acquire treasury stock for various reasons:

1. To reissue the shares to officers and employees under bonus and stock compensation plans.
2. To increase trading of the company's stock in the securities market in the hopes of enhancing its market value.
3. To have additional shares available for use in the acquisition of other companies.
4. To reduce the number of shares outstanding and thereby increase earnings per share.
5. To rid the company of disgruntled investors, perhaps to avoid a takeover, as illustrated in the **Ford Motor Company** Feature Story.

HELPFUL HINT
Treasury stock is so named because the company often holds the shares in its treasury for safekeeping.

HELPFUL HINT
Treasury shares do not have dividend rights or voting rights.

Many corporations have treasury stock. One survey of 600 companies in the United States found that 65 percent have treasury stock.[4] Specifically, **The Gillette Company** recently reported 299 million treasury shares, **The Coca-Cola Company** 994.7 million shares, and **United Airlines** 14.9 million shares.

PURCHASE OF TREASURY STOCK

Treasury stock is generally accounted for by **the cost method**. This method uses the cost of the shares purchased to value the treasury stock. Under the cost method, **Treasury Stock is debited for the price paid to reacquire the shares.**

The same amount is credited to Treasury Stock when the shares are disposed of. To illustrate, assume that on January 1, 2002, the stockholders' equity section of Mead, Inc. has 100,000 shares of $5 par value common stock outstanding (all

[4] *Accounting Trends & Techniques 2000* (New York: American Institute of Certified Public Accountants).

ACCOUNTING IN ACTION *Business Insight*

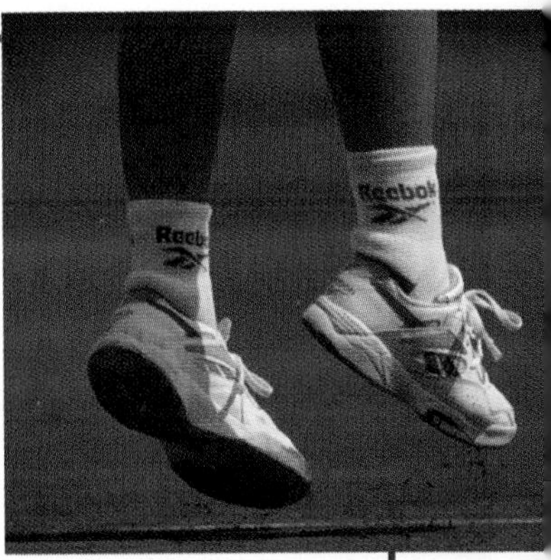

In a bold (and some would say risky) move in late 1996, **Reebok** bought back nearly a *third* of its shares. This repurchase of shares dramatically reduced Reebok's available cash. In fact, the company borrowed significant funds to accomplish the repurchase. In a press release, management stated that it was repurchasing the shares because it believed its stock was severely underpriced. The repurchase of so many shares was meant to signal management's belief in good future earnings.

Skeptics, however, suggested that Reebok's management was repurchasing shares to make it less likely that the company would be acquired by another company (in which case Reebok's top managers would likely lose their jobs). By depleting its cash, Reebok became a less likely acquisition target. Acquiring companies like to purchase companies with large cash reserves so they can pay off debt used in the acquisition.

issued at par value) and Retained Earnings of $200,000. The stockholders' equity section before purchase of treasury stock is as follows.

Illustration 14-9

Stockholders' equity with no treasury stock

MEAD, INC. Balance Sheet (partial)	
Stockholders' equity	
Paid-in capital	
Common stock, $5 par value, 100,000 shares issued and outstanding	$500,000
Retained earnings	200,000
Total stockholders' equity	$700,000

On February 1, 2002, Mead acquires 4,000 shares of its stock at $8 per share. The entry is:

Feb. 1	Treasury Stock	32,000	
	Cash		32,000
	(To record purchase of 4,000 shares of treasury stock at $8 per share)		

A	=	L	+	SE
−32,000				−32,000

Note that Treasury Stock is debited for the cost of the shares purchased. Is the original paid-in capital account, Common Stock, affected? No, because the number of issued shares does not change. In the stockholders' equity section of the balance sheet, treasury stock is deducted from total paid-in capital and retained earnings. Treasury Stock is a contra stockholders' equity account.

The stockholders' equity section of Mead, Inc. after purchase of treasury stock is as follows.

Illustration 14-10

Stockholders' equity with treasury stock

MEAD, INC. Balance Sheet (partial)	
Stockholders' equity	
Paid-in capital	
Common stock, $5 par value, 100,000 shares issued and 96,000 shares outstanding	$500,000
Retained earnings	200,000
Total paid-in capital and retained earnings	700,000
Less: Treasury stock (4,000 shares)	**32,000**
Total stockholders' equity	$668,000

Thus, the acquisition of treasury stock reduces stockholders' equity.

In the balance sheet, both the number of shares issued (100,000) and the number in the treasury (4,000) are disclosed. The difference between these two amounts is the number of shares of stock outstanding (96,000). The term **outstanding stock** means the number of shares of issued stock that are being held by stockholders.

Some maintain that treasury stock should be reported as an asset because it can be sold for cash. Under this reasoning, unissued stock should also be shown as an asset, clearly an erroneous conclusion. Rather than being an asset, treasury stock reduces stockholder claims on corporate assets. This effect is correctly shown by reporting treasury stock as a deduction from total paid-in capital and retained earnings.

DISPOSAL OF TREASURY STOCK

Treasury stock is usually sold or retired. The accounting for its sale is different when treasury stock is sold above cost than when it is sold below cost.

Sale of Treasury Stock above Cost

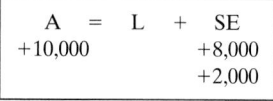

HELPFUL HINT

Treasury stock transactions are classified as capital stock transactions. As in the case when stock is issued, the income statement is not involved.

If the selling price of the treasury shares is equal to cost, the sale of the shares is recorded by a debit to Cash and a credit to Treasury Stock. When the selling price of the shares is greater than cost, the difference is credited to Paid-in Capital from Treasury Stock.

To illustrate, assume that 1,000 shares of treasury stock of Mead, Inc., previously acquired at $8 per share, are sold at $10 per share on July 1. The entry is as follows.

A	=	L	+	SE
+10,000				+8,000
				+2,000

July 1	Cash	10,000	
	Treasury Stock		8,000
	Paid-in Capital from Treasury Stock		2,000
	(To record sale of 1,000 shares of treasury stock above cost)		

The $2,000 credit in the entry would not be considered a gain on sale of treasury stock for two reasons: (1) Gains on sales occur when **assets** are sold, and treasury stock is not an asset. (2) A corporation does not realize a gain or suffer a loss from stock transactions with its own stockholders. Thus, paid-in capital arising from the sale of treasury stock should not be included in the measurement of net income. Paid-in Capital from Treasury Stock is listed separately on the balance sheet as a part of paid-in capital.

Sale of Treasury Stock below Cost

When treasury stock is sold below its cost, the excess of cost over selling price is usually debited to Paid-in Capital from Treasury Stock. Thus, if Mead, Inc. sells an additional 800 shares of treasury stock on October 1 at $7 per share, the entry is as follows.

Oct. 1	Cash	5,600	
	Paid-in Capital from Treasury Stock	800	
	Treasury Stock		6,400
	(To record sale of 800 shares of treasury stock below cost)		

A	=	L	+	SE
+5,600				−800
				+6,400

Observe the following from the two sales entries: (1) Treasury Stock is credited at cost in each entry. (2) Paid-in Capital from Treasury Stock is used for the difference between cost and the resale price of the shares. And (3) the original paid-in capital account, Common Stock, is not affected. **The sale of treasury stock increases both total assets and total stockholders' equity.**

After posting the foregoing entries, the treasury stock accounts will show the following balances on October 1.

Illustration 14-11
Treasury stock accounts

Treasury Stock

Feb. 1	32,000	July 1	8,000
		Oct. 1	6,400
Oct. 1 Bal.	17,600		

Paid-in Capital from Treasury Stock

Oct. 1	800	July 1	2,000
		Oct. 1 Bal.	1,200

When the credit balance in Paid-in Capital from Treasury Stock is eliminated, any additional excess of cost over selling price is debited to Retained Earnings. To illustrate, assume that Mead, Inc. sells its remaining 2,200 shares at $7 per share on December 1. The excess of cost over selling price is $2,200 [2,200 × ($8 − $7)]. In this case, $1,200 of the excess is debited to Paid-in Capital from Treasury Stock. The remainder is debited to Retained Earnings. The entry is:

Dec. 1	Cash	15,400	
	Paid-in Capital from Treasury Stock	1,200	
	Retained Earning	1,000	
	Treasury Stock		17,600
	(To record sale of 2,200 shares of treasury stock at $7 per share)		

A	=	L	+	SE
+15,400				−1,200
				−1,000
				+17,600

BEFORE YOU GO ON...

REVIEW IT

1. What is treasury stock, and why do companies acquire it?
2. How is treasury stock recorded?
3. Where is treasury stock reported in the financial statements? Does a company record gains and losses on treasury stock transactions? Explain.
4. How many shares of treasury stock did **Lands' End** have at January 28, 2000 and at January 29, 1999? What caused the change between 1999 and 2000? The answers to these questions are provided on page 598.

DO IT

Santa Anita Inc. purchases 3,000 shares of its $50 par value common stock for $180,000 cash on July 1. The shares are to be held in the treasury until resold. On November 1, the corporation sells 1,000 shares of treasury stock for cash at $70 per share. Journalize the treasury stock transactions.

ACTION PLAN

- Record the purchase of treasury stock at cost.
- When treasury stock is sold above its cost, credit the excess of the selling price over cost to Paid-in Capital from Treasury Stock.
- When treasury stock is sold below its cost, debit the excess of cost over selling price to Paid-in Capital from Treasury Stock.

SOLUTION

July 1	Treasury Stock	180,000	
	Cash		180,000
	(To record the purchase of 3,000 shares at $60 per share)		
Nov. 1	Cash	70,000	
	Treasury Stock		60,000
	Paid-in Capital from Treasury Stock		10,000
	(To record the sale of 1,000 shares at $70 per share)		

Related exercise material: BE14-6, E14-2, E14-4, E14-7, and E14-8.

THE NAVIGATOR

PREFERRED STOCK

STUDY OBJECTIVE 5

Differentiate preferred stock from common stock.

To appeal to more potential investors, a corporation may issue an additional class of stock, called preferred stock. **Preferred stock** has contractual provisions that give it a preference or priority over common stock in certain areas. Typically, preferred stockholders have a priority as to (1) distributions of earnings (dividends) and (2) assets in the event of liquidation. However, they generally do not have voting rights.

Like common stock, preferred stock may be issued for cash or for noncash assets. The entries for these transactions are similar to the entries for common stock. When a corporation has more than one class of stock, each paid-in capital account title should identify the stock to which it relates. For example, a company might have the following accounts: Preferred Stock, Common Stock, Paid-in Capital in Excess of Par Value—Preferred Stock, and Paid-in Capital in Excess of Par Value—Common Stock. Assume that Stine Corporation issues 10,000 shares of $10 par value preferred stock for $12 cash per share. The entry to record the issuance is:

A	=	L	+	SE
+120,000				+100,000
				+20,000

Cash	120,000	
Preferred Stock		100,000
Paid-in Capital in Excess of Par Value–Preferred Stock		20,000
(To record the issuance of 10,000 shares of $10 par value preferred stock)		

Preferred stock may have either a par value or no-par value. In the stockholders' equity section of the balance sheet, preferred stock is shown first because of its dividend and liquidation preferences over common stock.

Various features associated with the issuance of preferred stock, including dividend preferences, liquidation preferences, convertibility, and callability, are discussed on the following pages.

DIVIDEND PREFERENCES

As noted earlier, **preferred stockholders have the right to share in the distribution of corporate income before common stockholders**. For example, if the dividend rate on preferred stock is \$5 per share, common shareholders will not receive any dividends in the current year until preferred stockholders have received \$5 per share. The first claim to dividends does not, however, guarantee the payment of dividends. Dividends depend on many factors, such as adequate retained earnings and availability of cash.

The per share dividend amount is stated as a percentage of the preferred stock's par value or as a specified amount. For example, **Crane Company** specifies a 3¾ percent dividend on its \$100 par value preferred (\$100 × 3¾% = \$3.75 per share). **DuPont** has both a \$4.50 and a \$3.50 series of no-par preferred stock.

I hope there is some money left when it's my turn.

Preferred stockholders Common stockholders

Dividend Preference

Cumulative Dividend

Preferred stock often contains a **cumulative dividend** feature. This means that preferred stockholders must be paid both current-year dividends and any unpaid prior-year dividends before common stockholders receive dividends. When preferred stock is cumulative, preferred dividends not declared in a given period are called **dividends in arrears**.

To illustrate, assume that Scientific-Leasing has 5,000 shares of 7 percent, \$100 par value, cumulative preferred stock outstanding. The annual dividend is \$35,000 (5,000 × \$7 per share), but dividends are two years in arrears. In this case preferred stockholders are entitled to receive the following dividends in the current year.

HELPFUL HINT
The cumulative dividend feature is often critical in investors' acceptance of a preferred stock issue. Investors are much less interested in a noncumulative preferred stock because a dividend passed in any year is lost forever.

Illustration 14-12
Computation of total dividends to preferred stock

Dividends in arrears (\$35,000 × 2)	\$ 70,000
Current-year dividends	35,000
Total preferred dividends	**\$105,000**

No distribution can be made to common stockholders until this entire preferred dividend is paid. In other words, dividends cannot be paid to common stockholders while any preferred stock is in arrears.

ACCOUNTING IN ACTION *Business Insight*

Dividends in arrears can extend for fairly long periods of time. **Long Island Lighting Company's** directors voted at one time to make up some \$390 million in preferred dividends that had been in arrears for nearly ten years and to resume normal quarterly preferred payments. The announcement resulted from an agreement between the company and New York State. The company agreed to abandon a nuclear power plant in exchange for sizable rate increases over the next ten years.

Dividends in arrears are not considered a liability. No payment obligation exists until a dividend is declared by the board of directors. However, the amount of dividends in arrears should be disclosed in the notes to the financial statements. Doing so enables investors to assess the potential impact of this commitment on the corporation's financial position.

Companies that are unable to meet their dividend obligations are not looked upon favorably by the investment community. As a financial officer noted in discussing one company's failure to pay its cumulative preferred dividend for a

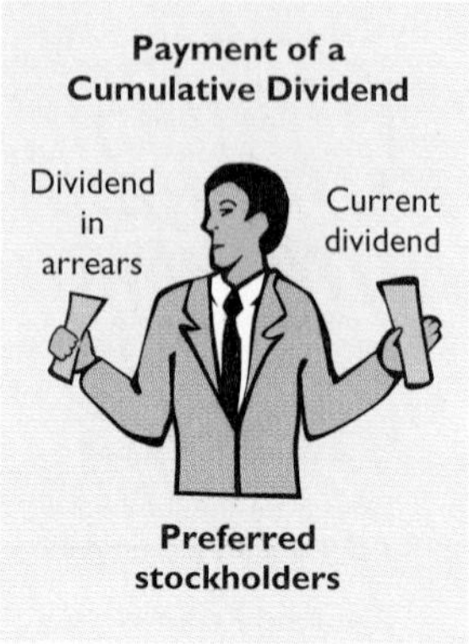

period of time, "Not meeting your obligations on something like that is a major black mark on your record." The accounting entries for preferred stock dividends are explained in Chapter 15.

LIQUIDATION PREFERENCE

Most preferred stocks also have a preference on corporate assets if the corporation fails. This feature provides security for the preferred stockholder. The preference to assets may be for the par value of the shares or for a specified liquidating value. **Commonwealth Edison's** preferred stock entitles the holders to receive $31.80 per share, plus accrued and unpaid dividends, in the event of involuntary liquidation. The liquidation preference establishes the respective claims of creditors and preferred stockholders.

CONVERTIBLE PREFERRED STOCK

Preferred stock is enhanced as an investment by adding a conversion privilege. **Convertible preferred stock** provides for the exchange of preferred stock into common stock, at a specified ratio, at the stockholder's option.

Convertible preferred stock is purchased by investors who want the greater security of a preferred stock, but who also want to be able to capture the market value of the common stock if it increases significantly. To illustrate, assume that Ross Industries issues, at par value, 1,000 shares of $100 par value convertible preferred stock. One share of preferred is convertible into 10 shares of $5 par value common (current price $9 per share). At this point, holders of the preferred would not want to convert. Their preferred stock is worth $100,000 (1,000 × $100), and the common stock is worth only $90,000 (10,000 × $9). However, if the price of the common stock increases above $10 per share, conversion would be advantageous for the preferred holders.

In recording the conversion, it is customary to transfer the amount paid in on the preferred stock to appropriate common stock accounts. To illustrate, assume that the 1,000 shares of Ross Industries $100 par preferred are issued at $105 and are converted into 10,000 shares of common stock ($5 par) when the market values per share of the two classes of stock are $101 and $12, respectively. The entry to record the conversion is:

A	=	L	+	SE
				−100,000
				−5,000
				+50,000
				+55,000

Preferred Stock	100,000	
Paid-in Capital in Excess of Par Value—Preferred Stock	5,000	
Common Stock		50,000
Paid-in Capital in Excess of Par Value—Common Stock		55,000
(To record conversion of 1,000 shares of preferred stock into 10,000 shares of $5 par value common stock)		

The market values of the shares at the time of the transaction are not considered in recording the transaction. The reason is that the exchange of shares is made directly through the corporation, and the corporation has not received any assets equal to fair market value. **Therefore, the conversion of preferred stock does not result in either gain or loss to the corporation.** If the preferred stock was issued for more than its par value, the paid-in capital in excess of the par value on the preferred stock should be eliminated.

CALLABLE PREFERRED STOCK

Many preferred stocks are issued with a call feature. A **callable preferred stock** grants the issuing corporation the right to purchase the stock from stockholders at specified future dates and prices. The call feature enables a corporation to eliminate the preferred stock when it is advantageous to do so. The **call (or redemption) price** is frequently slightly above the par or stated value of the shares. Often shares that are callable are also convertible. Sometimes companies will call their preferred shares to induce investors to convert those preferred shares into common stock.

STATEMENT PRESENTATION AND ANALYSIS

STUDY OBJECTIVE 6

Prepare a stockholders' equity section.

In the stockholders' equity section of the balance sheet, paid-in capital and retained earnings are reported. The specific sources of paid-in capital are identified. Within paid-in capital, two classifications are recognized:

1. **Capital stock.** This category consists of preferred and common stock. Preferred stock is shown before common stock because of its preferential rights. Par value, shares authorized, shares issued, and shares outstanding are reported for each class of stock.
2. **Additional paid-in capital.** This includes the excess of amounts paid in over par or stated value and paid-in capital from treasury stock.

PRESENTATION

The stockholders' equity section of Connally Inc. in Illustration 14-13 includes most of the accounts discussed in this chapter. The disclosures pertaining to Connally's common stock indicate that: 400,000 shares are issued; 100,000 shares are unissued (500,000 authorized less 400,000 issued); and 390,000 shares are outstanding (400,000 issued less 10,000 shares in treasury).

ALTERNATIVE TERMINOLOGY
Paid-in capital is sometimes called *contributed capital.*

Illustration 14-13
Stockholders' equity section

CONNALLY INC.
Balance Sheet (partial)

Stockholders' equity		
Paid-in capital		
Capital stock		
9% preferred stock, $100 par value, callable at $120, cumulative, 10,000 shares authorized, 6,000 shares issued and outstanding		$ 600,000
Common stock, no par, $5 stated value, 500,000 shares authorized, 400,000 shares issued, and 390,000 outstanding		2,000,000
Total capital stock		2,600,000
Additional paid-in capital		
In excess of par value—preferred stock	$ 30,000	
In excess of stated value—common stock	860,000	
From treasury stock	140,000	
Total additional paid-in capital		1,030,000
Total paid-in capital		3,630,000
Retained earnings		1,058,000
Total paid-in capital and retained earnings		4,688,000
Less: Treasury stock—common (10,000 shares) (at cost)		(80,000)
Total stockholders' equity		$4,608,000

In published annual reports, the individual sources of additional paid-in capital are often combined and reported as a single amount, as shown in Illustration 14-14. In addition, authorized shares are sometimes not reported.

Illustration 14-14

Published stockholders' equity section

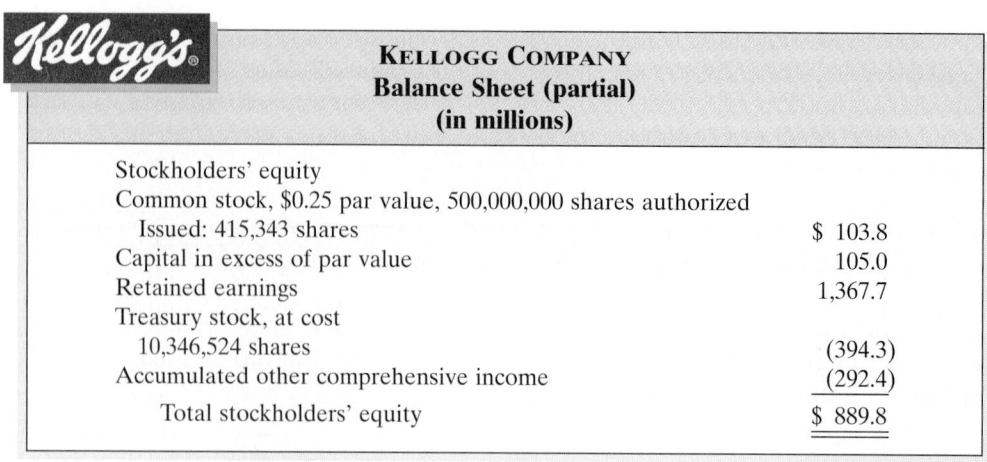

KELLOGG COMPANY
Balance Sheet (partial)
(in millions)

Stockholders' equity	
Common stock, $0.25 par value, 500,000,000 shares authorized	
Issued: 415,343 shares	$ 103.8
Capital in excess of par value	105.0
Retained earnings	1,367.7
Treasury stock, at cost	
10,346,524 shares	(394.3)
Accumulated other comprehensive income	(292.4)
Total stockholders' equity	$ 889.8

In practice, the term "capital surplus" is sometimes used in place of additional paid-in capital and "earned surplus" in place of retained earnings. The use of the term "surplus" suggests that an excess amount of funds is available. Such is not necessarily the case. Therefore, **the term "surplus" should not be employed in accounting**. Unfortunately, a number of financial statements still do use it.

ANALYSIS—BOOK VALUE PER SHARE

STUDY OBJECTIVE 7

Compute book value per share.

You have learned about a number of per share amounts in this chapter. Another per share amount of some importance is **book value per share**. It represents **the equity a common stockholder has in the net assets of the corporation** from owning one share of stock. Remember that the net assets of a corporation must be equal to total stockholders' equity. Therefore, the formula for computing book value per share when a company has only one class of stock outstanding is:

Illustration 14-15

Book value per share formula

Total Stockholders' Equity ÷ Number of Common Shares Outstanding = Book Value per Share

Thus, if Marlo Corporation has total stockholders' equity of $1,500,000 (common stock $1,000,000 and retained earnings $500,000) and 50,000 shares of common stock outstanding, book value per share is $30 ($1,500,000 ÷ 50,000).

When a company has both preferred and common stock, the computation of book value is a bit more complex. Since preferred stockholders have a prior claim on net assets over common stockholders, their equity must be deducted from total stockholders' equity. Then we can determine the stockholders' equity that applies to the common stock. The computation of book value per share involves the following steps.

1. **Compute the preferred stock equity.** This equity is equal to the sum of the call price of preferred stock plus any cumulative dividends in arrears. If the preferred stock does not have a call price, the par value of the stock is used.
2. **Determine the common stock equity.** Subtract the preferred stock equity from total stockholders' equity.

3. **Determine book value per share.** Divide common stock equity by shares of common stock outstanding.

Illustration

We will use the stockholders' equity section of Connally Inc. shown in Illustration 14-13. Connally's preferred stock is callable at $120 per share and cumulative. Assume that dividends on Connally's preferred stock were in arrears for one year, $54,000 (6,000 × $9). The computation of preferred stock equity (Step 1) is:

Illustration 14-16

Computation of preferred stock equity—Step 1

Call price (6,000 shares × $120)	$720,000
Dividends in arrears (6,000 shares × $9)	54,000
Preferred stock equity	**$774,000**

The computation of book value (Steps 2 and 3) is as follows.

Illustration 14-17

Computation of book value per share with preferred stock—Steps 2 and 3

Total stockholders' equity	$4,608,000
Less: Preferred stock equity	**774,000**
Common stock equity	**$3,834,000**
Shares of common stock outstanding	**390,000**
Book value per share ($3,834,000 ÷ 390,000)	**$9.83**

Note that we used the call price of $120 instead of the par value of $100. Note also that the paid-in capital in excess of par value of preferred stock, $30,000, **is not assigned to the preferred stock equity**. Preferred stockholders ordinarily do not have a right to amounts paid-in in excess of par value. Therefore, such amounts are assigned to the common stock equity in computing book value.

Book Value versus Market Value

Be sure you understand that **book value per share may not equal market value per share**. Book value generally is based on recorded costs. Market value reflects the subjective judgments of thousands of stockholders and prospective investors about a company's potential for future earnings and dividends. Market value per share may exceed book value per share, but that fact does not necessarily mean that the stock is overpriced. The correlation between book value and the annual range of a company's market value per share is often remote, as indicated by the following recent data.

Illustration 14-18

Book and market values compared

Company	Book Value (year-end)	Market Range (for year)
Limited, Inc.	$9.99	$30.50–$50.13
H. J. Heinz Company	$5.02	$44.56–$61.75
Cisco Systems	$3.57	$21.94–$67.06
Lands' End	$9.82	$28.00–$83.50

Book value per share **is useful** in determining the trend of a stockholder's per share equity in a corporation. It is also significant in many contracts and in court cases where the rights of individual parties are based on cost information.

BEFORE YOU GO ON...

REVIEW IT

1. Identify the classifications within the paid-in capital section and the totals that are stated in the stockholders' equity section of a balance sheet.
2. What is the method for computing book value per share when there is (a) only one class of stock and (b) both preferred and common stock?

A LOOK BACK AT OUR FEATURE STORY

Refer back to the Feature Story about **Ford Motor Company** at the beginning of the chapter, and answer the following questions.

1. Why did Henry Ford originally choose to form a corporation rather than a sole proprietorship?
2. Why did Ford Motor Company repurchase all of its shares?
3. What advantages and disadvantages of being organized as a corporation are illustrated by Ford?

SOLUTION

1. Henry Ford wanted to take full advantage of mass-production. This would require large factories and many employees, which would in turn require considerable funds. The most efficient way to raise these funds was to issue stock.
2. Ford Motor Company initiated a massive treasury stock purchase when Henry Ford's vision was not consistent with the wishes of the shareholders.
3. The history of Ford Motor Company illustrates a number of the strengths and weaknesses of being formed as a corporation. Forming a corporation allowed for more efficient access to funds, and thus more rapid expansion. This was critical because in the early 1900s, many companies were trying to build cars for the U.S. market.

   However, by issuing shares, Henry Ford relinquished control over the firm. This led to a collision in 1916 when he believed that it was in the company's best interest to retain funds in the firm rather than to pay dividends. To the extent that outside shareholders are not as well-informed as a corporation's managers, the shareholders may force management to do things that hinder the firm's success.

THE NAVIGATOR

DEMONSTRATION PROBLEM

Additional Demonstration Problem

The Rolman Corporation is authorized to issue 1,000,000 shares of $5 par value common stock. In its first year, the company has the following stock transactions.

Jan. 10	Issued 400,000 shares of stock at $8 per share.
July 1	Issued 100,000 shares of stock for land. The land had an asking price of $900,000. The stock is currently selling on a national exchange at $8.25 per share.
Sept. 1	Purchased 10,000 shares of common stock for the treasury at $9 per share.
Dec. 1	Sold 4,000 shares of the treasury stock at $10 per share.

Instructions

(a) Journalize the transactions.

(b) Prepare the stockholders' equity section assuming the company had retained earnings of $200,000 at December 31.

SOLUTION TO DEMONSTRATION PROBLEM

(a) Jan. 10	Cash	3,200,000	
	Common Stock		2,000,000
	Paid-in Capital in Excess of Par Value		1,200,000
	(To record issuance of 400,000 shares of $5 par value stock)		
July 1	Land	825,000	
	Common Stock		500,000
	Paid-in Capital in Excess of Par Value		325,000
	(To record issuance of 100,000 shares of $5 par value stock for land)		
Sept. 1	Treasury Stock	90,000	
	Cash		90,000
	(To record purchase of 10,000 shares of treasury stock at cost)		
Dec. 1	Cash	40,000	
	Treasury Stock		36,000
	Paid-in Capital from Treasury Stock		4,000
	(To record sale of 4,000 shares of treasury stock above cost)		

ACTION PLAN

- When common stock has a par value, credit Common Stock for par value.
- Use fair market value in a noncash transaction.
- Debit and credit the Treasury Stock account at cost.
- Record differences between the cost and selling price of treasury stock in stockholders' equity accounts, not as gains or losses.

(b)

ROLMAN CORPORATION
Balance Sheet (partial)

Stockholders' equity		
Paid-in capital		
Capital stock		
Common stock, $5 par value, 1,000,000 shares authorized, 500,000 shares issued, 494,000 shares outstanding		$2,500,000
Additional paid-in capital		
In excess of par value	$1,525,000	
From treasury stock	4,000	
Total additional paid-in capital		1,529,000
Total paid-in capital		4,029,000
Retained earnings		200,000
Total paid-in capital and retained earnings		4,229,000
Less: Treasury stock (6,000 shares)		(54,000)
Total stockholders' equity		$4,175,000

SUMMARY OF STUDY OBJECTIVES

1. ***Identify the major characteristics of a corporation.*** The major characteristics of a corporation are separate legal existence, limited liability of stockholders, transferable ownership rights, ability to acquire capital, continuous life, corporation management, government regulations, and additional taxes.

2. ***Differentiate between paid-in capital and retained earnings.*** Paid-in capital is the total amount paid in on capital stock. It is often referred to as contributed capital. Retained earnings is net income retained in a corporation. It is often referred to as earned capital.

3. ***Record the issuance of common stock.*** When the issuance of common stock for cash is recorded, the par value of the shares is credited to Common Stock. The portion of the proceeds that is above or below par value is recorded in a separate paid-in capital account. When no-par common stock has a stated value, the entries are similar to those for par value stock. When no-par stock does not have a stated value, the entire proceeds from the issue become legal capital and are credited to Common Stock.

4. ***Explain the accounting for treasury stock.*** The cost method is generally used in accounting for treasury stock. Under this approach, Treasury Stock is debited at the price paid to reacquire the shares. The same amount is credited to Treasury Stock when the shares are sold. The difference between the sales price and cost is recorded in stockholders' equity accounts, not in income statement accounts.

5. ***Differentiate preferred stock from common stock.*** Preferred stock has contractual provisions that give it priority over common stock in certain areas. Typically, preferred stockholders have a preference (1) to dividends and (2) to assets in liquidation. They usually do not have voting rights. Also, preferred stock may be convertible and/or callable. A convertible preferred stock entitles the holder to convert those shares to common stock in a specified ratio. The callable feature grants to the issuing corporation the right to purchase the stock from stockholders at specified future dates and prices.

6. ***Prepare a stockholders' equity section.*** In the stockholders' equity section, paid-in capital and retained earnings are reported and specific sources of paid-in capital are identified. Within paid-in capital, two classifications are shown: capital stock and additional paid-in capital. If a corporation has treasury stock, the cost of treasury stock is deducted from total paid-in capital and retained earnings to obtain total stockholders' equity.

7. ***Compute book value per share.*** Book value per share represents the equity a common stockholder has in the net assets of a corporation from owning one share of stock. When there is only common stock outstanding, the formula for computing book value is: Total stockholders' equity ÷ Number of common shares outstanding = Book value per share.

THE NAVIGATOR

Key Term Matching Activity

GLOSSARY

Authorized stock The amount of stock that a corporation is authorized to sell as indicated in its charter. (p. 567).

Book value per share The equity a common stockholder has in the net assets of the corporation from owning one share of stock. (p. 582).

By-laws The internal rules and procedures for conducting the affairs of a corporation. (p. 564).

Callable preferred stock Preferred stock that grants the issuer the right to purchase the stock from stockholders at specified future dates and prices. (p. 580).

Charter A document that creates a corporation. (p. 564).

Convertible preferred stock Preferred stock that provides for the exchange of preferred stock into common stock, at a specified ratio, at the stockholder's option. (p. 580).

Corporation A business organized as a legal entity separate and distinct from its owners under state corporation law. (p. 560).

Cumulative dividend A feature of preferred stock entitling the stockholder to receive current and unpaid prior-year dividends before common stockholders receive dividends. (p. 579).

Legal capital The amount per share of stock that must be retained in the business for the protection of corporate creditors. (p. 569).

No-par value stock Capital stock that has not been assigned a value in the corporate charter. (p. 569).

Organization costs Costs incurred in the formation of a corporation. (p. 565).

Outstanding stock Capital stock that has been issued and is being held by stockholders. (p. 576).

Paid-in capital Total amount of cash and other assets paid in to the corporation by stockholders in exchange for capital stock. (p. 569).

Par value stock Capital stock that has been assigned a value per share in the corporate charter. (p. 568).

Preferred stock Capital stock that has contractual preferences over common stock in certain areas. (p. 578).

Privately held corporation A corporation that has only a few stockholders and whose stock is not available for sale to the general public. (p. 561).

Publicly held corporation A corporation that may have thousands of stockholders and whose stock is regularly traded on a national securities exchange. (p. 560).

Retained earnings Net income that is retained in the corporation. (p. 569).

Stated value The amount per share assigned by the board of directors to no-par stock that becomes legal capital per share. (p. 569).

Treasury stock A corporation's own stock that has been issued, fully paid for, and reacquired by the corporation but not retired. (p. 574).

Chapter 14 Self-Test

SELF-STUDY QUESTIONS

Answers are at the end of the chapter.

(SO 1) **1.** Which of the following is *not* a major advantage of a corporation?
a. Separate legal existence.
b. Continuous life.
c. Government regulations.
d. Transferable ownership rights.

2. A major disadvantage of a corporation is: (SO 1)
a. limited liability of stockholders.
b. additional taxes.
c. transferable ownership rights.
d. none of the above.

3. Which of the following statements is *false*? (SO 2)
a. Ownership of common stock gives the owner a voting right.

b. The stockholders' equity section begins with paid-in capital.
c. The authorization of capital stock does not result in a formal accounting entry.
d. Legal capital per share applies to par value stock but not to no-par value stock.

(SO 2) 4. The account Retained Earnings is:
a. a subdivision of paid-in capital.
b. net income retained in the corporation.
c. reported as an expense in the income statement.
d. closed to capital stock.

(SO 3) 5. ABC Corporation issues 1,000 shares of $10 par value common stock at $12 per share. In recording the transaction, credits are made to:
a. Common Stock $10,000 and Paid-in Capital in Excess of Stated Value $2,000.
b. Common Stock $12,000.
c. Common Stock $10,000 and Paid-in Capital in Excess of Par Value $2,000.
d. Common Stock $10,000 and Retained Earnings $2,000.

(SO 4) 6. XYZ, Inc. sells 100 shares of $5 par value treasury stock at $13 per share. If the cost of acquiring the shares was $10 per share, the entry for the sale should include credits to:
a. Treasury Stock $1,000 and Paid-in Capital from Treasury Stock $300.
b. Treasury Stock $500 and Paid-in Capital from Treasury Stock $800.
c. Treasury Stock $1,000 and Retained Earnings $300.
d. Treasury Stock $500 and Paid-in Capital in Excess of Par Value $800.

7. In the stockholders' equity section, the cost of treasury stock is deducted from: (SO 4)
a. total paid-in capital and retained earnings.
b. retained earnings.
c. total stockholders' equity.
d. common stock in paid-in capital.

8. Preferred stock may have priority over common stock *except* in: (SO 5)
a. dividends.
b. assets in the event of liquidation.
c. conversion.
d. voting.

9. Which of the following is *not* reported under additional paid-in capital? (SO 6)
a. Paid-in capital in excess of par value.
b. Common stock.
c. Paid-in capital in excess of stated value.
d. Paid-in capital from treasury stock.

10. The ledger of JFK, Inc. shows common stock, common treasury stock, and no preferred stock. For this company, the formula for computing book value per share is: (SO 7)
a. Total paid-in capital and retained earnings divided by the number of shares of common stock issued.
b. Common stock divided by the number of shares of common stock issued.
c. Total stockholders' equity divided by the number of shares of common stock outstanding.
d. Total stockholders' equity divided by the number of shares of common stock issued.

THE NAVIGATOR

QUESTIONS

1. Lil Carmen, a student, asks your help in understanding the following characteristics of a corporation: (a) separate legal existence, (b) limited liability of stockholders, and (c) transferable ownership rights. Explain these characteristics to Lil.
2. (a) Your friend Mark Federia cannot understand how the characteristic of corporation management is both an advantage and a disadvantage. Clarify this problem for Mark.
   (b) Identify and explain two other disadvantages of a corporation.
3. (a) The following terms pertain to the forming of a corporation: (1) charter, (2) by-laws, and (3) organization costs. Explain the terms.
   (b) Sally Fields believes a corporation must be incorporated in the state in which its headquarters office is located. Is Sally correct? Explain.
4. What are the basic ownership rights of common stockholders in the absence of restrictive provisions?
5. (a) What are the two principal components of stockholders' equity?
   (b) What is paid-in capital? Give three examples.
6. How do the financial statements for a corporation differ from the statements for a proprietorship?
7. The corporate charter of Letterman Corporation allows the issuance of a maximum of 100,000 shares of common stock. During its first two years of operations, Letterman sold 70,000 shares to shareholders and reacquired 7,000 of these shares. After these transactions, how many shares are authorized, issued, and outstanding?
8. Which is the better investment—common stock with a par value of $5 per share, or common stock with a par value of $20 per share? Why?
9. What factors help determine the market value of stock?
10. What effect does the issuance of stock at a price above par value have on the issuer's net income? Explain.
11. Why is common stock usually not issued at a price that is less than par value?
12. Land appraised at $80,000 is purchased by issuing 1,000 shares of $20 par value common stock. The market price of the shares at the time of the exchange, based on active trading in the securities market, is $95 per share. Should the land be recorded at $20,000, $80,000, or $95,000? Explain.

13. For what reasons might a company like **IBM** repurchase some of its stock (treasury stock)?
14. Cederno, Inc. purchases 1,000 shares of its own previously issued $5 par common stock for $12,000. Assuming the shares are held in the treasury, what effect does this transaction have on (a) net income, (b) total assets, (c) total paid-in capital, and (d) total stockholders' equity?
15. The treasury stock purchased in question 14 is resold by Cederno, Inc. for $14,500. What effect does this transaction have on (a) net income, (b) total assets, (c) total paid-in capital, and (d) total stockholders' equity?
16. (a) What are the principal differences between common stock and preferred stock?
    (b) Preferred stock may be cumulative. Discuss this feature.
    (c) How are dividends in arrears presented in the financial statements?
17. A preferred stockholder exercises her right to convert her convertible preferred stock into common stock. What effect does this have on the corporation's (a) total assets, (b) total liabilities, and (c) total stockholders' equity?
18. What is the formula for computing book value per share when a corporation has only common stock?
19. MCE Inc.'s common stock has a par value of $1, a book value of $29, and a current market value of $15. Explain why these amounts are all different.
20. Indicate how each of the following accounts should be classified in the stockholders' equity section.
    (a) Common stock
    (b) Paid-in capital in excess of par value
    (c) Retained earnings
    (d) Treasury stock
    (e) Paid-in capital from treasury stock
    (f) Paid-in capital in excess of stated value
    (g) Preferred stock

BRIEF EXERCISES

List the advantages and disadvantages of a corporation. (SO 1)

BE14-1 Ron Weiland is studying for his accounting midterm examination. Identify for Ron the advantages and disadvantages of the corporate form of business organization.

Prepare closing entries for a corporation. (SO 2)

BE14-2 At December 31, Chavez Corporation reports net income of $575,000. Prepare the entry to close net income.

Prepare entries for issuance of par value common stock. (SO 3)

BE14-3 On May 10, Walters Corporation issues 1,000 shares of $10 par value common stock for cash at $16 per share. Journalize the issuance of the stock.

Prepare entries for issuance of no-par value common stock. (SO 3)

BE14-4 On June 1, Rickey Martin Inc. issues 2,000 shares of no-par common stock at a cash price of $7 per share. Journalize the issuance of the shares assuming the stock has a stated value of $1 per share.

Prepare entries for issuance of stock in a noncash transaction. (SO 3)

BE14-5 Henning Inc.'s $10 par value common stock is actively traded at a market value of $15 per share. Henning issues 5,000 shares to purchase land advertised for sale at $85,000. Journalize the issuance of the stock in acquiring the land.

Prepare entries for treasury stock transactions. (SO 4)

BE14-6 On July 1, Iron Mountain Corporation purchases 500 shares of its $5 par value common stock for the treasury at a cash price of $8 per share. On September 1, it sells 300 shares of the treasury stock for cash at $11 per share. Journalize the two treasury stock transactions.

Prepare entries for issuance of preferred stock. (SO 5)

BE14-7 Omar Inc. issues 5,000 shares of $100 par value preferred stock for cash at $112 per share. Journalize the issuance of the preferred stock.

Prepare stockholders' equity section. (SO 6)

BE14-8 Alzado Corporation has the following accounts at December 31: Common Stock, $10 par, 5,000 shares issued, $50,000; Paid-in Capital in Excess of Par Value $10,000; Retained Earnings $39,000; and Treasury Stock—Common, 500 shares, $11,000. Prepare the stockholders' equity section of the balance sheet.

Compute book value per share. (SO 7)

BE14-9 The balance sheet for Tanner Inc. shows the following: total paid-in capital and retained earnings $870,000, total stockholders' equity $830,000, common stock issued 44,000 shares, and common stock outstanding 40,000 shares. Compute the book value per share.

EXERCISES

Journalize issuance of common stock. (SO 3)

E14-1 During its first year of operations, Bono Corporation had the following transactions pertaining to its common stock.

Jan. 10 Issued 70,000 shares for cash at $5 per share.
July 1 Issued 40,000 shares for cash at $7 per share.

Instructions

(a) Journalize the transactions, assuming that the common stock has a par value of $5 per share.

(b) Journalize the transactions, assuming that the common stock is no-par with a stated value of $1 per share.

Journalize issuance of common and preferred stock and purchase of treasury stock. (SO 3, 4, 5)

E14-2 Armada Co. had the following transactions during the current period.

Mar. 2	Issued 5,000 shares of $1 par value common stock to attorneys in payment of a bill for $26,000 for services rendered in helping the company to incorporate.
June 12	Issued 60,000 shares of $1 par value common stock for cash of $375,000.
July 11	Issued 1,000 shares of $100 par value preferred stock for cash at $108 per share.
Nov. 28	Purchased 2,000 shares of treasury stock for $80,000.

Instructions

Journalize the transactions.

Journalize noncash common stock transactions. (SO 3)

E14-3 As an auditor for the CPA firm of Arnez and Ball, you encounter the following situations in auditing different clients.

1. Desi Corporation is a closely held corporation whose stock is not publicly traded. On December 5, the corporation acquired land by issuing 5,000 shares of its $20 par value common stock. The owners' asking price for the land was $120,000, and the fair market value of the land was $113,000.
2. Lucille Corporation is a publicly held corporation whose common stock is traded on the securities markets. On June 1, it acquired land by issuing 20,000 shares of its $10 par value stock. At the time of the exchange, the land was advertised for sale at $250,000. The stock was selling at $12 per share.

Instructions

Prepare the journal entries for each of the situations above.

Journalize treasury stock transactions. (SO 4)

E14-4 On January 1, 2002, the stockholders' equity section of Anita Corporation shows: Common stock ($5 par value) $1,500,000; paid-in capital in excess of par value $1,000,000; and retained earnings $1,200,000. During the year, the following treasury stock transactions occurred.

Mar. 1	Purchased 50,000 shares for cash at $15 per share.
July 1	Sold 10,000 treasury shares for cash at $17 per share.
Sept. 1	Sold 8,000 treasury shares for cash at $14 per share.

Instructions

(a) Journalize the treasury stock transactions.

(b) Restate the entry for September 1, assuming the treasury shares were sold at $11 per share.

Journalize preferred stock transactions and indicate statement presentation. (SO 5, 6)

E14-5 Abdella Corporation is authorized to issue both preferred and common stock. The par value of the preferred is $50. During the first year of operations, the company had the following events and transactions pertaining to its preferred stock.

Feb. 1	Issued 30,000 shares for cash at $51 per share.
July 1	Issued 12,000 shares for cash at $57 per share.

Instructions

(a) Journalize the transactions.

(b) Post to the stockholders' equity accounts.

(c) Indicate the financial statement presentation of the related accounts.

Journalize conversion of preferred stock (SO 5)

E14-6 Omar Corporation has 10,000 shares of $100 par value preferred stock outstanding. Each share is convertible into 5 shares of $15 par value common stock. When the market values of the two classes of stock are $110 and $25, respectively, 2,200 shares of preferred stock are converted into common stock. The preferred stock was issued at par.

Instructions

(a) Journalize the conversion of the 2,200 shares.

(b) Repeat (a) assuming that market values at conversion are $105 and $25, respectively.

(c) Repeat (a) assuming each share is convertible into 8 shares of $10 par value common stock.

Prepare correct entries for capital stock transactions.
(SO 3, 4, 5)

E14-7 Swartz Corporation recently hired a new accountant with extensive experience in accounting for partnerships. Because of the pressure of the new job, the accountant was unable to review his textbooks on the topic of corporation accounting. During the first month, the accountant made the following entries for the corporation's capital stock.

May 2	Cash	120,000	
	Capital Stock		120,000
	(Issued 10,000 shares of $5 par value common stock at $12 per share)		
10	Cash	600,000	
	Capital Stock		600,000
	(Issued 10,000 shares of $50 par value preferred stock at $60 per share)		
15	Capital Stock	14,000	
	Cash		14,000
	(Purchased 1,000 shares of common stock for the treasury at $14 per share)		
31	Cash	7,500	
	Capital Stock		2,500
	Gain on Sale of Stock		5,000
	(Sold 500 shares of treasury stock at $15 per share)		

Instructions

On the basis of the explanation for each entry, prepare the entry that should have been made for the capital stock transactions.

Answer questions about stockholders' equity section.
(SO 3, 4, 5, 6)

E14-8 The stockholders' equity section of Chile Corporation at December 31 is as follows.

CHILE CORPORATION
Balance Sheet (partial)

Paid-in capital	
Preferred stock, cumulative, 10,000 shares authorized, 6,000 shares issued and outstanding	$ 600,000
Common stock, no par, 750,000 shares authorized, 600,000 shares issued	1,800,000
Total paid-in capital	2,400,000
Retained earnings	1,258,000
Total paid-in capital and retained earnings	3,658,000
Less: Treasury stock (15,000 common shares)	(64,000)
Total stockholders' equity	$3,594,000

Instructions

From a review of the stockholders' equity section, as chief accountant, write a memo to the president of the company answering the following questions.

(a) How many shares of common stock are outstanding?
(b) Assuming there is a stated value, what is the stated value of the common stock?
(c) What is the par value of the preferred stock?
(d) If the annual dividend on preferred stock is $36,000, what is the dividend rate on preferred stock?
(e) If dividends of $72,000 were in arrears on preferred stock, what would be the balance in Retained Earnings?

Prepare a stockholders' equity section and compute book value.
(SO 6, 7)

E14-9 In a recent year, the stockholders' equity section of the **Aluminum Company of America (Alcoa)** showed the following (in alphabetical order): additional (paid-in) capital $680.5, common stock $88.3, preferred stock $66.0, and retained earnings $3,750.2. All dollar data are in millions.

The preferred stock has 660,000 shares authorized, with a par value of $100 and an annual $3.75 per share cumulative dividend preference. At December 31, all authorized preferred stock is issued and outstanding. There are 300 million shares of $1 par value common stock authorized, of which 88.3 million are outstanding at December 31.

Instructions

(a) Prepare the stockholders' equity section, including disclosure of all relevant data.

(b) Compute the book value per share of common stock, assuming there are no preferred dividends in arrears. (Round to two decimals.)

Classify stockholders' equity accounts.
(SO 6)

E14-10 The ledger of Springer Corporation contains the following accounts: Common Stock, Preferred Stock, Treasury Stock—Common, Paid-in Capital in Excess of Par Value—Preferred Stock, Paid-in Capital in Excess of Stated Value—Common Stock, Paid-in Capital from Treasury Stock, and Retained Earnings.

Instructions

Classify each account using the following table headings.

	Paid-in Capital			
Account	**Capital Stock**	**Additional**	**Retained Earnings**	**Other**

Compute book value per share with preferred stock.
(SO 7)

E14-11 At December 31, Castle Corporation has total stockholders' equity of $4,000,000. Included in this total are preferred stock $500,000 and paid-in capital in excess of par value—preferred stock $50,000. There are 10,000 shares of $50 par value 10% cumulative preferred stock outstanding. At year-end, 250,000 shares of common stock are outstanding.

Instructions

Compute the book value per share of common stock, under each of the following assumptions.

(a) There are no preferred dividends in arrears, and the preferred stock does not have a call price.

(b) Preferred dividends are 1 year in arrears, and the preferred stock has a call price of $60 per share.

PROBLEMS: SET A

Journalize stock transactions, post, and prepare paid-in capital section.
(SO 3, 5, 6)

Peachtree

P14-1A Tiger Corporation was organized on January 1, 2002. It is authorized to issue 10,000 shares of 8%, $100 par value preferred stock, and 500,000 shares of no-par common stock with a stated value of $2 per share. The following stock transactions were completed during the first year.

Jan. 10	Issued 80,000 shares of common stock for cash at $3 per share.
Mar. 1	Issued 5,000 shares of preferred stock for cash at $105 per share.
Apr. 1	Issued 24,000 shares of common stock for land. The asking price of the land was $90,000. The fair market value of the land was $80,000.
May 1	Issued 80,000 shares of common stock for cash at $4 per share.
Aug. 1	Issued 10,000 shares of common stock to attorneys in payment of their bill of $50,000 for services rendered in helping the company organize.
Sept. 1	Issued 10,000 shares of common stock for cash at $5 per share.
Nov. 1	Issued 1,000 shares of preferred stock for cash at $109 per share.

Instructions

(a) Journalize the transactions.

(b) Post to the stockholders' equity accounts. (Use J5 as the posting reference.)

(c) Prepare the paid-in capital section of stockholders' equity at December 31, 2002.

(c) Total paid-in capital $1,374,000

Journalize and post treasury stock transactions, and prepare stockholders' equity section.
(SO 4, 6)

P14-2A Gore Corporation had the following stockholders' equity accounts on January 1, 2002: Common Stock ($5 par) $500,000, Paid-in Capital in Excess of Par Value $200,000, and Retained Earnings $100,000. In 2002, the company had the following treasury stock transactions.

Mar. 1	Purchased 5,000 shares at $7 per share.
June 1	Sold 1,000 shares at $12 per share.
Sept. 1	Sold 2,000 shares at $9 per share.
Dec. 1	Sold 1,000 shares at $6 per share.

Gore Corporation uses the cost method of accounting for treasury stock. In 2002, the company reported net income of $50,000.

Instructions

(a) Journalize the treasury stock transactions, and prepare the closing entry at December 31, 2002, for net income.

(b) Treasury Stock $7,000
(c) Total stockholders' equity $851,000

(b) Open accounts for (1) Paid-in Capital from Treasury Stock, (2) Treasury Stock, and (3) Retained Earnings. Post to these accounts using J10 as the posting reference.

(c) Prepare the stockholders' equity section for Gore Corporation at December 31, 2002.

Journalize and post transactions, prepare stockholders' equity section, and compute book value.
(SO 2, 3, 4, 5, 6, 7)

P14-3A The stockholders' equity accounts of Notah Begay Corporation on January 1, 2002, were as follows.

Preferred Stock (12%, $50 par cumulative, 10,000 shares authorized)	$ 400,000
Common Stock ($1 stated value, 2,000,000 shares authorized)	1,000,000
Paid-in Capital in Excess of Par Value—Preferred Stock	100,000
Paid-in Capital in Excess of Stated Value—Common Stock	1,450,000
Retained Earnings	1,816,000
Treasury Stock—Common (10,000 shares)	40,000

During 2002, the corporation had the following transactions and events pertaining to its stockholders' equity.

Feb. 1	Issued 20,000 shares of common stock for $100,000.
Apr. 14	Sold 6,000 shares of treasury stock—common for $28,000.
Sept. 3	Issued 5,000 shares of common stock for a patent valued at $25,000.
Nov. 10	Purchased 1,000 shares of common stock for the treasury at a cost of $6,000.
Dec. 31	Determined that net income for the year was $402,000.

The preferred stock has a call price of $55 per share. No dividends were declared during the year.

Instructions

(a) Journalize the transactions and the closing entry for net income.

(b) Enter the beginning balances in the accounts, and post the journal entries to the stockholders' equity accounts. (Use J5 for the posting reference.)

(c) Total stockholders' equity $5,275,000

(c) Prepare a stockholders' equity section at December 31, 2002, including the disclosure of the preferred dividends in arrears.

(d) Compute the book value per share of common stock at December 31, 2002. (Round to two decimals.)

Journalize and post preferred stock transactions, and prepare stockholders' equity section.
(SO 2, 5, 6)

Peachtree

P14-4A Roberto Moreno Corporation is authorized to issue 10,000 shares of $100 par value, 10% convertible preferred stock and 125,000 shares of $5 par value common stock. On January 1, 2002, the ledger contained the following stockholders' equity balances.

Preferred Stock (5,000 shares)	$500,000
Paid-in Capital in Excess of Par Value—Preferred	75,000
Common Stock (70,000 shares)	350,000
Paid-in Capital in Excess of Par Value—Common	700,000
Retained Earnings	300,000

During 2002, the following transactions occurred.

Feb. 1	Issued 1,000 shares of preferred stock for land having a fair market value of $125,000.
Mar. 1	Issued 1,000 shares of preferred stock for cash at $125 per share.
July 1	Holders of 2,000 shares of preferred stock, purchased at $110 per share, converted the shares into common stock. Each share of preferred was convertible into 8 shares of common stock. Market values were preferred stock $122 and common stock $17.
Sept. 1	Issued 400 shares of preferred stock for a patent. The asking price of the patent was $60,000. Market values were preferred stock $125 and patent indeterminable.
Dec. 1	Holders of 1,000 shares of preferred stock, purchased at $130 per share, converted the shares into common stock. Each share of preferred was convertible into 8 shares of common stock. Market values were preferred stock $134 and common stock $16.
Dec. 31	Net income for the year was $260,000. No dividends were declared.

Instructions

(a) Journalize the transactions and the closing entry for net income.
(b) Enter the beginning balances in the accounts, and post the journal entries to the stockholders' equity accounts. (Use J2 for the posting reference.)
(c) Prepare a stockholders' equity section at December 31, 2002.

(c) Total stockholders' equity $2,485,000

Prepare stockholders' equity section and compute book value.
(SO 6, 7)

P14-5A The following stockholders' equity accounts arranged alphabetically are in the ledger of Servia Corporation at December 31, 2002.

Common Stock ($5 stated value)	$2,500,000
Paid-in Capital from Treasury Stock	10,000
Paid-in Capital in Excess of Stated Value—Common Stock	1,600,000
Paid-in Capital in Excess of Par Value—Preferred Stock	739,000
Preferred Stock (8%, $50 par, noncumulative)	800,000
Retained Earnings	2,448,000
Treasury Stock—Common (10,000 shares)	130,000

Instructions

(a) Prepare a stockholders' equity section at December 31, 2002.
(b) Compute the book value per share of the common stock, assuming the preferred stock has a call price of $60 per share.

(a) Total stockholders' equity $7,967,000
(b) $14.30

Prepare entries for stock transactions and stockholders' equity section.
(SO 3, 4, 5, 6)

P14-6A Bush Corporation has been authorized to issue 20,000 shares of $100 par value, 10%, noncumulative preferred stock and 1,000,000 shares of no-par common stock. The corporation assigned a $2.50 stated value to the common stock. At December 31, 2002, the ledger contained the following balances pertaining to stockholders' equity.

Preferred Stock	$ 120,000
Paid-in Capital in Excess of Par Value—Preferred	28,000
Common Stock	1,000,000
Paid-in Capital in Excess of Stated Value—Common	2,850,000
Treasury Stock—Common (1,000 shares)	11,000
Paid-in Capital from Treasury Stock	1,500
Retained Earnings	82,000

The preferred stock was issued for land having a fair market value of $148,000. All common stock issued was for cash. In November, 1,500 shares of common stock were purchased for the treasury at a per share cost of $11. In December, 500 shares of treasury stock were sold for $14 per share. No dividends were declared in 2002.

Instructions

(a) Prepare the journal entries for the:
  (1) Issuance of preferred stock for land.
  (2) Issuance of common stock for cash.
  (3) Purchase of common treasury stock for cash.
  (4) Sale of treasury stock for cash.
(b) Prepare the stockholders' equity section at December 31, 2002.

(b) Total stockholders' equity $4,070,500

PROBLEMS: SET B

Journalize stock transactions, post, and prepare paid-in capital section.
(SO 3, 5, 6)

P14-1B Argentina Corporation was organized on January 1, 2002. It is authorized to issue 20,000 shares of 6%, $50 par value preferred stock, and 500,000 shares of no-par common stock with a stated value of $1 per share. The following stock transactions were completed during the first year.

Jan. 10	Issued 100,000 shares of common stock for cash at $3 per share.
Mar. 1	Issued 10,000 shares of preferred stock for cash at $52 per share.
Apr. 1	Issued 25,000 shares of common stock for land. The asking price of the land was $90,000. The company's estimate of fair market value of the land was $85,000.
May 1	Issued 75,000 shares of common stock for cash at $4 per share.

Aug. 1 Issued 10,000 shares of common stock to attorneys in payment of their bill for $50,000 for services provided in helping the company organize.
Sept. 1 Issued 5,000 shares of common stock for cash at $6 per share.
Nov. 1 Issued 2,000 shares of preferred stock for cash at $54 per share.

Instructions

(a) Journalize the transactions.
(b) Post to the stockholders' equity accounts. (Use J1 as the posting reference.)
(c) Prepare the paid-in capital section of stockholders' equity at December 31, 2002.

(c) Total paid-in capital $1,393,000

Journalize and post treasury stock transactions, and prepare stockholders' equity section. (SO 4, 6)

P14-2B Hassan Corporation had the following stockholders' equity accounts on January 1, 2002: Common Stock ($1 par) $400,000, Paid-in Capital in Excess of Par Value $500,000, and Retained Earnings $100,000. In 2002, the company had the following treasury stock transactions.

Mar. 1 Purchased 5,000 shares at $6 per share.
June 1 Sold 1,000 shares at $10 per share.
Sept. 1 Sold 2,000 shares at $8 per share.
Dec. 1 Sold 1,000 shares at $5 per share.

Hassan Corporation uses the cost method of accounting for treasury stock. In 2002, the company reported net income of $50,000.

Instructions

(a) Journalize the treasury stock transactions, and prepare the closing entry at December 31, 2002, for net income.
(b) Open accounts for (1) Paid-in Capital from Treasury Stock, (2) Treasury Stock, and (3) Retained Earnings. Post to these accounts using J12 as the posting reference.
(c) Prepare the stockholders' equity section for Hassan Corporation at December 31, 2002.

(b) Treasury Stock $6,000
(c) Total stockholders' equity $1,051,000

Journalize and post transactions, prepare stockholders' equity section, and compute book value. (SO 2, 3, 4, 5, 6, 7)

P14-3B The stockholders' equity accounts of Chen Corporation on January 1, 2002, were as follows.

Preferred Stock (10%, $100 par noncumulative, 5,000 shares authorized)	$ 300,000
Common Stock ($5 stated value, 300,000 shares authorized)	1,000,000
Paid-in Capital in Excess of Par Value—Preferred Stock	20,000
Paid-in Capital in Excess of Stated Value—Common Stock	425,000
Retained Earnings	488,000
Treasury Stock—Common (5,000 shares)	40,000

During 2002, the corporation had the following transactions and events pertaining to its stockholders' equity.

Feb. 1 Issued 4,000 shares of common stock for $25,000.
Mar. 20 Purchased 1,000 additional shares of common treasury stock at $8 per share.
June 14 Sold 4,000 shares of treasury stock—common for $34,000.
Sept. 3 Issued 2,000 shares of common stock for a patent valued at $13,000.
Dec. 31 Determined that net income for the year was $240,000.

Instructions

(a) Journalize the transactions and the closing entry for net income.
(b) Enter the beginning balances in the accounts and post the journal entries to the stockholders' equity accounts. (Use J1 as the posting reference.)
(c) Prepare a stockholders' equity section at December 31, 2002.
(d) Compute the book value per share of common stock at December 31, 2002, assuming the preferred stock does not have a call price.

(c) Total stockholders' equity $2,497,000

Journalize and post preferred stock transactions, and prepare stockholders' equity section. (SO 2, 5, 6)

P14-4B Clinton Corporation is authorized to issue 10,000 shares of $100 par value, 10%, convertible preferred stock and 200,000 shares of $5 par value common stock. On January 1, 2002, the ledger contained the following stockholders' equity balances.

Preferred Stock (4,000 shares)	$400,000
Paid-in Capital in Excess of Par Value—Preferred	60,000
Common Stock (70,000 shares)	350,000
Paid-in Capital in Excess of Par Value—Common	700,000
Retained Earnings	300,000

During 2002, the following transactions occurred.

Feb. 1	Issued 1,000 shares of preferred stock for land having a fair market value of $125,000.
Mar. 1	Issued 1,000 shares of preferred stock for cash at $120 per share.
July 1	Holders of 2,000 shares of preferred stock purchased at $115 per share converted the shares into common stock. Each share of preferred was convertible into 10 shares of common stock. Market values were preferred stock $122 and common stock $15.
Sept. 1	Issued 400 shares of preferred stock for a patent. The asking price of the patent was $60,000. Market values were preferred stock $125 and patent, indeterminable.
Dec. 1	Holders of 1,000 shares of preferred stock purchased at $120 per share converted the shares into common stock. Each share of preferred was convertible into 10 shares of common stock. Market values were preferred stock $125 and common stock $16.
Dec. 31	Net income for the year was $210,000. No dividends were declared.

Instructions

(a) Journalize the transactions and the closing entry for net income.

(b) Enter the beginning balances in the accounts, and post the journal entries to the stockholders' equity accounts. (Use J2 as the posting reference.)

(c) Prepare a stockholders' equity section at December 31, 2002.

(c) Total stockholders' equity $2,315,000

Prepare stockholders' equity section and compute book value.
(SO 6, 7)

P14-5B The following stockholders' equity accounts arranged alphabetically are in the ledger of Iceland Corporation at December 31, 2002.

Common Stock ($10 stated value)	$1,500,000
Paid-in Capital from Treasury Stock	6,000
Paid-in Capital in Excess of Stated Value—Common Stock	920,000
Paid-in Capital in Excess of Par Value—Preferred Stock	288,400
Preferred Stock (8%, $100 par, noncumulative)	400,000
Retained Earnings	1,276,000
Treasury Stock—Common (8,000 shares)	88,000

Instructions

(a) Prepare a stockholders' equity section at December 31, 2002.

(b) Compute the book value per share of the common stock, assuming the preferred stock has a call price of $110 per share.

(a) Total stockholders' equity $4,302,400

BROADENING YOUR PERSPECTIVE

FINANCIAL REPORTING AND ANALYSIS

FINANCIAL REPORTING PROBLEM: Lands' End, Inc.

BYP14-1 The stockholders' equity section for **Lands' End, Inc.** is shown in Appendix A. You will also find data relative to this problem on other pages of the appendix.

Instructions

(a) What is the par or stated value per share of Lands' End's common stock?

(b) What percentage of Lands' End's authorized common stock was issued at January 28, 2000? (Round to the nearest full percentage.)

(c) How many shares of common stock were outstanding at January 28, 2000, and at January 29, 1999?

(d) What was book value per share at January 28, 2000, and at January 29, 1999?

(e) What was the high and low market price per share in the fourth quarter of fiscal 2000, as reported under Note 14?

COMPARATIVE ANALYSIS PROBLEM: Lands' End vs. Abercrombie & Fitch

LANDS' END DIRECT MERCHANTS

BYP14-2 **Lands' End's** financial statements are presented in Appendix A. **Abercrombie & Fitch's** financial statements are presented in Appendix B.

Instructions

- **(a)** Based on the information contained in these financial statements, compute the 2000 book value per share for each company.
- **(b)** Compare the market value per share for each company to the book value per share at year-end 2000. Assume that the market value of Abercrombie & Fitch's stock was $32.25 at year-end 2000.
- **(c)** Why are book value and market value per share different?

INTERPRETING FINANCIAL STATEMENTS: A Global Focus

BYP14-3 Investors with less than a controlling interest in a company are considered minority stockholders. The September 13, 1999, issue of *The Wall Street Journal* included an article by Namju Cho entitled "Minority Shareholders Lag in Emerging Markets."

Instructions

Read the article and answer the following questions.

- **(a)** What are three weaknesses of many companies in emerging markets that contribute to those companies' lack of response to stockholders?
- **(b)** What approach is Edward Schneider taking to try to improve the treatment of stockholders in Latin America?
- **(c)** Why is it in the interest of emerging markets to react to stockholder concerns?

EXPLORING THE WEB

www.wiley.com/college/weygandt

BYP 14-4 SEC filings of publicly traded companies are available to view online.

Address: **http//biz.yahoo.com/i** ***(or go to www.wiley.com/college/weygandt)***

Steps:

1. Pick a company and type in the company's name.
2. Choose **Quote**.

Instructions

Answer the following questions.

- **(a)** What company did you select?
- **(b)** What is its stock symbol?
- **(c)** What was the stock's trading range today?
- **(d)** What was the stock's trading range for the year?

CRITICAL THINKING

GROUP DECISION CASE

BYP14-5 The stockholders' meeting for Chow Corporation has been in progress for some time. The chief financial officer for Chow is presently reviewing the company's financial statements and is explaining the items that comprise the stockholders' equity section of the balance sheet for the current year. The stockholders' equity section of Chow Corporation at December 31, 2002, is as follows.

CHOW CORPORATION
Balance Sheet (partial)
December 31, 2002

Paid in capital		
Capital stock		
Preferred stock, authorized 1,000,000 shares cumulative, $100 par value, $8 per share, 6,000 shares issued and outstanding		$ 600,000
Common stock, authorized 5,000,000 shares, $1 par value, 3,000,000 shares issued, and 2,700,000 outstanding		3,000,000
Total capital stock		3,600,000
Additional paid-in capital		
In excess of par value—preferred stock	$ 50,000	
In excess of par value—common stock	25,000,000	
Total additional paid-in capital		25,050,000
Total paid-in capital		28,650,000
Retained earnings		900,000
Total paid-in capital and retained earnings		29,550,000
Less: Common treasury stock (300,000 shares)		9,300,000
Total stockholders' equity		$20,250,000

At the meeting, stockholders have raised a number of questions regarding the stockholders' equity section.

Instructions
With the class divided into groups, answer the following questions as if you were the chief financial officer for Chow Corporation.

(a) "What does the cumulative provision related to the preferred stock mean?"
(b) "I thought the common stock was presently selling at $29.75, but the company has the stock stated at $1 per share. How can that be?"
(c) "Why is the company buying back its common stock? Furthermore, the treasury stock has a debit balance because it is subtracted from stockholders' equity. Why is treasury stock not reported as an asset if it has a debit balance?"
(d) "Why is it necessary to show additional paid-in capital? Why not just show common stock at the total amount paid in?"

COMMUNICATION ACTIVITY

BYP14-6 Paul Tracey, your uncle, is an inventor who has decided to incorporate. Uncle Paul knows that you are an accounting major at U.N.O. In a recent letter to you, he ends with the question, "I'm filling out a state incorporation application. Can you tell me the difference in the following terms: (1) authorized stock, (2) issued stock, (3) outstanding stock, (4) preferred stock?"

Instructions
In a brief note, differentiate for Uncle Paul among the four different stock terms. Write the letter to be friendly, yet professional.

ETHICS CASE

BYP14-7 The R&D division of Nakona Chemical Corp. has just developed a chemical for sterilizing the vicious Brazilian "killer bees" which are invading Mexico and the southern states of the United States. The president of Nakona is anxious to get the chemical on the market to boost Nakona's profits. He believes his job is in jeopardy because of decreasing sales and profits. Nakona has an opportunity to sell this chemical in Central American countries, where the laws are much more relaxed than in the United States.

The director of Nakona's R&D division strongly recommends further testing in the laboratory for side-effects of this chemical on other insects, birds, animals, plants, and even humans. He cautions the president, "We could be sued from all sides if the chemical has tragic side-effects that we didn't even test for in the labs." The president answers, "We can't wait an additional year for your lab tests. We can avoid losses from such lawsuits by establishing a separate wholly owned corporation to shield Nakona Corp. from such lawsuits. We can't lose any more than our investment in the new corporation, and we'll invest just the patent covering this chemical. We'll reap the benefits if the chemical works and is safe, and avoid the losses from lawsuits if it's a disaster." The following week Nakona creates a new wholly owned corporation called Marques Inc., sells the chemical patent to it for $10, and watches the spraying begin.

Instructions

(a) Who are the stakeholders in this situation?
(b) Are the president's motives and actions ethical?
(c) Can Nakona shield itself against losses of Marques Inc.?

Answers to Self-Study Questions

1. c **2.** b **3.** d **4.** b **5.** c **6.** a **7.** a **8.** d **9.** b **10.** c

Answers to *Lands' End* Review It Question 3, p. 573 and Question 4, p. 577

LANDS' END DIRECT MERCHANTS

3. The par value of Lands' End's common stock is $0.001 per share. On January 28, 2000, Lands' End had issued 40,221,000 shares.

4. Treasury shares held at Lands' End on January 28, 2000, were 10,070,868, and on January 29, 1999, were 10,317,118, as shown in "Note 2. Shareholders' Investment."

Remember to go back to the Navigator box on the chapter-opening page and check off your completed work.

CORPORATIONS: DIVIDENDS, RETAINED EARNINGS, AND INCOME REPORTING

15

THE NAVIGATOR ✓

- Understand *Concepts for Review* ❑
- Read *Feature Story* ❑
- Scan *Study Objectives* ❑
- Read *Preview* ❑
- Read text and answer *Before You Go On* *p.* 609 ❑ *p.* 614 ❑ *p.* 619 ❑ *p.* 622 ❑
- Work *Demonstration Problem* ❑
- Review *Summary of Study Objectives* ❑
- Answer *Self-Study Questions* ❑
- Complete *Assignments* ❑

CONCEPTS FOR REVIEW

Before studying this chapter, you should know or, if necessary, review:

a. Why it is important to distinguish between paid-in capital and retained earnings. (Ch. 14, p. 569)

b. The significance of legal capital in accounting for capital stock transactions. (Ch. 14, pp. 568–569)

c. The form and content of the stockholders' equity section of the balance sheet. (Ch. 14, pp. 581–582)

d. The rights of cumulative preferred stockholders to dividends. (Ch. 14, pp. 579–580)

☑ THE NAVIGATOR

FEATURE STORY

What's Cooking?

What major U.S. corporation got its start almost 30 years ago with a waffle iron? Hint: It doesn't sell food. Another hint: Swoosh. Another hint: "Just do it." That's right, **Nike**. In 1971 Nike cofounder Bill Bowerman put a piece of rubber into a kitchen waffle iron, and the trademark waffle sole was born.

Nike was cofounded by Bowerman and Phil Knight, a member of Bowerman's University of Oregon track team. Each began in the shoe business independently during the early 1960s. Bowerman got his start by making hand-crafted running shoes for his university track team. Knight, after completing graduate school, started a small business importing low-cost, high-quality shoes from Japan. In 1964 the two joined forces. Each contributed $500, and formed Blue Ribbon Sports, a partnership. At first they marketed Japanese shoes. It wasn't until 1971 that the company began manufacturing its own line of shoes. With the new shoes came a new corporate name—Nike—the Greek goddess of victory. It is hard to imagine that the company that now enlists promoters such as Tiger Woods, Mia Hamm, and Michael Jordan at one time had part-time employees selling shoes out of car trunks.

By 1980 Nike was sufficiently established that it was able to issue its first stock to the public. In that same year it also created a stock ownership program that allowed its employees to share in the company's success. Since then Nike has enjoyed phenomenal growth. Sales in 1999 were $8.8 billion. Its dividend per share to shareholders has increased every year for the last 11 years.

Nike is not alone in its quest for the top of the sport shoe world. Reebok pushes Nike every step of the way. It's a race to see who will dominate the sports shoe industry. Currently Nike is outpacing Reebok. But is the race over? Probably not. The shoe market is fickle, with new styles becoming popular almost daily. Reebok's unwillingness to give up the race was boldly stated in its recent ad campaign, "This is my planet." Whether one of these two giants does eventually take control of the planet remains to be seen. Meanwhile the shareholders sit anxiously in the stands as this Olympic-size drama unfolds.

☑ THE NAVIGATOR

www.nike.com
www.reebok.com

STUDY OBJECTIVES

After studying this chapter, you should be able to:

1. Prepare the entries for cash dividends and stock dividends.
2. Identify the items that are reported in a retained earnings statement.
3. Prepare and analyze a comprehensive stockholders' equity section.
4. Describe the form and content of corporation income statements.
5. Indicate the statement presentation of material items not typical of regular operations.
6. Compute earnings per share.

☑ THE NAVIGATOR

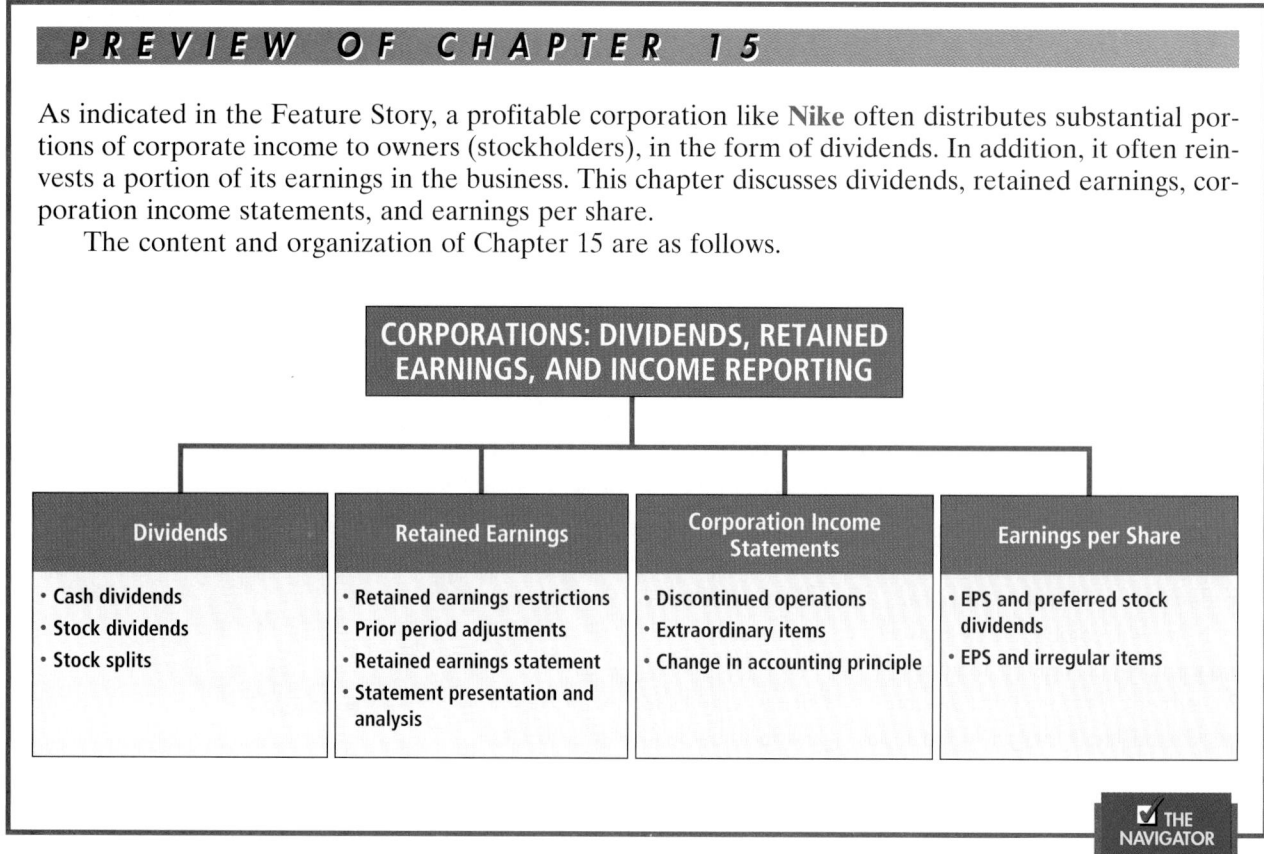

PREVIEW OF CHAPTER 15

As indicated in the Feature Story, a profitable corporation like **Nike** often distributes substantial portions of corporate income to owners (stockholders), in the form of dividends. In addition, it often reinvests a portion of its earnings in the business. This chapter discusses dividends, retained earnings, corporation income statements, and earnings per share.

The content and organization of Chapter 15 are as follows.

CORPORATIONS: DIVIDENDS, RETAINED EARNINGS, AND INCOME REPORTING

- **Dividends**
  - Cash dividends
  - Stock dividends
  - Stock splits
- **Retained Earnings**
  - Retained earnings restrictions
  - Prior period adjustments
  - Retained earnings statement
  - Statement presentation and analysis
- **Corporation Income Statements**
  - Discontinued operations
  - Extraordinary items
  - Change in accounting principle
- **Earnings per Share**
  - EPS and preferred stock dividends
  - EPS and irregular items

THE NAVIGATOR

DIVIDENDS

STUDY OBJECTIVE 1

Prepare the entries for cash dividends and stock dividends.

A **dividend is a distribution by a corporation to its stockholders on a pro rata (proportional) basis.** Potential buyers and sellers of stock are very interested in a company's dividend policies and practices. Dividends can take four forms: cash, property, scrip (a promissory note to pay cash), or stock. Cash dividends predominate in practice. Also, stock dividends are declared with some frequency. These two forms of dividends will be the focus of discussion in this chapter.

Dividends may be expressed in two ways: (1) as a percentage of the par or stated value of the stock, or (2) as a dollar amount per share. In the financial press, **dividends are generally reported quarterly as a dollar amount per share.** For example, **Boeing Company's** quarterly dividend rate is 14 cents a share, **Ford Motor Company's** is 50 cents, and **Nike's** is 12 cents.

CASH DIVIDENDS

A **cash dividend** is a pro rata distribution of cash to stockholders. For a corporation to pay a cash dividend, it must have:

1. **Retained earnings.** The legality of a cash dividend depends on the laws of the state in which the company is incorporated. Payment of cash dividends from retained earnings is legal in all states. In general, cash dividend distributions based only on common stock (legal capital) are illegal. Statutes vary considerably with respect to cash dividends based on paid-in capital in excess of par or stated value. Many states permit such dividends. A dividend declared out of paid-in capital is termed a **liquidating dividend**. The amount originally paid in by stockholders is being reduced or "liquidated" by such a dividend.

2. **Adequate cash.** The legality of a dividend and the ability to pay a dividend are two different things. For example, **Nike**, with retained earnings of $3,067 million, could legally declare a dividend of $3,067 million. But Nike's cash balance is only $198 million. In order to pay a $3,067 million dividend, Nike would need to raise additional cash through the sale of other assets or through additional financing.

   Before declaring a cash dividend, a company's board of directors must carefully consider both current and future demands on the company's cash resources. In some cases, current liabilities may make a cash dividend inappropriate. In other cases, a major plant expansion program may warrant only a relatively small dividend.
3. **A declaration of dividends.** A company does not pay dividends unless its board of directors decides to do so, at which point the board "declares" the dividend. The board of directors has full authority to determine the amount of income to be distributed in the form of a dividend and the amount to be retained in the business. Dividends do not accrue like interest on a note payable, and they are not a liability until declared.

The amount and timing of a dividend are important issues. The payment of a large cash dividend could lead to liquidity problems for the enterprise. On the other hand, a small dividend or a missed dividend may cause unhappiness among stockholders. Many of them expect to receive a reasonable cash payment from the company on a periodic basis. Many companies declare and pay cash dividends quarterly.

ACCOUNTING IN ACTION *Business Insight*

In order to remain in business, companies must honor their interest payments to creditors, bankers, and bondholders. The payment of dividends to stockholders is another matter. Many companies can survive, even thrive, without such payouts. In fact, some managements consider dividend payments unnecessary, or even harmful. Pay your creditors, by all means. But, fork over perfectly good cash to stockholders? "Why give money to those strangers?" is the response of one company president.

Investors must keep an eye on the company's dividend policy and understand what it may signal. For most companies, regular boosts in the face of irregular earnings can be a warning signal of financial trouble. Companies with high dividends and rising debt may be borrowing money to pay shareholders. Low dividends sometimes indicate an expectation by management of low future earnings. Or, they may indicate a policy of retaining earnings for corporate expansion that will result in a higher stock price in the future.

Entries for Cash Dividends

Three dates are important in connection with dividends: (1) the declaration date, (2) the record date, and (3) the payment date. Normally, there are two to four weeks between each date. Accounting entries are required on two of the dates—the declaration date and the payment date.

HELPFUL HINT
What is the effect of the *declaration* of a cash dividend on (1) total stockholders' equity, (2) total liabilities, (3) total assets? Answer: (1) Decrease, (2) increase, (3) no effect.

On the **declaration date**, the board of directors formally declares (authorizes) the cash dividend and announces it to stockholders. Declaration of a cash dividend **commits the corporation to a legal obligation**. The obligation is binding and cannot be rescinded. An entry is required to recognize the decrease in retained earnings and the increase in the liability Dividends Payable. To illustrate, assume that on December 1, 2002, the directors of Media General declare a 50¢ per share cash dividend on 100,000 shares of $10 par value common stock. The dividend is $50,000 (100,000 × 50¢). The entry to record the declaration is:

A	=	L	+	SE
		+50,000		−50,000

Declaration Date

Dec. 1	Retained Earnings	50,000	
	Dividends Payable		50,000
	(To record declaration of cash dividend)		

Dividends Payable is a current liability: it will normally be paid within the next several months.

Instead of debiting Retained Earnings, the account Dividends may be debited. This account provides additional information in the ledger. Also, a company may have separate dividend accounts for each class of stock. When a dividend account is used, its balance is transferred to Retained Earnings at the end of the year by a closing entry. Whichever account is used for the dividend declaration, the effect is the same: retained earnings is decreased and a current liability is increased. For homework problems, you should use the Retained Earnings account for recording dividend declarations.

At the **record date**, ownership of the outstanding shares is determined for dividend purposes. The records maintained by the corporation supply this information. In the interval between the declaration date and the record date, the corporation updates its stock ownership records. For Media General, the record date is December 22. No entry is required on this date because the corporation's liability recognized on the declaration date is unchanged.

HELPFUL HINT
Between the declaration date and record date, the number of shares outstanding should remain the same. The purpose of the record date is to identify the persons or entities that will receive the dividend, not to determine the amount of the dividend liability.

Record Date

Dec. 22	No entry necessary		

On the **payment date**, dividend checks are mailed to the stockholders and the payment of the dividend is recorded. Assuming that the payment date is January 20 for Media General, the entry on that date is:

A	=	L	+	SE
−50,000		−50,000		

Payment Date

Jan. 20	Dividends Payable	50,000	
	Cash		50,000
	(To record payment of cash dividend)		

Note that payment of the dividend reduces both current assets and current liabilities. It has no effect on stockholders' equity. The **cumulative effect** of the **declaration and payment** of a cash dividend is to **decrease both stockholders' equity and total assets**. Illustration 15-1 (on the next page) summarizes the three important dates associated with dividends.

Allocating Cash Dividends between Preferred and Common Stock

As explained in Chapter 14, preferred stock has priority over common stock in regard to dividends. Preferred stockholders must be paid any unpaid prior-year dividends before common stockholders receive dividends.

Illustration 15-1

Key dividend dates

To illustrate, assume that at December 31, 2002, IBR Inc. has 1,000 shares of 8%, $100 par value cumulative preferred stock. It also has 50,000 shares of $10 par value common stock outstanding. The dividend per share for preferred stock is $8 ($100 par value × 8%). The required annual dividend for preferred stock is therefore $8,000 (1,000 × $8). At December 31, 2002, the directors declare a $6,000 cash dividend. In this case, the entire dividend amount goes to preferred stockholders because of their dividend preference. The entry to record the declaration of the dividend is:

Dec. 31	Retained Earnings	6,000	
	Dividends Payable		6,000
	(To record $6 per share cash dividend to preferred stockholders)		

A	=	L	+	SE
		+6,000		−6,000

Because of the cumulative feature, dividends of $2 per share are in arrears on preferred stock for 2002. These dividends must be paid to preferred stockholders before any future dividends can be paid to common stockholders. Dividends in arrears should be disclosed in the financial statements.

At December 31, 2003, IBR declares a $50,000 cash dividend. The allocation of the dividend to the two classes of stock is as follows.

Illustration 15-2

Allocating dividends to preferred and common stock

Total dividend		$50,000
Allocated to preferred stock		
Dividends in arrears, 2002 (1,000 × $2)	**$2,000**	
2003 dividend (1,000 × $8)	**8,000**	10,000
Remainder allocated to common stock		$40,000

The entry to record the declaration of the dividend is:

Dec. 31	Retained Earnings	50,000	
	Dividends Payable		50,000
	(To record declaration of cash dividends of $10,000 to preferred stock and $40,000 to common stock)		

A	=	L	+	SE
		+50,000		−50,000

What if IBR's preferred stock were not cumulative? In that case preferred stockholders would have received only $8,000 in dividends in 2003. Common stockholders would have received $42,000.

STOCK DIVIDENDS

A **stock dividend** is a pro rata distribution to stockholders of the corporation's own stock. Whereas a cash dividend is paid in cash, a stock dividend is paid in stock. **A stock dividend results in a decrease in retained earnings and an increase in paid-in capital.** Unlike a cash dividend, a stock dividend does not decrease total stockholders' equity or total assets.

To illustrate, assume that you have a 2% ownership interest in Cetus Inc.; you own 20 of its 1,000 shares of common stock. If Cetus declares a 10% stock dividend, it would issue 100 shares (1,000 × 10%) of stock. You would receive 2 shares (2% × 100). Would your ownership interest change? No, it would remain at 2% (22 ÷ 1,100). **You now own more shares of stock, but your ownership interest has not changed.** Illustration 15-3 shows the effect of a stock dividend for stockholders.

Illustration 15-3

Effect of stock dividend for stockholders

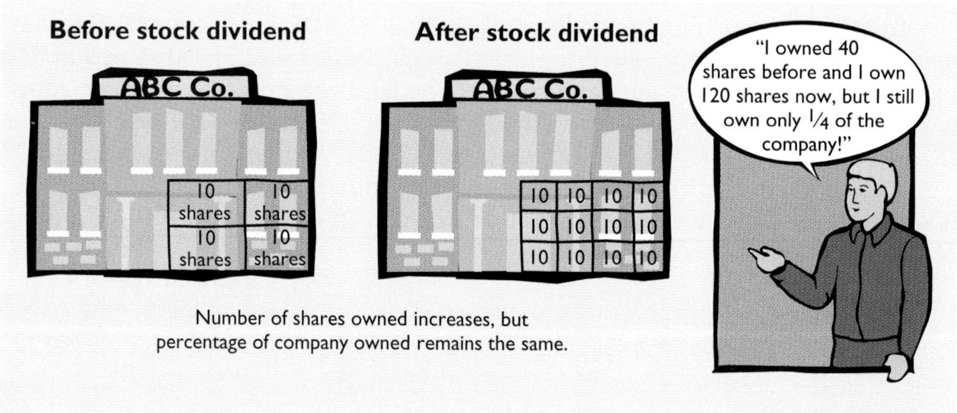

From the company's point of view, no cash has been disbursed, and no liabilities have been assumed by the corporation. What are the purposes and benefits of a stock dividend? Corporations issue stock dividends generally for one or more of the following reasons.

1. To satisfy stockholders' dividend expectations without spending cash.
2. To increase the marketability of the corporation's stock. When the number of shares outstanding increases, the market price per share decreases. Decreasing the market price of the stock makes it easier for smaller investors to purchase the shares.
3. To emphasize that a portion of stockholders' equity has been permanently reinvested in the business (and is unavailable for cash dividends).

The size of the stock dividend and the value to be assigned to each dividend share are determined by the board of directors when the dividend is declared. The per share amount must be at least equal to the par or stated value in order to meet legal requirements.

The accounting profession distinguishes between a **small stock dividend** (less than 20–25% of the corporation's issued stock) and a **large stock dividend** (greater than 20–25%). For small stock dividends, it recommends that the directors assign the **fair market value per share**. This treatment is based on the assumption that a small stock dividend will have little effect on the market price of the outstanding shares. Many stockholders consider small stock dividends to be distributions of earnings equal to the fair market value of the shares distributed. The amount to be assigned for a large stock dividend is not specified by the accounting profession. **Par or stated value per share** is normally assigned. Small stock dividends predominate in practice. Thus, we will illustrate only the entries for small stock dividends.

Entries for Stock Dividends

To illustrate the accounting for small stock dividends, assume that Medland Corporation has a balance of $300,000 in retained earnings. It declares a 10% stock dividend on its 50,000 shares of $10 par value common stock. The current fair market value of its stock is $15 per share. The number of shares to be issued is 5,000 (10% × 50,000). Therefore the total amount to be debited to Retained Earnings is $75,000 (5,000 × $15). The entry to record the declaration of the stock dividend is as follows.

Retained Earnings	75,000	
Common Stock Dividends Distributable		50,000
Paid-in Capital in Excess of Par Value		25,000
(To record declaration of 10% stock dividend)		

A	=	L	+	SE
				−75,000
				+50,000
				+25,000

Note that Retained Earnings is debited for the fair market value of the stock issued ($15 × 5,000). Common Stock Dividends Distributable is credited for the par value of the dividend shares ($10 × 5,000), and the excess over par ($5 × 5,000) is credited to Paid-in Capital in Excess of Par Value.

Common Stock Dividends Distributable is a **stockholders' equity account**. It is not a liability because assets will not be used to pay the dividend. If a balance sheet is prepared before the dividend shares are issued, the distributable account is reported under Paid-in capital, as an addition to common stock issued:

Paid-in capital		
Common stock	$500,000	
Common stock dividends distributable	**50,000**	$550,000

Illustration 15-4
Statement presentation of common stock dividends distributable

When the dividend shares are issued, Common Stock Dividends Distributable is debited, and Common Stock is credited as follows.

Common Stock Dividends Distributable	50,000	
Common Stock		50,000
(To record issuance of 5,000 shares in a stock dividend)		

A	=	L	+	SE
				−50,000
				+50,000

Effects of Stock Dividends

How do stock dividends affect stockholders' equity? They **change the composition of stockholders' equity**, because a portion of retained earnings is transferred to paid-in capital. However, **total stockholders' equity remains the same**. Stock dividends also have no effect on the par or stated value per share. But the number of shares outstanding increases, and the book value per share decreases. These effects are shown for Medland Corporation in Illustration 15-5.

Illustration 15-5

Stock dividend effects

	Before Dividend	After Dividend
Stockholders' equity		
Paid-in capital		
Common stock, $10 par	$500,000	$550,000
Paid-in capital in excess of par value	—	25,000
Total paid-in capital	500,000	575,000
Retained earnings	300,000	225,000
Total stockholders' equity	**$800,000**	**$800,000**
Outstanding shares	**50,000**	**55,000**
Book value per share	**$ 16.00**	**$ 14.55**

In this example, total paid-in capital is increased by $75,000, and retained earnings is decreased by the same amount. Note also that total stockholders' equity remains unchanged at $800,000.

STOCK SPLITS

A stock split, like a stock dividend, involves the issuance of additional shares to stockholders according to their percentage ownership. **A stock split results in a reduction in the par or stated value per share.** The purpose of a stock split is to increase the marketability of the stock by lowering its market value per share. A lower market value also makes it easier for the corporation to issue additional stock.

The effect of a split on market value is generally inversely proportional to the size of the split. For example, after a recent 2-for-1 stock split, the market value of **Nike's** stock fell from $111 to approximately $55. The lower market value stimulated market activity, and within one year the stock was trading above $100 again.

HELPFUL HINT

A stock split changes the par value per share but does not affect any balances in stockholders' equity.

In a stock split, the number of shares is increased in the same proportion that par or stated value per share is decreased. For example, in a 2-for-1 split, one share of $10 par value stock is exchanged for two shares of $5 par value stock. **A stock split does not have any effect on total paid-in capital, retained earnings, or total stockholders' equity.** But the number of shares outstanding increases and book value per share decreases. These effects are shown in Illustration 15-6 for Medland Corporation, assuming that it splits its 50,000 shares of common stock on a 2-for-1 basis.

Illustration 15-6

Stock split effects

	Before Stock Split	After Stock Split
Stockholders' equity		
Paid-in capital		
Common stock	$500,000	$500,000
Paid-in capital in excess of par value	-0-	-0-
Total paid-in capital	500,000	500,000
Retained earnings	300,000	300,000
Total stockholders' equity	**$800,000**	**$800,000**
Outstanding shares	**50,000**	**100,000**
Book value per share	**$16.00**	**$8.00**

A stock split does not affect the balances in any stockholders' equity accounts. Therefore **it is not necessary to journalize a stock split**.

The significant differences between stock splits and stock dividends are shown in Illustration 15-7.

Item	Stock Split	Stock Dividend
Total paid-in capital	No change	Increase
Total retained earnings	No change	Decrease
Total par value (common stock)	No change	Increase
Par value per share	Decrease	No change

Illustration 15-7
Differences between the effects of stock splits and stock dividends

ACCOUNTING IN ACTION *Business Insight*

A handful of U.S. companies have no intention of keeping their stock trading in a range accessible to mere mortals. These companies never split their stock, no matter how high their stock price gets. The king is investment company **Berkshire Hathaway's** Class A stock, which sells for a pricey $53,400—per share! The company's Class B stock is a relative bargain at roughly $1,700 per share. Other "premium" stocks are **A. D. Makepeace** at $9,000 and **Mechanics Bank** of Richmond, California, at $11,000.

BEFORE YOU GO ON...

REVIEW IT

1. What entries are made for cash dividends on (a) the declaration date, (b) the record date, and (c) the payment date?
2. Distinguish between a small and large stock dividend, and indicate the basis for valuing each kind of dividend.
3. Contrast the effects of a small stock dividend and a 2-for-1 stock split on (a) stockholders' equity, (b) outstanding shares, and (c) book value per share.

DO IT

Sing CD Company has had 5 years of record earnings. Due to this success, the market price of its 500,000 shares of $2 par value common stock has tripled from $15 per share to $45. During this period, paid-in capital remained the same at $2,000,000. Retained earnings increased from $1,500,000 to $10,000,000. President Joan Elbert is considering either (1) a 10% stock dividend or (2) a 2-for-1 stock split. She asks you to show the before-and-after effects of each option on (a) retained earnings and (b) book value per share.

ACTION PLAN

- Calculate the stock dividend's effect on retained earnings by multiplying the number of new shares times the market price of the stock (or par value for a large stock dividend).
- Recall that a stock dividend increases the number of shares without affecting total equity, thus decreasing the book value per share.
- Recall that a stock split only increases the number of shares outstanding and decreases the par value per share.

SOLUTION

(a) **(1)** The stock dividend amount is $2,250,000 [(500,000 × 10%) × $45]. The new balance in retained earnings is $7,750,000 ($10,000,000 − $2,250,000).

(2) The retained earnings balance after the stock split would be the same as it was before the split: $10,000,000.

(b) The book value effects are as follows:

	Original Balances	After Dividend	After Split
Paid-in capital	$ 2,000,000	$ 4,250,000	$ 2,000,000
Retained earnings	10,000,000	7,750,000	10,000,000
Total stockholders' equity	$12,000,000	$12,000,000	$12,000,000
Shares outstanding	500,000	550,000	1,000,000
Book value per share	$24	$21.82	$12

Related exercise material: BE15-2, BE15-3, E15-3, E15-4, E15-5, E15-6, and E15-7.

THE NAVIGATOR

RETAINED EARNINGS

STUDY OBJECTIVE 2

Identify the items that are reported in a retained earnings statement.

As you learned in Chapter 14, **retained earnings** is net income that is retained in the business. The balance in retained earnings is part of the stockholders' claim on the total assets of the corporation. It does not, though, represent a claim on any specific asset. Nor can the amount of retained earnings be associated with the balance of any asset account. For example, a $100,000 balance in retained earnings does not mean that there should be $100,000 in cash. The reason is that the cash resulting from the excess of revenues over expenses may have been used to purchase buildings, equipment, and other assets. To illustrate that retained earnings and cash may be quite different, Illustration 15-8 shows recent amounts of retained earnings and cash in selected companies.

Illustration 15-8

Retained earnings and cash balances

Company	(in millions) Retained Earnings	Cash
Walt Disney Co.	$12,281	$414
Sears, Roebuck and Co.	5,952	729
The Home Depot	7,941	168
Amazon.com	(882)	117

HELPFUL HINT

Remember that Retained Earnings is a stockholders' equity account, whose normal balance is a credit.

Remember from Chapter 14 that when a company has net profit, the net income that is retained in the business is recorded in retained earnings by means of a closing entry. This entry debits Income Summary and credits Retained Earnings.

However, when expenses exceed revenues, a **net loss** results. A net loss is debited to Retained Earnings in a closing entry. This is done even if it results in a debit balance in Retained Earnings. **Net losses are not debited to paid-in capital accounts.** To do so would destroy the distinction between paid-in and earned capital. A debit balance in Retained Earnings is identified as a **deficit**. It is reported as a deduction in the stockholders' equity section, as shown below.

Illustration 15-9

Stockholders' equity with deficit

Balance Sheet (partial)

Stockholders' equity	
Paid-in capital	
Common stock	$800,000
Retained earnings (deficit)	**(50,000)**
Total stockholders' equity	$750,000

RETAINED EARNINGS RESTRICTIONS

The balance in retained earnings is generally available for dividend declarations. Some companies state this fact. For example, in the notes to its financial statements, **Lockheed Martin Corporation** states:

LOCKHEED MARTIN CORPORATION
Notes to the Financial Statements

At December 31, retained earnings were unrestricted and available for dividend payments.

Illustration 15-10

Disclosure of unrestricted retained earnings

In some cases, there may be **retained earnings restrictions**. These make a portion of the retained earnings balance currently unavailable for dividends. Restrictions result from one or more of the following causes: legal, contractual, or voluntary.

1. **Legal restrictions.** Many states require a corporation to restrict retained earnings for the cost of treasury stock purchased. The restriction keeps intact the corporation's legal capital that is being temporarily held as treasury stock. When the treasury stock is sold, the restriction is lifted.
2. **Contractual restrictions.** Long-term debt contracts may restrict retained earnings as a condition for the loan. The restriction limits the use of corporate assets for payment of dividends. Thus, it increases the likelihood that the corporation will be able to meet required loan payments.
3. **Voluntary restrictions.** The board of directors may voluntarily create retained earnings restrictions for specific purposes. For example, the board may authorize a restriction for future plant expansion. By reducing the amount of retained earnings available for dividends, more cash may be available for the planned expansion.

Retained earnings restrictions are generally disclosed in the notes to the financial statements. For example, **Pratt & Lambert**, a leading producer of paint, had the following note in a recent financial statement.

PRATT & LAMBERT
Notes to the Financial Statements

Note D: Long-term Debt and Retained Earnings Loan agreements contain, among other covenants, a restriction on the payment of dividends, which limits future dividend payments to $20,565,000 plus 75% of future net income.

Illustration 15-11

Disclosure of restriction

PRIOR PERIOD ADJUSTMENTS

Suppose that a corporation's books have been closed and the financial statements have been issued. The corporation then discovers that a material error has been made in reporting net income of a prior year. How should this situation be recorded in the accounts and reported in the financial statements?

The correction of an error in previously issued financial statements is known as a **prior period adjustment**. The correction is made directly to Retained Earnings because the effect of the error is now in this account: The net income for the prior period has been recorded in retained earnings through the journalizing and posting of closing entries.

To illustrate, assume that General Microwave discovers in 2002 that it understated depreciation expense in 2001 by $300,000 due to computational errors. These errors overstated both net income for 2001 and the current balance in retained earnings. The entry for the prior period adjustment, assuming all tax effects are ignored, is as follows.

A	=	L	+	SE
−300,000				−300,000

	Debit	Credit
Retained Earnings	300,000	
Accumulated Depreciation		300,000
(To adjust for understatement of depreciation in a prior period)		

A debit to an income statement account in 2002 would be incorrect because the error pertains to a prior year.

Prior period adjustments are reported in the retained earnings statement.[1] They are added (or deducted, as the case may be) from the beginning retained earnings balance. This results in an adjusted beginning balance. Assuming General Microwave has a beginning balance of $800,000 in retained earnings, the prior period adjustment is reported as follows.

Illustration 15-12

Statement presentation of prior period adjustments

General Microwave
Retained Earnings Statement (partial)

Balance, January 1, as reported	$800,000
Correction for overstatement of net income in prior period (depreciation error)	**(300,000)**
Balance, January 1, as adjusted	$500,000

Again, reporting the correction in the current year's income statement would be incorrect because it applies to a prior year's income statement.

RETAINED EARNINGS STATEMENT

The **retained earnings statement** shows the changes in retained earnings during the year. The statement is prepared from the Retained Earnings account. Transactions and events that affect retained earnings are tabulated in account form as shown in Illustration 15-13.

Illustration 15-13

Debits and credits to retained earnings

Retained Earnings

Debits	Credits
1. Net loss	1. Net income
2. Prior period adjustments for overstatement of net income	2. Prior period adjustments for understatement of net income
3. Cash dividends and stock dividends	
4. Some disposals of treasury stock	

As indicated, net income increases retained earnings, and a net loss decreases retained earnings. Prior period adjustments may either increase or decrease retained earnings. Both cash dividends and stock dividends decrease retained earnings.

[1] A complete retained earnings statement is shown in Illustration 15-14 on the next page.

The circumstances under which treasury stock transactions decrease retained earnings are explained in Chapter 14, pages 576–579.

A complete retained earnings statement for Graber Inc., based on assumed data, is as follows.

Illustration 15-14

Retained earnings statement

GRABER INC.
Retained Earnings Statement
For the Year Ended December 31, 2002

Balance, January 1, as reported		$1,050,000
Correction for understatement of net income in prior period (inventory error)		50,000
Balance, January 1, as adjusted		1,100,000
Add: Net income		360,000
		1,460,000
Less: Cash dividends	$100,000	
Stock dividends	200,000	300,000
Balance, December 31		$1,160,000

STATEMENT PRESENTATION AND ANALYSIS

Presentation

STUDY OBJECTIVE 3

Prepare and analyze a comprehensive stockholders' equity section.

The stockholders' equity section of Graber Inc.'s balance sheet is presented in Illustration 15-15. Note the following: (1) "Common stock dividends distributable" is shown under "Capital stock," in "Paid-in capital." (2) A retained earnings restriction is disclosed in the notes.

Illustration 15-15

Comprehensive stockholders' equity section

GRABER INC.
Balance Sheet (partial)

Stockholders' equity		
Paid-in capital		
Capital stock		
9% Preferred stock, $100 par value, cumulative, callable at $120, 10,000 shares authorized, 6,000 shares issued and outstanding		$ 600,000
Common stock, no par, $5 stated value, 500,000 shares authorized, 400,000 shares issued and 390,000 outstanding	$2,000,000	
Common stock dividends distributable	**50,000**	2,050,000
Total capital stock		2,650,000
Additional paid-in capital		
In excess of par value—preferred stock	30,000	
In excess of stated value—common stock	1,050,000	
Total additional paid-in capital		1,080,000
Total paid-in capital		3,730,000
Retained earnings **(see Note R)**		1,160,000
Total paid-in capital and retained earnings		4,890,000
Less: Treasury stock—common (10,000 shares)		80,000
Total stockholders' equity		$4,810,000

Note R: Retained earnings is restricted for the cost of treasury stock, $80,000.

INTERNATIONAL NOTE

In Switzerland, there are no specific disclosure requirements for stockholders' equity. But Swiss companies typically disclose separate categories of capital on the balance sheet.

Instead of presenting a detailed stockholders' equity section in the balance sheet and a retained earnings statement, many companies prepare a **stockholders' equity statement**. This statement shows the changes in each stockholders' equity account and in total that have occurred during the year. An example of a stockholders' equity statement is illustrated in **Lands' End's** financial statements in Appendix A.

Analysis

Profitability from the viewpoint of the common stockholder can be measured by the **return on common stockholders' equity**. This ratio shows how many dollars of net income were earned for each dollar invested by the stockholders. It is computed by dividing net income available to common stockholders (which is net income minus preferred stock dividends) by average common stockholders' equity. To illustrate, **Lands' End's** beginning-of-the-year and end-of-the-year common stockholders' equity were \$242.5 and \$296.2 million respectively. Its net income was \$48.0 million, and no preferred stock was outstanding. The return on common stockholders' equity ratio is computed as follows.

Illustration 15-16

Return on common stockholders' equity ratio and computation

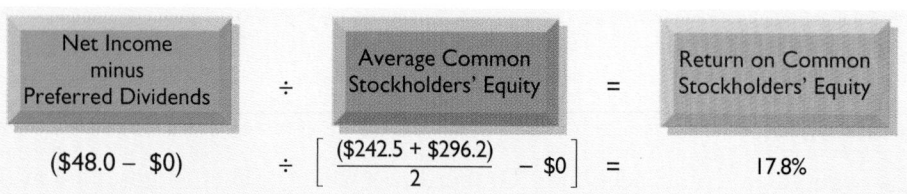

Net Income minus Preferred Dividends	÷	Average Common Stockholders' Equity	=	Return on Common Stockholders' Equity
(\$48.0 − \$0)	÷	$\left[\frac{(\$242.5 + \$296.2)}{2} - \$0\right]$	=	17.8%

As shown above, if a company has preferred stock, the amount of **preferred dividends** is deducted from net income to compute income available to common stockholders. Also, the par value of preferred stock is deducted from total average stockholders' equity to arrive at the amount of common stockholders' equity.

BEFORE YOU GO ON...

REVIEW IT

1. How are retained earnings restrictions generally reported?
2. What is a prior period adjustment, and how is it reported?
3. What are the principal sources of debits and credits to Retained Earnings?
4. How are stock dividends distributable reported in the stockholders' equity section?
5. Explain the return on common stockholders' equity ratio.

DO IT

Vega Corporation has retained earnings of \$5,130,000 on January 1, 2002. During the year, Vega earns \$2,000,000 of net income. It declares and pays a \$250,000 cash dividend. In 2002, Vega records an adjustment of \$180,000 due to the understatement of 2001 depreciation expense from a mathematical error. Prepare a retained earnings statement for 2002.

ACTION PLAN

- Recall that a retained earnings statement begins with retained earnings, as reported at the end of the previous year.
- Add or subtract any prior period adjustments to arrive at the adjusted beginning figure.
- Add net income and subtract dividends declared to arrive at the ending balance in retained earnings.

SOLUTION

VEGA CORPORATION Retained Earnings Statement For the Year Ended December 31, 2002	
Balance, January 1, as reported	$5,130,000
Correction for overstatement of net income in prior period (depreciation error)	(180,000)
Balance, January 1, as adjusted	4,950,000
Add: Net income	2,000,000
	6,950,000
Less: Cash dividends	250,000
Balance, December 31	$6,700,000

Related exercise material: BE15-4 and E15-8.

THE NAVIGATOR

CORPORATION INCOME STATEMENTS

STUDY OBJECTIVE 4

Describe the form and content of corporation income statements.

Income statements for **corporations are the same as the statements for proprietorships or partnerships except for one thing: the reporting of income taxes**. For income tax purposes, corporations are a separate legal entity. As a result, **income tax expense** is reported in a separate section of the corporation income statement before net income. The condensed income statement for Leads Inc. in Illustration 15-17 shows a typical presentation. Note that the corporation reports income before income taxes as one line item and income tax expense as another.

Illustration 15-17

Income statement with income taxes

LEADS INC. Income Statement For the Year Ended December 31, 2002	
Sales	$800,000
Cost of goods sold	600,000
Gross profit	200,000
Operating expenses	50,000
Income from operations	150,000
Other revenues and gains	10,000
Other expenses and losses	(4,000)
Income before income taxes	**156,000**
Income tax expense	**46,800**
Net income	$109,200

HELPFUL HINT

Corporations may also use the single-step form of income statement discussed in Chapter 5.

Income tax expense and the related liability for income taxes payable are recorded as part of the adjusting process. Using the data above for Leads Inc., the adjusting entry for income tax expense at December 31, 2002, would be:

Income Tax Expense	46,800	
Income Taxes Payable		46,800
(To record income taxes for 2002)		

A	=	L	+	SE
		+46,800		−46,800

Another illustration of income taxes is presented in the income statement of **Lands' End** in Appendix A.

The income statements we have studied so far provide insight into a company's income-related activities. In studying such statements, the user may ask: (1) Are the results typical for this company? (2) Are the results a reasonable indicator of the company's future earnings?

To provide answers to these questions, accountants have concluded that **material items not typical of regular operations** should also be reported. These items are reported in the income statement immediately before net income. The nontypical items include (1) discontinued operations, (2) extraordinary items, and (3) changes in accounting principle. These "irregular" items are reported net of income taxes. Thus, the income tax expense (or tax savings) is shown for income before income taxes and for each of the listed irregular items. The general concept is "let the tax follow income or loss."

DISCONTINUED OPERATIONS

STUDY OBJECTIVE 5

Indicate the statement presentation of material items not typical of regular operations.

Discontinued operations refers to the disposal of a **significant segment** of a business. Examples are the cessation of an entire activity and the elimination of a major class of customers. **Kmart's** decision to terminate its interest in four business activities, including **PACE Membership Warehouse** and **PayLess Drug Stores Northwest**, was reported as discontinued operations. On the other hand, the phasing out of a model such as the **GM** Chevette or part of a line of business is not considered to be a disposal of a segment.

Following the disposal of a significant segment, the income statement should report both income from continuing operations and income (or loss) from discontinued operations. **The income (loss) from discontinued operations consists of two parts: the income (loss) from operations and the gain (loss) on disposal of the segment.**

To illustrate, assume that during 2002 Acro Energy Inc. has income before income taxes of $800,000. During 2002 Acro discontinued and sold its unprofitable chemical division. The loss in 2002 from chemical operations (net of $60,000 taxes) was $140,000. The loss on disposal of the chemical division (net of $30,000 taxes) was $70,000. Assuming a 30% tax rate on income, the income statement presentation is shown below.

Illustration 15-18

Statement presentation of discontinued operations

ACRO ENERGY INC.
Income Statement (partial)
For the Year Ended December 31, 2002

Income before income taxes		$800,000
Income tax expense		240,000
Income from continuing operations		560,000
Discontinued operations		
Loss from operations of chemical division, net of $60,000 income tax saving	**$140,000**	
Loss from disposal of chemical division, net of $30,000 income tax saving	**70,000**	**210,000**
Net income		$350,000

HELPFUL HINT

Observe the dual disclosures: (1) The results of operations of the discontinued division must be eliminated from the results of continuing operations. (2) The disposal of the operation must also be reported.

Note that the caption "Income from continuing operations" is used and that a new section "Discontinued operations" is added. **Within the new section, both the operating loss and the loss on disposal are reported net of applicable income taxes.** This presentation clearly indicates the separate effects of continuing operations and discontinued operations on net income.

EXTRAORDINARY ITEMS

Extraordinary items are events and transactions that meet two conditions: They are (1) **unusual in nature and** (2) **infrequent in occurrence.** To be "unusual," the item should be abnormal and only incidentally related to the company's customary activities. To be "infrequent," the item should not be reasonably expected to recur in the foreseeable future. Both criteria must be evaluated in terms of the company's operating environment. Thus, **Weyerhaeuser Co.** reported the $36 million in damages to its timberland caused by the volcanic eruption of Mount St. Helens as an extraordinary item. The eruption was both unusual and infrequent. In contrast, Florida-Citrus Company does not report frost damage to its citrus crop as an extraordinary item. Frost damage is not viewed as infrequent. Illustration 15-19 shows the classification of extraordinary and ordinary items.

Illustration 15-19

Examples of extraordinary and ordinary items

Extraordinary items

1. Effects of major casualties (acts of God), if rare in the area.

2. Expropriation (takeover) of property by a foreign government.

3. Effects of a newly enacted law or regulation, such as a condemnation action.

4. Destruction of property by fire or explosion.

Ordinary items

1. Effects of major casualties (acts of God), frequent in the area.

2. Write-down of inventories or write-off of receivables.

3. Losses attributable to labor strikes.

4. Gains or losses from sales of property, plant, or equipment.

ACCOUNTING IN ACTION *Business Insight*

In the recession of the early 1990s, many companies closed plants and reduced their work forces. The costs incurred in these activities are called plant restructuring costs. Such costs are reported as other expenses and losses in the income statement. They are not considered an extraordinary item because plant closings are neither unusual nor infrequent in many industries.

Plant restructuring costs often have a significant effect on net income. For example, **Union Pacific Corp.** had a $585 million after-tax charge, of which $492 million applied to the disposal of 7,100 miles of the Union Pacific Railroad.

Extraordinary items are reported net of taxes in a separate section of the income statement immediately below discontinued operations. To illustrate, assume that in 2002 a foreign government expropriated property held as an investment by Acro Energy Inc. If the loss is $70,000 before applicable income taxes of $21,000, the income statement will report a deduction of $49,000 as shown in Illustration 15-20.

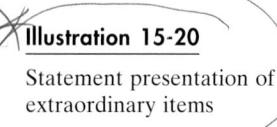

Illustration 15-20

Statement presentation of extraordinary items

ACRO ENERGY INC.
Income Statement (partial)
For the Year Ended December 31, 2002

Income before income taxes		$800,000
Income tax expense		240,000
Income from continuing operations		560,000
Discontinued operations		
Loss from operations of chemical division, net of $60,000 income tax saving	$140,000	
Loss from disposal of chemical division, net of $30,000 income tax saving	70,000	210,000
Income before extraordinary item		350,000
Extraordinary item		
Expropriation of investment, net of $21,000 income tax saving		**49,000**
Net income		$301,000

HELPFUL HINT
If there are no discontinued operations, the third line of the income statement would be labeled "Income before extraordinary item."

When there is an extraordinary item to report, the caption "Income before extraordinary item" is added immediately before the section for the extraordinary item. This presentation clearly indicates the effect of the extraordinary item on net income.

What if a transaction or event meets one (but not both) of the criteria for an extraordinary item? In that case it is reported under either "Other revenues and gains" or "Other expenses and losses" at its gross amount (not net of tax). This is true, for example, of gains (losses) resulting from the sale of property, plant, and equipment, as explained in Chapter 10. It has become quite common for companies to use the label "Non-recurring charges" for losses that do not meet the extraordinary item criteria.

CHANGE IN ACCOUNTING PRINCIPLE

For ease of comparison, financial statements are expected to be prepared on a basis **consistent** with the preceding period. Where a choice of accounting principles is available, the principle initially chosen should be consistently applied from period to period. A **change in accounting principle** occurs when the principle used in the current year is different from the one used in the preceding year. Examples include a change in depreciation methods (declining-balance to straight-line) and a change in inventory costing methods (FIFO to average cost). When is a change in accounting principle permitted? When two conditions are met: (1) Management can show that the new principle is preferable to the old principle, and (2) the effects of the change are clearly disclosed in the income statement.

When a change in accounting principle has occurred:

1. The new principle should be used in reporting the results of operations of the current year.

2. The cumulative effect of the change on all prior year income statements should be disclosed net of applicable taxes in a special section immediately preceding net income.

To illustrate, assume that at the beginning of 2002, Acro Energy Inc. changes from the straight-line method of depreciation to the declining-balance method for equipment purchased on January 1, 1999. The cumulative effect on prior year income statements (statements for 1999–2001) is to increase depreciation expense and decrease income before income taxes by $24,000. Assuming a 30 percent tax rate, the net-of-tax effect of the change is $16,800 ($24,000 × 70%). The income statement presentation for the change in accounting principle is shown in Illustration 15-21.

Illustration 15-21

Statement presentation of cumulative effect of change in accounting principle

ACRO ENERGY INC.
Income Statement (partial)
For the Year Ended December 31, 2002

Income before income taxes		$800,000
Income tax expense		240,000
Income from continuing operations		560,000
Discontinued operations		
Loss from operations of chemical division, net of $60,000 income tax saving	$140,000	
Loss from disposal of chemical division, net of $30,000 income tax saving	70,000	210,000
Income before extraordinary item and cumulative effect of change in accounting principle		350,000
Extraordinary item		
Expropriation of investment, net of $21,000 income tax saving		49,000
Cumulative effect of change in accounting principle		
Effect on prior years of change in depreciation method, net of $7,200 income tax saving		**16,800**
Net income		$284,200

HELPFUL HINT

If a company does not have either discontinued operations or extraordinary items, the label "Income before cumulative effect of change in accounting principle" is used in place of "Income from continuing operations."

The income statement for Acro Energy will also show depreciation expense for the current year. The amount is based on the new depreciation method. The caption "Income before extraordinary item and cumulative effect of change in accounting principle" is inserted immediately following the effects of discontinued operations. This presentation clearly indicates the cumulative effect of the change on prior years' income.

A complete income statement showing all material items not typical of regular operations is illustrated in the Demonstration Problem (pages 622–623).

ETHICS NOTE

Changes in accounting principle should result in financial statements that are more informative for statement users. They should not be used to artificially improve the reported performance or financial position of the corporation.

BEFORE YOU GO ON...

REVIEW IT

1. What is the unique feature of a corporation income statement?
2. What are the similarities and differences in reporting material items not typical of regular operations?
3. Did **Lands' End** report any of the three types of irregular items in its 2000 income statement? The answer to this question is provided on page 637.

LANDS' END DIRECT MERCHANTS

DO IT

In its proposed 2002 income statement, AIR Corporation reports income before income taxes $400,000, extraordinary loss from fire $100,000, income taxes (30%) $90,000, and net income $210,000. Prepare a correct income statement, beginning with income before income taxes.

ACTION PLAN

- Recall that a fire loss is unusual because it meets the criteria of being both unusual and infrequent.
- Disclose the income tax effect of each component of income, beginning with income before any irregular items.
- Report irregular items net of any income tax effect.

SOLUTION

AIR CORPORATION
Income Statement (partial)

Income before income taxes	$400,000
Income tax expense (30%)	120,000
Income before extraordinary item	280,000
Extraordinary loss from fire, net of $30,000 income tax saving	70,000
Net income	$210,000

Related exercise material: BE15-6, BE15-7, BE15-8, E15-12, and E15-13.

THE NAVIGATOR

EARNINGS PER SHARE

STUDY OBJECTIVE 6

Compute earnings per share.

Earnings data are frequently reported in the financial press. They are widely used by stockholders and potential investors in evaluating the profitability of a company. A convenient measure of earnings is **earnings per share (EPS)**, which indicates the net income earned by each share of outstanding **common stock**.

EPS AND PREFERRED DIVIDENDS

When a corporation has both preferred and common stock, the current year's dividend declared on preferred stock is subtracted from net income to arrive at **income available to common stockholders**. The formula for computing EPS is:

Illustration 15-22

Earnings per share

Net Income minus Preferred Dividends ÷ Weighted Average of Common Shares Outstanding = Earnings per Share

To illustrate, assume that Rally Inc. reports net income of $211,000 on its 102,500 weighted average common shares.[2] During the year it also declares a $6,000 dividend on its preferred stock. Therefore, the amount Rally has available

[2] The calculation of the weighted average of common shares outstanding is discussed in advanced accounting courses.

for common stock dividends is $205,000 ($211,000 − $6,000). Earnings per share is $2 ($205,000 ÷ 102,500). If the preferred stock is cumulative, the dividend for the current year is deducted whether or not it is declared. Remember that **earnings per share is reported only for common stock.**

Investors often attempt to link earnings per share to the market price per share of a company's stock.[3] Because of the importance of earnings per share, most companies are required to report it on the face of the income statement. Generally this amount is simply reported below net income on the statement. For Rally Inc. the presentation would be:

Illustration 15-23

Basic earnings per share disclosure

RALLY INC.
Income Statement (partial)

Net income	$211,000
Earnings per share	**$2.00**

ACCOUNTING IN ACTION Business Insight

When a company publicly announces its latest earnings per share figure, a change in the company's stock price will often result. The change in stock price will be most pronounced if the company's net income figure differs from what investors were expecting. When **Yahoo!** recently announced earnings per share that exceeded investor expectations, its stock price jumped 14 percent in a single day. When retail giant **Costco Wholesale Corporation** announced earnings per share only 1 cent below analysts' expectations, its stock price fell 22 percent in a single day. To avoid "earnings surprises" and the resultant wide swings in share prices, companies continually try to keep investors informed.

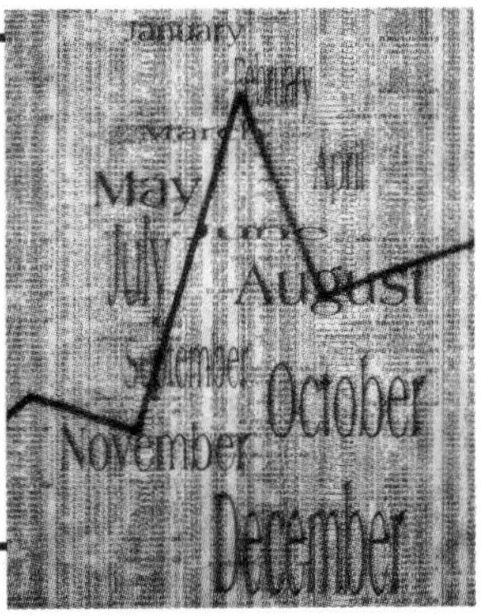

EPS AND IRREGULAR ITEMS

When the income statement contains any of the irregular items described earlier, EPS should be disclosed for each component. Assuming that Acro Energy had 100,000 shares of common stock outstanding during the year, the additional EPS disclosures for the income statement in Illustration 15-21 would be as shown below.

Illustration 15-24

Additional earnings per share disclosures

ACRO ENERGY INC.
Income Statement (partial)
For the Year Ended December 31, 2002

Net income	$284,200
Earnings per share	
Income from continuing operations	**$5.60**
Loss from discontinued operations	**(2.10)**
Income before extraordinary item and cumulative effect of change in accounting principle	**3.50**
Extraordinary loss	**(.49)**
Cumulative effect of change in accounting principle	**(.17)**
Net income	**$2.84**

[3]The ratio of the market price per share to the earnings per share is referred to as the *price-earnings (P-E) ratio.* This ratio is reported in *The Wall Street Journal* and in other newspapers for common stocks listed on major stock exchanges.

These disclosures enable decision makers to recognize the effects on EPS of income from continuing operations, as separate from income (or loss) from irregular items. **Earnings per share from continuing operations is generally the most useful per share amount.** It represents the results of continuing and ordinary business activity. Thus, it provides the best basis for predicting future operating results.

BEFORE YOU GO ON...

REVIEW IT

1. Explain the components of the formula for computing earnings per share when there is only common stock and outstanding shares are unchanged during the year.
2. What effects may preferred stock have on the formula for computing earnings per share?

A LOOK BACK AT OUR FEATURE STORY

Refer back to the Feature Story about **Nike** at the beginning of the chapter, and answer the following questions.

1. Nike's stock has split numerous times in recent years. What is the likely reason for these splits?
2. Prepare the quarterly journal entry (accounts and amount) recorded by a Nike shareholder when he or she receives a dividend of $1,000 from Nike.
3. Nike has increased its cash dividend per share every year for the past 11 years. What issues must it consider when deciding the level of the dividend payment?

SOLUTION

1. Nike's stock experienced a rapid increase in value. To keep the stock in an affordable price range for the average investor, management has split the stock a number of times.
2. The entry to record receipt of a dividend each quarter is:

Cash	1,000	
Dividend Revenue		1,000
(To record quarterly dividend revenue)		

3. Nike should consider the adequacy of its cash, the adequacy of its retained earnings, the level of its future earnings, and its ability to maintain the dividend level in the future.

THE NAVIGATOR

DEMONSTRATION PROBLEM

Additional Demonstration Problem

The events and transactions of Dever Corporation for the year ending December 31, 2002, resulted in the following data.

Cost of goods sold	$2,600,000
Net sales	4,400,000
Other expenses and losses	9,600
Other revenues and gains	5,600
Selling and administrative expenses	1,100,000
Income from operations of plastics division	70,000
Gain from disposal of plastics division	500,000
Loss from tornado disaster (extraordinary loss)	600,000
Cumulative effect of changing from straight-line depreciation to double-declining-balance (increase in depreciation expense)	300,000

Analysis reveals that:

1. All items are before the applicable income tax rate of 30%.
2. The plastics division was sold on July 1.
3. All operating data for the plastics division have been segregated.
4. There were 100,000 shares of common stock outstanding during the year.

Instructions
Prepare an income statement for the year, including the presentation of earnings per share data.

SOLUTION TO DEMONSTRATION PROBLEM

DEVER CORPORATION
Income Statement
For the Year Ended December 31, 2002

Net sales		$4,400,000
Cost of goods sold		2,600,000
Gross profit		1,800,000
Selling and administrative expenses		1,100,000
Income from operations		700,000
Other revenues and gains	$ 5,600	
Other expenses and losses	9,600	4,000
Income before income taxes		696,000
Income tax expense ($696,000 × 30%)		208,800
Income from continuing operations		487,200
Discontinued operations		
Income from operations of plastics division, net of $21,000 income taxes ($70,000 × 30%)	49,000	
Gain from disposal of plastics division, net of $150,000 income taxes ($500,000 × 30%)	350,000	399,000
Income before extraordinary item and cumulative effect of change in accounting principle		886,200
Extraordinary item		
Tornado loss, net of $180,000 income tax saving ($600,000 × 30%)		420,000
Cumulative effect of change in accounting principle		
Effect on prior years of change in depreciation method, net of $90,000 income tax saving ($300,000 × 30%)		210,000
Net income		$256,200
Earnings per share		
Income from continuing operations		$4.87
Gain from discontinued operations		3.99
Income before extraordinary item and cumulative effect of change in accounting principle		8.86
Extraordinary loss		(4.20)
Cumulative effect of change in accounting principle		(2.10)
Net income		$2.56

ACTION PLAN

- Report material items not typical of operations in separate sections, net of taxes.
- Associate income taxes with the item that affects the taxes.
- Apply the corporate tax rate to income before income taxes to determine tax expense.
- Recall that all data presented in determining income before income taxes are the same as for unincorporated companies.

THE NAVIGATOR

SUMMARY OF STUDY OBJECTIVES

1. ***Prepare the entries for cash dividends and stock dividends.*** Entries for both cash and stock dividends are required at the declaration date and at the payment date. At the declaration date the entries are: cash dividend—debit Retained Earnings, and credit Dividends Payable; small stock dividend—debit Retained Earnings, credit Paid-in Capital in Excess of Par (or Stated) Value, and credit Common Stock Dividends Distributable. At the payment date, the entries for cash and stock dividends are: cash dividend—debit Dividends Payable and credit Cash; small stock dividend—debit Common Stock Dividends Distributable and credit Common Stock.

2. ***Identify the items that are reported in a retained earnings statement.*** Each of the individual debits and credits to retained earnings should be reported in the retained earnings statement. Additions consist of net income and prior period adjustments to correct understatements of prior years' net income. Deductions consist of net loss, adjustments to correct overstatements of prior years' net income, cash and stock dividends, and some disposals of treasury stock.

3. ***Prepare and analyze a comprehensive stockholders' equity section.*** A comprehensive stockholders' equity section includes all stockholders' equity accounts. It consists of two sections: paid-in capital and retained earnings. It should also include notes to the financial statements that explain any restrictions on retained earnings and any dividends in arrears. One measure of profitability is the return on common stockholders' equity. It is calculated by dividing net income minus preferred stock dividends by average common stockholders' equity.

4. ***Describe the form and content of corporation income statements.*** The form and content of corporation income statements are similar to the statements of proprietorships and partnerships with one exception: Income taxes or income tax expense must be reported in a separate section before net income in the corporation's income statement.

5. ***Indicate the statement presentation of material items not typical of regular operations.*** Material items not typical of regular operations are reported net of taxes in sections on the income statement immediately before net income. These items include (a) discontinued operations, (b) extraordinary items, and (c) changes in accounting principle.

6. ***Compute earnings per share.*** Earnings per share is computed by dividing net income by the weighted average number of common shares outstanding during the period. When preferred stock dividends exist, they must be deducted from net income in order to calculate EPS.

THE NAVIGATOR

Key Term Matching Activity

GLOSSARY

Cash dividend A pro rata distribution of cash to stockholders. (p. 602).

Change in accounting principle The use of a principle in the current year that is different from the one used in the preceding year. (p. 618).

Declaration date The date the board of directors formally declares a dividend and announces it to stockholders. (p. 603).

Deficit A debit balance in retained earnings. (p. 610).

Discontinued operations The disposal of a significant segment of a business. (p. 616).

Dividend A distribution by a corporation to its stockholders on a pro rata (proportional) basis. (p. 602).

Earnings per share The net income earned by each share of outstanding common stock. (p. 620).

Extraordinary items Events and transactions that are unusual in nature and infrequent in occurrence. (p. 617).

Liquidating dividend A dividend declared out of paid-in capital. (p. 602).

Payment date The date dividend checks are mailed to stockholders. (p. 604).

Prior period adjustment The correction of an error in previously issued financial statements. (p. 611).

Record date The date when ownership of outstanding shares is determined for dividend purposes. (p. 604).

Retained earnings Net income that is retained in the business. (p. 610).

Retained earnings restrictions Circumstances that make a portion of retained earnings currently unavailable for dividends. (p. 611).

Retained earnings statement A financial statement that shows the changes in retained earnings during the year. (p. 612).

Return on common stockholders' equity A measure of profitability that shows how many dollars of net income were earned for each dollar invested by the owners; computed as net income minus preferred dividends divided by average common stockholders' equity. (p. 614).

Stock dividend A pro rata distribution to stockholders of the corporation's own stock. (p. 606).

Stockholders' equity statement A statement that shows the changes in each stockholders' equity account and in total stockholders' equity during the year. (p. 614).

Stock split The issuance of additional shares of stock to stockholders according to their percentage ownership; is accompanied by a reduction in the par or stated value per share. (p. 608).

Chapter 15 Self-Test

SELF-STUDY QUESTIONS

Answers are at the end of the chapter.

(SO 1) 1. Entries for cash dividends are required on the:
   a. declaration date and the payment date.
   b. record date and the payment date.
   c. declaration date, record date, and payment date.
   d. declaration date and the record date.

(SO 1) 2. Which of the following statements about small stock dividends is true?
   a. A debit to Retained Earnings for the par value of the shares issued should be made.
   b. A small stock dividend decreases total stockholders' equity.
   c. Market value per share should be assigned to the dividend shares.
   d. A small stock dividend ordinarily will have no effect on book value per share of stock.

(SO 2) 3. All *but one* of the following is reported in a retained earnings statement. The exception is:
a. cash and stock dividends.
b. net income and net loss.
c. some disposals of treasury stock below cost.
d. sales of treasury stock above cost.

(SO 2) 4. A prior period adjustment is:
a. reported in the income statement as a nontypical item.
b. a correction of an error that is made directly to retained earnings.
c. reported directly in the stockholders' equity section.
d. reported in the retained earnings statement as an adjustment of the ending balance of retained earnings.

(SO 3) 5. In the stockholders' equity section, Common Stock Dividends Distributable is reported as a(n):
a. deduction from total paid-in capital and retained earnings.
b. addition to additional paid-in capital.
c. deduction from retained earnings.
d. addition to capital stock.

(SO 4) 6. Corporation income statements may be the same as the income statements for unincorporated companies *except* for:
a. gross profit.
b. income tax expense.
c. operating income.
d. net sales.

(SO 3) 7. The return on common stockholders' equity is defined as:
a. Net income divided by total assets.
b. Cash dividends divided by average common stockholders' equity.
c. Income available to common stockholders divided by average common stockholders' equity.
d. None of these is correct.

8. In reporting discontinued operations, the income statement should show in a special section: (SO 5)
a. gains and losses on the disposal of the discontinued segment.
b. gains and losses from operations of the discontinued segment.
c. Both (a) and (b).
d. Neither (a) nor (b).

9. The Rand Corporation has income before taxes of $400,000 and an extraordinary loss of $100,000. If the income tax rate is 25% on all items, the income statement should show income before extraordinary items and extraordinary items, respectively, of: (SO 5)
a. $325,000 and $100,000.
b. $325,000 and $75,000.
c. $300,000 and $100,000.
d. $300,000 and $75,000.

10. The income statement for Nadeen, Inc. shows income before income taxes $700,000, income tax expense $210,000, and net income $490,000. If Nadeen has 100,000 shares of common stock outstanding throughout the year, earnings per share is: (SO 6)
a. $7.00.
b. $4.90.
c. $2.10.
d. No correct answer is given.

THE NAVIGATOR

QUESTIONS

1. (a) What is a dividend? (b) "Dividends must be paid in cash." Do you agree? Explain.
2. Mike Horn maintains that adequate cash is the only requirement for the declaration of a cash dividend. Is Mike correct? Explain.
3. (a) Three dates are important in connection with cash dividends. Identify these dates, and explain their significance to the corporation and its stockholders.
   (b) Identify the accounting entries that are made for a cash dividend and the date of each entry.
4. De Masi Inc. declares a $40,000 cash dividend on December 31, 2002. The required annual dividend on preferred stock is $12,000. Determine the allocation of the dividend to preferred and common stockholders assuming the preferred stock is cumulative and dividends are 1 year in arrears.
5. Contrast the effects of a cash dividend and a stock dividend on a corporation's balance sheet.
6. Veena Gall asks, "Since stock dividends don't change anything, why declare them?" What is your answer to Veena?
7. Noriega Corporation has 20,000 shares of $10 par value common stock outstanding when it announces a 2-for-1 split. Before the split, the stock had a market price of $140 per share. After the split, how many shares of stock will be outstanding? What will be the approximate market price per share?
8. The board of directors is considering either a stock split or a stock dividend. They understand that total stockholders' equity will remain the same under either action. However, they are not sure of the different effects of the two types of actions on other aspects of stockholders' equity. Explain the differences to the directors.
9. What is a prior period adjustment, and how is it reported in the financial statements?
10. ABC Corporation has a retained earnings balance of $210,000 on January 1. During the year, a prior period adjustment of $90,000 is recorded because of the understatement of depreciation in the prior period. Show the retained earnings statement presentation of these data.
11. What is the purpose of a retained earnings restriction? Identify the possible causes of retained earnings restrictions.
12. How are retained earnings restrictions generally reported in the financial statements?

13. Identify the events that result in credits and debits to retained earnings.

14. Shwu Chen believes that both the beginning and ending balances in retained earnings are shown in the stockholders' equity section. Is Shwu correct? Discuss.

15. David Sokol, who owns many investments in common stock, says, "I don't care what a company's net income is. The balance sheet tells me everything I need to know!" How do you respond to David?

16. What is the unique feature of a corporation income statement? Illustrate this feature, using assumed data.

17. Why is it important to report discontinued operations separately from income from continuing operations?

18. You are considering investing in Alou Transportation. The company reports 2002 earnings per share of $6.50 on income before extraordinary items and $4.75 on net income. Which EPS figure would you consider more relevant to your investment decision? Why?

19. Leeds Inc. reported 2001 earnings per share of $3.20 and had no extraordinary items. In 2002, EPS on income before extraordinary items was $2.99, and EPS on net income was $3.49. Is this a favorable trend?

20. Indicate which of the following items would be reported as an extraordinary item in Childs Corporation's income statement.
    (a) Loss from damages caused by volcano eruption.
    (b) Loss from sale of temporary investments.
    (c) Loss attributable to a labor strike.
    (d) Loss caused when manufacture of a product was prohibited by the Food and Drug Administration.
    (e) Loss from flood damage. (The nearby Black River floods every 2 to 3 years.)
    (f) Write-down of obsolete inventory.
    (g) Expropriation of a factory by a foreign government.

21. When studying for an accounting test, a fellow student says, "Changes in accounting principle are reported in the retained earnings statement." Is your friend correct, or should he study harder?

22. Why must preferred stock dividends be subtracted from net income in computing earnings per share?

BRIEF EXERCISES

Prepare entries for a cash dividend. (SO 1)

BE15-1 Weaner Corporation has 50,000 shares of common stock outstanding. It declares a $2 per share cash dividend on November 1 to stockholders of record on December 1. The dividend is paid on December 31. Prepare the entries on the appropriate dates to record the declaration and payment of the cash dividend.

Prepare entries for a stock dividend. (SO 1)

BE15-2 Romano Corporation has 80,000 shares of $10 par value common stock outstanding. It declares a 10% stock dividend on December 1 when the market value per share is $16. The dividend shares are issued on December 31. Prepare the entries for the declaration and payment of the stock dividend.

Show before and after effects of a stock dividend. (SO 1)

BE15-3 The stockholders' equity section of Herrera Corporation consists of common stock ($10 par) $1,000,000 and retained earnings $300,000. A 10% stock dividend (10,000 shares) is declared when the market value per share is $14. Show the before and after effects of the dividend on the following.

(a) The components of stockholders' equity.
(b) Shares outstanding.
(c) Book value per share.

Prepare a retained earnings statement. (SO 2)

BE15-4 For the year ending December 31, 2002, Fritz Inc. reports net income $150,000 and dividends $85,000. Prepare the retained earnings statement for the year assuming the balance in retained earnings on January 1, 2002, was $220,000.

Compute return on common stockholders' equity. (SO 3)

BE15-5 Tara Corporation reported net income of $170,000, declared dividends on common stock of $50,000, and had an ending balance in retained earnings of $360,000. Stockholders' equity was $700,000 at the beginning of the year and $820,000 at the end of the year. Compute the return on common stockholders' equity.

Prepare income statement including extraordinary items. (SO 5)

BE15-6 An inexperienced accountant for Ervay Corporation showed the following in the income statement: income before income taxes and extraordinary item $300,000, and extraordinary loss from flood (before taxes) $70,000. The extraordinary loss and taxable income are both subject to a 25% tax rate. Prepare a correct income statement.

Prepare discontinued operations section of income statement. (SO 5)

BE15-7 On June 30, Ingram Corporation discontinued its operations in Mexico. During the year, the operating loss was $300,000 before taxes. On September 1, Ingram disposed of the Mexico facility at a pretax loss of $160,000. The applicable tax rate is 35%. Show the discontinued operations section of the income statement.

BE15-8 On January 1, 2002, Jimenez Inc. changed from the straight-line method of depreciation to the declining-balance method. The cumulative effect of the change was to increase prior years' depreciation by $70,000 and 2002 depreciation by $8,000. Show the change in accounting principle section of the 2002 income statement, assuming the tax rate is 30%.

Prepare change in accounting principle section of income statement.
(SO 5)

BE15-9 Klumpe Corporation's income statement shows the following: income from continuing operations $580,000, loss from discontinued operations $200,000, extraordinary loss $90,000 (both net of taxes), and cumulative effect of a change in accounting principle that increases net income $30,000. Show the earnings per share data in the income statement assuming that there are 200,000 shares of common stock outstanding at December 31.

Show earnings per share data in income statement.
(SO 6)

BE15-10 Lumley Corporation reports net income of $370,000 and a weighted average of 200,000 shares of common stock outstanding for the year. Compute the earnings per share of common stock.

Compute earnings per share.
(SO 6)

BE15-11 Income and common stock data for Lumley Corporation are presented in BE15-10. Assume also that Lumley has cumulative preferred stock dividends for the current year of $20,000 that were declared and paid. Compute the earnings per share of common stock.

Compute earnings per share with cumulative preferred stock.
(SO 6)

EXERCISES

E15-1 On January 1, Garza Corporation had 75,000 shares of no-par common stock issued and outstanding. The stock has a stated value of $5 per share. During the year, the following occurred.

Journalize cash dividends; indicate statement presentation.
(SO 1)

Apr. 1	Issued 15,000 additional shares of common stock for $17 per share.
June 15	Declared a cash dividend of $1 per share to stockholders of record on June 30.
July 10	Paid the $1 cash dividend.
Dec. 1	Issued 2,000 additional shares of common stock for $19 per share.
15	Declared a cash dividend on outstanding shares of $1.30 per share to stockholders of record on December 31.

Instructions

(a) Prepare the entries, if any, on each of the three dividend dates.

(b) How are dividends and dividends payable reported in the financial statements prepared at December 31?

E15-2 Romano Corporation was organized on January 1, 2001. During its first year, the corporation issued 2,000 shares of $50 par value preferred stock and 100,000 shares of $10 par value common stock. At December 31, the company declared the following cash dividends: 2001, $6,000, 2002, $12,000, and 2003, $28,000.

Allocate cash dividends to preferred and common stock.
(SO 1)

Instructions

(a) Show the allocation of dividends to each class of stock, assuming the preferred stock dividend is 9% and not cumulative.

(b) Show the allocation of dividends to each class of stock, assuming the preferred stock dividend is 10% and cumulative.

(c) Journalize the declaration of the cash dividend at December 31, 2003, under part (b).

E15-3 On January 1, 2002, Tinker Corporation had $1,000,000 of common stock outstanding that was issued at par. It also had retained earnings of $750,000. The company issued 50,000 shares of common stock at par on July 1 and earned net income of $400,000 for the year.

Journalize stock dividends.
(SO 1)

Instructions

Journalize the declaration of a 15% stock dividend on December 10, 2002, for the following independent assumptions.

1. Par value is $10, and market value is $16.
2. Par value is $5, and market value is $20.

E15-4 On October 31, the stockholders' equity section of Salita Company consists of common stock $800,000 and retained earnings $1,000,000. Salita is considering the following two courses of action: (1) declaring a 5% stock dividend on the 80,000, $10 par value shares outstanding, or

Compare effects of a stock dividend and a stock split.
(SO 1)

(2) effecting a 2-for-1 stock split that will reduce par value to $5 per share. The current market price is $14 per share.

Instructions

Prepare a tabular summary of the effects of the alternative actions on the components of stockholders' equity, outstanding shares, and book value per share. Use the following column headings: Before Action, After Stock Dividend, and After Stock Split.

Compute book value per share; indicate account balances after a stock dividend. (SO 1, 3)

E15-5 On October 1, Sipio Corporation's stockholders' equity is as follows.

Common stock, $10 par value	$200,000
Paid-in capital in excess of par value	25,000
Retained earnings	75,000
Total stockholders' equity	$300,000

On October 1, Sipio declares and distributes a 10% stock dividend when the market value of the stock is $17 per share.

Instructions

(a) Compute the book value per share (1) before the stock dividend and (2) after the stock dividend. (Round to two decimals.)

(b) Indicate the balances in the three stockholders' equity accounts after the stock dividend shares have been distributed.

Indicate the effects on stockholders' equity components. (SO 1, 2, 3)

E15-6 During 2002, Flores Corporation had the following transactions and events.

1. Declared a cash dividend.
2. Issued par value common stock for cash at par value.
3. Completed a 3-for-1 stock split in which $15 par value stock was changed to $5 par value stock.
4. Declared a small stock dividend when the market value was higher than par value.
5. Made a prior period adjustment for overstatement of net income.
6. Issued the shares of common stock required by the stock dividend declaration in item no. 4 above.
7. Paid the cash dividend in item no. 1 above.
8. Issued par value common stock for cash above par value.

Instructions

Indicate the effect(s) of each of the foregoing items on the subdivisions of stockholders' equity. Present your answer in tabular form with the following columns. Use (I) for increase, (D) for decrease, and (NE) for no effect. Item no. 1 is given as an example.

	Paid-in Capital		
Item	**Capital Stock**	**Additional**	**Retained Earnings**
1	NE	NE	D

Prepare correcting entries for dividends and a stock split. (SO 1)

E15-7 Before preparing financial statements for the current year, the chief accountant for O'Dell Company discovered the following errors in the accounts.

1. The declaration and payment of $30,000 cash dividend was recorded as a debit to Interest Expense $30,000 and a credit to Cash $30,000.
2. A 10% stock dividend (1,000 shares) was declared on the $10 par value stock when the market value per share was $14. The only entry made was: Retained Earnings (Dr.) $10,000 and Dividend Payable (Cr.) $10,000. The shares have not been issued.
3. A 4-for-1 stock split involving the issue of 400,000 shares of $5 par value common stock for 100,000 shares of $20 par value common stock was recorded as a debit to Retained Earnings $2,000,000 and a credit to Common Stock $2,000,000.

Instructions

Prepare the correcting entries at December 31.

Prepare a retained earnings statement. (SO 2)

E15-8 On January 1, 2002, Mayes Corporation had retained earnings of $550,000. During the year, Mayes had the following selected transactions.

1. Declared cash dividends $120,000.
2. Corrected overstatement of 2001 net income because of depreciation error $20,000.

3. Earned net income $350,000.
4. Declared stock dividends $60,000.

Instructions
Prepare a retained earnings statement for the year.

Prepare a stockholders' equity section.
(SO 3)

E15-9 The following accounts appear in the ledger of Byung-Kee Inc. after the books are closed at December 31.

Common Stock, no par, $1 stated value, 400,000 shares authorized; 300,000 shares issued	$ 300,000
Common Stock Dividends Distributable	75,000
Paid-in Capital in Excess of Stated Value—Common Stock	1,200,000
Preferred Stock, $5 par value, 8%, 40,000 shares authorized; 30,000 shares issued	150,000
Retained Earnings	700,000
Treasury Stock (10,000 common shares)	74,000
Paid-in Capital in Excess of Par Value—Preferred Stock	244,000

Instructions
Prepare the stockholders' equity section at December 31, assuming retained earnings is restricted for plant expansion in the amount of $100,000.

Calculate ratios to evaluate earnings performance.
(SO 3, 6)

E15-10 The following financial information is available for Goldberg Corporation.

	2002	2001
Average common stockholders' equity	$1,200,000	$900,000
Dividends paid to common stockholders	50,000	30,000
Dividends paid to preferred stockholders	20,000	20,000
Net income	200,000	140,000
Market price of common stock	20	15

The weighted average number of shares of common stock outstanding was 80,000 for 2001 and 100,000 for 2002.

Instructions
Calculate earnings per share and return on common stockholders' equity for 2002 and 2001.

Calculate ratios to evaluate earnings performance.
(SO 3, 6)

E15-11 This financial information is available for Port City Corporation.

	2002	2001
Average common stockholders' equity	$1,800,000	$1,900,000
Dividends paid to common stockholders	90,000	70,000
Dividends paid to preferred stockholders	20,000	20,000
Net income	230,000	180,000
Market price of common stock	20	25

The weighted number of shares of common stock outstanding was 180,000 for 2001 and 150,000 for 2002.

Instructions
Calculate earnings per share and return on common stockholders' equity for 2002 and 2001.

Prepare a correct income statement.
(SO 4, 5)

E15-12 For its fiscal year ending October 31, 2002, Sass Corporation reports the following partial data.

Income before income taxes	$640,000
Income tax expense (30% × $540,000)	162,000
Income before extraordinary items	478,000
Extraordinary loss from fire	100,000
Net income	$378,000

The fire loss is considered an extraordinary item. The income tax rate is 30% on all items.

Instructions

(a) Prepare a correct income statement, beginning with income before income taxes.

(b) Explain in memo form why the income statement data are misleading.

Prepare income statement.
(SO 4, 5)

E15-13 Rizzo Corporation has income from continuing operations of $240,000 for the year ended December 31, 2002. It also has the following items (before considering income taxes).

1. An extraordinary fire loss of $80,000.
2. A gain of $50,000 on the discontinuance of a division.
3. A cumulative change in an accounting principle that resulted in an increase in prior years' depreciation of $35,000.
4. A correction of an error in last year's financial statements that resulted in a $20,000 understatement of 2001 net income.

Assume all items are subject to income taxes at a 30% tax rate.

Instructions

(a) Prepare an income statement, beginning with income from continuing operations.

(b) Indicate the statement presentation of any item not included in (a) above.

Compute earnings per share under different assumptions.
(SO 6)

E15-14 At December 31, 2002, Shields Corporation has 2,000 shares of $100 par value, 8%, preferred stock outstanding and 100,000 shares of $10 par value common stock issued. Shields's net income for the year is $547,000.

Instructions

Compute the earnings per share of common stock under the following independent situations. (Round to two decimals.)

(a) The dividend to preferred stockholders was declared. There has been no change in the number of shares of common stock outstanding during the year.

(b) The dividend to preferred stockholders was not declared. The preferred stock is cumulative. Shields held 10,000 shares of common treasury stock throughout the year.

PROBLEMS: SET A

Prepare dividend entries and stockholders' equity section.
(SO 1, 3)

Peachtree

P15-1A On Janury 1, 2002, Hayslett Corporation had the following stockholders' equity accounts.

Common Stock ($20 par value, 65,000 shares issued and outstanding)	$1,300,000
Paid-in Capital in Excess of Par Value	200,000
Retained Earnings	600,000

During the year, the following transactions occurred.

Feb. 1	Declared a $1 cash dividend per share to stockholders of record on February 15, payable March 1.
Mar. 1	Paid the dividend declared in February.
Apr. 1	Announced a 4-for-1 stock split. Prior to the split, the market price per share was $36.
July 1	Declared a 5% stock dividend to stockholders of record on July 15, distributable July 31. On July 1, the market price of the stock was $13 per share.
31	Issued the shares for the stock dividend.
Dec. 1	Declared a $0.50 per share dividend to stockholders of record on December 15, payable January 5, 2003.
31	Determined that net income for the year was $350,000.

Instructions

(a) Journalize the transactions and the closing entry for net income.

(b) Enter the beginning balances, and post the entries to the stockholders' equity accounts. (*Note:* Open additional stockholders' equity accounts as needed.)

(c) Prepare a stockholders' equity section at December 31.

(c) Total stockholders' equity $2,248,500

Journalize and post transactions; prepare retained earnings statement and stockholders' equity section.
(SO 1, 2, 3)

Peachtree

P15-2A The stockholders' equity accounts of Greene Company at January 1, 2002, are as follows.

Preferred Stock, 9%, $50 par	$600,000
Common Stock, $2 par	500,000
Paid-in Capital in Excess of Par Value—Preferred Stock	200,000
Paid-in Capital in Excess of Par Value—Common Stock	300,000
Retained Earnings	800,000

There were no dividends in arrears on preferred stock. During 2002, the company had the following transactions and events.

July	1	Declared a $0.50 cash dividend on common stock.
Aug.	1	Discovered $45,000 understatement of 2001 depreciation. Ignore income taxes.
Sept.	1	Paid the cash dividend declared on July 1.
Dec.	1	Declared 10% stock dividend on common stock when the market value of the stock was $18 per share.
	15	Declared a 9% cash dividend on preferred stock payable January 15, 2003.
	31	Determined that net income for the year was $385,000.
	31	Recognized a $200,000 restriction of retained earnings for plant expansion.

Instructions

(a) Journalize the transactions, events, and closing entries.

(b) Enter the beginning balances in the accounts, and post to the stockholders' equity accounts. (*Note:* Open additional stockholders' equity accounts as needed.)

(c) Prepare a retained earnings statement for the year.

(d) Prepare a stockholders' equity section at December 31, 2002.

(c) Ending balance $511,000
(d) Total stockholders' equity $2,561,000

Prepare retained earnings statement and stockholders' equity section, and compute earnings per share.
(SO 1, 2, 3, 6)

P15-3A The post-closing trial balance of Jajoo Corporation at December 31, 2002, contains the following stockholders' equity accounts.

Preferred Stock (15,000 shares issued)	$ 750,000
Common Stock (250,000 shares issued)	2,500,000
Paid-in Capital in Excess of Par Value—Preferred	250,000
Paid-in Capital in Excess of Par Value—Common	400,000
Common Stock Dividends Distributable	200,000
Retained Earnings	1,053,000

A review of the accounting records reveals the following.

1. No errors have been made in recording 2002 transactions or in preparing the closing entry for net income.
2. Preferred stock is $50 par, 10%, and cumulative; 15,000 shares have been outstanding since January 1, 2001.
3. Authorized stock is 20,000 shares of preferred, 500,000 shares of common with a $10 par value.
4. The January 1 balance in Retained Earnings was $1,170,000.
5. On July 1, 20,000 shares of common stock were sold for cash at $16 per share.
6. On September 1, the company discovered an understatement error of $60,000 in computing depreciation in 2001. The net of tax effect of $42,000 was properly debited directly to Retained Earnings.
7. A cash dividend of $250,000 was declared and properly allocated to preferred and common stock on October 1. No dividends were paid to preferred stockholders in 2001.
8. On December 31, an 8% common stock dividend was declared out of retained earnings on common stock when the market price per share was $16.
9. Net income for the year was $495,000.
10. On December 31, 2002, the directors authorized disclosure of a $200,000 restriction of retained earnings for plant expansion. (Use Note X.)

Instructions

(a) Reproduce the Retained Earnings account for the year.

(b) Prepare a retained earnings statement for the year.

(c) Prepare a stockholders' equity section at December 31.

(b) Retained earnings: $1,053,000
(c) Total stockholders' equity, $5,153,000

(d) Compute the earnings per share of common stock using 240,000 as the weighted average shares outstanding for the year.
(e) Compute the allocation of the cash dividend to preferred and common stock.

Prepare income statement with discontinued operations and extraordinary loss, and compute earnings per share.
(SO 4, 5, 6)

P15-4A Knight Corporation owns a number of cruise ships and a chain of hotels. The hotels, which have not been profitable, were discontinued on September 1, 2002. The 2002 operating results for the company were as follows.

Operating revenues	$12,850,000
Operating expenses	8,700,000
Operating income	$ 4,150,000

Analysis discloses that these data include the operating results of the hotel chain, which were: operating revenues $3,000,000 and operating expenses $4,000,000. The hotels were sold at a gain of $500,000 before taxes. This gain is not included in the operating results. During the year, Knight suffered an extraordinary fire loss of $800,000 before taxes, which is not included in the operating results. In 2002, the company had other revenues and gains of $100,000, which are not included in the operating results. The corporation is in the 30% income tax bracket.

Instructions

(a) Net income $2,765,000

(a) Prepare a condensed income statement.
(b) Compute the earnings per share data that should appear in the income statement. Assume weighted average shares of stock equaled 440,000. (Round to two decimals.)

Prepare income statement with nontypical items, and compute earnings per share data.
(SO 4, 5, 6)

P15-5A The ledger of McGrath Corporation at December 31, 2002, contains the following summary data.

Net sales	$1,700,000	Cost of goods sold	$1,000,000
Selling expenses	120,000	Administrative expenses	130,000
Other revenues and gains	20,000	Other expenses and losses	28,000

Your analysis reveals the following additional information that is not included in the above data.

1. The entire puzzles division was discontinued on August 31. The income from operations for this division before income taxes was $50,000. The puzzles division was sold at a loss of $70,000 before income taxes.
2. On May 15, company property was expropriated for an interstate highway. The settlement resulted in an extraordinary gain of $90,000 before income taxes.
3. During the year, McGrath changed its depreciation method from double-declining balance to straight-line. The cumulative effect of the change on prior years' net income was an increase of $60,000 before taxes. (Assume that depreciation under the new method is correctly included in the ledger data.)
4. The income tax rate on all items is 30%.

Instructions

(a) Net income: $400,400

(a) Prepare an income statement for the year ended December 31, 2002. Use the format illustrated in the Demonstration Problem (p. 623).
(b) Prepare the earnings per share data that should appear in the income statement. Assume there were 100,000 shares of common stock outstanding throughout the year.

PROBLEMS: SET B

Prepare dividend entries and stockholders' equity section.
(SO 1, 3)

P15-1B On January 1, 2002, Harris Corporation had the following stockholders' equity accounts.

Common Stock ($10 par value, 70,000 shares issued and outstanding)	$700,000
Paid-in Capital in Excess of Par Value	200,000
Retained Earnings	540,000

During the year, the following transactions occurred.

Jan. 15	Declared a $1 cash dividend per share to stockholders of record on January 31, payable February 15.
Feb. 15	Paid the dividend declared in January.

Apr. 15	Declared a 10% stock dividend to stockholders of record on April 30, distributable May 15. On April 15, the market price of the stock was $13 per share.
May 15	Issued the shares for the stock dividend.
July 1	Announced a 2-for-1 stock split. The market price per share prior to the announcement was $15. (The new par value is $5.)
Dec. 1	Declared a $0.50 per share cash dividend to stockholders of record on December 15, payable January 10, 2003.
31	Determined that net income for the year was $250,000.

Instructions

(a) Journalize the transactions and the closing entry for net income.

(b) Enter the beginning balances, and post the entries to the stockholders' equity accounts. (*Note:* Open additional stockholders' equity accounts as needed.)

(c) Prepare a stockholders' equity section at December 31.

(c) Total stockholders' equity $1,543,000

P15-2B The stockholders' equity accounts of Greco Inc., at January 1, 2002, are as follows.

Journalize and post transactions, and prepare retained earnings statement and stockholders' equity section. (SO 1, 2, 3)

Preferred Stock, $100 par, 9%	$500,000
Common Stock, $5 par	900,000
Paid-in Capital in Excess of Par Value—Preferred Stock	100,000
Paid-in Capital in Excess of Par Value—Common Stock	200,000
Retained Earnings	500,000

There were no dividends in arrears on preferred stock. During 2002, the company had the following transactions and events.

July 1	Declared a $0.50 cash dividend on common stock.
Aug. 1	Discovered a $72,000 overstatement of 2001 depreciation. Ignore income taxes.
Sept. 1	Paid the cash dividend declared on July 1.
Dec. 1	Declared a 10% stock dividend on common stock when the market value of the stock was $12 per share.
15	Declared a 9% cash dividend on preferred stock payable January 31, 2003.
31	Determined that net income for the year was $380,000.

Instructions

(a) Journalize the transactions and the closing entry for net income.

(b) Enter the beginning balances in the accounts and post to the stockholders' equity accounts. (*Note:* Open additional stockholders' equity accounts as needed.)

(c) Prepare a retained earnings statement for the year.

(d) Prepare a stockholders' equity section at December 31, 2002.

(c) Ending balance $601,000
(d) Total stockholders' equity $2,517,000

P15-3B The ledger of Healy Corporation at December 31, 2002, after the books have been closed, contains the following stockholders' equity accounts.

Prepare retained earnings statement and stockholders' equity section, and compute earnings per share. (SO 1, 2, 3, 6)

Preferred Stock (10,000 shares issued)	$1,000,000
Common Stock (400,000 shares issued)	2,000,000
Paid-in Capital in Excess of Par Value—Preferred	200,000
Paid-in Capital in Excess of Stated Value—Common	1,100,000
Common Stock Dividends Distributable	100,000
Retained Earnings	2,590,000

A review of the accounting records reveals the following.

1. No errors have been made in recording 2002 transactions or in preparing the closing entry for net income.
2. Preferred stock is 10%, $100 par value, noncumulative, and callable at $125. Since January 1, 2001, 10,000 shares have been outstanding; 20,000 shares are authorized.
3. Common stock is no-par with a stated value of $5 per share; 600,000 shares are authorized.
4. The January 1 balance in Retained Earnings was $2,450,000.
5. On October 1, 100,000 shares of common stock were sold for cash at $8 per share.
6. A cash dividend of $600,000 was declared and properly allocated to preferred and common stock on November 1. No dividends were paid to preferred stockholders in 2001.

7. On December 31, a 5% common stock dividend was declared out of retained earnings on common stock when the market price per share was $7.
8. Net income for the year was $880,000.
9. On December 31, 2002, the directors authorized disclosure of a $100,000 restriction of retained earnings for plant expansion. (Use Note A.)

Instructions

(b) Retained earnings: $2,590,000
(c) Total stockholders' equity: $6,990,000

(a) Reproduce the Retained Earnings account (T-account) for the year.
(b) Prepare a retained earnings statement for the year.
(c) Prepare a stockholders' equity section at December 31.
(d) Compute the earnings per share of common stock using 325,000 as the weighted average shares outstanding for the year.
(e) Compute the allocation of the cash dividend to preferred and common stock.

Prepare income statement with discontinued operations and an extraordinary loss; compute earnings per share.
(SO 4, 5, 6)

P15-4B Kee Hau Corporation owns a number of travel agencies and a chain of motels in the Northwest. Its condensed operating results for 2002 show the following.

Operating revenues	$14,800,000
Operating expenses	10,700,000
Income from operations	$ 4,100,000

An additional analysis of the data indicate that the travel agencies are very profitable, but the motel chain has been unprofitable. Through September 30, the motels lost $500,000 from operating revenues of $4,200,000 and operating expenses of $4,700,000. On October 1, the motel operation was discontinued and sold at a loss of $1,000,000 before taxes. The motel operating results are included in income from operations, but the loss on disposal is not included in the operating results shown above.

During the year, the corporation had other expenses and losses of $80,000, which are not included in the operating results. In November, a condemnation action was taken against the company to obtain property for a new national park. As a result, the corporation suffered an extraordinary loss of $800,000 before taxes. That loss is not included in the operating results. The corporation is in a 30% tax bracket.

Instructions

(a) Net income $1,554,000

(a) Prepare a condensed income statement for the year.
(b) Compute all of the earnings per share amounts that should appear on the income statement. Assume weighted average shares of stock equaled 400,000. (Round to two decimals.)

Prepare expanded income statement; compute earnings per share data.
(SO 4, 5, 6)

P15-5B The ledger of Haak Corporation at December 31, 2002, contains the following summary data.

Net sales	$1,400,000	Cost of goods sold	$800,000
Selling expenses	110,000	Administrative expenses	140,000
Other revenues and gains	40,000	Other expenses and losses	30,000

Your analysis reveals the following additional information that is not included in the above data.

1. The entire ceramics division was discontinued on August 31. The loss from operations for this division before income taxes was $150,000. The ceramics division was sold at a gain of $60,000 before income taxes.
2. On July 12, a fire occurred in one plant. The fire resulted in an extraordinary loss of $90,000 before income taxes.
3. During the year, Haak changed its depreciation method from straight-line to declining balance. The cumulative effect of the change on prior years' net income was a decrease of $30,000 before taxes. (Assume that depreciation under the new method is correctly included in the ledger data.)
4. The income tax rate on all items is 30%.

Instructions

(a) Net income: $105,000

(a) Prepare an income statement for the year ended December 31, 2002. Use the format illustrated in the Demonstration Problem (page 623).
(b) Prepare the earnings per share data that should appear in the income statement. Assume there were 100,000 shares of common stock outstanding throughout the year.

BROADENING YOUR PERSPECTIVE

FINANCIAL REPORTING AND ANALYSIS

FINANCIAL REPORTING PROBLEM: Lands' End, Inc.

BYP15-1 The financial statements of **Lands' End, Inc.** are presented in Appendix A.

Instructions

Refer to Lands' End's financial statements and answer the following questions.

(a) What amount did Lands' End pay in dividends in the year ended January 28, 2000? What is the company's dividend policy? (*Hint:* Read the section entitled "Liquidity and capital resources" in Management's Discussion and Analysis.)

(b) Lands' End reported nonrecurring charges or credits in its income statement. What was the nature of these nonrecurring charges and credits? How did these items differ from discontinued operations?

COMPARATIVE ANALYSIS PROBLEM: Lands' End vs. Abercrombie & Fitch

BYP15-2 **Lands' End's** financial statements are presented in Appendix A. **Abercrombie & Fitch's** financial statements are presented in Appendix B.

Instructions

(a) Compute earnings per share and return on common stockholders' equity for both companies for the year ending in January 2000. Assume Lands' End's weighted average shares were 30,085,000 and Abercrombie & Fitch's weighted average shares were 103,175,170. Can these measures be used to compare the profitability of the two companies? Why or why not?

(b) What was the total amount of dividends paid by each company in 2000?

(c) Did either company report one of the three types of irregular items on its income statement? If so, what was the nature of the irregular item?

INTERPRETING FINANCIAL STATEMENTS: A Global Focus

BYP15-3 **BFGoodrich Company** is a worldwide diversified manufacturer of tires, vinyl products, specialty chemicals, and aerospace products. Selected financial data, in millions of dollars, for a recent 2-year period were as follows.

	Current Year	Prior Year
Sales	$2,416.7	$2,023.5
Total operating income	298.0	200.7
Income from continuing operations	209.9	83.6
Income (loss) from discontinued operations (net of taxes)	(16.9)	(4.4)
Extraordinary items (net of taxes)		25.8
Cumulative effect of change in method of accounting for taxes	2.7	
Net income	195.7	105.0
Dividends on preferred stock	8.8	9.8
Dividends on common stock	43.3	37.0
Income retained in the business at end of year	548.9	405.3

The notes to the company's financial statements indicate that the weighted average number of common shares outstanding (in thousands of shares) was 25,179 for the current year and 23,651 for the prior year. In addition, the stockholders' equity section of the balance sheet shows that at December 31 of the current year there were 25,554,627 shares of common stock issued and 352,396 shares of common stock held in the treasury.

Instructions

(a) Present the earnings per share data for the company for each year.
(b) Comment on the relative importance of material nontypical items in each year.
(c) Discuss how you would factor these nontypical items into your prediction of next year's net income for BFGoodrich.
(d) Prepare a retained earnings statement for the current year.
(e) What was the total dividend per share of common stock for the current year?

EXPLORING THE WEB

BYP15-4 Use the stockholders' equity section of an annual report and identify the major components.

Address: **www.reportgallery.com** ***(or go to www.wiley.com/college/weygandt)***

Steps:

1. From Report Gallery Homepage, choose **Library of Annual Reports**.
2. Select a particular company.
3. Choose **Annual Report**.
4. Follow instructions below.

Instructions

Answer the following questions.

(a) What is the company's name?
(b) What classes of capital stock has the company issued?
(c) For each class of stock:
  (1) How many shares are authorized, issued, and/or outstanding?
  (2) What is the par value?
(d) What are the company's retained earnings?
(e) Has the company acquired treasury stock? How many shares?

CRITICAL THINKING

GROUP DECISION CASE

BYP15-5 General Dynamics develops, produces, and supports innovative, reliable, and highly sophisticated military and commercial products. In July of a recent year, the corporation announced that its Quincy Shipbuilding Division (Quincy) will be closed following the completion of the Maritime Prepositioning Ship construction program.

Prior to discontinuance, the operating results of Quincy were net sales \$246.8 million, income from operations before income taxes \$28.3 million, and income taxes \$12.5 million. The corporation's loss on disposition of Quincy was \$5.0 million, net of \$4.3 million income tax benefits.

From its other operating activities, General Dynamics' financial results were net sales \$8,163.8 million, cost of goods sold \$6,958.8 million, and selling and administrative expenses \$537.0 million. In addition, the corporation had interest expense of \$17.2 million and interest revenue of \$3.6 million. Income taxes were \$282.9 million.

General Dynamics had an average of 42.3 million shares of common stock outstanding during the year.

Instructions

With the class divided into groups, answer the following.

(a) Prepare the income statement for the year, assuming that the year ended on December 31, 2002. Show earnings per share data on the income statement. All dollars should be stated in millions, except for per share amounts. (For example, \$8 million would be shown as \$8.0)
(b) In the preceding year, Quincy's earnings were \$51.6 million before income taxes of \$22.8 million. For comparative purposes, General Dynamics reported earnings per share of \$0.61 from discontinued operations for Quincy in the preceding year.

(1) What was the average number of common shares outstanding during the preceding year?

(2) If earnings per share from continuing operations was $7.47, what was income from continuing operations during the preceding year? (Round to two decimals.)

COMMUNICATION ACTIVITY

BYP15-6 In the past year, Alameda Corporation declared a 10% stock dividend, and Butte, Inc. announced a 2-for-1 stock split. Your parents own 100 shares of each company's $50 par value common stock. During a recent phone call, your parents ask you, as an accounting student, to explain the difference between the two events.

Instructions

Write a letter to your parents that explains the effects of the two events to them as stockholders and the effects of each event on the financial statements of each corporation.

ETHICS CASE

BYP15-7 Flambeau Corporation has paid 60 consecutive quarterly cash dividends (15 years). The last 6 months, however, have been a cash drain on the company, as profit margins have been greatly narrowed by increasing competition. With a cash balance sufficient to meet only day-to-day operating needs, the president, Vince Ramsey, has decided that a stock dividend instead of a cash dividend should be declared. He tells Flambeau's financial vice president, Janice Rahn, to issue a press release stating that the company is extending its consecutive dividend record with the issuance of a 5% stock dividend. "Write the press release convincing the stockholders that the stock dividend is just as good as a cash dividend," he orders. "Just watch our stock rise when we announce the stock dividend; it must be a good thing if that happens."

Instructions

(a) Who are the stakeholders in this situation?

(b) Is there anything unethical about Ramsey's intentions or actions?

(c) What is the effect of a stock dividend on a corporation's stockholders' equity accounts? Which would you rather receive as a stockholder—a cash dividend or a stock dividend? Why?

Answers to Self-Study Questions

1. a **2.** c **3.** d **4.** b **5.** d **6.** b **7.** c **8.** c **9.** d **10.** b

Answers to *Lands' End* Review It Question 3, p. 619

In its 2000 income statement Lands' End did not report any of the three types of irregular items. It did, however, report "Non-recurring charges and credits."

LANDS' END DIRECT MERCHANTS

Remember to go back to the Navigator box on the chapter-opening page and check off your completed work.

16 LONG-TERM LIABILITIES

THE NAVIGATOR ✓

- Understand *Concepts for Review* ❑
- Read *Feature Story* ❑
- Scan *Study Objectives* ❑
- Read *Preview* ❑
- Read text and answer *Before You Go On* *p.* 645 ❑ *p.* 652 ❑ *p.* 655 ❑ *p.* 659 ❑
- Work *Demonstration Problems* ❑
- Review *Summary of Study Objectives* ❑
- Answer *Self-Study Questions* ❑
- Complete *Assignments* ❑

CONCEPTS FOR REVIEW

Before studying this chapter, you should know or, if necessary, review:

a. What is a long-term liability? What is a current liability? (Ch. 4, pp. 153–154 and Ch. 11, p. 446)

b. How to record adjusting entries for interest expense and interest payable. (Ch. 3, p. 101)

c. How to record entries for the issuance of notes payable and related interest expense. (Ch. 11, p. 447)

THE NAVIGATOR

FEATURE STORY

UK Builds with Bonds

Every year, hundreds of colleges construct new buildings. Where do most schools get the money for these expensive projects? From long-term bonds, which are obligations in which the issuer of the bond promises to repay the loan amount plus interest on or before a specified date.

The **University of Kentucky** (UK) has issued "revenue" bonds to build buildings on the 23,000-student Lexington campus, and on 14 community college campuses throughout the state. These bonds pledge the school's revenues as collateral to guarantee payment of the bonds. At one time the outstanding debt on the Lexington campus buildings was $137 million. The total debt on the community college buildings equaled $121 million. The bonds generally have maturities ranging from ten to twenty years.

Additional "guarantees" for bond purchasers are the ratings given the bonds by professional rating agencies. "Our bonds are rated AA– by Standard & Poor's Corp.," says Henry Clay Owen, UK's treasurer. "That's well above investment grade," he says. "We always have a very good market for our bonds. People in Kentucky identify very closely with the university. Even though the bonds are rated AA–, they trade at AAA [the top bond rating] because they're so easy to sell."

One advantage for investors: the bonds' interest revenue is exempt

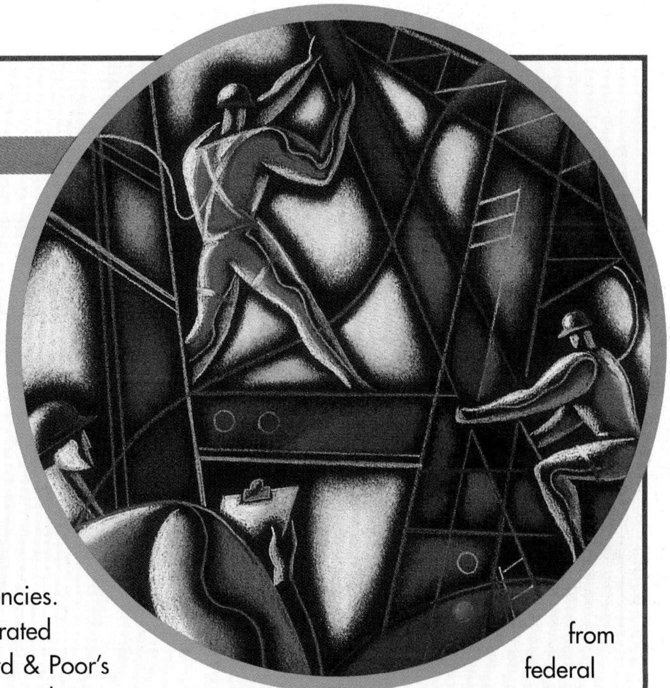

from federal income tax and from state tax for in-state investors. So, an issue offering 6 percent is the equivalent of 10 percent to individuals in the top tax bracket. "I would feel very comfortable buying UK bonds because it's inconceivable to me that there would ever be a default," says Owen.

THE NAVIGATOR

STUDY OBJECTIVES

After studying this chapter, you should be able to:

1. Explain why bonds are issued.
2. Prepare the entries for the issuance of bonds and interest expense.
3. Describe the entries when bonds are redeemed or converted.
4. Describe a bond sinking fund.
5. Describe the accounting for long-term notes payable.
6. Contrast the accounting for operating and capital leases.
7. Identify the methods for the presentation and analysis of long-term liabilities.

THE NAVIGATOR

PREVIEW OF CHAPTER 16

As you can see from the Feature Story, the **University of Kentucky** has chosen to issue long-term bonds to fund its building projects. The UK bonds are classified as **long-term liabilities** because they are obligations that are expected to be paid after one year. In this chapter we will explain the accounting for the major types of long-term liabilities reported on the balance sheet. These liabilities may be bonds, long-term notes, or lease obligations.

The content and organization of Chapter 16 are as follows.

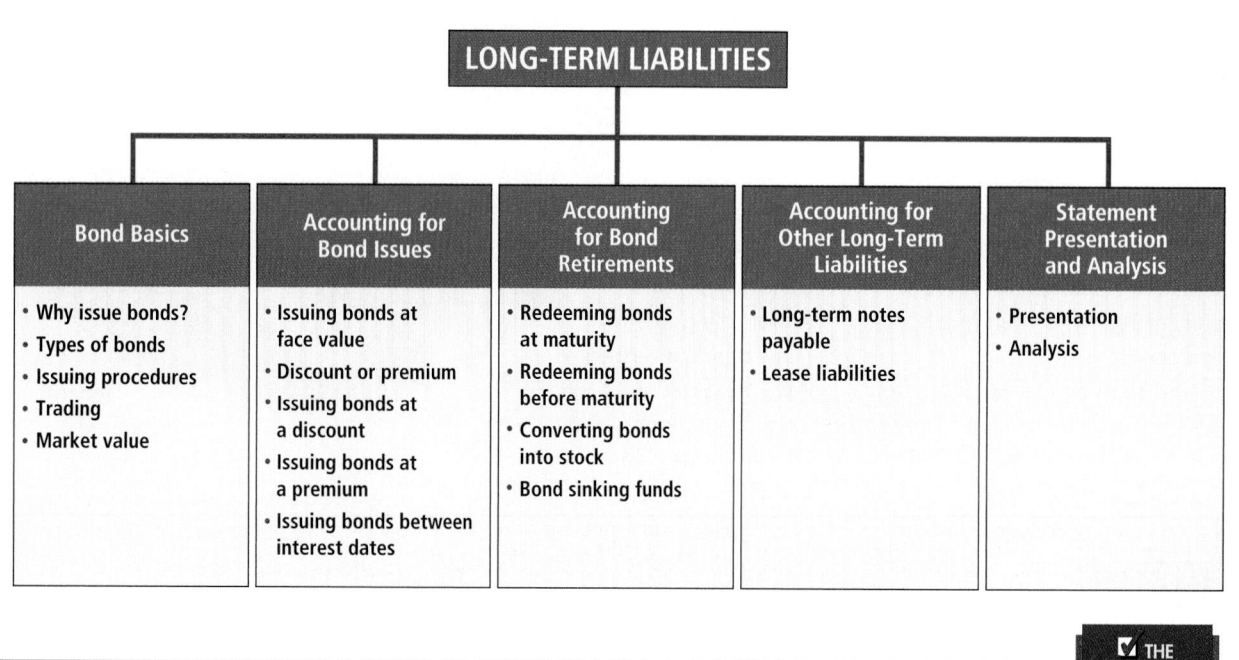

LONG-TERM LIABILITIES

Bond Basics	Accounting for Bond Issues	Accounting for Bond Retirements	Accounting for Other Long-Term Liabilities	Statement Presentation and Analysis
• Why issue bonds? • Types of bonds • Issuing procedures • Trading • Market value	• Issuing bonds at face value • Discount or premium • Issuing bonds at a discount • Issuing bonds at a premium • Issuing bonds between interest dates	• Redeeming bonds at maturity • Redeeming bonds before maturity • Converting bonds into stock • Bond sinking funds	• Long-term notes payable • Lease liabilities	• Presentation • Analysis

THE NAVIGATOR

BOND BASICS

Bonds are a form of interest-bearing notes payable. They are issued by corporations, universities, and governmental agencies. Bonds, like common stock, are sold in small denominations (usually a thousand dollars or thousand-dollar multiples). As a result, bonds attract many investors.

WHY ISSUE BONDS?

STUDY OBJECTIVE 1

Explain why bonds are issued.

A corporation may use long-term financing other than bonds, such as notes payable and leasing. These other forms of financing involve finding an individual, a company, or a financial institution willing to supply the needed funds. Notes payable and leasing are therefore seldom sufficient to furnish the funds needed for plant expansion and major projects like new buildings. To obtain **large amounts of long-term capital**, corporate management usually must decide whether to issue common stock (equity financing) or bonds.

From the standpoint of the corporation seeking long-term financing, bonds offer the following advantages over common stock:

Illustration 16-1

Advantages of bond financing over common stock

Bond Financing	Advantages
	1. **Stockholder control is not affected.** Bondholders do not have voting rights, so current owners (stockholders) retain full control of the company.
	2. **Tax savings result.** Bond interest is deductible for tax purposes; dividends on stock are not.
	3. **Earnings per share may be higher.** Although bond interest expense reduces net income, earnings per share on common stock often is higher under bond financing because no additional shares of common stock are issued.

To illustrate the potential effect on earnings per share, assume that Microsystems, Inc. is considering two plans for financing the construction of a new \$5 million plant. Plan A involves issuance of 200,000 shares of common stock at the current market price of \$25 per share. Plan B involves issuance of \$5 million, 12% bonds at face value. Income before interest and taxes on the new plant will be \$1.5 million. Income taxes are expected to be 30%. Microsystems currently has 100,000 shares of common stock outstanding. The alternative effects on earnings per share are shown in Illustration 16-2.

Illustration 16-2

Effects on earnings per share—stocks vs. bonds

	Plan A Issue Stock	Plan B Issue Bonds
Income before interest and taxes	\$1,500,000	\$1,500,000
Interest (12% × \$5,000,000)	—	600,000
Income before income taxes	1,500,000	900,000
Income tax expense (30%)	450,000	270,000
Net income	\$1,050,000	\$ 630,000
Outstanding shares	300,000	100,000
Earnings per share	**\$3.50**	**\$6.30**

Note that net income is \$420,000 less (\$1,050,000 − \$630,000) with long-term debt financing (bonds). However, earnings per share is higher because there are 200,000 fewer shares of common stock outstanding.

The major disadvantages resulting from the use of bonds are that interest must be paid on a periodic basis and the principal (face value) of the bonds must be paid at maturity. A company with fluctuating earnings and a relatively weak cash position may have great difficulty making interest payments when earnings are low.

INTERNATIONAL NOTE

The priority of bondholders' versus stockholders' rights varies across countries. In Japan, Germany, and France stockholders and employees are given priority, with liquidation of the firm to pay creditors seen as a last resort. In Britain creditors' interests are put first—the courts are quick to give control of the firm to creditors.

TYPES OF BONDS

Bonds may have many different features. Types of bonds commonly issued are described on the next page.

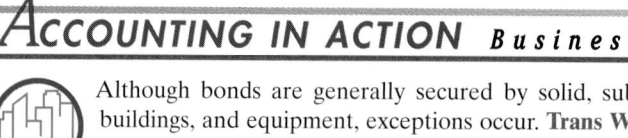

ACCOUNTING IN ACTION *Business Insight*

Although bonds are generally secured by solid, substantial assets like land, buildings, and equipment, exceptions occur. **Trans World Airlines Inc.** (TWA) at one time decided to issue $300 million of high-yielding 5-year bonds. TWA's bonds would be secured by a grab bag of assets, including some durable spare parts, but also a lot of disposable items that TWA had in its warehouses, such as light bulbs and gaskets. Some called the planned TWA bonds "light bulb bonds." As one financial expert noted: "You've got to admit that some security is better than none." Another noted, "They're digging pretty far down the barrel."

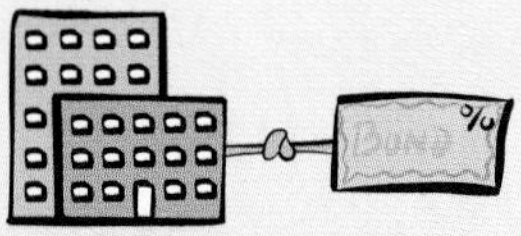

Secured Bonds

Unsecured Bonds

Secured and Unsecured Bonds

Secured bonds have specific assets of the issuer pledged as collateral for the bonds. A bond secured by real estate, for example, is called a **mortgage bond**. A bond secured by specific assets set aside to retire the bonds is called a **sinking fund bond**. (This type of bond is discussed later in the chapter). **Unsecured bonds** are issued against the general credit of the borrower. These bonds, called **debenture bonds**, are used extensively by large corporations with good credit ratings. For example, in a recent annual report, **DuPont** reported over $2 billion of debenture bonds outstanding.

Term and Serial Bonds

Bonds that mature (are due for payment) at a single specified future date are called **term bonds**. In contrast, bonds that mature in installments are called **serial bonds**. For example, **Caterpillar Inc.** debentures due in 2007 are term bonds. Caterpillar's debentures due between 2001 and 2007 are serial bonds (maturing annually).

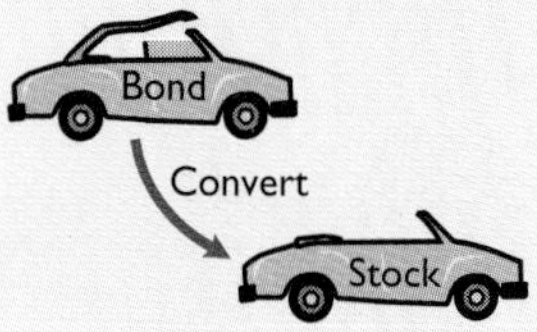

Convertible Bonds

Registered and Bearer Bonds

Bonds issued in the name of the owner are called **registered bonds**. Interest payments on registered bonds are made by check to bondholders of record. Bonds not registered are called **bearer** (or **coupon**) **bonds**. Holders of bearer bonds must send in coupons to receive interest payments. Coupon bonds may be transferred directly to another party. In contrast, the transfer of registered bonds requires cancellation of the bonds by the corporation and the issuance of new bonds. Most bonds issued today are registered bonds.

Callable Bonds

Convertible and Callable Bonds

Bonds that can be converted into common stock at the bondholder's option are called **convertible bonds**. Bonds subject to retirement at a stated dollar amount prior to maturity at the option of the issuer are known as **callable bonds**.

ISSUING PROCEDURES

State laws grant corporations the power to issue bonds. Within the corporation, approval by both the board of directors and stockholders is usually required. **In authorizing the bond issue, the board of directors must stipulate the number of bonds to be authorized, total face value, and contractual interest rate.** The total bond authorization often exceeds the number of bonds originally issued. This gives the corporation the flexibility it needs to meet future cash requirements.

The **face value** is the amount of principal the issuer must pay at the maturity date. The **contractual interest rate**, often referred to as the **stated rate**, is the rate used to determine the amount of cash interest the borrower pays and the investor receives. Usually the contractual rate is stated as an annual rate. Interest is generally paid semiannually.

The terms of the bond issue are set forth in a legal document called a **bond indenture**. In addition to the terms, the indenture summarizes the rights of the bondholders and their trustees, as well as the obligations of the issuing company. The **trustee** (usually a financial institution) keeps records of each bondholder, maintains custody of unissued bonds, and holds conditional title to pledged property.

After the bond indenture is prepared, **bond certificates** are printed. The indenture and the certificate are separate documents. As shown in Illustration 16-3, a bond certificate provides information such as the following: name of the issuer, face value, contractual interest rate, and maturity date. Bonds are generally sold through an investment company that specializes in selling securities.

Illustration 16-3
Bond certificate

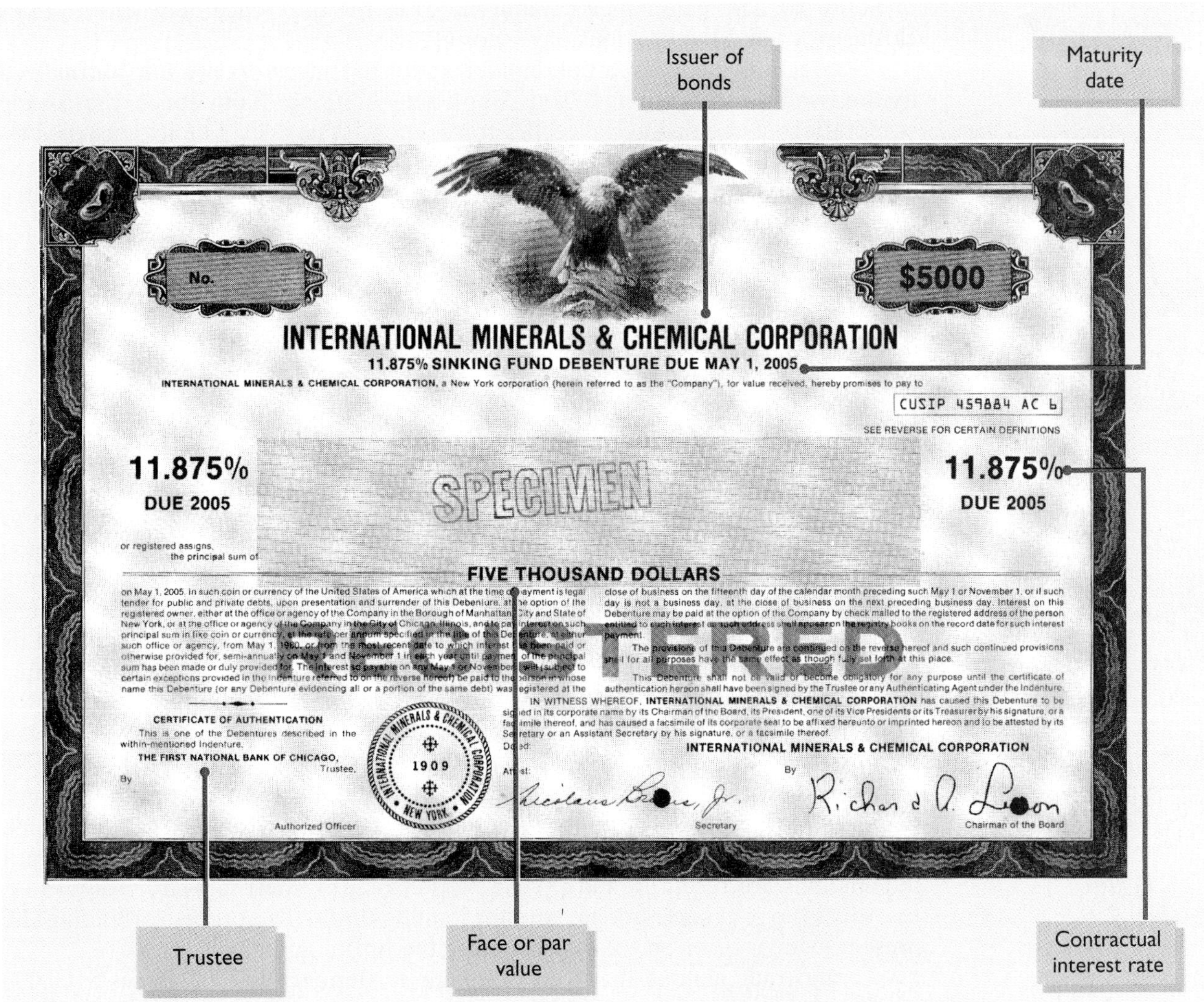

BOND TRADING

Corporate bonds, like capital stock, are traded on national securities exchanges. Thus, bondholders have the opportunity to convert their holdings into cash at any time by selling the bonds at the current market price.

Bond prices are quoted as a percentage of the face value of the bond, which is usually $1,000. A $1,000 bond with a quoted price of 97 means that the selling price of the bond is 97% of face value, or $970. Bond prices and trading activity are published daily in newspapers and the financial press, as illustrated by the following.

Illustration 16-4

Market information for bonds

Bonds	Current Yield	Volume	Close	Net Change
Kmart $8\frac{3}{8}$ 17	8.4	35	$100\frac{1}{4}$	$+\frac{7}{8}$

HELPFUL HINT
(1) What is the price of a $1,000 bond trading at $95\frac{1}{4}$?
(2) What is the price of a $1,000 bond trading at $101\frac{7}{8}$?
Answers: (1) $952.50.
(2) $1,018.75.

This bond listing indicates that **Kmart Corporation** has outstanding $8\frac{3}{8}$%, $1,000 bonds that mature in 2017. They currently yield an 8.4% return. On this day, 35 bonds were traded. At the close of trading, the price was $100\frac{1}{4}$% of face value, or $1,002.50. The net change column indicates the difference between the day's closing price and the previous day's closing price.

Transactions between a bondholder and other investors **are not journalized by the issuing corporation**. If Tom Smith sells bonds to Faith Jones, the issuing corporation does not journalize the transaction. (The issuer or its trustee does keep records of the names of bondholders in the case of registered bonds.) A corporation makes journal entries **only when it issues or buys back bonds**, and when bondholders convert bonds into common stock.

DETERMINING THE MARKET VALUE OF BONDS

Same dollars at different times are not equal.

If you were an investor wanting to purchase a bond, how would you determine how much to pay? To be more specific, assume that Coronet, Inc. issues a zero-interest bond (pays no interest) with a face value of $1,000,000 due in 20 years. For this bond, the only cash you receive is a million dollars at the end of 20 years. Would you pay a million dollars for this bond? We hope not! A million dollars received 20 years from now is not the same as a million dollars received today.

The reason you should not pay a million dollars for Coronet's bond relates to what is called the **time value of money**. If you had a million dollars today, you would invest it. From that investment, you would earn interest such that at the end of 20 years, you would have much more than a million dollars. If someone is going to pay you a million dollars 20 years from now, you would want to find its equivalent today. In other words, you would want to determine how much must be invested today at current interest rates to have a million dollars in 20 years. That amount, that must be invested today at a given rate of interest over a specified time, is called **present value**.

The present value of a bond is the value at which it should sell in the marketplace. Market value therefore is a function of the three factors that determine present value: (1) the dollar amounts to be received, (2) the length of time until the amounts are received, and (3) the market rate of interest. The **market interest rate** is the rate investors demand for loaning funds. The process of finding the present value is referred to as **discounting** the future amounts.

To illustrate, assume that Kell Company on January 1, 2002, issues $100,000 of 9% bonds, due in 5 years, with interest payable annually at year-end. The purchaser of the bonds would receive two types of cash inflows: (1) **principal** of

$100,000 to be paid at maturity, and (2) five $9,000 **interest payments** ($100,000 × 9%) over the term of the bonds. The time diagram depicting both cash flows is shown below.

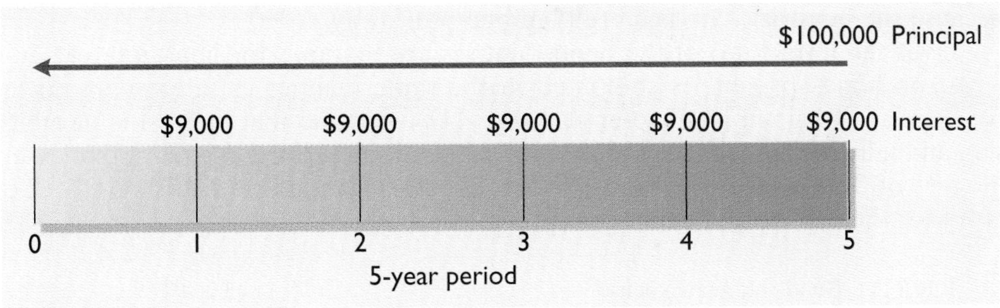

Illustration 16-5
Time diagram depicting cash flows

The present values of these amounts are as shown in Illustration 16-6.

Illustration 16-6
Computing the market price of bonds

Present value of $100,000 received in 5 years	$ 64,993
Present value of $9,000 received annually for 5 years	35,007
Market price of bonds	**$100,000**

Tables are available to find the present value numbers to be used, or these values can be determined mathematically.[1] Further discussion of time value of money computations is provided in Appendix C near the end of the book.

BEFORE YOU GO ON...

REVIEW IT

1. What are the advantages of bond versus stock financing?
2. What are secured versus unsecured bonds, term versus serial bonds, registered versus bearer bonds, and callable versus convertible bonds?
3. Explain the terms face value, contractual interest rate, and bond indenture.
4. Explain why you would prefer to receive $1 million today rather than 5 years from now.

THE NAVIGATOR

ACCOUNTING FOR BOND ISSUES

STUDY OBJECTIVE 2
Prepare the entries for the issuance of bonds and interest expense.

Bonds may be issued at face value, below face value (at a discount), or above face value (at a premium). They also are sometimes issued between interest dates.

ISSUING BONDS AT FACE VALUE

To illustrate the accounting for bonds, assume that on January 1, 2002, Devor Corporation issues 1,000, 10-year, 9%, $1,000 bonds at 100 (100% of face value). The entry to record the sale is:

[1] For those knowledgeable in the use of present value tables, the computations in this example are: $100,000 × .64993 = $64,993, and $9,000 × 3.88965 = $35,007 (rounded).

A =	L +	SE
+1,000,000	+1,000,000	

Jan. 1	Cash	1,000,000	
	Bonds Payable		1,000,000
	(To record sale of bonds at face value)		

Bonds payable are reported in the long-term liabilities section of the balance sheet because the maturity date is more than one year away.

Over the term (life) of the bonds, entries are required for bond interest. Interest on bonds payable is computed in the same manner as interest on notes payable, as explained in Chapter 11 (page 447). Assume that interest is payable semiannually on January 1 and July 1 on the bonds described above. In that case, interest of $45,000 ($1,000,000 × 9% × 6/12) must be paid on July 1, 2002. The entry for the payment, assuming no previous accrual of interest, is:

A =	L +	SE
−45,000		−45,000

July 1	Bond Interest Expense	45,000	
	Cash		45,000
	(To record payment of bond interest)		

At December 31, an adjusting entry is required to recognize the $45,000 of interest expense incurred since July 1. The entry is:

A =	L +	SE
	+45,000	−45,000

Dec. 31	Bond Interest Expense	45,000	
	Bond Interest Payable		45,000
	(To accrue bond interest)		

Bond interest payable is classified as a current liability, because it is scheduled for payment within the next year. When the interest is paid on January 1, 2003, Bond Interest Payable is debited and Cash is credited for $45,000.

DISCOUNT OR PREMIUM ON BONDS

In the previous illustrations, we assumed that the contractual (stated) interest rate paid on bonds and the market (effective) interest rate were the same. The contractual interest rate is the rate applied to the face (par) value to arrive at the interest paid in a year. The market interest rate is the rate investors demand for loaning funds to the corporation. When the contractual interest rate and the market interest rate are the same, bonds sell at face value, as shown above.

However, market interest rates change daily. They are influenced by the type of bond issued, the state of the economy, current industry conditions, and the company's performance. The contractual and market interest rates often differ. As a result, bonds sell below or above face value.

To illustrate, suppose that investors have one of two options: (1) purchase bonds that have a market interest rate of 10%, or (2) purchase bonds that have a contractual interest rate of 8%. If the bonds are of equal risk, investors will select the 10% investment. To make the investments equal, investors will demand a rate of interest higher than the 8% contractual interest rate. But investors cannot change the contractual interest rate. What they can do is to pay less than the face value for the bonds. By paying less for the bonds, investors can obtain the market rate of interest. In these cases, **bonds sell at a discount.**

On the other hand, the market interest rate may be **lower** than the contractual interest rate. In that case investors will have to pay more than face value for the bonds. That is, if the market interest rate is 8% and the contractual interest rate is 9%, the issuer will require more funds from the investor. In these cases, **bonds sell at a premium**. These relationships are shown graphically in Illustration 16-7 (on the next page).

Issuing bonds at an amount different from face value is quite common. By the time a company prints the bond certificates and markets the bonds, it will be a coincidence if the market rate and the contractual rate are the same. Thus, the sale of bonds at a discount does not mean that the issuer's financial strength is suspect. Nor does the sale of bonds at a premium indicate exceptional financial strength.

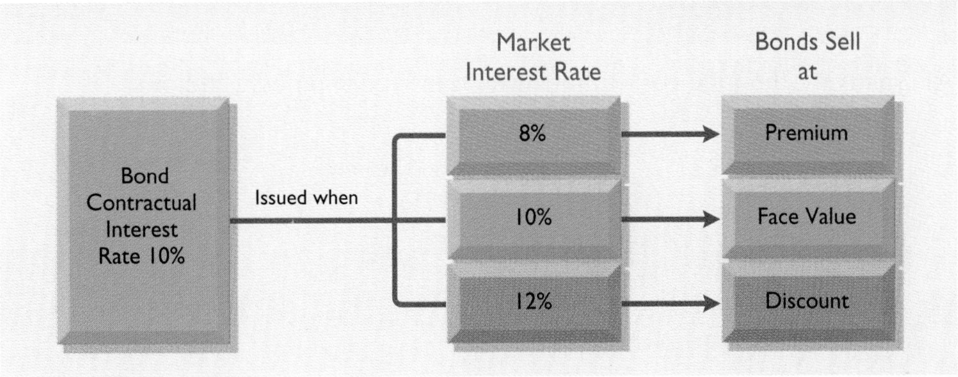

Illustration 16-7

Interest rates and bond prices

ISSUING BONDS AT A DISCOUNT

To illustrate the issuance of bonds at a discount, assume that on January 1, 2002, Candlestick, Inc. sells $100,000, 5-year, 10% bonds for $92,639 (92.639% of face value). Interest is payable on July 1 and January 1. The entry to record the issuance is:

Jan. 1	Cash	92,639	
	Discount on Bonds Payable	7,361	
	Bonds Payable		100,000
	(To record sale of bonds at a discount)		

A	=	L	+	SE
+92,639		−7,361		
		+100,000		

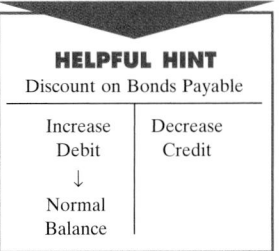

HELPFUL HINT

Discount on Bonds Payable

Increase Debit	Decrease Credit
↓ Normal Balance	

Although Discount on Bonds Payable has a debit balance, **it is not an asset**. Rather, it is a **contra account**. This account is **deducted from bonds payable** on the balance sheet, as illustrated below.

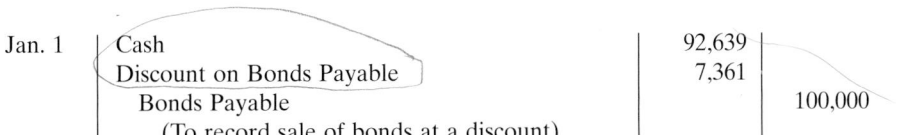

CANDLESTICK, INC.
Balance Sheet (partial)

Long-term liabilities		
Bonds payable	$100,000	
Less: Discount on bonds payable	**7,361**	$92,639

Illustration 16-8

Statement presentation of discount on bonds payable

The $92,639 represents the **carrying (or book) value** of the bonds. On the date of issue this amount equals the market price of the bonds.

The issuance of bonds below face value, at a discount, causes the total cost of borrowing to differ from the bond interest paid. That is, at maturity the issuing corporation must pay not only the contractual interest rate over the term of the bonds, but also the face value (rather than the issuance price). Therefore, the difference between the issuance price and face value of the bonds—the discount—is an **additional cost of borrowing. This additional cost should be recorded as bond interest expense over the life of the bonds.** The total cost of borrowing $92,639 for Candlestick, Inc. is $57,361, computed as follows.

HELPFUL HINT

Carrying value (book value) of bonds issued at a discount is determined by subtracting the balance of the discount account from the balance of the Bonds Payable account.

Illustration 16-9

Total cost of borrowing—bonds issued at a discount

Bonds Issued at a Discount	
Semiannual interest payments ($100,000 × 10% × 1/2 = $5,000; $5,000 × 10)	$50,000
Add: Bond discount ($100,000 − $92,639)	7,361
Total cost of borrowing	**$57,361**

Alternatively, the total cost of borrowing can be computed as follows.

Illustration 16-10

Alternative computation of total cost of borrowing—bonds issued at a discount

Bonds Issued at a Discount	
Principal at maturity	$100,000
Semiannual interest payments ($5,000 × 10)	50,000
Cash to be paid to bondholders	150,000
Cash received from bondholders	92,639
Total cost of borrowing	**$ 57,361**

Amortizing Bond Discount

To comply with the matching principle, bond discount should be allocated systematically to each accounting period that benefits from the use of the cash proceeds.

One method is the **straight-line method of amortization**. It allocates the same amount to interest expense in each interest period.[2] The formula for determining bond discount amortization is shown in Illustration 16-11.

Illustration 16-11

Formula for straight-line method of bond discount amortization

Bond Discount ÷ Number of Interest Periods = Bond Discount Amortization

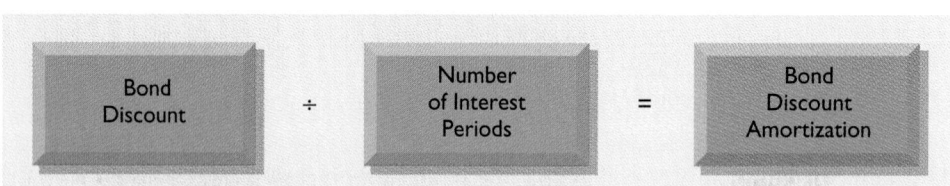

In this example, the bond discount amortization is $736 ($7,361 ÷ 10). The entry to record the payment of bond interest and the amortization of bond discount on the first interest date (July 1, 2002) is:

A	=	L	+	SE
−5,000		+736		−5,736

July 1	Bond Interest Expense	5,736	
	Discount on Bonds Payable		736
	Cash		5,000
	(To record payment of bond interest and amortization of bond discount)		

At December 31, the adjusting entry is:

A	=	L	+	SE
		+736		−5,736
		+5,000		

Dec. 31	Bond Interest Expense	5,736	
	Discount on Bonds Payable		736
	Bond Interest Payable		5,000
	(To record accrued bond interest and amortization of bond discount)		

[2]Another method, the effective-interest method, is discussed in the appendix at the end of this chapter.

Over the term of the bonds, the balance in Discount on Bonds Payable will decrease annually by the same amount until it has a zero balance at maturity. Thus, the carrying value of the bonds at maturity will be equal to the face value.

Preparing a bond discount amortization schedule as shown in Illustration 16-12 is useful. The schedule shows interest expense, discount amortization, and the carrying value of the bond for each interest period. The interest expense recorded each period for the Candlestick bond is $5,736. Also note that the carrying value of the bond increases $736 each period until it reaches its face value $100,000 at the end of period 10.

ALTERNATIVE TERMINOLOGY
The amount in the Discount on Bonds Payable account is often referred to as *Unamortized Discount on Bonds Payable.*

Illustration 16-12
Bond discount amortization schedule

CANDLESTICK, INC.
Bond Discount Amortization
Straight-Line Method—Semiannual Interest Payments

Semiannual Interest Periods	(A) Interest to Be Paid (5% × $100,000)	(B) Interest Expense to Be Recorded (A) + (C)	(C) Discount Amortization ($7,361 ÷ 10)	(D) Unamortized Discount (D) − (C)	(E) Bond Carrying Value ($100,000 − D)
Issue date				$7,361	$ 92,639
1	$ 5,000	$ 5,736	$ 736	6,625	93,375
2	5,000	5,736	736	5,889	94,111
3	5,000	5,736	736	5,153	94,847
4	5,000	5,736	736	4,417	95,583
5	5,000	5,736	736	3,681	96,319
6	5,000	5,736	736	2,945	97,055
7	5,000	5,736	736	2,209	97,791
8	5,000	5,736	736	1,473	98,527
9	5,000	5,736	736	737	99,263
10	5,000	5,737*	737*	-0-	100,000
	$50,000	$57,361	$7,361		

Column **(A)** remains constant because the face value of the bonds ($100,000) is multiplied by the semiannual contractual interest rate (5%) each period.
Column **(B)** is computed as the interest paid (Column A) plus the discount amortization (Column C).
Column **(C)** indicates the discount amortization each period.
Column **(D)** decreases each period by the same amount until it reaches zero at maturity.
Column **(E)** increases each period by the amount of discount amortization until it equals the face value at maturity.

*One dollar difference due to rounding.

We have highlighted columns (A), (B), and (C) in the amortization schedule to emphasize their importance. These three columns provide the numbers for each period's journal entries. They are the primary reason for preparing the schedule. Column (A) provides the amount of the credit to Cash. Column (B) shows the debit to Bond Interest Expense. And column (C) is the credit to Discount on Bonds Payable.

ISSUING BONDS AT A PREMIUM

To illustrate the issuance of bonds at a premium, we now assume the Candlestick, Inc. bonds described above are sold for $108,111 (108.111% of face value) rather than for $92,639.

The entry to record the sale is:

Jan. 1	Cash	108,111	
	Bonds Payable		100,000
	Premium on Bonds Payable		8,111
	(To record sale of bonds at a premium)		

A	=	L	+	SE
+108,111		+100,000		
		+8,111		

Premium on bonds payable is **added to bonds payable** on the balance sheet, as shown below.

Illustration 16-13

Statement presentation of bond premium

CANDLESTICK, INC. Balance Sheet (partial)		
Long-term liabilities		
Bonds payable	$100,000	
Add: Premium on bonds payable	**8,111**	$108,111

HELPFUL HINT

Premium on Bonds Payable

Decrease Debit	Increase Credit ↓ Normal Balance

The sale of bonds above face value causes the total cost of borrowing to be **less than the bond interest paid**. The bond premium is considered to be **a reduction in the cost of borrowing**. It should be credited to Bond Interest Expense over the life of the bonds. The total cost of borrowing $108,111 for Candlestick, Inc. is computed as follows.

Illustration 16-14

Total cost of borrowing—bonds issued at a premium

Bonds Issued at a Premium	
Semiannual interest payments	
($100,000 × 10% × ½ = $5,000; $5,000 × 10)	$50,000
Less: Bond premium ($108,111 − $100,000)	8,111
Total cost of borrowing	**$41,889**

Alternatively, the cost of borrowing can be computed as follows.

Illustration 16-15

Alternative computation of total cost of borrowing—bonds issued at a premium

Bonds Issued at a Premium	
Principal at maturity	$100,000
Semiannual interest payments ($5,000 × 10)	50,000
Cash to be paid to bondholders	150,000
Cash received from bondholders	108,111
Total cost of borrowing	**$ 41,889**

Amortizing Bond Premium

The formula for determining bond premium amortization under the straight-line method is presented in Illustration 16-16.

Illustration 16-16

Formula for straight-line method of bond premium amortization

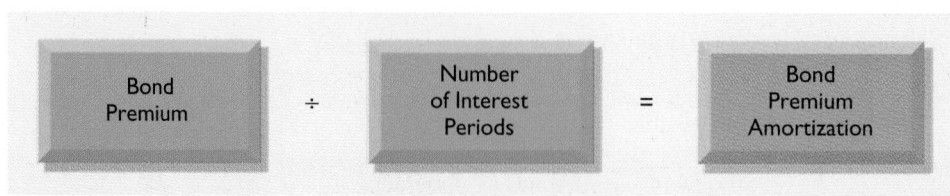

Bond Premium ÷ Number of Interest Periods = Bond Premium Amortization

In our example, the premium amortization for each interest period is $811 ($8,111 ÷ 10). The entry to record the first payment of interest on July 1 is:

July 1	Bond Interest Expense	4,189	
	Premium on Bonds Payable	811	
	Cash		5,000
	(To record payment of bond interest and amortization of bond premium)		

A	=	L	+	SE
−5,000		−811		−4,189

At December 31, the adjusting entry is:

Dec. 31	Bond Interest Expense	4,189	
	Premium on Bonds Payable	811	
	Bond Interest Payable		5,000
	(To record accrued bond interest and amortization of bond premium)		

A	=	L	+	SE
		−811		−4,189
		+5,000		

Over the term of the bonds, the balance in Premium on Bonds Payable will decrease annually by the same amount until it has a zero balance at maturity.

Preparing a bond premium amortization schedule as shown in Illustration 16-17 is useful. It shows interest expense, premium amortization, and the carrying value of the bond. The interest expense recorded each period for the Candlestick bond is $4,189. Also note that the carrying value of the bond decreases $811 each period until it reaches its face value $100,000 at the end of period 10.

Illustration 16-17

Bond premium amortization schedule

CANDLESTICK, INC.
Bond Premium Amortization
Straight-Line Method—Semiannual Interest Payments

Semiannual Interest Periods	(A) Interest to Be Paid (5% × $100,000)	(B) Interest Expense to Be Recorded (A) − (C)	(C) Premium Amortization ($8,111 ÷ 10)	(D) Unamortized Premium (D) − (C)	(E) Bond Carrying Value ($100,000 + D)
Issue date				$8,111	$108,111
1	$ 5,000	$ 4,189	$ 811	7,300	107,300
2	5,000	4,189	811	6,489	106,489
3	5,000	4,189	811	5,678	105,678
4	5,000	4,189	811	4,867	104,867
5	5,000	4,189	811	4,056	104,056
6	5,000	4,189	811	3,245	103,245
7	5,000	4,189	811	2,434	102,434
8	5,000	4,189	811	1,623	101,623
9	5,000	4,189	811	812	100,812
10	5,000	4,188*	812*	-0-	100,000
	$ 50,000	$41,889	$8,111		

Column **(A)** remains constant because the face value of the bonds ($100,000) is multiplied by the semiannual contractual interest rate (5%) each period.
Column **(B)** is computed as the interest paid (Column A) less the premium amortization (Column C).
Column **(C)** indicates the premium amortization each period.
Column **(D)** decreases each period by the same amount until it reaches zero at maturity.
Column **(E)** decreases each period by the amount of premium amortization until it equals the face value at maturity.

*One dollar difference due to rounding.

Similar to Illustration 16-12, page 649, columns (A), (B), and (C) provide information for the required journal entries.

ISSUING BONDS BETWEEN INTEREST DATES

Bonds are often issued between interest payment dates. **When this occurs, the issuer requires the investor to pay the market price for the bonds plus accrued interest since the last interest date.** At the next interest date, the corporation will return the accrued interest to the investor by paying the full amount of interest due on outstanding bonds.

To illustrate, assume that Deer Corporation sells $1,000,000, 9% bonds at face value plus accrued interest on March 1. Interest is payable semiannually on July 1 and January 1. The accrued interest is $15,000 ($1,000,000 × 9% × 2/12). The total proceeds on the sale of the bonds, therefore, are $1,015,000. The entry to record the sale is:

A	=	L	+	SE
+1,015,000		+1,000,000		
		+15,000		

Mar. 1	Cash	1,015,000	
	Bonds Payable		1,000,000
	Bond Interest Payable		15,000
	(To record sale of bonds at face value plus accrued interest)		

At the first interest date, it is necessary to do two things with regard to bond interest: (1) Eliminate the bond interest payable balance. And (2) recognize interest expense for the 4 months (March 1–June 30) the bonds have been outstanding. Interest expense in this example is $30,000 ($1,000,000 × 9% × 4/12). The entry on July 1 for the $45,000 interest payment is:

A	=	L	+	SE
−45,000		−15,000		−30,000

July 1	Bond Interest Payable	15,000	
	Bond Interest Expense	30,000	
	Cash		45,000
	(To record payment of bond interest)		

Why does the issuer, Deer Corporation, collect interest at the time of issuance and then return it at the time of payment? The rationale: Collection of accrued interest at the issuance date allows the company to pay a full period's (6 months') interest to all bondholders at the next interest payment date. Deer Corporation as the issuer does not have to determine the individual amount of interest due each holder based on the time each bond has been outstanding. If bonds are not sold "with accrued interest," the issuer would have to keep track of the purchaser and the date of purchase to ensure that each bondholder received the correct amount of interest. It is both simpler and less expensive for the issuer to sell the bonds "with accrued interest."

BEFORE YOU GO ON...

REVIEW IT

1. What entry is made to record the issuance of bonds payable of $1 million at 100? At 96? At 102?
2. Why do bonds sell at a discount? At a premium? At face value?
3. Explain the accounting for bonds sold between interest dates.

DO IT

A bond amortization table shows (a) interest to be paid $50,000, (b) interest expense to be recorded $52,000, and (c) amortization $2,000. Answer the following questions: (1) Were the bonds sold at a premium or a discount? (2) After recording the interest expense, will the bond carrying value increase or decrease?

ACTION PLAN

- Understand the effects that the amortization of bond discount and bond premium have on bond interest expense and on the carrying value of the bonds.
- Remember that bond discount amortization increases both bond interest expense and the carrying value of the bond.
- Remember that bond premium amortization decreases both bond interest expense and the carrying value of the bond.

SOLUTION: The bond amortization table indicates that interest expense is $2,000 greater than the interest paid. This difference is equal to the amortization amount. Thus, (1) the bonds were sold at a discount. (2) The interest entry will decrease Discount on Bonds Payable and increase the carrying value of the bonds.

Related exercise material: BE16-2, BE16-3, BE16-4, BE16-5, E16-2, E16-3, E16-4, and E16-5.

THE NAVIGATOR

ACCOUNTING FOR BOND RETIREMENTS

STUDY OBJECTIVE 3

Describe the entries when bonds are redeemed or converted.

Bonds may be retired either when they are redeemed by the issuing corporation or when they are converted into common stock by bondholders. The appropriate entries for these transactions are explained in the following sections.

REDEEMING BONDS AT MATURITY

Regardless of the issue price of bonds, the book value of the bonds at maturity will equal their face value. This can be seen in Illustrations 16-12 and 16-17: The carrying value of the bonds at the end of their 5-year life ($100,000) is equal to the face value of the bonds.

Assuming that the interest for the last interest period is paid and recorded separately, the entry to record the redemption of the Candlestick bonds at maturity is:

Bonds Payable	100,000	
Cash		100,000
(To record redemption of bonds at maturity)		

A	=	L	+	SE
−100,000		−100,000		

REDEEMING BONDS BEFORE MATURITY

Bonds may be redeemed before maturity. A company may decide to retire bonds before maturity to reduce interest cost and remove debt from its balance sheet. A company should retire debt early only if it has sufficient cash resources.

When bonds are retired before maturity, it is necessary to: (1) Eliminate the carrying value of the bonds at the redemption date. (2) Record the cash paid. (3) Recognize the gain or loss on redemption. The carrying value of the bonds is the face value of the bonds less unamortized bond discount or plus unamortized bond premium at the redemption date.

HELPFUL HINT

Question: A bond is redeemed prior to its maturity date. Its carrying value exceeds its redemption price. Will the retirement result in a gain or a loss on redemption?
Answer: Gain.

To illustrate, assume that Candlestick, Inc. has sold its bonds at a premium, per Illustration 16-17. At the end of the eighth period Candlestick retires these bonds at 103 after paying the semiannual interest. The carrying value of the bonds at the redemption date is $101,623. (See the bond premium amortization schedule in Illustration 16-17.) The entry to record the redemption at the end of the eighth interest period (January 1, 2006) is:

Jan. 1	Bonds Payable	100,000	
	Premium on Bonds Payable	1,623	
	Loss on Bond Redemption	1,377	
	Cash		103,000
	(To record redemption of bonds at 103)		

A	=	L	+	SE
−103,000		−100,000		−1,377
		−1,623		

Note that the loss of $1,377 is the difference between the cash paid of $103,000 and the carrying value of the bonds of $101,623. Losses (gains) on bond redemption are reported in the income statement as extraordinary items.

CONVERTING BONDS INTO COMMON STOCK

Convertible bonds have features that are attractive both to bondholders and to the issuer. The conversion often gives bondholders an opportunity to benefit if the market price of the common stock increases substantially. Until conversion, though, the bondholder receives interest on the bond. For the issuer, the bonds sell at a higher price and pay a lower rate of interest than comparable debt securities without the conversion option. Many corporations, such as **USAir**, **USX Corp.**, and **DaimlerChrysler Corporation**, have convertible bonds outstanding.

HELPFUL HINT
The method of recording this conversion of bonds to stock is called the **book value method**. The book value of the bonds is removed from the liability accounts and recorded as common stock and related paid-in capital.

When bonds are converted into common stock and the conversion is recorded, the current market prices of the bonds and the stock are ignored. Instead, the **carrying value** of the bonds is transferred to paid-in capital accounts. **No gain or loss is recognized**. To illustrate, assume that on July 1 Saunders Associates converts $100,000 bonds sold at face value into 2,000 shares of $10 par value common stock. Both the bonds and the common stock have a market value of $130,000. The entry to record the conversion is:

A	=	L	+	SE
		−100,000		+20,000
				+80,000

July 1	Bonds Payable	100,000	
	Common Stock		20,000
	Paid-in Capital in Excess of Par Value		80,000
	(To record bond conversion)		

Note that the current market price of the bonds and stock ($130,000) is not considered in making the entry. This method of recording the bond conversion is often referred to as the **carrying (or book) value method**.

BOND SINKING FUNDS

STUDY OBJECTIVE 4
Describe a bond sinking fund.

Many bond issues require the borrower to make periodic cash contributions to a sinking (redemption) fund over the life of the bonds. A **sinking fund** is cash or other assets set aside to retire debt. In other words, it is like a savings account that is used to pay back bondholders. **A sinking fund makes the bonds more attractive to investors, because it enhances the likelihood that the bonds will be redeemed at maturity.** For example, **Texaco** and **Alcoa** have sinking funds for their bonds. Such bonds are often referred to as **sinking fund bonds**.

Sinking funds are usually under the control of a trustee, such as a bank or a trust company. The trustee may be permitted to invest the periodic deposits in high-quality income-producing securities. **It is expected that the deposits plus the earnings from the investments will equal the face value of the bonds at maturity.** Shortly before the maturity date, the trustee sells the securities and uses the total cash in the fund to redeem the bonds. Any excess cash in the fund is returned to the bond issuer.

The bond sinking fund is reported as a single amount in the investments section of the balance sheet. Bond sinking fund revenue is classified as "other revenues and gains" in the income statement.

The bond contract may also require the corporation to establish a restriction on its retained earnings. As explained in Chapter 15, this restriction is reported as a note in the financial statements.

BEFORE YOU GO ON...

REVIEW IT

1. Explain the accounting for redemption of bonds at maturity, before maturity by payment in cash, and by conversion into common stock.
2. Did **Lands' End** redeem any of its debt during the fiscal year ended January 28, 2000? (*Hint:* To find information related to this question, examine Lands' End's statement of cash flows. The answer to this question is provided on page 679.)
3. What is the purpose of the bond sinking fund? Where is a bond sinking fund reported in the financial statements?

DO IT

R & B Inc. issued $500,000, 10-year bonds at a premium. Prior to maturity, when the carrying value of the bonds is $508,000, the company retires the bonds at 102. Prepare the entry to record the redemption of the bonds.

ACTION PLAN

- Determine and eliminate the carrying value of the bonds.
- Record the cash paid.
- Compute and record the gain or loss (which is the difference between the first two items).

SOLUTION: There is a loss on redemption: The cash paid, $510,000 ($500,000 × 102%), is greater than the carrying value of $508,000. The entry is:

Bonds Payable	500,000	
Premium on Bonds Payable	8,000	
Loss on Bond Redemption	2,000	
Cash		510,000
(To record redemption of bonds at 102)		

Related exercise material: BE16-6, E16-3, E16-4, and E16-6.

THE NAVIGATOR

ACCOUNTING FOR OTHER LONG-TERM LIABILITIES

Other common types of long-term obligations are notes payable and lease liabilities. The accounting for these liabilities is explained in the following sections.

LONG-TERM NOTES PAYABLE

STUDY OBJECTIVE 5

Describe the accounting for long-term notes payable.

The use of notes payable in long-term debt financing is quite common. Long-term notes payable are similar to short-term interest-bearing notes payable except that the terms of the notes exceed one year. In periods of unstable interest rates, the interest rate on long-term notes may be tied to changes in the market rate. Examples are the 8.03% adjustable-rate notes issued by **General Motors** and the floating-rate notes issued by **American Express Company**.

A long-term note may be secured by a **mortgage** that pledges title to specific assets as security for a loan. **Mortgage notes payable** are widely used by individuals to purchase homes and by many small and some large companies to acquire plant assets. Approximately 18 percent of **McDonald's** long-term debt relates to mortgage notes on land, buildings, and improvements. Mortgage loan terms may stipulate either a fixed or an adjustable interest rate. Typically, the terms require the borrower to make installment payments over the term of the loan. Each payment consists of (1) interest on the unpaid balance of the loan and (2) a reduction of loan principal. The interest decreases each period, while the portion applied to the loan principal increases.

Mortgage notes payable are recorded initially at face value. Subsequent entries are required for each installment payment. To illustrate, assume that Porter Technology Inc. issues a $500,000, 12%, 20-year mortgage note on December 31, 2002, to obtain needed financing for a new research laboratory. The terms provide for semiannual installment payments of $33,231 (not including real estate taxes and insurance). The installment payment schedule for the first 2 years is as follows.

Illustration 16-18

Mortgage installment payment schedule

Semiannual Interest Period	(A) Cash Payment	(B) Interest Expense (D) × 6%	(C) Reduction of Principal (A) − (B)	(D) Principal Balance (D) − (C)
Issue date				$500,000
1	$33,231	$30,000	$3,231	496,769
2	33,231	29,806	3,425	493,344
3	33,231	29,601	3,630	489,714
4	33,231	29,383	3,848	485,866

HELPFUL HINT
Electronic spreadsheets can create a schedule of installment loan payments. You can put in the data for your own mortgage loan and get information that really hits home.

The entries to record the mortgage loan and first installment payment are as follows.

A	=	L	+	SE
+500,000		+500,000		

Dec. 31	Cash	500,000	
	Mortgage Notes Payable		500,000
	(To record mortgage loan)		

A	=	L	+	SE
−33,231		−3,231		−30,000

June 30	Interest Expense	30,000	
	Mortgage Notes Payable	3,231	
	Cash		33,231
	(To record semiannual payment on mortgage)		

In the balance sheet, the reduction in principal for the next year is reported as a current liability. The remaining unpaid principal balance is classified as a long-term liability. At December 31, 2003, the total liability is $493,344. Of that amount, $7,478 ($3,630 + $3,848) is current, and $485,866 ($493,344 − $7,478) is long-term.

ACCOUNTING IN ACTION e Business Insight

Mortgage.com, a pioneer in one of the Web's more promising ideas, recently exited the online home-lending business and laid off most of its 618 employees. A study of Internet consumers showed that only 4 percent of them have applied online for a mortgage, and fewer than 1 percent have closed a loan. "The fact is, there is still a lot about getting a mortgage that can't be done online," says Dianne Glossman, an analyst with UBS Marburg. Although a recent change in federal law allows people to send their signatures electronically, "in most cases, you still need to sign paper documents, someone to visit the property and appraise it, and these loans still usually need to be closed in person."

SOURCE: Excerpts from Aaron Elstein, "Mortgage.com Plans to Cease Its Lending and Pare Its Staff," *The Wall Street Journal*, November 1, 2000. Reprinted by permission of the Wall Street Journal. © 2000 Dow Jones & Co, Inc. All Rights Reserved Worldwide.

LEASE LIABILITIES

STUDY OBJECTIVE 6

Contrast the accounting for operating and capital leases.

As indicated in Chapter 10, a lease is a contractual arrangement between a lessor (owner of the property) and a lessee (renter of the property). It grants the right to use specific property for a period of time in return for cash payments. Leasing is big business. An estimated $125 billion of capital equipment was leased in a recent year. This represents approximately one-third of equipment financed that year. The two most common types of leases are operating leases and capital leases.

Operating Leases

The renting of an apartment and the rental of a car at an airport are examples of operating leases. **In an operating lease the intent is temporary use of the property by the lessee. The lessor continues to own the property.** The lease (or rental) payments are recorded as an expense by the lessee and as revenue by the lessor. For example, assume that a sales representative for Western Inc. leases a car from Hertz Car Rental at the Los Angeles airport and that Hertz charges a total of $275. The entry by the lessee, Western Inc., is:

Car Rental Expense	275	
Cash		275
(To record payment of lease rental charge)		

A	=	L	+	SE
−275				−275

The lessee may incur other costs during the lease period. For example, in the case above, the lessee may pay for gas and oil. These costs are also reported as an expense.

Capital Leases

In most lease contracts, a periodic payment is made by the lessee and is recorded as rent expense in the income statement. But, in some cases, the lease contract transfers substantially all the benefits and risks of ownership to the lessee. Such a lease is in effect a purchase of the property. This type of lease is called a capital lease. Its name comes from the fact that the present value of the cash payments for the lease are capitalized and recorded as an asset. Illustration 16-19 indicates the major difference between an operating and a capital lease.

HELPFUL HINT
A capital lease situation is one that, although legally a rental case, is *in substance* an installment purchase by the lessee. Accounting standards require that substance over form be used in such a situation.

Illustration 16-19
Types of leases

Operating lease
U-Drive Corp.
"Have it back by 6:00 Sunday."
"OK!"
Lessor has substantially all of the benefits and risks of ownership
Capital lease
"Only 3 more payments and this baby is ours!"
Replace Drum
Lessee has substantially all of the benefits and risks of ownership

The lessee must record a lease **as an asset**—that is, as a capital lease—if **any one** of the following conditions exists:

1. **The lease transfers ownership of the property to the lessee.** *Rationale:* If during the lease term the lessee receives ownership of the asset, the leased asset should be reported as an asset on the lessee's books.
2. **The lease contains a bargain purchase option.** *Rationale:* If during the term of the lease the lessee can purchase the asset at a price substantially below its fair market value, the lessee will exercise this option. Thus, the lease should be reported as a leased asset on the lessee's books.

3. **The lease term is equal to 75% or more of the economic life of the leased property.** *Rationale:* If the lease term is for much of the asset's useful life, the asset should be recorded by the lessee.
4. **The present value of the lease payments equals or exceeds 90% of the fair market value of the leased property.** *Rationale:* If the present value of the lease payments is equal to or almost equal to the fair market value of the asset, the lessee has essentially purchased the asset. As a result, the leased asset should be recorded on the books of the lessee.

To illustrate, assume that Gonzalez Company decides to lease new equipment. The lease period is 4 years; the economic life of the leased equipment is estimated to be 5 years. The present value of the lease payments is $190,000, which is equal to the fair market value of the equipment. There is no transfer of ownership during the lease term, nor is there any bargain purchase option.

In this example, Gonzalez has essentially purchased the equipment. Conditions 3 and 4 have been met. First, the lease term is 75% or more of the economic life of the asset. Second, the present value of cash payments is equal to the equipment's fair market value. The entry to record the transaction is as follows.

A	=	L	+	SE
+190,000		+190,000		

Leased Asset—Equipment	190,000	
Lease Liability		190,000
(To record leased asset and lease liability)		

The leased asset is reported on the balance sheet under plant assets. The lease liability is reported on the balance sheet as a liability. **The portion of the lease liability expected to be paid in the next year is reported as a current liability. The remainder is classified as a long-term liability.**

Most lessees do not like to report leases on their balance sheets. Why? Because the lease liability increases the company's total liabilities. This, in turn, may make it more difficult for the company to obtain needed funds from lenders. As a result, companies attempt to keep leased assets and lease liabilities off the balance sheet by not meeting any of the four conditions mentioned above. The practice of keeping liabilities off the balance sheet is referred to as **off-balance sheet financing**.

STUDY OBJECTIVE 7

Identify the methods for the presentation and analysis of long-term liabilities.

STATEMENT PRESENTATION AND ANALYSIS

PRESENTATION

Long-term liabilities are reported in a separate section of the balance sheet immediately following current liabilities, as shown in Illustration 16-20.

Illustration 16-20

Balance sheet presentation of long-term liabilities

LAX CORPORATION
Balance Sheet (partial)

Long-term liabilities		
Bonds payable 10% due in 2009	$1,000,000	
Less: Discount on bonds payable	80,000	$ 920,000
Mortgage notes payable, 11%, due in 2015 and secured by plant assets		500,000
Lease liability		540,000
Total long-term liabilities		$1,960,000

Alternatively, summary data may be presented in the balance sheet with detailed data (interest rates, maturity dates, conversion privileges, and assets pledged as collateral) shown in a supporting schedule. The current maturities of long-term debt should be reported under current liabilities if they are to be paid from current assets.

ANALYSIS

Long-term creditors and stockholders are interested in a company's long-run solvency. Of particular interest is the company's ability to pay interest as it comes due and to repay the face value of the debt at maturity. Debt to total assets and times interest earned are two ratios that provide information about debt-paying ability and long-run solvency.

The **debt to total assets ratio** measures the percentage of the total assets provided by creditors. It is computed, as shown in the formula below, by dividing total debt (both current and long-term liabilities) by total assets. The higher the percentage of debt to total assets, the greater the risk that the company may be unable to meet its maturing obligations.

The **times interest earned ratio** indicates the company's ability to meet interest payments as they come due. It is computed by dividing income before income taxes and interest expense by interest expense.

To illustrate these ratios, we will use data from **Lands' End's** 2000 annual report. The company had total liabilities of \$160 million, total assets of \$456 million, interest expense of \$1.9 million, income taxes of \$28.2 million, and net income of \$48 million. Lands' End's debt to total assets ratio and times interest earned ratio are shown graphically below, along with their computations.

Illustration 16-21

Debt to total assets and times interest earned ratios, with computations

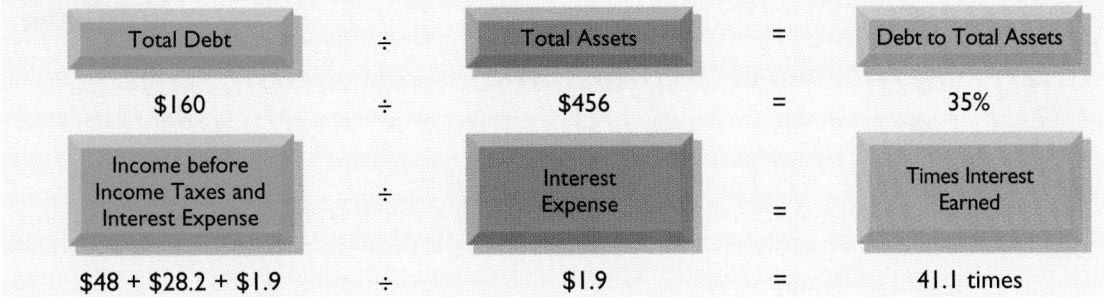

Total Debt	÷	Total Assets	=	Debt to Total Assets
\$160	÷	\$456	=	35%
Income before Income Taxes and Interest Expense	÷	Interest Expense	=	Times Interest Earned
\$48 + \$28.2 + \$1.9	÷	\$1.9	=	41.1 times

Lands' End has a relatively low debt to total assets percentage of 35%; its interest coverage of 41.1 times appears extremely safe.

BEFORE YOU GO ON...

REVIEW IT

1. Explain the accounting for long-term mortgage notes payable.
2. What is the difference in accounting for an operating lease versus a capital lease? Explain the four conditions used to determine whether the lease contract transfers substantially all the benefits and risks of ownership.
3. What ratios may be computed to analyze a company's long-run solvency?

A LOOK BACK AT OUR FEATURE STORY

Refer back to the Feature Story about the **University of Kentucky** at the beginning of the chapter, and answer the following questions.

1. The University of Kentucky's bonds are rated AA− by Standard & Poor's and A1 by Moody's Investor Service. Why is it important to the University of Kentucky that its bonds have a high bond rating?
2. Explain the meaning of the tax-exempt status of the University of Kentucky bonds. What does it mean to say that "a recent issue offering 6% is the equivalent of 10% to those individuals in the top tax bracket"?
3. Why does the state use bonds to finance the buildings rather than taking the funds out of general revenues?

SOLUTION

1. Having a high (good) bond rating is as important to a university as it is to a business corporation. A high bond rating indicates that the bonds are less risky. They are thus more attractive to purchasers. A lower interest rate results, and the cost to the issuer of the bonds is less.
2. Because the University of Kentucky bonds are tax exempt, bondholders do not have to pay federal or state (in-state residents only) income tax on the interest received. To earn an after-tax return of 6%, a person in the maximum tax bracket would have to receive interest equal to approximately 10% on taxable bonds [10% − (40% × 10%)].
3. Financing the buildings through the issuance of bonds spreads the cost of the buildings over many years and more equitably distributes the costs to a broader base of taxpayers. Future taxpayers pay for the buildings as they are used, rather than the taxpayers of one year absorbing the cost out of general revenues in the year of construction.

THE NAVIGATOR

DEMONSTRATION PROBLEM

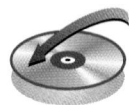

Additional Demonstration Problem

Snyder Software Inc. has successfully developed a new spreadsheet program. To produce and market the program, the company needed $2.0 million of additional financing. On December 31, 2002, Snyder borrowed money as follows.

1. Snyder issued $500,000, 11%, 10-year convertible bonds. The bonds sold at face value and pay semiannual interest on January 1 and July 1. Each $1,000 bond is convertible into 30 shares of Snyder's $20 par value common stock.
2. Snyder issued $1.0 million, 10%, 10-year bonds for $885,301. Interest is payable semiannually on January 1 and July 1. Snyder uses the straight-line method of amortization.
3. Snyder also issued a $500,000, 12%, 15-year mortgage note payable. The terms provide for semiannual installment payments of $36,324 on June 30 and December 31.

Instructions

1. For the convertible bonds, prepare journal entries for:
   (a) The issuance of the bonds on January 1, 2003.
   (b) Interest expense on July 1 and December 31, 2003.
   (c) The payment of interest on January 1, 2004.
   (d) The conversion of all bonds into common stock on January 1, 2004, when the market value of the common stock was $67 per share.
2. For the 10-year, 10% bonds:
   (a) Journalize the issuance of the bonds on January 1, 2003.
   (b) Prepare a bond discount amortization schedule for the first six interest periods.
   (c) Prepare the journal entries for interest expense and amortization of bond discount in 2003.

(d) Prepare the entry for the redemption of the bonds at 101 on January 1, 2006, after paying the interest due on this date.

3. For the mortgage note payable:
(a) Prepare the entry for the issuance of the note on December 31, 2002.
(b) Prepare a payment schedule for the first four installment payments.
(c) Indicate the current and noncurrent amounts for the mortgage note payable at December 31, 2003.

SOLUTION TO DEMONSTRATION PROBLEM

1. (a) 2003

Jan. 1	Cash	500,000	
	Bonds Payable		500,000
	(To record issue of 11%, 10-year convertible bonds at face value)		

(b) 2003

July 1	Bond Interest Expense	27,500	
	Cash ($500,000 × 0.055)		27,500
	(To record payment of semiannual interest)		
Dec. 31	Bond Interest Expense	27,500	
	Bond Interest Payable		27,500
	(To record accrual of semiannual bond interest)		

(c) 2004

Jan. 1	Bond Interest Payable	27,500	
	Cash		27,500
	(To record payment of accrued interest)		

(d)

Jan. 1	Bonds Payable	500,000	
	Common Stock		300,000*
	Paid-in Capital in Excess of Par Value		200,000
	(To record conversion of bonds into common stock) *($500,000 ÷ $1,000 = 500 bonds; 500 × 30 = 15,000 shares; 15,000 × $20 = $300,000)		

ACTION PLAN

- Compute interest semiannually (six months).
- Record the accrual and payment of interest on appropriate dates.
- Record the conversion of the bonds into common stock by removing the book (carrying) value of the bonds from the liability account.

2. (a) 2003

Jan. 1	Cash	885,301	
	Discount on Bonds Payable	114,699	
	Bonds Payable		1,000,000
	(To record issuance of bonds at a discount		

(b)

Semiannual Interest Period	Interest to Be Paid	Interest Expense to Be Recorded	Discount Amortization	Unamortized Discount	Bond Carrying Value
Issue date				$114,699	$885,301
1	$50,000	$55,735	$5,735	108,964	891,036
2	50,000	55,735	5,735	103,229	896,771
3	50,000	55,735	5,735	97,494	902,506
4	50,000	55,735	5,735	91,759	908,241
5	50,000	55,735	5,735	86,024	913,976
6	50,000	55,735	5,735	80,289	919,711

ACTION PLAN

- Record the discount on bonds issued as a contra liability account.
- Compute interest expense and bond discount amortization using the straight-line method.
- Record the amortization of bond discount as an increase in interest expense.
- Compute the loss on bond redemption as the excess of the cash paid over the carrying value of the redeemed bonds.

(c) 2003

Date	Account	Debit	Credit
July 1	Bond Interest Expense	55,735	
	Discount on Bonds Payable		5,735
	Cash		50,000
	(To record payment of semiannual interest and amortization of bond discount)		
Dec. 31	Bond Interest Expense	55,735	
	Discount on Bonds Payable		5,735
	Bond Interest Payable		50,000
	(To record accrual of semiannual interest and amortization of bond discount)		

(d) 2006

Date	Account	Debit	Credit
Jan. 1	Bonds Payable	1,000,000	
	Loss on Bond Redemption	90,289*	
	Discount on Bonds Payable		80,289
	Cash		1,010,000
	(To record redemption of bonds at 101)		
	*($1,010,000 – $919,711)		

ACTION PLAN

- Compute periodic interest expense on a mortgage note, recognizing that as the principal amount decreases, so does the interest expense.
- Record mortgage payments, recognizing that each payment consists of (1) interest on the unpaid loan balance and (2) a reduction of the loan principal.

THE NAVIGATOR

3. (a) 2002

Date	Account	Debit	Credit
Dec. 31	Cash	500,000	
	Mortgage Notes Payable		500,000
	(To record issuance of mortgage note payable)		

(b)

Semiannual Interest Period	**Cash Payment**	**Interest Expense**	**Reduction of Principal**	**Principal Balance**
Issue date				$500,000
1	$36,324	$30,000	$6,324	493,676
2	36,324	29,621	6,703	486,973
3	36,324	29,218	7,106	479,867
4	36,324	28,792	7,532	472,335

(c) Current liability $14,638 ($7,106 + $7,532)
Long-term liability $472,335

SUMMARY OF STUDY OBJECTIVES

1. *Explain why bonds are issued.* Bonds may be sold to many investors, and they offer the following advantages over common stock: (a) stockholder control is not affected, (b) tax savings result, (c) earnings per share of common stock may be higher.

2. *Prepare the entries for the issuance of bonds and interest expense.* When bonds are issued, Cash is debited for the cash proceeds, and Bonds Payable is credited for the face value of the bonds. Also, Bond Interest Payable is credited if there is accrued interest. The accounts Premium on Bonds Payable or Discount on Bonds Payable are used to show the bond premium or bond discount. Bond discount and bond premium are amortized by the straight-line method.

3. *Describe the entries when bonds are redeemed or converted.* When bonds are redeemed at maturity, Cash is credited and Bonds Payable is debited for the face value of the bonds. When bonds are redeemed before maturity, it is necessary to (a) eliminate the carrying value of the bonds at the redemption date, (b) record the cash paid, and (c) recognize the gain or loss on redemption. When bonds are converted to common stock, the carrying (or book) value of the bonds is transferred to appropriate paid-in capital accounts; no gain or loss is recognized.

4. ***Describe a bond sinking fund.*** A bond sinking fund is cash or other assets set aside to retire the bonds.

5. ***Describe the accounting for long-term notes payable.*** Each payment consists of (1) interest on the unpaid balance of the loan and (2) a reduction of loan principal. The interest decreases each period, while the portion applied to the loan principal increases.

6. ***Contrast the accounting for operating and capital leases.*** For an operating lease, lease (rental) payments are recorded as an expense by the lessee (renter). For a capital lease, the lessee records the asset and related obligation at the present value of the future lease payments.

7. ***Identify the methods for the presentation and analysis of long-term liabilities.*** The nature and amount of each long-term debt should be reported in the balance sheet or in the notes accompanying the financial statements. Stockholders and long-term creditors are interested in a company's long-run solvency. Debt to total assets and times interest earned are two ratios that provide information about debt-paying ability and long-run solvency.

☑ THE NAVIGATOR

Key Term Matching Activity

GLOSSARY

Bearer (coupon) bonds Bonds not registered. (p. 642).

Bond certificate A legal document that indicates the name of the issuer, the face value of the bonds, and such other data as the contractual interest rate and maturity date of the bonds. (p. 643).

Bond indenture A legal document that sets forth the terms of the bond issue. (p. 643).

Bonds A form of interest-bearing notes payable issued by corporations, universities, and governmental entities. (p. 640).

Callable bonds Bonds that are subject to retirement at a stated dollar amount prior to maturity at the option of the issuer. (p. 642).

Capital lease A contractual arrangement that transfers substantially all the benefits and risks of ownership to the lessee so that the lease is in effect a purchase of the property. (p. 657).

Contractual interest rate Rate used to determine the amount of interest the borrower pays and the investor receives. (p. 643).

Convertible bonds Bonds that permit bondholders to convert them into common stock at their option. (p. 642).

Debenture bonds Bonds issued against the general credit of the borrower. Also called unsecured bonds. (p. 642).

Debt to total assets ratio A solvency measure that indicates the percentage of total assets provided by creditors; computed as total debt divided by total assets. (p. 659).

Face value Amount of principal the issuer must pay at the maturity date of the bond. (p. 643).

Long-term liabilities Obligations expected to be paid after one year. (p. 640).

Market interest rate The rate investors demand for loaning funds to the corporation. (p. 644).

Mortgage bond A bond secured by real estate. (p. 642).

Mortgage note payable A long-term note secured by a mortgage that pledges title to specific assets as security for a loan. (p. 655).

Operating lease A contractual arrangement giving the lessee temporary use of the property, with continued ownership of the property by the lessor. (p. 657).

Registered bonds Bonds issued in the name of the owner. (p. 642).

Secured bonds Bonds that have specific assets of the issuer pledged as collateral. (p. 642).

Serial bonds Bonds that mature in installments. (p. 642).

Sinking fund Cash or other assets set aside to retire debt. (p. 654).

Sinking fund bonds Bonds secured by specific assets set aside to retire them. (p. 642).

Straight-line method of amortization A method of amortizing bond discount or bond premium that allocates the same amount to interest expense in each period. (p. 648).

Term bonds Bonds that mature at a single specified future date. (p. 642).

Times interest earned ratio A solvency measure that indicates a company's ability to meet interest payments; computed by dividing income before income taxes and interest expense by interest expense. (p. 659).

Unsecured bonds Bonds issued against the general credit of the borrower. Also called debenture bonds. (p. 642).

APPENDIX *Effective-Interest Amortization*

The straight-line method of amortization presented in the chapter has a conceptual deficiency: It does not completely satisfy the matching principle. Under the straight-line method, interest expense as a percentage of the carrying value of the bonds varies each interest period. We can see this by looking at data from four of the interest periods of the bond amortization schedule shown in Illustration 16-12.

Illustration 16A-1

Interest percentage rates under straight-line method

Semiannual Interest Period	Interest Expense to Be Recorded (A)	Bond Carrying Value (B)	Interest Expense as a Percentage of Carrying Value (A) ÷ (B)
1	$5,736	$92,639	6.19%
2	5,736	93,375	6.14%
3	5,736	94,111	6.09%
10	5,736	99,263	5.78%

STUDY OBJECTIVE 8

Contrast the effects of the straight-line and effective-interest methods of amortizing bond discount and bond premium.

Note that interest expense as a percentage of carrying value declines in each interest period. To comply with the matching principle, interest expense as a percentage of carrying value should not change over the life of the bonds. This percentage is referred to as the **effective-interest rate**. It is established when the bonds are issued and remains constant in each interest period.

The effective-interest method of amortization better satisfies the matching principle. Under the **effective-interest method**, the amortization of bond discount or bond premium results in periodic interest expense equal to a constant percentage of the carrying value of the bonds. The effective-interest method results in varying amounts of amortization and interest expense per period but **a constant percentage rate**. The straight-line method results in **constant amounts of amortization and interest expense** per period but a varying percentage rate.

The following steps are required under the effective-interest method.

1. Compute the **bond interest expense**. To do so, multiply the carrying value of the bonds at the beginning of the interest period by the effective-interest rate.
2. Compute the **bond interest paid** (or accrued). To do so, multiply the face value of the bonds by the contractual interest rate.
3. Compute the **amortization amount**. To do so, determine the difference between the amounts computed in steps (1) and (2).

These steps are graphically depicted in Illustration 16A-2.

Illustration 16A-2

Computation of amortization—effective-interest method

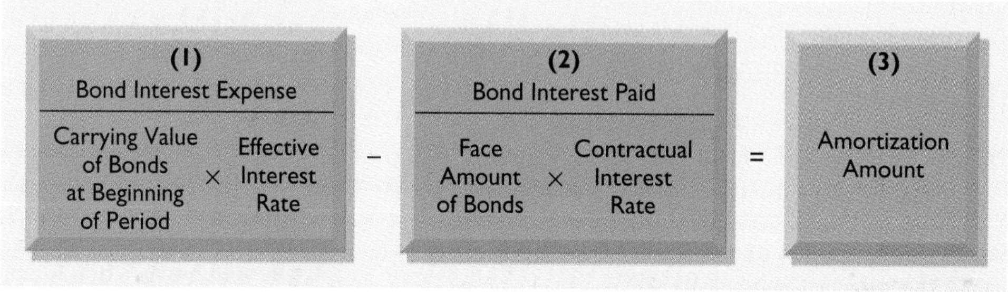

The straight-line and effective-interest methods result in the same total amount of interest expense over the term of the bonds. Also, interest expense each period is generally comparable in amount. However, **when the amounts are materially different, the effective-interest method is required under generally accepted accounting principles (GAAP).**

AMORTIZING BOND DISCOUNT

To illustrate the effective-interest method of bond discount amortization, assume that Candlestick, Inc. (as per this chapter pages 647–648) issues $100,000 of 10%, 5-year bonds on January 1, 2002, with interest payable each July 1 and January 1. The bonds sell for $92,639 (92.639% of face value). This sales price results in bond discount of $7,361 ($100,000 − $92,639) and an effective-interest rate of 12%. (Note that the $92,639 can be proven by time value of money techniques as shown in Appendix C at the end of this book.) A bond discount amortization schedule as shown in Illustration 16A-3 facilitates the recording of interest expense and the discount amortization. Note that interest expense as a percentage of carrying value remains constant at 6%. Illustration 16A-3 may be compared with Illustration 16-12 (page 649) to see the differences between the straight-line and the effective-interest amortization methods on a bond discount.

Illustration 16A-3

Bond discount amortization schedule

CANDLESTICK, INC.
Bond Discount Amortization
Effective-Interest Method—Semiannual Interest Payments
10% Bonds Issued at 12%

Semiannual Interest Periods	(A) Interest to Be Paid (5% × $100,000)	(B) Interest Expense to Be Recorded (6% × Preceding Bond Carrying Value)	(C) Discount Amortization (B) − (A)	(D) Unamortized Discount (D) − (C)	(E) Bond Carrying Value ($100,000 − D)
Issue date				$7,361	$ 92,639
1	$ 5,000	$ 5,558 (6% × $92,639)	$ 558	6,803	93,197
2	5,000	5,592 (6% × $93,197)	592	6,211	93,789
3	5,000	5,627 (6% × $93,789)	627	5,584	94,416
4	5,000	5,665 (6% × $94,416)	665	4,919	95,081
5	5,000	5,705 (6% × $95,081)	705	4,214	95,786
6	5,000	5,747 (6% × $95,786)	747	3,467	96,533
7	5,000	5,792 (6% × $96,533)	792	2,675	97,325
8	5,000	5,840 (6% × $97,325)	840	1,835	98,165
9	5,000	5,890 (6% × $98,165)	890	945	99,055
10	5,000	5,945* (6% × $99,055)	945	-0-	100,000
	$50,000	$57,361	$7,361		

Column **(A)** remains constant because the face value of the bonds ($100,000) is multiplied by the semiannual contractual interest rate (5%) each period.
Column **(B)** is computed as the preceding bond carrying value times the semiannual effective-interest rate (6%).
Column **(C)** indicates the discount amortization each period.
Column **(D)** decreases each period until it reaches zero at maturity.
Column **(E)** increases each period until it equals face value at maturity.
*$2 difference due to rounding.

For the first interest period, the computations of bond interest expense and the bond discount amortization are:

Illustration 16A-4

Computation of bond discount amortization

Bond interest expense ($92,639 × 6%)	$5,558
Contractual interest ($100,000 × 5%)	5,000
Bond discount amortization	**$ 558**

The entry to record the payment of interest and amortization of bond discount by Candlestick, Inc. on July 1, 2002, is:

July 1	Bond Interest Expense	5,558	
	Discount on Bonds Payable		558
	Cash		5,000
	(To record payment of bond interest and amortization of bond discount)		

A	=	L	+	SE
−5,000		+558		−5,558

For the second interest period, bond interest expense will be $5,592 ($93,197 × 6%), and the discount amortization will be $592. At December 31, the following adjusting entry is made.

A	=	L	+	SE
		+592		−5,592
		+5,000		

Dec. 31	Bond Interest Expense	5,592	
	Discount on Bonds Payable		592
	Bond Interest Payable		5,000
	(To record accrued interest and amortization of bond discount)		

Total bond interest expense for 2002 is $11,150 ($5,558 + $5,592). On January 1, payment of the interest is recorded by a debit to Bond Interest Payable and a credit to Cash.

AMORTIZING BOND PREMIUM

HELPFUL HINT

When a bond sells for $108,111, it is quoted as 108.111% of face value. Note that $108,111 can be proven as shown in Appendix C.

The amortization of bond premium by the effective-interest method is similar to the procedures described for bond discount. For example, assume that Candlestick, Inc. issues $100,000, 10%, 5-year bonds on January 1, 2002, with interest payable on July 1 and January 1. In this case, the bonds sell for $108,111. This sales price results in bond premium of $8,111 and an effective-interest rate of 8%. The bond premium amortization schedule is shown in Illustration 16A-5.

Illustration 16A-5 may be compared with Illustration 16-17 (page 651) to see the difference between the straight-line and the effective-interest amortization methods on a bond premium.

Illustration 16A-5

Bond premium amortization schedule

CANDLESTICK, INC.
Bond Premium Amortization
Effective-Interest Method—Semiannual Interest Payments
10% Bonds Issued at 8%

Semiannual Interest Periods	(A) Interest to Be Paid (5% × $100,000)	(B) Interest Expense to Be Recorded (4% × Preceding Bond Carrying Value)	(C) Premium Amortization (A) − (B)	(D) Unamortized Premium (D) − (C)	(E) Bond Carrying Value ($100,000 + D)
Issue date				$8,111	$108,111
1	$ 5,000	$ 4,324 (4% × $108,111)	$ 676	7,435	107,435
2	5,000	4,297 (4% × $107,435)	703	6,732	106,732
3	5,000	4,269 (4% × $106,732)	731	6,001	106,001
4	5,000	4,240 (4% × $106,001)	760	5,241	105,241
5	5,000	4,210 (4% × $105,241)	790	4,451	104,451
6	5,000	4,178 (4% × $104,451)	822	3,629	103,629
7	5,000	4,145 (4% × $103,629)	855	2,774	102,774
8	5,000	4,111 (4% × $102,774)	889	1,885	101,885
9	5,000	4,075 (4% × $101,885)	925	960	100,960
10	5,000	4,040* (4% × $100,960)	960	–0–	100,000
	$50,000	$41,889	$8,111		

Column (A) remains constant because the face value of the bonds ($100,000) is multiplied by the semiannual contractual interest rate (5%) each period.
Column (B) is computed as the carrying value of the bonds times the semiannual effective-interest rate (4%).
Column (C) indicates the preminum amortization each period.
Column (D) decreases each period until it reaches zero at maturity.
Column (E) decreases each period until it equals face value at maturity.

*$2 difference due to rounding.

For the first interest period, the computations of bond interest expense and the bond premium amortization are:

Bond interest expense ($108,111 × 4%)	$4,324
Contractual interest ($100,000 × 5%)	5,000
Bond premium amortization	**$ 676**

Illustration 16A-6

Computation of bond premium amortization

The entry on the first interest date is:

July 1	Bond Interest Expense	4,324	
	Premium on Bonds Payable	676	
	Cash		5,000
	(To record payment of bond interest and amortization of bond premium)		

A	=	L	+	SE
−5,000		−676		−4,324

For the second interest period, interest expense will be $4,297, and the premium amortization will be $703. Total bond interest expense for 2002 is $8,621 ($4,324 + $4,297).

TECHNOLOGY IN ACTION

The amortization schedule is an excellent example of an accounting computation efficiently and effectively performed by an electronic spreadsheet. Once the selling price, face amount, contractual rate of interest, effective rate of interest, and number of interest periods are determined and entered into the spreadsheet, all of the computations until maturity can be performed by the computer. Remember that all the data needed for the adjusting entries can be taken directly from the amortization schedule.

DEMONSTRATION PROBLEM

Additional Demonstration Problem

Gardner Corporation issues $1,750,000, 10-year, 12% bonds on January 1, 2002, at $1,820,000 to yield 10%. The bonds pay semiannual interest July 1 and January 1. Gardner uses the effective-interest method of amortization.

Instructions

(a) Prepare the journal entry to record the issuance of the bonds.

(b) Prepare the journal entry to record the payment of interest on July 1, 2002.

ACTION PLAN

- Compute interest expense by multiplying bond carrying value at the beginning of the period by the effective-interest rate.
- Compute credit to cash (or bond interest payable) by multiplying the face value of the bonds by the contractual interest rate.
- Compute bond premium or discount amortization, which is the difference between (1) and (2).
- Interest expense increases when the effective-interest method is used for bonds issued at a discount. The reason is that a constant percentage is applied to an increasing book value to compute interest expense.

SOLUTION TO DEMONSTRATION PROBLEM

(a) 2002

Jan. 1	Cash	1,820,000	
	Bonds Payable		1,750,000
	Premium on Bonds Payable		70,000
	(To record issuance of bonds at a premium)		

(b) 2002

July 1	Bond Interest Expense	91,000*	
	Premium on Bonds Payable	14,000**	
	Cash		105,000
	(To record payment of semiannual interest and amortization of bond premium)		
	*($1,820,000 × 5%)		
	**($105,000 − $91,000)		

SUMMARY OF STUDY OBJECTIVE FOR APPENDIX

8. ***Contrast the effects of the straight-line and effective-interest methods of amortizing bond discount and bond premium.*** The straight-line method of amortization results in a constant amount of amortization and interest expense per period but a varying percentage rate. In contrast, the effective-interest method results in varying amounts of amortization and interest expense per period but a constant percentage rate of interest. The effective-interest method generally results in a better matching of expenses with revenues. When the difference between the straight-line and effective-interest method is material, the use of the effective-interest method is required under GAAP.

GLOSSARY FOR APPENDIX

Effective-interest method of amortization A method of amortizing bond discount or bond premium that results in periodic interest expense equal to a constant percentage of the carrying value of the bonds. (p. 664).

Effective-interest rate Rate established when bonds are issued that remains constant in each interest period. (p. 664).

***Note:** All asterisked Questions, Exercises, and Problems relate to material in the appendix to the chapter.

Chapter 16 Self-Test

SELF-STUDY QUESTIONS

Answers are at the end of the chapter.

(SO 1) **1.** The term used for bonds that are unsecured is:
a. callable bonds.
b. indenture bonds.
c. debenture bonds.
d. bearer bonds.

(SO 2) **2.** Karson Inc. issues 10-year bonds with a maturity value of $200,000. If the bonds are issued at a premium, this indicates that:
a. the contractual interest rate exceeds the market interest rate.
b. the market interest rate exceeds the contractual interest rate.
c. the contractual interest rate and the market interest rate are the same.
d. no relationship exists between the two rates.

(SO 2) **3.** On January 1, Hurley Corporation issues $500,000, 5-year, 12% bonds at 96 with interest payable on July 1 and January 1. The entry on July 1 to record payment of bond interest and the amortization of bond discount using the straight-line method will include a:
a. debit to Interest Expense $30,000.
b. debit to Interest Expense $60,000.
c. credit to Discount on Bonds Payable $4,000.
d. credit to Discount on Bonds Payable $2,000.

(SO 2) **4.** For the bonds issued in question 3, above, what is the carrying value of the bonds at the end of the third interest period?
a. $486,000.
b. $488,000.
c. $472,000.
d. $464,000.

(SO 2) **5.** When the interest payment dates of a bond are May 1 and November 1, and a bond issue is sold on June 1, the amount of cash received by the issuer will be:
a. decreased by accrued interest from June 1 to November 1.
b. decreased by accrued interest from May 1 to June 1.
c. increased by accrued interest from May 1 to June 1.
d. increased by accrued interest from June 1 to November 1.

6. Gester Corporation retires its $100,000 face value bonds at 105 on January 1, following the payment of semiannual interest. The carrying value of the bonds at the redemption date is $103,745. The entry to record the redemption will include a: (SO 3)
a. credit of $3,745 to Loss on Bond Redemption.
b. debit of $3,745 to Premium on Bonds Payable.
c. credit of $1,255 to Gain on Bond Redemption.
d. debit of $5,000 to Premium on Bonds Payable.

7. Colson Inc. converts $600,000 of bonds sold at face value into 10,000 shares of common stock, par value $1. Both the bonds and the stock have a market value of $760,000. What amount should be credited to Paid-in Capital in Excess of Par as a result of the conversion? (SO 3)
a. $10,000.
b. $160,000.
c. $600,000.
d. $590,000.

8. Sanger Company has a bond sinking fund in the amount of $400,000. Where should this amount be reported on the balance sheet? (SO 4)
a. Investments section.
b. Current assets section.
c. Current liabilities section.
d. Long-term liabilities section.

9. Andrews Inc. issues a $497,000, 10% 3-year mortgage note on January 1. The note will be paid in three annual installments of $200,000, each payable at the end of the year. What is the amount of interest expense that (SO 5)

should be recognized by Andrews Inc. in the second year?
a. $16,567.
b. $49,740.
c. $34,670.
d. $347,600.

(SO 6) **10.** Lease A does not contain a bargain purchase option, but the lease term is equal to 90 percent of the estimated economic life of the leased property. Lease B does not transfer ownership of the property to the lessee by the end of the lease term, but the lease term is equal to 75 percent of the estimated economic life of the leased property. How should the lessee classify these leases?

	Lease A	Lease B
a.	Operating lease	Capital lease
b.	Operating lease	Operating lease
c.	Capital lease	Operating lease
d.	Capital lease	Capital lease

***11.** On January 1, Besalius Inc. issued $1,000,000, 9% bonds for $939,000. The market rate of interest for these bonds is 10%. Interest is payable annually on December 31. Besalius uses the effective-interest method of amortizing bond discount. At the end of the first year, Besalius should report unamortized bond discount of: (SO 8)
a. $54,900.
b. $57,100.
c. $51,610.
d. $51,000.

***12.** On January 1, Dias Corporation issued $1,000,000, 14%, 5-year bonds with interest payable on July 1 and January 1. The bonds sold for $1,098,540. The market rate of interest for these bonds was 12%. On the first interest date, using the effective-interest method, the debit entry to Bond Interest Expense is for: (SO 8)
a. $60,000.
b. $76,898.
c. $65,912.
d. $131,825.

THE NAVIGATOR

QUESTIONS

1. (a) What are long-term liabilities? Give three examples. (b) What is a bond?
2. (a) As a source of long-term financing, what are the major advantages of bonds over common stock? (b) What are the major disadvantages in using bonds for long-term financing?
3. Contrast the following types of bonds: (a) secured and unsecured, (b) term and serial, (c) registered and bearer, and (d) convertible and callable.
4. The following terms are important in issuing bonds: (a) face value, (b) contractual interest rate, (c) bond indenture, and (d) bond certificate. Explain each of these terms.
5. Describe the two major obligations incurred by a company when bonds are issued.
6. Assume that Bedazzled Inc. sold bonds with a par value of $100,000 for $104,000. Was the market interest rate equal to, less than, or greater than the bonds' contractual interest rate? Explain.
7. Elizabeth Hurley and Brendan Fraser are discussing how the market price of a bond is determined. Elizabeth believes that the market price of a bond is solely a function of the amount of the principal payment at the end of the term of a bond. Is she right? Discuss.
8. If a 10%, 10-year, $800,000 bond is issued at par and interest is paid semiannually, what is the amount of the interest payment at the end of the first semiannual period?
9. If the Bonds Payable account has a balance of $900,000 and the Discount on Bonds Payable account has a balance of $60,000, what is the carrying value of the bonds?
10. Explain the straight-line method of amortizing discount and premium on bonds payable.
11. Genji Corporation issues $300,000 of 8%, 5-year bonds on January 1, 2002, at 104. Assuming that the straight-line method is used to amortize the premium, what is the total amount of interest expense for 2002?
12. Which accounts are debited and which are credited if a bond issue originally sold at a premium is redeemed before maturity at 97 immediately following the payment of interest?
13. Kishwaukee Corporation is considering issuing a convertible bond. What is a convertible bond? Discuss the advantages of a convertible bond from the standpoint of (a) the bondholders and (b) the issuing corporation.
14. The financial statements of Macon Inc. disclose that it has a bond sinking fund. What is a bond sinking fund? What is its purpose?
15. Dan Dial, a friend of yours, has recently purchased a home for $125,000, paying $25,000 down and the remainder financed by a 10.5%, 20-year mortgage, payable at $998.38 per month. At the end of the first month, Dan receives a statement from the bank indicating that only $123.38 of principal was paid during the month. At this rate, he calculates that it will take over 67 years to pay off the mortgage. Is he right? Discuss.
16. (a) What is a lease agreement? (b) What are the two most common types of leases? (c) Distinguish between the two types of leases.
17. Waubonsee Company rents a warehouse on a month-to-month basis for the storage of its excess inventory. The company periodically must rent space when its production greatly exceeds actual sales. What is the nature of this type of lease agreement, and what accounting treatment should be used?

18. Alvarez Company entered into an agreement to lease 12 computers from Estes Electronics Inc. The present value of the lease payments is $186,300. Assuming that this is a capital lease, what entry would Alvarez Company make on the date of the lease agreement?

19. In general, what are the requirements for the financial statement presentation of long-term liabilities?

***20.** Diane Leto is discussing the advantages of the effective-interest method of bond amortization with her accounting staff. What do you think Diane is saying?

***21.** Graham Corporation issues $500,000 of 9%, 5-year bonds on January 1, 2002, at 104. If Graham uses the effective-interest method in amortizing the premium, will the annual interest expense increase or decrease over the life of the bonds? Explain.

BRIEF EXERCISES

Compare bond versus stock financing
(SO 1)

BE16-1 Grambling Inc. is considering two alternatives to finance its construction of a new $2 million plant.

(a) Issuance of 200,000 shares of common stock at the market price of $10 per share.
(b) Issuance of $2 million, 8% bonds at par.

Complete the following table, and indicate which alternative is preferable.

	Issue Stock	Issue Bond
Income before interest and taxes	$800,000	$800,000
Interest expense from bonds		
Income before income taxes	$	$
Income tax expense (30%)		
Net income	$	$
Outstanding shares		500,000
Earnings per share		

Prepare entries for bonds issued at face value.
(SO 2)

BE16-2 Existenz Corporation issued 2,000, 8%, 5-year, $1,000 bonds dated January 1, 2002, at 100.

(a) Prepare the journal entry to record the sale of these bonds on January 1, 2002.
(b) Prepare the journal entry to record the first interest payment on July 1, 2002 (interest payable semiannually), assuming no previous accrual of interest.
(c) Prepare the adjusting journal entry on December 31, 2002, to record interest expense.

Prepare entries for bonds issued at a discount.
(SO 2)

BE16-3 Verdi Company issues $2 million, 10-year, 9% bonds at 96, with interest payable on July 1 and January 1. The straight-line method is used to amortize bond discount.

(a) Prepare the journal entry to record the sale of these bonds on January 1, 2002.
(b) Prepare the journal entry to record interest expense and bond discount amortization on July 1, 2002, assuming no previous accrual of interest.

Prepare entries for bonds issued at a premium.
(SO 2)

BE16-4 Puccini Inc. issues $3 million, 5-year, 10% bonds at 102, with interest payable on July 1 and January 1. The straight-line method is used to amortize bond premium.

(a) Prepare the journal entry to record the sale of these bonds on January 1, 2002.
(b) Prepare the journal entry to record interest expense and bond premium amortization on July 1, 2002, assuming no previous accrual of interest.

Prepare entries for bonds issued between interest dates.
(SO 2)

BE16-5 Bizet Inc. has outstanding $2 million, 10-year, 9% bonds with interest payable on July 1 and January 1. The bonds were dated January 1, 2002, but were issued on May 1, 2002, at face value plus accrued interest.

(a) Prepare the journal entry to record the sale of the bonds on May 1, 2002.
(b) Prepare the journal entry to record the interest payment on July 1, 2002.

Prepare entry for redemption of bonds.
(SO 3)

BE16-6 The balance sheet for Bravo Company reports the following information on July 1, 2002.

Long-term liabilities		
Bonds payable	$1,000,000	
Less: Discount on bonds payable	60,000	$940,000

Bravo decides to redeem these bonds at 102 after paying semiannual interest. Prepare the journal entry to record the redemption on July 1, 2002.

BE16-7 Fleckstones Inc. issues a $600,000, 10%, 10-year mortgage note on December 31, 2002, to obtain financing for a new building. The terms provide for semiannual installment payments of $48,146. Prepare the entry to record the mortgage loan on December 31, 2002, and the first installment payment.

Prepare entries for long-term notes payable.
(SO 5)

BE16-8 Prepare the journal entries that the lessee should make to record the following transactions.

Contrast accounting for operating and capital lease.
(SO 6)

1. The lessee makes a lease payment of $80,000 to the lessor in an operating lease transaction.
2. Yoakam Company leases a new building from Chang Construction, Inc. The present value of the lease payments is $600,000. The lease qualifies as a capital lease.

BE16-9 Presented below are long-term liability items for Ravinia Company at December 31, 2002. Prepare the long-term liabilities section of the balance sheet for Ravinia Company.

Prepare statement presentation of long-term liabilities.
(SO 7)

Bonds payable, due 2004	$600,000
Lease liability	50,000
Notes payable, due 2007	80,000
Discount on bonds payable	45,000

***BE16-10** Presented below is the partial bond discount amortization schedule for Savion Glover Corp. Savion Glover uses the effective-interest method of amortization.

Use effective-interest method of bond amortization.
(SO 8)

Semiannual Interest Periods	Interest to Be Paid	Interest Expense to Be Recorded	Discount Amortization	Unamortized Discount	Bond Carrying Value
Issue date				$62,311	$937,689
1	$45,000	$46,884	$1,884	60,427	939,573
2	45,000	46,979	1,979	58,448	941,552

Instructions

(a) Prepare the journal entry to record the payment of interest and the discount amortization at the end of period 1.
(b) Explain why interest expense is greater than interest paid.
(c) Explain why interest expense will increase each period.

EXERCISES

E16-1 Flypaper Airlines is considering two alternatives for the financing of a purchase of a fleet of airplanes. These two alternatives are:

Compare two alternatives of financing—issuance of common stock vs. issuance of bonds.
(SO 1)

1. Issue 60,000 shares of common stock at $45 per share. (Cash dividends have not been paid nor is the payment of any contemplated).
2. Issue 13%, 10-year bonds at par for $2,700,000.

It is estimated that the company will earn $500,000 before interest and taxes as a result of this purchase. The company has an estimated tax rate of 30% and has 90,000 shares of common stock outstanding prior to the new financing.

Instructions

Determine the effect on net income and earnings per share for these two methods of financing.

E16-2 On January 1, Anyswing Company issued $100,000, 10%, 10-year bonds at par. Interest is payable semiannually on July 1 and January 1.

Prepare entries for issuance of bonds, and payment and accrual of bond interest.
(SO 2)

Instructions

Present journal entries to record the following.

(a) The issuance of the bonds.
(b) The payment of interest on July 1, assuming that interest was not accrued on June 30.
(c) The accrual of interest on December 31.

E16-3 Pimpernel Company issued $400,000, 9%, 20-year bonds on January 1, 2002, at 103. Interest is payable semiannually on July 1 and January 1. Pimpernel uses straight-line amortization for bond premium or discount.

Prepare entries to record issuance of bonds, payment of interest, amortization of premium, and redemption at maturity.
(SO 2, 3)

Instructions

Prepare the journal entries to record the following.

(a) The issuance of the bonds.

(b) The payment of interest and the premium amortization on July 1, 2002, assuming that interest was not accrued on June 30.

(c) The accrual of interest and the premium amortization on December 31, 2002.

(d) The redemption of the bonds at maturity, assuming interest for the last interest period has been paid and recorded.

Prepare entries to record issuance of bonds, payment of interest, amortization of discount, and redemption at maturity.
(SO 2, 3)

E16-4 Jim Brickman Company issued $300,000, 11%, 10-year bonds on December 31, 2001, for $280,000. Interest is payable semiannually on June 30 and December 31. Jim Brickman Company uses the straight-line method to amortize bond premium or discount.

Instructions

Prepare the journal entries to record the following.

(a) The issuance of the bonds.

(b) The payment of interest and the discount amortization on June 30, 2002.

(c) The payment of interest and the discount amortization on December 31, 2002.

(d) The redemption of the bonds at maturity, assuming interest for the last interest period has been paid and recorded.

Prepare entries to record issuance of bonds between interest dates, and payment and accrual of interest.
(SO 2)

E16-5 On April 1, Blue Man Company issued $120,000, 10%, 10-year bonds dated January 1 at par plus accrued interest. Interest is payable semiannually on July 1 and January 1.

Instructions

Present journal entries to record the following.

(a) The issuance of the bonds.

(b) The payment of interest on July 1, assuming that interest was not accrued on June 30.

(c) The accrual of interest on December 31.

Prepare entries for redemption of bonds and conversion of bonds into common stock.
(SO 3)

E16-6 Presented below are three independent situations.

1. Apollo Corporation retired $130,000 face value, 12% bonds on June 30, 2002, at 101. The carrying value of the bonds at the redemption date was $107,500. The bonds pay semiannual interest, and the interest payment due on June 30, 2002, has been made and recorded.
2. Buju Inc. retired $150,000 face value, 12.5% bonds on June 30, 2002, at 96. The carrying value of the bonds at the redemption date was $151,000. The bonds pay semiannual interest, and the interest payment due on June 30, 2002, has been made and recorded.
3. Eden Company has $80,000, 8%, 12-year convertible bonds outstanding. These bonds were sold at face value and pay semiannual interest on June 30 and December 31 of each year. The bonds are convertible into 30 shares of Eden $5 par value common stock for each $1,000 worth of bonds. On December 31, 2002, after the bond interest has been paid, $20,000 face value bonds were converted. The market value of Eden common stock was $44 per share on December 31, 2002.

Instructions

For each independent situation above, prepare the appropriate journal entry for the redemption or conversion of the bonds.

Prepare entries to record mortgage note and installment payments.
(SO 5)

E16-7 J. Lopez Co. receives $150,000 when it issues a $150,000, 10%, mortgage note payable to finance the construction of a building at December 31, 2002. The terms provide for semiannual installment payments of $10,000 on June 30 and December 31.

Instructions

Prepare the journal entries to record the mortgage loan and the first two installment payments.

Prepare entries for operating lease and capital lease.
(SO 6)

E16-8 Presented below are two independent situations.

1. Speedy Car Rental leased a car to D'Onofrio Company for one year. Terms of the operating lease agreement call for monthly payments of $500.
2. On January 1, 2002, Knapp Inc. entered into an agreement to lease 20 computers from Guinn Electronics. The terms of the lease agreement require three annual rental payments of $60,000 (including 10% interest) beginning December 31, 2002. The present value of the three rental payments is $149,211. Knapp considers this a capital lease.

Instructions

(a) Prepare the appropriate journal entry to be made by D'Onofrio Company for the first lease payment.

(b) Prepare the journal entry to record the lease agreement on the books of Knapp Inc. on January 1, 2002.

E16-9 The adjusted trial balance for Wesley Snipes Corporation at the end of the current year contained the following accounts.

Prepare long-term liabilities section.
(SO 7)

Bond Interest Payable	$ 9,000
Lease Liability	59,500
Bonds Payable, due 2010	150,000
Premium on Bonds Payable	32,000
Bond Sinking Fund	241,600

Instructions

(a) Prepare the long-term liabilities section of the balance sheet.

(b) Indicate the proper balance sheet classification for the account(s) listed above that do not belong in the long-term liabilities section.

***E16-10** Tagawa Corporation issued $650,000, 9%, 10-year bonds on January 1, 2002, for $609,497. This price resulted in an effective interest rate of 10% on the bonds. Interest is payable semiannually on July 1 and January 1. Tagawa uses the effective-interest method to amortize bond premium or discount.

Prepare entries for issuance of bonds, payment of interest, and amortization of discount using effective-interest method
(SO 8)

Instructions

Prepare the journal entries to record the following. (Round to the nearest dollar.)

(a) The issuance of the bonds.

(b) The payment of interest and the discount amortization on July 1, 2002, assuming that interest was not accrued on June 30.

(c) The accrual of interest and the discount amortization on December 31, 2002.

***E16-11** Matiko Company issued $600,000, 11%, 10-year bonds on January 1, 2002, for $637,387. This price resulted in an effective interest rate of 10% on the bonds. Interest is payable semiannually on July 1 and January 1. Matiko uses the effective-interest method to amortize bond premium or discount.

Prepare entries for issuance of bonds, payment of interest, and amortization of premium using effective-interest method.
(SO 8)

Instructions

Prepare the journal entries to record the following. (Round to the nearest dollar).

(a) The issuance of the bonds.

(b) The payment of interest and the premium amortization on July 1, 2002, assuming that interest was not accrued on June 30.

(c) The accrual of interest and the premium amortization on December 31, 2002.

PROBLEMS: SET A

P16-1A Sherrick Electric sold $4,000,000, 10%, 10-year bonds on January 1, 2002. The bonds were dated January 1 and pay interest July 1 and January 1. Sherrick Electric uses the straight-line method to amortize bond premium or discount. The bonds were sold at 104. Assume no interest is accrued on June 30.

Prepare entries to record issuance of bonds, interest accrual, and amortization for 2 years.
(SO 2, 7)

Instructions

(a) Prepare the journal entry to record the issuance of the bonds on January 1, 2002.

(b) Prepare a bond premium amortization schedule for the first 4 interest periods.

(c) Prepare the journal entries for interest and the amortization of the premium in 2002 and 2003.

(d) Show the balance sheet presentation of the bond liability at December 31, 2003.

(b) Amortization $8,000
(d) Premium on bonds payable $128,000

P16-2A Perabo Company sold $2,500,000, 12%, 10-year bonds on July 1, 2002. The bonds were dated July 1, 2002, and pay interest July 1 and January 1. Perabo Company uses the straight-line method to amortize bond premium or discount. Assume no interest is accrued on June 30.

Prepare entries to record issuance of bonds, interest, and amortization of bond premium and discount.
(SO 2, 7)

(a) Amortization $5,000
(b) Amortization $2,500
(c) Premium on bonds payable $95,000
Discount on bonds payable $47,500

Instructions

(a) Prepare all the necessary journal entries to record the issuance of the bonds and bond interest expense for 2002, assuming that the bonds sold at 104.
(b) Prepare journal entries as in part (a) assuming that the bonds sold at 98.
(c) Show balance sheet presentation for each bond issue at December 31, 2002.

Prepare entries to record interest payments, premium amortization, and redemption of bonds.
(SO 2, 3)

P16-3A The following is taken from the Mike Sondgeroth Company balance sheet.

MIKE SONDGEROTH COMPANY
Balance Sheet (partial)
December 31, 2002

Current liabilities		
Bond interest payable (for 6 months from July 1 to December 31)		$ 180,000
Long-term liabilities		
Bonds payable, 12% due January 1, 2013	$3,000,000	
Add: Premium on bonds payable	200,000	$3,200,000

Interest is payable semiannually on January 1 and July 1. The bonds are callable on any semiannual interest date. Sondgeroth uses straight-line amortization for any bond premium or discount. From December 31, 2002, the bonds will be outstanding for an additional 10 years (120 months).

Instructions

(a) Journalize the payment of bond interest on January 1, 2003
(b) Prepare the entry to amortize bond premium and to pay the interest due on July 1, 2003, assuming no accrual of interest on June 30.
(c) Assume that on July 1, 2003, after paying interest, Mike Sondgeroth Company calls bonds having a face value of $1,200,000. The call price is 101. Record the redemption of the bonds.
(d) Prepare the adjusting entry at December 31, 2003, to amortize bond premium and to accrue interest on the remaining bonds.

(b) Amortization $10,000
(c) Gain $64,000
(d) Amortization $6,000

Prepare installment schedule and journal entries for a mortgage note payable.
(SO 5)

P16-4A Carol Dunn Electronics issues an $800,000, 12%, 10-year mortgage note on December 31, 2001. The proceeds from the note are to be used in financing a new research laboratory. The terms of the note provide for semiannual installment payments, exclusive of real estate taxes and insurance, of $69,748. Payments are due June 30 and December 31.

Instructions

(a) Prepare an installment payment schedule for the first 2 years.
(b) Prepare the entries for (1) the loan and (2) the first two installment payments.
(c) Show how the total mortgage liability should be reported on the balance sheet at December 31, 2002.

(b) June 30 Mortgage Notes Payable $21,748
(c) Current liability—2002: $50,338

Analyze three different lease situations and prepare journal entries.
(SO 6)

P16-5A Presented below are three different lease transactions that occurred for Choi Inc. in 2002. Assume that all lease contracts start on January 1, 2002. In no case does Choi receive title to the properties leased during or at the end of the lease term.

	Lessor		
	Shirley Delivery	**Mall Co.**	**Snipes Auto**
Type of property	Computer	Delivery equipment	Automobile
Yearly rental	$ 6,000	$ 4,200	$ 3,700
Lease term	6 years	4 years	2 years
Estimated economic life	7 years	7 years	5 years
Fair market value of lease asset	$33,000	$19,000	$11,000
Present value of the lease rental payments	$31,000	$13,000	$ 6,400
Bargain purchase option	None	None	None

Instructions

(a) Which of the leases above are operating leases and which are capital leases? Explain.
(b) How should the lease transaction for Mall Co. be recorded in 2002?
(c) How should the lease transaction for Shirley Delivery be recorded on January 1, 2002?

***P16-6A** On July 1, 2002, Edmonds Corporation issued $5,000,000 face value, 12%, 10-year bonds at $5,623,112. This price resulted in an effective-interest rate of 10% on the bonds. Edmonds uses the effective-interest method to amortize bond premium or discount. The bonds pay semiannual interest July 1 and January 1.

Prepare entries to record issuance of bonds, payment of interest, and amortization of bond premium using effective-interest method.
(SO 2)

Instructions

(Round all computations to the nearest dollar.)

(a) Prepare the journal entry to record the issuance of the bonds on July 1, 2002.

(b) Prepare the journal entry to record the accrual of interest and the amortization of the premium on December 31, 2002.

(b) Amortization $18,844

(c) Prepare the journal entry to record the payment of interest and the amortization of the premium on July 1, 2003, assuming no accrual of interest on June 30.

(c) Amortization $19,787

(d) Prepare the journal entry to record the accrual of interest and the amortization of the premium on December 31, 2003.

(d) Amortization $20,776

(e) Prepare an amortization table through December 31, 2003 (3 interest periods) for this bond issue.

***P16-7A** On July 1, 2002, Algonquin Company issued $3,000,000 face value, 10%, 10-year bonds at $2,655,888. This price resulted in an effective-interest rate of 12% on the bonds. Algonquin uses the effective-interest method to amortize bond premium or discount. The bonds pay semiannual interest July 1 and January 1.

Prepare entries to record issuance of bonds, payment of interest, and amortization of discount using effective-interest method. In addition, answer questions.
(SO 2, 8)

Instructions

(Round all computations to the nearest dollar.)

(a) Prepare the journal entries to record the following transactions.
- **(1)** The issuance of the bonds on July 1, 2002.
- **(2)** The accrual of interest and the amortization of the discount on December 31, 2002.
- **(3)** The payment of interest and the amortization of the discount on July 1, 2003, assuming no accrual of interest on June 30.
- **(4)** The accrual of interest and the amortization of the discount on December 31, 2003.

(a) (3) Amortization $9,914
(a) (4) Amortization $10,509

(b) Show the proper balance sheet presentation for the liability for bonds payable on the December 31, 2003, balance sheet.

(b) $2,685,664

(c) Provide the answers to the following questions in letter form.
- **(1)** What amount of interest expense is reported for 2003?
- **(2)** Would the bond interest expense reported in 2003 be the same as, greater than, or less than the amount that would be reported if the straight-line method of amortization were used?
- **(3)** Determine the total cost of borrowing over the life of the bond.
- **(4)** Would the total bond interest expense be greater than, the same as, or less than the total interest expense that would be reported if the straight-line method of amortization were used?

PROBLEMS: SET B

P16-1B Closet Company sold $3,000,000, 9%, 20-year bonds on January 1, 2002. The bonds were dated January 1, 2002, and pay interest on January 1 and July 1. Closet Company uses the straight-line method to amortize bond premium or discount. The bonds were sold at 98. Assume no interest is accrued on June 30.

Prepare entries to record issuance of bonds, interest accrual, and amortization for 2 years.
(SO 2, 7)

Instructions

(a) Prepare the journal entry to record the issuance of the bonds on January 1, 2002.

(b) Prepare a bond discount amortization schedule for the first 4 interest periods.

(b) Amortization $1,500

(c) Prepare the journal entries for interest and the amortization of the discount in 2002 and 2003.

(d) Discount on bonds payable $54,000

(d) Show the balance sheet presentation of the bond liability at December 31, 2003.

P16-2B Nathan K. Corporation sold $2,500,000, 8%, 10-year bonds on January 1, 2002. The bonds were dated January 1, 2002, and pay interest on July 1 and January 1. Nathan K. Corporation uses the straight-line method to amortize bond premium or discount. Assume no interest is accrued on June 30.

Prepare entries to record issuance of bonds, interest, and amortization of bond premium and discount.
(SO 2, 7)

Instructions

(a) Prepare all the necessary journal entries to record the issuance of the bonds and bond interest expense for 2002, assuming that the bonds sold at 103.

(a) Amortization $3,750

(b) Prepare journal entries as in part (a) assuming that the bonds sold at 96.

(b) Amortization $5,000

(c) Premium on bonds payable $67,500
Discount on bonds payable $90,000

(c) Show balance sheet presentation for each bond issue at December 31, 2002.

Prepare entries to record interest payments, discount amortization, and redemption of bonds.
(SO 2, 3)

P16-3B The following is taken from the Becky Corp. balance sheet.

BECKY CORPORATION
Balance Sheet (partial)
December 31, 2002

Current liabilities		
Bond interest payable (for 6 months from July 1 to December 31)		$ 120,000
Long-term liabilities		
Bonds payable, 10%, due January 1, 2013	$2,400,000	
Less: Discount on bonds payable	90,000	$2,310,000

Interest is payable semiannually on January 1 and July 1. The bonds are callable on any semiannual interest date. Becky uses straight-line amortization for any bond premium or discount. From December 31, 2002, the bonds will be outstanding for an additional 10 years (120 months).

Instructions

(Round all computations to the nearest dollar).

(a) Journalize the payment of bond interest on January 1, 2003.

(b) Amortization $4,500

(b) Prepare the entry to amortize bond discount and to pay the interest due on July 1, 2003, assuming that interest was not accrued on June 30.

(c) Loss $33,375

(c) Assume that on July 1, 2003, after paying interest, Becky Corp. calls bonds having a face value of $600,000. The call price is 102. Record the redemption of the bonds.

(d) Amortization $3,375

(d) Prepare the adjusting entry at December 31, 2003, to amortize bond discount and to accrue interest on the remaining bonds.

Prepare installment payments schedule and journal entries for a mortgage note payable.
(SO 5)

P16-4B Gere Electronics issues an $800,000, 10%, 10-year mortgage note on December 31, 2002, to help finance a plant expansion program. The terms provide for semiannual installment payments, not including real estate taxes and insurance, of $64,193. Payments are due June 30 and December 31.

Instructions

(a) Prepare an installment payment schedule for the first 2 years.

(b) June 30 Mortgage Notes Payable $24,193
(c) Current liability—2003: $54,679

(b) Prepare the entries for (1) the mortgage loan and (2) the first two installment payments.

(c) Show how the total mortgage liability should be reported on the balance sheet at December 31, 2003.

Analyze three different lease situations and prepare journal entries.
(SO 6)

P16-5B Presented below are three different lease transactions in which Coyote Enterprises engaged in 2002. Assume that all lease transactions start on January 1, 2002. In no case does Coyote receive title to the properties leased during or at the end of the lease term.

	Lessor		
	Winona Co.	**Ryder Co.**	**Wiley Inc.**
Type of property	Bulldozer	Truck	Furniture
Bargain purchase option	None	None	None
Lease term	4 years	6 years	3 years
Estimated economic life	8 years	7 years	5 years
Yearly rental	$13,000	$12,000	$ 4,000
Fair market value of leased asset	$80,000	$58,000	$27,500
Present value of the lease rental payments	$48,000	$50,000	$12,000

Instructions

(a) Identify the leases above as operating or capital leases. Explain.

(b) How should the lease transaction for Ryder Co. be recorded on January 1, 2002?

(c) How should the lease transaction for Wiley Inc. be recorded in 2002?

Prepare entries to record issuance of bonds, payment of interest, and amortization of bond discount using effective-interest method.
(SO 8)

***P16-6B** On July 1, 2002, Godzilla Satellites issued $2,700,000 face value, 9%, 10-year bonds at $2,531,760. This price resulted in an effective-interest rate of 10% on the bonds. Godzilla uses the effective-interest method to amortize bond premium or discount. The bonds pay semiannual interest July 1 and January 1.

Instructions
(Round all computations to the nearest dollar.)

(a) Prepare the journal entry to record the issuance of the bonds on July 1, 2002.

(b) Prepare the journal entry to record the accrual of interest and the amortization of the discount on December 31, 2002. (b) Amortization $5,088

(c) Prepare the journal entry to record the payment of interest and the amortization of the discount on July 1, 2003, assuming that interest was not accrued on June 30. (c) Amortization $5,342

(d) Prepare the journal entry to record the accrual of interest and the amortization of the discount on December 31, 2003. (d) Amortization $5,610

(e) Prepare an amortization table through December 31, 2003 (3 interest periods) for this bond issue.

Prepare entries to record issuance of bonds, payment of interest, and amortization of premium using effective-interest method. In addition, answer questions.
(SO 8)

***P16-7B** On July 1, 2002, Michelle Pfeiffer Chemical Company issued $2,000,000 face value, 12%, 10-year bonds at $2,249,245. This price resulted in a 10% effective-interest rate on the bonds. Pfeiffer uses the effective-interest method to amortize bond premium or discount. The bonds pay semiannual interest on each July 1 and January 1.

Instructions
(Round all computations to the nearest dollar.)

(a) Prepare the journal entries to record the following transactions.

(1) The issuance of the bonds on July 1, 2002.

(2) The accrual of interest and the amortization of the premium on December 31, 2002. (a) (2) Amortization $7,538

(3) The payment of interest and the amortization of the premium on July 1, 2003, assuming no accrual of interest on June 30. (a) (3) Amortization $7,915

(4) The accrual of interest and the amortization of the premium on December 31, 2003. (a) (4) Amortization $8,310

(b) Show the proper balance sheet presentation for the liability for bonds payable on the December 31, 2003, balance sheet. (b) $2,225,482

(c) Provide the answers to the following questions in letter form.

(1) What amount of interest expense is reported for 2003?

(2) Would the bond interest expense reported in 2003 be the same as, greater than, or less than the amount that would be reported if the straight-line method of amortization were used?

(3) Determine the total cost of borrowing over the life of the bond.

(4) Would the total bond interest expense be greater than, the same as, or less than the total interest expense if the straight-line method of amortization were used?

BROADENING YOUR PERSPECTIVE

FINANCIAL REPORTING AND ANALYSIS

FINANCIAL REPORTING PROBLEM: Lands' End, Inc.

LANDS' END DIRECT MERCHANTS

BYP16-1 Refer to the financial statements of **Lands' End, Inc.** and the Notes to Consolidated Financial Statements in Appendix A.

Instructions

(a) What was Lands' End's total long-term debt (excluding deferred income taxes) at January 28, 2000? What was the increase/decrease in total long-term debt (excluding deferred income taxes) from the prior year? What does Note 5 to the financial statements say about long-term debt?

(b) What does Lands' End lease (see Note 6)? How does Lands' End classify and account for its leases?

(c) What was the total rent expense under leases for the year ended January 28, 2000? Do the assets under these leases appear on the balance sheet? What is the total "future fiscal year commitments under these leases as of January 28, 2000"?

COMPARATIVE ANALYSIS PROBLEM: Lands' End vs. Abercrombie & Fitch

LANDS' END DIRECT MERCHANTS

BYP16-2 **Lands' End's** financial statements are presented in Appendix A. **Abercrombie & Fitch's** financial statements are presented in Appendix B.

Instructions

(a) Based on the information contained in these financial statements, compute the following 2000 ratios for each company.
  (1) Debt (excluding "deferred income taxes" and "other long-term liabilities") to total assets.
  (2) Times interest earned.

(b) What conclusions concerning the companies' long-run solvency can be drawn from these ratios?

(c) Which company has reported the greater amount of future minimum rental commitments? (Abercrombie & Fitch reported a total of $520,342.)

INTERPRETING FINANCIAL STATEMENTS: A Global Focus

BYP16-3 Apache Corporation is an international, independent energy enterprise engaged in the exploration, development, production, gathering, processing, and marketing of natural gas and crude oil. Its corporate headquarters are located in Houston, Texas, and it has operations in North America, Australia, Egypt, Poland and the People's Republic of China.

The 1994 annual report of Apache Corporation disclosed the following information in its management discussion section.

APACHE CORPORATION
Management Discussion

In May 1994, Apache issued 9.25% bonds due 2002 in the principal amount of $100 million. The proceeds of $99 million from the offering were used to reduce bank debt, to pay off the 9.5% convertible debentures due 1996, and for general corporate purposes. In December 1994, the company privately placed 3.93% convertible notes due 1997 in the principal amount of $75 million. The notes are not redeemable before maturity and are convertible into Apache common stock at the option of the holders at any time prior to maturity, at a conversion price of $27 per share. Proceeds from the sale of the notes were used for the repayment of bank debt.

Instructions

(a) Identify the face amount, contractual interest rate, and selling price of the newly issued bonds due in 2002. Explain whether the bonds sold at a premium or a discount.

(b) For what purposes has Apache Corporation been incurring more debt?

EXPLORING THE WEB

BYP16-4 Bond or debt securities pay a stated rate of interest. This rate of interest is dependent on the risk associated with the investment. **Moody's Investment Service** provides rating for companies that issue debt securities.

Address: **www.moodys.com** ***(or go to www.wiley.com/college/weygandt)***

Steps: From Moody's homepage, (1) choose **SiteMap**, (2) choose **About Moody's**.

Instructions

(a) What year did Moody's introduce the first bond rating?

(b) List three basic principles Moody's uses in rating bonds.

(c) What is the definition of Moody's Aaa rating on long-term taxable debt?

CRITICAL THINKING

GROUP DECISION CASE

BYP16-5 On January 1, 2001, Remmers Corporation issued $3,000,000 of 5-year, 8% bonds at 96; the bonds pay interest semiannually on July 1 and January 1. By January 1, 2003, the market rate of interest for bonds of risk similar to those of Remmers Corporation had risen. As a result the market value of these bonds was $2,500,000 on January 1, 2003—below their carrying value. Jackie Remmers, president of the company, suggests repurchasing all of these bonds in the open market at the $2,500,000 price. To do so the company will have to issue $2,500,000 (face value) of new 10-year, 12% bonds at par. The president asks you, as controller, "What is the feasibility of my proposed repurchase plan?"

Instructions

With the class divided into groups, answer the following.

(a) What is the carrying value of the outstanding Remmers Corporation 5-year bonds on January 1, 2003? (Assume straight-line amortization.)

(b) Prepare the journal entry to retire the 5-year bonds on January 1, 2003. Prepare the journal entry to issue the new 10-year bonds.

(c) Prepare a short memo to the president in response to her request for advice. List the economic factors that you believe should be considered for her repurchase proposal.

COMMUNICATION ACTIVITY

BYP16-6 Hal Adelman, president of the Adelman Corporation, is considering the issuance of bonds to finance an expansion of his business. He has asked you to (1) discuss the advantages of bonds over common stock financing, (2) indicate the type of bonds he might issue, and (3) explain the issuing procedures used in bond transactions.

Instructions

Write a memo to the president, answering his request.

ETHICS CASE

BYP16-7 Ron Gant is the president, founder, and majority owner of Newman Medical Corporation, an emerging medical technology products company. Newman is in dire need of additional capital to keep operating and to bring several promising products to final development, testing, and production. Ron, as owner of 51% of the outstanding stock, manages the company's operations. He places heavy emphasis on research and development and on long-term growth. The other principal stockholder is Judy Costello who, as a nonemployee investor, owns 40% of the stock. Judy would like to deemphasize the R&D functions and emphasize the marketing function, to maximize short-run sales and profits from existing products. She believes this strategy would raise the market price of Newman's stock.

All of Ron's personal capital and borrowing power is tied up in his 51% stock ownership. He knows that any offering of additional shares of stock will dilute his controlling interest because he won't be able to participate in such an issuance. But, Judy has money and would likely buy enough shares to gain control of Newman. She then would dictate the company's future direction, even if it meant replacing Ron as president and CEO.

The company already has considerable debt. Raising additional debt will be costly, will adversely affect Newman's credit rating, and will increase the company's reported losses due to the growth in interest expense. Judy and the other minority stockholders express opposition to the assumption of additional debt, fearing the company will be pushed to the brink of bankruptcy. Wanting to maintain his control and to preserve the direction of "his" company, Ron is doing everything to avoid a stock issuance. He is contemplating a large issuance of bonds, even if it means the bonds are issued with a high effective-interest rate.

Instructions

(a) Who are the stakeholders in this situation?

(b) What are the ethical issues in this case?

(c) What would you do if you were Ron?

Answers to Self-Study Questions

1. c **2.** a **3.** d **4.** a **5.** c **6.** b **7.** d **8.** a **9.** c **10.** d
***11.** b ***12.** c

Answer to *Lands' End* Review It Question 2, p. 655

An examination of Lands' End's statement of cash flows indicates the following reduction of debt: payment of short-term debt, $27.2 million.

LANDS' END DIRECT MERCHANTS

Remember to go back to the Navigator box on the chapter-opening page and check off your completed work.

17

INVESTMENTS

THE NAVIGATOR ✓

- Understand *Concepts for Review* ❑
- Read *Feature Story* ❑
- Scan *Study Objectives* ❑
- Read *Preview* ❑
- Read text and answer *Before You Go On*
  p. 686 ❑ *p.* 691 ❑ *p.* 696 ❑
- Work *Demonstration Problem* ❑
- Review *Summary of Study Objectives* ❑
- Answer *Self-Study Questions* ❑
- Complete *Assignments* ❑

CONCEPTS FOR REVIEW

Before studying this chapter, you should know or, if necessary, review:

a. How to record the issuance of bonds. (Ch. 16, pp. 645–652)

b. How to compute and record interest. (Ch. 3, p. 101, Ch. 9, p 376, and Ch. 16, pp. 645–646)

c. How to record amortization of bond discount and bond premium using the straight-line method. (Ch. 16, pp. 648–651)

d. Where short-term and long-term investments are classified on a balance sheet. (Ch. 4, pp. 151–152)

☑ THE NAVIGATOR

FEATURE STORY

Is There Anything Else We Can Buy?

In a rapidly changing world you must change rapidly or suffer the consequences. In business, change requires investment.

A case in point is found in the entertainment industry. Technology is bringing about innovations so quickly that it is nearly impossible to guess which technologies will last and which will soon fade away. For example, will both satellite TV and cable TV survive, or will just one succeed, or will both be replaced by something else? Or consider the publishing industry. Will paper newspapers and magazines be replaced by online news via the World Wide Web? If you are a publisher, you have to make your best guess about what the future holds and invest accordingly.

Time Warner Corporation lives at the center of this arena. It is not an environment for the timid, and Time Warner's philosophy is anything but timid. It might be characterized as, "If we can't beat you, we will buy you." Its mantra is "invest, invest, invest." A list of Time Warner's holdings gives an idea of its reach. Magazines: *People, Time, Life, Sports Illustrated, Fortune*. Book publishers: Time-Life Books, Book-of-the-Month Club, Little, Brown & Co, Sunset Books. Music: Warner Bros. Records, Reprise, Atlantic, Rhino, Elektra, and Asylum, representing such artists as Hootie and the Blowfish, Tori Amos, Eric Clapton, and Madonna. Television and movies: Warner Bros. ("ER" and "Friends"), HBO, and movies like *Austin Powers* and *The Matrix*. And, in 1996 Time Warner merged with Turner Broadcasting, so it now owns TNT, CNN, and Turner's library of thousands of classic movies. Even before the Turner merger, Time Warner owned more information and entertainment copyrights and brands than any other company in the world.

So what has Time Warner's aggressive acquisition spree meant for the bottom line? It has left Time Warner with huge debt and massive interest costs. Also, some of the acquisitions have not come cheap, resulting in large amounts of reported goodwill and goodwill amortization. At the time this book went to press, Time Warner was involved in its largest deal to date—a merger with **America Online (AOL)**. Although it is being billed as a merger of equals, it is AOL's phenomenal growth and astronomical stock price that made this merger possible. This demonstrates that, in the corporate acquisition food chain, no company is too large to be devoured.

www.timewarner.com

☑ THE NAVIGATOR

STUDY OBJECTIVES

After studying this chapter, you should be able to:

1. Discuss why corporations invest in debt and stock securities.
2. Explain the accounting for debt investments.
3. Explain the accounting for stock investments.
4. Describe the use of consolidated financial statements.
5. Indicate how debt and stock investments are valued and reported on the financial statements.
6. Distinguish between short-term and long-term investments.

☑ THE NAVIGATOR

PREVIEW OF CHAPTER 17

Time Warner's management believes in aggressive growth through investing in the stock of existing companies. Besides purchasing stock, companies also purchase other securities such as bonds issued by corporations or by governments. Investments can be purchased for a short or long period of time, as a passive investment, or with the intent to control another company. As you will see in this chapter, the way in which a company accounts for its investments is determined by a number of factors.

The content and organization of Chapter 17 are as follows.

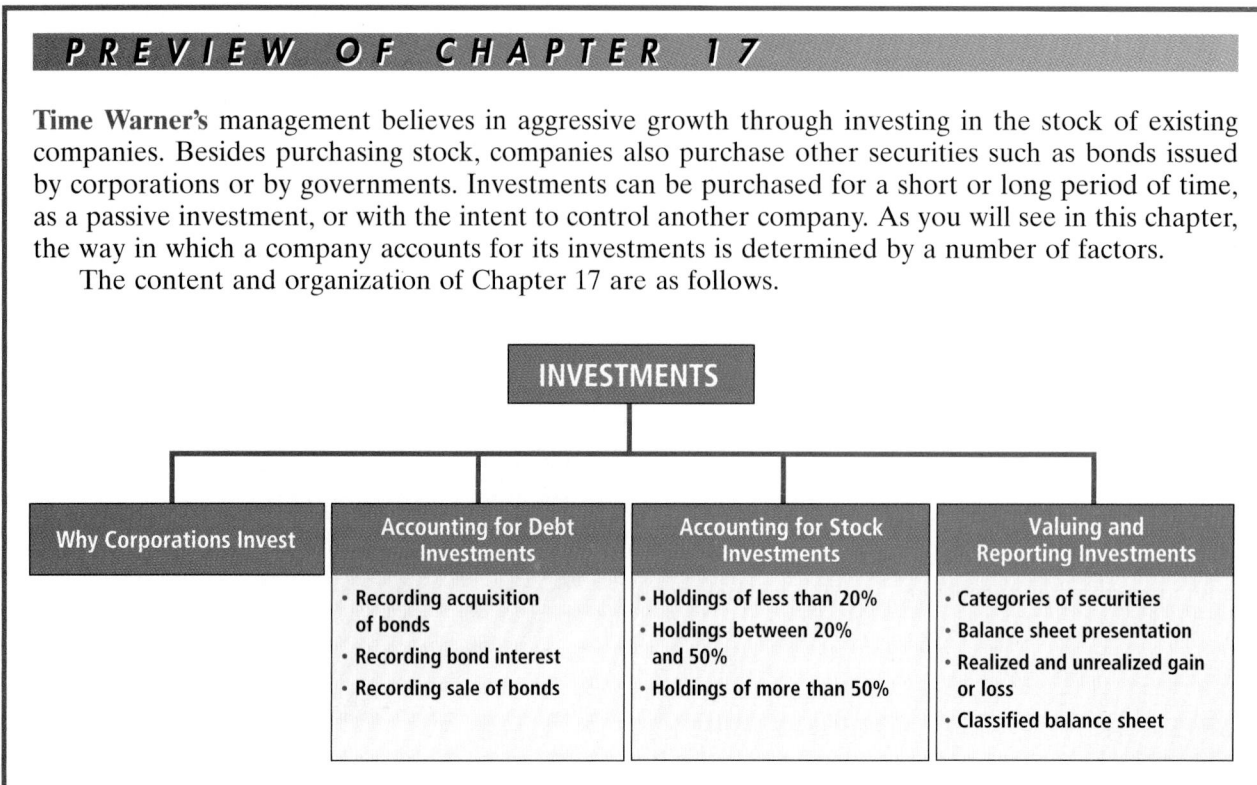

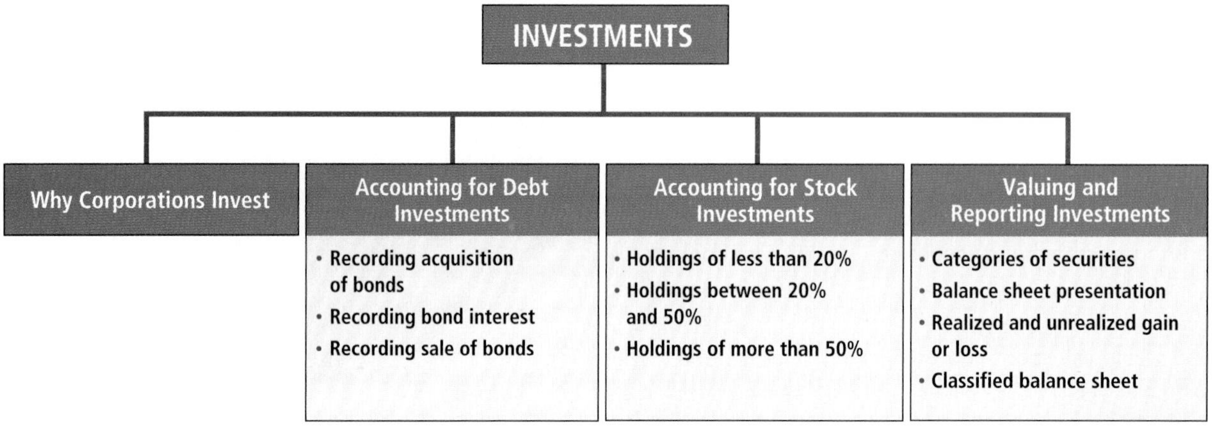

WHY CORPORATIONS INVEST

STUDY OBJECTIVE 1

Discuss why corporations invest in debt and stock securities.

Corporations purchase investments in debt or stock securities generally for one of three reasons. First, a corporation may **have excess cash** that it does not need for the immediate purchase of operating assets. For example, many companies experience seasonal fluctuations in sales. A Cape Cod marina has more sales in the spring and summer than in the fall and winter. The reverse is true for an Aspen ski shop. At the end of an operating cycle, many companies have cash on hand that is temporarily idle until the start of another operating cycle. These companies may invest the excess funds to earn a greater return than they would get by just holding the funds in the bank. The role that such temporary investments play in the operating cycle is depicted in Illustration 17-1.

Excess cash may also result from economic cycles. For example, when the economy is booming, **General Motors** generates considerable excess cash. It uses some of this cash to purchase new plant and equipment and pays out some of the cash in dividends. But it may also invest excess cash in liquid assets in anticipation of a future downturn in the economy. It can then liquidate these investments during a recession, when sales slow down and cash is scarce.

When investing excess cash for short periods of time, corporations invest in low-risk, highly liquid securities—most often short-term government securities. It is generally not wise to invest short-term excess cash in shares of common stock because stock investments can experience rapid price changes. If you did invest

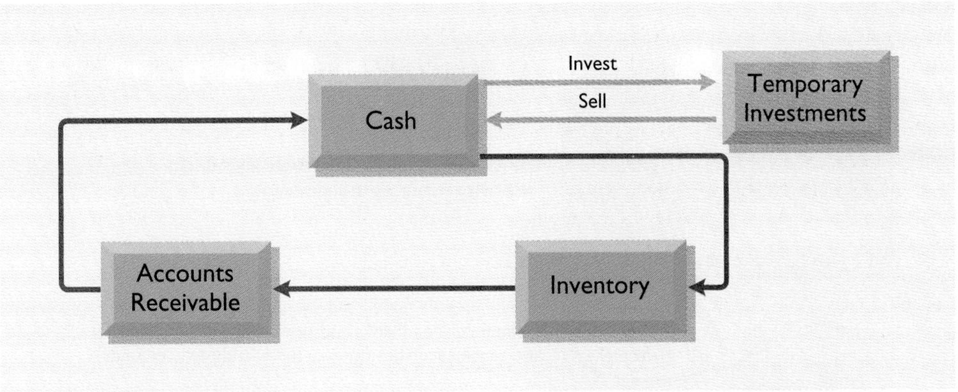

Illustration 17-1

Temporary investments and the operating cycle

your short-term excess cash in stock and the price of the stock declined significantly just before you needed cash again, you would be forced to sell your stock investment at a loss.

A second reason some companies such as banks purchase investments is to generate **earnings from investment income**. Although banks make most of their earnings by lending money, they also generate earnings by investing in debt and equity securities. But loan demand varies both seasonally and with changes in the economic climate. Thus, when loan demand is low, a bank must find other uses for its cash. Bank regulators severely limit the ability of banks to invest in common stock because of the risk involved. Therefore, most investments held by banks are debt securities.

Pension funds and mutual funds are corporations that also regularly invest to generate earnings. However, they do so for **speculative reasons**. They are speculating that the investment will increase in value and thus result in positive returns. Therefore, they invest primarily in the common stock of other corporations. These investments are passive in nature. The pension fund or mutual fund does not usually take an active role in controlling the affairs of the companies in which they invest.

Companies also invest for **strategic reasons**. A company may purchase a noncontrolling interest in another company in a related industry in which it wishes to establish a presence. For example, **Time Warner** initially purchased an interest of less than 20 percent in **Turner Broadcasting** to have a stake in Turner's expanding business opportunities. Similarly, Canadian giant **Seagram** purchased a significant interest in Time Warner. (Not even a huge corporation like Time Warner is at the top of the corporate "food-chain.") Or, a company can exercise some influence over a customer or supplier by purchasing a significant, but not controlling, interest in that company.

A corporation may also choose to purchase a controlling interest in another company. This might be done to enter a new industry without incurring the tremendous costs and risks associated with starting from scratch. Or a company might purchase another company in its same industry. The purchase of a company that is in your industry, but involved in a different activity, is called a **vertical acquisition**. For example, **Nike** might purchase a chain of athletic shoe stores, such as **The Athlete's Foot**. In a **horizontal acquisition** you purchase a company that does the same activity as your company. For example, Nike might purchase **Reebok**.

In summary, businesses invest in other companies for the reasons shown in Illustration 17-2.

Illustration 17-2

Why corporations invest

Reason	Typical Investment
To house excess cash until needed 	Low-risk, high-liquidity, short-term securities such as government-issued securities
To generate earnings 	Debt securities (banks and other financial institutions); and stock securities (mutual funds and pension funds)
To meet strategic goals 	Stocks of companies in a related industry or in an unrelated industry that the company wishes to enter

ACCOUNTING IN ACTION *Business Insight*

In the two months prior to approval by the federal government of the **Time Warner/Turner** deal, as approval appeared more certain, Time Warner's stock price increased by 30 percent. Although investors were applauding the strength of the combined entity, many analysts were very concerned about the mega-corporation's ability to control costs. The Time Warner deal and other acquisitions resulted in a $17.5 billion mountain of debt on Time Warner's balance sheet.

Observers were also interested to see how the two corporate cultures would merge. Ted Turner had been openly critical of Time Warner's management for running a loose ship, with far too much being spent on unnecessary extravagances such as corporate jets. Time Warner executives privately responded that if Mr. Turner was really concerned, he might consider taking a cut in his salary of $10 million a year.

ACCOUNTING FOR DEBT INVESTMENTS

STUDY OBJECTIVE 2

Explain the accounting for debt investments.

Debt investments are investments in government and corporation bonds. In accounting for debt investments, entries are required to record (1) the acquisition, (2) the interest revenue, and (3) the sale.

RECORDING ACQUISITION OF BONDS

At acquisition, the cost principle applies. Cost includes all expenditures necessary to acquire these investments, such as the price paid plus brokerage fees (commissions), if any. Assume, for example, that Kuhl Corporation acquires 50 Doan Inc. 12%, 10-year, $1,000 bonds on January 1, 2002, for $54,000, including brokerage fees of $1,000. The entry to record the investment is:

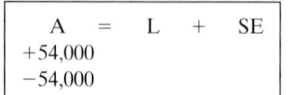

A	=	L	+	SE
+54,000				
−54,000				

Jan. 1	Debt Investments	54,000	
	Cash		54,000
	(To record purchase of 50 Doan Inc. bonds)		

RECORDING BOND INTEREST

The bonds pay interest of $3,000 semiannually on July 1 and January 1 ($50,000 × 12% × ½). The entry for the receipt of interest on July 1 is:

July 1	Cash	3,000	
	Interest Revenue		3,000
	(To record receipt of interest on Doan Inc. bonds		

A	=	L	+	SE
+3,000				+3,000

If Kuhl Corporation's fiscal year ends on December 31, it is necessary to accrue the interest of $3,000 earned since July 1. The adjusting entry is:

Dec. 31	Interest Receivable	3,000	
	Interest Revenue		3,000
	(To accrue interest on Doan Inc. bonds)		

A	=	L	+	SE
+3,000				+3,000

Interest Receivable is reported as a current asset in the balance sheet; Interest Revenue is reported under "other revenues and gains" in the income statement.

When the interest is received on January 1, the entry is:

Jan. 1	Cash	3,000	
	Interest Receivable		3,000
	(To record receipt of accrued interest)		

A	=	L	+	SE
+3,000				
−3,000				

A credit to Interest Revenue at this time would be incorrect. Why? Because the interest revenue was earned and accrued in the preceding accounting period.

RECORDING SALE OF BONDS

When the bonds are sold, it is necessary to credit the investment account for the cost of the bonds. Any difference between the net proceeds from the sale (sales price less brokerage fees) and the cost of the bonds is recorded as a gain or loss.

Assume, for example, that Kuhl Corporation receives net proceeds of $58,000 on the sale of the Doan Inc. bonds on January 1, 2003, after receiving the interest due. Since the securities cost $54,000, a gain of $4,000 has been realized. The entry to record the sale is:

Jan. 1	Cash	58,000	
	Debt Investments		54,000
	Gain on Sale of Debt Investments		4,000
	(To record sale of Doan Inc. bonds)		

A	=	L	+	SE
+58,000				+4,000
−54,000				

The gain on sale of debt investments is reported under "other revenues and gains" in the income statement.

The accounting for short-term debt investments and for long-term debt investments is similar. The major exception is when bonds are purchased at a premium or discount. For short-term investments, the bond premium or discount is not amortized to interest revenue because the bonds are held for a short period of time. A misstatement of interest revenue for such a period is not considered material. For long-term investments, any bond premium or discount is amortized to interest revenue over the remaining term of the bonds. Like the issuer of the bonds, the investor uses either the straight-line or the effective-interest method of amortization. The effective-interest method is required under GAAP when the annual amounts of the two methods are materially different.

BEFORE YOU GO ON...

REVIEW IT

1. Why might a company make investments in debt or stock securities?
2. What entries are required in accounting for debt investments?
3. How does the accounting for a short-term debt investment differ from that for a long-term debt investment?

DO IT

Waldo Corporation had the following transactions pertaining to debt investments.

Jan. 1	Purchased 30 10%, $1,000 Hillary Co. bonds for $30,000, plus brokerage fees of $900. Interest is payable semiannually on July 1 and January 1.
July 1	Received semiannual interest on Hillary Co. bonds.
July 1	Sold 15 Hillary Co. bonds for $15,000, less $400 brokerage fees.

(a) Journalize the transactions, and (b) prepare the adjusting entry for the accrual of interest on December 31.

ACTION PLAN

- Record bond investments at cost.
- Record interest when received and/or accrued.
- When bonds are sold, credit the investment account for the cost of the bonds.
- Record any difference between the cost and the net proceeds as a gain or loss.

SOLUTION

(a)	Jan. 1	Debt Investments	30,900	
		Cash		30,900
		(To record purchase of 30 Hillary Co. bonds)		
	July 1	Cash	1,500	
		Interest Revenue ($30,000 × .10 × 6/12)		1,500
		(To record receipt of interest on Hillary Co. bonds)		
	July 1	Cash	14,600	
		Loss on Sale of Debt Investments	850	
		Debt Investments ($30,900 × 15/30)		15,450
		(To record sale of 15 Hillary Co. bonds)		
(b)	Dec. 31	Interest Receivable	750	
		Interest Revenue ($15,000 × .10 × 6/12)		750
		(To accrue interest on Hillary Co. bonds)		

Related exercise material: BE17-1 and E17-1.

THE NAVIGATOR

ACCOUNTING IN ACTION e Business Insight

Amazon.com's Web site receives many "hits" each day. Because of this Amazon earns significant revenue by allowing other companies to advertise there. Many of them pay with stock in their company (since dot-coms often have very little cash). When Amazon receives the stock, it debits Investment in XYZ Company and credits Unearned Revenue for the market value of the shares on the day they are received. It then recognizes revenue over the life of the advertising agreement. In the future, Amazon hopes to do more cash deals and fewer stock deals.

ACCOUNTING FOR STOCK INVESTMENTS

STUDY OBJECTIVE 3

Explain the accounting for stock investments.

We buy stock of another co.

Stock investments are investments in the capital stock of corporations. When a company holds stock (and/or debt) of several different corporations, the group of securities is identified as an **investment portfolio**.

The accounting for investments in common stock is based on the extent of the investor's influence over the operating and financial affairs of the issuing corporation (commonly called the **investee**). Illustration 17-3 shows the guidelines for three levels of influence.

Illustration 17-3

Accounting guidelines for stock investments

Investor's Ownership Interest in Investee's Common Stock	Presumed Influence on Investee	Accounting Guidelines
Less than 20%	Insignificant	Cost method
Between 20% and 50%	Significant	Equity method
More than 50%	Controlling	Consolidated financial statements

The presumed influence may be negated by extenuating circumstances. For example, a company that acquires a 25% interest in another company in a "hostile" takeover may not have significant influence over the investee. Companies are required to use judgment instead of blindly following the guidelines.[1] On the following pages we will explain the application of each guideline.

HOLDINGS OF LESS THAN 20%

In accounting for stock investments of less than 20%, the cost method is used. Under the **cost method**, the investment is recorded at cost, and revenue is recognized only when cash dividends are received.

Recording Acquisition of Stock Investments

At acquisition, the cost principle applies. Cost includes all expenditures necessary to acquire these investments such as the price paid plus any brokerage fees (commissions). Assume, for example, that on July 1, 2002, Sanchez Corporation acquires 1,000 shares (10% ownership) of Beal Corporation common stock. Sanchez pays $40 per share plus brokerage fees of $500. The entry for the purchase is:

July 1	Stock Investments	40,500	
	Cash		40,500
	(To record purchase of 1,000 shares of Beal Corporation common stock)		

A	=	L	+	SE
+40,500				
−40,500				

[1]Among the questions that are considered in determining an investor's influence are these: (1) Does the investor have representation on the investee's board? (2) Does the investor participate in the investee's policy-making process? (3) Are there material transactions between the investor and investee? (4) Is the common stock held by other stockholders concentrated or dispersed?

Recording Dividends

During the time the stock is held, entries are required for any cash dividends received. If a $2.00 per share dividend is received by Sanchez Corporation on December 31, the entry is:

A	=	L	+	SE
+2,000				+2,000

Dec. 31	Cash (1,000 × $2)	2,000	
	Dividend Revenue		2,000
	(To record receipt of a cash dividend)		

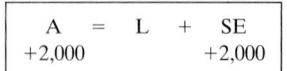

Dividend Revenue is reported under "other revenues and gains" in the income statement. Unlike interest on notes and bonds, dividends do not accrue. Therefore, adjusting entries are not made to accrue dividends.

Recording Sale of Stock

When stock is sold, the difference between the net proceeds from the sale (sales price less brokerage fees) and the cost of the stock is recognized as a gain or a loss. Assume that Sanchez Corporation receives net proceeds of $39,500 on the sale of its Beal stock on February 10, 2003. Because the stock cost $40,500, a loss of $1,000 has been incurred. The entry to record the sale is:

A	=	L	+	SE
+39,500				−1,000
−40,500				

Feb. 10	Cash	39,500	
	Loss on Sale of Stock Investments	1,000	
	Stock Investments		40,500
	(To record sale of Beal common stock)		

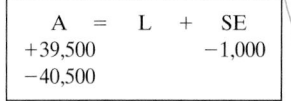

The loss account is reported under "other expenses and losses" in the income statement. A gain on sale is shown under "other revenues and gains."

HELPFUL HINT
The entries for investments in common stock also apply to investments in preferred stock.

HOLDINGS BETWEEN 20% AND 50%

When an investor company owns only a small portion of the shares of stock of another company, the investor cannot exercise control over the investee. But, when an investor owns between 20% and 50% of the common stock of a corporation, it is presumed that the investor has significant influence over the financial and operating activities of the investee. The investor probably has a representative on the investee's board of directors. Through that representative, the investor begins to exercise some control over the investee. The investee company in some sense becomes part of the investor company. For example, even prior to purchasing all of Turner Broadcasting, **Time Warner** owned 20% of Turner and could exercise significant control over major decisions made by Turner.

Companies with stock holdings between 20% and 50% in an investee use an approach called the equity method. Under the **equity method**, **the investor records its share of the net income of the investee in the year when it is earned.** An alternative might be to delay recognizing the investor's share of net income until a cash dividend is declared. But that approach would ignore the fact that the investor and investee are, in some sense, one company, making the investor better off by the investee's earned income.

Under the equity method, the investment in common stock is initially recorded at cost. After that, the investment account is **adjusted annually** to show the investor's equity in the investee. Each year, the investor does the following: (1) It increases (debits) the investment account and increases (credits) revenue for its share of the investee's net income.[2] (2) The investor also decreases (credits) the

[2]Or, the investor increases (debits) a loss account and decreases (credits) the investment account for its share of the investee's net loss.

investment account for the amount of dividends received. The investment account is reduced for dividends received because the net assets of the investee are decreased when a dividend is paid.

> **HELPFUL HINT**
> Under the equity method revenue is recognized on the accrual basis—i.e., when it is earned by the investee.

Recording Acquisition of Stock Investments

Assume that Milar Corporation acquires 30% of the common stock of Beck Company for $120,000 on January 1, 2002. The entry to record this transaction is:

Jan. 1	Stock Investments	120,000	
	Cash		120,000
	(To record purchase of Beck common stock)		

A	=	L	+	SE
+120,000				
−120,000				

Recording Revenue and Dividends

For 2002, Beck reports net income of $100,000. It declares and pays a $40,000 cash dividend. Milar is required to record (1) its share of Beck's income, $30,000 (30% × $100,000) and (2) the reduction in the investment account for the dividends received, $12,000 ($40,000 × 30%). The entries are:

(1)

Dec. 31	Stock Investments	30,000	
	Revenue from Investment in Beck Company		30,000
	(To record 30% equity in Beck's 2002 net income)		

A	=	L	+	SE
+30,000				+30,000

(2)

Dec. 31	Cash	12,000	
	Stock Investments		12,000
	(To record dividends received)		

A	=	L	+	SE
+12,000				
−12,000				

After posting the transactions for the year, the investment and revenue accounts will show the following.

Illustration 17-4
Investment and revenue accounts after posting

Stock Investments

Jan. 1	120,000	Dec. 31	**12,000**
Dec. 31	**30,000**		
Dec. 31 Bal.	138,000		

Revenue from Investment in Beck Company

		Dec. 31	**30,000**

During the year, the investment account has increased by $18,000. This $18,000 is Milar's 30% equity in the $60,000 increase in Beck's retained earnings ($100,000 − $40,000). In addition, Milar will report $30,000 of revenue from its investment, which is 30% of Beck's net income of $100,000. Note that the difference between reported revenue under the cost method and reported revenue under the equity method can be significant. For example, Milar would report only $12,000 of dividend revenue (30% × $40,000) if the cost method were used.

HOLDINGS OF MORE THAN 50%

> **STUDY OBJECTIVE 4**
> Describe the use of consolidated financial statements.

A company that owns more than 50% of the common stock of another entity is known as the **parent company**. The entity whose stock is owned by the parent company is called the **subsidiary (affiliated) company**. Because of its stock ownership, the parent company has a **controlling interest** in the subsidiary.

When a company owns more than 50% of the common stock of another company, **consolidated financial statements** are usually prepared. Consolidated financial statements present the total assets and liabilities controlled by the parent company. They also present the total revenues and expenses of the subsidiary companies. Consolidated statements are prepared **in addition to** the financial statements for the parent and individual subsidiary companies. When Time Warner had a 20% investment in Turner, this investment was reported in a single line item—Other Investments—in Time-Warner's balance sheet. After the merger, Time Warner instead consolidated Turner's results with its own. Under this approach, the individual assets and liabilities of Turner are included with those of Time Warner: its plant and equipment are added to Time Warner's plant and equipment, its receivables are added to Time Warner's receivables, and so on.

HELPFUL HINT
If parent (A) has three wholly owned subsidiaries (B, C, & D), there are four separate legal entities. But, from the viewpoint of the shareholders of the parent company, there is only one economic entity.

ACCOUNTING IN ACTION *Business Insight*

Time Warner, Inc. owns 100% of the common stock of **Home Box Office (HBO) Corporation**. The common stockholders of Time Warner elect the board of directors of the company, who, in turn, select the officers and managers of the company. Time Warner's board of directors controls the property owned by the corporation, which includes the common stock of HBO. Thus, they are in a position to elect the board of directors of HBO and, in effect, control its operations. These relationships are graphically illustrated here.

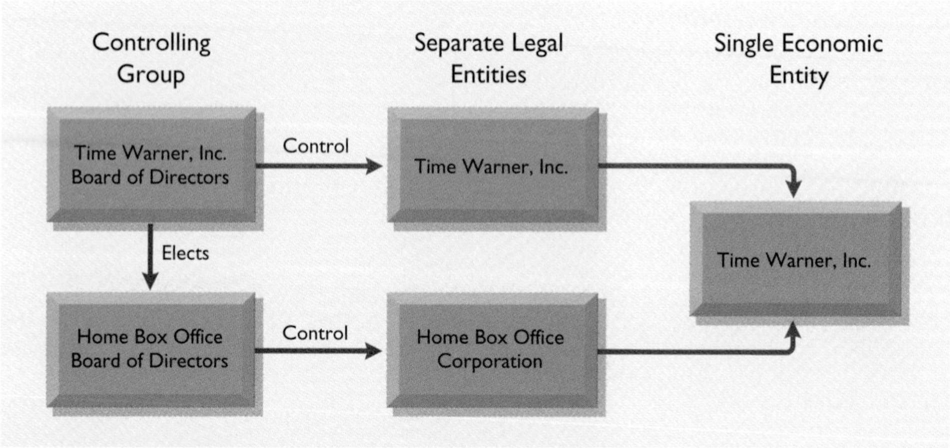

Consolidated statements are useful because they indicate the magnitude and scope of operations of the companies under common control. For example, regulators and the courts undoubtedly used the consolidated statements of **AT&T** to determine whether a breakup of AT&T was in the public interest. Listed below are three companies that prepare consolidated statements and some of the companies they have owned. Note that one, **Walt Disney**, is Time Warner's arch rival.

Beatrice Foods	American Brands, Inc.	The Walt Disney Company
Tropicana Frozen Juices	American Tobacco Company	Capital Cities/ABC, Inc.
Switzer Candy Company	Master Lock Company	Disneyland, Disney World
Samsonite Corporation	Pinkerton's Security Service	Mighty Ducks
Dannon Yogurt Company	Titleist Golf Company	Anaheim Angels
		ESPN

BEFORE YOU GO ON...

▶ *REVIEW IT*

1. What are the accounting entries for stock investments of less than 20%?
2. What entries are made under the equity method when (a) the investor receives a cash dividend from the investee and (b) the investee reports net income for the year?
3. What is the purpose of consolidated financial statements?
4. What does **Lands' End** state regarding its accounting policy involving consolidated financial statements? The answer to this question is provided on page 713.

LANDS' END DIRECT MERCHANTS

▶ *DO IT*

Presented below are two independent situations.

1. Rho Jean Inc. acquired 5% of the 400,000 shares of common stock of Stillwater Corp. at a total cost of $6 per share on May 18, 2002. On August 30, Stillwater declared and paid a $75,000 dividend. On December 31, Stillwater reported net income of $244,000 for the year.
2. Debbie, Inc. obtained significant influence over North Sails by buying 40% of North Sails' 60,000 outstanding shares of common stock at a cost of $12 per share on January 1, 2002. On April 15, North Sails declared and paid a cash dividend of $45,000. On December 31, North Sails reported net income of $120,000 for the year.

Prepare all necessary journal entries for 2002 for (1) Rho Jean Inc. and (2) Debbie, Inc.

ACTION PLAN

- Presume that the investor has relatively little influence over the investee when an investor owns less than 20% of the common stock of another corporation. In this case, net income earned by the investee is not considered a proper basis for recognizing income from the investment by the investor.
- Presume significant influence for investments of 20%–50%. Therefore, record the investor's share of the net income of the investee.

SOLUTION

(1) May 18	Stock Investments (20,000 × $6)	120,000	
	Cash		120,000
	(To record purchase of 20,000 shares of Stillwater Co. stock)		
Aug. 30	Cash	3,750	
	Dividend Revenue ($75,000 × 5%)		3,750
	(To record receipt of cash dividend)		
(2) Jan. 1	Stock Investments (60,000 × 40% × $12)	288,000	
	Cash		288,000
	(To record purchase of 24,000 shares of North Sails' stock)		
Apr. 15	Cash	18,000	
	Stock Investments ($45,000 × 40%)		18,000
	(To record receipt of cash dividend)		
Dec. 31	Stock Investments ($120,000 × 40%)	48,000	
	Revenue from Investment in North Sails		48,000
	(To record 40% equity in North Sails' net income)		

Related exercise material: BE17-2, BE17-3, E17-1, E17-2, E17-3, E17-4, and E17-5.

THE NAVIGATOR

VALUING AND REPORTING INVESTMENTS

STUDY OBJECTIVE 5

Indicate how debt and stock investments are valued and reported on the financial statements.

The value of debt and stock investments may fluctuate greatly during the time they are held. For example, in one 12-month peroid, the stock price of **Digital Equipment Corporation** hit a high of $76.50 and a low of $28.37. In light of such price fluctuations, how should investments be valued at the balance sheet date? Valuation could be at cost, at fair value (market value), or at the lower of cost or market value. Many people argue that fair value offers the best approach because it represents the expected cash realizable value of securities. **Fair value** is the amount for which a security could be sold in a normal market. Others counter that, unless a security is going to be sold soon, the fair value is not relevant because the price of the security will likely change again.

CATEGORIES OF SECURITIES

For purposes of valuation and reporting at a financial statement date, debt and stock investments are classified into three categories of securities:

1. **Trading securities** are securities bought and held primarily for sale in the near term to generate income on short-term price differences.
2. **Available-for-sale securities** are securities that may be sold in the future.
3. **Held-to-maturity securities** are debt securities that the investor has the intent and ability to hold to maturity.

The valuation guidelines for these securities are shown in Illustration 17-5. **These guidelines apply to all debt securities and all stock investments in which the holdings are less than 20%.**

Illustration 17-5

Valuation guidelines

Trading
"We'll sell within ten days."
At fair value with changes reported in net income
Available-for-sale
"We'll hold the stock for a while to see how it performs."
At fair value with changes reported in the stockholders' equity section
Held-to-maturity
"We intend to hold these bonds until maturity."
At amortized cost[3]

Trading Securities

Trading securities are held with the intention of selling them in a short period (generally less than a month). Trading means frequent buying and selling. Trading securities are reported at fair value, and changes from cost are reported as part of net income. The changes are reported as **unrealized gains or losses** because the securities have not been sold. The unrealized gain or loss is the difference between the **total cost** of trading securities and their **total fair value.**

[3]This category is provided for completeness. The accounting and valuation issues related to held-to-maturity securities are discussed in more advanced accounting courses.

Illustration 17-6 shows the cost and fair values for investments classified as trading securities for Pace Corporation on December 31, 2002. Pace has an unrealized gain of $7,000 because total fair value ($147,000) is $7,000 greater than total cost ($140,000).

Illustration 17-6

Valuation of trading securities

Trading Securities, December 31, 2002

Investments	Cost	Fair Value	Unrealized Gain (Loss)
Yorkville Company bonds	$ 50,000	$ 48,000	$(2,000)
Kodak Company stock	90,000	99,000	9,000
Total	$140,000	$147,000	$ 7,000

HELPFUL HINT

The fact that trading securities are short-term investments increases the likelihood that they will be sold at fair value (the company may not be able to time their sale) and the likelihood that there will be realized gains or losses.

Fair value and unrealized gain or loss are recorded through an adjusting entry at the time financial statements are prepared. In the entry, a valuation allowance account, Market Adjustment—Trading, is used to record the difference between the total cost and the total fair value of the securities. The adjusting entry for Pace Corporation is:

Dec. 31	Market Adjustment—Trading	7,000	
	Unrealized Gain—Income		7,000
	(To record unrealized gain on trading securities)		

A	=	L	+	SE
+7,000				+7,000

The use of a Market Adjustment—Trading account enables the company to maintain a record of the investment cost. Actual cost is needed to determine the gain or loss realized when the securities are sold. The Market Adjustment—Trading balance is added to the cost of the investments to arrive at a fair value for the trading securities.

The fair value of the securities is the amount reported on the balance sheet. The unrealized gain is reported in the income statement in the "other revenues and gains" section. The term "Income" is used in the account title to indicate that the gain affects net income.

When the total cost of the trading securities is greater than total fair value, an unrealized loss has occurred. In such a case, the adjusting entry is a debit to Unrealized Loss—Income and a credit to Market Adjustment—Trading. The unrealized loss is reported under "other expenses and losses" in the income statement.

The market adjustment account is carried forward into future accounting periods. No entries are made to this account during the period. At the end of each reporting period, the balance in the account is adjusted to the difference between cost and fair value. For trading securities, the Unrealized Gain (Loss)—Income account is closed at the end of the reporting period.

HELPFUL HINT

An unrealized gain or loss is reported in the income statement because of the likelihood that the securities will be sold at fair value since they are short-term investments.

Available-for-Sale Securities

As indicated earlier, available-for-sale securities are held with the intent of selling them sometime in the future. If the intent is to sell the securities within the next year or operating cycle, the securities are classified as current assets in the balance sheet. Otherwise, they are classified as long-term assets in the investments section of the balance sheet.

Available-for-sale securities are also reported at fair value. The procedure for determining fair value and the unrealized gain or loss for these securities is the same as for trading securities. To illustrate, assume that Elbert Corporation has two securities that are classified as available-for-sale. Illustration 17-7 provides information on their valuation. There is an unrealized loss of $9,537 because total cost ($293,537) is $9,537 more than total fair value ($284,000).

ETHICS NOTE

Some managers appear to hold their available-for-sale securities that have experienced losses, while selling those that have gains, thus increasing income. Do you think this is ethical?

Illustration 17-7

Valuation of available-for-sale securities

Available-for-Sale Securities, December 31, 2002			
Investments	**Cost**	**Fair Value**	**Unrealized Gain (Loss)**
Campbell Soup Corporation 8% bonds	$ 93,537	$103,600	$10,063
Hershey Corporation stock	200,000	180,400	(19,600)
Total	$293,537	$284,000	**$(9,537)**

Both the adjusting entry and the reporting of the unrealized gain or loss for available-for-sale securities differ from those illustrated for trading securities. The differences result because these securities are not going to be sold in the near term. Thus, prior to actual sale it is more likely that changes in fair value may reverse either unrealized gains or losses. Therefore, an unrealized gain or loss is not reported in the income statement. Instead, it is reported as a **separate component of stockholders' equity**. In the adjusting entry, the market adjustment account is identified with available-for-sale securities; the unrealized gain or loss account is identified with stockholders' equity. The adjusting entry to record the unrealized loss of $9,537 for Elbert Corporation is as follows:

A	=	L	+	SE
−9,537				−9,537

Dec. 31	Unrealized Loss—Equity	9,537	
	Market Adjustment—Available-for-Sale		9,537
	(To record unrealized loss on available-for-sale securities)		

If total fair value exceeds total cost, the adjusting entry would have a debit to the market adjustment account and a credit to an unrealized gain or loss account.

For available-for-sale securities, the unrealized gain or loss account is carried forward to future periods. At each future balance sheet date, it is adjusted with the market adjustment account to show the difference between cost and fair value at that time.

BALANCE SHEET PRESENTATION

In the balance sheet, investments are classified as either short-term or long-term.

Short-Term Investments

STUDY OBJECTIVE 6

Distinguish between short-term and long-term investments.

Short-term investments are securities held by a company that are (1) **readily marketable** and (2) **intended to be converted into cash** within the next year or operating cycle, whichever is longer. Investments that do not meet **both criteria** are classified as long-term investments.

HELPFUL HINT

Trading securities are always classified as short-term. Available-for-sale securities can be either short-term or long-term.

READILY MARKETABLE. **An investment is readily marketable when it can be sold easily whenever the need for cash arises.** Short-term paper[4] meets this criterion. It can be readily sold to other investors. Stocks and bonds traded on organized securities exchanges, such as the New York Stock Exchange, are readily marketable. They can be bought and sold daily. In contrast, there may be only a limited market for the securities issued by small corporations, and no market for the securities of a privately held company.

INTENT TO CONVERT. **Intent to convert means that management intends to sell the investment within the next year or operating cycle, whichever is longer.** Generally, this criterion is satisfied when the investment is considered a resource that will be used whenever the need for cash arises. For example, a ski resort may invest idle cash during the summer months with the intent to sell the securities to

[4]Short-term paper includes (1) certificates of deposit (CDs) issued by banks, (2) money market certificates issued by banks and savings and loan associations, (3) Treasury bills issued by the U.S. government, and (4) commercial paper issued by corporations with good credit ratings.

buy supplies and equipment shortly before the next winter season. This investment is considered short-term even if lack of snow cancels the next ski season and eliminates the need to convert the securities into cash as intended.

Because of their high liquidity, short-term investments are listed immediately below cash in the current assets section of the balance sheet. They are reported at fair value. For example, Pace Corporation would report its trading securities as shown in Illustration 17-8.

Illustration 17-8

Presentation of short-term investments

PACE CORPORATION Balance Sheet (partial)	
Current assets	
Cash	$ 21,000
Short-term investments, at fair value	147,000

HELPFUL HINT
In a recent survey of 600 large U.S. companies, over 400 reported short-term investments.

Long-Term Investments

Long-term investments are generally reported in a separate section of the balance sheet immediately below current assets, as shown later in Illustration 17-11. Long-term investments in available-for-sale securities are reported at fair value. Investments in common stock accounted for under the equity method are reported at equity.

PRESENTATION OF REALIZED AND UNREALIZED GAIN OR LOSS

Gains and losses on investments, whether realized or unrealized, must be presented in the financial statements. In the income statement, gains and losses are reported in the nonoperating activities section under the categories listed in Illustration 17-9. Interest and dividend revenue are also reported in that section.

Illustration 17-9

Nonoperating items related to investments

Other Revenue and Gains	Other Expenses and Losses
Interest Revenue	Loss on Sale of Investments
Dividend Revenue	Unrealized Loss—Income
Gain on Sale of Investments	
Unrealized Gain—Income	

As indicated earlier, an unrealized gain or loss on available-for-sale securities is reported as a separate component of stockholders' equity. To illustrate, assume that Dawson Inc. has common stock of $3,000,000, retained earnings of $1,500,000, and an unrealized loss on available-for-sale securities of $100,000. The statement presentation of the unrealized loss is shown in Illustration 17-10.

Illustration 17-10

Unrealized loss in stockholders' equity section

DAWSON INC. Balance Sheet (partial)	
Stockholders' equity	
Common stock	$3,000,000
Retained earnings	1,500,000
Total paid-in capital and retained earnings	4,500,000
Less: **Unrealized loss on available-for-sale securities**	**(100,000)**
Total stockholders' equity	$4,400,000

Note that the loss decreases stockholders' equity. The cost of treasury stock is presented in the same way. An unrealized gain would be added to stockholders' equity. Reporting the unrealized gain or loss in the stockholders' equity section serves two important purposes: (1) It reduces the volatility of net income due to fluctuations in fair value. (2) It informs the financial statement user of the gain or loss that would occur if the securities were sold at fair value.

A recent accounting standard requires that items such as this, which affect stockholders' equity but are not included in the calculation of net income, must be reported as part of a more inclusive measure called *comprehensive income*. Comprehensive income is discussed in more advanced courses.

CLASSIFIED BALANCE SHEET

Many sections of classified balance sheets have been presented in this and preceding chapters. The classified balance sheet in Illustration 17-11 on page 697 includes, in one place, key topics from previous chapters: the issuance of par value common stock, restrictions of retained earnings, issuance of long-term bonds, and bond sinking funds. From this chapter, the statement includes (highlighted in red) short-term and long-term investments. The investments in short-term securities are considered trading securities. The long-term investments in stock of less than 20% owned companies are considered available-for-sale securities. Illustration 17-11 also includes a long-term investment reported at equity and descriptive notations within the statement, such as the basis for valuing merchandise and two notes to the statement.

BEFORE YOU GO ON...

REVIEW IT

1. What is the proper valuation and reporting of trading and available-for-sale securities on a balance sheet?
2. Explain how the unrealized gain or loss for both trading and available-for-sale securities is reported.
3. Explain where short-term and long-term investments are reported on a balance sheet.

A LOOK BACK AT OUR FEATURE STORY

Refer back to the Feature Story about **Time Warner Corporation** at the beginning of the chapter, and answer the following questions.

1. For what reason(s) is Time Warner investing in equity securities (stocks)?
2. Would you expect Time Warner to prepare consolidated financial statements for the many companies it owns? Explain your answer.
3. What has Time Warner's aggressive acquisition spree meant for its bottom line?

SOLUTION

1. Time Warner is investing for strategic reasons. As indicated in the Feature Story, the company's attitude is, "If we can't beat you, we will buy you." Time Warner is diversifying because it is not sure what industries will be successful in the future. As a result, Time Warner now owns more information and entertainment copyrights and brands than any other company in the world.
2. When a company owns more than 50% of the common stock of another company, consolidated financial statements are usually prepared. Because Time Warner owns over 50% of the companies mentioned in the Feature Story, Time Warner would consolidate these subsidiary companies with its own.
3. To date, Time Warner's acquisition spree has left it with huge debt and massive interest costs. In addition, some of the acquisitions have not come cheap, resulting in large amounts of reported goodwill and goodwill amortization.

THE NAVIGATOR

Illustration 17-11

Classified balance sheet

PACE CORPORATION
Balance Sheet
December 31, 2002

Assets

Current assets			
Cash			$ 21,000
Short-term investments, at fair value			**147,000**
Accounts receivable		$ 84,000	
Less: Allowance for doubtful accounts		4,000	80,000
Merchandise inventory, at FIFO cost			43,000
Prepaid insurance			23,000
Total current assets			314,000
Investments			
Bond sinking fund		100,000	
Investments in stock of less than 20% owned companies, at fair value		**50,000**	
Investment in stock of 20–50% owned company, at equity		**150,000**	
Total investments			300,000
Property, plant, and equipment			
Land		200,000	
Buildings	$800,000		
Less: Accumulated depreciation	200,000	600,000	
Equipment	180,000		
Less: Accumulated depreciation	54,000	126,000	
Total property, plant, and equipment			926,000
Intangible assets			
Goodwill (Note 1)			170,000
Total assets			$1,710,000

Liabilities and Stockholders' Equity

Current liabilities		
Accounts payable		$185,000
Bond interest payable		10,000
Federal income taxes payable		60,000
Total current liabilities		255,000
Long-term liabilities		
Bonds payable, 10%, due 2013	$ 300,000	
Less: Discount on bonds	10,000	
Total long-term liabilities		290,000
Total liabilities		545,000
Stockholders' equity		
Paid-in capital		
Common stock, $10 par value, 200,000 shares authorized, 80,000 shares issued and outstanding	800,000	
Paid-in capital in excess of par value	100,000	
Total paid-in capital	900,000	
Retained earnings (Note 2)	255,000	
Total paid-in capital and retained earnings	1,155,000	
Add: Unrealized gain on available-for-sale securities	**10,000**	
Total stockholders' equity		1,165,000
Total liabilities and stockholders' equity		$1,710,000

Note 1. Goodwill is amortized by the straight-line method over 40 years.

Note 2. Retained earnings of $100,000 is restricted for plant expansion.

Additional Demonstration Problem

DEMONSTRATION PROBLEM

In its first year of operations, DeMarco Company had the following selected transactions in stock investments that are considered trading securities.

June 1	Purchased for cash 600 shares of Sanburg common stock at $24 per share, plus $300 brokerage fees.
July 1	Purchased for cash 800 shares of Cey common stock at $33 per share, plus $600 brokerage fees.
Sept. 1	Received a $1 per share cash dividend from Cey Corporation.
Nov. 1	Sold 200 shares of Sanburg common stock for cash at $27 per share, less $150 brokerage fees.
Dec. 15	Received a $0.50 per share cash dividend on Sanburg common stock.

At December 31, the fair values per share were: Sanburg $25 and Cey $30.

Instructions

(a) Journalize the transactions.

(b) Prepare the adjusting entry at December 31 to report the securities at fair value.

ACTION PLAN

- Include the price paid plus brokerage fees in the cost of the investment.
- Compute the gain or loss on sales as the difference between net selling price and the cost of the securities.
- Base the adjustment to fair value on the total difference between the cost and the fair value of the securities.

SOLUTION TO DEMONSTRATION PROBLEM

(a) June	1	Stock Investments	14,700	
		Cash		14,700
		(To record purchase of 600 shares of Sanburg common stock)		
July	1	Stock Investments	27,000	
		Cash		27,000
		(To record purchase of 800 shares of Cey common stock)		
Sept.	1	Cash	800	
		Dividend Revenue		800
		(To record receipt of $1 per share cash dividend from Cey Corporation)		
Nov.	1	Cash	5,250	
		Stock Investments		4,900
		Gain on Sale of Stock Investments		350
		(To record sale of 200 shares of Sanburg common stock)		
Dec.	15	Cash	200	
		Dividend Revenue		200
		(To record receipt of $0.50 per share dividend from Sanburg Corporation)		
(b) Dec.	31	Unrealized Loss—Income	2,800	
		Market Adjustment—Trading		2,800
		(To record unrealized loss on trading securities)		

Investment	Cost	Fair Value	Unrealized Gain (Loss)
Sanburg common stock	$ 9,800	$10,000	$ 200
Cey common stock	27,000	24,000	(3,000)
Totals	$36,800	$34,000	$(2,800)

THE NAVIGATOR

SUMMARY OF STUDY OBJECTIVES

1. *Discuss why corporations invest in debt and stock securities.* Corporations invest for three primary reasons: (a) They have excess cash. (b) They view investments as a significant revenue source. (c) They have strategic goals such as gaining control of a competitor or moving into a new line of business.

2. *Explain the accounting for debt investments.* Entries for investments in debt securities are required when the bonds are purchased, interest is received or accrued, and the bonds are sold. The accounting for long-term investments in bonds is the same as for temporary investments in bonds, except that bond premium and bond discount must be amortized.

3. *Explain the accounting for stock investments.* Entries for investments in common stock are required when the stock is purchased, dividends are received, and stock is sold. When ownership is less than 20%, the cost method is used. When ownership is between 20% and 50%, the equity method should be used. When ownership is more than 50%, consolidated financial statements should be prepared.

4. *Describe the use of consolidated financial statements.* When a company owns more than 50% of the common stock of another company, consolidated financial statements are usually prepared. These statements are useful because they indicate the magnitude and scope of operations of the companies under common control.

5. *Indicate how debt and stock investments are valued and reported on the financial statements.* Investments in debt and stock securities are classified as trading, available-for-sale, or held-to-maturity securities for valuation and reporting purposes. Trading securities are reported in current assets at fair value, with changes from cost reported in net income. Available-for-sale securities are also reported at fair value, with the changes from cost reported in stockholders' equity. Available-for-sale securities are classified as short-term or long-term depending on their expected realization.

6. *Distinguish between short-term and long-term investments.* Short-term investments are securities, held by a company, that are (a) readily marketable and (b) intended to be converted to cash within the next year or operating cycle, whichever is longer. Investments that do not meet both criteria are classified as long-term investments.

THE NAVIGATOR

Key Term Matching Activity

GLOSSARY

Available-for-sale securities Securities that may be sold in the future. (p. 692).

Consolidated financial statements Financial statements that present the assets and liabilities controlled by the parent company and the aggregate profitability of the affiliated companies. (p. 689).

Controlling interest Ownership of more than 50% of the common stock of another entity. (p. 689).

Cost method An accounting method in which the investment in common stock is recorded at cost, and revenue is recognized only when cash dividends are received. (p. 687).

Debt investments Investments in government and corporation bonds. (p. 684).

Equity method An accounting method in which the investment in common stock is initially recorded at cost, and the investment account is then adjusted annually to show the investor's equity in the investee. (p. 688).

Fair value Amount for which a security could be sold in a normal market. (p. 692).

Held-to-maturity securities Debt securities that the investor has the intent and ability to hold to their maturity date. (p. 692).

Investment portfolio A group of stocks in different corporations held for investment purposes. (p. 687).

Long-term investments Investments that are not readily marketable and that management does not intend to convert into cash within the next year or operating cycle, whichever is longer. (p. 694).

Parent company A company that owns more than 50% of the common stock of another entity. (p. 689).

Short-term investments Investments that are readily marketable and intended to be converted into cash within the next year or operating cycle, whichever is longer. (p. 694).

Stock investments Investments in the capital stock of corporations. (p. 687).

Subsidiary (affiliated) company A company in which more than 50% of its stock is owned by another company. (p. 689).

Trading securities Securities bought and held primarily for sale in the near term to generate income on short-term price differences. (p. 692).

Chapter 17 Self-Test

SELF-STUDY QUESTIONS

Answers are at the end of the chapter.

(SO 2) **1.** Debt investments are initially recorded at:
a. cost.
b. cost plus accrued interest.
c. fair value.
d. None of the above.

2. Hanes Company sells debt investments costing $26,000 for $28,000, plus accrued interest that has been recorded. In journalizing the sale, credits are to: (SO 2)
a. Debt Investments and Loss on Sale of Debt Investments.
b. Debt Investments, Gain on Sale of Debt Investments, and Bond Interest Receivable.

c. Stock Investments and Bond Interest Receivable.
d. No correct answer given.

(SO 3) **3.** Pryor Company receives net proceeds of $42,000 on the sale of stock investments that cost $39,500. This transaction will result in reporting in the income statement a:
a. loss of $2,500 under "other expenses and losses."
b. loss of $2,500 under "operating expenses."
c. gain of $2,500 under "other revenues and gains."
d. gain of $2,500 under "operating revenues."

(SO 3) **4.** The equity method of accounting for long-term investments in stock should be used when the investor has significant influence over an investee and owns:
a. between 20% and 50% of the investee's common stock.
b. 20% or more of the investee's common stock.
c. more than 50% of the investee's common stock.
d. less than 20% of the investee's common stock.

(SO 4) **5.** Which of the following statements is *not true*? Consolidated financial statements are useful to:
a. determine the profitability of specific subsidiaries.
b. determine the total profitability of enterprises under common control.
c. determine the breadth of a parent company's operations.
d. determine the full extent of total obligations of enterprises under common control.

(SO 5) **6.** At the end of the first year of operations, the total cost of the trading securities portfolio is $120,000. Total fair value is $115,000. The financial statements should show:
a. a reduction of an asset of $5,000 and a realized loss of $5,000.
b. a reduction of an asset of $5,000 and an unrealized loss of $5,000 in the stockholders' equity section.
c. a reduction of an asset of $5,000 in the current assets section and an unrealized loss of $5,000 in "other expenses and losses."
d. a reduction of an asset of $5,000 in the current assets section and a realized loss of $5,000 in "other expenses and losses."

7. In the balance sheet, Unrealized Loss—Equity is reported as a: (SO 5)
a. contra asset account.
b. contra stockholders' equity account.
c. loss in the income statement.
d. loss in the retained earnings statement.

8. Short-term debt investments must be readily marketable and be expected to be sold within: (SO 6)
a. 3 months from the date of purchase.
b. the next year or operating cycle, whichever is shorter.
c. the next year or operating cycle, whichever is longer.
d. the operating cycle.

THE NAVIGATOR

QUESTIONS

1. What are the reasons that corporations invest in securities?

2. (a) What is the cost of an investment in bonds?
(b) When is interest on bonds recorded?

3. Juan Ortiz is confused about losses and gains on the sale of debt investments. Explain to Juan (a) how the gain or loss is computed, and (b) the statement presentation of the gains and losses.

4. Wendall Company sells Hurley's bonds costing $40,000 for $45,000, including $2,000 of accrued interest. In recording the sale, Wendall books a $5,000 gain. Is this correct? Explain.

5. What is the cost of an investment in stock?

6. To acquire Parin Corporation stock, R. Scope pays $60,000 in cash, plus $1,500 broker's fees. What entry should be made for this investment, assuming the stock is readily marketable?

7. (a) When should a long-term investment in common stock be accounted for by the equity method? (b) When is revenue recognized under this method?

8. Maxwell Corporation uses the equity method to account for its ownership of 30% of the common stock of Warren Packing. During 2002 Warren reported a net income of $80,000 and declares and pays cash dividends of $10,000. What recognition should Maxwell Corporation give to these events?

9. What constitutes "significant influence" when an investor's financial interest is below the 50% level?

10. Distinguish between the cost and equity methods of accounting for investments in stocks.

11. What are consolidated financial statements?

12. What are the valuation guidelines for investments at a balance sheet date?

13. Mary Carne is the controller of Nakoma Inc. At December 31, the company's investments in trading securities cost $74,000. They have a fair value of $70,000. Indicate how Mary would report these data in the financial statements prepared on December 31.

14. Using the data in question 13, how would Mary report the data if the investment were long-term and the securities were classified as available-for-sale?

15. Kaston Company's investments in available-for-sale securities at December 31 show total cost of $195,000 and total fair value of $205,000. Prepare the adjusting entry.

16. Using the data in question 15, prepare the adjusting entry assuming the securities are classified as trading securities.

17. What is the proper statement presentation of the account Unrealized Loss—Equity (Available-for-Sale Security)?

18. What purposes are served by reporting Unrealized Gains (Losses)—Equity in the stockholders' equity section?

19. Francis Wholesale Supply owns stock in Chen Corporation. Francis intends to hold the stock indefinitely because of some negative tax consequences if sold. Should the investment in Chen be classified as a short-term investment? Why or why not?

BRIEF EXERCISES

BE17-1 Phelps Corporation purchased debt investments for $49,800 on January 1, 2002. On July 1, 2002, Phelps received cash interest of $2,490. Journalize the purchase and the receipt of interest. Assume that no interest has been accrued.

Journalize entries for debt investments.
(SO 2)

BE17-2 On August 1, McClain Company buys 1,000 shares of Morgan common stock for $35,000 cash, plus brokerage fees of $600. On December 1, McClain sells the stock investments for $38,000 in cash. Journalize the purchase and sale of the common stock.

Journalize entries for stock investments.
(SO 3)

BE17-3 Harmon Company owns 25% of Hook Company. For the current year Hook reports net income of $180,000 and declares and pays a $50,000 cash dividend. Record Harmon's equity in Hook's net income and the receipt of dividends from Hook.

Record transactions under the equity method of accounting.
(SO 3)

BE17-4 The cost of the trading securities of Michelle Company at December 31, 2002, is $64,000. At December 31, 2002, the fair value of the securities is $61,000. Prepare the adjusting entry to record the securities at fair value.

Prepare adjusting entry using fair value.
(SO 5)

BE17-5 For the data presented in BE17-4, show the financial statement presentation of the trading securities and related accounts.

Indicate statement presentation using fair value.
(SO 5, 6)

BE17-6 Duggan Corporation holds as a long-term investment available-for-sale stock securities costing $72,000. At December 31, 2002, the fair value of the securities is $66,000. Prepare the adjusting entry to record the securities at fair value.

Prepare adjusting entry using fair value.
(SO 5)

BE17-7 For the data presented in BE17-6, show the financial statement presentation of the available-for-sale securities and related accounts. Assume the available-for-sale securities are noncurrent.

Indicate statements presentation using fair value.
(SO 5, 6)

BE17-8 Saber Corporation has the following long-term investments: (1) Common stock of Kubek Co. (10% ownership) held as available-for-sale securities, cost $108,000, fair value $120,000. (2) Common stock of Ely Inc. (30% ownership), cost $210,000, equity $250,000. (3) A bond sinking fund of $150,000. Prepare the investments section of the balance sheet.

Prepare investments section of balance sheet.
(SO 5, 6)

EXERCISES

E17-1 Jorge Corporation had the following transactions pertaining to debt investments.

Journalize debt investment transactions and accrue interest.
(SO 2)

Jan. 1	Purchased 60 10%, $1,000 Weston Co. bonds for $60,000 cash plus brokerage fees of $900. Interest is payable semiannually on July 1 and January 1.
July 1	Received semiannual interest on Weston Co. bonds.
July 1	Sold 30 Weston Co. bonds for $32,000 less $400 brokerage fees.

Instructions

(a) Journalize the transactions.

(b) Prepare the adjusting entry for the accrual of interest at December 31.

E17-2 Puff Daddy Company had the following transactions pertaining to stock investments.

Journalize stock investment transactions.
(SO 3)

Feb. 1	Purchased 600 shares of GET common stock (2%) for $7,000 cash, plus brokerage fees of $200.
July 1	Received cash dividends of $1 per share on GET common stock.
Sept. 1	Sold 300 shares of GET common stock for $4,000, less brokerage fees of $100.
Dec. 1	Received cash dividends of $1 per share on GET common stock.

Instructions

(a) Journalize the transactions.

(b) Explain how dividend revenue and the gain (loss) on sale should be reported in the income statement.

E17-3 Torre Inc. had the following transactions pertaining to investments in common stock.

Journalize transactions for investments in stocks.
(SO 3)

Jan. 1	Purchased 1,500 shares of Parker Corporation common stock (5%) for $105,000 cash plus $2,100 broker's commission.
July 1	Received a cash dividend of $9 per share.
Dec. 1	Sold 500 shares of Parker Corporation common stock for $37,000 cash, less $800 broker's commission.
Dec. 31	Received a cash dividend of $9 per share.

Instructions

Journalize the transactions.

Journalize and post transactions, and contrast cost and equity method results.
(SO 3)

E17-4 On January 1 Lionel Corporation purchased a 25% equity in Bellingham Corporation for $150,000. At December 31 Bellingham declared and paid a $60,000 cash dividend and reported net income of $200,000.

Instructions

(a) Journalize the transactions.
(b) Determine the amount to be reported as an investment in Bellingham stock at December 31.

Journalize entries under cost and equity methods.
(SO 3)

E17-5 Presented below are two independent situations.

1. Roscoe Cosmetics acquired 10% of the 200,000 shares of common stock of Ling Fashion at a total cost of $13 per share on March 18, 2002. On June 30, Ling declared and paid a $75,000 dividend. On December 31, Ling reported net income of $122,000 for the year. At December 31, the market price of Ling Fashion was $14 per share. The stock is classified as available-for-sale.
2. Juan, Inc., obtained significant influence over Orlando Corporation by buying 30% of Orlando's 30,000 outstanding shares of common stock at a total cost of $9 per share on January 1, 2002. On June 15, Orlando declared and paid a cash dividend of $35,000. On December 31, Orlando reported a net income of $80,000 for the year.

Instructions

Prepare all the necessary journal entries for 2002 for (a) Roscoe Cosmetics and (b) Juan, Inc.

Prepare adjusting entry to record fair value, and indicate statement presentation.
(SO 5, 6)

E17-6 At December 31, 2002, the trading securities for Yanu, Inc. are as follows.

Security	Cost	Fair Value
A	$17,500	$16,000
B	12,500	14,000
C	23,000	19,000
	$53,000	$49,000

Instructions

(a) Prepare the adjusting entry at December 31, 2002, to report the securities at fair value.
(b) Show the balance sheet and income statement presentation at December 31, 2002, after adjustment to fair value.

Prepare adjusting entry to record fair value, and indicate statement presentation.
(SO 5, 6)

E17-7 Data for investments in stock classified as trading securities are presented in E17-6. Assume instead that the investments are classified as available-for-sale securities. They have the same cost and fair value. The securities are considered to be a long-term investment.

Instructions

(a) Prepare the adjusting entry at December 31, 2002, to report the securities at fair value.
(b) Show the statement presentation at December 31, 2002, after adjustment to fair value.
(c) M. Lieberman, a member of the board of directors, does not understand the reporting of the unrealized gains or losses. Write a letter to Mr. Lieberman explaining the reporting and the purposes that it serves.

Prepare adjusting entries for fair value, and indicate statement presentation for two classes of securities.
(SO 5, 6)

E17-8 Chaney Company has the following data at December 31, 2002.

Securities	Cost	Fair Value
Trading	$120,000	$124,000
Available-for-sale	100,000	94,000

The available-for-sale securities are held as a long-term investment.

Instructions

(a) Prepare the adjusting entries to report each class of securities at fair value.
(b) Indicate the statement presentation of each class of securities and the related unrealized gain (loss) accounts.

PROBLEMS: SET A

P17-1A Willow Carecenters Inc. provides financing and capital to the health-care industry, with a particular focus on nursing homes for the elderly. The following selected transactions relate to bonds acquired as an investment by Willow, whose fiscal year ends on December 31.

Journalize debt investment transactions and show financial statement presentation.
(SO 2, 5, 6)

2002

Jan.	1	Purchased at par $5,000,000 of Friendship Nursing Centers, Inc., 10-year, 10% bonds dated January 1, 2002, directly from Friendship.
July	1	Received the semiannual interest on the Friendship bonds.
Dec.	31	Accrual of interest at year-end on the Friendship bonds.

(Assume that all intervening transactions and adjustments have been properly recorded and that the number of bonds owned has not changed from December 31, 2002, to December 31, 2004.)

2005

Jan.	1	Received the semiannual interest on the Friendship bonds.
Jan.	1	Sold $2,500,000 Friendship bonds at 106. The broker deducted $10,000 for commissions and fees on the sale.
July	1	Received the semiannual interest on the Friendship bonds.
Dec.	31	Accrual of interest at year-end on the Friendship bonds.

Instructions

(a) Journalize the listed transactions for the years 2002 and 2005.

(a) Gain on sale of debt investment $140,000

(b) Assume that the fair value of the bonds at December 31, 2002, was $5,500,000. These bonds are classified as available-for-sale securities. Prepare the adjusting entry to record these bonds at fair value.

(c) Show the balance sheet presentation of the bonds and interest receivable at December 31, 2002. Assume the investments are considered long-term. Indicate where any unrealized gain or loss is reported in the financial statements.

P17-2A In January 2002, the management of Harris Company concludes that it has sufficient cash to permit some short-term investments in debt and stock securities. During the year, the following transactions occurred.

Journalize investment transactions, prepare adjusting entry, and show statement presentation.
(SO 2, 3, 5, 6)

Peachtree

Feb.	1	Purchased 400 shares of Alpha common stock for $21,800, plus brokerage fees of $600.
Mar.	1	Purchased 800 shares of Omega common stock for $20,000, plus brokerage fees of $400.
Apr.	1	Purchased 40 $1,000, 12% Pep bonds for $40,000, plus $1,000 brokerage fees. Interest is payable semiannually on April 1 and October 1.
July	1	Received a cash dividend of $0.60 per share on the Alpha common stock.
Aug.	1	Sold 200 shares of Alpha common stock at $58 per share less brokerage fees of $200.
Sept.	1	Received a $1 per share cash dividend on the Omega common stock.
Oct.	1	Received the semiannual interest on the Pep bonds.
Oct.	1	Sold the Pep bonds for $41,000 less $1,000 brokerage fees.

At December 31, the fair value of the Alpha common stock was $55 per share. The fair value of the Omega common stock was $23 per share.

Instructions

(a) Journalize the transactions and post to the accounts Debt Investments and Stock Investments. (Use the T-account form.)

(a) Gain on stock sale $200

(b) Prepare the adjusting entry at December 31, 2002, to report the investment securities at fair value. All securities are considered to be trading securities.

(c) Show the balance sheet presentation of investment securities at December 31, 2002.

(d) Identify the income statement accounts and give the statement classification of each account.

P17-3A On December 31, 2002, Melanie Associates owned the following securities, held as a long-term investment. The securities are not held for influence or control of the inves tee.

Journalize transactions and adjusting entry for stock investments.
(SO 3, 5, 6)

Common Stock	Shares	Cost
Carson Co.	6,000	$90,000
Pirie Co.	5,000	45,000
Scott Co.	1,500	30,000

On this date, the total fair value of the securities was equal to its cost. In 2003, the following transactions occurred.

July 1	Received $1 per share semiannual cash dividend on Pirie Co. common stock.
Aug. 1	Received $0.50 per share cash dividend on Carson Co. common stock.
Sept. 1	Sold 1,000 shares of Pirie Co. common stock for cash at $8 per share, less brokerage fees of $200.
Oct. 1	Sold 800 shares of Carson Co. common stock for cash at $17 per share, less brokerage fees of $500.
Nov. 1	Received $1 per share cash dividend on Scott Co. common stock.
Dec. 15	Received $0.50 per share cash dividend on Carson Co. common stock.
31	Received $1 per share semiannual cash dividend on Pirie Co. common stock.

At December 31, the fair values per share of the common stocks were: Carson Co. $16, Pirie Co. $8, and Scott Co. $18.

Instructions

(a) Journalize the 2003 transactions and post to the account Stock Investments. (Use the T-account form.)

(b) Unrealized loss $1,800

(b) Prepare the adjusting entry at December 31, 2003, to show the securities at fair value. The stock should be classified as available-for-sale securities.

(c) Show the balance sheet presentation of the investments at December 31, 2003. At this date, Melanie Associates has common stock $1,500,000 and retained earnings $1,000,000.

Prepare entries under the cost and equity methods, and tabulate differences.
(SO 3)

P17-4A Handy Services acquired 25% of the outstanding common stock of Quarles Company on January 1, 2002, by paying $800,000 for the 40,000 shares. Quarles declared and paid $0.50 per share cash dividends on March 15, June 15, September 15, and December 15, 2002. Quarles reported net income of $360,000 for the year. At December 31, 2002, the market price of Quarles common stock was $28 per share.

Instructions

(a) Prepare the journal entries for Handy Services for 2002 assuming Handy cannot exercise significant influence over Quarles. (Use the cost method and assume that Quarles' common stock should be classified as a trading security.)

(b) Prepare the journal entries for Handy Services for 2002, assuming Handy can exercise significant influence over Quarles. Use the equity method.

(c) In tabular form, indicate the investment and income statement account balances at December 31, 2002, under each method of accounting.

Journalize stock investment transactions and show statement presentation.
(SO 3, 5, 6)

P17-5A The following securities are in Hi-Tech Company's portfolio of long-term available-for-sale securities at December 31, 2002.

	Cost
1,000 shares of Awixa Corporation common stock	$52,000
1,400 shares of HAL Corporation common stock	84,000
800 shares of Renda Corporation preferred stock	33,600

On December 31, 2002, the total cost of the portfolio equaled total fair value. Hi-Tech had the following transactions related to the securities during 2003.

Jan. 20	Sold 1,000 shares of Awixa Corporation common stock at $56 per share less brokerage fees of $600.
28	Purchased 400 shares of $70 par value common stock of Mintor Corporation at $78 per share, plus brokerage fees of $480.
30	Received a cash dividend of $1.15 per share on HAL Corp. common stock.

Feb. 8	Received cash dividends of $0.40 per share on Renda Corp. preferred stock.
18	Sold all 800 shares of Renda Corp. preferred stock at $30.00 per share less brokerage fees of $360.
July 30	Received a cash dividend of $1.00 per share on HAL Corp. common stock.
Sept. 6	Purchased an additional 800 shares of $10 par value common stock of Mintor Corporation at $82 per share, plus brokerage fees of $800.
Dec. 1	Received a cash dividend of $1.50 per share on Mintor Corporation common stock.

At December 31, 2003, the fair values of the securities were:

HAL Corporation common stock	$64 per share
Mintor Corporation common stock	$72 per share

Hi-Tech Company uses separate account titles for each investment, such as "Investment in HAL Corporation Common Stock."

Instructions

(a) Prepare journal entries to record the transactions.

(a) Loss on sale $9,960

(b) Post to the investment accounts. (Use T accounts.)

(c) Prepare the adjusting entry at December 31, 2003, to report the portfolio at fair value.

(c) Unrealized loss $6,080

(d) Show the balance sheet presentation at December 31, 2003.

Prepare a balance sheet.
(SO 5, 6)

P17-6A The following data, presented in alphabetical order, are taken from the records of Scheer Corporation.

Accounts payable	$ 250,000
Accounts receivable	140,000
Accumulated depreciation—building	180,000
Accumulated depreciation—equipment	52,000
Allowance for doubtful accounts	6,000
Bonds payable (10%, due 2013)	500,000
Bond sinking fund	150,000
Buildings	950,000
Cash	72,000
Common stock ($10 par value; 500,000 shares authorized, 150,000 shares issued)	1,500,000
Dividends payable	80,000
Equipment	275,000
Goodwill	200,000
Income taxes payable	120,000
Investment in Lotto common stock (10% ownership), at cost	278,000
Investment in Portico common stock (30% ownership), at equity	230,000
Land	500,000
Market adjustment—available-for-sale securities (Dr)	8,000
Merchandise inventory	170,000
Notes payable (due 2003)	70,000
Paid-in capital in excess of par value	200,000
Premium on bonds payable	40,000
Prepaid insurance	16,000
Retained earnings	163,000
Short-term stock investment, at fair value (and cost)	180,000
Unrealized gain—available-for-sale securities	8,000

The investment in Lotto common stock is considered to be a long-term available-for-sale security.

Instructions

Prepare a balance sheet at December 31, 2002.

Total assets $2,931,000

PROBLEMS: SET B

Journalize debt investment transactions and show financial statement presentation.
(SO 2, 5, 6)

P17-1B Marvel Davis Farms is a grower of hybrid seed corn for DeKalb Genetics Corporation. It has had two exceptionally good years and has elected to invest its excess funds in bonds. The following selected transactions relate to bonds acquired as an investment by Marvel Davis Farms, whose fiscal year ends on December 31.

2002

Jan. 1	Purchased at par $1,000,000 of Sycamore Corporation 10-year, 9% bonds dated January 1, 2002, directly from the issuing corporation.
July 1	Received the semiannual interest on the Sycamore bonds.
Dec. 31	Accrual of interest at year-end on the Sycamore bonds.

(Assume that all intervening transactions and adjustments have been properly recorded and the number of bonds owned has not changed from December 31, 2002, to December 31, 2004.)

2005

Jan. 1	Received the semiannual interest on the Sycamore bonds.
Jan. 1	Sold $500,000 Sycamore bonds at 114. The broker deducted $7,000 for commissions and fees on the sale.
July 1	Received the semiannual interest on the Sycamore bonds.
Dec. 31	Accrual of interest at year-end on the Sycamore bonds.

Instructions

(a) Gain on sale of debt investments $63,000

(a) Journalize the listed transactions for the years 2002 and 2005.

(b) Assume that the fair value of the bonds at December 31, 2002, was $960,000. These bonds are classified as available-for-sale securities. Prepare the adjusting entry to record these bonds at fair value.

(c) Show the balance sheet presentation of the bonds and interest receivable at December 31, 2002. Assume the investments are considered long-term. Indicate where any unrealized gain or loss is reported in the financial statements.

Journalize investment transactions, prepare adjusting entry, and show statement presentation.
(SO 2, 3, 5, 6)

P17-2B In January 2002, the management of Wolfe Company concludes that it has sufficient cash to purchase some short-term investments in debt and stock securities. During the year, the following transactions occurred.

Feb. 1	Purchased 800 shares of LRT common stock for $32,000, plus brokerage fees of $800.
Mar. 1	Purchased 500 shares of IMA common stock for $15,000, plus brokerage fees of $300.
Apr. 1	Purchased 40 $1,000, 12% CAL bonds for $40,000, plus $1,200 brokerage fees. Interest is payable semiannually on April 1 and October 1.
July 1	Received a cash dividend of $0.60 per share on the LRT common stock.
Aug. 1	Sold 300 shares of LRT common stock at $42 per share, less brokerage fees of $350.
Sept. 1	Received a $1 per share cash dividend on the IMA common stock.
Oct. 1	Received the semiannual interest on the CAL bonds.
Oct. 1	Sold the CAL bonds for $44,000, less $1,000 brokerage fees.

At December 31, the fair value of the LRT common stock was $39 per share. The fair value of the IMA common stock was $30 per share.

Instructions

(a) Journalize the transactions and post to the accounts Debt Investments and Stock Investments. (Use the T-account form.)

(b) Unrealized loss $1,300

(b) Prepare the adjusting entry at December 31, 2002, to report the investments at fair value. All securities are considered to be trading securities.

(c) Show the balance sheet presentation of investment securities at December 31, 2002.

(d) Identify the income statement accounts and give the statement classification of each account.

Journalize transactions and adjusting entry for stock investments.
(SO 3, 5, 6)

P17-3B On December 31, 2002, Appolo Associates owned the following securities, held as long-term investments.

Common Stock	Shares	Cost
Abbot Co.	1,000	$50,000
Burns Co.	6,000	36,000
Costello Co.	1,200	24,000

On this date, the total fair value of the securities was equal to its cost. The securities are not held for influence or control over the investees. In 2003, the following transactions occurred.

July	1	Received $1 per share semiannual cash dividend on Burns Co. common stock.
Aug.	1	Received $0.50 per share cash dividend on Abbot Co. common stock.
Sept.	1	Sold 1,000 shares of Burns Co. common stock for cash at $7 per share, less brokerage fees of $100.
Oct.	1	Sold 600 shares of Abbot Co. common stock for cash at $56 per share, less brokerage fees of $600.
Nov.	1	Received $1 per share cash dividend on Costello Co. common stock.
Dec.	15	Received $0.50 per share cash dividend on Abbot Co. common stock.
	31	Received $1 per share semiannual cash dividend on Burns Co. common stock.

At December 31, the fair values per share of the common stocks were: Abbot Co. $47, Burns Co. $6, and Costello Co. $19.

Instructions

(a) Journalize the 2003 transactions and post to the account Stock Investments. (Use the T-account form.)

(a) Gain on sale, $900 and $3,000

(b) Prepare the adjusting entry at December 31, 2003, to show the securities at fair value. The stock should be classified as available-for-sale securities.

(c) Show the balance sheet presentation of the investments at December 31, 2003. At this date, Appolo Associates has common stock $2,000,000 and retained earnings $1,200,000.

Prepare entries under the cost and equity methods and tabulate differences.
(SO 3)

P17-4B Wet Concrete acquired 25% of the outstanding common stock of Hawkins, Inc. on January 1, 2002, by paying $1,200,000 for 50,000 shares. Hawkins declared and paid an $0.80 per share cash dividend on June 30 and again on December 31, 2002. Hawkins reported net income of $800,000 for the year. At December 31, 2002, the market price of Hawkins' common stock was $30 per share.

Instructions

(a) Prepare the journal entries for Wet Concrete for 2002 assuming Wet cannot exercise significant influence over Hawkins. (Use the cost method and assume Hawkins' common stock should be classified as available-for-sale.)

(a) Total dividend revenue $80,000

(b) Prepare the journal entries for Wet Concrete for 2002, assuming Wet can exercise significant influence over Hawkins. (Use the equity method.)

(b) Revenue from investments $200,000

(c) In tabular form, indicate the investment and income account balances at December 31, 2002, under each method of accounting.

Journalize stock transactions and show statement presentation.
(SO 3, 5, 6)

P17-5B The following are in Sammy Sosa Company's portfolio of long-term available-for-sale securities at December 31, 2002.

	Cost
500 shares of McGwire Corporation common stock	$26,000
700 shares of B. Ruth Corporation common stock	42,000
400 shares H. Aaron Corporation preferred stock	16,800

On December 31, the total cost of the portfolio equaled total fair value. Sammy Sosa Company had the following transactions related to the securities during 2003.

Jan.	7	Sold 500 shares of McGwire Corporation common stock at $56 per share, less brokerage fees of $700.
Jan.	10	Purchased 200 shares, $70 par value common stock of Mantle Corporation at $78 per share, plus brokerage fees of $240.
	26	Received a cash dividend of $1.15 per share on B. Ruth Corporation common stock.

Feb. 2	Received cash dividends of $0.40 per share on H. Aaron Corporation preferred stock.
10	Sold all 400 shares of H. Aaron Corporation preferred stock at $35.00 per share less brokerage fees of $180.
July 1	Received a cash dividend of $1.00 per share on B. Ruth Corporation common stock.
Sept. 1	Purchased an additional 400 shares of the $70 par value common stock of Mantle Corporation at $75 per share, plus brokerage fees of $400.
Dec. 15	Received a cash dividend of $1.50 per share on Mantle Corporation common stock.

At December 31, 2003, the fair values of the securities were:

B. Ruth Corporation common stock	$63 per share
Mantle Corporation common stock	$72 per share

Sosa uses separate account titles for each investment, such as Investment in B. Ruth Corporation Common Stock.

Instructions

(a) Loss on sale $2,980

(c) Unrealized loss $940

(a) Prepare journal entries to record the transactions.
(b) Post to the investment accounts. (Use T accounts.)
(c) Prepare the adjusting entry at December 31, 2003, to report the portfolio at fair value.
(d) Show the balance sheet presentation at December 31, 2003.

Prepare a balance sheet. (SO, 5, 6)

P17-6B The following data, presented in alphabetical order, are taken from the records of Webb Corporation.

Accounts payable	$ 240,000
Accounts receivable	90,000
Accumulated depreciation—building	180,000
Accumulated depreciation—equipment	52,000
Allowance for doubtful accounts	6,000
Bonds payable (10%, due 2015)	400,000
Bond sinking fund	360,000
Buildings	900,000
Cash	112,000
Common stock ($5 par value; 500,000 shares authorized, 300,000 shares issued)	1,500,000
Discount on bonds payable	20,000
Dividends payable	50,000
Equipment	275,000
Goodwill	200,000
Income taxes payable	120,000
Investment in Saratoga Inc. stock (30% ownership), at equity	240,000
Land	500,000
Merchandise inventory	170,000
Notes payable (due 2003)	70,000
Paid-in capital in excess of par value	200,000
Prepaid insurance	16,000
Retained earnings	250,000
Short-term stock investment, at fair value (and cost)	185,000

Instructions

Total assets $2,810,000

Prepare a balance sheet at December 31, 2002.

COMPREHENSIVE PROBLEM: CHAPTERS 13 TO 17

PART I

Monique Bergeron and her two colleagues Jared Nimitz and Rosaline Soileau are personal trainers at an upscale health spa/resort in Tampa, Florida. They want to start a health club that specializes in health plans for people in the 50+ age range. The growing population in this age range and strong consumer interest in the health benefits of physical activity have convinced them they can profitably operate their own club. In addition to many other decisions, they need to determine what type of business organization they want. Jared believes there are more advantages to the corporate form than a partnership, but he hasn't yet convinced Monique and Rosaline. They have come to you, a small business consulting specialist, seeking information and advice regarding the choice of starting a partnership versus a corporation.

Instructions

(a) Prepare a memo (dated May 26, 2000) that describes the advantages and disadvantages of both partnerships and corporations. Advise Monique, Jared, and Rosaline regarding which organizational form you believe would better serve their purposes. Make sure to include reasons supporting your advice.

PART II

After deciding to incorporate, each of the three investors receives 20,000 shares of $1 par common stock on June 12, 2000, in exchange for their co-owned building ($180,000 market value) and $120,000 total cash they contributed to the business. The next decision that Monique, Jared, and Rosaline need to make is how to obtain financing for renovation and equipment. They understand the difference between equity securities and debt securities, but do not understand the tax, net income, and earnings per share consequences of equity versus debt financing on the future of their business.

Instructions

(b) Prepare notes for a discussion with the three entrepreneurs in which you will compare the consequences of using equity versus debt financing. As part of your notes, show the differences in interest and tax expense assuming $1,400,000 is financed with common stock, and then alternatively with debt. Assume that when common stock is used, 140,000 shares will be issued. When debt is used, assume the interest rate on debt is 9%, the tax rate is 32%, and income before interest and taxes is $160,000. (You may want to use an electronic spreadsheet.)

PART III

During the discussion about financing, Rosaline mentions that one of her clients, Antonio Sandoval, has approached her about buying a significant interest in the new club. Having an interested investor sways the three to issue equity securities to provide the financing they need. On July 21, 2000, Mr. Sandoval buys 140,000 shares at a price of $10 per share.

The club, LifePath Fitness, opens on January 12, 2001, and after a slow start, begins to produce the revenue desired by the owners. The owners decide to pay themselves a stock dividend, since cash has been less than abundant since they opened their doors. The 5% stock dividend is declared by the owners on July 27, 2001. The market value of the stock is $1.50 on the declaration date. The date of record is July 31, 2001 (there have been no changes in stock ownership since the initial issuance), and the issue date is August 15, 2001. By the middle of the fourth quarter of 2001, the cash flow of LifePath Fitness has improved to the point that the owners feel ready to pay themselves a cash dividend. They declare a $0.01 cash dividend on December 4, 2001. The record date is December 14, 2001, and the payment date is December 24, 2001.

Instructions

(c) **(1)** Record all of the transactions related to the common stock of LifePath Fitness during the years 2000 and 2001. **(2)** Indicate how many shares are issued and outstanding after the stock dividend is issued.

PART IV

Since the club opened, a major concern has been the pool facilities. Although the existing pool is adequate, Monique, Jared, and Rosaline all desire to make LifePath a cutting-edge facility. Until the end of 2001, financing concerns prevented this improvement. However, because there has been steady growth in clientele, revenue, and income since the fourth quarter of 2001, the owners have explored possible financing options. They are hesitant to issue stock and change the ownership mix because they have been able to work together as a team with great effectiveness. They have formulated a plan to issue secured term bonds to raise the needed $500,000 for the pool facilities. By the end of April 2002 everything was in place for the bond issue to go ahead. On June 1, 2002, the bonds were issued for $463,200. The bonds pay semiannual interest of $3\frac{1}{2}$% (7% annual) on December 1 and June 1 of each year. The bonds mature in 10 years, and amortization is computed using the straight-line method.

Instructions

(d) Record (1) the issuance of the secured bonds, (2) the interest payment made on December 1, 2002, (3) the adjusting entry required at December 31, 2002, and (4) the interest payment made on June 1, 2003.

PART V

Mr. Sandoval's purchase of LifePath Fitness was done through his business. The investment has always been accounted for using the cost method on his firm's books. However, early in 2003 he decided to take his company public. He is preparing an IPO (initial public offering), and he needs to have the firm's financial statements audited. One of the issues to be resolved is to restate the investment in LifePath Fitness using the equity method, since Mr. Sandoval's ownership percentage is greater than 20%.

Instructions

(e) (1) Give the entries that would have been made on Sandoval's books if the equity method of accounting for investments had been used since the initial investment. Assume the following data for LifePath.

	2000	2001	2002
Net income	$19,000	$70,000	$105,000
Total cash dividends	$ 2,100	$25,000	$ 50,000

(2) Compute the balance in the LifePath Investment account at the end of 2003.

BROADENING YOUR PERSPECTIVE

FINANCIAL REPORTING AND ANALYSIS

FINANCIAL REPORTING PROBLEM: Lands' End, Inc.

BYP17-1 The annual report of **Lands' End, Inc.** is presented in Appendix A.

Instructions

(a) See Note 1 to the financial statements and indicate what the consolidated financial statements include.

(b) Using Lands' End's consolidated statement of cash flows, determine how much was spent for capital acquisitions during the current year.

COMPARATIVE ANALYSIS PROBLEM: Lands' End vs. Abercrombie & Fitch

BYP17-2 **Lands' End's** financial statements are presented in Appendix A. **Abercrombie & Fitch's** financial statements are presented in Appendix B.

Instructions

(a) Based on the information contained in these financial statements, determine each of the following for each company.

   (1) Cash used for investing (investment) activities for the current year (from the statement of cash flows).

   (2) Cash used for capital expenditures during the current year.

(b) Each of Lands' End's financial statements is labeled "consolidated." What has been consolidated? That is, from the contents of Lands' End's annual report, identify by name the corporations that have been consolidated (parent and subsidiaries).

INTERPRETING FINANCIAL STATEMENTS: A Global Focus

BYP17-3 **Xerox Corporation** has a 50% investment interest in a joint venture with the Japanese corporation Fuji, called **Fuji Xerox**. Xerox accounts for this investment using the equity method. The following additional information regarding this investment was taken from Xerox's 1998 annual report (in millions).

Investment in Fuji Xerox per balance sheet	$ 1,354
Fuji Xerox net income	108
Xerox total assets	30,024
Xerox total liabilities	25,167
Fuji Xerox total assets	6,279
Fuji Xerox total liabilities	3,757

Instructions

(a) What alternative approaches are available for accounting for long-term investments in stock? Discuss whether Xerox is correct in using the equity method to account for this investment.

(b) Under the equity method, how does Xerox reports its investment in Fuji Xerox? If Xerox owned a majority of Fuji Xerox, it then would have to consolidate Fuji Xerox instead of using the equity method. Discuss how this would change Xerox's financial statements. That is, in what way and by how much would assets and liabilities change?

(c) The use of 50% joint ventures is becoming a fairly common practice. Why might companies like Xerox prefer to participate in a joint venture rather than own a majority share?

EXPLORING THE WEB

BYP17-4 The **Securities and Exchange Commission (SEC)** is the primary regulatory agency of U.S. financial markets. Its job is to ensure that the markets remain fair for all investors. The following SEC site provides useful information for investors.

Address: **www.sec.gov/consumer/weisktc.htm** *(or go to www.wiley.com/college/weygandt)*

Steps:

1. Go to the site shown above.
2. Choose **Glossary**.

Instructions

Using the glossary, find the definition of the following terms.

(a) Ask price.
(b) Margin account.
(c) Prospectus.
(d) Yield.

BYP17-5 Most publicly traded companies are analyzed by numerous analysts. These analysts often don't agree about a company's future prospects. In this exercise you will find analysts' ratings about companies and make comparisons over time and across companies in the same industry. You will also see to what extent the analysts experienced "earnings surprises." Earnings surprises can cause changes in stock prices.

Address: **biz.yahoo.com/i** *(or go to www.wiley.com/college/weygandt)*

Steps:

1. Choose a company.
2. Use the index to find the company's name.
2. Choose **Research**.

Instructions

(a) How many brokers rated the company?
(b) What percentage rated it a strong buy?
(c) What was the average rating for the week?
(d) Did the average rating improve or decline relative to the previous week?
(e) How do the brokers rank this company among all the companies in its industry?
(f) What was the amount of the earnings surprise during the last quarter?

CRITICAL THINKING

GROUP DECISION CASE

BYP17-6 At the beginning of the question and answer portion of the annual stockholders' meeting of Purdy Corporation, stockholder Manor Newby asks, "Why did management sell the holdings in Pepco Company at a loss when this company has been very profitable during the period its stock was held by Purdy?"

Since president Tony Garcia has just concluded his speech on the recent success and bright future of Purdy, he is taken aback by this question and responds, "I remember we paid $1,100,000 for that stock some years ago, and I am sure we sold that stock at a much higher price. You must be mistaken."

Newby retorts, "Well, right here in footnote number 7 to the annual report it shows that 240,000 shares, a 30% interest in Pepco, were sold on the last day of the year. Also, it states that Pepco earned $550,000 this year and paid out $150,000 in cash dividends. Further, a summary statement indicates that in past years, while Purdy held Pepco stock, Pepco earned $1,240,000 and paid out $440,000 in dividends. Finally, the income statement for this year shows a loss on the sale of Pepco stock of $180,000. So, I doubt that I am mistaken."

Red-faced, president Garcia turns to you.

Instructions

With the class divided into groups, answer the following.

(a) What dollar amount did Purdy receive upon the sale of the Pepco stock?

(b) Explain why both stockholder Newby and president Garcia are correct.

COMMUNICATION ACTIVITY

BYP17-7 Ramon Corporation has purchased two securities for its portfolio. The first is a stock investment in Tierney Corporation, one of its suppliers. Ramon purchased 10% of Tierney with the intention of holding it for a number of years, but has no intention of purchasing more shares. The second investment was a purchase of debt securities. Ramon purchased the debt securities because its analysts believe that changes in market interest rates will cause these securities to increase in value in a short period of time. Ramon intends to sell the securities as soon as they have increased in value.

Instructions

Write a memo to Deno Constantine, the chief financial officer, explaining how to account for each of these investments. Explain what the implications for reported income are from this accounting treatment.

ETHICS CASE

BYP17-8 Cartwright Financial Services Company holds a large portfolio of debt and stock securities as an investment. The total fair value of the portfolio at December 31, 2002, is greater than total cost. Some securities have increased in value and others have decreased. Ann Dearing, the financial vice president, and Sue Kelso, the controller, are in the process of classifying for the first time the securities in the portfolio.

Dearing suggests classifying the securities that have increased in value as trading securities in order to increase net income for the year. She wants to classify the securities that have decreased in value as long-term available-for-sale securities, so that the decreases in value will not affect 2002 net income.

Kelso disagrees. She recommends classifying the securities that have decreased in value as trading securities and those that have increased in value as long-term available-for-sale securities. Kelso argues that the company is having a good earnings year and that recognizing the losses now will help to smooth income for this year. Moreover, for future years, when the company may not be as profitable, the company will have built-in gains.

Instructions

(a) Will classifying the securities as Dearing and Kelso suggest actually affect earnings as each says it will?

(b) Is there anything unethical in what Dearing and Kelso propose? Who are the stakeholders affected by their proposals?

(c) Assume that Dearing and Kelso properly classify the portfolio. Assume, at year-end, that Dearing proposes to sell the securities that will increase 2002 net income, and that Kelso proposes to sell the securities that will decrease 2002 net income. Is this unethical?

Answers to Self-Study Questions

1. a **2.** b **3.** c **4.** a **5.** a **6.** c **7.** b **8.** c

Answer to Lands' End Review It Question 4, page 691

In Note 1, the following statement is made regarding the consolidation policy of Land's End: "The consolidated financial statements include the accounts of the company and its subsidiaries after elimination of intercompany accounts and transactions."

Remember to go back to the Navigator box on the chapter-opening page and check off your completed work.

THE STATEMENT OF CASH FLOWS

18

THE NAVIGATOR ✓

- Understand *Concepts for Review* ❑
- Read *Feature Story* ❑
- Scan *Study Objectives* ❑
- Read *Preview* ❑
- Read text and answer *Before You Go On* *p.* 722 ❑ *p.* 732 ❑ *p.* 745 ❑ *p.* 750 ❑
- Work *Demonstration Problem* ❑
- Review *Summary of Study Objectives* ❑
- Answer *Self-Study Questions* ❑
- Complete *Assignments* ❑

CONCEPTS FOR REVIEW

Before studying this chapter, you should know or, if necessary, review:

a. The difference between the accrual basis and the cash basis of accounting. (Ch. 3, pp. 89–90)

b. The major items included in a corporation's balance sheet. (Ch. 17, pp. 694–697)

c. The major items included in a corporation's income statement. (Ch. 15, pp. 615–622)

☑ THE NAVIGATOR

FEATURE STORY

"Cash Is Cash, and Everything Else Is Accounting"

For Gerald Biby, vice president and chief financial officer of **Kilian Community College** in Sioux Falls, South Dakota, the statement of cash flows was the difference between being able to refinance a mortgage and being turned down by six local banks. "We recently wanted to refinance a $125,000 mortgage on a piece of property that we own," he says. "It was the statement of cash flows that finally showed our lender that we had the cash flow to service the debt."

As he explains, the traditional statement of cash flows for a not-for-profit, educational institution shows revenues and all expenditures, even the capital expenditures. According to this format, which the banks focused on initially, Kilian Community College was just breaking even. "In the business world, if we had spent $250,000 on a computer system, then we would have put that on a depreciation schedule. But in the non-profit arena, it's typical that the entire $250,000 is written off as an expense against the general fund." The statement of cash flows showed the bankers that one of the uses of funds was really the purchase of computer equipment that had several years of life.

The college's statement of cash flows has over 30 classifications including tuition, fees, bookstore revenues, and so on. The school has 250 students, charges $70 a credit hour (12 hours is a full-time schedule), and has five terms each year.

The bankers granted the refinancing when they saw that the college's sources of funds exceeded the loan repayments, including principal and interest, by a ratio of 3-to-1. Not only did the school get the loan, but it did so at a favorable rate. "We were able to cut the mortgage rate to prime plus 1 percent from prime plus 3 percent."

THE NAVIGATOR

STUDY OBJECTIVES

After studying this chapter, you should be able to:

1. Indicate the primary purpose of the statement of cash flows.
2. Distinguish among operating, investing, and financing activities.
3. Prepare a statement of cash flows using the indirect method.
4. Prepare a statement of cash flows using the direct method.
5. Analyze the statement of cash flows.

THE NAVIGATOR

PREVIEW OF CHAPTER 18

As the story about **Kilian Community College** indicates, the balance sheet, income statement, and retained earnings statement do not always show the whole picture of the financial condition of a company or institution. In fact, looking at the three traditional financial statements of some well-known companies, a thoughtful investor might have questions like the following: How did **Eastman Kodak** finance cash dividends of $649 million in a year in which it earned only $17 million? How could **Delta Airlines** purchase new planes costing $900 million in a year in which it reported a net loss of $86 million? How did the companies that spent a fantastic $3.4 trillion on merger deals in 1999 (over 36 percent more than the 1998 total) finance those deals? Answers to these and similar questions can be found in this chapter, which presents the **statement of cash flows**.

The content and organization of Chapter 18 are as follows.

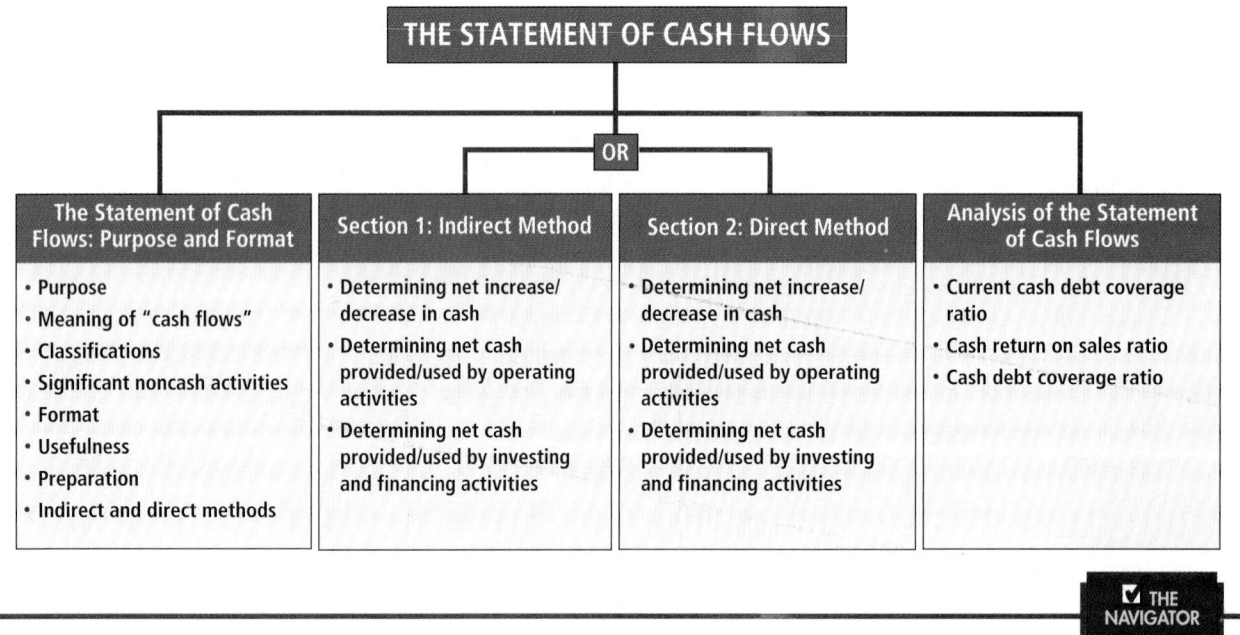

THE STATEMENT OF CASH FLOWS

The Statement of Cash Flows: Purpose and Format
- Purpose
- Meaning of "cash flows"
- Classifications
- Significant noncash activities
- Format
- Usefulness
- Preparation
- Indirect and direct methods

Section 1: Indirect Method (OR)
- Determining net increase/decrease in cash
- Determining net cash provided/used by operating activities
- Determining net cash provided/used by investing and financing activities

Section 2: Direct Method
- Determining net increase/decrease in cash
- Determining net cash provided/used by operating activities
- Determining net cash provided/used by investing and financing activities

Analysis of the Statement of Cash Flows
- Current cash debt coverage ratio
- Cash return on sales ratio
- Cash debt coverage ratio

THE NAVIGATOR

THE STATEMENT OF CASH FLOWS: PURPOSE AND FORMAT

The three basic financial statements we've studied so far present only fragmentary information about a company's cash flows (cash receipts and cash payments). For example, **comparative balance sheets** show the increase in property, plant, and equipment during the year. But they do not show how the additions were financed or paid for. The **income statement** shows net income. But it does not indicate the amount of cash generated by operating activities. Similarly, the **retained earnings statement** shows cash dividends declared but not the cash dividends paid during the year. None of these statements presents a detailed summary of the net change in cash as a result of operating, investing, and financing activities during the period.

STUDY OBJECTIVE 1

Indicate the primary purpose of the statement of cash flows.

PURPOSE OF THE STATEMENT OF CASH FLOWS

The primary purpose of the statement of cash flows is to provide information about an entity's cash receipts and cash payments during a period. A secondary objective is to provide information about its operating, investing, and financing activities.[1] The **statement of cash flows** reports the cash receipts, cash payments, and net change in cash resulting from operating, investing, and financing activities during a period. It does so in a format that reconciles the beginning and ending cash balances.

Reporting the causes of changes in cash helps investors, creditors, and other interested parties understand what is happening to a company's most liquid resource—its cash. As the opening story about **Kilian Community College** demonstrates, a statement of cash flows helps us understand what is happening. It provides answers to the following simple, but important, questions about an enterprise.

1. Where did the cash come from during the period?
2. What was the cash used for during the period?
3. What was the change in the cash balance during the period?

MEANING OF "CASH FLOWS"

The statement of cash flows is generally prepared using "**cash and cash equivalents**" as its basis. Cash equivalents are short-term, highly liquid investments that are both:

1. Readily convertible to known amounts of cash, and
2. So near their maturity that their market value is relatively insensitive to changes in interest rates.

Generally, only investments with original maturities of three months or less qualify under this definition. Examples of cash equivalents are Treasury bills, commercial paper (short-term corporate notes), and money market funds. All typically are purchased with cash that is in excess of immediate needs.

Note that since cash and cash equivalents are viewed as the same, transfers between cash and cash equivalents are not treated as cash receipts and cash payments. That is, such transfers are not reported in the statement of cash flows. The term "cash" when used in this chapter includes cash and cash equivalents.

CLASSIFICATION OF CASH FLOWS

STUDY OBJECTIVE 2

Distinguish among operating, investing, and financing activities.

The statement of cash flows classifies cash receipts and cash payments as operating, investing, and financing activities. Transactions and other events characteristic of each kind of activity are described in the list below.

1. **Operating activities** include the cash effects of transactions that create revenues and expenses. They thus enter into the determination of net income.
2. **Investing activities** include (a) acquiring and disposing of investments and productive long-lived assets, and (b) lending money and collecting the loans.
3. **Financing activities** include (a) obtaining cash from issuing debt and repaying the amounts borrowed, and (b) obtaining cash from stockholders and providing them with a return on their investment.

The category of operating activities is the most important. As noted above, it shows the cash provided by company operations. This source of cash is generally considered to be the best measure of a company's ability to generate sufficient cash to continue as a going concern.

[1]"Statement of Cash Flows," *Statement of Financial Accounting Standards No. 95* (Stamford, Conn.: FASB, 1987).

Illustration 18-1 below lists typical cash receipts and cash payments within each of the three classifications. **Study the list carefully**. It will prove very useful in solving homework exercises and problems.

Illustration 18-1

Typical receipts and payments classified by business activity and shown in the statement of cash flows

Operating activities

Investing activities

Financing activities

Types of Cash Inflows and Outflows

Operating activities

Cash inflows:
- From sale of goods or services.
- From returns on loans (interest received) and on equity securities (dividends received).

Cash outflows:
- To suppliers for inventory.
- To employees for services.
- To government for taxes.
- To lenders for interest.
- To others for expenses.

Investing activities

Cash inflows:
- From sale of property, plant, and equipment.
- From sale of debt or equity securities of other entities.
- From collection of principal on loans to other entities.

Cash outflows:
- To purchase property, plant, and equipment.
- To purchase debt or equity securities of other entities.
- To make loans to other entities.

Financing activities

Cash inflows:
- From sale of equity securities (company's own stock).
- From issuance of debt (bonds and notes).

Cash outflows:
- To stockholders as dividends.
- To redeem long-term debt or reacquire capital stock.

HELPFUL HINT

Operating activities generally relate to changes in current assets and current liabilities. Investing activities generally relate to changes in noncurrent assets. Financing activities relate to changes in long-term liabilities and stockholders' equity accounts.

As you can see, some cash flows related to investing or financing activities are classified as operating activities. For example, receipts of investment revenue (interest and dividends) are classified as operating activities. So are payments of interest to lenders. Why are these considered operating activities? **Because these items are reported in the income statement, where results of operations are shown.**

Note the following general guidelines: (1) Operating activities involve income determination (income statement) items. (2) Investing activities involve cash flows resulting from changes in investments and long-term asset items. (3) Financing activities involve cash flows resulting from changes in long-term liability and stockholders' equity items.

SIGNIFICANT NONCASH ACTIVITIES

Not all of a company's significant activities involve cash. Examples of significant noncash activities are:

1. Issuance of common stock to purchase assets.
2. Conversion of bonds into common stock.
3. Issuance of debt to purchase assets.
4. Exchanges of plant assets.

Significant financing and investing activities that do not affect cash are not reported in the body of the statement of cash flows. However, these activities are reported in either a **separate schedule** at the bottom of the statement of cash flows or in a **separate note or supplementary schedule** to the financial statements.

The reporting of these noncash activities in a separate schedule satisfies the **full disclosure principle**. In solving homework assignments you should present significant noncash investing and financing activities in a separate schedule at the bottom of the statement of cash flows. (See lower section of Illustration 18-2, at the bottom of this page, for an example.)

HELPFUL HINT
Do not include noncash investing and financing activities in the body of the statement of cash flows. Report this information in a separate schedule.

ACCOUNTING IN ACTION *Business Insight*

Net income is not the same as net cash provided by operating activities. The differences are illustrated by the following results from recent annual reports for the same fiscal year (all data are in millions of dollars).

Company	Net Income	Net Cash from Operations
Kmart Corporation	$ 518	$1,237
Wal-Mart Stores, Inc.	4,430	7,580
Gap Inc.	1,127	1,478
J.C. Penney Company, Inc.	594	1,058
Sears, Roebuck & Co.	1,048	3,090
The May Department Stores Company	849	1,505

Note the disparity among the companies that engaged in similar types of retail merchandising.

FORMAT OF THE STATEMENT OF CASH FLOWS

The general format of the statement of cash flows is the three activities discussed previously—operating, investing, and financing—plus the significant noncash investing and financing activities. A widely used form of the statement of cash flows is shown in Illustration 18-2.

Illustration 18-2
Format of statement of cash flows

COMPANY NAME
Statement of Cash Flows
Period Covered

Cash flows from operating activities		
(List of individual items)	XX	
Net cash provided (used) by operating activities		XXX
Cash flows from investing activities		
(List of individual inflows and outflows)	XX	
Net cash provided (used) by investing activities		XXX
Cash flows from financing activities		
(List of individual inflows and outflows)	XX	
Net cash provided (used) by financing activities		XXX
Net increase (decrease) in cash		XXX
Cash at beginning of period		XXX
Cash at end of period		XXX
Noncash investing and financing activities		
(List of individual noncash transactions)		XXX

As illustrated, the cash flows from operating activities section always appears first. It is followed by the investing activities and the financing activities sections.

Note also that **the individual inflows and outflows from investing and financing activities are reported separately**. Thus, cash outflow for the purchase of property, plant, and equipment is reported separately from the cash inflow from the sale of property, plant, and equipment. Similarly, the cash inflow from the issuance of debt securities is reported separately from the cash outflow for the retirement of debt. If a company did not report the inflows and outflows separately, it would obscure the investing and financing activities of the enterprise. This would make it more difficult to assess future cash flows.

The reported operating, investing, and financing activities result in either net cash **provided or used** by each activity. The amounts of net cash provided or used by each activity then are totaled. The result is the net increase (decrease) in cash for the period. This amount is then added to or subtracted from the beginning-of-period cash balance. This gives the end-of-period cash balance. Finally, any significant noncash investing and financing activities are reported in a separate schedule, usually at the bottom of the statement.

USEFULNESS OF THE STATEMENT OF CASH FLOWS

The information in a statement of cash flows should help investors, creditors, and others assess the following aspects of the firm's financial position.

1. **The entity's ability to generate future cash flows.** By examining relationships between items in the statement of cash flows, investors and others can make predictions of the amounts, timing, and uncertainty of future cash flows better than they can from accrual basis data.
2. **The entity's ability to pay dividends and meet obligations.** If a company does not have adequate cash, employees cannot be paid, debts settled, or dividends paid. Employees, creditors, and stockholders should be particularly interested in this statement, because it alone shows the flows of cash in a business.
3. **The reasons for the difference between net income and net cash provided (used) by operating activities.** Net income provides information on the success or failure of a business enterprise. However, some are critical of accrual basis net income because it requires many estimates. As a result, the reliability of the number is often challenged. Such is not the case with cash. Many readers of the statement of cash flows want to know the reasons for the difference between net income and net cash provided by operating activities. Then they can assess for themselves the reliability of the income number.
4. **The cash investing and financing transactions during the period.** By examining a company's investing and financing transactions, a financial statement reader can better understand why assets and liabilities changed during the period.

In summary, the information in the statement of cash flows is useful in answering the following questions.

How did cash increase when there was a net loss for the period?

How were the proceeds of the bond issue used?

How was the expansion in the plant and equipment financed?

Why were dividends not increased?

How was the retirement of debt accomplished?

How much money was borrowed during the year?

Is cash flow greater or less than net income?

ETHICS NOTE

Many investors believe that "Cash is cash and everything else is accounting." That is, they feel that cash flow is less susceptible to management manipulation than traditional accounting measures such as net income. Though we would discourage reliance on cash flows to the exclusion of accrual accounting, comparing cash from operations to net income can reveal important information about the "quality" of reported net income. Such a comparison can reveal the extent to which net income provides a good measure of actual performance.

HELPFUL HINT

Income from operations and cash flow from operating activities are different. Income from operations is based on accrual accounting; cash flow from operating activities is prepared on a cash basis.

PREPARING THE STATEMENT OF CASH FLOWS

The statement of cash flows is prepared differently from the three other basic financial statements. First, it is not prepared from an adjusted trial balance. The statement requires detailed information concerning the changes in account balances that occurred between two periods of time. An adjusted trial balance will not provide the necessary data. Second, the statement of cash flows deals with cash receipts and payments. As a result, **the accrual concept is not used in the preparation of a statement of cash flows**.

The information to prepare this statement usually comes from three sources:

- **Comparative balance sheets.** Information in the comparative balance sheets indicates the amount of the changes in assets, liabilities, and stockholders' equities from the beginning to the end of the period.
- **Current income statement.** Information in this statement helps determine the amount of cash provided or used by operations during the period.
- **Additional information.** Such information includes transaction data that are needed to determine how cash was provided or used during the period.

Preparing the statement of cash flows from these data sources involves three major steps, explained in Illustration 18-3.

Illustration 18-3

Three major steps in preparing the statement of cash flows

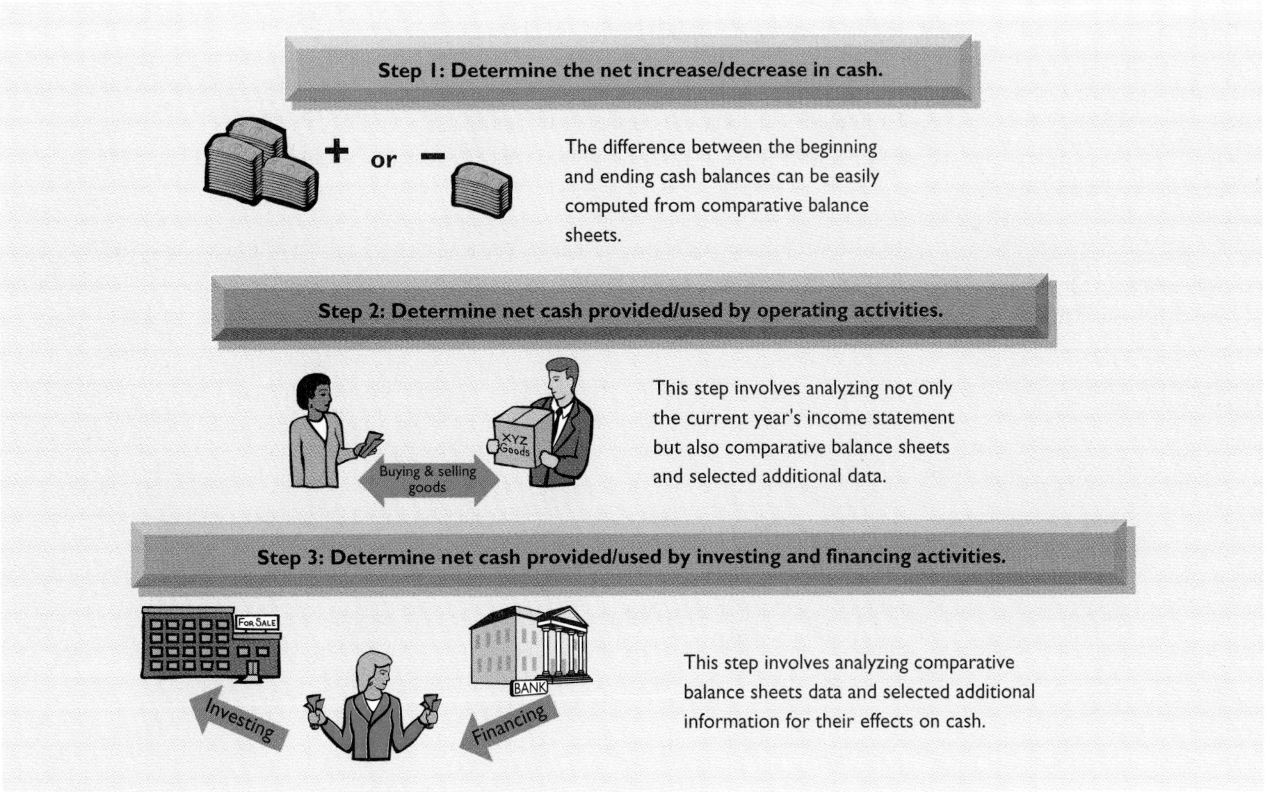

Step 1: Determine the net increase/decrease in cash.
+ or −
The difference between the beginning and ending cash balances can be easily computed from comparative balance sheets.
Step 2: Determine net cash provided/used by operating activities.
XYZ Goods
Buying & selling goods
This step involves analyzing not only the current year's income statement but also comparative balance sheets and selected additional data.
Step 3: Determine net cash provided/used by investing and financing activities.
For Sale
BANK
Investing
Financing
This step involves analyzing comparative balance sheets data and selected additional information for their effects on cash.

INDIRECT AND DIRECT METHODS

In order to perform step 2, **the operating activities section must be converted from an accrual basis to a cash basis**. This conversion may be done by either of two methods: (1) the indirect method or (2) the direct method. **Both methods arrive at the same total amount** for "Net cash provided by operating activities." They differ in disclosing the items that comprise the total amount.

Usage of Methods

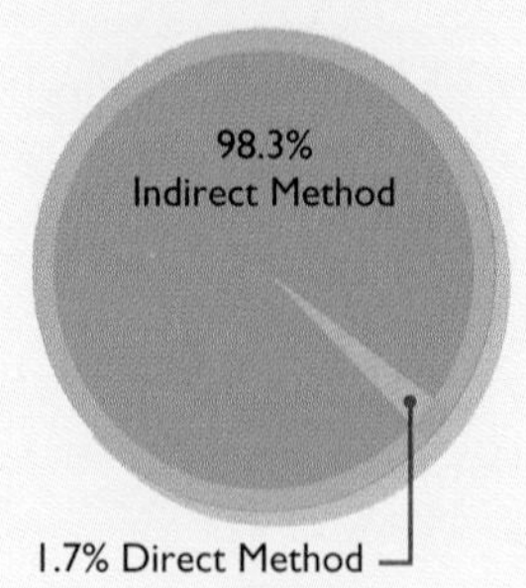

The indirect method is used extensively in practice, as shown in the nearby chart.[2] Companies (98%) favor the indirect method for two reasons: (1) It is easier to prepare, and (2) it focuses on the differences between net income and net cash flow from operating activities.

A minority of companies favor the direct method. This method shows operating cash receipts and payments, and so it is more consistent with the objective of a statement of cash flows. The FASB has expressed a preference for the direct method, but allows the use of either method. When the direct method is used, the net cash flow from operating activities as computed using the indirect method must also be reported in a separate schedule.

BEFORE YOU GO ON...

▶ *REVIEW IT*

1. What is the primary purpose of a statement of cash flows?
2. What are the major classifications of cash flows on the statement of cash flows?
3. Why is the statement of cash flows useful? What key information does it convey?
4. What are the three major steps in preparing a statement of cash flows?

▶ *DO IT*

During its first week of existence, Plano Molding Company had the following transactions.

1. Issued 100,000 shares of $5 par value common stock for $800,000 cash.
2. Borrowed $200,000 from Sandwich State Bank, signing a 5-year note bearing 8% interest.
3. Purchased two semi-trailer trucks for $170,000 cash.
4. Paid employees $12,000 for salaries and wages.
5. Collected $20,000 cash for services rendered.

Classify each of these transactions by type of cash flow activity.

INTERNATIONAL NOTE

International accounting requirements are quite similar in most respects with regard to the cash flow statement. Some interesting exceptions: In Japan, operating and investing activities are combined. In Australia, the direct method is mandatory. In Spain, the indirect method is mandatory. Also, in a number of European and Scandinavian countries a cash flow statement is not required at all, although in practice most publicly traded firms provide one.

ACTION PLAN

- Identify the three types of activities used to report all cash inflows and outflows.
- Report as operating activities the cash effects of transactions that create revenues and expenses and enter into the determination of net income.
- Report as investing activities transactions that (a) acquire and dispose of investments and productive long-lived assets, and (b) lend money and collect loans.
- Report as financing activities transactions that (a) obtain cash from issuing debt and repay the amounts borrowed, and (b) obtain cash from stockholders and pay them dividends.

SOLUTION

1. Financing activity.
2. Financing activity.
3. Investing activity.
4. Operating activity.
5. Operating activity.

Related exercise material: BE18-3, BE18-5, E18-1, and E18-6.

THE NAVIGATOR

On the following pages, in two separate sections, we describe the use of the two methods. Section 1 illustrates the indirect method. Section 2 illustrates the direct method. These sections are independent of each other. *Only one or the other* needs to be covered in order to understand and prepare the statement of cash flows. When you have finished the section assigned by your instructor, turn to the next topic—"Analysis of the Statement of Cash Flows" (on page 748).

[2] *Accounting Trends and Techniques* survey of 600 companies indicated that 590 use the indirect method and 10 use the direct method.

SECTION 1 *Statement of Cash Flows— Indirect Method*

To explain and illustrate the indirect method, we will use the transactions of the Computer Services Company for two years, 2002 and 2003, to prepare annual statements of cash flows. We will show basic transactions in the first year, with additional transactions added in the second year.

STUDY OBJECTIVE 3

Prepare a statement of cash flows using the indirect method.

FIRST YEAR OF OPERATIONS—2002

Computer Services Company started on January 1, 2002. At that time it issued 50,000 shares of $1.00 par value common stock for $50,000 cash. The company rented its office space and furniture and performed consulting services throughout the first year. The comparative balance sheets at the beginning and end of 2002, showing changes in each account, appear in Illustration 18-4. The income statement and additional information for Computer Services Company are shown in Illustration 18-5.

Illustration 18-4

Comparative balance sheets, 2002, with increases and decreases

COMPUTER SERVICES COMPANY
Comparative Balance Sheets

Assets	Dec. 31, 2002	Jan. 1, 2002	Change Increase/Decrease
Cash	$34,000	$-0-	$34,000 Increase
Accounts receivable	30,000	-0-	30,000 Increase
Equipment	10,000	-0-	10,000 Increase
Total	$74,000	$-0-	
Liabilities and Stockholders' Equity			
Accounts payable	$ 4,000	$-0-	$ 4,000 Increase
Common stock	50,000	-0-	50,000 Increase
Retained earnings	20,000	-0-	20,000 Increase
Total	$74,000	$-0-	

HELPFUL HINT

Although each of the balance sheet items increased, their individual effects are not the same. Some of these increases are cash inflows, and some are cash outflows.

Illustration 18-5

Income statement and additional information, 2002

COMPUTER SERVICES COMPANY
Income Statement
For the Year Ended December 31, 2002

Revenues	$85,000
Operating expenses	40,000
Income before income taxes	45,000
Income tax expense	10,000
Net income	$35,000

Additional information:
1. A dividend of $15,000 was declared and paid during the year.
2. The equipment was purchased at the end of 2002. No depreciation was taken in 2002.

STEP 1: DETERMINE THE NET INCREASE/ DECREASE IN CASH

To prepare a statement of cash flows, the first step is to **determine the net increase or decrease in cash**. This is a simple computation. For example, Computer Services Company had no cash on hand at the beginning of 2002. It had $34,000 on hand at the end of 2002. Thus, the change in cash for 2002 was an increase of $34,000.

HELPFUL HINT
You may wish to insert immediately into the statement of cash flows the beginning and ending cash balances and the increase/decrease in cash necessitated by these balances. The net increase/decrease is the target amount. The net cash flows from the three classes of activity must equal the target amount.

STEP 2: DETERMINE NET CASH PROVIDED/USED BY OPERATING ACTIVITIES

To determine net cash provided by operating activities under the indirect method, **net income is adjusted for items that did not affect cash**. A useful starting point is to understand **why** net income must be converted. Under generally accepted accounting principles, most companies use the accrual basis of accounting. As you have learned, this basis requires that revenue be recorded when earned and that expenses be recorded when incurred. Earned revenues may include credit sales that have not been collected in cash. Expenses incurred may not have been paid in cash. Thus, under the accrual basis of accounting, net income is not the same as net cash provided by operating activities. Therefore, under the indirect method, net income must be adjusted to convert certain items to the cash basis.

The **indirect method** (or reconciliation method) starts with net income and converts it to net cash provided by operating activities. In other words, **the indirect method adjusts net income for items that affected reported net income but did not affect cash**. Illustration 18-6 shows this adjustment. That is, noncash charges in the income statement are added back to net income. Likewise, noncash credits are deducted. The result is net cash provided by operating activities.

Illustration 18-6

Net income versus net cash provided by operating activities

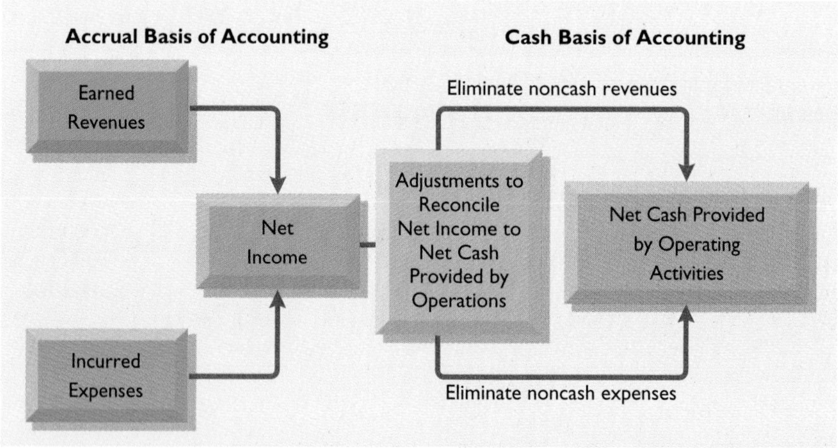

A useful starting point in identifying the adjustments to net income is the current asset and current liability accounts other than cash. Those accounts—receivables, payables, prepayments, and inventories—should be analyzed for their effects on cash.

Increase in Accounts Receivable

When accounts receivable increase during the year, revenues on an accrual basis are higher than revenues on a cash basis. In other words, operations of the period led to revenues, **but not all of these revenues resulted in an increase in cash**. Some of the revenues resulted in an increase in accounts receivable.

Illustration 18-7 shows that Computer Services Company had $85,000 in revenues, but it collected only $55,000 in cash. To convert net income to net cash provided by operating activities, the increase of $30,000 in accounts receivable must be deducted from net income.

Illustration 18-7

Analysis of accounts receivable

Accounts Receivable				
1/1/02	Balance	-0-	**Receipts from customers**	**55,000**
	Revenues	**85,000**		
12/31/02	Balance	30,000		

Increase in Accounts Payable

In the first year, operating expenses incurred on account were credited to Accounts Payable. When accounts payable increase during the year, operating expenses on an accrual basis are higher than they are on a cash basis. For Computer Services, operating expenses reported in the income statement were $40,000. But, since Accounts Payable increased $4,000, only $36,000 ($40,000 − $4,000) of the expenses were paid in cash. To adjust net income to net cash provided by operating activities, the increase of $4,000 in accounts payable must be added to net income. A T-account analysis indicates that payments to creditors are less than operating expenses.

Illustration 18-8

Analysis of accounts payable

Accounts Payable				
Payments to creditors	**36,000**	1/1/02	Balances	-0-
			Operating expenses	**40,000**
		12/31/02	Balance	4,000

For Computer Services, the changes in accounts receivable and accounts payable were the only changes in current asset and current liability accounts. This means that any other revenues or expenses reported in the income statement were received or paid in cash. Thus, the income tax expense of $10,000 was paid in cash, and no adjustment of net income is necessary.

The operating activities section of the statement of cash flows for Computer Services Company is shown in Illustration 18-9.

Illustration 18-9

Presentation of net cash provided by operating activities, 2002—indirect method

COMPUTER SERVICES COMPANY
Statement of Cash Flows—Indirect Method (partial)
For the Year Ended December 31, 2002

Cash flows from operating activities		
Net income		$35,000
Adjustments to reconcile net income to net cash provided by operating activities:		
Increase in accounts receivable	$(30,000)	
Increase in accounts payable	4,000	(26,000)
Net cash provided by operating activities		**$ 9,000**

STEP 3: DETERMINE NET CASH PROVIDED/USED BY INVESTING AND FINANCING ACTIVITIES

The third and final step in preparing the statement of cash flows begins with a study of the balance sheet. We look at it to determine changes in noncurrent accounts. The change in each noncurrent account is then analyzed to determine the effect, if any, the change had on cash.

In Computer Services Company, the three noncurrent accounts are Equipment, Common Stock, and Retained Earnings. All three have increased during the year. What caused these increases? No transaction data are given in the balance sheet for the increases in Equipment of $10,000 and Common Stock of $50,000. In solving your homework, you should assume that **any unexplained differences in noncurrent accounts involve cash**. Thus, the increase in Equipment is assumed to be a purchase of equipment for $10,000 cash. This purchase of equipment is reported as a cash outflow in the investing activities section of the statement of cash flows. The increase in Common Stock is assumed to result from the issuance of common stock for $50,000 cash. The issuance of common stock is reported as an inflow of cash in the financing activities section.

What caused the net increase of $20,000 in the Retained Earnings account? First, net income increased retained earnings by $35,000. Second, the additional information provided below the income statement in Illustration 18-5 indicates that a cash dividend of $15,000 was declared and paid.

This analysis can also be made directly from the Retained Earnings account in the ledger of Computer Services Company, as shown in Illustration 18-10.

Illustration 18-10

Analysis of retained earnings

Retained Earnings					
12/31/02	**Cash dividend**	**15,000**	1/1/02	Balance	–0–
			12/31/02	**Net income**	**35,000**
			12/31/02	Balance	20,000

The $20,000 increase in Retained Earnings in 2002 is a **net** change. When a net change in a noncurrent balance sheet account has occurred during the year, it generally is necessary to report the individual items that cause the net change. Therefore, the $35,000 increase due to net income is reported in the operating activities section. The cash dividend paid is reported in the financing activities section.

STATEMENT OF CASH FLOWS—2002

We now can prepare the statement of cash flows. The statement starts with the operating activities, followed by the investing activities, and then the financing activities. The 2002 statement of cash flows for Computer Services is shown in Illustration 18-11.

Computer Services' statement of cash flows for 2002 shows the following: Operating activities **provided** $9,000 cash. Investing activities **used** $10,000 cash. Financing activities **provided** $35,000 cash. The increase in cash of $34,000 reported in the statement of cash flows agrees with the increase of $34,000 shown as the change in the cash account in the comparative balance sheets.

Illustration 18-11

Statement of cash flows, 2002—indirect method

COMPUTER SERVICES COMPANY
Statement of Cash Flows—Indirect Method
For the Year Ended December 31, 2002

Cash flows from operating activities		
Net income		$35,000
Adjustments to reconcile net income to net cash provided by operating activities:		
Increase in accounts receivable	$(30,000)	
Increase in accounts payable	4,000	(26,000)
Net cash provided by operating activities		9,000
Cash flows from investing activities		
Purchase of equipment	(10,000)	
Net cash used by investing activities		(10,000)
Cash flows from financing activities		
Issuance of common stock	50,000	
Payment of cash dividends	(15,000)	
Net cash provided by financing activities		35,000
Net increase in cash		34,000
Cash at beginning of period		-0-
Cash at end of period		$34,000

SECOND YEAR OF OPERATIONS—2003

Illustrations 18-12 and 18-13 present information related to the second year of operations for Computer Services Company.

Illustration 18-12

Comparative balance sheets, 2003, with increases and decreases

COMPUTER SERVICES COMPANY
Comparative Balance Sheets
December 31

Assets	**2003**	**2002**	**Change Increase/Decrease**
Cash	$ 56,000	$34,000	$ 22,000 Increase
Accounts receivable	20,000	30,000	10,000 Decrease
Prepaid expenses	4,000	-0-	4,000 Increase
Land	130,000	-0-	130,000 Increase
Building	160,000	-0-	160,000 Increase
Accumulated depreciation—building	(11,000)	-0-	11,000 Increase
Equipment	27,000	10,000	17,000 Increase
Accumulated depreciation—equipment	(3,000)	-0-	3,000 Increase
Total	$383,000	$74,000	
Liabilities and Stockholders' Equity			
Accounts payable	$ 59,000	$ 4,000	$ 55,000 Increase
Bonds payable	130,000	-0-	130,000 Increase
Common stock	50,000	50,000	-0-
Retained earnings	144,000	20,000	124,000 Increase
Total	$383,000	$74,000	

Illustration 18-13

Income statement and additional information, 2003

COMPUTER SERVICES COMPANY
Income Statement
For the Year Ended December 31, 2003

Revenues		$507,000
Operating expenses (excluding depreciation)	$261,000	
Depreciation expense	15,000	
Loss on sale of equipment	3,000	279,000
Income from operations		228,000
Income tax expense		89,000
Net income		$139,000

Additional information:

1. In 2003, the company declared and paid a $15,000 cash dividend.
2. The company obtained land through the issuance of $130,000 of long-term bonds.
3. A building costing $160,000 was purchased for cash. Equipment costing $25,000 was also purchased for cash.
4. During 2003, the company sold equipment with a book value of $7,000 (cost $8,000, less accumulated depreciation $1,000) for $4,000 cash.

STEP 1: DETERMINE THE NET INCREASE/ DECREASE IN CASH

To prepare a statement of cash flows from this information, the first step is to **determine the net increase or decrease in cash**. As indicated from the information presented, cash increased $22,000 ($56,000 − $34,000).

STEP 2: DETERMINE NET CASH PROVIDED/USED BY OPERATING ACTIVITIES

As in step 2 in 2002, net income on an accrual basis must be adjusted to arrive at net cash provided/used by operating activities. Explanations for the adjustments to net income for Computer Services in 2003 follow.

HELPFUL HINT

Decrease in accounts receivable indicates that cash collections were greater than sales.
Increase in accounts receivable indicates that sales were greater than cash collections.
Increase in prepaid expenses indicates that the amount paid for the prepayments exceeded the amount that was recorded as an expense.
Decrease in prepaid expenses indicates that the amount recorded as an expense exceeded the amount of cash paid for the prepayments.
Increase in accounts payable indicates that expenses incurred exceed the cash paid for expenses that period.

Decrease in Accounts Receivable

Accounts receivable decreases during the period because cash receipts are higher than revenues reported on the accrual basis. To adjust net income to net cash provided by operating activities, the decrease of $10,000 in accounts receivable must be added to net income.

Increase in Prepaid Expenses

Prepaid expenses increase during a period because cash paid for expenses is higher than expenses reported on the accrual basis. Cash payments have been made in the current period, but expenses (as charges to the income statement) have been deferred to future periods. To adjust net income to net cash provided by operating activities, the $4,000 increase in prepaid expenses must be deducted from net income. An increase in prepaid expenses results in a decrease in cash during the period.

Increase in Accounts Payable

Like the increase in 2002, the 2003 increase of $55,000 in accounts payable must be added to net income to convert to net cash provided by operating activities.

Depreciation Expense

During 2003, the company reported depreciation expense of $15,000. Of this amount, $11,000 related to the building and $4,000 to the equipment. These two amounts were determined by analyzing the accumulated depreciation accounts in the balance sheets.

INCREASE IN ACCUMULATED DEPRECIATION—BUILDING. The Accumulated Depreciation—Building account increased $11,000. This change represents the depreciation expense on the building for the year. **Depreciation expense is a noncash charge. So it is added back to net income** in order to arrive at net cash provided by operating activities.

INCREASE IN ACCUMULATED DEPRECIATION—EQUIPMENT. The Accumulated Depreciation—Equipment account increased $3,000. But this change does not represent depreciation expense for the year. The additional information at the bottom of the income statement indicates why not: This account was decreased (debited $1,000) as a result of the sale of some equipment. Thus depreciation expense for 2003 was $4,000 ($3,000 + $1,000). That amount is added to net income to determine net cash provided by operating activities. The T-account below provides information about the changes that occurred in this account in 2003.

Illustration 18-14
Analysis of accumulated depreciation—equipment

Accumulated Depreciation—Equipment

Accumulated depreciation on equipment sold	1,000	1/1/03	Balance	-0-
			Depreciation expense	**4,000**
		12/31/03	Balance	3,000

Depreciation expense on the building ($11,000) plus depreciation expense on the equipment ($4,000) equals the depreciation expense of $15,000 reported in the income statement.

Other charges to expense that do not require the use of cash, such as the amortization of intangible assets and depletion expense, are treated in the same way as depreciation. Depreciation and similar noncash charges are frequently listed in the statement of cash flows as the first adjustments to net income.

Loss on Sale of Equipment

In the income statement, Computer Services Company reported a $3,000 loss on the sale of equipment (book value $7,000, less cash proceeds $4,000). The loss reduced net income but **did not reduce cash**. So the loss is **added to net income** in determining net cash provided by operating activities.[3]

As a result of the previous adjustments, net cash provided by operating activities is $218,000, as computed in Illustration 18-15.

---

[3] If a gain on sale occurs, a different situation results. To allow a gain to flow through to net cash provided by operating activities would be double-counting the gain—once in net income and again in the investing activities section as part of the cash proceeds from sale. As a result, a gain is deducted from net income in reporting net cash provided by operating activities.

Illustration 18-15

Presentation of net cash provided by operating activities, 2003—indirect method

COMPUTER SERVICES COMPANY
Statement of Cash Flows—Indirect Method (partial)
For the Year Ended December 31, 2003

Cash flows from operating activities		
Net income		$139,000
Adjustments to reconcile net income to net cash provided by operating activities:		
Depreciation expense	$15,000	
Loss on sale of equipment	3,000	
Decrease in accounts receivable	10,000	
Increase in prepaid expenses	(4,000)	
Increase in accounts payable	55,000	79,000
Net cash provided by operating activities		**$218,000**

STEP 3: DETERMINE NET CASH PROVIDED/USED BY INVESTING AND FINANCING ACTIVITIES

The next step involves analyzing the remaining changes in balance sheet accounts to determine net cash provided (used) by investing and financing activities.

Increase in Land

As indicated from the change in the Land account and the additional information, land of $130,000 was purchased through the issuance of long-term bonds. The issuance of bonds payable for land has no effect on cash. But it is a significant noncash investing and financing activity that merits disclosure in a separate schedule.

Increase in Building

As the additional data indicate, an office building was acquired for $160,000 cash. This is a cash outflow reported in the investing section.

Increase in Equipment

The Equipment account increased $17,000. The additional information explains that this was a net increase that resulted from two transactions: (1) a purchase of equipment of $25,000 and (2) the sale for $4,000 of equipment costing $8,000. These transactions are classified as investing activities. Each transaction should be reported separately. Thus the purchase of equipment should be reported as an outflow of cash for $25,000. The sale should be reported as an inflow of cash for $4,000. The T-account below shows the reasons for the change in this account during the year.

Illustration 18-16

Analysis of equipment

Equipment

1/1/03	Balance	10,000	Cost of equipment sold	8,000
	Purchase of equipment	**25,000**		
12/31/03	Balance	27,000		

The following entry shows the details of the equipment sale transaction.

A	=	L	+	OE
+4,000				−3,000
+1,000				
−8,000				

Cash	4,000	
Accumulated Depreciation	1,000	
Loss on Sale of Equipment	3,000	
Equipment		8,000

Increase in Bonds Payable

The Bonds Payable account increased $130,000. As indicated in the additional information, land was acquired from the issuance of these bonds. This noncash transaction is reported in a separate schedule at the bottom of the statement.

HELPFUL HINT
When stocks or bonds are issued for cash, the actual proceeds will appear in the statement of cash flows as a financing inflow (rather than the par value of the stocks or face value of bonds).

Increase in Retained Earnings

Retained earnings increased $124,000 during the year. This increase can be explained by two factors: (1) Net income of $139,000 increased retained earnings. (2) Dividends of $15,000 decreased retained earnings. Net income is adjusted to net cash provided by operating activities in the operating activities section. Payment of the dividends is a **cash outflow that is reported as a financing activity**.

HELPFUL HINT
It is the **payment** of dividends, not the declaration, that appears in the cash flow statement.

STATEMENT OF CASH FLOWS—2003

Combining the previous items, we obtain a statement of cash flows for 2003 for Computer Services Company as presented in Illustration 18-17.

Illustration 18-17
Statement of cash flows, 2003—indirect method

COMPUTER SERVICES COMPANY
Statement of Cash Flows—Indirect Method
For the Year Ended December 31, 2003

Cash flows from operating activities		
Net income		$139,000
Adjustments to reconcile net income to net cash provided by operating activities:		
Depreciation expense	$ 15,000	
Loss on sale of equipment	3,000	
Decrease in accounts receivable	10,000	
Increase in prepaid expenses	(4,000)	
Increase in accounts payable	55,000	79,000
Net cash provided by operating activities		218,000
Cash flows from investing activities		
Purchase of building	(160,000)	
Purchase of equipment	(25,000)	
Sale of equipment	4,000	
Net cash used by investing activities		(181,000)
Cash flows from financing activities		
Payment of cash dividends	(15,000)	
Net cash used by financing activities		(15,000)
Net increase in cash		22,000
Cash at beginning of period		34,000
Cash at end of period		$ 56,000
Noncash investing and financing activities		
Issuance of bonds payable to purchase land		$130,000

HELPFUL HINT
Note that in the investing and financing activities sections, positive numbers indicate cash inflows (receipts), and negative numbers indicate cash outflows (payments).

SUMMARY OF CONVERSION TO NET CASH PROVIDED BY OPERATING ACTIVITIES—INDIRECT METHOD

As shown in the previous illustrations, the statement of cash flows prepared by the indirect method starts with net income. It then adds (or deducts) items not affecting cash, to arrive at net cash provided by operating activities. The additions and deductions consist of (1) changes in specific current assets and current liabilities and (2) noncash charges reported in the income statement. A summary of the adjustments for current assets and current liabilities is provided in Illustration 18-18.

Illustration 18-18

Adjustments for current assets and current liabilities

Current Assets and Current Liabilities	Adjustments to Convert Net Income to Net Cash Provided by Operating Activities: Add to Net Income a(n):	Deduct from Net Income a(n):
Accounts receivable	Decrease	Increase
Inventory	Decrease	Increase
Prepaid expenses	Decrease	Increase
Accounts payable	Increase	Decrease
Accrued expenses payable	Increase	Decrease

HELPFUL HINT

1. An increase in a current asset is deducted from net income.
2. A decrease in a current asset is added to net income.
3. An increase in a current liability is added to net income.
4. A decrease in a current liability is deducted from net income.

Adjustments for the noncash charges reported in the income statement are made as shown in Illustration 18-19.

Illustration 18-19

Adjustments for noncash charges

Noncash Charges	Adjustments to Convert Net Income to Net Cash Provided by Operating Activities
Depreciation expense	Add
Patent amortization expense	Add
Depletion expense	Add
Loss on sale of asset	Add

BEFORE YOU GO ON...

REVIEW IT

1. What is the format of the operating activities section of the statement of cash flows using the indirect method?
2. Where is depreciation expense shown on a statement of cash flows using the indirect method?
3. Where are significant noncash investing and financing activities shown in a statement of cash flows? Give some examples.
4. Which method of computing net cash provided by operating activities does **Lands' End** use? What single item used the largest amount of cash outflow for Lands' End in the fiscal year ended January 28, 2000? The answers to these questions are provided on page 777.

DO IT

Presented below is information related to Reynolds Company. Use it to prepare a statement of cash flows using the indirect method.

REYNOLDS COMPANY
Comparative Balance Sheets
December 31

Assets	**2003**	**2002**	**Change Increase/Decrease**
Cash	$ 54,000	$ 37,000	$ 17,000 Increase
Accounts receivable	68,000	26,000	42,000 Increase
Inventories	54,000	–0–	54,000 Increase
Prepaid expenses	4,000	6,000	2,000 Decrease
Land	45,000	70,000	25,000 Decrease
Buildings	200,000	200,000	–0–
Accumulated depreciation—buildings	(21,000)	(11,000)	10,000 Increase
Equipment	193,000	68,000	125,000 Increase
Accumulated depreciation—equipment	(28,000)	(10,000)	18,000 Increase
Totals	$569,000	$386,000	
Liabilities and Stockholders' Equity			
Accounts payable	$ 23,000	$ 40,000	$ 17,000 Decrease
Accrued expenses payable	10,000	–0–	10,000 Increase
Bonds payable	110,000	150,000	40,000 Decrease
Common stock ($1 par)	220,000	60,000	160,000 Increase
Retained earnings	206,000	136,000	70,000 Increase
Totals	$569,000	$386,000	

REYNOLDS COMPANY
Income Statement
For the Year Ended December 31, 2003

Revenues		$890,000
Cost of goods sold	$465,000	
Operating expenses	221,000	
Interest expense	12,000	
Loss on sale of equipment	2,000	700,000
Income from operations		190,000
Income tax expense		65,000
Net income		$125,000

Additional information:

1. Operating expenses include depreciation expense of $33,000 and charges from prepaid expenses of $2,000.
2. Land was sold at its book value for cash.
3. Cash dividends of $55,000 were declared and paid in 2003.
4. Interest expense of $12,000 was paid in cash.
5. Equipment with a cost of $166,000 was purchased for cash. Equipment with a cost of $41,000 and a book value of $36,000 was sold for $34,000 cash.
6. Bonds of $10,000 were redeemed at their book value for cash. Bonds of $30,000 were converted into common stock.
7. Common stock ($1 par) of $130,000 was issued for cash.
8. Accounts payable pertain to merchandise suppliers.

ACTION PLAN

- Determine the net increase/decrease in cash.
- Determine net cash provided/used by operating activities by adjusting net income for items that did not affect cash.
- Determine net cash provided/used by investing activities.
- Determine net cash provided/used by financing activities.

SOLUTION

REYNOLDS COMPANY
Statement of Cash Flows—Indirect Method
For the Year Ended December 31, 2003

Cash flows from operating activities		
Net income		$125,000
Adjustments to reconcile net income to net cash provided by operating activities:		
Depreciation expense	$ 33,000	
Increase in accounts receivable	(42,000)	
Increase in inventories	(54,000)	
Decrease in prepaid expenses	2,000	
Decrease in accounts payable	(17,000)	
Increase in accrued expenses payable	10,000	
Loss on sale of equipment	2,000	(66,000)
Net cash provided by operating activities		59,000
Cash flows from investing activities		
Sale of land	25,000	
Sale of equipment	34,000	
Purchase of equipment	(166,000)	
Net cash used by investing activities		(107,000)
Cash flows from financing activities		
Redemption of bonds	(10,000)	
Sale of common stock	130,000	
Payment of dividends	(55,000)	
Net cash provided by financing activities		65,000
Net increase in cash		17,000
Cash at beginning of period		37,000
Cash at end of period		$ 54,000
Noncash investing and financing activities		
Conversion of bonds into common stock		$ 30,000

HELPFUL HINT

1. Determine net cash provided/used by operating activities, recognizing that operating activities generally relate to changes in current assets and current liabilities.
2. Determine net cash provided/used by investing activities, recognizing that investing activities generally relate to changes in noncurrent assets.
3. Determine net cash provided/used by financing activities, recognizing that financing activities generally relate to changes in long-term liabilities and stockholders' equity accounts.

Related exercise material: BE18-1, BE18-2, BE18-4, E18-2, E18-3, E18-4, and E18-5.

THE NAVIGATOR

Note: This concludes Section 1 on preparation of the statement of cash flows using the indirect method. Unless your instructor assigns Section 2, you should turn to the concluding section of the chapter, "Analysis of the Statement of Cash Flows," on page 748.

SECTION 2 *Statement of Cash Flows— Direct Method*

To explain and illustrate the direct method, we will use the transactions of Juarez Company for two years, 2002 and 2003, to prepare annual statements of cash flow. We will show basic transactions in the first year, with additional transactions added in the second year.

STUDY OBJECTIVE 4

Prepare a statement of cash flows using the direct method.

FIRST YEAR OF OPERATIONS—2002

Juarez Company began business on January 1, 2002. At that time it issued 300,000 shares of $1 par value common stock for $300,000 cash. The company rented office and sales space along with equipment. The comparative balance sheets at the beginning and end of 2002, showing changes in each account, appear in Illustration 18-20. The income statement and additional information for Juarez Company are shown in Illustration 18-21.

Illustration 18-20

Comparative balance sheet, 2002, with increases and decreases

JUAREZ COMPANY
Comparative Balance Sheet

Assets	**Dec. 31, 2002**	**Jan. 1, 2002**	**Change Increase/Decrease**
Cash	$159,000	$–0–	$159,000 Increase
Accounts receivable	15,000	–0–	15,000 Increase
Inventory	160,000	–0–	160,000 Increase
Prepaid expenses	8,000	–0–	8,000 Increase
Land	80,000	–0–	80,000 Increase
Total	$422,000	$–0–	
Liabilities and Stockholders' Equity			
Accounts payable	$ 60,000	$–0–	$ 60,000 Increase
Accrued expenses payable	20,000	–0–	20,000 Increase
Common stock	300,000	–0–	300,000 Increase
Retained earnings	42,000	–0–	42,000 Increase
Total	$422,000	$–0–	

Illustration 18-21

Income statement and additional information, 2002

JUAREZ COMPANY
Income Statement
For the Year Ended December 31, 2002

Revenues	$780,000
Cost of goods sold	450,000
Gross profit	330,000
Operating expenses	170,000
Income before income taxes	160,000
Income tax expense	48,000
Net income	$112,000

Additional information:
1. Dividends of $70,000 were declared and paid in cash.
2. The accounts payable increase resulted from the purchase of merchandise.

The three steps cited on page 721 for preparing the statement of cash flows are used in the direct method.

STEP 1: DETERMINE THE NET INCREASE/ DECREASE IN CASH

The comparative balance sheets for Juarez Company show a zero cash balance at January 1, 2002, and a cash balance of $159,000 at December 31, 2002. Thus, the change in cash for 2002 was a net increase of $159,000.

STEP 2: DETERMINE NET CASH PROVIDED/USED BY OPERATING ACTIVITIES

Under the **direct method**, net cash provided by operating activities is computed by **adjusting each item in the income statement** from the accrual basis to the cash basis. To simplify and condense the operating activities section, **only major classes of operating cash receipts and cash payments are reported**. For these major classes, the difference between cash receipts and cash payments is the net cash provided by operating activities. These relationships are as shown in Illustration 18-22.

Illustration 18-22

Major classes of cash receipts and payments

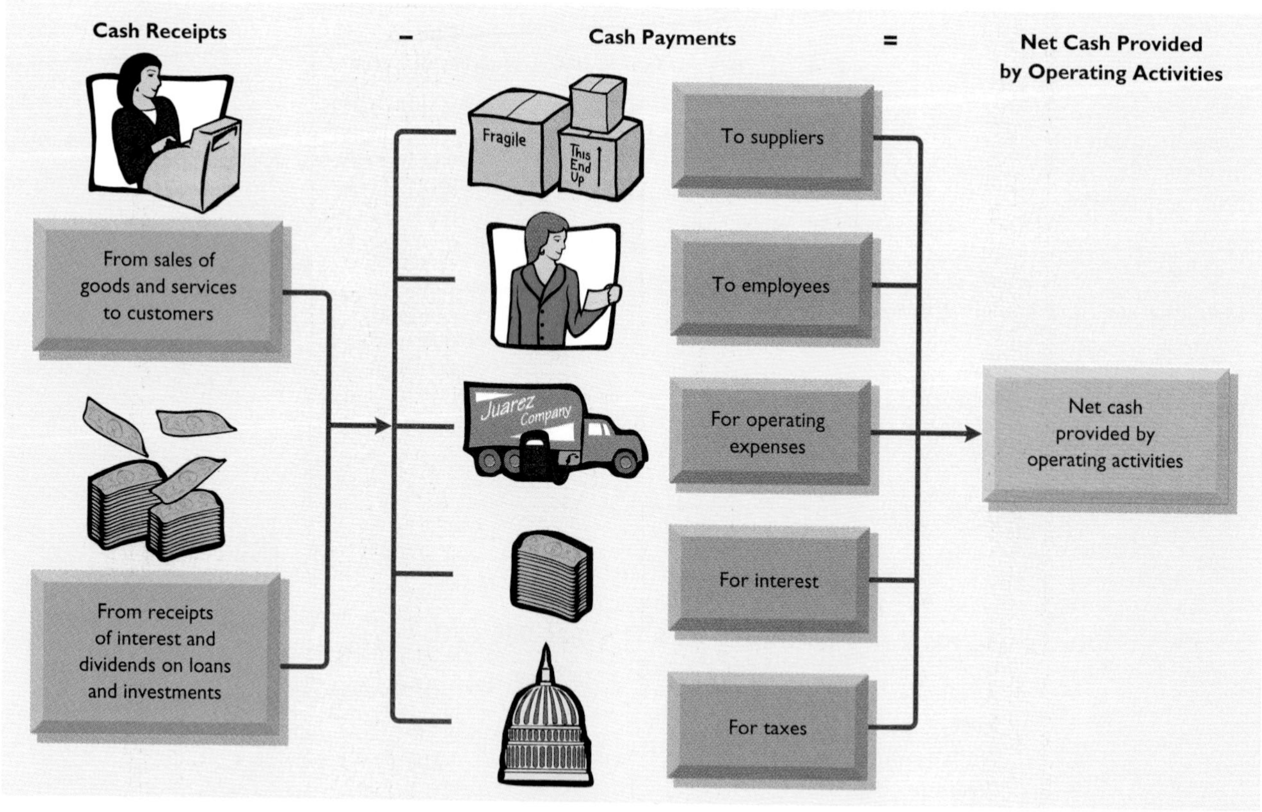

An efficient way to apply the direct method is to analyze the items reported in the income statement in the order in which they are listed. Cash receipts and cash payments related to these revenues and expenses are then determined. The direct method adjustments for Juarez Company in 2002 to determine net cash provided by operating activities are presented on the following pages.

Cash Receipts from Customers

The income statement for Juarez Company reported revenues from customers of $780,000. How much of that was cash receipts? To answer that, it is necessary to consider the change in accounts receivable during the year. When accounts receivable increase during the year, revenues on an accrual basis are higher than cash receipts from customers. Operations led to revenues, but not all of these revenues resulted in cash receipts. To determine the amount of cash receipts, the increase in accounts receivable is deducted from sales revenues. On the other hand, there may be a decrease in accounts receivable. That would occur if cash receipts from customers exceeded sales revenues. In that case, the decrease in accounts receivable is added to sales revenues.

For Juarez Company, accounts receivable increased $15,000. Thus, cash receipts from customers were $765,000, computed as follows.

Illustration 18-23

Computation of cash receipts from customers

Revenues from sales	$780,000
Deduct: Increase in accounts receivable	15,000
Cash receipts from customers	**$765,000**

Cash receipts from customers may also be determined from an analysis of the Accounts Receivable account, as shown in Illustration 18-24.

Illustration 18-24

Analysis of accounts receivable

Accounts Receivable

1/1/02	Balance	-0-	**Receipts from customers**	**765,000**
	Revenues from sales	780,000		
12/31/02	Balance	15,000		

HELPFUL HINT

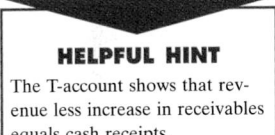

The T-account shows that revenue less increase in receivables equals cash receipts.

The relationships among cash receipts from customers, revenues from sales, and changes in accounts receivable are shown in Illustration 18-25.

Illustration 18-25

Formula to compute cash receipts from customers—direct method

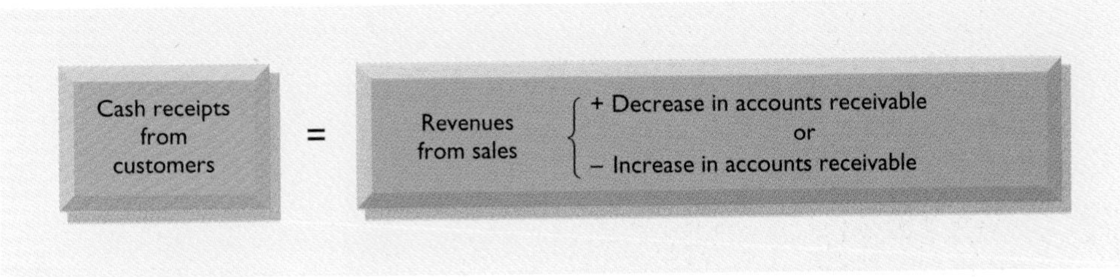

Cash Payments to Suppliers

Juarez Company reported cost of goods sold of $450,000 on its income statement. How much of that was cash payments to suppliers? To answer that, it is first necessary to find purchases for the year. To find purchases, cost of goods sold is adjusted for the change in inventory. When inventory increases during the year, purchases for the year have exceeded cost of goods sold. As a result, to determine the amount of purchases, the increase in inventory is added to cost of goods sold.

In 2002, Juarez Company's inventory increased $160,000. Purchases are computed as follows.

Illustration 18-26
Computation of purchases

Cost of goods sold	$450,000
Add: Increase in inventory	160,000
Purchases	**$610,000**

After purchases are computed, cash payments to suppliers can be determined. This is done by adjusting purchases for the change in accounts payable. When accounts payable increase during the year, purchases on an accrual basis are higher than they are on a cash basis. As a result, to determine cash payments to suppliers, an increase in accounts payable is deducted from purchases. On the other hand, there may be a decrease in accounts payable. That would occur if cash payments to suppliers exceed purchases. In that case, the decrease in accounts payable is added to purchases.

For Juarez Company, cash payments to suppliers were $550,000, computed as follows.

Illustration 18-27
Computation of cash payments to suppliers

Purchases	$610,000
Deduct: Increase in accounts payable	60,000
Cash payments to suppliers	**$550,000**

Cash payments to suppliers may also be determined from an analysis of the Accounts Payable account as shown in Illustration 18-28.

Illustration 18-28
Analysis of accounts payable

Accounts Payable

Payments to suppliers	**550,000**	1/1/02 Balance	–0–
		Purchases	610,000
		12/31/02 Balance	60,000

HELPFUL HINT
The T-account shows that purchases less increase in accounts payable equals payments to suppliers.

The relationships among cash payments to suppliers, cost of goods sold, changes in inventory, and changes in accounts payable are shown in the following formula.

Illustration 18-29
Formula to compute cash payments to suppliers—direct method

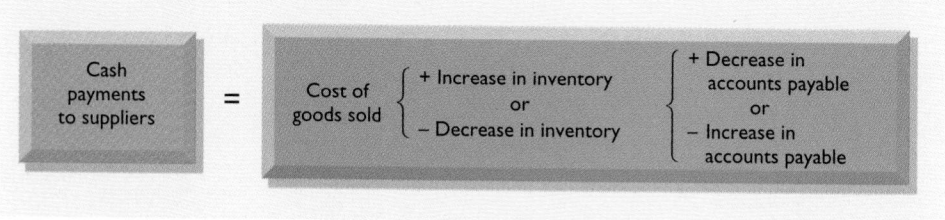

Cash payments to suppliers = Cost of goods sold { + Increase in inventory or – Decrease in inventory } { + Decrease in accounts payable or – Increase in accounts payable }

Cash Payments for Operating Expenses

HELPFUL HINT
Decrease in accounts receivable indicates that cash collections were greater than sales.
Increase in accounts receivable indicates that sales were greater than cash collections.

Operating expenses of $170,000 were reported on Juarez's income statement. How much of that amount was cash paid for operating expenses? To answer that, we need to adjust this amount for any changes in prepaid expenses and accrued expenses payable. For example, when prepaid expenses increased $8,000 during the year, cash paid for operating expenses was $8,000 higher than operating expenses reported on the income statement. To convert operating expenses to cash payments for operating expenses, the increase must be added to operating expenses.

On the other hand, if prepaid expenses decrease during the year, the decrease must be deducted from operating expenses.

Operating expenses must also be adjusted for changes in accrued expenses payable. When accrued expenses payable increase during the year, operating expenses on an accrual basis are higher than they are in a cash basis. As a result, to determine cash payments for operating expenses, an increase in accrued expenses payable is deducted from operating expenses. On the other hand, a decrease in accrued expenses payable is added to operating expenses because cash payments exceed operating expenses.

Juarez Company's cash payments for operating expenses were $158,000, computed as follows.

Increase in prepaid expenses indicates that the amount paid for the prepayments exceeded the amount that was recorded as an expense.
Decrease in prepaid expenses indicates that the amount recorded as an expense exceeded the amount of cash paid for the prepayments.
Increase in accounts payable indicates that expenses incurred exceed the cash paid for expenses that period.

Illustration 18-30

Computation of cash payments for operating expenses

Operating expenses	$170,000
Add: Increase in prepaid expenses	8,000
Deduct: Increase in accrued expenses payable	(20,000)
Cash payments for operating expenses	**$158,000**

The relationships among cash payments for operating expenses, changes in prepaid expenses, and changes in accrued expenses payable are shown in the following formula.

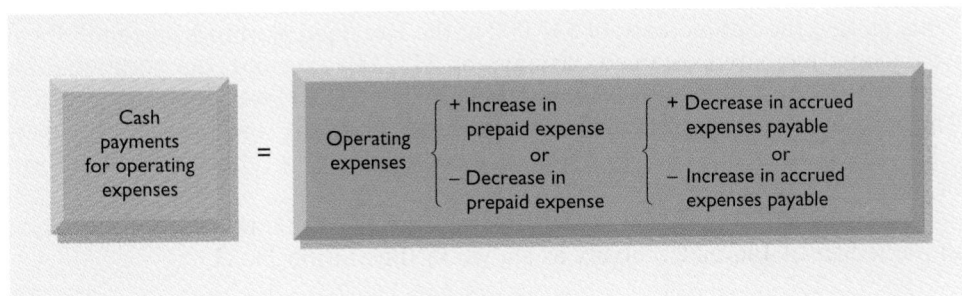

Illustration 18-31

Formula to compute cash payments for operating expenses—direct method

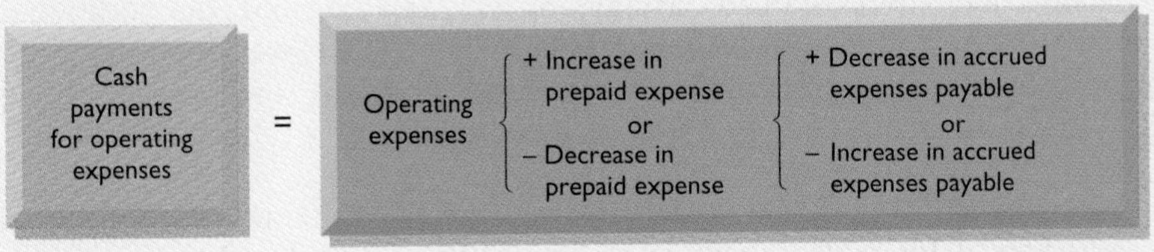

Cash Payments for Income Taxes

The income statement for Juarez shows income tax expense of $48,000. This amount equals the cash paid. The comparative balance sheets indicated no income taxes payable at either the beginning or end of the year.

All of the revenues and expenses in the 2002 income statement have now been adjusted to a cash basis. The operating activities section of the statement of cash flows is as follows.

Illustration 18-32

Operating activities section—direct method

JUAREZ COMPANY
Statement of Cash Flows—Direct Method (partial)
For the Year Ended December 31, 2002

Cash flows from operating activities		
Cash receipts from customers		$765,000
Cash payments:		
To suppliers	$550,000	
For operating expenses	158,000	
For income taxes	48,000	756,000
Net cash provided by operating activities		**$ 9,000**

STEP 3: DETERMINE NET CASH PROVIDED/USED BY INVESTING AND FINANCING ACTIVITIES

HELPFUL HINT
This is the same procedure used under the indirect method. The investing and financing activities are measured and reported the same under both methods.

Preparing the investing and financing activities sections of the statement of cash flows begins by determining the changes in noncurrent accounts reported in the comparative balance sheets. The change in each account is then analyzed to determine the effect, if any, the change had on cash.

Increase in Land

No additional information is given for the increase in land. In such case, you should assume that the increase affected cash. In solving homework problems, you should assume that **any unexplained differences in noncurrent accounts involve cash**. The purchase of land is an investing activity. Thus, an outflow of cash of $80,000 for the purchase of land should be reported in the investing activities section.

Increase in Common Stock

As indicated earlier, 300,000 shares of $1 par value stock were sold for $300,000 cash. The issuance of common stock is a financing activity. Thus, a cash inflow of $300,000 from the issuance of common stock is reported in the financing activities section.

Increase in Retained Earnings

HELPFUL HINT
It is the **payment** of dividends, not the declaration, that appears on the cash flow statement.

What caused the net increase of $42,000 in the Retained Earnings account? First, net income increased retained earnings by $112,000. Second, the additional information section indicates that a cash dividend of $70,000 was declared and paid. The adjustment of revenues and expenses to arrive at net cash provided by operations was done in step 2 above. The cash dividend paid is reported as an outflow of cash in the financing activities section.

This analysis can also be made directly from the Retained Earnings account in the ledger of Juarez Company as shown in Illustration 18-33.

Illustration 18-33
Analysis of retained earnings

Retained Earnings					
12/31/02	**Cash dividend**	**70,000**	1/1/02	Balance	–0–
			12/31/02	**Net income**	**112,000**
			12/31/02	Balance	42,000

The $42,000 increase in Retained Earnings in 2002 is a net change. When a net change in a noncurrent balance sheet account has occurred during the year, it generally is necessary to report the individual items that cause the net change.

STATEMENT OF CASH FLOWS—2002

We can now prepare the statement of cash flows. The operating activities section is reported first, followed by the investing and financing activities sections. The statement of cash flows for Juarez Company for 2002 is shown in Illustration 18-34.

The statement of cash flows shows the following: Operating activities **provided** $9,000 of the net increase in cash. Investing activities **used** $80,000 of cash. Financing activities **provided** $230,000 of cash. The $159,000 net increase in cash for the year agrees with the increase in cash of $159,000 reported in the comparative balance sheets.

Illustration 18-34

Statement of cash flows, 2002—direct method

JUAREZ COMPANY
Statement of Cash Flows—Direct Method
For the Year Ended December 31, 2002

Cash flows from operating activities		
Cash receipts from customers		$765,000
Cash payments:		
To suppliers	$550,000	
For operating expenses	158,000	
For income taxes	48,000	756,000
Net cash provided by operating activities		9,000
Cash flows from investing activities		
Purchase of land	(80,000)	
Net cash used by investing activities		(80,000)
Cash flows from financing activities		
Issuance of common stock	300,000	
Payment of cash dividend	(70,000)	
Net cash provided by financing activities		230,000
Net increase in cash		159,000
Cash at beginning of period		-0-
Cash at end of period		$159,000

HELPFUL HINT
Note that in the investing and financing activities sections, positive numbers indicate cash inflows (receipts), and negative numbers indicate cash outflows (payments).

SECOND YEAR OF OPERATIONS—2003

Illustrations 18-35 and 18-36 present information related to the second year of operations for Juarez Company.

Illustration 18-35

Comparative balance sheets, 2003, with increases and decreases

JUAREZ COMPANY
Comparative Balance Sheets
December 31

Assets	**2003**	**2002**	**Change Increase/Decrease**
Cash	$191,000	$159,000	$ 32,000 Increase
Accounts receivable	12,000	15,000	3,000 Decrease
Inventory	130,000	160,000	30,000 Decrease
Prepaid expenses	6,000	8,000	2,000 Decrease
Land	180,000	80,000	100,000 Increase
Equipment	160,000	-0-	160,000 Increase
Accumulated depreciation—equipment	(16,000)	-0-	16,000 Increase
Total	$663,000	$422,000	
Liabilities and Stockholders' Equity			
Accounts payable	$ 52,000	$ 60,000	$ 8,000 Decrease
Accrued expenses payable	15,000	20,000	5,000 Decrease
Income taxes payable	12,000	-0-	12,000 Increase
Bonds payable	90,000	-0-	90,000 Increase
Common stock	400,000	300,000	100,000 Increase
Retained earnings	94,000	42,000	52,000 Increase
Total	$663,000	$422,000	

Illustration 18-36

Income statement and additional information, 2003

JUAREZ COMPANY
Income Statement
For the Year Ended December 31, 2003

Revenues		$975,000
Cost of goods sold	$660,000	
Operating expenses (excluding depreciation)	176,000	
Depreciation expense	18,000	
Loss on sale of store equipment	1,000	855,000
Income before income taxes		120,000
Income tax expense		36,000
Net income		$ 84,000

Additional information:
1. In 2003, the company declared and paid a $32,000 cash dividend.
2. Bonds were issued at face value for $90,000 in cash.
3. Equipment costing $180,000 was purchased for cash.
4. Equipment costing $20,000 was sold for $17,000 cash when the book value of the equipment was $18,000.
5. Common stock of $100,000 was issued to acquire land.

STEP 1: DETERMINE THE NET INCREASE/ DECREASE IN CASH

The comparative balance sheets show a beginning cash balance of $159,000 and an ending cash balance of $191,000. Thus, there was a net increase in cash in 2003 of $32,000.

STEP 2: DETERMINE NET CASH PROVIDED/USED BY OPERATING ACTIVITIES

Cash Receipts from Customers

Revenues from sales were $975,000. Since accounts receivable decreased $3,000, cash receipts from customers were greater than sales revenues. Cash receipts from customers were $978,000, computed as follows.

Illustration 18-37

Computation of cash receipts from customers

Revenues from sales	$975,000
Add: Decrease in accounts receivable	3,000
Cash receipts from customers	**$978,000**

Cash Payments to Suppliers

The conversion of cost of goods sold to purchases and purchases to cash payments to suppliers is similar to the computations made in 2002. For 2003, purchases are computed using cost of goods sold of $660,000 from the income statement and the decrease in inventory of $30,000 from the comparative balance sheets. Purchases are then adjusted by the decrease in accounts payable of $8,000. Cash payments to suppliers were $638,000, computed as follows.

Illustration 18-38

Computation of cash payments to suppliers

Cost of goods sold	$660,000
Deduct: Decrease in inventory	30,000
Purchases	630,000
Add: Decrease in accounts payable	8,000
Cash payments to suppliers	**$638,000**

Cash Payments for Operating Expenses

Operating expenses (exclusive of depreciation expense) for 2003 were reported at $176,000. This amount is then adjusted for changes in prepaid expenses and accrued expenses payable to determine cash payments for operating expenses.

As shown in the comparative balance sheets, prepaid expenses decreased $2,000 during the year. This means that $2,000 was allocated to operating expenses (thereby increasing operating expenses), but cash payments did not increase by that $2,000. To determine cash payments for operating expenses, the decrease in prepaid expenses is deducted from operating expenses.

Accrued operating expenses decreased $5,000 during the period. As a result, cash payments were higher by $5,000 than the amount reported for operating expenses. The decrease in accrued expenses payable is added to operating expenses. Cash payments for operating expenses were $179,000, computed as follows.

Operating expenses, exclusive of depreciation	$176,000
Deduct: Decrease in prepaid expenses	(2,000)
Add: Decrease in accrued expenses payable	5,000
Cash payments for operating expenses	**$179,000**

Illustration 18-39

Computation of cash payments for operating expenses

Depreciation Expense and Loss on Sale of Equipment

Operating expenses are shown exclusive of depreciation. Depreciation expense in 2003 was $18,000. Depreciation expense is not shown on a statement of cash flows because it is a noncash charge. If the amount for operating expenses includes depreciation expense, operating expenses must be reduced by the amount of depreciation to determine cash payments for operating expenses.

The loss on sale of equipment of $1,000 is also a noncash charge. The loss on sale of equipment reduces net income, but it does not reduce cash. Thus, the loss on sale of equipment is not reported on a statement of cash flows.

Other charges to expense that do not require the use of cash, such as the amortization of intangible assets and depletion expense, are treated in the same manner as depreciation.

Cash Payments for Income Taxes

Income tax expense reported on the income statement was $36,000. Income taxes payable, however, increased $12,000. This increase means that $12,000 of the income taxes have not been paid. As a result, income taxes paid were less than income taxes reported in the income statement. Cash payments for income taxes were, therefore, $24,000 as shown below.

Income tax expense	$36,000
Deduct: Increase in income taxes payable	12,000
Cash payments for income taxes	**$24,000**

Illustration 18-40

Computation of cash payments for income taxes

The relationships among cash payments for income taxes, income tax expense, and changes in income taxes payable are shown in the following formula.

Illustration 18-41

Formula to compute cash payments for income taxes—direct method

Cash payments for income taxes	=	Income tax expense	+ Decrease in income taxes payable or – Increase in income taxes payable

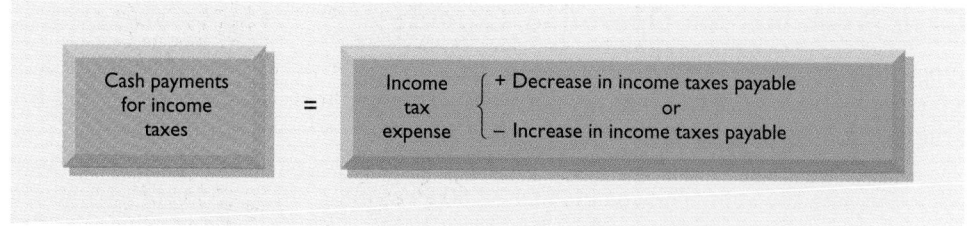

STEP 3: DETERMINE NET CASH PROVIDED/USED BY INVESTING AND FINANCING ACTIVITIES

Increase in Land

Land increased $100,000. The additional information section indicates that common stock was issued to purchase the land. The issuance of common stock for land has no effect on cash. But it is a **significant noncash investing and financing transaction**. This transaction requires disclosure in a separate schedule at the bottom of the statement of cash flows.

Increase in Equipment

The comparative balance sheets show that equipment increased $160,000 in 2003. The additional information in Illustration 18-36 indicates that the increase resulted from two investing transactions: (1) Equipment costing $180,000 was purchased for cash. And (2) equipment costing $20,000 was sold for $17,000 cash when its book value was $18,000. The relevant data for the statement of cash flows is the cash paid for the purchase and the cash proceeds from the sale. For Juarez Company, the investing activities section will show the following: The $180,000 purchase of equipment as an outflow of cash, and the $17,000 sale of equipment also as an inflow of cash. The two amounts **should not be netted. Both individual outflows and inflows of cash should be shown.**

The analysis of the changes in equipment should include the related Accumulated Depreciation account. These two accounts for Juarez Company are shown in Illustration 18-42.

Illustration 18-42

Analysis of equipment and related accumulated depreciation

Equipment

1/1/03	Balance	–0–	Cost of equipment sold	20,000
	Cash purchase	**180,000**		
12/31/03	Balance	160,000		

Accumulated Depreciation—Equipment

Sale of equipment	2,000	1/1/03	Balance	–0–
			Depreciation expense	18,000
		12/31/03	Balance	16,000

Increase in Bonds Payable

Bonds Payable increased $90,000. The additional information in Illustration 18-36 indicated that bonds with a face value of $90,000 were issued for $90,000 cash. The issuance of bonds is a financing activity. For Juarez Company, there is an inflow of cash of $90,000 from the issuance of bonds.

Increase in Common Stock

The Common Stock account increased $100,000. The additional information indicated that land was acquired from the issuance of common stock. This transaction is a **significant noncash investing and financing transaction** that should be reported separately at the bottom of the statement.

Increase in Retained Earnings

The $52,000 net increase in Retained Earnings resulted from net income of $84,000 and the declaration and payment of a cash dividend of $32,000. **Net income is not reported in the statement of cash flows under the direct method.** Cash dividends paid of $32,000 are reported in the financing activities section as an outflow of cash.

STATEMENT OF CASH FLOWS—2003

The statement of cash flows for Juarez Company is shown in Illustration 18-43.

Illustration 18-43

Statement of cash flows, 2003—direct method

JUAREZ COMPANY
Statement of Cash Flows—Direct Method
For the Year Ended December 31, 2003

Cash flows from operating activities		
Cash receipts from customers		$978,000
Cash payments:		
To suppliers	$638,000	
For operating expenses	179,000	
For income taxes	24,000	841,000
Net cash provided by operating activities		137,000
Cash flows from investing activities		
Purchase of equipment	(180,000)	
Sale of equipment	17,000	
Net cash used by investing activities		(163,000)
Cash flows from financing activities		
Issuance of bonds payable	90,000	
Payment of cash dividends	(32,000)	
Net cash provided by financing activities		58,000
Net increase in cash		32,000
Cash at beginning of period		159,000
Cash at end of period		$191,000
Noncash investing and financing activities		
Issuance of common stock to purchase land		$100,000

BEFORE YOU GO ON...

REVIEW IT

1. What is the format of the operating activities section of the statement of cash flows using the direct method?
2. Where is depreciation expense shown on a statement of cash flows using the direct method?
3. Where are significant noncash investing and financing activities shown on a statement of cash flows? Give some examples.

DO IT

Presented below is information related to Reynolds Company. Use it to prepare a statement of cash flows using the direct method.

REYNOLDS COMPANY
Comparative Balance Sheets
December 31

Assets	2003	2002	Change Increase/Decrease
Cash	$ 54,000	$ 37,000	$ 17,000 Increase
Accounts receivable	68,000	26,000	42,000 Increase
Inventories	54,000	–0–	54,000 Increase
Prepaid expenses	4,000	6,000	2,000 Decrease
Land	45,000	70,000	25,000 Decrease
Buildings	200,000	200,000	–0–
Accumulated depreciation—buildings	(21,000)	(11,000)	10,000 Increase
Equipment	193,000	68,000	125,000 Increase
Accumulated depreciation—equipment	(28,000)	(10,000)	18,000 Increase
Totals	$569,000	$386,000	
Liabilities and Stockholders' Equity			
Accounts payable	$ 23,000	$ 40,000	$ 17,000 Decrease
Accrued expenses payable	10,000	–0–	10,000 Increase
Bonds payable	110,000	150,000	40,000 Decrease
Common stock ($1 par)	220,000	60,000	160,000 Increase
Retained earnings	206,000	136,000	70,000 Increase
Totals	$569,000	$386,000	

REYNOLDS COMPANY
Income Statement
For the Year Ended December 31, 2003

Revenues		$890,000
Cost of goods sold	$465,000	
Operating expenses	221,000	
Interest expense	12,000	
Loss on sale of equipment	2,000	700,000
Income from operations		190,000
Income tax expense		65,000
Net income		$125,000

Additional information:

1. Operating expenses include depreciation expense of $33,000 and charges from prepaid expenses of $2,000.
2. Land was sold at its book value for cash.
3. Cash dividends of $55,000 were declared and paid in 2003.
4. Interest expense of $12,000 was paid in cash.
5. Equipment with a cost of $166,000 was purchased for cash. Equipment with a cost of $41,000 and a book value of $36,000 was sold for $34,000 cash.
6. Bonds of $10,000 were redeemed at their book value for cash. Bonds of $30,000 were converted into common stock.
7. Common stock ($1 par) of $130,000 was issued for cash.
8. Accounts payable pertain to merchandise suppliers.

ACTION PLAN

- Determine the net increase/decrease in cash.
- Determine net cash provided/used by operating activities by adjusting each item in the income statement from the accrual basis to the cash basis.
- Determine net cash provided/used by investing activities.
- Determine net cash provided/used by financing activities.

SOLUTION

REYNOLDS COMPANY
Statement of Cash Flows—Direct Method
For the Year Ended December 31, 2003

Cash flows from operating activities		
Cash receipts from customers		$848,000[a]
Cash payments:		
To suppliers	$536,000[b]	
For operating expenses	176,000[c]	
For interest expense	12,000	
For income taxes	65,000	789,000
Net cash provided by operating activities		59,000
Cash flows from investing activities		
Sale of land	25,000	
Sale of equipment	34,000	
Purchase of equipment	(166,000)	
Net cash used by investing activities		(107,000)
Cash flows from financing activities		
Redemption of bonds	(10,000)	
Sale of common stock	130,000	
Payment of dividends	(55,000)	
Net cash provided by financing activities		65,000
Net increase in cash		17,000
Cash at beginning of period		37,000
Cash at end of period		$ 54,000
Noncash investing and financing activities		
Conversion of bonds into common stock		$ 30,000

Computations:

[a]$848,000 = $890,000 − $42,000
[b]$536,000 = $465,000 + $54,000 + $17,000
[c]$176,000 = $221,000 − $33,000 − $2,000 − $10,000

Technically, an additional schedule reconciling net income to net cash provided by operating activities should be presented as part of the statement of cash flows when using the direct method.

HELPFUL HINT

1. Determine net cash provided/used by operating activities, recognizing that each item in the income statement must be adjusted to the cash basis.
2. Determine net cash provided/used by investing activities, recognizing that investing activities generally relate to changes in noncurrent assets.
3. Determine net cash provided/used by financing activities, recognizing that financing activities generally relate to changes in long-term liabilities and stockholders' equity accounts.

Related exercise material: BE18-6, BE18-7, BE18-8, E18-7, E18-8, E18-9, and E18-10.

THE NAVIGATOR

Note: This concludes Section 2 on preparation of the statement of cash flows using the direct method. You should now proceed to the concluding section of the chapter, "Analysis of the Statement of Cash Flows."

ANALYSIS OF THE STATEMENT OF CASH FLOWS

STUDY OBJECTIVE 5

Analyze the statement of cash flows.

The statement of cash flows provides information about a company's financial health that is not evident from the balance sheet or the income statement. Bankers, creditors, and other users of the statement of cash flows are as concerned with cash flow from operations as they are with net income because they are interested in a company's ability to pay its bills. Does accrual accounting conceal cash flow problems? What can be learned about a company and its management from the statement of cash flows?

In the following discussion of cash flow analysis, we use financial information from the fiscal 2000 annual report of **Gap Inc.** (manufacturer and retailer of Gap, Banana Republic, and Old Navy brands). Gap Inc. reported the following relevant information:

Illustration 18-44

Gap Inc. data used in cash flow analysis

GAP INC.

($ in millions)	**Fiscal 2000**	**Fiscal 1999**
Current liabilities	$ 1,753	$1,553
Total liabilities	2,956	2,390
Net sales	11,635	9,054
Net cash provided by operating activities	1,478	1,394

As with the balance sheet and the income statement, ratio analysis of the statement of cash flows can evaluate Gap Inc.'s liquidity, profitability, and solvency. Three cash flow ratios that contribute to these evaluations are (a) the current cash debt coverage ratio, (b) the cash return on sales ratio, and (c) the cash debt coverage ratio. Each of these ratios uses net cash provided by operating activities as the numerator.

CURRENT CASH DEBT COVERAGE RATIO

HELPFUL HINT

Recall that the current ratio is current assets divided by current liabilities.

A disadvantage of the current ratio is that it employs year-end balances of current asset and current liability accounts. These year-end balances may not be representative of what the company's current position was during most of the year. A ratio that partially corrects for this problem is the ratio of net cash provided by operating activities to average current liabilities, referred to as the **current cash debt coverage ratio**. Because it uses net cash provided by operating activities during the period, rather than a balance at a point in time, it may provide a better representation of **liquidity**. Using Gap Inc.'s financial data, the current cash debt coverage ratio is computed as follows.

Illustration 18-45

Current cash debt coverage ratio

Net Cash Provided by Operating Activities ÷ Average Current Liabilities = Current Cash Debt Coverage Ratio

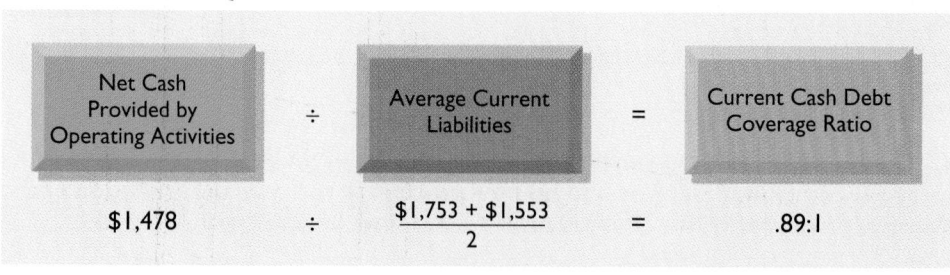

$$\$1{,}478 \div \frac{\$1{,}753 + \$1{,}553}{2} = .89:1$$

This ratio indicates that for every dollar of debt due during the year, \$0.89 of cash was generated from operations to pay that debt.

CASH RETURN ON SALES RATIO

One measure of profitability under accrual accounting is the profit margin ratio. This ratio is defined as net income divided by net sales and measures net income generated by each dollar of sales. The cash-based ratio that is the counterpart of the profit margin ratio is the **cash return on sales ratio**. It is computed by dividing net cash provided by operating activities by net sales. For Gap Inc., this ratio is computed as follows.

ALTERNATIVE TERMINOLOGY
The cash return on sales ratio is sometimes referred to as *cash flow margin*.

Illustration 18-46
Cash return on sales ratio

Net Cash Provided by Operating Activities	÷	Net Sales	=	Cash Return on Sales
\$1,478	÷	\$11,635	=	13%

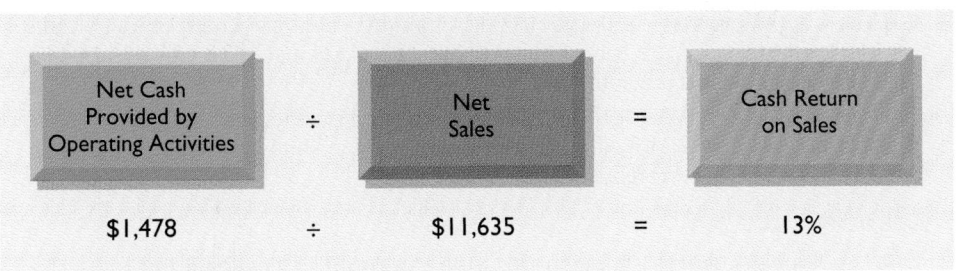

Some difference is to be expected between similar cash and accrual accounting ratios. But significant differences should be investigated. When Gap Inc.'s cash return on sales of 13% is compared with its profit margin of 9.7%, it appears that Gap Inc. is efficient at turning sales into cash—since its cash flow margin is greater than its profit margin (accrual basis).

CASH DEBT COVERAGE RATIO

One measure of long-term **solvency** is the debt to total assets ratio. The cash basis measure of solvency is the **cash debt coverage ratio**. It is the ratio of net cash provided by operating activities to average total liabilities. This ratio demonstrates a company's ability to repay its liabilities from net cash provided by operating activities, without having to liquidate the assets employed in its operations. Gap Inc.'s cash debt coverage ratio is computed as follows.

Illustration 18-47
Cash debt coverage ratio

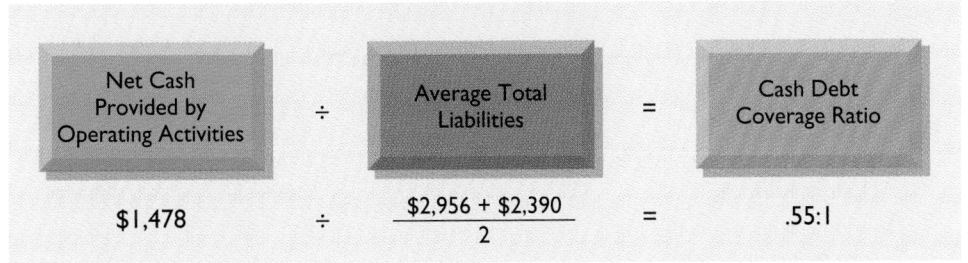

Net Cash Provided by Operating Activities	÷	Average Total Liabilities	=	Cash Debt Coverage Ratio
\$1,478	÷	$\frac{\$2,956 + \$2,390}{2}$	=	.55:1

This ratio indicates that for every dollar of total debt, \$0.55 of cash was generated from operations to pay that debt.

The three cash-based ratios presented here show that **Gap Inc.** is efficiently generating cash. Its cash flow coverage ratios are in line with industry averages. These ratios indicate that the company is liquid, profitable, and solvent.

BEFORE YOU GO ON...

REVIEW IT

1. Why might an analyst want to supplement accrual-based ratios with cash-based ratios?
2. What cash-basis ratios may be prepared to evaluate liquidity, profitability, and solvency?

A LOOK BACK AT OUR FEATURE STORY

Refer back to the Feature Story at the beginning of the chapter about Gerald Biby's attempt to refinance **Kilian Community College's** mortgage, and answer the following questions.

1. How was the purchase of the $250,000 computer system presented on the "traditional educational institution financial statement" so that it negatively affected Biby's ability to refinance the mortgage?
2. How was the purchase of the $250,000 computer system presented on the statement of cash flows? How did the preparation of the statement of cash flows aid Biby in securing the refinancing of the mortgage?

SOLUTION

1. A traditional financial statement for a not-for-profit, educational institution reports receipts as revenues. It expenses all expenditures, even capital expenditures such as the $250,000 computer system. The traditional financial statement reported the entire $250,000 as an expense in one year, making it look like the college was just breaking even.
2. The statement of cash flows classified the computer purchase as an investing activity. It therefore showed the bankers that one of the uses of funds was the purchase of computer equipment that had several years of life. In addition, the bankers noted from the statement of cash flows that the college's cash flows from operating activities exceeded the cash outflows for financing activities (the loan repayments, including principal and interest) by a ratio of 3-to-1.

THE NAVIGATOR

DEMONSTRATION PROBLEM

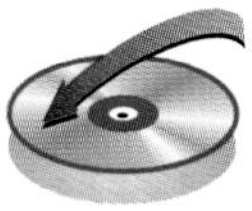

Additional Demonstration Problem

The income statement for the year ended December 31, 2002, for John Kosinski Manufacturing Company contains the following condensed information.

JOHN KOSINSKI MANUFACTURING COMPANY
Income Statement

Revenues		$6,583,000
Operating expenses (excluding depreciation)	$4,920,000	
Depreciation expense	880,000	5,800,000
Income before income taxes		783,000
Income tax expense		353,000
Net income		$ 430,000

Included in operating expenses is a $24,000 loss resulting from the sale of machinery for $270,000 cash. Machinery was purchased at a cost of $750,000.

The following balances are reported on Kosinski's comparative balance sheets at December 31.

JOHN KOSINSKI MANUFACTURING COMPANY
Comparative Balance Sheets (partial)

	2002	2001
Cash	$672,000	$130,000
Accounts receivable	775,000	610,000
Inventories	834,000	867,000
Accounts payable	521,000	501,000

Income tax expense of $353,000 represents the amount paid in 2002. Dividends declared and paid in 2002 totaled $200,000.

Instructions

(a) Prepare the statement of cash flows using the indirect method.

OR

(b) Prepare the statement of cash flows using the direct method.

SOLUTION TO DEMONSTRATION PROBLEM

(a)

JOHN KOSINSKI MANUFACTURING COMPANY
Statement of Cash Flows—Indirect Method
For the Year Ended December 31, 2002

Cash flows from operating activities		
Net income		$ 430,000
Adjustments to reconcile net income to net cash provided by operating activities:		
Depreciation expense	$880,000	
Loss on sale of machinery	24,000	
Increase in accounts receivable	(165,000)	
Decrease in inventories	33,000	
Increase in accounts payable	20,000	792,000
Net cash provided by operating activities		1,222,000
Cash flows from investing activities		
Sale of machinery	270,000	
Purchase of machinery	(750,000)	
Net cash used by investing activities		(480,000)
Cash flows from financing activities		
Payment of cash dividends		(200,000)
Net increase in cash		542,000
Cash at beginning of period		130,000
Cash at end of period		$ 672,000

ACTION PLAN

- Apply the same data to the preparation of a statement of cash flows under both the indirect and direct methods.
- Note the similarities of the two methods: Both methods report the same information in the investing and financing sections.
- Note the differences between the two methods: The cash flows from operating activities sections report different information (but the amount of net cash provided by operating activities is the same for both methods).

(b)

JOHN KOSINSKI MANUFACTURING COMPANY
Statement of Cash Flows—Direct Method
For the Year Ended December 31, 2002

Cash flows from operating activities		
Cash receipts from customers		$6,418,000*
Cash payments:		
For operating expenses	$4,843,000**	
For income taxes	353,000	5,196,000
Net cash provided by operating activities		1,222,000
Cash flows from investing activities		
Sale of machinery	270,000	
Purchase of machinery	(750,000)	

Net cash used by investing activities	(480,000)
Cash flows from financing activities	
Payment of cash dividends	(200,000)
Net increase in cash	542,000
Cash at beginning of period	130,000
Cash at end of period	$ 672,000

Direct Method Computations:

* Computation of cash receipts from customers:	
Revenues per the income statement	$6,583,000
Less increase in accounts receivable	165,000
Cash receipts from customers	$6,418,000
** Computation of cash payments for operating expenses:	
Operating expenses per the income statement	$4,920,000
Deduct loss from sale of machinery	(24,000)
Deduct decrease in inventories	(33,000)
Deduct increase in accounts payable	(20,000)
Cash payments for operating expenses	$4,843,000

THE NAVIGATOR

SUMMARY OF STUDY OBJECTIVES

1. *Indicate the primary purpose of the statement of cash flows.* The primary purpose of the statement of cash flows is to provide information about the cash receipts and cash payments during a period. A secondary objective is to provide information about the operating, investing, and financing activities during the period.

2. *Distinguish among operating, investing, and financing activities.* Operating activities include the cash effects of transactions that enter into the determination of net income. Investing activities involve cash flows resulting from changes in investments and long-term asset items. Financing activities involve cash flows resulting from changes in long-term liability and stockholders' equity items.

3. *Prepare a statement of cash flows using the indirect method.* The preparation of a statement of cash flows involves three major steps: (1) Determine the net increase or decrease in cash. (2) Determine net cash provided (used) by operating activities. (3) Determine net cash flows provided (used) by investing and financing activities. Under the indirect method, accrual basis net income is adjusted to net cash provided by operating activities.

4. *Prepare a statement of cash flows using the direct method.* The preparation of the statement of cash flows involves three major steps: (1) Determine the net increase or decrease in cash. (2) Determine net cash provided (used) by operating activities. (3) Determine net cash flows provided (used) by investing and financing activities. To determine net cash provided by operating activities, the direct method reports cash receipts less cash payments.

5. *Analyze the statement of cash flows.* The statement of cash flows can be used for cash-based ratio analysis. The current cash debt coverage ratio measures liquidity. The cash return on sales ratio measures profitability. The cash debt coverage ratio measures solvency.

THE NAVIGATOR

Key Term Matching Activity

GLOSSARY

Cash debt coverage ratio A cash-basis measure of solvency; computed as net cash provided by operating activities divided by average total liabilities. (p. 749).

Cash return on sales ratio A cash-basis measure of profitability; computed as net cash provided by operating activities divided by net sales. Also called *cash flow margin.* (p. 749).

Current cash debt coverage ratio A cash-basis measure of liquidity; computed as net cash provided by operating activities divided by average current liabilities. (p. 748).

Direct method A method of determining the net cash provided by operating activities by adjusting each item in the income statement from the accrual basis to the cash basis. (p. 736).

Financing activities Cash flow activities that include (a) obtaining cash from issuing debt and repaying the amounts borrowed and (b) obtaining cash from stockholders and providing them with a return on their investment. (p. 717).

Indirect method A method of preparing a statement of cash flows in which net income is adjusted for items that did not affect cash, to determine net cash provided by operating activities. (p. 724).

Investing activities Cash flow activities that include (a) acquiring and disposing of investments and productive long-lived assets and (b) lending money and collecting on those loans. (p. 717).

Operating activities Cash flow activities that include the cash effects of transactions that create revenues and expenses and thus enter into the determination of net income. (p. 717).

Statement of cash flows A financial statement that provides information about the cash receipts and cash payments of an entity during a period, classified as operating, investing, and financing activities, in a format that reconciles the beginning and ending cash balances. (p. 717).

APPENDIX *Using a Work Sheet to Prepare the Statement of Cash Flows—Indirect Method*

When preparing a statement of cash flows, numerous adjustments of net income may be necessary. In such cases, **a work sheet is often used to assemble and classify the data that will appear on the statement**. The work sheet is merely an aid in the preparation of the statement. Its use is optional. The skeleton format of the work sheet for preparation of the statement of cash flows is shown in Illustration 18A-1.

STUDY OBJECTIVE 6

Explain the guidelines and procedural steps in using a work sheet to prepare the statement of cash flows using the indirect method.

Illustration 18A-1

Format of work sheet

XYZ COMPANY
Work Sheet
Statement of Cash Flows
For the Year Ended . . .

Balance Sheet Accounts	End of Last Year Balances	Reconciling Items Debits	Reconciling Items Credits	End of Current Year Balances
Debit balance accounts	XX	XX	XX	XX
	XX	XX	XX	XX
Totals	XXX			XXX
Credit balance accounts	XX	XX	XX	XX
	XX	XX	XX	XX
Totals	XXX			XXX
Statement of Cash Flows Effects				
Operating activities				
Net income		XX		
Adjustments to net income		XX	XX	
Investing activities				
Receipts and payments		XX	XX	
Financing activities				
Receipts and payments		XX	XX	
Totals		XXX	XXX	
Increase (decrease) in cash		(XX)	XX	
Totals		XXX	XXX	

The following guidelines are important in using a work sheet.

1. In the balance sheet accounts section, **accounts with debit balances are listed separately from those with credit balances.** This means, for example, that Accumulated Depreciation is listed under credit balances and not as a contra account under debit balances. The beginning and ending balances of each account are entered in the appropriate columns. The transactions that caused the change in the account balance during the year are entered as reconciling items in the two middle columns.

   After all reconciling items have been entered, each line pertaining to a balance sheet account should "foot across." That is, the beginning balance plus or minus the reconciling item(s) must equal the ending balance. When this agreement exists for all balance sheet accounts, all changes in account balances have been reconciled.

2. The bottom portion of the work sheet consists of the operating, investing, and financing activities sections. It provides the information necessary to prepare the formal statement of cash flows. **Inflows of cash are entered as debits in the reconciling columns. Outflows of cash are entered as credits in the reconciling columns.** Thus, in this section, the sale of equipment for cash at book value is entered as a debit under investing activities. Similarly, the purchase of land for cash is entered as a credit under investing activities.

3. **The reconciling items shown in the work sheet are not entered in any journal or posted to any account.** They do not represent either adjustments or corrections of the balance sheet accounts. They are used only to facilitate the preparation of the statement of cash flows.

PREPARING THE WORK SHEET

As in the case of work sheets illustrated in earlier chapters, the preparation of a work sheet involves a series of prescribed steps. The steps in this case are:

1. Enter in the balance sheet accounts section the balance sheet accounts and their beginning and ending balances.

2. Enter in the reconciling columns of the work sheet the data that explain the changes in the balance sheet accounts other than cash and their effects on the statement of cash flows.

3. Enter on the cash line and at the bottom of the work sheet the increase or decrease in cash. This entry should enable the totals of the reconciling columns to be in agreement.

To illustrate the preparation of a work sheet, we will use the 2003 data for Computer Services Company. Your familiarity with these data should help you understand the use of a work sheet. For ease of reference, the comparative balance sheets, income statement, and selected data for 2003 are presented in Illustrations 18A-2 and 18A-3.

Illustration 18A-2

Comparative balance sheets, 2003, with increases and decreases

COMPUTER SERVICES COMPANY
Comparative Balance Sheets
December 31

Assets	**2003**	**2002**	**Change Increase/Decrease**
Cash	$ 56,000	$34,000	$ 22,000 Increase
Accounts receivable	20,000	30,000	10,000 Decrease
Prepaid expenses	4,000	–0–	4,000 Increase
Land	130,000	–0–	130,000 Increase
Building	160,000	–0–	160,000 Increase
Accumulated depreciation—building	(11,000)	–0–	11,000 Increase
Equipment	27,000	10,000	17,000 Increase
Accumulated depreciation—equipment	(3,000)	–0–	3,000 Increase
Totals	$383,000	$74,000	
Liabilities and Stockholders' Equity			
Accounts payable	$ 59,000	$ 4,000	55,000 Increase
Bonds payable	130,000	–0–	130,000 Increase
Common stock	50,000	50,000	–0–
Retained earnings	144,000	20,000	124,000 Increase
Totals	$383,000	$74,000	

Illustration 18A-3

Income statement and additional information, 2003

COMPUTER SERVICES COMPANY
Income Statement
For the Year Ended December 31, 2003

Revenues		$507,000
Operating expenses (excluding depreciation)	$261,000	
Depreciation expense	15,000	
Loss on sale of equipment	3,000	279,000
Income from operations		228,000
Income tax expense		89,000
Net income		$139,000

Additional information:

1. In 2003, the company declared and paid a $15,000 cash dividend.
2. The company obtained land through the issuance of $130,000 of long-term bonds.
3. A building costing $160,000 was purchased for cash. Equipment costing $25,000 was also purchased for cash.
4. During 2003, the company sold equipment with a book value of $7,000 (cost $8,000, less accumulated depreciation $1,000) for $4,000 cash.

DETERMINING THE RECONCILING ITEMS

Several approaches may be used to determine the reconciling items. For example, the changes affecting net cash provided by operating activities can be completed first, and then the effects of financing and investing transactions can be determined. Or, the balance sheet accounts can be analyzed in the order in which they are listed on the work sheet. We will follow this latter approach for Computer Services, except for cash. As indicated above, **cash is handled last.**

Accounts Receivable

The decrease of $10,000 in accounts receivable means that cash collections from revenues are higher than the revenues reported in the income statement. To convert net income to net cash provided by operating activities, the decrease of $10,000 is added to net income. The entry in the reconciling columns of the work sheet is:

(a)	Operating—Decrease in Accounts Receivable	10,000	
	Accounts Receivable		10,000

Prepaid Expenses

An increase of $4,000 in prepaid expenses means that expenses deducted in determining net income are less than expenses that were paid in cash. The increase of $4,000 must be deducted from net income in determining net cash provided by operating activities. The work sheet entry is:

(b)	Prepaid Expenses	4,000	
	Operating—Increase in Prepaid Expenses		4,000

Land

HELPFUL HINT
These amounts are asterisked in the work sheet to indicate that they result from a significant noncash transaction.

The increase in land of $130,000 resulted from a purchase through the issuance of long-term bonds. This transaction should be reported as a significant noncash investing and financing activity. The work sheet entry is:

(c)	Land	130,000	
	Bonds Payable		130,000

Building

The cash purchase of a building for $160,000 is an investing activity cash outflow. The entry in the reconciling columns of the work sheet is:

(d)	Building	160,000	
	Investing—Purchase of Building		160,000

Equipment

The increase in equipment of $17,000 resulted from a cash purchase of $25,000 and the sale of equipment costing $8,000. The book value of the equipment was $7,000, the cash proceeds were $4,000, and a loss of $3,000 was recorded. The work sheet entries are:

(e)	Equipment	25,000	
	Investing—Purchase of Equipment		25,000
(f)	Investing—Sale of Equipment	4,000	
	Operating—Loss on Sale of Equipment	3,000	
	Accumulated Depreciation—Equipment	1,000	
	Equipment		8,000

Accounts Payable

The increase of $55,000 in accounts payable must be added to net income to determine net cash provided by operating activities. The following work sheet entry is made.

(g)	Operating—Increase in Accounts Payable	55,000	
	Accounts Payable		55,000

Bonds Payable

The increase of $130,000 in this account resulted from the issuance of bonds for land. This is a significant noncash investing and financing activity. Work sheet entry (c) above is the only entry necessary.

Accumulated Depreciation—Building, and Accumulated Depreciation—Equipment

The increases in these accounts of $11,000 and $4,000, respectively, resulted from depreciation expense. Depreciation expense is a **noncash charge that must be added to net income** to determine net cash provided by operating activities. The work sheet entries are:

(h)	Operating—Depreciation Expense—Building	11,000	
	Accumulated Depreciation—Building		11,000
(i)	Operating—Depreciation Expense—Equipment	4,000	
	Accumulated Depreciation—Equipment		4,000

Retained Earnings

The $124,000 increase in retained earnings resulted from net income of $139,000 and the declaration and payment of a $15,000 cash dividend. Net income is included in net cash provided by operating activities, and the dividends are a financing activity cash outflow. The entries in the reconciling columns of the work sheet are:

(j)	Operating—Net Income	139,000	
	Retained Earnings		139,000
(k)	Retained Earnings	15,000	
	Financing—Payment of Dividends		15,000

Disposition of Change in Cash

The firm's cash increased $22,000 in 2003. The final entry on the work sheet, therefore, is:

(l)	Cash	22,000	
	Increase in Cash		22,000

As shown in the work sheet, the increase in cash is entered in the reconciling credit column as a **balancing** amount. This entry should complete the reconciliation of the changes in the balance sheet accounts. Also, it should permit the totals of the reconciling columns to be in agreement. When all changes have been explained and the reconciling columns are in agreement, the reconciling columns are ruled to complete the work sheet. The completed work sheet for Computer Services Company is shown in Illustration 18A-4.

Illustration 18A-4

Completed work sheet—indirect method

COMPUTER SERVICES COMPANY
Work Sheet
Statement of Cash Flows
For the Year Ended December 31, 2003

Balance Sheet Accounts	Balance 12/31/02	Reconciling Items Debit	Reconciling Items Credit	Balance 12/31/03
Debits				
Cash	34,000	(l) 22,000		56,000
Accounts receivable	30,000		(a) 10,000	20,000
Prepaid expenses	–0–	(b) 4,000		4,000
Land	–0–	(c) 130,000*		130,000
Building	–0–	(d) 160,000		160,000
Equipment	10,000	(e) 25,000	(f) 8,000	27,000
Total	74,000			397,000
Credits				
Accounts payable	4,000		(g) 55,000	59,000
Bonds payable	–0–		(c) 130,000*	130,000
Accumulated depreciation—building	–0–		(h) 11,000	11,000
Accumulated depreciation—equipment	–0–	(f) 1,000	(i) 4,000	3,000
Common stock	50,000			50,000
Retained earnings	20,000	(k) 15,000	(j) 139,000	144,000
Total	74,000			397,000
Statement of Cash Flows Effects				
Operating activities				
Net income		(j) 139,000		
Decrease in accounts receivable		(a) 10,000		
Increase in prepaid expenses			(b) 4,000	
Increase in accounts payable		(g) 55,000		
Depreciation expense—building		(h) 11,000		
Depreciation expense—equipment		(i) 4,000		
Loss on sale of equipment		(f) 3,000		
Investing activities				
Purchase of building			(d) 160,000	
Purchase of equipment			(e) 25,000	
Sale of equipment		(f) 4,000		
Financing activities				
Payment of dividends			(k) 15,000	
Totals		583,000	561,000	
Increase in cash			(l) 22,000	
Totals		583,000	583,000	

*Significant noncash investing and financing activity.

PREPARING THE STATEMENT

The statement of cash flows is prepared primarily from the data that appear in the work sheet under "Statement of Cash Flows Effects." The reconciling columns should also be scanned for any asterisked items that designate significant noncash activities. The formal statement was shown in Illustration 18-17.

SUMMARY OF STUDY OBJECTIVE FOR APPENDIX

6. *Explain the guidelines and procedural steps in using a work sheet to prepare the statement of cash flows using the indirect method.* When there are numerous adjustments, a work sheet can be a helpful tool in preparing the statement of cash flows. Key guidelines for using a work sheet are: (1) List accounts with debit balances separately from those with credit balances. (2) In the reconciling columns in the bottom portion of the work sheet, show cash inflows as debits and cash outflows as credits. (3) Do not enter reconciling items in any journal or account, but use them only to help prepare the statement of cash flows.

The steps in preparing the work sheet are: (1) Enter beginning and ending balances of balance sheet accounts. (2) Enter debits and credits in reconciling columns. (3) Enter the increase or decrease in cash in two places as a balancing amount.

***Note:** All **asterisked** Questions, Exercises, and Problems relate to material in the appendix to the chapter.

Chapter 18 Self-Test

SELF-STUDY QUESTIONS

Answers are at the end of the chapter.

(SO 1) **1.** Which of the following is *incorrect* about the statement of cash flows?
a. It is a fourth basic financial statement.
b. It provides information about cash receipts and cash payments of an entity during a period.
c. It reconciles the ending cash account balance to the balance per the bank statement.
d. It provides information about the operating, investing, and financing activities of the business.

(SO 2) **2.** The statement of cash flows classifies cash receipts and cash payments by the following activities:
a. operating and nonoperating.
b. investing, financing, and operating.
c. financing, operating, and nonoperating.
d. investing, financing, and nonoperating.

(SO 2) **3.** An example of a cash flow from an operating activity is:
a. payment of cash to lenders for interest.
b. receipt of cash from the sale of capital stock.
c. payment of cash dividends to the company's stockholders.
d. None of the above.

(SO 2) **4.** An example of a cash flow from an investing activity is:
a. receipt of cash from the issuance of bonds payable.
b. payment of cash to repurchase outstanding capital stock.
c. receipt of cash from the sale of equipment.
d. payment of cash to suppliers for inventory.

(SO 2) **5.** Cash dividends paid to stockholders are classified on the statement of cash flows as:
a. operating activities.
b. investing activities.
c. a combination of the above.
d. financing activities.

6. An example of a cash flow from a financing activity is: (SO 2)
a. receipt of cash from sale of land.
b. issuance of debt for cash.
c. purchase of equipment for cash.
d. None of the above.

7. Which of the following about the statement of cash flows (SO 2) is *incorrect?*
a. The direct method may be used to report cash provided by operations.
b. The statement shows the cash provided (used) for three categories of activity.
c. The operating section is the last section of the statement.
d. The indirect method may be used to report cash provided by operations.

Questions 8 and 9 apply only to the indirect method.

8. Net income is $132,000. During the year, accounts (SO 3) payable increased $10,000, inventory decreased $6,000, and accounts receivable increased $12,000. Under the indirect method, net cash provided by operations is:
a. $102,000.
b. $112,000.
c. $124,000.
d. $136,000.

9. Noncash charges that are added back to net income in (SO 3) determining cash provided by operations under the indirect method do *not* include:
a. depreciation expense.

b. an increase in inventory.
c. amortization expense.
d. loss on sale of equipment.

Questions 10 and 11 apply only to the direct method.

(SO 4) **10.** The beginning balance in accounts receivable is $44,000. The ending balance is $42,000. Sales during the period are $129,000. Cash receipts from customers are:
a. $127,000.
b. $129,000.
c. $131,000.
d. $141,000.

(SO 4) **11.** Which of the following items is reported on a cash flow statement prepared by the direct method?
a. Loss on sale of building.
b. Increase in accounts receivable.
c. Depreciation expense.
d. Cash payments to suppliers.

12. The statement of cash flows should *not* be used to evaluate an entity's ability to: (SO 3)
a. earn net income.
b. generate future cash flows.
c. pay dividends.
d. meet obligations.

***13.** In a work sheet for the statement of cash flows, a decrease in accounts receivable is entered in the reconciling columns as a credit to Accounts Receivable and a debit in the: (SO 5)
a. investing activities section.
b. operating activities section.
c. financing activities section.
d. None of the above.

THE NAVIGATOR

QUESTIONS

1. (a) What is the statement of cash flows? (b) Alice Weiseman maintains that the statement of cash flows is an optional financial statement. Do you agree? Explain.
2. What questions about cash are answered by the statement of cash flows?
3. What are "cash equivalents"? How do cash equivalents affect the statement of cash flows?
4. Distinguish among the three types of activities reported in the statement of cash flows.
5. What are the major sources (inflows) of cash in a statement of cash flows? What are the major uses (outflows) of cash?
6. Why is it important to disclose certain noncash transactions? How should they be disclosed?
7. Wilma Flintstone and Barny Rublestone were discussing the presentation format of the statement of cash flows of Rock Candy Co. At the bottom of Rock Candy's statement of cash flows was a separate section entitled "Noncash investing and financing activities." Give three examples of significant noncash transactions that would be reported in this section.
8. Why is it necessary to use comparative balance sheets, a current income statement, and certain transaction data in preparing a statement of cash flows?
9. Contrast the advantages and disadvantages of the direct and indirect methods. Are both methods acceptable? Which method is preferred by the FASB? Which method is more popular?
10. When the total cash inflows exceed the total cash outflows in the statement of cash flows, how and where is this excess identified?
11. Describe the indirect method for determining net cash provided by operating activities.
12. Why is it necessary to convert accrual-based net income to cash-basis income when preparing a statement of cash flows?
13. The president of Styx Company is puzzled. During the year, the company experienced a net loss of $800,000, yet its cash increased $300,000 during the same period. Explain to the president how this situation could occur.
14. Identify five items that are adjustments to reconcile net income to net cash provided by operating activities under the indirect method.
15. Why and how is depreciation expense reported in a statement prepared using the indirect method?
16. Why is the statement of cash flows useful?
17. During 2002, Joe Pesci Company converted $1,600,000 of its total $2,000,000 of bonds payable into common stock. Indicate how the transaction would be reported on a statement of cash flows, if at all.
18. Describe the direct method for determining net cash provided by operating activities.
19. Give the formulas under the direct method for computing (a) cash receipts from customers and (b) cash payments to suppliers.
20. Kim Bassinger Inc. reported sales of $2 million for 2002. Accounts receivable decreased $200,000 and accounts payable increased $325,000. Compute cash receipts from customers, assuming that the receivable and payable transactions related to operations.
21. Why is depreciation expense not reported in the direct-method cash flow from operating activities section?
22. Give an example of one accrual-based ratio and one cash-based ratio to measure these characteristics of a company: (a) liquidity, (b) solvency, and (c) profitability.

*23. Why is it advantageous to use a work sheet when preparing a statement of cash flows? Is a work sheet required to prepare a statement of cash flows?

BRIEF EXERCISES

BE18-1 Titanic Co. reported net income of $2.5 million in 2002. Depreciation for the year was $260,000, accounts receivable decreased $350,000, and accounts payable decreased $310,000. Compute net cash provided by operating activities using the indirect approach.

Compute cash provided by operating activities—indirect method.
(SO 3)

BE18-2 The net income for Robin Williams Co. for 2002 was $250,000. For 2002, depreciation on plant assets was $60,000, and the company incurred a loss on sale of plant assets of $10,000. Compute net cash provided by operating activities under the indirect method.

Compute cash provided by operating activities—indirect method.
(SO 3)

BE18-3 Each of the following items must be considered in preparing a statement of cash flows for Rudy Boesch Co. for the year ended December 31, 2002. For each item, state how it should be shown in the statement of cash flows for 2002.

Indicate statement presentation of selected transactions.
(SO 2)

(a) Issued bonds for $200,000 cash.
(b) Purchased equipment for $180,000 cash.
(c) Sold land costing $20,000 for $20,000 cash.
(d) Declared and paid a $50,000 cash dividend.

BE18-4 The comparative balance sheets for Survivor Company show the following changes in noncash current asset accounts: accounts receivable decrease $75,000, prepaid expenses increase $12,000, and inventories increase $30,000. Compute net cash provided by operating activities using the indirect method, assuming that net income is $220,000.

Compute net cash provided by operating activities using indirect method.
(SO 3)

BE18-5 Classify the following items as an operating, investing, or financing activity. Assume all items involve cash unless there is information to the contrary.

Classify items by activities.
(SO 2)

(a) Purchase of equipment.
(b) Sale of building.
(c) Redemption of bonds.
(d) Depreciation.
(e) Payment of dividends.
(f) Issuance of capital stock.

BE18-6 Kate Winslet Co. has accounts receivable of $14,000 at January 1, 2002, and $24,000 at December 31, 2002. Sales revenues for 2002 were $470,000. What is the amount of cash receipts from customers in 2002?

Compute receipts from customers using direct method.
(SO 4)

BE18-7 Amistad Company reported income taxes of $90,000 in its 2002 income statement and income taxes payable of $14,000 at December 31, 2001 and $9,000 at December 31, 2002. What amount of cash payments was made for income taxes during 2002?

Compute cash payments for income taxes using direct method.
(SO 4)

BE18-8 DiCaprio Company reports operating expenses of $100,000 excluding depreciation expense of $15,000 for 2002. During the year prepaid expenses decreased $6,600, and accrued expenses payable increased $2,400. Compute the cash payments for operating expenses in 2002.

Compute cash payments for operating expenses using direct method.
(SO 4)

BE18-9 The T accounts for Equipment and the related Accumulated Depreciation for Sharon Stone Company at the end of 2002 are as follows.

Determine cash received in sale of equipment.
(SO 3, 4)

Equipment

Beg. bal.	80,000	Disposals	22,000
Acquisitions	41,600		
End. bal.	99,600		

Accumulated Depreciation

Disposals	5,500	Beg. bal.	44,500
		Depr.	12,000
		End. bal.	51,000

Sharon Stone Company's income statement reported a loss on the sale of equipment of $4,900. What amount was reported on the statement of cash flows as "cash flow from sale of equipment"?

BE18-10 The following T account is a summary of the cash account of Amy Company.

Identify financing activity transactions.
(SO 2)

Cash (Summary Form)

Balance, 1/1/02	8,000		
Receipts from customers	364,000	Payments for goods	200,000
Dividends on stock investments	6,000	Payments for operating expenses	140,000
Proceeds from sale of equipment	36,000	Interest paid	10,000
Proceeds from issuance of bonds payable	200,000	Taxes paid	8,000
		Dividends paid	45,000
Balance, 12/31/02	211,000		

For Amy Company what amount of net cash provided (used) by financing activities should be reported in the statement of cash flows?

Calculate cash-based ratios. (SO 5)

BE18-11 Matt Damon Company reported cash from operations of $450,000, net sales $1,500,000, average current liabilities of $150,000, and average total liabilities of $225,000. Calculate these ratios.

(a) Current cash debt coverage ratio.
(b) Cash debt coverage ratio.
(c) Cash return on sales ratio.

Indicate entries in work sheet. (SO 6)

***BE18-12** Using the data in BE18-8, indicate how the changes in prepaid expenses and accrued expenses payable should be entered in the reconciling columns of a work sheet. Assume that beginning balances were: prepaid expenses $18,600 and accrued expenses payable $8,200.

EXERCISES

Classify transactions by type of activity. (SO 2)

E18-1 Barbara Eden Corporation had the following transactions during 2002.

1. Issued $50,000 par value common stock for cash.
2. Collected $16,000 of accounts receivable.
3. Declared and paid a cash dividend of $25,000.
4. Sold a long-term investment with a cost of $15,000 for $15,000 cash.
5. Issued $200,000 par value common stock upon conversion of bonds having a face value of $200,000.
6. Paid $18,000 on accounts payable.
7. Purchased a machine for $30,000, giving a long-term note in exchange.

Instructions
Analyze the transactions above and indicate whether each transaction resulted in a cash flow from **(a)** operating activities, **(b)** investing activities, **(c)** financing activities, or **(d)** noncash investing and financing activities.

Prepare the operating activities section—indirect method. (SO 3)

E18-2 Porky Company reported net income of $195,000 for 2002. Porky also reported depreciation expense of $35,000, and a loss of $5,000 on the sale of equipment. The comparative balance sheets show an increase in accounts receivable of $15,000 for the year, an $8,000 increase in accounts payable, and a decrease in prepaid expenses $4,000.

Instructions
Prepare the operating activities section of the statement of cash flows for 2002 using the indirect method.

Prepare the operating activities section—indirect method. (SO 3)

E18-3 The current sections of Depeche Mode Co. balance sheets at December 31, 2001 and 2002, are presented below.

DEPECHE MODE CO.
Comparative Balance Sheets (partial)
December 31

	2002	2001
Current assets		
Cash	$105,000	$ 99,000
Accounts receivable	110,000	89,000
Inventory	171,000	186,000
Prepaid expenses	27,000	32,000
Total current assets	$413,000	$406,000
Current liabilities		
Accrued expenses payable	$ 15,000	$ 5,000
Accounts payable	$ 85,000	$ 92,000
Total current liabilities	$100,000	$ 97,000

Depeche Mode's net income for 2002 was $163,000. Depreciation expense was $30,000.

Instructions

Prepare the net cash provided by operating activities section of Depeche Mode's statement of cash flows for the year ended December 31, 2002, using the indirect method.

Prepare a partial statement of cash flows—indirect method. (SO 3)

E18-4 Presented below are three accounts that appear in the general ledger of Wesley Snipes Co. during 2002.

Equipment

Date		Debit	Credit	Balance
Jan. 1	Balance			160,000
July 31	Purchase of equipment	70,000		230,000
Sept. 2	Cost of equipment constructed	53,000		283,000
Nov. 10	Cost of equipment sold		45,000	238,000

Accumulated Depreciation—Equipment

Date		Debit	Credit	Balance
Jan. 1	Balance			71,000
Nov. 10	Accumulated depreciation on equipment sold	30,000		41,000
Dec. 31	Depreciation for year		24,000	65,000

Retained Earnings

Date		Debit	Credit	Balance
Jan. 1	Balance			105,000
Aug. 23	Dividends (cash)	14,000		91,000
Dec. 31	Net income		57,000	148,000

Instructions

From the postings in the accounts above, indicate how the information is reported on a statement of cash flows by preparing a partial statement of cash flows using the indirect method. The loss on sale of equipment was $4,000.

Prepare a statement of cash flows—indirect method. (SO 3, 5)

E18-5 Comparative balance sheets for Eddie Murphy Company are presented below.

EDDIE MURPHY COMPANY
Comparative Balance Sheets
December 31

Assets	**2002**	**2001**
Cash	$ 63,000	$ 22,000
Accounts receivable	85,000	76,000
Inventories	180,000	189,000
Land	75,000	100,000
Equipment	260,000	200,000
Accumulated depreciation	(66,000)	(42,000)
Total	$597,000	$545,000
Liabilities and Stockholders' Equity		
Accounts payable	$ 34,000	$ 47,000
Bonds payable	150,000	200,000
Common stock ($1 par)	214,000	164,000
Retained earnings	199,000	134,000
Total	$597,000	$545,000

Additional information:

1. Net income for 2002 was $125,000.
2. Cash dividends of $60,000 were declared and paid.
3. Bonds payable amounting to $50,000 were redeemed for cash $50,000.
4. Common stock was issued for $50,000 cash.

5. Depreciation expense was $24,000.
6. Sales for the year were $978,000.

Instructions

(a) Prepare a statement of cash flows for 2002 using the indirect method.
(b) Compute the following cash-basis ratios.
   (1) Current cash debt coverage ratio.
   (2) Cash return on sales ratio.
   (3) Cash debt coverage ratio.

Classify transactions by type of activity.
(SO 2)

E18-6 An analysis of comparative balance sheets, the current year's income statement, and the general ledger accounts of Oprah Winfrey Corp. uncovered the following items. Assume all items involve cash unless there is information to the contrary.

1. Issuance of capital stock.
2. Amortization of patent.
3. Issuance of bonds for land.
4. Payment of interest on notes payable.
5. Conversion of bonds into common stock.
6. Sale of land at a loss.
7. Receipt of dividends on investment in stock.
8. Purchase of land.
9. Payment of dividends.
10. Sale of building at book value.
11. Exchange of land for patent.
12. Depreciation.
13. Redemption of bonds.
14. Receipt of interest on notes receivable.

Instructions

Indicate how the above items should be classified in the statement of cash flows using the following four major classifications: operating activity (indirect method), investing activity, financing activity, and significant noncash investing and financing activity.

Compute cash provided by operating activities—direct method.
(SO 4)

E18-7 Satchmo Company has just completed its first year of operations on December 31, 2002. Its initial income statement showed that Satchmo had revenues of $137,000 and operating expenses of $88,000. Accounts receivable at year-end were $42,000. Accounts payable at year-end were $33,000. Assume that accounts payable related to operating expenses. Ignore income taxes.

Instructions

Compute net cash provided by operating activities using the direct method.

Compute cash payments—direct method.
(SO 4)

E18-8 The income statement for Mel Gibson Company shows cost of goods sold $325,000 and operating expenses (exclusive of depreciation) $250,000. The comparative balance sheets for the year show that inventory increased $6,000, prepaid expenses decreased $6,000, accounts payable (merchandise suppliers) decreased $8,000, and accrued expenses payable increased $4,000.

Instructions

Using the direct method, compute (a) cash payments to suppliers and (b) cash payments for operating expenses.

Compute cash flow from operating activities—direct method.
(SO 2, 4)

E18-9 The 2002 accounting records of Winona Ryder Co. reveal the following transactions and events.

Payment of interest	$ 6,000	Collection of accounts receivable	$180,000
Cash sales	38,000	Payment of salaries and wages	65,000
Receipt of dividend revenue	14,000	Depreciation expense	18,000
Payment of income taxes	15,000	Proceeds from sale of aircraft	812,000
Net income	38,000	Purchase of equipment for cash	22,000
Payment of accounts payable for merchandise	90,000	Loss on sale of aircraft	3,000
Payment for land	74,000	Payment of dividends	14,000
		Payment of operating expenses	20,000

Instructions

Prepare the cash flows from operating activities section using the direct method. (Not all of the above items will be used.)

Calculate cash flows—direct method.
(SO 4)

E18-10 The following information is taken from the 2002 general ledger of Richard Gere Company.

Rent	Rent expense	$ 33,000
	Prepaid rent, January 1	7,900
	Prepaid rent, December 31	3,000
Salaries	Salaries expense	$ 54,000
	Salaries payable, January 1	5,000
	Salaries payable, December 31	8,000

Sales	Revenue from sales	$180,000
	Accounts receivable, January 1	12,000
	Accounts receivable, December 31	7,000

Instructions

In each of the above cases, compute the amount that should be reported in the operating activities section of the statement of cash flows using the direct method.

E18-11 Presented here is information for two companies in the same industry: Morgan Corporation and Erin Corporation.

Compare two companies by using cash-based ratios. (SO 5)

	Morgan Corporation	Erin Corporation
Cash provided by operations	$300,000	$300,000
Average current liabilities	50,000	100,000
Average total liabilities	200,000	250,000
Net income	200,000	200,000
Sales	400,000	800,000

Instructions

Using the cash-based ratios presented in this chapter, compare the (a) liquidity, (b) solvency, and (c) profitability of the two companies.

***E18-12** Information for Eddie Murphy Company is presented in E18-5.

Prepare a work sheet. (SO 6)

Instructions

Use the data in E18-5 to prepare a work sheet for a statement of cash flows for 2002. Enter the reconciling items directly on the work sheet, presenting the entries alphabetically.

PROBLEMS: SET A

P18-1A The income statement of Rebecca Sherrick Company is shown below.

Prepare the operating activities section—indirect method. (SO 3)

REBECCA SHERRICK COMPANY
Income Statement
For the Year Ended December 31, 2002

Sales		$7,100,000
Cost of goods sold		
Beginning inventory	$1,700,000	
Purchases	5,430,000	
Goods available for sale	7,130,000	
Ending inventory	1,920,000	
Cost of goods sold		5,210,000
Gross profit		1,890,000
Operating expenses		
Selling expenses	380,000	
Administrative expense	525,000	
Depreciation expense	75,000	
Amortization expense	30,000	1,010,000
Net income		$ 880,000

Additional information:

1. Accounts receivable increased $490,000 during the year.
2. Prepaid expenses increased $170,000 during the year.
3. Accounts payable to merchandise suppliers increased $40,000 during the year.
4. Accrued expenses payable decreased $180,000 during the year.

Instructions

Prepare the operating activities section of the statement of cash flows for the year ended December 31, 2002, for Rebecca Sherrick Company using the indirect method.

Net cash used $35,000

Prepare the operating activities section—direct method.
(SO 4)

Net cash used $35,000

P18-2A Data for Rebecca Sherrick Company are presented in P18-1A.

Instructions

Prepare the operating activities section of the statement of cash flows using the direct method.

Prepare the operating activities section—direct method.
(SO 4)

P18-3A The income statement of Dreamworks International Co. for the year ended December 31, 2002, reported the following condensed information.

Revenue from fees	$470,000
Operating expenses	280,000
Income from operations	190,000
Income tax expense	47,000
Net income	$143,000

Dreamworks' balance sheet contained the following comparative data at December 31.

	2002	2001
Accounts receivable	$55,000	$40,000
Accounts payable	32,000	41,000
Income taxes payable	6,000	4,000

Dreamworks has no depreciable assets. (Accounts payable pertains to operating expenses.)

Instructions

Net cash provided $121,000

Prepare the operating activities section of the statement of cash flows using the direct method.

Prepare the operating activities section—indirect method.
(SO 3)
Net cash provided $121,000

P18-4A Data for Dreamworks International Co. are presented in P18-3A.

Instructions

Prepare the operating activities section of the statement of cash flows using the indirect method.

Prepare a statement of cash flows—indirect method.
(SO 3, 5)

P18-5A The financial statements of Jim Carrey Company appear below.

JIM CARREY COMPANY
Comparative Balance Sheets
December 31

Assets		2002		2001
Cash		$ 24,000		$ 13,000
Accounts receivable		20,000		14,000
Merchandise inventory		38,000		35,000
Property, plant, and equipment	$70,000		$78,000	
Less: Accumulated depreciation	(30,000)	40,000	(24,000)	54,000
Total		$122,000		$116,000
Liabilities and Stockholders' Equity				
Accounts payable		$ 26,000		$ 33,000
Income taxes payable		15,000		20,000
Bonds payable		20,000		10,000
Common stock		25,000		25,000
Retained earnings		36,000		28,000
Total		$122,000		$116,000

JIM CARREY COMPANY
Income Statement
For the Year Ended December 31, 2002

Sales		$240,000
Cost of goods sold		180,000
Gross profit		60,000
Selling expenses	$24,000	
Administrative expenses	10,000	34,000
Income from operations		26,000
Interest expense		2,000
Income before income taxes		24,000
Income tax expense		7,000
Net income		$ 17,000

Additional information:

1. Dividends of $9,000 were declared and paid.
2. During the year equipment was sold for $10,000 cash. This equipment cost $15,000 originally and had a book value of $10,000 at the time of sale.
3. All depreciation expense, $11,000, is in the selling expense category.
4. All sales and purchases are on account.
5. Additional equipment was purchased for $7,000 cash.

Instructions

(a) Net cash provided by operating activities $7,000

(a) Prepare a statement of cash flows using the indirect method.
(b) Compute the following cash-basis ratios.
  (1) Current cash debt coverage ratio.
  (2) Cash return on sales ratio.
  (3) Cash debt coverage ratio.

Prepare a statement of cash flows—direct method
(SO 4, 5)

P18-6A Data for the Jim Carrey Company are presented in P18-5A. Further analysis reveals the following.

1. Accounts payable pertains to merchandise creditors.
2. All operating expenses except for depreciation are paid in cash.

Instructions

(a) Prepare a statement of cash flows using the direct method.
(b) Compute the following cash-basis ratios.
  (1) Current cash debt coverage ratio.
  (2) Cash return on sales ratio.
  (3) Cash debt coverage ratio.

(a) Net cash provided by operating activities $7,000

Prepare a statement of cash flows—indirect method.
(SO 3)

P18-7A Condensed financial data of Tom Cruise Company appear below.

TOM CRUISE COMPANY
Comparative Balance Sheets
December 31

Assets	**2002**	**2001**
Cash	$ 92,700	$ 47,250
Accounts receivable	90,800	57,000
Inventories	121,900	102,650
Investments	84,500	87,000
Plant assets	250,000	205,000
Accumulated depreciation	(49,500)	(40,000)
	$590,400	$458,900

Liabilities and Stockholders' Equity	2002	2001
Accounts payable	$ 57,700	$ 48,280
Accrued expenses payable	12,100	18,830
Bonds payable	100,000	70,000
Common stock	250,000	200,000
Retained earnings	170,600	121,790
	$590,400	$458,900

TOM CRUISE COMPANY
Income Statement Data
For the Year Ended December 31, 2002

Sales		$297,500
Gain on sale of plant assets		8,750
		306,250
Less:		
Cost of goods sold	$99,460	
Operating expenses (excluding depreciation expense)	14,670	
Depreciation expense	49,700	
Income taxes	7,270	
Interest expense	2,940	174,040
Net income		$132,210

Additional information:

1. New plant assets costing $92,000 were purchased for cash during the year.
2. Investments were sold at cost.
3. Plant assets costing $47,000 were sold for $15,550, resulting in a gain of $8,750.
4. A cash dividend of $83,400 was declared and paid during the year.

Net cash provided by operating activities $122,800
Investing activities used $73,950

Instructions

Prepare a statement of cash flows using the indirect method.

Prepare a statement of cash flows—direct method.
(SO 4)
Cash receipts from customers $263,700
Investing activities used $73,950

P18-8A Data for Tom Cruise Company are presented in P18-7A. Further analysis reveals that accounts payable pertains to merchandise creditors.

Instructions

Prepare a statement of cash flows for Tom Cruise Company using the direct method.

Prepare a statement of cash flows—indirect method.
(SO 3, 5)

P18-9A Presented below are the comparative balance sheets for Nicolas Cage Company at December 31.

NICOLAS CAGE COMPANY
Comparative Balance Sheets
December 31

Assets	2002	2001
Cash	$ 45,000	$ 57,000
Accounts receivable	72,000	64,000
Inventory	132,000	140,000
Prepaid expenses	12,140	16,540
Land	125,000	150,000
Equipment	200,000	175,000
Accumulated depreciation—equipment	(60,000)	(42,000)
Building	250,000	250,000
Accumulated depreciation—building	(75,000)	(50,000)
	$701,140	$760,540

Liabilities and Stockholders' Equity	2002	2001
Accounts payable	$ 38,000	$ 45,000
Bonds payable	235,000	265,000
Common stock, $1 par	280,000	250,000
Retained earnings	148,140	200,540
	$701,140	$760,540

Additional information:

1. Operating expenses include depreciation expense of $70,000 and charges from prepaid expenses of $4,400.
2. Land was sold for cash at cost.
3. Cash dividends of $79,290 were paid.
4. Net income for 2002 was $26,890.
5. Equipment was purchased for $65,000 cash. In addition, equipment costing $40,000 with a book value of $13,000 was sold for $14,000 cash.
6. Bonds were converted at face value by issuing 30,000 shares of $1 par value common stock.
7. Net sales in 2002 were $367,000.

Instructions

(a) Prepare a statement of cash flows for 2002 using the indirect method.

(b) Compute the following cash-basis ratios for 2002.

(1) Current cash debt coverage ratio.

(2) Cash return on sales ratio.

(3) Cash debt coverage ratio.

(a) Net cash provided by operating activities $93,290

***P18-10A** Data for Tom Cruise Company are presented in P18-7A.

Prepare a work sheet
(SO 6)

Instructions

Prepare a work sheet for a statement of cash flows. Enter the reconciling items directly in the work sheet columns, identifying the debit and credit amounts alphabetically.

Total reconciling columns $610,210

PROBLEMS: SET B

P18-1B The income statement of Barbara Streisand Company is shown below.

Prepare the operating activities section—indirect method.
(SO 3)

BARBARA STREISAND COMPANY
Income Statement
For the Year Ended November 30, 2002

Sales		$6,900,000
Cost of goods sold		
Beginning inventory	$2,000,000	
Purchases	4,300,000	
Goods available for sale	6,300,000	
Ending inventory	1,600,000	
Cost of goods sold		4,700,000
Gross profit		2,200,000
Operating expenses		
Selling expenses	450,000	
Administrative expenses	700,000	1,150,000
Net income		$1,050,000

Additional information:

1. Accounts receivable decreased $280,000 during the year.
2. Prepaid expenses increased $150,000 during the year.
3. Accounts payable to suppliers of merchandise decreased $200,000 during the year.
4. Accrued expenses payable decreased $100,000 during the year.
5. Administrative expenses include depreciation expense of $70,000.

Net cash provided $1,350,000

Instructions

Prepare the operating activities section of the statement of cash flows for the year ended November 30, 2002, for Barbara Streisand Company using the indirect method.

Prepare the operating activities section—direct method.
(SO 4)
Net cash provided $1,350,000

P18-2B Data for Barbara Streisand Company are presented in P18-1B.

Instructions

Prepare the operating activities section of the statement of cash flows using the direct method.

Prepare the operating activities section—direct method.
(SO 4)

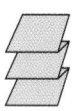

P18-3B George Clooney Company's income statement for the year ended December 31, 2002, contained the following condensed information.

Revenue from fees		$900,000
Operating expenses (excluding depreciation)	$624,000	
Depreciation expense	60,000	
Loss on sale of equipment	26,000	710,000
Income before income taxes		190,000
Income tax expense		40,000
Net income		$150,000

Clooney's balance sheet contained the following comparative data at December 31.

	2002	2001
Accounts receivable	$47,000	$57,000
Accounts payable	41,000	36,000
Income taxes payable	4,000	9,000

(Accounts payable pertains to operating expenses.)

Net cash provided $246,000

Instructions

Prepare the operating activities section of the statement of cash flows using the direct method.

Prepare the operating activities section—indirect method.
(SO 3)
Net cash provided $246,000

P18-4B Data for George Clooney Company are presented in P18-3B.

Instructions

Prepare the operating activities section of the statement of cash flows for George Clooney Company using the indirect method.

Prepare a statement of cash flows—indirect method.
(SO 3, 5)

P18-5B The financial statements of Frank B. Robinson Company appear below:

FRANK B. ROBINSON COMPANY
Comparative Balance Sheets
December 31

Assets	2002	2001
Cash	$ 29,000	$ 13,000
Accounts receivable	28,000	14,000
Merchandise inventory	25,000	35,000
Property, plant, and equipment	60,000	78,000
Accumulated depreciation	(20,000)	(24,000)
Total	$122,000	$116,000
Liabilities and Stockholders' Equity		
Accounts payable	$ 27,000	$ 23,000
Income taxes payable	5,000	8,000
Bonds payable	27,000	33,000
Common stock	18,000	14,000
Retained earnings	45,000	38,000
Total	$122,000	$116,000

FRANK B. ROBINSON COMPANY
Income Statement
For the Year Ended December 31, 2002

Sales		$220,000
Cost of goods sold		180,000
Gross profit		40,000
Selling expenses	$14,000	
Administrative expenses	10,000	24,000
Income from operations		16,000
Interest expense		2,000
Income before income taxes		14,000
Income tax expense		4,000
Net income		$ 10,000

Additional information:

1. Dividends declared and paid were $3,000.
2. During the year equipment was sold for $8,500 cash. This equipment cost $18,000 originally and had a book value of $8,500 at the time of sale.
3. All depreciation expense is in the selling expense category.
4. All sales and purchases are on account.

Instructions

(a) Prepare a statement of cash flows using the indirect method.
(b) Compute the following cash-basis ratios.
 (1) Current cash debt coverage ratio.
 (2) Cash return on sales ratio.
 (3) Cash debt coverage ratio.

(a) Net cash provided by operating activities $12,500

P18-6B Data for the Frank B. Robinson Company are presented in P18-5B. Further analysis reveals the following.

Prepare a statement of cash flows—direct method.
(SO 4, 5)

1. Accounts payable pertain to merchandise suppliers.
2. All operating expenses except for depreciation were paid in cash.

Instructions

(a) Prepare a statement of cash flows for Frank B. Robinson Company using the direct method.
(b) Compute the following cash-basis ratios.
 (1) Current cash debt coverage ratio.
 (2) Cash return on sales ratio.
 (3) Cash debt coverage ratio.

(a) Cash receipts from customers $206,000

P18-7B The financial statements of Bruce Willis Company appear below.

Prepare a statement of cash flows—indirect method.
(SO 3)

BRUCE WILLIS COMPANY
Comparative Balance Sheets
December 31

Assets	2002	2001
Cash	$ 23,000	$ 11,000
Accounts receivable	24,000	33,000
Merchandise inventory	20,000	29,000
Prepaid expenses	15,000	13,000
Land	40,000	40,000
Property, plant, and equipment	210,000	225,000
Less: Accumulated depreciation	(55,000)	(67,500)
Total	$277,000	$283,500

Liabilities and Stockholders' Equity	2002	2001
Accounts payable	$ 9,000	$ 18,500
Accrued expenses payable	9,500	7,500
Interest payable	1,000	1,500
Income taxes payable	3,000	2,000
Bonds payable	50,000	80,000
Common stock	125,000	105,000
Retained earnings	79,500	69,000
Total	$277,000	$283,500

BRUCE WILLIS COMPANY
Income Statement
For the Year Ended December 31, 2002

Revenues		
Sales	$600,000	
Gain on sale of plant assets	2,500	$602,500
Less: Expenses		
Cost of goods sold	500,000	
Operating expenses (excluding depreciation)	60,000	
Depreciation expense	7,500	
Interest expense	5,000	
Income tax expense	9,000	581,500
Net income		$ 21,000

Additional information:

1. Plant assets were sold at a sales price of $37,500.
2. Additional equipment was purchased at a cost of $40,000.
3. Dividends of $10,500 were paid.
4. All sales and purchases were on account.
5. Bonds were redeemed at face value.
6. Additional shares of stock were issued for cash.

Net cash provided by operating activities $35,000
Investing activities used $2,500

Instructions
Prepare a statement of cash flows for Bruce Willis Company for the year ended December 31, 2002, using the indirect method.

Prepare a statement of cash flows—direct method.
(SO 4)

P18-8B Data for Bruce Willis Company is presented in P18-7B. Further analysis reveals the following.

1. Accounts payable relates to merchandise creditors.
2. All operating expenses, except depreciation expense, were paid in cash.

Net cash provided by operating activities $35,000. Investing activities used $2,500

Instructions
Prepare a statement of cash flows for Bruce Willis Company for the year ended December 31, 2002, using the direct method.

Prepare a statement of cash flows—indirect method.
(SO 3, 5)

P18-9B Presented below are the comparative balance sheets for Dennis Weigle Company as of December 31.

DENNIS WEIGLE COMPANY
Comparative Balance Sheets
December 31

Assets	2002	2001
Cash	$ 39,000	$ 45,000
Accounts receivable	49,500	52,000
Inventory	151,450	142,000
Prepaid expenses	16,780	21,000
Land	100,000	130,000
Equipment	228,000	155,000
Accumulated depreciation—equipment	(45,000)	(35,000)
Building	200,000	200,000
Accumulated depreciation—building	(60,000)	(40,000)
	$679,730	$670,000

Liabilities and Stockholders' Equity		
Accounts payable	$ 38,730	$ 40,000
Bonds payable	250,000	300,000
Common stock, $1 par	200,000	150,000
Retained earnings	191,000	180,000
	$679,730	$670,000

Additional information:

1. Operating expenses include depreciation expense of $42,000.
2. Land was sold for cash at book value.
3. Cash dividends of $27,000 were paid.
4. Net income for 2002 was $38,000.
5. Equipment was purchased for $95,000 cash. In addition, equipment costing $22,000 with a book value of $10,000 was sold for $8,100 cash.
6. Bonds were converted at face value by issuing 50,000 shares of $1 par value common stock.
7. Net sales for 2002 totaled $420,000.

Instructions

(a) Prepare a statement of cash flows for the year ended December 31, 2002, using the indirect method.

(a) Net cash from operating activities $77,900

(b) Compute the following cash-basis ratios for 2002.
  (1) Current cash debt coverage ratio.
  (2) Cash return on sales ratio.
  (3) Cash debt coverage ratio.

***P18-10B** Data for Bruce Willis Company are presented in P18-7B.

Prepare a work sheet. (SO 6)

Instructions

Prepare a work sheet for a statement of cash flows for 2002. Enter the reconciling entries directly on the work sheet, presenting the entries alphabetically.

Total reconciling items $231,500

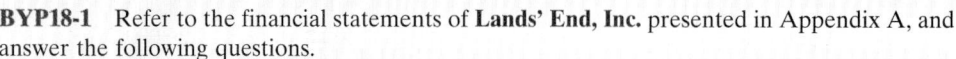

BROADENING YOUR PERSPECTIVE

FINANCIAL REPORTING AND ANALYSIS

FINANCIAL REPORTING PROBLEM: Lands' End, Inc.

BYP18-1 Refer to the financial statements of **Lands' End, Inc.** presented in Appendix A, and answer the following questions.

(a) What was the amount of net cash provided by operating activities for the year ended January 28, 2000? For the year ended January 29, 1999?

(b) What was the amount of increase or decrease in cash and cash equivalents for the year ended January 28, 2000? For the year ended January 29, 1999?

(c) Which method of computing net cash provided by operating activities does Lands' End use?

(d) From your analysis of the 2000 statement of cash flows, did the change in accounts receivable require or provide cash? Did the change in inventories require or provide cash? Did the change in accounts payable require or provide cash?

(e) What was the net outflow or inflow of cash from investing activities for the year ended January 28, 2000?

(f) What was the amount of interest paid in the year ended January 28, 2000? What was the amount of income taxes paid in the year ended January 28, 2000?

COMPARATIVE ANALYSIS PROBLEM: Lands' End vs. Abercrombie & Fitch

BYP18-2 **Lands' End's** financial statements are presented in Appendix A. **Abercrombie & Fitch's** financial statements are presented in Appendix B.

Instructions

(a) Based on the information contained in these financial statements, compute the following 2000 ratios for each company.

(1) Current cash debt coverage ratio.

(2) Cash return on sales ratio.

(3) Cash debt coverage ratio.

(b) What conclusions concerning the management of cash can be drawn from these data?

INTERPRETING FINANCIAL STATEMENTS: A Global Focus

BYP18-3 The statement of cash flows has become a commonly provided financial statement by companies throughout the world. It is interesting to note, however, that its format does vary across countries. The following statement of cash flows is from the 1998 financial statements of **Saint-Gobain** (Paris, France). Saint-Gobain, one of the top 100 industrial companies in the world, is a leading producer of flat glass, reinforcements, glass packaging, insulation, building materials, pipe, abrasives, high-performance plastics, and industrial ceramics.

Instructions

(a) What similarities to U.S. cash flow statements do you notice in terms of general format, as well as terminology?

(b) What differences do you notice in terms of general format, as well as terminology?

SAINT-GOBAIN

SAINT-GOBAIN GROUP
Consolidated Statements of Cash Flows

(in millions of euro)	1998	1997
Cash flow from operating activities		
Net operating income	1,096	920
Profit on sale of non-current assets	(394)	(307)
Depreciation and amortization (note 14)	1,136	1,037
Dividends from associated companies	74	43
Sources from operations	**1,912**	**1,693**
(Increase) decrease in stocks	(174)	(41)
(Increase) decrease in trade accounts receivable	(59)	(241)
Increase (decrease) in trade accounts payable	79	79
Changes in income taxes payable and deferred taxes	14	3
Change in provisions	(48)	4
Cash provided by operating activities	**1,724**	**1,497**
Cash flow from investing activities		
Acquisition of fixed assets	(1,288)	(1,353)
Investments in consolidated companies (note 2)	(1,349)	(850)
Investments in unconsolidated companies	(382)	(244)
Total expenditure on fixed assets and investments	**(3,019)**	**(2,447)**
Cash (debt) acquired (note 2)	(19)	(17)
Acquisition of treasury stock	(344)	(3)
Disposal of fixed and intangible assets	25	55
Disposal of investments	1,107	814
(Cash) debt disposed of (note 2)	3	(125)
(Increase) decrease in deferred charges and other intangible assets	(68)	(48)
(Increase) decrease in deposits, long term receivables	9	31
(Increase) decrease in receivables related to investing activities	(124)	37
Cash used for investing activities	**(2,430)**	**(1,703)**
Cash flow from financing activities		
Issue of share capital	105	265
Minority interests in share capital increases of subsidiaries	4	4
(Decrease) increase in long term debt	132	541
Dividends paid	(248)	(221)
Dividends paid to minority shareholders of consolidated subsidiaries	(44)	(82)
Cash provided by (used for) financing activities	**(51)**	**507**
Net effect of exchange rate fluctuations on cash and cash equivalents	(9)	(39)
Increase (decrease) in cash and cash equivalents (net)	**(766)**	**262**
Net cash and cash equivalents at the beginning of the year	(92)	(354)
Net cash and cash equivalents at the end of the year	**(858)**	**(92)**

EXPLORING THE WEB

BYP18-4 ***Purpose:*** Learn about the SEC.

Address: **www.sec.gov/index.html** ***(or go to www.wiley.com/college/weygandt)***

Steps:

1. From the SEC homepage, choose **About the SEC**.

Instructions
Answer the following questions.

(a) How many enforcement actions does the SEC take each year against securities law violators? What are typical infractions?

(b) After the Depression, Congress passed the Securities Acts of 1933 and 1934 to improve investor confidence in the markets. What two "common sense" notions are these laws based on?

(c) Who was the President of the United States at the time of the creation of the SEC? Who was the first SEC Chairperson?

BYP18-5 ***Purpose:*** Use the Internet to view SEC filings.

Address: **biz.yahoo.com/i** ***(or go to www.wiley.com/college/weygandt)***

Steps:

1. Type in a company name.
2. Choose **SEC filings** (this will take you to Yahoo-Edgar Online).

Instructions
Answer the following questions.

(a) What company did you select?

(b) What other recent SEC filings are available for your viewing?

(c) Which filing is the most recent? What is the date?

CRITICAL THINKING

GROUP DECISION CASE

BYP18-6 Greg Rhoda and Debra Sondgeroth are examining the following statement of cash flows for K.K. Bean Trading Company for the year ended January 31, 2001.

K.K. BEAN TRADING COMPANY
Statement of Cash Flows
For the Year Ended January 31, 2001

Sources of cash	
From sales of merchandise	$390,000
From sale of capital stock	420,000
From sale of investment (purchased below)	80,000
From depreciation	55,000
From issuance of note for truck	20,000
From interest on investments	6,000
Total sources of cash	971,000
Uses of cash	
For purchase of fixtures and equipment	340,000
For merchandise purchased for resale (all sold)	258,000
For operating expenses (including depreciation)	160,000
For purchase of investment	75,000
For purchase of truck by issuance of note	20,000
For purchase of treasury stock	10,000
For interest on note payable	3,000
Total uses of cash	866,000
Net increase in cash	$105,000

Greg claims that K.K. Bean's statement of cash flows is an excellent example of a superb first year, with cash increasing $105,000. Debra replies that it was not a superb first year—but rather, that the year was an operating failure. She says that the statement was incorrectly presented and that $105,000 is not the actual increase in cash. The cash balance at the beginning of the year was $140,000.

Instructions

With the class divided into groups, answer the following.

(a) With whom do you agree, Greg or Debra? Explain your position.

(b) Using the data provided, prepare a statement of cash flows in proper form using the indirect method. The only noncash items in the income statement are depreciation and the gain from the sale of the investment.

COMMUNICATION ACTIVITY

BYP18-7 Arnold Byte, the owner-president of Computer Services Company, is unfamiliar with the statement of cash flows which you, as his accountant, prepared. He asks for further explanation.

Instructions

Write him a brief memo explaining the form and content of the statement of cash flows as shown in Illustration 18-17 on page 731.

ETHICS CASE

BYP18-8 Puebla Corporation is a medium-sized wholesaler of automotive parts. It has ten stockholders, who have been paid a total of $1 million in cash dividends for eight consecutive years. The policy of the Board of Directors requires that in order for this dividend to be declared, net cash provided by operating activities as reported in Puebla's current year's statement of cash flows must be in excess of $1 million. President and CEO Phil Monat's job is secure so long as he produces annual operating cash flows to support the usual dividend.

At the end of the current year, controller Rick Rodgers presents president Monat with some disappointing news: The net cash provided by operating activities is calculated, by the indirect method, to be only $970,000. The president says to Rick, "We must get that amount above $1 million. Isn't there some way to increase operating cash flow by another $30,000?" Rick answers, "These figures were prepared by my assistant. I'll go back to my office and see what I can do." The president replies, "I know you won't let me down, Rick."

Upon close scrutiny of the statement of cash flows, Rick concludes that he can get the operating cash flows above $1 million by reclassifying a $60,000, 2-year note payable listed in the financing activities section as "Proceeds from bank loan—$60,000." He will report the note instead as "Increase in payables—$60,000" and treat it as an adjustment of net income in the operating activities section. He returns to the president saying, "You can tell the Board to declare their usual dividend. Our net cash flow provided by operating activities is $1,030,000." "Good man, Rick! I knew I could count on you," exults the president.

Instructions

(a) Who are the stakeholders in this situation?

(b) Was there anything unethical about the president's actions? Was there anything unethical about the controller's actions?

(c) Are the Board members or anyone else likely to discover the misclassification?

Answers to Self-Study Questions

1. c **2.** b **3.** a **4.** c **5.** d **6.** b **7.** c **8.** d **9.** b **10.** c
11. d **12.** a **13.** b

Answer to Lands' End Review It Question 4, p. 732

Lands' End uses the indirect method of computing net cash provided by operating activities. The largest single item of cash outflow for Lands' End in the fiscal year ended January 28, 2000, is "Cash paid for capital additions" $28.013 million.

Remember to go back to the Navigator box on the chapter-opening page and check off your completed work.

FINANCIAL STATEMENT ANALYSIS

19

THE NAVIGATOR ✓

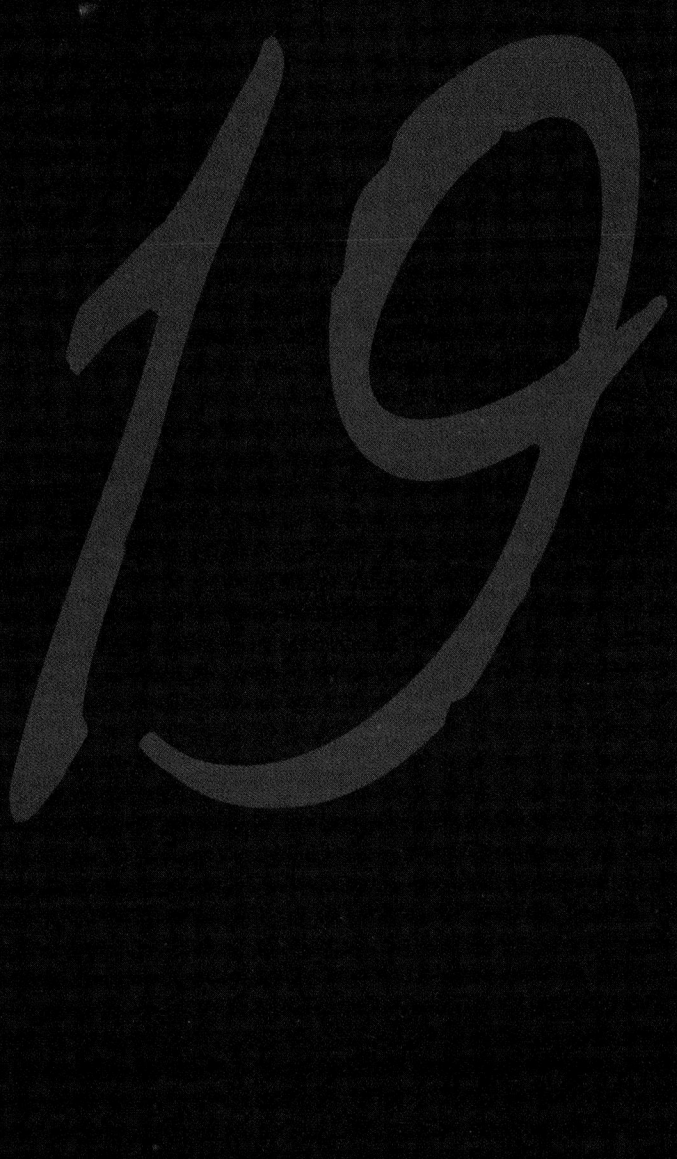

- Understand *Concepts for Review* ❑
- Read *Feature Story* ❑
- Scan *Study Objectives* ❑
- Read *Preview* ❑
- Read text and answer *Before You Go On* *p.* 787 ❑ *p.* 804 ❑ *p.* 805 ❑
- Work *Demonstration Problem* ❑
- Review *Summary of Study Objectives* ❑
- Answer *Self-Study Questions* ❑
- Complete *Assignments* ❑

CONCEPTS FOR REVIEW

Before studying this chapter, you should know or, if necessary, review:

a. The contents and classification of a corporate balance sheet. (Ch. 4, pp. 151–156)

b. The contents and classification of a corporate income statement. (Ch. 5, pp. 197–202)

c. Who are the various users of financial statement information. (Ch. 1, pp. 3–5)

d. How to compute earnings per share (EPS). (Ch. 15, pp. 620–622)

e. How the liquidity of a company is determined. (Ch. 4, p. 154)

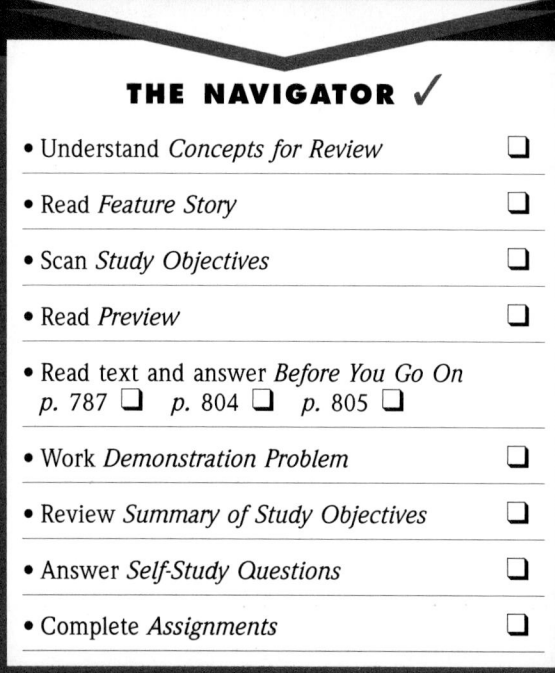

☑ THE NAVIGATOR

FEATURE STORY

"Follow that Stock!"

If you thought cab drivers with cell phones were scary, how about a cab driver with a trading desk in the front seat?

When a stoplight turns red or traffic backs up, New York City cabby Carlos Rubino morphs into a day trader, scanning real-time quotes of his favorite stocks as they spew across a PalmPilot mounted next to the steering wheel. "It's kind of stressful," he says. "But I like it."

Itching to know how a particular stock is doing? Mr. Rubino is happy to look up quotes for passengers. **Yahoo!**, **Amazon.com**, and **America Online** are the most requested ones. He even lets customers use his **Hitachi** Traveler laptop to send urgent e-mails from the back seat. Aware of a new local law prohibiting cabbies from using cell phones while they're driving, Mr. Rubino extends that rule to his trading. "I stop the cab at the side of the road if I have to make a trade," he says. "Safety first."

Originally from São Paulo, Brazil, Mr. Rubino has been driving his cab since 1987, and started trading stocks a few years ago. His curiosity grew as he began to educate himself by reading business publications. The Wall Street brokers he picks up are usually impressed with his knowledge, he says. But the feeling generally isn't mutual. Some of them "don't know much," he says. "They buy what people tell them to buy—they're like a toll collector."

Mr. Rubino is an enigma to his fellow cab drivers. A lot of his colleagues say they want to trade too. "But cab drivers are a little cheap," he says. "The [real-time] quotes cost $100 a month. The wireless Internet access is $54 a month."

Will he give up his brokerage firm on wheels for a stationary job? Not likely. Though he claims a 70 percent return on his investments in recent months, he says he makes $1,300 and up a week driving his cab—more than he does trading. Besides, he adds, "Why go somewhere and have a boss?"

Source: Excerpted from Barbara Boydston, "With this Cab, People Jump in and Shout, 'Follow that Stock!'," *The Wall Street Journal*, August 18, 1999, p. C1. Reprinted by permission of the Wall Street Journal © 1999 Dow Jones & Company, Inc. All Rights Reserved Worldwide.

THE NAVIGATOR

STUDY OBJECTIVES

After studying this chapter, you should be able to:

1. Discuss the need for comparative analysis.
2. Identify the tools of financial statement analysis.
3. Explain and apply horizontal analysis.
4. Describe and apply vertical analysis.
5. Identify and compute ratios, and describe their purpose and use in analyzing a firm's liquidity, profitability, and solvency.
6. Recognize the limitations of financial statement analysis.

THE NAVIGATOR

PREVIEW OF CHAPTER 19

An important lesson can be learned from the Feature Story: Experience is the best teacher. By now you have learned a significant amount about financial reporting by U.S. corporations. Using some of the basic decision tools presented in this book, you can perform a rudimentary analysis on any U.S. company and draw basic conclusions about its financial health. Although it would not be wise for you to bet your life savings on a company's stock relying solely on your current level of knowledge, we strongly encourage you to practice your new skills wherever possible. Only with practice will you improve your ability to interpret financial numbers.

Before unleashing you on the world of high finance, we will present a few more important concepts and techniques, as well as provide you with one more comprehensive review of corporate financial statements. We use all of the decision tools presented in this text to analyze a single company—**Sears, Roebuck and Co.,** one of the country's oldest and largest retail store chains.

The content and organization of Chapter 19 are as follows.

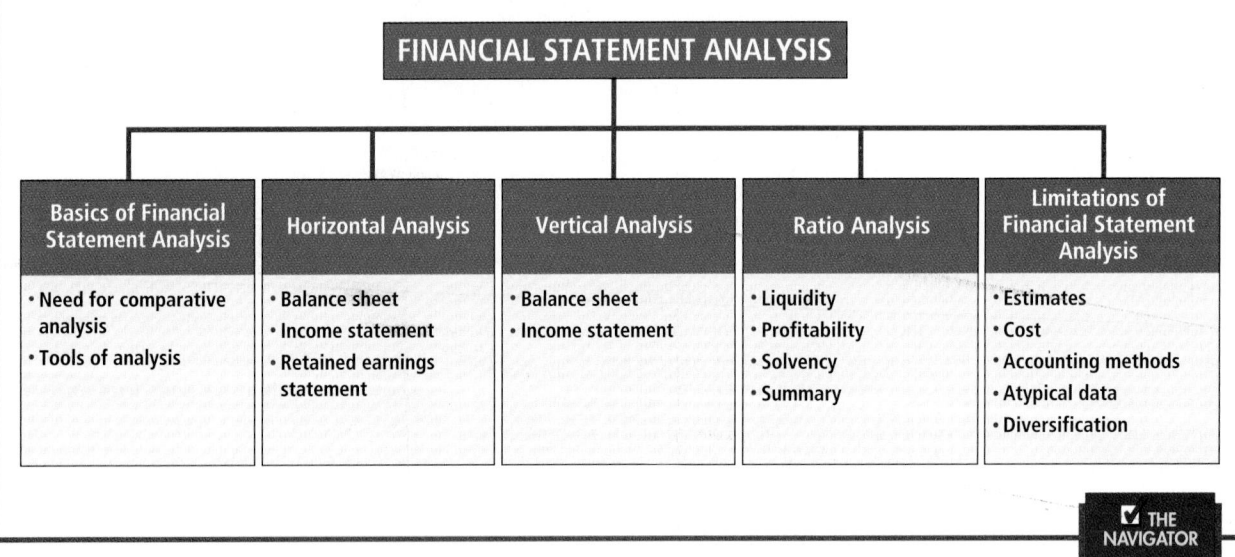

FINANCIAL STATEMENT ANALYSIS

Basics of Financial Statement Analysis	Horizontal Analysis	Vertical Analysis	Ratio Analysis	Limitations of Financial Statement Analysis
• Need for comparative analysis • Tools of analysis	• Balance sheet • Income statement • Retained earnings statement	• Balance sheet • Income statement	• Liquidity • Profitability • Solvency • Summary	• Estimates • Cost • Accounting methods • Atypical data • Diversification

THE NAVIGATOR

BASICS OF FINANCIAL STATEMENT ANALYSIS

Analyzing financial statements involves evaluating three characteristics of a company: its liquidity, its profitability, and its solvency. A **short-term creditor**, such as a bank, is primarily interested in the ability of the borrower to pay obligations when they come due. The liquidity of the borrower is extremely important in evaluating the safety of a loan. A **long-term creditor**, such as a bondholder, however, looks to profitability and solvency measures that indicate the company's ability to survive over a long period of time. Long-term creditors consider such measures as the amount of debt in the company's capital structure and its ability to meet interest payments. Similarly, **stockholders** are interested in the profitability and solvency of the company. They want to assess the likelihood of dividends and the growth potential of the stock.

STUDY OBJECTIVE 1

Discuss the need for comparative analysis.

NEED FOR COMPARATIVE ANALYSIS

Every item reported in a financial statement has significance. When **Sears, Roebuck and Co.** reports cash of $729 million on its balance sheet, we know the company had that amount of cash on the balance sheet date. But, we do not know whether the amount represents an increase over prior years, or whether it is adequate in relation to the company's need for cash. To obtain such information, it is necessary to compare the amount of cash with other financial statement data.

Comparisons can be made on a number of different bases. Three are illustrated in this chapter.

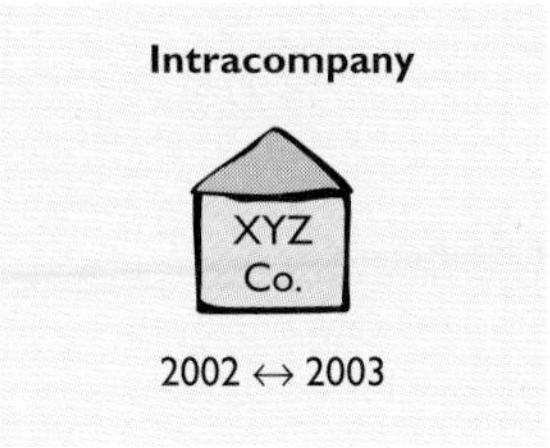

1. **Intracompany basis.** This basis compares an item or financial relationship **within a company** in the current year with the same item or relationship in one or more prior years. For example, Sears, Roebuck and Co. can compare its cash balance at the end of the current year with last year's balance to find the amount of the increase or decrease. Likewise, Sears can compare the percentage of cash to current assets at the end of the current year with the percentage in one or more prior years. Intracompany comparisons are useful in detecting changes in financial relationships and significant trends.

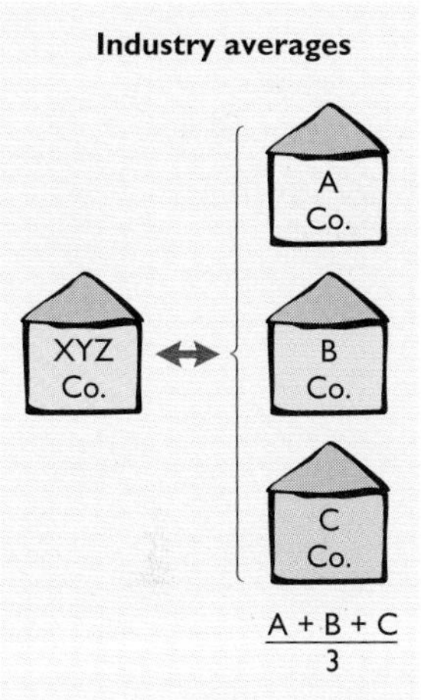

2. **Industry averages.** This basis compares an item or financial relationship of a company with **industry averages** (or **norms**) published by financial ratings organizations such as **Dun & Bradstreet**, **Moody's**, and **Standard & Poor's**. For example, Sears's net income can be compared with the average net income of all companies in the retail chain-store industry. Comparisons with industry averages provide information as to a company's relative performance within the industry.

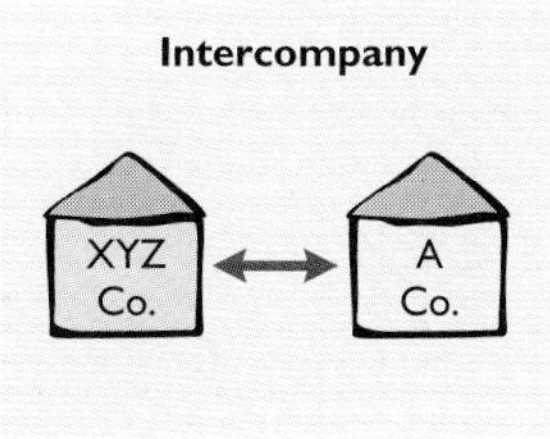

3. **Intercompany basis.** This basis compares an item or financial relationship of one company with the same item or relationship in **one or more competing companies**. The comparisons are made on the basis of the published financial statements of the individual companies. For example, Sears's total sales for the year can be compared with the total sales of its major competitors such as **Kmart** and **Wal-Mart**. Intercompany comparisons are useful in determining a company's competitive position.

TOOLS OF FINANCIAL STATEMENT ANALYSIS

STUDY OBJECTIVE 2

Identify the tools of financial statement analysis.

Various tools are used to evaluate the significance of financial statement data. Three commonly used tools are these:

- **Horizontal analysis** evaluates a series of financial statement data over a period of time.
- **Vertical analysis** evaluates financial statement data by expressing each item in a financial statement as a percent of a base amount.
- **Ratio analysis** expresses the relationship among selected items of financial statement data.

Horizontal analysis is used primarily in intracompany comparisons. Two features in published financial statements facilitate this type of comparison: First, each of the basic financial statements is presented on a comparative basis for a minimum of two years. Second, a summary of selected financial data is presented for a series of five to ten years or more. Vertical analysis is used in both intra- and intercompany comparisons. Ratio analysis is used in all three types of comparisons. In the following sections, we will explain and illustrate each of the three types of analysis.

HORIZONTAL ANALYSIS

STUDY OBJECTIVE 3

Explain and apply horizontal analysis.

Horizontal analysis, also called **trend analysis**, is a technique for evaluating a series of financial statement data over a period of time. Its purpose is to determine the increase or decrease that has taken place. This change may be expressed as either an amount or a percentage. For example, the recent net sales figures of **Sears, Roebuck and Co.** are as follows. (Yes, that's $41 **billion** 71 million in 1999.)

Illustration 19-1

Sears, Roebuck and Co.'s net sales

SEARS

SEARS, ROEBUCK AND CO.
Net Sales (in millions)

1999	1998	1997	1996	1995
$41,071	$41,575	$41,574	$38,064	$34,835

If we assume that 1995 is the base year, we can measure all percentage increases or decreases from this base period amount as follows.

Illustration 19-2

Formula for horizontal analysis of changes since base period

$$\text{Change since base period} = \frac{\text{Current year amount} - \text{Base year amount}}{\text{Base year amount}}$$

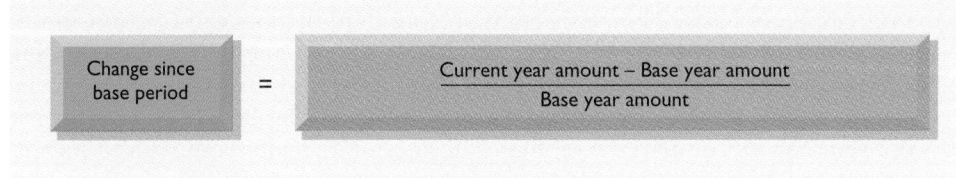

For example, we can determine that net sales for Sears increased from 1995 to 1996 approximately 9.3% [($38,064 − $34,835) ÷ $34,835]. Similarly, we can determine that net sales increased from 1995 to 1999 more than 17.9% [($41,071 − $34,835) ÷ $34,835].

Alternatively, we can express current year sales as a percentage of the base period. This is done by dividing the current year amount by the base year amount, as shown below.

Illustration 19-3

Formula for horizontal analysis of current year in relation to base year

$$\text{Current results in relation to base period} = \frac{\text{Current year amount}}{\text{Base year amount}}$$

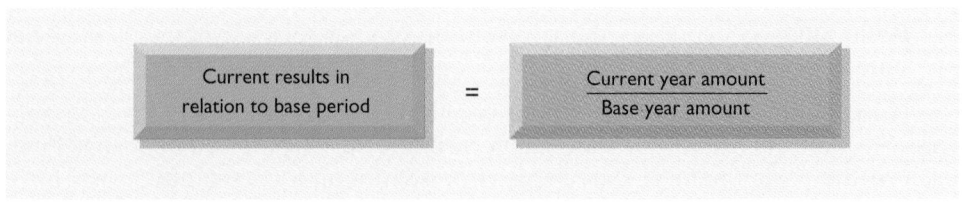

Illustration 19-4 presents this analysis for Sears for a five-year period using 1995 as the base period.

SEARS

Illustration 19-4

Horizontal analysis of Sears, Roebuck and Co.'s net sales in relation to base period

SEARS, ROEBUCK AND CO.
Net Sales (in millions)
in relation to base period 1995

1999	1998	1997	1996	1995
$41,071	$41,575	$41,574	$38,064	$34,835
117.9%	119.3%	119.3%	109.3%	100%

BALANCE SHEET

To further illustrate horizontal analysis, we will use the financial statements of Quality Department Store Inc. It is a downtown, full-line department store in a southeastern city of 55,000 people. A horizontal analysis of its two-year condensed balance sheets, showing dollar and percentage changes, is presented in Illustration 19-5.

Illustration 19-5

Horizontal analysis of balance sheets

QUALITY DEPARTMENT STORE INC.
Condensed Balance Sheets
December 31

			Increase or (Decrease) during 1999	
	1999	1998	Amount	Percent
Assets				
Current assets	$1,020,000	$ 945,000	**$ 75,000**	**7.9%**
Plant assets (net)	800,000	632,500	**167,500**	**26.5%**
Intangible assets	15,000	17,500	**(2,500)**	**(14.3%)**
Total assets	$1,835,000	$1,595,000	**$240,000**	**15.0%**
Liabilities				
Current liabilities	$ 344,500	$ 303,000	**$ 41,500**	**13.7%**
Long-term liabilities	487,500	497,000	**(9,500)**	**(1.9%)**
Total liabilities	832,000	800,000	**32,000**	**4.0%**
Stockholders' Equity				
Common stock, $1 par	275,400	270,000	**5,400**	**2.0%**
Retained earnings	727,600	525,000	**202,600**	**38.6%**
Total stockholders' equity	1,003,000	795,000	**208,000**	**26.2%**
Total liabilities and stockholders' equity	$1,835,000	$1,595,000	**$240,000**	**15.0%**

HELPFUL HINT

It is difficult to comprehend the significance of a change when only the dollar amount of change is examined. When the change is expressed in percentage form, it is easier to grasp the true magnitude of the change.

The comparative balance sheets in Illustration 19-5 show that a number of significant changes have occurred in Quality Department Store's financial structure from 1998 to 1999. In the assets section, plant assets (net) increased $167,500, or 26.5%. In the liabilities section, current liabilities increased $41,500, or 13.7%. In the stockholders' equity section, retained earnings increased $202,600, or 38.6%. This suggests that the company expanded its asset base during 1999 and **financed this expansion primarily by retaining income** rather than assuming additional long-term debt.

INCOME STATEMENT

Presented in Illustration 19-6 is a horizontal analysis of the two-year condensed income statements of Quality Department Store Inc. for the years 1999 and 1998.

Illustration 19-6

Horizontal analysis of income statements

QUALITY DEPARTMENT STORE INC.
Condensed Income Statements
For the Years Ended December 31

			Increase or (Decrease) during 1999	
	1999	**1998**	**Amount**	**Percent**
Sales	$2,195,000	$1,960,000	$235,000	12.0%
Sales returns and allowances	98,000	123,000	(25,000)	(20.3%)
Net sales	2,097,000	1,837,000	260,000	14.2%
Cost of goods sold	1,281,000	1,140,000	141,000	12.4%
Gross profit	816,000	697,000	119,000	17.1%
Selling expenses	253,000	211,500	41,500	19.6%
Administrative expenses	104,000	108,500	(4,500)	(4.1%)
Total operating expenses	357,000	320,000	37,000	11.6%
Income from operations	459,000	377,000	82,000	21.8%
Other revenues and gains				
Interest and dividends	9,000	11,000	(2,000)	(18.2%)
Other expenses and losses				
Interest expense	36,000	40,500	(4,500)	(11.1%)
Income before income taxes	432,000	347,500	84,500	24.3%
Income tax expense	168,200	139,000	29,200	21.0%
Net income	$ 263,800	$ 208,500	$ 55,300	26.5%

HELPFUL HINT
Note that though the amount column is additive (the total is $55,300), the percentage column is not additive (26.5% is not the total). A separate percentage has been calculated for each item.

Horizontal analysis of the income statements shows the following changes:

1. Net sales increased $260,000, or 14.2% ($260,000 ÷ $1,837,000).
2. Cost of goods sold increased $141,000, or 12.4% ($141,000 ÷ $1,140,000).
3. Total operating expenses increased $37,000, or 11.6% ($37,000 ÷ $320,000).

Overall, gross profit and net income were up substantially. Gross profit increased 17.1%, and net income, 26.5%. Quality's profit trend appears favorable.

RETAINED EARNINGS STATEMENT

A horizontal analysis of Quality Department Store's comparative retained earnings statements is presented in Illustration 19-7. Analyzed horizontally, net income increased $55,300, or 26.5%, whereas dividends on the common stock increased only $1,200, or 2%. We saw in the horizontal analysis of the balance sheet that ending retained earnings increased 38.6%. As indicated earlier, the company retained a significant portion of net income to finance additional plant facilities.

Illustration 19-7

Horizontal analysis of retained earnings statements

QUALITY DEPARTMENT STORE INC.
Retained Earnings Statements
For the Years Ended December 31

			Increase or (Decrease) during 1999	
	1999	1998	Amount	Percent
Retained earnings, Jan. 1	$525,000	$376,500	**$148,500**	**39.4%**
Add: Net income	263,800	208,500	**55,300**	**26.5%**
	788,800	585,000	**203,800**	
Deduct: Dividends	61,200	60,000	**1,200**	**2.0%**
Retained earnings, Dec. 31	$727,600	$525,000	**$202,600**	**38.6%**

Horizontal analysis of changes from period to period is relatively straightforward and is quite useful. But complications can occur in making the computations. If an item has no value in a base year or preceding year and a value in the next year, no percentage change can be computed. Similarly, if a negative amount appears in the base or preceding period and a positive amount exists the following year (or vice versa), no percentage change can be computed.

VERTICAL ANALYSIS

STUDY OBJECTIVE 4

Describe and apply vertical analysis.

Vertical analysis, also called **common size analysis**, is a technique for evaluating financial statement data that expresses each item within a financial statement as a percent of a base amount. On a balance sheet we might say that current assets are 22% of total assets (total assets being the base amount). Or on an income statement, we might say that selling expenses are 16% of net sales (net sales being the base amount).

BALANCE SHEET

Presented in Illustration 19-8 on page 786 is the vertical analysis of Quality Department Store Inc.'s comparative balance sheets. The base for the asset items is **total assets**. The base for the liability and stockholders' equity items is **total liabilities and stockholders' equity**.

Vertical analysis shows the relative size of each category in the balance sheet. It also can show the **percentage change** in the individual asset, liability, and stockholders' equity items. For example, we can see that current assets decreased from 59.2% of total assets in 1998 to 55.6% in 1999 (even though the absolute dollar amount increased $75,000 in that time). Plant assets (net) have increased from 39.7% to 43.6% of total assets. Retained earnings have increased from 32.9% to 39.7% of total liabilities and stockholders' equity. These results reinforce the earlier observations that **Quality is choosing to finance its growth through retention of earnings rather than through issuing additional debt**.

INCOME STATEMENT

Vertical analysis of Quality's income statements is shown in Illustration 19-9. We see that cost of goods sold as a percentage of net sales declined 1% (62.1% vs.

Illustration 19-8

Vertical analysis of balance sheets

QUALITY DEPARTMENT STORE INC.
Condensed Balance Sheets
December 31

	1999		1998	
	Amount	**Percent**	**Amount**	**Percent**
Assets				
Current assets	$1,020,000	55.6%	$ 945,000	59.2%
Plant assets (net)	800,000	43.6%	632,500	39.7%
Intangible assets	15,000	0.8%	17,500	1.1%
Total assets	$1,835,000	100.0%	$1,595,000	100.0%
Liabilities				
Current liabilities	$ 344,500	18.8%	$ 303,000	19.0%
Long-term liabilities	487,500	26.5%	497,000	31.2%
Total liabilities	832,000	45.3%	800,000	50.2%
Stockholders' Equity				
Common stock, $1 par	275,400	15.0%	270,000	16.9%
Retained earnings	727,600	39.7%	525,000	32.9%
Total stockholders' equity	1,003,000	54.7%	795,000	49.8%
Total liabilities and stockholders' equity	$1,835,000	100.0%	$1,595,000	100.0%

HELPFUL HINT
The formula for calculating these balance sheet percentages is:

$$\frac{\text{Each item on B/S}}{\text{Total assets}} = \%$$

61.1%) and total operating expenses declined 0.4% (17.4% vs. 17.0%). As a result, it is not surprising to see net income as a percent of net sales increase from 11.4% to 12.6%. Quality appears to be a profitable enterprise that is becoming even more successful.

Illustration 19-9

Vertical analysis of income statements

QUALITY DEPARTMENT STORE INC.
Condensed Income Statements
For the Years Ended December 31

	1999		1998	
	Amount	**Percent**	**Amount**	**Percent**
Sales	$2,195,000	104.7%	$1,960,000	106.7%
Sales returns and allowances	98,000	4.7%	123,000	6.7%
Net sales	2,097,000	100.0%	1,837,000	100.0%
Cost of goods sold	1,281,000	61.1%	1,140,000	62.1%
Gross profit	816,000	38.9%	697,000	37.9%
Selling expenses	253,000	12.0%	211,500	11.5%
Administrative expenses	104,000	5.0%	108,500	5.9%
Total operating expenses	357,000	17.0%	320,000	17.4%
Income from operations	459,000	21.9%	377,000	20.5%
Other revenues and gains				
Interest and dividends	9,000	0.4%	11,000	0.6%
Other expenses and losses				
Interest expense	36,000	1.7%	40,500	2.2%
Income before income taxes	432,000	20.6%	347,500	18.9%
Income tax expense	168,200	8.0%	139,000	7.5%
Net income	$ 263,800	12.6%	$ 208,500	11.4%

HELPFUL HINT
The formula for calculating these income statement percentages is:

$$\frac{\text{Each item on I/S}}{\text{Net sales}} = \%$$

An associated benefit of vertical analysis is that it enables you to compare companies of different sizes. For example, Quality's main competitor is a Sears store in a nearby town. Using vertical analysis, the condensed income statements of the small local retail enterprise, Quality Department Store Inc., can be more meaningfully compared with the 1999 income statement of the giant international retailer, **Sears, Roebuck and Co.**, as shown in Illustration 19-10.

Illustration 19-10

Intercompany income statement comparison

CONDENSED INCOME STATEMENTS
(in thousands)

	Quality Department Store Inc.		Sears, Roebuck and Co.[1]	
	Dollars	**Percent**	**Dollars**	**Percent**
Net sales	$2,097	100.0%	$41,071,000	100.0%
Cost of goods sold	1,281	61.1%	27,212,000	66.3%
Gross profit	816	38.9%	13,859,000	33.7%
Selling and administrative expenses	357	17.0%	10,137,000	24.7%
Income from operations	459	21.9%	3,722,000	9.0%
Other expenses and revenues (including income taxes)	195	9.3%	2,269,000	5.5%
Net income	$ 264	12.6%	$ 1,453,000	3.5%

Sears' net sales are 19,585 times greater than the net sales of relatively tiny Quality Department Store. But vertical analysis eliminates this difference in size. The percentages show that Quality's and Sears's gross profit rates were somewhat comparable at 38.9% and 33.7%. However, the percentages related to income from operations were significantly different at 21.9% and 9.0%. This disparity can be attributed to Quality's selling and administrative expense percentage (17%) which is much lower than Sears's (24.7%). Although Sears earned net income more than 5,500 times larger than Quality's, Sears's net income as a **percent of each sales dollar** (3.5%) is only 28% of Quality's (12.6%).

BEFORE YOU GO ON...

REVIEW IT

1. What are the different tools that might be used to compare financial information?
2. What is horizontal analysis?
3. What is vertical analysis?
4. Identify the specific sections in **Lands' End's** 1999 Annual Report where horizontal and vertical analysis of financial data is presented. The answer to this question is provided on page 824.

LANDS' END DIRECT MERCHANTS

DO IT

Summary financial information for Rosepatch Company is as follows.

	December 31, 2002	**December 31, 2001**
Current assets	$234,000	$180,000
Plant assets (net)	756,000	420,000
Total assets	$990,000	$600,000

[1] Sears, Roebuck and Co., *1999 Annual Report* (Hoffman Estates, Illinois).

Compute the amount and percentage changes in 2002 using horizontal analysis, assuming 2001 is the base year.

ACTION PLAN

- Find the percentage change by dividing the amount of the increase by the 2001 amount (base year).

SOLUTION

	Increase in 2002	
	Amount	**Percent**
Current assets	$ 54,000	30% [($234,000 − $180,000) ÷ $180,000]
Plant assets (net)	336,000	80% [($756,000 − $420,000) ÷ $420,000]
Total assets	$390,000	65% [($990,000 − $600,000) ÷ $600,000]

Related exercise material: BE19-1, BE19-3, BE19-4, BE19-6, E19-1, E19-3, and E19-4.

THE NAVIGATOR

RATIO ANALYSIS

STUDY OBJECTIVE 5

Identify and compute ratios, and describe their purpose and use in analyzing a firm's liquidity, profitability, and solvency.

Ratio analysis expresses the relationship among selected items of financial statement data. A **ratio** expresses the mathematical relationship between one quantity and another. The relationship is expressed in terms of either a percentage, a rate, or a simple proportion. To illustrate, in 1999 **Nike, Inc.**, had current assets of $3,265 million and current liabilities of $1,446 million. The relationship is determined by dividing current assets by current liabilities. The alternative means of expression are:

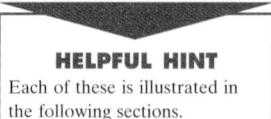

HELPFUL HINT
Each of these is illustrated in the following sections.

Percentage:	Current assets are 226% of current liabilities.
Rate:	Current assets are 2.26 times greater than current liabilities.
Proportion:	The relationship of current assets to liabilities is 2.26 : 1.

TECHNOLOGY IN ACTION

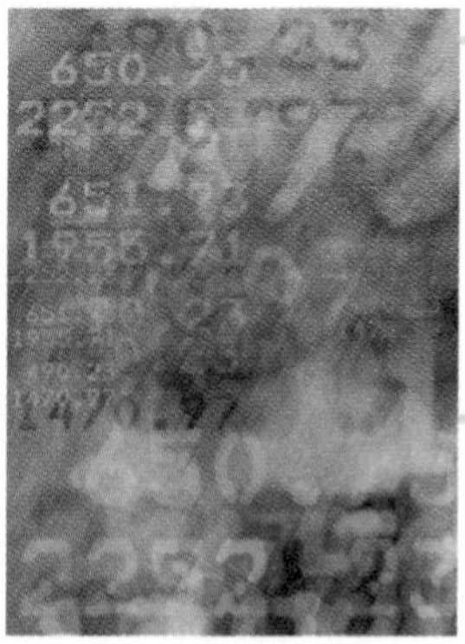

Many general ledger accounting programs include financial ratios as routine output. All the ratio computations presented in this chapter can be done with electronic spreadsheets as well. Also, many software programs are written specifically for financial statement analysis. These are written for both general purpose use and for use in specific industries. For example, financial institutions routinely use over 60 ratios geared specifically to the banking industry.

For analysis of the primary financial statements, ratios can be used to evaluate liquidity, profitability, and solvency. These classifications are described and pictured in Illustration 19-11.

Ratios can provide clues to underlying conditions that may not be apparent from individual financial statement components. However, a single ratio by itself is not very meaningful. Accordingly, in the discussion of ratios we will use the following types of comparisons.

1. **Intracompany comparisons** for two years for Quality Department Store.
2. **Industry average comparisons** based on median ratios for department stores.

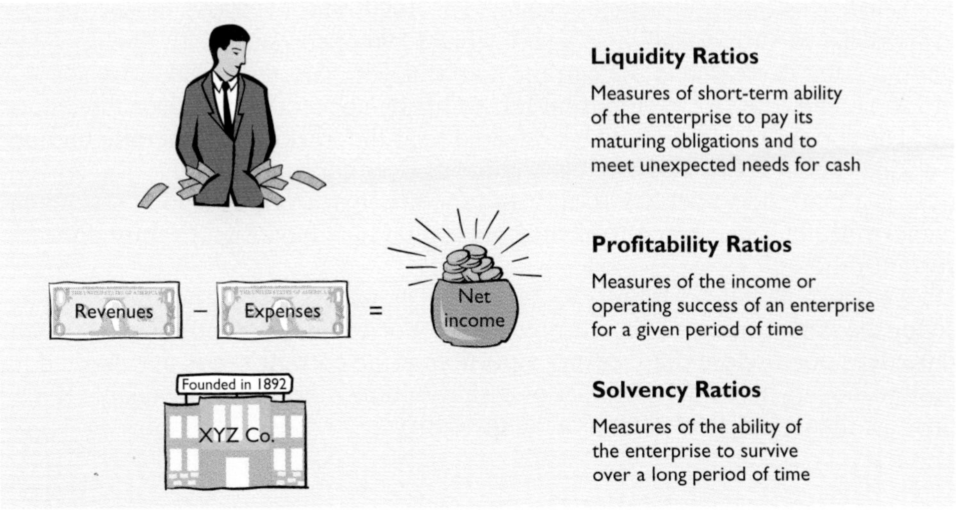

Liquidity Ratios
Measures of short-term ability of the enterprise to pay its maturing obligations and to meet unexpected needs for cash
Revenues
Expenses
Net income
Profitability Ratios
Measures of the income or operating success of an enterprise for a given period of time
Founded in 1892
XYZ Co.
Solvency Ratios
Measures of the ability of the enterprise to survive over a long period of time

Illustration 19-11
Financial ratio classifications

3. **Intercompany comparisons** based on **Sears, Roebuck and Co.** as Quality Department Store's principal competitor.

LIQUIDITY RATIOS

Liquidity ratios measure the short-term ability of the enterprise to pay its maturing obligations and to meet unexpected needs for cash. Short-term creditors such as bankers and suppliers are particularly interested in assessing liquidity. The ratios that can be used to determine the enterprise's short-term debt-paying ability are the current ratio, the acid-test ratio, the current cash debt coverage ratio, receivables turnover, and inventory turnover.

1. Current Ratio

The **current ratio** is a widely used measure for evaluating a company's liquidity and short-term debt-paying ability. The ratio is computed by dividing current assets by current liabilities.

The 1999 and 1998 current ratios for Quality Department Store and comparative data are shown in Illustration 19-12.

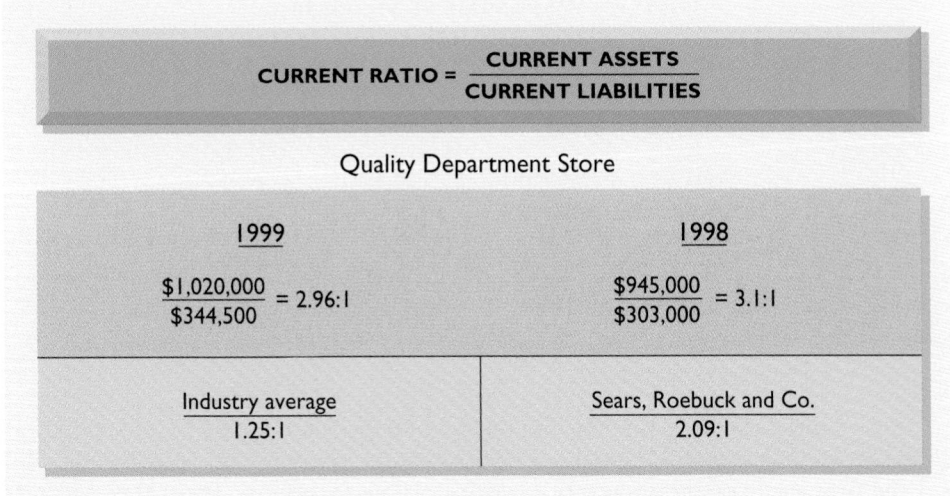

$$\text{CURRENT RATIO} = \frac{\text{CURRENT ASSETS}}{\text{CURRENT LIABILITIES}}$$

Quality Department Store

1999	1998
$\frac{\$1,020,000}{\$344,500} = 2.96:1$	$\frac{\$945,000}{\$303,000} = 3.1:1$
Industry average 1.25:1	Sears, Roebuck and Co. 2.09:1

Illustration 19-12
Current ratio

HELPFUL HINT
Can any corporation operate successfully without working capital? Yes, if it has very predictable cash flows and solid earnings. A surprising number of companies, including **Whirlpool**, **American Standard**, and **Campbell's Soup**, are pursuing this goal. The rationale: Less money tied up in working capital means more money to invest in the business.

What does the ratio actually mean? The 1999 ratio of 2.96:1 means that for every dollar of current liabilities, Quality has $2.96 of current assets. Quality's current ratio has decreased in the current year. But, compared to the industry average of 1.25:1, and Sears's 2.09:1 current ratio, Quality appears to be reasonably liquid.

The current ratio is sometimes referred to as the **working capital ratio** because **working capital** is the excess of current assets over current liabilities. The current ratio is a more dependable indicator of liquidity than working capital. Two companies with the same amount of working capital may have significantly different current ratios.

The current ratio is only one measure of liquidity. It does not take into account the composition of the current assets. For example, a satisfactory current ratio does not disclose the fact that a portion of the current assets may be tied up in slow-moving inventory. A dollar of cash would be more readily available to pay the bills than a dollar of slow-moving inventory.

ACCOUNTING IN ACTION *Business Insight*

The apparent simplicity of the current ratio can have real-world limitations. An addition of equal amounts to both the numerator and the denominator causes the ratio to decrease. Assume, for example, that a company has $2,000,000 of current assets and $1,000,000 of current liabilities. Its current ratio is 2:1. If it purchases $1,000,000 of inventory on account, it will have $3,000,000 of current assets and $2,000,000 of current liabilities. Its current ratio will decrease to 1.5:1. If, instead, the company pays off $500,000 of its current liabilities, it will have $1,500,000 of current assets and $500,000 of current liabilities, and its current ratio will increase to 3:1. Any trend analysis should be done with care, since the ratio is susceptible to quick changes and is easily influenced by management.

2. Acid-Test Ratio

ALTERNATIVE TERMINOLOGY The acid-test ratio is also called the *quick ratio.*

The **acid-test (quick) ratio** is a measure of a company's immediate short-term liquidity. It is computed by dividing the sum of cash, short-term investments, and net receivables by current liabilities. Thus, it is an important complement to the current ratio. For example, assume that the current assets of Quality Department Store for 1999 and 1998 consist of the following items.

Illustration 19-13

Current assets of Quality Department Store

QUALITY DEPARTMENT STORE INC.
Balance Sheet (partial)

	1999	1998
Current assets		
Cash	**$ 100,000**	**$155,000**
Short-term investments	**20,000**	**70,000**
Receivables (net)	**230,000**	**180,000**
Inventory	620,000	500,000
Prepaid expenses	50,000	40,000
Total current assets	$1,020,000	$945,000

net sale base value.

Total assets everything else on the balance sheet

Cash, short-term investments, and receivables (net) are highly liquid compared to inventory and prepaid expenses. The inventory may not be readily saleable, and the prepaid expenses may not be transferable to others. Thus, the acid-test ratio measures **immediate** liquidity. The 1999 and 1998 acid-test ratios for Quality Department Store and comparative data are as follows.

Illustration 19-14

Acid-test ratio

$$\text{ACID-TEST RATIO} = \frac{\text{CASH + SHORT-TERM INVESTMENTS + RECEIVABLES (NET)}}{\text{CURRENT LIABILITIES}}$$

Quality Department Store

1999	1998
$\frac{\$100,000 + \$20,000 + \$230,000}{\$344,500} = 1.0:1$	$\frac{\$155,000 + \$70,000 + \$180,000}{\$303,000} = 1.3:1$
Industry average 0.27:1	Sears, Roebuck and Co. 1.39:1

The ratio has declined in 1999. Is an acid-test ratio of 1.0:1 adequate? When compared with the industry average of 0.27:1 and Sears's of 1.39:1, Quality's acid-test ratio seems adequate.

3. Current Cash Debt Coverage Ratio

A disadvantage of the current and acid-test ratios is that they use year-end balances of current asset and current liability accounts. These balances may not represent the company's current position during most of the year. A ratio that partially corrects for this problem is the **current cash debt coverage ratio**. It is calculated by dividing net cash provided by operating activities by average current liabilities. Because it uses net cash provided by operating activities rather than a balance at a point in time, it may provide a better idea of a company's liquidity.

Assume that Quality Department Store's statement of cash flows shows net cash flows provided by operating activities of $404,000 in 1999 and $340,000 in 1998. Current liabilities at January 1, 1998, are $290,000. The current cash debt coverage ratio for Quality Department Store and comparative data are as follows.

Illustration 19-15

Current cash debt coverage ratio

$$\text{CURRENT CASH DEBT COVERAGE RATIO} = \frac{\text{NET CASH PROVIDED BY OPERATING ACTIVITIES}}{\text{AVERAGE CURRENT LIABILITIES}}$$

Quality Department Store

1999	1998
$\frac{\$404,000}{\left[\frac{\$303,000 + \$344,500}{2}\right]} = 1.25:1$	$\frac{\$340,000}{\left[\frac{\$290,000 + \$303,000}{2}\right]} = 1.15:1$
Industry average 1.1:1	Sears, Roebuck and Co. 0.264:1

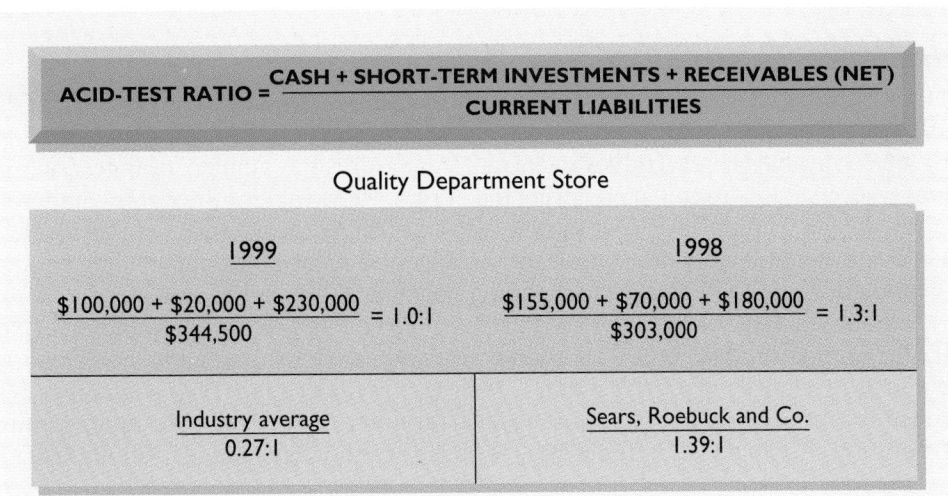

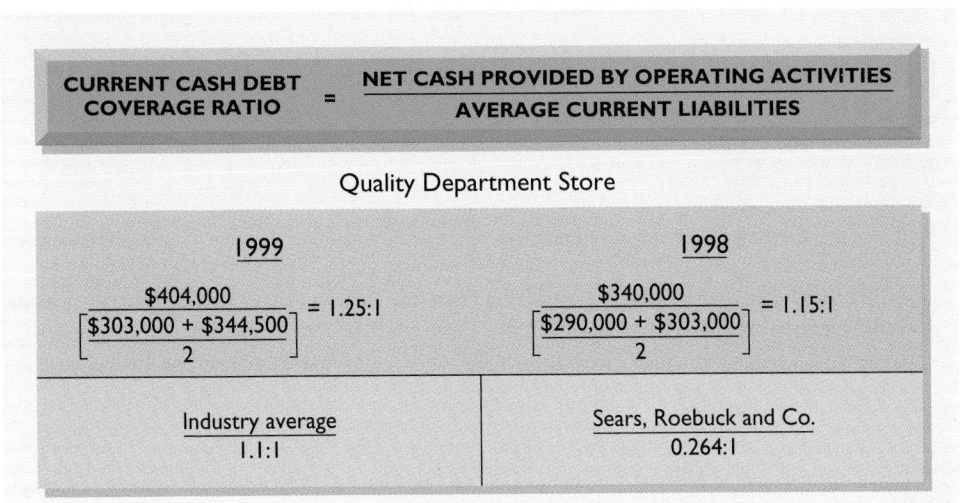

The ratio increased in 1999. Is the coverage adequate? Probably so. Quality's operating cash flow coverage of average current liabilities is slightly greater than the industry average. Sears's current cash debt coverage ratio in 1999 was 0.264:1.

4. Receivables Turnover

Liquidity may be measured by how quickly certain assets can be converted to cash. How liquid, for example, are the receivables? The ratio used to assess the liquidity of the receivables is **receivables turnover**. It measures the number of times, on average, receivables are collected during the period. Receivables turnover is computed by dividing net credit sales (net sales less cash sales) by the average net receivables. Unless seasonal factors are significant, average net receivables outstanding can be computed from the beginning and ending balances of the net receivables.[2]

Assuming that all sales are credit sales and the balance of receivables (net) at the beginning of 1998 is $200,000, the receivables turnover for Quality Department Store and comparative data are shown in Illustration 19-16. Quality's receivables turnover improved in 1999. The turnover of 10.2 times compares quite favorably with Sears's 2.39 times but is inferior to the department store industry's average of 13.7 times.

Illustration 19-16
Receivables turnover

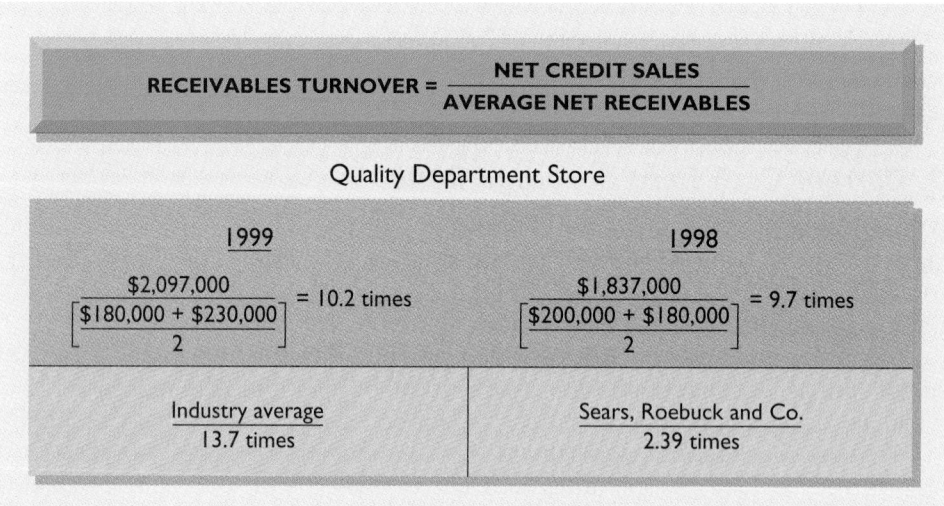

$$\text{RECEIVABLES TURNOVER} = \frac{\text{NET CREDIT SALES}}{\text{AVERAGE NET RECEIVABLES}}$$

Quality Department Store

1999	1998
$\frac{\$2,097,000}{\left[\frac{\$180,000 + \$230,000}{2}\right]} = 10.2 \text{ times}$	$\frac{\$1,837,000}{\left[\frac{\$200,000 + \$180,000}{2}\right]} = 9.7 \text{ times}$
Industry average 13.7 times	Sears, Roebuck and Co. 2.39 times

ACCOUNTING IN ACTION Business Insight

In some cases, receivables turnover may be misleading. Some companies, especially large retail chains, encourage credit and revolving charge sales. They may even slow collections in order to earn a healthy return on the outstanding receivables at interest rates of 18% to 22%. This may explain why **Sears's** turnover is only 2.39 times. In general, however, the faster the turnover, the greater the reliance that can be placed on the current and acid-test ratios for assessing liquidity.

A popular variant of the receivables turnover ratio is to convert it to an **average collection period** in terms of days. This is done by dividing the receivables turnover ratio into 365 days. For example, the receivables turnover of 10.2 times is divided into 365 days to obtain approximately 35.8 days. This means that re-

[2]If seasonal factors are significant, the average receivables balance might be determined by using monthly amounts.

ceivables are collected on average every 36 days, or about every 5 weeks. The average collection period is frequently used to assess the effectiveness of a company's credit and collection policies. The general rule is that the collection period should not greatly exceed the credit term period (the time allowed for payment).

5. Inventory Turnover

Inventory turnover measures the number of times on average the inventory is sold during the period. Its purpose is to measure the liquidity of the inventory. The inventory turnover is computed by dividing cost of goods sold by the average inventory. Unless seasonal factors are significant, average inventory can be computed from the beginning and ending inventory balances.

Assuming that the inventory balance for Quality Department Store at the beginning of 1998 was $450,000, its inventory turnover and comparative data are as shown in Illustration 19-17. Quality's inventory turnover declined slightly in 1999. The turnover of 2.3 times is relatively low compared with the industry average of 6.2 and Sears's 5.14. Generally, the faster the inventory turnover, the less cash that is tied up in inventory and the less the chance of inventory obsolescence.

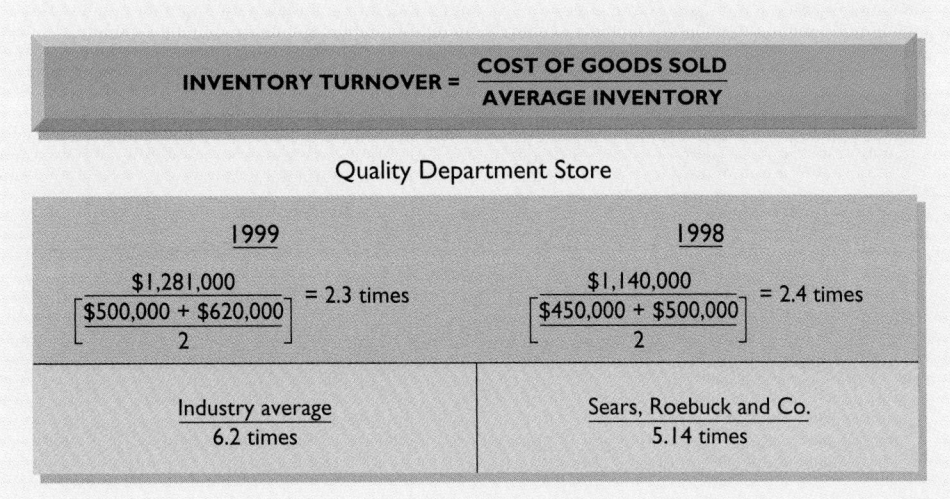

Illustration 19-17

Inventory turnover

$$\text{INVENTORY TURNOVER} = \frac{\text{COST OF GOODS SOLD}}{\text{AVERAGE INVENTORY}}$$

Quality Department Store

1999	1998
$\frac{\$1{,}281{,}000}{\left[\frac{\$500{,}000 + \$620{,}000}{2}\right]} = 2.3$ times	$\frac{\$1{,}140{,}000}{\left[\frac{\$450{,}000 + \$500{,}000}{2}\right]} = 2.4$ times
Industry average 6.2 times	Sears, Roebuck and Co. 5.14 times

A variant of inventory turnover is the **average days to sell the inventory**. It is calculated by dividing the inventory turnover into 365. For example, Quality's 1999 inventory turnover of 2.3 times divided into 365 is approximately 159 days. An average selling time of 159 days is also relatively high compared with the industry average of 59 days (365 ÷ 6.2) and Sears's 71 days (365 ÷ 5.14).

ACCOUNTING IN ACTION *Business Insight*

Inventory turnover ratios vary considerably among industries. For example, grocery store chains have a turnover of 10 times and an average selling period of 37 days. In contrast, jewelry stores have an average turnover of 1.3 times and an average selling period of 281 days. Even within a company there may be significant differences in inventory turnover among different types of products. Thus, in a grocery store the turnover of perishable items such as produce, meats, and dairy products will be faster than the turnover of soaps and detergents.

PROFITABILITY RATIOS

Profitability ratios measure the income or operating success of an enterprise for a given period of time. Income, or the lack of it, affects the company's ability to obtain debt and equity financing. It also affects the company's liquidity position and the company's ability to grow. As a consequence, both creditors and investors are interested in evaluating earning power—profitability. Profitability is frequently used as the ultimate test of management's operating effectiveness.

6. Profit Margin

ALTERNATIVE TERMINOLOGY
Profit margin is also called the *rate of return on sales.*

Profit margin is a measure of the percentage of each dollar of sales that results in net income. It is computed by dividing net income by net sales. Quality Department Store's profit margin and comparative data are shown in Illustration 19-18.

Illustration 19-18
Profit margin

$$\text{PROFIT MARGIN ON SALES} = \frac{\text{NET INCOME}}{\text{NET SALES}}$$

Quality Department Store

1999	1998
$\frac{\$263,800}{\$2,097,000} = 12.6\%$	$\frac{\$208,500}{\$1,837,000} = 11.4\%$
Industry average 3.67%	Sears, Roebuck and Co. 3.96%

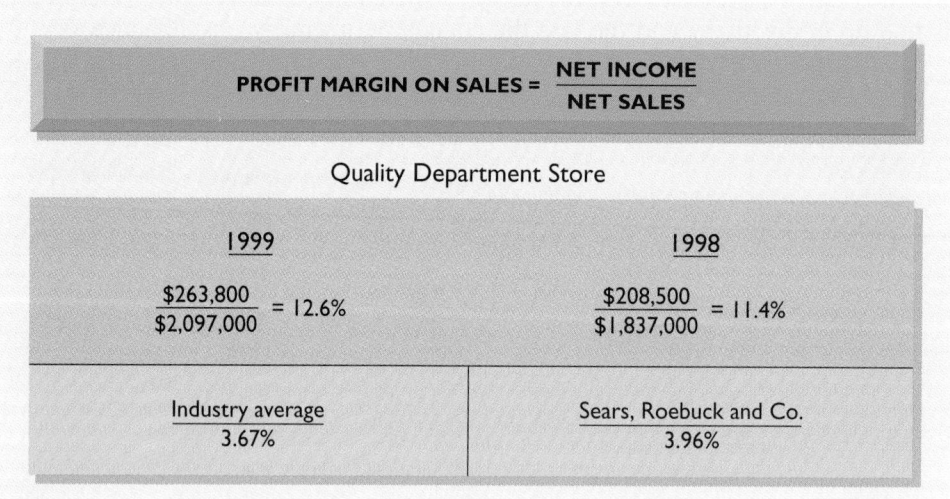

Quality experienced an increase in its profit margin from 1998 to 1999. Its profit margin is unusually high in comparison with the industry average of 3.67% and Sears's 3.96%.

High-volume (high inventory turnover) enterprises such as grocery stores (**Safeway** or **Kroger**) and discount stores (**Kmart** or **Wal-Mart**) generally experience low profit margins. In contrast, low-volume enterprises such as jewelry stores (**Tiffany & Co.**) or airplane manufacturers (**Boeing Co.**) have high profit margins.

7. Cash Return on Sales

Profit margin, discussed above, is an accrual-based ratio, using net income as the numerator. The cash-basis counterpart is the **cash return on sales**. It uses net cash provided by operating activities as the numerator and net sales as the denominator. The difference between these two ratios relates to differences between accrual-basis accounting and cash-basis accounting, that is, differences in the timing of revenue and expense recognition. Using net cash provided by operating activities of $404,000 in 1999 and $340,000 in 1998, Quality Department Store's cash return on sales is computed as shown in Illustration 19-19.

Illustration 19-19

Cash return on sales

$$\text{CASH RETURN ON SALES} = \frac{\text{NET CASH PROVIDED BY OPERATING ACTIVITIES}}{\text{NET SALES}}$$

Quality Department Store

1999	1998
$\frac{\$404,000}{\$2,097,000} = 19.3\%$	$\frac{\$340,000}{\$1,837,000} = 18.5\%$
Industry average 6.2%	Sears, Roebuck and Co. 9.0%

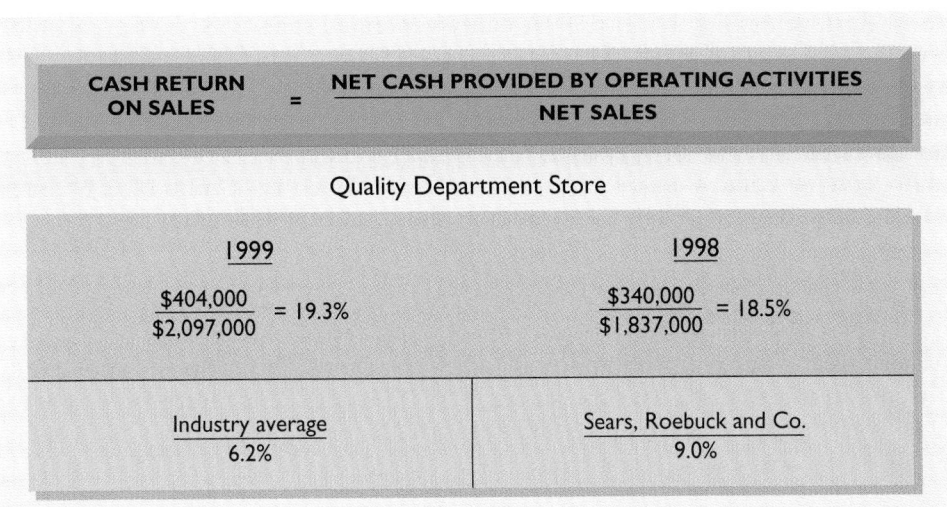

Quality's cash return on sales is considerably higher than its profit margin on sales. The difference of 6.7% in 1999 (19.3% − 12.6%) is due to more noncash charges than noncash credits in the income statement. Quality appears to have a very healthy cash return on sales.

8. Asset Turnover

Asset turnover measures how efficiently a company uses its assets to generate sales. It is determined by dividing net sales by average assets. The resulting number shows the dollars of sales produced by each dollar invested in assets. Unless seasonal factors are significant, average total assets can be computed from the beginning and ending balance of total assets. Assuming that total assets at the beginning of 1998 were $1,446,000, the 1999 and 1998 asset turnover for Quality Department Store and comparative data are as follows.

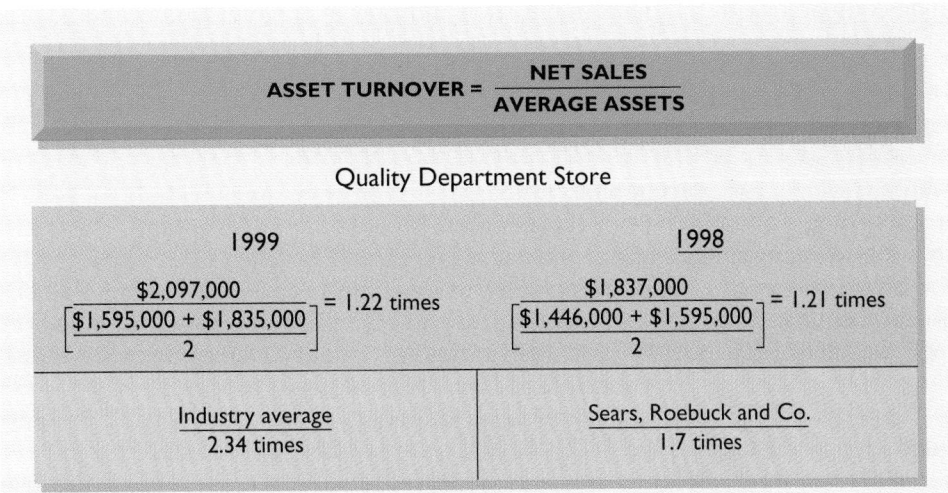

Illustration 19-20

Asset turnover

$$\text{ASSET TURNOVER} = \frac{\text{NET SALES}}{\text{AVERAGE ASSETS}}$$

Quality Department Store

1999	1998
$\frac{\$2,097,000}{\left[\frac{\$1,595,000 + \$1,835,000}{2}\right]} = 1.22 \text{ times}$	$\frac{\$1,837,000}{\left[\frac{\$1,446,000 + \$1,595,000}{2}\right]} = 1.21 \text{ times}$
Industry average 2.34 times	Sears, Roebuck and Co. 1.7 times

Asset turnover shows that in 1999 Quality generated sales of $1.22 for each dollar it had invested in assets. The ratio changed little from 1998 to 1999. Quality's asset turnover is below the industry average of 2.34 times and also below Sears's ratio of 1.7 times.

Asset turnover ratios vary considerably among industries. For example, a large utility company like **Consolidated Edison** (New York) has a ratio of 0.49 times, and the large grocery chain **Kroger Stores** has a ratio of 4.34 times.

9. Return on Assets

An overall measure of profitability is **return on assets**. This ratio is computed by dividing net income by average assets. The 1999 and 1998 return on assets for Quality Department Store and comparative data are shown below.

Illustration 19-21

Return on assets

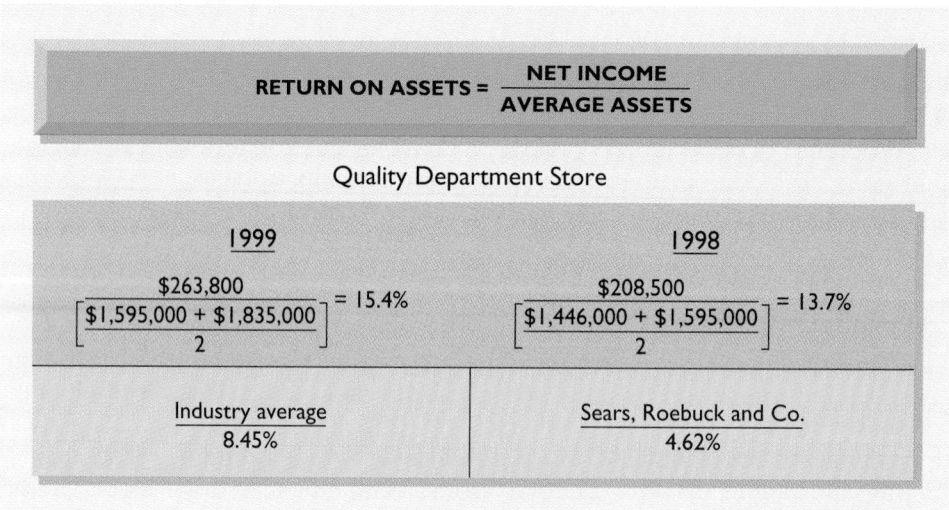

$$\text{RETURN ON ASSETS} = \frac{\text{NET INCOME}}{\text{AVERAGE ASSETS}}$$

Quality Department Store

1999	1998
$\frac{\$263,800}{\left[\frac{\$1,595,000 + \$1,835,000}{2}\right]} = 15.4\%$	$\frac{\$208,500}{\left[\frac{\$1,446,000 + \$1,595,000}{2}\right]} = 13.7\%$
Industry average 8.45%	Sears, Roebuck and Co. 4.62%

Quality's return on assets improved from 1998 to 1999. Its return of 15.4% is very high, compared with the department store industry average of 8.45% and Sears's 4.62%.

10. Return on Common Stockholders' Equity

Another widely used profitability ratio is **return on common stockholders equity**. It measures profitability from the common stockholders' viewpoint. This ratio shows how many dollars of net income were earned for each dollar invested by the owners. It is computed by dividing net income by average common stockholders' equity. Assuming that common stockholders' equity at the beginning of 1998 was $667,000, the 1999 and 1998 ratios for Quality Department Store and comparative data are shown in Illustration 19-22 on page 797.

Quality's rate of return on common stockholders' equity is high at 29.3%, considering an industry average of 22.4% and a rate of 24.6% for Sears.

When preferred stock is present, **preferred dividend** requirements are deducted from net income to compute income available to common stockholders.

Illustration 19-22

Return on common stockholders' equity

$$\text{RETURN ON COMMON STOCKHOLDERS' EQUITY} = \frac{\text{NET INCOME}}{\text{AVERAGE COMMON STOCKHOLDERS' EQUITY}}$$

Quality Department Store

1999	1998
$\dfrac{\$263{,}800}{\left[\dfrac{\$795{,}000 + \$1{,}003{,}000}{2}\right]} = 29.3\%$	$\dfrac{\$208{,}500}{\left[\dfrac{\$667{,}000 + \$795{,}000}{2}\right]} = 28.5\%$
Industry average 22.4%	Sears, Roebuck and Co. 24.6%

Similarly, the par value of preferred stock (or call price, if applicable) must be deducted from total stockholders' equity to determine the amount of common stock equity used in this ratio. The ratio then appears as follows.

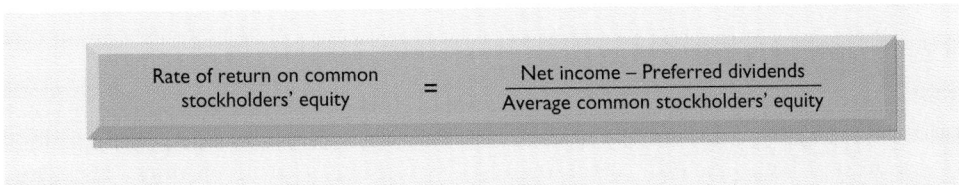

Illustration 19-23

Return on common stockholders' equity with preferred stock

$$\text{Rate of return on common stockholders' equity} = \frac{\text{Net income} - \text{Preferred dividends}}{\text{Average common stockholders' equity}}$$

Note that Quality's rate of return on stockholders' equity (29.3%) is substantially higher than its rate of return on assets (15.4%). The reason is that Quality has made effective use of **leverage** or **trading on the equity** at a gain. Trading on the equity at a gain means that the company has borrowed money at a lower rate of interest than it is able to earn by using the borrowed money. Leverage enables Quality Department Store to use money supplied by nonowners to increase the return to the owners. A comparison of the rate of return on total assets with the rate of interest paid for borrowed money indicates the profitability of trading on the equity. Quality Department Store earns more on its borrowed funds than it has to pay in the form of interest. Thus the return to stockholders exceeds the return on the assets, benefiting from the positive leveraging.

ALTERNATIVE TERMINOLOGY
Trading on the equity is also called *leveraging*.

11. Earnings per Share (EPS)

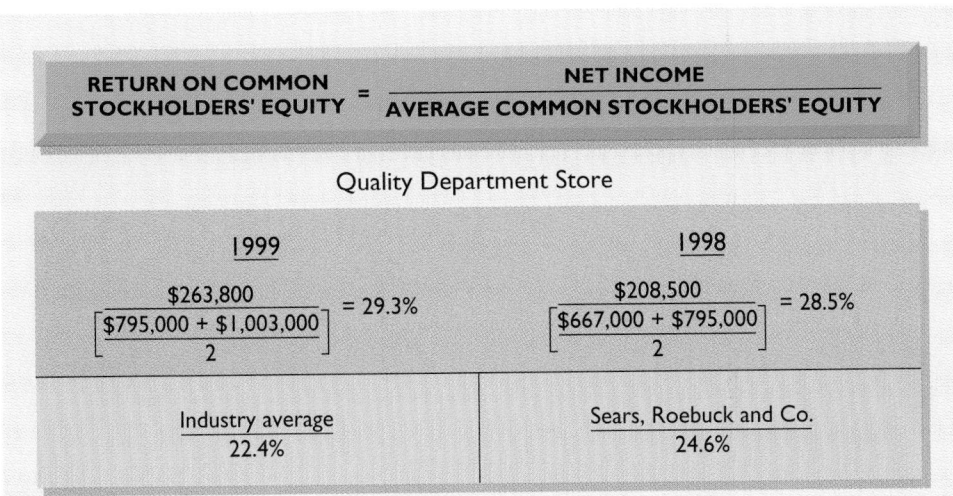

Earnings per share (EPS) is a measure of the net income earned on each share of common stock. It is computed by dividing net income by the number of weighted average common shares outstanding during the year. A measure of net income earned on a per share basis provides a useful perspective for determining profitability. Assuming that there is no change in the number of outstanding shares during 1998 and that the 1999 increase occurred midyear, the net income per share for Quality Department Store for 1999 and 1998 is computed as shown in Illustration 19-24 on page 798.

Illustration 19-24

Earnings per share

$$\text{EARNINGS PER SHARE} = \frac{\text{NET INCOME}}{\text{WEIGHTED AVERAGE COMMON SHARES OUTSTANDING}}$$

Quality Department Store

1999	1998
$\frac{\$263{,}800}{\left[\frac{270{,}000 + 275{,}400}{2}\right]} = \$.97$	$\frac{\$208{,}500}{270{,}000} = \$.77$

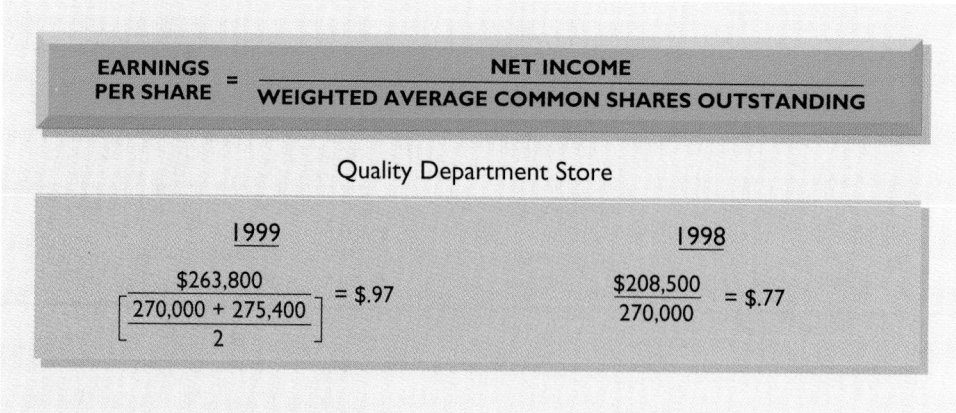

Note that no industry or Sears data are presented. Such comparisons are not meaningful because of the wide variations in the number of shares of outstanding stock among companies. The only meaningful EPS comparison is an intracompany trend comparison: Quality's earnings per share increased 20 cents per share in 1999. This represents a 26% increase over the 1998 earnings per share of 77 cents.

The terms "earnings per share" and "net income per share" refer to the amount of net income applicable to each share of **common stock**. Therefore, in computing EPS, if there are preferred dividends declared for the period, they must be deducted from net income to determine income available to the common stockholders.

12. Price-Earnings Ratio

The **price-earnings (P-E) ratio** is an oft-quoted measure of the ratio of the market price of each share of common stock to the earnings per share. The price-earnings (P-E) ratio reflects investors' assessments of a company's future earnings. It is computed by dividing the market price per share of the stock by earnings per share. Assuming that the market price of Quality Department Store Inc. stock is $8 in 1998 and $12 in 1999, the price-earnings ratio is computed as follows.

Illustration 19-25

Price-earnings ratio

$$\text{PRICE-EARNINGS RATIO} = \frac{\text{MARKET PRICE PER SHARE OF STOCK}}{\text{EARNINGS PER SHARE}}$$

Quality Department Store

1999	1998
$\frac{\$12.00}{\$\ .97} = 12.4 \text{ times}$	$\frac{\$8.00}{\$\ .77} = 10.4 \text{ times}$
Industry average 18 times	Sears, Roebuck and Co. 8 times

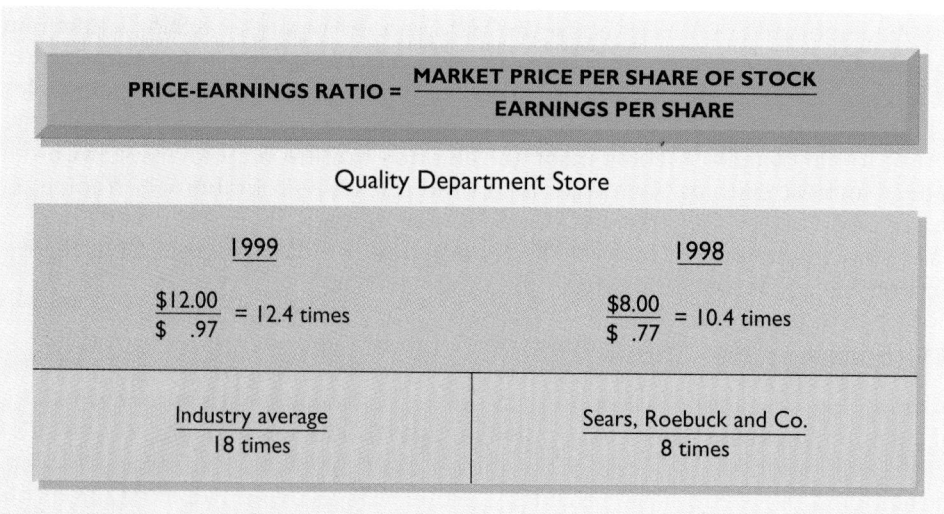

In 1999 each share of Quality's stock sold for 12.4 times the amount that was earned on each share. Quality's price-earnings ratio is lower than the industry average of 18 times, but it is higher than the ratio of 8 times for Sears. The average price-earnings ratio for the stocks that constitute the Dow-Jones industrial average on the New York Stock Exchange in December 2000 was an unusually high 20 times.

ACCOUNTING IN ACTION *Business Insight*

For the stock of some companies, investors are willing to pay over 20 times the current per share earnings. They feel the company's future growth in earnings will provide an adequate (or superior) return on the investment. Examples of companies with price-earnings ratios over 20 are **Oracle** (37), **Microsoft** (38), **Coca-Cola** (77), and **Gillette Co.** (38). Examples of companies with low price-earnings ratios are **Ford Motor** (7), **General Motors** (8), and **United Airlines** (6).

13. Payout Ratio

The **payout ratio** measures the percentage of earnings distributed in the form of cash dividends. It is computed by dividing cash dividends by net income. Companies that have high growth rates generally have low payout ratios because they reinvest most of their net income into the business. The 1999 and 1998 payout ratios for Quality Department Store are computed as follows.

Illustration 19-26
Payout ratio

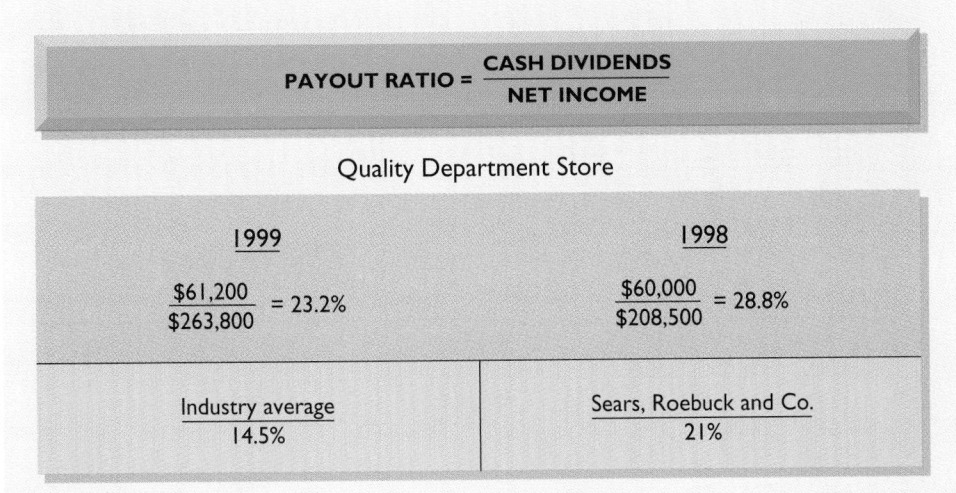

$$\text{PAYOUT RATIO} = \frac{\text{CASH DIVIDENDS}}{\text{NET INCOME}}$$

Quality Department Store

1999	1998
$\frac{\$61,200}{\$263,800} = 23.2\%$	$\frac{\$60,000}{\$208,500} = 28.8\%$
Industry average 14.5%	Sears, Roebuck and Co. 21%

Quality's payout ratio is comparable to Sears's payout ratio of 21%. As indicated earlier (page 783), Quality apparently has decided to fund its purchase of plant assets through retention of earnings.

ACCOUNTING IN ACTION *Business Insight*

Many companies with stable earnings have high payout ratios. For example, **Baltimore Gas and Electric** had an 84% payout ratio over a recent five-year period. **Omega Healthcare's** dividends exceeded net income over the same period. Conversely, companies that are expanding rapidly, such as **Toys "R" Us**, **Microsoft**, and **Tellabs Inc.** have never paid a cash dividend.

SOLVENCY RATIOS

Solvency ratios measure the ability of the company to survive over a long period of time. Long-term creditors and stockholders are particularly interested in a company's ability to pay interest as it comes due and to repay the face value of debt at maturity. Debt to total assets, times interest earned, and cash debt coverage are three ratios that provide information about debt-paying ability.

14. Debt to Total Assets Ratio

The **debt to total assets ratio** measures the percentage of the total assets provided by creditors. It is computed by dividing total debt (both current and long-term liabilities) by total assets. This ratio indicates the company's degree of leverage. It also provides some indication of the company's ability to withstand losses without impairing the interests of creditors. The higher the percentage of debt to total assets, the greater the risk that the company may be unable to meet its maturing obligations. The 1999 and 1998 ratios for Quality Department Store and comparative data are as follows.

Illustration 19-27

Debt to total assets ratio

$$\text{DEBT TO TOTAL ASSETS} = \frac{\text{TOTAL DEBT}}{\text{TOTAL ASSETS}}$$

Quality Department Store

1999	1998
$\frac{\$832,000}{\$1,835,000} = 45.3\%$	$\frac{\$800,000}{\$1,595,000} = 50.2\%$
Industry average 38%	Sears, Roebuck and Co. 81.5%

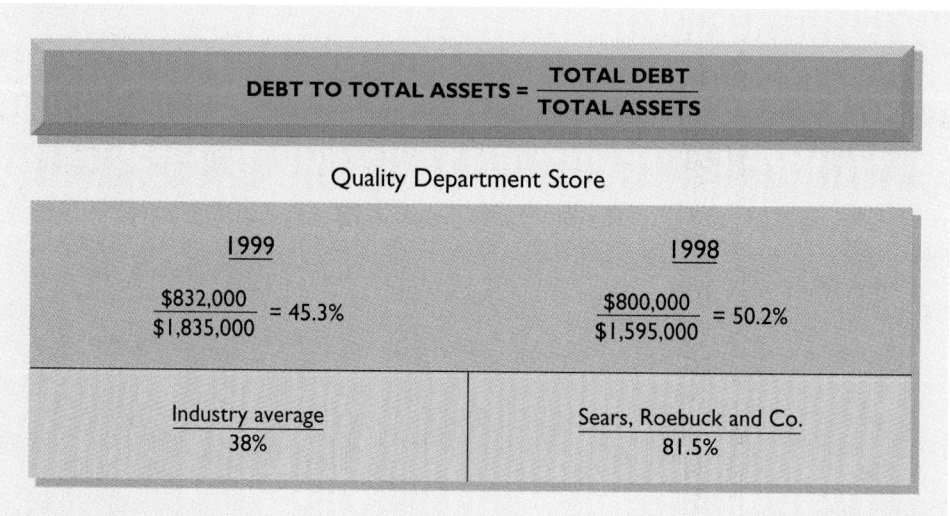

A ratio of 45.3% means that creditors have provided 45.3% of Quality Department Store's total assets. Quality's 45.3% is above the industry average of 38%. But it is considerably below the high 81.5% ratio of Sears. The lower the ratio, the more equity "buffer" there is available to the creditors. Thus, from the creditors' point of view, a low ratio of debt to total assets is usually desirable.

The adequacy of this ratio is often judged in the light of the company's earnings. Generally, companies with relatively stable earnings (such as public utilities) have higher debt to total assets ratios than cyclical companies with widely fluctuating earnings (such as many high-tech companies).

ACCOUNTING IN ACTION *Business Insight*

Examples of total debt to total assets ratios for selected companies are:

	Total Debt to Total Assets as a Percent
Toys "R" Us	56%
The Coca-Cola Company	56%
Merck & Co.	63%
Kellogg Company	83%
Bob Evans Farms	31%
Eastman Kodak	72%

Another means used in practice to measure leverage is the **debt to equity ratio**. It is computed by dividing total liabilities by total stockholders' equity. It shows the relative use of borrowed funds (total liabilities) as compared to resources invested by the owners. This ratio may be computed in several ways. Debt may be defined to include only the noncurrent portion of the liabilities. Also, intangible assets may be excluded from owners' equity (resulting in tangible net worth). Therefore, care should be taken when making comparisons using this ratio.

15. Times Interest Earned

Times interest earned provides an indication of the company's ability to meet interest payments as they come due. It is computed by dividing income before interest expense and income taxes by interest expense. The 1999 and 1998 ratios for Quality Department Store and comparative data are shown in Illustration 19-28. Note that times interest earned uses income before income taxes and interest expense. This represents the amount available to cover interest. For Quality Department Store the 1999 amount of $468,000 is computed by taking the income before income taxes of $432,000 and adding back the $36,000 of interest expense.

ALTERNATIVE TERMINOLOGY
Times interest earned is also called *interest coverage.*

Illustration 19-28
Times interest earned

$$\text{TIMES INTEREST EARNED} = \frac{\text{INCOME BEFORE INCOME TAXES AND INTEREST EXPENSE}}{\text{INTEREST EXPENSE}}$$

Quality Department Store

1999	1998
$\frac{\$468,000}{\$36,000} = 13$ times	$\frac{\$388,000}{\$40,500} = 9.6$ times
Industry average 8.19 times	Sears, Roebuck and Co. 3.09 times

Quality's interest expense is well covered at 13 times, compared with the industry average of 8.19 times and Sears's 3.09 times.

ACCOUNTING IN ACTION e-Business Insight

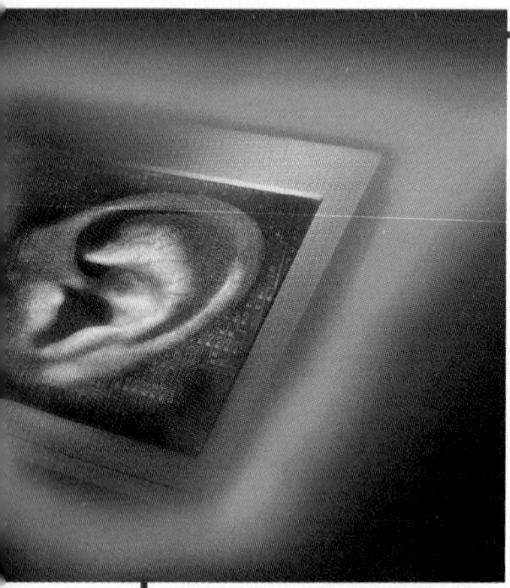

Today, investors have access to information provided by corporate managers that used to be available only to professional analysts. Corporate managers have always made themselves available to security analysts for questions at the end of every quarter. Now, because of a combination of new corporate disclosure requirements by the Securities and Exchange Commission and technologies that make communication to large numbers of people possible at a very low price, the average investor can listen in on these discussions. For example, one individual investor, Matthew Johnson, a **Nortel Networks** local area network engineer in Belfast, Northern Ireland, "stayed up past midnight to listen to **Apple Computer's** recent Internet conference call. Hearing the company's news 'from the dog's mouth,' he says 'gave me better information' than hunting through chat-rooms."

SOURCE: Jeff D. Opdyke, "Individuals Pick Up on Conference Calls," *The Wall Street Journal*, November 20, 2000.

16. Cash Debt Coverage Ratio

The ratio of net cash provided by operating activities to average total liabilities is the **cash debt coverage ratio**. This ratio is a cash-basis measure of **solvency**. It demonstrates a company's ability to repay its liabilities from cash generated by operating activities, without having to liquidate assets. Using Quality's net cash provided by operating activities of $404,000 in 1999 and $340,000 in 1998 and assuming total liabilities of $740,000 on January 1, 1998, the cash debt coverage ratios are as follows.

Illustration 19-29

Cash debt coverage ratio

$$\text{CASH DEBT COVERAGE RATIO} = \frac{\text{NET CASH PROVIDED BY OPERATING ACTIVITIES}}{\text{AVERAGE TOTAL LIABILITIES}}$$

Quality Department Store

1999	1998
$\dfrac{\$404,000}{\left[\dfrac{\$800,000 + \$832,000}{2}\right]} = .495 \text{ times}$	$\dfrac{\$340,000}{\left[\dfrac{\$740,000 + \$800,000}{2}\right]} = .442 \text{ times}$

Industry average	Sears, Roebuck and Co.
0.38 times	0.12 times

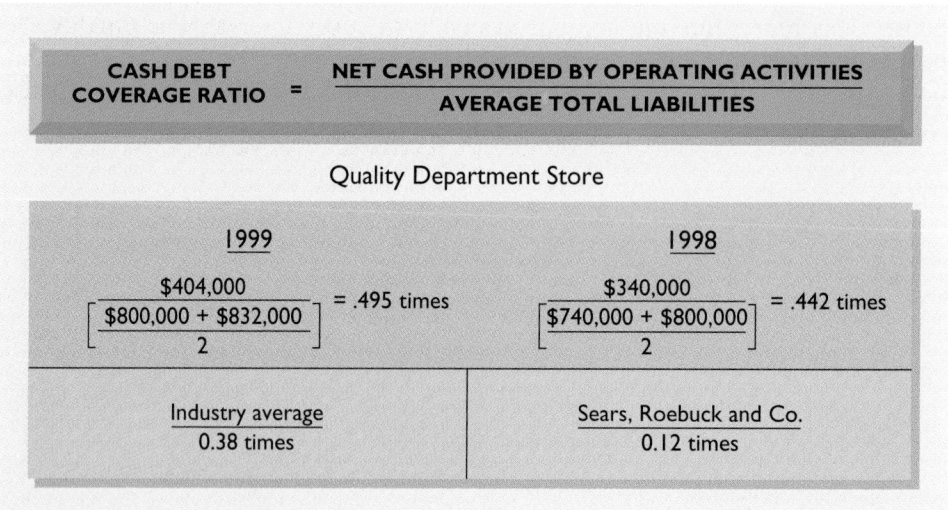

Based on net cash generated from operations in 1999, it would take Quality approximately two years to generate enough cash to pay off all its liabilities. This assumes that all of the net cash generated is used for that purpose only. Quality's cash debt coverage ratio is superior to that of the retail industry and of Sears.

SUMMARY OF RATIOS

A summary of the ratios discussed in the chapter is presented in Illustration 19-30. The summary includes the formula and purpose or use of each ratio.

Illustration 19-30

Summary of liquidity, profitability, and solvency ratios

Ratio	Formula	Purpose or Use
Liquidity Ratios		
1. Current ratio	$\frac{\text{Current assets}}{\text{Current liabilities}}$	Measures short-term debt-paying ability.
2. Acid-test (quick) ratio	$\frac{\text{Cash + Short-term investments + Receivables (net)}}{\text{Current liabilities}}$	Measures immediate short-term liquidity.
3. Current cash debt coverage ratio	$\frac{\text{Net cash provided by operating activities}}{\text{Average current liabilities}}$	Measures short-term debt-paying ability (cash basis).
4. Receivables turnover	$\frac{\text{Net credit sales}}{\text{Average net receivables}}$	Measures liquidity of receivables.
5. Inventory turnover	$\frac{\text{Cost of goods sold}}{\text{Average inventory}}$	Measures liquidity of inventory.
Profitability Ratios		
6. Profit margin	$\frac{\text{Net income}}{\text{Net sales}}$	Measures net income generated by each dollar of sales.
7. Cash return on sales	$\frac{\text{Net cash provided by operating activities}}{\text{Net sales}}$	Measures net cash flow generated by each dollar of sales.
8. Asset turnover	$\frac{\text{Net sales}}{\text{Average assets}}$	Measures how efficiently assets are used to generate sales.
9. Return on assets	$\frac{\text{Net income}}{\text{Average assets}}$	Measures overall profitability of assets.
10. Return on common stockholders' equity	$\frac{\text{Net income}}{\text{Average common stockholders' equity}}$	Measures profitability of owners' investment.
11. Earnings per share (EPS)	$\frac{\text{Net income}}{\text{Weighted average common shares outstanding}}$	Measures net income earned on each share of common stock.
12. Price-earnings (P-E) ratio	$\frac{\text{Market price per share of stock}}{\text{Earnings per share}}$	Measures the ratio of the market price per share to earnings per share.
13. Payout ratio	$\frac{\text{Cash dividends}}{\text{Net income}}$	Measures percentage of earnings distributed in the form of cash dividends.
Solvency Ratios		
14. Debt to total assets ratio	$\frac{\text{Total debt}}{\text{Total assets}}$	Measures the percentage of total assets provided by creditors.
15. Times interest earned	$\frac{\text{Income before income taxes and interest expense}}{\text{Interest expense}}$	Measures ability to meet interest payments as they come due.
16. Cash debt coverage ratio	$\frac{\text{Net cash provided by operating activities}}{\text{Average total liabilities}}$	Measures the long-term debt-paying ability (cash basis).

BEFORE YOU GO ON...

REVIEW IT

1. What are liquidity ratios? Explain the current ratio, acid-test ratio, current cash debt coverage ratio, receivables turnover, and inventory turnover.
2. What are profitability ratios? Explain the profit margin, cash return on sales, asset turnover ratio, return on assets, return on common stockholders' equity, earnings per share, price-earnings ratio, and payout ratio.
3. What are solvency ratios? Explain the debt to total assets ratio, times interest earned, and cash debt coverage ratio.

DO IT

Selected financial data for Drummond Company at December 31, 2002, are as follows: cash $60,000; receivables (net) $80,000; inventory $70,000; current liabilities $140,000. Compute the current and acid-test ratios.

ACTION PLAN

- Use the formula for the current ratio: Current assets ÷ Current liabilities.
- Use the formula for the acid-test ratio: Cash + Short-term investments + Receivables (net) ÷ Current liabilities.

SOLUTION: The current ratio is 1.5:1 ($210,000 ÷ $140,000). The acid-test ratio is 1:1 ($140,000 ÷ $140,000).

Related exercise material: BE19-7, BE19-8, BE19-9, BE19-10, BE19-11, E19-5, E19-6, and E19-7.

THE NAVIGATOR

LIMITATIONS OF FINANCIAL STATEMENT ANALYSIS

STUDY OBJECTIVE 6

Recognize the limitations of financial statement analysis.

Significant business decisions are frequently made using one or more of the analytical tools illustrated in this chapter. But, you should be aware of the limitations of these tools and of the financial statements on which they are based.

ESTIMATES

Financial statements contain numerous estimates. Estimates are used in determining the allowance for uncollectible receivables, periodic depreciation, the costs of warranties, and contingent losses. To the extent that these estimates are inaccurate, the financial ratios and percentages are inaccurate.

COST

Traditional financial statements are based on cost. They are not adjusted for price-level changes. Comparisons of unadjusted financial data from different periods may be rendered invalid by significant inflation or deflation. For example, a five-year comparison of Sears's revenues might show a growth of 36%. But this growth trend would be misleading if the general price level had increased significantly during the same period.

ALTERNATIVE ACCOUNTING METHODS

Companies vary in the generally accepted accounting principles they use. Such variations may hamper comparability. For example, one company may use the FIFO method of inventory costing; another company in the same industry may use LIFO. If inventory is a significant asset to both companies, it is unlikely that their current ratios are comparable. For example, if **General Motors Corporation** had used FIFO instead of LIFO in valuing its inventories, its inventories would have been 26% higher. This difference would significantly affect the current ratio (and other ratios as well). In addition to differences in inventory costing methods, differences also exist in reporting such items as depreciation, depletion, and amortization. These differences in accounting methods might be detectable from reading the notes to the financial statements. But, adjusting the financial data to compensate for the different methods is difficult, if not impossible in some cases.

INTERNATIONAL NOTE

In many industries competition is global. To evaluate a firm's standing, an investor or analyst must make comparisons to firms from other countries. But, given the many differences in accounting practices, these comparisons can be both difficult and misleading.

ATYPICAL DATA

Fiscal year-end data may not be typical of the financial condition during the year. Firms frequently establish a fiscal year-end that coincides with the low point in operating activity or in inventory levels. Therefore, certain account balances (cash, receivables, payables, and inventories) may not be representative of the balances in the accounts during the year.

ETHICS NOTE

When investigating diversified firms, investors are often most interested to learn about the results of particular divisions. Firms are required to disclose the results of distinct lines of business separately if they are a material part of operations. Unfortunately, shifting revenues and expenses across divisions to achieve desired results reduces the usefulness of this information for financial statement analysis.

DIVERSIFICATION OF FIRMS

Diversification in U.S. industry also limits the usefulness of financial analysis. Many firms today are so diversified that they cannot be classified by a single industry—they are true conglomerates. Others appear to be comparable but are not.

BEFORE YOU GO ON...

REVIEW IT

1. What are some limitations of financial statement analysis?
2. Give examples of alternative accounting methods that hamper comparability.
3. In what way does diversification limit the usefulness of financial statement analysis?

A LOOK BACK AT OUR FEATURE STORY

Refer back to the Feature Story about cabby Carlos Rubino at the beginning of the chapter, and answer the following questions.

1. In what ways has cabby Carlos Rubino joined the technological revolution?
2. What extra service does Rubino provide his passengers?
3. What is the monthly cost of Rubino's quotes and Internet access?

SOLUTION

1. Cabby Rubino carries in his cab an Hitachi Traveler laptop computer and a wireless cell phone.
2. Rubino provides real-time stock quotes using his wireless Internet access to **Yahoo!**, **Amazon.com**, and **America Online**. He also gladly provides his own stock tips and investment advice.
3. Rubino pays $100 a month for access to real-time quotes and $54 a month for wireless Internet access (plus he has the investment cost in his laptop computer and his cell phone).

THE NAVIGATOR

Additional Demonstration Problem

DEMONSTRATION PROBLEM

The condensed financial statements ot The Estée Lauder Companies, Inc., for the years ended June 30, 1998 and 1997, are presented below.

THE ESTÉE LAUDER COMPANIES, INC.
Balance Sheets
June 30

	(in millions) 1998	1997
Assets		
Current assets		
Cash and cash equivalents	$ 277.5	$ 255.6
Accounts receivable (net)	497.8	471.7
Inventories	513.2	440.6
Prepaid expenses and other current assets	166.1	143.2
Total current assets	1,454.6	1,311.1
Property, plant, and equipment (net)	335.8	265.0
Investments	27.7	25.9
Intangibles and other assets	694.7	271.1
Total assets	$2,512.8	$1,873.1
Liabilities and Stockholders' Equity		
Current liabilities	$ 837.4	$ 759.5
Long-term liabilities	619.0	565.9
Stockholders' equity—common	1,056.4	547.7
Total liabilities and stockholders' equity	$2,512.8	$1,873.1

THE ESTÉE LAUDER COMPANIES, INC.
Income Statements
For the Year Ended June 30

	(in millions) 1998	1997
Revenues	$3,618.0	$3,381.6
Costs and expenses		
Cost of goods sold	819.5	765.1
Selling and administrative expenses	2,357.6	2,224.6
Interest expense	38.1	52.4
Total costs and expenses	3,215.2	3,042.1
Income before income taxes	402.8	339.5
Income tax expense	166.0	165.3
Net income	$ 236.8	$ 174.2

Instructions

Compute the following ratios for 1998 and 1997.

(a) Current ratio.
(b) Inventory turnover. (Inventory on 6/30/96 was $452.8.)
(c) Profit margin ratio.
(d) Return on assets. (Assets on 6/30/96 were $1,779.4.)
(e) Return on common stockholders' equity. (Equity on 6/30/96 was $394.2.)
(f) Debt to total assets ratio.
(g) Times interest earned.

SOLUTION TO DEMONSTRATION PROBLEM

	1998	1997
(a) Current ratio:		
\$1,454.6 ÷ \$837.4 =	1.7:1	
\$1,311.1 ÷ \$759.5 =		1.7:1
(b) Inventory turnover:		
\$819.5 ÷ [(\$513.2 + \$440.6) ÷ 2] =	1.7 times	
\$765.1 ÷ [(\$440.6 + \$452.8) ÷ 2] =		1.7 times
(c) Profit margin:		
\$236.8 ÷ \$3,618.0 =	6.5%	
\$174.2 ÷ \$3,381.6 =		5.2%
(d) Return on assets:		
\$236.8 ÷ [(\$2,512.8 + \$1,873.1) ÷ 2] =	10.8%	
\$174.2 ÷ [(\$1,873.1 + \$1,779.4) ÷ 2] =		9.5%
(e) Return on common stockholders' equity:		
\$236.8 ÷ [(\$1,056.4 + \$547.7) ÷ 2] =	30%	
\$174.2 ÷ [(\$547.7 + \$394.2) ÷ 2] =		37%
(f) Debt to total assets ratio:		
(\$837.4 + \$619.0) ÷ \$2,512.8 =	58%	
(\$795.5 + \$565.9) ÷ \$1,873.1 =		71%
(g) Times interest earned:		
(\$236.8 + \$166.0 + \$38.1) ÷ \$38.1 =	11.6 times	
(\$174.2 + \$165.3 + \$52.4) ÷ \$52.4 =		7.5 times

ACTION PLAN

- Remember that the current ratio includes all current assets. The acid-test ratio uses only cash, temporary investments, and net receivables.
- Use average balances for turnover ratios like inventory, receivables, and assets.
- Remember that return on assets is greater or smaller than return on common stockholders' equity depending on cost of debt.

THE NAVIGATOR

SUMMARY OF STUDY OBJECTIVES

1. ***Discuss the need for comparative analysis.*** There are three bases of comparison: (1) Intracompany, which compares an item or financial relationship with other data within a company. (2) Industry, which compares company data with industry averages. (3) Intercompany, which compares an item or financial relationship of a company with data of one or more competing companies.

2. ***Identify the tools of financial statement analysis.*** Financial statements can be analyzed horizontally, vertically, and with ratios.

3. ***Explain and apply horizontal (trend) analysis.*** Horizontal analysis is a technique for evaluating a series of data over a period of time to determine the increase or decrease that has taken place, expressed as either an amount or a percentage.

4. ***Describe and apply vertical analysis.*** Vertical analysis is a technique that expresses each item within a financial statement in terms of a percentage of a relevant total or a base amount.

5. ***Identify and compute ratios, and describe their purpose and use in analyzing a firm's liquidity, profitability, and solvency.*** The formula and purpose of each ratio was presented in Illustration 19-30.

6. ***Recognize the limitations of financial statement analysis.*** The usefulness of analytical tools is limited by the use of estimates, the cost basis, the application of alternative accounting methods, atypical data at year-end, and the diversification of firms.

THE NAVIGATOR

Key Term Matching Activity

GLOSSARY

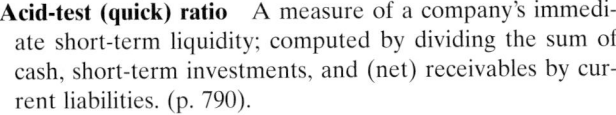

Acid-test (quick) ratio A measure of a company's immediate short-term liquidity; computed by dividing the sum of cash, short-term investments, and (net) receivables by current liabilities. (p. 790).

Asset turnover A measure of how efficiently a company uses its assets to generate sales; computed by dividing net sales by average assets. (p. 795).

Cash debt coverage ratio A cash-basis measure of long-term debt-paying ability; computed as net cash provided by operating activities divided by average total liabilities. (p. 802).

Cash return on sales A measure of the cash generated by each dollar of sales; computed as net cash provided by operating activities divided by net sales. (p. 794).

Current cash debt coverage ratio A cash-basis measure of short-term debt-paying ability; computed as net cash provided by operating activities divided by average current liabilities. (p. 791).

Current ratio A measure used to evaluate a company's liquidity and short-term debt-paying ability; computed by dividing current assets by current liabilities. (p. 789).

Debt to total assets ratio Measures the percentage of total assets provided by creditors; computed by dividing total debt by total assets. (p. 800).

Earnings per share (EPS) The net income earned by each share of common stock; computed by dividing net income by the weighted average common shares outstanding. (p. 797).

Horizontal analysis A technique for evaluating a series of financial statement data over a period of time, to determine the increase (decrease) that has taken place, expressed as either an amount or a percentage. (p. 782).

Inventory turnover A measure of the liquidity of inventory; computed by dividing cost of goods sold by average inventory. (p. 793).

Leverage See Trading on the equity.

Liquidity ratios Measures of the short-term ability of the enterprise to pay its maturing obligations and to meet unexpected needs for cash. (p. 789).

Payout ratio Measures the percentage of earnings distributed in the form of cash dividends; computed by dividing cash dividends by net income. (p. 799).

Price-earnings (P-E) ratio Measures the ratio of the market price of each share of common stock to the earnings per share; computed by dividing the market price of the stock by earnings per share. (p. 798).

Profit margin Measures the percentage of each dollar of sales that results in net income; computed by dividing net income by net sales. (p. 794).

Profitability ratios Measures of the income or operating success of an enterprise for a given period of time. (p. 794).

Ratio An expression of the mathematical relationship between one quantity and another. The relationship may be expressed either as a percentage, a rate, or a simple proportion. (p. 788).

Ratio analysis A technique for evaluating financial statements that expresses the relationship between selected financial statement data. (p. 788).

Receivables turnover A measure of the liquidity of receivables; computed by dividing net credit sales by average net receivables. (p. 792).

Return on assets An overall measure of profitability; computed by dividing net income by average assets. (p. 796).

Return on common stockholders' equity Measures the dollars of net income earned for each dollar invested by the owners; computed by dividing net income by average common stockholders' equity. (p. 796).

Solvency ratios Measures of the ability of the enterprise to survive over a long period of time. (p. 800).

Times interest earned Measures a company's ability to meet interest payments as they come due; computed by dividing income before interest expense and income taxes by interest expense. (p. 801).

Trading on the equity (leverage) Borrowing money at a lower rate of interest than can be earned by using the borrowed money. (p. 797).

Vertical analysis A technique for evaluating financial statement data that expresses each item within a financial statement as a percent of a base amount. (p. 785).

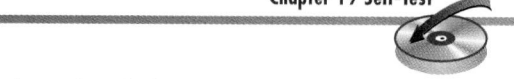

Chapter 19 Self-Test

SELF-STUDY QUESTIONS

Answers are at the end of the chapter.

(SO 1) 1. Comparisons of data within a company are an example of the following comparative basis:
a. Industry averages.
b. Intracompany.
c. Intercompany.
d. Both (b) and (c).

(SO 2) 2. In horizontal analysis, each item is expressed as a percentage of the:
a. net income amount.
b. stockholders' equity amount.
c. total assets amount.
d. base year amount.

(SO 4) 3. In vertical analysis, the base amount for depreciation expense is generally:
a. net sales.
b. depreciation expense in a previous year.
c. gross profit.
d. fixed assets.

(SO 4) 4. The following schedule is a display of what type of analysis?

	Amount	Percent
Current assets	$200,000	25%
Property, plant, and equipment	600,000	75%
Total assets	$800,000	

a. Horizontal analysis.
b. Differential analysis.
c. Vertical analysis.
d. Ratio analysis.

5. Earlville Corporation reported net sales of $300,000, $330,000, and $360,000 in the years, 2000, 2001, and 2002, respectively. If 2000 is the base year, what is the trend percentage for 2002? (SO 3)
a. 77%.
b. 108%.
c. 120%.
d. 130%.

6. Which of the following measures is an evaluation of a firm's ability to pay current liabilities? (SO 5)
a. Acid-test ratio.
b. Current ratio.
c. Both (a) and (b).
d. None of the above.

7. A measure useful in evaluating the efficiency in managing inventories is: (SO 5)
a. inventory turnover.
b. average days to sell inventory.
c. Both (a) and (b).
d. None of the above.

8. Which of the following is *not* a liquidity ratio? (SO 5)
a. Current ratio.
b. Asset turnover.
c. Inventory turnover.
d. Receivables turnover.

(SO 5) 9. Yorkville Corporation reported net income $24,000, net sales $400,000, and average assets $600,000 for 2002. The 2002 profit margin was:
a. 6%.
b. 12%.
c. 40%.
d. 200%.

10. Which of the following is generally *not* considered to be a limitation of financial analysis? (SO 6)
a. Use of estimates.
b. Use of ratio analysis.
c. Use of cost.
d. Use of alternative accounting methods.

THE NAVIGATOR

QUESTIONS

1. (a) Tom Truemper believes that the analysis of financial statements is directed at two characteristics of a company: liquidity and profitability. Is Tom correct? Explain.
   (b) Are short-term creditors, long-term creditors, and stockholders interested primarily in the same characteristics of a company? Explain.
2. (a) Distinguish among the following bases of comparison: (1) intracompany, (2) industry averages, and (3) intercompany.
   (b) Give the principal value of using each of the three bases of comparison.
3. Two popular methods of financial statement analysis are horizontal analysis and vertical analysis. Explain the difference between these two methods.
4. (a) If DeKalb Company had net income of $480,000 in 2002 and it experienced a 24.5% increase in net income for 2003, what is its net income for 2003?
   (b) If six cents of every dollar of DeKalb's revenue is net income in 2002, what is the dollar amount of 2002 revenue?
5. What is a ratio? What are the different ways of expressing the relationship of two amounts? What information does a ratio provide?
6. Name the major ratios useful in assessing (a) liquidity and (b) solvency.
7. Roger Holloway is puzzled. His company had a profit margin of 10% in 2002. He feels that this is an indication that the company is doing well. Loren Foelske, his accountant, says that more information is needed to determine the firm's financial well-being. Who is correct? Why?
8. What do the following classes of ratios measure? (a) Liquidity ratios. (b) Profitability ratios. (c) Solvency ratios.
9. What is the difference between the current ratio and the acid-test ratio?
10. Seneca Company, a retail store, has a receivables turnover of 4.5 times. The industry average is 12.5 times. Does Seneca have a collection problem with its receivables?
11. Which ratios should be used to help answer the following questions?
    (a) How efficient is a company in using its assets to produce sales?
    (b) How near to sale is the inventory on hand?
    (c) How many dollars of net income were earned for each dollar invested by the owners?
    (d) How able is a company to meet interest charges as they fall due?
12. The price-earnings ratio of **General Motors** (automobile builder) was 8, and the price-earnings ratio of **Microsoft** (computer software) was 38. Which company did the stock market favor? Explain.
13. What is the formula for computing the payout ratio? Would you expect this ratio to be high or low for a growth company?
14. Holding all other factors constant, indicate whether each of the following changes generally signals good or bad news about a company.
    (a) Increase in profit margin.
    (b) Decrease in inventory turnover.
    (c) Increase in the current ratio.
    (d) Decrease in earnings per share.
    (e) Increase in price-earnings ratio.
    (f) Increase in debt to total assets ratio.
    (g) Decrease in times interest earned.
15. The return on total assets for Matson Corporation is 7.6%. During the same year Matson's return on common stockholders' equity is 12.8%. What is the explanation for the difference in the two rates?
16. Which two ratios do you think should be of greatest interest to:
    (a) A pension fund considering the purchase of 20-year bonds?
    (b) A bank contemplating a short-term loan?
    (c) A common stockholder?
17. (a) What is meant by trading on the equity?
    (b) How would you determine the profitability of trading on the equity?
18. Downing Inc. has net income of $210,000, weighted average shares of common stock outstanding of 50,000, and preferred dividends for the period of $40,000. What is Downing's earnings per share of common stock? Downing Sherrick, the president of Downing Inc., believes the computed EPS of the company is high. Comment.
19. Identify and briefly explain five limitations of financial analysis.
20. Explain how the choice of one of the following accounting methods over the other raises or lowers a company's net income during a period of continuing inflation.
    (a) Use of FIFO instead of LIFO for inventory costing.
    (b) Use of a 6-year life for machinery instead of a 9-year life.
    (c) Use of straight-line depreciation instead of accelerated declining-balance depreciation.
21. What three ratios are dependent on cash-basis data? That is, what ratios use data from the statement of cash flows?

BRIEF EXERCISES*

Prepare horizontal analysis. (SO 3)

BE19-1 Using the following data from the comparative balance sheet of Hal Adelman Company, illustrate horizontal analysis.

	December 31, 2003	December 31, 2002
Accounts receivable	$ 520,000	$ 400,000
Inventory	$ 840,000	$ 600,000
Total assets	$3,500,000	$2,800,000

Prepare vertical analysis. (SO 4)

BE19-2 Using the same data presented above in BE19-1 for Hal Adelman Company, illustrate vertical analysis.

Calculate percentage of change. (SO 3)

BE19-3 Net income was $500,000 in 2001, $400,000 in 2002, and $504,000 in 2003. What is the percentage of change from **(a)** 2001 to 2002 and **(b)** 2002 to 2003? Is the change an increase or a decrease?

Calculate net income. (SO 3)

BE19-4 If Domingo Company had net income of $700,000 in 2003 and it experienced a 25% increase in net income over 2002, what was its 2002 net income?

Calculate change in net income. (SO 4)

BE19-5 Vertical analysis (common size) percentages for Veronica Company's sales, cost of goods sold, and expenses are shown below.

Vertical Analysis	2003	2002	2001
Sales	100.0	100.0	100.0
Cost of goods sold	58.2	62.4	64.5
Expenses	25.0	26.6	28.5

Did Veronica's net income as a percent of sales increase, decrease, or remain unchanged over the 3-year period? Provide numerical support for your answer.

Calculate change in net income. (SO 3)

BE19-6 Horizontal analysis (trend analysis) percentages for Flatt Company's sales, cost of goods sold, and expenses are shown below.

Horizontal Analysis	2003	2002	2001
Sales	96.2	106.8	100.0
Cost of goods sold	102.0	97.0	100.0
Expenses	110.6	95.4	100.0

Did Flatt's net income increase, decrease, or remain unchanged over the 3-year period?

Calculate liquidity ratios. (SO 5)

BE19-7 Selected condensed data taken from a recent balance sheet of Becky Farms are as follows.

BECKY FARMS
Balance Sheet (partial)

Cash	$ 8,241,000
Marketable securities	1,947,000
Accounts receivable	12,545,000
Inventories	14,814,000
Other current assets	5,371,000
Total current assets	$42,918,000
Total current liabilities	$40,844,000

What are the **(a)** working capital, **(b)** current, and **(c)** acid-test ratios?

Calculate profitability ratios. (SO 5)

BE19-8 Crear Corporation has net income of $13.5 million and net revenue of $90 million in 2002. Its assets were $12 million at the beginning of the year and $18 million at the end of the year. What are **(a)** Crear's asset turnover and **(b)** profit margin?

---

*Follow the rounding procedures used in the chapter.

BE19-9 The following data are taken from the financial statements of Geiss Company.

Evaluate collection of accounts receivable.
(SO 5)

	2003	2002
Accounts receivable (net), end of year	$ 560,000	$ 540,000
Net sales on account	3,850,000	3,100,000

Terms for all sales are 1/10, n/60.

(a) Compute for each year (1) the receivables turnover and (2) the average collection period. **(b)** What conclusions about the management of accounts receivable can be drawn from these data? At the end of 2001, accounts receivable (net) was $490,000.

BE19-10 The following data are from the income statements of Shirley Denson Company.

Evaluate management of inventory.
(SO 5)

	2003	2002
Sales	$6,420,000	$6,240,000
Beginning inventory	980,000	860,000
Purchases	4,540,000	4,661,000
Ending inventory	1,020,000	980,000

(a) Compute for each year (1) the inventory turnover and (2) the average days to sell the inventory. **(b)** What conclusions concerning the management of the inventory can be drawn from these data?

BE19-11 Nofftz Company has owners' equity of $400,000 and net income of $50,000. It has a payout ratio of 20% and a rate of return on assets of 16%. How much did Nofftz pay in cash dividends, and what were its average assets?

Calculate profitability ratios.
(SO 5)

BE19-12 Selected data taken from the 2002 financial statements of Lester Fredrick Manufacturing Company are as follows.

Calculate cash-basis liquidity, profitability, and solvency ratios.
(SO 5)

Net sales for 2002	$6,860,000
Current liabilities, January 1, 2002	180,000
Current liabilities, December 31, 2002	240,000
Net cash provided by operating activities	720,000
Total liabilities, January 1, 2002	1,500,000
Total liabilities, December 31, 2002	1,300,000

Compute the following ratios at December 31, 2002: **(a)** current cash debt coverage ratio, **(b)** cash return on sales, and **(c)** the cash debt coverage ratio.

EXERCISES*

E19-1 Financial information for Merlynn Inc. is presented below.

Prepare horizontal analysis.
(SO 3)

	December 31, 2003	December 31, 2002
Current assets	$125,000	$100,000
Plant assets (net)	400,000	330,000
Current liabilities	91,000	70,000
Long-term liabilities	144,000	95,000
Common stock, $1 par	155,000	115,000
Retained earnings	135,000	150,000

Instructions
Prepare a schedule showing a horizontal analysis for 2003 using 2002 as the base year.

*Follow the rounding procedures used in the chapter.

Prepare vertical analysis.
(SO 4)

E19-2 Operating data for Enid Corporation are presented below.

	2003	2002
Sales	$800,000	$600,000
Cost of goods sold	472,000	390,000
Selling expenses	120,000	72,000
Administrative expenses	80,000	54,000
Income tax expense	38,400	25,200
Net income	89,600	58,800

Instructions

Prepare a schedule showing a vertical analysis for 2003 and 2002.

Prepare horizontal and vertical analyses.
(SO 3, 4)

E19-3 The comparative balance sheets of Ricky Corporation are presented below.

RICKY CORPORATION
Comparative Balance Sheets
December 31

	2003	2002
Assets		
Current assets	$ 76,000	$ 80,000
Property, plant, and equipment (net)	99,000	90,000
Intangibles	20,000	40,000
Total assets	$195,000	$210,000
Liabilities and stockholders' equity		
Current liabilities	$ 40,800	$ 48,000
Long-term liabilities	138,000	150,000
Stockholders' equity	16,200	12,000
Total liabilities and stockholders' equity	$195,000	$210,000

Instructions

(a) Prepare a horizontal analysis of the balance sheet data for Ricky Corporation using 2002 as a base. (Show the amount of increase or decrease as well.)

(b) Prepare a vertical analysis of the balance sheet data for Ricky Corporation in columnar form for 2003.

Prepare horizontal and vertical analyses.
(SO 3, 4)

E19-4 The comparative income statements of Sondgeroth Corporation are shown below.

SONDGEROTH CORPORATION
Comparative Income Statements
For the Years Ended December 31

	2003	2002
Net sales	$600,000	$500,000
Cost of goods sold	450,000	420,000
Gross profit	150,000	80,000
Operating expenses	57,200	44,000
Net income	$ 92,800	$ 36,000

Instructions

(a) Prepare a horizontal analysis of the income statement data for Sondgeroth Corporation using 2002 as a base. (Show the amounts of increase or decrease.)

(b) Prepare a vertical analysis of the income statement data for Sondgeroth Corporation in columnar form for both years.

E19-5 **Nordstrom, Inc.** operates department stores in numerous states. Selected financial statement data for the year ending January 31, 2000, are as follows.

Compute liquidity ratios and compare results. (SO 5)

NORDSTROM

NORDSTROM, INC.
Balance Sheet (partial)

(in millions)	End-of-Year	Beginning-of-Year
Cash and cash equivalents	$ 27	$ 242
Short-term investments	26	-0-
Receivables (net)	617	587
Merchandise inventory	798	750
Prepaid expenses	97	74
Total current assets	$1,565	$1,659
Total current liabilities	$807	$779

For the year, net sales were $5,124, and cost of goods sold was $3,360. Net cash provided by operating activities was $378.

Instructions

(a) Compute the five liquidity ratios at the end of the current year.

(b) Using the data in the chapter, compare Nordstrom's liquidity with (1) that of **Sears, Roebuck and Co.**, and (2) the industry averages for department stores.

E19-6 Sycamore Incorporated had the following transactions occur involving current assets and current liabilities during February 2002.

Perform current and acid-test ratio analysis. (SO 5)

Feb. 3 Accounts receivable of $15,000 are collected.
7 Equipment is purchased for $25,000 cash.
11 Paid $3,000 for a 3-year insurance policy.
14 Accounts payable of $12,000 are paid.
18 Cash dividends of $6,000 are declared.

Additional information:

1. As of February 1, 2002, current assets were $140,000, and current liabilities were $50,000.
2. As of February 1, 2002, current assets included $15,000 of inventory and $5,000 of prepaid expenses.

Instructions

(a) Compute the current ratio as of the beginning of the month and after each transaction.

(b) Compute the acid-test ratio as of the beginning of the month and after each transaction.

E19-7 Bobbette Company has the following comparative balance sheet data.

Compute selected ratios. (SO 5)

BOBBETTE COMPANY
Balance Sheets
December 31

	2002	2001
Cash	$ 15,000	$ 30,000
Receivables (net)	65,000	60,000
Inventories	60,000	50,000
Plant assets (net)	205,000	180,000
	$345,000	$320,000
Accounts payable	$ 50,000	$ 60,000
Mortgage payable (15%)	100,000	100,000
Common stock, $10 par	140,000	120,000
Retained earnings	55,000	40,000
	$345,000	$320,000

Additional information for 2002:

1. Net income was $25,000.
2. Sales on account were $420,000. Sales returns and allowances were $20,000.
3. Cost of goods sold was $198,000.
4. Net cash provided by operating activities was $33,000.

Instructions
Compute the following ratios at December 31, 2002.

(a) Current.
(b) Acid-test.
(c) Receivables turnover.
(d) Inventory turnover.
(e) Cash return on sales.
(f) Cash debt coverage.
(g) Current cash debt coverage.

Compute selected ratios.
(SO 5)

E19-8 Selected comparative statement data for Li Na Products Company are presented below. All balance sheet data are as of December 31.

	2003	2002
Net sales	$800,000	$720,000
Cost of goods sold	480,000	40,000
Interest expense	7,000	5,000
Net income	56,000	42,000
Accounts receivable	120,000	100,000
Inventory	85,000	75,000
Total assets	600,000	500,000
Total common stockholders' equity	450,000	325,000

Instructions
Compute the following ratios for 2003.

(a) Profit margin.
(b) Asset turnover.
(c) Return on assets.
(d) Return on common stockholders' equity.

Compute selected ratios.
(SO 5)

E19-9 The income statement for Laura Wilkinson, Inc., appears below.

LAURA WILKINSON, INC.
Income Statement
For the Year Ended December 31, 2002

Sales	$400,000
Cost of goods sold	230,000
Gross profit	170,000
Expenses (including $20,000 interest and $24,000 income taxes)	100,000
Net income	$ 70,000

Additional information:

1. Common stock outstanding January 1, 2002, was 30,000 shares.
2. The market price of Laura Wilkinson, Inc. stock was $15 in 2002.
3. Cash dividends of $21,000 were paid, $5,000 of which were to preferred stockholders.
4. Net cash provided by operating activities was $92,000.

Instructions
Compute the following ratios for 2002.

(a) Earnings per share.
(b) Price-earnings.
(c) Payout.
(d) Times interest earned.
(e) Cash return on sales.

E19-10 Alverez Corporation experienced a fire on December 31, 2003, in which its financial records were partially destroyed. It has been able to salvage some of the records and has ascertained the following balances.

Compute amounts from ratios.
(SO 5)

	December 31, 2003	December 31, 2002
Cash	$ 30,000	$ 10,000
Receivables (net)	72,500	126,000
Inventory	200,000	180,000
Accounts payable	50,000	90,000
Notes payable	30,000	60,000
Common stock, $100 par	400,000	400,000
Retained earnings	113,500	101,000

Additional information:

1. The inventory turnover is 3.6 times.
2. The return on common stockholders' equity is 22%. The company had no additional paid-in capital.
3. The receivables turnover is 9.4 times.
4. The return on assets is 20%.
5. Total assets at December 31, 2002, were $605,000.

Instructions

Compute the following for Alverez Corporation.

(a) Cost of goods sold for 2003.
(b) Net sales (credit) for 2003.
(c) Net income for 2003.
(d) Total assets at December 31, 2003.

PROBLEMS*

P19-1 Comparative statement data for Sara Company and Reiling Company, two competitors, appear below. All balance sheet data are as of December 31, 2003, and December 31, 2002.

Prepare vertical analysis and comment on profitability.
(SO 4, 5)

	Sara Company		Reiling Company	
	2003	2002	2003	2002
Net sales	$1,549,035		$339,038	
Cost of goods sold	1,080,490		238,006	
Operating expenses	292,275		79,000	
Interest expense	6,800		2,252	
Income tax expense	41,230		6,650	
Current assets	325,975	$312,410	83,336	$ 79,467
Plant assets (net)	521,310	500,000	139,728	125,812
Current liabilities	66,325	75,815	35,348	30,281
Long-term liabilities	108,500	90,000	29,620	25,000
Common stock, $10 par	500,000	500,000	120,000	120,000
Retained earnings	172,460	146,595	38,096	29,998

Instructions

(a) Prepare a vertical analysis of the 2003 income statement data for Sara Company and Reiling Company in columnar form.
(b) Comment on the relative profitability of the companies by computing the return on assets and the return on common stockholders' equity ratios for both companies.

*Follow the rounding procedures used in the chapter.

Compute ratios from balance sheet and income statement.
(SO 5)

P19-2 The comparative statements of Westphal Tool Company are presented below.

WESTPHAL TOOL COMPANY
Income Statement
For the Year Ended December 31

	2002	2001
Net sales	$1,818,500	$1,750,500
Cost of goods sold	1,005,500	996,000
Gross profit	813,000	754,500
Selling and administrative expense	506,000	479,000
Income from operations	307,000	275,500
Other expenses and losses		
Interest expense	27,000	19,000
Income before income taxes	280,000	256,500
Income tax expense	84,000	77,000
Net income	$ 196,000	$ 179,500

WESTPHAL TOOL COMPANY
Balance Sheets
December 31

Assets	2002	2001
Current assets		
Cash	$ 60,100	$ 64,200
Marketable securities	54,000	50,000
Accounts receivable (net)	107,800	102,800
Inventory	123,000	115,500
Total current assets	344,900	332,500
Plant assets (net)	625,300	520,300
Total assets	$970,200	$852,800
Liabilities and Stockholders' Equity		
Current liabilities		
Accounts payable	$160,000	$145,400
Income taxes payable	43,500	42,000
Total current liabilities	203,500	187,400
Bonds payable	200,000	200,000
Total liabilities	403,500	387,400
Stockholders' equity		
Common stock ($5 par)	280,000	300,000
Retained earnings	286,700	165,400
Total stockholders' equity	566,700	465,400
Total liabilities and stockholders' equity	$970,200	$852,800

On April 1, 2002, 4,000 shares were repurchased and canceled. All sales were on account. Net cash provided by operating activities for 2002 was $270,000.

Instructions
Compute the following ratios for 2002. (Weighted average common shares in 2002 were 57,000.)

(a) Earnings per share.
(b) Return on common stockholders' equity.
(c) Return on assets.
(d) Current.
(e) Acid-test.
(f) Receivables turnover.
(g) Inventory turnover.
(h) Times interest earned.
(i) Asset turnover.
(j) Debt to total assets.
(k) Current cash debt coverage.
(l) Cash return on sales.
(m) Cash debt coverage.

P19-3 Condensed balance sheet and income statement data for Terry Duffy Corporation appear below.

Perform ratio analysis, and evaluate financial position and operating results.
(SO 5)

TERRY DUFFY CORPORATION
Balance Sheets
December 31

	2003	2002	2001
Cash	$ 25,000	$ 20,000	$ 18,000
Receivables (net)	50,000	45,000	48,000
Other current assets	90,000	85,000	64,000
Investments	75,000	70,000	45,000
Plant and equipment (net)	400,000	370,000	358,000
	$640,000	$590,000	$533,000
Current liabilities	$ 75,000	$ 80,000	$ 70,000
Long-term debt	80,000	85,000	50,000
Common stock, $10 par	340,000	300,000	300,000
Retained earnings	145,000	125,000	113,000
	$640,000	$590,000	$533,000

TERRY DUFFY CORPORATION
Income Statement
For the Year Ended December 31

	2003	2002
Sales	$740,000	$700,000
Less: Sales returns and allowances	40,000	50,000
Net sales	700,000	650,000
Cost of goods sold	420,000	400,000
Gross profit	280,000	250,000
Operating expenses (including income taxes)	236,000	218,000
Net income	$ 44,000	$ 32,000

Additional information:

1. The market price of Duffy's common stock was $4.00, $5.00, and $7.95 for 2001, 2002, and 2003, respectively.
2. All dividends were paid in cash.
3. On July 1, 2003, 4,000 shares of common stock were issued.

Instructions

(a) Compute the following ratios for 2002 and 2003.
   (1) Profit margin.
   (2) Asset turnover.
   (3) Earnings per share. (Weighted average common shares in 2003 were 32,000.)
   (4) Price-earnings.
   (5) Payout.
   (6) Debt to total assets.

(b) Based on the ratios calculated, discuss briefly the improvement or lack thereof in financial position and operating results from 2002 to 2003 of Terry Duffy Corporation.

Compute ratios, and comment on overall liquidity and profitability.
(SO 5)

P19-4 Financial information for Mexicalli Company is presented below.

MEXICALLI COMPANY
Balance Sheets
December 31

Assets	2003	2002
Cash	$ 70,000	$ 65,000
Short-term investments	45,000	40,000
Receivables (net)	94,000	90,000
Inventories	130,000	125,000
Prepaid expenses	25,000	23,000
Land	130,000	130,000
Building and equipment (net)	190,000	175,000
	$684,000	$648,000
Liabilities and Stockholders' Equity		
Notes payable	$100,000	$100,000
Accounts payable	45,000	42,000
Accrued liabilities	40,000	40,000
Bonds payable, due 2006	150,000	150,000
Common stock, $10 par	200,000	200,000
Retained earnings	149,000	116,000
	$684,000	$648,000

MEXICALLI COMPANY
Income Statement
For the Years Ended December 31

	2003	2002
Sales	$850,000	$790,000
Cost of goods sold	620,000	575,000
Gross profit	230,000	215,000
Operating expenses	194,000	180,000
Net income	$ 36,000	$ 35,000

Additional information:

1. Inventory at the beginning of 2002 was $115,000.
2. Receivables at the beginning of 2002 were $88,000.
3. Total assets at the beginning of 2002 were $630,000.
4. No common stock transactions occurred during 2002 or 2003.
5. All sales were on account.

Instructions

(a) Indicate, by using ratios, the change in liquidity and profitability of Mexicalli Company from 2002 to 2003. (*Note:* Not all profitability ratios can be computed.)

(b) Given below are three independent situations and a ratio that may be affected. For each situation, compute the affected ratio (1) as of December 31, 2003, and (2) as of December 31, 2004, after giving effect to the situation. Net income for 2004 was $40,000. Total assets on December 31, 2004, were $700,000.

Situation	Ratio
(1) 18,000 shares of common stock were sold at par on July 1, 2004.	Return on common stockholders' equity
(2) All of the notes payable were paid in 2004. The only change in liabilities was that the notes payable were paid.	Debt to total assets
(3) Market price of common stock was $9 on December 31, 2003, and $12.80 on December 31, 2004.	Price-earnings ratio

P19-5 Selected financial data of two intense competitors in a recent year are presented below.

Compute selected ratios, and compare liquidity, profitability, and solvency for two companies.
(SO 5)

	(in millions) Kmart Corporation	Wal-Mart Stores, Inc.
Income Statement Data for Year		
Net sales	$34,025	$82,494
Cost of goods sold	25,992	65,586
Selling and administrative expenses	7,701	12,858
Interest expense	494	706
Other income (net)	572	918
Income taxes	114	1,581
Net income	$ 296	$ 2,681
Balance Sheet Data (End-of-Year)		
Current assets	$ 9,187	$15,338
Property, plant, and equipment (net)	7,842	17,481
Total assets	$17,029	$32,819
Current liabilities	$ 5,626	$ 9,973
Long-term debt	5,371	10,120
Total stockholders' equity	6,032	12,726
Total liabilities and stockholders' equity	$17,029	$32,819
Beginning-of-Year Balances		
Total assets	$17,504	$26,441
Total stockholders' equity	6,093	10,753
Other Data		
Average net receivables	$ 1,570	$ 695
Average inventory	7,317	12,539
Net cash provided by operating activities	351	3,106
Average current liabilities	5,720	10,110
Average total liabilities	11,230	20,160

Instructions

(a) For each company, compute the following ratios.

(1) Current.
(2) Receivables turnover.
(3) Inventory turnover.
(4) Profit margin.
(5) Asset turnover.
(6) Return on assets.
(7) Return on common stockholders' equity.
(8) Debt to total assets.
(9) Times interest earned.
(10) Current cash debt coverage.
(11) Cash return on sales.
(12) Cash debt coverage.

(b) Compare the liquidity, profitability, and solvency of the two companies.

Compute numerous ratios. (SO 5)

P19-6 The comparative statements of Johansen Company are presented below.

JOHANSEN COMPANY
Income Statement
For Year Ended December 31

	2003	2002
Net sales (all on account)	$600,000	$520,000
Expenses		
Cost of goods sold	415,000	354,000
Selling and administrative	120,800	114,800
Interest expense	7,200	6,000
Income tax expense	18,000	14,000
Total expenses	561,000	488,800
Net income	$ 39,000	$ 31,200

JOHANSEN COMPANY
Balance Sheets
December 31

Assets	2003	2002
Current assets		
Cash	$ 21,000	$ 18,000
Marketable securities	18,000	15,000
Accounts receivable (net)	92,000	74,000
Inventory	84,000	70,000
Total current assets	215,000	177,000
Plant assets (net)	423,000	383,000
Total assets	$638,000	$560,000
Liabilities and Stockholders' Equity		
Current liabilities		
Accounts payable	$112,000	$110,000
Income taxes payable	23,000	20,000
Total current liabilities	135,000	130,000
Long-term liabilities		
Bonds payable	130,000	80,000
Total liabilities	265,000	210,000
Stockholders' equity		
Common stock ($5 par)	150,000	150,000
Retained earnings	223,000	200,000
Total stockholders' equity	373,000	350,000
Total liabilities and stockholders' equity	$638,000	$560,000

Additional data:
The common stock recently sold at $19.50 per share.

Instructions
Compute the following ratios for 2003.

(a) Current.
(b) Acid-test.
(c) Receivables turnover.
(d) Inventory turnover.
(e) Profit margin.
(f) Asset turnover.
(g) Return on assets.
(h) Return on common stockholders' equity.
(i) Earnings per share.
(j) Price-earnings.
(k) Payout.
(l) Debt to total assets.
(m) Times interest earned.

P19-7 Presented below is an incomplete income statement and an incomplete comparative balance sheet of Windsor Corporation.

Compute missing information given a set of ratios.
(SO 5)

WINDSOR CORPORATION
Income Statement
For the Year Ended December 31, 2003

Sales	$11,000,000
Cost of goods sold	?
Gross profit	?
Operating expenses	1,665,000
Income from operations	?
Other expenses and losses	
Interest expense	?
Income before income taxes	?
Income tax expense	560,000
Net income	$?

WINDSOR CORPORATION
Balance Sheets
December 31

Assets	**2003**	**2002**
Current assets		
Cash	$ 450,000	$ 375,000
Accounts receivable (net)	?	950,000
Inventory	?	1,720,000
Total current assets	?	3,045,000
Plant assets (net)	4,620,000	3,955,000
Total assets	$?	$7,000,000
Liabilities and Stockholders' Equity		
Current liabilities	$?	$ 825,000
Long-term notes payable	?	2,800,000
Total liabilities	?	3,625,000
Common stock, $1 par	3,000,000	3,000,000
Retained earnings	400,000	375,000
Total stockholders' equity	3,400,000	3,375,000
Total liabilities and stockholders' equity	$?	$7,000,000

Additional information:

1. The receivables turnover for 2003 is 10 times.
2. All sales are on account.
3. The profit margin for 2003 is 14.5%.
4. Return on assets is 22% for 2003.
5. The current ratio on December 31, 2003, is 3.2.
6. The inventory turnover for 2003 is 4.8 times.

Instructions

Compute the missing information given the ratios above. Show computations. (*Note*: Start with one ratio and derive as much information as possible from it before trying another ratio. List all missing amounts under the ratio used to find the information.)

BROADENING YOUR PERSPECTIVE

FINANCIAL REPORTING AND ANALYSIS

FINANCIAL REPORTING PROBLEM: Lands' End, Inc.

LANDS' END DIRECT MERCHANTS

BYP19-1 Your parents are considering investing in **Lands' End, Inc.**, common stock. They ask you, as an accounting expert, to make an analysis of the company for them. Fortunately, excerpts from a current annual report of Lands' End are presented in Appendix A of this textbook. Note that all amounts omit 000's (i.e., all dollar amounts are in thousands).

Instructions

(Follow the approach in the chapter for rounding numbers.)

(a) Make a 5-year trend analysis, using 1996 as the base year, of (1) net sales and (2) net income. Comment on the significance of the trend results.

(b) Compute for 2000 and 1999 the (1) profit margin, (2) asset turnover, (3) return on assets, and (4) return on common stockholders' equity. How would you evaluate Lands' End's profitability? Total assets at December 31, 1998, were $4,334.7, and total stockholders' equity at December 31, 1998, was $2,427.1.

(c) Compute for 2000 and 1999 the (1) debt to total assets and (2) times interest earned ratio. How would you evaluate Lands' End's long-term solvency?

(d) What information outside the annual report may also be useful to your parents in making a decision about Lands' End, Inc.?

COMPARATIVE ANALYSIS PROBLEM: Lands' End vs. Abercrombie & Fitch

LANDS' END DIRECT MERCHANTS

BYP19-2 **Lands' End's** financial statements are presented in Appendix A. **Abercrombie & Fitch's** financial statements are presented in Appendix B.

Instructions

(a) Based on the information contained in these financial statements, determine each of the following for each company.

(1) The percentage increase (decrease) in (i) net sales and (ii) net income from 1999 to 2000.

(2) The percentage increase in (i) total assets and (ii) total stockholders' (shareholders') equity from 1999 to 2000.

(3) The earnings per share and price-earnings ratio for 2000. Abercrombie & Fitch's common stock had a market price of $29.62 at the end of fiscal-year 2000.

(b) What conclusions concerning the two companies can be drawn from these data?

INTERPRETING FINANCIAL STATEMENTS: A Global Focus

BYP19-3 In England, the railroads were run by the government until recently. Five years ago, **Railtrack Group PLC** became a publicly traded company. The largest railroad company in the United States is **Burlington Northern Railroad Company**. The following data were taken from the 1998 financial statements of each company.

	Railtrack Group (pounds in millions)		Burlington Northern (dollars in millions)	
Financial Highlights	**1998**	**1997**	**1998**	**1997**
Cash and short-term investments	£ 380	£ 26	$ 95	$ -0-
Accounts receivable	434	402	676	632
Total current assets	909	521	1,357	1,197
Total assets	7,095	5,760	22,725	21,199
Current liabilities	1,128	1,209	2,175	2,089
Total liabilities	3,882	2,888	14,497	14,176
Total stockholders' equity	3,213	2,872	8,228	7,023
Sales	2,573		8,936	
Operating costs	2,102		6,781	

	Railtrack Group (pounds in millions)		Burlington Northern (dollars in millions)	
Financial Highlights	**1998**	**1997**	**1998**	**1997**
Interest expense	£ 93		$ 293	
Income tax expense	3		733	
Net income	425		1,206	
Cash provided by operations	988		2,107	

Instructions

(a) Calculate the following 1998 liquidity ratios and discuss the relative liquidity of the two companies.
(1) Current ratio.
(2) Acid-test.
(3) Current cash debt coverage.
(4) Receivables turnover.

(b) Calculate the following 1998 solvency ratios and discuss the relative solvency of the two companies.
(1) Debt to total assets.
(2) Times interest earned.
(3) Cash debt coverage.

(c) Calculate the following 1998 profitability ratios and discuss the relative profitability of the two companies.
(1) Asset turnover.
(2) Profit margin.
(3) Return on assets.
(4) Return on common stockholders' equity.

(d) What other issues must you consider when comparing these two companies?

EXPLORING THE WEB

BYP19-4 The Management Discussion and Analysis section of an annual report addresses corporate performance for the year, and sometimes uses financial ratios to support its claims.

Address: **www.ibm.com/financialguide** ***(or go to www.wiley.com/college/weygandt)***

Steps:

1. From IBM's Financial Guide, choose **Guides Contents**.
2. Choose **Anatomy of an Annual Report**.

Instructions

Using the information from the above site, answer the following questions.

(a) What are the optional elements that are often included in an annual report?
(b) What are the elements of an annual report that are required by the SEC?
(c) Describe the contents of the Management Discussion.
(d) Describe the contents of the Auditors' Report.
(e) Describe the contents of the Selected Financial Data.

CRITICAL THINKING

GROUP DECISION CASE

BYP19-5 As the CPA for Latino Manufacturing Inc., you have been asked to develop some key ratios from the comparative financial statements. This information is to be used to convince creditors that the company is solvent and will continue as a going concern. The data requested and the computations developed from the financial statements follow.

	2000	**1999**
Current ratio	3.1 times	2.1 times
Acid-test ratio	.8 times	1.4 times
Asset turnover	2.8 times	2.2 times
Sales to stockholders' equity	2.3 times	2.7 times
Net income	Up 32%	Down 8%
Earnings per share	$3.30	$2.50
Book value per share	Up 8%	Up 11%

Instructions

With the class divided into groups, answer the following.

(a) Latino Manufacturing Inc. asks you to prepare a list of brief comments stating how each of these items supports the solvency and going-concern potential of the business. The company wishes to use these comments to support its presentation of data to its creditors. You are to prepare the comments as requested, giving the implications and the limitations of each item separately. Then prepare a collective inference that may be drawn from the individual items about Latino's solvency and going-concern potential.

(b) What warnings should you offer these creditors about the limitations of ratio analysis for the purpose stated here?

COMMUNICATION ACTIVITY

BYP19-6 Carol Dunn is the CEO of Midwest Electronics. Dunn is an expert engineer but a novice in accounting. She asks you to explain (1) the bases for comparison in analyzing Midwest's financial statements, and (2) the limitations, if any, in financial statement analysis.

Instructions

Write a letter to Carol Dunn that explains the bases for comparison and the limitations of financial statement analysis.

ETHICS CASE

BYP19-7 Andy Manion, president of Manion Industries, wishes to issue a press release to bolster his company's image and maybe even its stock price, which has been gradually falling. As controller, you have been asked to provide a list of twenty financial ratios along with some other operating statistics relative to Manion Industries' first quarter financials and operations.

Two days after you provide the ratios and data requested, Manny Alomar, the public relations director of Manion, asks you to prove the accuracy of the financial and operating data contained in the press release written by the president and edited by Manny. In the news release, the president highlights the sales increase of 25% over last year's first quarter and the positive change in the current ratio from 1.5:1 last year to 3:1 this year. He also emphasizes that production was up 50% over the prior year's first quarter.

You note that the press release contains only positive or improved ratios and none of the negative or deteriorated ratios. For instance, no mention is made that the debt to total assets ratio has increased from 35% to 55%, that inventories are up 89%, and that while the current ratio improved, the acid-test ratio fell from 1:1 to .5:1. Nor is there any mention that the reported profit for the quarter would have been a loss had not the estimated lives of Manion's plant and machinery been increased by 30%. Manny emphasized, "The prez wants this release by early this afternoon."

Instructions

(a) Who are the stakeholders in this situation?

(b) Is there anything unethical in president Manion's actions?

(c) Should you as controller remain silent? Does Manny have any responsibility?

Answers to Self Study Questions

1. b **2.** d **3.** a **4.** c **5.** c **6.** c **7.** c **8.** b **9.** a **10.** b

Answer to Lands' End Review It Question 4, p. 787

Lands' End presents horizontal analyses in its "Financial Highlights" section and its Management's Discussion and Analysis section. Vertical analysis is used in schedules presented in the Management's Discussion and Analysis section (page A10 especially).

Remember to go back to the Navigator box on the chapter-opening page and check off your completed work.

20

MANAGERIAL ACCOUNTING

THE NAVIGATOR ✓

- Understand *Concepts for Review* ❑
- Read *Feature Story* ❑
- Scan *Study Objectives* ❑
- Read *Preview* ❑
- Read text and answer *Before You Go On* *p.* 831 ❑ *p.* 833 ❑ *p.* 843 ❑
- Work *Demonstration Problems* ❑
- Review *Summary of Study Objectives* ❑
- Answer *Self-Study Questions* ❑
- Complete *Assignments* ❑

CONCEPTS FOR REVIEW

Before studying this chapter, you should know or, if necessary, review:

a. The cost principle. (Ch. 1, p. 10)

b. Ethics in accounting. (Ch. 1, p. 9)

c. The computation of cost of goods sold. (Ch. 6, pp. 231–232)

d. The adjusting and closing process used in a merchandising firm. (Ch. 5, pp. 195–197)

e. The use of a work sheet in the preparation of financial statements. (Ch. 4, pp. 137–140 and Ch. 5, pp. 205–206)

✓ THE NAVIGATOR

FEATURE STORY

What a Difference a Day Makes

In January 1998 **Compaq Computer** had just become the largest seller of personal computers, and it was *Forbes* magazine's "company of the year." Its chief executive, Eckhard Pfeiffer, was riding high. But during the next two years Compaq lost $2 billion. The company was in chaos, and Mr. Pfeiffer was out of a job. What happened?

First, Dell happened. **Dell Computer** pioneered a new way of making and selling personal computers. Its customers "custom design" their computer over the Internet or phone. Dell reengineered its "supply chain": It coordinated its efforts with its suppliers and streamlined its order-taking and production process, and it can ship a computer within two days of taking an order. Personal computers lose 1 percent of their value every week they sit on a shelf. Thus, having virtually no inventory is a great advantage to Dell. Compaq tried to adopt Dell's approach, but with limited success.

The second shock to Compaq came when it acquired a company even larger than itself—**Digital Equipment**. Digital was famous as much for its technical service as it was for its products. Mr. Pfeiffer believed that the purchase of Digital, with its huge and respected technical sales force, opened new opportunities for Compaq as a global service company. Now it could sell to and service high-end corporate customers. But combining the two companies proved to be hugely expensive and extremely complicated.

Managers are evaluated on the results of their decisions. In the long run, it may turn out that Mr. Pfeiffer had great strategic vision and made a good decision. But, in a world that wants results at "Internet speed," Compaq's board of directors wasn't willing to wait and see. Managers in today's rapidly changing global environment often must make decisions that determine their company's fate, and their own. The remaining chapters of this text discuss techniques used to assist managers in making these decisions.

www.compaq.com
www.dell.com

THE NAVIGATOR

STUDY OBJECTIVES

After studying this chapter, you should be able to:

1. Explain the distinguishing features of managerial accounting.
2. Identify the three broad functions of management.
3. Define the three classes of manufacturing costs.
4. Distinguish between product and period costs.
5. Explain the difference between a merchandising and a manufacturing income statement.
6. Indicate how cost of goods manufactured is determined.
7. Explain the difference between a merchandising and a manufacturing balance sheet.

THE NAVIGATOR

PREVIEW OF CHAPTER 20

Beginning with this chapter, we turn our attention to issues illustrated in the Feature Story about **Compaq Computer**. To this point in the text, we have described the form and content of **financial statements** for **external users** such as stockholders and creditors. These statements represent the principal end-product of financial accounting. The remaining chapters of this textbook focus primarily on the preparation of **reports** for **internal users**, such as the managers and officers of a company. These reports are an integral part of managerial accounting. Managerial accounting provides techniques for assisting management in making decisions and tools for evaluating the effectiveness of those decisions.

The content and organization of Chapter 20 are as follows.

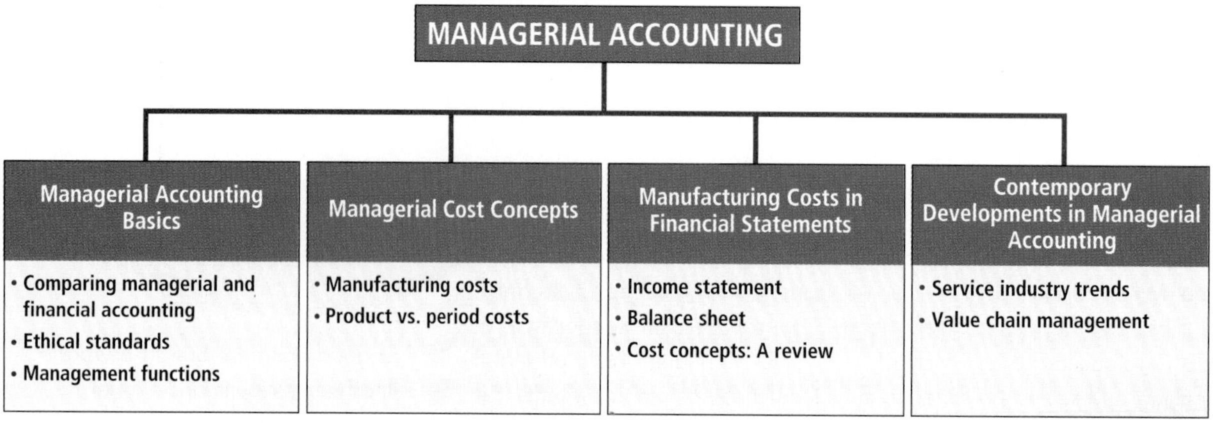

THE NAVIGATOR

MANAGERIAL ACCOUNTING BASICS

Managerial accounting, also called management accounting, is a field of accounting that provides economic and financial information for managers and other internal users. The activities that are part of managerial accounting (and the chapters in which they are discussed) are as follows:

1. Explaining manufacturing and nonmanufacturing costs and how they are reported in the financial statements (Chapter 20).
2. Computing the cost of providing a service or manufacturing a product (Chapters 21 and 22).
3. Determining the behavior of costs and expenses as activity levels change and analyzing cost–volume–profit relationships within a company (Chapter 23).
4. Assisting management in profit planning and formalizing these plans in the form of budgets (Chapter 24).
5. Providing a basis for controlling costs and expenses by comparing actual results with planned objectives and standard costs (Chapters 25 and 26).
6. Accumulating and presenting relevant data for management decision making (Chapter 27).

Managerial accounting applies to all types of businesses—service, merchandising, and manufacturing. It also applies to all forms of business organizations—proprietorships, partnerships, and corporations. Managerial accounting is needed in not-for-profit entities as well as in profit-oriented enterprises.

Not long ago, the managerial accountant was primarily engaged in cost accounting—collecting and reporting manufacturing costs to management. Today, the managerial accountant's responsibilities extend to **strategic cost management**—

providing managers with data on the efficient use of company resources in both manufacturing and service industries.

COMPARING MANAGERIAL AND FINANCIAL ACCOUNTING

STUDY OBJECTIVE 1

Explain the distinguishing features of managerial accounting.

There are both similarities and differences between managerial and financial accounting. First, each field of accounting deals with the economic events of an enterprise. Thus, their interests overlap. For example, determining the unit cost of manufacturing a product is part of managerial accounting. Reporting the total cost of goods manufactured and sold is part of financial accounting. In addition, both managerial and financial accounting require that a company's economic events be quantified and communicated to interested parties.

The principal differences between financial accounting and managerial accounting are summarized in Illustration 20-1. The diverse needs for economic data among interested parties are responsible for many of the differences.

Illustration 20-1

Differences between financial and managerial accounting

Financial Accounting		Managerial Accounting
• External users: stockholders, creditors, and regulators.	**Primary Users of Reports**	• Internal users: officers, department heads, managers, and supervisors.
• Classified financial statements. • Issued quarterly and annually.	**Types and Frequency of Reports**	• Internal reports. • Issued as frequently as needed.
• General-purpose information for all users.	**Purpose of Reports**	• Special-purpose information for a particular user for a specific decision.
• Pertains to business as a whole and is highly aggregated (condensed). • Limited to double-entry accounting system and cost data. • Reporting standard is generally accepted accounting principles.	**Content of Reports**	• Pertains to subunits of the business and may be very detailed. • May extend beyond double-entry accounting system to any type of relevant data. • Reporting standard is relevance to the decision to be made.
• Annual independent audit by certified public accountant.	**Verification Process**	• No independent audits.

ETHICAL STANDARDS FOR MANAGERIAL ACCOUNTANTS

We have emphasized throughout the textbook the importance of ethics in business and in accounting. Managerial accountants recognize that they have an ethical obligation to their companies and the public. To provide guidance for managerial accountants, the Institute of Management Accountants (IMA) has developed a code of ethical standards, entitled *Standards of Ethical Conduct for Management Accountants*. This code divides the managerial accountants' responsibilities into four areas: (1) competence, (2) confidentiality, (3) integrity, and (4) objectivity. The code states that management accountants should not commit acts in violation of these standards. Nor should they condone such acts by others within their organizations.

HELPFUL HINT
The IMA code of ethical standards is provided in Appendix D.

MANAGEMENT FUNCTIONS

STUDY OBJECTIVE 2

Identify the three broad functions of management.

The management of an organization performs three broad functions. They are:

1. Planning.
2. Directing and motivating.
3. Controlling.

In performing these functions, managers must make decisions that have a significant impact on the organization.

Planning requires management to look ahead and to establish objectives. These objectives are often diverse: maximizing short-term profits and market share, maintaining a commitment to environmental protection, contributing to social programs. A key objective of management is to add **value** to the business under its control. Value is usually measured by the trading price of the company's stock and by the potential selling price of the company.

Directing and **motivating** involves coordinating a company's diverse activities and human resources to produce a smooth-running operation. This function relates to implementing planned objectives and providing necessary incentives. For example, in manufacturers such as **Campbell Soup Company**, **General Motors**, and **Compaq Computer**, purchasing, manufacturing, warehousing, and selling must be coordinated. Service corporations such as **American Airlines**, **Federal Express**, and **AT&T** must coordinate scheduling, sales, and equipment and supply acquisitions. Directing also involves selecting executives, appointing managers and supervisors, and hiring and training employees. Most companies prepare **organization charts** to show the interrelationship of activities and the delegation of authority and responsibility within the company.

The third management function, **controlling**, is the process of keeping the firm's activities on track. In controlling operations, managers determine whether planned goals are being met. When there are deviations from targeted objectives, they must decide what changes are needed to get back on track.

How do managers achieve control? A smart manager in a small operation should make personal observations, ask good questions, and know how to evaluate the answers. But such a system in a large organization would be chaotic. Imagine the president of **Compaq Computer** attempting to determine whether planned objectives are being met without some record of what has happened and what is expected to occur. Thus, a formal system of evaluation is typically used in large businesses. It would include such items as budgets, responsibility centers, and performance evaluation reports.

Decision making is not a separate management function. Rather, it is the outcome of the exercise of good judgment in planning, directing, motivating, and controlling.

You are now ready to study specific applications of managerial accounting. As you study the managerial chapters, you will encounter many new terms, concepts, and reports. At the same time, you will find some new uses and interpretations of a number of familiar financial accounting terms.

ACCOUNTING IN ACTION *e* Business Insight

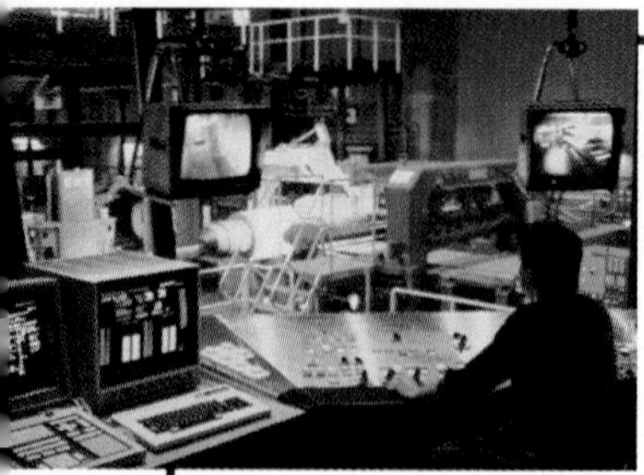

The trend toward more automated and computerized factories has changed the way managers and employees interact. For one thing, managers have fewer direct labor employees to supervise because fewer are needed on the line. Instead of standing in one spot all day, employees and managers have become more mobile, monitoring the computers that handle the production, and involving themselves in a variety of jobs.

Recently, two technology giants, **General Electric** and **Cisco Systems**, joined forces to build computerized infrastructures for manufacturers. Their goal is to improve productivity by making better use of data generated by factory-automation equipment. Ultimately their systems should provide a closer link between the factory and corporate offices. They believe the market for such systems will be $3 billion by 2003.

BEFORE YOU GO ON...

▶ *REVIEW IT*

1. Compare financial accounting and managerial accounting, identifying the principal differences.
2. Identify and discuss the three broad functions of management.

THE NAVIGATOR

MANAGERIAL COST CONCEPTS

To perform the three management functions effectively, management needs information. One very important type of information is related to costs. For example, questions such as the following should be asked.

1. What costs are involved in making a product or providing a service?
2. If production volume is decreased, will costs decrease?
3. What impact will automation have on total costs?
4. How can costs best be controlled?

To answer these questions, management needs reliable and relevant cost information. We now explain and illustrate the costs that management uses.

MANUFACTURING COSTS

STUDY OBJECTIVE 3

Define the three classes of manufacturing costs.

Manufacturing consists of activities and processes that convert raw materials into finished goods. Contrast this type of operation with merchandising, which sells merchandise in the form in which it is purchased. Manufacturing costs are typically classified as shown in Illustration 20-2.

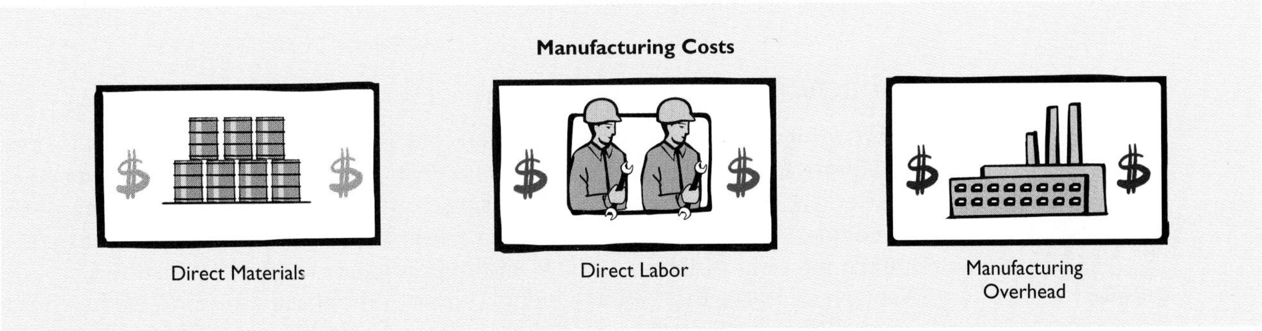

Illustration 20-2

Classifications of manufacturing costs

Direct Materials

To obtain the materials that will be converted into the finished product, the manufacturer purchases raw materials. **Raw materials** are the basic materials and parts used in the manufacturing process. For example, steel, plastics, and tires are raw materials in making cars.

Raw materials that can be physically and directly associated with the finished product during the manufacturing process are called **direct materials**. Examples include flour in the baking of bread, syrup in the bottling of soft drinks, and steel in the making of automobiles. In the Feature Story, direct materials for computers include plastic, glass, hard drives, and processing chips.

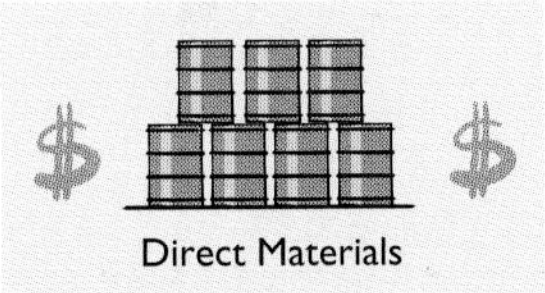

HELPFUL HINT
A manufacturer uses masking tape to protect certain sections of its product while other sections are painted. The tape is removed and thrown away when the paint is dry. Is the tape a direct or an indirect material? Answer: Indirect.

But some raw materials cannot be easily associated with the finished product. These are considered indirect materials. **Indirect materials** (1) do not physically become part of the finished product, such as lubricants and polishing compounds, or (2) cannot be traced because their physical association with the finished product is too small in terms of cost, such as cotter pins and lock washers. Indirect materials are accounted for as part of **manufacturing overhead**.

Direct Labor

The work of factory employees that can be physically and directly associated with converting raw materials into finished goods is considered **direct labor**. Bottlers in a soft drink plant, bakers in a bakery, and typesetters in a print shop are employees whose activities are usually classified as direct labor. In contrast, the wages of maintenance people, time-keepers, and supervisors are usually identified as **indirect labor**. Their efforts have no physical association with the finished product, or it is impractical to trace the costs to the goods produced. Like indirect materials, indirect labor is classified as **manufacturing overhead**.

ACCOUNTING IN ACTION *Business Insight*

For the first time, a closely watched study of productivity reported that a U.S. manufacturer, **Ford**, outperformed the North American plants of its Japanese rivals. It also reported that productivity at **General Motors** had improved the most of all auto makers. On a per car basis, GM spends $1,979 on labor and benefits, Ford spends $1,667, and **Nissan**, the most efficient of all North American operators, spends just $1,055. If GM were as efficient as Nissan it would reduce labor spending by $5.3 billion.

SOURCE: Karen Lundegaard, "Ford Plant, GM Receive High Marks in Study of Auto Makers' Productivity," *The Wall Street Journal*, June 16, 2000.

Manufacturing Overhead

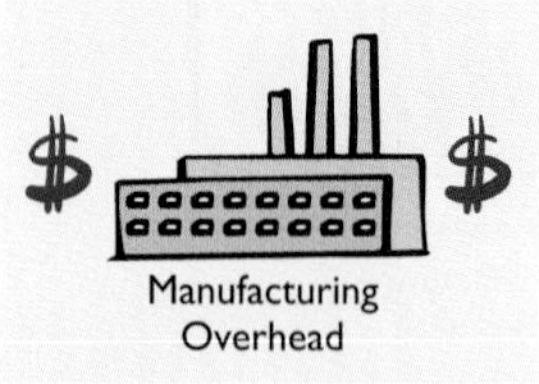

Manufacturing overhead consists of costs that are indirectly associated with the manufacture of the finished product. These costs may also be manufacturing costs that cannot be classified as direct materials or direct labor. Manufacturing overhead includes indirect materials, indirect labor, depreciation on factory buildings and machines, and insurance, taxes, and maintenance on factory facilities.

ALTERNATIVE TERMINOLOGY
Terms such as *factory overhead, indirect manufacturing costs,* and *burden* are sometimes used instead of manufacturing overhead.

One study found the following magnitudes of the three different product costs in terms of the total product cost: direct materials 54.4 percent, direct labor 12.9 percent, and manufacturing overhead 32.6 percent. Note that the direct labor component is the smallest. This component of product cost is dropping substantially because of automation. In some companies, direct labor has become as little as 5 percent of the total cost.

Allocating materials and labor costs to specific products is fairly straightforward. But dealing with overhead presents problems. How much of the purchasing agent's salary is attributable to the hundreds of products made in the same plant? What about the grease that keeps the machines humming, or the computers that make sure paychecks come out on time? Boiled down to its simplest form, the question becomes: Which products cause which costs? In subsequent chapters we show various methods of allocating overhead to products.

PRODUCT VERSUS PERIOD COSTS

STUDY OBJECTIVE 4

Distinguish between product and period costs.

Each of the manufacturing cost components (direct materials, direct labor, and manufacturing overhead) are product costs. As the term suggests, **product costs** are costs that are a necessary and integral part of producing the finished product. Under the matching principle, these costs do not become expenses until the finished goods inventory is sold. The expense is cost of goods sold. Direct materials and direct labor are often referred to as **prime costs** because of their direct association with the manufacturing of the finished product. Also, because direct labor and manufacturing overhead are incurred in converting raw materials into finished goods, these two cost elements are often referred to as **conversion costs**.

ALTERNATIVE TERMINOLOGY
Product costs are also called *inventoriable costs*.

Period costs are costs that are identified with a specific time period rather than with a salable product. These are nonmanufacturing costs. Period costs include selling and administrative expenses. They are deducted from revenues in the period in which they are incurred.

The foregoing relationships and cost terms are summarized in Illustration 20-3. Our main concern in this chapter is with product costs.

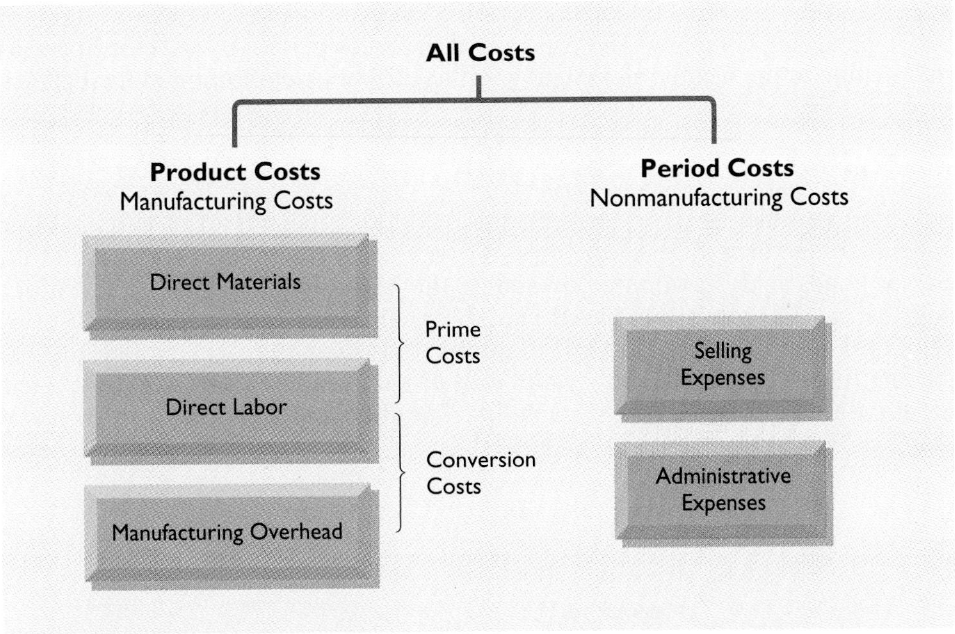

Illustration 20-3
Product versus period costs

ETHICS NOTE
An unethical manager may choose to inflate the company's earnings by absorbing period costs (such as selling and administrative expenses not pertaining to production) in the ending inventory balances.

BEFORE YOU GO ON...

REVIEW IT

1. What are the major cost classifications involved in manufacturing a product?
2. What are product and period costs, and what is their relationship to the manufacturing process?

DO IT

In making bicycles, a company has the following costs: tires, salaries of employees who put tires on the wheels, factory building depreciation, wheel nuts, spokes, salary of factory foreman, handle bars, and salaries of factory maintenance employees. Classify each cost as direct materials, direct labor, or manufacturing overhead.

ACTION PLAN

- Classify as direct materials any raw materials that can be physically and directly associated with the finished product.

- Classify as direct labor the work of factory employees that can be physically and directly associated with the finished product.
- Classify as manufacturing overhead any costs that are indirectly associated with the finished product.

SOLUTION: Tires, spokes, and handle bars are direct materials. Salaries of employees who put tires on the wheels are direct labor. All of the other costs are manufacturing overhead.

Related exercise material: BE20-4, BE20-5, BE20-7, E20-1, and E20-2.

THE NAVIGATOR

MANUFACTURING COSTS IN FINANCIAL STATEMENTS

STUDY OBJECTIVE 5

Explain the difference between a merchandising and a manufacturing income statement.

The financial statements of a manufacturing company are very similar to those of a merchandising company. The principal differences pertain to the cost of goods sold section in the income statement and the current assets section in the balance sheet.

INCOME STATEMENT

Under a periodic inventory system, the income statements of a merchandiser and a manufacturer differ in the cost of goods sold section. For a merchandiser, cost of goods sold is computed by adding the beginning merchandise inventory and the **cost of goods purchased** and subtracting the ending merchandise inventory. For a manufacturer, cost of goods sold is computed by adding the beginning finished goods inventory and **cost of goods manufactured** and subtracting the ending finished goods inventory. The different components are shown graphically below.

Illustration 20-4

Cost of goods sold components

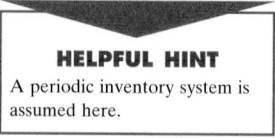

HELPFUL HINT

A periodic inventory system is assumed here.

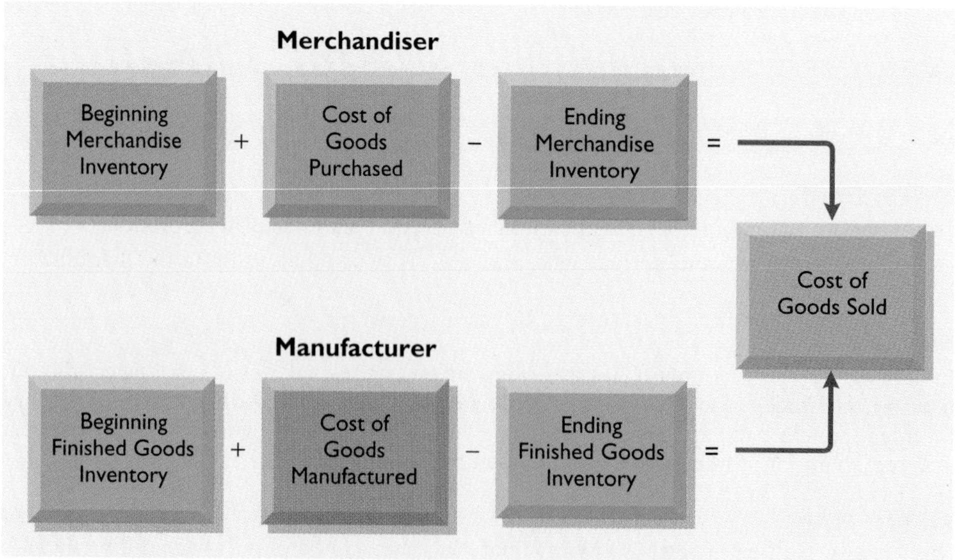

The cost of goods sold sections for merchandising and manufacturing companies presented below illustrate the different presentations.

Illustration 20-5

Cost of goods sold sections of merchandising and manufacturing income statements

Merchandise Company **Income Statement (partial)** **For the Year Ended December 31, 2002**		**Manufacturing Company** **Income Statement (partial)** **For the Year Ended December 31, 2002**	
Cost of goods sold		Cost of goods sold	
Merchandise inventory, January 1	**$ 70,000**	**Finished goods inventory, January 1**	**$ 90,000**
Cost of goods purchased	**650,000**	**Cost of goods manufactured (see Illustration 20-7)**	**370,000**
Cost of goods available for sale	720,000	Cost of goods available for sale	460,000
Merchandise inventory, December 31	**400,000**	**Finished goods inventory, December 31**	**80,000**
Cost of goods sold	$320,000	Cost of goods sold	$380,000

The other sections of an income statement are similar for merchandisers and manufacturers.

A number of accounts are involved in determining the cost of goods manufactured. To eliminate excessive detail, it is customary to show in the income statement only the total cost of goods manufactured. The details are presented in a Cost of Goods Manufactured Schedule. The form and content of this schedule are shown in Illustration 20-7 (page 836).

Determining the Cost of Goods Manufactured

STUDY OBJECTIVE 6

Indicate how cost of goods manufactured is determined.

An example may help show how the cost of goods manufactured is determined. Assume that **Compaq Computer** has a number of computers in various stages of production on January 1. In total, these partially completed units are called **beginning work in process inventory**. The costs assigned to beginning work in process inventory are based on the **manufacturing costs incurred in the prior period**.

The manufacturing costs incurred in the current year are used first to complete the work in process on January 1. They then are used to start the production of other computers. The sum of the direct materials costs, direct labor costs, and manufacturing overhead incurred in the current year is the **total manufacturing costs** for the current period.

HELPFUL HINT

Does the amount of "total manufacturing costs for the current year" include the amount of "beginning work in process inventory?" Answer: No.

We now have two cost amounts: (1) the cost of the beginning work in process and (2) the total manufacturing costs for the current period. The sum of these costs is the **total cost of work in process** for the year.

At the end of the year, some computers may be only partially completed. The costs of these units become the cost of the **ending work in process inventory**. To find the **cost of goods manufactured**, we subtract this cost from the total cost of work in process. The determination of the cost of goods manufactured is shown graphically in Illustration 20-6.

Illustration 20-6

Cost of goods manufactured formula

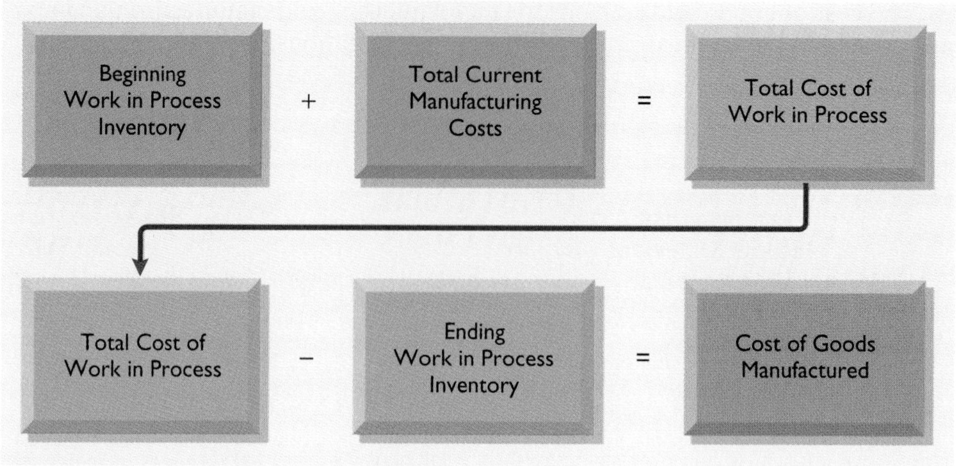

Cost of Goods Manufactured Schedule

An internal report shows each of the cost elements shown in Illustration 20-6. This report is called the **cost of goods manufactured schedule**. The schedule for Olsen Manufacturing Company (using assumed data) is shown in Illustration 20-7. Note that the schedule presents detailed data for direct materials and for manufacturing overhead.

Illustration 20-7

Cost of goods manufactured schedule

OLSEN MANUFACTURING COMPANY
Cost of Goods Manufactured Schedule
For the Year Ended December 31, 2002

Work in process, January 1			$ 18,400
Direct materials			
Raw materials inventory, January 1	$ 16,700		
Raw materials purchases	152,500		
Total raw materials available for use	169,200		
Less: Raw materials inventory, December 31	22,800		
Direct materials used		$146,400	
Direct labor		175,600	
Manufacturing overhead			
Indirect labor	14,300		
Factory repairs	12,600		
Factory utilities	10,100		
Factory depreciation	9,440		
Factory insurance	8,360		
Total manufacturing overhead		54,800	
Total current manufacturing costs			376,800
Total cost of work in process			395,200
Less: Work in process, December 31			25,200
Cost of goods manufactured			$370,000

Review Illustration 20-6 and then examine the cost of goods manufactured schedule in Illustration 20-7. You should be able to distinguish between "total current manufacturing costs" and "cost of goods manufactured." The difference is the effect of the change in work in process during the period.

BALANCE SHEET

The balance sheet for a merchandising company shows just one category of inventory. In contrast, the balance sheet for a manufacturer may have three inventory accounts. They are:

STUDY OBJECTIVE 7

Explain the difference between a merchandising and a manufacturing balance sheet.

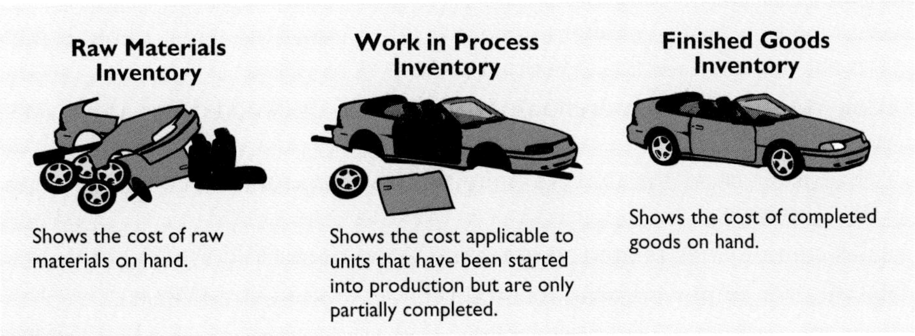

Raw Materials Inventory
Work in Process Inventory
Finished Goods Inventory
Shows the cost of raw materials on hand.
Shows the cost applicable to units that have been started into production but are only partially completed.
Shows the cost of completed goods on hand.

Illustration 20-8

Inventory accounts for a manufacturer

Finished Goods Inventory is to a manufacturer what Merchandise Inventory is to a merchandiser. It represents the goods that are available for sale.

The current assets sections presented in Illustration 20-9 contrast the presentations of inventories for merchandising and manufacturing companies. Manufacturing inventories are generally listed in the order of their liquidity—the order in which they are expected to be realized in cash. Thus, finished goods inventory is listed first. The remainder of the balance sheet is similar for the two types of companies.

Illustration 20-9

Current assets sections of merchandising and manufacturing balance sheets

MERCHANDISING COMPANY Balance Sheet December 31, 2002	
Current assets	
Cash	$100,000
Receivables (net)	210,000
Merchandise inventory	**400,000**
Prepaid expenses	22,000
Total current assets	$732,000

MANUFACTURING COMPANY Balance Sheet December 31, 2002		
Current assets		
Cash		$180,000
Receivables (net)		210,000
Inventories		
Finished goods	**$80,000**	
Work in process	**25,200**	
Raw materials	**22,800**	**128,000**
Prepaid expenses		18,000
Total current assets		$536,000

Each step in the accounting cycle for a merchandiser applies to a manufacturer. For example, prior to preparing financial statements, adjusting entries are required. The adjusting entries are essentially the same as those of a merchandiser. The closing entries are also similar for manufacturers and merchandisers.

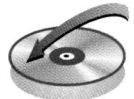

Chapter 20—Accounting Cycle (Work Sheet) for a Manufacturing Company

COST CONCEPTS—A REVIEW

You have learned a number of cost concepts in this chapter. Because many of these concepts are new, we believe an extended example will help illustrate how they are used. Assume that Northridge Company manufactures and sells pre-hung metal doors. Recently, it has decided to start selling pre-hung wood doors also.

An old warehouse that the company owns will be used to manufacture the new product. Northridge identifies the following costs associated with manufacturing and selling the pre-hung wood doors.

1. The material cost (wood) for each door is $10.
2. Labor costs involved in constructing a wood door are $8 per door.
3. Depreciation on the new equipment used to make the wood doors using the straight-line method is $25,000 per year.
4. Property taxes on the warehouse used to make the wood doors are $6,000 per year.
5. Advertising costs for the pre-hung wood doors total $2,500 per month or $30,000 per year.
6. Sales commissions related to pre-hung wood doors sold are $4 per door.
7. Salaries for employees who maintain the warehouse are $28,000.
8. The salary of the plant manager in charge of pre-hung wood doors is $70,000.
9. The cost of shipping pre-hung wood doors is $12 per door sold.

These manufacturing and selling costs can be assigned to the various categories shown in Illustration 20-10.

Illustration 20-10

Assignment of costs to cost categories

	Product Costs					
Cost Item	**Direct Materials**	**Direct Labor**	**Manufacturing Overhead**	**Period Costs**	**Prime Costs**	**Conversion Costs**
1. Material cost ($10) per door	X				X	
2. Labor costs ($8) per door		X			X	X
3. Depreciation on new equipment ($25,000 per year)			X			X
4. Property taxes ($6,000 per year)			X			X
5. Advertising costs ($30,000 per year)				X		
6. Sales commissions ($4 per door)				X		
7. Maintenance salaries ($28,000 per year)			X			X
8. Salary of plant manager ($70,000)			X			X
9. Cost of shipping pre-hung doors ($12 per door)				X		

Remember that total manufacturing costs are the sum of the product costs—direct materials, direct labor, and manufacturing overhead. If Northridge Company produces 10,000 pre-hung wood doors the first year, the total manufacturing costs would be:

Illustration 20-11

Computation of total manufacturing costs

Cost Number and Item	Manufacturing Cost
1. Material cost ($10 × 10,000)	$100,000
2. Labor cost ($8 × 10,000)	80,000
3. Depreciation on new equipment	25,000
4. Property taxes	6,000
7. Maintenance salaries	28,000
8. Salary of plant manager	70,000
Total manufacturing costs	**$309,000**

Knowing the total manufacturing costs, Northridge can compute the manufacturing cost per unit, assuming 10,000 units: The cost to produce one pre-hung wood door is $30.90 ($309,000 ÷ 10,000 units).

The cost concepts above will be used extensively in subsequent chapters. Study Illustration 20-10 carefully. If you do not understand any of these classifications, go back and reread the appropriate section in this chapter.

CONTEMPORARY DEVELOPMENTS IN MANAGERIAL ACCOUNTING

Since the 1970s, the competitive environment for U.S. businesses has changed significantly. Within the United States, for example, the airline, financial services, and telecommunications industries have been deregulated. Global competition has intensified, particularly in the automotive and electronics industries. Today, business managers demand from managerial accountants different and better information than they needed just a few years ago. Factors such as those discussed below will contribute to the expanding role of managerial accounting in the twenty-first century.

SERVICE INDUSTRY TRENDS

The Feature Story notes that at the peak of its success as a personal computer manufacturer, **Compaq** purchased **Digital Equipment**. Its management believes that the future of computing lies in providing computer services, rather than in manufacturing hardware. In fact, during the most recent decade, the U.S. economy in general shifted toward an emphasis on providing services, rather than goods. Today over 50 percent of U.S. workers are employed by service companies, and that percentage is projected to increase in coming years. Much of this chapter has focused on manufacturers. But most of the techniques that you will learn in this course are equally applicable to service entities.

In some respects, the challenges for managerial accounting are greater in service companies than in manufacturing companies. Further complicating matters in recent years, many service industries have been deregulated (for example: trucking, airlines, telecommunications, and banking). In a deregulated environment the information provided by managerial accounting is even more important. Illustration 20-12 presents examples of questions faced by service-company managers.

Illustration 20-12

Service industries and companies and the managerial accounting questions they face

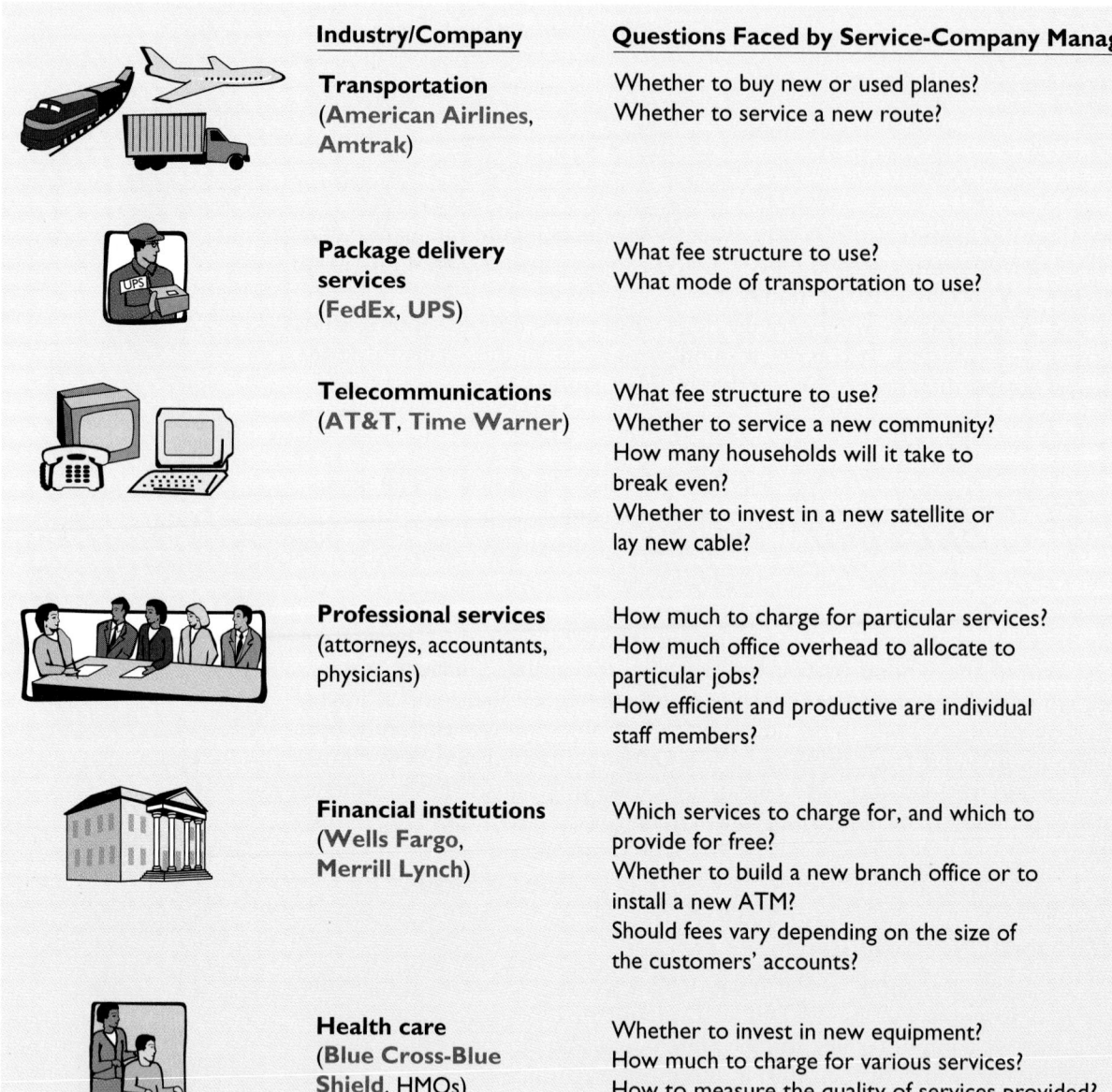

	Industry/Company	Questions Faced by Service-Company Managers
	**Transportation** (American Airlines, Amtrak)	Whether to buy new or used planes? Whether to service a new route?
	**Package delivery services** (FedEx, UPS)	What fee structure to use? What mode of transportation to use?
	**Telecommunications** (AT&T, Time Warner)	What fee structure to use? Whether to service a new community? How many households will it take to break even? Whether to invest in a new satellite or lay new cable?
	**Professional services** (attorneys, accountants, physicians)	How much to charge for particular services? How much office overhead to allocate to particular jobs? How efficient and productive are individual staff members?
	**Financial institutions** (Wells Fargo, Merrill Lynch)	Which services to charge for, and which to provide for free? Whether to build a new branch office or to install a new ATM? Should fees vary depending on the size of the customers' accounts?
	**Health care** (Blue Cross-Blue Shield, HMOs)	Whether to invest in new equipment? How much to charge for various services? How to measure the quality of services provided?

Managers of service companies look to managerial accounting to answer these questions. In some instances the managerial accountant may need to develop new systems for measuring the cost of serving individual customers. In others, he or she may need new operating controls to improve the quality and efficiency of specific services. Many of the examples we present in subsequent chapters will be based on service companies.

ACCOUNTING IN ACTION *Business Insight*

At **South Central Bell (Telephone)**, management accountants have shed their scorekeeping image. A corporate reorganization plan challenged the accountants to "show their stuff." They took on the roles of interpreter, advisor, and partner. To do so, they had to understand what the accounting numbers mean, relate the numbers to business activity, and recommend alternative courses of action. In addition, they evaluate alternatives and make decisions to maximize business efficiency.

VALUE CHAIN MANAGEMENT

The **value chain** is the term that describes all activities associated with providing a product or service. The value chain includes activities such as research and development, ordering raw materials, manufacturing, marketing, delivery, and customer relations. Each of these activities should be designed and operated so that they add value to the product or service. A critical component of the value chain is the supply chain. The **supply chain** is all of the activities from receipt of an order to delivery of a product or service. A number of factors affect efforts to manage the value chain and supply chain.

Technological Change

Many companies now employ **enterprise resource planning (ERP)** software systems to manage their value chain. ERP systems provide a comprehensive, centralized, integrated source of information used to manage all major business processes, from purchasing to manufacturing to human resource records. In large companies, an ERP system might replace as many as 200 individual software packages. For example, an ERP system can eliminate the need for individual software packages for personnel, inventory management, receivables, and payroll. Because the value chain extends beyond the walls of the company, ERP systems often collect and provide information from and to the company's major suppliers, customers, and business partners.

TECHNOLOGY IN ACTION

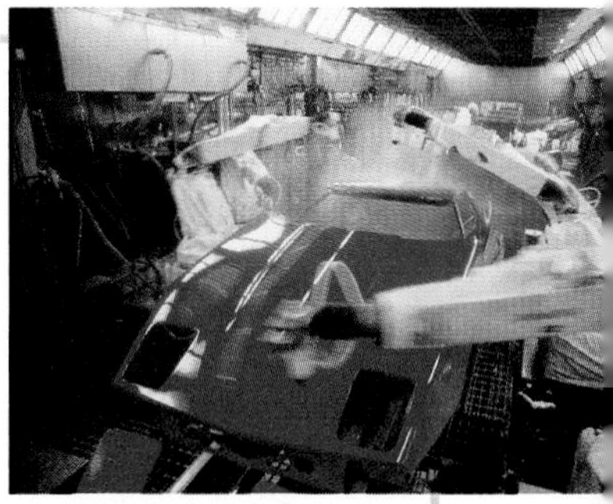

Through **computer-integrated manufacturing (CIM)**, many companies can now manufacture products that are untouched by human hands. An example is the use of robotic equipment in the steel and automobile industries. Automation significantly reduces direct labor costs in many cases. The worker simply monitors the manufacturing process by watching instrument panels.

Also, the widespread use of computers has greatly reduced the cost of accumulating, storing, and reporting managerial accounting information. Computers now make it possible to do more detailed costing of products, processes, and services than was possible under manual processing.

Technology is also affecting the value chain through business-to-business e-commerce on the Internet. The Internet has dramatically changed the way corporations do business with one another. It enables customers and suppliers to share information nearly instantaneously. In addition, it has changed the marketplace, often having the effect of cutting out the "middle man." Industries such as the automobile, airline, hotel, and electronics industries have made commitments to purchase some or all of their supplies and raw materials in the huge business-to-business electronic marketplaces. For example, **Hilton Hotels** recently committed to purchase as much as $1.5 billion of bed sheets, pest control services, and other items from **PurchasePro.com**.

Just-in-Time Inventory Methods

Many companies have significantly lowered inventory levels and costs using **just-in-time (JIT) inventory** methods. Under a just-in-time method, goods are manufactured or purchased just in time for use. As noted in the Feature Story, **Dell Computer** is famous for having developed a system for making computers in response to individual customer requests. Even though each computer is custom-made to meet each customer's particular specifications, it takes Dell less than 48 hours to assemble the computer and put it on a truck. By integrating its information systems with those of its suppliers, Dell reduced its inventories to nearly zero. This is a huge advantage in an industry where products become obsolete nearly overnight.

Quality

JIT inventory systems require an increased emphasis on product quality. If products are produced only as they are needed, it is very costly for the company to have to stop production because of defects or machine breakdowns. Many companies have installed **total quality management (TQM)** systems to reduce defects in finished products. The goal is to achieve zero defects. These systems require timely data on defective products, rework costs, and the cost of honoring warranty contracts. Often this information is used to help redesign the product in a way that makes it less prone to defect. Or it may be used to reengineer the production process to reduce setup time and decrease the potential for error. TQM systems also provide information on nonfinancial measures such as customer satisfaction, number of service calls, and time to generate reports. Attention to these measures, which employees can control, leads to increased profitability.

ACCOUNTING IN ACTION *Business Insight*

When it comes to total quality management, few companies go to greater lengths than **Chiquita Brands International**. Grocery store customers are very picky about bananas—bad bananas are consistently the number one grocery store complaint. Because bananas often account for up to 3 percent of a grocery store's sales, Chiquita goes to great lengths to protect the popular fruit. While bananas are in transit from Central America, "black box" recording devices attached to shipping crates ensure that they are kept in an environment of 90 percent humidity and an unvarying 55-degree temperature. Upon arrival in the U.S. bananas are ripened in airtight warehouses that use carefully monitored levels of ethylene gas. Regular checks are made of each warehouse using ultrasonic detectors that can detect leaks the size of a pinhole. Says one grocery store executive, "No other item in the store has this type of attention and resources devoted to it."

SOURCE: Devon Spurgeon, "When Grocers in U.S. Go Bananas Over Bad Fruit, They Call Laubenthal," *The Wall Street Journal*, August 14, 2000, p. A1.

Focus on Activities

As discussed earlier, overhead costs have become an increasingly large component of product and service costs. By definition, overhead costs cannot be directly traced to individual products. But to determine each product's cost, overhead must be allocated to the various products. In order to obtain more accurate product costs, many companies now allocate overhead using **activity-based costing (ABC)**. Under ABC, overhead is allocated based on each product's use of activities in making the product. For example, the company can keep track of the cost of setting up machines for each batch of a production process. Then a particular product can be allocated part of the total set-up cost based on the number of set-ups that product required. Activity-based costing is beneficial because it results in more accurate product costing and in more careful scrutiny of all activities in the supply chain. For example, if a product's cost is high because it requires a high number of set-ups, management will be motivated to determine how to produce the product using the optimal number of machine set-ups.

BEFORE YOU GO ON...

REVIEW IT

1. How does the content of an income statement for a merchandiser differ from that for a manufacturer?
2. How are the work in process inventories reported in the cost of goods manufactured schedule?
3. How does the content of the balance sheet for a merchandiser differ from that for a manufacturer?

A LOOK BACK AT OUR FEATURE STORY

Refer back to the Feature Story about **Compaq Computer** at the beginning of the chapter, and answer the following questions.

1. Relate the management functions discussed in the chapter to the manufacturing of computers.
2. Identify some of the likely manufacturing overhead costs incurred by a computer manufacturer.

SOLUTION

1. Manufacturing computers involves **planning**, that is, establishing production and marketing objectives; **directing** employees into a production work force; implementing planned objectives by coordinating purchasing, manufacturing, warehousing, and selling functions; and **motivating** and **controlling** activities and operations through supervision, training, evaluation, reporting, and analysis.
2. A computer manufacturer would likely incur overhead costs such as indirect materials (supplies, lubricants, etc.); indirect labor (supervisors, maintenance, etc.); depreciation of factory buildings and machinery; and factory insurance, taxes, and utilities.

THE NAVIGATOR

DEMONSTRATION PROBLEM 1

Additional Demonstration Problem

Superior Manufacturing Company has the following cost and expense data for the year ending December 31, 2002.

Raw materials, 1/1/02	$ 30,000	Insurance, factory	$ 14,000
Raw materials, 12/31/02	20,000	Property taxes, factory building	6,000
Raw materials purchased	205,000	Sales (net)	1,500,000
Indirect materials	15,000	Delivery expenses	100,000
Work in process, 1/1/02	80,000	Sales commissions	150,000
Work in process, 12/31/02	50,000	Indirect labor	90,000
Finished goods, 1/1/02	110,000	Factory machinery rent	40,000
Finished goods, 12/31/02	120,000	Factory utilities	65,000
Direct labor	350,000	Depreciation, factory building	24,000
Factory manager's salary	35,000	Administrative expenses	300,000

Instructions

(a) Prepare a cost of goods manufactured schedule for Superior Company for 2002.
(b) Prepare an income statement for Superior Company for 2002.
(c) Assume that Superior Company's ledgers show the balances of the following current asset accounts: Cash $17,000, Accounts Receivable (net) $120,000, Prepaid Expenses $13,000, and Short-term Investments $26,000. Prepare the current assets section of the balance sheet for Superior Company as of December 31, 2002.

SOLUTION TO DEMONSTRATION PROBLEM 1

ACTION PLAN

- Start with beginning work in process as the first item in the cost of goods manufactured schedule.
- Sum direct materials used, direct labor, and total manufacturing overhead to determine total current manufacturing costs.
- Sum beginning work in process and total current manufacturing costs to determine total cost of work in process.
- Cost of goods manufactured is the total cost of work in process less ending work in process.
- In the cost of goods sold section of the income statement, show beginning and ending finished goods inventory and cost of goods manufactured.
- In the balance sheet, list manufacturing inventories in the order of their expected realization in cash, with finished goods first.

(a)

SUPERIOR MANUFACTURING COMPANY
Cost of Goods Manufactured Schedule
For the Year Ended December 31, 2002

Work in process, 1/1			$ 80,000
Direct materials			
Raw materials inventory, 1/1	$ 30,000		
Raw materials purchased	205,000		
Total raw materials available for use	235,000		
Less: Raw materials inventory, 12/31	20,000		
Direct materials used		$215,000	
Direct labor		350,000	
Manufacturing overhead			
Indirect labor	90,000		
Factory utilities	65,000		
Factory machinery rent	40,000		
Factory manager's salary	35,000		
Depreciation on building	24,000		
Indirect materials	15,000		
Factory insurance	14,000		
Property taxes	6,000		
Total manufacturing overhead		289,000	
Total current manufacturing costs			854,000
Total cost of work in process			934,000
Less: Work in process, 12/31			50,000
Cost of goods manufactured			$884,000

(b)

SUPERIOR MANUFACTURING COMPANY
Income Statement
For the Year Ended December 31, 2002

Sales (net)		$1,500,000
Cost of goods sold		
Finished goods inventory, January 1	$110,000	
Cost of goods manufactured	884,000	
Cost of goods available for sale	994,000	
Less: Finished goods inventory, December 31	120,000	
Cost of goods sold		874,000
Gross profit		626,000
Operating expenses		
Administrative expenses	300,000	
Sales commissions	150,000	
Delivery expenses	100,000	
Total operating expenses		550,000
Net income		$ 76,000

(c)

SUPERIOR MANUFACTURING COMPANY
Balance Sheet (partial)
December 31, 2002

Current assets		
Cash		$ 17,000
Short-term investments		26,000
Accounts receivable (net)		120,000
Inventories		
Finished goods	$120,000	
Work in process	50,000	
Raw materials	20,000	190,000
Prepaid expenses		13,000
Total current assets		$366,000

THE NAVIGATOR

DEMONSTRATION PROBLEM 2

Additional Demonstration Problem

Giant Company specializes in manufacturing different models of racing bicycles. A new model, the Jaguar, has been well accepted. As a result, the company has established a separate manufacturing facility to produce these bicycles. The company produces 1,000 bicycles per month. Giant's monthly manufacturing cost and other expenses data related to these bicycles are as follows.

1. Rent on manufacturing equipment (lease cost) — $2,000/month
2. Insurance on manufacturing building — $750/month
3. Raw materials (frames, tires, etc.) — $80/bicycle
4. Utility costs for manufacturing facility — $1,000/month
5. Supplies for general office — $800/month
6. Wages for assembly line workers in manufacturing facility — $30/bicycle
7. Depreciation on office equipment — $650/month
8. Miscellaneous materials (lubricants, solders, etc.) — $1.20/bicycle
9. Property taxes on manufacturing building — $2,400/year
10. Manufacturing supervisor's salary — $3,000/month
11. Advertising for bicycles — $30,000/year
12. Sales commissions — $10/bicycle
13. Depreciation on manufacturing building — $1,500/month

Instructions

(a) Prepare an answer sheet with the following column headings.

	Product Costs					
Cost Item	**Direct Materials**	**Direct Labor**	**Manufacturing Overhead**	**Period Costs**	**Prime Costs**	**Conversion Costs**

Enter each cost item on your answer sheet, placing an "X" mark under the appropriate headings.

(b) Compute total manufacturing costs for the month.

ACTION PLAN

- Remember the definitions of: Prime costs = Direct materials + Direct labor. Conversion costs = Direct labor + Manufacturing overhead costs incurred in converting raw materials into finished goods.
- Make sure you are doing the computations for the appropriate period: month, year, unit, etc.
- Recall that period costs are not manufacturing costs and, therefore, are not inventoriable.
- Recall that product costs are manufacturing costs and are inventoriable.

THE NAVIGATOR

SOLUTION TO DEMONSTRATION PROBLEM 2

(a)

Cost Item	Product Costs: Direct Materials	Direct Labor	Manufacturing Overhead	Period Costs	Prime Costs	Conversion Costs
1. Rent on equipment ($2,000/month)			X			X
2. Insurance on manufacturing building ($750/month)			X			X
3. Raw materials ($80/bicycle)	X				X	
4. Manufacturing utilities ($1,000/month)			X			X
5. Office supplies ($800/month)				X		
6. Wages for workers ($30/bicycle)		X			X	X
7. Depreciation on office equipment ($650/month)				X		
8. Miscellaneous materials ($1.20/bicycle)			X			X
9. Property taxes on building ($2,400/year)			X			X
10. Manufacturing supervisor's salary ($3,000/month)			X			X
11. Advertising cost ($30,000/year)				X		
12. Sales commissions ($10/bicycle)				X		
13. Depreciation on manufacturing building ($1,500/month)			X			X

(b)

Cost Item	Manufacturing Cost
Rent on equipment	$ 2,000
Insurance	750
Raw materials ($80 × 1,000)	80,000
Manufacturing utilities	1,000
Labor ($30 × 1,000)	30,000
Miscellaneous materials ($1.20 × 1,000)	1,200
Property taxes ($2,400 ÷ 12)	200
Manufacturing supervisor's salary	3,000
Depreciation on building	1,500
Total manufacturing costs	$119,650

SUMMARY OF STUDY OBJECTIVES

1. ***Explain the distinguishing features of managerial accounting.*** The distinguishing features of managerial accounting are:

Primary users of reports—internal users, who are officers, department heads, managers, and supervisors in the company.

Type and frequency of reports—internal reports that are issued as frequently as the need arises.

Purpose of reports—to provide special-purpose information for a particular user for a specific decision.

Content of reports—pertains to subunits of the business and may be very detailed; may extend beyond double-entry accounting system; the reporting standard is relevance to the decision being made.

Verification of reports—no independent audits.

2. ***Identify the three broad functions of management.*** The three functions are planning, directing and motivating, and controlling. Planning requires management to look ahead and to establish objectives. Directing and motivating involves coordinating the diverse activities and human resources of a company to produce a smooth-running operation. Controlling is the process of keeping the activities on track.

3. ***Define the three classes of manufacturing costs.*** Manufacturing costs are typically classified as either (1) direct materials, (2) direct labor, or (3) manufacturing overhead. Raw materials that can be physically and directly associated with the finished product during the manufacturing process are called direct materials. The work of factory employees that can be physically and directly associated with converting raw materials into finished goods is considered direct labor. Manufacturing overhead consists of costs that are indirectly associated with the manufacture of the finished product.

4. ***Distinguish between product and period costs.*** Product costs are costs that are a necessary and integral part of producing the finished product. Product costs are also called inventoriable costs. Under the matching principle, these costs do not become expenses until the inventory to which they attach is sold. Period costs are costs that are identified with a specific time period rather than with a salable product. These costs relate to nonmanufacturing costs and therefore are not inventoriable costs.

5. ***Explain the difference between a merchandising and a manufacturing income statement.*** The difference between a merchandising and a manufacturing income statement is in the cost of goods sold section. A manufacturing cost of goods sold section shows beginning and ending finished goods inventories and the cost of goods manufactured.

6. ***Indicate how cost of goods manufactured is determined.*** The cost of the beginning work in process is added to the total manufacturing costs for the current year to arrive at the total cost of work in process for the year. The ending work in process is then subtracted from the total cost of work in process to arrive at the cost of goods manufactured.

7. ***Explain the difference between a merchandising and a manufacturing balance sheet.*** The difference between a manufacturing and a merchandising balance sheet is in the current assets section. In the current assets section of a manufacturing company's balance sheet, three inventory accounts are presented: finished goods inventory, work in process inventory, and raw materials inventory.

THE NAVIGATOR

Key Term Matching Activity

GLOSSARY

Activity-based costing (ABC) A method of allocating overhead based on each product's use of activities in making the product. (p. 842).

Conversion costs Direct labor and manufacturing overhead costs incurred in converting raw materials into finished goods. (p. 833).

Cost of goods manufactured Total cost of work in process less the cost of the ending work in process inventory. (p. 835).

Direct labor The work of factory employees that can be physically and directly associated with converting raw materials into finished goods. (p. 832).

Direct materials Raw materials that can be physically and directly associated with manufacturing the finished product. (p. 831).

Enterprise resource planning (ERP) system Software that provides a comprehensive, centralized, integrated source of information used to manage all major business processes. (p. 841).

Indirect labor Work of factory employees that has no physical association with the finished product, or for which it is impractical to trace the costs to the goods produced. (p. 832).

Indirect materials Raw materials that do not physically become part of the finished product or cannot be traced because their physical association with the finished product is too small. (p. 832).

Just-in-time (JIT) inventory Inventory system in which goods are manufactured or purchased just in time for use. (p. 842).

Managerial accounting A field of accounting that provides economic and financial information for managers and other internal users. (p. 828).

Manufacturing overhead Manufacturing costs that are indirectly associated with the manufacture of the finished product. (p. 832).

Period costs Costs that are identified with a specific time period and charged to expense as incurred. (p. 833).

Prime costs Direct materials and direct labor. (p. 833).

Product costs Costs that are a necessary and integral part of producing the finished product. (p. 833).

Supply chain All activities from receipt of an order to delivery of a product or service. (p. 841).

Total cost of work in process Cost of the beginning work in process plus total manufacturing costs for the current period. (p. 835).

Total manufacturing costs The sum of direct materials, direct labor, and manufacturing overhead incurred in the current period. (p. 835).

Total quality management (TQM) Systems implemented to reduce defects in finished products with the goal of achieving zero defects. (p. 842).

Value chain All activities associated with providing a product or service. (p. 841).

Chapter 20 Self-Test

SELF-STUDY QUESTIONS

Answers are at the end of the chapter.

(SO 1) **1.** Managerial accounting:
a. is governed by generally accepted accounting principles.
b. places emphasis on special-purpose information.
c. pertains to the entity as a whole and is highly aggregated.
d. is limited to cost data.

(SO 1) **2.** Which of the following is *not* one of the categories in *Standards of Ethical Conduct for Management Accountants?*
a. Confidentiality. c. Integrity.
b. Competence. d. Independence.

(SO 2) **3.** The management of an organization performs several broad functions. They are:
a. planning, directing and motivating, and selling.
b. planning, directing and motivating, and controlling.
c. planning, manufacturing, and controlling.
d. directing and motivating, manufacturing, and controlling.

(SO 3) **4.** Direct materials are a:

	Conversion Cost	Manufacturing Cost	Prime Cost
a.	Yes	Yes	No
b.	No	Yes	Yes
c.	Yes	Yes	Yes
d.	No	No	No

(SO 4) **5.** Indirect labor is a:
a. nonmanufacturing cost.
b. prime cost.
c. product cost.
d. period cost.

6. Which of the following costs would be included in manufacturing overhead of a computer manufacturer? (SO 3)
a. The cost of the $3\frac{1}{2}$-inch disk drives.
b. The wages earned by computer assemblers.
c. The cost of the memory chips.
d. Depreciation on testing equipment.

7. Which of the following is *not* an element of manufacturing overhead? (SO 3)
a. Sales manager's salary.
b. Plant manager's salary.
c. Factory repairman's wages.
d. Product inspector's salary.

8. For the year, Redder Company has cost of goods manufactured of $600,000, beginning finished goods inventory of $200,000, and ending finished goods inventory of $250,000. The cost of goods sold is: (SO 5)
a. $450,000. c. $550,000.
b. $500,000. d. $600,000.

9. A cost of goods manufactured schedule shows beginning and ending inventories for: (SO 6)
a. raw materials and work in process only.
b. work in process only.
c. raw materials only.
d. raw materials, work in process, and finished goods.

10. In a manufacturer's balance sheet, three inventories may be reported: (1) raw materials, (2) work in process, and (3) finished goods. Indicate in what sequence these inventories generally appear on a balance sheet. (SO 7)
a. (1), (2), (3) c. (3), (1), (2)
b. (2), (3), (1) d. (3), (2), (1)

THE NAVIGATOR

QUESTIONS

1. (a) "Managerial accounting is a field of accounting that provides economic information for all interested parties." Do you agree? Explain.
(b) Pat Gonzalez believes that managerial accounting serves only manufacturing firms. Is Pat correct? Explain.

2. Distinguish between managerial and financial accounting as to (a) primary users of reports, (b) types and frequency of reports, and (c) purpose of reports.

3. How does the content of reports and the verification of reports differ between managerial and financial accounting?

4. (a) Identify the four categories of ethical standards for management accountants.
(b) Is the responsibility of the management accountant limited to only his or her own acts? Explain.

5. Karen Gish is studying for the next accounting mid-term examination. Summarize for Karen what she should know about management functions.

6. "Decision making is management's most important function." Do you agree? Why or why not?

7. Sue Sablow is studying for her next accounting examination. Explain to Sue what she should know about the differences between the income statements for a manufacturing and for a merchandising company.

8. Bob Jackson is unclear as to the difference between the balance sheets of a merchandising company and a manufacturing company. Explain the difference to Bob.

9. How are manufacturing costs classified?

10. Gene Toni claims that the distinction between direct and indirect materials is based entirely on physical association with the product. Is Gene correct? Why?

11. Jane Diaz is confused about the differences between a product cost and a period cost. Explain the differences to Jane.

12. Amy Victor asks your help with the terms (a) prime costs and (b) conversion costs. Distinguish between the terms.

13. In Jamaica Molding Company, direct materials are $12,000, direct labor is $15,000, and manufacturing overhead is $9,000. What is the amount of (a) prime costs and (b) conversion costs?

14. Identify the differences in the cost of goods sold section of an income statement between a merchandising company and a manufacturing company.

15. The determination of the cost of goods manufactured involves the following factors: (A) beginning work in process inventory, (B) total manufacturing costs, and (C) ending work in process inventory. Identify the meaning of x in the following formulas:
(a) $A + B = x$
(b) $A + B - C = x$

16. Sajjad Manufacturing has beginning raw materials inventory $12,000, ending raw materials inventory $18,000, and raw materials purchases $180,000. What is the cost of direct materials used?

17. Jam Manufacturing Inc. has beginning work in process $27,200, direct materials used $240,000, direct labor $200,000, total manufacturing overhead $150,000, and ending work in process $32,000. What are total manufacturing costs?

18. Using the data in Q17, what are (a) the total cost of work in process and (b) the cost of goods manufactured?

19. In what order should manufacturing inventories be listed in a balance sheet?

BRIEF EXERCISES

BE20-1 Complete the following comparison table between managerial and financial accounting.

Distinguish between managerial and financial accounting.
(SO 1)

	Financial Accounting	Managerial Accounting
Primary users		
Type of reports		
Frequency of reports		
Purpose of reports		
Reporting standards		
Verification		

BE20-2 The Institute of Management Accountants has promulgated ethical standards for managerial accountants. Identify the four specific standards.

Identify ethical standards.
(SO 1)

BE20-3 Listed below are three functions of the management of an organization:

Identify the three management functions.
(SO 2)

1. Planning 2. Directing and motivating 3. Controlling

Identify each of the following statements that best describes each of the above functions.

(a) ____ require(s) management to look ahead and to establish objectives. A key objective of management appears to be to add value to the business.

(b) ____ involve(s) coordinating the diverse activities and human resources of a company to produce a smooth-running operation. This function relates to the implementation of planned objectives.

(c) ____ is the process of keeping the activities on track. Management must determine whether goals are being met and what changes are necessary when there are deviations.

BE20-4 Determine whether each of the following costs should be classified as direct materials (DM), direct labor (DL), or manufacturing overhead (MO).

Classify manufacturing costs.
(SO 3)

(a) ____ Frames and tires used in manufacturing bicycles.
(b) ____ Wages paid to production workers.
(c) ____ Insurance on factory equipment and machinery.
(d) ____ Depreciation on factory equipment.

Classify manufacturing costs. (SO 3)

BE20-5 Indicate whether each of the following costs of an automobile manufacturer would be classified as direct materials, direct labor, or manufacturing overhead:

(a) ____ Windshield.
(b) ____ Engine.
(c) ____ Wages of assembly line worker.
(d) ____ Depreciation of factory machinery.
(e) ____ Factory machinery lubricants.
(f) ____ Tires.
(g) ____ Steering wheel.
(h) ____ Salary of painting supervisor.

Identify product and period costs. (SO 4)

BE20-6 Identify whether each of the following costs should be classified as product costs or period costs.

(a) ____ Manufacturing overhead.
(b) ____ Selling expenses.
(c) ____ Administrative expenses.
(d) ____ Advertising expenses.
(e) ____ Direct labor.
(f) ____ Direct material.

Classify manufacturing costs. (SO 3, 4)

BE20-7 Presented below are Hyde Company's monthly manufacturing cost data related to its personal computer products.

(a) Utilities for manufacturing equipment	$116,000
(b) Raw material (CPU, chips, etc.)	$ 85,000
(c) Depreciation on manufacturing building	$880,000
(d) Wages for production workers	$191,000

Enter each cost item in the following table, placing an "X" under the appropriate headings.

	Product Costs				
	Direct Materials	**Direct Labor**	**Factory Overhead**	**Prime Costs**	**Conversion Costs**
(a)					
(b)					
(c)					
(d)					

Compute total manufacturing costs and total cost of work in process. (SO 6)

BE20-8 Buslik Manufacturing Company has the following data: direct labor $242,000, direct materials used $180,000, total manufacturing overhead $208,000, and beginning work in process $25,000. Compute **(a)** total manufacturing costs and **(b)** total cost of work in process.

Prepare current assets section. (SO 7)

BE20-9 In alphabetical order below are current asset items for Ivy Company's balance sheet at December 31, 2002. Prepare the current assets section (including a complete heading).

Accounts receivable	$200,000
Cash	62,000
Finished goods	75,000
Prepaid expenses	38,000
Raw materials	68,000
Work in process	87,000

Determine missing amounts in computing total manufacturing costs. (SO 6)

BE20-10 Presented below are incomplete 2002 manufacturing cost data for Hyun Corporation. Determine the missing amounts.

	Direct Materials Used	**Direct Labor Used**	**Factory Overhead**	**Total Manufacturing Costs**
(a)	$35,000	$61,000	$ 50,000	?
(b)	?	$75,000	$120,000	$296,000
(c)	$55,000	?	$111,000	$300,000

Determine missing amounts in computing cost of goods manufactured. (SO 6)

BE20-11 Use the same data from BE20-10 above and the data below. Determine the missing amounts.

	Total Manufacturing Costs	**Work in Process (1/1)**	**Work in Process (12/31)**	**Cost of Goods Manufactured**
(a)	?	$120,000	$86,000	?
(b)	$296,000	?	$98,000	$321,000
(c)	$300,000	$463,000	?	$715,000

EXERCISES

Classify costs into three classes of manufacturing costs. (SO 3)

E20-1 Presented below is a list of costs and expenses usually incurred by Iguana Corporation, a manufacturer of furniture, in its factory.

1. Salaries for assembly line inspectors.
2. Insurance on factory machines.
3. Property taxes on the factory building.
4. Factory repairs.
5. Upholstery used in manufacturing furniture.
6. Wages paid to assembly line workers.
7. Factory machinery depreciation.
8. Glue, nails, paint, and other small parts used in production.
9. Factory supervisors' salaries.
10. Wood used in manufacturing furniture.

Instructions

Classify the above items into the following categories: **(a)** direct materials, **(b)** direct labor, and **(c)** manufacturing overhead.

Determine the total amount of various types of costs. (SO 3, 4)

E20-2 Honmura Company reports the following costs and expenses in May.

Factory utilities	$ 8,500	Direct labor	$69,100
Depreciation on factory equipment	12,650	Sales salaries	49,400
Depreciation on delivery trucks	3,500	Property taxes on factory building	2,500
Indirect factory labor	48,900	Repairs to office equipment	1,300
Indirect materials	89,800	Factory repairs	2,000
Direct materials used	137,600	Advertising	18,000
Factory manager's salary	8,000	Office supplies used	2,640

Instructions

From the information, determine the total amount of:

(a) Prime costs.
(b) Manufacturing overhead.
(c) Conversion costs.
(d) Product costs.
(e) Period costs.

Classify various costs into different cost categories. (SO 3, 4)

E20-3 Karpman Company is a manufacturer of personal computers. Various costs and expenses associated with its operations are as follows.

1. Property taxes on the factory building.
2. Production superintendents' salaries.
3. Memory boards and chips used in assembling computers.
4. Depreciation on the factory equipment.
5. Salaries for assembly line quality control inspectors.
6. Sales commissions paid to sell personal computers.
7. Electrical wiring in assembling computers.
8. Wages of workers assembling personal computers.
9. Soldering materials used on factory assembly lines.
10. Salaries for the night security guards for the factory building.

The company intends to classify these costs and expenses into the following categories: **(a)** direct materials, **(b)** direct labor, **(c)** manufacturing overhead, and **(d)** period costs.

Instructions

List the items (1)–(10). For each item, indicate the cost category to which the item belongs.

Determine missing amounts in cost of goods manufactured schedule.
(SO 5, 6)

E20-4 The cost of goods manufactured schedule shows each of the cost elements. Complete the following schedule for Salazar Manufacturing Company.

SALAZAR MANUFACTURING COMPANY
Cost of Goods Manufactured Schedule
For the Year Ended December 31, 2002

Work in process (1/1)			$ 200,000
Direct materials			
Raw materials inventory (1/1)	$?		
Add: Raw materials purchases	158,000		
Less: Raw materials inventory (12/31)	7,500		
Direct materials used		$190,000	
Direct labor		?	
Manufacturing overhead			
Indirect labor	$ 18,000		
Factory depreciation	36,000		
Factory utilities	68,000		
Total overhead		122,000	
Total manufacturing costs			?
Total cost of work in process			$?
Less: Work in process (12/31)			81,000
Cost of goods manufactured			$560,000

Determine the missing amount of different cost items.
(SO 6)

E20-5 Manufacturing cost data for Hermes Company are presented below.

	Case A	Case B	Case C
Direct materials used	(a)	$68,400	$130,000
Direct labor	$ 57,000	86,000	(g)
Manufacturing overhead	42,500	81,600	102,000
Total manufacturing costs	180,650	(d)	253,700
Work in process 1/1/02	(b)	16,500	(h)
Total cost of work in process	221,500	(e)	327,000
Work in process 12/31/02	(c)	9,000	70,000
Cost of goods manufactured	185,275	(f)	(i)

Instructions
Indicate the missing amount for each letter.

Determine the missing amount of different cost items, and prepare a condensed cost of goods manufactured schedule.
(SO 5, 6)

E20-6 Incomplete manufacturing cost data for Hollis Company for 2002 are presented as follows.

	Direct Materials Used	Direct Labor Used	Manufacturing Overhead	Total Manufacturing Costs	Work in Process 1/1	Work in Process 12/31	Cost of Goods Manufactured
(1)	$117,000	$140,000	$ 77,000	(a)	$30,000	(b)	$360,000
(2)	(c)	200,000	132,000	$440,000	(d)	$40,000	470,000
(3)	80,000	100,000	(e)	255,000	60,000	80,000	(f)
(4)	70,000	(g)	75,000	294,000	45,000	(h)	270,000

Instructions
(a) Indicate the missing amount for each letter.
(b) Prepare a condensed cost of goods manufactured schedule for situation (1) for the year ended December 31, 2002.

Prepare a cost of goods manufactured schedule and a partial income statement.
(SO 5, 6)

E20-7 Issey Corporation has the following cost records for June 2002.

Indirect factory labor	$ 4,500	Factory utilities	$ 400
Direct materials used	20,000	Depreciation, factory equipment	1,400
Work in process, 6/1/02	3,000	Direct labor	25,000
Work in process, 6/30/02	3,500	Maintenance, factory equipment	1,300
Finished goods, 6/1/02	5,000	Indirect materials	2,200
Finished goods, 6/30/02	7,500	Factory manager's salary	3,000

Instructions

(a) Prepare a cost of goods manufactured schedule for June 2002.

(b) Prepare an income statement through gross profit for June 2002 assuming net sales are $98,100.

Indicate in which schedule or financial statement(s) different cost items will appear.
(SO 5, 6, 7)

E20-8 Hippo Manufacturing Company produces blankets. From its accounting records it prepares the following schedule and financial statements on a yearly basis.

(a) Cost of goods manufactured schedule
(b) Income statement
(c) Balance sheet

The following items are found in its ledger and accompanying data.

1. Direct labor
2. Raw materials inventory, 1/1
3. Work in process inventory, 12/31
4. Finished goods inventory, 1/1
5. Indirect labor
6. Depreciation on factory machinery
7. Work in process, 1/1
8. Finished goods inventory, 12/31
9. Factory maintenance salaries
10. Cost of goods manufactured
11. Depreciation on delivery equipment
12. Cost of goods available for sale
13. Direct materials used
14. Heat and electricity for factory
15. Repairs to roof of factory building
16. Cost of raw materials purchases

Instructions

List the items (1)–(16). For each item, indicate by using the appropriate letter or letters, the schedule and/or financial statement(s) in which the item will appear.

Prepare a cost of goods manufactured schedule, and present the ending inventories of the balance sheet.
(SO 5, 6, 7)

E20-9 An analysis of the accounts of Lanier Manufacturing reveals the following manufacturing cost data for the month ended June 30, 2002.

Inventories	Beginning	Ending
Raw materials	$9,000	$11,100
Work in process	5,000	8,000
Finished goods	8,000	6,000

Costs incurred:

Raw materials purchases $64,000, direct labor $50,000, manufacturing overhead $19,900. The specific overhead costs were: indirect labor $5,500, factory insurance $4,000, machinery depreciation $4,000, machinery repairs $1,800, factory utilities $3,100, miscellaneous factory costs $1,500.

Instructions

(a) Prepare the cost of goods manufactured schedule for the month ended June 30, 2002.

(b) Show the presentation of the ending inventories on the June 30, 2002, balance sheet.

Determine the amount of cost to appear in various accounts, and indicate in which financial statements these accounts would appear.
(SO 5, 6, 7)

E20-10 Jazz Motor Company manufactures automobiles. During September 2002 the company purchased 5,000 head lamps at a cost of $9 per lamp. Jazz withdrew 4,650 lamps from the warehouse during the month. Fifty of these lamps were used to replace the head lamps in autos used by traveling sales staff. The remaining 4,600 lamps were put in autos manufactured during the month.

Of the autos put into production during September 2002, 90% were completed and transferred to the company's storage lot. Of the cars completed during the month, 70% were sold by September 30.

Instructions

(a) Determine the cost of head lamps that would appear in each of the following accounts at September 30, 2002: Raw Materials, Work in Process, Finished Goods, Cost of Goods Sold, and Selling Expenses.

(b) Write a short memo to the chief accountant, indicating whether and where each of the accounts in (a) would appear on the income statement or on the balance sheet at September 30, 2002.

PROBLEMS: SET A

Classify manufacturing costs into different categories and compute the unit cost.
(SO 3, 4)

P20-1A Snapper Company specializes in manufacturing a unique model of bicycle helmet. The model is well accepted by consumers, and the company has enough orders to keep the factory production at 10,000 helmets per month (80% of its full capacity). Snapper's monthly manufacturing cost and other expense data are as follows.

Rent on factory equipment	$ 6,000
Insurance on factory building	1,500
Raw materials (plastics, polystyrene, etc.)	70,000
Utility costs for factory	900
Supplies for general office	300
Wages for assembly line workers	46,000
Depreciation on office equipment	800
Miscellaneous materials (lubricants, solders, etc.)	1,100
Factory manager's salary	5,700
Property taxes on factory building	400
Advertising for helmets	11,000
Sales commissions	7,000
Depreciation on factory building	1,500

Instructions

(a) Prepare an answer sheet with the following column headings:

	Product Costs					
Cost Item	Direct Materials	Direct Labor	Manufacturing Overhead	Period Costs	Prime Costs	Conversion Costs

Enter each cost item on your answer sheet, placing the dollar amount under the appropriate headings. Total the dollar amounts in each of the columns.

(b) Compute the cost to produce one helmet.

Classify manufacturing costs into different categories and compute the unit cost.
(SO 3, 4)

P20-2A Galex Company, a manufacturer of stereo systems, started its production in October 2002. For the preceding 3 years Galex had been a retailer of stereo systems. After a thorough survey of stereo system markets, Galex decided to turn its retail store into a stereo equipment factory.

Raw materials cost for a stereo system will total $70 per unit. Workers on the production lines are on average paid $10 per hour. A stereo system usually takes 5 hours to complete. In addition, the rent on the equipment used to assemble stereo systems amounts to $4,500 per month. Indirect materials cost $5 per system. A supervisor was hired to oversee production; her monthly salary is $2,700.

Janitorial costs were $1,300 monthly. Advertising costs for the stereo system will be $8,500 per month. The factory building depreciation expense is $7,200 per year. Property taxes on the factory building will be $6,000 per year.

Instructions

(a) Prepare an answer sheet with the following column headings:

	Product Costs					
Cost Item	Direct Materials	Direct Labor	Manufacturing Overhead	Period Costs	Prime Costs	Conversion Costs

Assuming that Galex manufactures, on average, 1,300 stereo systems per month, enter each cost item on your answer sheet, placing the dollar amount per month under the appropriate headings. Total the dollar amounts in each of the columns.

(b) Compute the cost to produce one stereo system.

P20-3A Incomplete manufacturing costs, expenses, and selling data for two different cases are as follows.

Indicate the missing amount of different cost items, and prepare a condensed cost of goods manufactured schedule, an income statement, and a partial balance sheet.
(SO 5, 6, 7)

	Case	
	1	**2**
Direct Materials Used	$ 7,600	$ (g)
Direct Labor	6,000	8,000
Manufacturing Overhead	5,000	4,000
Total Manufacturing Costs	(a)	19,000
Beginning Work in Process Inventory	1,000	(h)
Ending Work in Process Inventory	(b)	3,000
Sales	24,500	(i)
Sales Discounts	2,500	1,400
Cost of Goods Manufactured	16,000	22,000
Beginning Finished Goods Inventory	(c)	3,300
Goods Available for Sale	18,000	(j)
Cost of Goods Sold	(d)	(k)
Ending Finished Goods Inventory	3,400	2,500
Gross Profit	(e)	7,000
Operating Expenses	2,500	(l)
Net Income	(f)	3,000

Instructions

(a) Indicate the missing amount for each letter.
(b) Prepare a condensed cost of goods manufactured schedule for Case 1.
(c) Prepare an income statement and the current assets section of the balance sheet for Case 1. Assume that in Case 1 the other items in the current assets section are as follows: Cash $4,000, Receivables (net) $15,000, Raw Materials $600, and Prepaid Expenses $400.

P20-4A The following data were taken from the records of Gamma Manufacturing Company for the fiscal year ended June 30, 2002.

Prepare a cost of goods manufactured schedule, a partial income statement, and a partial balance sheet.
(SO 5, 6, 7)

Raw Materials Inventory 7/1/01	$ 48,000	Factory Insurance	$ 4,600
Raw Materials Inventory 6/30/02	39,600	Factory Machinery Depreciation	15,000
Finished Goods Inventory 7/1/01	96,000	Freight-in on Raw Materials Purchased	8,600
Finished Goods Inventory 6/30/02	95,900	Factory Utilities	24,600
Work in Process Inventory 7/1/01	19,800	Office Utilities Expense	8,650
Work in Process Inventory 6/30/02	17,600	Sales	547,000
Direct Labor	147,250	Sales Discounts	4,200
Indirect Labor	24,460	Plant Manager's Salary	29,000
Accounts Receivable	27,000	Factory Property Taxes	9,600
		Factory Repairs	1,400
		Raw Materials Purchases	89,800
		Cash	32,000

Instructions

(a) Prepare a cost of goods manufactured schedule.
(b) Prepare an income statement through gross profit.
(c) Prepare the current assets section of the balance sheet at June 30, 2002.

Totals
(a) $364,910
(b) $177,790
(c) $212,100

P20-5A Istanbul Company is a manufacturer of computers. Its controller resigned in October 2002. An inexperienced assistant accountant has prepared the following income statement for the month of October 2002.

Prepare a cost of goods manufactured schedule and a correct income statement.
(SO 5, 6)

ISTANBUL COMPANY
Income Statement
For the Month Ended October 31, 2002

Sales (net)		$780,000
Less: Operating expenses		
Raw materials purchased	$260,000	
Direct labor cost	190,000	
Advertising expense	92,000	
Selling and administrative salaries	75,000	
Rent on factory facilities	60,000	
Depreciation on sales equipment	45,000	
Depreciation on factory equipment	35,000	
Indirect labor cost	25,000	
Factory utilities	12,000	
Factory insurance	8,000	802,000
Net loss		$(22,000)

Prior to October 2002 the company had been profitable every month. The company's president is concerned about the accuracy of the income statement. As his friend, you have been asked to review the income statement and make necessary corrections. After examining other manufacturing cost data, you have acquired additional information as follows.

1. Inventory balances at the beginning and end of October were:

	October 1	October 31
Raw materials	$18,000	$31,000
Work in process	16,000	14,000
Finished goods	30,000	48,000

2. Only 70% of the utilities expense and 60% of the insurance expense apply to factory operations. The remaining amounts should be charged to selling and administrative activities.

Instructions

(a) CGM $572,200
(b) NI $7,000

(a) Prepare a schedule of cost of goods manufactured for October 2002.
(b) Prepare a correct income statement for October 2002.

PROBLEMS: SET B

Classify manufacturing costs into different categories and compute the unit cost.
(SO 3, 4)

P20-1B Kanjo Company specializes in manufacturing motorcycles. The company has enough orders to keep the factory production at 1,000 motorcycles per month. Kanjo's monthly manufacturing cost and other expense data are as follows.

Maintenance costs on factory building	$ 300
Factory manager's salary	5,000
Advertising for motorcycles	10,000
Sales commissions	5,000
Depreciation on factory building	700
Rent on factory equipment	5,000
Insurance on factory building	3,000
Raw materials (frames, tires, etc.)	20,000
Utility costs for factory	800
Supplies for general office	200
Wages for assembly line workers	40,000
Depreciation on office equipment	500
Miscellaneous materials (lubricants, solders, etc.)	1,000

Instructions

(a) Prepare an answer sheet with the following column headings.

	Product Costs					
Cost Item	**Direct Materials**	**Direct Labor**	**Manufacturing Overhead**	**Period Costs**	**Prime Costs**	**Conversion Costs**

Enter each cost item on your answer sheet, placing the dollar amount under the appropriate headings. Total the dollar amounts in each of the columns.

(b) Compute the cost to produce one motorcycle.

P20-2B Match Company, a manufacturer of tennis rackets, started production in November 2002. For the preceding 5 years Match had been a retailer of sports equipment. After a thorough survey of tennis racket markets, Match decided to turn its retail store into a tennis racket factory.

Classify manufacturing costs into different categories and compute the unit cost.
(SO 3, 4)

Raw materials cost for a tennis racket will total $20 per racket. Workers on the production lines are paid on average $13 per hour. A racket usually takes 2 hours to complete. In addition, the rent on the equipment used to produce rackets amounts to $1,000 per month. Indirect materials cost $3 per racket. A supervisor was hired to oversee production; her monthly salary is $3,500.

Janitorial costs are $1,200 monthly. Advertising costs for the rackets will be $6,000 per month. The factory building depreciation expense is $8,400 per year. Property taxes on the factory building will be $4,320 per year.

Instructions

(a) Prepare an answer sheet with the following column headings.

	Product Costs					
Cost Item	**Direct Materials**	**Direct Labor**	**Manufacturing Overhead**	**Period Costs**	**Prime Costs**	**Conversion Costs**

Assuming that Match manufactures, on average, 2,000 tennis rackets per month, enter each cost item on your answer sheet, placing the dollar amount per month under the appropriate headings. Total the dollar amounts in each of the columns.

(b) Compute the cost to produce one racket.

P20-3B Incomplete manufacturing costs, expenses, and selling data for two different cases are as follows.

Indicate the missing amount of different cost items, and prepare a condensed cost of goods manufactured schedule, an income statement, and a partial balance sheet.
(SO 5, 6, 7)

	Case	
	1	**2**
Direct Materials Used	$ 8,300	$ (g)
Direct Labor	3,000	4,000
Manufacturing Overhead	4,000	5,000
Total Manufacturing Costs	(a)	22,000
Beginning Work in Process Inventory	1,000	(h)
Ending Work in Process Inventory	(b)	2,000
Sales	21,500	(i)
Sales Discounts	1,500	1,200
Cost of Goods Manufactured	12,800	21,000
Beginning Finished Goods Inventory	(c)	4,000
Goods Available for Sale	17,300	(j)
Cost of Goods Sold	(d)	(k)
Ending Finished Goods Inventory	1,200	2,500
Gross Profit	(e)	6,000
Operating Expenses	2,700	(l)
Net Income	(f)	2,800

Instructions

(a) Indicate the missing amount for each letter.

(b) Prepare a condensed cost of goods manufactured schedule for Case 1.

(c) Prepare an income statement and the current assets section of the balance sheet for Case 1. Assume that in Case 1 the other items in the current assets section are as follows: Cash $3,000, Receivables (net) $10,000, Raw Materials $700, and Prepaid Expenses $200.

(b) CGM $12,800
(c) Total current assets $18,600

Prepare a cost of goods manufactured schedule, a partial income statement, and a partial balance sheet.
(SO 5, 6, 7)

P20-4B The following data were taken from the records of Mauro Manufacturing Company for the year ended December 31, 2002.

Raw Materials Inventory 1/1/02	$ 45,000	Factory Insurance	$ 5,400
Raw Materials Inventory 12/31/02	44,200	Factory Machinery Depreciation	7,700
Finished Goods Inventory 1/1/02	85,000	Freight-in on Raw Materials Purchased	3,900
Finished Goods Inventory 12/31/02	77,800	Factory Utilities	15,900
Work in Process Inventory 1/1/02	9,500	Office Utilities Expense	8,600
Work in Process Inventory 12/31/02	8,000	Sales	475,000
Direct Labor	145,100	Sales Discounts	3,500
Indirect Labor	19,100	Plant Manager's Salary	30,000
Accounts Receivable	27,000	Factory Property Taxes	6,100
		Factory Repairs	800
		Raw Materials Purchases	64,600
		Cash	28,000

Totals
(a) $300,900
(b) $163,400
(c) $185,000

Instructions

(a) Prepare a cost of goods manufactured schedule.
(b) Prepare an income statement through gross profit.
(c) Prepare the current assets section of the balance sheet at December 31.

Prepare a cost of goods manufactured schedule and a correct income statement.
(SO 5, 6)

P20-5B Chelsea Company is a manufacturer of toys. Its controller, Ruth Chelsea, resigned in August 2002. An inexperienced assistant accountant has prepared the following income statement for the month of August 2002.

CHELSEA COMPANY
Income Statement
For the Month Ended August 31, 2002

Sales (net)		$670,000
Less: Operating expenses		
Raw materials purchased	$200,000	
Direct labor cost	150,000	
Advertising expense	75,000	
Selling and administrative salaries	70,000	
Rent on factory facilities	60,000	
Depreciation on sales equipment	55,000	
Depreciation on factory equipment	35,000	
Indirect labor cost	20,000	
Factory utilities	10,000	
Factory insurance	5,000	680,000
Net loss		$ (10,000)

Prior to August 2002 the company had been profitable every month. The company's president is concerned about the accuracy of the income statement. As her friend, you have been asked to review the income statement and make necessary corrections. After examining other manufacturing cost data, you have acquired additional information as follows.

1. Inventory balances at the beginning and end of August were:

	August 1	August 31
Raw materials	$19,500	$33,000
Work in process	25,000	21,000
Finished goods	40,000	62,000

2. Only 60% of the utilities expense and 70% of the insurance expense apply to factory operations; the remaining amounts should be charged to selling and administrative activities.

Instructions

(a) CGM $465,000
(b) NI $21,500

(a) Prepare a cost of goods manufactured schedule for August 2002.
(b) Prepare a correct income statement for August 2002.

BROADENING YOUR PERSPECTIVE

GROUP DECISION CASE

BYP20-1 Intermix Manufacturing Company specializes in producing fashion outfits. On July 31, 2002, a tornado touched down at its factory and general office. The inventories in the warehouse and the factory were totally damaged due to heavy rain and moisture. The general office nearby was completely destroyed. Next morning, through a careful search of the disaster site, however, Ed Loder, the company's controller, and Susan Manning, the cost accountant, were able to recover a small part of manufacturing cost data for the current month.

"What a horrible experience," sighed Ed. "And the worst part is that we may not have enough records to use in filing an insurance claim."

"It was terrible," replied Susan. "However, I managed to recover some of the manufacturing cost data that I was working on yesterday afternoon. The data indicate that our direct labor cost in July totaled $250,000 and that we had purchased $345,000 of raw materials. Also, I recall that the raw materials used for July was $350,000. But I'm not sure this information will help. The rest of our records are blown away."

"Well, not exactly," said Ed. "I was working on the year-to-date income statement when the tornado warning was announced. My recollection is that our sales in July were $1,250,000 and our gross profit ratio has been 40% of sales. Also, I can remember that our cost of goods available for sale was $790,000 for July."

"Maybe we can work something out from this information!" exclaimed Susan. "My experience tells me that our manufacturing overhead is usually 60% of direct labor."

"Hey, look what I just found," cried Susan. "It's a copy of this June's balance sheet, and it shows that our inventories as of June 30 are Finished goods $36,000, Work in process $22,000, and Raw materials $19,000."

"Super," yelled Ed. "Let's go work something out."

In order to file an insurance claim Intermix Company must determine the amount of its inventories as of July 31, 2002, the date of the tornado touchdown.

Instructions

With the class divided into groups, determine the amount of cost in the Raw Materials, Work in Process, and Finished Goods inventory accounts as of the date of the tornado touchdown.

MANAGERIAL ANALYSIS

BYP20-2 Tennis, Anyone? is a fairly large manufacturing company located in the southern United States. The company manufactures tennis rackets, tennis balls, tennis clothing, and tennis shoes, all bearing the company's distinctive logo, a large green question mark on a white flocked tennis ball. The company's sales have been increasing over the past 10 years.

The tennis racket division has recently implemented several advanced manufacturing techniques. Robot arms hold the tennis rackets in place while glue dries, and machine vision systems check for defects. The engineering and design team uses computerized drafting and testing of new products. The following managers work in the tennis racket division.

Wayne Gryer, Sales Manager (supervises all sales representatives)
Tommye Stevens, technical specialist (supervises computer programmers)
Martie Lefever, cost accounting manager (supervises cost accountants)
Jack Marler, production supervisor (supervises all manufacturing employees)
Tina Roy, engineer (supervises all new product design teams)

Instructions

(a) What are the primary information needs of each manager?
(b) Which, if any, financial accounting report(s) is each likely to use?
(c) Name one special-purpose management accounting report that could be designed for each manager. Include the name of the report, the information it would contain, and how frequently it should be issued.

REAL-WORLD FOCUS

BYP20-3 **Anchor Glass Container Corporation** the third largest manufacturer of glass containers in the U.S., supplies beverage and food producers and consumer products manufacturers nationwide. Parent company **Consumers Packaging Inc.** (*Toronto Stock Exchange:* CGC) is a leading international designer and manufacturer of glass containers.

The following management discussion appeared in a recent annual report of Anchor Glass.

Anchor Glass Container

ANCHOR GLASS CONTAINER CORPORATION
Management Discussion

Cost of Products Sold Cost of products sold as a percentage of net sales was 89.3% in the current year compared to 87.6% in the prior year. The increase in cost of products sold as a percentage of net sales principally reflected the impact of operational problems during the second quarter of the current year at a major furnace at one of the Company's plants, higher downtime, and costs and expenses associated with an increased number of scheduled capital improvement projects, increases in labor, and certain other manufacturing costs (with no corresponding selling price increases in the current year). Reduced fixed costs from the closing of the Streator, Illinois, plant in June of the current year and productivity and efficiency gains partially offset these cost increases.

Instructions
What factors affect the costs of products sold at Anchor Glass Container Corporation?

EXPLORING THE WEB

www.wiley.com/college/weygandt

BYP20-4 **The Institute of Management Accountants (IMA)** is the largest organization of its kind in the world, dedicated to excellence in the practice of management accounting and financial management.

Address:* www.imanet.org *(or go to www.wiley.com/college/weygandt)

Instructions
At the IMA's home page, locate the answers to the following questions.

(a) How many members does the IMA have, and what are their job titles?
(b) What are some of the benefits of joining the IMA as a student?
(c) Use the chapter locator function to locate the IMA chapter nearest you, and find the name of the chapter president.

COMMUNICATION ACTIVITY

BYP20-5 Refer to Problem 20-5B and add the following requirement.

Prepare a letter to the president of the company, Marie Klinger, describing the changes you made. Explain clearly why net income is different after the changes. Keep the following points in mind as you compose your letter.

1. This is a letter to the president of a company, who is your friend. The style should be generally formal, but you may relax some requirements. For example, you may call the president by her first name.

2. Executives are very busy. Your letter should tell the president your main results first (for example, the amount of net income).
3. You should include brief explanations so that the president can understand the changes you made in the calculations.

ETHICS CASE

BYP20-6 Carlos Morales, controller for Tredway Industries, was reviewing production cost reports for the year. One amount in these reports continued to bother him—advertising. During the year, the company had instituted an expensive advertising campaign to sell some of its slower-moving products. It was still too early to tell whether the advertising campaign was successful.

There had been much internal debate as how to report advertising costs. The vice president of finance argued that advertising costs should be reported as a cost of production, just like direct materials and direct labor. He therefore recommended that this cost be identified as manufacturing overhead and reported as part of inventory costs until sold. Others disagreed. Morales believed that this cost should be reported as an expense of the current period, based on the conservatism principle. Others argued that it should be reported as Prepaid Advertising and reported as a current asset.

The president finally had to decide the issue. He argued that these costs should be reported as inventory. His arguments were practical ones. He noted that the company was experiencing financial difficulty and expensing this amount in the current period might jeopardize a planned bond offering. Also, by reporting the advertising costs as inventory rather than as prepaid advertising, less attention would be directed to it by the financial community.

Instructions

(a) Who are the stakeholders in this situation?
(b) What are the ethical issues involved in this situation?
(c) What would you do if you were Carlos Morales?

Answers to Self-Study Questions

1. b **2.** d **3.** b **4.** b **5.** c **6.** d **7.** a **8.** c **9.** a **10.** d

Remember to go back to the Navigator box on the chapter-opening page and check off your completed work.

JOB ORDER COST ACCOUNTING

21

THE NAVIGATOR ✓

- Understand *Concepts for Review* ❑
- Read *Feature Story* ❑
- Scan *Study Objectives* ❑
- Read *Preview* ❑
- Read text and answer *Before You Go On* *p.* 866 ❑ *p.* 876 ❑ *p.* 881 ❑
- Work *Demonstration Problem* ❑
- Review *Summary of Study Objectives* ❑
- Answer *Self-Study Questions* ❑
- Complete *Assignments* ❑

CONCEPTS FOR REVIEW

Before studying this chapter, you should know or, if necessary, review:

a. How a perpetual inventory system works. (Ch. 5, pp. 187–196)

b. The three classifications of manufacturing costs. (Ch. 20, pp. 831–832)

c. The difference between product and period costs. (Ch. 20, p. 833)

d. The form and content of a cost of goods manufactured schedule. (Ch. 20, pp. 835–836)

✓ THE NAVIGATOR

FEATURE STORY

"... And We'd Like It in Red"

Western States Fire Apparatus, Inc., of Cornelius, Oregon, is one of the few U.S. companies that makes fire trucks. The company builds about 25 trucks per year. Founded in 1941, the company is run by the children and grandchildren of the original founder.

"We buy the chassis, which is the cab and the frame," says Susan Scott, the company's bookkeeper. "In our computer, we set up an account into which all of the direct material that is purchased for that particular job is charged." Other direct materials include the water pump—which can cost $10,000—the lights, the siren, ladders, and hoses.

As for direct labor, the production workers fill out job sheets that tell what jobs they worked on. Usually, the company is building four trucks at any one time. On payday, the controller allocates the payroll to the appropriate job record.

Indirect materials, such as nuts and bolts, wiring, lubricants, and abrasives, are allocated to each job in proportion to direct material dollars. Other costs, such as insurance and supervisors' salaries, are allocated based on direct labor hours. "We need to allocate overhead in order to know what kind of price we have to charge when we submit our bids," she says.

Western gets orders through a "blind-bidding" process. That is, Western submits its bid without knowing the bid prices made by its competitors. "If we bid too low, we won't make a profit. If we bid too high, we don't get the job."

Regardless of the final price for the truck, the quality had better be first-rate. "The fire departments let you know if they don't like what you did, and you usually end up fixing it."

THE NAVIGATOR

STUDY OBJECTIVES

After studying this chapter, you should be able to:

1. Explain the characteristics and purposes of cost accounting.
2. Describe the flow of costs in a job order cost accounting system.
3. Explain the nature and importance of a job cost sheet.
4. Indicate how the predetermined overhead rate is determined and used.
5. Prepare entries for jobs completed and sold.
6. Distinguish between under- and overapplied manufacturing overhead.

THE NAVIGATOR

PREVIEW OF CHAPTER 21

The Feature Story about **Western States Fire Apparatus** described the manufacturing costs used in making a fire truck. This chapter illustrates how these manufacturing costs would be assigned to specific jobs, such as the manufacture of individual fire trucks. We begin the discussion in this chapter with an overview of the flow of costs in a job order cost accounting system. We then use a case study to explain and illustrate the documents, entries, and accounts in this type of cost accounting system.

The content and organization of Chapter 21 are as follows.

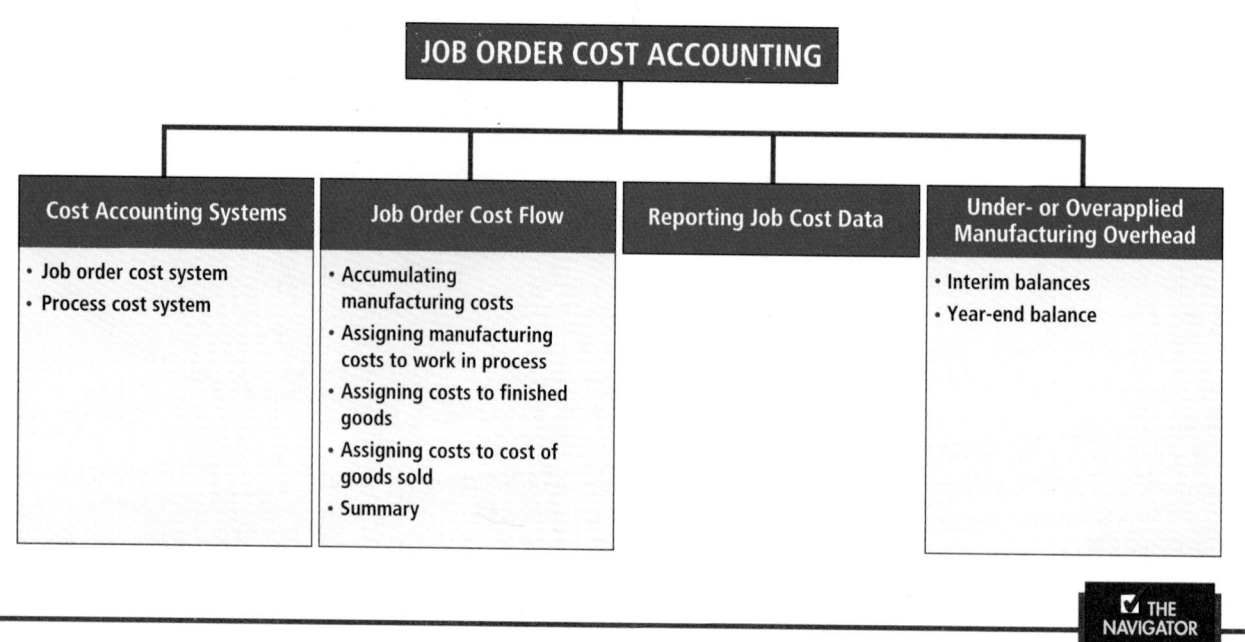

JOB ORDER COST ACCOUNTING

- **Cost Accounting Systems**
  - Job order cost system
  - Process cost system
- **Job Order Cost Flow**
  - Accumulating manufacturing costs
  - Assigning manufacturing costs to work in process
  - Assigning costs to finished goods
  - Assigning costs to cost of goods sold
  - Summary
- **Reporting Job Cost Data**
- **Under- or Overapplied Manufacturing Overhead**
  - Interim balances
  - Year-end balance

THE NAVIGATOR

COST ACCOUNTING SYSTEMS

STUDY OBJECTIVE 1

Explain the characteristics and purposes of cost accounting.

Cost accounting involves the measuring, recording, and reporting of product costs. From the data accumulated, both the total cost and the unit cost of each product is determined.

A **cost accounting system** consists of accounts for the various manufacturing costs. These accounts are fully integrated into the general ledger of a company. **An important feature of a cost accounting system is the use of a perpetual inventory system.** Such a system **provides immediate, up-to-date information on the cost of a product**. There are two basic types of cost accounting systems: (1) a job order cost system and (2) a process cost system. Although cost accounting systems differ widely from company to company, most are based on one of these two traditional product costing systems.

JOB ORDER COST SYSTEM

Under a **job order cost system**, costs are assigned to each **job** or to each **batch** of goods. An example of a job would be the manufacture of a high-speed drilling machine. An example of a batch would be the printing of 225 wedding invitations. Jobs or batches may be completed to fill a specific customer order or to replenish inventory.

An important feature of job order costing is that each job (or batch) has its own distinguishing characteristics. For example, each house is custom built, each motion picture is unique, and each printing job is different. **The objective is to compute the cost per job.** At each point in the manufacturing process, the job and its associated costs can be identified. A job order cost system measures costs for each completed job, rather than for set time periods. The recording of costs in a job order cost system is shown in Illustration 21-1.

Illustration 21-1

Job order cost system

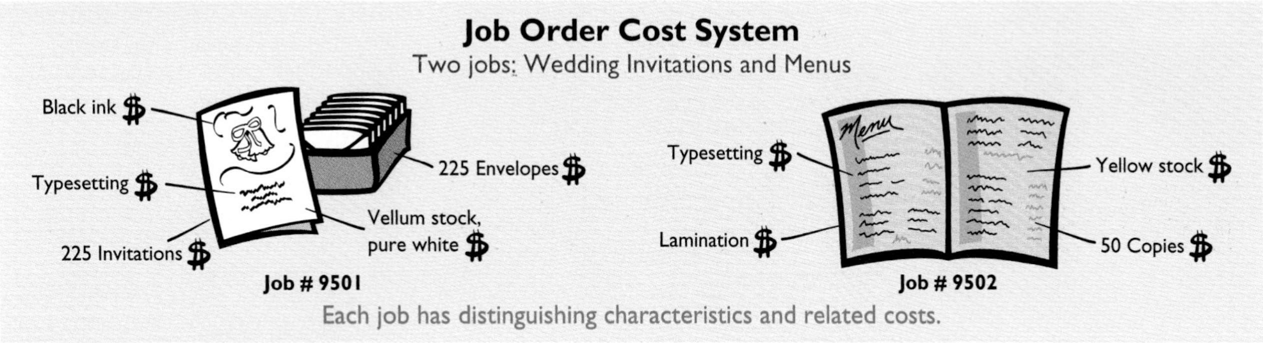
Job Order Cost System
Two jobs: Wedding Invitations and Menus
Black ink $
Typesetting $
225 Invitations $
225 Envelopes $
Vellum stock, pure white $
Job # 9501
Typesetting $
Lamination $
Menu
Yellow stock $
50 Copies $
Job # 9502
Each job has distinguishing characteristics and related costs.

PROCESS COST SYSTEM

A **process cost system** is used when a series of connected manufacturing processes or departments produce a large volume of similar products. Production is continuous to ensure that adequate inventories of the finished product(s) are on hand. A process cost system is used in the manufacture of cereal, the refining of petroleum, and the production of automobiles. Process costing accumulates product-related costs **for a period of time** (such as a week or a month) instead of assigning costs to specific products or job orders. In process costing, the costs are assigned to departments or processes for a set period of time. The recording of costs in a process cost system is shown in Illustration 21-2. The process cost system will be discussed further in Chapter 22.

Illustration 21-2

Process cost system

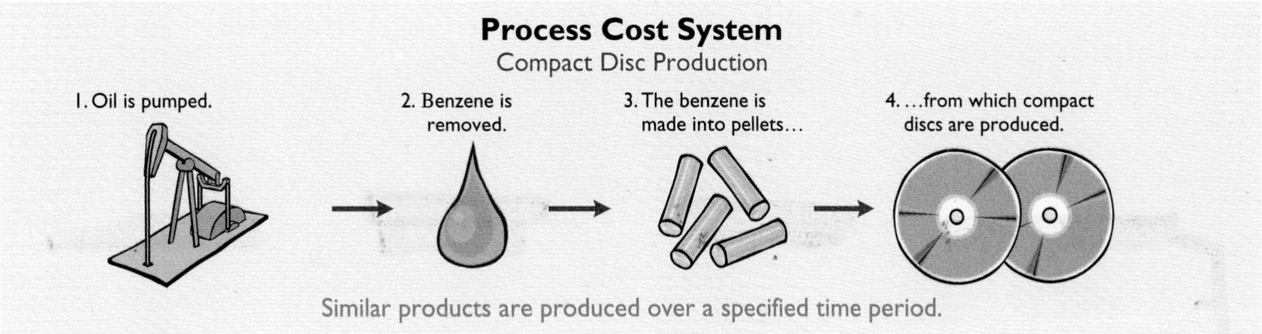
Process Cost System
Compact Disc Production
1. Oil is pumped.
2. Benzene is removed.
3. The benzene is made into pellets...
4. ...from which compact discs are produced.
Similar products are produced over a specified time period.

A company may use both types of cost systems. For example, **General Motors** uses process cost accounting for its standard model cars, such as Saturns and Corvettes, and job order cost accounting for a custom-made limousine for the President of the United States. The objective of both systems is to provide unit cost information for product pricing, cost control, inventory valuation, and financial statement presentation. End-of-period inventory values are computed by using unit cost data.

ACCOUNTING IN ACTION *Business Insight*

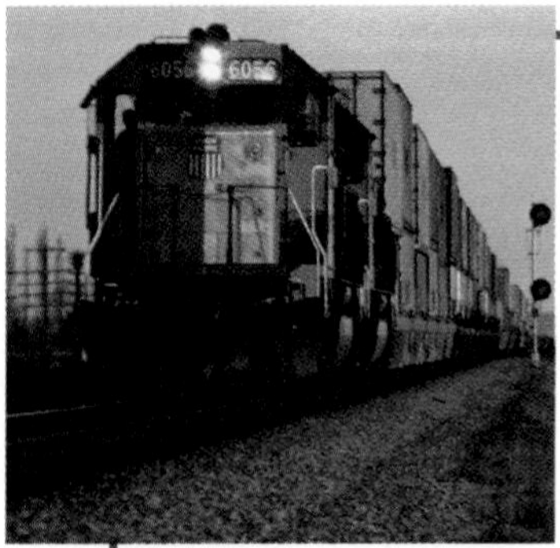

Many companies suffer from poor cost accounting. As a result, they sometimes make products they ought not to be selling at all and buy others that they could more profitably make themselves. Also, inaccurate cost data lead companies to misallocate capital and frustrate efforts by plant managers to improve efficiency.

For example, consider a diversified company in the business of rebuilding diesel locomotives. The managers thought they were making money, but a consulting firm found that costs had been seriously underestimated. The company bailed out of the business, and not a moment too soon. Says the consultant who advised the company: "The more contracts it won, the more money it lost."

BEFORE YOU GO ON...

REVIEW IT

1. What is cost accounting?
2. What is a cost accounting system?
3. How does a job order cost system differ from a process cost system?

THE NAVIGATOR

JOB ORDER COST FLOW

STUDY OBJECTIVE 2

Describe the flow of costs in a job order cost accounting system.

The flow of costs (direct materials, direct labor, and manufacturing overhead) in job order cost accounting parallels the physical flow of the materials as they are converted into finished goods. As shown in Illustration 21-3, manufacturing costs are assigned to the Work in Process Inventory account. When a job is completed, the cost of the job is transferred to Finished Goods Inventory. Later when the goods are sold, their cost is transferred to Cost of Goods Sold.

Illustration 21-3

Flow of costs in job order cost accounting

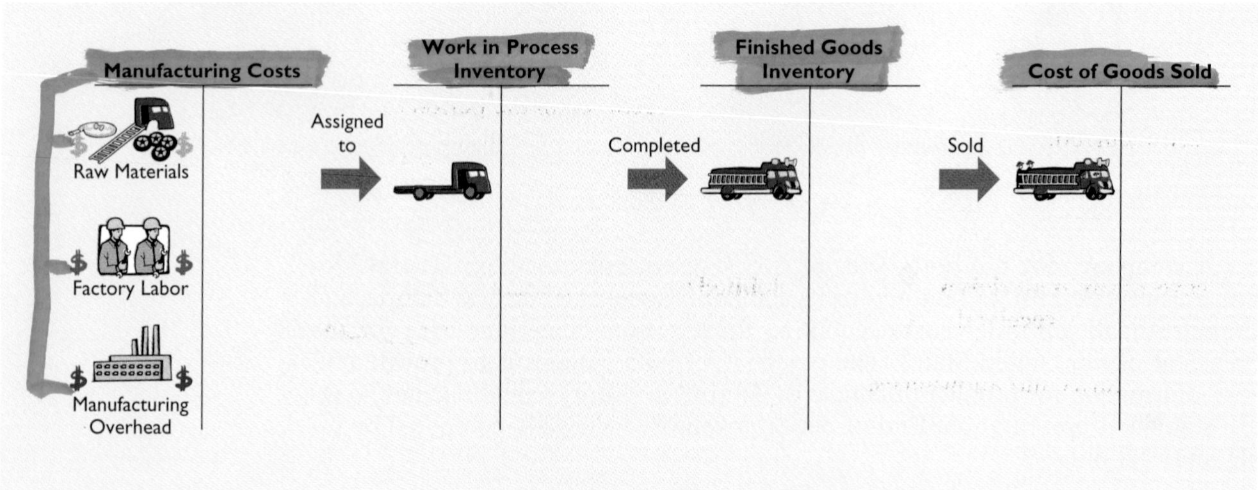

Illustration 21-3 provided a basic overview of the flow of costs in a manufacturing setting. A more detailed presentation of the flow of costs is shown in Illustration 21-4. It indicates that there are two major steps in the flow of costs: (1) *accumulating* the manufacturing costs incurred and (2) *assigning* the accumulated costs to the work done. As shown, manufacturing costs incurred are accumulated in entries 1–3 by debits to Raw Materials Inventory, Factory Labor, and Manufacturing Overhead. When these costs are incurred no attempt is made to associate the costs with specific jobs. The remaining entries (entries 4–8) assign manufacturing costs incurred. On the following pages we will use a case study to explain how a job order system operates.

Illustration 21-4

Job order cost accounting system

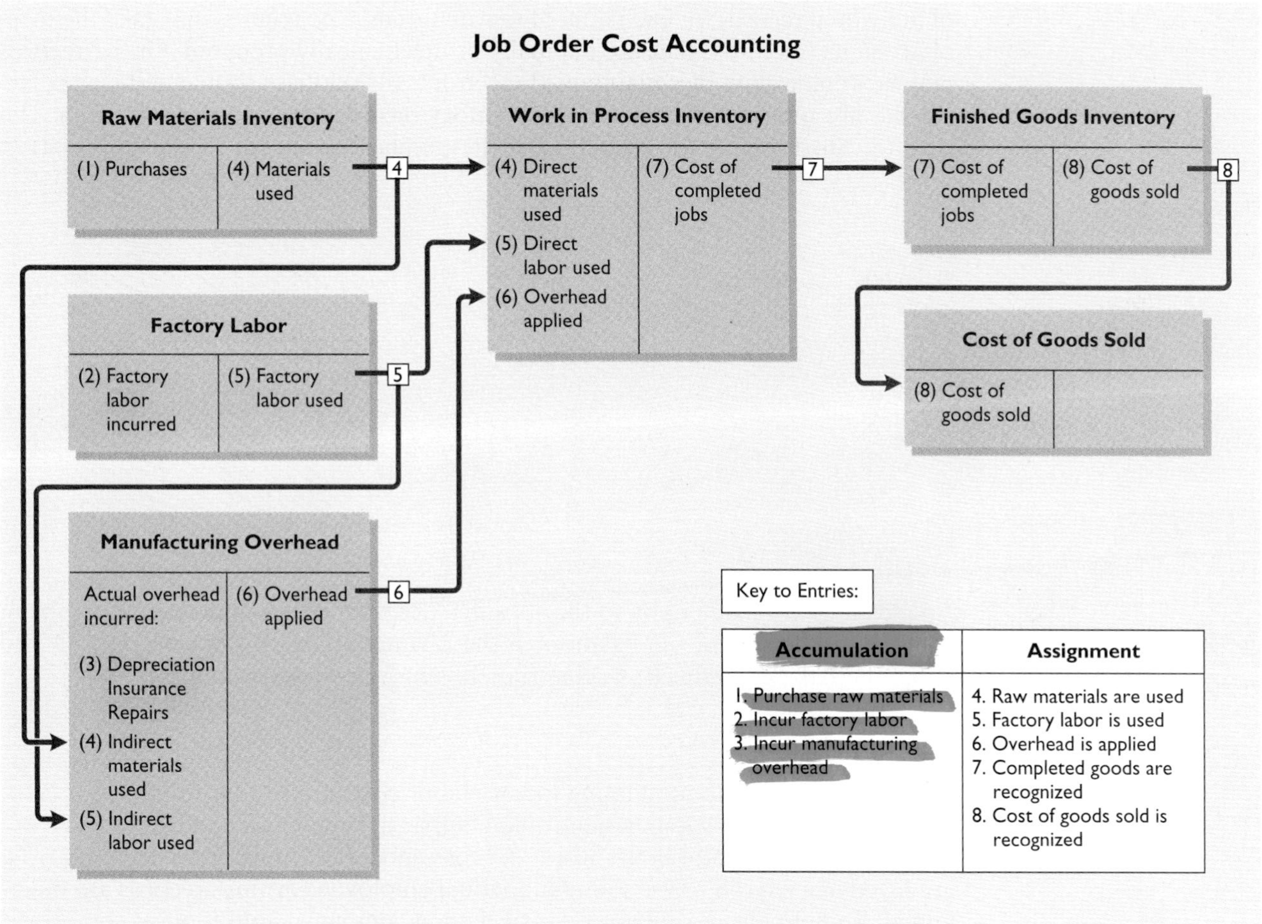

ACCUMULATING MANUFACTURING COSTS

In a job order cost system, manufacturing costs are recorded in the period in which they are incurred. To illustrate, we will use the January transactions of Wallace Manufacturing Company, which makes tools and dies.

Raw Materials Costs

The costs of raw materials purchased are debited to Raw Materials Inventory when the materials are received. This account is debited for the invoice cost and freight costs chargeable to the purchaser. It is credited for purchase discounts taken and purchase returns and allowances. **No effort is made at this point to associate the cost of materials with specific jobs or orders.** The procedures for ordering, receiving, recording, and paying for raw materials are similar to the purchasing procedures of a merchandising company.

To illustrate, assume that Wallace Manufacturing purchases 2,000 handles (Stock No. AA2746) at $5 per unit ($10,000) and 800 modules (Stock No. AA2850) at $40 per unit ($32,000) for a total cost of $42,000 ($10,000 + $32,000). The entry to record this purchase on January 4 is:

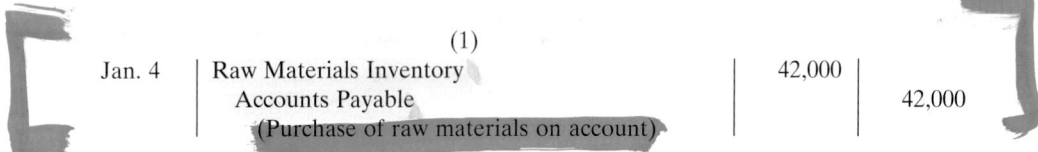

(1)

Jan. 4	Raw Materials Inventory	42,000	
	Accounts Payable		42,000
	(Purchase of raw materials on account)		

Raw Materials Inventory is a control account. The subsidiary ledger consists of individual records for each item of raw materials. The records may take the form of accounts (or cards) that are manually or mechanically prepared. Or the records may be kept as data files maintained electronically on disks or magnetic tape. The records are referred to as **materials inventory records** (or **stores ledger cards**). The card for Stock No. AA2746 following the purchase is shown in Illustration 21-5.

Illustration 21-5

Materials inventory card

Item: Handles — Part No: AA2746

	Receipts			Issues			Balance		
Date	Units	Cost	Total	Units	Cost	Total	Units	Cost	Total
1/4	2,000	$5	$10,000				2,000	$5	$10,000

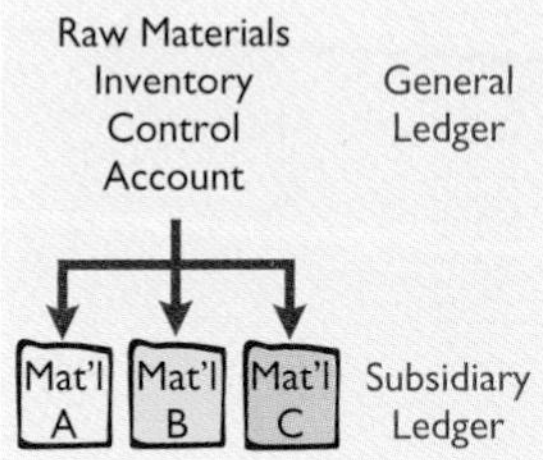

Postings are made daily to the subsidiary ledger. After all postings have been completed, the sum of the balances in the raw materials subsidiary ledger should equal the balance in the Raw Materials Inventory control account.

Factory Labor Costs

The procedures for accumulating factory labor costs are similar to those for computing the payroll for a merchandising company. Time clocks and time cards are used to determine total hours worked; gross and net earnings for each employee are listed in a payroll register; and individual employee earnings records are maintained. To help ensure the accuracy of data, a company should follow the principles of internal control for payrolls described in Chapter 11.

In a manufacturing company, the cost of factory labor consists of (1) gross earnings of factory workers, (2) employer payroll taxes on such earnings, and (3) fringe benefits (such as sick pay, pensions, and vacation pay) incurred by the employer. **Labor costs are debited to Factory Labor when they are incurred.**

To illustrate, assume that Wallace Manufacturing incurs $32,000 of factory labor costs. Of that amount, $27,000 relates to wages payable and $5,000 relates to payroll taxes payable in January. The entry is:

(2)

Jan. 31	Factory Labor	32,000	
	Factory Wages Payable		27,000
	Employer Payroll Taxes Payable		5,000
	(To record factory labor costs)		

Factory labor is subsequently assigned to work in process and manufacturing overhead, as explained later in the chapter.

Manufacturing Overhead Costs

A company may have many types of overhead costs. These costs may be recognized **daily**, as in the case of machinery repairs and the use of indirect materials and indirect labor. Or overhead costs may be recorded **periodically** through adjusting entries. Property taxes, depreciation, and insurance are recorded periodically, for example. Using assumed data, a summary entry for manufacturing overhead in Wallace Manufacturing Company is:

	(3)		
Jan. 31	Manufacturing Overhead	13,800	
	Utilities Payable		4,800
	Prepaid Insurance		2,000
	Accounts Payable (for repairs)		2,600
	Accumulated Depreciation		3,000
	Property Taxes Payable		1,400
	(To record overhead costs)		

Manufacturing Overhead is a control account. The subsidiary ledger consists of individual accounts for each type of cost, such as Factory Utilities, Factory Insurance, and Factory Repairs.

ASSIGNING MANUFACTURING COSTS TO WORK IN PROCESS

STUDY OBJECTIVE 3

Explain the nature and importance of a job cost sheet.

As shown in Illustration 21-4, assigning manufacturing costs to work in process results in the following entries: (1) **Debits** are made to Work in Process Inventory. (2) **Credits** are made to Raw Materials Inventory, Factory Labor, and Manufacturing Overhead. Journal entries to assign costs to work in process are usually made and posted **monthly.**

An essential accounting record in assigning costs to jobs is a **job cost sheet** shown in Illustration 21-6. A job cost sheet is a form used to record the costs chargeable to a specific job and to determine the total and unit costs of the completed job.

Illustration 21-6

Job cost sheet

Job Cost Sheet

Job No. ______________ Quantity ______________

Item ______________ Date Requested ______________

For ______________ Date Completed ______________

Date	Direct Materials	Direct Labor	Manufacturing Overhead

Cost of completed job	
Direct materials	$ ______
Direct labor	______
Manufacturing overhead	______
Total cost	$ ______
Unit cost (total dollars ÷ quantity)	$ ______

ETHICS NOTE

The misallocation of costs in a job order system can be a serious legal and ethical problem. For example, the Department of Defense sued General Dynamics Corporation at one time for over-allocating production costs that were not related to the underlying contract for U.S. Navy nuclear submarines.

Postings to job cost sheets are made daily, directly from supporting documents.

A separate job cost sheet is kept for each job. The job cost sheets constitute the subsidiary ledger for the Work in Process Inventory account. **Each entry to Work in Process Inventory must be accompanied by a corresponding posting to one or more job cost sheets.**

ACCOUNTING IN ACTION — e-Business Insight

General Motors recently launched a new Internet-based ordering system intended to deliver custom vehicles in between 15 to 20 days instead of the 55 to 60 days it previously took. Customers interested in a GM car can search online to see if any dealers have a car with the options they want. If not, the customer uses an online program to configure a car with the desired options and then places the order. While this online approach could potentially provide savings for automakers by reducing inventory costs, some people are skeptical. One auto analyst stated, "I don't think it's going to lead to a massive change in the way vehicles are built and sold in the next 10 years."

SOURCE: Karen Lundegaard, "GM Tests Web-Based Ordering System, Seeking to Slash Custom-Delivery Time," *The Wall Street Journal*, November 17, 2000.

Raw Materials Costs

HELPFUL HINT Approvals are an important part of a materials requisition slip because they help to establish individual accountability over inventory.

Raw materials costs are assigned when the materials are issued by the storeroom. To achieve effective internal control over the issuance of materials, the storekeeper should receive a written authorization before materials are released to production. Such authorization for issuing raw materials is made on a prenumbered **materials requisition slip**. This form is signed by an authorized employee such as a department supervisor. The materials issued may be used directly on a job, or they may be considered indirect materials. As shown in Illustration 21-7, the requisition should indicate the quantity and type of materials withdrawn and the account to be charged. Direct materials will be charged to Work in Process Inventory, and indirect materials to Manufacturing Overhead.

Illustration 21-7

Materials requisition slip

Wallace Manufacturing Company
Materials Requisition Slip

Deliver to: Assembly Department — Req. No. R247
Charge to: Work in Process—Job No. 101 — Date: 1/6/02

Quantity	Description	Stock No.	Cost per Unit	Total
200	Handles	AA2746	$5.00	$1,000

Requested by *Bruce Howart* — Received by *Herb Crowley*
Approved by *Kap Shin* — Costed by *Heather Remmers*

HELPFUL HINT The internal control principle of documentation includes prenumbering to enhance accountability.

The requisition is prepared in duplicate. A copy is retained in the storeroom as evidence of the materials released. The original is sent to accounting, where the cost per unit and total cost of the materials used are determined. Any of the inventory costing methods (FIFO, LIFO, or average cost) may be used in costing the requisitions. After the requisition slips have been costed, they are posted daily to the materials inventory records. Also, **requisitions for direct materials are posted daily to the individual job cost sheets**.

Periodically, the requisitions are sorted, totaled, and journalized. For example, if $24,000 of direct materials and $6,000 of indirect materials are used in Wallace Manufacturing in January, the entry is:

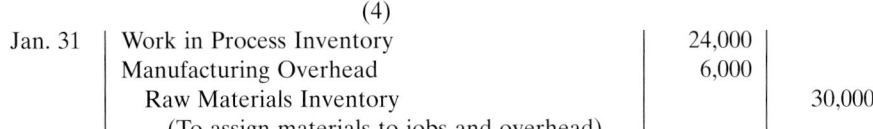

	(4)		
Jan. 31	Work in Process Inventory	24,000	
	Manufacturing Overhead	6,000	
	Raw Materials Inventory		30,000
	(To assign materials to jobs and overhead)		

The requisition slips show total direct materials costs of $12,000 for Job No. 101, $7,000 for Job No. 102, and $5,000 for Job No. 103. The posting of requisition slip R247 and other assumed postings to the job cost sheets for materials are shown in Illustration 21-8. After all postings have been completed, the sum of the direct materials columns of the job cost sheets should equal the direct materials debited to Work in Process Inventory.

Illustration 21-8

Job cost sheets—direct materials

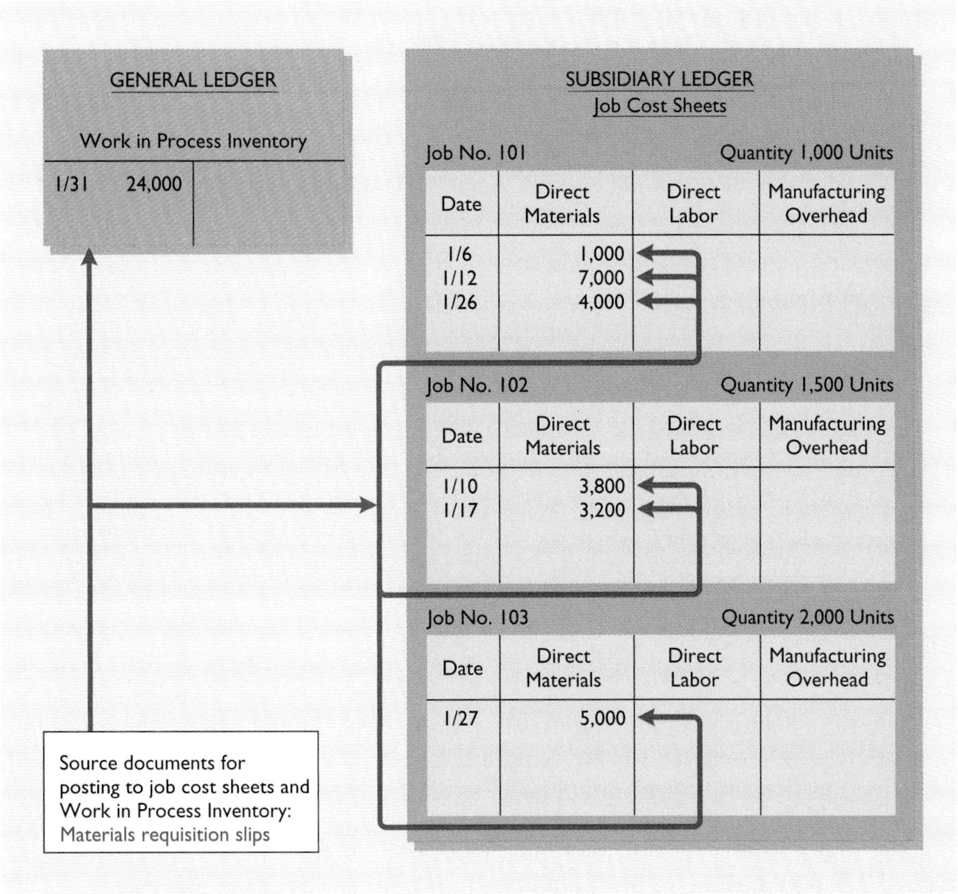

HELPFUL HINT

Postings to control accounts are made monthly, and postings to job cost sheets are made daily.

The materials inventory record for Part No. AA2746 is shown in Illustration 21-9. It shows the posting of requisition slip R247 and an assumed requisition slip for 760 handles costing $3,800 on January 10 for Job 102.

Illustration 21-9

Materials inventory card following issuances

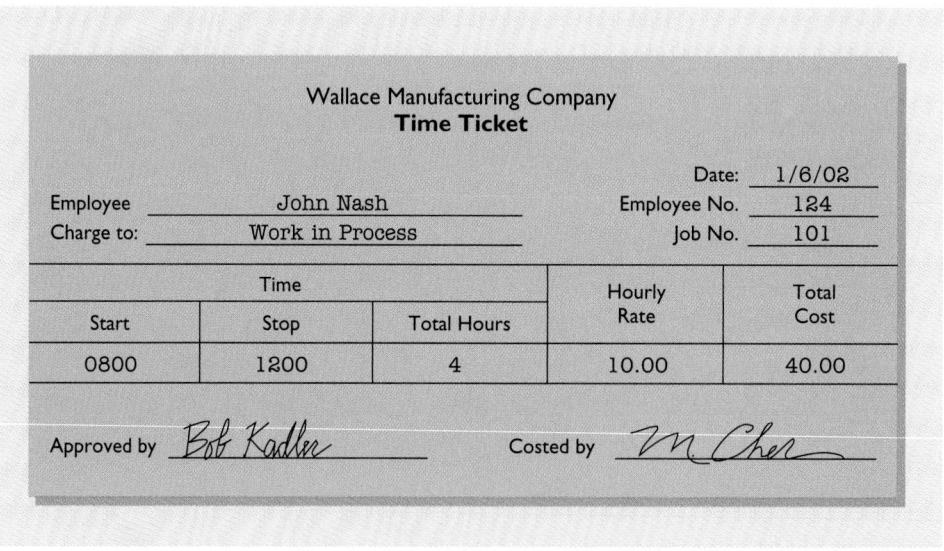

Item: Handles — Part No: AA2746

	Receipts			Issues			Balance		
Date	Units	Cost	Total	Units	Cost	Total	Units	Cost	Total
1/4	2,000	$5	$10,000				2,000	$5	$10,000
1/6				200	$5	$1,000	1,800	$5	9,000
1/10				760	$5	3,800	1,040	$5	5,200

Factory Labor Costs

Factory labor costs are assigned to jobs on the basis of time tickets prepared when the work is performed. The time ticket should indicate the employee, the hours worked, the account and job to be charged, and the total labor cost. The account Work in Process Inventory is debited for direct labor, and Manufacturing Overhead is debited for indirect labor. When direct labor is involved the job number must be indicated, as shown in Illustration 21-10. All time tickets should be approved by the employee's supervisor.

Illustration 21-10

Time ticket

Wallace Manufacturing Company
Time Ticket

Date: 1/6/02
Employee: John Nash — Employee No. 124
Charge to: Work in Process — Job No. 101

Time			Hourly Rate	Total Cost
Start	Stop	Total Hours		
0800	1200	4	10.00	40.00

Approved by Bob Kadler — Costed by M Chen

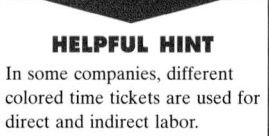

HELPFUL HINT
In some companies, different colored time tickets are used for direct and indirect labor.

The time tickets are later sent to the payroll department. There, the total time reported for an employee for a pay period is reconciled with total hours worked, as shown on the employee's time card. Then the employee's hourly wage rate is applied, and the total labor cost is computed. Finally, the time tickets are sorted, totaled, and journalized. For example, if the $32,000 total factory labor cost consists of $28,000 of direct labor and $4,000 of indirect labor, the entry is:

	(5)		
Jan. 31	Work in Process Inventory	28,000	
	Manufacturing Overhead	4,000	
	Factory Labor		32,000
	(To assign labor to jobs and overhead)		

As a result of this entry, Factory Labor is left with a zero balance, and gross earnings are assigned to the appropriate manufacturing accounts.

Let's assume that the labor costs chargeable to Wallace's three jobs are $15,000, $9,000, and $4,000. The Work in Process Inventory and job cost sheets after posting are shown in Illustration 21-11. As in the case of direct materials, the postings to the direct labor columns of the job cost sheets should equal the posting of direct labor to Work in Process Inventory.

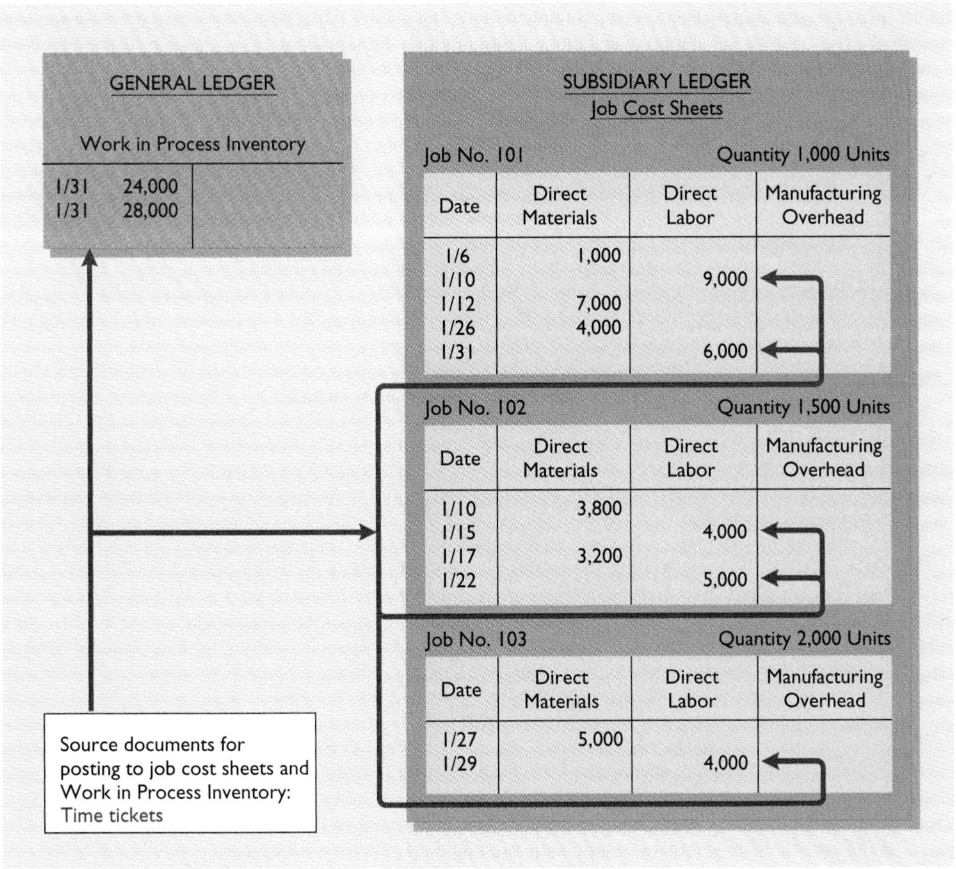

Illustration 21-11

Job cost sheets—direct labor

HELPFUL HINT

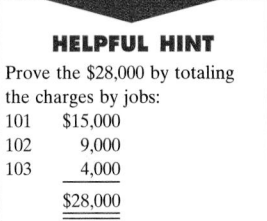

Prove the $28,000 by totaling the charges by jobs:

101	$15,000
102	9,000
103	4,000
	$28,000

Manufacturing Overhead Costs

STUDY OBJECTIVE 4

Indicate how the predetermined overhead rate is determined and used.

We've seen that direct materials and direct labor can be applied to specific jobs. In contrast, manufacturing overhead relates to production operations **as a whole**. As a result, overhead costs cannot be assigned to specific jobs on the basis of actual costs incurred. Instead, manufacturing overhead is assigned to work in process and to specific jobs **on an estimated basis through the use of a predetermined overhead rate**.

TECHNOLOGY IN ACTION

A job cost computer program provides summaries of material and labor costs by job. The program accumulates costs by jobs, provides data to accounts receivable for billings, assigns overhead costs, and provides up-to-date management reports. The reports generated by such systems are basically the same as those shown for Wallace Manufacturing. The major difference between manual and computerized systems is the time involved in converting data into information and in getting feedback (reports) to management.

The **predetermined overhead rate** is based on the relationship between estimated annual overhead costs and expected annual operating activity. This relationship is expressed in terms of a common **activity base**. The activity may be stated in terms of direct labor costs, direct labor hours, machine hours, or any other measure that will provide an equitable basis for applying overhead costs to jobs. The predetermined overhead rate is established at the beginning of the year. The formula for a predetermined overhead rate is:

Illustration 21-12

Formula for predetermined overhead rate

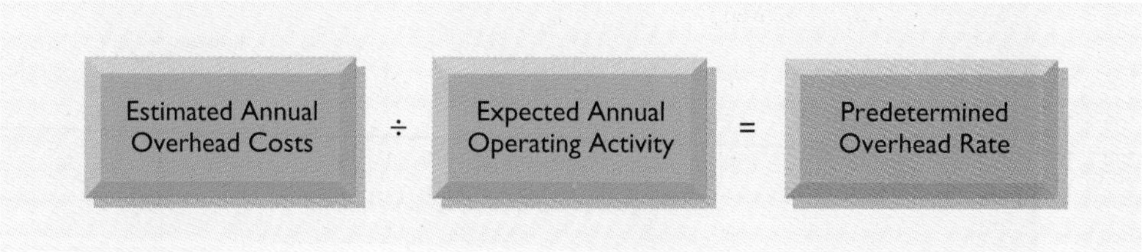

HELPFUL HINT

In contrast to overhead, actual costs for direct materials and direct labor are used to assign costs to Work in Process.

We indicated earlier that overhead relates to production operations as a whole. In order to know what "the whole" is, the logical thing would be to wait until the end of the year's operations, when all costs for the period would be available. But as a practical matter, that wouldn't work: managers could not wait that long before having information about product costs. Instead, using a predetermined overhead rate enables a cost to be determined for the job immediately. Illustration 21-13 indicates how manufacturing overhead is assigned to work in process.

Illustration 21-13

Using predetermined overhead rates

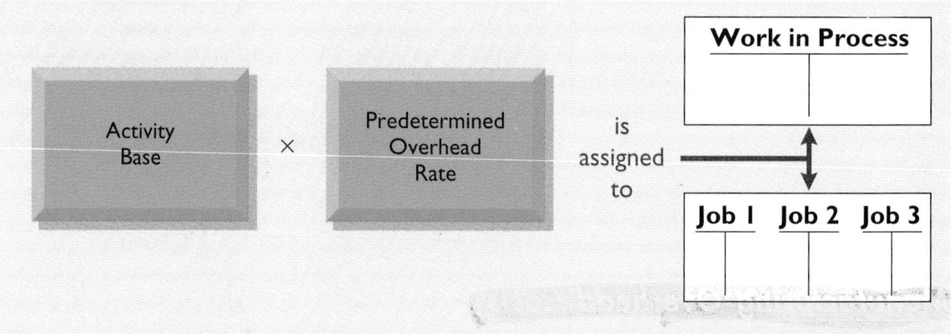

Wallace Manufacturing uses direct labor cost as the activity base. Assuming that annual overhead costs are expected to be \$280,000 and that \$350,000 of direct labor costs are anticipated for the year, the overhead rate is 80%, computed as follows:

$$\$280{,}000 \div \$350{,}000 = 80\%$$

This means that for every dollar of direct labor, 80 cents of manufacturing overhead will be assigned to a job. The use of a predetermined overhead rate enables the company to determine the approximate total cost of each job **when the job is completed**.

Historically, direct labor costs or direct labor hours have often been used as the activity base. The reason was the relatively high correlation between direct labor and manufacturing overhead. In recent years, **there has been a trend toward use of machine hours as the activity base, due to increased reliance on automation in manufacturing operations.**

A company may use more than one activity base. For example, if a job order is manufactured in more than one factory department, each department may have its own overhead rate. In the Feature Story about fire trucks, two bases were used in assigning overhead to jobs: direct materials dollars for indirect materials, and direct labor hours for such costs as insurance and supervisors' salaries.

For Wallace Manufacturing, the total amount of manufacturing overhead is assigned to work in process. It then is **charged to jobs when direct labor costs are assigned**. Overhead applied for January is $22,400 ($28,000 × 80%). This application is recorded through the following entry.

	(6)		
Jan. 31	Work in Process Inventory	22,400	
	Manufacturing Overhead		22,400
	(To assign overhead to jobs)		

The overhead assigned to each job will be 80 percent of the direct labor cost of the job for the month. After posting, the Work in Process Inventory account and the job cost sheets will appear as shown in Illustration 21-14. Note that the debit of $22,400 to Work in Process Inventory equals the sum of the overhead assigned to jobs: Job 101 $12,000 + Job 102 $7,200 + Job 103 $3,200.

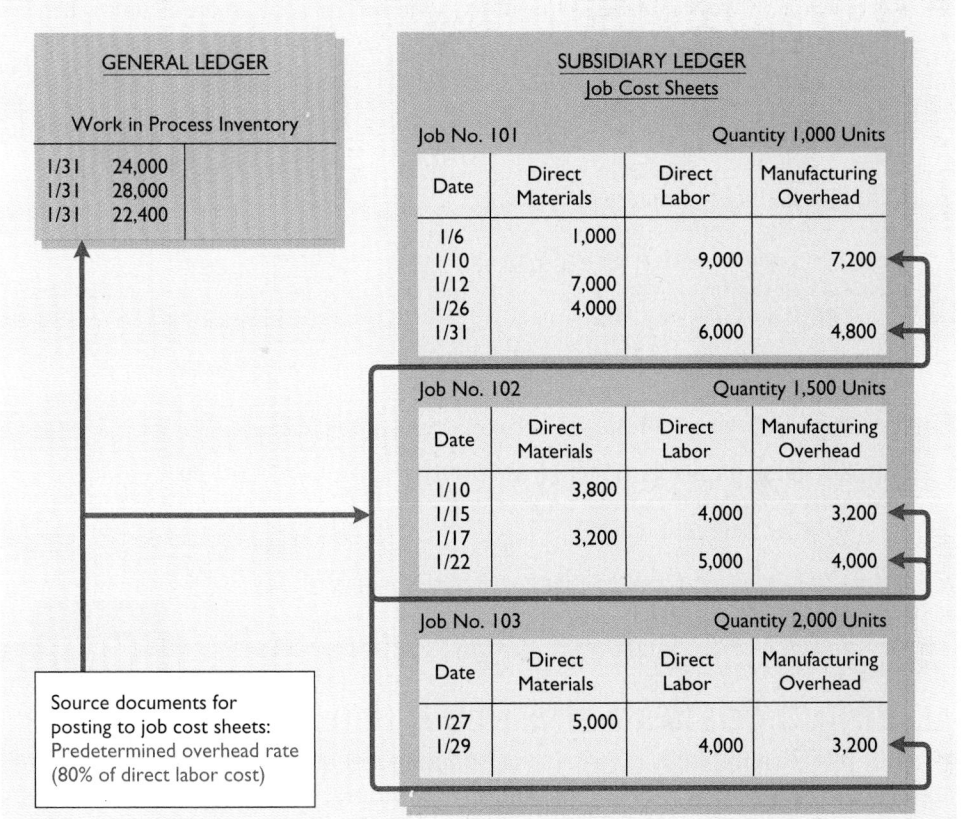

Illustration 21-14

Job cost sheets—manufacturing overhead applied

GENERAL LEDGER

Work in Process Inventory

1/31	24,000	
1/31	28,000	
1/31	22,400	

SUBSIDIARY LEDGER

Job Cost Sheets

Job No. 101 — Quantity 1,000 Units

Date	Direct Materials	Direct Labor	Manufacturing Overhead
1/6	1,000		
1/10		9,000	7,200
1/12	7,000		
1/26	4,000		
1/31		6,000	4,800

Job No. 102 — Quantity 1,500 Units

Date	Direct Materials	Direct Labor	Manufacturing Overhead
1/10	3,800		
1/15		4,000	3,200
1/17	3,200		
1/22		5,000	4,000

Job No. 103 — Quantity 2,000 Units

Date	Direct Materials	Direct Labor	Manufacturing Overhead
1/27	5,000		
1/29		4,000	3,200

Source documents for posting to job cost sheets:
Predetermined overhead rate (80% of direct labor cost)

At the end of each month, **the balance in Work in Process Inventory should equal the sum of the costs shown on the job cost sheets of unfinished jobs**. Assuming that all jobs are unfinished, proof of the agreement of the control and subsidiary accounts in Wallace Manufacturing is shown below.

Illustration 21-15

Proof of job cost sheets to work in process inventory

Work in Process Inventory			Job Cost Sheets	
Jan. 31	24,000		No. 101	$39,000
31	28,000		102	23,200
31	22,400		103	12,200
	74,400	←		**$74,400**

BEFORE YOU GO ON...

▶ *REVIEW IT*

1. What source documents are used in assigning manufacturing costs to Work in Process Inventory?
2. What is a job cost sheet, and what is its primary purpose?
3. What is the formula for computing a predetermined overhead rate?

▶ *DO IT*

Danielle Company is working on two job orders. The job cost sheets show the following:
Direct materials—Job 120 $6,000, Job 121 $3,600
Direct labor—Job 120 $4,000, Job 121 $2,000
Manufacturing overhead—Job 120 $5,000, Job 121 $2,500
Prepare the three summary entries to record the assignment of costs to Work in Process from the data on the job cost sheets.

ACTION PLAN

- Recognize that Work in Process Inventory is the control account for all unfinished job cost sheets.
- Debit Work in Process Inventory for the materials, labor, and overhead charged to the job cost sheets.
- Credit the accounts that were debited when the manufacturing costs were accumulated.

SOLUTION: The three summary entries are:

Work in Process Inventory ($6,000 + $3,600)	9,600	
Raw Materials Inventory		9,600
(To assign materials to jobs)		
Work in Process Inventory ($4,000 + $2,000)	6,000	
Factory Labor		6,000
(To assign labor to jobs)		
Work in Process Inventory ($5,000 + $2,500)	7,500	
Manufacturing Overhead		7,500
(To assign overhead to jobs)		

Related exercise material: BE21-3, BE21-4, BE21-7, E21-2, E21-3 E21-7, and E21-8.

THE NAVIGATOR

STUDY OBJECTIVE 5

Prepare entries for jobs completed and sold.

ASSIGNING COSTS TO FINISHED GOODS

When a job is completed, the costs are summarized and the lower portion of the applicable job cost sheet is completed. For example, if we assume that Job No. 101 is completed on January 31, the job cost sheet will show the following.

Illustration 21-16

Completed job cost sheet

Job Cost Sheet

Job No.	101	Quantity	1,000
Item	Magnetic Sensors	Date Requested	February 5
For	Tanner Company	Date Completed	January 31

Date	Direct Materials	Direct Labor	Manufacturing Overhead
1/6	$ 1,000		
1/10		$ 9,000	$ 7,200
1/12	7,000		
1/26	4,000		
1/31		6,000	4,800
	$12,000	$15,000	$12,000

Cost of completed job	
Direct materials	$ 12,000
Direct labor	15,000
Manufacturing overhead	12,000
Total cost	$ 39,000
Unit cost ($39,000 ÷ 1,000)	$ 39.00

When a job is finished, an entry is made to transfer its total cost to finished goods inventory. The entry for Wallace Manufacturing is:

	(7)		
Jan. 31	Finished Goods Inventory	39,000	
	Work in Process Inventory		39,000
	(To record completion of Job No. 101)		

Finished Goods Inventory is a control account. It controls individual finished goods records in a finished goods subsidiary ledger. Postings to the receipts columns are made directly from completed job cost sheets. The finished goods inventory record for Job No. 101 is shown in Illustration 21-17.

Illustration 21-17

Finished goods record

Item: Magnetic Sensors — Job No: 101

	Receipts			Issues			Balance		
Date	Units	Cost	Total	Units	Cost	Total	Units	Cost	Total
1/31	1,000	$39	$39,000				1,000	$39	$39,000
2/2				1000	$39	$39,000			—0—

ASSIGNING COSTS TO COST OF GOODS SOLD

Cost of goods sold is recognized when each sale occurs. To illustrate the entries when a completed job is sold, assume that on January 31 Wallace Manufacturing sells on account Job 101, costing $39,000, for $50,000.

The entries are:

	(8)		
Jan. 31	Accounts Receivable	50,000	
	Sales		50,000
	(To record sale of Job No. 101)		
31	Cost of Goods Sold	39,000	
	Finished Goods Inventory		39,000
	(To record cost of Job No. 101)		

The units sold, the cost per unit, and the total cost of goods sold for each job sold are recorded in the issues section of the finished goods record, as shown in Illustration 21-17.

SUMMARY OF JOB ORDER COST FLOWS

A completed flow chart for a job order cost accounting system is shown in Illustration 21-18. All postings are keyed to entries 1–8 in Wallace Manufacturing's accounts presented in the cost flow graphic in Illustration 21-4. Illustration 21-19 provides a summary of the flow of documents in a job order cost system.

Illustration 21-18

Flow of costs in a job order cost system

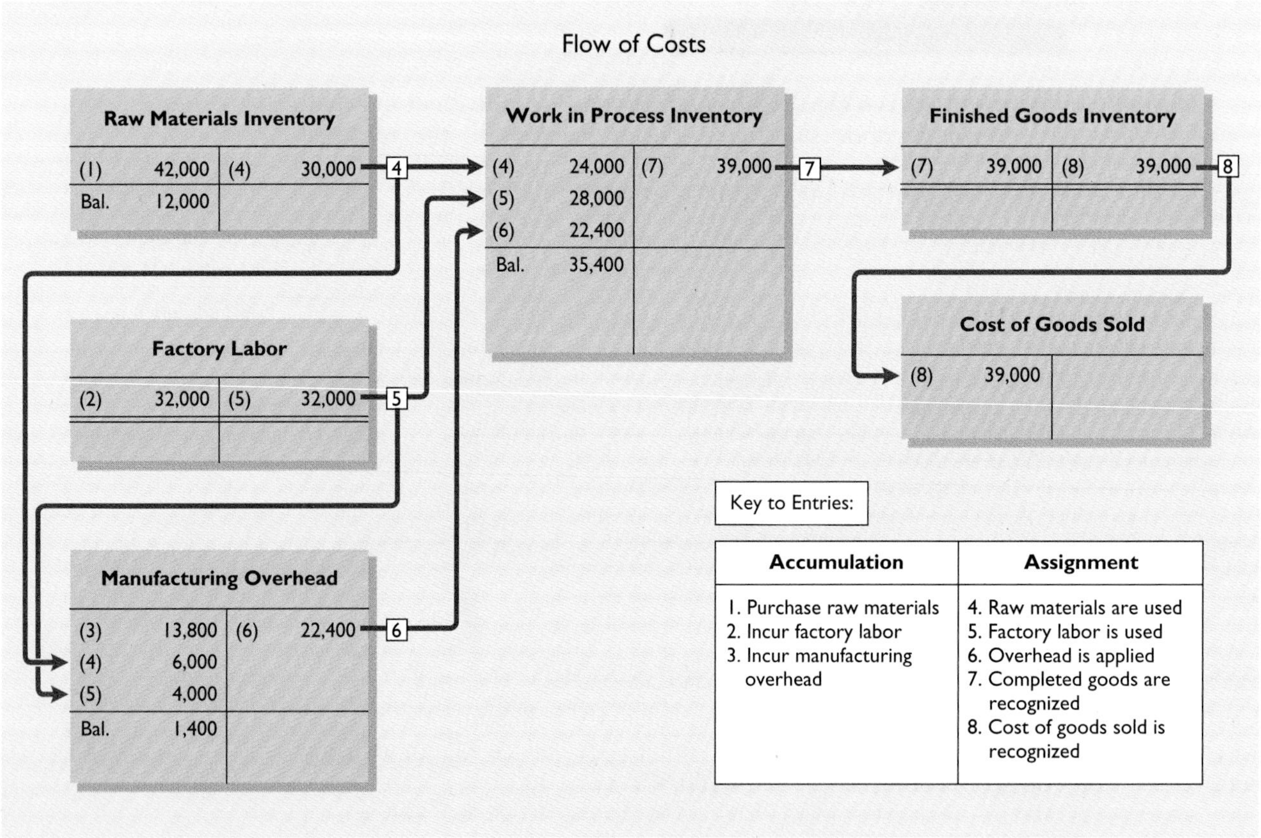

Illustration 21-19

Flow of documents in a job order cost system

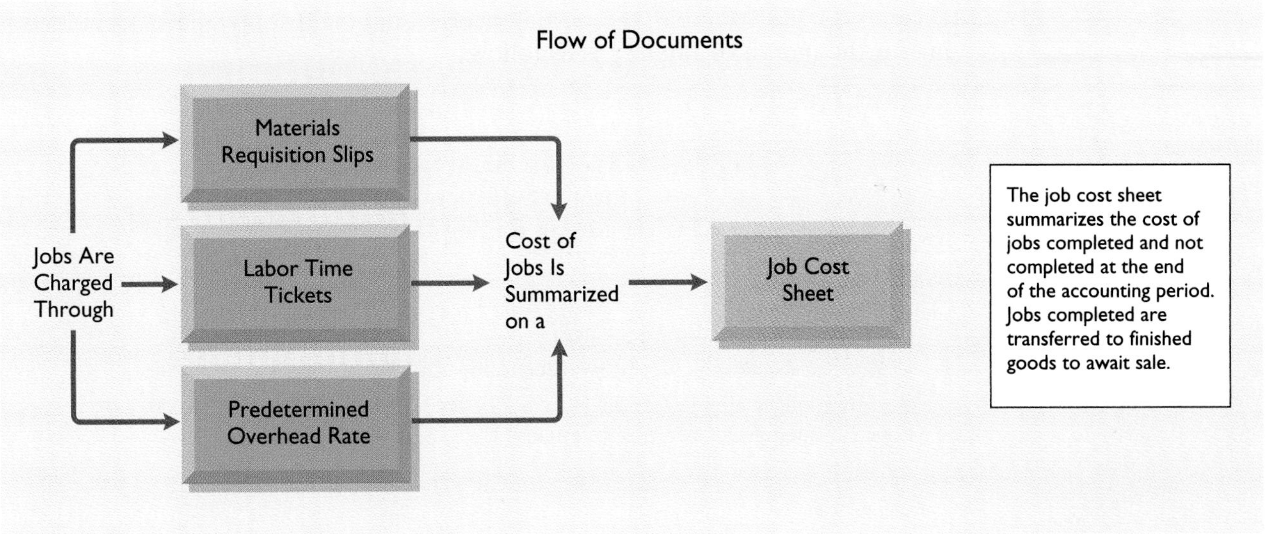

The job cost sheet summarizes the cost of jobs completed and not completed at the end of the accounting period. Jobs completed are transferred to finished goods to await sale.

TECHNOLOGY IN ACTION

With the increased sophistication of microcomputers, small manufacturers can now use micros to perform (1) computer-aided manufacturing (CAM), (2) computer-aided testing (CAT), (3) computer-aided design (CAD), (4) electronic data interchange (EDI), and (5) materials requirement planning (MRP). For a small investment, manufacturers can now use software with capabilities only dreamed about a few years ago.

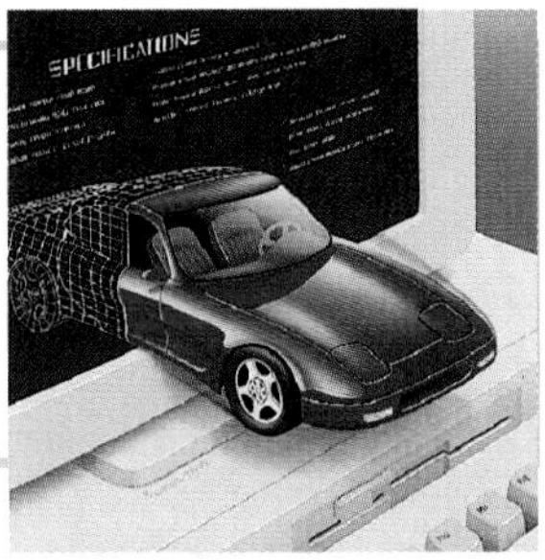

REPORTING JOB COST DATA

At the end of a period, financial statements are prepared that present aggregate data on all jobs manufactured and sold. The cost of goods manufactured schedule in job order costing is the same as in Chapter 20 with one exception: **Manufacturing overhead applied is shown, rather than actual overhead costs. This amount is added to direct materials and direct labor to determine total manufacturing costs.** The schedule is prepared directly from the Work in Process Inventory account. A condensed schedule for Wallace Manufacturing Company for January is as follows.

HELPFUL HINT
Monthly financial statements are usually prepared for management use only.

Illustration 21-20

Cost of goods manufactured schedule

WALLACE MANUFACTURING COMPANY
Cost of Goods Manufactured Schedule
For the Month Ended January 31, 2002

Work in current process, January 1		$ -0-
Direct materials used	$24,000	
Direct labor	28,000	
Manufacturing overhead applied	**22,400**	
Total current manufacturing costs		74,400
Total cost of work in process		74,400
Less: Work in process, January 31		35,400
Cost of goods manufactured		$39,000

Note that the cost of goods manufactured ($39,000) agrees with the amount transferred from Work in Process Inventory to Finished Goods Inventory in journal entry no. 7 in Illustration 21-18.

The income statement and balance sheet are the same as those illustrated in Chapter 20. For example, the partial income statement for Wallace Manufacturing for the month of January is as follows.

Illustration 21-21

Partial income statement

WALLACE MANUFACTURING
Income Statement (partial)
For the Month Ending January 31, 2002

Sales		$50,000
Cost of goods sold		
Finished goods inventory, January 1	$ -0-	
Cost of goods manufactured (See Illustration 21-20)	**39,000**	
Cost of goods available for sale	39,000	
Less: Finished goods inventory, January 31	-0-	
Cost of goods sold		39,000
Gross profit		$11,000

UNDER- OR OVERAPPLIED MANUFACTURING OVERHEAD

STUDY OBJECTIVE 6

Distinguish between under- and overapplied manufacturing overhead.

When Manufacturing Overhead has a **debit balance,** overhead is said to be underapplied. **Underapplied overhead** means that the overhead assigned to work in process is less than the overhead incurred. Conversely, when manufacturing overhead has a **credit balance**, overhead is overapplied. **Overapplied overhead** means that the overhead assigned to work in process is greater than the overhead incurred. These concepts are shown in Illustration 21-22.

Manufacturing Overhead	
Actual (Costs incurred)	Applied (Costs assigned)

If actual is *greater* than applied, manufacturing overhead is underapplied.

If actual is *less* than applied, manufacturing overhead is overapplied.

Illustration 21-22

Under- and overapplied overhead

INTERIM BALANCES

The existence of under- or overapplied overhead at the end of a month is expected. It usually does not require corrective action by management. Monthly differences between actual and applied overhead will usually be offsetting over the course of the year.

When monthly financial statements are prepared, under- or overapplied overhead is reported on the balance sheet. **Underapplied overhead is shown as a prepaid expense in the current assets section. Overapplied overhead is reported as unearned revenue in the current liabilities section.**

YEAR-END BALANCE

At the end of the year, all manufacturing overhead transactions are complete. There is no further opportunity for offsetting events to occur. Accordingly, any balance in Manufacturing Overhead is eliminated by an adjusting entry. Usually, under- or overapplied overhead is considered to be an **adjustment to cost of goods sold**. Thus, **underapplied overhead is debited to Cost of Goods Sold. Overapplied overhead is credited to Cost of Goods Sold**. To illustrate, assume that Wallace Manufacturing has a $2,500 credit balance in Manufacturing Overhead at December 31. The adjusting entry for the overapplied overhead is:

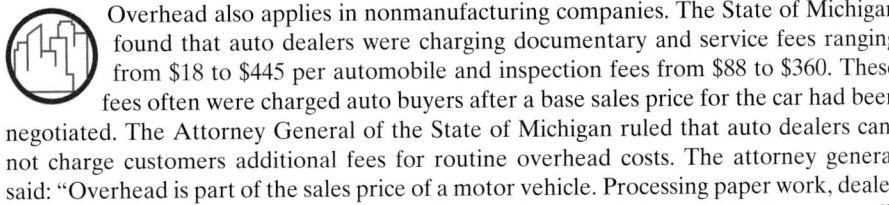

Dec. 31	Manufacturing Overhead	2,500	
	Cost of Goods Sold		2,500
	(To transfer overapplied overhead to cost of goods sold)		

After this entry is posted, Manufacturing Overhead will have a zero balance. In preparing an income statement for the year, the amount reported for cost of goods sold will be the account balance **after the adjustment** for either under- or overapplied overhead.

ACCOUNTING IN ACTION *Business Insight*

Overhead also applies in nonmanufacturing companies. The State of Michigan found that auto dealers were charging documentary and service fees ranging from $18 to $445 per automobile and inspection fees from $88 to $360. These fees often were charged auto buyers after a base sales price for the car had been negotiated. The Attorney General of the State of Michigan ruled that auto dealers cannot charge customers additional fees for routine overhead costs. The attorney general said: "Overhead is part of the sales price of a motor vehicle. Processing paper work, dealer incurred costs, and inspection fees to qualify cars for extended warranty plans are ordinary overhead expenses."

Conceptually, it can be argued that under- or overapplied overhead at the end of the year should be allocated among ending work in process, finished goods, and cost of goods sold. However, most management accountants do not believe allocation is worth the cost and effort. The bulk of the under- or overapplied amount will be allocated to cost of goods sold anyway, because most of the jobs will be sold during the year.

BEFORE YOU GO ON...

REVIEW IT

1. When are entries made to record the completion and sale of a job?
2. What costs are included in total manufacturing costs in the cost of goods manufactured schedule?
3. How is under- or overapplied manufacturing overhead reported in monthly financial statements?

A LOOK BACK AT OUR FEATURE STORY

Refer back to the Feature Story about **Western States Fire Apparatus, Inc.** at the beginning of the chapter, and answer the following questions.

1. Would you expect Western States to use a job order or a process cost system? Why?
2. Is the flow of costs consistent with the cost flow used in the text? Explain.
3. On what basis does Western States allocate its overhead?
4. Why is the allocation of costs important to Western States Fire Apparatus?

SOLUTION

1. Western States uses job cost sheets. Thus, we know that the company uses a job order cost system. The use of a job order system makes sense because each job is custom built to fill a specific customer order, and each has its own distinguishing characteristics.
2. Western States follows the approach used in the text: it accumulates material, labor, and overhead costs and then assigns these costs to specific jobs and work in process.
3. Western States' overhead includes indirect materials (such as nuts and bolts, wiring, lubricants, and abrasives), which are allocated to each job in proportion to direct material costs. Its overhead also includes other costs such as insurance and supervisors' salaries, which are assigned based on direct labor hours.
4. Western States engages in blind-bidding to win contracts. In order to avoid over- or underbidding, the firm must have precise knowledge about costs.

THE NAVIGATOR

DEMONSTRATION PROBLEM

Additional Demonstration Problem

During February, Cardella Manufacturing works on two jobs: A16 and B17. Summary data concerning these jobs are as follows.

Manufacturing Costs Incurred:

Purchased $54,000 of raw materials on account.
Factory labor $76,000, plus $4,000 employer payroll taxes.
Manufacturing overhead exclusive of indirect materials and indirect labor $59,800.

Assignment of Costs:

Direct materials:	Job A16 $27,000, Job B17 $21,000
Indirect materials:	$3,000
Direct labor:	Job A16 $52,000, Job B17 $26,000
Indirect labor:	$2,000

Manufacturing overhead rate: 80% of direct labor costs.

Job A16 was completed and sold on account for $150,000. Job B17 was only partially completed.

Instructions

(a) Journalize the February transactions in the sequence followed in the chapter.
(b) What was the amount of under- or overapplied manufacturing overhead?

ACTION PLAN

- In accumulating costs, debit three accounts: Raw Materials Inventory, Factory Labor, and Manufacturing Overhead.
- When Work in Process Inventory is debited, credit one of the three accounts in strategy (1), above.
- Debit Finished Goods Inventory for the cost of completed jobs. Debit Cost of Goods Sold for the cost of jobs sold.
- Overhead is underapplied when Manufacturing Overhead has a debit balance.

SOLUTION TO DEMONSTRATION PROBLEM

(a) **1.**

Feb. 28	Raw Materials Inventory	54,000	
	Accounts Payable		54,000
	(Purchase of raw materials on account)		

Date	Account Titles and Explanation	Debit	Credit
	2.		
Feb. 28	Factory Labor	80,000	
	Factory Wages Payable		76,000
	Employer Payroll Taxes Payable		4,000
	(To record factory labor costs)		
	3.		
28	Manufacturing Overhead	59,800	
	Accounts Payable, Accumulated Depreciation, and Prepaid Insurance		59,800
	(To record overhead costs)		
	4.		
28	Work in Process Inventory	48,000	
	Manufacturing Overhead	3,000	
	Raw Materials Inventory		51,000
	(To assign raw materials to production)		
	5.		
28	Work in Process Inventory	78,000	
	Manufacturing Overhead	2,000	
	Factory Labor		80,000
	(To assign factory labor to production)		
	6.		
28	Work in Process Inventory	62,400	
	Manufacturing Overhead		62,400
	(To assign overhead to jobs—80% × $78,000)		
	7.		
28	Finished Goods Inventory	120,600	
	Work in Process Inventory		120,600
	(To record completion of Job A16: direct materials $27,000, direct labor $52,000, and manufacturing overhead $41,600)		
	8.		
28	Accounts Receivable	150,000	
	Cost of Goods Sold	120,600	
	Sales		150,000
	Finished Goods Inventory		120,600
	(To record sale of Job A16)		

(b) Manufacturing Overhead has a debit balance of $2,400 as shown below.

Manufacturing Overhead

(3)	59,800	(6)	62,400
(4)	3,000		
(5)	2,000		
Bal.	2,400		

Thus, manufacturing overhead is underapplied for the month.

THE NAVIGATOR

SUMMARY OF STUDY OBJECTIVES

1. ***Explain the characteristics and purposes of cost accounting.*** Cost accounting involves the procedures for measuring, recording, and reporting product costs. From the data accumulated, the total cost and the unit cost of each product is determined. The two basic types of cost accounting systems are job order cost and process cost.

2. ***Describe the flow of costs in a job order cost accounting system.*** In job order cost accounting, manufacturing costs are first accumulated in three accounts: Raw Materials Inventory, Factory Labor, and Manufacturing Overhead. The accumulated costs are then assigned to Work in Process Inventory and eventually to Finished Goods Inventory and Cost of Goods Sold.

3. ***Explain the nature and importance of a job cost sheet.*** A job cost sheet is a form used to record the costs chargeable to a specific job and to determine the total and unit cost of the completed job. Job cost sheets constitute the subsidiary ledger for the Work in Process Inventory control account.

4. ***Indicate how the predetermined overhead rate is determined and used.*** The predetermined overhead rate is based on the relationship between estimated annual overhead costs and expected annual operating activity. This is expressed in terms of a common activity base, such as direct labor cost. The rate is used in assigning overhead costs to work in process and to specific jobs.

5. ***Prepare entries for jobs completed and sold.*** When jobs are completed, the cost is debited to Finished Goods Inventory and credited to Work in Process Inventory. When a job is sold the entries are: (a) Debit Cash or Accounts Receivable and credit Sales for the selling price, and (b) debit Cost of Goods Sold and credit Finished Goods Inventory for the cost of the goods.

6. ***Distinguish between under- and overapplied manufacturing overhead.*** Underapplied manufacturing overhead means that the overhead assigned to work in process is less than the overhead incurred. Overapplied overhead means that the overhead assigned to work in process is greater than the overhead incurred.

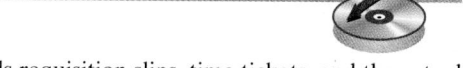

THE NAVIGATOR

Key Term Matching Activity

GLOSSARY

Cost accounting An area of accounting that involves the measuring, recording, and reporting of product costs. (p. 864).

Cost accounting system Manufacturing cost accounts that are fully integrated into the general ledger of a company. (p. 864).

Job cost sheet A form used to record the costs chargeable to a job and to determine the total and unit costs of the completed job. (p. 869)

Job order cost system A cost accounting system in which costs are assigned to each job or batch. (p. 864).

Materials requisition slip A document authorizing the issuance of raw materials from the storeroom to production. (p. 870).

Overapplied overhead A situation in which overhead assigned to work in process is greater than the overhead incurred. (p. 880).

Predetermined overhead rate A rate based on the relationship between estimated annual overhead costs and expected annual operating activity, expressed in terms of a common activity base. (p. 874).

Process cost system A system of accounting used by companies that manufacture relatively homogeneous products through a series of continuous processes or operations. (p. 865).

Time ticket A document that indicates the employee, the hours worked, the account and job to be charged, and the total labor cost. (p. 872).

Underapplied overhead A situation in which overhead assigned to work in process is less than the overhead incurred. (p. 880).

Chapter 21 Self-Test

SELF-STUDY QUESTIONS

Answers are at the end of the chapter.

(SO 1) **1.** Cost accounting involves the measuring, recording, and reporting of:
a. product costs.
b. future costs.
c. manufacturing processes.
d. managerial accounting decisions.

(SO 2) **2.** In accumulating raw materials costs, the cost of raw materials purchased in a perpetual system is debited to:
a. Raw Materials Purchases.
b. Raw Materials Inventory.
c. Purchases.
d. Work in Process.

(SO 2) **3.** When incurred, factory labor costs are debited to:
a. Work in Process.
b. Factory Wages Expense.
c. Factory Labor.
d. Factory Wages Payable.

(SO 3) **4.** The source documents for assigning costs to job cost sheets are:
a. invoices, time tickets, and the predetermined overhead rate.
b. materials requisition slips, time tickets, and the actual overhead costs.
c. materials requisition slips, payroll register, and the predetermined overhead rate.
d. materials requisition slips, time tickets, and the predetermined overhead rate.

5. In recording the issuance of raw materials in a job order cost system, it would be *incorrect* to: (SO 3)
a. debit Work in Process Inventory.
b. debit Finished Goods Inventory.
c. debit Manufacturing Overhead.
d. credit Raw Materials Inventory.

6. The entry when direct factory labor is assigned to jobs is a debit to: (SO 3)
a. Work in Process Inventory and a credit to Factory Labor.
b. Manufacturing Overhead and a credit to Factory Labor.
c. Factory Labor and a credit to Manufacturing Overhead.
d. Factory Labor and a credit to Work in Process Inventory.

(SO 4) 7. The formula for computing the predetermined manufacturing overhead rate is estimated annual overhead costs divided by an expected annual operating activity, expressed as:
a. direct labor cost.
b. direct labor hours.
c. machine hours.
d. any of the above.

(SO 4) 8. In Cleo Company, the predetermined overhead rate is 80% of direct labor cost. During the month, $210,000 of factory labor costs are incurred, of which $180,000 is direct labor and $30,000 is indirect labor. Actual overhead incurred was $200,000. The amount of overhead debited to Work in Process Inventory should be:
a. $120,000.
b. $144,000.
c. $168,000.
d. $160,000.

9. In BAC Company, Job No. 26 is completed at a cost of $4,500 and later sold for $7,000 cash. A correct entry is: (SO 5)
a. Debit Finished Goods Inventory $7,000 and credit Work in Process Inventory $7,000.
b. Debit Cost of Goods Sold $7,000 and credit Finished Goods Inventory $7,000.
c. Debit Finished Goods Inventory $4,500 and credit Work in Process Inventory $4,500.
d. Debit Accounts Receivable $7,000 and credit Sales $7,000.

10. In preparing monthly financial statements, overapplied overhead is reported in the balance sheet as a(an): (SO 6)
a. prepaid expense.
b. unearned revenue.
c. noncurrent asset.
d. noncurrent liability.

THE NAVIGATOR

QUESTIONS

1. Hal Adelman is studying for an accounting midterm examination. What should Hal know about how management may use job cost data?
2. (a) Marc Tucci is not sure about the differences between cost accounting and a cost accounting system. Explain the difference to Marc. (b) What is an important feature of a cost accounting system?
3. (a) Distinguish between the two types of cost accounting systems. (b) May a company use both types of cost accounting systems?
4. What type of industry is likely to use a job order cost system? Give some examples.
5. What type of industry is likely to use a process cost system? Give some examples.
6. Your roommate asks your help in understanding the major steps in the flow of costs in a job order cost system. Identify the steps for your roommate.
7. There are three inventory control accounts in a job order system. Identify the control accounts and their subsidiary ledgers.
8. What source documents are used in accumulating direct labor costs?
9. "Entries to manufacturing overhead normally are only made daily." Do you agree? Explain.
10. Phil Remmers is confused about the source documents used in assigning materials and labor costs. Identify the documents and give the entry for each document.
11. What is the purpose of a job cost sheet?
12. Indicate the source documents that are used in charging costs to specific jobs.
13. Differentiate between a "materials inventory record" and a "materials requisition slip" as used in a job order cost system.
14. John Simon believes actual manufacturing overhead should be charged to jobs. Do you agree? Why or why not?
15. What relationships are involved in computing a predetermined overhead rate?
16. How can the agreement of Work in Process Inventory and job cost sheets be verified?
17. Pam Smith believes that the cost of goods manufactured schedule in job order cost accounting is the same as in manufacturing accounting. Is Pam correct? Explain.
18. Greg Carnes is confused about under- and overapplied manufacturing overhead. Define the terms for Greg, and indicate the balance in the manufacturing overhead account applicable to each term.
19. "Under- or overapplied overhead is reported in the income statement when monthly financial statements are prepared." Do you agree? If not, indicate the proper presentation.
20. "At the end of the year, under- or overapplied overhead is closed to Income Summary." Is this correct? If not, indicate the customary treatment of this account.

BRIEF EXERCISES

BE21-1 Sinason Tool & Die begins operations on January 1. Because all work is done to customer specifications, the company decides to use a job cost accounting system. Prepare a flow chart of a typical job order system with arrows showing the flow of costs. Identify the eight transactions.

Prepare a flowchart of a job order cost accounting system, and identify transactions.
(SO 2)

Prepare entries in accumulating manufacturing costs.
(SO 2)

BE21-2 During the first month of operations, Sinason Tool & Die accumulated the following manufacturing costs: raw materials $3,000 on account, factory labor $4,000 of which $3,600 relates to factory wages payable and $400 relates to payroll taxes payable, and utilities payable $2,000. Prepare separate journal entries for each type of manufacturing cost.

Prepare entry for the assignment of raw materials costs.
(SO 2)

BE21-3 In January, Sinason Tool & Die requisitions raw materials for production as follows: Job 1 $900, Job 2 $1,200, Job 3 $200, and general factory use $600. Prepare a summary journal entry to record raw materials used.

Prepare entry for the assignment of factory labor costs.
(SO 2)

BE21-4 Factory labor data for Sinason Tool & Die is given in BE21-2. During January, time tickets show that the factory labor of $4,000 was used as follows: Job 1 $1,200, Job 2 $1,600 Job 3 $700, and general factory use $500. Prepare a summary journal entry to record factory labor used.

Prepare job cost sheets.
(SO 3)

BE21-5 Data pertaining to job cost sheets for Sinason Tool & Die are given in BE21-3 and BE21-4. Prepare the job cost sheets for each of the three jobs. (*Note:* You may omit the column for Manufacturing Overhead.)

Compute predetermined overhead rates.
(SO 4)

BE21-6 Carlos Company estimates that annual manufacturing overhead costs will be $400,000. Estimated annual operating activity bases are: direct labor cost $500,000, direct labor hours 50,000, and machine hours 100,000. Compute the predetermined overhead rate for each activity base.

Assign manufacturing overhead to production.
(SO 4)

BE21-7 During the first quarter, Carlos Company incurs the following direct labor costs: January $40,000, February $30,000, and March $50,000. For each month, prepare the entry to assign overhead to production using a predetermined rate of 80% of direct labor cost.

Prepare entries for completion and sale of completed jobs.
(SO 5)

BE21-8 In March, Santana Company completes Jobs 10 and 11. Job 10 cost $20,000 and Job 11 $32,000. On March 31, Job 10 is sold to the customer for $35,000 in cash. Journalize the entries for the completion of the two jobs and the sale of Job 10.

Indicate statement classification of under- or overapplied overhead.
(SO 6)

BE21-9 On September 30, balances in Manufacturing Overhead are: Wendy Company—debit $1,800, Mahmoud Company—credit $3,000. Indicate how each company should report its balance at September 30, assuming each company prepares annual financial statements on December 31.

Prepare adjusting entries for under- and overapplied overhead.
(SO 6)

BE21-10 At December 31, balances in Manufacturing Overhead are: Sanchez Company—debit $1,000, Gomez Company—credit $900. Prepare the adjusting entry for each company at December 31, assuming the adjustment is made to cost of goods sold.

EXERCISES

Prepare entries for factory labor.
(SO 2)

E21-1 The gross earnings of the factory workers for Cerrato Company during the month of January are $90,000. The employer's payroll taxes for the factory payroll are $9,000. The fringe benefits to be paid by the employer on this payroll are $4,000. Of the total accumulated cost of factory labor, 85% is related to direct labor and 15% is attributable to indirect labor.

Instructions

(a) Prepare the entry to record the factory labor costs for the month of January.
(b) Prepare the entry to assign factory labor to production.

Prepare journal entries for manufacturing costs.
(SO 2, 3, 4, 5)

E21-2 Alvarez Manufacturing uses a job order cost accounting system. On May 1, the company has a balance in Work in Process Inventory of $3,200 and two jobs in process: Job No. 429 $2,000, and Job No. 430 $1,200. During May, a summary of source documents reveals the following.

Job Number	Materials Requisition Slips	Labor Time Tickets
429	$2,500	$ 2,400
430	2,000	3,000
431	4,400	7,600
General use	800	1,200
	$9,700	$14,200

Alvarez Manufacturing applies manufacturing overhead to jobs at an overhead rate of 80% of direct labor cost. Job No. 429 is completed during the month.

Instructions

(a) Prepare summary journal entries to record the requisition slips, time tickets, the assignment of manufacturing overhead to jobs, and the completion of Job No. 429.

(b) Post the entries to Work in Process Inventory, and prove the agreement of the control account with the job cost sheets.

Analyze a job cost sheet and prepare entries for manufacturing costs.
(SO 2, 3, 4, 5)

E21-3 A job order cost sheet for Stan Free Company is shown below.

Job No. 92			For 2,000 Units
Date	Direct Materials	Direct Labor	Manufacturing Overhead
Beg. bal. Jan. 1	5,000	6,000	3,900
8	6,000		
12		8,000	6,000
25	2,000		
27		4,000	3,000
	13,000	18,000	12,900

Cost of completed job:	
Direct materials	$13,000
Direct labor	18,000
Manufacturing overhead	12,900
Total cost	$43,900
Unit cost ($43,900 ÷ 2,000)	$21.95

Instructions

(a) On the basis of the foregoing data answer the following questions.

(1) What was the balance in Work in Process Inventory on January 1 if this was the only unfinished job?

(2) If manufacturing overhead is applied on the basis of direct labor cost, what overhead rate was used in each year?

(b) Prepare summary entries at January 31 to record the current year's transactions pertaining to Job No. 92.

Analyze costs of manufacturing and determine missing amounts.
(SO 2, 5)

E21-4 Manufacturing cost data for Lopez Company, which uses a job order cost system, are presented below.

	Case A	Case B	Case C
Direct materials	$ (a)	$83,000	$ 63,150
Direct labor used	50,000	90,000	(h)
Manufacturing overhead applied	42,500	(d)	(i)
Total manufacturing costs	185,650	(e)	287,000
Work in process 1/1/02	(b)	15,500	18,000
Total cost of work in process	201,500	(f)	(j)
Work in process 12/31/02	(c)	11,800	(k)
Cost of goods manufactured	192,300	(g)	262,000

Instructions

Indicate the missing amount for each letter. Assume that in all cases manufacturing overhead is applied on the basis of direct labor cost and the rate is the same.

Compute the manufacturing overhead rate and under- or overapplied overhead.
(SO 4, 6)

E21-5 Ramirez Company applies manufacturing overhead to jobs on the basis of machine hours used. Overhead costs are expected to total $275,000 for the year, and machine usage is estimated at 125,000 hours.

In January, $26,000 of overhead costs are incurred and 12,000 machine hours are used. For the remainder of the year, $274,000 of overhead costs are incurred and 118,000 machine hours are worked.

Instructions

(a) Compute the manufacturing overhead rate for the year.

(b) What is the amount of under- or overapplied overhead at January 31? How should this amount be reported in the financial statements prepared on January 31?

(c) What is the amount of under- or overapplied overhead at December 31?

(d) Assuming the under- or overapplied overhead for the year is not allocated to inventory accounts, prepare the adjusting entry to assign the amount to cost of goods sold.

Analyze job cost sheet and prepare entry for completed job.
(SO 2, 3, 4, 5)

E21-6 A job cost sheet of Serrano Company is given below.

Job Cost Sheet

JOB NO. 469 — Quantity 2,000
ITEM White Lion Cages — Date Requested 7/2
FOR Tesla Company — Date Completed 7/31

Date	Direct Materials	Direct Labor	Manufacturing Overhead
7/10	825		
12	900		
15		440	572
22		380	494
24	1,600		
27	1,500		
31		540	702

Cost of completed job:	
Direct materials	______
Direct labor	______
Manufacturing overhead	______
Total cost	______
Unit cost	______

Instructions

(a) Answer the following questions.

(1) What are the source documents for direct materials, direct labor, and manufacturing overhead costs assigned to this job?

(2) What is the predetermined manufacturing overhead rate?

(3) What are the total cost and the unit cost of the completed job?

(b) Prepare the entry to record the completion of the job.

Prepare entries for manufacturing costs.
(SO 2, 4, 5)

E21-7 Tejada Corporation incurred the following transactions.

1. Purchased raw materials on account $46,300.
2. Raw Materials of $36,000 were requisitioned to the factory. An analysis of the materials requisition slips indicated that $8,800 was classified as indirect materials.
3. Factory labor costs incurred were $64,900, of which $59,000 pertained to factory wages payable and $5,900 pertained to employer payroll taxes payable.
4. Time tickets indicated that $60,000 was direct labor and $4,900 was indirect labor.
5. Overhead costs incurred on account were $80,500.
6. Manufacturing overhead was applied at the rate of 150% of direct labor cost.
7. Goods costing $88,000 were completed and transferred to finished goods.
8. Finished goods costing $68,000 to manufacture were sold on account for $103,000.

Instructions

Journalize the transactions. (Omit explanations.)

Prepare entries for manufacturing costs.
(SO 2, 3, 4, 5)

E21-8 Barajas Printing Corp. uses a job order cost system. The following data summarize the operations related to the first quarter's production.

1. Materials purchased on account $172,000, and factory wages incurred $87,300.
2. Materials requisitioned and factory labor used by job:

Job Number	Materials	Factory Labor
A20	$ 32,240	$18,000
A21	42,920	26,000
A22	36,100	15,000
A23	39,270	25,000
General factory use	4,470	3,300
	$155,000	$87,300

3. Manufacturing overhead costs incurred on account $39,500.
4. Depreciation on machinery and equipment $14,550.
5. Manufacturing overhead rate is 75% of direct labor cost.
6. Jobs completed during the quarter: A20, A21, and A23.

Instructions

Prepare entries to record the operations summarized above. (Prepare a schedule showing the individual cost elements and total cost for each job in item 6.)

Prepare a cost of goods manufactured schedule and partial financial statements.
(SO 2, 5)

E21-9 At May 31, 2002, the accounts of Corrales Manufacturing Company show the following.

1. May 1 inventories—finished goods $12,600, work in process $14,700, and raw materials $8,200.
2. May 31 inventories—finished goods $10,500, work in process $17,900, and raw materials $7,100.
3. Debit postings to work in process were: direct materials $62,400, direct labor $32,000, and manufacturing overhead applied $64,000.
4. Sales totaled $200,000.

Instructions

(a) Prepare a condensed cost of goods manufactured schedule.
(b) Prepare an income statement for May through gross profit.
(c) Indicate the balance sheet presentation of the manufacturing inventories at May 31, 2002.

Compute work in process and finished goods from job cost sheets.
(SO 3, 5)

E21-10 Mendoza Company begins operations on April 1. Information from job cost sheets shows the following.

Job Number	Manufacturing Costs Assigned		
	April	May	June
10	$5,200	$4,400	
11	4,100	3,900	$3,000
12	1,200		
13		4,700	4,500
14		3,900	3,600

Job 12 was completed in April. Job 10 was completed in May. Jobs 11 and 13 were completed in June. Each job was sold for 60% above its cost in the month following completion.

Instructions

(a) What is the balance in Work in Process Inventory at the end of each month?
(b) What is the balance in Finished Goods Inventory at the end of each month?
(c) What is the gross profit for May, June, and July?

PROBLEMS: SET A

Prepare entries in a job cost system and job cost sheets.
(SO 2, 3, 4, 5)

P21-1A Don Tidrick Manufacturing uses a job order cost system and applies overhead to production on the basis of direct labor costs. On January 1, 2002, Job No. 50 was the only job in process. The costs incurred prior to January 1 on this job were as follows: direct materials $20,000, direct labor $12,000, and manufacturing overhead $21,000. As of January 1, Job No. 49 had been completed at a cost of $90,000 and was part of finished goods inventory. There was a $15,000 balance in the Raw Materials inventory account.

During the month of January, Don Tidrick Manufacturing began production on Jobs 51 and 52, and completed Jobs 50 and 51. Jobs 49 and 50 were also sold on account during the month for $122,000 and $158,000, respectively. The following additional events occurred during the month.

1. Purchased additional raw materials of $90,000 on account.
2. Incurred factory labor costs of $63,000. Of this amount $13,000 related to employer payroll taxes.
3. Incurred manufacturing overhead costs as follows: indirect materials $14,000; indirect labor $15,000; depreciation expense $19,000, and various other manufacturing overhead costs on account $23,000.
4. Assigned direct materials and direct labor to jobs as follows.

Job No.	Direct Materials	Direct Labor
50	$10,000	$ 6,000
51	39,000	24,000
52	30,000	18,000

Instructions

(a) Calculate the predetermined overhead rate for 2002, assuming Don Tidrick Manufacturing estimates total manufacturing overhead costs of $1,050,000, direct labor costs of $700,000, and direct labor hours of 20,000 for the year.

(b) Open job cost sheets for Jobs 50, 51, and 52. Enter the January 1 balances on the job cost sheet for Job No. 50.

(c) Prepare the journal entries to record the purchase of raw materials, the factory labor costs incurred, and the manufacturing overhead costs incurred during the month of January.

(d) Prepare the journal entries to record the assignment of direct materials, direct labor, and manufacturing overhead costs to production. In assigning manufacturing overhead costs, use the overhead rate calculated in (a). Post all costs to the job cost sheets as necessary.

(e) Job 50, $78,000
Job 51, $99,000

(e) Total the job cost sheets for any job(s) completed during the month. Prepare the journal entry (or entries) to record the completion of any job(s) during the month.

(f) Prepare the journal entry (or entries) to record the sale of any job(s) during the month.

(g) What is the balance in the Finished Goods Inventory account at the end of the month? What does this balance consist of?

(h) What is the amount of over- or underapplied overhead for the month? How would this be reported on the financial statements for the month of January?

Prepare entries in a job cost system and partial income statement.
(SO 2, 3, 4, 5, 6)

P21-2A For the year ended December 31, 2002, the job cost sheets of Chicago Company contained the following data.

Job Number	Explanation	Direct Materials	Direct Labor	Manufacturing Overhead	Total Costs
7640	Balance 1/1	$25,000	$24,000	$28,800	$ 77,800
	Current year's costs	34,000	36,000	43,200	113,200
7641	Balance 1/1	11,000	18,000	21,600	50,600
	Current year's costs	40,000	48,000	57,600	145,600
7642	Current year's costs	48,000	55,000	66,000	169,000

Other data:

1. Raw materials inventory totaled $15,000 on January 1. During the year, $140,000 of raw materials were purchased on account.
2. Finished goods on January 1 consisted of Job No. 7638 for $87,000 and Job No. 7639 for $92,000.
3. Job No. 7640 and Job No. 7641 were completed during the year.
4. Job Nos. 7638, 7639, and 7641 were sold on account for $530,000.
5. Manufacturing overhead incurred on account totaled $115,000.
6. Other manufacturing overhead consisted of indirect materials $14,000, indirect labor $20,000, and depreciation on factory machinery $8,000.

Instructions

(a) Prove the agreement of Work in Process Inventory with job cost sheets pertaining to unfinished work.
(b) Prepare the adjusting entry for manufacturing overhead, assuming the balance is allocated entirely to Cost of Goods Sold.
(c) Determine the gross profit to be reported for 2002.

P21-3A Peoria Inc. is a construction company specializing in custom patios. The patios are constructed of concrete, brick, fiberglass, and lumber, depending upon customer preference. On June 1, 2002, the general ledger for Peoria Inc. contains the following data.

Prepare entries in a job cost system and cost of goods manufactured schedule.
(SO 2, 3, 4, 5)

Raw Materials Inventory	$4,200	Manufacturing Overhead Applied	$32,640
Work in Process Inventory	$5,900	Manufacturing Overhead Incurred	$31,650

Subsidiary data for Work in Process Inventory on June 1 are as follows.

Job Cost Sheets

	Customer Job		
Cost Element	**Rockford**	**Aurora**	**Moline**
Direct materials	$ 600	$ 800	$ 900
Direct labor	320	540	580
Manufacturing overhead	480	810	870
	$1,400	$2,150	$2,350

A summary of materials requisition slips and time tickets for June shows the following.

Customer Job	Materials Requisition Slips	Time Tickets
Rockford	$ 800	$ 450
Elgin	2,000	800
Aurora	500	360
Moline	1,300	800
Rockford	300	250
	4,900	2,660
General use	1,500	1,200
	$6,400	$3,860

During June, raw materials purchased on account were $3,900, and all wages were paid. Additional overhead costs consisted of depreciation on equipment $700 and miscellaneous costs of $400 incurred on account. Overhead was charged to jobs at the same rate that was used in May. The patios for customers Rockford, Aurora, and Moline were completed during June and sold for a total of $18,900. Each customer paid in full.

Instructions

(a) Journalize the June transactions.
(b) Post the entries to Work in Process Inventory.
(c) Reconcile the balance in Work in Process Inventory with the costs of unfinished jobs.
(d) Prepare a cost of goods manufactured schedule for June.

(d) Cost of goods manufactured $13,450

P21-4A Urbana Manufacturing Company uses a job order cost system in each of its three manufacturing departments. Manufacturing overhead is applied to jobs on the basis of direct labor cost in Department D, direct labor hours in Department E, and machine hours in Department K.

Compute predetermined overhead rate, apply overhead and indicate statement presentation of under- or overapplied overhead.
(SO 4, 6)

In establishing the predetermined overhead rates for 2003 the following estimates were made for the year.

	Department D	Department E	Department K
Manufacturing overhead	$1,170,000	$1,500,000	$960,000
Direct labor costs	$1,500,000	$1,250,000	$450,000
Direct labor hours	100,000	120,000	40,000
Machine hours	400,000	500,000	120,000

During January, the job cost sheets showed the following costs and production data.

	Department D	Department E	Department K
Direct materials used	$140,000	$126,000	$78,000
Direct labor costs	$120,000	$110,000	$37,500
Manufacturing overhead incurred	$98,000	$129,000	$80,000
Direct labor hours	8,000	11,000	3,500
Machine hours	34,000	45,000	10,400

Instructions

(a) Compute the predetermined overhead rate for each department.
(b) Compute the total manufacturing costs assigned to jobs in January in each department.
(c) Compute the under- or overapplied overhead for each department at January 31.
(d) Indicate the statement presentation of the under- or overapplied overhead at January 31.
(e) If the amount in (d) was the same at December 31, how would it be reported in the year-end financial statements?

Analyze manufacturing accounts and determine missing amounts.
(SO 2, 3, 4, 5, 6)

P21-5A Florida Boot Corporation's fiscal year ends on November 30. The following accounts are found in its job order cost accounting system for the first month of the new fiscal year.

Raw Materials Inventory

Dec. 1	Beginning balance	(a)	Dec. 31	Requisitions	14,850
31	Purchases	19,225			
Dec. 31	Ending balance	7,975			

Work in Process Inventory

Dec. 1	Beginning balance	(b)	Dec. 31	Jobs completed	(f)
31	Direct materials	(c)			
31	Direct labor	8,100			
31	Overhead	(d)			
Dec. 31	Ending balance	(e)			

Finished Goods Inventory

Dec. 1	Beginning balance	(g)	Dec. 31	Cost of goods sold	(i)
31	Completed jobs	(h)			
Dec. 31	Ending balance	(j)			

Factory Labor

Dec. 31	Factory wages	10,800	Dec. 31	Wages assigned	(k)

Manufacturing Overhead

Dec. 31	Indirect materials	1,900	Dec. 31	Overhead applied	(m)
31	Indirect labor	(l)			
31	Other overhead	1,245			

Other data:

1. On December 1, two jobs were in process: Job No. 154 and Job No. 155. These jobs had combined direct materials costs of $9,750 and direct labor costs of $12,000. Overhead was applied at a rate that was 75% of direct labor cost.
2. During December, Job Nos. 156, 157, and 158 were started. On December 31, Job No. 158 was unfinished. This job had charges for direct materials $3,800 and direct labor $4,400, plus manufacturing overhead. All jobs, except for Job No. 158, were completed in December.
3. On December 1, Job No. 153 was in the finished goods warehouse. It had a total cost of $5,000. On December 31, Job No. 157 was the only job finished that was not sold. It had a cost of $4,000.
4. Manufacturing overhead was $230 overapplied in December.

Instructions

List the letters (a) through (m) and indicate the amount pertaining to each letter.

PROBLEMS: SET B

Prepare entries in a job cost system and job costs sheets.
(SO 2, 3, 4, 5, 6)

P21-1B Han Wu Manufacturing uses a job order cost system and applies overhead to production on the basis of direct labor hours. On January 1, 2002, Job No. 25 was the only job in process. The costs incurred prior to January 1 on this job were as follows: direct materials $10,000; direct labor $6,000; and manufacturing overhead $10,500. Job No. 23 had been completed at a cost of $45,000 and was part of finished goods inventory. There was a $5,000 balance in the Raw Materials inventory account.

During the month of January, the company began production on Jobs 26 and 27, and completed Jobs 25 and 26. Jobs 23 and 25 were sold on account during the month for $67,000 and $74,000, respectively. The following additional events occurred during the month.

1. Purchased additional raw materials of $45,000 on account.
2. Incurred factory labor costs of $31,500. Of this amount $6,500 related to employer payroll taxes.
3. Incurred manufacturing overhead costs as follows: indirect materials $10,000; indirect labor $7,500; depreciation expense $12,000; and various other manufacturing overhead costs on account $15,000.
4. Assigned direct materials and direct labor to jobs as follows.

Job No.	Direct Materials	Direct Labor
25	$ 5,000	$ 3,000
26	20,000	12,000
27	15,000	9,000

5. The company uses direct labor hours as the activity base to assign overhead. Direct labor hours incurred on each job were as follows: Job No. 25, 200; Job No. 26, 800; and Job No. 27, 600.

Instructions

(a) Calculate the predetermined overhead rate for the year 2002, assuming Han Wu Manufacturing estimates total manufacturing overhead costs of $500,000, direct labor costs of $300,000, and direct labor hours of 20,000 for the year.

(b) Open job cost sheets for Jobs 25, 26, and 27. Enter the January 1 balances on the job cost sheet for Job No. 25.

(c) Prepare the journal entries to record the purchase of raw materials, the factory labor costs incurred, and the manufacturing overhead costs incurred during the month of January.

(d) Prepare the journal entries to record the assignment of direct materials, direct labor, and manufacturing overhead costs to production. In assigning manufacturing overhead costs, use the overhead rate calculated in (a). Post all costs to the job cost sheets as necessary.

(e) Total the job cost sheets for any job(s) completed during the month. Prepare the journal entry (or entries) to record the completion of any job(s) during the month.

(e) Job 25, $39,500
Job 26, $52,000

(f) Prepare the journal entry (or entries) to record the sale of any job(s) during the month.
(g) What is the balance in the Work in Process Inventory account at the end of the month? What does this balance consist of?
(h) What is the amount of over- or underapplied overhead for the month? How would this be reported on the financial statements for the month of January?

Prepare entries in a job cost system and partial income statement.
(SO 2, 3, 4, 5, 6)

P21-2B For the year ended December 31, 2002, the job cost sheets of Ying Chen Company contained the following data.

Job Number	Explanation	Direct Materials	Direct Labor	Manufacturing Overhead	Total Costs
7650	Balance 1/1	$18,000	$20,000	$25,000	$ 63,000
	Current year's costs	22,000	30,000	37,500	89,500
7651	Balance 1/1	12,000	18,000	22,500	52,500
	Current year's costs	28,000	40,000	50,000	118,000
7652	Current year's costs	40,000	60,000	75,000	175,000

Other data:

1. Raw materials inventory totaled $20,000 on January 1. During the year, $100,000 of raw materials were purchased on account.
2. Finished goods on January 1 consisted of Job No. 7648 for $98,000 and Job No. 7649 for $62,000.
3. Job No. 7650 and Job No. 7651 were completed during the year.
4. Job Nos. 7648, 7649, and 7650 were sold on account for $390,000.
5. Manufacturing overhead incurred on account totaled $120,000.
6. Other manufacturing overhead consisted of indirect materials $12,000, indirect labor $18,000 and depreciation on factory machinery $19,500.

Instructions

(a) Prove the agreement of Work in Process Inventory with job cost sheets pertaining to unfinished work.
(b) Prepare the adjusting entry for manufacturing overhead, assuming the balance is allocated entirely to cost of goods sold.
(c) Determine the gross profit to be reported for 2002.

Prepare entries in a job cost system and cost of goods manufactured schedule.
(SO 2, 3, 4, 5)

P21-3B Richard E. Baker is a contractor specializing in custom-built jacuzzis. On May 1, 2002, his ledger contains the following data.

Raw Materials Inventory	$30,000
Work in Process Inventory	12,400
Manufacturing Overhead	2,500 (dr.)

The Manufacturing Overhead account has debit totals of $12,500 and credit totals of $10,000. Subsidiary data for Work in Process Inventory on May 1 include:

Job Cost Sheets

Job by Customer	Direct Materials	Direct Labor	Manufacturing Overhead
Engstrom	$2,500	$2,000	$1,500
Hendricks	2,000	1,200	900
Keys	900	800	600
	$5,400	$4,000	$3,000

A summary of materials requisition slips and time tickets for the month of May reveals the following.

Job by Customer	Materials Requisition Slips	Time Tickets
Engstrom	$ 500	$ 400
Hendricks	600	1,000
Keys	2,300	1,300
Bennett	2,400	3,300
	5,800	6,000
General use	1,500	2,600
	$7,300	$8,600

During May, the following costs were incurred: (a) raw materials purchased on account $5,000, (b) labor paid $8,600, (c) manufacturing overhead paid $1,400. Overhead was charged to jobs on the basis of direct labor cost at the same rate as in the previous month.

The jacuzzis for customers Engstrom, Hendricks, and Keys were completed during May. Each jacuzzi was sold for $12,500 cash.

Instructions

(a) Prepare journal entries for the May transactions.
(b) Post the entries to Work in Process Inventory.
(c) Reconcile the balance in Work in Process Inventory with the costs of unfinished jobs.
(d) Prepare a cost of goods manufactured schedule for May.

(d) Cost of goods manufactured $20,525

P21-4B Hopkins Manufacturing uses a job order cost system in each of its three manufacturing departments. Manufacturing overhead is applied to jobs on the basis of direct labor cost in Department A, direct labor hours in Department B, and machine hours in Department C.

Compute predetermined overhead rates, apply overhead, and indicate statement presentation of under- or overapplied overhead.
(SO 4, 6)

In establishing the predetermined overhead rates for 2002 the following estimates were made for the year.

	Department		
	A	B	C
Manufacturing overhead	$900,000	$760,000	$780,000
Direct labor cost	$600,000	$100,000	$600,000
Direct labor hours	50,000	50,000	40,000
Machine hours	100,000	120,000	150,000

During January, the job cost sheets showed the following costs and production data.

	Department		
	A	B	C
Direct materials used	$92,000	$86,000	$64,000
Direct labor cost	$48,000	$35,000	$50,400
Manufacturing overhead incurred	$76,000	$54,000	$64,500
Direct labor hours	4,000	3,500	4,200
Machine hours	8,000	10,500	12,600

Instructions

(a) Compute the predetermined overhead rate for each department.
(b) Compute the total manufacturing costs assigned to jobs in January in each department.
(c) Compute the under- or overapplied overhead for each department at January 31.
(d) Indicate the statement presentation of the under- or overapplied overhead at January 31.
(e) If the amount in (d) was the same at December 31, how would it be reported in the year-end financial statements?

Analyze manufacturing cost accounts and determine missing amounts.
(SO 2, 3, 4, 5, 6)

P21-5B Devona Company's fiscal year ends on June 30. The following accounts are found in its job order cost accounting system for the first month of the new fiscal year.

Raw Materials Inventory

July 1	Beginning balance	19,000	July 31	Requisitions	(a)
31	Purchases	90,400			
July 31	Ending balance	(b)			

Work in Process Inventory

July 1	Beginning balance	(c)	July 31	Jobs completed	(f)
31	Direct materials	75,000			
31	Direct labor	(d)			
31	Overhead	(e)			
July 31	Ending balance	(g)			

Finished Goods Inventory

July 1	Beginning balance	(h)	July 31	Cost of goods sold	(j)
31	Completed jobs	(i)			
July 31	Ending balance	(k)			

Factory Labor

July 31	Factory wages	(l)	July 31	Wages assigned	(m)

Manufacturing Overhead

July 31	Indirect materials	8,900	July 31	Overhead applied	91,000
31	Indirect labor	16,000			
31	Other overhead	(n)			

Other data:

1. On July 1, two jobs were in process: Job No. 4085 and Job No. 4086, with costs of $17,000 and $8,200, respectively.
2. During July, Job Nos. 4087, 4088, and 4089 were started. On July 31, only Job No. 4089 was unfinished. This job had charges for direct materials $2,000 and direct labor $1,500, plus manufacturing overhead.
3. On July 1, Job No. 4084, costing $135,000, was in the finished goods warehouse. On July 31, Job No. 4088, costing $143,000, was in finished goods.
4. Manufacturing overhead was applied at the rate of 130% of direct labor cost. Overhead was $3,000 underapplied in July.

Instructions

List the letters (a) through (n) and indicate the amount pertaining to each letter. Show computations.

BROADENING YOUR PERSPECTIVE

GROUP DECISION CASE

BYP21-1 Du Page Products Company uses a job order cost system. For a number of months there has been an ongoing rift between the sales department and the production department concerning a special-order product, TC-1. TC-1 is a seasonal product that is manufactured in batches of 1,000 units. TC-1 is sold at cost plus a markup of 40% of cost.

The sales department is unhappy because fluctuating unit production costs significantly affect selling prices. Sales personnel complain that this has caused excessive customer complaints and the loss of considerable orders for TC-1.

The production department maintains that each job order must be fully costed on the basis of the costs incurred during the period in which the goods are produced. Production personnel maintain that the only real solution to the problem is for the sales department to increase sales in the slack periods.

Sandra Devona, president of the company, asks you as the company accountant to collect quarterly data for the past year on TC-1. From the cost accounting system, you accumulate the following production quantity and cost data.

	Quarter			
Costs	**1**	**2**	**3**	**4**
Direct materials	$100,000	$220,000	$ 80,000	$200,000
Direct labor	60,000	132,000	48,000	120,000
Manufacturing overhead	105,000	123,000	97,000	125,000
Total	$265,000	$475,000	$225,000	$445,000
Production in batches	5	11	4	10
Unit cost (per batch)	$ 53,000	$ 43,182	$ 56,250	$ 44,500

Instructions

With the class divided into groups, answer the following questions.

(a) What manufacturing cost element is responsible for the fluctuating unit costs? Why?

(b) What is your recommended solution to the problem of fluctuating unit cost?

(c) Restate the quarterly data on the basis of your recommended solution.

MANAGERIAL ANALYSIS

BYP21-2 In the course of routine checking of all journal entries prior to preparing month-end reports, Sally Weber discovered several strange entries. She recalled that the president's son Jeff had come in to help out during an especially busy time and that he had recorded some journal entries. She was relieved that there were only a few of his entries, and even more relieved that he had included rather lengthy explanations. The entries Jeff made were:

1.

Work in Process Inventory	20,000	
Cash		20,000

(This is for materials put into process. I don't find the record that we paid for these, so I'm crediting Cash, because I know we'll have to pay for them sooner or later.)

2.

Manufacturing Overhead	12,000	
Cash		12,000

(This is for bonuses paid to salespeople. I know they're part of overhead, and I can't find an account called "Non-factory Overhead" or "Other Overhead" so I'm putting it in Manufacturing Overhead. I have the check stubs, so I know we paid these.)

3.

Wages Expense	120,000	
Cash		120,000

(This is for the factory workers' wages. I have a note that payroll taxes are $8,000. I still think that's part of wages expense, and that we'll have to pay it all in cash sooner or later, so I credited Cash for the wages and the taxes.)

4.

Work in Process Inventory	3,000	
Raw Materials Inventory		3,000

(This is for the glue used in the factory. I know we used this to make the products, even though we didn't use very much on any one of the products. I got it out of inventory, so I credited an inventory account.)

Instructions

(a) How should Jeff have recorded each of the four events?

(b) If the entry was not corrected, which financial statements (income statement or balance sheet) would be affected? What balances would be overstated or understated?

REAL-WORLD FOCUS

BYP21-3 Founded in 1970, **Parlex Corporation** is a world leader in the design and manufacture of flexible interconnect products. Utilizing proprietary and patented technologies, Parlex produces custom flexible interconnects including flexible circuits, polymer thick film, laminated cables, and value-added assemblies for sophisticated electronics used in automotive, telecommunications, computer, diversified electronics, and aerospace applications. In addition to manufacturing sites in Methuen, Massachusetts; Salem, New Hampshire; Cranston, Rhode Island; San Jose, California; Shanghai, China; Isle of Wight, UK; and Empalme, Mexico, Parlex has logistic support centers and strategic alliances throughout North America, Asia, and Europe.

The following information was provided in the company's annual report.

PARLEX COMPANY
Notes to the Financial Statements

The Company's products are manufactured on a job order basis to customers' specifications. Customers submit requests for quotations on each job, and the Company prepares bids based on its own cost estimates. The Company attempts to reflect the impact of changing costs when establishing prices. However, during the past several years, the market conditions for flexible circuits and the resulting price sensitivity haven't always allowed this to transpire. Although still not satisfactory, the Company was able to reduce the cost of products sold as a percentage of sales to 85% this year versus 87% that was experienced in the two immediately preceding years. Management continues to focus on improving operational efficiency and further reducing costs.

Instructions

(a) Parlex management discusses the job order cost system employed by their company. What are several advantages of using the job order approach to costing?

(b) Contrast the products produced in a job order environment, like Parlex, to those produced when process cost systems are used.

EXPLORING THE WEB

BYP21-4 The Institute of Management Accountants sponsors a certification for management accountants, allowing them to obtain the title of Certified Management Accountant.

Address: **www.imanet.org** ***(or go to www.wiley.com/college/weygandt)***

Steps:

1. Go to the site shown above.
2. Choose **Certification**.

Instructions

(a) What are the objectives of the certification program?
(b) What is the "experience requirement"?
(c) How many hours of continuing education are required, and what types of courses qualify?

COMMUNICATION ACTIVITY

BYP21-5 You are the management accountant for Modine Manufacturing. Your company does custom carpentry work and uses a job order cost accounting system. Modine sends detailed job cost sheets to its customers, along with an invoice. The job cost sheets show the date materials were used, the dollar cost of materials, and the hours and cost of labor. A predetermined overhead application rate is used, and the total overhead applied is also listed.

Cindy Ross is a customer who recently had custom cabinets installed. Along with her check in payment for the work done, she included a letter. She thanked the company for including the detailed cost information but questioned why overhead was estimated. She stated that she would be interested in knowing exactly what costs were included in overhead, and she thought that other customers would, too.

Instructions

Prepare a letter to Ms. Ross (address: 123 Cedar Lane, Altoona, Kansas 66651) and tell her why you did not send her information on exact costs of overhead included in her job. Respond to her suggestion that you provide this information.

ETHICS CASE

BYP21-6 NIU Printing provides printing services to many different corporate clients. Although NIU bids most jobs, some jobs, particularly new ones, are often negotiated on a "cost-plus" basis. Cost-plus means that the buyer is willing to pay the actual cost plus a return (profit) on these costs to NIU.

Cathrine Traynor, controller for NIU, has recently returned from a meeting where NIU's president stated that he wanted her to find a way to charge most costs to any project that was on a cost-plus basis. The president noted that the company needed more profits to meet its stated goals this period. By charging more costs to the cost-plus projects and therefore less cost to the jobs that were bid, the company should be able to increase its profits for the current year.

Cathrine knew why the president wanted to take this action. Rumors were that he was looking for a new position and if the company reported strong profits, the president's opportunities would be enhanced. Cathrine also recognized that she could probably increase the cost of certain jobs by changing the basis used to allocate manufacturing overhead.

Instructions

(a) Who are the stakeholders in this situation?
(b) What are the ethical issues in this situation?
(c) What would you do if you were Cathrine Traynor?

Answers to Self-Study Questions

1. a **2.** b **3.** c **4.** d **5.** b **6.** a **7.** d **8.** b **9.** c **10.** b

Remember to go back to the Navigator box on the chapter-opening page and check off your completed work.

THE NAVIGATOR ✓

- Understand *Concepts for Review* ❑
- Read *Feature Story* ❑
- Scan *Study Objectives* ❑
- Read *Preview* ❑
- Read text and answer *Before You Go On* *p.* 907 ❑ *p.* 916 ❑ *p.* 921 ❑
- Work *Demonstration Problem* ❑
- Review *Summary of Study Objectives* ❑
- Answer *Self-Study Questions* ❑
- Complete *Assignments* ❑

CONCEPTS FOR REVIEW

Before studying this chapter, you should know or, if necessary, review:

a. The three manufacturing cost elements. (Ch. 20, pp. 831–832)

b. How manufacturing costs are accumulated in the accounts. (Ch. 21, pp. 867–869)

c. How manufacturing costs are assigned to work in process, finished goods, and cost of goods sold. (Ch. 21, pp. 869–876)

d. The flow of costs and supporting documents in a job order cost accounting system. (Ch. 21, pp. 878–879)

THE NAVIGATOR

FEATURE STORY

Ben & Jerry's Tracks Its Mix-Ups

At one time, one of the fastest growing companies in the nation was **Ben & Jerry's Homemade, Inc.**, based in Waterbury, Vermont. The ice cream company that started out of a garage in 1978 is now a public company.

Making ice cream is a process—a movement of product from a mixing department to a prepping department to a pint department. The mixing department is where the ice cream is created. The prep area is where extras such as cherries and walnuts are added to make plain ice cream into "Cherry Garcia." And the pint department is where the ice cream is actually put into containers. As the product is processed from one department to the next, the appropriate materials, labor, and overhead are added to it.

"The incoming ingredients from the shipping and receiving departments are stored in certain locations, either in a freezer or dry warehouse," says Beecher Eurich, staff accountant. "As ingredients get added, so do the costs associated with them." How much ice cream is actually produced? Running the plant around the clock, 24,000 pints are produced per 8-hour shift, or 72,000 pints per day.

Using a process costing system, Eurich can tell you how much a certain batch of ice cream costs to make—its materials, labor, and overhead in each of the production departments. She generates reports for the production department heads, but makes sure not to overdo it. "You can get bogged down in numbers," says Eurich. "If you're generating a report that no one can use, then that's a waste of time." More likely, though, Ben & Jerry's production people want to know how efficient they are. Why? Many own stock in the company.

www.benjerry.com

THE NAVIGATOR

STUDY OBJECTIVES

After studying this chapter, you should be able to:

1. Understand who uses process cost systems.
2. Explain the similarities and differences between job order cost and process cost systems.
3. Explain the flow of costs in a process cost system.
4. Make the journal entries to assign manufacturing costs in a process cost system.
5. Compute equivalent units.
6. Explain the four steps necessary to prepare a production cost report.
7. Prepare a production cost report.
8. Explain just-in-time (JIT) processing.
9. Explain activity-based costing (ABC).

THE NAVIGATOR

PREVIEW OF CHAPTER 22

The cost accounting system used by companies such as **Ben & Jerry's** is called a **process cost accounting** system. In contrast to job order cost accounting, which focuses on the individual job, process cost accounting focuses on the processes involved in mass-producing products that are identical or very similar in nature. The primary objective of the chapter is to explain and illustrate process cost accounting.

The content and organization of Chapter 22 are as follows.

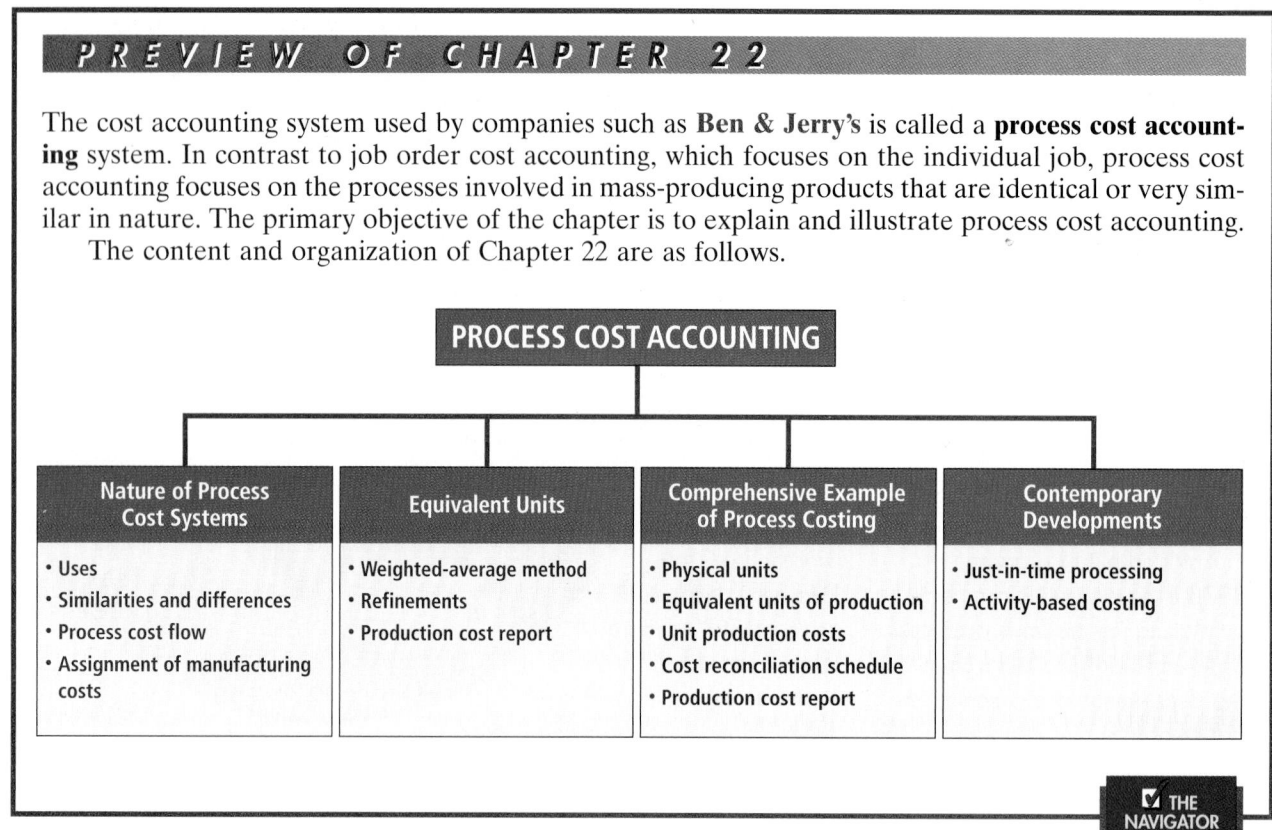

PROCESS COST ACCOUNTING

Nature of Process Cost Systems
- Uses
- Similarities and differences
- Process cost flow
- Assignment of manufacturing costs

Equivalent Units
- Weighted-average method
- Refinements
- Production cost report

Comprehensive Example of Process Costing
- Physical units
- Equivalent units of production
- Unit production costs
- Cost reconciliation schedule
- Production cost report

Contemporary Developments
- Just-in-time processing
- Activity-based costing

THE NAVIGATOR

THE NATURE OF PROCESS COST SYSTEMS

USES OF PROCESS COST SYSTEMS

STUDY OBJECTIVE 1

Understand who uses process cost systems.

Process cost systems are used to apply costs to similar products that are mass-produced in a continuous fashion. Ben & Jerry's uses a process cost system: Production of the ice cream, once it begins, continues until the ice cream emerges, and the processing is the same for the entire run—with precisely the same amount of materials, labor, and overhead. Each finished pint of ice cream is indistinguishable from another.

A company such as **USX** uses process costing in the manufacturing of steel. **Kellogg** and **General Mills** use process costing for cereal production. **ExxonMobil** uses process costing for its oil refining. And **Sherwin Williams** uses process costing for its paint products. At a bottling company like **Coca-Cola**, the manufacturing process begins with the blending of the beverages. Next the beverage is dispensed into bottles that are moved into position by automated machinery. The bottles are then capped, packaged, and forwarded to the finished goods warehouse. This process is shown in Illustration 22-1.

Illustration 22-1

Manufacturing processes

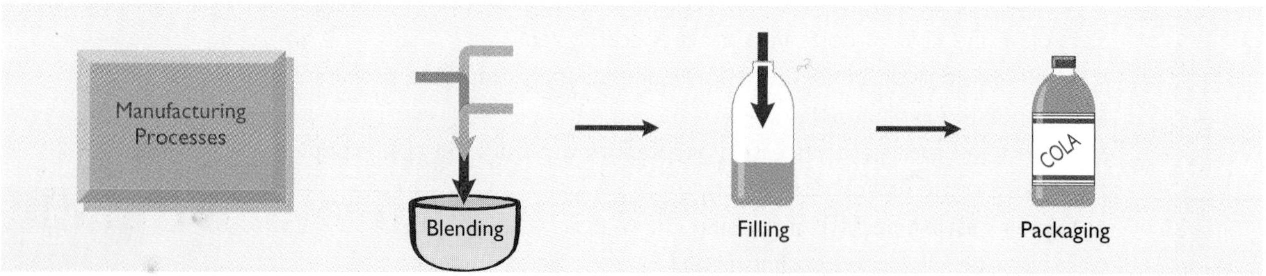

For Coca-Cola, as well as the other companies just mentioned, once the production begins, it continues until the finished product emerges, and each unit of finished product is like every other unit.

In comparison, costs in a job order cost system are assigned to a specific job. Examples are the construction of a customized home, the making of a motion picture, or the manufacturing of a specialized machine. Illustration 22-2 provides examples of companies that primarily use either a process cost system or a job order cost system.

Illustration 22-2

Process cost and job order cost companies and products

Process Cost System Company	Product	Job Order Cost System Company	Product
Coca-Cola, PepsiCo	Soft drinks	Young & Rubicam, J. Walter Thompson	Advertising
ExxonMobil, Shell Oil	Oil	Walt Disney, Warner Brothers	Motion pictures
Intel, Advanced Micro Devices	Computer chips	Center Ice Consultants, Ice Pro	Ice rinks
Dow Chemical, DuPont	Chemicals	Kaiser, Mayo Clinic	Patient health care

SIMILARITIES AND DIFFERENCES BETWEEN JOB ORDER COST AND PROCESS COST SYSTEMS

STUDY OBJECTIVE 2

Explain the similarities and differences between job order cost and process cost systems.

In a job order cost system, costs are assigned to each job. In a process cost system, costs are tracked through a series of connected manufacturing processes or departments, rather than by individual jobs. Thus, process cost systems are used when a large volume of uniform or relatively homogeneous products are produced. The basic flow of costs in these two systems is shown in Illustration 22-3.

Illustration 22-3

Job order cost and process cost flow

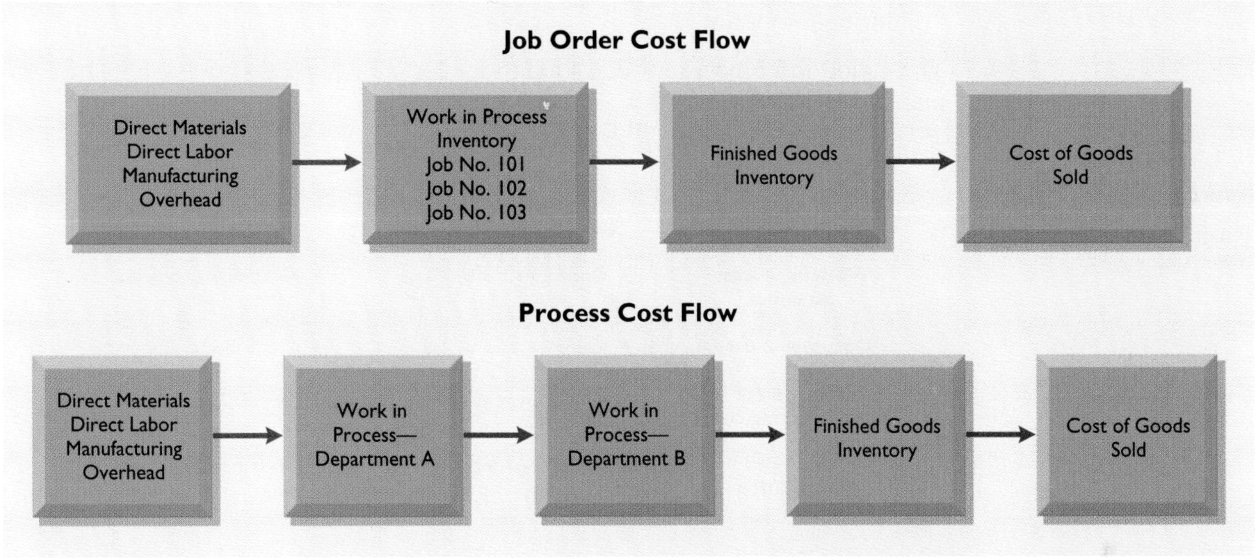

The basic similarities and differences between these two systems are highlighted in the following analysis.

Similarities

Job order cost and process cost systems are similar in three ways:

1. **The manufacturing cost elements.** Both a job order cost and a process cost system track the same three manufacturing cost elements—direct materials, direct labor, and manufacturing overhead.
2. **The accumulation of the costs of materials, labor, and overhead.** In both costing systems, all raw materials are debited to Raw Materials Inventory; all factory labor is debited to Factory Labor; and all manufacturing overhead costs are debited to Manufacturing Overhead.
3. **The flow of costs.** As noted above, all manufacturing costs are accumulated by debits to Raw Materials Inventory, Factory Labor, and Manufacturing Overhead. These costs are then assigned to the same accounts in both costing systems—Work in Process, Finished Goods Inventory, and Cost of Goods Sold. **The methods of assigning costs, however, differ significantly.** These differences are explained and illustrated later in the chapter.

Differences

The differences between a job order cost and a process cost system are as follows.

1. **The number of work in process accounts used.** In a job order cost system, only one work in process account is used. In a process cost system, multiple work in process accounts are used; separate accounts are maintained for each production department or manufacturing process.
2. **Documents used to track costs.** In a job order cost system, costs are charged to individual jobs and summarized in a job cost sheet. In a process cost system, costs are summarized in a production cost report for each department.
3. **The point at which costs are totaled.** In a job order cost system, total costs are determined when the job is completed. In a process cost system, total costs are determined at the end of a period of time, such as a month or year.
4. **Unit cost computations.** In a job order cost system, the unit cost is the total cost per job divided by the units produced. In a process cost system, the unit cost is total manufacturing costs for the period divided by the units produced during the period.

The major differences between a job order cost and a process cost system are summarized in Illustration 22-4.

Illustration 22-4

Job order versus process cost systems

Features	Job Order Cost System	Process Cost System
Work in process accounts	• One for each job	• One for each process
Documents used	• Job cost sheets	• Production cost reports
Determination of total manufacturing costs	• Each job	• Each period
Unit-cost computations	• Cost of each job ÷ Units produced for the job	• Total manufacturing costs ÷ Units produced during the period

PROCESS COST FLOW

STUDY OBJECTIVE 3

Explain the flow of costs in a process cost system.

Illustration 22-5 shows the flow of costs in the process cost system for Tyler Company. Tyler Company manufactures automatic can openers that are sold to retail outlets. Manufacturing consists of two processes: machining and assembly. In the Machining Department, the raw materials are shaped, honed, and drilled. In the Assembly Department, the parts are assembled and packaged.

Illustration 22-5

Flow of costs in process cost system

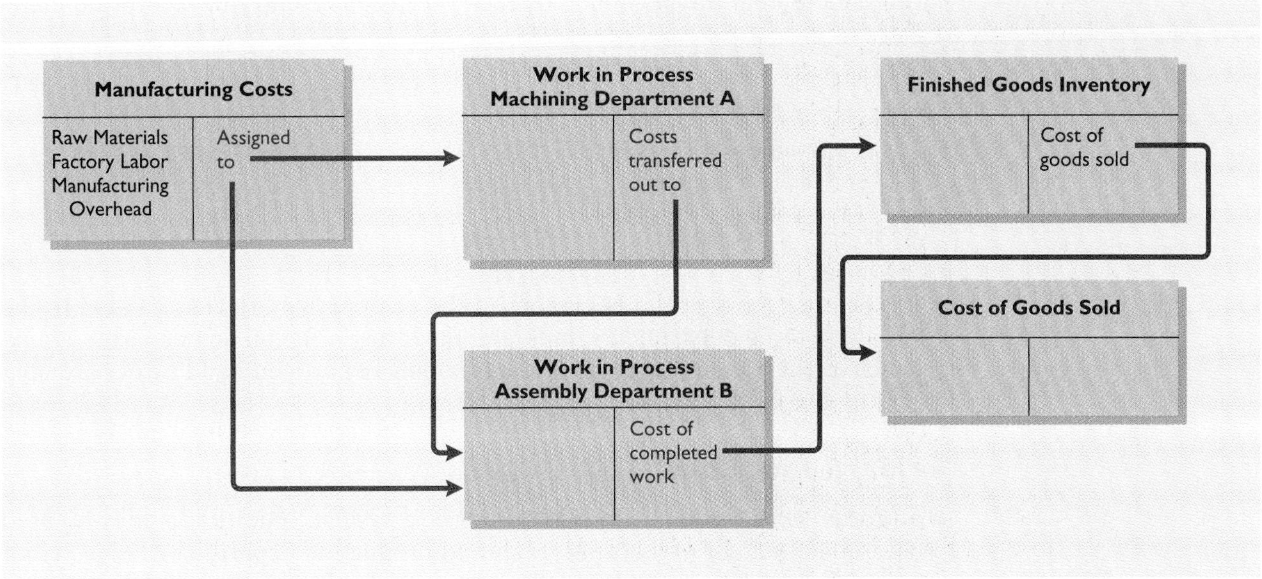

As the flow of costs indicates, materials, labor, and manufacturing overhead can be added in both the Machining and Assembly Departments. When the Machining Department finishes its work, the partially completed units are transferred to the Assembly Department. In the Assembly Department, the goods are finished and are then transferred to the finished goods inventory. Upon sale, the goods are removed from the finished goods inventory. Within each department, a similar set of activities is performed on each unit processed.

ASSIGNMENT OF MANUFACTURING COSTS— JOURNAL ENTRIES

STUDY OBJECTIVE 4

Make the journal entries to assign manufacturing costs in a process cost system.

As indicated earlier, the accumulation of the costs of materials, labor, and manufacturing overhead is the same in a process cost system as in a job order cost system. All raw materials are debited to Raw Materials Inventory when the materials are purchased. All factory labor is debited to Factory Labor when the labor costs are incurred. And overhead costs are debited to Manufacturing Overhead as they are incurred. However, the assignment of the three manufacturing cost elements to Work in Process in a process cost system is different from a job order cost system. Here we'll look at how these manufacturing cost elements are assigned in a process cost system.

Materials Costs

All raw materials issued for production are a materials cost to the producing department. Materials requisition slips may be used in a process cost system, but

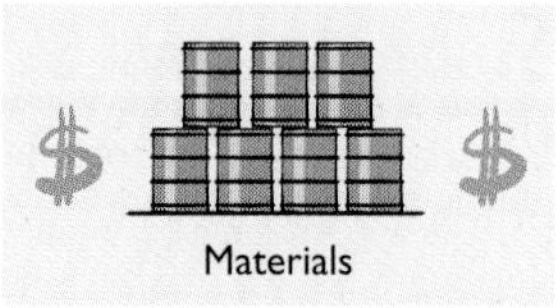

fewer requisitions are generally required than in a job order cost system, because the materials are used for processes rather than for specific jobs. Requisitions are issued less frequently in a process cost system because the requisitions are for larger quantities.

Materials are usually added to production at the beginning of the first process. However, in subsequent processes, other materials may be added at various points. For example, in the manufacture of **Hershey** candy bars, the chocolate and other ingredients are added at the beginning of the first process, and the wrappers and cartons are added at the end of the packaging process. At Tyler Company, materials are entered at the beginning of each process. The entry to record the materials used is:

Work in Process—Machining	XXXX	
Work in Process—Assembly	XXXX	
Raw Materials Inventory		XXXX
(To record materials used)		

In the Feature Story at the beginning of the chapter, materials are added to the ice cream in three departments: milk and flavoring in the mixing department; extras such as cherries and walnuts in the prepping department; and cardboard containers in the pinting (packaging) department.

Factory Labor Costs

In a process cost system, as in a job order cost system, time tickets may be used to determine the cost of labor assignable to production departments. Since labor costs are assigned to a process rather than a job, the labor cost chargeable to a process can be obtained from the payroll register or departmental payroll summaries.

All labor costs incurred within a producing department are a cost of processing the raw materials. Thus, labor costs for the Machining Department will include the wages of employees who shape, hone, and drill the raw materials. The entry to assign these costs for Tyler Company is:

Work in Process—Machining	XXXX	
Work in Process—Assembly	XXXX	
Factory Labor		XXXX
(To assign factory labor to production)		

Manufacturing Overhead Costs

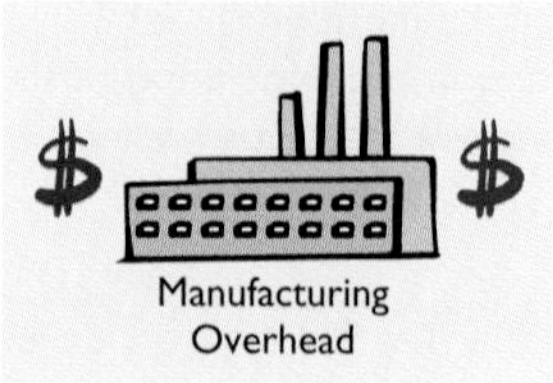

The objective in assigning overhead in a process cost system is to allocate the overhead costs to the production departments on an objective and equitable basis. That basis is the activity that "drives" or causes the costs. A primary driver of overhead costs in continuous manufacturing operations is **machine time used,** not direct labor. Thus, **machine hours are widely used** in allocating manufacturing overhead costs. The entry to allocate overhead to the two processes is:

Work in Process—Machining	XXXX	
Work in Process—Assembly	XXXX	
Manufacturing Overhead		XXXX
(To assign overhead to production)		

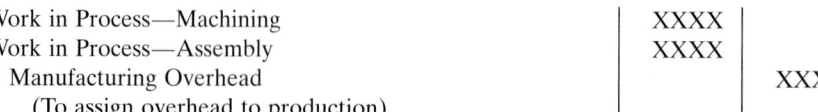

ACCOUNTING IN ACTION *Business Insight*

In one of **Caterpillar's** automated cost centers, work is fed into the cost center, processed by robotic machines, and transferred to the next cost center without human intervention. One person tends all of the machines and spends more time maintaining machines than operating them. In such cases, overhead rates based on direct labor hours may be misleading. Surprisingly, some companies continue to assign manufacturing overhead on the basis of direct labor despite the fact that there is no cause-and-effect relationship between labor and overhead.

Transfer to Next Department

At the end of the month, an entry is needed to record the cost of the goods transferred out of the department. In this case, the transfer is to the Assembly Department, and the following entry is made:

Work in Process—Assembly	XXXXX	
Work in Process—Machining		XXXXX
(To record transfer of units to the Assembly Department)		

Transfer to Finished Goods

The units completed in the Assembly Department are transferred to the finished goods warehouse. The entry for this transfer is as follows.

Finished Goods Inventory	XXXXX	
Work in Process—Assembly		XXXXX
(To record transfer of units to finished goods)		

Transfer to Cost of Goods Sold

When finished goods are sold, the entry to record the cost of goods sold is as follows.

Cost of Goods Sold	XXXXX	
Finished Goods Inventory		XXXXX
(To record cost of units sold)		

BEFORE YOU GO ON...

REVIEW IT

1. What type of manufacturing companies might use a process cost accounting system?
2. What are the principal similarities and differences between a job order cost system and a process cost system?

DO IT

Ruth Company manufactures ZEBO through two processes: Blending and Bottling. In June, raw materials used were Blending $18,000 and Bottling $4,000. Factory labor costs were Blending $12,000 and Bottling $5,000. Manufacturing overhead costs were Blending $6,000 and Bottling $2,500. Units completed at a cost of $19,000 in the Blending Department are transferred to the Bottling Department. Units completed at a cost of $11,000 in the Bottling Department are transferred to Finished Goods. Journalize the assignment of these costs to the two processes and the transfer of units as appropriate.

ACTION PLAN

- In process cost accounting, keep separate work in process accounts for each process.
- When the costs are assigned to production, debit the separate work in process accounts.
- Transfer cost of completed units to the next process or to Finished Goods.

SOLUTION: The entries are:

Work in Process—Blending	18,000	
Work in Process—Bottling	4,000	
Raw Materials Inventory		22,000
(To record materials used)		
Work in Process—Blending	12,000	
Work in Process—Bottling	5,000	
Factory Labor		17,000
(To assign factory labor to production)		
Work in Process—Blending	6,000	
Work in Process—Bottling	2,500	
Manufacturing Overhead		8,500
(To assign overhead to production)		
Work in Process—Bottling	19,000	
Work in Process—Blending		19,000
(To record transfer of units to the Bottling Department)		
Finished Goods Inventory	11,000	
Work in Process—Bottling		11,000
(To record transfer of units to finished goods)		

Related exercise material: BE22-1, BE22-2, BE22-3, E22-7, and E22-10.

THE NAVIGATOR

EQUIVALENT UNITS

STUDY OBJECTIVE 5

Compute equivalent units.

Suppose you were asked to compute the cost of instruction at your college per full-time equivalent student. You are provided the following information.

Illustration 22-6

Information for full-time student example

Costs:	
Total cost of instruction	$900,000
Student population:	
Full-time students	900
Part-time students	1,000

Part-time students take 60 percent of the classes of a full-time student during the year. To compute the number of full-time equivalent students per year, you would make the following computation.

Illustration 22-7

Full-time equivalent unit computation

Full-time Students	+	Equivalent Units of Part-time Students	=	Full-time Equivalent Students
900	+	(60% × 1,000)	=	1,500

The cost of instruction per full-time equivalent student is therefore the total cost of instruction ($900,000) divided by the number of full-time equivalent students (1,500), which is $600 ($900,000 ÷ 1,500).

In a process cost system, the same idea, called equivalent units of production, is used. **Equivalent units of production** measure the work done during the period, expressed in fully completed units. This concept is used to determine the cost per unit of completed product.

WEIGHTED-AVERAGE METHOD

The formula to compute equivalent units of production is as follows.

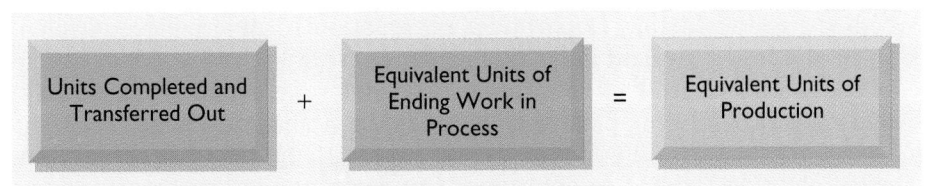

Illustration 22-8

Equivalent units of production formula

Units Completed and Transferred Out	+	Equivalent Units of Ending Work in Process	=	Equivalent Units of Production

To better understand this concept of equivalent units, consider the following two examples.

> **Example 1:** The Blending Department's entire output during the period consists of ending work in process of 4,000 units which are 60 percent complete as to materials, labor, and overhead. The equivalent units of production for the Blending Department are therefore 2,400 units (4,000 × 60%).

> **Example 2:** The Packaging Department's output during the period consists of 10,000 units completed and transferred out, and 5,000 units in ending work in process which are 70 percent completed. The equivalent units of production are therefore 13,500 [10,000 + (5,000 × 70%)].

This method of computing equivalent units is referred to as the **weighted-average method**. It considers the degree of completion (weighting) of the units completed and transferred out and the ending work in process. It is the method most widely used in practice. A lesser used method, called the FIFO method, is discussed in advanced cost accounting courses.

REFINEMENTS ON THE WEIGHTED-AVERAGE METHOD

Kellogg Company has produced Eggo® Waffles since 1970. Three departments are used to produce these waffles: Mixing, Baking, and Freezing and Packaging. In the Mixing Department dry ingredients, including flour, salt, and baking powder, are mixed with liquid ingredients, including eggs and vegetable oil, to make waffle batter. Information related to the Mixing Department at the end of June is provided in Illustration 22-9.

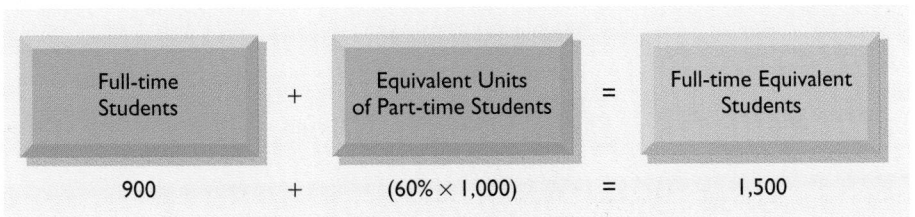

Illustration 22-9

Information for Mixing Department

Mixing Department

		Percentage Complete	
	Physical Units	**Materials**	**Conversion Costs**
Work in process, June 1	100,000	100%	70%
Started into production	800,000		
Total units	900,000		
Units transferred out	700,000		
Work in process, June 30	200,000	100%	60%
Total units	900,000		

HELPFUL HINT
Question: When are separate unit cost computations needed for materials and conversion costs? Answer: Whenever the two types of costs do not occur in the process at the same time.

Illustration 22-9 indicates that the beginning work in process is 100 percent complete as to materials cost and 70 percent complete as to conversion costs. In other words, both the dry and liquid ingredients (materials) are added at the beginning of the process to make Eggo® Waffles. The conversion costs (labor and overhead) related to the mixing of these ingredients were incurred uniformly and are 70 percent complete. The ending work in process is 100 percent complete as to materials cost and 60 percent complete as to conversion costs.

We then use the Mixing Department information to determine equivalent units. **In computing equivalent units, the beginning work in process is not part of the equivalent units of production formula.** The units transferred out to the Baking Department are fully complete as to both materials and conversion costs. The ending work in process is fully complete as to materials, but only 60 percent complete as to conversion cost. **Two equivalent unit computations are therefore necessary:** one for materials and the other for conversion costs. Illustration 22-10 shows these computations.

Illustration 22-10

Computation of equivalent units—Mixing Department

	Equivalent Units	
	Materials	**Conversion Costs**
Units transferred out	700,000	700,000
Work in process, June 30		
200,000 × 100%	200,000	
200,000 × 60%		120,000
Total equivalent units	900,000	820,000

The earlier formula used to compute equivalent units of production can be refined to show the computations for materials and for conversion costs, as follows.

Illustration 22-11

Refined equivalent unit of production formula

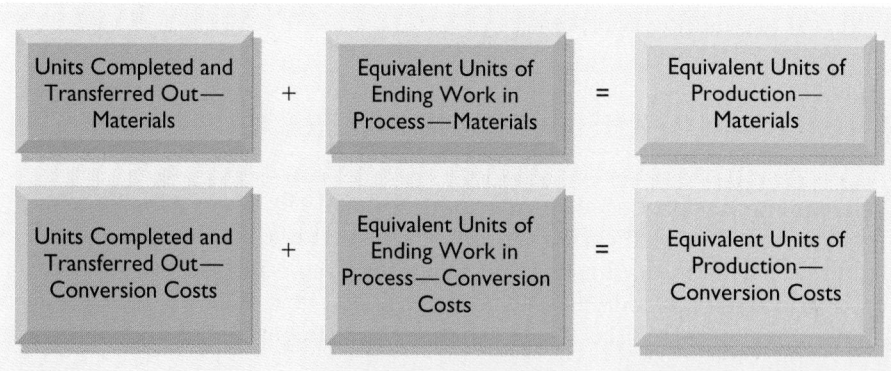

Units Completed and Transferred Out—Materials + Equivalent Units of Ending Work in Process—Materials = Equivalent Units of Production—Materials

Units Completed and Transferred Out—Conversion Costs + Equivalent Units of Ending Work in Process—Conversion Costs = Equivalent Units of Production—Conversion Costs

PRODUCTION COST REPORT

STUDY OBJECTIVE 6

Explain the four steps necessary to prepare a production cost report.

As mentioned earlier, a production cost report is prepared for each department in a process cost system. A **production cost report** is the key document used by management to understand the activities in a department. It shows the production quantity and cost data related to that department. For example, in producing Eggo® Waffles, **Kellogg Company** would have three production cost reports: Mixing, Baking, and Freezing and Packaging. Illustration 22-12 shows the flow of costs to make an Eggo® Waffle and the related production cost reports for each department.

Illustration 22-12

Flow of costs in making Eggo® Waffles

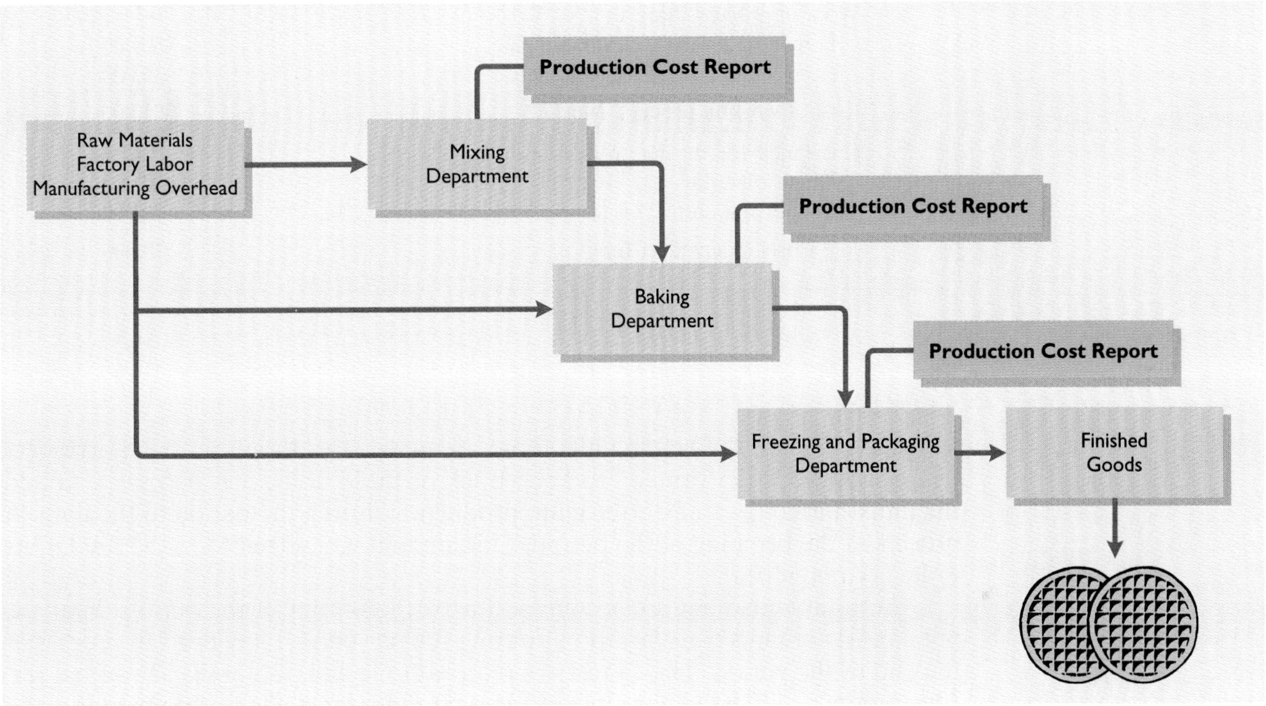

In order to be ready to complete a production cost report, the company must perform four steps:

1. Compute the physical unit flow.
2. Compute the equivalent units of production.
3. Compute unit production costs.
4. Prepare a cost reconciliation schedule.

As a whole, these four steps make up the process costing system. The next section explores these steps in an extended example.

COMPREHENSIVE EXAMPLE OF PROCESS COSTING

Assumed data for the Mixing Department at **Kellogg Company** for the month of June are shown in Illustration 22-13. We will use this information to complete a production cost report for the Mixing Department.

Illustration 22-13

Unit and cost data—Mixing Department

Mixing Department	
Units:	
Work in process, June 1	100,000
Direct materials: 100% complete	
Conversion costs: 70% complete	
Units started into production during June	800,000
Units completed and transferred out to Baking Department	700,000
Work in process, June 30	200,000
Direct materials: 100% complete	
Conversion costs: 60% complete	
Costs:	
Work in process, June 1	
Direct materials: 100% complete	$50,000
Conversion costs: 70% complete	35,000
Cost of work in process, June 1	$85,000
Costs incurred during production in June	
Direct materials	$400,000
Conversion costs	170,000
Costs incurred in June	$570,000

COMPUTE THE PHYSICAL UNIT FLOW (STEP 1)

Physical units are the actual units to be accounted for during a period, irrespective of any work performed. To keep track of these units, it is necessary to add the units started (or transferred) into production during the period to the units in process at the begining of the period. This amount is referred to as the **total units to be accounted for**.

The total units then are accounted for by the output of the period. The output consists of units transferred out during the period and any units in process at the end of the period. This amount is referred to as the **total units accounted for**. Illustration 22-14 shows the flow of physical units for Kellogg Company for the month of June for the Mixing Department.

Illustration 22-14

Physical unit flow—Mixing Department

Mixing Department	Physical Units
Units to be accounted for	
Work in process, June 1	100,000
Started (transferred) into production	800,000
Total units	**900,000**
Units accounted for	
Completed and transferred out	700,000
Work in process, June 30	200,000
Total units	**900,000**

The records indicate that 900,000 units must be accounted for in the Mixing Department. Of this sum, 700,000 units were transferred to the Baking Department and 200,000 units were still in process.

COMPUTE EQUIVALENT UNITS OF PRODUCTION (STEP 2)

Once the physical flow of the units is established, it is necessary to measure the Mixing Department's productivity in terms of equivalent units of production. In the Mixing Department, materials are added at the beginning of the process, and conversion costs are incurred uniformly during the process. Thus, two computations of equivalent units are required: one for materials and one for conversion costs. The equivalent unit computation is as follows.

HELPFUL HINT
Materials are not always added at the beginning of the process. For example, materials are sometimes added uniformly during the process.

Illustration 22-15
Computation of equivalent units—Mixing Department

	Equivalent Units	
	Materials	**Conversion Costs**
Units transferred out	700,000	700,000
Work in process, June 30		
200,000 × 100%	200,000	
200,000 × 60%		120,000
Total equivalent units	**900,000**	**820,000**

Remember that the beginning work in process is ignored in this computation.

COMPUTE UNIT PRODUCTION COSTS (STEP 3)

Armed with the knowledge of the equivalent units of production, we can now compute the unit production costs. **Unit production costs** are costs expressed in terms of equivalent units of production. When equivalent units of production are different for materials and conversion costs, three unit costs are computed: (1) materials, (2) conversion, and (3) total manufacturing.

The computation of total materials cost related to Eggo® Waffles is as follows.

Illustration 22-16
Materials cost computation

Work in process, June 1	
Direct materials cost	$ 50,000
Costs added to production during June	
Direct materials cost	400,000
Total materials cost	**$450,000**

The computation of unit materials cost is as follows.

Illustration 22-17
Unit materials cost computation

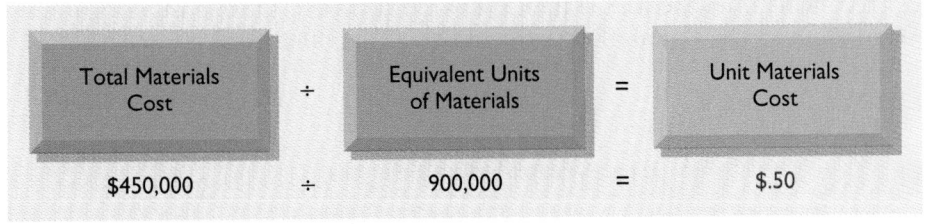

Total Materials Cost	÷	Equivalent Units of Materials	=	Unit Materials Cost
$450,000	÷	900,000	=	$.50

The computation of total conversion costs is as follows.

Illustration 22-18
Conversion costs computation

Work in process, June 1	
Conversion costs	$ 35,000
Costs added to production during June	
Conversion costs	170,000
Total conversion costs	**$205,000**

The computation of unit conversion cost is as follows.

Illustration 22-19
Unit conversion cost computation

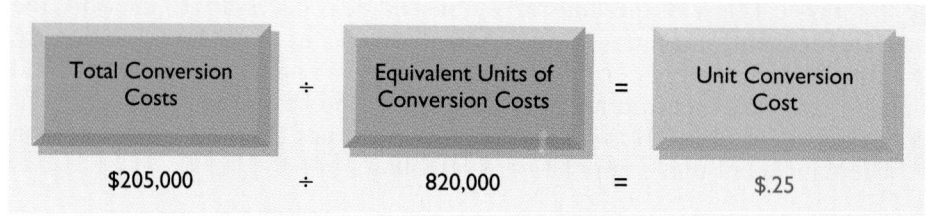

Total Conversion Costs	÷	Equivalent Units of Conversion Costs	=	Unit Conversion Cost
$205,000	÷	820,000	=	$.25

Total manufacturing cost per unit is therefore computed as follows.

Illustration 22-20
Total manufacturing cost per unit

Unit Materials Cost	+	Unit Conversion Cost	=	Total Manufacturing Cost per Unit
$.50	+	$.25	=	$.75

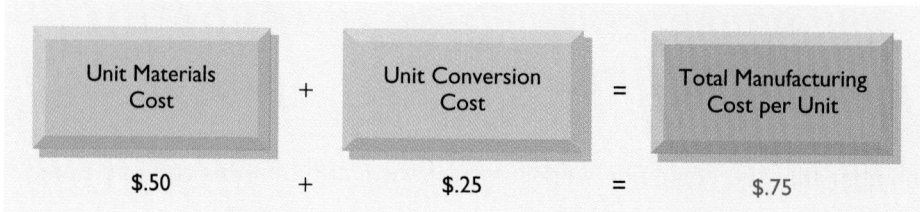

PREPARE A COST RECONCILIATION SCHEDULE (STEP 4)

We are now ready to determine the cost of goods transferred out of the Mixing Department to the Baking Department and the costs in ending work in process. The total costs that were charged to the Mixing Department in June are as follows.

Illustration 22-21
Costs charged to Mixing Department

Costs to be accounted for	
Work in process, June 1	$ 85,000
Started into production	570,000
Total costs	$655,000

The total costs charged to the Mixing Department in June are therefore $655,000. A cost reconciliation schedule is then prepared to assign these costs to (1) units transferred out to the Baking Department and (2) ending work in process.

Illustration 22-22
Cost reconciliation schedule—Mixing Department

Mixing Department
Cost Reconciliation Schedule

Costs accounted for		
Transferred out (700,000 × $0.75)		$525,000
Work in process, June 30		
Materials (200,000 × $0.50)	$100,000	
Conversion costs (120,000 × $0.25)	30,000	130,000
Total costs		$655,000

The total manufacturing cost per unit, $0.75, is used in costing the units completed and transferred to the Baking Department. In contrast, the unit cost of materials and the unit cost of conversion are needed in costing units in process. The **cost reconciliation schedule** shows that the **total costs accounted for** (Illustration 22-22) equal the **total costs to be accounted for** (see Illustration 22-21).

PREPARING THE PRODUCTION COST REPORT

STUDY OBJECTIVE 7

Prepare a production cost report.

At this point, we are ready to prepare the production cost report for the Mixing Department. As indicated earlier, this report is an internal document for management that shows production quantity and cost data for a production department.

There are four steps in preparing a production cost report. They are: (1) Prepare a physical unit schedule. (2) Compute equivalent units. (3) Compute unit costs. (4) Prepare a cost reconciliation schedule. The production cost report for the Mixing Department is shown in Illustration 22-23. The four steps are identified in the report.

Illustration 22-23

Production cost report

Mixing Department
Production Cost Report
For the Month Ended June 30, 2002

	Physical Units	Equivalent Units: Materials	Equivalent Units: Conversion Costs	
	Step 1	Step 2		
QUANTITIES				
Units to be accounted for				
Work in process, June 1	100,000			
Started into production	800,000			
Total units	900,000			
Units accounted for				
Transferred out	700,000	700,000	700,000	
Work in process, June 30	200,000	200,000	120,000	(200,000 × 60%)
Total units	900,000	900,000	820,000	

COSTS		Materials	Conversion Costs	Total
Unit costs Step 3				
Costs in June	(a)	$450,000	$205,000	$655,000
Equivalent units	(b)	900,000	820,000	
Unit costs [(a) ÷ (b)]		$0.50	$0.25	$0.75
Costs to be accounted for				
Work in process, June 1				$ 85,000
Started into production				570,000
Total costs				$655,000
Cost Reconciliation Schedule Step 4				
Costs accounted for				
Transferred out (700,000 × $0.75)				$525,000
Work in process, June 30				
Materials (200,000 × $0.50)			$100,000	
Conversion costs (120,000 × $0.25)			30,000	130,000
Total costs				$655,000

HELPFUL HINT
What are the two self-checks in the report? Answer: (1) Total physical units accounted for must equal the total units to be accounted for. (2) Total costs accounted for must equal the total costs to be accounted for.

HELPFUL HINT
Because production cost reports are used as the basis for evaluating department productivity and efficiency, the units, costs, and computations reported therein should be independently accumulated and analyzed to prevent misstatements by department managers.

Production cost reports provide a basis for evaluating the productivity of a department. In addition, the cost data can be used to assess whether unit costs and total costs are reasonable. By comparing the quantity and cost data with predetermined goals, top management can also judge whether current performance is meeting planned objectives.

FINAL COMMENTS

Companies often use a combination of a process cost and a job order cost system, called **operations costing**. Operations costing is similar to process costing in that standardized methods are used to manufacture the product. At the same time, the product may have some customized, individual features that require the use of a job order cost system. Consider, for example, the automobile manufacturer **Ford Motor Company**. Each automobile at a given plant goes through the same assembly line, but different materials (such as seat coverings, paint, and tinted glass) may be used for different automobiles. Similarly, **Kellogg's** Pop-Tarts Toaster Pastries® go through numerous processes—mixing, filling, baking, frosting, and packaging. The pastry dough, however, comes in three flavors—plain, chocolate, and graham—and fillings include Smucker's® real fruit, chocolate fudge, vanilla creme, brown sugar cinnamon, and S'mores.

A cost–benefit tradeoff occurs as a company decides which costing system to use. A job order system, for example, provides detailed information related to the cost of the product. Because each job has its own distinguishing characteristics, an accurate cost per job can be provided. This information is useful in controlling costs and pricing products. However, the cost of implementing a job order cost system is often expensive because of the accounting costs involved.

On the other hand, for a company like **Intel**, which makes computer chips, is there a benefit in knowing whether the cost of the one hundredth chip produced is different from the one thousandth chip produced? Probably not. An average cost of the product will suffice for control and pricing purposes. In summary, when deciding to use one of these systems, or a combination system, a company must weigh the cost of implementing the system against the benefits from the additional information provided.

BEFORE YOU GO ON...

REVIEW IT

1. How do physical units differ from equivalent units of production?
2. What are the formulas for computing unit costs of production?
3. How are costs assigned to units transferred out and in process?
4. What are the four sections of a production cost report?
5. What is operations costing, and in what circumstances would a manufacturer use operations costing instead of process costing?
6. Describe the cost-benefit tradeoff involved in deciding what costing system to use.

DO IT

In March, Rodayo Manufacturing had the following unit production costs: materials $6 and conversion costs $9. On March 1, it had zero work in process. During March, 12,000 units were transferred out, and 800 units that were 25 percent complete as to conversion costs and 100 percent complete as to materials were in ending work in process at March 31. Assign the costs to the units transferred out and in process.

ACTION PLAN

- Assign the total manufacturing cost of $15 per unit to the 12,000 units transferred.
- Assign the materials cost and conversion cost based on equivalent units of production to units in process.

SOLUTION: The assignment of costs is as follows:

Costs accounted for		
Transferred out (12,000 × $15)		$180,000
Work in process, March 31		
Materials (800 × $6)	$4,800	
Conversion costs (200[a] × $9)	1,800	6,600
Total costs		$186,600

[a]800 × 25%

Related exercise material: BE22-4, BE22-5, BE22-6, BE22-7, BE22-8, E22-1, E22-2, E22-4, E22-6, E22-8, E22-9, and E22-10.

THE NAVIGATOR

CONTEMPORARY DEVELOPMENTS

As indicated in Chapter 20, two contemporary developments in managerial accounting are just-in-time processing and activity-based costing. We explain these innovations in the following sections.

JUST-IN-TIME PROCESSING

STUDY OBJECTIVE 8

Explain just-in-time (JIT) processing.

Traditionally, continuous process manufacturing has been based on a **just-in-case** philosophy: Inventories of raw materials are maintained **just in case** some items are of poor quality or a key supplier is shut down by a strike. Subassembly parts are manufactured and stored **just in case** they are needed later in the manufacturing process. Finished goods are completed and stored **just in case** unexpected and rush customer orders are received. This philosophy often results in a **"push approach"**: Raw materials and subassembly parts are pushed through each process. Traditional processing often results in the buildup of extensive manufacturing inventories.

Primarily in response to foreign competition, many U.S. firms have switched to **just-in-time (JIT) processing**. JIT manufacturing is dedicated to producing the right products (or parts) at the right time as they are needed. Under JIT processing, raw materials are received **just in time** for use in production, subasssembly parts are completed **just in time** for use in finished goods, and finished goods are completed **just in time** to be sold. Illustration 22-24 shows the sequence of activities in just-in-time processing.

Illustration 22-24

Just-in-time processing

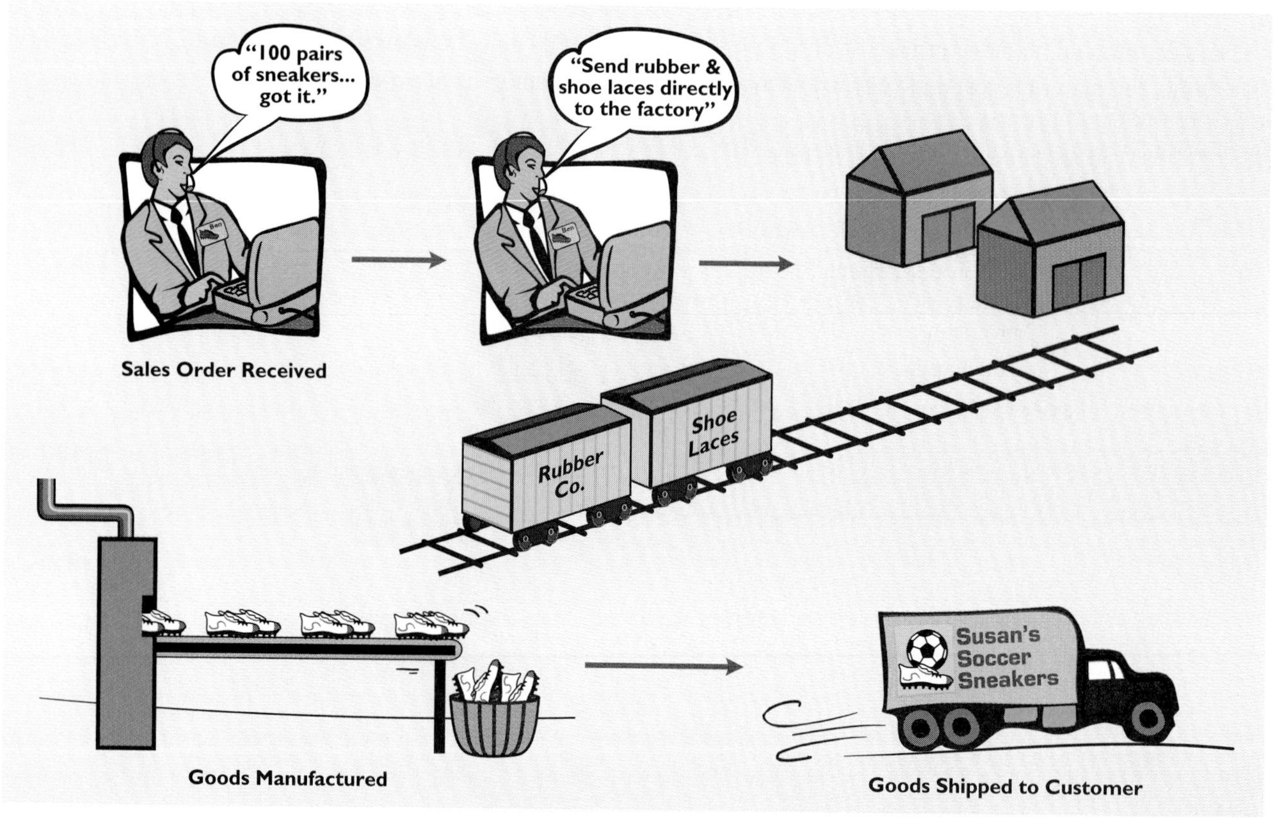

Objective of JIT Processing

A primary objective of JIT is to eliminate all manufacturing inventories. Inventories are considered to have an adverse effect on net income because they tie up funds and storage space that could be made available for more productive purposes. JIT strives to eliminate inventories by using a **"pull approach"** in manufacturing: At the final process (work station) a signal is sent via a computer to the next preceding work station. This signal indicates the exact materials (parts and subassemblies) needed to complete the production of a specified product for a specified time period (such as an eight-hour shift). The preceding process, in turn,

ACCOUNTING IN ACTION — e Business Insight

Electronic data interchange (EDI) is the electronic transmission of routine, repetitive business documents directly between computer systems of separate companies doing business with each other. **Gerber Products Company** uses EDI to coordinate its inventory control efforts with those of its grocery store customers. An EDI application feeds data to Gerber on sales of its products. The data are used by the company's supply chain management software to schedule new deliveries and to aid in forecasting production needs. In addition, events such as in-store promotions are automatically sent to Gerber inventory managers.

SOURCE: Excerpts from E. Turban, R. K. Rainer, Jr., and R. E. Potter, *Introduction to Information Technology* (New York: John Wiley and Sons, 2001), p. 199.

sends its signal to other processes back up the line. The goal is a smooth continuous flow in the manufacturing process and no buildup of inventories at any point.

Elements of JIT Processing

There are three important elements in JIT processing:

1. A company must have **dependable suppliers**. Suppliers must be willing to deliver on short notice exact quantities of raw materials according to precise quality specifications (even including multiple deliveries within the same day). Suppliers must also be willing to deliver the raw materials at specified work stations rather than at a central receiving department. This type of purchasing requires constant and direct communication. Such communication is facilitated by an online computer linkage between the company and its suppliers.
2. A **multiskilled workforce** must be developed. Under JIT, machines are often strategically grouped around work cells or work stations. Much of the work is automated. As a result, one worker may have the responsibility to operate and maintain several different types of machines.
3. A **total quality control system** must be established throughout the manufacturing operations. Total quality control means **no defects**. Since only required quantities are signaled by the **pull approach**, any defects at any work station will shut down operations at subsequent work stations. Total quality control requires continuous monitoring by both employees and supervisors at each work station.

Benefits of JIT Processing

The major benefits of JIT processing are:

1. Manufacturing inventories are significantly reduced or eliminated.
2. Product quality is enhanced.
3. Rework costs and inventory storage costs are reduced or eliminated.
4. Production cost savings are realized from the improved flow of goods through the processes.

One of the major accounting benefits of JIT is the elimination of raw materials and work in process inventory accounts. In place of these accounts is **one account**, Raw and In-Process Inventory. All materials and conversion costs are charged to this account. Because of the reduction (or elimination) of in-process inventories, the computation of equivalent units of production is simplified.

ACCOUNTING IN ACTION *Business Insight*

JIT first hit the United States in the early 1980s when it was adopted by automobile companies to meet foreign competition. It is now being successfully used in many companies, including **General Electric**, **Caterpillar**, and **Harley-Davidson**. The effects in most cases have been dramatic. For example, after using JIT for two years, a major division of **Hewlett-Packard** found that work-in-process inventories (in dollars) were down 82 percent, scrap/rework costs were down 30 percent, space utilization was down 40 percent, and labor efficiency improved 50 percent. As indicated, JIT not only reduces inventory but also enables a manufacturer to produce a better product faster and with less waste.

ACTIVITY-BASED COSTING

STUDY OBJECTIVE 9

Explain activity-based costing (ABC).

Activity-based costing (ABC) is a development in product costing that has received much attention in recent years. **Activity-based costing** focuses on the activities performed in producing a product. An ABC system is similar to conventional costing systems in accounting for direct materials and direct labor, but it differs in regard to manufacturing overhead.

In a conventional cost system, a **single unit-level** basis is used to allocate overhead costs to products. The basis may be direct labor or machine hours used to manufacture the product. The assumption in this approach is that as volume of units produced increases, so does the cost of overhead. However, in some cases, the overhead cost is unrelated to the number of units produced.

In ABC, the cost of a product is equal to the sum of the costs of all activities performed to manufacture it. ABC recognizes that to have accurate and meaningful cost data, **more than one basis** of allocating activity costs to products is needed.

In selecting the allocation basis, ABC seeks to identify the **cost drivers** that measure the activities performed on the product. A cost driver may be any factor that has a direct cause–effect relationship with the resources consumed. Examples of activities and possible cost drivers are as follows.

Illustration 22-25

Activities and cost drivers in ABC

Activity	Cost Driver
Ordering raw materials	Ordering hours; number of orders
Receiving raw materials	Receiving hours; number of shipments
Materials handling	Number of requisitions; weight of materials; handling hours
Production scheduling	Number of orders
Machine setups	Setup hours; number of setups
Machining (fabricating, assembling, etc.)	Machine hours
Quality control inspections	Number of inspections
Factory supervision	Number of employees

Two important assumptions must be met in order to obtain accurate product costs under ABC:

1. All overhead costs related to the activity must be driven by the cost driver used to assign costs to products.
2. All overhead costs related to the activity should respond proportionally to changes in the activity level of the cost driver.

For example, if there is little or no correlation between changes in the cost driver and consumption of the overhead cost, inaccurate product costs are inevitable. A case example in the use of ABC is explained and illustrated in the appendix at the end of this chapter.

Activity-based costing may be used with either a job order or a process cost accounting system. The primary benefit of ABC is more accurate and meaningful product costing. Also, improved cost data about an activity can lead to reduced costs for the activity. In sum, ABC makes managers realize that it is activities and not products that determine the profitability of a company.

ACCOUNTING IN ACTION *International Insight*

Contrary to popular opinion, ABC was not a Japanese invention. ABC was developed in France in the 1950s, but most Japanese corporations have used a form of ABC since that time. In Japan, ABC is called "target costing." Exhaustive market research is done on a new product to determine a price the market will accept. This becomes the target cost that designers, engineers, and production managers must meet. The use of target costing has resulted in products that are priced properly and profitably and that promptly win market share.

BEFORE YOU GO ON...

REVIEW IT

1. What are the principal accounting effects of just-in-time (JIT) processing?
2. What are the primary differences between activity-based costing (ABC) and traditional costing?

A LOOK BACK AT OUR FEATURE STORY

Refer back to the Feature Story about **Ben & Jerry's Homemade Inc.** at the beginning of the chapter, and answer the following questions.

1. How many processes are used by Ben & Jerry's to make ice cream? Identify the processes.
2. Why does Ben & Jerry's use a process costing system rather than a job order system?
3. How does the production report satisfy the needs of the department heads?

SOLUTION

1. The three processes used by Ben & Jerry's to make ice cream are (1) mixing, (2) prepping, and (3) pinting.
2. Ben & Jerry's uses a process costing system because making ice cream is continuous process manufacturing. It is mass production of many homogeneous units. Making ice cream fits the process manufacturing characteristics: (1) once production begins, it continues until the finished product emerges, and (2) the finished products will all have been processed in the same manner with precisely the same amount of materials, labor, and overhead. Each finished pint of ice cream is indistinguishable one from another.
3. The production report provides current cost data that can be compared with previous cost data and with budget expectations so that efficiency can be evaluated. The production report shows how much was processed and at what cost. These data are needed by department heads to manage and control production.

THE NAVIGATOR

DEMONSTRATION PROBLEM

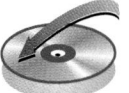

Additional Demonstration Problem

Essence Company manufactures a high-end after-shave lotion, called Eternity, in 10-ounce plastic bottles. Because the market for after-shave lotion is highly competitive, the company is very concerned about keeping its costs under control. Eternity is manufactured through three processes: mixing, filling, and corking. Materials are added at the beginning of the process, and labor and overhead are incurred uniformly throughout each process. The company uses a weighted-average method to cost its product. A partially completed production cost report for the month of May for the Mixing Department is shown on the next page.

ESSENCE COMPANY
Mixing Department
Production Cost Report
For the Month Ended May 31, 2002

QUANTITIES	Physical Units	Equivalent Units: Materials	Equivalent Units: Conversion Costs	
Units to be accounted for	Step 1	Step 2		
Work in process, May 1	1,000			
Started into production	2,000			
Total units	3,000			
Units accounted for				
Transferred out	2,200	?	?	
Work in process, May 31	800	?	?	
Total units	3,000	?	?	
COSTS		**Materials**	**Conversion Costs**	**Total**
Unit costs Step 3				
Costs in May	(a)	?	?	?
Equivalent units	(b)	?	?	
Unit costs [(a) ÷ (b)]		?	?	?
Costs to be accounted for				
Work in process, May 1				$ 56,300
Started into production				119,320
Total costs				$175,620
Cost Reconciliation Schedule Step 4				
Costs accounted for				
Transferred out				?
Work in process, May 31				
Materials			?	
Conversion costs			?	?
Total costs				?

Additional information:

Work in process, May 1, 1000 units		
Materials cost, 1,000 units (100% complete)	$49,100	
Conversion costs, 1,000 units (70% complete)	7,200	$ 56,300
Materials cost for May, 2,000 units		$100,000

Work in process, May 31, 800 units, 100% complete as to materials and 50% complete as to conversion costs.

Instructions

(a) Prepare a production cost report for the Mixing Department for the month of May.

(b) Prepare the journal entry to record the transfer of goods from the Mixing Department to the Filling Department.

(c) Explain why Essence Company is using a process cost system to account for its costs.

SOLUTION

(a) A completed production cost report for the Mixing Department is shown on the next page. Computations to support the amounts reported follow the report.

ESSENCE COMPANY
Mixing Department
Production Cost Report
For the Month Ended May 31, 2002

QUANTITIES	Physical Units	Equivalent Units: Materials	Equivalent Units: Conversion Costs
Units to be accounted for	Step 1	Step 2	
Work in process, May 1	1,000		
Started into production	2,000		
Total units	3,000		
Units accounted for			
Transferred out	2,200	2,200	2,200
Work in process, May 31	800	800	400 (800 × 50%)
Total units	3,000	3,000	2,600

COSTS		Materials	Conversion Costs	Total
Unit costs Step 3				
Costs in May	(a)	$149,100	$26,520	$175,620
Equivalent units	(b)	3,000	2,600	
Unit costs [(a) ÷ (b)]		$49.70	$10.20	$59.90
Costs to be accounted for				
Work in process, May 1				$ 56,300
Started into production				119,320
Total costs				$175,620
Cost Reconciliation Schedule Step 4				
Costs accounted for				
Transferred out (2,200 × $59.90)				$131,780
Work in process, May 31				
Materials (800 × $49.70)			$39,760	
Conversion costs (400 × $10.20)			4,080	43,840
Total costs				$175,620

Additional computations to support production cost report data:
Materials cost—$49,100 + $100,000
Conversion costs—$7,200 + $19,320 ($119,320 − $100,000)

(b) Work in Process—Filling	131,780	
Work in Process—Mixing		131,780

(c) Process cost systems are used to apply costs to similar products that are mass-produced in a continuous fashion. Essence Company uses a process cost system: production of the after-shave lotion, once it begins, continues until the after-shave lotion emerges. The processing is the same for the entire run—with precisely the same amount of materials, labor, and overhead. Each bottle of Eternity after-shave lotion is indistinguishable from another.

ACTION PLAN

- Compute the physical unit flow—that is, the total units to be accounted for.
- Compute the equivalent units of production.
- Compute the unit production costs, expressed in terms of equivalent units of production.
- Prepare a cost reconciliation schedule, which shows that the total costs accounted for equal the total costs to be accounted for.

THE NAVIGATOR

SUMMARY OF STUDY OBJECTIVES

1. *Understand who uses process cost systems.* Process cost systems are used by companies that mass-produce similar products in a continuous fashion. Once production begins, it continues until the finished product emerges. Each unit of finished product is indistinguishable from every other unit.

2. *Explain the similarities and differences between job order cost and process cost systems.* Job order cost systems are similar to process cost systems in three ways: (1) Both systems track the same cost elements—direct materials, direct labor, and manufacturing overhead. (2) Costs are accumulated in the same accounts—Raw Materials Inventory, Factory Labor, and Manufacturing Overhead. (3) Accumulated costs are assigned to the same accounts—Work in Process, Finished Goods Inventory, and Cost of Goods Sold. However, the method of assigning costs differs significantly.

There are four main differences between the two cost systems: (1) A process cost system uses separate accounts for each production department or manufacturing process, rather than only one work in process account used in a job order cost system. (2) In a process cost system, costs are summarized in a production cost report for each department. In a job cost system, costs are charged to individual jobs and summarized in a job cost sheet. (3) Costs are totaled at the end of a time period in a process cost system and at the completion of a job in a job cost system. (4) In a process cost system, unit cost is calculated as: Total manufacturing costs for the period ÷ Units produced during the period. Unit cost in a job cost system is: Total cost per job ÷ Units produced.

3. ***Explain the flow of costs in a process cost system.*** Manufacturing costs for raw materials, labor, and overhead are assigned to work in process accounts for various departments or manufacturing processes. The costs of units completed in a department are transferred from one department to another as those units move through the manufacturing process. The costs of completed work are transferred to Finished Goods Inventory. When inventory is sold, costs are transferred to Cost of Goods Sold.

4. ***Make the journal entries to assign manufacturing costs in a process cost system.*** Entries to assign the costs of raw materials, labor, and overhead consist of a credit to Raw Materials Inventory, Factory Labor, and Manufacturing Overhead, and a debit to Work in Process for each of the departments doing the processing. Entries to record the cost of goods transferred to another department are a credit to Work in Process for the department whose work is finished and a debit to the department to which the goods are transferred. The entry to record units completed and transferred to the warehouse is a credit for the department whose work is finished and a debit to Finished Goods Inventory. Finally, the entry to record the sale of goods is a credit to Finished Goods Inventory and a debit to Cost of Goods Sold.

5. ***Compute equivalent units.*** Equivalent units of production measure work done during a period, expressed in fully completed units. This concept is used to determine the cost per unit of completed product. Equivalent units are the sum of units completed and transferred out plus equivalent units of ending work in process.

6. ***Explain the four steps necessary to prepare a production cost report.*** The four steps to complete a production cost report are: (1) Compute the physical unit flow—that is, the total units to be accounted for. (2) Compute the equivalent units of production. (3) Compute the unit production costs, expressed in terms of equivalent units of production. (4) Prepare a cost reconciliation schedule, which shows that the total costs accounted for equal the total costs to be accounted for.

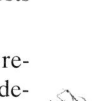

7. ***Prepare a production cost report.*** The production cost report contains both quantity and cost data for a production department. There are four sections in the report: (1) number of physical units, (2) equivalent units determination, (3) unit costs, and (4) cost reconciliation schedule.

8. ***Explain just-in-time (JIT) processing.*** JIT is a manufacturing technique dedicated to producing the right products at the right time as needed. One of the principal accounting effects is that a Raw and In-Process Inventory account replaces both the raw materials and work in process inventory accounts.

9. ***Explain activity-based costing (ABC).*** ABC is a method of product costing that focuses on the activities performed to produce products. It assigns the cost of the activities to products by using cost drivers that measure the activities performed. The primary objective of ABC is accurate and meaningful product costs.

THE NAVIGATOR

Key Term Matching Activity

GLOSSARY

Activity-based costing A cost accounting system that focuses on the activities performed in manufacturing a specific product. (p. 920).

Cost reconciliation schedule A schedule that shows that the total costs accounted for equal the total costs to be accounted for. (p. 915).

Equivalent units of production A measure of the work done during the period, expressed in fully completed units. (p. 909).

Just-in-time processing A processing system dedicated to producing the right products (or parts) as they are needed. (p. 917).

Operations costing A combination of a process cost and a job order cost system, in which products are manufactured primarily by standardized methods, with some customization. (p. 916).

Physical units Actual units to be accounted for during a period, irrespective of any work performed. (p. 912).

Process cost systems An accounting system used to apply costs to similar products that are mass-produced in a continuous fashion. (p. 902).

Production cost report An internal report for management that shows both production quantity and cost data for a production department. (p. 911).

Total units (costs) accounted for The sum of the units (costs) transferred out during the period plus the units (costs) in process at the end of the period. (pp. 912, 915).

Total units (costs) to be accounted for The sum of the units (costs) started (or transferred) into production during the period plus the units (costs) in process at the beginning of the period. (pp. 912, 915).

Unit production costs Costs expressed in terms of equivalent units of production. (p. 913).

Weighted-average method Method used to compute equivalent units of production which considers the degree of completion (weighting) of the units completed and transferred out and the ending work in process. (p. 909).

APPENDIX *Case Example of Traditional Costing versus Activity-Based Costing*

PRODUCTION AND COST DATA

STUDY OBJECTIVE 10

Apply activity-based costing to specific company data.

In this appendix we'll look at a case example of activity-based costing and compare that approach to traditional costing. Assume that Atlas Company produces two products, Product X and Product Y. Product X is a high-volume item totaling 25,000 units annually. Product Y is a low-volume item totaling only 5,000 units per year. Both products require one hour of direct labor for completion. Therefore, total direct labor hours are 30,000 (25,000 + 5,000). Expected annual manufacturing overhead costs are \$900,000. The overhead rate is \$30 (\$900,000 ÷ 30,000) per direct labor hour.

The direct materials cost per unit is \$40 for Product X and \$30 for Product Y. The direct labor cost is \$12 per unit for each product.

UNIT COSTS UNDER TRADITIONAL COSTING

The unit cost for each product under traditional costing is shown below.

Illustration 22A-1

Units costs—traditional costing

	Product	
Manufacturing Costs	**X**	**Y**
Direct materials	\$40	\$30
Direct labor	12	12
Overhead	30	30
Total unit cost	\$82	\$72

DETERMINING OVERHEAD RATES UNDER ABC

Analysis reveals that Atlas Company's expected annual overhead costs of \$900,000 relate to three activities—machine setups, machining, and inspections. The cost driver and overhead rate for each activity are shown in Illustration 22A-2.

Illustration 22A-2

Computing overhead rates—ABC

Activity	Cost Driver	Total Expected Overhead Cost	Total Expected Use of Driver	Overhead Rate
Machine setups	Number of setups	\$300,000	1,500	\$200
Machining	Machine hours	500,000	50,000	10
Inspections	Number of inspections	100,000	2,000	50

ASSIGNING OVERHEAD COSTS TO PRODUCTS UNDER ABC

In assigning costs, it is necessary to know the expected number of cost drivers for each product. Because of its low volume, Product Y requires more setups and inspections than Product X. The expected number of cost drivers for each product is as follows.

Illustration 22A-3

Expected number of cost drivers

Cost Driver	Product X	Product Y	Total Usage
Number of machine setups	500	1,000	1,500
Machine hours	30,000	20,000	50,000
Number of inspections	500	1,500	2,000

Using these data, the assignment of the expected annual overhead cost to each product is as follows.

Illustration 22A-4

Assignment of overhead costs to products

	Product X		Product Y		
Activity	**Number**	**Cost**	**Number**	**Cost**	**Total Cost**
Machine setups ($200)	500	$100,000	1,000	$200,000	$300,000
Machining ($10)	30,000	300,000	20,000	200,000	500,000
Inspections ($50)	500	25,000	1,500	75,000	100,000
Total assigned costs (a)		$425,000		$475,000	$900,000
Units produced (b)		25,000		5,000	
Overhead cost per unit [(a) ÷ (b)]		$17		$95	

These data show that under ABC, overhead costs are shifted from the high-volume product (Product X) to the low-volume product (Product Y). This shift results in more accurate costing for two reasons:

1. Low-volume products often require special handling, such as more machine setups and inspections, than high-volume products. This is true for Atlas Company. Thus, the low-volume product frequently is responsible for more overhead costs per unit than a high-volume product.

2. The overhead costs incurred by the low-volume product often are disproportionate to a traditional allocation base. For example, direct labor hours is usually a poor cost driver for assigning overhead costs to low-volume products. When overhead is properly assigned in ABC, it will usually increase the unit cost of low-volume products.

TECHNOLOGY IN ACTION

Many software packages designed especially for ABC costing are available for a personal computer or computer network. EASYABC developed by **ABC Technologies** includes three modules: overhead, activity, and cost object. The overhead module contains the overhead costs that are to be allocated to activities. In the activity module a user identifies the activities that are consumed by products. In the final module, the user defines the cost object such as a product, a customer, a product line, or any combination of the three. EASYABC also generates reports.

COMPARING UNIT COSTS

A comparison of unit manufacturing costs under traditional costing and ABC shows the following significant differences:

Illustration 22A-5

Comparison of unit product costs

	Traditional Costing		ABC	
	Product		Product	
Manufacturing Costs	X	Y	X	Y
Direct materials	$40	$30	$40	$ 30
Direct labor	12	12	12	12
Overhead	30	30	17	95
Total	$82	$72	$69	$137

The comparison shows that unit costs under traditional costing have been significantly distorted. The cost of Product X has been overstated $13 per unit ($82 − $69). The cost of Product Y has been understated $65 per unit ($137 − $72). The differences are attributable to how manufacturing overhead is assigned. A likely consequence of the differences is that Atlas Company has been overpricing Product X and possibly losing market share to competitors. It also has been sacrificing profitability by underpricing Product Y.

As illustrated in the above case, ABC involves the following steps.

1. Identify the major activities that pertain to the manufacture of specific products.
2. Accumulate manufacturing overhead costs by activities.
3. Identify the cost driver(s) that accurately measure(s) each activity's contribution to the finished product.
4. Assign manufacturing overhead costs for each activity to products, using the cost driver(s).

BENEFITS AND LIMITATIONS OF ACTIVITY-BASED COSTING

We have already seen that a primary benefit of ABC is more accurate product costing. In addition, ABC offers the following other benefits:

1. **Control over overhead costs** is enhanced. Many overhead costs are incurred directly by activities. Thus, managers become more aware of their responsibility to control the activities that generate the costs.
2. **Better management decisions** can be made. More accurate product costing should contribute to setting selling prices that will achieve desired profitability levels. The cost data also should be helpful in deciding whether to discontinue or expand a product line or whether to make or buy a component.

The principal disadvantages of ABC generally focus on two factors. First, **the expense of obtaining the cost data** required by the system is relatively high. ABC requires data that are not normally generated within a company. Examples of such data are the number of setups, inspections, orders placed, and orders received. In addition, many computations are involved in assigning overhead costs to individual products.

ACCOUNTING IN ACTION *Business Insight*

ABC enabled **Digital Communications Associates**, a computer hardware and software manufacturer, to discover why profit margins slipped from 18.6 percent to 8 percent over a three-year period. Digital boiled down 600 production activities to 136. ABC helped Digital and its 1,300 employees to bring costs under control.

Second, **ABC does not eliminate arbitrary assignments** of overhead. For example, plant-wide overhead costs such as depreciation, insurance, and property taxes on the factory building should be allocated to the activity centers in determining the cost of a product. With ABC, these allocations may be more difficult to do accurately because of the increased number of activity centers. As a result, accuracy of product costs could be adversely affected.

SUMMARY OF STUDY OBJECTIVE FOR APPENDIX

10. *Apply activity-based costing to specific company data.* In applying ABC, it is necessary to compute the overhead rate for each activity by dividing total expected overhead by the total expected usage of the cost driver. The overhead cost for each activity is then assigned to products on the basis of each product's use of the cost driver.

*Note: All **asterisked** Questions, Exercises, and Problems relate to material contained in the appendix to the chapter.

Chapter 22 Self-Test

SELF-STUDY QUESTIONS

Answers are at the end of the chapter.

(SO 1) **1.** Which of the following items is *not* a characteristic of a process cost system?
a. Once production begins, it continues until the finished product emerges.
b. The products produced are heterogeneous in nature.
c. The focus is on continually producing homogeneous products.
d. When the finished product emerges, all units have precisely the same amount of materials, labor, and overhead.

(SO 2) **2.** Indicate which of the following statements is *not* correct.
a. Both a job order and a process cost system track the same three manufacturing cost elements—direct materials, direct labor, and manufacturing overhead.
b. In a job order cost system, only one work in process account is used, whereas in a process cost system, multiple work in process accounts are used.
c. Manufacturing costs are accumulated the same way in a job order and in a process cost system.
d. Manufacturing costs are assigned the same way in a job order and in a process cost system.

(SO 3) **3.** In a process cost system, costs are assigned only:
a. to one work in process account.
b. to work in process and finished goods inventory.
c. to work in process, finished goods, and cost of goods sold.
d. to work in process accounts.

4. In making the journal entry to assign raw materials costs: (SO 4)
a. the debit is to Finished Goods Inventory.
b. the debit is often to two or more work in process accounts.
c. the credit is generally to two or more work in process accounts.
d. the credit is to Finished Goods Inventory.

5. The Mixing Department's output during the period consists of 20,000 units completed and transferred out, and 5,000 units in ending work in process 60% complete as to materials and conversion costs. Beginning inventory is 1,000 units, 40% complete as to materials and conversion costs. The equivalent units of production are: (SO 5)
a. 22,600.
b. 23,000.
c. 24,000.
d. 25,000.

6. In RYZ Company, there are zero units in beginning work in process, 7,000 units started into production, and 500 units in ending work in process 20% completed. The physical units to be accounted for are: (SO 6)
a. 7,000.
b. 7,360.
c. 7,600.
d. 7,340.

7. Stock Company has 2,000 units in beginning work in process, 20% complete as to conversion costs, 23,000 units transferred out to finished goods, and 3,000 units in ending work in process $33\frac{1}{3}\%$ complete as to conversion costs. The beginning and ending inventory is fully complete as to materials costs. Equivalent units for materials and conversion costs are, respectively: (SO 6)

a. 22,000, 24,000.
b. 24,000, 26,000.
c. 26,000, 24,000.
d. 26,000, 26,000.

(SO 6) **8.** Fortner Company has no beginning work in process; 9,000 units are transferred out and 3,000 units in ending work in process are one-third finished as to conversion costs and fully complete as to materials cost. If total materials cost is $60,000, the unit materials cost is:
a. $5.00.
b. $5.45 rounded.
c. $6.00.
d. No correct answer is given.

(SO 6) **9.** Largo Company has unit costs of $10 for materials and $30 for conversion costs. If there are 2,500 units in ending work in process, 40% complete as to conversion costs, and fully complete as to materials cost, the total cost assignable to the ending work in process inventory is:
a. $45,000.
b. $55,000.
c. $75,000.
d. $100,000.

(SO 7) **10.** A production cost report
a. is an external report.
b. shows costs charged to department and costs acounted for.
c. shows equivalent units of production but not physical units.
d. contains six sections.

11. Just-in-time processing (JIT): (SO 8)
a. strives to eliminate inventories.
b. uses a pull approach in manufacturing.
c. Neither of the above.
d. Both (a) and (b).

12. Activity-based costing (ABC): (SO 9)
a. can be used only in a process cost system.
b. focuses on units of production.
c. focuses on activities performed to produce a product.
d. uses only a single basis of allocation.

***13.** The overhead rate for Machine Setups is $100 per setup. Products A and B have 80 and 60 setups, respectively. The overhead assigned to each product is: (SO 10)
a. Product A $8,000, Product B $8,000.
b. Product A $8,000, Product B $6,000.
c. Product A $6,000, Product B $6,000.
d. Product A $6,000, Product B $8,000.

THE NAVIGATOR

QUESTIONS

1. Identify which costing system—job order or process cost—the following companies would use: (a) **Quaker Oats**, (b) **Ford Motor Company**, (c) **Kinko's Print Shop**, and (d) **Warner Bros. Motion Pictures**.
2. Contrast the primary focus of job order cost accounting and of process cost accounting.
3. What are the similarities between a job order and a process cost system?
4. Your roommate is confused about the features of process cost accounting. Identify and explain the distinctive features for your roommate.
5. Tina Turner believes there are no significant differences in the flow of costs between job order cost accounting and process cost accounting. Is Turner correct? Explain.
6. (a) What source documents are used in assigning (1) materials and (2) labor to production?
   (b) What criterion and basis are commonly used in allocating overhead to processes?
7. At Kun Company, overhead is assigned to production departments at the rate of $15 per machining hour. In July, machine hours were 3,000 in the Machining Department and 2,400 in the Assembly Department. Prepare the entry to assign overhead to production.
8. Kent Krause is uncertain about the steps used to prepare a production cost report. State the procedures that are required in the sequence in which they are performed.
9. Alan Bruski is confused about computing physical units. Explain to Alan how physical units to be accounted for and physical units accounted for are determined.
10. What is meant by the term "equivalent units of production"?
11. How are equivalent units of production computed?
12. Sandy Company had zero units of beginning work in process. During the period, 9,000 units were completed, and there were 600 units of ending work in process. What were the units started into production?
13. Cesska Co. has zero units of beginning work in process. During the period 12,000 units were completed, and there were 600 units of ending work in process one-fifth complete as to conversion cost and 100% complete as to materials cost. What were the equivalent units of production for (a) materials and (b) conversion costs?
14. Hipp Co. started 3,000 units for the period. Its beginning inventory is 800 units one-fourth complete as to conversion costs and 100% complete as to materials cost. Its ending inventory is 400 units one-fifth complete as to conversion cost and 100% complete as to materials costs. How many units were transferred out this period?
15. Gruber Company transfers out 14,000 units and has 2,000 units of ending work in process that are 25% complete. Materials are entered at the beginning of the process and there is no beginning work in process. Assuming unit materials costs of $3 and unit conversion costs of $9, what are the costs to be assigned to units (a) transferred out and (b) in ending work in process?
16. (a) Jane Jelk believes the production cost report is an external report for stockholders. Is Jane correct? Explain.
    (b) Identify the sections in a production cost report.

17. What purposes are served by a production cost report?
18. At Apex Company, there are 800 units of ending work in process that are 100% complete as to materials and 40% complete as to conversion costs. If the unit cost of materials is $4 and the costs assigned to the 800 units is $6,600, what is the per-unit conversion cost?
19. What is the difference between operations costing and a process costing system?
20. How does a company decide whether to use a job order or a process cost system?
21. (a) Describe the philosophy and approach of just-in-time processing.
(b) Identify the major elements of JIT processing.
22. (a) What are the principal differences between activity-based costing (ABC) and traditional product costing?
(b) What assumptions must be met for ABC costing to be useful?
23. Hoy Co. identifies the following activities that pertain to manufacturing overhead: Materials Handling, Machine Setups, Factory Machine Maintenance, Factory Supervision, and Quality Control. For each activity identify an appropriate cost driver.
*24. (a) Identify the steps that pertain to activity-based costing.
(b) What are the advantages of ABC costing?

BRIEF EXERCISES

Journalize entries for accumulating costs.
(SO 4)

BE22-1 Table Manufacturing purchases $50,000 of raw materials on account, and it incurs $40,000 of factory labor costs. Journalize the two transactions on March 31 assuming the labor costs are not paid until April.

Journalize the assignment of materials and labor costs.
(SO 4)

BE22-2 Data for Table Manufacturing are given in BE22-1. Supporting records show that (a) the Assembly Department used $24,000 of raw materials and $28,000 of the factory labor, and (b) the Finishing Department used the remainder. Journalize the assignment of the costs to the processing departments on March 31.

Journalize the assignment of overhead costs.
(SO 4)

BE22-3 Factory labor data for Table Manufacturing are given in BE22-2. Manufacturing overhead is assigned to departments on the basis of 200% of labor costs. Journalize the assignment of overhead to the Assembly and Finishing Departments.

Compute physical units of production.
(SO 6)

BE22-4 Burrand Manufacturing Company has the following production data for selected months.

			Ending Work in Process	
Month	**Beginning Work in Process**	**Units Transferred Out**	**Units**	**% Complete as to Conversion Cost**
January	–0–	30,000	5,000	40%
March	–0–	40,000	4,000	75
July	–0–	40,000	10,000	25

Compute the physical units for each month.

Compute equivalent units of production.
(SO 5)

BE22-5 Using the data in BE22-4, compute equivalent units of production for materials and conversion costs, assuming materials are entered at the beginning of the process.

Compute unit costs of production.
(SO 6)

BE22-6 In Caroline Company, total material costs are $48,000, and total conversion costs are $60,000. Equivalent units of production are materials 10,000 and conversion costs 12,000. Compute the unit costs for materials, conversion costs, and total manufacturing costs.

Assign costs to units transferred out and in process.
(SO 6)

BE22-7 Sota Company has the following production data for April: units transferred out 40,000, and ending work in process 5,000 units that are 100% complete for materials and 40% complete for conversion costs. If unit materials cost is $8 and unit conversion cost is $12, determine the costs to be assigned to the units transferred out and the units in ending work in process.

Compute unit costs.
(SO 6)

BE22-8 Production costs chargeable to the Finishing Department in June in Madlock Company are materials $9,000, labor $20,000, overhead $18,000. Equivalent units of production are materials 20,000 and conversion costs 19,000. Compute the unit costs for materials and conversion costs.

Prepare cost reconciliation schedule.
(SO 6)

BE22-9 Data for Madlock Company are given in BE22-8. Production records indicate that 18,000 units were transferred out, and 2,000 units in ending work in process were 50% complete as to conversion cost and 100% complete as to materials. Prepare a cost reconciliation schedule.

BE22-10 The Smelting Department of Darlinda Manufacturing Company has the following production and cost data for November.

Compute equivalent units of production.
(SO 5)

Production: Beginning work in process 2,000 units that are 100% complete as to materials and 20% complete as to conversion costs; units transferred out 8,000 units; and ending work in process 2,000 units that are 100% complete as to materials and 40% complete as to conversion costs.

Compute the equivalent units of production for **(a)** materials and **(b)** conversion costs for the month of November.

***BE22-11** Dooley Company identifies three activities in its manufacturing process: machine setups, machining, and inspections. Estimated annual overhead cost for each activity is $180,000, $300,000, and $70,000, respectively. The cost driver for each activity and the expected annual usage are: number of setups 1,000, machine hours 25,000, and number of inspections 1,400. Compute the overhead rate for each activity.

Compute overhead rates for activities.
(SO 10)

EXERCISES

E22-1 In Kam Company, materials are entered at the beginning of each process. Work in process inventories, with the percentage of work done on conversion costs, and production data for its Sterilizing Department in selected months during 2002 are as follows.

Compute physical units and equivalent units of production.
(SO 5, 6)

	Beginning Work in Process			Ending Work in Process	
Month	**Units**	**Conversion Cost %**	**Units Transferred Out**	**Units**	**Conversion Cost %**
January	–0–	—	7,000	2,000	60
March	–0–	—	12,000	3,000	30
May	–0–	—	16,000	4,000	80
July	–0–	—	10,000	1,500	40

Instructions

(a) Compute the physical units for January and May.
(b) Compute the equivalent units of production for (1) materials and (2) conversion costs for each month.

E22-2 The Cutting Department of Bjerg Manufacturing has the following production and cost data for July.

Determine equivalent units, unit costs, and assignment of costs.
(SO 5, 6)

Production

1. Transferred out 8,000 units.
2. Started 1,000 units that are 40% complete as to conversion costs and 100% complete as to materials at July 31.

Costs	
Beginning work in process	$ –0–
Materials	45,000
Labor	14,700
Manufacturing overhead	18,900

Materials are entered at the beginning of the process. Conversion costs are incurred uniformly during the process.

Instructions

(a) Determine the equivalent units of production for (1) materials and (2) conversion costs.
(b) Compute unit costs and prepare a cost reconciliation schedule.

E22-3 The Sanding Department of Copa Furniture Company has the following production and manufacturing cost data for March 2002.

Prepare a production cost report.
(SO 5, 6, 7)

Production: 12,000 units finished and transferred out; 3,000 units started that are 100% complete as to materials and 30% complete as to conversion costs.

Manufacturing costs: Materials $33,000; labor $30,000; overhead $35,790.

Instructions

Prepare a production cost report.

Determine equivalent units, unit costs, and assignment of costs.
(SO 5, 6)

E22-4 The Blending Department of Battle Company has the following cost and production data for the month of April.

Costs:	
Work in process, April 1	
Direct materials: 100% complete	$100,000
Conversion costs: 20% complete	70,000
Cost of work in process, April 1	$170,000
Costs incurred during production in April	
Direct materials	$ 800,000
Conversion costs	350,000
Costs incurred in April	$1,150,000

Units transferred out totaled 8,000. Ending work in process was 1,000 units that are 100% complete as to materials and 40% complete as to conversion costs.

Instructions

(a) Compute the equivalent units of production for (1) materials and (2) conversion costs for the month of April.
(b) Compute the unit costs for the month.
(c) Determine the costs to be assigned to the units transferred out and in ending work in process.

Explain the production cost report.
(SO 7)

E22-5 Larry Lair has recently been promoted to production manager, and so he has just started to receive various managerial reports. One of the reports he has received is the production cost report that you prepared. It showed that his department had 1,000 equivalent units in ending inventory. His department has had a history of not keeping enough inventory on hand to meet demand. He has come to you, very angry, and wants to know why you credited him with only 1,000 units when he knows he had at least twice that many on hand.

Instructions

Explain to him why his production cost report showed only 1,000 equivalent units in ending inventory. Write an informal memo. Be kind and explain very clearly why he is mistaken.

Answer questions on costs and production.
(SO 3, 5, 6)

E22-6 The ledger of Tombert Company has the following work in process account.

Work in Process—Painting

5/1	Balance	3,590	5/31	Transferred out	?
5/31	Materials	6,060			
5/31	Labor	2,500			
5/31	Overhead	1,650			
5/31	Balance	?			

Production records show that there were 700 units in the beginning inventory, 30% complete, 1,100 units started, and 1,300 units transferred out. The beginning work in process had materials cost of $2,040 and conversion costs of $1,550. The units in ending inventory were 40% complete. Materials are entered at the beginning of the painting process.

Instructions

(a) How many units are in process at May 31?
(b) What is the unit materials cost for May?
(c) What is the unit conversion cost for May?
(d) What is the total cost of units transferred out in May?
(e) What is the cost of the May 31 inventory?

Journalize transactions for two processes.
(SO 4)

E22-7 Yellowknife Manufacturing Company has two production departments: Cutting and Assembly. July 1 inventories are Raw Materials $4,200, Work in Process — Cutting $2,900, Work in Process — Assembly $10,600, and Finished Goods $31,000. During July, the following transactions occurred.

1. Purchased $56,300 of raw materials on account.
2. Incurred $56,000 of factory labor. (Credit Wages Payable.)

3. Incurred $70,000 of manufacturing overhead; $36,000 was paid and the remainder is unpaid.
4. Requisitioned materials for Cutting $15,700 and Assembly $8,900.
5. Used factory labor for Cutting $29,000 and Assembly $27,000.
6. Applied overhead at the rate of $20 per machine hour. Machine hours were Cutting 1,640 and Assembly 1,720.
7. Transferred goods costing $77,600 from the Cutting Department to the Assembly Department.
8. Transferred goods costing $134,900 from Assembly to Finished Goods.
9. Sold goods costing $130,000 for $200,000 on account.

Instructions

Journalize the transactions. (Omit explanations.)

Compute equivalent units, unit costs, and costs assigned.
(SO 5, 6)

E22-8 The Polishing Department of Medina Manufacturing Company has the following production and manufacturing cost data for September. Materials are entered at the beginning of the process.

Production: Beginning inventory 1,600 units that are 100% complete as to materials and 30% complete as to conversion costs; units started during the period are 12,000; ending inventory of 3,000 units 10% complete as to conversion costs.

Manufacturing costs: Beginning inventory costs, comprised of $20,000 of materials and $43,180 of conversion costs; materials costs added in Polishing during the month, $177,200; labor and overhead applied in Polishing during the month, $100,080 and $257,860, respectively.

Instructions

(a) Compute the equivalent units of production for materials and conversion costs for the month of September.
(b) Compute the unit costs for materials and conversion costs for the month.
(c) Determine the costs to be assigned to the units transferred out and in process.

Prepare a production cost report.
(SO 5, 6, 7)

E22-9 The Welding Department of Tomlin Manufacturing Company has the following production and manufacturing cost data for February 2002. All materials are added at the beginning of the process.

Manufacturing Costs			Production Data	
Beginning work in process			Beginning work in process	15,000 units
Materials	$18,000			1/10 complete
Conversion costs	14,175	$32,175	Units transferred out	49,000
Materials		180,000	Units started	60,000
Labor		35,100	Ending work in process	26,000
Overhead		64,545		1/5 complete

Instructions

Prepare a production cost report for the Welding Department for the month of February.

Journalize transactions.
(SO 3, 4)

E22-10 Mary Lou Company manufactures pizza sauce through two production departments: Cooking and Canning. In each process, materials and conversion costs are incurred evenly throughout the process. For the month of April, the work in process accounts show the following debits.

	Cooking	Canning
Beginning work in process	$ –0–	$ 4,000
Materials	15,000	6,000
Labor	8,500	7,000
Overhead	29,500	21,800
Costs transferred in		45,000

Instructions

Journalize the April transactions.

Compute overhead rates and assign overhead using ABC.
(SO 10)

***E22-11** Amend Instrument Inc. manufactures two products: missile range instruments and space pressure gauges. During January, 50 range instruments and 300 pressure gauges were produced, and overhead costs of $81,000 were incurred. An analysis of overhead costs reveals the following activities.

Activity	Cost Driver	Total Cost
1. Materials handling	Number of requisitions	$30,000
2. Machine setups	Number of setups	27,000
3. Quality inspections	Number of inspections	24,000

The cost driver volume for each product was as follows.

Cost Driver	Instruments	Gauges	Total
Number of requisitions	400	600	1,000
Number of setups	150	300	450
Number of inspections	200	400	600

Instructions

(a) Determine the overhead rate for each activity.

(b) Assign the manufacturing overhead costs for January to the two products using activity-based costing.

(c) Write a memo to the president of Amend Instrument, explaining the benefits of activity-based costing.

PROBLEMS: SET A

Complete four steps necessary to prepare a production cost report.
(SO 5, 6, 7)

P22-1A Zion Company manufactures bowling balls through two processes: Molding and Packaging. In the Molding Department, the urethane, rubber, plastics, and other materials are molded into bowling balls. In the Packaging Department, the balls are placed in cartons and sent to the finished goods warehouse. All materials are entered at the beginning of each process. Labor and manufacturing overhead are incurred uniformly throughout each process. Production and cost data for the Molding Department during June 2002 are presented below.

Production Data	June
Beginning work in process units	–0–
Units started into production	22,000
Ending work in process units	2,000
Percent complete—ending inventory	45%
Cost Data	
Materials	$286,000
Labor	114,000
Overhead	136,800
Total	$536,800

Instructions

(a) Prepare a schedule showing physical units of production.

(b) Determine the equivalent units of production for materials and conversion costs.

(c) Compute the unit costs of production.

(d) Determine the costs to be assigned to the units transferred and in process for June.

(e) Prepare a production cost report for the Molding Department for the month of June only.

Complete four steps necessary to prepare a production cost report.
(SO 5, 6, 7)

P22-2A Stein Industries Inc. manufactures in separate processes furniture for homes. In each process, materials are entered at the beginning, and conversion costs are incurred uniformly. Production and cost data for the first process in making two products in two different manufacturing plants are as follows.

Production Data—July	Cutting Department Plant 1 T12-Tables	Plant 2 C10-Chairs
Work in process units, July 1	–0–	–0–
Units started into production	20,000	18,000
Work in process units, July 31	1,000	500
Work in process percent complete	60	80
Cost Data — July		
Work in process, July 1	$ –0–	$ –0–
Materials	380,000	288,000
Labor	190,000	118,100
Overhead	104,000	96,700
Total	$674,000	$502,800

Instructions

(a) For each plant:

(1) Compute the physical units of production.

(2) Compute equivalent units of production for materials and for conversion costs.

(3) Determine the unit costs of production.

(4) Show the assignment of costs of units transferred out and in process.

(b) Prepare the production cost report for Plant 1 for July 2002.

Journalize transactions. (SO 3, 4)

P22-3A Vargas Company manufactures its product, Vitadrink, through two manufacturing processes: Mixing and Packaging. All materials are entered at the beginning of each process. On October 1, 2002, inventories consisted of Raw Materials $26,000, Work in Process—Mixing $0, Work in Process—Packaging $250,000, and Finished Goods $89,000. The beginning inventory for Packaging consisted of 10,000 units that were 50% complete as to conversion costs and fully complete as to materials. During October, 50,000 units were started into production in the Mixing Department and the following transactions were completed.

1. Purchased $400,000 of raw materials on account.
2. Issued raw materials for production: Mixing $210,000 and Packaging $45,000.
3. Incurred labor costs of $329,800.
4. Used factory labor: Mixing $182,500 and Packaging $56,400.
5. Incurred $790,000 of manufacturing overhead on account.
6. Applied indirect manufacturing overhead on the basis of $25 per machine hour. Machine hours were 28,000 in Mixing and 7,000 in Packaging.
7. Transferred 45,000 units from Mixing to Packaging at a cost of $999,000.
8. Transferred 53,000 units from Packaging to Finished Goods at a cost of $1,455,000.
9. Sold goods costing $1,640,000 for $2,500,000 on account.

Instructions

Journalize the October transactions.

Assign costs and prepare production cost report. (SO 5, 6, 7)

P22-4A Elite Company has several processing departments. Costs charged to the Assembly Department for November 2002 totaled $2,129,000 as follows.

Work in process, November 1		
Materials	$69,000	
Conversion costs	48,150	$ 117,150
Materials added		1,405,000
Labor		225,920
Overhead		380,930

Production records show that 30,000 units were in beginning work in process 30% complete as to conversion costs, 640,000 units were started into production, and 25,000 units were in ending work in process 40% complete as to conversion costs. Materials are entered at the beginning of each process.

Instructions

(a) Determine the equivalent units of production and the unit costs for the Assembly Department.

(b) Determine the assignment of costs to goods transferred out and in process.

(c) Prepare a production cost report for the Assembly Department.

Determine equivalent units and unit costs and assign costs.
(SO 5, 6, 7)

P22-5A Sprague Company manufactures basketballs. Materials are added at the beginning of the production process and conversion costs are incurred uniformly. Production and cost data for the month of July 2002 are as follows.

Production Data—Basketballs	**Units**	**Percent Complete**
Work in process units, July 1	500	60%
Units started into production	1,600	
Work in process units, July 31	600	40%

Cost Data—Basketballs		
Work in process, July 1		
Materials	$750	
Conversion costs	600	$1,350
Direct materials		2,400
Direct labor		1,580
Manufacturing overhead		1,300

Instructions

(a) Calculate the following.

(1) The equivalent units of production for materials and conversion.

(2) The unit costs of production for materials and conversion costs.

(3) The assignment of costs to units transferred out and in process at the end of the accounting period.

(b) Prepare a production cost report for the month of July for the basketballs.

Compute equivalent units and complete production cost report.
(SO 5, 7)

P22-6A Taylor Processing Company uses a weighted-average process costing system and manufactures a single product—a premium rug shampoo and cleaner. The manufacturing activity for the month of October has just been completed. A partially completed production cost report for the month of October for the mixing and cooking department is shown below.

TAYLOR PROCESSING COMPANY
Mixing and Cooking Department
Production Cost Report
For the Month Ended October 31

		Equivalent Units	
QUANTITIES	**Physical Units**	**Materials**	**Conversion Costs**
Units to be accounted for			
Work in process, October 1 (all materials, 70% conversion costs)	20,000		
Started into production	160,000		
Total units	180,000		
Units accounted for			
Transferred out	140,000	?	?
Work in process, October 31 (50% materials, 25% conversion costs)	40,000	?	?
Total units accounted for	180,000	?	?

COSTS	Materials	Conversion Costs	Total
Unit costs			
Costs in October	$240,000	$90,000	$330,000
Equivalent units	?	?	
Unit costs	$?	+ $?	= $?
Costs to be accounted for			
Work in process, October 1			$ 30,000
Started into production			300,000
Total costs			$330,000

Cost Reconciliation Schedule		
Costs accounted for		
Transferred out		$?
Work in process, October 31		
Materials	?	
Conversion costs	?	?
Total costs		?

Instructions

(a) Prepare a schedule that shows how the equivalent units were computed so that you can complete the "Quantities: Units accounted for" equivalent units section shown in the production cost report above, and compute October unit costs.

(b) Complete the "Cost Reconciliation Schedule" part of the production cost report above.

Assign overhead to products using ABC. (SO 10)

***P22-7A** Becky Electronics manufactures two large-screen television models: the Royale which sells for $1,500, and a new model, the Majestic, which sells for $1,200. The production cost per unit for each model in 2002 was as follows.

	Royale	Majestic
Direct materials	$ 700	$420
Direct labor ($20 per hour)	100	80
Manufacturing overhead ($40 per DLH)	200	160
Total per unit cost	$1,000	$660

In 2002, Becky manufactured 30,000 units of the Royale and 10,000 units of the Majestic. The overhead rate of $40 per direct labor hour was determined by dividing total expected manufacturing overhead of $7,600,000 by the total direct labor hours (190,000) for the two models.

The gross profit on the model was: Royale $500 ($1,500 − $1,000) and Majestic $540 ($1,200 − $660). Because of this difference, management is considering phasing out the Royale model and increasing the production of the Majestic model.

Before finalizing its decision, management asks the controller, Rebecca Sherrick, to prepare an analysis using activity-based costing. Rebecca accumulates the following information about overhead for the year ended December 31, 2002.

Activity	Cost Driver	Total Cost	Cost Driver Volume	Overhead Rate
Purchase orders	Number of orders	$1,200,000	30,000	$40
Machine setups	Number of setups	900,000	15,000	60
Machining	Machine hours	4,800,000	160,000	30
Quality control	Number of inspections	700,000	35,000	20

The cost driver volume for each product was:

Cost Driver	Royale	Majestic	Total
Purchase orders	10,000	20,000	30,000
Machine setups	5,000	10,000	15,000
Machine hours	100,000	60,000	160,000
Inspections	10,000	25,000	35,000

Instructions

(a) Assign the total 2002 manufacturing overhead costs to the two products using activity-based costing (ABC).

(b) What was the cost per unit and gross profit of each model using ABC costing?

(c) Are management's future plans for the two models sound?

PROBLEMS: SET B

Complete four steps necessary to prepare a production cost report.
(SO 5, 6, 7)

P22-1B Acquatic Corporation manufactures water skis through two processes: Molding and Packaging. In the Molding Department fiberglass is heated and shaped into the form of a ski. In the Packaging Department, the skis are placed in cartons and sent to the finished goods warehouse. Materials are entered at the beginning of both processes. Labor and manufacturing overhead are incurred uniformly throughout each process. Production and cost data for the Molding Department for January 2002 are presented below.

Production Data	January
Beginning work in process units	–0–
Units started into production	42,500
Ending work in process units	2,500
Percent complete—ending inventory	40%
Cost Data	
Materials	$552,500
Labor	117,000
Overhead	170,000
Total	$839,500

Instructions

(a) Compute the physical units of production.

(b) Determine the equivalent units of production for materials and conversion costs.

(c) Compute the unit costs of production.

(d) Determine the costs to be assigned to the units transferred out and in process.

(e) Prepare a production cost report for the Molding Department for the month of January.

Complete four steps necessary to prepare a production cost report.
(SO 5, 6, 7)

P22-2B Freedo Corporation manufactures in separate processes refrigerators and freezers for homes. In each process, materials are entered at the beginning and conversion costs are incurred uniformly. Production and cost data for the first process in making two products in two different manufacturing plants are as follows.

	Stamping Department	
Production Data—June	**Plant A R12 Refrigerators**	**Plant B F24 Freezers**
Work in process units, June 1	–0–	–0–
Units started into production	20,000	20,000
Work in process units, June 30	2,000	2,500
Work in process percent complete	75	60
Cost Data—June		
Work in process, June 1	$ –0–	$ –0–
Materials	840,000	700,000
Labor	223,500	251,000
Overhead	420,000	319,000
Total	$1,483,500	$1,270,000

Instructions

(a) For each plant:

(1) Compute the physical units of production.

(2) Compute equivalent units of production for materials and for conversion costs.

(3) Determine the units costs of production.

(4) Show the assignment of costs to units tranferred out and in process.

(b) Prepare the production cost report for Plant A for June 2002.

P22-3B Pepi Company manufactures a nutrient, Everlife, through two manufacturing processes: Blending and Packaging. All materials are entered at the beginning of each process. On August 1, 2002, inventories consisted of Raw Materials $5,000, Work in Process—Blending $0, Work in Process—Packaging $3,945, and Finished Goods $7,500. The beginning inventory for Packaging consisted of 500 units, two-fifths complete as to conversion costs and fully complete as to materials. During August, 9,000 units were started into production in Blending, and the following transactions were completed.

Journalize transactions.
(SO 3, 4)

1. Purchased $25,000 of raw materials on account.
2. Issued raw materials for production: Blending $16,930 and Packaging $7,140.
3. Incurred labor costs of $18,770.
4. Used factory labor: Blending $13,320 and Packaging $5,450.
5. Incurred $41,500 of manufacturing overhead on account.
6. Applied manufacturing overhead at the rate of $35 per machine hour. Machine hours were Blending 900 and Packaging 300.
7. Transferred 8,200 units from Blending to Packaging at a cost of $54,940.
8. Transferred 8,600 units from Packaging to Finished Goods at a cost of $74,490.
9. Sold goods costing $62,000 for $90,000 on account.

Instructions

Journalize the August transactions.

P22-4B Wang Company has several processing departments. Costs charged to the Assembly Department for October 2002 totaled $1,347,200 as follows.

Assign costs and prepare production cost report.
(SO 5, 6, 7)

Work in process, October 1		
Materials	$29,000	
Conversion costs	26,200	$ 55,200
Materials added		1,071,000
Labor		90,000
Overhead		131,000

Production records show that 25,000 units were in beginning work in process 40% complete as to conversion cost, 415,000 units were started into production, and 35,000 units were in ending work in process 20% complete as to conversion costs. Materials are entered at the beginning of each process.

Instructions

(a) Determine the equivalent units of production and the unit costs for the Assembly Department.

(b) Determine the assignment of costs to goods transferred out and in process.

(c) Prepare a production cost report for the Assembly Department.

P22-5B Clemente Company manufactures bicycles and tricycles. For both products, materials are added at the beginning of the production process, and conversion costs are incurred uniformly. Production and cost data for the month of May are as follows.

Determine equivalent units and unit costs and assign costs.
(SO 5, 6, 7)

Production Data—Bicycles	Units	Percent Complete
Work in process units, May 1	500	80%
Units started in production	1,000	
Work in process units, May 31	600	9.5%

Cost Data—Bicycles

Work in process, May 1		
Materials	$10,000	
Conversion costs	9,280	$ 19,280
Direct materials		50,000
Direct labor		18,140
Manufacturing overhead		30,000

Instructions

(a) Calculate the following.
   (1) The equivalent units of production for materials and conversion.
   (2) The unit costs of production for materials and conversion costs.
   (3) The assignment of costs to units transferred out and in process at the end of the accounting period.

(b) Prepare a production cost report for the month of May for the bicycles.

Compute equivalent units and complete production cost report.
(SO 5, 7)

P22-6B Magic Cleaner Company uses a weighted-average process costing system and manufactures a single product—an all-purpose liquid cleaner. The manufacturing activity for the month of March has just been completed. A partially completed production cost report for the month of March for the mixing and blending department is shown below.

MAGIC CLEANER COMPANY
Mixing and Blending Department
Production Cost Report
For the Month Ended March 31

QUANTITIES	Physical Units	Equivalent Units: Materials	Equivalent Units: Conversion Costs
Units to be accounted for			
Work in process, March 1 (40% materials, 20% conversion costs)	10,000		
Started into production	100,000		
Total units	110,000		
Units accounted for			
Transferred out	95,000	?	?
Work in process, March 31 (2/3 materials, 1/3 conversion costs)	15,000	?	?
Total units accounted for	110,000	?	?

COSTS	Materials		Conversion Costs		Total
Unit costs					
Costs in March	$170,100		$98,000		$268,100
Equivalent units	?		?		
Unit costs	$?	+	$?	=	$?
Costs to be accounted for					
Work in process, March 1					$ 15,700
Started into production					252,400
Total costs					$268,100

Cost Reconciliation Schedule

Costs accounted for		
Transferred out		$?
Work in process, March 31		
Materials	?	
Conversion costs	?	?
Total costs		?

Instructions

(a) Prepare a schedule that shows how the equivalent units were computed so that you can complete the "Quantities: Units accounted for" equivalent units section shown in the production cost report above, and compute March unit costs.

(b) Complete the "Cost Reconciliation Schedule" part of the production cost report above.

BROADENING YOUR PERSPECTIVE

GROUP DECISION CASE

BYP22-1 English Bay Beach Company manufactures suntan lotion, called Surtan, in 11-ounce plastic bottles. Surtan is sold in a competitive market. As a result, management is very cost-conscious. Surtan is manufactured through two processes: mixing and filling. Materials are entered at the beginning of each process and labor and manufacturing overhead occur uniformly throughout each process. Unit costs are based on the cost per gallon of Surtan using the weighted-average costing approach.

On June 30, 2002, Sara Simmons, the chief accountant for the past 20 years, opted to take early retirement. Her replacement, Joe Jacobs, had extensive accounting experience with motels in the area but only limited contact with manufacturing accounting.

During July, Joe correctly accumulated the following production quantity and cost data for the Mixing Department.

> Production quantities: Work in process, July 1, 8,000 gallons 75% complete; started into production 100,000 gallons; work in process, July 31, 5,000 gallons 20% complete. Materials are added at the beginning of the process.
>
> Production costs: Beginning work in process $88,000, comprised of $21,000 of materials costs and $67,000 of conversion costs; incurred in July: materials $600,000, conversion costs $785,800.

Joe then prepared a production cost report on the basis of physical units started into production. His report showed a production cost of $14.738 per gallon of Surtan. The management of English Bay Beach was surprised at the high unit cost. The president comes to you, as Sara's top assistant, to review Joe's report and prepare a correct report if necessary.

Instructions

With the class divided into groups, answer the following questions.

(a) Show how Joe arrived at the unit cost of $14.738 per gallon of Surtan.

(b) What error(s) did Joe make in preparing his production cost report?

(c) Prepare a correct production cost report for July.

MANAGERIAL ANALYSIS

BYP22-2 Logan Furniture Company manufactures living room furniture through two departments: Framing and Upholstering. Materials are entered at the beginning of each process. For May, the following cost data are obtained from the two work in process accounts.

	Framing	Upholstering
Work in process, May 1	$ –0–	$?
Materials	420,000	?
Conversion costs	210,000	330,000
Costs transferred in	–0–	550,000
Costs transferred out	550,000	?
Work in process, May 31	80,000	?

Instructions

Answer the following questions.

(a) If 3,000 sofas were started into production on May 1 and 2,500 sofas were transferred to Upholstering, what was the unit cost of materials for May in the Framing Department?

(b) Using the data in (a) above, what was the per unit conversion cost of the sofas transferred to Upholstering?

(c) Continuing the assumptions in (a) above, what is the percentage of completion of the units in process at May 31 in the Framing Department?

REAL-WORLD FOCUS

BYP22-3 **General Microwave Corp.** is engaged primarily in the design, development, manufacture, and marketing of microwave, electronic, and fiber optic test equipment, components, and subsystems. A substantial portion of the company's microwave product is sold to manufacturers and users of microwave systems and equipment for applications in the defense electronics industry.

General Microwave Corp. reports the following information in one of the notes to its financial statements.

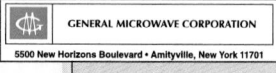

GENERAL MICROWAVE CORPORATION
5500 New Horizons Boulevard • Amityville, New York 11701

GENERAL MICROWAVE CORPORATION
Notes to the Financial Statement

Work in process inventory reflects all accumulated production costs, which are comprised of direct production costs and overhead, reduced by amounts attributable to units delivered. Work in process inventory is reduced to its estimated net realizable value by a charge to cost of sales in the period [in which] excess costs are identified. Raw materials and finished goods inventories are reflected at the lower of cost or market.

Instructions

(a) What types of manufacturing costs are accumulated in the work in process inventory account?

(b) What types of information must General Microwave have to be able to compute equivalent units of production?

(c) How does General Microwave assign costs to the units transferred out of work in process that are completed?

EXPLORING THE WEB

www.wiley.com/college/weygandt

BYP22-4 Search the Internet and find the Web sites of two manufacturers that you think are likely to use process costing. Are there any specifics included in their Web sites that confirm the use of process costing for each of these companies?

COMMUNICATION ACTIVITY

BYP22-5 Catherine Harper was a good friend of yours in high school and is from your home town. While you chose to major in accounting when you both went away to college, she majored in marketing and management. You have recently been promoted to accounting manager for the Snack Foods Division of Clark Enterprises, and your friend was promoted to regional sales manager for the same division of Clark. Catherine recently telephoned you. She explained that she was familiar with job cost sheets, which had been used by the Special Projects division where she had formerly worked. She was, however, very uncomfortable with the production cost reports prepared by your division. She faxed you a list of her particular questions. These included the following.

1. Since Clark occasionally prepares snack foods for special orders in the Snack Foods Division, why don't we track costs of the orders separately?
2. What is an equivalent unit?
3. Why am I getting four production cost reports? Isn't there only one Work in Process account?

Instructions

Prepare a memo to Catherine. Answer her questions, and include any additional information you think would be helpful. You may write informally, but be careful to use proper grammar and punctuation.

ETHICS CASE

BYP22-6 R. B. Robin Company manufactures a high-tech component that passes through two production processing departments, Molding and Assembly. Department managers are partially compensated on the basis of units of products completed and transferred out relative to units of product put into production. This was intended as encouragement to be efficient and to minimize waste.

Barb Crusmer is the department head in the Molding Department, and Wayne Terrago is her quality control inspector. During the month of June, Barb had three new employees who were not yet technically skilled. As a result, many of the units produced in June had minor molding defects. In order to maintain the department's normal high rate of completion, Barb told Wayne to pass through inspection and on to the Assembly Department all units that had defects nondetectable to the human eye. "Company and industry tolerances on this product are too high anyway," says Barb. "Less than 2% of the units we produce are subjected in the market to the stress tolerance we've designed into them. The odds of those 2% being any of this month's units are even less. Anyway, we're saving the company money."

Instructions

(a) Who are the potential stakeholders involved in this situation?
(b) What alternatives does Wayne have in this situation? What might the company do to prevent this situation from occurring?

Answers to Self-Study Questions

1. b **2.** d **3.** c **4.** b **5.** b **6.** a **7.** c **8.** a **9.** b **10.** b **11.** d
12. c **13.** b

Remember to go back to the Navigator box on the chapter-opening page and check off your completed work.

23

COST-VOLUME-PROFIT RELATIONSHIPS

THE NAVIGATOR ✓

- Understand *Concepts for Review* ❑
- Read *Feature Story* ❑
- Scan *Study Objectives* ❑
- Read *Preview* ❑
- Read text and answer *Before You Go On* *p.* 952 ❑ *p.* 959 ❑ *p.* 964 ❑
- Work *Demonstration Problem* ❑
- Review *Summary of Study Objectives* ❑
- Answer *Self-Study Questions* ❑
- Complete *Assignments* ❑

CONCEPTS FOR REVIEW

Before studying this chapter, you should know or, if necessary, review:

a. The three manufacturing cost elements. (Ch. 20, pp. 831–832)

b. The difference between product and period costs. (Ch. 20, p. 833)

c. The income statement for a manufacturing company. (Ch. 20, pp. 835–836)

THE NAVIGATOR

FEATURE STORY

Growing by Leaps and Leotards

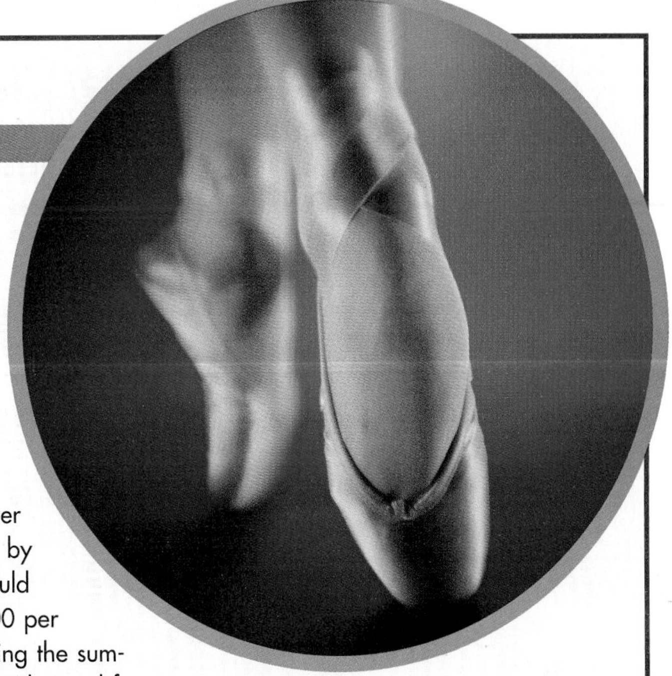

When the last of her three children went off to school, Amy began looking for a job. At this same time, her daughter asked to take dance classes. The nearest dance studio was over 20 miles away, and Amy didn't know how she would balance a new job and driving her daughter to dance class. Suddenly it hit her—why not start her own dance studio?

Amy sketched out a business plan: A local church would rent its basement for $6 per hour. The size of the basement limited the number of students she could teach, but the rent was low. Insurance for a small studio was $50 per month. Initially she would teach classes only for young kids since that was all she felt qualified to do. She thought she could charge $2.50 for a one-hour class. There was room for 8 students per class. She wouldn't get rich—but at least it would be fun, and she didn't have much at risk.

Amy soon realized that the demand for dance classes far exceeded her capacity. She began to consider renting a bigger space in which she could serve as many as 15 students per class. But her rent would also increase significantly. Also, rather than paying rent by the hour, she would have to pay $600 per month, even during the summer months when demand for dance classes was low. She also would have to pay utilities—roughly $70 per month.

However, with a bigger space Amy could offer classes for teens and adults. Teens and adults would pay a higher fee—$5 per hour—though the number of students per class would have to be smaller, probably only 8 per class. She would hire a part-time instructor at about $18 per hour to teach advanced classes. Insurance costs would increase to $100 per month. In addition, she would need a part-time administrator at $100 per month to keep records. Amy also realized she could increase her income by selling dance supplies such as shoes, towels, and leotards.

Amy laid out a new business plan based on these estimates. If she failed, she stood to lose real money. Convinced she could make a go of it, she made the big plunge.

Within 10 years of starting her business in a church basement Amy had over 800 students, seven instructors, two administrators, and a facility with three separate studios.

THE NAVIGATOR

STUDY OBJECTIVES

After studying this chapter, you should be able to:

1. Distinguish between variable and fixed costs.
2. Explain the significance of the relevant range.
3. Explain the concept of mixed costs.
4. List the five components of cost-volume-profit analysis.
5. Indicate what contribution margin is and how it can be expressed.
6. Identify the three ways to determine the break-even point.
7. Define margin of safety, and give the formulas for computing it.
8. Give the formulas for determining sales required to earn target net income.
9. Describe the essential features of a cost-volume-profit income statement.

THE NAVIGATOR

PREVIEW OF CHAPTER 23

As the Feature Story indicates, to manage any size business you must understand how costs respond to changes in sales volume and the effect of costs and revenues on profits. A prerequisite to understanding cost-volume-profit (CVP) relationships is knowledge of how costs behave. In this chapter, we first explain the considerations involved in cost behavior analysis. Then we discuss and illustrate CVP analysis and variable costing.

The content and organization of Chapter 23 are as follows.

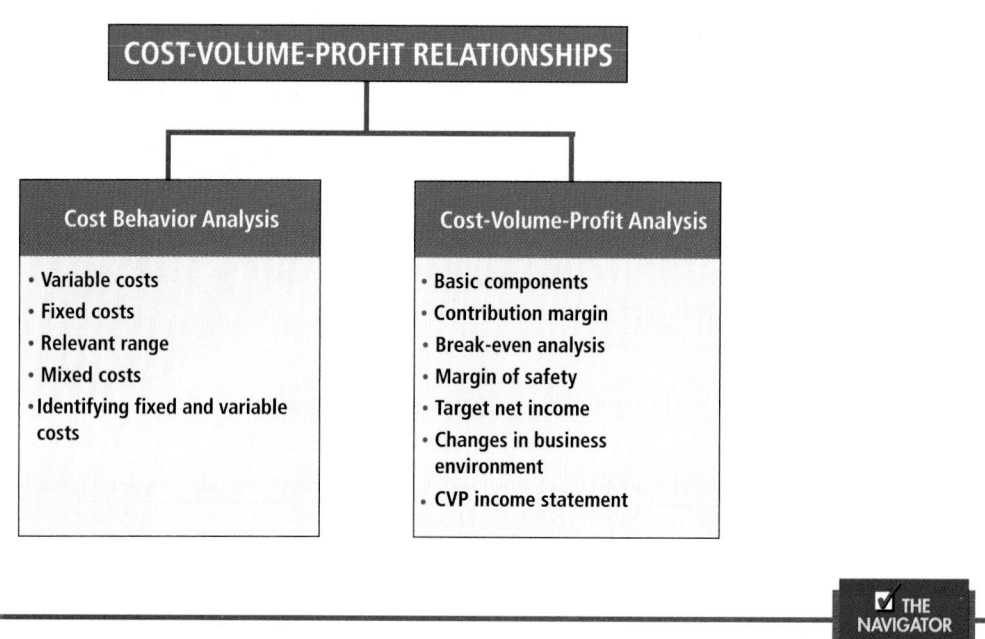

COST-VOLUME-PROFIT RELATIONSHIPS

Cost Behavior Analysis
- Variable costs
- Fixed costs
- Relevant range
- Mixed costs
- Identifying fixed and variable costs

Cost-Volume-Profit Analysis
- Basic components
- Contribution margin
- Break-even analysis
- Margin of safety
- Target net income
- Changes in business environment
- CVP income statement

THE NAVIGATOR

COST BEHAVIOR ANALYSIS

Cost behavior analysis is the study of how specific costs respond to changes in the level of business activity. As you might expect, some costs change, and others remain the same. A knowledge of cost behavior helps management plan operations and decide between alternative courses of action. Cost behavior analysis applies to all types of entities, as the story about Amy's dance studio indicates.

The starting point in cost behavior analysis is measuring the key business activities. Activity levels may be expressed in terms of sales dollars (in a retail company), miles driven (in a trucking company), room occupancy (in a hotel), or dance classes taught (by a dance studio). Many companies use more than one measurement base. A manufacturer, for example, may use direct labor hours or units of output for manufacturing costs and sales revenue or units sold for selling expenses.

For an activity level to be useful in cost behavior analysis, changes in the level or volume of activity should be correlated with changes in costs. The activity level selected is referred to as the activity (or volume) index. The **activity index** identifies the activity that causes changes in the behavior of costs. With an appropriate activity index, it is possible to classify the behavior of costs in response to changes in activity levels into three categories: variable, fixed, or mixed.

STUDY OBJECTIVE 1

Distinguish between variable and fixed costs.

VARIABLE COSTS

Variable costs are costs that vary **in total** directly and proportionately with changes in the activity level. If the level increases 10 percent, total variable costs will increase 10 percent. If the level of activity decreases by 25 percent, variable costs will decrease 25 percent. Examples of variable costs include direct materials and direct labor for a manufacturer; cost of goods sold, sales commissions, and freight-out for a merchandiser; and gasoline in airline and trucking companies. A variable cost may also be defined as a cost that **remains the same *per unit* at every level of activity**.

To illustrate the behavior of a variable cost, assume that Damon Company manufactures radios that contain a $10 digital clock. The activity index is the number of radios produced. As each radio is manufactured, the total cost of the clocks increases by $10. As shown in part (a) of Illustration 23-1, total cost of the clocks will be $20,000 if 2,000 radios are produced, and $100,000 when 10,000 radios are produced. We also can see that a variable cost remains the same per unit as the level of activity changes. As shown in part (b) of Illustration 23-1, the unit cost of $10 for the clocks is the same whether 2,000 or 10,000 radios are produced.

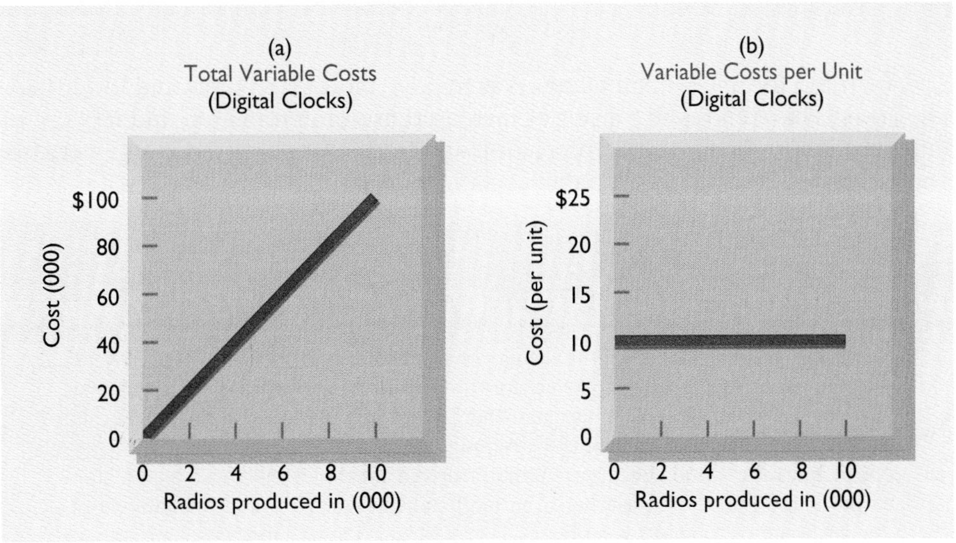

Illustration 23-1

Behavior of total and unit variable costs

HELPFUL HINT

True or false: Variable cost per unit changes directly and proportionately with changes in activity. Answer: False. Per unit cost remains constant at all levels of activity.

Companies that rely heavily on labor to manufacture a product or to render a service are likely to have many variable costs. In contrast, companies that use a high proportion of machinery and equipment in producing revenue, such as public utilities, may have few variable costs.

FIXED COSTS

Fixed costs are costs that **remain the same in total** regardless of changes in the activity level. Examples include property taxes, insurance, rent, supervisory salaries, and depreciation on buildings and equipment. Because total fixed costs remain constant as activity changes, it follows that **fixed costs *per unit* vary inversely with activity: As volume increases, unit cost declines, and vice versa**.

To illustrate the behavior of fixed costs, assume that Damon Company leases its productive facilities at a cost of $10,000 per month. Total fixed costs of the facilities will remain constant at every level of activity, as shown in part (a) of Illustration 23-2. But, on a per unit basis, the cost of rent will decline as activity increases, as shown in part (b) of Illustration 23-2. At 2,000 units, the unit cost is $5 ($10,000 ÷ 2,000). When 10,000 radios are produced, the unit cost is only $1 ($10,000 ÷ 10,000).

Illustration 23-2

Behavior of total and unit fixed costs

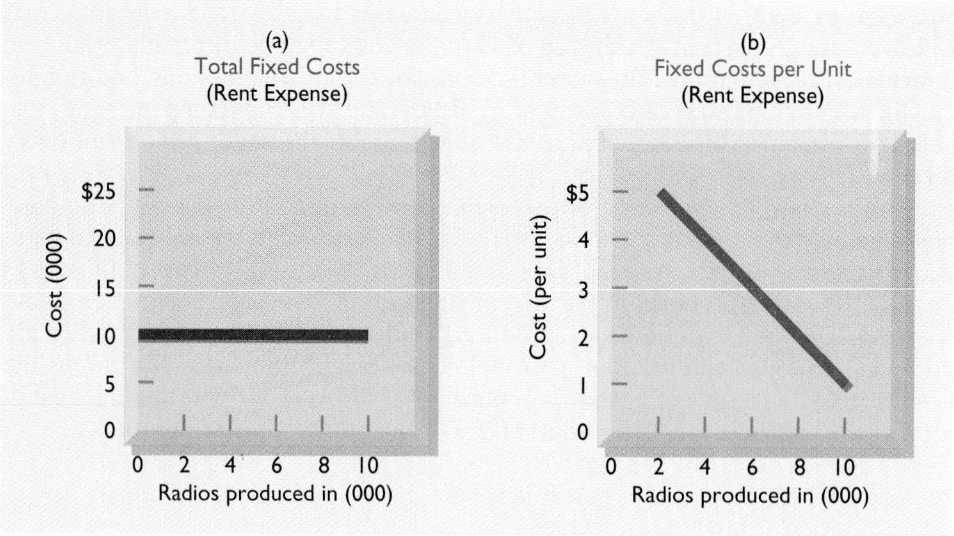

The trend for many manufacturers is to have more fixed costs and fewer variable costs. This trend is the result of increased use of automation and less use of employee labor. As a result, depreciation and lease charges (fixed costs) increase, whereas direct labor costs (variable costs) decrease.

ACCOUNTING IN ACTION *Business Insight*

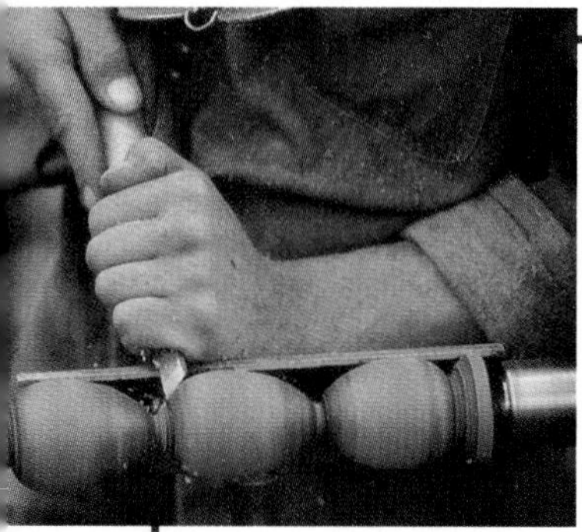

When Thomas Moser quit teaching communications at Bates College 25 years ago, he turned to what he loved doing—furniture woodworking. Today he has over 120 employees. In a business where profit margins are seldom thicker than wood shavings, cost control is everything. Moser keeps no inventory; a 50 percent deposit buys the wood. Because computer-driven machines cut most of the standardized parts and joints, "we're free to be inefficient in assembly and finishing work, where the craft is most obviously expressed," says Moser. Direct labor costs are a manageable 30 percent of revenues. By keeping a tight lid on costs and running an efficient operation, Moser is free to spend most of his time doing what he enjoys most—designing furniture.

SOURCE: Excerpts from "Out of the Woods," *Forbes,* April 5, 1999, p. 74.

RELEVANT RANGE

STUDY OBJECTIVE 2

Explain the significance of the relevant range.

In Illustrations 23-1 and 23-2, straight lines were drawn throughout the entire activity index for total variable costs and total fixed costs. In essence, the assumption was made that the costs were **linear**. It is now necessary to ask: Is the straight-line relationship realistic? Does the linear assumption produce useful data for CVP analysis?

In most business situations, a straight-line relationship **does not exist** for variable costs throughout the entire range of possible activity. At abnormally low levels of activity, it may be impossible to be cost efficient. Small-scale operations may not allow the company to obtain quantity discounts for raw materials or to use specialized labor. In contrast, at abnormally high levels of activity, labor costs may increase sharply because of overtime pay. Also at high activity levels, materials costs may jump significantly because of excess spoilage caused by worker fatigue. As a result, in the real world, the relationship between the behavior of a variable cost and changes in the activity level is often **curvilinear,** as shown in part (a) of Illustration 23-3.

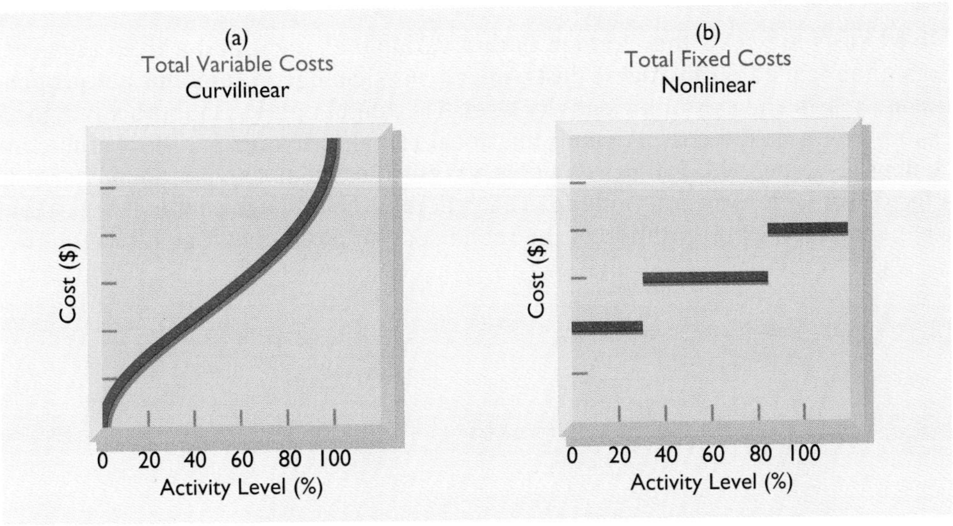

Illustration 23-3

Nonlinear behavior of variable and fixed costs

Total fixed costs also do not have a straight-line relationship over the entire range of activity. Some fixed costs will not change. But it is possible for management to change other fixed costs. For example, in the Feature Story the dance studio's rent was originally variable and then became fixed at a certain amount. It then increased to a new fixed amount when the size of the studio increased beyond a certain point. An example of the behavior of total fixed costs through all potential levels of activity is shown in part (b) of Illustration 23-3.

For most companies, operating at almost zero or at 100 percent capacity is the exception rather than the rule. Instead, companies often operate over a somewhat narrower range, such as 40–80 percent of capacity. The range over which a company expects to operate during a year is called the **relevant range** of the activity index. Within the relevant range, as shown in both diagrams in Illustration 23-4, a straight-line relationship generally exists for both variable and fixed costs.

HELPFUL HINT

Fixed costs that may be changeable include research, such as new product development, and management training programs.

ALTERNATIVE TERMINOLOGY

The relevant range is also called the *normal* or *practical range.*

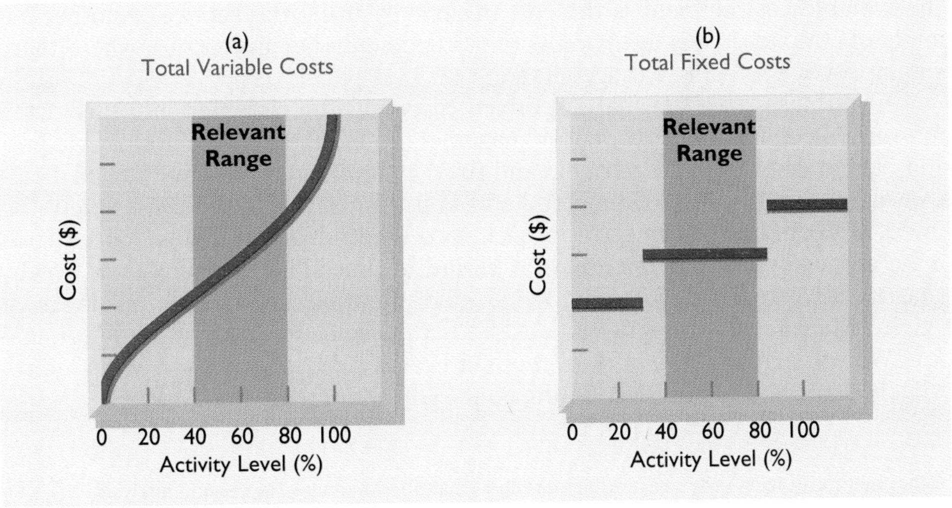

Illustration 23-4

Linear behavior within relevant range

As you can see, although the straight-line relationship may not be completely realistic, **the linear assumption produces useful data for CVP analysis as long as the level of activity remains within the relevant range.**

MIXED COSTS

STUDY OBJECTIVE 3

Explain the concept of mixed costs.

Mixed costs are costs that contain both a variable element and a fixed element. Sometimes called **semivariable costs, mixed costs change in total but not proportionately with changes in the activity level.** The rental of a U-Haul truck is a good example of a mixed cost. Assume that local rental terms for a 17-foot truck, including insurance, are \$50 per day plus 50 cents per mile. The per diem charge is a fixed cost with respect to miles driven, whereas the mileage charge is a variable cost. The graphic presentation of the rental cost for a one-day rental is as follows.

Illustration 23-5

Behavior of a mixed cost

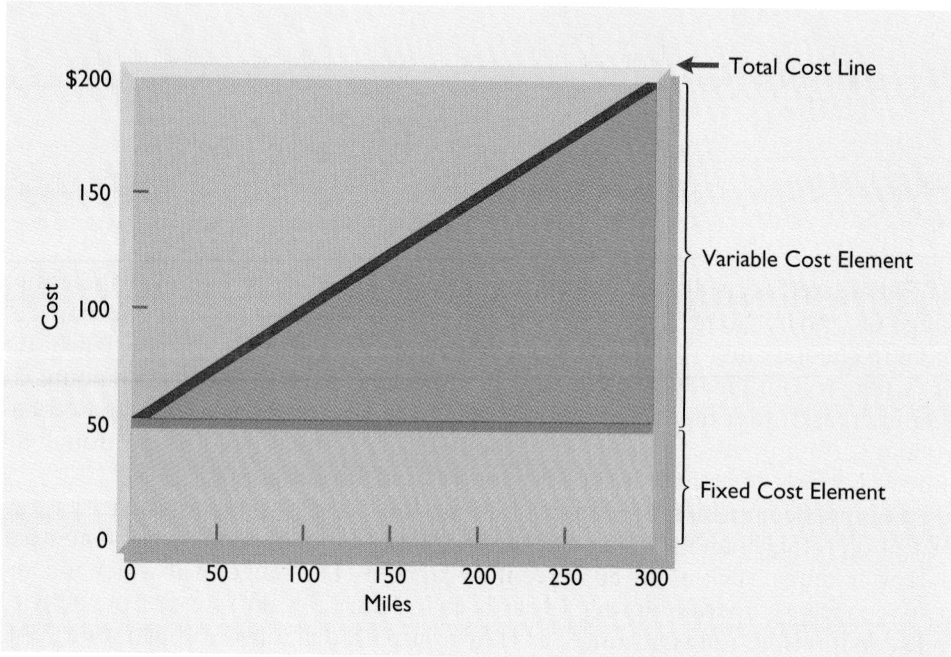

In this case, the fixed cost element is the cost of having the service available. The variable cost element is the cost of actually using the service. Another example of a mixed cost is utility costs (electric, telephone, and so on), where there is a flat service fee plus a usage charge.

For purposes of CVP analysis, **mixed costs must be classified into their fixed and variable elements**. How does management make the classification? One possibility is to determine the variable and fixed components each time a mixed cost is incurred. But because of time and cost constraints, this approach is rarely followed. Instead, the customary approach is to determine variable and fixed costs on an **aggregate basis at the end of a period of time**. The company does this by using its past experience with the behavior of the mixed cost at various levels of activity. Management may use any of several methods in making the determination. We will explain the **high-low method** here. Other methods are more appropriately explained in cost accounting courses.[1]

[1]Other methods include the scatter diagram method and least squares regression analysis.

High-Low Method

The **high-low method** uses the total costs incurred at the high and low levels of activity. The difference in costs between the high and low levels represents variable costs, since only the variable cost element can change as activity levels change. The steps in computing fixed and variable costs under this method are as follows.

1. **Determine variable cost per unit from the following formula.**

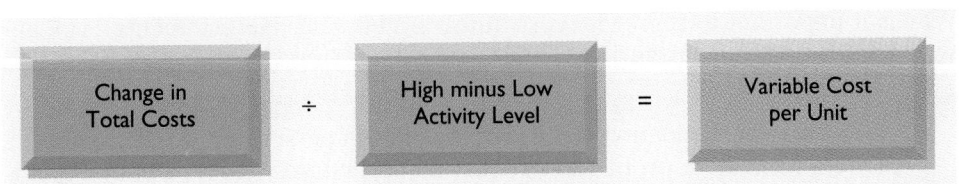

Illustration 23-6

Formula for variable cost per unit using high-low method

Change in Total Costs	÷	High minus Low Activity Level	=	Variable Cost per Unit

To illustrate, assume that Metro Transit Company has the following maintenance costs and mileage data for its fleet of buses over a 4-month period.

Illustration 23-7

Assumed maintenance costs and mileage data

Month	Miles Driven	Total Cost	Month	Miles Driven	Total Cost
January	**20,000**	**$30,000**	March	35,000	$49,000
February	40,000	48,000	April	**50,000**	**63,000**

The high and low levels of activity are 50,000 miles in April and 20,000 miles in January. The maintenance costs at these two levels are $63,000 and $30,000, respectively. The difference in maintenance costs is $33,000 ($63,000 − $30,000) and the difference in miles is 30,000 (50,000 − 20,000). Therefore, for Metro Transit, variable cost per unit is $1.10, computed as follows.

$$\$33{,}000 \div 30{,}000 = \$1.10$$

2. **Determine the fixed cost by subtracting the total variable cost at either the high or the low activity level from the total cost at that activity level.**

For Metro Transit, the computations are shown in Illustration 23-8.

Illustration 23-8

High-low method computation of fixed costs

	Activity Level	
	High	**Low**
Total cost	$63,000	$30,000
Less: Variable costs		
50,000 × $1.10	55,000	
20,000 × $1.10		22,000
Total fixed costs	$ 8,000	$ 8,000

Maintenance costs are therefore $8,000 per month plus $1.10 per mile. For example, at 45,000 miles, estimated maintenance costs would be $8,000 fixed and $49,500 variable (45,000 × $1.10).

The high-low method generally produces a reasonable estimate for analysis. However, it does not produce a precise measurement of the fixed and variable elements in a mixed cost because other activity levels are ignored in the computation.

IMPORTANCE OF IDENTIFYING VARIABLE AND FIXED COSTS

Why is it important to segregate costs into variable and fixed elements? The answer may become apparent if we look at the following four business decisions.

1. If **American Airlines** is to make a profit when it reduces all domestic fares by 30 percent, what reduction in costs or increase in passengers will be required? **Answer:** To make a profit when it cuts domestic fares by 30 percent, American Airlines will have to increase the number of passengers or cut its variable costs for those flights. Its fixed costs will not change.
2. If **Ford Motor Company** meets the United Auto Workers' demands for higher wages, what increase in sales revenue will be needed to maintain current profit levels? **Answer:** Higher wages to UAW members at Ford Motor Company will increase the variable costs of manufacturing automobiles. To maintain present profit levels, Ford will have to cut other variable costs or increase the price of its automobiles.
3. If **USX Corp.'s** program to modernize plant facilities reduces the work force by 50 percent, what will be the effect on the cost of producing one ton of steel? **Answer:** The modernizing of plant facilities at USX Corp. changes the proportion of fixed and variable costs of producing one ton of steel. Fixed costs increase because of higher depreciation charges whereas variable costs decrease due to the reduction in the number of steelworkers.
4. What happens if **Kellogg Company** increases its advertising expenses but can't increase prices because of competitive pressure? **Answer:** Sales volume must be increased to cover three items: (1) the increase in advertising, (2) the variable cost of the increased sales volume, and (3) the desired additional net income.

BEFORE YOU GO ON...

REVIEW IT

1. What are the effects on (a) a variable cost and (b) a fixed cost due to a change in activity?
2. What is the relevant range, and how do costs behave within this range?
3. What are the steps in applying the high-low method to mixed costs?

DO IT

Helena Company reports the following total costs at two levels of production.

	10,000 units	20,000 units
Direct materials	$20,000	$40,000
Maintenance	8,000	10,000
Depreciation	4,000	4,000

Classify each cost as either variable, fixed, or mixed.

ACTION PLAN
- Recall that a variable cost varies in total directly and proportionately with each change.
- Recall that a fixed cost remains the same in total with each change.
- Recall that a mixed cost changes in total but not proportionately with each change.

SOLUTION: Direct materials is a variable cost. Maintenance is a mixed cost. Depreciation is a fixed cost.

Related exercise material: BE23-1, E23-1, and E23-2.

THE NAVIGATOR

COST-VOLUME-PROFIT ANALYSIS

STUDY OBJECTIVE 4

List the five components of cost-volume-profit analysis.

Cost-volume-profit (CVP) analysis is the study of the effects of changes in costs and volume on a company's profits. CVP analysis is important in profit planning. It also is a critical factor in such management decisions as setting selling prices, determining product mix, and maximizing use of production facilities.

BASIC COMPONENTS

CVP analysis considers the interrelationships among the components shown in Illustration 23-9.

Illustration 23-9

Components of CVP analysis

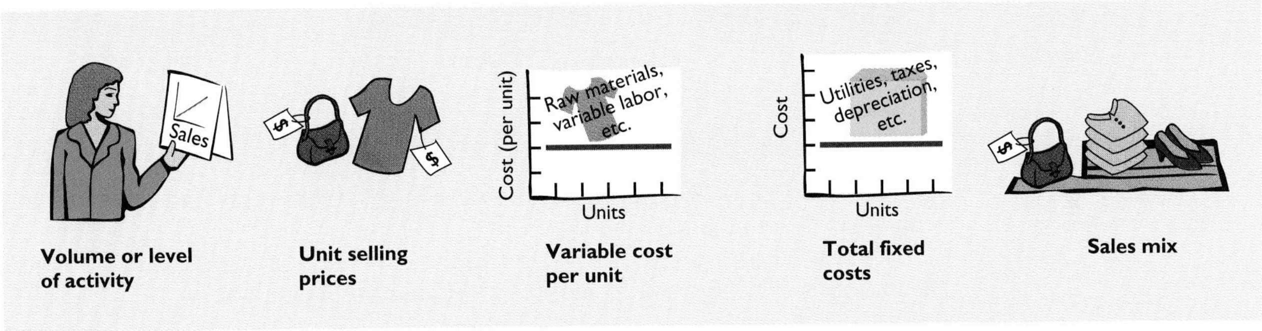

The following assumptions underlie each CVP analysis.

1. The behavior of both costs and revenues is linear throughout the relevant range of the activity index.
2. All costs can be classified with reasonable accuracy as either variable or fixed.
3. Changes in activity are the only factors that affect costs.
4. All units produced are sold.
5. When more than one type of product is sold, the sales mix will remain constant. That is, the percentage that each product represents of total sales will stay the same. Sales mix complicates CVP analysis because different products will have different cost relationships. In this text we assume a single product. Technical issues of addressing sales mix problems are dealt with in advanced accounting courses.

When these five assumptions are not valid, the results of CVP analysis may be inaccurate.

In the applications of CVP analysis that follow, we will assume that the term "cost" includes **all** costs and expenses pertaining to production and sale of the product. That is, **cost includes manufacturing costs plus selling and administrative expenses**. We will use Vargo Video Company as an example. Relevant data for the videocassette recorders (VCRs) made by this company are as follows.

Illustration 23-10

Assumed selling price and cost data for Vargo Video

Unit selling price	$500
Unit variable costs	$300
Total monthly fixed costs	$200,000

CONTRIBUTION MARGIN

STUDY OBJECTIVE 5

Indicate what contribution margin is and how it can be expressed.

One of the key relationships in CVP analysis is **contribution margin (CM)**. **Contribution margin is the amount of revenue remaining after deducting variable costs.** For example, if we assume that Vargo Video sells 1,000 VCRs in one month, sales are $500,000 (1,000 × $500) and variable costs are $300,000 (1,000 × $300). Thus, contribution margin is $200,000, computed as follows.

Illustration 23-11

Formula for and computation of contribution margin

Sales	−	Variable Costs	=	Contribution Margin
$500,000	−	$300,000	=	$200,000

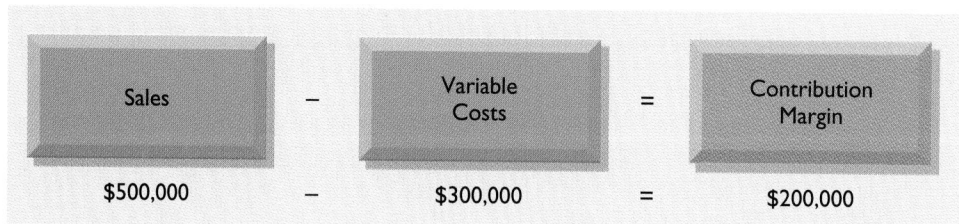

This contribution margin is then available to cover fixed costs and to contribute income for the company.

Views differ as to the best way to express contribution margin. Some favor a per unit basis. The formula for **contribution margin per unit** is:

Illustration 23-12

Formula for contribution margin per unit

Unit Selling Price	−	Unit Variable Costs	=	Contribution Margin per Unit

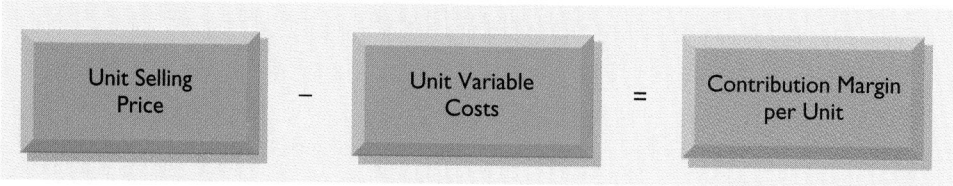

At Vargo Video, the contribution margin per unit is $200, computed as follows.

$$\$500 - \$300 = \$200$$

Contribution margin per unit indicates that for every VCR sold, Vargo will have $200 to cover fixed costs and contribute to income. Since fixed costs are $200,000, Vargo Video must sell 1,000 VCRs ($200,000 ÷ $200) before there is any income. Above that sales volume, every sale will contribute $200 to income. Thus, if 1,500 units are sold, income will be $100,000 (500 × $200).

Others prefer to use a **contribution margin ratio**. The ratio formula is:

Contribution Margin per Unit ÷ Unit Selling Price = Contribution Margin Ratio

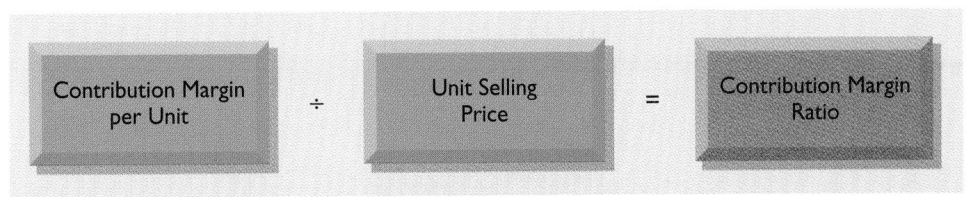

Illustration 23-13
Formula for contribution margin ratio

At Vargo Video, the ratio is 40 percent, as shown below.

$$\$200 \div \$500 = 40\%$$

The CM ratio of 40 percent means that 40 cents of each sales dollar ($1 × 40%) is available to apply to fixed costs and to contribute to income.

The contribution margin ratio is helpful in determining the effect on income of changes in sales. To illustrate, if Vargo Video wants to know the effect of a $50,000 increase in sales, they simply multiply $50,000 by the CM ratio (40%) to determine that income will increase $20,000.

HELPFUL HINT
The same ratio results from dividing total CM by total sales; i.e., $200,000 ÷ $500,000 = 40%.

BREAK-EVEN ANALYSIS

STUDY OBJECTIVE 6
Identify the three ways to determine the break-even point.

A second key relationship in CVP analysis is the level of activity at which total revenues equal total costs (both fixed and variable). This level of activity is called the **break-even point**. At this volume of sales, the company will realize no income and will suffer no loss. The process of finding the break-even point is called **break-even analysis**. Knowledge of the break-even point is useful to management when it decides whether to introduce new product lines, change sales prices on established products, or enter new market areas.

The break-even point can be:

1. Computed from a mathematical equation.
2. Computed by using contribution margin.
3. Derived from a cost-volume-profit (CVP) graph.

The break-even point can be expressed **either in sales dollars or sales units.**

ACCOUNTING IN ACTION — e-Business Insight

The Internet is wringing inefficiencies out of nearly every industry. While commercial aircraft spend roughly 4,000 hours a year in the air, chartered aircraft spend only 500 hours flying. That means that they are sitting on the ground—not making any money—nearly 90 percent of the time. Enter **flightserve.com**. For about the same cost as a first-class ticket, flightserve.com matches up executives with charter flights in small "private jets." The executive gets a more comfortable ride and can avoid the hassle of big airports. Flightserve.com says that the average charter jet has eight seats. When all eight seats are full, the company has an 80 percent profit margin. It breaks even at an average of 3.3 full seats per flight.

SOURCE: "Jet Set Go," *The Economist*, March 18, 2000, p. 68.

Mathematical Equation

In its simplest form, the equation for break-even sales is:

Illustration 23-14

Break-even equation

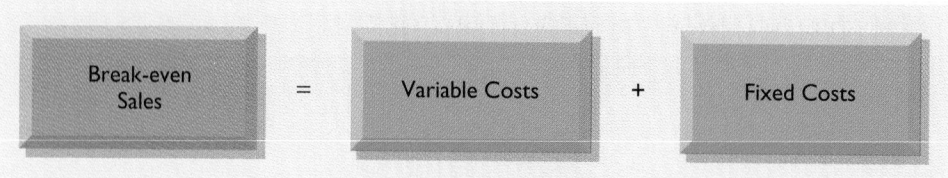

Break-even Sales = Variable Costs + Fixed Costs

The break-even point **in dollars** is found by expressing **variable costs as a percentage of unit selling price**. For Vargo Video, the percentage is 60 percent ($300 ÷ $500). The computation to determine sales dollars at the break-even point is:

Illustration 23-15

Computation of break-even point in dollars

$$X = .60X + \$200{,}000$$
$$.40X = \$200{,}000$$
$$X = \mathbf{\$500{,}000}$$

where:

X = sales dollars at the break-even point
.60 = variable costs as a percentage of unit selling price
$200,000 = total fixed costs

Therefore, sales must be $500,000 for Vargo Video to break even.

The break-even point **in units** can be computed directly from the mathematical equation by **using unit selling prices** and **unit variable costs**. The computation is:

Illustration 23-16

Computation of break-even point in units

$$\$500X = \$300X + \$200{,}000$$
$$\$200X = \$200{,}000$$
$$X = \mathbf{1{,}000\ units}$$

where:

X = sales volume
$500 = unit selling price
$300 = variable cost per unit
$200,000 = total fixed costs

Thus, Vargo Video must sell 1,000 units to break even. The accuracy of the computations can be proved as follows.

Illustration 23-17

Break-even proof

Sales (1,000 × $500)		$500,000
Total costs:		
Variable (1,000 × $300)	$300,000	
Fixed	200,000	500,000
Net income		**$ -0-**

Contribution Margin Technique

We know that contribution margin equals total revenues less variable costs. It follows that at the break-even point, **contribution margin must equal total fixed costs**. On the basis of this relationship, we can compute the break-even point using either the contribution margin per unit or the contribution margin ratio.

When the contribution margin per unit is used, the formula to compute break-even point in units is as follows.

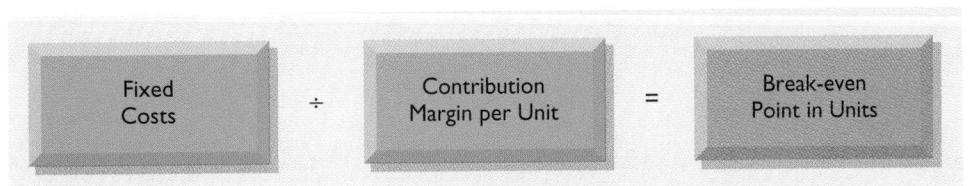

Illustration 23-18

Formula for break-even point in units using contribution margin

Fixed Costs	÷	Contribution Margin per Unit	=	Break-even Point in Units

For Vargo Video, the contribution margin per unit is \$200, as explained earlier. Thus, the break-even point in units is:

$$\$200{,}000 \div \$200 = 1{,}000 \text{ units}$$

When the contribution margin ratio is used, the formula to compute break-even point in dollars is:

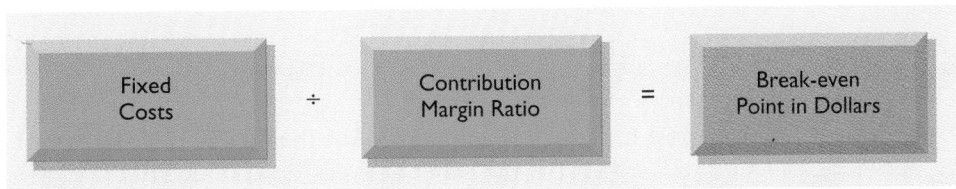

Illustration 23-19

Formula for break-even point in dollars using contribution margin ratio

Fixed Costs	÷	Contribution Margin Ratio	=	Break-even Point in Dollars

We know that the contribution margin ratio for Vargo Video is 40 percent. Thus, the break-even point in dollars is:

$$\$200{,}000 \div 40\% = \$500{,}000$$

Graphic Presentation

An effective way to find the break-even point is to prepare a break-even graph. Because this graph also shows costs, volume, and profits, it is referred to as a **cost-volume-profit (CVP) graph**.

As shown in the CVP graph in Illustration 23-20, sales volume is recorded along the horizontal axis. This axis should extend to the maximum level of expected sales. Both total revenues (sales) and total costs (fixed plus variable) are recorded on the vertical axis.

The construction of the graph, using the data for Vargo Video, is as follows.

1. Plot the total-revenue line, starting at the zero activity level. For every VCR sold, total revenue increases by \$500. For example, at 200 units, sales are \$100,000. At the upper level of activity (1,800 units), sales are \$900,000. Note that the revenue line is assumed to be linear throughout the full range of activity.

Illustration 23-20

CVP graph

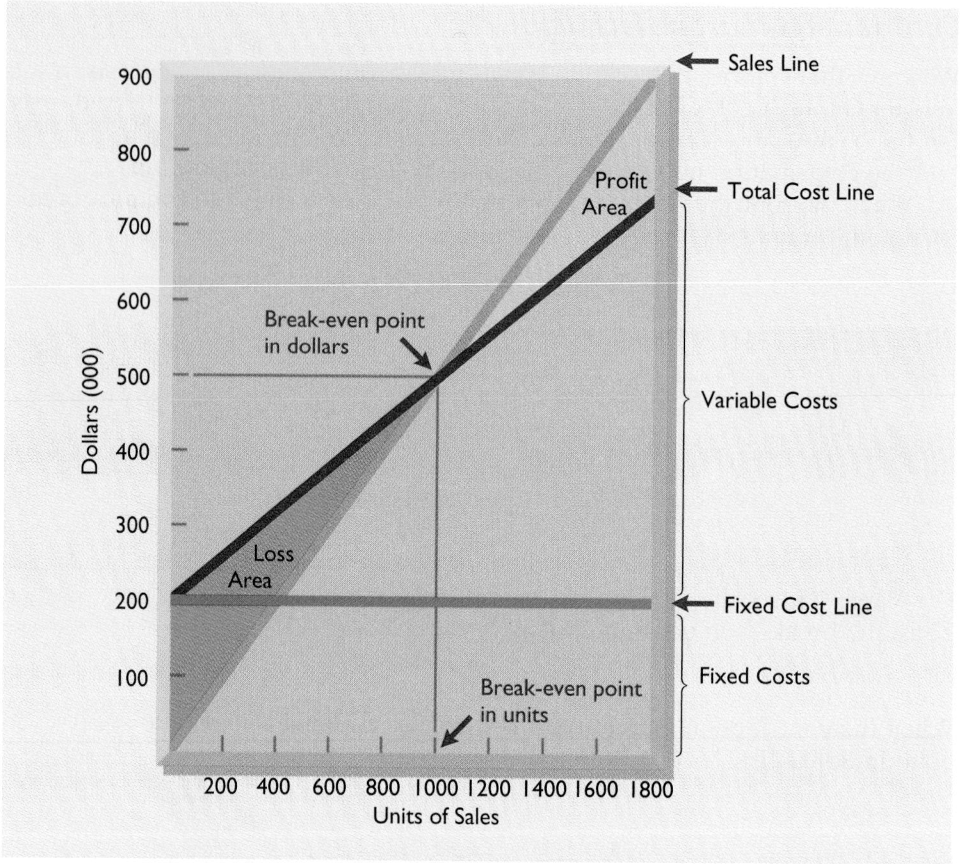

2. Plot the total fixed cost using a horizontal line. For the VCRs, this line is plotted at \$200,000. The fixed cost is the same at every level of activity.
3. Plot the total cost line. This starts at the fixed-cost line at zero activity. It increases by the variable cost at each level of activity. For each VCR, variable costs are \$300. Thus, at 200 units, total variable cost is \$60,000, and the total cost is \$260,000. At 1,800 units total variable cost is \$540,000, and total cost is \$740,000. On the graph, the amount of the variable cost can be derived from the difference between the total cost and fixed cost lines at each level of activity.
4. Determine the break-even point from the intersection of the total cost line and the total revenue line. The break-even point in dollars is found by drawing a horizontal line from the break-even point to the vertical axis. The break-even point in units is found by drawing a vertical line from the break-even point to the horizontal axis. For the VCRs, the break-even point is \$500,000 of sales, or 1,000 units. At this sales level, Vargo Video will cover costs but make no profit.

The CVP graph also shows both the net income and net loss areas. Thus, the amount of income or loss at each level of sales can be derived from the total sales and total cost lines.

A CVP graph is useful because the effects of a change in any element in the CVP analysis can be quickly seen. For example, a 10 percent increase in selling price will change the location of the total revenue line. Likewise, the effects on total costs of wage increases can be quickly observed.

TECHNOLOGY IN ACTION

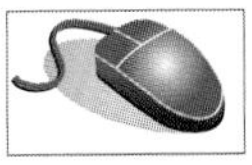

Computer graphics are a valuable companion to an increasing number of computer software packages. Graphs can be instantly changed to provide visual "what if" analysis. This can all be done in color for either video or hard copy output.

Current technology allows for stunning graphs in a variety of different formats (pie charts, bar, stacked bar, two-dimensional, three-dimensional, etc.). In the appropriate situation, a graph can literally be worth a thousand words.

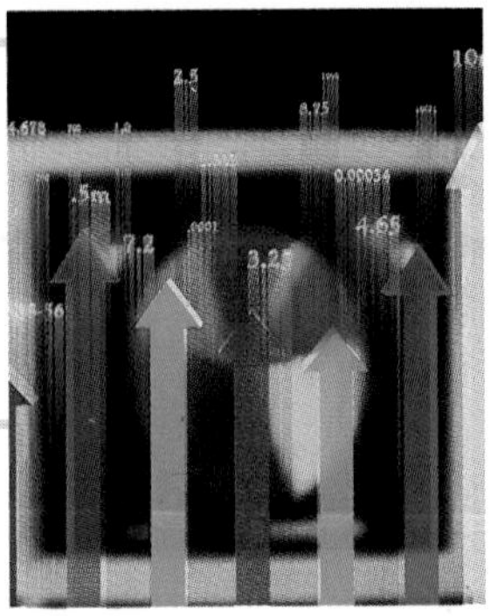

BEFORE YOU GO ON...

REVIEW IT

1. What are the assumptions that underlie each CVP application?
2. What is contribution margin, and how can it be expressed?
3. How can the break-even point be determined?

DO IT

Lombardi Company has a unit selling price of \$400, variable costs per unit of \$240, and fixed costs of \$160,000. Compute the break-even point in units using (a) a mathematical equation and (b) contribution margin per unit.

ACTION PLAN

- Apply the equation: Break-even sales = Variable costs + Fixed costs.
- Apply the formula: Fixed costs ÷ Contribution margin per unit = Break-even point in units.

SOLUTION: (a) The equation is \$400X = \$240X + \$160,000. The break-even point in units is 1,000 (\$160,000 ÷ \$160X). (b) Contribution margin per unit is \$160 (\$400 − \$240). The formula is \$160,000 ÷ \$160, and the break-even point in units is 1,000.

Related exercise material: BE23-5, BE23-6, E23-3, E23-4, E23-5, E23-6, and E23-7.

THE NAVIGATOR

MARGIN OF SAFETY

STUDY OBJECTIVE 7

Define margin of safety, and give the formulas for computing it.

The margin of safety is another relationship that may be calculated in CVP analysis. Margin of safety is the difference between actual or expected sales and sales at the break-even point. This relationship measures the "cushion" that management has, allowing it to still break even if expected sales fail to materialize. The margin of safety may be expressed in dollars or as a ratio.

The formula for stating the **margin of safety in dollars** is:

Actual (Expected) Sales	−	Break-even Sales	=	Margin of Safety in Dollars

Illustration 23-21

Formula for margin of safety in dollars

Assuming that actual (expected) sales for Vargo Video are \$750,000, the computation is:

$$\$750,000 - \$500,000 = \$250,000$$

The formula and computation for determining the **margin of safety ratio** are:

Illustration 23-22

Formula for margin of safety ratio

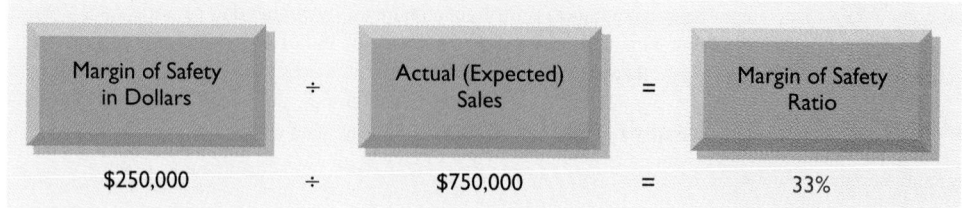

Margin of Safety in Dollars	÷	Actual (Expected) Sales	=	Margin of Safety Ratio
$250,000	÷	$750,000	=	33%

The higher the dollars or the percentage, the greater the margin of safety. The adequacy of the margin of safety should be evaluated by management in terms of such factors as the vulnerability of the product to competitive pressures and to downturns in the economy.

ACCOUNTING IN ACTION *Business Insight*

Computation of break-even and margin of safety is important for various types of businesses. Consider how the promoter for the Rolling Stones' tour used the break-even point and margin of safety. For example, one outdoor show should bring 70,000 individuals for a gross of $2.45 million. The promoter guarantees $1.2 million to the Rolling Stones. In addition, 20 percent of gross, or approximately $500,000, goes to the stadium in which the performance is staged. Add another $400,000 for other expenses such as ticket takers, parking attendants, advertising, and so on. This leaves $350,000 to the promoter per show, if it sells out. At 75 percent, the promoter breaks about even. At 50 percent, the promoter loses hundreds of thousands of dollars. However, the promoter also shares in sales of T-shirts and memorabilia for which the promoter will net over $7 million during the tour. From a successful Rolling Stones' tour, the promoter could make $35 million!

TARGET NET INCOME

STUDY OBJECTIVE 8

Give the formulas for determining sales required to earn target net income.

Management usually sets an income objective for individual product lines. This objective is called **target net income**. It indicates the sales necessary to achieve a specified level of income. The sales necessary to achieve target net income can be determined from each of the approaches used to determine break-even sales.

Mathematical Equation

We know that at the break-even point no profit or loss results for the company. By adding a factor for target net income to the break-even equation, we obtain the following formula for determining required sales.

Illustration 23-23

Formula for required sales to meet target net income

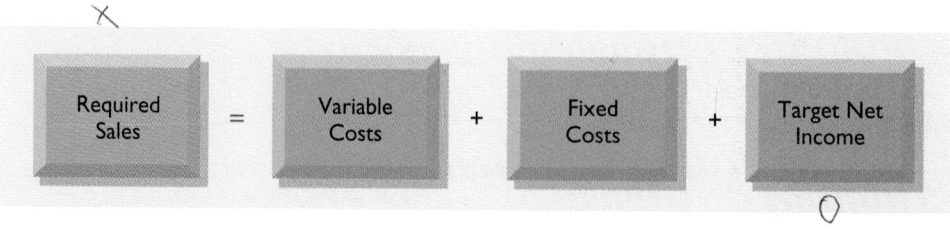

Required Sales	=	Variable Costs	+	Fixed Costs	+	Target Net Income

Required sales may be expressed in **either sales dollars or sales units**. Assuming that target net income is \$120,000 for Vargo Video, the computation of required sales in dollars is as follows.

$$X = .60X + \$200{,}000 + \$120{,}000$$
$$.40X = \$320{,}000$$
$$X = \mathbf{\$800{,}000}$$

where:

X = required sales
.60 = variable costs as a percentage of unit selling price
\$200,000 = total fixed costs
\$120,000 = target net income

Illustration 23-24

Computation of required sales

HELPFUL HINT

Alternatively, the required sales units can be computed directly by using unit prices in the equation: $\$500X = \$300X + \$200{,}000 + \$120{,}000$; $\$200X = \$320{,}000$, or 1,600 units.

The sales volume in units at the targeted income level is found by dividing the sales dollars by the unit selling price (\$800,000 ÷ \$500) = 1,600 units.

Contribution Margin Technique

As in the case of break-even sales, the sales required to meet a target net income can be computed in either dollars or units. The formula using the contribution margin ratio is as follows:

Fixed Costs + Target Net Income ÷ Contribution Margin Ratio = Required Sales

Illustration 23-25

Formula for required sales in dollars using contribution margin ratio

The computation for Vargo Video is as follows.

$$\$320{,}000 \div 40\% = \$800{,}000$$

Graphic Presentation

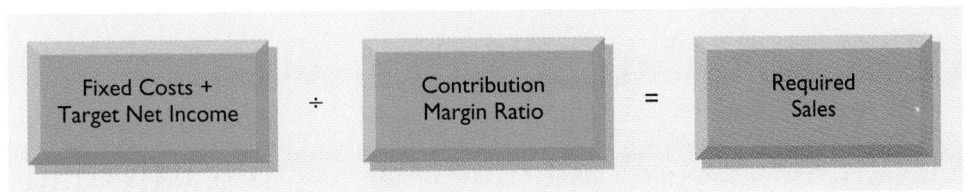

The CVP graph in Illustration 23-20 (on page 958) can also be used to find the sales required to meet target net income. In the profit area of the graph, the distance between the sales line and the total cost line at any point equals net income. Required sales are found by analyzing the differences between the two lines until the desired net income is found.

CVP AND CHANGES IN THE BUSINESS ENVIRONMENT

When the IBM personal computer (PC) was introduced, it sold for \$2,500. Today the same type of computer sells for much less. Recently, when oil prices rose, the break-even point for airline and trucking companies rose dramatically. Because of lower prices for imported steel, the demand for domestic steel dropped significantly. The point should be clear: Business conditions change rapidly, and management must respond intelligently to these changes. CVP analysis can help.

To illustrate how CVP analysis can be used in responding to change, we will look at three independent situations that might occur at Vargo Video. Each case is based on the original VCR sales and cost data, which were:

Illustration 23-26

Original VCR sales and cost data

Unit selling price	$500
Unit variable cost	$300
Total fixed costs	$200,000
Break-even sales	$500,000 or 1,000 units

CASE I. A competitor is offering a 10% discount on the selling price of its VCRs. Management must decide whether to offer a similar discount. **Question:** What effect will a 10 percent discount on selling price have on the break-even point for VCRs? **Answer:** A 10 percent discount on selling price reduces the selling price per unit to $450 [$500 − ($500 × 10%)]. Variable costs per unit remain unchanged at $300. Thus, the contribution margin per unit is $150. Assuming no change in fixed costs, break-even sales are 1,333 units, computed as follows.

Illustration 23-27

Computation of break-even sales in units

Fixed Costs	÷	Contribution Margin per Unit	=	Break-even Sales
$200,000	÷	$150	=	1,333 units (rounded)

For Vargo Video, this change would require monthly sales to increase by 333 units, or 33⅓ percent, in order to break even. In reaching a conclusion about offering a 10 percent discount to customers, management must determine how likely it is to achieve the increased sales. Also, management should estimate the possible loss of sales if the competitor's discount price is not matched.

CASE II. To meet the threat of foreign competition, management invests in new robotic equipment that will lower the amount of direct labor required to make the VCRs. It is estimated that total fixed costs will increase 30 percent and that variable cost per unit will decrease 30 percent. **Question**: What effect will the new equipment have on the sales volume required to break even? **Answer**: Total fixed costs become $260,000 [$200,000 + (30% × $200,000)]. The variable cost per unit becomes $210 [$300 − (30% × $300)]. The new break-even point is approximately 900 units, computed as follows.

Illustration 23-28

Computation of break-even sales in units

Fixed Costs	÷	Contribution Margin per Unit	=	Break-even Sales
$260,000	÷	($500 − $210)	=	900 units (rounded)

These changes appear to be advantageous for Vargo Video. The break-even point is reduced by 10 percent, or 100 units.

CASE III. Vargo's principal supplier of raw materials has just announced a price increase. The higher cost is expected to increase the variable cost of VCRs by $25 per unit. Management would like to hold the line on the selling price of VCRs. It plans a cost-cutting program that will save $17,500 in fixed costs per month. Vargo is currently realizing monthly net income of $80,000 on sales of 1,400 VCRs. **Question**: What increase in sales will be needed to maintain the same level of net income? **Answer**: The variable cost per unit increases to $325 ($300 + $25). Fixed costs are reduced to $182,500 ($200,000 − $17,500). Because of the change in variable cost, the variable cost becomes 65 percent of sales ($325 ÷ $500). Using the equation for target net income, we find that required sales are $750,000, computed as follows.

Required Sales	=	**Variable Costs**	+	**Fixed Costs**	+	**Target Net Income**
X	=	$.65X$	+	\$182,500	+	\$80,000
$.35X$	=	\$262,500				
X	=	**\$750,000**				

Illustration 23-29

Computation of required sales

To achieve the required sales, 1,500 VCRs will have to be sold (\$750,000 ÷ \$500), an increase of 100 units. If this does not seem to be a reasonable expectation, management will either have to make further cost reductions or accept less net income if the selling price remains unchanged.

ACCOUNTING IN ACTION e Business Insight

When analyzing an Internet business, the so-called "conversion rate" is closely watched. It is calculated by dividing the number of people who actually take action at an Internet site (e.g., buy something) by the total number of people who visit the site. Average conversion rates are from 3 to 5 percent. A rate below 2 percent is poor, while a rate above 10 percent is great.

Conversion rates have an obvious effect on break-even point. Suppose you spend \$10,000 on your site, and you attract 5,000 visitors. If you get a 2 percent conversion rate (100 purchases), your site costs \$100 per purchase (\$10,000 ÷ 100). A 4 percent conversion rate gets you down to a cost of \$50 per transaction, and an 8 percent conversion rate gets you down to \$25. Studies have shown that conversion rates increase if the site has an easy-to-use interface, fast-performing screens, a convenient ordering process, and advertising that is both clever and clear.

SOURCE: J. William Gurley, "The One Internet Metric That Really Counts," *Fortune,* March 6, 2000, p. 392.

CVP INCOME STATEMENT

STUDY OBJECTIVE 9

Describe the essential features of a cost-volume-profit income statement.

As you have learned, cost behavior and contribution margin are key factors in CVP analysis. Because management makes its decisions on these factors, it often wants the results of these decisions reported in a similar format. This has led to the development **for internal use only** of a **CVP** or **contribution margin format** for the income statement. The **CVP income statement** classifies costs and expenses as variable or fixed. It also specifically reports contribution margin in the body of the statement. In contrast, the income statement traditionally prepared for external use does not disclose the behavior of costs and expenses. In the traditional statement, costs and expenses are classified only by function, such as cost of goods sold, selling expenses, and administrative expenses.

To illustrate the CVP income statement, we will assume that Vargo Video reaches its target net income of \$120,000 (see Illustration 23-24 on page 961). The following information is obtained on the \$680,000 of costs that were incurred in June.

Illustration 23-30

Assumed cost and expense data

	Variable	**Fixed**	**Total**
Cost of goods sold	\$400,000	\$120,000	\$520,000
Selling expenses	60,000	40,000	100,000
Administrative expenses	20,000	40,000	60,000
	\$480,000	\$200,000	\$680,000

Illustration 23-31

Traditional versus CVP income statements

The traditional and CVP income statements for Vargo are shown side-by-side for comparative purposes in Illustration 23-31.

VARGO VIDEO COMPANY
Income Statements
For the Month Ended June 30, 2002

Traditional Format			CVP Format		
Sales		$800,000	Sales		$800,000
Cost of goods sold		520,000	Variable expenses		
Gross profit		280,000	Cost of goods sold	$400,000	
Operating expenses			Selling expenses	60,000	
Selling expenses	$100,000		Administrative expenses	20,000	
Administrative expenses	60,000		Total variable expenses		480,000
Total operating expenses		160,000	**Contribution margin**		**320,000**
Net income		$120,000	Fixed expenses		
			Cost of goods sold	120,000	
			Selling expenses	40,000	
			Administrative expenses	40,000	
			Total fixed expenses		200,000
			Net income		$120,000

Note that net income is the same ($120,000) in both statements. The major difference is the format for the expenses: The CVP statement classifies costs and expenses as either variable or fixed. Another difference is that the traditional statement shows gross profit, whereas the CVP statement shows contribution margin. Study the CVP format carefully. It will be used in remaining chapters, and it is often used in business in internal reporting to management.

BEFORE YOU GO ON...

REVIEW IT

1. What is the formula for computing the margin of safety (a) in dollars and (b) as a ratio?
2. How does a CVP income statement differ from a traditional income statement?

A LOOK BACK AT OUR FEATURE STORY

Refer back to the Feature Story about Amy's dance studio at the beginning of the chapter, and answer the following questions.

1. What are some variable costs that Amy's dance studio might incur?
2. What are some fixed costs that Amy's dance studio might incur?
3. Why is it important to segregate costs into variable and fixed costs when analyzing profitability?

SOLUTION

1. Some variable costs are instructors' wages, dance towels, dance shoes, and leotards.
2. Some fixed costs are insurance, depreciation, rent, utilities, administrative salaries, and maintenance and repairs.

3. For Amy to determine whether to increase the size of her studio, she must understand how changes in volume affect changes in revenues and costs. For example, when advertising expense is increased, it may increase volume and profit, or it may increase volume but not generate any additional profit. By segregating costs into variable and fixed, Amy can determine what dollar impact a change in sales revenue will have on overall profit.

THE NAVIGATOR

DEMONSTRATION PROBLEM

Additional Demonstration Problem

Mabo Company makes calculators that sell for \$20 each. For the coming year, management expects fixed costs to total \$220,000 and variable costs to be \$9.00 per unit.

Instructions:

(a) Compute break-even sales in dollars using the mathematical equation.
(b) Compute break-even sales using the contribution margin (CM) ratio.
(c) Compute the margin of safety percentage assuming actual sales are \$500,000.
(d) Compute the sales required to earn net income of \$165,000.

SOLUTION TO DEMONSTRATION PROBLEM

(a) Break-even sales = Variable costs + Fixed costs

$$X = .45X + \$220{,}000$$
$$.55X = \$220{,}000$$
$$X = \$400{,}000$$

(b) Contribution margin per unit = Unit selling price − Unit variable costs

$$\$11 = \$20 - \$9$$

Contribution margin ratio = Contribution margin per unit ÷ Unit selling price

$$55\% = \$11 \div \$20$$

Break-even sales = Fixed cost ÷ Contribution margin ratio

$$X = \$220{,}000 \div 55\%$$
$$X = \$400{,}000$$

(c)
$$\text{Margin of safety} = \frac{\text{Actual sales} - \text{Break-even sales}}{\text{Actual sales}} = \frac{\$500{,}000 - \$400{,}000}{\$500{,}000} = 20\%$$

(d) Required sales = Variable costs + Fixed costs + Net income

$$X = .45X + \$220{,}000 + \$165{,}000$$
$$.55X = \$385{,}000$$
$$X = \$700{,}000$$

THE NAVIGATOR

ACTION PLAN

- Know the formulas.
- Recognize that variable costs change with sales volume; fixed costs do not.
- Avoid computational errors.
- Prove your answers.

SUMMARY OF STUDY OBJECTIVES

1. *Distinguish between variable and fixed costs.* Variable costs are costs that vary in total directly and proportionately with changes in the activity index. Fixed costs are costs that remain the same in total regardless of changes in the activity index.

2. *Explain the significance of the relevant range.* The relevant range is the range of activity in which a company expects to operate during a year. It is important in CVP analysis because the behavior of costs is linear throughout the relevant range.

3. *Explain the concept of mixed costs.* Mixed costs increase in total but not proportionately with changes in the activity level. For purposes of CVP analysis, mixed costs must be classified into their fixed and variable elements. One method that management may use is the high-low method.

4. *List the five components of cost-volume-profit analysis.* The five components of CVP analysis are (a) volume or level of activity, (b) unit selling prices, (c) variable cost per unit, (d) total fixed costs, and (e) sales mix.

5. *Indicate what contribution margin is and how it can be expressed.* Contribution margin is the amount of revenue remaining after deducting variable costs. It can be expressed as a per unit amount or as a ratio.

6. *Identify the three ways to determine the break-even point.* The break-even point can be (a) computed from a mathematical equation, (b) computed by using a contribution margin technique, and (c) derived from a CVP graph.

7. *Define margin of safety, and give the formulas for computing it.* Margin of safety is the difference between actual or expected sales and sales at the break-even point. The formulas for margin of safety are: Actual (expected) sales − Break-even sales = Margin of safety in dollars; Margin of safety in dollars ÷ Actual (expected) sales = Margin of safety ratio.

8. *Give the formulas for determining sales required to earn target net income.* One formula is: Required sales = Variable costs + Fixed costs + Target net income. Another formula is: Fixed costs + Target net income ÷ Contribution margin ratio = Required sales.

9. *Describe the essential features of a cost-volume-profit income statement.* The CVP income statement classifies costs and expenses as variable or fixed and reports contribution margin in the body of the statement.

THE NAVIGATOR

Key Term Matching Activity

GLOSSARY

Activity index The activity that causes changes in the behavior of costs. (p. 946).

Break-even point The level of activity at which total revenues equal total costs. (p. 955).

Contribution margin (CM) The amount of revenue remaining after deducting variable costs. (p. 954).

Cost behavior analysis The study of how specific costs respond to changes in the level of business activity. (p. 946).

Cost-volume-profit (CVP) analysis The study of the effects of changes in costs and volume on a company's profits. (p. 953).

Cost-volume-profit (CVP) graph A graph showing the relationship between costs, volume, and profits. (p. 957).

Cost-volume-profit (CVP) income statement A statement for internal use that classifies costs and expenses as fixed or variable and reports contribution margin in the body of the statement. (p. 963).

Fixed costs Costs that remain the same in total regardless of changes in the activity level. (p. 947).

High-low method A mathematical method that uses the total costs incurred at the high and low levels of activity. (p. 951).

Margin of safety The difference between actual or expected sales and sales at the break-even point. (p. 959).

Mixed costs Costs that contain both a variable and a fixed cost element and change in total but not proportionately with changes in the activity level. (p. 950).

Relevant range The range of the activity index over which the company expects to operate during the year. (p. 949).

Target net income The income objective for individual product lines. (p. 960).

Variable costs Costs that vary in total directly and proportionately with changes in the activity level. (p. 946).

APPENDIX *Variable Costing*

STUDY OBJECTIVE 10

Explain the difference between absorption costing and variable costing.

In the earlier managerial chapters, both variable and fixed manufacturing costs have been classified as product costs. In job order costing, for example, a job is assigned the costs of direct materials, direct labor, and both variable and fixed manufacturing overhead. This costing approach is referred to as full or **absorption costing**. It is so named because all manufacturing costs are charged to, or absorbed by, the product.

An alternative approach is to use variable costing. Under **variable costing** only direct materials, direct labor, and variable manufacturing overhead costs are considered product costs. Fixed manufacturing overhead costs are recognized as period costs (expenses) when incurred. The difference between absorption costing and variable costing is graphically shown as follows.

Illustration 23A-1

Difference between absorption costing and variable costing

Selling and administrative expenses are period costs under both absorption and variable costing.

To illustrate the computation of unit production cost under absorption and variable costing, assume that Premium Products Corporation manufactures a polyurethane sealant called Fix-it for car windshields. Relevant data for Fix-it in January 2002, the first month of production, are as follows.

Illustration 23A-2

Sealant sales and cost data for Premium Products Corporation

Selling price	$20 per unit.
Units	Produced 30,000; sold 20,000; beginning inventory zero.
Variable unit costs	Manufacturing $9 (direct materials $5, direct labor $3, and variable overhead $1). Selling and administrative expenses $2.
Fixed costs	Manufacturing overhead $120,000. Selling and administrative expenses $15,000.

The per unit production cost under each costing approach is:

Illustration 23A-3

Computation of per unit production cost

Type of Cost	Absorption Costing	Variable Costing
Direct materials	$ 5	$5
Direct labor	3	3
Variable manufacturing overhead	1	1
Fixed manufacturing overhead ($120,000 ÷ 30,000 units produced)	**4**	**0**
Total unit cost	**$13**	**$9**

The total unit cost is $4 ($13 − $9) higher for absorption costing. This occurs because fixed manufacturing costs are a product cost under absorption costing. They are a period cost under variable costing and so are expensed, instead. Based on these data, each unit sold and each unit remaining in inventory is costed at $13 under absorption costing and at $9 under variable costing.

EFFECTS OF VARIABLE COSTING ON INCOME

The income statements under the two costing approaches are shown in Illustrations 23A-4 and 23A-5. The traditional income statement format is used with absorption costing. The cost-volume-profit format is used with variable costing. Computations are inserted parenthetically in the statements to facilitate your understanding of the amounts.

Illustration 23A-4

Absorption costing income statement

HELPFUL HINT
This is the traditional statement that would result from job order and processing costing explained in Chapters 21 and 22.

PREMIUM PRODUCTS COMPANY
Income Statement
For the Month Ended January 31, 2002
(Absorption Costing)

Sales (20,000 units × $20)		$400,000
Cost of goods sold		
Inventory, January 1	$ -0-	
Cost of goods manufactured (30,000 units × $13)	390,000	
Cost of goods available for sale	390,000	
Inventory, January 31 (10,000 units × $13)	**130,000**	
Cost of goods sold (20,000 units × $13)		260,000
Gross profit		140,000
Selling and administrative expenses		
(Variable 20,000 units × $2 + fixed $15,000)		55,000
Income from operations		**$ 85,000**

Income from operations under absorption costing shown in Illustration 23A-4 is $40,000 higher than under variable costing ($85,000 − $45,000) shown in Illustration 23A-5.

As highlighted in the two income statements, there is a $40,000 difference in the ending inventories ($130,000 under absorption costing versus $90,000 under variable costing). Under absorption costing, $40,000 of the fixed overhead costs (10,000 units × $4) have been deferred to a future period as a product cost. In contrast, under variable costing the entire fixed manufacturing costs are expensed when incurred.

Illustration 23A-5

Variable costing income statement

HELPFUL HINT
Note the difference in the computation of the ending inventory: $9 per unit here, $13 per unit above.

PREMIUM PRODUCTS COMPANY
Income Statement
For the Month Ended January 31, 2002
(Variable Costing)

Sales (20,000 units × $20)		$400,000
Variable expenses		
Variable cost of goods sold		
Inventory, January 1	$ -0-	
Variable manufacturing costs (30,000 units × $9)	270,000	
Cost of goods available for sale	270,000	
Inventory, January 31 (10,000 units × $9)	**90,000**	
Variable cost of goods sold	180,000	
Variable selling and administrative expenses		
(20,000 units × $2)	40,000	
Total variable expenses		220,000
Contribution margin		180,000
Fixed expenses		
Manufacturing overhead	120,000	
Selling and administrative expenses	15,000	
Total fixed expenses		135,000
Income from operations		**$ 45,000**

As shown, when units produced exceed units sold, income under absorption costing is higher. When units produced are less than units sold, income under absorption costing is lower. The reason is that the cost of the **ending inventory will be higher under absorption costing** than under variable costing. For example, if 30,000 units of Fix-it are sold in February and only 20,000 units are produced, income from operations will be $40,000 less under absorption costing because of the $40,000 difference in the ending inventories.

When units produced and sold are the same, income from operations will be equal under the two costing approaches. In this case, there is no increase in ending inventory. So fixed overhead costs of the current period are not deferred to future periods through the ending inventory.

The foregoing effects of the two costing approaches on income from operations may be summarized as follows.

Illustration 23A-6

Summary of income effects

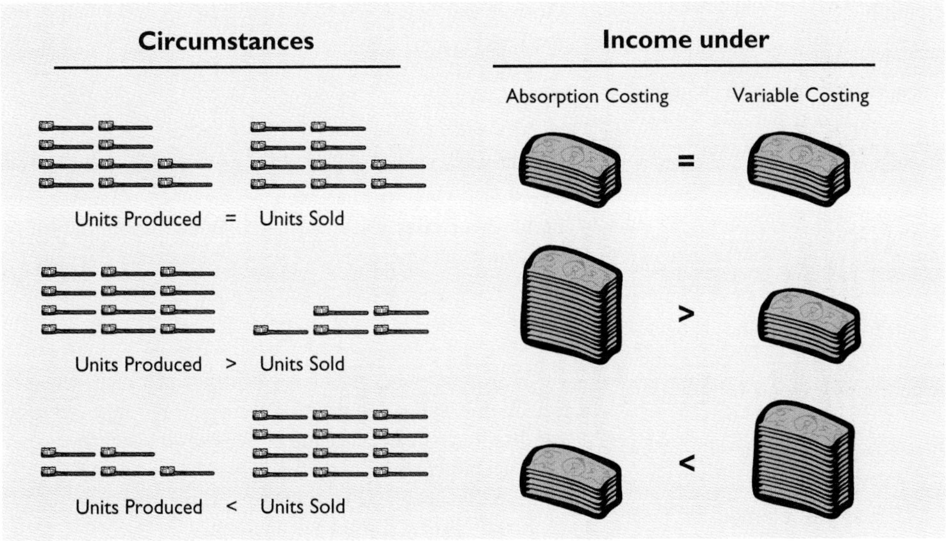

RATIONALE FOR VARIABLE COSTING

The rationale for variable costing centers on the purpose of fixed manufacturing costs. That purpose is **to have productive facilities available for use**. These costs are incurred whether a company operates at zero or at 100 percent of capacity. Thus, proponents of variable costing argue that these costs should be expensed in the period in which they are incurred.

Supporters of absorption costing defend the assignment of fixed manufacturing overhead costs to inventory. They say that these costs are as much a cost of getting a product ready for sale as direct materials or direct labor. Accordingly, these costs should not be matched with revenues until the product is sold.

The use of variable costing is acceptable **only for internal use by management**. It cannot be used in determining product costs in financial statements prepared in accordance with generally accepted accounting principles because it understates inventory costs. To comply with the matching principle, a company must use absorption costing for its work in process and finished goods inventories. Similarly, absorption costing must be used for income tax purposes.

SUMMARY OF STUDY OBJECTIVE FOR APPENDIX

10. *Explain the difference between absorption costing and variable costing.* Under absorption costing, fixed manufacturing costs are product costs. Under variable costing, fixed manufacturing costs are period costs.

GLOSSARY FOR APPENDIX

Absorption costing A costing approach in which all manufacturing costs are charged to the product. (p. 966).

Variable costing A costing approach in which only variable manufacturing costs are product costs, and fixed manufacturing costs are period costs (expenses). (p. 966).

*Note: All **asterisked** Questions, Exercises, and Problems relate to material contained in the appendix to the chapter.

Chapter 23 Self-Test

SELF-STUDY QUESTIONS

Answers are at the end of the chapter.

(SO 1) **1.** Variable costs are costs that:
a. vary in total directly and proportionately with changes in the activity level.
b. remain the same per unit at every activity level.
c. Neither of the above.
d. Both (a) and (b) above.

(SO 2) **2.** The relevant range is:
a. the range of activity in which variable costs will be curvilinear.
b. the range of activity in which fixed costs will be curvilinear.
c. the range over which the company expects to operate during a year.
d. usually from zero to 100% of operating capacity.

(SO 3) **3.** Mixed costs consist of a:
a. variable cost element and a fixed cost element.
b. fixed cost element and a controllable cost element.
c. relevant cost element and a controllable cost element.
d. variable cost element and a relevant cost element.

(SO 4) **4.** One of the following is *not* involved in CVP analysis. That factor is:
a. sales mix.
b. unit selling prices.
c. fixed costs per unit.
d. volume or level of activity.

(SO 5) **5.** Contribution margin:
a. is revenue remaining after deducting variable costs.
b. may be expressed as contribution margin per unit.
c. is selling price less cost of goods sold.
d. Both (a) and (b) above.

(SO 6) **6.** Gossen Company is planning to sell 200,000 pliers for $4 per unit. The contribution margin ratio is 25%. If Gossen will break even at this level of sales, what are the fixed costs?
a. $100,000.
b. $160,000.
c. $200,000.
d. $300,000.

7. Marshall Company had actual sales of $600,000 when break-even sales were $420,000. What is the margin of safety ratio? (SO 7)
a. 25%.
b. 30%.
c. $33\frac{1}{3}$%.
d. 45%.

8. The mathematical equation for computing required sales to obtain target net income is: Required sales = (SO 8)
a. Variable costs + Target net income.
b. Variable costs + Fixed costs + Target net income.
c. Fixed costs + Target net income.
d. No correct answer is given.

9. Cournot Company sells 100,000 wrenches for $12 a unit. Fixed costs are $300,000, and net income is $200,000. What should be reported as variable expenses in the CVP income statement? (SO 9)
a. $700,000.
b. $900,000.
c. $500,000.
d. $1,000,000.

***10.** Under variable costing, fixed manufacturing costs are classified as: (SO 10)
a. period costs.
b. product costs.
c. both (a) and (b).
d. neither (a) nor (b).

THE NAVIGATOR

QUESTIONS

1. (a) What is cost behavior analysis?
(b) Why is cost behavior analysis important to management?

2. (a) Jenny Beason asks your help in understanding the term "activity index." Explain the meaning and importance of this term for Jenny.

(b) State the two ways that variable costs may be defined.

3. Contrast the effects of changes in the activity level on total fixed costs and on unit fixed costs.

4. R.E. Leon claims that the relevant range concept is important only for variable costs.
(a) Explain the relevant range concept.
(b) Do you agree with R.E.'s claim? Explain.

5. "The relevant range is indispensable in cost behavior analysis." Is this true? Why or why not?

6. Bart Gomez is confused. He does not understand why rent on his apartment is a fixed cost and rent on a Hertz rental truck is a mixed cost. Explain the difference to Bart.

7. How should mixed costs be classified in CVP analysis? What approach is used to effect the appropriate classification?

8. At the high and low levels of activity during the month, direct labor hours are 90,000 and 40,000, respectively. The related costs are $175,000 and $100,000. What are the fixed and variable costs at any level of activity?

9. "Cost-volume-profit (CVP) analysis is based entirely on unit costs." Do you agree? Explain.

10. Patty Dye defines contribution margin as the amount of profit available to cover operating expenses. Is there any truth in this definition? Discuss.

11. Doolin Company's Speedo pocket calculator sells for $40. Variable costs per unit are estimated to be $24. What are the contribution margin per unit and the contribution margin ratio?

12. "Break-even analysis is of limited use to management because a company cannot survive by just breaking even." Do you agree? Explain.

13. Total fixed costs are $22,000 for Froelich Inc. It has a contribution margin per unit of $15, and a contribution margin ratio of 20%. Compute the break-even sales in dollars.

14. Linda Fearn asks your help in constructing a CVP graph. Explain to Linda how (a) the break-even point is plotted, and (b) the level of activity and dollar sales at the break-even point are determined.

15. Define the term "margin of safety." If Hancock Company expects to sell 1,500 units of its product at $12 per unit, and break-even sales for the product are $12,000, what is the margin of safety ratio?

16. Jung Company's break-even sales are $600,000. Assuming fixed costs are $240,000, what sales dollars are needed to achieve a target net income of $56,000?

17. What are the similarities and differences between a CVP income statement and a traditional income statement?

18. The traditional income statement for Reeves Company shows sales $900,000, cost of goods sold $600,000, and operating expenses $200,000. Assuming all costs and expenses are 70% variable and 30% fixed, prepare a CVP income statement through contribution margin.

*19. Distinguish between absorption costing and variable costing.

*20. (a) What is the major rationale for the use of variable costing? (b) Discuss why variable costing may not be used for financial reporting purposes.

BRIEF EXERCISES

BE23-1 Monthly production costs in Obianwu Company for two levels of production are as follows.

Classify costs as variable, fixed, or mixed.
(SO 1, 3)

Cost	2,000 units	4,000 units
Indirect labor	$10,000	$20,000
Supervisory salaries	5,000	5,000
Maintenance	3,000	4,000

Indicate which costs are variable, fixed, and mixed, and give the reason for each answer.

BE23-2 For Lundy Company, the relevant range of production is 40–80% of capacity. At 40% of capacity, a variable cost is $2,000 and a fixed cost is $4,000. Diagram the behavior of each cost within the relevant range assuming the behavior is linear.

Diagram the behavior of costs within the relevant range.
(SO 2)

BE23-3 For Skole Company, a mixed cost is $40,000 plus $8 per direct labor hour. Diagram the behavior of the cost using increments of 1,000 hours up to 5,000 hours on the horizontal axis and increments of $20,000 up to $80,000 on the vertical axis.

Diagram the behavior of a mixed cost.
(SO 3)

BE23-4 Sass Company accumulates the following data concerning a mixed cost, using miles as the activity level.

Determine variable and fixed cost elements using the high-low method.
(SO 3)

	Miles Driven	Total Cost		Miles Driven	Total Cost
January	8,000	$14,100	March	8,500	$15,000
February	7,500	13,400	April	8,200	14,400

Compute the variable and fixed cost elements using the high-low method.

Determine missing amounts for contribution margin. (SO 5)

BE23-5 Determine the missing amounts.

	Unit Selling Price	Unit Variable Costs	Contribution Margin per Unit	Contribution Margin Ratio
1.	$250	$160	(a)	(b)
2.	$500	(c)	$150	(d)
3.	(e)	(f)	$360	30%

Compute the break-even point. (SO 6)

BE23-6 Low Company has a unit selling price of $400, variable costs per unit of $280, and fixed costs of $150,000. Compute the break-even point using (a) the mathematical equation and (b) contribution margin per unit.

Compute the margin of safety and the margin of safety ratio. (SO 7)

BE23-7 For Koren Company actual sales are $1,200,000 and break-even sales are $900,000. Compute **(a)** the margin of safety in dollars and **(b)** the margin of safety ratio.

Compute sales for target net income. (SO 8)

BE23-8 For Bianco Company, variable costs are 75% of sales, and fixed costs are $180,000. Management's net income goal is $60,000. Compute the required sales needed to achieve management's target net income of $60,000. (Use the mathematical equation approach.)

Prepare CVP income statement. (SO 9)

BE23-9 Friedman Manufacturing Inc. has sales of $1,800,000 for the first quarter of 2002. In making the sales, the company incurred the following costs and expenses.

	Variable	Fixed
Cost of goods sold	$760,000	$540,000
Selling expenses	95,000	60,000
Administrative expenses	79,000	66,000

Prepare a CVP income statement for the quarter ended March 31, 2002.

Compute net income under absorption and variable costing. (SO 10)

***BE23-10** Gigliuto Company's fixed overhead costs are $4 per unit, and its variable overhead costs are $8 per unit. In the first month of operations, 50,000 units are produced, and 45,000 units are sold. Write a short memo to the chief financial officer explaining which costing approach will produce the higher income and what the difference will be.

EXERCISES

Define and classify variable, fixed, and mixed costs. (SO 1, 3)

E23-1 Fox Company manufactures a single product. Annual production costs incurred in the manufacturing process are shown below for two levels of production.

	Costs Incurred			
Production in Units	5,000		10,000	
Production Costs	Total Cost	Cost/Unit	Total Cost	Cost/Unit
Direct materials	$8,250	$1.65	$16,500	$1.65
Direct labor	9,500	1.90	19,000	1.90
Utilities	1,400	.28	2,300	.23
Rent	4,000	.80	4,000	.40
Maintenance	800	.16	1,100	.11
Supervisory salaries	1,000	.20	1,000	.10

Instructions

(a) Define the terms variable costs, fixed costs, and mixed costs.
(b) Classify each cost above as either variable, fixed, or mixed.

Determine fixed and variable costs using the high-low method and prepare graph. (SO 1, 3)

E23-2 The controller of Getty Industries has collected the following monthly expense data for use in analyzing the cost behavior of maintenance costs.

Month	Total Maintenance Costs	Total Machine Hours
January	$2,900	3,000
February	3,000	4,000
March	3,600	6,000
April	4,500	7,900
May	3,200	5,000
June	4,900	8,000

Instructions

(a) Determine the fixed and variable cost components using the high-low method.

(b) Prepare a graph showing the behavior of maintenance costs, and identify the fixed and variable cost elements. Use 2,000 unit increments and $1,000 cost increments.

Compute contribution margin, break-even point, and margin of safety.
(SO 5, 6, 7)

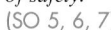

E23-3 In the month of June, Andrea's Beauty Salon gave 2,500 haircuts, shampoos, and permanents at an average price of $30. During the month, fixed costs were $18,000 and variable costs were 70% of sales.

Instructions

(a) Determine the contribution margin in dollars, per unit, and as a ratio.

(b) Using the contribution margin technique, compute the break-even point in dollars and in units.

(c) Compute the margin of safety in dollars and as a ratio.

Prepare a CVP graph and compute break-even point and margin of safety.
(SO 6, 7)

E23-4 Ewing Company estimates that variable costs will be 50% of sales, and fixed costs will total $800,000. The selling price of the product is $4.

Instructions

(a) Prepare a CVP graph, assuming maximum sales of $3,200,000. (*Note*: Use $400,000 increments for sales and costs and 100,000 increments for units.)

(b) Compute the break-even point in (1) units and (2) dollars.

(c) Compute the margin of safety in (1) dollars and (2) as a ratio, assuming actual sales are $2 million.

Compute variable cost per unit, contribution margin ratio, and increase in fixed costs.
(SO 5)

E23-5 In 2002, Donnin Company had a break-even point of $350,000 based on a selling price of $7 per unit and fixed costs of $140,000. In 2003, the selling price and the variable cost per unit did not change, but the break-even point increased to $455,000.

Instructions

(a) Compute the variable cost per unit and the contribution margin ratio for 2002.

(b) Compute the increase in fixed costs for 2003.

Compute various components to derive target net income under different assumptions.
(SO 6, 8)

E23-6 Jain Company had $150,000 of net income in 2002 when the selling price per unit was $150, the variable costs per unit were $90, and the fixed costs were $750,000. Management expects per unit data and total fixed costs to remain the same in 2003. The president of Jain Company is under pressure from stockholders to increase net income by $60,000 in 2003.

Instructions

(a) Compute the number of units sold in 2002.

(b) Compute the number of units that would have to be sold in 2003 to reach the stockholders' desired profit level.

(c) Assume that Jain Company sells the same number of units in 2003 as it did in 2002. What would the selling price have to be in order to reach the stockholders' desired profit level?

Compute net income under different alternatives.
(SO 8)

E23-7 Gomez Company reports the following operating results for the month of August: Sales $300,000 (units 5,000); variable costs $210,000; and fixed costs $80,000. Management is considering the following independent courses of action to increase net income.

1. Increase selling price by 10% with no change in total variable costs.
2. Reduce variable costs to 65% of sales.
3. Reduce fixed costs by $10,000.

Instructions

Compute the net income to be earned under each alternative. Which course of action will produce the highest net income?

Prepare a CVP income statement before and after changes in business environment. (SO 9)

E23-8 Halko Company had sales in 2002 of $1,500,000 on 60,000 units. Variable costs totaled $720,000, and fixed costs totaled $500,000.

A new raw material is available that will decrease the variable costs per unit by 20% (or $2.40). However, to process the new raw material, fixed operating costs will increase by $50,000. Management feels that one-half of the decline in the variable costs per unit should be passed on to customers in the form of a sales price reduction. The marketing department expects that this sales price reduction will result in a 5% increase in the number of units sold.

Instructions

Prepare a CVP income statement for 2002, assuming the changes are made as described.

Compute total product cost and prepare an income statement using variable costing. (SO 10)

***E23-9** Wu Equipment Company manufactures and distributes industrial air compressors. The following costs are available for the year ended December 31, 2002. The company has no beginning inventory. In 2002, 1,500 units were produced, but only 1,200 units were sold. The unit selling price was $4,500. Costs and expenses were:

Variable costs per unit	
Direct materials	$ 800
Direct labor	1,500
Variable manufacturing overhead	300
Variable selling and administrative expenses	70
Annual fixed costs and expenses	
Manufacturing overhead	$1,200,000
Selling and administrative expenses	100,000

Instructions

(a) Compute the manufacturing cost of one unit of product using variable costing.
(b) Prepare a 2002 income statement for Wu Company using variable costing.

PROBLEMS: SET A

Determine variable and fixed costs, compute break-even point, prepare a CVP graph, and determine net income. (SO 1, 3, 5, 6)

P23-1A Joe Vida owns the Peace Barber Shop. He employs five barbers and pays each a base rate of $1,200 per month. One of the barbers serves as the manager and receives an extra $600 per month. In addition to the base rate, each barber also receives a commission of $3.50 per haircut.

Other costs are as follows.

Advertising	$200 per month
Rent	$800 per month
Barber supplies	$0.30 per haircut
Utilities	$175 per month plus $0.20 per haircut
Magazines	$25 per month

Joe currently charges $10 per haircut.

Instructions

(a) Determine the variable cost per haircut and the total monthly fixed costs.
(b) Compute the break-even point in units and dollars.
(c) Prepare a CVP graph, assuming a maximum of 1,800 haircuts in a month. Use increments of 300 haircuts on the horizontal axis and $3,000 on the vertical axis.
(d) Determine net income, assuming 1,500 haircuts are given in a month.

Prepare a CVP income statement, compute break-even point, contribution margin ratio, margin of safety ratio, and sales for target net income. (SO 5, 6, 7, 8, 9)

P23-2A Tyson Company bottles and distributes NO-KAL, a diet soft drink. The beverage is sold for 40 cents per 16-ounce bottle to retailers, who charge customers 60 cents per bottle. At full (100%) plant capacity, management estimates the following revenues and costs.

Net sales	$1,800,000	Selling expenses—variable	$80,000
Direct materials	400,000	Selling expenses—fixed	65,000
Direct labor	280,000	Administrative expenses—variable	20,000
Manufacturing overhead—variable	300,000	Administrative expenses—fixed	52,000
Manufacturing overhead—fixed	283,000		

Instructions

(a) Prepare a CVP income statement for 2002 based on management's estimates.
(b) Compute the break-even point in (1) units and (2) dollars.
(c) Compute the contribution margin ratio and the margin of safety ratio. (Round to full percents.)
(d) Determine the sales required to earn net income of $150,000.

Compute break-even point under alternative courses of action.
(SO 5, 6)

P23-3A Cruz Manufacturing's sales slumped badly in 2002. For the first time in its history, it operated at a loss. The company's income statement showed the following results from selling 600,000 units of product: Net sales $2,400,000; total costs and expenses $2,600,000; and net loss $200,000. Costs and expenses consisted of the following.

	Total	Variable	Fixed
Cost of goods sold	$2,100,000	$1,440,000	$ 660,000
Selling expenses	300,000	72,000	228,000
Administrative expenses	200,000	48,000	152,000
	$2,600,000	$1,560,000	$1,040,000

Management is considering the following independent alternatives for 2003.

1. Increase unit selling price 25% with no change in costs, expenses, and sales volume.
2. Change the compensation of salespersons from fixed annual salaries totaling $210,000 to total salaries of $70,000 plus a 4% commission on net sales.
3. Purchase new automated equipment that will change the proportion between variable and fixed cost of goods sold to 60% variable and 40% fixed.

Instructions

(a) Compute the break-even point in dollars for 2002.
(b) Compute the break-even point in dollars under each of the alternative courses of action. (Round to nearest full percent.) Which course of action do you recommend?

Compute break-even point and margin of safety ratio, and prepare a CVP income statement before and after changes in business environment.
(SO 6, 7, 9)

P23-4A Lois Baiser is the advertising manager for Value Shoe Store. She is currently working on a major promotional campaign. Her ideas include the installation of a new lighting system and increased display space that will add $44,000 in fixed costs to the $280,000 currently spent. In addition, Lois is proposing that a 5% price decrease ($40 to $38) will produce a 20% increase in sales volume (20,000 to 24,000). Variable costs will remain at $20 per pair of shoes. Management is impressed with Lois's ideas but concerned about the effects that these changes will have on the break-even point and the margin of safety.

Instructions

(a) Compute the current break-even point in units, and compare it to the break-even point in units if Lois's ideas are used.
(b) Compute the margin of safety ratio for current operations and after Lois's changes are introduced. (Round to nearest full percent.)
(c) Prepare a CVP income statement for current operations and after Lois's changes are introduced. Would you make the changes suggested?

Prepare income statements under absorption and variable costing.
(SO 10)

***P23-5A** AFN produces plastic that is used for injection molding applications such as gears for small motors. In 2002, the first year of operations, AFN produced 4,000 tons of plastic and sold 3,000 tons. In 2003, the production and sales results were exactly reversed. In each year, selling price per ton was $2,000, variable manufacturing costs were 15% of the sales price of units produced, variable selling expenses were 10% of the selling price of units sold, fixed manufacturing costs were $2,400,000, and fixed administrative expenses were $600,000.

Instructions

(a) Prepare comparative income statements for each year using variable costing.
(b) Prepare comparative income statements for each year using absorption costing.
(c) Reconcile the differences each year in income from operations under the two costing approaches.
(d) Comment on the effects of production and sales on net income under the two costing approaches.

PROBLEMS: SET B

Determine variable and fixed costs, compute break-even point, prepare a CVP graph, and determine net income.
(SO 1, 3, 5, 6)

P23-1B The College Barber Shop employs four barbers. One barber, who also serves as the manager, is paid a salary of $2,000 per month. The other barbers are paid $1,400 per month. In addition, each barber is paid a commission of $4 per haircut. Other monthly costs are: store rent $800 plus 60 cents per haircut, depreciation on equipment $500, barber supplies 40 cents per haircut, utilities $300, and advertising $200. The price of a haircut is $10.

Instructions

(a) Determine the variable cost per haircut and the total monthly fixed costs.
(b) Compute the break-even point in units and dollars.
(c) Prepare a CVP graph, assuming a maximum of 1,800 haircuts in a month. Use increments of 300 haircuts on the horizontal axis and $3,000 increments on the vertical axis.
(d) Determine the net income, assuming 1,800 haircuts are given in a month.

Prepare a CVP income statement, compute break-even point, contribution margin ratio, margin of safety ratio, and sales for target net income.
(SO 5, 6, 7, 8, 9)

P23-2B Corbin Company bottles and distributes LO-KAL, a fruit drink. The beverage is sold for 50 cents per 16-ounce bottle to retailers, who charge customers 70 cents per bottle. At full (100%) plant capacity, management estimates the following revenues and costs.

Net sales	$2,000,000	Selling expenses—variable	$ 90,000
Direct materials	360,000	Selling expenses—fixed	150,000
Direct labor	650,000	Administrative expenses—variable	30,000
Manufacturing overhead—variable	270,000	Administrative expenses—fixed	70,000
Manufacturing overhead—fixed	260,000		

Instructions

(a) Prepare a CVP income statement for 2002 based on management's estimates.
(b) Compute the break-even point in (1) units and (2) dollars.
(c) Compute the contribution margin ratio and the margin of safety ratio.
(d) Determine the sales required to earn net income of $240,000.

Compute break-even point under alternative courses of action.
(SO 5, 6)

P23-3B Griffey Manufacturing had a bad year in 2002. For the first time in its history it operated at a loss. The company's income statement showed the following results from selling 60,000 units of product: Net sales $1,500,000; total costs and expenses $1,740,000; and net loss $240,000. Costs and expenses consisted of the following.

	Total	Variable	Fixed
Cost of goods sold	$1,200,000	$780,000	$420,000
Selling expenses	420,000	75,000	345,000
Administrative expenses	120,000	45,000	75,000
	$1,740,000	$900,000	$840,000

Management is considering the following independent alternatives for 2003.

1. Increase unit selling price 20% with no change in costs, expenses, and sales volume.
2. Change the compensation of salespersons from fixed annual salaries totaling $200,000 to total salaries of $40,000 plus a 5% commission on net sales.
3. Purchase new high-tech factory machinery that will change the proportion between variable and fixed cost of goods sold to 50:50.

Instructions

(a) Compute the break-even point in dollars for 2002.
(b) Compute the break-even point in dollars under each of the alternative courses of action. Which course of action do you recommend?

Compute break-even point and margin of safety ratio, and prepare a CVP income statement before and after changes in business environment.
(SO 6, 7, 9)

P23-4B Barb Tsai is the advertising manager for Thrifty Shoe Store. She is currently working on a major promotional campaign. Her ideas include the installation of a new lighting system and increased display space that will add $35,000 in fixed costs to the $225,000 currently spent. In addition, Barb is proposing that a 6 2/3% price decrease (from $30 to $28) will produce an increase in sales volume from 17,000 to 22,000 units. Variable costs will remain at $15 per pair of shoes. Management is impressed with Barb's ideas but concerned about the effects that these changes will have on the break-even point and the margin of safety.

Instructions

(a) Compute the current break-even point in units, and compare it to the break-even point in units if Barb's ideas are used.

(b) Compute the margin of safety ratio for current operations and after Barb's changes are introduced. (Round to nearest full percent.)

(c) Prepare a CVP income statement for current operations and after Barb's changes are introduced. Would you make the changes suggested?

Prepare income statements under absorption and variable costing.
(SO 10)

***P23-5B** Zaki Metal Company produces the steel wire that goes into the production of paper clips. In 2002, the first year of operations, Zaki produced 40,000 miles of wire and sold 30,000 miles. In 2003, the production and sales results were exactly reversed. In each year, selling price per mile was $80, variable manufacturing costs were 25% of the sales price, variable selling expenses were $6.00 per mile sold, fixed manufacturing costs were $1,200,000, and fixed administrative expenses were $200,000.

Instructions

(a) Prepare comparative income statements for each year using variable costing.

(b) Prepare comparative income statements for each year using absorption costing.

(c) Reconcile the differences each year in income from operations under the two costing approaches.

(d) Comment on the effects of production and sales on net income under the two costing approaches.

BROADENING YOUR PERSPECTIVE

GROUP DECISION CASE

BYP23-1 Cedeno Company has decided to introduce a new product.The new product can be manufactured by either a capital-intensive method or a labor-intensive method. The manufacturing method will not affect the quality of the product. The estimated manufacturing costs by the two methods are as follows.

	Capital-Intensive	Labor-Intensive
Raw materials	$5 per unit	$5.50 per unit
Direct labor	$6 per unit	$7.20 per unit
Variable overhead	$3 per unit	$4.80 per unit
Fixed manufacturing costs	$2,440,000	$1,390,000

Cedeno's market research department has recommended an introductory unit sales price of $30. The incremental selling expenses are estimated to be $500,000 annually plus $2 for each unit sold, regardless of manufacturing method.

Instructions

With the class divided into groups, answer the following.

(a) Calculate the estimated break-even point in annual unit sales of the new product if Cedeno Company uses the:

(1) capital-intensive manufacturing method.

(2) labor-intensive manufacturing method.

(b) Determine the annual unit sales volume at which Cedeno Company would be indifferent between the two manufacturing methods.

(c) Explain the circumstance under which Cedeno should employ each of the two manufacturing methods.

(CMA adapted)

MANAGERIAL ANALYSIS

BYP23-2 The condensed income statement for the Rivera and Santos partnership for 2002 is as follows.

RIVERA AND SANTOS COMPANY
Income Statement
For the Year Ended December 31, 2002

Sales (200,000 units)		$1,200,000
Cost of goods sold		800,000
Gross profit		400,000
Operating expenses		
Selling	$320,000	
Administrative	160,000	480,000
Net loss		($80,000)

A cost behavior analysis indicates that 75% of the cost of goods sold are variable, 50% of the selling expenses are variable, and 25% of the administrative expenses are variable.

Instructions

(Round to nearest unit, dollar, and percentage, where necessary. Use the CVP income statement format in computing profits.)

(a) Compute the break-even point in total sales dollars and in units for 2002.

(b) Rivera has proposed a plan to get the partnership "out of the red" and improve its profitability. She feels that the quality of the product could be substantially improved by spending $0.55 more per unit on better raw materials. The selling price per unit could be increased to only $6.50 because of competitive pressures. Rivera estimates that sales volume will increase by 30%. What effect will Rivera's plan have on the profits and the break-even point in dollars of the partnership?

(c) Santos was a marketing major in college. He believes that sales volume can be increased only by intensive advertising and promotional campaigns. He therefore proposed the following plan as an alternative to Rivera's. (1) Increase variable selling expenses to $0.85 per unit, (2) lower the selling price per unit by $0.20, and (3) increase fixed selling expenses by $20,000. Santos quoted an old marketing research report that said that sales volume would increase by 50% if these changes were made. What effect will Santos's plan have on the profits and the break-even point in dollars of the partnership?

(d) Which plan should be accepted? Explain your answer.

REAL-WORLD FOCUS

BYP23-3 The **Coca-Cola Company** hardly needs an introduction. A line taken from the cover of a recent annual report says it all: If you measured time in servings of Coca-Cola, "a billion Coca-Cola's ago was yesterday morning." On average, every U.S. citizen drinks 363 8-ounce servings of Coca-Cola products each year. Coca-Cola's primary line of business is the making and selling of syrup to bottlers. These bottlers then sell the finished bottles and cans of Coca-Cola to the consumer.

In the annual report of Coca-Cola, the following information was provided.

THE COCA-COLA COMPANY
Management Discussion

Our gross margin declined to 61 percent in 1995 from 62 percent in 1994, primarily due to costs for materials such as sweeteners and packaging.

The increases [in selling expenses] in 1996 and 1995 were primarily due to higher marketing expenditures in support of our Company's volume growth.

We measure our sales volume in two ways: (1) gallon shipments of concentrates and syrups and (2) unit cases of finished product (bottles and cans of Coke sold by bottlers).

Instructions
Answer the following questions.

(a) Are sweeteners and packaging a variable cost or a fixed cost? What is the impact on the contribution margin of an increase in the per unit cost of sweeteners or packaging? What are the implications for profitability?

(b) In your opinion, are marketing expenditures a fixed cost, variable cost, or mixed cost to The Coca-Cola Company? Give justification for your answer.

(c) Which of the two measures cited for measuring volume represents the activity index as defined in this chapter? Why might Coca-Cola use two different measures?

EXPLORING THE WEB

BYP23-4 **Ganong Bros. Ltd.**, located in St. Stephen, New Brunswick, is Canada's oldest independent candy company. Its products are distributed worldwide. In 1885, Ganong invented the popular "chicken bone," a cinnamon flavored, pink, hard candy jacket over a chocolate center. The home page of Ganong, listed below, includes information about the company and its products.

Address: **www.pcsolutions.nb.ca/ganong/times.htm** ***(or go to www.wiley.com/college/weygandt)***

Instructions
Read the description of "chicken bones," and answer the following.

(a) Describe the steps in making "chicken bones."

(b) Identify at least two variable and two fixed costs that are likely to affect the production of "chicken bones."

COMMUNICATION ACTIVITY

BYP23-5 Your roommate asks your help on the following questions about CVP analysis formulas.

(a) How can the mathematical equation for break-even sales show both sales dollars and sales units?

(b) How do the formulas differ for contribution margin per unit and contribution margin ratio?

(c) How can contribution margin be used to determine break-even sales in dollars and in units?

Instructions
Write a memo to your roommate stating the relevant formulas and answering each question.

ETHICS CASE

BYP23-6 Donny Blake is an accountant for Swenson Company. Early this year Donny made a highly favorable projection of sales and profits over the next 3 years for Swenson's hot-selling computer PLEX. As a result of the projections Donny presented to senior management, they decided to expand production in this area. This decision led to dislocations of some plant personnel who were reassigned to one of the company's newer plants in another state. However, no one was fired, and in fact the company expanded its work force slightly.

Unfortunately Donny rechecked his computations on the projections a few months later and found that he had made an error that would have reduced his projections substantially. Luckily, sales of PLEX have exceeded projections so far, and management is satisfied with its decision. Donny, however, is not sure what to do. Should he confess his honest mistake and jeopardize his possible promotion? He suspects that no one will catch the error because sales of PLEX have exceeded his projections, and it appears that profits will materialize close to his projections.

Instructions

(a) Who are the stakeholders in this situation?

(b) Identify the ethical issues involved in this situation.

(c) What are the possible alternative actions for Donny? What would you do in Donny's position?

Answers to Self-Study Questions

1. d **2.** c **3.** a **4.** c **5.** d **6.** c **7.** b **8.** b **9.** a **10.** a

Remember to go back to the Navigator box on the chapter-opening page and check off your completed work.

24

BUDGETARY PLANNING

THE NAVIGATOR ✓

- Understand *Concepts for Review* ❑
- Read *Feature Story* ❑
- Scan *Study Objectives* ❑
- Read *Preview* ❑
- Read text and answer *Before You Go On* *p.* 986 ❑ *p.* 997 ❑ *p.* 1000 ❑
- Work *Demonstration Problem* ❑
- Review *Summary of Study Objectives* ❑
- Answer *Self-Study Questions* ❑
- Complete *Assignments* ❑

CONCEPTS FOR REVIEW

Before studying this chapter, you should know or, if necessary, review:

a. The meaning of the management function of planning. (Ch. 20, p. 830)

b. The difference between variable costs and fixed costs. (Ch. 23, pp. 946–948)

THE NAVIGATOR

FEATURE STORY

Big Red's Biennial Budget

Every university has a budget. Usually, there's a capital budget for big projects such as new buildings, and there's an operating budget for the day-to-day expenditures.

At the **University of Nebraska**, the operating budget request takes up four volumes totaling nearly 900 pages. Because the university is funded by the state of Nebraska, the budget must be submitted to the state legislature for approval. That means the university has to pay lobbyists to plead its case with legislators. The budget is due September 15th of every other year. The lawmakers consider it during their sessions, which begin in January.

As you might expect, increases in expenses are resisted because money is tight. "Roughly 70 percent of our budget goes toward salaries," says Paula Boroff, budget officer at the Omaha campus. "A university is a very labor-intensive institution," she observes. The total budget for a recent fiscal year is about $95 million, reflecting a 1 percent cut in state funds from the prior year.

One budget item of interest to students is the "remission" category. That's where scholarships are funded. "This year, the budget for honor students and needy students is nearly $2 million—$1,994,488 to be exact," says Boroff, who recently received her MBA from the University of Nebraska graduate school. "Of our 16,000 students, we had 8,274 on some kind of aid," she says.

THE NAVIGATOR

STUDY OBJECTIVES

After studying this chapter, you should be able to:

1. Indicate the benefits of budgeting.
2. State the essentials of effective budgeting.
3. Identify the budgets that comprise the master budget.
4. Describe the sources for preparing the budgeted income statement.
5. Explain the principal sections of a cash budget.
6. Indicate the applicability of budgeting in nonmanufacturing companies.

THE NAVIGATOR

PREVIEW OF CHAPTER 24

As the Feature Story about the **University of Nebraska** indicates, budgeting is an integral part of our society. As a student, you budget your study time and your money. Families budget income and expenses. Governmental agencies budget revenues and expenditures. Business enterprises use budgets in planning and controlling their operations.

Our primary focus in this chapter is budgeting—specifically, how budgeting is used as a *planning tool* by management. Through budgeting, it should be possible for management to maintain enough cash to pay creditors, to have sufficient raw materials to meet production requirements, and to have adequate finished goods to meet expected sales.

The content and organization of Chapter 24 are as follows.

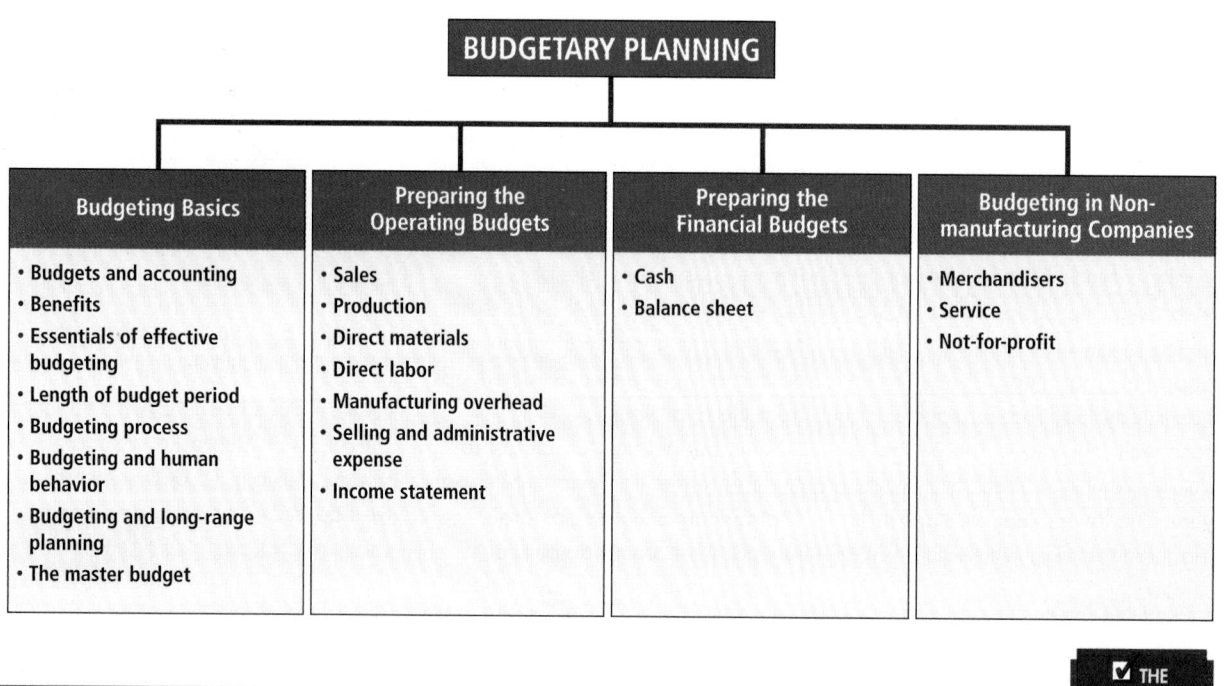

BUDGETARY PLANNING

Budgeting Basics	Preparing the Operating Budgets	Preparing the Financial Budgets	Budgeting in Nonmanufacturing Companies
• Budgets and accounting • Benefits • Essentials of effective budgeting • Length of budget period • Budgeting process • Budgeting and human behavior • Budgeting and long-range planning • The master budget	• Sales • Production • Direct materials • Direct labor • Manufacturing overhead • Selling and administrative expense • Income statement	• Cash • Balance sheet	• Merchandisers • Service • Not-for-profit

THE NAVIGATOR

BUDGETING BASICS

One of management's major responsibilities is planning. As explained in Chapter 20, **planning** is the process of establishing enterprise-wide objectives. A successful organization makes both long-term and short-term plans. These plans set forth the objectives of the company and the proposed means of accomplishing them.

A **budget** is a formal written statement of management's plans for a specified future time period, expressed in financial terms. It normally represents the primary means of communicating agreed-upon objectives throughout the organization. Once adopted, a budget becomes an important basis for evaluating performance. It promotes efficiency and serves as a deterrent to waste and inefficiency. We consider the role of budgeting as a **control device** in Chapter 25.

BUDGETING AND ACCOUNTING

Accounting information makes major contributions to the budgeting process. From the accounting records, historical data on revenues, costs, and expenses can be obtained. These data may be helpful in formulating future budget goals.

Normally, accountants have the responsibility for expressing management's budgeting goals in financial terms. In this role, they translate management's plans and communicate the budget to all areas of responsibility. Accountants also prepare periodic budget reports that provide the basis for measuring performance and comparing actual results with planned objectives. The budget itself, and the administration of the budget, however, are entirely management responsibilities.

TECHNOLOGY IN ACTION

In large firms, the computer is an essential tool in the budgeting process. Entire computer programs are designed to aid in budget preparation. These systems can also be integrated into the general ledger. They can provide a complete reporting package for monitoring budgeted versus actual results. Packages with similar features are available for microcomputers, so even small companies can adopt the budgeting practices found in major companies.

A powerful feature of many spreadsheet packages is the ability to merge and consolidate budget data as they flow up the organizational chain of command.

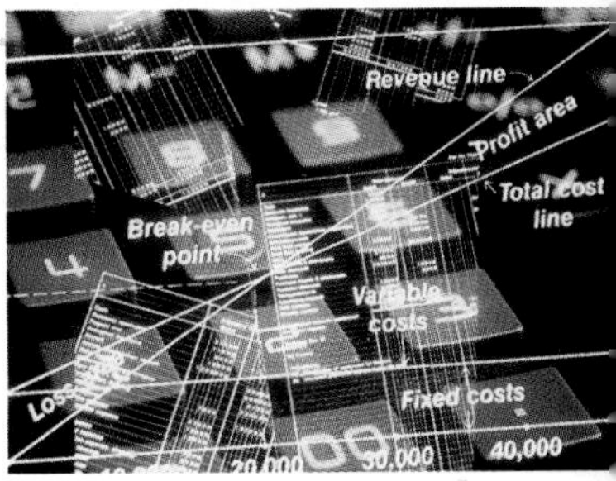

THE BENEFITS OF BUDGETING

STUDY OBJECTIVE 1
Indicate the benefits of budgeting.

The primary benefits of budgeting are:

1. It requires all levels of management to **plan ahead** and to formalize their goals on a recurring basis.
2. It provides **definite objectives** for evaluating performance at each level of responsibility.
3. It creates an **early warning system** for potential problems. With early warning, management has time to make changes before things get out of hand.
4. It facilitates the **coordination of activities** within the business. It does this by correlating the goals of each segment with overall company objectives. Thus, production and sales promotion can be integrated with expected sales.
5. It results in greater **management awareness** of the entity's overall operations and the impact on operations of external factors, such as economic trends.
6. It **motivates personnel** throughout the organization to meet planned objectives.

A budget is an aid to management; it is not a substitute for management. A budget cannot operate or enforce itself. The benefits of budgeting will be realized only when budgets are carefully prepared and properly administered by management.

ESSENTIALS OF EFFECTIVE BUDGETING

STUDY OBJECTIVE 2
State the essentials of effective budgeting.

Effective budgeting depends on a **sound organizational structure.** In such a structure, authority and responsibility for all phases of operations are clearly defined. Budgets based on **research and analysis** should result in realistic goals that will contribute to the growth and profitability of a company. And, the effectiveness of a budget program is directly related to its **acceptance by all levels of management**.

Once the budget has been adopted, it should be an important tool for evaluating performance. Variations between actual and expected results should be systematically and periodically reviewed to determine their cause(s). However, individuals should not be held responsible for variations that are beyond their control.

LENGTH OF THE BUDGET PERIOD

As indicated in the Feature Story about the **University of Nebraska** budget, the budget period is not necessarily one year in length. **A budget may be prepared for any period of time.** Various factors influence the length of the budget period. These factors include the type of budget, the nature of the organization, the need for periodic appraisal, and prevailing business conditions. For example, cash may be budgeted monthly, and a plant expansion budget may cover a ten-year period.

The budget period should be long enough to provide an attainable goal under normal business conditions. Ideally, the time period should minimize the impact of seasonal or cyclical fluctuations. On the other hand, the budget period should not be so long that reliable estimates are impossible.

The **most common budget period is one year**. The annual budget, in turn, is often supplemented by monthly and quarterly budgets. Many companies use **continuous twelve-month budgets**. These budgets drop the month just ended and add a future month. One advantage of continuous budgeting is that it keeps management planning a full year ahead.

THE BUDGETING PROCESS

The development of the budget for the coming year generally starts several months before the end of the current year. The budgeting process usually begins with the collection of data from each organizational unit of the company. Past performance is often the starting point from which future budget goals are formulated.

The budget is developed within the framework of a **sales forecast**. This forecast shows potential sales for the industry and the company's expected share of such sales. Sales forecasting involves a consideration of various factors: (1) general economic conditions, (2) industry trends, (3) market research studies, (4) anticipated advertising and promotion, (5) previous market share, (6) changes in prices, and (7) technological developments. The input of sales personnel and top management are essential to the sales forecast.

In many companies, responsibility for coordinating the preparation of the budget is assigned to a **budget committee**. The committee ordinarily includes the president, treasurer, chief accountant (controller), and management personnel from each of the major areas of the company, such as sales, production, and research. The budget committee serves as a review board where managers can defend their budget goals and requests. Differences are reviewed, modified if necessary, and reconciled. The budget is then put in its final form by the budget committee, approved, and distributed.

BUDGETING AND HUMAN BEHAVIOR

A budget can have a significant impact on human behavior. It may inspire a manager to higher levels of performance. Or, it may discourage additional effort and pull down the morale of a manager. Why do these diverse effects occur? The answer is found in how the budget is developed and administered.

In **developing the budget**, each level of management should be invited to participate. The overall goal is to reach agreement on a budget that the manager considers fair and achievable. When this objective is met, the budget will have a positive effect on the manager. In contrast, if the manager views the budget as being unfair and unrealistic, he or she may feel discouraged and uncommitted to the budget goals. The risk of having unrealistic budgets is generally greater when the budget is developed from top management down to lower management than vice versa. Illustration 24-1 graphically displays the appropriate flow of budget data from bottom to top in an organization.

Illustration 24-1
Flow of budget data from lower levels of management to top

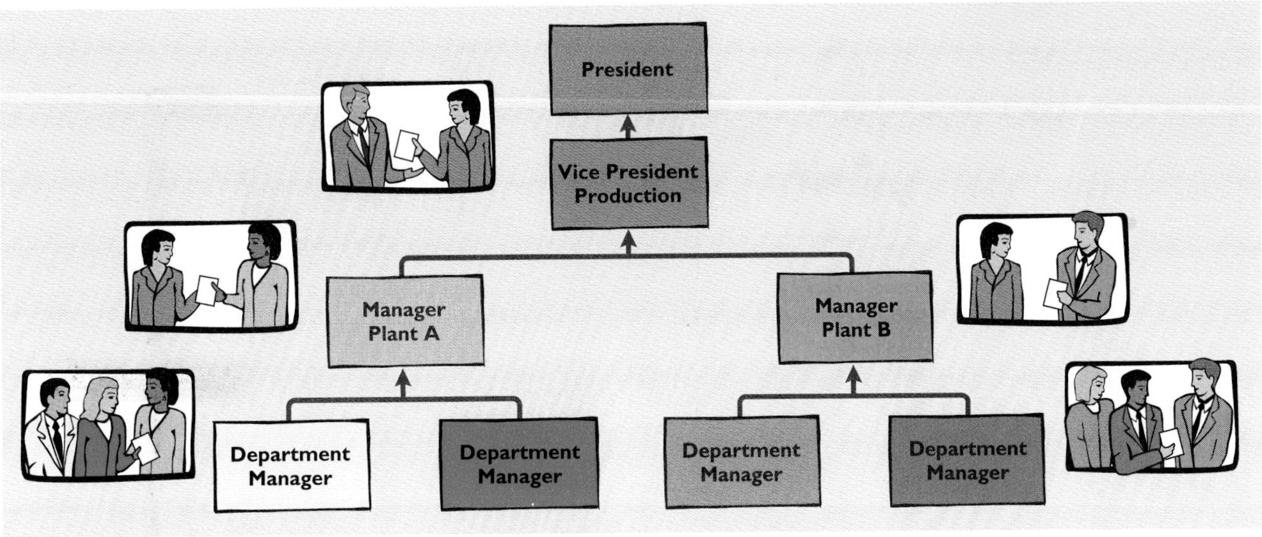

Administering the budget relates to how the budget is used by top management. As explained earlier, the budget should have the complete support of top management. The budget also should be an important basis for evaluating performance. The effect of an evaluation will be positive when top management tempers criticism with advice and assistance. In contrast, a manager is likely to respond negatively if the budget is used exclusively to assess blame.

A budget may be used improperly as a pressure device to force improved performance. Or, it can be used as a positive aid in achieving projected goals. In sum, a budget can become a manager's friend or a foe.

ETHICS NOTE
Unrealistic budgets can lead to unethical employee behavior such as cutting corners on the job or distorting internal financial reports.

BUDGETING AND LONG-RANGE PLANNING

In business, you may hear talk about the need for long-range planning. Budgeting and long-range planning are not the same. One important difference is the **time period involved**. The maximum length of a budget is usually one year, and budgets are often prepared for shorter periods of time, such as a month or a quarter. In contrast, long-range planning usually encompasses a period of at least five years.

A second significant difference is in **emphasis**. Budgeting focuses on achieving specific short-term goals, such as meeting annual profit objectives. **Long-range planning**, on the other hand, identifies long-term goals, selects strategies to achieve those goals, and develops policies and plans to implement the strategies. In long-range planning, management also considers anticipated trends in the economic and political environment and how the company should cope with them.

The final difference between budgeting and long-range planning pertains to the **amount of detail presented**. Budgets, as you will see in this chapter, can be very detailed. Long-range plans contain considerably less detail. The data in long-range plans are intended more for a review of progress toward long-term goals than as a basis of control for achieving specific results. The primary objective of long-range planning is to develop the best strategy to maximize the company's performance over an extended future period.

HELPFUL HINT
In comparing a budget with a long-range plan: (1) Which has more detail? (2) Which is done for a longer period of time? (3) Which is more concerned with short-term goals?
Answer: (1) Budget. (2) Long-range plan. (3) Budget.

THE MASTER BUDGET

STUDY OBJECTIVE 3

Identify the budgets that comprise the master budget.

The term "budget" is actually a shorthand term to describe a variety of budget documents. All of these documents are combined into a master budget. The **master budget** is a set of interrelated budgets that constitutes a plan of action for a specified time period. The individual budgets included in a master budget are pictured in Illustration 24-2.

Illustration 24-2

Components of the master budget

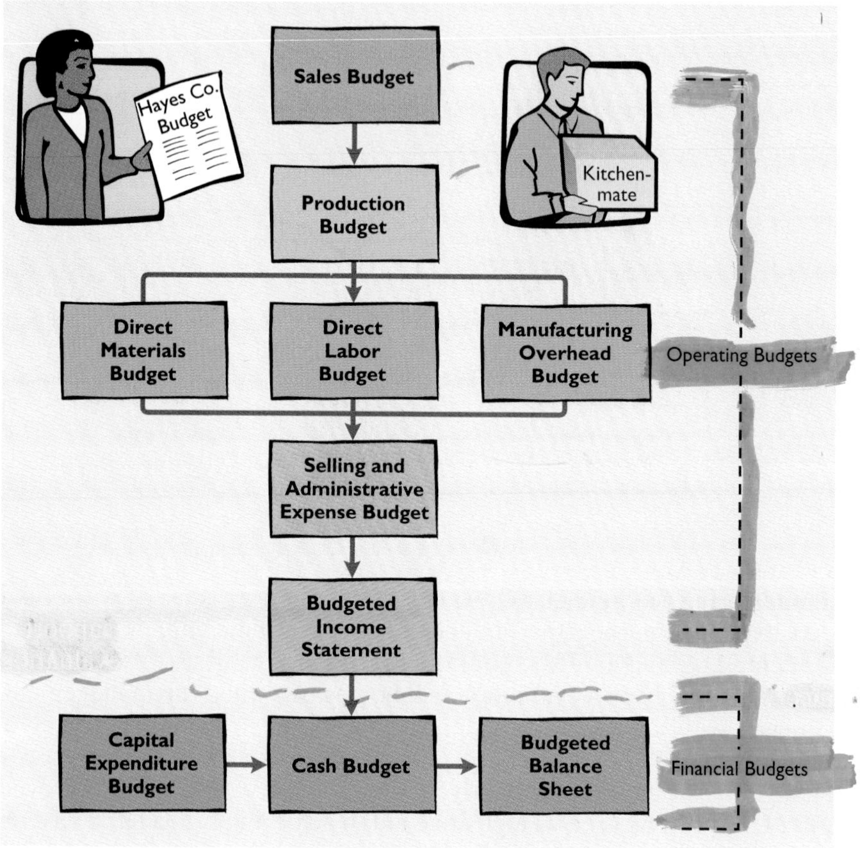

As the illustration shows, the master budget contains two classes of budgets. **Operating budgets** are the individual budgets that result in the preparation of the budgeted income statement. These budgets establish goals for the company's sales and production personnel. In contrast, **financial budgets** are the cash budget and the budgeted balance sheet. These budgets focus primarily on the cash resources needed to fund expected operations and planned capital expenditures.

The master budget is prepared in the sequence shown in Illustration 24-2. The operating budgets are developed first, beginning with the sales budget. Then the financial budgets are prepared. We will explain and illustrate each budget shown in Illustration 24-2 except the capital expenditure budget. This budget is discussed under the topic Capital Budgeting in Chapter 27.

BEFORE YOU GO ON...

REVIEW IT

1. What are the benefits of budgeting?
2. What are the factors essential to effective budgeting?
3. How does the budget process work?
4. How does budgeting differ from long-range planning?
5. What is a master budget?

THE NAVIGATOR

PREPARING THE OPERATING BUDGETS

A case study of Hayes Company will be used in preparing the operating budgets. Hayes manufactures and sells a single product, Kitchen-mate. The budgets will be prepared by quarters for the year ending December 31, 2002. Hayes Company begins its annual budgeting process on September 1, 2001, and it completes the budget for 2002 by December 1, 2001.

SALES BUDGET

As shown in the master budget in Illustration 24-2, **the sales budget is the first budget prepared**. Each of the other budgets depends on the sales budget. The **sales budget** is derived from the sales forecast. It represents management's best estimate of sales revenue for the budget period. An inaccurate sales budget may adversely affect net income. For example, an overly optimistic sales budget may result in excessive inventories that may have to be sold at reduced prices. In contrast, an unduly conservative budget may result in loss of sales revenue due to inventory shortages.

The sales budget is prepared by multiplying the expected unit sales volume for each product by its anticipated unit selling price. For Hayes Company, sales volume is expected to be 3,000 units in the first quarter with 500-unit increments in each succeeding quarter. Based on a sales price of $60 per unit, the sales budget for the year, by quarters, is shown in Illustration 24-3.

HELPFUL HINT
For a retail or manufacturing company, what is the starting point in preparing the master budget, and why? Answer: Preparation of the sales budget is the starting point for the master budget. It sets the level of activity for other functions such as production and purchasing.

Illustration 24-3
Sales budget

HAYES COMPANY
Sales Budget
For the Year Ending December 31, 2002

	Quarter 1	Quarter 2	Quarter 3	Quarter 4	Year
Expected unit sales	3,000	3,500	4,000	4,500	15,000
Unit selling price	× $60	× $60	× $60	× $60	× $60
Total sales	$180,000	$210,000	$240,000	$270,000	$900,000

Some companies classify the anticipated sales revenue as cash or credit sales and by geographical regions, territories, or salespersons.

PRODUCTION BUDGET

The **production budget** shows the units that must be produced to meet anticipated sales. Production requirements are determined from the following formula.[1]

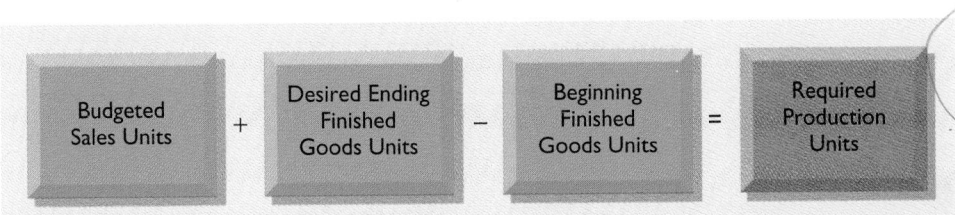

Illustration 24-4
Production requirements formula

Budgeted Sales Units + Desired Ending Finished Goods Units − Beginning Finished Goods Units = Required Production Units

[1] This formula ignores any work in process inventories, which are assumed to be nonexistent in Hayes Company.

A realistic estimate of ending inventory is essential in scheduling production requirements. Excessive inventories in one quarter may lead to cutbacks in production and employee layoffs in a subsequent quarter. On the other hand, inadequate inventories may result either in added costs for overtime work or in lost sales. Hayes Company believes it can meet future sales requirements by maintaining an ending inventory equal to 20 percent of the next quarter's budgeted sales volume. For example, the ending finished goods inventory for the first quarter is 700 units (20% × anticipated second-quarter sales of 3,500 units). The production budget is shown in Illustration 24-5.

Illustration 24-5

Production budget

HAYES COMPANY
Production Budget
For the Year Ending December 31, 2002

	Quarter				
	1	**2**	**3**	**4**	**Year**
Expected unit sales (Illustration 24-3)	3,000	3,500	4,000	4,500	
Add: Desired ending finished goods units[a]	700	800	900	1,000[b]	
Total required units	3,700	4,300	4,900	5,500	
Less: Beginning finished goods units	600[c]	700	800	900	
Required production units	**3,100**	**3,600**	**4,100**	**4,600**	**15,400**

[a]20% of next quarter's sales
[b]Expected 2003 first-quarter sales, 5,000 units × 20%
[c]20% of estimated first-quarter 2002 sales units

The production budget, in turn, provides the basis for determining the budgeted costs for each manufacturing cost element, as explained in the following pages.

ACCOUNTING IN ACTION *Business Insight*

Wrong move, wrong time, poor planning. When **Fruit of the Loom Inc.** saw underwear and apparel sales slowing, it cut back production sharply. Too sharply, in fact: almost overnight, demand soared. Caught with its shorts down, the company hired back thousands of workers and frantically increased production. The mistimed production cuts contributed to a 43 percent fall in first-quarter profits. For the year, Fruit stood to lose $200 million in sales, and analysts expected an 11 percent drop in profits for the year.

SOURCE: Business Week, June 6, 1994, p. 38.

DIRECT MATERIALS BUDGET

The **direct materials budget** shows both the quantity and cost of direct materials to be purchased. The quantities of direct materials are derived from the following formula.

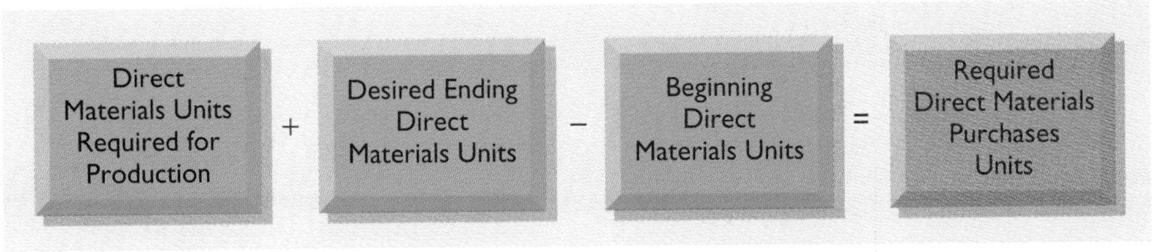

Illustration 24-6

Formula for direct materials quantities

The budgeted cost of direct materials to be purchased is then computed by multiplying the required units of direct materials by the anticipated cost per unit.

The desired ending inventory is again a key component in the budgeting process. For example, inadequate inventories could result in temporary shutdowns of production. Because of its close proximity to suppliers, Hayes Company has found that an ending inventory of raw materials equal to 10 percent of the next quarter's production is sufficient. The manufacture of each Kitchen-mate requires 2 pounds of raw materials, and the expected cost per pound is $4. The direct materials budget is shown in Illustration 24-7.

Illustration 24-7

Direct materials budget

HAYES COMPANY
Direct Materials Budget
For the Year Ending December 31, 2002

	Quarter 1	Quarter 2	Quarter 3	Quarter 4	Year
Units to be produced (Illustration 24-5)	3,100	3,600	4,100	4,600	
Direct materials per unit	× 2	× 2	× 2	× 2	
Total pounds needed for production	6,200	7,200	8,200	9,200	
Add: Desired ending direct materials (pounds)[a]	720	820	920	1,020[b]	
Total materials required	6,920	8,020	9,120	10,220	
Less: Beginning direct materials (pounds)	620[c]	720	820	920	
Direct materials purchases	6,300	7,300	8,300	9,300	
Cost per pound	× $4	× $4	× $4	× $4	
Total cost of direct materials purchases	**$25,200**	**$29,200**	**$33,200**	**$37,200**	**$124,800**

[a] 10% of next quarter's production
[b] Estimated 2003 first-quarter pounds needed for production, 10,200 × 10%
[c] 10% of estimated first-quarter pounds needed for production

TECHNOLOGY IN ACTION

The successful manufacturers of the twenty-first century will be fully computerized. A crucial step on the way is material requirements planning (MRP) systems. Early MRP systems accepted a sales forecast and computed how much materials, inventory, people, and machinery a company needed to manufacture the product. Current MRP systems link the company's manufacturing resource planning with its financial management. This new capability creates a powerful system of control over the entire business planning and operating process. With MRP, management can make decisions on facts rather than on "hunches" and "instinct."

DIRECT LABOR BUDGET

Like the direct materials budget, the **direct labor budget** contains the quantity (hours) and cost of direct labor necessary to meet production requirements. Direct labor hours are determined from the production budget. At Hayes Company, two hours of direct labor are required to produce each unit of finished goods. The anticipated hourly wage rate is $10. These data are shown in Illustration 24-8. The direct labor budget is critical in maintaining a labor force that can meet the expected levels of production.

Illustration 24-8

Direct labor budget

HELPFUL HINT
An important assumption here is that the company can add to and subtract from its work force as needed so that the $10 per hour labor cost applies to a wide range of possible production activity.

HAYES COMPANY
Direct Labor Budget
For the Year Ending December 31, 2002

	Quarter 1	Quarter 2	Quarter 3	Quarter 4	Year
Units to be produced (Illustration 24-5)	3,100	3,600	4,100	4,600	
Direct labor time (hours) per unit	× 2	× 2	× 2	× 2	
Total required direct labor hours	6,200	7,200	8,200	9,200	
Direct labor cost per hour	× $10	× $10	× $10	× $10	
Total direct labor cost	**$62,000**	**$72,000**	**$82,000**	**$92,000**	**$308,000**

MANUFACTURING OVERHEAD BUDGET

The **manufacturing overhead budget** shows the expected manufacturing overhead costs for the budget period. As shown in Illustration 24-9, **this budget distinguishes between variable and fixed overhead costs**. Hayes Company expects variable costs to fluctuate with production volume on the basis of the following rates per direct labor hour: indirect materials $1.00, indirect labor $1.40, utilities $0.40, and maintenance $0.20. Thus, for 6,200 direct labor hours, budgeted indirect materials are $6,200 (6,200 × $1), and budgeted indirect labor is $8,680 (6,200 × $1.40). Hayes also recognizes that some maintenance is fixed. The amounts reported for fixed costs are assumed.

At Hayes Company, overhead is applied to production on the basis of direct labor hours. Thus, as shown in Illustration 24-9, the annual rate is $8 per hour ($246,400 ÷ 30,800).

SELLING AND ADMINISTRATIVE EXPENSE BUDGET

Hayes Company combines its operating expenses into one budget, the **selling and administrative expense budget**. This budget projects anticipated selling and administrative expenses for the budget period. In this budget, as in the preceding one, expenses are classified as either variable or fixed. In this case, the variable expense rates per unit of sales are sales commissions $3.00 and freight-out $1.00. Variable expenses per quarter are based on the unit sales from the sales budget (Illustration 24-3). For example, sales in the first quarter are expected to be 3,000 units. Thus, Sales Commissions Expense is $9,000 (3,000 × $3), and Freight-out is $3,000 (3,000 × $1). Fixed expenses are based on assumed data. The selling and administrative expense budget is shown in Illustration 24-10.

Illustration 24-9

Manufacturing overhead budget

HAYES COMPANY
Manufacturing Overhead Budget
For the Year Ending December 31, 2002

	Quarter 1	Quarter 2	Quarter 3	Quarter 4	Year
Variable costs					
Indirect materials	$ 6,200	$ 7,200	$ 8,200	$ 9,200	$ 30,800
Indirect labor	8,680	10,080	11,480	12,880	43,120
Utilities	2,480	2,880	3,280	3,680	12,320
Maintenance	1,240	1,440	1,640	1,840	6,160
Total variable	18,600	21,600	24,600	27,600	92,400
Fixed costs					
Supervisory salaries	20,000	20,000	20,000	20,000	80,000
Depreciation	3,800	3,800	3,800	3,800	15,200
Property taxes and insurance	9,000	9,000	9,000	9,000	36,000
Maintenance	5,700	5,700	5,700	5,700	22,800
Total fixed	38,500	38,500	38,500	38,500	154,000
Total manufacturing overhead	**$57,100**	**$60,100**	**$63,100**	**$66,100**	**$246,400**
Direct labor hours	**6,200**	**7,200**	**8,200**	**9,200**	**30,800**
Manufacturing overhead rate per direct labor hour ($246,400 ÷ 30,800)					**$8.00**

Illustration 24-10

Selling and administrative expense budget

HAYES COMPANY
Selling and Administrative Expense Budget
For the Year Ending December 31, 2002

	Quarter 1	Quarter 2	Quarter 3	Quarter 4	Year
Variable expenses					
Sales commissions	$ 9,000	$10,500	$12,000	$13,500	$ 45,000
Freight-out	3,000	3,500	4,000	4,500	15,000
Total variable	12,000	14,000	16,000	18,000	60,000
Fixed expenses					
Advertising	5,000	5,000	5,000	5,000	20,000
Sales salaries	15,000	15,000	15,000	15,000	60,000
Office salaries	7,500	7,500	7,500	7,500	30,000
Depreciation	1,000	1,000	1,000	1,000	4,000
Property taxes and insurance	1,500	1,500	1,500	1,500	6,000
Total fixed	30,000	30,000	30,000	30,000	120,000
Total selling and administrative expenses	**$42,000**	**$44,000**	**$46,000**	**$48,000**	**$180,000**

budget very close
why?
should be @ 0

ACCOUNTING IN ACTION e-Business Insight

Good budgeting depends on good information. And good information is what e-business is all about. As manufacturers, suppliers, and customers become electronically linked, each benefits by being better informed. **Dell Computer** not only is directly linked to **Solectron**, one of its main suppliers, but also to **Texas Instruments**, one of the main suppliers of parts to Solectron. This linking takes a lot of guesswork out of planning and budgeting for all three companies.

To further improve planning and budgeting, Dell hopes that some day everyone in its industry will anonymously provide their up-to-the-minute production and sales information at a central, electronic exchange. A centralized database such as this would provide valuable information about the supply and demand of computer goods in the marketplace. This information might dramatically improve sales projections, leading to significant improvements in the budgeting process.

SOURCE: "E-Management," *The Economist*, November 11, 2000.

BUDGETED INCOME STATEMENT

STUDY OBJECTIVE 4

Describe the sources for preparing the budgeted income statement.

The **budgeted income statement** is the important end-product of the operating budgets. This budget indicates the expected profitability of operations for the budget period. The budgeted income statement provides the basis for evaluating company performance.

As you would expect, this budget is prepared from the various operating budgets. For example, to find the cost of goods sold, it is first necessary to determine the total unit cost of producing one Kitchen-mate, as follows.

Illustration 24-11

Computation of total unit cost

Cost of One Kitchen-mate

Cost Element	Illustration	Quantity	Unit Cost	Total
Direct materials	24-7	2 pounds	$ 4.00	$ 8.00
Direct labor	24-8	2 hours	$10.00	20.00
Manufacturing overhead	24-9	2 hours	$ 8.00	16.00
Total unit cost				**$44.00**

Cost of goods sold can then be determined by multiplying the units sold by the unit cost. For Hayes Company, budgeted cost of goods sold is $660,000 (15,000 × $44). All data for the statement are obtained from the individual operating budgets except the following: (1) interest expense is expected to be $100 and (2) income taxes are estimated to be $12,000. The budgeted income statement is shown in Illustration 24-12.

Illustration 24-12

Budgeted income statement

HAYES COMPANY Budgeted Income Statement For the Year Ending December 31, 2002	
Sales (Illustration 24-3)	$900,000
Cost of goods sold (15,000 × $44)	660,000
Gross profit	240,000
Selling and administrative expenses (Illustration 24-10)	180,000
Income from operations	60,000
Interest expense	100
Income before income taxes	59,900
Income tax expense	12,000
Net income	$ 47,900

PREPARING THE FINANCIAL BUDGETS

As shown in Illustration 24-2, the financial budgets consist of the capital expenditure budget, the cash budget, and the budgeted balance sheet. The capital expenditure budget is discussed in Chapter 27; the other budgets are explained in the following sections.

CASH BUDGET

STUDY OBJECTIVE 5

Explain the principal sections of a cash budget.

The **cash budget** shows anticipated cash flows. Because cash is so vital, this budget is considered to be the most important output in preparing financial budgets. The cash budget contains three sections (cash receipts, cash disbursements, and financing) and the beginning and ending cash balances, as shown in Illustration 24-13.

Illustration 24-13

Basic form of a cash budget

ANY COMPANY Cash Budget	
Beginning cash balance	$X,XXX
Add: Cash receipts (Itemized)	X,XXX
Total available cash	X,XXX
Less: Cash disbursements (Itemized)	X,XXX
Excess (deficiency) of available cash over cash disbursements	X,XXX
Financing	X,XXX
Ending cash balance	$X,XXX

The **cash receipts section** includes expected receipts from the company's principal source(s) of revenue. These are usually cash sales and collections from customers on credit sales. This section also shows anticipated receipts of interest and dividends, and proceeds from planned sales of investments, plant assets, and the company's capital stock.

The **cash disbursements section** shows expected cash payments. Such payments include direct materials, direct labor, manufacturing overhead, and selling and administrative expenses. This section also includes projected payments for income taxes, dividends, investments, and plant assets.

The **financing section** shows expected borrowings and the repayment of the borrowed funds plus interest. This section is needed when there is a cash deficiency or when the cash balance is below management's minimum required balance.

HELPFUL HINT

Why is the cash budget prepared after the other budgets are prepared? Answer: Because the information generated by the other budgets dictates the need for inflows and outflows of cash.

Data in the cash budget must be prepared in sequence. The ending cash balance of one period becomes the beginning cash balance for the next period. Data for preparing the cash budget are obtained from other budgets and from information provided by management. In practice, cash budgets are often prepared for the year on a monthly basis.

ACCOUNTING IN ACTION *Business Insight*

Douglas Roberson, president of **Atlantic Network**, woke up one morning to find that his company was out of cash. At that point, Roberson realized that managing cash flow is different from simply accumulating sales. He says: "If you don't do serious projections about how much cash you will need to handle sales—and how long it will take to collect on invoices—you can end up out of business no matter how fast you are growing." In fact, Roberson says, fast growth makes cash flow problems worse because the company can be spending cash on supplies and payroll at an accelerated pace while waiting 45 days or longer to collect receivables.

To minimize detail, we will assume that Hayes Company prepares an annual cash budget by quarters. The cash budget for Hayes Company is based on the following assumptions.

1. The January 1, 2002, cash balance is expected to be $38,000.
2. Sales (Illustration 24-3): 60 percent are collected in the quarter sold and 40 percent are collected in the following quarter. Accounts receivable of $60,000 at December 31, 2001, are expected to be collected in full in the first quarter of 2002.
3. Short-term investments are expected to be sold for $2,000 cash in the first quarter.
4. Direct materials (Illustration 24-7): 50 percent are paid in the quarter purchased and 50 percent are paid in the following quarter. Accounts payable of $10,600 at December 31, 2001, are expected to be paid in full in the first quarter of 2002.
5. Direct labor (Illustration 24-8): 100 percent is paid in the quarter incurred.
6. Manufacturing overhead (Illustration 24-9) and selling and administrative expenses (Illustration 24-10): All items except depreciation are paid in the quarter incurred.
7. Management plans to purchase a truck in the second quarter for $10,000 cash.
8. Hayes makes equal quarterly payments of its estimated annual income taxes.
9. Loans are repaid in the earliest quarter in which there is sufficient cash (i.e., when the cash on hand exceeds the $15,000 minimum required balance).

In preparing the cash budget, it is useful to prepare schedules for collections from customers (assumption No. 2, above) and cash payments for direct materials (assumption No. 4, above). The schedules are shown in Illustrations 24-14 and 24-15.

Illustration 24-14

Collections from customers

Schedule of Expected Collections from Customers

	Quarter			
	1	2	3	4
Accounts receivable, 12/31/01	$ 60,000			
First quarter ($180,000)	108,000	$ 72,000		
Second quarter ($210,000)		126,000	$ 84,000	
Third quarter ($240,000)			144,000	$ 96,000
Fourth quarter ($270,000)				162,000
Total collections	$168,000	$198,000	$228,000	$258,000

Illustration 24-15

Payments for direct materials

Schedule of Expected Payments for Direct Materials

	Quarter 1	2	3	4
Accounts payable, 12/31/01	$10,600			
First quarter ($25,200)	12,600	$12,600		
Second quarter ($29,200)		14,600	$14,600	
Third quarter ($33,200)			16,600	$16,600
Fourth quarter ($37,200)				18,600
Total payments	$23,200	$27,200	$31,200	$35,200

The cash budget for Hayes Company is shown in Illustration 24-16. The budget indicates that $3,000 of financing will be needed in the second quarter to maintain a minimum cash balance of $15,000. Since there is an excess of available cash over disbursements of $22,500 at the end of the third quarter, the borrowing is repaid in this quarter plus $100 interest.

Illustration 24-16

Cash budget

HAYES COMPANY
Cash Budget
For the Year Ending December 31, 2002

	Assumption	Quarter 1	2	3	4
Beginning cash balance	1	$ 38,000	$ 25,500	$ 15,000	$ 19,400
Add: Receipts					
Collections from customers	2	168,000	198,000	228,000	258,000
Sale of securities	3	2,000	0	0	0
Total receipts		170,000	198,000	228,000	258,000
Total available cash		208,000	223,500	243,000	277,400
Less: Disbursements					
Direct materials	4	23,200	27,200	31,200	35,200
Direct labor	5	62,000	72,000	82,000	92,000
Manufacturing overhead	6	53,300[1]	56,300	59,300	62,300
Selling and administrative expenses	6	41,000[2]	43,000	45,000	47,000
Purchase of truck	7	0	10,000	0	0
Income tax expense	8	3,000	3,000	3,000	3,000
Total disbursements		182,500	211,500	220,500	239,500
Excess (deficiency) of available cash over disbursements		25,500	12,000	22,500	37,900
Financing					
Borrowings		0	3,000	0	0
Repayments—plus $100 interest	9	0	0	3,100	0
Ending cash balance		$ 25,500	$ 15,000	$ 19,400	$ 37,900

[1]$57,100 − $3,800 depreciation
[2]$42,000 − $1,000 depreciation

A cash budget contributes to more effective cash management. It can show when additional financing will be necessary well before the actual need arises. And, it can indicate when excess cash will be available for investments or other purposes.

BUDGETED BALANCE SHEET

The **budgeted balance sheet** is a projection of financial position at the end of the budget period. This budget is developed from the budgeted balance sheet for the preceding year and the budgets for the current year. Pertinent data from the budgeted balance sheet at December 31, 2001, are as follows.

Building and equipment	$182,000	Common stock	$225,000
Accumulated depreciation	$ 28,800	Retained earnings	$ 46,480

The budgeted balance sheet at December 31, 2002, is shown below.

Illustration 24-17

Budgeted balance sheet

HAYES COMPANY
Budgeted Balance Sheet
December 31, 2002

Assets		
Cash		$ 37,900
Accounts receivable		108,000
Finished goods inventory		44,000
Raw materials inventory		4,080
Buildings and equipment	$192,000	
Less: Accumulated depreciation	48,000	144,000
Total assets		$337,980
Liabilities and Stockholders' Equity		
Accounts payable		$ 18,600
Common stock		225,000
Retained earnings		94,380
Total liabilities and stockholders' equity		$337,980

The computations and sources of the amounts are explained below.

Cash: Ending cash balance $37,900, shown in the cash budget (Illustration 24-16).

Accounts receivable: 40 percent of fourth-quarter sales $270,000, shown in the schedule of expected collections from customers (Illustration 24-14).

Finished goods inventory: Desired ending inventory 1,000 units, shown in the production budget (Illustration 24-5) times the total unit cost $44 (shown in Illustration 24-11).

Raw materials inventory: Desired ending inventory 1,020 pounds, times the cost per pound $4, shown in the direct materials budget (Illustration 24-7).

Buildings and equipment: December 31, 2001, balance $182,000, plus purchase of truck for $10,000.

Accumulated depreciation: December 31, 2001, balance $28,800, plus $15,200 depreciation shown in manufacturing overhead budget (Illustration 24-9) and $4,000 depreciation shown in selling and administrative expense budget (Illustration 24-10).

Accounts payable: 50 percent of fourth-quarter purchases $37,200, shown in schedule of expected payments for direct materials (Illustration 24-15).

Common stock: Unchanged from the beginning of the year.

Retained earnings: December 31, 2001, balance $46,480, plus net income $47,900, shown in budgeted income statement (Illustration 24-12).

TECHNOLOGY IN ACTION

After the budgeting data are entered into the computer, the various budgets (sales, cash, etc.) can be prepared, as well as the budgeted financial statements. Management can also manipulate the budgets in "what if" (sensitivity) analyses based on different hypothetical assumptions. For example, suppose that sales were budgeted to be 10 percent higher in the coming quarter. What impact would the change have on the rest of the budgeting process and the financing needs of the business? The computer can quickly "play out" the impact of the various assumptions on the budgets. Armed with these analyses, management can make more informed decisions about the impact of various projects. They also can anticipate future problems and business opportunities. Budgeting is one of the top uses of electronic spreadsheets. Template versions of every one of the Hayes Company budgets shown in this chapter could easily be prepared.

BEFORE YOU GO ON...

REVIEW IT

1. What are the two classifications of the individual budgets in the master budget?
2. What is the sequence for preparing the budgets that comprise the operating budgets?
3. Identify some of the source documents that would be used in preparing each of the operating budgets.
4. What are the three principal sections of the cash budget?
5. Obviously, **Lands' End** does not present its detailed budgets in its 2000 Annual Report. But, in the "Business outlook" in its Management Discussion and Analysis section, what expectations does Lands' End have about 2001 first-quarter and first-half operations? The answer to this question is provided on page 1016.

DO IT

In Martian Company, management wants to maintain a minimum monthly cash balance of $15,000. At the beginning of March, the cash balance is $16,500, expected cash receipts for March are $210,000, and cash disbursements are expected to be $220,000. How much cash, if any, must be borrowed to maintain the desired minimum monthly balance?

ACTION PLAN

- Write down the basic form of the cash budget, starting with the beginning cash balance, adding cash receipts for the period, deducting cash disbursements, and identifying the needed financing to achieve the desired minimum ending cash balance.
- Insert the data given into the outlined form of the cash budget.

SOLUTION

MARTIAN COMPANY
Cash Budget
For the Month Ending March 31, 2002

Beginning cash balance	$ 16,500
Add: Cash receipts for March	210,000
Total available cash	226,500
Less: Cash disbursements for March	220,000
Excess of available cash over cash disbursements	6,500
Financing	8,500
Ending cash balance	$ 15,000

To maintain the desired minimum cash balance of $15,000, Martian Company must borrow $8,500 of cash.

Related exercise material: BE24-9 and E24-9.

BUDGETING IN NONMANUFACTURING COMPANIES

STUDY OBJECTIVE 6

Indicate the applicability of budgeting in nonmanufacturing companies.

Budgeting is not limited to manufacturers. Budgets may also be used by merchandisers, service enterprises, and not-for-profit organizations.

MERCHANDISERS

As in manufacturing operations, the sales budget for a merchandiser is both the starting point and the key factor in the development of the master budget. The major differences between the master budgets of a merchandiser and a manufacturer are these: (1) A merchandiser **uses a merchandise purchases budget instead of a production budget.** (2) A merchandiser **does not use the manufacturing budgets (direct materials, direct labor, and manufacturing overhead).** The merchandise purchases budget shows the estimated cost of goods to be purchased to meet expected sales. The formula for determining budgeted merchandise purchases is:

Illustration 24-18

Merchandise purchases formula

Budgeted Cost of Goods Sold + Desired Ending Merchandise Inventory − Beginning Merchandise Inventory = Required Merchandise Purchases

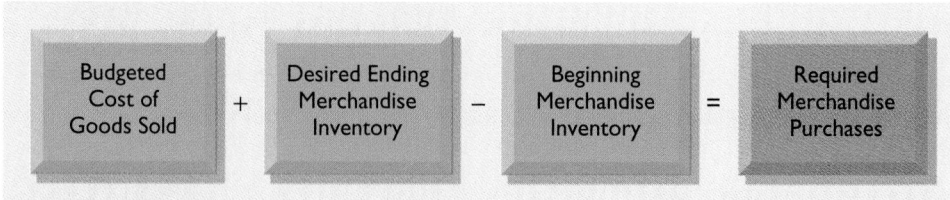

To illustrate, assume that the budget committee of Lima Company is preparing the merchandise purchases budget for July. It estimates that budgeted sales will be $300,000 in July and $320,000 in August. Cost of goods sold is expected to be 70 percent of sales. The company's desired ending inventory is 30 percent of the following month's cost of goods sold. Required merchandise purchases for July are $214,200, computed as follows.

Illustration 24-19

Computation of required merchandise purchases

Budgeted cost of goods sold (budgeted sales for July, $300,000 × 70%)	$210,000
Desired ending merchandise inventory (budgeted cost of goods sold for August, $320,000 × 70% × 30%)	67,200
Total	277,200
Less: Beginning merchandise inventory (budgeted sales for July, $300,000 × 70% × 30%)	63,000
Required merchandise purchases for July	**$214,200**

When a merchandiser is departmentalized, separate budgets are prepared for each department. For example, a grocery store may start by preparing sales budgets and purchases budgets for each of its major departments, such as meats, dairy, and produce. These budgets are then combined into a master budget for the store. When a retailer has branch stores, separate master budgets are prepared for each store. Then these budgets are incorporated into master budgets for the company as a whole.

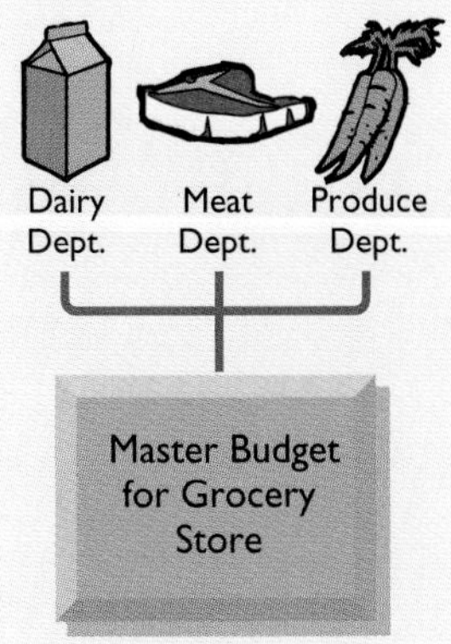

Departmentalized budgets

SERVICE ENTERPRISES

In service enterprises, such as a public accounting firm, a law office, or a medical practice, the critical factor in budgeting is **coordinating professional staff needs with anticipated services**. If a firm is overstaffed, several problems may result: (1) Labor costs will be disproportionately high. (2) Profits will be lower because of the additional salaries. (3) Staff turnover may increase because of lack of challenging work. In contrast, if an enterprise is understaffed, revenue may be lost because existing and prospective client needs for service cannot be met. Also, professional staff may seek other jobs because of excessive work loads.

Budget data for service revenue may be obtained from **expected output** or **expected input**. When output is used, it is necessary to determine the expected billings of clients for services rendered. In a public accounting firm, for example, output would be the sum of its billings in auditing, tax, and consulting services. When input data are used, each professional staff member is required to project his or her billable time. Billing rates are then applied to billable time to produce expected service revenue.

ACCOUNTING IN ACTION *Business Insight*

Lucy Carter, managing partner of a small CPA firm in Nashville, uses formal budgets as the principal tool for keeping cash flow on an even keel throughout the year. The firm budgets annually for both revenues and expenses on a month-by-month basis. For example, the revenue budget is derived from chargeable-hour goals set by the staff. The firm sets a threshold of 1,800 hours for each staff member and 1,700 hours for each manager. Each month the budget is compared with the financial statements, and adjustments are made if necessary.

NOT-FOR-PROFIT ORGANIZATIONS

Budgeting is just as important for not-for-profit organizations as for profit-oriented enterprises. The budget process, however, is significantly different. In most cases not-for-profit entities budget **on the basis of cash flows (expenditures and receipts), rather than on a revenue and expense basis**. Further, the starting point in the process is usually expenditures, not receipts. For the not-for-profit entity, management's task generally is to find the receipts needed to support the planned expenditures. This was the case for the University of Nebraska in the Feature Story. The activity index is also likely to be significantly different. For example, in a not-for-profit entity, such as a university, budgeted faculty positions may be based on full-time equivalent students or credit hours expected to be taught in a department.

For some governmental units, the budget must be approved by voters. In other cases, such as state governments and the federal government, legislative approval is required. After the budget is adopted, it must be strictly followed. Overspending is often illegal. In governmental budgets, authorizations tend to be on a line-by-line basis. That is, the budget for a municipality may have a specified authorization for police and fire protection, garbage collection, street paving, and so on. The line-item authorization of governmental budgets significantly limits the amount of discretion management can exercise. The city manager often cannot use savings from one line item, such as street paving, to cover increased spending in another line item, such as snow removal.

BEFORE YOU GO ON...

REVIEW IT

1. What is the formula for computing required merchandise purchases?
2. How does budgeting in service and not-for-profit organizations differ from budgeting for manufacturers and merchandisers?

A LOOK BACK AT OUR FEATURE STORY

Refer back to the Feature Story about the **University of Nebraska** budget at the beginning of the chapter, and answer the following questions.

1. How does the length of the budget period for the University of Nebraska compare with the guidelines given for businesses in the chapter?
2. What is the difference between a capital budget and an operating budget?
3. Who do you believe sits on the budget committee at your college or university?

SOLUTION

1. The University of Nebraska must submit its budget to the state legislature on September 15 *every other year*. Thus, the length of the budget period is two years. For businesses, the length of the budget period is normally one year, and for some items, such as cash, monthly budgets may be prepared.
2. A capital budget is for big projects, such as buildings, which span more than a year. An operating budget is established to plan for day-to-day expenditures.
3. The budget committee at many universities consists of key officers and the deans of the various colleges. Key officers would be the president, vice president for academic affairs (sometimes called the provost), and the vice president of finance.

THE NAVIGATOR

DEMONSTRATION PROBLEM

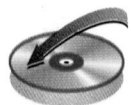

Additional Demonstration Problem

The Soroco Company is preparing its master budget for 2002. Relevant data pertaining to its sales and production budgets are as follows:

Sales: Sales for the year are expected to total 1,200,000 units. Quarterly sales are 20%, 25%, 30%, and 25% respectively. The sales price is expected to be $50 per unit for the first three quarters and $55 per unit beginning in the fourth quarter. Sales in the first quarter of 2003 are expected to be 10% higher than the budgeted sales volume for the first quarter of 2002.

Production: Management desires to maintain ending finished goods inventories at 25% of the next quarter's budgeted sales volume.

Instructions

Prepare the sales budget and production budget by quarters for 2002.

ACTION PLAN

- Know the form and content of the sales budget.
- Prepare the sales budget first as the basis for the other budgets.
- Determine the units that must be produced to meet anticipated sales.
- Determine the budgeted cost for each manufacturing cost element.
- Know how to compute the beginning and ending finished goods units.

SOLUTION TO DEMONSTRATION PROBLEM

SOROCO COMPANY
Sales Budget
For the Year Ending December 31, 2002

	Quarter				
	1	**2**	**3**	**4**	**Year**
Expected unit sales	240,000	300,000	360,000	300,000	1,200,000
Unit selling price	× $50	× $50	× $50	× $55	—
	$12,000,000	$15,000,000	$18,000,000	$16,500,000	$61,500,000

SOROCO COMPANY
Production Budget
For the Year Ending December 31, 2002

	Quarter				
	1	**2**	**3**	**4**	**Year**
Expected unit sales	240,000	300,000	360,000	300,0000	
Add: Desired ending finished goods units	75,000	90,000	75,000	66,000[1]	
Total required units	315,000	390,000	435,000	366,000	
Less: Beginning finished goods units	60,000[2]	75,000	90,000	75,000	
Units to be produced	255,000	315,000	345,000	291,000	1,206,000

[1]Estimated first-quarter 2003 sales volume 240,000 + (240,000 × 10%) = 264,000; 264,000 × 25%.
[2]25% of estimated first-quarter 2002 sales units.

THE NAVIGATOR

SUMMARY OF STUDY OBJECTIVES

1. ***Indicate the benefits of budgeting.*** The primary advantages of budgeting are that it (a) requires management to plan ahead, (b) provides definite objectives for evaluating performance, (c) creates an early warning system for potential problems, (d) facilitates coordination of activities, (e) results in greater management awareness, and (f) motivates personnel to meet planned objectives.

2. ***State the essentials of effective budgeting.*** The essentials of effective budgeting are (a) sound organizational structure, (b) research and analysis, and (c) acceptance by all levels of management.

3. ***Identify the budgets that comprise the master budget.*** The master budget consists of the following budgets: (a) sales, (b) production, (c) direct materials, (d) direct labor, (e) manufacturing overhead, (f) selling and administrative expense, (g) budgeted income statement, (h) capital expenditure budget, (i) cash budget, and (j) budgeted balance sheet.

4. ***Describe the sources for preparing the budgeted income statement.*** The budgeted income statement is prepared from (a) the sales budget, (b) the budgets for direct materials, direct labor, and manufacturing overhead, and (c) the selling and administrative expense budget.

5. ***Explain the principal sections of a cash budget.*** The cash budget has three sections (receipts, disbursements, and financing) and the beginning and ending cash balances.

6. ***Indicate the applicability of budgeting in nonmanufacturing companies.*** Budgeting may be used by merchandisers for development of a master budget. In service enterprises budgeting is a critical factor in coordinating staff needs with anticipated services. In not-for-profit organizations, the starting point in budgeting is usually expenditures, not receipts.

THE NAVIGATOR

Key Term Matching Activity

GLOSSARY

Budget A formal written statement of management's plans for a specified future time period, expressed in financial terms. (p. 982).

Budget committee A group responsible for coordinating the preparation of the budget. (p. 984).

Budgeted balance sheet A projection of financial position at the end of the budget period. (p. 996).

Budgeted income statement An estimate of the expected profitability of operations for the budget period. (p. 992).

Cash budget A projection of anticipated cash flows. (p. 993).

Direct labor budget A projection of the quantity and cost of direct labor to be incurred to meet production requirements. (p. 990).

Direct materials budget An estimate of the quantity and cost of direct materials to be purchased. (p. 988).

Financial budgets Individual budgets that indicate the cash resources needed for expected operations and planned capital expenditures. (p. 986).

Long-range planning A formalized process of selecting strategies to achieve long-term goals and developing policies and plans to implement the strategies. (p. 985).

Manufacturing overhead budget An estimate of expected manufacturing overhead costs for the budget period. (p. 990).

Master budget A set of interrelated budgets that constitutes a plan of action for a specific time period. (p. 986).

Merchandise purchases budget The estimated cost of goods to be purchased by a merchandiser to meet expected sales. (p. 998).

Operating budgets Individual budgets that result in a budgeted income statement. (p. 986).

Production budget A projection of the units that must be produced to meet anticipated sales. (p. 987).

Sales budget An estimate of expected sales for the budget period. (p. 987).

Sales forecast The projection of potential sales for the industry and the company's expected share of such sales. (p. 984).

Selling and administrative expense budget A projection of anticipated selling and administrative expenses for the budget period. (p. 990).

Chapter 24 Self-Test

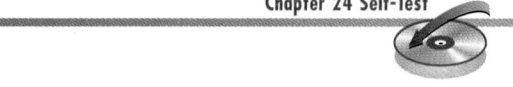

SELF-STUDY QUESTIONS

Answers are at the end of the chapter.

(SO 1) **1.** The benefits of budgeting include *all but one* of the following:
a. Management can plan ahead.
b. An early warning system is provided for potential problems.
c. It enables disciplinary action to be taken at every level of responsibility.
d. The coordination of activities is facilitated.

(SO 2) **2.** The essentials of effective budgeting do *not* include:
a. top-down budgeting.
b. management acceptance.
c. research and analysis.
d. sound organizational structure.

(SO 2) **3.** Compared to budgeting, long-range planning generally has the:
a. same amount of detail.
b. longer time period.
c. same emphasis.
d. same time period.

(SO 3) **4.** A sales budget is:
a. derived from the production budget.
b. management's best estimate of sales revenue for the year.
c. not the starting point for the master budget.
d. prepared only for credit sales.

(SO 3) **5.** The formula for the production budget is budgeted sales in units plus:
a. desired ending merchandise inventory less beginning merchandise inventory.
b. beginning finished goods units less desired ending finished goods units.
c. desired ending direct materials units less beginning direct materials units.
d. desired ending finished goods units less beginning finished goods units.

6. Direct materials inventories are kept in pounds in Byrd Company, and the total pounds of direct materials needed for production is 9,500. If the beginning inventory is 1,000 pounds and the desired ending inventory is 2,200 pounds, the total pounds to be purchased is: (SO 3)
a. 9,400. c. 9,700.
b. 9,500. d. 10,700.

7. The formula for computing the direct labor cost budget is to multiply the direct labor cost per hour by the: (SO 3)
a. total required direct labor hours.
b. physical units to be produced.
c. equivalent units to be produced.
d. No correct answer is given.

8. Each of the following budgets is used in preparing the budgeted income statement *except* the: (SO 4)
a. sales budget.
b. selling and administrative budget.
c. capital expenditure budget.
d. direct labor budget.

9. Expected direct materials purchases in Read Company are $70,000 in the first quarter and $90,000 in the second quarter. Forty percent of the purchases are paid in cash as incurred, and the balance is paid in the following quarter. The budgeted cash payments for purchases in the second quarter are: (SO 5)

a. $96,000.
b. $90,000.
c. $78,000.
d. $72,000.

(SO 6) 10. The budget for a merchandiser differs from a budget for a manufacturer because:
a. a merchandise purchases budget replaces the production budget.
b. the manufacturing budgets are not applicable.
c. None of the above.
d. Both (a) and (b) above.

THE NAVIGATOR

QUESTIONS

1. (a) What is a budget?
(b) How does a budget contribute to good management?
2. Valerie Flynn and Ken Leask are discussing the benefits of budgeting. They ask you to identify the primary advantages of budgeting. Comply with their request.
3. Lorraine Scott asks your help in understanding the essentials of effective budgeting. Identify the essentials for Lorraine.
4. (a) "Accounting plays a relatively unimportant role in budgeting." Do you agree? Explain.
(b) What responsibilities does management have in budgeting?
5. What criteria are helpful in determining the length of the budget period? What is the most common budget period?
6. Mary Miller maintains that the only difference between budgeting and long-range planning is time. Do you agree? Why or why not?
7. Distinguish between a master budget and a sales forecast.
8. What budget is the starting point in preparing the master budget? What may result if this budget is inaccurate?
9. "The production budget shows both unit production data and unit cost data." Is this true? Explain.
10. Wheaton Company has 8,000 beginning finished goods units. Budgeted sales units are 160,000. If management desires 20,000 ending finished goods units, what are the required units of production?
11. In preparing the direct materials budget for Dukane Company, management concludes that required purchases are 54,000 units. If 50,000 direct materials units are required in production and there are 7,000 units of beginning direct materials, what is the desired units of ending direct materials?
12. The production budget of Hinsdale Company calls for 90,000 units to be produced. If it takes 30 minutes to make one unit and the direct labor rate is $14 per hour, what is the total budgeted direct labor cost?
13. Villanova Company's manufacturing overhead budget shows total variable costs of $168,000 and total fixed costs of $147,000. Total production in units is expected to be 160,000. It takes 15 minutes to make one unit, and the direct labor rate is $15 per hour. Express the manufacturing overhead rate as (a) a percentage of direct labor cost, and (b) an amount per direct labor hour.
14. Westphal Company's variable selling and administrative expenses are 15% of net sales. Fixed expenses are $60,000 per quarter. The sales budget shows expected sales of $200,000 and $250,000 in the first and second quarters, respectively. What are the total budgeted selling and administrative expenses for each quarter?
15. For Advent Company, the budgeted cost for one unit of product is direct materials $10, direct labor $20, and manufacturing overhead 80% of direct labor cost. If 25,000 units are expected to be sold at $77 each, what is the budgeted gross profit?
16. Indicate the supporting schedules used in preparing a budgeted income statement through gross profit for a manufacturer.
17. Identify the three sections of a cash budget. What balances are also shown in this budget?
18. Andrew Manion Company has credit sales of $500,000 in January. Past experience suggests that 45% is collected in the month of sale, 50% in the month following the sale, and 4% in the second month following the sale. Compute the cash collections from January sales in January, February, and March.
19. What is the formula for determining required merchandise purchases for a merchandiser?
20. How may expected revenues in a service enterprise be computed?

BRIEF EXERCISES

BE24-1 Sharon Livingston Manufacturing Company uses the following budgets: Balance Sheet, Capital Expenditure, Cash, Direct Labor, Direct Materials, Income Statement, Manufacturing Overhead, Production, Sales, and Selling and Administrative. Prepare a diagram of the interrelationships of the budgets in the master budget. Indicate whether each budget is an operating or a financial budget.

Prepare a diagram of a master budget.
(SO 3)

BE24-2 Emil Company estimates that unit sales will be 10,000 in quarter 1; 12,000 in quarter 2; 14,000 in quarter 3; and 15,000 in quarter 4. Using a sales price of $70 per unit, prepare the sales budget by quarters for the year ending December 31, 2002.

Prepare a sales budget.
(SO 3)

Prepare a production budget for 2 quarters.
(SO 3)

BE24-3 Sales budget data for Emil Company are given in BE24-2. Management desires to have an ending finished goods inventory equal to 30% of the next quarter's expected unit sales. Prepare a production budget by quarters for the first 6 months of 2002.

Prepare a direct materials budget for 1 month.
(SO 3)

BE24-4 Korenewych Company has 1,200 pounds of raw materials in its December 31, 2002, ending inventory. Required production for January and February are 4,000 and 5,000 units, respectively. Two pounds of raw materials are needed for each unit, and the estimated cost per pound is $6. Management desires an ending inventory equal to 15% of next month's materials requirements. Prepare the direct materials budget for January.

Prepare a direct labor budget for 2 quarters.
(SO 3)

BE24-5 For Shawn Green Company, units to be produced are 5,000 in quarter 1 and 6,000 in quarter 2. It takes 1.8 hours to make a finished unit, and the expected hourly wage rate is $12 per hour. Prepare a direct labor budget by quarters for the 6 months ending June 30, 2002.

Prepare a manufacturing overhead budget.
(SO 3)

BE24-6 For John Dunham Inc. variable manufacturing overhead costs are expected to be $20,000 in the first quarter of 2002 with $3,000 increments in each of the remaining three quarters. Fixed overhead costs are estimated to be $35,000 in each quarter. Prepare the manufacturing overhead budget by quarters for the year.

Prepare a selling and administrative expense budget.
(SO 3)

BE24-7 Chudzick Company classifies its selling and administrative expense budget into variable and fixed components. Variable expenses are expected to be $25,000 in the first quarter, and $5,000 increments are expected in the remaining quarters of 2002. Fixed expenses are expected to be $40,000 in each quarter. Prepare the selling and administrative expense budget by quarters for 2002.

Prepare a budgeted income statement for the year.
(SO 4)

BE24-8 Bitterman Company has completed all of its operating budgets. The sales budget for the year shows 50,000 units and total sales of $2,000,000. The total unit cost of making one unit of sales is $28. Selling and administrative expenses are expected to be $300,000. Income taxes are estimated to be $50,000. Prepare a budgeted income statement for the year ending December 31, 2002.

Prepare data for a cash budget.
(SO 5)

BE24-9 Jorie Aloisio Industries expects credit sales for January, February, and March to be $200,000, $275,000, and $310,000, respectively. It is expected that 70% of the sales will be collected in the month of sale, and 30% will be collected in the following month. Compute cash collections from customers for each month.

Determine required merchandise purchases for 1 month.
(SO 6)

BE24-10 Maggie Sharrer Wholesalers is preparing its merchandise purchases budget. Budgeted sales are $400,000 for April and $450,000 for May. Cost of goods sold is expected to be 75% of sales. The company's desired ending inventory is 20% of the following month's cost of goods sold. Compute the required purchases for April.

EXERCISES

Prepare a sales budget for 2 quarters.
(SO 3)

E24-1 L. Quick Electronics Inc. produces and sells two models of pocket calculators, XQ-103 and XQ-104. The calculators sell for $12 and $20, respectively. Because of the intense competition Quick faces, management budgets sales semiannually. Its projections for the first 2 quarters of 2002 are as follows.

	Unit Sales	
Product	**Quarter 1**	**Quarter 2**
XQ-103	30,000	27,000
XQ-104	12,000	13,000

No changes in selling prices are anticipated.

Instructions
Prepare a sales budget for the 2 quarters ending June 30, 2002. List the products and show for each quarter and for the 6 months, units, selling price, and total sales by product and in total.

Prepare quarterly production budgets.
(SO 3)

E24-2 S. Stahl Company produces and sells two types of automobile batteries, the heavy-duty HD-240 and the long-life LL-250. The 2002 sales budget for the two products is as follows.

Quarter	HD-240	LL-250
1	5,000	10,000
2	7,000	18,000
3	8,000	20,000
4	10,000	35,000

The January 1, 2002, inventory of HD-240 and LL-250 units is 3,500 and 6,000, respectively. Management desires an ending inventory each quarter equal to 60% of the next quarter's sales. Sales in the first quarter of 2003 are expected to be 30% higher than sales in the same quarter in 2002.

Instructions
Prepare separate quarterly production budgets for each product by quarters for 2002.

Prepare a direct materials purchases budget.
(SO 3)

E24-3 Gosh-by-Golly Industries has adopted the following production budget for the first 4 months of 2003.

Month	Units	Month	Units
January	10,000	March	6,000
February	8,000	April	4,000

Each unit requires 5 pounds of raw materials costing $1.50 per pound. On December 31, 2002, the ending raw materials inventory was 25,000 pounds. Management wants to have a raw materials inventory at the end of the month equal to 50% of next month's production requirements.

Instructions
Prepare a direct materials purchases budget by months for the first quarter.

Prepare production and direct materials budgets by quarters for 6 months.
(SO 3)

E24-4 The W. Sublette Company budget committee has reached agreement on the following data for the 6 months ending June 30, 2003.

Sales units:	First quarter 5,000; second quarter 8,000
Ending raw materials inventory:	40% of the next quarter's production requirements
Ending finished goods inventory:	20% of the next quarter's expected sales units

The ending raw materials and finished goods inventories at December 31, 2002, follow the same percentage relationships to production and sales that occur in 2003. Three pounds of raw materials are required to make each unit of finished goods. Raw materials purchased are expected to cost $4 per pound. Sales of 7,000 units and required production of 7,250 units are expected in the third quarter of 2003.

Instructions
(a) Prepare a production budget by quarters for the 6 months.
(b) Prepare a direct materials budget by quarters for the 6 months.

Prepare a direct labor budget.
(SO 3)

E24-5 Twyla, Inc., is preparing its direct labor budget for 2002 from the following production budget based on a calendar year.

Quarter	Units	Quarter	Units
1	20,000	3	35,000
2	25,000	4	30,000

Each unit requires 1.5 hours of direct labor.

Instructions
Prepare a direct labor cost budget for 2002. Wage rates are expected to be $14 for the first 2 quarters and $16 for quarters 3 and 4.

Prepare a manufacturing overhead budget for the year.
(SO 3)

E24-6 Vincent Nathan Company is preparing its manufacturing overhead budget for 2002. Relevant data consist of the following.

Units to be produced (by quarters): 10,000, 12,000, 14,000, 16,000.

Direct labor: Time is 1.5 hours per unit.

Variable overhead costs per direct labor hour: Indirect materials $0.70; indirect labor $1.20; and maintenance $0.30.

Fixed overhead costs per quarter: Supervisory salaries $35,000; depreciation $12,000; and maintenance $9,000.

Instructions
Prepare the manufacturing overhead budget for the year, showing quarterly data.

Prepare a selling and administrative expense budget for 2 quarters.
(SO 3)

E24-7 Marcum Company combines its operating expenses for budget purposes in a selling and administrative expense budget. For the first 6 months of 2002, the following data are available.

1. Sales: 15,000 units quarter 1; 18,000 units quarter 2.
2. Variable costs per dollar of sales: Sales commissions 5%, delivery expense 2%, and advertising 3%.
3. Fixed costs per quarter: Sales salaries $10,000, office salaries $6,000, depreciation $4,200, insurance $1,500, utilities $800, and repairs expense $600.
4. Unit selling price: $20.

Instructions
Prepare a selling and administrative expense budget by quarters for the first 6 months of 2002.

Prepare a budgeted income statement for the year.
(SO 3, 4)

E24-8 Longhead Company has accumulated the following budget data for the year 2002.

1. Sales: 30,000 units, unit selling price $80.
2. Cost of one unit of finished goods: Direct materials 3 pounds at $5 per pound, direct labor 3 hours at $12 per hour, and manufacturing overhead $6 per direct labor hour.
3. Inventories (raw materials only): Beginning, 10,000 pounds; ending, 15,000 pounds.
4. Raw materials cost: $5 per pound.
5. Selling and administrative expenses: $150,000.
6. Income taxes: 30% of income before income taxes.

Instructions
Prepare a budgeted income statement for 2002. Show the computation of cost of goods sold.

Prepare a cash budget for 2 months.
(SO 5)

E24-9 Campagna Company expects to have a cash balance of $46,000 on January 1, 2002. Relevant monthly budget data for the first 2 months of 2002 are as follows.

Collections from customers: January $80,000, February $150,000.

Payments to suppliers: January $40,000, February $75,000.

Direct labor: January $30,000, February $45,000. Wages are paid in the month they are incurred.

Manufacturing overhead: January $21,000, February $30,000. These costs include depreciation of $1,000 per month. All other overhead costs are paid as incurred.

Selling and administrative expenses: January $15,000, February $20,000. These costs are exclusive of depreciation. They are paid as incurred.

Sales of marketable securities in January are expected to realize $10,000 in cash. Campagna Company has a line of credit at a local bank that enables it to borrow up to $25,000. The company wants to maintain a minimum monthly cash balance of $20,000.

Instructions
Prepare a cash budget for January and February.

Prepare a purchases budget and budgeted income statement for a merchandiser.
(SO 6)

E24-10 In May 2002, the budget committee of Sherrick Stores assembles the following data in preparation of budgeted merchandise purchases for the month of June.

1. Expected sales: June $500,000, July $600,000.
2. Cost of goods sold is expected to be 65% of sales.
3. Desired ending merchandise inventory is 40% of the following (next) month's cost of goods sold.
4. The beginning inventory at June 1 will be the desired amount.

Instructions
(a) Compute the budgeted merchandise purchases for June.
(b) Prepare the budgeted income statement for June through gross profit on sales.

PROBLEMS: SET A

Prepare budgeted income statement and supporting budgets.
(SO 3, 4)

P24-1A Oakbrook Farm Supply Company manufactures and sells a pesticide called Snare. The following data are available for preparing budgets for Snare for the first 2 quarters of 2003.

1. Sales: Quarter 1, 35,000 bags: quarter 2, 50,000 bags. Selling price is $60 per bag.
2. Direct materials: Each bag of Snare requires 5 pounds of Gumm at a cost of $3 per pound and 8 pounds of Tarr at $1.50 per pound.
3. Desired inventory levels:

Type of Inventory	January 1	April 1	July 1
Snare (bags)	8,000	12,000	18,000
Gumm (pounds)	9,000	10,000	13,000
Tarr (pounds)	14,000	20,000	25,000

4. Direct labor: Direct labor time is 15 minutes per bag at an hourly rate of $12 per hour.
5. Selling and administrative expenses are expected to be 8% of sales plus $175,000 per quarter.
6. Income taxes are expected to be 30% of income from operations.

Your assistant has prepared two budgets: (1) The manufacturing overhead budget shows expected costs to be 150% of direct labor cost. (2) The direct materials budget for Tarr shows the cost of Tarr to be $477,000 in quarter 1 and $679,500 in quarter 2.

Instructions

Prepare the budgeted income statement for the first 6 months and all required supporting budgets by quarters. (*Note:* Use variable and fixed in the selling and administrative expense budget).

Net income $986,650
Standard cost per bag $34.50

Prepare sales, production, direct materials, direct labor, and income statement budgets.
(SO 3, 4)

P24-2A Joe Dunham Inc. is preparing its annual budgets for the year ending December 31, 2003. Accounting assistants furnish the following data.

	Product JB 50	Product JB 60
Sales budget:		
Anticipated volume in units	480,000	180,000
Unit selling price	$20.00	$25.00
Production budget:		
Desired ending finished goods units	25,000	15,000
Beginning finished goods units	30,000	10,000
Direct materials budget:		
Direct materials per unit (pounds)	2	3
Desired ending direct materials pounds	30,000	15,000
Beginning direct materials pounds	40,000	10,000
Cost per pound	$3.00	$4.00
Direct labor budget:		
Direct labor time per unit	0.4	0.6
Direct labor rate per hour	$11.00	$11.00
Budgeted income statement:		
Total unit cost	$12.00	$20.00

An accounting assistant has prepared the detailed manufacturing overhead budget and the selling and administrative expense budget. The latter shows selling expenses of $660,000 for product JB 50 and $360,000 for product JB 60, and administrative expenses of $420,000 for product JB 50 and $340,000 for product JB 60. Income taxes are expected to be 30%.

Instructions

Prepare the following budgets for the year. Show data for each product. Quarterly budgets should not be prepared.

(a) Sales
(b) Production
(c) Direct materials
(d) Direct labor
(e) Income statement (*Note*: Income taxes are not allocated to the products.)

(a) Total sales $14,100,000
(b) Required production units: JB 50, 475,000 JB 60, 185,000
(c) Total cost of direct materials purchases $5,060,000
(d) Total direct labor cost $3,311,000
(e) Net income $2,072,000

Prepare sales and production budgets and compute cost per unit under two plans.
(SO 3, 4)

P24-3A Hindu Industries had sales in 2002 of $6,300,000 and gross profit of $1,500,000. Management is considering two alternative budget plans to increase its gross profit in 2003.

Plan A would increase the selling price per unit from $9.00 to $9.40. Sales volume would decrease by 5% from its 2002 level. Plan B would decrease the selling price per unit by $0.50. The marketing department expects that the sales volume would increase by 150,000 units.

At the end of 2002, Hindu has 30,000 units of inventory on hand. If Plan A is accepted, the 2003 ending inventory should be equal to 4% of the 2003 sales. If Plan B is accepted, the ending inventory should be equal to 40,000 units. Each unit produced will cost $1.60 in direct labor, $2.00 in direct materials, and $0.90 in variable overhead. The fixed overhead for 2003 should be $1,800,000.

Instructions

(c) Unit cost: Plan A $7.22
Plan B $6.59
(d) Gross profit:
Plan A $1,449,700
Plan B $1,623,500

(a) Prepare a sales budget for 2003 under each plan.
(b) Prepare a production budget for 2003 under each plan.
(c) Compute the production cost per unit under each plan. Why is the cost per unit different for each of the two plans? (Round to two decimals.)
(d) Which plan should be accepted? (*Hint:* Compute the gross profit under each plan.)

Prepare cash budget for 2 months.
(SO 5)

P24-4A Yaeger Company prepares monthly cash budgets. Relevant data from operating budgets for 2003 are:

	January	**February**
Sales	$360,000	$400,000
Direct materials purchases	125,000	130,000
Direct labor	90,000	100,000
Manufacturing overhead	70,000	75,000
Selling and administrative expenses	79,000	86,000

All sales are on account. Collections are expected to be 50% in the month of sale, 30% in the first month following the sale, and 20% in the second month following the sale. Sixty percent (60%) of direct material purchases are paid in cash in the month of purchase, and the balance due is paid in the month following the purchase. All other items above are paid in the month incurred except for selling and administrative expenses that include $1,000 of depreciation per month.

Other data:
1. Credit sales: November 2002, $260,000; December 2002, $300,000.
2. Purchases of direct materials: December 2002, $100,000.
3. Other receipts: January — Collection of December 31, 2002, notes receivable $15,000; February—Proceeds from sale of securities $6,000.
4. Other disbursements: February—Withdrawal of $5,000 cash for personal use of owner, Dewey Yaeger.

The company's cash balance on January 1, 2003, is expected to be $70,000. The company wants to maintain a minimum cash balance of $50,000.

(a) January:
collections $322,000
payments $115,000
(b) Ending cash balance:
January $54,000
February $50,000

Instructions

(a) Prepare schedules for (1) expected collections from customers and (2) expected payments for direct materials purchases.
(b) Prepare a cash budget for January and February in columnar form.

Prepare purchases and income statement budgets for a merchandiser.
(SO 6)

P24-5A The budget committee of Henning Company collects the following data for its San Miguel Store in preparing budgeted income statements for May and June 2003.
1. Sales for May are expected to be $600,000. Sales in June and July are expected to be 10% higher than the preceding month.
2. Cost of goods sold is expected to be 70% of sales.
3. Company policy is to maintain ending merchandise inventory at 25% of the following month's cost of goods sold.
4. Operating expenses are estimated to be:

Sales salaries	$25,000 per month
Advertising	5% of monthly sales
Delivery expense	3% of monthly sales
Sales commissions	4% of monthly sales
Rent expense	$5,000 per month
Depreciation	$800 per month
Utilities	$600 per month
Insurance	$500 per month

5. Income taxes are estimated to be 30% of income from operations.

Instructions

(a) Prepare the merchandise purchases budget for each month in columnar form.

(b) Prepare budgeted income statements for each month in columnar form. Show in the statements the details of cost of goods sold.

(a) Purchases: May $430,500
June $473,550
(b) Net income:
May $53,270
June $60,830

P24-6A East Asian Industries' balance sheet at December 31, 2002, is presented below.

Prepare budgeted income statement and balance sheet.
(SO 3, 4)

EAST ASIAN INDUSTRIES
Balance Sheet
December 31, 2002

Assets

Current assets		
Cash		$ 7,500
Accounts receivable		82,500
Finished goods inventory (2,000 units)		30,000
Total current assets		120,000
Property, plant, and equipment		
Equipment	$40,000	
Less: Accumulated depreciation	10,000	30,000
Total assets		$150,000

Liabilities and Stockholders' Equity

Liabilities		
Notes payable		$ 25,000
Accounts payable		45,000
Total liabilities		70,000
Stockholders' equity		
Common stock	$50,000	
Retained earnings	30,000	
Total stockholders' equity		80,000
Total liabilities and stockholders' equity		$150,000

Additional information accumulated for the budgeting process is as follows.

Budgeted data for the year 2003 include the following.

	4th Qtr. of 2003	Year 2003 Total
Sales budget (8,000 units at $35)	$80,000	$280,000
Direct materials used	17,000	72,400
Direct labor	8,500	38,600
Manufacturing overhead applied	10,000	42,000
Selling and administrative expenses	18,000	76,000

To meet sales requirements and to have 2,500 units of finished goods on hand at December 31, 2003, the production budget shows 8,500 required units of output. The total unit cost of production is expected to be $18. East Asian Industries uses the first-in, first-out (FIFO) inventory costing method. Selling and administrative expenses include $4,000 for depreciation on equipment. Interest expense is expected to be $3,500 for the year. Income taxes are expected to be 30% of income before income taxes.

All sales and purchases are on account. It is expected that 60% of quarterly sales are collected in cash within the quarter and the remainder is collected in the following quarter. Direct materials purchased from suppliers are paid 50% in the quarter incurred and the remainder in the following quarter. Purchases in the fourth quarter were the same as the materials used. In 2003, the company expects to purchase additional equipment costing $24,000. It expects to pay $8,000 on notes payable plus all interest due and payable to December 31 (included in interest expense $3,500, above). Accounts payable at December 31, 2003, includes amounts due suppliers (see above) plus other accounts payable of $7,500. In 2003, the company expects to declare and pay a $5,000 cash dividend. Unpaid income taxes at December 31 will be $5,000. The company's cash budget shows an expected cash balance of $29,750 at December 31, 2003.

Instructions

Net income $43,750
Total assets $156,750

Prepare a budgeted income statement for 2003 and a budgeted balance sheet at December 31, 2003. In preparing the income statement, you will need to compute cost of goods manufactured (materials + labor + overhead) and finished goods inventory (December 31, 2003).

PROBLEMS: SET B

Prepare a budgeted income statement and supporting budgets.
(SO 3, 4)

P24-1B Alcorn Farm Supply Company manufactures and sells a fertilizer called Basic II. The following data are available for preparing budgets for Basic II for the first 2 quarters of 2002.

1. Sales: Quarter 1, 50,000 bags; quarter 2, 70,000 bags. Selling price is $60 per bag.
2. Direct materials: Each bag of Basic II requires 5 pounds of Crup at a cost of $3 per pound and 10 pounds of Dert at $1.50 per pound.
3. Desired inventory levels:

Type of Inventory	January 1	April 1	July 1
Basic II (bags)	10,000	15,000	20,000
Crup (pounds)	9,000	12,000	15,000
Dert (pounds)	15,000	20,000	25,000

4. Direct labor: Direct labor time is 15 minutes per bag at an hourly rate of $10 per hour.
5. Selling and administrative expenses are expected to be 10% of sales plus $150,000 per quarter.
6. Income taxes are expected to be 30% of income from operations.

Your assistant has prepared two budgets: (1) The manufacturing overhead budget shows expected costs to be 100% of direct labor cost. (2) The direct materials budget for Dert which shows the cost of Dert to be $832,500 in quarter 1 and $132,500 in quarter 2.

Instructions

Net income $1,386,000
Standard cost per bag $35.00

Prepare the budgeted income statement for the first 6 months of 2002 and all required supporting budgets by quarters. (*Note:* Use variable and fixed in the selling and administrative expense budget.)

Prepare sales, production, direct materials, direct labor, and income statement budgets.
(SO 3, 4)

P24-2B Borealis Inc. is preparing its annual budgets for the year ending December 31, 2002. Accounting assistants furnish the following data.

	Product LN 35	Product LN 40
Sales budget:		
Anticipated volume in units	300,000	150,000
Unit selling price	$20.00	$30.00
Production budget:		
Desired ending finished goods units	30,000	25,000
Beginning finished goods units	20,000	15,000

	LN 35	LN 40
Direct materials budget:		
Direct materials per unit (pounds)	2	3
Desired ending direct materials pounds	50,000	20,000
Beginning direct materials pounds	40,000	10,000
Cost per pound	$2.00	$3.00
Direct labor budget:		
Direct labor time per unit	0.5	0.75
Direct labor rate per hour	$9.00	$9.00
Budgeted income statement:		
Total unit cost	$10.00	$20.00

An accounting assistant has prepared the detailed manufacturing overhead budget and the selling and administrative expense budget. The latter shows selling expenses of $460,000 for product LN 35 and $440,000 for product LN 40, and administrative expenses of $420,000 for product LN 35 and $380,000 for product LN 40. Income taxes are expected to be 30%.

(a) Total sales $10,500,000
(b) Required production units: LN 35, 310,000 LN 40, 160,000
(c) Total cost of direct materials purchases $2,730,000
(d) Total direct labor cost $2,475,000
(e) Net income $1,960,000

Instructions

Prepare the following budgets for the year. Show data for each product. Quarterly budgets should not be prepared.

(a) Sales
(b) Production
(c) Direct materials
(d) Direct labor
(e) Income statement (*Note:* Income taxes are not allocated to the products.)

Prepare sales and production budgets and compute cost per unit under two plans.
(SO 3, 4)

P24-3B David Chambers Industries has sales in 2002 of $5,250,000 (656,250 units) and gross profit of $1,587,500. Management is considering two alternative budget plans to increase its gross profit in 2003.

Plan A would increase the selling price per unit from $8.00 to $8.60. Sales volume would decrease by 10% from its 2002 level. Plan B would decrease the selling price per unit by 5%. The marketing department expects that the sales volume would increase by 100,000 units.

At the end of 2002, Chambers has 75,000 units on hand. If Plan A is accepted, the 2003 ending inventory should be equal to 87,500 units. If Plan B is accepted, the ending inventory should be equal to 100,000 units. Each unit produced will cost $2.00 in direct materials, $1.50 in direct labor, and $0.50 in variable overhead. The fixed overhead for 2003 should be $965,000.

Instructions

(a) Prepare a sales budget for 2003 under (1) Plan A and (2) Plan B.
(b) Prepare a production budget for 2003 under (1) Plan A and (2) Plan B.
(c) Compute the cost per unit under (1) Plan A and (2) Plan B. Explain why the cost per unit is different for each of the two plans. (Round to two decimals.)
(d) Which plan should be accepted? (*Hint:* Compute the gross profit under each plan.)

(c) Unit cost: Plan A $5.60, Plan B $5.24
(d) Gross profit: Plan A $1,771,875 Plan B $1,784,750

Prepare cash budget for 2 months.
(SO 5)

P24-4B Flypaper Company prepares monthly cash budgets. Relevant data from operating budgets for 2003 are:

	January	February
Sales	$350,000	$400,000
Direct materials purchases	95,000	110,000
Direct labor	100,000	115,000
Manufacturing overhead	60,000	75,000
Selling and administrative expenses	75,000	85,000

All sales are on account. Collections are expected to be 60% in the month of sale, 30% in the first month following the sale, and 10% in the second month following the sale. Thirty percent (30%) of direct material purchases are paid in cash in the month of purchase, and the balance due is paid in the month following the purchase. All other items above are paid in the month incurred. Depreciation has been excluded from manufacturing overhead and selling and administrative expenses.

Other data:

1. Credit sales: November 2002, $200,000; December 2002, $280,000.
2. Purchases of direct materials: December 2002, $90,000.
3. Other receipts: January—Collection of December 31, 2002, interest receivable $3,000; February—Proceeds from sale of securities $5,000.
4. Other disbursements: February—payment of $20,000 for land.

(a) January:
collections $314,000
payments $91,500
(b) Ending cash balance:
January $50,500
February $50,000

The company's cash balance on January 1, 2003, is expected to be $60,000. The company wants to maintain a minimum cash balance of $50,000.

Instructions

(a) Prepare schedules for (1) expected collections from customers and (2) expected payments for direct materials purchases.

(b) Prepare a cash budget for January and February in columnar form.

Prepare purchases and income statement budgets for a merchandiser.
(SO 6)

P24-5B The budget committee of Oriental Company collects the following data for its Westwood Store in preparing budgeted income statements for July and August 2002.

1. Expected sales: July $400,000, August $450,000, September $500,000.
2. Cost of goods sold is expected to be 75% of sales.
3. Company policy is to maintain ending merchandise inventory at 30% of the following month's cost of goods sold.
4. Operating expenses are estimated to be:

Sales salaries	$20,000 per month
Advertising	4% of monthly sales
Delivery expense	2% of monthly sales
Sales commissions	3% of monthly sales
Rent expense	$3,000 per month
Depreciation	$700 per month
Utilities	$500 per month
Insurance	$300 per month

5. Income taxes are estimated to be 30% of income from operations.

(a) Purchases: July $311,250
August $348,750
(b) Net income: July $27,650
August $33,250

Instructions

(a) Prepare the merchandise purchases budget for each month in columnar form.

(b) Prepare budgeted income statements for each month in columnar form. Show the details of cost of goods sold in the statements.

BROADENING YOUR PERSPECTIVE

GROUP DECISION CASE

BYP24-1 Castle Corporation operates on a calendar-year basis. It begins the annual budgeting process in late August when the president establishes targets for the total dollar sales and net income before taxes for the next year.

The sales target is given first to the marketing department. The marketing manager formulates a sales budget by product line in both units and dollars. From this budget, sales quotas by product line in units and dollars are established for each of the corporation's sales districts. The marketing manager also estimates the cost of the marketing activities required to support the target sales volume and prepares a tentative marketing expense budget.

The executive vice president uses the sales and profit targets, the sales budget by product line, and the tentative marketing expense budget to determine the dollar amounts that can be devoted to manufacturing and corporate office expense. The executive vice president prepares the budget for corporate expenses. She then forwards to the production department the product-line sales budget in units and the total dollar amount that can be devoted to manufacturing.

The production manager meets with the factory managers to develop a manufacturing plan that will produce the required units when needed within the cost constraints set by the executive vice president. The budgeting process usually comes to a halt at this point because the production department does not consider the financial resources allocated to be adequate.

When this standstill occurs, the vice president of finance, the executive vice president, the marketing manager, and the production manager meet together to determine the final budgets for each of the areas. This normally results in a modest increase in the total amount available for manufacturing costs and cuts in the marketing expense and corporate office expense budgets. The total sales and net income figures proposed by the president are seldom changed. Although the participants are seldom pleased with the compromise, these budgets are final. Each executive then develops a new detailed budget for the operations in his or her area.

None of the areas has achieved its budget in recent years. Sales often run below the target. When budgeted sales are not achieved, each area is expected to cut costs so that the president's profit target can be met. However, the profit target is seldom met because costs are not cut enough. In fact, costs often run above the original budget in all functional areas (marketing, production, and corporate office).

The president is disturbed that Castle has not been able to meet the sales and profit targets. He hired a consultant with considerable experience with companies in Castle's industry. The consultant reviewed the budgets for the past 4 years. He concluded that the product-line sales budgets were reasonable and that the cost and expense budgets were adequate for the budgeted sales and production levels.

Instructions

With the class divided into groups, answer the following.

(a) Discuss how the budgeting process employed by Castle Corporation contributes to the failure to achieve the president's sales and profit targets.

(b) Suggest how Castle Corporation's budgeting process could be revised to correct the problems.

(c) Should the functional areas be expected to cut their costs when sales volume falls below budget? Explain your answer. (CMA adapted.)

MANAGERIAL ANALYSIS

BYP24-2 Thebeau & Lewis Inc. manufactures ergonomic devices for computer users. Some of their more popular products include glare screens (for computer monitors), keyboard stands with wrist rests, and carousels that allow easy access to floppy disks. Over the past 5 years, they experienced rapid growth, with sales of all products increasing 20% to 50% each year.

Last year, some of the primary manufacturers of computers began introducing new products with some of the ergonomic designs, such as glare screens and wrist rests, already built in. As a result, sales of Thebeau & Lewis's accessory devices have declined somewhat. The company believes that the disk carousels will probably continue to show growth, but that the other products will probably continue to decline. When the next year's budget was prepared, increases were built in to research and development so that replacement products could be developed or the company could expand into some other product line. Some product lines being considered are general-purpose ergonomic devices including back supports, foot rests, and sloped writing pads.

The most recent results have shown that sales decreased more than was expected for the glare screens. As a result, the company may have a shortage of funds. Top management has therefore asked that all expenses be reduced 10% to compensate for these reduced sales. Summary budget information is as follows.

Raw materials	$240,000
Direct labor	110,000
Insurance	50,000
Depreciation	90,000
Machine repairs	30,000
Sales salaries	50,000
Office salaries	80,000
Factory salaries (indirect labor)	50,000
Total	$700,000

Instructions

Using the information above, answer the following questions.

(a) What are the implications of reducing each of the costs? For example, if the company reduces raw materials costs, it may have to do so by purchasing lower-quality materials. This may affect sales in the long run.

(b) Based on your analysis in (a), what do you think is the best way to obtain the $70,000 in cost savings requested? Be specific. Are there any costs that cannot or should not be reduced? Why?

REAL-WORLD FOCUS

BYP24-3 **Network Computing Devices Inc.** was founded in 1988 in Mountain View, Calif. The company develops software products such as X-terminals, Z-mail, PC X-ware, and related hardware products. Presented below is a discussion by management in its annual report.

NCD

NETWORK COMPUTING DEVICES, INC.
Management Discussion

The Company's operating results have varied significantly, particularly on a quarterly basis, as a result of a number of factors, including general economic conditions affecting industry demand for computer products, the timing and market acceptance of new product introductions by the Company and its competitors, the timing of significant orders from large customers, periodic changes in product pricing and discounting due to competitive factors, and the availability of key components, such as video monitors and electronic subassemblies, some of which require substantial order lead times. The Company's operating results may fluctuate in the future as a result of these and other factors, including the Company's success in developing and introducing new products, its product and customer mix, and the level of competition which it experiences. The Company operates with a small backlog. Sales and operating results, therefore, generally depend on the volume and timing of orders received, which are difficult to forecast. The Company has experienced slowness in orders from some customers during the first quarter of each calendar year due to budgeting cycles common in the computer industry. In addition, sales in Europe typically are adversely affected in the third calendar quarter as many European customers reduce their business activities during the month of August.

Due to the Company's rapid growth rate and the effect of new product introductions on quarterly revenues, these seasonal trends have not materially impacted the Company's results of operations to date. However, as the Company's product lines mature and its rate of revenue growth declines, these seasonal factors may become more evident. Additionally, the Company's international sales are denominated in U.S. dollars, and an increase or decrease in the value of the U.S. dollar relative to foreign currencies could make the Company's products less or more competitive in those markets.

Instructions

(a) Identify the factors that affect the budgeting process at Network Computing Devices Inc.
(b) Explain the additional budgeting concerns created by the international operations of the company.

www.wiley.com/college/weygandt

EXPLORING THE WEB

BYP24-4 The opportunities for business consulting in the areas of corporate planning, budgeting, and strategy are almost limitless as new, more powerful software continues to be developed. This exercise takes you to the Web site of **CP Corporate Planning**, a European consulting firm.

Address: **www.corporate-planning.com/home/fse_home.html** *(or go to www.wiley.com/college/weygandt)*

Steps:

Go to the site above.

Instructions

Choose three case studies, and in each case identify the problem the company faced and how the situation was resolved.

Communication Activity

BYP24-5 In order to better serve their rural patients, Drs. Jim and Jeff Howell (brothers) began giving safety seminars. Especially popular were their "emergency-preparedness" talks given to farmers. Many people asked whether the "kit" of materials the doctors recommended for common farm emergencies was commercially available.

After checking with several suppliers, the doctors realized that no other company offered the supplies they recommended in their seminars, packaged in the way they described. Their wives, Marie and Pam, agreed to make a test package by ordering supplies from various medical supply companies and assembling them into a "kit" that could be sold at the seminars. When these kits proved a runaway success, the sisters-in-law decided to market them. At the advice of their accountant, they organized this venture as a separate company, called Life Protection Products (LPP), with Marie Howell as CEO and Pam Howell as Secretary-Treasurer.

LPP soon started receiving requests for the kits from all over the country, as word spread about their availability. Even without advertising, LPP was able to sell its full inventory every month. However, the company was becoming financially strained. Marie and Pam had about $100,000 in savings, and they invested about half that amount initially. They believed that this venture would allow them to make money. However, at the present time, only about $30,000 of the cash remains, and the company is constantly short of cash.

Marie Howell has come to you for advice. She does not understand why the company is having cash flow problems. She and Pam have not even been withdrawing salaries. However, they have rented a local building and have hired two more full-time workers to help them cope with the increasing demand. They do not think they could handle the demand without this additional help.

Marie is also worried that the cash problems mean that the company may not be able to support itself. She has prepared the cash budget shown on the next page. All seminar customers pay for their products in full at the time of purchase. In addition, several large companies have ordered the kits for use by employees who work in remote sites. They have requested credit terms and have been allowed to pay in the month following the sale. These large purchasers amount to about 25% of the sales at the present time. LPP purchases the materials for the kits about 2 months ahead of time. Marie and Pam are considering slowing the growth of the company by simply purchasing less materials, which will mean selling fewer kits.

The workers are paid in cash weekly. Marie and Pam need about $15,000 cash on hand at the beginning of the month to pay for purchases of raw materials. Right now they have been using cash from their savings, but as noted, only $30,000 is left.

The cash budget that Marie Howell has given you is shown at the top of the next page.

Instructions

Write a response to Marie Howell. Explain why LPP is short of cash. Will this company be able to support itself? Explain your answer. Make any recommendations you deem appropriate.

LIFE PROTECTION PRODUCTS
Cash Budget
For the Quarter Ending June 30, 2003

	April	May	June
Cash balance, beginning	$15,000	$15,000	$15,000
Cash received			
From prior month sales	5,000	7,500	12,500
From current sales	15,000	22,500	37,500
Total cash on hand	35,000	45,000	65,000
Cash payments			
To employees	3,000	3,000	3,000
For products	25,000	35,000	45,000
Miscellaneous expenses	5,000	6,000	7,000
Postage	1,000	1,000	1,000
Total cash payments	34,000	45,000	56,000
Cash balance	$ 1,000	$ 0	$ 9,000
Borrow from savings	$14,000	$15,000	$ 1,000
Borrow from bank?	$ 0	$ 0	$ 7,000

ETHICS CASE

BYP24-6 You are an accountant in the budgetary, projections, and special projects department of American Bare Conductor, Inc., a large manufacturing company. The president, Robert Boey, asks you on very short notice to prepare some sales and income projections covering the next 2 years of the company's much heralded new product lines. He wants these projections for a series of speeches he is making while on a 2-week trip to eight East Coast brokerage firms. The president hopes to bolster American Bare's stock sales and price.

You work 23 hours in 2 days to compile the projections, hand deliver them to the president, and are swiftly but graciously thanked as he departs. A week later you find time to go over some of your computations and discover a miscalculation that makes the projections grossly overstated. You quickly inquire about the president's itinerary and learn that he has made half of his speeches and has half yet to make. You are in a quandary as to what to do.

Instructions

(a) What are the consequences of telling the president of your gross miscalculations?
(b) What are the consequences of *not* telling the president of your gross miscalculations?
(c) What are the ethical considerations to you and the president in this situation?

Answers to Self-Study Questions

1. c **2.** a **3.** b **4.** b **5.** d **6.** d **7.** a **8.** c **9.** c **10.** d

Answer to Lands' End Review It Question 5, page 997

Lands' End offers the following general expectation: "For the first half of fiscal 2001, the company anticipates a sales increase in the mid-single digits, together with a strong increase in earnings. The first quarter is expected to show flat sales on 5 percent fewer pages mailed, with somewhat weaker earnings. . . The company anticipates that the fourth quarter will represent the largest improvement over the prior year in both sales and earnings."

Remember to go back to the Navigator box on the chapter-opening page and check off your completed work.

BUDGETARY CONTROL AND RESPONSIBILITY ACCOUNTING

25

THE NAVIGATOR ✓

- Understand *Concepts for Review* ❑
- Read *Feature Story* ❑
- Scan *Study Objectives* ❑
- Read *Preview* ❑
- Read text and answer *Before You Go On* *p.* 1030 ❑ *p.* 1038 ❑ *p.* 1043 ❑
- Work *Demonstration Problem* ❑
- Review *Summary of Study Objectives* ❑
- Answer *Self-Study Questions* ❑
- Complete *Assignments* ❑

CONCEPTS FOR REVIEW

Before studying this chapter, you should know or, if necessary, review:

a. The meaning and scope of the management function of controlling. (Ch. 20, p. 830)

b. The cost elements that produce a total cost per unit of finished goods. (Ch. 20, pp. 831–833)

c. How variable costs differ from fixed costs. (Ch. 23, pp. 946–950)

✓ THE NAVIGATOR

FEATURE STORY

"If Money Is Low, We'll Take the Bus"

Virtually every department on a college campus develops a budget and then compares that budget to the amount actually spent. As the school term progresses, the person in charge of the budget can see how well the department is doing compared to expectations.

One of the most expensive departments on campus is the athletic department. That fact usually rankles the academic department heads. They argue that a university exists first and foremost to educate. But the money for sports is often justified because the sports teams—particularly at big schools—generate large incomes from television contracts that can then be used for a variety of educational purposes.

At the **University of Nevada, Las Vegas**, each athletic team has its own budget and its own financial statements. This financial information "shows what the teams have spent for the month and for the year to date, and how the actual expenditures compare to the budget," says Merv Gupton, athletic accounting manager. The biggest budget items: scholarships for student athletes, payroll, and travel costs.

UNLV sports teams include football, basketball, tennis, baseball, softball, soccer, track, cross country, golf, and swimming. Travel costs are usually the most uncontrollable item in the budget. What if you get two-thirds through the season and run out of money? "One sports team might be able to help out another," says Gupton. Or more likely, "if a coach is running low on money, the team won't fly—it'll take the bus."

THE NAVIGATOR

STUDY OBJECTIVES

After studying this chapter, you should be able to:

1. Describe the concept of budgetary control.
2. Evaluate the usefulness of static budget reports.
3. Explain the development of flexible budgets and the usefulness of flexible budget reports.
4. Describe the concept of responsibility accounting.
5. Indicate the features of responsibility reports for cost centers.
6. Identify the content of responsibility reports for profit centers.
7. Explain the basis and formula used in evaluating performance in investment centers.

THE NAVIGATOR

PREVIEW OF CHAPTER 25

The Feature Story indicates not only that budgets are necessary for an athletic department, but also that they can be used to control the department's activities. For example, if you were the athletic director at **UNLV**, you might require periodic updates from each coach, showing actual and budgeted expenses.

In contrast to Chapter 24, we now consider how budgets are used by management to control operations. This chapter focuses on two aspects of management control: (1) budgetary control and (2) responsibility accounting.

The content and organization of Chapter 25 are as follows.

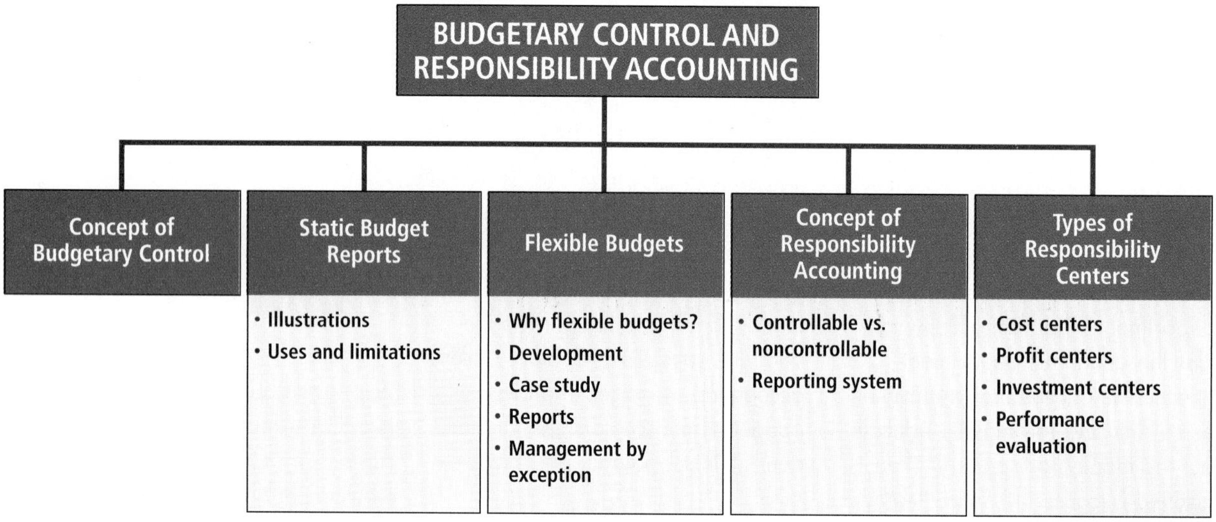

THE NAVIGATOR

CONCEPT OF BUDGETARY CONTROL

STUDY OBJECTIVE 1

Describe the concept of budgetary control.

One of management's major functions is to control company operations. Control consists of the steps taken by management to see that planned objectives are met. We now ask: How do budgets contribute to control of operations?

The use of budgets in controlling operations is known as **budgetary control**. Such control takes place by means of **budget reports** that compare actual results with planned objectives. The use of budget reports is based on the belief that planned objectives lose much of their potential value without some monitoring of progress along the way. Just as your professors give midterm exams to evaluate your progress, so top management requires periodic reports on the progress of department managers toward their planned objectives.

Budget reports provide management with feedback on operations. The feedback for a crucial objective, such as having enough cash on hand to pay bills, may be made daily. For other objectives, such as meeting budgeted annual sales and operating expenses, monthly budget reports may suffice. Budget reports can be prepared as frequently as needed. From these reports, management analyzes any differences between actual and planned results and determines their causes. Management then may take corrective action, or it may decide to modify future plans.

Budgetary control involves the following activities.

Illustration 25-1

Budgetary control

Budgetary control works best when a company has a formalized reporting system. The system should do the following: (1) Identify the name of the budget report, such as the sales budget or the manufacturing overhead budget. (2) State the frequency of the report, such as weekly or monthly. (3) Specify the purpose of the report. And (4) indicate the primary recipient(s) of the report. The following schedule illustrates a partial budgetary control system for a manufacturing company. Note the frequency of the reports and their emphasis on control. For example, there is a daily report on scrap and a weekly report on labor.

Illustration 25-2

Budgetary control reporting system

Name of Report	Frequency	Purpose	Primary Recipient(s)
Sales	Weekly	Determine whether sales goals are being met	Top management and sales manager
Labor	Weekly	Control direct and indirect labor costs	Vice president of production and production department managers
Scrap	Daily	Determine efficient use of materials	Production manager
Departmental overhead costs	Monthly	Control overhead costs	Department manager
Selling expenses	Monthly	Control selling expenses	Sales manager
Income statement	Monthly and quarterly	Determine whether income objectives are being met	Top management

STATIC BUDGET REPORTS

STUDY OBJECTIVE 2

Evaluate the usefulness of static budget reports.

You learned in Chapter 24 that the master budget formalizes management's planned objectives for the coming year. When used in budgetary control, each budget included in the master budget is considered to be static. A **static budget** is a projection of budget data at one level of activity. Data for different levels of activity are ignored. As a result, actual results are always compared with budget data at the activity level used in developing the master budget.

ILLUSTRATIONS

To illustrate the role of a static budget in budgetary control, we will use selected data prepared for Hayes Company in Chapter 24. Budget and actual sales data for the Kitchen-mate product in the first and second quarters of 2002 are as follows.

Illustration 25-3

Budget and actual sales data

Sales	First Quarter	Second Quarter	Total
Budgeted	$180,000	$210,000	$390,000
Actual	179,000	199,500	378,500
Difference	$ 1,000	$ 10,500	$ 11,500

The sales budget report for Hayes Company's first quarter is shown below. The right-most column reports the difference between the budgeted and actual amounts.

Illustration 25-4

Sales budget report—first quarter

ALTERNATIVE TERMINOLOGY
The difference between budget and actual is sometimes called a *budget variance.*

HAYES COMPANY
Sales Budget Report
For the Quarter Ended March 31, 2002

Product Line	Budget	Actual	Difference Favorable F Unfavorable U
Kitchen-mate[a]	$180,000	$179,000	$1,000 U

[a] In practice, each product line would be included in the report.

The report shows that sales are $1,000 under budget—an unfavorable result. This difference is less than 1 percent of budgeted sales ($1,000 ÷ $180,000 = .0056). Top management's reaction to unfavorable differences is often influenced by the materiality (significance) of the difference. Since the difference of $1,000 is immaterial in this case, we will assume that Hayes Company management takes no specific corrective action.

The budget report for the second quarter is presented in Illustration 25-5. It contains one new feature: cumulative year-to-date information. This report indicates that sales for the second quarter were $10,500 below budget. This is 5 percent of budgeted sales ($10,500 ÷ $210,000). Top management may now conclude that the difference between budgeted and actual sales requires investigation.

Illustration 25-5

Sales budget report—second quarter

HAYES COMPANY
Sales Budget Report
For the Quarter Ended June 30, 2002

	Second Quarter			Year-to-Date		
Product Line	Budget	Actual	Difference Favorable F Unfavorable U	Budget	Actual	Difference Favorable F Unfavorable U
Kitchen-mate	$210,000	$199,500	$10,500 U	$390,000	$378,500	$11,500 U

Management's analysis should start by asking the sales manager the cause(s) of the shortfall. The need for corrective action should be considered. For example, management may decide to spur sales by offering sales incentives to customers or by increasing the advertising of Kitchen-mates. Or, if management concludes that a downturn in the economy is responsible for the lower sales, it may modify planned sales and profit goals for the remainder of the year.

USES AND LIMITATIONS

From these examples, you can see that a master sales budget is useful in evaluating the performance of a sales manager. It is now necessary to ask: Is the master budget appropriate for evaluating a manager's performance in controlling costs? Recall that in a static budget, data are not modified or adjusted, regardless of changes in activity. It follows, then, that a static budget is appropriate in evaluating a manager's effectiveness in controlling costs when:

1. The actual level of activity closely approximates the master budget activity level, and/or
2. The behavior of the costs in response to changes in activity is fixed.

A static budget report is, therefore, appropriate for **fixed manufacturing costs** and for **fixed selling and administrative expenses**. But, as you will see shortly, static budget reports may not be a proper basis for evaluating a manager's performance in controlling variable costs.

Static budgets are best for fixed costs and expenses

FLEXIBLE BUDGETS

STUDY OBJECTIVE 3

Explain the development of flexible budgets and the usefulness of flexible budget reports.

In contrast to a static budget, which is based on one level of activity, a **flexible budget** projects budget data for various levels of activity. In essence, **the flexible budget is a series of static budgets at different levels of activity**. The flexible budget recognizes that the budgetary process is more useful if it is adaptable to changed operating conditions.

Flexible budgets can be prepared for each of the types of budgets included in the master budget. For example, **Marriott Hotels** can budget revenues and net income on the basis of 60 percent, 80 percent, and 100 percent of room occupancy. Similarly, **American Van Lines** can budget its operating expenses on the basis of various levels of truck miles driven. Likewise, the bottling department of **Coca-Cola** can budget manufacturing costs on the basis of 70 percent, 80 percent, and 100 percent of direct labor costs or machine hours. In the following pages, we will illustrate a flexible budget for manufacturing overhead.

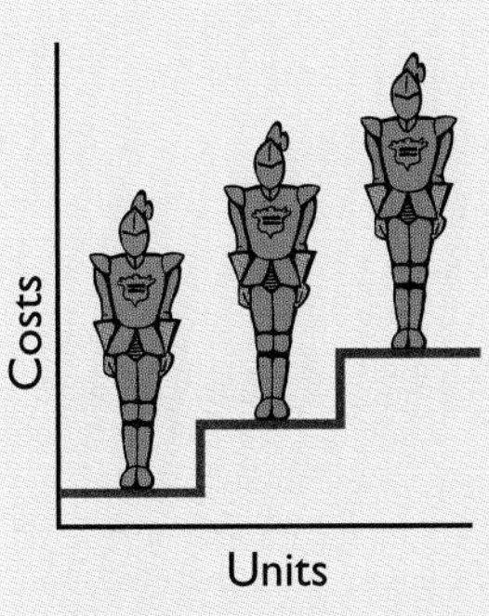

Flexible budgets are static budgets at different activity levels

WHY FLEXIBLE BUDGETS?

Assume that you are the manager in charge of manufacturing overhead in the Forging Department of Barton Steel. In preparing the manufacturing overhead budget for 2002, you prepare the following static budget based on a production volume of 10,000 units of steel ingots.

Illustration 25-6

Static overhead budget

BARTON STEEL
Manufacturing Overhead Budget (Static)
Forging Department
For the Year Ended December 31, 2002

Budgeted production in units (steel ingots)	10,000
Budgeted costs	
Indirect materials	$ 250,000
Indirect labor	260,000
Utilities	190,000
Depreciation	280,000
Property taxes	70,000
Supervision	50,000
	$1,100,000

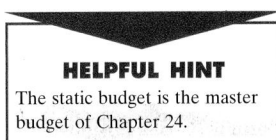

HELPFUL HINT
The static budget is the master budget of Chapter 24.

HELPFUL HINT
Which of the following is likely to be of little use when costs are variable—the static budget or the flexible budget? Answer: The static budget.

Fortunately for the company, the demand for steel ingots has increased, and 12,000 units are produced and sold during the year, rather than 10,000. You are elated: Increased sales means increased profitability, which should mean a bonus or a raise for you and the employees in your department. Unfortunately, a comparison of Forging Department actual and budgeted costs has put you on the spot. The budget report is shown below.

Illustration 25-7
Static overhead budget report

BARTON STEEL
Manufacturing Overhead Budget Report (Static)
Forging Department
For the Year Ended December 31, 2002

	Budget	Actual	Difference Favorable F Unfavorable U
Production in units	10,000	12,000	
Costs			
Indirect materials	$ 250,000	$ 295,000	$ 45,000 U
Indirect labor	260,000	312,000	52,000 U
Utilities	190,000	225,000	35,000 U
Depreciation	280,000	280,000	–0–
Property taxes	70,000	70,000	–0–
Supervision	50,000	50,000	–0–
	$1,100,000	$1,232,000	$132,000 U

HELPFUL HINT
A static budget will not work if a company has substantial variable costs.

This comparison uses budget data based on the original activity level (10,000 steel ingots). It indicates that the Forging Department is significantly **over budget** for three of the six overhead costs. And, there is a total unfavorable difference of $132,000, which is 12 percent over budget ($132,000 ÷ $1,100,000). Your supervisor is very unhappy! Instead of sharing in the company's success, you may find yourself looking for another job. What went wrong?

When you calm down and carefully examine the manufacturing overhead budget, you identify the problem: The budget data are not relevant! At the time the budget was developed, the company anticipated that only 10,000 units of steel ingots would be produced, **not** 12,000 ingots. Comparing actual with budgeted variable costs is meaningless. As production increases, the budget allowances for variable costs should increase both directly and proportionately. The variable costs in this example are indirect materials, indirect labor, and utilities.

Analyzing the budget data for these costs at 10,000 units, you arrive at the following per unit results.

Illustration 25-8
Variable costs per unit

Item	Total Cost	Per Unit
Indirect materials	$250,000	$25
Indirect labor	260,000	26
Utilities	190,000	19
	$700,000	$70

You then can calculate the budgeted variable costs at 12,000 units as follows.

Illustration 25-9
Budgeted variable costs, 12,000 units

Item	Computation	Total
Indirect materials	$25 × 12,000	$300,000
Indirect labor	26 × 12,000	312,000
Utilities	19 × 12,000	228,000
		$840,000

Because fixed costs do not change in total as activity changes, the budgeted amounts for these costs remain the same. The budget report based on the flexible budget for **12,000 units** of production is shown in Illustration 25-10. (Compare this with Illustration 25-7.)

Illustration 25-10
Flexible overhead budget report

BARTON STEEL
Manufacturing Overhead Budget Report (Flexible)
Forging Department
For the Year Ended December 31, 2002

	Budget	Actual	Difference Favorable F Unfavorable U
Production in units	12,000	12,000	
Variable costs			
Indirect materials	$ 300,000	$ 295,000	$5,000 F
Indirect labor	312,000	312,000	-0-
Utilities	228,000	225,000	3,000 F
Total variable	840,000	832,000	8,000 F
Fixed costs			
Depreciation	280,000	280,000	-0-
Property taxes	70,000	70,000	-0-
Supervision	50,000	50,000	-0-
Total fixed	400,000	400,000	-0-
Total costs	$1,240,000	$1,232,000	$8,000 F

This report indicates that the Forging Department is below budget—a favorable difference. Instead of worrying about being fired, you may be in line for a bonus or a raise after all! As this analysis shows, the only appropriate comparison is between actual costs at 12,000 units of production and budgeted costs at 12,000 units. Flexible budget reports provide this comparison.

DEVELOPING THE FLEXIBLE BUDGET

The flexible budget uses the master budget as its basis. To develop the flexible budget, management should take the following steps.

1. Identify the activity index and the relevant range of activity.
2. Identify the variable costs, and determine the budgeted variable cost per unit of activity for each cost.

3. Identify the fixed costs, and determine the budgeted amount for each cost.
4. Prepare the budget for selected increments of activity within the relevant range.

The activity index chosen should be one that significantly influences the costs that are being budgeted. For manufacturing overhead costs, for example, the activity index is usually the same as the index used in developing the predetermined overhead rate—that is, direct labor hours or machine hours. For selling and administrative expenses, the activity index usually is sales or net sales.

The choice of the increment of activity is largely a matter of judgment. For example, if the relevant range is 8,000 to 12,000 direct labor hours, increments of 1,000 hours may be selected. The flexible budget is then prepared for each increment within the relevant range.

FLEXIBLE BUDGET—A CASE STUDY

To illustrate the flexible budget, we will use Fox Manufacturing Company. Fox's management wants to use a **flexible budget for monthly comparisons** of actual and budgeted manufacturing overhead costs of the Finishing Department. The master budget for the year ending December 31, 2002, shows expected annual operating capacity of 120,000 direct labor hours and the following overhead costs.

Illustration 25-11

Master budget data

Variable Costs		Fixed Costs	
Indirect materials	$180,000	Depreciation	$180,000
Indirect labor	240,000	Supervision	120,000
Utilities	60,000	Property taxes	60,000
Total	$480,000	Total	$360,000

The four steps for developing the flexible budget are applied as follows.

Step 1. Identify the activity index and the relevant range of activity. The activity index is direct labor hours. Management concludes that the relevant range is 8,000–12,000 direct labor hours per month.

Step 2. Identify the variable costs, and determine the budgeted variable cost per unit of activity for each cost. There are three variable costs. The variable cost per unit is found by dividing each total budgeted cost by the direct labor hours used in preparing the master budget (120,000 hours). For Fox Manufacturing, the computations are:

Illustration 25-12

Computation of variable costs per direct labor hour

Variable Cost	Computation	Variable Cost per Direct Labor Hour
Indirect materials	$180,000 ÷ 120,000	**$1.50**
Indirect labor	240,000 ÷ 120,000	**2.00**
Utilities	60,000 ÷ 120,000	**0.50**
Total		**$4.00**

Step 3. Identify the fixed costs, and determine the budgeted amount for each cost. There are three fixed costs. Since Fox desires **monthly budget data**, the budgeted amount is found by dividing each annual budgeted cost by 12. For Fox Manufacturing, the monthly budgeted fixed costs are: depreciation $15,000, supervision $10,000, and property taxes $5,000.

Step 4. Prepare the budget for selected increments of activity within the relevant range. Management decides to prepare the budget in increments of 1,000 direct labor hours.

The flexible budget is shown in Illustration 25-13.

Illustration 25-13

Flexible monthly overhead budget

FOX MANUFACTURING COMPANY
Flexible Monthly Manufacturing Overhead Budget
Finishing Department
For the Year 2002

Activity level					
Direct labor hours	8,000	9,000	10,000	11,000	12,000
Variable costs					
Indirect materials	$12,000	$13,500	$15,000	$16,500	$18,000
Indirect labor	16,000	18,000	20,000	22,000	24,000
Utilities	4,000	4,500	5,000	5,500	6,000
Total variable	32,000	36,000	40,000	44,000	48,000
Fixed costs					
Depreciation	15,000	15,000	15,000	15,000	15,000
Supervision	10,000	10,000	10,000	10,000	10,000
Property taxes	5,000	5,000	5,000	5,000	5,000
Total fixed	30,000	30,000	30,000	30,000	30,000
Total costs	$62,000	$66,000	$70,000	$74,000	$78,000

From the budget, the following formula may be used to determine total budgeted costs at any level of activity.

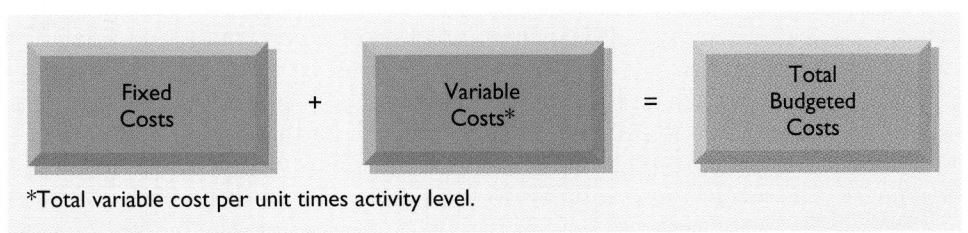

Illustration 25-14

Formula for total budgeted costs

Fixed Costs + Variable Costs* = Total Budgeted Costs

*Total variable cost per unit times activity level.

HELPFUL HINT

Using the data given for the Fox Manufacturing Company, what amount of total costs would be budgeted for 10,600 direct labor hours?

Answer:

Fixed	$30,000
Variable (10,600 × $4)	42,400
Total	$72,400

For Fox Manufacturing, fixed costs are $30,000, and total variable cost per unit is $4.00. Thus, at 9,000 direct labor hours, total budgeted costs are $66,000 [$30,000 + ($4.00 × 9,000)]. Similarly, at 8,622 direct labor hours, total budgeted costs are $64,488 [$30,000 + ($4.00 × 8,622)].

Total budgeted costs can also be shown graphically, as in Illustration 25-15. In the graph, the activity index is shown on the horizontal axis, and costs are indicated on the vertical axis. The graph highlights two of the 1,000 increments (10,000 and 12,000). As shown, total budgeted costs are \$70,000 [\$30,000 + (\$4.00 × 10,000)] and \$78,000 [\$30,000 + (\$4.00 × 12,000)], respectively.

Illustration 25-15

Graphic flexible budget data highlighting 10,000 and 12,000 activity levels

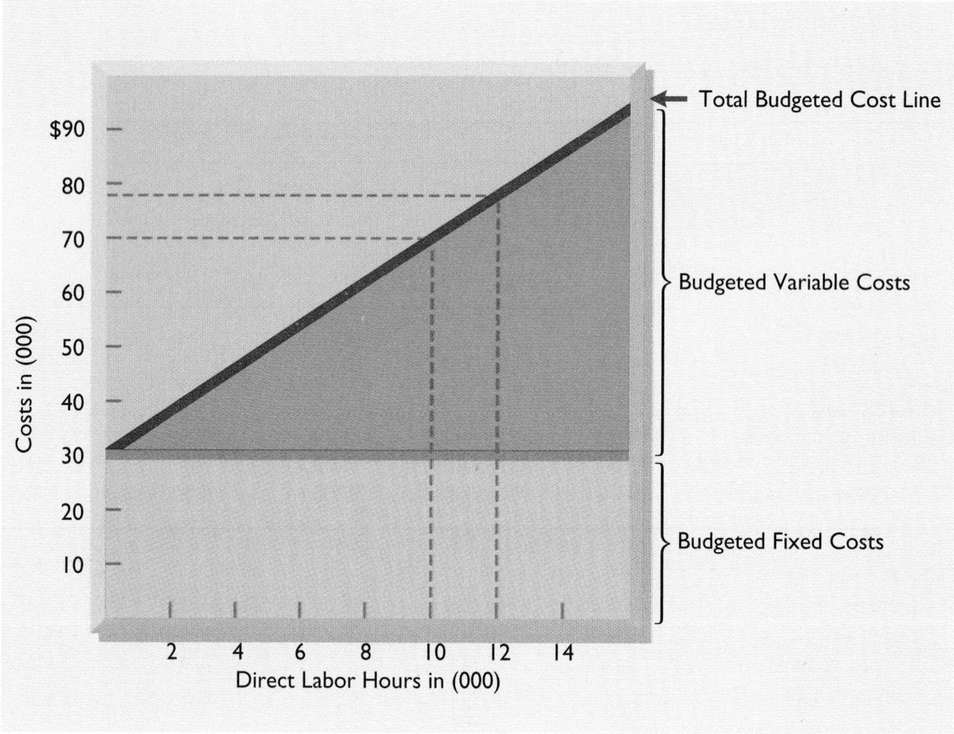

HELPFUL HINT

An assembly department is a production department, and a maintenance department is a service department, as explained on page 1035.

FLEXIBLE BUDGET REPORTS

Flexible budget reports are another type of internal report produced by managerial accounting. The flexible budget report consists of two sections: (1) production data for a selected activity index, such as direct labor hours, and (2) cost data for variable and fixed costs. The report provides a basis for evaluating a manager's performance in two areas: production control and cost control. Flexible budget reports are widely used in production and service departments.

A budget report for the Finishing Department of Fox Company for the month of January is shown in Illustration 25-16 (on page 1029). In this month, 8,800 direct labor hours were expected but 9,000 hours were worked. The budget data are based on the flexible budget for 9,000 hours in Illustration 25-13. The actual cost data are assumed.

How appropriate is this report in evaluating the Finishing Department manager's performance in controlling overhead costs? The report clearly provides a reliable basis. Both actual and budget costs are based on the activity level worked during January. Since variable costs generally are incurred directly by the department, the difference between the budget allowance for those hours and the actual costs are the responsibility of the department manager.

Illustration 25-16

Flexible overhead budget report

FOX MANUFACTURING COMPANY **Flexible Manufacturing Overhead Budget Report** **Finishing Department** **For the Month Ended January 31, 2002**				
Direct labor hours (DLH)				**Difference**
Expected	8,800	**Budget at**	**Actual Costs**	**Favorable F**
Actual	9,000	**9,000 DLH**	**9,000 DLH**	**Unfavorable U**
Variable costs				
Indirect materials		**$13,500**	$14,000	$ 500 U
Indirect labor		**18,000**	17,000	1,000 F
Utilities		**4,500**	4,600	100 U
Total variable		**36,000**	35,600	400 F
Fixed costs				
Depreciation		**15,000**	15,000	-0-
Supervision		**10,000**	10,000	-0-
Property taxes		**5,000**	5,000	-0-
Total fixed		**30,000**	30,000	-0-
Total costs		**$66,000**	$65,600	$ 400 F

From the standpoint of production control, the report shows a 200-hour difference between expected direct labor hours and actual hours. This difference is favorable if actual production orders required 9,000 direct labor hours. The difference is unfavorable if actual production orders required only 8,800 direct labor hours. In either case, the budget for purposes of cost control is based on 9,000 direct labor hours.

In subsequent months, other flexible budget reports will be prepared. For each month, the budget data are based on the actual activity level attained. In February that level may be 11,000 direct labor hours, in July 10,000, and so on.

MANAGEMENT BY EXCEPTION

Management by exception means that top management's review of a budget report is focused either entirely or primarily on differences between actual results and planned objectives. This approach enables top management to focus on problem areas. Management by exception does not mean that top management will investigate every difference. For this approach to be effective, there must be guidelines for identifying an exception. The usual criteria are materiality and controllability.

Materiality

Without quantitative guidelines, management would have to investigate every budget difference regardless of the amount. Materiality is usually expressed as a percentage difference from budget. For example, management may set the percentage difference at 5 percent for important items and 10 percent for other items. All differences either over or under budget by the specified percentage will be investigated. Costs over budget warrant investigation to determine why they were not controlled. Likewise, costs under budget merit investigation to determine whether costs critical to profitability are being curtailed. For example, if maintenance costs are budgeted at $80,000 but only $40,000 is spent, major unexpected breakdowns in productive facilities may occur in the future.

Alternatively, a company may specify a single percentage difference from budget for all items and supplement this guideline with a minimum dollar limit. For example, the exception criteria may be stated at 5 percent of budget or more than $10,000.

Controllability of the Item

Exception guidelines are more restrictive for controllable items than for items that are not controllable by the manager. In fact, there may be no guidelines for noncontrollable items. For example, a large unfavorable difference between actual and budgeted property tax expense may not be flagged for investigation because the only possible causes are an unexpected increase in the tax rate or in the assessed value of the property. An investigation into the difference will be useless: the manager cannot control either cause.

BEFORE YOU GO ON...

REVIEW IT

1. What is the meaning of budgetary control?
2. When is a static budget appropriate for evaluating a manager's effectiveness in controlling costs?
3. What is a flexible budget?
4. How is a flexible budget developed?
5. What are the criteria used in management by exception?

DO IT

Your roommate asks your help in understanding how total budgeted costs are computed at any level of activity. Compute total budgeted costs at 30,000 direct labor hours, assuming that in the flexible budget graph, the fixed cost line and the total budgeted cost line intersect the vertical axis at $36,000 and that the total budget cost line is $186,000 at an activity level of 50,000 direct labor hours.

ACTION PLAN

- Apply the formula: Fixed costs + Variable costs (Total variable costs per unit × Activity level) = Total budgeted costs.

SOLUTION: Using the graph, fixed costs are $36,000, and variable costs are $3 per direct labor hour [($186,000 − $36,000) ÷ 50,000]. Thus, at 30,000 direct labor hours, total budgeted costs are $126,000 [$36,000 + ($3 × 30,000)].

Related exercise material: BE25-3, BE25-4, BE25-5, E25-1, E25-2, E25-3, E25-4, E25-5, E25-6, and E25-7.

THE NAVIGATOR

THE CONCEPT OF RESPONSIBILITY ACCOUNTING

STUDY OBJECTIVE 4

Describe the concept of responsibility accounting.

Like budgeting, responsibility accounting is an important part of management accounting. **Responsibility accounting** involves accumulating and reporting costs (and revenues, where relevant) on the basis of the manager who has the authority to make the day-to-day decisions about the items. Under responsibility accounting, a manager's performance is evaluated on matters directly under that manager's control. Responsibility accounting can be used at every level of management in which the following conditions exist.

1. Costs and revenues can be directly associated with the specific level of management responsibility.
2. The costs and revenues are controllable at the level of responsibility with which they are associated.
3. Budget data can be developed for evaluating the manager's effectiveness in controlling the costs and revenues.

Levels of responsibility for controlling costs are depicted in Illustration 25-17.

Illustration 25-17

Responsibility for controllable costs at varying levels of management

Under responsibility accounting, any individual who has control and is accountable for a specified set of activities can be recognized as a responsibility center. Thus, responsibility accounting may extend from the lowest level of control to the top strata of management. Once responsibility has been established, the effectiveness of the individual's performance is first measured and reported for the specified activity. It is then reported upward throughout the organization.

Responsibility accounting is especially valuable in a decentralized company. **Decentralization** means that the control of operations is delegated to many managers throughout the organization. The term **segment** is sometimes used to identify an area of responsibility in decentralized operations. Under responsibility accounting, segment reports are prepared periodically such as monthly, quarterly, and annually, to evaluate managers' performance.

HELPFUL HINT
All companies use responsibility accounting. Without some form of responsibility accounting, there would be chaos in discharging management's control function.

Responsibility accounting is an essential part of any effective system of budgetary control. The reporting of costs and revenues under responsibility accounting differs from budgeting in two respects.

1. A distinction is made between controllable and noncontrollable items.
2. Performance reports either emphasize or include only items controllable by the individual manager.

Responsibility accounting applies to both profit and not-for-profit entities. The former seek to maximize net income. The latter wish to minimize the cost of providing services.

ACCOUNTING IN ACTION *Business Insight*

Since devising its budgeting and control system, **JKL, Inc.**, a large New York advertising agency, has become aware of which specific customer accounts are unprofitable and the reasons why. As a result, the agency has dropped several unprofitable accounts that otherwise would have gone unnoticed. Account managers now feel responsible for the profitability of their accounts. They carefully monitor actual hours spent on each account to make sure the account is being managed and run as efficiently as possible. For example, an account manager noticed a large amount of supervisory creative time was being spent on one account. Further investigation showed that the supervisors, rather than the creative department, were doing the actual creative work. The account manager pointed this out, and a junior creative team was appointed to the account, saving JKL a great deal of money.

CONTROLLABLE VERSUS NONCONTROLLABLE REVENUES AND COSTS

All costs and revenues are controllable at some level of responsibility within a company. This truth underscores the adage by the CEO of any organization that "the buck stops here." Under responsibility accounting, the critical issue is **whether the cost or revenue is controllable at the level of responsibility with which it is associated.**

A cost is considered to be **controllable** at a given level of managerial responsibility if the manager has the power to incur it within a given period of time. From this criterion, it follows that:

> **HELPFUL HINT**
> Are there more or fewer controllable costs as you move to higher levels of management? Answer: More.

1. All costs are controllable by top management because of the broad range of its authority.
2. Fewer costs are controllable as one moves down to each lower level of managerial responsibility because of the manager's decreasing authority.

> **HELPFUL HINT**
> The longer the time span, the more likely that the cost becomes controllable.

In general, **costs incurred directly by a level of responsibility are controllable at that level**. In contrast, costs incurred indirectly and allocated to a responsibility level are considered to be **noncontrollable** at that level.

RESPONSIBILITY REPORTING SYSTEM

A **responsibility reporting system** involves the preparation of a report for each level of responsibility in the company's organization chart. To illustrate such a system, we will use the partial organization chart and production departments of Francis Chair Company in Illustration 25-18.

The responsibility reporting system begins with the lowest level of responsibility for controlling costs and moves upward to each higher level. The connections between levels are detailed in Illustration 25-19 (on page 1034). A brief description of the four reports for Francis Chair Company is as follows.

1. **Report D** is typical of reports that go to managers at the lowest level of responsibility shown in the organization chart—department managers. Similar reports are prepared for the managers of the Fabricating, Assembling, and Enameling Departments.
2. **Report C** is an example of reports that are sent to plant managers. It shows the costs of the Chicago plant that are controllable at the second level of responsibility. In addition, Report C shows summary data for each department that is controlled by the plant manager. Similar reports are prepared for the Detroit and St. Louis plant managers.

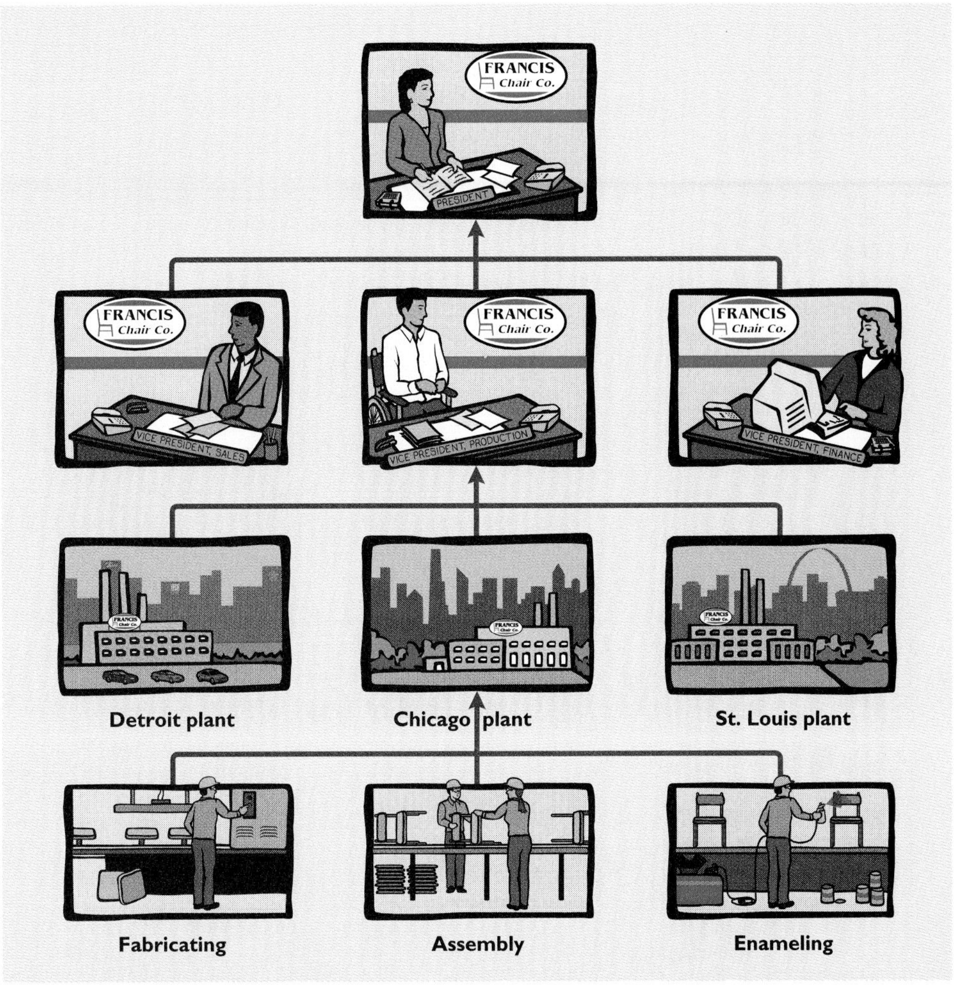

Illustration 25-18

Partial organization chart

Report A
President sees summary data of vice presidents.

Report B
Vice president sees summary of controllable costs in his/her functional area.

Report C
Plant manager sees summary of controllable costs for each department in the plant.

Report D
Department manager sees controllable costs of his/her department.

3. **Report B** illustrates the reports at the third level of responsibility. It shows the controllable costs of the vice president of production and summary data on the three assembly plants for which this officer is responsible.
4. **Report A** is typical of the reports that go to the top level of responsibility—the president. This report shows the controllable costs and expenses of this office and summary data on the vice presidents that are accountable to the president.

A responsibility reporting system permits management by exception at each level of responsibility. And, each higher level of responsibility can obtain the detailed report for each lower level of responsibility. For example, the vice president of production in the Francis Chair Company may request the Chicago plant manager's report because this plant is $5,300 over budget.

This type of reporting system also permits comparative evaluations. In Illustration 25-19, the Chicago plant manager can easily rank the department managers' effectiveness in controlling manufacturing costs. Comparative rankings provide further incentive for a manager to control costs. For example, the Detroit plant manager will want to continue to be No. 1 in the report to the vice president of production. The Chicago plant manager will not want to remain No. 3 in future reporting periods.

Illustration 25-19

Responsibility reporting system

Report A
President sees summary data of vice presidents.

REPORT A

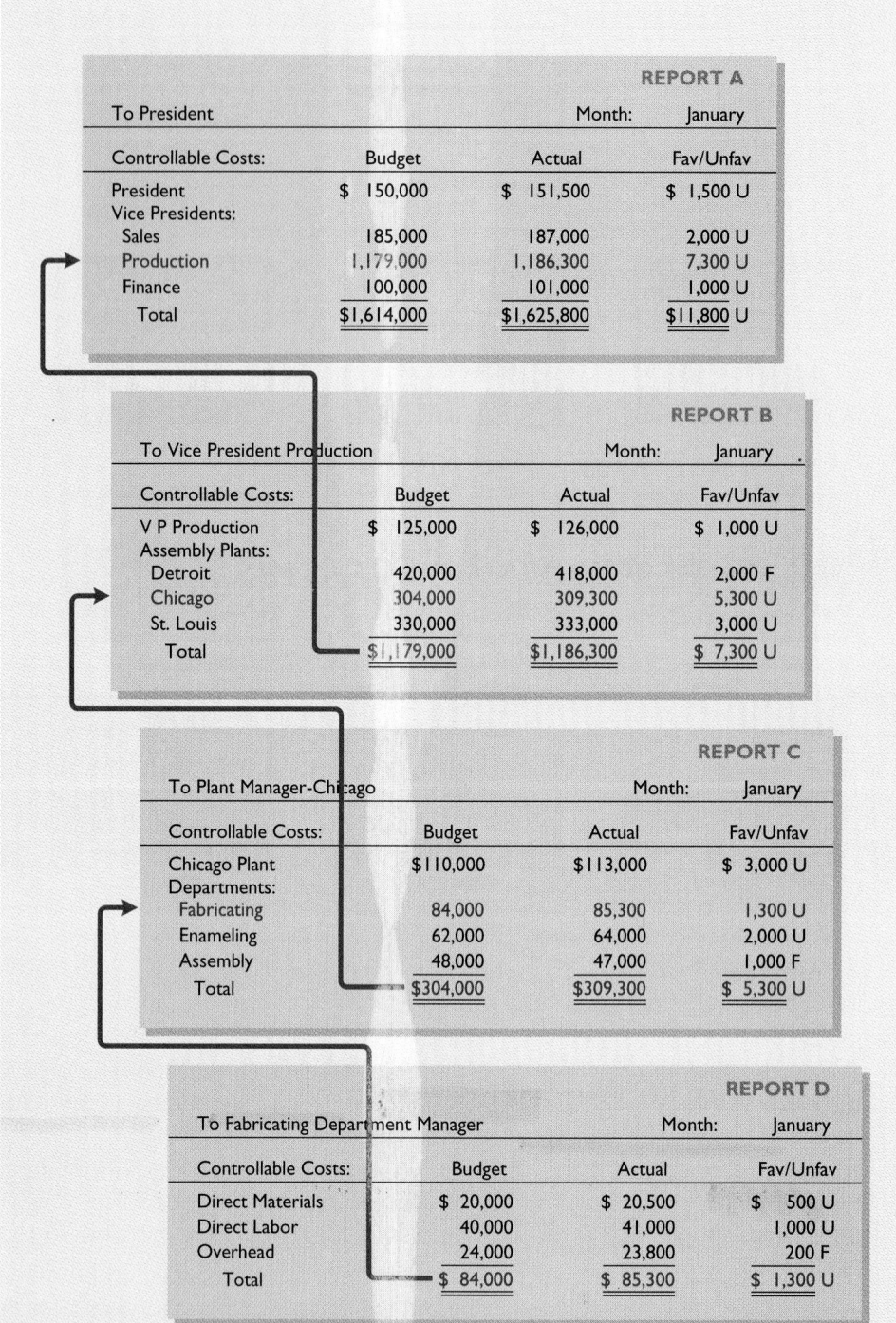

To President — Month: January

Controllable Costs:	Budget	Actual	Fav/Unfav
President	$ 150,000	$ 151,500	$ 1,500 U
Vice Presidents:			
Sales	185,000	187,000	2,000 U
Production	1,179,000	1,186,300	7,300 U
Finance	100,000	101,000	1,000 U
Total	$1,614,000	$1,625,800	$11,800 U

Report B
Vice president sees summary of controllable costs in his/her functional area.

REPORT B

To Vice President Production — Month: January

Controllable Costs:	Budget	Actual	Fav/Unfav
V P Production	$ 125,000	$ 126,000	$ 1,000 U
Assembly Plants:			
Detroit	420,000	418,000	2,000 F
Chicago	304,000	309,300	5,300 U
St. Louis	330,000	333,000	3,000 U
Total	$1,179,000	$1,186,300	$ 7,300 U

Report C
Plant manager sees summary of controllable costs for each department in the plant.

REPORT C

To Plant Manager-Chicago — Month: January

Controllable Costs:	Budget	Actual	Fav/Unfav
Chicago Plant	$110,000	$113,000	$ 3,000 U
Departments:			
Fabricating	84,000	85,300	1,300 U
Enameling	62,000	64,000	2,000 U
Assembly	48,000	47,000	1,000 F
Total	$304,000	$309,300	$ 5,300 U

Report D
Department manager sees controllable costs of his/her department.

REPORT D

To Fabricating Department Manager — Month: January

Controllable Costs:	Budget	Actual	Fav/Unfav
Direct Materials	$ 20,000	$ 20,500	$ 500 U
Direct Labor	40,000	41,000	1,000 U
Overhead	24,000	23,800	200 F
Total	$ 84,000	$ 85,300	$ 1,300 U

ACCOUNTING IN ACTION — e Business Insight

In Chapter 20 we discussed enterprise resource planning (ERP) software packages that collect all information regarding the results of the supply chain. A recent innovation is to attach enterprise application systems (EAS) to ERP systems. EAS systems are budgeting and planning tools. By attaching an EAS system called Hyperion Pillar to its ERP system, **Fujitsu Computer Products of America** found that it could more easily compare its budgeted amounts to its actual results. It also reduced its typical time spent on planning and budgeting from 6 to 8 weeks down to 10 to 15 days. Finally, the new system has enabled the company to respond quickly to new developments. For example, in 1999, the software forewarned the company of a potential oversupply problem, and provided recommendations for changes in staffing and capital needs.

SOURCE: Russ Banham, "Better Budgets," *Journal of Accountancy*, February 2000, p. 37.

TYPES OF RESPONSIBILITY CENTERS

There are three basic types of responsibility centers: cost centers, profit centers, and investment centers. These centers indicate the degree of responsibility the manager has for the performance of the center.

A **cost center** incurs costs (and expenses) but does not directly generate revenues. Managers of cost centers have the authority to incur costs. They are evaluated on their ability to control costs. **Cost centers are usually either production departments or service departments.** The former participate directly in making the product. The latter provide only support services. In a **Ford Motor Company** automobile plant, the welding, painting, and assembling departments are production departments; the maintenance, cafeteria, and human resources departments are service departments. All of them are cost centers.

A **profit center** incurs costs (and expenses) and also generates revenues. Managers of profit centers are judged on the profitability of their centers. Examples of profit centers include the individual departments of a retail store, such as clothing, furniture, and automotive products, and branch offices of banks.

> **HELPFUL HINT**
> (1) Is the jewelry department of **Marshall Field's** department store a profit center or a cost center? (2) Is the props department of a movie studio a profit center or a cost center?
> Answers: (1) Profit center. (2) Cost center.

Like a profit center, an **investment center** incurs costs (and expenses) and generates revenues. In addition, an investment center has control over the investment funds available for use. Managers of investment centers are evaluated on both the profitability of the center and the rate of return earned on the funds invested. Investment centers are often associated with subsidiary companies. For example, **General Mills's** product lines include cereals, helper dinner mixes, fruit snacks, popcorn, and yogurt. The manager of the investment center (product line) is able to control or significantly influence investment decisions pertaining to such matters as plant expansion and entry into new market areas. These three types of responsibility centers are depicted in Illustration 25-20.

The evaluation of a manager's performance in each type of responsibility center is explained in the remainder of this chapter.

Illustration 25-20

Types of responsibility centers

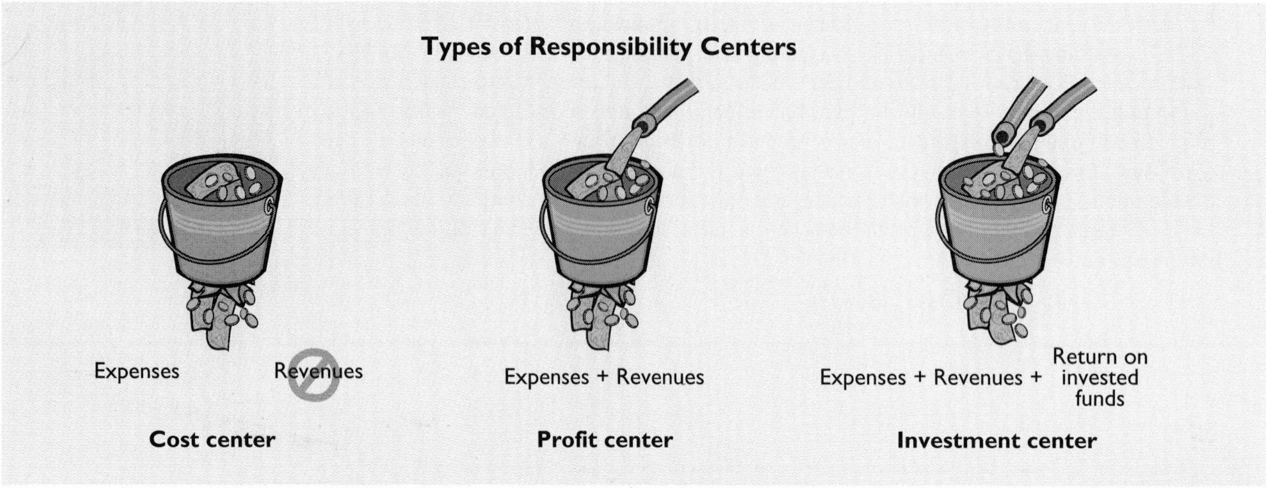

RESPONSIBILITY ACCOUNTING FOR COST CENTERS

STUDY OBJECTIVE 5

Indicate the features of responsibility reports for cost centers.

The evaluation of a manager's performance for cost centers is based on his or her ability to meet budgeted goals for controllable costs. **Responsibility reports for cost centers compare actual controllable costs with flexible budget data.**

A responsibility report is illustrated in Illustration 25-21. The report is adapted from the budget report for Fox Manufacturing Company in Illustration 25-16 on page 1029. It assumes that the Finishing Department manager is able to control all manufacturing overhead costs except depreciation, property taxes, and his own monthly salary of $6,000. The remaining $4,000 of supervision costs are assumed to apply to other supervisory personnel within the Finishing Department, whose salaries are controllable by the manager.

Illustration 25-21

Responsibility report for a cost center

FOX MANUFACTURING COMPANY
Finishing Department
Responsibility Report
For the Month Ended January 31, 2002

Controllable Cost	Budget	Actual	Difference: Favorable F / Unfavorable U
Indirect materials	$13,500	$14,000	**$ 500 U**
Indirect labor	18,000	17,000	**1,000 F**
Utilities	4,500	4,600	**100 U**
Supervision	**4,000**	**4,000**	**–0–**
	$40,000	$39,600	**$ 400 F**

Only controllable costs are included in the report, and no distinction is made between variable and fixed costs. The responsibility report continues the concept of management by exception. In this case, top management may request an explanation of the $1,000 favorable difference in indirect labor and/or the $500 unfavorable difference in indirect materials.

RESPONSIBILITY ACCOUNTING FOR PROFIT CENTERS

To evaluate the performance of a manager of a profit center, detailed information is needed about both controllable revenues and controllable costs. The operating revenues earned by a profit center, such as sales, are controllable by the manager. All variable costs (and expenses) incurred by the center are also controllable by the manager because they vary with sales. However, to determine the controllability of fixed costs, it is necessary to distinguish between direct and indirect fixed costs.

STUDY OBJECTIVE 6

Identify the content of responsibility reports for profit centers.

Direct and Indirect Fixed Costs

A profit center may have both direct and indirect fixed costs. **Direct fixed costs** are costs that relate specifically to one center and are incurred for the sole benefit of that center. Examples of such costs include the salaries established by the profit center manager for supervisory personnel and the cost of a timekeeping department for the center's employees. Since these fixed costs can be traced directly to a center, they are also called **traceable costs. Most direct fixed costs are controllable by the profit center manager.**

In contrast, **indirect fixed costs** pertain to a company's overall operating activities and are incurred for the benefit of more than one profit center. Indirect fixed costs are allocated to profit centers on some type of equitable basis. For example, property taxes on a building occupied by more than one center may be allocated on the basis of square feet of floor space used by each center. Or, the costs of a company's human resources department may be allocated to profit centers on the basis of the number of employees in each center. Because these fixed costs apply to more than one center, they are also called **common costs. Most indirect fixed costs are not controllable by the profit center manager.**

Responsibility Report

The responsibility report for a profit center shows budgeted and actual **controllable revenues and costs**. The report is prepared using the cost-volume-profit income statement explained in Chapter 23. In the report:

1. Controllable fixed costs are deducted from contribution margin.
2. The excess of contribution margin over controllable fixed costs is identified as **controllable margin**.
3. Noncontrollable fixed costs are not reported.

The responsibility report for the manager of the Marine Division, a profit center of Mantle Manufacturing Company, is shown in Illustration 25-22. For the year, the Marine Division also had $60,000 of indirect fixed costs that were not controllable by the profit center manager.

Controllable margin is considered to be the best measure of the manager's performance **in controlling revenues and costs**. This report shows that the manager's performance was below budgeted expectations by approximately 10 percent ($36,000 ÷ $360,000). Top management would likely investigate the causes of this unfavorable result. Note that the report does not show the Marine Division's non-

Illustration 25-22

Responsibility report for profit center

MANTLE MANUFACTURING COMPANY Marine Division Responsibility Report For the Year Ended December 31, 2002			
			Difference
	Budget	**Actual**	**Favorable F Unfavorable U**
Sales	$1,200,000	$1,150,000	$50,000 U
Variable costs			
Cost of goods sold	500,000	490,000	10,000 F
Selling and administrative	160,000	156,000	4,000 F
Total	660,000	646,000	14,000 F
Contribution margin	540,000	504,000	36,000 U
Controllable fixed costs			
Cost of goods sold	100,000	100,000	–0–
Selling and administrative	80,000	80,000	–0–
Total	180,000	180,000	–0–
Controllable margin	**$ 360,000**	**$ 324,000**	**$36,000** U

HELPFUL HINT

Recognize that we are emphasizing financial measures of performance. These days companies are also making an effort to stress nonfinancial performance measures such as product quality, labor productivity, market growth, materials' yield, manufacturing flexibility, and technological capability.

ETHICS NOTE

Responsibility reports are helpful tools for evaluating managerial performance. Too much emphasis on profits or investments, however, can be harmful because it ignores other important performance issues such as quality and social responsibility.

controllable fixed costs of $60,000. These costs would be included in a report on the profitability of the profit center.

Responsibility reports for profit centers may also be prepared monthly. In addition, they may include cumulative year-to-date results.

BEFORE YOU GO ON...

REVIEW IT

1. What conditions are essential for responsibility accounting?
2. What is involved in a responsibility reporting system?
3. What is the primary objective of a responsibility report for a cost center?
4. How does contribution margin differ from controllable margin in a responsibility report for a profit center?

DO IT

Midwest Division operates as a profit center. It reports the following actual results for the year: Sales $1,700,000, variable costs $800,000, controllable fixed costs $400,000, noncontrollable fixed costs $200,000. Annual budgeted amounts were $1,500,000, $700,000, $400,000, and $200,000, respectively. Prepare a responsibility report for the Midwest Division for December 31, 2002.

ACTION PLAN

- Deduct variable costs from sales to show contribution margin.
- Deduct controllable fixed costs from the contribution margin to show controllable margin.
- Do not report noncontrollable fixed costs.

SOLUTION

MIDWEST DIVISION
Responsibility Report
For the Year Ended December 31, 2002

	Budget	Actual	Difference Favorable F Unfavorable U
Sales	$1,500,000	$1,700,000	$200,000 F
Variable costs	700,000	800,000	100,000 U
Contribution margin	800,000	900,000	100,000 F
Controllable fixed costs	400,000	400,000	-0-
Controllable margin	$ 400,000	$ 500,000	$100,000 F

Related exercise material: BE25-7 and E25-9.

THE NAVIGATOR

RESPONSIBILITY ACCOUNTING FOR INVESTMENT CENTERS

STUDY OBJECTIVE 7

Explain the basis and formula used in evaluating performance in investment centers.

As explained earlier, an investment center manager can control or significantly influence the investment funds available for use. Thus, the primary basis for evaluating the performance of a manager of an investment center is **return on investment (ROI)**. The return on investment is considered to be superior to any other performance measurement because it shows the **effectiveness of the manager in utilizing the assets at his or her disposal**.

Return on Investment (ROI)

The formula for computing ROI for an investment center, together with assumed illustrative data, is shown in Illustration 25-23. Both factors in the formula are controllable by the investment center manager. Operating assets consist of current assets and plant assets used in operations by the center and controlled by the manager. Nonoperating assets such as idle plant assets and land held for future use are excluded. Average operating assets are usually based on the cost or book value of the assets at the beginning and end of the year.

Investment Center Controllable Margin (In dollars)	÷	Average Investment Center Operating Assets	=	Return on Investment (ROI)
$1,000,000	÷	$5,000,000	=	20%

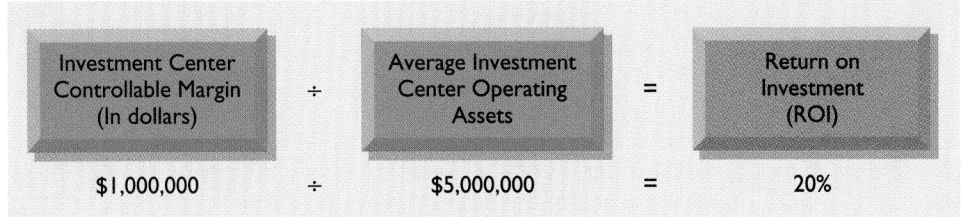

Illustration 25-23
ROI formula

Responsibility Report

The scope of the investment center manager's responsibility significantly affects the content of the performance report. Since an investment center is an independent entity for operating purposes, **all fixed costs are controllable by its manager**. For example, the manager is responsible for depreciation on investment center assets. Therefore, more fixed costs are identified as controllable in the performance report for an investment center manager than in a performance report for a profit center manager. The report also shows budgeted and actual ROI below controllable margin.

To illustrate this responsibility report, we will now assume that the Marine Division of Mantle Manufacturing Company is an investment center. It has budgeted and actual average operating assets of $2,000,000. We now will assume that the manager can control the $60,000 of fixed costs that were not controllable when the division was a profit center. The responsibility report is shown in Illustration 25-24.

Illustration 25-24

Responsibility report for investment center

MANTLE MANUFACTURING COMPANY
Marine Division
Responsibility Report
For the Year Ended December 31, 2002

	Budget	Actual	Difference Favorable F Unfavorable U
Sales	$1,200,000	$1,150,000	$50,000 U
Variable costs			
Cost of goods sold	500,000	490,000	10,000 F
Selling and administrative	160,000	156,000	4,000 F
Total	660,000	646,000	14,000 F
Contribution margin	540,000	504,000	36,000 U
Controllable fixed costs			
Cost of goods sold	100,000	100,000	-0-
Selling and administrative	80,000	80,000	-0-
Other fixed costs	**60,000**	**60,000**	**-0-**
Total	240,000	240,000	-0-
Controllable margin	**$ 300,000**	**$ 264,000**	**$36,000 U**
Return on investment	15% (a)	13.2% (b)	1.8% U (c)

(a) $\frac{\$300,000}{\$2,000,000}$ (b) $\frac{\$264,000}{\$2,000,000}$ (c) $\frac{\$36,000}{\$2,000,000}$

The report shows that the manager's performance based on ROI was 12 percent below budget expectations (1.8% ÷ 15%). Top management would likely want an explanation of the reasons for this unfavorable result.

Improving ROI

The manager of an investment center can improve ROI in two ways: (1) increase controllable margin, and/or (2) reduce average operating assets. To illustrate, we will use the following assumed data for the Marine Division of Mantle Manufacturing.

Sales	$2,000,000
Variable cost	1,100,000
Contribution margin (45%)	900,000
Controllable fixed costs	300,000
Controllable margin (a)	$ 600,000
Average operating assets (b)	$5,000,000
Return on investment (a) ÷ (b)	12%

Illustration 25-25
Assumed data for Marine Division

INCREASING CONTROLLABLE MARGIN. Controllable margin can be increased by increasing sales or by reducing variable and controllable fixed costs as follows.

1. **Increase sales 10 percent.** Sales will increase $200,000 ($2,000,000 × .10). Assuming no change in the contribution margin percentage of 45 percent, contribution margin will increase $90,000 ($200,000 × .45). Controllable margin will increase by the same amount because controllable fixed costs will not change. Thus, controllable margin becomes $690,000 ($600,000 + $90,000). The new ROI is 13.8 percent, computed as follows.

$$\text{ROI} = \frac{\text{Controllable margin}}{\text{Average operating assets}} = \frac{\$690{,}000}{\$5{,}000{,}000} = 13.8\%$$

Illustration 25-26
ROI computation—increase in sales

An increase in sales benefits both the investment center and the company if it results in new business. It would not benefit the company if the increase was achieved at the expense of other investment centers.

2. **Decrease variable and fixed costs 10 percent.** Total costs will decrease $140,000 [($1,100,000 + $300,000) × .10]. This reduction will result in a corresponding increase in controllable margin. Thus, controllable margin becomes $740,000 ($600,000 + $140,000). The new ROI is 14.8 percent, computed as follows.

$$\text{ROI} = \frac{\text{Controllable margin}}{\text{Average operating assets}} = \frac{\$740{,}000}{\$5{,}000{,}000} = 14.8\%$$

Illustration 25-27
ROI computation—decrease in costs

This course of action is clearly beneficial when waste and inefficiencies are eliminated. But, a reduction in vital costs such as required maintenance and inspections is not likely to be acceptable to top management.

REDUCING AVERAGE OPERATING ASSETS. Assume that average operating assets are reduced 10 percent or $500,000 ($5,000,000 × .10). Average operating assets become $4,500,000 ($5,000,000 − $500,000). Since controllable margin remains unchanged at $600,000, the new ROI is 13.3 percent, computed as follows.

$$\text{ROI} = \frac{\text{Controllable margin}}{\text{Average operating assets}} = \frac{\$600{,}000}{\$4{,}500{,}000} = 13.3\%$$

Illustration 25-28
ROI computation—decrease in operating assets

Reductions in operating assets may or may not be prudent. It is beneficial to eliminate overinvestment in inventories and to dispose of excessive plant assets. However, it is unwise to reduce inventories below expected needs or to dispose of essential plant assets.

Judgmental Factors in ROI

The return on investment approach includes two judgmental factors:

1. **Valuation of operating assets.** Operating assets may be valued at acquisition cost, book value, appraised value, or market value. The first two bases are readily available from the accounting records.
2. **Margin (income) measure.** This measure may be controllable margin, income from operations, or net income.

Each of the alternative values for operating assets can provide a reliable basis for evaluating a manager's performance as long as it is consistently applied between reporting periods. However, the use of income measures other than controllable margin will not result in a valid basis for evaluating the performance of an investment center manager.

PRINCIPLES OF PERFORMANCE EVALUATION

Performance evaluation is at the center of responsibility accounting. **Performance evaluation** is a management function that compares actual results with budget goals. It is based on internal reports prepared by the managerial accountant. Performance evaluation involves both behavioral and reporting principles.

Behavioral Principles

The human factor is critical in evaluating performance. Behavioral principles include the following.

1. **Managers of responsibility centers should have direct input into the process of establishing budget goals of their area of responsibility.** Without such input, managers may view the goals as unrealistic or arbitrarily set by top management. Such views adversely affect the managers' motivation to meet the targeted objectives.
2. **The evaluation of performance should be based entirely on matters that are controllable by the manager being evaluated.** Criticism of a manager on matters outside his or her control reduces the effectiveness of the evaluation process. It leads to negative reactions by a manager and to doubts about the fairness of the company's evaluation policies.
3. **Top management should support the evaluation process.** As explained earlier, the evaluation process begins at the lowest level of responsibility and extends upward to the highest level of management. Managers quickly lose faith in the process when top management ignores, overrules, or bypasses established procedures for evaluating a manager's performance.
4. **The evaluation process must allow managers to respond to their evaluations.** Evaluation is not a one-way street. Managers should have the opportunity to defend their performance. Evaluation without feedback is both impersonal and ineffective.
5. **The evaluation should identify both good and poor performance.** Praise for good performance is a powerful motivating factor for a manager. This is especially true when a manager's compensation includes rewards for meeting budget goals.

Reporting Principles of Performance Evaluation

Performance evaluation under responsibility accounting should be based on certain reporting principles. These principles pertain primarily to the internal reports that provide the basis for evaluating performance. Performance reports should:

1. Contain only data that are controllable by the manager of the responsibility center.
2. Provide accurate and reliable budget data to measure performance.
3. Highlight significant differences between actual results and budget goals.
4. Be tailor-made for the intended evaluation.
5. Be prepared at reasonable intervals.

BEFORE YOU GO ON...

REVIEW IT

1. What is the formula for computing return on investment (ROI)?
2. Identify three actions a manager may take to improve ROI.
3. What responsibility centers (investment type) might **Lands' End** be utilizing in determining ROI? (*Hint:* Review "Management's Discussion and Analysis.") The answer to this question is provided on page 1061.

LANDS' END DIRECT MERCHANTS

A LOOK BACK AT OUR FEATURE STORY

Refer back to the Feature Story at the beginning of the chapter about the athletic department of **UNLV**, and answer the following questions.

1. Would you expect a static or a flexible budget to be used in comparing actual and budgeted expenditures for each team?
2. Which of the biggest budget items are variable and which are fixed?
3. What is the relationship, if any, of the budgets used at UNLV and the allocation of cash to each team?

SOLUTION

1. At the time of preparing the budget, if a sports team has a fixed schedule of games (meets) along with a fixed number of players and coaches, a static budget might be sufficient. That is, if the predetermined activity level is static or fixed, the budget may be static. However, if the activity level (games/meets along with the roster size, number of scholarships, and coaches) is flexible and not predeterminable, a flexible budget tied to the activity driver is necessary in order to evaluate budget compliance at different activity levels.
2. The biggest variable expense is travel cost, which varies with distance, the number in the traveling party, and number of trips. Once the coaches, trainers, and managers are hired, payroll is a fixed cost for the season. Scholarships, once the number of in-state and out-of-state scholarships has been granted, is also a fixed cost for the season.
3. Once approved, the budget becomes the basis for the appropriation of funds and the allocation of cash to each team. Cash is allocated to each team in accordance with the approved budget. The budget sets the limits and the categories of expenditures.

THE NAVIGATOR

DEMONSTRATION PROBLEM

Glenda Company uses a flexible budget for manufacturing overhead based on direct labor hours. For 2002 the master overhead budget for the Packaging Department at normal capacity of 300,000 direct labor hours was as follows.

Additional Demonstration Problem

Variable Costs		Fixed Costs	
Indirect labor	$360,000	Supervision	$ 60,000
Supplies and lubricants	150,000	Depreciation	24,000
Maintenance	210,000	Property taxes	18,000
Utilities	120,000	Insurance	12,000
	$840,000		$114,000

During July, 24,000 direct labor hours were worked when 25,000 hours were expected to be worked. The company incurred the following variable costs in July: indirect labor $30,200, supplies and lubricants $11,600, maintenance $17,500, and utilities $9,200. Actual fixed overhead costs were the same as monthly budgeted fixed costs.

Instructions

Prepare a flexible budget report for the Packaging Department for July.

ACTION PLAN

- Use budget data for actual direct labor hours worked.
- Classify each cost as variable or fixed.
- Determine the difference between budgeted and actual costs.
- Identify the difference as favorable or unfavorable.
- Determine the difference in total variable costs, total fixed costs, and total costs.

SOLUTION TO DEMONSTRATION PROBLEM

GLENDA COMPANY
Manufacturing Overhead Budget Report (Flexible)
Packaging Department
For the Month Ended July 31, 2002

Direct labor hours (DLH) Expected 25,000 Actual 24,000	Budget 24,000 DLH	Actual Costs 24,000 DLH	Difference Favorable F Unfavorable U
Variable costs			
Indirect labor	$28,800	$30,200	$1,400 U
Supplies and lubricants	12,000	11,600	400 F
Maintenance	16,800	17,500	700 U
Utilities	9,600	9,200	400 F
Total variable	67,200	68,500	1,300 U
Fixed costs			
Supervision	5,000	5,000	–0–
Depreciation	2,000	2,000	–0–
Property taxes	1,500	1,500	–0–
Insurance	1,000	1,000	–0–
Total fixed	9,500	9,500	–0–
Total costs	$76,700	$78,000	$1,300 U

THE NAVIGATOR

SUMMARY OF STUDY OBJECTIVES

1. *Describe the concept of budgetary control.* Budgetary control consists of (a) preparing periodic budget reports that compare actual results with planned objectives, (b) analyzing the differences to determine their causes, (c) taking appropriate corrective action, and (d) modifying future plans, if necessary.

2. *Evaluate the usefulness of static budget reports.* Static budget reports are useful in evaluating the progress toward planned sales and profit goals. They are also appropriate in assessing a manager's effectiveness in controlling fixed costs and expenses when (a) actual activity closely approximates the master budget activity level and/or (b) the behavior of the costs in response to changes in activity is fixed.

3. *Explain the development of flexible budgets and the usefulness of flexible budget reports.* To develop the flexible budget it is necessary to:

(a) Identify the activity index and the relevant range of activity.

(b) Identify the variable costs, and determine the budgeted variable cost per unit of activity for each cost.

(c) Identify the fixed costs, and determine the budgeted amount for each cost.

(d) Prepare the budget for selected increments of activity within the relevant range.

Flexible budget reports permit an evaluation of a manager's performance in controlling production and costs.

4. *Describe the concept of responsibility accounting.* Responsibility accounting involves accumulating and reporting revenues and costs on the basis of the individual manager who has the authority to make the day-to-day decisions about the items. The evaluation of a manager's performance is based on the matters directly under the manager's control. In responsibility accounting, it is necessary to distinguish between controllable and noncontrollable fixed costs and to identify three types of responsibility centers: cost, profit, and investment.

5. *Indicate the features of responsibility reports for cost centers.* Responsibility reports for cost centers compare actual costs with flexible budget data. The reports show only controllable costs, and no distinction is made between variable and fixed costs.

6. *Identify the content of responsibility reports for profit centers.* Responsibility reports show contribution margin, controllable fixed costs, and controllable margin for each profit center.

7. *Explain the basis and formula used in evaluating performance in investment centers.* The primary basis for evaluating performance in investment centers is return on investment (ROI). The formula for computing ROI for investment centers is: Controllable margin (in dollars) ÷ Average operating assets.

Key Term Matching Activity

GLOSSARY

Budgetary control The use of budgets to control operations. (p. 1020).

Controllable costs Costs that a manager has the authority to incur within a given period of time. (p. 1032).

Controllable margin Contribution margin less controllable fixed costs. (p. 1037).

Cost center A responsibility center that incurs costs but does not directly generate revenues. (p. 1035).

Decentralization Control of operations is delegated to many managers throughout the organization. (p. 1031).

Direct fixed costs Costs that relate specifically to a responsibility center and are incurred for the sole benefit of the center. (p. 1037).

Flexible budget A projection of budget data for various levels of activity. (p. 1023).

Indirect fixed costs Costs that are incurred for the benefit of more than one profit center. (p. 1037).

Investment center A responsibility center that incurs costs, generates revenues, and has control over the investment funds available for use. (p. 1035).

Management by exception The review of budget reports by top management focused entirely or primarily on differences between actual results and planned objectives. (p. 1029).

Noncontrollable costs Costs incurred indirectly and allocated to a responsibility center that are not controllable at that level. (p. 1032).

Profit center A responsibility center that incurs costs and also generates revenues. (p. 1035).

Responsibility accounting A part of management accounting that involves accumulating and reporting revenues and costs on the basis of the manager who has the authority to make the day-to-day decisions about the items. (p. 1030).

Responsibility reporting system The preparation of reports for each level of responsibility in the company's organization chart. (p. 1032).

Return on investment (ROI) A measure of management's effectiveness in utilizing assets at its disposal in an investment center. (p. 1039).

Segment An area of responsibility in decentralized operations. (p. 1031).

Static budget A projection of budget data at one level of activity. (p. 1021).

Chapter 25 Self-Test

SELF-STUDY QUESTIONS

Answers are at the end of the chapter.

(SO 1) **1.** Budgetary control involves all but one of the following:
- a. modifying future plans.
- b. analyzing differences.
- c. using static budgets.
- d. determining differences between actual and planned results.

(SO 2) **2.** A static budget is useful in controlling costs when cost behavior is:
- a. mixed.
- b. fixed.
- c. variable.
- d. linear.

(SO 3) **3.** At zero direct labor hours in a flexible budget graph, the total budgeted cost line intersects the vertical axis at $30,000. At 10,000 direct labor hours, a horizontal line drawn from the total budgeted cost line intersects the vertical axis at $90,000. Fixed and variable costs may be expressed as:
- a. $30,000 fixed plus $6 per direct labor hour variable.
- b. $30,000 fixed plus $9 per direct labor hour variable.
- c. $60,000 fixed plus $3 per direct labor hour variable.
- d. $60,000 fixed plus $6 per direct labor hour variable.

4. At 9,000 direct labor hours, the flexible budget for indi- (SO 3)
rect materials is $27,000. If $28,000 of indirect materials costs are incurred at 9,200 direct labor hours, the flexible budget report should show the following difference for indirect materials:
- a. $1,000 unfavorable.
- b. $1,000 favorable.
- c. $400 favorable.
- d. $400 unfavorable.

(SO 4) 5. Under responsibility accounting, the evaluation of a manager's performance is based on matters that the manager:
a. directly controls.
b. directly and indirectly controls.
c. indirectly controls.
d. has for shared responsibility with another manager.

(SO 4) 6. Responsibility centers include:
a. cost centers.
b. profit centers.
c. investment centers.
d. all of the above.

(SO 5) 7. Responsibility reports for cost centers:
a. distinguish between fixed and variable costs.
b. use static budget data.
c. include both controllable and noncontrollable costs.
d. include only controllable costs.

(SO 6) 8. In a responsibility report for a profit center, controllable fixed costs are deducted from contribution margin to show:
a. profit center margin.
b. controllable margin.
c. net income.
d. income from operations.

9. In the formula for return on investment (ROI), the factors for controllable margin and operating assets are, respectively: (SO 7)
a. controllable margin percentage and total operating assets.
b. controllable margin dollars and average operating assets.
c. controllable margin dollars and total assets.
d. controllable margin percentage and average operating assets.

10. A manager of an investment center can improve ROI by: (SO 7)
a. increasing average operating assets.
b. reducing sales.
c. increasing variable costs.
d. reducing variable and/or controllable fixed costs.

THE NAVIGATOR

QUESTIONS

1. (a) What is budgetary control?
(b) Tony Crespino is describing budgetary control. What steps should be included in Tony's description?
2. The following purposes are part of a budgetary reporting system: (a) Determine efficient use of materials. (b) Control overhead costs. (c) Determine whether income objectives are being met. For each purpose, indicate the name of the report, the frequency of the report, and the primary recipient(s) of the report.
3. How may a budget report for the second quarter differ from a budget report for the first quarter?
4. Don Cox questions the usefulness of a master sales budget in evaluating sales performance. Is there justification for Don's concern? Explain.
5. Under what circumstances may a static budget be an appropriate basis for evaluating a manager's effectiveness in controlling costs?
6. "A flexible budget is really a series of static budgets." Is this true? Why?
7. The static manufacturing overhead budget based on 40,000 direct labor hours shows budgeted indirect labor costs of $56,000. During March, the department incurs $66,000 of indirect labor while working 45,000 direct labor hours. Is this a favorable or unfavorable performance? Why?
8. A static overhead budget based on 40,000 direct labor hours shows Factory Insurance $6,500 as a fixed cost. At the 50,000 direct labor hours worked in March, factory insurance costs were $6,200. Is this a favorable or unfavorable performance? Why?
9. Kate Coulter is confused about how a flexible budget is prepared. Identify the steps for Kate.
10. Alou Company has prepared a graph of flexible budget data. At zero direct labor hours, the total budgeted cost line intersects the vertical axis at $25,000. At 10,000 direct labor hours, the line drawn from the total budgeted cost line intersects the vertical axis at $85,000. How may the fixed and variable costs be expressed?
11. The flexible budget formula is fixed costs $40,000 plus variable costs of $2 per direct labor hour. What is the total budgeted cost at (a) 9,000 hours and (b) 12,345 hours?
12. What is management by exception? What criteria may be used in identifying exceptions?
13. What is responsibility accounting? Explain the purpose of responsibility accounting.
14. Ann Wilkins is studying for an accounting examination. Describe for Ann what conditions are necessary for responsibility accounting to be used effectively.
15. Distinguish between controllable and noncontrollable costs.
16. How do responsibility reports differ from budget reports?
17. What is the relationship, if any, between a responsibility reporting system and a company's organization chart?
18. Distinguish among the three types of responsibility centers.
19. (a) What costs are included in a performance report for a cost center? (b) In the report, are variable and fixed costs identified?
20. How do direct fixed costs differ from indirect fixed costs? Are both types of fixed costs controllable?
21. Lori Quan is confused about controllable margin reported in an income statement for a profit center. How is this margin computed, and what is its primary purpose?
22. What is the primary basis for evaluating the performance of the manager of an investment center? Indicate the formula for this basis.
23. Explain the ways that ROI can be improved.
24. Indicate two behavioral principles that pertain to (a) the manager being evaluated and (b) top management.

BRIEF EXERCISES

BE25-1 For the quarter ended March 31, 2002, Russo Company accumulates the following sales data for its product, Garden-Tools: $315,000 budget; $302,000 actual. Prepare a static budget report for the quarter.

Prepare static budget report.
(SO 2)

BE25-2 Data for Russo Company are given in BE25-1. In the second quarter, budgeted sales were $380,000, and actual sales were $389,000. Prepare a static budget report for the second quarter and for the year to date.

Prepare static budget report for 2 quarters.
(SO 2)

BE25-3 In Maltz Company, direct labor is $20 per hour. The company expects to operate at 10,000 direct labor hours each month. In January 2002, direct labor totaling $207,000 is incurred in working 10,400 hours. Prepare (a) a static budget report and (b) a flexible budget report. Evaluate the usefulness of each report.

Show usefulness of flexible budgets in evaluating performance.
(SO 3)

BE25-4 Gomez Company expects to produce 1,200,000 units of Product XX in 2002. Monthly production is expected to range from 80,000 to 120,000 units. Budgeted variable manufacturing costs per unit are: direct materials $5, direct labor $6, and overhead $9. Prepare a flexible manufacturing budget for the relevant range value using 20,000 unit increments.

Prepare a flexible budget for variable costs.
(SO 3)

BE25-5 Data for Gomez Company are given in BE25-4. In March 2002, the company incurs the following costs in producing 100,000 units: direct materials $520,000, direct labor $590,000, and variable overhead $915,000. Prepare a flexible budget report for March. Were costs controlled?

Prepare flexible budget report.
(SO 3)

BE25-6 In the Assembly Department of Rado Company, budgeted and actual manufacturing overhead costs for the month of April 2002 were as follows.

Prepare a responsibility report for a cost center.
(SO 5)

	Budget	Actual
Indirect materials	$15,000	$14,500
Indirect labor	20,000	20,800
Utilities	10,000	10,750
Supervision	5,000	5,000

All costs are controllable by the department manager. Prepare a responsibility report for April for the cost center.

BE25-7 Savage Manufacturing Company accumulates the following summary data for the year ending December 31, 2002, for its Water Division which it operates as a profit center: sales—$2,000,000 budget, $2,080,000 actual; variable costs—$1,000,000 budget, $1,050,000 actual; and controllable fixed costs—$300,000 budget, $307,000 actual. Prepare a responsibility report for the Water Division.

Prepare a responsibility report for a profit center.
(SO 6)

BE25-8 For the year ending December 31, 2002, Stoker Company accumulates the following data for the Plastics Division which it operates as an investment center: contribution margin—$700,000 budget, $715,000 actual; controllable fixed costs—$300,000 budget, $295,000 actual. Average operating assets for the year were $1,600,000. Prepare a responsibility report for the Plastics Division beginning with contribution margin.

Prepare a responsibility report for an investment center.
(SO 7)

BE25-9 For its three investment centers, Chow Company accumulates the following data:

Compute return on investment using the ROI formula.
(SO 7)

	I	II	III
Sales	$2,000,000	$3,000,000	$ 4,000,000
Controllable margin	1,200,000	2,400,000	3,200,000
Average operating assets	6,000,000	8,000,000	10,000,000

Compute the return on investment (ROI) for each center.

BE25-10 Data for the investment centers for Chow Company are given in BE25-9. The centers expect the following changes in the next year: (I) increase sales 10%; (II) decrease costs $200,000; (III) decrease average operating assets $400,000. Compute the expected return on investment (ROI) for each center. Assume center I has a contribution margin percentage of 80%.

Compute return on investment under changed conditions.
(SO 7)

EXERCISES

Prepare flexible manufacturing overhead budget.
(SO 3)

E25-1 Voss Company uses a flexible budget for manufacturing overhead based on direct labor hours. Variable manufacturing overhead costs per direct labor hour are as follows.

Indirect labor	$1.00
Indirect materials	0.50
Utilities	0.30

Fixed overhead costs per month are: Supervision $4,000, Depreciation $1,500, and Property Taxes $800. The company believes it will normally operate in a range of 7,000–10,000 direct labor hours per month.

Instructions

Prepare a monthly flexible manufacturing overhead budget for 2002 for the expected range of activity, using increments of 1,000 direct labor hours.

Prepare flexible budget reports for manufacturing overhead costs, and comment on findings.
(SO 3)

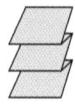

E25-2 Using the information in E25-1, assume that in July 2002, Voss Company incurs the following manufacturing overhead costs.

Variable Costs		Fixed Costs	
Indirect labor	$8,700	Supervision	$4,000
Indirect materials	4,300	Depreciation	1,500
Utilities	2,500	Property taxes	800

Instructions

(a) Prepare a flexible budget performance report, assuming that the company worked 9,000 direct labor hours during the month. The company expected to work 9,000 direct labor hours.

(b) Prepare a flexible budget performance report, assuming that the company worked 8,500 direct labor hours during the month. The company expected to work 8,500 direct labor hours.

(c) Comment on your findings.

Prepare flexible selling expense budget.
(SO 3)

E25-3 Samano Company uses flexible budgets to control its selling expenses. Monthly sales are expected to range from $170,000 to $200,000. Variable costs and their percentage relationship to sales are: Sales Commissions 5%, Advertising 4%, Traveling 3%, and Delivery 2%. Fixed selling expenses will consist of Sales Salaries $30,000, Depreciation on Delivery Equipment $7,000, and Insurance on Delivery Equipment $1,000.

Instructions

Prepare a monthly flexible budget for each $10,000 increment of sales within the relevant range for the year ending December 31, 2002.

Prepare flexible budget reports for selling expenses.
(SO 3)

E25-4 The actual selling expenses incurred in March 2002 by Samano Company are as follows.

Variable Expenses		Fixed Expenses	
Sales commissions	$9,200	Sales salaries	$30,000
Advertising	7,000	Depreciation	7,000
Travel	5,100	Insurance	1,000
Delivery	3,500		

Instructions

(a) Prepare a flexible budget performance report for March using the budget data in E25-3, assuming that March sales were $170,000. Expected and actual sales are the same.

(b) Prepare a flexible budget performance report, assuming that March sales were $180,000. Expected sales and actual sales are the same.

(c) Comment on the importance of using flexible budgets in evaluating the performance of the sales manager.

Prepare flexible budget and responsibility report for manufacturing overhead.
(SO 3, 5)

E25-5 Sanchez Company's manufacturing overhead budget for the first quarter of 2002 contained the following data.

Variable Costs		Fixed Costs	
Indirect materials	$12,000	Supervisory salaries	$30,000
Indirect labor	10,000	Depreciation	7,000
Utilities	8,000	Property taxes and insurance	8,000
Maintenance	5,000	Maintenance	5,000

Actual variable costs were: indirect materials $14,200, indirect labor $9,600, utilities $8,700, and maintenance $4,200. Actual fixed costs equaled budgeted costs except for property taxes and insurance, which were $8,300.

All costs are considered controllable by the production department manager except for depreciation, and property taxes and insurance.

Instructions

(a) Prepare a flexible overhead budget report for the first quarter.

(b) Prepare a responsibility report for the first quarter.

Prepare flexible budget report, and answer question. (SO 2, 3)

E25-6 As sales manager, Todd Keyser was given the following static budget report for selling expenses in the Clothing Department of Pace Company for the month of October.

PACE COMPANY
Clothing Department
Budget Report
For the Month Ended October 31, 2002

	Budget	Actual	Difference Favorable F Unfavorable U
Sales in units	8,000	10,000	2,000 F
Variable costs			
Sales commissions	$ 2,000	$ 2,500	$ 500 U
Advertising expense	800	850	50 U
Travel expense	4,400	4,900	500 U
Free samples given out	1,000	1,300	300 U
Total variable	8,200	9,550	1,350 U
Fixed costs			
Rent	1,500	1,500	-0-
Sales salaries	1,200	1,200	-0-
Office salaries	800	800	-0-
Depreciation—autos (sales staff)	500	500	-0-
Total fixed	4,000	4,000	-0-
Total costs	$11,800	$13,550	$1,350 U

As a result of this budget report, Todd was called into the president's office and congratulated on his fine sales performance. He was reprimanded, however, for allowing his costs to get out of control. Todd knew something was wrong with the performance report that he had been given. However, he was not sure what to do, and comes to you for advice.

Instructions

(a) Prepare a budget report based on flexible budget data to help Todd.

(b) Should Todd have been reprimanded? Explain.

State total budgeted cost formulas, and prepare flexible budget graph. (SO 3)

E25-7 Lockwood Company has two production departments, Fabricating and Assembling. At a department managers' meeting, the controller uses flexible budget graphs to explain total budgeted costs. Separate graphs based on direct labor hours are used for each department. The graphs show the following.

1. At zero direct labor hours, the total budgeted cost line and the fixed cost line intersect the vertical axis at $50,000 in the Fabricating Department and $45,000 in the Assembling Department.

2. At normal capacity of 50,000 direct labor hours, the line drawn from the total budgeted cost line intersects the vertical axis at $160,000 in the Fabricating Department, and $110,000 in the Assembling Department.

Instructions

(a) State the total budgeted cost formula for each department.
(b) Compute the total budgeted cost for each department, assuming actual direct labor hours worked were 53,000 and 47,000, in the Fabricating and Assembling Departments, respectively.
(c) Prepare the flexible budget graph for the Fabricating Department, assuming the maximum direct labor hours in the relevant range is 100,000. Use increments of 10,000 direct labor hours on the horizontal axis and increments of $50,000 on the vertical axis.

Prepare reports in a responsibility reporting system.
(SO 4)

E25-8 Loebs Company's organization chart includes the president; the vice president of production; three assembly plants—Dallas, Atlanta, and Tucson; and two departments within each plant—Machining and Finishing. Budget and actual manufacturing cost data for July 2002 are as follows:

Finishing Department—Dallas: Direct materials $41,000 actual, $46,000 budget; direct labor $83,000 actual, $82,000 budget; manufacturing overhead $51,000 actual, $49,200 budget.

Machining Department—Dallas: Total manufacturing costs $218,000 actual, $214,000 budget.

Atlanta Plant: Total manufacturing costs $426,000 actual, $421,000 budget.

Tucson Plant: Total manufacturing costs $494,000 actual, $499,000 budget.

The Dallas plant manager's office costs were $95,000 actual and $92,000 budget. The vice president of production's office costs were $132,000 actual and $130,000 budget. Office costs are not allocated to departments and plants.

Instructions

Using the format on page 1034, prepare the reports in a responsibility system for:

(a) The Finishing Department—Dallas.
(b) The plant manager—Dallas.
(c) The vice president of production.

Compute missing amounts in responsibility reports for three profit centers, and prepare a report.
(SO 6)

E25-9 Haven Manufacturing Inc. has three divisions which are operated as profit centers. Operating data for the divisions listed alphabetically are as follows.

Operating Data	Women's Shoes	Men's Shoes	Children's Shoes
Contribution margin	$270,000	(3)	$160,000
Controllable fixed costs	100,000	(4)	(5)
Controllable margin	(1)	$ 90,000	96,000
Sales	600,000	450,000	(6)
Variable costs	(2)	310,000	250,000

Instructions

(a) Compute the missing amounts. Show computations.
(b) Prepare a responsibility report for the Women's Shoe Division assuming (1) the data are for the month ended June 30, 2002, and (2) all data equal budget except variable costs which are $10,000 over budget.

Compute ROI for current year and for possible future changes.
(SO 7)

E25-10 The Hackcraft Division of Nunez Company reported the following data for the current year.

Sales	$3,000,000
Variable costs	1,800,000
Controllable fixed costs	600,000
Average operating assets	6,000,000

Top management is unhappy with the investment center's return on investment (ROI). It asks the manager of the Hackcraft Division to submit plans to improve ROI in the next year. The manager believes it is feasible to consider the following independent courses of action.

1. Increase sales by $320,000 with no change in the contribution margin percentage.
2. Reduce variable costs by $100,000.
3. Reduce average operating assets by 5%.

Instructions

(a) Compute the return on investment (ROI) for the current year.

(b) Using the ROI formula, compute the ROI under each of the proposed courses of action. (Round to one decimal.)

PROBLEMS: SET A

Prepare flexible budget and budget report for manufacturing overhead.
(SO 3)

P25-1A Tick Company estimates that 360,000 direct labor hours will be worked during the coming year, 2002, in the Packaging Department. On this basis, the following budgeted manufacturing overhead cost data are computed for the year.

Fixed Overhead Costs		Variable Overhead Costs	
Supervision	$ 90,000	Indirect labor	$144,000
Depreciation	60,000	Indirect materials	90,000
Insurance	27,000	Repairs	54,000
Rent	36,000	Utilities	108,000
Property taxes	18,000	Lubricants	18,000
	$231,000		$414,000

It is estimated that direct labor hours worked each month will range from 27,000 to 36,000 hours.

During October, 27,000 direct labor hours were worked and the following overhead costs were incurred.

Fixed overhead costs: Supervision $7,500, Depreciation $5,000, Insurance $2,225, Rent $3,000, and Property taxes $1,500.

Variable overhead costs: Indirect labor $11,760, Indirect materials, $6,400, Repairs $4,000, Utilities $8,550, and Lubricants $1,640.

Instructions

(a) Prepare a monthly flexible manufacturing overhead budget for each increment of 3,000 direct labor hours over the relevant range for the year ending December 31, 2002.

(b) Prepare a flexible budget report for October, when 27,500 direct labor hours were expected.

(c) Comment on management's efficiency in controlling manufacturing overhead costs in October.

(a) Total costs: DLH 27,000, $50,300, DLH 36,000, $60,650
(b) Total $1,275 U

Prepare flexible budget, budget report, and graph for manufacturing overhead.
(SO 3)

P25-2A Wahlen Company manufactures tablecloths. Sales have grown rapidly over the past 2 years. As a result, the president has installed a budgetary control system for 2002. The following data were used in developing the master manufacturing overhead budget for the Ironing Department, which is based on an activity index of direct labor hours.

Variable Costs	Rate per Direct Labor Hour	Annual Fixed Costs	
Indirect labor	$0.40	Supervision	$30,000
Indirect materials	0.50	Depreciation	18,000
Factory utilities	0.30	Insurance	12,000
Factory repairs	0.20	Rent	24,000

The master overhead budget was prepared on the expectation that 480,000 direct labor hours will be worked during the year. In June, 42,000 direct labor hours were worked and 42,000 were expected. At that level of activity, actual costs were as follows.

Variable—per direct labor hour: Indirect labor $0.43, Indirect materials $0.50, Factory utilities $0.32, and Factory repairs $0.24.

Fixed: same as budgeted.

Instructions

(a) Prepare a monthly flexible manufacturing overhead budget for the year ending December 31, 2002, assuming production levels range from 35,000 to 50,000 direct labor hours. Use increments of 5,000 direct labor hours.

(b) Prepare a budget performance report for June comparing actual results with budget data based on the flexible budget.

(c) Were costs effectively controlled? Explain.

(a) Total costs: 35,000 DLH, $56,000, 50,000 DLH, $77,000
(b) Budget $65,800
Actual $69,580

(d) State the formula for computing the total budgeted costs for Wahlen Company.
(e) Prepare the flexible budget graph, showing total budgeted costs at 35,000 and 45,000 direct labor hours. Use increments of 5,000 direct labor hours on the horizontal axis and increments of $10,000 on the vertical axis.

State total budgeted cost formula, and prepare flexible budget reports for 2 time periods.
(SO 2, 3)

P25-3A Nigh Company uses budgets in controlling costs. The August 2002 budget report for the company's Assembling Department is as follows.

NIGH COMPANY
Budget Report
Assembling Department
For the Month Ended August 31, 2002

Manufacturing Costs	Budget	Actual	Difference Favorable F Unfavorable U
Variable costs			
Direct materials	$ 48,000	$ 47,000	$1,000 F
Direct labor	78,000	74,100	3,900 F
Indirect materials	24,000	24,200	200 U
Indirect labor	18,000	17,500	500 F
Utilities	15,000	14,900	100 F
Maintenance	9,000	9,200	200 U
Total variable	192,000	186,900	5,100 F
Fixed costs			
Rent	10,000	10,000	–0–
Supervision	17,000	17,000	–0–
Depreciation	7,000	7,000	–0–
Total fixed	34,000	34,000	–0–
Total costs	$226,000	$220,900	$5,100 F

The budget data in the report are based on the master budget for the year, which assumed that 720,000 units would be produced. The Assembling Department manager is pleased with the report and expects a raise, or at least praise for a job well done. The company president, however, is unhappy with the results for August, because only 58,000 units were produced. (*Hint:* The budget amounts above are one-twelfth of the master budget.)

Instructions

(a) State the total monthly budgeted cost formula.

(b) Budget $219,600

(b) Prepare a budget report for August using flexible budget data. Why does this report provide a better basis for evaluating performance than the report based on static budget data? Assume 62,000 units were expected to be produced.

(c) Budget $238,800
Actual $239,590

(c) In September, 64,000 units were produced when 65,000 were expected. Prepare the budget report using flexible budget data, assuming (1) each variable cost was 10% higher than its actual cost in August, and (2) fixed costs were the same in September as in August.

Prepare responsibility report for a profit center.
(SO 6)

P25-4A Lococo Manufacturing Inc. operates the Patio Furniture Division as a profit center. Operating data for this division for the year ended December 31, 2002, are as follows.

	Budget	Difference from Budget
Sales	$2,500,000	$50,000 F
Cost of goods sold		
Variable	1,300,000	43,000 F
Controllable fixed	200,000	5,000 U
Selling and administrative		
Variable	220,000	7,000 U
Controllable fixed	50,000	2,000 U
Noncontrollable fixed costs	70,000	4,000 U

In addition, Lococo Manufacturing incurs $180,000 of indirect fixed costs that were budgeted at $175,000. Twenty percent (20%) of these costs are allocated to the Patio Furniture Division.

Instructions

(a) Prepare a responsibility report for the Patio Furniture Division for the year.

(b) Comment on the manager's performance in controlling revenues and costs.

(c) Identify any costs excluded from the responsibility report and explain why they were excluded.

(a) Contribution margin $86,000 F
Controllable margin $79,000 F

P25-5A Kurian Manufacturing Company manufactures a variety of tools and industrial equipment. The company operates through three divisions. Each division is an investment center. Operating data for the Home Division for the year ended December 31, 2002, and relevant budget data are as follows.

Prepare responsibility report for an investment center, and compute ROI.
(SO 7)

	Actual	Comparison with Budget
Sales	$1,500,000	$100,000 favorable
Variable cost of goods sold	700,000	100,000 unfavorable
Variable selling and administrative expenses	125,000	25,000 unfavorable
Controllable fixed cost of goods sold	170,000	On target
Controllable fixed selling and administrative expenses	100,000	On target

Average operating assets for the year for the Home Division were $2,000,000 which was also the budgeted amount.

Instructions

(a) Prepare a responsibility report (in thousands of dollars) for the Home Division.

(b) Evaluate the manager's performance. Which items will likely be investigated by top management?

(c) Compute the expected ROI in 2003 for the Home Division, assuming the following changes.

(1) Variable cost of goods sold is decreased by 6%.

(2) Average operating assets are decreased by 10%.

(3) Sales are increased by $200,000, and this increase is expected to increase contribution margin by $90,000.

(a) Controllable margin: Budget $430; Actual $405

P25-6A Tilg Company uses a responsibility reporting system. It has divisions in Denver, Seattle, and San Diego. Each division has three production departments: Cutting, Shaping, and Finishing. The responsibility for each department rests with a manager who reports to the division production manager. Each division manager reports to the vice president of production. There are also vice presidents for marketing and finance. All vice presidents report to the president.

In January 2002, controllable actual and budget manufacturing overhead cost data for the departments and divisions were as follows.

Prepare reports for cost centers under responsibility accounting, and comment on performance of managers.
(SO 4)

Manufacturing Overhead	Actual	Budget
Individual costs—Cutting Department—Seattle		
Indirect labor	$ 73,000	$ 70,000
Indirect materials	46,700	46,000
Maintenance	20,500	18,000
Utilities	20,100	17,000
Supervision	31,000	30,000
	$ 191,300	$ 181,000
Total costs		
Shaping Department—Seattle	$ 158,000	$ 148,000
Finishing Department—Seattle	210,000	208,000
Denver division	676,000	673,000
San Diego division	722,000	715,000
	$1,766,000	$1,744,000

Additional overhead costs were incurred as follows: Seattle division production manager—actual costs $52,500, budget $51,000; vice president of production—actual costs $65,000, budget $64,000; president—actual costs $76,400, budget $74,200. These expenses are not allocated.

The vice presidents who report to the president, other than the vice president of production, had the following expenses.

Vice president	Actual	Budget
Marketing	$133,600	$130,000
Finance	107,000	105,000

(a) (1) $10,300 U
(2) $23,800 U
(3) $34,800 U
(4) $42,600 U

Instructions

(a) Using the format on page 1034, prepare the following responsibility reports.
 (1) Manufacturing overhead—Cutting Department manager—Seattle division.
 (2) Manufacturing overhead—Seattle division manager.
 (3) Manufacturing overhead—vice president of production.
 (4) Manufacturing overhead and expenses—president.

(b) Comment on the comparative performances of:
 (1) Department managers in the Seattle division.
 (2) Division managers.
 (3) Vice presidents.

PROBLEMS: SET B

Prepare flexible budget and budget report for manufacturing overhead.
(SO 3)

P25-1B Greish Company estimates that 240,000 direct labor hours will be worked during 2002 in the Assembly Department. On this basis, the following budgeted manufacturing overhead data are computed.

Variable Overhead Costs		Fixed Overhead Costs	
Indirect labor	$ 72,000	Supervision	$ 72,000
Indirect materials	48,000	Depreciation	36,000
Repairs	24,000	Insurance	9,600
Utilities	19,200	Rent	7,200
Lubricants	9,600	Property taxes	6,000
	$172,800		$130,800

It is estimated that direct labor hours worked each month will range from 18,000 to 24,000 hours.

During January, 20,000 direct labor hours were worked and the following overhead costs were incurred.

Variable Overhead Costs		Fixed Overhead Costs	
Indirect labor	$ 6,200	Supervision	$ 6,000
Indirect materials	3,600	Depreciation	3,000
Repairs	1,600	Insurance	800
Utilities	1,250	Rent	700
Lubricants	830	Property taxes	500
	$13,480		$11,000

(a) Total costs: 18,000 DLH, $23,860; 24,000 DLH, $28,180
(b) Budget, $25,300
Actual, $24,480

Instructions

(a) Prepare a monthly flexible manufacturing overhead budget for each increment of 2,000 direct labor hours over the relevant range for the year ending December 31, 2002.

(b) Prepare a manufacturing overhead budget report for January, assuming 20,500 direct labor hours were expected.

(c) Comment on management's efficiency in controlling manufacturing overhead costs in January.

Prepare flexible budget, budget report, and graph for manufacturing overhead.
(SO 3)

P25-2B Juds Manufacturing Company produces one product, Kebo. Because of wide fluctuations in demand for Kebo, the Assembly Department experiences significant variations in monthly production levels.

The annual master manufacturing overhead budget is based on 300,000 direct labor hours. In July 27,500 labor hours were worked, and 27,500 hours were expected to be worked. The master manufacturing overhead budget for the year and the actual overhead costs incurred in July are as follows.

Overhead Costs	Master Budget (annual)	Actual in July
Variable		
Indirect labor	$ 360,000	$32,000
Indirect materials	210,000	17,000
Utilities	90,000	8,100
Maintenance	60,000	5,400
Fixed		
Supervision	192,000	16,000
Depreciation	120,000	10,000
Insurance and taxes	60,000	5,000
Total	$1,092,000	$93,500

Instructions

(a) Prepare a monthly flexible overhead budget for the year ending December 31, 2002, assuming monthly production levels range from 22,500 to 30,000 direct labor hours. Use increments of 2,500 direct labor hours.

(a) Total costs: 22,500 DLH, $85,000; 30,000 DLH, $103,000

(b) Prepare a budget performance report for the month of July 2002 comparing actual results with budget data based on the flexible budget.

(b) Budget $97,000 Actual $93,500

(c) Were costs effectively controlled? Explain.

(d) State the formula for computing the total monthly budgeted costs in Juds Company.

(e) Prepare the flexible budget graph showing total budgeted costs at 25,000 and 27,500 direct labor hours. Use increments of 5,000 on the horizontal axis and increments of $10,000 on the vertical axis.

P25-3B Lorch Company uses budgets in controlling costs. The May 2002 budget report for the company's Packaging Department is as follows.

State total budgeted cost formula, and prepare flexible budget reports for 2 time periods.
(SO 2, 3)

LORCH COMPANY
Budget Report
Packaging Department
For the Month Ended May 31, 2002

Manufacturing Costs	Budget	Actual	Difference: Favorable F / Unfavorable U
Variable costs			
Direct materials	$ 30,000	$ 32,000	$2,000 U
Direct labor	50,000	53,000	3,000 U
Indirect materials	15,000	15,200	200 U
Indirect labor	12,500	13,000	500 U
Utilities	7,500	7,100	400 F
Maintenance	5,000	5,200	200 U
Total variable	120,000	125,500	5,500 U
Fixed costs			
Rent	9,000	9,000	–0–
Supervision	9,000	9,000	–0–
Depreciation	5,000	5,000	–0–
Total fixed	23,000	23,000	–0–
Total costs	$143,000	$148,500	$5,500 U

The budget amounts in the report were on the master budget for the year, which assumed that 600,000 units would be produced. (*Hint:* The budget amounts above are one-twelfth of the master budget for the year.)

The company president was displeased with the department manager's performance. The department manager, who thought he had done a good job, could not understand the unfavorable results. In May, 55,000 units were produced.

Instructions

(b) Budget $155,000

(c) Budget $119,000
Actual $123,400

(a) State the total budgeted cost formula.
(b) Prepare a budget report for May using flexible budget data. Why does this report provide a better basis for evaluating performance than the report based on static budget data? Assume 57,000 units were expected to be produced in the Packaging Department.
(c) In June, 40,000 units were produced when 39,000 were expected. Prepare the budget report using flexible budget data, assuming (1) each variable cost was 20% less in June than its actual cost in May, and (2) fixed costs were the same in the month of June as in May.

Prepare responsibility report for a profit center.
(SO 6)

P25-4B Peters Manufacturing Inc. operates the Home Appliance Division as a profit center. Operating data for this division for the year ended December 31, 2002, are as follows.

	Budget	Difference from Budget
Sales	$2,400,000	$100,000 U
Cost of goods sold		
Variable	1,200,000	57,000 U
Controllable fixed	200,000	10,000 F
Selling and administrative		
Variable	240,000	8,000 F
Controllable fixed	60,000	6,000 U
Noncontrollable fixed costs	50,000	2,000 U

In addition, Peters Manufacturing incurs $150,000 of indirect fixed costs that were budgeted at $155,000. Twenty percent (20%) of these costs are allocated to the Home Appliance Division. None of these costs are controllable by the division manager.

Instructions

(a) Contribution margin $149,000 U
Controllable margin $145,000 U

(a) Prepare a responsibility report for the Home Appliance Division (a profit center) for the year.
(b) Comment on the manager's performance in controlling revenues and costs.
(c) Identify any costs excluded from the responsibility report and explain why they were excluded.

Prepare responsibility report for an investment center, and compute ROI.
(SO 7)

P25-5B Ridder Manufacturing Company manufactures a variety of garden and lawn equipment. The company operates through three divisions. Each division is an investment center. Operating data for the Lawnmower Division for the year ended December 31, 2002, and relevant budget data are as follows.

	Actual	Comparison with Budget
Sales	$2,800,000	$200,000 unfavorable
Variable cost of goods sold	1,400,000	150,000 unfavorable
Variable selling and administrative expenses	300,000	50,000 favorable
Controllable fixed cost of goods sold	270,000	On target
Controllable fixed selling and administrative expenses	130,000	On target

Average operating assets for the year for the Lawnmower Division were $4,000,000 which was also the budgeted amount.

Instructions

(a) Controllable margin: Budget $1,000; Actual $700

(a) Prepare a responsibility report (in thousands of dollars) for the Lawnmower Division.
(b) Evaluate the manager's performance. Which items will likely be investigated by top management?
(c) Compute the expected ROI in 2003 for the Lawnmower Division, assuming the following changes.
  (1) Variable cost of goods sold is decreased by 15%.
  (2) Average operating assets are decreased by 20%.
  (3) Sales are increased by $500,000 and this increase is expected to increase contribution margin by $200,000.

BROADENING YOUR PERSPECTIVE

GROUP DECISION CASE

BYP25-1 Green Pastures is a 400-acre farm on the outskirts of the Kentucky Bluegrass, specializing in the boarding of broodmares and their foals. A recent economic downturn in the thoroughbred industry has led to a decline in breeding activities, and it has made the boarding business extremely competitive. To meet the competition, Green Pastures planned in 2002 to entertain clients, advertise more extensively, and absorb expenses formerly paid by clients such as veterinary and blacksmith fees.

The budget report for 2002 is presented below. As shown, the static income statement budget for the year is based on an expected 21,900 boarding days at $25 per mare. The variable expenses per mare per day were budgeted: Feed $5, Veterinary fees $3, Blacksmith fees $0.30, and Supplies $0.40. All other budgeted expenses were either semifixed or fixed.

During the year, management decided not to replace a worker who quit in March, but it did issue a new advertising brochure and did more entertaining of clients.[1]

GREEN PASTURES
Static Budget Income Statement
Year Ended December 31, 2002

	Actual	Master Budget	Difference
Number of mares	52	60	8*
Number of boarding days	18,980	21,900	2,920*
Sales	$379,600	$547,500	$167,900*
Less variable expenses:			
Feed	104,390	109,500	5,110
Veterinary fees	58,838	65,700	6,862
Blacksmith fees	6,074	6,570	496
Supplies	7,402	8,760	1,358
Total variable expenses	176,704	190,530	13,826
Contribution margin	202,896	356,970	154,074*
Less fixed expenses:			
Depreciation	40,000	40,000	–0–
Insurance	11,000	11,000	–0–
Utilities	12,000	14,000	2,000
Repairs and maintenance	10,000	11,000	1,000
Labor	88,000	96,000	8,000
Advertisement	12,000	8,000	4,000*
Entertainment	7,000	5,000	2,000*
Total fixed expense	180,000	185,000	5,000
Net income	$ 22,896	$171,970	$149,074*

*Unfavorable.

Instructions

With the class divided into groups, answer the following.

(a) Based on the static budget report:

(1) What was the primary cause(s) of the loss in net income?

[1] Data for this case are based on Hans Sprohge and John Talbott, "New Applications for Variance Analysis," *Journal of Accountancy* (AICPA, New York), April 1989, pp. 137–141.

(2) Did management do a good, average, or poor job of controlling expenses?
(3) Were management's decisions to stay competitive sound?

(b) Prepare a flexible budget report for the year.

(c) Based on the flexible budget report, answer the three questions in part (a) above.

(d) What course of action do you recommend for the management of Green Pastures?

MANAGERIAL ANALYSIS

BYP25-2 Lakenvelder Dutch manufactures expensive watch cases sold as souvenirs. Three of its sales departments are: Retail Sales, Wholesale Sales, and Outlet Sales. The Retail Sales Department is a profit center. The Wholesale Sales Department is a cost center. Its managers merely take orders from customers who purchase through the company's wholesale catalog. The Outlet Sales Department is an investment center, because each manager is given full responsibility for an outlet store location. The manager can hire and discharge employees, purchase, maintain, and sell equipment, and in general is fairly independent of company control.

Rena Worthington is a manager in the Retail Sales Department. Winston Hillhouse manages the Wholesale Sales Department. Oscar Hadley manages the Golden Gate Club outlet store in San Francisco. The following are the budget responsibility reports for each of the three departments.

Budget

	Retail Sales	Wholesale Sales	Outlet Sales
Sales	$ 750,000	$ 400,000	$200,000
Variable costs			
Cost of goods sold	150,000	100,000	25,000
Advertising	100,000	30,000	5,000
Sales salaries	75,000	15,000	3,000
Printing	10,000	20,000	5,000
Travel	20,000	30,000	2,000
Fixed costs			
Rent	50,000	30,000	10,000
Insurance	5,000	2,000	1,000
Depreciation	75,000	100,000	40,000
Investment in assets	$1,000,000	$1,200,000	$800,000

Actual Results

	Retail Sales	Wholesale Sales	Outlet Sales
Sales	$ 750,000	$ 400,000	$200,000
Variable costs			
Cost of goods sold	195,000	120,000	26,250
Advertising	100,000	30,000	5,000
Sales salaries	75,000	15,000	3,000
Printing	10,000	20,000	5,000
Travel	15,000	20,000	1,500
Fixed costs			
Rent	40,000	50,000	12,000
Insurance	5,000	2,000	1,000
Depreciation	80,000	90,000	60,000
Investment in assets	$1,000,000	$1,200,000	$800,000

Instructions

(a) Determine which of the items should be included in the responsibility report for each of the three managers.

(b) Compare the budgeted measures with the actual results. Decide which results should be called to the attention of each manager.

REAL-WORLD FOCUS

BYP25-3 **Computer Associates International, Inc.**, the world's leading business software company, delivers the end-to-end infrastructure to enable e-business through innovative technology, services, and education. CA has 19,000 employees worldwide and had revenue of over $6 billion for the fiscal year ended March 31, 2000.

Presented below is information from the company's annual report.

COMPUTER ASSOCIATES INTERNATIONAL
Management Discussion

The Company has experienced a pattern of business whereby revenue for its third and fourth fiscal quarters reflects an increase over first- and second-quarter revenue. The Company attributes this increase to clients' increased spending at the end of their calendar year budgetary periods and the culmination of its annual sales plan. Since the Company's costs do not increase proportionately with the third- and fourth-quarters' increase in revenue, the higher revenue in these quarters results in greater profit margins and income. Fourth-quarter profitability is traditionally affected by significant new hirings, training, and education expenditures for the succeeding year.

Instructions

(a) Why don't the company's costs increase proportionately as the revenues increase in the third and fourth quarters?

(b) What type of budgeting seems appropriate for the Computer Associates situation?

EXPLORING THE WEB

BYP25-4 Genelle and Doug have recorded the story of their wedding planning. They are on a strict budget and need help in preparing what they call "a somewhat flexible budget."

Address: **www.wednet.com/inspire/wedstory/story1.htm**
(or go to www.wiley.com/college/weygandt)

Steps:

1. Go to Genelle and Doug's Web site, and read about their trials and tribulations in planning a wedding.
2. Review the **Planning and Budgeting** section in "Part 1" of their story. They mention that this is a "somewhat flexible budget" for 250 guests, totalling $7,150. They would like to reduce their total costs to $7,000, if at all possible.

Instructions

Recast Genelle and Doug's budget into a truly flexible budget so that they can see the effects on their total costs of reducing the number of invited guests to 225 or 200.

Communication Activity

BYP25-5 The manufacturing overhead budget for Reebles Company contains the following items.

Variable expenses	
Indirect materials	$25,000
Indirect labor	12,000
Maintenance expenses	10,000
Manufacturing supplies	6,000
Total variable	$53,000
Fixed expenses	
Supervision	$17,000
Inspection costs	1,000
Insurance expenses	2,000
Depreciation	15,000
Total fixed	$35,000

The budget was based on an estimated 2,000 units being produced. During the past month, 1,500 units were produced, and the following costs incurred.

Variable expenses	
Indirect materials	$25,200
Indirect labor	13,500
Maintenance expenses	8,200
Manufacturing supplies	5,100
Total variable	$52,000
Fixed expenses	
Supervision	$19,300
Inspection costs	1,200
Insurance expenses	2,200
Depreciation	14,700
Total fixed	$37,400

Instructions

(a) Determine which items would be controllable by Ed Lopat, the production manager.

(b) How much should have been spent during the month for the manufacture of the 1,500 units?

(c) Prepare a flexible manufacturing overhead budget report for Mr. Lopat.

(d) Prepare a responsibility report. Include only the costs that would have been controllable by Mr. Lopat. In an attached memo, describe clearly for Mr. Lopat the areas in which his performance needs to be improved.

Ethics Case

BYP25-6 National Products Corporation participates in a highly competitive industry. In order to meet this competition and achieve profit goals, the company has chosen the decentralized form of organization. Each manager of a decentralized investment center is measured on the basis of profit contribution, market penetration, and return on investment. Failure to meet the objectives established by corporate management for these measures has not been acceptable and usually has resulted in demotion or dismissal of an investment center manager.

An anonymous survey of managers in the company revealed that the managers feel the pressure to compromise their personal ethical standards to achieve the corporate objectives. For example, at certain plant locations there was pressure to reduce quality control to a level which could not assure that all unsafe products would be rejected. Also, sales personnel were encouraged to use questionable sales tactics to obtain orders, including gifts and other incentives to purchasing agents.

The chief executive officer is disturbed by the survey findings. In his opinion such behavior cannot be condoned by the company. He concludes that the company should do something about this problem.

Instructions

(a) Who are the stakeholders (the affected parties) in this situation?
(b) Identify the ethical implications, conflicts, or dilemmas in the above described situation.
(c) What might the company do to reduce the pressures on managers and decrease the ethical conflicts?

(CMA adapted)

Answers to Self-Study Questions

1. c **2.** b **3.** a **4.** d **5.** a **6.** d **7.** d **8.** b **9.** b **10.** d

Answer to Lands' End Review It Question 3, p. 1043

In its Management's Discussion and Analysis under the heading "Segment results," Lands' End reports that it has three business segments consisting of Core (regular monthly and prospecting catalogs, First Person, and Beyond Buttondowns), Specialty (Kids, Corporate Sales, and Coming Home catalogs), and International (foreign-based operations in Japan, the United Kingdom and Germany).

Remember to go back to the Navigator box on the chapter-opening page and check off your completed work.

26

PERFORMANCE EVALUATION THROUGH STANDARD COSTS

THE NAVIGATOR ✓

- Understand *Concepts for Review* ❑
- Read *Feature Story* ❑
- Scan *Study Objectives* ❑
- Read *Preview* ❑
- Read text and answer *Before You Go On* *p.* 1070 ❑ *p.* 1081 ❑ *p.* 1086 ❑
- Work *Demonstration Problem* ❑
- Review *Summary of Study Objectives* ❑
- Answer *Self-Study Questions* ❑
- Complete *Assignments* ❑

CONCEPTS FOR REVIEW

Before studying this chapter, you should know or, if necessary, review:

a. The flow of costs in a job order and process cost accounting system. (Ch. 21, pp. 866–867, and Ch. 22, p. 905)

b. How manufacturing overhead is applied to work in process. (Ch. 21, pp. 873–876)

c. The management by exception principle. (Ch. 25, p. 1029)

d. How to prepare a flexible manufacturing overhead budget. (Ch. 25, pp. 1026–1027)

THE NAVIGATOR

FEATURE STORY

Highlighting Performance Efficiency

There's a very good chance that the highlighter you're holding in your hand was made by **Sanford**, a maker of permanent markers and other writing instruments. Sanford, headquartered in Illinois, annually sells hundreds of millions of dollars' worth of ACCENT highlighters, fine-point pens, Sharpie permanent markers, Expo dry-erase markers for overhead projectors, and other writing instruments.

Since Sanford makes literally billions of writing utensils per year, the company must keep tight control over manufacturing costs. A very important part of Sanford's manufacturing process is determining how much direct materials, labor, and overhead should cost. These costs are then compared to actual costs to assess performance efficiency. Raw materials for Sanford's markers include a barrel, plug, cap, ink reservoir, and a nib (tip). These parts are assembled by machine to produce thousands of units per hour. A major component of manufacturing overhead is machine maintenance—some fixed, some variable.

"Labor costs are associated with material handling and equipment maintenance functions. Although the assembly process is highly automated, labor is still required to move raw materials to the machine and to package the finished product. In addition, highly skilled technicians are required to service and maintain each piece of equipment," says Mike Orr, vice president, operations.

Labor rates are predictable because the hourly workers are covered by a union contract. The story is the same with the fringe benefits and some supervisory salaries. Even volume levels are fairly predictable—demand for the product is high—so fixed overhead is efficiently absorbed. Raw material standard costs are based on the previous year's actual prices plus any anticipated inflation. Lately, though, inflation has been so low that the company is considering any price increase in raw material to be unfavorable because its standards will remain unchanged.

www.sanfordcorp.com

THE NAVIGATOR

STUDY OBJECTIVES

After studying this chapter, you should be able to:

1. Distinguish between a standard and a budget.
2. Identify the advantages of standard costs.
3. Describe how standards are set.
4. State the formulas for determining direct materials and direct labor variances.
5. State the formulas for determining manufacturing overhead variances.
6. Discuss the reporting of variances.
7. Enumerate the features of a standard cost accounting system.

THE NAVIGATOR

PREVIEW OF CHAPTER 26

In this chapter we continue the study of controlling costs. Here we consider additional measures that permit the evaluation of performance.

The content and organization of Chapter 26 are as follows.

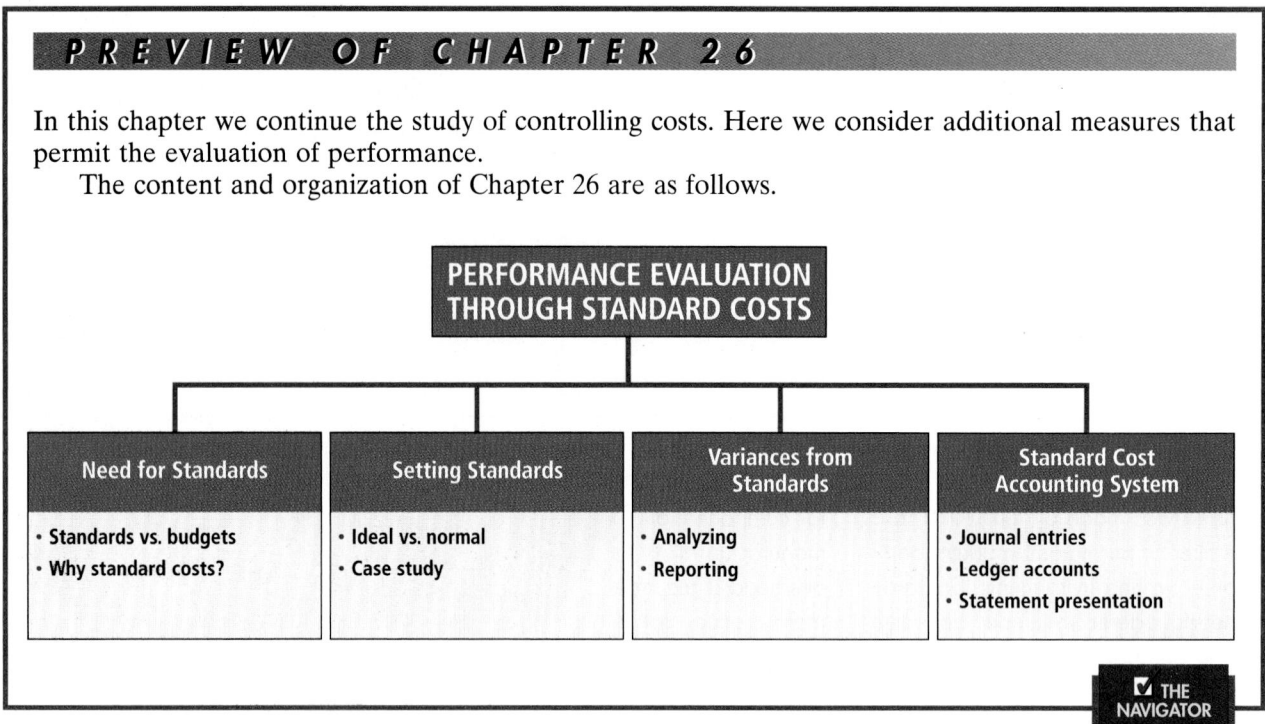

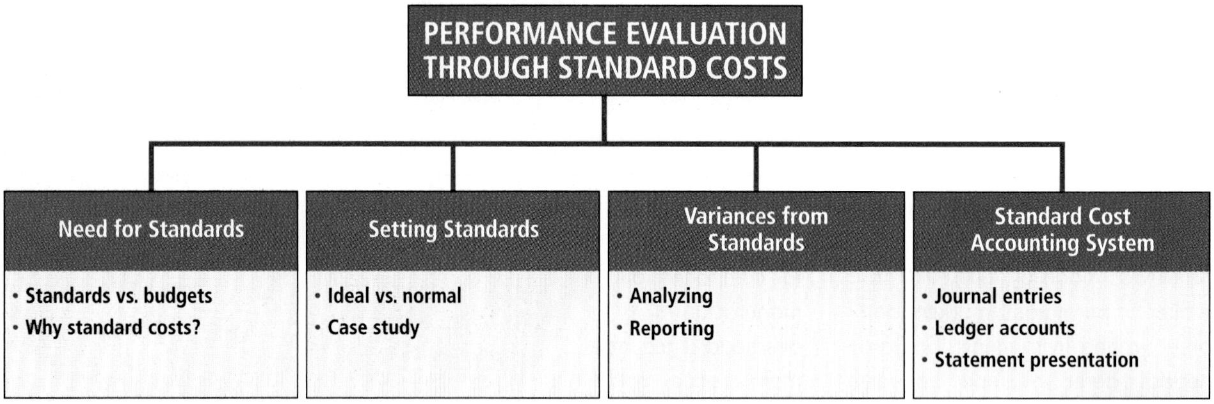

THE NAVIGATOR

THE NEED FOR STANDARDS

Standards are a fact of life. You met the admission standards for the school you are attending. The vehicle that you drive had to meet certain governmental emissions standards. The hamburgers and salads you eat in a restaurant have to meet certain health and nutritional standards before they can be sold. The reason for standards in these cases is very simple: They help to ensure that overall product quality is high. Without standards, quality control is lost.

Standards are also common in business. Those imposed by government agencies are often called **regulations**. They include the Fair Labor Standards Act, the Equal Employment Opportunity Act, and a multitude of environmental standards. Standards established internally by a company may extend to personnel matters, such as employee absenteeism and ethical codes of conduct, quality control standards for products, and standard costs for goods and services. In managerial accounting, **standard costs** are predetermined unit costs, which are used as measures of performance.

We will focus on manufacturing operations in the remainder of this chapter. But you should also recognize that standard costs also apply to many other types of businesses. For example, a fast-food restaurant such as **McDonald's** knows the price it should pay for pickles, beef, buns, and other ingredients. It also knows how much time it should take an employee to flip hamburgers. If too much is paid for pickles or too much time is taken to prepare Big Macs, the deviations are noticed and corrective action is taken. Standard costs also may be used in not-for-profit enterprises such as universities, charitable organizations, and governmental agencies.

DISTINGUISHING BETWEEN STANDARDS AND BUDGETS

STUDY OBJECTIVE 1

Distinguish between a standard and a budget.

In concept, **standards** and **budgets** are essentially the same. Both are predetermined costs, and both contribute to management planning and control. There is a difference, however, in the way the terms are expressed. A standard is a **unit** amount. A budget is a **total** amount. Thus, it is customary to state that the standard cost of direct labor for a unit of product is $10. If 5,000 units of the product are produced, the $50,000 of direct labor is the **budgeted** labor cost. A standard is the budgeted cost per unit of product. A standard is therefore concerned with each individual cost component that makes up the entire budget.

There are important accounting differences between budgets and standards. Except in the application of manufacturing overhead to jobs and processes, budget data are not journalized in cost accounting systems. In contrast, as will be illustrated in the chapter, standard costs may be incorporated into cost accounting systems. Also, a company may report its inventories at standard cost in its financial statements, but it would not report inventories at budgeted costs.

WHY STANDARD COSTS?

STUDY OBJECTIVE 2

Identify the advantages of standard costs.

Standard costs offer a number of advantages to an organization, as shown in Illustration 26-1. These advantages will be realized only when standard costs are carefully established and prudently used. Using standards solely as a means of placing blame can have a negative effect on managers and employees. In an effort to minimize this effect, many companies offer wage incentives to those who meet their standards.

Illustration 26-1

Advantages of standard costs

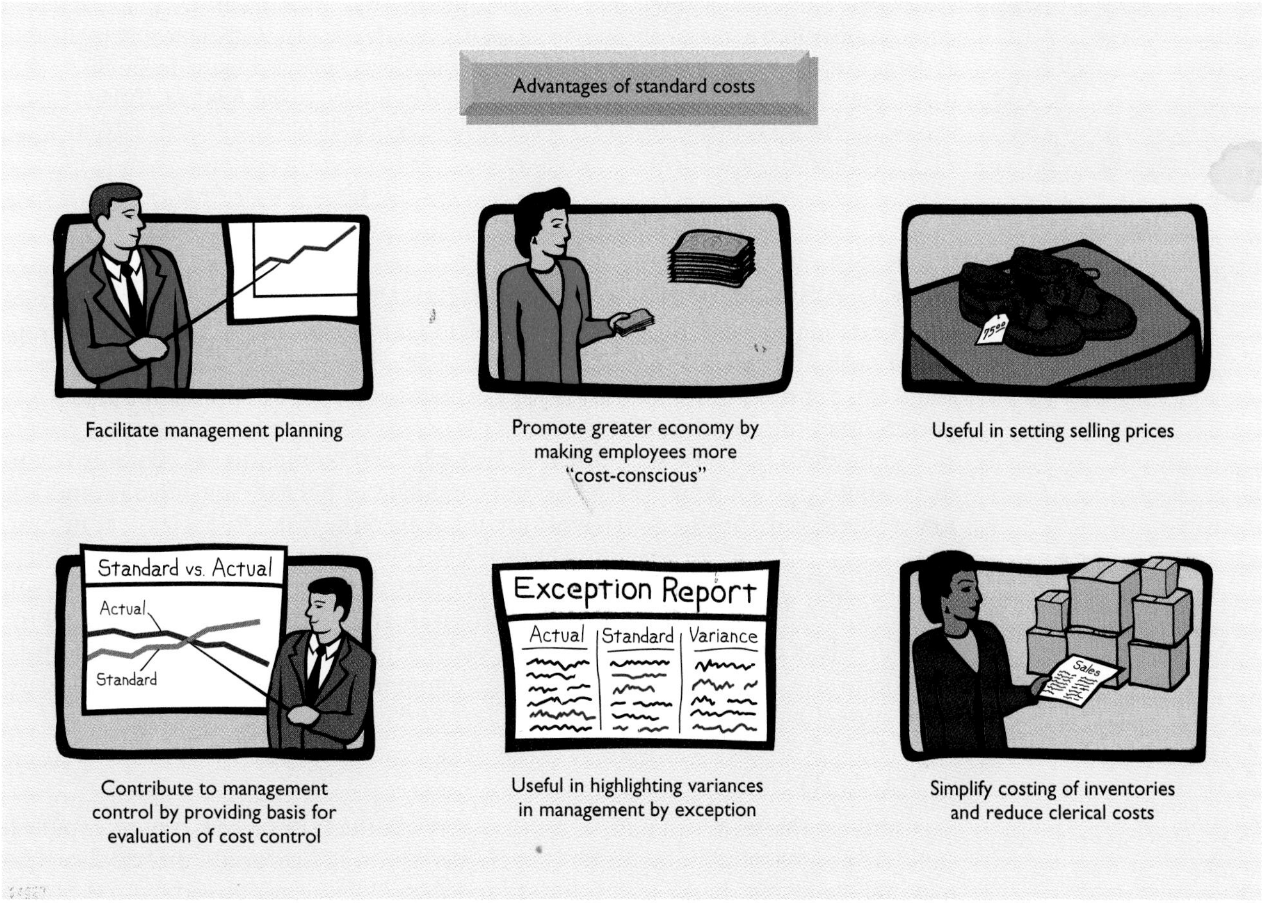
Advantages of standard costs
Facilitate management planning
Promote greater economy by making employees more "cost-conscious"
Useful in setting selling prices
Standard vs. Actual
Actual
Standard
Contribute to management control by providing basis for evaluation of cost control
Exception Report
Actual
Standard
Variance
Useful in highlighting variances in management by exception
Sales
Simplify costing of inventories and reduce clerical costs

SETTING STANDARD COSTS—A DIFFICULT TASK

STUDY OBJECTIVE 3

Describe how standards are set.

The setting of standard costs to produce a unit of product is a difficult task. It requires input from all persons who have responsibility for costs and quantities. To determine the standard cost of direct materials, management may have to consult purchasing agents, product managers, quality control engineers, and production supervisors. In setting the cost standard for direct labor, pay rate data are obtained from the payroll department, and the labor time requirements may be determined by industrial engineers. The managerial accountant provides input into the standards-setting process by accumulating historical cost data and by knowing how costs respond to changes in activity levels. The decision as to what the standard cost should be is, of course, a management responsibility.

To be effective in controlling costs, standard costs need to be current at all times. Thus, standards should be under continuous review. They should be changed whenever it is determined that the existing standard is not a good measure of performance. Circumstances that may warrant revision of a standard include changed wage rates resulting from a new union contract, a change in product specifications, or the implementation of a new manufacturing method.

TECHNOLOGY IN ACTION

Computerized standard cost systems represent one of the most complex accounting systems to develop and maintain. The standard cost system must be fully integrated into the general ledger. It must allow for the creation and timely maintenance of the database of standard usage and costs for every product. It must perform variance computations. And it must also produce variance reports by product, department, or employee. With the increased use of automation and robotics, the computerized standard cost system may even be tied directly into these systems to gather variance information.

IDEAL VERSUS NORMAL STANDARDS

Standards may be set at one of two levels: ideal or normal. **Ideal standards** represent optimum levels of performance under perfect operating conditions. **Normal standards** represent efficient levels of performance that are attainable under expected operating conditions.

Some managers believe ideal standards will stimulate workers to ever-increasing improvement. However, most managers believe that ideal standards lower the morale of the entire workforce because they are so difficult, if not impossible, to meet. Very few companies use ideal standards.

Most companies that use standards set them at a normal level. Properly set, normal standards should be **rigorous but attainable**. Normal standards allow for rest periods, machine breakdowns, and other "normal" contingencies in the production process. It will be assumed in the remainder of this chapter that standard costs are set at a normal level.

ETHICS NOTE

When standards are set too high, employees sometimes feel pressure to consider unethical practices to meet these standards.

A CASE STUDY

To establish the standard cost of producing a product, it is necessary to establish standards for each manufacturing cost element—direct materials, direct labor, and manufacturing overhead. The standard for each element is derived from the standard price to be paid and the standard quantity to be used. To illustrate, we will look at a case study of how standard costs are set. In this extended example, we will assume that Xonic, Inc. wishes to use standard costs to measure performance in filling an order for 1,000 gallons of Weed-O, a liquid weed killer.

Direct Materials

The **direct materials price standard** is the cost per unit of direct materials that should be incurred. This standard should be based on the purchasing department's best estimate of the **cost of raw materials**. This is frequently based on current purchase prices. The price standard should also include an amount for related costs such as receiving, storing, and handling. The materials price standard per pound of material for Xonic's weed killer is:

Item	Price
Purchase price, net of discounts	$2.70
Freight	0.20
Receiving and handling	0.10
Standard direct materials price per pound	**$3.00**

Illustration 26-2

Setting direct materials price standard

The **direct materials quantity standard** is the quantity of direct materials that should be used per unit of finished goods. This standard is expressed as a physical measure, such as pounds, barrels, or board feet. In setting the standard, management should consider both the quality and quantity of materials required to manufacture the product. The standard should include allowances for unavoidable waste and normal spoilage. The standard quantity per unit for Xonic, Inc. is as follows.

Item	Quantity (Pounds)
Required materials	3.5
Allowance for waste	0.4
Allowance for spoilage	0.1
Standard direct materials quantity per unit	**4.0**

Illustration 26-3

Setting direct materials quantity standard

The standard direct materials cost per unit is the standard direct materials price times the standard direct materials quantity. For Xonic, Inc., the standard direct materials cost per gallon of Weed-O is $12.00 ($3.00 × 4.0 pounds).

Direct Labor

The **direct labor price standard** is the rate per hour that should be incurred for direct labor. This standard is based on current wage rates, adjusted for anticipated changes such as cost of living adjustments (COLAs). The price standard also generally includes employer payroll taxes and fringe benefits, such as paid holidays and vacations. For Xonic, Inc., the direct labor price standard is as follows.

ALTERNATIVE TERMINOLOGY

The direct labor price standard is also called the *direct labor rate standard.*

Illustration 26-4

Setting direct labor price standard

Item	Price
Hourly wage rate	$ 7.50
COLA	0.25
Payroll taxes	0.75
Fringe benefits	1.50
Standard direct labor rate per hour	**$10.00**

ALTERNATIVE TERMINOLOGY
The direct labor quantity standard is also called the *direct labor efficiency standard.*

The **direct labor quantity standard** is the time that should be required to make one unit of the product. This standard is especially critical in labor-intensive companies. Allowances should be made in this standard for rest periods, cleanup, machine setup, and machine downtime. For Xonic, Inc., the direct labor quantity standard is as follows.

Illustration 26-5

Setting direct labor quantity standard

Item	Quantity (Hours)
Actual production time	1.5
Rest periods and cleanup	0.2
Setup and downtime	0.3
Standard direct labor hours per unit	**2.0**

The standard direct labor cost per unit is the standard direct labor rate times the standard direct labor hours. For Xonic, Inc., the standard direct labor cost per gallon of Weed-O is $20 ($10.00 × 2.0 hours).

Manufacturing Overhead

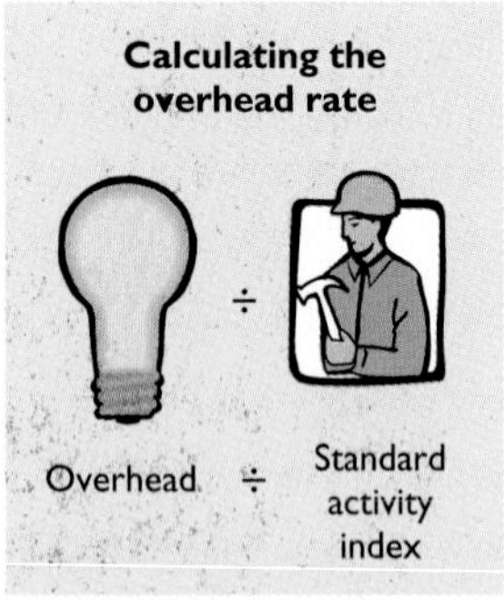

For manufacturing overhead, a **standard predetermined overhead rate** is used in setting the standard. This overhead rate is determined by dividing budgeted overhead costs by an expected standard activity index. For example, the index may be standard direct labor hours or standard machine hours. Xonic, Inc. uses standard direct labor hours as the activity index. The company expects to produce 13,200 gallons of Weed-O during the year at normal capacity. Since it takes 2 direct labor hours for each gallon, total standard direct labor hours are 26,400 (13,200 × 2). At this level of activity, overhead costs are expected to be $132,000. Of that amount, $79,200 are variable and $52,800 are fixed. The standard predetermined overhead rates are computed as shown in Illustration 26-6.

Illustration 26-6

Computing predetermined overhead rates

Budgeted Overhead Costs	Amount	÷	Standard Direct Labor Hours	=	Overhead Rate per Direct Labor Hour
Variable	$ 79,200		26,400		**$3.00**
Fixed	52,800		26,400		**2.00**
Total	$132,000		26,400		**$5.00**

The standard manufacturing overhead rate per unit is the predetermined overhead rate times the activity index quantity standard. For Xonic, Inc., which uses direct labor hours as its activity index, the standard manufacturing overhead rate per gallon of Weed-O is $10 ($5 × 2 hours).

Total Standard Cost per Unit

Now that the standard quantity and price have been established per unit of product, the total standard cost can be determined. The total standard cost per unit is the sum of the standard costs of direct materials, direct labor, and manufacturing overhead. For Xonic, Inc., the total standard cost per gallon of Weed-O is $42, as shown on the following standard cost card.

Illustration 26-7

Standard cost per gallon of Weed-O

Product: Weed-O | **Unit Measure: Gallon**

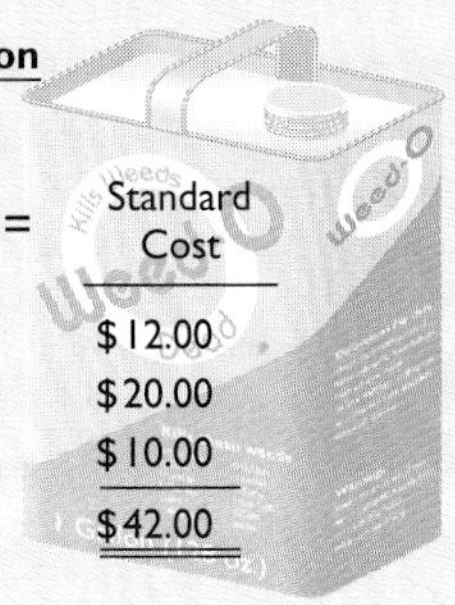

Manufacturing Cost Elements	Standard Quantity	×	Standard Price	=	Standard Cost
Direct materials	4 pounds		$ 3.00		$ 12.00
Direct labor	2 hours		$ 10.00		$ 20.00
Manufacturing overhead	2 hours		$ 5.00		$ 10.00
					$ 42.00

A standard cost card is prepared for each product. This card provides the basis for determining variances from standards.

ACCOUNTING IN ACTION *Business Insight*

Setting standards can be difficult. Consider **Susan's Chili Factory**, which manufactures and sells chili. The cost of manufacturing Susan's chili consists of the costs of raw materials, labor to convert the basic ingredients to chili, and overhead. We will use material cost as an example. Three standards need to be developed: (1) What should be the formula (mix) of ingredients for one gallon of chili? (2) What should be the normal wastage (or shrinkage) for the individual ingredients? (3) What should be the standard cost for the individual ingredients that go into the chili?

Susan's Chili Factory also illustrates how standard costs can be used by management in controlling costs. Suppose that summer droughts have reduced crop yields. As a result, prices have doubled for beans, onions, and peppers. In this case, actual costs will be significantly higher than standard costs, which will cause management to evaluate the situation. Management might decide to increase the price charged for a gallon of chili. It might reexamine the product mix to see if other types of ingredients can be used. Or it might curtail production until ingredients can be purchased at or near standard costs. Similarly, assume that poor maintenance caused the onion-dicing blades to become dull. As a result, usage of onions to make a gallon of chili tripled. Because this deviation is quickly highlighted through standard costs, corrective action can be promptly taken.

SOURCE: Adapted from David R. Beran, "Cost Reduction Through Control Reporting," *Management Accounting*, April 1982, pp. 29–33.

BEFORE YOU GO ON...

REVIEW IT

1. How do standards differ from budgets?
2. What are the advantages of standard costs to an organization?
3. Distinguish between normal standards and ideal standards. Which standard is more widely used? Why?

DO IT

The management of Arapahoe Company has decided to use standard costs. Management asks you to explain the components used in setting the standard cost per unit for direct materials, direct labor, and manufacturing overhead.

ACTION PLAN

- Differentiate between the two components of each standard: price and quantity.

SOLUTION: The standard direct materials cost per unit is the standard direct materials price times the standard direct materials quantity. The standard direct labor cost per unit is the standard direct labor rate times the standard direct labor hours. The standard manufacturing overhead rate per unit is the standard predetermined overhead rate times the activity index quantity standard.

Related exercise material: BE26-2, BE26-3, and E26-1.

THE NAVIGATOR

VARIANCES FROM STANDARDS

ALTERNATIVE TERMINOLOGY In business, the term *variance* is also used to indicate differences between total budgeted and total actual costs.

One of the major management uses of standard costs is to identify variances from standards. **Variances** are the differences between total actual costs and total standard costs. To illustrate, we will assume that in producing 1,000 gallons of Weed-O in the month of June, Xonic, Inc. incurred the following costs.

Illustration 26-8

Actual production costs

Direct materials	$13,020
Direct labor	20,580
Variable overhead	6,500
Fixed overhead	4,400
Total actual costs	$44,500

Total standard costs are determined by multiplying the units produced by the standard cost per unit. The total standard cost of Weed-O is $42,000 (1,000 gallons × $42). Thus, the total variance is $2,500, as shown below.

Illustration 26-9

Computation of total variance

Actual costs	$44,500
Standard costs	42,000
Total variance	**$ 2,500**

Note that the variance is expressed in total dollars and not on a per unit basis.

When actual costs exceed standard costs, the variance is **unfavorable**. The $2,500 variance in June for Weed-O is unfavorable. An unfavorable variance has a negative connotation. It suggests that too much was paid for one or more of the manufacturing cost elements or that the elements were used inefficiently.

If actual costs are less than standard costs, the variance is **favorable**. A favorable variance has a positive connotation. It suggests efficiencies in incurring manufacturing costs and in using direct materials, direct labor, and manufacturing overhead. However, be careful: A favorable variance could be obtained by using inferior materials. In printing wedding invitations, for example, a favorable variance could result from using an inferior grade of paper. Or, a favorable variance might be achieved in installing tires on an automobile assembly line by tightening only half of the lug bolts. The point should be obvious: A variance is not favorable if quality control standards have been sacrificed.

ANALYZING VARIANCES

To interpret properly the significance of a variance, you must analyze it to determine the underlying factors. Analyzing variances begins by determining the cost elements that comprise the variance. **For each manufacturing cost element, a total dollar variance is computed. Then this variance is analyzed into a price variance and a quantity variance.** The relationships are shown graphically as follows.

Illustration 26-10

Variance relationships

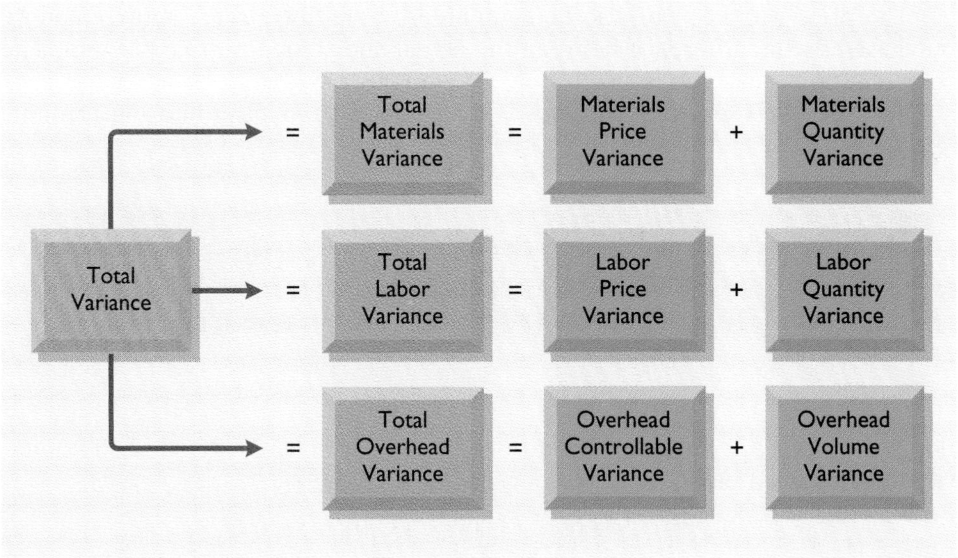

Each of the variances is explained below.

STUDY OBJECTIVE 4

State the formulas for determining direct materials and direct labor variances.

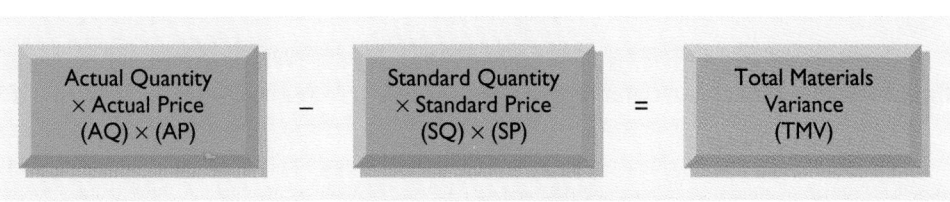

Direct Materials Variances

In completing the order for 1,000 gallons of Weed-O, Xonic used 4,200 pounds of direct materials. These were purchased at a cost of $3.10 per unit. The **total materials variance** is computed from the following formula.

Illustration 26-11

Formula for total materials variance

$$\begin{array}{c}\text{Actual Quantity}\\ \times\text{ Actual Price}\\ (\text{AQ})\times(\text{AP})\end{array} - \begin{array}{c}\text{Standard Quantity}\\ \times\text{ Standard Price}\\ (\text{SQ})\times(\text{SP})\end{array} = \begin{array}{c}\text{Total Materials}\\ \text{Variance}\\ (\text{TMV})\end{array}$$

For Xonic, Inc., the total materials variance is $1,020 ($13,020 − $12,000) unfavorable as shown below.

$$(4{,}200 \times \$3.10) - (4{,}000 \times \$3.00) = \$1{,}020 \text{ U}$$

Next, the total variance is analyzed to determine the amount attributable to price (costs) and to quantity (use). The **materials price variance** is computed from the following formula.[1]

Illustration 26-12

Formula for materials price variance

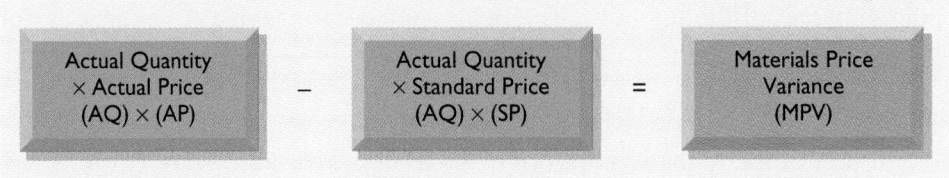

Actual Quantity × Actual Price (AQ) × (AP)	−	Actual Quantity × Standard Price (AQ) × (SP)	=	Materials Price Variance (MPV)

For Xonic, Inc., the materials price variance is $420 ($13,020 − $12,600) unfavorable as shown below.

$$(4{,}200 \times \$3.10) - (4{,}200 \times \$3.00) = \$420 \text{ U}$$

HELPFUL HINT
The alternative formula is:
AQ × AP−SP = MVP

The price variance can also be computed by multiplying the actual quantity purchased by the difference between the actual and standard price per unit. The computation in this case is 4,200 × ($3.10 − $3.00) = $420 U.

The **materials quantity variance** is determined from the following formula.

Illustration 26-13

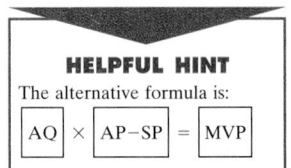

Formula for materials quantity variance

Actual Quantity × Standard Price (AQ) × (SP)	−	Standard Quantity × Standard Price (SQ) × (SP)	=	Materials Quantity Variance (MQV)

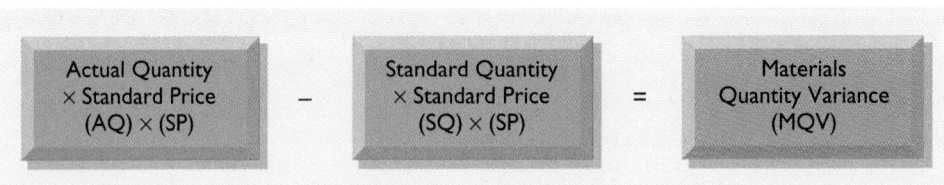

For Xonic, Inc., the materials quantity variance is $600 ($12,600 − $12,000) unfavorable, as shown below.

$$(4{,}200 \times \$3.00) - (4{,}000 \times \$3.00) = \$600 \text{ U}$$

HELPFUL HINT
The alternative formula is:
SP × AQ−SQ = MQV

This variance can also be computed by applying the standard price to the difference between actual and standard quantities used. The computation in this example is $3.00 × (4,200 − 4,000) = $600 U.

The total materials variance of $1,020(U), therefore, consists of the following.

Illustration 26-14

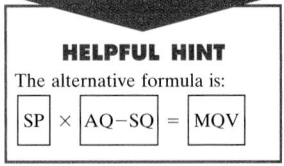

Summary of materials variance

Materials price variance	$ 420 U
Materials quantity variance	600 U
Total materials variance	**$1,020 U**

A matrix is sometimes used to analyze a variance. **When the matrix is used, the formulas for each cost element are computed first and then the variances.** The

[1]We will assume that all materials purchased during the period are used in production and that no units remain in inventory at the end of the period.

completed matrix for the direct materials variance for Xonic, Inc. is shown in Illustration 26-15. The matrix provides a convenient structure for determining each variance.

Illustration 26-15

Matrix for direct materials variance

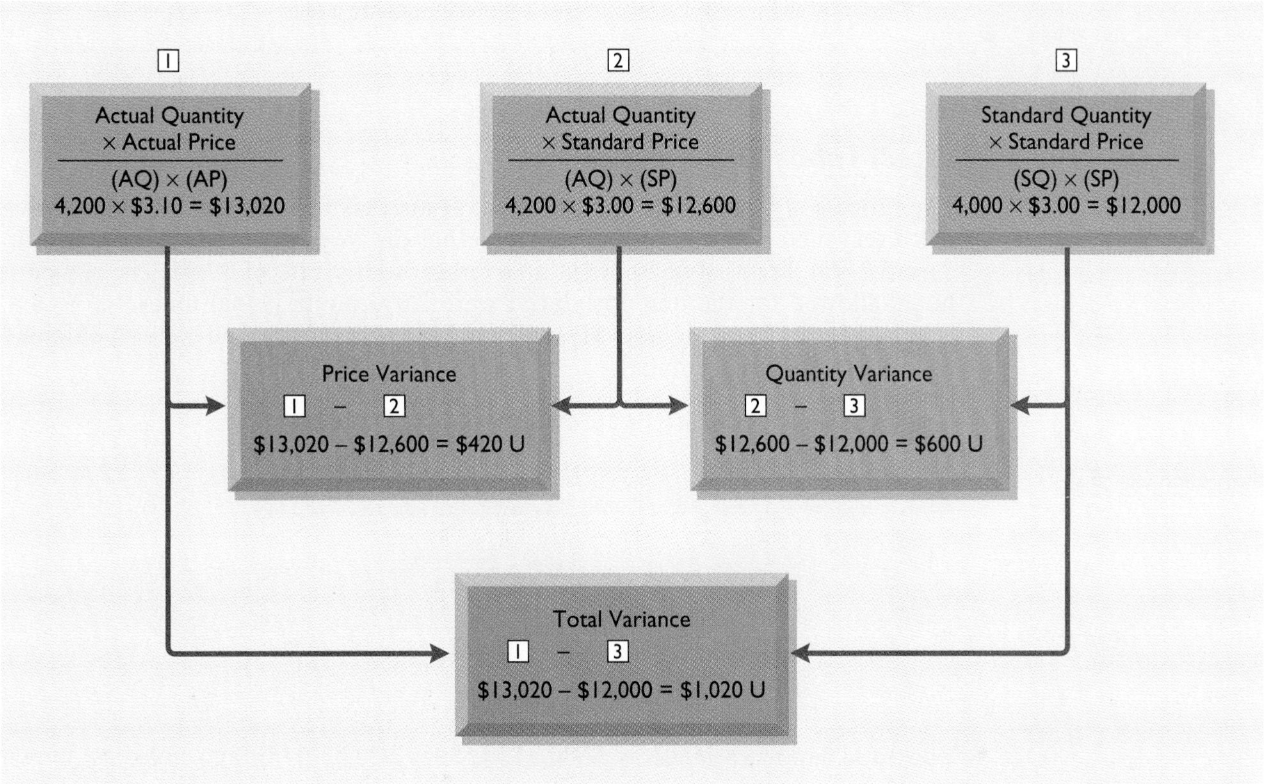

CAUSES OF MATERIALS VARIANCES. What are the causes of a variance? The causes may relate to both internal and external factors. **The investigation of a materials price variance usually begins in the purchasing department.** Many factors affect the price paid for raw materials. These include the delivery method used, availability of quantity and cash discounts, and the quality of the materials requested. To the extent that these factors have been considered in setting the price standard, the purchasing department should be responsible for any variances.

However, a variance may be beyond the control of the purchasing department. Sometimes, for example, prices may rise faster than expected. Moreover, actions by groups over which the company has no control, such as the OPEC nations' oil price increases, may cause an unfavorable variance. There are also times when a production department may be responsible for the price variance. This may occur when a rush order forces the company to pay a higher price for the materials.

The starting point for determining the cause(s) of an unfavorable **materials quantity variance** is in the **production department**. If the variances are due to inexperienced workers, faulty machinery, or carelessness, the production department would be responsible. However, if the materials obtained by the purchasing department were of inferior quality, then the purchasing department should be responsible.

ACCOUNTING IN ACTION *e* **Business Insight**

If purchase price variances are used as a basis for measuring performance, purchasing departments often will continually search for the lowest-cost item. However, this basis can become counterproductive if it leads to late deliveries of the goods or the purchase of inferior-quality goods.

Direct Labor Variances

The process of determining direct labor variances is the same as for determining the direct materials variances. In completing the Weed-O order, Xonic, Inc. incurred 2,100 direct labor hours at an average hourly rate of $9.80. The standard hours allowed for the units produced were 2,000 hours (1,000 units × 2 hours). The standard labor rate was $10 per hour. The **total labor variance** is obtained from the following formula.

Illustration 26-16

Formula for total labor variance

Actual Hours × Actual Rate (AH) × (AR)	−	Standard Hours × Standard Rate (SH) × (SR)	=	Total Labor Variance (TLV)

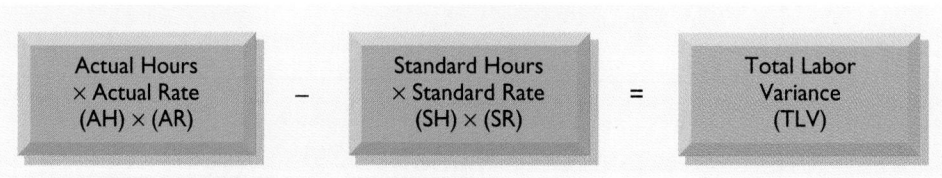

The total labor variance is $580 ($20,580 − $20,000) unfavorable, as shown below.

(2,100 × $9.80) − (2,000 × $10.00) = $580 U

The formula for the **labor price variance** is:

Illustration 26-17

Formula for labor price variance

Actual Hours × Actual Rate (AH) × (AR)	−	Actual Hours × Standard Rate (AH) × (SR)	=	Labor Price Variance (LPV)

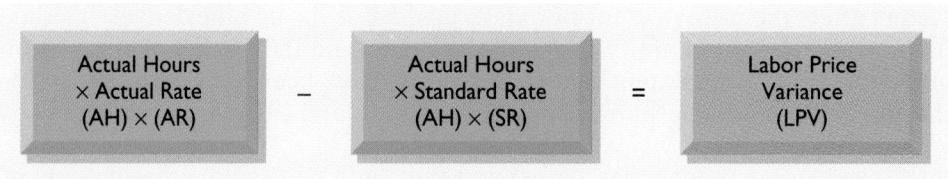

HELPFUL HINT
The alternative formula is:
AH × AR−SR = LPV

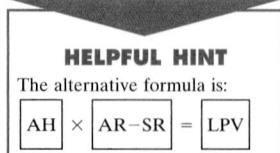

For Xonic, Inc., the labor price variance is $420 ($20,580 − $21,000) favorable as shown below.

(2,100 × $9.80) − (2,100 × $10.00) = $420 F

This variance can also be computed by multiplying actual hours worked by the difference between the actual pay rate and the standard pay rate. The computation in this example is 2,100 × ($10.00 − $9.80) = $420 F.

The **labor quantity variance** is derived from the following formula.

the Weed-O order, the standard hours allowed are 2,000. The predetermined overhead rate is $5 per direct labor hour. Thus, overhead applied is $10,000 (2,000 × $5). Note that actual hours of direct labor (2,100) are not used in applying manufacturing overhead.

The formula for the total overhead variance is:

Illustration 26-22
Formula for total overhead variance

Actual Overhead − Overhead Applied* = Total Overhead Variance

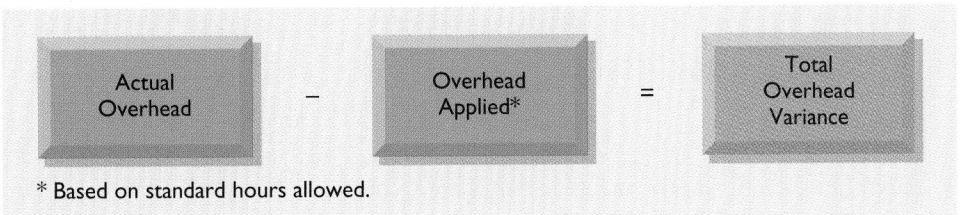

* Based on standard hours allowed.

Thus, for Xonic, Inc., the total overhead variance is $900 unfavorable as shown below:

$10,900 − $10,000 = $900 U

The overhead variance is generally analyzed through a price variance and a quantity variance. The name usually given to the price variance is the **overhead controllable variance**, whereas the quantity variance is referred to as the **overhead volume variance**.

OVERHEAD CONTROLLABLE VARIANCE. The **overhead controllable variance** shows whether overhead costs were effectively controlled. To compute this variance, actual overhead costs incurred are compared with budgeted costs for the **standard hours allowed**. The budgeted costs are determined from the flexible manufacturing overhead budget. The budget for Xonic, Inc. is as follows.

ALTERNATIVE TERMINOLOGY
The overhead controllable variance is also called the *budget* or *spending variance*.

Illustration 26-23
Flexible budget using standard direct labor hours

XONIC, INC.
Flexible Manufacturing Overhead Budget

Activity Index				
Standard direct labor hours	1,800	**2,000**	2,200	2,400
Costs				
Variable costs				
Indirect materials	$1,800	**$ 2,000**	$ 2,200	$ 2,400
Indirect labor	2,700	**3,000**	3,300	3,600
Utilities	900	**1,000**	1,100	1,200
Total variable	5,400	**6,000**	6,600	7,200
Fixed costs				
Supervision	3,000	**3,000**	3,000	3,000
Depreciation	1,400	**1,400**	1,400	1,400
Total fixed	4,400	**4,400**	4,400	4,400
Total costs	$9,800	**$10,400**	$11,000	$11,600

As shown, the budgeted costs for 2,000 standard hours are $10,400 ($6,000 variable and $4,400 fixed).[2]

The formula for the overhead controllable variance is:

Illustration 26-24

Formula for overhead controllable variance

Actual Overhead − Overhead Budgeted* = Overhead Controllable Variance

* Based on standard hours allowed.

The overhead controllable variance for Xonic, Inc. is $500 unfavorable as shown below.

$10,900 − $10,400 = $500 U

Most controllable variances are associated with variable costs, which are controllable costs. Fixed costs are usually known at the time the budget is prepared. At Xonic, Inc., the variance is accounted for by comparing the actual variable overhead costs ($6,500) with the budgeted variable costs ($6,000).

Management can compare actual and budgeted overhead for each manufacturing overhead cost that contributes to the controllable variance. In addition, cost and quantity variances can be developed for each overhead cost, such as indirect materials and indirect labor.

OVERHEAD VOLUME VARIANCE. The **overhead volume variance** indicates whether plant facilities were efficiently used. The formula for computing the volume variance is as follows.

Illustration 26-25

Formula for overhead volume variance

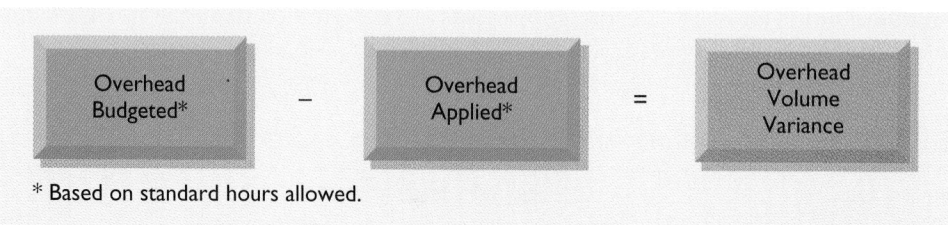

Overhead Budgeted* − Overhead Applied* = Overhead Volume Variance

* Based on standard hours allowed.

Both the factors in this formula have been explained above. The overhead budgeted is the same as the amount used in computing the controllable variance, or $10,400 in our example. Overhead applied of $10,000 is the amount used in determining the total overhead variance. For Xonic Inc. the overhead volume variance is $400 unfavorable as shown below.

$10,400 − $10,000 = $400 U

We can analyze the volume variance in even more detail. As shown in the flexible manufacturing overhead budget, the budgeted overhead of $10,400 consists of $6,000 variable and $4,400 fixed. As shown in Illustration 26-6 (page 1068), the predetermined overhead rate of $5 consists of $3 variable and $2 fixed. The detailed analysis, therefore, is:

[2]The flexible budget formula is: fixed costs $4,400 plus variable costs $3 per hour. Thus, total budgeted costs are $4,400 + ($3 × 2,000), or $10,400.

Illustration 26-26
Detailed analysis of overhead volume variance

Overhead budgeted		
Variable costs	$6,000	
Fixed costs	**4,400**	$10,400
Overhead applied		
Variable costs (2,000 × $3)	6,000	
Fixed costs (2,000 × $2)	**4,000**	10,000
Overhead volume variance—unfavorable		$ 400

This analysis indicates that **the overhead volume variance relates solely to fixed costs** (fixed costs budgeted $4,400 − fixed costs applied $4,000). Thus, **the volume variance measures the amount that fixed overhead costs are under- or overapplied.**

We have already established that total fixed costs remain the same at every level of activity within the relevant range. A predetermined overhead rate based on normal capacity is used in applying overhead. **It follows that if the standard hours allowed are less than the standard hours at normal capacity, fixed overhead costs will be underapplied.** In contrast, **if production exceeds normal capacity, fixed overhead costs will be overapplied.**

An alternative formula for computing the overhead volume variance is shown in Illustration 26-27.

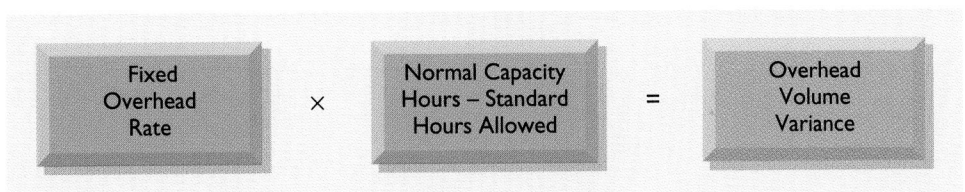

Illustration 26-27
Alternative formula for overhead volume variance

Fixed Overhead Rate × Normal Capacity Hours − Standard Hours Allowed = Overhead Volume Variance

In Xonic, Inc. normal capacity is 26,400 hours for the year, or 2,200 hours for a month (26,400 ÷ 12). The fixed overhead rate is $2 per hour. Thus, the volume variance is $400 unfavorable as shown below.

$$\$2 \times (2{,}200 - 2{,}000) = \$400\ \text{U}$$

The total overhead variance of $900 unfavorable for Xonic, Inc., therefore, consists of the following.

Illustration 26-28
Summary of overhead variance

Overhead controllable variance	$500 U
Overhead volume variance	400 U
Total overhead variance	**$900 U**

The results can also be obtained from the matrix in Illustration 26-29 shown on the next page.

In computing the overhead variances, it is important to remember the following.

1. Standard hours allowed are used in each of the variances.
2. Budgeted costs for the controllable variance are derived from the flexible budget.
3. The controllable variance generally pertains to variable costs.
4. The volume variance pertains solely to fixed costs.

Illustration 26-29

Matrix for manufacturing overhead variance

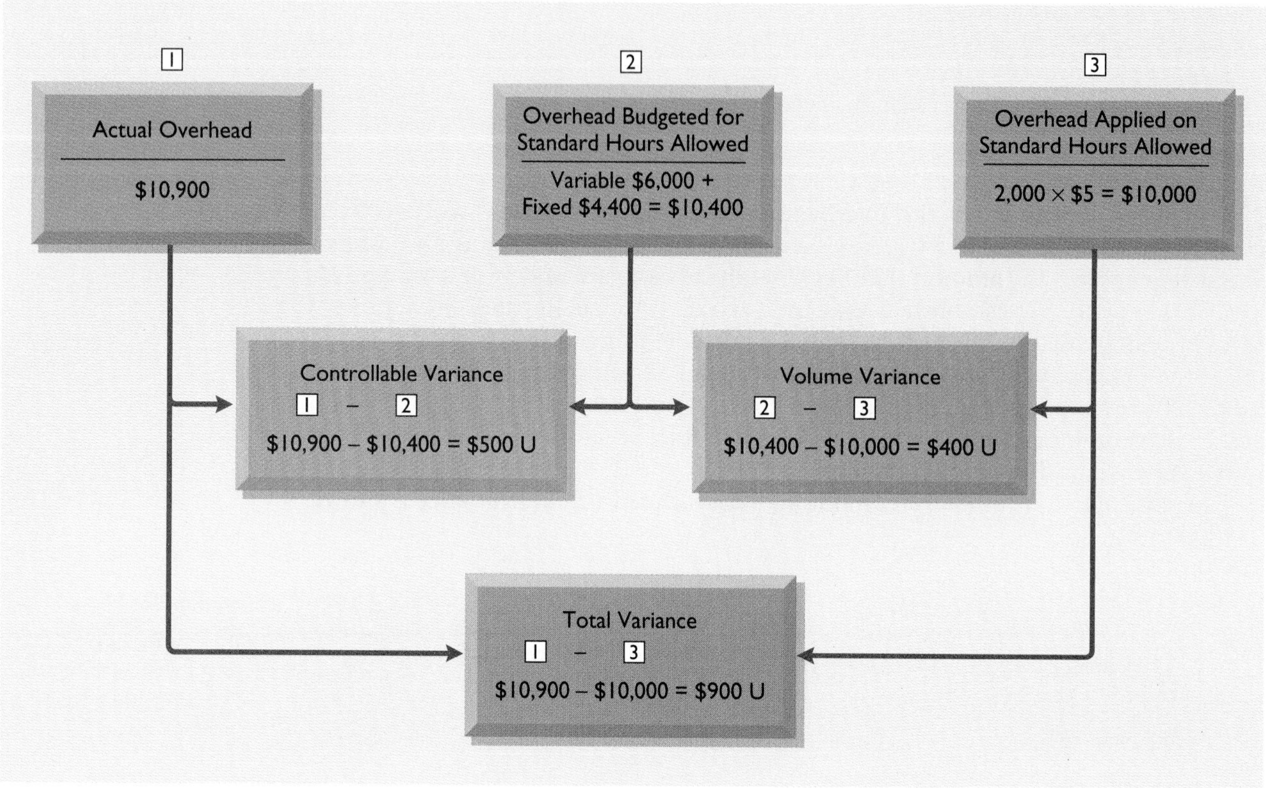

CAUSES OF MANUFACTURING OVERHEAD VARIANCES. Since the **controllable variance** relates to variable manufacturing costs, the responsibility for the variance rests with the **production department**. The cause of an unfavorable variance may be: (1) **higher than expected use** of indirect materials, indirect labor, and factory supplies, or (2) **increases in indirect manufacturing costs**, such as fuel and maintenance costs.

The **overhead volume variance** is the responsibility of the **production department** if the cause is inefficient use of direct labor or machine breakdowns. When the cause is a **lack of sales orders**, the responsibility rests **outside** the production department.

REPORTING VARIANCES

STUDY OBJECTIVE 6

Discuss the reporting of variances.

All variances should be reported to appropriate levels of management as soon as possible. The sooner management is informed, the sooner problems can be evaluated and corrective actions taken if necessary.

The form, content, and frequency of variance reports vary considerably among companies. One approach is to prepare a weekly report for each department that has primary responsibility for cost control. Under this approach, materials price variances are reported to the purchasing department, and all other variances are reported to the production department that did the work. The following report for Xonic, Inc., with the materials for the Weed-O order listed first, illustrates this approach.

Illustration 26-30

Materials price variance report

XONIC, INC.
Variance Report—Purchasing Department
For Week Ended June 8, 2002

Type of Materials	Quantity Purchased	Actual Price	Standard Price	Price Variance	Explanation
× 100	4,200 lbs.	$3.10	$3.00	$420 U	Rush order
× 142	1,200 units	2.75	2.80	60 F	Quantity discount
A 85	600 doz.	5.20	5.10	60 U	Regular supplier on strike
Total price variance				**$420 U**	

The explanation column is completed after consultation with the purchasing department manager.

Variance reports facilitate the principle of "management by exception" explained in Chapter 25. For example, the vice president of purchasing can use the report shown above to evaluate the effectiveness of the purchasing department manager. Or, the vice president of production can use production department variance reports to determine how well each production manager is controlling costs. In using variance reports, top management normally looks for **significant variances**. These may be judged on the basis of some quantitative measure, such as more than 10 percent of the standard or more than $1,000.

BEFORE YOU GO ON...

REVIEW IT

1. What are the formulas for computing the total, price, and quantity variances for direct materials?
2. What are the formulas for computing the total, price, and quantity variances for direct labor?
3. What are the formulas for computing the total, controllable, and volume variances for manufacturing overhead?

DO IT

The standard cost of Product XX includes two units of direct materials at $8.00 per unit. During July, 22,000 units of direct materials are purchased at $7.50 and used to produce 10,000 units. Compute the total, price, and quantity variances for materials.

ACTION PLAN

Use the formulas for computing each of the materials variances:

- Total materials variance $= (AQ \times AP) - (SQ \times SP)$
- Materials price variance $= (AQ \times AP) - (AQ \times SP)$
- Materials quantity variance $= (AQ \times SP) - (SQ \times SP)$

SOLUTION: Substituting amounts into the formulas, the variances are:

Total materials variance = (22,000 × \$7.50) − (20,000 × \$8.00) = \$5,000 unfavorable.

Materials price variance = (22,000 × \$7.50) − (22,000 × \$8.00) = \$11,000 favorable.

Materials quantity variance = (22,000 × \$8.00) − (20,000 × \$8.00) = \$16,000 unfavorable.

Related exercise material: BE26-4, BE26-5, BE26-6, BE26-7, BE26-8, E26-2, E26-3, E26-4, E26-6, E26-7, E26-8, E26-9, and E26-12.

THE NAVIGATOR

STANDARD COST ACCOUNTING SYSTEM

STUDY OBJECTIVE 7

Enumerate the features of a standard cost accounting system.

A **standard cost accounting system** is a double-entry system of accounting. In this system, standard costs are used in making entries, and variances are formally recognized in the accounts. A standard cost system may be used with either job order or process costing. At this point, we will explain and illustrate a **standard cost, job order cost accounting system**. The system is based on two important assumptions: (1) Variances from standards are recognized at the earliest opportunity. (2) The Work in Process account is maintained exclusively on the basis of standard costs. In practice, there are many variations among standard cost systems. The system described here should prepare you for systems you see in the "real world."

JOURNAL ENTRIES

We will use the transactions of Xonic, Inc. to illustrate the journal entries. Note as you study the entries that the major difference between the entries here and those for the job order cost accounting system in Chapter 21 is the **variance accounts**.

1. Purchase raw materials on account for \$13,020 when the standard cost is \$12,600.

Raw Materials Inventory	12,600	
Materials Price Variance	420	
Accounts Payable		13,020
(To record purchase of materials)		

The inventory account is debited for actual quantities at standard cost. This enables the perpetual materials records to show actual quantities. The price variance, which is unfavorable, is debited to Materials Price Variance.

2. Incur direct labor costs of \$20,580 when the standard labor cost is \$21,000.

Factory Labor	21,000	
Labor Price Variance		420
Wages Payable		20,580
(To record direct labor costs)		

Like the raw materials inventory account, Factory Labor is debited for actual hours worked at the standard hourly rate of pay. In this case, the labor variance is favorable. Thus, Labor Price Variance is credited.

3. Incur actual manufacturing overhead costs of \$10,900.

Manufacturing Overhead	10,900	
Accounts Payable/Cash/Acc. Depreciation		10,900
(To record overhead incurred)		

The controllable overhead variance is not recorded at this time. It depends on standard hours applied to work in process. This amount is not known at the time overhead is incurred.

4. Issue raw materials for production at a cost of $12,600 when the standard cost is $12,000.

Work in Process Inventory	12,000	
Materials Quantity Variance	600	
Raw Materials Inventory		12,600
(To record issuance of raw materials)		

Work in Process Inventory is debited for standard materials quantities used at standard prices. The variance account is debited because the variance is unfavorable. Raw Materials Inventory is credited for actual quantities at standard prices.

5. Assign factory labor to production at a cost of $21,000 when standard cost is $20,000.

Work in Process Inventory	20,000	
Labor Quantity Variance	1,000	
Factory Labor		21,000
(To assign factory labor to jobs)		

Work in Process Inventory is debited for standard labor hours at standard rates. The unfavorable variance is debited to Labor Quantity Variance. The credit to Factory Labor produces a zero balance in this account.

6. Applying manufacturing overhead to production $10,000.

Work in Process Inventory	10,000	
Manufacturing Overhead		10,000
(To assign overhead to jobs)		

Work in Process Inventory is debited for standard hours allowed multiplied by the standard overhead rate.

7. Transfer completed work to finished goods $42,000.

Finished Goods Inventory	42,000	
Work in Process Inventory		42,000
(To record transfer of completed work to finished goods)		

In this example, both inventory accounts are at standard cost.

8. The 1,000 gallons of Weed-O are sold for $60,000.

Accounts Receivable	60,000	
Cost of Goods Sold	42,000	
Sales		60,000
Finished Goods Inventory		42,000
(To record sale of finished goods and the cost of goods sold)		

Cost of Goods Sold is debited at standard cost. Gross profit, in turn, is the difference between sales and the standard cost of goods sold.

9. Recognize unfavorable overhead variances: controllable, $500; volume, $400.

Overhead Controllable Variance	500	
Overhead Volume Variance	400	
Manufacturing Overhead		900
(To recognize overhead variances)		

Prior to this entry, a debit balance of $900 existed in Manufacturing Overhead. This entry therefore produces a zero balance in the Manufacturing Overhead account. The information needed for this entry is often not available until the end of the accounting period.

LEDGER ACCOUNTS

The cost accounts for Xonic, Inc., after posting the entries, are shown in Illustration 26-31 on the next page. Note that six variance accounts are included in the ledger. The remaining accounts are the same as those illustrated for a job order cost system in Chapter 21, in which only actual costs were used.

STATEMENT PRESENTATION OF VARIANCES

In income statements **prepared for management** under a standard cost accounting system, **cost of goods sold is stated at standard cost and the variances are separately disclosed**, as shown in Illustration 26-32 on the next page. The statement shown is based entirely on the production and sale of Weed-O. It assumes selling and administrative costs of $3,000. Observe that each variance is shown, as well as the total net variance. In this example, variations from standard costs reduced net income by $2,500.

In financial statements prepared for stockholders and other external users, standard costs may be used. The costing of inventories at standard costs is in accordance with generally accepted accounting principles when there are no significant differences between actual costs and standard costs. **Hewlett-Packard** and **Jostens, Inc.**, for example, report their inventories at standard costs. However, if there are significant differences between actual and standard costs, inventories and cost of goods sold must be reported at actual costs.

It is also possible to show the variances in an income statement prepared in the contribution margin format. To do so, it is necessary to analyze the overhead variances into variable and fixed components. This type of analysis is explained in cost accounting textbooks.

Illustration 26-31
Cost accounts with variances

Raw Materials Inventory	
(1) 12,600	(4) 12,600

Materials Price Variance	
(1) 420	

Work in Process Inventory	
(4) 12,000	(7) 42,000
(5) 20,000	
(6) 10,000	

Factory Labor	
(2) 21,000	(5) 21,000

Materials Quantity Variance	
(4) 600	

Finished Goods Inventory	
(7) 42,000	(8) 42,000

Manufacturing Overhead	
(3) 10,900	(6) 10,000
	(9) 900

Labor Price Variance	
	(2) 420

Cost of Goods Sold	
(8) 42,000	

Labor Quantity Variance	
(5) 1,000	

Overhead Controllable Variance	
(9) 500	

Overhead Volume Variance	
(9) 400	

HELPFUL HINT
All debit balances in variance accounts indicate unfavorable variances; all credit balances indicate favorable variances.

Illustration 26-32
Variances in income statement for management

XONIC, INC.
Income Statement
For the Month Ended June 30, 2002

Sales		$60,000
Cost of goods sold (at standard)		42,000
Gross profit (at standard)		18,000
Variances		
Materials price	**$ 420**	
Materials quantity	**600**	
Labor price	**(420)**	
Labor quantity	**1,000**	
Overhead controllable	**500**	
Overhead volume	**400**	
Total variance unfavorable		**2,500**
Gross profit (actual)		15,500
Selling and administrative expenses		3,000
Net income		$12,500

BEFORE YOU GO ON...

REVIEW IT

1. Does a debit balance in a variance account indicate favorable or unfavorable performance?
2. What entry is made to recognize overhead variances in the accounts?
3. How are standard costs and variances reported in income statements prepared for management?

A LOOK BACK AT OUR FEATURE STORY

Refer back to the data in the Feature Story about **Sanford** at the beginning of the chapter, and answer the following questions.

1. Should standard unit costs be based on normal or ideal manufacturing activity?
2. What factor is critical in controlling costs? How might Sanford improve its control over this factor?
3. For internal reporting to top management, should Sanford report actual costs, standard costs, or both? Why?
4. In financial statements for stockholders, should Sanford report actual costs, standard costs, or both? Why?

SOLUTION

1. Normal standards are more widely used because they represent an efficient level of performance that is attainable under expected operating conditions. Most managers believe that because ideal standards are so difficult to meet, they lower morale.
2. The critical factor in controlling costs is the efficiency of the machine operator. However, excess labor time is often due to malfunctioning equipment. Management admits that this factor is difficult to control. The following steps may reduce or eliminate malfunctions: (1) increase maintenance on the equipment, and (2) purchase new equipment.
3. Both standard costs and actual costs should be reported to top management. Differences between the two costs should also be reported. Then, by scanning the differences, management can quickly identify those that are significant. This approach follows the principle of "management by exception." When a significant variance is identified, management can investigate the cause and take corrective action.
4. For financial statements, actual costs should be used. Standard costs are permissible but only if standard costs are not significantly different from actual costs. GAAP requires the use of actual costs if standard costs are not current and comparable to actual costs.

THE NAVIGATOR

DEMONSTRATION PROBLEM

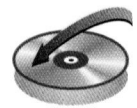

Additional Demonstration Problem

Manlow Company makes a cologne called Allure. The standard cost for one bottle of Allure is as follows.

	Standard					
Manufacturing Cost Elements	**Quantity**	×	**Price**	=	**Cost**
Direct materials	6 oz.	×	$ 0.90	=	$ 5.40
Direct labor	0.5 hrs.	×	$12.00	=	6.00
Manufacturing overhead	0.5 hrs.	×	$ 4.80	=	2.40
					$13.80

During the month, the following transactions occurred in manufacturing 10,000 bottles of Allure.

1. 58,000 ounces of materials were purchased at $1.00 per ounce.
2. All the materials purchased were used to produce the 10,000 bottles of Allure.
3. 4,900 direct labor hours were worked at a total labor cost of $56,350.
4. Variable manufacturing overhead incurred was $15,000 and fixed overhead incurred was $10,400.

The manufacturing overhead rate of $4.80 is based on a normal capacity of 5,200 direct labor hours. The total budget at this capacity is $10,400 fixed and $14,560 variable.

Instructions

Compute the total variance and the variances for each of the manufacturing cost elements.

SOLUTION TO DEMONSTRATION PROBLEM

Total Variance

Actual costs incurred:	
Direct materials	$ 58,000
Direct labor	56,350
Manufacturing overhead	25,400
	139,750
Standard cost (10,000 × $13.80)	138,000
Total variance	$ 1,750 (U)

Direct Materials Variances

Total	=	$58,000 (58,000 × $1.00)	−	$54,000 (60,000 × $0.90)	=	$4,000 U
Price	=	$58,000 (58,000 × $1.00)	−	$52,200 (58,000 × $0.90)	=	$5,800 U
Quantity	=	$52,200 (58,000 × $0.90)	−	$54,000 (60,000 × $0.90)	=	$1,800 F

Direct Labor Variances

Total	=	$56,350 (4,900 × $11.50)	−	$60,000 (5,000 × $12.00)	=	$3,650 F
Price	=	$56,350 (4,900 × $11.50)	−	$58,800 (4,900 × $12.00)	=	$2,450 F
Quantity	=	$58,800 (4,900 × $12.00)	−	$60,000 (5,000 × $12.00)	=	$1,200 F

Overhead Variances

Total	=	$25,400 ($15,000 + $10,400)	−	$24,000 (5,000 × $4.80)	=	$1,400 U
Controllable	=	$25,400 ($15,000 + $10,400)	−	$24,400 ($14,000 + $10,400)	=	$1,000 U
Volume	=	$24,400 ($14,000 + $10,400)	−	$24,000 (5,000 × $4.80)	=	$ 400 F

ACTION PLAN

- Check to make sure the total variance and the sum of the individual variances are equal.
- Find the price variance first, then the quantity variance.
- Base budgeted overhead costs on flexible budget data.
- Base overhead applied on standard hours allowed.
- Ignore actual hours worked in computing overhead variances.
- Relate the overhead volume variance solely to fixed costs.

THE NAVIGATOR

SUMMARY OF STUDY OBJECTIVES

1. ***Distinguish between a standard and a budget.*** Both standards and budgets are predetermined costs. The primary difference is that a standard is a unit amount, whereas a budget is a total amount. A standard may be regarded as the budgeted cost per unit of product.

2. ***Identify the advantages of standard costs.*** Standard costs offer a number of advantages. They (a) facilitate management planning, (b) promote greater economy and efficiency, (c) are useful in setting selling prices, (d) contribute to management control, (e) permit "management by exception,"

and (f) simplify the costing of inventories and reduce clerical costs.

3. ***Describe how standards are set.*** The direct materials price standard should be based on the delivered cost of raw materials plus an allowance for receiving and handling. The direct materials quantity standard should establish the required quantity plus an allowance for waste and spoilage.

The direct labor price standard should be based on current wage rates and anticipated adjustments such as COLAs. It also generally includes payroll taxes and fringe benefits. Direct labor quantity standards should be based on required production time plus an allowance for rest periods, cleanup, machine setup, and machine downtime.

For manufacturing overhead, a standard predetermined overhead rate is used. It is based on an expected standard activity index such as standard direct labor hours or standard direct labor cost.

4. ***State the formulas for determining direct materials and direct labor variances.*** The formulas for the direct materials variances are:

$$\begin{pmatrix}\text{Actual quantity}\\ \times\ \text{Actual price}\end{pmatrix} - \begin{pmatrix}\text{Standard quantity}\\ \times\ \text{Standard price}\end{pmatrix} = \text{Total materials variance}$$

$$\begin{pmatrix}\text{Actual quantity}\\ \times\ \text{Actual price}\end{pmatrix} - \begin{pmatrix}\text{Actual quantity}\\ \times\ \text{Standard price}\end{pmatrix} = \text{Materials price variance}$$

$$\begin{pmatrix}\text{Actual quantity}\\ \times\ \text{Standard price}\end{pmatrix} - \begin{pmatrix}\text{Standard quantity}\\ \times\ \text{Standard price}\end{pmatrix} = \text{Materials quantity variance}$$

The formulas for the direct labor variances are:

$$\begin{pmatrix}\text{Actual hours}\\ \times\ \text{Actual rate}\end{pmatrix} - \begin{pmatrix}\text{Standard hours}\\ \times\ \text{Standard rate}\end{pmatrix} = \text{Total labor variance}$$

$$\begin{pmatrix}\text{Actual hours}\\ \times\ \text{Actual rate}\end{pmatrix} - \begin{pmatrix}\text{Actual hours}\\ \times\ \text{Standard rate}\end{pmatrix} = \text{Labor price variance}$$

$$\begin{pmatrix}\text{Actual hours}\\ \times\ \text{Standard rate}\end{pmatrix} - \begin{pmatrix}\text{Standard hours}\\ \times\ \text{Standard rate}\end{pmatrix} = \text{Labor quantity variance}$$

5. ***State the formulas for determining manufacturing overhead variances.*** The formulas for the manufacturing overhead variances are:

$$\text{Actual overhead} - \text{Overhead applied} = \text{Total overhead variance}$$

$$\text{Actual overhead} - \text{Overhead budgeted} = \text{Overhead controllable variance}$$

$$\text{Overhead budgeted} - \text{Overhead applied} = \text{Overhead volume variance}$$

6. ***Discuss the reporting of variances.*** Variances are reported to management in variance reports. The reports facilitate management by exception by highlighting significant differences.

7. ***Enumerate the features of a standard cost accounting system.*** In a standard cost accounting system, standard costs are journalized and posted, and separate variance accounts are maintained in the ledger. When differences between actual costs and standard costs do not differ significantly, inventories may be reported at standard costs.

Key Term Matching Activity

GLOSSARY

Direct labor price standard The rate per hour that should be incurred for direct labor. (p. 1067).

Direct labor quantity standard The time that should be required to make one unit of product. (p. 1068).

Direct materials price standard The cost per unit of direct materials that should be incurred. (p. 1067).

Direct materials quantity standard The quantity of direct materials that should be used per unit of finished goods. (p. 1067).

Ideal standards Standards based on the optimum level of performance under perfect operating conditions. (p. 1066).

Labor price variance The difference between the actual hours times the actual rate and the actual hours times the standard rate for labor. (p. 1074).

Labor quantity variance The difference between actual hours times the standard rate and standard hours times the standard rate for labor. (p. 1074).

Materials price variance The difference between the actual quantity times the actual price and the actual quantity times the standard price for materials. (p. 1072).

Materials quantity variance The difference between the actual quantity times the standard price and the standard quantity times the standard price for materials. (p. 1072).

Normal standards Standards based on an efficient level of performance that are attainable under expected operating conditions. (p. 1066).

Overhead controllable variance The difference between actual overhead incurred and overhead budgeted for the standard hours allowed. (p. 1077).

Overhead volume variance The difference between overhead budgeted for the standard hours allowed and the overhead applied. (p. 1078).

Standard cost accounting system A double-entry system of accounting in which standard costs are used in making entries and variances are recognized in the accounts. (p. 1082).

Standard costs Predetermined unit costs which are used as measures of performance. (p. 1064).

Standard hours allowed The hours that should have been worked for the units produced. (p. 1076).

Standard predetermined overhead rate An overhead rate determined by dividing budgeted overhead costs by an expected standard activity index. (p. 1068).

Total labor variance The difference between actual hours times the actual rate and standard hours times the standard rate for labor. (p. 1074).

Total materials variance The difference between the actual quantity times the actual price and the standard quantity times the standard price of materials. (p. 1071).

Total overhead variance The difference between actual overhead costs and overhead costs applied to work done. (p. 1076).

Variances The difference between total actual costs and total standard costs. (p. 1070).

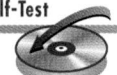

Chapter 26 Self-Test

SELF-STUDY QUESTIONS

Answers are at the end of the chapter.

(SO 1) 1. Standards differ from budgets in that:
   a. budgets but not standards may be used in valuing inventories.
   b. budgets but not standards may be journalized and posted.
   c. budgets are a total amount and standards are a unit amount.
   d. only budgets contribute to management planning and control.

(SO 2) 2. The advantages of standard costs include all of the following *except:*
   a. management by exception may be used.
   b. management planning is facilitated.
   c. they may simplify the costing of inventories.
   d. management must use a static budget.

(SO 3) 3. The setting of standards is:
   a. a managerial accounting decision.
   b. a management decision.
   c. a worker decision.
   d. preferably set at the ideal level of performance.

(SO 4) 4. Each of the following formulas is correct except:
   a. Labor price variance = (Actual hours × Actual rate) − (Actual hours × Standard rate).
   b. Overhead controllable variance = Actual overhead − Overhead budgeted.
   c. Materials price variance = (Actual quantity × Actual cost) − (Standard quantity × Standard cost).
   d. Overhead volume variance = Overhead budgeted − Overhead applied.

(SO 4) 5. In producing product AA, 6,300 pounds of direct materials were used at a cost of $1.10 per pound. The standard was 6,000 pounds at $1 per pound. The direct materials quantity variance is:
   a. $330 unfavorable.
   b. $300 unfavorable.
   c. $600 unfavorable.
   d. $630 unfavorable.

6. In producing product ZZ, 14,800 direct labor hours were used at a rate of $8.20 per hour. The standard was 15,000 hours at $8.00 per hour. Based on these data, the direct labor: (SO 4)
   a. quantity variance is $1,600 favorable.
   b. quantity variance is $1,600 unfavorable.
   c. price variance is $2,960 favorable.
   d. price variance is $3,000 unfavorable.

7. Which of the following is *correct* about overhead variances? (SO 5)
   a. The controllable variance generally pertains to fixed overhead costs.
   b. The volume variance pertains solely to variable overhead costs.
   c. Standard hours actually worked are used in each variance.
   d. Budgeted overhead costs are based on the flexible overhead budget.

8. The formula for computing the total overhead variance is: (SO 5)
   a. actual overhead less overhead applied.
   b. overhead budgeted less overhead applied.
   c. actual overhead less overhead budgeted.
   d. No correct answer given.

9. Which of the following is *incorrect* about variance reports? (SO 6)
   a. They facilitate "management by exception."
   b. They should only be sent to the top level of management.
   c. They should be prepared as soon as possible.
   d. They may vary in form, content, and frequency among companies.

10. Which of the following is *incorrect* about a standard cost accounting system? (SO 7)
   a. It is applicable to job order costing.
   b. It is applicable to process costing.
   c. It is a single-entry system.
   d. It keeps separate accounts for each variance.

THE NAVIGATOR

QUESTIONS

1. (a) "Standard costs are the expected total cost of completing a job." Is this correct? Explain.
   (b) "A standard imposed by a governmental agency is known as a regulation." Do you agree? Explain.

2. (a) Explain the similarities and differences between standards and budgets.
   (b) Contrast the accounting for standards and budgets.

3. Standard costs facilitate management planning. What are the other advantages of standard costs?
4. Contrast the roles of the management accountant and management in setting standard costs.
5. Distinguish between an ideal standard and a normal standard.
6. What factors should be considered in setting (a) the materials price standard and (b) the materials quantity standard?
7. "The objective in setting the direct labor quantity standard is to determine the aggregate time required to make one unit of product." Do you agree? What allowances should be made in setting this standard?
8. How is the predetermined overhead rate determined when standard costs are used?
9. What is the difference between a favorable cost variance and an unfavorable cost variance?
10. In each of the following formulas, supply the words that should be inserted for each number in parentheses.
    (a) (Actual quantity × (1)) − (Standard quantity × (2)) = Total materials variance
    (b) ((3) × Actual price) − (Actual quantity × (4)) = Materials price variance
    (c) (Actual quantity × (5)) − ((6) × Standard price) = Materials quantity variance
11. In the direct labor variance matrix, there are three factors: (1) Actual hours × Actual rate, (2) Actual hours × Standard rate, and (3) Standard hours × Standard rate. Using the numbers, indicate the formulas for each of the direct labor variances.
12. Dant Company's standard predetermined overhead rate is $6.00 per direct labor hour. For the month of June, 26,000 actual hours were worked, and 27,500 standard hours were allowed. Normal capacity hours were 28,000. How much overhead was applied?
13. If the $6.00 per hour overhead rate in question 12 consists of $4.00 variable, and actual overhead costs were $163,000, what is the overhead controllable variance for June? Is the variance favorable or unfavorable?
14. Using the data in questions 12 and 13, what is the overhead volume variance for June? Is the variance favorable or unfavorable?
15. What is the purpose of computing the overhead volume variance? What is the basic formula for this variance?
16. Ellen Landis does not understand why the overhead volume variance indicates that fixed overhead costs are under- or overapplied. Clarify this matter for Ellen.
17. Stan LaRue is attempting to outline the important points about overhead variances on a class examination. List four points that Stan should include in his outline.
18. How often should variances be reported to management? What principle may be used with variance reports?
19. What circumstances may cause the purchasing department to be responsible for both an unfavorable materials price variance and an unfavorable materials quantity variance?
20. (a) Explain the basic features of a standard cost accounting system. (b) What type of balance will exist in the variance account when (1) the materials price variance is unfavorable and (2) the labor quantity variance is favorable?
21. (a) How are variances reported in income statements prepared for management? (b) May standard costs be used in preparing financial statements for stockholders? Explain.

BRIEF EXERCISES

Distinguish between a standard and a budget. (SO 1)

BE26-1 Tumbo Company uses both standards and budgets. For the year, estimated production of Product X is 500,000 units. Total estimated cost for materials and labor are $1,200,000 and $1,600,000. Compute the estimates for (a) a standard cost and (b) a budgeted cost.

Set direct materials standard. (SO 3)

BE26-2 Nurmi Company accumulates the following data concerning raw materials in making one gallon of finished product: (1) Price—net purchase price $3.50, freight-in $0.20 and receiving and handling $0.10. (2) Quantity—required materials 2.6 pounds, allowance for waste and spoilage 0.4 pounds. Compute the following.

(a) Standard direct materials price per gallon.
(b) Standard direct materials quantity per gallon.
(c) Total standard material cost per gallon.

Set direct labor standard. (SO 3)

BE26-3 Labor data for making one gallon of finished product in Nurmi Company are as follows: (1) Price—hourly wage rate $10.00, payroll taxes $0.80, and fringe benefits $1.20. (2) Quantity—actual production time 1.6 hours, rest periods and clean up 0.25 hours, and setup and downtime 0.15 hours. Compute the following.

(a) Standard direct labor rate per hour.
(b) Standard direct labor hours per gallon.
(c) Standard labor cost per gallon.

BE26-4 Nadia Company's standard materials cost per unit of output is $8 (2 pounds × $4.00). During July, the company purchases and uses 3,300 pounds of materials costing $13,365 in making 1,500 units of finished product. Compute the total, price, and quantity materials variances.

Compute direct materials variances.
(SO 4)

BE26-5 Kimiko Company's standard labor cost per unit of output is $18 (2 hours × $9.00 per hour). During August, the company incurs 1,850 hours of direct labor at an hourly cost of $9.60 per hour in making 1,000 units of finished product. Compute the total, price, and quantity labor variances.

Compute direct labor variances.
(SO 4)

BE26-6 In October, Hilo Company reports 21,000 actual direct labor hours, and it incurs $98,000 of manufacturing overhead costs. Standard hours allowed for the work done is 20,000 hours. The predetermined overhead rate is $5.00 per direct labor hour. Compute the total manufacturing overhead variance.

Compute total manufacturing overhead variance.
(SO 5)

BE26-7 Some overhead data for Hilo Company are given in BE26-6. In addition, the flexible manufacturing overhead budget shows that budgeted costs are $4.00 variable per direct labor hour and $25,000 fixed. Compute the manufacturing overhead controllable variance.

Compute the manufacturing overhead controllable variance.
(SO 5)

BE26-8 Using the data in BE26-6 and BE26-7, compute the manufacturing overhead volume variance.

Compute overhead volume variance.
(SO 5)

BE26-9 Journalize the following transactions for Nashua Manufacturing.

(a) Purchased 6,000 units of raw materials on account for $11,700. The standard cost was $12,000.
(b) Issued 5,600 units of raw materials for production. The standard units were 5,800.

Journalize materials variances.
(SO 7)

BE26-10 Journalize the following transactions for Harlem Manufacturing.

(a) Incurred direct labor costs of $24,000 for 3,000 hours. The standard labor cost was $24,300.
(b) Assigned 3,000 direct labor hours costing $24,000 to production. Standard hours were 3,100.

Journalize labor variances.
(SO 7)

EXERCISES

E26-1 Robin Ritz manufactures and sells homemade wine, and he wants to develop a standard cost per gallon. The following are required for production of a 50-gallon batch.

Compute standard materials costs.
(SO 3)

3,000 ounces of grape concentrate at $0.05 per ounce
54 pounds of granulated sugar at $0.30 per pound
70 lemons at $0.60 each
50 yeast tablets at $0.25 each
50 nutrient tablets at $0.20 each
2,500 ounces of water at $0.0043 per ounce

Robin estimates that 4% of the grape concentrate is wasted, 10% of the sugar is lost, and 20% of the lemons cannot be used.

Instructions
Compute the standard cost of the ingredients for one gallon of wine. (Carry computations to three decimal places.)

E26-2 The standard cost of Product B manufactured by Lopez Company includes three units of direct materials at $5.00 per unit. During June, 30,000 units of direct materials are purchased at a cost of $4.80 per unit, and 27,200 units of direct materials are used to produce 9,000 units of Product B.

Compute materials price and quantity variances.
(SO 4)

Instructions
(a) Compute the materials price and quantity variances.
(b) Repeat (a), assuming the purchase price is $5.10 and the quantity used is 26,400 units.

E26-3 Napier Company's standard labor cost of producing one unit of Product DD is 3.9 hours at the rate of $12.00 per hour. During August, 40,800 hours of labor are incurred at a cost of $12.10 per hour to produce 10,000 units of Product DD.

Compute labor price and quantity variances.
(SO 4)

Instructions
(a) Compute the labor price and quantity variances.
(b) Repeat (a), assuming the standard is 4.2 hours of direct labor at $12.20 per hour.

Compute materials and labor variances.
(SO 4)

E26-4 Kayjay Inc., which produces a single product, has prepared the following standard cost sheet for one unit of the product.

Direct materials (8 pounds at $2.50 per pound)	$20.00
Direct labor (3 hours at $12.00 per hour)	$36.00

During the month of April, the company manufactures 250 units and incurs the following actual costs.

Direct materials (1,900 pounds)	$5,035
Direct labor (700 hours)	$8,050

Instructions

Compute the total, price, and quantity variances for materials and labor.

Journalize entries for materials and labor variances.
(SO 7)

E26-5 Data for Kayjay Inc. are given in E26-4.

Instructions

Journalize the entries to record the materials and labor variances.

Compute the materials and labor variances and list reasons for unfavorable variances.
(SO 4, 6)

E26-6 The following direct materials and direct labor data pertain to the operations of Juan Manufacturing Company for the month of August.

Costs		Quantities	
Actual labor rate	$13.00 per hour	Actual hours incurred and used	4,200 hours
Actual materials price	$128.00 per ton	Actual quantity of materials purchased and used	1,230 tons
Standard labor rate	$12.00 per hour	Standard hours used	4,300 hours
Standard materials price	$130.00 per ton	Standard quantity of materials used	1,200 tons

Instructions

(a) Compute the total, price, and quantity variances for materials and labor.

(b) Provide two possible explanations for each of the unfavorable variances calculated above, and suggest where responsibility for the unfavorable result might be placed.

Compute manufacturing overhead variances and interpret findings.
(SO 5)

E26-7 The following information was taken from the annual manufacturing overhead cost budget of SooTech Company.

Variable manufacturing overhead costs	$33,000
Fixed manufacturing overhead costs	$19,800
Normal production level in hours	16,500
Normal production level in units	4,125

During the year, 4,000 units were produced, 16,100 hours were worked, and the actual manufacturing overhead was $54,000. Actual fixed manufacturing overhead costs equaled budgeted fixed manufacturing overhead costs. Overhead is applied on the basis of direct labor hours.

Instructions

(a) Compute the total, fixed, and variable predetermined manufacturing overhead rates.

(b) Compute the total, controllable, and volume overhead variances.

(c) Briefly interpret the overhead controllable and volume variances computed in (b).

Compute overhead variances and journalize transactions and adjusting entry.
(SO 5, 7)

E26-8 Manufacturing overhead data for the production of Product H by Fierello Company are as follows.

Overhead incurred for 51,000 actual direct labor hours worked	$213,000
Overhead rate (variable $3.00; fixed $1.00) at normal capacity of 54,000 direct labor hours	$ 4.00
Standard hours allowed for work done	51,000

Instructions

(a) Compute the total, controllable, and volume overhead variances.

(b) Journalize the incurrence of the overhead costs and the application of overhead to the job, assuming a standard cost accounting system is used.
(c) Prepare the adjusting entry for the overhead variances.

Prepare a variance report for direct labor. (SO 4, 6)

E26-9 During March 2002, Tenza Tool & Die Company worked on four jobs. A review of direct labor costs reveals the following summary data.

Job Number	Actual Hours	Actual Costs	Standard Hours	Standard Costs	Total Variance
A257	220	$ 4,400	226	$4,520	$ 120 F
A258	450	10,350	430	8,600	1,750 U
A259	300	6,150	300	6,000	150 U
A260	116	2,088	110	2,200	112 F
Total variance					$1,668 U

Analysis reveals that Job A257 was a repeat job. Job A258 was a rush order that required overtime work at premium rates of pay. Job A259 required a more experienced replacement worker on one shift. Work on Job A260 was done for one day by a new trainee when a regular worker was absent.

Instructions
Prepare a report for the plant supervisor on direct labor cost variances for March. The report should have columns for (1) Job No., (2) Actual Hours, (3) Standard Hours, (4) Labor Quantity Variance, (5) Actual Rate, (6) Standard Rate, (7) Labor Price Variance, and (8) Explanations.

Prepare income statement for management. (SO 7)

E26-10 Alvarez Company uses a standard cost accounting system. During January, the company reported the following manufacturing variances.

Materials price variance	$1,250 debit	Labor quantity variance	$ 725 debit
Materials quantity variance	700 credit	Overhead controllable	200 credit
Labor price variance	525 debit	Overhead volume	1,000 debit

In addition, 6,000 units of product were sold at $8.00 per unit. Each unit sold had a standard cost of $5.00. Selling and administrative expenses were $9,000 for the month.

Instructions
Prepare an income statement for management for the month ending January 31, 2002.

Journalize entries in a standard cost accounting system. (SO 7)

E26-11 DeSoto Company installed a standard cost system on January 1. Selected transactions for the month of January are as follows.

1. Purchased 18,000 units of raw materials on account at a cost of $4.50 per unit. Standard cost was $4.00 per unit.
2. Issued 18,000 units of raw materials for jobs that required 17,600 standard units of raw materials.
3. Incurred 15,200 actual hours of direct labor at an actual rate of $4.80 per hour. The standard rate is $5.00 per hour. (Credit Wages Payable)
4. Performed 15,200 hours of direct labor on jobs when standard hours were 15,400.
5. Applied overhead to jobs at the rate of 100% of direct labor cost for standard hours allowed.

Instructions
Journalize the January transactions.

Answer questions concerning missing entries and balances. (SO 4, 5, 7)

E26-12 Amand Company uses a standard cost accounting system. Some of the ledger accounts have been destroyed in a fire. The controller asks your help in reconstructing some missing entries and balances.

Instructions
Answer the following questions.

(a) Materials Price Variance shows a $3,000 favorable balance. Accounts Payable shows $126,000 of raw materials purchases. What was the amount debited to Raw Materials Inventory for raw materials purchased?

(b) Materials Quantity Variance shows a $3,000 unfavorable balance. Raw Materials Inventory shows a zero balance. What was the amount debited to Work in Process Inventory for direct materials used?

(c) Labor Price Variance shows a $1,500 unfavorable balance. Factory Labor shows a debit of $152,000 for wages incurred. What was the amount credited to Wages Payable?

(d) Factory Labor shows a credit of $152,000 for direct labor used. Labor Quantity Variance shows a $900 unfavorable balance. What was the amount debited to Work in Process for direct labor used?

(e) Overhead applied to Work in Process totaled $165,000. If the total overhead variance was $1,300 unfavorable, what was the amount of overhead costs debited to Manufacturing Overhead?

(f) Overhead Controllable Variance shows a debit balance of $1,500. What was the amount and type of balance (debit or credit) in Overhead Volume Variance?

PROBLEMS: SET A

Compute variances, and prepare income statement. (SO 4, 5, 7)

P26-1A Ellison Manufacturing Corporation accumulates the following data relative to jobs started and finished during the month of June 2002.

Costs and Production Data	Actual	Standard
Raw materials purchases, 10,500 units	$23,100	$20,000
Raw materials units used	10,500	10,000
Direct labor payroll	$122,100	$120,000
Direct labor hours worked	14,800	15,000
Manufacturing overhead incurred	$182,500	
Manufacturing overhead applied		$184,500
Machine hours expected to be used at normal capacity		42,500
Budgeted fixed overhead for June		$46,750
Variable overhead rate per hour		$3.00

Overhead is applied on the basis of standard machine hours. Three hours of machine time are required for each direct labor hour. The jobs were sold for $400,000. Selling and administrative expenses were $40,000.

Instructions

(a) Compute all of the variances for direct materials, direct labor, and manufacturing overhead.

(b) Prepare an income statement for management. Ignore income taxes.

Compute variances. (SO 4, 5, 7)

P26-2A Moore Corporation manufactures a single product. The standard cost per unit of product is shown below.

Direct materials—1 pound plastic at $7.00 per pound	$ 7.00
Direct labor—1.5 hours at $12.00 per hour	18.00
Variable manufacturing overhead	11.25
Fixed manufacturing overhead	3.75
Total standard cost per unit	$40.00

The predetermined manufacturing overhead rate is $10 per direct labor hour ($15.00 ÷ 1.5). This rate was computed from a master manufacturing overhead budget based on normal production of 90,000 direct labor hours (60,000 units) for the year. The master budget showed total variable costs of $675,000 and total fixed costs of $225,000. Actual costs for October in producing 5,000 units were as follows.

Direct materials (5,100 pounds)	$ 36,720
Direct labor (7,000 hours)	86,100
Variable overhead	56,170
Fixed overhead	19,680
Total manufacturing costs	$198,670

The purchasing department normally buys the quantities of raw materials that are expected to be used in production each month. Raw materials inventories, therefore, can be ignored.

Instructions

Compute all of the materials, labor, and overhead variances.

Compute variances, journalize entries, and identify significant variances.
(SO 4, 5, 6, 7)

P26-3A Novall Clothiers is a small company that manufactures tall-men's suits. The company has used a standard cost accounting system. In May 2003, 11,300 suits were produced.

The following standard and actual cost data applied to the month of May when normal capacity was 14,000 direct labor hours.

Cost Element	Standard (per unit)	Actual
Direct materials	8 yards at \$4.50 per yard	\$375,150 for 91,500 yards (\$4.10 per yard)
Direct labor	1.2 hours at \$13.00 per hour	\$204,450 for 14,500 hours (\$14.10 per hour)
Overhead	1.2 hours at \$6.00 per hour (fixed \$3.50; variable \$2.50)	\$49,000 fixed overhead \$36,000 variable overhead

Overhead is applied on the basis of direct labor hours. At normal capacity, budgeted fixed overhead costs were \$49,000, and budgeted variable overhead was \$35,000.

Instructions

(a) Compute the total, price, and quantity variances for (1) materials and (2) labor, and the total, controllable, and volume variances for manufacturing overhead.

(b) Journalize the entries to record the variances assuming (1) all purchases of materials were on account, and (2) Wages Payable was credited for factory labor incurred.

(c) Which of the materials and labor variances should be investigated if management considers a variance of more than 7% from standard to be significant?

Journalize and post standard cost entries, and prepare income statement.
(SO 4, 5, 7)

P26-4A Walton Corporation uses standard costs with its job order cost accounting system. In January, an order (Job No. 12) for 2,000 units of Product B was received. The standard cost of one unit of Product B is as follows.

Direct materials	3 pounds at \$1.00 per pound	\$ 3.00
Direct labor	1 hour at \$8.00 per hour	8.00
Overhead	2 hours (variable \$4.00 per machine hour; fixed \$2.25 per machine hour)	12.50
Standard cost per unit		\$23.50

Normal capacity for the month was 4,200 machine hours. During January, the following transactions applicable to Job No. 12 occurred.

1. Purchased 6,250 pounds of raw materials on account at \$1.06 per pound.
2. Requisitioned 6,250 pounds of raw materials for Job No. 12.
3. Incurred 2,200 hours of direct labor at a rate of \$7.80 per hour.
4. Worked 2,200 hours of direct labor on Job No. 12.
5. Incurred manufacturing overhead on account \$25,800.
6. Applied overhead to Job No. 12 on basis of standard machine hours used.
7. Completed Job No. 12.
8. Billed customer for Job No. 12 at a selling price of \$70,000.
9. Incurred selling and administrative expenses on account \$2,000.

Instructions

(a) Journalize the transactions.

(b) Post to the job order cost accounts.

(c) Prepare the entry to recognize the overhead variances.

(d) Prepare the January 2003 income statement for management.

Answer questions about variances.
(SO 4, 5, 7)

P26-5A Calpine Manufacturing Company uses a standard cost accounting system. In 2002, 32,000 units were produced. Each unit took several pounds of direct materials and $1\frac{1}{4}$ standard hours of direct labor at a standard hourly rate of \$12.00. Normal capacity was 50,000 direct labor hours. During the year, 133,000 pounds of raw materials were purchased at \$0.92 per pound. All pounds purchased were used during the year.

Instructions

(a) If the materials price variance was $3,990 favorable, what was the standard materials price per pound?

(b) If the materials quantity variance was $1,710 unfavorable, what was the standard materials quantity per unit?

(c) What were the standard hours allowed for the units produced?

(d) If the labor quantity variance was $7,200 unfavorable, what were the actual direct labor hours worked?

(e) If the labor price variance was $6,000 favorable, what was the actual rate per hour?

(f) If total budgeted manufacturing overhead was $340,000 at normal capacity, what was the predetermined overhead rate?

(g) What was the standard cost per unit of product?

(h) How much overhead was applied to production during the year?

(i) If the fixed overhead rate was $2.00, what was the overhead volume variance?

(j) If the overhead controllable variance is $3,000 unfavorable, what were the total variable overhead costs incurred?

(k) Using one or more answers above, what were the total costs assigned to work in process?

PROBLEMS: SET B

Compute variances, and prepare income statement.
(SO 4, 5, 7)

P26-1B Onasis Manufacturing Company uses a standard cost accounting system. In July 2002, it accumulates the following data relative to jobs started and finished.

Cost and Production Data	Actual	Standard
Raw materials		
Units purchased	17,500	
Units used	17,500	18,000
Unit cost	$3.40	$3.00
Direct labor		
Hours worked	2,900	3,000
Hourly rate	$11.80	$12.00
Manufacturing overhead		
Incurred	$87,500	
Applied		$97,500

Manufacturing overhead was applied on the basis of direct labor hours. Normal capacity for the month was 2,800 direct labor hours. At normal capacity, budgeted overhead costs were: variable $56,000 and fixed $35,000.

Jobs finished during the month were sold for $240,000. Selling and administrative expenses were $25,000.

Instructions

(a) Compute all of the variances for direct materials, direct labor, and manufacturing overhead.

(b) Prepare an income statement for management. Ignore income taxes.

Compute variances.
(SO 4, 5, 7)

P26-2B Flesch Corporation manufactures a single product. The standard cost per unit of product is as follows.

Direct materials—2 pounds of plastic at $5.00 per pound	$10.00
Direct labor—2 hours at $12.00 per hour	24.00
Variable manufacturing overhead	12.00
Fixed manufacturing overhead	6.00
Total standard cost per unit	$52.00

The master manufacturing overhead budget for the year based on normal productive capacity of 180,000 direct labor hours (90,000 units) shows total variable costs of $1,080,000 and total fixed costs of $540,000. Overhead is applied on the basis of direct labor hours. Actual costs for November in producing 7,700 units were as follows.

Direct materials (15,000 pounds)	$ 72,000
Direct labor (14,900 hours)	183,270
Variable overhead	88,990
Fixed overhead	44,000
Total manufacturing costs	$388,260

The purchasing department normally buys the quantities of raw materials that are expected to be used in production each month. Raw materials inventories, therefore, can be ignored.

Instructions

Compute all of the materials, labor, and overhead variances.

Compute variances, journalize entries, and identify significant variances.
(SO 4, 5, 6, 7)

P26-3B True-Value Clothiers manufactures women's business suits. The company uses a standard cost accounting system. In March 2002, 12,000 suits were made. The following standard and actual cost data applied to the month of March when normal capacity was 15,000 direct labor hours.

Cost Element	Standard (per unit)	Actual
Direct materials	5 yards at $7.00 per yard	$424,800 for 59,000 yards ($7.20 per yard)
Direct labor	1.0 hours at $12.00 per hour	$127,680 for 11,400 hours ($11.20 per hour)
Overhead	1.0 hours at $9.30 per hour (fixed $6.30; variable $3.00)	$90,000 fixed overhead $42,000 variable overhead

Overhead is applied on the basis of direct labor hours. At normal capacity, budgeted fixed overhead costs were $94,500, and budgeted variable overhead costs were $45,000.

Instructions

(a) Compute the total, price, and quantity variances for (1) materials and (2) labor, and compute the total, controllable, and volume variances for manufacturing overhead.
(b) Journalize the entries to record the variances assuming (1) all purchases of materials were on account, and (2) Wages Payable was credited for factory labor incurred.
(c) Which of the materials and labor variances should be investigated if management considers a variance of more than 6% from standard to be significant?

Journalize and post standard cost entries, and prepare income statement.
(SO 4, 5, 7)

P26-4B Pomona Manufacturing Company uses standard costs with its job order cost accounting system. In January, an order (Job 84) was received for 4,000 units of Product D. The standard cost of 1 unit of Product D is as follows.

Direct materials—1.4 pounds at $4.00 per pound	$ 5.60
Direct labor—1 hour at $9.00 per hour	9.00
Overhead—1 hour (variable $7.40; fixed $10.00)	17.40
Standard cost per unit	$32.00

Overhead is applied on the basis of direct labor hours. Normal capacity for the month of January was 4,500 direct labor hours. During January, the following transactions applicable to Job No. 84 occurred.

1. Purchased 6,200 pounds of raw materials on account at $3.50 per pound.
2. Requisitioned 6,200 pounds of raw materials for production.
3. Incurred 3,900 hours of direct labor at $9.25 per hour.
4. Worked 3,900 hours of direct labor on Job No. 84.
5. Incurred $73,650 of manufacturing overhead on account.
6. Applied overhead to Job No. 84 on the basis of direct labor hours.
7. Transferred Job No. 84 to finished goods.
8. Billed customer for Job No. 84 at a selling price of $250,000.
9. Incurred selling and administrative expenses on account $61,000.

Instructions

(a) Journalize the transactions.
(b) Post to the job order cost accounts.
(c) Prepare the entry to recognize the overhead variances.
(d) Prepare the income statement for management for January 2002.

Answer questions about variances.
(SO 4, 5, 7)

P26-5B Oaks Manufacturing Company uses a standard cost accounting system. In 2002, 36,000 units were produced. Each unit took several pounds of direct materials and $1\frac{1}{4}$ standard hours of direct labor at a standard hourly rate of $12.00. Normal capacity was 42,000 direct labor hours. During the year, 132,000 pounds of raw materials were purchased at $0.90 per pound. All pounds purchased were used during the year.

Instructions

(a) If the materials price variance was $6,600 unfavorable, what was the standard materials price per pound?
(b) If the materials quantity variance was $2,550 favorable, what was the standard materials quantity per unit?
(c) What were the standard hours allowed for the units produced?
(d) If the labor quantity variance was $8,400 unfavorable, what were the actual direct labor hours worked?
(e) If the labor price variance was $9,140 favorable, what was the actual rate per hour?
(f) If total budgeted manufacturing overhead was $319,200 at normal capacity, what was the predetermined overhead rate?
(g) What was the standard cost per unit of product?
(h) How much overhead was applied to production during the year?
(i) If the fixed overhead rate was $2.50, what was the overhead volume variance?
(j) If the overhead controllable variance was $3,000 favorable, what were the total variable overhead costs incurred?
(k) Using selected answers above, what were the total costs assigned to work in process?

BROADENING YOUR PERSPECTIVE

GROUP DECISION CASE

BYP26-1 Gates Professionals, a management consulting firm, specializes in strategic planning for financial institutions. Bob Menard and Alice Chavez, partners in the firm, are assembling a new strategic planning model for use by clients. The model is designed for use on most microcomputers and replaces a rather lengthy manual model currently marketed by the firm. To market the new model Bob and Alice will need to provide clients with an estimate of the number of labor hours and computer time needed to operate the model. The model is currently being test marketed at five small financial institutions. These financial institutions are listed below, along with the number of combined computer/labor hours used by each institution to run the model one time.

Financial Institutions	Computer/Labor Hours Required
Midland National	25
First State	45
Financial Federal	40
Pacific America	30
Lakeview National	30
Total	170
Average	34

Any company that purchases the new model will need to purchase user manuals to access and operate the system. Also required are specialized computer forms that are sold only by

Gates Professionals. User manuals will be sold to clients in cases of 20, at a cost of $400 per case. One manual must be used each time the model is run because each manual includes a nonreusable computer accessed password for operating the system. The specialized computer forms are sold in packages of 250, at a cost of $75 per package. One application of the model requires the use of 50 forms. This amount includes two forms that are generally wasted in each application due to printer alignment errors. The overall cost of the strategic planning model to user clients is $12,000. Most clients will use the model four times annually.

Gates Professionals must provide its clients with estimates of ongoing costs incurred in operating the new strategic planning model. They would like to provide this information in the form of standard costs.

Instructions

With the class divided into groups, answer the following.

(a) What factors should be considered in setting a standard for computer/labor hours?
(b) What alternatives for setting a standard for computer/labor hours might be used?
(c) What standard for computer/labor hours would you select? Justify your answer.
(d) Determine the standard materials cost associated with the user manuals and computer forms for each application of the strategic planning model.

MANAGERIAL ANALYSIS

BYP26-2 Mo Vaugh and Associates is a medium-sized company located near a large metropolitan area in the Midwest. The company manufactures cabinets of mahogany, oak, and other fine woods for use in expensive homes, restaurants, and hotels. Although some of the work is custom, many of the cabinets are a standard size.

One such non-custom model is called Luxury Base Frame. Standard production is 1,000 units. Each unit has a direct labor hour standard of 5 hours. Overhead is applied to production based on standard direct labor hours. During the most recent month, only 900 units were produced; 4,500 direct labor hours were allowed for standard production, but only 4,000 hours were used. Standard and actual overhead costs were as follows.

	Standard (1,000 units)	Actual (900 units)
Indirect materials	$ 12,000	$ 12,300
Indirect labor	43,000	51,000
(Fixed) Manufacturing supervisors salaries	22,000	22,000
(Fixed) Manufacturing office employees salaries	13,000	11,500
(Fixed) Engineering costs	27,000	25,000
Computer costs	10,000	10,000
Electricity	2,500	2,500
(Fixed) Manufacturing building depreciation	8,000	8,000
(Fixed) Machinery depreciation	3,000	3,000
(Fixed) Trucks and forklift depreciation	1,500	1,500
Small tools	700	1,400
(Fixed) Insurance	500	500
(Fixed) Property taxes	300	300
Total	$143,500	$149,000

Instructions

(a) Determine the overhead application rate.
(b) Determine how much overhead was applied to production.
(c) Calculate the controllable overhead variance and the overhead volume variance.
(d) Decide which overhead variances should be investigated.
(e) Discuss causes of the overhead variances. What can management do to improve its performance next month?

Real-World Focus

BYP26-3 **Glassmaster Co.** was incorporated in 1946 as Koolvent Metal Awning Company. Its current name was adopted in 1982 to reflect the more general nature of its products. The company is organized as two divisions and one subsidiary. One division focuses on the manufacture of filaments such as fishing line and sewing thread; the other division manufactures antennas and specialty fiberglass products. Its subsidiary manufactures flexible steel wire controls and molded control panels.

The annual report of Glassmaster provides the following information.

Glassmaster® Company

GLASSMASTER COMPANY
Management Discussion

Gross profit margins for the year improved to 20.9% of sales compared to last year's 18.5%. All operations reported improved margins due in large part to improved operating efficiencies as a result of cost reduction measures implemented during the second and third quarters of the fiscal year and increased manufacturing throughout due to higher unit volume sales. Contributing to the improved margins was a favorable materials price variance due to competitive pricing by suppliers as a result of soft demand for petrochemical-based products. This favorable variance is temporary and will begin to reverse itself as stronger worldwide demand for commodity products improves in tandem with the economy. Partially offsetting these positive effects on profit margins were competitive pressures on sales prices of certain product lines. The company responded with pricing strategies designed to maintain and/or increase market share.

Instructions

(a) Is it apparent from the information whether Glassmaster utilizes standard costs?
(b) Do you think the price variance experienced should lead to changes in standard costs for the next fiscal year?

www.wiley.com/college/weygandt

Exploring the Web

BYP26-4 Computer manufacturer **Hewlett-Packard's** Web site provides information about Hewlett-Packard's 25,000 electronic products and services, its worldwide operations, and its financial picture.

Address:* www.hp.com/ *(or go to www.wiley.com/college/weygandt)

Steps:

1. Choose **HP Financials**.
2. Choose the current **Annual Report**.
3. Review the Summary of Significant Accounting Policies in the Notes to the Financial Statements.

Instructions

(a) At what cost does Hewlett-Packard report its inventories?
(b) What inventory costing method does standard cost approximate for Hewlett-Packard?
(c) Has the lower-of-cost-or-market rule been applied to the Hewlett-Packard inventories?
(d) Why do you suppose that Hewlett-Packard accounts for and reports its inventories at standard cost?

Communication Activity

BYP26-5 The setting of standards is critical to the effective use of standards in evaluating performance.

Instructions
Explain the following in a memo to your instructor.

(a) The comparative advantages and disadvantages of ideal versus normal standards.
(b) The factors that should be included in setting the price and quantity standards for direct materials, direct labor, and manufacturing overhead.

Ethics Case

BYP26-6 At Lofton Manufacturing Company, production workers in the Painting Department are paid on the basis of productivity. The labor time standard for a unit of production is established through periodic time studies conducted by the Fisher Management Department. In a time study, the actual time required to complete a specific task by a worker is observed. Allowances are then made for preparation time, rest periods, and clean-up time. Dion Young is one of several veterans in the Painting Department.

Dion is informed by Fisher Management that he will be used in the time study for the painting of a new product. The findings will be the basis for establishing the labor time standard for the next 6 months. During the test, Dion deliberately slows his normal work pace in an effort to obtain a labor time standard that will be easy to meet. Because it is a new product, the Fisher Management representative who conducted the test is unaware that Dion did not give the test his best effort.

Instructions

(a) Who was benefited and who was harmed by Dion's actions?
(b) Was Dion ethical in the way he performed the time study test?
(c) What measure(s) might the company take to obtain valid data for setting the labor time standard?

Answers to Self-Study Questions

1. c **2.** d **3.** b **4.** c **5.** b **6.** a **7.** d **8.** a **9.** b **10.** c

Remember to go back to the Navigator box on the chapter-opening page and check off your completed work.

27

INCREMENTAL ANALYSIS AND CAPITAL BUDGETING

THE NAVIGATOR ✓

- Understand *Concepts for Review* ❑
- Read *Feature Story* ❑
- Scan *Study Objectives* ❑
- Read *Preview* ❑
- Read text and answer *Before You Go On* *p.* 1112 ❑
- Work *Demonstration Problem 1* ❑
- Read text and answer *Before You Go On* *p.* 1122 ❑
- Work *Demonstration Problem 2* ❑
- Review *Summary of Study Objectives* ❑
- Answer *Self-Study Questions* ❑
- Complete *Assignments* ❑

CONCEPTS FOR REVIEW

Before studying this chapter, you should know or, if necessary, review:

a. The difference between variable and fixed costs. (Ch. 23, pp. 946–948)

b. The meaning of the term contribution margin. (Ch. 23, pp. 954–955)

c. How to use present value tables. (Appendix C)

THE NAVIGATOR

FEATURE STORY

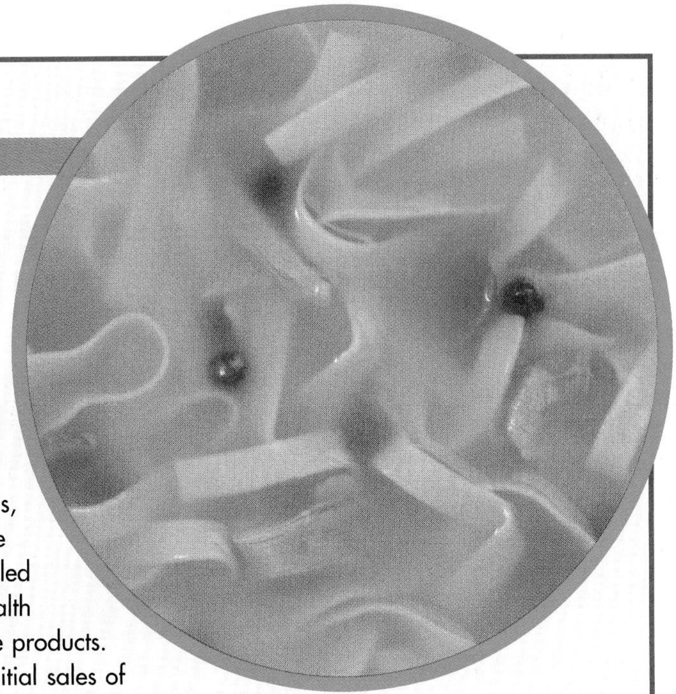

Soup Is Good Food

When you hear the word *Campbell's*, what is the first thing that comes to mind? Soup. Campbell's *is* soup. It sells 38 percent of all the soup—including homemade—consumed in the United States. But can a company survive on soup alone? In an effort to expand its operations and to lessen its reliance on soup, **Campbell Soup Company** began searching for an additional line of business in 1990. Campbell's management believed it saw an opportunity in convenient meals that were low in fat, nutritionally rich, and had therapeutic value for heart patients and diabetics. This venture would require a huge investment—but the rewards were potentially tremendous.

The initial investment required building food labs, hiring nutritional scientists, researching prototype products, constructing new production facilities, and marketing the new products. Management predicted that with an initial investment of roughly $55 million, the company might generate sales of $200 million per year.

By 1994 the company had created 24 meals, and an extensive field-study revealed considerable health benefits from the products. Unfortunately, initial sales of the new product line, called Intelligent Quisine, were less than stellar. In 1997 a consulting firm was hired to evaluate whether the project should be continued. Product development of the new line was costing $20 million per year—a sum that some managers felt could be better spent developing new products in other divisions, or expanding overseas operations. In 1998 the project was discontinued.

Campbell's was not giving up on growth, but simply had decided to refocus its efforts on soup. The company's annual report stated management's philosophy: "Soup will be our growth engine." Campbell's is now selling off many of its non-soup businesses and in a recent year introduced twenty new soup products.

THE NAVIGATOR

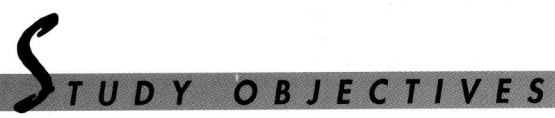

Source: Vanessa O'Connell, "Food for Thought: How Campbell Saw a Breakthrough Menu Turn into Leftovers," *The Wall Street Journal,* October 6, 1998.

www.campbellsoup.com

STUDY OBJECTIVES

After studying this chapter, you should be able to:

1. Identify the steps in management's decision-making process.
2. Describe the concept of incremental analysis.
3. Identify the relevant costs in accepting an order at a special price.
4. Identify the relevant costs in a make-or-buy decision.
5. Give the decision rule for whether to sell or process materials further.
6. Identify the factors to be considered in retaining or replacing equipment.
7. Explain the relevant factors in deciding whether to eliminate an unprofitable segment.
8. Determine which products to make and sell when resources are limited.
9. Contrast the annual rate of return and cash payback techniques in capital budgeting.
10. Distinguish between the net present value and internal rate of return methods.

THE NAVIGATOR

PREVIEW OF CHAPTER 27

An important purpose of management accounting is to provide relevant information for decision making. Examples of these decisions include the following: (1) **Campbell Soup's** decision to produce "therapeutic meals" rather than some other food product. (2) **Boeing's** strategic decisions to spend $5 billion to build a plane for the 21st century—the B-777—and to cancel development of a larger version of the B-747. (3) **The Coca-Cola Company's** decision to spend $750 million to build twelve plants in Russia.

This chapter begins with an explanation of management's decision-making process. It then considers the topics of incremental analysis and capital budgeting.

The content and organization of Chapter 27 are as follows.

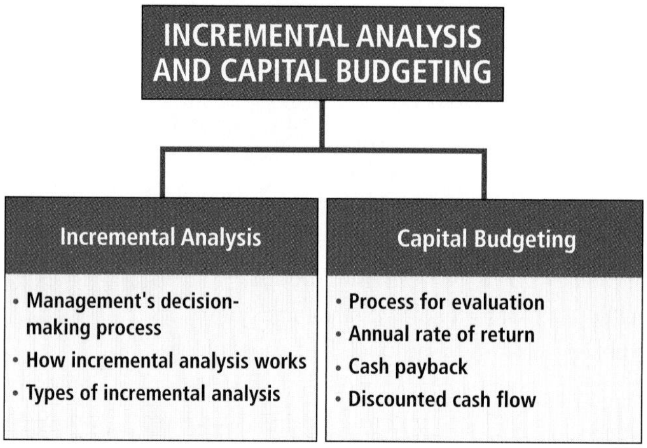

THE NAVIGATOR

SECTION 1 *Incremental Analysis*

MANAGEMENT'S DECISION-MAKING PROCESS

STUDY OBJECTIVE 1

Identify the steps in management's decision-making process.

Making decisions is an important management function. Management's decision-making process does not always follow a set pattern, because decisions vary significantly in their scope, urgency, and importance. It is possible, though, to identify some steps that are frequently involved in the process. These steps are shown in Illustration 27-1.

Accounting's contribution to the decision-making process occurs primarily in Steps 2 and 4. In Step 2, for each possible course of action, relevant revenue and cost data are provided. These show the expected overall effect on net income. In Step 4, internal reports are prepared that review the actual impact of the decision.

In making business decisions, management ordinarily considers both financial and nonfinancial information. **Financial** information is related to revenues and costs and their effect on the company's overall profitability. **Nonfinancial** information relates to such factors as the effect of the decision on employee turnover, the environment, or the overall image of the company in the community. Although the nonfinancial information can be as important as the financial information, we will focus primarily on financial information that is relevant to the decision.

Illustration 27-1

Management's decision-making process

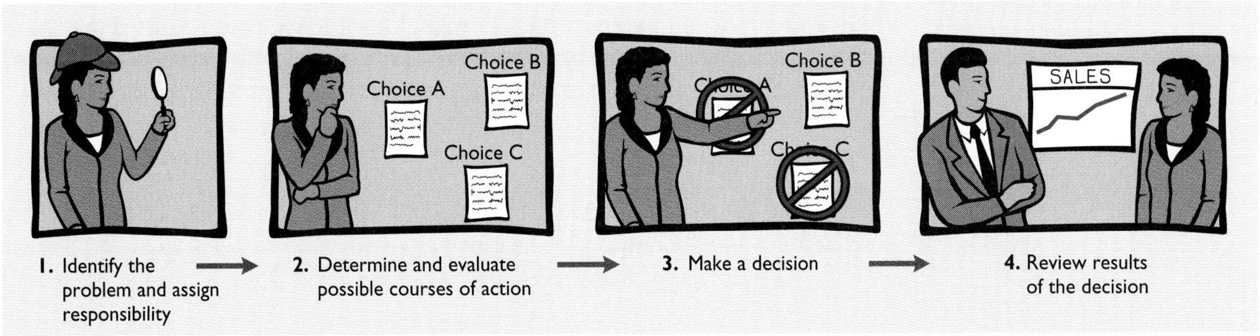
Choice A
Choice B
Choice C
SALES
1. Identify the problem and assign responsibility
2. Determine and evaluate possible courses of action
3. Make a decision
4. Review results of the decision

STUDY OBJECTIVE 2

Describe the concept of incremental analysis.

Decisions involve a choice among alternative courses of action. Suppose that you were deciding whether to purchase or lease an IBM PC for use in doing your accounting homework. The financial data relate to the cost of leasing versus the cost of purchasing. For example, leasing would involve periodic lease payments; purchasing would require "up-front" payment of the purchase price. In other words, the financial data relevant to the decision are the data that would vary among the possible alternatives. The process used to identify the financial data that change under alternative courses of action is called **incremental analysis**. In some cases, you will find that when you use incremental analysis, both costs **and** revenues will change. In other cases, only costs **or** revenues will change.

ALTERNATIVE TERMINOLOGY
Incremental analysis is also called *differential analysis* because the analysis focuses on differences.

Just as your decision to buy or lease a PC will affect your future, similar decisions—on a larger scale—will affect a company's future. Incremental analysis identifies the probable effects of those decisions on future earnings. Such analysis inevitably involves estimates and uncertainty. Gathering data for incremental analyses may involve market analysts, engineers, and accountants. In quantifying the data, the accountant is expected to produce the most reliable information available at the time the decision must be made.

HOW INCREMENTAL ANALYSIS WORKS

The basic approach in incremental analysis is illustrated in the following example.

Illustration 27-2

Basic approach in incremental analysis

	Alternative A	Alternative B	Net Income Increase (Decrease)
Revenues	$125,000	$110,000	**$ (15,000)**
Costs	100,000	80,000	**20,000**
Net income	$ 25,000	$ 30,000	**$ 5,000**

In this example, alternative B is being compared with alternative A. The net income column shows the differences between the alternatives. In this case, incremental revenue will be $15,000 less under alternative B than under alternative A. But a $20,000 incremental cost saving will be realized.[1] Thus, alternative B will produce $5,000 more net income than alternative A.

[1] Although income taxes are sometimes important in incremental analysis, they are ignored in the chapter for simplicity's sake.

Incremental analysis sometimes involves changes that at first glance might seem contrary to your intuition. For example, sometimes variable costs **do not** change under the alternative courses of action. Also, sometimes fixed costs **do** change. For example, direct labor, normally a variable cost, is not an incremental cost in deciding between two new factory machines if each asset requires the same amount of direct labor. In contrast, rent expense, normally a fixed cost, is an incremental cost in a decision to continue occupancy of a building or to purchase or lease a new building.

TYPES OF INCREMENTAL ANALYSIS

A number of different types of decisions involve incremental analysis. The more common types of decisions are whether to:

1. Accept an order at a special price.
2. Make or buy.
3. Sell or process further.
4. Retain or replace equipment.
5. Eliminate an unprofitable business segment.
6. Allocate limited resources.

We will consider each of these types of analysis in the following pages.

ACCEPT AN ORDER AT A SPECIAL PRICE

STUDY OBJECTIVE 3

Identify the relevant costs in accepting an order at a special price.

Sometimes, a company may have an opportunity to obtain additional business if it is willing to make a major price concession to a specific customer. To illustrate, assume that Sunbelt Company produces 100,000 automatic blenders per month, which is 80 percent of plant capacity. Variable manufacturing costs are $8 per unit. Fixed manufacturing costs are $400,000, or $4 per unit. The blenders are normally sold directly to retailers at $20 each. Sunbelt has an offer from Mexico Co. (a foreign wholesaler) to purchase an additional 2,000 blenders at $11 per unit. Acceptance of the offer would not affect normal sales of the product, and the additional units can be manufactured without increasing plant capacity. What should management do?

If management makes its decision on the basis of the total cost per unit of $12 ($8 + $4), the order would be rejected, because costs ($12) would exceed revenues ($11) by $1 per unit. However, since the units can be produced within existing plant capacity, the special order **will not increase fixed costs.** The relevant data for the decision, therefore, are the variable manufacturing costs per unit of $8 and the expected revenue of $11 per unit. Thus, as shown in Illustration 27-3, Sunbelt will increase its net income by $6,000 by accepting this special order.

HELPFUL HINT

This is a good example of different costs for different purposes. In the long-run all costs are relevant, but for this decision only costs that change are relevant.

Illustration 27-3

Incremental analysis—accepting an order at a special price

	Reject Order	Accept Order	Net Income Increase (Decrease)
Revenues	$-0-	$22,000	**$22,000**
Costs	-0-	16,000	**(16,000)**
Net income	$-0-	$ 6,000	**$ 6,000**

Two points should be emphasized: First, it is assumed that sales of the product in other markets would not be affected by this special order. If other sales were affected, then Sunbelt would have to consider the lost sales in making the decision. Second, if Sunbelt is operating at full capacity, it is likely that the special order would be rejected. Under such circumstances, the company would have to expand plant capacity. In that case, the special order would have to absorb these additional fixed manufacturing costs, as well as the variable manufacturing costs.

MAKE OR BUY

STUDY OBJECTIVE 4

Identify the relevant costs in a make-or-buy decision.

When a manufacturer assembles component parts in producing a finished product, management must decide whether to make or buy the components. For example, **General Motors Corporation** may either make or buy the batteries, tires, and radios used in its cars. Similarly, **Zenith Corporation** may make or buy the electronic circuitry, cabinets, and speakers for its television sets. The decision to make or buy components should be made on the basis of incremental analysis.

To illustrate the analysis, assume that Baron Company incurs the following annual costs in producing 25,000 ignition switches for motor scooters.

Illustration 27-4

Annual product cost data

Direct materials	$ 50,000
Direct labor	75,000
Variable manufacturing overhead	40,000
Fixed manufacturing overhead	60,000
Total manufacturing costs	$225,000
Total cost per unit ($225,000 ÷ 25,000)	**$9.00**

Or, Baron Company may purchase the ignition switches from Ignition, Inc. at a price of $8 per unit. The question again is, "What should management do?"

At first glance, it appears that management should purchase the ignition switches for $8, rather than make them at a cost of $9. However, a review of operations indicates that if the ignition switches are purchased from Ignition, Inc., all of Baron's variable costs but only $10,000 of its fixed manufacturing costs will be eliminated. Thus, $50,000 of the fixed manufacturing costs will remain if the ignition switches are purchased. The relevant costs for incremental analysis are as follows.

Illustration 27-5

Incremental analysis—make or buy

	Make	Buy	Net Income Increase (Decrease)
Direct materials	$ 50,000	$ -0-	**$ 50,000**
Direct labor	75,000	-0-	**75,000**
Variable manufacturing costs	40,000	-0-	**40,000**
Fixed manufacturing costs	60,000	50,000	**10,000**
Purchase price (25,000 × $8)	-0-	200,000	**(200,000)**
Total annual cost	$225,000	$250,000	**$ (25,000)**

ETHICS NOTE

In the make-or-buy decision it is important for management to take into account the social impact of their choice. For instance, buying may be the most economically feasible solution, but such action could result in the closure of a manufacturing plant that employs many good workers.

This analysis indicates that Baron Company will incur $25,000 of additional cost by buying the ignition switches. Therefore, Baron should continue to make the ignition switches, even though the total manufacturing cost is $1 higher than the purchase price. The reason is that if the company purchases the ignition switches, it will still have fixed costs of $50,000 to absorb.

The foregoing analysis is complete only if the productive capacity used to make the ignition switches cannot be converted to another purpose. If there is an opportunity to use this productive capacity in some other manner, then this opportunity cost must be considered. **Opportunity cost** is the potential benefit that may be obtained by following an alternative course of action.

To illustrate, assume that through buying the switches, Baron Company can use the released productive capacity to generate additional income of $28,000. This lost income is an additional cost of continuing to make the switches in the make-or-buy decision. This opportunity cost therefore is added to the "Make" column, for comparison. As shown, it is now advantageous to buy the ignition switches.

Illustration 27-6

Incremental analysis—make or buy, with opportunity cost

	Make	Buy	Net Income Increase (Decrease)
Total annual cost	$225,000	$250,000	$(25,000)
Opportunity cost	28,000	-0-	28,000
Total cost	$253,000	$250,000	$ 3,000

The qualitative factors in this decision include the possible loss of jobs for employees who produce the ignition switches. In addition, management must assess how long the supplier will be able to satisfy the company's quality control standards at the quoted price per unit.

ACCOUNTING IN ACTION *Business Insight*

In the bicycle industry, nearly all bikes of quality are made with **Shimano** parts. This dominance by a single supplier has made bikes a sort of commodity. That is, if all bikes are made from the same parts, then what does it matter what brand of bike you buy? As a consequence, the majority of profits go to Shimano, with bike manufacturers that use Shimano parts having to accept an increasingly small profit margin.

To break this trend, and increase its profit margins, **Cannondale Corporation** has decided to take "the approach that we manufacture the whole bicycle, not just taking a frame and putting somebody's parts on it." Similar steps are being taken by **Trek Bicycle Corporation** and **Specialized Bicycle Components Inc.** These companies recognize that they are taking a risk. In order to compete with Shimano, they will have to dramatically step up their research and development efforts and significantly increase their efficiency in the manufacture of parts. This will be difficult given Shimano's huge volume advantage.

SOURCE: Ross Kerber, "Bike Maker Faces a Tactical Shift," *The Wall Street Journal*, October 12, 1998, p. B1.

SELL OR PROCESS FURTHER

STUDY OBJECTIVE 5

Give the decision rule for whether to sell or process materials further.

Many manufacturers have the option of selling products at a given point in the production cycle or continuing to process with the expectation of selling them at a higher price. For example, a bicycle manufacturer such as **Schwinn** could sell its 10-speed bicycles to retailers either unassembled or assembled, and a furniture manufacturer such as **Ethan Allen** could sell its dining room sets to furniture stores either unfinished or finished. The sell-or-process further decision should be made on the basis of incremental analysis. The basic decision rule is: **Process further as long as the incremental revenue from such processing exceeds the incremental processing costs.**

Assume, for example, that Woodmasters Inc. makes tables. The cost to manufacture an unfinished table is $35, computed as follows.

Illustration 27-7

Per unit cost of unfinished table

Direct material	$15
Direct labor	10
Variable manufacturing overhead	6
Fixed manufacturing overhead	4
Manufacturing cost per unit	**$35**

The selling price per unfinished unit is $50. Woodmasters currently has unused productive capacity that is expected to continue indefinitely. Management concludes that some of this capacity can be used to finish the tables and sell them at $60 per unit. For a finished table, direct materials will increase $2 and direct labor costs will increase $4. Variable manufacturing overhead costs will increase by $2.40 (60% of direct labor). No increase is anticipated in fixed manufacturing overhead. The incremental analysis on a per unit basis is as follows.

Illustration 27-8

Incremental analysis—sell or process further

	Sell	Process Further	Net Income Increase (Decrease)
Sales per unit	$50.00	$60.00	**$10.00**
Cost per unit			
Direct materials	15.00	17.00	**(2.00)**
Direct labor	10.00	14.00	**(4.00)**
Variable manufacturing overhead	6.00	8.40	**(2.40)**
Fixed manufacturing overhead	4.00	4.00	**-0-**
Total	$35.00	$43.40	**$(8.40)**
Net income per unit	$15.00	$16.60	**$ 1.60**

HELPFUL HINT

Current net income is known. Net income from processing further is an estimate. In making its decision, management could add a "risk" factor for the estimate.

It would be advantageous for Woodmaster to process the tables further. The incremental revenue of $10.00 from the additional processing is $1.60 higher than the incremental processing costs of $8.40.

RETAIN OR REPLACE EQUIPMENT

STUDY OBJECTIVE 6

Identify the factors to be considered in retaining or replacing equipment.

Management often has to decide whether to continue using an asset or replace it. To illustrate, assume that Jeffcoat Company has a factory machine with a book value of $40,000 and a remaining useful life of 4 years. A new machine is available that costs $120,000. It is expected to have zero salvage value at the end of its 4-year useful life. If the new machine is acquired, variable manufacturing costs are expected to decrease from $160,000 to $125,000 annually, and the old unit will be scrapped. The incremental analysis for the 4-year period is as follows.

Illustration 27-9

Incremental analysis—retain or replace equipment

	Retain Equipment	Replace Equipment	Net Income Increase (Decrease)
Variable manufacturing costs	$640,000[a]	$500,000[b]	**$140,000**
New machine cost		120,000	**(120,000)**
Total	$640,000	$620,000	**$ 20,000**

[a](4 years × $160,000)
[b](4 years × $125,000)

In this case, it would be to the company's advantage to replace the equipment. The lower variable manufacturing costs due to replacement more than offset the cost of the new equipment.

One other point should be mentioned regarding Jeffcoat's decision: **The book value of the old machine does not affect the decision.** Book value is a **sunk cost**, which is a cost that cannot be changed by any present or future decision. Sunk costs **are not relevant in incremental analysis.** In this example, if the asset is retained, book value will be depreciated over its remaining useful life. Or, if the new unit is acquired, book value will be recognized as a loss of the current period. Thus, the effect of book value on current and future earnings is the same regardless of the replacement decision. **Any trade-in allowance or cash disposal value of the existing asset, however, is relevant** to the decision, because this value will not be realized if the asset is continued in use.

ELIMINATE AN UNPROFITABLE SEGMENT

STUDY OBJECTIVE 7

Explain the relevant factors in deciding whether to eliminate an unprofitable segment.

Management sometimes must decide whether to eliminate an unprofitable business segment. Again, the key is to focus on the data that change under the alternative courses of action. To illustrate, assume that Martina Company manufactures tennis racquets in three models: Pro, Master, and Champ. Pro and Master are profitable lines. Champ (highlighted in color in the table below) operates at a loss. Condensed income statement data are:

Illustration 27-10

Segment income data

	Pro	Master	Champ	Total
Sales	$800,000	$300,000	**$100,000**	$1,200,000
Variable expenses	520,000	210,000	**90,000**	820,000
Contribution margin	280,000	90,000	**10,000**	380,000
Fixed expenses	80,000	50,000	**30,000**	160,000
Net income	$200,000	$ 40,000	**$ (20,000)**	$ 220,000

It might be expected that total net income will increase by $20,000 to $240,000 if the unprofitable line of racquets is eliminated. However, **net income may decrease if the Champ line is discontinued.** The reason is that the fixed expenses allocated to the Champ racquets will have to be absorbed by the other products. To illustrate, assume that the $30,000 of fixed costs applicable to the unprofitable segment are allocated 2/3 and 1/3 to the Pro and Master product lines, respectively. Fixed expenses will increase to $100,000 ($80,000 + $20,000) in the Pro line and to $60,000 ($50,000 + $10,000) in the Master line. The revised income statement is:

HELPFUL HINT

A decision to discontinue a segment based solely on the bottom line—net loss—is inappropriate.

Illustration 27-11

Income data after eliminating unprofitable product line

	Pro	Master	Total
Sales	$800,000	$300,000	$1,100,000
Variable expenses	520,000	210,000	730,000
Contribution margin	280,000	90,000	370,000
Fixed expenses	**100,000**	**60,000**	160,000
Net income	$180,000	$ 30,000	**$ 210,000**

Total net income has decreased $10,000 ($220,000 − $210,000). This result is also obtained in the following incremental analysis of the Champ racquets.

Illustration 27-12

Incremental analysis—eliminating an unprofitable segment

	Continue	Eliminate	Net Income Increase (Decrease)
Sales	$ 100,000	$ -0-	**$(100,000)**
Variable expenses	90,000	-0-	**90,000**
Contribution margin	10,000	-0-	**(10,000)**
Fixed expenses	30,000	30,000	**-0-**
Net income	$ (20,000)	$(30,000)	**$ (10,000)**

The loss in net income is attributable to the contribution margin ($10,000) that will not be realized if the segment is discontinued.

In deciding on the future status of an unprofitable segment, management should consider the effect of elimination on related product lines. It may be possible for continuing product lines to obtain some or all of the sales lost by the discontinued product line. In some businesses, services or products may be linked—for example, free checking accounts at a bank, or coffee at a donut shop. In addition, management should consider the effect of eliminating the product line on employees who may have to be discharged or retrained.

ACCOUNTING IN ACTION *Business Insight*

In 1994 **Quaker Oats** paid $1.7 billion for one of America's hottest new beverage companies. While some observers thought that Quaker Oats had overpaid, Quaker's management believed it was an exciting purchase because it would make a great strategic partner for Quaker Oats' famous sport drink—Gatorade. For a variety of reasons, the acquisition didn't work out. One of those reasons was that at about the same time, several other major beverage manufacturers decided to begin producing and selling competing fruit and tea drinks. Worse yet, the processing methods used by these other manufacturers appeared to allow them to produce their drinks much more inexpensively. Only a few years after purchasing the beverage company, Quaker Oats sold it and took a $1.4 billion loss. Management stated that by selling this division, the company could reduce its debt burden and focus on its cereal brands and Gatorade.

ALLOCATE LIMITED RESOURCES

Everyone's resources are limited. For a company, the limited resource may be floor space in a retail department store, or raw materials, direct labor hours, or machine capacity in a manufacturing company. When a company has limited resources,

STUDY OBJECTIVE 8

Determine which products to make and sell when resources are limited.

management must decide which products to make and sell in order to maximize net income.

To illustrate, assume that Collins Company manufactures deluxe and standard pen and pencil sets. The limiting resource is machine capacity, which is 3,600 hours per month. Relevant data consist of the following.

Illustration 27-13

Contribution margin and machine hours

	Deluxe Sets	Standard Sets
Contribution margin per unit	$8	$6
Machine hours required	4	2

HELPFUL HINT

CM alone is not enough in this decision. The key factor is CM per limited resource.

The deluxe sets may appear to be more profitable: they have a higher contribution margin ($8) than the standard sets ($6). However, note that the standard sets take fewer machine hours to produce than the deluxe sets. Therefore, it is necessary to find the **contribution margin per unit of limited resource**, in this case, contribution margin per machine hour. This is obtained by dividing the contribution margin per unit of each product by the number of units of the limited resource required for each product. The computation shows that the standard sets have a higher contribution margin per unit of limited resource.

Illustration 27-14

Contribution margin per unit of limited resource

	Deluxe Sets	Standard Sets
Contribution margin per unit (a)	$8	$6
Machine hours required (b)	4	2
Contribution margin per unit of limited resource [(a) ÷ (b)]	**$2**	**$3**

If Collins Company can increase machine capacity from 3,600 hours to 4,200 hours, the additional 600 hours could be used to produce either the standard or deluxe pen and pencil sets. The total contribution margin under each alternative is found by multiplying the machine hours by the contribution margin per unit of limited resource as shown below.

Illustration 27-15

Incremental analysis—computation of total contribution margin

	Produce Deluxe Sets	Produce Standard Sets
Machine hours (a)	600	600
Contribution margin per unit of limited resource (b)	$2	$3
Contribution margin [(a) × (b)]	**$1,200**	**$1,800**

From this analysis, we can see that to maximize net income, all of the increased capacity should be used to make and sell the standard sets.

BEFORE YOU GO ON...

REVIEW IT

1. Give three examples of how incremental analysis might be used.
2. What is the decision rule in deciding to sell or process products further?
3. How may the elimination of an unprofitable segment decrease the overall net income of a company?
4. What is the critical factor in allocating limited resources?

DO IT

Cobb Company incurs a cost of $28 per unit, of which $18 is variable, to make a product that normally sells for $42. A foreign wholesaler offers to buy 5,000 units at $25 each. Cobb will incur shipping costs of $1 per unit. Compute the net income (loss) Cobb will realize by accepting the special order, assuming Cobb has excess operating capacity. Should Cobb Company accept the special order?

ACTION PLAN

- Identify all revenues that will change as a result of accepting the order.
- Identify all costs that will change as a result of accepting the order, and net this amount against the change in revenues.

SOLUTION

	Reject	**Accept**	**Net Income Increase (Decrease)**
Revenues	$–0–	$125,000	$125,000
Costs	–0–	95,000*	(95,000)
Net income	$–0–	$ 30,000	$ 30,000

*(5,000 × $18) + (5,000 × $1)

Given the result of the above analysis, Cobb Company should accept the special order.

Related exercise material: BE27-2, BE27-3, and E27-1.

THE NAVIGATOR

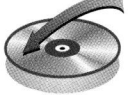

DEMONSTRATION PROBLEM 1

Additional Demonstration Problem

Juanita Company must decide whether to make or buy some of its components. The costs of producing 50,000 electrical cords for its floor lamps are as follows.

Direct materials	$60,000	Variable overhead	$12,000
Direct labor	30,000	Fixed overhed	8,000

Instead of making the electrical cords at an average cost per unit of $2.20 ($110,000 ÷ 50,000), the company has an opportunity to buy the cords at $2.15 per unit. If the cords are purchased, all variable costs and one-half of the fixed costs will be eliminated.

Instructions

(a) Prepare an incremental analysis showing whether the company should make or buy the electrical cords.

(b) Will your answer be different if the released productive capacity will generate additional income of $25,000?

SOLUTION TO DEMONSTRATION PROBLEM 1

ACTION PLAN

- Look for the costs that change.
- Ignore the costs that do not change.
- Use the format in the chapter for your answer.
- Recognize that opportunity cost can make a difference.

(a)

	Make	**Buy**	**Net Income Increase (Decrease)**
Direct materials	$ 60,000	$ –0–	$ 60,000
Direct labor	30,000	–0–	30,000
Variable manufacturing costs	12,000	–0–	12,000
Fixed manufacturing costs	8,000	4,000	4,000
Purchase price	–0–	107,500	(107,500)
Total cost	$110,000	$111,500	$ (1,500)

This analysis indicates that Juanita Company will incur $1,500 of additional costs if it buys the electrical cords.

(b)

	Make	Buy	Net Income Increase (Decrease)
Total cost	$110,000	$111,500	$ (1,500)
Opportunity cost	25,000		25,000
Total cost	$135,000	$111,500	$ 23,500

THE NAVIGATOR

Yes, the answer is different because the analysis shows that net income will be increased by $23,500 if the electrical cords are purchased.

SECTION 2 *Capital Budgeting*

Individuals make capital expenditures when they buy a new home, car, or television set. Similarly, businesses make capital expenditures when they modernize plant facilities or expand operations. Companies like **Campbell Soup** must constantly determine how to invest their resources. Other examples: Hollywood studios recently built 25 new sound stage projects to allow for additional filming in future years. **Starwood Hotels and Resorts Worldwide, Inc.** committed a total of $1 billion in 1998 and 1999 to renovate its existing hotel properties, while at roughly the same time, the hotel industry canceled about $2 billion worth of *new* construction scheduled through the year 2000. And **Union Pacific Resources Group Inc.** announced that it would cut its 1998 capital budget by 19 percent in order to use the funds to reduce its outstanding debt.

In business, as for individuals, the amount of possible capital expenditures usually exceeds the funds available for such expenditures. Thus, the resources available must be allocated (budgeted) among the competing alternatives. The process of making capital expenditure decisions in business is known as **capital budgeting**. Capital budgeting involves choosing among various capital projects to find the one(s) that will maximize a company's return on investment.

PROCESS FOR EVALUATION

Many companies follow a standard process in capital budgeting. At least once a year, proposals for projects are requested from each department. The proposals are screened by a capital budgeting committee, which submits its findings to the officers of the company. The officers, in turn, select the projects they believe to be most worthy of funding. They submit this list to the board of directors. Ultimately, the directors approve the capital expenditure budget for the year.

The involvement of top management and the board of directors in the process demonstrates the importance of capital budgeting decisions. These decisions often have a significant impact on a company's future profitability. In fact, poor capital budgeting decisions have led to the bankruptcy of some companies. Accounting data are indispensable in assessing the probable effects of capital expenditures.

To provide management with relevant data for capital budgeting decisions, you should be familiar with the quantitative techniques that may be used. The three most common techniques are: (1) annual rate of return, (2) cash payback, and (3) discounted cash flow. To illustrate the three quantitative techniques, assume that Tappan Company is considering an investment of $130,000 in new equipment. The new equipment is expected to last 10 years. It will have zero salvage value at the end of its useful life. The straight-line method of depreciation is used for accounting purposes. The expected annual revenues and costs of the new product that will be produced from the investment are:

Sales		$200,000
Less: Costs and expenses		
Manufacturing costs (exclusive of depreciation)	$145,000	
Depreciation expenses ($130,000 ÷ 10)	13,000	
Selling and administrative expenses	22,000	180,000
Income before income taxes		20,000
Income tax expense		7,000
Net income		$ 13,000

Illustration 27-16

Estimated annual net income from capital expenditure

ANNUAL RATE OF RETURN

STUDY OBJECTIVE 9

Contrast the annual rate of return and cash payback techniques in capital budgeting.

The **annual rate of return technique** is based directly on accounting data. It indicates **the profitability of a capital expenditure** by dividing expected annual net income by the average investment. The formula for computing annual rate of return is shown in Illustration 27-17.

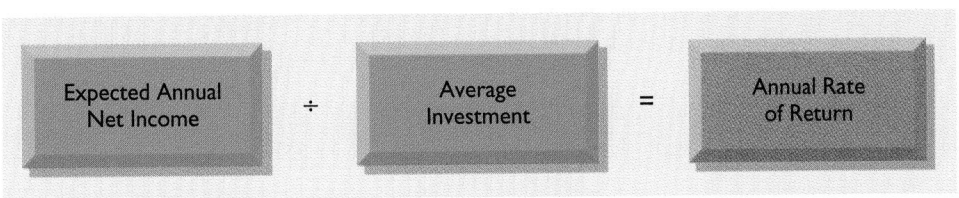

Expected Annual Net Income ÷ Average Investment = Annual Rate of Return

Illustration 27-17

Annual rate of return formula

Expected annual net income is obtained from the projected income statement. Tappan Company's expected annual net income is $13,000. Average investment is derived from the following formula.

$$\text{Average investment} = \frac{\text{Original investment} + \text{Value at end of useful life}}{2}$$

Illustration 27-18

Formula for computing average investment

The value at the end of useful life is equal to the asset's salvage value, if any. For Tappan Company, average investment is $65,000 [($130,000 + $0) ÷ 2]. The expected annual rate of return for Tappan Company's investment in new equipment is therefore 20 percent, computed as follows:

$$\$13{,}000 \div \$65{,}000 = 20\%$$

Management then compares this annual rate of return with its required minimum rate of return for investments of similar risk. The minimum rate of return (also called the **hurdle rate** or **cutoff rate**) is generally based on the company's **cost of capital**. The cost of capital is the rate of return that management expects to pay on all borrowed and equity funds. It does not relate to the cost of funding a specific project. The decision rule is: **A project is acceptable if its rate of return is greater than management's minimum rate of return. It is unacceptable when the reverse is true.** When the rate of return technique is used in deciding among several acceptable projects, **the higher the rate of return for a given risk, the more attractive the investment.**

The principal advantages of this technique are simplicity of calculation and management's familiarity with the accounting terms used in the computation. A major limitation of the annual rate of return approach is that it does not consider the time value of money. For example, no consideration is given as to whether cash inflows will occur early or late in the life of the investment. As explained in Appendix C, recognition of the time value of money can make a significant difference between the future value and the present value of an investment.

HELPFUL HINT

A capital budgeting decision based on only one technique may be misleading. It is often wise to analyze the investment from a number of different perspectives.

CASH PAYBACK

The **cash payback technique** identifies the time period required to recover the cost of the capital investment from the annual cash inflow produced by the investment. The formula for computing the cash payback period is:

Illustration 27-19
Cash payback formula

Cost of Capital Investment	÷	Annual Cash Inflow	=	Cash Payback Period

HELPFUL HINT
Annual cash inflow can also be approximated by net cash provided by operating activities from the statement of cash flows.

Annual (or **net**) **cash inflow** is approximated by taking net income and adding back depreciation expense. Depreciation expense is added back because depreciation on the capital expenditure does not involve an annual outflow of cash. Accordingly, the depreciation deducted in determining net income must be added back to determine annual cash inflows. In the Tappan Company example, annual cash inflow is $26,000, as shown below.

Illustration 27-20
Computation of annual cash inflow

Net income	$13,000
Add: Depreciation expense	13,000
Annual cash inflow	**$26,000**

The cash payback period in this example is therefore 5 years, computed as follows.

$$\$130{,}000 \div \$26{,}000 = 5 \text{ years}$$

The evaluation of the payback period is often related to the expected useful life of the asset. For example, assume that at Tappan Company a project is unacceptable if the payback period is longer than 60 percent of the asset's expected useful life. The 5-year payback period in this case is 50 percent of the project's expected useful life. Thus, the project is acceptable. It follows that when the payback technique is used to decide among acceptable alternative projects, **the shorter the payback period, the more attractive the investment**. This is true for two reasons: (1) The earlier the investment is recovered, the sooner the cash funds can be used for other purposes. And (2) the risk of loss from obsolescence and changed economic conditions is less in a shorter payback period.

The cash payback technique may be useful as an initial screening tool. It also may be the most critical factor in the capital budgeting decision for a company that desires a fast turnaround of its investment because of a weak cash position. Like the annual rate of return, cash payback is relatively easy to compute and understand.

However, cash payback should not ordinarily be the only basis for the capital budgeting decision because it ignores the expected profitability of the project. To illustrate, assume that Projects A and B have the same payback period, but Project A's useful life is double the useful life of Project B's. Project A's earning power, therefore, is twice as long as Project B's. A further disadvantage of this technique is that it ignores the time value of money.

STUDY OBJECTIVE 10
Distinguish between the net present value and internal rate of return methods.

DISCOUNTED CASH FLOW

The **discounted cash flow technique** is generally recognized as the best conceptual approach to making capital budgeting decisions. This technique considers both the estimated total cash inflows from the investment and the time value of money.

The expected total cash inflow consists of the sum of the annual cash inflows plus the estimated liquidation proceeds when the asset is sold for salvage at the end of its useful life. But because liquidation proceeds are generally immaterial, they are ignored in subsequent discussions.

Two methods are used with the discounted cash flow technique: (1) net present value and (2) internal rate of return. Before we discuss the methods, we recommend that you examine Appendix C if you need a review of present value concepts.

NET PRESENT VALUE METHOD

Under the **net present value method**, cash inflows are discounted to their present value and then compared with the capital outlay required by the investment. The difference between these two amounts is referred to as **net present value**. The interest rate to be used in discounting the future cash inflows is the required minimum rate of return. The decision rule is this: **A proposal is acceptable when net present value is zero or positive**. This means that the rate of return on the investment equals or exceeds the required rate of return. When net present value is negative, the project is unacceptable. Illustration 27-21 shows the net present value decision criteria.

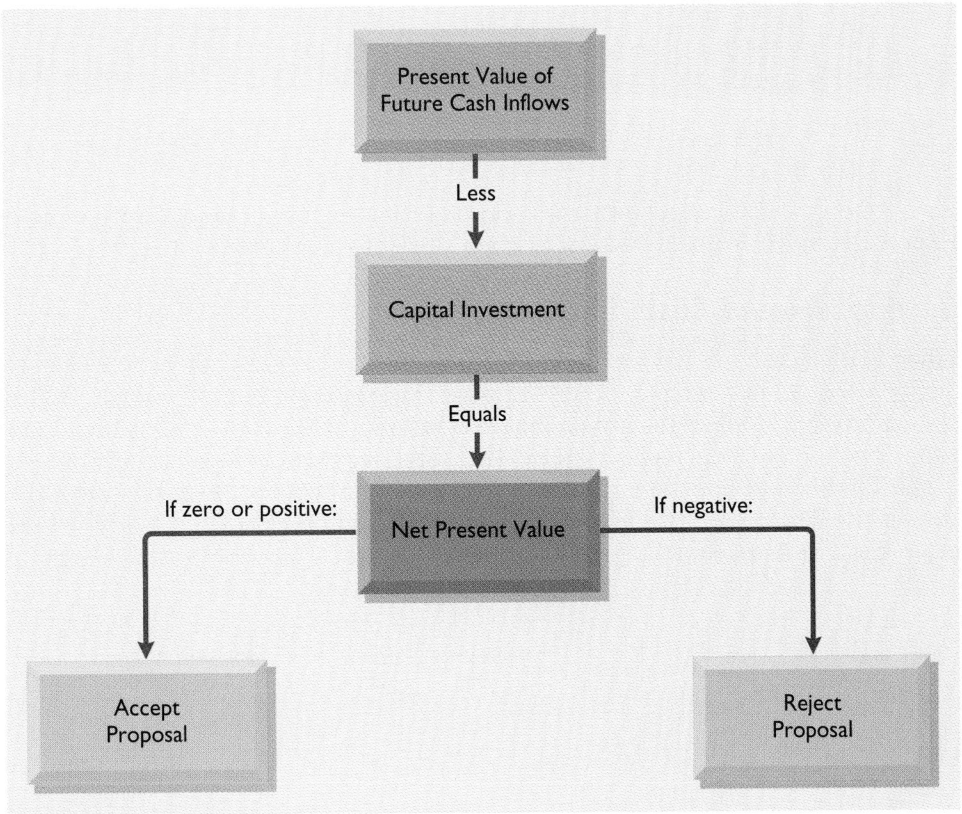

Illustration 27-21

Net present value decision criteria

When making a selection among acceptable proposals, **the higher the positive net present value, the more attractive the investment**. The application of this method to two cases is described in the next two sections. In each case, we will assume that the investment has no salvage value.

> **ETHICS NOTE**
>
> Discounted future cash flows may not take into account all of the important considerations needed to make an informed capital budgeting decision. Other issues, for example, could include worker safety, product quality, and environmental impact.

Equal Annual Cash Flows

Tappan Company's annual cash inflows are $26,000. If we assume this amount **is uniform over the asset's useful life**, the present value of the annual cash inflows can be computed by using the present value of an annuity of 1 for 10 periods (in Table 2, Appendix C). The computations at rates of return of 12 percent and 15 percent, respectively, are:

Illustration 27-22

Present value of annual cash inflows

	Present Values at Different Discount Rates	
	12%	15%
Discount factor for 10 periods	5.65022	5.01877
Present value of cash inflows:		
$26,000 × 5.65022	**$146,906**	
$26,000 × 5.01877		**$130,488**

The analysis of the proposal by the net present value method is as follows:

Illustration 27-23

Computations of net present value

	12%	15%
Present value of future cash inflows	$146,906	$130,488
Capital investment	130,000	130,000
Positive (negative) net present value	**$ 16,906**	**$ 488**

HELPFUL HINT

The ABC Co. expects equal cash flows over an asset's 5-year useful life. What discount factor should be used in determining present values if management wants (1) a 12 percent return or (2) a 15 percent return? Answer: Using Table 2, the factors are (1) 3.60478 and (2) 3.35216.

The proposed capital expenditure is acceptable at a required rate of return of both 12 percent and 15 percent because the net present values are positive.

Unequal Annual Cash Inflows

When annual cash inflows are unequal, we cannot use annuity tables to calculate their present value. Instead, tables showing the **present value of a single future amount must be applied to each annual cash inflow**. To illustrate, assume that Tappan Company management expects the same aggregate annual cash inflow ($260,000) but a declining market demand for the new product over the life of the equipment. The present value of the annual cash flows is calculated as follows using Table 1 in Appendix C.

Illustration 27-24

Computing present value of unequal annual cash inflows

		Discount Factor		Present Value	
Year	Assumed Annual Cash Inflows	12%	15%	12%	15%
	(1)	(2)	(3)	(1) × (2)	(1) × (3)
1	$ 36,000	.89286	.86957	$ 32,143	$ 31,305
2	32,000	.79719	.75614	25,510	24,196
3	29,000	.71178	.65752	20,642	19,068
4	27,000	.63552	.57175	17,159	15,437
5	26,000	.56743	.49718	14,753	12,927
6	24,000	.50663	.43233	12,159	10,376
7	23,000	.45235	.37594	10,404	8,647
8	22,000	.40388	.32690	8,885	7,192
9	21,000	.36061	.28426	7,573	5,969
10	20,000	.32197	.24719	6,439	4,944
	$260,000			**$155,667**	**$140,061**

Therefore, the analysis of the proposal by the net present value method is as follows.

Illustration 27-25

Analysis of proposal using net present value method

	12%	15%
Present value of future cash inflows	$155,667	$140,061
Capital investment	130,000	130,000
Positive (negative) net present value	**$ 25,667**	**$ 10,061**

In this example, the present values of the cash inflows are greater than the $130,000 capital investment. Thus, the project is acceptable at both a 12 percent and 15 percent required rate of return. The difference between the present values using the 12 percent rate under equal cash inflows ($146,906) and unequal cash inflows ($155,667) is due to the pattern of the inflows.

ACCOUNTING IN ACTION *Business Insight*

Inaccurate trend forecasting and market positioning are often more detrimental to a capital budget decision than using the wrong discount rate. **Ampex** patented the VCR, but failed to see its market potential. **Westinghouse** made the same mistake with flat-screen video display. More often, companies adopt projects or businesses but later discontinue them in response to market changes. **Texas Instruments** announced it would stop manufacturing computer chips, after investing to become one of the world's leading suppliers. The company has dropped out of some twelve business lines in recent years.

SOURCE: World Research Advisory Inc. (London), August 1998, page 4.

INTERNAL RATE OF RETURN METHOD

The internal rate of return method finds the **interest yield of the potential investment**. The internal rate of return is the rate that will cause the present value of the proposed capital expenditure to equal the present value of the expected annual cash inflows. The determination of the internal rate of return involves two steps.

Step 1. Compute the internal rate of return factor. The formula for this factor is:

Illustration 27-26

Formula for internal rate of return factor

Capital Investment ÷ Annual Cash Inflows = Internal Rate of Return Factor

The computation for the Tappan Company, assuming equal annual cash inflows[2] is:

$$\$130,000 \div \$26,000 = 5.0$$

[2]When annual cash inflows are equal, the internal rate of return factor is the same as the cash payback period.

Step 2. Use the factor and the present value of an annuity of 1 table to find the internal rate of return. Table 2 of Appendix C is used in this step. The internal rate of return is found by locating the discount factor that is closest to the internal rate of return factor for the time period covered by the annual cash flows.

In Tappan Company, the annual cash inflows are expected to continue for 10 years. Thus, it is necessary to read across the period-10 row in Table 2 to find the discount factor. Row 10 is reproduced below for your convenience.

TABLE 2
PRESENT VALUE OF AN ANNUITY OF 1

(n) Periods	5%	6%	8%	9%	10%	11%	12%	15%
10	7.72173	7.36009	6.71008	6.41766	6.14457	5.88923	5.65022	**5.01877**

In this case, the closest discount factor to 5.0 is 5.01877, which represents an interest rate of approximately 15 percent. The rate of return can be further determined by interpolation, but since we are using estimated annual cash flows such precision is seldom required.

The internal rate of return that has been determined is then compared to management's required minimum rate of return. The decision rule is: **Accept the project when the internal rate of return is equal to or greater than the required rate of return. Reject the project when the internal rate of return is less than the required rate.** These relationships are shown graphically in Illustration 27-27. Assuming the minimum required rate of return is 10 percent for Tappan Company, the project is acceptable because the 15 percent internal rate of return is greater than the required rate.

The internal rate of return method is widely used in practice. Most managers find the internal rate of return easy to interpret.

Illustration 27-27

Internal rate of return decision criteria

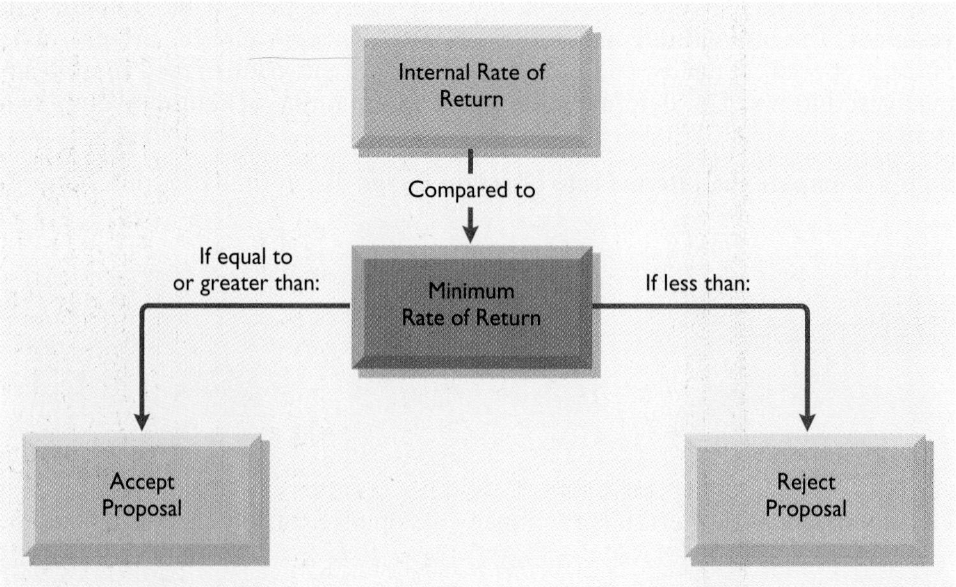

ACCOUNTING IN ACTION *Business Insight*

Which capital budgeting methods are used the most? One survey asked financial officers which method they used in considering expenditures for factory automation. Internal rate of return and cash payback were the most popular methods. Subjective evaluation—though not, strictly speaking, a capital budgeting method—also turned out to be popular with finance professionals.

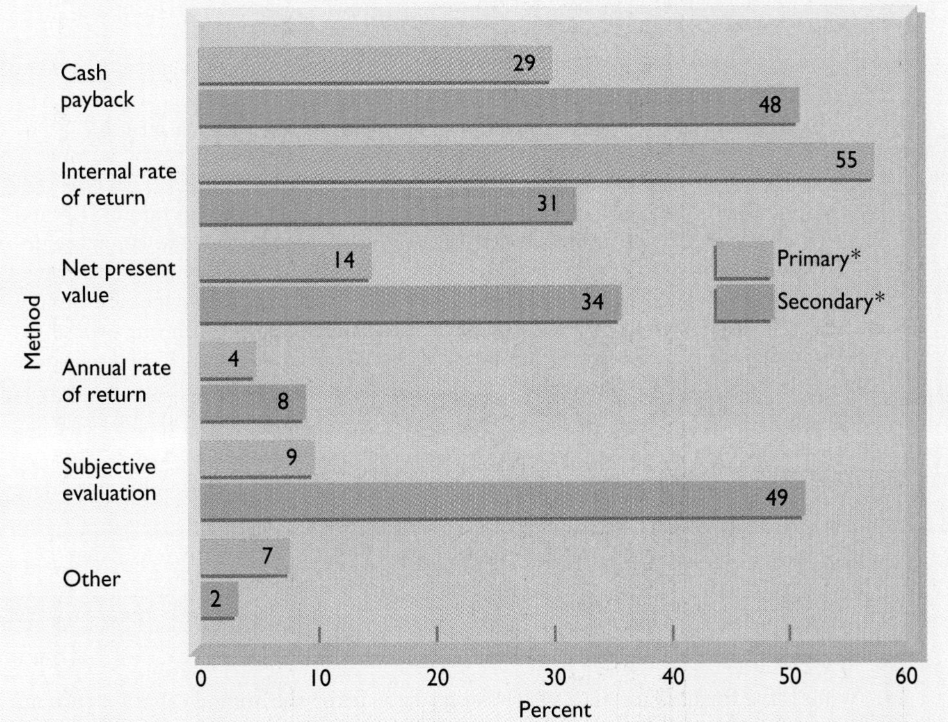

*The percentages in each column sum to more than 100% because some respondents indicated the use of more than one primary technique and many respondents use more than one secondary technique.

SOURCE: James A. Hendricks, "Applying Cost Accounting to Factory Automation," *Management Accounting.*

COMPARISON OF DISCOUNTED CASH FLOW METHODS

A comparison of the two discounted cash flow methods—net present value and internal rate of return—is presented in Illustration 27-28. When properly used, either method will provide management with relevant quantitative data for making capital budgeting decisions.

Illustration 27-28

Comparison of discounted cash flow methods

Item	Net Present Value	Internal Rate of Return
1. Objective	Compute net present value (a dollar amount).	Compute internal rate of return (a percentage).
2. Decision rule	If net present value is zero or positive, accept the proposal. If net present value is negative, reject the proposal.	If internal rate of return is equal to or greater than the minimum required rate of return, accept the proposal. If internal rate of return is less than the minimum rate, reject the proposal.

ACCOUNTING IN ACTION e Business Insight

One reason that e-business is changing the face of business so quickly is that the cost of the necessary hardware and software has fallen so rapidly. For example, an executive at **General Electric (GE)** reports that the company developed software for its own electronic-auction site for only $15,000. In discussing e-business related capital expenditures, a GE executive in Europe noted, "the incremental investment required is extraordinarily small compared with our overall investment. A $300 million investment for a company making $4 billion to $5 billion is [just a few] weeks of cash flow." He added that the cash payback period on these projects is a few months, rather than years. Thus, GE experienced almost "instant" productivity gains.

SOURCE: "E-Management: Inside the Machine," *The Economist*, November 11, 2000.

BEFORE YOU GO ON...

REVIEW IT

1. What is the formula for and the decision rule in using the annual rate of return method?
2. What is the formula for the cash payback method?
3. When is a proposal acceptable under (a) the net present value method and (b) the internal rate of return method?
4. What does **Lands' End** report as its return on average assets for 2000? (See Lands' End's 11-year summary of selected financial data.) Since 1990, what has been the trend in Lands' End's return on average assets? The answer to this question is provided on page 1138.

A LOOK BACK AT OUR FEATURE STORY

Refer back to the Feature Story about **Campbell Soup Company** at the beginning of the chapter, and answer the following questions.

1. What decisions faced by Campbell Soup Company might benefit from incremental analysis?
2. In what ways does the story about Campbell Soup demonstrate the statement, "Capital budgeting is only as good as its inputs"?

SOLUTION

1. Campbell Soup's decisions that might benefit from incremental analysis would be: (a) the decision whether to accept an order at a special price (e.g., a large order from the armed forces); (b) retain or replace processing equipment; (c) eliminate an unprofitable business segment, such as "Intelligent Quisine"; (d) allocate limited processing resources.

2. Capital budgeting decisions are based on many assumptions and estimates about future costs and revenues. The analysis surrounding Campbell's decision to invest in the "Intelligent Quisine" project demonstrates that effective capital budgeting is only as good as the accuracy of these assumptions and estimates. If management underestimates costs, or overestimates revenues, the company will invest in projects that will not be profitable.

THE NAVIGATOR

DEMONSTRATION PROBLEM 2

Sierra Company is considering a long-term capital investment project called ZIP. The project will require an investment of $120,000, and it will have a useful life of 4 years. Annual net income for ZIP is expected to be: Year 1, $12,000; Year 2, $10,000; Year 3, $8,000; and Year 4, $6,000. Depreciation is computed by the straight-line method with no salvage value. The company's cost of capital is 12%.

Additional Demonstration Problem

Instructions

(Round all computations to two decimal places.)

(a) Compute the annual rate of return for the project.

(b) Compute the cash payback period for the project. (Round to two decimals.)

(c) Compute the net present value for the project. (Round to nearest dollar.)

(d) Should the project be accepted? Why?

SOLUTION TO DEMONSTRATION PROBLEM 2

(a) $9,000 ($36,000 ÷ 4) ÷ $60,000 ($120,000 ÷ 2) = 15%

(b) $120,000 ÷ $39,000 ($9,000 + $30,000) = 3.08 years

(c)

Year	Discount Factor	Cash Inflow	Present Value
1	.89286	$42,000	$ 37,500
2	.79719	40,000	31,888
3	.71178	38,000	27,048
4	.63552	36,000	22,879
			119,315
		Capital investment	120,000
		Negative net present value	$ (685)

(d) The annual rate of return of 15% is good. However, the cash payback period is 77% of the project's useful life, and net present value is negative. The recommendation is to reject the project.

ACTION PLAN

- To compute annual rate of return, divide expected annual net income by average investment.
- To compute cash payback, divide cost of the investment by annual cash inflows.
- Recall that annual cash inflow equals annual net income plus annual depreciation expense.
- Be careful to use the correct discount factor in using the net present value method.

THE NAVIGATOR

SUMMARY OF STUDY OBJECTIVES

1. *Identify the steps in management's decision-making process.* Management's decision-making process consists of (a) identifying the problem or opportunity, (b) assigning responsibility for the decision, (c) determining possible courses of action, (d) developing data relevant to each course of action, (e) making the decision, and (f) reviewing the results of the decision.

2. *Describe the concept of incremental analysis.* Incremental analysis is the process that is used to identify financial data that change under alternative courses of action. These data are relevant to the decision because they will vary in the future among the possible alternatives.

3. *Identify the relevant costs in accepting an order at a special price.* The relevant information in accepting an order at a special price is the difference between the variable manufacturing costs to produce the special order and expected revenues.

4. *Identify the relevant costs in a make-or-buy decision.* In a make-or-buy decision, the relevant costs are (a) the variable manufacturing costs that will be saved, (b) the purchase price, and (c) opportunity costs.

5. *Give the decision rule for whether to sell or process materials further.* The decision rule for whether to sell or process materials further is: Process further as long as the incremental revenue from processing exceeds the incremental processing costs.

6. ***Identify the factors to be considered in retaining or replacing equipment.*** The factors to be considered in determining whether equipment should be retained or replaced are the effects on variable costs and the cost of the new equipment. Also, any disposal value of the existing asset must be considered.

7. ***Explain the relevant factors in deciding whether to eliminate an unprofitable segment.*** In deciding whether to eliminate an unprofitable segment, it is necessary to determine the contribution margin, if any, produced by the segment and the disposition of the segment's fixed expenses.

8. ***Determine which products to make and sell when resources are limited.*** When a company has limited resources, it is necessary to find the contribution margin per unit of limited resource. Then multiply this amount by the units of limited resource to determine which product maximizes net income.

9. ***Contrast the annual rate of return and cash payback techniques in capital budgeting.*** The annual rate of return is obtained by dividing expected annual net income by the average investment. The higher the rate of return, the more attractive the investment. The cash payback technique identifies the time period to recover the cost of the investment. The formula is: Cost of capital expenditure divided by estimated annual cash inflow equals cash payback period. The shorter the payback period, the more attractive the investment.

10. ***Distinguish between the net present value and internal rate of return methods.*** Under the net present value method, the present value of future cash inflows is compared with the capital investment to determine net present value. The decision rule is: Accept the project if net present value is zero or positive. Reject the investment if net present value is negative.

Under the internal rate of return method, the objective is to find the interest yield of the potential investment. The decision rule is: Accept the project when the internal rate of return is equal to or greater than the required rate of return. Reject the project when the internal rate of return is less than the required rate.

THE NAVIGATOR

Key Term Matching Activity

GLOSSARY

Annual rate of return technique The determination of the profitability of a capital expenditure by dividing expected annual net income by the average investment. (p. 1115).

Capital budgeting The process of making capital expenditure decisions in business. (p. 1114).

Cash payback technique A capital budgeting technique that identifies the time period required to recover the cost of a capital investment from the annual cash inflow produced by the investment. (p. 1116).

Cost of capital The rate of return that management expects to pay on all borrowed and equity funds. (p. 1115).

Discounted cash flow technique A capital budgeting technique that considers both the estimated total cash inflows from the investment and the time value of money. (p. 1116).

Incremental analysis The process of identifying the financial data that change under alternative courses of action. (p. 1105).

Internal rate of return The rate that will cause the present value of the proposed capital expenditure to equal the present value of the expected annual cash inflows. (p. 1119).

Internal rate of return method A method used in capital budgeting that results in finding the interest yield of the potential investment. (p. 1119).

Net present value The difference that results when the original capital outlay is subtracted from the discounted cash inflows. (p. 1117).

Net present value method A method used in capital budgeting in which cash inflows are discounted to their present value and then compared to the capital outlay required by the investment. (p. 1117).

Opportunity cost The potential benefit that may be obtained from following an alternative course of action. (p. 1108).

Sunk cost A cost that cannot be changed by any present or future decision. (p. 1110).

Chapter 27 Self-Test

SELF-STUDY QUESTIONS

Answers are at the end of the chapter.

(SO 1) **1.** Three of the steps in management's decision process are: (1) Review results of decision. (2) Develop data relevant to each course of action. (3) Make the decision. The steps are prepared in the following order.
a. (1), (2), (3).
b. (3), (2), (1).
c. (2), (1), (3).
d. (2), (3), (1).

(SO 2) **2.** Incremental analysis is the process of identifying the financial data that:
a. do not change under alternative courses of action.
b. change under alternative courses of action.
c. are mixed under alternative courses of action.
d. No correct answer is given.

3. It costs a company $14 of variable costs and $6 of fixed costs to produce product A that sells for $30. A foreign buyer offers to purchase 3,000 units at $18 each. If the special offer is accepted and produced with unused capacity, net income will: (SO 3)
a. decrease $6,000.
b. increase $6,000.
c. increase $12,000.
d. increase $9,000.

(SO 4) **4.** In a make-or-buy decision, relevant costs are:
a. manufacturing costs that will be saved.
b. the purchase price of the units.
c. opportunity costs.
d. all of the above.

(SO 5) **5.** The decision rule in a sell-or-process-further decision is: Process further as long as the incremental revenue from process exceeds:
a. incremental processing costs.
b. variable processing costs.
c. fixed processing costs.
d. No correct answer is given.

(SO 6) **6.** In a decision to retain or replace equipment, the book value of the old equipment is a(n):
a. opportunity cost.
b. sunk cost.
c. incremental cost.
d. marginal cost.

(SO 7) **7.** If an unprofitable segment is eliminated:
a. net income will always increase.
b. variable expenses of the eliminated segment will have to be absorbed by other segments.
c. fixed expenses allocated to the eliminated segment will have to be absorbed by other segments.
d. net income will always decrease.

8. If the contribution margin per unit is $15 and it takes 3.0 machine hours to produce the unit, the contribution margin per unit of limited resource is: (SO 8)
a. $25.
b. $5.
c. $45.
d. No correct answer is given.

9. Which of the following is *incorrect* about the annual rate of return technique? (SO 9)
a. The calculation is simple.
b. The accounting terms used are familiar to management.
c. The timing of the cash inflows is not considered.
d. The time value of money is considered.

10. A positive net present value means that the: (SO 10)
a. project's rate of return is less than the cutoff rate.
b. project's rate of return exceeds the required rate of return.
c. project's rate of return equals the required rate of return.
d. project is unacceptable.

THE NAVIGATOR

QUESTIONS

1. What steps are frequently involved in management's decision-making process?
2. Your roommate, Terry Duffy, contends that accounting contributes to most of the steps in management's decision-making process. Is your roommate correct? Explain.
3. "Incremental analysis involves the accumulation of information concerning a single course of action. "Do you agree? Why?
4. Stan Free asks your help concerning the relevance of variable and fixed costs in incremental analysis. Help Stan with his problem.
5. What data are relevant in deciding whether to accept an order at a special price?
6. Mike Muzzillo Company has an opportunity to buy parts at $7 each that currently cost $10 to make. What manufacturing costs are relevant to this make-or-buy decision?
7. Define the term "opportunity cost." How may this cost be relevant in a make-or-buy decision?
8. What is the decision rule in deciding whether to sell a product or process it further?
9. Your roommate, Loren Foelske, is confused about sunk costs. Explain to your roommate the meaning of sunk costs and their relevance to a decision to retain or replace equipment.
10. Cindy Tisinai Inc. has one product line that is unprofitable. What circumstances may cause overall company net income to be lower if the unprofitable product line is eliminated?
11. How is the contribution margin per unit of limited resources computed?
12. Describe the process a company may use in screening and approving the capital expenditure budget.
13. Your classmate, Jana Kingston, is confused about the factors that are included in the annual rate of return technique. What is the formula for this technique?
14. Jose Trevino is trying to understand the term "cost of capital." Define the term, and indicate its relevance to the decision rule under the annual rate of return technique.
15. Charles Barth claims the formula for the cash payback technique is the same as the formula for the annual rate of return technique. Is Charles correct? What is the formula for the cash payback technique?
16. What are the advantages and disadvantages of the cash payback technique?
17. Two types of present value tables may be used with the discounted cash flow technique. Identify the tables and the circumstance(s) when each table should be used.
18. What is the decision rule under the net present value method?
19. Identify the steps required in using the internal rate of return method.
20. Roger Holloway Company uses the internal rate of return method. What is the decision rule for this method?

BRIEF EXERCISES

Identify the steps in management's decision-making process.
(SO 1)

BE27-1 The steps in management's decision-making process are listed in random order below. Indicate the order in which the steps should be executed.

— Make decision.
— Identify the opportunity or problem.
— Assign responsibility for decision.
— Review results of decision.
— Determine possible courses of action.
— Develop data relevant to each course of action.

Determine incremental changes.
(SO, 2)

BE27-2 Diehl Company is considering two alternatives. Alternative A will have sales of $150,000 and costs of $100,000. Alternative B will have sales of $185,000 and costs of $125,000. Compare Alternative A to Alternative B showing incremental revenues, costs, and net income.

Determine whether to accept a special order.
(SO 3)

BE27-3 In Armanda Company it costs $30 per unit ($20 variable and $10 fixed) to make a product that normally sells for $45. A foreign wholesaler offers to buy 4,000 units at $23 each. Armanda will incur special shipping costs of $1 per unit. Assuming that Armanda has excess operating capacity, indicate the net income (loss) Armanda would realize by accepting the special order.

Determine whether to make or buy a part.
(SO 4)

BE27-4 Sparrow Manufacturing incurs unit costs of $8 ($5 variable and $3 fixed) in making a sub-assembly part for its finished product. A supplier offers to make 10,000 of the part at $6.00 per unit. If the offer is accepted, Sparrow will save all variable costs but no fixed costs. Prepare an analysis showing the total cost saving, if any, Sparrow will realize by buying the part.

Determine whether to sell or process further.
(SO 5)

BE27-5 Kleckner Inc. makes unfinished bookcases that it sells for $60. Production costs are $30 variable and $10 fixed. Because it has unused capacity, Kleckner is considering finishing the bookcases and selling them for $70. Variable finishing costs are expected to be $6 per unit with no increase in fixed costs. Prepare an analysis on a per unit basis showing whether Kleckner should sell unfinished or finished bookcases.

Determine whether to retain or replace equipment.
(SO 6)

BE27-6 Alice Company has a factory machine with a book value of $90,000 and a remaining useful life of 4 years. A new machine is available at a cost of $200,000. This machine will have a 4-year useful life with no salvage value. The new machine will lower annual variable manufacturing costs from $600,000 to $440,000. Prepare an analysis showing whether the old machine should be retained or replaced.

Determine whether to eliminate an unprofitable segment.
(SO 7)

BE27-7 Kansas, Inc. manufactures golf clubs in three models. For the year, the Eagle line has a net loss of $20,000 from sales $200,000, variable expenses $180,000, and fixed expenses $40,000. If the Eagle line is eliminated, $25,000 of fixed costs will remain. Prepare an analysis showing whether the Eagle line should be eliminated.

Show allocation of limited resources.
(SO 8)

BE27-8 In Seabee Company, data concerning two products are: Contribution margin per unit—Product A $9, Product B $12; machine hours required for one unit—Product A 2, Product B 3. Compute the contribution margin per unit of limited resource for each product.

Compute the cash payback period for a capital investment.
(SO 9)

BE27-9 Satina Company is considering purchasing new equipment for $400,000. It is expected that the equipment will produce annual net income of $24,000 over its 10-year useful life. Annual depreciation will be $40,000. Compute the payback period.

Compute net present value of an investment.
(SO 10)

BE27-10 Desi Company accumulates the following data concerning a proposed capital investment: cash cost $225,000, annual cash inflow $42,000, present value factor of cash inflows for 10 years 5.65 (rounded). Determine the net present value, and indicate whether the investment should be made.

EXERCISES

Make incremental analysis for special order.
(SO 3)

E27-1 Cortez Company manufactures toasters. For the first 8 months of 2003, the company reported the following operating results while operating at 75% of plant capacity.

Sales (400,000 units)	$4,000,000
Cost of goods sold	2,400,000
Gross profit	1,600,000
Operating expenses	900,000
Net income	$ 700,000

Cost of goods sold was 70% variable and 30% fixed. Operating expenses were 60% variable and 40% fixed.

In September, Cortez Company receives a special order for 25,000 toasters at $6.00 each from Alazar Company of Mexico City. Acceptance of the order would result in $3,000 of shipping costs but no increase in fixed operating expenses.

Instructions

(a) Prepare an incremental analysis for the special order.

(b) Should Cortez Company accept the special order? Why or why not?

Make incremental analysis for make-or-buy decision.
(SO 4)

E27-2 Roland Inc. has been manufacturing its own shades for its table lamps. The company is currently operating at 100% of capacity. Variable manufacturing overhead is charged to production at the rate of 50% of direct labor cost. The direct materials and direct labor cost per unit to make the lamp shades are $4.00 and $6.00, respectively. Normal production is 40,000 table lamps per year.

A supplier offers to make the lamp shades at a price of $13.50 per unit. If Roland Inc. accepts the supplier's offer, all variable manufacturing costs will be eliminated, but the $40,000 of fixed manufacturing overhead currently being charged to the lamp shades will have to be absorbed by other products.

Instructions

(a) Prepare the incremental analysis for the decision to make or buy the lamp shades.

(b) Should Roland Inc. buy the lamp shades?

(c) Would your answer be different in (b) if the productive capacity released by not making the lamp shades could be used to produce income of $35,000?

Make incremental analysis for further processing of materials.
(SO 5)

E27-3 Sandy Santiago recently opened her own basketweaving studio. She sells finished baskets in addition to the raw materials needed by customers to weave baskets of their own. Sandy has put together a variety of raw material kits, each including materials at various stages of completion. Unfortunately, owing to space limitations, Sandy is unable to carry all varieties of kits originally assembled and must choose between two basic packages.

The basic introductory kit includes undyed, uncut reeds (with dye included) for weaving one basket. This basic package costs Sandy $12 and sells for $27. The second kit, called Stage 2, includes cut reeds that have already been dyed. With this kit the customer need only soak the reeds and weave the basket. Sandy is able to produce the second kit by using the basic materials included in the first kit and adding one hour of her own time, which she values at $18 per hour. Because she is more efficient at cutting and dying reeds than her average customer, Sandy is able to make two kits of the dyed reeds, in one hour, from one kit of undyed reeds. The kit of dyed and cut reeds sells for $34.

Instructions

Determine whether Sandy's basketweaving shop should carry the basic introductory kit with undyed and uncut reeds, or the Stage 2 kit with reeds already dyed and cut. Prepare an incremental analysis to support your answer.

Make incremental analysis for retaining or replacing equipment.
(SO 6)

E27-4 Cheng Enterprises uses a word processing computer to handle its sales invoices. Lately, business has been so good that it takes an extra 3 hours per night, plus every third Saturday, to keep up with the volume of sales invoices. Management is considering updating its computer with a faster model that would eliminate all of the overtime processing.

	Current Machine	New Machine
Original purchase cost	$15,000	$21,000
Accumulated depreciation	6,000	—
Estimated operating costs	20,000	16,000
Useful life	5 years	5 years

If sold now, the current machine would have a salvage value of $3,000. If operated for the remainder of its useful life, the current machine would have zero salvage value. The new machine is expected to have zero salvage value after 5 years.

Instructions

Should the current machine be replaced? (Ignore the time value of money.)

Make incremental analysis concerning elimination of division.
(SO 7)

E27-5 Amy O'Neil, a recent graduate of Rolling's accounting program, evaluated the operating performance of Winser Company's six divisions. Amy made the following presentation to

Winser's Board of Directors and suggested the Ketchum Division be eliminated. "If the Ketchum Division is eliminated," she said, "our total profits would increase by $16,870."

	The Other Five Divisions	Ketchum Division	Total
Sales	$1,664,200	$ 98,200	$1,762,400
Cost of goods sold	978,520	76,470	1,054,990
Gross profit	685,680	21,730	707,410
Operating expenses	527,940	38,600	566,540
Net income	$ 157,740	$(16,870)	$ 140,870

In the Ketchum Division, cost of goods sold is $56,000 variable and $20,470 fixed, and operating expenses are $14,000 variable and $24,600 fixed. None of the Ketchum Division's fixed costs will be eliminated if the division is discontinued.

Instructions

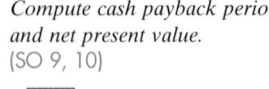

Is Amy right about eliminating the Ketchum Division? Prepare a schedule to support your answer.

Compute contribution margin and determine the product to be manufactured.
(SO 8)

E27-6 Stein Company manufactures and sells three products. Relevant per unit data concerning each product are given below.

	Product A	Product B	Product C
Selling price	$8	$12	$14
Variable costs and expenses	$4	$ 9	$12
Machine hours to produce	2	1	2

Instructions

(a) Compute the contribution margin per unit of the limited resource (machine hour) for each product.

(b) Assuming 3,000 additional machine hours are available, which product should be manufactured?

(c) Prepare an analysis showing the total contribution margin if the additional hours are (1) divided equally among the products, and (2) allocated entirely to the product identified in (b) above.

Compute cash payback period and annual rate of return.
(SO 9)

E27-7 Henning Service Center just purchased an automobile hoist for $11,000. The hoist has a 5-year life and an estimated salvage value of $960. Installation costs were $2,900, and freight charges were $660. Henning uses straight-line depreciation.

The new hoist will be used to replace mufflers and tires on automobiles. Henning estimates that the new hoist will enable his mechanics to replace four extra mufflers per week. Each muffler sells for $65 installed. The cost of a muffler is $35, and the labor cost to install a muffler is $10.

Instructions

(a) Compute the payback period for the new hoist.

(b) Compute the annual rate of return for the new hoist. (Round to one decimal.)

Compute cash payback period and net present value.
(SO 9, 10)

E27-8 Jimmy Castle Manufacturing Company is considering three new projects, each requiring an equipment investment of $23,000. Each project will last for 3 years and produce the following cash inflows.

Year	AA	BB	CC
1	$ 7,500	$ 9,500	$13,000
2	9,000	9,500	9,000
3	15,000	9,500	11,000
Total	$31,500	$28,500	$33,000

The equipment's salvage value is zero. Castle uses straight-line depreciation. Castle will not accept any project with a payback period over 2 years. Castle's minimum required rate of return is 15%.

Instructions

(a) Compute each project's payback period, indicating the most desirable project and the least desirable project using this method. (Round to two decimals.)

(b) Compute the net present value of each project. Does your evaluation change? (Round to nearest dollar.)

Compute annual rate of return, cash payback period, and net present value.
(SO 9, 10)

E27-9 Hinckley Company is considering a capital investment of $150,000 in additional productive facilities. The new machinery is expected to have a useful life of 5 years with no salvage value. Depreciation is by the straight-line method. During the life of the investment, annual net income and cash inflows are expected to be $12,000 and $42,000, respectively. Hinckley has a 15% cost of capital rate, which is the minimum acceptable rate of return on the investment.

Instructions

(Round to two decimals.)

(a) Compute (1) the annual rate of return and (2) the cash payback period on the proposed capital expenditure.

(b) Using the discounted cash flow technique, compute the net present value.

Determine internal rate of return.
(SO 10)

E27-10 Tucci Company is considering three capital expenditure projects. Relevant data for the projects are as follows.

Project	Investment	Annual Income	Life of Project
22A	$240,000	$15,000	6 years
23A	270,000	21,400	9 years
24A	288,000	20,000	8 years

Annual income is constant over the life of the project. Each project is expected to have zero salvage value at the end of the project. Tucci Company uses the straight-line method of depreciation.

Instructions

(a) Determine the internal rate of return for each project. Round the internal rate of return factor to three decimals.

(b) If Tucci Company's minimum required rate of return is 11%, which projects are acceptable?

PROBLEMS: SET A

Make incremental analysis for special order, and identify nonfinancial factors in decisions.
(SO 3)

P27-1A Ramos Company is currently producing 16,000 units per month, which is 80% of its production capacity. Variable manufacturing costs are currently $11.00 per unit. Fixed manufacturing costs are $48,000 per month. Ramos pays a 9% sales commission to its sales people, has $30,000 in fixed administrative expenses per month, and is averaging $320,000 in sales per month.

A special order received from a foreign company would enable Ramos Company to operate at 100% capacity. The foreign company offered to pay 75% of Ramos's current selling price per unit. If the order is accepted, Ramos will have to spend an extra $2.00 per unit to package the product for overseas shipping. Also, Ramos Company would need to lease a new stamping machine to imprint the foreign company's logo on the product, at a monthly cost of $2,500. The special order would require a sales commission of $3,000.

Instructions

(a) Compute the number of units involved in the special order and the foreign company's offered price per unit.

(b) What is the manufacturing cost of producing one unit of Ramos's product for regular customers?

(c) Prepare an incremental analysis of the special order. Should management accept the order?

(d) What is the lowest price that Ramos could accept for the special order to earn net income of $1.20 per unit?

(e) What nonfinancial factors should management consider in making its decision?

Make incremental analysis related to make or buy; consider opportunity cost, and identify nonfinancial factors.
(SO 4)

P27-2A The management of Mendez Manufacturing Company has asked for your assistance in deciding whether to continue manufacturing a part or to buy it from an outside supplier. The part, called Tropica, is a component of Mendez's finished product.

An analysis of the accounting records and the production data revealed the following information for the year ending December 31, 2002.

1. The Machinery Department produced 36,000 units of Tropica.
2. Each Tropica unit requires 10 minutes to produce. Three people in the Machinery Department work full time (2,000 hours per year) producing Tropica. Each person is paid $11.00 per hour.
3. The cost of materials per Tropica unit is $2.00.
4. Manufacturing costs directly applicable to the production of Tropica are: indirect labor, $5,500; utilities, $1,300; depreciation, $1,600; property taxes and insurance, $1,000. All of the costs will be eliminated if Tropica is purchased.
5. The lowest price for a Tropica from an outside supplier is $3.70 per unit. Freight charges will be $0.30 per unit, and a part-time receiving clerk at $8,500 per year will be required.
6. If Tropica is purchased, the excess space will be used to store Mendez's finished product. Currently, Mendez rents storage space at approximately $0.60 per unit stored per year. Approximately 4,500 units per year are stored in the rented space.

Instructions

(a) Prepare an incremental analysis for the make-or-buy decision. Should Mendez make or buy the part? Why?

(b) Prepare an incremental analysis, assuming the released facilities can be used to produce $10,000 of net income in addition to the savings on the rental of storage space. What decision should now be made?

(c) What nonfinancial factors should be considered in the decision?

Compute contribution margin, and prepare incremental analysis concerning elimination of divisions.
(SO 7)

P27-3A Sorrento Manufacturing Company has four operating divisions. During the first quarter of 2002 the company reported total income from operations of $61,000 and the following results for the divisions.

	Division			
	Boston	**Miami**	**San Diego**	**Tacoma**
Sales	$450,000	$730,000	$920,000	$520,000
Cost of goods sold	380,000	480,000	576,000	430,000
Selling and administrative expenses	120,000	207,000	246,000	120,000
Income (loss) from operations	$(50,000)	$ 43,000	$ 98,000	$(30,000)

Analysis reveals the following percentages of variable costs in each division.

	Boston	**Miami**	**San Diego**	**Tacoma**
Cost of goods sold	95%	80%	90%	90%
Selling and administrative expenses	80	60	70	60

Discontinuance of any division would save 60% of the fixed costs and expenses for that division.

Top management is deeply concerned about the unprofitable divisions (Boston and Tacoma). The consensus is that one or both of the divisions should be eliminated.

Instructions

(a) Compute the contribution margin for the two unprofitable divisions.

(b) Prepare an incremental analysis concerning the possible elimination of (1) the Boston Division and (2) the Tacoma Division. What course of action do you recommend for each division?

(c) Prepare a columnar condensed income statement using the CVP format for Sorrento Manufacturing Company, assuming (1) the Boston Division is eliminated, and (2) the unavoidable fixed costs and expenses of the Boston Division are allocated 30% to Miami, 50% to San Diego, and 20% to Tacoma.

(d) Compare the total income from operations with the Boston Division ($61,000) to total income from operations without this division.

P27-4A The Shmi Corporation is considering three long-term capital investment proposals. Relevant data on each project are as follows.

Compute rate of return, cash payback, and net present value.
(SO 9, 10)

	Project		
	Brown	Red	Yellow
Capital investment	$160,000	$200,000	$250,000
Annual net income:			
Year 1	25,000	20,000	31,000
2	16,000	20,000	24,000
3	13,000	20,000	23,000
4	10,000	20,000	22,000
5	8,000	20,000	20,000
Total	$ 72,000	$100,000	$120,000

Salvage value is expected to be zero at the end of each project. Depreciation is computed by the straight-line method. The company's minimum rate of return is the company's cost of capital which is 12%.

Instructions

(a) Compute the average annual rate of return for each project. (Round to two decimals.)
(b) Compute the cash payback period for each project. (Round to two decimals.)
(c) Compute the net present value for each project. (Round to nearest dollar.)
(d) Rank the projects on each of the foregoing bases. Which project do you recommend?

P27-5A Tammy Schipper is managing director of the Village Day Care Center. Village is currently set up as a full-time child care facility for children between the ages of 12 months and 6 years. Tammy is trying to determine whether the center should expand its facilities to incorporate a newborn care room for infants between the ages of 6 weeks and 12 months. The necessary space already exists. An investment of $20,000 would be needed, however, to purchase cribs, high chairs, etc. The equipment purchased for the room would have a 5-year useful life with zero salvage value.

Compute annual rate of return, cash payback, and net present value.
(SO 9, 10)

The newborn nursery would be staffed to handle 12 infants on a full-time basis. The parents of each infant would be charged $150 weekly, and the facility would operate 52 weeks of the year. Staffing the nursery would require two full-time specialists and five part-time assistants at an annual cost of $74,000. Food, diapers, and other miscellaneous supplies are expected to total $14,000 annually.

Instructions

(a) Determine (1) annual net income and (2) cash inflow for the new nursery.
(b) Compute (1) the annual rate of return and (2) the cash payback period for the new nursery. (Round to two decimals.)
(c) Assuming that Village can borrow the money needed for expansion at 12%, compute the net present value of the new room. (Round to the nearest dollar.)
(d) What should Tammy conclude from these computations?

PROBLEMS: SET B

P27-1B High-Five Inc. manufactures basketballs for the National Basketball Association (NBA). For the first 6 months of 2003, the company reported the following operating results while operating at 90% of plant capacity.

Make incremental analysis for special order, and identify nonfinancial factors in decision.
(SO 3)

	Amount	Per Unit
Sales	$4,500,000	$50.00
Cost of goods sold	3,600,000	40.00
Selling and administrative expenses	360,000	4.00
Net income	$ 540,000	$ 6.00

Fixed costs for the period were: Cost of goods sold $900,000, and selling and administrative expenses $180,000.

In July, normally a slack manufacturing month, High-Five receives a special order for 5,000 basketballs at $34 each from the Italian Basketball Association (IBA). Acceptance of the order would increase variable selling and administrative expenses $0.40 per unit because of shipping costs but would not increase fixed costs and expenses.

Instructions

(a) Prepare an incremental analysis for the special order.
(b) Should High-Five Inc. accept the special order?
(c) What is the minimum selling price on the special order to produce net income of $3.00 per ball?
(d) What nonfinancial factors should management consider in making its decision?

Make incremental analysis related to make or buy; consider opportunity cost, and identify nonfinancial factors.
(SO 4)

P27-2B The management of Oswego Manufacturing Company is trying to decide whether to continue manufacturing a part or to buy it from an outside supplier. The part, called WISCO, is a component of the company's finished product.

The following information was collected from the accounting records and production data for the year ending December 31, 2003.

1. 7,000 units of WISCO were produced in the Machining Department.
2. Variable manufacturing costs applicable to the production of each WISCO unit were: direct materials $4.75, direct labor $4.80, indirect labor $0.45, utilities $0.35.
3. Fixed manufacturing costs applicable to the production of WISCO were:

Cost Item	Direct	Allocated
Depreciation	$1,600	$ 900
Property taxes	400	200
Insurance	900	600
	$2,900	$1,700

All variable manufacturing and direct fixed costs will be eliminated if WISCO is purchased. Allocated costs will have to be absorbed by other production departments.

4. The lowest quotation for 7,000 WISCO units from a supplier is $77,000.
5. If WISCO units are purchased, freight and inspection costs would be $0.30 per unit, and receiving costs totaling $750 per year would be incurred by the Machining Department.

Instructions

(a) Prepare an incremental analysis for WISCO. Your analysis should have columns for (1) Make WISCO, (2) Buy WISCO, and (3) Net Income Increase/Decrease.
(b) Based on your analysis, what decision should management make?
(c) Would the decision be different if Oswego Company has the opportunity to produce $5,000 of net income with the facilities currently being used to manufacture WISCO? Show computations.
(d) What nonfinancial factors should management consider in making its decision?

Compute contribution margin, and prepare incremental analysis concerning elimination of divisions.
(SO 7)

P27-3B Steffan Manufacturing Company has four operating divisions. During the first quarter of 2003, the company reported aggregate income from operations of $165,000 and the following divisional results.

	Division			
	I	II	III	IV
Sales	$490,000	$410,000	$300,000	$200,000
Cost of goods sold	300,000	250,000	270,000	180,000
Selling and administrative expenses	60,000	80,000	35,000	60,000
Income (loss) from operations	$130,000	$ 80,000	$ (5,000)	$ (40,000)

Analysis reveals the following percentages of variable costs in each division.

	I	II	III	IV
Cost of goods sold	70%	80%	75%	90%
Selling and administrative expenses	40	50	60	70

Discontinuance of any division would save 50% of the fixed costs and expenses for that division.

Top management is very concerned about the unprofitable divisions (III and IV). Consensus is that one or both of the divisions should be discontinued.

Instructions

(a) Compute the contribution margin for Divisions III and IV.

(b) Prepare an incremental analysis concerning the possible discontinuance of (1) Division III and (2) Division IV. What course of action do you recommend for each division?

(c) Prepare a columnar condensed income statement for Steffan Manufacturing, assuming Division IV is eliminated. Use the CVP format. Division IV's unavoidable fixed costs are allocated equally to the continuing divisions.

(d) Reconcile the total income from operations ($165,000) with the total income from operations without Division IV.

Compute rate of return, cash payback, and net present value.
(SO 9, 10)

P27-4B The Oslo Corporation is considering three long-term capital investment proposals. Each investment has a useful life of 5 years. Relevant data on each project are as follows.

	Project Tic	Project Tac	Project Toe
Capital investment	$160,000	$180,000	$200,000
Annual net income:			
Year 1	13,000	18,000	27,000
2	13,000	17,000	22,000
3	13,000	16,000	21,000
4	13,000	12,000	18,000
5	13,000	9,000	12,000
Total	$ 65,000	$ 72,000	$100,000

Depreciation is computed by the straight-line method with no salvage value. The company's cost of capital is 15%.

Instructions

(a) Compute the annual rate of return for each project. (Round to two decimals.)

(b) Compute the cash payback period for each project. (Round to two decimals.)

(c) Compute the net present value for each project. (Round to nearest dollar.)

(d) Rank the projects on each of the foregoing bases. Which project do you recommend?

Compute annual rate of return, cash payback, and net present value.
(SO, 9, 10)

P27-5B Sara Donish is an accounting major at a midwestern state university located approximately 60 miles from a major city. Many of the students attending the university are from the metropolitan area and visit their homes regularly on the weekends. Sara, an entrepreneur at heart, realizes that few good commuting alternatives are available for students doing weekend travel. She believes that a weekend commuting service could be organized and run profitably from several suburban and downtown shopping mall locations. Sara has gathered the following investment information.

1. Six used vans would cost a total of $66,000 to purchase and would have a 3-year useful life with negligible salvage value. Sara plans to use straight-line depreciation.
2. Ten drivers would have to be employed at a total payroll expense of $50,000.
3. Other annual out of pocket expenses associated with running the commuter service would include Gasoline $12,000, Maintenance $2,800, Repairs $3,500, Insurance $3,200, Advertising $1,500. (Exclude interest expense.)
4. Sara has visited several financial institutions to discuss funding for her new venture. The best interest rate she has been able to negotiate is 12%. Use this rate for cost of capital.
5. Sara expects each van to make nine round trips weekly and carry an average of five students each trip. The service is expected to operate 30 weeks each years. Each student will be charged $12.00 for a round-trip ticket.

Instructions

(a) Determine the annual (1) net income, and (2) cash inflow for the commuter service.

(b) Compute (1) the annual rate of return, and (2) the cash payback period. (Round to two decimals.)

(c) Compute the net present value of the commuter service. (Round to the nearest dollar.)

(d) What should Sara conclude from these computations?

COMPREHENSIVE PROBLEM: CHAPTERS 20 TO 27

You would like to start a business manufacturing a unique model of bicycle helmet. In preparation for an interview with the bank to discuss your financing needs, you develop answers to the following questions. A number of assumptions are required; clearly note all assumptions that you make.

Instructions

(a) Identify the types of costs that would likely be involved in making this product.

(b) Set up five columns as indicated.

	Product Costs			
Item	Direct Materials	Direct Labor	Manufacturing Overhead	Period Costs

Classify the costs you identified in (a) into the manufacturing cost classifications of product costs (direct materials, direct labor, and manufacturing overhead) and period costs.

(c) Assign hypothetical monthly dollar figures to the costs you identified in (a) and (b).

(d) Assume you have no raw materials or work in process beginning or ending inventories. Prepare a projected cost of goods manufactured schedule for the first month of operations.

(e) Project the number of helmets you expect to produce the first month of operations. Compute the cost to produce one bicycle helmet. Review the result to ensure it is reasonable; if not, return to part (c) and adjust the monthly dollar figures you assigned accordingly.

(f) What type of cost accounting system will you likely use—job order or process costing?

(g) Explain how you would assign costs in either the job order or process costing system you plan to use.

(h) Classify your costs as either variable or fixed costs. For simplicity, assign all costs to either variable or fixed, assuming there are no mixed costs, using the format shown.

Item	Variable Costs	Fixed Costs	Total Costs

(i) Compute the unit variable cost, using the production number you determined in (e).

(j) Project the number of helmets you anticipate selling the first month of operations. Set a unit selling price, and compute both the contribution margin per unit and the contribution margin ratio.

(k) Determine your break-even point in dollars and in units.

(l) Prepare projected operating budgets (sales, production, direct materials, direct labor, manufacturing overhead, selling and administrative expense, and income statement).

Assumptions will be required for each of the following:

Direct materials budget:	Quantity of direct materials required to produce one helmet; cost per unit of quantity; desired ending direct materials (assume none).
Direct labor budget:	Direct labor time required per helmet; direct labor cost per hour.
Budgeted income statement:	Income tax expense is 45% of income from operations.

(m) Prepare a cash budget for the month.

Assume the percentage of sales that will be collected from customers is 75%, and the percentage of direct materials that will be paid in the current month is 75%.

(n) Determine a relevant range of activity, using the number of helmets produced as your activity index. Recast your manufacturing overhead budget into a flexible monthly budget for two additional activity levels.

(o) Identify one potential cause of materials, direct labor, and manufacturing overhead variances for your product.

(p) Assume that you wish to purchase production equipment that costs $720,000. Determine the cash payback period, utilizing the monthly cash flow that you computed in part (m) multiplied by 12 months (for simplicity).

(q) Identify any non-quantitative factors that should be considered before commencing your business venture.

BROADENING YOUR PERSPECTIVE

GROUP DECISION CASE

BYP27-1 Barrister Company is considering the purchase of a new machine. The invoice price of the machine is $115,000, freight charges are estimated to be $4,000, and installation costs are expected to be $6,000. Salvage value of the new equipment is expected to be zero after a useful life of 4 years. Existing equipment could be retained and used for an additional 4 years if the new machine is not purchased. At that time, the salvage value of the equipment would be zero. If the new machine is purchased now, the existing machine would be scrapped. Barrister's accountant, Diane Gallup, has accumulated the following data regarding annual sales and expenses with and without the new machine.

1. Without the new machine, Barrister can sell 11,000 units of product annually at a per unit selling price of $100. If the new unit is purchased, the number of units produced and sold would increase by 20%. The selling price would remain the same.
2. The new machine is faster than the old machine, and it is more efficient in its usage of materials. With the old machine the gross profit rate will be 26.5% of sales. With the new machine the rate will be 28% of sales.
3. Annual selling expenses are $180,000 with the current equipment. Because the new equipment would produce a greater number of units to be sold, annual selling expenses are expected to increase by 10% if it is purchased.
4. Annual administrative expenses are expected to be $100,000 with the old machine and $113,000 with the new machine.
5. The current book value of the existing machine is $36,000. Barrister uses straight-line depreciation.
6. Barrister's management wants a minimum rate of return of 15% on its investment and a payback period of no more than 3 years.

Instructions

With the class divided into groups, answer the following. (Ignore income tax effects.)

(a) Prepare an incremental analysis for the 4 years showing whether Barrister should keep the existing machine or buy the new machine.
(b) Calculate the annual rate of return for the new machine. (Round to two decimals.)
(c) Compute the payback period for the new machine. (Round to two decimals.)
(d) Compute the net present value of the new machine. (Round to the nearest dollar.)
(e) On the basis of the foregoing data, would you recommend that Barrister buy the machine? Why?

MANAGERIAL ANALYSIS

BYP27-2 Sanchez Company manufactures private-label small electronic products, such as alarm clocks, calculators, kitchen timers, stopwatches, and automatic pencil sharpeners. Some of the products are sold as sets, and others are sold individually. Products are studied as to their sales potential, and then cost estimates are made. The Engineering Department develops production plans, and then production begins. The company has generally had very successful product introduction. Only two products introduced by the company have been discontinued.

One of the products currently sold is a multi-alarm alarm clock. The clock has four alarms that can be programmed to sound at various times and for varying lengths of time. The company has experienced a great deal of difficulty in making the circuit boards for the clocks. The production process has never operated smoothly. The product is unprofitable at the present time, primarily because of warranty repairs and product recalls. Two models of the clocks were recalled, for example, because they sometimes caused an electric shock when the alarms were being shut off. The Engineering Department is attempting to revise the manufacturing process, but the revision will take another 6 months at least.

The clocks were very popular when they were introduced, and since they are private-label, the company has not suffered much from the recalls. Presently, the company has a very large order for several items from Kmart Stores. The order includes 5,000 of the multi-alarm clocks. When the company suggested that Kmart purchase the clocks from another manufacturer, Kmart threatened to rescind the entire order unless the clocks were included.

The company has therefore investigated the possibility of having another company make the clocks for them. The clocks were bid for the Kmart order, based on an estimated $5 cost to manufacture, as follows.

Circuit board, 1 each @ $1.00	$1.00
Plastic case, 1 each @ $0.50	0.50
Alarms, 4 @ $0.15 each	0.60
Labor, 15 minutes @ $10/hour	2.50
Overhead, $1.60 per labor hour	0.40

Sanchez could purchase clocks to fill the Kmart order for $9 from Silver Star, a Korean manufacturer with a very good quality record. Silver Star has offered to reduce the price to $7.50 after Sanchez has been a customer for 6 months, placing an order of at least 1,000 units per month. If Sanchez becomes a "preferred customer" by purchasing 15,000 units per year, the price would be reduced still further to $4.50.

Alpha Products, a local manufacturer, has also offered to make clocks for Sanchez. They have offered to sell 5,000 clocks for $3 each. However, Alpha Products has been in business for only 6 months. They have experienced significant turnover in their labor force, and the local media have reported that the owners may soon face tax evasion charges. The owner of Alpha Products is an electronic engineer, however, and the quality of the clocks is likely to be good.

If Sanchez decides to purchase the clocks from either Silver Star or Alpha, all the costs to manufacturer could be avoided, except a total of $5,000 in overhead costs for machine depreciation. The machinery is fairly new, and has no alternate use.

Instructions

(a) What is the difference in profit under each of the alternatives if the clocks are to be sold for $12.50 each to Kmart?

(b) What are the most important nonfinancial factors that Sanchez should consider when making this decision?

(c) What should Sanchez do in regard to the Kmart order? What should it do in regard to continuing to manufacture the multi-alarm alarm clocks? Be prepared to defend your answer.

REAL-WORLD FOCUS

BYP27-3 Founded in 1983, the **Beverly Hills Fan Company** is located in Woodland Hills, California. With 23 employees and sales of less than $10 million, the company is relatively small. Management feels that there is potential for growth in the upscale market for ceiling fans and lighting. They are particularly optimistic about growth in Mexican and Canadian markets.

Presented below is information from the president's letter in the company's annual report.

BEVERLY HILLS FAN COMPANY
President's Letter

An aggressive product development program was initiated during the past year resulting in new ceiling fan models planned for introduction in 1993. Award winning industrial designer Ron Rezek created several new fan models for the Beverly Hills Fan and L.A. Fan lines, including a new Showroom Collection, designed specifically for the architectural and designer markets. Each of these models has received critical acclaim, and order commitments for 1993 have been outstanding. Additionally, our Custom Color and special order fans continued to enjoy increasing popularity and sales gains as more and more customers desire fans that match their specific interior decors. Currently, Beverly Hills Fan Company offers a product line of over 100 models of contemporary, traditional, and transitional ceiling fans.

Instructions

(a) What points did the company management need to consider before deciding to offer the special-order fans to customers?

(b) How would incremental analysis be employed to assist in this decision?

EXPLORING THE WEB

BYP27-4 **Campbell Soup Company** is an international provider of soup products. Management is very interested in continuing to grow the company in its core business, while "spinning off" those businesses that are not part of its core operation.

Address: **www.campbellsoups.com** ***(or go to www.wiley.com/college/weygandt)***

Steps:

1. Go to the home page of Campbell Soup Company at the address shown above.
2. Choose **Financial Center**.
3. Choose **Financial Reports**.
4. Choose the 2000 annual report, or the current annual report if 2000 is no longer available.

Instructions

Review the financial statements and management's discussion and analysis, and answer the following questions.

(a) What was the total amount reported as "Purchase of Plant Assets" in the 2000 statement of cash flows? How does this amount compare with the previous year?

(b) What range of interest rates does the company report on its long-term liabilities in the notes to its financial statements?

(c) Assume that this year's capital expenditures are expected to increase cash flows by $35 million. What is the expected internal rate of return (IRR) for these capital expenditures? (Assume a 10-year period for the cash flows.)

COMMUNICATION ACTIVITY

BYP27-5 Refer back to Exercise 27-7 to address the following.

Instructions

Prepare a memo to Mary Ann Griffin, your supervisor. Show your calculations from E27-7, parts **(a)** and **(b)**. In one or two paragraphs, discuss important nonfinancial considerations. Make any assumptions you believe to be necessary. Make a recommendation, based on your analysis.

ETHICS CASE

BYP27-6 Bristle Brush Company operates in a state where corporate taxes and workmen's compensation insurance rates have recently doubled. Bristle's president has assigned you the task of preparing an economic analysis and making a recommendation about whether to move the company's entire operation to Missouri. The president is slightly in favor of such a move because Missouri is his boyhood home, and he also owns a fishing lodge there.

You have just completed building your dream house, moved in, and sodded the lawn. Your children are all doing well in school and sports and, along with your spouse, want no part of a move to Missouri. If the company does move, so will you because your town is a one-industry community, and you and your spouse will have to move to have employment. Moving when everyone else does will cause you to take a big loss on the sale of your house. The same hardships will be suffered by your coworkers, and the town will be devastated.

In compiling the costs of moving versus not moving, you have latitude in the assumptions you make, the estimates you compute, and the discount rates and time periods you project. You are in a position to influence the decision singlehandedly.

Instructions

(a) Who are the stakeholders in this situation?
(b) What are the ethical issues in this situation?
(c) What would you do in this situation?

Answers to Self-Study Questions

1. d **2.** b **3.** c **4.** d **5.** a **6.** b **7.** c **8.** b **9.** d **10.** b

Answer to Lands' End Review It Question 4, p. 1122

LANDS' END DIRECT MERCHANTS

Lands' End's return on average assets for 2000 was 11%. Lands' End's return on average assets was 18% in 1990. It has bounced between a high of 18% and a low of 7% during this 10-year period.

Remember to go back to the Navigator box on the chapter-opening page and check off your completed work.

Appendixes A–D

APPENDIX A

SPECIMEN FINANCIAL STATEMENTS: Lands' End, Inc.

THE ANNUAL REPORT

Once each year a corporation communicates to its stockholders and other interested parties by issuing a complete set of audited financial statements. The **annual report**, as this communication is called, summarizes the financial results of its operations for the year and its plans for the future. Many annual reports have become attractive, multicolored, glossy public relations pieces containing pictures of corporate officers and directors as well as photos and descriptions of new products and new buildings. Yet the basic function of every annual report is to report **financial information**, almost all of which is a product of the corporation's accounting system.

The content and organization of corporate annual reports have become fairly standardized. Excluding the public relations part of the report (pictures and products), the following items are the traditional financial portions of the annual report:

Financial Highlights
Letter to the Stockholders
Auditor's Report
Management Discussion and Analysis
Financial Statements and Accompanying Notes
Five- or Ten-Year Summary

In this appendix we illustrate current financial reporting with a comprehensive set of corporate financial statements. They have been prepared in accordance with generally accepted accounting principles and audited by an international independent certified public accounting firm. We are grateful for permission to use the actual financial statements and other accompanying financial information from the annual report of a large, publicly held company, **Lands' End, Inc.**

FINANCIAL HIGHLIGHTS

The financial highlights section is usually presented inside the front cover or on the first two pages of the annual report. This section generally reports the total or per share amounts for five to ten financial items for the current year and one or more previous years. Financial items from the income statement and the balance sheet that typically are presented are sales, income from continuing operations, net income, net income per share, dividends per common share, and the amount of capital expenditures. The financial highlights section from Lands' End's Annual Report is shown below.

Financial Highlights

LANDS' END DIRECT MERCHANTS

Lands' End, Inc. & Subsidiaries

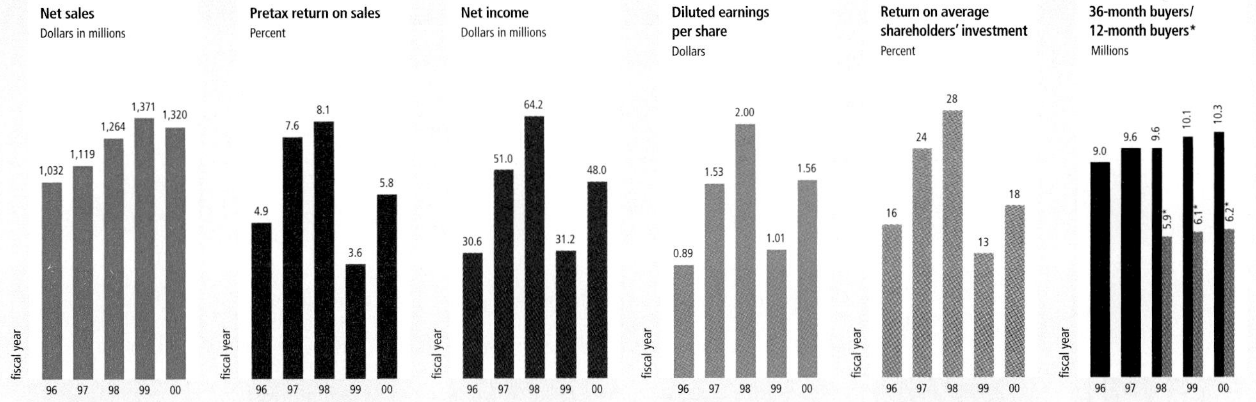

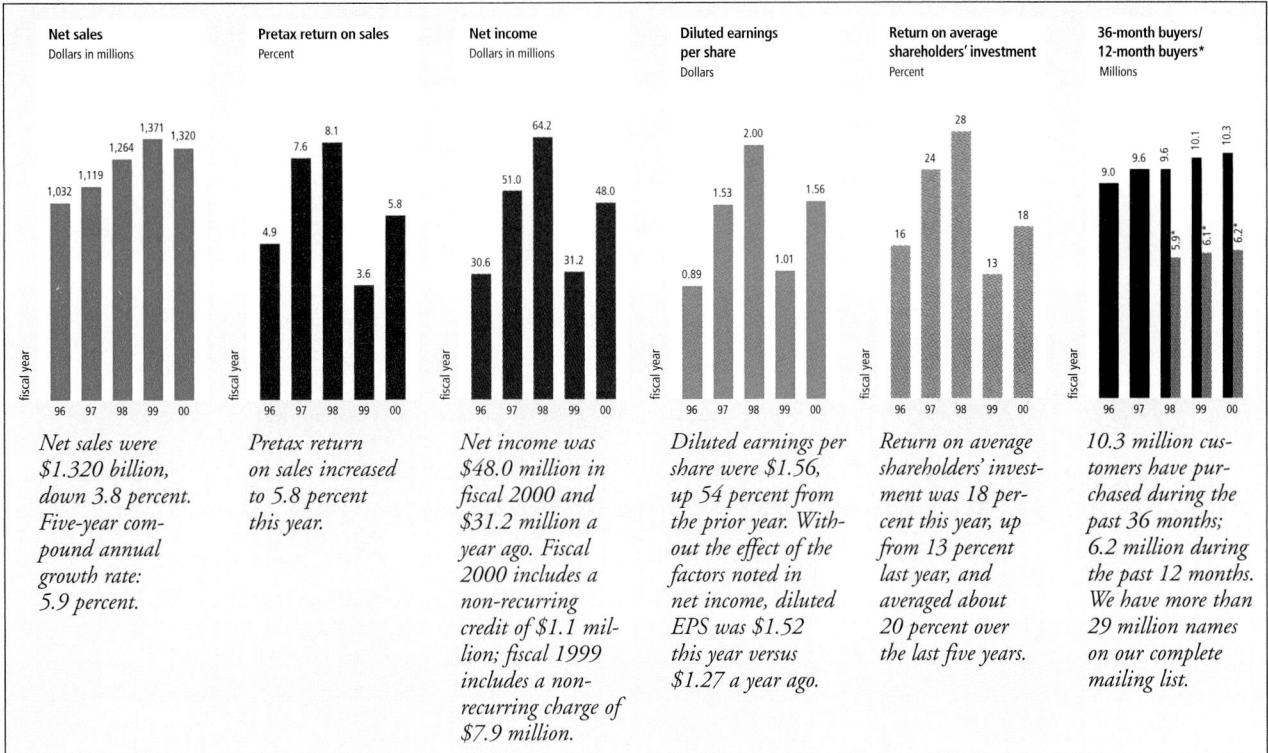

Net sales were $1.320 billion, down 3.8 percent. Five-year compound annual growth rate: 5.9 percent.

Pretax return on sales increased to 5.8 percent this year.

Net income was $48.0 million in fiscal 2000 and $31.2 million a year ago. Fiscal 2000 includes a non-recurring credit of $1.1 million; fiscal 1999 includes a non-recurring charge of $7.9 million.

Diluted earnings per share were $1.56, up 54 percent from the prior year. Without the effect of the factors noted in net income, diluted EPS was $1.52 this year versus $1.27 a year ago.

Return on average shareholders' investment was 18 percent this year, up from 13 percent last year, and averaged about 20 percent over the last five years.

10.3 million customers have purchased during the past 36 months; 6.2 million during the past 12 months. We have more than 29 million names on our complete mailing list.

As shown above, Lands' End chose to present its financial highlights using bar graphs accompanied with narrative describing current-year results and comparisons.

LETTER TO THE STOCKHOLDERS

Nearly every annual report contains a letter to the stockholders from the Chairman of the Board or the President (or both). This letter typically discusses the company's accomplishments during the past year. It also highlights significant events

Dear Shareholder

Lands' End has completed a challenging year of planned transition. While net sales for fiscal 2000 were down about 4 percent to $1.320 billion, we are pleased with our earnings of $48 million. Before non-recurring items, our earnings per diluted share improved by almost 20 percent. The year is explained in full in the Management's Discussion and Analysis section of this annual report.

Last year in my letter to shareholders, I outlined the steps that we would take to put our company on the right track for long-term growth and improved profitability. These steps included reinvigorating our merchandise offering and creative presentation, a more disciplined approach to inventory and SKU management, reduction of unprofitable circulation, improved sourcing and gross profit margins, and an energetic focus on growing our e-commerce business.

In terms of these goals, the year overall was most satisfactory. The company transformed itself from a U.S. catalog company to a global direct merchant selling through multiple channels of distribution. We were recognized by FORTUNE® magazine as one of the top 10 companies that "get it" when it comes to e-commerce, and we have built the largest, most successful, acclaimed and profitable apparel Web site. We managed our inventory masterfully through the transition, clearing out the old merchandise without excessive markdowns and bringing in the new merchandise, all while maintaining our high standard for initial fulfillment – our measure of outstanding customer service. We made great strides in resourcing our products and, as a result, expect strong margin performance this coming year. We have rationalized our circulation plans and now have a profitable platform on which to build. We augmented our existing talented staff with new, strong and talented executives who together have reinvigorated our company. And for the third year in a row, we were recognized as one of the "100 Best Companies to Work For" in the United States – and we have done all of this while increasing profitability.

Inventory at year-end was down to $162 million, 26 percent below last year, and SKUs were down from 110,000 to 92,000 at year-end. Throughout the year, our initial fulfillment rate was at the very high level that we require for excellent customer service.

This pivotal year is now behind us. We accomplished a lot and learned a lot, and necessary course corrections have been made for this coming year. While it's too early to know with absolute certainty, our early spring business indications are indeed promising.

We have a number of terrific growth opportunities in the year ahead. We believe that we can advance all of our businesses, including the core catalog. But especially noteworthy such as mergers and acquisitions, new products, operating achievements, business philosophy, changes in officers or directors, financing commitments, expansion plans, and future prospects. The letter to the stockholders signed by David F. Dyer, President and Chief Executive Officer of Lands' End, is shown on pages A4 to A6.

are the prospects for our Internet and Corporate Sales business-to-business divisions.

To begin with, Internet sales last year were \$138 million, more than double the \$61 million of the previous year. From all reports we have seen to date, Lands' End remains the world's largest apparel Web site. Even after full expense allocation, Internet sales in the past year were more profitable than our catalog sales.

Based on results from fall 1999, circulation tests to Internet buyers confirmed the synergistic relationship of our catalog to the Web. We know that withholding catalogs from Internet buyers does not generate online sales. We believe that a smaller catalog (fewer pages) with sufficient mailing frequency may produce the best results over time. Still, we will continue to refine our tests to determine the optimum frequency and pages for keeping our Internet customers apprised of Lands' End's exciting new products.

The Internet was the fastest growing source of new customer names to our file last year. It is less costly to bring these customers to the Lands' End file through e-commerce than through printed media. About 20 percent of our Internet buyers are totally new to Lands' End.

As for our Corporate Sales business-to-business division, it should continue its double-digit growth increases this coming year. Nine out of 10 Fortune 500 companies have purchased business apparel from the Lands' End Corporate Sales division. Last year we achieved about \$140 million in sales, and we just announced plans to develop an additional facility in Stevens Point, Wisconsin, in anticipation of the future planned growth. The new site will be fully operational in time for the 2001 peak season.

David F. Dyer

Corporate Sales is one of our most profitable businesses. We are uniquely positioned to provide a respected brand and a high-quality embroidery product featuring very rapid turnaround even for larger orders. We are exploring the possibility of broadening our product line beyond apparel.

Earlier this year, we launched a transaction-enabled Corporate Sales Web site. For large customers, we can now create online custom company stores. We currently have seven custom company stores online and expect to have about 30 more by year-end. For example, we just announced an agreement with Saturn to provide their dealers, employees and customers with logo apparel.

In addition to our Internet and Corporate Sales business, our other specialty businesses – kids' apparel and home furnishings – are planned for nice growth this year. Finally, we believe that our reinvigorated merchandise and creative presentation will also revitalize our core business.

As for our FY 2001 plans and goals, we seek a balance of top line sales growth and bottom line profit. Circulation is planned up 6 percent for the year and sales somewhat higher, which will occur largely in the fourth quarter when we cut back circulation too aggressively last year. In the fourth quarter of this year, we will add back a post-Thanksgiving mailing and reinstate the January catalog.

Gross profit is planned to improve by about 225 basis points due to better sourcing and more normalized liquidations. We have cleared the deck of old merchandise. We have negotiated more effectively with our vendors for lower costs.

We plan to invest about a third of our gross profit improvement in Internet advertising and national advertising. Our capital expenditures are planned at about $50 million, the large majority of which is focused on systems for our call centers, the Internet and Corporate Sales. Our goal is to achieve about a 7.5 percent pretax profit on net sales.

"We have a leading direct-to-consumer infrastructure that positions us perfectly for future e-commerce growth."

These are exciting times for our company. We believe that Lands' End possesses the necessary key attributes to position us for success in the digital age.

Lands' End is a trusted, nationally recognized brand with a very loyal customer base. We are dedicated to provide outstanding customer service. We have very high standards for product quality. We control the distribution of our product, and our primary categories of apparel and home textiles offer sufficient margin to produce good profit. We have a leading direct-to-consumer infrastructure that positions us perfectly for future e-commerce growth.

And, most important of all, we at Lands' End are passionate about our company and our customers, and we'll work hard to create our future success.

Thanks for being a shareholder.

David F. Dyer

David F. Dyer
President and Chief Executive Officer

AUDITOR'S REPORT

All publicly held corporations, as well as many other enterprises and organizations (both profit and not-for-profit, large and small) engage the services of independent certified public accountants who will provide an objective, expert report on their financial statements. Based on a comprehensive examination of the company's accounting system and records, and of the financial statements, the outside CPA issues the auditor's report.

The standard auditor's report consists of three pieces of information, expressed in separate sentences or paragraphs: (1) a responsibilities statement, (2) a scope statement, and (3) the opinion. In the **responsibilities statement**, the auditor identifies who and what was audited and indicates the responsibilities of management and the auditor relative to the financial statements. In the **scope statement**, the auditor states that the audit was conducted in accordance with generally accepted auditing standards and discusses the nature and limitations of the audit. In the **opinion statement**, the auditor expresses an informed opinion as to (1) the fairness of the financial statements and (2) their conformity with generally accepted accounting principles. The **Report of Arthur Andersen, Independent Public Accountants**, appearing in Lands' End's Annual Report is shown below.

To the Board of Directors and Shareholders of
Lands' End, Inc.:

We have audited the accompanying consolidated balance sheets of Lands' End, Inc. (a Delaware corporation) and its subsidiaries as of January 28, 2000, and January 29, 1999, and the related consolidated statements of operations, shareholders' investment and cash flows for each of the three years in the period ended January 28, 2000. These financial statements are the responsibility of the company's management. Our responsibility is to express an opinion on these financial statements based on our audits.

We conducted our audits in accordance with generally accepted auditing standards. Those standards require that we plan and perform the audit to obtain reasonable assurance about whether the financial statements are free of material misstatement. An audit includes examining, on a test basis, evidence supporting the amounts and disclosures in the financial statements. An audit also includes assessing the accounting principles used and significant estimates made by management, as well as evaluating the overall financial statement presentation. We believe that our audits provide a reasonable basis for our opinion.

In our opinion, the financial statements referred to above present fairly, in all material respects, the financial position of Lands' End, Inc. and subsidiaries as of January 28, 2000, and January 29, 1999, and the results of their operations and their cash flows for each of the three years in the period ended January 28, 2000, in conformity with generally accepted accounting principles.

Arthur Andersen LLP

Arthur Andersen LLP

Milwaukee, Wisconsin
March 3, 2000

The auditor's report issued on Lands' End's financial statements is **unqualified** or "clean." That is, it contains no qualifications or exceptions. The auditor conformed completely with generally accepted auditing standards in performing the audit, and the financial statements conformed in all material respects with generally accepted accounting principles.

When the financial statements do not conform with generally accepted accounting principles, the auditor must issue a **qualified** opinion and describe the exception. If the lack of conformity with GAAP is sufficiently material, the auditor is compelled to issue an **adverse** or negative opinion. An adverse opinion means that the financial statements do not present fairly the company's financial condition and/or the results of the company's operations at the dates and for the periods reported.

In circumstances where the auditor is unable to perform all the auditing procedures necessary to reach a conclusion as to the fairness of the financial statements, a **disclaimer** must be issued. In these rare instances, the auditor must report the reason for failure to reach a conclusion on the fairness of the financial statements.

Companies strive to obtain an unqualified auditor's report. Hence, only infrequently are you likely to encounter anything other than this type of opinion on the financial statements.

MANAGEMENT'S REPORT

A relatively recent addition to corporate annual reports is the statement made by management about its role in and responsibility for the accuracy and integrity of the financial statements. Lands' End's management letter is entitled **Management's Responsibility for Financial Statements**. In it the Chief Executive Officer along with the Chief Financial Officer, on behalf of management, do the following: They (1) assume primary responsibility for the financial statements and the related notes, (2) outline and assess the company's internal control system, (3) declare the financial statements in conformity with generally accepted accounting principles, and (4) comment on the audit by the certified public accountant and the composition and role of the Audit Committee of the Board of Directors. Lands' End's management report is presented below.

Management's Responsibility for Financial Statements

The management of Lands' End, Inc. and its subsidiaries has the responsibility for preparing the accompanying financial statements and for their integrity and objectivity. The statements were prepared in accordance with generally accepted accounting principles applied on a consistent basis. The consolidated financial statements include amounts that are based on management's best estimates and judgments. Management also prepared the other information in the annual report and is responsible for its accuracy and consistency with the consolidated financial statements.

The company's consolidated financial statements have been audited by Arthur Andersen LLP, independent certified public accountants. Management has made available to Arthur Andersen LLP all the company's financial records and related data, as well as the minutes of shareholders' and directors' meetings. Furthermore, management believes that all representations made to Arthur Andersen LLP during its audit were valid and appropriate.

Management of the company has established and maintains a system of internal control that provides for appropriate division of responsibility, reasonable assurance as to the integrity and reliability of the consolidated financial statements, the protection of assets from unauthorized use or disposition, the prevention and detection of fraudulent financial reporting, and the maintenance of an active program of internal audits. Management believes that, as of January 28, 2000, the company's system of internal control is adequate to accomplish the objectives discussed herein.

Two directors of the company, not members of management, serve as the audit committee of the board of directors and are the principal means through which the board supervises the performance of the financial reporting duties of management. The audit committee meets with management, the internal audit staff and the company's independent auditors to review the results of the audits of the company and to discuss plans for future audits. At these meetings, the audit committee also meets privately with the internal audit staff and the independent auditors to assure its free access to them.

David F. Dyer
Chief Executive Officer

Stephen A. Orum
Executive Vice President and Chief Financial Officer

MANAGEMENT'S DISCUSSION AND ANALYSIS

The **management's discussion and analysis (MD&A)** section covers three financial aspects of a company: its results of operations, its ability to pay near-term obligations, and its ability to fund operations and expansion. Management must highlight favorable or unfavorable trends and identify significant events and uncertainties that affect these three factors. This discussion obviously involves a number of subjective estimates and opinions. The MD&A section of Lands' End's annual report is presented on the following pages.

Management's Discussion and Analysis

LANDS' END DIRECT MERCHANTS

Lands' End, Inc. & Subsidiaries

The company planned fiscal year 2000 as a transition year in which it reduced unprofitable mailings, reduced expenses and liquidated excess inventory to prepare for a reinvigorated and new merchandise offering.

For fiscal 2000, sales declined 3.8 percent. The decrease in net sales was primarily from the company's core business segment, offset in part by growth in the specialty business. Net income increased 54 percent to $48 million in fiscal 2000. Net income includes an after-tax non-recurring credit of $1.1 million for fiscal 2000, compared with an after-tax non-recurring charge of $7.9 million in fiscal 1999.

Consolidated statements of operations presented as a percentage of net sales

For the period ended	**January 28, 2000**	January 29, 1999	January 30, 1998
Net sales	**100.0%**	100.0%	100.0%
Cost of sales	**55.1**	55.0	53.4
Gross profit	**44.9**	45.0	46.6
Selling, general and administrative expenses	**39.0**	39.7	38.8
Non-recurring charge (credit)	**(0.1)**	0.9	–
Income from operations	**6.0**	4.4	7.8
Interest income (expense), net	**(0.1)**	(0.6)	–
Gain on sale of subsidiary	**–**	–	0.6
Other	**(0.1)**	(0.2)	(0.3)
Income before income taxes	**5.8**	3.6	8.1
Income tax provision	**2.2**	1.3	3.0
Net income	**3.6%**	2.3%	5.1%

Segment net sales

(Amounts in millions)	**January 28, 2000 Amount**	**% of Net Sales**	January 29, 1999 Amount	% of Net Sales	January 30, 1998 Amount	% of Net Sales
Core	**$ 780**	**59%**	$ 861	63%	$ 825	66%
Specialty	**397**	**30%**	364	27%	307	24%
International	**143**	**11%**	146	10%	132	10%
Total net sales	**$1,320**	**100%**	$1,371	100%	$1,264	100%

Segment income (loss) before income taxes

(Amounts in millions)	**January 28, 2000 Amount**	**% of Net Sales**	January 29, 1999 Amount	% of Net Sales	January 30, 1998 Amount	% of Net Sales
Core	**$ 33**	**2.5 %**	$ 27	2.0 %	$ 59	4.7%
Specialty	**43**	**3.3 %**	23	1.7 %	30	2.4%
International	**2**	**0.2 %**	5	0.3 %	8	0.6%
Other	**(2)**	**(0.2)%**	(5)	(0.4)%	5	0.4%
Income before income taxes	**$ 76**	**5.8 %**	$ 50	3.6 %	$ 102	8.1%

Results of operations for fiscal 2000, compared with fiscal 1999

Net sales decreased by 3.8 percent

Net sales for the year just ended totaled $1.320 billion, compared with $1.371 billion in the prior year, a decrease of 3.8 percent. This decrease was greater than anticipated, even with the planned reduction in catalog pages mailed during the year. The specialty business segment had the strongest performance for fiscal 2000, with sales up about 9 percent to $396.3 million, due in large part to another successful year for our Corporate Sales business-to-business division, which now accounts for about $140 million in sales. Sales for the core business segment were $780.3 million, down 9 percent from the prior year, due largely to an 18 percent page circulation reduction. Sales for the international business segment were $143.2 million, slightly down from $146 million last year. Lower inventory levels throughout the year resulted in a first-time fulfillment of about 88 percent.

Sales for November and December, the two most important months of our critical holiday season, were down almost 15 percent from the prior year. This was due principally to the planned strategy of mailing fewer catalog pages to reduce unprofitable mailings, the elimination of a full-size catalog at Thanksgiving time, and a lower level of liquidation sales compared with the prior year when catalog mailings and promotional pricing were aggressively increased to clear excess inventory. In January, the company traditionally mails its January full-price primary catalog, as well as an end-of-season clearance catalog. This year these two mailings were combined into one book, with only a small presentation devoted to full-price merchandise, resulting in a 30 percent page reduction and a 24 percent decline in sales for the month of January.

Our Internet sales at *www.landsend.com* more than doubled in fiscal 2000, with sales of $138 million, compared with $61 million in fiscal 1999. We continue to find that more than 20 percent of our Internet buyers are new to Lands' End, and believe this channel will continue to be an important growth opportunity for us.

Gross profit margin

Gross profit for the year just ended was $593 million, or 44.9 percent of net sales, compared with $617 million, or 45.0 percent of net sales, for the prior year. During the first nine months of fiscal 2000, gross profit margin was running well below the prior year, due primarily to a higher level of liquidated merchandise sales at steeper markdowns. However, in the fourth quarter, gross profit margin was strong due to higher initial margins as a result of improved sourcing and the lower level of liquidations. Liquidations were about 12 percent of total net sales in fiscal 2000, compared with 10 percent in the prior year.

In fiscal 2000, the cost of inventory purchases was down 2.7 percent, compared with inflation of 0.5 percent in fiscal 1999. This reduction was a result of deflation, as well as more efficient negotiations with our suppliers. As a result, the LIFO reserve was reduced by $5.9 million in fiscal 2000.

Selling, general and administrative expenses

Selling, general and administrative (SG&A) expenses decreased 5.3 percent to $515 million in fiscal 2000, compared with $544 million in the prior year. The decrease was due to a reduction in the number of catalog pages mailed, somewhat offset by relatively higher fulfillment costs. As a percentage of sales, SG&A was 39.0 percent in fiscal 2000 and 39.7 percent in the prior year. The decrease in the SG&A ratio was primarily the result of the reduction in the number of pages mailed and greater overall catalog productivity (sales per page). The number of full-price catalogs mailed totaled 236 million in fiscal 2000, down 9 percent from the prior year, while the total number of pages mailed decreased by about 17 percent.

The cost of producing and mailing catalogs represented about 37 percent and 43 percent of total SG&A in fiscal 2000 and 1999, respectively.

Depreciation and amortization expense was $20.7 million, up 10.6 percent from the prior year, related primarily to additional computer hardware and software, and buildings. Rental expense was $15.5 million, down 0.8 percent from fiscal 1999, as a result of three store closings.

Utilization of credit lines decreased

Inventory decreased to $162 million in fiscal 2000, down 26 percent from $220 million in the prior year. As a result of lower inventory levels and reduced purchases of treasury stock, borrowing decreased under our short-term lines of credit. Interest expense decreased to $1.9 million in fiscal 2000, compared to $7.7 million in fiscal 1999. We spent $28 million in capital expenditures and purchased about $4.5 million in treasury stock. Our lines of credit peaked at $53 million in fiscal 2000, compared with a peak of $257 million in the prior year. At January 28, 2000, the company's foreign subsidiaries had short-term debt outstanding of $11.7 million and domestic operations had no outstanding borrowings. No long-term debt was outstanding at fiscal year-end 2000.

Net income increased

Net income for fiscal 2000 was $48.0 million, up 54 percent from the $31.2 million earned in fiscal 1999. Diluted earnings per share for the year just ended were $1.56, compared with $1.01 per share for the prior year. In the third and fourth quarters of fiscal 1999, the company had after-tax non-recurring charges of $0.9 million and $7.0 million, respectively, or $0.26 per share for the entire fiscal year. Fiscal 2000 includes an addition to after-tax net income of $1.1 million, or $0.04 per share, from the reversal of a portion of that non-recurring charge. Before the effect of these adjustments, net income for the year just ended was $46.9 million, or $1.52 per diluted share, compared with fiscal 1999 net income of $39.1 million, or $1.27 per share. The diluted weighted average number of common shares outstanding was 30.9 million for fiscal 2000 and 30.8 million for fiscal 1999.

Segment results

The company has three business segments consisting of Core (regular monthly and prospecting catalogs, First Person, and Beyond Buttondowns), Specialty (Kids, Corporate Sales, and Coming Home catalogs) and International (foreign-based operations in Japan, United Kingdom and Germany). "Other" includes corporate expenses, intercompany eliminations, other income and deduction items that are not allocated to segments. (See Note 12.)

The core segment's net sales were $780.3 million or 59 percent of total net sales in fiscal 2000, which represents a decrease of $80.6 million from the prior year. Within the core operating segment, sales from the monthly and prospecting full-price catalogs were down from the prior year due principally to a planned reduction in circulation and pages mailed. Total pages circulated were down 18 percent in the core segment.

The specialty segment's net sales were $396.3 million or 30 percent of total net sales in fiscal 2000, which represents an increase of $31.8 million from the prior year. This sales increase was mainly from our Corporate Sales business-to-business division.

The international segment's net sales were $143.2 million or 11 percent of total net sales in fiscal 2000, which represents a decrease of $2.7 million from the prior year. The decrease was due mainly to lower sales for the United Kingdom and Japan.

Income (loss) before income taxes for the segments were: core increased by $5.4 million to $32.7 million in fiscal 2000 from $27.3 million in the prior year; specialty increased by $20.1 million to $43.1 million in fiscal 2000 from $23.0 million in the prior year; and international decreased by $2.4 million to $2.3 million in fiscal 2000 from $4.7 million last year. The core and specialty segments' increase in income before income taxes was primarily the result of the company's strategy to reduce circulation and focus on catalog productivity. In addition, both core and specialty segments incurred non-recurring credits of $0.5 million and $1.3 million, respectively. This compares to fiscal 1999 non-recurring charges of $7.6 million and $5.0 million allocated to core and specialty, respectively. International's decrease in income before income taxes was attributed mainly to its sales decrease in the United Kingdom and Japan.

Adoption of SFAS 133

The company adopted SFAS 133 at the beginning of the third quarter of fiscal 2000. For the company's cash flow hedges, changes in fair value are recognized in shareholders' investment as other comprehensive income to the extent determined to be effective until the hedged item is recognized in earnings. For fiscal 2000, $0.6 million of gains were included in other comprehensive income. Prior to the adoption of SFAS 133 for fiscal 2000, $0.7 million of losses were recognized in other expenses. For fiscal 2000, $0.8 million of losses were recognized in other expenses compared to $1.9 million of losses in fiscal 1999. Pursuant to this standard, the ineffective portion of cash flow hedges, as well as certain changes related to the company's option contracts, are reflected in earnings as the changes occur. These changes resulted in a $0.1 million non-cash charge for fiscal 2000. Results of operations will continue to be affected by changes in fair value for these contracts, the amount and timing of which cannot be predicted.

Results of operations for fiscal 1999, compared with fiscal 1998

Net sales grew by 8.5 percent

Net sales for fiscal 1999 totaled $1.371 billion, compared with $1.264 billion in the prior year, an increase of 8.5 percent. The increase in sales was due primarily to additional catalogs and pages mailed to customers. The growth in sales came from all of the company's operating segments. In fiscal 1999, our company expanded the number of reported operating segments to three: core, specialty and international. Prior to this, only domestic and foreign segments were disclosed. (See Note 12.)

Within the core operating segment, sales from the monthly and prospecting full-price catalogs were down from the prior year despite an increase in pages circulated. The specialty segment has a higher operating profit compared with the core and international segments, due principally to higher gross profit margins and relatively lower costs of catalog advertising.

Fiscal 1999 inventory was $220 million, down 9 percent from $241 million in fiscal 1998. Inventory throughout most of the year was higher as we experienced softening sales, especially in the third quarter. To correct this, we instituted price rollbacks, price reductions and some promotional pricing in the fourth quarter. This helped increase sales, but also had a negative effect on the gross profit margin. Higher inventory levels throughout the year allowed the company to achieve a first-time fulfillment of 91 percent.

Gross profit margin decreased

Gross profit for fiscal 1999 was $617 million, or 45.0 percent of net sales, compared with $588 million, or 46.6 percent of net sales, for the prior year. The decrease in gross profit margin was due primarily to more steep markdowns on higher sales of liquidated merchandise, especially in the fourth quarter when we aggressively addressed our overstock situation, as well as from lower initial markups. Liquidations were about 10 percent of total net sales in fiscal 1999, compared with 8 percent in the prior year.

In fiscal 1999, inflationary pressure was low, and costs of inventory purchases increased 0.5 percent, compared with 1.2 percent in fiscal 1998.

Selling, general and administrative expenses

Selling, general and administrative (SG&A) expenses rose 11.1 percent to $544 million in fiscal 1999, compared with $490 million in the prior year. As a percentage of sales, SG&A was 39.7 percent in fiscal 1999 and 38.8 percent in fiscal 1998. The increase in the SG&A percentage was mainly the result of lower productivity in the catalogs due to an increase in pages and catalogs mailed and a weaker response from customers. Additional factors increasing the SG&A percentage were relatively higher salaries and benefits, higher Year 2000 expenses, and increased investment in the Internet site. This was partially offset by lower bonus and profit-sharing expense due to lower profitability. The number of full-price catalogs mailed totaled 259 million in fiscal 1999, up 12 percent from the prior year, while the total number of pages mailed increased by about 10 percent.

Over the past two years, catalog circulation had increased 22 percent and page circulation by 38 percent. This level of circulation was due in part to our efforts to clear excess inventory in the fourth quarter. Starting with fall of 1999, we will circulate fewer catalogs and pages to reduce less profitable mailings. This will have a negative effect on sales growth, but is expected to have a positive impact on operating profit margins by increasing catalog productivity, or sales per page.

The cost of producing and mailing catalogs represented about 43 percent and 41 percent of total SG&A in fiscal 1999 and 1998, respectively.

Depreciation and amortization expense was $18.7 million, up 23.8 percent from the prior year, primarily because of additional equipment, computer hardware and software, and buildings. Rental expense was $15.6 million, up 15.7 percent, due mainly to increased computer-related rentals.

In fiscal 1999, we recorded a non-recurring charge of $12.6 million. This charge includes costs associated with severance payments due to organizational changes, liquidation of the Willis & Geiger division, closing of three outlet stores and the termination of a licensing agreement with MontBell Co. Ltd.

Utilization of credit lines increased

Because of higher inventory levels and lower profits throughout the year, there was additional borrowing under our short-term lines of credit, increasing our interest expense to $7.7 million in fiscal 1999. In addition, we spent $47 million in capital expenditures and purchased about $36 million in treasury stock. Our lines of credit peaked at $257 million in October 1998, compared with a peak of $118 million in the prior year. At January 29, 1999, the company's foreign subsidiaries had short-term debt outstanding of $17.1 million and domestic operations had borrowings of $21.8 million. No long-term debt was outstanding at January 29, 1999.

Net income decreased

Net income for fiscal 1999 was $31.2 million, down 51 percent from the $64.2 million earned in fiscal 1998. Diluted earnings per share for fiscal 1999 were $1.01, compared with $2.00 per share for the prior year. The diluted weighted average number of common shares outstanding was 30.8 million for fiscal 1999 and 32.1 million for fiscal 1998.

The fiscal 1999 results include an after-tax non-recurring charge of $7.9 million, or $0.26 per share. In the first quarter of fiscal 1998 the company had an after-tax gain of $4.9 million, or $0.15 per share, from the sale of its majority interest in The Territory Ahead. Before the effect of these adjustments, net income for fiscal 1999 was $39.1 million, or $1.27 per share, compared with $59.2 million, or $1.85 per share, in fiscal 1998.

Segment results

The core segment's net sales were $860.9 million or 63 percent of total net sales in fiscal year 1999, which represents an increase of $36.0 million from the prior year. Within the core operating segment, sales from the monthly and prospecting full-price catalogs were down from the prior year despite an increase in pages circulated.

The specialty segment's net sales were $364.6 million or 27 percent of total net sales in fiscal year 1999, which represents an increase of $57.6 million from the prior year. The specialty segment has a higher operating profit, compared with the core and international segments, due principally to higher gross profit margins and relatively lower catalog advertising costs.

The international segment's net sales were $145.9 million or 10 percent of total net sales in fiscal year 1999, which represents an increase of $14.1 million from the prior year.

Income before income taxes for the segments was: core decreased by $32.1 million to $27.3 million in fiscal year 1999 from $59.4 million in the prior year; specialty decreased by $7.2 million to $23.0 million in fiscal year 1999 from $30.2 million in the prior year; and international decreased by $3.0 million to $4.7 million in fiscal year 1999 from $7.7 million in the prior year. The decreases in the segments' income before income taxes were the result of steep markdowns on a higher portion of liquidated merchandise, and higher expenses resulting from lower productivity of the catalogs. In fiscal 1999, both the core and specialty segments incurred non-recurring charges of $7.6 million and $5.0 million, respectively.

The Christmas season is our busiest

Our business is highly seasonal. The fall/winter season is a five-month period ending in December. In the longer spring/summer season, orders are fewer and the merchandise offered generally has lower unit selling prices than products offered in the fall/winter season. As a result, net sales are usually substantially greater in the fall/winter season, and SG&A as a percentage of net sales is usually higher in the spring/summer season. Additionally, as we continue to refine our marketing efforts by experimenting with the timing of our catalog mailings, quarterly results may fluctuate.

Nearly 34 percent of our annual sales came in the fourth quarter of fiscal 2000, compared with about 40 percent in fiscal 1999. Approximately 59 percent and 82 percent of before-tax profit was realized in the same quarter of fiscal 2000 and 1999, respectively.

Liquidity and capital resources

To date, the bulk of our working capital needs have been met through funds generated from operations and from short-term bank loans. Our principal need for working capital has been to meet peak inventory requirements associated with our seasonal sales pattern. In addition, our resources have been used to make asset additions and purchase treasury stock. During fiscal 2000 we entered into a new domestic credit facility providing unsecured credit totaling $200 million. As of January 28, 2000, the only reduction of this facility was $28.7 million of outstanding letters of credit. The company also maintains foreign credit lines for use in foreign operations totaling the equivalent of approximately $54 million, of which $11.7 million was used at January 28, 2000.

Since fiscal 1990, the company's board of directors has authorized the purchase of a total of 12.7 million shares of the company's common stock. A total of 0.1 million, 1.1 million and 1.5 million shares have been purchased in the fiscal years ended January 28, 2000, January 29, 1999 and January 30, 1998, respectively. As of January 28, 2000, 11.6 million shares have been purchased, and there is a balance of 1.1 million shares authorized to be purchased by the company.

The board of directors from time to time evaluates its dividend practice. Given our current authorization to buy back additional shares, the payment of cash dividends is not planned for the foreseeable future.

Capital investment

Capital investment was about $28 million in fiscal 2000. Major projects included computer hardware and software and distribution center equipment.

In the coming year, we plan to invest about $50 million in capital expenditures, investing primarily in our information technology. We believe that our cash flow from operations and borrowings under our current credit facilities will provide adequate resources to meet our capital requirements and operational needs for the foreseeable future.

Other matters

Year 2000

We began to address the Year 2000 issue (possibility that some date-sensitive computer software will not correctly process two-digit year references and other date-related functions) in 1996, and established a Year 2000 project office in 1997. The project office worked with our information systems department and outside consultants to identify and assess the Year 2000 readiness of our internal computer systems and microprocessors and, where appropriate, to remediate and test them. The project office also worked with our buyers, quality assurance and other personnel to assess the readiness of our suppliers.

We completed substantially all the identification, assessment, remediation and testing of significant internal systems (mainframe, mid-range and personal computers, and embedded hardware and software in our warehouses and other operations) by the fourth quarter of 1999, and have encountered no material Year 2000-related problems in those systems. We have also encountered no material problems in the ability of our product vendor and supply base to deliver goods and services. Although we believe no further significant Year 2000 contingencies exist, contingency plans developed throughout 1999 remain available for implementation in the event such problems were to develop.

Cost: The total cost of our Year 2000 efforts is expected to be approximately $21 million, which is being expensed as incurred except for $1.2 million of hardware replacement costs that has been capitalized. About $3.4 million of the total amount was incurred through the end of fiscal 1998. An additional $8.9 million was spent in fiscal 1999, and $8.7 million was incurred in fiscal 2000. We currently expect total expenditures of less than $100,000 in fiscal 2001. The timing and amount of these future expenditures are forward-looking and subject to uncertainties relating to our ongoing assessment of the Year 2000 issue, as well as the occurrence and response to any problem that may arise. Our Year 2000 expenses have been part of our annual budgets for information services. Accordingly, other technology development projects have been delayed to the extent that resources have been devoted to the Year 2000 project.

Market risk disclosure

The company uses derivative instruments to hedge, and therefore attempts to reduce its exposure to the effects of currency fluctuations on cash flows. The company is subject to foreign currency risk related to its transactions with operations in the United Kingdom, Japan, Germany and with foreign third-party vendors. The company's foreign currency risk management policy is to hedge the majority of merchandise purchases by foreign operations and from foreign third-party vendors, which includes forecasted transactions, through the use of foreign exchange forward contracts and options to minimize this risk. The company's policy is not to speculate in derivative instruments for profit on the exchange rate price fluctuation, trade in currencies for which there are no underlying exposures, or enter into trades for any currency to intentionally increase the underlying exposure. Derivative instruments used as hedges must be effective at reducing the risk associated with the exposure being hedged and must be designated as a hedge at the inception of the contract.

As of January 28, 2000, the company had net outstanding foreign currency forward contracts totaling about $46 million and options totaling $4 million. Based on the anticipated cash flows and outflows for the next 12 months and the foreign currency derivative instruments in place at January 28, 2000, a hypothetical 10 percent strengthening of the U.S. dollar relative to all other currencies would adversely affect the expected fiscal 2001 cash flows by $2.1 million.

The company is subject to the risk of fluctuating interest rates in the normal course of business, primarily as a result of its short-term borrowing and investment activities at variable interest rates. As of January 28, 2000, the company had no outstanding financial instruments related to its debt or investments. At January 28, 2000, a sensitivity analysis was performed for its short-term debt and investments that have interest rate risk. The company has determined that a 10 percent change in the company's weighted average interest rates would have no material effect on the consolidated financial statements.

Possible future changes

A 1992 Supreme Court decision confirmed that the Commerce Clause of the United States Constitution prevents a state from requiring the collection of its use tax by a mail order company unless the company has a physical presence in the state. However, there continues to be uncertainty due to inconsistent application of the Supreme Court decision by state and federal courts. The company attempts to conduct its operations in compliance with its interpretation of the applicable legal standard, but there can be no assurance that such compliance will not be challenged.

In recent challenges, various states have sought to require companies to begin collection of use taxes and/or pay taxes from previous sales. The company has not received assessments from any state.

The Supreme Court decision also established that Congress has the power to enact legislation that would permit states to require collection of use taxes by mail order companies. Congress has from time to time considered proposals for such legislation. The company anticipates that any legislative change, if adopted, would be applied only on a prospective basis.

In October 1998, The Internet Tax Freedom Act was signed into law. Among the provisions of this Act is a three-year moratorium on multiple and discriminatory taxes on electronic commerce. An Advisory Commission on Electronic Commerce has been appointed to study and report back to Congress on whether, and if so, how, electronic commerce should be taxed. We are monitoring the activities of the Commission, as well as any proposed changes in the sales and use tax laws and policies in general.

Business outlook

In the year just ended, one of the company's major initiatives had been to revamp its merchandise line. Beginning with the spring line this year, more new and enhanced products are being offered to customers than ever before. Due to changes in sourcing and more successful negotiations with its vendors, the company expects an improvement in gross profit margin of about 225 basis points for fiscal 2001. About one-third of the increased margin dollars will be invested in additional Internet and national advertising.

Another major initiative for the year just ended was to reduce unprofitable mailings, and as the company anniversaries these significant cuts, beginning with this year's second quarter, it will focus on growth from a more productive base. Our circulation strategy for fiscal 2001 will include an increase of about 6 percent in page circulation for the year, most of which will take place in the fourth quarter. Due to improved merchandise offerings and more compelling creative presentations, the company expects sales to improve somewhat more than the 6 percent increase in page circulation. Based on these expectations, the company's goal is to achieve about a 7.5 percent pretax profit on net sales. Because of circulation changes currently planned, the company anticipates fluctuating quarterly comparisons with the prior year for both sales and earnings.

For the first half of fiscal 2001, the company anticipates a sales increase in the mid-single digits, together with a strong increase in earnings. The first quarter is expected to show flat sales on 5 percent fewer pages mailed, with somewhat weaker earnings. The sales comparison trend excludes the impact of the discontinued Willis & Geiger business, which accounted for $11 million in sales in the first quarter of fiscal 2000. In the second quarter of fiscal 2001, the company plans to increase circulation and anticipates strong sales for that period.

The company anticipates that the fourth quarter will represent the largest improvement over the prior year in both sales and earnings, in light of the planned merchandise introductions and the current circulation strategy for the last half of fiscal 2001.

Statement regarding forward-looking information

Statements in this report (including, but not limited to, the president's letter and Management's Discussion and Analysis) that are not historical, including, without limitation, statements regarding our goals for fiscal 2001 sales, gross profit margin, pretax profit and earnings, as well as anticipated sales trends and future development of our business strategy, are considered forward-looking in this report. As such, these statements are subject to a number of risks and uncertainties. Future results may be materially different from those expressed or implied by these statements due to a number of factors. Currently, we believe that the principal factors that create uncertainty about our future results are the following: customer response to our new merchandise introductions, circulation changes and other initiatives; general economic or business conditions, both domestic and foreign; effects of shifting patterns of e-commerce versus catalog purchases; costs associated with printing and mailing catalogs; dependence on consumer seasonal buying patterns; and fluctuations in foreign currency exchange rates. Our future results could, of course, be affected by other factors as well.

The company does not undertake to publicly update or revise its forward-looking statements even if experience or future changes make it clear that any projected results expressed or implied therein will not be realized.

Lands' End *Direct Merchants*

As a leading global direct merchant, we are dedicated to offering exceptional quality products at prices that represent honest value, backed by the best customer service in the industry. *Guaranteed. Period.*®

Our **core business** segment is composed of adult apparel offered through our regular monthly and prospecting catalogs and our two catalogs of classic clothing for the workplace – *First Person* for women and *Beyond Buttondowns* for men. Sales in our core business segment were $780 million in fiscal 2000 and $861 million in fiscal 1999.

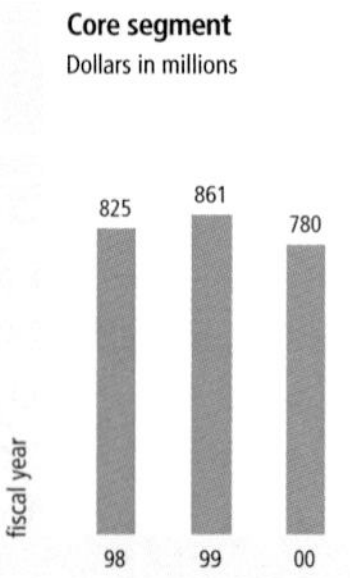

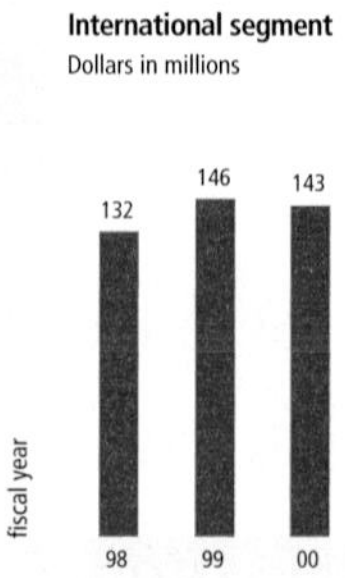

Our **international business** segment includes operations in Japan, Germany and the United Kingdom. These catalogs are written in local languages and denominated in local currencies. International segment sales were $143 million in fiscal 2000 and $146 million in fiscal 1999.

Our **specialty business** segment contains three catalogs – *Kids*, a collection of comfortable casual clothing for children; *Corporate Sales*, our business-to-business catalog offering the Lands' End brand as an option for company incentives, rewards, gifts and group apparel; and *Coming Home*, featuring products for the home. Sales in this segment were $397 million in fiscal 2000 and $364 million in fiscal 1999.

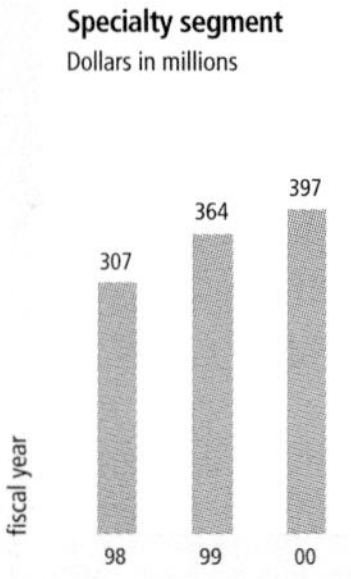

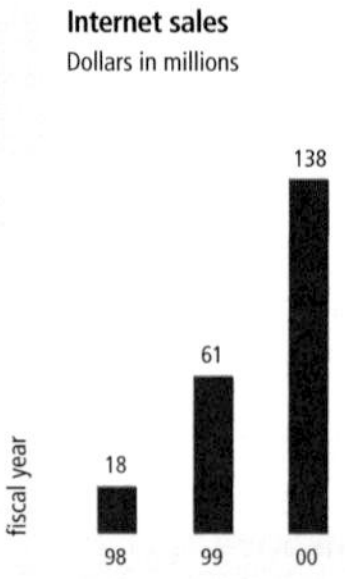

landsend.com is our Lands' End Web site, where we have expanded our Direct Merchant concept for the growing number of customers who prefer cybershopping. All of our products are available on the Web. Internet sales were $138 million in fiscal 2000 and $61 million in fiscal 1999. All Internet, export and liquidation sales are included in the respective business segment figures.

FINANCIAL STATEMENTS AND ACCOMPANYING NOTES

The standard set of financial statements consists of: (1) a comparative income statement (statement of operations) for three years, (2) a comparative balance sheet for two years, (3) a comparative statement of cash flows for three years, (4) a statement of stockholders' equity (or shareholders' investment) for three years, and (5) a set of accompanying notes that are considered an integral part of the financial statements. The auditor's report, unless stated otherwise, covers the financial statements and the accompanying notes. The financial statements and accompanying notes plus some supplementary data for Lands' End, Inc. appear on the following pages.

Consolidated Statements of Operations

Lands' End, Inc. & Subsidiaries

	For the period ended		
(In thousands, except per share data)	**January 28, 2000**	January 29, 1999	January 30, 1998
Net sales	**$1,319,823**	$1,371,375	$1,263,629
Cost of sales	**727,291**	754,661	675,138
Gross profit	**592,532**	616,714	588,491
Selling, general and administrative expenses	**515,375**	544,446	489,923
Non-recurring charge (credit)	**(1,774)**	12,600	–
Income from operations	**78,931**	59,668	98,568
Other income (expense):			
Interest expense	**(1,890)**	(7,734)	(1,995)
Interest income	**882**	16	1,725
Gain on sale of subsidiary	–	–	7,805
Other	**(1,679)**	(2,450)	(4,278)
Total other income (expense), net	**(2,687)**	(10,168)	3,257
Income before income taxes	**76,244**	49,500	101,825
Income tax provision	**28,210**	18,315	37,675
Net income	**$ 48,034**	$ 31,185	$ 64,150
Basic earnings per share	**$ 1.60**	$ 1.02	$ 2.01
Diluted earnings per share	**$ 1.56**	$ 1.01	$ 2.00
Basic weighted average shares outstanding	**30,085**	30,471	31,851
Diluted weighted average shares outstanding	**30,854**	30,763	32,132

LANDS' END DIRECT MERCHANTS

Consolidated Balance Sheets

Lands' End, Inc. & Subsidiaries

(In thousands)	January 28, 2000	January 29, 1999
Assets		
Current assets:		
Cash and cash equivalents	$ 76,413	$ 6,641
Receivables, net	17,753	21,083
Inventory	162,193	219,686
Prepaid advertising	16,572	21,357
Other prepaid expenses	5,816	7,589
Deferred income tax benefits	10,661	17,947
Total current assets	289,408	294,303
Property, plant and equipment, at cost:		
Land and buildings	102,776	102,018
Fixtures and equipment	175,910	154,663
Leasehold improvements	4,453	5,475
Total property, plant and equipment	283,139	262,156
Less – accumulated depreciation and amortization	117,317	101,570
Property, plant and equipment, net	165,822	160,586
Intangibles, net	966	1,030
Total assets	$ 456,196	$ 455,919
Liabilities and shareholders' investment		
Current liabilities:		
Lines of credit	$ 11,724	$ 38,942
Accounts payable	74,510	87,922
Reserve for returns	7,869	7,193
Accrued liabilities	43,754	54,392
Accrued profit sharing	2,760	2,256
Income taxes payable	10,255	14,578
Total current liabilities	150,872	205,283
Deferred income taxes	9,117	8,133
Shareholders' investment:		
Common stock, 40,221 shares issued	402	402
Donated capital	8,400	8,400
Additional paid-in capital	29,709	26,994
Deferred compensation	(236)	(394)
Accumulated other comprehensive income	2,675	2,003
Retained earnings	454,430	406,396
Treasury stock, 10,071 and 10,317 shares at cost, respectively	(199,173)	(201,298)
Total shareholders' investment	296,207	242,503
Total liabilities and shareholders' investment	$ 456,196	$ 455,919

The accompanying notes to consolidated financial statements are an integral part of these consolidated balance sheets.

LANDS' END DIRECT MERCHANTS

Consolidated Statements of Shareholders' Investments

Lands' End, Inc. & Subsidiaries

(Dollars in thousands)	Comprehensive Income	Common Stock	Donated Capital	Additional Paid-in Capital	Deferred Compensation	Accumulated Other Comprehensive Income	Retained Earnings	Treasury Stock	Total
Balance, Jan. 31, 1997		$402	$8,400	$26,230	$(1,370)	$ 378	$311,061	$(122,096)	$223,005
Purchase of treasury stock		–	–	–	–	–	–	(45,899)	(45,899)
Issuance of treasury stock		–	–	–	–	–	–	409	409
Tax benefit of stock options exercised		–	–	227	–	–	–	–	227
Deferred compensation expense		–	–	–	323	–	–	–	323
Comprehensive income:									
Net income	$64,150	–	–	–	–	–	64,150	–	64,150
Other comprehensive income:									
Foreign currency translation adjustments	497	–	–	–	–	497	–	–	497
Comprehensive income	$64,647								
Balance, Jan. 30, 1998		$402	$8,400	$26,457	$(1,047)	$ 875	$375,211	$(167,586)	$242,712
Purchase of treasury stock		–	–	–	–	–	–	(35,557)	(35,557)
Issuance of treasury stock		–	–	–	–	–	–	1,845	1,845
Tax benefit of stock options exercised		–	–	537	–	–	–	–	537
Deferred compensation expense		–	–	–	653	–	–	–	653
Comprehensive income:									
Net income	$31,185	–	–	–	–	–	31,185	–	31,185
Other comprehensive income:									
Foreign currency translation adjustments	1,128	–	–	–	–	1,128	–	–	1,128
Comprehensive income	$32,313								
Balance, Jan. 29, 1999		$402	$8,400	$26,994	$ (394)	$2,003	$406,396	$(201,298)	$242,503
Purchase of treasury stock		–	–	–	–	–	–	(4,516)	(4,516)
Issuance of treasury stock		–	–	–	–	–	–	6,641	6,641
Tax benefit of stock options exercised		–	–	2,715	–	–	–	–	2,715
Deferred compensation expense		–	–	–	158	–	–	–	158
Comprehensive income:									
Net income	$48,034	–	–	–	–	–	48,034	–	48,034
Other comprehensive income:									
Foreign currency translation adjustments	92	–	–	–	–	92	–	–	92
Unrealized gain on forward contracts and options	580	–	–	–	–	580	–	–	580
Comprehensive income	$48,706								
Balance, Jan. 28, 2000		$402	$8,400	$29,709	$ (236)	$2,675	$454,430	$(199,173)	$296,207

The accompanying notes to consolidated financial statements are an integral part of these consolidated statements.

LANDS' END DIRECT MERCHANTS

Consolidated Statements of Cash Flows

Lands' End, Inc. & Subsidiaries

	For the period ended		
(In thousands)	**January 28, 2000**	January 29, 1999	January 30, 1998
Cash flows from (used for) operating activities:			
Net income	**$ 48,034**	$ 31,185	$ 64,150
Adjustments to reconcile net income to net cash flows from operating activities–			
Non-recurring charge (credit)	**(1,774)**	12,600	–
Depreciation and amortization	**20,715**	18,731	15,127
Deferred compensation expense	**158**	653	323
Deferred income taxes	**8,270**	(5,948)	(1,158)
Pre-tax gain on sale of subsidiary	–	–	(7,805)
Loss on disposal of fixed assets	**926**	586	1,127
Changes in assets and liabilities excluding the effects of divestitures:			
Receivables, net	**3,330**	(5,640)	(7,019)
Inventory	**57,493**	21,468	(104,545)
Prepaid advertising	**4,785**	(2,844)	(7,447)
Other prepaid expenses	**1,773**	(2,504)	(1,366)
Accounts payable	**(13,412)**	4,179	11,616
Reserve for returns	**676**	1,065	944
Accrued liabilities	**(7,664)**	6,993	8,755
Accrued profit sharing	**504**	(2,030)	1,349
Income taxes payable	**(4,323)**	(5,899)	(1,047)
Other	**3,387**	1,665	64
Net cash flows from (used for) operating activities	**122,878**	74,260	(26,932)
Cash flows from (used for) investing activities:			
Cash paid for capital additions	**(28,013)**	(46,750)	(47,659)
Proceeds from sale of subsidiary	–	–	12,350
Net cash flows used for investing activities	**(28,013)**	(46,750)	(35,309)
Cash flows from (used for) financing activities:			
Proceeds from (payment of) short-term debt	**(27,218)**	6,505	21,242
Purchases of treasury stock	**(4,516)**	(35,557)	(45,899)
Issuance of treasury stock	**6,641**	1,845	409
Net cash flows used for financing activities	**(25,093)**	(27,207)	(24,248)
Net increase (decrease) in cash and cash equivalents	**69,772**	303	(86,489)
Beginning cash and cash equivalents	**6,641**	6,338	92,827
Ending cash and cash equivalents	**$ 76,413**	$ 6,641	$ 6,338
Supplemental cash flow disclosures:			
Interest paid	**$ 1,890**	$ 7,693	$ 1,995
Income taxes paid	**21,078**	27,857	39,337

The accompanying notes to consolidated financial statements are an integral part of these consolidated statements.

Notes to Consolidated Financial Statements

Note 1. Summary of significant accounting policies

Nature of business
Lands' End, Inc. (the company) is a direct marketer of traditionally styled apparel, domestics (primarily bedding and bath items), soft luggage and other products. The company manages its business in three operating segments consisting of core, specialty and international, based principally on type of catalog focusing on customer needs and markets served. The company's primary market is the United States, and other markets include Europe, the Pacific Basin area and Canada.

Principles of consolidation
The consolidated financial statements include the accounts of the company and its subsidiaries after elimination of intercompany accounts and transactions.

Year-end
The company's fiscal year is comprised of 52-53 weeks ending on the Friday closest to January 31. Fiscal 2000 ended on January 28, 2000, fiscal 1999 ended on January 29, 1999, and fiscal 1998 ended on January 30, 1998. All three years were comprised of 52 weeks.

Use of estimates
The preparation of financial statements in conformity with generally accepted accounting principles requires management to make estimates and assumptions that affect the reported amounts of assets and liabilities and disclosure of contingent assets and liabilities at the date of the financial statements and the reported amounts of revenues and expenses during the reporting periods. Actual results could differ from those estimates.

Inventory
Inventory, primarily merchandise held for sale, is stated at last-in, first-out (LIFO) cost, which is lower than market. If the first-in, first-out (FIFO) method of accounting for inventory had been used, inventory would have been approximately $21.0 million and $26.9 million higher than reported at January 28, 2000 and January 29, 1999, respectively.

Advertising
The company expenses the costs of advertising for magazines, television, radio and other media the first time the advertising takes place, except for direct-response advertising, which is capitalized and amortized over its expected period of future benefits.

Direct-response advertising consists primarily of catalog production and mailing costs that are generally amortized within three months from the date catalogs are mailed. Advertising costs reported as prepaid assets were $16.6 million and $21.4 million as of January 28, 2000 and January 29, 1999, respectively. Advertising expense was $225.0 million, $262.9 million and $226.7 million for fiscal years ended January 28, 2000, January 29, 1999 and January 30, 1998, respectively.

Depreciation
Depreciation expense is calculated using the straight-line method over the estimated useful lives of the assets, which are 20 to 30 years for buildings and land improvements and five to 10 years for leasehold improvements and furniture, fixtures, equipment and software. The company provides one-half year of depreciation in the year of addition and retirement.

Intangibles
Intangible assets consist primarily of trademarks, as well as their associated goodwill that is being amortized over 15 years on a straight-line basis.

Reserve for losses on customer returns
At the time of sale, the company provides a reserve equal to the gross profit on projected merchandise returns, based on its prior returns experience.

Financial instruments with off-balance-sheet risk
The company uses import letters of credit to purchase foreign-sourced merchandise. The letters of credit are primarily U.S. dollar-denominated and are issued through third-party financial institutions to guarantee payment for such merchandise within agreed-upon time periods. At January 28, 2000, the company had outstanding letters of credit of approximately $28.7 million, all of which had expiration dates of less than one year.

The counterparties to the financial instruments discussed above are primarily large financial institutions; management believes the risk of counterparty nonperformance on these financial instruments is not significant.

Foreign currency translations and transactions
Financial statements of the foreign subsidiaries are translated into U.S. dollars in accordance with the provisions of Statement of Financial Accounting Standards (SFAS) No. 52. Translation adjustments are recorded in accumulated other comprehensive income, which is a component of stockholders' equity. Foreign currency transaction gains and losses, recorded as other income and expense on the consolidated statements of operations, included losses of $0.8 million, $1.9 million and $3.8 million in fiscal 2000, 1999 and 1998, respectively.

Fair values of financial instruments
The fair value of financial instruments does not materially differ from their carrying values.

Reclassifications
Certain financial statement amounts have been reclassified to be consistent with the fiscal 2000 presentation.

Note 2. Shareholders' investment

Capital stock

The company currently has 160 million shares of $0.01 par value common stock. The company is authorized to issue 5 million shares of preferred stock, $0.01 par value. The company's board of directors has the authority to issue shares and to fix dividend, voting and conversion rights, redemption provisions, liquidation preferences, and other rights and restrictions of the preferred stock. No preferred shares have been issued.

Treasury stock

The company's board of directors has authorized the purchase of a total of 12.7 million shares of the company's common stock. A total of 11.6 million, 11.4 million and 10.3 million shares had been purchased as of January 28, 2000, January 29, 1999 and January 30, 1998, respectively.

Treasury stock activity in terms of shares was as follows:

For the period ended	January 28, 2000	January 29, 1999	January 30, 1998
Beginning balance	10,317,118	9,281,138	7,778,258
Purchase of stock	122,400	1,144,460	1,533,880
Issuance of stock	(368,650)	(108,480)	(31,000)
Ending balance	10,070,868	10,317,118	9,281,138

Earnings per share

A reconciliation of the basic and diluted per share computations is as follows:

(In thousands, except per share data)	January 28, 2000	January 29, 1999	January 30, 1998
Net income	$48,034	$31,185	$64,150
Basic weighted average shares of common stock outstanding	30,085	30,471	31,851
Incremental shares from assumed exercise of stock options	769	292	281
Diluted weighted average shares of common stock outstanding	30,854	30,763	32,132
Basic earnings per share	$ 1.60	$ 1.02	$ 2.01
Diluted earnings per share	$ 1.56	$ 1.01	$ 2.00

As of January 28, 2000, 130,000 shares of common stock with exercise prices ranging from $46.56 to $66.13 per share were not included in the computation of diluted EPS, because the options' exercise prices were greater than the average market price of the common shares during fiscal 2000.

Stock awards and grants

The company has a restricted stock award plan. Under the provisions of the plan, a committee of the company's board of directors may award shares of the company's common stock to its officers and key employees. Such shares vest over a five- or 10-year period on a straight-line basis from the date of the award.

The granting of these awards and grants has been recorded as deferred compensation based on the fair market value of the shares at the date of grant. Compensation expense under these plans is recorded as shares vest. The balance of the awards and grants totaled 17,960 shares, 31,000 shares and 77,000 shares for the period ended January 28, 2000, January 29, 1999 and January 30, 1998, respectively.

Stock options

The company has 5.5 million shares of common stock and 0.4 million shares of treasury shares that may be issued pursuant to the exercise of options granted under the company's Stock Option Plan (for employees) and the Non-Employee Director Stock Option Plan, respectively.

Under the company's stock option plans, options are granted at the discretion of a committee of the company's board of directors to officers, key employees of the company, and members of the board of directors of the company who are not also employed by the company. No option may have an exercise price less than the fair market value per share of the common stock at the date of the grant.

Activity under the stock option plans was as follows:

	Options	Average Exercise Price	Exercisable Options
Balance at January 31, 1997	1,150,400	$18.49	193,140
Granted	347,917	$33.45	
Exercised	(31,000)	$13.21	
Forfeited	–	–	
Balance at January 30, 1998	1,467,317	$21.42	350,107
Granted	1,874,000	$23.73	
Exercised	(108,480)	$17.01	
Forfeited	(541,330)	$22.35	
Balance at January 29, 1999	2,691,507	$23.41	473,597
Granted	591,000	$38.64	
Exercised	(368,650)	$18.02	
Forfeited	(137,840)	$32.17	
Balance at January 28, 2000	2,776,017	$26.94	1,371,397

Notes to Consolidated Financial Statements

The range of options outstanding as of January 28, 2000 is as follows:

Price Range Per Share	Number of Options Shares Outstanding/Exercisable	Weighted Average Exercise Price Outstanding/Exercisable	Weighted Average Remaining Contractual Life *(In years)*
$15.00–$29.99	1,490,600/1,237,230	$19.58/$19.36	8.2
$30.00–$44.99	1,155,417/ 129,167	33.16/ 32.48	9.0
Over $45.00	130,000/ 5,000	56.01/ 57.56	9.5
	2,776,017/1,371,397	$26.94/$20.73	8.6

The options above generally have a 10-year term. Options granted under the company's Stock Option Plan generally vest from six months to five years; options granted under the Non-Employee Director Stock Option Plan vest over a period from zero to two years.

Stock-based compensation

As permitted by SFAS No. 123, "Accounting for Stock-Based Compensation," the company accounts for its stock-based compensation plans as presented by APB Opinion No. 25 and related interpretations. Accordingly, compensation costs related to the stock awards and grants were $0.2 million, $0.7 million and $0.3 million in fiscal 2000, 1999 and 1998, respectively. These compensation costs are recorded in Deferred Compensation in the Shareholders' investment section of the Consolidated Balance Sheet.

Had compensation cost for the company's options granted after January 27, 1995 been determined consistent with the provisions of SFAS No. 123, the company's net income and earnings per share would have been reduced to the following pro forma amounts:

(In thousands, except per share data)	January 28, 2000	January 29, 1999	January 30, 1998
Net income			
As reported	$48,034	$31,185	$64,150
Pro forma	$42,378	$26,429	$62,511
Basic earnings per share			
As reported	$ 1.60	$ 1.02	$ 2.01
Pro forma	$ 1.41	$ 0.87	$ 1.96
Diluted earnings per share			
As reported	$ 1.56	$ 1.01	$ 2.00
Pro forma	$ 1.38	$ 0.86	$ 1.95

The fair value of each option grant was estimated as of the date of grant using the Black-Scholes pricing model. The resulting compensation cost was amortized over the vesting period.

The option grant fair values and assumptions used to determine such value are as follows:

Options granted during	2000	1999	1998
Weighted average grant-date fair value	$19.74	$11.21	$17.02
Assumptions:			
Risk-free interest rate	5.58%	4.74%	6.10%
Expected volatility	38.55%	35.86%	37.30%
Expected term (in years)	7.0	7.0	7.0

Note 3. Income taxes

Earnings before income taxes consisted of the following :

(In thousands)	2000	1999	1998
United States	$ 78,050	$ 44,499	$ 95,909
Foreign	(1,806)	5,001	5,916
Total	$ 76,244	$ 49,500	$101,825

The components of the provision for income taxes for each of the periods presented are as follows (in thousands):

Period ended	January 28, 2000	January 29, 1999	January 30, 1998
Current:			
Federal	$19,984	$21,026	$31,335
State	473	1,752	4,449
Foreign	(517)	1,485	3,049
Deferred	8,270	(5,948)	(1,158)
	$28,210	$18,315	$37,675

The difference between income taxes at the statutory federal income tax rate of 35 percent and income tax reported in the statements of operations is as follows (in thousands):

Period ended	January 28, 2000 Amount	%	January 29, 1999 Amount	%	January 30, 1998 Amount	%
Tax at statutory federal tax rate	$26,685	35%	$17,325	35%	$35,640	35%
Foreign taxes (excess over statutory rate)	22	–	263	–	1,130	1
State income taxes, net of federal benefit	907	1	1,306	3	3,999	4
Tax credits and other	596	1	(579)	(1)	(3,094)	(3)
	$28,210	37%	$18,315	37%	$37,675	37%

Under the liability method prescribed by SFAS No. 109, "Accounting for Income Taxes," deferred taxes are provided based upon enacted tax laws and rates applicable to the periods in which taxes become payable.

Notes to Consolidated Financial Statements

Temporary differences that give rise to deferred tax assets and liabilities as of January 28, 2000 and January 29, 1999 are as follows (in thousands):

Period ended	January 28, 2000	January 29, 1999
Deferred tax assets:		
Catalog advertising	$ (4,968)	$ (3,914)
Inventory	8,233	9,198
Employee benefits	4,231	7,937
Reserve for returns	2,912	2,661
Foreign operating loss carryforwards	124	686
Valuation allowance	(124)	(686)
Other	253	2,065
Total	$10,661	$17,947
Deferred tax liabilities:		
Depreciation	$ 8,581	$ 8,141
Other	536	(8)
Total	$ 9,117	$ 8,133

The valuation allowance required under SFAS No. 109 has been established for the deferred income tax benefits related to certain subsidiary loss carryforwards, which management currently estimates may not be realized. These carryforwards do not expire.

Note 4. Lines of credit

During fiscal 2000, the company entered into a new domestic credit facility providing unsecured credit totaling $200 million. There were no short-term borrowings as of January 28, 2000, compared to $21.8 million outstanding at January 29, 1999.

In addition, the company has unsecured lines of credit with various foreign banks totaling the equivalent of approximately $54 million for its wholly owned subsidiaries. There was $11.7 million outstanding at January 28, 2000, compared with $17.1 million as of January 29, 1999.

The following table summarizes certain information regarding these short-term borrowings:

(Dollars in millions)	2000	1999	1998
Maximum amount of borrowings	$53	$257	$118
Average amount of borrowings	$33	$134	$ 38
Weighted average interest rate during year	4.96%	5.77%	5.25%
Weighted average interest rate at year-end	3.43%	5.42%	5.27%

Note 5. Long-term debt

There was no long-term debt as of January 28, 2000 and January 29, 1999.

Note 6. Leases

The company leases store and office space and equipment under various leasing arrangements. The leases are accounted for as operating leases. Total rental expense under these leases was $15.5 million, $15.6 million and $13.5 million for the years ended January 28, 2000, January 29, 1999 and January 30, 1998, respectively.

Total future fiscal year commitments under these leases as of January 28, 2000 are as follows (in thousands):

2001	$ 7,900
2002	5,702
2003	3,568
2004	1,960
2005	1,473
Thereafter	6,337
	$26,940

Note 7. Retirement plan

The company has a retirement plan, which covers most regular employees and provides for annual contributions at the discretion of the board of directors. Also included in the plan is a 401(k) feature that allows employees to make contributions, and the company matches a portion of those contributions. Total expense provided under this plan was $5.2 million, $4.8 million and $6.6 million for the years ended January 28, 2000, January 29, 1999 and January 30, 1998, respectively.

Note 8. Postretirement benefits

In January 1998, the company implemented a plan to provide health insurance benefits for eligible retired employees. These insurance benefits will be funded through insurance contracts, a group benefit trust or general assets of the company. The assets were contributed to the plan in January 2000 and January 1999. The cost of these insurance benefits is recognized as the eligible employees render service.

Notes to Consolidated Financial Statements

The following table presents the change in the benefit obligation and plan assets in fiscal years 2000 and 1999:

(In thousands)	**2000**	1999
Change in benefit obligation:		
Benefit obligation at beginning of year	**$ 5,731**	$ 4,419
Service cost	**767**	630
Interest cost	**385**	308
Plan participants' contributions	**16**	13
Actuarial (gain)/loss	**(1,448)**	376
Benefits paid	**(57)**	(15)
Implementation of plan	**–**	–
Benefit obligation at end of year	**$ 5,394**	$ 5,731
Change in plan assets:		
Fair value of plan assets at beginning of year	**$ 1,978**	$ –
Actual return on plan assets	**58**	–
Employer contributions	**1,970**	1,980
Plan participants' contributions	**16**	13
Benefits paid	**(57)**	(15)
Fair value of plan assets at end of year	**$ 3,965**	$ 1,978
Net amount recognized:		
Funded status	**$(1,429)**	$(3,753)
Unrecognized net actuarial (gain)/loss	**(985)**	373
Unrecognized prior service cost	**3,783**	4,052
Prepaid benefit cost	**$ 1,369**	$ 672
Weighted-average assumptions at end of year:		
Discount rate	**8.00%**	6.75%
Expected return on plan assets	**7.50%**	7.50%

The components of net periodic benefit cost for the years ended January 28, 2000 and January 29, 1999 were as follows:

(In thousands)	**2000**	1999
Service cost	**$ 767**	$ 630
Interest cost	**385**	308
Expected return on plan assets	**(148)**	–
Amortization of prior service cost	**269**	270
Postretirement benefit cost	**$1,273**	$1,208

For measurement purposes, a 6.5 percent annual rate of increase in the per capita cost of covered health care benefits was assumed for fiscal year 2001. The rate was assumed to decrease gradually to 5 percent for fiscal year 2004 and remain at that level thereafter.

Assumed health care cost trend rates have a significant effect on the amounts reported for the health care plan. A 1 percentage point change in assumed health care cost trend rates would have the following effects:

(In thousands)	Service and Interest Costs	Postretirement Benefit Obligation
1 percent increase	$ 66	$ 252
1 percent decrease	(56)	(216)

Note 9. Non-recurring charge and related reversal

During fiscal year 1999, in connection with changes in executive management, the company announced a Plan designed to reduce administrative and operational costs stemming from duplicative responsibilities and certain non-profitable operations. This Plan included the reduction of staff positions, the closing of three outlet stores, the liquidation of the Willis & Geiger operations and the termination of a licensing agreement with MontBell Co. Ltd. A non-recurring charge of $12.6 million was recorded in fiscal 1999 related to these matters.

Below is a summary of related costs for the periods ended January 28, 2000:

(In thousands)	Balance January 29, 1999	Cost Incurred	Charges Reversed	**Balance January 28, 2000**
Severence costs	$ 6,700	$(5,693)	$ –	**$1,007**
Asset impairments	3,199	(2,057)	(1,111)	**31**
Facility exit costs and other	2,590	(1,820)	(663)	**107**
Total	$12,489	$(9,570)	$ (1,774)	**$1,145**

For the year ended January 28, 2000, the company executed the Plan and incurred costs totaling $9.6 million. In addition, there was a reversal of $1.8 million of the reserves recorded in fiscal 1999. Those included $0.7 million for better than expected lease termination settlements related to fiscal 2000 store closings, and $1.1 million for better than anticipated sell-through of Willis & Geiger inventory liquidations. Based on these two factors, there was an addition to net income of $1.1 million, or $0.04 per share, in the year ended January 28, 2000. The balance of $1.1 million, predominantly severance, will be paid in fiscal 2001.

Note 10. Divestitures

Willis & Geiger

During fiscal 2000, the company completed the liquidation of its Willis & Geiger inventory and fixed assets. The company retains the Willis & Geiger tradename.

The Territory Ahead

During the first quarter of fiscal 1998, the company sold its majority interest in The Territory Ahead to The International Cornerstone Group, Inc. of Boston, Massachusetts, resulting in an after-tax gain of $4.9 million. The after-tax gain was recorded in the first quarter of fiscal 1998.

Sales and results of operations of The Territory Ahead and Willis & Geiger were not material to the consolidated financial statements.

Notes to Consolidated Financial Statements

Note 11. Sales and use tax

A 1992 Supreme Court decision confirmed that the Commerce Clause of the United States Constitution prevents a state from requiring the collection of its use tax by a mail order company unless the company has a physical presence in the state. However, there continues to be uncertainty due to inconsistent application of the Supreme Court decision by state and federal courts. The company attempts to conduct its operations in compliance with its interpretation of the applicable legal standard, but there can be no assurance that such compliance will not be challenged.

In recent challenges, various states have sought to require companies to begin collection of use taxes and/or pay taxes from previous sales. The company has not received assessments from any state. The amount of potential assessments, if any, cannot be reasonably estimated.

The Supreme Court decision also established that Congress has the power to enact legislation that would permit states to require collection of use taxes by mail order companies. Congress has from time to time considered proposals for such legislation. The company anticipates that any legislative change, if adopted, would be applied only on a prospective basis.

In October 1998, The Internet Tax Freedom Act was signed into law. Among the provisions of this Act is a three-year moratorium on multiple and discriminatory taxes on electronic commerce. An Advisory Commission on Electronic Commerce has been appointed to study and report back to Congress on whether and, if so, how electronic commerce should be taxed.

We are monitoring the activities of the Commission, as well as any proposed changes in the sales and use tax laws and policies in general.

Note 12. Segment disclosure

The company organizes and manages its business segments (core, specialty and international) based on type of catalog, which focuses on specific customer needs and markets served. Certain catalogs are combined for purposes of assessing financial performance. Each business segment is separately evaluated by executive management with financial information reviewed to assess performance. The company evaluates the performance of its business segments based on net income before income taxes. The accounting policies of the company's segments are the same as those described in Note 1. The company is not dependent upon any single customer or group of customers, the loss of which would have a material effect on the company.

Core

The core segment is composed of adult apparel offered through our regular monthly catalogs, tailored catalogs and prospector catalogs. Sales for these catalogs that are received via the Internet, liquidation or export channels are included in this core segment. The regular monthly catalogs contain a full assortment of classically inspired, traditionally styled casual wear for adults. Some of these products include dress shirts, jeans, mesh knit shirts, women's knits, sweaters, outerwear and turtlenecks. The prospecting catalog is a condensed version of our monthly catalog featuring some of the company's best-selling products. The prospector catalogs are sent to active buyers, to those on the house file who have been inactive or have yet to make a purchase and to prospective customers. The tailored catalogs are Beyond Buttondowns, offering a broad assortment of fine tailored clothing for men, and First Person, featuring women's finely tailored clothing suitable for the workplace.

Specialty

The specialty segment is composed of Kids, Coming Home and Corporate Sales catalogs. Sales for these catalogs that are received via the Internet, liquidation or export channels are included in this specialty segment. The specialty catalogs have been developed over the years in response to customer requests for additional merchandise and are used to target specific needs that are important to Lands' End customers. The specialty businesses include the Kids catalog, which offers a collection of clothing for children of all ages. In addition, there is a uniform catalog that targets the growing uniform trend in many public and private schools. The Coming Home catalog offers home products, primarily bedding and bath items. The Corporate Sales catalog is a business-to-business catalog that utilizes the company's embroidery capabilities to design and apply unique emblems and logos on Lands' End product for corporations, clubs, teams and other groups.

International

The international segment consists of foreign-based operations located in Japan, the United Kingdom and Germany, which include catalogs, Internet and liquidation channels. Catalogs are denominated in local currencies and written in native languages. There are phone and distribution centers located in both Japan and the United Kingdom. Germany has its own phone and customer service center, but orders are packed and shipped from the distribution center in the United Kingdom.

Segment sales represent sales to external parties. Segment income before income taxes is revenue less direct and allocable operating expenses, which includes interest expense and interest income. Segment identifiable assets are those that are directly used in or identified with segment operations. "Other" includes corporate expenses, inter-company eliminations, and other income and deduction items that are not allocated to segments.

Notes to Consolidated Financial Statements

Lands' End, Inc. & Subsidiaries

Pertinent financial data by operating segment for the three years ended January 28, 2000 are as follows:

	Fiscal year ended January 28, 2000				
(In thousands)	**Core**	**Specialty**	**International**	**Other**	**Consolidated**
Net sales	**$780,298**	**$396,327**	**$143,198**	**$ –**	**$1,319,823**
Income (loss) before income taxes[1]	**$ 32,725**	**$ 43,144**	**$ 2,348**	**$(1,973)**	**$ 76,244**
Identifiable assets	**$262,397**	**$133,276**	**$ 60,523**	**$ –**	**$ 456,196**
Depreciation and amortization	**$ 12,165**	**$ 6,179**	**$ 2,371**	**$ –**	**$ 20,715**
Capital expenditures	**$ 17,573**	**$ 8,925**	**$ 1,515**	**$ –**	**$ 28,013**
Interest expense	**$ 848**	**$ 430**	**$ 612**	**$ –**	**$ 1,890**
Interest income	**$ 547**	**$ 278**	**$ 57**	**$ –**	**$ 882**

	Fiscal year ended January 29, 1999				
(In thousands)	Core	Specialty	International	Other	Consolidated
Net sales	$860,891	$364,576	$145,908	$ –	$1,371,375
Income (loss) before income taxes[2]	$ 27,305	$ 23,016	$ 4,655	$(5,476)	$ 49,500
Identifiable assets	$273,929	$116,007	$ 65,983	$ –	$ 455,919
Depreciation and amortization	$ 11,310	$ 5,323	$ 2,098	$ –	$ 18,731
Capital expenditures	$ 24,828	$ 10,514	$ 11,408	$ –	$ 46,750
Interest expense	$ 3,910	$ 2,296	$ 1,528	$ –	$ 7,734
Interest income	$ 11	$ 5	$ –	$ –	$ 16

	Fiscal year ended January 30, 1998				
(In thousands)	Core	Specialty	International	Other	Consolidated
Net sales	$824,854	$306,986	$131,789	$ –	$1,263,629
Income before income taxes	$ 59,356	$ 30,225	$ 7,672	$ 4,572	$ 101,825
Identifiable assets	$275,764	$102,630	$ 55,078	$ –	$ 433,472
Depreciation and amortization	$ 9,805	$ 3,813	$ 1,509	$ –	$ 15,127
Capital expenditures	$ 27,585	$ 10,266	$ 9,808	$ –	$ 47,659
Interest expense	$ 714	$ 351	$ 930	$ –	$ 1,995
Interest income	$ 1,257	$ 468	$ –	$ –	$ 1,725

(1) Includes non-recurring credits of $0.5 million and $1.3 million allocated to the core and specialty segments, respectively.
(2) Includes non-recurring charges of $7.6 million and $5.0 million allocated to the core and specialty segments, respectively.
(3) Fiscal years 1999 and 1998 have been restated to conform to fiscal 2000 presentation.

Pertinent financial data by geographical location for the three years ended January 28, 2000 are as follows:

	Net Sales			Identifiable Assets		
(In thousands)	**Jan. 28, 2000**	Jan. 29, 1999	Jan. 30, 1998	**Jan. 28, 2000**	Jan. 29, 1999	Jan. 30, 1998
United States	**$1,176,625**	$1,225,467	$1,131,840	**$395,673**	$389,936	$378,394
Other countries	**143,198**	145,908	131,789	**60,523**	65,983	55,078
Total	**$1,319,823**	$1,371,375	$1,263,629	**$456,196**	$455,919	$433,472

Notes to Consolidated Financial Statements

Lands' End, Inc. & Subsidiaries

Note 13. Derivative instruments and hedging activities

The company's sales of merchandise to its subsidiaries in the United Kingdom, Japan and Germany are denominated in the subsidiary's local currency. To a lesser extent, the company has export sales to customers in Canada. The company incurs third-party expenses related to the Canadian export business, some of which are denominated in Canadian dollars. Accordingly, the future U.S. Dollar-equivalent cash flows may vary due to changes in related foreign currency exchange rates. To reduce that risk, the company enters into foreign currency forward contracts and purchases foreign currency put options. The company's sales to its foreign subsidiaries and its third-party purchases are on open account with settlement within approximately one month. Accordingly, the settlement dates of the forward contracts and put options fall approximately one month after the date of forecasted sales or purchases. The company has no other freestanding or embedded derivative instruments.

As of July 31, 1999, the company adopted the Financial Accounting Standards Board's (FASB's) Statement of Financial Accounting Standards No. 133, "Accounting for Derivative Instruments and Hedging Activities" (Statement 133). Statement 133 unifies accounting and financial reporting standards for forward contracts, put options, other derivative instruments and related hedging activities. Statement 133 requires, in part, that the company report all derivative instruments in the statement of financial position as assets or liabilities at their fair value. The treatment of subsequent changes in fair value depends on whether hedge accounting is available. Prior to the adoption of Statement 133 for fiscal 2000, a loss of $0.7 million was recognized in other expenses. For fiscal 2000, a loss of $0.8 million was recognized in other expenses, compared with a loss of $1.9 million in fiscal 1999. Before the effective date of Statement 133, hedge accounting was not available for the company's forward contracts. Those contracts were reported in the statement of financial position as assets or liabilities at their fair value and changes in fair value were reported currently in earnings. Hedge accounting for the company's put options involved reporting the put options initially at the amount of the premium paid, with amortization of the premium over the option period. Subsequent gains or losses on the put options through the date of the sale to the foreign subsidiary were deferred until the date the consolidated entity (through the foreign subsidiary) sold the merchandise to a third party. At the date merchandise is sold to a foreign subsidiary, the hedging relationship is terminated and subsequent gains and losses on the put option (including unamortized premium) were reported currently in earnings.

As part of its adoption of Statement 133 on July 31, 1999, the company designated all of its hedging relationships anew. Both forward contracts and put options can qualify for cash flow hedge accounting under Statement 133 if applicable hedging criteria are met. Under Statement 133's cash flow hedging model, gains and losses on the derivative instrument that occur through the date the company sells merchandise to a subsidiary or purchases from a foreign third party are deferred in a component of equity (accumulated other comprehensive income) to the extent the hedging relationship is effective. The maximum hedging period (the period between the company's designation and culmination of a hedging relationship) of the company's cash flow hedges is 24 months.

As required by Statement 133, the company assesses hedge effectiveness at least quarterly. The effectiveness of put options is assessed based on changes in intrinsic value of the options due to changes in spot foreign exchange rates. Because they are excluded from the company's assessment of hedge effectiveness, the company reports currently in earnings changes in the fair value of put options due to changes in time value of the options. For the year ended January 28, 2000, a net loss of $0.1 million was recognized in other expense due to hedge ineffectiveness and fair value changes excluded from the company's effectiveness assessments.

To the extent the company must discontinue cash flow hedge accounting because it is probable that original forecasted sales will not occur, Statement 133 requires that the company immediately reclassify the net gain or loss from accumulated other comprehensive income into earnings. During fiscal 2000, net losses of $0.2 million were so reclassified.

At the date merchandise is sold to a foreign subsidiary or purchased from a foreign third party, the hedging relationship is terminated and subsequent gains and losses on the hedging derivative instrument are reported currently in earnings. At the date of the ultimate sale of the merchandise by the foreign subsidiary to a third party or purchase from a foreign third party, the gain or loss previously deferred in equity is reclassified into earnings. The company estimates that net hedging gains of $0.1 million will be reclassified from accumulated other comprehensive income into earnings within the 12 months between January 29, 2000 and January 26, 2001.

Upon the company's adoption of Statement 133 on July 31, 1999, the company adjusted the carrying amount of the two put option contracts as assets at their fair value of $34 thousand. Because the put options had previously qualified in a cash-flow-type hedging relationship prior to adoption of Statement 133, an immaterial cumulative-effect-type transition adjustment and an immaterial transition adjustment related to the ineffective portion of the put options were reported in accumulated other comprehensive income and other expense, respectively. No transition adjustment was needed for the forward contracts, which were already being reported at their fair value with changes in fair value reported currently in earnings.

Notes to Consolidated Financial Statements

Lands' End, Inc. & Subsidiaries

Note 14. Consolidated quarterly analysis (unaudited)

(In thousands, except per share data)	Fiscal 2000 1st Qtr.	Fiscal 2000 2nd Qtr.	Fiscal 2000 3rd Qtr.	Fiscal 2000 4th Qtr.	Fiscal 1999 1st Qtr.	Fiscal 1999 2nd Qtr.	Fiscal 1999 3rd Qtr.	Fiscal 1999 4th Qtr.
Net sales	$289,609	$254,616	$325,970	$449,628	$268,587	$239,194	$322,422	$541,172
Gross profit	125,434	118,216	140,813	208,069	124,740	115,478	145,262	231,234
Pretax income	10,332	7,068	13,890	44,954	8,266	(97)	551	40,780
Net income	$ 6,509	$ 4,453	$ 8,751	$ 28,321	$ 5,208	$ (61)	$ 347	$ 25,691
Basic earnings per share	$ 0.22	$ 0.15	$ 0.29	$ 0.94	$ 0.17	$ 0.00	$ 0.01	$ 0.85
Diluted earnings per share	$ 0.21	$ 0.14	$ 0.28	$ 0.92	$ 0.17	$ 0.00	$ 0.01	$ 0.84
Common shares outstanding	30,110	30,060	30,149	30,149	30,961	30,236	30,239	30,142

(In dollars)								
Market price of shares outstanding:								
Market high	39 15/16	49 1/2	78 7/16	83 1/2	44 1/8	37 5/8	30 3/8	32 7/16
Market low	28 1/8	37 9/16	39 9/16	28	35	26 1/8	15 3/8	16 3/4

Quarterly earnings per share amounts are based on the weighted average common shares outstanding for each quarter and, therefore, might not equal the amount computed for the total year.

FIVE- OR TEN-YEAR SUMMARY

Usually presented in close proximity to the audited financial statements is a five- or ten-year summary of selected financial data. From such a summary, one can determine trends and growth patterns over a fairly long period of time. Lands' End presents eleven years of selected financial data that includes operating data, financial position data, and selected statistics and ratios.

Eleven-Year Consolidated Financial Summary (unaudited)

The following selected financial data have been derived from the company's consolidated financial statements, which have been audited by Arthur Andersen LLP, independent public accountants. The information set forth below should be read in conjunction with "Management's Discussion and Analysis" and the consolidated financial statements and notes thereto included elsewhere herein.

(In thousands, except per share data)	2000	1999	1998
Income statement data:			
Net sales	$1,319,823	$1,371,375	$1,263,629
Pretax income	76,244	49,500	101,825
Percent to net sales	5.8%	3.6%	8.1%
Net income before cumulative effect of change in accounting	48,034	31,185	64,150
Cumulative effect of accounting change	–	–	–
Net income	48,034	31,185	64,150
Per share of common stock: [1]			
Basic earnings per share before cumulative effect of change in accounting	$ 1.60	$ 1.02	$ 2.01
Cumulative effect of change in accounting	–	–	–
Basic earnings per share	$ 1.60	$ 1.02	$ 2.01
Diluted earnings per share	$ 1.56	$ 1.01	$ 2.00
Cash dividends per share	$ –	$ –	$ –
Common shares outstanding	30,149	30,142	30,979
Balance sheet data:			
Current assets	$ 289,408	$ 294,303	$ 299,146
Current liabilities	150,872	205,283	182,013
Property, plant, equipment and intangibles, net	166,788	161,616	134,326
Total assets	456,196	455,919	433,472
Noncurrent liabilities	9,117	8,133	8,747
Shareholders' investment	296,207	242,503	242,712
Other data:			
Net working capital	$ 138,536	$ 89,020	$ 117,133
Capital expenditures	28,013	46,750	48,228
Depreciation and amortization expense	20,715	18,731	15,127
Return on average shareholders' investment	18%	13%	28%
Return on average assets	11%	7%	16%

(1) Net income per share was computed after giving retroactive effect to the two-for-one stock split in May 1994.

(2) Effective January 30, 1993, the company adopted Statement of Financial Accounting Standards (SFAS) No. 109 "Accounting for Income Taxes," which was recorded as a change in accounting principle at the beginning of fiscal 1994 with an increase to net income of $1.3 million or $0.04 per share.

LANDS' END DIRECT MERCHANTS

Lands' End, Inc. & Subsidiaries

Fiscal year							
1997	1996	1995	1994[2]	1993	1992	1991	1990
$1,118,743	$1,031,548	$992,106	$869,975	$733,623	$683,427	$601,991	$544,850
84,919	50,925	59,663	69,870	54,033	47,492	29,943	47,270
7.6%	4.9%	6.0%	8.0%	7.4%	7.0%	4.1%	8.7%
50,952	30,555	36,096	42,429	33,500	28,732	14,743	29,071
–	–	–	1,300	–	–	–	–
50,952	30,555	36,096	43,729	33,500	28,732	14,743	29,071
$ 1.54	$ 0.89	$ 1.03	$ 1.18	$ 0.92	$ 0.77	$ 0.38	$ 0.73
–	–	–	0.04	–	–	–	–
$ 1.54	$ 0.89	$ 1.03	$ 1.22	$ 0.92	$ 0.77	$ 0.38	$ 0.73
$ 1.53	$ 0.89	$ 1.02	$ 1.21	$ 0.91	$ 0.76	$ 0.37	$ 0.73
$ –	$ –	$ –	$ 0.10	$ 0.10	$ 0.10	$ 0.10	$ 0.10
32,442	33,659	34,826	35,912	36,056	36,944	38,436	39,762
$ 272,039	$ 222,089	$198,168	$192,276	$137,531	$131,273	$107,824	$ 99,714
145,566	114,744	102,717	91,049	67,315	74,548	60,774	43,915
106,006	101,408	99,444	81,554	74,272	74,527	77,576	67,218
378,045	323,497	297,612	273,830	211,803	205,800	185,400	166,932
9,474	7,561	5,767	5,496	5,100	4,620	7,800	8,413
223,005	201,192	189,128	177,285	139,388	126,632	116,826	114,604
$ 126,473	$ 107,345	$ 95,451	$101,227	$ 70,216	$ 56,725	$ 47,050	$ 55,799
17,992	14,780	27,005	16,958	9,965	5,347	17,682	25,160
13,558	12,456	10,311	8,286	7,900	7,428	7,041	5,251
24%	16%	20%	28%	25%	23%	13%	28%
15%	10%	13%	18%	16%	15%	8%	18%

SPECIMEN FINANCIAL STATEMENTS: Abercrombie & Fitch Co.

Abercrombie & Fitch Co.

FINANCIAL SUMMARY

(Thousands except per share and per square foot amounts, ratios and store and associate data)

Fiscal Year	1999	1998	1997	1996	1995*	1994	1993
Summary of Operations							
Net Sales	$1,042,056	$815,804	$521,617	$335,372	$235,659	$165,463	$110,952
Gross Income	$ 465,583	$343,951	$201,080	$123,766	$ 79,794	$ 56,820	$ 30,562
Operating Income (Loss)	$ 242,064	$166,958	$ 84,125	$ 45,993	$ 23,798	$ 13,751	$ (4,064)
Operating Income (Loss) as a Percentage of Sales	23.2%	20.5%	16.1%	13.7%	10.1%	8.3%	(3.7%)
Net Income (Loss)	$ 149,604	$102,062	$ 48,322	$ 24,674	$ 14,298	$ 8,251	$ (2,464)
Net Income (Loss) as a Percentage of Sales	14.4%	12.5%	9.3%	7.4%	6.1%	5.0%	(2.2%)
Per Share Results (1)							
Net Income (Loss) Per Basic Share	$ 1.45	$ .99	$ .47	$ .27	$ .17	$ .10	$ (.03)
Net Income (Loss) Per Diluted Share	$ 1.39	$ .96	$ .47	$ .27	$ .17	$ .10	$ (.03)
Weighted Average Diluted Shares Outstanding	107,641	106,202	102,956	91,520	86,000	86,000	86,000
Other Financial Information							
Total Assets	$ 458,166	$319,161	$183,238	$105,761	$ 87,693	$ 58,018	$ 48,882
Return on Average Assets	38%	41%	33%	26%	20%	15%	(4%)
Capital Expenditures	$ 83,824	$ 41,876	$ 29,486	$ 24,323	$ 24,526	$ 12,603	$ 4,694
Long-Term Debt	–	–	$ 50,000	$ 50,000	–	–	–
Shareholders' Equity (Deficit)	$ 311,094	$186,105	$ 58,775	$ 11,238	$(22,622)	$(37,070)	$(45,341)
Comparable Store Sales Increase	10%	35%	21%	13%	5%	15%	6%
Retail Sales Per Average Gross Square Foot	$ 512	$ 483	$ 376	$ 306	$ 290	$ 284	$ 243
Stores and Associates at End of Year							
Total Number of Stores Open	250	196	156	127	100	67	49
Gross Square Feet	2,174,000	1,791,000	1,522,000	1,229,000	962,000	665,000	499,000
Number of Associates	11,300	9,500	6,700	4,900	3,000	2,300	1,300

**Fifty-three week fiscal year.*

(1) Per share amounts reflect the two-for-one stock split on the Company's Class A Common Stock, paid on June 15, 1999.

Abercrombie & Fitch Co.

CONSOLIDATED STATEMENTS OF INCOME

(Thousands except per share amounts)	1999	1998	1997
Net Sales	$1,042,056	$815,804	$521,617
Cost of Goods Sold, Occupancy and Buying Costs	576,473	471,853	320,537
Gross Income	465,583	343,951	201,080
General, Administrative and Store Operating Expenses	223,519	176,993	116,955
Operating Income	242,064	166,958	84,125
Interest (Income)/ Expense, Net	(7,270)	(3,144)	3,583
Income Before Income Taxes	249,334	170,102	80,542
Provision for Income Taxes	99,730	68,040	32,220
Net Income	$ 149,604	$102,062	$ 48,322
Net Income Per Share:			
Basic	$ 1.45	$ .99	$ .47
Diluted	$ 1.39	$ .96	$ .47

The accompanying Notes are an integral part of these Consolidated Financial Statements.

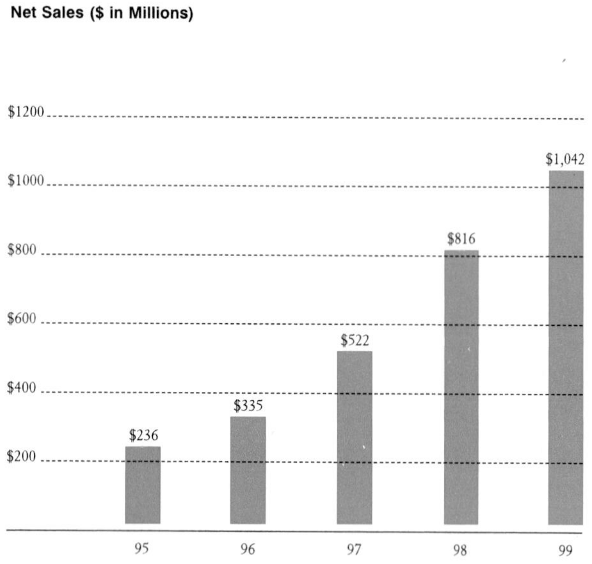

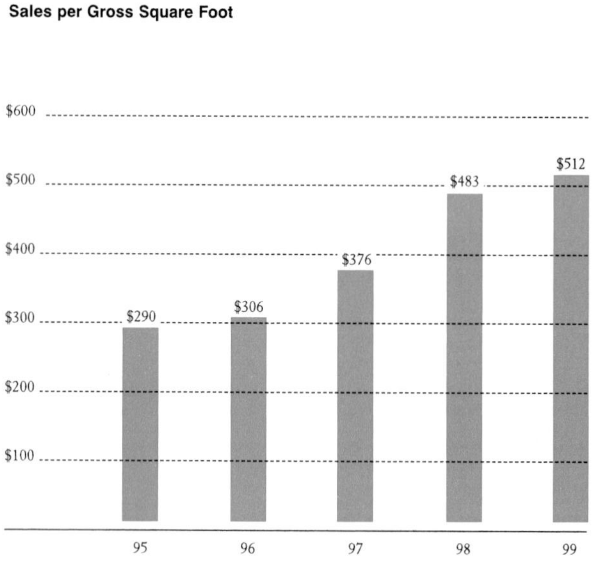

Abercrombie & Fitch Co.

CONSOLIDATED BALANCE SHEETS

(Thousands)	January 29, 2000	January 30, 1999
Assets		
Current Assets		
Cash and Equivalents	$147,908	$163,564
Marketable Securities	45,601	–
Accounts Receivable	11,447	4,101
Inventories	75,262	43,992
Other	19,999	6,578
Total Current Assets	300,217	218,235
Property and Equipment, Net	146,403	89,558
Deferred Income Taxes	11,060	10,854
Other Assets	486	631
Total Assets	$458,166	$319,278
Liabilities and Shareholders' Equity		
Current Liabilities		
Accounts Payable	$ 18,714	$ 24,759
Accrued Expenses	85,373	63,882
Income Taxes Payable	33,779	33,704
Total Current Liabilities	137,866	122,345
Other Long-Term Liabilities	9,206	10,828
Shareholders' Equity		
Common Stock	1,033	1,033
Paid-In Capital	147,305	143,626
Retained Earnings	192,735	43,131
	341,073	187,790
Less: Treasury Stock, at Average Cost	(29,979)	(1,685)
Total Shareholders' Equity	311,094	186,105
Total Liabilities and Shareholders' Equity	$458,166	$319,278

The accompanying Notes are an integral part of these Consolidated Financial Statements.

Abercrombie & Fitch Co.

CONSOLIDATED STATEMENTS OF SHAREHOLDERS' EQUITY

	Common Stock					
(Thousands)	Shares Outstanding	Par Value	Paid-In Capital	Retained Earnings (Deficit)	Treasury Stock, at Average Cost	Total Shareholders' Equity
Balance, February 1, 1997	102,100	$1,022	$117,469	$(107,253)	–	$ 11,238
Purchase of Treasury Stock	(100)	–	–	–	$ (929)	(929)
Net Income	–	–	–	48,322	–	48,322
Stock Options, Restricted Stock and Other	18	–	(8)	–	152	144
Balance, January 31, 1998	102,018	$1,022	$117,461	$ (58,931)	$ (777)	$ 58,775
Purchase of Treasury Stock	(490)	–	–	–	(11,240)	(11,240)
Net Income	–	–	–	102,062	–	102,062
Issuance of Common Stock	1,200	11	25,870	–	–	25,881
Stock Options, Restricted Stock and Other	86	–	295	–	10,332	10,627
Balance, January 30, 1999	102,814	$1,033	$143,626	$ 43,131	$ (1,685)	$ 186,105
Purchase of Treasury Stock	(1,510)	–	–	–	(50,856)	(50,856)
Net Income	–	–	–	149,604	–	149,604
Stock Options, Restricted Stock and Other	700	–	3,679	–	22,562	26,241
Balance, January 29, 2000	102,004	$1,033	$147,305	$ 192,735	$(29,979)	$ 311,094

The accompanying Notes are an integral part of these Consolidated Financial Statements.

Operating Income (%)

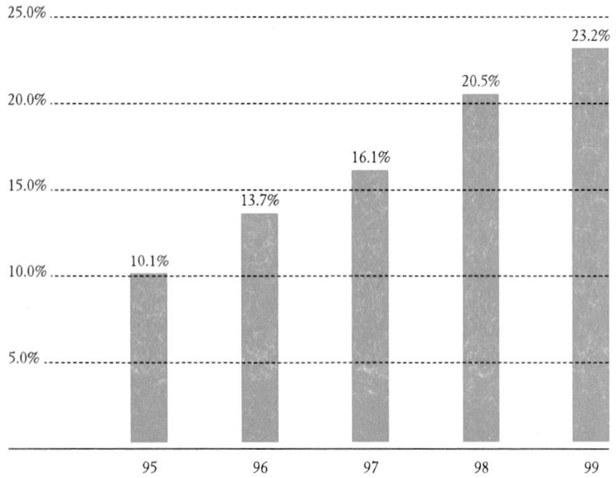

Earning Per Diluted Share

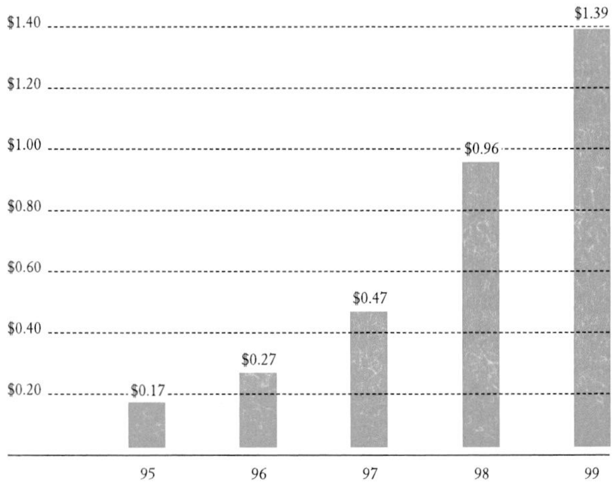

Abercrombie & Fitch Co.

CONSOLIDATED STATEMENTS OF CASH FLOWS

(Thousands)	1999	1998	1997
Cash Flows from Operating Activities			
Net Income	$149,604	$102,062	$ 48,322
Impact of Other Operating Activities on Cash Flows			
Depreciation and Amortization	27,721	20,946	16,342
Non Cash Charge for Deferred Compensation	5,212	11,497	6,219
Change in Assets and Liabilities			
Inventories	(31,270)	(10,065)	1,016
Accounts Payable and Accrued Expenses	15,446	37,530	22,309
Income Taxes	(131)	10,758	4,606
Other Assets and Liabilities	(12,773)	355	1,381
Net Cash Provided by Operating Activities	153,809	173,083	100,195
Investing Activities			
Capital Expenditures	(83,824)	(41,876)	(29,486
Proceeds from Maturities of Marketable Securities	11,332	–	–
Purchase of Marketable Securities	(56,933)	–	–
Note Receivable	(1,500)	–	–
Net Cash Used for Investing Activities	(130,925)	(41,876)	(29,486
Financing Activities			
Settlement of Balance with The Limited	–	23,785	–
Decrease in Receivable from The Limited	–	–	(29,202
Net Proceeds from Issuance of Common Stock	–	25,875	–
Repayment of Long-Term Debt	–	(50,000)	–
Purchase of Treasury Stock	(50,856)	(11,240)	(929
Other Changes in Shareholders' Equity	12,316	1,270	144
Net Cash Used for Financing Activities	(38,540)	(10,310)	(29,987
Net Increase/(Decrease) in Cash and Equivalents	(15,656)	120,897	40,722
Cash and Equivalents, Beginning of Year	163,564	42,667	1,945
Cash and Equivalents, End of Year	$147,908	$163,564	$ 42,667

The accompanying Notes are an integral part of these Consolidated Financial Statements.

APPENDIX C

PRESENT VALUE CONCEPTS

Business enterprises borrow and invest large sums of money. Both of these types of transactions involve the use of **present value computations**. A present value computation is based on the concept of the **time value of money**. For example, would you rather be given $1,000 today or be given $1,000 a year from today? If you get the $1,000 today and invest it to earn 10% per year, the $1,000 will accumulate to $1,100 ($1,000 plus the $100 interest) one year from today. The $1,000 received today is the present value amount that is equivalent to $1,100 one year from now. The present value, therefore, is based on three variables: (1) the dollar amount to be received (the future amount), (2) the length of time until the amount is received (the number of periods), and (3) the interest rate (the discount rate). The process of determining the present value is referred to as **discounting the future amount**. The relationship of these fundamental variables is depicted in the following time diagram.

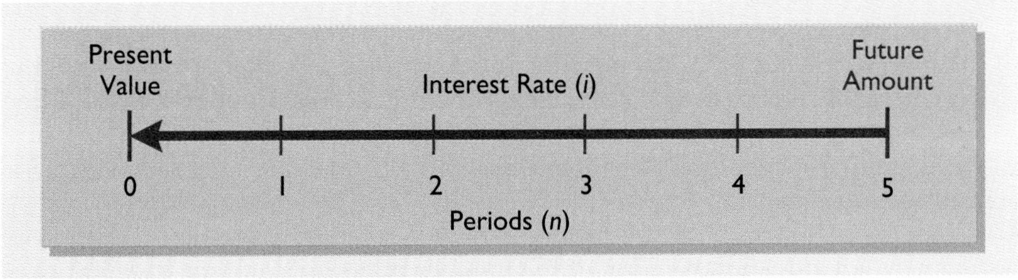

Illustration C-1
Time diagram

To better understand the variables involved in present value analysis, we encourage you to use time diagrams such as the one in Illustration C-1.

In this textbook, present value computations are used in measuring several items. For example, in Chapter 16, to determine the market price of a bond, the present value of the principal and interest payments is computed. In addition, finding the amount to be reported for notes payable and lease liability involves present value computations. And, in Chapter 27, the discounted cash flow technique and the net present value method for capital budget decisions use present value computations.

PRESENT VALUE OF A SINGLE FUTURE AMOUNT

To illustrate present value concepts, assume that you are willing to invest a sum of money that will yield $1,000 at the end of one year. In other words, what amount would you need to invest today to have $1,000 one year from now? If you want a 10% rate of return, the investment or present value is $909.09 ($1,000 ÷ 1.10). The computation of this amount is shown in Illustration C-2.

Present value × (1 + interest rate)	= Future amount
Present value × (1 + 10%)	= $1,000
Present value	= $1,000 ÷ 1.10
Present value	**= $909.09**

Illustration C-2
Present value computation—$1,000 discounted at 10% for 1 year

The future amount ($1,000), the discount rate (10%), and the number of periods (1) are known. The variables in this situation can be depicted in the time diagram in Illustration C-3 on the next page.

Illustration C-3

Finding present value if discounted for one period

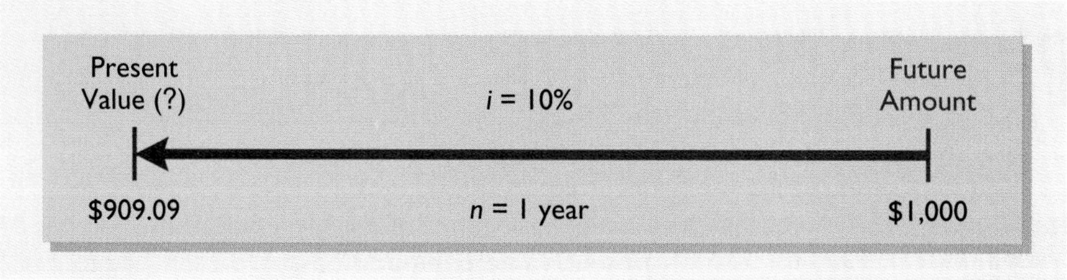

If the single future amount of $1,000 is to be received **in 2 years** and discounted at 10%, its present value is $826.45 [($1,000 ÷ 1.10) ÷ 1.10], depicted as follows.

Illustration C-4

Finding present value if discounted for two periods

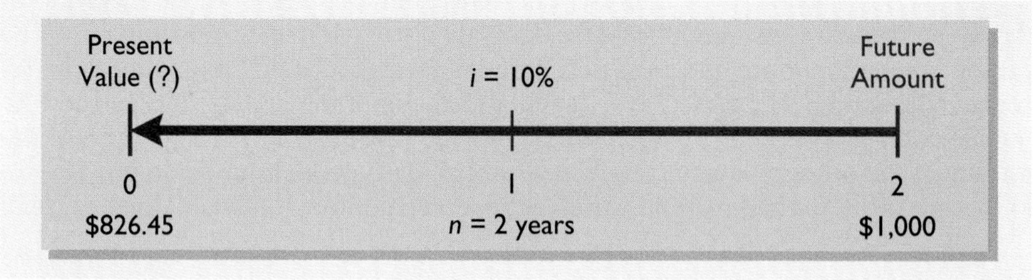

The present value of 1 may also be determined through tables that show the present value of 1 for *n* periods. In Table C-1 below, *n* is the number of discounting periods involved. The percentages are the periodic interest rates or discount rates, and the 5-digit decimal numbers in the respective columns are the factors for the present value of 1.

When Table C-1 is used, the future amount is multiplied by the present value factor specified at the intersection of the number of periods and the discount rate. For example, the present value factor for 1 period at a discount rate of 10% is .90909, which equals the $909.09 ($1,000 × .90909) computed in Illustration C-2.

TABLE C-1
Present Value of 1

(*n*) Periods	4%	5%	6%	8%	9%	10%	11%	12%	15%
1	.96154	.95238	.94340	.92593	.91743	.90909	.90090	.89286	.86957
2	.92456	.90703	.89000	.85734	.84168	.82645	.81162	.79719	.75614
3	.88900	.86384	.83962	.79383	.77218	.75132	.73119	.71178	.65752
4	.85480	.82270	.79209	.73503	.70843	.68301	.65873	.63552	.57175
5	.82193	.78353	.74726	.68058	.64993	.62092	.59345	.56743	.49718
6	.79031	.74622	.70496	.63017	.59627	.56447	.53464	.50663	.43233
7	.75992	.71068	.66506	.58349	.54703	.51316	.48166	.45235	.37594
8	.73069	.67684	.62741	.54027	.50187	.46651	.43393	.40388	.32690
9	.70259	.64461	.59190	.50025	.46043	.42410	.39092	.36061	.28426
10	.67556	.61391	.55839	.46319	.42241	.38554	.35218	.32197	.24719
11	.64958	.58468	.52679	.42888	.38753	.35049	.31728	.28748	.21494
12	.62460	.55684	.49697	.39711	.35554	.31863	.28584	.25668	.18691
13	.60057	.53032	.46884	.36770	.32618	.28966	.25751	.22917	.16253
14	.57748	.50507	.44230	.34046	.29925	.26333	.23199	.20462	.14133
15	.55526	.48102	.41727	.31524	.27454	.23939	.20900	.18270	.12289
16	.53391	.45811	.39365	.29189	.25187	.21763	.18829	.16312	.10687
17	.51337	.43630	.37136	.27027	.23107	.19785	.16963	.14564	.09293
18	.49363	.41552	.35034	.25025	.21199	.17986	.15282	.13004	.08081
19	.47464	.39573	.33051	.23171	.19449	.16351	.13768	.11611	.07027
20	.45639	.37689	.31180	.21455	.17843	.14864	.12403	.10367	.06110

For 2 periods at a discount rate of 10%, the present value factor is .82645, which equals the $826.45 ($1,000 × .82645) computed previously.

Note that **a higher discount rate produces a smaller present value**. For example, using a 15% discount rate, the present value of $1,000 due one year from now is $869.57. At 10%, it is $909.09. You also should recognize that **the further removed from the present the future amount is, the smaller the present value**. For example, using the same discount rate of 10%, the present value of $1,000 due **in 5 years** is $620.92. The present value of $1,000 due in **1** year is $909.09.

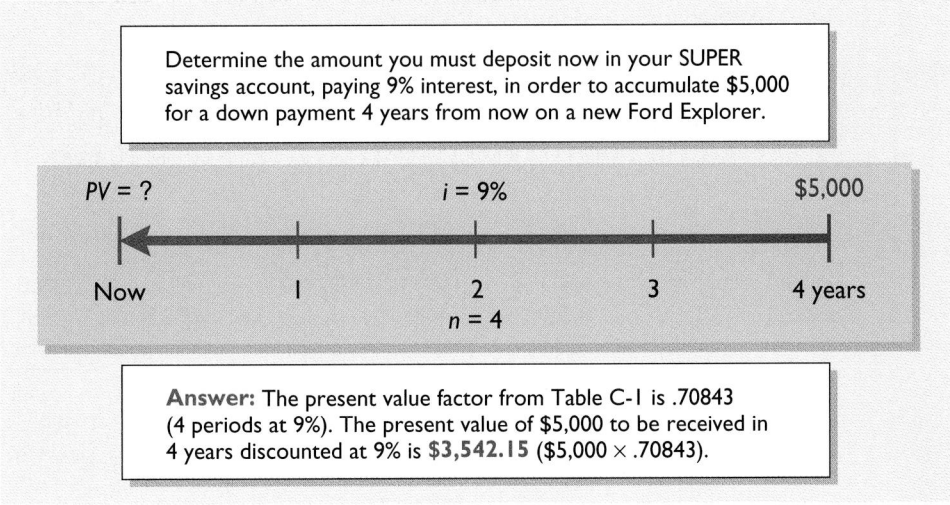

The following two demonstration problems (Illustrations C-5 and C-6) illustrate how to use Table C-1.

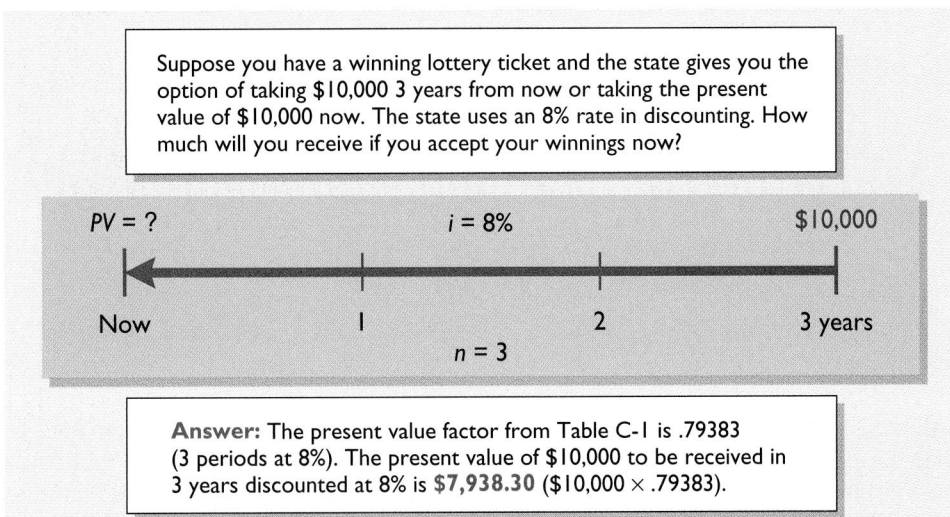

Illustration C-5

Demonstration Problem—Using Table C-1 for PV of 1

Suppose you have a winning lottery ticket and the state gives you the option of taking $10,000 3 years from now or taking the present value of $10,000 now. The state uses an 8% rate in discounting. How much will you receive if you accept your winnings now?

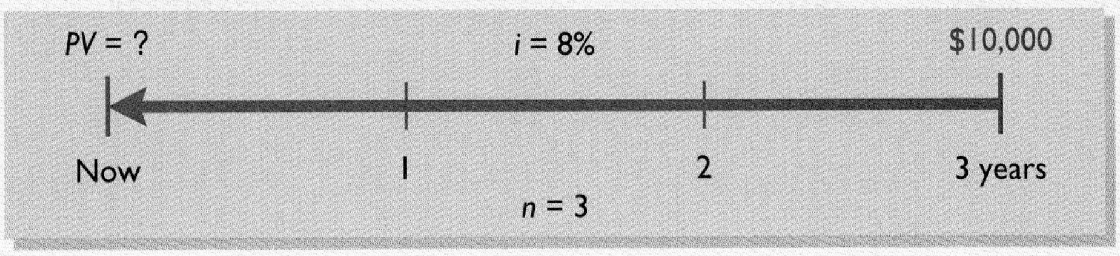

Answer: The present value factor from Table C-1 is .79383 (3 periods at 8%). The present value of $10,000 to be received in 3 years discounted at 8% is **$7,938.30** ($10,000 × .79383).

Illustration C-6

Demonstration Problem—Using Table C-1 for PV of 1

Determine the amount you must deposit now in your SUPER savings account, paying 9% interest, in order to accumulate $5,000 for a down payment 4 years from now on a new Ford Explorer.

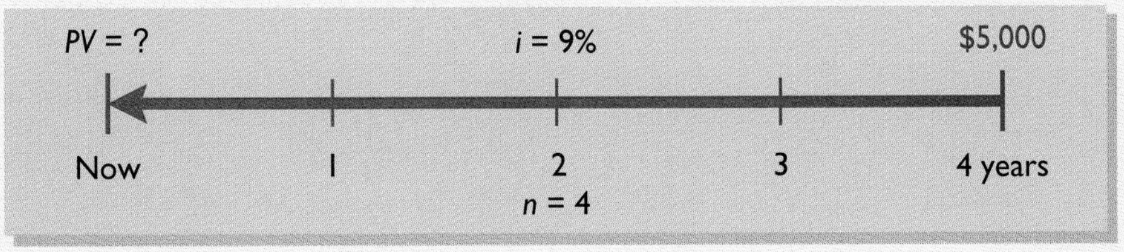

Answer: The present value factor from Table C-1 is .70843 (4 periods at 9%). The present value of $5,000 to be received in 4 years discounted at 9% is **$3,542.15** ($5,000 × .70843).

PRESENT VALUE OF A SERIES OF FUTURE AMOUNTS (ANNUITIES)

The preceding discussion involved the discounting of only a single future amount. Businesses and individuals frequently engage in transactions in which a series of equal dollar amounts are to be received or paid periodically. Examples of a series of periodic receipts or payments are loan agreements, installment sales, mortgage notes, lease (rental) contracts, and pension obligations. These series of periodic receipts or payments are called **annuities**. In computing the present value of an annuity, it is necessary to know (1) the discount rate, (2) the number of discount periods, and (3) the amount of the periodic receipts or payments. To illustrate the computation of the present value of an annuity, assume that you will receive $1,000 cash annually for 3 years and the discount rate is 10%. This situation is depicted in the following time diagram.

Illustration C-7

Time diagram for a 3-year annuity

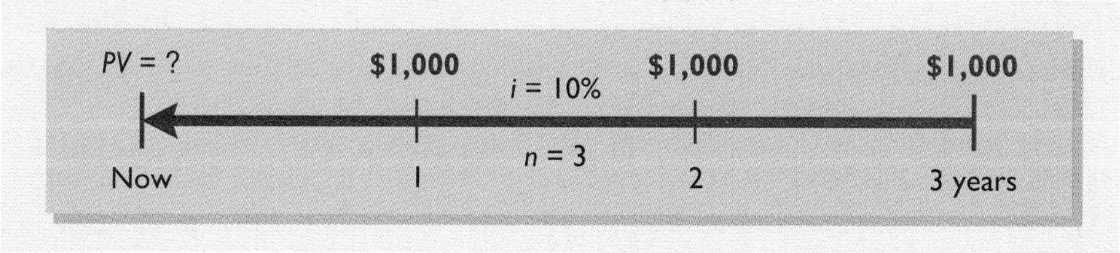

The present value in this situation may be computed as follows.

Illustration C-8

Present value of a series of future amounts computation

Future Amount	×	Present Value of 1 Factor at 10%	=	Present Value
$1,000 (1 year away)		.90909		$ 909.09
1,000 (2 years away)		.82645		826.45
1,000 (3 years away)		.75132		751.32
		2.48686		$2,486.86

This method of calculation is required when the periodic cash flows are not uniform in each period. When the future receipts are the same in each period, there are two other ways to compute present value. First, the annual cash flow can be multiplied by the sum of the three present value factors. In the example above, $1,000 × 2.48686 equals $2,486.86. Second, annuity tables may be used. As illustrated in Table C-2 below, these tables show the present value of 1 to be received periodically for a given number of periods.

TABLE C-2
Present Value of an Annuity of 1

(n) Periods	4%	5%	6%	8%	9%	10%	11%	12%	15%
1	.96154	.95238	.94340	.92593	.91743	.90909	.90090	.89286	.86957
2	1.88609	1.85941	1.83339	1.78326	1.75911	1.73554	1.71252	1.69005	1.62571
3	2.77509	2.72325	2.67301	2.57710	2.53130	2.48685	2.44371	2.40183	2.28323
4	3.62990	3.54595	3.46511	3.31213	3.23972	3.16986	3.10245	3.03735	2.85498
5	4.45182	4.32948	4.21236	3.99271	3.88965	3.79079	3.69590	3.60478	3.35216
6	5.24214	5.07569	4.91732	4.62288	4.48592	4.35526	4.23054	4.11141	3.78448
7	6.00205	5.78637	5.58238	5.20637	5.03295	4.86842	4.71220	4.56376	4.16042
8	6.73274	6.46321	6.20979	5.74664	5.53482	5.33493	5.14612	4.96764	4.48732
9	7.43533	7.10782	6.80169	6.24689	5.99525	5.75902	5.53705	5.32825	4.77158
10	8.11090	7.72173	7.36009	6.71008	6.41766	6.14457	5.88923	5.65022	5.01877
11	8.76048	8.30641	7.88687	7.13896	6.80519	6.49506	6.20652	5.93770	5.23371
12	9.38507	8.86325	8.38384	7.53608	7.16073	6.81369	6.49236	6.19437	5.42062
13	9.98565	9.39357	8.85268	7.90378	7.48690	7.10336	6.74987	6.42355	5.58315
14	10.56312	9.89864	9.29498	8.24424	7.78615	7.36669	6.98187	6.62817	5.72448
15	11.11839	10.37966	9.71225	8.55948	8.06069	7.60608	7.19087	6.81086	5.84737
16	11.65230	10.83777	10.10590	8.85137	8.31256	7.82371	7.37916	6.97399	5.95424
17	12.16567	11.27407	10.47726	9.12164	8.54363	8.02155	7.54879	7.11963	6.04716
18	12.65930	11.68959	10.82760	9.37189	8.75563	8.20141	7.70162	7.24967	6.12797
19	13.13394	12.08532	11.15812	9.60360	8.95012	8.36492	7.83929	7.36578	6.19823
20	13.59033	12.46221	11.46992	9.81815	9.12855	8.51356	7.96333	7.46944	6.25933

From Table C-2 you can see that the present value factor of an annuity of 1 for three periods at 10% is 2.48685.[1] This present value factor is the total of the three individual present value factors as shown in Illustration C-8. Applying this amount to the annual cash flow of $1,000 produces a present value of $2,486.85.

The following demonstration problem (Illustration C-9) illustrates how to use Table C-2.

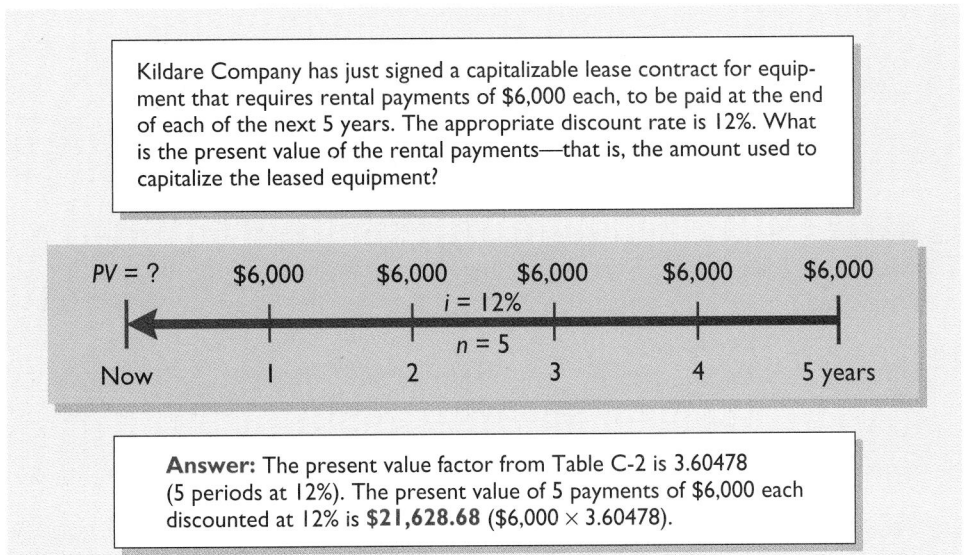

Illustration C-9

Demonstration Problem— Using Table C-2 for PV of an annuity of 1

Kildare Company has just signed a capitalizable lease contract for equipment that requires rental payments of $6,000 each, to be paid at the end of each of the next 5 years. The appropriate discount rate is 12%. What is the present value of the rental payments—that is, the amount used to capitalize the leased equipment?

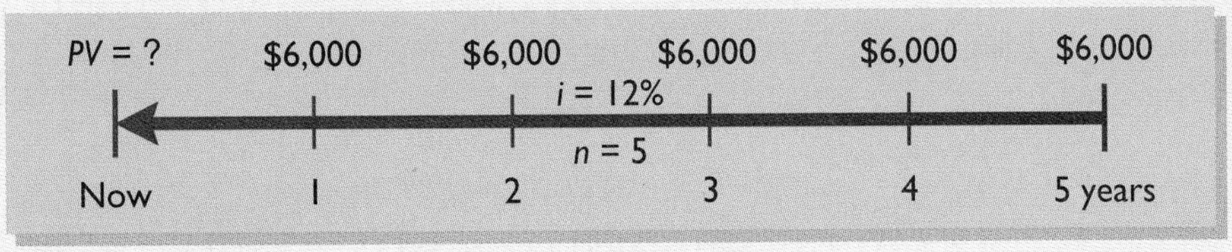

Answer: The present value factor from Table C-2 is 3.60478 (5 periods at 12%). The present value of 5 payments of $6,000 each discounted at 12% is **$21,628.68** ($6,000 × 3.60478).

TIME PERIODS AND DISCOUNTING

In the preceding calculations, the discounting has been done on an annual basis using an annual interest rate. Discounting may also be done over shorter periods of time, such as monthly, quarterly, or semiannually. When the time frame is less than one year, it is necessary to convert the annual interest rate to the shorter time frame. Assume, for example, that the investor in Illustration C-8 received $500 **semiannually** for 3 years instead of $1,000 annually. In this case, the number of periods becomes 6 (3 × 2), the discount rate is 5% (10% ÷ 2), the present value factor from Table C-2 is 5.07569, and the present value of the future cash flows is $2,537.85 (5.07569 × $500). This amount is slightly higher than the $2,486.86 computed in Illustration C-8 because interest is computed twice during the same year. That is, interest is earned on the first half year's interest.

COMPUTING THE PRESENT VALUE OF A BOND

The present value (or market price) of a bond is a function of three variables: (1) the payment amounts, (2) the length of time until the amounts are paid, and (3) the discount rate.

The first variable (dollars to be paid) is made up of two elements: (1) a series of interest payments (an annuity) and (2) the principal amount (a single sum). To

[1]The difference of .00001 between 2.48686 amd 2.48685 is due to rounding.

compute the present value of the bond, both the interest payments and the principal amount must be discounted. This is done in two different computations. The time diagrams for a bond due in 5 years are shown in Illustration C-10.

Illustration C-10

Time diagram for the present value of a bond

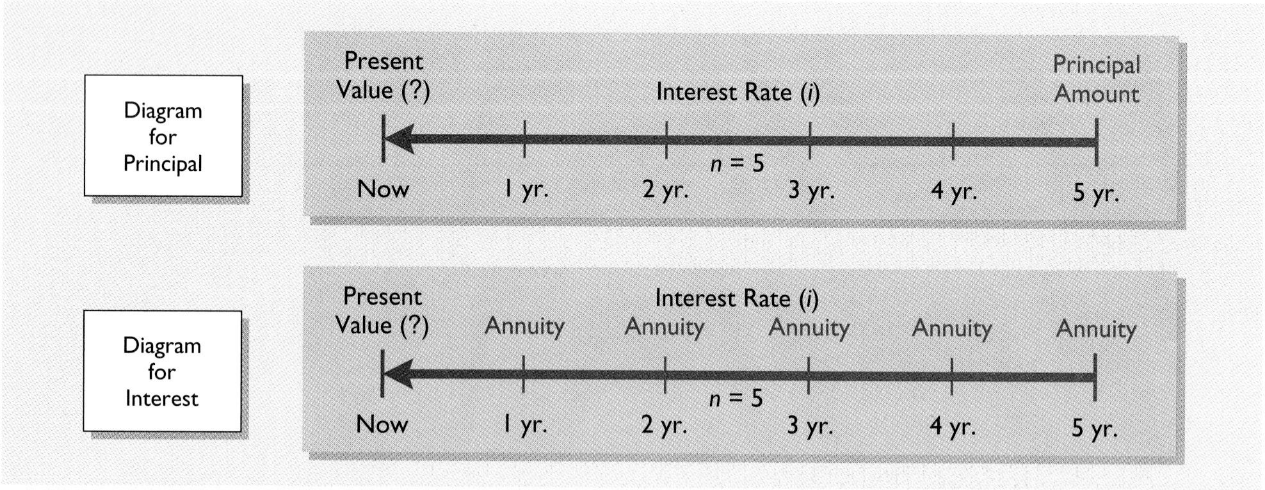

When the investor's discount rate is equal to the bond's contractual interest rate, the present value of the bonds will equal the face value of the bonds. To illustrate, assume a bond issue of 10%, 5-year bonds with a face value of $100,000 with interest payable **semiannually** on January 1 and July 1. If the discount rate is the same as the contractual rate, the bonds will sell **at face value**. In this case, the investor will receive (1) $100,000 at maturity and (2) a series of ten $5,000 interest payments [($100,000 × 10%) ÷ 2] over the term of the bonds. The length of time is expressed in terms of interest periods (in this case, 10) and the discount rate per interest period (5%). The following time diagram (Illustration C-11) depicts the variables involved in this discounting situation.

Illustration C-11

Time diagram for the present value of a 10%, 5-year bond paying interest semiannually

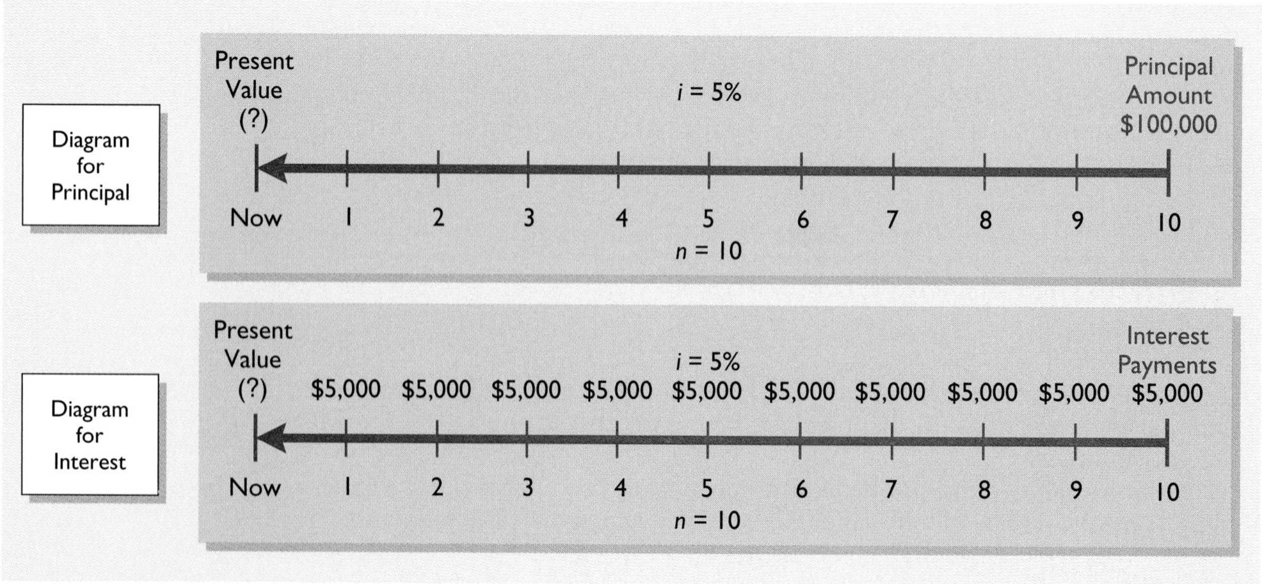

The computation of the present value of these bonds is shown below.

Illustration C-12
Present value of principal and interest (face value)

10% Contractual Rate—10% Discount Rate	
Present value of principal to be received at maturity	
$100,000 × PV of 1 due in 10 periods at 5%	
$100,000 × .61391 (Table C-1)	$ 61,391
Present value of interest to be received periodically over the term of the bonds	
$5,000 × PV of 1 due periodically for 10 periods at 5%	
$5,000 × 7.72173 (Table C-2)	38,609*
Present value of bonds	**$100,000**

*(Rounded).

Now assume that the investor's required rate of return is 12%, not 10%. The future amounts are again $100,000 and $5,000, respectively. But now a discount rate of 6% (12% ÷ 2) must be used. The present value of the bonds is $92,639, as computed below.

Illustration C-13
Present value of principal and interest (discount)

10% Contractual Rate—12% Discount Rate	
Present value of principal to be received at maturity	
$100,000 × .55839 (Table C-1)	$55,839
Present value of interest to be received periodically over the term of the bonds	
$5,000 × 7.36009 (Table C-2)	36,800
Present value of bonds	**$92,639**

If the discount rate is 8% and the contractual rate is 10%, the present value of the bonds is $108,111, computed as follows.

Illustration C-14
Present value of principal and interest (premium)

10% Contractual Rate—8% Discount Rate	
Present value of principal to be received at maturity	
$100,000 × .67556 (Table C-1)	$ 67,556
Present value of interest to be received periodically over the term of the bonds	
$5,000 × 8.11090 (Table C-2)	40,555
Present value of bonds	**$108,111**

TECHNOLOGY IN ACTION

As discussed in this appendix, the selling price of bonds can be determined by present value formulas. Many computer spreadsheets and computer programs can perform the discounting functions given the basic information of the situation.

USE OF CALCULATORS TO SOLVE PRESENT VALUE PROBLEMS

The above discussion relied on present value tables in solving present value problems. Electronic hand-held calculators may also be used to compute present values without the use of these tables. Some calculators, especially the "business" or "financial" type calculators, have present value (PV) functions that allow you to calculate present values by merely punching in the proper amount, discount rate, periods, and pressing the PV key. Whether you use a calculator or tables to solve present value problems, you should make sure that you fully understand the important concepts that underlie the calculations.

BRIEF EXERCISES (Use Tables to Solve Exercises)

Using present value tables.

BEC-1 For each of the following cases, indicate (a) to what interest rate columns and (b) to what number of periods you would refer in looking up the discount rate.

1. In Table C-1 (present value of 1):

	Annual Rate	Number of Years Involved	Discounts Per Year
(a)	12%	6	Annually
(b)	10%	15	Annually
(c)	8%	8	Semiannually

2. In Table C-2 (present value of an annuity of 1):

	Annual Rate	Number of Years Involved	Number of Payments Involved	Frequency of Payments
(a)	12%	20	20	Annually
(b)	10%	5	5	Annually
(c)	8%	4	8	Semiannually

Determining present values.

BEC-2 **(a)** What is the present value of $10,000 due 8 periods from now, discounted at 8%? **(b)** What is the present value of $10,000 to be received at the end of each of 6 periods, discounted at 9%?

Compute the present value of a single-sum investment.

BEC-3 Hernandez Company is considering an investment that will return a lump sum of $500,000 5 years from now. What amount should Hernandez Company pay for this investment in order to earn a 15% return?

Compute the present value of a single-sum investment.

BEC-4 Pizzeria Company earns 11% on an investment that will return $875,000 8 years from now. What is the amount Pizzeria should invest now in order to earn this rate of return?

Compute the present value of a single-sum noninterest-bearing note.

BEC-5 Slurpy Company sold a 5-year, noninterest-bearing $27,000 note receivable to Valley Inc. Valley wishes to earn 12% over the remaining 4 years of the note. How much cash will Slurpy receive upon sale of the note?

Compute the present value of a single-sum noninterest-bearing note.

BEC-6 Roberto Company issues a 3-year, zero-interest-bearing $66,000 note. The interest rate used to discount the zero-interest-bearing note is 8%. What are the cash proceeds that Roberto Company should receive?

Compute the present value of an annuity investment.

BEC-7 Bob Skabo Company is considering investing in an annuity contract that will return $20,000 annually at the end of each year for 15 years. What amount should Skabo Company pay for this investment if it earns a 6% return?

Compute the present value of an annuity investment.

BEC-8 Donald R. Hughes Enterprises earns 11% on an investment that pays back $110,000 at the end of each of the next 4 years. What is the amount Donald R. Hughes Enterprises invested to earn the 11% rate of return?

BEC-9 Dick Way Railroad Co. is about to issue $100,000 of 10-year bonds paying a 12% interest rate, with interest payable semiannually. The discount rate for such securities is 10%. How much can Dick Way expect to receive for the sale of these bonds?

Compute the present value of bonds.

BEC-10 Assume the same information as BEC-9 except that the discount rate is 12% instead of 10%. In this case, how much can Dick Way expect to receive from the sale of these bonds?

Compute the present value of bonds.

BEC-11 Cheryl Countryman Company receives a $50,000, 6-year note bearing interest of 11% (paid annually) from a customer at a time when the discount rate is 12%. What is the present value of the note received by Cheryl Countryman Company?

Compute the present value of a note.

BEC-12 Michael Mooney Enterprises issued 10%, 8-year, $2,000,000 par value bonds that pay interest semiannually on October 1 and April 1. The bonds are dated April 1, 2002, and are issued on that date. The discount rate of interest for such bonds on April 1, 2002, is 12%. What cash proceeds did Michael Mooney receive from issuance of the bonds?

Compute the present value of bonds.

BEC-13 Barney Googal owns a garage and is contemplating purchasing a tire retreading machine for $16,280. After estimating costs and revenues, Barney projects a net cash flow from the retreading machine of $2,790 annually for 8 years. Barney hopes to earn a return of 11% on such investments. What is the present value of the retreading operation? Should Barney Googal purchase the retreading machine?

Compute the value of a machine for purposes of making a purchase decision.

BEC-14 Hung-Chao Yu Company issues a 10%, 6-year mortgage note on January 1, 2002, to obtain financing for new equipment. Land is used as collateral for the note. The terms provide for semiannual installment payments of $112,825. What were the cash proceeds received from the issuance of the note?

Compute the present value of a note.

BEC-15 Denice Rode Company is considering purchasing equipment. The equipment will produce the following cash flows: Year 1, $30,000; Year 2, $40,000; Year 3, $50,000. Rode requires a minimum rate of return of 15%. What is the maximum price Rode should pay for this equipment?

Compute the maximum price to pay for a machine.

BEC-16 If Josey Rodriquez invests $1,827 now, she will receive $10,000 at the end of 15 years. What annual rate of interest will Josey earn on her investment? (*Hint*: Use Table C-1.)

Compute the interest rate on a single sum.

BEC-17 Jeri Delaney has been offered the opportunity of investing $24,719 now. The investment will earn 15% per year and at the end of that time will return Jeri $100,000. How many years must Jeri wait to receive $100,000? (*Hint*: Use Table C-1.)

Compute the number of periods of a single sum.

BEC-18 Janice Rahn purchased an investment for $11,469.92. From this investment, she will receive $1,000 annually for the next 20 years, starting one year from now. What rate of interest will Janice's investment be earning for her? (*Hint*: Use Table C-2.)

Compute the interest rate on an annuity.

BEC-19 Amy Sanchez invests $8,851.37 now for a series of $1,000 annual returns, beginning one year from now. Amy will earn a return of 8% on the initial investment. How many annual payments of $1,000 will Amy receive? (*Hint*: Use Table C-2.)

Compute the number of periods of an annuity.

APPENDIX D

STANDARDS OF ETHICAL CONDUCT FOR MANAGEMENT ACCOUNTANTS

Management accountants have an obligation to the organizations they serve, their profession, the public, and themselves to maintain the highest standards of ethical conduct. In recognition of this obligation, the **Institute of Management Accountants**, formerly the National Association of Accountants, has published and promoted the following standards of ethical conduct for management accountants. Adherence to these standards is integral to achieving the *Objectives of Management Accounting.*[1] Management accountants shall not commit acts contrary to these standards nor shall they condone the commission of such acts by others within their organizations.

COMPETENCE

Management accountants have a responsibility to:

- Maintain an appropriate level of professional competence by ongoing development of their knowledge and skills.
- Perform their professional duties in accordance with relevant laws, regulations, and technical standards.
- Prepare complete and clear reports and recommendations after appropriate analyses of relevant and reliable information.

CONFIDENTIALITY

Management accountants have a responsibility to:

- Refrain from disclosing confidential information acquired in the course of their work except when authorized, unless legally obligated to do so.

[1]Institute of Management Accountants, formerly National Association of Accountants, *Statements on Management Accounting: Objectives of Management Accounting,* Statement No. 1B, June 17, 1982.

- Inform subordinates as appropriate regarding the confidentiality of information acquired in the course of their work and monitor their activities to assure the maintenance of that confidentiality.
- Refrain from using or appearing to use confidential information acquired in the course of their work for unethical or illegal advantage either personally or through third parties.

Integrity

Management accountants have a responsibility to:

- Avoid actual or apparent conflicts of interest and advise all appropriate parties of any potential conflict.
- Refrain from engaging in any activity that would prejudice their ability to carry out their duties ethically.
- Refuse any gift, favor, or hospitality that would influence or would appear to influence their actions.
- Refrain from either actively or passively subverting the attainment of the organization's legitimate and ethical objectives.
- Recognize and communicate professional limitations or other constraints that would preclude responsible judgment or successful performance of an activity.
- Communicate unfavorable as well as favorable information and professional judgments or opinions.
- Refrain from engaging in or supporting any activity that would discredit the profession.

Objectivity

Management accountants have a responsibility to:

- Communicate information fairly and objectively.
- Disclose fully all relevant information that could reasonably be expected to influence an intended user's understanding of the reports, comments, and recommendations presented.

PHOTO CREDITS

Chapter 1
Opener: Warren Bolster/Stone. Page 5: Gary Hunter/Stone. Page 6: Jean Miele/The Stock Market. Page 8: Mike Cressy/Stock Illustration Source. Page 11: Roger Boehm/Stock Illustration Source. Page 24: Will Crocker/The Image Bank. Page 39: Courtesy of Nestle S.A.

Chapter 2
Opener: Rod Long/Stone. Page 50: Simon Battensby/Stone. Page 53: Mike Stewart/Corbis Sygma. Page 55: Joe Bator/The Stock Market. Page 62: Nora Hope/Stock Illustration Source. Page 66: Frank Wing/Stock, Boston/PNI.

Chapter 3
Opener: T. Kevin Smyth/The Stock Market. Page 90: ©AP/Wide World Photos. Page 94: Romily Lockyer/The Image Bank. Page 98: Dennis Galante/Stone. Page 103: Peter Poulides/Stone.

Chapter 4
Opener: Matthias Kulka/The Stock Market. Page 137: William Whitehurst/The Stock Market. Page 142: Marc Francoeur/Liaison Agency, Inc. Page 144: M. Tcherevkoff/The Image Bank. Page 150: Miguel S. Salmeron/FPG International. Page 152: Leland Bobbe/Stone. Page 153 (top): John Fiordalisi/SUPERSTOCK. Page 153 (bottom): Zigy Kaluzny/Stone. Page 154 (top): Courtesy United Airlines. Page 154 (bottom): Courtesy Consolidated Freightways. Page 155: The Dell logo is a registered trademark of Dell Computer Corporation in the United States and other countries. Page 162: John Riley/Stone. Page 179: Courtesy Holmen.

Chapter 5
Opener: Rob Colvin/©2000 Artville, Inc. Page 186: Michael Simpson/FPG International. Page 190: Ed Honowitz/Stone. Page 191: Gregory Heislerban/The Image Bank. Page 193: Thierry Dosogne/The Image Bank. Page 201: Steve Taylor/Stone.

Chapter 6
Opener: Chris Noble/Stone. Page 226: John Turner/Stone. Page 227: Tom Tracey/FPG International. Page 241: Michael Rosenfeld/Stone. Page 242 (top): Courtesy The Quaker Oats Company. Page 242 (bottom): Bob Krist/Stone. Page 271 (top): Courtesy Fuji Photo Film U.S.A, Inc. Page 271 (bottom): Kodak corporate symbol is a trademark of Eastman Kodak Company. Used with permission.

Chapter 7
Opener: Elle Schuster/The Image Bank. Page 278: W. Cody/CORBIS. Page 281: Earl Glass/Stock, Boston/PNI.

Chapter 8
Opener: Robert Stanton/Stone. Page 319: Gary Buss/FPG International. Page 321: Ken Straiton/The Stock Market. Page 322: R. Michael Stuckey/Comstock, Inc. Page 324: Sean Kane/Stock Illustration Source. Page 330: Michael Murphy/The Image Bank. Page 334: Miachel A. Keller/The Stock Market. Page 336: J.W. Burkey/Stone. Page 341: Kodak corporate symbol is a trademark of Eastman Kodak Company. Used with permission.

Chapter 9
Opener: ©PhotoDisc. Page 364: David Gould/The Image Bank. Page 369: ©Zefa/Stock Imagery. Page 370: ©Yemi/Stock Illustration Source. Page 377: Brad Hamann/Stock Illustration Source. Page 379: ©Telegraph Colour Library/FPG International.

Chapter 10
Opener: Stewart Cohen/Stone. Page 405: Greg Probst/Stone. Page 411: Thierry Cariou/The Stock Market. Page 421: ©Schnepf/Liaison Agency, Inc. Page 422: Courtesy Grand Metropolitan. Page 441: Courtesy J Sainsbury.

Chapter 11
Opener: John Turner/Stone. Page 448: Ed Honowitz/Stone. Page 452: Peter Gridley/FPG International. Page 453: ©The Image Bank. Page 455: James Noble/The Stock Market. Page 463: ©1994 Turner & Devries/The Image Bank. Page 476: "Polaroid" is a registered trademark of the Polaroid Corporation.

Chapter 12
Opener: Andrew Olney/Stone. Page 489: Lonny Kalfus/Stone. Page 491: Comstock, Inc. Page 497: Henry Sims/The Image Bank. Page 498: Doug Armand/Stone. Page 499: Barbara Nessim/Stock Illustration Source. Page 503: Olney Vasan/Stone.

Chapter 13
Opener: ©2000 Razor & Tie Direct, LLC. Page 522: Jude Maceren/Stock Illustration Source. Page 524: Denis Scott/The Stock Market. Page 528: Robert Cattan/Index Stock.

Chapter 14
Opener: Rick Graves/Stone. Page 563: Stephen Johnson/Stone. Page 564: ©Josh Sohm; Chromosohm, Inc./CORBIS. Page 566: ©AP/Wide World Photos. Page 568 (top): Lands' End is a registered trademark of Lands' End, Inc. Used with permission. Page 568 (bottom): Seth Resnick/Stock, Boston/PNI. Page 575: Alex Fevzer/CORBIS. Page 579: Jaime Salles/The Stock Market. Page 582: The Kellogg's logo is a registered trademark of the Kellogg Corporation. Used with permission. All rights reserved.

Chapter 15
Opener: Gregg Adams/Stone. Page 603: Sandra Baker/Stone. Page 609: John Labbe/The Image Bank. Page 611 (top): David Madison/Stone. Page 611 (bottom): Ken Whitmore/Stone. Page 617: Andy Sacks/Stone. Page 621: Charles Thomaidis/Stone.

Chapter 16
Opener: Leon Zeritsky/Stock Illustration Source. Page 642: ©AP/Wide World Photos. Page 656: Andy Levine/Stock Illustration Source. Page 667: Ken Whitmore/Stone. Page 678: Information supplied courtesy of Apache Corporation.

Chapter 17
Opener: ©Photofest. Page 684: ©AP/Wide World Photos. Page 686: D. Boone/CORBIS.

Chapter 18
Opener: John Lund/Stone. Page 719: Jonathan Elderfield/Liaison Agency, Inc. Page 748: ©William Waldron. Page 775: Compliments of Saint-Gobaine.

Chapter 19
Opener: Jerry Driendl/FPG International. Page 782 & 783: Sears, Roebuck and Co. Page 788: Don Bishop/©2000 Artville, Inc. Page 790: Nora Good/Masterfile. Page 792: Christopher Morris/Black Star. Page 793: Jay Ahrend/FoodPix. Page 799 (top): Michael Skott/The Image Bank. Page 799 (bottom): Eric Sander/Liaison Agency, Inc. Page 801: Laurie Rubin/The Image Bank. Page 802: Mark Wiens/Stone. Page 806: Jan Cobb/The Image Bank. Page 813: Courtesy Nordstrom.

Chapter 20
Opener: Andrew Olney/Stone. Page 830: ©Premium Stock/CORBIS. Page 832: ©Paul A. Souders/CORBIS. Page 841 (top): Eric Kamp/Index Stock. Page 841 (bottom): Andrew Sacks/Stone. Page 842: Shaun Egan/Stone. Page 860: Courtesy Anchor Glass Container Corporation.

Chapter 21
Opener: Karen Beard/Stone. Page 866: David Frazier/Stone. Page 870: James Porto/FPG International. Page 874: Ed Honowitz/Stone. Page 879: Robert Tinney/The Stock Market. Page 881: Richard Pasley/Stock, Boston/PNI. Page 898: Courtesy Parlex Corporation. The information was provided in the company's annual report.

Chapter 22
Opener: John Burwell/FoodPix. Page 907: John Wilkinson/CORBIS. Page 918: Chip Simons/FPG International. Page 919: Jennie Oppenheimer/Stock Illustration Source. Page 921: Herrmann/Starke/The Stock Market. Page 926: Trish Burgio/Stock Illustration Source. Page 928: Margie & Howard Fullmer/Stock Illustration Source. Page 942: Courtesy General Microwave.

Chapter 23
Opener: Dave Crosier/Stone. Page 948: Martin Schreiber/Stone. Page 955: ©CORBIS. Page 959: Cyberimage/Stone. Page 960: Yael/Retna. Page 963: Micheal Simpson/FPG International.

Chapter 24
Opener: Courtesy University of Nebraska. Page 983: Gary Conner/Index Stock. Page 988: Peter Zeray/Photonica. Page 989: Donald C. Johnson/The Stock Market. Page 992: Ralph Mercer/Stone. Page 994: Larry Gilpin/Stone. Page 997: Paul Muns/Stock Illustration Source. Page 999: Mark Wiens/Stone. Page 1014: Courtesy Network Computing Devices, Inc.

Chapter 25
Opener: Michael Simpson/FPG International. Page 1032: Chet Phillips/©2000 Artville, Inc. Page 1035: ©EyeWire. Page 1059: Courtesy Computer Associates International, Inc.

Chapter 26
Opener: Dick Luria/FPG International. Page 1066: Garry Gay/The Image Bank. Page 1069: John Syoboda/FoodPix. Page 1074: Michel Tchervkoff/The Image Bank. Page 1076: Courtesy United Parcel Service. Page 1100: Courtesy Glassmaster Company.

Chapter 27
Opener: Burke & Triolo/©2000 Artville, Inc. Page 1108: Ed Eckstein/CORBIS. Page 1111: Courtesy Snapple Beverage Group. Page 1119: Tim Jonke/The Image Bank. Page 1122: Ken Ross/Liaison Agency, Inc.

COMPANY INDEX

SUBJECT INDEX